Bookman's
Price Index

ISSN 0068-0141

Bookman's Price Index

VOLUME 52

A Guide to the Values of Rare and Other Out of Print Books

Edited by
Anne F. McGrath

GALE

an International Thomson Publishing company I(T)P®

Editor: Anne F. McGrath

Coordinating Editors: Nancy Franklin, Charles B. Montney

Production Director: Mary Beth Trimper
Production Assistant: Deborah Milliken

Art Director: Cynthia Baldwin
Keyliner: C.J. Jonik

The editor would like to acknowledge the diligence of Patricia Burdette in the preparation of this and previous BPI volumes. Without her many hours of keying and proofing, these volumes might never see the light of day.

While every effort has been made to ensure the reliability of the information presented in this publication, Gale Research does not guarantee the accuracy of the data contained herein. Gale accepts no payment for listing; and inclusion in the publication of any organization, agency, institution, publication service, or individual does not imply endorsement of the editors or publisher. Errors brought to the attention of the publisher and verified to the satisfaction of the publisher will be corrected in future editions.

⊚™ This book is printed on acid-free paper that meets the minimum requirements of American National Standard for Information Sciences—Permanence Paper for Printed Library Materials, ANSI Z39.48-1984.

Library of Congress Catalog Card Number 64-8723
ISBN 0-8103-6444-1
ISSN 0068-0141

Printed in the United States of America

I(T)P™
Gale Research, an International Thomson Publishing Company.
ITP logo is a trademark under license.

Contents

Introduction

The *Bookman's Price Index*, established in 1964, is published twice a year as an index to both the prices and availability of antiquarian books in the United States, Canada, and the British Isles.

Each issue of the BPI reports the prices and availability of over 25 thousand different antiquarian books. Thus, in the course of an average calendar year, the BPI reports the prices and availability of some 50 thousand antiquarian books that are important to readers in the North Atlantic portion of the English-speaking community.

The present issue of the BPI, Volume 52, is the first of the two issues for 1996.

Definition of Antiquarian Books

An antiquarian book is one that is, or has been, traded on the antiquarian book market. It is, or was, traded there because it is important (or in demand) and scarce.

Importance, in the case of antiquarian books, is national. American, Canadian, and British readers buy and sell the artifacts of their own literature and history, science and art, as well as a select number of books that document the Continental and Classical origins of certain aspects of their cultures. There are special enthusiasms, too, like children's books, and sporting books, and books that are important principally for their physical beauty; but even the books of these special enthusiasms reflect the national preoccupations of English-speaking readers.

Scarcity means that the number of copies of any book that might come onto the market is measured, at most, in scores, and that only a dozen or a half-dozen, at most, come onto the market during any calendar year.

Lots of important books are not scarce, and lots of scarce books are not important. And, despite the word antiquarian, age is no guarantee of either scarcity or importance. Conversely, many books that are less than a generation old bring a handsome price on the market.

The antiquarian books that do appear on the North Atlantic market are a small percentage of the world's entire antiquarian book market, and, necessarily, they are the tiniest fraction of the total number of books published over the centuries.

Despite their thin ranks and scant number, antiquarian books are not outrageously expensive. They range in price from $100 to $500, with most clustering between $100 and $200, and precious few enjoying four-figure prominence.

Prices Reported in the BPI

The prices reported in the *Bookman's Price Index* are established by some 175-200 antiquarian booksellers in the United States, Canada, and the British Isles. By drawing information from a large number of antiquarian booksellers across English-speaking North America, as well as the British Isles, the BPI is able to report broad, consistent, and reliable market patterns in the whole North Atlantic English-speaking community.

Within the ranks of the antiquarian booksellers whose prices are reported in the BPI, the group most interesting is the specialist dealers whose stock is limited to books in a single subject such as law, or psychiatry, or maritime studies, or horticulture. Such specialists provide readers of the BPI with information that is available nowhere else.

The prices that all of these antiquarian booksellers report are retail prices that they have established on the basis of their working experience and familiarity with current market conditions, including supply and demand and the effect upon price of the general physical condition of a book, as well as such extraordinary factors as the presence of important autographs.

The willingness of the various antiquarian booksellers to publish their prices in direct comparison with the prices of all other antiquarian booksellers serves as a general indication of the reliability of the prices reported in the BPI as well as the probity of the antiquarian booksellers. These prices are public market prices, not private deals.

Availability of Books in the BPI

Every one of the books in the *Bookman's Price Index* was recently available in one of the shops of the antiquarian booksellers whose catalogs are included in this volume of the BPI. It was upon the basis of a hands-on appraisal of each book that an antiquarian bookseller established its price. Thus, the prices reported in the BPI are actual prices for specific books rather than approximate prices for probable or possible books.

While a particular book may no longer be in the shop of the antiquarian bookseller who established its price, the fact that the book stood on the shelf there recently means that the book is still to be found on the market and that the antiquarian bookseller who established its price may have access to another copy of the same book, or that a different antiquarian bookseller may price another copy of the book in the following issue of the BPI. Thus, by reporting prices of actual books, and their real availability, the *Bookman's Price Index* serves as an index to the general market availability of a particular antiquarian book.

Conversely, the BPI is an index to the absence of certain antiquarian books from the market: books not priced in the BPI may be presumed to be generally unavailable on the antiquarian book market. (The BPI makes no effort to predict what such unavailable books might be worth if they were perhaps to someday come on the market; the BPI reports only what is going on in the market, not what might go on.)

For example, if a reader were to search the six most recent issues of the BPI for the price of the first edition of Edgar Allan Poe's *Tamerlane*, he might not find it and could safely conclude that a first edition of *Tamerlane* was not generally available during the past three years. If on the other hand, the same reader were to make a similar search for a first edition of *Salem's Lot* by Poe's spiritual son Stephen King, he might discover that *Salem's Lot* has been found in the shops from time to time and that it is worth about $500, give or take a few dollars, depending on condition.

The Importance of Condition

Condition is critical in antiquarian books as in any other antiquarian artifact. The condition of all of the books priced in the *Bookman's Price Index* is stated in elaborate detail because it is impossible to understand or justify the price of any antiquarian book without full knowledge of its condition.

Arrangement of the BPI

The books priced in the *Bookman's Price Index* are arranged in a single main alphabet according to the name of the author: in cases of personal authorship, the author's last name; in cases of books produced by corporate bodies such as governments of countries or states, the name of that corporation; in cases of anonymous books, the title; and in cases of anonymous classics such as the *Arabian Nights*, by customary title.

All names of authors, or titles, are standardized according to the usage of American libraries, thus gathering all works by an author.

The works of an author are arranged under his name in alphabetical sequence according to the first word of the title, excepting initial articles. However, editions of an author's collected works are listed, out of alphabetical sequence, at the end of the list of his individual works.

Different editions of a single work are arranged according to date of publication, with the earlier preceding the later even though this sequence sometimes disrupts alphabetical regularity. In such cases, the editor has sought to consult the reader's convenience rather than any rigid consistency.

The reasons for the occasional disruption of alphabetical regularity are two: the first reason is that in reporting prices, the antiquarian booksellers sometimes refer to a book elliptically, leaving unknown the complete title. The second reason is that certain books change title without changing substance. The most obvious example of this particular editorial problem is the Bible. Title pages of Bibles can begin with such words as Complete, Holy, Sacred, New, Authorized, and so on; it is still the same book. Therefore all English Bibles appear, under the heading BIBLES-ENGLISH, in chronological order. Following the title of each book is its imprint: the place and date of publication and the name of the publisher (or the name of the printer in cases of certain books produced prior to the late eighteenth century).

Description of the Condition of Books

Following the author, title, and imprint of each book is a thorough description of the physical condition of the book. While the antiquarian booksellers do not always apply a standard formula in describing the condition of a book, they generally include, as appropriate, most of the following details:

Edition: The BPI reports which edition of a book is being priced when this information is critical, as in cases when several editions were published in one year. If an edition was published in more than one issue, or state, the BPI distinguishes among them and identifies them either by the order in which they appeared, or by the physical peculiarities that characterize them. When necessary, the BPI even describes those obscure details called points that are used to distinguish among issues or states. The points are often minute and consist of such details as one misspelled word buried in the text. Finally, the BPI identifies limited editions, stating the number of copies in the press run and, if necessary, the types of paper used and the specific number assigned to the book being priced.

Physical Size: The BPI describes the height and the bulk of each book. Height is usually described in the traditional language of the antiquarian book trade: folio, for a tall book; quarto (4to) for a medium-size book; and octavo (8vo) or duodecimo (12mo) for a smaller book. Miniature books are usually described in inches top to bottom and left to right. The bulk of a book is described by stating its pagination, a custom that operates to assure the reader that the book in question is complete.

Illustrations: Since many antiquarian books are more valuable for their illustrations than for their text, the BPI describes such illustrations carefully, sometimes in considerable detail, as in the case of a book with hand-colored plates.

Binding: All bindings are described fully as to the material used, be it paper, cloth or leather, and even as to the type and color of the material and the time at which it was applied. ("Contemporary tan calf" means that a binding of cattle hide was made for the book contemporaneously with its printing.) Decorations of the binding are also described, and in the cases of twentieth century books, the presence or absence of the dust jacket is always noted.

Authors' Signatures: These are always cited, as they have a significant effect on the price of a book.

General Physical Condition, Specific Flaws, and Relative Scarcity: Usually, the BPI provides some advice on the general condition of a book, by stating that its condition is good, very good, or fine. Additionally, specific flaws are usually listed; some of them are significant, as in the case of a missing leaf or a worn binding, while others are very minor, as in the case of a worm hole in an ancient tome.

Availability: Frequently the BPI will point out that certain books are of unusual scarcity or rarity. As all antiquarian books are by definition scarce, a special remark that a book is uncommonly scarce should be noted carefully.

Prices: Following the description, the BPI gives the price of the book along with the name of the antiquarian bookseller who established the price and provided the physical description. Accompanying the antiquarian bookseller's name is the number of the catalog in which he published the price and description of the book, plus the item number of the book in the catalog. The addresses of the antiquarian booksellers whose prices are reported in the BPI are listed in the front matter of the book, in the section entitled Dealers Represented in This Volume.

Association Copies, Fine Bindings, and Fore-edge Paintings

Following the main section of the *Bookman's Price Index* are three small sections of association copies of books, books in fine bindings, and books decorated with fore-edge paintings. The books in these three sections take on additional interest and value because of features peculiar to them that are not found in other copies of the same books. Their value, or some portion of it, derives from factors not inherent in the text and not identifiable through the name of the author, thereby requiring that they be isolated so that readers can search them out according to the factors that create, or influence, their worth: association, binding or fore-edge painting.

All books priced and described in one of the special sections are also priced and described in the main section of the BPI, thus permitting the reader to compare an ordinary copy of a book with one that enjoys added attraction because of a unique feature.

Association Copies: Certain antiquarian books acquire added value because of their association with a prominent owner. For instance, an ordinary eighteenth century book would take on enormous extra worth if it had once belonged to George Washington. Association copies of books priced in the special section of the BPI are arranged according to the name of the person with whom the book was associated rather than according to the name of the author. (The same book is listed in the main body of the BPI under the name of the author.)

Fine Bindings: Some books are valuable because custom bindings were applied to them alone, and not to other copies of the same book. In the Fine Bindings section of the BPI, books are gathered under the name of the binder, when known, and then listed according to author. (Each of the books so listed is also listed under the name of the author in the main section of the BPI.)

Fore-edge Paintings: Fore-edge paintings are original watercolor drawings upon the vertical edges of the leaves of a book. The book is laid flat with the front cover open so that the vertical edges of the leaves slant a little when the painting is applied; when the book is closed, the painting is not visible. These unusual examples of book decoration are gathered in the Fore-edge section under the year of publication of the book, and then arranged according to the name of the author. Generally, fore-edge paintings are not signed and dated, and it is often difficult if not impossible, to be sure a fore-edge painting was executed in the year of publication of the book. When there is conclusive evidence as to the name of the artist and the date of a fore-edge painting, the book is listed under the year in which the painting was executed. (All books listed in the Fore-edge section are also listed in the main section of the BPI under the name of the author.)

Errors in the BPI

The two volumes of the BPI that appear each year combine to include about 14,000,000 letters and numerals. The editor makes every effort to get them all right, and she asks the reader to be understanding about an occasional typo.

Dealers Represented in Volume 52

RICHARD H. ADELSON
North Pomfret, VT 05053

CHARLES AGVENT
Rd 2, Box 377a
Mertztown, PA 19539

ANACAPA HOUSE
1727 Anacapa Street
Santa Barbara, CA 93101

HUGH ANSON-
 CARTWRIGHT
229 College Street
Toronto
Ontario M5T 1R4
Canada

ANTIC HAY RARE
 BOOKS
P. O. Box 2185
Asbury Park, NJ 07712

ANTIPODEAN BOOKS,
 MAPS & PRINTS
P. O. Box 189
Cold Spring, NY 10516

APPELFELD GALLERY
1372 York Avenue
New York, NY 10021

ARCHEOLOGIA
707 Carlston Ave.
Oakland, CA 94610

ARGONAUT BOOK SHOP
786-792 Sutter Street
San Francisco, CA 94109

ARGOSY BOOK STORE,
 INC.
116 East 59th Street
New York, NY 10022

DAVID ARONOVITZ
781 Snell Road
Rochester, MI 48306

ASH RARE BOOKS
25 Royal Exchange
Threadneedle Street
London EC3V 3LP
England

GENE W. BAADE - BOOKS
 ON THE WEST
824 Lynnwood Ave., N.E.
Renton, WA 98056

NELSON BALL,
 BOOKSELLER
31 Willow Street
Paris, Ontario N3L 2K7
Canada

BANNATYNE BOOKS LTD.
6 Bedford Road
London N8 8HL
England

BEASLEY BOOKS
1533 West Oakdale
Chicago, IL 60657

BEELEIGH ABBEY BOOKS
Beeleigh Abbey
Maldon
Essex CM9 6LL
England

BELLA LUNA BOOKS
P.O. Box 260425
Highlands Ranch, CO 80126

STEVEN C. BERNARD
15011 Plainfield Lane
Darnestown, MD 20874

BETWEEN THE COVERS
132 Kings Highway East
Haddonfield, NJ 08033

DAVID BICKERSTETH
4 Southend, Bassingbourn
Royston
Hertfordshire SC8 5NG
England

BLACKWELL'S RARE
 BOOKS
38 Holywell Street
Oxford OX1 3SW
England

BLUE MOUNTAIN BOOKS
 & MANUSCRIPTS, LTD.
P.O. Box 363
Catskill, NY 12414

BLUE RIVER BOOKS
6219 N. Guilford Ave.
Indianapolis, IN 46220

BOHLING BOOK COMPANY
P. O. Box 204
Decatur, MI 49045

THE BOOK BLOCK
8 Loughlin Avenue
Cos Cob, CT 06807

BOOKPRESS, LTD.
411 W. Duke of
   Gloucester St.
P.O. Box KP
Willliamsburg, VA 23187

BOOK TIME
456 South Main Street
Orange, CA 92668

BOOKWORM & SILVERFISH
P. O. Box 639
Wytheville, VA 24382

MARILYN BRAITERMAN
20 Whitfield Road
Baltimore, MD 21210

BRANNAN BOOKS
P. O. Box 475
Garberville, CA 95542

BROMER BOOKSELLERS
607 Boylston St.
Boston, MA 02116

JAMES BURMESTER
Manor House Farmhouse
North Stoke
Bath BA19AT
England

ANDREW CAHAN:
   BOOKSELLER
3000 Blueberry Lane
Chapel Hill, NC 27516

THE CAPTAIN'S
   BOOKSHELF, INC.
P. O. Box 2258
31 Page Avenue
Asheville, NC 28802

BEV CHANEY JR. BOOKS
73 Croton Ave.
Ossining, NY 10562

CHAPEL HILL RARE
   BOOKS
P. O. Box 456
Carrboro, NC 27510

JENS J. CHRISTOFFERSEN
   RARE BOOKS
221 South Barry Avenue
P.O. Box 246
Marmaroneck, NY 10543

ROY W. CLARE
47 Woodshire South
P. O. Box 136
Getzville, NY 14068

ROBERT CLARK
6a King Street
Jericho
Oxford OX2 6DF
England

J. M. COHEN, RARE BOOKS
2 Karin Court
New Platz, NY 12561

NEIL COURNOYER,
   BOOKSELLER
Box 4193 Station E
Ottawa
Ontario K1S 5B2
Canada

CLAUDE COX, OLD AND
   RARE BOOKS
College Gateway Bookshop
3 & 5 Silent Street
Ipswich IPI 1TF
England

JAMES CUMMINS,
   BOOKSELLER
P. O. Box 232
Pottersville, NJ 07979

L. CLARICE DAVIS
P.O. Box 56054
Sherman Oaks, CA 91413

DAWSON'S BOOK SHOP
535 N. Larchmont Boulevard
Los Angeles, CA 90004

THOMAS DORN
P. O. Box 2585
Decatur, GA 30031

DRAMATIS PERSONAE
   BOOKSELLERS
P.O. Box 1070
Sheffield, MA 10257

JOHN DRURY, (RARE
   BOOKS) LTD.
Strandlands, Wrabness
Manningtree
Essex CO11 2TX
England

DUMONT BOOKS & MAPS
   OF THE WEST
301 E. Palace Ave.
P. O. Box 10250
Santa Fe, NM 87504

THE EARLY WEST
Box 9292
College Station, TX 77842

HARLAND H. EASTMAN
66 Main Street
Springvale, ME 04083

ELTON ENGINEERING
   BOOKS
27 Mayfield Ave.
London W4 1PN
England

FAMILY ALBUM
R. R. 1, Box 42
Glen Rock, PA 17327

JOSEPH J. FELCONE INC.
P.O. Box 366
Princeton, NJ 08540

JAMES FENNING
12 Glenview,
Rochestown Ave.
Dun Loughaire
County Dublin
Ireland

SIMON FINCH RARE
BOOKS
Clifford Chambers
10 New Bond Street
London W1Y 9PF
England

H. M. FLETCHER
201 Cardamom Building
31 Shad Thames
London SE1 2YR
England

FOREST BOOKS
Knipton
Grantham
Lincs NG32 1RF
England

FREEDOM BOOKSHOP
Box 247 Maple St.
Freedom, NH 03836

W. BRUCE FYE
1607 North Wood Avenue
Marshfield, WI 54449

JOHN GACH BOOKS
5620 Waterloo Road
Columbia, MD 21045

ROBERT GAVORA,
BOOKSELLER
4514 East Burnside St.
Portland, OR 97215

R. A. GEKOSKI
Pied Bull Yard
15a Bloomsbury Square
London WC1A 2LP
England

BENNETT GILBERT
P. O. Box 46056
Los Angeles, CA 90046

EDWIN V. GLASER,
RARE BOOKS
P.O. Box 1765
Sausalito, CA 94966

GLENN BOOKS
4503 Genessee, 2nd Floor
Kansas City, MO 64111

JAMES TAIT GOODRICH
La Casa Vista Grande
125 Tweed Blvd
Upper Grandview-on-Hudson
NY 10960

WILLIAM A. GRAF - BOOKS
717 Clark Street
Iowa City, IO 52240

DAVID A. H. GRAYLING
Lyvennet, Crosby Ravensworth
Penrith
Cumbria CA10 3JP
England

ROBIN GREER
29 Oxbury Avenue
London SW6 5SP
England

HARTFIELD FINE AND
RARE BOOKS
117 Dixboro Road
Ann Arbor, MI 48105

TIMOTHY HAWLEY
915 S. Third St.
Louisville, KY 40203

ROBERT G. HAYMAN,
ANTIQUARIAN BOOKS
Box 188
Carey, OH 43316

MICHAEL D. HEASTON CO.
5614 Wagon Train Rd.
P. O. Box 91147
Austin, TX 78749

JOSHUA HELLER RARE
BOOKS, INC.
P. O. Box 39114
Washington, DC 20016

JOHN HENLY,
BOOKSELLER
Brooklands, Walderton
Chichester
West Sussex PO18 9EE
England

HERITAGE BOOKSHOP
8540 Melrose Avenue
Los Angeles, CA 90069

HERMITAGE BOOKSHOP
290 Fillmore Street
Denver, CO 80206

PETER MURRAY HILL
(RARE BOOKS)
10 Beverley Gardens, Stamford
Lincolnshire PE9 2UD
England

IAN HODGKINS & CO. LTD
Upper Vatch Mill
The Vatch, Slad, Stroud
Gloucester GL6 7JY
England

R. F. G. HOLLETT & SON
6 Finkle Street
Sedbergh, Cumbria LA10 5BZ
England

DAVID HOLLOWAY,
    BOOKSELLER
7430 Grace St.
Springfield, VA 22150

DAVID J. HOLMES
230 S. Broad Street, 3rd Fl.
Philadelphia, PA 19102

HOULE RARE BOOKS &
    AUTOGRAPHS
7260 Beverly Boulevard
Los Angeles, CA 90036

HOWES BOOKSHOP, LTD.
Trinity Hall
Braybrooke Terrace
Hastings
East Sussex TN34 1HQ
Wales

C. P. HYLAND
c/o H & S Associates
Barclays Bank Building
High Street, Chepstow
Gwent NP6 5QX
Wales

JAMES S. JAFFE, RARE
    BOOKS
367 West Lancaster Ave.
Haverford, PA 19041

MARJORIE JAMES
The Old School
Oving, Chichester
West Sussex PO20 6DG
England

JANUS BOOKS
P. O. Box 40787
Tucson, AZ 85717

JARNDYCE, ANTIQUARIAN
    BOOKSELLERS
46 Great Russell Street
Bloomsbury
London WC1B 3PA
England

C. R. JOHNSON RARE
    BOOK COLLECTIONS
53 Duncan Terrace
London N1 8AG
England

JOHN JOHNSON
R.R. 1, Box 513
No. Barrington, VT 05257

PRISCILLA JUVELIS - RARE
    BOOKS
1166 Massachussetts Ave.
Cambridge, MA 02138

K BOOKS ANTIQUARIAN
    BOOKSELLERS
Waplington Hall
Allerthorpe
York YO4 4RS
England

KENNETH KARMIOLE
    BOOKSELLER, INC.
509 Wilshire Boulevard
P.O. Box 464
Santa Monica, CA 90406

JOHN K. KING
901 Lafayette Boulevard
Detroit, MI 48226

KNOLLWOOD BOOKS
P.O. Box 197
Oregon, WI 53575

LAKIN & MARLEY RARE
    BOOKS
P. O. Box 1209
Mill Valley, CA 94942

MAGGIE LAMBETH
Star Route 4
Box 361
Blanco, TX 78606

LAME DUCK BOOKS
90 Moraine St.
Jamaica Plains, NY 02130

ANTHONY W. LAYWOOD
Knipton, Grantham
Lincolnshire, NG32 1RF
England

LEFT BANK BOOKS
P. O. Box 728
Long Beach, CA 90801

JOHN LEWCOCK,
    BOOKSELLER
6 Chewells Lane
Haddenham, Ely
Cambridgeshire CB6 3SS
England

LIMESTONE HILLS BOOK
    SHOP
P. O. Box 1125
Glen Rose, TX 76043

KEN LOPEZ, BOOKSELLER
51 Huntington Road
Hadley, MA 01035

ROBERT F. LUCAS
P. O. Box 63
Blandford, MA 01008

STEPHEN C. LUNSFORD
P. O. Box 3023
Blaine, WA 98230

STEPHEN LUPACK
449 New Hanover Ave.
St. Meriden, CT 06451

LYMAN BOOKS
P. O. Box 853
E. Otis, MA 01029

M & S RARE BOOKS
P.O. Box 2594
East Side Station
Providence, RI 02906

MACDONNELL RARE
    BOOKS
9307 Glenlake Drive
Austin, TX 78730

MAGGS BROS., LTD.
50 Berkeley Square
London W1X 6EL
England

MAGNUM OPUS RARE
    BOOKS
P.O. Box 1301
Charlottesville, VA 22902

JOSEPH D. MANCEVICE,
    INC.
P. O. Box 413
West Side Station
Worcester, MA 01602

MARLBOROUGH RARE
    BOOKS LTD.
144-146 New Bond Street
London W1Y 9FD
England

DAVID MASON
342 Queen Street West
Toronto
Ontario M5V 2A2
Canada

MCGOWAN BOOK CO.
P. O. Box 16325
Chapel Hill, NC 48226

METACOMET BOOKS
P.O. Box 2479
Providence, RI 02906

MEYER BOSWELL
    BOOKS, INC.
2141 Mission Street
San Francisco, CA 94110

MIDDLE EARTH BOOKS
P. O. Box 81906
Rochester Hills, MI 48308

EDWARD MORRILL & SON
27 Country Club Road
Newton Centre, MA 02159

W. M. MORRISON BOOKS
15801 La Hacienda
Austin, TX 78734

HOWARD S. MOTT, INC.
P.O. Box 309
170 S. Main
Sheffield, MA 01257

MOUNTAINEERING BOOKS
6 Bedford Road
London N8 8HL
England

J. B. MUNS, FINE ARTS
    BOOKS
1162 Shattuck Avenue
Berkeley, CA 94707

19TH CENTURY SHOP
1047 Hollins Street
Baltimore, MD 21223

OCTOBER FARM
2609 Branch Road
Raleigh, NC 27610

ORACLE BOOKS
P. O. Box 2488
Reston, VA 22090

ORPHEUS BOOKS
11522 N.E. 20th Street
Bellevue, WA 98004

PARKER BOOKS OF
    THE WEST
see
DUMONT MAPS & BOOKS
    OF THE WEST

PARMER BOOKS
7644 Forrestal Road
San Diego, CA 92120

IAN PATTERSON
221 Bateman Street
Cambridge CB1 2NB
England

PETERSFIELD BOOKSHOP
16a Chapel Street, Petersfield
Hampshire GU32 3DS
England

PETTLER & LIEBERMAN,
    BOOKSELLER
8033 Sunset Blvd., #977
Los Angeles, CA 90046

PHILLIP J. PIRAGES
2205 Nutt Tree Lane
P.O. Box 504
McMinnville, OR 97128

POLYANTHOS PARK
    AVENUE BOOKS
P.O. Box 343
Huntington, NY 11743

QUILL & BRUSH
P.O. Box 5365
Rockville, MD 20848

P. R. RAINSFORD
23 A Manvers St.
Bath BA1 1JW
England

WILLIAM REEVES
  BOOKSELLER, LTD.
1a Norbury Crescent
London SW16 4JR
England

REVERE BOOKS
P.O. Box 420
Revere, PA 18953

ALICE ROBBINS,
  BOOKSELLER
3002 Round Hill Road
Greensboro NC 27408

ROCKLAND BOOKS
1706 Rockland Avenue
Victoria, B. C. V8S 1W8
Canada

PAULETTE ROSE
360 E. 72nd Street
New York, NY 10021

ROSTENBERG & STERN -
  RARE BOOKS
40 E. 88th Street
New York, NY 10128

BERTRAM ROTA, LTD.
31 Long Acre
Covent Garden
London WC2E 9LT
England

KEN SANDERS, BOOKS
P. O. B. 26707
Salt Lake City, UT 84126

ORRIN SCHWAB - BOOKS
P. O. Box 4502
Logan, UT 84323

BUD SCHWESKA,
  BOOKSELLER
P. O. Box 754010
Parkside Station
Forest Hills, NY 11375

SECOND LIFE BOOKS
P.O. Box 242
55 Quarry Road
Lanesborough, MA 01237

SHERWOOD FINE BOOKS
5911 E. Spring St.
Suite 402
Long Beach, CA 90808

TIMOTHY P. SLONGO,
  BOOKS
714 E. Yoke St.
Indianapolis, IN 46203

A. SOKOL
Flat 5, 4 Mount Street
London W1Y 5AA
England

HENRY SOTHERAN LTD.
2 Sackville Street
Picadilly
London W1X 2DP
England

KEN SPELMAN ANTI-
  QUARIAN BOOKSELLERS
70 Micklegate
York YO1 1LF
England

BARBARA STONE
135 Kings Road, Chelsea
London SW3 4PW
England

G. W. STUART, JR.,
  RARE BOOKS
204 Madison Ave.
Yuma, AZ 85364

RAYMOND M. SUTTON, JR.
430 Main Street
P.O. Box 330
Williamsburg, KY 40769

T. A. SWINFORD,
  BOOKSELLER
7136 Main Street
Scottsdale, AZ 85251

TAURUS BOOKS
P. O. Box 716
Northampton, MA 01061

THOMAS THORP, ANTI-
  QUARIAN BOOKSELLER
9 George Street
St. Albans
Hertfordshire AL3 4ER
England

CHARLES W. TRAYLEN
Castle House
49-50 Quarry Street
Guildford
Surrey GU1 3UA
England

TREBIZOND RARE BOOKS
P.O. Box 2430
8 New Preston Hill Road
New Preston, CT 06777

ULYSSES BOOKSHOP
31 & 40 Museum Street
Bloomsbury
London WC1A 1LH
England

VIRGO BOOKS
Little Court, South Wraxall
Bradford-on-Avon
Wiltshire BA15 2SE
England

JEFF WEBER RARE BOOKS
1923 Foothill Drive
P.O. Box 3368 - 91221
Glendale, CA 01201

GRAHAM WEINER
78 Roseberry Road
London N10 2LA
England

WHELDON & WESLEY,
    LTD.
Lytton Lodge, Codicote
Hitchin
Hertfordshire SG4 8TE
England

IAN WILKINSON
Gothic House, Barker Gate
Nottingham NG1 1JU
England

WORDS ETCETERA
Hinton Lodge
Crown Road, Marnhull
Dorset DT10 1LN
England

WORLDWIDE
    ANTIQUARIAN
P.O. Box 391
Cambridge, MA 02141

XIMENES: RARE BOOKS,
    INC.
19 East 69th Street
New York, NY 10021

Bookman's
Price Index

A

ABC for Tiny Schools. Los Angeles: 1975. 3/4 x 1/2 inches; (30)ff; large calligraphic style letters, burnt orange leather with gilt title on spine; very fine, tiny bookplate of Abraham Horodisch.   Bromer Booksellers 87-202 1996 $150.00

THE A, B, C. With the Church of England Catechism. Philadelphia: printed by Young. Stewart and M'Cullock, 1785. 12mo; 6 leaves, uncut and partially unopened; some ruffling to edges, but generally as fine a copy of this fragile piece as one could hope to find. Rosenbach 99; Evans 19208.   Priscilla Juvelis 95/1-59 1996 $3,500.00

ABBADIE, JACQUES   The History of the Late Conspiracy Against the King and the Nation. London: printed for Daniel Brown, and Tho. Bennet, 1696. 1st edition in English; 8vo; contemporary calf., spine rubbing, spine bit worn, lacks label; very good. Wing A52.   Ximenes 108-1 1996 $200.00

ABBEY, EDWARD   Appalachian Wilderness: the Great Smokey Mountains. New York: Dutton, 1970. 1st edition; folio; fine in fine dust jacket, with tiny tear at crown, beautiful copy.   Between the Covers 42-2 1996 $150.00

ABBEY, EDWARD   Appalachian Wilderness. New York: Dutton, 1970. 1st edition; Photograph by Eliot Porter; near fine, brief gift inscription on front pastedown; near fine, one small stain price clipped.   Bella Luna 7-4 1996 $150.00

ABBEY, EDWARD   Black Sun. New York: Simon & Schuster, 1971. 1st edition; fine in fine dust jacket.   Book Time 2-2 1996 $165.00

ABBEY, EDWARD   Desert Solitaire. New York: McGraw-Hill Co., 1968. 1st edition; drawings by Peter Parnall; name and date on flyleaf, otherwise near fine in dust jacket which is slightly worn at spine ends. Steven C. Bernard 71-1 1996 $300.00

ABBEY, EDWARD   Fire On the Mountain. New York: Dial, 1962. 1st edition; some slight fraying to cloth at spine extremities, otherwise near fine in very good dust jacket with few small internally tape repaired edge tears and modest rubbing and hint of paper clip mark along upper edge of front panel, quite scarce, particularly signed; inscribed by author. Ken Lopez 74-1 1996 $1,250.00

ABBEY, EDWARD   The Fool's Progress. New York: Holt, 1988. 1st edition; original cloth, fine in fine dust jacket with one very tiny tear; inscribed by author.   Beasley Books 82-1 1996 $125.00

ABBEY, EDWARD   Good News. New York: Dutton, 1980. 1st edition; very near fine in dust jacket; signed by author in 1980.   Lame Duck Books 19-2 1996 $200.00

ABBEY, EDWARD   The Hidden Canyon. New York: Viking, 1977. 1st edition; fine copy in near fine dust jacket, slight wear at tips, stain inside jacket panel, signed by J. Blaustein.   Book Time 2-793 1996 $150.00

ABBEY, EDWARD   Jonathan Troy. New York: Dodd, Mead, 1954. 1st edition; author's first book; very near fine in very good dust jacket with couple of chips to head of spine and tape repair to verso; inscribed by author to a collector; scarce, not often found inscribed.   Lame Duck Books 19-1 1996 $3,000.00

ABBEY, EDWARD   The Journey Home. New York: E. P. Dutton, 1977. 1st edition; xiv, 242 pages; black cloth spine, rust paper covered boards, fine in fine dust jacket, signed by author, absolutely beautiful copy.   Orpheus Books 17-41 1996 $300.00

ABBEY, EDWARD   The Monkey Wrench Gang. Philadelphia and New York: J. B. Lippincott Co., 1975. 1st edition; 9 x 6 inches; 352 pages; black boards with red cloth spine, dust jacket; very nice.   Dawson's Books Shop 528-1 1996 $150.00

ABBEY, EDWARD   The Monkey Wrench Gang. Philadelphia: New York: Lippincott, 1975. 1st edition; remainder stripe close to spine on bottom edge, else about fine in very good dust jacket with several very short tears and a couple of small nicks, scarce.   Between the Covers 42-1 1996 $125.00

ABBEY, EDWARD   Slickrock. The Canyon Country of Southeast Utah. San Francisco: Sierra Club, 1971. Folio; photographs; fine in bright white fine dust jacket.   Thomas Dorn 9-1 1996 $250.00

ABBEY, EDWARD   Sunset Canyon. London: Talmy, Franklin, 1972. 1st U.K. edition; fine, in fine dust jacket.   Bella Luna 7-8 1996 $125.00

ABBEY, EDWARD   Vox Clamantis in Desierto. Santa Fe: Rydal Press, 1989. Publisher's over run; very fine.   Bella Luna 7-10 1996 $100.00

ABBEY, JOHN ROLAND   Catalogue of Valuable Printed Books and Fine Bindings, from the Celebrated Collection of... London: 1965-70. 4to; volumes 1-6 (of 9), xii, 279; ii, 134; viii, 233 + 10 index; iv, 52; 179; 52 pages; 216 plates; original boards and wrappers, lacking only price list to part 4.   Thomas Thorp 489-1 1996 £80.00

ABBEY, JOHN ROLAND   Life in England in Aquatint and Lithography 1770-1860. London: privately printed at the Curwen Press, 1953. Limited to 400 numbered copies, 4to; xxii, 428 pages; color frontispiece, 32 collotype plates, 50 text illustrations; brown half morocco, gilt panelled spine in 6 compartments, top edge gilt, double red and green morocco lettering pieces; handsome copy.   Thomas Thorp 489-3 1996 £400.00

ABBEY, JOHN ROLAND   Life in England in Aquatint and Lithography, 1770-1860. London: Curwen Press, 1953. 1st edition; limited to 400 numbered copies; 4to; colored frontispiece, 32 collotype plates, 50 illustrations in text; original brown cloth, red morocco spine label, headcaps and corners mildly bumped, upper hinge slightly cracked, Major Abbey's own copy with his booklabel.   Maggs Bros. Ltd. 1191-63 1996 £320.00

ABBEY, JOHN ROLAND   Scenery of Great Britain and Ireland in Aquatint and Lithography 1770-1860. London: privately printed at the Curwen Press, 1952. Limited edition of 500 numbered copies; 4to; xx, 399 pages; color frontispiece, 34 collotype plates, 54 text illustrations; brown half morocco, gilt panelled spine in 6 compartments, red and green morocco double lettering pieces, top edge gilt, handsome set. Thomas Thorp 489-2 1996 £400.00

ABBEY, JOHN ROLAND   Travel in Aquatint and Lithography 1770-1860. Folkestone & London: Dawsons of Pall Mall, 1972. Reprint of original edition of 1956-57. 4to; 2 volumes; original cloth, colored frontispiece, 36 plates, 52 illustrations in text; brown cloth, dust jackets, (1 with small tear);   Maggs Bros. Ltd. 1191-64 1996 £120.00

ABBOTT, CHARLES   A Treatise of the Law Relative to Merchant Ships and Seamen (etc.). London: ptd. for E. and R. Brooke and J. Rider...and J. Butterworth, 1802. 1st edition; new quarter calf, definite embrowning, ex-library, usable copy.   Meyer Boswell SL26-1 1996 $275.00

ABBOTT, CHARLES C.   Primitive History; or Illustrations of the Handiwork, in Stone, Bone and Clay of the Native Races of the Northern Atlantic Seaboard of America. Salem: George A. Bates, 1881. 1st edition; 8vo; viii, 560 pages, ads, 429 text illustrations; cloth; near fine. Metacomet Books 54-1 1996 $125.00

ABBOTT, EDWIN   Flatland, a Romance of Many Dimensions. San Francisco: Arion Press, 1980. One of 275 numbered copies; page size 14 x 7 inches; printed on T.H. Saunders hot-press finish mouldmade, each signed by artist/publisher, Andrew Hoyem and author Ray Bradbury; 14 line drawings and 10 diecuts by Hoyem; watercolors added by hand; bound accordion fold with 56 folded panels, aluminum covers in hinged and clasped aluminum container. Fine in original mailing carton except for thin scratch on back about 6 inches long;   Priscilla Juvelis 95/1-6 1996 $1,200.00

ABBOTT, MAUDE E.   Classified and Annotated Bibliography of Sir William Osler's Publications. Montreal: Medical Museum, McGill University, 1939. 2nd edition; 8vo; xiii, (ii), 163 pages; frontispiece, plate, 16 figures; blue cloth, very good; bookplate of Elmer Belt.   Jeff Weber 31-102 1996 $120.00

ABE, KOBO   The Woman in the Dunes. New York: Knopf, 1964. 1st U.S. edition; illustrations by author's wife, Michi; near fine in very good+, lightly spine tanned dust jacket.   Lame Duck Books 19-3 1996 $125.00

A'BECKETT, GILBERT ABBOTT 1811-1856　The Comic History of England. (with) The Comic History of Rome. London: Bradbury & Evans, 1847-8 & n.d. 1st editions; tall octavo; 3 volumes, half titles present, pages xii, 308; xvii, 310, 304; illustrations by John Leech, 30 hand colored steel engraved plates and more than 300 woodcuts in text; elegant black crushed morocco, elaborate triple gilt rules, spine decorations and dentelles, marbled endpapers, top edge gilt, handsome set; slight rubbing to hinges, but unusually fine set. Tooley 297, 298. Hartfield 48-A1　1996 $495.00

ABEEL, DAVID　Journal of a Residence in China, and the Neighboring Countries... New York: J. Abeel Williamson, 1836. 2nd edition; 12mo; 378 pages; original cloth, paper spine label, cloth faded.　Kenneth Karmiole 1NS-73　1996 $100.00

ABERCROMBIE, LASCELLES　Lyrics and Unfinished Poems. Newtown: Gregynog Press, 1940. Limited to 175 numbered copies; 4to; xii, 83 pages; original black morocco backed marbled boards, spine gilt, edges uncut.　Thomas Thorp 489-4　1996 £125.00

ABERCROMBIE, P.　Cumbrian Regional Planning Scheme, Prepared for the Cumbrian Regional Joint Advisory Scheme. Liverpool University Press, 1932. 1st edition; large 4to; pages xviii, 220; frontispiece, 25 maps and diagrams, 18 plates; original cloth backed boards, dust jacket little torn and defective; title little spotted.　R.F.G. Hollett & Son　78-652　1996 £85.00

ABERNETHY, JOHN　The Surgical and Physiological Works of... London: Longman, et al, 1830. octavo; 4 volumes; volumes 1 and 2 in early quarter sheep, volumes 3 and 4 in original sheep with new cloth backs; ex-library with usual markings, other than some foxing internally, a good set. Iowa 731-32.　James Tait Goodrich K40-2　1996 $195.00

ABERNETHY, JOHN　Surgical Observations on Injuries of the Head; and On Miscellaneous Subjects. Philadelphia: printed for Thomas Dobson, 1811. 162 pages; frontispiece; original boards, uncut, spine chipped, hinges cracked, front inner hinge repaired); Austin, Early American Medical Imprints 3.　Kenneth Karmiole 1NS-175　1996 $150.00

ABERT, JAMES WILLIAM　Report of the Secretary of War...A Report and Map of the Examination of New Mexico. Washington: Senate Executive Document 23, 1848. 1st edition; 132 pages; 24 plates, large folding map; original printed yellow wrappers, minor chipping and neatly rebacked; tall, untrimmed copy, some foxing to map, plates quite crisp and clean; fine; formerly the copy of Lindley Eberstadt; presentation copy from U.S. Senator Roger Sherman Baldwin to Yale Library. Goetzmann pp. 144-49; Streeter Sale 168; Howes A11; Graff 5. Michael D. Heaston 23-1　1996 $1,850.00

ABERT, JAMES WILLIAM　Western America in 1846-1847. San Francisco: John Howell Books, 1966. 2nd edition, limited to 3000 copies; folio; (12), 116 pages; colored frontispiece, 13 colored plates, 2 plans, 2 folding maps, text illustrations; tan cloth, gilt, very fine.　Argonaut Book Shop　113-3　1996 $100.00

ABRAHAM, GEORGE D.　Motor Ways in Lakeland. London: Methuen & Co., 1913. 1st edition; 8vo; pages xi, 307, 30, 24 illustrations and map; original cloth, gilt, spine rather faded, small snag to head and upper hinge; fore-edge and endpapers little spotted; presentation copy, inscribed by author.　R.F.G. Hollett & Son　78-656　1996 £65.00

ABRAMS, ALBERT　Transactions of the Antiseptic Club. New York: 1895. 1st edition; 205 pages; numerous woodcut illustrations; original binding, backstrip soiled and spotted.　W. Bruce Fye　71-12　1996 $100.00

ACADEMY OF PACIFIC COAST HISTORY　Publications. Berkeley: University of California, 1910-11. Large 8vo; 2 volumes; (10), 358; (12), 358 pages; 9 plates; contemporary black calf over buckram, gilt spine. Kenneth Karmiole 1NS-61　1996 $100.00

ACADEMY OF PACIFIC COAST HISTORY　Publications. Berkeley: University of California Press, 1910-19. 5 volumes; numerous maps, illustrations; bound from original parts in three quarter morocco and cloth, gilt lettered spines, very fine set.　Argonaut Book Shop 113-4 1996 $500.00

ACADEMY OF SCIENCE OF ST. LOUIS　Transactions. 1857-91. 5 volumes; 726 pages, 21 plates; 602 pages, 13 plates; 602, 286 pages, plates 2-5; 688, 134 pages, 13 plates; 629, 66 pages, 15 plates; later red cloth, all ex-library.　Bookworm & Silverfish 280-1　1996 $450.00

AN ACCOUNT Of All the Manors, Messuages, Lands, Tenements and Hereditaments in the Different Counties of England and Wales, Held by lease from the Crown. London: printed by Stafford and Davenport for S. Hooper & Messrs. Robinsons, 1787. 1st edition; oblong folio; contemporary tree calf, gilt, spine gilt. Fine, handsome copy. Kress B1147.　Ximenes 108-96　1996 $350.00

AN ACCOUNT of the Ceremony in Westminster Hall on Thursday May 9th, 1935... Cambridge University Press, 1935. Small 4to; printed in black, red, blue and green on Head's handmade; 2 photos; decorative initials; full blue morocco gilt, covers just little spotted, but very nice in cloth wrapper and matching slipcase.　Bertram Rota 272-63　1996 £50.00

ACCOUNT of the County Stock Levied and raised by the County of Cumberland, and Of Other Sums Cararied to the Credit Thereof, for the Year Ending at the Easter Quarter Sessions, 1849... Carlisle: C. Thurnam, 1849. 8vo; 42 pages; disbound as issued, outer leaves trifle creased and dusty.　R.F.G. Hollett & Son 78-658　1996 £65.00

AN ACCOUNT of the New Sheriffs, Holding Their Office. Made Public Upon Reason of Conscience, Respecting Themselves and Others, in Regard to the Act for Corporations. London: printed for Thos. Snowden, 1680. Folio; 4 pages; uncut, disbound. Wing A333.　H. M. Fletcher 121-33　1996 £65.00

AN ACCOUNT of the Origin, Progress and Consequences of the Late Discontents of the Army on the Madras Establishment. London: printed for T. Cadell, and W. Davies, 1810. 1st edition; 8vo; original pale blue boards, drab paper backstrip, printed paper label (slight wear), fine copy in original condition. 5 copies in NUC.　Ximenes 109-162　1996 $375.00

AN ACCOUNT of the Proceedings at the Guild-Hall of the City of London, on Saturday September 12, 1679. London: 1679. Folio; 4 pages; disbound, Wing A356b.　H. M. Fletcher　121-34　1996 £75.00

AN ACCOUNT of the Rise and Progress of the Indian or Spasmodic Cholera; with a Particular Description of the Symptoms Attending the Disease. New Haven: L.H. Young, 1832. 1st edition; 12mo; 48 pages; folding map, one fold torn without loss; original printed wrappers, early corners frayed, foxed. B&B 10790.　M & S Rare Books　60-447　1996 $125.00

ACCUM, FREDERICK　A Practical Treatise on Gas-Light... London: printed by G. Hayden for R. Ackermann, 1815. 1st edition; 8vo; (2), iii, v, (1), 186 pages, 7 hand colored plates, 2 of which are folding, and 2 woodcuts; contemporary half morocco, rebacked with original red morocco spine label laid down; bookplate removed from front pasatedown, few scuff marks on binding, else fine, uncut; Singer Hist. of Tech. IV 268-274; Zeitlinger 22; Honeyman Sale I 10.　Edwin V. Glaser 121-1　1996 $2,400.00

AN ACCURATE Account of the Trial of William Corder for the Murder of Maria Marten...To Which are Added, An Explantory Preface and Fifty-Three of the Letters Sent by Various Ladies, in Answer to Corder's Matrimonial Advertisements... London: Pubished by George Foster, n.d., c. 1828. 2nd edition; 12mo; the printer appears to have left off the page number 14 as the consecutive pages are 13 to 15 and text appears continuous, pages 52 to 57 are out of order, some light spotting and browning; contemporary calf, red morocco label, upper joint starting, some knocking of corners and rubbing, generally light, without portrait; signature and address of H. J. Kirby on free endpaper, cropped signature of Jane Waldo on title.　James Cummins 14-140　1995 $200.00

ACHAD, FRATER　The Egyptian Revival: or the Evercoming Sun in the Light of the Tarot. Chicago: 1923. 1st edition; iimited to 1001 copies, this being number 8; signed; cloth, very good+.　Middle Earth 77-Addendum-432　1996 $245.00

ACHEBE, CHINUA　Things Fall Apart. New York: McDowell, Obolensky, 1959. 1st American edition; advance review copy with publisher's slip laid in; very good plus in very good dust jacket with light edge wear. Thomas Dorn　9-7　1996 $100.00

ACHILLES TATIUS　De Dlitophontis et leucippes Amoribus Libri VIII. Heidelberg: Commelin, 1606. 8vo; title within border, 1 f., 396 ff. num.; contemporary Parisian crimson morocco, covers panelled gilt with outer and inner triple rule, border empty, panel decorated to a fanfare pattern of compartments outlined by a single and double fillet and filled with small tools, background of gyrate and leafy spray tools, central oval panel empty, flat spine similarly patterned, titled later at head and foot, all edges gilt, later endpapers, corners soft, two pairs of ties gone, preserved in cloth box. From the collection of "Potier, Paris, 1853"; Sir Edward Sullivan with his ex-libris, his sale, lot 14 Sotheby's May 19, 1890; J. R. Abbey with his ex-libris, his sale lot, Sotheby's June 21, 1965 to H. M. Fletcher.　Marlborough 160-11　1996 $2,100.00

ACHILLES TATIUS   The Loves of Clitophon and Leucippe. Oxford: printed by William Turner for John Allam, 1638. 1st edition of this translation; crown 8vo; A8, a4, B-R8, lacking frontispiece, contemporary sheep roughly rebacked. STC 91.   H. M. Fletcher 121-57 1996 £285.00

ACKERMANN, RUDOLPH 1764-1834   The History of the Abbey Church of St. Peter's Westminster, Its Antiquities and Monuments. London: 1812. Large 4to; 2 volumes; xviii pages; 1 f. (binders), 330 pages, 3 ff. (index), half title, title, 275 pages, 2 ff. with aquatint portrait, engraved plan, color aquatint frontispiece and 80 colored aquatint plates, half morocco, rebound, using original gilt spines, top edge gilt. Abbey Scenery 213; Tooley pp. 1-5.   Marlborough 162-103 1996 £500.00

ACKERMANN, RUDOLPH 1764-1834   The History of the Charter-House. London: Ackermann, 1816. Large 4to; title, 332 pages, engraved aquatint portrait proof to frontispiece in laid india paper, 5 hand colored aquatint plates; red straight grain morocco, marbled boards (worn), contemporary red morocco label, gilt lettered, gilt roll tool border; some offsetting, otherwise finely coored early issue. Pencil note suggests this is "The Rev. P. Fisher's copy, master of the Charter-House to whom this work is dedicated". Bookplate of W. Russell Button.   Marlborough 162-1 1996 £350.00

ACKERMANN, RUDOLPH 1764-1834   The History of the Colleges of Winchester, Eton and Westminster, with the Charter-House, the Schools of St. Paul's, Merchant Taylor's and Rugby and the Free-School of Christ's Hospital. London: Ackermann, 1816. 4to; 3ff. (lacks binder's leaf), pages 56, 72, 40, 32, 43, 34, 27, 22, 48 hand colored aquatint plates, plate 26 in second state, few plates offset, as usual; later red straight grain morocco gilt, all edges gilt, by Frost. Abbey scenery 438. Marlborough 162-2 1996 £3,500.00

ACKERMANN, RUDOLPH 1764-1834   A History of the University of Cambridge, Its Colleges, Halls and Public Buildings. London: R. Ackermann, 1815. 4to; 2 volumes, xii pages (lacks binder's leaf), 296, 3 ff; 2 ff, 324 pages, 4 ff; 95 hand colored aquatint plates; contemporary green straight grain morocco, gilt, elaborate gilt and blindstamped borders, later rebacked (green calf in contemporary style, minimal offsetting), all edges gilt; good crisp set; on J. Whatman paper, 1812. Abbey Scenery 80. Tooley 5; Prideaux p. 126.   Marlborough 162-3 1996 £5,000.00

ACKERMANN, RUDOLPH 1764-1834   A History of the University of Oxford, Its Colleges, Halls and Public Buildings. London: Ackermann, 1814. 4to; (lacks half title i/ii), iii-xiv, 1 f. first issue list of plates, xxv, 275 pages, 3 ff. index (lacks half title), title, 262 pages, 3 ff. index, 115 plates (all hand colored aquatints, except pl. 2, 65 are views and the rest costume plates and portraits of the Founders), plates 1, 39, 50, 74 an d78 are 1st state plates, 15, 84 and 94 in second state; half burgundy morocco by Sangorski, all edges gilt. Abbey Scenery 280; Tooley p. 14.   Marlborough 162-4 1996 £3,500.00

ACKERMANN, RUDOLPH 1764-1834   A History of the University of Oxford, Its Colleges, Halls and Public Buildings. London: R. Ackermann, 1814. 4to; 2 volumes; pages xiv, (ii), 275, (1) (blank), (6) (index); (iv), 262, (6) (index); 2 frontispieces, 62 plates, aquatints, 6 with double views, all hand colored, 17 colored line and stipple plates, uncolored stipple engraved portrait, half titles present, plates and text in excellent state, although plates offset, expert paper repair to blank fore-margins of two leaves in gathering Hh, volume 2, corner of last leaf volume 2 creased, wide margins; early 20th century three quarter crushed polished blue morocco, for Henry Sotheran, backstrips with gilt decorated raised bands, lettered direct in second and third compartments, remainder gilt panelled, pale blue cloth sides, marbled endpapers, red markers, entirely untrimmed; excellent; bookplate of Thomas Ramsden of Middton Tower, King's Lynn. Abbey Scenery 278-280; Clary 113; Cordeaux-Merry Univ. 25; Tooley 5.   Blackwell's B112-219 1996 £3,200.00

ACKERMANN, RUDOLPH 1764-1834   Microcosm of London. London: Ackermann, 1808-10. Large 4to; 3 volumes; woodcut title, engraved title, half title, 1 f. contents, pages i-iv, 231; woodcut title, engraved title, half title, 1 f. contents, pages iii-vi, 239; woodcut title, engraved title, half title, 1 f. contents, pages iii-iv, 280, 3 ff. index, 104 hand colored aquatint plates after Rowlandson and Pugin; original wrappers (to parts 2-4, 6-8; 11, 14-16; 20, 21, 24-26) bound in; one or two tears and repairs, some offsetting, foxing, near contemporary black half morocco, gilt panelled spines, raised bands, all edges gilt, slight wear to edges; fine tall copy with wide margins; fine set.   Marlborough 162-104 1996 £8,500.00

ACKROYD, PETER   Country Life. London: Ferry Press, 1978. One of 350 copies; tall stapled wrappers, little rust on staples and one corner little bumped, still very near fine; inscribed by author to American Poet Howard Moss.   Between the Covers 42-3 1996 $475.00

ACKROYD, PETER   London Lickpenny. London: Ferry Press, 1973. Limited to 500 copies, this one of 26, this letter G, signed by author, with additional holograph poem; wrappers, near fine.   Virgo Books 48-2 1996 £120.00

ACLAND, HENRY W.   The Oxford Museum. London: Smith, Elder and Co., 1859. 1st edition; 8vo; 112, 4 pages ads; 1 folding plan and lithograph plate; contemporary mauve blindstamped and gilt lettered cloth, corners of boards slightly bumped, otherwise clean copy. Wise 83.   Sotheran PN32-170 1996 £148.00

ACOSTA, JOSE DE   Historia Natural Y Moral De Las Indias. Seville: Juan de Leon Leon, 1590. 1st Spanish Language edition; 4to; 536, (36) pages; contemporary vellum, title lightly soiled, overall very clean, this copy contains final 2 leaves, but does not contain the license leaf with errata (not found in all copies); Palau 1980.   Kenneth Karmiole 1NS-147 1996 $4,000.00

ACTON, HAROLD   Memoirs of an Aesthete. London: 1948. 1st edition; very good in dust jacket torn at head and foot of spine, also torn on corners.   Words Etcetera 94-6 1996 £55.00

ACTON, WILLIAM   Prostitution, Considered In Its Moral, Social and Sanitary Aspects, in London and Other Large Cities. London: John Churchill, 1857. 1st edition; 8vo; ix, (3), 189, 3 pages, 32 pages of publisher's ads at end; original dark brown cloth embossed in blind, spine rather worn and frayed at head and foot, internally very good, complete with half title.   John Drury 82-1 1996 £150.00

ADAIR, JOHN   Hints on the Culture of Ornamental Plants in Ireland. London: 1878. 8vo; cloth, very good, scarce.   C. P. Hyland 216-1 1996 £75.00

ADAIR, ROBERT   Sketch of the Character of the Late Duke of Devonshire. London: printed by William Bulmer and Co., 1811. 1st edition; one of 50 copies; small 4to; 28 pages, half title, engraved portrait (offset onto title); contemporary half calf, neatly rebacked; Martin, Privately printed books p. 197.   James Burmester 29-2 1996 £90.00

ADAIR, ROBERT   Sketch of the Character of the Late Duke of Devonshire. London: printed by William Bulmer, 1811. One of 50 copies; 4to; pages 28; mezzotint portrait offset on tile; printed on Furness & Co. paper dated 1804; contemporary dark blue straight grained morocco, elaborately decorated in gold and blind, blue watered silk endpapers similarly decorated, all edges gilt, hinges and edges worn, upper hinge cracked and weak, but held on cords; very good; bookplate and stamp of the Writers Library to which it was donated by Alexander Fullerton. Claude Cox 107-25 1996 £65.00

ADAM, R. B.   The R. B. Adam Library Relating to Dr. Samuel Johnson and His Era. London: Oxford University, 1929. Limited to 500 copies; 4to; 3 volumes; plates, facsimiles; original binding, fine in dust jackets with darkened spines and slipcase.   Charles Agvent 4-759 1996 $400.00

ADAM, W.   The Gem of the Peak; or Matlock Bath and its Vicinity. Derby: Henry Mozley & Sons; W. Adam, Matlock Bath; Goodwin, Bakewell... 1845. 4th edition; 12mo; folding map as frontispiece, folding intaglio map, 8 tinted lithograph paltes; illustrations in text; original cloth, spine slightly faded, uncut, nice.   Anthony W. Laywood 108-147 1996 £90.00

ADAMS, ANDREW LEITH   Field and Forest Rambles. London: 1873. frontispiece and title, few text illustrations; folding map; original cloth; excellent copy.   David A.H. Grayling MY95Orn-1 1996 £70.00

ADAMS, ANDREW LEITH   Wanderings of a Naturalist in India. Edinburgh: Edmonston & Douglas, 1867. 1st edition; 8vo; xi, 333 pages; c half calf, raised bands, gilt compartments, leather labels, fine.   David Mason 71-89 1996 $160.00

ADAMS, ANSEL   Born Free and Equal. New York: 1944. 1st edition; photos; wrappers, very rare, spine faded and chipped at base.   J. B. Muns 154-1 1996 $600.00

ADAMS, ANSEL   Making a Photograph: an Introduction to Photography. London: & New York: Studio Publications, 1935. 1st edition; 96 pages; 32 tipped in photographic plates by Adams; black cloth and illustrated boards in somewhat worn but presentable dust jacket, bookplate on front pastedown endpaper with glue residue offset on front free endpaper; overall very good.   Blue River Books 9-1 1996 $150.00

ADAMS, ANSEL   My Camera in the National Parks. Yosemite: 1950. 1st edition; folio; 30 photos with text; dust jacket torn, signed.   J. B. Muns 154-2 1996 $500.00

ADAMS, ANSEL   The Pageant of History and the Panorama of Today in Northern California. San Francisco; American Trust Co., 1954. 1st edition; thin folio; superb fine screen halftone reproductions of photos by Adams; stiff pictorial wrappers, spiral bound; very fine, with scarce illustrated cardboard slipcase. Scarce in this condition.   Argonaut Book Shop 113-6 1996 $225.00

ADAMS, ANSEL   The Portfolios. New York Graphic Society, 1977. 1st printing; illustrations; dust jacket.   J. B. Muns 154-5 1996 $100.00

ADAMS, ANSEL   Sierra Nevada: the John Muir Trail. Berkeley: 1938. Limited to 500 signed and numbered copies; 50 tipped in half tones, in handsome slipcase, mint, rare.   J. B. Muns 154-6 1996 $3,200.00

ADAMS, ANSEL   Taos Pueblos. Boston: New York Graphic Society, 1977. Limited edition, signed; slipcase, half leather; mint.   J. B. Muns 154-10 1996 $1,200.00

ADAMS, ANSEL   Yosemite and the Range of Light. New York Graphic Society, 1979. Oblong 4to; signed; dust jacket.   J. B. Muns 154-7 1996 $300.00

ADAMS, ANSEL   Yosemite and the Range of Light. New York Graphic Society, 1979. 1st edition; dust jacket; not signed.   J. B. Muns 154-8 1996 $175.00

ADAMS, ANSEL   Yosemite and the Range of Light. Boston: 1979. 1st edition; 12.5 x 15.5 inches; 116 photos; cloth, one corner bumped, else good in worn dust jacket, label signed by Adams.   John K. King 77-574 1996 $195.00

ADAMS, DANIEL   The Medical and Agricultural Register, for the Years 1806 and 1807. Boston: Loring and Manning et al, 1806-07. Volume I 1-24, all published; contemporary leather backed boards, front endpaper little loose,, otherwise nice, tight copy; scarce complete run. Imprints 10842.   Second Life Books 103-2 1996 $400.00

ADAMS, EDWARD   The Polychromatic Ornament of Italy. London: G. W. Nickisson, n.d. 1846. 1st edition; 4to; iv, 16 pages, 11 chromlithographic plates; original cloth spine, boards; the original wrappers are very worn with some thumbing and foxing, very faint waterstains on top and bottom margins of a few plates, not affecting illustrations. RIBA 729.   Bookpress 75-1 1996 $585.00

ADAMS, FRANCIS COLBURN   Our World; or, the Democrat's Rule. London: Sampson, Low, Son and Co., 1855. 1st English edition; 8vo; 2 volumes; original grey green cloth, traces of rubbing; fine, very rare edition; cf. Wright li 13; cf. Hamitlon 199 (American printing).   Ximenes 109-1 1996 $850.00

ADAMS, FREDERICK B.   Bookbindings by T. J. Cobden-Sanderson. An Exhibition at the Pierpont Morgan Library. New York: Pierpont Morgan Library, 1969. 1st edition; 4to; 36 full page plates; 32 pages; cloth, original printed wrappers bound in. Scarce.   Forest Books 74-2 1996 £70.00

ADAMS, FREDERICK UPHAM   John Henry Smith. A Humorous Romance of Outdoor Life. New York: Doubleday Page, 1905. 1st edition; illustrations by A. B. Frost; patched of light rubbing to fore edge and extremities, still near fine with splendid pictorial label by Frost. Captain's Bookshelf 38-7 1996 $125.00

ADAMS, GEORGE   Astronomical and Geographical Essays... London: printed for the author by R. Hindmarsh, 1790. 2nd edition; 8vo; 599 pages + 15 page catalog; rebound in modern leather and marbled endpapers, gilt spine titling, corner torn from titlepage, previous owner's name written and stamped in several places on prelim pages, scattered light foxing, otherwise good copy.   Knollwood Books 70-14 1996 $400.00

ADAMS, GEORGE   Essays on the Microscope. London: 1798. 2nd edition; 4to; 2 volumes; with volume of 32 plates; covers detached, contents clean.   Petersfield Bookshop FH58-131 1996 £275.00

ADAMS, H. G.   The Smaller British Birds, with Descriptions of their Nests, Eggs, Habits, Etc. London: 1894. Royal 8vo; pages iv, 252, 32 colored plates; original cloth. Signature on titlepage partly erased. Wheldon & Wesley 207-620 1996 £60.00

ADAMS, HENRY 1838-1918   Democarcy an American Novel. New York: 1880. 1st edition; original decorated mustard cloth; very good+. Stephen Lupack 83- 1996 $125.00

ADAMS, HENRY 1838-1918   Democracy. An American Novel. London: Macmillan and Co., 1882. 1st English edition; 8vo; 280 pages; contemporary pebbled green cloth (trial binding?). Very scarce.   M & S Rare Books 60-101 1996 $200.00

ADAMS, HENRY 1838-1918   The Education of Henry Adams. Boston: Limited Editions Club, 1942. Copy number 904 from a total edition of 1500 numbered copies signed by Samuel Chamberlain; etchings by Samuel Chamberlain; fine in newly made slipcase.   Hermitage SP95-930 1996 $100.00

ADAMS, J. N.   A Bibliography of Nineteenth Century Legal Literature. London: Avero Publications Ltd., & Chadwyck-Healey Ltd., 1992-95. 3 volumes.   Meyer Boswell SL25-1 1996 $2,195.00

ADAMS, JAMES   The Dartmoor Prison; or, a Faithful Narrative of the Massacre of American Seamen. To which is Added a Sketch of the Treatment of Prisoners, During the Late War, by the British Government. Pittsburgh: printed by S. Engles, 1816. 1st edition; 16mo; 84 pages; contemporary calf backed boards, spine cracked, moderate waterstaining and considerable browning throughout. Rare. S&S 36676; not in Sabin. M & S Rare Books 60-427 1996 $750.00

ADAMS, JAMES H.   Message of His Excellency James H. Adams to the Legislature of South Carolina, at Session in 1855. Columbia: R. W. Gibbes, Printer to the Senate, 1855. 8vo; 17 pages; printed wrappers, unopened and fine. Not listed in Turnbull.   Andrew Cahan 47-184 1996 $100.00

ADAMS, JEREMY DUQUESNAY   A Leaf from the Letters of St. Jerome First Printed by Sixtus Riessinger, Rome c. 1466-1467. Los Angeles: London: Zeitlin & Ver Brugge, H. M. Fletcher, 1981. Colophon: "300 copies set in Monotype Janson and Printed letterpress on Frankfurt Cream paper by Patrick Reagh and Vance Gerry, Los Angeles, California, June 1981". (probably closer to 200 copies); folio; 30 pages, specimen leaf printed by Riessinger inserted in pocket at end; quarter vellum, marbled boards, as new.   H. M. Fletcher 121-1 1996 £125.00

ADAMS, JOHN 1735-1826   An Address to the Convention for Framing a New Constitution of Government, for the State of Massachusetts Bay to Their Constituents. Boston: White and Adams, 1780. 1st edition; 12mo; 18 pages, with half title; crudely sewn, half title damaged at inner margin and resewn further in half title, also soiled, good margins to text, but corners clipped and some erratic trimming to outer margins. Evans 16843.   M & S Rare Books 60-371 1996 $650.00

ADAMS, JOHN 1735-1826   A Defence of the Constitutions of Government of the United States of America, Against the Attack of M. Turgot in His Letter to Dr. Price, Dated the Twenty-Second Day of March, 1778. London: John Stockdale, 1794. New edition; 8vo; 3 volumes, plate, portrait, 8, xxxii, 392; (2), 451, (1); (2), 528, (36) pages, bound without half titles; early 19th century calf, from the library of Francies Mary Richardson Currer with her bookplate in each volume. Sabin 235; Goldsmiths 15903.   C. R. Johnson 37-49 1996 £350.00

ADAMS, JOHN QUINCY 1767-1848   Discurso del Ex-President de los Estados Unidos...en la Camara de Representantes de Washington. mayo 25 de 1836. Mejico: 1836. 1st edition; 22 pages; sewn as issued, minor foxing, very good, laid in half morocco slipcase; rare. Streeter Texas 847.   Michael D. Heaston 23-2 1996 $600.00

ADAMS, JOHN S.   Answers to Seventeen Objections Against Spiratul Intercourse and Inquiries Relating to the Manifestions of the Present Time. New York: Fowlers & Wells, 1853. 1st edition; 12mo; 86 pages; original cloth.   M & S Rare Books 60-411 1996 $125.00

ADAMS, JULIUS J.   Challenge: a Study in Negro Leadership. New York: Wendell Malliet Co., 1949. 1st edition; fine in lightly worn, very good plus dust jacket with few small chips; inscribed by author to Justice Frances E. Rivers.   Between the Covers 43-240 1996 $165.00

ADAMS, NATHANIEL   Annals of Portsmouth (New Hampshire), Comprising a Period of Two Hundred Years from the First Settlement of the Town... Portsmouth: pub. by the author, 1825. 8vo; 400 pages; original mottled calf, green spine label, extremities rubbed. Howes A70. Kenneth Karmiole 1NS-8 196 $100.00

ADAMS, RAMON F.   The Adams One-Fifty: a Checklist of the 150 Most Important Books on Western Outlaws and Lawmen (with) Six Score: the 120 Best Books on the Range Cattle Industry. Austin: Jenkins Pub. Co., 1976. 1st edition; quarto; 2 volumes; illustrations; printed boards with publisher's slipcase with printed paper label, slipcase slightly worn, else very fine set.   Argonaut Book Shop 113-15 1996 $250.00

ADAMS, RAMON F.   Burs Under the Saddle: a Second Look at Books and Histories of the West. Norman: University of Oklahoma Press, 1964. 1st edition; vii, 610 pages; original tan cloth, gilt lettered spine, very fine with dust jacket.   Argonaut Book Shop 113-7 1996 $225.00

ADAMS, RAMON F.   More Burs Under the Saddle: Books and Histories of the West. Norman: University of Oklahoma Press, 1979. 1st edition; xv, 182 pages; original cloth, very fine with dust jacket. Argonaut Book Shop 113-11 1996 $100.00

ADAMS, RAMON F.   The Old-Time Cowhand. New York: Macmillan Co., 1961. Special first edition, one of 350 numbered copies, signed by author and by artist; x, 354 pages; black and white drawings by Nick Eggenhofer; pictorial cloth stamped in brown, gilt lettering on spine, very fine with publisher's slipcase (paper label on slipcase). Six Guns 12. Argonaut Book Shop 113-12 1996 $225.00

ADAMS, RAMON F.   Six-Guns and Saddle Leather. Norman: University of Oklahoma Press, 1954. 1st edition; xiii, 426 pages; fine, with printed dust jacket.   Argonaut Book Shop 113-14 1996 $125.00

ADAMS, RAMON F.   Six-Guns and Saddle Leather. Norman: University of Oklahoma Press, 1954. 1st edition; 8vo; fine in faintly worn dust jacket.   Glenn Books 36-1 1996 $125.00

ADAMS, RAMON F.   Six-Guns and Saddle Leather, a Bibliography of Books and Pamphlets on Western Outlaws and Gunman. Norman: University of Oklahoma, 1954. 1st edition; xiii, 426 pages; facsimiles of titlepages; original cloth, dust jacket; very good/very good plus, jacket with some wear; Jenkins BTB B3.   Bohling Book Co. 192-109 1996 $100.00

ADAMS, THOMAS   A Study of Rural Conditions and Problems in Canada. Ottawa: Commission of Conservation, Canada, 1917. 25.5 cm; (xi), 281 pages; illustrations, portraits, folding maps and plans; gilt stamped brown cloth; very good.   Rockland Books 38-2 1996 $100.00

ADAMS, W. H. DAVENPORT   Windsor Castle and the Water-Way Thither. London: Marcus Ward & Co., 1880. 4to; 144 pages; 74 illustrations, 12 chromolithographs; contemporary half leather, cloth, raised bands; some light rubbing at extremities, otherwise fine with nice color plates.   David Mason 71-18 1996 $240.00

ADCOCK, ST. JOHN   Wonderful London. London: Fleetway House, 1926-27. 1st edition; post 4to; 3 volumes: (8), 384; (viii) 385-768; (viii), 770-1152 pages; colored frontispiece, over 1200 photogravure illustrations, folding map; original binding, gilt, few very minor marks, but very good set.   Ash Rare Books Zenzybyr-1 1996 £65.00

ADDISON, C. G.   The Knights Templars. London: 1853. 3rd edition; 8vo; vii, 315 pages, tinted lithos; half calf, small library label with 'withdraw stamp', no other markings; very good, neat Government Crest on spine and front board.   K Books 442-320 1996 £55.00

ADDISON, G. A.   Indian Reminiscences or the Bengal Moofussul Miscellany Chiefly Written by... London: Edward Bull, 19 Holles St., 1837. 1st edition; 8vo; half title, (v-vii),, (ix-xv), 3-6, 7-399 pages, Notice to the Public to face title, bookplate removed from front pastedown leaving some traces; full speckled calf, gilt ruled borders, upper hinge partially cracked, gilt tooling to compartments, raised bands to spine, title label missing from spine, edges speckled, marbled endpapers. Good copy. Beeleigh Abbey BA56-32 1996 £175.00

ADDISON, JOSEPH 1672-1719   The Miscellaneous Works in Verse and Prose... London: for J. and R. Tonson, 1765. 8vo; 4 volumes; frontispiece in volume 1, frontispiece in volume 2, contemporary finely spirnkled tan calf, smooth spines ruled across in gilt, red morocco lettering pieces, black oval numbering pieces, blue sprinkled edges; little rubbing, unobtrusive marks to foot of spine of volumes 3 and 4 where old shelf labels removed, excellent set; ex-Coventry City Libraries with bookplates etc. on front and back pastedowns (no borrowing recorded) and with ink library stamp on blank verso of each title, presented to the library by John Gulson.   Simon Finch 24-1 1996 £200.00

ADDISON, JOSEPH 1672-1719   Remarks on Several Parts of Italy, &c. in the Years 1701, 1702, 1703. London: printed for Jacob Tonson, 1705. 1st edition; 8vo; contemporary speckled calf, spine gilt, spine rubbed, but sound; nice copy, complete with half title. Pine Coffin 701.2; CBEL II 1100.   Ximenes 108-2 1996 $350.00

ADDISON, JOSEPH 1672-1719   Remarks on Several Parts of Italy, etc. In the Years 1701-1703. London: J. and R. Tonson, 1736. 12mo; 304 pages, plus index; original polished calf boards, panelled in blind, recent handsome rebacking, raised bands, gilt and blind tooling, gilt on red leather label; occasional engraved decorations in text, very good. CBEL II 604.   Hartfield 48-L1 1996 $295.00

ADDISON, THOMAS   A Collection of the Published Writings. London: 1868. 1st edition; 242 pages; original binding.   W. Bruce Fye 71-19 1996 $250.00

THE ADDRESSES of the Freeholders of the County of Middlesex, Made and Delivered in Writing the Third Day of This Instant March 1680 at Hampstead Heath Unto Sir William Roberts Kt. and Bt. and William Ranton, Esq. after they were Declared to be... London: ptd. for Francis Smith, at the Elephant and Castle in Cornhill, 1680. Folio; 2 pages; disbound; Wing A548.   H. M. Fletcher 121-41 1996 £65.00

ADE, GEORGE   The Girl Proposition: a Bunch of He and She Fables. New York: Russell & Russell, 1908. 1st edition; 16mo; attractive pictorial label on front pastedown; near fine; signed by Ade in 1909.   Captain's Bookshelf 38-8 1996 $100.00

ADLER, ALFRED   The Neurotic Constitution: Outlines of a Comparative Individualistic Psychology and Psychotherapy. New York: Moffat, Yard and Co., 1916. 1st edition in English; 8vo; blue cloth, gilt spine; very good; Smith Ely Jelliffe's copy, signed on titlepage, with his bookplate and long note opposite titlepage about translation. Grinstein 405.   John Gach 150-4 1996 $125.00

ADLER, JANKEL   Jankel Adler. London: Nicholson & Watson, 1948. 1st edition; quarto; 38 full page reproductions, of which 13 are in color; original binding, top edge dusty, endpapers browned, upper hinge cracked, page edges slightly browned, good in chipped, torn, creased, rubbed, marked and dusty, internally sellotape marked dust jacket darkened at edges and missing a few small pieces.   Ulysses 39-2 1996 £110.00

ADLER, JEREMY   To Cythera! Alphabox Press, 1993. One of only 30 numbered copies, signed by author and artist, each plate numbered, signed and dated; folio; text printed in 14 pt. Fournier on Arches at Libanus Press, Marlborough; unbound leaves laid into blue morocco and Ingres folder, lettered in blind, fine in slipcase.   Bertram Rota 272-14 1996 £750.00

ADLER, JEREMY   Triplets: 24 Poems. Alphabox Press, 1980. One of 40 numbered copies, this one of 30 for sale, signed by author and artist, each plate numbered and signed; 4to; text set by author and printed at Fachhochschule Aachen; unbound leaves in patterned paper box with printed label; fine.   Bertram Rota 272-13 1996 £400.00

ADOLPHUS, JOHN   Memoirs of John Bannister. London: Richard Bentley, 1839. Thick 8vo; 2 volumes; extra illustrated with approximately 140 plates, an original wash drawing of the Surrey Theatre by Thomas H. Shepherd; choicely bound in full crimson morocco, 3 line gilt border, fully gilt spine in 6 compartments, morocco doublures, all edges gilt, by Riveire.   Charles W. Traylen 117-60 1996 £950.00

AELIANUS, CLAUDIUS   De Historia Animalium Libri XVII. Leyden: Guliel. Rovillium, 1575. Reissue of 1562 printing; Small 8vo; (16), 668, (37) pages; woodcut device on title, woodcut headpieces and initials; contemporary vellum, lightly browned, very good. Casey Wood p. 180; BMC 195; Durling 41 for 1562 printing;   Edwin V. Glaser 121-2 1996 $750.00

AESOPUS   Baby's Own Aesop. London: Routledge, 1887. 1st edition; colored illustrations by Walter Crane, printed by Edmund Evans; cloth backed glazed pictorial boards, corners knocked, spine slightly rubbed, else very nice. Masse 36.   Barbara Stone 70-4 1996 £125.00

AESOPUS   Fables of Aesop and Other Eminent Mytholgoists. London: ptd. for R. Sare, B. Took, M. Gillyflower, A. and J. Churchill,... 1694. 2nd edition; folio; engraved frontispiece and portrait; 18th century blindstamped calf, rebacked, binding rubbed and worn at edges, some pale dampstaining but still nice.   Barbara Stone 70-5 1996 £275.00

AESOPUS   The Fables of Aesopus and Others. London: 1818. One of 500 copies only, signed by artist; wood engravings by Thomas Bewick; 19th century brown calf, gilt borders to covers and gilt panelling to spine with morocco title label, calf little rubbed in places but generally an extremely handsome volume. Roscoe 456.   Words Etcetera 94-185 1996 £650.00

AESOPUS   Aesop's Fables. London: Murray, 1848. 1st edition thus, by the Rev. Thomas James; octavo; xxv, 232, 12 pages; black and white illustrations by Tenniel; morocco, gilt stamped spine; light foxing to titlepages, else fine.   Bromer Booksellers 90-144 1996 $400.00

AESOPUS   Aesop's Fables. London: Dent, 1895. 12mo; drawings in black and white by Charles Robinson; green cloth pictorially stamped in gilt, silk ties, cloth, slightly dusty, esle nice; very scarce.   Barbara Stone 70-1 1996 £110.00

AESOPUS   The Fables of Aesop. Waltham St. Lawrence: Golden Cockrel Press, 1926. Limited to 350 copies; small quarto; 94 pages; wood engravings by Celia M. Fiennes; unopened in cloth backed boards; extremely fine.   Bromer Booksellers 87-73 1996 $300.00

AESOPUS   Aesop's Fables. Hampstead: privately printed, 1964. Small 4to; with 8 unsigned lino cut illustrations in black and white mounted on different colored card pages; cream hessian backed green boards; fine. Barbara Stone 70-2 1996 £75.00

AESOPUS   Aesop's Frog Fables. Santa Cruz: Peter and Donna Thomas, 1990. Number 33 of a limited edition of 50 numbered copies; printed on handmade paper by Peter Thomas; illustrations by Donna Thomas printed in green and black on light green and light blue paper; full dark green suede, spine with raised bands, upper cover stamped in silver, uncut and partly unopened; fine in publisher's gilt stamped green boards, slipcase.   Barbara Stone 70-3 1996 £150.00

AESOPUS   Aesop's Frog Fables. Santa Cruz: Peter and Donna Thomas, 1990. One of 50 copies, page size 7 3/8 x 5 1/3 inches; printed on handmade paper by Peter Thomas, illustrated by Donna Thomas and handprinted and bound by Peter and Donna Thomas; pond-blue paper has the text printed in black with frog-green titles; full frog green suede with title stamped on front panel in green, lighter green handmade paper flyleaves, housed in green board slipcase with title in gilt.   Priscilla Juvelis 95/1-58 1996 $125.00

AESOPUS   The Little Esop. London: Tilt and Bogue, ca. 1835. 2 15/16 x 2 1/2 inches; 191 pages; 48 wood engravings; half speckled calf by Arthur S. Colley, with gold tooling, spine in five compartments and morocco label, all edges gilt, original cloth cover with gilt stamp showing Aesop telling a tale to a child, bound in; Bondy p. 67; Welsh 62.   Bromer Booksellers 90-194 1996 $500.00

AESOPUS   Some of Aesop's Fables with Modern Instances. London: Macmillan, 1883. 1st edition thus; 4to; illustrations by Randolph Caldecott; tan cloth pictorially stamped in brown with cover design by Caldecott, little plate spotting to prelims, else very fresh.   Barbara Stone 70-6 1996 £95.00

AESOPUS   Twelve Fables. New York: Museum of Modern Art, 1954. Limited to 975 copies, signed by artist, author and printer, Joseph Blumenthal; quarto; (13)ff.: printed in red and black with striking illustrations on every page by Antonio Frasconi; cloth backed illustrated boards, slipcase; fine.   Bromer Booksellers 90-39 1996 $250.00

AESOPUS   Twelve Fables of Aesop. New York: Museum of Modern Art, 1954. One of 975 copies, signed by Frasconi, Wescott and Blumethal; quarto; (32) pages; each of the fables boldly illustrated with linoleum blocks by Frasconi; cloth backed boards printed with repeating design from a Frasconi cut, spine lightly faded, else fine, original slipcase with printed paper label, which is lightly bubbled and rubbed at edges. Artist and the Book 111.   Bromer Booksellers 87-72 1996 $225.00

AETHELGIFU   The Will of Aethelgifu. Oxford: Roxburgh Club, 1968. Limited edition, printed for presentation to members only; folio; 92 pages; publisher's brown morocco backed cloth, top edge gilt, others uncut; fine.   Thomas Thorp 489-6 1996 £150.00

AFTER Ffity Years: a Lincoln Day Program. Cincinnati: Feedmen's Aid Society of the Methodist Episcopal Church... n.d., c. 1905. illustrations by Mildred Marion Coughlin; stapled wrappers, slight splits at edges of extremely fragile decorated wrappers, very good or better, very fragile, presumably few have survived in this condition.   Between the Covers 43-358 1996 $150.00

AGATE, JAMES   Here's Richness! London: 1942. One of limited edition of 100 copies, signed by author, and Osbert Sitwell who signed foreword; 271 pages; three quarter morocco, minor wear on head and foot of spine, very good, attractive copy.   Lyman Books 21-10 1996 $200.00

AGATE, JAMES   A Shorter Ego. Autobiography. London: 1946. Limited to 110 numbered sets, each signed by Agate; 2 volumes, 230, 230 pages; half morocco, top edge gilt, others uncut; spine sunned, otherwise fine.   Lyman Books 21-9 1996 $150.00

AGEE, JAMES 1909-1955   Let Us Now Praise Famous Men. Boston: Houghton Mifflin Co., 1941. 1st edition; 8vo; xvi, 471 pages, 31 photos; very good in price clipped dust jacket, that has very slight wear to spine ends and is slightly dusty on rear panel; scarce.   Andrew Cahan 47-71 1996 $550.00

AGEE, JAMES 1909-1955   Permit Me Voyage. New Haven: Yale University Press, 1934. 1st edition; 8vo; original cloth, dust jacket; fine in very slighly rubbed jacket which shows faint dampstain to lower portion of spine. Author's scarce first book.   James S. Jaffe 34-1 1996 $650.00

AGNER, DWIGHT   The Books of WAD - A Bibliography of the Books Designed by W. A. Dwiggins. Baton Rouge: The Press of Nightowl, 1974. One of approximately 190 numbered copies, printed on 70 pound Curtis Colophon - there were also 16 copies on damped Worthy Hand and Arrows paper; handset in Eric Gill's Monotype Joanna; titlepage and decorations by W. A. Dwiggins; bound by Robert Burlen and Son, cloth backed marbled paper boards, tail of spine and bottom corners slightly bumped, near fine. From the library of James D. Hart.   Ulysses 39-165 1996 £185.00

AGRICOLA, GEORGIUS   De Re Metallica. London: 1912. Folio; pages xxxi, 640; 270 woodcut illustrations, many full page, short split in upper hinge, otherwise fine, bound in vellum; inscribed by H. C. Hoover to S. T. Bloomline, Esq.   John Henly 27-636 1996 £550.00

AGRICOLA, GEORGIUS   De Re Metallica. London: published for the translators by the Mining Magazine, 1912. 4to; 640 pages; 270 woodcut illustrations; uncut, bound in full vellum, soiled, 2 inch cut to lower hinge, endpaper soiled, possibly a bookplate removed, internally nice, clean copy. Inscribed by Herbert Hoover.   Second Life Books 103-6 1996 $600.00

AGRICOLA, GEORGIUS   De Re Metallica. New York: 1950. Dover edition; imperial 8vo; pages xxxi, 638, 270 woodcut illustrations; cloth, dust jacket, fine.   John Henly 27-635 1996 $65.00

AGRIPPA VON NETTESHEIM, HEINRICH CORNELIUS 1486?-1535 Fourth Book of Occult Philosophy: of Geomancy, Magical Elements of Peter De Abano, Astronomical Geomancy, the Nature of Spirits, Arbatel of Magick. London: Askin, 1978. Reprint of 1655 edition, limited to 500 copies; this number 121; 8vo; xvi, 217 pages; handsomely bound, fine. Middle Earth 77-207 1996 $245.00

AGUILAR, GRACE   The Jewish Faith: its Spiritual Consolation, Moral Guidance and Immortal Hope. Philadelphia: L. Johnson, 1864. American Stereotype edition; 8vo; (446) pages; three quarter calf over marbled boards, gilt lettered spine, extremities lightly scuffed, some color renewed on spine, sign of label removed on front free endpaper, still quite nice; scarce.   Paulette Rose 16-189 1996 $800.00

AHLBERG, HAKON   Swedish Architecture of the Twentieth Century. New York: Scribner's, 1925. 1st edition; folio; xvi, 41, (5) pages; 152 plates; cloth, number on spine, covers lightly rubbed.   Bookpress 75-145 1996 $375.00

AHMED, ROLLO   I Rise: the Life Story of a Negro. London: John Long, 1937. 1st edition; small owner name and some foxing to a couple of prelim pages, else fine, very good dust jacket with small hole on spine and osme small tears.   Between the Covers 43-243 1996 $150.00

AIKEN, CONRAD   Blue Voyage. New York: Scribners, 1927. 1st edition; near fine in near fine dust jacket with just a little edge wear; Thomas Dorn 9-9 1996 $150.00

AIKEN, CONRAD   Bring! Bring! and Other Stories. New York: Boni & Liveright, 1925. 1st edition; fine in nice, near fine dust jacket that is little spine faded and with some small nicks and tears, attractive example of the fragile jacket.   Between the Covers 42-6 1996 $125.00

AIKEN, CONRAD   Costumes by Eros. New York: Charles Scribner's Sons, 1928. 1st edition; very good in slightly chipped dust jacket. Hermitage SP95-1122 1996 $100.00

AIKEN, CONRAD   Senlin: a Biography. London: Hogarth Press, 1925. 1st edition; signed by author; covers slightly rubbed, otherwise fine; Woolmer 55.   James S. Jaffe 34-2 1996 $250.00

AIKIN, JOHN 1747-1822   Annals of the Reign of King George the Third. London: printed for Longman et al, 1816. 1st edition; 9 1/4 x 6 inches; 2 volumes, pages 287/288 misbound between 272/273 in volume 2; contemporary flamed calf boards and black roan spines, covers framed with decorative rules, marbled endpapers, 2 covers slightly affected by worm, minor loss of patina or leather, boards litle marked but bindings both pleasing in design and very well preserved, bright spines and no significant wear to joints or extremities; excellent copy internally.   Phillip J. Pirages 33-2 1996 $275.00

AIKIN, JOHN 1747-1822   Essays On Song-Writing: with a Collection of Such English Songs as are Most Eminent for Poetical Merit. London: printed for Joseph Johnson, 1772. 8vo; contemporary sheep, spine and joints worn, some rubbing, usual marginal browning of endpapers, otherwise very clean and pleasant copy; from the Lonsdale Library with her bookplate.   James Cummins 14-189 1996 $250.00

AIKIN, JOHN 1747-1822   The Woodland Companion. London: 1802. 1st edition; 8vo; ages (3), 92; 28 double page engraved plates; contemporary quarter calf, worn and scuffed, some spine splitting, although the book is solid, occasional brown spots, only affecting, 1 plate, name on title.   Raymond M. Sutton VII-406 1996 $285.00

AIKIN, JOHN 1747-1822   The Woodland Companion. London: 1820. 3rd edition; 12mo; pages (3), 92, 28 double page engraved plates; contemporary quarter leather with marbled boards, very rubbed and worn, head of spine perished, hinges somewhat tender, missing top portion of title repaired, flyleaf and small upper corner of contents missing with institutional bookplate.   Raymond M. Sutton VII-405 1996 $145.00

AINSLIE, WHITELAW   Observations on the Cholera Morbus of India. London: 1825. 1st edition; 8vo; original boards, uncut, spine rather worn; on front flyleaf is ms. note of some 40 lines by author giving his latest thoughts; Royal Society of Edinburgh copy, inscribed to them by author. Maggs Bros. Ltd. 1190-362 1996 £180.00

AINSWORTH, WILLIAM HARRISON 1805-1882   Cardinal Pole; or, the Days of Philip and Mary. London: 1863. 1st edition; 3 volumes; shaken in bindings, library label at head of upper cover of each volume.   Words Etcetera 94-9 1996 £55.00

AINSWORTH, WILLIAM HARRISON 1805-1882   Crichton. New York: Harper & Bros., 1837. 1st American edition, same year as first English; 2 volumes; original lavender patterned muslin, remains of old library label on covers, worn, spines faded, original printed paper spine labels rubbed, minor foxing, light waterstain or two. scarce.   G. W. Stuart 59-2 1996 $150.00

AINSWORTH, WILLIAM HARRISON 1805-1882   Jack Sheppard. London: Richard Bentley, 1839. 1st edition; 8 x 5 1/4 inches; 3 volumes; 27 engraved plates by George Cruikshank, as well as portrait of Ainsworth in volume 1, with half title in volume 3 (no others called for), fly title from 1 mistakenly bound at front as a half title; half title somewhat soiled, few additional leaves slightly smudged, small nick on one spine, one or two other quite trivial imperfections; lovely crimson crushed morocco by Riviere & Son, French fillet frame on covers, spines beautifully gilt in compartments, with central floral ornament surrounded by circles, stars, flowers and folaige, top edge gilt, other edges untrimmed, fine filligree gilt inner dentelles, front hinge of volume 1 with neat cosmetic repair, original cloth covers and spines bound in at rear of each volume; fine copy in extremely handsome binding.   Phillip J. Pirages 33-3 1996 $575.00

AINSWORTH, WILLIAM HARRISON 1805-1882   James the Second; or the Revolution of 1688. London: Henry Colburn, 1848. 1st edition; 12mo; 3 volumes; original grey boards, green cloth spines, printed paper labels, trifle rubbed, some wear to corners, labels little brown and slightly chipped, but wholly legible; rare; very good. Sadleir 15; Wolff 54; CBEL III 912.   Ximenes 108-3 1996 $900.00

AINSWORTH, WILLIAM HARRISON 1805-1882   Rookwood: a Romance. London: Richard Bentley, 1834. 1st edition; octavo; 3 volumes; bound without half titles to volumes 2 and 3, note on flyleaf of volume 1, name on title to volumes 2 and 3, author's presentation inscription to Henry Colburn, his former publisher on half title of volume 1, bookplate removed from each volume; contemporary half calf, scuffed; interesting presentation set. Sadleir 26.   G. W. Stuart 59-3 1996 $650.00

AIR Service Medical. Washington: 1919. 1st edition; 446 pages; more than 100 photographic illustrations; original binding; scarce.   W. Bruce Fye 71-25 1996 $300.00

AITKEN, JAMES   The Trial (at large) of James Hill; Otherwise, James Hind; Otherwise James Actzen; for...Setting fire to the Rope-House, in His Majesty's Dock-Yard at Portsmouth.. London: sold by G. Kearsley and Martha Gurney, n.d. 1777. 1st edition; folio; recent marbled boards, cloth spine; very good, rare. Adams 77-8; Sabin 31840; Howes H484. Ximenes 109-2 1996 $900.00

AITKEN, JOHN   Principles of Midwifery, or Puerperal Medicine. London: for John Murray, 1786. 3rd edition; 8vo; 210 pages, 8 pages; frontispiece, portrait, 31 folding copperplates; original half calf, covers detached, spine splitting and worn at head and tail, endpapers loose, ex-library.   Argosy 810-4 1996 $300.00

AITON, W.   Hortus Kewensis; or, a Catalogue of the Plants Cultivated in the Royal Botanic Garden at Kew. London: 1810-13. 2nd edition; 8vo; 5 volumes; new cloth, blindstamp on titlepages with library marks on reverse, some very limited slight foxing.   Wheldon & Wesley 207-1 1996 £400.00

AITON, W.   A Treatise on the Origin, Qualities and Cultivation of Moss Earth. Glasgow: 1805. 8vo; pages (iv), 178, (2); boards, morocco back, nice ex-library with stamps.   Wheldon & Wesley 207-1869 1996 £85.00

AKEHURST, B. C.   Tobacco. London: 1981. 2nd edition; 8vo; 788 pages; illustrations; cased.   Wheldon & Wesley 207-1870 1996 £88.00

AKENSIDE, MARK 1721-1770   An Ode to the Country Gentlemen of England. London: printed for R. and J. Dodsley, and sold by M. Cooper, 1758. 1st edition; 4to; modern panelled calf, spine and inner dentelles gilt, by Dulau & Co. (slight rubbing); very good, bookplate of Lord Esher. Rothschild 25; Iolo Williams p. 93; CBEL II 637.   Ximenes 109-3 1996 $125.00

AKENSIDE, MARK 1721-1770   The Pleasures of Imagination. London: R. Dodsley, 1744. 3rd edition, same year as first; tall octavo; pages 142; early mottled calf, gilt rules and decorations, titlepage in red and black, vignette engraving after Boitard. Name of first owner dated 1744 on flyleaf and comments in same hand scattered throughout; nice. Foxon A141; Williams p. 77.   Hartfield 48-L4 1996 $285.00

AKHMATOVA, ANNA   Forty Seven Love Poems. London: Jonathan Cape, 1927. One of 300 numbered copies; author's first book in the U.K., printed on handmade paper; black and whtie frontispiece photo of author; loose frontispiece tissue guard creased and spotted; original binding, covers slightly cocked, spine slightly darkened, very good in nicked, rubbed and dusty, slightly marked and creased dust jacket browned at spine and edges and missing, small piece at head of spine. Ulysses 39-4 1996 £325.00

ALABAMA. LAWS, STATUTES, ETC.   An Act of the General Assembly of Alabama to Aid in Arresting Deserters and Stragglers from the Army, Adopted at the Called Session, 1864, Held in the City of Montgomery, Commencing on the Twenty-sixth Day of September A.D., 1864. Montgomery: 1864. 1st edition; 4 pages; shows creases where folded, few traces of glue, yet very good, rare. Parrish & Willingham 2617. Not in Crandall.   McGowan Book Co. 65-110 1996 $650.00

ALARCON, FRANCISCO X.   De Amor Oscuro?Of Dark Love. Santa Cruz: Moving Parts Press, 1993. 1st edition; one of 70 signed copies; page size 14 x 7 1/4 inches; on Frankfurt Cream paper; drawings by Ray Rice; yellow iris bookcloth over boards, publisher's slipcase in yellow cloth and blue paper printed in black with title in Spanish and English; Priscilla Juvelis 95/1-182 1996 $280.00

ALARCON, PEDRO ANTONIO DE   The Three Cornered Hat. New York: H. bittner, 1944. One of 500 copies; octavo; 151 pages; printed by Victor and Jacob Hammer at the Wells College Press; 21 hand colored woodcuts by Fritz Kredel; fine, unopened copy in slightly darkened dust jacket torn and chipped at extremities.   Bromer Booksellers 90-161 1996 $100.00

ALASKAN BOUNDARY TRIBUNAL   Proceedings of the Alaskan Boundary Tribunal, Convened at London,...with Respect to the Boundary Line Between the Territory of Alaska and the British Possessions in North America. Washington: 1904. Volumes I-VII; some in original wrappers, others in original cloth, all have minor to moderate wear. Stephen Lunsford 45-3 1996 $300.00

ALBEE, EDWARD   The American Dream. New York: Coward McCann, 1961. 1st edition; rine in fine dust jacket.   Sherwood 3-16 1996 $135.00

ALBEE, EDWARD   A Delicate Balance. New York: Atheneum, 1966. Stated first edition; very fine in perfect dust jacket, exceptional copy. Sherwood 3-18 1996 $100.00

ALBEE, EDWARD   Delicate Balance. New York: Atheneum, 1966. 1st edition; fine in dust jacket, signed by author.   Left Bank Books 2-2 1996 $100.00

ALBEE, EDWARD   Tiny Alice. New York: 1965. 1st edition; fine in near fine dust jacket, laid in is TLS, signed by author, in typed envelope. Lyman Books 21-479 1996 $125.00

ALBEE, EDWARD   Who's Afraid of Virginia Woolf? New York: Atheneum, 1962. 1st edition; 8 1/2 x 5 1/2 inches; 6 p.l., 242 pages, (1) leaf; original cloth, dust jacket; particularly fine and desirable copy, in very fine jacket. inscribed by author for Robert A. Wilson.   Phillip J. Pirages 33-4 1996 $150.00

ALBEE, EDWARD   The Zoo Story, The Death of Bessie Smith & The Sandbox. New York: Coward McCann, 1960. 1st edition; author's first regularly published book; fine in later issue dust jacket (price changed to $3.50), wrapper has library catalog number on spine, else fine. Sherwood 3-15 1996 $130.00

ALBEE, FRED HOUDLETT   Bone-Graft Surgery. Philadelphia: W. B. Saunders, 1917. 1st reprinting; 417 pages; original binding, bit rubbed, spine faded, internally quite clean. GM 5757.   James Tait Goodrich K40-4 1996 $125.00

ALBERTI, RAFAEL   El Negro Motherwell. New York: Tyler, 1982. One of 51 copies only; page size 15 x 15, 15 x 25 3/4 and 15 x 37 3/4 inches; on paper handmade at the Tyler Graphics Ltd. paper mill, each signed and numbered by artist; natural color buckram cloth, device which holds the pages together as a book, has detachable bar which permits the pages to be removed for exhibition or custom binding purposes.   Priscilla Juvelis 95/1-181 1996 $22,500.00

ALBERTUS MAGNUS 1193?-1280   Compendium Theologice Veritatis. Venice: Pietro Quarengi, Oct. 23, 1510. Small 4to; ff. (96); later vellum over marbled boards, library card pocket removed from rear pastedown and front free endpaper lacking, crack to lower front hinge, but still very sound copy. Rare.   Kenneth Karmiole 1NS-4 1996 $650.00

ALBIN, ELEAZAR   A Natural History of English Song-Birds and Such of the Foreign as are Usually Brought Over and Esteemed for Their Singing. London: printed for R. ware, 1741. 2nd edition; 8vo; 23 engraved plates; contemporary calf, rubbed, hinges cracked, label.   Anthony W. Laywood 109-2 1996 £135.00

ALBO, JOSEPH   (Hebrew:) Sefer Ha-Ikkarim.... Venice: P. & L. Bragadini, 1618. 1st edition; folio; 292 pages; few woodcut text diagrams; contemporary goat, panelled and decorated in blind and by branding; fine. Very rare. Furst I.32; Rosenthal I.594; not in NUC or BM STC.   Bennett Gilbert LL29-43 1996 $2,250.00

ALBUCASIS   Albucasis On Surgery and Instruments. Los Angeles: University of California Press, 1973. 8vo; 850 pages; ; as new in dust jacket.   James Tait Goodrich K40-5 1996 $125.00

ALBUCASIS   On Surgery and Instruments. London: 1973. 1st edition; 850 pages; original binding, dust jacket. GM 5550.   W. Bruce Fye 71-27 1996 $125.00

ALBUM Vilmorin, the Vegetable Garden. London: 1986. Full size reproductions of the complete set of 35 plates of garden vegetables; giant folio sized color plates in portolio.   Raymond M. Sutton VII-1 1996 $375.00

THE ALBUM. New York: F. & R. Lockwood, 1824. 1st edition; 8vo; 156 pages; vignette-title; original two toned boards, printed paper label, both boards detached (but present), uncut, very tall, large paper copy. Shoemaker 15057; BAL 496 and 1589.   M & S Rare Books 60-110 1996 $600.00

ALCOCK, C. W.   Famous Cricketers and Cricket Grounds. London: Hudson & Kearns, 1895. 1st edition; folio; pages (iv), (288), pages numbered in ink, many photographic illustrations; original cloth, gilt, spine and edges of covers faded, otherwise very good.   Sotheran PN32-72 1996 £248.00

ALCOCK, JOHN   Harmonia Festi, or a Collection of Canons; Cheerful and Serious Glees and Catches. Ptd. for the author and sold by him at Lichfield, 1791. 1st edition; oblong 4to; initialled by author on title, 4 page list of subscribers, 59 pages of engraved music; modern cloth, nice, clean copy.   Anthony Laywood 108-21 1996 £90.00

ALCOTT, LOUISA MAY 1832-1888   Hospital Sketches. Boston: James Redpath, 1863. 1st edition; 12mo; 102, (2) pages; original plain slate-green cloth, covers with blind rules but no title, only title on spine, neither author nor publisher's name appears. BAL 145, 2nd printing.   M & S Rare Books 60-104 1996 $350.00

ALCOTT, LOUISA MAY 1832-1888   Jack and Jill. Boston: Roberts Bros., 1880. 1st edition; original blue pictorial cloth, gilt, very fine, fresh copy. BAL 195.   Mac Donnell 12-2 1996 $200.00

ALCOTT, LOUISA MAY 1832-1888   Jo's Boys, and How they Turned Out. Boston: Roberts Bros., 1886. 1st edition; 1st state (bulks 1 1/16 inches); original brown cloth, gilt, front hinge paper beginning to crack, else fine, bright copy. BAL 211.   Mac Donnell 12-3 1996 $100.00

ALCOTT, LOUISA MAY 1832-1888   Little Women. Boston: Roberts Bros., 1868/69. 1st edition; part 1st is first printing with price $1.25 printed on third page of terminal ads; part 2nd is in first state, with no notice for Little Women, part first at p. iv; octavo; 2 volumes, 341 pages, plus (6) pages ads; 359 pages plus (8) pages of ads; illustrations by May Alcott; bound in gilt stamped cloth, light rubbing to extremities of part second, spine slightly cocked, else fine set, partial removal of bookplate in volume 1, pair housed in leather backed cloth drop back box. BAL 158-159; Grolier American 74; Peter Parley to Penrod p. 30. Bromer Booksellers 87-104 1996 $7,500.00

ALDAN, DAISY   The Destruction of Cathedrals and Other Poems. Paris/New York: Two Cities Press, 1963. 1st edition; decorated wrapeprs; neara fine, inscribed by author, laid in is chatty one page ALS to recipient.   Captain's Bookshelf 38-9 1996 $100.00

ALDER, J.   The British Tunicata. London: Ray Society, 1905-12. 8vo; 3 volumes, 3 portraits, 66 plates; original cloth, dust jackets (worn); very nice, volume 2 has been very slightly affected by damp.   Wheldon & Wesley 207-1228 1996 £120.00

ALDERTON, D.   The Atlas of Parrots. London: 1991. Royal 4to; 544 pages, over 300 colored illustrations and photos; hardcover.   Wheldon & Wesley 207-621 1996 £85.00

ALDIN, CECIL   Scarlet to M. F. H. New York: Charles Scribner's Sons, 1933. 1st American edition; large 4to; 151 pages; illustrations by Cecil Aldin; slight fading and wear to head of spine, otherwise fine in worn dust jacket lacking upper 3 inches of spine panel.   Hermitage SP95-889 1996 $125.00

ALDIN, CECIL   The Twins. London: Henry Frowde, 1910. 1st edition; 4to; 24 fine full color plates by Aldin; original green cloth backed boards lettered in gilt, onlaid colored plate to upper cover, pictorial endpapers. Sotheran PN32-101 1996 £298.00

ALDINGTON, RICHARD   The Colonel's Daughter. London: Chatto & Windus, 1931. Signed limited edition of 210 numbered copies; 8vo; green buckram cloth, near fine, some sunning and with minor evidence of label removal from lower spine.   Antic Hay 101-16 1996 $125.00

ALDINGTON, RICHARD   Last Straws. Paris: Hours Press, 1930. Signed, limited edition of 200 numbered copies printed on Haut Vidalon paper, out of a total edition of 200 numbered copies; 4to; green 'suede' cloth, very good, covers with some discoloration and wear.   Antic Hay 101-18 1996 $125.00

ALDINGTON, RICHARD   Roads to Glory. London: Chatto & Windus, 1930. Signed limited edition, 360 numbered copies; 8vo; cloth and boards, near fine, little wear and foxing.   Antic Hay 101-21 1996 $125.00

ALDINGTON, RICHARD   Stepping Heavenwards. Florence: George Orioli, 1931. Limited edition, 242/808 signed copies; corners bumped, otherwise very good, unopened, in clean dust jacket and good slipcase. Virgo Books 48-4 1996 $50.00

ALDISS, BRIAN   The Brighfount Diaries. London: Faber, 1955. 1st edition; 8vo; pages 200; original pale blue cloth, backstrip lettered in yellow, dust jacket designed by Pearl Falconer, fine.   Blackwell's B112-2 1996 £65.00

ALDISS, BRIAN   Space Time and Nathaniel. London: Faber & Faber, 1957. 1st edition; very good+ in dust jacket; with author's inscribed business card laid in.   Aronovitz 57-3 1996 $175.00

ALDRICH, THOMAS A.   The History of Battery A, First Regiment Rhode Island Light Artillery in the War to Preserve the Union 1861-1865. Providence: 1904. 1st edition; 408 pages, frontispiece, photos; pictorial cloth; inscribed/signed copy, very good+. Dornbusch RI 19.   T. A. Swinford 49-9 1996 $175.00

ALDRIN, EDWIN E.   Return to Earth. New York: Random House, 1973. 1st edition; 8vo; black and white photos and facsimiles; very good in dust jacket; signed by Aldrin for Hal Levinson.   George J. Houle 68-6 1996 $150.00

ALECHINSKY, PIERRE   Pierre Alechinsky. New York: Abrams, 1977. Folio; 258 pages; profusely illustrated, much in color; cloth, dust jacket. Brannan Books 43-6 1996 $120.00

ALEMBERT, JEAN LEROND D' 1717-1783   Traite de Dynamique, Dans Lequel les Loix de L'Equilibre & du Mouvement des Corps sont Reduites au Plus Petit Nombre Possible. Paris: Chez David, 1758. 2nd edition; 4to; (12), xl, 272, xiii pages, 5 folding plates, several woodcut head and tailpieces, contemporary mottled calf, gilt compartmented spine with raised bands, marbled endpapers, red edges; front joint started, corners bit rubbed, unobtrusive library blindstamp on title, attractive, near fine. PMM 195 for 1st ed. of 1743;   Edwin V. Glaser 121-3 1996 $1,250.00

ALEMBIC PRESS   Specimens of Wood Type Held at the Alembic Press. Oxford: Alembic Press, 1993. 1st edition; limited to 100 copies; large oblong folio; 50 folios printed on rectos only with 3 leaves of introduction and list of specimens, printed in various colors (generally two per specimen) on 120 gsm Rivioli paper; in 3 hole interscrew binding of silk cloth backed printed boards.   Claude Cox 107-1 1996 £100.00

ALEXANDER, W. B.   Birds of the Ocean, a Handbook for Voyagers Containing Descriptions of All the Sea-Birds of the World... New York: G. P. Putnam's sons, 1928. 1st edition; xxiii, 428 pages + ads; 140 illustrations; black cloth, gilt titles, some wear and spotting to covers, interior is very good. Spence 11.   Parmer Books Nat/Hist-067190 1996 $125.00

ALFRED, H. J.   Views of the Thames...Marlow Weir, Near Marlow Bridge, Bisham Abbey, Temple Lock, Hurley Harleyford. London: M. & N. Hanhart lithographers, 1857. Oblong folio; engraved vignette on upper wrapper, 6 tinted lithographs by Alfred; disbound, original printed drab wrappers, margins a trifle dusty, some small tears.   Marlborough 162-5 1996 £1,500.00

ALGAE Abstracts. A Guide to Literature Up to 1974. New York: 1973-76. 4to; 3 volumes, 2168 pages; cloth, dust jacket.   John Johnson 135-335 1996 $100.00

ALGAROTTI, FRANCESCO   An Essay on Painting. London: L. Davis & C. Reymers, 1764. 1st English edition; small8vo; vii, (i), 186, (4) pages ads; recent quarter calf, marbled boards; very good; signature of Wm. Curran at head of titlepage and second signature of Thos. Andrews.   Ken Spelman 30-10 1996 £220.00

ALGAROTTI, FRANCESCO   The Philosophy of Sir Isaac Newton Explained in Six Dialogues on Light and Colours Between a Lady and the Author. Glasgow: Robert Urie, 1765. Foolscap 8vo; (2), xiv, 17-280 pages, ad leaf, errata slip pasted onto final page, contents leaf (i.e. pp. xv-xvi) misbound as in one other copy we have handled; contemporary calf green gilt label, joints and head and tial of spine expertly repaired, some browning to prelim and final few leaves; very good.   Ken Spelman 30-11 1996 £360.00

ALGREN, NELSON   Chicago: City on the Make. Garden City: Doubleday, 1951. 1st edition; fine in dust jacket (priced clipped), with few traces of wear, signed by author.   Captain's Bookshelf 38-10 1996 $150.00

ALINDER, J.   Roy De Carava Photographs. Friends of Photo, 1981. 1st edition; large square 4to; illustrations, dust jacket slightly chipped, signed and inscribed by De Carava.   J. B. Muns 154-91 1996 $100.00

ALISON, ARCHIBALD   Essays on the Nature and Principles of Taste. Edinburgh: David Willison, 1825. 6th edition; 8vo; 2 volumes, xxix, (i), 376 pages; vi, 447 pages, half titles; 19th century half calf, attractive gilt panelled spines and green gilt labels.   Ken Spelman 30-59 1996 £220.00

ALISON, ARCHIBALD   The Principles of Population, and Their Connection with Human Happiness. Edinburgh: William Blackwood and Sons, London: Thomas Cadell, 1840. 1st edition; 8vo; 2 volumes, xix, (1), 572; viii, 544 pages, complete with two half titles; contemporary half calf, gilt spines with raised bands and labels; very good. Goldsmiths 31429; Kress C5068; Williams I 218; not in Einaudi.   John Drury 82-4 1996 £450.00

ALISON, ARCHIBALD   The Principles of Population, and Their Connection with Human Happiness. Edinburgh: William Blackwood, Thomas Cadell, London, 1840. 1st edition; 8vo; 2 volumes, lacking half titles; contemporary half calf, spines dry, one joint tender, spine labels renewed; McCulloch p. 261; Kress C5068.   James Burmester 29-5 1996 £325.00

ALKEN, HENRY   Military Occurrences. N.P.: n.d., c. 1820. 52 of 56 hand colored etched plates, lacks ms. and printed titles; all plates inlaid within a bordered panel on grey paper, with facing blank, 37 of first 38 plates have a manuscript title within an elaborate panel border and 1 other has a title caption in pencil, final 14 have an elaborate panel border but no captions, plates all in fine condition, near mint, offsetting to facing blank only, plates all on Whatman paper; full straight grain green morocco, slightly rubbed, corners bumped, elaborate gilt panels and decorative cornerpieces to boards, gilt tooled compartments to spine, gilt title to spine, raised bands, all edges gilt, marbled endpapers; very scarce. Abbey Life 349.   Beeleigh Abbey BA/56-131 1996 £3,500.00

ALKEN, HENRY   Qualified Horses and Unqualified Riders, or the Reverse of Sporting Phrases, from the Work Intitled Indispensable Accomplishments by Ben Tally-Ho. London: by S. & J. Fuller, 1815. 1st edition; 1st issue; oblong folio; etched titlepage, 7 etched plates in original hand coloring (watermarked 1815), uncut in original brown printed wrappers, stab stitched as issued, wrappers little frayed, small piece missing from blank margin of plate 6, generally in fine condition, half morocco slipcase. Schwerdt I p. 20; Tooley no. 44; Siltzer p. 69.   H. M. Fletcher 121-127 1996 £2,800.00

ALKEN, HENRY   The Sporting Repository. London: printed for W. Lewis, 21 Finch Lane for Thomas McLean, 26 Haymarket, 1822. 1st and only edition; 8vo; text 1-537 pages, addenda 537-540; hand colored etched frontispiece, 18 hand colored plates, new endpapers and prelims, text heavily browned, some light foxing to margins of a few plates, margins also slightly grubby, however plate imprint in good condition, occasional light offsetting to letterpress; full dark green morocco, triple gilt rule borders to boards, elaborate gilt tooling to panelled spine, gilt title to spine, raised bands to spine, gilt tooled inner dentelles, corners slightly bumped, top edge gilt.   Beeleigh Abbey BA56-234 1996 £950.00

ALLBEURY, TED   Show Me a Hero. Bristol: Scorpion Press, 1992. 1/20 deluxe lettered copies; quarter bound in goatskin with raised bands; signed by author and Len Deighton who provided author appreciation; fine.   Quill & Brush 102-6 1996 $450.00

ALLBEURY, TED   Show Me a Hero. Bristol: Scorpion Press, 1992. 1/99 signed, numbered copies; fine in quarter bound leather, marbled paper boards, textured colored endpapers and colored top edges. Quill & Brush 102-78 1996 $125.00

ALLEN PRESS   The Allen Press Bibliography. Book Club of California, 1985. One of 750 copies; folio; printed by offset lithography in black and red, illustrations in full color; new material printed letterpress in black, red, grey and blue in Monotype Van Dijck at the Tamal Land Press, typography by Lewis Allen; full brown cloth, decorated in blind on upper cover; fine.   Bertram Rota 272-10 1996 £150.00

ALLEN PRESS   The Allen Press Bibliography. San Francisco; Book Club of California, 1985. Limited to 750 copies; folio; 114 pages, plus index; mint.   Argonaut Book Shop 113-20 1996 $225.00

ALLEN, CHARLES   A New and Improved Roman History, from the Foundation of the City of Rome, to its Final Dissolution as the Seat of Empire, in the Year of Christ 476... London: printed for J. Johnson, 1798. 2nd edition; 12mo; 4 engravings by William Blake; contemporary half calf, spine gilt, trifle rubbed; margins trimmed bit close, shaving the odd headline and imprint of two of the plates, generally very good fresh copy. Bentley 416.   Ximenes 108-4 1996 $1,250.00

ALLEN, CHARLES   The Polite Lady; or, a Course of Female Education. London: John Newbery, 1760. 1st edition; 162 x 98mm; 287 pages; frontispiece, 40 numbered letters; full speckled calf, spine with raised bands decorated in gilt, very skilfully rebacked and corners repaired, very good. Osborne 693.   Marjorie James 19-165 1996 £950.00

ALLEN, FRANCIS   The Complete English Dictionary... London: printed for J. Wilson and J. Fell and J. Coot, 1765. Sole edition; 12mo; mark on title, small tears in fore edge, 2 pages ads with small hole in inner margin; rebound in half seckled calf, marbled boards, red label. Alston V236.   Jarndyce 103-103 1996 £650.00

ALLEN, G. M.   The Mammals of China and Mongolia. Pt. I. New York: 1938. 1st edition; 8vo; all published; plates and maps; original cloth. Maggs Bros. Ltd. 1190-659 1996 £115.00

ALLEN, H. WARNER   A History of Wine. London: Faber & Faber, 1961. 1st edition; demy 8vo; 304 pages; plates; bound in elegant recent half morocco by Bayntun-Riviere of Bath, top edge gilt, fine.   Ash Rare Books Zenzybyr-2 1996 £195.00

ALLEN, HENRY T.   Report of an Expedition to the Copper, Tanana and Koyukuk Rivers, in the Territory of Alaska, in the Year 1885. Washington: 1887. 1st edition; 8vo; 172 pages + 29 plates and 5 large folding maps; original dark cloth, light wear and fading, waterstains along top margins of several pages and plates throughout, maps generally very good, save for some light foxing.   Blue River Books 9-7 1996 $165.00

ALLEN, IRA   A Concise Summary of the Second Volume of the Olive Branch, a Book... Philadelphia: Thomas T. Stiles, 1806. 12mo; 15 pages, removed; S&S 9821; Howes A143, this ed. not listed.   M & S Rare Books 60-273 1996 $1,500.00

ALLEN, IRA   A Narrative of the Transactions Relative to the Capture of the American Ship Olive Branch. Philadelphia? 1804. 1st edition of volume 2; 8vo; 368 pages, uncut and unopened, trace of boards on spine, otherwise lacking, one leaf torn without loss, two quarter inch holes driven through leaves at inner margin affecting a letter or two, except for nail holes a clean and appealing copy. Howes A143; S&S 5684; Mallary 32a.   M & S Rare Books 60-274 1996 $1,250.00

ALLEN, JAMES   Schoolcraft and Allen Expedition to Northwest Indians. Washington: House War Dept. Document 323, 1834. 1st edition; 68 pages; folding map; later cloth, morocco label; Becker Wagner Camp 47a; Field 1366; Graff 3703; Streeter Sale 1793.   Michael D. Heaston 23-15 1996 £450.00

ALLEN, JOHN   Modern Judaism; or, a Brief Account of the Opinions, Traditions, Rites and Ceremonies of the Jews in Modern Times. London: printed for T. Hamilton, and Oliphant, Waugh & Innes, Edinburgh, 1816. 1st edition; 8vo; xiv, 434 pages, fine engraved frontispiece, uncut in original blue boards, drab spine, printed label, piece missing from foot of spine. Uncommon. Roth, Magna Bib. Anglo-Judaica p. 397.   James Burmester 29-6 1996 £175.00

ALLEN, L. F.   The American Herd Book 1846... Buffalo: 1846. 8vo; 4 plates (browned), pages xxiv, (9-) 240; half leather, spine and corners worn, covers spotted, light to moderate foxing.   Raymond M. Sutton VII-815 1996 $145.00

ALLEN, REGINALD   The First Night Gilbert and Sullivan. New York: printed at the Gallery Press for Limited Editions Club, 1958. Limited to 1500 copies; 12 x 8 1/4 inches; 488 pages; set in Monotype Bell and Victorian display types on Curtis Bethany paper; contemporary drawings, half red velvet with dark green leather label, green linen sides, gold stamped, accompanied by a boxed set of 27 facsimiles or original programs with index, fine in slipcase which has split at outer edge. Complete librettos of the 14 operas; newsletter laid in.   Taurus Books 83-114 1996 £65.00

ALLEN, WILLIAM A.   Adventures with Indians and Game or Twenty Years in the Rockies. Chicago: 1903. 1st edition; 302 pages; frontispiece, photos; cloth/boards, top edge gilt, new spine; nice; scarce. Howes A16a5; 6 guns 36; Graff 44; Jennewein 102.   T. A. Swinford 49-13 1996 $200.00

ALLESTREE, RICHARD   The Government of the Tongue. Oxford: at the Theater, 1674. 1st edition; 2nd impression; 8vo; in half sheets, pages (xvi); 224; contemporary 'sombre' binding, dark brown morocco, elaborately decorated in blind with a background of fine parallel lines and some cross-hatching forming a 'cottage-roof' pattern, then decorated with tulips, fruit, rosettes and other tools, spine in compartments with darkened maroon morocco label gilt, some wear at joints and corners, marbled endpapers, inner hinges split, imprimatur leaf pasted to front free endpaper and with inscription erased, some light staining and soiling, but very good, and interestingly bound copy. Wing A1134; Madan 3002.   Simon Finch 24-2 1996 £550.00

ALLFREY, PHYLLIS SHAND   In Circles. Poems. London: Raven Press, 1940. Number 261 of an edition of 300, signed by poet; 20 pages; wrappers, sewn; nice, scarce; with additional inscription in her hand to Peter Abrahams.   Ian Patterson 9-23 1996 £75.00

ALLIN, THOMAS   Mechanics' Institutions Defended on Christian Principles. Sheffield: printed for the Mechanics' Inst. by Timothy Scott, 1833. 1st edition; 8vo; 24 pages, inner margins stabbed; recent linen backed marbled boards, lettered; very good.   John Drury 82-5 1996 £60.00

ALLINGHAM, HELEN   Happy England as Painted. London: A. & C. Black, 1904. 1st edition; portrait, 80 colored plates; blue decorated cloth, few slight damp marks to binding.   Petersfield Bookshop FH58-20 1996 £180.00

ALLINGHAM, MARGERY   Mr. Campion: Criminologist - Seven Important Episodes from the Casebook of Albert Campion. New York: Pub. for the Crime Club Inc. by Doubleday Doran & Co., 1937. 1st edition; original binding, two edges of two or three pages nicked, endpaper gutters browned, head and tail of spine and corners bumped and slightly rubbed, covers slightly marked, very good in nicked, chipped, rubbed, creased and dusty, slightly soiled and torn dust jacket, missing small pieces at head of spine.   Ulysses 39-8 1996 £250.00

ALLINGHAM, WILLIAM   The Ballad Book. London: 1879. 1st edition; 8vo; cloth, piece torn from top of first preface leaf, otherwise good Ex-Milltown Park Library.   C. P. Hyland 216-4 1996 £70.00

ALLISON, DOROTHY   Bastard Out of Carolina. New York: Dutton, 1992. 1st edition; fine in fine dust jacket; signed.   Book Time 2-5 1996 $150.00

ALLISON, DRUMMOND   The Poems of Drummond Allison. Whiteknights Press, University of Reading, 1978. One of 200 numbered copies; original binding, patterned endpapers, loosely inserted are: a slightly soiled publicity leaflet for this book and an 'editorial errata' slip, listing errors arising from misreading of the original manuscripts; fore-edge of upper cover darkened, covers very slightly marked, cover edges very slightly rubbed, very good, issued without dust jacket. Bookplate of the literary agent John Johnson.   Ulysses 39-9 1996 £65.00

ALLISON, DRUMMOND   The Yellow Night - Poems - 1940-41-42-43. London: Fortune Press, 1944. 1st edition; frontispiece, 3 other drawings; original binding, gilt lettering on spine oxidised, covers slightly marked, head and tail of spine & corners bumped, bottom edges of covers slightly worn, front free endpaper partially browned from insertion of small newspaper clipping, very good in nicked, rubbed and spotted, slightly creased, chipped, marked and dusty dust jacket browned at spine; bookplate of literary agent John Johnson.   Ulysses 39-654 1996 £155.00

ALLIX, PIERRE   Reflections Upon the Opinions of Some Modern Divines, Concerning the Nature of Government in General and that of England in Particular. London: Richard Chiswell, 1689. 1st edition; 4to; (12), 112, (8), 113-284 (i.e. 148) pages; fore-edges of title and following leaf cropped and with marginal tears (but no loss of printed surface), recently bound in quarter calf and marbled sides, spine lettered in gilt; good, with half title/licence leaf. Wing R733; not in Goldsmiths.   John Drury 82-6 1996 £195.00

ALLMAN, GEORGE JOHNSTON   Greek Geometry from Thales to Euclid. Dublin: Hodges, Figgis & Co., 1889. 1st edition; 8vo; xii, 237, (2 ad) pages; frontispiece, figures in text; original cloth, few faint library marks, but very good. Zeitlinger, 3rd Supplement 485.   Edwin V. Glaser 121-4 1996 $100.00

ALLOM, THOMAS 1804-1872   Lake and Mountain Scenery. London: printing and publishing, n.d. Oblong 8vo; title an 32 steel engraved plates, frontispiece trifle spttted; original blindstamped cloth, gilt, all edges gilt, very nice.   R.F.G. Hollett & Son 78-666 1996 £120.00

ALLOM, THOMAS 1804-1872   Westmorland, Cumberland and Durham and Northumberland. London: Fisher Son and Co., 1832. 4to; pages 220, vignette on title, 215 steel engraved plates, most original tissues retained; old half calf, gilt with broad riased bands, trifle rubbed, little scattered spotting, but excellent clean and sound set.   R.F.G. Hollett & Son 78-665 1996 £495.00

ALLOM, THOMAS 1804-1872   Westmorland, Cumberland, Durham and Northumberland Illustrated from Original Drawings... London: F. Fisher, etc., n.d. 1832. 4to; pages 220; vignette on title, 215 steel engraved plates; old panelled calf, gilt, little scrapedd, handsomely rebacked in matching calf, gilt with raised bands, little occasional browning and spotting, very good, sound.   R.F.G. Hollett & Son 78-664 1996 £475.00

ALLSTON, WASHINGTON   Outlines and Sketches... Boston: Stephen H. Perkins, 1850. 1st edition; oblong folio; engraved title, loose and stained, page of text and 18 plates with paper plate guards, all generally very clean with very light outer edge dampstaining; original cloth, worn at tips, front cover separated, leather spine almost gone, internally generally very good, uncommon.   Freedom Bookshop 14-6 1996 $325.00

ALLSTON, WASHINGTON   The Sylphs of the Seasons, with Other POems. Boston: 1813. 1st American edition; 12mo; 168 pages; original plain boards, foxed; very good. Printed on thin paper. BAL 494; Wegelin 845; S&S 27701.   M & S Rare Books 60-105 1996 $200.00

ALLWOOD, PHILIP   Literary Antiquities of Greece; as Developed in an Attempt to Ascertain Principles for a New Analysis of the Greek Tongue...(with) Remarks On some Observations Edited in "The British Critic" Relating to a Work Lately Published... London: ptd. by J. Davis... 1799/1800. 1st editions; 4to; 2 volumes in one; 1st title with 4 plates & leaf of errata; the 4 page list of subscribers not preserved; 2nd title with half title, frontispiece map and errata leaf; contemporary tree calf, covers with attractive red mottled borders framed in gilt, spine stained dark and ruled in gilt, red morocco label (slight cracking of joints); both titles very scarce; fine in striking and very handsome binding; armorial bookplate of Lord Newark. not in Blackmer.   Ximenes 109-4 1996 $650.00

ALMACK, EDWARD   Fine Old Bindings with Other Interesting Miscellanea in Edward Almack's Library. London: Blades, East & Blades, 1913. Limited to 200 copies; 52 paltes; white and maroon cloth, headcaps mildly bumped, very minor offset from chromolithographs, but none of the usual sticking; good copy. Schmidt Kunsemuller 1188.   Maggs Bros. Ltd. 1191-1 1996 £475.00

ALMANAC for the Year 1386. London: printed for the Proprietor by C. Stower Hackney, 1812. 74 pages, 2 hand colored plates, red morocco backed roan, spine gilt in compartments, bit worn at extremities, top of spine slightly split.   Maggs Bros. Ltd. 1191-135 1996 £265.00

ALMANACH der Wiener Werkstatte. Vienna & Leipzig: Bruder Rosenbaum, 1911. Square 12mo; each page with decorataive border of green lines and black dots; orange and gold linen in a geometric pattern designed by Josef Hoffman; fine.   Marilyn Braiterman 15-207 1996 $1,000.00

ALMANACH. Paris: Le Breton, 1778. contemporary crimson morocco, covers gilt with placque by Dubuisson, spine with five raised bands, panels with gilt fleur-de-lys or lettering, all edges gilt, blue silk endpapers, the bookseller Larcher's striking engraved (1756) label on blank leaf before title, head of spine neatly repaired.   Marlborough 160-25 1996 £600.00

ALMANACK 1929. London: Lanston Monotype Corp., 1928. 1st edition; 8vo; pages (48), printed in red and black, 12 wood engravings and 4 page essay by Eric Ravilious; 6 pages specimen at end; original buckram backed boards, slightly soiled, lettered in gold; uncommon Ravilious item.   Claude Cox 107-134 1996 £180.00

ALMANACK for 1793. London: Company of Stationers, 1793. Original red morocco gilt cottage style binding with silver floriated medallions on upper and lower corners; along fore-edge, extending from medallions, are silver loops through which a silver locking pin slides; unusual gilt pastepaper endpapers with leather accordian pleats forming calling card pockets on pastedowns, text clean and unmarked, binding has some light rubbing, but elaborate gilt tooling is bright, small volume has lovely patina.   Glenn Books 36-3 1996 $600.00

ALMANACK for the Year of Christ 1850. London: 1849. 58 x 33 mm; 13 ff., engraved throughout, folding plate mounted at 2 leaves; original brown morocco, gilt, all edges gilt, covers gilt with beige, green and red onlays, spine gilt with knot and cord pattern, matching contemporary slipcase; excellent condition.   Marlborough 160-60 1996 £225.00

ALPINUS, PROSPER   De Plantis Aegyptis Liber...De Balsamo, Dialogvs (etc.). Venice: Francesco Franceschi, 1592. 1st edition of first work, 2nd edition of the second; 4to; ff. (iv), 80, (viii), Roman letter, woodcut printer's device on main titlepage (repeated on 2nd), many woodcuts of plants, mostly full page, woodcut initials and ornaments, titlepage bit dusty, frayed at edges and reinforced in gutter, light yellowing in parts, some outer margins lightly waterstained, small pieces torn from upper edges of last 4 leaves, without loss; contemporary calf, neatly rebacked, gilt double fillets & spine, outer corners worn; inscription recording gift by Richard Richardson of North Bierley to Thos. Knowlton 7.2. 1748/9 on endpaper. BM STC It. p. 20; Adams A803; Index Aurel 103.853; Pritzel 163; A. Sokol XXV-3 1996 $2,850.00

ALSOP, RICHARD   The Echo. New York: Noah Bailey, 1807. 1st edition; 8vo; 15, 331, (10) pages, index; 8 engraved plates; full contemporary calf, some browning and foxing, but very good. BAL 1315; Wegelin 1266; S&S 11971. Sabin 21778.   M & S Rare Books 60-106 1996 $425.00

ALSTON, E. R.   Biologia Centrali-Americana: Mammalia. London: 1879-82. 4to; pages xx, 220, 22 plates; buckram; now very scarce; from the collection of Jan Coldewey.   Wheldon & Wesley 207-11 1996 £800.00

ALSTON, J. W.   Hints to Young Practioners in the Study of Landscape Painting. London: Longman, c. 1808. 3rd edition; 8vo; (6), 67, (1), (14) pages ads dated Dec. 1st 1808, etched title with aquatint view and 5 aquatint plates (one with additional contemporary hand coloring); worn original linen backed boards, some browning to text; uncut.   Ken Spelman 30-28 1996 £85.00

ALTHAMER, ANDREAS   Diallage, Hoc Est. Conciliatio Locorum Scripturae... Nuremberg: Fridericus Pepyus, 1527. 8vo; ff. (4), 99, (7), index, title within woodcut border, woodcut printer's device below colophon; later (18th century?) tan marbled boards, spine quite chipped, waterstain along half inch strip of bottom margin.   Kenneth Karmiole 1NS-7 1996 $450.00

ALVAREZ, J. M.   Instituciones De Derecho Real De Castilla Y De Indias...Para El Curso, De Los Discipulos De P. A. Jose Martinez, En Taso De Nuevo Mexico.... Taos: Martinez, 1842. 1st edition; (10), 168 pages; 3 and one third leaves in expert facsimile; contemporary full leather, very simple and somewhat crudely bound by a local artisan, few leaves including title professionally repaired; very good, very rare. Wagner New Mexico Spanish Press 20.   Michael D. Heaston 23-262 1996 $12,000.00

AMANTIUS, BARTHOLOMAEUS   Flores Celebriorum Sententiarum Graecarum ac Latinarum, Definitionum, Item Virtutem et Vitiorum, Omnium Exemplorum, Proverbiorum, Apopthegmatum, Apologorum, Similium et Dissimilium... Dillingen: Sebaldus Mayer, 1556. 1st (only?) edition; folio; (48), 478 pages, woodcut printer's device on title and historiated initials, numerous passages in Greek; small tear in one leaf without loss of text, marginal dampstain on last 3 leaves; early ownership inscription in top blank margin whited out; contemporary calf backed wooden boards, rebacked with original spine preserved (lacking clasps); rare. Bucher, Dillingen 48; VD 16, A-2152; Jocher I 327.   Jeffrey D. Mancevice 20-1 1996 $750.00

AMBERLEY   The Amberley Papers - the Letters and Diaries of Lord and Lady Amberley. London: Hogarth Press, 1937. 1st edition; 2 volumes; 20 black and white plates; original binding, top edges dusty, prelims and edges slightly spotted, free endpapers partially browned, heads and tails of spine and corners slightly bumped, covers slightly marked, cover edges slightly rubbed, very good in worn, torn and soiled, defective and dusty, slightly creased dust jackets browned at spines and edges, lacking pieces at heads and tails of spine and with extrensive internal repairs.   Ulysses 39-301 1996 £295.00

AN AMERICAN ABC by Maud and Miska Petersham. New York: Macmillan, 1941. 1st edition; 4to; 26 full page colored lithographs with texxt on facing pages; blue cloth, gilt, fresh copy.   Barbara Stone 70-8 1996 £85.00

AMERICAN Decorative Papermakers. The Work and Specimens of Twelve Craft Artists. Mattapoisett: Busyhaus Publications, 1983. One of 200 special hardcover copies; oblong 4to; 66 pages; 10 original tipped in marbled paper samples, photos, 4 woodblock illustrations; quarter morocco over cloth, gilt spine.   Kenneth Karmiole 1NS-203 1996 $125.00

AMERICAN JEWISH PUBLICATION SOCIETY   Constitution and By-Laws...(Founded on the 9th of Heshvan 5606) Adopted at Philadelphia, on Sunday, Nov. 30, 1845, Kislev 1, 5606. Philadelphia: C. Sherman 5606 1845. 1st edition; 12mo; 11 pages; contemporary plain wrappers, library stamp on front wrapper and title, otherwise fine; Not in Rosenbach; Wolf 158; singerman 0881.   M & S Rare Books 60-354 1996 $600.00

AMERICAN Journal of the Medical Sciences. Volume I. Philadelphia: 1827. 2nd edition; 496 pages; cloth backed marbled boards, ex-library.   W. Bruce Fye 71-38 1996 $100.00

THE AMERICAN Jurist and Law Magazine. Volume I. Boston: Freeman & Bolles, Court St., Corner of Brattle Street, 1829. 1st two issues; contemporary quarter sheep, quite rubbed, one joint cracking, sound. Meyer Boswell SL27-140 1996 $250.00

AMERICAN MEDICAL ASSOCIATION   Code of Ethics...Adopted...1847. Philadelphia: T. K. and P. G. Collins, 1848. 1st edition; 12mo; 30 pages; removed from binder, cloth remains on edges.   M & S Rare Books 60-442 1996 $250.00

THE AMERICAN Stage of To-Day. New York: P. F. Collier & son, 1910. 1st edition; folio; profusely illustrated; modern cloth.   Dramatis Personae 37-2 1996 $120.00

THE AMERICAN Star. Richmond: Peter Cottom, 1817. 2nd edition; 12mo; (ii), 215, (1) pages; later full morocco, scarce, minor foxing, some waterstains.   The Bookpress 75-374 1996 $250.00

AMERICAN TYPE FOUNDERS CO.   Wood-Type. Boston: American Type Founders Co., n.d., ca. 1900. Small folio; 126 pages; original wrappers, lightly soiled, otherwise fine.   Glenn Books 36-275 1996 $100.00

AMERICAN WATER COLOR SOCIETY   Illustrated Catalogue Twentieth Annual Exhibition of the American Water Color Society Held at the Galleries of the National Academy of Design... New York: American Water Color Society, 1887. 4to; (1st general exhibition in which a work by Frederic Remington appeared); wrappers, slight edge browning, tiny chip lower right corner front cover, nice appearing, very good plus copy, uncommon.   Freedom Bookshop 14-9 196 $250.00

AMERICAN WATER COLOR SOCIETY   Illustrations of Pictures and Catalogue of the twenty-Second Annual Exhibition. New York: 1889. Wrappers; near fine.   Freedom Bookshop 14-11 1996 $100.00

AMES, B.   Drawings of Florida Orchids. Ormond, 1947. 1st edition; limited to 325 copies; tall 8vo; (4), 190 pages; 63 plates; stiff wrappers, some spine and edge fading, some chipping to edges of wrappers, uncommon edition.   Raymond M. Sutton VI-852 1996 $100.00

AMES, JOSEPH   A Catalogue of English Heads; or, an Account of About Two Thousand Prints, Describing What Is Peculiar On Each... London: printed by W. Faden for the editor and sold by J. Robinson, 1748. 1st edition; 8vo; (4), 182 pages; later portrait mounted onto prelim blank in form of frontispiece; titlepage dusty and some minor soiling, but good; contemporary calf, double gilt banded spine and original gilt label, rear joint expertly repaired towards head; scarce.   Ken Spelman 30-6 1996 £140.00

AMES, JOSEPH   Typographical Antiquities; or an Historical Account of the Origin and Progress of Printing in Great Britain and Ireland... London: 1785-90. 4to; 3 volumes; 8 plates, illustrations in text, later black cloth, purple and gilt spine labels, occasional spotting throughout (mainly in preface & middle of volume 3), some offset from plates and browning to some plates. De Ricci p. 49.   Maggs Bros. Ltd. 1191-172 1996 £400.00

AMES, NATHANIEL 1708-1764   An Astronomical Diary, or an Almanack for 1761. Boston: John Draper, Richard Draper, Green & Russell & Edes & Gill, Thomas &.. 1760. 24 pages; Drake 3126; Evans 8529.   Blue River Books 9-10 1996 $100.00

AMES, O.   Orchidaceae. Boston: 1908. 1st printing; tall 8vo; pages viii, 99; 34 sepia plates; cloth backed boards, light foxing to endpapers, small tear to contents page; rare.   Raymond M. Sutton VI-859 1996 $165.00

AMES, O.   Orchidaceae, Illustrations and Studies of the Fmaily Orchidaceae. Boston: 1915. Tall 8vo; pages xiv, 271; folding map; cloth backed boards, endpapers foxed, occasional foxing in gutters of text. Raymond M. Sutton VI-860 1996 $100.00

AMES, O.   Orchids of Guatemala. Chicago: 1952-53. 8vo; pages iv, 728; nearly 200 line drawings; 2 volumes; cloth.   Wheldon & Wesley 207-1785 1996 £80.00

AMHURST, NICHOLAS   A Collection of Poems on Several Occasions, Publish'd in the Craftsman. London: printed for R. Francklin, 1731. 1st bookform edition; 8vo; in 4's; pages (iv), 76; modern half brown calf, smooth backstrip divided by gilt rules and gilt lettered direct, marbled boards. Foxon D39.   Blackwell's B112-3 1996 £95.00

AMHURST, NICHOLAS   Terrae-Filius; or, the Secret History of the University of Oxford... London: printed for R. Francklin, Under Tom's Coffee House, 1726. Crown 8vo; 2 volumes in 1; titlepages in red and black, frontispiece by W. Hogarth in volume 1, 1st title rather soiled, 2nd title cropped at head; contemporary half vellum, marbled boards, worn. Halkett & Laing 6 p. 18.   H. M. Fletcher 121-82 1996 £115.00

AMHURST, NICHOLAS   Terrae-Filius: or, the Secret History of the University of Oxford... London: printed for R. Francklin, 1726. 1st edition in book from; 12mo; 2 volumes, bound in 1, f, xxiii, 354 pages; original panelled calf, rubbed, lacking label.   David Bickersteth 133-93 1996 £110.00

AMHURST, NICHOLAS   Terrae-Filius; or, the Secret History of Oxford; in Several Essays. London: printed for R. Francklin, 1754. 3rd edition; 8vo; contemporary calf, worn, some light marginal browning and spotting, endpapers browned, front free endpaper loose.   James Cummins 14-148 1996 $150.00

AMIS, KINGSLEY 1922-   The Anti-Death League. London: Gollancz, 1966. 1st edition; 8vo; cloth in dust jacket, near fine, small tear to front flap fold of jacket; signed and dated (1966) by Amis on titlepage. Antic Hay 101-44 1996 $100.00

AMIS, KINGSLEY 1922-   The Crime of the Century. New York: Mysterious Press, 1989. Limited to 100 copies, signed by author; fine in slipcase.   Words Etcetera 94-23 1996 £50.00

AMIS, KINGSLEY 1922-   I Like It Here. New York: Harcourt Brace, 1958. 1st edition; small 8vo; cloth in dust jacket, near fine, minor wear (shot tears), dust jacket; signed by author.   Antic Hay 101-49 1996 $100.00

AMIS, KINGSLEY 1922-   Lucky Jim. London: Gollancz, 1953. 1st edition; 8vo; green boards, dust jacket lightly rubbed at several corners and head of spine, some faint discoloration at edges of inner flaps; very attractive, fine copy.   James S. Jaffe 34-4 1996 $1,750.00

AMIS, KINGSLEY 1922-   Lucky Jim. Garden City: Doubleday, 1954. 1st American edition; author's first book; near fine in price clipped dust jacket, mildly spine darkened; very scarce, particularly in nice condition; inscribed by author.   Ken Lopez 74-4 1996 $650.00

AMIS, KINGSLEY 1922-   One Fat Englishman. London: Penguin Books, 1966. Paperback; 12mo; pages 173, (iv) ads, autograph inscription of John Lennon and Yoko Ono Lennon on first page, loosely inserted memo on headed writing paper "Waiting for a plane at Heathrow on 29th December 1969 to take us to Moscow, we met John Lennon & Yoko. They very kindly signed the book..."   Simon Finch 24-153 1996 £185.00

AMIS, MARTIN   Invasion of the Space Invaders. London: Hutchinson, 1982. 1st edition; quarto; very near fine in illustrated glossy wrappers; scarce.   Lame Duck Books 19-38 1996 $250.00

AMIS, MARTIN   Invasion of the Space Invaders. London: Hutchinson, 1982. 1st edition; quarto; numerous illustrations, almost all in color; wrappers, fore edge very slightly thumbed, near fine.   Ulysses 39-12 1996 £95.00

AMIS, MARTIN   The Rachel Papers. New York: Knopf, 1973. 1st American edition; author's first book; fine in fine, price clipped dust jacket, with very slight slant to spine.   Book Time 2-8 1996 $175.00

AMIS, MARTIN   The Rachel Papers. New York: Alfred A. Knopf, 1974. 1st U.S. edition; author's first book; near fine in dust jacket which has tiny tear at top edge of front panel and minor crease on front flap. Steven C. Bernard 71-7 1996 $100.00

AMMAN, JOST   Stand Und Orden der H. Romischen Catholischen Kirchen, Darinn aller Geistlichen Personen, H. Ritter und Dero Verwandten Herkommen, Constitution Regeln, Habit und Kleidung, Beneben Schonen und Kunstlichen Figurn Fleissig Beschrieben... Frankfurt a.m.: Sigmund Feyerabend, 1585. 1st German edtiion; small 4to; 102 fine woodcuts; full crushed dark brown morocco with triple gilt fillet borders, spine with five raised bands and one small tool in each of four compartments, the other two reserved for the title, board edges gilt, inner gilt dentelles, all edges gilt, by Mansell, successors to Hayday, fine, exceedingly scarce. Splendid copy. Becker 40a; Brunet I 234; Colas 120; Fairfax Murray German Books p.33.   Book Block 32-71 1996 $4,500.00

AMSDEN, CHARLES AVERY   Navajo Weaving, It's Technique and History. Albuquerque: University of New Mexico, 1949. 1st edition; 263 pages; foldout insert, original decorated cloth, heavy rubbing at extremities; titlepage with original bookseller's sticker, not affecting text; very good.   Ken Sanders 8-Nat. Amer. 1996 $175.00

AMSINCK, PAUL   Tunbridge Wells and Its Neighbourhood. London: Miller and Lloyd, 1810. Large 4to; half title, title, 4 ff., 183 pages; frontispiece, 30 etched plates, 12 engraved text vignettes; russia gilt, little rubbed; scarce.   Marlborough 162-6 1996 £480.00

AMUCHASTEGUI, AXEL   Some Birds and Mammals of Africa. London: 1979. Limited to 500 copies; folio; 62 pages; 14 fine colored plates; quarter blue morocco, gilt, gilt top.   Wheldon & Wesley 207-2 196 £380.00

AMUCHASTEGUI, AXEL   Some Birds and Mammals of South America. London: Tryon Gallery, 1966. Limited edition of 300 copies; this coyp being "File Copy only, ex series"; folio; printed on pure rag paper; publisher's buckram, spine and covers little waterstained, but internally fine.   Thomas Thorp 489-8 1996 £125.00

AMUCHASTEGUI, AXEL   Some Birds and Mammals of South America. London: Tryon Gallery, 1971. Limited to 505 copies, this being a 'file copy only, ex series'; this copy signed by artist; 540 x 350 mm; pritned on pure rag paper; publisher's buckram, spine lettered gilt, top edge gilt, fine in slightly worn cloth slipcase.   Thomas Thorp 489-9 1996 £180.00

ANACREON   Five Odes of Anacreon. Tern Press, 1985. One of 75 numbered copies, signed by artist; suqare folio; printed in yellow and shades of brown in Caslon on Zerkall; five etchings by Nicholas Parry; half cloth, marbled boards; fine.   Bertram Rota 272-463 1996 £60.00

ANACREON   Odes Done into English. London: Nonesuch Press, 1923. One of 725 numbered copies; 8vo; printed in Garamond on Perusia handmade; 7 engravings on copper by Stephen Gooden; quarter parchment with gold paper boards, somewhat soiled and rubbed, internally nice, name on flyleaf, bookplate by Reynolds Stone.   Bertram Rota 272-314 1996 £60.00

ANACREON   29 Odes. London: Gerald Howe, 1926. Limited edition, number 61 of 105 copies; full vellum, very fine in custom full green morocco solander case, spine and edges of case faded to brown. Hermitage SP95-866 1996 $500.00

THE ANCIENT British Drama. (with) The Modern British Drama. London: William Miller, 1810/11. Sole editions(?). royal 8vo. in fours; 8 volumes; half titles, pages xi, (i) 595, (iv) 614; (iv), 598, (2); half titles, pages vi, (ii), 688; iv, 602; (iv), vii, (i), 668; (vi), 648; viii, 668; uniformly bound in contemporary half white vellum, minor wear to some extremities, smooth backstrips darkened, divided into compartments by narrow arrow head rolls, red leather title label in second compartments, dark blue volume labels in fourth, remainder with small concave sided octagonal ornament in centre, drab boards, blue sprinkled edges, light damage to front endpaper of volume i, bookplate of Lord Londesborough in each volume, generally excellent.   Blackwell's B112-88 1996 £350.00

ANCIENT Maya Paintings of Bonampak Mexico. Washington: Carnegie Inst. of Washington, 1955. 8vo. and folio; 2 parts, (iii), 36 pages, 1 figure, 1 map, 3 large folding plates in color (loose in folder as issued); wrappers, folder tattered.   Archaeologia Luxor-4335 1996 $125.00

ANDERDON, J.   The River Dove, with Some Quiet Thoughts on the Happy Practice of Angling. London: 1847. contemporary cloth, gilt borders, some worming to hinges, not affecting contents, all edges gilt, apart from worming, a most excellent copy.   David A.H. Grayling 3/95-400 1996 £50.00

ANDERSEN, HANS CHRISTIAN 1805-1875   The Fairy Tales of Hans Christian Andersen. London: George Newnes, 1899. 1st edition thus; large 4to; 320 pages, with upwards of 400 illustrations; cream and blue buckram decorated in gilt, covers slightly soiled, otherwise very good. Marjorie James 19-203 1996 £125.00

ANDERSEN, HANS CHRISTIAN 1805-1875   Fairy Tales. London: Hodder & Stoughton, 1924. 1st edition; 1st printing; 4to; 12 tissue guarded plates by Kay Nielsen; original green moire cloth, elaborate pictorial gilt cover.   Glenn Books 36-195 1996 $1,050.00

ANDERSEN, HANS CHRISTIAN 1805-1875   Fairy Tales. London: George G. Harrap & Co., 1932. Limited to 525 numbered copies, signed by artist; quarto; 287 pages; 12 color plates with descriptive tissue guards, 59 drawings in black and white by Arthur Rackham; original full vellum over boards with front cover and spine stamped in gilt, top edge gilt, others uncut, pictorial endpapers, boards bit bowed, otherwise fine, unopened copy in original publisher's cardboard slipcase. Latimore & Haskell p. 68.   Heritage Book Shop 196-209 1996 $2,250.00

ANDERSEN, HANS CHRISTIAN 1805-1875   The Improvisatore; or, Life in Italy. London: Ward, Lock & Tyler, ca. 1857. 8vo; 2 volumes in one, xxx, 340 pages, continuously paginated; 47 actual plates; original vellum, vellum bit marked, otherwise good; scarce.   K Books 442-28 1996 £100.00

ANDERSEN, HANS CHRISTIAN 1805-1875   The Sand-Hills of Jutland. Ticknor & Fields, 1860. 1st American edition; spine somewhat lightened, some light wear to spine extremities, otherwise tight, very good copy. Aronovitz 57-8 1996 $175.00

ANDERSEN, HANS CHRISTIAN 1805-1875   Stories from Hans Andersen. London: Hodder & Stoughton, 1911. Edition deluxe, limited to 750 numbered copies, signed by artist; large quarto; viii, 250 pages; 28 mounted color plates by Edmund Dulac; bound by Zaehnsdorf in full green morocco, front cover decoratively stamped in gilt, gilt lettered spine with raised bands, gilt board edges and turn-ins, top edge gilt, others uncut, marbled endpapers, little light foxing and browning, otherwise fine.   Heritage Book Shop 196-208 1996 $2,250.00

ANDERSEN, HANS CHRISTIAN 1805-1875   Stories from Hans Andersen. London: Geographia, n.d. 1920's. 4to; 80 pages; 6 color plates; grey boards, large embossed color pictorial onlay, illustrated endpapers; extremities rubbed, else very good.   Marjorie James 19-185 1996 £55.00

ANDERSEN, K.   Catalogue of the Chiroptera in the Collection of the British Museum. London: 1912. 8vo; pages ci, 854, 85 text figures; new cloth.   Wheldon & Wesley 207-537 1996 £80.00

ANDERSON, AENEAS   A Narrative of the British Embassy to China, in the Years 1792, 1793 and 1794... Dublin: for P. Byrne, 1796. 2nd edition; 8vo; xxiv, 304 pages; half morocco, marbled boards, marbled endpapers, richly gilt spine, slightly rubbed, minor foxing, otherwise very good, all edges marbled.   Worldwide Antiquarian 162-15 1996 $275.00

ANDERSON, ALEX D.   The Silver Country; or, the Great Southwest. New York: G. P. Putnam's Sons, 1877. 1st edition; 221 pages; folding map; original pictorial brown cloth with map of New Spain on front cover, bit of light rubbing to extremities, minor wear to corners; fine. Cowan p. 14; raines p. 9.   Argonaut Book Shop 113-23 1996 $125.00

ANDERSON, ARTHUR J. O.   Florentine Codex. Santa Fe: School of American Research and the University of Utah, 1950-69. Limited to 1000 copies; 4to; 13 parts in 11 volumes; 1669 pages, over 1700 illustrations; original cloth, several corners bumped; very scarce; J. A. Bennyhoff's light pencil annotations in several volumes, his stamp in most volumes. Archaeologia Luxor-4214 1996 $650.00

ANDERSON, GEORGE WILLIAM   A New, Authentic and Complete Collection of Voyages Round the World... London: Alex. Hogg, 1784. Thick folio; 655, (5) pages; portrait, large folding map, 155 engraved plates, maps and charts; contemporary calf, rebacked, extremities, bit worm, front hinge cracking, occasional offsetting and foxing, few minor marginal tears. Hill, Pacific Voyages 5.   Joseph J. Felcone 64-13 1996 $1,000.00

ANDERSON, HENRY   An Enquiry Into the Natural Right of Mankind to Debate Freely Concerning Religion. London: C. Davis and G. Hawkins, 1737. 1st and only edition; 8vo; viii, (2), 357, (1) page, errata at foot of last page of text, ads on verso; contemporary calf, gilt, raised bands, label, bit worn, joints cracking, otherwise good. From the 18th century library of John Campbell, 4th Earl of Loudoun. 3 copies in NUC.   John Drury 82-7 1996 £300.00

ANDERSON, HENRY   The Medical and Surgical Aspects of Aviation. London: 1919. 1st edition; 255 pages; photographic plates; original binding, skilfully recased, ex-library. GM 2137.5.   W. Bruce Fye 71-41 1996 $300.00

ANDERSON, J.   The New Practical Gardener and Modern Horticulturist. London: c. 1870. 8vo; pages iv, 988, 27 chromolithographed plates, 12 plain plates; half calf, gilt, color plate of grapes is slightly foxed.   John Henly 27-272 1996 £180.00

ANDERSON, J. M.   Prodromus of South African Megafloras, Devonian to Lower Cretaceous. Rotterdam: 1985. 4to; 423 pages; 2 colored maps, about 2000 photos; cloth.   Wheldon & Wesley 207-1306 1996 £109.00

ANDERSON, JOHN 1833-1900   Mandalay to Momien: a Narrative of the Two Expeditions to Western China of 1868 and 1875. London: Macmillan & Co., 1876. 1st edition; demy 8vo; xvi, (480) pages; plates, folding maps; original decorative cloth, gilt, by Burn and Co., with their ticket, covers little worn, nicked and marked, but good copy still, bookplate of Hooker's Son, Joseph Symonds Hooker.   Ash Rare Books Zenzybyr-3 1996 £450.00

ANDERSON, POUL   Brain Wave. London: Heinemann, 1955. 1st British and 1st hard cover edition; signed by author; bright very good+ copy in dust jacket. Most uncommon.   Aronovitz 57-12 1996 $375.00

ANDERSON, POUL   Tau Zero. New York: Doubleday, 1970. 1st edition; signed by author; very fine in fine dust jacket.   Aronovitz 57-15 1996 $165.00

ANDERSON, POUL   Twilight World. Torquil/D-M, 1961. 1st edition; signed by author; just about fine in very good dust jacket with some light wear and tear.   Aronovitz 57-13 1996 $115.00

ANDERSON, POUL   The Worlds of Poul Anderson. Boston: Gregg Press, 1978. 1st editions; 7 volumes; all fine in dust jackets.   Robert Gavora 61-2 1996 $200.00

ANDERSON, R.   Ballads in the Cumberland Dialect... Wigton: E. Rook, 1815. 2nd edition; 8vo; pages vi, 258; modern half levant morocco, gilt. R.F.G. Hollett & Son 78-312 1996 £85.00

ANDERSON, R.   Ballads in the Cumberland Dialect... Wigton: printed by R. Hetherton, 1808. 1st edition; 8vo; pages vi, 258, untrimmed; engraved frontispiece; original boards, recased.   R.F.G. Hollett & Son 78-311 1996 £120.00

ANDERSON, R.   Cumberland Ballads. Wigton: William Robertson, n.d., c. 1830. 8vo; pages x, 138; frontispiece; original printed boards, little rubbed and soiled.   R.F.G. Hollett & Son 78-314 1996 £65.00

ANDERSON, SHERWOOD 1876-1941   Dark Laughter. New York: Boni & Liveright, 1925. Limited to 350 numbered copies, signed by Sherwood Anderson; 8vo; 319 pages, title decorations in blue; white parchment backed black boards, spine spotted, titled in gilt on spine and red on front cover, black slipcase, rubbed, broken at top with color pictorial paper label; fine in very good slipcase.   Blue Mountain SP95-86 1996 $125.00

ANDERSON, SHERWOOD 1876-1941   Nearer the Grass Roots. San Francisco: Westgate Press, 1929. One of 500 numbered copies, signed by author; tiny bump to bottom of pages, still a superb copy in very scarce original glassine dust jacket.   Between the Covers 42-10 1996 $275.00

ANDERSON, SHERWOOD 1876-1941   Nearer the Grass Roots. (and) An Account of a Journey-Elizabethon. San Francisco: Westgate Press, 1929. 1st edition as such; limited to 500 numbered and signed copies; 8vo; 35 pages, titlepage vignette, color woodcuts; cloth backed patterned paper over boards, bright copy with slightest of wear; near fine.   Andrew Cahan 47-18 1996 $125.00

ANDERSON, SHERWOOD 1876-1941   Tar: a Midwest Childhood. N.P.: Boni & Liveright, 1926. Limited edition, number 90 of 350 numbered copies, signed by author; 8vo; titlepage printed in black and ochre; Japan vellum over patterned boards, spine with brown printed paper label (slight stains to Japan vellum), very good in publisher's tan board slipcase (worn).   George J. Houle 68-2 1996 $250.00

ANDERSON, SHERWOOD 1876-1941   Tar - a Midwest Childhood. New York: 1926. 1st edition; decorated cloth, very near fine.   Stephen Lupack 83- 1996 $150.00

ANDERSON, SHERWOOD 1876-1941   Windy McPherson's Son. New York: John Lane, 1916. 1st edition; author's first book; near fine, handsome bookplate, slightly faded at spine and lacking the rare dust jacket.   Captain's Bookshelf 38-12 1996 $300.00

ANDERSON, SHERWOOD 1876-1941   Winesburg, Ohio. New York: Huebsch, 1919. 1st edition; 1st issue; 8vo; yellow cloth with printed label on spine, head of spine bumped and very slightly rubbed, otherwise fine, bright copy.   James S. Jaffe 34-5 1996 $500.00

ANDERSON, WALTER   The History of Coresus in IV Parts. Edinburgh: printed by Hamilton, Balfour and Neill, 1755. 1st edition; 12mo; contemporary calf, spine gilt; very fine; rare; early armorial bookplate of George Baillie and signed on titlepage by Grizel (Grisell) Baillie, daughter of the well-known Scottish poetess.   Ximenes 109-7 1996 $900.00

ANDRE, R.   A Dream of the Zoo. London: Perry & Co., Ltd., n.d., ca. 1880. 1st edition; 8vo; 14 pages; 13 color printed plates, extra color pictorial orange limp wrappers; very light wear.   Robin Greer 94A-7 1996 £120.00

ANDREAE, BERNARD   The Art of Rome. New York: Harry N. Abrams, 1977. Folio; 655 pages, 900 illustrations; original cloth, dust jacket, slipcase.   Archaeologia Luxor-2898 1996 $250.00

ANDREW, W. P.   India and Her Neighbours. London: Wm. H. Allen, 1878. 1st edition; tall 8vo; (xviii), 413, (40) pages ads dated Aug. 1878; 2 large folding maps, tear in one map repaired on rear with archival tape, short tear in second map, spine faded, otherwise near fine.   David Mason 71-90 1996 $160.00

ANDREWES, LANCELOT   XCVI Sermons. London: George Miller for Richard Badger, 1629. 1st edition; folio; pages (xii), 1008, 168, 22, (ii), mainly Roman letter, large engraved printer's device and ornament on main titlepage, the former repeated (slightly modified) in smaller size on 2nd titlepage, many large woodcut initials and engraved ornaments, slight waterstaining to upper portions and fore edges in parts, small hole in 1 leaf with loss but not affecting legibility; contemporary calf, bit worn and scratched, foot of front hinge and head of spine split, gilt title label; autograph of Robert? Whitfield of Chartham, Kent & erases name (pierced) dated 1875, otherwise good copy. STC 606. McKerrow 222; this edition not in Lowndes. 4 copies in NUC.   A. Sokol XXV-4 1996 £750.00

ANDREWS, ALICE E.   Christopher C. Andrews, Pioneer in Forestry Conservation in the United States for Sixty Years a Dominant Influence in the Public Affairs of Minnesota: Lawyer, Editor, Diplomat, General in the Civil War: Recollections 1829-1822. Cleveland: 1928. 1st edition; 327 pages; frontispiece, plates; cloth, very good+. Dornbusch MN 35.   T. A. Swinford 49-22 1996 $125.00

ANDREWS, BERT   In the Shadow of the Great White Way: Images from the Black Theatre. New York: Thunders Mouth Press, 1989. 1st edition; folio; photos; fine in very lightly rubbed dust jacket; nicely inscribed by Andrews.   Between the Covers 43-449 1996 $100.00

ANDREWS, E. WYLLYS   The Archaeology of Southwestern Campeche. Washington: Carnegie Inst., 1943. 8vo; frontispiece, 100 pages, 28 plates; wrappers.   Archaeologia Luxor-4215 1996 $125.00

ANDREWS, H. C.   Coloured Engravings of Heaths... London: 1802-09. Folio; volumes 1-3, 216 exceptionally fine hand colored plates; contemporary calf, neatly rebacked, plates fine; half title to volume 1 creased and neatly strengthened.   Wheldon & Wesley 207-3 1996 £3,000.00

ANDREWS, L.   Grammar of the Hawaiian Language. Honolulu: printed at the Mission Press, 1854. 1st edition; 8vo; 156 pages; text browned; contemporary limp cloth, rebacked.   Anthony W. Laywood 108-148 1996 £225.00

ANDREWS, R. C.   Ends of the Earth. 1929. illustrations; excellent copy.   David Grayling J95Biggame-470 1996 £55.00

ANDREWS, R. MC CANTS   John Merrick: a Biographical Sketch. Durham: Seeman Printery, 1920. 1st edition; 229 pages; spine bit sunned and some wear to extremities of spine, about very good. Work p. 475.   Between the Covers 43-245 1996 $185.00

ANDREWS, STEPHEN PEARL 1812-1886   Discoveries in Chinese or the Symbolism of the Primitive Characters of the Chinese System of Writing. New York: Charles B. Norton, 1854. 1st edition; near fine.   Captain's Bookshelf 38-39 1996 $150.00

ANDREWS, WILLIAM   The Doctor in History, Literature, Folk-Lore, Etc. London: 1896. 1st edition; 287 pages; original binding; very scarce. Osler 4323.   W. Bruce Fye 71-44 1996 $175.00

ANDREWS, WILLIAM LORING   The Heavenly Jerusalem: a Mediaeval Song of the Joys of the Church Triumphant. New York: Scribner, 1908. 1st edition; beautiful copy in decorated French-fold wrappers and worn slipcase, rare printed outer wrapper chipped, but present.   Captain's Bookshelf 38-13 1996 $125.00

ANDRIC, IVO   Bosnian Story. London: Lincolns-Prager, 1961. 1st English edition; signed by author, very uncommon thus; small owner's label front free paper, else fine in near fine dust jacket.   Thomas Dorn 9-14 1996 $350.00

ANDRY, NICHOLAS   An Account of the Breeding of Worms in Human Bodies... London: H. Rhodes, 1701. 1st edition; 8vo; xl, (iv), 120 pages, 12-176 numbered leaves, 177-266, (xxvi) pages, 5 plates; later sheep, very good.   The Bookpress 75-376 1996 $600.00

ANGEL, JOSEPH K.   A Treatise on the Law of Watercourses with an Appendix Containing forms of Declaration. Boston: Charles C. Little and James Brown, 1840. 3rd edition; contemporary quarter calf, worn, joint cracking; presentation copy.   Meyer Boswell SL27-5 1996 $250.00

ANGEL, ROBERT J.   Designs for An Iron Roof. London: Royal Inst. of British Architects, 1891. Folio; 4 hand colored plates, 1 text leaf; half morocco, covers slightly rubbed, else very good.   Bookpress 75-147 1996 $485.00

ANGELINI BONTEMPI, GIOVANNI ANDREA   Historia Della Ribellione D'Ungheria. Dresden: Seyffert, 1672. 1st edition; 12mo; 372 pages; 4 full page engravings, typographic and woodcut ornaments; contemporary full vellum, text browning, but very good. Apponyi 966.   Bennett Gilbert LL29-2 1996 $950.00

ANGELIO, PIETRO DA BARGA   Poemata Omnia. Diligenter ab Ipso Recognita... Rome: ex typogr. Francisci Zannetti, 1585. 2nd edition; 8vo; 2 volumes in 1; pages (xxii), 424 (p. 424 misnumbered 124), (xvi), 180, italic letter, 5 plates Greek, Roman dedications and index, separate titlepage to each volume, large engraved woodcut printer's device (stag) on each, 1 full page engraving signed Aliprandus Capriolus, large woodcut initials and ornaments; 17th century polished calf, rebacked, later gilt spine remounted; old owner's autograph on second titlepage, wormtrail through blank lower margin in last third of volume, text untouched, final leaf lightly foxed, otherwise very good; bookplate of Chatsworth library. BM STC It. p. 28; Adams A1105; Index Aurel 105.684 and 105.685.   A. Sokol XXV-5 1996 £850.00

ANGELO, VALENTI   Valenti Angelo: Author - Illustrator - Printer. San Francisco: Book Club of California, 1976. 1st edition; limited to 400 copies printed by Andrew Hoyem and signed by Angelo; folio; 97 pages; 43 plates, mostly in color; cloth backed decorated boards, paper spine label, very fine. Original announcement laid in.   Argonaut Book Shop 113-24 1996 $600.00

ANGELOU, MAYA   Gather Together in My Name. New York: Random House, 1974. 1st edition; 8 1/2 x 5 3/4 inches; 3 p.l., 214 pages, (1) leaf; original cloth, dust jacket; signed and inscribed by author for David Mitchell. Very fine in like jacket.   Phillip J. Pirages 33-10 1996 $100.00

ANGELOU, MAYA   I Know Why the Caged Bird Sings. New York: Random House, 1969. 1st edition; small name, couple of very small spots to topstain, otherwise fine in dust jacket with two internal repairs; bright, attractive copy of author's first book.   Between the Covers 43-1 1996 $250.00

ANGELOU, MAYA   I Know Why the Caged Bird Sings. New York: Random House, 1969. 1st edition; author's first book; fine in dust jacket. Steven C. Bernard 71-28 1996 $150.00

ANGELOU, MAYA   I Know Why the Caged Bird Sings. New York: Random House, 1969. 1st edition; 8 1/2 x 5 3/4 inches; 3 p.l., 281, (1) pages; original cloth, dust jacket, with Christmas card from author laid in; very fine in like jacket; inscribed and signed by author for Pat Magarick.   Phillip J. Pirages 33-12 1996 $150.00

ANGELOU, MAYA   Oh Pray My Wings Are Gonna Fit Me Well. New York: Random House, 1975. 1st edition; 8 1/2 x 5 3/4 inches; ix, (1) 67 pages; original cloth backed boards, dust jacket; extremely fine in like jacket; inscribed and signed by author for David Mitchell.   Phillip J. Pirages 33-13 1996 $100.00

ANGELOU, MAYA   Wouldn't Take Nothing For My Journey Now. New York: Random House, 1993. 1st edition; one of 500 (#113) numbered and signed by author; 8vo; 141 pages; maroon cloth, maroon slipcase; fine; signed by author.   Robert F. Lucas 42-3 1996 $100.00

ANGIOLIERE, CECCO   Sonette. Officina Bodoni, 1944. One of 165 numbered copies; 4to; printed in 16 pt. Griffo roman and italic on Magnani handmade; quarter linen, patterned sides, printed label on spine, very nice, fresh copy in slipcase; rare.   Bertram Rota 272-343 1996 £650.00

THE ANGLER'S Guide: Containing Easy Instructions for the Youthful Beginner, with Several Obsevations on Fishing, Pointing Out the Proper Times and Seasons for the Different Kinds of Fish... London: Joseph Smith, 1828. Small 8vo; frontispiece; printed boards, boards soiled, nearly all of backstrip missing; with specially made folding box. Petersfield Bookshop FH58-295 196 £260.00

ANGULO, JAIME DE   Coyote Man and Old Dcotor Loon. San Francisco: Turtle Island Foundation, 1973-74. 1st edition; one of 1000 printed sets; cloth, spines faded, otherwise fine set.   James S. Jaffe 34-6 1996 $250.00

ANGUS, H. F.   British Columbia and the United States: The North Pacific slope from Fur Trade to Aviation. Toronto/New Haven/London: Ryerson Press/Yale and Oxford University Presses, 1942. 25cm; xv, 408 pages; maps; fine in mildly chipped dust jacket, uncut and unopened; beautiful copy. Lowther 1819; Strahern 12; E&L 86.   Rockland Books 38-6 1996 $125.00

ANNALS of Medical History. 1917-28. First Series, 10 volumes, illustrations; various cloth bindings, some volumes ex-library, good to very good. GM 6658.   W. Bruce Fye 71-48 1996 $400.00

ANNUAL Abstract of the Sinking Fund, for Michaelmas 1718, When it Was First Stated to Parliament, to the 10th of October, 1763. London: ptd. for R. Davis, J. Newbery, L. Davis and C. Reymers, C. Henderson.. 1764. 1st edition; 4to; original boards, rebacked, uncut, nice. Kress 6155; Goldsmith 9995; Higgs 3233.   Anthony W. Laywood 108-121 1996 £135.00

ANNUNZIO, GABRIELE D' 1863-1938   The Daughter of Jorio: a Pastoral Tragedy. Boston: Little Brown and Co., 1907. 1st American edition; 8vo; xxxvii, (v), 206, (i) pages; frontispiece and 5 plates; pictorial yellow tan cloth, titled with vignette in gilt on spine and titled on front cover above elaborate gilt illustration of an angel, the whole framed in gilt, in original pictorial tan dust jacket (very slightly soiled, 2 tiny tears at top), with matching illustration in orange, top edge gilt; fine in near fine dust jacket, beautiful unopened copy in wonderful binding.   Blue Mountain SP95-95 1996 $150.00

ANNUNZIO, GABRIELE D' 1863-1938   Episcopo and Company. Chicago: Herbert S. Stone & Co., 1896. 1st English language publication of any of D'Annunzio's works; 8vo; xiii, (i), 122, (iii) pages, deckle edged, title vignette in brown; near fine, green cloth titled in gilt on spine and front cover with gilt vignette within gilt ruled frame on front and rear covers, top edge gilt; near fine.   Blue Mountain SP95-94 1996 $125.00

ANNUNZIO, GABRIELE D' 1863-1938   The Flame of Life. Boston: Page, 1900. 1st edition; fine in attractive printed dust jacket that is splitting along edge of front panel and flap, with several very small nicks, uncommon in jacket.   Between the Covers 42-124 1996 $225.00

ANSORGE, W. J.   Under the African Sun: A Description of Native Races in Uganda, Sporting Adventures and Other Experiences. New York: Longmans, Green and Co., 1899. 1st American edition; 134 illustrations from photos by author, 2 colored plates; foxing, but photos and plates are largely unaffected, spine mdoerately skewed with two small ink spots, otherwise very good, loosk better than it sounds.   Hermitage SP95-1090 1996 $225.00

ANSTED, DAVID THOMAS   The Channel Islands. London: 1893. 3rd edition; 8vo; 476 pages; maps, illustrations; original green cloth, gilt lettered, very good.   K Books 442-32 1996 £50.00

ANSTED, DAVID THOMAS   Scenery, Science and Art: Being Extracts from the Notebook of a Geologist and Mining Engineer. London: John Van Voorst, 1854. 1st edition; 8vo; viii, 323, 4 page publisher's ads; 4 tinted lithographs, 21 woodcut text figures; modern half calf, red morocco label.   Thomas Thorp 489-10 1996 £120.00

ANSTED, DAVID THOMAS   Scenery, Science and Art: Being Extracts from the Note-Book of a Geologist and Mining Engineer. London: 1854. 1st edition; 8vo; pages viii, 323, 4 ads; 4 tinted litho plates, 21 woodcut text figures; cloth, lower joint starting to split.   John Henly 27-384 1996 £85.00

ANSTEY, CHRISTOPHER   The New Bath Guide; or, Memoirs of the B---r--d Family. (with) On the Much Lamented Death of the Marquis of Tavistock. (with) The Patriot, a Pindaric Address to Lord Buckhorse. Cambridge: Fletcher & Hodson sold also by J. Dodsley, J. Wilson...(2nd title London: J. Dodsley), 1766/67/67. 2nd edition of first 2 titles, 1st edition of 3rd; 8vo. and 4to; 139; 7; 44 pages; contemporary calf, stained and rather rubbed, spine in compartments with raised bands and gilt rules, lacking label, joints cracked, first few leaves little browned at edges, last page browned, but very good.   Simon Finch 24-3 1996 £120.00

ANSTEY, JOHN   The Pleader's Guide, a Didactic Poem: Containing the Conduct of a Suit at Law... London: printed for T. Cadell and W. Davies, Strand, 1804. 4th edition; contemporary speckled calf, worn, joints cracked, usable copy.   Meyer Boswell SL25-6 1996 $125.00

ANTAL, FREDERICK   Hogarth and His Place in European Art. London: Routledge & Kegan Paul, 1962. 26 x 19 cm; xxi, 270 pages; 152 plates; original cloth, in dust jacket.   Rainsford A54-320 1996 £55.00

ANTHONY Askabouts Pleasant Exercises for Little Minds: or a New and Entertaining Riddle Book for Young Masters and Misses. London: printed and sold by T. Batchelor, c. 1810. 60 x 94mm; pages 16; 1 woodcut to each page, untrimmed; sewn into later blue wrapper, excellent. Blackwell's B112-57 1996 £125.00

ANTHONY, EDWARD   The Fairies Up to Date. London: Butterworth, 1928. 1st edition; small 4to; more than 90 pages of colored illustrations by Jean De Bosschere; blue cloth gilt, few pages carelessly opened, spine darkened, else fresh copy; very scarce.   Barbara Stone 70-33 1996 £135.00

ANTHONY, GORDON   Russian Ballet: Camera Studies. London: Bles, 1939. 1st edition; thick folio; 96 tipped in photos; dust jacket slightly creased and chipped.   J. B. Muns 154-17 1996 $250.00

THE ANTI-Weesils. A Poem. London: printed and are to be sold by Randal Taylor, 1691. 1st edition; small 4to; disbound; fine. Wing A3516; Macdonald Dryden p. 269.   Ximenes 109-230 1996 $300.00

ANTON, JAMES   Retrospect of a Military Life. c. 1840. 8vo; xv, 381 pages; frontispiece and vignette titlepage; cloth, very good.   C. P. Hyland 216-7 1996 £75.00

ANTONINUS, BROTHER 1912-   The Blowing of the Seed. New Haven: Henry W. Wenning, One of 218 copies, signed by Everson; quarter calf, batik boards, fine; inscribed by well known bookseller and publisher, Henry Wenning, to a book scout.   Bev Chaney, Jr. 23-198 1996 $200.00

ANTONINUS, BROTHER 1912-   The Hazards of Holiness. Poems 1957-1960. Garden City: Doubleday & Co., 1962. 1st edition; near fine in lightly soiled dust jacket; inscribed by author. Front pastedown bears the rubber stamp "A Personal Reading Copy for Our Bookseller Friends.." Left Bank Books 2-31 1996 $100.00

ANTONINUS, BROTHER 1912-   On Printing: a Collection of Essays. San Francisco: Book Club of California, 1992. One of 400 copies; foolscap 8vo; illustrations and fold-out broadside; cloth, printed label, fine. Bertram Rota 272-52 1996 £50.00

ANTONINUS, BROTHER 1912-   X War Elegies. Waldport: Untide Press, 1943. 1st edition, 1st issue with black and yellow lettering; printed in an edition of 1000 copies; illustrations by Kemper Normalnd Jur.; wrappers faded at edges (common flaw with this title), otherwise very good fragile.   Left Bank Books 2-30 1996 $225.00

ANTONINUS, BROTHER 1912-   The Year's Declension. Berkeley: 1961. One of 100 copies; 11 1/4 x 8 inches; printed by Kenneth Carpenter on the Berkeley Albion; woodcut decorations; signed by Antoninus; binding spotted, otherwise near fine.   Timothy Hawley 115-199 1996 $200.00

APHORISMS for Youth, with Observations and Reflections, Religious, Moral, Critical and Characteristic... London: Lackington, Allen, 1801. Sole edition; small 8vo; 200 pages; frontispiece, tissue guard, early owner's name, lacks half title (?); finely bound in contemporary marbled brown calf, smooth backstrip divided by wide gilt roundel and lozenge bands, between dotted rolls, red morocco label in second compartment, remaining compartments with dotted line saltire and central foliate stars, seme other small tools, sides with border of fillet, lozenge and star roll, fillet and open twist roll, fillet on board edges, ball roll on turn-ins, marbled endpapers and edges, lilac silk marker, fine. Scarce. From the library of Marcus Gage.   Blackwell's B112-64 1996 £250.00

APHTHONIUS   Progymnasmata...cum Scholiss R. Lorichii. Amsterdam: L. Elzevir, 1642. 12mo; engraved title, printed title, 5 ff. index, 1 f. blank, 400 pages; contemporary plain calf, covers gilt with arms of F. A. de Thou, spine gilt in five panels, raised bands, de Thou monogram in four panels, all edges red, plain endpapers;   Marlborough 160-12 1996 £900.00

APIANUS, PETRUS   La Cosmographie... Paris: Par Vivant Gaultherot, 1553. Quarto; 70 leaves; half page woodcut on title, double page woodcut world map, numerous woodcut illustrations, including five half page woodcuts carrying ten (of 12?) woodcut volvelles; decorative woodcut initials; later quarter sheep over marbled boards, spine lettered in gilt, edges sprinkled red, several leaves with paper repairs, mostly marginal, but costing some letters and a small portion of one cut, overall very good. STC French 20. Shirley 84n.   Heritage Book Shop 196-176 1996 $3,750.00

APPARITIONS. Northridge: Lord John Press, 1981. 1st edition; one of 50 deluxe copies (from a total of 350) signed by each poet; silver stamped black cloth, without dust jacket, as issued; fine.   Captain's Bookshelf 38-1 1996 $125.00

APPENDIX to the Comment on the Petition of the British Inhabitants of Bengal, Bahar and Orissa to Parliament. N.P.: London, 1780? 1st edition; 4to; 60 pages; disbound;   Anthony W. Laywood 109-70 1996 £60.00

APPENDIX to the Comment on the Petition of the British Inhabitants of Bengal, Bahar and Orissa to Parliament. N.P.: London, n.d. 1780. 1st edition; 4to; (4), 24, 8, 8, 8, 8; disbound.   Anthony Laywood 108-76 1996 £85.00

APPERLEY, CHARLES JAMES 1777-1843   Hunting Reminiscences. London: Rudolph Ackermann, 1843. 1st edition; royal 8vo; (x), 332 pages; engraved plates and illustrations, engraved maps; original pictorial cloth, gilt, little very light wear, few faint marks and creases, but very good, scarce. Not in Podeschi.   Ash Rare Books Zenzybyr-5 1996 £245.00

APPERLEY, CHARLES JAMES 1777-1843   Memoirs of the Life of the Late John Mytton... London: Kegan, Paul Trench, ca. 1900. Tall 8vo; 20 color illustrations; green cloth, as issued, slight wear.   Appelfeld Gallery 54-170 1996 $125.00

APPERLEY, CHARLES JAMES 1777-1843   Remarks on the Condition of Hunters. London: M. A. Pittman, 1831. 1st edition; demy 8vo; (viii), (504) pages; contemporary half calf, gilt with horses, some wear, hinges slightly split, little bumped, few minor marks and flaws, but nice in attractive contemporary binding. Podeschi 138.   Ash Rare Books Zenzybyr-4 1996 £250.00

APPERSON, G. L.   A Jane Austen Dictionary. London: Cecil Palmer, 1932. 1st edition; 7 1/8 x 4 3/4 inches; pages x, 151, 2 pages ads; light tan cloth, black titling to backstrip, fine copy in slightly dust soiled dust jacket, scarce. Gilson M544.   Ian Hodgkins 78-85 1996 £68.00

APPERT, FRANCOIS   The Art of Preserving All Kinds of Animal and Vegetable Substances for Several Years. London: Black, Parry and Kingsbury, 1812. 2nd English edition; 8vo; 164 pages, page of ads and one folding plate; uncut in modern cloth backed boards; fine. Rare. Second Life Books 103-12 1996 $500.00

APPLE Pie ABC. New York: McLoughlin, 1897. 4to; 6 full page chromo litho illustrations plus 8 pages of illustrations printed in red and black; stif colored pictorial wrappers; very nice.   Barbara Stone 70-9 1996 £95.00

APULEIUS   Les Amours de Psyche et de Cupidan, avec la Poeme d'Adonis. Paris: Didot le Jeune, 1795. 1st of this edition; 4to; portrait of LaFontaine by Audouin after Rigault and 8 engraved plates after Moreau le Jeune, each with original tissue guard; contemporary polished calf, ornamental gilt tooled borders on covers, gilt spines, blue silk moire doublures and flyleaves, somewhat rubbed, one corner weak, top of spine repaired; handsome book. Cohen Ricci 583; Lewine 283; Gordon Ray 56; Brunet III 762.   Marilyn Braiterman 15-147 1996 $1,500.00

APULEIUS   De Cupidis et Psyches Amoribus Fbula Anilis. London: Hacon & Ricketts, 1901. One of 310 copies; folip; pages xxx, (2); printed on handmade paper, large initial, border and five fine wood engraved illustrations by Ricketts; original holland backed blue boards, paper label, uncut; light browning on two leaves, otherwise very good. Tomkinson 33.   Claude Cox   107-170   1996 £150.00

APULEIUS   The Golden Ass, or The Transformation of Lucius. London: Folio Society, 1960. One of 250 numbered and specially bound copies, signed by artist, of which in fact only 79 copies were issued; 9 lithographs and endpapers by Michael Ayrton; full decorated gilt leather covers, top edge gilt, covers slightly rubbed and marked, near fine. Ulysses   39-27   1996 £225.00

APULEIUS   Operum, Secunda Pars. Basle: per Henricum Petri, 1560. Early collected edition; 8vo; pages 404, (lxxiii), text in Roman letter, index in italic, woodcut initials, printed side notes, 2 or 3 small marginal tears, occasional old but later marginalia; most attractive contemporary calf, probably Lyonese, gilt arabesques on each cover, gilt florets in 6 compartments on spine, single gilt rule at borders of covers; rare. Not in BM STC Germ. Adams A 1365; not in Wellcome, Durling, Nissen.   A. Sokol XXV-6   1996 £750.00

ARABIAN NIGHTS   Ali Baba and the Forty Thieves. Chicago: 1962. Limited to 400 copies; 2 1/2 x 1 15/16 inches; 46 pages; printed in brown and black on Dutch handmade paper by John Enschede, first book of the Press to be printed offset and only 100 copies were actually bound up, full brown leather, cover design in gilt, all edges gilt; extremely fine.   Bromer Booksellers   90-177   1996 $100.00

ARABIAN NIGHTS   Arabian Nights. London: Cassell, Petter and Galpin, n.d., c. 1870. 4to; hundreds of engravings on wood after drawings by various artists; three quarter green morocco, sand grained green cloth boards, spine in compartments tooled in gilt, little spotting to relims, else very fresh copy.   Barbara Stone   70-17   1996 £125.00

ARABIAN NIGHTS   The Arabian Nights. London: Constable & Co., n.d. 1912. 1st edition; xi, 299 pages; decorated half title, color frontispiece and 19 color plates mounted on dark brown paper with captioned tissue guards, title vignette, 26 full page, 71 text illustrations and 27 pictorial headpieces by Rene Bull; purple cloth gilt, small onlaid extra color plate, top edge purple, endpaper foxed, head of spine snagged.   Robin Greer 94A-21   1996 £175.00

ARABIAN NIGHTS   The Arabian Nights Tales from the Thousand and One Nights. London: Hodder & Stoughton, 1924. 1st edition illustrated by Detmold; 4to; pages viii, 240; 12 absolutely stunning mounted colored plates behind tissue guards by E. J. Detmold; original white cloth, elaborately and pictorialy gilt, glorious copy in very fine, sparkling condition, very scarce.   Sotheran PN32-111   1996 £950.00

ARABIAN NIGHTS   Stories from the Arabian Nights. London: Hodder & Stoughton, 1907. Limited to 350 copies, numbered and signed by artist; quarto; xvi, 133 pages; 50 mounted color plates by Edmund Dulac; with descriptive tissue guards; bound by Sangorski & Sutcliffe in full orange morocco decoratively stamped in gilt on front cover, gilt lettered spine with raised bands, gilt board edges and turn-ins, top edge gilt, others uncut, marbled endpapers; fine.   Heritage Book Shop 196-210   1996 $2,250.00

ARAGO, DOMINIQUE FRANCOIS JEAN   Life of James Watt... Edinburgh: Adam and Charles Black, 1839. 1st edition in English; 8vo; 142 pages, complete with half title and 8 pages of publisher's ads at end; original cloth, printed label on upper cover, uncut, fine. Kress C4779; Not in Goldsmiths or Williams.   John Drury 82-8   1996 £75.00

ARAGO, JACQUES   Promenade Autour du Monde, Pendant les Annees 1817, 1818, 1819 and 1820, sur Les Corvettes du Roi l'Uranie et la Physicienne... Paris: Leblanc, 1822. 1st edition; 8vo; 2 volumes; with 4to. atlas volume; atlas with engraved map and 25 lithographed plates; uncut; 1st title in contemporary light blue paper boards, ms. spine labels, rubbed but sound, original tan boards, printed paper side label, bit rubbed; fine set. Hill p. 7-10; Ferguson 850; Sabin 1867; Borba de Moraes I 44.   Ximenes   109-10   1996 $3,500.00

ARAGON, LOUIS   Henri Matisse: a Novel. New York: Harcourt Brace Jovanovich, 1972. 4to; 2 volumes, 356; 366 pages; 155 color plates, 541 monochrome illustrations; cloth, dust jackets, slipcase. Freitag 6199. Brannan 43-395   1996 $275.00

ARATUS   Phenomena. Lexington; King Library Press, 1975. Number 30 of 75 copies; 10.5 x 8 inches; 200dcuts, printed in black with brown; orange decorative paste paper over boards, printed paper label on spine, errata slip laid in. Upper joint of the extremely fragile binding has cracks at head and foot, otherwise fine (hinges unaffected by hairline cracks in binding), in fine dust jacket. Printers Choice 50.   Joshua Heller   21-148   1996 $200.00

ARBER, A.   Herbals, Their Origin and Evolution. Cambridge: 1938. 2nd edition; royal 8vo; pages xxiv, 326, 27 plates and 131 text figures; cloth, without front flyleaf, otherwise nice, clean copy.   Wheldon & Wesley 207-201   1996 £75.00

ARBLAY, FRANCES BURNEY D' 1752-1840   Brief Reflections Relative to the Emigrant French Clergy... London: printed by T. Davison for Thomas Cadell, 1793. 1st edition; 8vo; full red crushed levant, gilt, spine and inner dentelles gilt, top edge gilt, fine. Rothschild 549; CBEL II 971. Ximenes   108-50   1996 $750.00

ARBLAY, FRANCES BURNEY D' 1752-1840   Camilla or a Picture of Youth. London: T. Payne, T. Cadell etc., 1802. Small octavo; 5 volumes, approximately 350 pages each; sympatheticaly rebound in grey line with leather spines, gilt on red leather labels; attractive set. Rothschild 551 (for first ed.).   Hartfield   48-L16   1996 $495.00

ARBLAY, FRANCES BURNEY D' 1752-1840   Cecillia, or Memoirs of an Heiress. London: J. F. Dove, n.d. 1825. 8vo; 2 volumes, pages 480, 480; extra engraved titles and frontispieces by Heath after Corbould; elegant blue grained morocco, raised bands, spine extra gilt in compartments, gilt fillets and inner dentelles, endpapers and all ages marbled; attractive set.   Hartfield   48-L17   1996 $295.00

ARBLAY, FRANCES BURNEY D' 1752-1840   Diary and Letters of Madame D'Arblay. London: Colburn, 1854. Octavo; 7 volumes; portrait frontispiece, holograph ms. foldout in volume 1; bound by Leighton in dark blue cloth, pretty set. CBEL II 527.   Hartfield   48-A3   1996 $295.00

ARBLAY, FRANCES BURNEY D' 1752-1840   Diary and Letters of Madame D'Arblay. Swan Sonnenscheim and Co., 1892. 8vo; 4 volumes, finely bound in contemporary green half morocco gilt, top edge gilt, spines of 2 volumes lightly rubbed, edges spotted, but nice set. Thomas Thorp   489-50   1996 £150.00

ARBLAY, FRANCES BURNEY D' 1752-1840   Evelina, or the History of a Young Lady's Introduction to the World. London: J. F. Dove, n.d. 1825? 8vo; 426 pages; elegant blue grained morocco, raised bands, spine extra gilt in compartments, gilt fillets and inner dentelles, endpapers and all edges marbled; attractive set.   Hartfield   48-L18 1996 $195.00

ARBUTHNOT, JOHN   Tables of the Grecian, Roman and Jewish Measures, Weights and Coins. London: Ralph Smith, n.d. 1705? 1st edition; small oblong 4to; 14 leaves, engraved throughout, title within a cartouche and signed 'Sturt sculpsit', 29 tables; contemporary cottage panelled calf, neatly rebacked, very good; early 18th century ownership inscriptions of Thomas and Elizabeth Wrottesley. Not in Goldsmith or Kress.   John Drury 82-9   1996 £250.00

ARCANGELI, FRANCESCO   Graham Sutherland. New York: Abrams, 1975. Folio; 41 pages text, 230 plates, 117 in color; cloth, dust jacket. Freitag 9235.   Brannan   43-629   1996 $135.00

ARCE, HECTOR   Groucho. New York: Putnam, 1979. 1st edition; thick 8vo; illustrations; dust jacket, very good; from Cukor's library with his Paul Landacre bookplate.   George J. Houle   68-92   1996 $175.00

ARCHBALD, ROBERT W.   Proceedings of the United States Senate and the House of Representatives in the Trial of Impeachment of Robert W. Archbald, Additional Circuit Judge of the United States from the Third Judicial Circuit. Washington: GPO, 1913. 3 volumes; ex-library, worn and soiled, usable set.   Meyer Boswell SL25-116   1996 $150.00

ARCHER, G.   The Birds of British Somaliland and the Gulf of Aden. London: 1937-61. Imperial 8vo; 4 maps, 23 plain and 34 colored plates; half red morocco, gilt; very fine, very scarce; from the collection of Jan Coldewey.   Wheldon & Wesley   207-4   1996 £1,000.00

ARCHER, THOMAS   The Frogs' Parish Clerk; and His Adventures in Strange Lands. London: Sampson Low, Son and Marston, 1866. 1st edition; 104 pages; 18 fine engraved illustrations, signed "GS", perhaps George Augustus Sala; original mauve embossed cloth, gilt, vignette on front board, all edges gilt; extremities lightly rubbed, very nice. Osborne p. 962/3.   Robert Clark   38-245   1996 £85.00

ARCHER, W. G.   Indian Paintings from the Punjab Hills. London: Sotheby Parke Bernet, 1973. 1st edition; small folio; 2 volumes, frontispiece, xxxiv, 448; vi, 335 pages; cloth, dust jacket lightly chipped and soiled, else fine.   The Bookpress 75-377   1996 $225.00

THE ARCTIC World: its Plants Animals and Natural Phenomena. London: 1876. 4to; pages viii, 276, 16 plates, 112 woodcut text engravings; pictorial cloth, gilt, top edge gilt, slight foxing, otherwise fine. John Henly 27-151 1996 £75.00

ARDINGER, RICHARD "What Thou Lovest Well Remains", 100 Years of Ezra Pound. Boise: Limberlost Press, 1986. One of 26 copies, signed by all 22 contributors; fine issued without dust jacket. Bella Luna 7-472 1996 $350.00

ARDITTI, J. Fundamentals of Orchid Biology. London: 1992. 8vo; 704 pages; numerous illustrations; cloth. Wheldon & Wesley 207-1786 1996 £80.00

ARDIZZONE, EDWARD Nicholas and the Fast Moving Diesel. London: Eyre and Spottiswoode, 1947. 1st edition; folio; 40 chalk drawings in color and line made on the plate with titlepage and vignette, lettering throughout in cursive script by Ardizzone; yellow boards with color drawing and lettering on front cover, boards little dusty, else very nice, very scarce. Barbara Stone 70-18 1996 £250.00

ARDIZZONE, EDWARD Tim and Lucy Go to Sea. London: Oxford University Press, 1938. 1st edition; folio; 32 pages printed rectos only, hand lettered text; illustrations in color by author; cloth backed pictorial boards, extremities just rubbed, else very fresh copy of a very scarce title. Barbara Stone 70-19 1996 £275.00

ARETINO, PIETRO La Vita di Maria Vergine. Venice: Francesco Marcolini, c. 1540? Small 8vo; 180 unnumbered leaves, italic letter, woodcut medallion on titlepage repeated at end, corner of 1 leaf repaired without loss; 18th century French crushed red morocco, gilt triple fillets, edges and spine, marbled endpapers, all edges gilt; very good; autograph of Pierre Gauthier, Aretino's biographer on fly. Index Aurel 107.069. Brunet 1416. A. Sokol XXV-7 1996 £1,950.00

ARGENTERIO, GIOVANNI 1513-1572 De Morbis Lib. XIIII...ex secunda hac aeditione. Lyon: J. Forus for J. Giunta's heirs, 1558. 2nd edition in this form; 8vo; (10) leaves, 662 pages, (27) leaves, woodcut printer's device on title and woodcut initials; some early marginal annotations, light dampstaining and browning; 19th century calf backed marbled boards, spine damaged but sound. I. A. 107-232. Baudrier VI 291; Durling 265; Wellcome I 403. Jeffrey D. Mancevice 20-2 1996 $425.00

ARGUS, ARABELLA Further Adventures of Jemmy Donkey; Interspersed with Biographical Sketches of the Horse. London: William Darton, 1821. 1st edition; 12mo; 154, (2 ad) pages, engraved frontispiece, 2 engraved plates; original roan backed marabled boards; Osborne p. 858. James Burmester 29-7 1996 £65.00

ARIAS, P. E. A History of 1000 Years of Greek Vase Paintings. New York: Harry N. Abrams, 1962. Folio; 410 pages, 329 plates; original cloth; signed presentation copy. Archaeologia Luxor-2911 1996 $375.00

ARIOSTO, LODOVICO La Lena Comedia... Venice: Gabriel Giolito, 1551. New edition; 12mo; 36 leaves, woodcut printer's devices on title and at end; light dampstain (darker on endpapers), 19th century morocco, gilt, edges gilt (lightly rubbed). Adams A1632; Gamba 73. Jeffrey D. Mancevice 20-3 1996 $375.00

ARIOSTO, LODOVICO Orlando Furioso. London: printed for otridge & Son, et al, 1799. 8vo; 5 volumes in 3; engraved frontispiece to each volume, portrait of translator and additional plate in Volume III engraved by William Blake., this set has been extra illustrated with numerous plates from a continental edition of the same poem, printed ca. 1774; some of the inserted plates are engraved by Bartolozzi; 19th century half vellum, spines gilt, contrasting red and black morocco labels, spines bit soiled; plates lightly browned, but very good. Bentley 417D; CBEL II 842. Ximenes 108-7 1996 $250.00

ARISTAENETUS The Love Epistles of Aristaenetus. London: printed for J. Wilkie, 1771. 1st edition; 8vo; bound without half title and final leaf of ads (as often), otherwise very good; full dark blue morocco, gilt, spine and inner dentelles, gilt, all edges gilt, slight rubbing to upper joint; Iolo Williams p. 210; Rothschild 1843; CBEL II 817. Ximenes 109-263 1996 $350.00

ARISTOCRACY. A Novel. New York: D. Appleton & Co., Sept. 15, 1888. 1st edition; 8vo; original orange printed wrappers with ads on inner and back wrappers, plus 14 pages publisher's ads at back, some tears of wrappers and rubbing; ownership signature removed from endpaper and page 147, few gatherings loose, good, rare in original wrappers. Wright III 126. James Cummins 14-144 1996 $100.00

ARISTOPHANES The Birds. London: Lion and Unicorn Press, 1971. Limited to 400 copies, this number 67; 4to; numerous illustrations in pen and wash by Quentin Blake; pictorial wrappers designed by Blake. Barbara Stone 70-31 1996 £55.00

ARISTOPHANES The Frogs. Oxford: ptd. for J. & J. Fletcher & sold by Messrs. Rivington; T. Payne...n.d. 1785. 1st edition in English; 4to; complete with half title; disbound; fine, uncommon. Ximenes 108-8 1996 $300.00

ARISTOPHANES The Frogs. New York: Joh. Enschede en Zoenen/Haarlem, 1937. Limited to 1500 copies, signed by artist; 4to; wood engravings by John Austen; original pictorial linen, brown board chemise and slipcase, fine in lightly dust soiled slipcase. James S. Jaffe 34-694 1996 $125.00

ARISTOPHANES Lysistrata. Fanfrolic Press, 1926. One of 725 numbered copies, signed by Jack Lindsay; large folio; headpieces and four full page illustrations by Norman Lindsay; printed on Batchelor's handmade at the Chiswick Press; half blue morocco, boards, gilt, leather just little scuffed in places and endpapers severely foxed, otherwise remarkably nice, fresh copy. Bertram Rota 272-141 1996 £275.00

ARISTOPHANES Lysistrata. New York: Limited Editions Club, 1934. Copy number 904 from a total edition of 1500 numbered copies, signed by Picasso; illustrations by Picasso; decorative paper covered boards, tissue jacket slightly chipped and torn, slightest of fading to spine of card liner and box lightly worn, overall fine, in very slightly worn slipcase. Hermitage SP95-932 1996 $3,750.00

ARISTOTELES 384-322 BC (Greek & Latin) De Coloribus Libellus. Florence: L. Torrentino, 1548. Editio princeps; 4to; 197, (1) pages, (1) leaf, two large historiated initials; contemporary limp vellum, small portion of upper blank margin torn away from first 2 leaves, not affecting text, some minor stains; early inscription at foot of titlepage of the Ciscalced Augustinians of Genoa. Cranz 108.139; Hoffmann I 289; Adams P 1958. Jeffrey D. Mancevice 20-4 1996 $1,750.00

ARISTOTELES 384-322 BC On the Parts of Animals. London: 1882. 1st English translation; 263 pages; original binding; GM 275. W. Bruce Fye 71-59 1996 $200.00

ARISTOTELES 384-322 BC De Poetica Liber. Oxford: Typographeo Clarendoniano, 1760. 8vo; (8), 132 pages, engraved very good vignette; original calf. Kenneth Karmiole 1NS-23 1996 $175.00

ARISTOTELES 384-322 BC Aristoteles Poetics; or, Discourses Concerning Tragic and Epic Imitation. London: printed for J. Dodsley & Messrs. Richardson & Urquhart, 1775. 1st edition of this anonymous translation; 8vo; disbound; half title present; very good. CBEL II 1489. Ximenes 108-9 1996 $250.00

ARISTOTELES 384-322 BC Politics and Poetics. Lunenburg: Printed for the members of the Limited Edtions Club, 1964. Number 417 of 1500 signed by Leonard Baskin; illustrations by Baskin; fine in publisher's slipcase. Hermitage SP95-933 1996 $250.00

ARISTOTELES 384-322 BC Problemata cum Commento...cum Petri de Apono...Commentarijs...Adiunctis Alexandri Aphrodisei: ac Plutarchi...Problematibus. Venice: Lucantonio Giunta, 15th Nov. 1518. One of the earliest 16th century editions; folio; ff. (xx), 282; gothic letter in 2 sizes, double columns, many woodcut initials (3 large white on black), 5 woodcut diagrams, small woodcut printer's device at end, light browning in parts, early annotations in 2 hands on endpapers and in margins, 4 lines crossed through; good copy in medieval antiphonal leaf over boards, rebacked in vellum, covers bit soiled, extensive 17th century textual annotations on endpapers. GM STC It. p. 55; this ed. not in Adams, NUC, Essling or Sander. A. Sokol XXV-8 1996 £1,500.00

ARISTOTELES 384-322 BC The Complete Works of Aristotle. London: 1984. 8vo; 2 volumes, 2457 pages; cloth. Wheldon & Wesley 207-139 1996 £60.00

ARISTOTLE, PSEUD. Aristotle's Compleat Master-Piece. London: sold by the Book Sllers, n.d., ca. 1710. 12th edition; 8vo; 153, (17) pages, printing defect on D3, folding plate and several text engravings; contemporary full calf. James Tait Goodrich K40-12 1996 $195.00

ARISTOTLE, PSEUD. The Works of Aristotle. London: L. Hawes and S. Crowder, 1772. Part 1 is the 30th edition, part 2 is the 12th edition, part 3 is 28th edition; 8vo; 4 parts with separate pagination 144; 156; (4); 156; 120 pages; frontispiece, first title bound in reverse, numerous text illustrations, pages foxed, with some heavy browning towards the rear third; recent rebinding in full calf. James Tait Goodrich K40-13 1996 $175.00

THE ARIZONA Republican Phoenix, Arizona, August 1892. Phoenix: Arizona Republican, 1892. 1st edition; 63 pages; illustrations and portraits; original pictorial wrappers; chipping, some wrapper text affected and last 4 page numbers, internal text fine with tears neatly repaired, very good.   Michael D. Heaston 23-16 1996 $1,200.00

ARMAN, MARK   A Legacy of Metal Types. Thaxted: The Workshop Press, 1987. 1st edition; one of 130 copies, numbered and signed by author/printer all on Goatskin Parchment paper and Abbey Mills Laid; page size 11 1/2 x 8 1/8 inches; handset in 14 pt. Caslon Old Face Roman and italic and hand printed and bound by author; with many tip-ins on various papers and inks; marbled paper over boards, brown linen spine; as new.   Priscilla Juvelis 95/1-245 1996 $350.00

ARMENINI, GIOVAN BATTISTA   De' Veri Precetti della Pittura. Ravenna: Francesco Teboldini for Tomaso Pasini in Bologna, 1587. 1st edition; 2nd issue; 4to; (10) leaves, 229, (3) pages, italic type, woodcut printer's device on titlepage; modern vellum, some foxing. Arntzen Rainwater H33; Chamberlain 1983; Borroni I 1674;   Jeffrey D. Mancevice 20-5 1996 $2,500.00

ARMES, GEORGE A.   Ups and Downs of an Army Officer. Washington: n.p., 1900. Large 8vo; xx, 784 pages, index, frontispiece, 106 text illustrations; original brown cloth, ornate silver stamped design, very nice, scarce. Howes A316.   Kenneth Karmiole 1NS-74 1996 $250.00

ARMITAGE, MERLE   Dance Memoranda. New York: 1947. 1st edition; photos; dust jacket.   J. B. Muns 154-325 1996 $125.00

ARMITAGE, MERLE   Martha Graham. Los Angeles: 1937. Limited edition; photos.   J. B. Muns 154-205 1996 $185.00

ARMITT, M. L.   Rydal. Kendal: Titus Wilson, 1916. 1st edition; large thick 8vo; xv, 728 pages, colored frontispiece, 14 illustrations, folding pedigree and additional map tipped in; modern half levant morocco, gilt. R.F.G. Hollett & Son 78-671 1996 £95.00

ARMITT, M. L.   Rydal. Kendal: Titus Wilson, 1916. 1st edition; 2nd issue with slip correcting the page number pasted in at last entry of list of illustrations; large thick 8vo; pages xv, 728; colored frontispiece, 14 illustrations, folding pedigree, additional map tipped in; uncut, original blue cloth, little worn, neatly recased, little spotting in one or two places; prospectus loosely inserted.   R.F.G. Hollett & Son 78-670 1996 £75.00

ARMOR, SAMUEL   History of Orange County, California. Los Angeles: 1911. 1st edition; 705 pages; photos, folding map, leather, nice; 6 Guns 76.   T. A. Swinford 49-28 1996 $350.00

ARMSTRONG, A. M.   The Place-Names of cumberland. Cambridge: University Press, 1950-52. 1st editions; 8vo; 3 volumes; pages 565, map in rear pocket; original cloth, gilt, slight wear to few edges.   R.F.G. Hollett & Son 78-672 1996 £65.00

ARMSTRONG, AMZI   A Syllabus of Lectures on the Visions of the Revelation. Morris-town: P. A. Johnson, 1815. 1st edition; 12mo; 238, (2) pages; full contemporary calf and label, small signature clipped from title; some browning. Gaustad p. 214; S&S 33882.   M & S Rare Books 60-270 1996 $125.00

ARMSTRONG, ELIZABETH   Robert Estienne, Royal Printer. Cambridge: the University Press, 1954. 1st edition; 4to; (xxii), 310 pages, 8 plates; cloth, dust jacket; fine.   The Bookpress 75-267 1996 $135.00

ARMSTRONG, HARRY   Principles and Practice of Aviation Medicine. Baltimore: 1941. 1st edition, reprinted; 496 pages; numerous photographic illustrations; original binding. GM 2137.10.   W. Bruce Fye 71-62 1996 $100.00

ARMSTRONG, JOHN 1709-1779   The Art of Preserving Health: a Poem. London: printed for A. Millar, 1744. 1st edition; 4to; (ii), 134 pages; recent half calf antique with new endpapers; Rothschild 56; Foxon A296; Osler 4335; Hayward 168.   David Bickersteth 133-3 1996 £125.00

ARMSTRONG, MARGARET   Western Wild Flowers. New York: and London: G. P. Putnam's sons, 1915. 1st edition; 8vo; author's first book; 596 pages, orange gilt stamped cloth with distinctive design by Armstrong of intertwining flowers and stems; minor wear to edges, generally very good+ copy.   Priscilla Juvelis 95/1-9 1996 $750.00

ARMSTRONG, MARTIN   Saint Hercules and Other Stories. Printed by Oliver Simon at the Curwen Press & pub. by The Fleuron Ltd. 1927. One of 310 numbered copies; 11 1/2 x 7 3/4 inches; 65 pages; drawings by Paul Nash; cloth backed decorated paper covered boards; worn and bumped, interior near fine. Ransom 23.   Timothy Hawley 115-213 1996 $100.00

ARMSTRONG, MARTIN   Saint Hercules and Other Stories. London: Fleuron, 1927. Limited to 310 copies; tall quarto; 65 pages; 4 pochoir colored images by Nash; cloth backed patterned boards; very fine. Ransom 2702.   Bromer Booksellers 90-205 1996 $375.00

ARMSTRONG, MOSTYN JOHN   An Actual Survey of the Great Post-Roads Between London and Edinburgh, with the country Three Miles, On Each Side, Drawn On a Scale of Half an Inch to a Mile. London: printed for and sold by author and the booksellers, August 1, 1776. 1st edition; 8vo; frontispiece, engraved titlepage, 44 very attractive engraved road maps, some with coloring in outline and each with facing leaf of letterpress; enhanced by the presence of an appealing engraved leaf of ads, virtually a trade card, printed in sepia; contemporary half calf, spine gilt, slight wear; few small stains, but fine. Fordham Studies in Carto-Bib. p. 45.   Ximenes 109-12 1996 $750.00

ARMSTRONG, WALTER   Sir Henry Raeburn. London: Heinemann, 1901. Limited edition; folio; pages ix, 121; 61 large and 8 small plates; original cloth, gilt, little marked, endpapers little spotted.   R.F.G. Hollett 76-6 1996 £120.00

ARMSTRONG, ZELLA   Notable Southern Families. Chattanooga & Bristol: 1974. Reprint of 1918-33 edition; 8vo; 6 volumes; plates; original cloth.   Howes Bookshop 265-1617 1996 £75.00

ARNALDI, ENEA, CONTE   Idea di Un Teatro Nelle Principali Sue Parti Simile a'Teatri Antichi. Venice: Antonio Veronese, 1762. 1st edition; 4to; (iv), xxxii, 82, (2) pages; 6 folding plates; later wrappers, very nice, unfortunately lacking a 58 page addendum to text; Berlin Cat. 2790. Bookpress 75-148 1996 $1,500.00

ARNAY, JEAN RODOLPHE D'   Della Vita Privata de' Romani. Napoli: Nella Stamperia Simoniana, 1763. 1st Italian translation; 8vo; 8 leaves, 400 pages, ?large and thick paper; contemporary Italian red morocco, fully gilt with large central lozenge and elaborate corner pieces of leafy scrolls with flowers and fleur-de-lys within wide ornamental borders, spine fully gilt, all edges gilt, very slight rubbing on hinges, but in fine condition.   H. M. Fletcher 121-84 1996 £650.00

ARNOBIUS   Disputationum Adversus Gentes. Rome: Priscianese, 1542. Editio Princeps; folio; 108ff; printed guide letters; old full vellum; very good. Ind. Aur. 108.890; Adams A1994.   Bennett Gilbert LL29-3 1996 $1,200.00

ARNOLD, CHANNING   The American Egypt: a Record of Travel in Yucatan. New York: Doubleday Page, 1909. Small 4to; frontispiece, xiv, 391 pages; 8 figures, 15 plates, 5 maps and plans; original cloth, top edge gilt.   Archaeologia Luxor-4221 1996 $125.00

ARNOLD, E. C.   The Birds of Eastbourne. Eastbourne: 1936. Imperial 8vo; 10 colored plates, other illustrations; original buckram, top of spine, very slightly snagged, contents lightly foxed; very scarce; inscribed by author to Clifford Bower.   David A.H. Grayling MY95Orn-89 1996 £65.00

ARNOLD, EDWIN   The Light of Asia; or the Great Renunciation. London: Ballantyne Press for Trubner & Co., 1889. One of 126 large paper copies; 7 1/4 x 5 3/4 inches; xviii, (2), (21)-240 pages; frontispiece, decorative initials and number of small illustrations in text, title printed in red and black, bookplate on flyleaf; very appealing auburn crushed levant morocco by Bayntun (for Brentano's), raised bands, gilt titling on spine, wide turn-ins decorated with triple gilt rules and corner ornaments, marbled endpapers, all edges gilt; very fine, only the most trivial imperfections, binding quite bright and essentially unworn;   Phillip J. Pirages 33-57 1996 $175.00

ARNOLD, J. B.   Nautical Archeology of Padre Island: The Spanish Shipwrecks of 1554. New York: Academic Press, 1978. 1st edition; 4to; 462 pages;illustrations; dust jacket.   Maggie Lambeth 30-23 1996 $100.00

ARNOLD, JOSIAS LYNDON   Poems. Providence: Carter & Wilkinson, 1797. 12mo; 142 pages; contemporary calf, gilt red morocco, extremities somewhat rubbed. Wegelin, Early American Poetry p. 8.   Kenneth Karmiole 1NS-24 1996 $125.00

ARNOLD, MATTHEW 1822-1888　　Empedocles on Etna: a Dramatic Poem... Portland: 1900. Limited to 450 copies on Kelmscott handmade paper; octavo; 51 pages, colored calligraphic lettering and ornate borders; faintly darkened to extremities and tail of spine chipped, else fine, crisp copy.　Bromer Booksellers 87-239　1996 $250.00

ARNOLD, MATTHEW 1822-1888　　Poems. London: Macmillan & Co., 1888. Crown 8vo; 3 volumes; slightly later white calf, for Bumpus, gilt and enamelled with roses, inner gilt dentelles, all edges gilt, few faint marks and scratches, little discolored with age, but still very pretty set. Ash Rare Books Zenzybyr-6　1996 £125.00

ARNOLD, MATTHEW 1822-1888　　The Popular Education of France, with Notices of That of Holland and Switzerland. London: Longman, Green, 1861. 1st edition; half title, contemporary half calf, rubbed, gilt block of General Assembly Library, New Zealand on front board and cancelled library label on endpapers.　Jarndyce 103-378　1996 £75.00

ARNOLD, MATTHEW 1822-1888　　The Works... London: Macmillan and Co., Ltd., Smith, Elder and Co., 1903. 1st complete collected edition, limited to 775 copies only; 8vo; 15 volumes; frontispiece in volume 1, general title and titles printed in red and black; contemporary half red crushed morocco, spines divided in 6 compartments, gilt lettered direct in two, others with gilt devices, red cloth sides, marbled endpapers, top edge gilt, others uncut, by Morrell; occasional very light spotting; fine. Simon Finch 24-4　1996 £950.00

ARNOLD, THOMAS　　Memorials of St. Edmund's Abbey. London: 189-92. 8vo; volumes I-II; without volume III published some years later; original cloth.　Howes Bookshop 265-1607　1996 £55.00

ARNOLD, WILLIAM HARRIS　　First Report of a Book-Collector. New York: Dodd, Mead, 1898. 1st trade edition; one of 220 copies; 12mo; printed in red and black at the Marion Press on handmade paper; original three quarter red cloth and boards, labels, gilt, uncut, very unusual binding with paper spine piece pasted onto full length of cloth spine before application of gilt cloth label; gilt rubbed from spine label, entirely uncut and unopened, nice copy of an extremely rare book. Mac Donnell 12-8　1996 $300.00

ARNOT, HUGO　　The History of Edinburgh...to Which is Added...Improvements of the city from the 1763 (sic) to the Present Period. Edinburgh: Creech, 1788. 4to; title, pages xii, 677, map, 19 engraved plates; calf, rebacked, some foxing.　Marlborough 162-7 1996 £335.00

ARNOTT, JAMES　　The House of Arnot and Some Of Its Branches. Edinburgh: T. & A. Constable, 1918. Small 4to; pages xi, 276; 18 plates; original cloth, gilt, over bevelled boards, little scratched and marked, extremities rather worn and frayed, tear to top of upper hinge repaired. Flyleaves foxed.　R.F.G. Hollett 76-7　1996 £65.00

ARNOW, HARRIETTE SIMPSON　　Hunter's Horn. New York: Macmillan, 1949. 1st edition; near fine in bright dust jacket with some edge wear to bottom of spine.　Anacapa House 5-15　1996 $135.00

ARONSON, J. K.　　An Account of the Foxglove and Medical Uses, 1785-1985.. London: 1985. 1st edition; 399 pages; original binding. GM 1836.　W. Bruce Fye 71-2286　1996 $125.00

ART in California. A Survey of American Art with Special Reference to Californian Painting, Sculpture, and Architecture. Irvine: Westphal Pub., 1988. New edition; 670 pages; 250 black and white illustrations; fine with slipcase.　Argonaut Book Shop 113-28　1996 $145.00

ART in Industry through the Ages. New Delhi: Navrang, 1982. 4to; 212 pages, 88 photographic plates, text illustrations; cloth, very good in dust jacket.　J. M. Cohen 35-1　1996 $165.00

ART Work of Seattle and Alaska. Racine: W. D. Harney, 1907. Large thick 4to; text and 80 leaves with one or two toned gravure reproductions of original photos on stiff leaves with tissue guards; original bevelled black calf, nicely rebacked in crimson calf with new spine label; fine, tight and clean, plates very fresh.　Marilyn Braiterman 15-159　1996 $675.00

ARTAMONOV, M. I.　　Treasures from Scythian Tombs in the Hermitage Museum, Leningrad. London: Thames and Hudson, 1969. Large 4to; 296 pages, 488 illustrations, 23 diagrams, 2 maps; original cloth, dust jacket. Archaeologia Luxor-2912　1996 $150.00

ARTEMIDORUS, DALDIANUS　　Oneirokriton Biblia Pente/de Somniorum Interpretatione Libre Quinque. Venetiis: Aldus Manutius, 1518. 1st edition; 8vo; (ii), (166) pages; crushed olive levant with Aldine gilt devices on both sides, slight edge rubbing, early ink notes and contemporary ms. index bound in at rear; pretty copy.　John Gach 150-15　1996 $5,000.00

ARTHUR, ELIZABETH　　Beyond the Mountain. New York: Harper, 1983. Uncorrected proof; wrappers; fine.　Between the Covers 42-16　1996 $125.00

ARTHUR, T. S.　　The Seamstress. A Tale of the To,es/ Philadelphia: R. G. Berford, 1843. 1st edition; 8vo; 48 pages; removed, tear in blank portion of title; rare. Wright i 153.　M & S Rare Books 60-113　1996 $100.00

ARTHUR, T. W.　　Arthur's Directory of Carlisle... Carlisle: A. Barnes Moss, 1880. 8vo; pages xvi, 192, xvii-l, 1; printed cloth from original binding bound in at end (damped); modern half red levant morocco, gilt. R.F.G. Hollett & Son 78-676　1996 £85.00

ARTHUR, T. W.　　Confessions of a Housekeeper. Philadelphia: Lippincott, Grambo & Co., 1851. 1st edition; 12mo; 213 pages; 12 illustrations; old calf backed boards, bookplate inside front cover. Wright II 89.　M & S Rare Books 60-112　1996 $450.00

ARTICLES Drawn Up by order of the Edinburgh Society, with the View to Render More Complete the Laws Concerning Highways, Bridges and Ferries. N.P.: n.d. Edinburgh: 1770? folio; 4 pages; uncut, very nice. C. R. Johnson 37-2　1996 £110.00

ARTISTS and Writers Protest Against the War in Viet Nam. N.P.: Artists and Writers Protest Inc., 1967. One of 500 copies; folio; original wrappers, dust jacket; mint.　James S. Jaffe 34-377　1996 $150.00

ARUNDELL, F. V. J.　　Discoveries in Asia Minor; Including a Description of the Ruins of Several Ancient Cities and Especially Antioch of Pisidia. London: Richard Bentley, 1834. 1st edition; tall 8vo; 2 volumes; xxiii, 355, vii, 439 pages; 10 plates, 1 folding map; contemporary green half leather, cloth stamped with floral pattern, raised bands; some minor foxing, page xv in volume 1 has been reinforced, otherwise attractive, near fine set.　David Mason 71-108　1996 $360.00

ASCH, SHOLEM　　The Nazarene. New York: Putnam, 1939. 1st edition; fine in lightly worn dust jacket, with couple of small chips at extremities and touch of darkening to spine, signed by author and dated in year of publication.　Between the Covers 42-18　1996 $100.00

ASCHAM, ROGER　　Disertissimi Viri rogeri Aschami...Familiarum Epistolarum Libri Tres.. London: Hatfield for Coldock, 1590/89. Thick 8vo; 2 volumes in 1; titles within typographical borders, calf rebacked, hole in title margin, some scribbling in margins. STC 829.　Rostenberg & Stern 150-77　1996 $675.00

ASCHAM, ROGER　　Toxophilus, the Schole, or Partitions, of Shooting. Wrexham: Reprinted by R. Marsh, 1788. 8vo; contemporary tree calf, spine rubbed, upper hinge cracked, small piece missing from head of spine, arms of Sir John Ingilby, Bart in gilt on upper cover.　Anthony Laywood 108-22　1996 £110.00

ASGILL, JOHN　　An Essay on a Registry for Title of Lands. London: printed in the year 1698. 8vo; 34 pages; recent marbled wrappers; Wing A3927; Kress 2064; Goldsmiths 3477.　C. R. Johnson 37-3　1996 £125.00

ASH, JOHN　　The Easiest Introduction to Dr. Lowth's English Grammar... London: printed for E. and C. Dilly, 1768. 24mo; 4 pages ads; contemporary sheep, rough blind borders, one corner worn, neatly rebacked, nice, clean copy. Alston I 157.　Jarndyce 103-12　1996 £120.00

ASHBEE, CHARLES ROBERT　　Conradin. London: Essex House Press, 1908. One of 250 copies; 10 1/2 x 8 inches; 2 p.l., 26 pages, (1) leaf (colophon); 6 full page illustrations by Mairet, woodcut initial, tailpiece; buckram backed blue printed paper boards, edges untrimmed, very slight fading to spine and to edges of covers, faint browning to endleaves, as usual, last two leaves somewhat foxed, otherwise very fine, especially clean.　Phillip J. Pirages 33-209　1996 $275.00

ASHBEE, CHARLES ROBERT   An Endeavour Towards the Teaching of John Ruskin and William Morris. London: Essex House Press, 1901. Limited to 300 numbered copies; 8vo; decorative titlepage and initials; stiff vellum, darkened; unopened, small stamp on pastedown and bottom of 1 text page, remnants of label on cover and library bookplate inside, very good.   Charles Agvent 4-910 1996 $200.00

ASHBEE, CHARLES ROBERT   Where the Great City Stands, a Study in New Civics. London: Essex House Press, 1917. 1st edition; folio; xii, 164, (4) pages; 121 illustrations on plates; cloth spine, boards, rear hinge internally cracked, tips worn, spine lightly sunned, decorated boards lightly rubbed, as usual.   Bookpress 75-149 1996 $450.00

ASHBERY, JOHN   Three Madrigals. New York: printed for Poet's Press, 1968. Limited edition, 131/150 copies, signed by author; pictorial wrappers; fine.   Polyanthos 22-22 1996 $125.00

ASHBY, PROFESSOR   Viola; the Redeemed. Boston: Gleason's Pub. Hall, 1845. 1st edition; 8vo; 66 pages; illustrations; removed. Wright I 192.   M & S Rare Books 60-114 1996 $150.00

ASHBY, W. ROSS   Design for a Brain. New York: John Wiley, 1952. 1st American edition; 8vo; ix, 260 pages; illustrations; original cloth, very good.   Edwin V. Glaser 121-11 1996 $150.00

ASHBY, W. ROSS   Design for a Brain... London: Chapman & Hall, 1960. 2nd edition; 8vo; ix, 286 pages; illustrations; original cloth, dust jacket, near fine.   Edwin V. Glaser 121-12 1996 $150.00

ASHE, ARTHUR R.   A Hard Road to Glory: A History of the African-American Athelete. New York: Armistad, 1993. Revised edition; 3 volumes; as new, dust jackets.   Between the Covers 43-257 1996 $125.00

ASHE, R. P.   Chronicles of Uganda. London: Hodder and Stoughton, 1894. 1st edition; tall 8vo; xiv, 480, (2) pages ads; original blue cloth, inner front hinge cracked, some rubbing to extremities, otherwise very good.   David Mason 71-2 1996 $100.00

ASHENDENE PRESS   A Chronological List, with Prices, of the Forty Books Printed at the Ashendene Press MDCCCXCV-MCMXXXV. Ashendene Press, 1935. Printed for private circulation only; 13 1/4 x 9 1/4 inches; (4) leaves; printed in red and black; original sewn printed blue wrappers; wrappers bit rumpled, faded and soiled, otherwise in excellent condition. Phillip J. Pirages 33-29 1996 $300.00

ASHFORD, FAITH   Poor Man's Pence. Ditching, Sussex: printed by Douglas Pepler, AD 1917. 1st edition; 16mo; pages (6), 84 + colophon title vignette of angel on horseback and 3 other wood engravings by Eric Gill, also winged lion, fish and lamb by Beedham (& others?), printed in Caslon on handmade paper; uncut, original printed brown sugar paper wrappers, little frayed along bottom (over-lapping) edge, otherwise very good. Gill 362 (variant - as Gleeson Lib. copy); Sewell 12.   Claude Cox 107-151 1996 £65.00

ASHFORD, FAITH   A Soul Cake. Verses. Ditchling: ptd. & pub. by Douglas Pepler, S. Dominic's Press, 1919. 1st edition; one of 240 copies printed; 200 x 136mm; pages (4), 53; Gill's Press device in red on title, printed on handmade paper; original printed brown sugar paper wrappers. Sewell 30.   Claude Cox 107-152 1996 £55.00

ASHFORD, FAITH   Things Unseen. A Book of Verse. Ditchling, Sussex: printed and published at S. Dominic's Press, 1924. 1st edition; 8vo; pages (4), 28, (2); printed on handmade paper; original printed drab wrappers, lower wrapper slightly frayed where protruding, but very good, uncut, scarce.   Claude Cox 107-153 1996 £50.00

ASHLEY, CLIFFORD W.   Whaleships of New Bedford. Sity Plates. Boston & New York: Houghton Mifflin, 1929. One of 1035 copies; 10.5 x 8.5 inches; red cloth, bit of wear at head of spine; interesting bookplate of William Van Rensselaer Irving.   Parmer Books O39Nautica-039139 1996 $275.00

ASHLEY, CLIFFORD W.   The Yankee Whaler. Boston and New York: Houghton Mifflin, 1926. 1st edition; one of 1625 copies; 4to; 379 pages, frontispiece and illustrations; gilt decorated cloth spine and printed boards, corners bumped, as usual, boards rubbed slightly, both inner hinges cracking, clean attractive spine and text, very good. Jenkins p. 77; Howes A356.   Robert F. Lucas 42-83 1996 $350.00

ASHLEY, CLIFFORD W.   The Yankee Whaler. Boston: Houghton Mifflin Co., 1926. One of 1625 copies; 10 7/8 x 8 3/8 inches; xxvi, 379 pages, photographic illustrations; printed beige boards with gold stamped linen spine, inner hinges weak, rubbing to boards.   Dawson's Books Shop 528-4 1996 $150.00

ASHLEY, WILLIAM H.   The West of William H. Ashley. Denver: The Old West Publishing Co., 1964. One of 250 numbered copies of the deluxe first edition, signed by editor, Dale Morgan; folio; liv, 341 pages; numerous plates, facsimiles, maps; original three quarter dark brown calf, gilt lettered red morocco spine label, very fine and bright, slipcase. Corey, Prelim Checklist p. 32; Saunders, Morgan Bib. 68.   Argonaut Book Shop 113-29 1996 $750.00

ASHLEY, WILLIAM H.   The West of William H. Ashley ... 1822-1838. Denver: The Old West Publishing Co., 1964. 1st trade edition; folio; liv, 341 pages; numerous plates, facsimiles and maps; pictorial cloth; very fine.   Argonaut Book Shop 113-30 1996 $225.00

ASHMOLE, ELIAS   The Antiquities of Berkshire. London: 1719. 1st edition; 8vo; 3 volumes; folding map by Hollar, 13 folding plates or tables; calf, spines repaired at head and foot, new labels. Pennington 658.   Marlborough 162-8 1996 £475.00

ASHMUN, JEHUDI   History of the American Colony in Liberia from December 1821 to 1823. Washington City: Way & Gideon, 1826. 1st edition; 8vo; 42 pages; removed, disbound; browned and somewhat brittle with minor chipping, library stamp on title, lacks map. Very scarce. LCP/HSP AFro Amer. Cat. 686; Shoemaker 23547; LCP Nego Hist. Cat. 37.   M & S Rare Books 60-362 1996 $300.00

ASHTON, DORE   Richard Lindner. New York: Abrams, 1969. Oblong 4to; 217 pages; 52 tipped in color plates, 135 monochrome illustrations; cloth, dust jacket. Freitag 5640.   Brannan 43-354 1996 $195.00

ASHTON, JAMES   The Book of Nature... New York: Wallis & Ashton, 1861. 1st edition; 18mo; 64 pages; 7 colored plates (of 8), of which one folding plate lacks flap; original flexible cloth, tears in text, but without loss; good. Very rare. Not in Howes.   M & S Rare Books 60-278 1996 $550.00

ASHTON, JOHN   Chap-Books of the Eighteenth Century. London: Chatto & Windus, 1882. 1st edition; 8vo; xvi, (488) pages, 32 page catalog; illustrations from woodcuts; original brown cloth, blocked in black and gilt, lightly rubbed, very good.   Robert Clark 38-220 1996 £60.00

ASHTON, JOHN   A History of English Lotteries Now for the First Time Written. London: Leadenhall Press, 1893. 1st edition; 8vo; (xii), (360), (16) pages; illustrations, 28 facsimile lottery bills printed on various colored papers tipped in; catalog at end; original buckram, printed paper labels, untrimmed; spine label rubbed, spine ends very slightly frayed; good.   Robert Clark 38-221 1996 £125.00

ASIMOV, ISAAC 1920-1992   Earth is Room Enough. New York: Doubleday, 1957. 1st edition; fine in near fine dust jacket.   Aronovitz 57-52 1996 $160.00

ASIMOV, ISAAC 1920-1992   Fantastic Voyage II. New York: Doubleday, 1987. 1st edition, 1/450 copies, signed by author; fine in slipcase. Aronovitz 57-63 1996 $125.00

ASIMOV, ISAAC 1920-1992   Foundation, Foundation & Empire. & Second Foundation. Gnome Press, 1951-53. 1st editions; 1st state bindings and dust jackets save for second state binding of volume 3); 3 volumes; all near fine (again save for volume 3 which is fine save for volume 3 which is fine save for tape shadows to covers and endpapers), in near fine dust jackets save for volume 2 whose dust jacket is very good with some light wear and chipping to head of spine, still very nice and most desirable.   Aronovitz 57-50 1996 $1,250.00

ASIMOV, ISAAC 1920-1992   Foundation. New York: Gnome Press, 1951. 1st edition; 8 1/4 x 5 1/2 inches; original cloth, dust jacket; excellent copy in very good jacket with nice front panel, spine and rear panel yellowed and somewhat wrinkled with five small chips and reinforced in four places on verso.   Phillip J. Pirages 33-33 1996 $125.00

ASIMOV, ISAAC 1920-1992   The Foundation Trilogy. New York: Doubleday, 1963. 1st edition; in one volume; signed by author; very good in lightly worn dust jacket.   Aronovitz 57-51 1996 $175.00

ASIMOV, ISAAC 1920-1992   Little Brothers. Pretentious Press, 1988. 1st edition; 1/126 copies signed by author, of which no copies were ever offered for sale; tipped in photos; fine in wrappers.   Aronovitz 57-65 1996 $395.00

ASIMOV, ISAAC 1920-1992   Lucky Starr and the Moons of Jupiter. New York: Doubleday, 1957. 1st edition; just about fine in very good+ dust jacket with some light wear.   Aronovitz 57-53 1996 $150.00

ASIMOV, ISAAC 1920-1992   The Naked Sun. London: 1958. 1st English edition; very good in dust jacket, trifle dust soiled on spine.   Words Etcetera 94-64 1996 £75.00

ASIMOV, ISAAC 1920-1992   Nightfall. New York: Doubleday, 1990. 1st edition; 1/750 copies, signed by author; fine in slipcase.   Aronovitz 57-67 1996 $100.00

ASIMOV, ISAAC 1920-1992   Nine Tomorrows. New York: Doubleday, 1959. 1st edition; fine in near fine dust jacket.   Aronovitz 57-54 1996 $160.00

ASIMOV, ISAAC 1920-1992   Pebble in the Sky. New York: Doubleday, 1950. 1st edition; very good+ in very good dust jacket with some wear to dust jacket spine extremities, and front flap fold.   Aronovitz 57-49 1996 $195.00

ASIMOV, ISAAC 1920-1992   The Robots of Dawn. Phantasia Press, 1983. 1st edition; 'Advance Copy - Phantasia Press' on half title; unbound signatures; very scarce. Inscribed by author.   Aronovitz 57-59 1996 $150.00

ASSOCIATION OF THE BAR OF THE CITY OF NEW YORK   Charter and Constitution of the Association of the Bar of the City of New York. New York: George F. Nesbitt and Co., 1873. 24 pages; blue printed wrpapers, ex-library, chipped but sound.   Meyer Boswell SL27-9 1996 $125.00

THE ASSYRIAN Dictionary of the Oriental Institute of the University of Chicago. Chicago: Oriental Institute, 1956-73. 4to; 12 volumes, 3990 pages; cloth, leather labels, several spines faded, bookplate.   Archaeologia Luxor-2542 1996 $450.00

ASTELL, MARY   Bart'lemy Fair; or, an Enquiry After Wit; in Which Due Respect is Had to a Letter Concerning Enthusiasm to My Lord. London: printed for R. Wilkin, 1709. 1st edition; 8vo; old boards, black morocco spine (slight wear); title bit dusty and slightly restored along blank inner margin, small hole in last leaf affecting a single word, which is clear from context. Uncommon. Rothschild 58.   Ximenes 109-13 1996 $1,250.00

ASTLE, THOMAS   The Origin and Progress of Writing, as Well Hieroglyphic as Elementary... London: printed for the author, sold by T. Payne & Son, &c., 1784. 1st edition; 4to; half title; rebound in half calf, marbled boards, red label, very good, extensive 18th century ms. marginal notes on pages 36-37 and 51, also on few other pages. Alston III 850.   Jarndyce 103-13 1996 $350.00

ASTLE, THOMAS   The Origin and Progress of Writing, as Well Hieroglyphic as Elementary, Illustrated by Engravings... London: printed by T. Bensley...for J. White, 1803. 2nd edition; 4to; (viii), xxiv, 240 pages; frontispiece, waterstained, offset to title, 9 folding dust jacket, 23 other plates, some browned, prelim and final leaves lightly foxed; contemporary tan calf, modern reback with raised bands between double gilt rules, original label laid down, sides with blind fillet and palmette roll border, drab endpapers, red sprinkled edges, corners rubbed. Bigmore & Wyman p. 20; Kennedy 2011. Alston III no. 850.   Blackwell's B112-7 1996 £200.00

ASTON, FRANCIS W.   Isotopes. London: Edward Arnold, 1922. 1st edition; 8vo; viii, 152 pages, 4 photographic plates, 21 figures and tables in text; original cloth, rubbed, some bubbling; lightly foxed in front and back, else very good. PMM 412; Norman Lib. 77 & 78. Stanitz Sale 21. Honeyman Sale I 156.   Edwin V. Glaser 121-13 1996 $250.00

ASTURIAS, MIGUEL ANGEL   The Talking Machine. Garden City: Doubleday, 1971. 1st U.S. edition; illustrations by Jacqueline Duheme; near fine in very good+ dust jacket; this copy inscribed by Asturias to one Leo Matarasso.   Lame Duck Books 19-43 1996 $1,500.00

ATCHISON, TOPEKA & SANTA FE RAILROAD   Plan of Re-Organization, Atchison, Topeka & Santa Fe Railroad Company. Circular No. 63 October 15, 1889. Boston: 1889. 1st edition; 19 pages; original white printed wrappers; fine. Railway Econ. Cat. p. 174; Hopkins Railway Library p. 35.   Michael D. Heaston 23-35 1996 $125.00

ATCHLEY, S. C.   Wild Flowers of Attica. Oxford: 1938. 4to; pages xix, 60; 22 colored plates; cloth, some wear at spine ends, some overall fading and light staining.   Raymond M. Sutton VI-656 1996 $115.00

ATGET   The Work... New York: MOMA, 1981-85. 1st edition; 4 volumes, complete set; illustrations; dust jackets.   J. B. Muns 154-22 1996 $500.00

ATHENAEUM CLUB, LONDON. LIBRARY   Catalogue of the Library. Together with the Supplement. London: printed for Members Only, 1845. Royal 8vo; 2 volumes; original half leather, joints rubbed, scarce.   Charles W. Traylen 117-1 1996 £85.00

ATHERTON, FAXON DEAN   The California Diary of Faxon Dean Atherton 1836-1839. San Francisco: California Historical Scoiety, 1964. One of 325 copies of the deluxe edition, numbered and signed by editor; gilt lettered and decorated cloth, very fine, slipcase; this edition quite scarce.   Argonaut Book Shop 113-32 1996 $125.00

ATHERTON, GERTRUDE   The Splendid Idle Forties New York: Macmillan Co., 1902. 1st edition; small 8vo; vii, (3), 389 pages; frontispiece, 7 plates; original red cloth, covers and spine decoratively and pictorially stamped in black, green, white, grey and gilt; very minor rubbing to spine ends; very fine. Scarce in this condition; Zamorano 80 1.   Argonaut Book Shop 113-33 1996 $200.00

ATKIN, G. DUCKWORTH   House Scraps. London: for the author 1887. One of 200 copies; 8vo; pages vi, 183, frontispiece, etched title, text illustrations; original maroon cloth.   Marlborough 162-105 1996 £100.00

ATKINSON, J. C.   A Glossary of the Cleveland Dialect; Explanatory, Derivative and Critical. London: John Russell Smith, 1868. 1st edition; 4to; 8 pages subscribers' list; original purple cloth, spine faded and slightly worn at head and tail; clean and sound, armorial bookplate of Wm. Scurfield Grey.   Jarndyce 103-61 1996 £95.00

ATKINSON, WILLIAM   The Physicians and Surgeons of the United States. Philadelphia: 1878. 1st edition; 788 pages; recent cloth, very scarce. GM 6715.1.   W. Bruce Fye 71-70 1996 $300.00

ATKYNS, ROBERT   An Enquiry into the Power of Dispensing with Penal Statutes. London: printed for Timothy Goodwin, 1689. 1st edition; folio; hole in title just affecting 2 letters, with final blank leaf Q2; 58 pages; disbound. Not in Sweet and Maxwell; Wing A4138; McAlpine IV p. 323.   Anthony W. Laywood 109-4 1996 £165.00

ATLANTIC & PACIFIC RAILROAD   Annual Report Atlantic and Pacific Railroad Company to the Stockholders, for the Fiscal Ending December 31st, 1874. New York: Evening Post Steam Presses, 1875. 1st edition; 79 pages, folding charts, 2 folding maps; original printed salmon wrappers, chipping to wrappers and spine, very good.   Michael D. Heaston 23-37 1996 $750.00

ATLAS Of Canada. Ottawa: Dept. of Mines and Technical Services, 1957. 53 x 42 cm; (vii), 110, two panel sheets in full color; grey and red cloth, bound with trip metal casings; very good, now quite scarce.   Rockland Books 38-10 1996 $150.00

ATLAS of the Lewis and Clark Expedition. Lincoln: 1983. 1st edition; folio; 126 facsimiles of original maps, most in original size; cloth; mint.   W. M. Morrison 436-132 1996 $300.00

ATLAS to Accompany the Monograph on the Geology of the Eureka District... Washington: 1883. Folio; comprising sheets 3-13 (of 13), inserted loose as issued; nice; original wrappers.   Edward Morrill 368-323 1996 $100.00

ATLEE, WASHINGTON L.   General and Differential Diagnosis of Ovarian Tumors, with Special Reference to the Operation of Ovariotomy. Philadelphia: 1873. 1st edition; tall 8vo; 482 pages; 39 illustrations; cloth, top of spine frayed. GM p. 938.   Argosy 810-24 1996 $300.00

ATTICUS BOOKS   William S. Burroughs - The Hombre Invisible. San Diego: Atticus Books, 1981. 1st edition; Catalogue 8; numerous black and white photos; wrappers. Burroughs has signed the catalog; spine browned, covers slightly marked and dusty, very good;   Ulysses 39-85 1996 £95.00

ATTLEE, CLEMENT   As it Happened. London: William Heinemann Ltd., 1954. Reprint; 16 pages of black and white photos, loosely inserted black and white photo taken at the same time a the photo in the book, piece of tissue paper has been stuck wtih masking tape over it and marked off with a view to including the photo in another book; original binding, edges browned, cover edges rubbed, head and tail of spine and corners slightly bumped, no dust jacket; presentation copy from author to Mannie Shinwell.   Ulysses 39-24 1996 £350.00

ATWATER, CALEB   An Essay on Education. Cincinnati: Printed by Kendall & Henry, 1841. 1st edition; 8vo; vii, 123 pages; revious owner's name stamp on title, otherwise very good, in contemporary cloth which shows moderate staining. American Imprints 41-309.   Andrew Cahan 47-69 1996 $275.00

ATWOOD, MARGARET   The Animals in that Country. Boston: Little Brown, 1968. 1st U.S. edition; near fine in very good+, lightly spine tanned dust jacket with short pen stroke to upper edge of front panel. Lame Duck Books 19-44 1996 $275.00

ATWOOD, MARGARET   Encounters with the Element Man. Concord: Ewert, 1982. One of 100 numbered copies out of a total printing of 160, signed by author and artist; illustration by Michael McCurdy, marbled wrappers; fine.   Anacapa House 5-23 1996 $100.00

ATWOOD, MARGARGET   Hurricane Hazel and Other Stories. Helsinki: Eurographica, 1987. 1st edition; one of 350 copies, signed and dated by author on titlepage; 8vo; on Michelangelo paper from Magnani paper mills in Peschia; printed by Tipografia Nobili in Pesaro; blue printed wrappers; fine.   Priscilla Juvelis 95/1-11 1996 $150.00

AUBESPIN, NICOLAS   La Cordeliere ou Tresor des Indulgences du Cordon St. Francois. Paris: Jean le Bouc, 1610. Very small 8vo; engraved title, 11 fine engraved plates by L. Gaultier, p. 97 torn without loss, very good with final colophon leaf; full early 17th brown morocco, boards elaborately gilt with outer panel enclosing large floral scrolls at corners surrounding a central symmetrical gilt arabesque, corners worn, flat spine symmetrically gilt, small wear at head. Good example of an early French binding.   Ian Wilkinson 95/1-32 1996 £260.00

AUBORN, A. D.'   The French Convert:...From the Errors and Supersitions of Popery to the Reformed Religion, by Means of a Protestant Gardener, Her Servant... Brookfield: E. Merriam for G. Merriam, 1798. 12mo; 112 pages; original calf backed boards, extremities rubbed, some text foxing. Evans 33322.   Kenneth Karmiole 1NS-29 1996 $150.00

AUBREY, JOHN   The Natural History and Antiquities of the County of Surrey; Begun in the Year 1673...and Continued to the Present Time. London: printed for E. Curll, 1718-23. 1st edition; 5 volumes, extra illustrated with 252 engraved, etched and aquatint plates; some offsetting and spotting, pages 3-16 in volume 3 supplied in ms.; contemporary calf, slightly rubbed, volumes 2 and 3 rebacked with original spines, all edges gilt, bookplates and ownership inscriptions on titles of William Roots. Note at beginning states "26 April/42 Lot. 59 - at Strawberrry Hill.." bt. by Bohn".   Anthony W. Laywood 109-5 1996 £850.00

AUBREY, JOHN   The Topographical Collections. Devizes, Bull, 1862. 1st edition; 4to; half title, pages xiii, 491, (1 p. errata), frontispiece, 42 engraved plates, 3 folding pedigrees and 2 folding plans, 1 hand colored text plan; contemporary half morocco, trifle rubbed, one or two tears to the folding plates; presentation copy with ink ms. corrections by J. E. Jackson to Viscount Barrington, tipped in at back is Jackson's printed appeal "Ten Pounds Reward. Folio Volume of Aubrey's Wiltshire Antiquities: an Original Manuscript Missing".   Marlborough 162-268 1996 £250.00

AUCASSIN ET NICOLETE   The Song Story of Aucassin and Nicolete. Elston Press, 1902. One of 240 copies; 6 1/2 x 5 inches; 2 p.l., 66, (2) pages, (1) leaf (colophon); printed in orange and black; elaborate woodcut borders and initials on first two pages of text; original cloth backed paper boards, paper label on spine, original printed paper dust jacket, spine of jacket partly perished, jacket in two pieces and slightly chipped along edges, text leaves very slightly browned at edges, but surprisingly fine nevertheless, volume very clean inside and out, jacket (in any form) an amazing surivival.   Phillip J. Pirages 33-200 1996 $250.00

AUCASSIN ET NICOLETTE   Aucassin and Nicolette. New York: n.d., ca. 1915. 1st edition; limited to 125 copies, number 61, signed by Evelyn Paul; small 4to; 124 pages, illuminated half title, frontispiece and title, 13 mounted color plates by M. R. Bocher, many text illustrations and decorations; full white vellum, gilt and color decorated, top edge gilt. Robin Greer 94A-65 1996 £350.00

AUCASSIN ET NICOLETTE   Aucassin and Nicolette. Prague: Limited Editions Club, 1931. Limited to 1500 copies; signed by artist; 4to; printed on handmade paper and bound in Czechoslovakia; illustrations by Vojtech Preissig; full tan silk, fine in near fine and uncommon dust jacket and very good slipcase.   Charles Agvent 4-817 1996 $150.00

AUCHINCLOSS, LOUIS   The Injustice Collectors. Boston: Houghton Mifflin Co., 1950. 1st edition; author's first book published under his own name; fine in lightly used dust jacket.   Priscilla Juvelis 95/1-12 1996 $100.00

AUDEN, WYSTAN HUGH 1907-1973   The Dance of Death. London: faber, 1933. 1st edition; one of 1200 copies; 8vo; green boards, dust jacket; very fine. B&M A4.   James S. Jaffe 34-12 1996 $350.00

AUDEN, WYSTAN HUGH 1907-1973   The Dyer's Hand and Other Essays. New York: Random House, 1962. 1st edition; original cloth; signed by author, fine in fine dust jacket but for very slight sunning and tiny edge tears.   Beasley Books 82-10 1996 $150.00

AUDEN, WYSTAN HUGH 1907-1973   Nones. New York: Random House, 1951. 1st edition; 8vo; cloth, dust jacket chipped at head of spine; fine. Signed by author. Bloomfield A32.   James S. Jaffe 34-13 1996 $225.00

AUDEN, WYSTAN HUGH 1907-1973   Selections from Poems by Auden. London: Petersburg Press, 1974. Edition B, one of 150 copies for the Americas numbered 15 and signed by Moore and accompanied by four original lithographs, each signed and numbered by the artist in matching folder, the whole preserved in cloth fall down-back box; bound in dark green linen; fine.   Sotheran PN32-171 1996 £1,100.00

AUDEN, WYSTAN HUGH 1907-1973   Three Songs for St. Cecilia's Day. New York: Caroline Newton, 1941. One of 250 privately printed copies; small octavo; very good plus in blue sewn wrappers.   Lame Duck Books 19-47 1996 $200.00

AUDEN, WYSTAN HUGH 1907-1973   Two Songs. New York: Phoenix Book Shop, 1968. 1st edition; one of 100 numbered copies, signed by Auden, out of a total edtiion of 126 copies; oblong 8vo; wrappers; fine. James S. Jaffe 34-14 1996 $250.00

AUDLEY, GEORGE ASHDOWN   The Art of Organ Building. Dodd, Mead and Co., 1905. Thick 4to; 2 volumes; iv, 600, 760 pages; frontispiece, 15 plates, 384 text figures and several tables; cloth, top edge gilt, others uncut, new endpapers, spines faded and covers stained.   Thomas Thorp 489-14 1996 £150.00

AUDLJO, JOHN   Journal of a Visit to Constantinople and some of the Greek Islands, in the Spring and Summer of 1833. London: Longmans, Rees, Orme, Brown, Green, Longman, 1835. 8vo; pages xii, 259; engraved titlepage, 2 (of 7) plates and 1 illustration in text; recent half morocco; very good; bookplate of Major R. S. Seton and of Larchmont Yacht Club.   Worldwide Antiquarian 151-60 1996 $165.00

AUDUBON, JOHN JAMES 1785-1851   The Viviparous Quadrupeds of North America. New York: Audubon, 1846-51. 1st two volumes of the 1st edition of text; 8vo; volumes 1-2 (of 3) of text only; 2 volumes; contemporary purple cloth, very stained and worn, printed labels almost flaked away, signature and bookplate of T. Tileston (Wells), an original subscriber.   Maggs Bros. Ltd. 1190-664 1996 £115.00

AUDUBON, JOHN WOODHOUSE   Audubon's Western Journal: 1849-1850. Cleveland: Arthur H. Clark Co., 1906. 1st edition; folding map, portrait, original drawings; bookplate, lower corners bumped, else fine. Hermitage SP95-694 1996 $200.00

AUER, H. A.   Camp Fires in the Yukon. Cincinnati: 1916. 1st edition; illustrations; lovely bright copy, scarce.   David Grayling J95Biggame-396 1996 £85.00

AUERBACH, ERNA   Nicholas Hilliard. London: Routledge and Kegan Paul, 1961. 25 x 19.5 cm; xxiv, 352 pages, 252 plates including 7 in color; original buckram.   Rainsford A54-315 1996 £90.00

AUGEREAN, YAROUTHIUN   A Brief Account of the Mechitaristican Society Founded on the Island of St. Lazaro. Venice: printed at the Press of the Same Armenian Academy, 1835. Large 12mo; frontispiece, portrait, 62 pages; original half crimson straight grained morocco, gilt, gilt edges; fine, fresh copy.   James Fenning 133-11 1996 £115.00

AUGUSTINUS DE ANCONA 1243-1328   Summa de Potestate Ecclesiasatica. Augsburg: Johann Schussler 6 March, 1473. 1st edition; folio; 470 leaves (first blank) and 4 line printed slip at fol. 153, gothic letter, initials, paragraph marks and initial strokes all supplied in red, broad margins with many uncut edges, pinholes still visible and last leaves and gutter of lower margin, but tall, clean and crisp copy; contemporary South German binding of blindstamped pigskin stained red over wooden boards, brass clasps and catches, ms. title in ink on lower edge, expertly rebacked, straps renewed. Goff A1363; Hain 960; BMC II 329; GKW 3050.   H. M. Fletcher   121-4   1996   £8,800.00

AUGUSTINUS, AURELIUS, SAINT, BP. OF HIPPO   De Civitate Dei. Basel: Michael Wenssler, 25, March 1479. Folio; 247 leaves (of 248, lacking final leaf blank), (some signatures scrambled), gothic letter, very handsome initials supplied in red and blue, few marginal annotations in early hand, few insignificant wormholes in first and last leaves, first and last leaf slightly spotted, few other minor stains; later (16-17 century?) speckled calf, rather worn, spine very wormed; generally tall, clean and crisp copy.   H. M. Fletcher   121-2   1996   £8,000.00

AUGUSTINUS, AURELIUS, SAINT, BP. OF HIPPO   The Confessions. Philadelphia: Lippincott, 1900. Number 95 of 150 copies for the U.S.; titlepage and text in red and black, frontispiece and initial engravings by Clemence Housman from desgins of Paul Woodroffe and her brother, Lawrence Housman; printed on fine handmade paper, uncut, top edge gilt, full vellum, gilt, yapped edges, ribbon ties, marbled endpapers; minor waterstains to two blank prelims, slight wear to vellum, text crisp and fine, very good copy of a handsome edition.   Hartfield   48-V2   1996 $185.00

AUGUSTINUS, AURELIUS, SAINT, BP. OF HIPPO   Explantio Psalmorum. Venice: Bernardinus Benalius 4 August, 1493.. Folio; 372 leaves, gothic letter, wormholes in first two leaves expertly mended, but affecting few letters, clean, tall and crisp copy in sympathetic binding of antique style blindstamped brown morocco over bevelled boards. On fol. 16 there are early records of ownership by members of the Pandulphini family, old library stamp of Museo Cavaleri. Goff A1273; BMC V 374; GKW 2910. H. M. Fletcher   121-3   1996   £2,200.00

AULARD, A.   The French Revolution: a Poltical History 1789-1804. London: 1910. Original edition; thick 8vo; 4 volumes; buckram, gilt tops, withdrawn from Girton College with neat ownership, spines slightly chafed.   Howes Bookshop   265-37   1996   £75.00

AULD, J. B.   A Poetical Essay on the First good and the First Fair. With Salutatory Addresses. New York: pub. by the Class, 1835. 1st edition; 8vo; 16 pages; sewn; light dust soiling. Rinderknecht 30138   M & S Rare Books   60-141   1996 $100.00

AULNOY, MARIE CATHERINE JUMELLE DE BERNEVILLE, COMTESSE D' d. 1705   Memoirs of the Court of France. London: printed for R. Bentley and T. Bennet, 1692. 1st edition in English; 8vo; contemporary mottled sheep, bit rubbed, remnants of old bookseller's description tipped to front cover; slight spotting, but nice copy, very scarce. Wing A4218a; Mish p. 79; CBEL II 982 and 1053.   Ximenes   109-18   1996 $600.00

AUNIGA, Ignacio. Rapida Ojeada al Estado de Sonora... Mexico: Ojeda, 1835. 1st edition; 66 pages; original plain white wrappers, very faint stain to several pages, fine copy laid in morocco slipcase. Howes Z25; Graff 4801. Becker Wagner Camp 58a.   Michael D. Heaston   23-27   1996 $2,250.00

AUNT LAURA   Christmas Stories. Buffalo: 1862. 2 1/8 x 1 1/2 inches; 64 pages; all edges gilt, faded violet cloth with elaborately gilt stamped front cover and spine; fine, owner's inscription. Welch 4299.   Bromer Booksellers   87-193   1996 $125.00

AUNT Louisa's Birthday Gift. London: Frederick Warne and Co., n.d., ca. 1875. 1st edition; quarto; 24 color printed plates; original green cloth decoratively stamped in gilt and blind on front cover, in gilt on spine, and in blind on back cover, light wear to extremities, back hinge starting, little minor soiling, bookplate; near fine. Osborne II p. 668. Heritage Book Shop   196-274   1996 $500.00

AURELIUS ANTONINUS, MARCUS, EMPEROR OF ROME 121-180 Meditations... London: M. Flesher, 1643. 1st greek and Latin edition printed in England; 8vo; 2 parts in one, (56), 344; 148, (4) pages; Greek and Latin text on opposing pages, title printed in red and black; contemporary vellum, soiled, spine hand lettered. Wing A4224. Kenneth Karmiole   1NS-30   1996 $350.00

AURORA County, South Dakota, and its Fertile Lands. Plankinton: Standard Print, ca. 1898. 1st edition; (28) pages, including wrappers; illustrations; original pictorial wrappers, small portion of back wrapper torn away, very good copy of a fragile item. Very scarce.   Michael D. Heaston   23-302   1996 $350.00

AUSCHER, E. S.   A History and Description of French Porcelain. London: 1905. Limited to 1250 numbered copies; 10 x 6 inches; 200 pages; 24 color plates and numerous other illustrations; top edge gilt, bookplate, moderately rubbed with back cover dent and scratch, titlepage detached.   John K. King   77-543   1996 $100.00

AUSTEN, JANE 1775-1817   Charades Etc. London: Pub. Spottiswoode & Co., n.d. 1895. 1st edition; 9 x 5 1/2 inches; 34 pages, illustrations; cream wrappers lettered in black and red on front, cased in dark red rexine backed paper covered boards; fine, scarce; John Sparrow's copy with his bookplate and signature. Gilson F2; Keynes 169; Chapman 31. Ian Hodgkins   78-4   1996   £130.00

AUSTEN, JANE 1775-1817   Emma. London: for John Murray, 1816. 1st edition; 12mo; 3 volumes, half titles; later red half roan, flat spines ruled and lettered in gilt, marbled boards, occasional light staining, wormholes at margins for much of volume 2 and at end of volume 3, some closed, occasionally touching text, but not affecting sense and mostly minor, 2 leaves in volume 3 with trivial tears, one repaired, withal very good and attractive copy. Gilson A8.   Simon Finch   24-7   1996   £5,000.00

AUSTEN, JANE 1775-1817   Emma. London: printed for John Murray, 1816. 1st edition; 12mo; 3 volumes; lacking half titles, outer corner torn from last leaf of volume 1 (not touching the text), usual general spotting and minor signs of use, attractively rebound in contemporary style dark blue quarter calf, spines gilt ruled. Gilson A8.   James Burmester 29-151   1996   £3,500.00

AUSTEN, JANE 1775-1817   Emma: a Novel. London: printed for John Murray, 1816. 1st edition; 12mo; 3 volumes; rebound by Bernard Middleton in period style full calf, spines fully gilt and with red morocco lettering pieces, inside dentelles, lacks half titles, some foxing, ownership inscription on titles, very good in sympathetic modern binding; Gilson A8. Sotheran   PN32-2   1996   £1,250.00

AUSTEN, JANE 1775-1817   Emma. London: Richard Bentley, 1866. New edition; 7 x 4 5/8 inches; frontispiece, pages iv, 435; light brown sand grain cloth, gilt titling and volume number on backstrip, double stamped blind border to both covers, dark green endpapers, uncut; some foxing to prelims, lower corners slightly worn, very good, scarce. Gilson D7 page 230; Keynes 28.   Ian Hodgkins   78-5   1996   £50.00

AUSTEN, JANE 1775-1817   Emma. New York: Limited Editions Club, 1964. 1st edition thus, limited to 1500 signed and numbered copies; 9 1/4 x 6 3/8 inches; pages xvi, 430, including colophon; 32 color illustrations; light grey cloth with embossed white medallion of author on front cover; fine in worn slipcase. Gilson E359.   Ian Hodgkins   78-12 1996   £85.00

AUSTEN, JANE 1775-1817   Lady Susan. London: Oxford University Press, 1925. Limited to 250 copies; 7 3/4 x 5 inches; large paper copy, pages vii, 173, 15 pages; white linen backed grey boards, printed paper title label, backstrip, spare label rear, uncut, title label slightly discolored; fine; initialled presentation copy from editor, R. W. Chapman to John Sparrow. Gilson F5; Keynes 176; Chapman 28.   Ian Hodgkins   78-13 1996   £125.00

AUSTEN, JANE 1775-1817   The Letters of... London: Richard Bentley & Son, 1884. 1st edition; 7 7/8 x 5 1/2 inches; 2 volumes, frontispiece in each volume, pages xv, 374, 2 pages ads; v, 366, 2 pages ads; dark olive green cloth, Austen's monogram in gilt on front covers, gilt titling to backstrip, bevelled boards, doneky brown endpapers, uncut, backstrips worn at top and bottom, slight trace of label to front covers, corners slightly worn, contents very good. Reginald Brimley Johnson's copy with his bookplate. Gilson g1; Keynes 165; Chapman 95.   Ian Hodgkins   78-66   1996   £180.00

AUSTEN, JANE 1775-1817   Letters to Her Sister Cassandra and Others. London: Oxford University Press, 1932. 1st edition; 8 7/8 x 5 3/4 inches; large paper copy, 2 volumes, frontispiece, 29 illustrations and 2 maps, pages xlv, 266, 33 notes; xxx, 267-509, 119 including appendix and index; grey cloth backed marbled boards, printed paper title labels, spare labels rear, uncut; slight foxing to prelims and last pages of both volumes, fine set in discolored and slightly worn dust jacket. Ian Hodgkins   78-67   1996   £240.00

AUSTEN, JANE 1775-1817   Mansfield Park: a Novel. London: (G. Sidney (vol. 1) C. Roworth (vol. 2 & 3), for T. Egerton, 1814. 1st edition; 12mo; 3 volumes, half titles and final ad leaf in volume 3; contemporary half calf, joints skilfully restored, smooth spines decorated in blind and lettered in gilt, marbled sides, endpapers and edges; gathering C of volume 2 partly sprung at lower stitches and with lower outer corner of C6 torn away without loss of text, very good. Gilson A6.   Simon Finch 24-6   1996   £4,000.00

AUSTEN, JANE 1775-1817   Northanger Abbey. New York: Limied Editions Club, 1971. Number 1029 of 1500 copies; signed by artist; illustrations by Clarke Hutton; fine in slipcase. Hermitage   SP95-934 1996 $100.00

AUSTEN, JANE 1775-1817   The Novels of... London: J. M. Dent & Co., 1892. 2nd edition thus; 6 3/4 x 4 1/4 inches; 10 volumes; illustrations by William Cooke, ornaments by F. C. Tilney; pale green cloth, gilt ornamental title piece top right of front cover, gilt titling and decoration on backstrips, top edge gilt, others uncut, printed ex-libris. Free endpapers discolored, very good set. Gilson E75.   Ian Hodgkins 78-60 1996 £195.00

AUSTEN, JANE 1775-1817   The Novels of. London: 1901. Clawton edition, salesman's dummy, limited to 10 copies; 8 1/8 x 5 1/2 inches; consisting of hand colored frontispiece by Lee Woodward Zeigler on handmade paper and 6 illustrations by C.E. and H.M. Brock printed in color on Japan vellum and 60 pages of text from "Mansfield Park: dark green crushed morocco with Art Nouveau gilt border design wtih inlay of Tudor Roses on covers, gilt decorated crimson crushed morocco doublures, edges in dark green crushed morocco decorated in gilt, backstrip laid in, gilt Art Nouveau design, red inlay Tudor Roses in panels, raised bands, gilt titling, crimson silk free endpapers, backstrip, corners and edges of boards rubbed and discolored to brown.   Ian Hodgkins 78-57 1996 £85.00

AUSTEN, JANE 1775-1817   The Novels Of.. New York: Society for English and French Literature, 1906. Limited to 500 numbered copies, this no. 135; 8 3/8 x 5 1/2 inches; 12 volumes; frontispiece and 2 illustrations in each volume; pale blue/grey cloth, thin leather title labels to backstrips, top edge gilt, others uncut; some title labels damaged and backstrips faded, some discoloration to prelims and small snag top of backstrip of one volume, contents fine. Gilson E106.   Ian Hodgkins 78-62 1996 £250.00

AUSTEN, JANE 1775-1817   The Novels of. New York: Frank S. Holby, 1906. Hampshire edition limited to 1000 numbered copies, copy number 413; 7 7/8 x 5 1/2 inches; 10 volumes; frontispiece and 2 illustrations in each volume; brown cloth with printed paper title label backstrips, top edge gilt, others uncut, title labels slightly discolored and chipped at edges; very good. Gilson E106.   Ian Hodgkins 78-63 1996 £245.00

AUSTEN, JANE 1775-1817   The Novels. London: J. M. Dent & Sons, 1922. 1st edition thus; 7 3/8 x 4 3/4 inches; 6 volumes, frontispiece and 15 color plates in each volume; illustrations by C. E. Brock; blue cloth, blindstamped decorated centre to each cover and gilt titling and decorated backstrip, decorated front pastedown; fine in worn dust jackets. Gilson E147.   Ian Hodgkins 78-64 1996 £175.00

AUSTEN, JANE 1775-1817   The Novels. Oxford: Clarendon Press, 1926. 2nd edition; 7 3/4 x 5 1/4 inches; 5 volumes; frontispiece to each volume, 44 illustrations and facsimiles; maroon cloth with circular gilt decoration to front cover, gilt titling to backstrips, uncut, backstrips slightly faded and two backstrips with crease down centre, pages 238 and 239 carelessly opened at fore edge with some loss of margin, very good set. Gilson E150.   Ian Hodgkins 78-65 1996 £125.00

AUSTEN, JANE 1775-1817   Persuasion. Philadelphia: Carey & Lea, 1832. 1st American edition; 7 1/4 x 4 1/2 inches; 2 volumes, pages 204, 36 page publisher's catalogue, 204; heavy foxing of section 4, pages 74/75 carelessly opened at top and two pages at top corners, ocassional light foxing contents of both volumes, rare in original brown linen backed drab boards (lacking title labels on backstrips), uncut, small leather booklabel of Charles Beecher Hogan, backstrips and boards marked and worn at corners and edges, volume 1 loose in its binding and has small piece torn from fore edge of title, lower edge of p. 133 at top corner page 119, sections 6, 8 and 9 foxed and occasional slight waterstain top corner of some pages, volume 2 has front free endpaper caught by glue at top edge and slightly torn, lacks 2nd front free e.p. & one of rear free e.p. Gilson B3 1250.   Ian Hodgkins 78-26 1996 £3,750.00

AUSTEN, JANE 1775-1817   Two Chapters of "Persuasion" Printed From Jane Austen's Autograph. London: Oxford University Press, 1926. Large paper copy, limited to 250 copies on handmade paper; 7 1/2 x 5 inches; pages viii, 39, 18 pages notes, bound in at front of book is 16 page facimile of the manuscript; white linen backed grey boards, printed paper title label backstrip, spare label rear, uncut, backstrip slightly discolored; fine. Gilson F8; Keynes 178; Chapman 29.   Ian Hodgkins 78-51 1996 £80.00

AUSTEN, JANE 1775-1817   Pride and Prejudice. New York: Pocket Books, 1940. 1st edition thus; 5 1/2 x 4 1/8 inches; pages v, 405; laminated color card covers, slight creasing of front cover, very good; scarce. Gilson E192.   Ian Hodgkins 78-31 1996 £55.00

AUSTEN, JANE 1775-1817   Pride and Prejudice New York: Doubleday, 1945. 1st edition thus, limited to 1000 copies, signed by artist; 9 5/8 x 6 1/2 inches; pages vi, 380; 10 single and 3 double page color plates and many black and white illustrations by Robert Ball; blue cloth, gilt decorated front cover, gilt decorated and pink printed title labels backstrip, top edge gilt, others uncut, backstrip slightly faded and discolored, covers slightly marked and corners of boards slightly bruised, very good. Gilson E207.   Ian Hodgkins 78-33 1996 £55.00

AUSTEN, JANE 1775-1817   Pride and Prejudice New York: Doubleday, 1945. 1st edition thus; 5 1/2 x 4 1/8 inches; pages v, 405; laminated color card covers, slight creasing on front cover, very good, scarce. Gilson E192.   Ian Hodgkins 78-31 1996 £55.00

AUSTEN, JANE 1775-1817   Sanditon. London: Oxford University press, 1925. Large paper copy, limited to 250 copies; 7 5/8 x 5 inches; printed on handmade paper, pages xi, 170, 34 notes; frontispiece; white linen backed grey boards, printed paper title label backstrip (spare label present), uncut; label discolored, slight marks, rear cover, very good. Gilson F6; Keynes 177; Chapman 30.   Ian Hodgkins 78-35 1996 £70.00

AUSTEN, JANE 1775-1817   Sense and Sensibility and Persuasion. New York: Derby & Jackson, 1857. 4th American edition; 7 1/4 x 4 3/4 inches; pages (iv), 522, 6 ads; titlepage with vignette; crimson morocco grain cloth with blindstamped decorated covers and titling backstrip, deep cream endpapers; faint inscription, engraved title slightly foxed and slight waterstain, some wear to top and bottom of backstrip and corners, very good, scarce. Gilson E21.   Ian Hodgkins 78-39 1996 £160.00

AUSTEN, JANE 1775-1817   Sense and Sensibility and Persuasion. New York: H. W. Derby, 1861. Re-issue of 4th American edition of 1857; engraved title with vignette, 522 pages; dark brown vertical ribbed cloth with elaborate blindstamped decorated covers, gilt titling and blindstamped decoration on backstrip, yellow endpapers, ex-library with stamp bottom of title and top of p. 5, top and bottom of backstrip worn, endpapers with some damage by removal of labels; contents very good. Gilson E21.   Ian Hodgkins 78-40 1996 £75.00

AUSTEN, JANE 1775-1817   Sense and Sensiblity and Persuasion. Boston: Ticknor & Fields, 1864. Re-issue of 1863 edition; 7 5/8 x 4 7/8 inches; pages (iii), 522; brown vertical ribbed cloth with blindstamped border and Central design containing publisher's initials to both covers, gilt titling to backstrip, yellow endpapers, original backstrip laid down, top rear corner worn away, waterstain top edge of pages and page 375/6 has stain thereon, contemporary inscription; very good. Gilson #28.   Ian Hodgkins 78-41 1996 £75.00

AUSTEN, JANE 1775-1817   Sir Charles Grandison, or the Happy Man. London: David Astor, 1981. Limited to 250 copies; 9 1/2 x 6 inches; pages iv, 53; 26; 8; facsimile olive green silk cloth, printed version in green marbled paper boards and foreword in green marbled wrappers, the 3 items with prospectus and review from TLS in cloth solander box with matching marbled paper pasted thereon, printed paper title label on front of box, fine set, scarce.   Ian Hodgkins 78-49 1996 £285.00

AUSTEN, JANE 1775-1817   The Watsons. London: Oxford University Press, 1927. Limited to 250 copies; 7 1/2 x 5 inches; pages vii, 121, 42; printed on handmade paper; frontispiece; white linen backed grey boards, printed paper title label backstrip, uncut and unopened, title label slightly discolored, corners very slightly bruised; fine; John Sparrow's copy with his bookplate. Gilson F10; Keynes 180; Chapman 26.   Ian Hodgkins 78-54 1996 £120.00

AUSTEN, JANE 1775-1817   The Watsons. London: Elkin Mathews & Marrot, 1928. 1st edition thus; 7 1/2 x 5 inches; pages (viii), 183; blue cloth backed grey boards, titling and decoration on front cover by Gower Parks, gilt titling to backstrip, uncut; fine in dust jacket. Gilson J10; Keynes 181; Chapman 27.   Ian Hodgkins 78-71 1996 £55.00

AUSTEN, JANE 1775-1817   The Works. London: Heffer & Sons, n.d. 1st edition; 7 volumes, all but on volume very good in dust jackets, 7th volume has dust jacket heavily repaired with adhesive tape.   Words Etcetera 94-67 1996 £70.00

AUSTEN, JANE 1775-1817   The Works of. London: Richard Bentley and Son, 1882. Steventon edition; limited to 375 copies on handmade paper; 7 3/4 x 5 3/8 inches; 6 volumes, frontispiece engraved in sepia in volumes 1-5, volume 6 has frontispiece portrait, 2 woodcuts; text printed in sepia with ruled border, rebound in crimson buckram, vellum title label with gilt titling on backstrips, top edge gilt, backstrips very slightly faded, engrs. foxed, lacking ad for Miss Ferrier's novels at end of volumes 1, 3 and 5; very good, scarce. Gilson D13.   Ian Hodgkins 78-59 1996 £250.00

AUSTEN, JANE 1775-1817   The Works Of... Boston: Little Brown & Co., 1898. 1st edition thus; 6 7/8 x 4 1/4 inches; 12 volumes; frontispiece in each volume; olive green silk cloth, gilt decorated title piece to front covers, gilt decorated and titling to backstrips, top edge gilt, others uncut, backstrips discolored to brown, endpapers discolored and neat initials top right corner of titlepages, very good, clean set. Gilson E76, p. 266.   Ian Hodgkins 78-61 1996 £195.00

AUSTEN-LEIGH, J. E.   A Memoir of Jane Austen. London: Richard Bentley & Son, 1879. 4th edition; 7 3/8 x 4 7/8 inches; pages x, 364; trace of label to front pastedown frontispiece, 4 illustrations; dark green cloth blindstamped, decorated boards, gilt titling and decorated backstrip, brown endpapers, traces of label to front pastedown, slight wear to top and bottom of backstrips, very good, clean copy. Gilson M130.   Ian Hodgkins 78-88 1996 £85.00

AUSTEN-LEIGH, M. A.   Personal Aspects of Jane Austen. London: John Murray, 1920. 1st edition; 2nd issue; 8 x 5 5/8 inches; frontispiece, 7 illustrations, pages viii, 171, including appendix; green cloth, black simple decoration to border on front cover, gilt titling to backstrip, uncut, gilt dull on backstrip, top corners of boards slightly bumped, inscription, some foxing to contents; very good. Gilson M393.   Ian Hodgkins 78-90 1996 £50.00

AUSTEN-LEIGH, W.   Jane Austen. Her Life and Letters, a Family Record. London: Smith, Elder, 1913. 1st edition; 8 1/2 x 5 1/2 inches; pages xv, 437, 2 pages ads; frontispiece, deep pink cloth, gilt titling to front cover and backstrip, some foxing to contents, very good, scarce; presentation copy from authors. Gilson M313; keynes 237; Chapman 120. Ian Hodgkins 78-91 1996 £135.00

AUSTER, PAUL   Auggie Wren's Christmas Story. New York: William Drentel, 1992. Limited edition, one of 100 copies, signed; printed at Libanus Press on mold made paper; quarter bound in buckram and marbled paper; lovely book.   Bev Chaney, Jr. 23-39 1996 $130.00

AUSTER, PAUL   City of Glass, Ghosts and The Locked Room. Los Angeles: Sun & Moon Press, 1985-86. 1st editions; volume one has light slant to spine, otherwise near fine in fine dust jacket, volumes 2 and 3 fine in dust jackets.   Thomas Dorn 9-15 1996 $375.00

AUSTER, PAUL   City of Glass, Ghosts and The Locked Room. Los Angeles: Sun and Moon Press, 1985/86. Uncorrected proof copies of the New York Trilogy; 3 volumes; wrappers; fine, very scarce.   Ken Lopez 74-16 1996 $2,000.00

AUSTER, PAUL   City of Glass, Ghosts and The Locked Room. Los Angeles: Sun and Moon, 1986/85/86. 1st editions; 3 volumes; volumes two and three signed, all near fine, in dust jacket.   Lame Duck Books 19-48 1996 $750.00

AUSTIN, MARY   The Land of Little Rain. Boston: 1950. 1st edition; dust jacket chipped at edges.   J. B. Muns 154-9 1996 $125.00

AN AUTHENTIC Account of the Conversion and Expereience of a Negro. London: printed by T. Wilkins, n.d., c. 1790. Unrecorded London imprint; 4 pages; uncut, folded leaves, as issued; very fine.   C. R. Johnson 37-38 1996 £60.00

AUTOGRAPH Leaves Of Our Country's Authors. Baltimore: Cushings & Bailey, 1864. 1st edition; quarto; original brown cloth, gilt, top edge gilt; spine ends worn, few light spots, otherwise clean, tight copy. BAL 2418, 13672, 20112.   Mac Donnell 12-130 1996 $750.00

AUTOGRAPHS for Freedom. Auburn & Rochester: Alden, Beardsley, 1854. 1st edition; with rare variant imprint (usually New York); original purple cloth, gilt, some fading, but very good.   Mac Donnell 12-42 1996 $165.00

AVEDON, RICHARD   Avedon: Photographs 1947-1977. New York: Farrar, Straus and Giroux, 1978. 1st edition; folio; pictorial boards and otuer translucent dust jacket; fine.   Left Bank Books 2-120 1996 $125.00

AVENARIUS, JOHANN   Hoc Est, Liber Radicum Seu Lexicon Ebraicum, in Quo Omnium Vocabulorum Biblicorum... Wittenberg: Heirs of Johannes Crato, 1589, colophon, 1588. 2nd edition; folio; (16), 860 pages, woodcut printer's device on title and much larger version on final leaf, text in Hebrew and Latin; titlepage backed at an early period; contemporary blindstamped pigskin dated '1597' with initials "M.I.M.M.", some minor worming, through binding and portions of text (mostly along bottom blank margin), only occasionally touching text, not affecting readability. Adams A2306.   Kenneth Karmiole 1NS-160 1996 $1,250.00

AVERILL, ESTHER   Daniel Boone, Historic Adventures of an American Hunter Among the Indians. Paris: Domino Press, 1931. Folio; lithographs in color by Rojankovsky; cloth backed colored pictorial boards; fine. Barbara Stone 70-185 1996 £150.00

AVERMAETE, ROGER   Frans Masereel. London: Thames and Hudson, 1977. Square folio; 318 pages, 518 illustrations, 8 in color; cloth, dust jacket, slipcase. Freitag 6113.   Brannan 43-392 1996 $275.00

AVERY, DAVID   A Poem on the Origin and Suppression of the Late Rebellion. Wilmantic: 1865. 1st edition; 12mo; 24 pages; original wrappers.   M & S Rare Books 60-136 1996 $125.00

AVICENNA   Canon Medicinae. E. Louvain: 1658. 12.5 x 8 inches; 2 volumes in 1; (12), 432, (8); 912), 311, (7); 71, (1) pages; contemporary vellum, binding worn, spine splitting at bottom, interior foxed, title detached but present, else good.   John K. King 77-726 1996 $495.00

AVILA, JUAN DE   Triumph Uber die Welt, Das Fleisch und den Teufel. Munich: Heinrich the Younger, 1601. 1st edition; 4to; 233 leaves; woodcut ornaments, title in red and black, fraktur throughout; contemporary limp vellum; fine, rare. Faber du Faur 2.892a. Dunnhaupt 1.207.13.   Bennett Gilbert LL29-8 1996 $2,250.00

AVITY, PIERRE D', SIEUR DE MONTMARTIN 1573-1635   Bannissement des Folles Amours, ou Sont Adioustes Quatre Beaux & Excellents Traictes, Tres Curieux & Memorables, Enrichis d'Excellentes Annotations & Beaux Commentaires. Lyon: Barthelemy Vincent, 1618. 1st edition; 8vo; (4), 106, (6) pages, (16), 160 pages, 16 leaves, 80 pages; printer's device on main title, repeated 4 times on special titlepages; contemporary vellum, some minor dampstains and occasional browning. Cioranescu 23606; Gay Lemonnyer I 356.   Jeffrey D. Mancevice 20-7 1996 $1,250.00

AWOONOR, KOFI   This Earth, My Brother... Garden City: Doubleday, 1971. 1st edition; near fine in attractive dust jacket, despite two inch edge-tear to front panel; inscribed by author to African-American Novelist Barry Beckham.   Lame Duck Books 19-7 1996 $150.00

AXELROD, H. R.   The Complete Coloured Lexicon of Cichlids. London: 1993. 4to; 864 pages; 300 colored drawings and nearly 2000 color photos; leather.   Wheldon & Wesley 207-948 1996 £70.00

AXSOME, RICHARD H.   The Prints of Frank Stella: a Catalogue Raisonne 1962-1982. New York: Hudson Hills, 1983. Square 4to; 192 pages; profusely illustrated, much in color; cloth, dust jacket.   Brannan 43-624 1996 $165.00

AYER, HANNAH PALFREY   A Legacy of New England. Letters of the Palfrey Family. N.P.: privately printed, 1950. Limited to 150 copies; 4to; 2 volumes, xviii, 401 pages; partly unopened, very nice, in original box (box partly dampstained and partly cracked).   Edward Morrill 369-511 1996 $100.00

AYLING, STEPHEN   Photographs from Sketches by Augustus Welby N. Pugin. London: S. Ayling, 1865. 1st edition; large 8vo; title leaf, 4 pages, 250 mounted photos; frontispiece; publisher's cloth, top edge gilt, light wear to covers, but very good set overall; bookplate of John Douglas. Gernsheim 274.   Bookpress 75-103 1996 $1,825.00

AYME, MARCEL   Five Short Stories by Marcel Ayme: The State of Grace. The Dwarf. Rue de l'Evangile. Legend of Poldevia. The Seven-League Boots. Newtown: Bird & Bull Press, 1994. One in an edition of 150 numbered copies; 10 x 8 inches; 100 pages; 10 wood engravings in blue and black by Gaylord Schanilec; printed on Arches mould made at Bird & Bull Press; blue cloth over board with blue leather title label on spine, red cloth slipcase with title label on spine, together with a grey card folder containing A companion to Five Short Stories by Marcel Ayme: Creating the Illustrations by Henry Morris, and an extra set of wood engravings, each in their own labeled folder; fine.   Joshua Heller 21-209 1996 $400.00

AYRES, ATLEE B.   Mexican Architecture. Domestic, Civil and Ecclesiastical. New York: William Helburn Inc., 1926. Folio; (160) pages; frontispiece + 150 plates, green gilt cloth, a nice copy.   Kenneth Karmiole 1NS-20 1996 $150.00

AYRTON, MICHAEL   Giovanni Pisano, Sculptor. London: Thames & Hudson, 1969. 28 x 26 cm; 248 pages; color frontispiece, 370 black and white plates, original cloth, in dust jacket, name on endpaper. Rainsford A54-464 1996 £95.00

AYRTON, MICHAEL   Giovanni Pisano: Sculptor. New York: Webright and Talley, 1969. 1st American edition; 248 pages; fine in dust jacket. Hermitage SP95-754 1996 $100.00

AYRTON, MICHAEL   Hogarth's Drawings - London Life in the 18th Century. Avalon Press, 1948. 1st edition; quarto; 78 black and white reproductions, many full page; buckram covers, top edge dusty, free endpapers partially browned, head and tail of spine and corners slightly bumped and faded, very good in nicked, chipped, rubbed, torn, marked and dusty, slightly soiled, internally repaired and price clipped dust jacket, browned internally at flaps and at spine and edges frayed at head of spine.   Ulysses 39-26 1996 £85.00

AYTOUN, WILLIAM EDMONSTOUNE   Lays of the Scottish Cavaliers and Other Poems. London: William Blackwood and Sons, 1881. 4to; pages (viii), 268; 68 illustrations; original cloth, gilt extra over bevelled boards, spine rather faded, little rucked at head, all edges gilt; odd mark, but very good.   R.F.G. Hollett 76-344 1996 £65.00

B

B., A.   A Narrative of the Atrocities Committed by the Crew of the Piratical Brig "El Defensor de Pedro" with a Brief Account of the Trial and Execution of the Pirates. London: Effingham Wilson, 1830. 1st edition; 8vo; fine lithographed frontispiece; half calf, gilt, spine gilt; rare. 4 copies in NUC.   Ximenes 109-19 1996 $450.00

BAAS, J. H.   Outlines of the History of Medicine and Medical Profession. New York: Vail, 1889. 1st English edition; 8vo; 1173 pages; original binding, lightly shaken, stamp on titlepage; internally very good. GM 6389.   James Tait Goodrich K40-17 1996 $275.00

THE BABACOMORI Land Grant. N.P.: ca. 1880? 1st edition; 11 pages; original printed pink wrappers, very good. Not in Adams Herd or Alliot Arizona.   Michael D. Heaston 23-17 1996 $1,200.00

BABBAGE, CHARLES 1792-1871   The Analytical Engine and Mechanical Notation. London: 1989. 253 pages, plates; cloth.   Graham Weiner C2-290 1996 £50.00

BABBAGE, CHARLES 1792-1871   Passages from the Life of a Philosopher. London: Longman, Green, Longman, Roberts & Green, 1864. 1st edition; demy 8vo; xii, 496, 24 pages; frontispiece; original binding, gilt, little very minor wear, top cover slightly creased, front endpaper cracking, touch shaken, few minor marks and occasional pencil annotations, but good, unrestored copy.   Ash Rare Books Zenzybyr-7 1996 £1,250.00

BABCOCK, PHILIP H.   Falling Leaves. Tales From a Gun Room. New York: Derrydale Press, 1937. 1st edition; one of 950 numbered copies; 8vo; illustrations by Aiden L. Ripley; very good with light rubbing to spine. Siegel 115; Frazier B1a.   Glenn Books 36-65 1996 $150.00

BABINGTON, CHURCHILL   Catalogue of the Birds of Suffolk. London: John Van Vorost, 1884-86. 1st edition; 8vo; pages 281; 6 photographic plates, one map, colored in outline; original green cloth, covers ruled in black, spine titled in gilt, vignette of bird. Mullens & Swann p. 32. Sotheran PN32-82 1996 £168.00

BABINGTON, CHURCHILL   The Influence of Christianity in Promoting the Abolition of Slavery in Europe. Cambridge: J. and J. J. Deighton, 1846. 1st edition; 8vo; viii, 199 pages; contemporary black morocco, fully gilt; fine presentation copy, inscribed by author, inscription rather faded. Headicar & Fuller III 487; Goldsmiths 34874; not in Kress.   John Drury 82-10 1996 £65.00

BABSON, GRACE   A Descriptive Catalogue of the Grace K. Babson Collection of the Works of Sir Isaac Newton and the Material Relating to Him in the Babson Inst. Library, Babson Park, Mass. Babson Park: 1950. 1st edition; limited to 750 copies; large 8vo; portrait, 19 plates; original cloth, uncut, nice.   Forest Books 74-198 1996 £50.00

BABTICOCHI, D.   Lesson for the Harpsichord or Piano Forte. London: printed for the author, c. 1770. Oblong folio; 9 pages; fine.   William Reeves 309-9615 1996 £62.00

BACH, RICHARD   Jonathan Livingston Seagull. New York: Macmillan, 1970. 1st edition; fine in dust jacket, extremely uncommon in first edition. Between the Covers 42-24 1996 $575.00

BACHE, A. D.   Safety Apparatus for Steam Boilers. Philadelphia: 1832. 1st edition; 8vo; 11 pages, illustrations; original printed wrappers. Inscribed presentation copy from author. B&B 11031;   M & S Rare Books 60-443 1996 $200.00

BACK, GEORGE 1796-1878   Narrative of the Arctic Land Expedition to the Mouth of the Great Fish River and Along the Shores of the Arctic Ocean in the Years 1833, 1834 and 1835. Philadelphia: 1836. 9 x 5.5 inches; 456 pages; folding map, ex-library, leather, covers detached, few pages with bad staining, foxing, etc.   John K. King 77-785 1996 $100.00

BACON, DELIA SALTER   The Bride of Fort Edward, Founded On an Incident of the Revolution. New York: S. Colman, 1839. 1st edition; 12mo; 174 pages; original cloth, printed paper label; BAL 556; Wright I 218; Rinderknecht 54088.   M & S Rare Books 60-115 1996 $125.00

BACON, EDWIN N.   Historic Pilgrimages in New England, Among Landmarks of Pilgrim and Puritan Days and of the Provincial and Revolutionary Periods. Boston: Silver, Burdett & Co., 1898. original pictorial cloth, showing definite wear but sound; Clarence Darrow's copy with his bookplate.   Meyer Boswell SL27-59 1996 $750.00

BACON, FRANCIS, VISCOUNT ST. ALBANS 1561-1626   The Essayes or Counsels Civill and Morall. New York: Limited Editions Club, 1944. Copy number 904 from a total edition of 1100 numbered copies; designed by Bruce Rogers, signed by Rogers; cloth backed decorative boards, fine in tissue jacket and very slightly worn drop lid box.   Hermitage SP95-935 1996 $175.00

BACON, FRANCIS, VISCOUNT ST. ALBANS 1561-1626   The Essayes, or Counsels, Civill and Moral... London: by John Haviland for Hanna Barret, and Richard Whitaker, 1625. 1st complete edition, 1st issue (last lifetime edition); 4to; (10), 340 pages; woodcut initials and headpieces; lacks initial blank A1, as usual, neat repair to running head of 2G3, with loss of a few letters; sprinkled calf, gilt, by Bedford; clean, fresh copy with good margins; Gibson 13; Pforzheimer 30 (2nd issue); STC 1147.   Joseph J. Felcone 64-2 1996 $3,000.00

BACON, FRANCIS, VISCOUNT ST. ALBANS 1561-1626   The Essays or Counsels, Civil and Moral, of Sir Francis Bacon... London: printed by Mr. Clark, 1680. 12mo; 4 leaves, 222 pages, 2 leaves of table, 4 leaves, 28 pages, TP for "Wisdom"; 5 leaves, 111 pages, 1 leaf of tables, contents in excellent condition; original calf, very worn, both covers present but detached.   Roy W. Clare XXIV-66 1996 $100.00

BACON, FRANCIS, VISCOUNT ST. ALBANS 1561-1626   Bacon's Essays and Colours of Good and Evil with Notes and Glossarial Index... Cambridge & London: Macmillan and Co., 1865. Golden Treasury Edition, Fourth Thousandth Impression; small 8vo; 388 pages of text; full red straight grain morocco, gilt rule borders, tiny corner ornaments to boards, gilt rule, title and small gilt leaf tools to panelled spine, all edges gilt, narrow inner gilt dentelles, marbled endpapers, ink inscription (Eton 1817), last leaf of text lightly foxed; a fine fore-edge painting of Eton College.   Beeleigh Abbey BA56-132 1996 £275.00

BACON, FRANCIS, VISCOUNT ST. ALBANS 1561-1626   Essays. London: Longmans, Green and Co., 1873. New edition; 8 3/4 x 6 inches; xxiv, 620 pages; extremely pretty contemporary flamed calf, gilt, by Riviere, covers with delicate twining floral border, raised bands, spine compartments handsomely gilt in antique style with large floral stamps at middle and scrolling foliage in corners, black morocco lettering piece, marbled edges and endpapers; especially fine, handsome binding bright with only negligible wear and virtually pristine internally.   Phillip J. Pirages 33-34 1996 $150.00

BACON, FRANCIS, VISCOUNT ST. ALBANS 1561-1626   The Essays: Colors of Good and Evil and Advancement of Learning. London: Macmillan, 1900. 8vo; titlepage printed in red and black; full dark blue calf by Sangorski & Sutcliffe, spine with raised bands, gilt stamped devices within gilt ruled compartments and gilt stamped red morocco label, covers triple ruled in gilt with floral designs in corners, gilt ruled edges and gilt stamped inner dentelles, grey silk bookmark, marbled endpapers, all edges gilt, slight rubbing to extremities; very good. George J. Houle 68-11 1996 $175.00

BACON, FRANCIS, VISCOUNT ST. ALBANS 1561-1626   The History of the Reigns of Henry the Seventh, Henry the Eighth, Edward the Sixth and Queen Mary... London: R. Scot, T. Basset, J. Wright, R. Chiswell and J. Edwyn, 1676. Folio; (16), 138, (12), 202 pages; frontispiece; original calf, spine somewhat chipped and rubbed. Gibson, Bacon 121. Wing B300. Kenneth Karmiole 1NS-32 1996 $350.00

BACON, FRANCIS, VISCOUNT ST. ALBANS 1561-1626   The History of the Reigns of Henry the Seventh, Henry the Eighth, Edward the Sixth and Queen Mary. London: R. Scot, 1676. 1st edition; folio; frontispiece, general title dated 1676, 3 divisional titles dated 1675, library stamp to title and prelims, occasional light spotting; full contemporary calf, little worn, rebacked, red morocco label. Wing B300.   Ian Wilkinson 95/1-27 1996 £190.00

BACON, FRANCIS, VISCOUNT ST. ALBANS 1561-1626   Letters of Sr. Francis Bacon, Baron of Verulam, Viscount St. Albany, and Lord High Chancellor of England. London: printed for Benj. Tooke, 1702. 1st edition; 4to; contemporary mottled calf, gilt, neatly rebacked, original label preserved, all edges gilt, corners worn; large paper; very good with errata leaf at end, few copies are known with leaf of dedication to the king, not present here, but it was meant to be called as William III died before publication. Presentation copy inscribed by Rob. Stephens for Edward Ward. Gibson 245   Ximenes 109-20 1996 $600.00

BACON, FRANCIS, VISCOUNT ST. ALBANS 1561-1626   Of the Advancement and Proficiencie of Learning; or the Partitions of Sciences... London: printed for Thomas Williams, 1674. Folio; frontispiece, final printer's note, library stamps; excellently rebound in full calf, label, very good. With contemporary signature of R. Sacvile ap. 15.75 pre. 6s. Wing B312; Gibson 142.   Jarndyce 103-388   1996 £240.00

BACON, FRANCIS, VISCOUNT ST. ALBANS 1561-1626   Of Studies. San Francisco: 1928. One of 50 copies; 6 3/4 x 4 1/8 inches; (10) pages; tan boards, paper cover label, rubbed area on front board.   Dawson's Books Shop   528-48   1996 $200.00

BACON, FRANCIS, VISCOUNT ST. ALBANS 1561-1626   Of Gardens. Northampton: Gehenna Press, 1959. One of 200 copies, signed by Baskin; 12mo; (12) ff.; original woodcuts to title and colophon by Leonard Baskin; stiff floral patterned wrappers with printed label; extremely fine.   Bromer Booksellers   90-44   1996 $350.00

BACON, FRANCIS, VISCOUNT ST. ALBANS 1561-1626   Of Gardens. Northampton: Gehenna Press, 1959. One of 200 copies, signed by Leonard Baskin; 12mo; printed in Italic, black and orange-brown; stiff wrappers, with illustrations on titlepage and colophon; hand sewn into thin boards and covered with Japanese decorated paper. Brook 19; Baskin 20.   Second Life Books   103-13   1996 $250.00

BACON, FRANCIS, VISCOUNT ST. ALBANS 1561-1626   Of Gardens. London: Fleece Press, 1993. One of 225 copies; large 4to; printed in Van Dijck, set at the Rocket Press, in black and olive green on Arches; Jane Mansfield's floral paper over boards, green cloth back; fine.   Bertram Rota   272-150   1996 £56.00

BACON, FRANCIS, VISCOUNT ST. ALBANS 1561-1626   Resuscitatio, or, Bringing Into Publick Light Severall Pieces of the Works, Civil, Historical, Philosophical and Theological, Hietherto Sleeping... London: By William Rawley...Sarah Griffin, for William Lee, 1657. 1st edition; folio; (xxiv), 282, (iv), 242, (ii) pages; frontispiece (mounted), 6 secondary titlepages, errata leaf Oo2, final leaf of list of Bacon's works/ads; early ms. index on blank leaf at end; contemporary calf, rebacked in blind, old plain reback; rubbed, joints cracked, upper corner of titlepage restored with part of border made good, well clear of text, small piece torn from upper corner of next twenty leaves, clear of text and border, localised staining on last two leaves; sound, clean copy. Wing B319; Gibson 226.   Robert Clark   38-1   1996 £280.00

BACON, FRANCIS, VISCOUNT ST. ALBANS 1561-1626   Sylva Sylvarum; or a Naturall Historie. London: William Lee, 1635. Folio; (18), 260, (28); (4), 48, (2) pages; frontispiece, added engraved titlepage; old calf, outer hinges cracked but holding, front hinge repaired with glue, top inch of spine chipped; bookplate.   Kenneth Karmiole   1NS-33   1996 $475.00

BACON, FRANCIS, VISCOUNT ST. ALBANS 1561-1626   Sylva Sylvarum, or, a Natural Histroy... London: 1664. 8th edition; folio; extra engraved title, title (frayed and remargined), frontispiece (inkstains to inner margin, outer one restored), title remargined at head with slight loss to rule, occasional old library stamp, generally a bit stained and spotted; recent amateurish calf. Gibson 178.   Graham Weiner   C2-354   1996 £50.00

BACON, FRANCIS, VISCOUNT ST. ALBANS 1561-1626   The Works of Francis Bacon... London: printed for a. Millar, 1765. 4to; 5 volumes; 4 steel engraved frontispieces, folding table; near contemporary full polished tan calf, gilt, spines with twin lettering pieces and 6 raised bands, panels with overall diaper pattern in gilt; each volume inscribed "To the Hawkshead Institute, John Ruskin, Brantwood, Candlemasm 1883"; each volume with armorial bookplate of J. W. Cuthbert.   R.F.G. Hollett & Son   78-318   1996 £1,200.00

BACON, ROGER   The Opus Majus of Roger Bacon. Philadelphia: University of Pennsylvania Press, 1928. 1st edition thus; 8vo; 2 volumes, xiii, 418; (10), (419)-840 pages; 8 plates, including frontispiece in each volume, 72 figures in text original cloth; near fine set.   Edwin V. Glaser   121-15   1996 $385.00

BADEN-POWELL, ROBERT STEVENSON SMYTH   Aids to Scouting for N.-C.O.'s & Men. London: Gale & Polden, n.d. 1900. Early (possibly second) issue; 16mo; 138 pages; original limp vellum red buckram printed in black, original pink endpapers with printed ads, over opened at third gathering, where previous owner has signed in ink along gutter, also signed on first page of text; near fine, scarce, very fragile. Heritage Book Shop   196-234   1996 $650.00

BADHAM, C. D.   A Treatise on the Esculent Funguses of England... London: 1863. 2nd edition; 8vo; pages xvi, 152; 12 hand colored plates from drawings by W. Fitch; original gilt decorated cloth, light wear, 3 plates with scientific names carefully written in ink.   Raymond M. Sutton   VII-2   1996 $325.00

BADIUS ASCENCIUS, JODOCUS 1462-1535   Stultiferae Naves Sensus Animosque Trahentes Mortis in Exitium. Paris: Thielmann Kerver for E. J. and G. Marnef, 1500. 1st edition; small 4to; 6 large woodcut illustrations; full crushed burgundy morocco du cap, spine with five raised bands and gilt titling, board edges gilt, inner gilt dentelles, all edges gilt, by Riviere, very top of front joint slightly cracked, nearly invisible paper remarging to few leaves; bookplates of Edward Rahir and Henri Burton.   Book Block   32-29   1996 $7,500.00

BAEDEKER, KARL   The United States with an Excursion into Mexico. Leipsic: 1893. 1st edition; 516 pages; 17 maps and 22 plans; original cloth, gilt, spine slightly faded, near fine.   Blue River Books   9-27   1996 $325.00

BAETA, HENRIQUE XAVIER   Comparative View of the Theories and Practice of Drs. Cullen, Brown and Darwin in the Treatment of Fever and of Acute Rheumatism. London: printed by Luke Hansard for J. Johnson, 1800. 1st edition (?only) edition; 8vo; pages viii, 55, wanting half title; recent paper wrapper; nice.   James Fenning   133-12   1996 £350.00

BAGEHOT, WALTER   The English Constitution... London: Henry S. King & Co., 1872. 2nd edition; 8vo; lxxi, (i), 291, (5) pages, complete with 2 final ad leaves; original blue cloth lettered in gilt and with geometric designs in black; very good, with Carlingford armorial bookplate.   John Drury   82-12   1996 £200.00

BAGEHOT, WALTER   Physics and Politics or Thoughts on the Application of the Principles of 'Natural Selection' and 'Inheritance' to Political Society. London: Henry S. King, 1872. 1st edition in book form; 8vo; (4), 224 pages, 32 page publisher's list at end, ad leaf before title; original red cloth embossed in black, spine lettered in gilt, very good. John Drury   82-11   1996 £175.00

BAGEHOT, WALTER   Some Articles on the Depreciation of Silver and On Topics Connected With It. London: Henry S. King and Co., 1877. 1st edition in book form; 8vo; viii, 136 pages, leaf of ads, original cloth, lettered in gilt, neatly rebacked, endpapers renewed; good. Hollander 3201; Masui p. 176; not in Einaudi.   John Drury   82-13   1996 £150.00

BAGGULEY, WILLIAM H.   Andrew Marvell 1621-1678 - Tercentenary Tributes. Humphrey Milford/Oxford University Press, 1922. 1st edition 14 black and white plates; original binding, head and tail of spine slightly bumped, very good in torn, marked and dusty, slightly creased, soiled and rubbed dust jacket, slightly browned at spine and edges.   Ulysses 39-171   1996 £65.00

BAGLEY, CLARENCE B.   History of King County, Washington. Chicago: Seattle: S. J. Clarke Publishing Co., 1929. 1st edition; quarto; xii, 889, 938, 940 pages; frontispiece in volumes 1 and 3, profusely illustrated; original black cloth, stamped in black and gilt, small nick to spine of volume 2, otherwise fine set. Smith 407.   Argonaut Book Shop   113-36   1996 $375.00

BAGLEY, GEORGE   A Guide to the Tongues, Antient and Modern; being Short and Comprehensive Grammars of the English, French, Italian, Spanish, German, Latin, Greek, Hebrew, with the Arabic, Chaldaic and Syriac Languages... Shrewsbury: ptd. & sold by Wm. Morris, Likewise sold by R.S. Kirby, London, 1804. Folio; errata slip, slightly dusted or damp marked at edges; original blue boards, cream paper spine, splitting of leading hinge, very good.   Jarndyce 103-16   1996 £400.00

BAGOT, JOSCELINE   Colonel James Grahme of Levens. Kendal: T. Wilson, 1886. 1st edition; 8vo; pages 48, with autotype illustrations; original printed parchment; very good, scarce.   R.F.G. Hollett & Son 78-97   1996 £55.00

BAGROW, LEO   A History of the Cartography of Russia Up to 1600. (with) A History of Russian Cartography Up to 1800. Ontario: The Walker Press, 1975. 1st edition; fine.   Hermitage SP95-1091   1996 $175.00

BAHR, JEROME   All Good Americans. New York: 1937. 1st edition; 7.5 x 5 inches; 273 pages; cloth, marker pen numbers, otherwise very good in edge frayed and rubbed dust jacket.   John K. King   77-202 1996 $100.00

BAIF, LAZARE DE   Annotationes in L. II. De Captivis, et Postliminio Reversis. In Quibus Tractatur De Re Navali. Paris: Robert Estienne 31 August, 1536. 1st edition; 4to; (4) leaves, 168 pages, (4) leaves, 203, (13) pages, Estienne's printer device on title, several fine large crible initials; 29 large woodcuts; 19th century half calf; wide margined copy with two early ms. entries at foot of title, one consisting of a presentation in Greek from Joseph Biennaios, probably a hellenization of the name 'Bienne'; Renouard, Estienne 44: 19; Brun p. 116; Armstrong 110.   Jeffrey D. Mancevice   20-8   1996 $1,650.00

BAILEY, D. M.   A Catalogue of the Lamps in the British Museum. Volume II: Roman Lamps Made in Italy. London: British Museum, 1980. 4to; xvii, 458 pages, 113 figures, 104 plates; original cloth, dust jacket. Archaeologia Luxor-2957 1996 $450.00

BAILEY, FLORENCE MERRIAM   Birds of New Mexico. New Mexico Dept. of Game & Fish, 1928. 1st edition; limited edition, 6/350 signed copies; lovely color plates; good, chipped spine, rubbed corners, all plates very good or better, top edge gilt. Beautiful book.   Parker Books of the West 30-8 1996 $295.00

BAILEY, HAROLD H.   The Birds of Florida. Maryland, U.S.A.: privately published by author, 1925. Small folio; 76 full page color plates; original cloth, light rubbing, corners slightly bumped.   David A.H. Grayling MY95Orn-3 1996 £120.00

BAILEY, J. M.   The Book of Ensilage; or, the New Dispensation for Farmers, Experience with "Ensilage" at "Winning Farm." Billerica: 1880. 1st edition; 8vo; pages 202, illustrated as - 26 pages; engraved plates and text figures; original decorative cloth, light rubbing, bookplate, pages tanned, light marginal dampstaining to text.   Raymond M. Sutton VII-824 1996 $145.00

BAILEY, NATHAN   An Universal Etymological English Dictionary. London: Ware, Innys and many others, 1753. 15th edition; very thick octavo; unpaginated, final leaf of book ads present; full sprinkled morocco, original panelled boards, nice blind fillets and decorations, professionally rebacked, raised bands, original gilt on red leather label laid down, two (partially overlapping) engraved armorial bookplates of Sir Armine Wodehouse Johnson and a later family member. Excellent copy. Cordell p. 10; CBEL II 930.   Hartfield 48-V11A 1996 $385.00

BAILEY, NATHANIEL   The Antiquities of London and Westminster. London: H. Tracy, 1722. 1st edition; 12mo; title, 2 ff., 244 pages, 1 f., engraved frontispiece; contemporary panelled sheep, rubbed. Marlborough 162-106 1996 £175.00

BAILEY, NATHANIEL   An Universal Etymological English Dictionary... London: printed for J. J. and P. Knapton, D. Midwinter & A Ward, &c., 1733. 6th edition; lasat leaf little fragile with loss in margins; rebound in plain half calf, red label. Alston V99.   Jarndyce 103-113 1996 £85.00

BAILEY, NATHANIEL   An Universal Etymological English Dictionary. London: printed for D. Midwinter, R. Ware... 1740. 9th edition; contemporary calf, hinges weak, edges rubbed. Alston V162.   Jarndyce 103-114 1996 £70.00

BAILEY, NATHANIEL   Universal Etymological English Dictionary. London: printed for R. Ware, J. & P. Knapton &c., 1749. 13th edition; 1 page ads; browning in preface; rebound in half calf, marbled boards, red label. Alston V 106.   Jarndyce 103-115 1996 l85.00

BAILEY, NATHANIEL   Universal Etymological English Dictionary. London: printed for R. Ware, J. & P. Knapton, T. Longman, 1751. 14th edition; lacks leading free endpaper; contemporary reversed calf, some wear, good, sound copy. Alston V 107.   Jarndyce 103-116 1996 £90.00

BAILEY, NATHANIEL   Universal Etymological English Dictionary. London: Printed for T. Osborne, 1763. 20th edition; slight stain at end, ink note on Bailey on following endpaper and letter re 'baby language' laid on verso of title; contemporary speckled calf, gilt borders, corners rubbed, spine little worn, hinges splitting, label. Alston V113.   Jarndyce 103-117 1996 £90.00

BAILEY, NATHANIEL   An Universal Etymological English Dictionary. London: printed for J. Buckland, W. Strahan, 1782. 24th edition; sheep, worn at head and tail of spine, hinges weakening; Alston V 121. Jarndyce 103-119 1996 £65.00

BAILEY, NATHANIEL   An Universal Etymological English Dictionary. London: printed for J. F. & C. Rivington, &c., 1790. 25th edition; handsomely rebound in half dark brown calf, gilt spine, red label, very good. Alston V124.   Jarndyce 103-120 1996 £110.00

BAILEY, WILLIAM   The Angler's Instructor, a Treatise on the Best Modes of Angling in English Rivers, Lakes and Ponds, and on the Habits of the Fish. London: 1857. 1st edition; original pictorial cloth, lovely copy.   David A.H. Grayling 3/95-568 1996 £120.00

BAILLIE, GEORGE   Memoirs of... London: 1822. fine binding of blindstamped straight grained green morocco, gilt inside dentelles, 2 page ALS from Lavina Spencer, close friend of editor, loosely inserted. Petersfield Bookshop FH58-108 1996 £150.00

BAILLIE, JOANNA   Metrical Legends of Exalted Characters. London: Longman, et al, 1821. 1st edition; 8vo; half title, prelim and final leaves foxed, some marginal foxing, pages xxxvi, 373; mid 19th century dark green morocco, joints rubbed, backstrip with raised bands, gilt lettered direct in second compartment, remainder gilt, marbled boards, corners slightly bumped, marbled endpapers, top edge gilt; good.   Blackwell's B112-8 1996 £90.00

BAILLIE, JOANNA   A Series of Plays: In Which It is Attempted to Delineate the Stronger Passions of the Mind, Each Passion Being the Subject of a Tragedy and a Comedy. London: 1802. 2nd edition of volume 1, 1st edition of volume 2; full calf, title labels inset on red morocco, good.   K Books 442-36 1996 £56.00

BAILLIE-GROHMAN, W. A.   Fifteen Years' Sport and Life in the Hunting Grounds of Western America and British Columbia. London: Horace Cox, 1900. 1st edition; 13 7/8 x 10 1/2 inches; 77 photos, 3 specially prepared maps, frontispiece, 3 color folding maps in rear pocket; green cloth shows light soiling and slight tan on spine, but little wear, endpapers split over rear hinge (no doubt owning to map pocket) and browned, photographic plate leaves foxed, mainly in margins, with stain or two in text and two text illustrations marked, overall sound, very good; armorial bookplate of George Barclay Rives, by Jos. Rith of Vienna. Riling (1951 ed.) 1488.   Magnum Opus 44-16 1996 $200.00

BAILLIE-GROHMAN, W. A.   Sport and Life in Western America and British Columbia. 1900. illustrations; original pictorial gift buckram, apart from odd fox mark on endpapers, a most remarkably fine copy. Very scarce.   David Grayling J95Biggame-397 1996 £250.00

BAINBRIDGE, H. C.   Peter Carl Faberge. Goldsmith & Jeweller to the Russian Imperial Court and the Principal Crowned Heads of Europe. London: Batsford, 1949. Limited to 1750 copies; thick 4to; 128 plates, 18 are in color; original cloth, dust jacket.   Charles W. Traylen 117-16 1996 £60.00

BAINES, EDWARD   History of the Cotton Manufacture in Great Britain... London: H. Fisher, R. Fisher and P. Jackson, n.d. 1835. 1st edition; 8vo; (4), 5-18, (9)-543, (1) pages; 18 plates, frontispiece; contemporary black half calf, gilt, rubbed, else very good. Kress C3905. Goldsmiths 29008; Williams il 119.   John Drury 82-15 1996 £175.00

BAINES, EDWARD   Yorkshire, Past and Present: a History and a Description of the Three Ridings of the Great County of York from the Earliest Ages to the Year 1870, with an Account of Its Manufactures, Commerce and Civil and Mechanical Engineering... London: 1863. 1st edition; 4to; 4 volumes; numerous finely engraved plates; elaborate gilt decorated purple cloth, fine example of a Victorian binding; very good. K Books 441-25 1996 £100.00

BAINES, THOMAS   The Gold Regions of South Eastern Africa. London: Edward Stanford; Port Elizabeth, Cape Colony; J., W.C. Mackay, 1877. 1st edition; 8vo; portrait, 3 mounted photo plates, other illustrations in text, folding map in pocket at end; original bright green pictorial coth, minor rubbing; fine. Theal p. 17.   Ximenes 109-23 1996 $500.00

BAINES, THOMAS   The Gold Regions of South Eastern Africa. London: 1877. photo illustrations, text engravings, folding map in rear pocket; original pictorial cloth, just very light rubbing; excellent copy.   David Grayling J95Biggame-7 1996 £250.00

BAINES, THOMAS   Lancashire and Cheshire, Past and Present...from the Earliest Age to the Present Time (1867). London: n.d. 1868. 1st edition; 4to; 4 volumes; many plates and portraits; original cloth, gilt extra, gilt edges.   Charles W. Traylen 117-367 1996 £115.00

BAIRD, S. F.   Reptiles of U. S. Pacific R. R. Exp. and Surveys. Washington: 1857-59. 4to; 42 plates; bound.   John Johnson 135-558 1996 $100.00

BAKER, D.   The Royal Gunroom at Sandringham. 1989. Folio; many colored and other illustrations; mint in dust jacket.   David Grayling J95Biggame-344 1996 £65.00

BAKER, DOROTHY   Young Man with a Horn. Boston: Houghton Mifflin Co., 1938. Later printing; moderately worn and soiled, about very good, lacking dust jacket; Langston Hughes' copy with his ownership signature. Between the Covers 43-21 1996 $200.00

BAKER, EDWARD   Sport in Bengal. How, When & Where to Seek It. London: 1887. folding colored map in pocket at rear, one very small tear, title and dedication leaf lightly foxed; finely bound in modern half calf, gilt borders.   David Grayling   J95Biggame-356   1996 £150.00

BAKER, EDWARD CHARLES STUART   The Game Birds of India, Burma and Ceylon. London: 1921-30. Royal 8vo; 3 volumes; 60 colored and 18 plain plates, 2 maps; volumes 1 and 2 in original half morocco, volume 3 in original cloth. Good, complete set, as usual spines of volumes 1 and 2 have faded slightly, paper of plates in volume 1 little browned. Wheldon & Wesley   207-6   196 £300.00

BAKER, EDWARD CHARLES STUART   The Indian Ducks and Their Allies. London: 1908. Royal 8vo; pages xi, 292; 30 colored plates by Gronvold, Lodge and Keulemans; original half morocco, trifle used, spine faded.   Wheldon & Wesley   207-5   1996 £330.00

BAKER, HARRIET   The Organ Grinder; or, Struggles After Holiness. Boston: Henry Hoyt, 1862. 1st edition; 12mo; 235 pages; frontispiece; original cloth; Not in Wright; 1 copy in NUC.   M & S Rare Books   60-116   1996 $100.00

BAKER, HENRY   The Microscope Made Easy. London: 1743. 2nd edition; 14 folding plates, contemporary calf, covers detached, contents very good.   Petersfield Bookshop   FH58-134   1996 £90.00

BAKER, HENRY   The Microscope Made Easy. London: 1743. 4th edition; 14 folding plates; contemporary calf, top of joints beginning to crack, contents very good.   Petersfield Bookshop   FH58-133   1996 £85.00

BAKER, INEZ   Yesterday in Hall County. Dallas: 1940. 1st edition; 219 pages; photos, decorated cloth, very good+. Scarce. Herd 196.   T. A. Swinford   49-45   1996 $100.00

BAKER, J. G.   Flora of Mauritius and the Seychelles. London: 1970. 8vo; 628 pages; cloth.   Wheldon & Wesley   207-1517   1996 £90.00

BAKER, NICHOLSON   The Mezzanine. London: Granta Books in association with Penguin Books, 1989. 1st edition; author's first book; near fine in very slightly creased and dusty dust jacket.   Ulysses 39-29   1996 £65.00

BAKER, NICHOLSON   Room Temperature. New York: Grove Weidenfeld, 1990. 1st edition; original cloth, fine in fine dust jacket; signed by author.   Beasley Books   82-16   1996 $100.00

BAKER, NICHOLSON   Vox. New York: RH, 1922. 1st edition; advance reading copy; wrappers and publisher's plain brown paper wrap-around dust jacket; fine.   Lame Duck Books   19-51   1996 $100.00

BAKER, NICHOLSON   Vox. New York: Random House, 1992. Advance uncorrected proofs; wrappers, fine in fine brown wrapping paper wrapper.   Beasley Books   82-15   1996 $100.00

BAKER, R. T.   The Hardwoods of Australia and Their Economics. Sydney: 1919. 4to; pages xvi, 522; colored frontispiece, 72 plates containing 136 colored photographic cross-sections of wood and 194 text figures; original cloth backed boards, light soiling, some scuffing to rear cover, wear to edges of covers, light browning to endpapers. Raymond M. Sutton   VII-425   1996 $150.00

BAKER, R. T.   A Research on the Pines of Australia. Sydney: 1910. 4to; pages xiv, 458; profusion of illustrations, 3 maps; original red cloth, professionally rebacked, light soiling, 3 edges darkened, edge of front cover bumped, endpapers renewed, marginal brown spots to half title. Raymond M. Sutton   VII-424   1996 $145.00

BAKER, RICHARD   A Chronicle of the Kings of England from the Time of the Romans Government unto the Raigne of Our Soveraigne Lord King Charles. London: for Daniel Frere, 1643. 1st edition; folio; (10), 181, (1), 163, (1), 108, 163, (36) pages, errata leaf present; portrait, engraved title; late 19th century full sprinkled calf, gilt, small repair at upper blank edge of portrait, fore-edge of engraved title bit darkened and neatly strengthened on verso, two margins neatly extended, few minor marginal repairs, clean and desirable copy, in very attractive binding; with 2 interesting B. M. Pickering letters laid in relating to Baker's book. Wing B501.   Joseph J. Felcone   64-3   1996 $800.00

BAKER, ROBERT   Remarks on the English Language, in the Nature of Vaugelas's Remarks on the French... London: printed for J. Bell, 1770. contemporary calf, wormed on hinges; Alston III 299-301.   Jarndyce 103-17   1996 £150.00

BAKER, SAMUEL WHITE   The Albert N'Yanza Great Basin of the Nile and Exploration of the Nile Sources. London: Macmillan and Co., 1874. New edition; 8vo; xxvii, 499, 60 pages ads dated Oct. 1873; original green cloth, occasional foxing, inner hinges cracked, some wear along spine, still very good.   David Mason   71-3   1996 $120.00

BAKER, SAMUEL WHITE   Explorations of the Nile Tributaries of Abyssinia. Hartford: O. D. Case & Co., 1868. 1st American edition; illustrations, 2 maps, one plate loose, edges rubbed with some fraying to head and foot of spine, still nice.   Hermitage SP95-1092   1996 $200.00

BAKER, THOMAS   Reflections Upon Learning, Wherein is Shown the Insuffiency Thereof, In Its Several Particulars. London: A. Bosvile, 1699. 1st edition; 8vo; (xvi), 248 pages, tear in foot of one leaf (F8) neatly repaired, but with loss of one or two letters on each page; contemporary ruled calf, upper joint cracked and wear to upper edge of boards, else very good, crisp copy. Wing B519; Alston III 203.   John Drury   82-16   1996 £275.00

BAKER, THOMAS BARWICK LLOYD   'War With Crime", Being a Selection of Reprinted Papers on Crime, Reformatories, etc. London: Longmans, Green and Co., 1889. 1st edition; 8vo; frontispiece, xxix, (1), 299 pages, 24 pages of publisher's ads; original green cloth lettered in gilt, foot of covers stained, internally very good.   John Drury   82-17 1996 £75.00

BALDWIN, C. L.   Quinquivara. New York: Gemor Press, 1944. 1st edition; limited to 300 copies; 8vo; (viii), 58, (v) pages; cover illustration and 6 engravings by Ian Hugo; pictorial white boards, illustration in black on front cover, in tissue dust jacket; fine. Presentation copy inscribed by author.   Blue Mountain   SP95-87   1996 $125.00

BALDWIN, JAMES 1924-   The Devil Finds Work. New York: Dial, 1976. 1st edition; fine in dust jacket; signed by author.   Lame Duck Books 19-14   1996 $200.00

BALDWIN, JAMES 1924-   The Fire Next Time. New York: Dial, 1963. 1st edition; some dampstaining top and bottom page, edges otherwise very good in lightly chipped dust jacket.   Sherwood   3-1   1996 $100.00

BALDWIN, JAMES 1924-   Giovanni's Room. New York: 1956. 1st edition; fine in dust jacket with small chip to spine top.   Stephen Lupack   83-   1996 $250.00

BALDWIN, JAMES 1924-   Go Tell It to the Mountain. New York: Knopf, 1953. Advance review copy; with reviewer's notes in pencil on verso of review slip and page numbers cited in his notes bear light marginal markings, also in red pencil; in custom clamshell box; near fine in dust jacket that is at least very good with small chip at spine and crown and rear hinge, but very little of spine fading; Nice copy, scarce.   Ken Lopez   74-21   1996 $2,500.00

BALDWIN, JAMES 1924-   Go Tell It On the Mountain. Franklin Center: Franklin Library, 1979. Limited edition; signed by author; illustrations by Burt Silverman; leather, top edge gilt, all edges with silk ribbon; very fine.   Left Bank Books   2-8   1996 $100.00

BALDWIN, JAMES 1924-   Gypsy and Other Poems. Leeds: Gehenna Press, 1989. Limited edition of 325 copies, this one of 50 with series of 6 etched portraits of Baldwin by Leonard Baskin, printed from copperplates and numbered and signed by artist; page size 11 7/8 x 8 7/8 inches; printed on Magnani paper; black pastepaper over boards, black morocco spine, housed in red silk clamshell box with black morcco labels on spine and front cover gilt tooled. Signed by Baskin.   Priscilla Juvelis   95/1-13A   1996 $3,000.00

BALDWIN, JAMES 1924-   Gypsy and Other Poems. Leeds: Gehenna Press, 1989. Limited edition of 275 copies, this one of 275 copies containing one etching of Baldwin by Baskin signed and numbered by artist; printed on Magnani paper; bound by Claudia Cohen in grey paper over boards, red morocco label on spine and front cover, signed by Baskin.   Priscilla Juvelis   95/1-13   1996 $375.00

BALDWIN, JAMES 1924-   Little Man Little Man. New York: Dial Press, 1976. 1st edition; review copy with publicity photo of Baldwin and prospectus laid in. illustrations by Yoran Cazac; pictorial boards; very fine with slight chip to bottom rear dust jacket.   Bromer Booksellers 87-29   1996 $110.00

BALDWIN, JAMES 1924-   Nothing Personal. New York: 1964. 1st edition; 14.5 x 11 inches; photos by Richard Avedon; boards, very minor tear at bottom of spine, otherwise very good in rubbed and stained slipcase.   John K. King 77-203 1996 $250.00

BALDWIN, JAMES 1924-   Nothing Personal. New York: Atheneum, 1964. 1st edition; Photos by Richard Avedon; some minor spotting to boards, otherwise near fine in publisher's box, which is also a bit spotted, but otherwise unworn.   Left Bank Books 2-119 1996 $200.00

BALDWIN, JAMES 1924-   Nothing Personal. New York: Atheneum, 1964. (84) pages, (2 folded) photos; white boards, slipcase; lightly soiled, some rubbing of spine and beginning to split at foot of outer front hinge, slipcase with some wear and soil.   Bohling Book Co. 192-625 1996 $150.00

BALDWIN, JAMES 1924-   The Price of the Ticket. New York: St. Martin's Press, 1985. 1/150 signed and numbered copies; fine in slipcase.   Bev Chaney, Jr. 23-45 1996 $175.00

BALE, JOHN   The First Two Partes of the Actes or Unchast Examples of the Englysh Votaries Taken Out of Their Owne Legenades (sic) and Chronycles of Johan Bale... London: Abraham Vele, 1551. Small folio; (viii) pages, folios 1-78, (iv) pages, folios 1-120, (viii) pages; old calf, gilt rule and centrepiece, rebacked and recornered with old spine laid down; library stamp on title and few in margins, few shoulder-notes very slightly cropped, some minor staining, occasional underlining. Good copy; all early editions are extremely scarce. STC 1273.5, incorporating STC 1273.   Robert Clark 38-2 1996 £1,250.00

BALFOUR, ALICE B.   Twelve Hundred Miles in a Waggon. London: 1895. illustrations; finely bound in mdoern half morocco, gilt; attractive. David Grayling J95Biggame-8 1996 £90.00

BALFOUR, FRANCIS   A Treatise on Putrid Intestinal Remitting Fevers, In Which the Laws of the Febrile State and Sol-Lunar Influence... Edinburgh: 1790. xxix, 148, (4) pages; folding table; card wrappers defective, small library stamp on titlepage, occasional marginal stain; inscribed by author.   Graham Weiner C2-356 1996 £50.00

BALFOUR-KINNEAR, G. P. R.   Flying Salmon. Spinning Salmon. London: 1973-38. 1st edition; 2 volumes; illustrations; finely bound in half calf, gilt rules, borders and motifs, marbled endpapers, apart from the lightest of foxing to second title, a fine set.   David A.H. Grayling 3/95-402 1996 £150.00

BALL, BENJAMIN LINCOLN   Three Days on the White Moutains... Boston: Nathaniel Noyes, 1856. 1st edition; 8vo; 72 pages; original printed wrappers, uncut; fine. Sabin 2933; Bent p. 2.   M & S Rare Books 60-432 1996 $1,000.00

BALL, C. L.   Manzenita a Flower of the Sierra Nevada. Winchester: ca. 1911. 1st edition; 11 pages; original printed wrappers with Manzanita stamped on front cover; fine. Not in Cowan or Rocq.   Michael D. Heaston 23-72 1996 $200.00

BALL, CHARLES   Fifty Years in Chains; or the Life of an American Slave. New York: H. Dayton; Indianapolis: Asher & Co., 1859. 8vo; 430 pages; original cloth; LCP/HSP Afro Amer. Cat. 812 for 1858 ed. Howes B69 for 1859 ed.   M & S Rare Books 60-279 1996 $150.00

BALL, ELIZA CRAUFURDD   The Christian Armour. New York: Charles Scribner & Co., 1866. 4to; 31 leaves, every page embellished in color and gold; full brown morocco over bevelled boards, heavily embossed in blind, richly gilt decorated on both covers, with sunken oval panels in which the title appears above and below a shield and sword, spine with five raised bands, much gilt decoration, but without title information, all edges gilt, inner dentelles, marbled endpapers; fine, original, unsophisticated copy; Marzo p. 49; Bennett p. 8; Waddleton Chronology p. 172.   Book Block 32-15 1996 $1,250.00

BALL, JAMES MOORE   The Sack-'Em-Up Men. Edinburgh: Oliver and Boyd, 1928. 8vo; 216 pages; 60 plates; original binding, spine sunned, else good, uncut.   James Tait Goodrich K40-21 1996 $125.00

BALL, JOHN   In the Heat of the Night. New York: Harper and Row, 1965. 1st edition; author's first book; fine in dust jackets with very light rubbing.   Quill & Brush 102-44 1996 $175.00

BALL, LUCILLE   Lucy's Notebook. N.P.: Phillip Morris & Co., ca. 1951-57. Large 8vo; , many in color, full page ad for Philip Morris cigarettes on inside of back wrapper; stiff color pictorial wrappers, upper cover with drawings of Lucy and Desi; very good, uncommon. George J. Houle 68-36 1996 $150.00

BALL, ROBERT S.   An Atlas of Astronomy... London: George Philip & Son, 1892. 1st edition; 7.5 x 8.5 inches; 57 pages text; 72 plates; gilt illustrated blue cloth, all edges gilt, extremities worn and fraying, few spots to rear boards, rear edge of spine fraying, scattered foxing, bookplate, dent in edge of rear board; good copy, attractive book. Knollwood Books 70-25 1996 $150.00

BALLANCE, CHARLES   Some Points in the Surgery of the Brain and its Membranes. London: 1907. 1st edition; 451 pages; original binding; Power 36; Courville 97; Walker 135.   W. Bruce Fye 71-81 1996 $500.00

BALLARD, C. R.   Kitchener. London: Faber & Faber, 1930. 1st edition; 17 sketch maps; original binding, top edge dusty, top corners of few pages creased, head and tail of spine slightly bumped, free endpapers partially browned, edges and endpapers slightly spotted, spine slightly spotted and darkened, very good in nicked and spotted, slightly torn, rubbed, marked and dusty price clipped dust jacket browned at spine and edges.   Ulysses 39-338 1996 £65.00

BALLARD, J. G.   The Atrocity Exhibition. London: J. Cape, 1970. 1st edition; just about fine in dust jacket, signed by author.   Aronovitz 57-78 1996 $250.00

BALLARD, J. G.   Concrete Island. London: Jonathan Cape Ltd., 1974. 1st edition; signed by author; head and tail of spine slightly bumped, original binding; near fine in dust jacket slightly crinkled at edges. Ulysses 39-30 1996 £125.00

BALLARD, J. G.   The Day of Creation. London: Gollancz, 1987. 1st edition; 1/100 copies; signed and numbered by author; fine in slipcase. Aronovitz 57-81 1996 $200.00

BALLARD, J. G.   High Rise. London: Cape, 1975. 1st edition; signed by author on titlepage, fine in price clipped dust jacket.   Virgo Books 48-14 1996 £85.00

BALLARD, J. G.   Low-Flying Aircraft and Other Stories. London: Jonathan Cape, 1976. 1st edition; original binding, tail of spine very slightly bumped, fine in very slightly creased dust jacket by Bill Botten; presentation copy from author.   Ulysses 39-31 1996 £155.00

BALLARD, J. G.   The Terminal Beach. London: Gollancz, 1964. 1st edition; top edge foxed, but very good plus copy in price clipped dust jacket, jacket spine is bit soiled, but much better copy than usually encountered, scarce.   Lame Duck Books 19-53 1996 $500.00

BALLOU, ADIN   After Reading Thoreau. Seal Harbor: the Printing Office at High Loft, 1979. One of 140 copies; octavo; 59 pages; drawings; bound by Gray Parrot in pictorial green paper boards with morocco label going the full length of the spine. Fine.   Bromer Booksellers 90-65 1996 $125.00

BALLOU, ADIN   History of the Town of Milford, Worcester County, Massachusetts, From Its First Settlement in 1881. Boston: 1882. 1st edition; 8vo; 2 volumes, 18, 1154 pages; large folding map, numerous plates; original cloth.   M & S Rare Books 60-280 1996 $200.00

BALLOU, MATURIN MURRAY   Due South, or Cuba Past and Present. Boston and New York: Houghton Mifflin, 1885. 1st edition; 8vo; 8 pages ads; ad leaf; original pictorial cloth, gilt, spine gilt; fine; presentation copy from author and recipient's signature both dated 1885. Trebizond 39-77 1996 $100.00

BALTIMORE MUSEUM OF ART   The History of Bookbinding 525-1950 A.D.: an Exhibition Held at the Baltimore Museum of Art, Nov. 12, 1957 to Jan. 12, 1958. Baltimore: 1957. 4to; 106 plates; original buckram, headcaps bumped, ex-library, shelf mark on spine. Brenni 347.   Maggs Bros. Ltd. 1191-31 1996 £90.00

BALTIMORE MUSEUM OF ART   The History of Bookbinding 525-1950 A.D.: an Exhibition Held at the Baltimore Museum of Art. Baltimore: Walters Art Gallery, 1957. 1st edition; 4to; xii, 275 pages; 106 plates; decorated cloth.   The Bookpress 75-308 1996 $150.00

BALZAC, HONORE   Eugenie Grandet. Limited Editions Club, 1960. One of 1500 numbered copies, signed by artist; 4to; hand colored illustrations by Rene ben Sussan; tan buckram with black leather insets, very nice bright copy in slipcase.   Bertram Rota 272-265 1996 £50.00

BANCROFT, EDWARD   An Essay on the Natural History of Guiana, in South America. London: 1769. 8vo; pages (4), (i-) iv, 402, (2), (ads 4 pages); frontispiece; modern buckram, ink stamps on verso of title, scattered foxing, slightly browned, call numbers on spine, from the University of Chicago Library.   Raymond M. Sutton VI-1 1996 $800.00

BANCROFT, EDWARD   Experimental Researches Concerning the Philosophy of Permanent Colours; and the Best Means of Producing Them, by Dyeing, Calico Printing &c. Philadelphia: Thomas Dobson, 1814. 1st American edition; 8vo; 2 volumes, (3), xlv, (2), 401, (2 ads); (3), 394, (2 ad) pages; early half morocco over marbled boards, binding bit shelfworn, some browning and foxing; very good set.   Edwin V. Glaser 121-15 1996 $385.00

BANCROFT, HUBERT HOWE 1832-1918   History of British Columbia 1792-1887. San Francisco: 1887. 1st edition; pages xxxi, 792, folding map; full sheep, light edge wear, else very good.   Stephen Lunsford 45-11 1996 $125.00

BANCROFT, HUBERT HOWE 1832-1918   History of British Columbia, 1792-1887. San Francisco: History Company, 1887. 1st edition; xxxi, 792 pages; folding map, text maps; newly bound in cloth, black spine label, fine.   Argonaut Book Shop 113-44 1996 $125.00

BANCROFT, HUBERT HOWE 1832-1918   History of California. Santa Barbara: Wallace Hebberd, 1963. Facsimile reprint; 7 volumes; mint set with dust jackets.   Argonaut Book Shop 113-45 1996 $350.00

BANCROFT, HUBERT HOWE 1832-1918   History of Mexico. San Francisco: 1883/85/86/87. 1st edition; 6 volumes, 702, 790, 780, 829, 812, 766 pages; maps; calf with leather label, nice. Howes B91.   T. A. Swinford 49-54 1996 $200.00

BANCROFT, HUBERT HOWE 1832-1918   History of the Life of William Gilpin. San Francisco: The History Co., 1889. 8vo; 62 pages; engraved portrait; original cloth, gilt, trifle bumped and scratched.   R.F.G. Hollett & Son 78-99 1996 £65.00

BANCROFT, HUBERT HOWE 1832-1918   History of Utah, 1540-1887. San Francisco: The History Company, Publishers, 1890. 1st separate deluxe special edition; xlvii, 808 pages; extra color lithographed title, 6 full page color lithographic plates, 5 steel engravings, eleven photo engravings, 22 maps; three quarter red maroon leatherette, cloth sides, gilt lettered spine, all edges gilt; fine. Flake 286.   Argonaut Book Shop 113-46 1996 $325.00

BANCROFT, HUBERT HOWE 1832-1918   The Works of...Volumes XV and XVI. North American States and Texas. San Francisco: 1887. 1st edition; 2 volumes 773, 824 pages; maps; calf with leather label, nice; Howes B91; Rader 200; Smith 531; Graff 155.   T. A. Swinford 49-53 1996 $175.00

BANCROFT, HUBERT HOWE 1832-1918   The Works of...Volume XXV. History of Nevada, Colorado and Wyoming. San Francisco: 1890. 1st edition; 820 pages; maps; calf, leather label, very good+. Six Guns 127; Herd 203.   T. A. Swinford 49-56 1996 $100.00

BANCROFT, HUBERT HOWE 1832-1918   The Works of...Volume XXVI. The History of Washington, Idaho and Montana. San Francisco: 1890. 1st edition; 836 pages; maps; full calf, leather label on spine, very good+. Graff 155; 6 Guns 128; Smith 530; Howes B91; Rader 200.   T. A. Swinford 49-50 1996 $100.00

BANCROFT, HUBERT HOWE 1832-1918   The Works of...Volumes XXIX & XXX. History of Oregon. San Francisco: 1886-87. 2 volumes, 789, 808 pages; maps; calf with leather label; nice. Smith 513; Graff 202; Howes B91.   T. A. Swinford 49-52 1996 $150.00

BANCROFT, HUBERT HOWE 1832-1918   The Works of...Volume XXXII. British Columbia. San Francisco: 1887. 1st edition; 792 pages; maps; full calf, leather label, very good+ Smith 511; Howes B91; Graff 202.   T. A. Swinford 49-51 1996 $100.00

BANCROFT, HUBERT HOWE 1832-1918   The Works of...Volume XXXIII. Alaska. San Francisco: 1886. 1st edition; 779 pages; maps; calf with leather label, nice. Scarce. Howes B91; Smith 509; Graff 202.   T. A. Swinford 49-55 1996 $100.00

BANCROFT, HUBERT HOWE 1832-1918   The Works of...Volume XXXIV. California Pastoral. San Francisco: 1888. 808 pages; full calf with leather label, very good+. Graff 1555; 6 Guns 129; Howes B91; Rader 200; Smith 530.   T. A. Swinford 49-49 1996 $100.00

BANCROFT, HUBERT HOWE 1832-1918   The Works of...Volume XXXV. California Inner Pocula. San Francisco: 1888. 1st edition; 830 pages; calf with leather label, nice. Wheat Gold Rush 10; Howes B91; Graff 202. T. A. Swinford 49-57 1996 $100.00

BANDELIER, ADOLPH F.   The Southwestern Journals of Adolph F. Bandelier. Albuquerque: University of New Mexico Press, 1966-75. 1st edition; 9 1/4 x 6 inches; 3 volumes, maps and illustrations; cloth, different for each volume, dust jackets, bit cocked.   Dawson's Books Shop 528-5 1996 $150.00

BANDELLO, MATTEO   The Novels. Ptd. for the Villon Society by Private Subscription & for Private... 1890. Limited edition; square 8vo; 6 volumes, printed on handmade large paper; attractively bound in dark blue levant half morocco, gilt, top edge gilt, others uncut, extremities very slightly rubbed and little minor spotting in volume 1, but fine, unopened set.   Thomas Thorp 489-16 1996 £120.00

BANDINELLI, RANUCCIO BIANCHI   Rome, the Center of Power: 500 B.C. to A.D. 200. New York: George Braziller, 1970. 4to; xii, 437 pages; 435 illustrations; 3 maps, 13 plans; original cloth.   Archaeologia Luxor-2962 1996 $200.00

BANKOFF, GEORGE   The Story of Plastic Surgery. London: 1952. 1st edition; 224 pages; original binding.   W. Bruce Fye 71-83 1996 $125.00

BANKS, JOHN   Vertue Betray'd: or, Anna Bullen. London: R. Bentley and M. Magnes, 1682. 1st edition; quarto; disbound, some embrowning, top edge lightly shaved, nice. Wing B667.   G. W. Stuart 59-4 1996 $350.00

BANKS, JONATHAN   The Life of the Right Reverend Father in God, Edw. Rainbow, D.D. Late Lord Bishop of Carlisle. London: printed by Samuel Roycroft for Robert Clavell, 1688. 1st edition; small 8vo; pages (xii), 112, 29; engraved frontispiece; modern calf, gilt, old spine label retained. Wing B669.   R.F.G. Hollett & Son 78-100 1996 £120.00

BANKS, JOSEPH   The Endeavour Journal of Joseph Banks 1768-1771. Sydney: Public Lib. Of New South Wales, Angus & Robertson Ltd., 1962. 8vo; 2 volumes, xxvii, 476 pages plus plates, 5 sketch maps, 40 black/white plates, 10 color plates, 6 illustrations; xvi, 406 pages + plates, 5 appendices, index, 6 color plates, 4 sketch maps, 40 black/white plates; burgundy cloth; dust jackets worn, slightly soiled at edges, else very good.   Parmer Books Nat/Hist-077361 1996 $480.00

BANKS, JOSEPH   Joseph Banks in Newfoundland and Labrador. London: 1971. 4to; pages xxviii,4 58, frontispiece, 8 colored maps, 12 colored plates, 96 pages of half tones; cloth.   Wheldon & Wesley 207-356 1996 £70.00

BANKS, W.   Stirling and the Scottish Lakes. Edinburgh: Banks & Co., n.d., c. 1860. Oblong 8vo; ornamental title, 26 steel engraved plates, 4 ad pages; publisher's purple cloth, decorated in blind and gilt, gilt edges, slightly worn and faded, little foxed.   Thomas Thorp 489-17 1996 £50.00

BANNATYNE CLUB   The Bannatyne Miscellany.... Edinburgh: printed 1827-36-55. 4to; complete set, 3 volumes; contemporary half red morocco, top edge gilt; fine; bookplates of Henry Drummond, Albury Park, Surrey. CBEL III 679.   Ximenes 108-14 1996 $650.00

BANNERMAN, DAVID ARMITAGE   Birds of the Atlantic Islands. London: 1963-68. Royal 8vo; 4 volumes; 11 maps, 47 colored and 54 plain plates and numerous text figures; cloth, good set although spines are slightly marked at foot.   Wheldon & Wesley 207-7 1996 £500.00

BANNERMAN, DAVID ARMITAGE   Birds of the Atlantic Islands. London: 1963-68. Large 4to; 4 volumes; colored and plain plates, text illustrations; apart from volume 1 lacking it's dust jacket, a mint set. David A.H. Grayling MY95Orn-5 1996 £480.00

BANNERMAN, DAVID ARMITAGE   The Birds of the British Isles. London: 1953-63. Imperial 8vo; 12 volumes; 387 colored plates by G. E. Lodge; cloth, dust jackets.   John Henly 27-5 1996 £330.00

BANNERMAN, DAVID ARMITAGE   The Birds of the British Isles. London: 1953. 12 volumes; numerous colored plates by George Lodge; corners of dust wrappers slightly torn and scuffed, otherwise fine set. David A.H. Grayling   MY95Orn-4   1996 £370.00

BANNERMAN, DAVID ARMITAGE   The Birds of the British Isles. London: 1956. 4to; Volume 5, 1 plain and 34 colored plates; cloth. Wheldon & Wesley   207-632   1996 £150.00

BANNERMAN, DAVID ARMITAGE   Birds of the Maltese Archipelago. London: 1976. 20 colored plates, other illustrations, maps; mint in dust jacket.   David A.H. Grayling MY95Orn-98   1996 £55.00

BANNERMAN, DAVID ARMITAGE   The Birds of West and Equatorial Africa. London: 1953. 8vo; 2 volumes; pages xiii, 1526; 30 color and 24 plain plates, numerous text illustrations; cloth, dust jackets chipped at head of spine, otherwise fine.   John Henly   27-4   1996 £112.00

BANNERMAN, DAVID ARMITAGE   The Birds of West and Equatorial Africa. London: 1953. 8vo; pages 1526, colored and 24 plain plates, 433 text figures; cloth.   Wheldon & Wesley   207-629   1996 £75.00

BANNERMAN, DAVID ARMITAGE   The Birds of West and Equatorial Africa. London: 1953. 2 volumes; many colored and plain plates, text illustrations; light marking on covers and lower cover of volume 2 is slightly bubbled, contents are excellent.   David A.H. Grayling MY95Orn-99   1996 £75.00

BANNERMAN, DAVID ARMITAGE   The History of the Birds of the Cape Verde Islands. London: 1968. 4to; pages xxxi, 458; 20 color and 31 plain plates; cloth, dust jacket.   John Henly   27-3   1996 £135.00

BANNERMAN, HELEN   Sambo and the Twins, a New Adventure of Little Black Sambo. New York: Stokes, 1936. 1st American edition; small octavo; 90 pages; 43 illustrations by author in color; color dust jacket by Bannerman, which is lightly chipped and soiled, else fine, bookplate. Bromer Booksellers   90-82   1996 $185.00

BANNERMAN, HELEN   The Story of Little Black Sambo. Garden City: Garden City Publishing, 1933. Octavo; (60) pages; 27 full page color images by Kurt Wiese, including movables by A. V. Warren; bright yellow cloth with pictorial paper label; bright and fine.   Bromer Booksellers   87-154   1996 $550.00

BANNET, IVOR   The Amazons. Waltham St. Lawrence: Golden Cockerel Press, 1948. Limited to 500 numbered copies; 4to; 253 pages; frontispiece, tailpiece, 8 full page wood engravings by Clifford Webb, 3 maps by Mina Greenhill; half morocco, designed by Christopher Sandford, spine gilt, top edge gilt, others uncut (spine very slightly faded).   Thomas Thorp   489-18   1996 £80.00

BANNING, KENDALL   Songs of the Love Unending: a Sonnet Sequence. Village Press, 1912. One of 375 copies; 10 1/4 x 6 3/4 inches; 1 p.l., 14, (2) pages; red device on title, device in colophon, decorative woodcut initial, frontispiece reproduction, order form laid in; original holland backed printed blue paper boards. Fine. Cary 77.   Phillip J. Pirages   33-500   1996 $200.00

BANNING, WILLIAM   Six Horses. New York: Century Co., 1930. 1st edition; xx, 410 pages; plates; original black cloth stamped in blind and lettered in orange-red; fine. Scarce. Six-Guns 134.   Argonaut Book Shop   113-50   1996 $100.00

BARAKA, AMIRI   Home: Social Essays. New York: Morrow, 1966. 1st edition; bookplate of a Morrow editor, else fine in near fine dust jacket with short tear at crown; inscribed twice by Jones to editor at Morrow, inscribed books by Jones are becoming increasingly less common. Between the Covers   43-142   1996 $175.00

BARAKA, AMIRI   The Dead Lectuer. New York: Grove Press, 1964. 1st edition; fine, dust jacket, signed by author, owner's signature. Captain's Bookshelf   38-128   1996 $125.00

BARAKA, AMIRI   Prefaceto a Twenty Volume Suicide Note. N.P.: Totem Press/Corinth, 1961. 1st edition; printed wrappers; inscribed by author.   Revere Books   4-25   1996 $125.00

BARBA, ALBARO ALONSO   Grundlicher Unterricht von den Metallen, Darinnen Beschrieben Wird, Wie Sie Werde in der Erden Generirt... Ephrata: J. Georg Zeisiger, 1763. 1st American edition; 8vo; 2 parts in 1, with separate titlepages, 198,, (4), 14 pages, full page woodcut illustrations, two large woodcut tailpieces and few smaller head and tailpieces; contemporary half sheep over boards, binding rubbed and worn along extremities with bit of erosion at top of spine, front hinge cracked, some occasional staining and browning, nevertheless, very good. Rare. Honeyman Sale I 201; Evans 9333. Rink Tech Amer 769. Edwin V. Glaser   121-17   1996 $2,200.00

BARBARUS, HERMOLAUS   Castigationes Plinae et Pomponii Melae. Venice: Eponymous Press, ca. 1493/94. Folio; 19th century polished quarter sheep, boards, joints cracked, somewhat worn, few notes in margins, minor underlining here and there, light soiling, quite decent and complete with initial leaf blank save for short title. Hain Copinger 2423; GW 3341; Goff B101.   G. W. Stuart   59-50   1996 $3,750.00

BARBAULD, ANNA, LAETITIA AIKIN 1743-1825   Poems. London: J. Johnson, 1773. 3rd edition, same year as the first; octavo; pages 138; full calf, raised bands, gilt, nicely rebacked, original label laid down; CBEL II 352; Pottle p. xxxiv.   Hartfield   48-L3   1996 $225.00

BARBER, H.   Furness and Cartmel Notes, or Jottings of Topographical, Ecclesiastical and Popular Antiquities and of Historical Circumstances... Ulverston: James Atkinson, 1894. 1st edition; 8vo; pages (viii), 391, illustrations; original cloth, gilt, over bevelled boards; fine.   R.F.G. Hollett & Son   78-684   1996 £85.00

BARBER, WILLIAM HENRY   The Case of Mr. W. H. Barber. London: published by Effingham Wilson, 1849. 2nd edition; 8vo; 116 pages; disbound; signature of C. R. Weld on title.   Anthony W. Laywood 108-149   1996 £135.00

BARBEY D'AUREVILLY, JULES AMEDEE 1808-1889   What Never Dies. A Romance. Privately printed, 1928. No. 16 of only 25 special copies with extra plates; 9 hand colored plates by Donald Denton, frontispiece in 2 states; three quarter morocco, gilt decorated spine with raised bands, little edge rubbed; fine.   Polyanthos   22-936   1996 $250.00

BARBOUR, JOHN   The Life and Acts of the Most Victorious Conqueror Robert Bruce, King of Scotland. Edinburgh: 1758. Small 4to; pages 443, uncut, printed in black letter with head and tailpieces, few leaves rather browned; old binders cloth, gilt, lower corners of boards damped; nice, unsophisticated copy. Inscription of William Ingram 1788, on title; signature of James Crawfurd on pastedown & inscription below of George Arbuthnot dated Feb. 1st 1831.   R.F.G. Hollett   76-13   1996 £95.00

BARBUT, JACQUES   The Genera Insectorum of Linnaeus Exemplified by Various Specimens of English Insects Drawn from Nature. London: J. Dixwell for J. Sewell, 1781. 1st edition; 4to; 20 brilliantly hand colored plates; full contemporary acid calf with enclosed thin ribbon border, on both covers, smooth rounded spine with gilt decoration and morocco lettering piece, light wear to extremities, but very attractive and sound. Nissen ZBI 220; Lisney 289.   Book Block   32-12   1996 $1,500.00

BARBUT, JAMES   The Genera Vermium Exemplified by Various Specimens of the Animals Contained in the Orders of the Intestina at Mollusca Linnaei. Drawn from Nature. London: printed for the author by James Dixwell, 1783. 1st edition; 4to; frontispiece, 2 page list of subscribers, 11 hand colored plates, some offsetting in text, text in English and French; contemporary tree calf, spine gilt, label, with Deschamps bookplates; nice copy. Nissen ZBI 221.   Anthony W. Laywood   109-6   1996 £425.00

BARCIA, D. A. GONZALEZ DE   Ensayo Cronologico, Para La Historia General De La Florida. Madrid: Nicolas Rodriguez Franco, 1723. 1st edition; folio; (40), 368, (54) pages; title printed in red and black; one folding table at p. 150; contemporary mottled calf over marbled boards, red leather spine label; fine. Howes B130 b; Sabin 3349; Palau 105049. Kenneth Karmiole   1NS-34   1996 $2,000.00

BARCLAY, JAMES   A Complete and Universal English Dictionary on a New Plan. London: printed for Richardson & Urquhart; W. Otridge &c., 1774. 1st edition; initial ad leaf; rebound in half speckled calf, retaining original red label. Alston V284.   Jarndyce   103-121   1996 £180.00

BARCLAY, JAMES   Barclay's Universal Dictionary. London: J. McGowan, c. 1820? 4to; plates; handsome contemporary half calf, elaborately gitl spine, very good.   Jarndyce   103-122   1996 £140.00

BARCLAY, JOHN   Argenia. Lugd. Bat.: ex Officina Elzeviriana, 1630. 3rd Elzevir edition; small 12mo; 690, (6) pages; including engraved title; short tear without loss in A2; contemporary vellum.   K Books   442-198 1996 £90.00

BARCLAY, JOHN   John Barclay, His Argenis. London: Felix Kyngston for Richard Meighen and Henry Seile, 1628. 1st edition of this new translation; 4to; (8), 490 pages; engraved headpieces, initials; old mottled calf, rebacked, morocco spine label, gilt, extremities lightly rubbed; bookplate of Edmund Gosse. STC 1393.   Kenneth Karmiole 1NS-37 1996 $450.00

BARCLAY, JOHN   Barclay, His Argenis. London: printed for Henry Seile, 1636. 2nd edition of this translation; 4to; 23 plates; contemporary calf, spine worn, front cover detached; the copy of Clara Reeve, 18th century novelist), with signature. Aside from binding, in very good condition. STC 1392.5. Esdaile p. 18; Mish p. 21.   Ximenes 109-24 1996 $750.00

BARCLAY, JOHN   Euphormionis Lusinini, Partes Quinq. London: Felix Kyngston for Richard Meighen and Henry Seile, 1628. 1st edition of this new translation, the second into English; 12mo; (10), 782 pages; endpapers and final blank lacking, overall nice copy in contemporary calf. STC 1397.   Kenneth Karmiole 1NS-36 1996 $200.00

BARCLAY, JOHN   Euphormionis Lusinini Sive...Satyricon. Lugd. Batavorum (Leiden): apud Elzevirios, 1637. Small 12mo; 717 pages, including engraved title, pages 207, 209 correctly numbered; full vellum, very good.   K Books 441-206 1996 £80.00

BARCLAY, JOHN   The Mirror of Minds or Barclay's Icon Animorum. London: I.B. for Thomas Walkley, 1633. 12mo; pages (xii), 380, roman letter, title backed long since, couple of minor tears not affecting text, perfectly acceptable copy; early 19th century calf gilt, upper cover loosening; armorial bookplates of W. Combes and Henry Batchellor Inman, autograph of "J. Mitford 1832" (probably the writer John Mitford 1781-1859). STC 1400. Lowndes 112.   A. Sokol XXV-10 1996 £500.00

BARCLAY, ROBERT 1648-1690   The Anarchy of the Ranters and Other Libertines, the Hierarchy of the Romanists, and Other Pretended Churches Equally Refused and Refuted in a Two-fold Apology for the Church and People of God... London: printed for Thomas Northcott in George Yard, 1691. 2nd edition; folio; 55 pages; disbound, excellent.   Roy W. Clare XXIV-6 1996 $250.00

BARCLAY, ROBERT 1648-1690   An Apology for the True Christian Divinity... Birmingham: Baskerville, 1765. 1st Bakserville printing; tall wide quarto; pages (xi), xiii, 504, (xvi), contemporary calf, rebacked, leather label, some wear, but nice, wide margined copy. With appropriate bookplate of Library Company of Philadelphia. Gaskell 30; Wing B720.   Hartfield 48-L5 1996 $395.00

BARCLAY, ROBERT 1648-1690   A Catechism and Confession of Faith...Bound with, the Ancient Testimony of the People Called Quakers... Philadelphia: Joseph James, 1788. 12mo; viii, 147, (3); 34 pages; 2 volumes bound as one; contemporary speckled calf, head of spine chipped, some light foxing, contemporary inscription in ink on front free endpaper, still good. Evans 20950.   The Bookpress 75-382 1996 $250.00

BARCLAY, ROBERT 1648-1690   Theologie vere Christianae Apologia. Londoni: apud Benjamin Clark, Roterodami, apud Isaac Naeranum, Francofurti... 1686. 4to; half title, errata leaf at end; contemporary calf, slightly rubbed. Wing 736a.   Anthony Laywood 108-2 1996 £135.00

BARCLAY, ROBERT 1648-1690   Truth Triumphant Through the Spiritual Warfare, Christian Labours and Writings. London: Thomas Northcott, 1692. 1st collected edition; folio; (ii), xxxviii, (xvi), 908, (xviii) pages; modern library buckram, number on spine, label on endpaper, few insignificant blindstamps, some page edges at beginning and end bit frayed, well clear of text. Sound, clean copy. Wing B740.   Robert Clark 38-4 1996 £125.00

BARD, J. P.   Microtextures of Igneous and Metamorphic Rocks. Amsterdam: 1986. 8vo; 278 pages; illustrations; hardbound.   Wheldon & Wesley 207-1309 1996 £72.75

BARDSLEY, SAMUEL ARGENT   Medical Reports of Cases and Experiments, with Observations, Chiefly Derived from Hospital Practice. London: 1807. 1st edition; 8vo; 336 pages; contemporary mottled calf, somewhat worn, hinges cracked, some waterstains, especially to prelims. Wellcome ii p. 100.   Argosy 810-34 1996 $600.00

BARETTI, GIUSEPPE MARC0 ANTONIO 1719-1789   A Journey from London to Genoa, through England, Portugal, Spain and France... Dublin: printed by T. Ewing... 1770. 12mo; 4 volumes bound in 2; contemporary calf, gilt spines, hinges little worn, good.   H. M. Fletcher 121-85 1996 £265.00

BARETTI, GIUSEPPE MARCO ANTONIO 1719-1789   An Account of the Manners and Customs of Italy, with Observations on the Mistakes of Some Travellers with Regard to that Country. London: Davies, Davis and Reymers, 1768. 1st edition; tall 8vo; 2 volumes in 1; pages xxi, 317; vii, 330; 2 engraved plates of music; recent fine binding in maroon polished morocco, raised bands, gilt, gilt on red leather label, marbled boards; excellent condition. CBEL II 745.   Hartfield 48-L6 1996 $395.00

BARETTI, GIUSEPPE MARCO ANTONIO 1719-1789   A Journey from London to Genoa, through England, Portugal, Spain and France. London: printed for T. Davies and L. Davis, 1770. 8vo; 4 volumes, piece missing from outer blank margin of L3 in volume 1 with no loss of text, 3 or 4 minor marginal tears; contemporary sprinkled calf, slightly rubbed, some hinges partly cracked, spines gilt, contrasting labels (one chipped), nice set.   Anthony Laywood 108-25 1996 £325.00

BARHAM, RICHARD HARRIS 1788-1845   The Ingoldsby Legends, or Mirth and Marvels. London: J. M. Dent, 1907. One of 560 copies on large paper, signed by artist; 4to; 24 mounted color plates and numerous drawings in tint and black and white by Arthur Rackham; full vellum with gilt stamped design and lettering on front cover and spine, gilt top. Preserved in half morocco folding box; fine.   Appelfeld Gallery 54-152 1996 $1,500.00

BARHAM, RICHARD HARRIS 1788-1845   The Ingoldsby Legends. London: Heineman, 1920. Early printing; 4to; 24 tipped in color plates by Arthur Rackham; also with 12 tinted plates and many many engravings; decorated cloth, some fraying to spine tips and edges, occasional foxing, very good   Charles Agvent 4-706 1996 $175.00

BARHAM, RICHARD HARRIS 1788-1845   Martin's Vagaries; Being a Sequel to "A Tale of a Tub"... London: A. H. Baily & Co., 1843. 1st edition; 8 x 5 inches, 48 pages; 2 plates, 1 textual illustration by George Cruikshank, text illustration repeated on original printed wrappers bound in at back; finely bound by Riviere in medium brown crushed morocco, covers framed with French fillet, spine handsomely gilt in compartments (with vertical title in elongated center compartment), turn-ins covered with lovely gilt filigree, gilt top, two edges rough trimmed, short portions at top of joints showing first signs of cracking, covers with few faint spots, slight wrinkling of a few leaves at fore edge, otherwise fine in very appealing binding. Cohn 516.   Phillip J. Pirages 33-149 1996 $250.00

BARING, M.   Orpheus in Mayfair and Other Stories and Sketches. Mills & Boon, 1909. 1st edition; slight fading to spine, but very good, author's first book of short stories; uncommon.   Aronovitz 57-86 1996 $135.00

BARING, THOMAS   Catalogue of the Library of Thomas Baring, Esq. at Sunninghill Park (later at Baring Court). London: 1914. 8vo; over 200 pages of typescript; full red morocco by Bickers & Son, gilt, all edges gilt.   Forest Books 74-168 1996 £110.00

BARKER, BENJAMIN   Francisco, or the Pirate of the Pacific. Boston: Gleason's Pub.Hall, 1845. 1st edition; 8vo; 58 pages; illustrations; original printed and colored pictorial wrappers, some mildew to lower margins, fraying. Wright I 269.   M & S Rare Books 60-118 1996 $100.00

BARKER, CLIVE   Books of Blood. London: Sphere, 1984. 1st hardcover edition; volumes 1 and 2; very fine in dust jacket; inscribed by author.   Robert Gavora 61-6 1996 $160.00

BARKER, CLIVE   Hellraiser. Anaheim: Graphitti, 1990. 1st edition; one of 500 numbered copies, signed by author and artists; volume 1; illustrations by John Bolton and Simon Bisley; very fine in dust jacket.   Robert Gavora 61-9 1996 $130.00

BARKER, CLIVE   Weaveworld. London: 1987. 1st edition; few leaves trifle creased at head, otherwise very good in dust jacket.   Words Etcetera 94-81 1996 £125.00

BARKER, CLIVE   Weaveworld. London: Collins, 1987. 1st British edition, and only edition with illustrations by author; very fine, issued without dust jacket, in slipcase with small bump at one corner.   Robert Gavora 61-12 1996 $195.00

BARKER, CLIVE   Weaveworld. New York: Poseidon, 1987. 1st edition; one of 500 numbered copies, signed by author; very fine in 3 mil mylar dust jacket with slipcase.   Robert Gavora 61-10 1996 $175.00

BARKER, CLIVE   Weaveworld. New York: Poseidon Press, 1987. Signed limited, numbered edition of 500 copies; 8vo; cloth, in original slipcase, fine.   Antic Hay 101-109 1996 $150.00

BARKER, GEORGE   Elegy On Spain. Manchester: Contemporary Bookshop, 1939. 1st edition; frontispiece; original binding, nice in only minimally rubbed dust jacket.   Ian Patterson 9-28 1996 £100.00

BARKER, MATTHEW HENRY 1790-1846   Jem Bunt: a Tale of the Land and the Ocean. London: Willoughby & Co., n.d. 1st edition; octavo; (8), 312, (8) pages; engraved vignette and 22 engraved plates; 3 original watercolor drawings signed by George Cruikshank, a proof of one of the illustrations with marginal drawings as well as an early proof for one of the drawings on engraved title; original blue blindstamped cloth decoratively stamped and lettered in gilt on front cvoer and spine, extremities lightly rubbed, front hinge cracked, but sound, occasional light foxing and browning; still, overall, a very good copy, housed in quarter navy blue morocco folding case, drawings protected in blue cloth slipcase.   Heritage Book Shop 196-165 1996 $1,250.00

BARKER, MATTHEW HENRY 1790-1846   Tough Yarns: a Series of Tall Tales and Sketches to Please all Hands. London: Effingham Wilson, 1835. 1st edition; small 8vo; 351 pages; 8 full page plates by Cruikshank; contemporary half black morocco with raised bands, gilt tooled spine panels, top edge gilt, rubbed, bookpalte, else very good. Chapel Hill 94-48 1996 $150.00

BARLA, JEAN BAPTISTE   Les Champignons de la Province de Nice et Principalement Les Especes Comestibles, Suspectes ou Veneneuses... Nice: 1859. Oblong 4to; pages lv, 138, (1); 49 colored lithographic plates; marbled boards, leather spine, tear to upper edge of spine; nice, rare.   Raymond M. Sutton VII-3 1996 $2,100.00

BARLAAM AND JOSAPHAT   Barlaam & Josaphat: a Christian Legend of the Buddha. 1986. One of 140 copies; 4to; prtined in black and red in handset Menhart unical and Garamond Bold on specially made Richard de Bas; black and white illustrations, initials hand colored by Dorothy Allen; cloth, fine.   Bertram Rota 272-12 1996 £180.00

BARLOW, JANE   The End of Elfintown. London: Macmillan and Co., 1894. 1st edition; titlepage, 8 full page black and white illustrations and various decorations by Laurence Housman; decorated cloth, gilt, all edges gilt, head and tail of spine and corners bumped and slightly worn, spine rubbed and darkened, endpapers and contents spotted; good. Ulysses 39-305 1996 £175.00

BARLOW, JANE   The End of Elfintown. London: Macmillan, 1898. 1st edition; 8vo; 78 pages; 8 plates and other illustrations; cloth gilt with repeating stylised pattern; very near fine, scarce in this condition. Marjorie James 19-125 1996 £225.00

BARLOW, JOEL   A Letter to the National Convention of France, on the Defects in the Constitution of 1791...To Which is Added The conspiracy of Kings, a Poem. New York: Thomas Greenleaf, 1793? 1st American edition of both titles; 8vo; 87 pages; recent three quarter cloth, some browning and foxing. BAL 880. Evans 25143; Wegelin 12.   M & S Rare Books 60-119 1996 $125.00

BARLOW, JOEL   The Vision of Columbus; a Poem in Nine Books. Hartford: printed by Hudson and Goodwin, for the author, 1787. 1st edition; full original calf shows rubbing, which has almost erased some gilt bands across spine, more noticeable at head of spine where leather is rubbed through at top of front joint, as you would expect, text paper has few minor stains from use, but just scattered foxing, however, top of title leaf has been irregularly torn away to remove and ownership signature; 12 pages of subscriber's names follow text, in this copy blank leaf in middle of ads has been excised & leaves following tipped to stub. BAL 865; Evans 20220.   Magnum Opus 44-17 1996 $300.00

BARLOW, PETER   A Treatise on the Strength of Timber, Cast and Malleable Iron, and Other Materials... London: John Weale, 1851. New edition; 8vo; xii, 516 pages; 7 folding engraved plates, 9 folding litho plates; publisher's cloth, neatly rejointed; contemporary ownership inscription, good, bright copy.   Elton Engineering 10-8 1996 £140.00

BARLOW, THOMAS   The Case Concerning Setting Up Images or Painting of them in Churches. London: James Roberts, 1714. Large 12mo; (2), 22 pages, interleaved and bound in marbled wrappers at the beginning of the 19th century; head of titlepage clipped but not affecting text; signature of Anth. Taylor, 1811, and leaf of manuscript transcriptions from Dugdale.   Ken Spelman 30-2 1996 £220.00

BARNARD, M. R.   Sketches of Life, Scenery and Sport in Norway. London: Horace Cox, 1871. 1st edition; 8vo; viii, 312 pages; original blue cloth, inner hinges cracked, small tear in rear spine gutter, still near fine. David Mason 71-129 1996 $120.00

BARNEBY, W. HENRY   Life and Labour in the Far, Far West; Being Notes of a Tour in the Western States, British Columbia, Manitoba and the North-West Territory. London: Paris: New York: Cassell & Co., 1884. 22.5 cm; xvi, 432, (8) pages; large full color map; gilt stamped red cloth, bit of cracking to inner hinges and slight depression on one side of spine; very good. Lowther 641; Peel 714.   Rockland Books 38-16 1996 $245.00

BARNES, A. C.   Mechanical Processes for the Extraction of Palm Oil. Lagos: 1925. Only edition; 8vo; 69 pages; 19 illustrations; half cloth and boards, corner wear, original wrappers bound in.   Raymond M. Sutton VII-829 1996 $125.00

BARNES, DJUNA 1892-   The Antiphon: a Play. London: Faber & Faber, 1958. 1st edition; some rubbing to spine, very good plus, lacking the dust jacket; inscribed by author to poet Charles Reznikoff. Between the Covers 42-29 1996 $1,000.00

BARNES, DJUNA 1892-   The Book. New York: Boni & Liveright, 1923. 1st edition; illustrations; original cloth, near fine with sunning; author's second book.   Beasley Books 82-20 1996 $125.00

BARNES, DJUNA 1892-   Ladies Almanack - showing Their Signs and Their Tides: Their Moons and Their Changes; the Seasons as it is With Them; Their Eclipses and Equinoxes... Paris: printed for the author and sold by Edward W. Titus, 1928. One of 1050 numbered copies; numerous black and white drawings, some full page, by author; pages unopened; printed by Imprimerie Darantiere at Dijon on Alfa paper; loosely inserted prospectus for the book; wrappers, prelims, edges and endpapers spotted, head and tail of spine and corners bumped, covers slightly dusty, very good.   Ulysses 39-33 1996 £575.00

BARNES, DJUNA 1892-   Ryder. New York: Liveright, 1928. 1st edition; illustrations by author; fine in nice, near fine dust jacket with small hole near front gutter some very slight loss at spinal extremities and faint stain on rear panel; pretty copy, uncommon in this condition.   Between the Covers 42-28 1996 $675.00

BARNES, DJUNA 1892-   The Selected Works. New York: FSG, 1962. 1st edition; fine in lightly worn very good plus dust jacket with couple of short tears, nicely inscribed by author in year of publication.   Between the Covers 42-30 1996 $650.00

BARNES, JULIAN   Duffy. London: Cape, 1980. 1st edition; fine in like dust jacket, signed by author using his pseudonym.   Lame Duck Books 19-55 1996 $250.00

BARNES, JULIAN   Duffy. London: Jonathan Cape, 1980. 1st edition; fine in price clipped dust jackets.   Quill & Brush 102-60 1996 $125.00

BARNES, JULIAN   Fiddle City. London: Jonathan Cape, 1981. 1st edition; spine ends very lightly bumped, otherwise fine in dust jackets. Quill & Brush 102-61 1996 $150.00

BARNES, JULIAN   Flaubert's Parrot. New York: Knopf, 1985. 1st American edition; fine in dust jacket with three tiny tears, nice, increasingly scarce.   Between the Covers 42-31 1996 $100.00

BARNES, JULIAN   Going to the Dogs. London: Viking, 1987. 1st edition; fine in near fine dust jacket. Signed.   Alice Robbins 15-20 1996 $100.00

BARNES, JULIAN   Talking It Over. New York: Alfred A. Knopf, 1991. Special advance issue; wit printed white wrappers, in black folding cardboard box; fine; signed on tipped in page.   Bev Chaney, Jr. 23-53 1996 $100.00

BARNES, R. G.   Babes in the African Wood. London: 1910. illustrations, contents foxed, otherwise very clean, in original cloth, scarce.   David Grayling J95Biggame-9 1996 £50.00

BARNES, WILLIAM   Hwomely Rhymes. A Second Collection of Poems in the Dorset Dialect. London: J. R. Smith, 1859. 1st edition; foolscap 8vo; usual brown cloth.   Charles W. Traylen 117-61 1996 £120.00

BARNES, WILLIAM   Tiew; or, a View of the Roots and Stems of the English as a Teutonic Tongue. London: John Russell Smith, 1862. half tile, 4 pages ads; uncut in original blue cloth, bit faded, slight wear to head and tail of spine, otherwise very good, scarce.   Jarndyce 103-18 1996 £150.00

BARNEY, JOSHUA   Report of the Survey Estimates, &c. of a Route from St. Louis to the Big Bend of the Red River. Wasahington: 1852. 59 pages; folding map; removed; nice. Howes B158.   Bohling Book Co. 192-112 1996 $110.00

BARNUM PHINEAS TAYLOR 1810-1896   Barnum's American Museum Illustrated. New York: 1840. 8vo; 32 pages, plus numerous ads; dozens of woodcuts engraved by Orr; original printed and pictorial front wrapper, lacks back wrapper, front wrapper frayed and lightly soiled. Early signature of Natchez owner. Sabin 3571 citing drop title on p. 1;   M & S Rare Books 60-282 1996 $275.00

BARON, JOHN   Scudamore Organs, Practical Hints Respecting Organs. London: Bell and Daldy, 1862. 2nd edition; 8vo; frontispiece, xxii, (ii), 112, (8) pages, 7 plates; publisher's cloth, light foxing on a few leaves, spine slighly sunned, else very good. From the library of architect James O'Byrne.   Bookpress 75-125 1996 $265.00

BARON, S.   A Description of the Kingdom of Tonqueen. c. 1734. Folio; 40 pages; 12 illustrations, on 7 engraved plates, map, 2 double page plates; modern sprinkled half calf, maroon morocco label, nice, crisp copy.   Thomas Thorp 489-19 1996 £120.00

BARONIO, GIUSEPPE   On Grafting in Animals. Boston: Countway Library, 1985. One of only 325 numbered copies; 8vo; 87, (4) pages, printed on Arches paper; illustrations; original printed boards, morocco spine with leather label; fine, untrimmed copy, very rare. GM 5736.   Edwin V. Glaser B122-12 1996 $225.00

BARR, ALWYN   Black Texans. Austin: Pemberton, 1973. 1st edition; 259 pages, dust jacket.   Maggie Lambeth 30-39 1996 $100.00

BARR, JOHN   Natural Wonders: Poems. Warwick Press, 1991. One of only 75 copies, signed by author and artist/printer; 8vo; printed in Monotype Spectrum in black and green on Frankfurt White paper; 8 hand colored drawings by Carol J. Blinn, bamboo lace paper inserts; green batik wrappers on vellum tapes; fine.   Bertram Rota 272-493 1996 £130.00

BARR, LOUISE FARROW   Presses of Northern California and Their Books 1900-1933. Berkeley: The Book Arts Club of the University of California, 1934. Limited to 400 copies; 1st edition;; 278 pages; original green cloth, leather spine label, spine faded, leather label lightly chipped, else fine, clean copy.   Argonaut Book Shop 113-54 1996 $325.00

BARR, NEVADA   Track of the Cat. New York: Putnam, 1993. Uncorrected proof; wrappers; fine, author's first book.   Between the Covers 42-472 1996 $275.00

BARR, NEVADA   Track of the Cat. New York: G. P. Putnam's Sons, 1993. 1st edition; new in dust jacket.   Steven C. Bernard 71-278 1996 $100.00

BARRA, E. I.   A Tale of Two Oceans; a New Story by an Old Californian. San Francisco: by the author, 1893. 1st edition; 198 pages, titlepage vignette, 6 illustrations; newly bound in three quarter leather; fine.   Argonaut Book Shop 113-55 1996 $225.00

BARRATT, JOSEPH   The Indian of New England, and the North-Eastern Provinces... Middletown: Charles H. Pelton, printer, 1851. 1st edition; 12mo; original pale blue printed wrappers; faint stains in lower blank margins, but very fine in original condition. Howes B168; Field 86; not in Sabin.   Ximenes 109-25 1996 $500.00

BARRERA, A. DE   Memoirs of Rachel. London: Hurst and Blackett, 1858. 1st edition; 8vo; 2 volumes; engraved portrait (spotted); contemporary green half calf; very nice; with contemporary bookplates of Lord Carew.   James Burmester 29-10 1996 £100.00

BARRERE, ALBERT   Argot and Slang; a New French and English Dictionary Of the Cant Words, Quaint Expressions, Slang Forms and Flash Phrases Used in the High and Low Life of Old and New Paris. London: Whittaker & Co., 1889. New edition; half title; original cream cloth spine, color wearing off from brown cloth sides; good copy.   Jarndyce 103-19 1996 £50.00

BARRETT, CHARLES RAYMOND BOOTH   Essex: Highways, Byways and Waterways. London: Lawrence & Bullen, 1892-93. 1st edition; 10 1/4 x 8 inches; xvi, 228; xvi, 232 pages; 2 volumes; fore edge and tail edge untrimmed, etched armorial border on titlepages, 18 tipped in etched plates, one additional plate, many illustrations in text; original cloth, gilt titling and decoration, binding with few trivial nicks, otherwise only very minor wear to corners and spine ends, fine, especially clean copy.   Phillip J. Pirages 33-36 1996 $225.00

BARRETT, EATON STANNARD   Woman, a Poem. London: printed for Henry Colburn, 1818. 2nd edition; small 8vo; half title, engraved frontispiece; contemporary full red straight grained morocco, gilt, spine and inner dentiles gilt, all edges gilt, slight rubbing; blank strip clipped from upper margin of titlepage, slight foxing, otherwise attractive copy.   Jackson p. 439; CBEL III 709.   Ximenes 109-26 1996 $150.00

BARRETT, FRANKLIN A.   Caughley and Coalport Porcelain. Leigh-on-Sea: 1951. 1st edition; limited to 500 numbered copies; 11 x 8 inches; 612 illustrations, 108 pages with index + plates; cloth. Minor wear.   John K. King 77-544 1996 $100.00

BARRETT, THOMAS J.   The Annals of Hampstead. London: Adam and Charles Black, 1912. Limited to 550 copies, signed by author; large 4to; 3 volumes; pages xxxvi, 306, frontispiece, 14 plates, 1 folding map, illustrations; xix, 299, frontispiece and 31 plates, some colored and mounted at large, 1 map, folding table in pocket, illustrations; xviii, 409, frontispiece and 18 plates, some colored and mounted at large, 3 maps, illustrations in text. publisher's decorated and titled cloth, all edges gilt.   Sotheran PN32-174 1996 £425.00

BARRETT, WILLIAM E.   The Lilies of the Field. London: Heinemann, 1963. 1st English edition; fine in dust jacket, signed by author, nicely inscribed by author; scarce issue of an uncommon book.   Between the Covers 42-32 1996 $150.00

BARRIE, JAMES MATTHEW 1860-1937   The Little Minister. London: Cassell and Co., 1891. 1st edition; crown 8vo; half titles and 16 page publisher's catalog; original cloth, gilt spines, unusually nice. Sadleir 167.   Charles W. Traylen 117-64 1996 £275.00

BARRIE, JAMES MATTHEW 1860-1937   Novels. Tales and Sketches. New York: & London: 1896. 8vo; 10 volumes; portrait from a photo; original silk cloth, gilt tops, spines little faded.   Charles W. Traylen 117-63 1996 £110.00

BARRIE, JAMES MATTHEW 1860-1937   Peter Pan in Kensington Gardens. London: Hodder & Stoughton, 1906. 1st edition; limited to 500 copies, signed by artist; quarto; xii, 126 pages, (49)ff; 50 color plates tipped in on heavy brown paper and one vignette by Arthur Rackham, front endpaper is map of Kensington Gardens, drawn by Arthur Rackham to Barrie's specifications; gilt stamped full vellum cover, slight bowing to covers else fine, top edge gilt, lacking ties. Latimore and Haskell p. 27; Hudson pp 61-70.   Bromer Booksellers 90-135 1996 $4,500.00

BARRIE, JAMES MATTHEW 1860-1937   Peter Pan in Kensington Gardens. H&S, n.d., ca. 1925. 16 tipped in full color illustrations by Arthur Rackham; gold-gilt pictorial cloth, spine little faded, else solid, very good.   Aronovitz 57-93 1996 $110.00

BARRIE, JAMES MATTHEW 1860-1937   Peter Pan or the Boy Who Would Not Grow Up. London: Hodder and Stoughton, 1928. 1st published edition; small 8vo; blue cloth, fine, paper labels, dust jacket bit sunned and rubbed at spine ends, title in red and black, contents fine.   Dramatis Personae 37-17 1996 $125.00

BARRIE, JAMES MATTHEW 1860-1937   Sentimental Tommy: the Story of His Boyhood. London: Paris: & Melbourne: Cassell and Co., 1896. 1st edition; 7 1/2 x 5 1/2 inches; viii, 452 pages, (2) leaves (ads, but without final, separate, 8 leaf section of ads); very pretty contemporary honey-brown three quarter calf by Zaehnsdorf, marbled sides and endpapers, spine densely gilt in compartments, top edge gilt; very fine copy, handsomely bound. Cutler 46.   Phillip J. Pirages 33-37 1996 $150.00

BARRIE, JAMES MATTHEW 1860-1937   A Tillyloss Scandal. New York: Lovell, Coryell & Co., 1893. 1st edition; 1st issue, with publisher's address listed as "43, 47 and 47 East Tenth Street"; small 8vo; blue cloth, top edge gilt, very good, bright, ink name on front endpaper; scarce variant, primarily issued in wrpapers;   Antic Hay 101-131 1996 $150.00

BARRIE, JAMES MATTHEW 1860-1937   When a Man's Single. London: Hodder & Stoughton, 1888. 1st British edition; small 8vo; gilt worked blue buckram cloth, top edge gilt, very good, in handsome green blue morocco leather and cloth gilt worked slipcase. Cutler 10.   Antic Hay 101-120 1996 $175.00

BARRINGTON, DAINES 1727-1800   Miscellanies. London: printed by J. Nichols; sold by B. White and J. Nichols, 1781. 1st edition; 4to; 2 plates, 2 maps, 5 genealogical tables; contemporary tree calf, spine gilt, neatly rebacked, original spine laid down; very desirable copy, from the library of historian Edward Gibbon with his booklabel. Sabin 3628; Howes B177; Hill pp. 13-14; Lada Mocarski 34.   Ximenes 109-27 1996 $2,500.00

BARRINGTON, DAINES 1727-1800   Miscellanies. London: printed by J. Nichols, 1781. 1st edition; 4to; viii, 557, (1) pages; contemporary quarter calf, marbled boards, original spine rehinged, edgewear, bookplate, inscriptions in pencil, else very good.   The Bookpress 75-383 1996 $875.00

BARRINGTON, DAINES 1727-1800   Observataions on the More Ancient Statutes, from Magna Charta... London: Printed by W. Bowyer and J. Nichols, 1775. contemporary calf, rebacked, some foxing, but good sound copy.   Meyer Boswell SL27-14 1996 $450.00

BARRINGTON, E.   "The Ladies"! A Shining Constellation of Wit and Beauty. Boston: Atlantic Monthly Press, 1922. 2nd impression; 8 1/8 x 5 1/2 inches; frontispiece, 7 illustrations; pages ix, 268; blue cloth, top edge gilt, others uncut; fine. Gilson J3.   Ian Hodgkins 78-72 1996 £50.00

BARRINGTON, JONAH   Historic Memoirs of Ireland; Comprising Secret Records of the National Convention, the Rebellion and the Union. 1835. New edition; 8vo; 2 volumes; 40 (ex 42) plates; worn half calf, text very good.   C. P. Hyland 216-19 1995 £95.00

BARRON, WILLIAM   A Just Defence of the Royal Martyr K. Charles I. London: A. Roper, 1699. 1st edition; 8vo; some spotting; late 18th century half calf, marbled boards, spine gilt.   Ian Wilkinson 95/1-28 1996 £125.00

BARRONS, JOHN R.   Ubet. Caldwell: 1934. 1st edition; 278 pages, illustrations; pictorial cloth, very good+. Six Guns 144; Herd 215; Howes B185; 6 Score 8.   T. A. Swinford 49-67 1996 $150.00

BARROW, JOHN   Mountain Ascents in Cumberland and Westmorland. London: Sampson Low, etc., 1886. 1st edition; pages viii, 208, 32, 10 illustrations and folding map; original pictorial cloth, gilt, extremities little rubbed. Neate B47.   R.F.G. Hollett & Son 78-285 1996 £140.00

BARROW, JOHN   Mountain Ascents in Cumberland and Westmorland. London: Sampson, Low, etc., 1886. 1st edition; 8vo; pages viii, 208, 32, 10 illustrations and folding map; original pictorial cloth, gilt, extremities little rubbed. Neate B47.   R.F.G. Hollett & Son 78-285 1996 £140.00

BARROW, JOHN   Travels in China...A Short Residence at the Imperial Palace of Yuen-Min-Yuen, and...a Subsequent Journey through the Country, from Pekin to Canton... Philadelphia: printed and sold by W. F. M'Laughlin, 1805. 1st American edition; 8vo; 422 pages; frontispiece foxed; later full sheep with morocco spine label, pages somewhat browned; but very good. Scarce.   Chapel Hill 94-148 1996 $275.00

BARRY, HANNAH   Night-Watchmen. New York: Viking, 1973. 1st edition; fine save for publisher's slash mark lower edge, in attractive dust jacket.   Bev Chaney, Jr. 23-298 1996 $100.00

BARRY, T. A.   Men and Memories of San Francisco in the Spring of '50. San Francisco; A. L. Bancroft & Co., 1873. 7 1/2 x 4 3/4 inches; 296 pages; blind and gold stamped green cloth, light spotting to binding and wear to extremities.   Dawson's Books Shop 528-6 1996 $150.00

BARTH, HENRY   Travels and Discoveries in North and Central Africa. Philadelphia: J. W. Bradley, 1859. 1st of this edition; 8vo; xxiv, (25)-538 pages, (6) ads; illustrations and folding map; original brown cloth, bookplate, some wear to spine ends and corners, otherwise near fine. David Mason 71-4 1996 $120.00

BARTH, JEAN BAPTISTE   A Manual of Auscultation and Percussion. Philadelphia: 1845. 1st edition; 12mo; original cloth;   Argosy 810-35 1996 $125.00

BARTH, JOHN 1930-   Chimera. New York: Random House, 1972. 1st edition; one of 300 copies, specially bound and signed by author; 8 1/2 x 5 3/4 inches; 6 p.l., (1 blank), 308 pages, (1) leaf; original cloth, publisher's slipcase, mint.   Phillip J. Pirages 33-38 1996 $100.00

BARTH, JOHN 1930-   The End of the Road. London: Secker & Warburg, 1962. 1st edition; fine in dust jacket.   Bev Chaney, Jr. 23-57 1996 $150.00

BARTH, JOHN 1930-   The Floating Opera. New York: Appleton-Century-Crofts, Inc., 1956. 1st edition; 8 1/4 x 5 3/4 inches; author's first book; 3 p.l., 280 pages; signed by author; original cloth, faint dampstains to cloth, faint but large dampstain on front endpapers, otherwise fine; scarce.   Phillip J. Pirages 33-40 1996 $225.00

BARTH, JOHN 1930-   Giles Goat-Boy; or, the Revised New Syllabus. Garden City: Doubleday and Co., 1966. 1st edition; one of 250 copies signed by author; 9 1/2 x 6 1/2 inches; 1 p.l., xxxi, (1) pages, (1) leaf, 710 pages; original cloth, in publisher's slipcase; virtually mint.   Phillip J. Pirages 33-42 1996 $150.00

BARTH, JOHN 1930-   Letters: a Novel. New York: G. P. Putnam's Sons, 1979. 1st edition, one of 500 copies signed and signed by author; 8 1/4 x 5 3/4 inches; 3 p.l., 280 pages; original cloth backed boards, in publisher's slipcase, a virtually mint copy.   Phillip J. Pirages 33-43 1996 $100.00

BARTH, JOHN 1930-   Lost in the Funhouse. Garden City: Doubleday and Co., 1968. 1st edition; 9 1/2 x 6 1/2 inches; x pages, (1) leaf, 201 pages; autographed by author; original cloth, dust jacket; extremely fine in fine jacket.   Phillip J. Pirages 33-44 1996 $100.00

BARTH, JOHN 1930-   The Sot-Weed Factor. Garden City: Doubleday & Co., 1960. 1st edition; 9 1/2 x 6 1/4 inches; 806 pages; signed by author with signed postcard from Barth, dated 25 April 1965; original cloth backed boards and dust jacket, cloth very slightly soiled, but excellent copy in very good jacket with minor edge wear, soiled back panel and four neat tape repairs on verso.   Phillip J. Pirages 33-47 1996 $300.00

BARTHELME, DONALD   Here in the Village. Northridge: Lord John Press, 1978. Limited edition, 12/50 special copies on Ingres paper, with collage by author as frontispiece; this copy additionally signed presentation from author; corners slightly rubbed, fine, issued without dust jacket.   Polyanthos 22-38 1996 $100.00

BARTHES, ROLAND   Erte. Parma: Ricci, 1972. Limited edition; folio; 181 pages; 80 tipped in color plates + illustrations; silk, boxed. Brannan 43-194 1996 $200.00

BARTHOLOMEW, ED   The Biographical Album of Western Gunfighters. Houston: Frontier, 1958. 1st edition; large oblong folio; photos; very good.   Parker Books of the West 30-9 1996 $180.00

BARTHOLOMEW, ED   Wyatt Earp. Toyahuale: 1963/64. 1st edition; 328, 335 pages; photos; frontispiece; cloth, very good. Howes B188; Graff 196. Mintz 23.   T. A. Swinford 49-69 1996 $350.00

BARTLETT, DAVID W.   What I Saw in London, or Men and Things in the Great Metropolis. Auburn and Buffalo: 1853. Sole edition; 8vo; frontispiece (foxed), original cloth, gilt spine. American Travellers Abroad B41.   Marlborough 162-108 1996 £125.00

BARTLETT, ELISHA   The History, Diagnosis and Treatment of Typhoid and Typhus Fever; with an Essay on the Diagnosis of Bilious Remittent and of Yellow Fever. Philadelphia: 1842. 1st edition; 393 pages; half leather, hinges weak, one missing from top of backstrip. Bloomfield (1958) 7; Bloomfield 286. Osler (1908) 131.   W. Bruce Fye 71-96 1996 $300.00

BARTLETT, FRED   Shoot Straight and Stay Alive. Limited to 1000 copies, signed by author; crown 4to; many illustrations;.   David Grayling J95Biggame-11 1996 £60.00

BARTLETT, HENRIETTA C.   A Census of Shakespeare's Plays in Quarto 1594-1709. New Haven: Yale University Press, 1916. 1st edition; one of 500 copies; folio; original boards, cloth back, paper label, fore and bottom edges uncut; fine; with Charles Beecher Hogan bookplate. Howard S. Mott 227-125 1996 $200.00

BARTLETT, WILLIAM HENRY 1809-1854   Jerusalem Revisited. London: Arthur Hall, Virtue and Co., 1855. Only edition; tall 8vo; 22 full page steel engravings, 18 text woodcuts; original gilt decorated cloth, spine gilt, light foxing to plates, but bright and clean.   Trebizond 39-78 1996 $200.00

BARTLETT, WILLIAM HENRY 1809-1854   The Scenery and Antiquities of Ireland. London: George Virtue, n.d., c. 1841. 1st edition; 4to; 2 volumes; map, 2 engraved title vignettes, 118 engraved plates; original three quarter crimson roan, corners and edges slightly rubbed in spots, gilt edges; well preserved set, with all tissue sheets.   Jens J. Christoffersen SL94-188 1996 $325.00

BARTLETT, WILLIAM HENRY 1809-1854   The Scenery and Antiquities of Ireland. London: James Virtue, 1855. 4to; 2 volumes; engraved vignette, printed titles, engraved map, 118 steel engraved plates; contemporary half morocco, gilt panelled spines and gilt tops, gilt edges; unusually clean copy, generall found foxed.   Charles W. Traylen 117-364 1996 £240.00

BARTOL, B. H.   A Treatise on the Marine Boilers of the United States. Philadelphia: R. W. Barnard and Sons, Printers, 1851. 143 pages; many line drawings and measurements; original embossed cloth worn and faded, some offsetting, occasional internal mark.   Parmer Books O39Nautica-039145 1996 $300.00

BARTOLI, DANIELLO   Del Suono de' Tremori Armonici e dell' Udito. Rome: Nicolo Angelo Tinassi, 1679. 1st edition; small 4to; (16), 330, (2) pages, woodcut figures and diagrams in text and a number of large woodcut initials and head and tailpieces; complete with half title and register leaf; earlyvellum, fine, crisp copy. Zeitlinger (2nd supp) 4395; Honeyman Sale I 233; Wellcome II 109.   Edwin V. Glaser 121-18 196 $2,800.00

BARTOLINI, ANNA MARIA   Effleurage. Leeds: Gehenna Press, 1989. One of 38 copies only; page size 10 x 13 7/8 inches; printed on Fabriano paper, each signed by Leonard Baskin, as publisher on colophon page and each of the 26 etchings by Barollini are signed in pencil and numbered. Grey paper with morocco edges.   Priscilla Juvelis 95/1-48 1996 $800.00

BARTON, ROSE   Familiar London. London: Adam and Charles Black, 1904. 61 color plates; very faint foxing to few pages, small stain to back cover, top edge gilt; rare.   Petersfield Bookshop FH58-178 1996 £220.00

BARTON, W. P. C.   Compendium Florae Philadelphicae; Containing a Description of the Indigenous and Naturalized Plants Found Within a Circuit of Ten Miles Around Philadelphia. Philadelphia: M. Carey and Son, 1818. 1st edition; 8vo; 2 volumes; half calf, Surgeons stamp on titles. Stafleu 325.   Maggs Bros. Ltd. 1190-62 1996 £160.00

BASHLINE, L. J.   America's Great Outdoors, The Story of the Eternal Romance Between Man and Nature. Chicago: 1976. 1st edition; 367 pages; photos, color photos, plates, illustrations; pictorial cloth, very good+; presentation copy by Gov. Babbitt, signed by most contributors.   T. A. Swinford 49-72 1996 $125.00

BASILIUS VALENTINUS   The Triumphal Chariot of Antimony... London: James Elliott, 1893. 1st edition thus; small 8vo; xxxiii, 204, (4 ads) pages; frontispiece, few full page figures in text; original cloth, top inch of frnt joint just starting, some light blistering to spine and front cover, very good. Duveen p. 49; Hoover 99; Osler 4149.   Edwin V. Glaser 121-19 1996 $225.00

BASILIUS, SAINT, THE GREAT, ABP. OF CAESAREA 330 ca. - 379 Orationes de Moribus XXIII. Simone Magistro Auctore. (with) Conciones de Vita et Moribus. Paris: Guil. Morel, 1556/58. 1st edition thus; 8vo; 2 works in 1, pages (iv), 417, (iii), (viii), 264,-, (iv), last leaf blank, first work Greek letter, second italic, printer's device on first title, naturalistic woodcut initials on second, first work bit age browned, first two leaves lightly washed, both generally rather good; contemporary dark calf, double head crowned eagle in centre of covers, rebacked to match. BM STC Fr. p.4 2; adams B349 (ii); Adams B353.   A. Sokol XXV-11 1996 £650.00

BASILIUS, SAINT, THE GREAT, ABP. OF CAESAREA 330 ca. - 379 Divi Basilii...Opera. Cologne: Godefridi Hiltorpi, 1523. 64 leaves of 180 only, printer's device ont itle bit stained and lower page corners frayed; new vellum type binding; pleasing typography.   K Books 442-40 1996 £50.00

BASKIN, LEONARD   Ars Anatomica. New York: 1972. Limited to 2500 copies; folio; 13 plates, with commentary laid into a slipcase; signed by Baskin.   W. Bruce Fye 71-100 1996 $350.00

BASKIN, LEONARD   Ars Anatomica, a Medical Fantasia. New York: Medicina Rara, 1972. Number 43 of 300 copies with double suite of the 13 lithographs, printed on specially watermarked paper; folio; signed by artist on colophon; small tear in one lower blank margin, loose in original morocco backed portfolio, slipcase.   Maggs Bros. Ltd. 1190-367 1996 £130.00

BASKIN, LEONARD   Jewish Artists of the Early and Late Renaissance. Northampton: Gehenna Press, 1993. Limited to 26 copies; 4to; portraits; geometric texts have been set in van Krimpen's Spectrum types and have been printed on a variety of Europgean handmade papers using an Albion handpress, portraits have been pulled on the same sheets as the letterpress; full green morocco with various color morocco onlays and gilt tooling and titling, matching clamshell case (by Claudia Cohen).   Book Block 32-49 1996 $7,500.00

BASKIN, LEONARD   Grotesques. Leeds: Gehenna Press, 1991. Limited to 26 copies; this one of 8 deluxe copies with an extra suite on ohter papers, a copperplate and watercolor; page size 9 5/8 x 12 7/8 inches; 41 original etchings, all but 3 printed in color; bound by Gray Parrot in green gilt stamped vellum, housed in black cloth clamshell box.   Priscilla Juvelis 95/1-102A 1996 $12,000.00

BASKIN, LEONARD   Grotesques. Lees: Gehenna Press, 1991. Limited to 26 copies, this one of 13 regular copies; page size 9 5/8 x 12 7/8 inches; on handmade Italian and French papers, each signed by the artist/author; 41 original etchings, all but 3 printed in color, bound by Gray Parrot, gilt stamped marbled paper over boards, designed by Baskin.   Priscilla Juvelis 95/1-102 1996 $7,500.00

BASKIN, LEONARD   Grotesques: Etchings and a Panegyrical Note. Northampton: Gehenna Press, 1991. One of 26 copies; large 4to; with a total of 48 etchings in various colors, printed on French and Italian papers, laid in is an original mounted watercolor grotesque signed by Mr. Baskin; hand marbled paper over boards with geometric gilt design on upper cover, incorporating the name of the book, spine with gilt lettered morocco label, preserved in sturdy cloth clamshell case with matching morocco label, binding and box by Gray Parrot.   Book Block 32-48 1996 $8,500.00

BASKIN, LEONARD   Icones Librorum Artifices. Northampton: Gehenna Press, 1988. One of just 32 copies (of an edition of 40 copies for sale), folio; 15 3/4 x 11 1/2 inches; printed in Arrighi type on a variety of dampened handmade English papers; 32 signed & numbered etched portraits, portraits are colored; quarter morocco over marbled sides, in custom clamshell case by Gray Parrot.   Book Block 32-50 1996 $11,500.00

BASKIN, LEONARD   To Colour Thought; a Lecture. New Haven: 1967. One of 300 numbered copies; 8vo; calligraphic half title designed by Crimilda Pontes; illustrations; printed in black and red in Dante; quarter brown morocco, fine.   Bertram Rota 272-350 1996 £220.00

BASKIN, R. N.   Reminiscences of Early Utah. Salt Lake City: 1914. 1st edition; 252 pages; frontispiece, photos; cloth; fine, scarce. 6 Guns 161; Howes B226; Graff 203.   T. A. Swinford 49-73 1996 $100.00

BASS, HEINRICH   Grundlicher Bericht von Banadagen... Leipzig: C. J. Eysseln, 1720. 1st edition; 8vo; 240 pages; frontispiece and 16 full page engravings, woodcut ornaments; contemporary calf; quite scarce. Blake 33.   Bennett Gilbert LL29-49 1996 $3,250.00

BASTABLE, C. FRANCIS   The Theory of International Trade with Some of Its Applications to Economic Policy. Dublin: Hodges, Figgis & Co., 1887. 1st edition; 8vo; viii, 176 pages, several annotations and emphasis marks in pencil; original cloth, very good. Batson p. 40; New Palgrave I 203.   John Drury 82-19 1996 £70.00

BATCHELOR, JOHN CALVIN   The Birth of the People's Republic of Antartica. New York: Dial, 1983. Uncorrected proof; wrappers; near fine, scarce.   Ken Lopez 74-24 1996 $200.00

BATCHELOR, JOHN CALVIN   The Further Adventures of Halley's Comet. N.P.: Congdon and Lattes, 1980. Uncorrected proof; 1st state, in blue wrappers, with pages reproduced from typescript, rather than typeset; author's first book, wrappers, spine darkened and mildly creased, else very good, uncommon proof.   Ken Lopez 74-23 1996 $350.00

BATE, C. S.   A History of British Sessile-Eyed Crustacea. London: 1863. royal 8vo; 2 volumes, numerous text illustrations, vignette tailpieces; cloth, spines worn, little faded, otherwise fine.   John Henly 27-74 1996 £60.00

BATEMAN, JAMES   A Second Century of Orchidaceous Plants Selected from the Subjects Published in "Curtis' Botanical Magazine"... London: 1867. 4to; pages viii, 100 hand colored lithographic plates by W. H. Fitch; original brown pebbled cloth, light overall soiling, some wear to edges, corners bumped, paper on interior hinges cracked, occasional foxing to text, plates quite clean and bright, in modern cloth bound clamshell box.   Raymond M. Sutton VI-2 1996 $5,000.00

BATES, EDWARD F.   History and Reminiscences of Denton County. Denton: 1918. 1st edition; 416 pages, frontispiece, plates, illustrations, map; cloth, very good+; Herd 222; 6 Guns 168.   T. A. Swinford 49-77 1996 $500.00

BATES, ELY   Rural Philosophy; or Reflections on Knowledge, Virtue and Happiness, Chiefly in Reference to a Life of Retirement in the Country. London: for Longman and Rees, Pater-noster Row, 1803. xxxi, 356 pages; contemporary tree calf, red label; very nice.   C. R. Johnson 37-70 1996 £200.00

BATES, GEORGE   Murder: Catalogue the Seventh of Rare and Interesting Books Illustrating the Development of the Detective and Mystery Story. London: George Bates, n.d. 1934. near fine copy with small chip at lower corner, short closed tear at spine and light soiling, quite scarce;   Janus Books 36-19 1996 $300.00

BATES, H. W.   Naturalist on the River Amazon. London: 1863. 1st edition; 2 volumes; 10 plates, 31 text illustrations, folding map, 32 pages end of volume 1, 774 pages; original brown cloth with design of Assai Palm in gilt on front covers, volume 2 with some pages loose, top and bottom of spines chipped, corners bumped.   John Johnson 135-8 1996 $500.00

BATES, HERBERT ERNEST 1905-1974   Achilles and the Twins. London: Dobson, 1964. 1st edition; colored illustrations by Carol Barker; very slight soiling to first two pages, back cover very slightly spotted, otherwise very good, in price clipped and slightly soiled and browned dust jacket; school prize bookplate on verso of f.e.p.   Virgo Books 48-22 1996 £80.00

BATES, HERBERT ERNEST 1905-1974   The Black Boxer. London: 1932. 1st edition; slight foxing to fore edges, otherwise very good in dust jacket browned on spine and minimally chipped at its head; inscribed by author for Alan W. Steele.   Words Etcetera 94-97 1996 £150.00

BATES, HERBERT ERNEST 1905-1974   Catherine Foster. New York: Viking Press, 1929. 1st American edition; cloth backed boards, gilt, slight discoloration at head of both covers, otherwise very good in dust jacket little browned on spine and with one closed tear, loosely inserted is a small 3 x 2 1/2 inch studio photo of Bates; inscribed by author for A. W. Steele.   Words Etcetera 94-90 1996 £160.00

BATES, HERBERT ERNEST 1905-1974   Charlotte's Row. London: 1931. 1st edition; near fine in dust jacket, superb copy, inscribed by author for Alan W. Steele.   Words Etcetera 94-94 196 £160.00

BATES, HERBERT ERNEST 1905-1974   Cut and Come Again. London: 1935. 1st edition; beautiful bright copy in dust jacket with minimal rubbing to extremities of lower edge of upper panel and head of spine. Inscribed by author for Alan W. Steele.   Words Etcetera 94-99 1996 £150.00

BATES, HERBERT ERNEST 1905-1974   Day's End and Other Stories. London: 1928. 1st edition; very good in dust jacket with browned spine and little chipped at head; inscribed by author for A. W. Steele. Words Etcetera 94-89 1996 £150.00

BATES, HERBERT ERNEST 1905-1974   The Fallow Land. London: 1932. 1st edition; minimal foxing, otherwise fine in dust jacket, rare thus; warmly inscribed by author for Alan W. Steele, with APCs Christmas Greeting from author.   Words Etcetera 94-96 1996 £150.00

BATES, HERBERT ERNEST 1905-1974   The Fallow Land. London: 1932. 1st edition; very good in dust jacket with slightly darkened spine. Words Etcetera 94-95 1996 £110.00

BATES, HERBERT ERNEST 1905-1974   Flowers and Faces. Waltham St. Lawrence: Golden Cockerel Press, 1935. 1st edition; limited to 325 copies, this being one of 259 copies in this binding; small 4to; 54 pages, printed on Batchelor handmade paper and signed by author; wood engraved border to title and 4 full page wood engravings by John Nash; original quarter green morocco, spine lettered in gilt, marbled cloth sides, top edge gilt, others uncut. Chanticleer 106.   Sotheran PN32-41 1996 £498.00

BATES, HERBERT ERNEST 1905-1974   The Flying Goat. London: 1939. 1st edition; very good in dust jacket with few short closed tears and minimal rubbing to head and foot of spine; Alan W. Steele's copy with his signature.   Words Etcetera 94-104 1996 £100.00

BATES, HERBERT ERNEST 1905-1974   The Great House. Snake River Press, 1984. One of only 25 numbered copies; square 4to; printed in black and light brown in Baskerville on Velin Cuve Rives; 1 double page and 2 full page colored lithographs by Geoffrey Trenaman; half morocco; fine.   Bertram Rota 272-436 1996 £65.00

BATES, HERBERT ERNEST 1905-1974   A House of Women. London: 1936. 1st edition; rust mark on inner hinge, otherwise very good in dust jacket worn on spine and chipped at head and foot and rubbed on two corners; inscribed by author for Alan W. Steele.   Words Etcetera 94-100 1996 £160.00

BATES, HERBERT ERNEST 1905-1974   Seven Tales and Alexander; Stories. London: Scholartis Press, 1929. 1st edition; cloth backed boards, somewhat worn and browned, dust jacket torn and defective, newscuttings of reviews, one by Arnold Bennett, loosely inserted, also loosely inserted 8 page pamphlet entitled Mr. H. E. Bates which has been reprinted from the Times of Jan. 24th 1935; inscribed at length by author for Alan W. Steele; with ALS to Steele.   Words Etcetera 94-92 1996 £160.00

BATES, HERBERT ERNEST 1905-1974   Seven Tales and Alexander: Stories. London: Scholartis Press, 1929. 1st edition; cloth backed boards, near fine in dust jacket; bookplate of Scott Cunningham. Words Etcetera 94-91 1996 £75.00

BATES, HERBERT ERNEST 1905-1974   Seven Tales and Alexander. New York: 1930. 1st American edition; canvas backed boards, very good in browned and chipped dust jacket; inscribed by author of Alan W. Steele.   Words Etcetera 94-93 1996 £150.00

BATES, HERBERT ERNEST 1905-1974   Something Short and Sweet: Stories. London: 1937. 1st edition; stunningly beautiful copy in bright and colorful dust jacket whose color appears not to have diminished since the day it was printed, with one minute closed tear.   Words Etcetera 94-101 1996 £125.00

BATES, HERBERT ERNEST 1905-1974   Spella Ho: a Novel. London: 1938. 1st edition; presentation inscription from author to Joan Hancock, Joan's own name written alongside a number of town names on endpapers, otherwise very good in scarce and bright dust jacket with wrap around band.   Words Etcetera 94-103 1996 £160.00

BATES, HERBERT ERNEST 1905-1974   Thirty One Selected Tales. London: 1947. 1st edition; very good in colorful and pictorial dust jacket which has a couple of short closed tears at foot of upper panel and one small snag at head of spine, uncommon thus.   Words Etcetera 94-114 1996 £60.00

BATES, HERBERT ERNEST 1905-1974   Through the Woods. London: Victor Gollancz, 1936. 1st edition; post 4to; wood engravings by Agnes Miller Parker; original binding, very good and clean copy in dust jacket, which bears an additional Parker wood engraving; Eads A27.   Ash Rare Books Zenzybyr-8 1996 £75.00

BATES, HERBERT ERNEST 1905-1974   The Two Sisters. London: Jonathan Cape, 1926. Only 1500 copies printed; 1st edition; 8vo; signed by author; cloth, in dust jacket, near fine, with tiny tear to head of spine, little discoloration to endpapers, as usual, some browning to edges and spine (little shallow chip head and few minor stains to spine), dust jacket.   Antic Hay 101-136 1996 $450.00

BATES, J. W.   Bryophytes and Lichens in a Changing Enivornment. London: 1992. 8vo; 400 pages, 5 plates, 65 text figures; cloth. Wheldon & Wesley 207-1602 1996 £60.00

BATES, JOHN CADWALLADER   Thomas Bates and the Kirklevington Shorthorns. Newcastle-upon-Tyne: Robert Redpath, 1897. 1st edition; large paper copy; half title, portrait, 5 plates, 32 vignettes in text, folding map at end; original cloth, gilt, inner hinges shaken, uncut, nice, bright copy.   Anthony W. Laywood 109-7 1996 £85.00

BATES, ROBERT H.   Mountain Man; the Story of Belmore Browne, Hunter, Explorer, Artist, Naturalist and Preserver of Our Northern Wilderness. Clinton: Amwell Press, 1988. Limited edition, 1 of 1000 copies, signed by author; full blue morocco like binding, decorated and stamped in gilt, mild bump to one corner of publisher's slipbox, else very fine.   Magnum Opus 44-98 1996 $100.00

BATES, WILLIAM   George Cruikshank; the Artist, the Humourist and the Man... Birmingham: 1878. Large paper copy, very limited number of copies printed; 8vo; (vi), 94 pages; illustrations, extra illustrated with 2 colored plates by Cruikshank, folding plate with 7 colored vignettes, several other folding plates, over a dozen engravings and two booklets; half calf, good.   K Books 441-31 1996 £150.00

BATES, WILLIAM C.   The Stars and Stripes in Rebeldom, a Series of Papers Written by Federal Prisoners (Privates) in Richmond, Tuscalossa, New Orleans, and Salisbury, N.C. Boston: T. O. H. P. Burnham, 1862. 1st edition, 2nd printing (?) ("second thousand"); 8vo; 137 pages, (6) pages publisher's ads, green cloth, light marginal damp stain toward rear of book, lacks rear free endpaper, good to very good.   Robert F. Lucas 42-15 1996 $125.00

BATESON, GREGOY   Steps to an Ecology of Mind: Collected Essays in Anthropology, Psychiatry, Evolution and Epistemology. San Francisco: Chandler Publishing Co., 1972. 8vo; (xxviii), 545, (3) pages; blue grey cloth, very good in dust jacket.   John Gach 150-24 1996 $125.00

BATESON, W.   Mendel's Principles of Heredity. Cambridge: 1913. 3rd impression; royal 8vo; pages xiv 396, 3 portraits, 6 colored plates, 38 text figures; cloth, inner joints cracking slightly.   Wheldon & Wesley 207-140 1996 £60.00

BATH, MARQUIS OF   Report on the Manuscripts of the Marquis of Bath at Longleat, Wiltshire. London: 1904-08. 8vo; 3 volumes; neatly bound in buckram, morocco lettering pieces.   Howes Bookshop 265-528 1996 £60.00

BATHURST, CHARLES   Lectures Read at a Mechanics' Institute in the Country. London: John W. Parker and Son, 1854. 1st edition; 8vo; xvii, (3), 392 pages, text figures, page xvii misnumbered 'vii' as described in NUC, a complete copy with half title and final 2 leaves of ads; original cloth with printed spine labels; rare; fine presentation copy inscribed by author.   John Drury 82-20 1996 £95.00

THE BATTLE of the Frogs and Mice. Libanus Press, 1988. One of 200 numbered copies; concertina fold, approximately 11 x 4 1/4 inches, printed in monotype Poliphilus and Antigone on Saunders mouldmade; illustrations by Fiona MacVicar; terracotta boards with rust cloth spine; fine.   Bertram Rota 272-252 996 £65.00

BATTY, ELIZABETH FRANCES   Italian Scenery. From Drawings Made in 1817. London: Rodwell & Martin, 1820. 1st edition; 11 3/4 x 9 1/2 inches; 5 p.l., 197, (1) pages; eng. title, vignette on final leaf, 60 fine engraved plates, all with tissue guards; very handsome contemporary rose colored hard grain mor., extra gilt by C. Smith, covers handsomely framed with 3 sets of parallel fillets enclosing 2 elegant scrolling floral borders, flat spines beautifully gilt in 2 compartments, top one with titling, elongated lower one composed of central vertical band of urn-like roll-tool flanked by gilt rules and pretty borders of acanthus leaves, board edges with triple gilt fillets, turn-ins with four gilt rules & corner ovals, endpapers of deep green coated stock, all edges gilt, spine evenly sunned to terra cotta color, minor scuffing or rubbing to edges, otherwise binding in excellent condition, with only trivial defects, very well executed, completely solid, and quite pretty; the majority of the plates with foxing, almost always very minor, but occasionally more noticeable (without ever being serious), otherwise fine internally, text clean & smooth.   Phillip J. Pirages 33-482 1996 $1,259.00

BATTY, ROBERT d. 1848   French Scenery, from Drawings Made in 1819. London: Rodwell & Martin, 1822. 1st edition; 11 3/4 x 9 1/2 inches; (64) leaves, half title called for in list of plates, not present; engraved title and 65 plates, tissue guards, separate texts in English and French; very handsome cont. rose colored hard grain mor. extra gilt by C. Smith, covers handsomely framed w/3 sets of parallel fillets enclosing 2 elegant scrolling floral borders, flat spines beautifully gilt in 2 compartments, top one with titling, elongated lower one composed of central and vertical band of urn-like roll-tool flanked by gilt rules & pretty borders of acanthus leaves, board edges with triple gilt fillets, turn-ins 2/4 gilt rules & corner ovals, endpapers of deep green coated stock, a.e.g.; most plates free from foxing; spine evenly faded to a terra cotta color, minor scuffing or rubbing to edges, otherwise binding in excellent condition, with only trivial defects.   Phillip J. Pirages 33-483 1996 $1,250.00

BATTY, ROBERT d. 1848   German Scenery. From Drawings made in 1820. London: Rodwell & Martin, 1823. 1st edition; 11 3/4 x 9 1/2 inches; (65) leaves; 61 fine engraved plates of views by Batty, tissue guards, with text in English and French; very handsome contemporary rose colored hard grain morocco, extra gilt by C. Smith, covers handsomely framed with 3 sets of parallel fillets enclosing two elegant scrolling floral borders, flat spines beautifully gilt in 2 compartments, top one with titling, elongated lower one composed of central vertical band of urn-like roll-tool flanked by gilt rules and pretty borders of acanthus leaves, board edges with triple gilt fillets, turn-ins with four gilt rules and corner ovals, endpapers of deep green coated stock, all edges gilt, spine evenly sunned to terra cotta color, minor scuffing or rubbing to edges, otherwise binding in excellent condition, with only trivial defects.   Phillip J. Pirages 33-484 1996 $3,500.00

BATTY, ROBERT d. 1848   German Scenery from Drawings Made in 1820. London: Rodwell & Martin, 1823. 1st edition; royal 8vo; ff. (iii), (60); engraved vignette titlepage, 60 engraved plates, engraved vignette plate; original black morocco, joints rubbed, backstrip with wide gilt decorated raised bands, lettered direct in second compartment, remainder blind panelled, paneled side with outer border of blind fillet, blind arabesque roll, single wide and triple narrow gilt fillets, inner blind border, gilt roll on board edges and turn-ins, marbled endpapers, gilt edges, very good, some slight foxing to prelim and final leaves and plates, but generally excellent.   Blackwell's B112-9 1996 £1,100.00

BATTY, ROBERT d. 1848   Scenery of the Rhine, Belgium and Holland. London: Robert Jennings, 1826. 1st edition; 11 3/4 x 9 1/2 inches; (65) leaves; engraved title, 61 fine engraved plates, text in English and French; very handsome cont. rose colored hard grain morocco, extra gilt by C. Smith, covers handsomely framed with 3 sets of parallel fillets enclosing two elegant scrolling floral borders, flat spines beautifully gilt in 2 compartments, top one with titling, elongated lower one composed of central vertical band of urn-like roll-tool flanked by gilt rules and pretty borders of acanthus leaves, board edges with triple gilt filelts, turn-ins with four gilt rules and corner ovals, endpapers of deep green coated stock, all edges gilt; spine evenly sunned to terra cotta color, minor scuffing or rubbing to edges, otherwise binding in excellent condition.   Phillip J. Pirages 33-485 1996 $3,000.00

BATTYE, CHRISTINE   The Brewhouse Private Press 1963-1983. Wymondham: Sycamore Press, 1984. Limited to 120 numbered copies; 4to; 180 pages; frontispiece, numerous line illustrations and photos; cloth, gilt, very slightly worn.   Thomas Thorp 489-20 1996 £80.00

BAUDELAIRE, CHARLES   Flowers of Evil. London: Limited Editions Club, 1940. Copy 904 from a total edition of 1500 numbered copies; 2 volumes; stone lithographs by Jacob Epstein; English text in brick red cloth and French facsimile in wrappers and tissue jacket, both near fine, slipcase to cloth volume rubbed, else near fine set.   Hermitage SP95-939 1996 $225.00

BAUDELAIRE, CHARLES   Flowers of Evil. New York: Limited Editions Club, 1971. Number 1029 of 1500 copies, signed by artist; 2 volumes; illustrations by Pierre-Yves Tremois; fine in slipcase.   Hermitage SP95-938 1996 $125.00

BAUDEMENT, EMILE   Les Races Bovines. Paris: Imprimerie Imperiale, 1861-62. 1st edition; oblong folio; 2 volumes, 74 pages; 5 hand colored maps, 87 fine lithograph plates; contemporary green half morocco, sides slightly scuffed, slightly foxed, one or two plates more heavily spotted.   Thomas Thorp 489-21 1996 £1,000.00

BAUDOUIN, ALEXANDRE   The Man of the World's Dictionary. London: J. Appleyard, 1822. 12mo; half title; half calf neatly rebacked; armorial bookplate of Sir Edward Watkins.   Jarndyce 103-123 1996 £75.00

BAUER, P. V.   The Excavations at Dura-Europos. Final Report IV. Part III: The Lamps. New Haven: Yale University Press, 1947. large 4to; vi, 84 pages, 38 figures, 16 plates, original cloth.   Archaeologia Luxor-3275 19964 $200.00

BAUERMAN, H.   Report of the Geology of the Country Near the Forty-Ninth Parallel of North Latitutde West of the Rocky Mountains. From Observations Made 1859-1861. Montreal: Dawson Bros., 1884. 23.5 cm; 42 pages; later wrappers; fine.   Rockland Books 38-19 1996 $125.00

BAUGHAN, PETER E.   North of Leeds. London: Roundhouse Books, 1966. 1st edition; thick 8vo; pages 500; 58 illustrations and 4 maps; original cloth, gilt, dust jacket, corners of flyleaf and half title creased, otherwise very good.   R.F.G. Hollett & Son 78-603 1996 £65.00

BAUHIN, CASPAR   Pinax Theatri Botanici...sive Index in Theophrasti Dioscoridis Plinii et Botanicorum Qui a Seculo Scripserunt Opera... Basel: 1623. 1st edition; large 8vo; pages (23), 522, (22 pages index, errata sheet; old vellum, soiled and stained, text browned as usual, inner hinges cracked, tear to title and last index page, professionally repaired, mild ex-library. PMM 121.   Raymond M. Sutton VII-4 1996 $4,200.00

BAUM, LYMAN FRANK   Aunt Jane's Nieces on Vacation. R&G, 1912. 1st edition; near fine in very good dust jacket with some fading to dust jacket spine and small closed tear to rear dust jacket panel; very scarce in dust jacket.   Aronovitz 57-96 1996 $325.00

BAUM, LYMAN FRANK   Bandit Jim Crow. Chicago: Reilly & Britton Co., 1906. 1st edition; illustrations by Maginel Wright Enright; color pictorial boards, covers slightly worn and soiled, otherwise very good. Steven C. Bernard 71-434 1996 $400.00

BAUM, LYMAN FRANK   Dorothy and the Wizard in Oz. Chicago: Reilly & Britton, 1908. 1st edition; 1st state with picture of Dorothy on ownership page, and Ozma on last page; quarto; 256 pages; 16 color plates and numerous black and white illustrations by John R. Neill; first binding state with "The Reilly & Brittton Co." on spine; very light foxing to title, chip to edge of cover, else fine in blue cloth with pictorial label on gold background. Hanff, Greene pp. 53-4.   Bromer Booksellers 90-83   1996 $750.00

BAUM, LYMAN FRANK   The Master Key. Indianapolis: Bowen-Merrill Co., 1901. 1st edition; 3rd state, with copyright notice having publisher's name measuring 1 25/32 inches in length; small octavo; 245 pages; 12 color plates, black and white illustrations; original olive green cloth stamped in gilt on front cover and spine, color pictorial label on front cover, back cover stamped in blind, light wear to extremities, slightly over opened at few gatherings, little minor soiling; near fine.   Heritage Book Shop 196-264   1996 $300.00

BAUM, LYMAN FRANK   Phoebe Daring. Chicago: The Reilly & Britton Co., 1912. 1st edition; illustrations by Joseph Pierre Nuyttens; spine skewed and darkened, but overall nice, with front decorative color panel bright and attractive.   Hermitage SP95-853   1996 $200.00

BAUM, LYMAN FRANK   The Road to Oz. Chicago: Reilly & Britton, 1909. 1st edition; 1st state; one of the first off the press with perfect type in the words "Toto on" (p. 34, line 4) & in the numeral '121' (page 121); quarto; 261 pages; illustrated with drawings by John Neill, including pictorial endpapers; printed on paper of 8 different colors; pictorial green cloth stamped in red, black and green, light smudging to cover, extremities lightly rubbed, else fine, all edges green. Hanff Greene pp. 57-59.   Bromer Booksellers 90-84   1996 $750.00

BAUM, LYMAN FRANK   The Wizard of Oz Waddle Book. New York: Blue Ribbon Books, Inc., 1934. 1st Blue Ribbon edition, second state; in light olive cloth and no imprint at base of spine; lacking Waddles, ink name on front free endpaper, spine very slightly skewed, otherwise very fine, bright copy. Greene & hanff 35.   Hermitage SP95-854   1996 $175.00

BAX, CLIFFORD   The Traveller's Tale. Oxford: 1921. 1st edition; original binding, top edge dusty, free endpapers browned, pastedowns partially browned, head and tail of spine and corners bumped, covers marked and slightly dusty; good; ownership signature of Ian Fleming. Ulysses 39-671   1996 £125.00

BAXTER   The Birds of Scotland. London: 1953. Imperial 8vo; 2 volumes; colored frontispieces by George Lodge, other plates; protected dust jackets. mint copy.   David A.H. Grayling MY95Orn-6   1996 £130.00

BAXTER, CHARLES   Shadow Play. New York: Norton, 1993. Advance reading copy; slight bend to one corner, still about fine in wrappers, as issued; briefly inscribed by author.   Between the Covers 42-38   1996 $125.00

BAXTER, CHARLES   Through the Safety Net. New York: Viking, 1985. 1st edition; fine in dust jacket, signed by author, uncommon, especially signed.   Between the Covers 42-37   1996 $175.00

BAXTER, RICHARD   The Grand Debate Between the Most Reverend the Bishops, & the Presbyterian Divines, Appointed by His Sacred Majesty...Review and Alteration of the Book of Common Prayer. (with) To the Kings Most Excellent Majesty. The Due Account, & Humble Petition of the... London: printed,, 1661/61. 4to; (viii), 148; (ii), 6 pages; bound together, 19th century half morocco, gilt lettering, rubbed, corners slightly worn, minor browning, few shoulder notes slightly cropped, good copies. Wing B1278a, T1499.   Robert Clark 38-5   1996 £160.00

BAXTER, RICHARD   Poetical Fragments: Heart-Imployment with God and It Self, The Concordant Discord of a Broken-Healed Heart. Sorrowing-Rejoicing. Fearing-Hoping, Dying-Living. London: Tho. Parkhurst, 1699. 3rd edition; 12mo; (viii), 100, (ii), 105-158, (xii) pages; contemporary sheep, ruled in blind, rebacked and recornered, slight adhesion marks on inner margin of title, minor soiling, little cropped, affecting few page numbers and catchwords, just touching one line of text (no loss of sense). Good copy; all early editions appear to be quite uncommon. Wing B1351.   Robert Clark 38-6   1996 £325.00

BAYARD, SAMUEL J.   A Sketch of the Life of Com. Robert F. Stockton; with...Extracts from the Defence of Col. J. C. Fremont. New York: Derby & Jackson, 1856. 1st edition; 131 pages, plus one leaf of ads, frontispiece; original brown embossed cloth, title in gilt on spine, minor fading to spine and some wear, fine; from the collection of Carl Wheat, with his bookplate. Howes B259; Becker Wagner Camp 271b. Tutorow Mex. Amer. War 3743.   Michael D. Heaston 23-39   1996 $250.00

BAYLDON, OLIVER   The Paper Makers Craft. Leicester: ptd. by Will Carter at Cambridge for the Twelve by Eight Press, 1965. Limited edition of less that 400 copies, this being copy number 363 signed by publisher, John Mason; thin folio; viii, 20 pages; printed on a variety of handmade papers; 8 illustrations on colored papers; original parchment gilt, gilt edges, uncut, dust jacket, fine.   Thomas Thorp 489-23   1996 £100.00

BAYLEY, JOHN   The History and Antiquities of the Tower of London, with Biographical Anecdotes of Royal and Distinguished Persons Deduced from Records, State-Papers and Manuscripts... London: for T. Cadell, 1812-25. Large 4to; 2 volumes; pages xiv, (ii), 272, xxxiv, (ii), 26 numbered engraved plates; vi, 671, (i, blank), cxxviii, (xviii), frontispiece; contemporary half morocco over marbled boards, marbled endpapers, good, clean copy, attractively bound.   Sotheran PN32-175   1996 £398.00

BAYLEY, JOHN   The History and Antiquities of the Tower of London, with Memoirs of Royal and Distinguished persons, Deduced from Records, State Papers and Manuscripts... London: for T. Cadell, 1821-25. Large 8vo; 2 volumes, half title, title, dedn., list of paltes, title and dedn., repeated, pages vii-xiv, list of plates repeated, pages 272, xxiv, 1 f. ad, frontispiece, double page map, 28 engraved plates (3-27, 3 n.n.); half title, title 2 ff., pages 273-674, xxxv-cxxviii, 9 ff. index; half brown morocco, spines faded and scuffed, top edge gilt. bookplates of Charles Lewes Dashwood. Adams 136.   Marlborough 162-110   1996 £550.00

BAYLISS, MARGUERITE   The Matriarchy of the American Turn 1875-1930. N.P.: Robert Gerry, 1931. 1st edition; original binding, shelfworn, scarce.   October Farm 36-318   1996 $295.00

BAYLOR, BYRD   Yes Is Better than No. New York: Charles Scribner's & sons, 1977. 1st edition; 187 pages; fine in price clipped dust jacket. Ken Sanders 8-382   1996 $175.00

BAYLY, LEWES   The Practice of Piety, Directing a Christian How to Walk that He May Please God. London: printed for Edward Brewster, 1685. 8vo; frontispiece (insignificant crack in printing block), engraved title (highly illustrated), 13 leaves, 1 lf. Book catalog, 548 pages, (lacking If Aal, a binder's omission), contents in very nice condition; 19th century half leather over marbled boards.   Roy W. Clare XXIV-3   1996 $250.00

BAYNES, HELTON GODWIN   Mythology of the Soul: A Research Into the Unconscious from Schizophrenic Dreams and Drawings. London: Routledge & Kegan Paul Ltd., 1955. Thick 8vo; xii, 939, (1) pages; 50 plates; blue cloth, very good in dust jacket.   John Gach 150-26   1996 $100.00

BAYNES, ROBERT H.   The Illustrated Book of Sacred Poems. London: Cassell, Petter and Galpin, n.d. ca. 1867. 1st edition; 8vo; viii, 391, (1) pages; illustrations; publisher's cloth, all edges gilt; spine lightly sunned, otherwise very good; from the library of Robin de Beaumont. Bookpress 75-5   1996 $145.00

BAZIN, GILLES AUGUSTINE   The Natural History of Bees. London: printed for J. and P. Knapton, 1744. Sole edition in English; tall 8vo; 8 leaves, 452, 16 pages; 12 folding plates in fine impression; recent calf in imitation of original with blind tooling, raised bands, red label, front flyleaf repaired, title leaf somewhat stained in margins, strengthened at gutter, last 8 leaves with very slight fraying.   Roy W. Clare XXIV-15   1996 $750.00

BEACH, JOSEPH WARREN   Body's Breviary. Pasadena: printed by Gregg Anderson for the Zamorano Club, 1930. Out of series copy; 7 1/8 x 4 3/4 inches; (iv), 30 pages + colophon; printed tan wrappers, uncut. Fullerton 19.   Dawson's Books Shop 528-50   1996 $200.00

BEACH, S. A.   The Apples of New York. Albany: 1905. 8vo; 2 volumes; pages xx, 409; iv, 360; 130 colored and 68 black and white plates, plus 9 text figures; original gilt stamped cloth, corners lightly bumped, name stamp on titles, very bright set.   Raymond M. Sutton VII-833   1996 $195.00

BEACH, WOOSTER   An Improved System of Midwifery, Adapted to the Reformed Practice of Medicine... New York: pub. and for Sale by the author, 1847. 1st edition; 4to; 272 pages; with 57 full page lithographs; original cloth, small pieces torn from margin of leaf of preface, some foxing, but overall very good.   M & S Rare Books 60-446   1996 $650.00

BEADLE, J. H.   Life in Utah. Philadelphia: National Publishing Co., 1870. 1st edition; 1st issue; 540 pages, plus 4 pages of ads; frontispiece, folding map, portraits, plates, illustrations; original green cloth, gilt lettered spine and cover, extremities slightly rubbed, else near fine. Flake 344.   Argonaut Book Shop 113-57   1996 $175.00

BEALE, JAMES   The Battle Flags of the Army of the Potomac at Gettysburg, Pennsylvania. July 1st, 2d and 3d, 1863. Philadelphia: James Beale, 1885. Number 66 of 125 copies, signed and numbered by James Beale; 35 leaves, 32 color plates; later cloth, 2 small ownership stamps, one small rubber library stamp, otherwise near fine with plates in superb condition. Nicholson p.69; Dornbusch I Mass. 161; Nevins I 4.   McGowan Book Co.   65-7   1996 $2,250.00

BEALS, CARLETON   The Crime of Cuba. Philadelphia: Lippincott, 1933. 1st edition; 8vo; 31 aquatone illustrations from photos by Walker Evans; silver stamped black cloth, dust jacket (slight wear), very good.   George J. Houle   68-111   1996 $450.00

BEAN, W. J.   Trees and Shrubs Hardy in the British Isles. London: 1936. 6th edition; 8vo; 3 volumes, including 1936 2nd edition supplement. pages xvi, 688; (7), 736; xiv, 517; 127 plates plus numerous drawings; cloth, light wear, slight joint crack in volume 2.   Raymond M. Sutton VII-434   1996 $125.00

BEAN, W. J.   Trees and Shrubs Hardy in the British Isles. London: 1981. 8th edition; 8vo; pages xvi, 784; 100 photos and 96 line drwings; cloth, small dent to front cover, dust jacket.   Raymond M. Sutton VII-436   1996 $115.00

BEAN, W. J.   Trees and Shrubs Hardy in the British Isles. London: 1989. 8th edition; 8vo; volume 1, A-C, 77 black and white photos, plus 84 line drawings, xx, 845 pages; cloth, dust jacket.   Raymond M. Sutton   VII-435   1996 $115.00

BEARD, GEORGE MILLER   A Practical Treatise on the Medical and Surgical Uses of Electricity. New York: William Wood & Co., 1875. 2nd edition; 8vo; (iv), (xxx), 794, (4) pages; 198 text woodcuts; panelled green cloth, gilt spine, moderate spotting to covers, joints and edges rubbed; good to very good. Cordasco 70-0209.   John Gach   150-28   1996 $250.00

BEARD, GEORGE MILLER   A Practical Treatise on Nervous Exhaustion (Neurasthenia): Its Symptoms, Nature, Sequences, and Treatment. New York: William Wood and Co., 1880. 1st edition; covers quite shelfworn, upper front board stained, good copy only. Wozniak 1992 #56.   John Gach   150-27   1996 $200.00

BEARD, JOHN R.   The Life of Toussaint L'Ouverture. The Negro Patriot of Hayti. London: Ingram, Cooke and Co., 1853. 1st edition; 8vo; 11, (1), 335, (1) pages; map and 7 plates; half title; original cloth, spine soiled; LCP/HSP Afro Amer. Cat. 989.   M & S Rare Books   60-284   1996 $250.00

BEARD, MARK   Manhattan Third Year Reader. New York: Vincent Fitz Gerald & Co., 1984. Out of series copy, one of 30 copies only, each signed by author; 35 linocuts pulled and assembled by the artist and publisher on 28 different papers; specially bound by Gerard Charriere in green morocco with rondel onlays on front and back panel, rondel is of white box calf with onlays including a smashed trash can on both covers.   Priscilla Juvelis   95/1-23   1996 $13,000.00

BEARD, MARK   New York Portfolio. New York: Vincent Fitz Gerald, n.d., ca. 1987. Signed, limited edition, one of 20 copies of this portfolio; image size 26 x 20 inches; 7 original mixed media prints: chine colle, hand collage, auqatint, etch, linoleum cut, on various handmade papers, each hand touched by artist with his holograph title on each print which is signed and numbered; housed in black board portfolio.   Priscilla Juvelis   95/1-24   1996 $3,000.00

BEARD, P.   The End of the Game. London: 1965. 1st edition; folio; many illustrations; very slightly frayed dust jacket; near mint.   David Grayling   J95Biggame-12   1996 $60.00

BEARDSLEY, GRACE HADLEY   The Negro in Greek and Roman Civilization. Baltimore: Johns Hopkins Press, 1929. 8vo; xii, 145 pages; 24 illustrations; original cloth, minor shelfwear at extremities.   Archaeologia   Luxor-2972   1996 $150.00

BEATIE, RUSSEL   Saddles. Norman: 1981. 1st edition; xv, 371 pages, photos, illustrations; dust jacket.   T. A. Swinford   49-84   1996 $100.00

BEATIE, RUSSEL H.   Saddles. Norman: 1981. 1st edition; 4to; 391 pages; illustrations/drawings by Niles and Osburn; photos; gilt stamped binding, fine in slightly worn dust jacket.   Gene W. Baade   1094-7   1996 $125.00

BEATON, CECIL   Winged Squadrons: Impressions of the Men of the R.A.F. & Fleet Air Arm. London: c. 1944. 1st edition; 67 photos of author; wrappers, slightly rubbed on spine, otherwise very good. Words Etcetera   94-129   1996 £55.00

BEATTIE, ANN   Chilly Scenes of Winter. New York: Doubleday, 1976. 1st edition; author's first novel, near fine in dust jacket with some edge wear, this copy signed by author.   Anacapa House   5-338   1996 $145.00

BEATTIE, ANN   Distortions. Garden City: Doubleday, 1976. 1st edition; 8vo; cloth backed boards, dust jacket, as new.   James S. Jaffe   34-16 1996 $100.00

BEATTIE, ANN   Jacklighting. Worcester: Metacom Press, 1981. 1st edition; one of 26 hardbound copies, signed by author; brown linen, dust jacket; mint.   Bromer Booksellers   90-3   1996 $125.00

BEATTIE, JAMES 1735-1803   An Essay on the Nature and Immutability of Truth, in Opposition to sophistry and Scepticism. London: ptd. for Edward and Charles Dilly, & A. Kincaid and W. Creech, Edin., 1786. 2nd edition; 8vo; 2 volumes in 1, ad leaf at end of volume 2; contemporary calf, spine gilt, label, fine.   Anthony W. Laywood   109-9   1996 £165.00

BEATTIE, WILLIAM 1793-1875   The Danube: its History, Scenery and Topography. London: Virtue and Co., ca. 1840's. 10 3/4 x 8 3/4 inches; 3 p.l., 236 pages; frontispiece, engraved title, 2 maps and 80 fine steel engraved plates by W. H. Bartlett, as well as many engravings in text; extremely fine contemporary scarlet half morocco, marbled sides, edges and endpapers, spine with wide raised bands decorated in gilt, as well as gilt rules, ornaments, and titling; few tiny marks on sides, two small smudges on spine but remarkably fine, with virtually no wear to binding and with only most trivial traces of foxing that often afflicts this work. Phillip J. Pirages   33-50   1996 $1,250.00

BEATTIE, WILLIAM 1793-1875   Scotland Illustrated in a Series of Views Taken Expressly for This Work by Messrs. London: George Virtue, 1838. 1st edition; 4to; 2 volumes; engraved vignette titlepages, printed titles, 200, 164 pages of text, 118 steel engraved plates, 1 folding map; original red leather backstrip with gilt emblematic tooling and title, red relief buckram boards, yellow endpapers; couple of plates badly foxed, rest have occasional minor foxing, map foxed and browned, hinges cracked, still good, tight copy. Holloway 22.   Beeleigh Abbey   BA/56-1 1996 £250.00

BEATTIE, WILLIAM 1793-1875   Scotland Illustrated, in A Series of Views Taken Expressly for this Work by Messrs. Allom, Bartlett, &c. London: George Virtue, 1842. 4to; 2 volumes; folding map, 112 steel engraved plates; old half calf, gilt, marbled boards, gilt panels and contrasting lettering pieces, hinges little rubbed, little light spotting or browning, mainly to plate margins, but very attractive, sound set. R.F.G. Hollett   76-20   1996 £275.00

BEATTIE, WILLIAM 1793-1875   Switzerland Illustrated in a Series of Views Taken Expressly for this Work. London: Virtue and Co., City And Ivy Lane, n.d. c. 1830-40. 4to; 2 volumes; Directors to Binder, 1-188 pages, 1-152 pages; 105 steel engraved plates, all tissue guarded and 1 large folding map, one plate misbound into volume 2 rather than volume 1, frontispiece and half titles foxed and browned, some plates have heavy foxing, whilst rest have sproadic foxing to margins, not affecting plates, owner's ink inscription; publisher's full tan morocco, elaboartely blind stamped blocking to boards, central gilt tooled motif to upper boards, gilt title and tooling to spines, raised bands to spines, corners bumped and worn, all edges gilt, hinges cracked and joints slightly worn, yellow endpapers.   Beeleigh Abbey   BA56-34   1996 £550.00

BEATTIE, WILLIAM 1793-1875   Switzerland Illustrated in a Series of Views Taken Expressly for this Work... London: George Virtue, 26, Ivy Lane Paternoster Row, 1836. 1st edition; 4to; Dedication leaf, To the Reader (iii-iv), Contents, Directions to the Binder, text 1-88 & 1-152 pages, 106 steel engraved plates, 1 large folding map, plates all in excellent condition with no foxing or offsetting, contemporary ink inscription; full green straight grain morocco, few scuff marks to binding, gilt arabesque design to boards, gilt titles and volume numbers to spines, raised bands, all edges gilt; handsome copy.   Beeleigh Abbey BA56-35   1996 £600.00

BEATTY, DAVID L.   Don't Tread On My Tire Rubber Sandals: a Tale of Vietnam. Boonville: Seven Oceans, 1969. 1st edition; signed by author; fine in dust jacket.   Thomas Dorn   9-27   1996 $100.00

BEATTY, RICHARD C.   A Vanderbilt Miscellany 1919-1944. Nashville: Vanderbilt University Press, 1944. 1st edition; lightly worn pictorial dust jacket, signed by Beatty; fine.   Captain's Bookshelf   38-2   1996 $100.00

BEAUCHAMPS, PIERRE FRANCOIS GODART DE   Recherches sur les Theatres de France, Depuis l'Annee Onze Cens Soixante-un, Jusques a Present. Paris: Prault, 1735. 1st edition; 4to; (12), 166, (2), 334, (2), 321, (1) pages; 2 folding tables, etched vignette on title, numerous large etched head and tailpieces, some slight foxing, contemporary mottled calf, gilt spine, some wear to head and tail of spine.   Jeffrey D. Mancevice 20-9 1996 $1,450.00

BEAUCLARK, TOPHAM   Bibliotheca Beauclerkiana. A Catalogue of the Large and Valuable Library of the Late Honourable Topham Beauclerk, F.R.S. Deceased. London: Samuel Paterson, 1781. 8vo; without half title and 8 pages of index; 231, 137 pages, interleaved throughout; contemporary calf, expertly rebacked, nice.   Forest Books 74-8 1996 £265.00

BEAUCLERK, CHARLES   Military Operations in Canada, 1837-8-9. Belleville: Mica Pub. Co., 1980. Limited to 100 copies; 38 cm; (vi), v, 24, (6) pages; frontispiece map, 6 full color plates, tissue guarded; fine in gilt stamped and decorated full leather, uncut; Boxed.   Rockland Books 38-20 1996 $225.00

BEAUFORT, DUKE OF   Driving. London: 1889. Limited to 250 copies; small 4to; large paper edition; portrait and numerous illustrations; beautifully bound in half red levant morocco, gilt top, by Zaehnsdorf. Charles W. Traylen 117-279 1996 £150.00

BEAUMONT, C.   New Paths. London: Beaumont, 1918. One of 30 copies (of a total edition of 130), with original color woodcut frontispiece signed and in 2 states and the decorations hand colored; this is copy number 4 signed by Rice; decorations by Anne Estelle Rice; original binding, spine frayed along edges seemingly a result of a binding defect, large bookplate of Pickford Waller designed by Haldane Macfall. Charles Agvent 4-1239 1996 $200.00

BEAUMONT, C. W.   The Mysterious Toyshop. London: Beaumont Press, 1924. 1st edition; crown 8vo; pages 32, (i); color printed illustrations; original quarter fawn buckram, backstrip gilt lettered, printed front cover label, decorated black boards, free endpapers lightly browned, untrimmed, excellent.   Blackwell's B112-10 1996 £50.00

BEAUMONT, FRANCIS 1584-1616   Comedies and Tragedies, Never Before Published. London: 1647. 1st collected edition; folio; half calf, rebacked, this copy lacks titlepage and portrait; scarce. CBEL I 632. Lyman Books 21-490 1996 $200.00

BEAUMONT, FRANCIS 1584-1616   A King and No King. London: n.p., 1661. small 4to; title within woodcut border; modern half calf, clean copy, fine. Wing B1590; Woodward & McManaway 49; Grego 360(f). Dramatis Personae 37-18 1996 $300.00

BEAUMONT, FRANCIS 1584-1616   The Maids Tragedy. London: printed for William Leake, 1650. 6th impression; small 4to; (36) pages; fine woodcut on title, outer side margin of title frayed and repaired, with loss of letters in two words of title and right hand ruled edge of woodcut, upper and lower margins throughout trimmed close, sometimes touching the headlines, and with loss on some pages of signatures and catchwords, few small wormholes in final fix leaves just touching the printed surface, side margin of some leaves repaired; recent quarter calf with marbled boards, old style endpapers. Wing B1595; Greg 357(f)II. David Bickersteth 133-4 1996 £180.00

BEAUMONT, ROBERTS   Colour in Woven Design. London: Whittaker, George Bell, 1890. 1st edition; 8vo; xxiv, 440, (32) pages; 32 color plates; cloth; very good.   Bookpress 75-6 1996 $275.00

BEAUMONT, WILLIAM 1785-1853   Experiments and Observations on the Gastric Juice and the Physiology of Digestion. Plattsburgh: F. P. Allen, 1833. 1st edition; 8vo; 280 pages, 3 wood engravings in text; 3 wood engravings in text; original boards, rebacked in cloth, paper spine label, replicating original; half morocco folding clamshell box; usual light foxing to prelims; early ownership signature of A. Clark; very good. GM 989; Norman Lib. 152.   Edwin V. Glaser B122-15 1996 $2,400.00

BEAUMONT, WILLIAM 1785-1853   Experiments and Observations on the Gastric Juice and the Physiology of Digestion. Plattsburgh: F. P. Allen, 1833. 1st edition; 8vo; 3 illustrations, 280 pages; modern half brown levant, some usual foxing. Osler 1972; GM 989.   Argosy 810-39 1996 $2,000.00

BEAUMONT, WILLIAM 1785-1853   Experiments and Observations on the Gastric Juice, and the Physiology of Digestion. Edinburgh: Maclachlan & Stewart, 1838. Reprinted from Plattsburgh Edition; 1st British edition; octavo; half title, xx, 319 pages plus ads; original binding, paper label, uncut, some wear to headpiece; very good. GM 989 for Plattsburgh edition.   James Tait Goodrich K40-23 1996 $775.00

BEAUMONT, WILLIAM 1785-1853   Experiments and Observations of Gastric Juice and the Physiology and Digestion. Boston: 1929. Facsimile of original edition of 1833, with biographical essay by Sir William Osler; 280 pages; original binding.   W. Bruce Fye 71-107 1996 $100.00

BEAUMONT, WILLIAM 1785-1853   The Physiology of Digestion with Experiments on the Gastric Juice. Burlington: Chauncey Goodrich, 1847. 2nd edition; small 4to; 303 pages, plus index; illustrations; publisher's blindstamped vertically ribbed brown cloth, spine titled in gilt, traces of bookplate on pastedown, slight chipping at head of spine, else very good.   Hermitage SP95-1075 1996 $375.00

THE BEAUTIES of the Court of King Charles the Second. London: for Henry Colburn by Richard Bentley, 1833. 1st edition; extra tall, wide folio; pages ix, 222; 21 engraved portraits after Sir Peter Lely, on India paper, 17 marked PROOF; splendid full red Turkey morocco binding by C. Lewis, elaborately gilt panels and spine decorations, wide gilt tooled dentelles, all edges gilt, marbled endpapers, slight wear, but elegant copy; nice. CBEL III 674.   Hartfield 48-L8 1996 $695.00

BEAUTY and the Beast. London: Sampson, Low, Marston Low and Searle, 1875. 1st edition thus, bound in variant binding; 4to; 10 chromolitho illustrations and in text wood engraved illustrations by Eleanor Boyle; apricot cloth pictorially stamped in black, two short repaired tears, scattered foxing, lacks 1 guard, cloth slightly marked, else clean, nice copy.   Barbara Stone 70-36 1996 £195.00

BEAVERBROOK, WILLIAM MAXWELL AIKEN   Don't Trust to Luck. London: London Express, ca. 1950. Revised; small 8vo; frontispiece; very good in dust jacket with few nicks and tears; signed and inscribed by author for Jack Warner.   George J. Houle 68-13 1996 $175.00

BEAZLEY, J. D.   Attic Black-Figure Vase-Painters. New York: Hacker Art Books, 1978. 8vo; xvi, 851 pages; original cloth, fine.   Archaeologia Luxor-2974 1996 $150.00

BEAZLEY, J. D.   Etruscan Vase-Painting. Oxford: Clarendon Press, 1947. 4to; xvi, 351 pages; 40 plates; original cloth, dust jacket (corner lightly bumped, signature).   Archaeologia Luxor-2977 1996 $450.00

BEAZLEY, J. D.   The Lewes House Collection of Ancient Gems. Oxford: Clarendon Press, 1920. Small 4to; xii, 124 pages, 10 plates; original boards, paper label (spine rubbed, corners lightly bumped, few pages of text foxed).   Archaeologia Luxor-2979 1996 $650.00

BECHSTEIN, LUDWIG   The Rabbit Catcher and Other Fairy Tales. New York: Macmillan, 1962. 1st trade edition; 4to; illustrations by Ugo Fontana; pictorial boards, issued without the dust jacket, covers slightly rubbed at extremities and one corner bumped, otherwise very good, scarce.   James S. Jaffe 34-319 1996 $175.00

BECK, THOMAS ALCOCK   Annales Furnesienses. London: Payne & Foss & M. A. Nattali, and Ulverston: S. Soulby, 1844. 1st edition; 250 copies; large 4to; pages xi, (ii), 403, cxl, 22 steel engraved plates, 1 chromolithograph, 3 tinted plates; margins of frontispiece and few other plates little spotted, titlepage trifle creased, fine, clean and sound copy; 19th century half morocco, gilt, raised bands and marbled boards, hinges and edges little rubbed;   R.F.G. Hollett & Son 78-693 1996 £375.00

BECKER, ROBERT H.   Disenos of California Ranchos. Maps of Thirty-Seven land Grants (1822-1846). San Francisco; Book Club of California, 1964. 1st edition; one of 400 copies; folio; 37 maps, including 24 folding, 27 in color, text illustrations; decorated boards with linen back, very fine and bright.   Argonaut Book Shop 113-60 1996 $500.00

BECKETT, SAMUEL 1906-1989   All that Fall. New York: 1957. Limited to 100 numbered copies; 8 x 5.5 inches; 59 pages; cloth backed boards; slight extremity discoloration, otherwise very good, specially bound.   John K. King 77-206 1996 $200.00

BECKETT, SAMUEL 1906-1989   All Strange Away. New York: Gotham Book Mart, 1976. 1st edition; limited to 226 copies, signed by author and artist; large 8vo; illustrations by Edward Gorey; quarter leather, pictorial boards, slipcase, as new.   James S. Jaffe 34-18 1996 $750.00

BECKETT, SAMUEL 1906-1989   How it Is. London: John Calder, 1964. 1st edition in English; 8 1/4 x 5 1/2 inches; original cloth, and dust jacket; fine in excellent jacket that is very slightly wrinkled along top and little soiled on back panel.   Phillip J. Pirages 33-52 1996 $100.00

BECKETT, SAMUEL 1906-1989   Malone Dies. New York: 1956. 1st American edition, limited to 500 numbered copies; 8 x 5.5 inches; 120 pages; cloth, very good.   John K. King   77-208   1996 $150.00

BECKETT, SAMUEL 1906-1989   Murphy. New York: Grove Press, 1958. Limited to 100 numbered copies, signed by author; cloth backed boards, very good in original acetate wrapper which is torn at foot of spine an with very small chip at head.   Words Etcetera   94-139   1996 £450.00

BECKETT, SAMUEL 1906-1989   Nohow On. New York: Limited Editions Club, 1989. Limited to 550 copies, signed by author and artist; 4to; 6 aquatints by Robert Ryman; full black niger morocco, black linen folding box, leather label on spine. Castleman, A Cent. of Artists Books 201. James S. Jaffe   34-19   1996 $3,500.00

BECKETT, SAMUEL 1906-1989   The North. London: Enitharmon Press, 1972. Number 6 of 125 copies numbered in press and signed by author, there were a further 12 ad personam copies; folio; 3 full page etchings by Avigdor Arikha; loose gatherings in folding wrapper and cloth case; fine in slightly dusty slipcase; presentation copy from author for Noel Lloyd and Geoffrey Palmer. Fine in slightly dusty slipcase.   Ulysses 39-38   1996 £650.00

BECKETT, SAMUEL 1906-1989   Nohow On. New York: Limited Editions Club, 1989. One of 550 copies; age size 7 1/4 x 10 3/4 inches; signed by author, artist; typeset in English Monotype Bodoni at Golgonooza Letterfoundry with new descending characters from punches cut by Daniel Carr; text printed at Shagbark Press, etchings printed on Arches at Wingate Studio and Renaissance Press; full black morocco with gold stamped title in black clamshell box.   Priscilla Juvelis   95/1-214   1996 $2,500.00

BECKETT, SAMUEL 1906-1989   Premier Amour. Paris: Le Editions de Minuit, 1970. 1st edition; trade issue; self wrappers; fine, signed by author.   Ken Lopez   74-26   1996 $650.00

BECKETT, SAMUEL 1906-1989   Proust. New York: n.d. 1957. 1st American edition, limited to 250 numbered copies, signed by author; 8 x 5.5 inches; 72 pages; cloth backed boards, tinge of discolor along extremities, very slight stain on fore edge, else very good.   John K. King   77-209   1996 $350.00

BECKETT, SAMUEL 1906-1989   The Unnamable. New York: Grove Press, 1958. Limited to 100 numbered copies; cloth backed boards, fine. Words Etcetera   94-138   1996 £120.00

BECKETT, SAMUEL 1906-1989   Waiting for Godot. London: Faber & Faber, 1956. 1st edition; original binding, top edge slightly dusty, endpapers partially browned, edges spotted, very good in nicked, creased and slightly spotted, rubbed and dusty dust jacket slightly browned at edges.   Ulysses   39-36   1996 £135.00

BECKETT, SAMUEL 1906-1989   Whoroscope. Paris: Hours Press, 1930. 1st edition; the first printing consisted of 300 copies, the first 100 signed by Becket, this one of the issue of 200, althought not called for, this copy signed; slim pamphlet in stapled wrappers, light crease to upper left corner, offsetting to rear wrapper, staples rusted, but nice, overall very good+ or better.   Lame Duck Books   19-57   1996 $3,750.00

BECKFORD, PETER   Thoughts Upon Hunting. Sarum: ptd. by E. Easton; sold by P. Elmsly, J. Robson, J. Debrett, London... 1782. New edition; small 4to; half title, 3 line errata to foot, contents and 358 pages of text; frontispiece by Bartolozzzi, 2 plates to rear; full dark red morocco, gilt rule and decorative gilt borders, fully gilt spine, marbled endpapers.   Beeleigh Abbey   BA/56-2   1996 $295.00

BECKFORD, WILLIAM 1760-1844   Biographical Memoirs of Extraordinary Painters. London: J. Robson, 1780. 1st edition; 1st issue; octavo; modern quarter morocco, usual foxing, complete with rare errata leaf; Chapman 1.   G. W. Stuart   59-14   1996 $950.00

BECKFORD, WILLIAM 1760-1844   Vathek. Paris: Perrin, 1893. 2nd edition; wrappers; very good+ or better; this copy inscribed by Stephane Mallarme.   Lame Duck Books   19-300   1996 $950.00

BECKFORD, WILLIAM 1760-1844   Vathek. London: Lonesuch Press, 1929. Limited to 1550 numbered copies; 8vo; pages iv, 172; printed on buff tinted laid paper, 10 lithographic illustrations in color by Marion V. Dorn; publisher's brick red boards, vellum spine, arabic gilt design on front cover, top edge gilt, others uncut, extremities trifle worn, but very nice.   Thomas Thorp   489-24   1996 £65.00

BECKHAM, BARRY   My Main Mother. New York: Walker, 1969. 1st edition; slight abrasion to the bottom of the front board, else near fine in lightly rubbed, very good dust jacket; inscribed by author to editor of his novel "Runner Mack". Author's first novel.   Between the Covers 43-26   1996 $350.00

BECKHAM, BARRY   Runner Mack. New York: Morrow, 1972. 1st edition; one corner slightly bumped, else fine in near fine dust jacket with two tiny tears; inscribed by author to his editor.   Between the Covers   43-28   1996 $350.00

BEDDOME, R. H.   The Ferns of Southern India. Madras: 1873. 2nd edition; 4to; pages xv, 88, xv, 272 plates of line drawings; buckram, slightly loose. Few plates torn and repaired, some pencil annotations. Rare original printing.   Wheldon & Wesley   207-1603   1996 £80.00

BEDDOME, R. H.   The Ferns of British India. New Delhi: 1973. 4to; 2 volumes, pages (4), 345, (4), (i)-vi; 345 plates; recent half calf, light wear, some corners bumped.   Raymond M. Sutton   VII-59   1996 $125.00

BEDE   The History of the Church of England. Antwerp: John Laet, 1565. 1st edition in English; (14), 192, (6) leaves; 3 woodcuts, contemporary vellum, title soiled, few minor defects, very good. STC 1778; PMM 16 (Latin ed.).   19th Century Shop   39-   1996 $10,000.00

BEDE   The History of the Church of Englande. Shakespeare Head Press, 1930. Limited to 475 copies; folio; pages xx, 479; printed in Cloister type in red and black on Batchelor's SHP handmade paper; woodcuts of the original edition have been engraved in wood in slightly larger size by Mr. John Farleigh; uncut, largely unopened in original natural calf backed marbled boards, vellum tips, lettered in gold; fine. Claude Cox   107-11   1996 £165.00

BEDFORD, GUNNING S.   The Principles and Practice of Obstetrics. New York: Wm. Wood, 1862. 2nd edition; 8vo; xxxvii, 731 pages, 100 text wood engravings; original binding, rebacked, original spine. Rutkow GY6.   James Tait Goodrich   K40-204   1996 $115.00

BEDFORDSHIRE GENERAL LIBRARY   Catalogue of the Bedfordshire General Library: Established in July, 1830. Bedford: Chas. F. Timaeus, 1831. 64 pages; half vellum, very worn, some very mild browning; booklabel of Woburn Abbey.   Maggs Bros. Ltd.   1191-32   1996 £225.00

BEDLOE, WILLIAM   The Excommunicated Prince; or the False Relic. London: printed for Tho. Parkhurst, D. Newman, Tho. Cockerill and Tho... 1679. 1st edition; folio; prelim license leaf; half calf; very good; the Sir Thomas Phillipps copy, with "M.H.C." in pencil on front flyleaf. Wing B1676.   Ximenes   109-29   1996 $350.00

BEEBE, CHARLES WILLIAM 1877-1962   Galapagos: World's End. New York: G. P. Putnam's Sons, 1924. 10.5 inches; xxi, 443 pages, 8 colored plates, 82 figures, wonderful colored double page igunana; cloth with gilt cover and spine titles, some wear, overall very good.   Parmer Books Nat/Hist-077114   1996 $100.00

BEEBE, CHARLES WILLIAM 1877-1962   A Monograph of the Pheasants. 1918-22. Reprint; 4to; 4 volumes in 2; 20 maps, 90 colored plates and 88 other illustrations; buckram;   Wheldon & Wesley 207-638   1996 £100.00

BEEBE, CHARLES WILLIAM 1877-1962   Pheasants, Their Lives and Homes. USA: 1936. 2 volumes in 1; color and other plates; original buckram; fine.   David A.H. Grayling   MY95Orn-7   1996 £100.00

BEEBE, CHARLES WILLIAM 1877-1962   Pheasants, their Lives and Homes. New York: 1937. Small 4to; 2 volumes in 1; 337 pages, 32 colored and 32 plain plates; original buckram, faded.   Wheldon & Wesley   207-639   1996 £90.00

BEEBE, CHARLES WILLIAM 1877-1962   Two Bird-Lovers in Mexico. Boston: Houghton Mifflin, 1905. 1st edition; 2nd issue; 8vo; xiii, 407, (8) pages; author's first book; photographs; original pictorial orange cloth, covers and spine somewhat darkened, bookplate, else very good in heavily chipped and tape repaired dust jacket. Very scarce in dust jacket. Chapel Hill   94-294   1996 $200.00

BEECHEY, FREDERICK WILLIAM 1796-1856   Narrative of a Voyage to the Pacific and Beering's Strait, to Co-Operate with the Polar Expeditions... London: Henry Colburn and Richard Bentley, 1831. 1st octavo edtion; 2 volumes, pages xxviii, 472; iv, 452, 3 maps, 23 plates; newly bound in full leather, gilt lettered leather labels, occasional very light foxing, else fine and exceptionally clean. Cowan p. 42; Hill Collection p. 19; Howes B309; Zamorano 80 4.   Argonaut Book Shop 113-63 1996 $1,750.00

BEECHEY, FREDERICK WILLIAM 1796-1856   Narrative of a Voyage to the Pacific and Beering's Strait, to Co-Operate with the Polar Expeditions... London: Henry Colburn and Richard Bentley, 1831. 21 cm; 2 volumes, xxvi, ll., 472 pages, frontispiece folding map, 2 other maps, portrait, 12 other plates; iv, 452 pages, 10 plates; half leather and marbled paper over boards, some wear and rubbing to binding, several plates age darkened, library bookplate, no other markings, overall very nice. Sabin 4347; Howes B309; Wickersham 6541; Cowan p. 19; Zamorano 4.   Parmer Books O39Nautica-047007 1996 $1,500.00

BEEDOME, R. H.   The Flora Sylvatica for Southern India... Dehra Dun: 1978. 4to; 2 volumes in 3, 800 pages, 360 plates; cloth.   Wheldon & Wesley 207-1821 1996 £90.00

BEEDOME, THOMAS   Select Poems Divine and Humane. London: Nonesuch Press, 1928. One of 1250 numbered copies; 8vo; printed in Janson types on Van Gelder; thonged limp parchment gilt, very nice copy in slipcase.   Bertram Rota 272-321 1996 £60.00

BEERBOHM, MAX 1872-1956   And Even Now. London: Heinemann, 1920. 1st edition; 8vo; green cloth with paper spine label, very good or better; Joseph Hergesheimer's copy with his name and address stamped in gilt on lower right hand corner of front cover.   Antic Hay 101-149 1996 $125.00

BEERBOHM, MAX 1872-1956   Around Theatres. London: Heinemann, 1924. Limited edition, 780 sets, 750 for sale; 2 volumes; edges spotted, offsetting and browning to endpapers, very slight foxing to prelims, otherwise very good in soiled and browned dust jackets, which are chipped at corners and ends of spine where several large chips are missing. Gallatin 22.   Virgo Books 48-27 1996 £400.00

BEERBOHM, MAX 1872-1956   Cartoons... London: Stephen Swift, n.d. 1901. 1st edition; folio; portfolio, (vi) pages, 15 color plates; portfolio worn, however the plates are very good.   The Bookpress 75-385 1996 $300.00

BEERBOHM, MAX 1872-1956   A Christmas Garland. London: William Heinemann, 1912. 1st edition; original decorated cloth, covers little darkened and worn, trifle foxed, otherwise bright copy; bookplates, in half morocco slipcase. Gallatin & Oliver 10.   David J. Holmes 52-11 1996 $250.00

BEERBOHM, MAX 1872-1956   Fifty Caricatures. London: Heinemann, 1913. 1st edition; 4to; pages vii, (plates), 2 (caricatures), (2) (ads), (1); 48 plates, each tipped to captioned brown card and 2 full page caricatures printed on rectos of white paper leaves, title printed in red, with none of the foxing usually found in this book; original diced mid-green cloth, gilt lettered backstrip and front cover, gilt Beerbohm caricature on front cover, excellent; Presentation copy and so blindstamped at head of titlepage; Gallatin & Oliver 12.   Blackwell's B112-27 1996 £85.00

BEERBOHM, MAX 1872-1956   Observations. London: Heinemann, 1926. 1st edition; 89/280 copies, signed by Max Beerbohm; large 4to; pages viii, color printed frontispiece, 51 monochrome plates, each with captioned tissue guard, extra tinted plate (issued with the limited issue and signed 'Max' at its tail margin), attached tissueguard and loosely inserted in pocket on rear pastedown; original bevel edged mid-green cloth, backstrip and front cover gilt lettered, faint foxing to pastedowns, gilt edges, dust jacket dust soiled and little creased, very good. Gallatin & Oliver 24a.   Blackwell's B112-28 1996 £295.00

BEERBOHM, MAX 1872-1956   A Survey. London: Heinemann, 1921. 1st edition; 197/275 copies, signed by Beerbohm; imperial 8vo; pages viii, color printed frontispiece, large titlepage cartoon and 51 monochrome plates, each tipped to tan backing card and each with captioned tissue guard; original bevel edged purple buckram, gilt lettering on faded backstrip and on front cover, endpapers browned, gilt edges, dust jacket faintly dust soiled, good.   Blackwell's B112-29 1996 £275.00

BEERBOHM, MAX 1872-1956   Zuleika Dobson. London: William Heinemann, 1911. 1st edition; 8vo; embossed smooth brown cloth, very good, scattered foxing, some rubbing and small stain, tiny nameplate to front pastedown.   Antic Hay 101-152 1996 $150.00

BEESON, HARVEY C.   Beeson's Inland Marine Directory. Chicago: 1894. Seventh Annual edition; 10 x 6.5 inches; 290 pages; photos; cloth, inner hinges cracked, 1 page of ads detached, spine ends badly chipped, covers worn.   John K. King 77-135 1996 $195.00

BEETON, ISABELLA MARY   The Book of Household Management. London: S. O. Beeton, 1861. 1st bookform edition, 1st issue printed by Cox and Wayman, with first line of errata correctly referring to p. 57 and not p. 657; plates are also first issue; small 8vo; pages xxxix, (i) (blank), 1112; chromolithographed frontispiece, illustrated additional titlepage, 11 colored plates, title at foot of frontispiece, cropped, waterstain in gutter margin of frontispiece and titlepages, some browning, small hole in N7 and N8, fore edges of 2Z1-2Z5 strengthened; early 20th century half brown russia, backstrip with rope roll decorated raised bands between double gilt rules, gilt lettered direct in second compartment, khaki linen sides, minor marks, very good. Bitting p. 32; Gernon 561; Simon 186.   Blackwell's B112-30 1996 £650.00

BEETON, ISABELLA MARY   Household Management, a Complete Cookery Book. London: 1923. New edition; 8vo; very thick (3 1/2 inches); nearly 700 illustrations, 32 colored plates; original cloth, very good.   K Books 441-33 1996 £70.00

BEETON, ISABELLA MARY   Mrs. Beeton's Dictionary of Every-Day Cookery. London: S. O. Beeton, 1865. 1st edition in book form, crown 8vo; bound from original parts published between September 1864 and March 1865; viii, (372), (ii) pages; contemporary half roan, somewhat rubbed and worn, lacks half title and final imprint leaf, discarded in binding, minor repairs, endpapers replaced, text somewhat thumbed and soiled, some small stains, etc., nicks to some edges, but reasonable copy of a scarce and fragile production.   Ash Rare Books Zenzybyr-10 1996 £195.00

BEEVER, J.   Practical Fly-Fishing: Founded on Nature... London: 1849. Half disbound, having one of the original royal blue/gilt covers still intact, housed in new quarter calf book box. Rare in any state, but especially with part of the original printed card covers preserved.   David A.H. Grayling 3/95-401 1996 £400.00

BEHAN, BRENDAN 1923-1964   The Quare Fellow. New York: 1956. Limited to 100 numbered copies, specially bound; 8 x 5.5 inches; 86 pages; cloth backed boards, extremities bit discolored, else very good.   John K. King 77-210 1996 $175.00

BEHRENS, CHARLES   Atomic Medicine. New York: 1949. 416 pages; original binding.   W. Bruce Fye 71-113 1996 $150.00

BEHRMAN, S. N.   The Second Man. Pub. for the Theatre Guild, 1927. 1st edition; thin boards, spotted, otherwise very good, tight copy; inscribed by author, scarce.   Lyman Books 21-491 1996 $100.00

BEINING, GUY   Stoma. New York: Red Ozier Press, 1984. 1st edition; one of 100 copies signed by author; thin 8vo; original wrappers; mint.   James S. Jaffe 34-557 1996 $150.00

BEKASSY, FERENC   Adriatica and Other Poems. London: 1925. 1st edition; marbled paper covered boards, head and foot of spine, trifle nicked, otherwise very good.   Words Etcetera 94-628 1996 £100.00

BELCHER, EDWARD   Narrative of a Voyage Round the World, Performed in Her Majesty's Ship Sulphur, During the Years 1836-1842. London: 1843. 1st edition; 8vo; 2 volumes; 3 folding maps, 19 engraved plates, illutrations in text; some plates very slightly foxed in margins; prize binding of full blue morocco, gilt extra. Very fine. Sabin 4490; Ferguson, Bib. of Australia 3564;   Charles W. Traylen 117-438 1996 £800.00

BELCHER, EDWARD 1799-1877   Narrative of a Voyage Round the World, Performed in Her Majesty's Ship Sulphur, during the Years 1836-1842... London: Henry Colburn, 1843. 8vo; 2 volumes; xxxviii, 1 l., 387 pages, 3 folding maps, 8 pages ads, vi, 1 l., 474 pages, plates; original embossed cloth with gilt spine titles; corners bumped, covers rubbed with some wear to cloth, especially at perimeters of spine; Hill p. 20; Sabin 4390; Howes B318.   Parmer Books O39Nautica-039160 1996 $1,250.00

BELCHER, HENRY   Illustrations of the Scenery on the Line of the Whitby and Pickering Railway... London: published for the Proprietors by Longman Rees, et al, 1836. 1st edition; 8vo; engraved title, 12 engraved plates, few wood engravings in text, some foxing on plates, otherwise fine in publisher's olive morocco grain cloth, blindstamped greek key borders, title blocked in gold on upper cover. Ottley 7085.   H. M. Fletcher 121-128 1996 £95.00

BELCHER, THOMAS   The Art of Boxing, or Science of Manual Defence, Clearly Displayed on Rational Principles Whereby Every Person May Easily Make Themselves Masters of that Manly Acquirement... London: printed by W. Mason, n.d. 1819. 1st edition; 12mo; woodcut frontispiece, 2 other plates, all rather crudely drawn; half calf, very rare. Hartley 135.   Ximenes 109-30 1996 $900.00

BELDEN, LEMUEL W.   An Account of Jane C. Rider, the Springfield Somnambulist: the Substance of Which Was Delivered as a Lecture Before the Springfield Lyceum, Jan. 22, 1834. Springfield: pub. by G. and C. Merriam, 1834. 1st edition; 16mo; 134, (6) pages + 4 pages of ads; publisher's tan cloth with paper spine label, covers rubbed, spine label lacking and gouge to base of spine, lightly foxed, modern bookplate, still attractive.   John Gach 150-33 1996 $285.00

BELDER, ROBERT DE   A Magnificent Collection of Botanical Books...fromt he Celebrated Library formed by Robert De Belder. London: 1987. Larage 8vo; 428 pages; illustrations; price list inserted; cloth; fine.   Graham Weiner C2-646 1996 £50.00

BELIDOR, B. F. DE   Architecture Hydraulique. Paris: Jombert, 1782/82/50/70. 4to; 2 parts, each in 2 volumes; (8), xii, 412 pages, engraved frontispiece, 44 folding engraved plates; (8), 423, (1), xxviii pages, 55 folding engraved plates; (8), xiv, (2), 412, xxxii pages, 60 folding engraved plates; viii, 480, xl pages, engraved frontispiece, 60 folding engraved plates; contemporary cats paw calf, gilt panelled spines, original red gilt labels, joints and head and tail of spines expertly repaired, together with some of the corners, some rubbing to gilt. Ken Spelman 30-61 1996 £2,600.00

BELL, A. MORTON   Locomotives. Their Construction, Maintenance and Operation, with Notes on Electric and Internal Combustion Locomotives. London: Virtue, 1946. 5th edition; 4to; 2 volumes; viii, 224; viii, (225)-452 pages; numerous illustrations, folding color frontispiece; original cloth, with locomotive motif embossed on front covers; very good.   Edwin V. Glaser 121-21 1996 $150.00

BELL, A. N.   Climatology and Mineral Waters of the United States. New York: 1885. 1st edition; 386 pages; charts and maps; original binding, Kelly Burrage 88.   W. Bruce Fye 71-120 1996 $125.00

BELL, CHARLES 1774-1842   Essays on the Anatomy of Expression in Painting. London: 1806. 1st edition; 4to; 186 pages; half leather, marbled boards, new endpapers; fine, large copy. BM 6604.92; Choulant Frank 343; Norman 170.   W. Bruce Fye 71-116 1996 $1,500.00

BELL, CHARLES 1774-1842   Essays on the Anatomy of Expression in Painting. London: printed for Longman, Hurst, Rees, and Orme, 1806. 1st edition; 4to; xii, 186 pages, 6 engraved plates, 26 engravings in text; contemporary calf, rebacked, original spine label and endpapers preserved, without half title and without final ad leaf, little light spotting near inner joint of front fly, titlepage and following two pages, and on endpapers; the copy of Sir Edwin Landseer". Gordon Taylor 6.   David Bickersteth 133-179 1996 £465.00

BELL, CHARLES 1774-1842   An Exposition of the Natural System of the Nerves of the Human Body. Philadelphia: 1825. 1st American edition; 8vo; 3 engraved plates, by author, 2 folding (one torn), several text figures, 165 pages; contemporary sheep, worn, front cover loose, ex-library.   Argosy 810-43 1996 $300.00

BELL, CHARLES 1774-1842   The Hand - its Mechanism and Vital Endowments as Evincing Design. London: 1833. 2nd edition; 314 pages; illustrations; half leather; GM 411.1. Norman 175.   W. Bruce Fye 71-117 1996 $400.00

BELL, CHARLES 1774-1842   Institutes of Surgery: Arranged in the Order of the Lectures Delivered in the University of Edinburgh. Philadelphia: Waldie, 1840. 8vo; 446 pages; contemporary quarter sheep and boards, quite worn with weak and cracked joints, occasional light foxing, else, clean, crisp internally.   James Tait Goodrich K40-25 1996 $145.00

BELL, CHARLES 1774-1842   Letters Concerning the Diseases of the Urethra. Boston: 1811. 1st American edition; 8vo; 6 plates engraved after Bell, partially colored; modern polished calf, text browned.   James Tait Goodrich K40-284 1996 $250.00

BELL, CHARLES DENT   The Four Seasons on the Lakes. London: Marcus Ward, n.d. 1878. 1st edition; large 4to; 16 leaves, printed on recto only; publisher's cloth, all edges gilt; light occasional foxing, but very good overall, scarce.   Bookpress 75-7 1996 $265.00

BELL, CHARLES DENT   The Four Seasons at the Lakes. London: Marcus Ward & Co., n.d., c. 1880. 4to; pages 16; lithographed in full color on thick card on rectos, tissue guarded; all edges gilt, original cloth, gilt over bevelled boards, fore edges and head and tail of spine little frayed; excellent copy.   R.F.G. Hollett & Son 78-694 1996 £140.00

BELL, HENRY   The Perfect Painter; or, a Compleat History of the Original Progress and Improvement of Painting. London: 1730. Small 8vo; (4), 138, (6) pages, frontispiece; contemporary calf, neatly rebacked, new gilt label; very good.   Ken Spelman 30-4 1996 £175.00

BELL, HORACE   Reminiscences of a Ranger, or Early Times in Southern California. Los Angeles: Yarnell, Caystile and Mathes, 1881. 1st edition; 9 x 5 5/8 inches; 457 pages; black and gold stamped green pictorial cloth, inner hinges just a little weak, light wear to tips and spine ends.   Dawson's Books Shop 528-8 1996 $350.00

BELL, JOHN   Report of the Importance and Economy of Sanitary Measures to Cities. New York: 1859. 243 pages; original binding, one inch piece missing from spine, free endpaper taped.   W. Bruce Fye 71-119 1996 $200.00

BELL, JOHN 1745-1831   British Theatre. London: printed for the proprietors, by Bunney and Cold, Shoe Lane, Fleet St. 1791-99. 12mo; volumes 1-30; 90 engraved half titles, 90 engraved frontispieces; full green straight grain morocco, corners only very slightly bumped, gilt tooled scrolled border to boards, gilt rule, title and volume number of spines, marbled endpapers; light foxing to a few pages, contemporary ink inscription to upper board of volume 28, fairly discreet and not very prominent to the naked eye, overall very handsome set.   Beeleigh Abbey BA56-134 1996 £750.00

BELL, JOHN 1763-1820   The Anatomy and Physiology of the Human Body. London: Longmans, et al, 1829. 7th edition; octavo; 3 volumes; xxxiv, 604; xvi, 592; xii, 471 pages; several woodcuts and text figures in text; original boards, uncut, title label of volume 1 lacking and one hinge cracked, volume 2 binding shaken, mild foxing and browning of text; despite binding defects, a nice, clean copy.   James Tait Goodrich K40-27 1996 $195.00

BELL, JOHN 1763-1820   The Principles of Surgery. New York: 1810. 1st American edition; 8vo; 562 pages; 7 engraved plates, numerous text engravings; contemporary full calf, spine quite worn with original labels lacking, text with usual foxing and browning. Austin 195.   James Tait Goodrich K40-28 1996 $195.00

BELL, MADISON SMARTT   The Washington Square Ensemble. New York: Viking, 1983. 1st edition; author's first book; top corners just slightly bumped, else fine in jacket with few light scratches (barely visible) to front panel.   Alice Robbins 15-25 1996 $125.00

BELL, MADISON SMARTT   The Washington Square Ensemble. New York: Viking, 1983. 1st edition; author's first book; fine in fine dust jacket.   Book Time 2-36 1996 $100.00

BELL, MALCOLM   Edward Burne-Jones: a Record and Review. London: 1892. Limited to 390 numbered copies; 13.5 x 10 inches; 130 pages; profusely illustrated with plates; cream buckram lettered in gilt, top edge gilt, covers soiled and darkened, contents loosening.   John K. King 77-587 1996 $185.00

BELL, QUENTIN   Virginia Woolf: a Biogrpahy. London: Hogarth Press, 1972. 1st edition; 2 volumes; very good in slightly soiled and chipped dust jackets.   Virgo Books 48-233 1996 £50.00

BELL, SAMUEL D.   Justice and Sheriff, Practical Forms for the Use of Justices of the Peace, Sheriffs, Coroners and Constables, Containing Forms of Proceedings (etc.). Concord: pub. by G. Parker Lyon, 1843. 1st edition; contemporary sheep, quite worn, one endpaper lacking(?), but sound.   Meyer Boswell SL26-12 1996 $150.00

BELL, SAUL   Henderson the Rain King. London: Weidenfeld & Nicolson, 1959. 1st British edition; near fine in attractively illustrated jacket.   Lame Duck Books 19-60 1996 $100.00

BELL, THOMAS   The Anatomy, Physiology and Diseases of the Teeth. London: 1835. 2nd edition; 8vo; 11 engraved full page plates; modern boards, foxed. Campbell 136; Weinberger p. 14.   Argosy 810-45 1996 $300.00

BELL, WALTER GEORGE   The Great Plague in London in 1665. London: 1924. 1st edition; 374 pages; illustrations; original binding, library stamp on endpapers; otherwise very good. Bloomfield (1958) 49. W. Bruce Fye 71-121 1996 $100.00

BELL, WILLIAM   Elegies. London: Fortune Press, n.d. 1st edition; (18 pages); on handmade paper; original binding, top edge slightly dusty, head and tail pf spine and corners bumped, free endpapers slightly browned, very good in nicked, rubbed and dusty dust jacket darkened at the spine and edges and missing a small piece at tail of spine; signed by author.   Ulysses 39-43 1996 £65.00

BELL, WILLIAM   Poetry from Oxford in Wartime. London: Fortune Press, 1945. 1st edition; original binding, top edge dusty, edges slightly spotted, front pastedown very slightly soiled, tail of spine and one corner very slightly bumped, very good in nicked, dusty and slightly rubbed, marked, spotted and soiled dust jacket browned at spine and edges; mounted on front pastedown is printed slip, denoting this book to have been from the library of John Masefield.   Ulysses 39-345 1996 £195.00

BELL, WILLIAM DALRYMPLE MAITLAND 1800-1851   Bell of Africa. London: 1960. 4to; illustrations; mint in laminated dust jacket.   David Grayling J95Biggame-17 1996 £70.00

BELL, WILLIAM DALRYMPLE MAITLAND 1800-1851   Karamojo Safari. London: 1949. original cloth, slightly discolored, light bumping, contents fine.   David Grayling J95Biggame-18 1996 £85.00

BELL, WILLIAM E.   Carpentery Made Easy; or, the Science and Art of Framing, on a New and Improved System. Philadelphia: Ferguson Bros., 1883. 2nd edition; 8vo; 152 pages; 44 plates, almost 200 figures in text; original cloth, several signatures loose, else very good. Hitchcock 88. Edwin V. Glaser 121-22 1996 $175.00

BELLARMINE, ROBERT   De Aeterna Felicitate Sanctorum. Rome: Zanetti, 1616. 1st edition; 12mo; 416 pages; woodcut and typographic ornaments; contemporary limp vellum; DeBacker-Sommervogel 1.1236. Bennett Gilbert LL29-9 1996 $500.00

BELLARMINO, ROBERTO FRANCISCO ROMOLO, SAINT   Institutiones Linguae Hebraicae, Postremo Recognitae ac Locupletae. Geneva: Franciscus Faber, 1619. 8vo; (4) leaves, 334 pages, 3 large folding tables, printer's device on title, Latin and Hebrew text; contemporary calf. De Backer Sommervogel I 1152; Steinschneider, Handbuch 194.12. Jeffrey D. Mancevice 20-12 1996 $575.00

BELLASIS, EDWARD   Westmorland Church Notes. Kendal: T. Wilson, 1889. Thick tall 8vo; 2 volumes; pages xii, 281; 340; contemporary full vellum gilt over bevelled boards, arms in gilt and black (slightly rubbed) on each lower board, spines little darkened, top edge gilt, untrimmed with frontispiece to volume 1, interleaved throughout; superb, unique set, rare.   R.F.G. Hollett & Son 78-695 1996 £450.00

THE BELLE Epoque of French Jewellery 1850-1910: Jewellery Making in Paris 1850-1910. London: 1991. 1st edition in English; large 4to; 327 pages; profusely illustrated in color; cloth, fine in dust jacket.   J. M. Cohen 35-46 1996 $125.00

BELLEGARDE, JEAN BAPTISTE MORVAN DE   Reflexions on Ridicule; or, What it Is that Makes a Man Ridiculous... London: printed for Tho. Newborough, D. Midwinter and Benj. Tooke, 1707. 2nd edition in English; 8vo; (xvi), 390, (xviii) pages; original panelled calf, rebacked, new morocco spine label, original endpapers preserved. Heltzel 136 (this ed.). David Bickersteth 133-6 1996 £150.00

BELLERS, FETTIPLACE   A Delineation of Universal Law: Being an Abstract of an Essay Towards Deducing the Elements of Universal Law... London: printed by J. Hughs for R. and J. Dodsley, 1754. 1st edition; 4to; name on title which is slightly soiled, small hole in first 6 leaves barely affecting text, 74 pages, ad leaf at end; disbound. Sweet & Maswell p. 592, 5.   Anthony W. Laywood 109-10 1996 £100.00

BELLEW, CHRISTOPHER D.   A Catalogue of Books in the Library of Christopher D. Bellew, Esq. Mount Bellew. Galway: Geo. Conolly, 1813. Only 15 copies printed; narrow folio; 64 pages; original paper backed blue wrappers with printed label on upper cover, some dampstaining to lower half of upper cover, spine mildly worn; scarce.   Maggs Bros. Ltd. 1191-33 1996 £3,250.00

BELLEW, CHRISTOPHER D.   Catalogue of the Mount Bellew Library, 1814. Dublin: ptd. at Hibernia Press Office by James Cumming & Co., 1814. 4to; 173 pages, last 5 pages wrongly paginated ending with p. 123; original paper backed wrappers, some repair to spine, paper printed label on upper cover, stained edges bit chewed, corners curling, uncut, 3 brown spots on title and some mild dampstaining to first few leaves, ms. press marks added to first two pages.   Maggs Bros. Ltd. 1191-34 1996 £3,000.00

BELLIN, JACQUES NICOLAS   Essai Geographique sur les Isles Britanniques Contenant une Description de l'Angleterre... Paris: De L'Imprimrie de Didot, 1757. 1st edition; small 4to; 1-471 pages, 22 vignette plates to letterpress, 18 maps, city plans, 2 large folding, maps, map of Ireland detached and loosely inserted, royal library stamp to engraved title, small part of upper right corner of front f.e.p. missing; full French mottled calf, gilt coat of arms of Louis XV and library stamp of Versailles to boards, triple gilt rule borders, gilt tooling to compartments, corners worn and bumped, marbled endpapers. Cox III p. 92.   Beeleigh Abbey BA/56-3 1996 £650.00

BELLOC, HILAIRE 1870-1953   The Bad Child's Book of Beasts. London: Duckworth, 1896. 1st edition; small 4to; over 30 illustrations; grey pictorial boards, printed in red and black, wear to spine, rubbed, good to very good.   George J. Houle 68-15 1996 $375.00

BELLOC, HILAIRE 1870-1953   Belinda - a Tale of Affection in Youth and Age. London: 1928. One of 165 numbered copies, signed by author; top edge gilt, parchment covers lettered in gilt, prelims, edges and endpapers slightly spotted, free endpapers browned, head and tail of spine and corners slightly bumped, covers spotted, very good. Ulysses 39-45 1996 £85.00

BELLOC, HILAIRE 1870-1953   Sonnets and Verse. London: Duckworth, 1923. Signed, limited edition of 525 numbered copies; 8vo; printed on handmade paper; blue cloth, top edge gilt, near fine.   Antic Hay 101-159 1996 $100.00

BELLOW, SAUL   The Adventures of Augie March. New York: Viking Press, 1953. 1st edition; thick 8vo; boards, dust jacket; fine in slightly rubbed and darkened jacket; signed by author.   James S. Jaffe 34-20 1996 $250.00

BELLOW, SAUL   The Adventures of Augie March. New York: Viking, 1953. 1st edition; fine in price clipped, chipped and slightly wrinkled dust jacket (2nd issue top, not stained orange).   Sherwood 3-29 1996 $125.00

BELLOW, SAUL   Dangling Man. New York: Vanguard Press, 1944. 1st edition; author's first book; small stain at foot of spine matching 1" piece missing from otherwise very good dust jacket, desirable copy of a difficult title.   Sherwood 3-27 1996 $450.00

BELLOW, SAUL   The Dean's December. New York: H&R, 1982. Uncorrected proof; green printed wrappers; spine mildly faded, else fine. Lame Duck Books 19-64 1996 $100.00

BELLOW, SAUL   The Dean's December. New York: Harper & Row, 1982. 1st edition; 1/500 signed and numbered copies; fine in slipcase. Bev Chaney, Jr. 23-76 1996 $150.00

BELLOW, SAUL   The Dean's December. New York: 1982. 1st edition; signed, limited edition of 500 copies; fine in glassine, near fine in slipcase.   Stephen Lupack 83- 1996 $100.00

BELLOW, SAUL   Henderson the Rain King. New York: Viking, 1956. 1st edition; 1st issue, top edge yellow; near fine in bright dust jacket with two unobtrusive small tears.   Thomas Dorn 9-28 1996 $125.00

BELLOW, SAUL   Henderson The Rain King. London: Weidenfeld & Nicholson, 1959. 1st English edition; 8vo; boards, dust jacket, spine cocked, otherwise fine in slightly rubbed and dusty jacket.   James S. Jaffe 34-21 1996 $150.00

BELLOW, SAUL   Henderson the Rain King. New York: Viking, 1959. 1st edition; fine in very good plus dust jacket with several short unobtrusive tears, small dampstain visible only on inside of dust jacket, nicer copy than is usually encountered.   Between the Covers 42-42 1996 $150.00

BELLOW, SAUL   Henderson the Rain King. New York: Viking, 1959. 1st edition; fine in dust jacket.   Sherwood 3-31 1996 $125.00

BELLOW, SAUL   Herzog. New York: Viking, 1964. 1st edition; fine in very near fine dust jacket and signed by author.   Ken Lopez 74-27 1996 $275.00

BELLOW, SAUL   Him with His Foot In His Mouth. New York: H&R, 1984. 1st edition; fine in dust jacket, signed by author.   Lame Duck Books 19-65 1996 $100.00

BELLOW, SAUL   Humboldt's Gift. New York: Viking, 1975. Advance reading copy, spine sunned, else near fine in printed wrappers with publisher's information laid in; signed by author.   Lame Duck Books 19-63 1996 $275.00

BELLOW, SAUL   Humboldt's Gift. New York: Viking, 1975. 1st edition; slight bump to foot of spine, else fine in dust jacket. this copy signed by Bellow, on tipped in leaf for members of The First Edition Circle, with bookmark laid in.   Lame Duck Books 19-62 1996 $125.00

BELLOW, SAUL   Nobel Lecture. New York: Targ Editions, 1979. 1st edition; one of 350 copies signed by author; designed and printed by Ronald Gordon at the Oliphant Press, designated as printer's copy on colophon; cream cloth, plain tissue dust jacket, which is torn at edges; mint.   Bromer Booksellers 90-4 1996 $100.00

BELLOW, SAUL   Seize the Day. New York: Viking, 1956. 1st edition; faint foxing at top edge of pages, else near fine in very good or better spine faded dust jacket with one inch edge tear to rear panel and several tiny tears to extremities.   Lame Duck Books 19-59 1996 $125.00

BELLOW, SAUL   Seize the Day. New York: Viking, 1956. 1st edition; fine in spine faded dust jacket.   Sherwood 3-30 1996 $125.00

BELLOW, SAUL   Something to Remember Me By. New York: Signet, 1991. Uncorrected proof of the first trade edition; tan printed wrappers; fine.   Lame Duck Books 19-72 1996 $100.00

BELLOW, SAUL   Something to Remember Me By. New York: Albondoconi, 1991. One of a limited first edition of 376 copies, numbered and signed by author; fine in quarter cloth and marbled paper covered boards.   Lame Duck Books 19-73 1996 $100.00

BELLOW, SAUL   To Jerusalem and Back. New York: Viking, 1976. 1st edition; cloth darkened at spine extremities, else fine in very near fine dust jacket and signed by author.   Ken Lopez 74-28 1996 $100.00

BELLOW, SAUL   The Victim. New York: Vanguard, 1947. 1st edition; bump to fore corner of rear panel, very faint tanning to spine, else near fine, small chip and light wear to head of spine, scarce in collectable condition.   Lame Duck Books 19-58 1996 $750.00

BELLOW, SAUL   The Victim. New York: Vanguard Press, 1947. 1st edition; fine in dust jacket with chips to head and foot of spine stairp, stains on front and rear flaps, otherwise very good; attractive copy. Sherwood 3-28 1996 $450.00

BELLOW, SAUL   The Victim. New York: 1947. 1st edition; author's second book; near fine in scarce dust jacket with 2 tears closed internally with archival tape.   Stephen Lupack 83- 1996 $225.00

BELLOWS, EMMA S.   George Bellows: His Lithographs. New York: Knopf, 1928. Revised edition; folio; 278 pages; 197 plates; cloth. Lucas p. 124. Freitag 591.   Brannan Books 43-50 1996 $175.00

BELLOWS, GEORGE   The Paintings of George Bellows. New York: Knopf, 1929. Limited edition; folio; unpaginated text, color frontispiece, 143 plates; vellum backed boards, dust jacket. Lucas p. 124; Freitag 592.   Brannan Books 43-51 1996 $295.00

BELLOWS, HENRY WHITNEY   An Address Upon the claims of the Drama, Delivered Before the President and Members of the American Dramatic Fund Society, 1857. London: pub. by J. W. Anson, T. H. Lacy; Sheffield, printer, n.d. 1857. 1st English edition; 8vo; disbound; very good, scarc edition; 3 copies in NUC; LAR 609 (not seen).   Ximenes 109-31 1996 $100.00

BELT, T.   Naturalist in Nicaragua. London: John Murray, 1874. 1st edition; 403 pages; 4 plates, text illustrations; half tooled leather, very nice.   John Johnson 135-12 1996 $200.00

BELZONI, GIOVANNI BATTISTA   Narrataive of the Operations and Recent Discoveries Within the Pyramids, Temples, Tombs and Excavations in Egypt and Nubia; and of a Journey to the Coast of the Red Sea, in Search of the Ancient Berenice; and Another to the Oasis of Jupiter Ammon. London: John Murray, 1820. 1st edition; 4to. (text) and large folio (plates); 2 volumes; pages xxii, 483, frontispiece, plate volume: xi, 44 plates on 34 sheets, mainly lithographs, some etchings, all but 4 colored, 2 folding; contemporary half calf, marbled boards, spine with some decoration in blind, calf of text volume darkened to match spine leather of plate volume, joints slightly cracked but nonetheless still firm, some rubbing to boards on both volumes, extremities bumped, some spotting to frontispiece and prelim leaves and rear endpaper of text volume, some slight browning to a few plates, tears to two of the plate leaves (not affecting images), nonetheless very good, with crisp and bright plates. Blackmer 166, 117; Gay 1940; Ibrahim-Hilmy p. 62. Sotheran PN32-157 1996 £4,500.00

BEMBO, PIETRO, CARDINAL 1470-1547   Historiae Venetae Libri XII. Venice: Sons of Aldus, 1551. Folio; fine title woodcut of Mercury & Pallas within frame of Cupids and Angels, Aldine Anchor at end, woodcut initials; gilt calf, rebacked, Aldine Anchors gilt impressed on both covers, "vigilantibus" bookticket of 3rd Earl of Gosford; large paper copy; The Renouard copy. Adams B597. Renouard 152 no. 17.   Rostenberg & Stern 150-75 1996 $3,500.00

BEMBO, PIETRO, CARDINAL 1470-1547   Rerum Venetarum Historiae Libri XII. Paris: Michael Vascosan, 1551. 2nd printing, same year as the first; wide quarto; pages xx, 311, (1 blank), ll. Vellum, as usual; early hand written titles on spine and bottom edge; 17th century ownership title on flyleaf, marginal notes in same neat hand; well preserved copy. Index Aurel 116 and 417; Adams B598; Thompson Hist. Writing I 504.   Hartfield 48-L8 1996 $1,250.00

BEMELMANS, LUDWIG   Madeline's Christmas. New York: Viking Kestrel, 1985. 1st edition in book form; colored illustrations by author; colored pictorial boards, fine in pictorial dust jacket.   Barbara Stone 70-24 1996 £75.00

BEMROSE, WILLIAM   Manual of Buhl-Work and Marquetry. London: Bemrose, n.d., ca. 1860. 1st edition; 4to; 26, (8) pages; 14 chromolithographic plates; publisher's cloth, covers lightly soiled, but very good, scarce.   Bookpress 75-8 1996 $485.00

BEMROSE, WILLIAM   Mosaicon; or, Paper Mosaic. London: Bemrose, n.d., ca. 1870. 2nd edition; 8vo; 16, 8 pages, 3 full color plates, 1 is folding; publisher's cloth, upper tip of title leaf has been torn, otherwise vine, bright copy.   Bookpress 75-9 1996 $225.00

BEN-GURION, DAVID   Israel: A Personal History. New York: Funk & Wagnalls, 1971. 1st edition; number 1085 of 2000 numbered copies, signed by author; small 4to; frontispiece, map, 32 pages of black and white photos; gilt stamped dark blue leatherette, watered silk endpapers, top edge gilt, fine, publisher's matching cloth slipcase.   George J. Houle 68-74 1996 $375.00

THE BENCH and Bar. Philadelphia: E. L. Carey and A. Hart, 1839. Patterned cloth, worn and chipped, definite foxing, usable.   Meyer Boswell SL25-142 1996 $250.00

BENCHLEY, PETER   The Deep. Garden City: Doubleday, 1976. 1st edition; later printing; 8vo; dust jacket with few nicks, tear to lower cover; very good; signed and inscribed by cast of the 1977 film, including Nick Nolte, Jacqueline Bisset, Robert Shaw and Lou Gossett. George J. Houle 68-16 1996 $450.00

BENCHLEY, PETER   Jaws. Garden City: Doubleday, 1974. 1st edition; fine in about fine all black dust jacket that has some light edgewear to bottom spine panel and small chip to heel of spine.   Bud Schweska 12-153 1996 $155.00

BENCI, FRANCESCO   Qvinqve Martyres. Cologne: gottfried Kempen in Officina Birckmannica, 1594. 1st German edition; 12mo; pages 210, mainly italic letter, woodcut printer's device on titlepage, woodcut initials, uniform light age browning, few leaves very slightly soiled or ink spotted (frayed at 1 edge), tears in 2 neatly repaired without loss, contemporary Jesuit ex-libris on titlepage, occasional early ms. annotation or mark, contemporary limp vellum with ties, generally good, preserving original bone or horn bobbles. This ed. not in BM STC German, Adams, NUC or JFB.   A. Sokol XXV-12 1996 £1,350.00

BENEDICT, PICKNEY   The Wrecking Yard. New York: Doubleday, 1992. Uncorrected proof, signed by author; printed cream colored wrappers; fine.   Thomas Dorn 9-30 1996 $100.00

THE BENEDICTINES of Stanbrook. Worcester: Stanbrook Abbey Press, 1957. Reprint; hand set in Perpetua type and printed on WSH handmade paper, hand painted initials in gold and 3 colors; parchment wrappers, titlepage very slightly creased and marked (production fault, near fine in bumped slipcase; loosely inserted is the Press's Christmas list for 1959, together with an order form; from the library of James D. Hart. Ulysses 39-552 1996 £65.00

BENET, STEPHEN VINCENT 1898-1943 Five Men and Pompey. Boston: Four Seas Co., 1915. 1st edition; 1st issue; octavo; author's first book; original boards, original printed purple paper wrappers (slightly faded, small chip at head of spine), quite nice and preserved in fine quarter citron morocco, gilt slipcase. G. W. Stuart 59-15 1996 $350.00

BENET, STEPHEN VINCENT 1898-1943 Five Men and Pompey. Boston: Four Seas, 1915. 1st edition; author's first book; boards and brown wrapper as issued; fine. Sherwood 3-46 1996 $150.00

BENET, STEPHEN VINCENT 1898-1943 John Brown's Body. Garden City: Doubleday Doran, 1928. 1st trade edition; fine in dust jacket with couple of tiny nicks and touch of soiling to the extremities of oatmeal colored dust jacket, beautiful copy. Between the Covers 42-44 1996 $135.00

BENET, STEPHEN VINCENT 1898-1943 John Brown's Body. New York: 1980. 10.5 x 7.25 inches; 360, (1) pages; original wood engravings by Barry Moser; bound in two-tone maroon and red cloths, orange paper title label, printed tan dust jacket, maroon cloth slipcase, brown ribbon marker,, top edge gilt. Fine. Joshua Heller 21-170 1996 $125.00

BENEZET, ANTHONY Some Historical Account of Guinea, Its Situation, Produce and the General Disposition of Its Inhabitants. London: Printed and sold by J. Phillips, 1788. New edition, in fact the second London edition, preceded by Philadelphia edition of 1771 and a London reprint of the following year; 8vo; disbound; half title present; fine. Sabin 4689. Ximenes 108-15 1996 $400.00

BENIOWSKI, BARTOMIEJ The Anti-Absurd or Phrenotypic English Pronouncing & Orthographical Dictionary. London: published by the author, 1845. half title, slight dampmarking, 2 parts; black embossed calf, rubbed with splits in leading hinge; scarce. Jarndyce 103-125 1996 £75.00

BENJAMIN BEN JOHAN, OF TUDELA Itinerarium Beniamini Tudelensis: In Quo Res memorabiles, Quas Ante Quadringentos Annos Totum Fere Terrarum Orbem Notatis... Antwerp: Christopher Plantin, 1575. 1st Latin translation; 8vo; 114, (14) page index; woodcut printer's device on title; contemporary vellum, spine lettered by hand, some old marginal waterstains (few leaves partly discolored), but overall an excellent copy in contemporary binding. Voet Plantin press 641. Kenneth Karmiole 1NS-135 1996 $2,000.00

BENJAMIN, ASHER The Architect, or Practical House Carpenter... Boston: Sanborn, Carter, Bazin & Co., 1847 (1857). 4to; 119 pages; 64 engraved plates, institutional blindstamp, otherwise good; buckram. Hitchcock 134 indicates this to be the 1857 printing. Andrew Cahan 47-19 1996 $285.00

BENJAMIN, ASHER The Builder's Guide... Boston: Perkins & Marvin, 1839. 1st edition; 4to; 83 pages, 66 plates; later half calf, contemporary marbled sides, lacking plate 7, with extra copy of plate 5, light foxing, else very good. Bookpress 75-10 1996 $875.00

BENJAMIN, S. G. W. Contemporary Art in Europe. New York: Harper & Bros., 1877. 1st edition; 8vo; 165, (8) pages; illustrations; publisher's gilt cloth, all edges gilt, both hinges internally cracked, covers and edges rubbed, else very good. Bookpress 75-11 1996 $125.00

BENNET, E. ARNOLD A Man From the North. London: & New York: John Lane, 1989. 1st edition; author's first book; elusive white lettering on spine and cover intact; brick red cloth showing only light soil and small faint dampspot, one chip in top margin of one leaf, otherwise text is fresh, housed in morocco backed slipcase with folding wrapper, some rubbing, still dignified, on slipcase spine. Nice copy, scarce; bookplate of Perry Molstad. Wolff 391; John Quinn 461. Magnum Opus 44-39 1996 $225.00

BENNET, S. S. R. Thirty Seven Bamboos Growing in India. Dehra Dun: 1990. Folio; pages 100; 37 colored plates; cloth. Raymond M. Sutton VII-440 1996 $190.00

BENNETT, ARNOLD 1867-1931 The Bright Island. London: Golden Cockerel Press, 1924. Signed, limited edition of 200 numbered copies; tall 8vo; full vellum binding, top edge gilt, near fine, covers somewhat warped, as usual. Antic Hay 101-160 1996 $150.00

BENNETT, ARNOLD 1867-1931 Clayhanger - Hilda Lessways - These Twain. London: 1910/11/16. 1st edition; 3 volumes; spines to first two volumes faded, head of spine to 2nd title little torn down edges, otherwise the three volumes are very good. Words Etcetera 94-162 1996 £65.00

BENNETT, ARNOLD 1867-1931 Elsie and the Child. London: Cassell, 1929. 89/100 copies (of an edition of 750 copies), signed by author and artist; 4to; pages (v), 87; 7 full page illustrations and 2 further illustrations in text by E. McKnight Kauffer, color stencilled; original fawn linen, backstrip and front cover lettered and decorated in fawn and brown, usual faint browning to free endpapers, top edge gilt, others untrimmed, tissue jacket little imperfect at front cover, head and rear cover tail with matching faint marking to cover, board slipcase with printed label, good. Emery 203. Blackwell's B112-32 1996 £250.00

BENNETT, ARNOLD 1867-1931 Lillian. London: Cassell, 1922. 1st edition; boards slightly rubbed, still near fine in striking, near fine dust jacket with couple of small nicks and tears at extremities, and little foxing on spine, very nice. Between the Covers 42-46 1996 $150.00

BENNETT, ARNOLD 1867-1931 The Old Wives' Tale. London: Chapman and Hall, 1908. 1st edition; small 8vo; decorative lavender cloth, in quarter morocco leather and cloth slipcase, with gilt worked spine and five raised bands, good, ink name, minor bubbling to cloth; autograph signature of author tipped to front pastedown. Antic Hay 101-161 1996 $425.00

BENNETT, ARNOLD 1867-1931 The Old Wives' Tale. Oxford: Limited Editions Club, 1941. Copy number 904 from a total edition of 1500 numbeed copies, signed by artist; 2 volumes; illustrations by John Austen; cloth backed paper covered boards and dust jackets, fine set in lightly worn publisher's slipcase. Hermitage SP95-940 1996 $100.00

BENNETT, E. T. The Gardens and Menagerie of the Zoological Society Delineated. London: 1830-31. 2 volumes; numerous fine engravings; apart from two very small tears to half title and title of volume 2, an attractive set, tastefully bound in modern half blue morocco. David A.H. Grayling MY95Orn-8 1996 £150.00

BENNETT, EMERSON Viola; or, Adventures in the Far Southwest. Philadelphia: T. B. Emerson & Bros., 306 Chestnust ST., 1852. Probable 3rd issue; 226 pages, 17, (15) pages ads; original pattern cloth with gilt title on spine, neatly rebacked with original spine and new endsheets, very good. Wright II 285 notes 2nd issue ca. 1854. Michael D. Heaston 23-40 1996 $175.00

BENNETT, FREDERICK DEBELL Narrative of a Whaling Voyage Round the Globe... London: Richard Bentley, 1840. 1st edition; 8 1/2 x 5 3/4 inches; 2 volumes; aquatint frontispiece in each volume, folding map, several illustrations in text; contemporary rose colored smooth calf, spines repaired with considerable skill, covers framed with decorative gilt and blind rules, spines attratively gilt in compartments with elaborate foliate and floral decoration, black morocco double labels, marbled edges and endpapers; bindings just little soiled and marked, but expertly restored, completely solid and rather pleasing, very fine internally. Bookplate in each volume, pres. inscription from Richard Crawley to Brownlow Cecil on his leaving Eton, May 1844. Hill p. 22; Sabin 4726; Ferguson 2936; Forster 7. Phillip J. Pirages 33-55 1996 $2,500.00

BENNETT, JOHN Letters to a Young Lady, on a Variety of Useful and Interesting Subjects, Calculated to Improve the Heart... London: T. Cadell and W. Davies, 1812. 4th edition; 2 volumes, half titles; uncut, contemporary marbled boards, green paper spines, ruled in gilt; attractive. Jarndyce 103-613 1996 £60.00

BENNETT, JOHN B. The Evil of Theatrical Amusements, Stated and Illustrated in a Sermon, Preached in the Wesleyan Methodist Chapel, Abbey St., Dublin, on Sunday, Nov. 4, 1838. London: John Mason; John Fannin and Co., Dublin, 1839. 2nd edition; 8vo; disbound; very good, rare. NUC notes 3 copies of the first printing; LAR 576 (not seen). Ximenes 109-32 1996 $150.00

BENNETT, LERONE Before the Mayflower: a History of the Negro in America 1619-1964. Chicago: Johnson Pub. Co., 1964. Revised edition; 435 pages; fine in lightly worn, very good plus dust jacket with small chip and bit of edgewear; signed by author. Between the Covers 43-263 1996 $125.00

BENNETT, LERONE   The Shaping of Black America. Chicago: Johnson Pub. Co., 1975. 1st edition; illustrations by Charles White; fine in attractive Charles White dust jacket with couple of short tears. Inscribed by Bennett and White. Great copy.   Between the Covers 43-268 1996 $500.00

BENNETT, LERONE   What Manner of Man: A Biography of Martin Luther King Jr. Chicago: Johnson Pub. Co., 1964. 1 fine in very good dust jacket with several small chips and tears; signed by author. Between the Covers 43-266 1996 $100.00

BENNETT, NATHANIEL   The Pacific Law Magazine. January 1867. San Francisco: F. Clarke, 1867. 1st edition; 1st issue; 24 pages; original printed sewn wrappers, very worn and chipped.   Meyer Boswell SL25-13 1996 $125.00

BENNETT, PAUL A.   Bouquet for B. R. New York: Typophiles, 1950. One of 600 copies; reproductions of 7 pages designed by Bruce Rogers, 6 black and white photos; original binding, very good in plain, unprinted tissue jacket which is nicked, creased and slightly torn and browned at spine and edges; from the library of James D. Hart, loosely inserted is postcard to him from Tyophiles.   Ulysses 39-506 1996 £55.00

BENNETT, R.   The Story of Bovril. Bovril: Private printing, 1953. 1st edition; 8vo; wood engravings by Robert Gibbings; cloth, dust jacket, fine, very scarce.   C. P. Hyland 216-266 1996 £120.00

BENNETT, T. P.   Architectural Design in Concrete. London: Ernest Benn, 1927. 4to; (ii), 24, (2) pages; 100 photo plates, publisher's cloth, lower joint split.   Elton Engineering 10-9 1996 £120.00

BENNETT, WHITMAN   A Practical Guide to American Nineteenth Century Color Plate Books. New York: Bennett Book Studios, 1949. 1st edition; 8vo; xxii, 133 pages, 8 page supplement and errata slip; cloth, fine.   The Bookpress 75-270 1996 $110.00

BENNION, ELISABETH   Antique Medical Instruments. London: 1979. 1st edition; 355 pages; original binding, dust jacket. GM 5813.11.   W. Bruce Fye 71-126 1996 $100.00

BENSON, C. E.   Crag and Hound in Lakeland. London: Hurst and Blackett, 1902. 1st edition; 8vo; pages xvi, 313, 6, untrimmed, 28 illustrations; original cloth, gilt, fore-edge little spotted. Very nice. R.F.G. Hollett & Son 78-632 1996 £60.00

BENSON, D. R.   Irene, Good-Night. New York: Targ Editions, 1982. 1st edition; one of 250 copies signed by Benson and Gorey; illustrations by Edward Gorey; bound in purple Japanese silk over boards, glassine jacket has the Gorey portrait of Ms. Adler in four colors.   Priscilla Juvelis 95/1-316 1996 $175.00

BENSON, E. F.   The Life of Alcibiades. London: 1928. 1st edition; some light foxing to prelims, otherwise very good.   Words Etcetera 94-163 1996 £55.00

BENSON, HENRY C.   Life Among the Choctaw Indians and Sketches of the Southwest. Cincinnati: pub. by L. Swormstedt & A. Poe, 1860. 1st edition; 314 pages; half morocco and cloth, gilt title on spine, very good. Howes B360a; Gilcrease Hargrett Cat. p. 116.   Michael D. Heaston 23-41 1996 $250.00

BENSON, STELLA   Twenty. New York: Macmillan, 1918. 1st edition; fine in attractive, very good plus dust jacket with one modest triangular chip on front panel, nice example of fragile jacket.   Between the Covers 42-47 1996 $125.00

BENSON, THOMAS   Vocabularium Anglo-Saxonicum, Lexico Gul. somneri. Oxford: Sam Smith, 1701. 1st edition; 8vo; folding engraved frontispiece, titlepage with engraved vignette, large paper copy, edges untrimmed, occasional faint staining; original paper backed blue boards, worn at edges, some soiling to upper board; scarce.   Ian Wilkinson 95/1-30 1996 £150.00

BENSON, WILLIAM   A Letter to Sir J--- B--- (Jacob Bancks), by Birth a Swede, but Naturaliz'd and a M---4 of the Present P---5... London: printed for A. Baldwin, 1711. 1st edition; 8vo; (viii), 40 pages, including half title, disbound.   David Bickersteth 133-7 1996 £65.00

BENTHAM, G.   Flora Australiensis: a Description of the Plants of the Australian Territory. London: 1863-78. 8vo; 7 volumes; new cloth. Wheldon & Wesley 207-8 1996 £350.00

BENTHAM, JEREMY 1748-1832   Benthamiana; or, Select Extracts from the Works of Jeremy Bentham. Edinburgh: William Tait; Simpkin, Marshall, London:, John Cumming, Dublin, 1843. 1st edition of this selection; 8vo; xxiv, 419 pages, engraved portrait, apparently lacking half title; rebound in boards, printed label.   James Burmester 29-15 1996 £50.00

BENTHAM, JEREMY 1748-1832   The Elements of the Art of Packing, as Applied to to Special Juries, Particularly in Cases of Libel Law. London: pub. by Effingham Wilson, 1821. 1st published edition; 8vo; (iv), vii, (i), 269, (4 ad) pages; original green cloth backed boards, printed label, top of spine frayed, old library label at foot.   James Burmester 29-11 1996 £400.00

BENTHAM, JEREMY 1748-1832   Emancipate Your Colonies! Addressed to the National Convention of France, Ao 1793, Shewing the Uselessness and Mischievousness of Distant Dependencies to an European State. London: ptd. by C. & W. Reynell for Robert Heward, 1830 & 1793. titlepage, 48, 2 pages; disbound; very nice. Kress c2445; Goldsmiths 26210; Muirhead p. 17.   C. R. Johnson 37-50 1996 £250.00

BENTHAM, JEREMY 1748-1832   An Introduction to the Principles of Morals and Legislation. London: printed for W. Pickering and E. Wilson, 1823. 2nd edition; 8vo; 2 volumes, half titles, engraved portrait (offset onto title), nicely rebound in contemporary style quarter calf; cf. PMM 237.   James Burmester 29-12 1996 £500.00

BENTHAM, JEREMY 1748-1832   Plan of Parliamentary Reform, in the form of a Catechism, with Reasons for Each Article, with an Introduction, Shewing the Necessity of Radical... London: printed for R. Hunter, 1817. 1st edition; 8vo; slightly later 19th century half calf, spine gilt, by J. Kelly, with his miniscule ticket; slight rubbing; very good.   Ximenes 108-16 1996 $750.00

BENTHAM, JEREMY 1748-1832   Plan of Parliamentary Reform, in the Form of a Catechism... London: T. J. Wooler, 1818. 2nd edition; 8vo; few spots and stains in text, later 19th century morocco backed boards, spine slightly worn.   Anthony W. Laywood 108-150 1996 £125.00

BENTHAM, JEREMY 1748-1832   Supply Without Burthen; or Escheat Vice Taxation: Being a Proposal for a Saving in Taxes by an Extension of the law of Escheat... to which is prefixed A Protest Against Law Taxes, Shewing the Peculiar Mischievousness of All Such Impositions... London: printed for J. Debrett, 1795/93. 1st edition; 8vo; disbound; scarce, complete and in excellent condition; signed on titlepage by Dudley North (1748-1829). Kress B2287.   Ximenes 108-17 1996 $1,500.00

BENTHAM, JEREMY 1748-1832   The Works of Jeremy Bentham. Edinburgh: William Tait, 107 Prince Street, 1843. 11 volumes; contemporary morocco, extra gilt, worn, joints cracked, clean only. Meyer Boswell SL25-14 1996 $1,500.00

BENTLEY, RICHARD   The Works. London: Francis MacPherson, 1836-38. 8vo; 3 volumes; xxii, 430; (iv), 402; xvi, 546 pages; half titles; contemporary calf, old rebacks, spines gilt, labels, rubbed, corners worn, small library stickers on spines, inoffensive blindstamp on corner of titles and many text pages, no other markings; uncommon; serviceable set.   Robert Clark 38-158 1996 £125.00

BENTLEY, WILLIAM   Catalogue of the Part of the Late Dr. Bentley's Library, Not Bequeathed to Literary Institutions, to be sold at Auction, on Wednesday and Thursday, June 14, and 15, 1820, at 9 o'clock A.M. and 3 P.M. at Blake & Cunningham's Office... Boston: printed by Crocker & Brewster, 1820. 8vo; disbound; very good. McKay 188; Shoemaker 397. Ximenes 108-10 1996 $500.00

BENTLY, JOHN   A Book of Discarded Things. London: Liver & Lights, 1992. 1st edition; one of 53 copies only, each unique, on various papers; page size 4 13/16 x 4 1/16 inches; letterpress by author, paper collages, ink stamps, photocopy; wood boards with collage of 'found' objects on front panel and paper collage of discarded items on back panel, red grosgrain ribbon ties, exposed spine;   Priscilla Juvelis 95/1-27 1996 $550.00

BEOWULF   Ellor-Gast. Eight Anglo-Saxon texts from Beowulf with translations by the Artist. Red Hen Press, 1986. One of 40 numbered copies, signed by artist, square folio; printed by Shirley Jones in dark green in handset 18 and 12 pt. Baskerville, the Anglo Saxon in red, on specially made Moulin du Verger; bound by Jan Ascoli in half dark green morocco, matching fore-edges, sides covered in coarsely textured handmade paper incorporating areas of fine black and green mesh; fine in cloth box.   Bertram Rota 272-235 1996 £900.00

BERBEROVA, NINA   The Italics Are Mine. New York: HB&W, 1969. 1st edition; very good+ in dust jacket; inscribed by author.   Lame Duck Books 19-74 1996 $650.00

BERENSON, BERNARD   Lorenzo Lotto. Paintings and Drawings. London: Phaidon Press, 1956. 27 x 19 cm; xiv, 477 pages; 400 illustrations; original cloth, in dust jacket, very slightly torn.   Rainsford A54-381 1996 £80.00

BERENSON, BERNARD   Three Essays in Method. Oxford University Press, 1927. 1st edition; 4to; xxii, 139 pages; frontispiece, 133 illustrations; original decorated cloth, spine chipped, ex-library with rubber stamps on f.e.p. and remains of label.   Rainsford A54-659 1996 £75.00

BERESFORD, J. D.   The Hampdenshire Wonder. S&J, 1911. 1st edition; good/very good; inscribed by author to a close friend at time of publication.   Aronovitz 57-117 1996 $375.00

BERGER, THOMAS   Crazy in Berlin. New York: Charles Scribners, 1958. 1st edition; near fine with some offsetting to free endpapers and neat signature, in crudely tape repaired and price clipped dust jacket. Bev Chaney, Jr. 23-81 1996 $100.00

BERGER, THOMAS   Little Big Man. New York: Dial, 1964. 1st edition; fine in very good dust jacket with few small edge tears, some crimping to spine (endemic to this title) and modest rubbing, nice, with much less of the fading to dust jacket spine than is usually the case; signed by author.   Ken Lopez 74-30 1996 $350.00

BERGER, THOMAS   Little Big Man. New York: Dial, 1964. 1st edition; near fine in like jacket, with some crimping to spine and bit of mild rubbing, much nicer than usual.   Ken Lopez 74-31 1996 $250.00

BERGERAT, EMILE   A Wild Sheep Chase. New York: Macmillan, 1894. 8vo; 315 pages; with original photos of author (signed by him) tipped in; original maroon cloth, small decoration in gilt on upper cover; marks on pastedown from removal of bookplate, newspaper clipping on endpaper, slight rubbing at spine ends, otherwise near fine.   David Mason 71-78 1996 $100.00

BERGMAN, S.   In Korean Wilds and Villages. London: 1938. 8vo; pages (vi), 232, map and numerous photos; cloth, faded.   Wheldon & Wesley 207-360 1996 £55.00

BERINGTON, SIMON   The Adventures of Sigr. Gaudentio di Lucca. London: printed for W. Innys and R. Manby and H. S. Cox, 1748. 2nd edition; 8vo; pages xii, 24, 291; contemporary calf, neatly rebacked, very light foxing in places, still very good.   James Fenning 133-23 1996 £145.00

BERKELEY, EDMUND CALLIS   Giant Brains; or Machines that Think. New York: John Wiley and Sons, 1949. 1st edition; 8vo; xvi, 270 pages; 77 figures in text; original cloth, very good. Sarrazin J1. Shiers 1099. Edwin V. Glaser 121-23 1996 $135.00

BERKELEY, G. F. H.   Italy in the Making 1815-48. Cambridge University Press, 1968. Octavo; 3 volumes; 14 maps, 2 folding in pocket; bukcram.   Howes Bookshop 265-63 1996 £65.00

BERKELEY, GEORGE CHARLES GRANTLEY FITZHARDINGE   Sandron Hall, or the Days of Queen Anne. London: Henry Colburn, 1840. 1st edition; 12mo; 3 volumes; later green morocco, gilt, spines gilt, some fading, slight rubbing; very good. Block p. 20; Wolff 408.   Ximenes 108-18 1996 $275.00

BERKELEY, GEORGE MONCK 1763-1793   Literary Relics: Containing Original Letters from King Charles II. King James II. The Queen of Bohemia, Swift, Berkeley, Addison, Steele, Congreve, the Duke of Ormond and Bishop Rundle. London: for C. Elliot and T. Kay and C. Elliot, Edinburgh, 1789. 1st edition; 8vo; pages lvi, 415, half title; uncut in original blue-grey paper boards, skilfully rebacked to style; presentation copy to the fourth Duke of Marlborough, with Berkeley's autograph inscription; presentation copy; bookplate and added ownership inscription of the fourth Duke's youngest son, Lord Francis Almeric Spencer. Teerink 120; Rothschild 385.   Simon Finch 24-222 1996 £175.00

BERKELEY, GEORGE, BP. OF CLOYNE 1685-1753   The Works of... Oxford: 1871. 8vo; 3 volumes, over 1500 pages; purple cloth, spines faded, otherwise good, sound set.   K Books 441-371 1996 £60.00

BERKELEY, GRANTLEY F.   Reminiscences of a Huntsman. London: Longman, Brown, Green and Longmans, 1854. 1st edition; octavo; xi, 415 pages, plus 24 pages ads; hand colored frontispiece and 3 engraved plates; bound by Riviere & Son, in full red levant morocco, gilt lettered spine with raised bands, gilt board edges and inner dentelles, top edge gilt, marbled endpapers, scattered light foxing; armorial bookplate; very good. Schwerdt I p. 61.   Heritage Book Shop 196-198 1996 $400.00

BERKELEY, M. J.   Handbook of British Mosses. London: 1863. 1st edition; 23 hand colored paltes, 1 plain plate; near fine.   David A.H. Grayling MY95Orn-9 1996 £50.00

BERKENHOUT, J.   Outlines of the Natural History of Great Britain and Ireland. London: 1769-72. 2nd and 3rd editions; 8vo; 3 volumes; contemporary calf backed boards, neatly rebacked, uncut. Rare. Wheldon & Wesley 207-9 1996 £300.00

BERKENHOUT, JOHN   Clavis Anglica Linguae Botanicae; or, a Botanical Lexicon. London: Cadell, 1789. 2nd edition; 8vo; ca. 300 pages; contemporary calf, speckled and somewhat rubbed, front hinge loose; foxed on titlepage, otherwise nice, clean copy. Henrey 442.   Second Life Books 103-21 1996 $225.00

BERLIN IRON BRIDGE CO.   The Berlin Iron Bridge Co., Engineers, Architects and Builders in Iron and Steel. East Berlin: n.d., c. 1895. Oblong 8vo; 317, (1) pages, many fine wood engraved illustrations; seemly modern cloth.   Elton Engineering 10-11 1996 £260.00

BERLIN IRON BRIDGE CO.   The Berlin Iron Bridge Company. A Trade Catalogue. East Berlin: Berlin Iron Bridge Co., 1889. Oblong 8vo; 127, (3) pages, final leaf in facsimile, many wood engraved illustrations; limp crimson leather boards, very worn, original printed front wrpaper bound in, original back wrapper in facsimile; from the library of J. G. James. Elton Engineering 10-10 1996 £150.00

BERLIN, IRON BRIDGE CO.   Berlin Bridges and Buildings. East Berlin: for the Company, 1898/99. 4to; 11 issues; original printed wrappers, lower wrapper of number 9/ll lacking; boxed.   Elton Engineering 10-12 1996 £280.00

BERLIN, ISAIAH   Historical Inevitability. London: Oxford University Press, 1954. 1st edition; wrappers, yapp edges creased, nicked and slightly chipped, covers slightly marked and creased, head and tail of spine and corners bumped; very good; presentation copy from author to John Sparrow.   Ulysses 39-48 1996 £95.00

BERNACCHI, L. C.   Saga of the 'Discovery'. London: and Glasgow: Blackie & Son Ltd., 1938. 8vo; xv, 240 pages, 3 maps, many photo plates; blue cloth, edges foxed, else very good. Spence 129.   Parmer Books Nat/Hist-051137 1996 $125.00

BERNAL, RALPH   Illustrated Catalogue of the Distinguished Collection of Works of Art and Vertu, from the Byzantine Period to that of Louis Seize Collected by the Late Ralph Bernal, Esq. London: for J. H. Burn, 1855. 4to; Large paper copy printed on thick paper, with additional general titlepage and frontispiece, (2), 357, (1), 66, (2) pages, frontispiece, plates, loosely inserted is a printed petition from P. Le Neve Foster of the Society for the Encouragement of Arts, Manufactures and Commerce, Requesting for the Collection to be Purchased for the Nations; there is also an associated letter from Le Neve Foster to Augustus Franks, keeper of the Dept. of British & Medieval Antiquities at the British Museum; although unsigned, this would suggest this is Frank's copy of the catalog; some occasional foxing, but good copy, bound by Riviere in later 19th century half brown morocco, several small repairs to joints and corners and also to the marbled paper on board edges.   Ken Spelman 30-46 1996 £360.00

BERNARD, AUGUSTE   Geofroy Tory, Painter and Engraver: First Royal Printer: Reformer of Orthography and Typography Under Francois I. 1969. Reprint of 1909 edition; small folio; pages (22), 332, (8); illustrations; original cloth, gilt, excellent copy.   James Fenning 133-340 1996 £55.00

BERNARD, CLAUDE   An Introduction to the Study of Experimental Medicine. New York: 1927. 1st English translation; 226 pages; original binding, ex-library, but fine. GM 1766.501.   W. Bruce Fye 71-134 1996 $100.00

BERNARD, DAVID   A Revelation of Free Masonry, As Published to the World by a Convention of Seceding Masons, Held at Le Roy, Genesee County, New York. Rochester: Weed & Heron, 1828. 1st edition; 16mo; 7, 107 pages; contemporary plain wrappers, last leaf torn with loss of perhaps a dozen words on recto, nicely rebacked. Shoemaker 32820. M & S Rare Books 60-369 1996 $450.00

BERNARD, M.   The Praise of Hell-or A Discovery of the Infernal World Describing the Advantages of that Place, with Regards to Its Situation, Antiquity and Duration, with a Particular Account of Its Inhabitants, Their Dresses, Customs, Manners, Occupations & Diversions... London: 1765. 1st edition in English; 19th century leather; nice.   Aronovitz 57-119 1996 $175.00

BERNARD, PHILIPPA   Antiquarian Books: a Companion for Booksellers, Librarians and Collectors. England: Scholar Press, 1994. 1st edition; small 4to; illustrations; boards, dust jacket. New.   James S. Jaffe 34-72 1996 $125.00

BERNARD, PIERRE JOSEPH   Oeuvres... Paris: P. Didot l'aine, 1797. 4 engraved plates after Pierre-Paul Prud-Hon; full morocco by Riviere, original wrappers bound in, light rubbing to joints, still a beautiful copy, handsomely bound. Cohen de Ricci 133-134; Lewine 54.   Marilyn Braiterman 15-170 1996 $1,750.00

BERNARDUS, CARTHUSIENSIS   Dialogus Virginis Mariae Misericordiam Elucidans. Leipzig: Melchior Lotter, 1497. Quarto; 19th century boards, lightly worn, bookplate, minor embrowning and waterstaining, final leaf backed, stamp partially removed on blank lower portion of short title leaf, few neat annotations and sentence here and there underlined. Hain 2841; GW 3903; Goff B361.   G. W. Stuart 59-51 1996 $3,500.00

BERNERS, GERALD HUGH TYRWHITT-WILSON   Percy Wallingford and Mr. Pidger. Oxford: Basil Blackwell, 1941. 1st edition; original binding, spine and cover edges browned, covers slightly marked, rubbed and dusty, very good.   Ulysses 39-49 1996 £125.00

BERNERS, JULIANA   A Treatyse of Fysshynge wyth an Angle. Ashendene Press, 1903. One of 20 copies for sale on vellum (there were also 150 on paper); 7 3/4 x 5 1/2 inches; 48 pages, plus 5 vellum blanks at front and 5 at back; one nearly full page reproduction of a 15th century woodcut, one initial in red, several small illustrations in text, device in colophon; contemporary black morocco by Katherine Adams (signed "K/A 1904" on rear turn-in), spine almost invisibly repaired (nature and extent of restoration are uncertain because the work is so skillfully done), raised bands, front cover and top spine compartment with gilt titling, gilt ruled turn-ins; fine.   Phillip J. Pirages 33-24 1996 $4,500.00

BERNHARD, RUTH   The Eternal Body: a Collection of 50 Nudes. Carmel: 1986. 1st edition; square large 4to; dust jacket partially sunned and rubbed at edges; elusive.   J. B. Muns 154-35 1996 $400.00

BERNHARDT, SARAH   Dans les Nuages. Impressions d'une Chaise. Paris: Charpentier, 1878. Quarto; illustrations by Georges Clarin; period half leather, rather worn; internally very good with original wrappers bound in; inscribed by Bernhardt.   Lame Duck Books 19-75 1996 $1,250.00

BERNOULLI, JAKOB   Ars Conjectandi, Opus Posthumum. Basel: Impensis Thurnisiorum, Fratrum, 1713. 1st edition; small quarto; (4), 306, 35, (1 errata) pages; 2 folding tables, 1 folding plate; 19th century full green calf, gilt single rule border on covers, gilt decorated spine wtih red morocco label, gilt board edges, few leaves slightly browned, otherwise excellent; ink signature of Theod. Dotrenge, and his handwritten notes at foot of page 78 and on recto and verso of back free endpaper. Dibner 110; Horblit 12; PMM 179.   Heritage Book Shop 196-177 1996 $9,500.00

BERNSTEIN, ALINE   Three Blue Suits. New York: Equinox Cooperative Press 1933. One of 600 copies only, signed by author; octavo; original cloth, original printed paper labels, very slightly worn, spine grifle sunned; fine, uncommon, author's first book.   G. W. Stuart 59-16 1996 $165.00

BEROALDO, FILIPPO   Declamatio Lepidissima Ebriosi, Scortatoris,, et Aleatoris de Vitiositate Disceptantium. Bologna: Benedictus Hectoris, 1499. 1st edition; quarto; modern vellum boards, inner blank edge of title leaf restored, few other inner blank margins guarded, minor spot or two, lightly washed, nice; rare. Hain 2965; GW 4130. Goff B 471.   G. W. Stuart 59-52 1996 $4,950.00

BEROALDUS, PHILIPPUS   Declamatio Lepidissima Ebriosi Scortatoris Aleatoris de Vitiositate Disceptanium. Bologna: a Benedicto Hectoris, 1499. 1st edition; 4to; 20 unnumbered leaves, Roman letter, 27 lines and headline per page, printed side notes, printer's large white on black device on rector of last, very good, clean, well margined copy; full modern calf antique, panels gilt and blind on covers; BMC VI 845; GKW 4131; Goff B472.   A. Sokol XXV-13 1996 $2,950.00

BERQUIN, ARNAUD   The Looking-Glass for the Mind; or Intellectual Mirror... London: printed for J. Harris, successor to E. Newbery, 1803. 9th edition; 12mo; 74 woodcuts by John Bewick, contemporary sheep, hinges cracked, label. Hugo 66; Pease 57.   Anthony W. Laywood 108-152 1996 £50.00

BERQUIN, ARNAULD   The Friend of Youth. London: printed for C. Dilly, J. Stockdale, T. and J. Egerton and W. Creech... 1788. 1st English edition; 12mo; 2 volumes; name on titles, engraved frontispieces (partly hand colored); contemporary sheep, rubbed, hinges cracked, labels. Anthony Laywood 108-28 1996 £110.00

BERRIGAN, DANIEL   Lost and Found. Montclair: Calliban Press, 1989. 1st edition; one of 125 numbered copie, signed by artist and author; printed on handmade paper from the Capelledes Paper Mill in Barcelona, in monotype Centaur and Arrighi; maps and drawings; bound in terracotta boards printed in black with Tim's drawing/map printed on front, fine.   Priscilla Juvelis 95/1-28 1996 $125.00

BERRIGAN, DANIEL   Lost and Found: a Story. Montclair: Caliban Press, 1989. One of 125 copies, numbered in the press, signed by author and artist; 8vo; printed in Centaur and Arrighi on Spanish handmade paper, boards with cloth spine, five colored illustrations by Timothy Ely; fine.   Bertram Rota 272-55 1996 £55.00

BERRY, DON   A Majority of Scoundrels: an Informal History of the Rocky Mountain Fur Company. New York: Harper & Bros., 1961. 1st edition; 432 pages; illustrations; folding maps in rear pocket; fine with lightly chipped dust jacket.   Argonaut Book Shop 113-67 1996 $125.00

BERRY, R. J.   The Natural History of Orkney. London: Collins, 1985. So called "Second issue" which is in fact the wrappered edition with cloth binding, issued when the smaller than usual print run of the first hard-back issue ran out; both issues scarce; pages 304, 20 colored plates, over 100 black and white plates and diagrams; original cloth, gilt, dust jacket.   R.F.G. Hollett 76-21 1996 £80.00

BERRY, R. J.   The Natural History of Shetland. London: Collins, 1980. 1st edition; very scarce true first issue; 8vo; pages 380, 29 colored and 44 black and whtie photos and 47 line drawings; mint, original cloth, gilt, dust jacket.   R.F.G. Hollett 76-22 1996 £130.00

BERRY, R. J.   The Natural History of Shetland. London: Collins, 1980. 1st edition; 2nd issue; 8vo; pages 380; 29 colored and 44 black and white photos and 47 line drawings; original cloth, gilt, dust jacket; scarce.   R.F.G. Hollett 76-23 1996 £85.00

BERRY, W. TURNER   Catalogue of Specimens of Printing Types by English and Scottish Printers and Founders 1665-1830. Oxford University Press, 1935. 4to; liv, 98 pages; 24 plates, original cloth backed boards, edges uncut.   Thomas Thorp 489-27 1 996 £100.00

BERRY, WENDELL   An Eastward Look. Berkeley: Sand Dollar, 1974. 1st edition; one of 25 copies, printed on mould made paper and signed by Berry out of a total edition of 376; thin 8vo; original wrappers; fine. James S. Jaffe 34-27 1996 $225.00

BERRY, WENDELL   Findings. Poems. Iowa City: Prairie Press, 1969. 1st edition; 8vo; cloth backed decorated boards, dust jacket; fine. James S. Jaffe 34-24 1996 $100.00

BERRY, WENDELL   The Memory of Old Jack. New York: Harcourt Brace Jovanovich, 1974. 1st edition; review copy with slip laid in; cloth, dust jacket; fine.   James S. Jaffe 34-28 1996 $150.00

BERRY, WENDELL   November Twenty-Six Nineteen Hundred Sixty Three. New York: Braziller, 1964. 1st edition; one of an unspecified number of copies, signed by Shahn and Berry; oblong large 8vo; 1 tipped in color plate, 12 black and white illustrations by Ben Shahn, white cloth, stamped black on spine and upper cover, fine, publisher's black cloth slipcase, with printed paper label. Bound by Haddon Craftsmen.   George J. Houle 68-76 1996 $350.00

BERRY, WENDELL   November Twenty-Six Nineteen Hundred Sixty Three. New York: Braziller, 1964. Limited edition (limitation not stated) with tipped in plate by Shahn and signed by author and artist; illustrations by Ben Shahn; fine in partially sun faded slipcase.   Ken Lopez 74-32 1996 $300.00

BERRY, WENDELL   November Twenty Six Nineteen Hundred Sixty Three. New York: Braziller, 1964. Limited edition; quarto; (16)ff; on handmade Fabriano paper, signed by author and artist; lettered by Shahn, with his drawings on each verso and one tipped in color plates; fine in linen boards lettered by Shahn, in slipcase with matching printed label.   Bromer Booksellers 90-222 1996 $225.00

BERRY, WENDELL   Sayings and Doings and an Eastward Look. Frankfort: Gnomon Press, 1990. 1st edition; one of 50 copies, signed by Berry; 8vo; cloth, as new.   James S. Jaffe 34-36 1996 $125.00

BERRY, WENDELL   There Is a Singing Around Me. Austin: Cold Mountain Press, 1976. 1st edition; one of 26 lettered copies; from a total edition of 326 copies; 8vo; printed on Iyo Glazed paper; bound in boards; as new.   James S. Jaffe 34-32 1996 $250.00

BERRY, WENDELL   Three Memorial Poems. Berkeley: Sand Dollar Books, 1977. 1st edition; one of 100 copies, signed by author; 8vo; cloth, printed labels, glassine dust jacket, fine in jacket with one closed tear.   James S. Jaffe 34-34 1996 $125.00

BERRYMAN, JOHN 1914-1972   Homage to Mistress Bradstreet. New York: Farrar, Straus and Cudahy, 1956. 1st edition; 1st printing; 10 illustrations by Ben Shahn; decorated boards, extremely fine, matching dust jacket. Stefanik A7.1.a.   Bromer Booksellers 90-6 1996 $250.00

BERRYMAN, JOHN 1914-1972   Homage to Mistress Bradstreet. New York: Farrar, Straus & Cudahy, 1956. 1st edition; 8vo; pictorial boards, dust jacket; very fine.   James S. Jaffe 34-39 1996 $175.00

BERRYMAN, JOHN 1914-1972   Homage to Mistress Bradstreet. New York: Farrar, Straus & Cudahy, 1956. 1st edition; pictures by Ben Shahn; beautiful copy in dust jacket, very fine.   Left Bank Books 2-11 1996 $165.00

BERRYMAN, JOHN 1914-1972   Love and Fame. New York: Farrar Straus Giroux, 1970. 1st edition; limited to 250 copies, signed by author; 8vo; marbled endpapers, cloth, all edges gilt, acetate dust jacket, slipcase; very fine.   James S. Jaffe 34-42 1996 $250.00

BERRYMAN, JOHN 1914-1972   Love and Fame. New York: Farrar, Straus & Giroux, 1970. 1/250 numbered copies, signed by Berryman; just a trace of rubbing to spine, otherwise fine, with tight hinges in publisher's box.   Left Bank Books 2-10 1996 $225.00

BERRYMAN, JOHN 1914-1972   Poems. Norfolk: New Directions, 1942. 1st edition; one of 500 copies of the hardbound issue; 8vo; fine in equally fine dust jacket.   Lakin & Marley 3-1 1996 $450.00

BERRYMAN, JOHN 1914-1972   77 Dream Songs. London: Faber & Faber, 1964. 1st British edition; fine in dust jacket, laid in is a 1967 Dublin Poetry Season program featuring Berryman; inscribed by author to poet Dan Gerber in 1967.   Captain's Bookshelf 38-16 1996 $300.00

BERTOLDI, GIUSEPPE   Memoirs of the Secret Societies of the South of Italy, Particulary the Carbonari. London: John Murray, 1821. 1st edition; demy 8vo; (xvi), (236), pages; frontispiece, 11 litho plates and facsimiles, some folding; contemporary calf, gilt, compartments worked in blind, lacks half title, little rubbed and marked, some slight browning, nonetheless a nice copy.   Ash Rare Books Zenzybyr-11 1996 £195.00

BERTRAM, JAMES G.   The Harvest of the Sea. London: John Murray, 1865. 1st edition; 8vo; xvi, 519 pages, including wood engraved frontispiece, wood engraved text illustrations, 32 page publisher's catalog at end, illustrations; original green cloth, blocked in gilt; excellent copy. James Burmester 29-16 1996 £90.00

BERTRAMUS   The Book of Bertram the Priest, Concerning the Body and Blood of Christ in the Sacrament... London: B. Griffin, to be sold by Sam. Keble, 1686. 3rd edition; 12mo; (xxxvi), 96, (viii) pages; frontispiece, 8 page catalog at end; contemporary sheep, ruled in blind, remains of old paper label; neat old repairs to spine ends, corners slightly worn, front endpaper renewed. Good copy. Wing B2049BA (Tulane only for this issue).   Robert Clark 38-7 1996 £90.00

BERVE, HELMUT   Greek Temples, Theaters and Shrines. New York: Harry N. Abrams, 1962. Folio; 508 pages; 154 figures, 212 plates (36 in color, tipped in); original cloth, dust jacket.   Archaeologia Luxor-2992 1996 $350.00

BESANCON, FRANCE.   Ordonnances, Reglemens et Status es Arts & Metiers de la Cite Royale de Besancon. Besancon: Louis Rigoine, 1689. 4to; 146 pages, (2) leaves, woodcut device on title, woodcut head and tailpieces; contemporary calf, rubbed. Rare.   Jeffrey D. Mancevice 20-13 1996 $1,600.00

BESANT, WALTER   London. New York: Harper & Bros., 1892. 1st American edition; demy 8vo; (xvi), (510) pages; contemporary half morocco, banded and gilt, top edge gilt, touch sunned, few leaves slightly bumped, but very good.   Ash Rare Books Zenzybyr-12 1996 £125.00

BESCHKE, WILLIAM   The Dreadful Sufferings and Thrilling Adventures of an Overland Party of Emigrants to California, Their Terrible conflicts with Savage Tribes of Indians!! St. Louis: Barclay & Co., 1850. 1st edition; 1st issue? 8vo; 60 pages; five full page text illustrations; original printed and pictorial wrappers; splendid copy. Howes B396; Graff 11; Wagner Camp 171.1. Wright I 308.   M & S Rare Books 60-120 1996 $5,000.00

BESSON, MAURICE   The Scourge of the Indies Buccaneers, Corsairs and Filibusters. London: George Routledge & Sons, 1929. Limited edition; one of 960 copies; quarto; 5 full page hand colored reproductions of antique plates, printed by letterpress on slick paper, maps, text illustrations; brick red cloth.   Glenn Books 36-24 1996 $175.00

BEST, THOMAS   A Concise Treatise on the Art of Angling. London: 1992. One of 175 copies; 2 color plates, text drawings; cloth backed boards title labels on spine and upper cover, printed on handmade paper; bound by Mary Parry.   David A.H. Grayling 3/95-571 1996 £75.00

BEST, THOMAS   A Concise Treatise on the Art of Angling... Market Drayton: Tern Press, 1992. One in an edition of 175 copies, numbered and signed by Mary Parry; 10 x 6.25 inches; etchings and printing by Nicholas Parry, Caslon type, arranged in style of original, set by Bill Hughes on Arches paper; bound by Mary Parry in green and yellow decorated paper with toning cloth spine, paper title label on front cover and spine, brown endpapers; fine.   Joshua Heller 21-250 1996 $145.00

BEST, WILLIAM   The Merit and Reward of a Good Intention. London: printed for W. Innys, 1742. 1st edition; 4to; disbound;; fine, outer edges uncut, very scarce. Sabin 5054; European Americana 742/15.   Ximenes 108-19 1996 $250.00

BESTER, A.   The Demolished Man. Shasta, 1953. 1st edition; fine in like white dust jacket with 3 short closed tears.   Aronovitz 57-120 1996 $350.00

BETHAM, MARY MATILDA   A Biographical Dictionary of the Celebrated Women of Every Age and Country. London: for B. Crosby & Co.; Tegg & Castleman, 1804. 1st edition; post 12mo. variant, the 22 line errata list is virtually identical to the 24 lines of the regular octavo; vi, 774 pages; frontispiece; contemporary half calf, red label, little worn, some slight wear and few marks, but good.   Ash Rare Books Zenzybyr-13 1996 £185.00

BETHEL, SLINGSBY   The Interest of the Princes and States of Europe. London: printed by J. M. for John Wickins, 1681. 2nd edition; small hole in L1 affecting a few letters, contemporary mottled calf, hinges cracked. Kress 1508 (1st ed.); Goldsmith 2439; Wing B2065.   Anthony Laywood 108-3 1996 £125.00

BETJEMAN, JOHN 1906-1984   Collected Poems. London: Murray, 1958. 1st edition; book near fine, jacket slightly chipped at top and bottom of spine, still very good.   Priscilla Juvelis 95/1-29 1996 $200.00

BETJEMAN, JOHN 1906-1984   Ghastly Good Taste. London: Chapman and Hall, 1933. 1st edition; 8vo; folding panorama, chart, xii, 136 pages + errata slip; publisher's cloth backed decorated pink boards, paper label on spine, boards and spine slightly worn, label on spine appears to be a spare one.   Thomas Thorp 489-28 1996 £60.00

BETJEMAN, JOHN 1906-1984   Ghastly Good Taste - or, a Depressing Story of the Rise and Fall of English Architecture. London: Anthony Blond Ltd., 1970. Re-issue; one of 200 numbere copies, signed by author; folding 9 foot panorama at rear; morocco backed boards, leather spine slightly rubbed and marked, near fine in slightly marked and bumped matching slipcase.   Ulysses 39-52 1996 £180.00

THE BETRAYL of the Left. London: Gollancz, LBC, 1941. 1st edition; paper boards; nice.   Ian Patterson 9-193 1996 £75.00

BETTERTON, THOMAS   The Life of Mr. Thomas Betterton, the Late Eminent Tragedian... London: Robert Gosling, 1710. Small 8vo; 2 parts in 1, 176, 88 pages; frontispiece; rebound in full blue morocco (circa 1900), gilt.   Kenneth Karmiole 1NS-237 1996 $200.00

BETTRIDGE, WILLIAM   A Brief History of the Church in Upper Canada... London: printed and Published by W. E. Painter, 1838. 1st edition; 8vo; 143 pages; disbound. Staton & Tremaine 2128.   David Bickersteth 133-137 1996 £55.00

BETTS, DORIS   The Gentle Insurrection and Other Stories. New York: G. P. Putnam's Sons, 1954. 1st edition; author's first book; very good+ in dust jacket which is slightly worn at spine ends and lightly soiled on rear panel.   Steven C. Bernard 71-23 1996 $125.00

BEURDELEY, MICHEL   The Chinese Collector Through the Centuries from the Han to the 20th Century. Fribourg: Ofice du Livre, 1966. 4to; 287 pages; 24 plates in color, 301 black and white illustrations; original linen over thick boards.   Howes Bookshop 265-2293 1996 £85.00

BEVERIDGE, ALBERT J.   The Life of John Marshall. Boston: Houghton Mifflin, 1919. 4 volumes; three quarter dark maroon morocco, bit rubbed, but attractive set.   Meyer Boswell SL26-14 1996 $450.00

BEVERIDGE, W. H.   Unemployment - a Problem of Industry. London: Longmans, Green and Co., 1931. Reprint; original binding, top edge dusty, covers rubbed and marked, free endpapers browned, spine darkened, head and tail of spine slightly bumped, free endpaeprs browned and spotted, very good; with ownership signature of J. H. Lascelles, dated Balliol 3.8.32. Bookplate of late owner.   Ulysses 39-53 1996 £65.00

BEVERLY, BOB   Hobo of the Rangeland. Lovingston: n.d. 1st edition; 27 pages; stiff paper wrpapers, very good+. Very Scarce. Herd 257. 6 Guns 206.   T. A. Swinford 49-99 1996 $250.00

BEWICK, ELIZABETH   Comfort Me with Apples and Other Poems. Florin Press, 1987. One of 135 numbered copies, signed by author and artist; narrow 4to; printed in black, with apple green on titlepage, in Joanna and Rockwell Light on English mouldmade; 9 wood engravings by Graham Williams; patterned cloth over boards, leather lettering piece, fine in slipcase.   Bertram Rota 272-154 1996 £85.00

BEWICK, THOMAS 1753-1828   A General History of Quadrupeds. Newcastle-upon-Tyne: 1790. 1st edition; 8vo; pages viii, 456, 200 figures, 103 vignettes, tailpieces, etc., half calf; rare; titlepage slighty foxed, but good, uncut, contemporary binding, very neatly rebacked.   Wheldon & Wesley 207-542 1996 £250.00

BEWICK, THOMAS 1753-1828   A General History of Quadrupeds. London: 1791. 2nd edition; pages x, 483, 212 figures of quadrupeds, 1 text figure and 103 vignettes and tailpieces; calf, rebacked, preserving label, 2 tears repaired at 284-85.   John Henly 27-35 1996 £90.00

BEWICK, THOMAS 1753-1828   A General History of Quadrupeds. London: 1811. 6th edition; many woodcuts; contents slightly browned/foxed, title and one one page bit grubby; nicely bound in modern half morocco.   David A.H. Grayling MY95Orn-462 1996 £120.00

BEWICK, THOMAS 1753-1828   History of British Birds. 2 volumes; numerous engravings; bookplates, otherwise extremely nice. Limestone Hills 41-148 1996 $225.00

BEWICK, THOMAS 1753-1828   History of British Birds. Newcastle-upon-Tyne: 1797. 2nd edition, but actually published in 1798; imperial 8vo; contemporary straight grain dark blue morocco, gilt. Indelicate woodcut at p. 285 has been partly inked over, but is not fully obscured.   Wheldon & Wesley 207-644 1996 £180.00

BEWICK, THOMAS 1753-1828   A History of British Birds. London: 1809-21. 3 volumes; many woodcuts, 4 pages of introduction in volume 1 have a corner tear repaired, which has browned; apart from this blemish, an attractive set, uniformly bound in modern half sprinkled calf. David A.H. Grayling MY95Orn-10 1996 £300.00

BEWICK, THOMAS 1753-1828   A History of British Birds. London: 1809. 8vo; 2 parts in 1 volume; binder's cloth, trifle loose, some signs of use, little browning and spotting. Roscoe 20.   Wheldon & Wesley 207-645 1996 £130.00

BEWICK, THOMAS 1753-1828   Thomas Bewick's ABC. New York: Triptych 1926. Limited to 99 copies; 2 1/8 x 1 3/4 inches; (31)ff.; 24 zinc etchings; bound in color patterned boards with original printed paper label; bookplate, fine, scarce.   Bromer Booksellers 90-176 1996 $350.00

BEWICK, THOMAS 1753-1828   The Watercolours and Drawings of Thomas Bewick. USA: 1981. Oblong 4to; numerous color and other illustrations; mint in original slipcase.   David A.H. Grayling MY95Orn-11 1996 £80.00

BEWICK, THOMAS 1753-1828   Wood Engravings. Newcastle-upon-Tyne: Charlotte Press, 1978. Limited to 250 copies; 5 original blocks; fine in original folder and envelope.   Words Etcetera 94-186 1996 £50.00

BIBLE. ARABIC - 1776   (Arabic Gospels). Lebanon: Convent of Mar Jouana, Mt. Kerouan, 1776. Folio; 2ff., 315 pages, printed in red and black with numerous ornaments, 4 engraved portraits; contemporary red goatskin, gilt and blindstamped (slightly rubbed); rare Lebanese monastic binding.   Marlborough 160-30 1996 £1,750.00

BIBLE. BLACKFOOT - 1890   The Gospel According to St. Matthew. London: British and Foreign Bible Society, 1890. 1st edition; 109 pages; original brown cloth over stiff boards, Matthew embossed on front cover, hinges repaired, fine overall.   Michael D. Heaston 23-53 1996 $225.00

BIBLE. CREE - 1876   The New Testament Translated Into the Cree Language. London: printed for the British and Foreign Bible Society, 1876. 8vo; pages (ii), 425; contemporary calf, hinges loose, section of spine missing, interior clean and crisp; inscribed by J. L. Colter, Ruperts House, 1877 to Prof. John Galbraith. Banks p. 38; Evans 80; Peel 437. Hugh Anson-Cartwright 87-309 1996 $275.00

BIBLE. ENGLISH -   The Large-Print Paragraph Bible...The New Testament. London: Samuel Bagster and Sons, n.d. 8vo; numerous colored maps and colored view; original publisher's roan, gilt lettered in gilt, gilt edges, covers worn, preserved in black cloth fall-down back box with leather label; Robert Louis Stevenson's copy with his Skerryvore bookplate and with his mother's inscription.   Sotheran PN32-53 1996 £998.00

BIBLE. ENGLISH - 1635   The Whole Booke of Psalmes Collected into English Meeter by T. Sternhold, I. Hopkins and Others. London: Imprinted for the Company of Stationers, 1635. 32mo; roman letter; contemporary ivory stain embroidered with scrolling and raised flowers in silver thread covered in colored silks, enhanced with sequins, few missing, all edges gilt, apart from some minor tear at extremities and some yellowing of satin through age, this delicate binding is in very fine condition; preserved in velvet lined cloth box.   H. M. Fletcher 121-78 1996 £2,000.00

BIBLE. ENGLISH - 1668   The Holy Bible Containing the Old Testament and the New... Cambridge: printed by John Field, 1668. 4to; contemporary black morocco, panelled in gilt, spine elaborately gilt, all edges gilt, some rubbing, but quite sound; some light soiling. D&M 697; Wing B2277.   Ximenes 109-33 1996 $1,250.00

BIBLE. ENGLISH - 1715   The Holy Bible. Edinburgh: Watson, 1715, colophon 1714. 8vo; engraved title, 348 ff. n.n.; black morocco panelled gilt, all edges gilt, corners little worn, edges little rubbed, some foxing, presumably a Scottish binding, but the distinctive cornerpieces are without record known to the N.L.S.; D&M 729.   Marlborough 160-28 1996 £90.00

BIBLE. ENGLISH - 1759   An Illustration of the New Testament... London: R. Goadby, 1759. Large folio; frontispiece, xliv, 1006 pages, 1 f., 8 pages, 67 engraved plates; old calf, rebacked; unusually fine and firm. Jens J. Christoffersen SL94-189 1996 $295.00

BIBLE. ENGLISH - 1780   The Bible in Miniature or a Concise History of the Old and New Testaments. London: E. Newbery, 1780. 1st edition; 3rd issue; 43 x 30 mm; 256 pages, titlepage, 14 engraved plates, no imprint on p. 256; highly decorated red gilt morocco with central oval leather onlay on upper and lower boards, containing sacred monogram "JHS", spine compartmented in gilt, all edges gilt, marbled endpapers. Near fine. Roscoe J28(3); Bondy 34.   Marjorie James 19-153 1996 £175.00

BIBLE. ENGLISH - 1780. The Bible in Miniuture (sic), or a Concise History of the Old and New Testaments. London: E. Newbery, 1780. 42 x 30mm; 256 pages; 2 engraved titlepages, 14 plates; contemporary black morocco, gilt dog-tooth roll border with floral cornerpieces, central oval red onlay, with sacred monogram in gilt, smooth spine divided into three gilt decorated panels, spot marbled endpapers, all edges gilt; early issue in good condition and in the scarcer variant black binding. Marlborough 160-27 1996 £950.00

BIBLE. ENGLISH - 1815 The Book of Psalms. London: Sold by F. C. & J. Rivington and Longman, Hurst, Rees, Orme & Brown, 1815. 8vo; 2 volumes, xxiv, 310; (2), 326, (2) pages, index; 19th century calf over marbled boards, gilt spines, boards, edges bit rubbed. Kenneth Karmiole 1NS-126 1996 $150.00

BIBLE. ENGLISH - 1815 The Holy Bible Containing the Old and New Testaments, and the Apocrypha. London: White, Cochrane & Co., 1815/14. 4to; 3 volumes; engravings by Richard Westall, engraved by Charles Heath, printed on heavy laid paper which is lightly foxed; full black straight grained morocco with pair of triple gilt fillet borders surrounding a decorative roll, inner central frame is composed of four corner flowerheads with leafy sprays radiating therefrom, connected to each other by three spaced gilt fillets, spine has five wide raised bands with gilt tooling and rather complex arabesque gilt tooling in four of the six compartments, handsome set with some minor superficial rubbing, board edges gilt, inner gilt dentelles, all edges gilt, signed with name of binder on verso of front free endleaf of volume 1: "CHARLES SMITH"; fine, bindings very handsome and extremely well executed. Book Block 32-46 1996 $1,650.00

BIBLE. ENGLISH - 1823 The Holy Bible, Containing the Old and New Testaments; Together with the Apocrypha. New York: Daniel D. Smith, 1823. Daniel Smith's Stereotype Edition; thick quarto; 770 pages; numerous engraved plates; contemporary full red morocco, spine gilt stamped, orange endpapers, flyleaves becoming loose), two scratches on back cover, but spectacular contemporary American period binding; very rare, extremely handsome, signatures and inscriptions, indicating early and long ownership by prominent Rhode Island family of Samuel Arnold. Hills 459; Shoemaker 11816. M & S Rare Books 60-286 1996 $750.00

BIBLE. ENGLISH - 1824 The Devotional Diamond Pocket Bible. (with) The Devotional Diamond Testament. London: printed by and for J. Jones/London: printed by and for J. White, ca. 1824/1816. 5 1/4 x 3 inches; bound in one volume, 874; 263, (1) pages, (1) leaf (ad); vignette, 44 engraved plates; very pleasing contemporary wrap-around binding of red straight grain morocco, spine with broad raised bands and compartments filled with massed ornate gilt tools, wrap-around flap secured by means of a tab in a loop on lower cover, all edges gilt; small loss of leather at top of spine, covers slightly discolored, spine gilt little muted, occasional spotting to plates, but solid. Herbert 1621. Phillip J. Pirages 33-56 1996 $275.00

BIBLE. ENGLISH - 1849 The Thumb Bible. London: Longman, 1849. 2 1/8 x 2 inches; bound in decoratively blindstamped brown leather with clasp, all edges red, small area of scuffing to rear cover, light rubbing to extremities, else near fine, bookplate. Bromer Booksellers 87-237 1996 $150.00

BIBLE. ENGLISH - 1861 The Sermon on the Mount. London: Day and Son, 1861. 1st edition thus; elephant folio; cromolithographic frontispiece, 26 pages; publisher's elborately gilt stamped full morocco, all edges gilt, some rubbing along edges and spine and half inch tear on left margin of frontispiece, not affecting illustration, otherwise very bright copy. McLean VBD p. 133; Color Printing in England no. 182. Bookpress 75-4 1996 $1,850.00

BIBLE. ENGLISH - 1861 The Sermon on the Mount. London: Day & Son, 1861. Large folio; frontispiece, titlepage and 24 most beautiful colored plates printed in chromolithography by Charles Bolt and W. R. Tymms; original elaborate brown morocco, gilt all over and gilt edges, loose in case as it is a 'stuck in' book. Charles W. Traylen 117-224 1996 £750.00

BIBLE. ENGLISH - 1865 The New Testament of Our Lord and Saviour Jesus Christ. London: John Murray, 1865. Small quarto; 2 volumes, 354, 441 pages; engravings, including many folding plates; all edges gilt, full crushed brown morocco, 6 panel spines elaborately gilt with raised bands, with only the slightest rubbing to extremities and incident foxing; bookplates of the Blackmore Museum Library, Salisbury, otherwise very good. Hermitage SP95-829 1996 $350.00

BIBLE. ENGLISH - 1887 The Song of Songs. Philadelphia: J. B. Lippincott Co., 1887. Number 45 of 250 copies; 13.25 x 9.5 inches; 47 pages; 26 etchings by Edmond Hedouin and Emile Boilvin from designs by Bida, printed chine colee, 12 black and white floral illustrations from designs by Gustave Greux, as well as decorative headpieces and initial letters to each verse; modern binding of black cloth boards with leather title labels on spine and front cover, edges of pages slightly darkened, some minor browning and marks, generally very good. Joshua Heller 21-52 1996 $550.00

BIBLE. ENGLISH - 1901 The Holy Bible, Containing the Old and New Testaments... Glasgow: 1901. 1 7/16 x 7/8 inches; 876 pages; several full page illustrations; gilt stamped red leather, housed in gold colored metal case with magnifying glass set in lid. Very fine. Bromer Booksellers 87-196 1996 $225.00

BIBLE. ENGLISH - 1903 The Parables from the Gospels. London: Vale Press, 1903. One of 310 copies; 8vo; 10 original woodcuts designed and engraved on wood by Charles Ricketts; full vellum; fine. Marilyn Braiterman 15-199 1996 $700.00

BIBLE. ENGLISH - 1903 The Parables from the Gospels. London: Printed at the Ballantyne Press, 1903. One in an edition of 310 copies; 8.5 x 6 inches; lxxv, (75) pages; 10 original woodcuts designed and engraved on wood by Charles Ricketts; full limp vellum, later thin board slipcase covered in gold paper; foxing, particularly on front and back endpapers, some light spotting, generally good. Ransom 40. Joshua Heller 21-274 1996 $450.00

BIBLE. ENGLISH - 1904 A Book of Songs and Poems from the Old Testament and the Apocrypha. Chelsea: Ashendene Press, 1904. Limited to 150 copies, this being a presentation copy signed by St. John Hornby, Christmas 1908. 8vo; 62, (2) pages, printed in red, blue and black; original vellum, gilt spine. Ashendene Bib. 18. Kenneth Karmiole 1NS-28 1996 $1,250.00

BIBLE. ENGLISH - 1923 The Book of Ruth. London: Nonesuch Press, 1923. Number 230 of 250 copies; 8vo; pages (18), printed in 12 pt. Caslon on handmade Van Gelder paper with large woodcut borders enlarged, printed in sepia; original batik boards and blue card slipcase with paper label; very good. Dreyfus 3. Claude Cox 107-102 1996 £220.00

BIBLE. ENGLISH - 1924 The Holy Bible and Apocrypha. London: Nonesuch Press, 1924-27. One of 1000 copies, the Apocrypha one of 1250 printed on japon; small folio; 5 volumes; parchment boards ornamented with gilt fleurons, foot of one spine bruised and few corners bumped, otherwise unusually nice, bright copy. Bertram Rota 272-317 1996 £380.00

BIBLE. ENGLISH - 1924 Genesis. London: Nonesuch Press, 1924. Limited edition; 329/375 copies; imperial 8vo; 28 leaves; printed on Zanders handmade paper; 12 wood engravings by Paul Nash; original black boards, backstrip and head of front cover gilt lettered, row of gilt stars at tail, faint rubbing to backstrip head and tail, faint browning to front endpapers, untrimmed, dust jacket little defective and with tape and tissue repairs, otherwise excellent. Dreyfus 14. Blackwell's B112-202 1996 £575.00

BIBLE. ENGLISH - 1924 Genesis. London: Nonesuch Press, 1924. 1st edition; 12 woodcuts by Paul Nash; boards, head and tail of spine and corners bumped and worn, covers marked, good, no dust jacket; presentation copy from Nash to his wife. Ulysses 39-435 1996 £2,250.00

BIBLE. ENGLISH - 1925 The Song of Songs. Waltham St. Lawrence: Golden Cockerel Press, 1925. One of 720 copies (of a total edition of 750); 10 1/2 x 7 3/4 inches; 2 p.l., 9-42 pages (2) leaves; woodcut vignette in red on title, colophon device, one engraved plate, 17 engravings in text, all by Eric Gill, initials in red; original white buckram, spine titled in gilt, edges untrimmed; front free endpaper slightly browned from paper previously laid in, otherwise remarkably fine, binding extraordinarily clean and text gloriously fresh, with fine impressions on the cuts. Small bookplate. Chanticleer 31; Gill 275; Tomkinson p. 97. Phillip J. Pirages 33-252 1996 $1,350.00

BIBLE. ENGLISH - 1925 The Song of Songs. Waltham St. Lawrence: Golden Cockerel Press, 1925. One of 750 numbered copies; 4to; printed in black and red on handmade paper; white buckram; free endpapers and rear blank discolored, as often, nice bright copy. Bertram Rota 272-165 1996 £500.00

BIBLE. ENGLISH - 1931 Canticum Canticorum Salomonis. Cranach Press, 1931. One of 200 copies (of a total of 268); 10 1/4 x 5 1/4 inches; (3)-31 pages, (1) leaf (colophon); 7 full page and 4 smaller woodcuts as well as woodcut initials all by Eric Gill; original vellum backed paper boards, original unadorned paper dust jacket and slipcase, bottom of slipcase spine sl. bumped, little chafing to case and dust jacket, few faint dots of foxing, but very fine. Schroder p. 11. Phillip J. Pirages 33-141 1996 $2,900.00

BIBLE. ENGLISH - 1932 The Wisdom of Jesus the Son of Sirach, Commonly Called Ecclesiasticus. Arundel Press, 1930. One of 328 copies; small folio; printed in Subiaco and Blado italic in black and red, 172 hand drawn initial letters in blue and green by Graily Hewitt and assistants; original full limp orange vellum, ties, spine just little faded, but exceptionally nice, fresh copy in slipcase. Bertram Rota 272-20 1996 £1,500.00

BIBLE. ENGLISH - 1932   The Wisdom of Jesus the Son of Sirach Commonly Called Ecclesiasticus. Ashendene Press, 1932. One of 250 paper copies for sale; there were also 21 vellum copies offered for sale; 11 1/2 x 8 inches; 4 p.l., 182 pages; printer's device in colophon, text in red and black, initials hand colored in blue and green by Graily Hewitt and his assistants; original orange vellum, silk ties, gilt titling on spine, publisher's original matching marbled slipcase; extremely fine. Hornby 38; Franklin pp. 186 ff.   Phillip J. Pirages 33-25 1996 $3,250.00

BIBLE. ENGLISH - 1933   The Book of Ruth. London: Nonesuch Press, 1933. One of 250 copies; slim 8vo; 18 pages printed within wide strapwork borders in sepia in a modification of William Caslon's type, stiff batik wrappers; fine in slipcase.   Marilyn Braiterman 15-153 1996 $500.00

BIBLE. ENGLISH - 1933   The Revelation of Saint John the Divine. Newtown: Gregynog Press, 1932, actually published 1933. One of 250 numbered copies; small folio; not paginated, printed on Japanese vellum, 41 wood engravings, titlepage and book design by Blair Hughes-Stanton, text printed in Tyrian red and black; original dark red Hermitage calf, titled in blind on upper cover and spine; very good in repaired slipcase. Harrop 24.   Sotheran PN32-43 1996 £1,250.00

BIBLE. ENGLISH - 1936   The Book of Ruth. San Francisco: Grabhorn Press, 1936. One of 150 copies; 12 pages of text illuminated by Valenti Angelo, with color frontispiece, signed by him in pencil; parchment covers, lettering on spine faded, covers slightly marked, very good in slightly worn slipcase covered with marbled paper.   Ulysses 39-240 1996 £225.00

BIBLE. ENGLISH - 1941   Ecclesiastaes, Reprinted from the Authorised Version. Rampant Lions Press, 1941. One of 150 numbered copies; small folio; printed in 16 pt. Bembo in black and red; woodcut initials by Reynolds Stone; wrappers, printed label, backstrip and wrappers faded and somewhat marked, but nice, very scarce. Bertram Rota 272-386 1996 £125.00

BIBLE. ENGLISH - 1947   The Book of Ruth. New York: Limited Edtiions Club, 1947. Copy number 904 from a total edition of 1950 numbered copies, signed by artist; illustrations by Arthur Szyk; three quarter leather and pictorial boards, slight rubbing to crown and heel of spine, else near fine in rubbed slipcase.   Hermitage SP95-941 1996 $225.00

BIBLE. ENGLISH - 1963   The Holy Bible. London: Nonesuch Press, 1963. 3 volumes; green cloth, gilt, fine in original acetate wrappers. Hermitage SP95-1055 1996 $175.00

BIBLE. ENGLISH - 1968   The Book of Ecclesiastes. New York: Limited Editions Club, 1968. Number 1029 of 1500 copies, signed by artist; illustrations by Edgar Miller; fine in slipcase.   Hermitage SP95-944 1996 $150.00

BIBLE. ENGLISH - 1970   The Jerusalem Bible. Garden City: Doubldeday, 1970. 4to; 358 pages, numerous color plates, maps, leatherette, boxed.   Brannan 43-145 1996 $200.00

BIBLE. ENGLISH - 1977   The Book of Jonah, Taken from the Authorised Version of King James I. Cambridge: privately printed at the Rampant Lions Press for Clover Hill Editions, 1977. Limited edition, 124/300 (of an edition of 470 copies); small folio; pages (ix), 33, (1); printed on barcham Green mouldmade paper, 13 wood engravings, including 4 large engravings and 4 illustrated half borders by David Jones, title and fly-title printed in green; original quarter dark green buckram, backstrip gilt lettered, patterned pale green boards, untrimmed; fine.   Blackwell's B112-239 1996 £125.00

BIBLE. ENGLISH - 1979   The Book of the Prophet Isaiah. New York: Limited Editions Club, 1979. One of 2000 numbered copies, signed by Chaim Gross and by Franklin Littell; watercolors by Chaim Gross; quarter leather and cloth in cardboard slipcase; fine, tiny spot on spine of box.   Between the Covers 42-236 1996 $175.00

BIBLE. ENGLISH - 1980   The Gospel According to Saint Mark Translated into English in 1380 by John Purvey. Tern Press, 1980. One in an edition of 150 copies, signed by Nicholas Parry; 15.5 x 10 inches; 44 pages; 7 wood engravings in black by Nicholas Parry; handset in Caslo and printed on Glastonbury; linen spine and cork over boards. Fine. Joshua Heller 21-232 1996 $150.00

BIBLE. ENGLISH - 1985   The Song of Songs by Solomon. Utrecht: Catharijne Press, 1985. Limited to 155 copies, signed by artist; 2 1/2 x 1 11/16 inches; 51 pages; engraved frontispiece; 6 large hand colored initial letters; bound in full vellum with title gilt stamped on cover by Luce Thurkow, top edge red, very fine.   Bromer Booksellers 87-201 1996 $100.00

BIBLE. ENGLISH - 1988   The Gospel According to Saint Mathew. Shropshire: Tern Press, 1988. One of 15 specials in an edition of 140 copies, signed by Nicholas Parry; 11.5 x 8.25 inches; 121 pages; titlepage border in blue, title in shades of blue and green; with handcut capitals for chapter headings in different colors, 24 etched lino and combined technique prints in different colors, set in Baskerville, printed on H. T. Saunders handmade paper; bound in colored decorative tapestry cloth in clamshell box, fine.   Joshua Heller 21-237 1996 $750.00

BIBLE. ENGLISH - 1988   Saint Matheu. Shropshire: Tern Press, 1988. One in an edition of 140 copies signed by Nicholas and Mary Parry; 11.5 x 8.25 inches; 121 pages; illustrations by Nicholas Parry; titlepage border in blue, title in shades of blue and green, handcut capitals for chapter headings in different colors, 24 etched lino and combined technique prints in different colors, set in Baskerville, printed on T. H. Saunders handmade paper; bound by Mary Parry in white woven linen, paper title label in green on spine. Fine.   Joshua Heller 21-236 1996 $275.00

BIBLE. ENGLISH - 1991   Cantica Canticori. Salamons Lovelist Song. Market Drayton: Tern Press, 1991. One of 100 thus, in a total edition of 110 copies, signed by Nicholas Parry and Mary Parry; 5.25 x 6.5 inches; etchings printed in relief in black and shades of brown by Nicholas Parry on Arches paper; bound by Mary Parry in floral printed cloth; fine. Joshua Heller 21-244 1996 $135.00

BIBLE. ENGLISH - 1994   The Book of Ruth. Market Drayton: Tern Press, Summer, 1994. One of 10 specials in an edition of 75 copies; 6 x 9.5 inches; 51 pages; printed on handmade paper with 20 original watercolor paintings in place of printed illustrations by Nicholas Parry and in gusset box; bound in Persian patterned linen in blue, pink and beige, printed label; fine.   Joshua Heller 21-264 1996 $500.00

BIBLE. ENGLISH - 1994   The Book of Ruth. Tern Press, March, 1994. 11.25 x 15.5 inches; 52 hand watercolor paintings together with calligraphy by Nicholas Parry, all on T. H. Saunders paper; signed by Nicholas Parry; bound by Mary Parry in green and red floral decorated cream linen over board, green leather and cream cloth drop back box; Joshua Heller 21-265 1996 $8,000.00

BIBLE. ENGLISH - 1994   The History of Susanna. Tern Press, 1994. Binding 14.4 x 11.25 inches, page size 14 x 11 inches, average image size 10 x 8 inches; 74 brilliantly colored original watercolor paintings and calligraphy; brown leather spine (leather 100 years old), mottled cream paper boards with painted paper title label on front board, boxed. Joshua Heller 21-266 1996 $8,500.00

BIBLE. FRENCH - 1738   Version du Nouveau Testament Selon La Vulgate... Paris: Chez J. B. Garnier, 1738. New edition; 8vo; 2 volumes, engraved frontispiece to volume 1, each page ruled in red, well margined; handsomely bound in full 18th century French brown morocco, triple gilt fillet to boards enclosing stylised fleurons at corners each board with large round elaborate gilt stamp of dual coat-of-arms, corners little worn, flat spines elaborately gilt in compartments with lettering direct, tiny wormhole to base of spine of volume 2, large red morocco doublures on inside of all boards, wide and elaborate gilt dentelle border, all edges gilt, marbled endpapers, magnificent contemporary French armorial bindings; bookplates of Mr. A. G-du Plessis and P de La Morandiere.   Ian Wilkinson 95/1-36 1996 £580.00

BIBLE. FRENCH - 1930   Ruth et Booz. Paris: Chez F. L. Schmied, 1930. One of 179 copies signed by artist; folio; 26 illustrations, engraved on wood and printed in colors; unbound signatures, as issued, in chemise and slipcase, slipcase splitting at lower edge, all else fine. Marilyn Braiterman 15-182 1995 $3,500.00

BIBLE. FRENCH - 1931   Cantique des Cantiques de Salomon. Cranach Press, 1931. One of 55 copies on Imperial Japanese paper, of a total edition of 163; 10 1/2 x 5 1/2 inches; 1 p.l. (blank), (3)-32 pages, (1) leaf (colophon); 7 full page and 4 smaller woodcuts as well as woodcut initials, all by Eric Gill, printed in blue and black; prospects for the English version laid in; fine sky blue levant morocco by Sangorski & Sutcliffe, gilt rule border on covers, front cover titled in gilt, top edge gilt, other edges untrimmed, in vellum backed suede lined folding cloth box, titled in gilt on spine, leather slightly faded right at edges of boards, very faint mottling to text (on most pages, but not at all noticeable, otherwise in extremely fine condition.   Phillip J. Pirages 33-142 1996 $5,500.00

BIBLE. FRENCH - 1952   Cantique des Cantiques. Paris: A. Krol, 1952. Limited to 236 copies; oblong octavo; 57 pages; engravings and woodcut initials by Burins de Abram Krol; bound in full Chinese red morocco by Denise Lubett in 1975, spine gilt tooled with design of grape vines, front cover with gilt tooled chalice, grape vines and deer, gilt tooled turquoise morocco doublures, all edges gilt, housed in felt lined morocco backed chemise with morocco trimmed slipcase, spine of chemise slightly faded, else extremely fine; presentation inscription from Krol.   Bromer Booksellers 87-166 1996 $2,000.00

BIBLE. GERMAN - 1926   Biblia, das 1st; Die Gantze Heilige Schrifft-Deudsch D. Martin Luther. Bremer Presse, 1926-28. One of 365 copies; 14 1/4 x 10 1/4 inches; 5 volumes; titles and initials by Anna Simons; one of a limited number of copies very finely bound in stately vellum by Frieda Thiersch (signed by her on rear turn-in), covers with single gilt rule frame, raised bands, gilt titling on backstrips, spine compartments ruled in gilt, top edge gilt, other edges untrimmed, in rather faded and partly defective paper slipcases, very slight discoloration in few places on vellum, but very fine, showing no signs of wear and virtually pristine internally.   Phillip J. Pirages 33-110 1996 $8,500.00

BIBLE. GREEK - 1568   Nouum Testamentum. Paris: Robert Estienne, 1568, 1569 at end; 7th Estienne edition; small 8vo; 2 volumes; pages (xxxii), 494, 342, (sl), Greek letter in 2 sizes, Roman dedication, woodcut printer's basilisk device on titlepages, 'Noli altum' device at end of volume 2, woodcut initials & ornaments, single line red borders throughout volume 2, fairly light waterstain in gutter of first 60 or so leaves of volume 1, light age yellowing, generally very good set; English red morocco richly gilt, c. 1700, all edges gilt; 18th century bookplates of William Trumbull; BMSTC Fr. p. 62; Adams B1670; Renouard 171.1. Brunet V 737.   A. Sokol XXV-68 1996 £985.00

BIBLE. GREEK - 1619   (Greek title, then) Novum Jesu Christi... Coloniae Allobrogum: apud Petrum de la Rouiere, 1619. 4to; 451 + blank, 16 pages, engraved title bit frayed at edges and last leaf bit frayed, some minor imperfections, priced accordingly; new old style half calf. K Books 442-364 1996 £160.00

BIBLE. GREEK - 1723   Novum Testamentum Graecum. Leipzig: Gleditsch, 1723. Folio; crimson morocco by Walther, with his label, all edges gilt, the Syston Park copy, with Thorold's pencil note "Chart Max/Walther" in front flyleaves.   Marlborough 160-29 1996 £500.00

BIBLE. GREEK - 1863   Noveum Testamentum Sinaiticum... Leipzig: Brockhaus, 1863. Large 4to; pages (82), 148, folding lithographed plate, fine edition of the Greek text; half red morocco, ex-library.   Family Album Tillers-624 1996 $140.00

BIBLE. LATIN - 1545   Biblia. Paris: Robert Estienne, 1545. 1st edition of Estienne's second 8vo. Bible; 8vo; ff. (xii) 156, 172, 116, 180 (recte) 128, (xl), small Roman letter, 1st word of title within woodcut border, woodcut printer's device below, text in 2 columns, all pages and columns framed in single red lines, date corrected in ms., lamp oil stains with 1 or 2 perforations at or near a few fore edges (no loss), occasional light browning, ownership note dated 1916 on fly, overall good copy; 19th century calf, gilt spine and centerpieces, slight wear, all edges gilt; BM STC Fr. p. 54; Adams B1037; Renouard 62.2. Darlow & Moule 6127;   A. Sokol XXV-14 1996 £1,250.00

BIBLE. LATIN - 1549   Biblia Sacra Iuxta Vulgatam Quam Dicunt Editionem. Paris: Charlotte Guillard & G. Desboys, 1549. 2nd edition of the revised 'Benedictione' Bible, named after editor, Joannes Benedictus (Jean Benoist); folio; (8) leaves, 214 pages, (1) blank leaf, (64) leaves, title unillustrated, except for cartouche enclosing the word "BIBLIA" which is xylographic, crible initials; 18th century calf, back gilt, worn, inner margin of title reinforced, last leaf backed, some dampstains; contemporary marginalia, ruled in red. BL STC French 54; Adams B1041; not in DM (cf. note to 6119).   Jeffrey D. Mancevice 20-14 1996 $2,750.00

BIBLE. LATIN - 1567   Novum I. C. Testamentum. Antwerp: Plantin, 1567. 16mo; 244ff. num., 20 ff. n.n.; contemporary brown calf, covers and spine a la fanfare, all edges gilt, worn, ties gone, attractive and still bright small scale fanfare binding.   Marlborough 160-1 1996 £1,500.00

BIBLE. POLYGLOT - 1543   Novum Testamentum Graece & Latine... Paris: sold by Joannem Roigny printed by Carola Guillard, 1543. 8vo; 2 parts in 1, ff. (12), 228; 168, (12); Greek and Latin; each page ruled in red, 18th century boards, rubbed, free endpapers lacking, some small worming, not affecting legiblity. DM 4613.   Kenneth Karmiole 1NS-40 1996 $650.00

BIBLE. POLYGLOT - 1940   The Song of Solomon. Jerusalem: Shulammite, ca. 1940's. Small folio; (52) pages, text in English and Hebrew; color plates mounted; bound in textured brown cloth with pictorially stamped brass plate laid into the front cover; gift inscription in Hebrew on front free endpaper, else fine.   Bromer Booksellers 87-254 1996 $475.00

BIBLE. POLYGLOT - 1965   The Ten Commandments. Los Angeles: 1965. 1 x 3/4 inches; text in Hebrew and English; handset and printed on vellum by Bela Blau; gilt stamped vellum with matching slipcase; very fine, bookplate.   Bromer Booksellers 87-190 1996 $350.00

BIBLE. WELSH - 1927   Llyfr y Pregeth-wr (The Book of Ecclesiastes). Newtown: Gregynog Press, 1927. One of 250 numbered copies; 4to; printed in Poliphilus in black and red on Batchelor handmade; limp blue buckram, gilt, spine faded as usual, otherwise very nice, crisp copy.   Bertram Rota 272-199 1996 £250.00

BIBLIOGRAPHICA. Papers on Books, Their History and Art. London: Kegan Paul, 1895-97. Thick 4to; 12 parts in 3 volumes, 65 plates and numerous illustrations; quarter morocco, bound by Zaehnsdorf (original wrappers bound in); fine set from the library of the late bookseller H. W. Edwards.   Charles W. Traylen 117-2 1996 £330.00

A BIBLIOGRAPHY of the Writings of Harvey Cushing Prepared on the Occasion of His Seventieth Birthday. Springfield: 1939. Limited to 500 copies; 8vo; xvi, 108 pages; original binding, fine, dust jacket.   James Tait Goodrich K40-103 1996 $150.00

A BIBLIOGRAPHY of the Writings of Harvey Cushing. Springfield: 1939. 1st edition; 2nd printing; 108 pages; original binding, dust jacket, "Neurosurgery" boldly stamped on free endpaper, private bookplate, otherwise fine. Rare.   W. Bruce Fye 71-459 1996 $250.00

BICK, EDGAR   Source Book of Orthopaedics. Baltimore: 1937. 1st edition; 376 pages; original binding.   W. Bruce Fye 71-154 1996 $150.00

BICKERSTAFF, LAURA M.   Pioneer Artists of Taos. Denver: Sage Books, 1955. 1st edition; fine in lightly worn and soiled dust jacket with half inch chip missing from top of spine; inscribed by author.   Hermitage SP95-755 1996 $200.00

BICKERSTAFFE, ISAAC   Love in a Village. London: for I. Walsh, n.d., c. 1762? Oblong folio; 62 pages of engraved music; disbound.   Dramatis Personae 37-23 1996 $125.00

BICKHAM, WILLIAM D.   From Ohio to the Rocky Mountains. Dayton: Journal Book & Job Printing House, 1879. Square 8vo; 178 pages; publisher's deluxe presentation binding of full brown morocco, hinges rubbed, but sound; presentation copy inscribed in 1879 to author's sister.   Kenneth Karmiole 1NS-9 1996 $275.00

BICKNELL, A. J.   Detail, Cottage and Constructive Architecture. New York: A. J. Bicknell & Co., 1873. 1st edition; small folio; frontispiece, (iv) pages, 75 plates; publisher's cloth; rebacked with original spine laid-on, covers worn, inscription in ink on front free endpaper, water damage along outer margin of early leaves, text handled.   Bookpress 75-12 1996 $350.00

BICKNELL, LES   13 Poetential Poems; the Incomplete Works. London: Oblivion Boys Press, 15th, Nov., 1986. One of 13 copies only, signed by artist and author; page size 8 1/4 x 5 7/8 inches; black and white photos, text printed in black, titlepage in purple, using various types on a variety of papers, organized into 13 booklets and colophon; all copies numbered and dated; in white chemise, housed in slipcase constructed of orange crate slats, decorated with numerous stapled-on, rubber stamped scraps and fold-overs.   Priscilla Juvelis 95/1-187 1996 $1,250.00

BICKNELL, LESLIE   The Art of Gravitating Upwards. London: Oblivion Boys, 1986. 1st edition; signed and limited to 20 copies; page size 12 5/8 x 11 inches; on handmade paper; 26 original blind embossed etchings, printed in Tempo bold condensed 24 pt. in black on recto and blue on verso; loose, as issued in white fold-over case;   Priscilla Juvelis 95/1-186 1996 $500.00

BICKNELL, LESLIE   Elsewhere. London: Oblivion Boys Press, 1987. 1st edition; one of 50 copies only, signed and numbered by artist and author; page size 14 3/4 x 11 inches; on Kent edition paper; 1 collograph, 9 linocuts, 250 rubber stamps, all hand collage; publisher's wooden boards over sewn text.   Priscilla Juvelis 95/1-30 1996 $500.00

BIDDLE, GEORGE   Boardman Robinson: Ninety Three Drawings. Colorado Springs: Fine Arts Center, 1937. 4to; 16 pages text + lithograph and 93 plates; cloth, dust jacket, slipcase, includes signed and numbered lithograph as frontispiece.   Brannan 43-558 1996 $195.00

BIDDLECOMBE, GEORGE   The Art of Rigging... London: Wilson, 1848. New edition; small 8vo; 131 pages; folding tables, 14 engraved plates, folding frontispiece, original gilt cloth, some marginal foxing, otherwise very good.   John Lewcock 30-154 1996 £125.00

BIDPAI   A Fable of Bidpai. Janus Press, 1974. One of 270 copies thus, in an edition of 300 copies, signed by artist; 10 x 7 inches; 20 pages; 14 wood engravings by Helen Siegl; designed and letterpress printed by Claire Van Vliet, text printed in black with title and colophon pages in blue, wood engravings printed in dark blue, light blue, green, orange or lavender on French-folded Hosokawa and handsewn into mustard Strathmore Beau Brilliant cover glued over light boards, binding and boxes by Claire Van Vliet and James Bicknell. Fine.   Joshua Heller 21-6 1996 $175.00

BIDPAI   Kalil and Dimna, or the Fables of Bidpai. Oxford: printed by W. Baxter, 1819. 1st English edition; 8vo; half title, original boards, rebacked, uncut.   Anthony W. Laywood 108-151 1996 £75.00

BIEBER, MARGARET   Ancient Copies: Contributions to the History of Greek and Roman Art. New York: New York University Press, 1977. 4to; xliv, 302 pages; 911 illustrations; original cloth, dust jacket. Archaeologia Luxor-3003 1996 $250.00

BIEBER, MARGARET   The Portraits of Alexander the Great. Philadelphia: American Philosophical Society, 1949. 4to; 53 pages, 27 plates; wrappers; very scarce; signed presentation.   Archaeologia Luxor-3002 1996 $150.00

BIEBER, MARGARET   The Sculpture of the Hellenistic Age. New York: Columbia University Press, 1961. Revised edition; folio; xi, 250 pages, 818 figures; original cloth, dust jacket, 1 corner lightly bumped. Archaeologia Luxor-3007 1996 $175.00

BIENS, P. C.   Goddelike Liefde-Vlammen Van een Boetvaardige, Geheiligde, Liefheebende... Amsterdam: J. Boekhalt, 1691. 1st edition; 8vo; 248 pages; 47 text emblematic engravings, engraved title plus 2 full page engraved frontispieces; contemporary vellum, fine in first binding. Not in NUC; Landwehr 458; Praz p. 379; not in Hecksher & Sherman. Bennett Gilbert LL29-33 1996 $1,250.00

BIERCE, AMBROSE 1842-1914   Black Beetles in Amber. San Francisco & New York: Western Authors Pub. Co., 1892. 1st edition; 8vo; 280 pages; frontispiece; original grey cloth, two part cloth box. The very fine Swann-Bradley Martin copy. Swann Sale 21 (1960).   M & S Rare Books 60-121 1996 $950.00

BIERCE, AMBROSE 1842-1914   The Cynic's Word Book. New York: Doubleday Page and Co., 1906. 1st edition; BAL state A (no priority) with no printer's imprint on p. (iv); octavo; v, 233 pages, frontispiece; original olive green cloth decoratively stamped and lettered in red and black on front cover and spine, top edge gilt, uncut, light wear to extremities, previous owner's ink signature; near fine, largely unopened. BAL 1124; Starrett 19.   Heritage Book Shop 196-225 1996 $325.00

BIERCE, AMBROSE 1842-1914   The Shadow on the Dial and other Essays. Robertson, 1909. 1st edition; fine in like dust jacket with some fading to dust jacket spine and margins of dust jacket panels; beautiful copy.   Aronovitz 57-124 1996 $200.00

BIERCE, AMBROSE 1842-1914   The Collected Works of Ambrose Bierce. New York: Neale Pub. Co., 1909-12. 8vo; 12 volumes, frontispiece; cream cloth over boards, paper spine label, waterstains to spine of volume 12, some occasional soiling to other spines, top edge gilt.   Kenneth Karmiole 1NS-42 196 $250.00

BIERMANN, A.   60 Photos. Berlin: Klinkhardt & Biermann, 1930. 1st edition; illustrations; wrappers.   J. B. Muns 154-38 1996 $300.00

BIGELOW, FRANK H.   Eclipse Meteorology and Allied Problems. Washington: USGPO, 1902. 4to; 166 pages; 43 charts and plates. good in blindstamped blue cloth, front board spotted and soiled, corners bumped and worn, small stain to bottom margin.   Knollwood Books 70-213 1996 $110.00

BIGELOW, HENRY JACOB   Ether and Chloroform. A Compendium of Their History Surgical Uses, Dangers, and Discovery, Anaesthetic Agents, Their Mode of Exhibition and Physiological Effects. Boston: 1848. Offprint; 27, 18 pages; original wrappers. GM 5730.   W. Bruce Fye 71-157 1996 $700.00

BIGELOW, HENRY JACOB   A Lecture Introductory to the Course of Surgery Delivered at the Massachusetts Medical College. Boston: 1850. 1st edition; 24 pages; wrappers.   W. Bruce Fye 71-159 1996 $100.00

BIGELOW, HENRY JACOB   The Mechanism of Dislocation and Fracture of the Hip. (and) Litholapaxy; or, Rapid Lithotrity with Evacuation. Boston: 1900. 8vo; 2 volumes in one; contemporary cloth, spine repaired. Cushing Collection B381; GM 4424 H. Winnett Orr 991. Argosy 810-57 1996 $150.00

BIGELOW, HENRY JACOB   Orthopedic Surgery and Other Medical Papers. Boston: 1900. 1st edition; original binding, scarce.   W. Bruce Fye 71-160 1996 $100.00

BIGELOW, HORATIO   An International System of Electro-Therapeutics. Philadelphia: 1895. 1st edition; 1179 pages; more than 200 woodcuts; original binding.   W. Bruce Fye 71-161 1996 $250.00

BIGELOW, JACOB 1787-1879   Brief Expositions of Rational Medicine: to Which is Prefixed the Paradise of Dcotros, a Fable. Boston: 1858. 1st edition; 69 pages; original binding. GM 2212.   W. Bruce Fye 71-162 1996 $125.00

BIGELOW, JACOB 1787-1879   Nature in Disease, Illustrated in Various Discourses and Essays. Boston: 1854. 1st edition; 391 pages; original binding, scarce. Kelly Burrage 97.   W. Bruce Fye 71-164 1996 $225.00

BIGELOW, JACOB 1787-1879   A Treatise on the Materia Medica, Intended as a Sequel to the Pharmacopoeia of the United States... Boston: 1822. 424 pages; recent quarter leather with marbled boards and new endpapers, library perforation stamp on title, scattered foxing. GM 1842; Kelly Burrage 97.   W. Bruce Fye 71-165 1996 $300.00

BIGELOW, JOHN   The Campaign of Chancellorsville a Strategic and Tactical Study. New Haven: Yale University Press, 1910. Number 534 of 1000 copies; xvi, 528 pages, errata, 39 maps, 3 sketches, 5 plans; later cloth, ex-libris, leaf comprising pages 101-2 in facsimile. Dornbusch III 1667. Nevins I 23.   McGowan Book Co. 65-8 1996 $150.00

BIGG, WILLIAM   The Ten day Tourist; or Sniffs of the Mountain Breeze. London: A. W. Bennett, 1865 2nd edition; 8vo; pages (iv), 170; original blindstamped cloth, gilt, spine little darkened, trifle snagged at head, few leaves slightly creased, scarce.   R.F.G. Hollett 76-24 1996 £85.00

BIGGERS, DON HAMPTON   A Biggers Chronicle: Consisting of a Reprint of the Extremely Rare History that Will Never Be Repeated by Lan Franks. Lubbock: Texas Technological College, 1961. One of 500 copies; 147 pages; plates from photos; two-tone red and black cloth; very fine.   Argonaut Book Shop 113-70 1996 $125.00

BIGGERS, DON HAMPTON   German Pioneers in Texas: a Brief History of Their Hardships, Struggles and Achievements. Fredericksburg: Press of the Fredericksburg Pub. Co., 1925. 1st edition; 230 pages; original light blue cloth, title stamped in black on front cover; fine. Jenkins Cracker Barrel Chronicles 1866; Adams Herd 259.   Michael D. Heaston 23-51 1996 $150.00

BIGLAND, JOHN   The History of Spain, from the Earliest Period the the close of the Year 1809. London: Longman, Hurst, Rees and Orme, 1810. 1st edition; 8vo; 2 volumes, xvii 468; viii, 517 pages; full contemporary calf, leather spine labels; ink name on title, front hinge of volume one tender with two inch crack, some wear at extremities, still nice set.   David Mason 71-150 1996 $240.00

BIGLAND, JOHN   A Natural History of Animals... Philadelphia: 1828. 1st edition; 8vo; 2 volumes; colored vignette titles, 22 hand colored plates, rather browned, as often; contemporary half roan, worn, one backstrip off, and cover detached; bookplate of Frances Meyers, later in the Bradley Martin collection.   Maggs Bros. Ltd. 1190-223 1996 £85.00

BIGMORE, E. C.   Bibliography of Printing. London: Bernard Quaritch, 1880-86. Limited large paper edition of 250 copies; small 4to; 3 volumes, xi, 449; vii, 412; vi, 115 pages; numerous text illustrations; contemporary quarter brown morocco, spines lettered gilt, crisp set. Pages mostly unopened.   Thomas Thorp 489-30 1996 £280.00

BIGSBY, J. J.   The Flora and Fauna of the Devonian and Carboniferous Periods. London: 1878. 8vo; pages x, (i), 447, folding table; cloth.   Wheldon & Wesley 207-1313 1996 £80.00

BIGSBY, JOHN J.   The Shoe and the Canoe or Pictures of Travel in the Canadas. London: 1850. 2 volumes, pages xv, 352, 7 plates, 3 maps; viii, 346, 13 plates, 2 maps; original cloth, rebaacked, original backstrips laid down, bright copy with all plates hand colored, some minor spotting, slight tears to inner margins of folding maps; TPL 1426. Stephen Lunsford   45-12   1996 $1,850.00

BILLINGS, JOHN S.   Description of the Johns Hopkins Hospital. Baltimore: 1890. 1st edition; 4to; 116 pages, plus 56 plates; photographic plates; recent quarter leather with marbled boards; very rare. GM 1627.   W. Bruce Fye   71-168   1996 $1,400.00

BILLINGS, JOHN S.   Hospitals, Dispensaries, and Nursing. New York: 1984. Facsimile of 1894 edition; 719 pages; numerous diagrams; original binding.   W. Bruce Fye   71-167   1996 $125.00

BILLINGS, JOHN S.   A Report on the Hygiene of the United States Army with Descriptions of Military Posts. New York: 1974. Facsimile of 1875 edition; 4to; 567 pages; plates, charts, maps; original binding. W. Bruce Fye   71-175   1996 $150.00

BILLINGS, ROBERT WILLIAM   Architectural Illustrations, History and Description of Carlisle Cathedral. London: Thomas and William Boone and R. W. Billings, 1840. 4to; pages vi, 92, complete with 45 steel engraved plates on heavy paper and vignette on title; modern three quarter morocco, gilt, very clean, bright copy.   R.F.G. Hollett & Son   78-4   1996   £185.00

BILLINGS, ROBERT WILLIAM   Architectural Illustrations, History and Description of Carlisle Cathedral. London: Thomas and William Boone and R. W. Billings, 1840. 4to; pages vi, 92, complete with 45 steel engraved plates on stiff cream paper and vignette on title; original cloth, gilt, lower corners of boards a trifle damped; few prelim text leaves and index leaves little stained, otherwise very good.   R.F.G. Hollett & Son   78-5   1996   £160.00

BILLINGS, ROBERT WILLIAM   The Baronial and Ecclesiastical Antiquities of Scotland. London: pub. for the author by William Blackwood and Son, 1845-52. 4to; 4 volumes in 2, 4 engraved titlepages and 60 steel engraved plates, all in very fine impressions; full olive/tan levant morocco gilt, boards panelled with multiple rules and wide formal roll with cornerpieces, spines with 5 raised bands and heavily gilt panels, slight rubbing to lower edge of one board, occasional spot or light mark, but superb set in handsome binding.   R.F.G. Hollett   76-25   1996   £475.00

BILLINGS, ROBERT WILLIAM   The Power of Form Applied to Geometric Tracery. Edinburgh: the author, 1851. 1st edition; 8vo; vi, 7-26 pages; 100 illustrations on plates; later half morocco, very good. Bookpress   75-13   1996 $175.00

BILLROTH, CHRISTIAN ALBERT THEODOR   General Surgical Pathology and Therapeutics in Fifty-One Lectures. New York: 1883. 8vo; 169 wood engraved woodcut prints; half sheepskin, rebacked; with signature of Charles E. Woodruff, well known American surgeon and ethnologist. GM 5608 (Berlin 1863 ed.).   Argosy   810-60   1996 $200.00

BILLROTH, THEODOR   The Medical Sciences in German Universities. New York: 1924. 1st English translation. 292 pages; original binding. GM 1766.603.   W. Bruce Fye   71-177   1996 $100.00

BILLY, JACQUES DE   Sonnets Spirituels. Paris: Chesneau & Poupy, 1577. 2nd edition, 16mo; 564 pages; printer's device, decorative initials; original full limp vellum, yapp edges, fine; 18th century book ticket; IA 119.363. not in NUC.   Bennett Gilbert   LL29-13   1996 $875.00

BINACHI, LEONARDO   A Text-Book of Psychiatry for Physicians and Students. New York: William Wood and Co., 1906. 1st American edition; thick 8vo; (xvi), 904 pages, 106 illustrations; panelled black cloth with gilt spine, titlepage stamp and spine numbers of the Hartford Retreat, rear pocket removed; with Jelliffe's name stamp to titlepage and front paste-down.   John Gach   150-41   1996 $125.00

BINGHAM, CLIFTON   Six and Twenty Boys and Girls. London: Blackie & Son, n.d. 1902. 4to; full page colored illustrations; glazed pictorial boards; two traces of pencil erasure, small tear in spine and extremities rubbed, else very good, very scarce.   Marjorie James   19-123   1996   £125.00

BINION, SAMUEL AUGUSTUS   Ancient Egypt or Mizraim. New York: Henry G. Allen & Co., 1887. Limited to 800 copies; this number 685; large folio; 2 volumes in 4, containing the complete set of 12 original parts; wood engraved titles with vignettes and 72 plates of which 37 are chromolithographs, 10 tinted, 22 wood engraved and 3 plans; publisher's yellow wrappers preserved within 4 later maroon cloth portfolios, few outer margins slightly creased, one or two plates very slightly affected by paper adhesion.   Thomas Thorp   489-31   1996   £1,800.00

BINKLEY, WILLIAM CAMPBELL   Expansionist Movement in Texas, 1836-1850. Berkeley: University of California, 1925. x, 253 pages; maps; printed wrappers; very good+, light wear to foot of spine.   Bohling Book Co.   191-9   1996 $200.00

BINKLEY, WILLIAM CAMPBELL   The Expansionist Movement in Texas: 1836-1850. Berkeley: University of California, 1925. 1st edition; 53 pages; wrappers, chipped,   Maggie Lambeth   30-53   1996 $125.00

BINYON, LAURENCE 1869-1943   Chinese Paintings in English Collections. Paris & Brussels: G. Van Oest, 1927. 1st edition; 4to; 70 pages; 64 full page collotype plates; original cloth, gilt, gilt top. Howes Bookshop   265-2294   1996   £85.00

BINYON, LAURENCE 1869-1943   The Followers of William Blake. Edward Calvert, Samuel Palmer, George Richmond & Their Circle. London: Halton & Truscott Smith, Ltd., Minton Balch & Co., New York, 1925. 1st edition; 4to; frontispiece and 79 plates; original light brown cloth, slight rubbing, very good. Bentley 1201.   Ximenes   108-20   1996 $200.00

BINYON, LAURENCE 1869-1943   Japanese Colour Prints. London: Ernest Benn, 1923. 4to; lvi, 237 pages; 46 plates; cloth.   Thomas Thorp   489-32   1996   £65.00

BINYON, LAURENCE 1869-1943   Poems. Oxford: Daniel Press, 1895. 1st edition; number 45 of 200 copies; large 8vo; pages (8), 52, (4); printed with Fell italic type on French (Rives, Isere) handmade paper; slight spotting on edges, otherwise very good, uncut in original printed grey wrappers with prospectus slip laid in; 2 ALS's from Dr. Daniel preserved in original postal envelope with penny violet stamp franked 'Oxford 11.45am SP 30 95'. Madan 35   Claude Cox   107-37   1996   £220.00

BIOGRAPHIA Dramatica; or, a Companion to the Playhouse. London: 1812. 3 volumes, published in 4, 799, 404, 475 pages; gilt etched full leather, spines and edges rubbed with label wear, hinges weakened, but very good, tight copies; minor foxing.   Lyman Books   21-48   1996 $100.00

BIOGRAPHICAL Souvenir of the State of Texas. Chicago: 1889. 1st edition; small folio; illustrations; full leather, all edges gilt, hinges repaired, original spine laid back down but dried out and cracked, otherwise nice, tight copy.   W. M. Morrison   436-17   1996 $325.00

BIOGRAPHIES of Physicians and Surgeons, Illustrated. Chicago: 1904. 4to; 708 pages; numerous portraits; full leather, front board nearly detached, contents fine. Rare.   W. Bruce Fye   71-178   1996 $300.00

BIRBECK, MORRIS   Notes On a Journey through France, From Dieppe Through Paris and Lyons, to the Pyrennees and Back through Toulouse, in July, August and September 1814... London: printed and sold by William Phillips, George Yard Lombard St... 1815. 2nd edition; 8vo; 3-115 pages, appendix 1-23 pages, 4 page publisher's catalog to rear; paper backed boards, original paper label to spine, partial loss of original backstrip with neat repair, joints rubbed, corners bumped; hinges cracked, owners bookplate, some light foxing to prelims.   Beeleigh Abbey   BA56-37   1996   £65.00

BIRCH, JONATHAN   Fifty-One Original Fables, with Morals and Ethical Index. London: Hamilton Adams, 1833. 1st edition; octavo; 251 pages; 85 original wood engravings designed by Robert Cruikshank, including full page frontispiece; bound by Tout in tan calf, gilt stamped to covers and elaborately gilt stamped to spine and dentelles, faint wear to edges of spine, else very fine, all edges gilt.   Bromer Booksellers   90-92   1996 $475.00

BIRCK, BETULEIUS   ...In M. T. Ciceronis Libros III. De Natura Deorum & Paradoxa, Commentarii,... Basel: Oporinus, 1550. 1st edition; 8vo; 448 pages; 2 folding woodcut charts and two folding printed tables, numerous printed charts, italic throughout, occasional Greek text; contemporary wallet-style vellum, fine. Signed presentation from author, name of presentee is effaced from the inscription, but signature and few other words are clear. NUC 58.328-329 (3 copies); VD16 B5565; Adams B847.   Bennett Gilbert   LL29-60   1996 $1,300.00

BIRINGUCCIO, VANNOCCIO   The Pirotechnia... New York: American Inst. of Mining and Metallurgical Engineers, 1942. 1st complete edition in English; 4to; xxvi, 476, (1) pages; illustrations; original parchment backed cloth, cloth spine label; fine, untrimmed copy. Duveen pp. 79-80.   Edwin V. Glaser   121-27   1996 $300.00

BIRLEY, ERIC   Research on Hadrian's Wall. Kendal: Titus Wilson, 1961. 1st edition; 8vo; pages (xvi), 318, 18 plates, 38 figures, plans, etc; original cloth, gilt, dust jacket; endpapers little browned.   R.F.G. Hollett & Son   78-6   1996 £55.00

THE BIRMINGHAM Six: an Appealling Vista. Dublin: Dec. 1990. Limited to 100 copies, signed by Seamus Heaney, Francis Stuart, Paul Durcan, Thomas Kinsella, Seamus Deane, Patrick Galvin, Louis le Brocquy; fine in dust jacket.   Words Etcetera   94-597   1996 £100.00

BIRNBAUM, MARTIN   Introductions: Painters, Sculptors and Graphic Artists. New York: Frederic Fairchild Sherman, 1919. 1st edition; 8vo; 137 pages, 32 black and white plates; cloth backed paper over boards, front cover water spotted, light occasional foxing, else very good; presented by author with self-caricature playing the violin.   Andrew Cahan   47-29   1996 $150.00

BIRNEY, EARLE   The Beginnings of Chaucer's Irony (an Essay). New York: Modern Language Association, n.d. ... Sept. 1939. Reprint; printed wrpapers; fine, rare; from the library of John Metcalf, with his ownership signature.   Nelson Ball   118-2   1996 $300.00

BIRNEY, EARLE   David and Other Poems. Toronto: Ryerson Press, 1942. Reprint; boards, dust jacket, fine in good jacket; from the library of John Metcalf, with his ownership signature.   Nelson Ball   118-8   1996 $100.00

BIRNEY, EARLE   Near False Creek Mouth (Poems). Toronto and Montreal: McClelland and Stewart, c. 1964. 1st edition; unpaginated; cloth, in dust jacket, scarce in cloth; fine; from the library of John Metcalf, with his ownership signature.   Nelson Ball   118-18   1996 $100.00

BIRNEY, EARLE   Now Is the Time (Poems). Toronto: Ryerson Press, 1945. 1st edition; 56 pages; boards, in dust jacket; author's signed presentation, inscribed with two lines of a poem in the book, author has changed a word in poem on page 49; about very good; from the library of John Metcalf, with his ownership signature.   Nelson Ball   118-19   1996 $150.00

BIRNEY, EARLE   The Strait of Anian. Selected Poems. Toronto: Ryerson Press, 1948. 1st edition; viii, 84 pages; boards, in dust jacket; inscribed and signed by author, fine in good jacket; from the library of John Metcalf, with his ownership signature.   Nelson Ball   118-24   1996 $100.00

THE BIRTH-Place, Home, Churches and Other Places Connected with the Author of "The Christian Year." Winchester: William Savage and London: James Parker & Co., 1867. 2nd edition; small thick 4to; viii, 204 pages, 32 albumen plates, numerous wood engravings; gilt decorated cloth, bevelled, all edges gilt, tips and edges rubbed, spine repaired; very good, prints bright and sharp; with bookplate of the library of the Berkshire Athenaeum, stamped withdrawn, accession numbers on verso of titlepage with no other markings.   Andrew Cahan   47-159   1996 $250.00

BISHOP, ELIZABETH 1911-   The Ballad of the Burglar of Babylon. New York: FSG, 1968. 1st edition; oblong quarto; woodcuts by Ann Grifalconi; fine in near fine price clipped dust jacket with few short, unobtrusive trears.   Between the Covers   42-517   1996 $225.00

BISHOP, ELIZABETH 1911-   The Complete Poems. New York: 1970. 3rd printing; fine/near fine. Inscribed by author to poet Edwin Honig.   Stephen Lupack   83-   1996 $150.00

BISHOP, ELIZABETH 1911-   Geography III. New York: FSG, 1976. 1st edition; very near fine in dust jacket; inscribed by author.   Lame Duck Books   19-78   1996 $675.00

BISHOP, ELIZABETH 1911-   Geography III. New York: Farrar, Straus & Giroux, 1976. 1st edition; thin 8vo; cloth, dust jacket; fine.   James S. Jaffe   34-43   1996 $125.00

BISHOP, ELIZABETH 1911-   Poems. North and South - A Cold Spring. Boston: Houghton Mifflin Co., 1955. 1st edition; very good+ or better in dust jacket with one inch tear to head of spine affecting front panel.   Lame Duck Books   19-76   1996 $275.00

BISHOP, ELIZABETH 1911-   Questions of Travel. New York: FSG, 1965. 1st edition; very fine in dust jacket.   Lame Duck Books   19-77   1996 $150.00

BISHOP, ISABELLA LUCY BIRD 1831-1904   The Yangtze Valley and Beyond... London: J. Murray, 1899. 1st edition; royal 8vo; pages 572; map, 116 half tone illustrations; neatly bound in cloth, contrasting morocco lettering piece, errata slip inserted at p. 1, some cockling of art paper contents due to slight exposure.   Howes Bookshop   265-2295   1996 £95.00

BISHOP, ISABELLA LUCY BIRD 1911-   Among the Tibetans. Chicago: Fleming H. Revell, 1894. 1st U.S. edition; 8vo; illustrations by Edward Whymper; original green cloth with figure in gilt on upper cover, name on pastedown, pages browned, otherwise fine, bright copy.   David Mason   71-53   1996 $120.00

BISHOP, ISABELLA LUCY BIRD 1911-   Korea and Her Neighbours. Chicago: Fleming H. Revell, 1898. 1st U.S. edition; 8vo; 480 pages, illustrations from photos by author and with folding map; original tan buckram decorated in yellow; fine.   David Mason   71-54   1996 $160.00

BISHOP, ISABELLA LUCY BIRD 1911-   Unbeaten Tracks in Japan. London: George Newnes, 1900. New edition; tall 8vo; xiv, 483 pages; folding map; original blue pictorial cloth, bevelled edges, all edges gilt; some light wear to extremities, otherwise near fine.   David Mason   71-55   1996 $160.00

BISHOP, ISABELLA LUCY BIRD 1911-   The Yangtze Valley and Beyond. New York: G. P. Putnam's, 1900. 1st U.S. edition; tall 8vo; xii, 410, (2), vii, 365, (2) pages ads; 2 volumes; illustrations and folding map at rear of volume 1; original blue cloth, gilt decoration, top edge gilt; some rubbing at foot of spines, otherwise fine set.   David Mason   71-56   1996 $240.00

BISHOP, J. LEANDER   A History of American Manufactures from 1608 to 1860. Philadelphia: Edward Young, 1861-64. 1st edition; 8vo; 2 volumes, 11, xii, (13)-642 (1); 826 pages; frontispiece in volume 2; original pebbled cloth; bindings dull, spine extremities rubbed, very good set.   Edwin V. Glaser   121-28   1996 $150.00

BISHOP, JOEL PRENTISS   Commentaries on the Law of Contracts Upon a New and Condensed Method. Chicago: T. H. Flood and Co., 1887. contemporary sheep, quite rubbed, but sound.   Meyer Boswell   SL27-19   1996 $125.00

BISHOP, JOEL PRENTISS   Practical Directions and forms for the Grand-Jury Room, Trial Court and Court of Appeal in Criminal Causes With... Boston: Little, Brown and Co., 1885. 1st edition; contemporary sheep, definitely rubbed and marked, but sound.   Meyer Boswell   SL25-16   1996 $175.00

BISHOP, RICHARD E.   Bishop's Wildfowl. USA: 1948. 1st edition; folio; many color plates, dry-points, etchings; full leather, all edges gilt, apart from lower spine being nicely chipped very good.   David A.H. Grayling   MY95Orn-12   1996 £130.00

BISHOP, W. J.   A Bio-Bibliography of Florence Nightingale. London: Dawsons, 1962. 15 illustrations; blue cloth, gilt lettering on spine, protective wwrappers.   Maggs Bros. Ltd.   1191-70   1996 £90.00

BISSCHOP, JAN DE   Paradigmata Graphices Variorum Artificum. Amsterdam: Nicholas Visscher, n.d., ca. 1671. Folio; fine suite of 157 etched plates in two parts, each with engraved title; contemporary half red morocco and paper boards, spine gilt, rubbed, edges worn; few minor marginal stains, but generally in excellent condition. Brunet II 1019 and III 401.   Ximenes   108-21   1996 $2,250.00

BISSET, ROBERT   The Life of Edmund Burke. London: printed and published by George Cawthorne and also by Messrs. .... 1798. 1st edition; 8vo; contemporary half calf, spine gilt; fine copy, complete with half title and frontispiece; Sabin 5648; CBEL II 1187.   Ximenes   108-22   1996 $275.00

BIXBY-SMITH, SARAH   Adobe Days. Cedar Rapids: Torch Press, 1925. 1st edition; 208 pages; original cloth backed boards, lettered on front cover, paper spine label, fine; very scarce thus, signed by author.   Argonaut Book Shop   113-74   1996 $150.00

BLACK'S Picturesque Guide to the English Lakes. Edinburgh: Adam and Charles Black, 1849. 3rd edition; 8vo; pages xxiv, 252; 2 steel engraved plates, edges dampstained, engraved vignette, 4 maps, 12 outline views; original blindstamped red cloth, gilt, rebacked in matching morocco gilt. Bicknell 123.3.   R.F.G. Hollett & Son   78-699   1996   £85.00

BLACK'S Picturesque Guide to the English Lakes. Edinburgh: 1858. 9th edition; 8vo; pages xxiv,, 232, 64, 26 illustrations by Birket Foster; original blindstamped green cloth, gilt, trifle shaken. From the library of Norman Nicholson, Lake District poet and author.   R.F.G. Hollett & Son   78-700   1996   £55.00

BLACK'S Picturesque Guide to the English Lakes. Edinburgh: Adam and Charles Black, 1879. 19th century; 8vo; pages xxv, 293, 112; illustrations by Birket Foster and views; original blindstamped green cloth, gilt; fine. Bicknell 123.19.   R.F.G. Hollett & Son   78-701   1996   £50.00

BLACK, HENRY   History and Antiquities of the Worshipful Company of Leatherselelrs... London: for Private Circualtion, 1871. Folio; title, chromolitho dedn., 3ff., 132 pages, 24 litho plates, 2 folding chromolitho facsimiles, one very large; black morocco gilt, armorial on upper cover, worn, some margins dusty.   Marlborough   162-111   1996   £450.00

BLACK, READING W.   The Life and Diary of Reading Black a History of Early Uvalde. Uvalde: privately printed for the El Progreso Club, 1934. 1st edition; 93 pages; frontispiece; map, plates, illustrations; original green pritned wrappers, fading to spine, very good. Jenkins Cracker Barrel Chronicles 4523.   Michael D. Heaston   23-52   1996 $200.00

BLACKADDER, H. HOME   Observations on Phagedaena Gangraenosa. Edinburgh: Balfour and Clarke, 1818. 8vo; xvi, 180 pages; original boards, worn about spine and joints, uncut, clean copy internally.   James Tait Goodrich   K40-48   1996 $150.00

BLACKBURN, HENRY   The Harz Mountains: a Tour in the Toy Country. London: Sampson Low & Co., 1873. 1st edition; small 4to; 7, 9-184, 13 pages of ads; frontispiece, title vignette, text map, 9 plates, 28 text illustrations; plain dark brown endpaper, dark green cloth, gilt lettering, black pictorial, very light wear; excellent copy of scarce title. Robin Greer   94A-24   1996   £180.00

BLACKBURN, ISAAC WRIGHT   Intracranial Tumors Among the Insane: a Study of Twenty-Nine Intracranial Tumors Found in Sixteen Hundred and Forty-Two Autopsies in Cases of Mental Disease. Washington: GPO, 1903. 1st edition; 8vo; 94, (2) pages, 71 plates; pebbled ruled green cloth with gilt spine, with spine numbers and titlepage stamp of Hartford Retreat; with author's printed complimentary slip and Jelliffe's name stamp and bookplate.   John Gach   150-47   1996 $125.00

BLACKBURN, JOHN   Description of a Parabolic Sounding Board, Erected in Attercliffe Church. London: for C. J. G. and F. Rivington, 1829. 8vo; 12 pages, engraved frontispiece and some wood engraved text illustrations; wrappers.   Elton Engineering   10-13   1996   £185.00

BLACKBURN, PAUL   Proensa. Majorca: Divers Press, 1953. 1st edition; thin 4to; decorated wrappers somewhat soiled, still a good copy, fragile spine has been neatly repaired; Michael McClure's copy with his ownership signature.   Captain's Bookshelf   38-17   1996 $100.00

BLACKBURN, PAUL   Two New Poems. Mt. Horeb: Perishable Press, 1969. 1st edition; one of only 10 copies printed in Palatino handmade Shadwell paper "none are for public distribution, but rather are for the poet and printer evenly divided"; oblong 8vo; embossed grey wrappers, very fine, rare. Inscribed by author, although not stated, this copy belonged to Walter Hamady, the printer-publisher.   James S. Jaffe   34-537   1996 $2,750.00

BLACKBURN, WILLIAM   A Duke Miscellany. Durham: Duke University, 1970. 1st edition; signed by Anne Tyler at her entry, The Feather Behind the Rock; unobtrusive bump to fore-edge of a number of pages, else fine in dust jacket.   Lame Duck Books   19-546   1996 $175.00

BLACKBURNE, E. L.   Suburban and Rural English Architecture, English and Foreign. London: James Hagger, n.d., ca. 1869. 4to; frontispiece, (ii), 117 pages; 89 plates; later quarter brown morocco; few leaves browned, with occasional light thumbing, else very good.   Bookpress   75-14   1996 $1,250.00

BLACKMER, HENRY MYRON   Greece and the Levant. The Catalogue of the Henry Myron Blackmer Collection of Books and manuscripts. London: 1989. Limited to 300 copies only; small folio; frontispiece, 16 color plates; grey cloth.   Maggs Bros. Ltd.   1191-55   1996   £600.00

BLACKMER, HENRY MYRON   The Library of Henry Myron Blackmer II, October 11, 12, 13, 1989. London: Sotheby's, 1989. 8vo; frontispiece, (xvi), 653 pages; profusely illustrated; original cloth.   Archaeologia Luxor-2949   1996 $150.00

BLACKMER, HENRY MYRON   The Library of Henry M. Blackmer II. London: Sotheby's, 11-13 Oct. 1989. 4to; 1515 lots, 135 plates; numerous illustrations in text; blue boards, picture on upper cover, price lists inserted loose.   Maggs Bros. Ltd.   1191-37   1996   £50.00

BLACKMORE, J.   Views on the Newcastle-Upon-Tyne and Carlisle Railway... Newcastle: Currie and Bowman; Carlisle: Thurnam, 1836/37. 1st edition; 8vo; 4 steel engraved plates; sewn and tissued guarded as issued. Ottley 7096.   R.F.G. Hollett & Son   78-698   1996   £65.00

BLACKMORE, R. D.   The Farm and Fruit of Old. London: Sampson Low, 1862. 1st edition; crown 8vo; vi, 57 pages; original cloth, front joint sprung, lower margins of A1-C8 stained), very scarce.   Thomas Thorp   489-33   1996   £100.00

BLACKMORE, RICHARD   Eliza, an Epick Poem. London: Awnsham and John Churchill, 1705. 1st edition; tall folio; pages 305 (12 index), (1), (4); handsome early panelled calf, nicely rebacked, raised bands, original leather label laid down, small repair to titlepage, else unusually fine, scarce. Lowndes I 201; Foxon B 249.   Hartfield   48-L9   1996 $395.00

BLACKMUR, R. P.   Dirty Hands or the True-Born Censor. Cambridge: Minority Press, 1930. 1st edition; thin 8vo; wrappers; fine.   James S. Jaffe   34-45   1996 $175.00

BLACKMUR, R. P.   The Double Agent. Essays in Craft and Elucieation. New York: Arrow Editions, 1935. 1st edition; 8vo; cloth, dust jacket, fine in lightly rubbed and spine darkened jacket.   James S. Jaffe   34-46   1996 $100.00

BLACKMUR, R. P.   The Expense of Greatness. New York: Arrow Editions, 1940. 1st edition; 8vo; boards, dust jacket, signed by author, spine faded, otherwise fine.   James S. Jaffe   34-48   1996 $150.00

BLACKMUR, R. P.   From Jordan's Delight. New York: Arrow Editions, 1937. 1st edition; 8vo; cloth, dust jacket price clipped, with new price stamped on inner front flap; fine.   James S. Jaffe   34-47   1996 $100.00

BLACKMUR, R. P.   The Second World. Cummington: Cummington Press, 1942. 1st edition; one of 300 copies; bottom edge of covers very lightly stained, otherwise fine in slightly chipped and spine faded jacket. James S. Jaffe   34-49 1 996 $125.00

BLACKMUR, R. P.   T. S. Eliot. N.P.: Hound and Horn, 1928. 1st edition; 8vo; wrappers chipped and worn, two internal tape mends, otherwise good; author's rare first book.   James S. Jaffe   34-44   1996 $225.00

BLACKSTONE, WILLIAM 1723-1780   An Analysis of the Laws of England. Oxford: printed at the Clarendon Press, 1762. 5th edition; 8vo; pages lxxvii, (7), 189, (15); contemporary calf, label supplied, nice, fresh copy; contemporary signature of William Hodder.   James Fenning   133-25   1996   £115.00

BLACKSTONE, WILLIAM 1723-1780   Commentaries on the Laws of England. Dublin: printed for John Exshaw, 1766-67-69-70. 1st Irish edition; 8vo; 4 volumes, 2 folding engraved plates, pages (4), iii, (4), 473; (8), 520, xix; (8), 455, xxvii; (60, 436, vii, (46), with half title to volume one (none others called for); contemporary calf, labels supplied, very good to nice. Contemporary signature of William Hodder.   James Fenning   133-26   1996   £1,250.00

BLACKSTONE, WILLIAM 1723-1780   Commentaries on the Laws of England. London: printed for W. Strahan, T. Cadell in the Strand, 1774. 6th edition; quarto; 4 volumes; modern three quarter sheep over marbled boards; handsome set.   Meyer Boswell   SL26-18   1996 $2,750.00

BLACKSTONE, WILLIAM 1723-1780   Commentaire sur le Code Criminel d'Angleterre. Paris: Chez Knapen Libraire Imprimeur de la Cour des Aides, 1776. quarter morocco, ex-faculty library, some wear, but pretty set.   Meyer Boswell   SL26-16   1996 $850.00

BLACKSTONE, WILLIAM 1723-1780   Commentaries on the Laws of England. London: for T. Cadell, 1791. 11th edition; contemporary calf, joints cracking, worn and rubbed, usable set.   Meyer Boswell   SL26-17   1996 $650.00

BLACKSTONE, WILLIAM 1723-1780   The Great Charter and Charter of the Forest, with Other Authentic Instruments to Which is Prefixed an Introductory Discourse, Containing the History of the Charters. Oxford: Clarendon Press, 1759. contemporary reverse calf, rebacked, good, fresh copy.   Meyer Boswell SL27-22 1996 $3,500.00

BLACKWALL, JOHN   A History of Spiders of Great Britain and Ireland. London: for the Society, 1861-64. Folio; 2 volumes; 29 plates, figures partly colored by hand, some foxing on plates; binder's cloth, red morocco labels on spines.   H. M. Fletcher 121-129 1996 £285.00

BLACKWELL, MISS   Poverty and Affluence. Brussels: imp. de G. Stapleaux, 1851. 1st edition; 12mo; 2 volumes in one, pages 190, (i), errata: 192; half titles; some foxing, chiefly marginal in first volume; contemporary red hard grain morocco, richly gilt, marbled endpapers, gilt edges, by Dodd and Peeling, Woburn; from the ducal library at Woburn with bookplate of Anna Maria, Duchess of Bedford. Rare.   Simon Finch 24-8 1996 £950.00

BLACKWELL, THOMAS   An Enquiry Into the Life and Writings of Homer. London: printed in the Year 1735. 1st edition; 8vo; (iv), 335, (lxxxi) pages; frontispiece, folding map, 12 engravings in text, rubbed, extremities bit worn, closed tears in map and p. 54; both repaired, without loss; contemporary calf, old reback, label; some minor soiling; sound copy; bookplate of classical scholar Robert Shackleton.   Robert Clark 38-159 1996 £100.00

BLACKWELL, THOMAS   An Enquiry into the Life and Writings of Homer. London: 1735. 1st edition; 8vo; pages (iv), 335, (i), (80); engraved vignette on titlepage (repairs to verso of gutter margin), folding map, engraved chapter headings and tailpieces, paper repair to fore margin of K1, otherwise internally fine; modern half dark brown calf, backstrip with raised bands, original label laid down, marbled paper sides; very good.   Blackwell's B112-156 1996 £80.00

BLACKWELL, THOMAS   An Enquiry into the Life and Writings of Homer. London: printed in the year 1736. 2nd edition; 8vo; frontispiece, vignette title, folding map, 12 engravings in text by Gravelot, with additional tailpieces; contemporary calf, gilt, spine rubbed, trifle rubbed; fine, complete with two leaves at end; CBEL II 2051.   Ximenes 108-23 1996 $250.00

BLADEN, MARTIN   Solon: Or, Philosophy No Defence Against Love. London: R. Smith and J. Nutt, 1705. 1st edition; quarto; morocco grained half cloth, gilt over boards, embrowed, top edge lightly shaved here and there, minor stains, large copy, complete with rare half title and with ads on verso.   G. W. Stuart 59-17 1996 $320.00

BLADES, WILLIAM   An Account of the German Morality Play Entitled Depositio Cornuti Typoraphici, as Performed in the 17th and 18th Centuries. London: Trubner & Co., 1885. 1st edition; xii, 116; half parchment, marbled paper sides, very good plus, ex-libris, spine repaired.   Taurus Books 83-96 1996 $100.00

BLADES, WILLIAM   The Biography and Typography of William Caxton, England's First Printer. London: & Strassburg: 1877. 8vo; viii, 383 pages, illustrations; new old style quarter calf, very good.   K Books 442-53 1996 $80.00

BLADES, WILLIAM   The Enemies of Books. London: Trubner & Co., 1880. 1st edition; 8 x 5 1/4 inches; 8 p.l., 110 pages, (1) leaf; frontispiece; 6 plates; green half morocco, marbled paper sides, raised bands, spine compartments with gilt rules, titling and ornaments, marbled endpapers; original paper wrappers bound in, leather faded, joints and extremities moderately rubbed, but binding entirely solid, otherwise excellent copy.   Phillip J. Pirages 33-88 1996 $100.00

BLAES, GERARD   Anatome Animalium, Terrestrium Variorum, Volatilium, Aquatilium, Serpentum, Insectorum, Ovorumque, Structuram Naturalem... Amstelodami: Joannis a Someren, 1681. 1st edition; 4to; 65 copperplates, 8496 pages; contemporary vellum, usual light foxing. GM 296; Cushing B434; Cole 829; Wellcome II 179;Wood 243.   Argosy 810-61 1996 $1,500.00

BLAIR, JOHN   The History of the Life, Adventures and Heroic Actions of the Celebrated Sir William Wallace, General and Governor of Scotland. New York: William W. Crawford, 1820. 1st American edition; 8vo; 236 pages; frontispiece; original printed boards; spine lacking, boards almost detached, moderate to heavy foxing, front board dampstained, binding or reading copy.   Robert F. Lucas 42-67 1996 $100.00

BLAIR, WILLIAM   An Opium-Eater in America and The Fraticide's Death. Aurora: Wells College Press, 1941. Number 22 of 150 copies for sale, plus 32 for presentation; 9.5 x 6.5 inches; 59 pages; designed by Victor and Jacob Hammer and presswork by Jacob Hammer; printed on Zurich Zerkall; blue grey boards, printed label on backstrip; very good Victor Hammer, Artist & Printer #3.   Joshua Heller 21-139 1996 $125.00

BLAKE, MARION ELIZABETH   Ancient Roman Construction in Italy from the Prehistoric Period to Augustus: a Chronological Study Based in Part Upon the Material Accumulated by the Late Dr. Esther Boise Van Deman. Washington: Carnegie Inst. of Washington, 1947. 4to; xxii, 421 pages, 57 plates; original cloth, minor shelfwear at edges, few small holes at inner joint of first two blank leaves, bookplate; with full signature of author. Scarce.   Archaeologia Luxor-3013 1996 $175.00

BLAKE, MARION ELIZABETH   Roman Construction in Italy from Tiberius through the Flavians. Washington: Carnegie Inst. of Washington, 1959. 4to; xvii, 195 pages, 31 plates, 6 plans; original cloth. Archaeologia Luxor-3015 1996 $150.00

BLAKE, MARION ELIZABETH   Roman Construction in Italy from Tiberius through the Flavians. Washington: Carnegie Inst. of Washington, 1959. 4to; xvii, 195 pages, 31 plates, 6 plans; stiff wrappers; with signature and stamp of Richard Brilliant at flyleaves.   Archaeologia Luxor-3016 1996 $125.00

BLAKE, MRS.   The Realities of Freemasonry. : 1879. 1st edition; 8vo; frontispiece; cloth, spine cloth cracked, text very good. ex-Wigan Library. C. P. Hyland 216-44 1996 £55.00

BLAKE, WILLIAM 1757-1827   America, a Prophecy. Edmonton: Muir, Muir, Druitt & Hughes, 1887. 1st colored facsimile, limited to 50 copies, signed by publisher, William Muir; folio; (18)ff; plates, beautifully hand colored; original printed blue wrappers with white spine, extremities of fragile wrappers show light wear, still fine, bright copy, rare, bookplate. Keynes 217k; Bentley 6.   Bromer Booksellers 87-36 1996 $1,250.00

BLAKE, WILLIAM 1757-1827   America. Taurus Press, 1977. One of 100 numbered copies, signed by artist; folio; linocut text and illustrations by Paul Peter Piech; printed in black and deep red, introduction in green, on green Strathmore laid; black cloth, linocut label; fine.   Bertram Rota 272-461 1996 £80.00

BLAKE, WILLIAM 1757-1827   Blake's Pencil Drawings: Second Series. London: Nonesuch Press, 1956. Number 8 of 1440 numbered copies; 4to; cloth, very nice bright copy in dust jacket.   Bertram Rota 272-336 1996 £90.00

BLAKE, WILLIAM 1757-1827   The Divine Image. New York: 1949. One of 25 copies; color titlepage design and 4 initials by Valenti Angelo, handmade paper; plain, unprinted wrappers; near fine; loosely inserted is a Christmas Card, not inscribed by bearing printed legend "Season's greetings. Maxine and Valenti Angelo".   Ulysses 39-15 1996 £95.00

BLAKE, WILLIAM 1757-1827   Europe, a Prophecy. Edmonton: Muir, Druitt & Hughes, 1887. Limited to 50 copies, signed by Publisher, William Muir; facsimile of first edition; folio; (16)ff; plates beautifully hand colored; original printed blue wrappers with white spine, extremities of fragile wrappers show light wear, still fine, bright copy of this rare facsimile; bookplate. Keynes 217; Bentley 34.   Bromer Booksellers 87-37 1996 $1,250.00

BLAKE, WILLIAM 1757-1827   Illustrations to Young's Night Thoughts Done in Water-Colour by William Blake. Cambridge: printed for the Fogg Museum of Art by the Press at Harvard College... 1927. One of 500 numbered copies; folio; loose, as issued, in blue cloth portfolio (some rubbing); very good.   Ximenes 108-24 1996 $250.00

BLAKE, WILLIAM 1757-1827   The Ladies Charity School-House Roll of Highgate; or a Subscription of Many Noble, Well Disposed Ladies for the Easie Carrying of It On. London: 1670. 8vo; drophead title, 292 pages, 1 f., lacks the 4 plates; contemporary black morocco, richly gilt, all over repeating pattern of 'drawer-handles', tulips, rosettes, dots, pointed leaves, etc., spine gilt in compartments, with presentation inscription "TO MAD'm SEMENS' in gilt in a panel on upper cover, all edges gilt, comb marbled endpapers, edges and hinges little worn; with stamp in blue of A. Ehrman, who formed the famous Broxbourne Library.   Marlborough 160-88 1996 £750.00

BLAKE, WILLIAM 1757-1827   Pencil Drawings by William Blake. London: Nonesuch Press, 1927. 1st edition; number 932 of 1550 copies; 4to; unpaginated; 82 reproductions; original half tan buckram and boards, very good, quite handsome.   Chapel Hill 94-37 1996 $200.00

BLAKE, WILLIAM 1757-1827   Poetical Sketches. London: Hacon & Ricketts, 1899. Limited to 210 copies on handmade paper; 8vo; pages xciii, + colophon, frontispiece, pictorial initials, 2 full page and one half page borders designed and cut on wood by Charles Ricketts', original blue boards, paper labels, backstrip darkened and little rubbed, but good, uncut copy. Etched pictorial library bookplate of Francis Edwin Murray.   Claude Cox 107-171 1996 £135.00

BLAKE, WILLIAM 1757-1827   Selections from the Writings of William Blake. London: Kegan Paul, 1893. 1st edition thus; 16mo; deluxe binding in full vellum, top edge gilt, printed in red and black; fine.   Captain's Bookshelf 38-18 1996 $100.00

BLAKE, WILLIAM 1757-1827   The Song of Los. Paris: Trianon Press, 1975. Facsimile edition, number 41 of 400 copies; folio; (12)ff., original half brown morocco and marbled boards, few small water spots on spine, else fine in publisher's slipcase of marbled boards edged with brown morocco.   Chapel Hill 94-38 1996 $285.00

BLAKE, WILLIAM 1757-1827   Songs of Innocence. London: Dent, 1912. 1st edition thus; 7 color plates by Charles and Mary Robinson; cloth pictorially stamped in colors and gilt, spine darkened, cloth slightly dusty, else nice.   Barbara Stone 70-182 1996 £55.00

BLAKE, WILLIAM 1757-1827   Visions of the Daughters of Albion. Pawlet: Banyan Press, 1957. One of 180 copies set and printed by Claude Fredericks for his friends at Christmas; folio; (6)fff; loose as issued in marbled paper folder; very fine.   Bromer Booksellers 90-7 1996 $175.00

BLAKE, WILLIAM 1757-1827   William Blake's Illustrations to Thornton's Pastorals of Virgil in Ambrose Phillips' Imitation of Virgil's First Eclogue. 1821. N.P.: privately printed, 1912. Limited to 25 copies, signed by photographer, quarto; (34)ff; reproductions, each of the 17 plates mounted onto heavy gray paper, facing mounted text from which the illustration is taken; unbound as issued, in plain brown wrapper; fine, rare. Keynes 235.   Bromer Booksellers 87-38 1996 $1,850.00

BLAKEMAN, ELISHA D'ALEMBERT   The Youth's Guide in Zion, and Holy Mother's Promises. Canterbury: 1842. 1st edition; 16mo; 35, (1) pages; original plain wrappers, fine. Richmond 85; MacLean 478; R&B 42-600.   M & S Rare Books 60-406 1996 $250.00

BLAKEMORE, TREVOR   The Art of Herbert Schmalz. London: George Allen & Co., 1911. 35 x 27 cm; xviii, 199 pages, 64 illustrations; original cloth, slightly damaged, spine cockled, top edge gilt, some foxing.   Rainsford A54-519 1996 £55.00

BLAKEY, ROBERT   Hints on Angling. London: 1846. Hand colored engraving of fish pasated on front endpaper; original pictorial cloth, spine repaired, corners rubbed.   David A.H. Grayling 3/95-602 1996 £75.00

BLAKSTON, W. A.   The Illustrated Book of Canaries and Cage-Birds. British and Foreign. London: Cassell, Petter & Galpin, 1877-80. Original edition; 4to; pages viii, 448, 56 colored plates; recent half calf, slight marginal stains and few slight signs of use; scarce original edition.   Wheldon & Wesley 207-650 1996 £175.00

BLALOCK, ALFRED   The Papers of Alfred Blalock. Baltimore: 1953. 1st edition; 2 volumes, 2026 pages; illustrations; original binding.   W. Bruce Fye 71-190 1996 $100.00

BLAMIRES, DAVID   Adults' Alphabets: Examples of English Press Alphabet Books from the Last Hundred Years... Hanborough Parrot Press, 1990. Of 170 numbered copies, signed by author, this one of only 25 selectively pochoir colored by Sylvia Stokeld; folio; printed in Souvenir on Zerkall; numerous illustrations; patterned cloth with printed labels; fine in slipcase.   Bertram Rota 272-223 1996 £136.00

BLANC, LOUIS   Letters on England. London: Sampson, Low, 1866. 1st edition; 2 volumes; quarter bound in leather over marbled paper covered boards, leather powdery and flaking, good to very good copies.   Beasley Books 82-803 1996 $150.00

BLANCHARD, JEAN PIERRE   Principles, History and Use of Air-Balloons. N.P.: 1993. One of 50 numbered hardbound copies of a total printing of 250; small 8vo; (2), ii, 63 pages, frontispiece and woodcut head and tailpieces, original calf backed marbled boards, gilt vignette on front cover, linen endpapers.   Edwin V. Glaser 121-29 1996 $135.00

BLANCHOT, MAURICE   Celui Qui ne m'Accompagnait Pas. Paris: Gallimard, 1953. 1st edition; review copy; wrappers with some foxing to lower border of front panel, in publisher's glassine; near fine, this copy warmly inscribed by author for Albert Camus, superb association.   Lame Duck Books 19-79 1996 $1,500.00

BLAND, HARCOURT   The Exposure Dissected, and the Foul Calumnies of Aitken & Co. Fully Established; or the Theatrical Profession Thoroughly Vindicated. Glasglow: Richard Stobbs, William Love, Peter Pollock (Edinburgh), 1857. 1st edition; 8vo; disbound; very good, rare. 1 copy in NUC; LAR 610.   Ximenes 109-34 1996 $150.00

BLAND, WILLIAM   Experimental Essays on the Principles of Construction in Arches, Piers, Buttresses &c. London: John Weale, 1839. 1st edition; 8vo; viii, 103, (1) pages, 8 page publisher catalog, many text illustrations; publisher's cloth, neatly rebacked, presentation inscription by author to a Mr. Austin, probably Henry Austin, the civil engineer, from the library of J. G. James.   Elton Engineering 10-14 1996 £135.00

BLANDFORD, GEORGE FIELDING   Insanity and Its Treatment: Lectures On the Treatment, Medical and Legal of Insane Patients... Philadelphia: Henry C. Lea, 1871. 1st American edition; 8vo; viii, (17)-471, (32 ads) pages; modern cloth; fine. Cordasco 70-0275.   Edwin V. Glaser B122-22 1996 $125.00

BLANDFORD, GEORGE FIELDING   Insanity and Its Treatment: Lectures on the Treatment, Medical and Legal, of Insane Patients. New York: William Wood and Co., 1886. 3rd American edition; 8vo; (x), 379, (1) pages, plus 9 plates; decorative russet cloth; fine.   John Gach 150-49 1996 $100.00

BLANFORD, W. T.   Scientific Results of the Second Yarkand Mission: Based Upon the Collections and Notes of the Late Ferdinand Stolickza. Mammalia. Calcutta: 1879. 4to; 94 pages; 29 paltes; binder's cloth; scarce. Linnean Society duplicate with small stamp on original wrappers (preserved in place) and titlepage, which bears inscription "The Linnean Society from the author".   Wheldon & Wesley 207-12 1996 £960.00

BLANTON, WYNDHAM   Medicine in Virginia in the Nineteenth Century. Richmond: 1933. 1st edition; 466 pages; original binding. GM 6588.   W. Bruce Fye 71-193 1996 $200.00

BLAQUIERE, EDWARD   Narrative of a Residence in Algiers... London: Henry Colburn and Richard Bentley, 1830. 2nd edition; 4to; pages 16, 467, 1 colored aquatint, 1 plan and map, spine faded, marbled boards, little rubbed, title and half title leaves trifle spotted, slight dampstaining to one corer of plan, nonetheless a handsome copy.   Sotheran PN32-158 1996 £498.00

BLASHILL, THOMAS   Sutton-in-Holderness, the Manor, the Berewic and the Village Community. Hull and London: 1896. Large papear copy; iv, iii, 302, xv, vii pages; well illustrated; half morocco; very good.   K Books 442-49 1996 £60.00

BLATCHFORD, ROBERT   Merrie England: a Series of Letters on the Labour Problem. London: Clarion Office and Walter Scott, 1893. 1st edition; small quarto; 101 pages; half leather, all edges gilt, head and tail of spine slightly chipped, edges of boards slightly marked; nice; inscribed "To Mr. S. Bamford with the compliments of the Clarion Board' and separately signed by author.   Ian Patterson 9-37 1996 £75.00

THE BLATHWAYT Atlas... Providence: Brown University Press, 1970. 1st edition; Large cloth portfolio and 8vo; dust jacket, bookplates, tape marks on half title leaf of portfolio from original packaging, else fine.   The Bookpress 75-386 1996 $525.00

BLATTER, E.   Beautiful Flowers of Kashmir. London: 1928-29. 8vo; 2 volumes, 1 plain and 63 colored plates; cloth, bindings damp stained, but contents unaffected.   Wheldon & Wesley 207-1523 1996 £75.00

BLATTY, WILLIAM PETER   The Exorcist. New York: Harper, 1971. 1st edition; fine in dust jacket with single tiny tear; inscribed by author in year of publication, scarce thus.   Between the Covers 42-51 1996 $175.00

BLAYLOCK, J.   Paper Dragons. Axolotl Press, 1986. 1st edition; 1/100 copies; signed by Blaylock and by Tim Powers; cloth.   Aronovitz 57-128 1996 $120.00

BLAZE DE BURY, MARIE PAULINE ROSE, BARONNE   Germania: its Courts, Camps and People. London: Henry Colburn, 1850. 1st edition; 8vo; 2 volumes; original blue grey cloth, slight traces of wear to ends of spine Fine set. Wolff I p. 103.   Ximenes 108-25 1996 $350.00

BLEGEN, CARL W.   Corinth. Volume XIII: The North Cemetery. Princeton: ASCSA, 1964. Folio; xv, 344 pages, 25 figures, 124 plates, 3 plans, corner lightly bumped; original cloth, spine faded.   Archaeologia Luxor-3189   1996 $450.00

BLESSINGTON, MARGARET POWER FARMER GARDINER, COUNTESS OF 1789-1849   The Idler in France. London: Henry Colburn, 1842. 2nd edition; 8vo; 356, 270, (2) pages ads; original purple cloth; spines very lightly faded, waterstain to rear board of volume one and upper board of volume two has made the affected area a bit lighter in color, still very nice, attractive copy;   David Mason 71-63   1996 $180.00

BLESSINGTON, MARGURERITE FARMER GARDINER, COUNTESS OF 1789-1849   The Idler in France. London: Henry Colburn, 1842. 1st edition of volume 1 and 2nd edition of volume 2; 8vo; 2 volumes; original blindstamped maroon cloth, spines faded and worn at ends; Robinson Wayward Women p. 83; CBEL III 711.   James Burmester 29-153   1996 £80.00

BLEULER, PAUL EUGEN   Dementia Praecox Oder Gruppen der Schizophrenien. Handbuch der Psychiatrie, Herausgegeben von G(ustav) Aschaffenburg Spezieller Teil, 4. Abteilung, 1. Halfte. Leizig und Wien: Franz Deuticke, 1911. 1st edition; 8vo; xii, 420 pages; early red buckram with leather spine label, titlepage stamp of Hartford Retreat; with Jelliffe's name stamp to titlepage and bookplate; GM Cat. 5 4957; Norman Catalog 245.   John Gach 150-53   1996 $1,000.00

BLEULER, PAUL EUGEN   Textbook of Psychiatry. New York: Macmillan Co., 1924. 1st American edition; 8vo; (xx), (636) pages, 51 text illustrations, embossed tan cloth, recased, head and foot of original spine cloth eroded, few tears to cloth, good to very good.   John Gach 150-55   1996 $125.00

BLEWETT, GEORGE   An Enquiry Whether a General Practice of Virtue Tends to the Wealth or Poverty, Benefit or Disadvantage of a People. London: printed for R. Wilkin, 1725. 8vo; pages viii, 218; clumsy repair to D4, otherwise fine, unpressed copy. Kress 3587; Goldsmiths 6404. Peter Murray Hill 185-8   1996 £700.00

BLEWITT, REGINALD JAMES   The Court of Chancery: a Satirical Poem. London: printed and published by J. Kay, 1 Welbeck St., 1827. three quarter calf, quite rubbed, front joint cracking, usable copy. Meyer Boswell SL26-19   1996 $350.00

BLIGH, WILLIAM 1754-1817   A Narrative of the Mutiny, on Board His Majesty's Ship Bounty; and the Subsequent Voyage of Part of the Crew, in the Ship's Boat, from Tofoa, One of the Friendly Islands, to Timor, a Dutch Settlement in the East Indies. London: printed for George Nicol, 1790. 1st edition; 4to; folding plan, 3 large folding maps; half red morocco and marbled boards, spine gilt; some foxing, but fine. Hill P. 26; Ferguson 71; Sabin 5908a. CBEL II 1481.   Ximenes 109-35 1996 $7,500.00

BLIGH, WILLIAM 1754-1817   A Voyage to the South Sea, Undertaken by Command of His Majesty, for the Purpose of Conveying the Bread-Fruit Tree to the West Indies, In His Majesty's Ship the Bounty... London: printed for George Nicol, 1792. 1st edition; 4to; frontispiece, 6 plans and charts; contemporary tree calf, rebacked, original spine laid down, spine gilt, slight restoration; some foxing of plates, but very good. Hill p. 27; Ferguson 125. Sabin 5910; CBEL II 1481.   Ximenes 109-36 1996 $6,000.00

BLIGH, WILLIAM 1754-1817   The Voyage of the Bounty's Launch as Related in William Bligh's Despatach to the Admiralty and Journal of John Fryer. London: Golden Cockerel Press, 1934. Limited to 300 copies; quarto; 86 pages; red and white cloth with original glassine wrapper; extremely fine. Chanticleer 95.   Bromer Booksellers 87-76 1996 $850.00

BLIGH, WILLIAM 1754-1817   A Voyage to the South Seas. Adelaide: Limited Editions Club, 1975. One of 2000 numbered copies, signed by Alan Villiers and Geoffrey C. Ingleton. illustrations by Ingleton; full pictorial cloth with leather label, slipcase; fine.   Hermitage SP95-943 1996 $150.00

BLISH, JAMES   Black Easter. New York: Doubleday, 1968. 1st edition; very good+/near fine in very good+ dust jacket.   Aronovitz 57-129 1996 $125.00

BLISH, JAMES   A Case of Conscience. London: Faber, 1958. 1st English and 1st hardcover edition; very good+/near fine in like dust jacket.   Aronovitz 57-130   1996 $395.00

BLISH, JAMES   Doctor Mirabilis. London: Faber & Faber, 1964. 1st edition; small 8vo; cloth in dust jacket; near fine, some tape residue and small tear to slip, in very good (small crease and moderate soil) dust jacket; signed presentation from author to his aunt and uncle, also with author's complimentary slip laid in.   Antic Hay 101-171 1996 $750.00

BLISS, CARLEY S.   A Leaf from the 1583 Rembert Dodoens Herbal Printed by Christopher Plantin, with a Short Essay by Carey S. Bliss. San Francisco: Book Club of California, 1977. One of 385 copies; 14 1/4 x 9 3/4 inches; 4 p.l., 28 pages, (2) leaves (blank, colophon); vignette in red on title, decorative initials, woodcut illustrations in margins, as well as few in text, 3 full page woodcut portraits, one half page portrait, one full page facsimile, title in red and black; tipped in original leaf containing five woodcut illustrations; original pictorial cloth, gilt titling on spine, in original plain dust jacket, this copy and original leaf in extremely fine condition.   Phillip J. Pirages 33-337 1996 $350.00

BLISS, D. E.   The Biology of the Crustacea. London: 1982-86. 8vo; 10 volumes; numerous illustrations; cloth.   Wheldon & Wesley 207-1233 1996 £960.00

BLISS, WILLIAM D. P.   The Encyclopedia of Social Reforms, Including Political Economy, Political Science, Sociology and Statistics. New York: Funk & Wagnalls, 1898. 2nd edition; original brown cloth, little rubbed, inner hinges splitting; scarce.   Jarndyce 103-127 1996 £120.00

BLITH, WALTER   The English Imrpover Improved or the Survey of Husbandry Surveyed Discovering the Improveableness of all Lands. London: printed for John Wright, at the Kings-head in the Old Bayley, 1652. 4to; folding engraved title, printed title, 25 leaves (prelims), 236 leaves (erratically paginated, 10 leaves (appendix and tables), 2 folding engraved plates (that at page 64 cropped at foot), 2 full page woodcuts, engraved title somewhat creased and soiled, cropped at fore-edge and foot and with inner margin renewed, old calf, spine very worn. Wing B3195; Fussell: Old English Farming Books p. 51 et seq.   H. M. Fletcher 121-58 1996 £550.00

BLOCH, ROBERT   Blood Runs Cold. S&S, 1961. 1st edition; near fine in very good+ dust jacket; wonderful association copy, inscribed by author for his agent Harry.   Aronovitz 57-136 1996 $375.00

BLOCH, ROBERT   Pleasant Dreams. Sauk City: Arkham House, 1960. 1st edition; just about fine in very good+ dust jacket, signed by author; formerly the author's agent's copy with his ownership stamp. Aronovitz 57-132 1996 $175.00

BLOCH, ROBERT   Psycho. Rivercity Press, 1976. 1/300 copies, this one specially signed by author; fine, rare pirated edition;   Aronovitz 57-134 1996 $475.00

BLOCH, ROBERT   The Scarf. New York: Dial, 1947. 1st edition; near fine with couple of insignificant dings to front cover and 1 tiny wormhole through entire book, dust jacket near fine with couple of tiny chips, very good, scarce.   Sherwood 3-55 1996 $125.00

BLOCK, LAWRENCE   The Sins of the Father. Arlington Heights: Dark Harvest, 1992. 1st hardcover edition; 1/400 copies; signed by Block and introducer, Stephen King; fine in fine dust jacket and slipcase.   Timothy P. Slongo 5-68 1996 $125.00

BLOCK, M. E.   Allgemeine Naturgeschichte der Fische. New York: 1993. Facsimile of first edition; text: 12 parts in 4 volumes, 4to; atlas of 432 colored plates; 2 volumes folio; together 6 volumes; art leather. Wheldon & Wesley 207-14 1996 £520.00

BLOGG, MINNIE WRIGHT   Bibliography of the Writings of Sir William Osler. Baltimore: Lord Baltimore Press, 1921. 1st separate edition; 8vo; 96 pages, frontispiece, blue cloth; fine; inscribed by author to Willard Goodwin, with his bookplate.   Jeff Weber 31-125 1996 $125.00

BLOMEFIELD, FRANCIS   A Supplement to Blomefield's Norfolk. London: Clement Ingleby, 1929. Limited to 350 numbered copies; thick 4to; 380 pages; 72 hand tipped plates, mostly colored, 27 hand tipped colored armorials, 14 folding pedigrees and tables, 9 illustrations in text; original buckram, gilt top, others untrimmed, spine trifle faded, but nice. Howes Bookshop 265-892 1996 £250.00

BLONDEL, JACQUES   Emily Bronte. Pub. Presses Universitaires de France, n.d. 1955. 1st edition; 10 x 6 3/8 inches; wrappers as issued, unopened and uncut, wrappers slightly used and dust soiled, very good, scarce.   Ian Hodgkins 78-276 1996 £85.00

BLONDUS, FLAVIUS   Roma Instaurata. De Origine et Gestis Venetorum. Italia Instaurata. Verona: Boninus de Bonini, I, 20 Dec. 1481/ II, 7 February, 1482. 1st collected edition; folio; 2 volumes in one; modern quarter vellum antique style, first several pages embrowned, minor mend to blank outer edge of first leaf, blank margins with some worming, last leaves with small wormholes, piercing text but not affecting legibility, else tall and clean with scattered notes by the early humanist Rocco di Carminati, whose ownership inscription occurs beneath the colophons and has been effaced, but is still Adentifiable. Hain Copinger 3243; GW 4423; Goff B702.   G. W. Stuart   59-53   1996 $6,750.00

BLOOMFIELD, ROBERT   The Farmer's Boy; a Rural Poem. London: printed for Vernor and Hood, 1800. 3rd edition; 8vo; xxxii, 128 pages, wood engraved frontispiece, 5 other plates, wood engraved vignettes at beginning of each part of the poem, uncut, original boards, pink paper spine largely defective, but fine, fresh copy, inscribed "From the author to Tho. Grant. 1800" and with loosely inserted letter, 3 pages from Grant to his mother.   David Bickersteth   133-138   1996 £160.00

BLOOMFIELD, ROBERT   The Horkey. London: Macmillan, 1882. 4to; color printed illustrations by George Cruikshank; cloth backed colored pictorial boards, corners rubbed, else fresh copy.   Barbara Stone   70-65   1996 £55.00

BLORE, EDWARD   The Monumental Remains of Nobe and Eminent Persons, Comprising The Sepulchral Antiquities of Great Britain, Engraved from Drawings... London: Harding, Lepard and Co., 1826. 1st edition; 8vo; 30 engraved plates; contemporary russia, neatly rebacked, spine gilt, lower corners slightly worn, little minor foxing; nice.   Robert Clark   38-225   1996 £70.00

THE BLOSSOMS Of Morality. London: E. Newbery, 1796. 2nd edition; 12mo; x, 221 pages; 47 woodcut vignettes by John Bewick, 19th century three quarter red morocco and marbled boards, extremities lightly rubbed, else fine. Roscoe J39(2); Hugo 87.   Bromer Booksellers   87-110   1996 $550.00

BLOUNT, THOMAS 1618-1679   Boscobel; or, the Compleat History of the most Miraculous Preservation of King Charles II. After the Battle of Worcester (and) Claustrum Regale Reseratum; or, the King's Concealment at Trent. London: printed for J. Wilford, 1725. 4th edition; 12mo; fine engraved title, portrait, printed title, 2 folding plates, neatly linen backed; sheep, rebacked, with Petworth House bookplate (?ca. 1910) of Viloet (Wyndham, nee Rawson, Lady) Leconfield.   Peter Murray Hill   185-35   1996 £65.00

BLOUNT, THOMAS 1618-1679   Boscobel; or, the Compleat History of the Most Miraculous Preservation of King Charles II after the Battle of Worcester, September 3rd, 1651...King's Concealment at Trent. London: printed for J. Wilford, 1725. 4th edition; 12mo; (22), 189 pages; 4 plates, 3 folding; new vellum type binding, bit browned throughout, minor damage to one plate.   K Books   441-46   1996 £60.00

BLOUNT, THOMAS 1618-1679   Fragmenta Antiquitatis, Antient Tenures of Land, and Jocular Customs of Some Mannors. London: the Assigns of Richard & Edward Atkins for Abel Roper (& 2 others) 1679. 1st edition; 8vo; (viii), 175, (xvii) pages; imprimatur leaf, final errata leaf; contemporary sheep; extremities worn, joints cracked but secure, lacks label, minor browning; sound. Wing B3333.   Robert Clark   38-72   1996 £125.00

BLOUNT, THOMAS 1618-1679   Glossographia; or a Dictionary, Interpreting the Hard Words of Whatsoever Language, Now Used In Our Refined English Tongue... London: by T. B. Printed by Tho. Newcomb, & are to be sold by John Martyn, 1670. 3rd edition; final errata leaf; contemporary calf, early repairs to corners, rebacked at another time, retaining earlier label. Alston V 50; Wing B3336.   Jarndyce   103-128   1996 £420.00

BLOUNT, THOMAS 1618-1679   Glossographia; or a Dictionary, interpreting the Hard Words of Whatsoever Language, Now used In our refined English Tongue... London: Ptd. by Tho. Newcomb, and are to be sold by Robert Boutler, 1674. 4th edition; final errata leaf, lacks free endpapers; contemporary calf, hinges cracking, but sound. Alston V 51; Wing B3337.   Jarndyce   103-129 1   1996 £350.00

BLOW, JOHN   Amphion Anglicus. A Work of Many Compositions, for One, Two, Three and Four Voices. London: William Pearson, for the author, and Henry Playford, 1700. Folio; (viii), viii, (ii), 216 pages; titlepage in red and black, printed music throughout, bound without portrait, as often; recent half calf, marbled boards, spine gilt, label; titlepage little soiled, some minor browning and soiling, very reasonable copy. Wing B3353; Day & Murrie 183.   Robert Clark   38-9   1996 £385.00

BLOWER, J. G.   Myriapoda. London: 1974. Royal 8vo; pages xxviii, 712; illustrations; cloth.   Wheldon & Wesley   207-1234   1996 £80.00

BLUMENTHAL, JOSEPH   Typographic Years: a Printer's Journey through a Half Century 1925-1975. Steinhour Press for the Grolier Club, 1982. One of 300 copies, signed by author; 9 1/2 x 6 1/4 inches; 6 p.l., 153, (1) pages, (1) leaf (colophon); device on title, several illustrations in text, some in brown, grey and black; very fine, inscribed and signed by author for Mimi Elkind, an impression of the Grolier Club 'centennial mark' laid in as well as printed note from publisher regarding the slipcase;   Phillip J. Pirages   33-278   1996 $125.00

BLUNDEN, EDMUND 1896-   Pastorals: A Book of Verses. London: Erskine Macdonald, 1916. 1st edition; one of 1000 copies; original wrappers; fine.   Priscilla Juvelis   95/1-33   1996 $140.00

BLUNDEN, EDMUND 1896-   Retreat. London: Richard Cobden Sanderson, 1928. 1st trade edition; original red cloth, label on spine, spine sunned, else fine in dust jacket, spine darkened and worn; inscribed for poet J. Redwood Anderson.   Priscilla Juvelis   95/1-34   1996 $150.00

BLUNDEN, EDMUND 1896-   To Nature. New Poems. London, Beaumont Press, 1923. 1st edition; 115/310 copies (of an edition 390 copies); crown 8vo; printed on handmade paper, pages (x), (2), (1) pages; titlepage printed in blue and brown, 2 color wood engr. medallion design on titlepage, initial letter to each poem, endpaper, and cover designs, all by Randolph Schwabe; original quarter fawn buckram, sunned backstrip gilt lettered, pale grey boards, overall apttern of flowers in green and yellow, endpapers lightly foxed, untrimmed, good. Inscribed by Blunden to Harold Massingham and his first wife. Blackwell's B112-13   1996 $75.00

BLUNDEN, EDMUND 1896-   To Themis. Poems on Famous Trials with Other Pieces. London: Beaumont Press, 1931. 1st edition; number 332 of 325 copies (of an edition of 405 copies); crown 8vo; pages 58, (1), printed on handmade paper, frontispiece, titlepage design and cover design by Randolph Schwabe; original quarter fawn buckram, backstrip gilt lettered, patterned yellow black and cream boards, untrimmed and partly unopened, tissue jacket, pristine; Kirkpatrick, Bibl. of Edmund Blunden A40a.   Blackwell's B112-14   1996 £50.00

BLUNT, A.   Drawings of G. B. Castiglione and Stefano Della Bella. London: 1954. 30 x 23 cm; 128 pages; 123 black and white illustrations; cloth.   Rainsford A54-588   1996 £60.00

BLUNT, A.   Roman Drawings of the XVII and XVIII Centuries. London: 1960. 30 x 23 cm; 197 pages, 66 black and white plates, 120 black and white illustrations; cloth.   Rainsford A54-590   1996 £65.00

BLUNT, R.   The Carlyle's Chelsea Home. London: G. Bell, 1895. small 4to; pages xvi, 98, 1 f. (ad), photogravure frontispiece, 23 plates, text illustrations, 4 ff., facsimile letter; quarter parchment, gilt decorated boards, spine bit foxed.   Marlborough   162-113   1996 £60.00

BLUNT, WILFRED 1901-   Flora Superba. London: 1971. Limited to 406 copies, signed by author, this copy un-numbered; folio; 16 colored plates; original morocco backed vellum boards by Zaehnsdorf (with cellotape stains around edges of pastedowns), all edges gilt. Raymond M. Sutton   VI-16   1996 $600.00

BLUNT, WILFRID SCAWEN 1840-1922   The Love Lyrics and Songs of Proteus...With the Love Sonnets of Proteus by the Same Author... Hammersmith: Kelmscott Press, 1892. Limited to 310 copies, this being one of 300 on paper; 8vo; pages (ii), vii, (i0, 251; printed in Golden type in red and black, 2 woodcut borders and numerous initials in red, printer's device; original vellum, spine lettered in gilt, uncut, booklabel and ownership inscription; excellent. Cockerell 3; Peterson A3.   Simon Finch   24-137   1996 £600.00

BLY, ROBERT   The Lion's Tail and Eyes, Poems Written Out of Laziness and Silence. Madison; Sixties Press, 1962. 1st edition; signed by Bly; stiff white wrappers, lightly used very good plus dust jacket; near fine.   Thomas Dorn   9-35   1996 $125.00

BLY, ROBERT   Mirabai Versions. New York: Red Ozier Press, 1980. 1st edition; one of 10 specially bound copies, hand colored by artist, signed by Bly, artist and binder; thin 8vo; illustrations by Ellen Lanyon; quarter vellum and boards by Gray Parrot; rare.   James S. Jaffe   34-559   1996 $1,000.00

BLY, ROBERT   Mirabai Versions. New York: Red Ozier Press, 1980. 1st edition; one of 220 copies, signed by Bly, Lanyon and printer-publishers, Steve Miller and Ken Botnick; thin 8vo; illustrations by Ellen Lanyon; original wrappers; mint, with prospectus signed by Miller and Botnick laid in.   James S. Jaffe   34-560   1996 $100.00

BLY, ROBERT   The Whole Moisty Night. New York: Red Ozier Press, 1983. Limited to 300 copies signed by author; square octavo; (12) pages; titlepage illustration by Barry Mosher; printed wrappers; extremely fine.   Bromer Booksellers 90-216 196 $150.00

BLY, ROBERT   This Tree Will Be Here a Thousand Years. New York: Harper & Row, 1979. Uncorrected proof of the first edition; wrappers, near fine, signed by Bly who has drawn a tree and written "Pine Tree!" with an arrow pointing to it, with inscription below.   Revere Books 4-47 1996 $100.00

BLY, ROBERT   The Traveller Who Repeats His Cry. New York: Red Ozier Press, 1982. 1st edition; one of 160 copies signed by Bly and Moser; small thin 8vo; illustration by Barry Moser; original wrappers; mint.   James S. Jaffe 34-561 1996 $150.00

BLY, ROBERT   Visiting Emily Dickinson's Grave and Other Poems. Madison: Red Ozier Press, 1979. 1st edition; one of 200 copies, signed by author and publishers, Steve Miller and Ken Botnick; 8vo; errata slip laid in; illustrations by Marta Anderson; original wrappers; mint. James S. Jaffe 34-558 1996 $175.00

BLY, ROBERT   The Whole Moisty Night. New York: Red Ozier Press, 1983. 1st edition; one of 300 copies, signed by author and artist; small thin 8vo; illustration by Barry Moser; original wrappers; mint, with separate titlepage and colophon leaf signed by Bly and Moser laid in; inscribed by Moser.   James S. Jaffe 34-562 1996 $100.00

BOAK, ARTHUR E. R.   Karanis: The Temples, Coin Boards, Botanical and Zoological Reports, Seasons 1924-31. Ann Arbor: University of Michigan Press, 1933. 4to; xii, 93 pages, 37 plates, 16 plans, 4 diagrams; original cloth.   Archaeologia Luxor-3030 1996 $125.00

BOAKE, BARCROFT   Where the Dead men Lie and Other Poems. Sydney: Angus and Robertson, 1896. 1st edition; 8vo; pages xiv, (ii), 208, 8 pages ads; original pale blue moire fine ribbed cloth, spine lettered across in gold, top edge gilt, bookseller's ticket of Dymock's Book Arcade, Sydney and neat ownership inscription of W. Fincham dated 1897; spine lightly rubbed, very good.   Simon Finch 24-10 1996 £260.00

BOARDEN, JAMES   The Life of Mrs. Jordan... London: Edward Bull, 1831. 1st edition; 8vo; 2 volumes; half brown morocco, gilt, spines elaborately gilt, all edges gilt, fine. LAR 3115; CBEL II 1127.   Ximenes 108-26 1996 $200.00

BOARDMAN, JOHN   Catalogue of the Engraved Gems and Finger Rings: I. Greek and Etruscan. Oxford: Clarendon Press, 1978. 8vo; xii, 122 pages, 64 plates; original cloth, dust jacket.   Archaeologia Luxor-3039 1996 $175.00

BOARDMAN, JOHN   The Cretan Collection in Oxford: The Dictaean Cave and Iron Age Crete. Oxford: Clarendon Press, 1961. 4to; frontispiece, xii, 180 pages, 57 figures, 48 plates; original cloth, dust jacket.   Archaeologia Luxor-3034 1996 $250.00

BOARDMAN, JOHN   Greek Art and Architecture. New York: Harry N. Abrams, 1967. Folio; 600 pages, 372 plates (52 in color, tipped in); 1 map; original cloth, lightly chipped dust jacket.   Archaeologia Luxor-3041 1996 $175.00

BOARDMAN, JOHN   Greek Gems and Finger Rings. London: Thames and Hudson, 1970. 4to; 458 pages, 318 figures, 1016 photos, 51 color plates; original cloth, slightly shelfworn dust jacket.   Archaeologia Luxor-3035 1996 $250.00

BOARDMAN, JOHN   Greek Gems and Finger Rings: Early Bronze Age to Late Classical. London: Thames & Hudson, 1970. 4to; 458 pages, 318 figures, 1016 photos, 51 color plates; original cloth, slightly shelfworn dust jacket.   Archaeologia Luxor-3035 1996 $250.00

BOAS, FRANZ   Anthropology and Modern Life. New York: Norton, 1928. 1st edition; bookplate mostly under front flap, else fine in good plus dust jacket lacking bottom inch of spine and with few small chips. Between the Covers 42-52 1996 $100.00

BOASZ, FRANZ   Kathlamet Texts: Bureau of American Ethnology Bulletin 26. Washington: GPO, 1901. 259 pages; green cloth.   Blue River Books 9-233 1996 $105.00

BOCCACCIO, GIOVANNI 1313-1375   Le Decameron. Lyons: Guillaume Rouille, 1558. 4th edition of this translation; 16mo; 1002 pages, 15 lls. (table), delicate head and tailpieces, decorated woodcut initials, 10 charming small oval woodcuts, corner of last leaf of table renewed affecting last lines of text on recto; 19th century olive morocco, all edges gilt, spines slightly scuffed. Brunet I 1006.   H. M. Fletcher 121-20 1996 £275.00

BOCCACCIO, GIOVANNI 1313-1375   Le Decameron. Paris: Martin Le Jeune, 1559. Early edition of the second French translation; small 8vo; ff. 341, (iii), Roman letter with some italic, woodcut printer's device on titlepage, woodcut initials, occasiona very light browning, some leaves lightly waterstained; contemporary polished calf, rebacked, blindstamped fillets, centre pieces and fleurons, gilt initials "I.L." on both covers, bit stained, edges worn; occasional very light browning, some leaves lightly waterstained; contemporary acquisition note above title; generally good. BM STC French p. 71; Adams B2162; Index Aurel 120.360.   A. Sokol XXV-16 1996 £1,450.00

BOCCACCIO, GIOVANNI 1313-1375   The Decameron, or Ten Days Entertainment.. London: R. Dodsely, 1741. 8vo; pages vii, (i), 591, woodcut on titlepage; contemporary sprinkled calf, rebacked, raised bands between gilt rules, gilt lettered red leather label, sides with blind double fillet border, hinges split, but firm, very good.   Blackwell's B112-42 1996 £75.00

BOCCACCIO, GIOVANNI 1313-1375   The Decameron. New York: Boni & Liveright, 1925. Limited edition; octavo; 2 volumes, xxix, 374; x, 355 pages; illustrations; original black cloth decoratively stamped in gilt and blind, yapp edges, fine set in dust jackets, lightly chipped with minor soiling.   Heritage Book Shop 196-212 1996 $150.00

BOCCACCIO, GIOVANNI 1313-1375   The Decameron. Garden City: Garden City Pub. Co. Inc., 1949. One in an edition of 1500 copies, signed by artist; 2 volumes, xvii, 309 pages, 18 full page two color illustrations; xv, 310-562 pages, 14 full page two color illustrations, vignettes, by Rockwell Kent; dark red cloth with title in gilt on spine, top edge gilt, board slipcase with decorated titlepages on both sides; slipcase worn at extremities, otherwise fine.   Joshua Heller 21-147 1996 $400.00

BOCCACCIO, GIOVANNI 1313-1375   Il Decamerone. London: printed for John Nicholson...James Knapton and Benj. Tooke, 1702. 8vo; engraved and printed titles, portrait (repaired, rehinged); pages (xxx, life, introduction, contents), 237 pages; part II title, pages 287; old calf, rebacked. Esdaile 24.5.   Peter Murray Hill 185-9 1996 £135.00

BOCCACCIO, GIOVANNI 1313-1375   The Nymphs of Fiesole. Verona: Officina Bodoni, 1952. One of 225 on Fabriano handmade paper; 4to; 23 woodcut illustrations by Bartolomeo di Giovanni reassembled and recut by Fritz Kredel, heliogravure facsimile of titlepage of original English edition; quarter vellum and purple paste-paper boards, spine slightly age darkened and bit rubbed along lower edges of boards, still a desirable copy, slipcase. Schmoller 102.   Marilyn Braiterman 15-154 1996 $1,500.00

BODDINGTON, MARY   Slight Reminiscences of the Rhine, Switzerland and a Corner of Italy. Philadelphia: Carey, Lea and Blanchard 1835. 1st U.S. edition; 8vo; xi, 216, vii, 212 pages; original cloth, paper spine labels, ex-library with bookplates on pastedowns, library labels reading "Quebec Library" on upper covers, with "Quebec Library" written in black on upper cover running from top to bottom, spine labels chipped, however, still a very good copy.   David Mason 71-80 1996 $132.00

BODE, WILHELM   Florentine Sculptors of the Renaissance. London: Methuen and Co., 1908. 1st edition; 96 black and white plates; green cloth, spine decoratively gilt, very light foxing to prelims, small ding to rear board, otherwise fine.   Hermitage SP95-758 1 996 $100.00

BODE, WINSTON   Portrait of Pancho: The Life of a Great Texan: J. Frank Dobie. Austin: Pemberton Press, 1965. Number 44 of 150 copies, signed by the author; xiii, 164 pages, many illustrations; full brown leather, glt title; fine.   Bohling Book Co. 191-12 1996 $300.00

BODENHEIMER, F. S.   Animal and Man in Bible Lands. Leiden: 1960-72. 4to; pages viii, 232, 2 tables; pages iii, 63, colored frontispiece, 27 plates and 312 paleographical maps and figures; cloth.   Wheldon & Wesley 207-361 1996 £68.00

BODIN, JEAN   De La Demonomanie des Sorciers. Antwerp: Arnold Coninx, 1586. Revised and much enlarged 4th edition; 8vo; pages (xxxii), 440, Roman letter with italic dedication and side notes; woodcut printer's device on top edge gilt, woodcut initials and ornaments; lightly age yellowed, early ms. ex libris on titlepage, 2 lines of early ms. in Spanish on verso of last leaf; 18th century calf, gilt borders and edges and richly gilt spine, worn at corners; good. Index Aurel 120.825; Caillet 1273. Brunet I 1025.   A. Sokol XXV-17 1996 £850.00

BODIN, JEAN   De Magorum Daemonomania, Seu Detestando Lamiarum ac Magorum Cum Satana Commercio, Libri IV. Francofurti: Officina Typographica Nicolai Bassaei, 1590. 8vo; 798 pages; later marbled boards, very scarce.   John Gach 150-58 1996 $850.00

BODINE, L.   Off the Face of the Earth. F.P. Co., 1894. 1st edition; advance edition; cloth covered boards; some soil and light wear to covers, else good/very good. Very scarce.   Aronovitz 57-144 1996 $125.00

BOECE, HECTOR   The Buik of the Cronicli of Scotland; or, a Metrical Version of the History of Hector Boece... London: 1858. 8vo; 3 volumes approximately 2000 pages; original cloth.   Howes Bookshop 265-1561 1996 £75.00

BOECKELMANN, ANDRIES   Nootwendig Bericht van Mr. Andries Boekelman, Chirurgyn, Breuck, en Vroetmeester der Stadt Amsterdam... Amsterdam: 1677. 1st edition; 12mo; 44 pamphlets; 19 bound together in contemporary boards, 25 bound separately;   Argosy 810-64 1996 $2,500.00

BOECKH, AUGUSTUS   The Public Economy of Athens; to Which is Added a Dissertation on the Silver Mines of Laurion. London: John W. Parker, 1842. 2nd edition; 8vo; xiii, (3), 688 pages, folding plate; contemporary calf, gilt, marbled edges, with University College, London, gilt prize stamp on sides; nice. Kress C5742; Goldsmiths 32521; McCulloch p. 356.   John Drury 82-24 1996 £55.00

BOELTER, HOMER H.   Portfolio of Hopi Kachinas. Hollywood: Homer H. Boelter, 1969. Limited to 1000, signed by author/artist; 61 pages, 15 color plates; with portfolio of 16 prints of plates in volume, all prints fine, portfolio folder has been ripped twice by fold under tab; fine in tan cloth; volume and portfolio in slipcase covered in tan cloth with some soiling and light fraying.   Ken Sanders 8-93 1996 $125.00

BOERSMA, J. S.   Athenian Building Policy from 561/0 to 405/4 BC. Groningen: Wolters-Noordhoff, 1970. 8vo; xi, 292 pages, numerous figures, 6 maps, 6 plans (in pocket at rear); original cloth. Archaeologia   Luxor-3045 1996 $125.00

BOETHIUS d. 524   Consolationis Philosophiae Libri Quinque. Glasgow: Excudebant Robertus et Andreas Foulis, 1751. 8vo; outer margins of title slightly browned, contemporary calf, upper hinge partly cracked, label, nice copy. Gaskell 184.   Anthony Laywood 108-60 1996 £75.00

BOETHIUS d. 524   Dialectica, in Qua Emendanda Tantam Adhibuit Martianvs Rota Diligentiam. Venice: Giacomo Simbeni, 1570. Folio; ff. 190 numbered in double columns, roman and italic letter, printer's woodcut device on titlepage, woodcut initials and diagrams, very slight waterstaining, mostly marginal, otherwise good; limp vellum, ties almost intact. BM STC It. Suppl. p.22; Adams B2303; Index Aurel 121.129.   A. Sokol XXV-18 1996 £975.00

BOETHIUS, AXEL   The Golden House of Nero: Some Aspects of Roman Architecture. Ann Arbor: University of Michigan Press, 1960. 4to; 195 pages, 109 figures; original cloth, dust jacket, blind embossed stamp on first 3 leaves.   Archaeologia Luxor-3028 1996 $125.00

BOETTICHER, ERNST   La Troie de Schliemann. Une Necropole a Incineration a la Maniere Assyro-Babylonienne. Louvain: Lefever, 1889. Offprint; 8vo; vii, 115 pages, 12 plates; half calf with 5 raised bands, marbled boards, spine chipped, bottom joint cracked but holding; from the collection of Heinrich Schliemann, and was acquired by Professor Akerstrom; with facsimile letter about acquisition; with remnants of Schliemann's paper private library label at foot of spine.   Archaeologia Luxor-3982 1996 $4,500.00

BOGAERT, LUDO VAN   First International Congress of Neurological Sciences...Brussels 21-28 July 1957. London: Pergamon, 1959. 4to; c. 2100 pages; 5 volumes; illustrations; original blue cloth; fine.   Edwin V. Glaser B122-23 1996 $300.00

BOGAN, LOUISE   The Blue Estuaries. Poems: 1923-68. New York: Farrar, Straus, Giroux, 1968. 1st edition; 8vo; cloth, dust jacket, mint. James S. Jaffe 34-67 1996 $125.00

BOGAN, LOUISE   This Body of Death. New York: MacBride, 1923. 1st edition; 8vo; fine in fine jacket, just lightly used, with two very short and tiny closed tears.   Lakin & Marley 3-2 1996 $750.00

BOGAN, LOUISE   Body of this Death. Poems. New York: Robert M. McBride, 1923. 1st edition; 8vo; author's first book; cloth backed boards, dust jacket; fine in slightly worn and faded jacket.   James S. Jaffe 34-59 1996 $350.00

BOGAN, LOUISE   Dark Summer. New York: Scribner's, 1929. 1st edition; near fine in about very good, spine faded dust jacket, with shallow chipping to extremities, inscribed by author.   Lame Duck Books 19-79 1996 $1,500.00

BOGAN, LOUISE   Dark Summer. New York: Scribner's, 1929. 1st edition; 8vo; cloth backed boards, printed labels, dust jacket; previous owner's signature, otherwise fine in somewhat rubbed jacket with spine faded as usual.   James S. Jaffe 34-60 1996 $225.00

BOGAN, LOUISE   Poems and New Poems. New York: Scribner's, 1941. 1st edition; 8vo; cloth, dust jacket, head and foot of spine somewhat discolored, otherwise good in chipped and worn jacket with several internal tape mends; inscribed by author with autograph postcard laid in.   James S. Jaffe 34-62 1996 $125.00

BOGAN, LOUISE   Selected Criticism - Poetry & Prose. London: Noonday Press, 1955. 1st edition; original binding, top edge dusty, front gutter slightly spotted, head and tail of spine and corners slightly bumped, very good in nicked, chipped, rubbed, marked and dusty, slightly creased dust jacket darkened at spine and edges; presentation copy from author to Isaac Singer.   Ulysses 39-56 1996 £135.00

BOGAN, LOUISE   The Sleeping Fury. New York: Scribner's, 1937. 1st edition; 8vo; cloth, dust jacket, light offsetting to front and back endsheets, otherwise fine in slightly chipped dust jacket.   James S. Jaffe 34-61 1996 $150.00

BOGG, EDMUND   Two Thousand Miles of Wandering in the Border Country, Lakeland and Ribblesdale. Leeds: the author; York: John Sampson, 1898. Combined edition; 4to; pages xxii, 364, 264, 350 illustrations; original half morocco, gilt with raised bands, joints cracked but sound, blind ownership stamps on flyleaves, very attractive. R.F.G. Hollett & Son 78-707 1996 £160.00

BOGG, EDMUND   Two Thousand Miles of Wandering in the Border, Country, Lakeland and Ribblesdale. Leeds: the author, York: John Sampson, 1898. 4to; pages xxii, 364, 264, 350 illustrations; contemporary half green morocco gilt, raised bands delineated with blind rules drawn over on to boards, each culminating in large gilt dot, few slight marks to green buckram boards. Handsome binding.   R.F.G. Hollett 76-29 1996 £160.00

BOHNY, NICHOLAS   The New Picture Book. Edinburgh: Edmonston and Douglas, 1858. 1st English edition; oblong 4to; printed title and preface leaf 36 lithographed leaves, each with 2 or more illustrations colored by hand, one leaf torn and neatly repaired, many of the others re-inserted skillfully on guards; publisher's pictorial hand colored boards, neatly rebacked in cloth, covers worn and soiled, some finger soiling and spotting internally, titlepage and preface dampstained along lower edge.   Thomas Thorp 489-34 1996 £180.00

BOHUN, WILLIAM   A Collection of Debates, Reports, Orders and Resolutions...Touching the Right of Electing Members to Serve in Parliament. London: printed for Bernard Lintott, at the Cross Keys, 1700? contemporary calf, definite wear, but fresh copy.   Meyer Boswell SL27-24 1996 $275.00

BOHUN, WILLIAM   The Law of Tithes... London: pritned by Elizabeth and R. Nutt and R. Gosling, etc., 1731. 2nd edition; contemporary calf, paper label, rubbed, but quite fresh.   Meyer Boswell SL26-20 1996 $450.00

BOHUN, WILLIAM   Privilegia Londini: or, the Laws, Customs and Priviledges of the City of London. London: for D. Brown and J. Walthoe, 1702. 1st edition; crown 8vo; (iv), (488) pages; recent calf, panelled and sprinkled in period style, red edges, text somewhat browned, little bumped, but good, minor faults notwithstanding.   Ash Rare Books Zenzybyr-14 1996 £245.00

BOHUN, WILLIAM   Privilegia Londini: or, the Rights, Liberties, Privileges, Laws and Customs of the City of London. London: printed for D. Browne, W. Mears, R. Gosling, 1723. contemporary calf, rebacked, definitely worn, sould only.   Meyer Boswell SL27-23 1996 $250.00

BOILEAU, D.   The Art of Working in Pasteboard, Upon Scientific Principles: To Which is Added, an Appendix... London: Boosey and Sons, 1827. 12mo; 114 pages + ad leaf; 8 folding plates; original green boards paper label on upper cover, expertly rebacked to match; very good, scarce.   Ken Spelman 30-40 1996 £95.00

BOILEAU, DANIEL   An Introduction to the Study of Political Economy; or Elementary View of the Man in Which the Wealth of Nations is Produced... London: printed for T. Cadell and W. Davies, 1811. 1st edition; 8vo; no half title, library stamp on title and in several places in text; new half calf, label. Kress B5791; Goldsmith 20201.   Anthony W. Laywood 108-153 1996 £235.00

BOILEAU-DESPREAUX, NICHOLAS   Oevvres. Glasgow: De L'Imprimerie De R. et A. Foulis, 1759. Octavo; 2 volumes; contemporary calf, spine ends chipped, joints cracked, one label gone from spine; bookplate of Sir John Trollope. Gaskell 364.   G. W. Stuart 59-18 1996 $195.00

BOITO, ARRIGO   Re Orso; Two Verse Legends. Milan: Officina Bodoni, 1948. One of 150 copies, numbered; royal 8vo; printed in 12 pt. Monotype Baskerville roman and italic, decorative capitals on Fabriano handmade; original glazed green boards, gilt, spine faded to white and somewhat rubbed along joints, sides unevenly faded and upper corners worn, but internally very nice, designated by a stamp on prelim blank as printed for Ottocaro Weiss; slipcase; very scarce.   Bertram Rota 272-344 1996 £600.00

BOIVIN, MARIE ANNE VICTORIE   Traite Pratique des Maladies de l'Uterus et de Ses Annexes. Bruxelles: Etablissement Encyclographique, 1834. 8vo; 2 volumes with atlas, xii, (1), 400 pages, with folding table, 330 pages; atlas with 39 legend leafs and 41 hand colored plates; in later quarter calf and marbled boards, with usual text foxing and occasional browning overall very good, clean, crisp set. GM 6028; Iowa 1280-1282.   James Tait Goodrich K40-52 1996 $1,750.00

THE BOKE of Noblesse Addressed to King Edward the Fourth on His Invasion of France in 1475. Roxburghe Club, 1860. 4to; titlepage in red and black; original quarter morocco.   Charles W. Traylen 117-69 1996 £120.00

THE BOKE of Noblesse. London: printed for the Roxburghe Club, by J. B. Nichols and Sons, 1890. 1st edition; 10 1/2 x 8 inches; 4 p.l., lx, 95, (1) pages; original roan backed reddish paper boards, gilt titling on spine, corners of paper boards slightly worn, just a tiny bit of rubbing to spine ends and chafing to covers, but binding entirely sound and pleasing, fine internally. Bookplates of C. H. St. John Hornby and John Roland Abbey.   Phillip J. Pirages 33-450 1996 $600.00

BOLAM, GEORGE   Birds of Northumberland and the Eastern Borders. Henry Hunter Blair, Alnwick, 1912. 1st edition; 8vo; pages xvii, 726; frontispiece and 27 photographic plates; original blue cloth, photographic plate mounted on upper cover, unusually nice, scarce. Mullens & Swann p. 77.   Sotheran PN32-83 1996 £198.00

BOLAM, GEORGE   Wild Life in Wales. London: 1913. Many photographic illustrations; light rubbing/marking to cvoers, light foxing, scarce.   David A.H. Grayling MY95Orn-363 1996 £50.00

BOLLI, H. M.   Plankton Stratigraphy. Cambridge: 1985. 4to; 2 volumes; pages (viii), 1032, numerous figures; wrappers.   Wheldon & Wesley 207-302 1996 £85.00

BOLTON, ARTHUR T.   The Architecture of Robert and James Adam 1758-1794. London: Country Life, 1922. Folio; 2 volumes; profusely illustrated; ex-library, labels to front endpapers and neat rubber stamp to verso of titlepages, binding slightly soiled and top of backstrips rubbed, contents very good.   Petersfield Bookshop FH58-2 1996 £200.00

BOLTON, CLAIRE   Awa Gami: Japanese Handmade Paper from Fuji Mills, Tokushima. London: 1992. One of 320 numbered copies; 8vo; printed in spectrum on Japanese handmade; blue and white batik Japanese-style wrappers; fine.   Bertram Rota 272-8 1996 £63.00

BOLTON, CLAIRE   A Winchester Bookshop and Bindery 1729-1991. London: 1991. One of 250 numbered copies; large 8vo; printed in Caslon on Rivoli paper; half cloth, boards, fine.   Bertram Rota 272-7 1996 £68.00

BOLTON, HEBERT EUGENE 1870-1953   Anza's California Expeditions. Berkeley: University of California Press, 1930. 1st edition; 5 volumes, 14 maps, 106 plates, 47 facsimiles; blue cloth, gilt lettering; very fine and bright set. Cowan p. 60; Howes B583; Zamorano 80 7.   Argonaut Book Shop 113-77 1996 $750.00

BOLTON, HERBERT EUGENE 1870-1953   Coronado on the Turquoise Trail: Knight of Pueblos and Plains. Albuquerque: University of New Mexico Press, 1949. 10 1/4 x 7 inches; xvi, 489 pages, foldout map; gold stamped dark red cloth.   Dawson's Books Shop 528-12 1996 $125.00

BOLTON, HERBERT EUGENE 1870-1953   Kino's Historical Memoir of Pimeria Alta, A Contemporary Account of the Beginnings of California, Sonora and Arizona. Berkeley: 1948. Reprint; 2 volumes, 329, 379 pages; folding map; cloth, very good_. Howes K169.   T. A. Swinford 49-122 1996 $125.00

BOLTON, HERBERT EUGENE 1870-1953   Rim of Christendom. A Biography of Eusebio Francisco Kino, Pacific Coast Pioneer. New York: 1936. 1st edition? 644 pages; illustrations and maps; cloth, very good in chipped, twice clipped but rather scarce dust jacket. Howes B587.   Gene W. Baade 1094-11 1996 $150.00

BOLTON, HERBERT EUGENE 1870-1953   Texas in the Middle Eighteenth Century: Studies in Spanish Colonial History and Administration. Berkeley: University of California Press, 1915. 1st edition; large 8vo; (10), 501 pages; plans, facsimiles, plates, maps (some folding), large folding map at rear; original printed grey wrappers, lettered on spine and front cover in black, minor chipping to lower rear wrapper, small piece from corner of rear wrapper lacking, else very fine, internally pristine and uncut, housed in custom made clamshell box, leather labels. Howes 589; Jenkins BTB 20; Rader 399; Rittenhouse 70.   Argonaut Book Shop 113-78 1996 $350.00

BOLTON, JOHN   Geological Fragments Collected Principally from Rambles Among the Rocks of Furness and Cartmel. Ulverston: 1869. 1st edition; 8vo; pages 264; 5 plates; modern half green levant morocco gilt with spine label and raised bands, handsome copy, scarce.   R.F.G. Hollett & Son 78-516 1996 £120.00

BOLTON, JOHN   Geological Fragments Collected Principally From Rambles Among the Rocks of Furness and Cartmel. Ulverstson: 1869. 1st edition; 8vo; pages 264, 5 plates; original blindstamped cloth, gilt. R.F.G. Hollett & Son 78-517 1996 £95.00

BOLTON, ROBERT   An Answer to the Question, Where Are Your Arguments Against What You Call, Lewdness, If You Make No Use of the Bible? London: printed for R. and J. Dodsley, 1755. viii, 48 pages; disbound; nice.   C. R. Johnson 37-39 1996 £125.00

BOLTON, ROBERT   Letters to a Young Nobleman. London: A. Millar, 1762. 1st edition; 8vo; pages (vi), 230, (1), half title, errata leaf at end; contemporary speckled calf, double fillet gilt border to sides, spine in compartments with raised bands, gilt rules and star and flower ornaments, maroon morocco label lettered in gilt, some wear, spine and joints skillfully repaired, D5 torn at outer blank margin, not affecting text, various markings and underlinings, mostly in pencil; very good; with Wilton Park booklabel.   Simon Finch 24-12 1996 £200.00

BONAVENTURA, PSEUDO   Diaeta Salutis. Paris: Pierre le Dru for Denis Roce, c. 1500. Crown 8vo; 152 leaves (1)-58), gothic letter, rubricated throughout, large woodcut device of Denis Roce, on titlepage, 18th century panelled calf; bookplate of Edward Garnett, inscribed "N. Irelondi' in rubrricator's ink. Capinger 1154; GKWW 4735; not in Goff, BMC, Polain or Oates.   Petersfield Bookshop FH58-44 1996 £2,500.00

BONAVENTURA, SAINT   Breuiloqui Theologie; Quo Omnis Laus. Paris: Gaspard Philippe for Jean Petit, ca. 1510. Small octavo; disbound, quite minor soiling, small metal cut of perhaps St. Bonaventure himself, with staff and book, as well as woodcut text illustration of the crucifixion; Goff B860.   G. W. Stuart 59-19 1996 $1,750.00

BONAVENTURA, SAINT   Stimulus Duini Amoris. Paris: Georg Wolf for Jean Petit, 1498-500. Small octavo; disbound, quite minor soiling, complete with lovely woodcut on final leaf, with Petit's woodcut device on title as well as on final leaf; Not in Hain; GW 4826; Goff B967.   G. W. Stuart 59-54 1996 $2,850.00

BONAVIA, DUCCIO   Mural Painting in Ancient Peru. Bloomington: Indiana University press, 1985. 4to; xi, 224 pages, 124 illustrations, 34 plates in color; original cloth, lightly tattered dust jacket.   Archaeologia Luxor-4295 1996 $125.00

BONAVIA, E.   The Cultivated Oranges and Lemons, Etc. of India and Ceylon. Dehra Dun: 1973. 8vo. and oblong 12mo; 2 volumes; xix, 384 pages; with atlas of illustrations, 259 plates; cloth, light rubbing. Raymond M. Sutton VII-842 1996 $110.00

BOND, JULIEN   Black Candidates: Southern Campaign Experiences. Atlanta: Voter Education Project/Southern Regional Council, 1969. 1st edition; stapled wrappers, slight soiling and light creases to corners of last few pages; else near fine.   Between the Covers 43-273 1996 $100.00

BOND, THOMAS   Topographical and Historical East and West Looe. London: Nichols, 1823. 8vo; pages iv, 308, frontispiece and 4 litho plates, 2 text engravings, 1 full page text illustration; later half calf, rubbed, some foxing of title and elsewhere.   Marlborough 162-9 1996 £220.00

BOND, W. H.   Eighteenth Century Studies in Honor of Donald F. Hyde. New York: Grolier Club, 1970. One of 1650 copies; 10 3/4 x 7 inches; xv, (1), 424, (1) leaf (colophon); device on title, several plates; very fine. Phillip J. Pirages 33-279 1996 $100.00

BOND, W. H.   The Houghton Library 1942-1967. Harvard College Library, 1967. Folio; xv, 256 pages; 10 color plates and over 250 monochrome illustrations; cloth.   Thomas Thorp 489-36 1996 £65.00

BONDT, JACOB DE   An Account of the Diseases, Natural History and Medicines of the East Indies. London: T. Noteman, 1769. 1st English edition; 8vo; xvi, 231 pages, with last leaf in facsimile; contemporary calf, newly rebacked; GM 2263 (1st Latin ed. of 1642).   James Tait Goodrich K40-53 1996 $250.00

BONE, D. D.   Fifty Years Reminiscences of Scottish Cricket. Glasgow: Aird and Coghill, 1898. 1st edition; 8vo; 290, (xiv) pages; 26 plates; original cloth, gilt, over bevelled boards, spine very faded, little marked, trifle shaken, but very good, scarce. Padwick 3187.   R.F.G. Hollett 76-31 1996 £120.00

BONE, DAVID W.   Merchantman Rearmed. London: Chatto & Windus, 1949. 1st edition; number 43 of 160 copies signed by David Bone; 4to; (2), 331, (1) pages; original drypoint etched frontispiece portrait signed by artist Muirhead Bone, who did the full page and in-text illustrations; original blue quarter morocco and cloth, top edge gilt, couple of small light damp spots on front cover, but very good; this copy with signed inscription from David Bone for Franklin Abbott laid in on separate sheet, dated 1949.   Chapel Hill 94-39 1996 $150.00

BONER, CHARLES   Chamois Hunting in the Mountains of Bavaria. London: Chapman and Hall 193, Piccadilly, 1853. 1st edition; 8vo; (iii-iv), (v-viii), 1-410 pages; chromo litho frontispiece, 5 chromo litho plates, 6 woodcut vignettes to letterpress; foxing to frontispiece and chromo lithographs, ms. ink inscription to prelim, binders stamp to front f.e.p., hinges cracked; bound by Bickers & Son, full strawberry calf, rebacked, original spine laid down, double gilt rule borders to boards, some wear to upper board, some slight loss of original backstrip, endpapers and edges uniformly marbled.   Beeleigh Abbey BA56-38 1996 £125.00

BONER, CHARLES   Chamois Hunting in the Mountains of Bavaria and the Tyrol. London: Chapman and Hall, 1860. 2nd edition; 8vo; xiii, 446 pages, 7 colored lithographed plates, 9 text illustrations; contemporary blue calf, rebacked, light spotting on paltes, but good.   David Bickersteth 133-139 1996 £160.00

BONFILS, WINIFRED BLACK   The Life and Personality of Phoebe Apperson Hearst. Privately printed for William Randolph Hearst, 1928. Number 4 of 1000 numbered copies; folio; printed on paper specially watermarked "Hearst" and "Nash"; parchment over boards, raised bands, gilt rules and lettering, covers little marked, but very nice. Bertram Rota 272-304 1996 £280.00

BONI, ALBERT   Photographic Literature. An International Bibliographic Guide to General and Specialized Literature on Photographic Processes.... New York: Morgan and Morgan, 1962. 1st edition; 4to; original cloth, dust jacket.   Forest Books 74-21 1996 £65.00

BONI, ALBERT   Photographic Literature: an International Bibliographical Guide. New York: 1962/72. 1st editions; 2 volumes, volume 1 in dust jacket, volume 2 wrappers, as issued, uncommon to find together.   J. B. Muns 154-41 1996 $350.00

BONNE Responce a Tous Propos,...Auquel est Contenu Grand Nombre de Prouerbes & Sentences Ioyeuses... Lyon: B. Rigaud, 1567. 8vo; 160 pages; woodcut ornaments; modern boards; fine. Bingen p. 38 no. 8; not in Baudrier; 1 copy in NUC.   Bennett Gilbert LL29-15 1996 $900.00

BONNEMAINS, JACQUELINE   Baudin in Australian Waters. The Artwork Of the French Voyage of Discovery to the Southern Lands 1800-1804. London: 1988. 300 colored and plain plates; cloth.   Wheldon & Wesley 207-362 1996 £105.00

BONNEMAINS, JACQUELINE   Baudin in Australian Waters. The Artwork of the French Voyage of Discvoery to the Southern Lands 1800-1804. Melbourne: Oxford University Press, 1988. 1st edition; super royal 4to; xii, 348 pages, 10 maps, frontispiece, 153 color illustrations, 185 black and white illustrations; blue cloth with silver titles, decorated endpapers; new in dust jacket.   Parmer Books Nat/Hist-067308 1996 $200.00

BONNER, CAMPBELL   Studies in Magical Amulets, Chiefly Graeco-Egyptian. Ann Arbor: University Michigan Press, 1950. 4to; xxiv, 334 pages, 25 plates; original cloth; signature.   Archaeologia Luxor-3051 1996 $450.00

BONNER, T. D.   The Life and Adventures of James P. Beckwourth, Mountaineer, Scout and Pioneer and Chief of the Crow Nation of Indians. New York: Harper & Bros., 1856. 1st edition; 7 3/8 x 4 7/8 inches; 537 pages + ad leaf at end, frontispiece, 11 full page illustrations; blindstamped red cloth, some chipping to spine, light wear to tips. Dawson's Books Shop 528-13 1996 $275.00

BONNEY, H. K.   Historic Notices in Reference to Fotheringhay. Oundle: T. Bell, 1821. 1st edition; 127 pages; engravings; half calf over marbled boards, spine decoratively gilt in unusual repeated wave pattern, joints lightly rubbed, else fine.   Hermitage SP95-1094 1996 $100.00

BONNOT DE MABLY, GABRIEL   Translations from the French. printed for the author, by W. Whittingham, Lynn, 1770. 1st edition of this translation; 4to; 3 parts in one; each part has separate signatures and pagination, 4 page list of subscribers, original boards, uncut, lacks backstrip, very nice.   Anthony Laywood 108-29 1996 £145.00

BONNYCASTLE, JOHN   An Introduction to Astronomy. London: 1796. 1st edition; 8.5 x 5 inches; 431 pages; 20 plates; old calf, spine label lacking, covers detached, few illustrations frayed from improper folding; John K. King 77-714 1996 $350.00

BONNYCASTLE, R. H.   Spanish America; or a Descriptive, Historical and Geographical Account of the Dominions of Spain in the Western Hemisphere Continental and Insular. Philadelphia: Abraham Small, 1819. 1st American edition; folding map, folding hand colored chart, browning throughout, more so to prelims, map creased incorrectly but intact with few tears just starting at a few folds, overall wear, but joints and hinges tight; presentable. Sabin 6333.   Hermitage SP95-696 1996 $400.00

BONOMI, JOSEPH   Ninevah and its Palaces. The Discoveries of Botta and Layard, Applied to the Elucidation of Holy Writ. London: Office of the Illustrated London Library, n.d. 1852. 1st edition; 8vo; frontispiece, map, 234 illustrations in text; original cloth, gilt, uncut, nice.   Anthony W. Laywood 108-154 1996 £50.00

BONOMI, JOSEPH   Nineveh and Its Palaces. London: Office of the Illustrated London Library, 1852. 1st edition; 8vo; 402 pages; over 200 in text illustrations; 19th century half calf and marbled boards with gilt tooled spine and morocco spine label; unobtrusive marginal dampstain at lower corner of first 100 or so pages, former owner's name and bookseller's ticket, but very good.   Chapel Hill 94-277 1996 $175.00

BONSAL, STEPHEN   Edward Fitzgerald Beale: a Pioneer in the Path of Empire 1822-1903. New York: G. P. Putnam's, Sons, 1912. 1st edition; 1 illustrations, 312 pages; overall light wear, otherwise fine; ink inscription, possibly authorial; Howes B608.   Hermitage SP95-697 1996 $200.00

BONTEMPS, ARNA   Cavalcade of the American Negro: Diamond Jubilee Exposition Authority. Chicago: Illinois Writer's Project, 1940. 1st edition; frontispiece; fine in perfect bound wrappers, mailing envelope present with Booker T. Washington stamp and special cachet for the American Negro Exposition at the Chicago Coliseum; rare with envelope. Between the Covers 43-274 1996 $200.00

BONTEMPS, ARNA   Drums at Dusk. New York: Macmillan, 1939. 1st edition; owner's name, small tear to spine in dust jacket with several shallow chips and faded spine, overall acceptable copy, very scarce. David Holloway 94D-3 1996 $200.00

BONTEMPS, ARNA   Mr. Kelso's Lion. Philadelphia: New York: Lippincott, 1970. 1st edition; illustrations by Len Ebert; about fine in very good plus dust jacket, price clipped with couple of not so grievous tears; scarce.   Between the Covers 43-224 1996 $100.00

BONTEMPS, ARNA   Slappy Hooper, the Wonderful Sign Painter. Boston: Houghton Mifflin Co., 1946. 1st edition; oblong quarto; illustrations by Ursula Koering; fine in attractive, near fine dust jacket with bit of unobtrusive foxing and couple of tears, neatly repaired internally; exceptionally scarce.   Between the Covers 43-222 1996 $650.00

BONTEMPS, ARNA   Slappy Hooper, the Wonderful Sign Painter. Boston: Houghton Mifflin, 1946. 1st edition; illustrations by Ursula Koering; original cloth, fine, with pieces of dust jacket laid in; this copy inscribed by Jack Conroy.   Beasley Books 82-182 1996 $100.00

THE BOOK of American Negro Poetry. New York: HB & Co., 1922. 1st edition; rubbing to edges of boards and some moderate darkening to spine label, otherwise very good, lacking dust jacket.   Between the Covers 43-7 1996 $100.00

A BOOK of Belgium's Gratitude. London: 1915. 1st edition; limited to 200 copies; large attractive book with many plates; white boards with gilt and green decoration, slight soiling, still very good to fine.   Bannatyne Books 19-B11 1996 £70.00

THE BOOK of Fate. A New and Complete System of Fortune Telling...In Seven Parts. New York: printed for the translator & sold by all booksellers, 1817. 1st American edition; 18mo; 210, (1) pages; frontispiece and half title; original printed boards, very rubbed and darkened, spine shot, very shaken, worming in magin through most of the book, chiefly in one line, some letters affected, especially early, some soiling of leaves, but generally quite good, obviously only a fair copy.   M & S Rare Books 60-320 1996 $500.00

A BOOK of Prayers. Philadelphia: Christ Church, 1964. 1st edition; limited to 300 copies; signed by artist; 8vo; woodcuts by Helen Siegl, loose sheets in portfolio; fine.   James S. Jaffe 34-295 1996 $350.00

THE BOOK of the Camp Fire Girls. New York: Camp Fire Books, 1936. 1st edition; octavo; 247 pages; original limp beige buckram, printed in dark brown and red, minimal soiling and fraying, bookplate; near fine. Heritage Book Shop 196-235 1996 $300.00

BOOLE, GEORGE   An Investigation of the Laws of Thought on which are Founded the Mathematical Theories of Logic and Probabilities. London: Macmillan, 1854. 1st edition; 8vo; v, iv, (1), 424, (1) pages, complete with errata and leaf of notes at end; skilful paper repair to upper outside 2 inches of title and dedicatory leaf; original pebbled green cloth, rubbed at edges; some foxing, very good, mostly unopened. Edwin V. Glaser 121-35 1996 $2,000.00

BOOLE, GEORGE   A Treatise on the Calculus of Finite Differences. Cambridge: Macmillan and Co., 1860. 1st edition; 8vo; (viii), 248 pages, 18 pages of ads at end; original cloth, rather worn, hinges shaken, sides stained; presentation copy, inscribed "From the author".   John Drury 82-27 1996 £90.00

BOONE, JAMES SHERGOLD   The Council of Ten. London: printed for the Proprietors and Published by Thomas Wilkie, 1822-23. 8vo; 12 numbers in 3 volumes; (iv), (476); iv, 484; (viii), 476 pages; contemporary half calf, marbled boards, double labels, corners slightly worn, foot of one spine chipped, good, complete set.   Robert Clark 38-226 1996 £110.00

BOOS, FRANK H.   The Cermaic Sculptures of Ancient Oaxaca. South Brunswick: A. S. Barnes, 1966. Folio; 488 pages, 458 figures; original cloth, tattered dust jacket, reinforced with clear tape.   Archaeologia Luxor-4300 1996 $200.00

BOOTH, ANDREW D.   Automatic Digital Calculators. London: Butterworths, 1953. 1st edition; 8vo; vii, 231 pages; frontispiece, 3 plates, numerous figures and tables. original cloth; very good. Sarrazin F4 for 2nd ed. of 1956; Shiers 1102.   Edwin V. Glaser 121-37 1996 $175.00

BOOTH, DAVID   The Principles of English Composition: Illustrated by Examples with Critical Remarks. London: Cochrane and Pickersgill, 1831. 1st edition; 12mo; (ii), vi, 351, (1) pages, half title, engraved prize label on endpaper; contemporary olive calf, joints rubbed.   James Burmester 29-17 1996 £60.00

BOOTH, G. R.   A Popular Treatise on the Strength and Application of Materials Used in Buildings in General Shewing the Advantages to Be Derived from the Principles of the Patent of Messrs. R. Witty & Co. in All Architectural and Engineering... London: Weale, 1836. 8vo; vi, 35, (1) pages, 1 engraved plate; seemly modern cloth; from the library of J. G. James.   Elton Engineering 10-15 1996 £195.00

BOOTH, HENRY   Free Trade, As It Affects the People, Addressed to a Reformed Parliament. Liverpool: printed by Wales & Baines, & sold by them, Bancks & Co.... 1833. 1st edition; 8vo; 40 pages; disbound. Kress C3420.   James Burmester 29-18 1996 £60.00

BOOTH, WILLIAM   In Darkest England and the Way Out. London: International Headquarters of the Salvation Army, 1890. 1st edition; 8vo; frontispiece, (vi), 285, (29) pages; publisher's cloth, spine slightly shaken, endpapers foxed, covers rubbed, wear along spine and tips.   The Bookpress 75-388 1996 $150.00

BOOTHBY, ROBERT   Recollections of a Rebel. London: Hutchison & Co. Ltd., 1978. 1st edition; color frontispiece and numerous black and white photos; original binding, top edge slightly dusty, head and tail of spine slightly bumped, very good in nicked and slightly creased and frayed dust jacket. Inscribed presentation from author for Manny Shinwell.   Ulysses 39-57 1996 £75.00

BOOTT, FRANCIS   A Letter Addressed to William Pratt, Esq... N.P.: Derby?: 1819. 1st edition; 8vo; recent half calf, very good. Appears to be the dedication copy (for Lucy Hardcastle of Derby) whom Boott married the following year, with pres. inscription, with few ms. corrections.   Ximenes 108-28 1996 $250.00

BORCHARDT, RUDOLF   Gartenphantasie. Bremer Presse, 1925. One of 300 copies; 9 3/4 x 6 3/4 inches; 3 p.l. (1 blank), 7-36 pages, (2) leaves (colophon blank); black and red decorated initial by Anna Simons, who also designed title, printed in black and red; very fine burgundy crushed morocco by Frieda Thiersch (signed on rear turn-in), simple gilt fillet on covers, raised bands, gilt ruled spine compartments, turn-ins ruled in gilt, edges gilt, in very nice fleece lined slipcase with matching morocco lip, exceptionally fine copy.   Phillip J. Pirages 33-111 1996 $1,850.00

BORDEN, SPENCER   The Arab Horse. New York: Doubleday, Page, 1906. 1st edition; 8vo; (20), 104 pages; numerous photographic illustrations; original green cloth with mounted cover illustration, top edge gilt, nearly fine in lightly edge chipped dust jacket. Rare in jacket. Chapel Hill 94-189 1996 $225.00

BORDEN, W. C.   The Use of the Roentgen Ray by the Medical Department of the United States Army in the War with Spain. Washington: 1900. 1st edition; 4to; 98 pages, plus 38 x-ray plates; original binding; John B. Murphy's copy with his autograph and bookplate. Kelly Burrage 892; Norman 267.   W. Bruce Fye 71-206 1996 $500.00

BORDEN, W. C.   The Use of the Rontgen Ray by the Medical Department of the United States Army in the War with Spain. Washington: GPO, 1900. 4to; 98 pages, x-rays; half calf, some rubbing, but overall very clean, tight copy. GM 2687.2.   James Tait Goodrich K40-54 1996 $295.00

BORDEON, LAURENT   The Management of the Tongue. London: printed by D. L. for H. Rhodes, 1707. 2nd edition in English; 8vo; contemporary sprinkled calf, spine gilt; fine copy.   Ximenes 108-29 1996 $250.00

BORDLEY, JAMES   Two Centuries of American Medicine, 1776-1976. Philadelphia: 1976. 1st edition; 844 pages; original binding. GM 65963. W. Bruce Fye 71-207 1996 $125.00

BORELLI, GIOVANNI ALPHONSO   Euclides Restitutus Denuo Limatus, Sive Prisce Geometriae Brevius & Facilius Contexta. (with) Elementa Conica Apollonii Paergei et Archimedis Opera Nova & Breviori Methodo Demonstrata... Rome: ex typographia Mascardi/Rome: apud Mascardum, 1679/79. 3rd edition of first title, 1st edition of 2nd title; 12mo; 2 volumes in one; 8 engraved plates; contemporary vellum (bit soiled), very good.   Ximenes 108-30 1996 $750.00

BORGES, JORGE LUIS   The Aleph and Other Stories 1933-1969. London: Cape, 1971. 1st English edition; near fine in dust jacket. Lame Duck Books 19-86 1996 $200.00

BORGES, JORGE LUIS   Ficciones - the Selected Essays and Short Stories of Jorge Luis Borges. London: Weidenfeld and Nicolson, 1962. 1st edition; original binding, top edge slightly spotted and dusty, very good in nicked and slightly rubbed, marked and dusty very slightly spotted dust jacket; inscription.   Ulysses 39-58 1996 £225.00

BORGES, JORGE LUIS   Ficciones. London: Weidenfeld & Nicolson, 1962. 1st British edition; ownership name, date and address and bookplate to front fly, light foxing to page edges and two diagonal creases to lower fore-edge of first few pages, overall very good or better in very good+, lightly soiled jacket with tape reinforcement to verso of spine, very scarce edition.   Lame Duck Books 19-84 1996 $250.00

BORGES, JORGE LUIS   Ficciones. New York: Limited Editions Club, 1984. 1st edition; one of 1500 numbered copies, signed by LeWitt; thick square 8vo; silkscreens by LeWitt; full black calf stamped in blind; fine in slipcase.   Captain's Bookshelf 38-22 1996 $500.00

BORGES, JORGE LUIS   Siete Poemas Sajones. Seven Saxon Poems. Verona: Plain Wrapper Press, 1974. Limited to 120 copies, signed by author and artist; folio; 37 pages; low relief images by Arnaldo Pomodoro; binding by Marcello Fornaro of unbleached vellum, inset with 3 striking gold plated bronze bas-relief plates by Pomodoro, mounted in recessed panels on front cover, housed in cloth covered wooden box, which also displays relief-etched brass panel by Pomodoro on front cover. Smyth 14.   Bromer Booksellers 87-253 1996 $8,000.00

BORLAND, R.   Border Raids and Reivers. Dalbeattie: Thomas Fraser, 1910. 2nd edition; 8vo; pages xvi, 310; original cloth, gilt.   R.F.G. Hollett 76-33 1996 £60.00

BORLAND, R.   Border Raids and Reivers. Dalbeattie: Thomas Fraser, 1910. 2nd edition; 8vo; pages xvi, 310; original cloth, gilt, spine faded. R.F.G. Hollett & Son 78-709 1996 £50.00

BORROMEO, CHARLES   Pasatorum Instructiones. Antwerp: Plantin, 1586. 1st separate edition; small 8vo; 376 pages; portrait, woodcut ornaments; contemporary vellum (darkened), light browning, very good. Rare. Voet I.421-423; not in Reulens, De Backer, NUC or BM STC. Bennett Gilbert LL29-16 1996 $1,100.00

BORROW, GEORGE HENRY 1803-1881   The Bible in Spain; or, the Journeys, Adventures and Imprisonments of an Englishman... London: John Murray, 1843. 1st edition; 1st issue; large 12mo; pages xxiv, 370, (2); viii, 398, (2); viii, 391, (1); 3 volumes; half titles and integral ads present, without ad slip tipped in at end of volume 3; margins slightly browned, otherwise internally excellent; contemporary half calf, minor rubbing, crushed polished black morocco title and volume labels, two on volume 2 slightly chipped, marbled boards, slightly rubbed, marbled edges; very good. Collie & Fraser A.2.a. Wise pp 69-72; Wolff 597. Blackwell's B112-44 1996 £170.00

BORROW, GEORGE HENRY 1803-1881   Lavengro; the Scholar - the Gypsy - the Priest. London: John Murray, 1851. 1st edition; 12mo; 3 volumes; frontispiece, half titles, 32 pages ads at end of volumes 1 and 2; original cloth, spines somewhat faded and nicked at head and foot, labels little chipped, uncut, occasional spotting; very good; bookplate of first Viscount Eversley; Wolff 598; Wise 11.   Simon Finch 24-14 1996 £175.00

BORROW, GEORGE HENRY 1803-1881   Lavengro. London: Limited Editions Club, 1936. Limited edition; 2 volumes; 16 lithographs in color and drawings by Barnett Freedman; dark maroon cloth, gilt, fine set in slightly rubbed pictorial dust jacket.   Barbara Stone 70-97 1996 £95.00

BORROW, GEORGE HENRY 1803-1881   Lavengro. New York: Limited Editions Club, 1936. One of 1500 copies, signed by artist, this copy unnumbered; 8vo; 2 volumes; cloth, spines somewhat faded and scuffed, prelims spotted, otherwise very nice in slipcase.   Bertram Rota 272-264 1996 £85.00

BORROW, GEORGE HENRY 1803-1881   The Romany Rye; a Sequel to 'Lavengro'... London: John Murray, 1857. 1st edition; 8vo; 2 volumes; pages xi, (i), 372, 32 (pub. cat. Feb. 1857); vii, (), 375, (1), (8) ads; original fine vertical ribbed dark green cloth, rubbed, wear to heads and feet of backstrips, printed paper labels very damaged (that for vol. 2 nearly all gone), triple blind fillet borders, corners bumped, brown endpapers, hinges weak, sound only; shaken, edges browned, occasional soiling; Collie & Fraser 1; Collie & Fraser A4; Wise 12; Wolff 599. Blackwell's B112-45 1996 £125.00

BORROW, GEORGE HENRY 1803-1881   Works. London: John Murray, 1914-23. Mixed issues, but from the same edition; 8vo; 6 volumes; illustrations; contemporary dark red half morocco, spines richly gilt in five compartments, gilt ruled sides, top edge gilt, joints on one volume slightly rubbed, and joints of another very skilfully repaired, otherwise fine set.   Thomas Thorp 489-38 1996 £150.00

BORROW, GEORGE HENRY 1803-1881   Works. London: John Murray, 1923-26. 8vo; 7 volumes; frontispieces and other illustrations; half red morocco, gilt panel spines, marbled endpapers, top edge gilt, by De Coverly; handsome set.   Sotheran PN32-3 1996 £750.00

BOSANQUET, S. R.   A New System of Logic and Development of the Principles of Truth and Reasoning. London: John W. Parker, 1839. 1st edition; 8vo; half title; original cloth, nice.   Anthony W. Laywood 108-155 1996 £125.00

BOSCO, HENRI   Sites et Mirages. Paris: Les Editions de la Cigogne, 1950. 1st edition; one of 225 copies and 25 hors commerce, this copy being number 90/185 on Velin de Rives, signed and inscribed by Bosco; 4to; half title, title, 144, (8), 47 illustrations, 24 watercolors, hand colored by Louis Calle, 23 drawings reproduced as woodcuts, loose as issued; publisher's folder and slipcase.   Sotheran PN32-176 1996 £950.00

BOSMAN, RICHARD   Hannah Duston. San Francisco: Arion Press, 1987. One of 400 copies, from a total issue of 425 all on Rives paper, 25 copies hors commerce, 400 ordinary issue; page size 16 1/2 x 12 1/2 inches; printed in handset in Kennerley Bold, woodcuts by Richard Bosman;   Priscilla Juvelis 95/1-42 1996 $500.00

BOSQUI, EDWARD   Memoirs of Edward Bosqui. Oakland: Holmes Book Co., 1952. Reprint of very rare 1904 first edition; limited to 350 copies; xxvii, 180 pages; colored frontispiece, 3 facimiles, 2 plates; original cloth backed decorated boards, paper spine label; fine. Scarce. Cowan p. 64; Howes B623.   Argonaut Book Shop 113-84 1996 $175.00

BOSSERT, H. T.   Ornament in Applied Art: Decorative Motives from the Arts of Asia, Primitive Europe, North Central and South America, Africa, Oceania and from the Peasant Arts of Europe. New York: E. Weyhe, 1924. Folio; xi, 35 pages; 2000 color illustrations on 122 plates; cloth, worn.   Thomas Thorp 489-39 1996 £85.00

BOSSUET, JACQUES   De Nova Quaestione Tractatus Tres. Paris: Anisson, 1698. 1st edition; 8vo; 472 pages; woodcut ornaments; contemporary full speckled calf, richly gilt spine; fine. Cior. 14113. Bennett Gilbert LL29-17 1996 $950.00

BOSWELL, C. S.   An Irish Precursor of Dante: A Study on the Vision of Heaven and Hell Ascribed to... Nutt, 1908. 1st edition; cloth; very good; author's own copy, inscribed and annotated.   C. P. Hyland 216-52 1996 £225.00

BOSWELL, JAMES 1740-1795   British Essays in Favour of the Brave Corsicans... London: for Edward and Charles Dilly, 1769. 1st edition; 12mo; pages (i-iv), half title and title, (ii), explanation of frontispiece, (v)-xviii, 136; contemporary calf, red morocco label, joints cracked but holding, good copy, protected in red morocco backed folding case; scarce. Pottle 45; Rothschild 448.   Simon Finch 24-15 1996 £1,800.00

BOSWELL, JAMES 1740-1795   Carminum Rariorum Macaronicarum Delectus: In Usum Ludorum Apollinarum... Edinburgi: Ex Typographia G. Ramsay, 1813. 8vo; pages 144, 14; blind tooled calf, rebacked. Theodore Martin's copy, with his presentation ALS to Eustace Grubbe.   Peter Murray Hill 185-12 1996 £95.00

BOSWELL, JAMES 1740-1795   Everybody's Boswell... London: G. Bell and Sons Ltd., 1930. Large paper edition, one of 350 numbered copies signed by artist; 54 full page black and white drawings with printed tissue guards by E. H. Shepard; buckram covers, top edge gilt, map on rear endpapers, free endpapers partially browned, pastedown edges browned, edges slightly spotted, very good in chipped, frayed and rubbed, slightly marked, creased and dusty dust jacket browned at spine and edges and with small piece missing from centre of spine.   Ulysses 39-531 1996 £145.00

BOSWELL, JAMES 1740-1795   Jacob Boswells, Esq. Historich-Geographische Beschreibung von Corsica Nebst Vielen Wichtigen Nachrichten und Anecdoten vom Pascal Paoli dem General der Corsen. Leipzig: Caspar Fritsch, 1769. 2nd edition; 8vo; folding map; contemporary half calf; slight foxing, but fine. Pottle 33.   Ximenes 108-31 1996 $1,500.00

BOSWELL, JAMES 1740-1795   The Journal of a Tour to the Hebrides with Samuel Johnson. Dublin: printed for Messrs.. White, Byrone and Cash, 1785. 1st Dublin edition; tall octavo; pages viii,, 524, (1); three quarter tree calf and linen, raised bands, green leather label, gilt, all edges marbled; fine, very scarce. Pottle 58.   Hartfield 48-L10 1996 $795.00

BOSWELL, JAMES 1740-1795   The Journal of a Tour to the Hebrides, with Samuel Johnson. London: printed by Henry Baldwin for Charles Dilly, 1785. 2nd edition; 8vo; 534 pages, (1) page ad; original full calf with morocco spine label, joints cracked externally but holding, else very good, crisp, clean copy.   Chapel Hill 94-135 1996 $150.00

BOSWELL, JAMES 1740-1795   The Journal of a Tour to Corsica & Memoirs of Pascal Paoli. Cambridge: Cambridge University Press, 1923. 1st edition; black and white portrait; cloth backed patterned paper boards, spare title label, top edge dusty, head and tail of spine and corners bumped and bruised, covers marked, rubbed, dusty and slightly soiled, free endpapers browned, very good; with pencilled ownership signature of B. H. Bronson, who has marked off several passages in the book, again in pencil.   Ulysses 39-60 1996 £55.00

BOSWELL, JAMES 1740-1795   The Life of Samuel Johnson, LL.D. Comprehending an Account of His Studies and Numerous Works, in Chronological Order... London: by Henry Baldwin, for Charles Dilly, 1791. 1st edition; 4to; 2 volumes, xii, (xvi), 516; (iv), 588; this copy has the misprint 'gve' on p. 135, volume 1, indicating that the inner forme of sheet S in that volume is in an earlier uncorrected state; frontispiece, 2 engraved facsimile plates; contemporary mottled calf, sides with narrow gilt borders, spines divided into panels with a metope and pentaglyph roll, gilt blazons in each panel, black morocco lettering pieces, circular numbering pieces, marbled endpapers; spines lightly rubbed and gilt slightly faded, but fine in modern brown morocco backed folding case; engraved armorial bookplates of Jonathan Pytts. Courtney & Nichol Smith pp. 172-173; Pottle 79; Rothschild 463.   Simon Finch 24-16 1996 £5,500.00

BOSWELL, JAMES 1740-1795   The Life of Samuel Johnson, LL.D. London: Henry Baldwin for Charles Dilly, 1791. 1st edition; 2nd state of the first printing with the word 'give' on p. 135 corrected and with all cancels and other points called for by Pottle (79); tall quarto; 2 volumes; stipple engraved portrait, handsomely rebound in period style morocco spines, marbled boards, gilt extra, double leather labels, fine, bright set. Rothschild 464 .   Hartfield 48-L11 1996 $4,250.00

BOSWELL, JAMES 1740-1795   The Life of Samuel Johnson, Including a Journal of His Tour to the Hebrides. London: John Murray, 1839. New edition; small 8vo; 10 volumes; over 50 engraved illustrations; fine grained blue quarter morocco leather and marbled boards, heavily gilt worked spines, top edge gilt, marbled endpapers, ribbon markers, very attractive set.   Antic Hay 101-175 1996 $500.00

BOSWELL, JAMES 1740-1795   The Life of Samuel Johnson, LL.D.... London: Bell and Daldy, York St., Convent Garden, 1872. Small 8vo; 10 volumes; half titles, 16 steel engraved plates, 1 etched plate; full polished tan calf, double gilt rule borders to boards, tiny gilt onrmaents to corners, gilt tooling to compartments, red and green morocco labels to spines, joints rubbed, corners slightly bumped, edges and endpaper uniformly marbled. Good set.   Beeleigh Abbey BA56-154 1996 £350.00

BOSWELL, JAMES 1740-1795   Life of Samuel Johnson. Oxford: Clarendon Press/New York: Macmillan, 1887. 1st of this important edition; tall 8vo; original green cloth, gilt titles, uncut, 14 portraits, maps and facsimiles, some folding; some wear but very good. Bookplate of Walter Brooks. Pottle 98.   Hartfield 48-V4a 1996 $395.00

BOSWELL, JAMES 1740-1795   Life of Samuel Johnson. London: privately printed for the Navarre Society, 1924. Reprinted from the first edition of 1791 with appendix; royal 8vo; 3 volumes; illustrations, portraits; pictorial cloth, gilt, top edge gilt; very good. Pottle 101. Hartfield 48-V4b 1996 $265.00

BOSWELL, JAMES 1740-1795   Life of Samuel Johnson. London: Dent, 1925. Tall 8vo; 3 volumes; 100 illustrations by Herbert Railton, plus many photogravures; titlepages in red and black; original cloth, gilt crests and titles; attractive set.   Hartfield 48-V4c 1996 $185.00

BOSWELL, JAMES 1740-1795   Life of Samuel Johnson. Limited Editions Club at the Curwen Press, 1938. Limited to 1500 copies; 3 volumes; tan cloth, leather labels, gilt, boxed; excellent set.   Hartfield 48-V4d 1996 $275.00

BOSWELL, JAMES 1740-1795   The Life of Samuel Johnson. New York: Heritage Press, 1963. 3 volumes; tan linen, red and gilt leather labels; boxed, fine.   Hartfield 48-V4e 1996 $185.00

BOSWELL, JAMES 1740-1795   The Principal Corrections and Additions to the First Edition of Mr. Boswell's Life of Dr. Johnson. London: Henry Baldwin for Charles Dilly, 1793. 1st edition; 4to; pages (ii), 42; contemporary speckled calf, gilt Greek key border to sides, flat spine with gilt rules, lacks label, rubbed, spine worn at head and tail, front joint cracked at head; very good copy; the Gell copy with ownership inscription of Philip and Dorothy Gell, Hopton, dated 2 Jan. 1793, few ms. corrigenda; Pottle 113.   Simon Finch 24-17 1996 £1,500.00

BOSWELL, ROBERT   Dancing in the Movies. University of Iowa, 1986. 1st edition; 1500 printed; author's first book; signed; fine copy in fine dust jacket.   Book Time 2-47 1996 $125.00

BOSWELL, ROBERT   Dancing in the Movies. Iowa City: University of Iowa, 1986. 1st edition; reportedly published in an edition of 1500 copies; fine in dust jacket, signed by Boswell.   Lame Duck Books 19-87 1996 $175.00

BOSWORTH, JOSEPH   An Anglo-Saxon Dictionary Based on the Manuscript Collections of the Late Joseph Bosworth. Oxford: Clarendon Press, 1882. 1st edition; 5 original parts; buff wrappers, corners little creased, repairs to hinges, spine defective pt. IV 2.   Jarndyce 103-130 1996 £95.00

BOSWORTH, JOSEPH   A Dictionary of the Anglo-Saxon Language, etc. London: Longman, 1838. 1st edition; thick 8vo; large folding hand colored engraved map; full contemporary crushed brown morocco, boards with gilt borders, inner gilt dentelles, spine with raised bands, large floral gilt devices in compartments, lower edge of upper board with unobtrusive stain, joints lightly rubbed, all edges gilt, excellent copy, scarce 1st edition.   Ian Wilkinson 95/1-41 1996 £130.00

BOSWORTH, JOSEPH   The Elements of Anglo-Saxon Grammar with Copious Notes, Illustrating the Structure of the Saxon and the Formation of the English Language. London: 1823. 1st edition; 8vo; xlvii, 330 pages, engraved table; half calf, new title label inset on red morocco; good. K Books 442-79 1996 £86.00

BOSWORTH, W.   Gardens of Kijkuit. Privately printed, 1919. Photos by Genthe, slight soiling on covers, rare.   J. B. Muns 154-122 1996 $275.00

THE BOTANICAL Keepsake: an Arrangement of British Plants. London: 1846. Crown 8vo; pages x, 233, ii, 28 hand colored plates; cloth, gilt, binding little faded, neatly rebacked preserving spine.   John Henly 27-191 1996 £98.00

BOTTA, CHARLES   History of the War of the Independence of the United States of America. New Haven: Published and Printed by Nathan Whiting, 1836. 8th edition; 2 volumes, 472, 468 pages; full calf with gilt designs on spine and black leather labels. Howes B636.   Blue River Books 9-11 1996 $150.00

BOTTOMLEY, GORDON   Chambers of Imagery, Together with Chambers of Imagery (Second Series). London: Elkin Mathews, 1907-12. 1st editions; small 8vo; 2 volumes; original wrappers, those of first volume slightly soiled, spine of second volume chipped. 1st volume initialled "L(ascelles) A(bercrombie) and signed and dated by author at end, some underlining by Abercrombie, 2nd volume inscribed by author for Abercrombie.   R.F.G. Hollett & Son 78-323 1996 £85.00

BOTTOMLEY, GORDON   King Lear's Wife; the Crier by Night; the Riding to Lithend; Midsummer Eve; Laodice and Danae. London: Constable and Co. Ltd., 101920. 1st edition; half title; original decorated boards, spine defective, uncut and unopened. With 4 page ALS from author.   Anthony W. Laywood 109-12 1996 £145.00

BOTTOMLEY, GORDON   Laodice and Danae. London: privately printed, 1909. 1st edition; 8vo; original wrappers, slightly creased and chipped at edges; few spots; presentation copy inscribed in author's hand to Daisy Rigby and John Gold.   R.F.G. Hollett & Son 78-326 1996 £55.00

BOTTOMLEY, GORDON   Midsummer Eve: a Play. Pear Tree Press, 1905. One of 120 copies; 8vo; printed in grey, old gold and Venetian red; boards with canvas back, very nice, bright, unopened copy.   Bertram Rota 272-365 1996 £100.00

BOTTOMLEY, GORDON   Scenes and Plays. London: Constable, 1929. Signed, limited edition of 100 numbered copies; 4to; white cloth, top edge gilt, near fine, minor soil to cloth, minor browning to endpapers. Antic Hay 101-176 1996 $125.00

BOUCHETTE, JOSEPH   The British Dominions in North America; or, a Topographical and Statistical Description of the Provinces of Lower and Upper Canada, New Brunswick, Nova Scotia, The Islands of Newfoundland, Prince Edward Island and Cape Breton; London: Longman, Rees, Orme, Brown, Green and Longman, 1832. 4to; 2 volumes; xxvi, 498, xi, 296 pages; 2 engraved frontispieces, 15 plates, 10 plans; recently rebacked with new spine, new spine labels, contemporary marbled boards; some offsetting from plates, occasional foxing but in fact fine.   David Mason 71-118 1996 $2,000.00

BOUCHETTE, JOSEPH   The British Dominions in North America: or a Topographical and Statistical Description of the Province of Lower and Upper Canada, New Brunswick, Nova Scotia... (with) A Topographical Dictionary of the Province of Lower Canada. London: Longman, Rees, Orme, Brown, Green and Longman... 1832. 1st edition; 4to; 3 volumes in 2; frontispieces, 18 plates, all plates in good condition, contemporary ink presentation inscription; rebound in modern half polished tan calf, marbled boards, raised bands to spines, green and maroon morocco labels to spines, gilt tooling to compartments, new endpapers and prelims, original prelims bound in. Very good. Abbey Travel 622; Sabin 6848; Gagnon 527.   Beeleigh Abbey BA56-40 1996 £650.00

BOUCHETTE, JOSEPH A Topographical Description of the Province of Lower Canada, with Remarks Upon Upper Canada, and On the Relative Connection of Both Provinces with the United States of America. London: W. Faden, 1815. 1st edition; large 8vo; frontispiece, 3 folding maps, 5 plans, 7 fine aquatint plates, 2 tables; plate, errata leaf; contemporary calf, spine gilt, morocco label, expertly recased; very fine, crisp, and clean copy. Sabin 6849; Lande 1591. Trebizond 39-80 196 $950.00

BOUDRYE, LOUIS NAPOLEON Historic Records of the Fifth New York Cavalry, First Ira Harris Guard. Albany: S. R. Gray, 1865. 1st edition; 358 pages; original cloth, wear to extremities, two plates jutting out just a bit, yet very good. Nevins I 56; Dornbusch I NY 99; Nicholson p. 93. McGowan Book Co. 65-10 1996 $225.00

BOUGAINVILLE, LOUIS ANTOINE DE A Voyage Round the World, Performed by Order of His Most Christian Majesty in the Years 1766, 1767, 1768, and 1769. London: printed for J. Nourse, 1772. 1st edition in English; Demy 4to; xxvii, 476 pages, 5 folding maps, 1 folding plate; xxviii, 476 pages, 5 folding charts, 1 folding plate; contemporary calf, gilt spine with raised bands, red morocco title label; skillfully rebacked with original backstrip preserved, some light offset; very minor marginal dampstain on last two blanks; fine, very clean and crisp copy of a scarce title. Spence 158; Hill p. 32; Sabin 6869. Parmer Books O39Nautica-039256 $6,000.00

BOUGEANT, GUILLAUME HYACINTHE Voyage Merveilleux du Prince Fan-Feredin dans La Romance. Paris: P. G. Le Mercier, 1735. 1st edition; 12mo; 290 pagesp woodcut ornaments, modern boards in mottled paper, backed by polished calf, gilt. Hartig & Soboul 47. Bennett Gilbert LL29-18 1996 $1,100.00

BOULENGER, G. A. Catalogue of the Lizards. London: 1885-87. 1st edition; 8vo; 3 volumes; 96 lithographed plates, last few plates of volume 1 bit stained, just touching figure on last plate; cloth, worn and used, backstrips flapping, one rear endpaper missing, signature of A. Thomson on titles. Maggs Bros. Ltd. 1190-668 1996 £145.00

BOURGADE, ARMAND Polichinelle. Le Diable Rosse. Paris: Capendu, ca. 1880. Folio; (7)ff., 6 brightly colored scenes set up as if in a small theater, complete with audience and accompanist, small tab at bottom of page is pulled to move the players on stage, some minor marginal repairs, none affecting the images; bound in cloth backed pictorial boards, rubbed at extremities, still fine, and bright example, movable book. Bromer Booksellers 87-144 1996 $1,100.00

BOURGEOIS, CONSTANT Voyage Pittoresque a la Grande Chartreuse. Paris: Delpech, 1821. Folio; 8 pages, 20 litho plates, contemporary diced russia gilt, armorial crests on spine, joints cracking, apart from little marginal foxing, fine. Marlborough 162-221 1996 £800.00

BOURGOING, JEAN FRANCOIS, BARON DE Travels in Spain; containing a New, Accurate and Comprehensive View of the Present State of that Country. London: printed for G. G. J. and J. Robinson, 1789. 1st edition in English; 8vo; 3 volumes; folding frontispiece map in volume 1, and 11 other folding engraved maps and plans; contemporary half calf, spines gilt; fine, half title, errata leaf in volume III. CBEL II 1427. Ximenes 109-38 1996 $850.00

BOURKE, JOHN G. The Snake-Dance of the Moquis of Arizona. New York: Charles Scribner's, 1884. 1st edition; "Printed in Edinburgh. some copies have N.Y. imprint"; 31 plates, several in color and one folding; original gilt decorated cloth, front hinges partially separated, half title and frontispiece nearly detached, covers bright but show wear, including 1 inch tear at top of spine, yet internally very good. Ken Sanders 8-94 1996 $300.00

BOURKE, ULICK J. The College Irish Grammar. 1856. 1st edition; 8vo; xxvii, 204 pages; original cloth, spine worn, text good. C. P. Hyland 216-54 1996 £65.00

BOURKE-WHITE, MARGARET Portrait of Myself. New York: 1963. dust jacket; inscribed by Bourke-White, signed twice. J. B. Muns 154-43 1996 $125.00

BOURRIT, MARC THEODORE A Relation of a Journey to the Glaciers, in the Dutchy of Savoy... Norwich: ptd. by Richard Beatniffe, 1775. 1st edition in English; 8vo; 3 engraved plates, engraved leaf of dedication; old marbled boards, vellum tips, recent calf spine, spine gilt; very scarce. Very good. Eddy & Fleeman 8; Neete Mountaineering and Its Lit. 101. Ximenes 109-39 1996 $1,250.00

BOUSSINGAULT, J. B. Rural Economy, In its Relations with Chemistry, Physics and Meteorology... New York: 1845. 8vo; pages iv, 507; contemporary half calf, rubbed, worn at corners and edges, spine ends partially perished, with foxing and page browning, some minor marginal dampstaining. From the library of William Summer (1815-1878). Raymond M. Sutton VII-844 1996 $125.00

BOUSSUET, FRANCOIS De Natura Aquatilium Carmen, in Universam Guilelmi Rondeletii... Lyons: Mathieu Bonhomme, 1558. 1st edition; 4to; 2 volumes in 1, (10), 240; 139 (i.e. 138) leaves, including inserted folding leaf (numbered 65) in second part; Bonhomme's Perseus device (Baudrier 2) on titlepages, woodcut medallion portrait of author preceding each part, 466 text woodcuts, woodcut ornaments and initials; occasional light dampstains generally confined to margins; 17th century sprinkled calf, gilt back, front joint cracked; contemporary ownership inscription on titlepage; Adams B2607; Baudrier X 257; BM STC French 80; Brunet I 1184. Jeffrey D. Mancevice 20-15 1996 $3,500.00

BOUTCHER, WILLIAM A Treatise on Forest-Trees... Edinburgh: printed by R. Fleming and sold by author... 1775. Quarto; on verso of titlepage is printed "Entered in Stationers-Hall, and each genuine copy is signed by" with signature of Will: Boutcher in brown ink; without additional engraved title found in few copies; original boards, uncut, paper spine, printed label renewed; engraved armorial bookplate of Robert Mascall. Henrey 476. Bradley IV p. 107. H. M. Fletcher 121-87 1996 £185.00

BOUTFLOWER, DOUGLAS SAMUEL The Boutflower Book. Newcastle-upon-Tyne: printed for the author, 1930. Large square 8vo; pages 98; 5 pedigrees; original cloth, gilt. R.F.G. Hollett & Son 78-119 1996 £55.00

BOVALLIUS, CARL Nicaraguan Antiquities. Stockholm: Swedish Society of Anthropology and Geography, 1886. 1st edition; large 4to; 50 pages, 4 lithographic plates, 2 maps; original printed boards, fine. Very scarce. Archaeologia Luxor-4302 1996 $450.00

BOWDEN, B. V. Faster than Thought: a Symposium on Digital Computing Machines. London: Isaac Pitman & Sons, 1957. 1st edition; 3rd printing; 8vo; xix, 416 pages, frontispiece, 18 plates, 2 folding charts, numerous illustrations to text; original cloth, dust jacket; fine. Sarrazin F3. Edwin V. Glaser 121-39 1996 $125.00

BOWDEN, CHARLES Street Signs Chicago. Chicago: Chicago Review Press, 1981. 1st edition; Fine in near fine dust jacket with crease inside flap; signed by author. Bella Luna 7-98 1996 $150.00

BOWDITCH, NATHANIEL INGERSOLL A History of the Massachusetts General Hospital. (with) A Continuation to 1872. Boston: 1872. 2nd edition; 734 pages; engraved plates; half leather; Osler 5704. W. Bruce Fye 71-209 1996 $250.00

BOWDITCH, NATHANIEL INGERSOLL A History of the Massachusetts General Hospital, (to August 5, 1851)...with a Continuation to 1872. Boston: printed by the Trustees from the Bowditch Fund, 1872. 2nd edition; 8vo; 734 pages and frontispiece and illustrations; original green cloth, minor wear, very good+; presentation bookplate from the Trustees of the Massachusetts General Hospital. Sabin 6999 (unpublished ed. of 1851). Robert F. Lucas 42-51 1996 $150.00

BOWDITCH, NATHANIEL INGERSOLL Memoir of Nathaniel Bowditch. Boston: Charles C. Little and James Brown, 1840. 2nd edition; approximately 11.25 x 9.25 inches; 2 portraits, 172 pages; covers faded, interior very good. Parmer Books O39Nautica-039068 1996 $250.00

BOWE, WILLIAM FORRESTER Notions of the Nature of Fever and of Nervous Action. W. Davison, for D. Lizars, Edinburgh; W. Davison, Alnwick... 1829. 1st edition; text slightly stained at beginning and end; original cloth backed boards, spine worn, uncut. Anthony W. Laywood 109-13 1996 £90.00

BOWEN, RICHARD LE BARON Archaeological Discoveries in South Arabia. Baltimore: John Hopkins Press, 1958. 4to; xvii, 315 pages; 214 photographic illustrations; text figures an folding plans; boards, cloth spine. Thomas Thorp 489-40 1996 £75.00

BOWEN, T. J. Grammar and Dictionary of the Yoruba Language. Washington: 1858. 4to; xxi, (2), 71, 136 pages; wrappers, ex-library. Bookworm & Silverfish 276-4 1996 $125.00

BOWER, ARCHIBALD A Faithful Account of Mr. Archibald Bower's Motives for Leaving His Office of Secretary to the Court of Inquisition; Including Also, a Relation of the Horrid Treatment of an Innocent Gentleman... London: printed for R. Griffiths, 1750. 1st edition; preferred impression, with 4 page editor's preface and press figure 7-3; 8vo; disbound; wanting half title, otherwise very good. ESTC locates 5 copies Ximenes 109-41 1996 $100.00

BOWER, JOHN Description of the Abbeys of Melrose and Old Melrose, with Their Traditions. Kelso: printed by Alexander Leadbetter fo the author, 1813. 1st edition; 8vo; pages 100; folding lithographed frontispiece; modern half levant morocco gilt, uncut. R.F.G. Hollett 76-34 1996 £85.00

BOWERBANK, J. S.   A Monograph of the British Spongladae. London: Ray Society, 1864. 2 volumes; 37 plates; original cloth, one joint repaired top of backstrip rubbed.   Petersfield Bookshop FH58-231 1996 £65.00

BOWERS, C. G.   Rhododendrons and Azaleas, Their Origins, Cultivation and Development. New York: 1936. 1st edition; 4to; pages xiv, (1), 549; 40 plates, plus 2 endpaper maps; cloth light scuffing of spine ends, inscribed by author.   Raymond M. Sutton VII-455 1996 $125.00

BOWIE, THEODORE   The Carrey Drawings of the Parthenon Sculptures. Bloomington: Indiana University Press, 1971. Oblong folio; xii, 98 pages; 35 illustrations; original cloth.   Archaeologia Luxor-3061 1996 $200.00

BOWLES'S Florist. London: printed for and sold by the Proprietor, Carington Bowles, at his Map.. 1777(98). Small 4to; pages 16 (of 20), with 60 hand colored engraved plates; modern quarter calf; rare. Lacks the last two leaves of text (pages 17-20), outer blank corners of the first four plates have been restored, some slight foxing on reverse of some plates and two marginal tears in last two plates have been neatly mended, otherwise the copy is in good condition.   Wheldon & Wesley 207-15 1996 £1,600.00

BOWLES, CARRINGTON   The Art of Drawing Without a Master from the French of Sieur P.B. London: for Carington Bowles, c. 1785. Unrecorded in ESTC; large 12mo; engraved titlepage, 19 engraved plates; recent boards; v.   Ken Spelman 30-19 1996 £185.00

BOWLES, CARRINGTON   Bowles's New London guide; Being an Alphabetical Index... London: printed for the Proprietor, n.d. ca 1790. 8vo; title, pages iii-viii, 70ff., n.n.; contemporary sheep, very slightly grazed.   Marlborough 162-115 1996 £140.00

BOWLES, CARRINGTON   The Draughtmen's Assistant; or, Drawing Made Easy; Wherein the Principles of the Art are Rendered Familiar: in Ten Instructive Lessons. London: printed for R. Sayer and J. Bennett, n.d., ca. 1776. 4to; in this copy plates II and III (of 5) are not present, and perhaps never were; old half calf, worn, spine perished, leaves loose; needs rebacking; plates all good strikes in excellent condition; Ximenes 109-43 1996 $1,500.00

BOWLES, JANE   In the Summer House. New York: 1954. 1st edition; author's first play; photos; top spine slightly rubbed, fine, dust jacket spine little sunned.   Polyanthos 22-140 1996 $125.00

BOWLES, PAUL   The Hours After Noon. London: Heinemann, 1959. 1st English edition; near fine in very good plus dust jacket with light surface chipping at spinal extremities, else bright; scarce; this copy came from the library of English actor Sir Ralph Richardson, and 2 pages of his pencil written notes on last blank page & back free e.p. Thomas Dorn 9-41 1996 $750.00

BOWLES, PAUL   The Hours After Noon. London: Heinemann, 1959. 1st edition; owner name and date to front endpaper, otherwise near fine in near fine dust jacket, very nice; uncommon.   Ken Lopez 74-39 1996 $450.00

BOWLES, PAUL   In Touch. New York: Farrar Straus, Giroux, 1994. 1/250 copies, signed; fine in slipcase.   Bev Chaney, Jr. 23-104 1996 $100.00

BOWLES, PAUL   In Touch: the Letters of Paul Bowles. New York: Farrar, Straus & Girous, 1994. 1st edition; one of 276 specially bound copies, signed by author; thick 8vo; cloth, slipcase; as new.   James S. Jaffe 34-80 1996 $150.00

BOWLES, PAUL   Let It Come Down. New York: RH, 1952. 1st edition; very good plus in dust jacket; inscribed by Bowles.   Thomas Dorn 9-40 1996 $300.00

BOWLES, PAUL   Let it Come Down. Santa Barbara: Black Sparrow, 1980. New edition, one of 350 numbered copies, signed by author; fine in unprinted glassine as issued.   Between the Covers 42-60 1996 $275.00

BOWLES, PAUL   Let It Come Down. Santa Barbara: Black Sparrow Press, 1980. Reissue with new preface, limited to 350 copies signed by author; 8vo; cloth backed decorated boards, acetate dust jacket; as new.   James S. Jaffe 34-77 1996 $100.00

BOWLES, PAUL   Next to Nothing: Collected Poems 1926-1977. Santa Barbara: Black Sparrow Press, 1981. 1st edition; limited to 300 copies, signed by author; 8vo; cloth backed decorated boards, acetate dust jacket, as new.   James S. Jaffe 34-78 1996 $100.00

BOWLES, PAUL   Once a Lady Was Here. New York: Schirmer, 1946. 1st edition; sheet music, unbound sheets, neat name stamp to front wrapper, 3 small shadows in internal margin where sheet was held in places, else fine copy of the first edition.   Between the Covers 42-58 1996 $175.00

BOWLES, PAUL   The Spider House. New York: Random, 1955. 1st printing; author's fourth book; fine in near fine dust jacket.   Sherwood 3-58 1996 $200.00

BOWLES, PAUL   The Spider's House. London: MacDonald and Co., 1957. 1st edition; original binding, top edge dusty, head of spine bumped, very good in nicked, marked and slightly creased, torn, rubbed and dusty, very slightly soiled dust jacket.   Ulysses 39-62 1996 £75.00

BOWLES, PAUL   The Spider's House. Santa Barbara: Black Sparrow Press, 1982. New edition; limited to 350 copies; 8vo; signed by author; cloth backed decorated boards, acetate dust jacket, as new.   James S. Jaffe 34-79 1996 $100.00

BOWLES, PAUL   Things Gone and Things Still Here. Santa Barbara: Black Sparrow Press, 1977. 1st edition; limited to 250 copies, signed by Bowles; 8vo; cloth backed decorated boards, acetate dust jacket; as new.   James S. Jaffe 34-76 1996 $100.00

BOWLES, PAUL   Too Far from Home. London: Peter Owen, 1994. Limited to 100 copies, signed by author; illustrations; fine in plain paper dust jacket.   Words Etcetera 94-198 1996 £85.00

BOWLES, PAUL   Two Poems. New York: Modern Editions Press, n.d. 1933. 1st edition; one of approximately 175 copies; 8vo; pale blue printed wrappers; edges of wrappers very slightly faded, otherwise fine; author's rare first book.   James S. Jaffe 34-75 1996 $4,500.00

BOWLES, PAUL   Up Above the World. New York: S&S, 1966. 1st edition; signed by author; near fine in very good plus dust jacket with light edge wear.   Thomas Dorn 9-42 1996 $150.00

BOWMAN, DAVID   Let the Dog Drive. New York: NYU Press, 1992. 1st edition; very small first printing of 1500 copies; fine in fine dust jacket.   Thomas Dorn 9-44 1996 $150.00

BOWMAN, DAVID   Let the Dog Drive. New York: NYU Press, 1993. 1st edition; reportedly only 1000 copies in first; fine in near fine dust jacket.   Book Time 2-566 1996 $110.00

BOWMAN, S. M.   Sherman and His Campaigns: a Military Biography. New York: Charles B. Richardson, 1865. 1st edition; thick 8vo; frontispiece, other full page engrave dplates, infrequent spotting; original brown buckram, rubbed, black morocco label, gilt; generally very good; bookplate of Edward Keppel Stephenson of Langham Hall, Suffolk.   Ian Wilkinson 95/1-4 1996 £65.00

BOWYER, GEORGE   Commentaries on the Constitutional Law of England. London: Owen Richards, 1846. 2nd edition; original cloth, quite worn, joints cracked, usable copy.   Meyer Boswell SL25-23 1996 $125.00

BOWYER, W.   The Origin of Printing: in Two Essays: I. The Substance of Dr. Middleton's Dissertation on the Origin of Printing in England; II. Mr. Meerman's Acocunt of the First Invention of the Art... London: Bowyer & Nichols, 1774. 1st edition; black half calf, marbled boards, gilt lettering on spine, worn round edges and headcaps, hinges and boards rubbed, some spotting mainly to first and last few leaves. Bigmore & Wyman p. 74.   Maggs Bros. Ltd. 1191-173 1996 £240.00

BOYCE, A. P.   Boyce's Modern Ornamenter and Interior Decorator. Boston: A. Williams & Co., 1874. Oblong 8vo; 20 plates of which 3 are chromlithographed, two printed in gold on blue background; scarce; most pages soiled, with some pencil annotations and sketches throughout, binding heavily worn and stained, nonetheless a usable copy. Glenn Books 36-200 1996 $250.00

BOYCE, CHARLES WILLIAM   A Brief History of the Twenty-Eighth Regiment New York State Volunteers First Brigade, FirstDivision, Twelfth Corps, Army of the Potomac... Buffalo: Matthews Northrup Co., 1896? 1st edition; 194 pages; original cloth; near fine; with long presentation from Wilbur J. Lawton, a member of Co. K. to his Son. Dornbusch I NY 286; Nicholson p. 95.   McGowan Book Co.   65-12 1996 $275.00

BOYD HARTE, GLYNN   Temples of Power: the Architecture of Electricity in London... Cygnet Press, 1979. One of 250 numbered copies, signed by Boyd Harte and by Gavin Stamp; oblong folio; text printed in Monotype Walbaum in deep blue at Curwen Press, lithographs at the Curwen Studio, on specially made Van Gelder; 'power station' patterned boards, designed by the artist, blue buckram back; fine in pictorial dust jacket, as issued.   Bertram Rota   272-120 9196 £150.00

BOYD, ROBERT   The Office, Powers and Jurisdiction of His Majesty's Justices of the Peace and Commissioners of Supply. Edinburgh: printed for the author and sold by E. Balfour and J. Murray, 1787. 1st edition; 4to; 2 volumes; contemporary calf, spines gilt, contrasting red and blue morocco labels, bit rubbed, but quite sound. Fine set.   Ximenes 108-32 1996 $400.00

BOYD, ROBERT   The Office, Powers and Jurisidiction of His Majesty's Justices of the Peace, and Commissioners of Supply... Edinburgh: printed for the author, sold by E. Balfour and J. Murray, 1787. 1st edition; 4to; xxvi, 510; (ii), (513)-1028, xx pages; 2 volumes; recent quarter calf, retaining old marbled boards, labels, corners worn, upper corners of title and following leaf repaired, well clear of text, some soiling and foxing. Robert Clark 38-186 1996 £165.00

BOYD, WILLIAM   Cork Ulysses. London: 1994. Limited to 60 copies, signed by author and artist; illustrations by Ian Beck; cloth backed patterned boards, fine.   Words Etcetera 94-200 1 996 £75.00

BOYD, WILLIAM   A Good Man in Africa. London: Hamish Hamilton, 1981. 1st edition; very near fine in dust jacket; scarce; inscribed by author.   Lame Duck Books 19-90 1996 $750.00

BOYD, WILLIAM   On the Yankee Station. London: Hamish Hamilton, 1981. 1st edition; fine in dust jacket; inscribed by author.   Lame Duck Books 19-91 1996 $750.00

BOYER, ABEL   The Complete French Master for Ladies and Gentlemen... London: printed for E. Ballard, 1764. 20th edition; few pages proud, following free endpaper torn away; full contemporary sheep, rubbed and scarred with slight worming at base of spine, red label; good, sound copy. Alston XII 191.   Jarndyce 103-28 1996 £50.00

BOYER, ABEL   Memoirs of the Life and Negotiations of Sir W. Temple... London: printed for W. Taylor, 1714. 1st edition; engraved portrait by Van der Gucht, some browning of text; contemporary calf, upper hinge partly cracked, label.   Anthony W. Laywood 109-14 1996 £85.00

BOYER, ALEXIS   The Lectures of Boyer Upon Diseases of the Bones. Philadelphia: 1805. 1st American edition; 8vo; 2 volumes in 1; 368 pages; 7 engraved plates; contemporary calf, signature on front flyleaf from which, upper section as been torn away. Austin 261.   Argosy 810-70 1996 $275.00

BOYER, C. S.   The Diatomaceae of Philadelphia and Vicinity. Philadelphia: 1916. 4to; 143 pages; frontispiece and 40 plates (with 700 drawings by author); original cloth, faded and soiled, worn at extremities, inner joint cracked, ex-library.   Raymond M. Sutton VII-76 1996 $125.00

BOYES, JOSEPH   On the Shoulders of Giants: Notable Names in Hand Surgery. Philadelphia: 1976. 1st edition; 222 pages; original binding. W. Bruce Fye 71-214 1996 $200.00

BOYLE, ELEANOR VERE   Child's Play. London: Addey & Co., n.d. 1852. 1st edition; pictorial title, 16 full page plates; green boards, title gilt, all edges gilt, heavy foxing, board edges worn.   Robin Greer 94A-19 1996 £140.00

BOYLE, ELEANOR VERE   A Dream Book. London: Sampson Low, Son and Marston, 1870. Folio; 12 drawings; three quarter crushed green morocco over pebbled green cloth, spine, slightly sunned with five raised bands and title in gilt, rare; stamped on front free endleaf "C. Gross, Binder to the Queen." The Duke of Northumberland's bookplate. Reid p. 253; Baskin p. 55.   Book Block 32-22 1996 $825.00

BOYLE, ELEANOR VERE   A Garden of Pleasure. London: Elliot Stock, 1895. 3rd edition; 175 x 105mm; pages xvi, 220, (2), frontispiece and other illustrations in line; contemporary full tan morocco, sides ruled into 9 sections with gold lines and dot at intersections, backstrip lettered and double ruled in compartments with small triple leafe ornaments in blind extending from 3 raised band, all edges gilt on the rough, signed "D(ouglas) C(ockerell) 1900", little rubbed but sound; bookplate of Frank Lawson of Ewelme Down.   Claude Cox 107-14 1996 £110.00

BOYLE, FREDERICK   The Golden Prime. London: Chapman and Hall, 1882. 1st edition; 8vo; 3 volumes, lacking half titles to volumes I and II, circulating library labels on endpapers, original blue green cloth, blocked in black, corners knocked; bright coy. 1 copy in NUC.   James Burmester 29-154 1996 £175.00

BOYLE, JACK   Boston Blackie. New York: H.K. Fly Co., 1919. 1st edition; author's first book; illustrations by W. H. D. Koerner; very good with page edges lightly soiled, small store sticker on front endpaper and light soiling on first few pages, otherwise nice, bright copy.   Quill & Brush 102-83 1996 $150.00

BOYLE, MARIE   Three Little Maids from School. London: Ernest Nister n.d., ca. 1890. 1st edition; 12 pages; 4 color plates and 8 sepia text illustrations by E. S. Hardy; beige cloth spine, extra color pictorial cream boards; light foxing, excellent copy.   Robin Greer 94A-62 1996 £65.00

BOYLE, P.   The Fashionable Court Guide, or Town Visting Director, for the year 1793. London: for P. boyle, 1793. 3rd edition; small 12mo; title, 5ff., pages 166, 1 f., 103 pages; contemporary sheep, worn, messy inscription deletion on front endpapers.   Marlborough 162-116 1996 £100.00

BOYLE, ROBERT 1627-1691   An Essay Of the Great Effects of Even Languid and Unheeded Motion. London: sold by Sam. Smith, 1690. Second re-issue, consisting of sheets of the first (1685) edition, that added matter and re-arrangement of the first re-issue (also 1685) and cancel titlepages to both parts, (Original stubs visible), with genuine blanks 17-8 between the parts and L8 at the end; contemporary sheep, rubbed, some wear to spine, tall and fresh, unpressed copy. Wing B3950.   Peter Murray Hill 185-14 1996 £650.00

BOYLE, ROBERT 1627-1691   The Martyrdom of Theodora and of Didymus. London: printed by H. Clark, for John Taylor, and Christopher Skegnes, 1687. 1st edition; 8vo; the issue with single rules beneath "Didymus" and "honour" on titlepage; contemporary calf, covers with gilt coronet and initials "M.C.", spine prettily gilt (light rubbing); very fine, scarce; complete with genuine blanks at beginning and end; signature of M. Carnarvon dated 1687. Wing B3986; Fulton 173; Esdaile p. 166; Mish p. 71.   Ximenes 109-47 1996 $5,000.00

BOYLE, ROBERT 1627-1691   Medicinal Experiments; or, a Collection of Choice and Safe Remedies for the Most Part Simple, and Easily Prepar'd... London: printed for w. Innys, 1712. 5th edition; 12mo; engraved portrait laid down, perforation stamp on title, accession number on A2, 12 pages of ads; modern cloth; bookplate of Mortimer Frank. Fulton 184.   Anthony Laywood 108-30 1996 £85.00

BOYLE, ROBERT 1627-1691   New Experiments and Observations Touching Cold, or an Experimental History of Cold, Begun. London: Richard Davis, 1683. 4to; (xxxviii), 104, (iv), 113-266, (iv), 267-324, (iv), 20, (ii), 29, (i) pages; 2 engraved plates; contemporary panelled calf, old neat reback, old spine laid down, spine gilt ruled, label; little rubbed. Very good. Wing B3997; Fulton 71.   Robert Clark 38-24 1996 £1,150.00

BOYLE, ROBERT 1627-1691   Occasional Reflections Upon Several Subjects. London: by W. wilson for Henry Herringman, 1665. 1st edition; small 8vo; (40), 80, 161-264, 230, (10) pages; title in red and black; contemporary calf, rebacked, original spine laid down; early portrait of Boyle tipped in on imprimatur leaf; very good; signature of Edward Bourne, dated 1768. Fulton 64; Wing B4005; Honeyman Sale I 464; Waller 19434; Neu 657.   Edwin V. Glaser 121-41 1996 $950.00

BOYLE, ROBERT 1627-1691   Of the Reconcileableness of Specifick Medicines to the Corpuscular Philosophy. London: printed for Sam. Smith, 1685. 1st edition; 8vo; early 18th century black morocco, elaborate gilt borders, spine gilt in five compartments, with coronet in middle, all edges gilt; splendid copy in handsome binding; some light bornwning, but most appealing association copy, binding executed for John Boyle, 5th Earl of Cork and Orrery, in exceptional condition. Wing B4013; Fulton 166.   Ximenes 109-48 1996 $5,000.00

BOYLE, ROBERT 1627-1691   The Sceptical Chymist: or Chymico-Physical Doubts and Paradoxes... London: 1680. 18mo; 101, 440, (27), 268 pages; later red cloth with gilt on black labels, extra set provided by Mr Lannon, library discard stamp on titlepage and one more leaf, no ad leaf present.   Bookworm & Silverfish 276-39 1996 $875.00

BOYLE, ROBERT 1627-1691   Some Considerations Touching the Usefulnesse of Experimental Naturall Philosophy, Propos'd in Familiar Discourses to a Friend, by Way of Invitation to the Study Of It. Oxford: printed by Hen. Hall, Printer to the University, for Ric. Davis, 1663. 1st edition; 4to; 2 parts in 1 volume, as issued; (xvi), 127, (viii), 417, (xvi index), errata leaf, collation as in Fulton with all half titles and part titles called for, except the longitudinal label and half title to part 1, which are both lacking, small marginal holes in R4 and S1 (not affecting text), otherwise very good. Contemporary calf, rebacked and recornered in period style by Bernard Middleton. Fulton 50; Wing B4029; Madan 2634; Wellcome II p. 221.   Sotheran PN32-4 1996 £2,995.00

BOYLE, ROBERT 1627-1691   Some Considerataions Touching the Usefulnesse of Experimental Natural Philosophy. (with) Some Considerations Touching the Usefulnesse of Experimental Naturall Philosophy...the Second Tome. Oxford: ptd. by Henry Hall for Ric. Davis, 1664/71. 2nd edition, 1st edition of 2nd Tome; 4to; (16), 126, (4), 416, (18) pages, tear on titlepage expertly repaired without loss, some staining; (26), 47, (5)-3 blank, 20, (4), 14, (2), 31, (3), 26, (2), 50, (1) pages; early marbled boards, rebacked and recornered with calf, morocco spine label; v. Fulton 52 & 53; Madan 2655 & 2882; Wing B4030 & B4031.   Edwin V. Glaser 121-40 1996 $1,500.00

BOYLE, ROBERT 1627-1691   Some Considerations Touching the Style of the H. Scriptures... London: printed for Henry Herringman, 1668. 3rd edition; 16mo; 21 leaves, 254 pages; library stamp in bottom margin of leaf 2, marginal tear in C2 just touching 2 letters, some very light marginal staining but contents very nice; original calf rebacked a long time ago (nice condition but binding does show some wear).   Roy W. Clare XXIV-4 1996 $350.00

BOYLE, ROBERT 1627-1691   Some Considerations About the Reconcileableness of Reason and Religion. London: printed by T. N. for H. Herringman, 1675. 1st edition; 8vo; contemporary sprinkled sheep, lightly rubbed; John Evelyn's copy, inscribed by Evelyn on blank facing titlepage. With signature of William Upcott dated 1816. Fulton 122; Wing B4024.   Ximenes 109-49 1996 $4,500.00

BOYLE, ROBERT 1627-1691   Tracts Consisting of Observations about the Saltness of the Sea: an Account of a Statical Hygroscope and Its Uses. London: E. Flesher for R. Davis, 1674. 1st edition; 8vo; (8), 52; (2), 6; (2); 5; (2), 11; (2), 39; (2), 5; (2), 11; (2), 27; (2), 14 pages; 9 parts in one with its separate title; modern cloth, morocco spine; very good.   Edwin V. Glaser 121-42 1996 $950.00

BOYLE, T. CORAGHESSAN   If the River Was Whiskey. New York: Viking, 1989. 1st edition; fine in dust jacket, without usual remainder mark, signed by author.   Between the Covers 42-65 1996 $100.00

BOYLE, T. CORAGHESSAN   Water Music. Atlantic Press, 1981. 1st edition; review copy with publisher slip laid in; fine in fine dust jacket.   Book Time 2-54 1996 $135.00

BOYLE, T. CORAGHESSAN   Water Music. Boston: Atlantic/Little Brown, 1981. 1st edition; advance review copy with slip laid in; fine in dust jacket, lovely copy, no remainder mark nor soil on dust jacket, as is usually found.   Between the Covers 42-64 1996 $150.00

BOYLE, T. CORAGHESSAN   World's End. New York: Viking, 1987. 1st edition; fine in dust jacket, signed by author.   Lame Duck Books 19-93 1996 $100.00

BOYNTON, H. W.   The Golfer's Rubaiyat. Chicago: Stone, 1901. 1st edition; small 8vo; lxxix pages; original red cloth backed green boards, extremities lightly rubbed, covers slightly soiled, else near fine, unopened.   Chapel Hill 94-214 1996 $125.00

BOYS, JOHN   A General View of the Agriculture of the County of Kent... London: for G. Nicol, 1796. 8vo; xiv, (2), 206 pages, errata leaf, folding hand colored map, 2 engraved plates, folding table; contemporary half russia; very good; Duke of Bedford's copy with Woburn Abbey bookplate.   Ken Spelman 30-62 1996 £225.00

BR Today: a Selection of His Books with Comments. New York: Grolier Club, 1982. One of 420 copies; 8 1/2 x 5 inches; xiv, 41, (1) pages, (1) leaf colophon; vignette on title; very fine.   Phillip J. Pirages 33-281 1996 $150.00

BRABOURNE, LORD   The Birds of South America. Volume I. Checklist. London: 1912. Imperial 8vo; pages xix, 504, colored map; buckram.   Wheldon & Wesley 207-655 1996 £75.00

BRACKENBURY, HENRY   The Ashanti War... Edinburgh & London: William Blackwood and Sons, 1874. 1st edition; 8vo; 2 volumes; half titles, (vii-ix), (x-xi), list of maps to volume 1, text 1-428 pages, (v-vi), list of maps to volume 2, text 1-367 pages, 54 pages publisher's catalog to rear, facsimile letter frontispiece to volume 1, map frontispiece to volume 2, 3 folding maps, large folding map to rear pocket of volume 2; original red embossed cloth, gilt title to spines, blindstamped tooling to boards, upper hinge to volume 1 cracked, owners ink signature to half title, pencil inscription, corners bumped, slightly worn.   Beeeleigh Abbey BA56-41 1996 £225.00

BRACKENRIDGE, HENRY MARIE 1786-1871   Istoria Della Guerra Fra Gli Stati Uniti d'America e L'Inghilterra Negli Anni MDCCCXII-XIII-XIV E XV. Milano: N. Bettoni, 1821. vii, 448 pages; folding map; three quarter leather, clean and tight, nice, lacking half titlepage. Howes B684 mention.   Bohling Book Co. 192-1 1996 $100.00

BRACKENRIDGE, HENRY MARIE 1786-1871   Views of Louisiana; Together with a Jouranl of the Voyage Up the Mississippi Rier in 1811. Pittsburgh: Cramer, Spear and Eichbahn, 1814. 1st edition; 8vo; full contemporary calf, scuffed, upper hinge tender. Howes B688; Wagner Camp 12; Streeter 1776; Hubach p. 43.   Glenn Books 36-36 1996 $875.00

BRACKETT, ALBERT G.   History of the United States Cavalry, from the Formation of the Federal Government to the 1st of June, 1863. New York: Harper & Bros., 1865. 1st edition; 337 pages, plus ads, 2 maps, illustrations; original blue cloth, title in gilt on spine, minor wear to extremities; very good. Graff 38 1. Howes B692; Becker Wagner Camp 41 1.   Michael D. Heaston 23-54 1996 $300.00

BRACKETT, L.   The Sword of Rhiannon. Boardman, 1955. 1st English, 1st separate and 1st hardcover edition; fine in near fine dust jacket with some light wear and tear.   Aronovitz 57-153 1996 $225.00

BRACTON, HENRY DE d. 1268   De Legibus et Consuetudinibus Angliae Libri Quinq. London: Apud Richardum Totellum, 1569. Early calf, rebacked, sound.   Meyer Boswell SL26-23 1996 $15,000.00

BRACTON, HENRY DE d. 1268   De Legibus et Consuetudinibus Angliae. Libri Quinque in Varios Tractatus Distincti. London: 1878-83. 8vo; 6 volumes; original and English translation; original cloth.   Howes Bookshop 265-1593 1996 £250.00

BRADBURY, JOHN   Travels In the Interior of America, in the Years 1809, 1810 and 1811. Liverpool: printed for the author, 1817. 1st edition; (i)-xii, (9)-364 pages; original contemporary full calf with title in gilt on spine, some wear, very good. Bradford 502; Butler Osage 1; Howes B695; Jones 784; Pilling 433.   Michael D. Heaston 23-55 1996 $2,000.00

BRADBURY, OSGOOD   The Old Distiller; a Tale of Truth. New York: Brognard & Co., 1851. 1st edition; 8vo; 46, (2) pages; original printed wrappers, corners turned, some foxing; very nice, unusual to find in wrappers (with vignette); Wright II 350 (one copy).   M & S Rare Books 60-123 1996 $200.00

BRADBURY, RAY 1920-   The Anthem Sprinters. Dial, 1963. 1st edition; uncommon hard-cover issue; fine in near fine dust jacket with some light rubbing; signed by author.   Aronovitz 57-159 1996 $185.00

BRADBURY, RAY 1920-   Dandelion Wine. RHD, 1957. 1st edition; near fine in very good+/near fine dust jacket, signed by author.   Aronovitz 57-157 1996 $125.00

BRADBURY, RAY 1920-   Dark Carnival. Sauk City: Arkham House, 1947. 1st edition; 1/3000 copies; signed by author; very good+ in like dust jacket, signed by author on bookplate laid in.   Aronovitz 57-154 1996 $695.00

BRADBURY, RAY 1920-   Dark Carnival. London: Hamish Hamilton, 1948. 1st edition; author's first book; original binding, prelims, edges and endpapers spotted, head and tail of spine and corners slightly bumped, very good in nicked and slightly creased, marked, rubbed, spotted and dusty dust jacket by Michael Ayrton, slightly darkened at edges.   Ulysses 39-63 1996 £225.00

BRADBURY, RAY 1920-   Death is a Lonely Business. New York: Knopf, 1985. 1st edition; uncorrected proof; wrappers; fine; signed by author.   Aronovitz 57-164 1996 $125.00

BRADBURY, RAY 1920-　Fahrenheit 451. Limited Editions Club, 1982. One of 2000 copies, signed by author and artist; 11 x 7 1/4 inches; xx pages, (3) leaves, 152 pages, (2) leaves; 4 color plates by Joseph Mugnaini; monthly newsletter of the Limited Editions Club and warning about fragility of the aluminum binding laid in; in remarkable original binding of heavy duty aluminum foil over boards, spine and front cover serigraphed in red, white and black, in matching lined publisher's slipcase, very fine.　Phillip J. Pirages　33-348　1996 $225.00

BRADBURY, RAY 1920-　The Golden Apples of the Sun. Garden City: Dobuleday & Co., 1953. 1st edition; drawings by Joe Mugnaini, very good+ in lightly soiled dust jacket.　Steven C. Bernard　71-378　1996 $175.00

BRADBURY, RAY 1920-　The Golden Apples of the Sun. New York: Doubleday, 1953. 1st edition; review copy with accompanying review slip laid in, scarce thus, signed by author; fine in very good+ dust jacket with 1 inch tear and associated wrinkle to upper left section of the rear dust jacket panel;　Aronovitz　57-156　1996 $235.00

BRADBURY, RAY 1920-　The Illustrated Man. New York: Doubleday, 1951. 1st edition; some foxing to endpapers, else near fine in like dust jacket with unfaded dust jacket spine, signed by author.　Aronovitz 57-155　1996 $295.00

BRADBURY, RAY 1920-　Long After Ecclesiastes; New Biblical Texts by Ray Bradbury. Santa Ana: Gold Stein Press, 1985. 1st edition; limited to 75 copies, signed by author and by D'Ambrosio; 2 13/16 x 2 1/2 inches; illustrated with embossed images and with serigraphs, poems printed over some of these images; bound, printed and designed by Joseph D'Ambrosio; bound in full gray morocco with silver foil inset, which resembles a stained glass window and is embossed with Hebrew lettering; extremely fine, with marbled slipcase.　Bromer Booksellers 87-206　1996 $450.00

BRADBURY, RAY 1920-　The Martian Chronicles. Garden City: Doubleday, 1950. 1st edition; corners bumped and small tape ghosts hidden under flaps, else fine in dust jacket with quarter inch tear, with bumping at corners and spine panel ends, very nice.　Robert Gavora 61-16　1996 $500.00

BRADBURY, RAY 1920-　The Martian Chronicles. Garden City: Doubleday, 1950. 1st edition; fine in dust jacket; signed by author for Steven Bernard.　Steven C. Bernard　71-381　1996 $100.00

BRADBURY, RAY 1920-　The Martian Chronicles. Limited Editions Club, 1974. One of 2000 copies, signed by author and artist; 10 3/4 x 8 inches; xviii, 309, (1) pages, (1) leaf (colophon); 11 color plates and several illustrations in text, by Joseph Mugnaini; original silver speckled black cloth, original tissue jacket, in publisher's matching slipcase; very fine.　Phillip J. Pirages　33-349　1996 $250.00

BRADBURY, RAY 1920-　The Martian Chronicles. Limited Editions Club, 1974. 1/2000 copies; fine in glassine dust jacket and slipcase; signed by author and artist, Joseph Mugniani.　Aronovitz　57-161　1996 $175.00

BRADBURY, RAY 1920-　The October Country. Rupert Hart-Davis, 1956. 1st English edition; 8vo; vi, 306 pages; drawings by Joe Mugnaini, cloth, dust jacket by artist (wrapper very slightly frayed and tiny faded area at head of spine).　Thomas Thorp　489-41　1996 $40.00

BRADBURY, RAY 1920-　The Silver Locusts. London: Rupert Hart-Davis, 1951. 1st British edition, 1st printing; 8vo; very good, some soil and wear to dust jacket.　Glenn Books　36-37　1996 $210.00

BRADBURY, RAY 1920-　Something Wicked this Way Comes. S&S, 1962. 1st edition; fine in very good+ dust jacket with some light wear and tear.　Aronovitz　57-158　1996 $195.00

BRADBURY, RAY 1920-　Something Wicked This Way Comes. New York: Simon & Schuster, 1962. 1st edition; near fine with light cloth wear on boards, in near fine dust jacket; inscribed by author.　Revere Books　4-59　1996 $125.00

BRADBURY, RAY 1920-　The Stories. New York: Alfred A. Knopf, 1980. 1st edition; 9 1/2 x 6 1/2 inches; 1 p.l., xx, 884 pages, (3) leaves; original cloth and dust jacket, signed by author; extremely fine in very near fine jacket.　Phillip J. Pirages　33-109　1996 $150.00

BRADE, DANIEL　Picturesque Sketches in Italy. London: B. T. Batsford, 1886. 1st edition; folio; pages 8, plus 28 photo lithographed drawings on 20 interleaved sheets, new endpapers; original decorated cloth, margins of upper board little soiled.　R.F.G. Hollett & Son　78-1402 1996 £150.00

BRADFIELD, WESLEY　Cameron Creek Village, A Site in the Mimbres Area in Grant County, New Mexico. Santa Fe: School of American Research, 1931. 127 pages; 108 plates; original blue cloth, wear at extremities, first flyleaves just starting; very good. Saunders NM 367. Ken Sanders　8-5　1996 $200.00

BRADFORD, JOHN　John Bradford's Historical &c Notes on Kentucky from the Western Miscellany. San Francisco: Grabhorn Press, 1932. Limited to 500 copies; 8vo; folding map frontispiece, (xvi), 205, (6) pages; chapter head vignettes, illustrated paper over boards; fine. Howes S1011; Grabhorn Bib. 170.　Andrew Cahan　47-103　1996 $150.00

BRADFORD, ROARK　Ol' Man Adam An' His Chillun. New York: London: Harper & Bros., 1928. 1st edition; author's first book; drawings by A. B. Walker; very good+ in very good price clipped dust jacket which is moderately chipped at folds and with several mended tears; signed by author for Mrs. B. G. Murray.　Steven C. Bernard　71-54 1996 $125.00

BRADFORD, THOMAS LINDSLEY　The Bibliographer's Manual of American History Containing an Account of All State, Territory, Town and County Histories Relating to the United States of North America, with Verbatim Copies of their Titles, and Useful Bibliographical Notes... Detroit: Gale Research Co., 1968. Reprint of original 1907 edition; 5 volumes.　Blue River Books　9-41　1996 $100.00

BRADLEY, DAVID　South Street. New York: Grossman/Viking, 1975. 1st edition; original cloth, fine but for store stamp, in fine price clipped dust jacket with tiny tear on one flap.　Beasley Books　82-183　1996 $150.00

BRADLEY, EDWARD 1827-1889　Glencreggan; or, a Highland Home in Canatire. London: Longman, Green, Longman and Roberts, 1861. 1st edition; 8vo; 2 volumes; xxviii, 271, xiv, 358, (2) pages ads; 8 chromolithograph plates, 3 maps in color and numerous other illustrations in text; original green cloth, inner front hinge of volume one cracked, otherwise fine set.　David Mason　71-136　1996 $320.00

BRADLEY, EDWARD 1827-1889　Photographic Pleasures; Popularly Portrayed with Pen and Pencil. London: McLean, 1853. 1st edition; 24 plates, including frontispiece and extra lithograph title; decorated gilt cover and spine, all edges gilt, ends of spine fraying, partially shaken with one signature loose, some foxing on plates and endpapers, scarce. J. B. Muns　154-33　1996 $600.00

BRADLEY, HELEN　And Miss Carter Wore Pink. London: Cape, 1971. 1st edition; oblong 4to; pages 32; illustrations in color; original cloth, gilt, dust jacket; presentation copy from author.　R.F.G. Hollett & Son 78-328　1996 £120.00

BRADLEY, HELEN　The Queen Who Came to Tea. London: Cape, 1978. 1st edition; oblong 4to; pages 32; illustrations in color; original cloth, gilt, dust jacket, Presentation inscription from author.　R.F.G. Hollett & Son　78-332　1996 £120.00

BRADLEY, RICHARD d. 1732　New Improvements of Planting and Gardening, Both Philosophical and Practical, Explaining the Motion of the Sap and Generation of Plants... London: Mears, 1717/17/18. 1st edition; 8vo; pages (xvi), 70, (2), 1 plate; (xvi), 136, 3 plates; (xii), 290, (2), 3 plates; title printed in red and black, some foxing and light staining; contemporary panelled calf, worn, especially on spine; very good, tight copy; bookplate of Henry Home Lord Kames; Henrey 494, 495, 496; PMM 356 (note).　Second Life Books　103-31　1996 $1,800.00

BRADSHAW'S Canals and Navigable Rivers of England and Wales. London: Blacklock, 1918. Large 8vo; 476 pages, 5 ff. ads, large folding map in pocket; cloth.　Marlborough　162-10　1996 £95.00

BRADSHAW, HERBERT C.　History of Prince Edward County, Virginia. Richmond: 1955. Large 8vo; xxii, 934 pages; photo illustrations; extremely scarce, library number on backstrip and marks inside to be expected. Bookworm & Silverfish　280-24　1996 $150.00

BRADSHAW, W. R.　The Goddess of Atvatabar. Douthitt, 1892. 1st edition; illustrations; pictorial cloth with unbroken hinges, rubbing and slight darkening to spine, else just about very good.　Aronovitz 57-171　1996 $185.00

BRADSTREET, ANNE   The Works of Anne Bradstreet in Prose and Verse. Charlestown: Abram E. Cutter, 1867. 1st edition thus, one of 250 numbered large paper copies initialled by Cutter; tall quarto; bevelled green cloth with paper spine label which is somewhat browned and chipped; near fine   Captain's Bookshelf 38-23 1996 $200.00

BRADSTREET, ANNE   The Works of Anne Bradstreet in Prose and Verse. Charlestown: Abram E. Cutter, 1867. 1st edition; small 4to; 76, 434 pages; frontispiece; original cloth, spine laid down, new paper label, new endpapers. With several items inserted 1) letter dated 1895 from De Vinne & Co. to the NEH & GS, 2) printed prospectus for this Ellis edition of 1867; 3) 'Announcement' from Abram E. Cutter.   M & S Rare Books 60-124 1996 $475.00

BRADSTREET, ROBERT   The Sabine Farm, a Poem:.... London: printed for J. Mawman,, 1810. 1st edition; 8vo; 7 etched plates; contemporary half red morocco, gilt, spine gilt; nice, uncommon; signature "Cobbold, Holy Wells", presumably the Ipswich poet Elizabeth Cobbold (or her husband). Jackson p. 344; not in Mills.   Ximenes 108-34 1996 $225.00

BRADY, WILLIAM   Glimpses of Texas: its Divisions, Resources, Development and Prospects. Houston: 1871. 1st edition; 104 pages; folding map; original printed wrappers, chipped, mild waterstaining to first few pages, very good, laid in half morocco and chemise case. Rare. Raines p. 30; Howes B714.   Michael D. Heaston 23-56 1996 $1,500.00

BRAEGGER, MARGRIT   Prince Mido. Bienne: 1951. 1st edition; small 4to; 16 color paltes and 10 color text illustrations; white limp boards, color pictorial.   Robin Greer 94A-83 1996 £75.00

BRAIN: a Journal of Neurology. Volume VI. London: Macmillan and Co., 1884. 8vo; (xii), 576 pages; 3 original photos, 3 folding plates; contemporary leather backed marbled boards with leather spine label; bookplate and stamp to title and several other pages of Hartford Retreat.   John Gach 150-69 1996 $250.00

BRAINARD, JOHN G. C.   The Literary Remains...with Sketch of His Life. Hartford: pub. by P. B. Goodsell, n.d., 1832. 1st edition; 12mo; original tan boards, purple cloth spine, printed paper label (boards bit spotted, slight soiling of spine); some foxing, otherwise nice, in what appears to be the earliest binding, with date on paper spine label. Currier pp. 21-2; BAL 1332 and 21678; Sabin 7332.   Ximenes 109-52 1996 $200.00

BRAINERD, CHAUNCEY NILES   My Diary; or Three Weeks on the Wing. New York: Egbert Bourne & Co., 1868. 1st edition; 8vo; original printed wrappers; fine; Sabin 7337.   Ximenes 108-35 1996 $350.00

BRAINERD, GEORGE W.   The Archaeological Ceramics of Yucatan. Berkeley and Los Angeles: University of California Press, 1958. 8vo; iv, 374 pages, 110 pages of figures, 3 plates, 24 maps, 24 charts; original cloth, small discoloration at spine.   Archaeologia Luxor-4303 1996 $125.00

BRAITHWAITE, GEORGE FOSTER   The Salmonidae of Westmorland, Angling Reminiscences and Leaves from an Angler's Note Book. Kendal: Atkinson and Pollitt, 1884. 1st edition; 8vo; pages (x), 188, 4 illustrations; original cloth, gilt, trifle marked, head of spine little rucked, very scarce. R.F.G. Hollett & Son 78-633 1996 £150.00

BRAITHWAITE, J. W.   Guide to Kirkby Stephen, Appleby, Brough Warcop, Ravenstonedale, Mallerstang, &c. Kirkby: Stephen J. W. Braithwaite, 1884. 1st edition; 8vo; pages 134, (38 local ads) on many colored paper, woodcut illustrations, colored folding map; original cloth, gilt, spine trifle faded;   R.F.G. Hollett & Son 78-733 1996 £60.00

BRAITHWAITE, ROBERT 1824-1917   The British Moss Flora. London: 1887-1905. Royal 8vo; 3 volumes; 128 plates; cloth, some foxing at ends and sporadically elsewhere.   John Henly 27-255 1996 £140.00

BRAIVE, M. F.   The Photograph: a Social History. New York: 1966. 1st edition; well illustrated; dust jacket.   J. B. Muns 154-48 1996 $225.00

BRAMHALL, JOHN   The Works... Dublin: Benjamin Tooke, 1677. Folio; (lvi), 137, (i), 1050, (iv) pages; titlepage in red and black, 14 secondary titlepages; contemporary panelled calf, spine gilt ruled; rubbed and scuffed, extremities little worn, joints cracked but firm, insignificant marginal wormhole; good. Wing B4211.   Robert Clark 38-25 1996 £150.00

BRAMSTON, JAMES   The Art of Politicks, in Imitation of Horace's Art of Poetry. London: printed for Lawton Gilliver, 8vo. in 4's; pages 47, (1); frontispiece, small oval engraving of Homer on titlepage, horse and initials 'C.M.', watermarks; modern marbled boards, slightly rubbed, excellent.   Blackwell's B112-46 1996 £120.00

BRANCH, DOUGLAS   The Cowboy and His Interpreters. New York: D. Appleton & Co., 1926. 1st edition; ix, (3), 278 pages; illustrations; original pictorial rust cloth stamped in black, front endpapers bit darkened from newspaper clipping, else fine with soiled and lightly worn pictorial dust jacket. Adams Herd 306; Adams Six Guns 259; Dobie p. 97, 159, 178. Argonaut Book Shop 113-91 1996 $150.00

BRAND, JOHN   Observataions on Popular Antiquities. London: Rivington and Many Others, 1813. 1st edition; very tall, wide quarto; Large paper edition; 2 volumes; half titles and index, pages xxvi, 486; xi, 731; elegant binding in full tan polished calf, spines skillfully rehinged, gilt extra, gauffered edges, elaborately gilt panelled in compartments; gilt crests of the Earl of Minto on front and back covers of both volumes, marbled edges and endpapers, splendid set. Lowndes I 241.   Hartfield 48-L12 1996 $695.00

BRANDEIS, LOUIS D.   Other People's Money and How the Bankers Use It. New York: Frederick A. Stokes Co., 1914. 1st edition; 8vo; author's first book; xv, (i), 223 pages; brown cloth, bumped, slightly spotted, titled in gilt on front cvoer and spine, spine darkened with gilt vignette on front cover, near fine internally. Very scarce.   Blue Mountain SP95-44 1996 $175.00

BRANDES, RAY   Troopers West: Military and Indian Affairs on the American Frontier. San Diego: Frontier Heritage Press, 1970. 1st edition; limited to 1000 numbered copies; quarto; xii, 206 pages; photos, maps, numerous drawings and color plates by Ted De Grazia; original cloth; fine, with dust jacket; presentation copy, signed and dated by De Grazia. Argonaut Book Shop 113-190 1996 $150.00

BRANDT, BILL   Camera in London. Focal Press, April, 1948. 1st edition; royal 8vo; 88 pages; 59 photographic plates; original pictorial boards, spine worn and chipped.   Thomas Thorp 489-42 1996 £50.00

BRANDT, BILL   Camera in London. London: Focal Press, 1948. 4to; 89 pages; 69 photo illustrations and 1 folding table; original cream boards, dust jacket, some creasing and nicks to dust jacket. Marlborough 162-117 1996 £90.00

BRANDT, BILL   The English at Home. New York: 1936. 1st edition; 63 photos; pictorial boards, slightly scratched, edges rubbed. Scarce.   J. B. Muns 154-49 1996 $300.00

BRANDT, BILL   Shadow of Light: A Collection of Photos from 1931 to the Present. New York: 1966. 1st edition; dust jacket.   J. B. Muns 154-50 1996 $225.00

BRANDT, H.   Arizona and Its Bird Life. Cleveland: 1951. 4to; 723 pages; 20 halftontes, 20 superb color plates; bound; small stain inner corner of first 50 pages, not affecting text.   John Johnson 135-499 1996 $175.00

BRANDT, J. H.   Asian Hunter. 1989. Limited to 1250 numbered copies; many illustrations; corners bumped, dust jacket slightly frayed, otherwise mint.   David Grayling J95Biggame-485 1996 £75.00

BRANDT, J. H.   Asian Hunter. Mesilla: 1991. Limited to 1250 numbered copies; 4to; 420 pages, 15 maps and over 140 photos; cloth. Wheldon & Wesley 207-363 1996 £87.00

BRANGWYN, FRANK   The British Empire Panels Designed for the House of Lords. London: F. Lewis, 1933. 1st edition; 4to; 52 plates (1 folding, 22 colored) pages 245, (2 ads); original binding, very good. James Fenning 133-32 1996 £55.00

BRANNER, R.   Manuscript Painting in Paris During the Reign of Saint Louis. A Study of Styles. Berkeley: University of California Press, 1977. 4to; c. 150 plates bearing 438 illustrations; blue cloth, dust jacket, mint. Maggs Bros. Ltd. 1191-138 1996 £55.00

BRANNON, G.   Graphic Delineations of the Most Prominent Objects in the Isle of Wight, Serving Equally the Purposes of a Useful Accompaniment to Any of the Un-Illustrated Local Guides... Isle of Wight: G. & A. Brannon, n.d. 1857. Small oblong 8vo; 16 pages; 30 engravings with paper guards, some slight foxing, original cloth backed pink floral embossed paper covered boards, printed title on upper cover, edges trifle rubbed. Holloway Steel Engravings 36.   Marlborough 162-11 1996 £150.00

BRASAVOLA, ANTONIO MUSA   In Octo Libros Aphorismorum Hippocratis & Galeni. Commentaria & Annotationes. Basel: Hieronymous Froben & Nikolaus Episcopius, 1541. 1st and only edition; 8vo; (8), 1, 1145, (153) pages, 2 text woodcuts; frontispiece (most likely original) tooled pigskin vellum over oak boards, tooled with filigrees, vignettes of scholars, small birds, done in various panels, spine skillfully repaired in the past and clasps also have been renewed and quite tastefully so, quite handsome 16th century binding, other than some foxing and browning internally, a remarkable clean and tight copy. Durling 690; Adams B2698; BMC 407; Iowa 228.   James Tait Goodrich K40-61 1996 $2,950.00

BRASCH, FREDERICK E.   Sir Isaac Newton 1727-1927. A Bicentenary Evaluation of His Work... Baltimore: Williams and Wilkins, 1928. 1st edition; 8vo; ix, 351, (4) pages; frontispiece; original cloth, dust jacket, top edge gilt, fine.   Edwin V. Glaser 121-233 1996 $100.00

BRASS, JOHN   The Art of Ready Reckoning; or Mental and Practical Arithmetic. Toronto: printed by Lovell and Gibson, 1851. 8vo; pages 80; original paper covered boards, cloth strip at spine, paper label, boards warped and stained, else very good. Bookplate of G. Ducharme, noted Canadian book collector.   Hugh Anson-Cartwright 87-378 1996 $100.00

BRASSAI   Seville en Fete. Paris: n.p., 1954. 1st edition; photos; cloth edges fading, near fine in very good dust jacket with uneven horizontal chip at spine crown and upper front panel; inscribed by author to Gloria Swanson in year of publication.   Ken Lopez 74-41 1996 $1,250.00

BRATHWAITE, RICHARD 1588-1673   Drunken Barnaby's Four Journeys to the North of England. London: printed for J. Harding, 1805.. 8vo; pages xix, 160, 6 engraved illustrations; old polished panelled calf, gilt extra, by R. P. Moore of Bedford.   R.F.G. Hollett & Son 78-337 1996 £120.00

BRATHWAITE, RICHARD 1588-1673   Drunken Barnaby's Four Journeys to the North of England. London: T. & J. Allman, 1822. New edition; 8vo; pages 203, (i), uncut, 4 lithographed plates by D. Dighton; modern half calf, gilt.   R.F.G. Hollett & Son 78-338 1996 £95.00

BRAUN, THOMAS   L'An. Poemes... Bruxelles: E. Lyon Claesen, 1847, but 1897. One of 1000 copies of the regular edition on wove paper, from an edition of 1070 copies; square large 4to; 16 full page color illustrations by Franz Melchers; stiff decorated boards, grained black leather spine, title stamped in black and small block, there are remarques of the artist and author applied to covers, preserved in custom clamshell case. Superb association copy. This was author's copy and was later in the Citroen Collection, it was given by author in 1945 to a fund in aid of Dutch artists and writers in distress. Harvard, Turn of Century 89; Rice Univ. 56.   Book Block 32-27 1996 $3,500.00

BRAUTIGAN, RICHARD   A Confederate General from Big Sur. New York: Grove, 1964. 1st edition; slight foxing to top edge, otherwise fine in near fine jacket, very nice, quite scarce, especially in this condition.   Ken Lopez 74-42 1996 $300.00

BRAUTIGAN, RICHARD   Dreaming of Babylon: a Private Eye Novel 1942. New York: Delacorte, 1977. 1st edition; fine in dust jacket with few tiny nicks, complimentary author card laid in, splendid association copy with author's warm contemporary presentation inscription to the Dan Gerbers on titlepage.   Captain's Bookshelf 38-24 1996 $750.00

BRAUTIGAN, RICHARD   In Watermelon Sugar. San Francisco: Four Seasons Foundation, 1968. 1st edition; issue in wrappers, signed by author in year of publication, light rubbing to front cover, else fine.   Ken Lopez 74-44 1996 $1,100.00

BRAUTIGAN, RICHARD   The Pill Versus the Springhill Mine Disaster. San Francisco: Four Seasons, 1968. 1st edition; wrappers, very good.   Ken Lopez 74-43 1996 $125.00

BRAY, ANNA ELIZA   Life of Thomas Stothard, R.A. London: John Murray, 1841. 8vo; 1 volume bound in 2, xxiv, 246 pages; many illustrations in text, also extra illustrated, each leaf of text being neatly mounted in larger sheet of stiff paper, thus enlarging the format of the book, & c. 125 illustrations of Stothard's work bound in; contemporary green morocco, gilt, all edges gilt, rubbed, spines slightly frayed at foot, few corners of mounting leaves torn, well clear of text or image; good.   Robert Clark 38-227 1996 £400.00

BRAY, ANNA ELIZA   Life of Thomas Stothard. London: John Murray, 1851. 4to; 1 volume bound in 2, xxiv, 128; 129-246, 16 page catalog; 55 illustrations, extra illustrated with 147 engravings by Stothard, including some with handwashed borders, 2 water colors, 8 pen and ink sketches; 2 original wrappers bound in, later crimson full levant morocco by Bayntun, gilt panelled sides and spines gilt in 6 compartments, gilt edges; fine.   Thomas Thorp 489-291 1996 £480.00

BRAY, CHARLES   The Philosophy of Necessity; or, Natural Law as Applicable to Moral, Mental and Social Science. London: Longman, Green, Longman & Roberts, 1863. 2nd edition; 8vo; viii, (4), 446 pages; occasional reader's emphasis marks and annotations in pencil, little light soiling here and there, original brown cloth, rebacked. Williams II 555 (1841 ed.); Headicar & Fuller III 62.   John Drury 82-30 1996 £250.00

BRAY, JOHN   Hull's Victory. Philadelphia: G. Willig's Musical Magazine, 1812-13. Small folio; 4 pages, printed on pages (2-3); removed, some offsetting; Wolfe, Secular Music in Amer. 3101.   M & S Rare Books 60-428 1996 $175.00

BRAY, WILLIAM   Sketch of a Tour into Derbyshire and Yorkshire, Including Part of Buckingham, Warwick, Northampton, Bedfordshire and Hertford-shires. London: printed for B. White. 1778. 1st edition; 8vo; iv, 251, (1) pages; contemporary tree calf, gilt greek-key pattern border, silk marker, expertly reacked and with new red gilt label; very good. Scarce.   Ken Spelman 30-63 1996 £220.00

BRAYLEY, EDWARD WEDLAKE 1773-1854   A Concise Account, Historical and Descriptive of Lambeth Palace. London: S. Gosnell, 1806. 4to; 3 ff., 87 pages; engraved title, 18 plates; contemporary russia, joints cracked, but firm. Adams 95.   Marlborough 162-118 1996 £125.00

BRAYLEY, EDWARD WEDLAKE 1773-1854   A Topographical History of the County of Surrey... Dorking: Robert Best Ede; London: Tilt & David Bogue, 1841-48. 1st edition; royal 8vo; 5 volumes; titles printed in red and black each with hand colored armorial, dedication leaves with engraved arms, 121 (mostly) steel engraved plates, double page facsimile letter, 5 engraved maps and plans, numerous wood engraved text illtrations; contemporary green half morocco and cloth, gilt decorated and panelled spines, gilt tops and marbled endpapers.   Charles W. Traylen 117-379 1996 £300.00

BRAYLEY, EDWARD WEDLAKE 1773-1854   A Topographical History of Surrey. Dorking: R. B. Ede, 1841. 1st edition; thick 4to; 5 volumes; titlepages printed in colors, 125 engraved plates (mostly foxed to certain degrees), a colored map; contemporary half green morocco, gilt edges, spines discolored; foxing is mostly on margins of plates.   Charles W. Traylen 117-380 1996 £350.00

BRAYLEY, EDWARD WEDLAKE 1773-1854   A Topographical History of Surrey. London: Virtue & Co., n.d., ca. 1860. 2nd edition; thick 4to; 4 volumes; 4 engraved vignette titlepages, 4 printed titlepages, 72 engraved plates of views, 2 of which are double paged and 5 colored lithograph maps; attractive set in contemporary half red morocco, gilt edges.   Charles W. Traylen 117-381 1996 £320.00

BRAYTON, ALICE   George Berkeley in Newport. Newport: printed by Anthoensen Press, 1954. 1st edition; 4to; xviii, 129 pages, plates; fine in slipcase.   Metacomet Books 54-14 1996 $110.00

BRAZEAL, BRAILSFORD R.   The Brotherhood of Sleeping Car Porters. New York: Harper, 1946. Early later printing; fine in dust jacket with couple of very small nicks and tears; signed by A. Philip Randolph, the president of the Union.   Between the Covers 43-395 1996 $450.00

BREAD and Puppet: St. Francis Preaches to the Birds. Janus Press, 1978. One in an edition of 100 unsigned, unnumbered copies; 14.375 x 13.125 inches; 28 unnumbered pages; 28 masonite relief cuts and masonite relief decoration by Peter Schumann, one woodcut made for this edition by Claire Van Vliet, designed by Peter Schumann and Claire Van Vliet, set and printed by Claire Van Vliet; hand colored by Van Vliet and Kaja McGowan and Solveig Schumann; titles, text and relief cuts printed in black, relief cuts hand colored with watercolors; printed on Promatco Antique Endleaf, folded in the Japanese manner; Stab-bound (with four screw posts that may be removed to display the entire sequence); in three quarter dark blue linen finish book cloth over boards, front cover with masonite relief cuts printed in black on Bologna red Fabriano Miliani Ingres used for decorative cover paper and author/title label on spine printed in black, endpapers in same red as Fabriano cover; fine.   Joshua Heller 21-15 1996 $450.00

BREAD and Puppet: the Dream of the Dirty Woman. Janus Press, 1980. One in an edition of 85 copies; 12.25 x 11.875 inches; 10 unnumbered pages; 4 masonite relief and collograph illustrations for an ATF rooster dec. on colophon page; designed, set & ptd. by Claire Van Vliet; titles in old brass & wood type & Trump Mediaeval italic, English text in Franklin Gothic, French text in Trump Mediaeval italic, character desingations & colophon in Trump Mediaeval roman, titles printed in silver and black, English text in brown, French in black; illustrations printed in white & gray with type decoration in silver; ptd. on grey paper with areas of dark gray, white, brown & yellow pupl that become a base of the illus.; between title and colophon pages a four double sheets; the 6 sheets are overlapped & attached to form one continuous accordion-folded sheet, housed in clamshell box covered and lined with natural linen with sides of grey linen finish book cloth, masonite relief dec. of tree trunks printed in grey on front and back covers, title printed in gray on spine; laid in 2 pages of photos of performance of the play & recording of performance. Fine. Joshua Heller 21-20 1996 $550.00

BREADALBANE, MARCHIONESS OF The High Tops of Black Mount. London: William Blackwood and sons, 1907. 8vo; pages ix, 242, 32, 38 plates from photos by Olive Mackenzie; original pictorial cloth, spine little faded. R.F.G. Hollett 76-36 1996 £85.00

BREAKENRIDGE, WILLIAM M. Helldorado. Bringing the Law to the Mesquite. Boston and New York: Houghton Mifflin, 1928. 1st edition; xix, 256 pages; frontispiece, numerous paltes and portraits from photos; original cloth; previous owner's name on endpaper, fine, clean copy with very elusive and pictorial dust jacket (jacket soiled and lightly worn, with one inch piece lacking from front fore-edge). Adams Herd 315; Six Guns 262. Argonaut Book Shop 113-93 1996 $150.00

BREE, C. R. A History of the Birds of Europe. London: 1875-76. 2nd edition; 8vo; 5 volumes, 253 plates, all but one colored; original purple cloth, dust jackets, printed in black on grey, front covers with vignette title the same as blocked in gilt on cloth, surrounded by a geometrical pattern ditto (but the effect is quite different), on the back ads for other Bell publications, volume numbers lettered on spines, one cloth spine faded, stamped signature of Thomas Bableton(?) on titles, later in the Bradley Martin collection. Maggs Bros. Ltd. 1190-549 1996 £650.00

BREEN, HUGH A Treatise on the Summation of Series. Belfast: printed by Joseph Smyth, 1827. 1st and only edition; 8vo; pages 104, 104 (bis)-163, including 3 page list of Armagh, Belfast, Dublin and Newry subscribers; contemporary half calf, gilt spine, by Scott of Armagh, with his ticket, nice. Remarkably scarce. James Fenning 133-33 1996 £395.00

BREES, S. C. A Glossary of Civil Engineering, Comprising Its Theory and Modern Practice. London: Tilt and Bogue, 1841. 1st edition; 8vo; 310 pages, 32 pages ads; original dark green cloth, ownership stamps and sticker, front inner hinge cracked, spine darkened and worn at extremities, else very good. Chapel Hill 94-185 1996 $150.00

BRENNAN, J. P. Scream at Midnight. Macabre House, 1963. 1st edition; 1/250 copies, signed by author; very good, without dust jacket, as issued. Aronovitz 57-174 1996 $175.00

BRERETON, AUSTIN The Lyceum and Henry Irving. London: Lawrence and Bullen and New York: McClure, Phillips & Co., 1903. 1st edition; number 21 of a limited edition of 100 copies on Japanese vellum, signed by Henry Irving and Ellen Terry beneath their portraits (frontispiece and page 272); 4to; illustrations; Japanese vellum covered boards, spine lettered in gilt; fine. Dramatis Personae 37-26 1996 $200.00

BRERETON, F. S. The Great Aeroplane. Blackie, 1911. near fine in bright pictorial cloth with very good dust jacket save for a thumb-nail size chip missing from upper right corner of front dust jacket panel, great copy, scarce in dust jacket. Aronovitz 57-175 1996 $125.00

BRESLAUER, BERNARD H. Bibliography, Its History and Development. New York: Grolier Club, 1984. One of 600 copies; 9 1/4 x 6 1/4 inches; 223, (1) (colophon) pages; several full page reproductions in text, prospectus laid in; very fine. Phillip J. Pirages 33-277 1 1996 $125.00

BRESSON, HENRI CARTIER The Europeans: Photographs. Simon & Schuster/Editions Verve, 1955. 1st edition; folio; profusely illustrated, magnificent book in very good condition with minimal wear, scarce. Words Etcetera 94-204 1996 £275.00

BRETON DE LA MARTINIERE, J. B. La Chine en Miniature, ou Choix de Costumes, Arts et Metiers de cet Empire Representes par 74 Gravures...a l'Usage de la Jeunesse. Paris: Nepveu, 1811. Small 8vo; 4 volumes; suite of colored plates; elegant black straight grain morocco with decorative gilt border on covers, smooth rounded spines with 6 compartments formed by double gilt rules, the second from top containing the title and fourth containing the volume numbers, other compartments are filled with dense combination of delicate tools and pointelles, all edges gilt, marbled and tinted endleaves, on pastedown of all four volumes are the bookplates of Henry W. Longfellow. Brunet I 1225. Book Block 32-8 1996 $4,750.00

BRETT, THOMAS An Account of Church-Government and Governours. London: John Wyat, 1701. 1st edition; 8vo; reddish brown turkey morocco in triple panel design wtih 2 line fillet and rolls, second panel contains ornamental fleurons in corners from which a single acorn tool is suspended, there are four larger fleurons midway along each side, innermost panel is intersected at each corner, spine with five raised bands and closely stamped decoration within the compartments (without title), board edges gilt decorated, inner gilt dentelles, all edges gilt, marbled endleaves, in absolutely fine condition; bookplate of J. L. Templer, Torrhill, Devon. Book Block 32-33 1996 $875.00

BREVAL, JOHN DURANT The History of the Most Illustrious House of Nassau, continued from the Tenth Century...to this Present Time. London: printed for R. Montagu, 1734. 8vo; pages (xii), '360' (but 378), (18 index); contemporary calf, rubbed, lacking label, portrait (foremargin shaved). Peter Murray Hill 185-15 1996 £75.00

BREVOORT, HENRY The Letters of Henry Brevoort to Washington Irving. Garden City: Putnam, 1916. One of 310 numbered copies, signed by publisher; 8vo; 2 volumes; portraits, facsimiles; original binding, fine in dust jackets. Charles Agvent 4-725 1996 $125.00

BREWER, FRANCES J. The Fables of Jean de La Fontaine. Los Angeles: Dawson's Bookshop, 1964. 1st edition; folio; titlepage printed in red and black; with 2 original folio leaves from the Memorial Edition of "Fables Choisies" printed in Paris by Charles-Antoine Jombert (1755-59); stiff grey wrappers, paper spine label, uncut, fine, green marbled board slipcase (worn); George J. Houle 68-79 1996 $395.00

BREWER, J. S. The Reign of Henry VIII from His Accession to the Death of Wolsey. London: J. Murray, 1884. Original edition; thick 8vo; 2 volumes, pages 636, 530; portrait; original cloth, nice copy. Conyers Read 473. Howes Bookshop 265-491 1996 £75.00

BREWER, S. S. The Jubilee Harp. Concord: Oliver Hart, Printer, 1855. 1st edition; 18mo; 323 pages; original cloth, some soiling; Not in NUC; Wellcome pp. 238-41. 2 copies in NUC. M & S Rare Books 60-271 1996 $325.00

BREWERTON, G. DOUGLAS The Automaton Regiment, or Infantry Soldiers Practical Instructor, for All Regimental Movements in the Field. New York: D. Van Nostrand, 1862. 1st edition; narrow 8vo; box with printed and pictorial label, box rubbed and cracking, very good. M & S Rare Books 60-304 1996 $2,500.00

BREWSTER, JOHN The Parochial History and Antiquities of Stockton Upon Tees; Including an Account of the Trade of the Town, the Navigation of the River, and of Such Parts in the Neighbourhood as Have Been Connected with that Place. Stockton: printed by R. Christopher, 1796. 1st edition; 4to; frontispiece (foxed on margins), 3 page list of subscribers, blank corner of Y2 torn away, 7 engraved plates; original boards, uncut, backstrip defective. Anthony Laywood 108-32 1996 £225.00

BREYMEYER, A. I. Grasslands, Systems, Analysis and Man. Cambridge: 1980. 8vo; pages xxiv, 950; hardbound (card pocuh on front pastedown, institutional stamp on rear pastedown). Raymond M. Sutton VI-72 1996 $135.00

THE BRIDAL Souvenir. London: Griffith & Farran, 1857. Small 4to; printed in colors and gold on 21 leaves, complete with mounted photo portrait frontispiece, now always present; original richly gilt cloth, edges gilt, designed by John Leighton, signed "J.L.", trivial wear at headbands, otherwise bright, fresh and attractive copy. James Fenning 133-322 1996 £95.00

BRIDGES, JAMES View of the Political State of Scotland, at Michaelmas, 1811... Edinburgh: ptd. by John Moir for Peter Hill and Archibald Constable, 1812. 1st edition; tall 8vo; clxxxix, 324, 16 pages ads; fine, recently rebound in half calf, cloth, raised bands, label; fine. David Mason 71-137 1996 $240.00

BRIDGES, JOHN   The Supremacie of Christian Princes, Over All Persons Throughout Their Dominions, In All Causes So Wel Ecclesiastical as Temporall, Both Against the Counterblast of Thomas Stapleton... London: ptd. by Henrie Bynneman for Humfrey Toye, 1573. 1st edition; small 4to; contemporary calf, covers decorated with central blindstamped lozenge (pieces missing from top and bottom of spine), fine, crisop copy, rare; STC 3737.   Ximenes 108-36 1996 $1,750.00

BRIDGES, JOHN HENRY   The Unity of Comte's Life and Doctrine. London: N. Trubner & Co., 1866. 1st edition; 8vo; 70 pages; recently bound in cloth, spine lettered in gilt; very good; Laine 373; Sorley pp. 263 & 364.   John Drury 82-31 1996 £175.00

BRIDGES, ROBERT 1844-1930   Eros and Psyche. A Poem in XII Measures. Newtown: Gregynog Press, 1935. Limited to 300 copies (including 15 in a special binding); 4to; pages (viii), 142, colophon, designs by Burne-Jones prepared for engraving by Dorothy Hawksley, 5 of which were cut on wood by Loyd Haberly and the remaining 19 by R. John Beedham, initial letters designed by Graily Hewitt and printed in green, text printed in red and black, few light foxing spots on covers, otherwise very good in original cloth slipcase (little soiled); original white pigskin, blocked in gilt on upper cover with circular design which incorporates hand tooling, spine lettered in gilt and with imitation bands and gilt ties, top edge gilt, others uncut. Harrop 33.   Sotheran PN32-42 1996 £798.00

BRIDGES, ROBERT 1844-1930   New Verse - Written in 1921 - With Other Poems of that Year and A Few Earlier Pieces. London: 1925. One of 106 numbered copies, signed by author; printed on handmade T. H. Saunders paper, pages unopened; mounted black and white frontispiece photo of author; full gilt vellum covers, pages unopened, top edge dusty, covers bowed, dusty and slightly marked, spine darkened, very good. Ulysses 39-73 1996 £75.00

BRIDGES, ROBERT 1844-1930   Peace. Printed for the first anniversary June 1st, 1903. 1st edition; c. 100 copies; 4to; pages (8); printed on Van Gelderhandmade paper, original printed blue-grey wrappers and later maroon linen, uncut; bookplate of Oliver Brett & his pencilled initials dated Dec. 1921. Madan 55.   Claude Cox 107-38 1996 £95.00

BRIDGES, ROBERT 1844-1930   Prometheus the Firegiver. Oxford: printed at the Private Press of H. Daniel, 1883. 1st edition; number 35 of 100 copies; 4to; pages (4), 72, hand miniated initial F in red, printed in small pica roman on Van Gelder handmade paper, uncut in original vellum backed blue boards, little scuffed; scarce; ownership signature of G. Molesworth of Simla.   Claude Cox 107-39 1996 £135.00

BRIDGES, ROBERT 1844-1930   The Testament of Beauty - a Poem in Four Books. Oxford: Oxford University Press, 1929. 1st edition; original binding, pages unopened, top edge dusty, head and tail of spine slightly bumped, spine browned, covers marked and dusty, cover edges slightly rubbed; very good; ownership signature of Ian Fleming.   Ulysses 39-672 1996 £160.00

BRIDGMAN, RICHARD WHALLEY   An Analytical Digested Index of the Reported Cases in the Several Courts of Equity, and the High Court of Parliament (in Both England and Ireland), from the Earliest Authentic Period to the Present Time. London: printed by S. Brooke, 35 Paternoster Row; 1813. 2nd edition; 3 volumes, quarter calf, boards, detached, ex-library, working set.   Meyer Boswell SL27-29 1996 $150.00

BRIDSON, G. D. R.   Plant, Animal and Anatomical Illustrataion in Art and Science... Winchester: 1990. 4to; pages xxxvii, 450; hardbound, dust jacket.   Raymond M. Sutton VI-1124 1996 $150.00

A BRIEF Account of the Tagore Family. Calcutta: I.C. Bose & Co., Stanhope Press, 1868. 1st edition; 8vo; contemporary Indian red morocco, covers elaborately decorated in gilt, spine and inner dentelles gilt, couple of very small rubbed spots; fine copy in handsome Indian binding; rare; not listed in NUC.   Ximenes 109-279 1996 $350.00

A BRIEF Collection Out of the Records of the City, Touching Elections of the Sheriffs of London and the County of Middlesex. London: printed by S. Roycroft, Printer to this Honourable City, 1682. Folio; 4 pages; uncut, disbound. Wing B4556.   H. M. Fletcher 121-28 1996 £70.00

BRIEF Deductions Relative to the Aid and Supply of the Executive Power, According to the Law of England. In Cases of Infancy, Delirium, or Other Incapacity of the King. London: printed for J. Debrett, 1788. 2nd edition; modern quarter calf over marbled boards, very nice, clean.   Meyer Boswell SL25-149 1996 $500.00

BRIEF Extracts from High Authorities Exposing the Evils of Vaccination: Great Medical Delusion of the 19th Century: Now Inciting Popular Imagination. Providence: 1891. 1st American edition; 188 pages; original binding.   W. Bruce Fye 71-225 1996 $100.00

BRIERLEY, HENRY   The Registers of the Parish Church of Skelton, Cumberland 1580-1812. Kendal: Titus Wilson, 1918. 8vo; pages xii, 226, frontispiece; original wrappers, edges trifle faded.   R.F.G. Hollett & Son 78-593 1996 £85.00

BRIGGS, GRACE M.   The Honnold Library. The William W. Clarey Oxford Collection. A Descriptive Catalogue. Oxford: printed for the Honnold Library at the University Press, 1956. 1st edition; one of 550 copies; original cloth, dust jacket slightly torn.   Forest Books 74-25 1996 £55.00

BRIGGS, GRACE M.   The William W. Clary Oxford Collection. A Descriptive Catalogue. Oxford Univ. Press for the Honnold Library, Claremont, California, 1956-65. Limited to 550 and 300 copies; 8vo; 2 volumes; (xxvi), (236); xiv, 324 pages; very good.   Robert Clark 38-265 1996 £75.00

BRIGGS, HAROLD E.   Frontiers of the Northwest. New York: D. Appleton-Century Co., 1940. 1st edition; xiv, 629 pages, frontispiece, 31 plates, 7 maps, map endpapers; gilt lettered brown cloth, owner's bookplate on inner cover, otherwise fine. Adams Herd 319; Reese Six Score 14; Six Guns 275.   Argonaut Book Shop 113-95 1996 $100.00

BRIGGS, JOHN   The Lonsdale Magazine, or, Provincial Repository... Kendal: J. Briggs, 1820-22. 8vo; 3 volumes; pages iv, 566; iv, 476; iv, 476, 26 aquatint plates, hand colored map, hand colored plan, 1 full page woodcut vignette, text illustrations; contemporary black blind ruled roan, edges worn, rebacked to match with raised bands and spine labels; little occasional spotting and offsetting, some plates little cropped, in volume two, but very good.   R.F.G. Hollett & Son 78-736 1996 £375.00

BRIGGS, JOHN   The Lonsdale Magazine, or Provincial Repository... Kendal: J. Briggs, 1820. 8vo; Volume 1 (only) of 3; plates, text illustrations; modern half levant morocco, gilt, little occasional spotting and browning.   R.F.G. Hollett & Son 78-737 1996 £120.00

BRIGGS, JOHN   The Lonsdale Magazine, or Provincial Repository... Kendal: J. Briggs, 1822. 8vo; paes iv, 476, 12 aquatint plates, woodcut; modern half levant morocco, little occasional spotting and browning. R.F.G. Hollett & Son 78-738 1996 £120.00

BRIGGS, JOHN   The Remains of John Briggs... Kirkby Lonsdale: Printed and sold by Arthur Foster, 1825. 1st edition; 8vo; pages 408, pagination little irregular as usual, but correct; near contemporary half calf gilt, raised bands and spine label, extremities rubbed and little scraped, one shortt marginal tear, otherwise very nice, clean and sound copy; rare. Bicknell 97.   R.F.G. Hollett & Son 78-339 1996 £275.00

BRIGGS, L. VERNON   Arizona and New Mexico 1882, California 1886, Mexico 1891. Boston: privately printed, 1932. 1st edition; x, 282 pages, 41 halftone plates, numerous woodcut illustrations; gilt lettered blue cloth, very mild foxing to endpapers, else very fine and uncut. Argonaut Book Shop 113-96 1996 $175.00

BRIGGS, L. VERNON   The Manner of Man That Kills: Spencer - Czolgosz - Richeson. Boston: Richard G. Badger, 1921. 1st edition; 8vo; (ii), 444 pages, 16 half tones; ruled straight grained green cloth, uncommon; inscribed.   John Gach 150-73 1996 $100.00

BRIGGS, MARTIN SHAW   Muhammadan Architecture in Egypt and Palestine. Oxford: Clarendon Press, 1924. 1st edition; large 4to; xv, 255 pages, frontispiece, plates; partially unopened, cloth, spine slightly sunned, otherwise very good.   Bookpress 75-159 1996 $325.00

BRIGHAM, AMARIAH   Remarks on the Influence of mental Cultivation and Mental Excitment Upon Health. Glasgow: 1836. 1st English edition; 12mo; 137 pages; original linen, near fine, scarce. Hunter MacAlpine pp. 821-25.   James Tait Goodrich K40-58 1996 $175.00

BRIGHT, JOHN   Public Addresses... London: Macmillan and Co., 1879. 1st edition; 8vo; xvi, 542 pages, final leaf of ads; original brown cloth, gilt, fine, partially unopened.   John Drury 82-32 1996 £50.00

BRIGHT, P. M.   A Monograph of the British Aberrations of the Chalk-Hill Blue Butterfly Lysandra Coridon. Bournemouth: 1938. Original issue; 4to; pages ix, 138, (4), 18 plates; morocco, little very light foxing, but nice, though without 6 pages of errata etc.   Wheldon & Wesley 207-1005 1996 £100.00

BRILLAT-SAVARIN, JEAN ANTHELME 1755-1826   The Handbook of Dining, or, How to Dine. London: Longman, Brown, 1859. 1st edition thus; large 12mo; pages xi (i.e. xvii), 244, prelims erratically numbered but apparently complete; recent boards; minor marginal waterstain, otherwise good to very good.   James Fenning 133-35 1996 £55.00

BRILLAT-SAVARIN, JEAN ANTHELME 1755-1826   Physiologie du Gout, a Handbook of Gastronomy. New York: J. W. Bouton, 1884. Later edition; crown 8vo; 52 original etchings on China paper; bound in burgundy morocco backed boards, boards rubbed, French signed binding, gilt panelled spine, top edge gilt.   Glenn Books 36-59 1996 $125.00

BRILLAT-SAVARIN, JEAN ANTHELME 1755-1826   The Physiology of Taste, or Meditations on Transcendental Gastronomy. London: Peter Davies, 1925. One of 750 copies; 11 x 7 1/2 inches; xx, 326 pages; 40 vignette headpieces by Andrew Johnson; original vellum backed marbled paper boards, gilt lettering on spine, untrimmed edges; corners just slightly chafed, vellum with hint of soiling, paper sides little yellowed and chafed, but binding entirely sound and not unappealing, fine internally. Phillip J. Pirages 33-113 1996 $225.00

BRILLIANT, RICHARD   The Arch of Septimius Severus in the Roman Forum. Roma: American Academy in Rome, 1967. 4to; 271 pages, 108 figures and 98 plates, 7 plans, original cloth, tattered dust jacket; signature.   Archaeologia Luxor-3072 1996 $250.00

BRILLIANT, RICHARD   Gesture and Rank in Roman Art. New Haven: Connecticut Academy of Arts and Sciences, 1963. Folio; 238 pages; 479 illustrations; wrappers, uncut.   Archaeologia Luxor-3071 19964 $150.00

BRIM, CHARLES   Medicine in the Bible, the Pentateuch Torah. New York: 1936. 1st edition; 384 pages; original binding; scarce. GM 6499   W. Bruce Fye 71-227 1996 $130.00

BRIN, D.   Startide Rising. Phantasia Press, 1985. 1st hardcover edition; fine in dust jacket, inscribed by author to fellow writer Robert Adams and his wife.   Aronovitz 57-177 1996 $120.00

BRIN, D.   The Uplift War. Phantasia Press, 1987. 1st edition; 1/26 lettered copies; bound in full red leather with holographic insert on front cover and signed by author; as new.   Aronovitz 57-178 1996 $775.00

BRINE, MARY D.   Grandma's Attic Treasures. New York: Dutton, 1893. Octavo; 94 pages; 8 color lithographs and numerous black and white figures; color illustrated boards, original dust jacket which is lightly chipped and browned; all edges gilt; extremely fine.   Bromer Booksellers 90-89 1996 $275.00

BRINKLEY, F.   Oriental Series. Japan (China). Its History, Arts and Literature. Boston and Tokyo: J. B. Millet Co., 1901-02. Limited edition, number 18 of 50 copies of the "Special Artists' Edition"; 8vo; 12 volumes; 221 plates, many tinted, part; original green half morocco, patterned boards, spines gilt, top edge gilt, others untrimmed, largely unopened; rubbed, slight wear to few corners. Good set.   Robert Clark 38-276 1996 £450.00

BRISTED, JOHN   The Resources of the United States of America; or, a View of the Agricultural, Commercial, Manufacturing, Financial, Political, Literary, Moral and Religious Capacity and Character of the American People. New York: James Eastburn & Co., 1818. 1st edition; 8vo; xvi, 505, (1) pages; occasional unobtrusive spotting, original half calf, gilt, sometime rebacked with original backstrip preserved, marbled sides; very good; from the library of Helen Strong Belknap and William Burke Belknap with their bookplate. Sabin 8050; Kress C24; not in Einaudi, Hollander, McCulloch or Masui.   John Drury 82-33 1996 £150.00

BRISTOL NATURALISTS' SOCIETY   Proceedings. Bristol: 1866-1940. 8vo; 14 volumes;; binder's cloth.   Charles W. Traylen 117-286 1996 £150.00

BRISTOL, CHARLES BIRD   Picturesque Old Bristol, a Series of Fifty-Two Etchings. Bristol: Frost and Reed, 1885. Unlettered Proof edition, limited to 125 numbered sets; 2 volumes; letterpress by John Taylor; handsomely bound in full black morocco with raised bands, tooled in spine compartments with floral figures and covers decorated with elaborately and handsomely tooled borders, all edges gilt, gilt dentelles, joints and extremities slightly rubbed, but very handsome. Hermitage SP95-909 1996 $1,000.00

BRISTOW, AMELIA   The Orphans of Lissau and Other Interesting Narratives... London: pub. by T. Gardiner & Son; sold also by the author, 1830. 1st edition; 8vo; 2 volumes; bound without half titles; contemporary half calf, spines gilt lettered, slight rubbing to spine and extremities, otherwise very nice; scarace. Block p. 27; not in Wolff, not in Roth; 3 copies in NUC.   Paulette Rose 16-192 1996 $400.00

BRITISH & FOREIGN BIBLE SOCIETY   Reports of the British and Foreign Bible Society, with Extracts of Correspondence, &c... London: printed for the Society by J. Tilling, 1805-16. 22cm; various pagination; gilt and blindstamped dark blue calf, all edges gilt; very good. This set given by the Society to (lady?) Olivia Bernard-Sparrow (came from Kimbolton Castle Lib.).   Rockland Books 38-29 1996 $1,500.00

BRITISH ASSOCIATION FOR THE ADVANCEMENT OF SCIENCE   Report of the 48th Meeting Held at Dublin, in August 1878. 1879. 1st edition; 8vo; illustrations; cloth; very good.   C. P. Hyland 216-63 1996 £50.00

BRITISH Columbia: its Resources and Capabilities: Reprinted from "Canada: a Memorial Volume." Montreal: 1889. 20 pages; illustrations; printed wrappers; very good. Lowther 813; Dionne IIII 2238.   Rockland Books 38-30 1996 $100.00

THE BRITISH Essayists. London: printed for Nichols and Son et al, 1817. 6 1/2 x 4 1/4 inches; 45 volumes; 17 frontispiece portraits; very pleasing contemporary mahogany straight grain half morocco, marbled paper sides, raised bands, hightlighted with gilt floral decorations, spine compartments with gilt rules, titling and scalloped panelleing enclosing small ornamental flower; boards bit chafed, minor rubbing to leather (which has been skillfully masked), but bindings still quite bright and generally very clean, with no significant wear to joints and surprisingly, no fading to spines, extremely fine, very fresh and clean set, extraordinarily well preserved internally, with only trivial imperfections. Phillip J. Pirages 33-114 1996 $2,400.00

BRITISH MUSEUM.   Catalogue of Birds. Volume 1. Accipitres or Diurnal Birds of Prey. London: British Museum, 1874. 8vo; 14 hand cocclored plates; original cloth, neatly repaired; good, ex-library with stamps on titlepage and verso of plates. Scarce.   Wheldon & Wesley 207-657 1996 £90.00

BRITISH MUSEUM.   Catalogue of Birds. Volume 4. Passeriformes, Cichlomorphae Part 1. London: 1879. 8vo; pages xvi, 495; 14 hand colored plates; original cloth, neatly rebacked, good ex-library with stamps on titlepage and verso of paltes.   Wheldon & Wesley 207-660 1996 £60.00

BRITISH MUSEUM.   Catalogue of Birds. Volume 10. Fringilliformes, Part I. London: 1885. 8vo; pages xiii, 681, 12 hand colored plates; original cloth, apart from tiny snag on rear joint, nice.   Wheldon & Wesley 207-662 1996 £100.00

BRITISH MUSEUM.   Catalogue of Birds. Volume 12. Fringilliformes, Part 3: Fringillidae. London: 1888. 8vo; pages xv, 871, 16 hand colored plates; original cloth, neatly repaired. Small stamp on titlepage and verso of paltes.   Wheldon & Wesley 207-663 1996 £75.00

BRITISH MUSEUM.   Catalogue of Birds. Volume 16. Upupae and Trochili. London: 1892. 8vo; pages xvi, 704, 14 colored plates; original cloth.   Wheldon & Wesley 207-664 1996 £100.00

BRITISH MUSEUM.   Catalogue of Birds. Volume 17. Leptosomatidae, Coraciidae, Meropidae, Alcedinidae, Momotidae, Todidae, Collidae. London: 1892. 8vo; pages xi, 523, 17 colored plates; original cloth, small tear in titlepage.   Wheldon & Wesley 207-665 1996 £100.00

BRITISH MUSEUM.   Catalogue of Birds. Volume 19. Scansores and Coccyges: Rhamphastidae, Galbulidae and Bucconidae. London: 1891. 8vo; pages xii, 485; 13 colored plates; original cloth.   Wheldon & Wesley 207-666 1996 £100.00

BRITISH MUSEUM.   Catalogue of Birds. Volume 21. Columbae. London: 1893. 8vo; pages xviii, 676, 15 colored plates; recently rebound in cloth.   Wheldon & Wesley 207-667 1996 £150.00

BRITISH MUSEUM.   Catalogue of Birds. Volume 22. Game Birds: Pterocletes, Gallinae, Opisthocomi and Hemipodii. London: 1893. 8vo; pages xvi, 585; 8 colored plates; original cloth, trifle worn.   Wheldon & Wesley 207-668 1996 £90.00

BRITISH MUSEUM. Catalogue of Birds. volume 23. Fulicariae (Rallidae and Heliornithidae) and Alectorides (Aramidae-Otididae). London: British Museum, 1894. 8vo; pages xiii, 353, 9 colored plates; original cloth. Nice copy. Wheldon & Wesley 207-669 1996 £75.00

BRITISH MUSEUM. Catalogue of Birds. Volume 26. Plataleae and Herodiones. London: 1898. 8vo; pages xvii, 688, 14 colored plates; original cloth, binding very slightly used, small water stain in upper right hand corner of plates, not affecting colored area. Wheldon & Wesley 207-670 1996 £100.00

BRITISH MUSEUM. Catalogue of Birds. Volume 27. Chenomorphae, Crypturi and Ratitae. London: British Museum, 1895. 8vo; pages xv, 636; 19 colored plates; original cloth; trifle used, small tear in blank flyleaf. Wheldon & Wesley 207-671 1996 £100.00

BRITISH MUSEUM. Catalogue of Carnivorous Pachydermatous and Edente Mammalia in the British Museum. 1869. illustrations; totally unopened, excellent copy, 2 neat library stamps on prelims. David Grayling J95Biggame-519 1996 £65.00

BRITISH MUSEUM. Catalogue of Printed Books. London: 1882-1900. Thick 4to; 42 volumes; binder's cloth; very good set, formerly in the Ministry of Defence, small library stamps on titlepages. Charles W. Traylen 117-5 1996 £375.00

BRITISH MUSEUM. Catalogue of the Books, Manuscripts, Maps and Drawings in the British Museum (Natural History). New York: 1991. Reprint; limited to 450 sets; 8vo; 8 volumes in 4; original cloth. Forest Books 74-26 1996 £225.00

BRITISH MUSEUM. Catalogue of the Books, Manuscripts, Maps and Drawings in the British Museum (Natural History). New York: 1992. Limited edition of 400 copies; 8vo; 8 volumes in 4; cloth. Raymond M. Sutton VI-1126 1996 $250.00

BRITISH MUSEUM. Catalogue of the Books, Manuscripts, Maps and Drawings in the British Museum. New York: Martino, 1992. Reprint of London 1903-33 edition; limited to 450 sets; 8vo; 8 volumes in 4; c. 4000 pages; original cloth. Edwin V. Glaser 121-226 1996 $250.00

BRITISH MUSEUM. Catalogue of the Fifty Manuscripts and Printed Books Bequeathed to the British Museum by Alfred H. Huth. London: printed for the Trustees, 1912. 4to; xvi, 130 pages; frontispiece, 18 plates, facsimiles in text; original red cloth, gilt lettering, rebacked, old backstrip laid down; cloth faded, edges slightly rubbed. W. W. Greg's copy with his signature. Robert Clark 38-266 1996 £65.00

BRITISH MUSEUM. Catalogue of the Fossil Sponges in the Geological Department of the British Museum (Natural History). London: 1883. 4to; pages viii, 248; 38 plates; cloth, rebacked; inscribed "From the author to P. Martin Duncan". John Henly 27-728 1996 £60.00

BRITISH MUSEUM. Catalogue of the Greek and Etruscan Vases in the British Museum. London: British Museum: 1893-1925. 8vo; 4 volumes in 5 parts; xliv, 228 pages, 309 figures and 16 plates; xxxi, 276 pages, 396 figures, 34 plates; 313 pages, 44 figures, 7 plates; 425 pages, 28 figures, 28 plates; 275 pages, 30 figures, 16 plates; original gilt lettered cloth. Archaeologia Luxor-3076 1996 $1,250.00

BRITISH MUSEUM. Catalogue of Birds. Volume 6. Cichlomorphae. Part 3. London: 1881. 8vo; pages xiii, 420, 18 hand colored plates; original cloth, neatly rebacked, good ex-library, stamps on titlepage and last plate. Wheldon & Wesley 207-661 1996 £130.00

BRITISH MUSEUM. Facsimiles of Biblical Manuscripts in the British Museum. London: by Order of the Trustees, 1900. Folio; 25 plates of facsimiles of manuscripts; original half green morocco, gilt. Charles W. Traylen 117-6 1996 £65.00

BRITISH MUSEUM. List of the Specimens of British Animals in the Collection, with Synonyms and References to Figures. London: British Museum, 1848-56. 12mo; 18 parts; original wrpapers. Wheldon & Wesley 207-364 1996 £60.00

BRITISH REINFORCED CONCRETE ENGINEERING CO. B.R.C. Structures. A Photographic Record of the Use of Reinforced Concrete in Modern Building Construction. London: B.R.C., 1923. 8vo; 7, (1) pages, 361, (3) pages of photo plates; boards. Elton Engineering 10-16 1996 £55.00

BRITISH SCHOOL OF ARCHAEOLOGY IN JERUSALEM Journal of the British School of Archaeology in Jerusalem. London: British School of Archaeology in Jerusalem, 1969. 4to; Volumes I-XXIII, in 23 volumes; original printed wrappers, very good set. Archaeologia Luxor-2381 1996 $950.00

BRITISH Sports and Sportsmen. Shooting and Deerstalking. London: 1913. Large thick folio; many illustrations; original buckram, corners very lightly rubbed and bumped. David A.H. Grayling 3/95-116 1996 £65.00

BRITISH Yachts and Yachtsmen. A Complete History of British Yachting from the Middle of the Seventeenth Century to the Present Day. London: Yachtsman Pub. Co., 1907. Very thick 4to; photos; full black leather. Petersfield Bookshop FH58-352 1996 £260.00

BRITTEN, F. J. Old Clocks and Watches & Their Makers...Different Styles of Clocks and Watches of Post in England and Abroad, to which is added a list of nearly 12 thousand makers. London: 1932. 6th edition; thick 8vo; 934 illustrations; original cloth, new black leather backstrip gilt, corners just little bumped. Petersfield Bookshop FH58-115 1996 £80.00

BRITTEN, F. J. Old English Clocks (The Wetherfield Collection). London: Antique Collectors Club, c. 1980. Thin 4to; 131 illustrations; full suede leather. Petersfield Bookshop FH58-3 1996 £60.00

BRITTEN, J. A Dictionary of English Plant Names. London: 1878-86. 8vo; pages xxviii, 618; half morocco, rare; good. Wheldon & Wesley 207-1467 1996 £100.00

BRITTON, JOHN A Brief Memoir of the Life and Writings of John Britton. London: by J. Moyes (not for sale) 1825. Large 8vo; 49, (1) pages, ad leaf, half title; original roan backed marbled boards with paper label on upper cover, very scarce. Ken Spelman 30-64 1996 £160.00

BRITTON, JOHN Britton (On the Laws of England). London: 1640. 2nd edition; modern calf, definite embrowning, sound. Meyer Boswell SL25-25 1996 $450.00

BRITTON, JOHN Graphic Illustration, with Historical and Descriptive Accounts of Toddington, Gloucestershire, the Seat of Lord Sudeley... London: for the author, 1840. One of only 23 copies with proof plates according to subscription list; 4to; (title with vignette), pages xvi, 46, viii, 3 text illustrations, 28 etched plates and plans, (proofs), tinted litho frontispiece, foxing to frontispiece and most plates); contemporary purple blindstamped gilt lettered cloth by Runting, spine faded, repaired splits at head and foot of spine. Harris p. 42. Marlborough 162-12 1996 £190.00

BRITTON, WILEY The Union Indian Brigade in the Civil War. Kansas City: 1922. 1st edition; 474 pages; plates, cloth, leather label, very good . Very scarce. Dornbusch II 26. T. A. Swinford 49-143 1996 $175.00

BROAD, AMOS The Trial of Amos Broad and His Wife on the Several Indictments for Assaulting and Beating Betty, a Slave, and Her Little Female Child Sarah, Aged Three Years. New York: Henry C. Southwick, 1809. 1st edition; 8vo; 31 pages; sewn, last signature detached, quite browned, some minor stain and dust soiling, corner torn from last leaf with loss of one letter in first 8 lines. very rare. LCP/HSP Afro Amer. Cat. 1616; S&S 18777; Sabin 8140. M & S Rare Books 60-287 1996 $1,500.00

BROADSIDE Ballads of the Restoration Period from the Jersey Collection Known as the Osterley Park Ballads. London: John Lane, the bodley Head, 1930. 1st edition; number 540 of 750 copies; large 4to; 248 pages; printed on heavy laid paper; white linen spine, marbled linen boards, uncut; corners slightly bumped, contents excellent. Hartfield 48-A2 1996 $295.00

BROCH, HERMANN James Joyce und die Gegenwart. Zurich: Reichner, 1936. 1st edition; wrappers; near fine; inscribed by author to Daniel Brody. Lame Duck Books 19-94 1996 $1,500.00

BROCKETT, JOSHUA ARTHUR Zipporah: the Maid of Midian. Chicago: Ustafrican B. P. & D. Co., 1926. 1st edition; boards slightly splayed and some small, light spotting to front board, thus very good. Between the Covers 43-36 1996 $285.00

BROCKETT, L. P.   Epidemic and Contagious Diseases: Their History, Symptoms, and Treatment Illustrated With the Best Colored Plates of the Various Contagious and Eruptive Diseases Ever Executed in this Country, and Other Fine Engravings. New York: 1873. 1st edition; 507 pages; full leather, rubbed.   W. Bruce Fye 71-233 1996 $250.00

BROCKMAN, CARL HEINRICH   Die Metallurgischen Krankheiten des Oberharzes. Osterode: Sorge, 1851. 1st edition; large 8vo; pages xiv, 376; dedication copy, contemporary red morocco, gilt crowned monogram of Ernst August, of Hanover, on upper cover, his arms, onlaid in color, on lower cover, both within ornamental rococo gilt and silvered borders, flat spine, gilt lettered within scrolling floral border, glazed endpapers, all edges gilt, fine royal binding of the period, enchanced by the use of silver.   Marlborough 160-63 1996 £1,350.00

BRODER, PATRICIA JANIS   The American West, The Modern Vision. New York: 1984. 1st edition; limited to 150 specially bound copies, each signed and numbered by author; this copy number 53; fine; original print by Scholder has been removed and book is priced accordingly.   T. A. Swinford 49-144 1996 $400.00

BRODER, PATRICIA JANIS   Shadows on Glass, the Indian World of Ben Wittick. Savage: Rowman and Littlefield, 1990. 224 pages; fine in dust jacket.   Ken Sanders 8-307 1996 $150.00

BRODIE, BENJAMIN COLLINS   Lectures Illustrative of Certain Local Nervous Affections. London: printed for Longman, Rees, Orme, Brown, Green & Longman, 1837. 1st edition; 8vo; iv, 88 pages, plus Longman catalog dated Feb. 1837 inserted at front; original drab boards, spine chipped (wtih base erose for about an inch), fine, uncut in original condition; scarce; with titlepage stamp of the Hartford Retreat; with Jelliffe's name stamp to titlepage and his bookplate. Norman Cat. 346. John Gach 150-76 1996 $375.00

BRODIGAN, THOMAS   A Botanical, Historical and Practical Treatise on the Tobacco Plant, in Which the Art of Growing and Curing Tobacco in the British Isles Is made Familiar to Every Capacity, as Deduced from the Observations of the Author in the United States... London: Longman et al, 1830. 1st edition; 8vo; pages 236; publisher's cloth (cut along the hinge), uncut and unopened. Scarce. Sabin 8183; Arents N1346; not in BMC, Kress or Goldsmith.   Second Life Books 103-34 1996 $600.00

BRODKEY, HAROLD   Stories in an Almost Classical Mode. New York: knopf, 1988. 1st edition; original cloth, fine in fine dust jacket, inscribed by author; laid in is an ALS on New Yorker letterhead.   Beasley Books 82-28 1996 $125.00

BRODSKY, JOSEPH   A Part of Speech. New York: Farrar, Straus, Giroux, 1980. 1st edition; 8vo; signed by author; cloth, dust jacket; mint. James S. Jaffe 34-88 1996 $125.00

BRODSKY, JOSEPH   Selected Poems. New York: Harper & Row, 1973. 1st American edition; 8vo; cloth backed boards, dust jacket; signed by author, fine in price clipped jacket.   James S. Jaffe 34-86 1996 $125.00

BRODSKY, JOSEPH   To Urania. New York: Farrar, Straus, Giroux, 1988. 1st edition; one of 150 specially bound copies signed by author; 8vo; blue cloth, slipcase; mint.   James S. Jaffe 34-90 1996 $150.00

BRODSKY, JOSEPH   Verses on the Winter Campaign 1980. London: Anvil Press Poetry, 1981. 1st edition; one of 250 copies, signed by author and translator, Alan Myers; small 8vo; printed wrappers, dust jacket; mint.   James S. Jaffe 34-89 1996 $150.00

BRODZKY, HORACE   Henri Gaudier-Brzeska - 1891-1915. London: Faber and Faber Ltd., 1933. 1st edition; 24 full page line drawings, 32 black and white plates and some drawings in text by artist; original binding, top edge dusty, head and tail of spine and corners slightly bumped, very good in torn, chipped and creased, slightly rubbed and dusty dust jacket, darkened at spine and edges.   Ulysses 39-221 1996 £95.00

BROGGER, A. W.   The Viking Ships, Their Ancestry and Evolution. Oslo: 1951. Special Private edition; 9.5 x 6.5 inches; 248 pages, with index; illustrations, full polished calf, minor foxing on f.e.p.'s from related present clippings, covers (especially outer joints) rubbed, slight chipping to top of spine.   John K. King 77-764 1996 $100.00

BROINOWSKI, G. J.   The Birds of Australia... Melbourne: 1887-91. Demy folio; 6 volumes in 3; 303 colored plates; original full morocco, gilt, gilt edges.   Wheldon & Wesley 207-16 1996 £2,000.00

BROKESBY, FRANCIS   The Life of Mr. Henry Dodwell; with an Account of His Works and an Abridgment of Several Of Them... London: Geo. James for Richard Smith, 1715. 1st edition; 8vo; (xxxviii), 638, (ii) pages; frontispiece, final ad leaf; contemporary panelled calf, neatly rebacked and recornered, spine gilt, label; some browning at beginning and end. Good.   Robert Clark 38-166 1996 £100.00

BROMFIELD, LOUIS   A Modern Hero. New York: Frederick A. Stokes, 1932. 1st edition; one of 250 signed and numbered copies; in original gold gilt dust jacket and publisher's box of marbled paper in grey, red, green, blue and black with red label on front cover; design on jacket is the same architectural design as that on Twenty-Four Hours which is in silver gilt, endpapers are gold gilt matching the jacket, spine of jacket is trifle sunned and there is one small ruffle to top of spine.   Priscilla Juvelis 95/1-44 1996 $100.00

BROMFIELD, LOUIS   Twenty-Four Hours. New York: Stokes, 1930. 1st edition; limited to 500 copies, signed by author; red cloth with white cloth spine and stamped in gold, dust jacket and endpapers have an Art Deco montage in black on silver background of New York City by P. S. Jobst; very fine in dust jacket and original slipcase, also in silver and black with red label. Bookplate of Theodore Lilienthal.   Bromer Booksellers 90-10 1996 $250.00

BROMFIELD, LOUIS   Twenty-Four Hours. New York: Frederick A. Stokes and Co., 1930. 1st edition; one of 5000 copies, signed and numbered by author; original silver gilt and black, title in red, art deco jacket and matching endpapers by P.S. Jonst, publisher's slipcase is handmade grey and black paper in deco design with label in red, box is slightly worn but intact, jacket shows some ruffling to top of spine and spine color is slightly sunned, still very good, rare in this condition as the gilt paper jacket did not wear well.   Priscilla Juvelis 95/1-45 1996 $100.00

BRON, WILLIAM   Careless Love and its Apostrophes. New York: Red Ozier Press, 1985. 1st edition; one of 40 specially bound copies, signed by author, out of a total edition of 175; small 8vo; cloth backed decorated boards; mint.   James S. Jaffe 34-563 1996 $150.00

BRONAUGH, W. C.   The Youngers' Fight for Freedom. Columbia: printed for the author, 1906. 1st edition; 8vo; original burgundy cloth with some slight wear. Scarce. Adams 283; Rader 495.   Glenn Books 36-289 1996 $125.00

BRONEER, OSCAR   Corinth. Volume I. Part IV: The South Stoa and Its Roman Successors. Princeton: ASCSA, 1954. 4to; frontispiece, xix, 167 figures, 55 plates, 22 plans; original cloth, spine faded.   Archaeologia Luxor-3182 1996 $200.00

BRONEER, OSCAR   The Lion Monument at Amphipolis. Cambridge: Harvard University Press, 1941. 8vo; xvii, 76 pages, 37 illustrations, 11 plates; original cloth; inscribed "To Bob from the writer".   Archaeologia Luxor-3113 1996 $125.00

BRONOWSKI, JACOB   For Wilhelmina, Queen of the Netherlands. Cambridge: W. Heffer & Sons, 1929. 1st edition; saddlestitched in wrappers, very faint stain to front wrapper, else fine, nicely inscribed by author.   Between the Covers 42-68 1996 $250.00

BRONOWSKI, JACOB   For Wilhelmina, Queen of the Netherlands. Cambridge: W. Heffer & Sons Ltd., 1929. 1st edition; author's first book; cover design and decoration by Raymond McGrath; original binding, spine and cover edges browned, top edge spotted; very good; loosely inserted is an advance review slip for a book called "Pyramid" by Lionel Birch, this is inscribed on verso by Bronowkski.   Ulysses 39-74 1996 £95.00

BRONTE, ANNE   The Tenant of Wildfell Hall. Shakespeare Head, 1931. 1st American edition thus, limited to 1000 copies, this copy no. 355; 9 1/8 x 6 1/8 inches; 2 volumes, frontispiece to each volume, plus 3 other illustrations, pages xi, 282; vi, 278; green buckram, printed paper title label on backstrips, uncut; fine.   Ian Hodgkins 78-251 1996 £145.00

BRONTE, CHARLOTTE 1816-1855   Jane Eyre. London: Smith, Elder and Co., 1847. 1st edition; 7 3/4 x 4 3/4 inches; 3 volumes, pages iv, 304, 32 pages publisher's ads dated October 1847; iv, 304, 32 pages ads dated Oct. 1847; iv, 304; iv, 311; maroon cloth with blindstamped decorated borders on covers, gilt titling to backstrips, rebound with original cloth sides laid down, red leather title label on backstrips, rebound with original cloth sides laid down, red leather title label on backstrips, contents have usual foxing, good, sound copy, very scarce; pencil signature of Gertrude Nussey on half title of each volume. Smith 2.   Ian Hodgkins 78-190 1996 £6,750.00

BRONTE, CHARLOTTE 1816-1855　　Jane Eyre. New York: Harper & Bros., 1848. 1st American edition, later issue; 9 1/8 x 5 1/2 inches; pages 174 (with Harper ad below text on p. 174), recent quarter dark blue calf with red leather title label on backstrip, foxing to contents, lacks 2 pages ads at rear, very good, scarce.　Ian Hodgkins 78-191 1996 £185.00

BRONTE, CHARLOTTE 1816-1855　　Jane Eyre. Paris: Hachette, 1859. Re-issue; 6 3/4 x 4 1/4 inches; vi, 459; pages; half crimson morocco, raised bands, gilt titling to backstrip, marbled boards and endpapers, slight foxing to contents, very good.　Ian Hodgkins 78-192 1996 £85.00

BRONTE, CHARLOTTE 1816-1855　　Jane Eyre. Paris: 1923. 1st edition thus, limited to 475 numbered copies (this no. 69); 15 1/4 x 11 inches; pages iv, 258 + colophon; 17 original lithographs by Ethel Gabain; loose in wrappers, as issued, uncut, wrappers foxed, and slight foxing to contents, very good.　Ian Hodgkins 78-197 1996 £190.00

BRONTE, CHARLOTTE 1816-1855　　The Complete Poems. London: Hodder & Stoughton, n.d. 1923. 1st collected edition; 8 1/2 x 6 inches; pages xxi, 224; blue cloth backed grey boards, gilt titling to backstrip, uncut and partly unopened, corners of boards slightly bumped, very good, scarce. Wise (1929) p. 33.　Ian Hodgkins 78-215 1996 £90.00

BRONTE, CHARLOTTE 1816-1855　　The Professor. London: Smith, Elder & Co., 1857. 1st edition; 1st printing; 8vo; 2 volumes, newly bound by Bayntun of Bath in full forest green morocco with gilt ruled covers, gilt panelled spine and gilt inner dentelles, all edges gilt, contents clean and bright, fine in every way. Sadleir 347; Parrish 96.　Glenn Books 36-38 1996 $1,200.00

BRONTE, CHARLOTTE 1816-1855　　The Professor, a Tale. London: Smith, Elder & Co., 1857. 1st edition; 7 1/2 x 5 1/4 inches; 2 volumes, 2 pages of ads in volume 1 and 8 in volume 2 (ads undated); contemporary polished calf very elaborately grained, ruled and stamped in gilt and blind, recently rebacked, spine with raised bands, thick and thin gilt rules, and red and green morocco labels, new endpapers, boards with hint of chafing, text with very minor smudges or creasing, but quite excellent. Passel A4.　Phillip J. Pirages 33-115 1996 $650.00

BRONTE, CHARLOTTE 1816-1855　　The Professor. New York: Harper and Bros., 1857. 1st American edition; 7 1/4 x 4 7/8 inches; pages (vii), 330, 6 pages publisher's ads at rear. reddish brown morocco grain cloth with blindstamped decorated border to both covers, gilt titling to backstrip, yellow endpapers (variant binding); backstrip worn at top and slightly worn at bottom, edges of covers and backstrip faded to brown, contents foxed, very good. Smith p. 172; NCBEL III 865.　Ian Hodgkins 78-202 1996 £265.00

BRONTE, CHARLOTTE 1816-1855　　The Professor...to which are Added The Poems of Currer, Ellis & Acton Bell. London: Smith, Elder & Co., 1860. 2nd edition; 6 7/8 x 4 1/4 inches; pages iv, 436, 8 pages ads; orange cloth with titling in black on backstrip and front cover, ads to rear cover and endpapers, recased and refurbished with original backstrip laid down, occasional foxing contents, very good in slipcase, scarce.　Ian Hodgkins 78-203 1996 £125.00

BRONTE, CHARLOTTE 1816-1855　　The Professor. New York: Carleton, 1865. Sub-edition of 1st American edition; 7 1/4 x 4 7/8 inches; frontispiece, pages (vii), 330, 8 pages ads; light reddish brown wavy grain cloth with double scalloped blind embossed border, central circular ornament, publisher's name on both covers, gilt rules and titling to backstrip, pale blue endpapers, top and bottom of backstrip worn and covers patchily faded, very good, clean copy, scarce. Smith p. 173. Ian Hodgkins 78-204 1996 £275.00

BRONTE, CHARLOTTE 1816-1855　　Shirley, a Tale. London: Smith, Elder & Co., 1857. 3rd edition; 6 3/4 x 4 3/8 inches; pages iv, 534, 6 pages ads for the Uniform edtiion; orange cloth, titling in black to front cover and backstrip, ads to rear cover and endpapers, backstrip discolored and faded, titling rubbed from front cover and small split to top rear joint, contents very good.　Ian Hodgkins 78-206 1996 £68.00

BRONTE, CHARLOTTE 1816-1855　　Shirley et Agnes Grey. Paris: Lib. Hachette et Cie, 1877. 2nd French edition thus; 7 x 4 3/8 inches; pages iii, 407; iii, 370; scarlet cloth backed dark red marbled boards, gilt titling to backstrips, foxing to contents, backstrips rubbed, very good, scarce. Ian Hodgkins 78-207 1996 £100.00

BRONTE, CHARLOTTE 1816-1855　　Shirley. London: Oxford University Press, 1979. Clarendon edition, 1st edition thus; 8 1/2 x 5 1/2 inches; pages xli, 835; dark blue cloth, gilt titling, fine in dust jacket.　Ian Hodgkins 78-209 1996 £60.00

BRONTE, CHARLOTTE 1816-1855　　The Twelve Adventurers and Other Stories. London: Hodder & Stoughton, n.d. 1925. Limited to 1000 copies; 8 1/2 x 6 inches; pages x, 214; blue cloth backed grey boards, gilt titling to backstrip, uncut; fine in very slightly used dust jacket.　Ian Hodgkins 78-219 1996 £110.00

BRONTE, CHARLOTTE 1816-1855　　Two Tales "The Secret Hart" & "Lily Hart". University of Missouri Press, 1978. 1st edition; limited to 300 numbered copies, signed by editor; 10 x 8 inches; frontispiece and 7 illustrations, 13 pages of facsimile ms., pages 144 including colohon; beige leather backed blue boards with portrait of author in white on front cover, gilt titling on backstrip, pale blue endpapers; fine in slipcase. Ian Hodgkins 78-221 1996 £78.00

BRONTE, CHARLOTTE 1816-1855　　Villette. New York: Harper & Bros., 1853. 1st American edition; 7 3/8 x 5 inches; 2 pages of reviews, iv, 502, 6, 6, 4 pages publisher's ads at rear; dark mauve morocco grain cloth with blindstamped decoration and publisher's monogram to both covers, gilt titling to backstrip, yellow endpapers, backstrip faded to brown with some wear to top and bottom, contents foxed, very good, scarce. Smith p. 152;　Ian Hodgkins 78-210 1996 £215.00

BRONTE, CHARLOTTE 1816-1855　　Villette. London: Smith, Elder and Co., 1855. 2nd edition, later issue; 6 3/4 x 4 3/8 inches; pages iv, 492, half dark brown calf, marbled boards, rebacked, occasional fox mark, bookplate, very good, rare. Walter Smith pp. 141-43.　Ian Hodgkins 78-212 1996 £235.00

BRONTE, CHARLOTTE 1816-1855　　Villette. New York: Harper & Bros., 1855. 2nd American edition; 7 3/8 x 4 7/8 inches; pages iv, 502; brown wavy grain cloth with blindstamped decorated border to both covers, gilt titling to backstrip, pale yellow endpapers, contents foxed and endpapers discolored, backstrip much faded and covers faded and some marks thereon, very good. Smith p. 153.　Ian Hodgkins 78-211 1996 £135.00

BRONTE, CHARLOTTE 1816-1855　　Villette. New York: Derby & jackson, 1857. 3rd American edition; 7 1/4 x 4 3/4 inches; pages iv, 502, 2 ads; blue grey vertical ribbed cloth, blindstamped decoration on covers, gilt titling to backstrip, pale yellow endpapers, covers faded, top and bottom of backstrip worn and corners with some wear, foxing to contents, good, scarce.　Ian Hodgkins 78-213 1996 £110.00

BRONTE, CHARLOTTE 1816-1855　　Villette. Shakespeare Head Press, 1931. 1st edition thus, limited to 1000 copies; 9 1/8 x 6 1/8 inches; 2 volumes, frontispiece to each volume and 4 other illustrations; pages vii,3 19; v, 313; orange cloth, uncut, name to free endpaper volume 1; very good.　Ian Hodgkins 78-252 1996 £135.00

BRONTE, CHARLOTTE 1816-1855　　Villette. New York: Houghton Mifflin, 1931. 1st American edition, large paper edition, limited to 500 numbered copies; 9 1/4 x 6 inches; 2 volumes; frontispiece to each volume and 5 illustrations, pages ix, 319; vii, 313; black buckram backed sage green boards, black leather title label with gilt titling on backstrips, uncut and unopened, title label on volume 1, broken away lower right corner, fine. Ian Hodgkins 78-253 1996 £125.00

BRONTE, EMILY 1818-1848　　Gondal's Queen. Austin: University of Texas, 1955. 1st edition; 9 x 6 1/8 inches; pages (xxxviii), 207; frontispiece, 4 illustrations; cream buckram, gilt titling on blue panel backstrip, very good; Elizabeth Nreman's copy with her bookplate and signature on endpapers.　Ian Hodgkins 78-222 1996 £68.00

BRONTE, EMILY 1818-1848　　The Complete Poems Of. London: Hodder & Stoughton, n.d. 1923. 1st edition thus; 8 1/4 x 6 inches; 4 facsimiles reproductions, pages xxiv, 196; blue cloth backed grey boards, gilt titling, uncut, bookplate, very good, scarce.　Ian Hodgkins 78-223 1996 £90.00

BRONTE, EMILY 1818-1848　　The Complete Poems Of. New York: Columbia University Press, 1941. 1st edition; 9 x 6 inches; frontispiece facsimile and 3 others, pages xxiii, 262; green cloth, gilt titling to front cover and backstrip, free endpapers slightly discolored, very good; Ian Hodgkins 78-225 1996 £55.00

BRONTE, EMILY 1818-1848　　Wuthering Heights. London: Hodder & Stoughton, 1911. 1st edition thus, limited to 1000 copies; 8 1/4 x 5 3/8 inches; frontispiece, pages xvii, 456; crimson buckram, gilt titling backstrip, top edge gilt, others uncut, backstrip discolored to brown, very good, scarce.　Ian Hodgkins 78-227 1996 £90.00

BRONTE, EMILY 1818-1848   Wuthering Heights. New York: Random House, 1931. 1st edition thus, limited to 450 numbered copies, signed by artist, (no. 417); 10 1/2 x 8 1/4 inches; pages xvii, 325; 12 wood engravings by Clare Leighton; black cloth with gilt decoration and titling on backstrip, top edge stained black, uncut and unopened, wear to corners and top of backstrip, top edge stained black, uncut and unopened; wear to corners and top of backstrip, contents fine.   Ian Hodgkins 78-230 1996 £195.00

BRONTE, EMILY 1818-1848   Wurthering Heights. Paris: Chez Jean Porson, 1947. 1st edition thus, limited to 300 copies (being one of 299 on Rives blanc - copy no. 288); 12 1/2 x 10 inches; pages vii, 241, iv; vii, 249, vi; (text in French); with rare original lithographs by Leon Masson; loose in original lithographic wrappers, preserved in cloth backed decoration and illustrated board folder with ties, cloth of folders faded; fine in original decorated slipcase.   Ian Hodgkins 78-234 1996 £315.00

BRONTE, EMILY 1818-1848   Wuthering Heights. London: Fraser Press, 1970. 1st edition thus, limited to 1560 copies; 8 3/4 x 5 1/4 inches; pages 360 + colophon; full green crushed levant morocco, all edges gilt, marbled endpapers, backstrip discolored to brown, very good.   Ian Hodgkins 78-238 1996 £65.00

BRONTE, THE SISTERS   The Novels of. London: Smith, Elder & Co., 1888-96. New edition; 7 x 4 3/4 inches; green cloth, gilt titling within gilt ruled box on backstrips, top edge gilt, others uncut, name to free endpapers and two volumes have new front free endpapers, very good set.   Ian Hodgkins 78-245 1996 £140.00

BRONTE, THE SISTERS   The Novels Of... Edinburgh: John Grant, 1907. Thornton Edition, re-issue; 8 1/4 x 5 1/2 inches; frontispiece in each volume and other illustrations, sage green buckram with gilt design and titling to backstrips, top edge gilt, others uncut, foxing to fore edge of pages on few volumes, dated name to front free endpaper all volumes, free endpapers partially discolored and some endpapers slightly foxed, very good in white dust jackets as issued.   Ian Hodgkins 78-247 1996 £550.00

BRONTE, THE SISTERS   Novels of the Sisters Bronte. Edinburgh: 1924. Thornton Edition; 8vo; 12 volumes; original cloth, gilt spines, contents lettered.   Charles W. Traylen 117-73 1996 £220.00

BRONTE, THE SISTERS   The Novels. London: Folio Society, 1991. Re-issue with new illustrations; 8 3/4 x 5 5/8 inches; black and white wood engravings; green moire silk cloth with gilt titling backstrips, preserved in matching slipcase; fine set.   Ian Hodgkins 78-248 1996 £90.00

BRONTE, THE SISTERS   Poems by Currer, Ellis and Acton Bell. London: Smith, Elder and Co., 1846/48. 1st edition; 2nd issue, with Smith, Elder titlepage; 8vo; pages iv, 165, (i) imprint, (i) ads; uncut in original olive green vertically ribbed cloth, covers stamped in blind with double line rectangular border enclosing decorative floral designs, harp in centre, spine with bands in blind, lettered in gold, cream endpapers; spine worn at head and tail, corners just bumped, extremities slightly sunned; good copy; early ownership inscription of Miss Lowe, bookplate of John Sallows Hubbard; Walter Smith, Bronte Sisters pp. 6-14.   Simon Finch 24-18 1996 £650.00

BRONTE, THE SISTERS   The Works of. London: Smith, Elder & Co., 1880/87. Re-issue; 7 3/4 x 5 1/4 inches; 7 volumes; frontispiece and title vignette to each volume + 24 full page illustrations; dark green sand grain cloth with black titling and design on front covers, gilt titling on backstrips, dark brown endpapers, one or two corners slightly bumped, some wear to top and bottom backstrips and occasional slight foxing to contents, very good.   Ian Hodgkins 78-243 1996 £255.00

BRONTE, THE SISTERS   The Works of... London: J. M. Dent & Co., 1893/98. Various issues; 6 3/4 x 4 1/4 inches; 12 volumes; illustrations by T. S. Greig and decorations by F. C. Tilney; scarlet buckram, gilt decorated and titling to backstrips, top edge gilt, uncut, backstrips faded and marks on some covers, free endpapers discolored, name on free endpapers in some volumes, very good.   Ian Hodgkins 78-244 1996 £125.00

BRONTE, THE SISTERS   The Complete Works. Basil Blackwell & Houghton Mifflin, 1931/33. Shakespeare Head press edition, American issue, known as the large paper edition, limited to 1000 copies, of which 500 copies are for America (copy no.1 46); 9 x 6 inches; 6 volumes; illustrations; black buckram backed grey boards, dark green leather title labels on backstrips, uncut; bookplates, boards marked and corners of boards slightly worn, slight wear to some labels, occasional slight foxing to contents, very good.   Ian Hodgkins 78-257 1996 £750.00

BRONTE, THE SISTERS   The Complete Works. London: Basil Blackwell, 1931/33. 1st edition thus, limited to 1000 copies; 9 x 6 1/4 inches; 11 volumes; illustrations; orange cloth, uncut; fine.   Ian Hodgkins 78-256 1996 £1,000.00

BRONTE, THE SISTERS   The Complete Works. London: Basil Blackwell, 1931/36. Limited edition; 9 x 6 1/4 inches; 13 volumes; illustrations; dust jackets, unopened; fine, 4 volumes without dust jackets, all in orange cloth, top edge gilt.   Ian Hodgkins 78-258 1996 £2,300.00

BRONTE, THE SISTERS   Wuthering Heights & Jane Eyre. New York: Random House, 1943. 1st edition thus; 9 5/8 x 7 3/8 inches; 2 volumes, title vignette and many full page wood engravings; pages xv, 213; vi, 343; dark green buckram backed pictorial boards, gilt titling to backstrip; fine in slightly worn original slipcase.   Ian Hodgkins 78-249 1996 £65.00

BROOK, H. M. BERNARD   Catalogue of the Madreporarian Corals in the British Museum. London: 1893-1928. 4to; 7 volumes; 13 lithograph and 229 collotype plates and 35 text figures; original cloth, small stamps on titlepages, but nice.   Wheldon & Wesley 207-1236 1996 £250.00

BROOK, ROBERT   Elements of Style in Furniture and Woodwork. London: the author, 1889. 1st edition; tall 4to; 36 pages; 50 plates; publisher's cloth, all edges gilt; recased in original gilt lettered cloth, smudging throughout, some pencilling and sketching, covers worn, else good.   Bookpress 75-160 1996 $165.00

BROOKE, FULKE GREVILLE   The Remains...Being Poems of Monarchy and Religion. London: printed by T. N. Herringman, 1670. 1st edition; 8vo; contemporary mottled calf, spine gilt, spine bit rubbed. Fine copy; from the Evelyn family library, complete with leaf of imprimatur. Wing B4900; Grolier 408; CBEL I 1057.   Ximenes 109-147 1996 $1,250.00

BROOKE, FULKE GREVILLE, 1ST BARON 1554-1628   Caelica. Newtown: Gregynog Press, 1936, i.e. 1937. One of 15 copies specially bound (of a total edition of 225); 9 1/4 x 6 1/4 inches; xiii, (1), 149, (1) pages, (1) leaf (colophon); title printed in red and black, initials and colophon in red; lovely heavy grained slate blue levant morocco by Gregynog Press Bindery (signed in gilt on rear turn-in by Blair Hughes-Stanton and George Fisher), dec. in all over design featuring a total of 16 inset vellum stars on covers and spine, vellum stars stained a sublte shade pink and connected by gilt and blind fillets, raised bands, gilt titling on spine, wide turn-ins with one blind and one gilt rule, top edge gilt, other edges untrimmed, in somewhat faded and soiled folding cloth box, with paper label on spine, except for faint shadow of leather turn-ins on facing flyleaves, an extremely fine copy, especially clean inside and out, showing no signs of use. Harrop 36.   Phillip J. Pirages 33-260 1996 $6,500.00

BROOKE, FULKE GREVILLE, 1ST BARON 1554-1628   The Remains...Being Poems of Monarchy and Religion. London: T. N. for Henry Herringman, 1670. 8vo; (viii), 205, (i) pages; imprimatur leaf; old sheep, rebacked, label; rubbed, corners worn, label chipped, paper flaw on lower edge of N3, just touching catchword. Good. Wing B4900.   Robert Clark 38-52 1996 £325.00

BROOKE, HENRY   The Fool of Quality; or History of Henry Earl of Moreland. London: printed for W. Johnston, 1767-70. Original mixed set, volumes 1 and 2 are 2nd edition, volumes 3-5 first edition; 12mo; 5 volumes, foxing to some sections; uniform contemporary sprinkled calf, red and green labels, gilt spines, joints of volume 1 just starting, but good, sound set. Hardy 271.   H. M. Fletcher 121-88 1996 £400.00

BROOKE, JOCELYN   The Crisis in Bulgaria or Ibsen to the Rescue. London: Chatto & Windus, 1956. 1st edition; numerous full page black and white drawings by author; original binding, free endpapers partially browned, head and tail of spine and corners slightly bumped, top edge slightly spotted and soiled, very good in nicked, rubbed and soiled, slightly torn, creased and dusty internally repaired dust jacket, browned at spine and edges.   Ulysses 39-76 1996 £55.00

BROOKE, RICHARD   Liverpool As It Was During the Last Quarter of the Eighteenth Century 1775-1800. Liverpool: J. Mawdlsey and Son, 1853. 8vo; 558 pages; 6 plates; original cloth blocked in blind, lettered in gilt on spine, small paper label at foot of spine, small library numbers in ink on blank verso of title and at foot of first page of preface, waterstain on one plate, but very good.   David Bickersteth 133-140 1996 £95.00

BROOKE, ROBERT   La Graunde Abridgement Collect & Escrie Per Le Iudge Tresreuerend Syr Robert Brooke, Chiualier... (with) La Seconde part... London: in aedibus Richardi Totell, 1573. 1st edition; modern three quarter morocco, worn, first title trimmed, usable.   Meyer Boswell SL26-28 1996 $2,750.00

BROOKE, RUPERT 1887-1915   1914 and Other Poems. London: 1915. 1st edition; spare title label at end, corners trifle bruised, otherwise very good.   Words Etcetera 94-206 1996 £150.00

BROOKES, RICHARD   The General Practice of Physic... London: J. Newbery, 1763. 4th edition; 8vo; 2 volumes; contemporary polished calf, worn, institutional stamps on titles, one leaf torn with loss of text, replaced in manuscript.   James Tait Goodrich K40-60 1996 $150.00

BROOKNER, ANITA   Jacques-Louis David. London: Chatto & Windus ltd., 1980. 1st edition; 178 page study; 4 color plates, black and white frontispiece, 112 black and white plates; original binding, upper cover very slightly marked, head and tail of spine slightly bumped, bottom edges of covers slightly rubbed, very good in slightly creased and marked dust jacket, slightly faded at spine.   Ulysses 39-77 1996 £55.00

BROOKS, BRYANT B.   Memoirs of Bryant B. Brooks: Cowboy, Trapper, Lumberman, Stockman, Oilman, Banker and Governor of Wyoming. Glendale: Arthur H. Clark Co., 1939. 1st edition; limited to 150 copies; remains of small stamp on half title, small puncture to top of rear board, otherwise clean, bright; Adams Rampaging Herd 332. Hermitage SP95-698 1996 $200.00

BROOKS, BRYANT B.   Memoirs Of...Cowboy, Trapper, Lumberman, Stockman, Oilman, Banker and Governor of Wyoming. Glendale: 1939. 1st edition; 370 pages, frontispiece, photos; cloth, very scarce. Herd 332. T. A. Swinford 49-146 1996 $300.00

BROOKS, CLEANTH   Modern Poetry and the Tradition. Chapel Hill: University of North Carolina Press, 1939. 1st edition; original binding, top edge dusty, spine and cover edges slightly marked, very good in nicked dusty and slightly rubbed dust jacket, browned at spine and edges. Ulysses 39-78 1996 £95.00

BROOKS, ELIZABETH   Prominent Women of Texas. Akron: Werner Co., 1896. 1st edition; 216 pages; illustrations, portraits.   Maggie Lambeth 30-63 1996 $135.00

BROOKS, GWENDOLYN   In the Mecca. New York: Harper, 1968. Uncorrected galley sheets printed on rectos only; little browning to bottom half of front leaf, else about fine; rare.   Between the Covers 43-37 1996 $375.00

BROOKS, GWENDOLYN   Report from Part One. Detroit: Broadside Press, 1972. 1st edition; photogrpahs; bookplate, corners slightly bumped, else fine without dust jacket, possibly issued without one. Between the Covers 43-277 1996 $100.00

BROOKS, GWENDOLYN   Selected Poems. New York: Harper and Row, 1963. 1st edition; lovely copy in like dust jacket.   Bev Chaney, Jr. 23-116 1996 $125.00

BROOKS, JOHN   A Discourse Delivered Before the Humane Society of the Commonwealth of Massachusetts, 9th June, 1795. Boston: T. Fleet, 1795. 1st edition; 8vo; 32 pages; removed; fore-edge of title chipped. Austin 278; Evans 28351.   M & S Rare Books 60-292 1996 $150.00

BROOKS, S. H.   Designs for Cottage and Villa Architecture. London: Thomas Kelly, 1839. 4to; viii, 148, (4) pages, 111 plates; later half calf, marbled boards; occasional foxing, plate 32 repaired, otherwise very good. Archer 23.1.   Bookpress 75-16 1996 $550.00

BROOKS, T.   The Sword of Shannara. RH, 1977. 1st edition; review copy with accompanying review slip laid in; author's first book; illustrations by Hildebrandt's; fine in dust jacket.   Aronovitz 57-180 1996 $200.00

BROOME, WILLIAM   Poems on Several Discoveries. London: printed for Bernard Lintot, 1727. 1st edition; 8vo; portrait; contemporary calf, gilt lined, head and foot of spine repaired, new label, fine, fresh and unpressed copy;   Peter Murray Hill 185-17 1996 £220.00

BROUGHAM & VAUX, HENRY PETER BROUGHAM, 1ST BARON 1778-1868 British Constitution. London: Charles Knight & Co., 1844. 1st separate edition; 8vo; ix, (1), 132 pages, erasure on titlepage, few neat pencilled annotations in text; original cloth, spine worn.   John Drury 82-34 1996 £50.00

BROUGHAM & VAUX, HENRY PETER BROUGHAM, 1ST BARON 1778-1868 Installation Address (as Chancellor of the University of Edinburgh) Delivered in the 18th May. Edinburgh: Adam and Charles Black, 1860. 8vo; 70 pages; original cloth, gilt, spine faded; short ALS from author with stamped envelope addressed in his hand and signed, dated May 1861, loosely inserted; armorial bookplate of R. I. Nugent-Dunbar of Machemore.   R.F.G. Hollett & Son 78-340 1996 £75.00

BROWN, ALEXANDER   The Genesis of the United States. Boston and New York: 1890. 1st edition; 2 volumes; forest green linen, with very tiny flecking, weight stressing 2 inner joints.   Bookworm & Silverfish 280-27 1996 $150.00

BROWN, ALFRED   Old Masterpieces in Surgery. Omaha: 1928. 1st edition; 263 pages; 57 plates; original binding; very scarce. Cushing B702.   W. Bruce Fye 71-238 1996 $200.00

BROWN, C. C.   Samuel Morris, a Spirit Filled Life. Kingswood: c. 1900. 16mo; 28 pages; wrappers, beginning to separate.   Bookworm & Silverfish 280-28 1996 $125.00

BROWN, CHARLES   Descriptive Pamphlet of Marysville, Kansas, the Commercial and Manufacturing Metropolis of the Great Blue Valley. Marysville: Paul Springer, Printer and Binder, ca. 1887. 1st edition; 24 pages, titlepage having map of region below title; illustrations; original printed blue wrappers repaired, some old tapes to wrappers, overall fine. Rare.   Michael D. Heaston 23-190 1996 $850.00

BROWN, D. S.   America in 48 Hours, India and Back in a Fortnight, Being Suggestions for Certain Improvements in the Construction of Steam Vessels. London: Trelawny Saunders, 1852. 2nd edition; 8vo; 20 pages; disbound.   Anthony W. Laywood 109-15 1996 £65.00

BROWN, EDMUND RANDOLPH   The Twenty-Seventh Indiana Volunteer Infantry in the War of the Rebellion, 1861 to 1865, First Division, 12th and 20th Corps, a History of its Recruiting, Organization, Camp Life, Marches and Battles, Together with a Roster of the Men Composing It... Monticello: Privately published, 1899. 1st edition; 640, (2) pages; later buckram, ex-libris, yet very nice. Nevins I 64; Coulter 54; Dornbusch I Indiana 101.   McGowan Book Co. 65-11 1996 $250.00

BROWN, EDWARD   A Brief Account of Some Travels in Divers Parts of Europe, Viz. Hungaria, Servia, Bulgaria, Macedonia, Thessaly, Austria, Styria, Carinthia, Carniola and Friuli. London: printed for Benj. Tooke and are to be sold by Tho. Sawbridge, 1687. 2nd edition; small folio; (iv), 222, (iv) pages, ad leaf, 8 leage engraved text illustrations, 16 engraved plates, original calf, rebacked, old spine label preserved, small rust hole in O1, affecting 2 letters on each page, slight wear on tips of outer corners of covers. Wing B5111.   David Bickersteth 133-10 1996 £420.00

BROWN, ERASTUS   The Trial of Cain, the First Murderer, in Poetry, by Rule of Court... N.P.: printed for the publisher, 1834. 1st edition; 16mo; 36 pages; sewn, as issued, uncut, slight soiling. Not in Imprints Survey. R&B 23576 recording 2 copies of NY ed.   M & S Rare Books 60-249 1996 $150.00

BROWN, FREDRIC   And the Gods Laughed. West Bloomfield: Phantasia Press, 1987. One of 475 specially bound copies, numbered and signed by author, and Mack Reynolds, collaborator on 6 of the short stories; fine in dust jacket, slipcase.   Quill & Brush 102-147 1996 $225.00

BROWN, FREDRIC   Angels and Spaceships. New York: Dutton, 1954. 1st edition; near fine in very bright dust jacket with light rubbing, minor edge wear and back panel slightly soiled.   Quill & Brush 102-115 1996 $250.00

BROWN, FREDRIC   Before She Kills. San Diego: McMillan, 1984. One of 350 copies, numbered and signed by William Nolan; fine in dust jacket.   Quill & Brush 102-138 1996 $100.00

BROWN, FREDRIC   Before She Kills. San Diego: Dennis McMillan, 1984. 1st edition; publisher's copy; fine in jacket, inscribed to publisher with drawing by William Nolan.   Janus Books 36-102 1996 $150.00

BROWN, FREDRIC   The Bloody Moonlight. New York: Dutton, 1949. 1st edition; near fine with ends lightly worn in very good bright dust jackets with light rubbing, few small closed tears and light creasing. Quill & Brush 102-96 1996 $250.00

BROWN, FREDRIC   Brother Monster. Miami Beach: McMillan, 1987. One of 400 copies numbered and signed by Harry Altshuler, author of introduction; fine in dust jacket.   Quill & Brush 102-148 1996 $100.00

BROWN, FREDRIC   The Case of the Dancing Sandwiches. New York: Dell Publishing, 1950. 1st edition; fine in pictorial wrpapers.   Quill & Brush 102-100 1996 $225.00

BROWN, FREDRIC   The Case of the Dancing Sandwiches. Volcano, Hawaii: McMillan 1985. One of 400 copies, numbered and signed by Lawrence Block, author of the introduction; fine in dust jacket.   Quill & Brush   102-140   1996 $100.00

BROWN, FREDRIC   Compliments of a Fiend. New York: Dutton, 1950. 1st edition; very good or better with light soiling and edge wear, dust jacket with soiling, light chipping and few closed tears.   Quill & Brush   102-101   1996 $225.00

BROWN, FREDRIC   The Dead Ringer. New York: Dutton, 1948. 1st edition; very good with long inscription in green ink on front endpaper and list of names on front pastedown (covered by flap), in very good dust jackets with soiling, light chipping & edge wear.   Quill & Brush   102-94   1996 $250.00

BROWN, FREDRIC   Death Has Many Doors. New York: Dutton, 1951. 1st edition; near fine in bright dust jacket with lightly rubbed edges and few small closed tears.   Quill & Brush   102-106   1996 $300.00

BROWN, FREDRIC   The Deep End. New York: Dutton, 1952. 1st edition; near fine with light discoloration on covers in bright dust jacket with light soiling and minor edge wear.   Quill & Brush   102-109   1996 $225.00

BROWN, FREDRIC   The Deep End. New York: 1952. 1st edition; 7.5 x 5 inches; 220 pages; boards; nice in slightly worn dust jacket.   John K. King   77-220   1996 $125.00

BROWN, FREDRIC   The Fabulous Clipjoint. New York: Dutton, 1947. 1st edition; advance proof; author's first book; dust jackets attached at spine as issued, very good with light soiling in dust jackets with rubbing, light creases, chipping and partially intact back flap.   Quill & Brush   102-92   1996 $750.00

BROWN, FREDRIC   The Fabulous Clipjoint. New York: Dutton, 1947. 1st edition; author's first book; acidic paper browning with age, spine extremities slightly frayed, thus not quite very good in substantially worn and externally tape repaired dust jacket, not a beautiful copy, but inscribed by author to his agent in year of publication.   Ken Lopez   74-47   1996 $750.00

BROWN, FREDRIC   The Fabulous Clipjoint. New York: Dutton, 1947. 1st edition; author's first book; very good with light soiling, rubbing and last few pages frayed, in very good dust jackets with soiling, light chipping, few closed tears and light creases.   Quill & Brush   102-93   1996 $450.00

BROWN, FREDRIC   The Far Cry. New York: Dutton, 1951. 1st edition; near fine in very good bright dust jacket with few small closed tears, light rubbing and edge wear.   Quill & Brush   102-107   1996 $200.00

BROWN, FREDRIC   The Five Day Nightmare. New York: Dutton, 1962. 1st edition; fine in very good or better dust jacket with light rubbing and edge wear.   Quill & Brush   102-131   1996 $200.00

BROWN, FREDRIC   The Freak Show Murders. Belen: McMillan, 1985. One of 350 copies, numbered and signed by Richard Lupoff, author of introduction; fine in dust jacket.   Quill & Brush   102-140   1996 $100.00

BROWN, FREDRIC   Here Comes a Candle. New York: Dutton, 1950. 1st edition; near fine, in very good price clipped dust jacket with soiling, light chipping, few small closed tears and light creases; near fine with bookplate of publisher Oswald Train.   Quill & Brush   102-102   1996 $250.00

BROWN, FREDRIC   His Name Was Death. New York: Dutton, 1954. 1st edition; near fine in very good or better dust jacket with soiling, light rubbing and few closed tears.   Quill & Brush   102-116   1996 $250.00

BROWN, FREDRIC   Homicide Sanitarium. San Antonio: McMillan, 1984. One of 300 copies, numbered and signed by Bill Pronzini, author of introduction; fine in dust jacket.   Quill & Brush   102-139   1996 $150.00

BROWN, FREDRIC   Homicide Sanitarium. San Antonio: Dennis McMillan, 1984. 1st edition; 1/300 numbered copies, signed by Pronzini; fine in jacket.   Janus Books   36-101   1996 $125.00

BROWN, FREDRIC   Knock Three-One-Two. London: T. V. Boardman & Co., 1959. 1st edition; fine in near fine dust jacket with very light rubbing and light soiling.   Quill & Brush   102-126   1996 $175.00

BROWN, FREDRIC   Knock, Three-One-Two. New York: Dutton, 1959. 1st edition; near fine in bright price clipped dust jacket, with light rubbing and edge wear.   Quill & Brush   102-125   1996 $250.00

BROWN, FREDRIC   The Late Lamented. New York: Dutton, 1959. 1st edition; near fine with light soiling in bright dust jacket with lightly rubbed edges and one small closed tear.   Quill & Brush   102-127   1996 $200.00

BROWN, FREDRIC   The Lenient Beast. New York: Dutton, 1956. 1st edition; very good or better in dust jacket with light soiling, few small closed tears and light rubbing.   Quill & Brush   102-120   1996 $150.00

BROWN, FREDRIC   The Lights in the Sky are Stars. New York: Dutton, 1953. 1st edition; near fine with light soiling and small store sticker on back pastedown, in very good or better dust jacket with rubbing, few small closed tears and back panel slightly soiled.   Quill & Brush   102-111   1996 $250.00

BROWN, FREDRIC   Madman's Holiday. Volcano, Hawaii: McMillan, 1985. One of 350 copies, numbered and signed by Newton Baird, author of introduction.   Quill & Brush   102-142   1996 $125.00

BROWN, FREDRIC   Martians, Go Home. New York: Dutton, 1955. 1st edition; fine with owner's name stamped on back endpaper, in lightly soiled dust jacket.   Quill & Brush   102-118   1996 $350.00

BROWN, FREDRIC   Mostly Murder. New York: Dutton, 1953. 1st edition; near fine with spine ends lightly worn in very good or better dust jacket with few small chips and light soiling, cover is very bright.   Quill & Brush   102-113   1996 $225.00

BROWN, FREDRIC   Mrs. Murphy's Underpants. New York: Dutton, 1963. 1st edition; fine in very good dust jacket with creases on tips and edges, few small closed tears.   Quill & Brush   102-132   1996 $175.00

BROWN, FREDRIC   Murder Can Be Fun. New York: Dutton, 1948. 1st edition; near fine in very good dust jackets with few small closed tears, light rubbing and light soiling.   Quill & Brush   102-95   1996 $250.00

BROWN, FREDRIC   The Murderers. New York: Dutton, 1961. 1st edition; fine in very good dust jacket with light rubbing, few creases and edge wear, otherwise very bright.   Quill & Brush   102-129 1996 $150.00

BROWN, FREDRIC   Night of the Jabberwock. New York: Dutton, 1950. 1st edition; fine with edges lightly worn in very good or better, bright dust jacket with edge wear, light soiling and rubbing.   Quill & Brush   102-103   1996 $300.00

BROWN, FREDRIC   The Office. New York: Dutton, 1958. 1st edition; fine in very good, bright dust jacket with light rubbing, edge wear and light soiling.   Quill & Brush   102-123   1996 $225.00

BROWN, FREDRIC   One for the Road. New York: Dutton, 1958. 1st edition; near fine in price clipped dust jacket with light soiling and edge wear.   Quill & Brush   102-124   1996 $250.00

BROWN, FREDRIC   Paradox Lost and Twelve Other Great Science Fiction Stories. New York: Random House, 1973. 1st edition; fine in lightly creased dust jacket with light soiling.   Quill & Brush   102-135   1996 $100.00

BROWN, FREDRIC   Pardon My Ghoulish Laughter. N.P.: McMillan, 1986. One of 400 copies, numbered and signed by Donald Westlake, author of introduction; fine in dust jacket.   Quill & Brush   102-143   1996 $100.00

BROWN, FREDRIC   Project Jupiter. London: T. V. Boardman, 1954. 1st British edition (pub. in the U.S. as The Lights in the Sky are Stars); fine with owner's name on front endpaper, in very good or better bright dust jacket with rubbing and edge wear.   Quill & Brush   102-117   1996 $200.00

BROWN, FREDRIC   Red is the Hue of Hell. Miami Beach: McMillan, 1986. One of 400 copies, numbered and signed by Walt Sheldon, author of introduction; fine in dust jacket.   Quill & Brush 102-144 1996 $100.00

BROWN, FREDRIC   Rogue in Space. New York: Dutton, 1957. 1st edition; fine in very good bright dust jacket with rubbing, light chipping and back panel slightly soiled.   Quill & Brush 102-121 1996 $250.00

BROWN, FREDRIC   Science Fiction Carnival. Chicago: Shasta Pub., 1953.. 1st edition; fine with light edge wear, in very good dust jacket with few small closed tears, spine ends lightly chipped and light soiling. Quill & Brush 102-114 1996 $150.00

BROWN, FREDRIC   The Screaming Mimi. New York: Dutton, 1949. 1st edition; near fine in lightly soiled dust jacket.   Quill & Brush 102-97 1996 $300.00

BROWN, FREDRIC   Sex Life on the Planet Mars. Miami Beach: McMillan, 1986. One of 400 copies numbered and signed by Charles Willeford, author of introduction; fine in dust jacket.   Quill & Brush 102-145 1996 $150.00

BROWN, FREDRIC   The Shaggy Dog and Other Murders. New York: Dutton, 1963. 1st edition; fine with very light unavoidable offset in near fine dust jacket with light soiling and edge wear.   Quill & Brush 102-133 1996 $250.00

BROWN, FREDRIC   Space On My Hands. Chicago: Shasta, 1951. 1st edition; some offsetting to spine cloth, but still near fine in near fine, mildly spine darkened jacket, very nice, signed by author.   Ken Lopez 74-49 1996 $500.00

BROWN, FREDRIC   Space on My Hands. Chicago: Shasta Pub., 1951. 1st edition; signed on front endpaper; fine in dust jacket.   Quill & Brush 102-108 1996 $400.00

BROWN, FREDRIC   Thirty Corpses Every Thursday. Belen: McMillan, 1986. One of 375 copies numbered and signed by William Campbell Gault, author of introduction; fine in dust jacket.   Quill & Brush 102-146 1996 $100.00

BROWN, FREDRIC   We All Killed Grandma. New York: Dutton, 1952. 1st edition; fine in very good dust jacket with light rubbing, edge wear, few small closed tears, light soiling.   Quill & Brush 102-110 1996 $200.00

BROWN, FREDRIC   The Wench is Dead. New York: Dutton, 1955. 1st edition; fine in near fine dust jacket with light edge wear.   Quill & Brush 102-119 1996 $225.00

BROWN, FREDRIC   What Mad Universe. New York: Dutton, 1949. 1st edition; foxing to page edges and offsetting to endpapers, overall very good in somewhat edgeworn jacket with closed tear on back panel; nice copy; inscribed by author, scarce signature.   Ken Lopez 74-48 1996 $1,000.00

BROWN, FREDRIC   What Mad Universe. New York: Dutton, 1949. 1st edition; very good with unavoidable offset, page eges lightly soiled and edges of boards lightly worn, dust jacket with light rubbing, few small chips and back panel slightly soiled.   Quill & Brush 102-99 1996 $250.00

BROWN, GEORGE MACKAY   In the Margins of Shakespeare. London: Old Stile Press, 1991. Limited to 220 copies, signed by author and artist; slim folio; wood engravings by Llewellyn Thomas; fine in slipcase. Words Etcetera 94-212 1996 £75.00

BROWN, J. WOOD   An Inquiry Into the Life and Legend of Michael Scot. Edinburgh: David Douglas, 1897. 1st edition; 8vo; xvi, 281, (1), 20 ads pages; frontispiece, title vignette and one plate; original cloth, very good, ex-library. bib. Astrologica 181; Duveen p. 540.   Edwin V. Glaser 121-45 1996 $100.00

BROWN, JAMES BALDWIN   Memoirs of the Public and Private Life of John Howard... London: printed for Rest Fenner, 1818. 1st edition; 4to; xxvi, xxi-xxvi, (i), 690, (2 errata) pages, engraved portrait (offset onto title), one engraved plate, contemporary rose calf, gilt, spine gilt, by J. Thompson of Bucklersbury, London; slight traces of rubbing, but very handsome.   James Burmester 29-20 1996 £250.00

BROWN, JOHN   Essays on the Characteristics. London: printed for C. Davis, 1751. 2nd edition; title in red and black, half title follows dedication page; contemporary calf, rebacked, label. Eddy 11.   Anthony W. Laywood 109-16 1996 £95.00

BROWN, JOHN   The History of the Rise and Progress of Poetry, Through Its Several Species. Newcastle: printed by J. White and T. Saint for L. Davis and C. Reymers, London, 1764. 1st edition; 8vo; contemporary calf, gilt, spine gilt; fine, complete with final leaf of ads; Eddy 85; CBEL II 827.   Ximenes 108-40 1996 $750.00

BROWN, JOHN   Thoughts on Civil Liberty, on Licentiousness and Faction. Newcastle-Upon-Tyne: printed by J. White and T. Saint, for L. Davis and C. Reymers, London, 1765. 1st edition; 8vo; contemporary calf, spine gilt, slight cracking of joints, lacks label; nice. Eddy 88; CBEL II 827.   Ximenes 108-41 1996 $600.00

BROWN, JOHN HENRY   History of Texas 1685-1892. St. Louis: L. E. Daniel, 1892. 1st edition; 2 volumes, 631, 591 pages; 25 illustrations, 2 maps; beautifully bound in new rust linen with full leather spines and gilt stamped black leather spine labels, marbled edges. Howes B856; Raines p. 32; Basic 22.   Maggie Lambeth 30-68 1996 $350.00

BROWN, JOHN HENRY   The Indian Wars and Pioneers of Texas. Austin: L. E. Daniell, n.d., 1896. 1st edition; folio; 124 pages; green cloth stamped in gilt and blind, head and foot of spine expertly repaired; fine. Howes B857.   Hermitage SP95-699 1996 $850.00

BROWN, LARRY   Facing the Music. Chapel Hill: Algonquin, 1988. 1st edition; fine in dust jacket; signed by author; author's first book. Lame Duck Books 19-95 1996 $125.00

BROWN, LARRY   Facing the Music. Chapel Hill: Algonquin, 1988. 1st edition; author's first book; fine in fine dust jacket. Signed.   Alice Robbins 15-49 1996 $100.00

BROWN, LEONARD   Poems of the Prairies. Des Moines: Mills & Co., 1865. 1st edition; 12mo; 216 pages; original cloth, very worn, sound. Sabin 8533 for 1866 and 1868 editions only.   M & S Rare Books 60-182 1996 $150.00

BROWN, MARCIA   Felice. New York: Scribner's, 1958. 1st edition; 4to; water color illustrations by author; beige coth stamped in pink and black, lower end of spine slightly rubbed, else very fresh in pictorial dust jacket; laid in is compliments card from author and small original watercolor drawing; inscribed dedication copy for Maria Cimino and her husband Will Lipkind.   Barbara Stone 70-40 1996 £250.00

BROWN, MARGARET WISE   Baby Animals. New York: Random House, 1941. 4to; illustrations in color and black and white by Mary Cameron; colored pictorial boards; fresh copy in pictorial dust jacket; scarce. Barbara Stone 70-42 1996 £75.00

BROWN, MONTY   Hunter Away. The Life and Times of Arthur Henry Neumann. 1850-1907. Limited to 875 numbered copies, signed by author; 4to; color and other illustrations; quality cloth binding, colored dust jacket.   David Grayling J95Biggame-35 1996 £75.00

BROWN, OLIVER MADOX   The Dwale Bluth, Hebditch's Legacy and Other Literary Remains. London: Tinsley Bros., 1876. 1st edition; 8vo; 2 volumes; 2 portraits; original rose cloth (trifle spotted, spines faded); very good; tipped in at front of first volume is a page of ms. from what appears to be some sort of children's story; on verso William Michael Rossetti has written "I regard the writing over-page as being that of Oliver Madox Brown in boyhood."   Ximenes 108-42 1996 $900.00

BROWN, P. HUME   Our Journall into Scotland anno domini 1629, 5th of November... Edinburgh: David Douglas, 1894. 8vo; pages 56, (xvi), facsimile and plan; original cloth, gilt, spine trifle faded.   R.F.G. Hollett & Son 78-747 1996 £75.00

BROWN, P. HUME   Our Journall into Scotland Anno Domini 1629, 5th of November, from Lowther. Edinburgh: David Douglas, 1894. 8vo; pages 56, (xvi), facsimile and plan; original cloth, gilt, spine trifle faded. R.F.G. Hollett 76-43 1996 £75.00

BROWN, PAUL   3 Rings a Circus Book. New York: Scribner, 1938. 1st edition; original binding; signed by author; very good in fair dust jacket. October Farm 36-68 1996 $195.00

BROWN, RICHARD The London Bookshop. Parts I and II. London: Private Libraries Association, 1971/77. One of 1500 and 200 copies, 1st editions; oblong 8vo; 95; 77 pages; cloth; fine. The Bookpress 75-276 1996 $100.00

BROWN, RICHARD The Rudiments of Drawing Cabinet and Upholstery Furniture... London: The author and J. Taylor, 1820. 1st edition; 4to; xii, 52 pages, 25 plates, 16 of which are hand colored; later quarter calf, very good; rare. Bookpress 75-17 1996 $3,500.00

BROWN, ROBERT The Book of the Landed Estate. Edinburgh: William Blackwood and Sons, 1869. 1st edition; 8vo; xiii, (i), 505, (1), 16 pages; contemporary quarter black calf, covers slightly sunned, else very good; Graham Pollard's copy. The Bookpress 75-391 1996 $385.00

BROWN, ROBERT NEAL RUDMOSE 1879- A Naturalist at the Poles. London: 1923. illustrations; original cloth, excellent, ex-library, single label and small stamps; very scarce. David A.H. Grayling MY95Orn-364 1996 £55.00

BROWN, SUSAN ANNA Home Topics: a Book of Practical Papers on House and hOme Matters. New York: Century Co., 1881. 1st edition; large 8vo; pages 564; illustrations; little worn brown cloth, hinges loose, good copy; ex-library. Not in BAL. Second Life Books 103-35 1996 $150.00

BROWN, T. J. The Stonyhurst Gospel of Saint John. Oxford: printed for the Roxburghe Club, 1969. Color frontispiece, 7 plates, 188 pages; quarter red morocco, gilt lettering on spine, maroon boards. Maggs Bros. Ltd. 1191-140 1996 £150.00

BROWN, THOMAS Brighton; or, the Styne. London: for the author, sold by Sherwood, Neely and Jones, 1818. 1st edition; 8vo; 3 volumes, half titles; contemporary half straight grain citron morocco, smooth spines with gilt bands, black morocco sides, marbled sides and endpapers, green sprinkled edges, sides lightly rubbed; excellent set, clean and fresh; engraved bookplates with baronial arms of the Stewart family, Charles William Stewart, Baron Stewart Block p. 28; not in Wolff. Simon Finch 24-20 1996 £750.00

BROWN, THOMAS On Dreams. London: De La More Press, n.d. Limited to only 21 numbered copies; 8vo; 14 pages, printed on real vellum; frontispiece, titlepage border, half title decoration; original designed boards, morocco spine, extremities slightly rubbed, some very slight soiling to leather on sides. Thomas Thorp 489-44 1996 £150.00

BROWN, THOMAS 1663-1704 Amusements Serious and Comical, Calculated for the Meridian of London. London: printed and sold by the Booksellers, 1702. 2nd edition; 8vo; old sheep, worn, old rebacking, former lending library label; scarce. Boyce, Tom Brown 32 and passim. Peter Murray Hill 185-18 1996 £150.00

BROWN, THOMAS 1663-1704 The Late Converts Exposed; or the Reasons of Mr. Brays's. London: printed for Thomas Bennet, 1690. 1st edition; small 4to; disbound; fine. Wing B5061; Macdonald 249; CBEL II 1044. Ximenes 109-53 1996 $750.00

BROWN, THOMAS 1663-1704 The Reasons of Mr. Joseph Hains the Player's Conversion and Re-Conversion. London: printed for Richard Baldwin, 1690. 1st edition; small 4to; disbound, titlepage slightly dusty, but very good. Wing B5071; LAR 3016; Macdonald 250a; CBEL II 1044. Ximenes 109-54 1996 $1,250.00

BROWN, THOMAS 1663-1704 The Works of Mr. Thomas Brown, Serious and Comical, in Prose and Verse. London: Edward Midwinter, 1730. 7th edition; small 8vo; 4 volumes; frontispieces, full page illustrations; headpieces and devices in text; three quarter gilt stamped brown morocco over marbled boards by Zaehnsdorf, spines with raised bands, gilt stamped floral devices, gilt ruled covers, matching marbled endpapers, minor rubbing; very good. George J. Houle 68-18 1996 $375.00

BROWN, THOMAS 1770-1851 The Reminiscences of an old Traveller Throughout Different Parts of Europe. Edinburgh: John Anderson, Jun. & Co., Simpkin, Marshall, London, 1840. 3rd edition; 8vo; viii, 270 pages; original plum ribbed cloth, gilt edges, spine faded; fine; inscribed "to the Royal Society of Edinburgh, by the author"; Pine Coffin 833/6. James Burmester 29-21 1996 £65.00

BROWN, W. Privilegia Parlaimentaria Senatus Consensu Sublata. Being Remarks Upon the Acts of Parliament...For Preventing any Inconveniences That May Happen by Privilege of Parliament. London: printed by the Assigns of Ricahrd and Edward Atkins, 1704. Modern quarter calf, some embrowning, ex-library library, sound. Meyer Boswell SL26-29 1996 $450.00

BROWN, WILLIAM LAWRENCE An Essay on the Natural Equality of Men. Philadelphia: John Ormrod, 1793. 1st American edition; 12mo; 191, (5) pages; contemporary calf, worn. The Bookpress 75-392 1996 $125.00

BROWNE, B. The Conquest of Mount McKinley. London: 1956. 1st reprint since first edition of 1913. 41 photos; fine in very good+ dust jacket. Moutaineering Books 8-B67 1996 £60.00

BROWNE, D. J. The Field Book of Manures; or the American Muck Book... New York: 1855. 8vo; pages xii, (5-) 422, (2 pages ads); 22 text figures; original cloth, some wear, rebacked, retaining original backstrip, light dampstaining to first 100 pages, name inked out on title, rear endpaper torn. Raymond M. Sutton VII-849 1996 $110.00

BROWNE, EDWARD 1644-1708 A Brief Account of some Travels in Divers Parts of Europe. London: Benjamin Tooke, 1685. 1st folio (2nd) edition; 16 engraved full page plates, 9 of them folding, 8 text illustrations, ad leaf; contemporary panelled calf, early rebacking, evidently retaining original morocco label; spine worn, label chipped, front hinges tender, internally fine. Cox I p. 88; Wing B5111. Trebizond 39-82 1996 $1,350.00

BROWNE, JAMES A History of the Highlands, and of the Highland Clan. London: A. Fullarton & Co., 1845. Large 8vo; 4 volumes; 40 engraved plates (some dampstained), numerous text woodcuts, folding map, hand colored in outline; original blindstamped cloth, gilt, little faded and rubbed; one joint cracked and rather roughly reparied, some damping in places. R.F.G. Hollett 76-44 1996 £65.00

BROWNE, JAMES A History of the Highlands and of the Highland Clans. Edinburgh: A. Fullarton & Co., 1859. Demy 8vo; 4 volumes bound in 2; plates, some colored, wood engravings in text; contemporary half calf, decorated in gilt and blind, some very minor wear, some occasional browning, but good, solid set. Ash Rare Books Zenzybyr-15 1996 £195.00

BROWNE, JAMES The History of Scotland, its Highlands, Regiments and Clans. Edinburgh: 1909. Caledonia edition, limited to 1000 numbered sets; 9.5 x 6 inches; 8 volumes; cloth, top edge gilt, bit rubbed, spine labels soiled, volume 2 stained. John K. King 77-840 1996 $150.00

BROWNE, JOHN HUTTON BALFOUR The Medical Jurisprudence of Insanity. San Francisco: Sumner Whitney & Co., 1880. 2nd U.S. edition; 8vo; (714) pages; contemporary legal sheepskin with red and black leather spine labels, joints cracked, head and foot of spine shelfworn, minor chipping to edges of front endleaves, good, uncommon. John Gach 150-79 1996 $175.00

BROWNE, JOHN ROSS 1821-1875 Letter from the Sec. of the Treasury Transmitting Report Upon the Mineral Resources West of the States and Territories West of the Rocky Mountains. Washington: GPO, 1867. 1st edition; purple cloth, spine faded, owner's name. Cowan p. 83. Blue River Books 9-47 1996 $135.00

BROWNE, MOSES Angling Sports: in Nine Piscatory Eclogues. London: Edward and Charles Dilly, 1773. 3rd edition; 8vo; frontispiece, 2 ms. marginal notes, pages xxxvii, (iii), 136; contemporary speckled calf, upper joint split, but still frim, smooth backstrip divided by gilt bands and dotted rolls, slight loss at head, red leather label, dated at foot, Bewick bookplate of Revd. H. Cotes Vicar Bedlington 1802. Excellent. Westwood and Satchell p. 43. Blackwell's B112-48 1996 £150.00

BROWNE, THOMAS 1605-1682 A Letter to a Friend Upon the Occasion of the Death of an Intimate Friend, Together with Christian Morals. Waltham St. Lawrence: Golden Cockerel Press, 1923. One of only 115 numbered copies; 4to; printed in black and red, cockerel device in gold; boards with holland back, printed label, lower corners somewhat worn and sides discolored (as often), internally nice, clean copy; scarce. Bertram Rota 272-163 1996 £125.00

BROWNE, THOMAS 1605-1682 Pseudodoxia Epidemica; or, Enquiries into Very Many Received Tenets, and Commonly Presumed Truths. London: Miller, 1650. 2nd edition; folio; (8), 329, (5) pages; later calf, gilt inner dentelles, light browning, crisp copy. James Tait Goodrich K40-65 1996 $595.00

BROWNE, THOMAS 1605-1682   Pseudodoxia Epidemica; or, Enquiries into Very Many Received Tenents, and Commonly Presumed Truths. London: by A. Miller for Edw. Dod and Nath. Ekins, 1650. 2nd edition; folio; (16), 329, (10) pages; modern half calf, in period style; fine, fresh wide margined copy. Keynes 74; Osler 4489; Wellcome II p. 253; Wing B5160.   Joseph J. Felcone 64-6 1996 $550.00

BROWNE, THOMAS 1605-1682   Pseudodoxia Epidemica....Whereunto are Now Added Two Disccourses the One Urn-Burial, or Sepulchrall Urns, later Found in Norfolk. The Other the Garden of Cyrus... London: printed for Edward Dod, and are to be sould by Andrew Crook, 1658. 4th edition; 4to; with rare longitudinal half-title leaf; new quarter calf, light browning of pages, else clean, crisp copy. Keynes 76.   James Tait Goodrich K40-66 1996 $450.00

BROWNE, THOMAS 1605-1682   Pseudodoxia Epidemica: of Unicornes Hornes. Williamsburg: Cheloniidae Press, 1984. 1st edition thus, state proof issue, one of 15 copies only, all on obsolete Whatman paper (blue white laid ca. 1962) from a total issue of 225, all signed by the artist, as follows: 15 state proof copies in full vellum nonadhesive limp binding with an original drawing and an extra suite of proofs of the etching, 60 deluxe copies in vellum binding and an extra suite, 150 regular copies on T.H. Saunders Laid; page size 9 1/2 x 7 inches; bound by Gray Parrot in full vellum, matching quarter vellum sleeve for extra suites, all housed in vellum and linen clamshell box. Illustrated with 16 wood engravings and one etching by Alan James Robinson. Text is set and cast in Van Dijk Monotype in black and blue; this copy inscribed by Robinson to the noted collectors Mimi and Arnold Elkind and is signed on colophon by printer and binder as well as Robinson.   Priscilla Juvelis 95/1-53 1996 $1,500.00

BROWNE, THOMAS 1605-1682   Religio Medici. Juxta Exempt Lug. Batavor, 1644. Paris pirated edition; 12mo; 124 leaves, contemporary full calf, joints cracked and weak, some light browning, else very good; defense is bound at end in this copy, with two original blanks not in Keynes 60, which has the defense bound at front; rare. Huston Cat. #95. Keynes 60.   James Tait Goodrich K40-69 1996 $595.00

BROWNE, THOMAS 1605-1682   Religio Medici. Leiden: Fr. Hackius, 1644. 2nd Latin edition; 12mo; 235, (4) pages; engraved titlepage; contemporary full vellum; rare. Keynes 61.   James Tait Goodrich K40-67 1996 $895.00

BROWNE, THOMAS 1605-1682   Religio Medici. Lugd. Batavorum: Apud Francifcum, 1650. 12mo; 120 leaves, engraved frontispiece; full contemporary calf, raised bands, tooled spine, armorial gilt stamp on front board, all edges gilt, front blanks loose, nice, clean copy; bookplate of Garth Huston and Courville Collection. Keynes 62.   James Tait Goodrich K40-68 1996 $395.00

BROWNE, THOMAS 1605-1682   Religio Medici. New York: Limited Editions Club, 1939. One of 1500 numbered copies, signed by Nash; 4to; printed in handset 18 pt. Cloister; marbled boards with holland spine, spine little discolored, but very nice fresh copy.   Bertram Rota 272-309 1996 £50.00

BROWNE, THOMAS 1605-1682   Urne Buriall and The Garden of Cyrus. London: Cassell, 1932. One of 215 numbered copies; folio; printed in Monotype Bembo, Centaur and New Hellenic on Barcham Green handmade; full vellum with brown morocco inlays, gilt, designed by Nash, executed by Sangorski & Sutcliffe; fine in slipcase.   Bertram Rota 272-102A 1996 £2,000.00

BROWNE, THOMAS 1605-1682   The Works. London: Chiswell etc., 1686. 1st collected edition; very tall thick 8vo; titlepage in red and black, full page engraved frontispiece, mounted; handsomely rebound in period style, full polished chestnut calf, original leather label laid down, titlepage somewhat dusty, contents fine and bright, splendid copy, scarce. Wing B5150. Keynes 201.   Hartfield 48-L13 1996 $895.00

BROWNE, THOMAS 1605-1682   Posthumous Works... London: E. Curll, 1712. 1st edition; 8vo; pages (iv), xl, 74, (4); 8; 16; 56; 64; frontispiece, 22 plates; contemporary 'Cambridge-pane' style binding, expertly rebacked, raised bands between gilt rules, panelled sides, blind ruled, slight surface wear to upper board, otherwise very good. Blackwell's B112-49 1996 £150.00

BROWNE, THOMAS 1605-1682   The Works of Sir Thomas Browne. Edinburgh: 1927. 3 volumes; cloth backed boards with leather labels; Keynes 207.   W. Bruce Fye 71-254 1996 $125.00

BROWNE, THOMAS fl. 1820   The Union Dictionary... London: printed for Wilkie & Robinson, &c., 1806. 2nd edition; name cut from head of title removing first word; contemporary tree calf, slightly wormed on back board and tail of leading hinge, red label; good, sound copy. Alston V349; this edition not in BL.   Jarndyce 103-132 1996 £75.00

BROWNE, THOMAS fl. 1820   The Union Dictionary; Containing All That is Truly Useful in the Dictionaries of Johnson, Sheridan and Walker... London: Wilkie & Robinson, 1810. 3rd edition; 12mo; slight wear to fore-edges in first gatherings, one wormhole in early gatherings barely affecting text; contemporary sheep, leading hinge splitting, spine worn at head.   Jarndyce 103-133 1996 £55.00

BROWNING SOCIETY   The Browning Society's Papers...Parts I-V, VII-XIII (all published). London: publisht (sic) for the Browning Society by N. Trubner and Co., 1881-91. 8vo; 12 parts in 3 volumes; contemporary half red morocco, spines rather scuffed; very good, scarce. Todd 104i; CEL III 444.   Ximenes 108-392 1996 $450.00

BROWNING, ELIZABETH BARRETT 1806-1861   Aurora Leigh. London: Chapman and Hall, 1857. 1st edition; 8vo; original green cloth, very slight rubbing; nice.. Barnes A11.   Ximenes 108-351 1996 $400.00

BROWNING, ELIZABETH BARRETT 1806-1861   Aurora Leigh. London: Chapman and Hall, 1857. 2nd edition; 8vo; original red cloth, spine evenly faded; contemporary booklabel of T. W. Falcon; fine, scarce. Barnes E12.   Ximenes 108-352 1996 $150.00

BROWNING, ELIZABETH BARRETT 1806-1861   Aurora Leigh. London: Chapman and Hall, 1857. 3rd edition; 8vo; original green cloth, very slight rubbing, slight foxing at beginning and end, but fine, scarce; contemporary bookplate of Thomas Aloysius Perry.   Ximenes 108-353 1996 $100.00

BROWNING, ELIZABETH BARRETT 1806-1861   Aurora Leigh. London: Chapman and Hall, 1859. 4th edition; 8vo; frontispiece (some foxing) original green cloth; signataure at front of Ellen Moore, dated Dec. 1859; fine, uncommon. Barnes A11b.   Ximenes 108-354 1996 $175.00

BROWNING, ELIZABETH BARRETT 1806-1861   The Battle of Marathon. London: for private distribution only, 1891. 1st edition thus; one of only 50 copies printed (along with 4 more on vellum); 8vo; half red morocco, spine gilt, top edge gilt, by Bayntun; fine. Barnes E191; cf. Barnes A1; CBEL III 436.   Ximenes 108-356 1996 $400.00

BROWNING, ELIZABETH BARRETT 1806-1861   Casa Guidi Windows. London: Chapman and Hall, 1851. 1st edition; small 8vo; original blue cloth, spine evenly faded; nice. Barnes A7.   Ximenes 108-357 1996 $200.00

BROWNING, ELIZABETH BARRETT 1806-1861   An Essay on Mind, With Other Poems. London: James Duncan, 1826. 1st edition; contemporary tree calf, gilt, spine gilt, little rubbed, slight crack in upper joint; very good; the copy of Alan Park Paton, signed by him. Barnes A2; Hayward 238.   Ximenes 108-358 1996 $2,500.00

BROWNING, ELIZABETH BARRETT 1806-1861   Leila. London: printed for private circulation only, 1913. 1st edition; printed by T. J. Wise in an edition of only 30 copies; 8vo; original tan printed wrappers; fine; Barnes B5; Todd 76d.   Ximenes 108-359 1996 $400.00

BROWNING, ELIZABETH BARRETT 1806-1861   Letters...Addressed to Richard Hengist Horne... London: Richard Bentley & Son, 1877. 1st edition; 8vo; 2 voumes; original purple cloth, spines evenly faded; slight cracking of inner hinges, but fine set; Barnes D7.   Ximenes 108-360 1996 $350.00

BROWNING, ELIZABETH BARRETT 1806-1861   Poems. London: Chapman and Hall, 1856. 4th edition; small 8vo; 3 volumes; original green cloth, signs of shelf stickers removed from foot of two spines; aside from small marks on two spines, a very good set. Barnes A10. Ximenes 108-362 1996 $125.00

BROWNING, ELIZABETH BARRETT 1806-1861   Poems Before Congress. London: Chapman and Hall, 1860. 1st edition; 8vo; publisher's catalog dated Feb. 1860 (not present in most copies); original red cloth, spine slightly spotted, traces of rubbing; very good. Barnes A12. Ximenes 108-363 1996 $125.00

BROWNING, ELIZABETH BARRETT 1806-1861   The Poetical Works. London: Smith, elder & Co., 1889-1890. One of 125 sets on larage and fine paper; large 8vo; 6 volumes; five frontispiece portraits, four other plates, one ms. facsimile; original tan buckram, cloth, printed paper labels, corner of one label chipped; fine. Barnes E169.   Ximenes 108-365 1996 $600.00

BROWNING, ELIZABETH BARRETT 1806-1861   A Selection from the Poetry. London: Chapman and Hall, 1866. 1st edition; 8vo; frontispiece; original purple brown cloth, elaborately decorated in gilt, bit rubbed; excellent copy. Barnes E49.   Ximenes 108-366 1996 $150.00

BROWNING, ELIZABETH BARRETT 1806-1861   A Selection from the Poetry....First Series (-Second Series). London: Smith, Elder & Co., 1884. New edition; 8vo; 2 volumes; original brown cloth, some rubbing, spines bit dull; first volume bit shaken, but very good set; presentation copy, inscribed by Robert Browning for William G. Kingsland, who has added another inscription passing the set on to his grandson. Barnes E145.   Ximenes 108-367 1996 $450.00

BROWNING, ELIZABETH BARRETT 1806-1861   The Seraphim and Other Poems. London: Saunders and Otley, 1838. 1st edition; 12mo; contemporary half green calf, spine gilt, slightly rubbed, bound without half title, but nice; armorial bookplates of Dorothea Stanley and Conon Williams. Baranes A4; CBEL III 436.   Ximenes 108-368 1996 $400.00

BROWNING, ELIZABETH BARRETT 1806-1861   Sonnets from the Portuguese. Venice: S. Rosen, 1906. 2 3/4 x 2 1/8 inches; 104 pages, printed in two colors, with attractive type ornaments decorating each sonnet; full vellum, hand painted in 3 colors and gold with title and fleur-de-lys, later white calf ties, covers lightly soiled, else fine. Bondy p. 122; Welsh 1481.   Bromer Booksellers 87-194 1996 $125.00

BROWNING, ELIZABETH BARRETT 1806-1861   Sonnets from the Portugese. Montagnola: Officina Bodoni, 1925. One of 225 copies printed; small 4to; printed on Fabriano handmade paper and set in Bodoni Catania; full vellum boards with gilt publisher's device and lettering, small rubbed spot on rear cover and natural mellowing to vellum, still fine copy; Ransom 9; Schmoller 12.   Marilyn Braiterman 15-155 1996 $750.00

BROWNING, ELIZABETH BARRETT 1806-1861   Two Poems. London: by Bradbury & Evans for Chapman and Hall, 1854. 1st edition; 8vo; pages 15, (i) imprint, text within ruled frame; original cream printed wrappers; very good. Ashley I 110; Warner Barnes, Bibl. of Elizabeth Barrett Browning A9.   Simon Finch 24-21 1996 £250.00

BROWNING, ROBERT   An Account of the Illness and Death of His Father, Robert Browning the Second. London: printed for private circulation only by Richard Clay & Sons Ltd., 1921. 1st edition; one of 30 copies printed for T. J. Wise; 8vo; original pink printed wrappers, cloth folding case, fine. Not in Todd.   Ximenes 108-370 1996 $250.00

BROWNING, ROBERT 1812-1889   Bells and Pomegranates. No I - Pippa Passes. (No. II-No. VIII). London: Edward Moxon, 1841-46. 8vo; complete set, 8 numbers in one volume; with all original printed wrappers carefully preserved at back, together with inserted ads which were issued with last two parts, as usual; Hayward 253.   Ximenes 108-373 1996 $3,750.00

BROWNING, ROBERT 1812-1889   Bells and Pomegranates. No. I Pippa Passes. (No. II-No. VIII). London: Edward Moxon, 1841-46. 8vo; 8 numbers in 1 volume, complete set, with 2 leaves of ads inserted at front; original black cloth, very fine; large Victorian bookplate of Lionel Cresswell. Hayward 253.   Ximenes 108-374 1996 $2,750.00

BROWNING, ROBERT 1812-1889   Dramatis Personae. Doves Press, 1910. One of 250 copies on paper (there were also 15 on vellum); 9 1/4 x 6 1/2 inches; 4 p.l., (2 of them blank), (9)-202 pages, (1) leaf (colophon); printed in black and red; fine deep blue morocco, elaborately decorated in gilt, covers with many cloverleafs (outlined in gold or else gouged out and filled with gold), emanating from swirling stalks and tendrils, author's name enclosed by wreath at center, spine compartments and turn-ins similarly decorated, purportedly a Doves Binding (signed "The Doves Bindery/19C-S12" on tear turn-in), but actually a fake.   Phillip J. Pirages 33-62 1996 $4,500.00

BROWNING, ROBERT 1812-1889   Dramatis Personae. London: T. J. Cobden-Sanderson at the Doves Press, 1910. Limited to 250 copies, large 8vo; 204 pages; printed in red and black; original vellum (Doves Bindery), gilt spine, slipcase.   Kenneth Karmiole 1NS-93 1996 $475.00

BROWNING, ROBERT 1812-1889   Gold Hair: a Legend of Pornic. N.P.: London: 1864. Wise forgery, probably printed ca. 1890; 8vo; folded sheets as issued, one short split, cloth folding case; bookplate of Oliver Brett, later Lord Esher, above which is pencilled note "Bought Gorfin 1924". Nice. Todd 86f.   Ximenes 108-377 1996 $450.00

BROWNING, ROBERT 1812-1889   Helen's Tower. N.P.: London: April 26, 1870, i.e. ca. 1897. Wise forgery; 4to; 2 leaves folded; cloth folding case; fine; from the collection of Oliver Brett, later Lord Esher. Not in Todd.   Ximenes 108-378 1996 $600.00

BROWNING, ROBERT 1812-1889   Letters from Robert Browning to Various Correspondents. London: privately printed, 1895-96. 1st edition; 8vo; 2 volumes; original plum cloth; fine set, armorial bookplates of Henry Cabot Lodge. Presentation copy, inscribed by Thomas James Wise for H. S. Nichols. Todd 87d; CBEL III 445.   Ximenes 108-379 1996 $500.00

BROWNING, ROBERT 1812-1889   Letters from Le Croisic. London: printed for private circulation only, 1917. 1st edition; one of 30 copies printed by T.J. Wise; 8vo; original pale mauve printed wrappers, cloth folding case; fine. Todd 96e.   Ximenes 108-380 1996 $250.00

BROWNING, ROBERT 1812-1889   Paracelsus. London: published by Effingham Wilson, 1835. 1st edition; small 8vo; full tan morocco, covers elaborately decorated with all over gilt floral pattern, spine and inner dentelles, all edges gilt, by the League of Women Binders; very rare, half title removed, otherwise very good. Hayward 252.   Ximenes 108-382 1996 $750.00

BROWNING, ROBERT 1812-1889   Pictor Ignotus, Fra Lippo Lippi, Andrea del Sarto. Waltham St. Lawrence: Golden Cockerel Press, 1925. Limited edition, 113/360 copies; imperial 8vo; pages 39, (1); printed in black and red on Arnold's handmade paper, 2 large capitals designed by Eric Gill and printed in red, letter "I" repeated, the letter "B" also repeated at centre of front cover; original quarter white parchment, backstrip gilt lettered, mid blue baords with Gill designed capital "B" at centre of front cover, minor fading and faint foxing to covers, untrimmed and unopened; good. Chanticleer 26; Gill, Corey & Mackenzie Eric Gill Bib. 322.   Blackwell's B112-119 1996 £85.00

BROWNING, ROBERT 1812-1889   The Pied Piper of Hamelin. London: 1898. Limited to 100 copies, signed by Harry Quilter; folio; 2 colored plates by Lemercier in Paris, and all the ornamental text and illustrations; printed on vellum; original calf, stamped in golt with 2 metal inlays on front cover, sunk and surrounded with gold, slight fading.   Charles W. Traylen 117-75 1996 £850.00

BROWNING, ROBERT 1812-1889   The Pied Piper of Hamelin. New York: Grosset and Dunlap, 1936. 1st edition thus, large 4to; lithographed illustrations in color and black and white, colored pictorial endpapers; cloth backed colored pictorial boards, lower end of backstrip faded, else very nice in original pictorial dust jacket.   Barbara Stone 70-88 1996 £65.00

BROWNING, ROBERT 1812-1889   The Pied Piper of Hamlin. Portland: Chamberlain Press, 1980. Limited to 150 copies signed by artist, this copy inscribed by her as well; octavo; (16) pages; illustrations by Sarah Chamberlain, with 11 wood engravings; with prospectus; marbled boards, leather spine label stamped in black, extremely fine.   Bromer Booksellers 87-119 1996 $250.00

BROWNING, ROBERT 1812-1889   Poems. London: Chapman and Hall, 1849. New edition, but in fact first collected edition; 8vo; 2 volumes; original brown cloth, very slight rubbing; first volume neatly recased, new endpapers, second volume bit shaken, but generally very good set. CBEL III 440.   Ximenes 108-382 1996 $150.00

BROWNING, ROBERT 1812-1889   The Poetical Works. London: Chapman and Hall, 1863. 3rd edition; 8vo; 3 volumes; original maroon cloth, slight rubbing. Firsrt volume bit shaken, but very nice set. CBEL III 440.   Ximenes 108-383 1996 $150.00

BROWNING, ROBERT 1812-1889   The Poetical Works. London: Smith, Elder & Co., 1868. 8vo; 6 volumes; original dark brown cloth; fine. CBEL II 440.   Ximenes 108-384 1996 $250.00

BROWNING, ROBERT 1812-1889   The Poetical Works. London: Smith, Elder & Co., 1888-94. One of 250 sets on large and fine paper; large 8vo; 17 volumes; 3 portraits, 2 other plates; original tan buckram cloth, printed paper labels, half of one label missing, few others slightly chipped; otherwise fine condition. CBEL III 440.   Ximenes 108-385 1996 $750.00

BROWNING, ROBERT 1812-1889   The Ring and the Book. London: Smith, Elder and Co., 1868-69. 1st edition; 8vo; 4 volumes; original green cloth, traces of rubbing; 1st binding, with volume II numbered "Vol. 2", fine set. CBEL III 443.   Ximenes 108-386 1996 $400.00

BROWNING, ROBERT 1812-1889   The Ring and the Book. London: Smith, Elder & Co., 1868. 1st edition; crown 8vo; 4 volumes; original dark green cloth, decorated in black and lettered in gilt.   Charles W. Traylen 117-76 1996 £125.00

BROWNING, ROBERT 1812-1889   The Ring and the Book. Boston: Fields, Osgood, 1869. 1st American edition; 12mo; decorative terra cotta cloth, very good, small bookplate.   Antic Hay 101-228 1996 $125.00

BROWNING, ROBERT 1812-1889   The Ring and the Book. Boston: Fields, Osgood and Co., 1869. 1st American edition; 8vo; 2 volumes; on verso of half titles this is described as the "author's edition, from advance sheets."; original orange brown cloth; fine set. CBEL III 443. Ximenes 108-387 1996 $100.00

BROWNING, ROBERT 1812-1889   The Ring and the Book. London: Smith, Elder and Co., 1872. 2nd edition; 8vo; 4 volumes; original dark brown cloth; fine set. CBEL III 443.   Ximenes 108-388 1996 $150.00

BROWNING, ROBERT 1812-1889   A Selection from the Works of Robert Browning. London: Edward Moxon & Co., 1865. 1st edition; square 8vo; portrait; original blue cloth, elaborately decorated in gilt, slightly rubbed at ends of spine; very good. CBEL III 440.   Ximenes 108-389 1996 $150.00

BROWNING, ROBERT 1812-1889   Some Poems. Eragny Press, 1904. One of 215 copies on paper, 200 of them for sale, there were also 11 vellum copies0; 8 1/2 x 5 1/2 inches; 64 page,s (3) leaves; partly printed in red; lovely frontispiece, large decorative red intials and device at end, all by Lucien and Esther Pissarro; original patterned paper boards, gilt titling on front cover, leaves untrimmed and mostly unopened, spine ends just a bit bumped, hint of discoloration, endpapers slightly browned, as always, otherwise extremely fine, binding usually clean. Phillip J. Pirages 33-201 1996 $1,100.00

BROWNING, ROBERT 1812-1889   Strafford: an Historical Tragedy. London: printed for Longman, Rees, Orme, Brown, Green & Longman, 1837. 1st edition; 8vo; full brown crushed levant, covers decorated in gilt with elaborate interlocking ruled border enclosed withing light brown inlaid morocco strips, intricate tan morocco doublures, with all over floral pattern in gilt, spine gilt, all edges gilt, by the Club Bindery, original drab wrappers, printed paper side label, bound in at end; fine in handsome binding. From the library of H. W. Poor, additional bookplate of Christine Alexander Graham. CBEL III 442.   Ximenes 108-391 1996 $850.00

BROWNING, ROBERT 1812-1889   The Works. London: Smith, Elder and Co., 1912. Limited edition, one of 526 sets, this being one of 500; 8vo; printed on antique laid paper, titles printed in red and black; frontispieces; green cloth, gilt stamped spine and front covers, top edge gilt, others uncut, spines little dulled and extremities slightly worn, but very good set.   Thomas Thorp 489-45 1996 £180.00

BROWNRIG, RALPH   Forty Sermons. London: published by William Martyn/R. Everingham, 1685. Folio; 2 volumes bound in 1; (xiv), 433, (i); (viii), 259, (i) pages; frontispiece; contemporary panelled calf, spine gilt ruled, label; rubbed, head of spine bit torn, short splits at head of joints, portrait and early leaves bit frayed around edges, not affecting text or image, minor soiling & marginal worming. Sound copy.   Robert Clark 38-26 1996 £100.00

BROWSE, LILLIAN   Barbara Hepworth - Sculptress. London: pub. for the Shenval Press by Faber & Faber, Ltd., 1946. 1st edition; 50 black and white plates; original binding, top edge dusty, head and tail of spine, corners and cover edges slightly bumped, spine and cover edges darkened, covers slightly marked and bowed, page edges slightly browned, good only, no dust jacket. Presentation copy from artist to E. H. Ramsden and Margot Eates, inscribed by her.   Ulysses 39-286 1996 £175.00

BROWSE, LILLIAN   William Nicholson. London: Hart-Davis, 1956. Small 4to; 144 pages text + 54 plates, 4 in color; boards, dust jacket. Freitag 7045.   Brannan 43-486 1996 $145.00

BRUCE, GEORGE   The Land Birds In and Around St. Andrews, Including a Condensed History of the British Land Birds... Dundee: John Leng & Co., 1895. 8vo; pages vii, 563; little spotting to first and final leaves; original pictorial cloth gilt, extremities minimally rubbed, little spotting to first and final leaves; inscribed by son of author for Mrs. J. A. Duthie.   R.F.G. Hollett 76-45 1996 £65.00

BRUCE, GEORGE   Poems and Songs, on Various Occasions. (with) Poems, Ballads and Songs on Various Occasions. Edinburgh: ptd. for the author, by Oliver & Boyd.... 1811/13. 1st edition; 8vo; 2 volumes; wood engraved illustrations; contemporary half green calf, spines gilt, spines little rubbed, one label largely missing, other chipped; very good, scarce. Ximenes 108-43 1996 $400.00

BRUCE, J. COLLINGWOOD   The Hand-Book to the Roman Wall. London: Longmans, Green and Co., Newcastle-upon-Tyne: Andrew Reid, 1885. 3rd edition; large paper copyp; 4to; pages viii, 272, frontispiece, 9 etched plates, 8 full page illustrations, large extending linen backed colored mpa, 137 text woodcuts; original green cloth, gilt, extremities minimally rubbed;   R.F.G. Hollett & Son 78-749 1996 £175.00

BRUCE, J. COLLINGWOOD   The Hand-Book to the Roman Wall. London: Longmans, Green and Co. and Newcastle-upon-Tyne: Andrew Reid, 1885. 3rd edition; 4to; pages viii, 272; frontispiece, 9 etched plates, 8 full page illustrations, colored map, 137 text woodcuts; original green cloth, gilt, trifle scratched and rubbed.   R.F.G. Hollett & Son 78-748 1996 £165.00

BRUCE, JAMES   Travels to Discover the Source of the Nile, in the Years 1768, 1769, 1770, 1771, 1772 and 1773. Edinburgh: Archibald Constable & Co., 1805. 2nd edition; 7 volumes 8vo. and atlas 4to.; plate volume contains 79 engraved plates and 3 large folding maps; contemporary calf, rubbed, uniformly rebacked, volume 8 (atlas) spine bit rubbed.   Kenneth Karmiole 1NS-241 1996 $1,250.00

BRUCE, JOHN   Report on the Arrangements Which Were Made...When Spain, By Its Armada, Projected the Invasion. London: State Paper Office, 1798. Demy 8vo; (iv), (98), (xiv), cccxxviii pages, 2 folding tables; bound in elegant recent full morocco, top edge gilt, trimmed close, shaving few sidenotes, otherwise very good state. Presentation copy signed by Bruce and inscribed to Henry Dundas, 1st Viscount Melville, Secretary of War. Ash Rare Books Zenzybyr-16 1996 £450.00

BRUEL, WALTER   Praxis Medicinae, or, the Physicians Practice. London: William Sheares, 1632. 1st edition; small 4to; (iv), 407, (4) pages; contemporary calf, rebacked, later endpapers; stamp on title from Royal College of Physicians' library with bookplate; scarce.   The Bookpress 75-393 1996 $1,250.00

BRUFF, J. GOLDSBOROUGH   Gold Rush. The Journals, Drawings and other Papers of J. Goldsborough Bruff. New York: Columbia University Press, 1949. lxxii, 794 pages; color frontispiece, plus numerous illustrations and facsimiles; slight remains from removed bookplate on inner front cover, overall fine.   Argonaut Book Shop 113-101 1996 $100.00

BRUGUIERE, FRANCIS   San Francisco. San Francisco: Crocker, 1918. 1st edition; dust jacket slightly chipped and soiled, most uncommon in dust jacket.   J. B. Muns 154-53 1996 $225.00

BRUMMER, ERNEST   The Ernest Brummer Collection. Volume II (only). Zurich: Galerie Koller, 1979. 4to; 435 pages; profusely illustrated (many in color), original cloth, dust jacket.   Archaeologia Luxor-2944 1996 $150.00

BRUNET, G.   Life of William Bedell, D.D., Bishop of Kilmore in Ireland. 1685. 1st London edition; 8vo; (2), 37, (260) pages; rebacked calf, very good.   C. P. Hyland 216-28 1996 £80.00

BRUSHFIELD, T. N.   A Bibliography of Sir Walter Raleigh, Knt. Exeter: James G. Commin, 1908. 2nd edition; frontispiece, 14 plates, several illustrations in text; red cloth, rubbed and faded, headcaps bumped. Maggs Bros. Ltd. 1191-72 1996 £65.00

BRUTON, JOHN HILL   Life and Correspondence of David Hume. Edinburgh: William Tait, 1846. 1st edition; 8vo; 2 volumes, xvii, (1), 480; vii, (1), 534 pages, bound without half titles; frontispiece, folding facsimile letter in volume 1, 2 facsimiles of Hume's holograph in volume 2; contemporary calf, gilt and panelled, contrasting labels and marbled edges by Hayday; fine; from the 19th century library of Lord Belper with his bookplate. Jessop p. 46; Mossner p. 636; not in Chuo.   John Drury 82-117 1996 £275.00

BRUYERE, L.   Etudes Relatives a l'Art des Constructions. Paris: Chez Bance Aine, 1823/28. Folio: 2 text volumes (12 parts) in 1 and atlas of plates; 12, 16, 15, (1), 8, 8, 20, 8 pages; (iv), 12, 4, 8, 19, (1), 5, (1), 8 pages; 184 engraved plates, lower margins of plates dampstained, not affecting printed surface; contemporary quarter calf, marbled boards, lower joint of atlas neatly repaired.   Elton Engineering 10-19 1996 £2,250.00

BRYAN, ASHLEY   The Ox of the Wonderful Horns and Other African Folktales. New York: Atheneum, 1971. 1st edition; thin quarto; tiny gift inscription on half title, else very nearly fine in very good plus dust jacket with one short but somewhat jagged tear on front panel and some light wear to extremities, signed by author.   Between the Covers 43-225 1996 $125.00

BRYAN, DOROTHY   Michael and Patsy on the Golf Links. London: John Lane, Bodley Head, 1934. 1st edition; oblong 4to; 32 pages; color title vignette, 39 illustrations, green endpapers with color pictorial board game; grey and green boards, red tinted pictorial, similar dust jacket; excellent copy.   Robin Greer 94A-43 1996 £65.00

BRYAN, EMMA LYON   1860-1865, A Romance of the Valley of Virginia. Harrisonburg: J. Taliaffero, 1892. 1st edition; 12mo; 228, (1) pages; original wrappers, text browned, as usual, bookplate, bottom of spine chipped, light cover wear, else very good. Wright 743.   The Bookpress 75-394 1996 $135.00

BRYAN, J. E.   Bulbs. London: 1989. 4to; 2 volumes; 760 pages; 864 colored illustrations; boards.   Wheldon & Wesley 207-1675 1996 £99.00

BRYAN, J. E.   Bulbs. London: 1989. 4to; 2 volumes, pages vii, 451; 300 color plates, distribution maps on endpapers.   John Henly 27-278 1996 £95.00

BRYAN, MICHAEL   Dictionary of Painters and Engravers. London: George Bell, 1909-10. 4to; 5 volumes; xii, 364; x, 292; xvi, 394; xvi, 310; xviii, 426 pages, including 5 pages of artist's monograms at end; modern half calf, spines richly gilt in 6 compartments, red and brown morocco double lettering pieces, top edge gilt, by Stoakley of Cambridge, slight fading to spines, otherwise superb set.   Thomas Thorp 489-46 1996 £350.00

BRYAN, WILLIAM ALANSON   Natural History of Hawaii. Honolulu: Hawaiian Gazette Co. Ltd., 1915. 1st edition; 10 x 6.75 inches; 596 pages, 117 plates; partial removal of some tipped in matter from the half title causing wrinkling to that page, else very nice copy; cloth.   Parmer Books Nat/Hist-067049 1996 $200.00

BRYANT, G. E.   The Chelsea Porcelain Toys, Scent-Bottles, Bonbonnieres, Etuis, Seals, and Statuettes, Made at the Chelsea Factory 1745-1769. London: Medici Society, 1925. Limited ot 656 signed and numbered copies; 63 plates, including 47 in color;   Petersfield Bookshop FH58-4 1996 £260.00

BRYANT, HENRY G.   The Peary Auxiliary Expediton of 1894. Philadelphia: 1895. 1st edition; 8vo; 77 pages; photographic illustrations; original printed wrappers, name on front wrapper, ink title on spine, light soiling, still very good, very scarce.   Chapel Hill 94-31 1996 $125.00

BRYANT, JACOB   A New System; or, an Analysis of Antient Mythology. London: printed for J. Walker; W. J. and J. Richardson, R. Faulder... 1807. 3rd edition; 8vo; 6 volumes; lii, 396; (iv), 498; (iv), 439; (iv), 473; (ii), 424; (iv), 418, (vi) pages; 41 plates, including 9 folding maps; full calf, rubbed, covers of 2 volumes detached, several joints split, spines chipped at extremities, gilt decorated spines with raised bands, gilt lettered leather labels; occasional ink marks and rules in margins, else very nice internally.   Blue Mountain SP95-155 1996 $295.00

BRYANT, WILLIAM CULLEN 1794-1878   Picturesque America. New York: D. Appleton & Co., 1872. Thick 4to; 2 volumes; 48 fine steel engraved plates and about 800 original wood engravings; contemporary half brown morocco, gilt; rare American edition.   Charles W. Traylen 117-422 1996 £375.00

BRYANT, WILLIAM CULLEN 1794-1878   Picturesque America. New York: D. Appleton and Co., 1872. 2 volumes, 568, 576 pages; over 900 pictures; original full leather, slightly scuffed. Very good.   Blue River Books 9-48 1996 $250.00

BRYANT, WILLIAM CULLEN 1794-1878   Poems. Cambridge: Hilliard and Metcalf, 1821. 1st edition; 1 one of 750 copies; 16mo; 44 pages; original drab printed boards, uncut, spine intact, with only minute chipping, few leaves slightly soiled, but not obtrusively; with 1823 ownership inscription; superb copy. Grolier American 100 32; BAl 1587. M & S Rare Books 60-125 1996 $2,000.00

BRYANT, WILLIAM CULLEN 1794-1878   Poems. New York: & London: D. Appleton & Co., 1872. 8vo; 590 pages; illustrations; brown cloth, bumped, rubbed and soiled, rebacked with upper portion of original spine laid down, titled in gilt on spine with title within, gilt device on front cover, all edges gilt, lacks rear endpaper, front endpaper chipped, hinges reinforced with black tape, few page edges creased and chipped, text printed within red ruled frame; good; inscribed to a namesake William Cullen Bryant.   Blue Mountain SP95-91 1996 $125.00

BRYCE, JAMES   The American Commonwealth. London: Macmillan, 1888. 1st edition; octavo; 3 volumes; folding map; original navy cloth, publisher's ink presentation stamp on title.   Howes Bookshop 265-97 1996 £65.00

BRYDGES, SAMUEL EGERTON, BART 1762-1837   Letters From the Continent. Kent: printed at the private press of Lee Priory by John Warwick, 1821. 1st edition; 8vo; 2 volumes in 1; 177, (178)-362 pages, 7 pages ads; full speckled calf by Riviere with a decorative gilt border, spine richly gilt in 6 compartments with 5 raised bands, extremities slightly rubbed, bookplates and short tipped in clipping, else tight, very good, one of the bookplates is that of John Sheepshanks, famous English art collector; very scarce, most likely issued in an edition of 250 copies.   Chapel Hill 94-255 1996 $450.00

BRYDGES, SAMUEL EGERTON, BART. 1762-1837   Opartisk Skildring af Lord Byron, Sasom Skald Och Menniska....(Impartial Account of Lord Byron...). Stockholm: hos Zacharias Hoeggstrom, 1831. 1st edition in Swedish; 12mo; original printed white printed wrappers, slight wear; fine in original condition; rare. cf. CBEL III 1271.   Ximenes 108-44 1996 $400.00

BRYDGES, SAMUEL EGERTON, BART. 1762-1837   Restituta; or, Titles, Extracts and Characters of Old Books in English Literature. London: printed by T. Bensley...for Longman, 1814. 8vo; 4 volumes; contemporary diced russia, sometime neatly rebacked with calf, gilt, morocco labels, no half titles present, names cut from extreme corners o titles, nevertheless a good set. With flowery 3 1/2 page address in Joseph Haslewood's hand sent from Conduit St. to Brydges at Geneva with the gift of a book (not the present one).   Peter Murray Hill 185-19 1996 £225.00

BRYDSON, A. P.   Some Records of two Lakeland Townships... London: Elliot Stock, n.d. 1st edition; 8vo; 204 pages; colored frontispiece, map, 42 plates; original blue cloth, gilt, extremities trifle rubbed, spine little faded; scarce, signed by author.   R.F.G. Hollett & Son 78-757 1996 £95.00

BRYDSON, A. P.   Some Records of Two Lakeland Townships (Blawith and Nibthwaite) Chiefly from Original Documents. London: Elliot Stock, n.d 1st edition; 8vo; pages 204, colored frontispiece map, 42 plates; original blue cloth, gilt, scarce.   R.F.G. Hollett & Son 78-756 1996 £87.50

BUCHAN, JOHN 1875-1940   The African Colony. London: 1903. 1st edition; very good/fine copy.   Bannatyne Books 19-A07 1996 £135.00

BUCHAN, JOHN 1875-1940   Andrew Jameson, Lord Ardwell. London: 1913. 1st edition; neara fine.   Bannatyne Books 19-A08 1996 £70.00

BUCHAN, JOHN 1875-1940   Balliol College War Memorial Book. London: 1924. 1st edition; 26 x 19; 2 volumes; many plates; very good. Bannatyne Books 19-B01 1996 £80.00

BUCHAN, JOHN 1875-1940   The Battle of Jutland. London: 1916. 1st edition; 45 pages; fragile white paper cover has been backed to strengthen it and rusting staples have been replaced, cover has some marks, but is reasonably clean; scarce.   Bannatyne Books 19-B03 1996 £50.00

BUCHAN, JOHN 1875-1940   The Blanket of the Dark. London: 1931. 1st edition; some moderate foxing, mainly of first few pages, otherwise fine, dust jacket with repairs of spine ends, some browning or soiling of white portions and lettering of back panel rubbed.   Bannatyne Books 19-B10 1996 £65.00

BUCHAN, JOHN 1875-1940   A Book of Escapes and Hurried Journeys. London: 1922. 1st edition; illustrations; pleasantly illustrated cloth, cloth little rubbed in places, otherwise very good.   Words Etcetera 94-222 1996 £50.00

BUCHAN, JOHN 1875-1940   A Book of the Horace Club. London: 1901. 1st edition; only 500 copies printed; some soiling of white vellum boards, otherwise very good.   Bannatyne Books 19-B14 1996 £65.00

BUCHAN, JOHN 1875-1940   Essays of Lord Bacon. London: 1894. 1st edition; inked comments on a few pages and removable pencil underlinings on others, some faint stains on rear board, still very good+. Bannatyne Books 19-E08 1996 £55.00

BUCHAN, JOHN 1875-1940   The Fifteenth (Scottish) Division. 1914-1919. London: 1926. 1st edition; one of the 18 loose maps in folder at rear is missing and has been replaced by a photocopy in color; very good+.   Bannatyne Books 19-F03 1996 £100.00

BUCHAN, JOHN 1875-1940   The Free Fishers. London: 1934. 1st edition; very good+ in dust jacket with some minor chipping at ends of spine repaired, some minor soiling.   Bannatyne Books 19-F17 1996 £75.00

BUCHAN, JOHN 1875-1940   The Gap in the Curtain. London: 1932. 1st edition; very good in dust jacket with repairs to ends of spine and back panell, some soiling and browning of white spine and back panel. Bannatyne Books 19-G01 1996 £70.00

BUCHAN, JOHN 1875-1940   Greenmantle. London: 1916. 1st edition; internal foxing, but externally very good to fine.   Bannatyne Books 19-G11 1996 £60.00

BUCHAN, JOHN 1875-1940   Grey Weather. London: 1899. 1st edition; some faint marks on boards and slight rubbing on front fixed endpaper, but nice, clean, very good copy.   Bannatyne Books 19-G13 1996 £160.00

BUCHAN, JOHN 1875-1940   The Half-Hearted. London: 1900. 1st edition; 375 pages; black cloth, gilt lettered, very slightly rubbed and little frayed (about half inch) on fore-edge of front board, but clean good copy.   K Books 441-74 1996 £95.00

BUCHAN, JOHN 1875-1940   History of the Great Way. London: 1921-22. 1st edition; maps; cloth with spine lettered in gilt, very good, bright set.   Words Etcetera 94-215 1996 £75.00

BUCHAN, JOHN 1875-1940   A History of the Great War. London: 1921-22. 1st edition; 4 volumes; spine of first 2 volumes slightly faded, very good, other 2 volumes very good+; bookplates.   Bannatyne Books 19-H06 1996 £75.00

BUCHAN, JOHN 1875-1940   The History of the South African Forces in France. London: 1920. 1st edition; some marks on boards, but good, sound, very good copy.   Bannatyne Books 19-H08 1996 £100.00

BUCHAN, JOHN 1875-1940   The House of the Four Winds. London: 1935. 1st edition; light foxing of a few pages and foxing of edges, very good in dust jacket with minor repairs, some mdoerate soiling of white portions.   Bannatyne Books 19-H14 1996 £80.00

BUCHAN, JOHN 1875-1940   The Island of Sheep. London: 1936. 1st edition; fine copy in much above average dust jacket with minor repairs at spine ends.   Bannatyne Books 19-I04 1996 £90.00

BUCHAN, JOHN 1875-1940   The Island of Sheep. London: Hodder & Stoughton, 1936. 1st edition; fine in lightly used dust jacket.   Priscilla Juvelis 95/1-306 1996 $150.00

BUCHAN, JOHN 1875-1940   John Burnet of Barnes. London: 1898. 1st edition; slight fading at top of rear panel and insignificant marks on front board, very good+.   Bannatyne Books 19-J09 1996 £140.00

BUCHAN, JOHN 1875-1940   The King's Grace. London: 1935. 1st edition; large limited edition of 500 copies, signed by author; 26 x 16; attractive book bound in white cloth with gilt lettering; fine in original light blue box with label, some soiling and one corner repaired. Bannatyne Books 19-K01 1996 £100.00

BUCHAN, JOHN 1875-1940   The Kirk in Scotland. London: 1930. 1st edition; near fine, cream colored dust jacket has minor repairs and some slight soiling, scarce in dust jacket.   Bannatyne Books 19-K04 1996 £60.00

BUCHAN, JOHN 1875-1940   The Last Secrets: the Final Mysteries of Exploration. London: 1923. 1st edition; illustrated cloth, cloth little worn at head of upper cover, hinge with spine otherwise very good.   Words Etcetera 94-223 1996 £60.00

BUCHAN, JOHN 1875-1940   The Lodge in the Wilderness. London: 1907. 2nd impression of 1906 1st edition; moderate foxing of first few pages, 4 line inscription; very good.   Bannatyne Books 19-L08 1996 £60.00

BUCHAN, JOHN 1875-1940   The Long Traverse. London: 1941. 1st edition; few faint marks on boards, quite usual with this item, but generally fine in above average dust jacket.   Bannatyne Books 19-L13 1996 £50.00

BUCHAN, JOHN 1875-1940   Lord Minto. A Memoir. London: 1924. 1st edition; very slight fading of spine and some foxing of edges, near fine. Bannatyne Books 19-L16 1996 £50.00

BUCHAN, JOHN 1875-1940   A Lost Lady of Old Years. London: 1899. 1st edition; nice, near fine copy.   Bannatyne Books 19-L18 1996 £150.00

BUCHAN, JOHN 1875-1940   The Marquis of Montrose. London: 1913. 1st edition; very slight fading of spine, but generally very good+, nice. Bannatyne Books 19-M05 1996 £60.00

BUCHAN, JOHN 1875-1940   Menin Gate Pilgrimage. St. Barnabas 1927. London: 1927. 1st edition; 20.5 x 27.5; 43 page booklet in hard covers; photos; light foxing to endpapers, very good/fine, very scarce. Bannatyne Books 19-M17 1996 £50.00

BUCHAN, JOHN 1875-1940   Mr. Standfast. London: 1919. 1st edition; slight foxing of edges, but otherwise near fine in very scarce dust jacket with small mark on spine, slight soiling of white rear panel.   Bannatyne Books 19-M31 1996 £200.00

BUCHAN, JOHN 1875-1940   Montrose and Leadership. London: 1930. 1st edition; 22 page pamphlet; very good to fine, scarce.   Bannatyne Books 19-M24 1996 £70.00

BUCHAN, JOHN 1875-1940   The Moon Endureth. London: 1912. 1st edition; 2 small marks on boards, otherwise near fine; presentation copy from author "With the author's complements/April 1912."   Bannatyne Books 19-M24 1996 £70.00

BUCHAN, JOHN 1875-1940   The Nine Brasenose Worthies. London: 1909. 1st edition; 30 pages, 10 plates; very scarce, some moderate fading of spines.   Bannatyne Books 19-N08 1996 £80.00

BUCHAN, JOHN 1875-1940   The Northern Muse. London: 1924. 1st edition; limited to 150 copies, signed by author; 24 x 16.5; gilt lettering on green leather label on vellum spine, with grey boards, some browning of boards and foxing of edges, otherwise fine, attractive bookplate.   Bannatyne Books 19-N09 1996 £120.00

BUCHAN, JOHN 1875-1940   Oxford and Cambridge. London: H. Fletcher, 1909. 1st edition; faint mark on front board and light foxing of half title, very good.   Bannatyne Books 19-O04 1996 £55.00

BUCHAN, JOHN 1875-1940   The Path of the King. London: 1921. 1st edition; slight fading of spine, but generally very good/fine in very scarce dust jacket with 2 cm. of spine damaged, but now restored. Bannatyne Books 19-P01 1996 £100.00

BUCHAN, JOHN 1875-1940   The Power-House. London: William Blackwood and Sons, 1916. 1st edition; original binding, top edge dusty, spine faded, head and tail of spine and corners slightly bumped, covers marked and slightly soiled, page edges browned, good, no dust jacket. Ulysses 39-80 1996 £95.00

BUCHAN, JOHN 1875-1940   Prester John. London: Thomas Nelson and Sons, 1910. 1st edition; 8 pages of ads; bright, only little wear to white enamel on spine, top edge dusty, head and tail of spine and one corner bumped, lower cover very slightly marked, edges slightly spotted, rear free endpaper partially browned, enamel blocking on spine slightly chipped and retouched, very good.   Ulysses 39-79 1996 £175.00

BUCHAN, JOHN 1875-1940   Prester John. London: 1910. 1st edition; scarce variant binding in decorated blue cloth with gilt lettering; much more attractive than the usual binding, slight foxing on edges of titlepage and following page, slight rubbing of spine ends, very nice, fine copy. Bannatyne Books 19-P10 1996 £85.00

BUCHAN, JOHN 1875-1940   Prince of Captivity. London: 1933. 1st edition; some foxing, but very good in dust jacket with some moderate soiling and browning of white spine and rear panel; portion of top of spine (2 x 1 cm) affecting the title, was missing and has been restored. Bannatyne Books 19-P16 1996 £50.00

BUCHAN, JOHN 1875-1940 Principles of Social Service. London: 1933. 1st edition; near fine, very scarce. Bannatyne Books 19-P18 1996 £75.00

BUCHAN, JOHN 1875-1940 Scholar Gipsies. London: 1896. 1st edition; tiny nick at top of spine repaired and some rubbing of base of spine, but clean, bright, above average copy. Generally very good/fine. Bannatyne Books 19-S04 1996 £150.00

BUCHAN, JOHN 1875-1940 Sick Heart River. London: 1941. 1st edition; some foxing of page edges, but generally fine in much above average dust jacket. Bannatyne Books 19-S13 1996 £50.00

BUCHAN, JOHN 1875-1940 Sir Quixote of the Moors. This appears to be a variant binding of the first U.S.A. edition; grey binding with black lettering rather than the more usual pictorial boards, one page is missing and has been replaced by a photocopy on matching aged paper. Bannatyne Books 19-S18 1996 £65.00

BUCHAN, JOHN 1875-1940 Sir Quixote of the Moors, Being Some Account of an Episode in the Life of the Sieur de Rohaine. London: T. Fisher Unwin, 1895. 1st edition; 8vo; 4 pages ads; fine, clean copy of author's first book. Rare. Charles W. Traylen 117-78 1996 £200.00

BUCHAN, JOHN 1875-1940 Sir Quixote of the Moors. London: 1895. 1st English edition; this copy has "Sir Quixote of the Moors' on the spine, with attractive decorative pattern on black cloth, variant bindings with similar decorative pattern, but with "Sir Quixote" only on the spine, exist with either pink, brown or black cloth; generally good, sound, very good good. Bannatyne Books 19-S17 1996 £150.00

BUCHAN, JOHN 1875-1940 Sir Walter Raleigh. London: 1911. 1st edition; colored plates; brown cloth, gilt lettering and decoration on picture insert on front board, near fine, no foxing. Bannatyne Books 19-S20 1996 £80.00

BUCHAN, JOHN 1875-1940 Sir Walter Raleigh. London: 1911. 1st edition; colored plates; attractive cream and gilt pictorial boards, very light soiling of boards and some foxing, mainly of first few pages, near fine. Bannatyne Books 19-S21 1996 £75.00

BUCHAN, JOHN 1875-1940 Sir Walter Scott. London: 1932. 1st edition; near fine in dust jacket with some slight soiling and minor repairs, bookplate of C. H. Wilkinson, with inscription by author for Wilkinson; very scarce with inscription and dust jacket. Bannatyne Books 19-S22 1996 £100.00

BUCHAN, JOHN 1875-1940 Some Eighteenth Century Byways and Other Essays. London: 1908. 1st edition; fine copy. Bannatyne Books 19-S26 1996 £100.00

BUCHAN, JOHN 1875-1940 Some Eighteenth Century Byways and other Essays. London: 1908. 1st edition; variant binding with black lettering on blue cloth, rather than gold on turquoise, foxing of page edges and slight marking or foxing on spine, but still very good. Bannatyne Books 19-S27 1996 £60.00

BUCHAN, JOHN 1875-1940 The Thirty-Nine Steps. London: 1915. 1st edition; clean, bright, very good copy, usual browning of page edges. Bannatyne Books 19-T04 1996 £120.00

BUCHAN, JOHN 1875-1940 Unchanging Germany. London: 1939. 1st edition; 23 x 15; 46 page pamphlet; soft covers, some surface damage to front cover but lettering unaffected, very good-, very scarce. Bannatyne Books 19-U01 1996 £75.00

BUCHANAN, DONALD W. James Wilson Morrice: a Biography. Toronto: Ryerson Press, c. 1936. 8vo; pages viii, 187; frontispiece, illustrations; cloth, fine in chipped and soiled dust jacket. Hugh Anson-Cartwright 87-299 1996 $125.00

BUCHANAN, GEORGE 1506-1582 Rervm Scoticarvm Historia. Edimbvrgi (but London?) ad exemplar Alexandri Arbuthneti Editum, 1583. Folio; 17th century mottled calf, very nice; contemporary bookplate of Marquess of Tweeddale. STC 3992. G. W. Stuart 59-21 1996 $850.00

BUCHANAN, JAMES The British Grammar; or, an Essay in Four Parts, Towards Speaking and Writing the English Language Grammatically and Inditing Elegantly. Oxford: at the Clarendon Press, 1913. original boards, very good in slightly worn dust jacket; "With the Author's Compliments" slip loosely inserted. Jarndyce 103-36 1996 £250.00

BUCHANAN, JAMES A New Pocket-Book for Young Gentlemen and Ladies; or, a Spelling Dictionary. London: printed for R. Baldwin, 1757. 12mo; 5 pages ads; contemporary sheep, slightly rubbed, hinges splitting, lacking following free endpaper; Alston IV 674. Jarndyce 103-134 1996 £280.00

BUCHANAN, JOHN LANE Travels in the Western Hebrides; from 1782 to 1790. London: printed for G. G. J. and J. Robinson, and J. Debrett, 1793. 1st edition; 8vo; original pale blue boards, bit soiled, neatly rebacked. half title present, very good, uncut copy. CBEL II 1406. Ximenes 108-45 1996 $300.00

BUCHANAN, ROBERT The Piper of Hamelin: Fantastic Opera in Two Acts. London: Chiswick Press, 1893. 1st edition; 7 1/4 x 5 1/2 inches; 1 p.l., 63, (1) pages; added engraved title and 12 plates by Hugh Thomson; fine chestnut brown morocco by Sangorski & Sutcliffe, front cover with gilt titling above charming gilt vignette of two dancing rats, their tales entwining a musical pipe, spine with raised bands, gilt ruled compartments, gilt titling, blind ruled extensions of the raised bands terminating on covers in finial of 3 leaves, turn-ins with triple gilt fillets, all edges gilt, in fine plush lined folding morocco case by Zaehnsdorf with raised bands and gilt spine titling; from the distinguished collections of Doris Benz and Paul Chevalier with their bookplates. Virtually flawless copy Phillip J. Pirages 33-69 1996 $600.00

BUCHANAN, ROBERT Saint Abe and His Seven Wives. London: Strahan & Co., 1872. 1st edition; 8vo; pages ix, 169, 4 (ads); original blue cloth, gilt, very good. James Fenning 133-37 1996 £55.00

BUCHANAN, ROBERT The Wandering Jew. London: Chatto & Windus, 1893. 1st edition; 12mo; 32 page publisher's catalog bound in at rear; blue cloth stamped in gilt and black, spine discolored to a darker blue, light wear to tips, generally good+ copy. Priscilla Juvelis 95/1-65 1996 $100.00

BUCHANAN, W. Memoirs of Painting, With a Chronological History of the Importation of Pictures by the Great Masters into England since the French Revolution. London: for R. Ackermann, 1824. 1st edition; 8vo; 2 volumes; xiv, 364; (2), 297 pages; contemporary half calf, marbled boards; very scarce; very good. Ken Spelman 30-38 1996 £220.00

BUCKE, CHARLES Amusements in Retirement; or, the Influence of Science, Literature and the Liberal arts, on the Manners and Happiness of Private Life. London: printed for Henry Colburn, 1818. 2nd edition; 8vo; xvii, (iii), 320, (2 ad) pages; later black half morocco, top edge gilt, others uncut, joints slightly rubbed; ownership inscription on title of Leigh Hunt, and his marginal annotations throughout. James Burmester 29-22 1996 £375.00

BUCKINGHAM, GEORGE VILLIERS, 2ND DUKE OF 1628-1687 Miscellaneous Works... London: printed for Sam. Briscoe and sold by J. Nutt, 1705. 2nd edition of the 1st volume (as often), 1st edition of second volume; 8vo; 2 volumes; frontispiece in each; contemporary calf, slight rubbing; fine set with signature on each titlepage of the Earl of Panmure. Case 232; Macdonald 313; CBEL III 343 and 758. Ximenes 109-55 1996 $500.00

BUCKINGHAM, JOHN SHEFFIELD, 1ST DUKE OF 1648-1721 The Works of John Sheffield, Earl of Mulgrave, Marquis of Normanby and Duke of Buckingham. London: printed for John Barber and sold by the booksellers of London &... 1723. 1st edition; 4to; 2 volumes; engraved monument plate, portrait, engraved ornaments; this set with the two essays in rather elegant ms. form, the titlepages of the two volumes have been reversed by binder; contemporary calf, rebacked, spines gilt, some wear to edges and corners; very good. Griffith 137; Foxon p. 724. Ximenes 109-56 196 $400.00

BUCKINGHAM, NASH Mark Right! Tales of Shooting and Fishing. New York: Derrydale Press, 1936. 1st edition; number 770 of 1250 copies; full page photographic illustrations; original maroon cloth with color pictorial centerpiece depicting quail, spine lightly rubbed and some page edges trifle browned, else bright, near fine, housed in custom cloth slipcase. Bookplate of Eugene V. Connett, owner of Derrydale Press. Chapel Hill 94-375 1996 $450.00

BUCKLAND WRIGHT, JOHN Bathers and Dancers: the White Line and Silhouette Engravings. London: Fleece Press, 1993. Limited to 180 copies; quarter bound in vellum and japanese wood veneer paper; mint in slipcase as issued. Words Etcetera 94-243 1996 £225.00

BUCKLER, BENJAMIN   A Complete Vindication of the Mallard of All-Souls College, Against the Injurious Suggestions of the Rev. Mr. (John) Pointer. London: printed for J. and J. Rivington and J. Fletcher in Oxford, 1751. 2nd edition; 8vo; 62, (ii) pages, engraved vignette, text engraving at end; disbound, crisp copy.   David Bickersteth 133-97 1996 £160.00

BUCKLER, BENJAMIN   A Philosophical Dialogue Concerning Decency. Oxford: ptd. for James Fletcher... sold by J. & J. Rivington, London, 1751. 4to; pages 47, (1); recent quarter calf, marbled sides;   Peter Murray Hill 185-28 1996 £300.00

BUCKLER, W.   The Larvae of the British Butterflies and Moths. London: Ray Society, 1886-1901. 8vo; 9 volumes; 164 colored plates; cloth, volume 1 used and endpaper stained, volumes 2-4 faded, ownership stamps inside covers of some volumes.   Wheldon & Wesley 207-17 1996 £400.00

BUCKLEY, MICHAEL J.   Day at the Farm; a Poem. San Francisco: Privately printed, 1937. Large 4to; printed in black with elaborate ornamental borders in ochre; boards with cloth spine, very nice in dust jacket.   Bertram Rota 272-307 1996 £50.00

BUCKTON, A.   Through Human Eyes: Poems. Daniel Press, 1901. One of 130 numbered copies; 4to; wrappers, tear in upper wrapper and yapp edges somewhat crumpled, but internally very nice, clean copy. Bertram Rota 272-122 1996 £75.00

BUCKTON, G. B.   Monograph of the British Cicadae or Tettigidae. (with) The Natural History of Eristalis Tenax or the Drone Fly. London: 1890-95. 8vo; 2 volumes, 82 plates, pages vi, 91, 9 plates; quarter calf, ex-library, with slip inserted "Mrs. Buckton is very sorry but owing to some unfortunate circumstances the Letter Press of Part 4 of the Cicadae is not to be found", titlepage to volume 2 is here the original wrapper.   Wheldon & Wesley 207-1009 1996 £125.00

BUCKTON, G. B.   The Natural History of Eristalis Tenax or the Drone-Fly. London: 1895. illustrations; presentation copy, inscribed by author, plus 2 page ALS tipped in.   Petersfield Bookshop FH58-222 1996 £55.00

BUERGER, GOTTFRIED AUGUST   Leonora. London: T. Bensley for J. Edwards and E. and S. Harding, 1796. 1st edition of the 1st English translation; folio; 44 pages; frontispiece, 4 full page and 4 half page engravings, all by Bartolozzi; untrimmed, modern three quarter morocco; fine.   Bennett Gilbert LL29-20 1996 $1,000.00

BUFFON, G. L. L. DE   Natural History, General and Particular. London: 1812. 8vo; 20 volumes; portrait and 681 (of 682) engraved plates; contemporary tree calf; there is an extra plate 152 in Quadrupeds not called for in list of plates; the missing plate is no. 211; some volumes rather worn with joints cracked; plates clean, some offsetting from plates on to text.   Wheldon & Wesley 207-18 1996 £440.00

BUHL, H.   Nanga Parbat Pilgrimage. London: 1956. 1st English edition; 17 plates; faint brownish marks on spine, otherwise very good. Moutaineering Books 8-B70 1996 £50.00

BUJOLD, L.   Barrayar. Easton Press, 1991. 1st edition; signed by author; full leather binding and publisher's shrink wrapper; fine. Aronovitz 57-198 1996 $120.00

BUJOLD, L.   The Vor Game. Easton Press, 1990. 1st edition; full leather, publisher's shrink wrap, signed by author; fine.   Aronovitz 57-196 1996 $150.00

BUKOWSKI, CHARLES   Barfly. Black Sparrow Press, 1987. One of 400 copies of a limited edition, signed twice with author's drawing; fine in acetate wrapper.   Book Time 2-66 1996 $150.00

BUKOWSKI, CHARLES   Confessions of a Man Insane Enough to Live With Beasts. Bensonville: Mimeo Press, 1965. 1st printing of a limited edition of 'no more than 500 copies'; mimeographed on multicolored pages; stapled wrappers; fine.   Ken Lopez 74-52 1996 $400.00

BUKOWSKI, CHARLES   Crucifix in a Deathhand. New Orleans: Loujon Press, 1965. 1/3100 copies; signed by author; pictorial wrappers; fine with wrap around band.   Left Bank Books 2-14 1996 $165.00

BUKOWSKI, CHARLES   The Curtains Are Waving and People Walk through the Afternoon Here and in Berlin and in New York City and Mexico. San Francisco: Black Sparrow Press, 1967. 1st edition; one of 122 copies, signed by poet; chestnut brown wrappers, subtly printed in silver and black; near mint.   Bromer Booksellers 90-11 1996 $750.00

BUKOWSKI, CHARLES   The Days Run Away Like Wild Horses Over the Hills. Santa Barbara: Black Sparrow, 1969. 1st edition; 1 of 250 numbered copies, signed by author; uncommon, fine in clear acetate. Thomas Dorn 9-55 1996 $300.00

BUKOWSKI, CHARLES   "Dear Mr. Bukowski..." San Luis Obispo: Garage Graphics, 1979. One of 50 copies only, numbered and signed by author; 6 1/2 x 8 1/2 inches; 11 notecards, 10 silkscreened drawings, the whole housed in facsimile envelope. Fine, scarce.   Ken Lopez 74-54 1996 $850.00

BUKOWSKI, CHARLES   Hollywood. Black Sparrow Press, 1989. One of 150 copies of a limited edition, signed, with author's drawing; fine in acetate wrapper.   Book Time 2-63 1996 $195.00

BUKOWSKI, CHARLES   Notes of a Dirty Old Man. North Hollywood: Essex House, 1969. Paperback original; wrappers; light stains along spine edges, otherwise very good. Owner name in pencil on first page. Ken Lopez 74-53 1996 $375.00

BUKOWSKI, CHARLES   Play the Piano Like a Percussion Instrument Until the Fingers Begin to Bleed a Bit. Santa Barbara: Black Sparrow Press, 1979. One of 300 numbered copies signed by author; fine in clear acetate.   Thomas Dorn 9-57 1996 $145.00

BUKOWSKI, CHARLES   Screams from the Balcony. Black Sparrow Press, 1993. One of 26 lettered copies, with author's drawings, signed; in acetate wrapper.   Book Time 2-65 1996 $250.00

BUKOWSKI, CHARLES   Shakespeare Never Did This. San Francisco: City Lights Books, 1979. 1st edition; fine in fine dust jacket and signed by author; scarce hardcover issue, which was reportedly limited to only a few hundred copies.   Ken Lopez 74-55 1996 $650.00

BUKOWSKI, CHARLES   There's No Business. Black Sparrow Press, 1984. Limited edition, number 67 of 426 copies, signed by author and artist; illustrations by R. Crumb; wrappers; fine.   Book Time 2-62 1996 $120.00

BULFINCH, S. G.   Poems. Charleston: James S. Burges, 1834. 1st edition; 18mo; 108 pages; original cloth, printed paper label on spine. R&B 23605.   M & S Rare Books 60-126 1996 $100.00

BULL, H. G.   Notes on the Birds of Herefordshire. London: 1888. 8vo; pages xxxi, 274; portrait; original decorated cloth. Rather foxed at beginning.   Wheldon & Wesley 207-677 1996 £55.00

BULL, ROGER, PSEUD.   Grobianus; or the Compleat Booby. London: printed for T. Cooper, 1739. 1st edition; 8vo; contemporary mottled calf, spine gilt, joints neatly repaired; very good; bookplate of Frances Mary Richardson Currer. Foxon B564; Teerink 1318; Rothschild 513; Cagle, Matter of Taste 645.   Ximenes 108-46 1996 $750.00

BULLEID, ARTHUR   The Meare Lake Village. Privately printed at Taunton Castle of the Somerset Arch. Soc., 1948-66. Limited edition; 4to; 3 volumes, xvi, 105; xii, 106-280; x, 281-419 pages; 64 plates, 88 figures, printed boards, border design based on an ornamental Glastonbury pot, cloth spines.   Thomas Thorp 489-47 1996 £50.00

BULLEIN, WILLIAM   Bulleins Bulwarke of Defence Againste All Sicknes, Sores and Woundes that Dooe Daily Assaulte mankinde... London: J. Kingston, 1562. 1st edition; small folio; (vi) pages, folios i-xc, (xviii) pages, folios (i)-xlviii, (viii) pages, folios i-(xlviii), (xxii) pages, folios xlix-lxxiii, (iv) pages; modern half calf, spine gilt marbled boards, lacks titlepage (made-up title bound in with wrong text), leaf of 'list of authors' in prelims & Q1; substantial loss and repairs to P6, Q2, Ii4, Aa1 (divisional title) & Ii4; margins repaired from M1 to end, affecting some shoulder-notes, text (slightly) & index leaves, few more minor marginal repairs, some staining and soiling, extensively annotated by an early owner (annotations much cropped by binder, few 19th century notes. STC 4033.   Robert Clark 38-27 1996 £750.00

BULLEN, A. H. Speculum Amantis: Love Poems of the 17th century, from Rare Song Books and Miscelalnies. London: privately printed, 1902. 1st edition; number 8 of 400 copies; octavo; pages 129; printed on fine laid paper; titlepage in red and black; beautiful binding by Zaehnsdorf in full polished maroon morocco, double gilt fillets, gilt extra to spine panels, raised bands, top edge gilt, uncut, marbled endpapers, inner gilt dentelles; fine. CBEL II 258. Hartfield 48-V44 1996 $135.00

BULLEN, GEORGE Caxton Celebration 1877. Catalogue of the Loan Collection of Antiquities, Curiosities and Appliances Connected with the Art of Printing, South Kensington. London: N. Truebner and Co., 1877. 7.75 x 5.75 inches; 472 pages; some pencil marks in text, dates written in ink on margins of Bibles section (helpful guide in using the book), covers show some wear, offset on titlepage, generally very good. Joshua Heller 21-197 1996 $100.00

BULLEN, HENRY LEWIS Nicolas Jenson, Printer of Venice: His Famous Type Designs and Some Comment Upon the Printing Types of Earlier Printers. San Francisco: Pritned by John Henry Nash, 1926. One of 207 copies; 16 1/2 x 10 3/4 inches; with leaf from the Jenson Printing of Plutarch's 'Lives' of 1478 laid in, leaf bit foxed, faint dampstain in lower margin, bottom edge little frayed and creased; original vellum backed marbled paper boards, leather spine label, the volume with foxing to endpapers and with portions of edges of binding darkened, top edge of text leaves also with two small grey spots, otherwise the leaf and volume in excellent condition, without any appreciable signs of use; inscribed by John Henry Nash for Mrs. T. J. Cobden-Sanderson. Goff P832; BMC V 178 (for leaf). Phillip J. Pirages 33-339 1996 $450.00

BULLER, FRANCIS An Introduction to the Law Relative to Trials at Nisi Prius. Dublin: printed for Elizabeth Lynch, 1773. 8vo; pages (8), 364, (56); contemporary calf, binding little worn at fore-edge, else very good to nice. James Fenning 133-38 1996 £185.00

BULLER, WALTER L. Birds of New Zealand. London: 1967. Revision of text of second edition of 1888; folio; pages xviii, 262, (1), 48 colored plates; cloth. Wheldon & Wesley 207-678 1996 £55.00

BULLER, WALTER L. A History of the Birds of New Zealand. London: 1967. Folio; 48 fine tipped in color plates by Keulemans; fine in slightly marked dust jacket. David A.H. Grayling MY95Orn-13 1996 £70.00

BULLINS, ED Five Plays. Indianapolis: New York: Bobbs Merrill, 1969. 1st edition; fine in lightly rubbed, near fine dust jacket. Between the Covers 43-45 1996 $100.00

BULLOCH, WILLIAM The History of Bacteriology. London: 1938. 1st edition; 422 pages; original binding. GM 2580. W. Bruce Fye 71-270 1996 $125.00

BULLOCK, W. Six Months Residence and Travels in Mexico... London: John Murray, Albemarle St., 1824. title, preface (iii-vii), (ix-xii), folding table, 1-523 pages, index 525-530 pages list of plates 531-2 pages, large folding frontispiece, sepia aquatint, 15 aquatints, 2 large folding maps to rear; half strawberry calf and marbled boards, corners bumped and worn, joints rubbed, gilt tooling to panelled spine, brown morocco label to spine, edges and endpapers uniformly marbled. Abbey Travel 666; Sabin 9140; Church V 1326. Beeleigh Abbey BA56-43 1996 £475.00

BULLOCK, WILLIAM A Companion to Mr. Bullock's Museum...of...Natural and Foreign Curiosities, Antiquities...Fine Arts...in the Great Room, 22 Piccadilly, London. London: printed for the Proprietor, 1811. 10th edition; 12mo; frontispiece, title, pages vi, (ii blank), 150, vi, (i ads); original mottled boards and printed label, backstrip damaged. Peter Murray Hill 185-20 1996 £90.00

BULMER, T., & CO. History, Topography and Directory of East Yorkshire (with Hull) Comprising Its Ancient and Modern History...Family History and Genealogical Descent. London: ca. 1890. 1st edition; 8vo; 1233 pages; lacks maps, new binders cloth. K Books 442-92 1996 £75.00

BULMER, T., & CO. History, Topography and Directory of Cumberland, Comprising Its History and Archaeology... Preston: T. Snape, 1901. 1st edition; thick 8vo; pages vii, 983, complete with loose large folding map; original half red calf, gilt, little rubbed, upper joint cracked, but sound. R.F.G. Hollett & Son 78-759 1996 £95.00

BULMER, T., & CO. History, Topography and Director of West Cumberland. Preston: T. Snape & Co., 1883. 1st edition; 8vo; pages (viii), 679, xix, (v), large folding colored map; original blindstamped green cloth, gilt, title little browned as usual. R.F.G. Hollett & Son 78-765 1996 £85.00

BULMER, T., & CO. History, Topography and Directory of East Cumberland... Manchester: T. Bulmer and Co., 1884. 2nd edition; 8vo; pages 700, xvi, (ii), large folding colored map; original blue cloth, gilt, rather rubbed and marked, upper joint trifle strained. R.F.G. Hollett & Son 78-762 1996 £75.00

BULMER, T., & CO. History, Topography and Directory of East Cumberland... Manchester: T. Bulmer & Co., 1884. 2nd edition; 8vo; pages 700, xvi, (ii); old binder's cloth, gilt, spine lettering faded. R.F.G. Hollett & Son 78-763 1996 £65.00

BULMER, T., & CO. History, Topography and Directory of West Cumberland... Preston: 1883. 1st edition; 8vo; pages (viii), 679, xix, (v), complete, large folding colored map; original blindstamped brown cloth, gilt; title little browned. R.F.G. Hollett & Son 78-764 1996 £85.00

BULMER, T., & CO. History, Topography and Directory of Westmorland. Preston: T. Snape & Co., c. 1906. 2nd edition; 8vo; pages (xii), 632, viii, first 2 leaves in facsimile; R.F.G. Hollett & Son 78-766 1996 £75.00

BULMER, T., & CO. History, Topography and Directory of Westmorland. Preston: T. Snape & Co., c. 1906. 2nd edition; 8vo; pages (xii), 632, viii, large folding colored map, half title trimmed to the print and laid down, last leaf rather browned; original cloth, gilt, recased. R.F.G. Hollett & Son 78-767 1996 £75.00

BULOW, ERNIE Navajo Taboos. Gallup: Buffalo Medicine Books, 1991. 1st edition; Near fine, light rubbing, in near fine dust jacket with minor creasing; signed by Tony Hillerman who provided introduction. Bella Luna 7-118 1996 $150.00

BULOW, ERNIE Navajo Taboos. New Mexico: Buffalo Medicine Books, 1991. 1/50 copies, numbered and signed by Bulow, Hillerman and Ernest Franklin; with original illustration hand colored by Franklin that appears in the book. Left Bank Books 2-55 1996 $375.00

BULOW, ERNIE Words, Weather and Wolfmen. Gallup: Southerwesterner, 1989. One of 350 numbered copies, signed by Hillerman, Ernest Franklin, the artist and Ernie Bulow; very fine in dust jacket. Quill & Brush 102-917 1996 $225.00

BULOW, ERNIE Words, Weather and Wolfmen. New Mexico: Southwesterner Books, 1989. One of 26 specially bound copies which include an original pen and ink drawing and have been signed and lettered A to Z, this is copy R, #18 signed by Hillerman, the artist Ernest Franklin and Ernie Bulow, who provides the interview. Fine in slipcase. Quill & Brush 102-916 1996 $600.00

BULSTRODE, WHITELOCKE An Essay on Transmigration, in Defence of Pythagoras. London: E. H. for Tho. Basset, 1692. 1st edition; small 8vo; (56), 192 pages; frontispiece, half title; later red morocco, gilt rules, all edges gilt, marbled endpapers; binding lightly scuffed at extremities; near fine. Duveen p. 108; Thorndike VIII 350. Edwin V. Glaser 121-48 1996 $450.00

BULWER, JOHN Anthropometamorphosis: Man Transform'd; or, the Artificial Changeling. London: for J. Hardesty, 1650. 1st edition; 12mo; (24), 24, 45-263, (44) pages, engraved portrait and engraved frontispiece, containing 21 curious heads; contemporary sprinkled calf, rebacked; nice, final leaf probably supplied from another copy. Wellcome II p. 270; Wing B546. Joseph J. Felcone 64-8 1996 $1,600.00

BULWER-LYTTON, HENRY France, Social, Literary, Political. (with) The Monarachy of the Middle Classes. New York: Harper & Bros./Paris: A. and W. Galignani and Co.; 1835/36. Mixed editions, but complete thus; large 12mo; 3 volumes; 8 folding tables or charts, 220, 223, xx, 350 pages, complete in spite of erratic page numbered in volumes 1 and 2, first 2 volumes in contemporary half calf, gilt, rubbed, final volume in contemporary green half roan gilt; mixed editions, but complete thus; very scarce. John Drury 82-36 1996 £125.00

BUMPUS, J. & E. Catalogue of an Exhibition. London: J. & E. Bumpus, 1934. Fine copy. Janus Books 36-20 1996 $100.00

BUNBURY, HENRY WILLIAM 1750-1811 Annals of Horsemanship. London: for John Stockdale, 1812. Royal 4to; (xiv), (82), (ii) pages; stipple engraved frontispiece and 16 plates, all with fine, bright and original hand color; original boards with paper label (giving variant prices for plain and colored copies), expertly rebacked in good match of the original backstrip, pastedowns replaced, but original flies retained, one bearing 1809 watermark, touch bumped, few very minor marks but very good. Ash Rare Books Zenzybyr-17 1996 £595.00

BUNBURY, HENRY WILLIAM 1750-1811   Annals of Horsemanship. London: printed for John Stockdale, 1812. Early edition; small folio; xix, 81 pages; 17 full page hand colored stipple engravings; three quarter brown morocco and marbled boards, top edge gilt, marbled endpapers, bookplate, extremities lightly rubbed, light offsetting from plates, few expertly repaired tears, else near fine.   Chapel Hill 94-43 1996 $750.00

BUNCE, JOHN THACKRAY   History of Old St. Martin's, Birmingham. London: Cornish Brothers; Hall & English, Birmingham, 1875. 1st edition; folio; half title, colored frontispiece, 8 plates (six colored), 4 page list of subscribers; original cloth, lacks most of spine, top edge gilt, clean internally.   Anthony W. Laywood 109-17 1996 £60.00

BUNIN, IVAN   Memoirs and Portraits. London: John Lehmann, Ltd., 1951. 1st edition; black and white frontispiece photo; original binding, top edge dusty, covers slightly bubbled and cocked, head and tail of spine bumped, very good in nicked, chipped and rubbed, slightly torn, frayed and dusty dust jacket, darkened at spine and edges.   Ulysses 39-82 1996 £65.00

BUNTING, BASIL   Collected Poems. London: Fulcrum Press, 1968. 1st trade edition; fine in lightly used price clipped dust jacket, signed by author.   Captain's Bookshelf 38-27 1996 $175.00

BUNTING, BASIL   Loquitur. London: Fulcrum Press, 1965. 1st edition; one of 200 copies bound thus, from a total edition of 1000; 4to; original cloth, dust jacket, fine.   James S. Jaffe 34-94 1996 $350.00

BUNTING, BASIL   The Pious Cat. London: Bertram Rota, 1986. One of 200 numbered copies, 4to; half cloth, boards, pictorial decoration on upper cover; fine.   Bertram Rota 272-447 1996 £50.00

BUNTING, BASIL   What the Chairman Told Tom. Cambridge: Pym-Randall, 1967. One of 200 numbered copies, signed by author; wrappers as issued, fine; although not called for this copy also signed by Tom Pickard.   Between the Covers 42-71 1996 $275.00

BUNTING, EDWARD   The Ancient Music of Ireland. 1840. 1st edition; 8vo; modern cloth, very good.   C. P. Hyland 216-67 1996 £140.00

BUNYAN, JOHN 1628-1688   The Jerusalem Sinner Saved; or, Good News for the Vilest of men... London: printed for John Marshall, 1715. 9th edition; 12mo; lacks portrait, one leaf of contents and 12 pages of ads at end; woodcuts in text, few outer blank margins expertly strengthened, finely bound in 19th century ful calf, spine gilt, label. Harrison p. 54.   Anthony Laywood 108-33 1996 £125.00

BUNYAN, JOHN 1628-1688   The Pilgrim's Progress. London: David Bogue, n.d., but mid or late 19th century. Thick tall 8vo; profusely illustrated with wood engravings; dark green full morocco leather binding, all edges gilt, five raised bands on spine, gilt tooling on covers and spine, gilt worked inner dentelles, marbled endpapers; handsome volume, near fine, some rubbing.   Antic Hay 101-240 1996 $150.00

BUNYAN, JOHN 1628-1688   The Pilgrim's Progress. London: Cassell, Petter and Galpin, 4to; engraved illustrations and decorations by H. C. Selous and M. Paolo Priolo; contemporary binding by Gray of Cambridge in full dark blue calf, spine in compartments, double gilt ruled, elaborately tooled in gilt on spine; fresh copy; armorial binding. Gleeson White, English Ills. The Sixties 123.   Barbara Stone 70-43 1996 £75.00

BUNYAN, JOHN 1628-1688   The Pilgrim's Progress and The Life and Death of Mr. Badman. London: Nonesuch Press, 1928. Limited edition, 882/1600 copies; crown 8vo; printed on Velin Arches mouldmade paper, pages 450, (1); 8 wood engraved plates by Karl Michel color stenciled at the Curwen Press, original marbled fawn, brown and blue linen, cream parchment label, free endpapers browned, fore-edges trifle foxed, top edge gilt on rough, others untrimmed, excellent. Dreyfus 55. Blackwell's B112-203 1996 £100.00

BUNYAN, JOHN 1628-1688   The Pilgrim's Progress. New York: Limited Editions Club, 1941. Copy 904 from a total edition of 1500 numbeed copies; watercolors by William Blake; fine in publisher's slipcase. Hermitage SP95-947 1996 $150.00

BUNYAN, JOHN 1628-1688   Solomons Temple spiritualiz'd, or Gospel-Light Fecht Out of the Temple at Jerusalem, to Let Us More Easily into the Glory of New Testament Truths. London: printed for Eliz. Smith, 1691. 2nd edition; 12mo; contemporary sheep, corners rubbed, excellent copy, in well preserved early binding; Harrison XLI; Wing B5596. Ximenes 109-57 1996 $1,500.00

BUNYARD, E.   Eggs of Rarer Limiccolae and Variations. London: 1994. Limited to 50 copies; 4to; pages 46, 33 colored plates; half morocco, gilt, slipcase.   Wheldon & Wesley 207-19 1996 £365.00

BUONAROTTI, MICHEL ANGELO 1475-1564   His Sonnets. Allen Press, 1991. One of 115 copies; 11 1/4 x 7 1/2 inches; 10 p.l., lxxvii, (1) pages; printed in red, blue and black, using Bembo and Solemnis types, on light brown handmade paper produced at Barcham Green Mill at Maidstone in 1980; attravie patterned hand blocked Italian cloth boards, gilt titled on spine, leaves untrimmed, mounted photo. As new.   Phillip J. Pirages 33-7 1996 $550.00

BUONAROTTI, MICHEL ANGELO 1475-1564   The Letters of Michelangelo. London: Peter Owne Ltd., 1963. One of 500 sets; quarto; 2 volumes; decorated gilt buckram covers, bottom corners of two pages in volume 2 slightly creased, one of the corners is also very slightly torn, heads and tails of spine bumped, 3 corners slightly bumped, covers slightly rubbed, near fine in slightly torn, bumped and worn slipcase, top edge gilt; presentation inscription from E. H. Ramsden, the editor. Ulysses 39-409 1996 £195.00

BURDSALL, R.   Men Against the Clouds. London: 1935. 1st edition; 47 photos, some folding, maps and chart; fading of boards, some foxing, still very good in scarce, very good+ dust jacket with minor repairs; photo of Minya Konka cut from copy of National Geographic magazine loosely inserted.   Moutaineering Books 8-B71 1996 £125.00

BURFORD, THOMAS   Six Landscapes from Original Paintings. London: Thos. Burford...July 2nd, 1779. Oblong 4to; suite of 6 engraved scenes, first plate bears title at foot of image; stitched as issued in sugar paper wrappers and priced 1/6 in top corner of first plate.   Ken Spelman 30-16 1996 £280.00

BURGER, JOHN F.   African Adventures. London: 1957. 1st edition; illustrations, some light foxing, otherwise near fine in protected dust jacket.   David Grayling J95Biggame-44 1996 £65.00

BURGER, JOHN F.   African Jungle Memories. London: 1958. illustrations, nice in frayed dust jacket.   David Grayling J95Biggame-43 1996 £55.00

BURGESS, EDWARD   English and American Yachts, Illustrating and Describing the Most Famous Yachts Now Sailing in English and American Waters. London: Chapman and Hall Ltd., 1888. 1st edition; oblong folio; pages (vi), 14, 50 photogravure plates, each with leaf of descriptive text, occasional slight spotting, but very good; original dark blue cloth, blocked in gilt.   Sotheran PN32-79 1996 £698.00

BURGESS, GELETT FRANK 1866-1951   Bayside Bohemia, Fin de Siecle San Francisco and Its Little Magazines. San Francisco; Book Club of California, 1954. 1st edition; one of 375 copies; illustrated with facsimiles; fine.   Hermitage SP95-832 1996 $125.00

BURGESS, GELETT FRANK 1866-1951   Goop Tales Alphabetically Told. New York: Stokes, 1904. 4to; numerous illustrations by Burgess, blue cloth pictorially stamped in white and gilt, fresh copy, scarce.   Barbara Stone 70-14 1996 £110.00

BURGESS, MOLLY   Still. New Jersey: Carolingian Press, 1975. Limited to2 5 copies, signed by Burgess; square octavo, (86)ff. of various papers, most being frenchfold; letterpress from zinc plates; bound oriental style with gold threads and housed in black folding box, each side of which is silk lined in different primary color, on cover is a gold painted circle, symbol of eternal light, box is clasped with mother-of-pearl; mint with prospectus.   Bromer Booksellers 87-42 1996 $1,750.00

BURGESS, N. G.   The Photograph Manual: a Practical Treatise Containing the Cartes De Visite Process and the Method of Taking Stereoscopic Pictures. New York: D. Appleton, 1865. 12th edition; 4.5 x 7 inches; 283 pages; ex-library in green cloth, usual library marks, otherwise very good.   Knollwood Books 70-279 1996 $100.00

BURGESS, RENATE   Portraits of Doctors & Scientists in the Wellcome Institute of the History of Medicine. Wellcome Inst., 1973. 1st edition; 4to; numerous illustrations; original cloth, dust jacket; from the library of W. R. Le Fanu, with Le Fanu's typescript review for "Medical History" and a TLS from author to Le Fanu.   Forest Books 74-30 1996 £55.00

BURGH, A.   Anecdotes of Music, Historical and Biographical in a Series of Letters from a Gentleman to His Daughter. 1814. 3 volumes; covers detached and worn, texts in good condition.   William Reeves 309-9719 1996 £83.00

BURGH, JAMES   The Art of Speaking. London: printed for T. Longman & J. Buckland, &c., 1775. 4th edition; half title 2 pages ads; contemporary speckled calf, rubbed, gilt spine worn at head and tail, red label; good, sound copy. Alston VI 338.   Jarndyce 103-37   1996 £120.00

BURGH, JAMES   The Dignity of Human Nature. London: printed by W. B. and sold by J. and P. Knapton, 1754. 4to; xxii, (2), 430 pages; contemporary calf, neatly rebacked.   C. R. Johnson 37-71   1996 £650.00

BURHANS, ROBERT D.   The First Special Service Force, a War History of the North Americas 1942-44. Washington: 1947. 1st edition; 9 x 6 inches; 376 pages; photos, maps; cloth, removal marks on endpapers, couple pages repaired, covers moderately rubbed, scarce. John K. King   77-849   1996 $200.00

BURKE, CLIFFORD   Bone Songs. Janus Press, 1992. One of 150 numbered and signed copies; 8 x 10 inches; 40 pages; printed on Royal Watercolor Society paper; bone and skull drawings by Ruth Fine; bound in new woven non-adhesive structure of MacGregor-Vinzani ivory abaca paper, boxing its two slipcases, one of Barcham Green's old British Mail bags, the other is drum vellum and cloth constructed without glue; fine. Joshua Heller 21-34   1996 $500.00

BURKE, CLIFFORD   Bone Songs. West Burke: Janus Press, 1992. 1st edition; one of 150 copies only, each signed and numbered by Burke, Fine and Claire Van Vliet; page size 8 x 10 inches; woven non-adhesive structure of MacGregor-Vinzani ivory calendered abaca paper, housed in two specially made slipcases, one of Barcham Green's old British Mail bags, the other drum vellum and both constructed without glue.   Priscilla Juvelis 95/1-136   1996 $500.00

BURKE, CLIFFORD   A Chiroxylographic Book. Anacortes: Margaret's Press, 1981. Calligraphic design printed on a sheet 14 x 66 inches, fodled, attached to red boards, housed in paper slipcase, title hand lettered on box spine; fine in original paper box.   Joshua Heller 21-166   1996 $100.00

BURKE, CLIFFORD   A Landscape With Cows In It. Janus Press, 1987. One in an edition of 150 copies, signed by author and artist; 9 irregularly sized pages, accordion folded, with irregularly sized 24 page pamphlet sewn between 7 and 8, all unnumbered; page sizes vary from 2.25 x 6 to 4.875 x 8 inches; accordion section in French-folded to contain linoleum cut, inserted so image is seen most clearly from verso, linoleum cut by Ruth Fine measuring 34.125 x 6.25 inches; designed and printed by Claire Van Vliet, titles handset, printed dry in black on Okawara and kozo natural pamphlet, housed in grey Kizuki wrappers over boards with author and title printed in black on spine, title on front cover, fine.   Joshua Heller 21-26   1996 $150.00

BURKE, EDMUND 1729-1797   An Account of the European Settlements in America. London: J. Dodsley, 1777. 6th edition; 8vo; 2 volumes, (8), xii, 324; xii, 308 pages; frontispiece, engraved folding map in each volume; contemporary calf over marbled boards, spines rubbed, small gouge in spine of volume 1 and spine label lacking on volume 2. Howes B974.   Kenneth Karmiole 1NS-58   1996 $175.00

BURKE, EDMUND 1729-1797   An Appeal from the New to the Old Whigs, in Consequence of some Late Discussions in Parliament, Relative to the Reflections on the French Revolution. London: printed for J. Dodsley, 1791. 1st edition; 1st impression; as described by Todd; 8vo; disbound; wanting half title, otherwise fresh copy. Todd 56a.   Ximenes 108-47   1996 £125.00

BURKE, EDMUND 1729-1797   A Letter from the Rt. Honourable Edmund Burke to His Grace the Duke of Portland on the Conduct of the Minority in Parliament. London: for the editor, and sold by J. Owen, 1797. 1st edition; 8vo; 94), 94, (2) pages; half title, final leaf of ads; contemporary drab wrappers, soiled, uncut, few internal stains. Todd 67a.   Kenneth Karmiole 1NS-59   1996 $150.00

BURKE, EDMUND 1729-1797   Observations on a Late State of the Nation. London: printed for J. Dodsley, 1769. 2nd edition; 8vo; half title, 155 pages; disbound. Todd 16b; Kress 6612; Goldsmith 10557; Higgs 4719; Sabin 56488;   Anthony Laywood 108-34   1996 £85.00

BURKE, EDMUND 1729-1797   On Conciliation with the Colonies and Other Papers on the American Revolution. Stinehour Press, Limited Editions Club, 1975. Copy #1715 of 2000 copies; tall quarto; 268 pages; 12 full page plates, 2 in color, 6 roundels to divisional titles and 8 tailpieces; wood engravings by Lynd Ward; colonial motif patterned cloth, gilt, dark brown spine label, matching slipcase; signed by artist. Hartfield 48-V6   1996 $185.00

BURKE, EDMUND 1729-1797   On Concilliation with the Colonies and Other Papers on the American Revolution. Lunenburg: The Stinehour Press for Limited Editions Club, 1975. 1st edition thus; number 218 of 2000 numbered copies, signed by Ward; large 8vo; wood engravings in mauve and black by Lynd Ward; patterned cloth spine with gilt stamped brown leather label, glassine dust jacket, very good to fine, publisher's brown board slipcase.   George J. Houle 68-148   1996 $175.00

BURKE, EDMUND 1729-1797   On Conciliation with the Colonies. New York: Limited Editions Club, 1975. Copy 417 of 2000 copies, signed by artist; wood engravings by Lynd Ward; fine in slipcase.   Hermitage SP95-948 1 1996 $125.00

BURKE, EDMUND 1729-1797   A Philosophical Enquiry into the Origin of Our Ideas of the Sublime and Beautiful. London: for J. Dodsley, 1782. 9th edition; 8vo; ix, (7), 342 pages; 19th century half calf, marbled boards, raised gilt bands; very good.   Ken Spelman 30-65   1996 £100.00

BURKE, EDMUND 1729-1797   A Philosophical Inquiry into the Origin of Our Ideas of the Subline and Beautiful. London: Thos. Tegg, 1810. Small 8vo; pages 172; frontispiece and titlepage vignette, uncut; original printed publisher's boards, engraved frontispiece and titlepage vignette, uncut; covers considerably worn, faded, but perfectly legible, contents excellent. Hartfield 48-L14   1996 £125.00

BURKE, EDMUND 1729-1797   Reflections on the Revolution in France, and On the Proceedings in Certain Societies in London Relative to that Event. Dublin: W. Watson (etc), 1790. iv, 356 pages; contemporary tree calf, red label; fine and attractive copy. Bookplate of Robert Wilmot and extensively annotated throughout in ink in margins by Robert Wilmot Horton, bookplate is probably that of Wilmot Horton's father, Wilmot added surname Horton when he married Anne Horton in 1806.   C. R. Johnson 37-51   196 £750.00

BURKE, EDMUND 1729-1797   Reflections on the Revolution in France, and on the Proceedings Against Certain Societies in London Relative to that Event. London: printed for J. Dodsley, 1790. 1st edition; 8vo; disbound; very good, clean copy. Todd 53; PMM 239; Grolier Hundred 63.   Ximenes 108-48   1996 $450.00

BURKE, EDMUND 1729-1797   Reflections on the Revolution in France and On the Proceedings In Certain Societies in London Relative to that Event. London: printed for J. Dodsley, in Pall Mall, 1790. 3rd edition; 8vo; (iii-iv), 1-364 pages; full speckled calf, tastefully rebacked, preserving original backstrip, decorative gilt border to boards, ornate gilt tooling to compartments, red morocco label to spine, corners slightly bumped; upper hinge cracked, otherwise good, tight copy.   Beeleigh Abbey BA56-44   1996 £125.00

BURKE, EDMUND 1729-1797   Speech...on Presenting to the House of Commons (on the 11th of February, 1780) a Plan for the Better Security of the Independence of Parliament and the Oeconomical Reformation of the Civil and Other Establishments. London: J. Dodsley, 1780. 1st (authorised) edition, 1st impression; 8vo; (4), 95 pages, complete with half title; recent quarter calf, spine gilt; very good. Kress B264; Goldsmiths 12068.   John Drury 82-37   1996 £350.00

BURKE, EDMUND 1729-1797   A Vindication of Natural Society... London: printed for R. and J. Dodsley, 1757. 2nd edition; 8vo; pages xii, 106; Todd 3 b, revised throughout, with Preface; unbound.   Peter Murray Hill 185-21   1996 £150.00

BURKE, EDMUND 1729-1797   The Work... Dublin: Cross, Wilson, Wogan et al, 1792-93. 1st collected edition; tall thick octavo; 3 volumes, pages 580, 655, 602; full tree calf, handsomely rebacked, gilt on red and black labels, raised bands, blind and gilt decorations; nice set, scarce. Hartfield 48-L15   1996 $695.00

BURKE, JAMES LEE   Black Cherry Blues. Boston: Little Brown, 1989. Advance reading copy; glossy illustrated wrappers, signed by author; very near fine.   Lame Duck Books 19-354   1996 $100.00

BURKE, JAMES LEE   Dixie City Jam. Hyperion, 1994. Special boxed edition limited to 1525 signed copies; as new.   Book Time 2-575 1996 $125.00

BURKE, JAMES LEE   Dixie City Jam. New York: Hyperion, 1994. One of 1525 specially bound copies, numbered and signed by author; original cloth, fine in fine slipcase, issued without dust jacket.   Beasley Books 82-255   1996 $125.00

BURKE, JAMES LEE   Half of Paradise. Boston: Houghton Mifflin, 1965. 1st edition; elusive first book remainder marks top and bottom of pages, otherwie near fine in very good, spine faded and price clipped dust jacket; quite presentable copy, signed by author.   Ken Lopez 74-60 1996 $1,000.00

BURKE, JAMES LEE   Half of Paradise. Boston: Houghton Mifflin, 1965. 1st edition; author's first book; faint dampstaining to portions of front and rear boards, else near fine in very good dust jacket with medium size patch of surface loss to front panel and dampstain to verso at head of spine, signed by author.   Lame Duck Books 19-98 1996 $850.00

BURKE, JAMES LEE   Half of Paradise. Fribourg: Houghton Mifflin, 1965. 1st edition; elusive first book; very slightly tender hinge, visible at titlepage, else near fine in near fine jacket, signed by author.   Ken Lopez 74-59 1996 $1,500.00

BURKE, JAMES LEE   Heaven's Prisoner's. New York: Holt, 1988. 1st edition; review copy; fine in dust jacket with publisher's ad laid in; inscribed by author.   Lame Duck Books 19-353 1996 $200.00

BURKE, JAMES LEE   Heaven's Prisoners. New York: Holt, 1988. 1st edition; review copy; fine in fine dust jacket, publicity brochure laid in; inscribed by author.   Ken Lopez 74-65 1996 $200.00

BURKE, JAMES LEE   In the Electric Mist with the Confederate Dead. New York: Hyperion, 1993. One of 150 numbered copies; signed by author; fine in slipcase.   Between the Covers 42-473 1996 $250.00

BURKE, JAMES LEE   In the Electric Mist With Confederate Dead. New York: Hyperion, 1993. One of 150 signed, numbered and specially bound copies; fine in slipcase.   Quill & Brush 102-171 1996 $200.00

BURKE, JAMES LEE   Lay Down My Sword and Shield. New York: Crowell, 1971. 1st edition; near fine in about very good dust jacket with closed two inch edge tear and medium size internal piece missing to rear panel, signed by author.   Lame Duck Books 19-100 1996 $1,000.00

BURKE, JAMES LEE   The Lost Get-Back Boogie. Baton Rouge: LSU, 1986. Uncorrected proof; printed yellow wrappers, small faint sticker ghost front cover, otherwise fine.   Thomas Dorn 9-61 1996 $600.00

BURKE, JAMES LEE   The Lost Get-Back Boogie. Baton Rouge: Louisiana State University Press, 1986. 1st edition; fine in lightly rubbed but unfaded price clipped dust jacket, signed by author.   Ken Lopez 74-62 1996 $300.00

BURKE, JAMES LEE   The Lost Get-Back Boogie. Baton Rouge: LSU, 1986. 1st edition; couple of light stains to bottom edge, else near fine in price clipped dust jacket which is somewhat rubbed along edges, signed by author.   Lame Duck Books 19-101 1996 $250.00

BURKE, JAMES LEE   The Lost Get-Back Boogie. Baton Rouge: Louisiana State University Press, 1986. 1st edition; fine in near fine price clipped dust jacket and signed by author.   Ken Lopez 74-63 1996 $250.00

BURKE, JAMES LEE   The Lost Get-Back Boogie. Baton Rouge: LSU, 1986. 1st trade edition; signed by author; fine in fine price clipped dust jacket.   Thomas Dorn 9-62 1996 $225.00

BURKE, JAMES LEE   The Lost Get-Back Boggie. Baton Rouge: Louisiana State University Press, 1986. 1st edition; fine in price clipped dust jacket, signed by author.   Bud Schweska 12-852 1996 $200.00

BURKE, JAMES LEE   The Neon Rain. New York: Henry Holt, 1987. 1st edition; fine in dust jacket with very light rubbing.   Quill & Brush 102-163 1996 $100.00

BURKE, JAMES LEE   The Neon Rain. New York: Holt, 1987. 1st edition; fine in dust jacket, signed by author.   Lame Duck Books 19-352 1996 $150.00

BURKE, JAMES LEE   The Neon Rain. New York: Henry Holt, 1987. 1st edition; author's first novel fine in fine dust jacket; signed by author. Bud Schweska 12-853 1996 $135.00

BURKE, JAMES LEE   The Neon Rain. New York: Henry Holt & Co., 1987. 1st edition; signed by Burke; new in dust jacket.   Steven C. Bernard 71-291 1996 $125.00

BURKE, JAMES LEE   The Neon Rain. New York: Holt, 1987. 1st edition; fine in fine dust jacket and signed by author.   Ken Lopez 74-64 1996 $125.00

BURKE, JAMES LEE   To the Bright and Shining Sun. New York: Scribner, 1970. 1st edition; scarce second book; fine in very near fine dust jacket with very slight spine fading, nice, uncommon, signed by author.   Ken Lopez 74-61 1996 $1,500.00

BURKE, JAMES LEE   To the Bright and Shining Sun. New York: Scribner's, 1970. 1st edition; near fine in dust jacket with occasional faint waterstaining to upper and lower edges visible on verso; signed by author.   Lame Duck Books 19-99 1996 $1,000.00

BURKE, JAMES LEE   To the Bright and Shining Sun. Huntington Beach: Cahill, 1992. Limited to 500 copies; illustrations by Jose Servello; fine in slipcase, signed by author.   Bella Luna 7-122 1996 $150.00

BURKE, JAMES LEE   To the Bright and Shining Sun. Huntington Beach: Cahill Publishing Co., 1992. 1st limited edition, one of 400 numbered copies, signed by author; quarter leather and cloth in slipcase, as new.   Between the Covers 42-72 1996 $125.00

BURKE, JAMES LEE   Two for Texas. New York: Pocket Books, 1982. 1st edition; pictorial paper wrappers with light edge wear, light rubbing and soiling; very good+, owner's "to do" list on inside front panel; inscribed to Dennis McMillan, from author.   Quill & Brush 102-162 1996 $100.00

BURKE, JAMES LEE   Winter Light. Huntington Beach: Cahill Publishing, 1992. One of 300 numbered copies, signed by author and artist; frontispiece by Phil Parks; full leather, as issued, fine.   Between the Covers 42-73 1996 $100.00

BURKE, JANE   Messages on Healing Understood to Have Been Dictated by William James, William Osler, Andrew Jackson Davis and Others and Received by Jane Revere Burke Sitting with Edward Martin. 1936. 71 pages; original binding; scarce.   W. Bruce Fye 71-1580 1996 $100.00

BURLAND, H.   The Gold Worshipers. Dillingham, 1906. 1st edition; covers exhibit some wear at hinges and eges, else a tight very good copy in just about like dust jacket, very scarce in dust jacket. Aronovitz 57-202 1996 $135.00

BURLEIGH, GEORGE S.   Elegiac Poem on the Death of Nathaniel Peabody Rogers. Hartford: Charter Oak Office, 1846. 1st edition; 18mo; 32 pages; original printed wrappers;   M & S Rare Books 60-250 1996 $150.00

BURLINGAME, MERRILL G.   The Montana Frontier. Helena: 1942. 1st edition; xiii, 482 pages, photos, maps, map endpapers, cloth, nice, scarce. 6 Guns 332. Herd 369.   T. A. Swinford 49-166 1996 $175.00

BURLINGTON FINE ARTS CLUB   An Exhibition of Ancient Greek Art. London: Burlington Fine Arts Club, 1904. Folio; xxxii, 265 pages; 112 photographic plates; full red morocco, 5 raised bands, top edge gilt, extremities and corners rubbed, titlepage wrinkled, contents fine. Archaeologia Luxor-3124 1996 $950.00

BURLINGTON FINE ARTS CLUB   Illustrated Catalogue of Illuminated Manuscripts. Exhibition Catalogue 269. London: 1908. Folio; 162 plates; brown cloth, gilt lettering on spine and upper cover, bit scuffed, spine bit faded, some very slight browning only to edges, crease on f.f.e.p., pencil annotations beside few exhibits referring to particular lots in the Aldenham sale 1937l Ownership inscription of Lord Kenyon.   Maggs Bros. Ltd. 1191-141 1996 £360.00

BURLINGTON FINE ARTS CLUB   The Venetian School: Pictures by Titian and His Contemporaries. privately printed, 1915. 4to; 47 plates, 7 pages of text; buckram, gilt, over bevelled boards, top edge gilt, very slightly faded, but fine.   Thomas Thorp 489-49 1996 £50.00

BURN, EDWARD   A Reply to the Reverend Dr. Priestley's Appeal to the Public, on the Subject of the Late Riots at Birmingham, in Vindication of the Clergy, and Oter Respectable Inhabitants...(with) Birmingham, Thurs. April 19, 1792. To the Public. Birmingham: ptd. by Thomas Pearson and sold by R. Baldwin, London, 1792. 8vo; 2 items, issued together; xvi, 125, (1); 4 pages; stabbed, uncut as issued in fine condition.   C. R. Johnson 37-52 1996 £150.00

BURN, J. H.   A Descriptive Catalogue of the London Traders, Tavern and Coffee-House Tokens...in the Seventeenth Century, Presented by Beaufoy. London: printed for...the City of London, 1855. 2nd edition; 8vo; portrait, plates; original cloth, uncut, fine.   Peter Murray Hill 185-101 1996 £75.00

BURN, RICHARD   The Justice of the Peace and Parish Officer. London: printed by Henry Lintot...for A. Millar, in the Strand, London,... 1755. 1st edition; modern quarter calf, original labels preserved, good, clean set.   Meyer Boswell SL27-30 1996 $1,250.00

BURN, RICHARD   The Justice of the Peace, and Parish Officer. London: printed by H. Woodfall and W. Strahan for A. Millar, 1764. 9th edition; 8vo; 3 volumes, pages xxvii, 612; 540; 568, (16); contemporary calf, two labels chipped and bindings, though very strong, just little worn at edges; internally nice.   James Fenning 133-39 1996 £115.00

BURN, ROBERT SCOT   The Practical Directory for the Improvement of Landed Property. Edinburgh: Paterson, 1882. 1st edition; tall 4to; 603 pages; illustrated with 77 plates and numerous woodcuts; publisher's cloth (rebacked preserving original spines), some shelf wear rear cover stained, some minor foxing, very good, clean set.   Second Life Books 103-41 1996 $250.00

BURN, ROBERT SCOTT   Modern Building and Architecture: a Series of Working Drawings and Practical Designs... Edinburgh: A. Fulalrton, n.d., c. 1869. Large folio; (iv), 247, (1) pages, 52 double page litho plates and many wood engraved illustrations; contemporary cloth, well rebacked with calf.   Elton Engineering 10-23 1996 £680.00

BURNABY, FREDERICK   On Horseback through Asia Minor. London: Sampson Low, Marston, Searle & Rivington, Crown Buildings, 188... 1877. 1st edition; 8vo; 2 volumes, (v-vii), (ix-xiii), (xv-xxxii), 1-352 pages; (v-xix), 1-322, 323-399; frontispiece to volume 1, 3 maps, errata slip tipped in, binders stamp to front f.e.p.; bound by Riviere, full polished tan calf, double gilt rule border to boards, elaborate gilt tooling to panelled spines, morocco labels to spines, corners bumped and worn, all edges gilt, marbled endpapers.   Beeleigh Abbey BA56-47 1996 £425.00

BURNET, GILBERT, BP. OF SALISBURY 1643-1715   The Abridgement of the History of the Reformation of the Church of England... London: printed by J. D. for Rich. Chiswell, 1683. 2nd edition; 8vo; engraved title, 15 leaves, 2 plates, 319 pages, 2 plates, 384 pages; contemporary rough calf, expertly rehinged, good, sound copy. Wing B5756.   H. M. Fletcher 121-59 1996 £60.00

BURNET, GILBERT, BP. OF SALISBURY 1643-1715   An Essay on the Memory of the Late Queen. London: printed for Ric. Chiswell, 1695. 1st edition; engrved portrait; contemporary panelled calf, rubbed, label. Wing B5783.   Anthony W. Laywood 109-18 1996 £50.00

BURNET, GILBERT, BP. OF SALISBURY 1643-1715   Bishop Burnet's History of His Own Time: With the Suppressed Passages of the First Volume, and Notes by the Earls of Dartmouth and Hardwicke, and Speaker Onslow, Hitherto Unpublished. Oxford: Clarendon Press, 1823. 6 volumes; (iii)-xxxii, (602); (ii), (480); (ii), 392; (ii), (562); (ii), (452); (ii), (460) pages; 2 frontispieces; contemporary calf, spines gilt, labels; gilt stamps of united services club on spines, labels on endpapers, rubbed, some wear to corners, joints internally strengthened.   Robert Clark 38-28 1996 £110.00

BURNET, GILBERT, BP. OF SALISBURY 1643-1715   The Memoires of the Lives and Actions of James and William, Dukes of Hamilton and Castleherald, &c. London: printed by J. Grover, for R. Royston, 1677. 1st edition; small folio; 436, (12) pages; engraved portraits. contemporary full calf, spine and covers worn, some loss of leather at spine, engraved 'Downfield' bookplate, else nice, crisp and clean internally, with few instances of neat marginalia in unidentified 17th century hand.   Chapel Hill 94-354 1996 $300.00

BURNET, GILBERT, BP. OF SALISBURY 1643-1715   Some Letters Containing, an Account of What Seemed Most Remarkable in Switzerland, Italy &c. Rotterdam: printed by Abraham Archer, Bookseller by the Exchange, 1686. New edition; 3-303 pages, addenda 305-6 pages, errata leaf; full calf, corners restored, joints cracked and tender, red morocco label to spines, gilt tooling to compartments, edges speckled, owner's bookplate to front pastedown, owner's ink inscription to first page of text and front f.e.p., crudely repaired, 2 previous catalog descriptions loosely inserted. Wing B5915; Cox I p. 110; Lowndes I p. 319.   Beeleigh Abbey BA56-46 1996 £65.00

BURNET, JOHN   Practical Hints on Colour in Painting, Illustrated by Examples fromt he Works of the Venetian, Flemish and Dutch Schools. London: printed for the Proprietor & sold by James Carpenter and Son, 1827. tall 4to; 8 inserted hand colored plates; boards, label, covers separated, ex-library with mark on front cover, bookplate and stamps, text and plates clean and nice.   Freedom Bookshop 14-7 1996 $125.00

BURNET, THOMAS   Essays Divine, Moral and Political. London: printed in the year 1714. 1st edition; 8vo; frontispiece; disbound; very good, scarce. Teerink 1082; Rothschild 2213.   Ximenes 108-49 1996 $450.00

BURNET, THOMAS   De Fide & Officiis Christianorum Liber. Londini: 1722. 4to; (iv), 223, (i) pages; contemporary blindstamped calf, rubbed, lacks label, short splits in joints, minor foxing. Sound copy.   Robert Clark 38-167 1996 £65.00

BURNET, THOMAS   The Sacred Theory of the Earth...With a Review of the Theory... London: H. Lintot, 1734. 4th English edition; 8vo; 2 volumes; portrait, engraved title, 13 engraved illustrations of which 10 are separate plates, and the other 3 printed in text, minor waterstains, one plate torn at fold; contemporary calf, bit worn, one label chipped, probably a Scottish binding, names Geo Ross 1758 and James Dowd(?) 1765 on titles.   Maggs Bros. Ltd. 1190-279 1996 £145.00

BURNETT, FRANCES HODGSON   Editha's Burglar. Boston: Jordan Marsh, 1888. 1st American and 1st separate edition; 4to; 14 full page illustrations by Henry Sandham, 2 pages of facsimile writing, ad leaf; original pictorial cloth, gilt; very good. BAL 2071 (2nd state of copyright page).   Trebizond 39-1 1996 $100.00

BURNETT, FRANCES HODGSON   Little Lord Fauntleroy. New York: Charles Scribner's Sons, 1886. 1st edition; square octavo; xi, 209 pages, plus (16) pages ads; illustrations; original brown cloth, pictorially stamped in red, black and gilt on front cover and spine, light wear to extremities, just slightly skewed, over opened at few gatherings, little minor soiling; very good.   Heritage Book Shop 196-265 1996 $350.00

BURNETT, FRANCES HODGSON   Queen Silver-Bell. London: Warne & Co., 1907. 1st English edition; small square 8vo; i, 94 pages, endpapers very browned, color frontispiece, 18 color plates, 1 text illustrations; brown cloth, onlaid extra color plate; very good.   Robin Greer 94A-23 1996 £68.00

BURNETT, PETER H.   Recollections and Opinions of an Old Pioneer. New York: D. Appleton and Co., 1880. 1st edition; 7 3/4 x 5 inches; xiv, 448 pages, 6 pages of ads; black and gold stamped dark yellow cloth, spotting to rear cover, rear free endpaper lacking, small amount of marginal staining. Zamorano 80 13.   Dawson's Books Shop 528-16 1996 $300.00

BURNETT, WILLIAM HICKLING   Views of Cintra. London: Joseph Dickinson, n.d., ca. 1835. 14 litho plates on india paper; mounted, printed by Hullmandel; original printed wrpapers, neatly rebacked, fitted morocco backed case. Small marginal dampstain on few plates not affecting iage. Not in Abbey.   Marlborough 162-224 1996 £2,800.00

BURNEY, CAROLINE   Seraphina; or, a Winter in Town. London: printed for J. F. Hughes, 1809. 1st edition; 12mo; 3 volumes; some foxing, contemporary marbled boards, neat new calf spines. Block p. 30; 2 copies in NUC.   James Burmester 29-156 1996 £1,500.00

BURNEY, CHARLES   Dr. Burney's Musical Tours in Europe. London: Oxford University Press, 1959. 1st edition; tall octavo; 2 volumes, pages 328, 268; portraits; tan buckram, gilt, map endpapers; fine in price clipped dust jackets.   Hartfield 48-V5 1996 $195.00

BURNEY, FRANCES   Tragic Dramas... London: printed by Thomas Davison, for the author and sold by J. Murray, 1818. 1st edition; 8vo; contemporary calf, panelled in blind, gilt borders, spine and inner dentelels gilt, marbled edges, some rubbing, spine dull; half title present, very good; bookplate of the Earl of Craven and later bookplate of Robert William Rogers. Stratman 719.   Ximenes 108-51 1996 $275.00

BURNEY, JAMES   A Chronological History of the North-Eastern Voyages of Discovery and of the Early Eastern Navigations of the Russians, by Captain James Burney, F.R.S. Amsterdam: N. Isreal, 1969. Facsimile edition; 22cm; viii, 310 pages; frontispiece, folding map and one other; gilt stamped mock cream vellum; fine. Sabin 9386; Smith 1283; Strathern 80.   Rockland Books 38-35 1996 $100.00

BURNEY, SARAH HARRIET		Traits of Nature... London: Henry Colburn, 1812. 1st edition; 12mo; 5 volumes; half titles, evidently not called for; contemporary quarter calf,gilt, marbled boards; bindings somewhat rubbed, but attractive, few leaves torn, with no loss, overall very good. Trebizond 39-11 1996 $375.00

BURNHAM, HAROLD B.		Keep Me Warm One Night: Early Handweaving in Eastern Canada. Toronto: University of Toronto Press, 1975. Large 4to; 387 pages, 491 items described and illustrated, 4 color plates; cloth, very good in dust jacket.		J. M. Cohen 35-9 1996 $100.00

BURNOUF, EMILE		Memoires sur l'Antiquite: l'Age du Bronze, Troie, Santorin, Delos, Ycenes, le Parthenon, les Courbes, les Propylees, un Faubourg d'Athenes. Paris: Masionneuve, 1879. 8vo; 340 pages, 4 plates; half calf, rubbed, 5 raised bands, marbled boards, bottom joint starting but holding; from the collection of Heinrich Schliemann, and was acquired by Professor Akerstrom; with facsimile letter about acquisition; inscribed "....Schliemann admiration et affection, Em. Burnouf." (closely cut at top edge by Schoemann's bookbinder), also noted on same page as acquired at "Athens Sept. 1955" in hand of Akerstrom. Archaeologia Luxor-3983 1996 $1,250.00

BURNS, ALLAN		Observations on the Surgical Anatomy of the Head and Neck. Edinburgh: 1811. 1st edition; 8vo; 8, 415 pages; 10 finely engraved plates; old calf, spine worn, upper hinge repaired, ex-library, lower margin of titlepage cut away removing date, else good. GM 3055. Argosy 810-83 1996 $600.00

BURNS, JOHN		Popular Directions for the Treament of the Diseases of Women and Children. London: Longman, 1811. 1st edition; 8vo; xviii, 363 pages; contemporary calf;lower cover spotted, light browning and occasional foxing; Wellcome II p. 276.		James Burmester 29-25 1996 £160.00

BURNS, R. F.		The Life and Times of the Rev. Robert Burns, D.D. Toronto: James Campbell & Son, 1872. 8vo; pages xvi 462, (ii) steel engraved frontispiece (offset on to title), engraved title, 2 woodcuts; original cloth, gilt extra over bevelled boards, spine little faded, all edges gilt, presentation copy from publisher to Rev. J. C. Burns (descendant of the subject). With APS from James C. Burns.		R.F.G. Hollett 76-50 1996 £65.00

BURNS, ROBERT 1759-1796		Aloway Kirk; or Tam o'Shanter. N.P.: Glasgow?: n.d. 1796? 8vo; this variant has 'doon' as the last word on page 2; half brown morocco gilt, spine gilt by Kerr & Richardson, Glasgow; fine.		Ximenes 109-58 1996 $750.00

BURNS, ROBERT 1759-1796		The Correspondence Between Burns and Clarinda. Edinburgh: William Tait, 1843. 1st authorised edition; 8vo; pages xii, 297, (2 ads); frontispiece, additional decorative titlepage; original binding; very good to nice. Egerer 449.		James Fenning 133-40 1996 £75.00

BURNS, ROBERT 1759-1796		The Jolly Beggars. Northampton: Gehenna Press, 1963. 11.25 x 9 inches; wood engraved portrait of Burns by Gillian Lewis printed from block; printed in black with red on Amalfi handmade Italian paper; brown cloth spine with paper title label, marbled paper boards, printed label on front cover, matching slipcase (rubbed); book fine. Gehenna Press, Work of 50 Years #34.		Joshua Heller 21-124 1996 $150.00

BURNS, ROBERT 1759-1796		The Letters of Robert Burns, Chronologically Arranged from Dr. Currie's Collection. London: John Sharpe, 1819. 5 1/4 x 3 1/2 inches; 2 volumes in one; engraved title for each volume; quite attractive contemporary wine colored straight grain morocco, covers with double gilt rule border, wide raised bands and spine compartments ornately gilt, spine slightly and evenly faded to a pleasing light brown, little foxing on engraved leaves, otherwise very fine, virtually no wear to binding, text extraordinarily clean and fresh.		Phillip J. Pirages 33-116 1996 $150.00

BURNS, ROBERT 1759-1796		Poems Chiefly in the Scottish Dialect... London: for A. Strahan, T. Cadell and W. Creech, Edinburgh, 1787. 1st London edition; 8vo; pages xlviii (including list of subscribers), 13-372; frontispiece; contemporary diced russia, thick single fillet gilt border to sides, spine in compartments with gilt rules, brown morocco label, marbled endpapers, spine slightly faded, small hole to lower cover), protected in quarter calf book-form box, spine ruled and lettered in gilt, red and brown morocco labels, excellent, clean copy. Gibson p. 6. Simon Finch 24-24 1996 £450.00

BURNS, ROBERT 1759-1796		Poems, Chiefly in the Scottish Dialect. New York: John Tiebout, 1799. 3rd American edition; 8vo; pages 5, (9)-306 pages; lacking covers, sound; CBEL II 974; not in Evans, Shipton Mooney or Bristol, not in NUC.		M & S Rare Books 60-127 1996 $375.00

BURNS, ROBERT 1759-1796		Poems Chiefly in the Scottish Dialect. Glasgow: ca. 1900. Reduced facsimile of first edition; 1 3/16 x 7/8 inches; 240 pages; printed wrappers, housed in silvertone locket with magnifying glass on cover, very fine. Spielmann 69.		Bromer Booksellers 87-197 1996 $185.00

BURNS, ROBERT 1759-1796		Poems and Letters in the Handwriting of Robert Burns. Saint Louis: printed for the Burns Club, 1908. Limited edition of 300 numbered copies; folio; printed on Dutch handmade paper; numerous tipped in plates or ms. facsimiles; original half paper parchment and boards; very good, some browning to spine; signed presentation copy from William K. Bixby, the principal owner of the manuscripts reproduced herein, to the Hon. Albert Douglass.		Antic Hay 101-262 1996 $185.00

BURNS, ROBERT 1759-1796		The Poetry. London: Blackie and Son, 1859 Small 4to; 2 volumes; pages cclxxvi, 149; xiv, 410; 2 engraved vignette titles, 49 engraved plates, rather foxed or spotted in places; contemporary half calf, gilt, trifle rubbed and marked.		R.F.G. Hollett 76-47 1996 £65.00

BURNS, ROBERT 1759-1796		The Poetry. London: Blackie and Son, 1861. Small 4to; 2 volumes; pages cclxxvi, 149; xiv, 410; 2 engraved vignettes and 49 engraved plates; contemporary half calf, raised bands, double spine labels, trifle rubbed, patterned boards little stained and marked; occasional spot or mark, but very clean internally.		R.F.G. Hollett 76-48 1996 £75.00

BURNS, ROBERT 1759-1796		The Poetry. Edinburgh: T. C. and E. C. Jack, 1896. 8vo; 4 volumes; portraits and facsimiles; original decorated cream cloth, gilt, spines trifle darkened, top edge gilt, untrimmed, very nice set.		R.F.G. Hollett 76-46 1996 £75.00

BURNS, ROBERT 1759-1796		Reliques...Consisting Chiefly of Original Letters, Poems and Critical Observataions on Scottish Songs. Philadelphia: pub. by R. H. Cromek, 1809. 12mo; 20, 294 pages; contemporary tree calf, leather label, slightly scuffed, but very nice. Ink signature of Jo(seph) Gratz, brother of Rebecca. S&S 17127.		M & S Rare Books 60-186 1996 $200.00

BURNS, ROBERT 1759-1796		Tam O'Shanter. London: Edward Arnold, 1902. Limited to 150 copies; octavo; 12 pages; printed entirely on vellum; frontispiece by William Strang and hand colored opening woodcut initial, initials that follow are rendered in colors and gold leaf by Florence Kingsford; full vellum over boards, blindstamped with rose logo and motto of this series "Soul is Form", very fine.		Bromer Booksellers 87-66 1996 $525.00

BURNS, ROBERT 1759-1796		The Works of Robert Burns. 1877. 8vo; 2 volumes, over 600 pages, over 80 engravings; half black calf, title labels inset on red morocco, very good.		K Books 442-95 1996 £100.00

BURNS, ROBERT 1759-1796		Complete Works. Edinburgh: 1883. Limited to 500 copies; large 8vo; 6 volumes; each volume with frontispiece and vignette, folding facsimile; original cloth.		Charles W. Traylen 117-81 1996 £60.00

BURNS, ROBERT 1869-1944		Sir Patric Spens, The Wife of Usher's Well and The Bonnie Rle of Moray. London: privately printed by Robert Burns, 1930. 1st edition; Number 4 in an edition of 12 copies, signed by Burns; 70 pages; 69 large photographic plates mounted on white paper comprising title vignette, 26 full page plates, 35 smaller illustrations and hand lettered text, handwritten limitation note; grey cloth.		Robin Greer 94A-22 1996 £350.00

BURNSIDE, HELEN MARION		A Birthday Present. London: Ernest Nister, n.d. ca. 1890. 1st edition; 12mo; 12 pages; 4 color plates and 8 sepia text illustrations by E. S. Hardy; red cloth, spine extra color pictorial cream boards, light foxing; excellent copy.		Robin Greer 94A-60 1996 £65.00

BURNSIDE, HELEN MARION		Wonderland Pictures. London: Nister No. 456, n.d., ca. 1890. Square 8vo; 6 full color circular transformation pictures in floral borders, operated by a ribbon, when ribbon is moved to side, a kaleidoscope pattern is revealed; colored pictorial boards, rear cover soiled, else very good.		Marjorie James 19-159 1996 £425.00

BURNSIDE, WESLEY M.		Maynard Dixon: Artist of the West. Provo: Brigham Young University Press, 1974. 10 1/2 x 13 inches; xvi, 237 pages; plethora of full page color reproductions, other illustrations in text; tan cloth boards, brown fabricoid spine in dust jacket, publisher's shrink wrap.		Dawson's Books Shop 528-17 1996 $150.00

BURNYEAT, JOHN   The Truth Exalted in the Writings of that Eminent and Faithful Servant of Christ, John Burnyeat... London: printed for Thomas Northcott, 1691. 1st edition; square 8vo; pages (i), 264; modern full polished calf, gilt, raised bands, boards ruled in blind in 17th century style, very damped and fragile in places, with number of edge repairs, title laid down, lacking all but last leaf of Penn's introduction, but with separate printing of verse on verso of leaf loosely inserted; scarce. R.F.G. Hollett & Son 78-341 1996 £65.00

BURR, AARON   The Private Journal of Aaron Burr, During His Residence of Four Years in Europe. New York: Harper & Bros., 1838. 1st edition; 2 volumes; green cloth, titled in gilt, moderate foxing, heaviest to prelims, joints and hinges tight, very respectable set. Hermitage SP95-1095 1996 $175.00

BURR, AARON   Reports of the Trials of Col. Aaron Burr...for Treason and for a Misdeameanor...in the Circuit Court of the United States. Philadelphia: Hopkins and Earle, 1808. 1st edition; 2 volumes, (x), 596, (iv), 539 pages; original calf, some wormholes along bottom edge of spine of volume 1, covers worn and peeling in places, scattered foxing, otherwise tight and sound set, usually seen in worse condition or rebound.   Metacomet Books 54-16 1996 $400.00

BURRANRD, G.   Big Game Hunting in the Himalayas and Tibet. 1925. illustrations; original blue cloth; fine.   David Grayling J95Biggame-492 1996 £125.00

BURRISH, ONSLOW   Batavia Illustrata; or, a View of the Policy and Commerce of the United Provinces... London: printed for W. Innys, J. Osborne (and 9 others), 1731. 2nd edition; 8vo; surface of last page slightly defective due to adhesion to facing flyleaf, contemporary calf, slightly worn, spine gilt, label. Kress 3740 and Goldsmith 6576. Anthony Laywood 108-35 1996 £275.00

BURROUGHS, EDGAR RICE 1875-1950   At the Earth's Core. Chicago: A. C. McClurg & Co., 1922. 1st edition; 9 black and white paltes by J. Allen St. John; piece torn from bottom corner of pages 239-240 (does not affect text), rear inner hinge cracked, few light spots to front cover, otherwise very good.   Steven C. Bernard 71-388 1996 $500.00

BURROUGHS, EDGAR RICE 1875-1950   The Beasts of Tarzan. Chicago: McClurg, 1916. 1st edition; illustrations, spine little sunned; near fine. Polyanthos 22-741 1996 $200.00

BURROUGHS, EDGAR RICE 1875-1950   Carson of Venus. Burroughs, 1939. 1st edition; very good+/near fine in bright very good dust jacket with some light wear and tear and chipping.   Aronovitz 57-211 1996 $195.00

BURROUGHS, EDGAR RICE 1875-1950   The Chessmen of Mars. London: Methuen, 1923. 1st English edition; St. John illustrations; small cloth loss at outer hinges, else bright very good+/near fine copy in very good dust jacket with some light wear and tear, quite scarce in dust jacket.   Aronovitz 57-208 1996 $1,175.00

BURROUGHS, EDGAR RICE 1875-1950   I Am a Barbarian. Tarzana: Burroughs, 1967. 1st edition; 8vo; black and white frontispiece, color jacket illustration by Jeff Jones; very good to fine, dust jacket. George J. Houle 68-19 1996 $150.00

BURROUGHS, EDGAR RICE 1875-1950   John Carter of Mars. New York: Canaveral Press, 1964. 1st edition; 1st binding (1500 copies); 8 full page black and white drawings by Reed Crandall; near fine in very slightly rubbed dust jacket.   Steven C. Bernard 71-392 1996 $100.00

BURROUGHS, EDGAR RICE 1875-1950   Llana of Gathol. Tarzana: Edgar Rice Burroughs, 1948. 1st edition; 8vo; full page black and white illustrations and color jacket design by John Coleman Burroughs; blue cloth, stamped in red on spine and upper cover, top edge stained brick red, uncut, color pictorial dust jacket; very good.   George J. Houle 68-20 1996 $250.00

BURROUGHS, EDGAR RICE 1875-1950   Llana of Gathol. Tarzana: 1948. 1st edition; 7.5 x 5 inches; 317 pages; illustrations by John Coleman Burroughs, cloth, good in slightly edge chipped and tape reinforced dust jacket.   John K. King 77-632 1996 $125.00

BURROUGHS, EDGAR RICE 1875-1950   A Princess of Mars. New York: Pratt Adlib Press, 1965. One of an edition of 500 signed by artist; large quarto; (8)ff. frenchfold; printed from relief plates hand etched by Rothbert, as Keepsake no. 9 of the Adlib Press; white on black illustrations; self wrappers; fine.   Bromer Booksellers 90-219 1996 $125.00

BURROUGHS, EDGAR RICE 1875-1950   Synthetic Men of Mars. Tarzana: ERB, Inc., 1940. 1st edition; 1st state (laminated) dust jacket; 5 black and white plates by John Coleman Burroughs; fine, bright, near fine dust jacket which is a bit soiled on rear panel.   Steven C. Bernard 71-396 1996 $500.00

BURROUGHS, EDGAR RICE 1875-1950   Tarzan and the Forbidden City. Burroughs, 1938. 1st edition; near fine in dust jacket.   Aronovitz 57-210 1996 $325.00

BURROUGHS, EDGAR RICE 1875-1950   Tarzan and the Foreign Legion. Tarzana: Edgar Rice Burroughs, 1947. 1st edition; 8vo; five full page black and white illustrations and color jacket design by John Coleman Burroughs; blue cloth stamped in red on spine and upper cover, top edge stained red, uncut, color pictorial dust jacket, very good to fine. George J. Houle 68-21 1996 $200.00

BURROUGHS, EDGAR RICE 1875-1950   Tarzan and the Golden Lion. Chicago: McClurg, 1923. 1st edition; 1st issue; very good in dust jacket, jacket moderately soiled and has archival repair which covers about one third of the lower spine, very scarce in dust jacket.   Captain's Bookshelf 38-28 1996 $750.00

BURROUGHS, EDGAR RICE 1875-1950   Tarzan of the Apes. Burt, 1917. 1st edition; bright, very good+/near fine copy in very good dust jacket save for some light wear to dust jacket spine extremities.   Aronovitz 57-204 1996 $225.00

BURROUGHS, EDGAR RICE 1875-1950   The Warlords of Mars. Chicago: 1919. 1st edition; 1st issue with 'W.F. Hall' on copyright page; bright, near fine copy.   Stephen Lupack 83- 1996 $150.00

BURROUGHS, JOHN ROLFE   Guardian of the Grasslands. Cheyenne: Pioneer Printing & Stationery Co., 1971. 1st edition; quarto; viii, 430 pages; color frontispiece, gilt lettered green cloth; very fine with pictorial dust jacket. Reese Adams One Fifty 22.   Argonaut Book Shop 113-106 1996 $150.00

BURROUGHS, RAYMOND DARWIN   The Natural History of the Lewis and Clark Expedition. N.P.: Michigan State University Press, c. 1961. 8vo; xii, 340 pages; black cloth, very good in lightly worn dust jacket. Parmer Books Nat/Hist-43084 1996 $125.00

BURROUGHS, WILLIAM S.   Dead Fingers Talk. C&B, 1963. 1st edition; signed by author; fine in near fine dust jacket.   Aronovitz 57-216 1996 $295.00

BURROUGHS, WILLIAM S.   Exterminator. New York: Viking Press, 1973. 1st edition; beautiful copy in price clipped dust jacket; signed by author.   Left Bank Books 2-17 1996 $100.00

BURROUGHS, WILLIAM S.   Junkie. New York: 1953. 1st edition; 6.5 x 4 inches; 149 pages; pictorial wrappers, bit stained, worn and wrinkled; author's first book.   John K. King 77-222 1996 $250.00

BURROUGHS, WILLIAM S.   The Last Words of Dutch Schultz. London: Cape Goliard Press, 1970. 1st edition; one of 100 copies, numbered and signed by author; 8vo; frontispiece by Kitaj; cloth, glassine dust jacket, mint.   James S. Jaffe 34-95 1996 $350.00

BURROUGHS, WILLIAM S.   The Naked Lunch. London: 1964. 1st English edition; very good in dust jacket.   Words Etcetera 94-253 1996 £50.00

BURROUGHS, WILLIAM S.   The Soft Machine. New York: Grove Press, 1966. 1st American edition; near fine in near fine dust jacket; inscribed by author.   Revere Books 4-65 1996 $100.00

BURROUGHS, WILLIAM S.   The Streets of Chance. New York: Ozier Press, 1981. 1st edition; one of 160 copies, signed by author and artist; 8vo; drawings by Howard Buchwald; decorated boards, with 2 prospectuses, one inscribed by publishers, Steve Miller and Ken Botnick, laid in, along with 2 postcards signed by Miller; mint.   James S. Jaffe 34-565 1996 $250.00

BURROWS, GEORGE MAN   An Inquiry into Certain Errors Relative to Insanity; and Their Consequences; Physical, Moral and Civil. London: printed for Thomas and George Underwood, 1820. ix, (1), 320 pages; original grey boards, uncut, paper label, spine defective at top, but very good. Hunter & Macalpine pp. 777-783.   C. R. Johnson 37-78 1996 £650.00

BURROWS, J. E.   Southern African Ferns and Fern Allies. Sandton: 1990. 4to; pages xiii, 359; colored frontispiece, 26 colored photos, 56 colored plates, 83 pages of line drawings, 300 distribution maps; cloth, dust jacket.   Raymond M. Sutton VII-91 1996 $135.00

BURRUS, ERNEST J.   Kino and the Cartography of Northwestern New Spain. Tucson: Arizona Pioneers' Historical Society, 1965. 750 copies printed; folio; 21 maps and plates, pages (10), 104; original binding, gilt, nice.   James Fenning 133-41 1996 $55.00

BURSILL, HENRY   Hand Shadows to be Thrown Upon the Wall. London: Griffith and Farran, 1860. 5th edition; 4to; 4 pages plus 18 hand colored plates of hand shadows, 4 page publisher's catalog bound in; original cloth backed pictorial boards, corners rubbed, very good, scarce.   J. M. Cohen 35-8 1996 $175.00

BURTON, GILBERT   The Life of Sir Philip Musgrave, Bart, of Hartley Castle, Westmorland and of Edenhall, Co. Cumberland, Governor of the City of Carlisle... Carlisle: Samuel Jefferson, 1840. 8vo; pages 56, (ii ads); printed on pale blue paper; original stiff wrappers, paper label.   R.F.G. Hollett & Son 78-126 1996 $65.00

BURTON, JOHN   Monasticon Eboracense; and the Ecclesiastical History of Yorkshire. York: printed for the author by N. Nickson, 1758. 1st edition; folio; 3 engraved folding plates, small hole in b1 and c1 with loss of a word; contemporary calf, slightly worn, hinges cracked, label chipped; bookplate of Hon. Constantine John Phipps, Marquess of Normanby.   Anthony W. Laywood 109-19 1996 £245.00

BURTON, MARIA AMPARO RUIZ   The Squatter and the Don. San Francisco: 1885. 1st edition; 8vo; 421 pages; original cloth, slightly scuffed; very scarce; Wright III 845.   M & S Rare Books 60-129 1996 $175.00

BURTON, RICHARD FRANCIS   The Jew, the Gypsy and El Islam. Chicago & New York: Stone, 1898. Tall 8vo; xix, 351 pages; frontispiece; original cloth, slightly rubbed, bookplate removed from inner front cover, otherwise very good, top edge gilt.   Worldwide Antiquarian 151-113 1996 $250.00

BURTON, RICHARD FRANCIS 1821-1890   Falconry in the Valley of the Indus. London: John Van Voorst, 1852. 1st edition; large 12mo; pages xvi, 17, (xiii ads), 1 tinted lithograph frontispiece by Joseph Wolf and 3 other tinted lithograph plates; original dark purple cloth, lettered in gilt, usual fading to spine, spine slightly chipped at the head and foot, slight foxing to frontispiece, front endpaper and half title, small tear to upper margin of pages vii (expertly repaired and not affecting text), otherwise good firm and clean copy, rare. Casada 34; Penzer 41.   Sotheran PN32-59 1996 £1,450.00

BURTON, RICHARD FRANCIS 1821-1890   The Kasidah of Haji Abdu El Yezdi. New York: Limited Editions Club, 1937. Copy number 904 from a total edition of 1500 numbered copies, signed by artist; illustrations and decorations by Valenti Angelo; full purple leather with tissue jacket, liner and slipcase; very nice.   Hermitage SP95-949 1996 $125.00

BURTON, RICHARD FRANCIS 1821-1890   Letters from the Battle-Fields of Paraguay. London: Tinsley Bros., 18 Catherine Steet, Strand, 1870. 1st edition; 2nd issue(?); 8vo; (vii-xvi), (xvii-xix), 1-481 pages, 483-491; frontispiece, 1 large folding map, previous owner's bookplate, some very light foxing to half title and prelims, otherwise good, tight copy, uncommon; half red straight grain morocco and marbled boards, gilt title and floral device to spine, raised bands to spine, top edge gilt, marbled endpapers (uniform with boards). Penzer p. 84.   Beeleigh Abbey BA56-48 1996 £550.00

BURTON, ROBERT 1577-1640   The Anatomy of Melancholy, What It Is. Oxford: John Lichfield and James Short for Henry Cripps, 1621. 1st edition; small 4to; pages (iv), 783, (8); contemporary Oxford calf, sides with triple rule border and central arabesque in blind, spine in compartments with raised bands, slightly rubbed, joints repaired at head and foot, headcaps and corners repaired, Gg3-6 and Rr8 from another copy, some worming at margins, occasionally affecting sidenotes; contemporary signature of Thomas Nicholson on rear pastedown endpaper, ms. annotations in outer margins and few underlinings, last leaf of text, errata leaf, rear free endpaper copiously annotated. STC 4159; Pforzheimer 119; PMM 120.   Simon Finch 24-25 1996 £12,000.00

BURTON, ROBERT 1577-1640   The Anatomy of Melancholy. Oxford: J. Litchfield & J. Short for H. Cripps, 1621. 1st edition; small 4to; with errata leaf (Ddd4) which is un folio'd, and the preceding leaf Ddd3; tiny hole in Hh6 affecting a few words; full crushed morocco with outer gilt fillet border inside of which is a blind fillet border, three quarter of an inch inside this outermost border are two sets of gilt and blind fillet borders, about one quarter inch apart and on the corners of this inner set of borders are four gilt fleurons, spine divided into six compartments by five raised bands, second and third of which contain the title information, others each contain a gilt fleuron and some gilt border decoration, board edges gilt with single gilt fillet, inner gilt fillets stamped at bottom of front turn-in, bound by Riviere & Son; in half morocco slipcase with inner chemise; with bookplates of T. G. Arthur and Mortimer L. Schiff. Grolier English 18; PMM 120; Maden/Oxford Books I, 115. II 90.   Book Block 32-52 1996 $14,500.00

BURTON, ROBERT 1577-1640   The Anatomy of Melancholy... London: 1800. 9th edition; 8vo; 2 volumes; later 19th century half polished calf and marbled boards, gilt tooling, raised bands, crisp, handsome binding. James Tait Goodrich K40-72 1996 $195.00

BURTON, ROBERT 1577-1640   The Anatomy of Melancholy, What It is, With All the Kinds, Causes, Symptoms, prognostics and Several Cures Of It. London: 1849. 748 pages; fine engraved frontispiece; original binding. W. Bruce Fye 71-277 1996 $100.00

BURTON, ROBERT 1577-1640   The Anatomy of Melancholy. New York: George H. Doran Co., 1927. One of 500 copies; 9 1/2 x 6 1/2 inches; 2 volumes; frontispiece facsimile in 2nd volume, decorative initials; half vellum over tan paper boards, flat spines ruled and titled in gilt, top edges gilt, other edges untrimmed; trivial soiling to bindings, otherwise fine.   Phillip J. Pirages 33-117 1996 $125.00

BURTON, WILLIAM   The Description of Leicester Shire. London: John White, 1622. 1st edition; folio; frontispiece laid down with some loss, engraved titlepage, frayed at edge and very small hole, lower right hand corner of prelim leaf torn away without loss, slight worming to inner margin of a few leaves not affecting text, correction to page numbers towards fear in ink, lacks folding map and final leaf, else complete; numerous woodcut arms in text; rebound in quarter brown moroco, morocco label, rare; title signed in ink "William Burton".   Ian Wilkinson 95/1-49 1996 £185.00

BURTON-ON-TRENT NATURAL HISTORY AND ARCHAEOLOGICAL SOCIETY Transactions of the Burton-on-Trent Natural History and Archaeological Society. London: Bemrose & Sons/ & Derby: John C. Perfect.../Burton on Trent 1889-1927. 8vo; 9 volumes in 4, numerous plates, plans and maps and illustrations in text; uniform half calf, original printed wrappres bound in, labels.   Anthony W. Laywood 109-20 1996 £165.00

BURY, ADRIAN   John Varley of the "Old Society". Leigh-on-Sea: F. Lewis, 1946. Limited edition, number 202 of 500 copies; 8vo; 85 pages, 3 color plates, 73 black and white plates; buckram.   Rainsford A54-560 1996 $65.00

BUSH & SON & MEISSNER   Illustrated Descriptive Catalogue of American Grape Vines, a Grape Growers' Manual. St. Louis: 1883. 3rd edition; 8vo; 153 pages; 2 chromolithgraphic plates, plus numerous engravings; original cloth, some wear and soiling, 2 contemporary sheets of notes taped to endpapers, some dampstaining to upper page corners, occasional pencil marks in text.   Raymond M. Sutton VII-859 1996 $200.00

BUSH, BENJAMIN   The Drunkard's Emblem; or, an Enquiry into the Effects of Ardent Spirits Upon the Human Body and Mind. Winchester: printed by Jonathan Foster, 1811. 12mo; disbound; very good; not in Austin, not in Shaw and Shoemaker.   Ximenes 108-314 1996 $350.00

BUSH, I. J.   Gringo Doctor. Caldwell: Caxton, 1939. 1st edition; 261 pages; illustrations; dust jacket. Six Guns 348.   Maggie Lambeth 30-75 1996 $100.00

BUSH, J.   Hibernia Curiosa: a Letter from a Gentleman in Dublin. London: 1769. 8vo; 6 folding plates; half sheep, needs recasing, but text very good.   C. P. Hyland 216-69 1996 £180.00

BUSH, JAMES   The Choice: or Lines on the Beatitudes. London: R. Saywell; Cockermouth: Bailey & Sons; Carlisle: C. Thurman, 1841. Square 8vo; pages 102; frontispiece foxed; full polished calf, gilt, edges rubbed; presentation copy inscribed by author to Mrs. Joshua Stranger.   R.F.(. Hollett & Son 78-342 1996 £65.00

BUTLER, A. W.   The Birds of Indiana, a Descriptive Catalogue of the Birds that Have Been Observed Within the State, with an Account of Their Habits. Indianapolis: 1898. 8vo; cloth, 673 pages, 5 plates, 112 figures; cloth.   Wheldon & Wesley 207-681 1996 £50.00

BUTLER, ARTHUR GARDINER   British Birds, with their nests and Eggs. London: n.d. 1896-99. Large 4to; 6 volumes, 318 plates, 24 colored plates, original cloth, gilt tops. Mullens and Swann p. 111.   Charles W. Traylen 117-288   1996 £90.00

BUTLER, ELIZABETH   A Memoir of the Very Rev. Richard Butler, Vicar of Trim. 1863. 8vo; quarter leather, good. Presentation copy to Lady Elizabeth Brownlow.   C. P. Hyland 216-71   1996 £110.00

BUTLER, GERALD   Kiss the Blood Off My Hands. New York: F&R, 1946. 1st English edition; light wear, few pages in middle of text, with slight bend, else about fine in near fine dust jacket with some rubbing and light wear on spine and tiny tear at base of front panel. Scarce. Between the Covers 42-475 1 996 $175.00

BUTLER, HOWARD CROSBY   Sardis. Volume I (only): The Excavations, Part I. 1910-1914. Leyden: E. J. Brill, 1922. Folio; xi, 213 pages with 192 illustrations and 5 plates, 3 folding maps; original cloth backed boards, two small tears at head of spine, boards lightly soiled.   Archaeologia Luxor-3958 1996 $650.00

BUTLER, HOWARD CROSBY   Sardis. Volume II: Architecture. Part I (only), The Temple of Artemis. Leyden: E. J. Brill, 1925. Folio; xiii, 146 pages, 135 illustrations, 3 plates; original cloth backed boards, minor discolorations to top board, scarce; atlas portfolio of 19 plates is not present.   Archaeologia Luxor-3959   1996 $450.00

BUTLER, JAMES D.   A September Scamper. N.P.: c. 1877. 1st edition; 32 pages; illustrations; original printed wrappers, minor staining, very good, rare. Adams Herd 387;   Michael D. Heaston 23-57   1996 $350.00

BUTLER, ROBERT OLEN   The Alleys of Eden. New York: Horizon, 1981. 1st edition; very near fine in dust jacket, signed by author. Lame Duck Books 19-103 1996 $250.00

BUTLER, ROBERT OLEN   The Alleys of Eden. New York: Horizon, 1981. 1st edition; 2 small splatter marks on front endpapers (binder's glue?), otherwise very fine in fine dust jacket, quite scarce.   Ken Lopez 74-69 1996 $250.00

BUTLER, ROBERT OLEN   The Alleys of Eden. New York: Horizon, 1981. 1st edition; previous owner name, otherwise near fine in near fine dust jacket, nice.   Ken Lopez 74-70   1996 $175.00

BUTLER, ROBERT OLEN   The Alleys of Eden. New York: Horizon Press, 1981. 1st edition; fine in near fine dust jacket which is very lightly rubbed on front panel.   Bud Schweska 12-1317 1996 $175.00

BUTLER, ROBERT OLEN   A Good Scent from a Strange Mountains. New York: Holt, 1990. Uncorrected proof; printed green wrappers with publisher's ads pasted and stapled to front wrapper, signed by author; fine.   Lame Duck Books 19-104   1996 $150.00

BUTLER, ROBERT OLEN   A Good Scent from a Strange Mountain. New York: Holt, 1992. 1st edition;, with a small printing of 7500 copies; signed by author; fine in dust jacket.   Thomas Dorn 9-67 1996 $100.00

BUTLER, ROBERT OLEN   A Good Scent from a Strange Mountain. New York: Holt, 1992. 1st edition; fine in dust jacket, signed by author. Between the Covers 42-74   1996 $150.00

BUTLER, ROBERT OLEN   A Good Scent from a Strange Mountain. New York: Henry Holt, 1992. 1st edition; first printing of 7500 copies; very fine in fine dust jacket, signed and dated 5-25-93 by author.   Bud Schweska 12-1321   1996 $100.00

BUTLER, ROBERT OLEN   On Distant Ground. New York: Knopf, 1985. 1st edition; review copy, fine in fine dust jacket.   Ken Lopez 74-72 1996 $125.00

BUTLER, ROBERT OLEN   Sun Dogs. New York: Horizon, 1982. Advance review copy with publisher's slip, signed by author; fine in near fine dust jacket.   Thomas Dorn 9-66 1996 $175.00

BUTLER, ROBERT OLEN   Sun Dogs. New York: Horizon, 1982. 1st edition; fine in near fine dust jacket.   Ken Lopez 74-71 1996 $125.00

BUTLER, ROBERT OLEN   Sun Dogs. New York: Horizon, 1982. 1st edition; fine in near fine dust jacket.   Ken Lopez 74-71 1996 $125.00

BUTLER, ROBERT OLEN   They Whisper. Huntington: Cahill, 1994. Limited edition; of a total of 150 copies, one of 26 lettered copies, signed by author; quarter leather and publisher's slipcase; fine.   Lame Duck Books 19-105 1996 $150.00

BUTLER, SAMUEL 1612-1680   Hudibras. London: T. Browne, et al, 1720. 3rd edition thus, with additions; 16mo; xiv, (19), 408 pages; frontispiece, 18 plates; contemporary half calf with morocco spine label, rear hinge reinforced internally, but nice.   Chapel Hill 94-139 1996 $200.00

BUTLER, SAMUEL 1612-1680   Hudibras. London: Baldwin, 1819. New edition; Large octavo; 3 volumes, pages lvi, 294, 390, 347; 4 pages ads; extra illustrated with more than 60 portrait engravings, numerous vignettes, tailpieces, etc.; full green polished morocco, blind and gilt fillets, raised bands, gilt in panels, later gilt on red leather labels, marbled endpapers, handsomely bound large paper set. Lowndes I 313. Hartfield 48-L20 1996 $695.00

BUTLER, SAMUEL 1612-1680   Hudibras... London: 1835. New edition; 8vo; 2 volumes, over 650 pages; portrait; half calf, raised bands, title labels inset on red and black morocco, good set.   K Books 441-81 1996 £60.00

BUTLER, SAMUEL 1835-1902   Alps and Actuaries of Piedmont and the Canton Ticino. London: David Bogue, 1882. Longmans reissue with cancel title and binding in lighter shade of brown; half title, frontispiece, illustrations; original brown cloth, bevelled edges; David Garnett's copy with his bookplate. With inscription "Given by Samuel Butler to Robert Singleton Garnett and Martha Garnett (nee Roscoe) on their marriage 25th June 1896". Hoppe 13 pp. 35-36.   Jarndyce CII-33 1996 £250.00

BUTLER, SAMUEL 1835-1902   Alps and Sanctuaries of Piedmont and the Canton Ticino. London: A. C. Fifield, 1913. New edition; 3 loosely inserted Fifield lists; red cloth, dust jacket, very good. Hoppe 13 p. 36. Jarndyce CII-34 1996 £50.00

BUTLER, SAMUEL 1835-1902   The Authoress of the Odyssey. London: A. C. Fifield, n.d. 1908 reissue using original sheets; Original pink cloth, spine faded. Hoppe 36 pp. 71-72.   Jarndyce CII-59 1996 £50.00

BUTLER, SAMUEL 1835-1902   The Authoress of the Odyssey. London: A. C. Fifield, n.d. binding variant with front cover roundel blocked in blind, rather than gilt, spine slightly darkened.   Jarndyce CII-60 1996 £50.00

BUTLER, SAMUEL 1835-1902   The Authoress of the Odyssey. London: Longmans, Green and Co., 1897. Scarce 1st issue with uncancelled ad showing John Murray as publisher of Butler's Life and Letters of Dr. Samuel Butler, this correction was made prior to publication; original light purple cloth, spine faded; Brackenburn bookplate of Hugh Walpole. Jarndyce CII-57 1996 £120.00

BUTLER, SAMUEL 1835-1902   The Authoress of the Odyssey. London: A. C. Fifield, 1897. 1st edition; tall 8vo; 275 pages; frontispiece and 16 illustrations; red cloth, blind and gilt, very good. CBEL III 729.   Hartfield 48-V7 1996 $195.00

BUTLER, SAMUEL 1835-1902   The Authoress of the Odyssey. London: Longmans, Green and Co., 1897. 2nd issue with cancelled ad not showing John Murray as publisher of Butler's Life and Letters of Dr. Samuel Butler; original light purple cloth, spine faded, very good. Hoppe 36.   Jarndyce CII-58 1996 £90.00

BUTLER, SAMUEL 1835-1902   Butleriana. Bloomsbury: Nonesuch Press, 1932. Number 658 of 800 copies; half green calf by Sangorski & Sutcliffe, top edge gilt, booklabel of Howell L. Davies.   Jarndyce CII-98 1996 £85.00

BUTLER, SAMUEL 1835-1902   Erewhon or Over the Range. London: Trubner and Co., 1872. half title; original brown cloth, bevelled boards; nice, bookplate. Hoppe 5.   Jarndyce CII-10 1996 £350.00

BUTLER, SAMUEL 1835-1902   Erewhon or Over the Range. London: Trubner and Co., 1872. 2nd edition; half title; original dark green cloth, very slightly rubbed; Hoppe 6.   Jarndyce CII-11 1996 £90.00

BUTLER, SAMUEL 1835-1902   Erewhon or Over the Range. London: 1872. 2nd edition; half dark blue morocco by Bumpus, top edge gilt. Jarndyce CII-13   1996 £75.00

BUTLER, SAMUEL 1835-1902   Erewhon or Over the Range. London: Trubner and Co., 1872. 2nd edition; original dark green cloth, rather rubbed.   Jarndyce CII-12   1996 £60.00

BUTLER, SAMUEL 1835-1902   Erewhon or Over the Range. London: Trubner and Co., 1872. 4th edition; half title; original brown cloth bevelled boards, rather badly faded and rubbed. Hoppe 5 p. 12. Jarndyce CII-14   1996 £60.00

BUTLER, SAMUEL 1835-1902   Erewhon or Over the Range. London: Trubner and Co., 1873. 5th edition; half title with "Notices of the Press' on reverse; original brown cloth, nice. Hoppe 5 p. 12.   Jarndyce CII-15   1996 £85.00

BUTLER, SAMUEL 1835-1902   Erewhon or Over the Range. London: David Bogue, 1880. 6th edition; half title, 32 page David Bogue Catalog dated 1879; original brown cloth; nice. Hoppe 5 p. 12.   Jarndyce CII-16   1996 £75.00

BUTLER, SAMUEL 1835-1902   Erewhon or Over the Range. London: Longmans, Green & Co., 1890. 8th edition; half title, original brown cloth, fine; inscribed by author for J. P. Anderson. Hoppe 5 p. 12.   Jarndyce CII-17   1996 £200.00

BUTLER, SAMUEL 1835-1902   Erewhon or Over the Range. London: Longmans, Green & Co., 1890. 8th edition; half title; original brown cloth, very good.   Jarndyce CII-18   1996 £60.00

BUTLER, SAMUEL 1835-1902   Erewhon. London: Grant Richards, 1901. New edition; half title, 1 page ads; original red cloth bit marked and spotted, ex-library copy with section cut from front free endpaper; Hoppe 41.   Jarndyce CII-73   1996 £65.00

BUTLER, SAMUEL 1835-1902   Erewhon. Newtown: Gregynog Press, 1923. Number 59 of 300 copies; pages (2), 266, (1); 27 illustrations by Blair Hughes-Stanton; original brown calf, by Gregynog bindery, binding lightly scratched, otherwise very good to nice.   James Fenning 133-140   1996 £135.00

BUTLER, SAMUEL 1835-1902   Erewhon. New York: Limited Editions Club, 1934. Limited to 1500 copies, signed by Kent; small 4to; illustrations by Rockwell Kent; decorated cloth, slipcase, spine bit faded, otherwise fine.   James S. Jaffe 34-695   1996 $225.00

BUTLER, SAMUEL 1835-1902   Erewhon Revisited. London: Grant Richards, 1901. 1st edition; Original red cloth, very good, with original glassine dust jacket slightly torn, booklabel. With errata slip before preface. Hoppe 40.   Jarndyce CII-66   1996 £200.00

BUTLER, SAMUEL 1835-1902   Erewhon Revisited. London: 1901. 1st edition; original red cloth, slightly rubbed, review from the Times Oct. 9 1901 affixed to endpapers, library label and small library stamp on verso of title and last page.   Jarndyce CII-67   1996 £120.00

BUTLER, SAMUEL 1835-1902   Essays on Life, Art and Science. London: Grant Richards, 1904. half title; original red cloth, little faded, top edge gilt, small 'Day's Library' ticket on front cover. Hoppe 43. Jarndyce CII-83   1996 £50.00

BUTLER, SAMUEL 1835-1902   Evolution Old and New... London: Hardwicke and Bogue, 1879. Half title; original brown cloth, bevelled edges; fine. Hoppe 11.   Jarndyce CII-27   1996 £250.00

BUTLER, SAMUEL 1835-1902   Evolution, Old and New. London: David Bogue, 1882. 2nd edition; half title, 32 page catalog of Bogue publications; original brown cloth, bevelled edges; fine. Hoppe 14. Jarndyce CII-28   1996 £120.00

BUTLER, SAMUEL 1835-1902   Ex Voto: an Acocunt of the Sacro Monte of New Jerusalem at VArallo-Sesia. London: Trubner and Co., 1888. Half title, frontipsiece, 20 colotype plates, 3 pages ads; original brown cloth, bevelled edges; fine. Hoppe 21, but with yellow, rather than slate colored endpapers..   Jarndyce CII-43   1996 £150.00

BUTLER, SAMUEL 1835-1902   Ex Voto; an Account of the Scaro Monte or New Jerusalem at Varallo-Sesia. London: Longmans, Green and Co., 1890. Longman's re-issue of 1890 with cancel title and with Longman's imprint on spine; half title, 20 collotype plates, 3 pages ads; original brown cloth, bevelled edges; fine. Hoppe 21 and 23.   Jarndyce CII-44   1996 £100.00

BUTLER, SAMUEL 1835-1902   Ex Voto; an Account of the Sacro Monte or New Jerusalem at Varallo Sesia... London: Longmans, Green and Co., 1890. Longman's reissue; original brown cloth slightly rubbed; Hardwicke Drummond Rawnsley's copy with his bookplate and his ms. description on his Crosthwaite Vicarage, Keswick headed notepaper. Jarndyce CII-46   1996 £75.00

BUTLER, SAMUEL 1835-1902   The Fair Haven. London: Trubner & Co., 1873. 2nd edition; half title, errata slip preceding Memoir; original green cloth, bevelled edges; nice. Hopee 8 p. 23.   Jarndyce CII-20   1996 £120.00

BUTLER, SAMUEL 1835-1902   A First Year in Canterbury Settlement. London: Longman, Green, Longman, Roberts and Green, 1863. half title, folding map, 32 page catalog (Jan. 1863); original plum cloth, affected by damp; inscribed by Butler's father, Thomas Butler. Hoppe 2. Hoppe 48 for 1914 ed.   Jarndyce CII-8   1996 £300.00

BUTLER, SAMUEL 1835-1902   A First Year in Canterbury Settlement. London: Longman, Green, Longman, Roberts and Green, 1863. Original plum cloth, faded and slightly worn at head and tail of spine; booklabels. Jarndyce CII-9   1996 £220.00

BUTLER, SAMUEL 1835-1902   Gavottes, Minuets, Fugues and Other Short Pieces for the Piano by Samuel Butler. London: and New York: Novello, Ewer and Co., 1885. Original blue-grey mottled paper wrappers, as issued, backstrip worn, otherwise good. Signed presentation from Henry Festing Jones to G. F. Hilder. Hoppe 19.   Jarndyce CII-40 1996 £150.00

BUTLER, SAMUEL 1835-1902   God the Known and God the Unknown. London: A. C. Fifeld, 1909. Half title; original blue cloth; booklabel and signature of R. N. Green-Armytage. Hoppe 46.   Jarndyce CII-89 1996 £60.00

BUTLER, SAMUEL 1835-1902   The Humour of Homer. Cambride: Metcalfe and Co., 1892. 43 pages; bound in contemporary blue morocco, gilt dentelles, original grey printed wrappers bound in, very good. Very rare. Hoppe 26.   Jarndyce CII-51   1996 £200.00

BUTLER, SAMUEL 1835-1902   The Humour of Homer and Other Essays. London: A. C. Fifeld, 1913. Portrait in photogravure; original blue cloth, dust jacket; inscribed presentation copy from editor to Serge Tomkeieff, 7th Jan. 1921. Hoppe 26 p. 56; Hoppe III 5.   Jarndyce CII-52   1996 £60.00

BUTLER, SAMUEL 1835-1902   Life and Habit. London: Trubner and Co., 1878. 2nd edition, reissue of the first edition sheets with reprinted first gathering; half title, original brown cloth, bevelled edges, author's own copy, signed; Bogue slip attached to leading free endpaper. Jarndyce CII-24   1996 £300.00

BUTLER, SAMUEL 1835-1902   Life and Habit. London: Trubner & Co., 1878. half title; original brown cloth, slight damp marking, inner hinges cracking. Hoppe 9.   Jarndyce CII-23   1996 £120.00

BUTLER, SAMUEL 1835-1902   The Life and Letters of Dr. Samuel Butler, Head-Master of Shrewsbury School 1798-1836... London: John Murray, 1896. 2 volumes; original dark plum cloth, very good, this copy in the primary binding with ornamental gilt circle on front cover. Hoppe 35.   Jarndyce CII-55   1996 £85.00

BUTLER, SAMUEL 1835-1902   The Life and Letters of Dr. Samuel Butler, Head-Master of Shrewsbury School. London: John Murray, 1896. 2 volumes; this copy in the remainder binding not seen by Hoppe, original plum cloth, faded, slight wear to heads of spines.   Jarndyce CII-56   1996 £60.00

BUTLER, SAMUEL 1835-1902   Luck, or Cunning, as the Main Means of Organic Modification? London: Trubner and Co., 1887. Half title, 2 pages Trubner ads; original brown cloth, very good. Hoppe 19.   Jarndyce CII-41   1996 £180.00

BUTLER, SAMUEL 1835-1902   Narcissus. London: Weekes and Co., 1888. Without wrappers mentioned by Hoppe; loosely inserted is an ALS from Festing Jones (presumably to G. F. Hilder). Signed presentation from Jones to Hilder; Hoppe 22.   Jarndyce CII-49 1996 £120.00

BUTLER, SAMUEL 1835-1902   The Note-books of Samuel Butler, Author of "Erewhon". London: A. C. Fifeld, 1912. 1st edition; half title, frontispiece, 6 pages ads; blue cloth, dust jacket. Hoppe 47.   Jarndyce CII-91 1996 £65.00

BUTLER, SAMUEL 1835-1902   On the Trapanese Origin of the Odyssey. Cambridge: Metcalfe and Co., 1893. contemporary blue morocco, gilt dentelles, original grey printed wrappers bound in, corrigendum slip; rare. Hoppe 27.   Jarndyce CII-54 1996 £350.00

BUTLER, SAMUEL 1835-1902   Seven Sonnets and a Psalm of Montreal. Cambrdige: printed for Private Circulation, 1904. contemporary purple morocco by Bramhall and Menzies with green printed wrappers bound in; fine. Hoppe 44.   Jarndyce CII-86 1996 £150.00

BUTLER, SAMUEL 1835-1902   Seven Sonnets and a Psalm of Montreal. Cambridge: printed for Private Circulation, 1904. contemporary purple morocco by Bramhall and Menzies with green printed wrappers bound in; fine.   Jarndyce CII-86 1996 £150.00

BUTLER, SAMUEL 1835-1902   Seven Sonnets and a Psalm of Montreal. Cambridge: printed for Private Circulation, 1904. Original wrappers, chipped and detached; inscribed by Festing Jones to Charles Strachey, with ALS from Festing Jones to Strachey.   Jarndyce CII-87 1996 £150.00

BUTLER, SAMUEL 1835-1902   Shakespeare's Sonnets Reconsidered. London: Longmans, Green and Co., 1899. Reprint of original 1609 edition; original green cloth; very good; inscribed presentation copy from author to T. T. Greg, who occupied rooms beneath Butler's at 15 Clifford's Inn Dated Dec. 1st. 1899; Booklabel of Robert P. Greg, later Lord Esher's copy, with bookplate, 2 small ms. corrections in Butler's hand on p. 15. Jarndyce CII-63 1996 £250.00

BUTLER, SAMUEL 1835-1902   Shakespeare's Sonnets Reconsidered. London: Longmans, Green and Co., 1899. In this copy ad leaf is bound in before title rather than at end, following p. xii is a slip with two additional errata not mentioned in Hoppe; original green cloth, slightly dulled.   Jarndyce CII-64 1996 £110.00

BUTLER, SAMUEL 1835-1902   Ulysses: a Dramatic Oratorio in Vocal Score... London: Weekes and Co., 1904. Original light brown paper wrappers slightly faded, otherwise very good, signed presentation from Festing Jones to G. F. Hilder. Hoppe 45.   Jarndyce CII-88 1996 £110.00

BUTLER, SAMUEL 1835-1902   Unconscious Memory. London: David bogue, 1880. half title, 32 page David Bogue catalog dated 1879, errata slip; original brown cloth. Hoppe 12.   Jarndyce CII-30 1996 £280.00

BUTLER, SAMUEL 1835-1902   The Way of All Flash. London: Grant Richards, 1903. 1500 copies were printed; half title; original red cloth, very slight marking, otherwise very good; pencil inscription for E. W. Greg from T. T. Greg.   Jarndyce CII-77 1996 £350.00

BUTLER, SAMUEL 1835-1902   The Way of All Flesh. New York: Limited Editions Club, 1936. Copy number 904 from a total edition of 1500 numbered copies, signed by Ward Johnson; 2 volumes, full leather, fine in publisher's slipcase.   Hermitage SP95-950 1 1996 £100.00

BUTLER, SAMUEL 1835-1902   The Collected Works. London: Jonathan Cape/New York: E. P. Dutton and Co., 1926. Shrewsbury edition; 20 volumes; original blue buckram with parchment spines, top edge gilt, other edges uncut. Hoppe 50.   Jarndyce CII-97 1996 £850.00

BUTLER, W. F.   The Campaign of the Cataracts. London: Sampson Low, Marston, Searle and Rivington, 1887. 1st edition; 8vo; 389 pages of text, black and white photographic frontispiece, 6 full page woodcut illustrations, 18 woodcuts to text, large folding map; half brown morocco, blind rule borders, gilt bands to panelled spine (spine faded), joints rubbed, marbled boards, edges and endpapers, upper hinge and spine cracked, corners worn.   Beeleigh Abbey BA56-49 1996 £150.00

BUTOR, MICHEL   Octal. Munich: Studio Bruckmann, 1972. 1st edition; one of 850 copies, signed by author and artist; folio; (29)ff; 9 large color lithographs by Victor Vasarely on Rives-Couronne, interleaved with texts of Butor's poems on grey paper, each covered with a clear Mylar sheet on which is printed in blue the German translation; loosely bound so prints can easily be removed for framing very fine in black cloth printed with Vasarely design in blue, protected by pritned clear mylar wrapper.   Bromer Booksellers 90-239 1996 $1,000.00

BUTTERWORTH, E.   Macaws. London: 1993. Double elephant; 12 life size colored etchings; buckram, in book box.   Wheldon & Wesley 207-20 1996 £25,000.00

BUTTRE, J. C.   Catalogue of Engravings by J. c. Buttre, Publisher, Engraver and Plate Printer. New York: ca. 1870. Square 12mo; 68 pages; 2 engraved plates; original printed wrappers, margins frayed;   M & S Rare Books 60-288 1996 $350.00

BUXTON, EDWARD NORTH   Short Stalks. 1892. illustrations; deluxe binding (seldom appears) of full pictorial gilt vellum, very lightly marked; contents fine.   David Grayling J95Biggame-496 1996 £120.00

BUXTON, EDWARD NORTH   Short Stalks; or Hunting Camps North and South, East and West. London: 1892. 1st edition; 8vo; 25 full page plates, many textual illustrations; modern red binder's red cloth; scarce. Charles W. Traylen 117-289 1996 £60.00

BUXTON, THOMAS FOWELL   The African Slave Trade. London: John Murray, 1839. 1st edition; 8vo; xv, (1), 240 pages, large folding map (two short tears but no loss), 8 pages of ads at end; original green cloth lettered in gilt; good. Williams II 447; Goldsmith's 31181; Kress C3818 (but 2nd ed. only).   John Drury 82-38 1996 £150.00

BYATT, A. S.   Degrees of Freedom - the Novels of Iris Murdoch. London: Chatto & Windus Ltd., 1965. 1st edition; original binding, top edge spotted and slightly dusty, edges slightly spotted, top edges of covers very slightly soiled, head and tail of spine bumped, very good in slightly spotted, creased and dusty dust jacket, faded at spine and edges.   Ulysses 39-87 1996 £85.00

BYATT, A. S.   The Game. London: Chatto & Windus, 1967. 1st edition; original binding, top edge dusty, endpapers faintly and partially browned, bottom edge partially browned, covers slightly bowed, very good in nicked, rubbed and slightly soiled and dusty dust jacket, browned at spine and edges.   Ulysses 39-88 1996 £145.00

BYATT, A. S.   The Game. London: Chatto & Windus, 1967. 1st edition; about mine in about very good dust jacket with several small flaws, little soiled and couple of small chips and tears and slightly tanned on spine.   Between the Covers 42-75 1996 $175.00

BYATT, A. S.   Shadow of a Sun. London: Chatto & Windus Ltd., 1964. 1st edition; author's first novel; original binding, top edge slightly dusty, edges and endpaper spotted, head and tail of spine slightly bumped, very good in nicked, spotted and slightly dusty, very slightly creased dust jacket browned at spine and edges.   Ulysses 39-86 1996 £225.00

BYATT, A. S.   The Virgin in the Garden. London: Chatto & Windus Ltd., 1978. 1st edition; small paper flaw on titlepage, head and tail of spine and corners bumped, very good in nicked, creased, marked and slightly dusty dust jacket.   Ulysses 39-89 1996 £55.00

BYERS, DOUGLAS S.   The Prehistory of the Tehuacan Valley. Austin and London: University of Texas Press, 1967-72. 4to; 5 volumes; viii, 331 pages, 188 figures and 38 tables; xiii, 258 pages, 175 figures, 32 tables; xii,3 06 pages, 158 figures, 72 tables; xii, 290 pages, 99 illustrations, 15 tables; xii, 529 apges; 201 illustrations, 44 tables; original cloth, dust jackets, volume 1 and 5 jackets tattered, volume 4 jacket lightly chipped. Archaeologia Luxor-4331 1996 $250.00

BYINGTON, LEWIS FRANCIS   The History of San Francisco. San Francisco; S. J. Clarke Publishing Co., 1931. 1st edition; large octavo; 3 volumes, pages 542, 492, 502; portraits, maps, plates; original blindstamped and gilt stamped cloth, very light spotting to rear cover of one volume, else fine and clean set. Quite scarce.   Argonaut Book Shop 113-109 1996 $250.00

BYINGTON, MARGARET F.   Homestead: The Households of a Mill Town. New York: Russell Sage Foundation, Charities Pub. Committee, 1910. 1st edition; 8vo; xv, 292 pages, (4) pages ads, folding panorama photo illustration, map, photo and text illustrations; photos; gilt titled cloth, rubbed, front inner hinge starting, some red underlining, else good. Andrew Cahan 47-86 1996 $125.00

THE BYNG Papers Selected from the Letters and Papers of Admiral Sir George Byng, First Viscount Torrington and His Son Admiral the Hon. John Byng. London: 1930-31. 2 volumes, 2 portraits; Petersfield Bookshop FH58-383 1996 £50.00

BYNG, JOHN The Trial of the Honoruable Admiral John Byng, at a Court Martial, as Taken by Mr. Charles Fearne, Judge Advocate of His Majesty's Fleet. London: R. Manby, 1757. 1st edition; tall folio; 130, 19 pages; full contemporary calf, upper joint cracked but firm, red morocco label; signature of B. Bentham dated 1757 to verso of title and final leaf; engraved bookplate of Sir Strafford N. Northcote (private secretary to Gladstone). Ian Wilkinson 95/1-147 1996 £240.00

BYRD, CECIL Bibliography of Indiana Imprints 1804-1853. Indianapolis: Indiana Historical Bur., 1955. 1st and only edition; 479 pages; blue cloth, some pencil notes on rear endpaper, otherwise very good. Blue River Books 9-172 1996 $195.00

BYRNE, OLIVER Spons' Dictionary of Engineering, Civil, Mechanical, Military and Naval... London: 1869-74. 10 x 7 inches; 8 volumes; 3131 pages with index; illustrations; cloth, volume 8 spine torn, some staining, otherwise good set. John K. King 77-716 1996 $250.00

BYROM, JOHN A Catalogue of the Library of the Late John Byrom, Esq. M.A., F.R.S., Formerly Fellow of Trinity College, Cambridge, Preserved at Kersall Cell, Lancashire. London: Printed for Private Circulation Only (Crompton & Ritchie), 1848. 1st edition; small 4to; frontispiece; ex-library with stamps; original buckram, slight tears to hinges. Rare. Forest Books 74-32 1996 £145.00

BYROM, JOHN The Universal English Short-hand; or, The Way of Writing English, In the Most Easy, Concise, Regular and Beautiful Manner, Applicable to Any Other Language. Manchester: printed by Joseph Harrop, 1767. Page 37 is an engraved plate, with 5 plates between pages 50 & 51 and 7 at end, library stamp at end and few pencil marks; excellently rebound in half calf, very good. Alston VIII 246. Jarndyce 103-38 1996 £120.00

BYRON, GEORGE ANSON Voyage of HMS Blonde to the Sandwich Islands in the Years 1824-1825. London: John Murray, 1826. (xii), 260 pages; folding frontispiece and folding map, 13 aquatint plates; early full gilt decorated calf, modern calf spine, with matching decoration, maroon label, marbled endpapers, all edges marbled, very good+. Hill p. 309; Judd 76. Antipodean 28-615 1996 $2,750.00

BYRON, GEORGE GORDON NOEL, 6TH BARON 1788-1824 Childe Harold's Pilgrimage. Paris: Harrison, 1931. One of 660 copies printed on Montgolfier Freres vellum, from a total issue of 725; page size 10 3/8 x 7 7/8 inches; text printed in 12 point Didot roman and 9 point Didot Italic (for the notes); Sir Francis Cyril Rose illustrated the text with 28 wash drawings printed in collotype by Daniel Jacomet, which was the artist's first appearance in book form; red cloth over boards, tan publisher's slipcase with label, book fine, box split at top and bottom edge. Priscilla Juvelis 95/1-118 1996 $100.00

BYRON, GEORGE GORDON NOEL, 6TH BARON 1788-1824 Correspondence of Lord Byron, with a Friend, Including His Letters to His Mother, Written from Portugal, Spain, Greece and the Shore of the Mediterranean, in 1809, 1810, 1811. Paris: pub. by A. and W. Galignani, 1825. 1st published and 1st complete edition; 12mo; 3 volumes in one; contemporary half green morocco, gilt, spine gilt, bit rubbed; some foxing and light browning, as usual, paper being mediocre, but attractive copy, complete with half titles, uncommon. Wise II 51-2; Chew pp. 209-11; CBEL III 291. Ximenes 108-52 1996 $600.00

BYRON, GEORGE GORDON NOEL, 6TH BARON 1788-1824 English Bards and Scotch Reviewers. London: printed for Charles Cawthorn, n.d. 1809. 1st edition; 12mo; half blue calf, traces of rubbing fine; signed on half title by George D'Oyly (1778-1846). Wise I 21; Hayward 219; CBEL III 277. Ximenes 108-53 1996 $750.00

BYRON, GEORGE GORDON NOEL, 6TH BARON 1788-1824 Hours of Idleness, a Series of Poems. Newark: printed and sold by S. and J. Ridge; sold also by B. Crosby & Co..., 1807. 1st edition; crown 8vo; pages (iii-xiii), (i) errata, 187; rebound without half title, skilfully washed and resized, full dark blue crushed morocco, sides ruled in gilt with triple fillet, spine richly gilt between raised bands, gilt lettered in two panels and with date at foot, inner dentelles richly gilt, marbled endpapers, gilt edges; by Riviere. Wise I pp. 7-8. Simon Finch 24-26 1996 £975.00

BYRON, GEORGE GORDON NOEL, 6TH BARON 1788-1824 Hours of Idleness: a Series of Poems, Original and Translated. (with) English Bards and Scotch Reviewers... London: ptd. for Sherwin and Co./London: ptd. for James Cawthorn, 1820/10. 1st title is unauthorized reprint of the 'sixth' edition, 2nd title is first of two authorized 4th editions; 8vo. and large 12mo; 2 volumes in one; contemporary calf, ruled in blind, spine gilt, minor rubbing; half titles present; Wise pp. 15 and 25. Ximenes 108-54 1996 $300.00

BYRON, GEORGE GORDON NOEL, 6TH BARON 1788-1824 The Island, or Christian and His Comrades. London: by C. H. Rennell for John Hunt, 1823. 1st edition; 8vo; 94 pages, with half title, without final ad leaf F8; full green straight grain morocco, sides with single gilt fillet, spine with raised bands, gilt motifs, lettered in gilt in two compartments, inner dentelles with double gilt fillet, comb marbled endpapers, top edge gilt, others uncut, by Bedford; fine copy; bookplate of Frederick S. Peck, bookseller's catalog description and note of acquisition by "J.H.S." dated 14 may 1946 tipped on binder's blank; fine, scarce. Simon Finch 24-28 1996 £600.00

BYRON, GEORGE GORDON NOEL, 6TH BARON 1788-1824 Letter to **** ******, on the Rev. W. L. Bowles' Strictures on the Life and Writings of Pope. London: John Murray, 1821. 1st edition; 2nd issue, with 6 page addenda here first added, also, leaf B5 (pp. 9-10) is a cancel; 8vo; pages 55, (1), 6, (2 blank); disbound, nice. James Fenning 133-44 1996 £185.00

BYRON, GEORGE GORDON NOEL, 6TH BARON 1788-1824 Letters and Journals of Lord Byron. London: John Murray, 1830. 1st edition; large 4to; 2 volumes; half title in volume 1 (as is correct), portrait to volume 2, slip advertising "Murray's Landscape Illustrations to Byron"; contemporary cloth, printed labels, uncut, wear to one hinge, covers slightly marked, spines faded, reading society labels on endpapers, internally fine. Peter Murray Hill 185-27 1996 £75.00

BYRON, GEORGE GORDON NOEL, 6TH BARON 1788-1824 Marino Faliero, Doge of Venice an Historical Tragedy. London: John Murray, 1821. 1st edition; 1st issue; 8 1/2 x 5 1/2 inches; xxi, (1), 261, (1) pages, (1) leaf (ads); pleasing probably contemporary diced calf, sides framed with double gilt fillets and decorative floral blind rule, central panel in blind with large arabesque at middle, raised bands, spine gilt in compartments, feautring large foliate stamp, dark blue double labels, marbled edges; leather little faded and slightly soiled, joints and extremities with minor rubbing, but solid and attractive binding in excellent condition, very fine internally; bookplate of Alexander Spiers of Elderslie. Phillip J. Pirages 33-118 1996 $165.00

BYRON, GEORGE GORDON NOEL, 6TH BARON 1788-1824 The Poetical Works of Lord Byron. New York: Johnson Fry, 1867. 1st edition thus; 4to; xxviii, 740 pages; 48 lovely full page steel engravings; original publisher's full red morocco with gilt decorated covers and gilt spine in 6 compartments, volume has been personalized with gilt lettering at foot of spine, extremities rubbed and spine slightly darkened, small embossed library stamps, else very good. Chapel Hill 94-108 1996 $150.00

BYRON, GEORGE GORDON NOEL, 6TH BARON 1788-1824 The Poetical Works. New York: 1867. 1st edition thus; quarto; numerous steel engravings; full leather with raised bands, gilt imprint, marbled endpapers and edges, near fine. Stephen Lupack 83- 1996 $125.00

BYRON, GEORGE GORDON NOEL, 6TH BARON 1788-1824 Poetical Works. London: Henry Frowde, 1896. 8vo; 924 pages, printed on India paper; full natural vellum over slightly flexible boards, upper cover and spine hand painted in bright colors and gold to a medieval design with birds, flowers and intertwined leaves forming a most agreeable all over pattern (lower cover is unadorned), all edges gilt, although without their ticket, the binding appears to be the work of the Royal School of Needlework; in absolutely fine condition. Book Block 32-34 1996 $675.00

BYRON, GEORGE GORDON NOEL, 6TH BARON 1788-1824 The Complete Poetical Works. Oxford: Clarendon Press, 1980-93. 8vo; 7 volumes; frontispieces, plates; original dark green cloth, gilt lettered, dust jackets; fine. Blackwell's B112-51 1996 £395.00

BYRON, GEORGE GORDON NOEL, 6TH BARON 1788-1824 The Prisoner of Chillon. London: Day & Son, 1865. 1st edition; folio; 20 chromolithographed leaves, printed on recto only; cloth, richly decorated in blue, gold and red; front cover slightly sunned, minor edgewear, else very good. Bookpress 75-18 1996 $585.00

BYRON, GEORGE GORDON NOEL, 6TH BARON 1788-1824 Sardanapaus - Two Foscarai - Cain. London: John Murray, 1821. 1st edition; 2nd variant issue that bears the title "Sardanapalus/A Tragedy" on titlepage, the other variant only has "Sardanapalus" on titlepage, but no priority established; rebound in tooled leather, bright gilt lettering; fine. Left Bank Books 2-18 1996 $285.00

BYRON, GEORGE GORDON NOEL, 6TH BARON 1788-1824 Sunset from the Parthenon. N.P.: Chevening?: 1875. 1st edition; 4to; contemporary half calf and marbled boards, spine gilt, trifle rubbed; leaf of heavily corrected ms. from an early version of Byron's "Curse of Minerva" reproduced in photographic facsimile, along with letterpress titlepage, leaf of explanation, fine copy; from the library of Duke of Bedford at Woburn Abbey. Not in Wise or NCBEL. Ximenes 108-55 1996 $400.00

BYRON, GEORGE GORDON NOEL, 6TH BARON 1788-1824   Werner, a Tragedy. London: John Murray, 1823. 1st edition; 1st issue; 8vo; pages viii, 188 and 7 pages Murray's ads dated Nov. 1822; endpapers and flyleaves lightly foxed, otherwise very good; complete with half title and without imprint and "The End" on p. 188; contemporary half calf. James Fenning 133-43 1996 £125.00

BYRON, GEORGE GORDON NOEL, 6TH BARON 1788-1824   The Works of... London: John Murray, 1823. Small 8vo; 5 volumes; contemporary russia, gilt, gilt edges, some trivial scratches, but fine and attractive set. Peter Murray Hill 185-24 1996 £275.00

BYRON, GEORGE GORDON NOEL, 6TH BARON 1788-1824   The Works. Philadelphia: R. W. Pomeroy, 1825. 1st of this edition; small 8vo; 8 volumes; Westall engravings; uncut, original publisher's boards, paper spines and labels renewed, some darkening of pages, but generally good, unusual in original state; early ticket of Cambridge bookseller. CBEL III 187.   Hartfield 48-L21 1996 $450.00

BYSSHE, EDWARD   The Art of English Poetry. London: R. Knaplock et al, 1702. 1st edition; octavo; 19th century cloth, bit worn, bookplate, name on title, title tipped to endpaper, quite foxed and embrowned, little underlining, few faint pencil marks on title; rare.   G. W. Stuart 59-22 1996 $750.00

BYSSHE, EDWARD   The Art of English Poetry. London: Sam Buckley, sold by Dan Midwinter, 1705. 2nd edition; octavo; contemporary calf, rebacked preserving original spine and red morocco label, verses written on front endpapers and few within the work itself, final portion a bit waterstained in lower edge, quite minor worming to blank lower edge of several leaves, name marked out on title and on half title, yet attractive, decent copy, usually found in wretched condition.   G. W. Stuart 59-23 1996 $365.00

BYSSHE, EDWARD   The Art of English Poetry. London: F. Clay, et al, 1737. 8th edition; octavo; 2 volumes; contemporary calf, joints cracking, spine ends chipped, bookplate, name on endpaper, nice.   G. W. Stuart 59-25 1996 $210.00

C

C., A.   The Lives of Dr. Edward Pocock, the Celebrated Orientalist... London: printed for F. C. and J. Rivington, 1816. 1st edition; 8vo; 2 volumes; contemporary calf, rubbed, contrasting labels.   Anthony W. Laywood   108-157   1996 £65.00

CABATON, ANTOINE   Java, Sumatra and Other Islands of the Dutch East Indies. London: T. Fisher Unwin, 1912. 2nd English edition; 8vo; pages xvi, 376, (4 ads); folding map, 32 plates containing 47 illustrations; recent quarter calf, gilt, top edge gilt, some light foxing in places, but very good.   James Fenning   133-46   1996 £85.00

CABELL, JAMES BRANCH 1879-1958   Branchiana, Being a Partial Account of the Branch Family in Virginia. Richmond: Whittet & Shepperson, 1907. One of 157 copies, signed by Cabell; (3 1 bl.), 177 pages, errata; 10 portraits; green cloth with gilt title and top, light soiling, copy number in limitation erased, else very good+. Haynes VA 2653.   Bohling Book Co.   191-937   1996 $250.00

CABELL, JAMES BRANCH 1879-1958   Chivalry. New York: Harper & Bros., 1909. 1st edition; 12 illustrations in color by Howard Pyle; remains of small bookplate on front pastedown, otherwise fine.   Hermitage SP95-895   1996 $125.00

CABELL, JAMES BRANCH 1879-1958   The Cords of Vanity. New York: McBride, 1920. 1st revised edition; neat name to front pastedown and spine gilt little tarnished, else near fine in about very good good dust jacket with hole on spine, some light chipping at extremities and some general soiling, still nice copy of a book seldom found in jacket.   Between the Covers   42-77   1996 $125.00

CABELL, JAMES BRANCH 1879-1958   Domnei: a Comedy of Woman Worship. New York: McBride, 1920. 1st edition; slight wear to spine ends, else fine in fine dust jacket with light horizontal crease, slightly darkened along center of jacket, otherwise fresh and bright with some slight wear at crown, lovely copy of a book seldom found in jacket. Between the Covers   42-76   1996 $150.00

CABELL, JAMES BRANCH 1879-1958   Gallantry: an Eighteenth Century Dizain in Ten Comedies, with an Afterpiece. New York: Harper, 1907. 1st edition; illustrations in color by Howard Pyle; grey cloth tooled in blind and stamped in white, silver and gilt, top edge gilt; beautiful copy. Captain's Bookshelf   38-30   1996 $100.00

CABELL, JAMES BRANCH 1879-1958   Jurgen. Waltham St. Lawrence: Golden Cockrel Press, 1949. Limited to 500 numbered copies; maroon morocco backed red cloth gilt, top edge gilt, morocco somewhat faded, otherwise very good.   Words Etcetera   94-493   1996 £110.00

CABELL, JAMES BRANCH 1879-1958   Ladies and Gentlemen. McBride, 1934. 1st edition; 2/153 copies specially bound and signed by author of which 120 were for sale; fine in very good box.   Aronovitz 57-221 1996 $135.00

CABELL, JAMES BRANCH 1879-1958   Something About Eve. New York: McBride, 1927. 1st edition; one of 850 large paper copies, signed by author; vellum backed boards, just about fine.   Captain's Bookshelf 38-31   1996 $100.00

THE CABINET Cyclopaedia. A Treatise on the Origin, Progressive Improvement and Present State of the Silk Manufacture. Philadelphia: Carey & Lea, 1832. 1st edition; 8vo; pages 276 + ad; 28 wood engravings in text; little worn linen backed boards, paper label, some foxing, some pencil scribbling on early blank and first page of contents. Not in Imprints.   Second Life Books   103-154   1996 $125.00

THE CABINET of the Scottish Muses; Selected from the Works of the Most Esteemed Bards of Caledonia. Edinburgh: printed by and for Oliver and Boyd, 1808. Small 8vo; 213 pages; woodcut frontispiece; modern full calf, gilt, boards tooled in blind, few slight marks and spots, one or two marginal blindstamps.   R.F.G. Hollett   76-51   1996 £165.00

CABLE, GEORGE WASHINGTON 1844-1925   Strange True Stories of Louisiana. New York: 1889. 1st edition; decorated cream cloth, near fine, usually found dirty and darkened.   Stephen Lupack 83-   1996 $125.00

CADDICK, JOHN   Illustrated Catalogue of Bricks, Finials, Roofing Ridge and Floor Tiles, Terra Metallic Garden Edging, Chimney Pots, Sanitary Ware &c. Stoke-on-Trent: John Caddick, n.d., c. 1870's. Small folio; (i)ff., and 31ff. of litho illustrations, numbered 1-30, 3 (4 chromolitho); original stiff printed wrappers; excellent;   Elton Engineering 10-24 1996 £95.00

CAESAR, GAIUS JULIUS 100-44 BC   Commentaries. Waltham St. Lawrence: Golden Cockerel Press, 1951. Limited edition of 320 numbered copies; 4to; printed on Arnold's mould made paper, 312 pages; wood engraved frontispiece, 3 vignettes, 10 large headpieces by Clifford Webb, publisher's blue buckram sides with red spine, gilt vignette on cover, edges uncut, very slightly faded and some feint markings on front cover. Cock-a-Hoop 188.   Thomas Thorp   489-51   1996 £100.00

CAESAR, GAIUS JULIUS 100-44 BC   The Eyght Bookes of Caius Iulius Caesar... London: Willyam Seres, 1565. 1st edition in English; octavo; modern polished calf antique style, blind tooled and roll stamped, minor soiling and embrowning within, with few side notes, page numerals and headlines cropped, leaf Eg with signature 'Jonathan Wrigley' dated 1711. Attractive copy. STC 18962; Pforzheimer 411.   G. W. Stuart 59-26 1996 $3,500.00

CAGE, JOHN   Empty Words. Writings '73-78. Middletown: Wesleyan University Press, 1979. 1st edition; small 4to; cloth, extremities trifle rubbed, otherwise fine in slightly rubbed and price clipped jacket with price written on inside front flap in ink.   James S. Jaffe 34-97   1996 $125.00

CAIN, JAMES M.   Galatea. New York: Alfred A. Knopf, 1953. 1st edition; signed by author; very good+ in dust jacket.   Steven C. Bernard   71-299   1996 $300.00

CAIN, JAMES M.   Loves Lovely Counterfeit. New York: Alfred A. Knopf, 1942. 1st edition; fine in near fine price clipped dust jacket, still very attractive copy with rich top edge stain.   Left Bank Books   2-19 1996 $145.00

CAIN, JAMES M.   Mildred Pierce. New York: Alfred A. Knopf, 1941. 1st edition; advance pre-publication copy; stiff paper wrappers, dust jacket attached to spine by publisher, spine cocked and worn at edges, otherwise very good, scarce in this advance format.   Steven C. Bernard   71-301   1996 $375.00

CAIN, JAMES M.   The Moth. New York: Knopf, 1948. 1st edition; fine in a near fine dust jacket with very light rubbing, slight soiling on back panel and very minor edge wear.   Quill & Brush   102-175   1996 $125.00

CAIN, JAMES M.   Serenade. New York: Alfred A. Knopf, 1937. 1st edition; fine in dust jacket sunned at spine, but overall bright.   Left Bank Books   2-20   1996 $250.00

CAIN, PAUL   Fast One. Garden City: Doubleday Doran, 1933. 1st edition; bit of uneven soiling, some slight fraying to extremities, very good, lacking dust jacket; rare.   Between the Covers 42-476   1996 $200.00

CAINE, CAESAR   Cleator and Cleator Moor: Past and Present. Kendal: Titus Wilson, 1916. 1st edition; thick 8vo; pages xviii, 475, (iv), uncut, 70 illustrations; modern buckram gilt, original backstrip and gilt emblem on upper board relaid; very nice.   R.F.G. Hollett & Son   78-775   1996 £145.00

CAINE, CAESAR   Cleator and Cleator Moor: Past and Present. Kendal: Titus Wilson, 1916. 1st edition; thick 8vo; pages xviii, 475, iv, 70 illustrations; original cloth, gilt.   R.F.G. Hollett & Son   78-774   1996 £120.00

CAINE, HALL   The Bondman. A New Saga. London: William Heinemann, 1890. 1st edition; 8vo; 3 volumes; original red cloth, spines little dull and very slightly rubbed; very good, attractive prize label on first pastedown and flyleaf; Sadleir 481; Wolff 1033; CBEL III 1042. Ximenes   109-60   1996 $450.00

CAINE, HALL   The Bondman Play. London: Daily Mail, 1906. 1st edition; small 8vo; 6 of the 15 photographic plates are signed by the respective performer of the original production at London's Theatre Royal, including Frank Cooper, Henry Neville, Marie Illington, Lionel Brough, Marjorie Day and Austin Melford; red cloth; very good, occasional foxing. Signed presentation from author to Charles Sharp. Antic Hay 101-264 196 $175.00

CAIRNES, J. E.   Essays in Political Economy. London: Macmillan and Co., 1873. 1st edition; 8vo; x, (2), 371 pages; original brown cloth, lettered in gilt; very good. New Palgrave I 311; Einaudi 785; Masui p. 116.   John Drury 82-40 1996 £125.00

CAIRNES, J. E.   Essays on Political Economy, Theoretical and Applied. London: Macmillan and Co., 1873. 1st edition; 8vo; name on half title and title, 59 pages publisher catalogue at end; original cloth, hinges and head and tail of spine little worn, uncut, partly unopened, generally clean. New Palgrave I p. 311; Einaudi 785.   Anthony W. Laywood 109-22 1996 £60.00

CAJETAN, TOMASO DE VIO   In Praedicabilia Porphyrii, Praedicamenta & Lbiros Posteriorum Analyticorum Aristotelis... Venice: apud Haeredem Hieronymi Scoti, 1599. Probably the latest revised edition; folio; pages (iv), 212, Roman and italic letter, double columsn, large oval woodcut portrait, woodcut initials and 3 diagrams; contemporary limp vellum, recased, 2 contemporary annotations on front cover, early ms. penitential prayer in Italian enclosed on separate slip; early owner's autograph deleted on titlepage, generally good. This ed. not in BM STC It., Adams or NUC. Not in Cranz/Schmitt.   A. Sokol XXV-19 1 1996 £985.00

CALCRAFT, JOHN WILLIAM   A Defence of the Stage, or an Inquiry into the Real Qualities of Theatrical Entertainments, Their scope and Tendency. Dublin: Milliken and Son, 1839. 1st edition; 8vo; small tear on upper blank margin of title; modern boards, printed paper label; Arnott and Robinson 580.   Anthony W. Laywood 108-156 1996 £75.00

CALDANI, LEOPOLDO   Icones Anatomicae, Quotquot Sunt Celbriores, ex Optimis Neotericorum Operibus Summa Diligentia Depromtae et Collectae. (with) Oconum Anatomicarum Explicatio. Pars Prima, Partis Secundae Sectio Prima et Alterqa. Partis Tertiae Sectio Prima et Altera. Venetiis: ex caccographia Josephi Picotti, 1801/2/4/5/8/14 1st title large folio in 3 volumes; contemporary quarter sheep; 2nd title in folio, 5 volumes, in quarter sheep, dampstaining affecting lower portion of binding and contents of first atlas volume and end of second atlas volume, otherwise very clean, crisp set; plates. Rare. Iowa 962 and Choulant pp. 327-328.   James Tait Goodrich K40-74 1996 $5,995.00

CALDERARI, OTTONE   Disegni et Scritti d'Architettura di ottone Calderari. Vicenza: Tipografia Paroni, 1808. 1st edition; large folio; (ii), 42 pages, 47 plates; 30, (6) pages, 43 plates; very attractive in contemporary quarter calf, marbled boards.   Bookpress 75-163 1996 $3,500.00

CALDERON DE LA BARCA, MARQUESA   Life in Mexico, During a Residence of two Years in that Country. London: Chapman & Hall, 1843. 1st English edition; 8vo; newly rebound in quarter calf and buckram, panelled spine and red label, new endpapers. Sabin 9889.   Charles W. Traylen 117-398 1996 £115.00

CALDERON, V. G.   The Lottery Ticket. Waltham St. Lawrence: Golden Cockerel Press, 1945. One of 400 numbered copies, this one of 100 specially bound; 8vo; printed in Bembo on Batchelor's handmade; 6 wood engravings by Dorothea Braby; half white morocco, lightly foxed, but nice, name on flyleaf.   Bertram Rota 272-181 1996 £55.00

CALDERWOOD, MRS.   Letters and Journals of Mrs. Calderwood of Polton... Edinburgh: David Douglas, 1884. 1st edition; 8vo; lviii, 386 pages; contemporary half green morocco, minor spotting on edges, smudges on titlepage, else very good.   The Bookpress 75-397 1996 $185.00

CALDWELL, ERSKINE PRESTON 1903-   Journeyman. New York: Viking, 1935. 1st edition; one of 1475 copies; a curious copy in custom full black morocco decorated with a red band (simulating design of the published book), with rules on spine, lettered in gilt; laid in are two 1 page TLS's from author.   Captain's Bookshelf 38-32 1996 $300.00

CALDWELL, ERSKINE PRESTON 1903-   Kneel to the Rising Sun, and Other Stories... New York: Viking, 1935. Limited edition, number 93 of 300 numbered copies, signed by author; 8vo; titlepage printed in brown and black; original brick red cloth, gilt stamped black morocco labels on spine and upper cover, yellow silk book mark, top edge gilt, uncut, small loss to upper edge of spine label; very good in publisher's tan board slipcase.   George J. Houle 68-23 1996 $275.00

CALDWELL, ERSKINE PRESTON 1903-   Molly Cottontail. Boston & Toronto: Little, Brown & Co., 1958. 1st edition; illustrations by William Sharp; scarce, some light browning of front and rear inner hinges, otherwise near fine in bright, fine dust jacket.   Steven C. Bernard 71-437 1996 $250.00

CALDWELL, ERSKINE PRESTON 1903-   Tenant Farmer. New York: Phalanx Press, 1935. 1st edition; original printed green wrappers; fine. Bromer Booksellers 90-13 1996 $225.00

CALDWELL, ERSKINE PRESTON 1903-   La Route au Tabac. Paris: Editions du Pre aux Cleres, 1946. 1st French edition; one of 10 special copies (from a total of 900) with extra set of the plates in sepia, laid in at rear; decorated wrappers and glassine dust jacket, housed in well worn original box; fine.   Captain's Bookshelf 38-33 1996 $450.00

CALDWELL, HARRY R.   Blue Tiger. 1925. illustrations, prelims bit foxed, spine slightly rubbed; scarce.   David Grayling J95Biggame-497 1996 £70.00

CALENDAR for 1894. New York: Colgate & Co., 1894. 2 1/8 x 1 5/8 inches; 12 pages; original color pictorial stitched wrappers; very good. George J. Houle 68-98 1996 $150.00

CALIFORNIA HISTORICAL SOCIETY   Papers of the California Historical Society: Volume I, Parts I and II. San Francisco: California Historical Society, 1887. 8vo; 2 volumes, xxxii, 94, (8), 440 pages; original printed wrappers, covers slightly worn, spines slightly darkened, else fine, uncut set.   Argonaut Book Shop 113-112 1996 $150.00

CALIFORNIA. STATE BOARD OF HEALTH   Second Biennial Report of the State Board of Health of California, for the Years 1871, 1872 and 1873. Sacramento: State Board of Health, 1873. 8 3/4 x 5 1/2 inches; (viii), 235 pages, 5 folding tables, 3 maps, 3 lithographic plates; dark blue cloth. On titlepage is ownership stamp of George Davidson of the U.S. Coast Survey.   Dawson's Books Shop 528-19 1996 $100.00

CALLAGHAN, MORLEY   No Man's Meat. Paris: Edward W. Titus, 1931. Signed, limited edition of 525 numbered copies; 8vo; cloth and boards; fine.   Antic Hay 101-269 1996 $275.00

CALLAHAN, HARRY   Harry Callaghan: Photographs. Santa Barbara: El Mochuelo Gallery, 1964. 1st edition; limited to 1500 copies, signed by Callahan; folio; 126 black and white photos; silver lettering on black cloth, endpapers discolored, otherwise near fine in slipcase.   Andrew Cahan 47-41 1996 $1,000.00

CALLAWAY, NICHOLAS   Georgia O'Keefe: One Hundred Flowers. New York: Alfred A. Knopf, 1987. 1st edition; folio; 100 color plates; cloth; fine in dust jacket.   James Cummins 14-145 1996 $100.00

CALLCOTT, MARIA GRAHAM   Three Months Passed in the Mountains East of Rome, During the Year 1819. London: printed for Longman; A. Constable, Edinburgh, 1820. 1st edition; 8vo; viii, 305, (1) pages, 6 aquatint plates; contemporary half calf, spine gilt, joints slightly cracked, but firm; Abbey Travel 168 (2nd ed. 1821).   James Burmester 29-57 1996 £300.00

CALLENDER, JAMES THOMSON   Deformities of Dr. Samuel Johnson. London: for the author, and sold by J. Stockdale & W. Creech, Edinburgh, 1782. 2nd edition; 8vo; in half sheets, 89 pages; modern dark brown quarter morocco, marbled boards with surface wear, few leaves with light stain at fore edge, but very good. Courtney & Nichol Smith p. 136.   Simon Finch 24-29 1996 £400.00

CALLIMACHUS   The Hymns of Callimachus. London: printed for the translator, 1755. Only edition; large 4to; engraved vignette on titlepage, 6 engraved headpieces; contemporary mottled calf, spine gilt, morocco label; fine; signature of Michael Woodhull dated 1760; bookplate. NCBEL II 652.   Trebizond 39-9 1996 $600.00

CALLIMACHUS   The Hymns of Callimachus. London: for the Translator, 1755. 1st edition; quarto; pages 212; recent marbled boards, fine rebinding, gilt on red leather label, minor flaws, but nice, tall copy, scarce. CBEL II 760.   Hartfield 48-L30 1996 $395.00

CALTHROP, HENRY   Reports of Special Cases Touching Several Customes and Liberties of the City of London, Whereunto is Annexed Divers Ancient Customes and Usages of the Said City of London. London: 1670. Modern calf, some embrowning and foxing, title cut close with loss of portion of the imprint, else sound.   Meyer Boswell SL25-30 1996 $450.00

CALVERLEY, WILLIAM SLATER   Notes On the Early Sculptured Crosses, Shrines and Monuments in the Present Diocese of Carlisle. Kendal: T. Wilson, 1899. 8vo; pages xviii, 319, portrait, numerous plates and illustrations; original brown cloth, gilt; scarce; labe reads "This book belonged to William Paton Ker, All Souls College, Oxford and in memory of him was given to Mary Wordsworth Higginbotham Dec. 1923."   R.F.G. Hollett & Son   78-12   1996 £95.00

CALVERT, ALBERT F.   Spain: an Historical Descriptive Account of Its Architecture, Landscape and Arts. London: Batsford, 1924. 2nd edition; 4to; 2 volumes, xxviii, 463; xx, 464-896, 28 pages; 46 color illustrations, over 1700 other illustrations and maps; original cloth, slightly rubbed and soiled, slightly affected by dampness, minor tears in spine, otherwise very good, top edge gilt.   Worldwide Antiquarian   151-116   1996 $125.00

CALVERT, F. CRACE   Lectures on Coal Tar Colours, and on Recent Improvements and Progress in Dyeing and Calico Printing. Philadelphia: Henry Carey Baird, ca. 1863. 1st American edition; 8vo; 64 pages, 24 pages ads; 27 original cloth samples tipped in; original flexible brown cloth with paper label, pencil marks on several pages, but crisp copy. Chapel Hill   94-407   1996 $350.00

CALVERT, GEORGE H.   Illustrations of Phrenology. Baltimore: William & Joseph Neal, 1832. 1st edition; 8vo; 192 pages; author's first book; 26 woodcuts; original green muslin lacking paper spine label, spine splitting and chipping at ends, early owner's signature on titlepage, modest foxing, else very good. American Imprints 11625; BAL 2393.   Chapel Hill   94-265   1996 $325.00

CALVERT, J.   The Gold Rocks of Great Britain and Ireland and a General Outline of the Gold Regions of the World. London: 1853. 8vo; pages xx, 324, ii, x; cloth, neatly rebacked preserving spine, library stamp on verso of title.   John Henly   27-406   1996 £136.00

CALVINO, ITALO   The Baron in the Trees. New York: RH, 1959. 1st American edition; fine in very good dust jacket with few small edge tears and slight darkening to spine.   Thomas Dorn   9-68   1996 $135.00

CALVINO, ITALO   The Nonexistent Knight and the Cloven Viscount. New York: RH, 1962. 1st American edition; fine in lightly used, very good plus dust jacket with small edge tear to bottom of back panel. Thomas Dorn   9-69   1996 $125.00

CALVINO, ITALO   The Silent Mr. Palomar. New York: Targ Editions, 1981. One of 250 copies on Fabriano's Roma; fine in glassine dust jacket; signed.   Lame Duck Books   19-108   1996 $150.00

CALVINO, ITALO   T Zero. New York: HBW, 1969. 1st American edition; fine in bright, fine dust jacket.   Thomas Dorn   9-71   1996 $125.00

CALVINO, ITALO   Time and the Hunter. London: Cape, 1970. 1st British edition; soiling to bottom edge, else near fine in dust jacket. Lame Duck Books   19-107   1996 $100.00

CAMBITOGLOU, ALEXANDER   Apulian Red-Figured Vase-Painters of the Plain Style. New York: Archaeological Inst. of America, 1961. 4to; text xv, 103 pages; plates: 41 loose plates; text and plates laid in to a Japanese style box (as issued), with ivory clasps (very slight shelfwear at bottom edges to box, interior fine).   Archaeologia   Luxor-3131   1996 $350.00

THE CAMBRIDGE Economic History of Europe. Cambridge University Press, 1963-67. Thick large 8vo; 4 volumes in 5; buckram, dust jacket; from the library of Philip Gaskell, librarian of Trinity.   Howes Bookshop 265-124   1996 £175.00

THE CAMBRIDGE History of Iran. Cambridge Universtiy Press, 1968-86. royal 8vo; 5 volumes in 6; illustrations; buckram, dust jackets.   Howes Bookshop   265-125   1996 £275.00

CAMBRIDGE Modern History. London: 1934. 13 volumes; full green cloth, very good.   Bookworm & Silverfish   280-32   1996 $250.00

CAMBRIDGE, RICHARD OWEN   The Scribleriad: an Heroic Poem. London: printed for R. Dodsley and sold by M. Cooper, 1751. 1st edition; 4to; xvi, 31, 31, 31, 32, 32, 27, (viii) pages; engraved frontispiece, 6 plates; original cloth, spine gilt, red morocco label, verso of final leaf little soiled, otherwise fine.   David Bickersteth   133-12 1996 £140.00

CAMBRIDGE, RICHARD OWEN   The Works of Richard Owen Cambridge, Esq... London: printed by Luke Hansard and sold by T. Cadell and W. Davies and ... 1803. 1st edition; 4to; 77 pages life and 507 pages text; frontispiece, 12 engraved plates, 1 facsimile; full calf, gilt rule enclosing blindstamped border, gilt title and blind tools to spine, upper hinge cracked, still good, tight copy.   Beeleigh Abbey   BA56-138 1996 £250.00

CAMDEN, WILLIAM   Reges, Reginae Nobiles & Alii in Ecclesia Collegiata B. Petri Westmonasterii Sepulti, Usque ad Annum Reparatae Salutis 1600. London: excudebat E. Bollifantus, 1600. 1st edition; small 4to; 19th century calf, gilt spine, all edges gilt, by C. Smith (minor rubbing); fine. STC 4518.   Ximenes   109-61   1996 $900.00

CAMERON, CHARLES   The Baths of the Romans Explained and Illustrated... London: George Scott for the Author, 1772. 1st edition; Large folio; text in English and French, engraved title, English title with engraved vignette, engraved dedication f., iv, 65 pages, French title, iv + 68 pages, 20 engraved text illustrations in duplicate, 76 plates, errata slip pasted on verso of last plate; sumptuously bound in near cont. Russian red mor., covers gilt panelled w/roll-tooled borders and corner ornaments, spine gilt in 7 compartments w/neo-classical motifs, green label, inner borders gilt, marbled endpapers, gilt edges, upper cover w/gilt stamp of arms, crest, supporters & motto: PRO RIGE (sic) ET PATRIA, of Cameron of Lochiel (to which Charles Cameron was not entitled) & the initials C.C.A.M.I.R. (Charles Cameron Architecte a Sa Majeste Imperiale Russe); Cameron's own copy, covers little rubbed and scratched, otherwise fine, sound and unrestored condition. Marlborough   160-35   1996 £15,000.00

CAMERON, VERNEY LOVETT   Across Africa. London: 1885. New edition; 8vo; xxviii, 569 pages, large folding map; well illustrated; blue cloth, gilt lettered, very good.   K Books   442-3   1996 £90.00

CAMERON. A Novel. London: Edward Bull, 1832. 1st edition; 12mo; 3 volumes; contemporary dark green moire cloth, ends of spines very slightly rubbed; possibly bound without half titles, but attractive, very scarce. Block p. 33; not in wolff.   Ximenes   109-118   1996 $475.00

CAMFIELD, WILLIAM A.   Francis Picabia, His Art, Life and Times. Princeton: Princeton University Press, 1979. 28.5 x 22 cm; xviii, 366 pages, 20 color and 452 black and white illustrations; original cloth, dust jacket, ex-library, very good.   Rainsford   A54-457   1996 £210.00

CAMPAN, JEAN LOUISE HENRIETTE   Memoirs of the Court of Marie Antoinette. London: H. S. Nichols, 1895. One of 500 copies; tall 8vo; 2 volumes; frontispiece in each volume; handsome three quarter red straight grain morocco, richly gilt panelled spines, raised bands, gilt tops; fine.   Appelfeld Gallery   54-104   1996 $200.00

CAMPANELLA, TOMMASO   De Sensv Rervm, et Magia. Libros Qvatvor. Paris: Du Bray, 1637. 2nd edition; 4to; vellum, slightly warped, light marginal dampstain; Cardinal Richelieu's arms on titlepage; Bon Pas stamp on title margin. Rare 2nd edition; Brunet I 1520; Thorndike VII 291-301.   Rostenberg & Stern   150-120   1996 $1,250.00

CAMPBELL, ALEXANDER   Speech of Sir Alexander Campbell on the Second Reading of a Bill to Incorporate the Pacific Railway Company in the Senate, Ottawa, Thursday Feb. 3, 1881. Ottawa: 1881. 15 pages; wrappers, as issued. Not in Lowther or Peel.   Stephen Lunsford   45-18 1996 $100.00

CAMPBELL, ARCHBIALD   A Journey from Edinburgh through Parts of North Britain Containing Remarks on Scotish Landscape... London: printed by A. Strahan for T. N.Longman, and O. Rees and Vernor & Hood, 1802. 4to; 2 volumes; pages xxiv, 408; vi, 394, 44 fine tinted aquatints; half hard grained morocco, gilt, spines slightly faded, hinges trifle rubbed or cracked; text lightly browned in places, occasional spot, but very good, clean set.   R.F.G. Hollett   76-55   1996 £480.00

CAMPBELL, ARCHIBALD 1726-1780   Lexiphanes, a Dialogue. London: printed for R. Faulder and J. Fielding, 1783. 3rd edition; 12mo; contemporary tree calf, neatly rebacked retaining original gilt spine strip and slightly chipped red label; armorial bookplate and booklabel of A. S. F. Gow, the classicist. Alston III 281.   Jarndyce   103-39   1996 £180.00

CAMPBELL, BEBE MOORE   Sweet Summer: Growing Up with and Without My Dad. New York: Putnams, 1989. 1st edition; fine in dust jacket, signed by author.   Between the Covers   43-280   1996 $100.00

CAMPBELL, BEBE MOORE   Your Blues Ain't Like Mine. New York: Putnam, 1992. 1st edition; fine in fine dust jacket, signed and dated in month of publication.   Book Time   2-500   1996 $125.00

CAMPBELL, DONALD   A Narrataive of the Extraordinary Adventures and Sufferings by Shipwreck and Imprisonment, or Donald Campbell, Esq. of Barbreck. London: Vernor & Hood, 1796. 18mo; xi, 276 pages; frontispiece; contemporary half morocco, edges rubbed, hinges tender, light foxing; otherwise good.   Worldwide Antiquarian 162-173 1996 $190.00

CAMPBELL, HELEN   Prisoners of Poverty Abroad. Boston: Roberts Bros., 1889. 1st edition; 8vo; original brown cloth; very fine.   Ximenes 108-58 1996 $150.00

CAMPBELL, J.   Who Goes There? Shasta Press, 1948. 1st edition; review copy with accompanying review slip laid in; very good+ in near fine dust jacket;   Aronovitz 57-226 1996 $275.00

CAMPBELL, J. RAMSEY   The Doll Who Ate His Mother. B-M, 1976. 1st edition; fine in dust jacket with one small tear; inscribed by author. Aronvitz 57-233 1996 $135.00

CAMPBELL, J. RAMSEY   The Face that Must Die. Santa Cruz: Scream Press, 1983. 1st U.S. edition and 1st hardcover; signed by author and artist, J. K. Potter; fine in fine dust jacket.   Bud Schweska 12-212 1996 $150.00

CAMPBELL, J. RAMSEY   The Inhabitant of the Lake and Less Welcome Tenants. Sauk City: Arkham House, 1964. 1st edition; fine in dust jacket, author's first book; inscription from author laid in. Aronovitz 57-231 1996 $125.00

CAMPBELL, J. RAMSEY   New Tales of the Cthulhu Mythos. Sauk City: ARkham House, 1980. 1st edition; (3647 copies); new in dust jacket. Steven C. Bernard 71-400 1996 $100.00

CAMPBELL, JOHN CAMPBELL, 1ST BARON 1779-1861   The Lives of the Lord Chancellors and Keepers of the Great Seal of England, from the Earliest Times Till the Reign of King George IV. London: John Murray, Albemarle Street, 1846-69. contemporary mottled calf, rebacked, spines extra gilt, pretty.   Meyer Boswell SL25-33 1996 $1,250.00

CAMPBELL, JOHN CAMPBELL, 1ST BARON 1779-1861   The Lives of the Chief Justices of England. New York: 1873-75. 6 volumes; green cloth, gilt, bit worn, but quite good set.   Meyer Boswell SL25-32 1996 $350.00

CAMPBELL, JOHN CAMPBELL, 1ST BARON 1779-1861   The Lives of the Chief Justices of England. From the Norman Conquest Till the Death of Lord Tenterden. Long Island: Edward Thomson Co., 1894-99. 5 volumes; many full page plates, some in color, others folding; vellum backed crimson boards, showing wear, still attractive, original crimson dust jackets, now faded.   Meyer Boswell SL26-37 1996 $850.00

CAMPBELL, JOHN L.   Idaho: Six Months in the New Gold Diggings. New York: Published by J. L. Campbell, 1864. 1st edition; (1)-52, 53-63 ads, (1-4 ads on mauve paper, vignette and four full page illustrations, frontispiece map; original yellow pictorial front wrapper with back wrapper having ad, wrappers printed yellow and are semi-glazed, title printed in red and black, slightly soiled, with few minor tears, cloth slipcase. From the collection of Edward Ayer with his booklabel. Smith 580; Streeter Sale 3301; Graff 560; Flake 1117; Mintz Trail 75.   Michael D. Heaston 23-78 1996 $12,500.00

CAMPBELL, KEN   Night Feet on Earth: a Poem. 1987. One of 50 copies, numbered and signed by Campbell; folio; printed in 4 colors on Saunders mouldmade; handbound in boards by Robert Hadrill; fine in slipcase.   Bertram Rota 272-74 1996 £200.00

CAMPBELL, THOMAS MONROE   The Movable School Goes to the Negro Farmer. Tuskegee Inst. Press, 1936. 1st edition; photos; just about fine in lightly worn, very good pictorial dust jacket with several small chips and tears, but which is attractive and intact. Nicely inscribed by author.   Between the Covers 43-281 1996 $225.00

CAMPBELL, WILLIAM   Materials for a History of the Reign of Henry VII, from Original Documents Preserved in the Public Record Office. London: 1873-77. 8vo; 2 volumes, pages 725; 688; original cloth. Howes Bookshop 265-1589 1996 £60.00

CAMPE, JOACHIM HEINRICH   Polar Scenes, Exhibited in the Voyages of Heemskirk and Barenz to the Northern Regions. London: J. Harris & Son, 1823. 12mo; 138, (2) pages; 36 copperplate engravings; original red calf over printed boards, boards somewhat rubbed and soiled. Osborne p. 179 (1822 imprint).   Kenneth Karmiole 1NS-69 1996 $150.00

CAMPEN, JACOB VAN   Afbeelding Van't Stadt Huys Van Amsterdam... Amsterdam: Dancker Danckerts, 1661. 1st edition; folio; frontispiece, (vi), 11, (1), 24 plates; contemporary vellum, light foxing on margins, as usual, minor chipping on frontispiece, bookplates on water damaged endpaper, small waterstain at base of spine, light cover wear, still respectable copy. Fowler 77; Berlin 2233.   Bookpress 75-164 1996 $2,950.00

CAMPER, CHARLES   Historical Record of the First Regiment Maryland Infantry. Washington: Gibson Bros., 1871. 1st edition; 332 pages; original cloth, bit of edage wear, else near fine. Scarce. Dornbusch II 489. Howes C104; Nicholson p. 135.   McGowan Book Co. 65-14 1996 $350.00

CAMPION, EDMUND   Edmundi Campiani Angli e Soc. Iesu Decem Rationes Propositae in Causa Fidei, et Opuscula Eius Selecta. Antwerp: ex officina Plantiniana Balthasaris Moreti, 1631. 1st edition; 12mo; contemporary calf, minor rubbing; titlepage bit soiled, else very good, inscription. Alsion and Rogers 170.   Ximenes 109-62 1996 $400.00

CAMPION, J. S.   On the Frontier, Reminiscences of Wild Sports, Personal Adventures and Strange Scenes. London: 1878. 372 pages, illustrations; modern leather spine, cloth, very good plus. Howes C105; Graff 566; Rader 583.   T. A. Swinford 49-180 1996 $200.00

CAMPION, THOMAS   Campion's Works. Oxford: Oxford University Press, 1909. 1st edition; original binding, spare title label, top edge dusty, covers slightly marked, rubbed and very slightly soiled, title label on spine browned and rubbed, head and tail of spine and corners slightly bumped, very good.   Ulysses 39-91 1996 £55.00

CAMPION, THOMAS   The Maske by Thomas Campion, as Produced at Hatfield Palace on May 30th and 31st 1924 for the Benefit of the Hertfordshire County Nursing Association. London: privately ptd. at the Cayme Press for the Chelsea Pub. Co., 1924. One of 500 copies; buckram backed boards; spine faded and slightly worn, head and tail of spine and corners slightly bumped and rubbed, covers slightly marked, endpaper edges and gutters browned, very good.   Ulysses 39-92 1996 £48.00

CAMUS, ALBERT   The Outsider. London: Hamish Hamilton, 1946. 1st English translation; owner bookplate and bookstore label to front pastedown, mild foxing, overall very good of this thin, fragile post war book, in very good spine darkened jacket with bit of chipping at extremities.   Ken Lopez 74-73 1996 $250.00

CAMUS, ALBERT   The Plague. London: Hamish Hamilton, 1948. 1st English translation; tiny bookstore label front pastedown, some fading to spine cloth, very good in very good jacket with small chips at spine crown, nice.   Ken Lopez 74-74 1996 $250.00

CANADA a Year of the Land. Ottawa: 1969. 1st edition; large oblong 4to; 260 color and black and white plates of the Canadian landscape; near fine in very good original slipcase.   Gene W. Baade 1094-20 1996 $150.00

CANADA At the Universal Exhibition of 1855. Toronto: 1856. 463 pages; illustrations, maps; original cloth, faded, but very good. TPL 3512. Stephen Lunsford 45-20 1996 $125.00

CANADA. PARLIAMENT   Parliamentary Debates on the Subject of the Confederation of the British North American Provinces, 3rd Session, 8th Provincial Parliament of Canada. Quebec: 1865. 10 x 6.5 inches; 1032 double column pages, lacks f.e.p., cloth, covers show wear.   John K. King 77-37 1996 $125.00

CANADA. PARLIAMENT   Report from the Select Committee On the Civil Government of Canada. Quebec: 1829. 9 x 6 inches; 377 pages; plain wrappers, front cover and title stained, minor foxing and staining, ink name rubber stamp, covers loose.   John K. King 77-40 1996 $150.00

CANADIAN Farming: an Encyclopedia of Agriculture,,, Toronto: C. Blackett Robinson, 1881. 22.5 cm. 432 pages; illustrations, foldouts; extra fine in gilt blindstamped deep blue cloth, lovely copy, now rare.   Rockland Books 38-39 1996 $225.00

CANADIAN NORTHERN RAILWAY   Homeseekers and Settler's Guide to Western Canada. Chicago: April, 1917. Pages 56 in double columns, folded to make a brochure, large folding map, many illustrations; fine in color lithographed covers, laid in "Important Amendment to Canadian Homestead Regulations" Toronto, March, 1917. Peel 2657 lists a later, shorter work of the same title.   Stephen Lunsford 45-22 1996 $150.00

CANADIAN PACIFIC RAILWAY   The Canadian Pacific. The New Highway to the East Across the Mountains Prairies and Rivers of Canada. Montreal: 1887. Quarto; pages 45, (3), map on inner rear cover; original wrappers with some repairs, but generally attractive. Rare. Lowther 743.   Stephen Lunsford 45-24 1996 $450.00

CANDLER, ALLEN D.   The Confederate Records of the State of Georgia. Atlanta: Chas. P. Byrd, 1909-11. 1st edition; volumes 1-4 and 6 (5 volumes, all published); volumes 1-3 are in original cloth, volumes 4 and 6 in later cloth, inner hinges cracked in volumes 1 and 2, otherwise very good. Nevins II 216; not in DeRenne; Rowland & Dorsey 375. McGowan Book Co. 65-15 1996 $1,250.00

CANETTI, ELIAS   Crowds and Power. London: Victor Gollancz, 1962. 1st British edition; light crease to front free endpaper, else near fine in dust jacket with minor soiling to rear panel; inscribed; books signed by Canetti are decidedly scarce.   Lame Duck Books 19-122 1996 $1,500.00

CANEVARI, DEMETRIO   De Ligno Sancto Commentarium, in Quo Praecipuae Qualitates Eius and Facultates Omnes Exacta Diligentia Exprimuntur... Rome: G. Facciotti, 1602. 1st edition; 8vo; 141, (2) pages; couple of tiny round wormholes mostly in blank margins; modern boards; very good. Aldin Landis 602/24; BM 17th Cent. Italian books 177;   Jeffrey D. Mancevice 20-17 1996 $1,450.00

CANINA, LUIGI   The Vicissitudes of the Eternal City; or, Ancient Rome... London: Richard Bentley, 1849. 1st edition; 8vo; folding map, xvi, (i), 343 pages, blocked in blind, lettered gilt on spine, little spotting at edges of many pages, but fine.   David Bickersteth 133-141 1996 £55.00

CANNEY, M.   University of London Library Catalogue of the Goldsmiths' Library of Economic Literature. Cambridge: Cambridge University Press, and Athlone Press, 1970-82. Large 4to; 4 volumes; cloth, dust jackets.   Maggs Bros. Ltd. 1191-73 1996 £300.00

CANNING, ELIZABETH   Genuine and Impartial Memoirs of Elizabeth Canning, Containing a Complete History of that Unfortunate Girl, from Her Birth to the Present Time, and Particularly Every Remarkable Occurrence from the Day of Her Absence, Jan. 1, 1753... London: printed for G. Woodfall, 1754. 1st edition; 12mo; contemporary calf, gilt, neatly rebacked, spine gilt; very good. Amory 62; Raven 267.   Ximenes 109-67 1996 $750.00

CANNING, ELIZABETH   A Refutation of Sir Crisp Gascoyne's Address to the Liverymen of London; by a Clear State of the Case of Elizabeth Canning, in a Narrative of Facts, Ranged in a Regular Series and Supported by the Information and Affidavits of Near Eighty... London: printed for J. Payne, 1754. 1st edition; folio; disbound; very good. Amory 67.   Ximenes 109-68 1996 $400.00

CANNING, ELIZABETH   The Trial of Elizabeth Caning, Spinster, for Wilful and Corrupt Perjury; at Justice Hall in the Old Bailey... London: ptd. by the authority & appointment of the Rt. Hon. Thomas Rawlinson.. nd1754. 1st edition; folio; disbound; some foxing, very good, rare. Amory 70.   Ximenes 109-69 1996 $750.00

CANNING, ELIZABETH   The Truth of the Case; or Canning and Squires Fairly Opposed. London: printed for M. Cooper, W. Reeve, and C. Sympson, 1753. 1st edition; 8vo; half calf, spine defective; rare, library bookplates and release stamps, couple of small embossed stamps, inner margin of titlepage strengthened on blank verso, otherwise very good. Ximenes 109-63 1996 $650.00

CANOE and Camp Cookery: a Practical Cook Book for Canoeists, Corinthian Sailors and Outers. New York: Forest and Stream Pub. Co., 1885. 1st edition; brown cloth stamped in gilt and black, light rubbing along edges, otherwise fine.   Hermitage SP95-874 1996 $100.00

CANTWELL, J. C.   Report on the Operations of the U.S. Revenue Steamer Nunivak on the Yukon River Station, Alaska, 1899-1901. Washington: 1902. 325 pages; illustrations; original cloth; about fine. Arctic 18403.   Stephen Lunsford 45-26 1996 $110.00

CAPA, ROBERT   Slightly Out of Focus. New York: Holt, 1947. Quarto; slightly soiled, else fine in lightly worn and unfaded dust jacket, with two small chips at edge of crown, nicer.   Between the Covers 42-528 1996 $100.00

CAPEK, KAREL   Meteor. London: Allen & Unwin, 1935. 1st English edition; near fine, very good in dust jacket; recipient's bookplate. Lame Duck Books 19-126 1996 $850.00

CAPES, WILLIAM WOLFE   Scenes of Rural Life in Hampshire. London: Macmillan & Co., 1901. 1st edition; post 8vo; (x), (348) pages; plates, tables, folding colored map; bound in smart recent half morocco, banded and gilt, top edge gilt, titlepage little browned, otherwise very good.   Ash Rare Books Zenzybyr-18 1996 £95.00

CAPETANAKIS, DEMETROIS   The Poetry of Demetrois Capetanakis... Janus Press, 1966. One of 100 numbered copies; 11 x 8 inches; 20 pages; designed, set and printed on Vandercook proofing press at the University of Wisconsin, Madison and bound by Claire Van Vliet; titles handset, printed in black with silver titles on Rives cuve velin and handsewn into grey Fabriano wrappers; fine.   Joshua Heller 21-3 1996 $125.00

THE CAPITOL Land Reservation in the Panhandle of Texas Now Offered for Sale...3,000 Acres Fine Agricultural or Grazing Land, Low Prices, Easy Terms Perfect Titles... Chicago: ca. 1901. 1st edition; 20 pages; illustrations and maps; original printed grey wrappers; very fine. not in Adams Herd.   Michael D. Heaston 23-85 1996 $850.00

CAPOTE, TRUMAN 1924-1985   Breakfast at Tiffany's. New York: 1958. 1st edition; original cloth, near fine/very good+.   Stephen Lupack 83- 1996 $150.00

CAPOTE, TRUMAN 1924-1985   The Grass Harp. New York: Random House, 1951. 1st edition; 1st state binding; very good in dust jacket with few nicks.   George J. Houle 68-24 1996 $150.00

CAPOTE, TRUMAN 1924-1985   The Grass Harp. New York: Random House, 1951. 1st edition; 8vo; cloth, dust jacket, first binding, spine very slightly darkened, otherwise fine in slightly rubbed jacket.   James S. Jaffe 34-102 1996 $125.00

CAPOTE, TRUMAN 1924-1985   The Grass Harp. New York: Random House, 1952. 1st edition; fine in fine dust jacket, very slightly darkened on spine; very scarce play version.   Ken Lopez 74-75 1996 $400.00

CAPOTE, TRUMAN 1924-1985   In Cold Blood. New York: Random, 1955. 1/500 numbered and signed copies printed on special paper and specially bound. fine in near fine slipcase.   Alice Robbins 15-59 1996 $350.00

CAPOTE, TRUMAN 1924-1985   Miriam. Mankato: Creative Education, Inc., 1982. 1st separate edition; signed by author; illustrations by Sandra Higashi; fine in ilustrated library binding, issued without dust jacket. Steven C. Bernard 71-438 1996 $175.00

CAPOTE, TRUMAN 1924-1985   Music for Chameleons. New York: Random House, 1980. 1st edition; limited to 350 copies signed by author; 8vo; cloth, slipcase; very fine.   James S. Jaffe 34-103 1996 $350.00

CAPOTE, TRUMAN 1924-1985   Observations. New York: Simon & Schuster, 1959. 1st edition; folio; 151 pages; photos by Richard Avedon; printed boards, glassine and faintly soiled matching slipcase; very fine. Bromer Booksellers 90-2 1996 $300.00

CAPOTE, TRUMAN 1924-1985   One Christmas. New York: Random House, 1/500 signed and numbered copies; fine in unopened slipcase. Bev Chaney, Jr. 23-127 1996 $300.00

CAPOTE, TRUMAN 1924-1985   Other Voices, Other Rooms. New York: Random House, 1949. 1st edition; 8vo; cloth, fine in dust jacket chipped at bottom of spine, with residue from two internal tape mends; author's first book.   James S. Jaffe 34-100 1996 $150.00

CAPOTE, TRUMAN 1924-1985   A Tree of Night and Other Stories. New York: Random House, 1949. 1st edition; fine in dust jacket with one short closed tear very attractive copy of author's second book.   Left Bank Books 2-21 1996 $175.00

CAPOTE, TRUMAN 1924-1985   A Tree of Night and Other Stories. New York: Random House, 1949. 1st edition; 8vo; black cloth, dust jacket, spine slightly bumped, otherwise fine in slightly edge worn dust jacket. James S. Jaffe 34-101 1996 $150.00

CAPPE, CATHARINE   Thoughts on Various Charitable and Other Important Institutions, and on the Best Mode of Conducting Them. York: ptd. by Thomas Wilson and Sons, for Longman & J. Hatchard... 1814. 1st edition; 8vo; viii, 110, (1 ad) pages; recent boards. very unccommon; 2 copies in NUC.   James Burmester 29-26 1996 £250.00

CAPPER, JOHN The Three Presidencies of India: a History of the Rise and Progress of the British Indian Possessions. London: Ingram, Cooke and Co., 1853. 8vo; (v-vi), (vii-x), (xi-xii), 1-479, appendix and index 483-492 pages; frontispiece, large folding map, 6 full page illustrations, 54 illustrations; full maroon morocco, gilt ruled borders to boards, gilt title and decorative tooling to spine, raised bands to spine, corners and edges slightly worn, all edges gilt, yellow endpapers; contemporary ink ms. presentation inscription to prelim, very nice. Beeleigh Abbey BA56-50 1996 £125.00

CAPPON, LESTER J. Virginia Newspapers 1821-1935. New York: and London: 1936. xiii, 299 pages; very good, ex-library with backstrip ends rubbed to fraying. Bookworm & Silverfish 280-256 1996 $100.00

CARACCIOLI, CHARLES The Antiquities of Arundel; the Peculiar Privilege of Its Castle and Lordship, With an Abstract of the Lives of the Earls of Arundel. London: for the author, 1766. Thick large 8vo; extra illustrated with about 60 engraved portraits; russia with old rebacking, all edges uncut, binding little rubbed, contents fine. Petersfield Bookshop FH58-180 1996 £180.00

CARACCIOLI, LOUIS ANTOINE DE Advice from a Lady of Quality to Her Children, in the Last Stage of a Lingering Illness. Boston: printed and sold by S. Hall, 1796. 2nd American edition; 12mo; dust jacket half red morocco, spine gilt, rubbed, but sound; some light browning, few stains, but very good, scarce. Evans 29954; Newberry, Courtesy Books II (this ed.). Ximenes 108-59 1996 $150.00

CARACCIOLUS, ROBERTUS Sermones Quadragesimales de Peccatis. Venice: Joannes & Gregorius de Gregoriis, de Forlivio 11 May, 1490. Quarto; 158 leaves, double column, gothic letter, first 6 lines at head of text printed in red, initial spaces with guide letters, printer's device on fol. 158 recto, some page numerals slightly cropped, slight browning on first and last leaves; 18th century vellum boards; from the collection of Thomas Crofts, then Michael Wodhull. Goff C162; Hain 4441; GKW 083; IGI 2466; not in BMC. H. M. Fletcher 121-6 1996 £1,800.00

CARBONE, LODOVICO L'Hvomo Givsto, o la Centvria delle Lodi Dell'Hvomo Christinao.... Venice: Giacomo Antonio Somasco, 1594. 1st edition thus? 4to; ff. (iv), 121, (iii), roman letter with italic dedication, table of contents and index, woodcut printer's device on top edge gilt, woodcut initials and ornaments; contemporary limp vellum, foot of spine little damaged; ms. title on lower edges; slightly later owner's autograph (crossed through) & 2 early library stamps on titlepage, early annotations on 4 pages, insignificant marginal waterstains at foot of some leaves, good copy. Index Aurel 131.981. A. Sokol XXV-20 1996 £395.00

CARDINALL, A. W. In Ashanti and Beyond. Selley, Service & Co., 1927. 8vo; 288, 8 pages publisher's catalog; map, 24 photograpphic illustrations; yellow cloth, vignette on upper cover, spine and upper portion of back cover, little darkened, otherwise fine. Thomas Thorp 489-53 1996 £65.00

CARDONNEL, ADAM DE Numismata Scotiae; or, a Series of the Scottish Coinage, from the Reign of William the Lion to the Union. Edinburgh: printed for George Nicol, 1786. 4to; (6), 158, 34 pages; 20 engraved plates; old calf over marbled boards, gilt spine, extremities chipped, edges bit rubbed, front outer hinge cracked, but quite sound. Kenneth Karmiole 1NS-200 1996 $250.00

CARDOZO, BENJAMIN N. Law Is Justice, Notable Opinions of Mr. Justice Cardozo. New York: Ad Press, 1938. Special deluxe first edition, limited to 20 copies, this number 16; three quarter blue morocco over marbled boards, marbled endpapers, top edge gilt showing some wear; generally well preserved. Meyer Boswell SL25-34 1996 $450.00

CARE, HENRY English Liberties: or, the Free-Born Subject's Inheritance... London: printed by George Larkin, or Benjamin Harris, 1680? contemporary sheep, quite rubbed, trimmed close but sound. Meyer Boswell SL26-58 1996 $650.00

CAREW, BAMPFYLDE MOORE The Surprising Adventures of...King of the Beggars. London: Newman, 1813. Revised edition; small 8vo; frontispiece, titlepage vignette and 2 engraved plates; brown cloth, gilt stamped leather spine label (light foxing0; good to very good. George J. Houle 68-25 1996 $125.00

CAREW, THOMAS 1595-1639 A Rapture. Waltham St. Lawrence: Golden Cockerel Press, 1927. One of 375 copies; 7 3/4 x 5 1/4 inches; 14 pages, (1) leaf (colophon); 2 engraved plates by J. E. Laboureur, device in colophon; original cloth backed patterned paper boards, dust jacket, fore edge and tail edge untrimmed, virtually perfect copy in extremely fine jacket that has one small tear neatly repaired on verso; small bookplate of Pamela Lister. Chanticleer 47. Phillip J. Pirages 33-244 1996 $250.00

CAREW, THOMAS 1595-1639 A Rapture. Waltham St. Lawrence: Golden Cockerel Press, 1927. One of 375 numbered copies; 8vo; half buckram with batik sides, spine little darkened, but nice in dust jacket. Bertram Rota 272-169 1996 £95.00

CAREY, JOHN Vegetable Gardening: an Essay. Rampant Lions Press, 1989. Of 500 numbered copies, this one of only 20 signed by author, 8vo; with an extra set of signed proofs of linocuts and specially bound; printed in Octavian with Joanna italic in black and green on Arches; five colored linocut by Clare Melinsky; half dark green morocco, proofs laid into lighter green card portfolio; fine in slipcase. Bertram Rota 272-398 1996 £125.00

CAREY, MATHEW Letters on the Colonization Society; and On Its Probable Results... Philadelphia: April 15, 1833. 7th edition; 8vo; 4, (3)-32 pages; map; original printed wrappers, fine. B&B 18111. M & S Rare Books 60-296 1996 $100.00

CAREY, WILLIAM A Grammar of the Mahratta Language to Which are Added Dialogues on Familiar Subjects. Serampore: printed at the Mission Press, 1825. 3rd edition; 8vo; half title; modern cloth, morocco spine label; prevasive light dampstaining, but very good, uncommon; early armorial bookplate of T. Latter, Bengal Army. Trebizond 39-106 1996 $325.00

CARLETON, GEORGE A Thankfvll Remembrance of Gods Mercy. London: I. D. for Mylbourne, 1625. 2nd edition; square 8vo; calf, morocco rebacked; tear in Ff1 without loss of text. STC 4641. Rostenberg & Stern 150-39 1996 $425.00

CARLETON, HENRY GUY The Thompson Street Poker Club. Paris: Brentano's, 1888. 1st Paris edition; 8vo; 48 pages; drawings by E. W. Kemble; original illustrated grey boards with green cloth spine, some rubbing and water spotting to boards, else very good. Wright III 910. Chapel Hill 94-123 1996 $125.00

CARLETON, JOHN WILLIAM Recreations in Shooting. London: Chapman & Hall, 1846. 1st edition; royal 12mo; xxviii, (308), 16 pages; wood engraved plates on tint backgrounds, illustrations in text; original pictorial cloth, gilt, expertly restored and repaired, few very minor marks, endpapers rejointed, but good. Ash Rare Books Zenzybyr-19 1996 £95.00

CARLETON, WILLIAM The Works of... New York: 1881. Collier's unabridged edition; 3 volumes; illustrations, volume 1 bit shaky, else good; unusual. C. P. Hyland 216-81 1996 £75.00

CARLILE, JAMES Thoughts on the Mixed Character of Government Institutions in Ireland, with Particular Reference to the New System of Education. London: B. Fellowes, 1833. 1st edition; 8vo; 47 pages; disbound; 2 copies in NUC. James Burmester 29-27 1996 £60.00

CARLISLE NATURAL HISTORY SOCIETY Transactions. Carlisle: The Society, 1909-28. 8vo; volumes 1-4; original wrappers, spine of first volume faded and chipped; scarce. R.F.G. Hollett & Son 78-518 1996 £150.00

CARLISLE, ANTHONY An Essay on the Disorders of Old Age, and On the Means for Prolonging Human Life. London: printed for Longman, Hurst, 1817. 1st edition; 8vo; titlepage printed in red and black, pages iv, 103; some foxing, but very good, contemporary half calf; armorial bookplate of Thomas Brownrigg. James Fenning 133-48 1996 £145.00

CARLL, LEWIS BUFFETT A Treatise on the Calculus of Variations. New York: John wiley, 1881. 1st edition; 8vo; xvii, 568 pages; original cloth, lacks front flyleaf, very good. Edwin V. Glaser 121-52 1996 $135.00

CARLSON, P. S. The Biology of Crop Productivity. London: 1980. 8vo; 471 pages; cloth. Wheldon & Wesley 207-1873 1996 £69.50

CARLTON, AMBROSE B. The Wonder Lands of the Wild With Sketches of the Mormons. N.P.: 1891. 1st edition; 346 pages; frontispiece, plates, decorated cloth, very good+. Scarce. Flake 1193. T. A. Swinford 49-184 1996 $150.00

CARLTON, AMBROSE B. The Wonderlands of the Wild West With Sketches of the Mormons. N.P.: 1891. 346, (2) pages, 19 plates and portraits, errata; blue cloth, gilt title, printed presentation slip, very good+. Flake 1193. Bohling Book Co. 191-765 1996 $200.00

CARLYLE, THOMAS 1795-1881   German Romance: Specimens of Its Chief Authors; With Biographical and Critical Notices. Edinburgh: William Tait and Charles Tait, London, 1827. 1st edition; 8vo; 4 volumes; (xvi), (338); (iv), 288, 281-(318); (iv), (310); (iv), 352 pages; half titles, no final blank in volume 3; original boards, backed with green cloth, printed paper labels, untrimmed, boards marked, minor wear at extremities, labels browned and chipped, vertical crack in one backstrip, little foxing, very reasonable set. Tarr A4.1.   Robert Clark 38-229 1996 £200.00

CARLYLE, THOMAS 1795-1881   History of Frederick II of Prussia: Called Frederick the Great. Leipzig: Tauchnitz, 1858-65. Copyright edition; small 8vo; 13 volumes in 9; three quarter tan calf over marbled boards, spines with raised bands, gilt stamped floral devices within gilt stamped compartments, gilt stamped red and green morocco labels, marbled endpapers and edges, some foxing, minor rubbing; very good. George J. Houle 68-26 1996 $275.00

CARLYLE, THOMAS 1795-1881   History of Friedrich II of Prussia, Called Frederick the Great. London: Chapman & Hall, c. 1890. Crown 8vo; 6 volumes in 3; portrait; full blue prize calf gilt by Bickers, gilt crest of University College school on sides.   Howes Bookshop 265-136 1996 £50.00

CARLYLE, THOMAS 1795-1881   Sartor Resartus; the Life and Opinions of Herr Teufelsdrockh. London: Saunders and Otley, 1838. 1st English published edition; contemporary morocco or pebble grained blue-green cloth lettered only on spine and doesn't match any of the binding variants noted by Tarr A5.4, either a trial, or more likely, a remainder binding; small chip or erosion at heel of spine, possibly recased as endpapers seem more recent, text doesn't seem cropped, though, and is relatively clean, few scattered fingermarks and stray foxy stains to the contrary, front hinge looks shaken, but feels okay; ownership signatures of Gordon Cecil Hartley (1923) and one other. Scarce.   Magnum Opus 44-23 1996 $250.00

CARLYLE, THOMAS 1795-1881   Sartor Resartus. London: George Bell & Sons, 1898. Limited edition of 150 copies, number 94, with extra plate at page 258; xxiii, 352 pages; frontispiece, 33 plates and 45 text illustrations by Edmund J. Sullivan; beige holland cloth, lettering in black and red; fine, many pages still unopened.   Robin Greer 94A-34 1996 £200.00

CARLYLE, THOMAS 1795-1881   Complete Works. Boston: 1884. Limited edition deluxe, one of 315 copies, numbered; 8vo; 24 volumes; printed on parchment linen paper, portrait; beautifully bound in half light brown polished calf, cloth sides, gilt tops; fine set.   Charles W. Traylen 117-85 1996 £600.00

CARMAN, BLISS 1861-1929   By the Aurelian Wall and Other Elegies. Boston, New York & London: Lamson, Wolffe and Co., 1898. 1st edition; 1st state; 8vo; 132 pages; title in 2 colors; green cloth titled in gilt on spine with title in gilt and black on front cover above gilt and black vignette, single ruled black frame, vertical slit along top half of inner edge of titlepage; otherwise near fine. From the library of Paul Lemperly, founder of Rowfant Club.   Blue Mountain SP95-92 1996 $150.00

CARMAN, BLISS 1861-1929   The Princess of the Tower, The Wise Men from the East and to the Winged Victory. Village Press, 1906. One of 58 copies on paper, signed by author; there were also 4 on vellum; 10 1/4 x 6 3/4 inches; 3 p.l., 5-18 pages, (1) leaf (colophon); decorative initial; original holland backed printed blue paper boards, edges untrimmed, two tiny stains on front cover, light foxing on two leaves only, otherwise very fine. Bookplate. Cary 35.   Phillip J. Pirages 33-501 1996 $250.00

CARMICHAEL, PHILIP   The Man from the Moon. New York: 1909. 296 pages; 4 color cover design, probably by Frank Watkins, 8 full page color and many monochromatic illustrations by him. Tightened, one illustration frayed at top; overall very good.   Bookworm & Silverfish 280-33 1996 $250.00

CARMON, EZRA   Special Report On the History and Present Condition of the Sheep Industry of the United States. Washington: 1892. 1st edition; 1000 pages; plates; cloth, very good+. Rare.   T. A. Swinford 49-185 1996 $350.00

CARNAN, T.   The Gentleman and Lady's Key to Polite-Literature, or a Compendious Dictionary of Fabulous History. London: T. Carnan, 1788. 8vo; vi, 250 pages; frontispiece; modern quarter calf, marbled boards, head of title replaced, small hole in text on page 31.   Robin Greer 94A-26 1996 £120.00

CARNE, JOHN   Syria, The Holy Land, Asia Minor, &c. London: Paris & America: Fisher, Son & Co., Ltd., n.d. c. 1836. 1st edition; 4to; 3 volumes in 1; 117 steel engraved plates and 2 steel engraved maps, all plates are in good condition, no foxing or offsetting, hinges cracked, but still good, tight copy; full red morocco, gilt rule border to boards, alternate blind and gilt tooled design to boards, gilt title and tooling to panelled spine, corners bumped and worn, joints rubbed, all edges gilt. Beeleigh Abbey BA56-51 1996 £350.00

CAROVE, FRIEDRICH WILHELM 1789-1852   The Story Without an End. London: Sampson, Low, Marston Searle and Rivington, 1868. 1st edition; 4to; tinted frontispiece and 15 chromo litho plates by Eleanor Boyle; green cloth pictorially stamped in gilt, occasional pale spotting, else bright, very fresh copy.   Barbara Stone 70-35 1996 £135.00

CARP, AUGUSTUS   Augustus Carp, by Himself. London: William Heiemann, 1924. 1st edition; several black and white illustrations; original binding, top edge dusty, head of spine split and worn, head and tail of spine and corners bumped, covers marked and slightly soiled, cover edges rubbed, free endpapers browned, good. With ownership signataure of Ian Fleming.   Ulysses 39-673 1996 £125.00

CARPENTER, W. B.   The Microscope and Its Revelations. London: 1901. 8vo; 2 volumes; 23 plates, nearly 900 wood engravings; original cloth.   Wheldon & Wesley 207-145 1996 £85.00

CARPENTIER, WILLIAM E.   Introduction to the Study of Foraminifera. London: Ray Society, 1862. Large 4to; 22 plates; limp boards, paper label, little rubbed.   Petersfield Bookshop FH58-224 1996 £100.00

CARPUE, J. C.   An Account of Two Successful Operations for Restoring a Lost Nose from the Integuments of the Forehead with Foreword and Biography By Frank McDowell. Birmingham: 1981. Facsimile of 1816 edition; 103 pages; full leather; GM 5737.   W. Bruce Fye 71-306 1996 $100.00

CARR, CALEB   The Alienist. New York: Random House, 1994. 1st edition; fine in dust jacket, signed by author.   Between the Covers 42-83 1996 $150.00

CARR, CALEB   Casing the Promised Land. New York: Harper & Row, 1980. 1st edition; Fine in fine dust jacket.   Bella Luna 7-139 1996 $150.00

CARR, JOHN   A Tour through Holland, Along the Right and Left Banks of the Rhine, to the South of Germany, in the Summer and Autumn of 1806. Philadelphia: Conrad & Co., 1807. 1st edition; tall 8vo; xiv, 301 pages, 5 leaves; contents fine; original calf, red label, binding fine except for 3 scratches which remove about 4 inches of surface leather, corners bumped, top of spine slightly chipped.   Roy W. Clare XXIV-76 1996 $200.00

CARR, JOHN DICKSON   The Cavalier's Cup. New York: Wm. Morrow & co., 1953. 1st edition; lower corners lightly bumped, still near fine in price clipped dust jacket with spine tips and corners only lightly worn. Quill & Brush 102-190 1996 $125.00

CARR, JOHN DICKSON   Death Turns the Tables. New York: Harper & Bros., 1941. 1st edition; with publisher's "Sporting Offer" printed on pale green tissue paper and tipped to p. 193 and rear endpaper, light unavoidable offset on hinges, otherwise very good in lightly soiled dust jacket with few small, rubbed chips and tears; light unavoidable offset on hinges, otherwise very good in lightly soiled dust jacket with few small rubbed chips and tears.   Quill & Brush 102-185 1996 $150.00

CARR, JOHN DICKSON   The Emperor's Snuff-Box. New York: Harper & Bros., 1942. 1st edition; precedes the first U.K. edition; original binding, head and tail of spine slightly bumped, very good in nicked, rubbed and creased, slightly marked and dusty dust jacket missing a small piece at tail of spine.   Ulysses 39-93 1996 £250.00

CARR, JOHN DICKSON   He Who Whispers. New York: Harper & Bros., 1946. 1st edition; fine in very good dust jacket with light rubbing, few small closed tears and light soiling on back panel.   Quill & Brush 102-186 1996 $100.00

CARR, JOHN DICKSON   My Late Wives. New York: Wm. Morrow & Co., 1946. 1st edition; spine extremities and corners lightly rubbed, otherwise fine in price clipped dust jacket with few short closed tears. Quill & Brush 102-187 1996 $100.00

CARR, JOHN DICKSON   Night at the Mocking Widow. New York: Wm. Morrow and Co., 1950. 1st edition; near fine in dust jacket with touch of rubbing, rear panel very lightly soiled, few tiny closed tears.   Quill & Brush   102-189   1996 $100.00

CARR, WILLIAM   The Dialect of Craven, in the West-Riding of the County of York, with a Copious Glossary... London: William Crofts; & Robinson & Hernaman, Leeds, 1828. 2nd edition; 2 volumes; half titles; original red brown cloth, spines dulled, paper labels.   Jarndyce 103-96 1996 £90.00

CARRINGTON, HENRY B.   Ab-Sa-Ra-Ka, Land of Massacre, Being the Experiences of An Officer's Life Out on the Plains with an Outine of Indian Operations and Conferences from 1865 to 1878. Philadelphia: 1878. xx, 383 pages, frontispiece, plates, folding map; pictorial cloth, very good+. Rader 601; Howes C175; Dustin 49. Luther 137.   T. A. Swinford 49-189   1996 $100.00

CARROLL, GEORGE D.   Diamonds from Brilliant Minds. New York: Dempsey & Carroll, 1881. 8vo; frontispiece, (iv), iv, 104, 18, 26, 12, 8, 6, 24, (5) pages, 14 plates, 7 of which have metallic embossed engravings; publisher's cloth, all edges gilt, two short tears on back cover, otherwise nice.   Bookpress   75-20   1996 $110.00

CARROLL, JIM   Living at the Movies. New York: Grossman, 1973. Uncorrected proof; top corner slightly bumped, else fine in wrappers. Between the Covers   42-84   1996 $175.00

CARROLL, JOHN M.   The Elanor Hinman Interviews On the Life and Death of Crazy Horse. N.P.: 1976. 1st edition; copy 25 of 126 copies; 48 pages, illustrations by Bjorkland, signed, fine; leather and marbled boards,   T. A. Swinford   49-190   1996 $150.00

CARROTHERS, JULIA D.   Japan's Year. Tokyo: T. Hasegawa, 1905. 1st edition; 9 3/4 x 7 1/4 inches; 76 pages, printed on one side only and unopened at fore edge; hand painted illustrations on nearly every page, many of them full leaf, as well as 3 inserted color plates on highly textured paper, done by 'Japanese artists'; fine original embroidered silk binding, featuring many bright flowers in several colors and considerable gold on black background, boards laced on with purple tasseled cords, double slipcases (somewhat worn and with obvious tape repairs); portions of the black silk background bit threadbare at some edges, but flowers in fine, bright condition, internally excellent.   Phillip J. Pirages 33-316   1996 $300.00

CARRUTH, HAYDEN   Loneliness, an Outburst of Hexasyllables. West Burke: Janus Press, 1976. Limited to 150 copies, signed by author and artist; octavo; (16) pages; frenchfold; two color relief prints by Claire Van Vliet; printed on Japanese paper, bound in blue cloth, extremely fine. Bromer Booksellers   87-103   1996 $175.00

CARRYL, GUY WETMORE   Grimm Tales Made Gay. Boston: Houghton Mifflin & Co., 1902. 1st edition; illustrations by Albert Levering; green cloth decoratively stamped in black and white; ink name on front free endpaper, light rubbing, else fine.   Hermitage   SP95-855   1996 $125.00

CARSON, HAMPTON L.   History of the Celebration of the One Hundredth Anniversary of the Promulgation of the Constitution of the United States. Philadelphia: J. B. Lippincott Co., 1889. Large thick 4to; 2 volumes; xii, 478; viii, 516 pages; 121 plates and 6 plans; blue cloth, gilt, bit soiled.   Kenneth Karmiole 1NS-10   1996 $125.00

CARSON, RACHEL   The Sea Around Us. New York: Limited Editions Club, 1980. Limited to 2000 copies, signed by Eisenstadt; 10 1/4 x 7 3/8 inches; 284 pages; color photos by alfred Eisenstadt; full black buckram, stamped in gold, fine in slightly faded slipcase, spine label lacking. Taurus Books   83-112   1996 $175.00

CARSON, RACHEL   Silent Spring. Boston: Houghton Mifflin, 1962. 1st edition; fine in lightly worn dust jacket, chipping to head and foot of spine panel.   Sherwood   3-81   1996 $135.00

CARSON, RACHEL   Under the Sea-Wind: a Naturalist's Picture of Ocean Life. New York: Simon & Schuster, 1942. 1st edition; small faint stain to preliminary page, else fine in about very good dust jacket with two moderate chips, the largest obliterating most of the word 'Schuster' on spine and with some dampstaining and scraping barely visible along top edge, author's scarce first book in decent condition.   Between the Covers   42-85   1996 $125.00

CARSON, THOMAS   Ranching, Sport and Travel. London: T. Fisher Unwin, 1911. 1st edition; 319 pages, 16 illustrations; original gilt pictorial blue cloth, rear inner hinge slightly cracked, light rubbing to extremities, else fine. Adams Herd 422; Howes C184.   Argonaut Book Shop 113-117   1996 $150.00

CARTER, ANGELA   The Donkey Prince. New York: Simon & Schuster, 1970. 1st U.S. edition; original cloth, fine in near fine dust jacket with little wear to rear panel.   Beasley Books   82-35   1996 $100.00

CARTER, ANGELA   Unicorn. Leeds: 1966. 150 copies printed; 14 mimeographed sheets; stapled into wrappers, light sporadic spotting, covers spotted, slightly marked and dusty, very good.   Ulysses   39-94 1996 £295.00

CARTER, CLARENCE EDWIN   The Territorial Papers of the United States: The Territory of Indiana 1800-1816. Washington: GPO, 1939. 2 volumes, 784, 496 pages; blue cloth.   Blue River Books   9-173   1996 $100.00

CARTER, ELIZABETH   Poems on Several Occasions. London: for John Rivington, 1762. 1st edition; 8vo; pages vi, (ii) errata leaf, 104; contemporary tree calf, flat spine with gilt urn motifs in compartments, red morocco label, sides bordered in gilt, marbled endpapers, yellow edges; pretty contemporary book label, upper joint just cracked, but still firm, lower joint tender, some negligible browning, attractive copy. Simon Finch   24-34   1996 £200.00

CARTER, ELIZABETH   Poems on Several Occasions. London: printed for John Rivington, 1762. 1st edition; small 8vo; pages vii, 104; contemporary calf serviceably rebacked; bookplate of Wm. Gery, of Bushmead.   Peter Murray Hill   185-29   1996 £95.00

CARTER, F.   Gold Like Glass. London: Twyn Barlwn Press, 1932. 1st edition; of 200 copies, this 1/20 copies with signed etching by author/artist; fine, quite scarce in this format.   Aronovitz   57-250   1996 $175.00

CARTER, HARRY   Fournier on Typefounding. London: printed at the Curwen Press for Soncino Press, 1930. 1st edition; one of 260 copies; 8vo; portrait, 16 double page facsimiles, original cloth, slightly faded and stained. Bookplate of Ruari McLean.   Forest Books   74-301   1996 £85.00

CARTER, HARVEY LEWIS   'Dear Old Kit' The Historical Christopher Carson. Norman: University of Oklahoma Press, 1968. 1st edition; xix, 250 pages; numerous illustrations, 5 maps; original cloth, very fine with dust jacket. Rittenhouse 105.   Argonaut Book Shop   113-118   1996 $125.00

CARTER, JIMMY   Always a Reckoning and other Poems. New York: Random House, 1995. 1st edition; signed by author; 8vo; illustrations by Sarah Elizabeth Chuldenko; cloth backed boards, dust jacket; new. James S. Jaffe   34-106   1996 $100.00

CARTER, JOHN 1905-1975   Binding Variants in English Publishing, 1820-1900. London: Constable, 1932. 1st edition; one of 500 copies; 8vo; xviii, 172 pages, 28 collotype plates; vellum spine, boards, some light sporadic foxing on blue paper used for text, as usual, else fine.   The Bookpress   75-278   1996 $110.00

CARTER, JOHN 1905-1975   An Enquiry Into the Nature of Certain Nineteenth Century Pamphlets. London: Constable & Co.,/New York: Charles Scribner's Sons, 1934. 1st edition; 9 x 6 inches; xii, 400 pages; 4 plates; original cloth and dust jacket, in vinyl chemise and contained in hardshell box with sliding top panel; jacket little faded and smudged, otherwise very fine.   Phillip J. Pirages   33-90   1996 $250.00

CARTER, JOHN 1905-1975   More Binding Variants. London: Constable, 1938. 1st edition; small 8vo; x, 52 pages; cloth, dust jacket slightly worn and chipped, else fine, scarce.   The Bookpress   75-279   1996 $100.00

CARTER, JOHN 1905-1975   Printing and the Mind of Man. London: Cassell and Co., 1967. 1st edition; fine in lightly soiled, price clipped dust jacket.   Hermitage   SP95-835   1 996 $320.00

CARTER, JOHN 1905-1975   Printing and the Mind of Man. London: Cassell and Co., New York: Holt, Rinehart and Winston, 1967. 1st edition; 12 1/2 x 9 inches; xxxiii, (1) pages, (1) leaf, 280 pages; many facsimiles in text; original cloth, dust jacket; hint of browning to spine of jacket, otherwise very fine.   Phillip J. Pirages   33-89   1996 $100.00

CARTER, JOSEPH COLEMAN   The Sculpture of the Sanctuary of Athena at Priene. London: Society of Antiquaries of London, 1983. 4to; xxiii, 267 pages, 31 figures; 47 paltes, 13 tables, diagrams; original cloth, dust jacket.   Archaeologia   Luxor-3137   1996 $150.00

CARTER, MATTHEW   A Most Trve and Exact Relation of that Unfortunate Expedition of Kent, Essex and Colchester. London: 1650. 1st edition; pott 8vo; (x), 214 pages; contemporary sheep, with label and date later additions, spine repaired at tips, but still little split along hinge, some wear, some marks, some chips, some browning, but good; with Fairfax of Cameron bookplate. Wing C662.   Ash Rare Books Zenzybyr-20 1996 £195.00

CARTER, ROBERT GOLDTHWAITE   Four Brothers in Blue or Sunshine and Shadows of the War of the Rebellion a Story of the Great Civil War from Bull Run to Appomatox. Washington: Gibson Bros., 1913. True 1st edition, limited to only 80 copies; xiii, (v)-509 pages; scarce issue; original cloth; very good to near fine; formerly the copy of Bell Wiley. Dornbusch I Mass. 5; Howes C191; Nevins I 67.   McGowan Book Co. 65-18 1996 $2,250.00

CARTER, SAMUEL   The Law of Executions, or, a Treatise Shewing and Explaining the Nature of Executions... London: printed by the Assigns of Richard and Edward Atkins etc., 1706. contemporary panelled calf, showing wear, clean copy.   Meyer Boswell SL25-36 1996 $450.00

CARTER, SAMUEL   Lex Custumaria; or, a Treatise of Copy-Hold Estates, in Respect of the Lord (and the) Copyholder. London: printed by the Assigns of Richard and Edward Atkins, 1696. Modern quarter calf, some embrowning, but sound.   Meyer Boswell SL26-32 1996 $450.00

CARTER, SEBASTIAN   A Printer's Dozen. Cambridge: Rampant Lions Press, 1993. One of 200 copies; page size 12 1/2 x 9 3/4 inches; on Arches Velin and Fabriano Ingres Verdastro; various types were used, woodcuts; quarter cloth with cockerell marbled paper boards, housed in matching paper over boards slipcase.   Priscilla Juvelis 95/1-203 1996 $275.00

CARTER, THOMAS FRANCIS   The Invention of Printing in China. New York: Columbia University Press, 1925. 1st edition; 8vo; xx, 282 pages, many plates; cloth, fine.   The Bookpress 75-280 1996 $125.00

CARTER, W. A.   Great Inducements to Those Who Desire to Ship Cattle by the U.P. Railroad. Fort Bridger: W'y Ty July 2, 1877. 1st edition; 4 page folder, printed on blue paper, printed on 2 pages; fine. Michael D. Heaston 23-86 1996 $650.00

CARTER, WILL   The First 10. Some Ground Covered at the Rampant Lions Press by Will Carter 1949-58. Cambridge: printed by Will Carter at the Rampant Lions Press, 1958. 1st edition; 4to; 9 colored printed specimens; original cloth backed boards; nice.   Forest Books 74-225 1996 £65.00

CARTHEW, THOMAS   Reports of Cases Adjudged in the Court of King's Bench, from the Third Year of King James the Second, to the Twelfth Year of King William the Third... London: 1741. 2nd edition; folio; pages (22), 520, (24), with licence leaf; contemporary calf, little worn at corners, label defective, binding strong, internally nice large copy, with some neat marginal notes in contemporary hand.   James Fenning 133-50 1996 £125.00

CARTIER-BRESSON, HENRI   Decisive Moment: Photography. New York: 1952. 1st edition; dust jacket, pamphlet laid in as issued, dust jacket slightly soiled, very good.   J. B. Muns 154-62 1996 $750.00

CARTIER-BRESSON, HENRI   The Decisive Moment. New York: Simon & Schuster, 1952. 1st American edition; folio; 126 photos in gravure, booklet laid in; bound in color printed boards designed by Matisse; few short tears at hinges have been expertly repaired, boards moderately soiled, else very good.   Andrew Cahan 47-42 1996 $425.00

CARTIER-BRESSON, HENRI   From One China to the Other. New York: 1956. 1st edition; dust jacket slightly chipped.   J. B. Muns 154-68 1996 $165.00

CARTIER-BRESSON, HENRI   Henri Cartier Bresson Photographer. New York Graphic Society, 1979. 1st American edition; oblong 4to; 155 phot illustrations; dust jacket.   J. B. Muns 154-63 1996 $100.00

CARTIER-BRESSON, HENRI   People of Moscow. New York: 1955. 1st edition; dust jacket chipped.   J. B. Muns 154-66 1996 $100.00

CARTIER-BRESSON, HENRI   World of Henri Cartier Bresson. New York: 1968. 1st edition; oblong 4to; dust jacket.   J. B. Muns 154-67 1996 4100.00

CARTWRIGHT, FAIRFAX L.   The Mystic Rose from the Garden of the King. London?: privately printed, 1898. 1st edition; small 4to; 315 pages; contemporary full polished calf by Zaehnsdorf, with raised bands, gilt tooled spine panels and borders, 19th century bookplate, but nice copy. Chapel Hill 94-109 1996 $200.00

CARTWRIGHT, JOHN   Give Us Our Rights! London: printed for Dilly, n.d. 1782. 1st edition; 8vo; modern boards, titlepage and last leaf backed (touching couple of letters), otherwise good.   Ximenes 109-71 1996 $125.00

CARTY, T. J.   A Dictionary of Literary Pseudonyms in the English Language. London: Mansell Pub., 1994. 1st edition; small 4to; 637 pages; original cloth; new.   Forest Books 74-35 1996 £60.00

CARUS WILSON, WILLIAM   The Children's Friend. Kirby Lonsdale: Arthur Foster, 1831-38. 8vo; volumes 8 to 15, 8 volumes in 4; numerous text woodcut vignettes; contemporary matching crimson roan gilt, extremities little rubbed; occasional patch of browning or spotting, but excellent run, scarce.   R.F.G. Hollett & Son 78-344 1996 £240.00

CARVER, NORMAN F.   Form and Space of Japanese Architecture. Tokyo: Skokokusha, 1955. 1st edition; 4to; 200 pages; photographs; cloth, dust jacket. inscription in ink on front free endpaper, else very good.   Bookpress 75-165 1996 $185.00

CARVER, RAYMOND   Carnations. Vineburg: Engdahl Typography, 1992. One of 26 copies (in an edition of 200), small quarto; quarterbound in cream colored leather and black cloth, cloth covered slipcase.   Lame Duck Books 19-128 1996 $300.00

CARVER, RAYMOND   Cathedral. New York: Knopf, 1983. Uncorrected proof; wrappers; small pen name on front cover, otherwise fine.   Ken Lopez 74-78 1996 $175.00

CARVER, RAYMOND   Cathedral. New York: Alfred A. Knopf, 1983. 1st edition; 228 pages; grey cloth spine, grey paper covered boards; fine in fine dust jacket.   Orpheus Books 17-114 1996 $100.00

CARVER, RAYMOND   Furious Seasons and Other Stories. Santa Barbara: Capra Press, 1977. This one of 1200 copies of the softcover issue; wrappers; fine.   Ken Lopez 74-77 1996 $175.00

CARVER, RAYMOND   If It Please You. Northridge: Lord John, 1984. One of 26 lettered copies; signed by author. boards, as issued, fine. Between the Covers 42-87 1996 $350.00

CARVER, RAYMOND   If it Please You. Northridge: Lord John Press, 1984. 1st edition; limited to 200 copies, signed by author; extremely fine. Bromer Booksellers 87-45 1996 $175.00

CARVER, RAYMOND   Intimacy. Concord: Ewart, 1987. One of 75 numbered copies, signed by author; cloth and paper covered boards. Between the Covers 42-90 1996 $350.00

CARVER, RAYMOND   Music. Concord: William B. Ewert, Pub., c.1985. Limited to 136 copies, this copy one of 26 lettered copies, specially bound and signed by author; 5 x 7 inches; stitched wrappers; very good.   John K. King 77-229 1996 $175.00

CARVER, RAYMOND   Near Klamath. Sacramento: English Club of Sacramento State College, 1968. 1st edition; wrappers; very good or better, with previous owner's name and two relatively inoffensive bookstore rubber stamps, one on inside front cover and one on titlepage; scarce and fragile.   Lame Duck Books 19-127 1996 $1,250.00

CARVER, RAYMOND   No Heroics, Please. New York: Vintage, 1992. Uncorrected proof; wrappers; fine.   Ken Lopez 74-82 1996 $125.00

CARVER, RAYMOND   Put Yourself in My Shoes. Santa Barbara: Capra Press, 1974. 1st edition; one of 75 numbered copies, signed by Carver; pictorial boards; fine.   Captain's Bookshelf 38-35 1996 $600.00

CARVER, RAYMOND   This Water. Concord: Ewart, 1985. One of 36 copies; signed by author, from a total edition of 136; cloth and paper covered boards, as issued; fine.   Between the Covers 42-88 1996 $375.00

CARVER, RAYMOND   Two Poems. Maryland: Scarab Press, 1982. Limited to 100 copies, signed by author; additionally signed on title; wrappers; fine.   Words Etcetera 94-268 1996 £150.00

CARVER, RAYMOND   Ultramarine. New York: Random House, 1986. 1st edition; fine in dust jacket, signed by author.   Between the Covers 42-89 1996 $150.00

CARVER, RAYMOND   What We Talk About When We Talk About Love. New York: Knopf, 1981. Uncorrected proof; lightly soiled, very near fine, scarce.   Between the Covers 42-86 1996 $500.00

CARVER, RAYMOND   Where I'm Calling From. New York: Atlantic Monthly, 1988. One of 250 numbered copies, signed by author; fine in white cloth stamped in red and gold, publisher's blue slipcase which is near fine.   Ken Lopez 74-81 1996 $350.00

CARWITHEN, I. B. S.   A View of the Brahminical Religion, In its Confirmation of the Truth of the Sacred History, and In Its Influence on the Moral Character... London: printed for Cadell and Davies, Strand; for J. M. Gutch, Bristol.. 1810. 1st edition; 8vo; (i-iii), errata leaf, 3-307 pages, notes 311-325 pages; title and first two leaves discreetly blindstamped with library stamp, rest of text clean; rebound in modern half calf, marbled boards, gilt title to panelled spine, new endpapers and prelims.   Beeleigh Abbey BA56-52 1996 £100.00

CARY, ROBERT   Palaeologia Chronica. A Chronological Account of Ancient Time. London: Printed by J. Darby for Richard Chiswell, 1677. Tall folio; 18 p.l., 271, 97 pages, errata; title in red and black (slightly discolored); name of 1859 owner in blank part of title; very worn calf, nicely rebacked (bottom corners very bumped), complete copy in fine condition.   Roy W. Clare XXIV-9 1996 $350.00

CARYLL, JOHN   Sir Salomon; or the Cautious Coxcomb; a Comedy. London: printed for H. Herringman, 1671. 1st edition; 4to; modern calf, bit rubbed; very good, complete with final blank; Wing C746; Woodward & McManaway 196; Pforzheimer 136; CBEL II 759/1523   Ximenes 109-72 1996 $600.00

CASA, GIOVANNI DELLA   The Refin'd Courtier, or, a Correction of Several Indencencies Crept Into Civil Conversation. London: ptd. for R. Royston & are to be sold by Matthew Gilliflower &... 1679. 2nd edition; 12mo; portrait, (xxiv), 233 pages, 2 pages of ads, final blank leaf; original cloth, outer side margin of portrait trimmed close to plate, surface of leather at foot of upper cover rubbed, wormhole near foot of inner margin in middle of the book and from pages 95 to 130 quite large and touching some letters; book is slightly loose in binding. Wing C795; Heltzel, Courtesy Books 293.   David Bickersteth 133-14 1996 £185.00

CASA, GIOVANNI DELLA   Rime, et Prose. Fiorenza: Appresso I. Giunti, 1564. 1st edition thus; 12mo; 296 pages; 19th century half morocco, bookplates, front board detached and rear hinge weak, else complete and internally bright; rare;   Chapel Hill 94-338 1996 $350.00

CASALIS, EUGENE   The Basutos; or, Twenty-Three Years in South Africa. London: James Nisbet and Co., 1861. 1st edition in English; 8vo; wood engraved frontispiece, numerous other illustrations; original magenta cloth, some rubbing, spine rather faded; very good.   Ximenes 109-73 1996 $500.00

CASANOVA   The Memoirs of Jacques Casa Nova De Seingalt. Limited Editions Club, 1940. Limited to 1500 numbered sets; royal 8vo; 8 volumes; designed boards, buckram spines, very good.   Thomas Thorp 489-57 1996 £50.00

CASCOYNE, CRISP   An Address to the Liverymen of the City of Lodon, from Sir Crisp Cascoyne, Knt. Late Lord Mayor, Relative to His Conduct in the Cases of Elizabeth Canning and Mary Squires. London: printed for James Hodges, 1754. 1st edition; folio; disbound; some foxing of titlepage, but very good, uncommon. Amory 51.   Ximenes 109-66 1996 $500.00

THE CASE Between the Lord Maryor and Commons of London Concerning the Election of Sheriffs for the Year Ensuing, Clearly Stated. London: printed for R. Read, 1682. Folio; 8 pages, uncut, disbound; Wing C857.   H. M. Fletcher 121-42 1996 £75.00

THE CASE of Mr. Benjamin Leech Bricklayer, at the Old Baily, the Fourteenth Day of October, 1682. London: printed for A. Green, 1682. Folio; 4 pages; uncut, disbound. Wing C953.   H. M. Fletcher 121-43 1996 £80.00

THE CASE of the British and Irish Manufacture of Linen, Threads and Tapes, Fairly Stated; In Answer to the Impartial Considerer. N.P.: n.p., n.d. 1738. Sole edition; folio; (4) pages, drop title on page one, docket title on one of the otherwise blank folded panels on page (4); 1st and 2nd pages with slit at centre fold, lower inner margin on all four pages cut away, but nowhere near the printed surface. Hansen 5163; not traced in Kress of Goldsmith.   David Bickersteth 133-15 1996 £150.00

THE CASE Of the Lord Mayor and Aldermen of London, Upon the Petition of some of the Common Council Men, Presented to the Honourable House of Commons, with His Lordships and the Aldermens Answer to the Charge Exhibited... London: printed for John Harris at the Harrow in the Poultrey, 1690. Folio; 2 pages, portraion of left margin cut away; disbound.   H. M. Fletcher 121-45 1996 £65.00

THE CASE of the Planters of Tobacco in Virginia. London: J. Roberts, 1733. 1st edition; small 4to; 64 pages; half sprinkled calf, some light rubbing to cover, else very good.   The Bookpress 75-471 1996 $850.00

CASH, J.   The British Freshwater Rhizopoda and Heliozoa. London: 1905-19. 8vo; volumes 1-4 (of 5), 63 plates; original cloth; slight waterstaining but contents unaffected; volumes 1 and 2 with presentation inscription by Cash to his son Walter.   Wheldon & Wesley 207-1242 1996 £175.00

CASH, W. J.   The Mind of the South. New York: Knopf, 1941. 1st edition; dust jacket with few small chips and slightly darkened spine; near fine, small nice private library stamp.   Captain's Bookshelf 38-36 1996 $350.00

CASIGLIONI, ARTURO   A History of Medicine. New York: 1947. 2nd edition; 1192 pages; original binding, GM 6418.   W. Bruce Fye 71-317 1996 $150.00

CASKEY, L. D.   Attic Vase Paintings in the Museum of Fine Arts, Boston. Boston: Museum of Fine Arts, 1931-63. Small folio; 3 volumes in 6 parts (text volumes in original printed wrappers, small chip to upper corner of volume 1), otherwise fine, plate volumes in original cloth backed portfolios with ties, in large folio; minor shelfwear to corners of portfolios, interior fine; text in original printed wrappers.   Archaeologia Luxor-3138 1995 $1,500.00

CASPAR, JOHANN LUDWIG   A Handbook of the Practice of Forensic Medicine Based Upon Personal Experience. London: New Sydenham Society, 1861. 1st edition in English; 8vo; 4 volumes, xvi, 317; vii, 331; x, 417; xvi, 364 pages; embossed Victorian cloth, joints and edges worn, spines to two volumes torn, good set only, uncommon.   John Gach 150-89 1996 $175.00

CASSINO, SAMUEL   The Naturalist's Directory 1884. Boston: 1884. 1st edition; 191 pages; original binding, waterstain affecting cover and endpapers, contents fine.   W. Bruce Fye 71-314 1996 $100.00

CASSON, STANLEY   Macedonia, Thrace and Illyria: Their Relations to Greece from the Earliest Times Down to the Time of Philip, Son of Amyntas. Oxford: Oxford University Press, 1926. 8vo; xx, 357 pages; 106 illustrations, 19 maps; original cloth; scarce; with signature of Clark Hopkins.   Archaeologia Luxor-3142 1996 $150.00

CASTENEDA, C. E.   A Report of the Spanish Archives in San Antonio. (Texas). San Antonio: Yanaguana Society, 1937. 1st edition; limited to 500 numbered copies; 167 pages; original maroon cloth with title stamped in black on spine and front cover; fine. Tate Indians of Texas 28. Jenkins BTB 222.1.   Michael D. Heaston 23-84 1996 $150.00

CASTERA, JEAN HENRI   History of Catherine II, Empress of Russia. London: printed for J. Stockdale, 1800. 8vo; 13 portraits and a view; recent half calf, old marbled sides; prelims erratically paginated.   Peter Murray Hill 185-30 1996 £60.00

CASTIGLIONE, BALDASSARE 1475-1529   Il Cortegiano. Lyons: Guillaume Rouille, 1553. 16mo; titlepage, 7 ff. n.n., pages 1-"457", 6 ff. n.n., ruled in red; a Parisian binding c. 1560, red mor. over stiff pasteboards, tooled in silver (now oxydised) to a pre-fanfare pattern of compartments outlined by a continuous fillet & w/azured tools, spine w/4 double bands, compartments dec. w/azured tools, title label added in 18th century, edges of bds. dec. w/lines & tooling in silver, edges black (originally silver?), pastedown w/2 endleaves at front (two at back), no watermark; covers are divided into compartments by a continuous fillet, as on fanfare bindings, but do no have the leafy sprays of the true fanfare; note by W. Kerney, 15.11. (18)88; Lord Amherst of Hackney, his sale, Sotheby's, 3 December 1908, lot 173.   Marlborough 160-2 1996 £4,800.00

CASTIGLIONE, BALDASSARE 1475-1529   Le Parfait Covrtisan. Lyons: Cloquemin, 1580 1579 at end. 1st edition of this translation; 8vo; printer's device on titlepage, text in parallel columns of Italian and French; boards and vellum; Brunet I 1630; STC French Books 94. Rostenberg & Stern 150-78 1996 $975.00

CASTIGLIONE, BALDASSARE 1475-1529   Les Quatre Livres du Courtisan du Conte Baltazar de Castillon. N.P.: n.d. ?Lyon: Denis de Harsy, c. 1537. 2nd edition in French; crown 8vo; printer's woodcut device, historiated initials first two leaves washed, resewn, rebound in red morocco in 16th century style, all edges gilt, with original gauffring still visible; good, clean copy.   H. M. Fletcher 121-21 1996 £2,700.00

CASTIGLIONI, ARTURO   A History of Medicine. New York: 1947. 2nd edition; 8vo; 1182 pages; 541 illustrations; cloth rubbed; internally very good.   James Tait Goodrich K40-78 1996 $150.00

A CATAECHISM of American Law. Philadelphia: S. C. Atkinson, 1852. 1st edition; 18mo; 8, 256 pages; original cloth, printed paper label (chipped), text lightly foxed, but very good. Not in Imprints Survey.   M & S Rare Books 60-358 1996 $325.00

A CATALOGUE of the Library at Knowsley Hall, Lancashire. London: privately printed at the Chiswick Press, London, 1893. 4to; 4 volumes; green quarater roan, green cloth boards, spines worn and rubbed, uncut, ex-library, small stamps on title.   Maggs Bros. Ltd. 1191-52 1996 £130.00

CATE, WIRT ARMISTEAD   Lucius Q. C. Lamar: Secession and Reunion. Chapel Hill: 1935. 1/425 copies, signed by author; 594 pages; cloth, some spotting to spine. Nevins II p. 44.   W. M. Morrison 436-273 1996 $150.00

CATESBY, MARK   The Natural History of Carolina, Florida and the Bahama Islands. Savannah: 1974. One of 500 sets; Folio; xvi, (1), 107, (1) pages; 50 unbound facsimile colored plates (with titlepage and letterpress) and descriptive catalogue, bound by hand, containing 220 figures of birds, beasts, fishes, serpents, insects and plants, along with colored endpaper maps; gilt lettered cloth, enclosed, along with suite of plates, in gilt lettered cloth bound clamshell box.   Raymond M. Sutton VI-4 1996 $1,500.00

CATHER, WILLA SIBERT 1873-1947   Death Comes for the Archbishop. New York: Knopf, 1927. 1st edition; fine in about very good dust jacket with two small chips and some darkening to spine, very uncommon. Between the Covers 42-93 1996 $550.00

CATHER, WILLA SIBERT 1873-1947   My Mortal Enemy. New York: Alfred A. Knopf, 1926. 1st edition; 123 pages; boards; in very slightly worn dust jacket, book fine.   Robert G. Hayman 11/95-23 1996 $125.00

CATHER, WILLA SIBERT 1873-1947   O Pioneers! Boston/New York: Houghton Mifflin, 1913. 1st edition; 1st issue binding; neat contemporary bookplate, fine with touch of rubbing, lacking printed dust jacket (in an old unprinted glasine jacket which we do not believe original but about which we are unsure enough not to discard), very nice, very uncommon. Between the Covers 42-92 1996 $450.00

CATHER, WILLA SIBERT 1873-1947   The Old Beauty and Others. New York: Alfred A. Knopf, Inc., 1948. 1st edition; original binding, top edge dusty, head and tail of spine slightly bumped, spine slightly faded, endpaper edges slightly browned, very good in slightly rubbed, creased and dusty dust jacket browned at spine and edges.   Ulysses 39-96 1996 £55.00

CATHER, WILLA SIBERT 1873-1947   The Professor's House. New York: Knopf, 1925. 1st edition; bright, fine copy in unsoiled, near fine white dust jacket, with two small edge tears to bottom of front panel, scarce in dust jacket.   Thomas Dorn 9-78 1996 $600.00

CATHER, WILLA SIBERT 1873-1947   Sapphira and the Slave Girl. New York: Knopf, 1940. Advance Salesman's dummy, printing only first 14 pages of the book, slight foxing to fore edge, fine in dust jacket with couple of short, barely noticeable tears, jacket has no text on flaps or rear panel and displays the printers color register on front flap and edge of rear panel; rare, especially in this condition.   Between the Covers 42-94 1996 $750.00

CATHER, WILLA SIBERT 1873-1947   Sapphira and the Slave Girl. New York: 1940. 1st edition; limited to 520 numbered copies, signed by author; 10 x 6 inches; 295 pages; cloth, top edge gilt, bit rubbed, spine slightly sunned, lacks dust jacket and slipcase.   John K. King 77-231 1996 $295.00

CATHERINE OF SIENA, SAINT   Dialogo de la Seraphica Vergine... Venice: C. Arrivabene, 1517. 2nd edition; 8vo; 504 pages; small title woodcut; early 20th century pigskin; very good. Essling 738; Sander 1818.   Bennett Gilbert LL29-21 1996 $1,500.00

CATHERWOOD, JOHN   A New Method of Curing the Apoplexy. London: printed by J. Darby for W. Taylor, 1715. 8vo; pages viii, 77 (blank between 58-59), contemporary quarter calf and marbled boards, recently rebacked, light foxing, otherwise very good.   James Tait Goodrich K40-80 1996 $595.00

CATHOLIC CHURCH. COUNCILS   Conciliorum Quatuor Generalium Niceni, Constantinopolitani, Ephesini & Calcedonensis. Paris: Francois Regnault May 1535. 1st pocket edition; 8vo; 2 volumes, (24), 326; (8), 222 leaves, gothic type, double columns, numerous ornamental initials, titles with historiated architectural woodcut borders; modern calf, blind ruled and gilt in Renaissance style, old stamps in lower margins of titles. Moreau IV no. 1266; Cioranesco 14989; Adams C2767.   Jeffrey D. Mancevice 20-18 1996 $1,250.00

CATHOLIC CHURCH. LITURGY & RITUAL. OFFICE   Officium B. Mariae Virginis, Nuper Reformatum... Antwerp: Ex Architypographia Plantiniana, 1731. 8vo; title in red and black with engraved vignette, 21 f., 741 pages, 2 ff. index, 16 engraved plates; contemporary crimson morocco covers gilt with five fold outer border, central panel with swags, arabesque corner-pieces and central lozenge w/similar tools filled with star, flower and other small tool decoration, spine gilt in 6 panels, raised bands, gilt, panels with stars and arabesques, all edges gilt and gauffered, marbled endpapers, corners little soft, some aging of paper, attractive and striking Low Countries binding - having some affinity with H. Davis Gift II 311 and Culot, Quatre Siecles de Reliure en Belgique 1500-1900 no. 54; with contemporary illegible signature, later in the library of Robert Hoe with his label.   Marlborough 160-50 1996 £1,200.00

CATHOLIC CHURCH. LITURGY & RITUAL. BREVIARY   Dirunal du Breviarie Romain. Lyon: Valfray, 1740. 4to; contemporary crimson morocco, covers gilt with wide floral border and corner-pieces, arms of Henri Thomassin de Mazangues, spine gilt in 6 panels with floral decoration, all edges gilt, rubbed, corners worn, old reback now cracked at foot of one joint.   Marlborough 160-38 1996 £450.00

CATHOLIC CHURCH. LITURGY & RITUAL. HOURS   Horae Dive Virginis Marie, Secundum Usum Romanum. Paris: Gillet Hardouyn for Germain Hardouyn, 1514. 8vo; printed on vellum in Roman type issued without usual woodcut borders, a total of 41 splendid miniatures, 16 being full page and 25 smaller, all painted in rich colors & dec. with gold, lg. illustrations enclosed within architectural gold borders & there are hundreds of lg. & sm. capitals & line fillers, illuminated in red, blue & gold; 18th century brown crushed morocco with single dotted gilt border and four similar fleurons on each cover, spine with five raised bands and dotted gilt decoration on bands and within compartments, title and date on applied label, slight rubbing, gold-on-red printed endleaves, all edges gilt, lacks title leaf and one text leaf, C3, but with Hardouyn's other full page woodcut device. Lacombe 251; Brunet Heures 243.   Book Block 32-2 1996 $12,500.00

CATHOLIC CHURCH. LITURGY & RITUAL. HOURS   Horae Beatae Virginis Mariae Juxta Ritum Sacri Originis Praedicatorum Jussu Editae. S. Dominic's Press, 1923. One of 200 copies; 4to; 14 wood engravings, printed in black and red on handmade paper; linen boards, corners bumped and covers somwhat soiled and marked, endpapers stained, but contents clean and fresh, but for a few marginal spots; very scarce. Bertram Rota 272-421 1996 £500.00

CATHOLIC CHURCH. LITURGY & RITUAL. MISSAL   Missale Secundum Morem Sancte Romane Ecclesie. Venice: Joannes Baptista Sessa, 1490 (1493-98). 8vo; 290 leaves, printed in red and black throughout, roman type, title in gothic, 34 lines and headline, two columns, sessa's cat-and-mouse printer's device (Kristeller 289) printed in red on title, with a different device (Kristeller 288) at end, also printed in red, woodcut capitals and red printed Lombards, musical notes on red printed staves, full page woodcut Crucifixion on fol. q4v; contemporary Venetian brown calf over wooden boards, blind tooled and gilt, paneled spines, central compartments filled with blind diagonal intersecting triple fillets, two ornamented brass clasps with catches, gilt and guaffered edges, head and foot of spine worn away, minor abrasions elsewhere; but fine, fresh copy in its first binding. Small piece cut out and replaced from the lower blank margin of title, not affecting any printing, old stamp deleted from lower blank margin of penultimate leaf verso, neat repairs to bottom margins of few leaves, excellent, tall & fresh copy; HC 11395; Weale p. 138; Rivoli 157.35; Sander 4755; IGI 6693.   Jeffrey Mancevice 20-57 1996 $16,500.00

CATHOLIC CHURCH. LITURGY & RITUAL. MISSAL   Missale ad Usum Insignis ac Famose Ecclesie Saru. Paris: T. Kerver, 1503. 8vo; lacking 2 leaves of calendar and some leaves from text; 2 parts in 1; each with own pagination, double column, Gothic letter printed in red and black, recot of 1st leaf and verso of last somewhat dusty, few old lamp oil spots, upper margin cut bit close, occasional marginal grease marks; mid 19th century Russia, spine remounted, decorated in blind on spine and covers; fine, exceptionally rare piece or early printing. STC 16177; Lowndes 1576.   A. Sokol XXV-65 1996 £3,850.00

CATHOLIC CHURCH. LITURGY & RITUAL. MISSAL Missale Romanum. Venice: Apud Nicolaum Pezzana, 1763. Tall large thick 8vo; title in red and black with large copper plate engraving, 3 full page three quarter, woodcut initial letters, printed in red and black throughout, several pages of musical notation in red and black, 2 or 3 leaves with slight marginal soiling, rest in very good condition; handsomely bound in full contemporary brown morocco, boards with outer gilt roll border, foliate cornerpieces in gilt, center of boards stamped with large and elaborate gilt heraldic coat of arms enclosing 2 griffins surmounted by 2 cherubs and a crown, elaborate foliate outer border, spine gilt in compartments with repeated acorn devices, upper cover with slight staining and gilt rubbed, lower cover extremely good and bright; magnificent 18th century armorial binding, probably Venetian. Ian Wilkinson 95/1-34 1996 £690.00

CATHOLIC CHURCH. LITURGY & RITUAL. MISSAL Missale Romanum ex Decreto Sacrosancti Concilii Tridentini Restitutum... Venice: Balleone, 1766. Folio; vignette title, pages v-xxxv, 436, cviii, engraved frontispiece, 2 other plates; boards, cvoers gilt w/multi-colored mor., calf & paper onlays in form of a broad crimson outer border gilt w/leafy sprays, L-shaped black corner-pieces, circular brown inlays, central panel w/mottled brown broad borders, blue corner & centre pieces, enclosing a blue background & sunken red & green oval centre-piece w/crimson surrounds gilt w/flower & other sm. tools, 6 brass corner & centre studs, spine w/4 raised bands, alternate red & brown panels similarly gilt, all edges gilt, marbled pastedowns, sl. rubbed, unobtrusively & skillfully rebacked, remarkable binding using at least 50 pieces of leather on each cover to produce a design which is at once technically proficient & refreshingly exuberant. Marlborough 160-47 1996 £6,000.00

CATHOLIC CHURCH. LITURGY & RITUAL. OFFICE L'Officio di Maria Vergine. Vienna: Voigt, 1672. 8vo; engraved title, printed title, portrait on verso, 18ff. n.n. with 1 full page text illustration, 595 pages (16 full pae engraved text illustrations); brown morocco gilt, all edges gilt, gauffered, (worn, corners soft, clasps gone). Covers gilt with broad outer border, central panel with corner decoration a l'evantail and central 25 part wheel within arabesque and other ornament, flat spine with repeated small tool ornaments, all edges gilt and gauffered, plain endpapers, unusual binding, possibly italian. Marlborough 160-22 1996 £550.00

CATHOLIC CHURCH. LITURGY & RITUAL. OFFICE Officium Beatae Mariae Virginis. Brescia: Policreto Turlino, 1583. 12mo; title, 16ff., n.n., pp. 1-578, 1 f. printed in red and black, 5 full page and many smaller woodcuts; brown goatskin, sides stamped with plaque of arabesque ornament on a gilt ground around an empty oval centre, spine with 3 double bands outlined by continuous foliate ornament in gilt, gilt rosette in each compartment, edges of boards plain, lacks two pairs of blue fabric ties, edges plain gilt, pastedown and one endleaf at each end, front endleaf detached, in sound unrestored condition, the binding may be from Lombardy or from Brescia; the copy of Henry Virtue-Tebbs, his sale, Sotheby's 25 June, 1900, lot 318. Marlborough 160-7 1996 £2,100.00

THE CATHOLIC Religion Vindicated. Being an Answer to a Sermon Preached by the Rev. Mr. Cuyler, in Poughkeepsie, on the 30th day of July 1812, the Day Set Apart for Fasting and Prayer in the State of New York... N.P.: New York:? printed for the author, 1813. 1st edition; 12mo; disbound; rare; some foxing, few page numbers shaved, otherwise very good. Shaw and Shoemaker 25037. Ximenes 108-61 1996 $100.00

CATLIN, GEORGE 1796-1872 North American Indians. Edinburgh: 1903. Reprint; Pages 298, 303; 400 plates, maps; original decorated cloth, edge wear, little loose, generlaly very good. Stephen Lunsford 45-27 1996 $175.00

CATLOW, AGNES Popular Field Botany. London: 1848. Small 8vo; 80 hand colored prints on 20 plates, backsrip rubbed and torn, contents very good. Petersfield Bookshop FH58-225 1996 £90.00

CATLOW, AGNES Sketching Rambles; or, Nature in the Alps and Apennines. London: James Hogg & Sons, c. 1861. 1st edition; 8vo; 2 volumes, xii, (2), 374; viii, (2), 368 pages; hand colored frontispieces, 18 tinted lithograph plates from sketches by author; modern quarter calf, m.e., (prelims of volume 1 slightly spotted), some plates with very small insignificant stain in one corner; Thomas Thorp 489-58 1996 £200.00

CATLOW, AGNES Sketching Rambles; or, Nature in the Alps and Apennines. London: James Hogg and Sons, n.d., 1861. 1st edition; octavo; 2 volumes; xii, 374, (2 ads), viii, (2), 368 pages; 2 hand colored lithographed frontispieces, 18 lithographed plates in sepia; original red blindstamped cloth decoratively stamped in gilt on front covers and spines, extremities lightly rubbed, spine slightly darkened; frontispiece to volume 1 slithly foxed, previous owner's ink presentation inscription in each volume. Heritage Book Shop 196-252 1996 $300.00

CATTAN, CHRISTOPHER DE The Geomancie of Maister Christopher Cattan Gentleman. London: by John Wolfe, 1591. 1st edition in English; small 4to; (18), 240, (4) pages, black letter, numerous woodcut figures, diagrams; modern red morocco, scuffed at spine ends, titlepage laid down, browned and stained, first few and last few leaves stained, tables at pages 166 and 168 trimmed close with some minor loss; numerous pages misnumbered, but collated complete, good, rare. Caillet 2093 for Paris 1st ed. Bib. Astr 216; STC 4864; Wellcome 1382. Edwin V. Glaser 121-55 1996 $2,500.00

CATTERMOLE, RICHARD The Great Civil War of Charles I and His Parliament. London: New York and Paris: Longman et al, 1845. 2nd edition; 9 1/4 x 6 1/2 inches; added engraved title and frontispiece in each volume, as well as 26 engraved plates; fine contemporary red half morocco, marbled paper sides, raised bands, spines gilt in compartments with attractive floral and foliate ornaments, marbled endpapers, all edges gilt; plate imprints located well away from engraved images, with result being the loss or cropping of approximately one third of these imprints, (text and plates, ironically, with very wide margins), very slight offsetting from engravings, leather corners with trivial rubbing, but virtually perfect copy otherwise; generally fine set in handsome binding. Phillip J. Pirages 33-119 1996 $275.00

CATULLUS, C. VALERIUS The Carmina... London: printed for the translators...for private subscribers only, 1894. 1 of 4 copies on Japanese vellum; royal 8vo; pages xxiii, (i), 313; 3 states of frontispiece, mounted on linen guards, each with light paper guard, half title with limitation statement on verso; excellent copy; red silk marker; contemporary crushed and polished red morocco, by Morrell, backstrip with raised bands, gilt lettered direct in second compartment, and at foot, remaining panels gilt with arabesque tools, joints slightly rubbed, and upper joint tender, sides panelled with outer and inner triple fillet border, inner border expanded at corners to contain arabesque corner ornaments & masks, single fillet on board edges, wide turn-ins & hinges with 3 fillets, pointille roll & corner ornaments, pale turquoise watered silk doublures & free endpapers, top edge gilt, remainder untrimmed. Blackwell's B112-53 1996 £550.00

CATULLUS, C. VALERIUS (Opera). Caius Valerius Catullus et in Eum Isaaci Vossi Observationes. N.P.: Leyde: Prostat apud Isaacum Littleburii Bibiloplam Londinensem, 1684. 1st edition by Vossius; and first edition of Catullus to be published in England; small 4to; 18th century French red morocco, gilt, spine and inner dentelles gilt, all edges gilt (attributed in pencil note to Derome); some foxing and light browning, but fine in elegant early binding; from the library of John Sparrow. Wing C1526. Ximenes 109-74 1996 $600.00

CATULLUS, C. VALERIUS Catullus, Tibullus and Propertius. Opera. Birmingham: Johannis Baskerville, 1772. Sole edition in this format; duodecimo; original calf, neatly rebacked, neat inscription, quite attractive. Gaskell 45. G. W. Stuart 59-5 1996 $150.00

CAUNTER, HOBART The Oriental Album, Lives of the Moghul Emperors. London: 1837. 1st edition; 8vo; 240 pages, 21 of 22 engravings after drawings by William Daniell (lacks the plate of the Mogul Trooper); embossed calf, gilt decorated, slightly rubbed, but good. K Books 441-95 1996 £60.00

A CAUTION Against Deceivers, with Respect to the Subordination of the Son of God; and a Defence of Several Eminent Divines. Exeter: printed by George Bishop and sold by Booksellers in Exon, n.d. 1719. 8vo; 21 pages; disbound. David Bickersteth 133-70 1996 £80.00

CAUX, J. W. DE The Herring and the Herring Fishery, with Chapters on Fishes and Fishing and Our Sea Fisheries in the Future. London: Adams, 1881. 1st edition; small 8vo; 159 pages, 4 ads; cloth, very good. John Lewcock 30-5 1996 £55.00

CAVAFY, C. P. Fourteen Poems By... London: Editions, Alecto, 1966. Edition B, one of 250 copies numbered 251-500, this copy numbered 363 and signed by artist; folio; 12 full page etchings interleaved with text, by David Hockney; publisher's cloth, slipcase. From Manet to Hockney 137. Sotheran PN32-187 1996 £1,800.00

CAVAFY, C. P. Three Poems of Cavafy. Tragara Press, 1980. Limited edition, this number 42 of 95 copies; 10 x 7 inches; 12 pages; wrappers; spine very slightly faded, otherwise very nice. Virgo Books 48-75 1996 £80.00

CAVALCANTI, GUIDO Le Rime: Ballate, Sonetti, Canzoni. Officina Bodoni, 1966. One of 165 numbered copies; 8vo; printed in Arrighi-Vicentino and Centaur in black and red on Fabriano; Cavalcanti arms in red and grey on titlepage; full vellum over boards, gilt, fine in slipcase. Bertram Rota 272-349 1996 £850.00

CAVALIER, JEAN   Memoirs of the Wars of the Cevennes, Under Col. Cavallier, in Defence of the Protestants Persecuted in that Country. Dublin: printed by J. Carson, for the author, 1726. 1st Dublin edition; 8 page list of subscribers, folding map (short tear), contemporary panelled calf, label chipped;   Anthony Laywood 108-37 1996 £90.00

CAVE, F. O.   Birds of the Sudan, Their Identification and Distribution. London: 1955. 8vo; pages xxvii, 444; 12 colored plates, 12 pages of photos and 2 maps; original cloth, clean ex-library.   Wheldon & Wesley 207-685 1996 £110.00

CAVE, WILLIAM   Primitive Christianity; or,t he Religion of the Ancient Christians in the First Ages of the Gospel. London: printed by J. G. for R. Chiswell, 1676. 3rd edition; 8vo; engraved title, contemporary calf, worn, joints expertly repaired. Wing C1600.   H. M. Fletcher 121-60 1996 £55.00

CAVENDISH, GEORGE 1500-1561?   The Negotiations of Thomas Woolsey, the Great Cardinall of England. London: Sheares, 1641. 1st edition; 4to; finely engraved frontispiece; calf, rebacked, rare; Chase Side House Library bookticket. Wing C1619.   Rostenberg & Stern 150-79 1996 $525.00

CAVENDISH-BRADSHAW, MARY ANNE   Memoirs of Maria, Countess d'Alva; Being Neither Novel Nor Romance, but Appertaining to Both. London: printed by J. Barnfield for William Miller, 1808. 1st edition; 8vo; 2 volumes; xvi, 384; (iv), 494 pages; engraved frontispieces, plate, half titles, some leaves dust soiled, occasional browning and offsetting, several marginal tears (not affecting text),, contemporary half roan, rubbed, heraldic stamp on spines of a muzzled bear under a coronet. Summers p. 410; not in Block.   James Burmester 29-157 1996 £750.00

CAVENESS, WILLIAM F.   Atlas of Electroencephalography in the Developing Monkey: Macaca Multatta. Palo Alto: Addison Wesley, 1962. 1st edition; 4to; illustrations; presentation copy.   Argosy 810-91 1996 $100.00

CAVERLEY, WILLIAM SLATER   Notes on the Early Sculptured Crosses, Shrines and Monuments in the Present Diocese of Carlisle... Kendal: T. Wilson, 1899. 8vo; pages xviii, 319; portrait, numerous plates and illustrations; original brown cloth, gilt, neatly recased, new endpapers; scarce.   R.F.G. Hollett & Son 78-11 1996 £85.00

CAVINESS, MADELINE HARRISON   The Early Stained Glass of Canterbury Cathedral. Princeton: Princeton University Press, 1977. 4to; pages 209; 4 plates in color, 218 black and white plates, several text figures; original cloth, dust jacket.   Howes Bookshop 265-2127 1996 £75.00

CAWEIN, MADISON J.   Accolon of Gaul with Other Poems. Louisville: John P. Morton, 1889. 1 of 500 copies; 8vo; 8, 164 pages; original cloth, uncut. Very fine. BAL 2988.   M & S Rare Books 60-131 1996 $100.00

CAWSTON, GEORGE   The Early Chartered Companies (A.D. 1296-1858). London: 1896. pages xi, 329; engraved frontispiece; original cloth, nice. Scarce.   Stephen Lunsford 45-28 1996 $125.00

CAWTHORN, JAMES   Poems. London: printed by W. Woodfall and sold by S. Bladon, 1771. 1st edition; 4to; disbound; fine, complete with final leaf of ads; CBEL II 646.   Ximenes 108-62 1996 $400.00

CAYLEY, CORNELIUS   The Seraphical Young Shepherd... London: printed and sold by H. Trapp, 1779. 2nd edition; 12mo; pages (xvi), 199, (v); new half calf.   Peter Murray Hill 185-31 1996 £50.00

CAYLEY, N.   Australian Parrots. Sydney: 1938. 1st edition; color and other plates; original cloth, lightly rubbed and bubbled, very light foxing; scarce.   David A.H. Grayling MY95Orn-15 1996 £75.00

CECIL, HENRY   Independent Witness. London: Michael Joseph, 1963. 1st edition; inscribed on front endpaper, fine in lightly soiled, otherwise near fine dust jacket.   Quill & Brush 102-227 1996 $100.00

CECIL, HENRY   Portrait of a Judge and Other Stories. London: Michael Joseph, 1964. 1st edition; inscribed, fine in near fine dust jacket with light soiling and very minor edge wear.   Quill & Brush 102-228 1996 $100.00

CELIZ, FRAY FRANCISCO   Diary of the Alarcon Expedition Into Texas, 1718-1719. Los Angeles: Quivira Society Pub., Volume 5, 1935. 1st edition; number 259 of 600 copies; 124 pages; map, photos.   Maggie Lambeth 30-87 1996 $200.00

CELLIER, ELIZABETH   The Tryal and Sentence of Elizabeth Cellier, for Writing, Printing and Publishing a Sandalous Libel, Called Malice Defeated...Saturday the 11th and Monday the 13th of Sept. 1680. London: Thomas Collins, 1680. 8vo; (iv), 9-39, (1) pages; imprimatur leaf; some staining, mostly marginal, last two leaves detached. Wing T2171.   Robert Clark 38-116 1996 £50.00

CELLINI, BENVENUTO   The Life... London: Sold by Hacon & Ricketts, Vale Press, 1900. Limited to 300 copies; folio; 2 volumes; pages clxxxvi, (2); clxxxviii, (2), colophon and press mark, initial and large woodcut border by Ricketts, light spotting on endpapers, otherwise good set; original holland backed blue boards, paper labels (browned and chipped on backstrips), little wear at corners. Tomkinson 30.   Claude Cox 107-172 1996 £210.00

CELLINI, BENVENUTO   The Life of Benvenuto Cellini. London: Ballantyne/Vale Press, 1900. Folio; 2 volumes in 1; 2 titlepages, 187, 188 pages of text; woodcut border and initial to first page of text; bound by C. and C. McLeish, full maroon morocco, gilt rule borders with decorative gilt cornerpieces, gilt panelled spine, top edge gilt, others untrimmed, inner gilt rule and repeat cornerpieces; T. E. Lawrence's copy with his pencilled initials to top right hand corner of front free endpaper. Beeleigh Abbey BA56-139 1996 £450.00

CELLINI, BENVENUTO   The Life of Benvenuto Cellini. Verona: Limited Editions Club, 1937. Copy number 904 from a total edition of 1500 numbered copies; signed by artist; illustrations by Fritz Kredel; fine in decorative cloth and printed dust jacket, publisher's slipcase. Hermitage SP95-952 1996 $150.00

CENNINI, CENNINO   A Treatise on Painting, Written in the Year 1437 and First Published in Italian in 1821. London: Edward Lumley, 1844. Royal 8vo; illuminated titlepage, fine illuminated plate in gold and colors and 8 plates in outline; contemporary morocco, gilt edges, presentation copy from the translator, Signor Tambroni, from the library of Viscount Eversley.   Charles W. Traylen 117-227 1996 £225.00

CERESOLO, CARLO F.   Petrisyndon Evolvens Nova Volucria, Quadrupedia et Serpentia... Bergamo: Rubei, 1680. 1st edition; 12mo; 330 pages; frontispiece; original stiff wrappers; fine. Not in NUC, BM STC, Piantinida or Michel.   Bennett Gilbert LL29-22 1996 $550.00

CERTAINE Sermons or Homilies Appoynted to Be Read in Churches, in the Time of the Late Queene Elizabeth for Famous Memory. London: John Norton, for Joyce Norton and Richard Whitaker, 1633. Folio; (viii), 98, (vi), 320, (iv) pages; contemporary vellum ruled in blind, title in woodcut border, secondary titlepage to second part, blank leaf present between two parts, colophon leaf; velium marked boards bit bowed, upepr joint repaired, titlepage and prelims bit dusty; sound.   Robert Clark 38-30 1996 £145.00

CERVANTES SAAVEDRA, MIGUEL DE 1547-1616   Don Quixote De La Mancha. London: printed for T. M'lean, Bookseller and Publisher, 1819. 8vo; 4 volumes; 24 hand colored engraved plates by J. H. Clark; later 19th century green calf over marbled boards, spines and extremities somewhat rubbed.   Kenneth Karmiole 1NS-64 1996 $250.00

CERVANTES SAAVEDRA, MIGUEL DE 1547-1616   Don Quixote de la Mancha. London: Nonesuch Press, 1930. One of 1475 numbered copies; 8vo; 2 volumes; 21 illustrations in photogravure and stencilled color by E. McKnight Kauffer; printed in Monotype Goudy Modern with hand engraved Goudy titling in terracotta, on Casinensis handmade; full natural niger morocco, spines uniformly darkened and sides somewhat spotted, as usual, otherwise nice, fresh copy in slipcase; laid in is a typed letter from the Press to a subscriber.   Bertram Rota 272-326 1996 £200.00

CERVANTES SAAVEDRA, MIGUEL DE 1547-1616   Journey to Parnassus. London: Kegan Paul, Chiswick Press printed, 1883. Crown 8vo; portrait, pages (2), lxxv, (2), 387; original binding, gilt, edges gilt, metal clasp, very good to nice; inscribed to John Blyth by James Gibson.   James Fenning 133-52 1996 £55.00

CESCINSKY, HERBERT   Early English Furniture and Woodwork. London: Waverley Book Co., 1922. 1st edition; folio; xvi, 382 pages; vii, 387 pages; 2 volumes; color frontispieces, with printed tissue guards, profusely illustrated with plans, sketches and photos; two-toned cloth with calf spine labels, top edge gilt, rubbed and stained, label on volume 1 chipped, owner's name and stamp, else very good.   Andrew Cahan 47-74 1996 $175.00

CHABERT, JOSEPH BERNARD DE   Voyage Fait par Ordre Du Roi En 1750 et 1751, Dans l'Amerique Septentrionale... Paris: Imprimerie Royale, 1753. 4to; (2), viii, 288, (10) pages, 6 engraved folding maps, charts; contemporary mottled calf, gilt spine, red morocco label; fine housed in red cloth slipcase; Dionn II 489; Lande 114; Sabin 11723.   Kenneth Karmiole 1NS-242 1996 $2,000.00

CHABOT, CHARLES   The Handwriting of Junius Professionally Investigated by... London: 1871. Thick 4to; lxxviii, 289 pages, upwards of 200 pages of facsimiles of Private Letters of Junius; red cloth, ex-library, some unobtrusive stamps, slightly frayed spine, otherwise good, scarce. K Books 442-314 1996 £65.00

CHABOT, FREDERICK C.   Texas Expeditions of 184. San Antonio: Artes Graficas, 1942. 1st edition; 4to; 76 pages; illustrations; wrappers. Maggie Lambeth 30-90 1996 $100.00

CHABOT, FREDERICK C.   Texas Letters. San Antonio: Yanaguana Society V, Number 108 of 250 copies; 188 pages;   Maggie Lambeth 30-91 1996 $100.00

CHADWICK, HENRY   Sports and Pastimes of American Boys: a Guide and Text-Book of Games of the Play-Ground the Parlor and the Field, Adapted Especially for American Youth. New York: George Routledge and Son, 1884. 1st edition; square 8vo; pages 303, 4 chromolithograph plates, many wood engraved illustrations, some of the full page, original chromolithographed pictorial boards, illustrating, on both covers, various outdoor sports; very nice with attractive covers clean and bright, though just a trifle rubbed at edges and spine.   Sotheran PN32-71 1996 £398.00

CHADWICK, NORA K.   Celt and Saxon: Studies in the Early British Border. 1963. 1st edition; cloth, dust jacket, very good.   C. P. Hyland 216-90 1996 £55.00

CHAFF, SANDRA   Women in Medicine: A Bibliography of the Literature on Women Physicians. Metuchen: 1977. 1st edition; 1124 pages; original binding.   W. Bruce Fye 71-330 1996 $200.00

CHAGALL, MARC   The Ceiling of the Paris Opera. New York: Frederick A. Praeger, 1966. 1st edition; original lithograph frontispiece, 6 color lithographs, sketches and drawings; folded final study in pocket at rear; very fine in dust jacket, glassine wrapper and slipcase.   Hermitage SP95-766 1996 $400.00

CHAILLU, PAUL   The Land of the Midnight Sun. New York: 1882. 2 volumes; original illustrated cloth, some minor spotting, else bright and internally fine.   Stephen Lunsford 45-50 1996 $135.00

CHALKLEY, LYMAN   Records of Augusta County, Virginia 1745-1800. Baltimore: 1966. 3 volumes; very good.   Bookworm & Silverfish 280-257 1996 $175.00

CHALLONER, RICHARD   Martyrs to the Catholic Faith. Memoirs of Missionary Priests and Other Catholics of Both Sexes That Have Suffered Death in England on Religious Accounts from the Year 1577 to 1684... Edinburgh: Thomas C. Jack, 1878. 8vo; 2 volumes bound in 1; (iii)-xlviii, 296, (ii), 325, (i) pages; 20 plates; original green blindstamped cloth, decorated gilt, all edges gilt, neatly rebacked with old backstrip laid down, good copy.   Robert Clark 38-168 1996 £75.00

CHALLONER, RICHARD   The True Principles of a Catholic. Philadelphia: Mathew Carey, 1789. 1st American edition; 12mo; disbound; clean tear in titlepage, but very good, very scarce. Evans 21730. Parsons, Catholic Americana 74.   Ximenes 108-64 1996 $200.00

CHALMERS, GEORGE 1742-1825   The Life of Mary, Queen of Scots... London: printed for John Murray by W. Bulmer & Co., 1818. 1st edition; 4to; 499, 502 pages; 2 volumes; frontispiece, engravings, some folding; contemporary full tan polished calf with gilt tooled spine panels and morocco spine labels; very good. Allibone I 362.   Chapel Hill 94-216 1996 $200.00

CHALMERS, P. R.   Birds Ashore and Aforeshore. London: 1935. Limited edition of 150 copies, signed by author and artist; large 4to; 16 colored plates, many black and white drawings; finely rebound in half green morocco; light foxing, nice.   David A.H. Grayling MY95Orn-16 1996 £160.00

CHALMERS, THOMAS   The Application of Christianity to the Commercial and ordinary Affairs of Life, in a Series of Discourses. Glasgow: printed by James Starke, for Chalmers and Collins, 1820. 1st edition; 8vo; ad leaf at end; contemporary half calf, some worming on hinges, label. Kress C497; Goldsmith 22737.   Anthony W. Laywood 108-158 1996 £75.00

CHALMERS, THOMAS   On Political Economy, in Connexion with the Moral State and Moral Prospects of society. Glasgow: printed for William Collins, 1832. 1st edition; 8vo; viii, 566 pages; very slight spotting of prelim leaves; contemporary dark blue half calf, spine gilt and lettered; very good. Kress C3079; Goldsmiths 27260; Williams I p. 198. McCulloch p. 19.   John Drury 82-42 1996 £450.00

CHALMERS, THOMAS   On Political Economy, in Connexion with the Moral State and Moral Prospects of Society. Columbus: Published by Isaac N. Whiting, 1833. 2nd American edition; 8vo; 443 pages; contemporary cloth with leather spine label, binding rubbed, some soil, worn mostly along spine, scattered foxing, few pencil marks; good, with prospectus tipped to front free endpaper; American Imprints 18171. Andrew Cahan 47-68 1996 $125.00

CHALMERS, THOMAS   On the Power, Wisdom and Goodness of God as Manifested in the Adaptation of External Nature to the Moral and Intellectual Constitution of Man. London: William Pickering, 1833. 2nd edition; 8vo; 2 volumes in one, xi, (3), 284; vi, 304 pages; contemporary dark blue half calf, spine gilt with raised bands, contrasting labels, marbled edges; very good, occasional foxing. Sorley p. 357.   John Drury 82-43 1996 £95.00

CHALMERS, THOMAS   A Sermon Delived in the Tron Church, Glasgow, on Wednesday, Nov. 19th, 1817, the day of the Funeral of Her Royal Highness the Princess Charlotte of Wales. Glasgow Printed by James Hederwick, 1817. 44 pages; contemporary quarter morocco, marbled boards, spine rubbed; fine, tall copy; inscribed to Mrs. Chalmers.   C. R. Johnson 37-40 1996 £250.00

CHAMBERLAIN, CHARLES   The Servant-Girl of the Period. New York: J. S. Redfield, 1873. 1st edition; 12mo; original grey printed wrappers, slight wear, trifle dusty; very good, scarce. Wright II 481.   Ximenes 109-75 1996 $125.00

CHAMBERLAIN, HENRY   A New and Compleat History and Survey of the Cities of London and Westminster, the Borough of Southark and parts Adjacent... London: J. Cooke, 1770. Folio; 4 ff., pages 5-682, 1 f. appendix, 4 ff. index, 68 engraved plates; contemporary calf, gilt spine, raised bands, label, bit worn, one or two scuff marks; signaature on titlepage for R. Watkins, 1774. Adams 48.   Marlborough 162-120 1996 £500.00

CHAMBERLAYNE, EDWARD   Angliae Notitia; or the Present State of England. Together with Divers Reflections Upon the Ancient State Thereof. London: ptd. by T. Newcomb for R. Littlebury, R. Scott and G. Wells... 1682. 14th and 11th editions respectively; 12mo; 1-344 pages; errata leaf; full calf, corners restored, rebacked with lighter more modern style calf, red morocco label to spine, corners bumped, hinges cracked; some occasional light foxing, owner's inscription, owner's bookplate. Wing C1830; Cox I 343; Lowndes' I 406. Cox III.   Beeleigh Abbey BA/56-4 1996 £65.00

CHAMBERLAYNE, JOHN   Magnae Britanniae Notitia; or, the Present State of Great Britain; with Divers Remarks Upon the Antient State Thereof... London: printed for B. and S. Tooke, 1723. Large thick 8vo; frontispiece, 2 ll., pages, vi, (xii), 672, 48; 12 extra pages '577-588'inserted between 576 and 577; calf, rebacked; good, fresh copy. Kress 3502.   Peter Murray Hill 185-32 1996 £85.00

CHAMBERLAYNE, JOHN   Memoirs of the Royal Academy of Sciences in Parish Epitomized. With Lives of the Late Members... London: printed for William and John Innys, 1721. 2nd edition; 8vo; pages (16), xxxv, 464, (4, Inny's booklist); contemporary calf. scarce.   Peter Murray Hill 185-33 1996 £120.00

CHAMBERS, DAVID   Gogmagog: Morris Cox & The Gogmagog Press. Pinner: Private Libraraies Asoc., 1991. One of 59 numbered copies, signed by Cox; 4to; specially bound, with 9 additional specimens leaves, quarter black morocco, black cloth sides, boldly lettered and striped in gilt; fine in slipcase.   Bertram Rota 272-162 1996 £150.00

CHAMBERS, ERNEST   Canada's Fertiel Northland. (with) Agriculture and Colonization Committee Maps to Accompany Evidence on Mr. R. E. Young, D.L.S. Before Said Committee Session 1907-08... Ottawa: 1907. pages 139, 16 photo illustrations; printed envelope containing 1 huge colored map and one slightly less huge map.   Stephen Lunsford 45-29 1996 $350.00

CHAMBERS, ROBERT   Ancient Sea-Margins, as Memorials of Changes in the Relative Level of Sea and Land. Edinburgh: W. & R. Chambers, London: W. S. Orr & Co., 1848. 1st edition; 8vo; 337 pages; lithograph frontispiece, in text illustrations and hand colored folding map; original olive green cloth, some dust soiling, else near fine.   Chapel Hill 94-211   1996 $125.00

CHAMBERS, ROBERT   A Biographical Dictionary of Eminent Scotsmen. Glasgow: 1835. 1st edition; 4 volumes; plates foxed; half leather, some hinges reinforced, backstrips rubbed, corners bumped.   W. Bruce Fye 71-332   1996 $200.00

CHAMBERS, ROBERT   The Book of Days, a Miscellany of Popular Antiquities in Connection with the Calendar Including Anecdote, Biography and History and Oddities of Human Life and Character. London: 1866. Reprint; 4to; 2 volumes, over 1600 pages; well illustrated; half calf, titles labels inset on red and black morocco, gilt tooled spine, handsome set. K Books 441-96 1996 £68.00

CHAMBERS, ROBERT   Minor Antiquities of Edinburgh. Edinburgh: William and Robert Chambers, 1833. 1st edition; small 8vo; (xl), 338 pages; illustrations, large folding map at rear; contemporary half calf, some tearing and chipping to map, otherwise nice.   David Mason 71-138 1996 $148.00

CHAMBERS, ROBERT   Traditons of Edinburgh. Edinburgh: Printed for W. and C. Tait, 1825. 1st edition; small 8vo; 2 volumes; 312, 300, vi; contemporary half calf, raised bands, labels; near fine set.   David Mason 71-139 1996 $148.00

CHAMBERS, ROBERT WILLIAM   Police!!! New York: Appleton, 1915. 1st edition; illustrations; bright, very good+ copy in nice dust jacket with some wear, tear, soiling and inner reinforcement, very scarce in dust jacket.   Aronovitz 57-252 1996 $125.00

CHAMBERS, WILLIAM   Chambers's Encyclopaedia; or a Dictionary of Universal Knowledge. London: William & Robert Chambers, 1895. New edition; 8vo; 10 volumes, half titles; color maps, illustrations; original maroon cloth, very good.   Jarndyce 103-135 1996 £110.00

CHAMBERS, WILLIAM   Chambers's Encyclopaeida; a Dictionary of Universal Knowledge. London: William & Robert Chambers, 1906. New edition; 10 volumes, half titles, color maps, illustrations; contemporary, probably publisher's, half maroon morocco, slight rubbing to volume 10, but very good set.   Jarndyce 103-136 1996 £140.00

CHAMBERS, WILLIAM   A Treatise on Civil Arachitecture, in which the Principles of that Art are Laid Down and Illustrated by a Great Number of Plates... London: for the author by J. Haberkirn, 1759. 1st edition; folio; (i), ii-iv, (1), 2-85, (86) pages; 50 engraved plates; recent half morocco, marbled boards, some even browning to paper and occasional offsetting from plates; very good. Harris 122.   Ken Spelman 30-66 1996 £1,200.00

CHAMBERS, WILLIAM   A Treatise on the Decorative Part of Civil Architecture. London: Priestly and Weale, 1825. Royal 8vo; pages liii, 514, (ii), portrait frontispiece, 54 engraved plates; recent tan half calf over marbled boards, marbled endpapers, light spotting to some plates. Harris 126.   Sotheran PN32-178 1996 £225.00

CHAMBLISS, J. E.   The Life and Labors of David Livingstone Covering His Entire Career in Southern and Central Africa. Philadelphia: Hubbard Bros., n.d. 1875. Tall 8vo; 805, (9) pages ads; profusely illustrated, folding map, small tear in map; original rust cloth pictorially decorated in gilt on upper cover and spine, some slight rubbing to spine ends, but in fact fine, bright copy of an attractive book.   David Mason 71-5 1996 $160.00

CHAMPOMIER, P. A.   Statement of the Sugar Crop, made in Louisiana in 1861-62. New Orleans: Cook, Young, 1862. 1st edition; small 8vo; pages x, 46; printed yellow wrappers, very good tight copy. Scarce. Crandall 2903; Parrish & Willingham 5236.   Second Life Books 103-59 1996 $375.00

CHANCE BROS.   Designs for Coloured Ornamental Windows. Birmingham: The Author, 1853. 1st edition; 8vo; (8) pages, 32 chromolithographic plates; later boards, scarce; very good.   Bookpress 75-21 1996 $785.00

CHANCE, JAMES FREDERICK   The Pattinson's of Kirklinton. privately printed, Witherby, 1899. Small 8vo; 35 pages; frontispiece; original cloth, front flyleaf removed; scarce.   R.F.G. Hollett & Son 78-130 1996 £65.00

CHANCELLOR, J. W.   Through the Visograph. Christopher Publishing Co., 1928. 1st edition; near fine in very good dust jacket.   Aronovitz 57-254 1996 $125.00

CHANDLER, RAYMOND 1886-1959   The Blue Dahlia. Carbondale & Edwardsville: Southern Illinois University Press, 1976. 1st edition; (1000 copies); photo illustrations; fine in dust jacket which is lightly rubbed on rear panel.   Steven C. Bernard 71-308 1996 $100.00

CHANDLER, RAYMOND 1886-1959   The Lady in the Lake. New York: Knopf, 1943. 1st edition; near fine in price clipped dust jacket with very light soiling and closed tear that has been professionally mended. Quill & Brush 102-248 1996 $1,250.00

CHANDLER, RAYMOND 1886-1959   Playback. London: Hamish Hamilton, 1958. 1st edition; fine with light unavoidable offset in very good dust jacket with edge wear, few small closed tears, light rubbing and very light soiling.   Quill & Brush 102-252 1996 $200.00

CHANDLER, RAYMOND 1886-1959   Playback. London: Hamish Hamilton, 1958. 1st edition; fine in price clipped dust jacket with some rubbing, few tiny chips and creasing.   Quill & Brush 102-253 1996 $150.00

CHANDLER, RAYMOND 1886-1959   Red Wind - a Collection of Short Stories. Cleveland and New York: World Publishing Co., 1946. 1st edition; original binding, covers slightly marked and rubbed, small soiled patch to lower cover, head and tail of spine, top corners and bottom edge of upper cover slightly bumped, very good in nicked, chipped, marked and dusty, slightly torn and rubbed dust jacket.   Ulysses 39-100 1996 £75.00

CHANDLER, RAYMOND 1886-1959   Red Wind. Cleveland: World Pub., 1946. 1st edition; previous owner's name on pastedown (under dust jacket flap), pages darkened, small rubbed spot on front cover, otherwise very good to fine in lightly soiled dust jacket with corners nicked and few short creased but closed tears.   Quill & Brush 102-249 1996 $100.00

CHANDLER, RAYMOND 1886-1959   The Simple Art of Murder. Boston: Houghton Mifflin; Cambridge: Riverside Press, 1950. 1st edition; color jacket illustrations by Boris Artzybasheff, dust jacket with 2 short tears; very good, fresh copy.   George J. Houle 68-28 1996 $750.00

CHANDLER, RAYMOND 1886-1959   Spanish Blood - a Collection of Short Stories. Cleveland and New York: World Publishing Co., 1946. 1st edition; original binding, covers slightly marked, rubbed and dusty, head and tail of spine slightly bumped, very good in nicked and slightly rubbed, creased and dusty dust jacket, slightly darkened at spine and edges.   Ulysses 39-99 1996 £75.00

CHANDLESS, WILLIAM   A Visit to Salt Lake; Being a Journey Across the Plains and A Residence in the Mormon Settlements at Utah. London: Smith, Elder and Co., 1857. 1st edition; 8 x 5 1/4 inches; xii,3 46 page,s plus 24 pages ads at rear; folding map; original elaborately embossed orange cloth, backstrip uniformly faded, touch o soil to binding, map somewhat creased (but fresh, clean and untorn), rear endpapers bit soiled, otherwise excellent copy, completely sound with only trivial defects internally. Graff 646; Wagner Camp 287.1. Howes C286.   Phillip J. Pirages 33-120 1996 $750.00

CHANLER, JOHN ARMSTRONG   Four Years Behind the Bards of "Bloomingdale", or the Bankruptcy of Law in New York. Roanoke Rapids: Palmetto Press, 1906. 1st edition; (x), 80, 322, 88 pages; cloth; reviews tipped onto rear endpaper, very good.   Metacomet Books 54-20 1996 $100.00

CHANNING, WILLIAM ELLERY   Poems. Boston: 1843. 1st edition; 12mo; 151 pages; full 20th century turquoise morocco binding, original paper label preserved on back endleaf; inscribed by author for Emma Lazarus; beneath is 1916 inscription "This vol. that came to me on the death of Josephine Lazarus from her private library I inscribed to my brother John f. Grabau."   M & S Rare Books 60-193 1996 $4,500.00

CHANSON DE ROLAND   The Song of Roland. New York: Limited Editions Club, 1938. Limited to 1500 copies signed by Angelo; 8vo; illustrated and hand illuminated by Valenti Angelo; quarter vellum and boards, slipcase, fine in partially faded slipcase.   James S. Jaffe 34-702 1996 $175.00

CHANSON DE ROLAND   The Song of Roland. New York: Limited Editions Club, 1938. Limited to 1500 copies; 4to; illustrations hand illuminated and colored by Valenti Angelo, who signs; boards/vellum spine; fine in lightly worn and sunned slipcse; with Monthly Letter. Charles Agvent 4-1022 1996 $135.00

CHANSON DE ROLAND   The Song of Roland, Done into English in the Original Measure by Charles Scott Moncrieff. New York: Limited Editions Club, 1938. One of 1500 numbered copies, signed by artist; illustrated and hand illuminated by Valenti Angelo; vellum backed paper covered boards, fine in gouged and slightly faded publisher's slipcase. Hermitage SP95-1039   1996 $100.00

CHANTREY, FRANCIS LEGATT   Illustrations of Derbyshire. London: Longman and Co., & Messrs. Rodwell and Martin, 1818-22. Folio; 22 engraved 'proof' plates by Chantrey on India paper; with 2 original drawings by Sir Francis Chantrey; contemporary half morocco rebacked. Anthony W. Laywood   108-159   1996 £150.00

CHAPELL, FRED   It is Time, Lord. New York: Atheneum, 1963. Author's first book; predominantly white dust jacket, unusually bright and clean, suffering only one small closed tear on rear panel and small stain at foot of spine visible only on verso; signed in green ink with "Best Wishes".   Captain's Bookshelf 38-38 1996 $275.00

CHAPIN, ANNA ALICE   The Everyday Fairy Book. London: J. Coker & Co., n.d. ca. 1930. Later printing; quarto; 159 pages; 7 color plates by Jessie Willcox Smith; original quarter red cloth over white boards, color pictorial inset to front cover, spine lettered in black, slightly over opened at few gatherings, little minor foxing, previous owner's ink presentation inscription dated 1930 on front free endpaper; Nudelman B20.   Heritage Book Shop   196-213   1996 $450.00

CHAPIN, J. P.   The Birds of the Belgian Congo. New York: 1932-54. Royal 8vo; 4 volumes; 73 plates, 328 text figures and map; modern cloth.   Wheldon & Wesley 207-21 1996 £575.00

CHAPIN, J. P.   The Birds of the Belgian Congo, Part I (General Survey and Struthioniformes to Turniciformes. New York: 1932. 8vo; pages x, 756; map, 11 plates and text figures; cloth, back cover slightly stained, original wrappers pasted on front cover and spine.   Wheldon & Wesley 207-688   1996 £75.00

CHAPIN, J. P.   The Birds of the Belgian Congo, Part 3... New York: 1953. royal 8vo; pages 821; 14 lates; original wrappers, spine worn. Wheldon & Wesley   207-689   1996 £75.00

CHAPIN, LON F.   Thirty Years in Pasadena: with an Historical Sketch of Previous Eras. N.P.: Southwest Publishing Co., 1929. 9 x 6 inches; volume 1 (all published), xvi, 134, (ii), 323, (5) pages + numerous full page photographic illustrations; gold stamped balck cloth, most of gold flaked off, some wear to spine extremities.   Dawson's Books Shop 528-56   1996 $100.00

CHAPIUS, ALFRED   Automata: a Historical and Technological Study. London: Batsford, 1958. 4to; 413 pages; 18 plates in color, 488 monochrome illustrations and text figures; cloth, gilt, dust jacket, fine in original carton.   Thomas Thorp 489-60 1996 £65.00

CHAPMAN, ABEL   Bird-Life of the Borders on Moorland and Sea With Faunal Notes Extending Over Forty Years. London: 1907. 2nd edition; 8vo; pages xii, 458; colored map and numerous illustrations; original buckram, neatly repaired.   Wheldon & Wesley 207-690 1996 £50.00

CHAPMAN, ABEL   The Gun at Home and Abroad: British Game Birds and Wildfowl. London: London & Counties Press Assoc. ltd., 1912. Subscriber's edition, limited to 950 numbered copies; 4to; 30 colored plates by George Lodge, 4 other plates, initials printed in red, little spotting, but very good.   Sotheran PN32-74 1996 £398.00

CHAPMAN, ABEL   Unexplored Spain. London: 1910. Royal 8vo; 200 illustrations from photos; green cloth, surface of cloth slightly glossy (?varnished), backstrip trifle rubbed, contents clean and sound. Petersfield Bookshop FH58-226 1996 £110.00

CHAPMAN, F. M.   The Warblers of North America. U.S.A.: 1907. 1st edition; 24 colored plates, many other plates; original blue cloth; excellent.   David A.H. Grayling MY95Orn-17 1996 £65.00

CHAPMAN, GEORGE   An Anthology of His Work. London: Nonesuch Press, 1934. 1st edition; number 287 of 700 copies; 8vo; pages (4), 147, printed at Cambridge in Centaur and Arrighi on Van Gelder paper; original decorated paper covered boards, paper label, decorated card folder, using Enid Marx's Curwen printed patterned paper and slipcase. Dreyfus 93.   Claude Cox 107-103 1996 £55.00

CHAPMAN, GEORGE   The Tragedie of Chabot Admiral of France; as it Was Presented by Her Majesties Servants, at the Private House in Drury Lane. London: printed by Thomas Cotes for Andrew Cooke and William Cooke, 1639. 1st edition; small thin 8vo; rebound in late 19th century quarter leather over marbled boards, top edge gilt, pages somewhat dusty, thus a very good copy.   Captain's Bookshelf 38-37 1996 $400.00

CHAPMAN, GEORGE   A Treatise on Education. London: published for the author & sold by Booksellers in town and country, 1790. 4th edition; half title, uncut and largely unopened in original blue boards, cream paper spine, hand lettered, some minor wear, but fine.   Jarndyce 103-409 1996 £380.00

CHAPMAN, GUY   A Passionate Prodigality - Fragments of Autobiography. New York: Chicago: & San Francisco: Holt, Rinehart and Winston, 1966. 1st U.S. edition; cloth backed boarads, top edge slightly dusty, fine in slightly dusty and very slightly rubbed dust jacket slighty browned at spine and edges.   Ulysses 39-653 1996 £75.00

CHAPMAN, KENNETH M.   The Pottery of Santo Domingo Pueblo, a Detailed Study of Its Decoration. Santa Fe: 1936. 1st edition; 192 pages; color plates, photos, illustrations, maps; printed wrappers, very good plus; very scarce.   T. A. Swinford 49-199 1996 $250.00

CHAPMAN, KENNETH M.   The Pottery of Santo Domingo Pueblo... Santa Fe: Laboratory of Anthropology, 1953. Limited to 1000 copies; folio; frontispiece, xiv, 192 pages, 34 figures, 73 illustrations, 6 plates; wrappers.   Archaeologia Luxor-4348 1996 $150.00

CHAPMAN, NATHANIEL   Elements of Therapeutics and Materia medica. Philadelphia: 1823-24. 8vo; 2 volumes; contemporary calf, rubbed.   Argosy 810-97 1996 $400.00

CHAPMAN, WILLIAM   Report on the Harbour of New Shoreham (Sussex). (and) Supplementary Report on the Efficacy of the Measure Prorposed fro the Improvement of the Harbour of New Shoreham. Brighton: Fleet, 1815/1815. 8vo; 25 pages, 1 f.; 16 pages, 1 large folding engraved plan; later wrappers, some marginal soiling to contents. Skempton 257 & 258; Jessop 1800 and Rennie 1810.   Marlborough 162-13 1996 £100.00

CHAPONE, HESTER   Miscellanies in Prose and Verse. London: printed for E. and C. Dilly and J. Walter, 1775. 1st edition; 8vo; hlaf title, ad leaf at end, new half calf, label.   Anthony Laywood 108-38 1996 £135.00

CHAR, RENE   Elizabeth Petite Fille. Ales: P.A.B., 1958. Ales: P.A.B., 1958. 1st edition; one of 75 copies only; numbered and paragraphed by publisher, Pierre Andre Benoit; page size 3 3/8 x 3 1/4 inches; printed on Rives, color drawing after Chart; bound by Jill Tarlau in full turquoise and bordeaux mottled snakeskin with onlays in same mottled snakeskin and turquoise box calf forming pinwheel on center of front panel with a bordeaux 'jewel' in center of pinwheel, simplified binding structure in center of pinwheel; original wrappers bound in, signed on lower front turn-in, housed in bordeaux and turquoise pastepaper over boards clamshell box, with turquoise spine, lined in bordeaux suede and morocco.   Priscilla Juvelis 95/1-51 1996 $1,750.00

CHARACTERS and Anecdotes Collected in the Reigns of William Rufus, Charles the Second, and King George the Third, by the Celebrated Wandering Jew of Jerusalem. London: J. Ridgway, 1791. 1st edition; tall 8vo; contemporary half calf, marbled boards, binding carefully rehinged and final leaf dusty, overall very good; scarce;   Trebizond 39-2 1996 $375.00

CHARACTERS And Anecdotes of the Court of Sweden. London: printed for Elizabeth Harlow, 1790. 1st edition; 8vo; 2 volumes; some foxing of text, contemporary half calf, rubbed, hinges cracked, piece measuring 1 inch missing from spine of volume 2, bookplates of Sir John Ingilby. Anthony W. Laywood 108-129 1996 £50.00

CHARAKA CLUB   Proccedings of... Volume 2. New York: Wood, 1906. Limited edition of 33/315 copies; 8vo; original linen backed boards, lightly soiled, internally fine.   James Tait Goodrich K40-85 1996 $150.00

CHARAKA CLUB   The Proceedings of the Charaka Club. Volume 4. New York: 1916. Limited edition; 153 pages; original binding; scarce. W. Bruce Fye 71-340 1996 $150.00

CHARAKA CLUB   The Proceedings of the Charaka Club. Volume 5. New York: 1919. Limited edition; 101 pages; original binding; scarce. W. Bruce Fye 71-341 1996 $150.00

CHARAKA CLUB   The Proceedings of the Charaka Club. Volume 9. New York: 1938. Limited edition; 204 pages; original binding.   W. Bruce Fye 71-343 1996 $125.00

CHARCOT, JEAN MARTIN   Clinical Lectures on the Diseases of Old Age. New York: William Wood and Co., 1881. 1st American edition; 8vo; (iv), (xvi), 280, (2) pages; stamped brown cloth, gilt spine. GM 2222 citing French ed. of 1867; Freeman 1979 p. 64.   John Gach 150-91 1996 $175.00

CHARCOT, JEAN MARTIN   Lectures on Bright's Diseases of the Kidneys, Delivered at the School of Medicine of Paris... New York: 1878. 1st edition in English; 8vo; 2 chromolitho plates and text illustrations; original cloth, top of spine worn.   Argosy 810-98 1996 $175.00

CHARCOT, JEAN MARTIN   Lectures on the Pathological Anatomy of the Nervous System. Diseases of the Spinal Cord. Cincinnati: Peter G. Thomson, 1881. 8vo; 165 pages; illustrations; original binding, with spine label, second signature starting to spring, overall clean copy, very scarce.   James Tait Goodrich K40-87 1996 $125.00

CHARCOT, JEAN MARTIN   Neue Vorlesungen Uber die Krankheiten des Nervensystems Insbesondere Uber Hysterie. Leipzig und Wien: Toeplitz & Deuticke, 1886. 8vo; (xii), (358) pages, 59 text illustrations; contemporary leather backed marbled boards, boards rubbed and scratched, very good. Grinstein 10670; Norman Cat. F152; Norman Freud Cat. 14. John Gach 150-92 1996 $1,000.00

CHARDON, FRANCIS A.   Chardon's Journal at Fort Clark, 1834-1839: Descriptive of Life on the Upper Missouri; a Fur Trader's Experiences Among the Mandans, Gros Ventres and Their Neighbors' of the Ravages of the Small-Pox Epidemic of 1837. Pierre: Lawrence K. Fox, 1932. 1st edition; xvii, 458 pages, 3 plates; fine, scarce Howes C303.   Argonaut Book Shop 113-1 1996 $225.00

CHARLES I, KING OF GREAT BRITAIN   His Majesties Declaration: to All His Loving Subjects, of the Causes Which Moved Him to Dissolve the Last Parliament. London: printed by Robert Barker, and by the assignes of John Bill, 1640. 1st edition; small 4to; in this copy titlepage has rose and thistle ornaments, signature B is correctly paginated, and last line of verso fo D4 begins 'ever'; old vellum, dusty; very good. STC 9262.   Ximenes 109-76 1996 $250.00

CHARLES, C. J.   Elizabethan Interiors. London: George Newnes, n.d. One of 800 copies; folio; 40 pages; 32 plates; half leather, spine and boards rubbed, tips worn, rubber stamp on front endpaper, and titlepage, otherwise very good.   Bookpress 75-167 1996 $150.00

CHARLEVOIS, PIERRE FRANCOIS XAVIER DE   Histoire et Description Generale de al Nouvelle France, avec le Journal Historique d'un Voyage fait par Ordre du Roi dans l'Amerique Septentrionnale... Paris: Chez Nyon Fils, 1744. 12mo; 6 volumes, 28 folding maps, 44 folding plates; contemporary mottled calf, spines fully gilt in the French manner, aside from minor extremity wear and few cracked hinges (but held very securely by cords), remarkably fine, fresh set, looks like it was never opened. Howes C307; Lande 126; TPL 188.   Joseph J. Felcone 64-9 1996 $2,800.00

CHARNOCK, JOHN   Biographical Memoirs of Lord Viscount Nelson, &c. &c. With Observations Critical and Explanatory. London: H. D. Symonds, 1806. 1st edition; 8vo; xviii, 430, 68 (appendix), 32 pages ads; frontispiece, engraved illustrations, 5 engraved battle plans, original grey boards, uncut, slight staining not affecting text, very good.   John Lewcock 30-141 1996 £185.00

CHARNOCK, JOHN   An History of Marine Architecture Including an Enlarged and Progressive View of the Nautical Regulations and Naval History, Both Civil and Military of all Nations... London: printed by Bye and Law for R. Faulder et al, 1800-02. 1st edition; 12 3/4 x 10 1/4 inches; 3 volumes; engraved title in first volume and 99 plates, 19 folding, some plates bound in wrong order, but present; recent smooth half calf, marbled paper sides, raised bands, green and morocco labels, spine with gilt rules, ornaments and titling, untrimmed copy; first leaf of text somewhat soiled, small hole in one folding plate and two prelim leaves (no loss), 9 plates with stab holes along fore edge, slight soiling or fraying at edges of few engravings, but in most ways fine, with excellent impressions of the plates, with spacious margins. Scott 474; Abbey Life 331; JCB Maritime Hist. 432. Lowndes I 422.   Phillip J. Pirages 33-122 1996 $3,750.00

CHARTERIS, LESLIE   The Saint Sees It Through. London: Hodder & Stoughton, 1947. 1st edition; very good with spine ends lightly worn and foxing on page edges; very good, bright contemporary with few closed tears, light creasing and soiling, one small chip on lower front cover and tape repair on verso.   Quill & Brush 102-262 1996 $100.00

CHARTERIS, LESLIE   X Esquire. London: Ward, Lock & Co., 1929. Early reprint; scarce in dust jacket, very good with light soiling and short inscription in pencil on front endpaper, in bright dust jacket with soiling, chipping and few creases.   Quill & Brush 102-260 1996 $350.00

THE CHARTERS of the British Colonies in America. Dublin: John Beatty, 1776. 1st Irish printing; thin 8vo; 142 pages; contemporary full brown calf, spine with raised bands, blindstamped label, label partly lacking, rubbing, upper joint starting; very good. Sabin 12162; USIANA C310. George J. Houle 68-1 1996 $850.00

CHARTERS, ANN   Scenes Along the Road. Photographs of the Desolation Angels 1944-1960. New York: Portents/Gotham Book Mart, 1970. 1st edition; limited to 50 specially bound copies, signed by Ginsberg; 8vo; cloth; mint.   James S. Jaffe 34-181 1996 $150.00

CHASE, FREDERICK   A History of Dartmouth College and the Town of Hanover, N.H. Cambridge: University Press/Concord: Rumford Press, 1891-1913. 1st edition; 2 volumes, xii, 682; viii, 725 pages; plates; cloth, very good. Howes C316.   Metacomet Books 54-200 1996 $200.00

CHASE, GEORGE H.   Catalogue of Arretine Pottery. Boston: Museum of Fine Arts, 1916. 4to; 112 pages; 2 figures, 30 plates; boards. Archaeologia   Luxor-3151 1996 $150.00

CHASE, PHILANDER   Bishop Chase's Address Delivered Before the Convention of the Protestant Espicopal Church, Springfield, Illinois, June 16, 1845. St. Louis: Daniel Davies, 1845. 1st edition; 8vo; 27 pages; frontispiece; original printed wrappers, foxed. Buck 382.   M & S Rare Books 60-341 1996 $225.00

CHASE, PHILANDER   Constitution and Canons of the Diocese of Illinois. Jubilee College: Jubilee Press, 1847. 1st edition; 8vo; 15 pages; sewn, self wrappers, unopened, as issued, title lightly spotted.   M & S Rare Books 60-342 1996 $200.00

CHASTEL, ANDRE   The Age of Humanism: Europe 1480-1530. London: Thames & Hudson, 1963. 1st English edition; folio; pages 347; 401 reproductions including 40 mounted colored plates; original cloth, dust jacket.   Howes Bookshop 265-174 1996 £60.00

CHATHAM, WILLIAM PITT, EARL OF   Anecdotes of the Life of the Right Honourable William Pitt. London: J. S. Jordan, 1793. 3rd edition; 8vo; 3 volumes; contemporary full flame calf with morocco spine labels, couple of joints little weak, corners bumped on volume 1, else very good.   Chapel Hill 94-226 1996 $200.00

CHATTERTON, ALFRED   Experiments on the Strength of Building Materials Used in Southern India. Madras: Government Press, 1900. Folio; 23, (1) pages, 1 litho chart; original printed wrappers, worn, ex-library of the Inst. Mech. E. with their withdrawal stamp; preserved in pamphlet case.   Elton Engineering 10-26 1996 £85.00

CHATTERTON, THOMAS 1752-1770   Poems, Supposed to Have Been Written at bristol by Thomas Rowley, and Others in the Fifteenth Century. London: for T. Payne and Son, 1778. 3rd edition; 1st edition; with Tyrwhitt's appendix; 8vo; pages (ii), xxvii, (i), 333; facsimile plate facing p. 288; contemporary full russia, flat spine gilt lettered direct, gilt edges, spine slightly darkened and rubbed, front joint tender at head, good firm copy; with ownership of Elizabeth Walpole and bookplate of Lord Walpole of Woolterton. Warren 4.   Simon Finch 24-35 1996 £120.00

CHATTERTON, THOMAS 1752-1770   The Rowley Poems. London: Hacon and Ricketts at the sign of the Dial, 1898. Limited to 210 copies; large 8vo; 2 volumes; full red morocco, extra wide gilt floral borders on upper covers, gold panelled spines in 6 compartments, gilt tops, other edges uncut, bound by Riviere for Henry Sotheran.   Charles W. Traylen 117-87 1996 £450.00

CHATTERTON, THOMAS 1752-1770   The Rowley Poems. London: Hacon & Ricketts, 1898. Limited tto 210 copies; 8vo; volume one only (of two); pages 141, (2); full page wild bryony border and large woodcut initials by Charles Ricketts; original red/grey patterned paper backed boards, green bird and rose pattern on sides, paper label, little rubbed at extremities; very good, unopened. Tomkinson 17. Vol. 1 only. Claude Cox 107-173 1996 £65.00

CHATWIN, BRUCE   The Attractions of France. London: Colophon Press, 1993. Limited to 176 copies, this being one of 26 copies bound in cloth; fine.   Words Etcetera 94-280 1996 £125.00

CHATWIN, BRUCE   In Patagonia. New York: Summit, 1977. 1st U.S. edition; fine in dust jacket.   Lame Duck Books 19-132 1996 $200.00

CHATWIN, BRUCE   In Patagonia. New York: Summit books, 1978. 1st edition; author's scarce first book; beautiful copy in dust jacket.   Bud Schweska 12-246 1996 $150.00

CHATWIN, BRUCE   The Morality of Things. Francestown: Typographeum, 1993. 1/175 copies; fine in grey cloth.   Alice Robbins 15-70 1996 $150.00

CHATWIN, BRUCE   On the Black Hill. London: Cape, 1982. 1st edition; fine in dust jacket.   Between the Covers 42-97 1996 $125.00

CHATWIN, BRUCE   Patagonia Revisited. London: Michael Russell, 1985. 1st edition; one of 250 copies, signed by authors; 8vo; illustrations by Kyffin Williams; decorated cloth, glassine dust jacket; mint.   James S. Jaffe 34-109 1996 $375.00

CHATWIN, BRUCE   The Songlines. Franklin Center: Franklin Library, 1987. Limited first edition with special message from Bruce Chatwin; red and black leather decorated in gold, all edges gilt; fine, signed.   Alice Robbins 15-67 1996 $275.00

CHATWIN, BRUCE   The Songlines. Franklin Center: Franklin Library, 1987. 1st edition; illustrations; marbled endpapers, all edges gilt; very fine.   Bev Chaney, Jr. 23-137 1996 $225.00

CHATWIN, BRUCE   The Songlines. Franklin Park: Franklin Library, 1987. 1st edition; full decorated and gilt stamped leather and signed by author; fine.   Lame Duck Books 19-133 1996 $275.00

CHATWIN, BRUCE   The Songlines. London: London Limited Editions, 1987. 1st edition; one of 150 specially bound copies, signed by author; 8vo; cloth backed marbled boards, glassine dust jacket, mint.   James S. Jaffe 34-108 1996 $375.00

CHATWIN, BRUCE   The Songlines. London: Cape, 1987. 1st edition; fine in dust jacket.   Lame Duck Books 19-134 1996 $200.00

CHATWIN, BRUCE   The Songlines. London: 1987. 1st edition; near fine in dust jacket.   Words Etcetera 94-279 1996 £65.00

CHATWIN, BRUCE   The Songlines. New York: Viking, 1987. 1st U.S. edition; fine in dust jacket; signed by author, most uncommon thus.   Lame Duck Books 19-135 1996 $450.00

CHAUCER, GEOFFREY 1340-1400   The Booke of the Duchesse... Lexington: Anvil Press, 1954. One of 225 numbered copies; handset and printed by Jacob Hammer, handmade paper, pages unopened; unprinted covers with title label on spine, original binding, top edge slightly dusty, spine browned, endpapers slightly browned and spotted, very good; from the library of James D. Hart.   Ulysses 39-261 1996 £100.00

CHAUCER, GEOFFREY 1340-1400   The Canterbury Tales. London: Philip Lee Warner, publisher to the Medici Society Limited, 1913. Limited edition, number 248 of 512 copies, this being one of 500 on paper; 4to; 3 volumes, titles printed in blue and black with portraits by Flint, lettering designed by Edith M. Engall, 36 mounted colored plates after Flint; original quarter holland, blue paper boards, slight soiling and light stain to volume I, top edge gilt, others uncut, silk bookmarks, corners little rubbed, but very good.   Simon Finch 24-195 1996 £500.00

CHAUCER, GEOFFREY 1340-1400   The Canterbury Tales. Waltham St. Lawrence: Golden Cockerel Press, 1929-31. One of 485 copies on paper (there were also 15 copies printed on vellum); 12 1/2 x 8 inches; 4 volumes, red and blue initials and very pleasing wood engraved borders (frequently historiated) by Eric Gill on every page except in last part of volume 4; original morocco backed patterned paper boards by Sangorski & Sutcliffe, raised bands, gilt titling, top edge gilt, others untrimmed; tips of corners artfully refurbished, spine of first volume bit darker than the others, small spot on one spine and several tiny faint spots on another, quite a small abrasion at very bottom of one cover, otherwise fine, virtually no wear to joints and spine ends, gilt still bright and with text virtually without defects. Excellent copy. Chanticleer 63; Gill 281.   Phillip J. Pirages 33-245 1996 $5,000.00

CHAUCER, GEOFFREY 1340-1400   The Canterbury Tales. Waltham St. Lawrence: Golden Cockerel Press, 1929-31. One of 485 numbered copies on Batachelor handmade paper, out of a total edition of 500 copies; folio; 4 volumes; 1 full page illustration, 29 decorative borders, tailpieces and line fillers and 61 initial letters (printed in black, red or blue), all engraved on wood by Eric Gill; bound by Sangorski & Sutcliffe in quarter niger morocco over patterned boards, gilt lettered spine with raised bands, top edge gilt, others uncut, light wear to extremities, slight discoloration to boards, small glue stains to endpapers where they touch the leather, little minor foxing, still near fine set overall, housed together in quarter reddish brown morocco slipcase. Chanticleer 63; Gill 281.   Heritage Book Shop 196-214 1996 $4,500.00

CHAUCER, GEOFFREY 1340-1400   Flower and the Leaf. London: Edward Arnold, 1902. Limited to 165 copies; octavo; 45 pages; printed entirely on vellum; hand colored illustrations and initials by Edith Harwood, 80 historiated initials; full vellum over boards, blindstamped with rose logo and motto of the series "Soul is Form", very fine. Crawford p. 385; Ashbee p. 71-72.   Bromer Booksellers 87-62 1996 $600.00

CHAUCER, GEOFFREY 1340-1400   The Pardoner's Tale. Chicago: Studio, 1966. Folio; 82 woodcut plates with text in right margin; titlepage and woodcut sheets loose in drop front cloth portfolio, as issued; Brannan Books 43-31 1996 $245.00

CHAUCER, GEOFFREY 1340-1400   The Parlement of Fowles. Boston; Riverside Press, 1904. One of 325 copies; narrow 8vo; printed in red and black in 'lettre batarde' with two large initial letters printed in blue and gold; boards; near fine, with added printed leaf about the writing of the book laid in; BR 30; Work of Bruce Rogers 105.   Marilyn Braiterman 15-176 1996 $300.00

CHAUCER, GEOFFREY 1340-1400   The Romaunt of the Rose. World's End Press, 1974. One of only 25 numbered copies, signed by artist; large folio; printed in handset Monotype Garamond italic on cream Saunders mouldmade; 7 original etchings by Ann Brunskill; full vellum, decorative endpapers; fine in slipcase.   Bertram Rota 272-500 1 1996 £700.00

CHAUCER, GEOFFREY 1340-1400   Troilus and Criseyde. Waltham St. Lawrence: Golden Cockerel Press, 1927. One of 225 copies; 12 1/2 x 7 3/4 inches; xi, (1), 310 pages, (1) leaf (blank), (1) p. (colophon); 5 full page wood engravings, fore margins of every text page with wood engraved borders, all by Eric Gill, printed in red, blue and black; original quarter russet moroccco by Sangorski & Sutcliffe, patterned paper sides, vellum tips, top edge gilt, slipcase, paper on front cover with small abrasions, spine slightly nicked and with portions of the leather darkened (as often happens with this book), but binding otherwise unworn, and a virtually faultless copy internally. Chanticleer 50; Ransom p. 297.   Phillip J. Pirages 33-246 1996 $5,500.00

CHAUCER, GEOFFREY 1340-1400   Troilus and Cressida. London: Limited Editions Club, 1939. Copy number 904 from a total edition of 1500 numbered copies, signed by printer, George W. Jones; cloth backed decorative boards, slipcase; fine.   Hermitage SP95-953 1996 $100.00

CHAUCER, GEOFFREY 1340-1400   The Works of... London: Colophon: by Robart Toye, 1550? 12 x 8 inches; (6), 355 leaves, lacks all before signature Aii (1 leaf?); 19th century leather, binding very worn, especially at spine joints and tips, front inner hinge cracked, first few leaves closely cropped at top affecting running heads and some text, top portion of leaves lightly stained, previous owner's name written in ink on several leaves, spine dated book as 1542, an obvious error; in spite of this litany of faults, this is not a bad copy, scarce.   John K. King 77-233 1996 $1,250.00

CHAUCER, GEOFFREY 1340-1400   The Woorkes... London: by Jhon Kyngston for Jhon Wight, 1561. 1st Stowe edition, and 5th collected edition; folio; ff. (x), 378, printed in double column; black letter, woodcut device of Chaucer's arms to titlepage, separate titlepage for Canterbury Tales, woodcut of Knight at head of first tale; modern brown crushed morocco, raised bands, gilt lettering, spine and sides elaborately decorated and panelled in black, old red sprinkled edges, slight scuff on upper cover, prelims with slight dampstaining at head, p2 with small hole affecting a few letters either side but not the sense, old pentrial on blank A6 verso, paper flaw at head of F1 affecting folio numeral only, occasional trivial stain, generally very good, paper clean and strong; STC 5076; Grolier LW 42; Pforzheiemr 176 for first issue.   Simon Finch 24-36 1996 £6,500.00

CHAUCER, GEOFFREY 1340-1400   The Works of Geoffrey Chaucer. Cleveland: World Pub. Co., 1958. Folio; xx pages, (2), 554 pages; 87 illustrations; elaborately blindstamped, gilt cream cloth, suggesting the original pigskin binding, dust jacket.   Kenneth Karmiole 1NS-65 1996 $150.00

CHAUNCY, HENRY   The Historical Antiquities of Hertfordshire...
London: for B. Griffin etc., 1700. 1st edition; limited to 500 copies; folio;
title, 4 ff., 601 pages, 11 ff., engraved portrait, folding map, 44 plates;
early 19th century dark blue morocco gilt, gilt inner borders, gilt edges
by J. Wright; extremities rubbed; very handsome. Wing C3741; Lowndes
p. 430.   Marlborough 162-14 1996 £2,200.00

CHAUNDLER, CHRISTINE   Arthur and His Knights. London: Nisbet, c.
1920. Small 4to; 8 mounted color plates and pictorial endpapers by
Thomas Mackenzie; tan cloth stamped pictorially in black and white
cloth, very nice, scarce.   '150 1996 £135.00

THE CHECKERBOARD. New York: Weyhe Gallery, 1930. 1st edition; 8vo;
15 pages; 6 original wood engravings or linoleum cuts by Wanda Gag;
illustrated wrappers; fine.   Andrew Cahan 47-76 1996 $150.00

CHEETHAM, JAMES   The Life of Thomas Paine. New York: Southwick
& Pelsue, 1809. 1st edition; 8vo; calf and boards; browned. Howes
C336.   Rostenberg & Stern 150-7 1996 $125.00

CHEEVER, HENRY T.   The Island World of the Pacific. Glasgow: ca.
1860. Foolscap 8vo; 304 pages; frontispiece; original cloth, somewhat
age browned.   K Books 442-104 1996 £56.00

CHEEVER, JOHN 1912-1984   The Day the Pig Fell Into the Well.
Northridge: Lord John Press, 1978. 1 of 26 lettered copies, signed; fine
as issued.   Bev Chaney, Jr. 23-142 1996 $375.00

CHEEVER, JOHN 1912-1984   The Enormous Radio. London: Golanz,
1953. 1st edition; fine in lightly used dust jacket that has two spine
chips.   Bev Chaney, Jr. 23-143 1996 $125.00

CHEEVER, JOHN 1912-1984   Excerpts from the Journals of John
Cheever. Ex Ophidia, 1986. One of 90 copies; 12 1/4 x 7 1/2 inches; 21,
(1) pages, (1) leaf; device on first leaf, title printed in red and black;
burnt orange crushed morocco, unadorned except for small gilt emblem
on spine, text printed on light brown untrimmed leaves, in publisher's
attractive folding cloth box; as new.   Phillip J. Pirages 33-211 1996
$450.00

CHEEVER, JOHN 1912-1984   Falconer. New York: Alfred A. Knopf,
1977. 1st edition; fine in dust jacket; signed.   Bev Chaney, Jr. 23-144
1996 $100.00

CHEEVER, JOHN 1912-1984   Homage to Shakespeare. Stevenson:
Country Squires Books, 1968. One of 50 copies of the first edition of the
1st separate publication of this early Cheever story; fine in dust jacket;
inscribed by author for Malcolm and Muriel Cowley.   Lame Duck
Books 19-138 1996 $1,500.00

CHEEVER, JOHN 1912-1984   The Stories of John Cheever. New York:
Knopf, 1978. 1st edition; natural paper flaw resulting in a small hole on
half title, else fine in especially fine and unrubbed dust jacket, signed by
Cheever.   Between the Covers 42-99 1996 $250.00

CHEEVER, JOHN 1912-1984   The Stories of John Cheever. New York:
Alfred A. Knopf, 1978. 1st edition; fine in dust jacket, signed.   Bev
Chaney, Jr. 23-147 1996 $125.00

CHEEVER, JOHN 1912-1984   The Wapshot Chronicle. Franklin Center:
Franklin Library, 1978. 1st edition; illustrations; fine, signed by author.
Bev Chaney, Jr. 23-148 1996 $100.00

CHEN, JULIE   River of Stars. Flying Fish Press, 1994. 2.875 x 2.875
inches; accordion fold; designed by Ed Hutchins and Julie Chen,
letterpress printed on three colors of handmade paper with book
structure masterminded by Ed Hutchins, the light grey, grey and dark
blue (with scattered stars and flecks) paper from three layers; light
paper boards, front with onlay of dark blue paper with stars, slipcase of
matching dark blue paper board with light gray paper title;   Joshua
Heller 21-122 1996 $125.00

CHENEY, JOHN   John Cheney and His Descendants. Banbury: printed
for private circulation (by Cheney & Sons), 1936. 1st edition; 4to; 70
plates, family tree and plans; original buckram, dust jacket, slightly torn,
boxed, nice.   Forest Books 74-40 1996 £85.00

CHENEY, PETER   Dark Hero. London: Collins, 1946. Number 90 of 250
signed numbered copies, presented to author by his publisers; near fine
with pages lightly aged and bookplate on front pastedown, in near fine
dust jacket with light edge wear and very light soiling.   Quill & Brush
102-265 1996 $100.00

CHEROKEE NATION   Laws of the Cherokee Nation: Adopted by the
Council at Various Periods. (and) The Constitution and Laws of the
Cherokee Nation: Passed at Tahlequah, Cherokee Nation, 1839-1851.
Tahlequah: Cherokee Advocate Office, 1852-52. 1st edition; 12mo; 179,
248 pages; sewn and sound, but lacking covers and endsheets, first title
browned, otherwise very fine. Hargrett, Const. & laws of the American
Indians 18.   M & S Rare Books 60-349 1996 $2,250.00

CHERRYH, C. J.   Cyteen. Warner Books, 1988. 1st edition;
uncorrected proof; signed by author; fine in wrappers.   Aronovitz
57-257 1996 $110.00

CHESELDEN, WILLIAM   The Anatomy of the Human Body. London:
William Bowyer, 1741. 6th edition; 8vo; frontispiece, 40 copperplates
engraved by Vandergucht; contemporary calf, recently rebacked, lower
outer corner of plate 38 torn with some loss, tape repair, some text
foxing and browning; GM 390.   James Tait Goodrich K40-88 1996
$195.00

CHESELDEN, WILLIAM   The Anatomy of the Human Body. London: J.
F. and C. Rivington et al, 1778. 11th edition; 8vo; frontispiece, plus 40
copperplates engraved by Vandergucht; contemporary calf, recently
rebacked, but not in matching leather, endpapers renewed, upper blank
margin of title repaired, some text foxing and browning, otherwise tight
functional copy (lacking? frontispiece). GM 390.   James Tait Goodrich
K40-89 1996 $135.00

CHESNEY, ALAN   The Johns Hopkins Hospital and the Johns Hopkins
University School of Medicine, a Chronicle. Baltimore: 1943/58/63. 1st
edition; 3 volumes; illustrations; original binding.   W. Bruce Fye
71-349 1996 $200.00

CHESNEY, CHARLES CORNWALLIS   The Russo-Turkish Campaigns of
1828 and 1829. London: Smith, Elder 7 Co., 1854. 2nd edition; 8vo; xl,
448 pages, 16 pages ads; 2 large folding color maps; original green
cloth, gilt, spine somewhat soiled.   Kenneth Karmiole 1NS-66 1996
$125.00

CHESNEY, GEORGE TOMKYNS   The Battle of Dorking: Reminiscences
of a Volunteer. London: Blackwoods, 1871. 1st edition; 8vo; 64 pages, 8
pages ads; illustrated lilac wrappers, slight wear to spine, but nice.
Ian Patterson 9-51 1996 £100.00

CHESNEY, GEORGE TOMKYNS   A True Reformer. Edinburgh &
London: William Blackwood and Sons, 1873. 1st edition; 8vo; 3 volumes;
original scarlet cloth, slight rubbing; fine, rare. Wolff 1195; Gupta, India in
English Fiction 445.   Ximenes 109-77 1996 $450.00

CHESNUTT, CHARLES W.   The Conjure Woman. Boston and New
York: Houghton, Mifflin and Co., 1899. 1st edition; 12mo; (4), 229, (1)
pages; original pictorial cloth; Wright III 1017.   M & S Rare Books
60-133 1996 $600.00

CHESTER PLAYS   The Chester Play of the Deluge. Waltham St.
Lawrence: Golden Cockerel Press, 1927. One of 275 copies; 12 3/4 x 10
inches; iv, 16 pages, (1) leaf (colophon); 10 wood engravings in text by
David Jones, tissues laid in between every page; original buckram, edges
untrimmed, gilt spine titling, spine slightly and evenly faded, otherwise
extremely fine.   Phillip J. Pirages 33-247 1996 $1,850.00

CHESTER PLAYS   The Chester Play of the Deluge. Waltham St.
Lawrence: Golden Cockerel Press, 1927. One of 275 numbered copies;
large 4to; printed in 18 pt. Caslon O.F. on handmade paper; full red
buckram, covers little faded and marked, internally nice, clean copy,
bookplate removed.   Bertram Rota 272-170 1996 £550.00

CHESTER, ALDEN   Courts and Lawyers of New York: a History
1609-1925. New York: American Historical Society, 1925. three quarter
buckram, gilt, showing some wear, but sound set.   Meyer Boswell
SL27-42 1996 $250.00

CHESTER, SAMUEL H.   Pioneer Days in Arkansas. Richmond:
published for the author, 1927. 1st edition; 68 pages; portraits; original
stiff printed wrappers, title stamped in black on front cover, minor
chipping to spine, very good; presentation copy from author.   Michael
D. Heaston 23-28 1996 $125.00

CHESTERFIELD, PHILIP DORMER STANHOPE, 4TH EARL OF 1694-1773 Letters...to His Son, Philip Stanhope, Esq... London: J. Dodsley, 1774. 1st edition; 4to; 2 volumes; pages (iv), vii, (I), 568; (iv), 606, (1); oval portrait frontispiece in volume 1 (offset), half titles with early owner's name printed at head (P. Gell, Hopton), errata leaf at end of volume 2, 1 underlining and ink marginal note; contemporary sprinkled tan calf, expertly rebacked in sprinkled russia to match, raised bands between double gilt rules, original red morocco title and green volume labels laid down, blind fillet border on sides, hinges split but very firm, endpapers stained by turn-ins, overall excellent; Gulick 2; Rothschild 596. Blackwell's B112-63 1996 £500.00

CHESTERFIELD, PHILIP DORMER STANHOPE, 4TH EARL OF 1694-1773 Lettres du Comte de Chesterfield a son fils Philippe Stanhope. Venice: Justin Pasquali, 1811. 1st Italian edition; 16mo; 6 volumes bound in 3; all half titles present; original vellum backed boards, boards rubbed, otherwise very fine, crisp set; very uncommon. Trebizond 39-3 1996 $425.00

CHESTERFIELD, PHILIP DORMER STANHOPE, 4TH EARL OF 1694-1773 The Life of the Late Earl of Chesterfield; or, the Man of the World....Essays...Poems...Substance of the system of Education Delivered in...Letters to His Son. London: printed for J. Bew, 1774. 1st edition; 12mo; 2 volumes; frontispiece; contemporary calf, slight wear to spines; Gulick 54. Peter Murray Hill 185-36 1996 £105.00

CHESTERFIELD, PHILIP STANHOPE, 2ND EARL OF Correspondence with Various Ladies... London: Fanfrolico Press, 1930. Number 333 of 480 copies; decorations by Jeanne Bellon; original blindstamped cloth, gilt titles; very good. Hartfield 48-A5 1996 $195.00

CHESTERTON, GEORGE LAVAL Peace, War and Adventure. London: Longman, Brown, Green and Longmans, 1853. 1st edition; 8vo; 2 volumes; original dark brown cloth, tiny rubbed spot at head of one spine; fine set in original binding, not a common title in any condition; Sabin 12551. Howes C354. Ximenes 109-78 1996 $550.00

CHESTERTON, GILBERT KEITH 1874-1936 The Ball and the Cross. London: Wells Gardner, Darton & Co., 1910. 1st British edition; 8vo; erratum slip tipped in on p. 93, and line 18 on p. 358 reading 'But Lord bless us and save us!''; decorative green cloth, top edge gilt; very good. Sullivan 17. Antic Hay 101-294 1996 $125.00

CHESTERTON, GILBERT KEITH 1874-1936 The Club of Queer Trades. London: 1905. 1st edition; illustrations by author; spine faded, extremities bumped, otherwise very good. Words Etcetera 94-285 1996 £50.00

CHESTERTON, GILBERT KEITH 1874-1936 The Club of Queer Trades. New York: Harper & Bros., 1905. 1st edition; top edge dusty, covers marked and slightly cocked and rubbed, head and tail of spine and corners bumped, lower hinge partially cracked, very good; stamp of the Wardroom, H.M.S. Donegal on front pastedown. Ulysses 39-101 1996 £125.00

CHESTERTON, GILBERT KEITH 1874-1936 The Collected Poems of G. K. Chesterton. London: Burns, Oates and Washbourne Ltd., 1927. 1st edition; original binding, top edge dusty, inscription, prelims, edges and endpapers spotted, head and tail of spine slgithly bumped, free endpapers partially browned, very good in nicked marked and slightly rubbed, creased and dusty, internally repaired dust jacket darkened at spine and edges. Ulysses 39-104 1996 £85.00

CHESTERTON, GILBERT KEITH 1874-1936 The End of the Roman Road - a Pageant of Wayfarers. Classic Press, 1924. 1st edition; 12mo; color frontispiece and black and white decorations to each page, each repeated four times by T. H. Robinson, marbled endpapers; original binding, top edge slightly dusty, covers slightly browned and spotted, tail of spine slightly bumped, very good in torn, chipped, creased, rubbed and dusty dust jacket slightly darkened at spine and edges, with internal sellotape mark, upper panel of dust jacket incorporates color frontispiece. Ulysses 39-102 1996 £75.00

CHESTERTON, GILBERT KEITH 1874-1936 The Man Who Was Thursday. D-M, 1908. 1st American edition; very good+ in bright very good+ near fine second printing dust jacket, quite scarce in any dust jacket. Aronovitz 57-259 1996 $275.00

CHESTERTON, GILBERT KEITH 1874-1936 The Return of Don Quixote. D-M, 1927. 1st American edition; fine in very bright dust jacket with several small chips. Aronovitz 57-260 1996 $125.00

CHESTERTON, GILBERT KEITH 1874-1936 The Return of Don Quixote. London: Chatto & Windus, 1927. 1st edition; 312 pages; original binding, top edge dusty, prelims, edges and endpapers spotted, head and tail of spine and corners bumped, covers marked, cover edges rubbed, free endpapers browned, spine slightly darkened, some semi-erased pencillings on rear pastaedown; inscription; good; with ALS from author to W. R. Titterton. Ulysses 39-105 1996 £145.00

CHESTERTON, GILBERT KEITH 1874-1936 William Cobbett. London: Hodder & Stoughton, n.d. 1925. 1st edition; 275 pages; original binding, top edge dusty, head and tail of spine slightly bumped, prelims, edges and endpapers spotted, endpapers browned, very good in nicked and slightly rubbed and dusty, very slightly creased, internally repaired dust jacket browned at spine and ends. Ulysses 39-103 1996 £65.00

CHETHAM, JAMES The Angler's Vade Mecum; or, a Compendious, Yet Full Discourse of angling... ptd. for William Battersby & are to be sold at his shop at Thavies... 1700. 3rd edition; 8vo; viii, 334 pages, ad leaf; contemporary sprinkled calf, neatly rebacked, old style, corners little worn, text slightly browned, two small splits in titlepage, but without loss. Thomas Thorp 489-66 1996 £450.00

CHETWOOD, WILLIAM RUFUS d. 1766 The Voyages, Dangerous Adventures and Imminent Escapes of Captain Richard Falconer... London: printed for W. Chetwood at Cato's Head, 1720. 1st edition; 8vo; (8), 72, 136, 180 pages; frontispiece, title printed in red and black; original panelled calf, rebacked, hinges rubbed and partly cracked, spine extremities worn. Howes C356. Kenneth Karmiole 1NS-243 1996 $500.00

CHEVALIER, MICHAEL Society, Manners and Politics in the United States... 1st edition in English, translated from the third Paris edition; 467 pages; cloth, small worn spot on front cover, some fading at top of both back and front covers, moderate foxing. Clark III 20; Howes C359. Monaghan 424a. Robert G. Hayman 11/95-24 1996 $150.00

CHEVREUL, M. E. The Principles of Harmony and Contrast of Colours, and Their Applications to the Arts. London: Longman, Brown, Green and Longmans, 1855. 2nd edition; 8vo; xxvii, (1), 403, 24 pages ads, 4 folding plates; original blue cloth, gilt lettered spine; slight wear to head of spine and corners, otherwise very good. scarce. Ken Spelman 30-48 1996 £90.00

CHEVREUL, M. E. The Principles of Harmony and Contrast of Colours and Their Applications to the Arts. London: Bell & Daldy, 1870. 3rd edition; small 8vo; xlvi, 465 pages; three engraved plates, 2 folding; binding rubbed. Bookpress 75-22 1996 $150.00

CHEYNE, GEORGE 1671-1743 The English Malady; or, a Treatise of Nervous Diseases of All Kinds as Spleen, Vapours, Lowness of Spirits, Hypochondriacal and Hysterical Dystempers &c. London: printed for G. Strahan and J. Leake, 1733. 1st edition; 8vo; (vi), xxxii, 370 pages, 3 ad leaves, original panelled calf, old blank paper label on spine, excellent copy. GM 4840; Hunter & Macalpine p. 351. David Bickersteth 133-181 1996 £680.00

CHICAGO, BURLINGTON & QUINCY RAILROAD Estes Park, Colorado and Its Environs. Denver: Barkhauson and Lester, n.d. 16 pages; illustrations; original green printed wrappers, with Estes Park Hotel featured on back wrapper; very good. Michael D. Heaston 23-98 1996 $100.00

CHICAGO, ROCK ISLAND & PACIFIC RAILROAD Merry Christmas With the Compliments of the General Ticket & Passenger Department of the Great Rock Island Route. Chicago: ca. 1880's. 16 pages; illustrations; original pictorial wrappers, spine neatly repaired, very good. Michael D. Heaston 23-94 1996 $200.00

CHILD, D. L. A Report of the Trial of Pedro Gilbert, Bernardo de Soto (et al)...Before the U.S. Circuit Court, on an Indictment Charging Them with the Commission of an Act of Piracy, on Board the Brig Mexican of Salem. Boston: Russell, Odiorne & Metcalf, 1834. 1st edition; 8vo; 80 pages; 10 line engravings inserted on somewhat smaller paper; removed, lacking wrappers. Sabin 69915; not in Imprints Survey. M & S Rare Books 60-397 1996 $275.00

CHILDERS, ERSKINE The Riddle of the Sands - a Record of Secret Service Recently Achieved. London: Smith, Elder & Co., 1903. 1st edition; 2 maps and 2 charts, 4 pages of publisher's ads at rear; original binding, top edge dusty, prelims, edges and endpapers spotted, free endpapers browned, enamel lettering at tail of the spine chipped, head and tail of spine and corners bumped, covers slightly marked and ruubbed, very good. Ulysses 39-106 1996 £1,800.00

A CHILDREN'S Sampler. Stamford: Ladies of the Distaff Side, 1950. 1st and only edition, limited (number unspecified); 8vo; , illustrations; yellow decorated cloth stamped in red with Bruce Roger's heart design title repeated on front cover, spine minutely faded, housed in publisher's red paper over boards slipcase, fine in lightly used box. Priscilla Juvelis 95/1-62 1996 $500.00

CHILDRESS, ALICE Like One of the Family: Conversations from a Domestic's Life. Brooklyn: Independence Pub., 1956. 1st edition; author's first book; slight rubbing at bottom of spine, else fine in lightly soiled near fine dust jacket. Between the Covers 43-51 1996 $150.00

CHIN KU CH'I KUAN The Affectionate Pair, of the History of Sung-Kin. London: for Black, Kingsbury, Parbury and Allen, 1820. 1st English translation; 12mo; pages iv, 104; uncut in original boards, spine hand lettered, spine cracked but holding firm, edges of boards rubbed, excellent copy; ownership inscription erased from front pastedown. Simon Finch 24-37 1996 £320.00

CHISHOLM, LOUEY The Golden Staircase. London: T. C. and E. C. Jack, 1906. 1st edition; xxxi, 361 pages; color frontispiece, title vignette and 15 color plates, gold decorated endpapers; white cloth, ornately gilt decorated, top edge gilt, very light wear. Excellent. Robin Greer 94A-81 1996 £125.00

CHISHULL, EDMUND Antiquities Asiaticae Christianam Aeram Antecedentes... London: Guil. Bowyer, 1728. Only edition; folio; text is Latin and Greek; 2 engraved plates, text illustrations; contemporary sheep, carefully rebacked with morocco label; discreet library blindstamp on titlepage, binding rather worn, internally fine, clean copy, scarce. Trebizond 39-90 1996 $825.00

CHITTENDEN, HIRAM MARTIN The American Fur Trade of the Far West... New York: The Press of the Pioneers Inc., 1935. Reprint of the 1902 first edition; 2 volumes, xxx, 482 + 483-1014 pages, frontispiece in volume 1, 15 plates, large folding map in rear pocket of volume 2, gilt lettered green cloth, spines slightly faded, else fine set. Argonaut Book Shop 113-131 1996 $275.00

CHITTENDEN, HIRAM MARTIN History of Early Steamboat Navigation on the Missouri River. New York: Francis P. Harper, 1903. 1st edition; limited to 950 copies; 8vo; 2 volumes, xiv, 248 pages; (viii), 249-461 pages, complete with 16 plates; light foxing on endpapers, stain in gutter of second volume affecting first few leaves, previous owner's name on endpapers, else very good. Howes C399. Andrew Cahan 47-190 1996 $450.00

CHITTENDEN, RUSSELL History of the Sheffield Scientific School of Yale Universtly 1846-1922. New Haven: 1928. 2 volumes, 610 pages; half leather. W. Bruce Fye 71-353 1996 $125.00

CHITTY, JOSEPH A Practical Treatise on the Law of Nations, Relative to the Legal Effect of War on the Commerce of Belligerents and Neutrals... Boston: published by Bradford and Read, 1812. Contemporary sheep, rebacked, worn and foxed, usable copy. Meyer Boswell SL25-40 1996 $350.00

CHIVERS, T. H. Nacoochee; or, the Beautiful Star with Other Poems. New York: W. E. Dean, 1837. 1st edition; 12mo; 10, (2), 143 pages; original reddish brown cloth, text foxed, but an excellent copy, on title is the early ownership stamp of a private owner. BAL 3227; Rinderknecht 43665; Streeter Sale I 358. Streeter 1267. M & S Rare Books 60-134 1996 $425.00

CHMURY, B. Anatol Petritzky. Theater-Trachten. Staatsverlag der Ukraine: 1929. One of 1500 copies; 4to; titlepage, captions and text in Russian and German; 56 plates mounted on gray art paper, of which 29 are spectacular color plates, in addition, there are 16 illustrations; grey sueded paper covered boards, back strip of fragile binding torn, but internally fine. Stunning work, scarce. Marilyn Braiterman 15-180 1996 $1,950.00

CHOISEUL STAINVILLE, ETIENNE FRANCOIS, DUC DE Memoire Historque sur la Negociation de la France & de l'Angleterre, Depuis le 26 Mars 1761 jusqu'au 20 Septembre de la meme annee, Avec les Pieces Justificatives. Paris: de l'Imprimerie Royale, 1761. 1st edition; 8vo; contemporary marbled wrappers; large paper copy; fine. Sabin 47516; Howes M507; TPL 338. Ximenes 109-79 1996 $2,500.00

CHOLMONDELEY-PENNELL, H. Fishing. London: Longmans, 1885. Large paper edition, limited to 250 numbered copies; 4to; frontispiece, few plates, numerous illustrations in text; original half morocco, gilt top, top and bottom of spine expertly repaired. Charles W. Traylen 117-291 1996 £175.00

CHOULANT, LUDWIG History and Bibliography of Anatomic Illustration. Chicago: 1920. 1st English translation; 435 pages; original binding; rare. GM 440. W. Bruce Fye 71-355 1996 $350.00

CHRETIEN, CHARLES P. An Essay on Logical Method. Oxford: John Henry Parker, 1848. 1st edition; 8vo; vi, (2), 220 pages, with 8 pages of publisher's ads at end, small cancelled ink stamp of Pembroke College, Oxford; original cloth, printed label on spine, fine. John Drury 82-44 1996 £90.00

CHRISTIAN, EWAN Architectural Illustrations of Skelton Church, Yorkshire. London: George Bell, 1846. 1st edition; folio; viii, 39, (1) pages, 17 plates; publisher's blindstamped cloth, respined, inscription in ink, occasional foxing and smudging, half inch tear in margin of plate 12, not affecting illustration, minor edgewear. Abbey Scenery 382. Bookpress 75-168 1996 $135.00

CHRISTIE, AGATHA 1891-1976 Absent in the Spring. London: Collins, 1944. 1st edition; crown 8vo; pages 160; original mid grey cloth, backstrip gilt lettered, owner's name on front free endpaper, dust jacket, excellent. Westwood & Satchell p. 14. Blackwell's B112-72 1996 £100.00

CHRISTIE, AGATHA 1891-1976 A Daughter's a Daughter. London: Heinemann, 1952. 1st edition; fine in near fine dust jacket with light rubbing, light creasing on spine ends and one very small closed tear on back panel. Quill & Brush 102-276 1996 $100.00

CHRISTIE, AGATHA 1891-1976 Death on the Nile. New York: Dodd, Mead & Co., 1938. Advance proof copy in blue printed paper wrappers, spine and edges darkened, covers lightly soiled, few nicks and tiny, closed tears, otherwise good to very good. Quill & Brush 102-266 1996 $350.00

CHRISTIE, AGATHA 1891-1976 Death Comes as the End. New York: Dodd, Mead, 1944. 1st edition; near fine with tips lightly bumped, in very good near fine dust jacket with few very small closed tears and very minor rubbing on edges and rear panel is lightly soiled. Quill & Brush 102-270 1996 $175.00

CHRISTIE, AGATHA 1891-1976 Destination Unknown. London: Collins, 1954. 1st edition; fine in price clipped dust jacket with very light edge wear. Quill & Brush 102-281 1996 $100.00

CHRISTIE, AGATHA 1891-1976 Evil Under the Sun. New York: Dodd, Mead & Co., 1941. Advance proof copy in pictorial wrappers with flaps; edges rubbed with front flap fold frayed and splitting at bottom, front cover loose but still attached, otherwise good to very good with covers nice and bright. Quill & Brush 102-267 1996 $300.00

CHRISTIE, AGATHA 1891-1976 The Hollow. London: Samuel French Ltd., 1952. 1st edition; tan pictorial paper wrappers, light soiling and edge wear, near fine. Quill & Brush 102-278 1996 $100.00

CHRISTIE, AGATHA 1891-1976 The Hound of Death and Other Stories. London: 1933. 1st edition; near fine in near fine dust jacket. Priscilla Juvelis 95/1-310 1996 $1,100.00

CHRISTIE, AGATHA 1891-1976 The Labours of Hercules. London: Crime Club, 1947. 1st edition; near fine with light soiling, in very good dust jacket with few closed tears, light chipping, rubbing and soiling. Quill & Brush 102-272 1996 $175.00

CHRISTIE, AGATHA 1891-1976 The Mousetrap. London: Samuel French, 1954. 1st play edition; 8vo; original pictorial wrappers with light wear to spine, very good, evidence of sticker removal on page 1 affecting a few letters. Glenn Books 36-48 1996 $300.00

CHRISTIE, AGATHA 1891-1976 The Moving Finger. London: Crime Club, 1943. 1st edition; very good with light soiling and spine ends light worn, in very good dust jacket with one chip on lower front panel, light chipping on spine, light rubbing and back panel slightly soiled. Quill & Brush 102-269 1996 $250.00

CHRISTIE, AGATHA 1891-1976 Murder at the Vicarage. London: Samuel French Ltd., 1950. 1st edition; tan paper wrappers, light soiling and wear. Quill & Brush 102-273 1996 $100.00

CHRISTIE, AGATHA 1891-1976   Murder is Easy. London: Collins, 1939. 1st edition; crown 8vo; pages 254 (2) (ads); original orange cloth, backstrip lettered in black, some dampstaining to fore-edges of covers, owner's name on front free endpaper, dust jacket with closed tear to rear joint fold and backstrip, good.   Blackwell's B112-73 1996 £550.00

CHRISTIE, AGATHA 1891-1976   The Murder of Roger Ackroyd. London: W. Collins Sons, 1926. Good copy, no dust jacket.   Limestone Hills 41-23 1996 $330.00

CHRISTIE, AGATHA 1891-1976   N or M? New York: Dodd, 1941. 1st U.S. edition; original cloth, fine but for faint sticker darkening on f.e.p., in very lightly used dust jacket with faint skinned mark on spine.   Beasley Books 82-258 1996 $175.00

CHRISTIE, AGATHA 1891-1976   The Pale Horse. London: Collins, 1961. 1st edition; fine in dust jacket.   Quill & Brush 102-286 1996 $100.00

CHRISTIE, AGATHA 1891-1976   Poirot and the Regatta Mystery. London: Vallancey Press, n.d., ca. 1941. 1st edition; 16 page pamphlet in green cardboard printed wrappers, near fine with minor edge wear and back panel is slightly soiled.   Quill & Brush 102-268 1996 $250.00

CHRISTIE, AGATHA 1891-1976   Ten Little Niggers. London: Samuel French Ltd., 1944. 1st edition; sea-green paper wrappers with very light soiling, first few pages lightly creased and owners name and date written in ink on inside front cover; near fine,   Quill & Brush 102-271 1996 $100.00

CHRISTIE, JAMES   A Disquisition Upon Etruscan Vases... London: printed for Private Distribution by William Bulmer, 1806. 1st edition; one of 100 copies; folio; 16 engraved plates, 5 engraed vignettes, full contemporary dark purple straight grained morocco, gilt stamped spine with raised bands and decorations in gilt, gilt bordered covers with devices in corners, gilt ruled inner dentelles, all edges gilt, slight spotting or offsetting, very good. Rare.   George J. Houle 68-30 1996 $1,750.00

CHRISTIE-MILLER, S.   Cataloue of the Library of S. Christie-Miller, esq. Britwell, Bucks. (1) Divinity; (2). Voyages and Travels; (3) British History. London: the Chiswick Press, 1873/76. 4to; 3 volumes in 1; contemporary blue half buckram, red and gilt spine label, top edge gilt, uncut; very rare. De Ricci p. 105-113.   Maggs Bros. Ltd. 1191-38 1996 £220.00

CHRISTMAS Story Book. New York: McLoughlin Bros., 1903. Quarto; chromolithographic frontispiece, black and white text illustrations; original grey cloth pictorially stamped in red, green, black, white and tan on front cover and lettered in black on spine, extremities lightly rubbed, slightly shaken, little minor soiling, previous owner's ink presentation inscription dated 1906 on recto of frontispiece; very good, overall.   Heritage Book Shop 196-275 1996 $100.00

THE CHRISTMAS Tale, a Poetical Address and Remonstrance to the Young Ministry. London: printed for R. Faulder, 1784. 1st edition; 4to; disbound; very scarce, nice, complete with half title; Jackson p. 105. Ximenes 108-294 1996 $350.00

CHRISTMAS Tales of Flanders. New York: Dodd, Mead & Co., 1917. 1st American edition; 4to; 12 color plates and numerous black and white illustrations and decorative devices by De Bosschere; navy blue cloth, gilt cover and spine, pictorial endleaves, few rear leaves creased and light wear to tail of spine, else fine, front panel and spine of dust jacket laid in.   Glenn Books 36-62 1996 $195.00

CHRISTMAS With the Poets. London: Bogue, 1851. 1st edition; engraved titlepage printed in two or 3 colors and gold, with additional hand colring, illustrations throughout printed in black and two or three neutral tints, all by Birket Foster, ornaments and initials printed in gold; full publisher's black morocco stamped in gilt on both boards, design of holly leaves and on spine with gilt devices, gilt dentelles, some light spotting, but very fresh, bright copy; McLean VBD 176.   Barbara Stone 70-94 1996 £150.00

CHRISTOPHER, A. B.   The Word Accomplished: Extracts. NdA Press, 1974. One of 75 numbered copies, signed by author and artist; each print numbered, signed and dated by artist; 16 colored etchings by Natalie d'Arbeloff; text set in 18 pt. Monotype Garamond and hand printed on one side only in folded sheets of Barcham Green mouldmade; unbound sheets in etched paper folder, preserved in quarter brown leather box, title embossed on spine, cream paper sides with intaglio design on upper cover; fine.   Bertram Rota 272-311 1996 £350.00

CHRONICA Monasterii S. Albani. London: 1863-76. 8vo; 12 volumes; facsimiles; original cloth.   Howes Bookshop 265-1575 1996 £300.00

CHRONICLES of Canada. Toronto: Glasgow, Brook & Co., 1914/15/16. 18cm; various pagination; averaging 150 to 250 pages each; color frontispieces, illustrations, portraits, maps, some folding; very good in gilt stamped and decorated blue leather, uncut with top edge gilt. Rockland Books 38-43 1996 $250.00

CHUBB, RALPH   A Fable of Love and War a Romantic Poem. Curridge: printed by E. R.Chubb, published by R. N. Chubb, 1925. Limited to 200 copies, this copy out of series; small 8vo; pages (iv), 36, (i) limitation notice, woodcut frontispiece, title vignette, full page plate, 2 smaller illustrations by Ralph Chubb; uncut in original drab wrappers, upper cover with title and small woodcut device printed in green, 3 small marks on upper cover, extremities very slightly frayed; very good. Simon Finch 24-38 1996 £200.00

CHUINARD, E. G.   Only One Man Died: the Medical Aspects of the Lewis and Clark Expedition. Glendale: Arthur H. Clark Co., 1979. 1st edition; one of 1020 copies; 444 pages, 18 illustrations; bookplate; very fine in pictorial dust jacket. Clark & Brunet 41.   Argonaut Book Shop 113-414 1996 $250.00

CHUINARD, E. G.   Only One Man Died. The Medical Aspects of the Lewis and Clark Expedition. Glendale: 1979. 1st edition; 444 pages; color frontispiece, illustrations; fine, in dust jacket.   T. A. Swinford 49-206 1996 $225.00

CHUINARD. E. G.   Only One Man Died: the Medical Aspects of the Lewis and Clark Expedition. Glendale: Arthur H. Clark Co., 1979. 1st edition; 9 1/4 x 6 inches; 444 pages, frontispiece, double page map and 14 pages of illustrations included in pagination; red cloth in dust jacket. Dawson's Books Shop 528-58 1996 $100.00

THE CHURCH and the Indians: the Trouble at Metlakahtla. Victoria: Daily Colonist, 1882. 23.5 cm; 8 pages; fine in self wrappers; Lowther 615. Rockland Books 38-150 1996 $100.00

CHURCH OF ENGLAND. BOOK OF COMMON PRAYER   Book of Common Prayer. Oxford: at the Theatre, 1680. 8vo; fine engraved architectural titlepage of the inteior of a church, top edge cut close occasionally touching running title, 3 leaves with lower right hand corner torn away with loss of a few letters only, generally fine, crisp and clean; finely bound in full 18th century black morocco, boards with gilt key-roll border, spine elaborately gilt with stars and urn devices, insignificant wear at extremities. Scarce. Wing B3660.   Ian Wilkinson 95/1-37 1996 £95.00

CHURCH OF ENGLAND. BOOK OF COMMON PRAYER   Book of Common Prayer. Oxford: by the University Printers, 1701. Large folio; ruled in red and black; contemporary black morocco, covers gilt and blindstamped with broad outer border of floral drawer handle and small tools, central panel with blindstamped leafy sprays and flowers, monograms gilt in each corner, centre gilt with Royal Arms (Queen Anne, Davenport p. 51), spine gilt in 8 panels with raised bands and one panel lettered direct, all edges gilt, corner soft, some gilt faded, but generally fresh, fine binding with both Royal Arms and monograms almost certainly by Robert Steel.   Marlborough 160-31 1996 £2,250.00

CHURCH OF ENGLAND. BOOK OF COMMON PRAYER   Book of Common Prayer. London: 1717. 8vo; 85 pages, engraved, frontispiece, portrait, 2 small and 16 half page text illustrations; contemporary black morocco, panelled blind with outer leafy border and central panel with arabesque and other small tools, spine with five raised bands, panels with repeated small tools, all edges gilt, endpapers marbled, covers with centre and cornerpieces of filigree silver.   Marlborough 160-56 1996 £1,500.00

CHURCH OF ENGLAND. BOOK OF COMMON PRAYER   The Book of Common Prayer and Administration of the Sacraments...Together with the Psalter... London: Engraven & Ptd. by the Permission of Mr. John Baskett, 1717. Octavo; xxii, 166, (ii) pages; vignette illustrations and decorative borders, volvelle on page v present, but lacking pointers, as usual, 4 page subscriber's list, contemporary black panelled morocco, decorated in gilt, gilt edges, neatly rebacked with old backstrip laid down; lightly rubbed, paper little browned, very nice.   Robert Clark 38-17 1996 £425.00

CHURCH OF ENGLAND. BOOK OF COMMON PRAYER   Book of Common Prayer. London: by the Assigns of His Majesty's Printer & of Henry Hills, deceased, 1729. large folio; engraved title (undated, but 1713/14), title, 12 ff. prelims, 278 ff. n.n., ruled in red throughout; dark blue morocco, covers gilt with broad double border, inner of alternating crowns and flowers spine gilt in 8 panels, raised bands gilt, panels with royal monogram, crowns and flowers, all edges gilt, marbled endpapers, gilt arms of King George I (d. 1727) on covers, corners little rubbed, ties gone, a fine royal binding on large paper; from the library of Dudley Alexander Sydney Cosby, Baron of Stradbally (Ireland) with his ex-libris and signature, ca. 1730.   Marlborough 160-33 1996 £1,250.00

CHURCH OF ENGLAND. BOOK OF COMMON PRAYER   The Book of Common Prayer, and Administration of the Sacraments and Other Rites and Ceremonies of the Church, According to the Use of the Church of England... London: Printed by Thomas Baskett, Printer to the King's most Excellent... 1751. Folio; 1-19 pages; frontispiece, text and title rubricated by hand; full black morocco, elaborate tooled border to boards, gilt coat of arms of George II to both bds., gilt title St. James's Chapel 1752, to upper bd., corners bumped, jts. sl. worn, crown & GR monograph to compartments, raised bands to spine, marbled endpapers; owner's bookplate, owner's pen inscription, some sproadic foxing; ms. inscription "This book which belonged originally to the Princess of Wales, was used by Members of the Royal Family in the Chapel of St. James, was bought of Mr. Bohn at Canterbury in June 1847 by Robert Jenkins, M.A. Rector & Vicar of Lyminge...June 1847 and given by him to Helen Constable Jenkins Easter Monday (March 29th) 1880." Beeleigh Abbey BA56-140 1996 £550.00

CHURCH OF ENGLAND. BOOK OF COMMON PRAYER   The Book of Common Prayer. Cambridge: John Baskerville, 1760. 1st edition; octavo; 347 leaves, unnumbered; this copy with border ornaments; handsome blue straight grained morocco, boards stamped with roll and fillet borders in gilt and blind, spine with four wide raised bands forming five compartments elaborately decorated in gilt and blind, inner dentelles decorated in gilt and blind, inner dentelles decorated with roll and fillet in gilt, foxing to prelims, otherwise very clean, with wide margins, joints and hinges tender, very handsome book. Cancel top edge gilt with border and price of 7s. 6d. from Gaskell's group 1; contains early cancels except F4 & none of the later cancels. Gaskell 42.   Hermitage SP95-828 1996 $1,000.00

CHURCH OF ENGLAND. BOOK OF COMMON PRAYER   The Book of Common Prayer and Administration of the Sacraments, and Other Rites and Ceremonies of the Church. Cambridge: 1760. 1st edition; 2nd impression; 8vo; text unpaginated; text surrounded by border of lozenge and star ornaments; full burgundy morocco, gilt tool scrolled border, elaborate gilt tooling to panelled spine, black morocco label to spine, joints rubbed, corners worn, all edges gilt; hinges cracked, library identification plate to front pastedown. Bookplate of William Wilberforce, ownership inscription.   Beeleigh Abbey BA56-133 1996 £250.00

CHURCH OF ENGLAND. BOOK OF COMMON PRAYER   The Book of Common Prayer. Cambridge: J. Baskerville, 1762. 12mo. in 6's; unpaginated; full crushed black morocco with raised bands, attractively gilt; fine. Gaskell 20.   Hermitage SP95-827 1997 $450.00

CHURCH OF ENGLAND. BOOK OF COMMON PRAYER   Book of Common Prayer. Cambridge: Baskerville, 1762. 8vo; typical binding of the period, dark blue morocco gilt, with broad urn-and-flower border, all edges gilt.   Marlborough 160-32 1996 £250.00

CHURCH OF ENGLAND. BOOK OF COMMON PRAYER   The Book of Common Prayer, and Administration of the Sacraments and Other Rites and Ceremonies of the Church... Oxford: printed by T. Wright and W. Gill, 1773. 8vo; unpaginated double column text; contemporary black panelled calf, ornately gilt tooled, some occasional text foxing.   Kenneth Karmiole 1NS-47 1996 $200.00

CHURCH OF ENGLAND. BOOK OF COMMON PRAYER   The Book of Common Prayer, and Adminsitration of the Sacraments and Other Rites and Ceremonies of the Church.... London: printed by John Jarvis for Joseph Good, 1791. 8vo; unpaginated; 10 copper engraved plates, contemporary black straight grained morocco gilt, marbled endpapers, all edges gilt.   Kenneth Karmiole 1NS-48 1996 $150.00

CHURCH OF ENGLAND. BOOK OF COMMON PRAYER   The Book of Common Prayer, and Administration of the Sacraments...with the Psalter or Psalms of David... Oxford: printed at the Clarendon Press, 1791. tall 8vo; (196)ff; contemporary full red straight grained morocco with gilt tooled spine and inner dentelles, gilt ruled borders, all edges gilt, bookplate removed, but crisp, near fine in lovely binding showing only minimal wear; very scarce.   Chapel Hill 94-106 1996 $175.00

CHURCH OF ENGLAND. BOOK OF COMMON PRAYER   The Book of Common Prayer...Together with the Psalter. Oxford: University Press, 1840. 8vo; crushed red morocco over bevelled boards decorated in blind, with panels and rules extending from the four sets of double raised bands on spine, which has title information stamped thereon in gilt, the top and bottom and fore edge have been elaborately decorated through the application of gilt, guaffering and illumination, each end contains a religious admonition lettered on a medieval style banderole, the painting and gauffering with its wide selection of tools and fields of pointelles, is of high quality and the decoration is in wonderfully fresh condition owing to presence of original leather slipcase, binding is signed Hayday on lower front turn-in.   Book Block 32-24 1996 $975.00

CHURCH OF ENGLAND. BOOK OF COMMON PRAYER   The Book of Common Prayer. London: William Pickering, 1853. 7 1/4 x 5 inches; (360 leaves, every page of text with wide panel borders, title leaf with elaborate border on recto, all in imitation of Richard Day's "Booke of Christian Prayers", commonly known as "Queen Elizabeth's Prayerbook" first printed in 1569; title in red and black; extremely attractive ornately gilt & blindstamped contemporary dark brown morocco by Cape, covers dominated by large diapered field of blindstamped fleurs-de-lis, spine similarly decorated in compartments between raised bands, one compartment titled in gilt, very handsome densely gilt inner dentelles, marbled endpapers, all edges gilt, light mottling or foxing here and there otherwise very fine, lovely binding bright, clean and virtually unworn; Keynes p. 74.   Phillip J. Pirages 33-418 1996 $650.00

CHURCH OF ENGLAND. BOOK OF COMMON PRAYER   Book of Common Prayer...Together with the Psalter... London: Bickers and Bush, 1863. 8vo; 360 leaves (unpaginated), title in red and black with wood engraved border, portrait of Elizabeth I on verso and wood engraved borders by Mary Byfield after Hans Holbein, Durer & others from Q. Elizabeth's Book of Christmas Prayers of 1569; later 19th century half vellum, marbled boards, double morocco labels, little chipped, but attractive, top edge gilt, others uncut; good copy. McLean VBD. Keynes p. 86.   Claude Cox 107-187 1996 £55.00

CHURCH OF ENGLAND. BOOK OF COMMON PRAYER   The Book of Common Prayer Together with the Psalter or Psalms of David. London: Peacock, Mansfield & Britton, n.d., ca. 1885. 8vo; full calf, front cover achieved in cuir-cisele with words DEVS DANTE OMNIA AMANDVS above an heraldic coat of arms featuring a lion holding a hatchet, the date 1 8 8 5 in four corners, and the initials HCW below; background is covered in blind pointelles and raised letters tinted with gilt, spine with 4 raised bands and cuir-cisele panels, 8 silver corner bosses and silver clasp with leather strap extending from lower cover to a stud on upper cover to a stud on upper cover, all edges handsomely gilt and gauffered, gilt decorated vellum pastedowns and free endleaves in same of pomegranates on a leafy stem, on lower edge of rear cover is a sm. cuir-cisele panel with words, ME FEC, and initials O.H., above and below a stylized binding, bird with both wings extended, the initials & logotype of Otto Hupp, graphic designer & publisher; laid in is ANS from former owner, Helen C. Waterhouse, whose initials appear on cover; splendid binding example.   Book Block 32-42 1996 $1,175.00

CHURCH OF ENGLAND. BOOK OF COMMON PRAYER   The Book of Common Prayer...Together with the Psalter. London: Oxford University Press, 1898. 2 3/8 x 1 7/8 inches; 688 pages; full gilt stamped black morocco with an unusual Art Nouveau cover in silver, showing flowering vines and the "IHS" symbol in center; very fine. Bondy p. 117; Welsh 1856.   Bromer Booksellers 87-207 1996 $325.00

CHURCH OF ENGLAND. BOOK OF COMMON PRAYER   The Book of Common Prayer...Together with the Psalter... London: Oxford University Press, 1898. 2 3/8 x 1 7/8 inches; 688 pages; full gilt stamped black morocco with intricate gilt dentelles red edges gilt, housed in original velvet lined morocco fitted case; contemporary inscription and bookplat of Abraham Horodisch. Bondy p. 117; Welsh 1856.   Bromer Booksellers 87-208 1996 $225.00

CHURCH OF ENGLAND. BOOK OF COMMON PRAYER   The Book of Common Prayer, and Administration of the Sacraments, and Other Rites and Ceremonies of the Church According to the Use of the Church of England in Canada. London: Society for Promoting Christian Knowledge, 1917. Small 8vo; pages viii, 299; translated into the Cree language; (mixed roman and syllabic characters). full calf, all edges gilt, inscribed, with ALS by revisor, J. A. Mackay; near mint.   Hugh Anson-Cartwright 87-305 1996 $300.00

CHURCH OF ENGLAND. BOOK OF COMMON PRAYR   The Book of Common Prayer. London: John Murray, 1845. 1st edition; 8vo; xl, 484 pages; vignettes, initials, borders and ornaments designed by Owen Jones; publisher's full calf, all edges gilt, tastefully respined using origin as an over-lay, modern title label, inner hinges strengthened, else very good.   Bookpress 75-71 1996 $685.00

CHURCH OF JESUS CHRIST OF LATTER-DAY SAINTS   Doctrine and Covenants of the Church of Jesus Christ of Latter-Day Saints. Nauvoo: printed by John Taylor, 1845. 3rd edition; 448 pages; front page and paper replaced, last page (448) has some restored text in facsimile where a chip had been in paper; original half leather spine and tips, gilt still remaining on spine, though somewhat dulled, very readable. Period style paper re-laid over front and back boards, period-style leather tips replaced on lower outer corners of boards; overall a beautiful copy. Rare.   Orrin Schwab 10-35 1996 $4,500.00

CHURCH, EDWARD   Notice on the Beet Sugar... Northampton: Butler, 1837. 1st edition; small 8vo; 54 pages + ad, linen backed printed boards, front cover separate, ex-library, numerals on spine and labels on rear pastedown, library stamp on titlepage.   Second Life Books 103-49 1996 $165.00

CHURCH, ELIHU DWIGHT 1835-1908   A Catalogue of Books Relating to the Discovery and Early History of North and South America Forming a Part of the Library of E. D. Church. New York: 1995. Reprint of 1907 edition, limited to 100 sets; 8vo; 5 volumes; illustrations; original cloth. Forest Books 74-41 1996 £125.00

CHURCH, ELIHU DWIGHT 1835-1908   The E. D. Church Library. A Catalogue of Books Relating to the Discovery and Early History of North and South America. New York: Peter Smith, 1951. 2nd edition; 8vo; 5 volumes; profusely illustrated, illustrations. Fine set.   Trebizond 39-79 1996 $875.00

CHURCH, THOMAS   The History of Philip's War, Commonly Called the Great Indian War of 1675 and 1676. Boston: printed by J. H. A. Frost, 1827. 1st edition thus with plates; 12mo; 360 pages; contemporary calf, label, some looseness in two gatherings, generally tight and nice, very good plus copy.   Freedom Bookshop 14-1 1996 $175.00

CHURCHILL, CHARLES   The Apology. London: printed for the author and sold by W. Flexney, 1761. 1st edition; 4to; disbound; half title present, several tears, especially in last leaf, but without loss of text; with contemporary acquisition notes of Will's Coffee House, Lincoln's Inn dated May 19, along with names of 3 borrowers.   Ximenes 108-67 1996 $150.00

CHURCHILL, RANDOLPH S.   Winston S. Churchill. London: Heinemann, 1966-88. Thick large 8vo; 18 volumes; numerous plates and illustrations from photos; very good set in dust jackets.   Howes Bookshop 265-1376 1996 £300.00

CHURCHILL, WINSTON LEONARD SPENCER 1874-1965   Arms and Convenant. Speeches. London: Harrap, 1938. 1st edition; 466 pages; blue cloth, nice.   Ian Patterson 9-90 1996 £125.00

CHURCHILL, WINSTON LEONARD SPENCER 1874-1965   A Catalogue of His Paintings. London: 1967. 1st edition; quarto; 502 paintings; fine in dust jacket with small chip at spine top; signed by Lady Clementine Spencer-Churchill.   Stephen Lupack 83- 1996 $225.00

CHURCHILL, WINSTON LEONARD SPENCER 1874-1965   Defending the West. London: Maurice Temple Smith Ltd., 1981. 1st edition; 4 maps, 8 figures, 3 tables and 4 black and white photos; original binding, fine in very slightly creased and marked dust jacket; presentation copy from author inscribed for Lord Shinwell.   Ulysses 39-110 1996 £55.00

CHURCHILL, WINSTON LEONARD SPENCER 1874-1965   Great Contemporaries. London: Macmillan & Co., 1942. Re-issue; rebound in half morocco with raised bands, marbled endpapers and top edge gilt, inscribed by Churchill for Emmanuel Shinwell.   Ulysses 39-108 1996 £2,500.00

CHURCHILL, WINSTON LEONARD SPENCER 1874-1965   Ian Hamilton's March. London: Longman, 1900. 1st edition; small 8vo; choicely bound in half crimson levant morocco, cloth sides, 5 raised bands, gold lettering and gold lion design, gilt top, bound by Bayntun.   Charles W. Traylen 117-88 1996 £280.00

CHURCHILL, WINSTON LEONARD SPENCER 1874-1965   London to Ladysmith via Pretoria. London: Longmans, 1900. 1st edition; small 8vo; 4 maps, 1 folding, also 4 plans, 32 pages of ads at end; choicely bound in half red levant morocco, cloth sides to match, 5 raised bands, gold lion ornaments on spine, gilt top, by Bayntun. Woods A4 p. 29. Charles W. Traylen 117-89 1996 £320.00

CHURCHILL, WINSTON LEONARD SPENCER 1874-1965   The River War. London: Longmans, Green and Co., 1899. 1st edition; 1st printing; 2 volumes; original dark blue cloth gilt, endpapers cracked, but hinges quite firm; excellent set in half blue morocco cases.   19th Century Shop 39- 1996 $5,800.00

CHURCHILL, WINSTON LEONARD SPENCER 1874-1965   The Second World War. London: Cassell and Co. Ltd., 1948-54. 1st English edition; 8vo; 6 volumes; fine in lightly chipped dust jackets. Woods A123b. Glenn Books 36-50 1996 $275.00

CHURCHILL, WINSTON LEONARD SPENCER 1874-1965   The Second World War. London: 1948-54. 1st edition; 6 volumes; illustrations; very good in dust jackets.   Words Etcetera 94-299 1996 £75.00

CHURCHILL, WINSTON LEONARD SPENCER 1874-1965   Secret Session Speeches. London: Cassell & Co., 1946. 1st edition; 16 black and white photos; original binding, top edge dusty, head and tail of spine and corners bumped, covers bowed and slightly marked, cover edges rubbed and darkened; good, no dust jacket; presentation copy from author for Emmanuel Shinwell.   Ulysses 39-109 1996 £2,500.00

CHURCHILL, WINSTON LEONARD SPENCER 1874-1965   The Story of the Malakand Field Force. London: Longmans, Green and Co., 1898. 1st edition; original apple green cloth, errata slip, some rubbing and light soiling, half morocco case; inscribed presentation copy from author dated Dec. 1898, presentation copies inscribed in the year of publication are rare   19th Century Shop 39- 1996 $12,000.00

CHURCHILL, WINSTON LEONARD SPENCER 1874-1965   Thoughts and Adventures. London: Thornton Butterworth Ltd., 1932. 1st edition; 8vo; moderate extremity wear, small library card front pastedown, sandy brown cloth. Woods A39(a).   Glenn Books 36-51 1996 $250.00

CHURCHILL, WINSTON LEONARD SPENCER 1874-1965   The World Crisis 1911-1914. London: Thornton Butterworth, 1923-31. 1st edition; octavo; 6 volumes; folding maps; original blue blindstamped cloth with gilt lettered spines, spine extremities lightly rubbed, edges foxed, other occasional foxing, armorial bookplate, very good. Woods A31a. Heritage Book Shop 196-186 1996 $2,000.00

CHURTON, E.   The Book Collector's Hand-Book: a Modern Library Companion. London: E. Churton, 1845. 1st edition; 8vo; (iv), 76, (4) pages, 24 page catalog; original green limp cloth, upper cover blocked in gilt, neatly rebacked; inscribed "With E. Churton's respects".   James Burmester 29-28 1996 £85.00

CHUTE, CAROLYN   The Beans of Egypt, Maine. New York: Ticknor & Fields, 1985. 1st edition; beautiful copy, signed by author. Ticknor and Fields file copy, so designated on front free endpaper.   Lame Duck Books 19-139 1996 $500.00

CHUTE, CAROLYN   The Beans of Egypt, Maine. New York: Ticknor & Fields, 1985. 1st edition; author's first book; small spot on fore edge, otherwise fine in fine dust jacket; warmly inscribed by author in 1988. Ken Lopez 74-84 1996 $500.00

CIARDI, JOHN   Homeward to America. New York: Holt, 1940. 1st edition; neat name, small smudge front pastedown, else fine in price clipped near fine dust jacket with some negligible rubbing, very nice, author's first book.   Between the Covers 42-100 1996 $125.00

CIBBER, COLLEY 1671-1757   An Apology for the Life of Mr. Colley Cibber, Comedian... London: printed by John Watts for the author, 1740. 1st edition; 4to; frontispiece; contemporary mottled calf, gilt, spine gilt, trifle rubbed; fine. LAR 2555; Rothschild 636; CBEL II 778.   Ximenes 108-68 1996 $650.00

CIBBER, COLLEY 1671-1757   An Apology for the Life of Colley Cibber... London: Golden Cockerel Press, 1925. One of 450 numbered sets; 2 volumes; original cloth backed boards, spines gilt, trifle dusty, else very good.   Hermitage SP95-877 1996 $150.00

CIBBER, COLLEY 1671-1757   An Apology for the Life of Colley Cibber, Comedian, and Late Patentee of the Theatre-Royal. Tyford; The Golden Cockerel Press, 1925. No. 89 of 450 copies; tall 8vo; 2 volumes; original cloth backed boards, titles and headlines in blue and black, deckled edges partially unopened. LAR 2568.   Dramatis Personae 37-32 1996 $150.00

CIBBER, COLLEY 1671-1757   A Letter from Mr. Cibber, to Mr. Pope, Inquiring Into the Motives that Might Induce Him to His Satyrical Works... (with) Another Occasional Letter from Mr. Cibber to Mr. Pope... London: printed and sold by W. Lewis, 1742/44. 1st editions; 8vo. in 4's; pages 66; 56; 2 works bound in one; half titles (browned in first title), small repair in gutter margin I1, lacks final blank in 1st title, 2nd title outer leaves browned; modern yellow ochre cloth, backstrip longitudinally gilt lettered, excellent.   Blackwell's B112-75 1996 £145.00

CIBBER, COLLEY 1671-1757   Plays. London: Tonson, Lintot, Mears, Chetwood, 1721. 1st edition; 4to; 2 volumes; contemporary morocco, spines replaced with later cloth.   Lyman Books 21-529 1996 $125.00

CIBBER, THEOPHILUS   The Lives and Characters of the Most Eminent Actors and Actresses of Great Britain and Ireland... London: printed for R. Griffiths, 1753. 1st edition; 8vo; pages xcix, xiv, 89, final blank leaf; original boards, uncut, large unopened, cloth folding case, minor wear to covers, but fine, unsophisticated copy; evidently the Britwell copy, with pencil shelfmark. LAR 2503.   Peter Murray Hill 185-38 1996 £475.00

CICERO, MARCUS TULLIUS 106-43 BC   Cicero's Books of Friendship, Old Age and Scipio's Dream. London: Chatto & Windus/Boston: John W. Luce and Co., 1907. 6 x 4 3/4 inches; xviii, 217, (1) pages; frontispiece; very pretty burgundy morocco, heavily gilt by Riviere and Son (for Brentano's), covers with intricate frame featuring elegant roses on elongated stems reaching into the corners, large massed clump of a dozen roses at center of each cover, with tendrils extending to the four sides of the front cover fame, spine with raised bands, gilt to fur sides of the cover frame, spine with raised bands, gilt decorated compartments, gilt titling, turn-ins with simple gilt rules and corner ornaments, marbled endpapers, gilt edges; couple of minor marks to covers, spine a shade darker than boards, otherwise fine, attractively bound, virtually pristine internally.   Phillip J. Pirages 33-60 1996 $175.00

CICERO, MARCUS TULLIUS 106-43 BC   Le Epistole Famigliari, Gia Tradotte, & Hora in Molti Luoghi Corrette da Aldo Mavito. Venice: Aldo Manuzio, 1573. One of the latest 16th century editions of this translation; small 8vo; pages (xxiv), 750, italic letter with Roman index and side notes, woodcut printer's device on titlepage, 2 tiny paper flaws just touching text; 17th century vellum over boards; early ex-libris 'Lobier' at foot of titlepage, very good. BM STC It. p. 179; Adams C1989; Index Aurel 139.397. Reounard 216.5.   A. Sokol XXV-21 1996 £950.00

CICERO, MARCUS TULLIUS 106-43 BC   M. T. Cicero de Oratore. Or His Three Dialogues Upon the Character and Qualifications of an Orator. London: printed for T. Waller, 1755. 2nd edition by William Guthrie; handsome contemporary mottled calf with unusual applied 'whirl' staining, gilt spine, red label. Alston VI 180 for 1st ed. of 1742.   Jarndyce 103-44 1996 £120.00

CICERO, MARCUS TULLIUS 106-43 BC   Phippicae. Francisci Mantvrantii Enarrationes in Philippicas. Venice: Ioannes Tacuinus de Tridino, 22nd March 1494. 2nd edition; small folio; 78 unnumbered leaves a-n6, Roman letter in 2 sizes, white on black woodcut initials, woodcut printer's device; contemporary scholarly annotations throughout, later ownership autograph of St. Peter's College, Strasbourg on titlepage, slight age yellowing, 3 tiny wormholes affecting single letters but not legibility in few leaves, otherwise very good; 17th century English polished speckled calf panelled in blind, spine gilt; bookplate of Viscount Mersey, Bignor Park. BMC V 528; Hain Coppinger 5139; Goff C557; GKW 6797. Graesse II 165.   A. Sokol XXV-22 1996 £2,250.00

CINDERELLA   Cinderella. New York: McLoughlin, 1888. full page chromo litho illustration and cover design by Richard Andre; colored pictorial wrappers, fresh copy.   Barbara Stone 70-15 1996 £55.00

CIPRIANI, G. B.   Cipriani's Rudiments of Drawing. London: Edward Orme, 1815. Re-issue of the 1786 issue of engraved titlepage; oblong folio; 6 stipple engraved plates by Bartolozzi, but with plates still dated Jan. 1st 1786, augmented with 3 plates of hands and legs dated Jan. 1st 1792, and 2 further plates dated Jan. 20th 1793; original grey wrappers, paper label on upper wrapper titled "Cipriani & Bartolozzi's Drawing Book of the Human Figure. New Edition - 1815", spine expertly repaired; inscription "Helen Spiers, from Mrs. Spiers, March 1824 Hinckly".   Ken Spelman 30-32 1996 £280.00

CISNEROS, FRANCISCO JAVIER   Ferro Carril de Antioquia (United States of Columbia). Report on the Construction of a Railway from Puerto Berrio to Barbosa, (State of Antioquia). New York: D. Van Nostrand, 1878. 8vo; 166 pages; 2 large folding maps; original purple cloth; presentation copy inscribed by author.   Kenneth Karmiole 1NS-240 1996 $150.00

CITINO, DAVID   A Letter of Columbus. Columbus: Logan Elm Press, 1990. One of 130 copies; page size 12 1/8 x 9 inches; on handmade paper, each copy signed by designer Robert Tauber, the author and the artist, Anthony Rice; 31 monoprints (off hand painted zinc plates); handset janson; titlepage calligraphy and initial letters hand drawn by Ann Woods; bound in handmade paper with goatskin spine, yap edges, housed in slipcase with paste papers made from anchor line and inlaid with cast paper bas-relief taken of the titlepage illustration.   Priscilla Juvelis 95/1-157 1996 $1,850.00

THE CITY Of London's Plea to the Quo Warranto, (an information) Brought Against Their Charter in Michaelmas Term, 1681. London: Randal Taylor, 1682. 1st edition; folio; (2), 16 pages, 17-20 numbered ll. + 21-31, (1) pages, text printed in double columns in Latin and English; recent cloth with late 19th century linen backed wrappers preserved; very good. Wing C 4360; Goss 2029; Sweet & Maxwell I 434(4); Goldsmiths 2497.   John Drury 82-45 1996 £125.00

THE CIVIL Record of Major General Winfield S. Hancock During His Administration in Louisiana and Texas. N.P.: 1871. 1st edition; 32 pages; original printed wrappers, 2 small rubber stamps of Wyoming Historical Geological Society, else very good or better, scarce.   McGowan Book Co. 65-19 1996 $250.00

CLAIBORNE, NATHANIEL HERBERT   Notes On the War in the South... Richmond: Pub. by William Ramsay, 1819. 1st edition; 12mo; contemporary tree calf, spine gilt; some light browning, but fine, binding especially well preserved. Not in Sabin; Howes C421; Shaw & Shoemaker 47622.   Ximenes 109-80 1996 $1,500.00

CLAIRMONT, CHRISTOPH W.   The Glass Vessels. New Haven: Dura-Europos Publications, 1963. Folio; xx, 152 pages; 4 figures, 37 plates; original cloth.   Archaeologia Luxor-3157 1996 $150.00

CLAIRMONT, CHRISTOPH W.   Gravestone and Epigram: Greek Memorials fromt he Archaic and Classical Period. Mainz on Rhein: Philipp von Zabern, 1970. 4to; xix, 185 pages, 37 plates; 2 corners lightly bumped; original cloth.   Archaeologia Luxor-3158 1996 $250.00

CLAMPITT, AMY   Manhattan. An Elegy and other Poems. Iowa City: University of Iowa Center for the Book, 1990. 1st edition; limited to 130 numbered copies, signed by Clampitt & Sunday; folio; woodcuts by Margaret Sunday; original woodcut decorated handmade paper boards, acetate dust jacket; new at publication price.   James S. Jaffe 34-115 1996 $850.00

CLAMPITT, AMY   Multitudes, Multitudes New York: Washington St. Press, 1973. 1st edition; 8vo; singed by author; author's first book; wrappers, head of spine trifle rubbed, otherwise mint.   James S. Jaffe 34-110 1996 $500.00

CLANCEY, P. A.   The Birds of Natal and Zululand. London: 1964. Imperial 8vo; 41 colored paltes, text figures and map; mint in dust jacket.   David A.H. Grayling MY95Orn-18 1996 £70.00

CLANCEY, P. A.   The Birds of Natal and Zululand. London: 1964. Royal 8vo; pages xxxiv, 511, 30 colored paltes, illustrations, map; cloth.   Wheldon & Wesley 207-692 1996 £60.00

CLANCY, TOM   Armored Cav. New York: Putnam, 1994. One of only 150 signed, numbered copies in slipcase; fine as issued.   Quill & Brush 102-311 1996 $175.00

CLANCY, TOM   Armored Cav. New York: Putnam's, 1994. Severely limited edition of only 150 copies; fine in slipcase and signed by author.   Bev Chaney, Jr. 23-151 1996 $185.00

CLANCY, TOM   Debt of Honor. New York: Putnam, 1994. One of 450 signed copies, limited; fine in slipcase.   Bev Chaney, Jr. 23-152 1996 $165.00

CLANCY, TOM   Debt of Honor. New York: Putnam, 1994. One of 450 signed, numbered copies in slipcase; fine as issued.   Quill & Brush 102-312 1996 $150.00

CLANCY, TOM   Patriot Games. New York: Putnam's Sons, 1987; 1st edition; 1st and second states, first state with errors on pp. 227-228 and 230-231; and second state with errors corrected; 2 volumes; both are fine in dust jackets.   Quill & Brush 102-304 1996 $125.00

CLANCY, TOM   Submarine A Guided Tour Inside a Nuclear Warship. New York: Putnam's Sons, 1993. One of 300 copies, signed, numbered and specially bound copies; fine in slipcase.   Quill & Brush 102-307 1996 $175.00

CLANCY, TOM   Submarine: a Guided Tour Inside a Nuclear Warship. New York: Putnam's, 1993. Special edition limited, 1 of 300 copies, signed by author; cloth, original clear acetate dust jacket has small scratch; about fine.   Magnum Opus 44-28 1996 $175.00

CLANCY, TOM   Without Remorse. New York: Putnam's, 1993. One of 600 signed, numbered and specially bound copies; fine in slipcase. Quill & Brush 102-308 1996 $175.00

CLANNY, W. REID   A Treatise on the Mineral Waters of Gilsland. Sunderland: G. Garbutt, 1816. 8vo; pages 79; uncut, top corner of title neatly repaired, original cloth backed boards, edges little worn, top corner of title neatly repaired. R.F.G. Hollett & Son 78-605 1996 £240.00

CLANRICARDE, ULICK DE BURGH, EARL OF   Memoirs of the Right Honourable the Marquis of Clanricarde, Lord Deputy General of Ireland. London: printed for James Woodman, 1722. 1st edition; 8vo; contemporary; fine, possibly on large paper; with Constable bookplate. Ximenes 108-71 1996 $500.00

CLAPHAM, RICHARD   Rough Shooting for the Man of Moderate Means with Some Notes on Game Preservation and Vermin Extermination. London: Heath Cranton, 1922. 1st edition; 8vo 160 pages; 17 plates; author's name and address in pencil on front free endpaper dated Jan 31st, 1922 and his holograph pencilled notes and alterations in places throughout; original cloth, gilt, rather damped, author's name and address and pencilled notes and alterations in places, trifle shaken, few marks. R.F.G. Hollett & Son 78-634 1996 £60.00

CLAPHAM, RICHARD   Sport on Fell, Beck & Tarn. London: Heath Cranton, 1924. 1st edition; 8vo; pages 164; illustrations; original cloth, gilt, dust jacket (trifle worn); fine in scarce wrapper. R.F.G. Hollett & Son 78-636 1996 £55.00

CLARE, JOHN 1793-1864   The Hue and Cry: a Tale of the Times. Market Drayton: Tern Press, 1990. One in an edition of 125 copies, numbered and signed by Nicholas Parry; 11.75 x 8 inches; illustrated printed and bound in gold colored toile fabric by Nicholas and Mary Parry; fine. Joshua Heller 21-241 1996 $175.00

CLARE, JOHN 1793-1864   John Clare: Verses for His Children. Market Drayton: Tern Press, 1993. One of 75 special copies, from an edition of 150, with blocks enhanced with watercolor by Nicholas Parry; 10.5 x 8 inches; printed on Lana paper, 36 half and quarter page and vignettes of relief printed etchings in dark gray by Nicholas Parry; bound in black and white floral printed William Morris cloth over board, grey endpapers, white paper title label; fine. Joshua Heller 21-260 1996 $295.00

CLARE, JOHN 1793-1864   John Clare: Verses for His Children. Market Drayton: Tern Press, 1993. One of 75 copies thus in an edition of 150 copies, signed by Nicholas Parry; 10.5 x 8 inches; 48 pages, printed on Lana paper, 36 half and quarter page and vignettes of relief printed etchings in dark grey by Nicholas Parry throughout; bound in black and white floral printed William Morris cloth over board, grey endpapers, white paper title label on front cover. Fine. Joshua Heller 21-259 1996 $135.00

CLARE, JOHN 1793-1864   Madrigals & Chronicles. London: Beaumont Press, 1924. 1st edition; number 339 of 310 copies (of an edition of 398 copies); crown 8vo; printed on handmade paper, 3 plates, tissue gaurds, 5 full page illustrations, title (printed in brown) and cover designs by Randolph Schwabe, titlepage lettering printed in green; original fawn buckram, backstrip gilt lettered, little sunned, pale grey boards with overall floral green and yellow pattern, corners rubbed, bookplate, untrimmed, good. Beaumont 18; Kirkpatrick Bib. of Edmund Blunden B14a. Blackwell's B112-15 1996 £50.00

CLARE, JOHN 1793-1864   Poems Descriptive of Rural Life and Scenery. London: for Taylor and Hessey and E. Drury, 1820. 1st edition; 12mo; pages xxxii, 222, (x) ads; errata slip between contents and first leaf of text; author's first book; uncut in contemporary boards, rebacked with calf retaining old leather label, new endpapers, some slight spotting, very good. Simon Finch 24-39 1996 £450.00

CLARE, JOHN 1793-1864   Poems Descriptive of Rural Life and Scenery. London: printed for Taylor and Hessey and E. Drury, 1820. 1st edition; 12mo; pages 'xxxii' (in fact 30), 222, (10); owner's name "Milly Miles 1827"; 19th century half calf, marbled sides, rebacked, original label; author's first book. Hayward 236. Peter Murray Hill 185-40 1996 £400.00

CLARE, JOHN 1793-1864   The Village Minstrel, and Other Poems... London: for Taylor and Hessey and E. Drury, Stamford, 1821. 1st edition; 12mo; 2 volumes, pages xxviii, 216, (iv) ads; (viii), 211, (v) ads; frontispiece in volume 1; uncut in original blue boards, skilfully rebacked, new printed spine labels, some occasional spotting and marking internally; early bookplates of P. Hussey. Tinker 673. Simon Finch 24-40 1996 £700.00

CLARE, JOHN 1793-1864   The Village Minstrel and Other Poems. London: printed for Taylor and Hessey, and E. Drury, Stamford, 1821. 1st edition; 12mo; 2 volumes; portrait, half calf, gilt borders, neatly rebacked, spines gilt; contemporary calf, gilt borders, neatly rebacked, spines gilt; bound without terminal ads, but very attractive set. CBEL III 357. Ximenes 108-72 1996 $900.00

CLARE, M.   The Motion of Fluids, Natural and Artificial; in Particular that of Air and Water... London: printed for A. Ward, J. and P. Knapton and 11 others, 1747. 3rd edition; 8vo; title little browned, 9 folding engraved plates, new half calf, label, nice. Anthony Laywood 108-40 1996 £235.00

CLAREMONT; or, the Undivided Household. Philadelphia: Parry and McMillan, 1857. 1st edition; 12mo; 206 pages; original cloth, rare. Wright II 530. M & S Rare Books 60-107 1996 $150.00

CLARENDON, EDWARD HYDE, 1ST EARL OF 1609-1674   The History of the Rebellion and Civil Wars in England. London: Oxford University Press, 1839. New edition; small 8vo; 7 volumes; original grey blindstamped cloth, spines gilt, slight wear to few extremities, spines faded and bit marked, sound, clean set. Robert Clark 38-32 1996 £100.00

CLARENDON, EDWARD HYDE, 1ST EARL OF 1609-1674   The History of the Rebellion and Civil Wars in England Begun in the Year 1641. Oxford University Press, c. 1930. Reissue of 1888 edition; crown 8vo; 6 volumes; cloth. Howes Bookshop 265-189 1996 £150.00

CLARENDON, EDWARD HYDE, 1ST EARL OF 1609-1674   The Proceedings in the House of Commons, Touching the Impeachment of Edward Late Earl of Clarendon, Lord High Chancellour of England... N.P.: London:? 1700. Mottled calf, very worn, repaired, usable copy; with ownership signature on first blank of Joshua Williams, noted scholar on rearl property. Meyer Boswell SL27-45 1996 $350.00

CLARENDON, EDWARD HYDE, 1ST EARL OF 1609-1674   Religion and Policy and the Countenance and Assistance Each Should Give the Other. Oxford: Clarendon Press, 1811. 2 volumes in 1; (xii), 420, (ii); (viii), (421)-711, (xxix) pages; frontispiece, half titles; recent half calf, marbled boards, spine gilt, label; good. Robert Clark 38-33 1996 £110.00

CLARK'S Guide and History to Rye, to Which is Added Its Political History, Interspersed with many Pleasing and Interesting Incidents. Rye, Sussex, 1861. 8vo; 195 pages; some minor staining, otherwise good, old style quarter calf. Scarce. K Books 441-108 1996 £50.00

CLARK, GEORGE ROGERS   Col. George Rogers Clark's Sketch of His Campaign in the Illinois in 1778-79. Cincinnati: Robert Clarke, 1869. 1st edition; large 8vo; frontispiece, (vi), (2), 119 pages; scarce. The Bookpress 75-399 1996 $325.00

CLARK, GODFREY, MRS.   Gleanings from an Old Portfolio... 1895-98. 1st edition; limited? 8vo; 12 plates; partly unopened; cloth, very good. C. P. Hyland 216-98 1996 £105.00

CLARK, J. W.   The Life and Letters of the Reverend Adam Sedgwick. Cambridge: at the University Press, 1980. 1st edition; 8vo; 2 volumes; xiii, 539; vii, 640 pages; illustrations; original cloth, very good, crisp set. Edwin V. Glaser 121-283 1996 $150.00

CLARK, JANE INGLIS   Pictures and Memories. London: Moray Press, 1938. Large 8vo; pages 91, 48 plates, 26 in color; original cloth over bevelled boards. Neate C52. R.F.G. Hollett 76-61 1996 £85.00

CLARK, JOSEPH G.   Lights and Shadows of Sailor Life, as Exemplified in Fifteen Years' Experience, Including the More Thrilling Events of the U. S. Exploring Expedition, and Reminiscences of an Eventful Life on the "Mountain Wave". Boston: 1848. 2nd edition; 7.5 x 4.5 inches; 324 pages; illustrations; cloth, spine defective. John K. King 77-767 1996 $125.00

CLARK, KENNETH   Henry Moore Drawings. New York: Harper & Row, 1974. 4to; 326 pages; 40 color plates, 264 monochrome illustrations; cloth, some spotting. Freitag 6698. Brannan 43-447 1996 $125.00

CLARK, L. J.   Wild Flowers of the Pacific Northwest from Alask to Northern California. Sidney: 1976. Royal 8vo; 616 pages; about 660 color photos; cloth. Wheldon & Wesley 207-1526 1996 £60.00

CLARK, LARRY   Tulsa. New York: Lustrum Press, 1971. 1st edition; dust jacket, rear panel with crease, signed.   J. B. Muns 154-74 1996 $450.00

CLARK, MARK WAYNE   From the Danube to the Yalu. New York: Harper, 1954. 1st edition; ("C-D"); 8vo; frontispiece, 34 black and white photos; dust jacket, nicks, tears and some rubbing, very good. Signed and inscribed by author.   George J. Houle 68-31 1996 $150.00

CLARK, ROBERT A.   The Arthur H. Clark Company: a Bibliography and History 1902-1992. Seattle: 1993. 1st edition; copy 192 of 500; 242 pages; photos; cloth; fine.   T. A. Swinford 49-212 1996 $200.00

CLARK, ROBERT A.   The Arthur H. Clark Company. A Bibliography and History 1902-1992. Spokane: 1993. Limited to 500 numbered copies; 244 pages; illustrations; gilt stamped cloth; fine, no dust jacket, as issued. Gene W. Baade 1094-32 1996 $200.00

CLARK, ROBERT STERLING   Through Shen-Kan: The Account of the Clark Expedtion in North China 1908-09. London: T. Fisher Unwin, 1912. 1st edition; frontispiece map plus folding map in pocket at rear, 6 color plates, 58 photographic plates; light overall soiling, some bubbling to cloth on both front and rear boards, otherwise very good.   Hermitage SP95-1096 1996 $450.00

CLARK, ROLAND   Gunner's Dawn. New York: Derrydale Press, 1937. 1st edition; limited to 1000 copies (950 for sale); 4to; iii, 125, original signed frontispiece etching by Clark, 4 color plates, 10 black and white plates; gilt stamped red cloth, excellent, uncut.   Taurus Books 83-53 1996 $600.00

CLARK, WALTER   The Papers of Walter Clark. Chapel Hill: University of North Carolina Press, 1948-50. 1st edition; 2 volumes; original cloth, near fine set. Dornbusch IV 1166; Thornton 2315.   McGowan Book Co. 65-22 1996 $125.00

CLARKE COUNTY HISTORICAL SOCIETY   Proceedings. 1941. Volumes I-X; wrappers.   Bookworm & Silverfish 276-201 1996 $125.00

CLARKE COUNTY HISTORICAL SOCIETY   Proceedings. N.P.: 1941-57. Volumes I-XIV, wrappers.   Bookworm & Silverfish 276-200 1996 $165.00

CLARKE, ADAM   The Bibliographical Miscellany; or, Supplement to the Bibliographical Dictionary. London: W. Baynes, 1806. 1st edition; 12mo; 2 volumes; some fading and browning; later brown cloth, slight rubbing to hinges; very good.   Jarndyce 103-137 1996 £50.00

CLARKE, ADAM   A Dissertation on the Use and Abuse of Tobacco. London: printed for G. Whitfield, 1798. 2nd edition; 8vo; contemporary ms. notes in some blank margins; 19th century limp cloth.   Anthony Laywood 108-41 1996 £175.00

CLARKE, ARTHUR   An Essay on Warm, Cold and Vapour Bathing with Practical Observations on Sea Bathing, Diseases of the Skin, Bilious, Liver Complaints and Dropsy. London: for Henry Colburn, 1820. 5th edition; 12mo; xii, 232 pages; original boards, backstrip worn, joints started; very good. Wellcome II 353.   Edwin V. Glaser B122-32 1996 $100.00

CLARKE, ARTHUR C.   Against the Fall of Night. Gnome Press, 1953. 1st edition; near fine in like dust jacket with some light wear and tear; author's first novel.   Aronovitz 57-267 1996 $150.00

CLARKE, ARTHUR C.   Against the Fall of Night. New York: Gnome, 1953. 1st edition; light rubbing at spine ends, else fine in dust jacket with only hint of wear at spine panel ends, very bright and attractive. Robert Gavora 61-17 1996 $200.00

CLARKE, ARTHUR C.   Childhood's End. S&J, 1954. 1st English edition; near fine in very good+ dust jacket.   Aronovitz 57-269 1996 $250.00

CLARKE, ARTHUR C.   The Coast of Coral. New York: harpers, 1956. 1st edition; uncorrected proof; rare thus; wrappers; very good. Aronovitz 57-271 1996 $150.00

CLARKE, ARTHUR C.   Expedition to Earth. Ballantine, 1953. 1st edition; fine in dust jacket, signed by author.   Aronovitz 57-268 1996 $475.00

CLARKE, ARTHUR C.   A Fall of Moondust. New York: HBW, 1961. 1st edition; fine in fine dust jacket with three tiny tears on rear panel; exceptionally nice.   Between the Covers 42-510 1996 $250.00

CLARKE, ARTHUR C.   Imperial Earth. London: Gollancz, 1975. 1st edition; uncorrected proof; wrappers and proof dust jacket; very good+, scarce.   Aronovitz 57-279 1996 $225.00

CLARKE, ARTHUR C.   Interplanetary Flight: an Introduction to Astronautics. New York: Harper, ca. 1951. 1st American edition (from English sheets), third printing; small 8vo; frontispiece, 16 pages of photos, 14 line drawings; dust jacket (few nicks, rubbing); very good copy of author's first book.   George J. Houle 68-7 1996 $150.00

CLARKE, ARTHUR C.   Interplanetary Flight. New York: Harpers, 1950. 1st edition; 3rd impression; tight, bright, very good+ copy; signed by author with his agent, Scott Meredith's bookplate, author's first book. Aronovitz 57-263 1996 $150.00

CLARKE, ARTHUR C.   The Other Side of the Sky. London: 1961. 1st edition; very good in dust jacket.   Words Etcetera 94-306 1996 £50.00

CLARKE, ARTHUR C.   Prelude to Mars. H-B, 1965. 1st edition; near fine in dust jacket.   Aronovitz 57-275 1996 $125.00

CLARKE, ARTHUR C.   Rama II. (with) The Garden of Rama. New York: Bantam, 189/91. 1st edition; just a hint of a lean, otherwise very fine in like dust jacket, both books have author signed bookplates from library of Arthur C. Clarke.   Bud Schweska 12-1362 1996 $150.00

CLARKE, ARTHUR C.   Reach for Tomorrow. London: Gollancz, 1962. 1st British edition; some light dust soiling, else just about fine in very good+ dust jacket.   Aronovitz 57-274 1997 $125.00

CLARKE, ARTHUR C.   Rendezvous with Rama. London: Gollancz, 1973. 1st edition; uncorrected proof; wrappers and proof dust jacket; fine.   Aronovitz 57-278 1996 $395.00

CLARKE, ARTHUR C.   Tales of Ten Worlds: 15 New Stories. London: 1963. 1st edition; very good in dust jacket with dust band down outside edge of upper panel.   Words Etcetera 94-307 1 996 £50.00

CLARKE, ARTHUR C.   2061: Odyssey Three. Ultramarine Press, 1988. 1st edition; 1/26 lettered copies, signed by author; full leather, marbled endpapers; as new.   Aronovitz 57-283 1996 $675.00

CLARKE, AUSTIN 1896-1974   Two Great a Vine - Poems and Satires Second Series. Dublin; The Bridge Press, 1958. 2nd impression; wrappers; head and tail of spine and corners slightly bumped, cover edges browned, very good; presentation from author for William Kean Seymour, loosely inserted 2 page TLS from author.   Ulysses 39-112 1996 £115.00

CLARKE, CHARLES G.   The Men of the Lewis and Clark Expedition. Glendale: Arthur H. Clark Co., 1970. 1st edition; 9 1/2 x 6 1/8 inches; 351 pages + frontispiece, 14 pages of illustrations; red cloth. Dawson's Books Shop 528-59 1996 $100.00

CLARKE, EDWARD DANIEL   Travels in Various Countries of Europe, Asia and Africa. 1810-23. 1st edition; 1st issue; 11 1/4 x 9 inches; 6 volumes; 187 engraved plates, 6 frontispieces, 5 plans, and 155 other plates on 154 leaves as well as many pleasing vignettes in text; extremely fine & attractive chestnut calf, heavily gilt, 1st 4 vols. contemporary, final 2 being especially fine replica bindings by Roger de Coverley, first volume skilfully rebacked w/orig. backstrip laid down, covers indentically framed w/wide dentelles incorporating repeated closely spaced arches & haning vines, spine compartments filled w/very complex ornament w/scrolling, foliate, fan shaped & geometrical element in blind & gilt (including seme portions), turn-ins ruled and ornamented gilt, all edges gilt, dec. on spines and turn-ins of final 2 volumes very much in keeping with, but sl. different from the other vols.; joints 3 vols sl. flaked, trivial marks to covers, but handsome bindings in v.f. condition, bright, clean & showing only minor signs of use, wormhole through 1st 8 leaves of vol. 2, little spotting/foxing; excellent set. Cox I 85.   Phillip J. Pirages 33-133 1996 $2,750.00

CLARKE, EDWARD DANIEL   Travels in Various Countries of Europe, Asia and Africa. Part the Third. Scandinavia. London: T. Cadell and W. Davies, 1819/23. 1st edition; 4to; in volumes 5 and 6, xii, (12), (1)-763, iv, (14), 555 pages; 30 copperplates (on 29 leaves) including 5 folding maps and plans, several vignettes in text, volume 2 contains 16 copperplates, including 4 folding maps and charts and 23 vignettes and cuts; contemporary half green morocco, marbled boards, raised bands, elaborate gilt compartments, all edges gilt; some occasional foxing to few plates (mostly in margins), some light foxing to folind plans, pieces of marble paper have been torn off at outer edge of boards of both volumes, however boards not damaged or worn. Still fine, attractive copy.   David Mason 71-131 1996 $520.00

CLARKE, EWAN   The Rustic: a Poem. London: printed by J. Swan for Thomas Ostell, 1805. 1st edition; 8vo; pages (ii), 119, (i); uncut, original boards, sometime rebacked in cloth, rather worn; scarce.   R.F.G. Hollett & Son 78-350 1996 £140.00

CLARKE, JAMES   A Survey of the Lakes of Cumberland, Westmorland and Lancashire... London: printed for the author, 1787. 1st edition; 1st issue; tall folio; pages xlii, 194, complete with 11 large folding plans and maps, 2 plates; modern half levant morocco gilt, marbled boards, contrasting lettering pieces on spine and upper board; little spotting or browning in places, few neat repairs to plans, but very good, sound. Bicknell 19.1. Upcott p. 122 (note).   R.F.G. Hollett & Son 78-799 1996 £1,250.00

CLARKE, JAMES   A Survey of the Lakes of Cumberland, Westmorland and Lancashire... London: printed for the edition, 1789. 2nd edition; tall folio; pages xlii, 194, complete with 11 large folding plans and maps, 2 plates; title rather spotted and little cut down, lower corner neatly repaired, few small tears to plates, but very good, sound copy with maps on much heavier paper than usual; modern quarter calf, gilt, marbled boards. Bicknell 192; Upcott p. 122 (note).   R.F.G. Hollett & Son 78-800 1996 £1,150.00

CLARKE, JAMES STANIER   The Progress of Maritime Discovery from the Earliest Period to the Close of the Eighteenth Century... London: A. Strahan, 1803. 1st edition; 4to; xxxv, ccxx, 491, 263 pages, 3 plates, 5 slightly foxed charts by Arrowsmith; contemporary gilt panelled calf, very good. Sabin 13419.   John Lewcock 30-137 1996 £325.00

CLARKE, MARY W.   David Gouverneur Burnet, First President of Texas. Austin: Pemberton, 1969. Number 33 of 67 copies; 303 pages; morocco; lacks Republic of Texas bond called for; book together with his original signature laid in separately.   Maggie Lambeth 30-107 1996 $375.00

CLARKE, SAMUEL 1675-1729   Remarks Upon a Book, Entituled, A Philosophical Enquiry Concerning Human Liberty. London: James Knapton, 1717. 1st edition; 8vo; 46, (2) pages, including final leaf of ads, title slightly browned, small ink stamp of private library in blank margin of one leaf, recently well bound in old style quarter calf, gilt; very good, rare.   John Drury 82-46 1996 £350.00

CLARKE, W. J.   Baseball. New York: Charles Scribner's Sons, 1915. 1st edition; small octavo; viii, 205 pages; 11 photographic plates, diagrams; original green cloth stamped in black on front cover and in gilt on spine, extremities lightly rubbed, scattered light foxing and browning; very good.   Heritage Book Shop 196-200 1996 $200.00

CLARKE, WILLIAM   Studies in Bird Migration. London: 1912. 2 volumes; photographic plates, maps; lightly rubbed, top edge gilt; excellent set.   David A.H. Grayling MY95Orn-19 1996 £85.00

CLARKE, WILLIAM   Three Courses and a Dessert. Branston: Vizetelly, 1830. 1st edition; 8vo; wood engraved frontispiece and 4 plates, 4 titlepage vignettes and numerous head and tailpieces by George Cruikshank, full polished calf, spine elaborately tooled in gilt, covers triple gilt ruled, gilt letter, red morocco spine labels; fine. Cohn 144.   Barbara Stone 70-64 1996 £135.00

CLARKSON, L.   Indian Summer, Autumn, Poems and Sketches. New York: E. P. Dutton & Co., 1881. 1st edition; 4to; (55) pages; publisher's gilt cloth, all edges gilt, scarce; front hinge internally cracked, light wear to tips and extremities of spine, as usual, else very good.   Bookpress 75-24 1996 $265.00

CLARKSON, THOMAS   An Essay on the Impolicy of the African Slave Trade. London: printed and sold by J. Phillips, 1788. 1st edition; 8vo; disbound. Short tear in titlepage, without surface loss, but nice. Sabin 13479-80; Ragatz p. 488.   Ximenes 108-74 1996 $350.00

CLARKSON, THOMAS   Memoirs of the Private and Public Life of William Penn. London: Longman, etc., 1813. 1st edition; tall thick octavo; 2 volumes, pages 520, 500, half titles present; handsome modern binding in full sueded tan calf, gilt titles and tooled borders; fine set. CBEL II 856; Lowndes I 440.   Hartfield 48-L66 1996 $295.00

CLAUDET, F. G.   Gold: Its Properties, Modes of Extraction, Values, &c. Vancouver: 1958. Reprinted from the rare 1871 original, limited to 275 numbered copies; 44 pages, facsimiles; quarter oasis morocco; fine. Lowther 379.   Stephen Lunsford 45-30 1996 $135.00

CLAUDIN, A.   The First Paris Press. An Account of the Books printed for G. Fichet and J. Heynlin in the Sorbonne 1470-1472. London: prtd. for the Bibliographical Society at Chiswick Press, 1898. 1st edition; 4to; frontispiece, 10 facsimiles; 100 pages; original printed wrappers, unopened, uncut;   Forest Books 74-46 1996 £75.00

CLAUSEN, J.   Experimental Studies on the Nature of Species. Washington: Carnegie Inst., 1940-58. 8vo; 4 parts in 1 volume; 1076 pages, illustrations; cloth.   Wheldon & Wesley 207-1404 1996 £60.00

CLAVELL, JAMES   Shogun. New York: Atheneum, 1975. 1st edition; fine in fine dust jacket with tiny tear on rear panel and hint of wrinkle at crown, especially nice, usually found in poor condition.   Between the Covers 42-104 1996 $150.00

CLAVERING, ROBERT   An Essay on the Construction and Building of Chimneys. London: printed for I. Taylor, 1779. 1st edition; 8vo; vii, 100 pages, 2 leaves of publisher's ads, padded at end with blank leaves; folding engraved plate, one printed folded table; moderna half calf, marbled boards, nice.   David Bickersteth 133-16 1996 £350.00

CLAXTON, FLORENCE   The Adventures of a Woman in Search of Her Rights. London: Thomas Owen, ca. 1865. 1st edition; oblong 4to; 100 original drawings by author; cloth backed pictorial paper boards; very good with boards showing light soiling and bumping, uncommon. Captain's Bookshelf 38-40 1996 $250.00

CLAY, ENID   The Constant Mistress. Waltham St. Lawrence: Golden Cockerel Press, 1934. Limited edition, 34/50 specially bound copies (of an edition of 300 copies); crown 8vo; pages 40, (1); printed on Batchelor's handmade paper and signed by author and artist, titlepage engraving and 5 other wood engravings by Eric Gill; with a set of proof pulls of all 6 of the wood engravings used in the book, pulls loosely inserted in pocket on rear pastedown; excellent in original mid-blue crushed morocco, faded backstrip gilt lettered covers lightly spoted, top edge gilt, others untrimmed;   Blackwell's B112-120 1996 £850.00

CLAY, FELIX   Modern School Buildings', Elementary and Secondary... London: B. T. Batsford, 1902. 1st edition; folio; half title; folding plans, plates, illustrations; original red cloth, slightly dulled.   Jarndyce 103-411 1996 £60.00

CLAY, JOHN   My Life on the Range. Chicago: 1924. 1st edition; 365 pages; illustrations; gilt stamped cloth, few formerly creased page corners, just a few page margins somewhat roughly opened and some light blemishes on covers, good to very good; scarce. Herd 475; 6 Guns 434; Dobie p. 98; Graff 748; Howes C470; Reese 19.   Gene W. Baade 1094-33 1996 $300.00

CLAY, JOHN   My Life on the Range. Chicago: 1924. 1st edition; 366 pages; photos; cloth, very good. Howes C470; Rader 841; 6 Guns 434; Herd 475; 6 Score 9.   T. A. Swinford 49-214 1996 $250.00

CLAYTON, ELLEN CREATHORNE   Queens of Song: Being Memoirs of Some of the Most Celebrated Female Vocalists... New York: Harper & Bros., 1865. 8vo; (xiv, 543 pages); green cloth, gilt lettered spine, very light wear to cloth, otherwie nice.   Paulette Rose 16-235 1996 $100.00

CLAYTON, ROBERT   The Speech of..., Lord Mayor Elect for the City of London, at the Guild-Hall of the Said City, to the Citizens There Assembled on 29th September 1679... London: printed for Tho. Collins, at the Middle Temple Gate in Fleetstreet, 1679. Folio; 4 pages; uncut, disbound. Wing C4615.   H. M. Fletcher 121-36 1996 £60.00

CLAYTON, W.   The Invisible Hand. A Tale. London: by Watats for Cadell & Davies and Hatchard, 1815. 1st edition; 12mo; pages (iv), 160, (ii), half title, final leaf with engraved vignette on recto and imprint on verso; contemporary calf, smooth spine richly gilt in compartments, black morocco label, sides with deep border in gilt, drab endpapers, rubbed, front inner hinge just cracked but still firm, good. Block p. 42. Simon Finch 24-41 1996 £100.00

CLECKLEY, HERVEY M.   The Mask of Sanity: an Attempt to Clarify Some Issues about the So-Called Psychopathic Personality. St. Louis: The C. V. Mosby Co., 1941. 1st edition; 8vo; 298, (6) pages, printed ruled red cloth; near fine in lightly chipped dust jacket.   John Gach 150-97   1996 $100.00

CLEEVE, BOURCHIER   A Scheme for Preventing a Further Increase of the National Debt and for Reducing the Same. London: R. and J. Dodsley, 1756. 2nd edition; quarto; 26, (2) pages ads; recent wrappers. Higgs 1275 note; Goldsmiths 9152; Kress 5499.   C. R. Johnson 37-5 1996 £75.00

CLEGG, SAMUEL   Architecture of Machinery: an Essay on Propriety of Form and Proportion, with a View to Assist and Improve Design. London: John Weale, Architectural Library, 1842. 4to; (xiii), 64 pages, 40 page publisher's catalog; 8 engraved plates, many wood engraved text figures; publisher's cloth, neatly rebacked, from the library of J. G. James.   Elton Engineering   10-30 1 996 £2,800.00

CLEGG, SAMUEL   Architecture of Machinery: an Essay on Propriety of Form and Proportion, with a View to Assist and Improve Design. London: John Weale, Architectural Library, 1842. 4to; (xiii), 64 pages, 40 page publisher's catalog, 8 engraved plates, many wood engraved text figures; publisher's cloth, neatly rebacked. From the library of J. G. James.   Elton Engineering   10-30   1996 £2,800.00

CLELAND, HENRY WILSON   On the History and Properties Chemical and Medical of Tobacco, a Probationary Essay Presented to the Faculty of Physicians and Surgeons, Glasgow... Glasgow: Bell and Bain, Printers, 1840. 1st edition; 4to; 68 pages; original printed wrappers, vignette of Sir Walter Raleigh on upper cover and portrait on lower cover, rubbed, little soiled, internally a nice, clean copy; Library of the New College printed presentation label with cancellation stamp on inner cover, lithographed title and dedication, another 'Sale. Duplicate' stamp. Presentation inscription from author's father for Professor Welch. Arents 1424; Wellcome II p.3 57.   Anthony W. Laywood   108-161   1996 £395.00

CLEMENS, SAMUEL LANGHORNE 1835-1910   The Adventures of Huckleberry Finn. London: Chatto & Windus, 1884. 1st edition; (true first edition, preceding the American); 1st issue; attractive, near fine.   Ken Lopez   74-442   1996 $1,750.00

CLEMENS, SAMUEL LANGHORNE 1835-1910   Adventures of Huckleberry Finn. New York: Limited Editions Club, 1942. Limited edition; 8vo; spine slightly darkened, original box worn and repaired, signed by artist, Thomas Hart Benton.   Glenn Books   36-269   1996 $500.00

CLEMENS, SAMUEL LANGHORNE 1835-1910   Adventures of Huckleberry Finn. West Hatfield: Pennyroyal Press, 1985. Limited to 350 copies, signed by Barry Moser and by Gray Parrot; this copy number one, with each illustration signed by Moser, a signed prospectus, and an original, inscribed full page pencil drawing of Samuel Clemens as frontispiece; large quarto; xxiii, (8), 419 pages; 49 wood engravings by Moser, with an extra suite of plates; bound by Parrot in gilt stamped dark green morocco, extra suite is in a buckram chemise, book and sutie being housed together in slipcase of matching buckram; extremely fine.   Bromer Booksellers   87-250   1996 $2,500.00

CLEMENS, SAMUEL LANGHORNE 1835-1910   The Adventures of Tom Sawyer. Hartford: The American Publishing Co., 1876. 1st edition; 2nd printing, issue B on wove paper; recased in original binding; fore-edge of frontispiece chipped in margin, minor wear to corners, but very good, all gilt bright; BAL 3369.   Captain's Bookshelf 38-210   1996 $500.00

CLEMENS, SAMUEL LANGHORNE 1835-1910   The Adventures of Tom Sawyer. Toronto: Belford Bros., 1876. 1st Canadian edition; 12mo; (4), 341, (5) pages, includes 4 pages of ads; original pictorial brown front wrapper, lacks back wrapper, slight damage to both front wrapper and last ad leaf, affecting small amount of ad text, paper spine mostly gone, but sound and clean. Rare edition. BAL 3609; Parley to Penrod pp. 43-4. American Grolier 100 79.   M & S Rare Books   60-139   1996 $4,500.00

CLEMENS, SAMUEL LANGHORNE 1835-1910   The Adventures of Tom Sawyer. Hartford: American Publishing Co.; A. Roman & Co., San Francisco, 1880. Later printing; 8vo; frontispiece, numerous wood engraved illustrations; original blue cloth, decorated in black and gilt, bit rubbed, inner hinges tender; very good. cf. BAL 3369.   Ximenes 108-75   1996 $400.00

CLEMENS, SAMUEL LANGHORNE 1835-1910   The Adventures of Tom Sawyer. Cambridge: Limited Editions Club, 1939. Limited edition; 8vo; illustrations by Thomas Hart Benton, signed by artist; very slight fading of cloth on spine, original box worn and repaired.   Glenn Books 36-271   1996 $450.00

CLEMENS, SAMUEL LANGHORNE 1835-1910   The American Claimant. New York: 1892. 1st edition; bit of wear to head and foot of spine, otherwise near fine and bright copy.   Stephen Lupack 83- 1996 $125.00

CLEMENS, SAMUEL LANGHORNE 1835-1910   The Celebrated Jumping Frog of Calaveras County, and Other Sketches. New York: C. H. Webb, 1867. 1st edition; 2nd state; 7 x 5 inches; 198 pages; original pictorial plum colored cloth (gilt frog located in lower left corner, corners and spine ends bit worn, sl. tears & losses in each place, joints sl. threadbare, more noticeably at top and bottom, but binding entirely solid, hinges undamaged, boards clean and only sl. chafed, gift inscription faintly offset on title, rough erasure in margin of one leaf, else fine internally; excellent copy. BAL 3310.   Phillip J. Pirages 33-135 1996 $2,500.00

CLEMENS, SAMUEL LANGHORNE 1835-1910   The Jumping Frog. Cheloniidae Press, 1985. One of 20 specially bound copies (of a total edition of 325), signed by binder; 8 3/4 x 5 3/4 inches; (26) leaves, on of them folding, printed in green & black; 15 signed or initialled wood engravings by Alan James Robinson, including frontispiece; including an additional complete suite of engravings, an additional suite of state-proof and working proof prints, & another paperbound copy of the book, with every engraving in the two separate suites inscribed "To Arnold and Mimi"; prospectus laid in; inscribed by artist to Arnold and Mimi Elkind; bound by Daniel Kelm in fine & whimsical tan crushed mor., both covers w/lg. inlaid recumbent mor. frog, in 2 colors, each doublure w/similar onlaid leaping frog, vol. contained in book well inside attractive & cleverly designed burlap folding box, which also has a pull out chemise (containing the extra engravings), housed in recess under book well; as new.   Phillip J. Pirages   33-123   1996 $2,250.00

CLEMENS, SAMUEL LANGHORNE 1835-1910   The Jumping Frog. Easthampton: Cheloniidae Press, 1985. Out of series copy with same binding that appears on State Proof Edition, which is limited to five copies only and one extra suite of the woodengravings and portrait etching of Twain as in the deluxe edition, which is limited to 50 copies, each signed and numbered by the artist, and has an inscribed copy of the prospectus, an inscribed drawing of the frog and is signed on the colophon by the artist and binder, the regular edition was limited to 250 copies and was bound in green paper wrappers, all edges were signed and numbered by the artist, Alan James Robinson; printed on Saunders paper in Centaur and Arrighi types, page size 22 x 14 cm; bound by Daniel Kelm, full undyed Oasis with onlays of the frog in repose-before the jump on the front panel and after the jump on the back panel, onlays in green oasis of the frog jumping are on front and back pastedowns; housed in linen clamshell box with pull-out portfolio for extra suite and drawing and prospectus with paper label on spine. Beautiful copy.   Priscilla Juvelis 95/1-57   1996 $2,250.00

CLEMENS, SAMUEL LANGHORNE 1835-1910   A Connecticut Yankee in King Arthur's Court. New York: 1889. 1st American edition, 1st issue; 8.5 x 6.5 inches; 575 pages; pictorial cloth, ink inscription, inner hinges badly cracked, f.e.p. and frontispiece detached, extremities beginning to fray, few pages with tears and tape repair.   John K. King 77-482 1996 $250.00

CLEMENS, SAMUEL LANGHORNE 1835-1910   The Gilded Age: a Tale of To-Day. Hartford: American Publishing Co., 1874. 1st edition; mixed issue; 9 x 6 inches; xvi, (17)-574 pages, (3) leaves (ads); frontispiece, plates, numerous illustrations; original gilt decorated cloth, front hinge reinforced with matching paper; spine ends and corners bit worn, but binding remarkably clean, smooth and unfaded, internally very nice, with intermittent minor discoloration.   Phillip J. Pirages 33-137 1996 $175.00

CLEMENS, SAMUEL LANGHORNE 1835-1910   Is Shakespeare Dead? New York: 1909. 1st edition; 1st state, with titlepage, with no inserted ad leaf at end and without publisher's note leaf after title; very near fine and very bright.   Stephen Lupack 83- 1996 $125.00

CLEMENS, SAMUEL LANGHORNE 1835-1910   Life on the Mississippi. Boston: James R. Osgood and Co., 1883. 1st edition; 2nd state, with tailpiece on p. 441 removed (at the request of Twain's wife) and caption on p. 443 reading "The St. Charles Hotel"; 8vo; frontispiece, more than 300 wood engraved illustrations; original brown cloth, decorated in black and gilt; fine. BAL 3411.   Ximenes 108-76   1996 $400.00

CLEMENS, SAMUEL LANGHORNE 1835-1910   Life on the Mississippi. Boston: 1883. 1st edition; intermeidate state with Twain in flame p. 441, but with "the St. Charles Hotel' in caption p. 443; lovely, very near fine copy, bright, tight and clean, uncommon in such fresh condition. Stephen Lupack 83- 1996 $300.00

CLEMENS, SAMUEL LANGHORNE 1835-1910   Life on the Mississippi. London: Chatto & Windus, 1883. 1st British edition, 1st issue, preceding the American edition; cloth very slightly faded on spine, mild foxing to fore edge, very good.   Ken Lopez 74-441   1996 $900.00

CLEMENS, SAMUEL LANGHORNE 1835-1910　Old Times On the Mississippi. Toronto: Belford Bros., 1876. 1st edition; 12mo; 157 (2) pages; original purple cloth, faded, stain on back cover. BAL 3368 reprint B.　M & S Rare Books　60-138　1996 $300.00

CLEMENS, SAMUEL LANGHORNE 1835-1910　The Tragedy of Pudd'nhead Wilson and the Comedy Those Extraordinary Twins. Hartford: 1894. 1st edition; 1st state, sheets bulk 1 1/8", facsimile signature on frontispiece is 7/16" wide, titlepage integral; original decorated rust brown cloth, very near fine.　Stephen Lupack　83-　1996 $350.00

CLEMENS, SAMUEL LANGHORNE 1835-1910　The Tragedy of Pudd'nhead Wilson and the Comedy Those Extraordinary Twins. Hartford; American Pub. Co., 1894. 1st edition; 1st state; 8vo; 432 pages; original cloth; very good, BAL 3442; Wright III 1102.　M & S Rare Books 60-140　1996 $250.00

CLEMENS, SAMUEL LANGHORNE 1835-1910　A Tramp Abroad. Hartford: American Pub. Co., London: Chatto & Windus, 1880. 1st edition; 2nd issue; 8 3/4 x 6 inches; xvi, (17)-631, (1) pages; plates, numerous in text; later half morocco, cloth sides, raised bands, gilt rules, titling and ornaments on spine, modern (repaired) slipcase; owner's stamp; very minor wear & fading to a completely sturdy and interesting binding, internally excellent, with only trivial defects, excellent copy. BAL 3386　Phillip J. Pirages　33-136　1996 $225.00

CLEMENS, SAMUEL LANGHORNE 1835-1910　A Tramp Abroad. Hartford: American Pub. Co., 1880. 1st edition; octavo; xvi, 17-631, (1 ads), inserted frontispiece in Blanck's State B (Sequence only suggested), inserted frontispiece in Blanck's first state, captioned 'Moses', five inserted plates, 28 plates inserted and included in pagination, text illustrations, sheets bulk 1 5/8 inches (Blanck's State A, no sequence established), edges sprinkled brown; original black blindstamped cloth decoratively stamped in gilt on front cover and spine (Blanck's State A, no sequence established), this copy has small '3' blindstamped beneath publishers device on back cover, hinges just starting, otherwise fine, especially clean and bright, protected in tan cloth slipcase and matching chemise. BAL 3386.　Heritage Book Shop 196-262　1996 $2,000.00

CLEMENS, SAMUEL LANGHORNE 1835-1910　Wapping Alice... Berkeley: Friends of the Bancroft Library, 1981. 1st edition; specially tipped in is an extra leaf bearing the printed legend "To James D. Hart in appreciation of all your efforts on behalf of Mark Twain project - May 1981" quarter morocco, loosely inserted slip of paper signed by staff of the Mark Twain Project; fine.　Ulysses　39-598　1996 £155.00

CLEMENS, SAMUEL LANGHORNE 1835-1910　The Writings of Mark Twain. New York: Gabriel Wells, 1922. Definitive Edition; limited to 1024 sets, signed by author as Mark Twain; octavo; 35 volumes; bound-in addendum states that the fly-leaf was signed by Clemens in 1906; cloth backed boards, printed paper label to spine, few volumes show faint rubbing to extremities or small blemishes to spines, still fine, partially unopened set, with uniform slight darkening to spines, bookplate present in each volume.　Bromer Booksellers　87-48　1996 $3,750.00

CLEMENS, SAMUEL LANGHORNE 1835-1910　A Yankee at the Court of King Arthur. C & W, 1889. 1st English edition; spine little lightened, small tear in cloth at rear hinge, else tight, bright, very good+ copy. Aronovitz　57-1201　1996 $185.00

CLEMENT, HAL　Needle. New York: Doubleday, 1950. 1st edition; very good in contemporary, author's first book, signed by author. Aronovitz　57-288　1996 $100.00

CLEMENT, LEWIS　Modern Wildfowling. London: 1880. engraved plates, some folding, text engravings; original ornate pictorial gilt cloth; near fine, scarce.　David A.H. Grayling　3/95-396　1996 £165.00

CLEMENT, LEWIS　Shooting and Fishing Trips, in England, France, Alsace, Belgium, Holland and Bavaria. London: 1876. 1st edition; 2 volumes; original cloth, slightly rubbed.　David A.H. Grayling　3/95-397 1996 £75.00

CLERGUE, LUCIEN　De Cape Qui Caresse et D'Epee Qui Foudroie L'Oeuvre de Picasso. Fata Morgana, 1992. 1st edition; limited to 30 copies, this copy numbered hors commerce, signed by author; folio; pages 22; 5 original portrait photos, all mounted at large and signed by photographer; publisher's scarlet cloth folder and slipcase.　Sotheran PN32-180　1996 £1,250.00

CLERIHEWS. Cambridge: Rampant Lions Press, 1938. Wrappers very slightly rubbed, spine moderately wrinkled, but excellent; autograph letter from Will Carter to John Rayner laid in.　R. A. Gekoski　19-116　1996 £75.00

CLERY, JEAN B.　A Journal of Occurrences at the Temple, During the Confinement of Louis XVI, King of France. Cork: printed by A. Edwards, 1798. Large 12mo; pages (2), 169, (1 blank), near contemporary half calf, gilt spine, with label, name torn from upper portion of title loosing, just the first letter of title, otherwise very good.　James Fenning 133-59　1996 £145.00

CLEVELAND, JOHN　Poems... (with) Cleveland Revived: Poems, Orations, Epistles and Other of His Genuine Incomparable Pieces. London: ptd. by S. G. for John Williams/London: ptd. for Nathaniel Brooks, 1668. 4th edition; 8vo; 2 volumes in one; contemporary calf, rebacked, front joint quite weak; very good, booklabel of John Sparrow. Wing C4697 and 4677; Morris P16 and CR4.　Ximenes　108-77　1996 $300.00

CLEVELAND, RAY L.　An Ancient South Arabian Necropolis. Baltimore: John Hopkins Press, 1965. 4to; 120 plates, several text illustrations, folding plan, xiii, 188 pages; boards, cloth spine.　Thomas Thorp 489-68　1996 £60.00

CLIFFORD, HENRY H.　California Pictorial Letter Sheets. Catalogue of the Collection of Henry H. Clifford. Austin: Dorothy Sloan, 1994. 1st edition; limited to 275 copies; folio; xvi, 106 pages, plus 132 photographic plates, some in color, some folding; full cloth, printed paper labels on spine and front cover, mint.　Argonaut Book Shop 113-139　1996 $250.00

CLIFFORD, MARTIN　A Treatise of Humane Reason. London: printed for Henry Brome, 1675. 1st edition; 12mo; license leaf before title; contemporary calf, rubbed, rebacked, label; inscription. Wing C4707. Anthony Laywood　108-5　1996 £325.00

CLINE, L.　God Head. New York: Viking, 1925. 1st edition; near fine in like dust jacket with some light wear to upper left corner of dust jacket spine; wonderful copy.　Aronovitz　57-290　1996 $150.00

CLINTON, DE WITT　An Address, to the Benefactors and Friends of the Free School Society of New York, Delivered on the Opening of that Institution in Their New and Spacious Building. New York: Collins and Perkins, 1810. 1st edition; 8vo; 20 pages; disbound, lacking thread, uncut, in original signatures, small owner's label on verso of title causing stain on recto. S&S 19789.　M & S Rare Books　60-322　1996 $175.00

CLINTON, DE WITT　A Discourse Delivered at Schenectady, July 22nd, 1823, Before the New York Alpha of the Phi Beta Kappa. New York: Websters and Skinners, 1823. 1st edition; 8vo; 47 pages; removed; foxed. Inscribed "from the author" to the naturalist (James E) De Kay. Shoemaker 12185.　M & S Rare Books　60-306　1996 $150.00

CLINTON, HENRY　Narrative of: Relative to His Conduct During Part of His Command of the King's Troops in North America; Particularly to that Which Respects the Unfortunate Issue of the Campaign in 1781. London: printed for J. Debrett, 1783. 6th edition; 112 pages; one third black leather and boards, bookplate of William L. Clements. Howes C496. Blue River Books　9-12　1996 $350.00

CLINTON-BAKER, H.　Illustrations of Conifers. Hertford: privately printed, 1909-35. Limited to 300 sets; 4to; 327 photographic plates; first 3 volumes in half brown morocco, emblematically gilt spines, gilt top, final volume in original boards, uncut, slight scuffing and wear, but nice set.　Maggs Bros. Ltd.　1190-9　1996 £450.00

CLIVE, ROBERT　Lord Clive's Speech in the House of Commons, 30th March, 1772, on the Motion Made for Leave to Bring a Bill, for the Better Regulation of the Affairs of the East India Co., and of Their Servants in India, and for the Due Administration... London: Printed for J. Walter, n.d. 1772. 1st edition; 4to; 61 pages, final blank H4; disbound. Anthony Laywood　108-42　1996 £125.00

CLODE, C. M.　Memorials of the Guild of Merchant Taylors of the Fraternity of St. John the Baptist, in the City of London... London: Harrison and sons, 1875. 1st edition; royal 8vo; title printed in red and black, xxxi, (1), 746 pages, 29 plates and plans; original blue half morocco, gilt, rubbed at edges and joints, otherwise very good. Presentation copy to Raymond Henry Thrupp.　John Drury　82-47 1996 £50.00

CLOUSTON, THOMAS SMITH　Neuroses of Development Being the Morison Lectures for 1890. Edinburgh: Oliver and Boyd/London: Simpkin, Marshall, Hamilton, Kent & Co. Ltd. 1891. 1st edition; 8vo; viii, 138 pages, 9 plates; panelled crimson cloth with gilt spine, spine faded and lightly worn at crown and foot, very good.　John Gach　150-99　1996 $285.00

CLOWES, FREDERIC   A Description of the East Window of S. Martin's, Windermere... Kendal: Atkinson & Pollitt, 1874. 8vo; pages 26, 6 pasted in photographic illustrations; original cloth, gilt, slightly marked and damped, extremities little rubbed, rather loose, extremely scarce. R.F.G. Hollett & Son 78-801 1996 £75.00

THE CLUB, in a Dialogue Between Father and Son. London: printed for the Proprietor by John Johnson, 1817. Reissue of 1723 edition, one of 200 large paper copies; small folio; 96 pages; numerous mounted India proof illustrations by John Thurston, modern half calf and marbled boards, prelims lightly foxed, catalogue description pasted to front flyleaf, else nice.   Chapel Hill 94-87 1996 $150.00

CLUM, WOODWORTH   Apache Agent, the Story of John Clum. Boston & New York: Houghton Mifflin Co., 1936. 1st edition; 299 pages; red cloth applied to spine, minor to extremes, corners starting to fray, endpaper becoming stained with foxing, no dust jacket. Saunders NM 2821.   Ken Sanders 8-110 1996 $100.00

CLUTTERBUCK, ROBERT HAWLEY   Notes on the Parishes of Fyfield, Kimton, Penton Mewsey, Weyhill and Wherwell, in the County of Hampshire. Salisbury: 1898. 1st edition; 8vo; portrait, 3 page list of subscribers; 7 plates; original cloth, uncut.   Anthony W. Laywood 109-26 1996 £68.00

CLUYSENAAR, J. P.   Chemin de Fer Dendre-et-Waes, et de Bruxelles vers Gand Par Alost. Batiments des Stations et Maisons de Garde. Brussels: Van der Kolk, 1855. 1st edition; small folio; 28, (1) pages, 33 color plates; contemporary quarter morocco (purple); small rubber stamp on titlepage, but very good. Scarce.   Bookpress 75-25 1996 $2,500.00

CLYMAN, JAMES   James Clyman, American Frontiersman, 1792-1881. San Francisco; California Historical Society, 1928. 1st edition in book form, limited to 300 copies; 247 pages; frontispiece portrait tipped in, full page portrait; full page facsimile and 3 maps; original blue cloth stamped in gilt on spine and front cover, two very small tape stains on front free endpaper,, otherwise fine copy.   Argonaut Book Shop 113-141 1996 $375.00

CLYMAN, JAMES   James Clyman, American Frontiersman. Portland: 1960. 2nd edition; pages 400, 17 maps and plates; original cloth, minor shelf wear, else near fine. Howes C81.   Stephen Lunsford 45-31 1996 $200.00

CLYNE, GERALDINE   The Jolly Jump-Ups See the Circus. Springfield: McLouglin Bros., 1944. 1st edition; 8vo; 6 stupendous pop-ups, cloth backed pictorial boards, edges bit rubbed, else fine.   Glenn Books 36-208 1996 $125.00

CLYNE, GERALDINE   The Jolly Jump-Ups On the Farm. Springfield: McLouglin Bros., 1940. 1st edition; 8vo; 6 pop up farm scenes; cloth backed pictorial boards, some light edgewear and one small tear to one pop-up, else fine.   Glenn Books 36-209 1996 $125.00

COALE, CHARLES B.   The Life and Adventures of Wilburn Waters... Richmond: 1878. xiv, 18-265 pages; well rubbed, reglued, missing f.f.e.p., scarce.   Bookworm & Silverfish 280-54 1996 $175.00

COALE, WILLIAM EDWARD   A Practical Essay on Aneurism. Boston: David Clapp, 1861. 1st edition; 8vo; 72 pages; author's interleaved copy, with his bookplate; contemporary half calf over marbled boards, hinges just a bit tender, but fine copy. Not in Cordasco.   Edwin V. Glaser B122-33 1996 $150.00

COARELLI, FILIPPO   Etruscan Cities. New York: G. P. Putnam, 1975. 4to; 336 pages; profusely illustrated, many in color; original cloth, dust jacket.   Archaeologia Luxor-3161 1996 $125.00

COATES, CHARLES   The History and Antiquities of Reading. London: printed for the author by J. Nichols and Son, 1802. 1st edition; 4to; (xiv), 464, (xciv) pages; folding plan, 8 aquatint plates, original mottled calf, rebacked, preserving original spine. Abbey Scenery 291.   David Bickersteth 133-142 1996 £120.00

COATES, HENRY   A Perthshire Naturalist: Charles Macintosh of Inver. London: T. Fisher Unwin, 1923. 1st edition; 8vo; pages xx, 244, 41 sepia illustrations, map, 14 musical illustrations, flyleaves lightly browned; scarce. Original two tone cloth, gilt.   R.F.G. Hollett 76-62 1996 £60.00

COATTS, MARGOT   Portable Pleasures: Picnics for All Seasons. Libanus Press, 1992. One of 250 numbered copies; large 8vo; printed in Fournier on Velin Arches; hand colored drawings by Ian Beck; special patterned boards, linen spine, printed label recessed in upper cover; fine. Bertram Rota 272-258 1996 £55.00

COBB, J. H.   Manual Containing Information Respecting the Growth of the Mulberry Tree... Boston: Carter Hendee & Babcock, 1831. Only printing; 8vo; 66 pages; frontispiece, 2 full page plates, one handcolored; original cloth backed printed boards, evidence of tape removal on front board, obscuring a couple of words, else nice, tight copy. Sabin 13847; American Imprints 6567 locates 5 copies.   Chapel Hill 94-297 1996 $150.00

COBBE, FRANCES POWER   Darwinism in Morals and Other Essays. London: 1872. 1st edition; 399 pages; original binding.   W. Bruce Fye 71-384 1996 $100.00

COBBE, FRANCES POWER   The Life of Frances Power Cobbe. 1894. 8vo; 2 volumes; portraits, plates; very good, scarce.   C. P. Hyland 216-104 1996 £75.00

COBBETT, WILLIAM 1763-1835   Advice to Young Men and (Incidentally) to Young Women, in the Mddle and Higher Ranks of Life. Andover: Printed by R. Bensley; and published by author, 183, Fleet St., 1829. 1st edition; 12mo; unpaginated; contemporary marbled boards, rebacked, occasional spotting. Pearl 171.   James Burmester 29-30 1996 £125.00

COBBETT, WILLIAM 1763-1835   The American Gardener; or a Treatise on the Situation, Soil, Fencing and Laying Out of Gardens, on the Making and Managing of Hot-Beds and Greenhouses... New York: Turner & Hayden, 1844. Later printing; 12mo; 230 pages; little foxed, but very nice, tight copy.   Second Life Books 103-51 1996 $125.00

COBBETT, WILLIAM 1763-1835   Cottage Economy... London: C. Clement, 1822. Possibly 1st book edition; large 12mo; engraved plate, (2), iv, (2), 120, (145)-166, (169)-207 pages, text set in 208 consecutive paragraphs, wanting publisher's ad leaf (pages 167-68); corner stains on few leaves; contemporary half calf, gilt, rubbed; very good. Pearl 115; Goldsmiths 23476; Kress C840; Attar 46.1. Perkins 360.   John Drury 82-49 1996 £125.00

COBBETT, WILLIAM 1763-1835   The English Gardener; or, a Treatise on the Situation, Soil, Enclosing and Laying-Out of Kitchen Gardens... London: Cobbett, 1838. some text illustrations, one foldout plate; Cloth backed boards, lacking paper label, some light foxing, very good. Second Life Books 103-52 1996 $235.00

COBBETT, WILLIAM 1763-1835   The English Gardener; or a Treatise on the Situation, Soil, Enclosing and Laying Out of Kitchen Gardens... London: A. Cobbett, 1845. 8vo; (4), 405, (7) pages; folding engraved plate, text little browned, occasional spotting, original cloth backed boards, printed paper label on spine, bit worn, good. Pearl 150.   John Drury 82-50 1996 £90.00

COBBETT, WILLIAM 1763-1835   A Grammar of the English Language, in a Series of Letters. London: printed for Thomas Dolby, 1819. 1st English edition; 12mo; 186, (4 ad) pages; uncut in original darb boards, neatly rebacked, printed label.   James Burmester 29-31 1996 £150.00

COBBETT, WILLIAM 1763-1835   A Grammar of the English Language... London: printed for the author, & sold by Thomas Dolby, 1819. 2nd edition; 3 pages ads, slight spotting caused by endpapers; uncut in original drab boards, splits in leading hinge, paper label slightly rubbed. Jarndyce 103-45 1996 £65.00

COBBETT, WILLIAM 1763-1835   A History of the Protestant 'Reformation', in England and Ireland... London: 1824-26. 1st edition; 12mo; titlepage and contents generally slightly browned, as usual, unpaginated, A1-Q12; contemporary half mid-brown calf, rebacked, corners repaired, smooth backstrip, divided by double gilt rules; dark green morocco label, sand grain purple cloth sides (slightly faded), recased, very good. Pearl 132.   Blackwell's B112-76 1996 £85.00

COBBETT, WILLIAM 1763-1835   Paper Against Gold; or, the History and Mystery of the Bank of England... London: sold by John Cobbett, Jan., 1822. 4th edition; 8vo; (2) pages, vii, 470 columns; later cloth backed boards, entirely uncut, excellent copy with wide margins. Pearl 81. This edition not in Kress, Goldsmith or Einaudi.   John Drury 82-48 1996 £125.00

COBBETT, WILLIAM 1763-1835   Rural Rides in the Counties of Surrey, Kent, Sussex, Hampshire, Wiltshire, Gloucestershire, Herefordshire, Worcestershire, Somersetshire, Oxfordshire, Berkshire, Essex, Suffolk, Norfolk and Hertfordshrie. London: William Cobbett, 1830. 1st edition; thick small 8vo; original boards, cloth spine, complete with original paper label (slightly damaged); few small fox marks but generally an excellent copy in original state.   Charles W. Traylen 117-90   1996 £600.00

COBBETT, WILLIAM 1763-1835   The Woodlands; or a Treatise on Preparing the Ground for Planting...of Forest Trees and Underwood. London: 1825. 1st edition; 8vo; pages (344), (2 ads); contemporary tree calf.   John Henly 27-347   1996 £110.00

COBBING, BOB   Poems for the Aircraft. Cambridge? n.p., n.d., c. 1965. One of 12 numbered copies; wrappers, inscribed by author inside upper cover, cover edges creased, browned, chipped, torn and slightly defective and soiled, text pages slightly creased; very good.   Ulysses 39-114   1996 £55.00

COBDEN, EDWARD   Poems on Several Occasions. London: printed for the benefit of a clergyman's widow... 1748. 1st edition; 8vo; contemporary calf, gilt, spine gilt (bit rubbed, top of spine little worn); very good. Foxon p. 129.   Ximenes 108-79   1996 $400.00

COBDEN-SANDERSON, THOMAS JAMES 1840-1922   The Arts and Crafts Movement Hammersmith: Hammersmith Pub. Society, 1905. 1st edition; (40) pages; vellum backed boards, spine darkened, some browning to paste-down and front free endpaper, otherwise fine, bright copy; with bookplate of publisher, Crosby Gaige.   Hermitage SP95-769 1996 $400.00

COBDEN-SANDERSON, THOMAS JAMES 1840-1922   The Journals of Thomas James Cobden-Sanderson 1879-1922. London: Macmillan, 1926. Limited edition of 1000 numbered copies; royal 8vo; 2 volumes: (9), 400; (9), 437 pages; frontispiece, 4 plates; cloth, dust jacket, uncut and partly unopened (spines of dust jackets slightly darkened), otherwise fine. Thomas Thorp 489-70   1996 £195.00

COBDEN-SANDERSON, THOMAS JAMES 1840-1922   London, A Paper Read at a Meeting of the Art Workers Guild...March 6, 1891. Doves Press, Presented to the Subscribers, 1906. One of 300 copies on paper (there were also five on vellum); 9 1/4 x 6 1/2 inches; 7, (1) pages; bound in fine deep blue morocco by Doves Bindery, cover frames of two spaced gilt fillets, enclosing a double strapwork panel, spine with raised bands, simple gilt ruled compartments and gilt lettering turn-ins with two gilt rules, rear turn-in signed '19 C-S 19'; slight mottling to text, otherwise an excellent copy in bright, appealing binding, without any significant wear.   Phillip J. Pirages   33-184   1996 $650.00

COBDEN-SANDERSON, THOMAS JAMES 1840-1922   London, a Paper Read at a Meeting of the Art Workers Guild...March 6, 1891. Doves Press, Presented to Subscribers, 1906. One of 300 copies on paper, (there were also five on vellum); 9 1/4 x 6 1/2 inches, 7, (1) pages; original flexible vellum, gilt spine titling, couple of minor spots on binding but very fine inside and out. Tomkinson p. 54-55.   Phillip J. Pirages 33-183   1996 $450.00

COBDEN-SANDERSON, THOMAS JAMES 1840-1922   London: a Paper Read at a Meeting of the Art-Workers Guild, March 6, 1891. London: Doves Press, 1906. One of 300 copies; small 4to; printed in black and red on handmade paper; limp vellum; very nice.   Bertram Rota 272-128   1996 £150.00

COBLENTZ, STANTON A.   Under the Triple Suns. Reading: Fantasy Press, 1955. 1st edition; number 157 of 300 numbered copies, signed by author; 8vo; dust jacket (small chip to spine head, nicks to edges), very good. Publisher's TNS laid in loose. Currey p. 119.   George J. Houle 68-32   1996 $150.00

COBURN, ALVIN LANGDON   Alvin Langdon Coburn Photographer. London: 1966. 1st edition; 11 x 8.5 inches; illustrations, 144 pages, cloth, endpapers slightly discolored, else very good in dust jacket with minor edge tears.   John K. King   77-577   1996 $150.00

COBURN, ALVIN LANGDON   Men of Mark. London: Duckworth & Co./New York: Mitchell Kennerley, 1913. 1st edition; 4to; 30 pages; plus 33 tipped in hand pulled photogravures with tissue guards; original linen with gilt title, tips and lower edge of binding bumped, spine soiled and darkened, light scattered foxing (only one spot on one gravure), attractive bookplate, else very good. Truthful lens 37.   Andrew Cahan 47-51   1996 $1,500.00

COBURN, ALVIN LANGDON   More Men of Mark. New York: Alfred A. Knopf, 1922. 1st edition; 4to; 23 pages; plus 33 collotypes with tissue guards; original linen backed patterned boards, rubbed and scraped, darkened along spine, front hinge slightly loose, though unattractive externally, the photos are fine.   Andrew Cahan   47-52   1996 $325.00

COBURN, J.   The Atlas of Snakes of the World. London: 1991. 4to; 591 pages, over 1400 color photos; hardcover.   Wheldon & Wesley 207-911 1996 £90.00

COCHRANE, CHARLES STUART   Journal of a Residence and Travels in Colombia During the years 1823 and 1824. London: Henry Colburn, 1825. 1st edition; 8vo; 2 volumes; 2 hand colored frontispiece engravings, large folding map, errata leaf; modern three quarter gilt stamped brown calf over matching cloth, spines with raised bands, gilt ruled compartments, marbled edges; very good to fine in brown cloth slipcase. Palau 55908; Sabin 14072.   George J. Houle   68-33 1996 $1,500.00

COCK-a-Hoop Being a Bibliography of the Golden Cockerel Press Sept. 1949-Dec. 1961. London: n.d. Limited edition of 300 copies, signed by compilers David Chambers and Christopher Sandford; title border and frontispiece by John Buckland Wright, other wood engravings; blue morocco backed patterned cloth, top edge gilt, fine.   Words Etcetera 94-489   1996 £150.00

COCKALORUM: a Sequel to Chanticleer and Pertelote. Waltham St. Lawrence: Golden Cockerel Press, 1948. One of 2250 copies (there was also a limited edition of 250 copies); 10 x 6 1/4 inches; 112 pages; frontispiece, border device on title, many illustrations; original cloth and dust jacket, virtually mint copy in fine jacket.   Phillip J. Pirages 33-248 1996 $100.00

COCKBURN, JAMES PATTISON   Swiss Scenery. London: Rodwell & Martin, 1820. 1st edition; 11 3/4 x 9 1/2 inches; vii, (1), 200 pages; engraved title, vignette on final page and 61 fine paltes, tissue guards; very handsome cont. rose colored hard grain morocco, extra gilt by C. Smith, covers handsomely framed with 3 sets of parallel fillets enclosing two elegant scrolling floral borders, flat spines brilliantly gilt in 2 compartments, top one with titling, elongated lower one composed of central vertical band of urn-like roll-tool flanked by gilt rules & pretty borders of acanthus leaves, board edges with triple gilt fillets, turn-ins with four gilt rules and corner ovals, endpapers of deep green coated stock, all edges gilt, spine evenly sunned to terra cotta, minor scuffing or rubbing to edges, otherwise binding in excellent condition. Foxing to plates.   Phillip J. Pirages   33-486   1996 $1,800.00

COCKERELL, SYDNEY M.   The Repairing of Books. London: Sheppard Press, 1958. 1st edition; 8vo; frontispiece, 33 illustrations; original cloth, dust jacket; Howard M. Nixon's copy.   Forest Books 74-48 1996 £55.00

COCKERMOUTH, KESWIC & PENRITH RAILWAY   Widening of Line and Additional Lands. Plans and Sections. Session 1893-4. Edinburgh: John Bartholomew, 1894. Atlas folio; plans; original cloth backed printed wrappers. Fine set.   R.F.G. Hollett & Son 78-606 196 £180.00

COCKRUM, WILLIAM   History of the Underground Railroad: as It Was Conducted by the Anti-Slavery League. Oakland City: 1915. 1st edition; 328 pages; very good in dust jacket.   Blue River Books 9-37 1996 $175.00

COCTEAU, JEAN   The Blood of a Poet - a Film. New York: Bodley Press, 1949. Landscape format, 47 page screenplay, numerous black and white stills; original binding, head and tail of spine and corners bumped and rubbed, corners also bruised, covers marked, rubbed and dusty, good.   Ulysses 39-118 1996 £80.00

COCTEAU, JEAN   Picasso. Les Contemporains. Paris: Chez Delamain, Boutelleau et Cie, 1923. 1st edition; small 8vo; pages 32, 15 black and white photo plates; quarter black calf by Semet & Plumelle, preserving original wrappers; inscribed by Cocteau.   Sotheran PN32-181 1996 £550.00

COCTEAU, JEAN   Le Livre Blanc. Paris: Maurice Sachs, 1928. True 1st edition; copy number VII, one of 31 copies only; 1-21 on Montval, I-X on Montval for the author; 4to; original wrappers, absolutely mint in protective chemise and etui. Rare.   Priscilla Juvelis 95/1-70 1996 $5,000.00

A CODE of Gentoo Laws, or Ordinations of the Pundits from a Persian Translation... London: n.p. 1777. 2nd edition; contemporary calf, rubbed, new label, clean copy.   Meyer Boswell SL25-107 1996 $450.00

A CODE of Gentoo Laws, or Ordinations of the Pundits. London: printed in the Year 1781. 3rd edition; 8vo; engraved plates; contemporary calf, spine gilt; fine.   Ximenes 108-176 1996 $250.00

A CODE of Laws for the Island of Jersey. St. Helier: privately printed, 1771. 1st edition; 8vo; folding table, text in English and French, some foxing of text in places; contemporary vellum, soiled. Sweet and Maxwell p. 586, 5.   Anthony W. Laywood   109-77   1996   £365.00

COE, MICHAEL D.   In the Land of the Olmec. Austin: University of Texas Press, 1980. 4to; 2 volumes, 416 pages, 512 figures; 198 pages and 104 figures and portfolio with 4 large folding maps; original cloth, slipcase bumped.   Archaeologia   Luxor-4365   1996 $150.00

COE, MICHAEL D.   Lords of the Underworld: Masterpieces of Classic Maya Ceramics. Princeton: Art Museum, 1978. 4to; 142 pages; 20 illustrations, 20 folding color plates; original cloth, dust jacket. Archaeologia   Luxor-4360   1996 $125.00

COETLOGON, DENNIS DE   Natural Sagacity the Principal Secret, If Not the Whole in Phsysick... London: printed for T. Cooper, 1742. 1st edition; 8vo; iv, 44 pages, sewed as issued, title and fianl leaf little dusty; David Bickersteth   133-184   1996   £250.00

COETZEE, J. M.   Dusklands. Johannesburg: Ravan Press, 1974. 1st edition; 8vo; author's scarce first book; cloth, in dust jacket, near fine, minor foxing, few small mends with clear tape, also little foxing, dust jacket.   Antic Hay   101-316   1996 $300.00

COFFEY, CHARLES   The Devil to Pay; or, The Wives Matamorphos'd. London: printed for J. Watts, 1731. 1st edition; 8vo; pages (viii), 31; new half calf, marbled sides, brown stains to last two leaves, music to the 18 songs; scarce.   Peter Murray Hill   185-3   1996   £185.00

COFFEY, JAMES V.   A Opinion of Court Denying Application for Probate of Will. San Francisco: 1911. 173 pages; three quarter crimson morocco, quite well preserved.   Meyer Boswell   SL25-47   1996 $125.00

COFFIN, CHARLES CARLETON   The Seat of Empire. Boston: Fields, Osgood and Co., 1870. 18.5 cm; viii, 232, (11) pages; frontispiece, illustrations, folding map in rear pocket; gilt stamped and decorated green cloth, with repaired backstrip and new endpapers, large map neatly repaired along few creases; Smith 1859; Graff 793; not in Peel or Lowther.   Rockland Books   38-46 1 996 $150.00

COFFIN, R. S.   Epistle to Joseph T. Buckingham, Esq. Boston: Printed for Public Information, 1826. 1st edition; 8vo; 12 pages; removed. Shoemaker 24144.   M & S Rare Books   60-291   1996 $200.00

COGAN, LEE   Negroes for Medicine: Report of a Macy Conference. Baltimore: 1968. 1st edition; 71 pages; original binding, dust jacket, autographed by Cogan.   W. Bruce Fye   71-386   1996 $100.00

COGAN, THOMAS   Ethical Questions; or Speculations on the Principal Subjects of Controversy in Moral Philosophy. London: T. Cadell and W. Davies, 1817. 1st edition; 8vo; vi, (2), 439, (1) pages; contemporary calf, gilt, marbled edges and gilt armorial stamp of Glasgow University on sides; very good, prize binding.   John Drury   82-51   1996   £250.00

COGGER, H. G.   Reptiles and Amphibians of Australia. Ithaca: 1992. 5th edition; royal 8vo; 775 pages, several hundred color photos, text figures, maps; cloth.   Wheldon & Wesley   207-913   1996   £72.00

COHEN, LEONARD   Selected Poems. New York: Viking, 1968. Uncorrected proof; spiral bound in wrappers, slight darkening to edge of pages, else near fine; this is poet Louis Simpson's copy with his pencil ownership signature, very scarce proof.   Between the Covers   42-106 1996 $375.00

COIT, DANIEL WADSWORTH   An Artist in El Dorado. The Drawings and Letters of. San Francisco: Book Club of California, 1937. 1st edition; limited to 325 copies; 4to; xi, (4), 2-31, (32-50) pages, plus 8 plates; linen backed blue boards, gilt lettered paper labels on cover and spine; very fine and bright copy.   Argonaut Book Shop   113-143   1996 $125.00

COKE, EDWARD 1552-1634   The First Part of the Institutes of the Lawes of England. London: printed by the Assignes of John More, 1629. 2nd edition; most probably bound at one point but to which the binding did not adhere and was lost, leaving original uncovered boards and spine and disclosing its structure, preserved in modern linen cloth box. Meyer Boswell   SL27-48   1996 $2,250.00

COKE, EDWARD 1552-1634   The Third Part of the Institutes of the Laws of England....(and) Fourth Part of the Institutes. London: printed for A. Crooke/London: printed by John Streater, etc., 1671. 5th edition; contemporary calf, new label, corner of first portrait torn away, not affecting image, else very fresh.   Meyer Boswell   SL25-49   1996 $1,500.00

COKE, EDWARD 1552-1634   La Size Part des Reports Sr. Edw. Coke Chiualer,, Chief Iustice del Common Banke (etc.). London: printed for the Societie of Stationers, 1607. contemporary vellum, worn, else very fresh; John Sparrow's copy.   Meyer Boswell   SL26-47   1996 $1,250.00

COKE, EDWARD 1552-1634   The Third (and Fourth) Part of the Institutes of the Laws of England... London: 1671-71. 5th edition; folio; 2 parts in 1 volume; portrait to each part, pages (10), 243, (18); (14), 364, (37); contemporary calf, label supplied, little wear at foot of spine, boards lightly scratched, blank corner of first portrait torn off (clear of engraved surface), lower outer corner of leaf E2 in pt. 3 torn off affecting a side note only slightly, otherwise quite nice, fresh copies. James Fenning   133-61   1996   £285.00

COKE, ROGER   A Detection of the Court and State of England During the Four Last Reigns, and the Inter-Reignm. London: n.p., 1696. 2nd edition; 8vo; 2 volumes in 1; (42), 134, 200; (2), 88, 208, 78 pages; recent black calf, old red leather spine label laid down; Wing C4974. Kenneth Karmiole   1NS-75   1996 $300.00

COKE, THOMAS   A History of the West Indies. Liverpool: Ptd. by Nuttall, Fisher & Dixon (vols. 2-3 Lon. Ptd. for author, 1808/10-11. 1st edition; 8 1/2 x 5 1/2 inches; 3 volumes; folding map and five plates; modern dark brown half mor., marbled paper sides, flat spines very elaborately gilt in antique style, green double labels, trivial wear to few corners, spine leather just sl. faded, sm. scar to lower cover of 3rd vol., otherwise binding very fine, virtually no signs of wear, caption to 1 plate partly cropped, text w/sl. foxing & hint of browning, plates, especially margins and versos a bit more noticeably foxed, panorama with extra vertical folds, 2 leaves with few passages marked or underlined in pencil, but quite good, internally nevertheless, text generally clean, smooth and still rather fresh. Sabin 14244; Palau 5a6271.   Phillip J. Pirages   33-139 1996 $1,250.00

COLBURN, ZERAH   Locomotive Engineering, and the Mechanism of Railways; a Treatise on the Principles and Construction of the Locomotive Engine, Railway Carriages and Railway Plant. London: William Collins, Sons & Co., 1871. 1st edition; folio; 2 volumes (one of text and one of illustrations), pages xiv, 320, 5 diagram plates, 59 double page engraved plates, showing plans, 240 wood engravings; some worming in inner margins of volume 2 (plate volume), this slight worm damage neatly repaired, otherwise nice, fresh copy; recently rebound in half dark green morocco, spines decorated in gilt, top edge gilt;   Sotheran PN32-6   1996   £598.00

COLCORD, CHARLES FRANCIS   The Autobiography of Charles Francis Colcord 1859-1934. Tulsa: 1970. Limited and private printing; royal 8vo; 245 pages; illustrations; gilt stamped cloth; presentation bookplate; near fine, no dust jacket, as issued. A modern rarity.   Gene W. Baade 1094-35   1996 $350.00

COLDSTREAM, J. N.   Greek Geometric Pottery: a Survey of Ten Local Styles and Their Chronology. London: Methuen, 1968. 4to; xxxix, 465 pages, 64 plates, 1 folding map (pocket at rear); original cloth, spine lightly faded, otherwise fine.   Archaeologia   Luxor-3163   1996 $650.00

COLDSTREAM, J. N.   Kythera: Excavations and Studies Conducted by the University of Pennsylvania Museum and the British School at Athens. London: Faber & Faber, 1972. 4to; 319 pages, 96 figures; 88 plates; original cloth, dust jacket.   Archaeologia   Luxor-3165   1996 $225.00

COLDSTREAM, W.   Illustrations of Some of the Grasses of the Southern Punjab... London: 1889. Folio; pages (5), 8; 40 lithographs in dark green with short descriptive letterpress; recent full calf, some foxing in front and back.   Raymond M. Sutton   VI-679   1996 $350.00

COLE, ALPHAEUS P.   Timothy Cole, Wood-Engraver. New York: Pioneer Associates, 1935. Limited edition; 4to; illustrations; original blue cloth, fine.   Glenn Books   36-287   1996 $100.00

COLE, F. J.   The Cole Library of Early Medicine and Zoology. Catalogue of Books and Pamphlets. Part 1. 1472-1800. Part 2. 1800 to Present Day and Supplement to Part 1. Reading: 1969/75. 4to; 2 volumes; original binding; as new.   James Tait Goodrich   K40-35   1996 $135.00

COLE, G. D. H.   The Murder at the Munition Works. New York: Macmillan, 1940. 1st U.S. edition; minor edge bumps, fine in bright near fine jacket with short closed tear, light edgewear, light scuffing.   Janus Books   36-123   1996 $125.00

COLE, JOHN   Historical Sketches of Scalby, Burniston and Cloughton. Scarborough: Cole, 1829. Small 8vo; pages 1-67, 1-14, 83-94, iv pages, index; frontispiece; contemporary half calf, spine bumped at head and foot.   Marlborough 162-15 1996 £100.00

COLE, WILLIAM A.   Chemical Literature 1700-1860. A Bibliography with Annotations, Detailed Descriptions, Comparisons and Locations. London: 4to; 600 pages; original cloth; new.   Forest Books 74-50 1996 £120.00

COLEBROOK, FRANK   William Morris: Master Printer. Yellow Barn Press, 1989. One of 155 copies; 10 1/4 x 7 1/2 inches; x pages, (1) leaf, 34 pages, (1) leaf (colophon); colored frontispiece, 2 wood engraved plates by John Depol, several small decorations in text, printed in brown and black; original cloth, paper labels on front cover and spine, fore edge and tail edge untrimmed, as new.   Phillip J. Pirages 33-519 1996 $175.00

COLEMAN, A. D.   The Grotesque in Photography. New York: 1977. 1st edition; dust jacket.   J. B. Muns 154-78 1996 $125.00

COLEMAN, EDMUND T.   Scenes From the Snow-Fields; Being Illustrations of the Upper Ice-World of Mount Blanc, from Sketches Made on the spot in the Years 1855, 1856, 1857, 1858; with Historical and Descriptive Remarks and a Comparison of the Chamonix and St. Gervais Routes. London: Longman, Brown, Green, Longmans, and Roberts, 1859. 1st edition; large folio; pages viii, 47, with 12 lithographs by Vincent Brooks, printed in color; original cloth, recased, original spine laid down, alpine floral design in blind on upper and lower boards, lettered in gilt; front endpaper foxed, dedication leaf soiled and frayed at edges, repaired, slight dampstaining at lower gutter, but not affecting text or plates, all plates in very clean and bright condition, good, rare. Neate C92.   Sotheran PN32-160 1996 £4,800.00

COLEMAN, WILLIAM   Studies in the History of Biology. Baltimore: 1977-84. 1st edition; Volumes 1-7 (all published); original binding.   W. Bruce Fye 71-392 1996 $150.00

COLENSO, JOHN WILLIAM   Ten Weeks in Natal. A Journal of a First Tour of Visitation Among the Colonists and Zulu Kafirs of Natal. Cambridge: Macmillan, 1855. 1st edition; small 8vo; xxxi, 271, 16, 16 pages ads dated "March 1855"; folding map; recently rebound with tan calf spine, paper boards, leather spine label fine.   David Mason 71-6 1996 $200.00

COLERIDGE, CHRISTABEL ROSE   Jack O'Lanthorn. London: Walter Smith and Innes, 1889. 1st edition; 8vo; 2 volumes; original red cloth, spines faded and rubbed, short splits in lower joints.   James Burmester 29-160 1996 £90.00

COLERIDGE, HARTLEY   Lives of Northern Worthies. London: Edward Moxon, 1852. 1st edition thus; 8vo; 3 volumes; original green cloth, minor rubbed mark at foot of one spine; fine set. Beddie 2190; CBEL III 372.   Ximenes 109-81 1996 $275.00

COLERIDGE, S. T., MRS.   Minnow Among Tritons. Mrs. S. T. Coleridge's Letters to Thomas Poole 1799-1834. London: Nonesuch Press, 1934. 1st edition; number 13 of 565 copies; crown 8vo; pages xxxvii, 186, (1), 4 plates, press device designed by Agnes Miller Parker, printed in brown; original pale blue bevel edged buckram, backstrip gilt lettered, free endpapers browned in part, untrimmed, Curwen Press dust jacket partly defective, neat tape repair, excellent. Dreyfus 94. Blackwell's B112-204 1996 £55.00

COLERIDGE, SAMUEL TAYLOR 1772-1834   Aids to Reflection in the Formation of a Manly Character on the Several Grounds of Prudence, Morality and Religion... London: by Thomas Davidson for Taylor and Hessey, 1825. 1st edition; 8vo; pages xii, (ii), 404, without errata; 19th century library calf, richly gilt, red and green morocco labels, top edge gilt, others uncut, one corner lightly bumped; excellent copy. Wise 58; Tinker 705.   Simon Finch 24-49 1996 £200.00

COLERIDGE, SAMUEL TAYLOR 1772-1834   Biographia Literaria; or Biographical Sketches of My Literary Life and Opinions. London: Rest Fenner, 1817. 1st edition; 8vo; 2 volumes bound in one; pages (iv), 296; (vi), 309, (i) ads; contemporary full calf, maroon morocco label, sides ruled in blind, spine with gilt bands, red sprinkled edges, by J. Carss & Co., Glasgow with their ticket, spine rubbed in places, first two leaves spotted; excellent copy. Wise, Coleridge 40; Tinker 696.   Simon Finch 24-47 1996 £900.00

COLERIDGE, SAMUEL TAYLOR 1772-1834   Biographia Literaria; or Biographical Sketches of My Literary Life and Opinions... London: Rest Fenner, 1817. 1st edition; 8vo; 2 volumes; (iv), 296; (iv), 309, (iii) pages; half titles present, 3 pages ads at end of volume 2, little foxing; contemporary blue half calf, neatly rebacked and recornered, gilt lettering; very nice set. Wise 40.   Robert Clark 38-231 1996 £450.00

COLERIDGE, SAMUEL TAYLOR 1772-1834   Biographia Literaria; or Biographical Sketches of My Literary Life and Opinions. London: by S. Curtis for Rest Fenner, 1817. 1st edition; ordinary paper copy; 8vo; 2 volumes, pages (iv), 296; (iv), 309, (i); ex-library in modern library cloth, 3 inkstamps to outer margins of text of each volume, occasional trivial spotting, but good firm set. Wise 40.   Simon Finch 24-48 1996 £250.00

COLERIDGE, SAMUEL TAYLOR 1772-1834   Christabel; Kubla Khan, a Vision; the Pains of Sleep. London: for John Murray by William Bulmer and Co., 1816. 1st edition; 1st printing; 8vo; pages vii, (i) blank, 64; with half title, without inserted ad leaves sometimes found at end; well rebound in full red crushed morocco, spine lettered in gilt with date at foot, raised bands, one line gilt rules, gilt inner dentelles, top edge gilt, by Wood of London; bookplate, ownership inscription, blindstamps on endleaves; fine. Ashley I 204; Corns & Sparke p. 56; Hayward 207; Tinker 693.   Simon Finch 24-46 1996 £1,600.00

COLERIDGE, SAMUEL TAYLOR 1772-1834   Confessions of an Inquiring Spirit. London: William Pickering, 1840. 1st edition; 12mo; 95 pages; three quarter gilt decorated brown morocco and marbled boards, minor rubbing, very good to fine.   Robert F. Lucas 42-23 1996 $125.00

COLERIDGE, SAMUEL TAYLOR 1772-1834   The Friend: a Series of Essays to Aid in the Formation of Fixed Principles in Politics, Morals and Religion. London: William Pickering, 1837. 3rd edition; 8vo; 3 volumes; original pebble grain blue cloth, printed paper spine labels, edges uncut; spines rubbed, good firm set; bookplates of Yatton Court, Herefordshire. Wise 23.   Simon Finch 24-45 1996 £150.00

COLERIDGE, SAMUEL TAYLOR 1772-1834   The Friend. London: William Pickering, 1844. 4th edition; 7 x 4 1/2 inches; 3 volumes; half title in each volume and ads at end of volumes 1 and 3; original pebble grain blue cloth over thin boards, paper spine labels; spines uniformly faded to a pleasing light blue, but fine, very clean and essentially unworn copy. Keynes p. 48.   Phillip J. Pirages 33-419 1996 $250.00

COLERIDGE, SAMUEL TAYLOR 1772-1834   Notes and Lectures Upon Shakespeare and some of the Old Poets and Dramatists. London: William Pickering, 1849. 1st edition; small 8vo; 2 volumes; full crushed green morocco, decorative gilt to spines, spines faded to brown, panelled gilt, decorative gilt dentelles and inner dentelles, bit of rubbing to extremities, all edges gilt, internally fine; handsomely bound set, inscribed to Michael Holroyd on dedication page. Jaggard p. 55. Keynes p. 59.   Dramatis Personae 37-37 1996 $150.00

COLERIDGE, SAMUEL TAYLOR 1772-1834   The Plot Discovered; or an Address to the People Against Minsterial Treason. Bristol: 1795. 1st edition; small 8vo; 52 pages; later calf, marbled boards, preserved in full brown crushed morocco folding case, title slightly dusty, tiny mark in lower outer corner affecting first four leaves, very good. Presentation copy with author's autograph inscription for John Pye Smith (1774-1851) non-conformist divine. Wise 4; Tinker 675.   Simon Finch 24-42 1996 £5,000.00

COLERIDGE, SAMUEL TAYLOR 1772-1834   Poems on Various Subjects... London: for G. G. and J. Robinson and J. Cottle, Bristol, 1796. 1st edition; small 8vo; pages (iii)-xvi, 188, (2) errata, verso blank, (1) ads; bound without half title; contemporary green half morocco, spine with triple gilt bands, lettered in gilt, gilt lyre motifs in compartments, marbled sides, extremities slightly rubbed; very good; bookplate of William Hales Symons. Wise 8; Hayward 206; Tinker 678. Simon Finch 24-43 1996 £1,200.00

COLERIDGE, SAMUEL TAYLOR 1772-1834   Poems. London: by N. Biggs for J. Cottle, Bristol and Messrs. Robinsons, London, 1797. 2nd edition; small 8vo; pages xx, 278; contemporary tree calf, spine gilt, black morocco label, rubbed, spine with vertical crack and chipped at foot, front joint cracked but held firm by cords, front free endpaper detached, stain at upper outer corner affecting first few leaves, still good; bookplate of Stafford C. Northcote, and earlier Northcote family inscription. Ashley I p. 199.   Simon Finch 24-44 1996 £400.00

COLERIDGE, SAMUEL TAYLOR 1772-1834   The Rime of the Ancient Mariner. Philadelphia: Henry Altemus, 1889. 1st edition thus; folio; (82)ff., 38 stunning full page engravings by Gustave Dore, plus frontispiece and 2 small vignettes; original green cloth, pictorial stamping in black, silver and gilt, remarkably fine, worn publisher's printed pictorial box, lacking one edge.   Chapel Hill 94-52 1996 $375.00

COLERIDGE, SAMUEL TAYLOR 1772-1834   The Rime of the Ancient Mariner. London: Chatto & Windus, n.d. 1949. 1st edition thus; 7 full page black and white drawings by Mervyn Peake; original binding, top edge dusty, spine slightly faded, tail of spine and corners slightly bumped, covers cocked, very good in nicked and rubbed, spotted and dusty dust jacket browned at spine and edges.   Ulysses 39-461 1996 £125.00

COLERIDGE, SAMUEL TAYLOR 1772-1834   The Rime of the Ancient Mariner. New York: Chilmark Press, 1964. One of 315 numbered copies; folio; printed in Monotype Bembo in black and olive green on pale grey paper handmade by Barcham Green, plates printed by Thos. Ross and Son, London; 10 engravings on copper by David Jones; cloth, fine in slightly rubbed slipcase; laid in is handsome 4 page offprint of Paul Standard's article on this edition ''The Making of a Book", with publisher's compliments slip.   Bertram Rota   272-390   1996 £300.00

COLERIDGE, SAMUEL TAYLOR 1772-1834   Sibylline Leaves: a Collection of Poems. London: Rest Fenner, 1817. 1st edition; (4), x, (2), 303 pages, (20) page Hatchard catalogue; original tan paper covered boards and spine, printed spine label, front cover detached, top of spine chipped, else fine, uncut. In gilt morocco backed slipcase. H. Buxton Forman's copy with his bookplate and signature. Wise, Coleridge 45. Joseph J. Felcone   64-11   1996 $1,400.00

COLERIDGE, SAMUEL TAYLOR 1772-1834   Specimens of the Table Talk of the Late Samuel Taylor Coleridge. London: John Murray, 1835. 1st edition; 8vo; 2 volumes, pages lxxi, 267; 364; frontispiece in each volume; contemporary half maroon morocco, marbled boards, edges and endpapers by Kerr and Richardson of Glasgow, extremities worn; bookplates; good set. Wise 78; Tinker 709.   Simon Finch   24-51   1996 £120.00

COLERIDGE, SAMUEL TAYLOR 1772-1834   Specimens of the Table Talk of the Late Samuel Taylor Coleridge. London: 1835. 1st edition; 2 volumes, half titles and ads; frontispieces; half calf, little edge rubbed; fine.   Polyanthos   22-212   1996 $150.00

COLES, C.   Game Birds. London: 1981. Folio; 117 pages; 24 fine color plates; cloth, dust jacket, slipcase, fine in mint condition.   John Henly 27-8   1996 £65.00

COLES, ELISHA   A Dictionary of English-Latin and Latin-English... London: J. Walthoe (& 20 others), 1730. 12th edition; contemporary calf, ruled in blind, rubbed, extremities worn, upper joint tender, internally very good. Reasonable copy.   Robert Clark   38-170   1996 £65.00

COLES, ELISHA   An English Dictionary, Explaining the Difficult Terms... London: printed for Peter Parker, 1684. 3rd edition; few paper flaws affecting few rods; good, clean copy, excellently rebound in half calf. Inscribed "Charles Wilkinson came to Ireland ye 28th of August 1690". Alston V65.   Jarndyce   103-138   1996 £250.00

COLES, ELISHA   An English Dictionary... London: printed for Peter Parker, 1692. Contemporary speckled calf, rubbed and marked, with repairs to spine and hinges, black label, inner hinges cracking. Alston V67; Wing C5074.   Jarndyce   103-139   1996 £180.00

COLES, ELISHA   An English Dictionary. London: printed by F. Collins for R. Bonwick et al, 1713. 4th edition; 8vo; unpaginated; original full sheep, joints repaired with tissue and inner margin of titlepage and first text leaf similarly repaired; else very good. Bookplate of General J. Watts de Peyster.   Chapel Hill   94-170   1996 $175.00

COLETTE, SIDONIE GABRIELLE 1873-1954   Break of Day. Limited Editions Club, 1983. One of 2000 copies, signed by artist; 11 1/4 x 9 1/4 inches; 3 p.l., (12 blank), vii-xiii, (1), 138 pages, (2) leaves; 3 original six color silkscreened plates, plus several illustrations by Francoise Gilot, half title and title pritned in blue and black, prospectus laid in. Original lovely blue silk titled in gilt on front cover and spine, publisher's slipcase, mint copy.   Phillip J. Pirages   33-352   1996 $150.00

COLLARD, WILLIAM   Proposed London and Paris Railway. Westminster: P. S. King and son Ltd., 1928. Quarto; viii, 292 pages; folding map; publisher's blue cloth, gilt, fine.   H. M. Fletcher   121-153 1996 £120.00

A COLLECTION of Hymns in the Oneida Language for the Use of Native Christians. Toronto: Wesleyan Missionary Society, 1855. 16mo; pages (iv), 245; contemporary calf, covers loose, library stamp on edges, interior very good. Banks p. 70; Evans 632; Pilling, Iroquoian p. 155; TPL 5687.   Hugh Anson-Cartwright   87-313   1996 $200.00

A COLLECTION of Hymns, in Muncey and English for the Use of the Native Indians. Toronto: printed for the Wesleyan Missionary Society, 1874. 12mo; pages 96 (i.e. 192) numbered in duplicate, with English and Muncey on facing pages; original cloth, ex-library, 2 inkstamps, bookplate and residue of label on spine, else clean, crisp copy. Banks p. 117; Evans 552; Pilling, Algonquin p. 220.   Hugh Anson-Cartwright 87-310   1996 $200.00

A COLLECTION of Poems. London: printed for Ralph Smith, 1702. 8vo; contemporary panelled calf, trifle rubbed, tiny chip to top of spine; fine, complete with 3 pages of bookseller's ads at end. Case 151(f). CBEL II 342.   Ximenes   108-290   1996 $300.00

A COLLECTION Of Some Writings of the Most Noted of the People Called Quakers, in their Times. Philadelphia: printed for the compiler, 1767. 1st edition; 8vo; sewn as issued; tear in upper margin of last leaf, catching a couple of letters, few minor stains, but excellent copy, entirely uncut, very scarce. Evans 10583; Sabin 66919.   Ximenes   108-303 1996 $500.00

COLLECTION of Sundry Publications, and Other Documents, in Relation to the Attack Made During the Late War Upon the Private Armed Brig General Armstrong of New York, Commanded by S. C. Reid, on the Night of the 26th of Sept. 1814, at the Island of... New York: J. Gray, 1833. 12mo; iv, 55 pages (55 misnumbered 45); later half leather and marbled boards; nice, some light foxing. Howes C582.   Bohling Book Co.   192-2   1996 $100.00

A COLLECTION of the Addresses, Songs and Other Papers Which Were Published During the Late Contested Election for the Borough of Grantham; Which Took Place on the 8th, 9th and 10th of March, 1820... Grantham: printed & published by S. Ridge, 1820. 8vo; 68 pages; 68 pages; waterstain on title, worming on inner blank margins, affecting text in places; original printed wrappers, spine defective.   Anthony W. Laywood   108-219   1996 £75.00

COLLET, COLLET DOBSON   History of the Taxes on Knowledge, Their Origin and Repeal. London: T. Fisher Unwin, 1899. 1st edition; 8vo; 2 volumes; portrait, occasional light spotting, original light cloth, spines faded, ends of spines slightly frayed, library labels on spines. McCoy, Fredom of the Press C441.   James Burmester   29-32   1996 £75.00

COLLIER, JANE   An Essay on the Art of Ingeniously Tormenting. London: Millar, 1753. 8vo; title, pages 234, etched plate by Gillray dated 1804, mounted before title; slightly later calf, covers decorated with single gilt rule, enclosing stencilled intertwining snakes in plain calf on mottled calf background, flat spine gilt, 3 labels missing, edges speckled beneath blue diamond pattern, marbled endpapers, by the Count de Caumont (ca. 1804) with his pink Gerrard St. label, covers worn and pitted, some loss of surface; worn and shabby, acid has removed much of the surface of the cover and spine is worn, but enough survives to make clear the imaginative purpose and some of the dramatic effect of this unique and historically important binding.   Marlborough   160-36 1996 £550.00

COLLIER, JANE   An Essay on the Art of Ingeniously Tormenting... London: printed for A. Millar, 1753. 1st edition; 8vo; frontispiece (margins browned); contemporary calf, rebacked, original red morocco label preserved; slight soiling, otherwise very good.   Ximenes   108-80   1996 $300.00

COLLIER, JANE   An Essay on the Art of Ingeniously Tormenting... London: William Miller, 1811. 5th edition; 8vo; pages viii, 229; frontispiece; original three quarter red polished morocco, raised bands, gilt and blind decorations in panels, marbled boards,   Hartfield   48-L24 1996 $265.00

COLLIER, JEREMY 1650-1726   A Short View of the Profaness and Immorality of the English Stage. London: G. Strahan, Williamson, Osborne, 1730. 5th edition; octavo; pages 437, (3 book ads), serviceable recent vinyl binding, raised bands, gilt on red leather label, old names on title, considerable foxing, not affecting text; good. Wing C 5265 for first ed.   Hartfield   48-L25   1996 $185.00

COLLIER, JOHN 1708-1786   A View of the Lancashire Dialect... London: printed for & sold by the booksellers in town and country, c. 1746. 12mo; later half calf, slightly chipped, leading hinge splitting; Alston IX 11-27.   Jarndyce   103-71   1996 £220.00

COLLIER, JOHN 1708-1786   The Miscellaneous Works of Tim Bobbin, Esq... Manchester: printed for the author & Mr. Haslingdon, &c., 1775. 1st edition of this collection; frontispiece torn at fore-edge and neatly repaired, 10 vigorous plates, 2 page errata at end; later drab boards, green cloth spine worn and repaired, paper label creased and chipped. Alston IX 29.   Jarndyce   103-72   1996 £90.00

COLLIER, JOHN 1901-   Fancies and Goodnights. New York: Doubleday & Co., 1951. 1st edition; original binding, bottom corners bumped, endpapers slightly sellotape marked, very good indeed in nicked, chipped, rubbed and dusty dust jacket slightly darkened at spine and edges.   Ulysses   39-119   1996 £125.00

COLLIER, JOHN 1901-   Green Thoughts. London: 1932. Limited to 550 numbered copies, printed at the Chiswick press, signed by author; 10 x 6 inches, 56 pages; top edge gilt, covers heavily rubbed and darkened. John K. King   77-237   1996 $100.00

COLLIER, JOHN 1901-   No Traveller Returns. London: 1931. 1st edition; limited to 210 numbered copies, signed by author; 9 x 6 inches; black suede cloth with stamped Art Deco motif to front cover stamped in gilt and green, top edge gilt, covers soiled, spine sunned, mild wear to spine and edges, endpapers darkened.   John K. King   77-238 1996 $125.00

COLLIER, JOHN 1901-   Witch's Money. New York: 1940. 1st edition; limited to 350 numbered copies, signed by author; 8 x 5.5 inches; 30 pages; cloth, covers bit discolored, back cover with paint spray spots, else good.   John K. King   77-239   1996 $125.00

COLLIER, JOHN 1901-   Witches Money. New York: Viking, 1940. 1st edition; limited to 350 numbered copies, signed by author for private distriction to friends of author and publisher; laid in is complimentary slip from publisher and slip advertising the forthcoming edition of Collier's stories in which Witches Money will appear, spine sunned, small rear corner dampstain, near fine in glassine dust jacket.   Robert Gavora   61-18   1996 $225.00

COLLIER, JOHN PAYNE   Punch and Judy. New York: Limited Editions Club, 1937. Copy number 904 from a total edition of 1500 numbered copies; collotype reproductions of the original etchings by George Cruikshank; full leather, fine in tissue jacket and board folder, slightly worn publisher's slipcase.   Hermitage SP95-954 1996 $125.00

COLLINGWOOD, W. G.   Coniston Tales. Ulverstn: Wm. Holmes, 1899. 1st edition; 8vo; pages (iv), 78; frontispiece, decorated title; original patterned boards, spine little darkened and cracked, scarce.   R.F.G. Hollett & Son   78-357   1996 £85.00

COLLINGWOOD, W. G.   The Lake Counties. London: Frederick Warne, 1932. Limited edition, one of 350 copies, signed; 4to; pages xvi, 368; 16 colored plates, large folding map; near fine, superior edition, original cloth, gilt, dust jacket.   R.F.G. Hollett & Son   78-805   1996 £250.00

COLLINGWOOD, W. G.   The Life and Work of John Ruskin. London: Methuen & Co., 1893. Number 208 of 300 numbered copies; square 4to; 2 volumes; pages xiv, 243; vi, 285; on handmade paper; mounted color frontispiece, 20 plates; contemporary three quarter tan speckled calf gilt by Cedric Chivers of Bath, spines tooled in blind, with elaborate art nouveau sunflower design within a single vertical panel bordered with single and dotted rule, top edge gilt; handsome set.   R.F.G. Hollett & Son   78-133   1996 £275.00

COLLINGWOOD, W. G.   The Memoirs of Sir Daniel Fleming. Kendal: Titus Wilson, 1928. 8vo; pages x, 131; portrait; original wrappers. R.F.G. Hollett & Son   78-134   1996 £65.00

COLLINGWOOD, W. G.   A Pilgrimage to the Saga-Steads of Iceland. Ulverston: W. Holmes, 1899. 1st edition; 8vo; pages x, 187, map, 151 illustrations and plates; original blue cloth, lettered in silver, little rubbed and marked. very nice, rare.   R.F.G. Hollett & Son   78-1403   1996 £275.00

COLLINS BAKER, C. H.   Crome. London: Methuen, 1921. Large 4to; portrait, 52 plates; original buckram (little rubbed).   Charles W. Traylen 117-12   1996 £90.00

COLLINS, A. FREDERICK   Experimental Television. Boston: Lothrop, Lee & Shepard, 1932. 1st edition; 8vo; xv, (6), 313 pages; frontispiece and over 185 illustrations; original pictorial cloth, bright, near fine. Edwin V. Glaser   121-66   1996 $225.00

COLLINS, ANTHONY 1676-1729   A Dissertation on Liberty and Necessity... London: J. Shuckburgh, 1729. 1st edition; 8vo; vii, (1), 23, (1) pages, small ink stamp of a private library on foot of title and last leaf, text bit browned, otherwise good, recently well bound in old style quarter calf, gilt; scarce. Sorley p. 344.   John Drury   82-54 1996 £350.00

COLLINS, ANTHONY 1676-1729   A Philosophical Enquiry Concerning Human Liberty. London: Robinson, 1717. Corrected version of the first edition of 1715; 8vo; title, pages vi, 1f., 114, 1 f., ruled in red; red morocco panelled gilt, with centre and side pieces built up from small tools, spirals, acorns, small drawer handles and others, spine gilt in 6 compartments, all edges gilt, comb-marbled endpapers, perhaps by Brindley. Armorial bookplate of Lindsay of Kirkforther.   Marlborough 160-37   1996 £1,100.00

COLLINS, ANTHONY 1676-1729   A Philosophical Inquiry Concerning Human Liberty. London: for R. Robinson, 1717. 2nd edition; 8vo; (2), vi, (2), 118 pages; very small private library stamp on title and occasionally elsewhere, recently well bound in old style quarter calf, gilt, very good. John Drury   82-53   1996 £300.00

COLLINS, ARTHUR   Letters and Memorials of State in the Reigns of Mary, Elizabeth, James, Charles I, Part of Charles II and Oliver's Usurpation. 1746. 1st edition; folio; 2 volumes; portrait; contemporary calf, hinges worn, text very good.   C. P. Hyland   216-844   1996 £350.00

COLLINS, ARTHUR   Proceedings, Precedents, and Arguments, on Claims and Controversies, Concerning Baronies by Writ, and Other Honours. London: pritned for Thomas Wotton, at the Queen's Head and Three Daggers, 1734. Folio; (4), 416, (12) pages, index; with copy with additional (5) page holograph index tipped in; contemporary calf, nicely rebacked, gilt calf spine label, covers worn, bookplate removed, two ownership signatures on title.   Kenneth Karmiole 1NS-76   1996 $400.00

COLLINS, R. M.   Chapters from the Unwritten History of the War Between the States; or, the Incidents in the Life of a Confederate Soldier in Camp, on the March, in the Great Battles and in Prison. St. Louis: Nixon-Jones Printing Co., 1893. 1st edition; 335 pages; frontispiece, illustrations; original brown cloth, title in gilt on spine, some rubbing and light wear, very good. Howes C597; Raines p. 82; Nevins Civil War Books I 72.   Michael D. Heaston   23-96   1996 $850.00

COLLINS, W.   The Young French Emigrants; or, the Orphans of Montmorency, a Tale for the Moral Instruction and Amusement of Youth of Both Sexes. London: published and sold by J. Souter and N. Hailes, (Denham, printer), 1823. 1st edition; 12mo; 2 volumes, (ii), 312; (ii), 322 pages; frontispiece, occasional foxing, small hole in B2 of volume 2, text legible, contemporary half calf, part of one joint eroded but firm. Block p. 43; not in NUC.   James Burmester   29-161   1996 £400.00

COLLINS, WILKIE 1824-1889   The Legacy of Cain. London: Chatto & Windus, 1889. 1st edition; 8vo; 3 volumes; original blue cloth, decorated in black and red, slight rubbing of spines; half titles imperceptibly excised, inner stitching of first volume trifle weak, very good, quite presentable; Sadleir 595; Woolf 1362; CBEL III 926.   Ximenes 109-82 1996 $400.00

COLLINS, WILKIE 1824-1889   Miss or Mrs? and Other Stories in Outline. London: Richard Bentley and Son, 1873. 1st edition in variant binding; 8vo; pages viii, 325, (2), blank, ad, lacking rear free endpaper; original green cloth, upper cover lettered in gilt and decorated in black, spines lettered and decorated in gilt, lower cover decorated in blind, rather worn, hinges broken, inscription, good. Sadleir 397; Wolff 1366. Simon Finch   24-52   1996 £480.00

COLLINS, WILKIE 1824-1889   The Woman in White. London: Sampson Low, 1861. New edition; 1st English one volume edition; 8vo; pages viii, 494, (1); mounted oval real photograph portrait frontispiece (faded), guarded, additional engraved vignette titlepage, half title, integral ad leaf at end, prelim leaves very slightly foxed; modern mid-Victorian style half mid brown calf, backstrip with gilt milled raised bands, dark green label in second compartment, remainder black panelled with central gilt ornaments, marbled boards, top edge gilt, excellent. Parrish p. 42. Blackwell's   B112-77   1996 £165.00

COLLINS, WILLIAM   The Poetical Works, Enriched and Elegant Engravings. London: printed by T. Bensley, 1798. 8vo; attractive stipple engravings; 19th century half calf, handsome printing.   Peter Murray Hill 185-42   1996 £55.00

COLLMANN, H.   The Britwell Handlist or Short-Title Catalogue of the Principal Volumes from the Time of Caxton to the Year 1800, Formerly in the Library of Britwell Court, Buckinghamshire. London: Bernard Quaritch, 1933. 4to; 2 volumes, 2 portrait frontispieces, 62 plates; original brown cloth. Besterman 919; Howard Hill 347.   Maggs Bros. Ltd.   1191-39 1996 £80.00

COLONIAL CHURCH & SCHOOL SOCIETY   Annual Report of the..., for Sending Out of Clergymen, Catechist's and Schoolmasters to the Colonies of Great Britain and to British Residents in Other Parts of the World. London: 1851. pages x, 98; original wrappers, minor stain to edge of wrappers, else near fine.   Stephen Lunsford   45-33   1996 $100.00

COLORADO   Laws of Gregory District Enacted February 18 & 20, 1860. Denver City: Wm. N. Byers & Co., 1860. 12 pages; original printed brown wrappers, very fine, with one ms. chagne in text, laid in half morocco slipcase. Choice copy, excessively rare. Allen Colorado Imprints 6.   Michael D. Heaston   23-103   1996 $8,500.00

COLPOYS, MRS. The Irish Excursion, or I Fea to Tell You. Dublin: printed for H. Colbert, W. Porter, J. Moore, J. Rice, 1801. 1st Irish edition; 12mo; 2 volumes, half titles present, some marginal foxing, contemporary speckled calf, contrasting labels, one label (of 6) missing, joints rubbed; rare. Brown, Ireland in Fiction 367; Block p. 43; cf. Blakey p. 199. James Burmester 29-162 1996 £675.00

COLQUHOUN, J. The Moor and the Loch. 1880. 2 volumes; frontispiece, engraved plates, text illustrations; original pictorial cloth, slight rubbing and upper hinges bit loose. David Grayling J95Biggame-247 1996 £65.00

COLTON, ROBERT Rambles in Sweden and Gottland; with Etchings by the Wayside. London: Richard Bentley, 1847. Only edition; 8vo; frontispiece, 2 other lithograph plates, vignette titlepage, 6 text woodcut vignettes, 3 pages of music; original embossed blue cloth, spine gilt; prior owner's bookplate; uncommon; binding somewhat rubbed, otherwise very good. Trebizond 39-91 1996 $175.00

COLTON, WALTER Deck and Port: or Incidents of a Cruise in the United States Frigate Congress to California. New York: A. S. Barnes & Co., 1850. 1st edition; 7 1/4 x 5 inches; 408 pages, frontispiece, 4 tinted lithograph plates, 20 page publisher's catalog at end; blindstamped brown cloth, wear to tips and spine ends and along rear joint, new endpapers, frontispiece backed. Dawson's Books Shop 528-60 1996 $125.00

COLTON, WALTER Land and Lee in the Bosphorous and Aegean, or Views of Athens and Constantinople. New York: A. S. Barnes & Co., 1851. 2nd edition; 7 1/4 x 4 7/8 inches; 366 pages + frontispiece, 1 plate, 11 page publisher's catalog at end; blind and gold stamped brown cloth, foxing, some wear to tips and spine ends, 1 inch crack along front joint. Dawson's Books Shop 528-61 1996 $100.00

COLTON, WALTER The Sea and the Sailor: Notes on France and Italy and Other Literary Remains of Rev. Walter Colton. New York: A. S. Barnes & Co., 1851. 7 1/4 5 inches; 437 pages, frontispiece, 1 engraved plate and 8 page publisher's catalog at end; blind and gold stamped blue cloth, unobtrusive crack in cloth along front joint not harming soundness. Dawson's Books Shop 528-62 1996 $100.00

COLTON, WALTER Three Years in California. New York: A. S. Barnes & Co., 1850. 7 1/4 x 4 3/4 inches; 456 pages, 6 lithographed plates, 6 engraved portraits and folding facsimile; blind and gold stamped red cloth, rebacked with original spine laid down, edge wear, sunning to spine, scattered foxing and spotting, 2 short tears to facsimile. Zamorano 80 number 20. Dawson's Books Shop 528-64 1996 $250.00

COLTON, WALTER Three Years in California. New York: 1850. 1st edition; 7.5 x 5 inches; 456 pages; illustrations; cloth, rather foxed, rear fly defective, covers worn, spine chipped, fold-out torn and repaired with thread. John K. King 77-24 1996 $100.00

COLUTHUS The Rape of Helen, from the Greek of Coluthus, with Miscellaneous Notes. London: printed for T. and J. Egerton, 1786. 1st edition translated by William Beloe; 4to; 59 pages; some browning of text; disbound. Anthony W. Laywood 109-27 1996 £135.00

COLVILE, EDEN London Correspondence Inward from Eden Colvile: 1849-1852. London: Hudson's Bay Records Society, 1956. Limited, numbered, uncut and unopened; very good to fine in decorated blue cloth. Rockland Books 38-47 1996 $150.00

COLVILLE, EDEN London Correspondence Inward from Eden Colville 1849-1852. London: 1956. Pages cxv, 300, illustrations, fine unopened copy. Stephen Lunsford 45-66 1996 $125.00

COLWELL, STEPHEN Politics for American Christians... Philadelphia: Lippincott, Grambo & Co., 1852. 1st edition; 8vo; (2), iv, (5)-134 pages; original cloth backed boards, paper boards rather worn, else very good. John Drury 82-55 1996 £75.00

COMBE, ANDREW Observations on Mental Derangement: Being an Application of the Principles of Phrenology to the Elucidation of the Causes, Symptoms, Nature and Treatment of Insanity. Boston: Marsh, Capen & Lyon, 1834. 1st American edition; 8vo; 336 pages; author's first book; original blue-green cloth, cloth somewhat soiled and with one abraded spot on front cover, owners' names, small inkstain along bottom edge of last few leaves, not touching text, very good, scarce. Chapel Hill 94-266 1996 $175.00

COMBE, WILLIAM 1742-1823 The English Dance of Death. London: published at R. Ackermann's Repository of Arts, 101, Strand, 1815-16. 1st edition; 8vo; 2 volumes; pages viii, (iv index), 296; (ii), (iv index); + 300; hand colored aquatint frontispiece, hand colored aquatint vignette on engraved titlepage, 72 fine hand colored aquatint plates by Thomas Rowlandson; contemporary marbled calf, rebacked to style, by Bernard Middleton; Tooley 411; Abbey Life 263. Sotheran PN32-46 1996 £1,250.00

COMBE, WILLIAM 1742-1823 The History of Johnny Quae Genus... London: Ackermann, 1822. 1st edition; 24 hand colored plates by Rowlandson, some brown offsetting onto text from some plates, otherwise exceptionally fine copy; full blue niger morocco with gilt borders on covers and gilt decorative panels on spine, by Riviere, all edges gilt, fine. Words Etcetera 94-1096 1996 £385.00

COMBE, WILLIAM 1742-1823 A History of the River Thames. London: printed by W. Bulmer and Co. for John and Josiah Boydell, 1794-96. Early issue,, with rare general titlepages; folio; watermark 1794; 2 volumes, plates; contemporary straight grain red morocco gilt, line borders, six double raised bands on spines, crest of G. W. Wentworth in gilt at foot of each spine, spines somewhat darkened, heads repaired; as usual, some foxing, in text leaves and one or two gatherings in volume 2 are quite severely affected, but plates are remarkably clean by comparison, with only minimal offsetting. Abbey Scenery 432; Tooley (Batsford 1954 no. 102. H. M. Fletcher 121-131 1996 £4,850.00

COMBE, WILLIAM 1742-1823 Journal of Sentimental Travels in the Provinces of France, Shortly Before the Revolution. London: by R. Ackermann, 1821. Octavo; title, 'Address' 2 pages, 291 pages, 18 colored aquatint plates by Thomas Rowlandson; half crushed red morocco, marbled boards, spine gilt by Riviere, front hinge unobtrusively repaired, top edge gilt, others uncut, plates clean and in fine impressions; fine. Abbey Travel 89. H. M. Fletcher 121-132 1996 £800.00

COMBE, WILLIAM 1742-1823 Journal of Sentimental Travels in the Southern Provinces of France, Shortly Before the Revolution. London: Ackermann, 1821. Re-issue; 8vo; 2 ff., 291 pages, 18 hand colored aquatint plates from designs by Rowlandson, remainder binding of orange cloth, gilt spine. Abbey Travel 89. Marlborough 162-225 1996 £600.00

COMBE, WILLIAM 1742-1823 The Tour of Doctor Syntax, in Search of the Picturesque; The Second Tour...in Search of Consolation; The Third Tour...In Search of a Wife. London: R. Ackermann, 1815-21. Although printed titles all state 'The Third Edition", this set is in fact the 9th edition of 1st tour, 3rd edition of 2nd and 3rd tours; large 8vo; 3 volumes; 2), iv, (2), 276; (6), 278; (6), 280 pages; 78 hand colored engraved plates by Thomas Rowlandson, 2 hand colored engraved titlepages; bound in 19th century half green morocco over pebbled green cloth, gilt, spines lightly faded, very attractive set, very clean plates, all edges gilt. Kenneth Karmiole 1NS-77 1996 $850.00

COMBE, WILLIAM 1742-1823 The Tour of Doctor Syntax in Search of the Picturesque. (with) The Tour of Doctor Syntax in Search of Consolation. (with) The Tour of Doctor Syntax in Search of a Wife. London: Nattali and Bon, 1817. 9th edition; 3 volumes; 80 fine hand colored plates by Thomas Rowlandson; 19th century three quarter calf over marbled boards, all edges marbled, extra gilt compartments with spine labels in red and black, very attractive, near fine set. Captain's Bookshelf 38-42 1996 $750.00

COMBE, WILLIAM 1742-1823 A Word in Season, to the Traders and Manufacturers of Great Britain. London: sold at the European Magazine Warehouse in Cowper's Court, Cornhill, 1792. 1st edition; 8vo; 16 pages; recent linen backed marbled boards, lettered; very good. Kress B2266; Goldsmiths 15437. This edition not in Black. John Drury 82-56 1996 £125.00

COMERFORD, T. The History of Ireland. Dublin: c. 1780. 3rd edition; illustrations; contemporary calf, good. C. P. Hyland 216-114 1996 £75.00

COMFORT, J. W. The Practice of Medicine on Thomsonian Principles...with Practical Directions for Administering a Thomsonian Course of Medicine... Philadelphia: Aaron Comfort, 1843. 1st edition; 8vo; 15, 514, (1) pages; full contemporary leather, label, frequent pencilled notes. R&B 3-1216. M & S Rare Books 60-444 1996 $300.00

THE COMIC Adventures of Old Mother Hubbard, and her Dog. London: Griffin and Farran, n.d. ca. 1860. 8vo; 15 pages; hand colored illustration; pictorial wrappers, covers soiled and chipped and worn at spine, else very good. Marjorie James 19-207 1996 £85.00

COMINES, PHILIPPE DE, SIEUR D'ARGENTON 1445-1511   The Historie of Philip De Commines, Knight, Lord of Argenton. London: Ar. Hatfield for I. Norton, 1601. 2nd edition; small folio; (16), 264 pages; elaborate woodcut titlepage, old panelled calf, rebacked, black morocco spine labels, binding extremities rubbed, titlepage slightly trimmed, former owner's signature. STC 5603.   Kenneth Karmiole 1NS-78 1996 $450.00

COMINES, PHILIPPE DE, SIEUR D'ARGENTON 1445-1511   The Memoirs of Philip De Commines, Lord of Argenton. London: Henry G. Bohn, 1855. 2nd, but preferred edition; small 8vo; 2 volumes, 399, 444 pages; frontispiece portraits; contemporary three quarter green polished calf with heavily gilt tooled spine panel florets, light and dark red morocco spine labels, raised bands, top edge gilt, slight discoloration on couple of covers, otherwise near fine. Lowndes p. 505.   Chapel Hill 94-110 1996 $125.00

COMINI, ALESSANDRA   Egon Schiele's Portraits. University of California Press, 1974. 4to; xxxii, 271 pages, more than 335 illustrations; cloth, dust jacket; fine.   Rainsford A54-518 1996 £120.00

COMMERCIAL CLUB OF NORTH YAKIMA   The Yakima Valley Washington. Yakima: Commercial Club, ca. 1904. 1st edition; (32) pages; illustrations; original grey printed wrappers, wrapper title; very good. Not in Smith or Soliday Sale.   Michael D. Heaston 23-349 1996 $100.00

COMPAGNO, L.   Sharks of the World. Rome: 1984. 4to; Volume 4, parts 1, 2; 655 pages; illustrations and maps; wrappers.   John Johnson 135-592 1996 $100.00

A COMPENDIOUS Geographical and Historical Grammar. (with) A Compendious Geographical Dictionary. London: Ptd. for W. Peacock and Sons... 1802/04. 2nd edition; 3rd edition; 12mo; 2 volumes, xxviii, 408, (8); 40, (408) pages; 22 folding engraved maps; uniformly bound in full red straight grain morocco, gilt, all edges gilt, marbled endpapers, light wear to extremities, front hinge of volume 1 cracked, but cords still sound, little faint offsetting from maps, previous owner's signature, bookplate, otherwise fine, housed in black cloth slipcase.   Heritage Book Shop 196-226 1996 $850.00

THE COMPLEAT Brewer; or, the Art and Mystery of Brewing Explained. London: printed for J. Coote, 1760. 1st edition; 12mo; no front free endpaper, margins of title browned; contemporary calf, hinges cracked, label.   Anthony Laywood 108-31 1996 £345.00

THE COMPLEAT Clerk, Containing the Best Forms of All Sorts of Presidents, for Conveyances and Assurances... London: printed by W. Rawlins, S. Roycroft and H. Sawbridge, 1683. 5th edition; modern quarter calf, dusty, frontispiece (defective), sound.   Meyer Boswell SL25-46 1996 $400.00

THE COMPLETE Art of Boxing According to the Modern Method... London: printed for M. Follingsby and M. Smith, 1788. 1st edition; 8vo; half title present, folding frontispiece; half dark green morocco, spine gilt, top edge gilt, slight rubbing; very rare. Magriel 6 reprint; Hartley 48; CBEL II 1563.   Ximenes 109-44 1996 $2,000.00

A COMPLETE Guide to the Leading Hotels... London: H. Herbert, 1873. Large 8vo; titlepage, xxii, 206 pages, chromolithographic borders, engraved vignettes, 1 map; originaal decorated gilt and blindstamped cloth, all edges gilt, contents little shaken.   Marlborough 162-164 1996 £300.00

A COMPLETE Guide to the Places of Amusement, Objects of Interests, Parks, Clubs, Markets, Docks, Leading Hotels... London: J. P. Segg & Co., 1897. 18th edition; large 8vo; xii, 244 pages, all within chromolithographc borders heightened with gold, numerous text illustrations, printed in purple, original decorated cloth, gilt, bit rubbed, small repair.   Marlborough 162-171 1996 £250.00

THE COMPLETE Letter-Writer. Edinburgh: printed by and for W. Darling, 1778. 12mo; contemporary sheep, rubbed and slightly chipped, hinges cracking, strip torn from tail of following free endpaper.   Jarndyce 103-272 1996 £70.00

THE COMPLETE Letter-Writer; or, Polite English Secretary... London: printed for Stanley Crowder & Benjamin Collins, Salisbury, 1772. 14th edition; 12mo; fore-edge of title frayed, not touching type border, corner torn from last leaf affecting on word of ad, slight staining; contemporary sheep, surface of boards wormed, spine rather roughly rebacked with green label, new endpapers. Alston III 258.   Jarndyce 103-271 1996 £60.00

THE COMPTON Marbling Portfolio of Patterns. London: 1992. One of 150 numbered copies; small 4to; printed in handset 14 pt. Kennerley on Rivoli paper, unbound sheets laid into cloth and marbled paper portfolio; fine.   Bertram Rota 272-9 1996 £54.00

COMRIE, JOHN   History of Scottish Medicine. London: 1932. 2nd edition; 852 pages, 2 volumes; illustrations; original binding.   W. Bruce Fye 71-398 1996 $175.00

COMSTOCK, F. G.   A Practical Treatise on Culture of Silk, Adapted to the Soil and Climate of the United States. Hartford: Gleason, 1839. 2nd edition; 8vo; pages 96; 4 wood engravings; linen backed printed boards, very good, little light foxing.   Second Life Books 103-58 1996 $125.00

COMSTOCK, MARY   Greek, Etruscan and Roman Bronzes in the Museum of Fine Arts. Greenwich: New York Graphic Society, 1971. 8vo; xxvii, 511 pages, profusely illustrated; original cloth, dust jacket; with signature of G. M. A. Hanfmann.   Archaeologia Luxor-3169 1995 $150.00

COMSTOCK, WILLIAM   Modern Architectural Designs and Details...in the Queen Anne, Eastlake, Elizabethan and Other Modernized Styles. New York: the author, 1881. 1st edition; small folio; (viii), xi pages, 80 plates; decorated cloth; both hinges internally strengthened, front cover rubbed and spotted, extremities of spine chipped.   Bookpress 75-28 1996 $350.00

THE CONCERNED Photographer. New York: Grossman, 1968/72. 2 volumes (complete), illustrations; dust jackets, slightly torn top of spine.   J. B. Muns 154-81 1996 $175.00

A CONCISE and Accurate Description of the University, Town and County of Cambridge... Cambridge: J. & J. Merrill, n.d. 1790. Small 8vo; title, (ii, contents), 149, 11 engraved plates, one plate shaved at outer margin; recent linen backed boards, new title label to upper board.   Sotheran PN32-177 1996 £180.00

CONDER, JOSIAH   The Associate Minstrels. London: George Ellerton for Thomas Conder, 1810. 1st edition; octavo; author's first book; contemporary half calf, worn, extremities very worn, joints cracked, few minor spots, engraved title embrowned; rare. Author's first book.   G. W. Stuart 59-27 1996 $300.00

CONEL, J. LE ROY   The Postnatal Development of the Human Cerebral Cortex. Cambridge: Harvard University Press, 1939-47. 1st edition; folio; 3 volumes, c. 435 pages; 310 plates; original cloth, volumes 2 and 3 in original dust jackets, fine set. Courville 443 cites first vol. only.   Edwin V. Glaser B122-34 1996 $450.00

CONFEDERATE STATES OF AMERICA   Journal of the Congress of the Confederate States of America, 1861-1865. Washington: GPO, 1904-05. 1st edition thus; 7 volumes; original half leather and cloth, boards detached on volume one, volume two is in later cloth, overall good set. Nicholson p. 438.   McGowan Book Co. 65-21 1996 $750.00

CONFEDERATE STATES OF AMERICA   Military Laws of the Confederate States, Embracing All the Legislation of Congress Appertaining to Military Affairs from the First to the Last Session Inclusive... Richmond: J. W. Randolph, 1863. 8vo; 92, xvi pages; peach cloth backed green paper over boards (large portions of paper rubbed away from boards, slight worming, slight worming, gilt lettered black paper label on front cover; some offsetting, few leaves closely cropped at top, as issued; near fine internally. Crandall 37.   Blue Mountain SP95-8 1996 $375.00

CONFEDERATE STATES OF AMERICA   Regulations for the Army of the Confederate States. Richmond: J. W. Randolph, 1862. Original cloth, worn, rebacked, new paper spine label, with errata, very tight, somewhat worn, paper browned and foxed through much of the book, faint ink inscription "H. Gibbon Carter, CS Army, Battery No. 8, June 10th, 1862". Very scarce. Parrish & Willingham 2361.   Glenn Books 36-58 1996 $1,700.00

CONFEDERATE STATES OF AMERICA. CONSTITUTION   The Constitution of the Confederate States of America, Adopted March 11, 1861. N.P.: 1861. 1st edition thus; 15, (1) pages; original self wrappers; near fine, truly rare. Housed in custom made case with leather spine and antique marbled paper sides. Confederate Hundred 15; In Tall Cotton 110 (note).   McGowan Book Co. 65-113 1996 $3,500.00

CONFUCIUS   The Analects of Confucius. Shanghai: Limited Editions Club, 1933. Limited edition; fine in Chinese redwood box with only one small split to lid and virtually no warping.   Hermitage SP95-957 1996 $250.00

CONFUCIUS   The Analects of Confucius. New York: printed at the Plantin Press for members of the Limited Ed. Club, 1970. One in an edition of 1500 copies, numbered and signed by artist; 11 x 7 inches; 131 pages; 22 illustrations in color by Tseng Yu-Ho; shaded orange cloth overlaid with gilt pattern, paper title label on spine, cream cloth drop-back box, Chinese calligraphy on front, red button and string tie, right hand corners of drop back box loose, else fine. Joshua Heller 21-154 1996 $150.00

CONFUCIUS   The Analects of Confucius. New York: Limited Editions Club, 1970. Number 330 of 1500 copies, signed by artist; paintings by Tseng Yu-Ho; Chinese brocade cloth, fine in publisher's slipcase. Hermitage SP95-958 1996 $135.00

CONFUCIUS   The Analects of Confucius. New York: Limited Editions Club, 1970. Number 1029 of 1500 copies; illustrations by Tseng Yu-Ho; Chinese silk, fine in clamshell slipcase. Hermitage SP95-956 1996 $125.00

CONGDON, LENORE O. KEENE   Caryatid Mirrors of Ancient Greece: Technical, Stylistic and Historical Considerations of an Archaic and Early Classical Bronze Series. Mainz am Rhein: Philipp von Zabern, 1981. Folio; xiv, 288 pages; 23 figures, 6 illustrations, 97 plates, 1 map; original cloth. Archaeologia Luxor-3171 1996 $375.00

CONGREGATIONAL CHURCH IN THE UNITED STATES   A Book of Plans for Churches and Parsonages...Comprising Designs by Upjohn, Renwick, Wheeler. New York: Daniel Burgess, 1853. 1st edition; folio; 58 pages; 45 plates; publisher's decorated blindstamped cloth, light sporadic foxing on some plates, front hinge internally strengthened, covers and joints slightly rubbed, tips worn. Hitchcock 282. The Bookpress 75-402 1996 $2,500.00

THE CONGRESS of the Beasts, Under the Mediation of the Goat, for Negotiating a Peace Between the Fox, the Ass Wearing a Lion's Skin, the Horse, the Tigress and Other Quadrupeds at War. London: for W. Webb, 1748. 1st edition; 12mo; disbound, trimmed close at head, affecting few headlines. Dramatis Personae 37-7 1996 $150.00

CONGREVE, CELIA   The Transvaal War Alphabet. Manchester: George Falkner, 1900. 168 x 260mm; text and illustrations, printed throughout in blue and red, illustration opposite letter and text, single stapled gathering (rusty), centre page detached; original stiff wrappers, blue and red printed illustration of shell burst on upper side incorporating title, map on lower side, khaki border to both, little rubbed, generally very good. Blackwell's B112-65 1996 £60.00

CONGREVE, WILLIAM 1670-1729   The Way of the World, a Comedy. London: for Jacob Tonson, 1700. 1st edition; 4to; (10), 89, (3) pages, wanting half title, minor worming in blank bottom margins, with bottom margins of last two leaves extended, with loss of type on final page (Tonson ad) only; in handsome modern design binding of full crimson goat, each cover with panel made up of blind tooled circles, marbled endpapers, by the Stonehouse Bindery; slightly imperfect, but very pleasing copy in tasteful design binding. Grolier English 100, 37; Tinker 734. Wing C5878. Joseph J. Felcone 64-12 1996 $900.00

CONGREVE, WILLIAM 1670-1729   The Works... Birmingham: by John Baskerville, for J. and R. Tonson, London: 1761. 1st edition; with cancelled sheets at beginning of volume 1 as ususal. Royal 8vo; 3 volumes; frontispiece, 5 engraved plates; contemporary mottled calf contrasting green double lettering pieces, spines decorated in gilt to a lattice pattern, sides with single gilt rules, ornaments in corners, marbled endpapers, rubbed, joints of volume 3 just beginning to crack at foot, still frim, headcap of same volume chipped, old scar to lower board of volume 2, lightly browned, especially at beginning of volume 1 (as usual), still nice set; contemporary bookplates. Gaskell 16. Simon Finch 24-54 1996 £380.00

CONN, GEORGE   De Dvplici Statv Religionis Apvd Scotos Libri Duo. Rome: Typis Vaticanis, 1628. 1st and only recorded edition; 4to; pages (xii), 176, (viii), Roman letter, red and black woodcut arms (of Cardinal Barberini) on titlepage, woodcut initials and ornaments; modern vellum over boards; some marginal oauter edges and top corners waterstained, varying degrees of browning, couple of small ink holes on 1 leaf just touching odd letter, perfedtly acceptable. BM STC 17th It. p. 252; Allison & Rogers 262; Brunet II 210. A. Sokol XXV-23 1996 £385.00

CONNELL, EVAN S.   The Diary of a Rapist. New York: S&S, 1966. 1st edition; near fine in dust jacket which is slightly discolored around edges, signed by author. Lame Duck Books 19-147 1996 $150.00

CONNELL, EVAN S.   Mrs. Bridge. New York: Viking, 1959. 1st edition; name to front free endpaper, otherwise fine in very good, bright dust jacket with two small tears at spine and wrinkle to bottom of front panel; uncommon signed. Thomas Dorn 9-84 1996 $225.00

CONNELL, EVAN S.   Son of the Morning Star. San Francisco: Northpoint, 1984. Small first printing; fine in fine dust jacket. Bud Schweska 12-265 1996 $175.00

CONNELL, EVAN S.   Son of the Morning Star. San Francisco: North Point, 1984. 1st edition; very fine in dust jacket, the first printing was quite small. Left Bank Books 2-22 1996 $100.00

CONNELLEY, WILLIAM ELSEY   Doniphan's Expedition and the Conquest of New Mexico and California. Kansas City: Bryant & Douglas Book and Stationary Co., 1907. Pages xiv, 670; illustrations, folding map; slight wear and fading to spine, else very good. Rittenhouse SFT 125; Graff 851; Howes C688. Dumont 28-100 1996 $175.00

CONNELLY, MARC   The Green Pastures. New York: Farrar & Rinehart, 1930. Limited to 550 numbered copies, signed by author and artist; 4to; xiii, (v), 150, (i) pages, clipping removed from rear pastedown, plate removed from front pastedown; color frontispiece, pictorial titlepage, 11 black and white plates, 2 chapter headings, 18 quarter page pictorial headpieces, 12 tailpiece vignettes; green paper covered boards, slightly rubbed at extremities, titled in gilt on spine with title and vignette in gilt on front cover, top edge gilt, clipping removed from rear pastedown, plate removed from front pastedown; lacks slipcase, else near fine. Blue Mountain SP95-68 1996 $175.00

CONNELLY, MICHAEL   The Black Echo. Boston: Little Brown, 1992. 1st edition; fine in dust jacket and wrap-around band, signed by author. Between the Covers 42-480 1996 $100.00

CONNETT, EUGENE V.   American Sporting Dogs. New York: D. Van Nostrand Co., Inc., 1948. 1st edition; large 8vo; xiv, 550 pages; profusely illustrated; rust cloth, gilt spine, fine. Kenneth Karmiole 1NS-80 1996 $100.00

CONNETT, EUGENE V.   Upland Game Bird Shooting. New York: Derrydale Press, 1930. One of 850 unnumbered copies, after 75 deluxe numbered copies; folio; original brown cloth, gilt decorations; fine. Siegel 45; Frazier C11a. Glenn Books 36-66 1996 $475.00

CONNOLLY, CYRIL 1903-1974   Enemies of Promise. London: 1938. 1st edition; nice bright copy. Words Etcetera 94-315 1996 £50.00

CONNOLLY, CYRIL 1903-1974   The Modern Movement: 100 Key Books from England, France and America 1880-1950. London: Andre Deutsch/Hamish Hamilton, 1965. 1st edition; very lightly used price clipped dust jacket. fine copy. Captain's Bookshelf 38-44 1996 $100.00

CONNOLLY, CYRIL 1903-1974   The Modern Movement. New York: Atheneum, 1966. 1st American edition; owner name under front flap, else fine in fine dust jacket. Ken Lopez 74-87 1996 $100.00

CONNOLLY, CYRIL 1903-1974   The Rock Pool. Paris: Obelisk Press, 1936. 1st edition; author's first book; original printed paper wrappers, lightly spotted or soiled, slight wear, nice, untrimmed copy. G. W. Stuart 59-28 1996 $350.00

CONNOLLY, CYRIL 1903-1974   The Unquiet Grave. Horizon, 1944. 1st edition; wrappers, little browned around edges and with nick at foot of spine, otherwise very good; Charles Osborne's copy with his signature on half title. Words Etcetera 94-316 1996 £60.00

CONOLLY, JOHN   An Inquiry Concerning the Indications of Insanity with Suggestions for the Better Protection and Care of the Insane. London: printed for John Taylor, 1830. 1st edition; 8vo; vi, 496 pages; modern beige cloth, leather label. Hunter & Macalpine p. 805. John Gach 150-106 1996 $950.00

CONOLLY, JOHN   The Treatment of the Insane Without Mechanical Restraints. London: Smith, Elder & Co., 1856. 1st edition; 8vo; xii, 380 pages plus publisher's catalog dated Oct. 1856; original embossed brown cloth, gilt spine, hinges strengthened and rebacked, original spine laid down, part of top and bottom of original spine chipped away; good to very good, very scarce; embossed and gold foil stamps of Hartford Retreat. GM 5 4933; Hunter & Macalpine p. 1030; Norman Cat. 506. John Gach 150-107 1996 $1,850.00

CONRAD, H. S.   The Waterlilies, a Monograph of the Genus Nymphaea. Washington: 1905. 4to; 12 colored and 18 black and white plates, plus 82 text figures; green cloth. Raymond M. Sutton VI-5 1996 $485.00

CONRAD, H. S.   The Waterlilies, a Monograph of the Genus Nymphaea. Bury St. Edmunds: 1991. Reprint; 4to; 336 pages; 30 plates; buckram.   Wheldon & Wesley 207-1679   1996 £95.00

CONRAD, JESSIE   A Handbook of Cookery for a Small House. London: Heinemann, 1923. 1st edition; 8vo; 135 pages; printed cloth, little browned endpaper, very good, tight copy.   Second Life Books 103-60   1996 $200.00

CONRAD, JOSEPH 1857-1924   Conrad's Manifesto: Preface to a Career. Philadelphia: 1966. Number 290 of 110 copies; woodblock portrait; marbed boards, fine in lightly soiled double publisher's slipcase. Hermitage SP95-876   1996 $225.00

CONRAD, JOSEPH 1857-1924   Last Essays. London: J. M. Dent, 1926. 1st edition; 8vo; embossed green cloth in dust jacket; near fine, some darkening, small chips and tears, dust jacket.   Antic Hay 101-332 1996 $125.00

CONRAD, JOSEPH 1857-1924   Letters from Conrad 1895-1924. London: Nonesuch, 1928. 1st English edition; very near fine in scarce, near fine dust jacket.   Stephen Lupack 83-   1996 $125.00

CONRAD, JOSEPH 1857-1924   Lord Jim. Edinburgh & London: 1900. 1st edition; very good+, some rubbing to head and foot of spine, some spotting to pale green cloth, now most uncommon.   Stephen Lupack 83-   1996 $750.00

CONRAD, JOSEPH 1857-1924   Lord Jim. New York: 1916. Standard dark blue Doubleday cloth, signed, near fine.   Stephen Lupack 83- 1996 $250.00

CONRAD, JOSEPH 1857-1924   The Nature of a Crime. London: Duckworth & Co., 1924. 1st edition; small 8vo; cloth, dust jacket, near fine, very minor wear (tiny tears) to jacket.   Antic Hay 101-341 1996 $125.00

CONRAD, JOSEPH 1857-1924   The Nature of a Crime. London: 1924. 1st edition; Very near fine in like dust jacket.   Stephen Lupack 83- 1996 $125.00

CONRAD, JOSEPH 1857-1924   Nostromo. London: 1904. 1st edition; near fine copy, scarce.   Stephen Lupack 83-   1996 $600.00

CONRAD, JOSEPH 1857-1924   Nostromo, a Tale of the Seaboard. Limited Editions Club, 1961. One of 1500 copies signed by artist; 11 1/2 x 8 3/4 inches; xxiii, (1), 376 pages, (1) leaf (colophon); colored plates and colored and black and white illustrations by Lima de Freitas; LEC newsletter laid in; original burlap backed linen boards, silver vignette on front cover, matching cloth label with silver titling on spine, original tissue jacket, in publisher's (somewhat chafed) silver slipcase, tissue jacket bit torn, otherwise mint.   Phillip J. Pirages 33-354 1996 $100.00

CONRAD, JOSEPH 1857-1924   One Day More. Garden City: Doubleday, Page, 1920. Number 9 of 377 copies, signed by author; light dampstaining of parchment spine, couple of small water sppots are more evident on front cover, at least very good copy.   Magnum Opus 44-30 1996 $225.00

CONRAD, JOSEPH 1857-1924   A Personal Record. New York: 1912. 1st U.S. edition; near fine, uncommon.   Stephen Lupack 83-   1996 $125.00

CONRAD, JOSEPH 1857-1924   The Point of Honor. New York: McClure, 1908. 1st separate edition, 1st state (with 'McClure' at base of spine); 8vo; color frontispiece and 3 color plates by Dan Sayre Groesbeck; original dark green pictorial cloth, upper cover printed in gilt and white, rubbing to spine ends and extremities.   George J. Houle 68-34 1996 $125.00

CONRAD, JOSEPH 1857-1924   The Rescue. London: Dent, 1920. 1st edition; fine in dust jacket with two very short tears, lovely copy. Between the Covers 42-107 1996 $500.00

CONRAD, JOSEPH 1857-1924   Romance. New York: McClure Phillips, 1904. 1st American edition; small 8vo; illustrations by Charles Macauley; decorative blue cloth; near fine, ink name to titlepage. Wise 14.   Antic Hay 101-340 1996 $125.00

CONRAD, JOSEPH 1857-1924   The Rover. London: T. Fisher Unwin, 1923. 1st edition; near fine in very good, lightly chipped and soiled dust jacket. Unwin promotional piece on Conrad laid in.   Captain's Bookshelf 38-45 1996 $150.00

CONRAD, JOSEPH 1857-1924   The Rover. London: 1923. 1st edition; 8 x 5 inches; 317 pages; cloth, f.e.p. frayed at top corner from strong erasure, else good in very badly chipped dust jacket.   John K. King 77-243 1996 $125.00

CONRAD, JOSEPH 1857-1924   The Secret Agent. London: 1923. Number 934 of 1000 copies, signed by author; tissue guarded portrait frontispiece; parchment backed paper boards, pages unopened, tail of spine bumped, very good in slightly dusty and creased dust jacket, slightly creased at edges and slightly darkened at spine.   Ulysses 39-120 1996 £325.00

CONRAD, JOSEPH 1857-1924   The Secret Agent. London: 1923. Signed limited edition; bit of rubbing and closed tear at foot of spine, otherwise fine, clean copy.   Stephen Lupack 83- 1996 $250.00

CONRAD, JOSEPH 1857-1924   The Secret Sharer. Limited Editions Club, 1985. One of 1500 copies, signed by artist; 4to; text printed in Monotype Van Dijck on Magnani, illustrations; indigo silk over boards, leather label on upper cover, fine copy in silk lined cloth bookform box, leather label on spine.   Bertram Rota 272-270 1996 £165.00

CONRAD, JOSEPH 1857-1924   Suspense. London: Dent, 1925. 1st edition; foxing to fore edge and some puckering to frontispiece, else about fine in near the dust jacket with small nick at crown and short tear on rear panel, nice, bright copy.   Between the Covers 42-109 1996 $350.00

CONRAD, JOSEPH 1857-1924   Tales of Hearsay. London: T. Fisher Unwin, 1925. 1st edition; slight foxing to fore edge, else fine in nice, near fine dust jacket with some very shallow nicks at base of front panel.   Between the Covers 42-108 1996 $375.00

CONRAD, JOSEPH 1857-1924   Collected Works. Garden City: 1925. Memorial Edition, limited to 499 numbered sets, this set with TLS from Conrad tipped in; 9 x 5.5 inches; 23 volumes, frontispieces; gilt stamped blue cloth, top edge gilt, volume 1 front inner hinge cracked, one paper label chipped, corner bumped, some wear, but nice set.   John K. King 77-242 1996 $1,250.00

CONROY, PAT   The Boo. Verona: McClure Press, 1970. 1st edition; author's first book; owner labels and name on front pastedown, offsetting to endpapers, not affecting inscriptions, overall near fine in spotted, but very good dust jacket; very scarce boo, particularly with contemporary signatures.   Ken Lopez 74-88 1996 $2,500.00

CONROY, PAT   The Great Santini. Boston: Houghton Mifflin Co., 1976. 1st edition; fine in very near fine dust jacket, with small nick at crown and short tear on rear panel; nice, bright copy.   Between the Covers 42-110 1 996 $150.00

CONROY, PAT   The Great Santini. Boston: Houghton Mifflin Co., 1976. 1st edition; fine in dust jacket.   Lame Duck Books 19-148 1996 $150.00

CONROY, PAT   The Great Santini. Boston: Houghton Mifflin, 1976. 1st edition; author's first novel; near fine in near fine dust jacket.   Bud Schweska 12-268 1996 $150.00

CONROY, PAT   The Great Santini. Boston: Houghton Mifflin, 1976. 1st edition; fine copy in fine dust jacket.   Ken Lopez 74-90 1996 $125.00

CONROY, PAT   The Prince of Tides. Special issue, 1/35 copies, signed.   Bev Chaney, Jr. 23-164 1996 $600.00

CONROY, PAT   The Water is Wide. Boston: Houghton Mifflin, 1972. 1st edition; advance review copy with publisher's review slip laid in; near fine in like jacket.   Ken Lopez 74-89 1996 $650.00

CONROY, PAT   The Water is Wide. Boston: Houghton Mifflin, 1972. 1st edition; author's second book; slight cocking of spine, otherwise near fine in near fine price clipped dust jacket that has few small specks on back panel.   Bud Schweska 12-267 1996 $275.00

CONSEQUENCES; a Complete Story in the Manner of the Old Parlour Game in Nine Chapters, Each by a Different Author. Waltham St. Lawrence: Golden Cockerel Press, 1932. One of 200 numbered copies on handmade paper, signed by all authors and artist; 8vo; frontispiece and titlepage vignette by Eric Ravilious; half blue morocco, patterned cloth sides, spine faded and rubbed at extremities, internally nice crisp copy, some browning in just a few margins; scarce.   Bertram Rota 272-175 1996 £120.00

CONSIDERATIONS Against Laying Any New Duty Upon Sugar; Wherein Is Particularly Shewn, that a New Imposition Will be Ruinous to the Sugar Colonies, Insufficient for the Purposes Intended and Greatly Conducive to the Aggrandizement of France. London: printed for J. Roberts, 1744. 1st edition; 8vo; half title, short tear on inner blank margin; 19th century half calf, hinges rubbed. Sabin 15940; Kress 4708; Goldsmith 8071; Hanson 5819.   Anthony W. Laywood 108-139 1996 £245.00

CONSIDERATIONS on the Acts of Parliament Relative to Highways in Scotland, and on the New Scheme of a Tax in Lieu of Statute-Labour. Edinburgh: printed for A. Kincaid and J. Bell, 1764. 1st edition; 8vo; title slightly soiled, 65 pages; disbound. Kress 6165; Not in Goldsmith; Higgs 3283.   Anthony W. Laywood 108-132 1996 £85.00

CONSIDERATIONS on the Expedience of Spanish War: Containing Reflections On the Late Demands of Spain; and on the Negociations of Mons. Bussy. London: printed for R. Griffiths, 1761. 44 pages; later three quarter leather and marbled boards, spine worn and scuffed, starting to split along front hinge, very good interior.   Bohling Book Co. 191-538 1996 $350.00

CONSIDERATIONS on the Political and Commercial Circumstances of Great Britain and Ireland. London: 1787. 1st London edition of Bradshaw 2291; 8vo; 101 pages; modern boards, very good.   C. P. Hyland 216-120 1996 £90.00

CONSIDERATIONS on Two Papers, Published at Antwerp, Respecting a Loan for 3,600,00 Guilders, to be Subscribed at the Houses of Messieurs J. E. Werbrouck and C. J. M. De Wolf, of that City. London: John Stockdale, 1791. 1st edition; 8vo; 74, (10) pages, including final 10 pages of publisher's ads; recently well bound in cloth backed marbled boards, lettered in gilt; early signature on title, else very good, rare. Kress B2054. Goldsmiths 14746.   John Drury 82-59 1996 £150.00

CONSIDERATIONS Upon a Proposal for Lowering the Interest of All the Redeemable National Debts to Three Per Cent...To give Immediate Ease to His Majesty's Subjects... London: printed for J. Purser, 1737. 8vo; pages 46; later wrappers. Kress 4332; Hanson 5043.   Peter Murray Hill 185-43 1996 £85.00

CONSIDERATIONS Upon the Intended Navigable Communication Between the firth of Forth and Clyde. N.P.: n.d. Edinburgh: 1767. Quarto; 21 pages; disbound. Kress 6423.   C. R. Johnson 37-6 1996 £125.00

CONSTABLE, HENRY   The Poems and Sonnets. Vale Press, 1897. One of 210 copies; 9 1/4 x 6 inches; ci, (1) pages, (1) leaf (colophon, limitation), elaborate woodcut vine border on first page of text as well as fine decorative woodcut initials by Charles Ricketts; absolutely splendid crimson morocco, heavily gilt, by Riviere & Son (very possibly contemporary), covers with very wide and animated borders of circuling gilt vines terminating in deeply gouged broad leaves & groups of flowers & emanating from a semis ground, raised bands decorated with 3 large gilt dots, six spine panels, two with titling, rest with leafy gilt vines like those on covers, turn-ins gilt ruled and with corner ornaments, top edge gilt, others untrimmed; nearly perfect copy in sumptuous binding. Armorial bookplate of M. C. D. Borden. Tomkinson p. 165.   Phillip J. Pirages 33-490 1996 $1,800.00

CONSTABLE, HENRY STRICKLAND   Doctors, Vaccination and Utilitarianism. London: 1873. 1st and apparently only edition; 8vo; pages vii, 239; original mauve cloth, gilt, nice, fresh copy.   James Fenning 133-69 1996 £55.00

CONSTABLE, JOHN   English Landscape Scenery. London: Henry G. Bohn, 1855. Folio; 4 pages, 40 full page engravings; early 20th century binder's cloth.   H. M. Fletcher 121-133 1996 £565.00

CONSTABLE, W. G.   Richard Wilson. London: Routledge & Kegan Paul, 1953. 25 x 19 cm; xiii,3 06 pages, 160 plates, cloth, front endpaper damaged.   Rainsford A54-585 1996 £90.00

CONSTABLE-MAXWELL, ANDREW   Catalogue of the Constable-Maxwell Collection of Ancient Glass. The Property of Mr. and Mrs. Andrew Constable-Maxwell... London: Sotheby Parke Bernet, 1979. 8vo; 209 pages; 355 illustrations, many in color; boards, dust jacket (2 corners bumped).   Archaeologia Luxor-2937 1996 $125.00

PHILADELPHIA SOCIETY FOR ALLEVIATING THE MISERIES OF PUBLIC PRISONS.   Constitution. Philadelphia: Joseph Cruikshank, 1806. 1st edition; 16mo; 8 pages; contemporary marbled wrappers, fine. With signature of Samuel G. Arnold, wealthy Providence businessman. S&S 11155.   M & S Rare Books 60-402 1996 $250.00

CONTRIBUTIONS to Medical and Biological Research Dedicated to Sir William Osler...In Honor of His Seventieth Birthday, July 12, 1919 by His Pupils and Co-Workers. New York: Hoeber, 1919. Limited to 1500 copies; 8vo; 2 volumes; frontispiece in volume 1; cloth, bit rubbed, inner hinge of volume 2 split.   James Tait Goodrich K40-216 1996 $125.00

CONTRIBUTIONS to the Medical Sciences in Honor of Dr. Emanuel Libman by His Pupils, Friends and Colleagues. New York: 1932. 1st edition; 3 volumes; original binding.   W. Bruce Fye 71-1285 1996 $125.00

CONWAY, MONCURE DANIEL   Testimonies Concerning Slavery. London: Chapman and Hall, 1864. 1st edition; 8vo; viii, 140 pages; original green cloth, embossed in blind and gilt; fine. Sabin 16222; Headicar & Fuller III 487.   John Drury 82-60 1996 £50.00

CONWAY, MONCURE DANIEL   Travels in South Kensington. New York: Harper, 1882. 1st edition; 8vo; frontispiece, (5)-234, (4) pages; numerous wood engravings; publisher's cloth, name in ink on blank leaf, paper beginning to yellow, else very nice, bright copy, scarce. Hitchcock 284. Bookpress 75-29 1996 $335.00

CONWAY, WILLIAM MARTIN   The Alps from End to End. London: Archibald Constable, 1895. 2nd edition; royal 8vo; xii, 403 pages; frontispiece, 99 full page plates; publisher's buckram backed cloth, gilt, top edge gilt, worn and faded, joints sprung, corner of frontispiece stained and little spotting throughout text. Cox 20.   Thomas Thorp 489-73 1996 £80.00

CONWAY, WILLIAM MARTIN   The Alps. London: 1904. Large paper edition limited to 300 copies, signed by publishers; 70 colored reproductions; yellow, green and white art-deco illustration and gilt lettering on cream boards, titlepage; few faint marks on back board and slight rubbing of top and bottom of spine, but above average near fine copy. Protected by transparent plastic cover.   Moutaineering Books 8-EC01 1996 £195.00

CONYBEARE, JOHN JOSIAS   Illustrations of Anglo-Saxon Poetry. London: printed for Harding and Lepard, 1826. 1st edition; 8vo; errata leaf at end; original cloth backed boards, head of spine missing, original printed paper label, uncut.   Anthony W. Laywood 108-163 1996 £75.00

COOK, C. H.   Among the Pimas; or, the Mission to the Pima and Maricopa Indians. Albany: printed for the Ladies' Union Mission School Association, 1893. 1st edition; 136 pages; photo plates; original light brown cloth stamped in black and gilt; very fine.   Argonaut Book Shop 113-147 1996 $125.00

COOK, DAVID J.   Hands Up; or Thirty-Five Years of Detective Life in the Mountains and Plains. Denver: 1897. 442 pages; plates, illustrations; cloth, nice, rare.   T. A. Swinford 49-236 1996 $175.00

COOK, DAVID J.   Hands Up; or, Thirty-Five Years of Detetive Life in the Muntains and on the Plains. Denver: 1897. 2nd edition; ii, 442 pages, including illustrations; maroon cloth with gilt title, very good, spine bit dull and frayed at ends. Howes C728; Adams Guns 483; Graff 862; Adams 150 #34; Wynar 7005.   Bohling Book Co. 192-130 1996 $150.00

COOK, E. B.   American Chess-Nuts: a Collection of Problems, by Composers of the Western World. New York: Adelmour W. King, 1868. 1st edition; 8vo; x, 527 pages, errata; half contemporary brown morocco, gilt, hinges rubbed with short split at top of front hinge, small chip to front free fly, else very good; presentation from editor, E. B. Cook, the owner of this volume has placed two small paper game boards at opposition to form an 8 pointed star ex-libris with his initials.   Andrew Cahan 47-45 1996 $285.00

COOK, FREDERICK   My Attainment of the Pole. New York: & London: 1912. Pages xx, 604; many illustrations; original cloth, light shelfwear, else very good; inscribed and signed by Cook.   Stephen Lunsford 45-34 1996 $150.00

COOK, HENRY   Pride, or The Heir of Craven. London: John W. Parker, 1841. 1st edition; 8vo; author's own copy, with his bookplate; pages (iii)-viii, 139, (i) blank, (i) ad; contemporary calf with double fillet gilt border to sides with rosette at each corner, spine decorated in compartments with floral ornaments, leaf sprays, etc., green morocco label, marbled endpapers, gilt edges, some wear to upper joint and head of spine skilfully repaired; bookplates of author and Sir William Augustus Fraser Bart. and leather booklabel of Joseph Widener.   Simon Finch 24-55   1996 £450.00

COOK, J.   Beautiful Seaweeds. Paisley: 1877. 1st edition; imperial 8vo; 226 pages, 35 natural specimens; original cloth; very scarce. Some offsetting but good.   Wheldon & Wesley 207-1610   1996 £150.00

COOK, JAMES 1728-1779   The Charts and Coastal Views of Captain Cook's Voyages: Volume 1. Hakluyt Society, 1988. 4to; nearly 350 reproductions of charts, views and drawings; cloth.   Wheldon & Wesley 207-373   1996 £100.00

COOK, JAMES 1728-1779   The Charts and Coastal Views of Captain Cook's Voyages the Voyage of the Endeavour 1768-1771. London: Hakluyt Society, 1988. 1st edition; 48cm; lxiv, 328 pages; tipped in frontispiece, 17 plates, 320 reproductions of charts and views; dark blue cloth, gilt titles and cover decoration, new in dust jacket.   Parmer Books O39Nautica-047013   1996 $225.00

COOK, JAMES 1728-1779   The Charts and Coastal Views of Captain Cook's Voyages. Volume 2. Hakluyt Society, 1992. 4to; 250 charts and views; cloth.   Wheldon & Wesley 207-374   1996 £125.00

COOK, JAMES 1728-1779   The Journals of Captain James Cook on His Voyages of Discovery. Glasgow: Hakluyt Society, 1961-69. 1st edition thus; thick 8vo Text and 15 inch portfolio of charts; pages (ii), cclxxxiv, (ii), 696; pages (iv), clxx, 1028; pages ccxxiv, (1)-718, pages (2), 723)-1648; portfolio pages viii 58 charts and views, 224 maps and illustrations in text volumes including 2 colored portraits, plus 49 maps, portraits and views; original gilt decorated blue buckram; scarce. Hill p. 383; Beddie 2106.   Parmer Books O39Nautica-039228   1996 $995.00

COOK, JAMES 1728-1779   Troisieme Voyage dy Capitaine Cook Autour du Monde... Lyon: chez J. F. Rolland, 1834. 8vo; 2 volumes; folding hand colored engraved map, folding plate, contemporary calf, title labels inset on red morocco; good.   K Books 442-155   1996 £150.00

COOK, JOHN R.   The Border and the Buffalo. Topeka: Crane & Co., 1907. 1st edition; original pictorial cloth, former owner's inscription on inside front cover, else very good.   Howes C730; Adams Sixguns 487. Ken Sanders 8-67   1996 $165.00

COOK, JOHN R.   The Border and the Buffalo an Untold Story of the Southwest Plains. Topeka: 1907. 1st edition; xii, 351 pages; frontispiece, photos, illustrations; pictorial cloth; nice. Scarce. Howes C730; Rader 905; 6 Guns 486; Graff 864.   T. A. Swinford 49-238   1996 $145.00

COOK, R. L.   The Concord Saunterer. Middlebury: Middlebury College Press, 1940. 1st edition; one of 600 copies; original printed boards, dust jacket, some pencilling in text, but fine in unusually nice jacket with just a few chips, fragile volume, scarce in decent shape due to materials used for binding and jacket. Boswell & Crouch 522 and 2069; BAL 20156; Borst C29.   Mac Donnell 12-137   1996 $100.00

COOK, THEODORE ANDREA   The Watercolor Drawings of the National Gallery. London: Cassell & Co., 1904. Limited edition, number 1179 of 1200 copies; 34 x 28 cm; vi, 88 pages, 58 color plates, frontispiece, 4 text illustrations; original cloth, slightly marked, some foxing;   Rainsford A54-558   1996 £85.00

COOKE, E. W.   Grotesque Animals, Invented, Drawn and Described. London: 1872. 4to; pages vi, 24 plates, decorated cloth, trifle used, neatly refixed, small tear in endpaper neatly repaired.   Wheldon & Wesley 207-429   1996 £180.00

COOKE, EDWARD   Chronica Juridicialia; or, A General Calendar of the Years of Our Lord God, and Those of the Several Kings of England, from the First Year of William the Conqueror... London: printed for H. Sawbridge and T. simmons, 1685. 1st edition; 8vo; with A1 blank, contemporary calf, hinges cracked, spine worn. Wing C5999.   Anthony Laywood 108-6   1996 £75.00

COOKE, GEORGE   Views in London and its Vicinity. London: Longman, 1834. 4to; 8 pages, 48 copperplate engravings; contemporary half calf, slightly rubbed at extremities. Adams 149; Anderson p. 212; cf. UCBA p. 326.   Marlborough 162-122   1996 £700.00

COOKE, GRACE MC GOWAN   Their First Formal Call. New York: Harper, 1906. 1st edition; octavo; 55 pages; 14 full page illustrations by Peter Newell; red cloth, with illustrated label and with rare printed glassine dust jacket which is lightly chipped; fine.   Bromer Booksellers 90-124   1996 $250.00

COOKE, JOHN ESTEN 1830-1886   The Virginia Comedians; or, Old Days in the Old Dominion. New York: D. Appleton, 1854. 1st edition; 12mo; 2 volumes, with ads; original cloth, spines and corners chipped, text browned. BAL 3711; Wright II 626.   M & S Rare Books 60-143 1996 $100.00

COOKE, M. C.   British Fresh-Water Algae, Exclusive of Desmidiae and Diatomaceae. London: 1882-84. 8vo; 2 volumes; 130 colored plates; binder's cloth, good ex-library, no stamps on plates.   Wheldon & Wesley 207-1612   1996 £130.00

COOKE, M. C.   Illustrations of British Fungi. London: 1881-91. 8vo; a collection of 494 (of 1198) colored plates; unbound.   Wheldon & Wesley 207-1611   1996 £400.00

COOKE, THOMAS   The Mournful Nuptials, or Love the Cure of All Woes, a Tragedy. London: printed for T. Cooper, 1739. 1st edition; 8vo; disbound; very scarce, very good, complete with final leaf of epilogue. Stratman 1273; CBEL II 542.   Ximenes 108-82   1996 $225.00

COOKE, THOMAS   The Universal Letter-Writer; or, New Art of Polite Correspondence. London: printed for A. Millar, W. Law, & R. Cater, & for Wilson, Spence... 1794. 12mo; frontispiece; contemporary red stained sheep, spine faded and rubbed, one hole, leading hinge splitting; Alston III 295, a York piracy.   Jarndyce 103-283   1996 £75.00

COOKE, WILLIAM   The Elements of Dramatic Criticism. London: printed for G. Kearsly and G. Robinson, 1775. 1st edition; 8vo; half title, engraved vignette on title, contemporary calf, hinges partly cracked, spine gilt, lacks label, nice clean copy. Arnott & Robinson 3716. Anthony Laywood 108-43   1996 £225.00

COOKE, WILLIAM   The Elements of Dramatic Criticism. London: for G. Kearsley and G. Robinson, 1775. 1st edition; engraved vignette to title; disbound, half title embrowned and chipped at edges, T. J. Spencer's copy with his bookticket and annotations.   Dramatis Personae 37-49 1996 $100.00

COOKE, WILLIAM   Poetical Essays on Several Occasions. London: for S. Smith, 1774. 1st edition; 4to; disbound, very good, rare. Jackson p. 32.   Ximenes 108-83   1996 $400.00

COOLIDGE, H. J.   A Revision of the Genus Gorilla. Cambridge: 1929. 4to; 87 pages, 2 maps and 21 plates; cloth.   Wheldon & Wesley 207-545   1996 £75.00

COOLIDGE, RICHARD   Statistical Report on the Sickness and Mortality in the Army of the United States... Washington: 1856. 1st edition; 4to; 703 pages; skilfully rebacked with leather label; GM 2163.1.   W. Bruce Fye 71-405   1996 $275.00

COOLIDGE, RICHARD   Statistical Report on the Sickness and Mortality in the Army of the United States...from January 1839 to January 1855. Washington: 1856. 4to; folding lithograph map; contemporary leather, skillfully rebacked saving original spine which is laid down, partial dampstaining. GM 2163.1.   James Tait Goodrich K40-92   1996 $125.00

COOLIDGE, RICHARD   Statistical Report on the Sickness and Mortality in the Army of the United States... Washington: 1860. 1st edition; 4to; 515 pages; hand colored folding map; original binding. GM 2163.1.   W. Bruce Fye 71-406   1996 $275.00

COOMARASWAMY, ANANADA   Myths of the Hindus and Buddhists. London: George Harrap, 1913. Limited to 75 copies, signed by publishers; 32 color illustrations; printed on Japanese vellum; full embossed vellum, top edge gilt, very good.   Words Etcetera 94-244 1996 £90.00

COOMBES, B. L.   These Poor Hands - the Autobiography of a Miner Working in South Wales. London: Victor Gollancz Ltd., 1939. 1st edition; original binding, head and tail of spine and one corner slightly bumped, gilt titles on spine oxidising, very good; presentation copy from author, inscribed, dedication copy, for John Lehmann.   Ulysses 39-123 1996 £85.00

COOMBS, ORDE   Drums of a Life: a Photographic Essay on the Black Man in America. Garden City: Anchor/Doubleday, 1974. 1st edition; photos by Chester Higgins; perfect bound wrappers as issued, couple of mild blemishes on front wrapper and little rubbing at extremities, thus very good; very nicely inscribed by the photographer.   Between the Covers 43-458 1996 $100.00

COONEY, LORAINE   Garden History of Georgia 1733-1933. Atlanta: Peachtree Garden Club, 1933. 1st edition; one of 1500 copies; 4to; (xx), 458 pages; cloth, minor light foxing on few leaves, covers handled, corners lightly bruised, still very good.   Bookpress 75-170 1996 $250.00

COOPER, B. B.   The Life of Sir Astley Cooper, Bart. London: 1843. 1st edition; 8vo; 2 volumes; portrait; slightly later calf, gilt spines, marbled edges and endpapers (similar pattern marble), by Riviere, trifle worn. Maggs Bros. Ltd. 1190-388 1996 £90.00

COOPER, DOUGLAS   Picasso: Carnet Catalan. Paris: Beggruen, 1958. Limited to 550 copies; oblong 8vo; 2 volumes, 34 pages text, 74 page facsimile of Picasso sketchbook; wrappers and boards, slipcase. Freitag 7484.   Brannan 43-511 1996 $200.00

COOPER, DOUGLAS   Picasso Theatre. New York: Abrams, 1968. Square 4to; 360 pages; 491 illustrations, 48 in color; cloth, acetate dust jacket. Freitag 7429.   Brannan 43-510 1996 $1,615.00

COOPER, DOUGLAS   The Work of Graham Sutherland. London: 1962. 4to; 97 pages, well illustrated; original decorated boards.   Rainsford A54-545 1996 £95.00

COOPER, G. H. C.   Colchester Town Hall. A Brief History. London: Marchants Press, 1988. 1st edition; limited to 50 numbered copies; 4to; pages (8), 33, colophon, 4 tipped in woodcut plates, decorative initials and endpaper decoration (printed in blue) by Eileen Clarke; cloth backed decorated boards and slipcase.   Claude Cox 107-32 1996 £55.00

COOPER, GEORGE   A Treatise of Distresses, Replevins and Avowries... London: printed by S. Richardson and C. Lintot, etc., 1761. 4th edition; modern quarater morocco, lightly embrowned, good, attractive copy. Sale 498a.   Meyer Boswell SL26-53 1996 $450.00

COOPER, J. W.   The Experienced Botanist or Indian Physician. Ebensburg: printed by Canan & Scott, 1833. xxiv, (25)-301 pages; leather, covers rubbed, free endpaper detached in front, altogether a tight and solid copy.   Robert G. Hayman 11/95-28 1996 $400.00

COOPER, JAMES FENIMORE 1789-1851   The Deerslayer: a Tale. London: Richard Bentley, 1841. 2nd edition; 8vo; 3 volumes, half titles, contemporary dark blue half calf, spines gilt, inoffensive old ms. shelf marks on lower labels; fine, attractive.   James Burmester 29-163 1996 £100.00

COOPER, JAMES FENIMORE 1789-1851   The Red Rover, a Tale. Paris: printed for Hector Bossange; Bobee et Hingray, Baudry, Galignani, 1827. 1st edition; 12mo; 3 volumes; contemporary gren calf, covers ruled in black with gilt pointing, spines gilt, marbled edges; rare. Some foxing, mostly at beginning and end of each volume, but fine, complete with half titles. BAL 3837; Spiller and Blackburn p. 54.   Ximenes 108-84 1996 $1,750.00

COOPER, JAMES FENIMORE 1789-1851   The Two Admirals. Philadelphia: Lea and Blanchard, 1842. 1st American edition; 8vo; 2 volumes, 236, 247 pages; original purple cloth, stained and darkened, spines faded, printed paper labels on spines, labels chipped, bookplate removed from pastedown of volume 1, else very nice, near fine set. BAL 3899.   Blue Mountain SP95-93 1996 $550.00

COOPER, JAMES FENIMORE 1789-1851   The Wept of Wish-ton-Wish, a Tale. Florence: printed by Molini at Dante's Head, 1829. 1st edition; 12mo; 3 volumes; contemporary half calf, marbled boards, spines gilt (traces of rubbing); rare; some foxing (as paper is not of good quality), but fine set, complete with half titles and with outer edges uncut. Spiller and Blackburn p. 61.   Ximenes 109-83 1996 $7,500.00

COOPER, JOHN GIBLERT   Epistles to the Great, from Aristippus in Retirement. (with) The Call of Aristippus. London: printed for R. and J. Dodsley, 1757/58. 1st edition; 4to; 2 volumes in one; marbled boards; very good, complete with half titles, very uncommon.   Ximenes 109-84 1996 $450.00

COOPER, JOHN GILBERT   Letters Concerning Taste. London: printed for R. and J. Dodsley, 1757. 3rd edition; 8vo; (16) 220 pages, half title; frontispiece; contemporary calf, neatly rebacked, corners repaired; good. Ken Spelman 30-67 1996 £160.00

COOPER, JOHN GILBERT   Poems on Several Subjects. London: for R. and J. Dodsley, 1764. 1st edition; 12mo; pages (iv), 139, (i) contents, folding frontispiece engraved by Wale after Grignion; contemporary tan sprinkled calf, red morocco lettering piece, red sprinkled edges, joints very slightly rubbed, some faint spotting of endleaves, otherwise fine. Simon Finch 24-56 1996 £165.00

COOPER, JOHN GILBERT   Poems on Several Subjects. London: printed for R. and J. Dodsley, 1764. 1st edition; 12mo; contemporary calf, spine gilt; slight foxing, but fine, scarce. Foxon p. 144.   Ximenes 109-85 1996 $400.00

COOPER, S.   Mandrake. H&S, 1964. 1st edition; author's first book; fine in near fine dust jacket.   Aronovitz 57-300 1996 $120.00

COOPER, THOMPSON   Men of Mark. London: Sampson Low, 1876-83. 1st edition; 4to; 7 volumes; 252 photos, each mounted on card, few of the mounts foxed, bound in original green cloth, elaborately blocked in black and gilt, spines gilt, gilt edges; fine, bright copy.   James Burmester 29-34 1996 £900.00

COOPER, W. HEATON   The Hills of Lakeland. London: Warne, 1938. Signed limited edition of 250 copies; 4to; pages xviii, 126; 16 colored plates; original cloth, gilt, dust jacket (top edge trifle chipped), top edge gilt, uncut;   R.F.G. Hollett & Son 78-816 1996 £225.00

COOPER, W. HEATON   The Hills of Lakeland. London: Warne, 1938. Limited edition of 250 copies; 4to; pages xviii, 126, 16 colored plates; original cloth, gilt, dust jacket (small tear to top edge), flyleaves little spotted and marked by tape, otherwise nice.   R.F.G. Hollett & Son 78-817 1996 £160.00

COOPER, W. HEATON   The Hills of Lakeland. London: Warne, 1946. Library edition; small 4to; pages xviii, 126, 16 colored plates; original cloth, gilt, dust jacket (top of spine defective).   R.F.G. Hollett & Son 78-818 1996 £55.00

COOPER, W. HEATON   Lakeland Portraits. London: Hodder & Stoughton, 1954. 1st edition; small 4to; 128 pages; 6 fine colored plates; original two tone cloth, gilt, dust jacket price clipped; signed.   R.F.G. Hollett & Son 78-821 1996 £65.00

COOPER, W. HEATON   The Lakes. London: Frederick Warne & Co., 1966. 1st edition; 4to; 17 colored plates, 64 drawings by author; original pictorial cloth, dust jacket.   R.F.G. Hollett & Son 78-822 1996 £60.00

COOPER, W. HEATON   The Lakes. London: Frederick Warne & Co., 1970. 2nd edition; 4to; pages xvii, 228, 17 colored plates and 64 drawings by author; original pictorial cloth, dust jacket (top edge little torn and chipped).   R.F.G. Hollett & Son 78-823 1996 £50.00

COOPER, W. HEATON   The Tarns of Lakeland. London: Warne, 1960. 1st edition; small 4to; pages xiv, 237, 16 colored plates; original cloth, gilt, dust jacket, few slight edge creases and tears.   R.F.G. Hollett & Son 78-824 1996 £50.00

COOPER, W. HEATON   The Tarns of Lakeland. Grasmere: Heaton Cooper Studio, 1970. 2nd edition; small 4to; pages xiv, 237; 16 colored plates; original cloth gilt, dust jacket, signed by author.   R.F.G. Hollett & Son 78-825 1996 £65.00

COOTE, EYRE   A Letter from Certain Gentlemen of the Council at Bengal, to the Honourable Secret Committee for Affairs of the Honourable United Company of Merchants of England Trading to the East Indies. London: printed for T. Becket and P. A. De Hondt, 1764. 1st edition; 4to; 25 pages, last leaf torn in blank margin, stitched as issued, uncut; Kress S4331; Goldsmith 9987; Higgs 3204.   Anthony Laywood 108-44 1996 £145.00

COOVER, ROBERT   The Origin of the Brunists. New York: Putnam, 1966. Advance reading copy; author's first novel; wrappers, some modest soiling, still near fine; signed by author.   Between the Covers 42-114 1996 $250.00

COOVER, ROBERT   Pricksongs and Descants. New York: Dutton, 1969. 1st edition; signed by author; near fine in dust jacket.   Lame Duck Books 19-149 1996 $125.00

COOVER, ROBERT   Pricksongs and Descants. New York: E. P. Dutton & Co., Inc., 1969. 1st edition; 256 pages; brown cloth spine, ivory cloth, fine in fine dust jacket, postcard inscribed by author laid in.   Orpheus Books 17-119 1996 $100.00

COOVER, ROBERT   Spanking the Maid. Bloomfield Hills: Bruccoli Clark, 1982. 1st edition; 1/600 numbered copies; maroon cloth spine, ornamental paper covered boards; fine, signed by author.   Orpheus Books 17-120 1996 $100.00

COPE, THOMAS   The Smokers's Text Book. Liverpool: Cope, 1889-90. 2 volumes (Nos. 1-14, complete); illustrations; three quarter gilt stamped brown morocco over marbled boards by Zaehnsdorf, spines with raised bands and decorative devices stamped in gilt and black within double gilt ruled compartments, gilt ruled covers, marbled endpapers, top edge gilt, uncut, very good to fine, scarce. With all original gilt decorated wrappers bound in.   George J. Houle 68-144 1996 $450.00

COPELAND, R. MORRIS   Country Life. Boston: Crosby and Nichols, 1863. 2nd edition; 8vo; frontispiece, x, 814 pages; publisher's blindstamped cloth, faint waterstain on lower edge, minor cover wear, else very good.   Bookpress 75-31 1996 $195.00

COPIES of the Letters Patent, the Bishop of London's Grant, and the Original Ordinances, Evidencing the Foundation of Sir Roger Cholmeley's Free Grammar School at Highgate, and referred to in a Bill Now Pending in Parliament... London: printed by C. M. Topping, 1822. 1st edition; 8vo; 28 pages; disbound.   James Burmester 29-72 1996 £65.00

COPINGER, W. A.   History and Records of the Smith-Carington Family from the Conquest to the Present Time. London: Henry Sotheran, 1907. Thick large 4to; 710 pages; 44 plates, illustrations and maps, many in photogravure; original strong half vellum, leather label, gilt top.   Howes Bookshop 265-2031 1996 £250.00

COPLEY, ESTHER HEWLETT   The Housekeeper's Guide, or a Plain and Pratical System of Domestic Cookery. London: Jackson & Walford, 1834. 1st edition; small 8vo; xi, (i), 407 pages; frontispiece, additional engraved title, 5 engraved plates, contemporary half calf; rare. Cagle, Matter of Taste 635.   James Burmester 29-35 1996 £225.00

COPPARD, ALFRED EDGAR 1878-1957   Count Stefan. Waltham St. Lawrence: Golden Cockerel Press, 1928. One of 600 numbered copies on handmade paper; 8vo; marbled boards, yellow buckram spine, fine in partially faded dust jacket.   Bertram Rota 272-172 1996 £80.00

COPPARD, ALFRED EDGAR 1878-1957   Crotty Shinkwin. Waltham St. Lawrence: Golden Cockerel Press, 1932. 1st edition; limited edition, 318/500 copies; 8vo; pages (ii), 68, (1); printed on Batchelor handmade paper, 7 wood engravings in text and wood engraved border to double titlepage, all by Robert Gibbings; original quarter mid-blue morocco, gilt lettered backstrip lightly faded, patterned pale and dark blue cloth, top edge gilt, others untrimmed; excellent. Chanticleer 84.   Blackwell's B112-121 1996 £85.00

COPPARD, ALFRED EDGAR 1878-1957   Emergency Exit. New York: Random House, 1934. Signed, limited edition of 350 numbered copies; 8vo; decorative buckram cloth; fine.   Antic Hay 101-348 1996 $100.00

COPPARD, ALFRED EDGAR 1878-1957   Fishmonger's Fiddle. London: Cape, 1925. 1st edition; signed on half title, some foxing and browning of endpapers and prelims, uncut, edges browned, some cracking to edges of spine - worming? lower back corner bumped, otherwise good in soiled and browned dust jacket nicked at corners and ends of spine, top edge of spine quarter inch missing.   Virgo Books 48-54 1996 £60.00

COPPARD, ALFRED EDGAR 1878-1957   Nixey's Harlequin. London: Cape, 1931. Limited edition, this number 89 copies from an edition of 304; printed on handmade paper, top edge gilt; full vellum, edges of pages slightly browned, covers spotted otherwise very good in glassine wrapper; from the library of Frederic Prokosch with his signature and bookplate   Virgo Books 48-56 1996 £60.00

COPPARD, ALFRED EDGAR 1878-1957   Tapster's Tapestry. Waltham St. Lawrence: Golden Cockerel Press, 1938. One of 75 copies, signed by author and artist; 8 3/4 x 6 1/2 inches; 3 p.l., (two blank), 5-58 pages, (1) leaf (colophon); device on title, 10 wood engravings by Gwenda Morgan; original morocco backed buckram boards by Sangorski & Sutcliffe, gilt titling on spine, top edge gilt, other edges untrimmed, extremely fine. Pertelote 137.   Phillip J. Pirages 33-249 1996 $225.00

COPPENS, CHARLES   Moral Principles and Medical Practice, the Basis of Medical Jurisprudence. Cincinnati: 1897. 1st edition; 222 pages; original binding.   W. Bruce Fye 71-410 1996 $100.00

COPPER, BASIL   The Black Death. Minneapolis: Fedogan & Bremer, 1991. 1st edition; one of 100 numbered copies, signed by author and artist; illustrations by Stefanie Kate Hawks; very fine in dust jacket with slipcase.   Robert Gavora 61-19 1996 $100.00

COPPER, BASIL   The Exploits of Solar Pons. Minneapolis: Fedogan & Bremer, 1993. One of 100 numbered copies, signed by author and artist; illustrations by Stefanie Hawks; very fine in dust jacket with slipcase.   Robert Gavora 61-20 1996 $100.00

COPPETTA DE' BECCUTI, FRANCESCO   Rime. Venice: D. & G. B. Guerra for Aldo Manuzio, 1580. 1st edition; small 8vo; pages (xvi), 190, lacking final blank, italic letter with Roman Index, woodcut printer's device on titlepage and at end, woodcut initials and ornaments, few early ms. annotations, fore edge of titlepage bit soiled, top outer corner of this and following leaf repaired, occasional spot, finger mark or similar blemish, good copy in attractive neo-Classical binding c. 1800, vellum over boards, gilt borders and title, morocco lettering pieces; engraved armorial bookplate of Jaffray. BM STC It. p. 77; Adams C2606; Gamba 372; Brunet II 261.   A. Sokol XXV-24 1996 £625.00

COPPINGER, JOSEPH   The American Practical Brewer and Tanner. New York: Van Winkle and Wiley, 1815. 1st edition; 8vo; iv, (3), (11)-246, (2) pages, plates and plans; later marbled boards, cloth spine, ex-library with old ink numerals on titlepage, some foxing and browning, good. Uncommon. Kress S6147.   Edwin V. Glaser 121-69 1996 $450.00

COPPOCK, PARSON   The Genuine Dying Speech of the Rev. Parson Coppock, Pretended Bishop of Carlisle... Carlisle: Thomas Harris, 1746. 1st edition; 8vo; 32 pages; half title, old wrappers bound in, modern full blind ruled calf, gilt; rare. Trifle soiled, cleaned throughout.   R.F.G. Hollett & Son 78-361 1996 £180.00

A COPY of the Poll for the Knights of the Shire for the County of Norfolk Taken at Norwich, March 23, 1768. Norwich: printed by J. course, 1768. 4to; 172 pages; contemporary half calf, rebacked, label, nice.   Anthony W. Laywood 108-99 1996 £245.00

COQUILLETTE, DANIEL R.   The Civilian Writers of Doctors' Commons, London, Three Centuries of Juristic Innovation in Comparative Commercial and International Law. Berlin: Duncker & Humblot, 1988. 303 pages; printed sewn wrappers.   Meyer Boswell SL27-53 1996 $115.00

CORBET, G. B.   Mammals of the Indo-Malayan Region, a Systematic Review. London: 1992. Royal 8vo; 350 pages; line drawings, text figures, 177 maps; cloth.   Wheldon & Wesley 207-547 1996 £60.00

CORBET, RICHARD   Poems... London: by J. C. for William Crook, 1672. 1st edition under this title; 12mo; pages (x), 138, (iv) ads, lacks initial blank and final ad leaf; Dragon woodcut device of William Crook on title; recent antique style mottled calf decorated in gilt, marbled endpapers, old gilt edges, quite closely trimmed all round, very occasionally just shaving headline, page numeral or catchword, title slightly dust soiled, good copy. Wing C6271; Grolier WP 199.   Simon Finch 24-57 1996 £500.00

CORBY, HERBERT   Hampdens Going Over. London: Nicholson and Watson - Editions Poetry, 1945. 1st edition; original binding, top edge dusty, head and tail of spine and corners slightly bumped, prelims, edges and endpapers slightly spotted, very good in nicked, spotted and slightly rubbed, marked and dusty dust jacket, slightly faded at spine and chipped at head of spine.   Ulysses 39-655 1996 £135.00

CORDASCO, FRANCESCO   American Medical Imprints 1820-1910. Totawa: 1985. 4to; 2 volumes, 1680 pages; original binding.   James Tait Goodrich K40-93 1996 $250.00

CORDASCO, FRANCESCO   American Medical Imprints 1820-1910. Totowa: 1985. 2 volumes, 1654 pages; original binding. GM 6786.28. JHM 40.486, 1985.   W. Bruce Fye 71-413 1996 $200.00

CORDELL, EUGENE F.　The Medical Annals of Maryland 1799-1899. Baltimore: 1903. 1st edition; large 8vo; 889 pages; 32 plates; cloth, uncut, unopened, fine.　The Bookpress 75-403　1996 $250.00

CORDER, E. M.　The Deer Hunter. New York: 1979. 1st hardcover edition; fine, near fine.　Stephen Lupack 83-　1996 $125.00

CORDER, WILLIAM　The Trial of William Corder...for the Murder of Maria Marten. London: printed for Knight and Lacey, 55 Paternoster Row, etc., 1828. Modern green morocco over marbled boards, embrowned but attractive.　Meyer Boswell SL26-172　1996 $350.00

CORELLI, M.　The Life Everlasting. H&S, 1911. 1st American edition; marvelous bright, tight, very good+ copy in very good dust jacket with some light wear and tear and thumb-nail size chip missing from the upper right corner of the rear dust jacket panel, very scarce in dust jacket, most desirable copy.　Aronovitz 57-301　1996 $135.00

CORK & ORREY, JOHN BOYLE, 5TH EARL OF 1707-1762　Letters from Italy, in the Years 1754 and 1755. London: printed for B. White, 1773. 1st edition; small 8vo; 267 pages; half tan calf and cloth boards, ca. 1900, with morocco spine label, one corner slightly skinned, still tight, near fine; a distinguished copy, with bookplate of noted Revolutionary figure Earl Charles Cornwallis, later owner's bookplate.　Chapel Hill 94-197　1996 $250.00

CORLE, EDWIN　Igor Stravinsky. Duell, Sloan & Pearce, 1949. 1st edition; black and white photos; original binding, head and tail of spine and corners bumped, very good in nicked, rubbed, marked and dusty dust jacket, borwned at spine and edges.　Ulysses 39-565　1996 £75.00

CORLETT, WILLIAM THOMAS　The Medicine Man of the American Indian and His Cultural Background. Springfield: Thomas, 1935. 8vo; ix, 369 pages; illustrations; cloth. GM 6461.　James Tait Goodrich K40-94　1996 $145.00

CORMACK, W. E.　Narrative of a Journey Across the Island of Newfoundland in 1822. London: Longmans, Green, 1928. 18.5 cm; xviii, 138 pages; frontispiece, illustrations, map; cloth boards, aged and with slight burn on lower right cover; very good. TPL 4868.　Rockland Books 38-49　1996 $125.00

CORNARO, LEWIS　Sure and Certain Methods of Attaining a Long and Healthful Life, etc. London: D. Midwinter, 1737. th edition; small 12mo; pages xviii, (2), 120; modern full black leather, raised bands, gilt rules and titles, original marbled endpapers; pretty copy. CBEL I 452.　Hartfield 48-L26　1996 $195.00

CORNELIUS, BROTHER　Keith, Old Master of California. New York: & Berkeley: 1942/57. 1st editions; 2 volumes, 631, 296 pages; frontispieces and 90 plates, including 16 in color; very fine set with dust jackets, jacket of volume 1 slightly soiled; presentation inscription, signed by author.　Argonaut Book Shop 113-381　1996 $400.00

CORNELIUS, BROTHER　Keith, Old Master of California. New York: & Berkeley: 1942/57. 1st editions; 2 volumes, volume 1 without dust jacket and not signed, volume 2 in fine condition with slightly chipped dust jacket.　Argonaut Book Shop 113-382　1996 $325.00

CORNELL, F. C.　The Glamour of Prospecting. London: 1920. xiv, 334 pages; folding map, illustrations; new binders cloth, good.　K Books 442-158　1996 £60.00

CORNER, E. J. H.　Wayside Trees of Malaya. Singapore: 1952. 2nd edition; tall 8vo; pages vii, 772; 2 volumes; 228 pages from photos and 259 text figures; cloth, occasional foxing in volume 1, dust jackets with some chipping and scuffing.　Raymond M. Sutton VII-499　1996 $125.00

CORNER, E. J. H.　Wayside Trees of Malaya. Singapore: 1952. 2nd edition; royal 8vo; 2 volumes, 259 text figures, 228 plates; cloth.　Wheldon & Wesley 207-1825　1996 £65.00

CORNER, WILLIAM　San Antonio De Bexar, a Guide and History. San Antonio: Bainbridge, 1890. 1st edition; 166 pages + 28 pages of ads; illustrations, photos; gilt stamped blue cloth, cover lightly faded.　Maggie Lambeth 30-115　1996 $165.00

CORNER, WILLIAM　San Antonio de Bexar. San Antonio: Bainbridge & Corner, 1890. 1st edition; large 8vo; 8, 166 pages + ads; profusely illustrated, map and photo affixed to endpapers, presumably as published; decorated cloth; bright, near fine copy.　Metacomet Books 54-28　1996 $100.00

CORNFORD, L. COPE　A Century of Sea Trading 1824-1924. London: A. & C. Black, 1924. 1st edition; 8vo; 182 pages, color plate; decorated cloth, very good.　John Lewcock 30-166　1996 £70.00

CORNISH, C. J.　The New Forest. 1894. Plates, text drawings; finely bound in tree calf, gilt borders and edges, spine gilt extra. Lovey copy of a scarce item.　David Grayling J95Biggame-248　1996 £80.00

CORNISH, C. J.　The New Forest. London: 1894. Imperia 8vo; plates by Lancelot Speed and others, text drawings; finely bound in tree calf, gilt borders and edges, spine gilt extra; lovely copy, scarce.　David A.H. Grayling MY95Orn-372　1996 £80.00

CORNISH, HENRY　Under the Southern Cross. Madras: at the 'Mail' Press, by J. J. Craen, 1879. 1st edition; demy 8vo; xiv, (370) pages, apparently the author's copy (or perhaps a proof copy), with 11 pages marked with ms. amendments and corrections; contemporary binder's cloth, with local ticket of Lawrence Asylum Press, Madras, covers little splash-marked, top edge little stained, some spotting and browning, mainly of edges, but sound. Ferguson 8704.　Ash Rare Books Zenzybyr-22　1996 £250.00

CORNWELL, PATRICIA　All That Remains. London: Little Brown, 1992. 1st edition; precedes U.S. edition; fine in dust jacket.　Quill & Brush 102-350　1996 $175.00

CORNWELL, PATRICIA　Body of Evidence. New York: Scribners, 1991. 1st edition; signed review copy with slip laid in; fine in dust jacket.　Quill & Brush 102-346　1996 $150.00

CORNWELL, PATRICIA　Body of Evidence. New York: Scribner's, 1991. 1st edition; Author's second book; fine in fine dust jacket; signed by author.　Bella Luna 7-166　1996 $100.00

CORNWELL, PATRICIA　Postmortem. London: Macdonald, 1990. 1st edition; author's firt book; fine in dust jacket.　Quill & Brush 102-348　1996 $200.00

CORNWELL, PATRICIA　Postmortem. New York: Scribners, 1990. 1st edition; author's first book; fine in dust jacket with review slip laid in.　Quill & Brush 102-353　1996 $650.00

THE CORONATION of Her Majesty Queen Elizabeth II, 1953. Worcester: 1953. Limited to 2000 copies; 2 3/4 x 1 15/16 inches; printed in red and black; luxuriously bound in red crushed morocco with double gilt rule and stamping by Sangorski & Sutcliffe, all edges gilt; very fine.　Bromer Booksellers 87-225　1996 $175.00

CORPORATION OF NORWICH　Notices and Illustrations of the Costume, Processions, Pageantry &c., Formerly Displayed by the Corporation of Norwich. Norwich: Charles Muskett, 1850. larage folio; 19 colored and 2 plain plates; contemporary half red morocco, mottled board sides; exceedingly rare; not in Abbey Cat.　Charles W. Traylen 117-371　1996 £400.00

CORREDOR-MATHEOS, J.　Miro's Posters. Barcelona: Poligrafa, 1987. Square 4to; 269 pages, 119 color plates; cloth, dust jacket. Freitag 6564.　Brannan 43-421　1996 $110.00

CORRELL, D. S.　Manual of the Vascular Plants of Texas. Richardson 1979. 8vo; pages xv, 1881; 3 maps; cloth.　Raymond M. Sutton VI-486　1996 $100.00

CORRIE, EDGAR　Letters on the Subject of the Scotch Distillery Laws. Liverpool: M'Creery, 1796. Half title, 23 pates; recent marbled wrappers; nice, inscribed presentation copy from author to Benjamin Bell.　C. R. Johnson 37-7　1996 £150.00

CORRY, JOHN　A Satirical View of London at the Commencement of the 19th Century. London: printed for G. Kearsley; T. Hurst, Ogilvy and Son, R. Ogle and... 1801. 1st edition; 8vo; contemporary half calf, spine gilt, slight rubbing; nice.　Ximenes 108-85　1996 $250.00

CORRY, JOSEPH   Observations Upon the Windward Coast of Africa, the Religion, Character, Customs &c. of the Natives. London: printed for G. and W. Nicol and James Apserne, by W. Bulmer & Co., 1807. 1st edition; 4to; frontispiece, 7 folding plates, all very attractively hand colored, engraved map; modern half calf, spine gilt, minor rubbing; occasional foxing, nice. Abbey Travel 278.   Ximenes 109-86 1996 $2,500.00

CORRY, TREVOR   Descriptive and Scenic Souvenir. The White Pass and Yukon Route. The Scenic Railway of the World... Seattle: 1900. 144 pages; large folding colored map, profusely illustrated with photos and ads; original printed wrappers; very good, very rare. Not in Wickersham. Stephen Lunsford 45-35 1996 $850.00

THE CORSICAN'S Downfall. The Rise, Name, Regin and Final Downfall of Napoleon, Alias Nicolais Buonaparte... Mansfield: printed and sold by B. Robinson for the author, published by Messrs... 1814. 1st edition; 8vo; 175, (1 errata) pages; old blindstamp on corner of first few leaves, recent boards, original printed wrapper laid down on upper cover. James Burmester 29-101 1996 £85.00

CORTAZAR, JULIO   End of the Game. New York: Pantheon, 1967. 1st U.S. edition; fine in unfaded dust jacket, scarce thus.   Lame Duck Books 19-152 1996 $250.00

CORTESE, JAMES   What the Owl Said. Janus Press, 1979. One in an edition of 150 pen numbered copies; 12 x 9 inches; 32 pages; 19 linoleum cut illustrations and one linecut decoration from a pen drawing by Claire Van Vliet, designed, set and printed by Van Vliet, titles printed in black and ochre, text in black, ochre and brown (wtih 6 red star asterisks on 12), linoleum cuts printed in blue, yellow, sap green and two shades of blue, white, dark blue and two shades of yellow; linecut decoration printed in blue, printed on Promatco Heavy Library Endlead; bound in natural Belgain linen over boards, Masonite cut decoration printed in tan on front and back covers; author/title label on spine printed in black on ochre Fabriano cover used also for endpapers; fine. Joshua Heller 21-18 1996 $350.00

CORY, WILLIAM JOHNSON   Lucretilis. Rampant Lions Press, 1951. One of 175 numbered copies; imperial 8vo; printed in handset 18 pt. Walbaum italic, titlepage in black and red, lettering by Will Carter; marbled boards, cloth spine and printed label, head and foot of spine just little rubbed, but very nice, scarce.   Bertram Rota 272-388 1996 £80.00

CORYATE, THOMAS 1577?-1617   Coryats Crudities Hastily gobbled Up in Five Moneths Travells In France, Savoy, Italy, Rhetia Commonly Called the Grisons Country, Helvetia Alias Switzerland, Some Parts of High Germany and the Netherlands. London: by William Stansby, 1611. 1st edition; thick 4to; engraved title (shaved slgihtly at head), engraved plates skillfully inlaid, and engraved plate of clock at Strasburg (shaved at head and foot), woodcut of Prince of Wales' feathers, text portrait of Emperor Frederick IV; errata leaf present; portrait of Prince Henry inserted; late 18th or early 19th century straight grain red morocco, blind tooled panel and gilt fillet on covers, spine tooled in gilt and blind, inner dentelles tooled in gilt and blind, edges gilt, by Charles Hering, with his binder's ticket on endpaper, neat marginal repair to F2; unusually nice. Pforzheimer 218; Grolier Langland to Wither 49; STC 5808.   Joseph J. Felcone 64-15 1996 $7,500.00

COSGRAVE, GEORGE   Early California Justice, The History of the United States District Court for the Southern District of California 1849-1944. San Francisco: Grabhorn Press, 1948. one of 400 copies; original red linen, spine faded and labels chipped, yet sound; titlepage slightly marked, otherwise quite nice.   Meyer Boswell SL26-54 1996 $175.00

COSTARD, GEORGE   The History of Astronomy, with Its Application to Geography, History and Chronology... London: ptd. by James Lister and sold by J. Newbery, 1767. 1st edition; 4to; no half title, double sided engraved plate (foxed), numerous illustrations in text, occasional spotting of text, errata leaf at end, new cloth backed boards, printed paper label. Houzeau and Lancaster 20; Roscoe A98; Welsh pp. 195-96.   Anthony Laywood 108-45 1996 £195.00

COSTELLO, LOUISA STUART   Specimens of the early Poetry of France. London: William Pickering, 1835. 1st edition; 8vo; pages xlix, (i), 298; 4 lithographs, hand colored in colors and gold after illuminated manuscripts; original blindstamped cloth, sometime rebacked retaining original backstrip, good, uncut, large mrgins, most attractive. McLean VBD p. 172; Keynes p. 61.   Claude Cox 107-191 1996 £135.00

THE COSTUME, Manners and Peculiarities of Different Inhabitants of the Globe. London: John Harris, ca. 1830. 6 1/2 x 4 inches; 1 p.l., 16 leaves (printed on one side only); each of the 16 numbered leaves containing a half page hand colored woodcut accompanied by a poem related to the illustration; later green cloth, titled in gilt on front cover, small tear at inner part of one woodcut (repaired with old paper on blank verso), one other minor marginal tear without loss, four leaves cut close at fore edge (with illustration or page number just slightly cropped, bit creased, rather thumbed; very rare. cf. Gumuchian 1881-82.   Phillip J. Pirages 33-125 1996 $200.00

COTES, ROGER   Hydrostatical and Pneumatical Lectures. Cambridge: printed by J. Bentham, for W. Thurlbourn, and sold by J. Beecroft... 1747. 2nd edition; 8vo; 5 folding plates; contemporary calf; fine. Ximenes 108-86 1996 $450.00

THE COTTAGE Fireside. Dublin: C. Bentham, 1821. 12mo; 180 pages; woodcut frontispiece, vignette, title, 3 full page and other smaller woodcut illustrations; half black morocco and marbled boards, covers show light wear, else near fine.   Bromer Booksellers 87-122 1996 $175.00

COTTERELL, CONSTANCE   Summer Holidays in North East England. London: c. 1895. Square 8vo; photos by Paynem Jennings; contemporary calf, fully gilt backstrip, marbled sides; fine.   Petersfield Bookshop FH58-189 1996 £72.00

COTTLE, JOSEPH   Malvern Hills, and Other Poems. London: printed for T. N. Longman and O. Rees, by Biggs and Cottle, 1802. 3rd edition; small 8vo; contemporary tree calf, spine gilt, spine rubbed, upper joint cracked; very good, scarce. 5 copies in NUC; CBEL III 374.   Ximenes 108-87 1996 $175.00

COTTLE, JOSEPH   A New Version of the Pslams of David. London: printed for T. N. Longman and O. Rees, by Biggs and Co., Bristol, 1801. 1st edition; small 8vo; contemporary tree calf, spine gilt, spine quite rubbed, lacks label; aside from the rubbed spine, very good, rare. CBEL III 374.   Ximenes 109-87 1996 $1,750.00

COTTON, ROBERT BRUCE 1571-1631   Cottoni Posthuma: Divers Choice Pieces of that Renowned Antiquary... London: for Richard Lowndes, and Matthew Gilliflower, 1672. 8vo; pages (iv), 351; contemporary sprinkled sheep, red morocco label (chipped), waste leaves from a contemporary Latin glossary used as endpapers, front joint just split at foot, D5-6 browned in fore-edge margin; good, firm copy. Wing C6485; Keynes, Donne pp. 96 and 292.   Simon Finch 24-58 1996 £130.00

COTTON, ROBERT BRUCE 1571-1631   The Danger Wherein the Kingdome Now Standeth and the Remedie. London: n.p., 1628. 1st edition; variant issue; 4to; Roman letter, title dusty, old ink splashed on 2 pages, light age yellowing, quarter calf, marbled boards; overall not a bad copy. STC 5863.2.   A. Sokol XXV-25 1996 £435.00

COUCH, JONATHAN   A History of the Fishes of the British Islands. London: George Bell, 1877. Royal 8vo; 4 volumes, 452 fine colored plates; original blue cloth, gilt emblem on upper covers. Clean copy, plates usually have some foxing.   Charles W. Traylen 117-293 1996 £650.00

COUCH, JONATHAN   A History of the Fishes of the British Islands. London: 1877. Royal 8vo; 4 volumes; 252 colored plates; original blue cloth, fine, clean copy, volume 4 neatly refixed in case.   Wheldon & Wesley 207-959a 1996 £600.00

COUES, E.   Monographs of North American Rodentia. Washington: 1887. 4to; pages xii, x, 1091, 7 plates; original cloth, trifle used. Good ex-library copy, slightly loose in binding.   Wheldon & Wesley 207-548 1996 £75.00

COUES, ELLIOTT   The History of the Lewis and Clark Expedtion. New York: 1893. 1st edition; 4 volumes, cxxxii, 1364 pages, frontispiece, folding map; three quarter leather (contemporary), nice. Beautiful set. Wagner Camp 13; Howes L317; Smith 5902; Graff 2478.   T. A. Swinford 49-244 1996 $750.00

COUES, ELLIOTT   New Light on the Early History of the Greater Northwest. Minneapolis: Ross & Haines, 1965. Reprint of rare 1897 edition, one of 1500 copies; 2 volumes; illustrations, maps, portraits, 3 section folding map plus folding facsimile; original cloth, gilt lettered spines; fine set with publisher's slipcase.   Argonaut Book Shop 113-149 1996 $175.00

COUES, ELLIOTT   On the Trail of a Spanish Pioneer: The Diary and Itinerary of Francisco Garces. New York: Francis P. Harper, 1900. One of 950 copies; 8 7/8 x 6 1/4 inches; 2 volumes, 18 maps, views and facsimiles; blue cloth, light wear to extremities, scratches to rear cover of volume 2; presentation inscription from publisher Harper and his son Lathrop Harper.   Dawson's Books Shop   528-66   1996 $325.00

COULSON, ELIZABETH KERR   Dante and Beatrice from 1282 to 1290. London: Henry S. King & Co., 1876. 1st edition; 8vo; 2 volumes, frontispiece in volume 1, 48 pages publisher's catalog at end of volume 2; original cloth, gilt, slightly worn, uncut; Not in Sadleir or Wolff. Anthony W. Laywood   108-212   1996 £90.00

COULTER, G. W.   Lake Tanganyika and Its Life. London: 1991. 4to; 352 pages, 2 colored and numerous plain illustrations, text figures; hardback.   Wheldon & Wesley   207-308   1996 £60.00

COULTER, HARRIS   Divided Legacy: a History of the Schism in Medical Thought. Washington: 1975-82. 3 volumes, 537, 785, 552 pages; original binding.   W. Bruce Fye   71-423   1996 $150.00

COUPER, ROBERT   The Tourifications of Malachi Meldrum, Esq. of Meldrum-Hall... Aberdeen: by J. Chalmers & Co. for J. Johnson, London: W. Creech, Edinburgh... 1803. 1st edition; 8vo; 2 volumes; pages (ii), 226; 256, (ii); errata leaf present, H6, volume 1, torn at margin where carelessly opened, not affecting text; uncut in original paper backed boards, printed labels, spines defective at ends, labels chipped.   Simon Finch   24-59   1996 £350.00

COURTENAY, JOHN   Juvenile Poems. London: printed by J. Jones, 1795. 1st edition; 8vo; disbound; fine, very rare; presentation copy inscribed to Dudley North. Jackson p. 200.   Ximenes   109-88   1996 $450.00

COURTENAY, JOHN   Philosophical Reflections on the Late Revolution in France, and the Conduct of the Dissenters in England; in a Letter to the Rev. Dr. Priestly. London: T. Becket, 1790. Half title, 94 pages; stabbed pamphlet as issued; uncut.   C. R. Johnson   37-54   1996 £75.00

COURTHION, PIERRE   Geoges Rouault. New York: Abrams, n.d. 4to; 489 pages; 832 illustrations, including 49 tipped in color plates; cloth, dust jacket. Freitag 8420.   Brannan   43-566   1996 $150.00

COURTHION, PIERRE   Georges Rouault. New York: Harry N. Abrams, 1961. 1st edition; 489 pages; fine in very lightly soiled dust jacket. Hermitage   SP95-811   1996 $125.00

COURTNEY, W. P.   Dodsleys Collection of Poetry, Its Contents and Contributors. London: Arthur L. Humphreys, printed for private circulation, 1910. Limited to 75 copies; small 8vo; half calf spine gilt in compartments, raised bands, red morocco, spine labels, headcaps, corners and joints bit worn.   Maggs Bros. Ltd.   1191-78   1996 £70.00

THE COURTSHIP, Merry Marriage and Pic-Nic of Cock Robin and Jenny Wren. London: Griffith and Farran, n.d. ca. 1850. Narrow 8vo; 17 pages; hand colored frontispiece and hand colored illustrations; printed green card wrappers, covers soiled, spine neatly overstitched, pages browned at edges, else very good.   Marjorie James   19-208   1996 £85.00

COUSE, ERWINA L.   Button Classics. Chicago: Lightner Publishing, 1942. 2nd edition; quarto; 249 pages; color and black and white illustrations; extremities rubbed, else near fine.   Bromer Booksellers   90-12   1996 $275.00

COUSIN, VICTOR   Report on the State of Public Instruction in Prussia... London: Effingham Wilson, 1834. 1st English edition; 5 folding plans; original boards, green cloth spine, paper label, very good. Jarndyce   103-455   1996 £90.00

COVENTRY, FRANCIS   The History of Pompey the Little, or the Life and Adventures of a Lap-dog. Waltham St. Lawrence: Golden Cockerel Press, 1926. Number 332 of 400 copies; 8vo; pages xvi, 225 + colophon; frontispiece and tailpiece wood engravings by David Jones; unopened, original buckram backed boards, backstrip darkened and slightly marked; good, uncut. Chanticleer 44.   Claude Cox   107-62   1996 £85.00

COVENY, CHRISTOPHER   Twenty Scenes from the Works of Dickens. Sydney: printed for Thomas H. Fielding, 1883. 4to; additional etched titlepage and 21 etched plates; 3 or 4 margins slightly stained, but not affecting engraved area, descriptive leaf adjacent to each plate; original half morocco, covers rubbed and worn.   Thomas Thorp   489-86   1996 £195.00

COVERTE, ROBERT   A True and Almost Incredible Report of an Englishman that...Travelled by Land Thorow Many Unknowne Kingdomes and Great Cities. London: by I.N. for Hugh Perry, 1631. 4to; pages (vi), 68, (ii), without first and last blanks, Black letter; woodcut ornaments and initials; 19th century calf, spine gilt; early autograph 'Burton' at head of title, running title shaved on couple of leaves; good, clean copy. STC 5897. Lowndes 539; JFB C529; not in Kress. 4 copies in NUC.   A. Sokol   XXV-26   1996 £2,450.00

COWAN, ROBERT ERNEST   A Bibliography of the Spanish Press of California, 1833-1845. San Francisco: Robert Ernest Cowan, 1919. 10 1/8 x 7 inches; 31 pages; printed white wrappers, mild overall soiling to wrappers.   Dawson's Books Shop   528-67   1996 $100.00

COWARD, NOEL 1899-1973   Bitter Sweet and Other Plays. Garden City: Doubleday, Doran, 1929. Signed, limited edition of 1000 numbered copies; gilt black cloth in (supplied) acetate dust jacket, very good, tasteful bookplate, both hinges appear to have been cracked at one time, but have been tightened.   Antic Hay   101-359   1996 $225.00

COWARD, NOEL 1899-1973   Peace In Our Time. Garden City: Doubleday, 1948. 1st American edition; small 8vo; cloth, in dust jacket with some minor wear; very good. Signed presentation from author. Antic Hay   101-360   1996 $175.00

COWARD, NOEL 1899-1973   The Vortex, a Play in Three Acts. London: Ernest Benn Ltd., 1925. 1st edition; 8vo; original bue cloth with printed labels on spine and upper cover; appears to have been issued without a protective dust jacket; lovely, near fine copy with light and even browning to pages and just little darkening to spine and spine label; presentation copy, inscribed to George Bernard Shaw's secretary, Blanche Patch, from Coward.   Lakin & Marley   3-8   1996 $850.00

COWDRY, E. V.   Arteriosclerosis: a Survey of the Problem. New York: 1933. 1st edition; 617 pages; original binding.   W. Bruce Fye   71-428   1996 $150.00

COWELL, JOHN   Institvtiones Ivris Anglicani, ad Methodvm et Seriem Institvtionvm Imperialium Compositae & Digestae. Frankfurt: Fitzer, 1630. 2nd edition; 8vo; vellum; Shaaber C359.   Rostenberg & Stern   150-43   1996 $500.00

COWELL, JOHN   The Interpreter; or Booke, Containing the Signification of Words. London: William Sheares, 1637. 2nd or 3rd edition; 4to; unpaginated, ff. (iv), 312; title printed within double ruled border, text printed in double column within borders, paper repair to corner of D4 affecting a few letters; contemporary sprinkled dark sheep, rebacked with slightly lighter calf, blind ruled, backstrip with modern red morocco gilt lettered label, endpapers lifted, very good. Cordell C130; Kennedy 8582. STC 5902.   Blackwell's   B112-79   1996 £475.00

COWLEY, ABRAHAM 1618-1667   The Works...Consisting of Those Which Were Formerly Printed and Those Which He Design'd for the Press, Now Published Out of the Authors Original Copies. London: J. M. for Henry Herringman, 1668. 1st collected edition, 1st issue; folio; (xlii), 41, (i), 80, (iv), 70 (=68), 154, 23, (i), 148 pages; frontispiece, 3 secondary titlepages; contemporary calf, neatly rebacked in morocco, label; two corners little worn, scattered minor browning and staining, good, clean copy. Wing C6649; Perkin B1.   Robert Clark   38-34   1996 £200.00

COWPER, H. S.   The Oldest Register Book of the Parish of Hawkshead in Lancashire. 1568-1704. London: Bemrose & Sons, 1897. 1st edition; large 8vo; pages civ, 453; 4 illustrations; original cloth, gilt, little worn and marked, lower boards bumped at corners; little spotting or browning in places, upper joint cracked.   R.F.G. Hollett & Son   78-578   1996 £120.00

COWPER, HENRY SWAINSON   Hawkshead: (The Northermost Parish of Lancashire) Its History, Archaeology, Industries, Folklore, Dialect, Etc. Etc. London: Bemrose & Sons, 1899. 1st edition; large 8vo; pages xvi, 580; 2 colored folding maps, 32 illustrations; original buckram gilt, spine and upper board edges rather faded, dust jacket (rather worn and repaired on reverse), top edge gilt, very good, sound copy, scarce in scarce wrapper.   R.F.G. Hollett & Son   78-832   1996 £210.00

COWPER, HENRY SWAINSON   Hawkshead. London: Bemrose & Sons, 1899. 1st edition; large 8vo; pages xvi, 580; 2 colored folding maps, 32 illustrations; original buckram gilt, little rubbed, spine and edges rather faded; joints strengthened, but very good, sound copy; ALS from P. Hildew loosely inserted.   R.F.G. Hollett & Son 78-833 1996 £195.00

COWPER, HENRY SWAINSON   Registers of the Parish of Aldingham in Furness 1542-1695; Registers of the Parish Church of Coniston, Lancashire 1599-1700. Wigan: Stowger & Son, 1907. 8vo; pages 161, 58, (ix), 2 plates; original cloth, gilt.   R.F.G. Hollett & Son 78-574 1996 £85.00

COWPER, WILLIAM 1731-1800   Olney Hymns in Three Books. London: printed and sold by W. Oliver, sold also by J. Buckland & J. Johnson, 1779. 1st edition; 12mo; full brown morocco, all edges gilt; not common; very narrow blank strip trimmed from top of titlepage, some foxing, but very good; contemporary clergyman has neatly annotated each hymn to indiate occasions of use. Russell 21. Rothschild 680. Ximenes 109-89 1996 $750.00

COWPER, WILLIAM 1731-1800   Poems. London: printed for J. Johnson, 1782. 1st edition; 8vo; few copies are known with preface by Rev. Newton, but these leaves were suppressed and are not present here; contemporary calf, gilt, spine gilt, rebacked, original spine laid down, corners restored; very good.   Ximenes 108-90 1996 $300.00

COWPER, WILLIAM 1731-1800   Poems. (with) The Task. London: Johnson, 1782/85. 1st editions; octavo; 2 volumes, 367, 359 pages; beautifully bound by Riviere and son in full dark blue morocco, covers outlined with a triple gilt rule, spine gilt in 6 compartments, showing elaborate floral devices, turn-ins richly gilt with floral border; housed together in morocco backed pull-off box; very fine; bookplates of H. Bradley Martin. Rothschild 681; Hayward I 191; Grolier English II 60. Bromer Booksellers 90-21 1996 $1,000.00

COWPER, WILLIAM 1731-1800   Poems... London: J. Johnson, 1786. 2nd edition; 8vo; 2 volumes bound together; half title in volume 2 (not called for in volume 1), pages (iv), 367, (1) blank; (viii), 359, (1); contemporary quarter dark brown calf, rubbed, smooth backstrip divided by gilt rules, red leather gilt lettered label, slight loss at head, marbled boards, modern calf tips, early owner's name on upper pastedown (D. Gel, Hopton), early owner's name (S. Gell, Hopton); generally excellent. Blackwell's B112-80 1996 £150.00

COWPER, WILLIAM 1731-1800   Poems. London: printed for J. Johnson, 1794-95. 6th edition; 8vo; 2 volumes; contemporary mottled calf, spines gilt, contrasting green and black morocco labels, very slight rubbing, tiny blemish on spine; fine and attractive set. Russell 78. Ximenes 108-91 1996 £400.00

COWPER, WILLIAM 1731-1800   Poems. London: J. Johnson, 1798. 1st illustrated edition; foolscap 8vo; no half titles, as issued, 2 volumes; pages (iv), x, 324; iv, (iv), 335, (1); 10 engraved plates; contemporary marbled calf, smooth backstrips divided by gilt rules, red and blue title and volume labels, crest and name (P. Gell) stamped on upper pastedown within wash shield surround, speckled edges; excellent. Russell 83.   Blackwell's B112-81 1996 £85.00

COWPER, WILLIAM 1731-1800   Poems. London: printed for J. Johnson and Co., 1812. 6 3/4 x 4 1/4 inches; 2 volumes; very pleasing contemporary blond straight grain morocco, sides framed with lovely latticework border in gilt and blind, raised bands, spines attractively gilt in compartments featuring multiple plain and decorative rules and large scrolling and floral ornament at center, all edges gilt, spines evenly darkened to pleasing honey brown, very slight rubbing at spine ends, otherwise an ornate and charming contemporary set in fine condition, nearly immaculate internally; armorial bookplate of John Mackenzie of Dunvegan and with presentation inscription from Lydia to Alice Rigby. Phillip J. Pirages 33-140 1996 $165.00

COWPER, WILLIAM 1731-1800   The Poetical Works... London: Henry G. Bohn, 1851. 8vo; pages xxiv, 516; frontispiece, extra engraved title (both foxed), 2 portraits and one view (slightly foxed), 18 engraved plates; contemporary green hard grained morocco, sides tooled with wide gilt dentelle order made up of a large number of individual tools, spine divided into six panels by raised bands, elaborately tooled in gilt, lettered in second panel, gilt inner dentelles, pale yellow endpapers, gilt edges, spine slightly darkened and rubbed at head and tail, handsome binding by John Wright; contemporary presentation inscription to Arthur Pemberton Lonsdale on his leaving Eton on front blank.   Simon Finch 24-61 1996 £180.00

COX, CHARLES E.   John Tobias, Sportsman. New York: Derrydale Press, 1937. 1st edition; one of 950 numbered copies; 8vo; illustrations by Aiden Ripley; near fine. Siegel 119; Frazier C15a.   Glenn Books 36-67 1996 $110.00

COX, EDWARD YOUNG   The Art of Garnishing Churches at Christmas and Other Festivals. London: Cox and Son, 1868. 8vo; (viii), 68, (12) pages, 27 plates, 4 are mounted photos; publisher's cloth, some cover wear, good copy only. Gernsheim 416.   Bookpress 75-100 1996 $375.00

COX, GEORGE   Black Gowns and Red Coats, or Oxford in 1834. London: James Ridgway and Sons, 1834. 1st edition of first part, 2nd edition of rest; 8vo; 6 parts in one volume; contemporary half red morocco; with leaf of ads at end of parts II and III; some foxing but in very good condition. Cordeaux and Merry 4959; Calry Oxford Collection 773; Jackson p. 578.   Ximenes 108-92 1996 $200.00

COX, GEORGE   Black Gowns and Red Coats, or Oxford in 1834. London: James Ridgway & Sons, 1834. Parts 2-6 state 'Second Edition'; 8vo; 6 parts in 1; 24, 32; 32; 24; 32, 30 pages; half contemporary red calf over marbled boards, bit rubbed.   Kenneth Karmiole 1NS-84 1996 $125.00

COX, ISAAC   The Annals of Trinity County. Eugene: printed for Harold C. Holmes, 1940. One of 350 copies; xxix, 265 pages; half cloth, boards, paper spine label, bookplate, owner's ink notation, otherwise fine with slipcase; presentation signed by printer, John Henry Nash, to Harry Butler, ink notation by Butler under presentation. Howes C819; Rocq 15151.   Argonaut Book Shop 113-150 1996 $165.00

COX, J. M.   A Cultural Table of Orchidaceous Plants. Sydney: 1946. Tall 8vo; pages (6), xiii, 378; 57 plates; cloth (light wear), dust jacket. Raymond M. Sutton VI-882 1996 $115.00

COX, JAMES   Historical and Biographical Record of the Cattle Industry and the Cattlemen of Texas and Adjacent Territory. New York: Antiquarian Press, 1959. Reprint of the excessively rare 1895 edition; one of 550 copies; folio; 2 volumes; 743 pages, plus colored frontispiece and numerous illustrations; original blind and gilt stamped cowhide and buckram, very fine set with slipcase. Adams 593; Dobie p. 100; Dykes Kid 29; Graff 891; Howes C820.   Argonaut Book Shop 113-151 1996 $300.00

COX, M. J.   The Snakes of Thailand and Their Husbandry. Melbourne: 1991. 8vo; 564 pages; 164 colored illustrations; hardbound.   Wheldon & Wesley 207-915 1996 £70.00

COX, MARY L.   History of Hale County Texas. Plainview: n.p., 1937. 1st edition; 230 pages; scarce. CBC 2140.   Maggie Lambeth 30-117 1996 $125.00

COX, MORRIS   Blind Drawings... Gogmagog Press, 1978. Of 75 numbered copies, signed by author and artist/printer, this is one of 30 with plates on 'akebi', 'sakura', 'nemu' and natural Japanese handmade papers, with original signed blind drawing as frontispiece; fine, laid in are original prospectus and Franklin's Christmas card reproducing one of the drawings.   Bertram Rota 272-160 1996 £450.00

COX, MORRIS   Blind Drawings... Gogmagog Press, 1978. Of 75 numbered copies, signed by author and artist/printer, this one of 40 with plates on 'mingei' colored handmade papers; small folio; 24 plates engraved from line drawings; half vellum, Japanese patterned paper sides; fine.   Bertram Rota 272-159 1996 £300.00

COX, MORRIS   Crash!: An Experiment in Blockmaking and Printing. Gogmagog Press, 1963. One of 80 copies; 8vo; boards, backstrip slightly faded and creased, but very nice, with variant proofs, unfolded and two spreads.   Bertram Rota 272-156 1996 £350.00

COX, MORRIS   An Impression of Autumn: a Landscape Panorama. Gogmagog Press, 1966. One of 100 numbered copies, signed by Cox; 8vo; original monotype printed boards; fine.   Bertram Rota 272-158 1996 £300.00

COX, MORRIS   An Impression of Winter: a Landscape Panorama. Gogmagog Press, 1965. One of 100 numbered copies, signed by Cox; 8vo; original monotype printed boards; fine.   Bertram Rota 272-157 1996 £300.00

COX, NICHOLAS   The Gentleman's Recreation. London: J. Dawks for N. Nolls, 1697. 4th edition; 8vo; (vi), 138, 91, 2-78, 71, (i), 90, (ii), 101, (ix) pages; frontispiece, 4 folding plates, corners little rubbed, first plate torn along lower edge with some loss of image; early 20th century antique style panelled calf, gilt, rebacked, preserving old decorated gilt spine and label; worming in lower margin of early leaves, affecting a few letters on some pages, minor staining and foxing, with these defects, still a pleasant copy. Wing C6707.   Robert Clark 38-35 1996 £175.00

COX, NICHOLAS   The Gentleman's Recreation. London: F. Collins for N. Cox, 1706. 5th edition; (8), 138; 90; 78; 72; 106; (2), 102 pages; frontispiece, 4 folding plates; 18th century polished calf, rebacked, red leather spine label, text somewhat browned, as usual.   Kenneth Karmiole 1NS-230 1996 $450.00

COX, PALMER   The Brownies Abroad. New York: 1899. 11th printing; 10 x 8 inches; 144 pages; drawings by Cox. glazed pictorial boards, extremities frayed some, still nice in rubbed and soiled dust jacket with slight spine chipping.   John K. King 77-591 1996 $150.00

COX, THOMAS   Westmorland. London: Sold by M. Nutt, 1720-21. Square 8vo; pages 46; folding engraved map; quarter roan gilt, hinges little rubbed, edge of final leaf trifle dusty.   R.F.G. Hollett & Son 78-836 1996 £85.00

COX, THOMAS   Westmorland. London: sold by E. and R. Nutt and T. Cox, 1731. Square 8vo; pages 46; folding engraved map, engraved chart, old cloth, gilt.   R.F.G. Hollett & Son 78-837 1996 £95.00

COX, WALLY   Ralph Makes Good. New York: Simon and Schuster, 1965. 1st edition; 1st printing; 8vo; color pictorial boards, with drawing by Cox; very good; author's second book, signed and inscribed by him. George J. Houle 68-39 1996 $125.00

COXE, DANIEL   A Description of the English Province, of Carolina, by the Spaniards Called Florida and by the French La Louisiane. St. Louis: Churchill and Harris, Printers, 1840. 1st American edition; 8vo; 6, 90 pages, large folding engraved map; folds of map weak and one entirely broken, map complete; modern buckram. Howes C826. Not in Imprints Survey; Clark I 68.   M & S Rare Books 60-331 1996 $600.00

COXE, JOHN REDMAN   The Philadelphia Medical Dictionary. Philadelphia: Thomas Dobson, 1817. 2nd edition; 8vo; viii, 433, (1 blank), (2) pages; later quarter calf; some minor and sporadic foxing, else very good; Austin 560.   The Bookpress 75-404 1996 $225.00

COXE, JOHN REDMAN   The Writings of Hippocrates and Galen Epitomised from the Original Latin Translations. Philadelphia: Lindsay & Blakiston, 1846. 8vo; xvi, 682 pages; original full sheep, rubbed, lacking spine label, occasional foxing, else good. Very scarce. Iowa 1288. James Tait Goodrich K40-95 1996 $175.00

COXE, WILIAM   A View of the Cultivation of Fruit Trees and the Management of Orchards and Cider. Philadelphia: 1817. 1st edition; 8vo; pages 253, (15); 77 wood engraved plates; contemporary tree calf, light wear and rubbing, some dark edge browning to title, occasional mild browning in text, including plates, minor foxing, rear blank leaves missing, bookplate with name removed.   Raymond M. Sutton VII-6 1996 $550.00

COZZENS, JAMES GOULD   Michael Scarlett. New York: A. & C. Boni, 1925. 1st edition; contemporary bookplate, fine in very good dust jacket with shallow chipping at upper extremities, half inch at deepest point (at one corner of crown), long tear along rear gutter; uncommon. Between the Covers 42-115 1996 $225.00

COZZENS, SAMUEL WOODWORTH   The Marvellous Country; or, Three Years in Arizona and New Mexico, the Apaches' Home...and a Description of the Author's Guide, Cochise, the Great Apache War Chief... Boston: Shepard and Gill, 1873. 1st edition; 532 pages; double frontispiece, 100 wood engraved illustrations; original three quarter morocco and marbled boards, light rubbing to extremities, owner's name on blank flyleaf, overall fine. Graff 898; Howes C838; larned 623. Argonaut Book Shop 113-153 1996 $225.00

CRABBE, GEORGE 1754-1832   The Library. A Poem. London: printed for J. Dodsley, 1783. 2nd edition; 4to; disbound; very good, complete with final blank; Barcham and Gatrell A4; Jackson p. 101; CBEL II 610. Ximenes 108-94 1996 $650.00

CRABBE, GEORGE 1754-1832   Peter Grimmes. London: Old Stile Press, 1985. 53/220 copies, royal 8vo; printed on St. Cuthbert's Mill paper and signed by artist; pages 35, (2); 19 linocuts printed in brown and green; original illustrated canvas of various hues of green, backstrip lettered in green, cloth and board slipcase, fine.   Blackwell's B112-215 1996 £50.00

CRABBE, GEORGE 1754-1832   The Poetical Works of the Rev. George Crabbe, with His Letters and Journals and His Life. London: John Murray, 1835. New edition; 8vo; 8 volumes; frontispieces; full scarlet diced calf, triple gilt rule border to boards, tiny ornamental gilt corner pieces, corners bumped, green morocco labels to spines, extensive gilt tooling to spine, uniform marbled edges and endpapers, some slight dampstaining to couple of volumes, some very light foxing to few pages. Lowndes I p. 545.   Beeleigh Abbey BA56-141 1996 £250.00

CRABBE, GEORGE 1754-1832   The Complete Poetical Works. Oxford: Clarendon Press, 1988. Sole edition; 8vo; 3 volumes, pages l, 820; v, (i), 1010; x, 540; 3 portrait frontispieces, illustrations; original blue cloth, gilt lettered, glassine jackets; excellent.   Blackwell's B112-82 1996 £165.00

CRABBE, GEORGE 1754-1832   The Works of the Rev. George Crabbe. London: John Murray, 1823. Small 8vo; 8 volumes; full black straight grain morocco, decorative gilt borders to covers, inner blind rule and corner ornaments, fully gilt decorated spines, gilt edges, narrow inner gilt dentelles, red endpapers, ink inscriptions to all volumes; each volume with a fore-edge painting of London, all paintings in bright clean state and in excellent condition; upper hinges cracked to volumes 2 and 8. Beeleigh Abbey BA/56-6 1996 £3,000.00

CRABBE, HARRIETTE   Edith Vernon; or, Contrasts of Character. London: Hope & Co., 1855. 1st edition; 8vo; 2 volumes; original green cloth, spines sunned, slightly rubbed; rare, very good. Not in Wolff. Ximenes 109-90 1996 $450.00

CRABTREE, ADAM   Animal Magnetism, Early Hypnotism and Psychical Research, 1766-1925. An Annotated Bibliography. New York: 1988. 1st edition; 522 pages; original binding; GM 5019.21.   W. Bruce Fye 71-430 1996 $100.00

CRACE, JIM   Continent. London: Heinemann, 1986. 1st edition; original cloth; fine in fine dust jacket; inscribed by author.   Beasley Books 82-43 1996 $100.00

A CRACKER Bon-Bon for Christmas Parties; Consisting of Christmas Tree Pieces for Private Representation. London: David Bogue, 1852. 1st edition; 8vo; pages iv, 3-99; pretty hand colored frontispiece and engraved characters; original red blindstamped cloth, gilt, all edges gilt, lovely copy.   Sotheran PN32-103 1996 £78.00

CRADOCK, JOSEPH   An Account of some of the Most Romantic Parts of North Wales. London: printed for T. Davies and T. Cadell, 1777. small 8vo; iv, 147, (1) pages, folding map and 3 engraved plates on 2 leaves; contemporary mottled calf, gilt panelled spine and red gilt label; very good, joints and head of spine expertly repaired.   Ken Spelman 30-68 1996 £220.00

CRAFTS, WILLIAM   A Selection, in Prose and Poetry, from the Miscellaneous Writings of the Late William Crafts. Charleston: C. C. Sebring and J. S. Burges, 1828. 1st edition; 8vo; 50, (1), 384 pages; original two toned paper covered boards, printed paper label on spine, some minor soiling and chipping of boards; Shoemaker 32846.   M & S Rare Books 60-144 1996 $150.00

CRAIG, EDWARD GORDON 1872-1966   Books and Theatres. London: 1925. 1st edition; 164 pages, 32 plates and 3 illustrations; moderate wear, but very good, acceptable copy; ownership signature of John Mason Brown. Note pasted in; signed by author.   Lyman Books 21-94 1996 $175.00

CRAIG, EDWARD GORDON 1872-1966   Gordon Craig's Paris Diary 1932-1933. Bird & Bull Press, 1982. One of 350 numbered copies; small 4to; 8 pages of colored facsimiles; printed in Baskerville, zodiacal devices in colors; half brown morocco, Japanese patterned paper sides, fine.   Bertram Rota 272-33 1996 £115.00

CRAIG, EDWARD GORDON 1872-1966   The Last Eight Years 1958-1966. Andoversford: Whittington Press, 1983. 1st edition; 93/250 copies (of an edition of 345 copies); 8vo; pages (vii), 49, (1), printed in brown on cream Sommerville laid paper and signed by Craig, plate by Dame Laura Knight tipped to form frontispiece, 4 wood engravings; original quarter mid brown canvas, printed label, marbled orange and yellow boards, untrimmed, fine.   Blackwell's B112-286 1996 £60.00

CRAIG, EDWARD GORDON 1872-1966   Woodcuts and Some Words. New York: E. P. Dutton and Co. Inc., 1924. 1st American edition bookplate to front pastedown, light foxing to prelims, some overall darkening, more so to spine, else very good. E.P. Dutton imprint pasted over London imprint on titlepage.   Hermitage SP95-771 1996 $100.00

CRAIG, MAURICE   Irish Bookbindings 1600-1800. London: Cassell, 1954. 1st edition; folio; 60 pages, 58 plates; cloth, fine, one tip bruised, else very good.   The Bookpress 75-283 1996 $385.00

CRAIG, MAURICE   Irish Bookbindings 1600-1800. London: Cassell & Co. Ltd., 1954. 1st edition; large 4to; colored frontispiece, 58 plates, upper cover slightly cockled, original cloth, spine gilt, top edge gilt. Forest Books 74-52 1996 £195.00

CRAIG, WILLIAM MARSHALL   Description of the Plates Representing the Intinerant Traders of London in Their Ordinary Costume... London: n.d., c. 1804. Small 4to; 31 hand colored etched plates each with facing page of descriptive text, all bar seven plates have a grey wash border, plates all in very good condition with no foxing, light offsetting to letterpress only, text watermarked 1803 & majority of plates watermarked Whatman 1804, plate 3 'Baskets' watermarked E. & P. 1801, title to plate 12 'Green Hasteds" rather than 'Green Hastings" given in Abbey, new endpapers and prelims; bound by Riviere, full modern French styled mottled calf, triple gilt rule borders to boards, elaborate gilt tooling to panelled spine, green morocco labels to spine raised bands, grey speckled endpapers, very handsome copy. Abbey Life 271.   Beeleigh Abbey BA56-235 1996 £1,500.00

CRAIK, DINAH MARIA MULOCK 1826-1887   John Halifax, Gentleman. London: Hurst and Blackett, 1586. 1st edition; 8vo; 3 volumes, no half titles, but none called for, 3 pages ads, and 24 page undated publisher's catalog at end of volume 1, one page of ads at end of volume 2, and one leaf of ads end of volume 3; drab endpapers; original brown wavy grain cloth blocked in blind on covers, lettered gilt on spines, Leighton Son & Hodge's ticket inside back cover of volume 1, small hole in outer side margins of one leaf of volume 3, just touching one letter at end of one line only, slight wear at head and foot of each spine, but excellent copy, without ownership marks or traces of labels. Sadleir 1812. Wolff 4996; Carter's A Binding.   David Bickersteth 133-160 1996 £260.00

CRAIK, GEORGE LILLIE   English Causes Celebres; or Reports of Remarkable Trials. London: Charles Knight & Co., Ludgate Street, 1844. three quarter morocco, spine gilt, embrowned, still pretty.   Meyer Boswell SL25-57 1996 $175.00

CRAIK, GEORGE LILLIE   The History of British Commerce, from the Earliest Times. London: Charles Knight & Co., 1844. 1st edition in book form; 12mo; 3 volumes, 272, 220, 284 pages, cancelled Board of Customs stamp on endpapers (but not elsewhere); contemporary dark blue half calf gilt, slightly rubbed, else very good set. Kress C6267. Goldsmiths 33719. Williams I 390.   John Drury 82-61 1996 £90.00

CRAIK, JOHN L.   The New Zealanders... London: Nattali, 1847. 12mo; pages iv, 424, map, text illustrations; modern cloth, leather label, Hocken p. 46.   Richard Adelson W94/95-224 1996 $175.00

CRAKES, SYLVESTER   Five Years a Captive Among the Black-Feet Indians. Columbus: Osgood & Pearce, 1858. 1st edition; 224 pages; frontispiece and plates; original black embossed cloth, title in gilt on spine, very good, exceedingly rare. Braislin sale 508; Howes C850; Graff 903; Ayer Supp. 37;   Michael D. Heaston 23-123 1996 $1,750.00

CRAMER, GABRIEL   Introduction a l'analyse des Lignes Courbes Algebriques. Geneva: chez les Freres Cramer & Cl. Philibert, 1750. 1st edition; 4to; xxiii, 680, (xii) pages, folding table at p. 672 and 33 folding plates in rear; title printed in red and black; original calf with richly gilt spine compartments and contrasting red morocco label with gilt floral devices at corners, binding cracked but quite sound; very good. Zeitlinger/Sotheran I 892; Honeyman Sale II 775.   Edwin V. Glaser 121-71 1996 $1,200.00

CRAMP, S.   Handbook of the Birds of Europe, the Middle East and North Africa. (Birds of Western Palearctic) Volume 4 Terns to Woodpeckers. Oxford: 1985. 4to; 960 pages; 98 color plates, numerous maps and figures; dust jacket.   John Johnson 135-505 1996 $100.00

CRAMP, STANLEY   Handbook of the Birds of Europe, the Middle East and North Africa. Volume I. Ostrich to Ducks. London: 1977. Many color and other plates; mint in dust jacket.   David A.H. Grayling MY95Orn-20 1996 l70.00

CRAMP, STANLEY   Handbook of the Birds of Europe, the Middle East and North Africa. Volume 2. Hawks to Bustards. London: 1980. Numerous color and other plates, maps, tables; fine in dust jacket. David A.H. Grayling MY95Orn-22 1996 £70.00

CRAMP, STANLEY   Handbook of the Birds of Europe, the Middle East & North Africa. Volume 2. Hawks to Bustards. London: 1980. Numerous color and other plates, maps, tables; no dust jacket, otherwise mint. David A.H. Grayling MY95Orn-23 1996 £65.00

CRAMP, STANLEY   Handbook of the Birds of Europe, the Middle East and North Africa. Volume 3. Waders to Gulls. London: 1983. Numerous color and other plates, maps, tables; mint in dust jacket.   David A.H. Grayling MY95Orn-25 1996 £70.00

CRAMP, STANLEY   Handbook of the Birds of Europe, the Middle East & North Africa. Volume 4. Terns to Woodpeckers. London: 1985. Numerous color and other plates, maps, tables, etc; mint in dust jacket David A.H. Grayling MY95Orn-24 1996 £70.00

CRAMP, STANLEY   Handbook of the Birds of Europe, the Middle East and North Africa. Volume 5. Tyrant Flycatchers to Thrushes. London: 1988. Many color and other plates; mint in dust jacket.   David A.H. Grayling MY95Orn-21 1996 £70.00

CRANBORNE, JAMES CECIL, VISCOUNT   Ten Weeks from Home in the Spring of 1857...Being Leaves from the Diary of a Blind Traveller. London: John Mitchell, 1858. 1st edition; 8vo; original pale green glazed printed wrappers, slight wear. Fine, rare. Not in Blackmer.   Ximenes 109-91 1996 $225.00

CRANDALL, NORMA   Emily Bronte. London: Rindge, Richard Smith, 1957. 1st edition; 8 1/2 x 5 1/2 inches; pages xv, 160; 4 page prospectus loosely inserted, frontispiece and one illustration; blue cloth, name label, very good in slightly worn and marked dust jacket, scarce. Ian Hodgkins 78-286 1996 £60.00

CRANE, E.   Bees and Beekeeping, Science, Practice and World Resources. Ithaca: 1990. 4to; pages xvii, 614; numerous illustrations; cloth, dust jacket.   Raymond M. Sutton VII-888 1996 $110.00

CRANE, HART 1899-1932   The Bridge. New York: Horace Liveright, 1930. 1st trade edition, 2nd edition, extensively revised and corrected; 8vo; frontispiece by Walker evans; original blue cloth, covers slightly rubbed, but very good; presentation copy inscribed by author for Paul Rosenfeld, important association copy.   James S. Jaffe 34-120 1996 $12,000.00

CRANE, HART 1899-1932   Voyages: Six Poems for White Buildings. New York: Museum of Modern Art, 1957. One of 1000 copies, including 25 hors commerce, all signed and numbered by Baskin on colophon; page size 9 1/2 x 11 inches; text on Amalfi paper; 7 original wood engravings on Moriki paper, 4 hors-texte and 3 in texte; blue wrappers housed in faded blue folding case; The Artist and the Book 16. Priscilla Juvelis 95/1-104 1996 $300.00

CRANE, LUCY   Art and the Formation of Taste: Six Lectures. London: Macmillan, 1882. 1st edition; 12mo; xiii, (i), 292, (4) pages; 6 plates; 13 in text illustrations; publisher's cloth, minor cover wear, else fine; Bookpress 75-32 1996 $275.00

CRANE, STEPHEN 1871-1900   The Black Riders and Other Lines. Boston: Copeland and Day, 1895. 1st edition; one of 500 copies; 12mo; white paper boards beautifully decorated with a lily motif in an art deco style, head of spine little rubbed, binding very slightly dusty, otherwise a fine copy, housed in quarter morocco clamshell slipcase; the Bradley Martin copy with his bookplate.   Captain's Bookshelf 38-47 1996 $1,500.00

CRANE, STEPHEN 1871-1900   Great Battles of the World. Philadelphia: 1901. 1st edition; illustrations by John Sloan; decorated covers gilt, top edge gilt, extremities little rubbed; fine.   Polyanthos 22-224 1996 $125.00

CRANE, STEPHEN 1871-1900   The Little Regiment and Other Episodes of the American Civil War. London: William Heinemann, 1897. 1st English edition; 8vo; 5, 150 pages, plus ads; original white stamped slate green cloth, binding slightly rubbed, but very good, with W. H. Smith & Son's Sub. Library London label pasted inside fron tcover. Very scarce.   M & S Rare Books 60-145 1996 $325.00

CRANE, STEPHEN 1871-1900   Maggie A Girl of the Streets. London: Limited Editions Club, 1974. Limited to 2000 copies, this number 394; signed by artist; illustrations by Sigmund Abeles; fine in slipcase. Hermitage SP95-964 1996 $100.00

CRANE, STEPHEN 1871-1900   The Open Boat and Other Stories. London: 1898. 1st English edition; spine dull and little rubbed at head and foot, otherwise very good, scarce.   Words Etcetera 94-331 1996 £75.00

CRANE, STEPHEN 1871-1900   The Red Badge of Courage. New York: Random House, 1931. Limited to 980 numbered copies; this copy label "Review"; folio; 142 pages, printed in red and black in handset Goudy Modern on Van Gelder paper; titlepage illustration, 24 headpieces and tailpiece by Valenti Angelo; quarter black cloth over blue decorative boards with red leather spine label stamped in gilt; fine in original black cloth slipcase. Grabhorn Bib. 154.   Heritage Book Shop 196-187 1996 $175.00

CRANE, THOMAS   London Town. London: Marcus Ward, 1883. 4to; 56 chromolithographic pages printed in colors on stiff paper; pictorial boards.   Marlborough 162-123 1996 £75.00

CRANE, WALTER 1845-1915   Eight Illustrations to Shakespeare's Two Gentlemen of Verona. Dallas: Dallastype Press, for J. M. Dent & Co., 1894. Limited edition of 650 numbered copies, signed by artist and engraver, title printed in red and black, elaborate border, 8 engravings on India paper, each with its own card window mount and protective glasine guard (this bearing a caption), loose as issued in foldover cloth box, lettered and decorated gilt (upper hinge of box split, several mounts slightly foxed, but engravings clean apart from two which are also slightly foxed);   Thomas Thorp 489-74 1996 £120.00

CRANE, WALTER 1845-1915   The First of May, a Fairy Masque; Presented in a Series of 52 Designs. Boston: James R. Osgood & Co., 1881. Apparently a facsimile reprint of the London proof edition, limited to 200 copies, signed by Crane, this is the first American edition; oblong 4to; original pictorial and printed boards, cloth shelfback, library stamp and release stamp, boards scuffed and slightly soiled.   M & S Rare Books 60-146 1996 $125.00

CRANE, WALTER 1845-1915   Flora's Feast. A Masque of Flowers. London: Cassell & Co., 1889. 1st edition; large 8vo; 40 pages, all with text and pictures in color, ad leaf, 8 page publisher's catalog; decorated endpapers, original pictorial boards with cloth spine, edges of covers little rubbed, name and date in ink on blank verso of front endpaper, good copy.   David Bickersteth 133-143 1996 £50.00

CRANE, WALTER 1845-1915   A Flower Wedding. London: Cassell, 1905. 1st edition; 40 pages colored illustrations printed on palges folded Japanese style; decorated by Walter Crane; cloth backed colored pictorial boards, edges rubbed, else nice.   Barbara Stone 70-59 1996 £85.00

CRANE, WALTER 1845-1915   Pan-Pipes a Book of Old Songs. London: George Routledge and Sons, 1884. 2nd edition; oblong 4to; pages (vii), 9-51; beautifully color printed throughout; original cloth backed brown pictorial boards, pictorial endpapers, small tear to front endpaper, excellent copy with cover unrubbed and not showing the usual wear to edges.   Sotheran PN32-106 1996 £128.00

CRANE, WALTER 1845-1915   Rumbo Rhymes or the Great Combine: a Satire. London: Harper, 1911. 1st edition; 24 color plates by Walter Crane; green pictorial cloth, top hinge starting to crack, else very fresh, bright, tight copy.   Barbara Stone 70-61 1996 £95.00

CRASHAW, RICHARD   Steps to the Temple. London: printed by T. W. for Humphrey Moseley, 1646, 1st edition; 12mo; early 19th century green cloth, hinges bit frayed, in red half morocco folding case; wanting blanks at beginning and end, but nice, fresh copy. Wing C6836; Hayward 82; Grolier 232.   Ximenes 109-92 1996 $4,750.00

CRAUFURD, QUINTIN   Sketches Chiefly Relating to the History, Religion, Learning and Manners of the Hindoos. With a Concise Account of the Present State of the Native Powers of Hindostan. London: printed for T. Cadell, in the Strand, 1790. 1st edition; 8vo; (iii-vii), 1-422 pages, errata leaf, 1 large folding plate to rear; full speckled calf, slight scoring to boards, corners bumped, red morocco label to spine, gilt title and tooled bands to spine, some light sporadic foxing to text, some slight foxing to title, armorial bookplate and private library indentification label. Halkett & Laing V 285.   Beeleigh Abbey BA56-57 1996 £125.00

CRAW, WILLIAM   Naval, Poetical Journal: in Twelve Letters. Kilmarnock: Printed by H. & S. Crawford for the author, 1807. 1st edition; 12mo; 144 pages, unbound gatherings, stitched as issued, first and last few leaves soiled, else very good, untrimmed. Rare.   Chapel Hill 94-355 1996 $125.00

CRAWFORD, ALAN   C. R. Ashbee, Architect, Designer and Romantic Socialist. New Haven: Yale University Press, 1985. 4to; (xii), 499 pages, 203 illustrations in text; cloth, dust jacket. Fine.   Bookpress 75-150 1996 $135.00

CRAWFORD, FRANCIS MARION 1854-1909   The Novels. New York: and London: Macmillan, 1894-1911. several first editions; 7 x 4 3/4 inches (two volumes slightly smaller); 42 volumes; several volumes with plates and/or illustrations; uniformly bound in attractive contemporary green crushed three quarter morocco, marbled sides and endpapers, spines handsomely gilt in compartments, top edge gilt, one hinge neatly reinforced with matching paper, little wear to top edge of two volumes, spines just slightly and little unevenly faded, 3 volumes with small dark spots, otherwise very pretty bindings in splendid condition, one tear into text, few other trivial tears, otherwise fine internally. Large engraved bookplate in each volume.   Phillip J. Pirages 33-147 1996 $1,250.00

CRAWFORD, J. MARSHALL   Mosby and His Men: a Record of the Adventures of that Renowned Ranger, John S. Mosby. New York: 1867. 1st edition; 7.5 x 5 inches; 375 pages; illustrations; cloth; ink inscription, covers rather worn with frayed spine.   John K. King 77-86 1996 $150.00

CRAWFORD, MEDOREM 1819-1891   An Account of His Trip Across the Plains with the Oregon Pioneers of 1842. Eugene: Star Job Office, 1897. 1st in this edition; 26 pages; stapled as issued, very good. Mintz Trail 110; Graff 914; Howes C874.   Michael D. Heaston 23-122 1996 $150.00

CRAWFORD, OSWALD   By Path and Trail. N.P.: Press of the "Intermountain Catholic", 1908. 1st edition; 225 pages; numerous plates from photos; original cloth, very minor rubbing to corners and spine ends; bookplate removed from inner cover, fine, quite scarce. Argonaut Book Shop 113-155 1996 $100.00

CRAWHALL, JOSEPH b. 1821   A Collection of Right Merrie Garlands for North Country Anglers. Newcastle-on-Tyne: George Rutland, 1864. 1st edition; 8vo; pages xvi, 312, ad leaf, various illustrations and decorations in text, including woodcuts; original morocco backed cloth, lettered in gold on backstrip, top edge gilt, others uncut, head of backstrip and corners rubbed, but good. Felver p. 19 et seq.   Claude Cox 107-34 1996 £65.00

CRAWHALL, JOSEPH b. 1821   Old Ffrendes Wyth Newe Faces. London: Field & Tuer, 1883. 4to; numerous hand colored woodcuts; printed boards, joints badly rubbed but sound, front cover foxed, some light foxing; presentation copy, inscribed on titlepage, 2 page ALS to a niece.   Petersfield Bookshop FH58-21 1996 £370.00

CRAWSHAY, RICHARD   The Birds of Tierra del Fuego. London: Bernard Quaritch, 1907. Limited to 300 copies; 4to; xl, 158 pages; 44 plates, 21 finelyhand colored lithographs by Keulemans, 1 map; morocco backed green cloth, gilt, top edge gilt, spine faded, very slight foxing to text page edges.   Thomas Thorp 489-75 1996 £850.00

CREASEY, JOHN   Murder London - New York. London: Hodder & Stoughton, 1958. 1st edition; fine in very good dust jacket with very light soiling; inscribed by author.   Quill & Brush 102-364 1996 $100.00

CREED, R. S.   Reflex Activity of the spinal Cord. Oxford: 1923. 1st edition; 8vo; 183 pages, plates and text illustrations; original cloth, spine rubbed and worn; Garriston/McHenry 230, 424, 483.   Argosy 810-123 1996 $150.00

CREIGHTON, C.   A History of Epidemics in Britian. Cambridge: 1891-94. 1st edition; 8vo; 2 volumes; cloth, bit worn and scuffed; Charles Singer's copy with his signature.   Maggs Bros. Ltd. 1190-391 1996 £80.00

CREIGHTON, CHARLES   A History of Epidemics in Britain from A.D. 664 to the Extinction of Plague. Cambridge: 1891. 1st edition; 706 pages; ex-library; original binding, GM 1680.   W. Bruce Fye 71-435 1996 $100.00

CREMONY, JOHN C.   Life Among the Apaches. San Francisco: A. Roman & Co., 1868. 1st edition; 322 pages; original pictorial brown cloth over stiff paper boards, title stamped in black on front cover, plain black cloth spine, some wear, but very good and tight; Edwards p. 45; Howes C879; Raines p. 57; Graff 915. Saunders 716.   Michael D. Heaston 23-126 1996 $500.00

CRESSON, JOSHUA   Meditations Written During the Prevalence of the Yellow Fever in the City of Philadelphia in the Year 1793. London: W. Phillips, 1803. 1st edition; 8vo; pages x, 26; original marbled wrappers; signature of Ann Dillwyn of the Quaker family. Not in Wellcome. Maggs Bros. Ltd. 1190-392 1996 £85.00

CREWDSON, ISAAC   A Beacon to the Society of Friends. London: Hamilton, Adams and Co., 1835. 1st edition; 8vo; original cloth, lather spine label.   R.F.G. Hollett & Son 78-362 1996 £85.00

CREWS, HARRY   Car. New York: Morrow, 1972 1st trade edition; fine in fine dust jacket.   Thomas Dorn 9-90 1996 $250.00

CREWS, HARRY   Car. New York: Morrow, 1972. 1st edition; uncorrected proof, signed by author; white wrappers, some soiling and use; very good.   Thomas Dorn 9-89 1996 $400.00

CREWS, HARRY   The Enthusiaast. Winston-Salem: Palaemon Press Ltd., 1981. One of limited edition of 200 copies, signed by him; new, issued, without dust jacket.   Steven C. Bernard 71-70 1996 $175.00

CREWS, HARRY   A Feast of Snakes. New York: Atheneum, 1976. 1st edition; near fine in very good dust jacket which shows some light dampstaining (mainly on its inside).   Pettler & Lieberman 28-64 1996 $100.00

CREWS, HARRY   The Gospel Singer. New York: Morrow, 1968. 1st edition; uncommon; page edges foxed, usual discoloration to endpages and cloth, overall very good in near fine jacket with small chip at upper rear spine fold; inscribed by author 3 days after publication.   Ken Lopez 74-91 1996 $850.00

CREWS, HARRY   The Gospel Singer. New York: Morrow, 1968. 1st edition; unsigned; very slight discoloration to endpapers, otherwise fine in fine dust jacket, very nice copy of scarce first book.   Ken Lopez 74-92 1996 $750.00

CREWS, HARRY   The Gospel Singer. New York: Morrow, 1968. 1st edition; author's first book; typical but only light acidic discoloration of pastedowns, else fine, bright copy in fine dust jacket.   Thomas Dorn 9-87 1996 $725.00

CREWS, HARRY   The Gospel Singer. New York: Wm. Morrow & Co., 1968. 1st edition; (4000 copies); author's first book; front and rear covers blotchy, pastedowns discolored, both flaws are common with this book, otherwise very good in fine dust jacket.   Steven C. Bernard 71-71 1996 $700.00

CREWS, HARRY   The Gypsy's Curse. New York: Knopf, 1974. 1st edition; becoming quite scarce, particularly in nice shape, this copy is fine in fine dust jacket.   Ken Lopez 74-94 1996 $125.00

CREWS, HARRY   The Gypsy's Curse. London: Secker & Warburg, 1975. 1st English edition; fine in bright, fine dust jacket.   Thomas Dorn 9-92 1996 $100.00

CREWS, HARRY   Karate is a Thing of the Spirit. New York: Morrow, 1971. 1st edition; fine in fine dust jacket, very nice.   Ken Lopez 74-93 1996 $250.00

CREWS, HARRY   Karate Is a Thing of the Spirit. New York: Wm. Morrow & Co., 1971. 1st edition; (5942 copies); signed by author; fine in dust jacket.   Steven C. Bernard 71-74 1996 $225.00

CREWS, HARRY   Karate Is a Thing of the Spirit. New York: Morrow, 1971. 1st edition; near fine in bright, close to fine dust jacket with few faint age spots.   Thomas Dorn 9-88 1996 $220.00

CREWS, HARRY   Karate Is a Thing of the Spirit. New York: Wm. Morrow & Co., 1971. 1st edition; (5942 copies); fine in dust jacket. Steven C. Bernard 71-73 1996 $175.00

CREWS, HARRY   The Knockout Artist. New York: Harper, 1988. Uncorrected proof; in wrappers, as issued, tiny tear to base of spine, else fine.   Between the Covers 42-116 1996 $100.00

CREWS, HARRY   Naked in Garden Hills. New York: Wm. Morrow & Co., 1969. 1st edition; (5500 copies); author's second book; former owner's name, address, phone number & date on flyleaf, edges worn, otherwise very good in 1st issue dust jacket which is lightly yellowed and spotted at top border of front and rear panels.   Steven C. Bernard 71-75 1996 $175.00

CREWS, HARRY   This Thing Don't Lead to Heaven. New York: Wm. Morrow & Co., 1970. 1st edition; (7500 copies); fine in very good+ price clipped dust jacket which has 3/4" internally mended tear at top edge of rear panel and top right corner of front panel.   Steven C. Bernard 71-77 1996 $150.00

CRICHTON, MICHAEL   The Andromeda Strain. London: Cape, 1969. 1st English edition; very good with light general wear in about very good dust jacket with some short tears and nicks at corners, uncommon edition.   Between the Covers 42-117 1996 $100.00

CRICHTON, MICHAEL   The Andromeda Strain. New York: Knopf, 1969. 1st edition; very near fine in very near fine dust jacket.   Ken Lopez 74-95 1996 $150.00

CRICHTON, MICHAEL   Dealing, or the Berkeley-to-Boston Forty-Brick Lost Bag Blues. New York: Knopf, 1971. 1st edition; usual slight darkening to edges of the paper covered boards, very small binding flaw, else about fine in very good, price clipped dust jacket with 2 inch snag tear on rear panel.   Between the Covers 42-119 1996 $125.00

CRICHTON, MICHAEL   Jurassic Park. New York: Knopf, 1990. Advance uncorrected proofs; wrappers; fine.   Beasley Books 82-45 1996 $125.00

CRIMINAL Trials Illustrative of the Tale Entitled "The Heart of Mid-Lothian" (by Sir Walter Scott), Published from the Original Record... Edinburgh: Constable, 1818. 8vo; pages 12 (ads), xxxvi, 344; untrimmed, engraved frontispiece. modern half calf, gilt, with spine label and marbled boards.   R.F.G. Hollett 76-68 1996 £85.00

CRIMP, W. SANTO   Sewage Disposal Works: a Guide to the Construction of Works for the Prevention of the Pollution by Sewage of Rivers and Estuaries. London: 1890. 1st edition; 277 pages; 33 lithographic folding plates, numerous woodcuts. original binding, inner hinges cracked, ex-library.   W. Bruce Fye 71-437 1996 $100.00

CRISP, F.   Mediaeval Gardens. London: 1924. Limited to 1000 copies; 4to; 2 volumes; 562 illustrations; buckram, uncut, fine, with defective dust jacket.   Wheldon & Wesley 207-1681 1996 £250.00

CRISP, QUENTIN   The Naked Civil Servant. New York: 1977. 1st American edition; near fine in dust jacket with one closed tear at foot of upper panel; presentation copy from author.   Words Etcetera 94-332 1996 £60.00

CRITTENDEN, H. H.   The Crittenden Memoirs. New York: 1936. 1st edition; 542 pages; frontispiece, photos; cloth; fine. 6 Guns 513; Adams 150 37.   T. A. Swinford 49-252 1996 $185.00

CROAL, THOMAS A.   Scottish Loch Scenery, Illustrated in a Series of Coloured Plates from drawings by A. F. Lydon. London: ca. 1882. 50 pages, 25 rather fine colored plates, title printed in red and black, original decorated boards, neatly and expertly respined, very good.   K Books 442-168 1996 £180.00

CROFF, G. B.   Model Suburban Architecture, Embodying Designs for Dwellings of Moderate Cost, Varying from $1400 to $5000, Together with Extensive and Elaborate Villas, Banking Houses, Club Houses, Hotels, Engine Houses and a Variety of Architectural Features... Saratoga Springs: 1870. 1st edition; large 4to; lithographic title, 43 lithographic plates; original green cloth, upper cover lettered in gilt; very good; Loosely inserted is a short ALS from author to Mr. M. L. Filley. Hitchcock 293.   John Drury 82-62 1996 £500.00

CROFT, HERBERT   The Abbey of Kilkhampton; or, Monumental Records for the Year 1960. Dublin: printed for W. Wilson, 1780. 1st Irish edition; 8vo; pages (4), 66, (4 index); recent wrappers, some light staining, but very good.   James Fenning 133-74 1996 £115.00

CROFT, JOHN   Memoirs of Harry Rowe; Constructed from Materials in an Old Box, After His Decease. York: ptd. by Wilson & Spence, sold by all booksellelrs...n.d. 1805. 1st edition; 12mo; portrait, 8 page subscribers, old half calf, gilt; very good, complete with half title; bookplate of J. Cresswell. 5 copies in NUC; LAR 1703 (not seen). Ximenes 109-93 1996 $750.00

CROKE, GEORGE   The Third Part (though first publish't) of the Reports of...During the First Sixteen Years Regin of King Charles the First. London: printed by W. Rawlins, 1683. Folio; engraved portrait, pages (30), 610, (66), licence leaf; minor old waterstain on first few leaves, but large and very good copy, strongly bound in recent boards, label. Wing C7020.   James Fenning 133-75 1996 £125.00

CROKER, JOHANN MELCHIOR   Der Wohl Anfuhrende Mahler... Jena: J. R. Croker, 1736. 1st enlarged edition; 8vo; 560 pages; frontispiece, 60 small text woodcuts, usual light browning; modern boards, gilt. Very rare.   Bennett Gilbert LL29-6 1996 $2,400.00

CROKER, THOMAS CROFTON   Narratives Illustrative of the Contests in Ireland in 1641 and 1690. London: Camden Society, 1841. 8vo; partly unopened, very good, cloth.   C. P. Hyland 216-128 196 £65.00

CROKER, THOMAS CROFTON   A Walk from London to Fulham. London: William Tegg, 1860. 8vo. (xviii), 256 pages, lacks half title, text illustrations; half morocco, respined.   Marlborough 162-124 1996 £100.00

CROLY, GEORGE   May Fair. London: Ainsworth, 1827. 1st edition; octavo; pages 194, (2); handsome binding by Riviere in full mottled calf, gilt extra, panelled spine, gilt decorated dentelles and panels, double leather labels, marbled endpapers, all edges gilt; unsuually attractive copy. CBEL III 231.   Hartfield 48-L27 1996 $195.00

CROLY, GEORGE   Salathiel - a Tale of the Past, the Present and the Future. Colburn, 1828. 1st edition; 3 volumes; leather and marbled boards, marbled endpapers; some light rubbing, else very good. Quite scarce.   Aronovitz 57-304 1996 $450.00

CROMARTY, GEORGE MAC KENZIE, 1ST EARL OF 1630-1714   A Vindication of Robert III, King of Scotland... Edinburgh: printed by the Heirs and Successors to Andrew Anderson, 1695. Small 4to; pages (iv), 48, 3 decorated initials, final leaf incorrectly paginated and small hole inserted to remove incorrect printing, title little soiled, library stamp of Alexander Gardyne, 1883 on verso; modern quarter calf, gilt, marbled boards. Wing C7027; Aldiss 3454.   R.F.G. Hollett 76-70 1996 £185.00

CROMBIE, JOHN   Cette Galere. Paris: 1991. Number 97 in an edition of 115 copies; 8 x 7.5 inches; colored illustrations, French text; specially bound by Jill Oriane Tarlau in light green leather with various colored leather onlays and inlays, with pieces of metallic embroidery and colored stones, various colored endpapers, all edges green, green decorated paper board chemise with light and dark green leather edges, slipcase of green decorated paper board with dark green leather trim, fine. Joshua Heller 21-229 1996 $1,400.00

CROMBIE, JOHN   The Colour Schemers. Paris: Kickshaws, 1982. 1st edition; one of 45 copies on Rives from a total issue of 235; 45 with extra printed signed and in special binding, 190 regular copies; 6 1/2 x 6 1/2 inches; original color printed wrappers.   Priscilla Juvelis 95/1-146 1996 $150.00

CROMMELYNCK, ALDO   Picasso 347. New York: Random, 1970. Folio; 2 volumes, 22 pages text, 347 reproductions; cloth.   Brannan 43-512 1996 $200.00

CROMPTON, SARAH   The Life of Robinson Crusoe in Short Words. London: James Hogg & Sons, n.d., 1859. 160 x 100mm; 124, 4 pages; frontispiece, 3 other full page hand colored engravings with tissue-guards by the Dalziel Bros.; red cloth gilt with title and vignette blindstamped in gilt; top and base of spine snagged, spine faded, else very good. Grant Collection no. 1292; Osborne 246.   Marjorie James 19-188 1996 £65.00

CROMWELL, THOMAS KITSON   Excursions in the County of Essex. London: for Longman, Hunt et al, 1818-19. 1st edition; 6 1/2 x 4 1/2 inches; 2 volumes; 2 engraved titles, 2 folding maps, 96 engraved plates; excellent early 19th century red smooth half calf, marbled sides, edges and endpapers, spine attractively gilt in compartments featuring stylized concentric squares, black morocco labels; 2 small portions of leather with loss of patina, minor wear to corners and edges, but bindings completely sound, scarcely worn, joints show virtually no wear, and rather pretty; 2 plates with marginal foxing, but splendid copy internally, extraordinarily bright and clean and with rich impressions of the engravings.   Phillip J. Pirages 33-148 1996 $450.00

CROMWELL, THOMAS KITSON   Excursions in the County of Essex... London: printed for Longman, Hurst, Rees, Orme and Brown,... 1818-19. Small 8vo; 2 volumes; (iii-iv), 1-216 pages, 217-224 pages, directions to binder, errata leaf, directions to binder, errata leaf, 1-190 pages, 191-197 pages; large folding map frontispiece to volume 1, 96 engraved copperplates and 1 large folding city plan of Colchester; half strawberry calf and marbled boards, corners worn, joints rubbed with slight loss to lower joint of volume 1, gilt tooling to compartments, black morocco labels to spines, board edges and endpapers, all uniformly marbled; bound by Birdsall; armorial bookplates, binder's ticket.   Beeleigh Abbey BA56-236 1996 £150.00

CROMWELL, THOMAS KITSON   Excursions in the County of Kent. London: Longman, 1822. 8vo; pages iv, 216, engraved title, 2 engraved folding maps, 52 engraved plates, 8 plates on 4 sheets tipped in; contemporary half calf, edges rubbed.   Marlborough 162-16 1996 £150.00

CROMWELL, THOMAS KITSON   History and Description of the Ancient Town and Borough of Colchester, in Essex. London: by Robert Jennings, Poultry and Swinborne and Walter, Colchester, 1825. Royal 8vo; large paper copy, 2 volumes in 1; 3-448, 449-472, errata leaf, frontispiece to both titles, 23 steel engraved plates, 3 facsimiles, 1 map, city plan, new endpapers and prelims, some light foxing occasionally, plates in good condition, good wide margins, newspaper cuttings relating to siege of Colchester loosely inserted. Modern dark brown half calf and marbled boards, maroon morocco label to spine, gilt tooling to compartments, edges gilt. Holloway 50.   Beeleigh Abbey BA/56-7 1996 £200.00

CRONE, RAINER   Andy Warhol. New York: Praeger, 1970. 4to; 331 pages, numerous illustrations, 16 in color; cloth, laminated dust jacket. Freitag 10108.   Brannan 43-666 1996 $650.00

CRONIN, A. J.   The Keys of the Kingdom. Boton: Little Brown, 1941. 1st edition; neat contemporary name and date, else fine in bright and fresh, fine dust jacket with couple of tiny tears and some insignificant rubbing, beautiful copy.   Between the Covers 42-121 1996 $200.00

CRONISE, TITUS FEY   The Natural Wealth of California. San Francisco: H. H. Bancroft & Co., N.Y., 113 William St., 1868. 1st edition; xvi, 696 pages; original green cloth, some wear along edges, overall very good. Blue River Books 9-57 1996 $150.00

CRONQUIST, A.   Integrated System of Classification of Flowering Plans. New York: 1981. 8vo; pages xviii, 1262; frontispiece, numerous text figures; cloth, light staining to front cover, 2 small nicks to edge of cover, names on edges of pages, few ink underlinings in outline section. Raymond M. Sutton VI-110 1996 $125.00

CROOKS, JOHN J.   A History of the Colony of Sierra Leone, Western Africa. Dublin: Browne and Nolan, 1903. 1st edition; crown 8vo; pages xiv, (1), 375; 2 folding maps; original binding, very good.   James Fenning 133-76 1996 £85.00

CROOKSHANK, EDGAR   History and Pathology of Vaccination. Volume 2. Selected Essays. London: 1889. 1st edition; 610 pages; original binding, scarce.   W. Bruce Fye 71-439 1996 $175.00

CROPPER, JAMES   Notes and Memories. Kendal: Bateman and Hewitson, 1900. Small 8vo; pages 211; 18 charming portraits, prospectus (little browned) loosely inserted; original cloth, gilt, all edges gilt, very scarce.   R.F.G. Hollett & Son 78-141 1996 £85.00

CROSBY'S Parliamentary Record of Elections in Great Britain and Ireland York: 1845. 8vo; cloth, very good.   C. P. Hyland 216-131 1996 £50.00

CROSBY, NICHOLS, LEE & CO.   Catalogue of...Publications. Boston: Crosby, Nicols, Lee and Co., 1860. 12mo; 177 pages; original printed wrappers, rebacked, wrappers slightly soiled, but very good. Not in Romaine.   M & S Rare Books 60-290 1996 $250.00

CROSS, HENRY P.   Little Black Sambo, an Operetta for Children. New York: 1936. (4), 53, (1) pages; nice scratchboard style cover illustration. Bookworm & Silverfish 276-23 1996 $175.00

CROSS, JOHN KEIR   The Other Passenger - 18 Strange Stories. London: John Westhouse Publishers Ltd., 1944. 1st edition; 8 color plates by Bruce Angrave; original binding, top edge dusty, prelims, edges and endpapers spotted, head and tail of spine slightly bumped, covers slightly marked, very good in nicked, rubbed and dust slightly torn, marked and creased dust jacket browned at spine and edges.   Ulysses 39-128 1996 £65.00

CROSS, THOMAS   The Autobiography of a Stage-Coachman. London: Hurst & Blackett, 1861. 1st edition; crown 8vo; 3 volumes, xii, (312); vi 312; (viii), 292 pages; frontispieces; bound (without half titles) in later half calf, banded and gilt, top edge gilt, few faint marks, but very good set.   Ash Rare Books Zenzybyr-23 1996 £245.00

CROUCH, NATHANIEL 1632?-1725?   A Journey to Jerusalem, Containing the Travels of Fourteen Englishmen in 1667, to the Holy Land... Hartford: printed by J. Babcock, 1796. 4th surviving American edition; 12mo; contemporary boards, leather spine, boards very rubbed, some foxing, but very good, very scarce. Evans 30301; Rosenbach 109 Trumbull 431.   Ximenes 108-95 1996 $350.00

CROUCH, NATHANIEL 1632?-1725?   A New View and Observations on the Ancient and Present State of London and Westminster... London: A. Bettesworth, Charles Hitch and J. Batley, 1730. 12mo; woodcut frontispiece, title, 2 ff., 1-240, 265-312, 145-240, 380-468, text woodcuts; contemporary mottled calf, joints cracking but firm, this coy lacks 2 final leaves of ads; armorial bookplate of Sir Roger Newdigate. Marlborough 162-125 1996 £220.00

CROWELL, MOSES   The Counsellor, or Every Man His Own Lawyer... Ithaca: printed by D. D. & A. Spencer, 1844. contemporary sheep, rubbed, quite sound.   Meyer Boswell SL25-60 1996 $225.00

CROWFIELD, CHRISTOPHER   The Chimney Corner. Boston: Houghton Mifflin, 1888. Reprint; 12mo; green cloth, fine; signed by Harriet Beecher Stowe with inscription.   Charles Agvent 4-1057 1996 $850.00

CROWFIELD, CHRISTOPHER   House and Home Papers. Boston: Ticknor and Fields, 1865. 1st edition; 8vo; three quarter calf, moderate rubbing; very good, tipped in sheet with inscription from Harriet Beecher Stowe.   Charles Agvent 4-1058 1996 $600.00

CROWLEY, ALEISTER   Clouds Without Water. London: privately printed, 1909. 1st edition; xxi, 144 pages; paper, needs rebinding, very good.   Middle Earth 77-39 1996 $275.00

CROWLEY, ALEISTER   The Confessions of Aleister Crowley - an Autobiography. London: Jonathan Cape Ltd., 1969. 1st edition; black and white frontispiece self portrait and 22 black and white plates; original binding, head and tail of spine slightly bumped, near fine in nicked and slightly rubbed, creased and dusty, price clipped dust jacket.   Ulysses 39-130 1996 £65.00

CROWLEY, ALEISTER   Konx Om Pax. Essays in Light. London: Felling-on-Tyne: & New York: Walter Scott.../Boleskine foyers, Inverness: Soc. for... 1907. Limited to 500 numbered copies, signed by author; small 4to; xii, 108 pages, 12 page publisher's catalog (slight offsetting from tissue gaurd), deckle-edged, frontispiece; cream cloth, very slightly soiled, with elaborate gilt ruled title, top edge gilt; fine. Inscribed by Crowley.   Blue Mountain SP95-129 1996 $1,250.00

CROWLEY, ALEISTER   Magick. London: published for subscribers only, 1929. 1st edition; 4to; top edge gilt, very good.   Words Etcetera 94-335 1996 £175.00

CROWLEY, ALEISTER   Rodin in Rime. London: for the author at the Chiswick Press, 1907. Limited edition of 488 copies on handmade paper, there were also 10 copies on China paper and 2 copies on vellum; 4to; pages 67; 7 full page lithographs after Rodin, printed in colors, printed on handmade paper in Chiswick Press fount; original white cloth, titled in gilt; inscribed by Crowley.   Sotheran PN32-45 1996 £498.00

CROWLEY, ALEISTER   The Tale of Archais - a Romance in Verse. London: Kegan Paul, Trench, Trubner & Co., 1898. 1st edition; printed on handmade paper; pages unopened; linen backed boards, top edge slightly dusty, edges and endpapers slightly spotted, head and tail of spine and corners bumped, corners also bruised, free endpapers browned, covers slightly marked, very good.   Ulysses 39-129 1996 £375.00

CROWLEY, JOHN   Aegypt. New York: Bantam, 1987. Advance review copy; fine in near fine dust jacket with light wear at spine crown; promotional sheet and review laid in; signed by author.   Ken Lopez 74-99 1996 $125.00

CROWLEY, JOHN   Aegypt. New York: Bantam, 1987. Advance Review copy, with photo and publisher's material laid in; fine in dust jacket.   Between the Covers 42-122 1996 $100.00

CROWLEY, JOHN   Beasts. Garden City: Doubleday, 1975. 1st edition; remainder speckling to bottom page edges, otherwise fine in fine dust jacket with touch of rubbing at spine crown, signed by author.   Ken Lopez 74-96 1996 $125.00

CROWLEY, JOHN   Beasts. Garden City: Doubleday, 1976. 1st edition; fine in dust jacket, signed by author.   Between the Covers 42-512 1996 $150.00

CROWLEY, JOHN   The Deep. Garden City: Doubleday, 1975. 1st edition; fine in very good or better dust jacket with single internal repair and faint horizontal crease running the length of the front panel; author's scarce first book.   Between the Covers 42-511 1996 $175.00

CROWLEY, JOHN   Engine Summer. London: Gollancz, 1980. 1st British edition; fine in fine dust jacket with one wrinkle on back panel, signed by author; scarce.   Ken Lopez 74-97 1996 $150.00

CROWLEY, JOHN   Little Big New York: Bantam, 1981. 1st edition; wrappers, near fine with some rubbing, particularly along spine folds; signed by author.   Ken Lopez 74-98 1996 $150.00

CROYDON, MICHAEL   Ivan Albright. New York: Abbeville, n.d. Folio; 308 pages, 140 plates, 88 in color and illustrations in text; cloth, dust jacket.   Brannan Books 43-5 1996 $120.00

CRUIKSHANK, GEORGE 1792-1878   Cruikshank's Water Colours. London: Black, 1903. 67 full page color plates by Cruikshank; original gilt stamped brown cloth, spine and upper cover with art nouveau design stamped in ochre and tan, spine ends worn, corners rubbed, very good. George J. Houle 68-40 1996 $150.00

CRUIKSHANK, GEORGE 1792-1878   Illustrations to Punch and Judy; Drawn and Engraved by George Cruikshank. London: for Septimus Prowett, 1828. 1st edition thus; large 8vo; 23 etched India proofs to a large paper, loose as issued, light dampstaining to upper left corner of all plates, intruding over plate work but only touching image in few places, some marginal dustiness, well away from images, else very good; original printed board portfolio, rubbed and soiled, split along leather spine into two. Cohn 145.   Dramatis Personae 37-51 1996 $400.00

CRUIKSHANK, GEORGE 1792-1878   London Characters. London: Robins, 1906. 12mo; title and 24 hand colored engraved plates; skillfully executed reissue with 20 (out of 24) impressions from the original plates and facsimile title; boards, red morocco slipcase by Root. Cohn 182. Marlborough 162-128 1996 £450.00

CRULL, JODOCUS   A Compleat History of the Affairs of Spain, From the First Treaty of Partition, to this Present Time. London: Jos. Barns, 1708. 2nd edition; 8vo; frontispiece; full contemporary panelled calf, joints repaired; annotations of Peter Collinson on front free endpaper, bookplate of John Cator.   Ian Wilkinson 95/1-86 1996 £175.00

CRUMLEY, JAMES   Dancing Bear. New York: Random House, 1983. 1st edition; fine in dust jacket, signed.   Quill & Brush 102-405 1996 $100.00

CRUMLEY, JAMES   The Muddy Ford. Northridge: Lord John Press, 1984. One of 200 copies, numbered and signed by author; fine, without slipcase as issued.   Quill & Brush 102-406 1996 $150.00

CRUMLEY, JAMES   The Muddy Fork: a Work in Progress. Northridge: Lord John Press, 1984. 1st edition; 1/50 deluxe specially bound, numbered copies, signed by author; fine, issued without jacket.   Janus Books 36-131 1996 $150.00

CRUMLEY, JAMES   The Muddy Fork and Other Things. Livingston: Clark City Press, 1991. One of reportedly only 10 copies of the uncorrected proof; off white, printed paper wrappers; fine.   Quill & Brush 102-409 1996 $350.00

CRUMLEY, JAMES   One to Count Cadence. New York: Random House, 1969. 1st edition; author's first book; lightly rubbed on bottom edge, front bottom corner lightly bumped, otherwise fine in fine dust jacket.   Bud Schweska 12-1326 1996 $280.00

CRUMLEY, JAMES   The Pigeon Shoot. Santa Barbara: Neville, 1987. Limited, signed edition; One of 26 (of 350 total); orange cloth boards, printed in red; fine.   Quill & Brush 102-407 1996 $125.00

CRUMLEY, JAMES   Whores. Missoula: Dennis McMillan Publications, 1988. One of 26 (of 501 total), signed, lettered copies; cover and endpapers by Joe Servello; bound in full goatskin morocco with gold stamped lettering and design and page edges marbled; fine; this copy inscribed to publisher from author.   Quill & Brush 102-408 1996 $750.00

CRUMLEY, JAMES   Whores. Missoula: Dennis McMillan, 1988. 1st edition; 1/450 numbered copies, signed by author; fine in jacket. Janus Books 36-132 1996 $150.00

CRUNDEN, JOHN   Convenient and Ornamental Architecture Consisting of Original Designs... London: I. Taylor, 1785. 4to; viii, 26 pages, 70 plates; contemporary calf, respined, lacking dedication leaf, endpapers renewed, corners worn, some light spots or marks, else very good; bookplate of Nathaniel Lloyd.   Bookpress 75-172 1996 $1,350.00

CRUTCHLEY, BROOKE   Two Men. Walter Lewis and Stanley Morison at Cambridge. Cambridge: Christmas, 1968. 1st edition; one of 500 copies; 8vo; pages vi, 48; many illustrations and facsimiles, 7 mounted pages from books; original buckram backed decorated boards, slipcase, fine.   Claude Cox 107-26 1996 £55.00

THE CRYSTAL Palace that Fox Built. A Pyramid of Rhyme. London: David Bogue, 1851. Small 8vo; 30 pages, 8 wood engraved plates; original decorative printed wrappers mounted on new boards.   Elton Engineering 10-59 1996 £165.00

CUBI Y SOLER, MARIANO   The English Translation: O Neuvo I Practico Sistema de Traduccion, Adaptado al Ingles Para los Que Hablan Espanol. Cambridge: Carlos Folsom, 1828. 1st edition; 8vo; original cloth backed boards, printed paper labels, rubbed, fraying and some staining; browned, some staining.   James Cummins 14-192 1996 $175.00

CUDWORTH, WILLIAM   Histories of Bolton and Bowling (Townships of Bradford), Historically and Topographically Treated. Bradford: pub. by subscription, 1891. 8vo; viii, 363 pages; illustrations; blue cloth, slightly rubbed, but good, sound copy.   K Books 442-170 1996 £180.00

CUDWORTH, WILLIAM   Life and Correspondence of Abraham Sharp, the Yorkshire Mathematician (sic) and Astronomer, and Assistant of Flamsteed, with Memorials of His Family and Associated Families. London: Sampson, Low, Thomas Brear, Bradford, 1889. 1st edition; 4to; xvi, 342, (2) pages; frontispiece and numerous illustrations, uncut, original half vellum; Signet Arms on covers.   James Burmester 29-38 1996 £85.00

CUJACIUS, JACOBUS   Recitationes Solemnes... Frankfurt am Main: Ex Officiana Paltheniana, 1597. 4to; 1182 pages + index, woodcut printer's device on title, name neatly cut away from title with no loss; 17th century blindstamped pigskin, little rubbed and soiled, but excellent example, some browning, foxing and ink annotations. Rare. Not in Adams.   K Books 441-144 1996 £250.00

CULLEN, COUNTEE   The Ballad of the Brown Girl. New York: Harper, 1927. Trade edition; original cloth, fine and lovely copy in worn box missing a piece on bottom edge.   Beasley Books 82-187 1996 $125.00

CULLEN, COUNTEE   Caroling Dusk: An Anthology of Verse by Negro Poets. New York: Harper, 1927. 1st edition; decoratraions by Aaron Douglas; slight scuffing to boards and some chipping to spine label, clean, very good plus copy, lacking dust jacket. Nicely inscribed by editor for Walter Grueninger.   Between the Covers 43-56 1996 $950.00

CULLEN, COUNTEE   Color. New York: Harper & Bros., 1925. 1st edition; 1st printing; 8vo; cloth backed decorated paper boards, spine bit darkened, some markings to text, inked poem on back endpaper, still nice, author's first book.   Glenn Books 36-61 1996 $125.00

CULLEN, COUNTEE   One Way to Heaven. New York: Harpers, 1932. 1st edition; short contemporary gift inscription and touch of rubbing to spine label, else about fine in very good price clipped dust jacket with faded spine and several very small chips at extremities.   Between the Covers 43-55 1996 $700.00

CULLEN, WILLIAM   Lectures on the Materia Medica... Philadelphia: Robert Bell, 1775. 1st American edition; 4to; viii, 512 pages; later calf, foxed, contemporary notes on endpapers; Jacob Kittredge's copy. Evans 14000; Austin 577.   The Bookpress 75-405 1996 $500.00

CULLEY, GEORGE   Observations on Live Stock... London: Wilkie, et al, 1807. 4th edition; 8vo; pages xx, 274, (6), index + 20 pages of ads, 2 engraved plates; uncut in original boards (backstrap chipped and part of label, joints cracked, plates foxed and stained, text lightly browned); Kress B5171; Goldsmith 19348; Fussell II p. 128.   Second Life Books 103-64 1996 $250.00

CULLING, LOUIS   The Complete Magick Curriculum of the Secret Order G. B. G. 1969. 1st edition; color frontispiece, x, 130 pages, illustrations; cloth, fine in very good+ dust jacket.   Middle Earth 77-251 1996 $145.00

CULLUM, GEORGE W.   Register of the Officers and Graduates of the U.S. Military Academy...from March 16, 1802, to January 1, 1850. New York: J. F. Trow, Printer, 1850. 1st edition; small octavo; 303 pages; original printed wrappers, spine shows wear, paper label with early ms. name pasted to blank rear cover, overall very good and complete.   Argonaut Book Shop 113-159 1996 $225.00

CULLYER, JOHN   The Gentleman and Farmer's Assistant Containing, First, Tables for Finding the content of Any Piece of Land... Norwich: printed for the author & sold by Stevenson & Matchen, 1798. 2nd edition; 12mo; xix, (i), 124 pages, diagrams in text; Cullyer's copyright signature at end of preface; contemporary calf, neataly rebacked, very good.   Ken Spelman 30-69 1996 £140.00

CULPEPPER, NICHOLAS 1616-1654   The Complete Herbal... London: 1835. 4to; pages vi, 398, frontispiece, 20 colored plates; half calf, joints cracked; frontispiece rather foxed with offset to titlepage.   Wheldon & Wesley 207-1901 1996 £100.00

CULPEPPER, NICHOLAS 1616-1654   The Complete Herbal. Birmingham 1953. Royal 8vo; pages x, 603; portrait and 16 colored plates; half morocco.   Wheldon & Wesley 207-1902 1996 £75.00

CULPEPPER, NICHOLAS 1616-1654   Culpeper's English Physician; and Complete Herbal. London: for the Proprietors, 1790. Later edition; 4to; xvi, 398, 256 pages; frontispiece, 29 hand colored plates, 12 plates printed in red; period style full calf, unobtrusive blindstamps on title and plates, occasional light foxing, still very good.   Chapel Hill 94-267 1996 $275.00

CULPEPPER, NICHOLAS 1616-1654   Culpeper's English Physician; and Complete Herbal... London: printed for the author, ca. 1794-98. Small 4to; 2 volumes in 1; 46 engraved plates, 3 tables in appendix; full contemporary brown calf, gilt stamped dark red morocco spine label, corners and edges rubbed, hinges and joints weak; very good.   George J. Houle 68-64 1996 $550.00

THE CUMBERLAND Foxhounds. Carlisle: C. Thurnam, n.d., c. 1877. 4to pages 44; original cloth, gilt, rather faded, original red wrappers (rather chipped and spotted on reverse) bound in, few neat alterations and corrections to text in contemporary hand; scarce.   R.F.G. Hollett & Son 78-639 1996 £75.00

CUMBERLAND, GEORGE   Thoughts on Outline, Sculpture and the System that Guided the Ancient Artists in Composing Their Figures and Groups... London: W. Wilson, St. Peter's Hill, Doctors' Commons, & so by Messr.... 1796. 1st edition; 4to; (4), iii, (i), 52 pages, engraved frontispiece, unsigned, 15 plates, 8 plates; uncut and unsophisticated in original limp boards, made from reversed sheets from another publication, which are almost invisible within their etruscan key pattern borders, backstrip and board edges worn, preserved in drop-lid box with paper label, some pages watermarked Whatman 1794; some light foxing to early text pages and endpapers, otherwise clean.   Ken Spelman 30-22 1996 £850.00

CUMBERLAND, RICHARD   Anecdotes of Eminent Painters in Spain, During the Sixteenth and Seventeenth Centuries... London: for J. Walter, 1782. Small 8vo; 2 volume,s (2), 225, (1) pages, 1 f. index; (2), 224 pages, 1 f. index; contemporary tree calf, greek-key pattern gilt borders expertly rebacked with new gilt labels. Very good.   Ken Spelman 30-18 1996 £220.00

CUMMINGS, BYRON   First Inhabitants of Arizona and the Southwest Tucson: Cummings Publication Council, 1953. 1st edition; ink stain slight affects margins of covers, with minor bleedover to endpapers, else very good to fine in dust jacket with minor creasing and light soiling.   Ken Sanders 8-14 1996 $125.00

CUMMINGS, BYRON   Kinishba. A Prehistoric Pueblo of the Great Pueblo Period. Hohokam: Museum Assn. & University of Arizona, Tucson, 1940. 1st edition; very good in dust jacket with chipping on edges, including half inch missing at top of spine, signed by author.   Ken Sanders 8-15 1996 $100.00

CUMMINGS, EDWARD ESTLIN 1894-1962   (no title) New York: Covici Friede, 1930. One of 491 numbered copies, signed by author; quarto; illustrations by author, issued without dust jacket; light soiling to board starts in hinges, otherwise near fine.   Beasley Books 82-46 1996 $250.00

CUMMINGS, EDWARD ESTLIN 1894-1962   Ciopw. New York: Covici Friede, 1931. One of 391 numbered copies, signed by author; quarto; illustrations by author, burlap covered boards, burlap covered boards; unusually nice with aesthetically well repaired front joint.   Beasley Books 82-47 1996 $750.00

CUMMINGS, EDWARD ESTLIN 1894-1962   Fairy Tales. New York: Harcourt Brace, and World, 1965. 1st edition; small 4to; illustrations in water color and pen wash by John Eaton; grey boards pictorially stamped in black, edges of boards just a little faded, else fresh in original pictorial dust jacket. Scarce.   Barbara Stone 70-66 1996 £75.00

CUMMINGS, EDWARD ESTLIN 1894-1962   Is 5. New York: Boni & Liveright, 1926. 1st edition; 8vo; cloth backed boards, dust jacket, previous bookseller's label on rear pastedown, covers somewhat rubbed and soiled, otherwise good, slightly rubbed and chipped dust jacket, rare in jacket.   James S. Jaffe 34-122 1996 $175.00

CUMMINGS, EDWARD ESTLIN 1894-1962   Ninety-five Poems. New York: Harcourt Brace, 1958. 1st edition; one of 300 copies, signed by poet; blue cloth, original slipcase bumped at one corner; very fine.   Bromer Booksellers 90-23 1996 $375.00

CUMMINGS, M. F.   Architecture. Designs for Street Fronts, Suburban Houses, and Cottages. Troy: the authors, 1867. 3rd edtion; small folio; (ii), ii, (4) pages; 52 plates; publisher's cloth, covers sunned and rubbed, head of spine chipped, front hinge internally strengthened, still respectable copy.   Bookpress 75-34 1996 $475.00

CUMMINS, ELLA STERLING   The Story of the Files: a Review of Californian Writers and Literature. San Francisco: and Chicago: World's Fair Commission of California, 1893. 1st edition; 8 1/2 x 5 1/2 inches; 460 pages + frontispiece, 2 errata slips, 3 ad leaves at beginning and 2 at end, illustrations in text; brown printed tan boards, only light wear to extremities. Zamorano 80 number 24.   Dawson's Books Shop 528-70 1996 $300.00

CUMMINS, MAUREEN   Aureole to Zingaresca. Inanna Press....Printed in the Fall of 1994. Printed in an edition of 50 copies; 8 x 12 inches; 35 pages; printed in Century Schoolbook with initial capitals from woodtype, both type and color woodblock illustrations were printed letterpress on thick handmade paper; bound into white wrappers that unfurl the title sweeping across its length, purple cloth slipcase, gilt title on spine. Fine. Joshua Heller 21-43 1996 $525.00

CUNARD, NANCY   Authors Take Sides on the Spanish War. London: Left Review, 1937. 1st edition; 28 pages; original wrappers rubbed and frayed on spine, single vertical crease, light foxing, very good.   Ian Patterson 9-104 1996 £60.00

CUNDALL, H. M.   Birket Foster R.W.S. London: A. & C. Black, 1906. Limited to 300 copies; signed by publisher, with additional etched frontispiece by artist; 4to; xx, 216 pages; frontispiece, 92 plates, text illustrations; publisher's white buckram over bevelled boards, design on spine and front cover in red and green, and gilt, top edge gilt, others uncut, binding somewhat soiled as usual, slightly worn at corners. Thomas Thorp 489-76 1996 £180.00

CUNDALL, JOSEPH   On Bookbindings, Ancient and Modern. London: 1881. Crown 4to; 28 plates; cloth, brown morocco spine, joints rubbed, some foxing as usual with this book.   Charles W. Traylen 117-13 1996 £150.00

CUNDY, N. W.   Inland Transit: The Practicability, Utility and Benefit of Railroads; the Comparative Attraction and Speed of Steam Engines, on a Railroad, Navigation and Turnpike Road... London: G. Herbert, 1834. 2nd edition; 161 pages; tables, charts, folding map, folding plate; cloth backed boards, fine in custom slipcase and cloth dust jacket. Lengthy presentation inscription from author on a separate piece of paper tipped onto front pastedown.   Hermitage SP95-1097 1996 $500.00

CUNELIUS, GEORGIUS   Facilis et Expeditus Modus Constituendarum Figurarum Coelestium, Seu, ut Volgo Vocant, Thematum Natalitiorum... Leipzig: Johannes Steinman, 1582. 1st edition; 4to; 23 pages; woodcut diagram, computations, 18th century marbled wrappers; rare. Zinner 3031; Houzeau Lancaster 4944.   Jeffrey D. Mancevice 20-22 1996 $450.00

CUNNINGHAM, A. B.   Murder at Deer Lick. New York: E. P. Dutton, 1939. 1st edition; very good with light discoloration on pages and covers rubbed, dust jacket with chipping and light soiling, but front panel very bright.   Quill & Brush 102-412 1996 $200.00

CUNNINGHAM, ALLAN   Songs: Chiefly in the Rural Language of Scotland. London: printed for the author by Smith & Davy, and sold by J. Hearne... 1813. 1st edition; 8vo; original drab boards, trifle soiled, slight crack in upper joint; fine copy in original condition. Jackson p. 373; CBEL III 717.   Ximenes 108-97 1996 $600.00

CUNNINGHAM, FRANK   General Stand Watie's Confederate Indians. San Antonio: The Naylor Co., 1959. 1st edition; xiv, (2), 242; photographic illustrations, primarily portraits; original cloth, very fine with lightly rubbed and spine faded pictorial dust jacket. Long presentation inscription signed by author; very scarce.   Argonaut Book Shop 113-160 1996 $150.00

CUNNINGHAM, FRANK   General Stand Watie's Confederate Indians. San Antonio: Naylor Co., 1959. 1st edition; xiv, 242 pages; original cloth, near fine in very good chipped. Nevins I 26. Dornbusch III 288. McGowan Book Co. 65-23 1996 $125.00

CUNNINGHAM, HENRY DUNCAN   The Capabilities and Advantages of Cunningham's Patent Mode of Reefing Topsails &c... Portsea, 1853. 8 pages text, 4 engraved plates, thick blindstamped cloth, backstrip just a little rubbed.   Petersfield Bookshop FH58-356 1996 £50.00

CURIOSITIES for the Ingenious: Selected from the Most Authentic Treasures of Nature, Science and Art, Biography, History and General Literature. London: printed for Thomas Boys, 1822. 2nd edition; 12mo; 12 engraved plates (some foxed); contemporary half calf, label. Anthony W. Laywood 109-32 1996 £60.00

THE CURIOSITIES Natural and Artificial, of the Island of Great Britain... London: printed for the Proprietors and sold by R. Snagg, n.d., c. 1780. 8vo; 6 volumes, allegorical frontispiece, 55 engraved plates; contemporary sprinkled calf, morocco labels, very sound set.   H. M. Fletcher 121-101 1996 £285.00

A CURIOUS Traveller. Being a Choice Collection of Very Remarkable Histories, Voyages, Travels, Etc. London: J. Rowland, 1742. 8vo; (4), 384, (4) pages; 8 copper engraved plates; contemporary mottled calf, rebacked, top of front hinge with 2 inch crack, but still perfectly sound; very scarce.   Kenneth Karmiole 1NS-244 1996 $350.00

CURLE, ALEXANDER O.   The Treasure of Trapain. Glasgow: Maclehose, Jackson and Co., 1923. 4to; pages xv, 131; 41 plates and 70 text figures; original green cloth, gilt, top edge gilt, uncut; presentation copy, inscribed by author.   R.F.G. Hollett 76-72 1996 £85.00

CURLE, RICHARD   Collecting American First Editions: Its Pitfalls and Its Pleasures. Indianapolis: Bobbs Merrill Co., 1930. 1st edition; one of 1250 copies, signed by author; 8 3/4 x 6 inches; 1 p.l., xviii pages, (1) leaf, 221 pages; frontispiece, 50 plates, title in red and black; original cloth, paper labels, top edge gilt, other edges untrimmed, few leaves unopened, in publisher's printed slipcase that has been carefully (and abundantly) reinforced with masking tape. Spine slightly and evenly faded, otherwise excellent. Webber p. 53.   Phillip J. Pirages 33-91 1996 $100.00

CURLE, RICHARD   Joseph Conrad's Last Day. London: privately printed, 1924. One of 100 numbered copies; 29 pages of text; wrappers, some internal spotting, tail of spine and bottom corners slightly bumped, very good.   Ulysses 39-121 1996 £125.00

CURLE, RICHARD   The Personality of Joseph Conrad. London: privately printed, 1925. One of 100 copies; wrappers, titlepage and edges slightly spotted, slightly creased; very good; presentation copy from author inscribed for John Hodgson.   Ulysses 39-122 1996 £135.00

CURRAN, JOHN PHILPOT   Speeches of John Philpot Curran, Esq. London: printed and published by I. Riley, New York, 1811. contemporary calf, rubbed and chipped, but good set.   Meyer Boswell SL27-56 1996 $225.00

CURRIER, THOMAS FRANKLIN   A Bibliography of Oliver Wendell Holmes. New York: New York University Press, 1953. 1st edition; 4to; xiii, 705, (1) pages; frontispiece, 24 full page illustrations; original cloth; fine.   Edwin V. Glaser B122-37 1996 $125.00

CURRIER, THOMAS FRANKLIN   A Bibliography of Oliver Wendell Holmes. New York: 1953. 1st edition; 708 pages; original binding.   W. Bruce Fye 71-1032 1996 $100.00

CURRY, EUGENE   Cath Mhuighe Leana, or The Battle of Magh Leana. London: 1855. 1st edition; 8vo; cloth, spine cloth chipped top and bottom, otherwise very good, 2 ALS's from Norman Moore to unnamed correspondent.   C. P. Hyland 216-133 1996 £125.00

CURRY-LINDAHL, K.   Bird Migration in Africa. London: 1981. 8vo; 2 volumes; cloth.   Wheldon & Wesley 207-704 1996 £99.00

CURTIN, L. S. M. Healing Herbs of the Upper Rio Grande. Santa Fe: Laboratory of Anthropology, 1947. 1st edition; pages (10), 281, (4 errata), paltes, map; good in worn, chipped dust jacket. Dumont 28-63 1996 $100.00

CURTIS, C. DENSMORE Sardis. Volume XIII: Jewlery and Gold Work. Part I, 1910-1914. Roma: Sindacato Italiano Arti Grafiche, 1925. Folio; 48 pages, 11 plates; original cloth backed boards, spine and boards chipped. Archaeologia Luxor-3960 1996 $200.00

CURTIS, EDWARD S. The North American Indian: The Southwest. Santa Fe: 1980. Limited to 228 copies; folio; 153 pages; stunning sepia photogravure of Curtis' self-portrait, text is letter press on Italian handmade paper, marbled endpapers; full calf, as new. Gene W. Baade 1094-38 1996 $250.00

CURTIS, EDWARD S. The North American Indian: the Southwest. Santa Fe: Classic Gravure, 1980. 1st edition thus, limited to 228 copies; folio; frontispiece; full leather by Roswell Bindery in Phoenix. Parker Books of the West 30-45 1996 $250.00

CURTIS, EDWARD S. Portraits from North American Indian Life. New York: Outerbridge & Lazard with American Museum of Natural History, 1972. 1st edition; oblong folio; xvi, 176 pages; 88 full page sepia toned plates from photogravures; cloth backed illustrated paper over boards; minor wear to bottom of spine, else very good. Andrew Cahan 47-59 1996 $150.00

CURTIS, GEORGE TICKNOR Life of Daniel Webster. New York: D. Appleton and Co., 1870. 3rd edition; 2 volumes; woodcut illustrations; contemporary three quarter morocco, bit worn, still attractive. Meyer Boswell SL27-240 1996 $250.00

CURTIS, GEORGE WILLIAM Washington Irving: a Sketch... New York: Grolier Club, 1891. 1st edition; one of 344 copies; full red calf, Grolier club emblem in gilt on front panel between triple gilt rules, top edge gilt; fine, somewhat worn slipcase. Captain's Bookshelf 38-120 1996 $150.00

CURTIS, JOHN Farm Insects; Being the Natural History and Economy of the Insects Injurious to the Field Crops of Great Britain and Ireland. Glasgow: Edinburgh: and London: 1860. Royal 8vo; 16 colored plates and 69 other illustrations; old half morocco, rebacked. Charles W. Traylen 117-296 1996 £75.00

CURTIS, JOHN Farm Insects. London: 1881. 15 color plates, large corner torn from endpaper and blank flyleaf, small nick to backstrip, otherwise very good and clean. Petersfield Bookshop FH58-235 1996 £52.00

CURTIS, PAUL A. Sportsmen All. New York: Derrydale Press, 1938. 1st edition; one of 950 numbered copies; 8vo; illustrations by Marguerite Kirmse; very good, one (of 3) front endpapers excised. Siegel 140; Frazier C16a. Glenn Books 36-68 1996 $125.00

CURTIS, WILLIAM E. Oklahoma Indian Territory and Texas. St. Louis: Frisco System, ca. 1905. 1st edition; 32 pages; frontispiece; original printed grey wrappers, title stamped in blue, minor soiling, fine. Gilcrease Hargrett p. 302. Michael D. Heaston 23-128 1996 $225.00

CURWEN PRESS A Specimen Book of Pattern Papers. London: published for the Curwen Press by the Leuron Ltd., 1928. One of 220 numbered copies; quarto; 31 whole patterned papers; decorated buckram covers, head and tail of spine and corners bumped, covers worn, free endpapers browned; good. Ulysses 39-135 1996 £1,750.00

CURWEN, ANNIE ISABEL Poems. Barrow-in-Furness: the Barrow Printing Co., 1899. 8vo; pages 284; frontispiece, full tan morocco, gilt, all edges gilt. R.F.G. Hollett & Son 78-368 1996 £65.00

CURWEN, J. SPENCER Memorials of John Curwen. London: J. Curwen & sons, 1882. 8vo; pages xii, 320; frontispiece; original cloth, gilt; scarce; signature of Kathleen Spencer Curwen on flyleaf. R.F.G. Hollett & Son 78-144 1996 £85.00

CURWEN, JOHN F. The Ancient Parish of Heversham with Milnthorpe... Kendal: Titus Wilson & Son, 1930. 1st (only) edition; 8vo; pages (iii), 89; 7 plates and illustrations; original cloth, rather mottled, uncut, few spots, but nice, very scarce. R.F.G. Hollett & Son 78-857 1996 £85.00

CURWEN, JOHN F. The Castles and Fortified Towers of Cumberland, Westmorland and Lancashire North of the Sands... Kendal: Titus Wilson, 1913. 1st edition; thick 8vo; pages xv, 527, 80 plates, illustrations and plans; original brown cloth, gilt; fine, extremely scarce. R.F.G. Hollett & Son 78-19 1996 £275.00

CURWEN, JOHN F. Historical Description of Levens Hall. Kendal: T. Wilson, 1898. Tall 8vo; 40 pages; illustrations; original cloth, gilt; R.F.G. Hollett & Son 78-864 1996 £55.00

CURWEN, JOHN F. Kirkbie Kendall. Kendal: T. Wilson, 1900. 1st edition; small 4to; 455 pages; illustrations; original cloth, gilt, extremities rubbed and worn. R.F.G. Hollett & Son 78-866 1996 £175.00

CURWEN, JOHN F. The Later Records Relating to North Westmorland or the Barony of Appleby. Kendal: Titus Wilson, 1932. 8vo; pages vi, (i), 428, frontispiece; original ribbed green cloth, gilt. R.F.G. Hollett & Son 78-867 1996 £140.00

CUSACK, M. F. A History of the Kingdom of Kerry. London: 1871. 1st edition; color map, 1 plate, many text illustrations; cloth. C. P. Hyland 216-135 1996 £90.00

CUSHING, H. Consecratio Medici and Other Papers. Boston: 1928. 2nd printing; 8vo; cloth, bit worn, elaborate inscription from author to Pat Leonard, July 16, 1919. with small ink sketch. Maggs Bros. Ltd. 1190-395 1996 £75.00

CUSHING, HARVEY WILLIAMS 1869-1939 A Bio Bibliography of Andreas Vesalius. New York: Schuman, 1943. Limited to 800 copies; 8vo; 228 pages; numerous illustrations; half green morocco and linen boards, armorial crest of Vesalius on front board, some light rubbing to binding, otherwise near fine. James Tait Goodrich K40-289 1996 $495.00

CUSHING, HARVEY WILLIAMS 1869-1939 The Harvey Cushing Collection of Books and Manuscripts. New York: 1943. 1st edition; 207 pages; original binding, ex-library with notation in white ink on front cover, library stamps on endpaper, but no library markings on titlepage or internally. W. Bruce Fye 71-460 1996 $100.00

CUSHING, HARVEY WILLIAMS 1869-1939 The Life of Sir William Osler. Oxford: Clarendon Press, 1925. 1st edition; 2nd impression; 8vo; 2 volumes, xiii, 685; x, 728 pages; frontispiece, plates, plate facing p. 31 foxed; blue cloth, very good. Jeff Weber 31-139 1996 $150.00

CUSHING, HARVEY WILLIAMS 1869-1939 The Life of Sir William Osler. Oxford: 1925. 1st edition; 1st impression; 8vo; 2 volumes; original binding, light shelf wear, lower corner of volume two repaired, good set. James Tait Goodrich K40-220 1996 $135.00

CUSHING, HARVEY WILLIAMS 1869-1939 The Life of Sir William Osler. Oxford: Clarendon Press, 1925. 1st edition; 3rd impression; 8vo; 2 volumes; xiii, 685; x, 728 pages; frontispiece, plates; blue cloth; very good; former owner's signature. Jeff Weber 31-140 1996 $150.00

CUSHING, HARVEY WILLIAMS 1869-1939 The Life of Sir William Osler. Oxford: Clarendon Press, 1925. 1st edition; 1st printing; 8vo; 2 volumes; illustrations; original blue cloth, very good set. M & S Rare Books 60-470 1996 $300.00

CUSHING, HARVEY WILLIAMS 1869-1939 The Life of Sir William Osler. Oxford: Clarendon Press, 1925. 2nd edition; 8vo; 2 volumes; navy blue cloth, joints and edges lightly rubbed, else very good; modern bookplate and warm inscription. Glenn Books 36-181 1996 $250.00

CUSHING, HARVEY WILLIAMS 1869-1939 The Life of Sir William Osler. Oxford: At the Clarendon Press, 1925. 1st edition; thick 8vo; (xvi), 685, (3), (xii), 728 pages, plus 44 plates; panelled blue cloth, joints and edges moderately rubbed, slight bubbling to cloth, very good set. John Gach 150-117 1996 $250.00

CUSHING, HARVEY WILLIAMS 1869-1939 The Life of Sir William Osler. Oxford: Clarendon Press, 1925. 1st edition; 8vo; 2 volumes; xiii, 685; x, 728 pages; frontispiece, plates, lacks front free endpaper; blue cloth, rubbed, otherwise very good. Waller 17451. Jeff Weber 31-13 1996 $200.00

CUSHING, HARVEY WILLIAMS 1869-1939   The Life of Sir William Osler. Oxford: Clarendon Press, 1925. 1st edition; 8vo; 2 volumes; xiii, 685; x, 728 pages; frontispiece, plates, blue cloth, outer hinges torn; Jeff Weber 31-138 1996 $150.00

CUSHING, HARVEY WILLIAMS 1869-1939   The Life of Sir William Osler. Oxford: Clarendon Press, 1926. 1st edition; 4th impression; 8vo; 2 volumes, xiii, 685; x, 728 pages; frontispiece, plates; blue cloth, printed dust jacket, jacket spine bit browned, else very good.   Jeff Weber 31-141 1996 $250.00

CUSHING, HARVEY WILLIAMS 1869-1939   The Pituitary Body and Its Disorders. Clinical States Produced by Disorders of the Hypophysis Cerebri. Philadelphia: 1912. 1st edition; 1st impression; 8vo; 341 pages; original binding, some shelf wear, spine partially varnished, endpapers renewed, stamp on title, internally quite clean. GM 3896.   James Tait Goodrich K40-99 1996 $495.00

CUSHING, HARVEY WILLIAMS 1869-1939   Studies in Intracranial Physiology and Surgery. The Third Circulation. The Hypophysis. The Gliomas. The Cameron Prize Lectures. Oxford Press, 1926. 8vo; original binding, very good, tight copy, scarce.   James Tait Goodrich K40-101 1996 $495.00

CUSHING, HARVEY WILLIAMS 1869-1939   Tumors Arising from the Blood-Vessels of the Brain. Angiomatous Malformations and Hemangioblastomas. Springfield: Thomas, 1928. One of 1000 copies; 8vo; 219 pages; illustrations; newly rebound in linen, early owner has done some pencil underlining of text in various parts, else clean, tight copy. Cushing Society 10.   James Tait Goodrich K40-97 1996 $395.00

CUSHMAN, HORATIO B.   A History of the Choctaw, Chickasaw and Natchez Indians. Greenville: 1899. 1st edition; 607 pages, frontispiece; cloth, very good+. Howes C976.   T. A. Swinford 49-258 1996 $250.00

CUST, ROBERT H. HOBART   The Life of Benvenuto Cellini. London: Bell, 1910. 2 volumes, xlii, 390 pages; xx, 533 pages, numerous plates; original gilt stamped cloth, top edge gilt, very good.   J. M. Cohen 35-11 1996 $125.00

THE CUSTER Battlefield National Cemetery. San Francisco: 1937. 1st edition; 6 pages; printed wrappers; nice.   T. A. Swinford 49-261 1996 $350.00

CUSTER, ELIZABETH B.   Following the Guidon. New York: Harper & Bros., 1899. 1st edition; green cloth stamped in gilt, blue, red, white and black, ink inscription to front flyleaf, some abrasion along leading edges of boards, occasional overall wear, still very nice, gilt and colors bright. Hermitage SP95-700 1996 $100.00

CUSTER, ELIZABETH B.   Tenting On the Plains. New York: 1887. 1st edition; 702 pages; frontispiece, illustrations; pictorial cloth, very good-. Very scarce. Rader 1009; Luther 15; Dustin 77. Smith 2186.   T. A. Swinford 49-262 1996 $175.00

CUTBUSH, JAMES   A System of Pyrotechny, Comprehending the Theory and Practice, with the Application of Chemistry. Philadelphia: Clara F. Cutbush, 1825. 1st edition; 8vo; 44, 612 pages; one plate; full contemporary calf, hinges weak, binding dry, some foxing but internally very good. Rink2158; shoemaker 20239.   M & S Rare Books 60-314 1996 $600.00

CUTBUSH, JAMES   A System of Pyrotechny, Comprehending the Theory and Practice, with the Application of Chemistry. Philadelphia: Clara F. Cutbush, 1825. 1st edition; 8vo; 44, 612 pages, one plate; full contemporary calf, signature clipped from title deleting word "A", edges stained yellow, foxed, very good. Rink 2158; Shoemaker 20239.   M & S Rare Books 60-451 1996 $600.00

CUTCHINS, JOHN A.   A Famous Command, the Richmond Light Infantry Blues. Richmond: 1934. Royal 8vo; xx, (2), 399 pages; endpaper reglued, 95 per cent intact; very good in dust jacket with chips at end of backstrip and one other chip.   Bookworm & Silverfish 276-65 1996 $125.00

CUTLER, CARL C.   A Descriptive Catalogue of the Marine Collection at India House. Middleton: India House, 1973. 2nd edition, limited to 1250 copies; 4to; xliv, 11, 144 pages; 12 color plates and 39 monochrome plates; as new in similar slipcase.   Parmer Books O39Nautica-039050 1996 $125.00

CUTLER, D. F.   Root Identification Manual of Trees and Shrubs. London: 1987. 8vo; 256 pages; 500 photos; hardback.   Wheldon & Wesley 207-1827 1996 £70.00

CUTLER, JERVIS   A Topographical Description of the State of Ohio, Indiana Territory, and Louisiana. Boston: 1812. 1st edition; 12mo; 219 pages (leaf 97-98 and page of errata in facsimile), lacks endleaves, some rubbing, sound; contemporary calf, leather label. Howes C984; Wagner Camp 10.   Edward Morrill 369-87 1996 $400.00

CUTLER, THOMAS W.   A Grammar of Japanese Ornament and Design... London: Batsford, 1880. 1st edition; folio; xi, (1), 31, (1) pages, 7 and 58 plates; pictorial publisher's cloth, white cloth cover is slightly soiled, overall very good, scarce thus.   Bookpress 75-35 1996 $1,250.00

CUTTER, G. W.   Buena Vista: and Other Poems. Cincinnati: Morgan and Overend, 1848. 1st edition; 12mo; 168 pages; frontispiece; original cloth, foxed.   M & S Rare Books 60-147 1996 $100.00

CUTTS, EDWARD L.   An Essay on the Christmas Decoration of Churches. London: John Crockford, 1859. 8vo; (vi), 67 pages; publisher's cloth, green cloth is slightly discolored along spine and edges, else very good.   Bookpress 75-36 1996 $150.00

CUTTS, EDWARD L.   A Manual for the Study of the Sepulchral Slabs and Crosses of the Middle Ages. London: John Henry Parker, 1849. 1st edition; 8vo; frontispiece, viii, 93 pages, 83 plates; publisher's cloth, some foxing, light cover wear to tips and extremities of spine. Bookpress 75-37 1996 $125.00

CUVIER, GEORGES, BARON 1769-1832   Animal Kingdom. London: Henderson, 1834. Pisces plate volume with 140 (of 148) plates, 139 hand colored, 6 (of 8) folding black and white plates, lacks front cover and titlepage and pages I-IV of table of contents; some foxing, sold as is. Nissan 1016.   John Johnson 135-583 1996 $200.00

CYNWAL, WILLIAM   In Defence of Woman. Waltham St. Lawrence: Golden Cockerel Press, 1960. Limited edition, 159/400 copies (of an edition of 500 copies); tall crown 8vo; 28 pages; printed on mouldmade paper, 10 full page color printed wood engravings; original mauve linen, backstrip lettering and Petts design on front cover, all gilt blocked, untrimmed, tissue jacket, fine. Cock-a-Hoop 210.   Blackwell's B112-122 1996 £80.00

CYPRIANUS, SAINT, BP. OF CARTHAGE   Opera. Stuttgart: printer of the Erwahlung Maximilians, n.d., c. 1486. Folio; repairs to last leaf, without loss of text, some worming towards end, mostly minor; contemporary calf over wooden boards, upper cover stamped with floral pattern within triple fillet, a hop-vine roll tool, interesting outer frame of a dog, deer, another dog and a dragon chasing through flowering shrubs, lower cover, with same floral pattern in larger panel, surrounded by two stylized rolls and an outer frame of intersecting triple fillets, rebacked, preserving some of the original spine, brass clasps and catches, spine bit worn; essentially a large fresh copy; the Eric Sexton copy. Goff C1014; GKW 7887; HC *5895; Proctor 2750; BMC III p. 675.   Ximenes 109-94 1996 $6,000.00

CZWIKLITZER, CHRISTOPHER   Picasso's Posters. New York: Random, 1970/71. Folio; 365 pages; 297 illustrations, including 53 tipped in color plates and other color illustrations; cloth, dust jacket. Freitag 7430. Brannan 43-513 1996 $290.00

D

D'ABRANTES, LAURE JUNOT, DUCHESS   Memoirs of Napoleon, His Court and Family. London: Richard Bentley, 1836. 1st English edition; 8vo; 2 volumes, 548, 520 pages; frontispiece, portraits; original purple cloth, spines faded, covers lightly spotted, but tight, very good set.   Chapel Hill 94-292 1996 $150.00

D'ABRERA, B.   Butterflies of the Neotropical Region. Part I. Papilionidae and Pieridae. Melbourne: 1981. 4to; pages xvi, 172, map, numerous color photos; cloth.   Wheldon & Wesley 207-1019 1 996 £180.00

DACIER, ANDRE   The Life of Pythagoras with His Symbols and Golden Verses. Together with the Life of Hierocles... London: for Jacob Tonson, 1707. 1st edition in English; 8vo; (2), xxxiv, 389, (14) pages; contemporary panelled calf, spine gilt, raised bands, red morocco spine label, ends of spine lightly scuffed, joints cracking; very good; bookplate of Stuart Rendel dated 1886; Waller 15871.   Edwin V. Glaser 121-259 1996 $850.00

DACUS, JOSEPH A.   Illustrated Lives and Adventures of Frank and Jesse James and the Younger Brothers, the Noted Western Outlaws. St. Louis: N. D. Thompson & Co., 1881. 2nd edition; 8vo; original brown cloth, gilt, binding nearly detached, except for some minor browning, this is a very good copy internally and cloth itself is quite good; large older bookplate. Howes D6; Graff 967; 6 Guns 539; Adams 150 #43; Rader 1019.   Glenn Books 36-202 1996 $125.00

DACUS, JOSEPH A.   Life and Adventures of Frank and Jesse James, the Noted Outlaws. St. Louis: W. S. Bryan et al, 1880. 12mo; 383, (1) pages, illustrations; original gilt stamped cloth, light wear and rubbing, front hinge cracked, scattered light foxing. Howes D6; Graff 967; Adams Guns 538; Adams 150 43. Adams Burs 104.   Bohling Book Co. 192-133 1996 $400.00

DAGGETT, DAVID   Count the Cost. An Address to the People of Connecticut, on Sundry Political Subjects, and Particularly on the Proposition for a New Constitution. Hartford: Hudson and Goodwin, 1804. 1st edition; 8vo; 21, 2 pages; sewn and uncut as issued, foxed. S&S 6109.   M & S Rare Books 60-315 1996 $125.00

DAGLEY, R.   Takings; or the Life of a Collegian. London: John Warren, 1821. Large 8vo; vii, (i), 184 pages, 26 etchings on tinted paper; late 19th century full polished calf, gilt panelled spine; externally a handsome copy, plates foxed and browned at margins.   Ken Spelman 30-36 1996 £95.00

DAGLISH, E. F.   The Birds of the British Islands. London: 1948. 4to; pages xviii, 222; 48 plates of which 25 are colored by hand; buckram, top edge gilt, fine.   John Henly 27-9 1996 £85.00

DAHL, ROALD   Boy. Tales of Childhood. New York: Farrar, Straus Giroux, 1984. 1st edition; limited to 200 copies, signed by author; 8vo; boards, slipcase; as new.   James S. Jaffe 34-124 1996 $225.00

DAHL, ROALD   The Witches. New York: Farrar Straus Giroux, 1983. 1st edition; limited to 300 copies, signed by author and artist; 8vo; pictures by Quentin Blake; cloth, slipcase; mint.   James S. Jaffe 34-123 1996 $250.00

DAHL, ROALD   Works London: 1991. Commemorative Edition, 60/500 sets; 8vo; 15 volumes; quarter dark blue morocco, backstrips gilt lettered, patterned white boards, top edge gilt, matching board slipcases and overall blue board slipcase, new set.   Blackwell's B112-85 1996 £1,000.00

DAHLBERG, EDWARD   Bottom Dogs. London: 1929. 1st trade edition; 8 x 5 inches; 285 pages; cloth, minor wear.   John K. King 77-258 1996 $125.00

DAHLBERG, EDWARD   The Confessions of... New York: 1971. 1st edition; limited to 200 numbered copies, signed by author; 8.5 x 5.5. inches; 312 pages; cloth, very good in slipcase.   John K. King 77-25 1996 $125.00

DAHLBERG, EDWARD   The Sorrows of Priapus. Norfolk: New Directions, 1957. 1st edition; one of 150 numbered copies, signed by author and by artist; large 8vo; printed on untrimmed mould-made Arches paper with full page and smaller illustrations printed in sanguine, by Ben Shahn; printed Japanese vellum over boards, fine in lightly worn slipcase.   Marilyn Braiterman 15-186 1996 $625.00

DAHLBERG, EDWARD   Those Who Perish. New York: John Day, 193 1st edition; in presumed first state (black linen) binding; sparse light foxing to page edges, spine faded, else very good+ in dust jacket with few small chips; briefly inscribed by author.   Lame Duck Books 19-155 1996 $275.00

DAIX, PIERRE   Picasso: the Blue and Rose Periods. Greenwich: New York Graphic Society, 1967. Folio; 348 pages, 61 tipped in color plates, 770 monochrome illustrations; cloth, dust jacket. Lucas p. 177; Freitag 7432.   Brannan 43-514 1996 $395.00

DALE, EDWARD EVERETT   The Range Cattle Industry. Norman: University of Oklahoma Press, 1930. 1st edition; small 4to; xvii, (4), 22-216 pages; frontispiece, title map, 16 text maps, 7 illustrations from photos and reproductions; green cloth, owner's name on endpaper, spine faded, foxing to titlepage, near fine in lightly worn and chipped dust jacket, spine of jacket reinforced on inside; Adams herd 639; Dibu p. 101; Howes D20; Rader 1036; Reese 6 Score 27.   Argonaut Book Shop 113-169 1996 $300.00

DALECHAMP, CALEB   Christian Hospitalitie Handled Common-Place-Wise in the Chappel of Trinity Colledge in Cambridge... Cambridge: printed by Tho. Buck, 1632. 1st edition; small 4to; modern half calf; very good. STC 6192.   Ximenes 108-99 1996 $750.00

DALECHAMP, JACQUES   Histoire Generale des Plantes. Lyon: 1653. 2nd French edition; folio; 2 volumes; pages (5), 960, (36); 120, 758, (22); quarter old sheep, extremities worn, some cracking to upper edge of spines, volume 1 title frayed and loose, volume 2 titled cropped on left side and mounted, occasinal minor dampstaining, some browning to text from offsetting, scattered foxing, corner missing to a preliminary page in volume 1, tears to corner of index, repaired with modern stickers, corner missing to Latin table, resulting in some loss of text, last 8 pages in both volumes frayed, soiled or with small tears. Raymond M. Sutton VI-7 1996 $2,850.00

DALI, SALVADOR   Les Diners De Gala. New York: Felicie, Inc., 1973. 4to; 320, (iii) pages; color pictorial endpapers and profuse color and black and white illustrations; color pictorial cloth, rubbed at extremities, in color pictorial dust jacket; near fine.   Blue Mountain SP95-23 199 $150.00

DALI, SALVADOR   50 Secrets of Magic Craftsmanship. New York: Dial, 1948. Folio; 192 pages, numerous illustrations, 3 in color; cloth, lengthy inscription, dust jacket.   Brannan 43-144 1996 $125.00

DALI, SALVADOR   50 Secrets of Magic Craftsmanship. New York: D Press, 1948. 1st American edition; 4to; 192 pages; color and black and white illustrations; black cloth, bumped, rubbed and soiled, titled in gilt on spine, with 'Dali' in gilt on front cover, in pictorial dust jacket (chipped and torn at edges); very good.   Blue Mountain SP95-22 1996 $125.00

DALL, W. H.   Notes on the Avifauna of the Aleutian Islands, from Unalashka, Eastward (West of Unalashka). Boston: 1868/73-74. Offprints 2 parts, pages 11, 12; wrappers bit worn and soiled, loosely inserted single leaf offprint by the same 'some remarks upon the natural history of Alaska'; blank margins bit defective.   Maggs Bros. Ltd. 1190-555 1996 £55.00

DALLAS in 1873. An Invitation to Immigrants. Dallas: Stone-Inge Books, 1980. Of an edition of 450 copies, this one of a few very special copie bound thus; 3 x 2 1/8 inches; 26 pages; sumptuous brown morocco with gold stamped title on front cover and gold star on rear cover, blindstamped stars at each corner of both covers, extremely fine. Bromer Booksellers 87-205 1996 $125.00

DALLAS, GEORGE   System of Stiles, as Now Practicable Within the Kingdom of Scotland; and Reduced to a Clear Method... Edinburgh: printed by the Heirs and Successors of Andrew Anderson, 1697. contemporary calf, very worn, embrowned, usable copy.   Meyer Boswell SL27-57 1996 $450.00

DALLAWAY, JAMES   History of the Western Division of the County of Sussex, Including the Rapes of Chichester, Arundel and Bramber, with the City and Diocese of Chichester. London: 1815-32. Large 4to; 4 volumes, numerous engraved maps and plates; contemporary polished calf gilt, neatly rebacked, volume 1 with original spine, remainders bound to match, gilt edges. with armorial ex-libris of James Comerford, noted collector of topographic books. Lowndes pp. 580-582.   Marlborough 162-17 1996 £2,400.00

DALRYMPLE, JOHN   An Essay Towards a General History of Feudal Property in Great Britain Under the Following Heads. London: printed for A. Millar, 1758. 2nd edition; 12mo; contemporary calf, hinges cracked. Sweet & Maxwell pp. 444, 5.   Anthony Laywood 108-47 1996 £165.00

DALTON, E. A.   History of Ireland from...Earliest Times to the Present Day. London: 1910. 2nd edition; 8vo; 4 volumes in 8; color and balck and white illustrations; cloth, very good.   C. P. Hyland 216-138 1996 £75.00

DALTON, JOHN   History of the College of Physicians and Surgeons in the City of New York: Medical Department of Columbia College. New York: 1888. 208 pages; original binding, scarce.   W. Bruce Fye 71-480 1996 $100.00

DALTON, MICHAEL   The Countrey Justice: Containing the Practice of the Justices of the Peace Out of Their Sessions. London: printed by H. Sawbridge, S. Roycroft and W. Rawlins, 1682. Unlettered contemporary calf, very well preserved.   Meyer Boswell SL26-59 1996 $750.00

DALTON, O. M.   The Treasure of the Oxus with Other Examples of Early Oriental Metal-Work. London: British Museum, 1964. 8vo; frontispiece, lxxvi, 82 pages, 81 figures, 41 plates; original cloth, dust jacket (2 corners lightly bumped).   Archaeologia Luxor-3232 1996 $125.00

DALY, CESAR   Les Theatres de La Place Du Chatelet, Theatre du Chatelet-Theatre Lyrique. Paris: Librairie Generale de l'Architecture, n.d., ca. 1865. 2nd edition; folio: (iv), 42, (4) pages, 64 plates; contemporary half morocco, all edges gilt, joints rubbed, bookplate, else bright copy. Bookpress 75-38 1996 $2,500.00

DALYELL, JOHN GRAHAM   Fragments of Scotish (sic) History. Edinburgh: printed for Archibald Constable, 1798. 1st edition; 4to; frontispiece and 3 engraved maps; contemporary calf, ruled in blind and gilt, spine gilt, all edges gilt, joints rubbed, but sound; frontispiece foxed, some light browning, but nice, scarce.   Ximenes 108-100 1996 $400.00

DALYELL, JOHN GRAHAM   Scottish Poems of the Sixteenth Century. Edinburgh: printed for Archibald Constable; & Messrs. Vernor & Hood, London, 1801. 1st edition; 8vo; 2 volumes; (iii-xi), (xiii-xiv), 5-152, 2-356, 357-380, errata leaf, publisher's catalog, separate half title to all poems; full polished calf, double blind rule and single gilt ruled border to boards, gilt title to spines, spines worn and rubbed, raised bands to spines, corners very slightly bumped, owner's bookplate to front pastedown of all volumes.   Beeleigh Abbey BA56-142 1996 £125.00

DAMPIER, WILLIAM 1652-1715   A New Voyage Round the World. London: Argonaut Press, 1927. Limited edition, number 503 of 975 copies; xxxvii, 376 pages, printed on Japon vellum, publisher's prospectus laid in; maps (part folded), plates; maroon cloth, vellum spine has been replaced with a printed paper backstrip to approximate the original, binding lightly worn, bumped corners, interior clean, tight, unopened. Cox Lit. of Travel, v. I p. 44; Hill, Pacific Voyages I p. 78. Bohling Book Co. 191-421 1996 $150.00

DAMPIER, WILLIAM 1652-1715   Voyages and Discoveries. London: Argonaut Press, 1931. One of 375 copies; 27cm; xxxv, 311 pages; 4 folding maps; vellum spine, burgundy cloth, gilt cover decorataions; near fine, mostly unopened. Hill p. 78.   Parmer Books O39Nautica-039174 1996 $250.00

DANA, C. L.   Contributions to Medical and Biological Research Dedicated to Sir William Osler, in Honour of His Seventieth Birthday, July 12, 1919, by His Pupils and Co-Workers. New York: 1919. Number 35 of 1600 copies; 8vo; 2 volumes; steel engraved plate; cloth bit marked. Maggs Bros. Ltd. 1190-396 1996 £85.00

DANA, C. W.   The Garden of the World. Boston: Wentworth and Co., 1856. Pages 396; illustrations; original stamped boards, extremities worn, damp to first few pages, generally tight and good. W-C 279a.1. Buck 564.   Dumont 28-66 1996 $135.00

DANA, CHARLES   Poetry and Doctors: a Catalogue of Poetical Works Written by Physicians with Biographical Notes. Woodstock: 1916. 1st edition; 83 pages; illustrations; original binding; inscribed by Henry Barton Jacobs to Thomas B. Futcher; rare.   W. Bruce Fye 71-484 1996 $250.00

DANA, CHARLES A.   Proudhon and His 'Bank of the People' Being a Defence of the Great French Anarchist, Showing the Evils of a specie Currency and That Interest on Capital Can and Ought to be Abolished by a System of Free and Mutual Banking. New York: Benj. R. Tucker, 1896. 1st edition; 16mo; 7, 67 pages, plus ads; original stiff wrappers.   M & S Rare Books 60-424 1996 $150.00

DANA, CHARLES LOOMIS   Contributions to Medical and Biological Research Dedicated to Sir William Osler, Bart, M.D., F.R.S. In Honour of His Seventieth Birthday July 12th, 1919. New York: Paul B. Hoeber, 1919. Limited to 1600 sets; thick 8vo; 2 volumes; pages (xxii), (650), 29 plates; (xiv), 651-1268, (2) pages, 25 plates; printed panelled blue buckram. John Gach 150-118 1996 $200.00

DANA, JAMES D.   Manual of Mineralogy and Lithology: Containing the Elements of the Science of Minerals and Rocks. London: Trubner & Co., 1879. 3rd edition; 8vo; pages viii, 474; many woodcuts; original green cloth, fine, bright, fresh and unopened copy.   James Fenning 133-79 1996 £85.00

DANA, JOHN COTTON   The Far North-West. Newark: 1906. Approximately 400 copies printed for members of the American Lib. Assoc. Quarto; pages 40, 63 plates; original wrappers, very nice. Wickersham 6433.   Stephen Lunsford 45-38 1996 $125.00

DANA, RICHARD HENRY 1815-1882   Two Years Before the Mast. Chicago: Lakeside Press, 1930. Limited to 1000 copies; small quarto; ix, 524 pages; designed and illustrated in color and black and white by Edward A. Wilson; gilt stamped cloth, top edge gilt, housed in decorated cloth slipcase; bookplate; extremely fine.   Bromer Booksellers 87-278 1996 $200.00

DANA, RICHARD HENRY 1815-1882   Two Years Before the Mast. Chicago: Lakeside Press, 1930. Limited to 1000 copies; octavo, ix, 524 pages; illustrations by E. A. Wilson; original blue cloth with white cloth backstrip, decoratively stamped in gilt on front cover and spine, spine bit soiled, otherwise fine in publisher's cardboard slipcase.   Heritage Book Shop 196-167 1996 $150.00

DANBY, FRANCIS   Three Views, Illustrative of the Scenery of Bristol and Its Vicinity. London: Rowney & Forster, 1823. Oblong folio; 3 lithographic plates, uncolored, original paper wrappers, one or two small marks. Not in Abbey.   Marlborough 162-18 1996 £1,600.00

DANDY, WALTER   Benign Tumors in the Third Ventricle of the Brain: Diagnosis and Treatment. Springfield: 1933. 8vo; 171 pages; numerous illustrations; original binding; virtually mint.   James Tait Goodrich K40-107 1996 $295.00

DANDY, WALTER   Intracranial Arterial Aneurysms. Ithaca: 1945. 2nd printing; 8vo; viii, 146 pages, 5 folding charts, numerous text illustrations; original binding; nice association copy, Bronson Ray's copy with his signature. Walker pp. 112-13.   James Tait Goodrich K40-109 1996 $395.00

DANDY, WALTER   Orbital Tumors Results Following the Transcranial Operative Attack. New York: 1941. 1st edition; 8vo; 168 pages; 100 illustrations; original binding, shelf worn, ex-library with spine label and some stamps on endpapers, internally very good, tight copy.   James Tait Goodrich K40-108 1996 $350.00

DANDY, WALTER   Selected Writings of Walter E. Dandy. Springfield: Thomas, 1957. 8vo; 789 pages; frontispiece; original binding.   James Tait Goodrich K40-111 1996 $135.00

DANGERFIELD, THOMAS   Dangerfield's Memoires, Digested Into Adventures, Receipts, and Expences. London: printed by J. Bennet, for Charles Brome, 1685. 1st edition; small 4to; recent paper boards, cloth spine; very good. Wing D194B; Mish p. 67.   Ximenes 109-95 1996 $900.00

DANIEL, GEORGE   Doctor Bolus; a Serio-comic-Bombastick-Operatick Interlude... London: printed for W. and J. Lowndes, 1818. 1st edition; 8vo; disbound; very good, scarce. CBEL III 1726.   Ximenes 109-96 1996 $100.00

DANIEL, GEORGE   Merrie England in the Olden Time. London: Richard Bentley, 1842. 1st separate edition; 8vo; 2 volumes, 292, 296 pages; frontispiece and 26 engravings; 19th century three quarter polished green calf by Zaehnsdorf with gilt tooled spine panel florets, red and brown morocco spine labels, raised bands, top edge gilt; near fine.   Chapel Hill 94-50 1996 $175.00

DANIEL, SAMUEL   The Collection of the History of England. London: by F. Leach, for Benj. Tooke, and Thomas Sawbridge, 1685. 5th edition; folio; (6), 262, (10), 263 pages; modern half calf, spine heavily gilt, by Bayntun, neat repair at inner margin of title, light overall foxing, occasional browning, otherwise very nice in fine binding. Wing D208.   Joseph J. Felcone 64-16 1996 $650.00

DANIEL-ROPS, HENRY   The Misted Mirror. London: Martin Secker, 1930. 1st edition; original binding, top edge dusty, prelims, edges and endpapers spotted, free endpapers partially browned, top corner of one page creased, rear pastedown, slightly bubbled, head and tail of spine bumped, covers rubbed at extremities, lower cover slightly marked, very good in slightly rubbed, creased and dusty dust jacket browned at spine and edges.   Ulysses 39-649 1996 £65.00

DANIELL, J. FREDERIC   Meteorological Essays and Observataions. London: 1827. 2nd edition; 9 x 5.5 inches; 643 pages, 6 charts; roughly attached to old boards covered in leather, very soiled, some staining. John K. King 77-718 1996 $100.00

DANIELL, L. E.   Texas: the Country and Its Men. London: pub. by the author, n.d. 796 pages; new gilt stamped black linen.   Maggie Lambeth 30-127 1996 $175.00

DANIELL, THOMAS   A Picturesque Voyage to India by the Way of China. London: T. Davison for Longman, 1810. Oblong 4to; titlepage, ii pages, 50 ff., 50 hand colored aquatint plates on thick paper, wash tinted borders, mounted on stubs, half calf, worn. few slight patches of foxing to margins, otherwise bright and clean. Abbey Travel 516; Colas 797; Mendelssohn I p. 413.   Marlborough 162-226 1996 £3,500.00

DANIELL, WILLIAM   Illustrations of the Island of Staffa, in a Series of Views... London: printed by Thomas Davison for Longman et al and W. Daniell, 1818. Oblong quarto; half title 1 l., title 1 l., text 6 lls., and 9 colored aquatint plates; original boards, printed paper label, green roan back, spine worn and joints split, some foxing in margins of few plates; bookseller's label "Sold by Manners & Miller, Edinburgh" at top of front board. Abbey Scenery 510; Tooley, English Books with Col. Plates 1935 p. 92.   H. M. Fletcher 121-134 1996 £775.00

DANIELLS, J. M.   The Life of Stonewall Jackson... New York: Charles Richardson, 1863. Reprinted from advance sheets of the Richmond edition (printed the same year); 8vo; engraved portraits, infrequent light spotting, 2 leaves slightly sprung, else good; original black cloth, worn at head of spine and corners, gilt lettering; inscription "Hd. Harvest 89 Regt., 11 April 1864."   Ian Wilkinson 95/1-5 1996 £65.00

DANTE, ALIGHIERI 1265-1321   Dante's Hell. Boston: Ticknor & Fields, 1857. 1st edition of this translation; 12mo; original quarter black roan and marbled boards, bit worn; some foxing at beginning and end, but very good; presentation copy, inscribed from translator to William C. Todd.   Ximenes 108-101 1996 $100.00

DANTE, ALIGHIERI 1265-1321   La Divina Commedia. Florence: 1919. 2 1/2 x 1 13/16 inches; 455 pages; bound in lavishly gilt stamped green calf, all edges red, spine slightly faded, original owner's notations on front free endpaper, else near fine. Bookplate. Bondy p. 100;   Bromer Booksellers 87-188 1996 $125.00

DANTE, ALIGHIERI 1265-1321   The Divine Comedy. New York: Limited Editions Club, 1932. One of 1500 numbered copies, signed by Mardersteig; small folio; printed in Monotype Bembo on San Marco paper; patterned cloth, very nice.   Bertram Rota 272-342 1996 £100.00

DANTE, ALIGHIERI 1265-1321   The Divine Comedy. printed by Hans Mardersteig at the Officina Bodoni for the LEC, 1933. Limited edition of 1500 numbered copies, signed by printer; 4to; xxi, 492 pages + colophon leaf; original patterned cloth, top edge gilt, others uncut, by Fortuny (occasional very slight spotting in text).   Thomas Thorp 489-79 1996 £150.00

DANTE, ALIGHIERI 1265-1321   In Defence of Woman. London: Nonesuch Press, 1928. Limited edition of 1475 numbered copies; folio;vo; (4), 327 pages, on Van Gelder mould made paper, 42 collotype illustrations pritned in sepia from drawings by Botticelli; publisher's orange vellum, gilt panelled sides with oval design in centre, spine gilt, top edge gilt, others uncut, spine faded and covers bowed as usual, fine, crisp copy internally.   Thomas Thorp 489-78 1996 £250.00

DANTE, ALIGHIERI 1265-1321   A Translation of the Inferno of Dante. London: printed by C. Dilly, 1785. 1st edition translated by Henry Boyd; 8vo; 2 volumes; original light blue boards, later paper spines, cloth case; fine, fresh copy, wholly uncut; uncommon. Cunningham, Divie Comedy in English pp. 14-16; CBEL III 370.   Ximenes 109-46 1996 $1,500.00

DANTE, ALIGHIERI 1265-1321   Dantes Inferno. Hopewell: Ecco Press, 1993. 1st edition; deluxe issue, limited to 125 copies, signed by each of the translators and with the original etching signed by Francesco Clemente laid in; small folio; frontispiece by Francesco Clemente; text was set in Monotype Dante & printed letterpress by Michael & Winifred Bixler on Rives heavyweight paper; quarter black calf and red silk over boards, slipcase by Claudia Cohen; handsome book, as new.   James S. Jaffe 34-244 1996 $1,500.00

DANTE, ALIGHIERI 1265-1321   The Stone Beloved. Austin: Kairos Press, 1986. One of 150 numbered copies, signed by artist, this one of only 25 with plates tinted in shades of brown and blue; folio; printed handset Romanee on Rives, lithographs printed by artist Peter Nickel; half vellum, grey paper boards, fine in slipcase.   Bertram Rota 272-237 1996 £385.00

DANTE, ALIGHIERI 1265-1321   Vita Nuova. Proemico di Benedetto Croce. Montagnola: Officina Bodoni, 1925. One of 225 copies on Fabriano handmade with watermark of the Press; folio; printed in 20 pt. Bodoni Casale roman and italic and 16 pt. Catania; maize buckram, gilt, exceptionally fine in original matching slipcase.   Bertram Rota 272-337 1996 £950.00

D'ARBELOFF, NATALIE   Philosophy: Seventeen Coloured Etchings/Aquatints. NdA Press, 1990. One of 18 numbered copies, signed by artist; approximately 3 1/2 x 9 inches; printed on Japanese Hodomura, versos hand colored in acrylics; sewn Japanese style between the artist's colored boards; fine in slipcase.   Bertram Rota 272-312 1996 £200.00

DARBY, WILLIAM   A Geographical Description of the State of Lousiana, the Southern Part of the State of Mississippi, and Territory of Alabama... New York: James Olmstead, 1817. 2nd edition; 356, (iii) pages; frontispiece; original full tree calf, rebacked with original spine and morocco label, usual foxing and offset, very good. Streeter Sale 4234; Hwoes D62; Clark Travels in Old south II 196.   Michael D. Heaston 23-131 1996 $1,500.00

DARIOT, CLAUDE   Dariotus Redivivus; or a Briefe Introduction to the Judgement of the Stars. London: for Andrew Kemb, 1653. 4to; (12), 303 pages, including woodcut frontispiece, 1 plate, many woodcut charts and diagrams including 3 with volvelles, title in red and black; very skillful period style modern full calf, imprint cut into, neat repair on A2, few small spots, otherwise very attractive; calligraphic signature of John Pillard, 1789. Wellcome II p. 432; Wing D257.   Joseph J. Felcone 64-1 1996 $1,000.00

DARLEY, GEORGE M.   Pioneering in the San Juan. Personal Reminiscences of Work Done in Southwestern Colorado During the "Great San Juan Excitement". Chicago: New York: Toronto: Fleming H. Revell Co., 1899. 1st edition; 8vo; (226) pages; illustrations; original pictorial grey cloth; very good to fine; Not in Graff Collection; not in Howes; Adams Six Guns 556.   Robert F. Lucas 42-24 1996 $150.00

DARLEY, GEORGE M.   Pioneering in the San Juan: Personal Reminiscences of Work Done in Southwestern Colorado During the "Great San Juan Excitment." Chicago: Fleming H. Revell Co., 1899. 7 1/2 x 5 inches; 226 pages + frontispiece, 12 pages of photographic illustrations; pictorial grey cloth stamped in blue and white.   Dawson's Books Shop 528-71 1996 $125.00

DARLING FOUNDATION OF NEW YORK STATE   Early American Silvermsith sand Silver. New York State Silversmiths. Eggertsville: Darling Foundation, 1964. Limited to 500 numbered copies; this copy with supplement bound in; 8vo; 228 pages; marks and several plates of silver objects; cloth, spine ends rubbed, lower extremities frayed, still very good. Scarce.   J. M. Cohen 35-17 1996 $375.00

DARLINGTON, W.   Memorials of John Bartram and Humphry Marshall, with Notices of Their Botanical Contemporaries. Philadelphia: 1849. 1st edition; 8vo; 2 plates of facsimile ms., 2 plates of houses; cloth, bit worn, rebacked; signature of M. H. Dickinson on title.   Maggs Bros. Ltd. 1190-230 1996 £55.00

DARROW, CLARENCE SEWARD 1857-1938   The Story of My Life. New York: Scribners, 1932. 1st edition; endpapers slightly darkened, else fine in very good dust jacket with couple of modest chips and with some not very noticeable dampstaining, mostly on spine.   Between the Covers 42-125 1996 $125.00

DARTMOUTH Verse. Portland: Mosher, 1925. owner's name and date (5/29/25) on front pastedown, spine slightly darkened, very good, without dust jacket.   Ken Lopez 74-147 1996 $100.00

DARWIN, BERNARD   The Tale of Mr. Tootleoo and the Cockiolly Bird. London: Nonesuch Press, 1925. 1st edition; oblong 4to; 22 full page colored illustrations; tan pictorial boards; fine.   Barbara Stone 70-68 1996 £110.00

DARWIN, CHARLES ROBEERT 1809-1882   Charles Darwin's Notebooks 1836-1844... Ithaca: 1987. 4to; pages viii, 747; cloth.   Wheldon & Wesley 207-226 1996 £85.00

DARWIN, CHARLES ROBERT 1809-1882   The Correspondence of Charles Darwin. Cambridge: 1985-93. 8vo; Volumes 1-8; illustrations; cloth.   Wheldon & Wesley 207-225 1996 £320.00

DARWIN, CHARLES ROBERT 1809-1882   The Descent of Man. Adelaide: Limited Editions Club, 1971. Number 1029 of 1500 copies, signed by the artist; drawings by Fritz Kredel; fine in slipcase.   Hermitage SP95-965 1996 $175.00

DARWIN, CHARLES ROBERT 1809-1882   The Different Forms of Flowers on Plants of the Same Species. London: 1877. 1st edition; only 1250 copies printed; 8vo; pages viii, 352, 15 text figures, 38 tables in text; with 32 pages of ads at end dated March 1877; original cloth; slightly foxed at beginning and end. Freeman 1277.   Wheldon & Wesley 207-1408 1996 £130.00

DARWIN, CHARLES ROBERT 1809-1882   Different Forms of Flowers on Plants of the Same Species. London: John Murray, 1877. 1st edition; 8, 352 pages; 22 pages ads not bound in, 15 figures; full tooled leather, tooled spines with school shield stamped in gold on front cover.. Freeman 1277.   John Johnson 135-188 1996 $150.00

DARWIN, CHARLES ROBERT 1809-1882   The Different Forms of Flowers on Plants of the Same Species. London: 1892. 4th thousand; 8vo; pages xxiv, 352, 15 text figures; original cloth, G.D.H. Carpenter's copy. Freeman 1286.   Wheldon & Wesley 207-1409 1996 £60.00

DARWIN, CHARLES ROBERT 1809-1882   The Expression of the Emotions in Man and Animals. London: John Murray, 1872. 1st edition; 2nd issue; 8vo; vi, 374, 4 (ad) pages, 7 heliotype plates, 3 folding, reproducing photos by Duchenne de Boulogne and Rejlander and 21 figures in text; later three quarter calf over marbled boards, raised spine bands; faded early signature on title, near fine. GM 4975; Freeman 1142; Waller 2298; Osler 1574; Blocker p. 100.   Edwin V. Glaser 121-77 1996 $450.00

DARWIN, CHARLES ROBERT 1809-1882   The Expression of the Emotions in Man and Animals. New York: Appleton, 1873. 1st American edition, 1st issue; 8vo; v, (1), 34, (14) ads pages; 7 heliotype plates, 3 folding, 21 figures in text; original decorated cloth, rubbed and bit frayed at extremities, early ownership signature on front free endpaper; very good. Freeman 1143; GM 4975.   Edwin V. Glaser 121-78 1996 $275.00

DARWIN, CHARLES ROBERT 1809-1882   The Formation of Vegetable Mould through the Action of Worms. London: 1881. 5th thousand; 8vo; pages vii, 326, (2); original cloth; from the collection of Samuel J. Fisher, then of Walter Garstang with his bookplate; some marginal annotation in pencil.   Wheldon & Wesley 207-1247 1996 £60.00

DARWIN, CHARLES ROBERT 1809-1882   Insectivorous Plants. London: 1875. 1st edition; 1st issue; 8vo; pages x, 462; original green cloth, short tear in front free endpaper, repaired; small ink marks on lower cover, some rubbing and wear, bookplate of the Conservatoire Botanique de Geneve, minor crack to two inner joints; inscribed "From the author" in hand of publisher's clerk; bookplate reads "Livres Provenant de la bibliotheque De Candolle, acquise par la Ville de Geneve en 1921, inseres la meme annee dans la bibliotheque du Conservatoire botanique de Geneve". Freeman 1217.   Raymond M. Sutton VI-8 1996 $1,450.00

DARWIN, CHARLES ROBERT 1809-1882   Life and Letters... London: 1887. 3rd edition; 8vo; 3 volumes; portraits; original cloth, little foxing, spine of volume 2 slightly worn. Freeman 1455.   Wheldon & Wesley 207-220 1996 £80.00

DARWIN, CHARLES ROBERT 1809-1882   Life and Letters of Charles Darwin... London: 1887. 3rd edition of volume 2; 3 volumes, 1206 pages, 7 plates; grey green cloth, volume 3 top of back hinge cracked, bindings worn; Freean 1452, 1455.   John Johnson 135-189 1996 $125.00

DARWIN, CHARLES ROBERT 1809-1882   The Life and Letters of Charles Darwin. New York: 1888. 8vo; 2 volumes; pages viii, 558; iv, (1), 562; 3 frontispieces, 3 engravings; original cloth, small tears to head of spine of volume 1, light rubbing; Freeman 1458.   Raymond M. Sutton VI-1134 1996 $145.00

DARWIN, CHARLES ROBERT 1809-1882   The Movements and Habits of Climbing Plants. London: 1891. 5th thousand; 8vo; pages x, 208; original cloth; G. D. H. Carpenter's copy with his signature.   Wheldon & Wesley 207-1407 1996 £60.00

DARWIN, CHARLES ROBERT 1809-1882   On the Origin of Species by Means of Natural Selection... London: John Murray, 1859. 1st edition; octavo; ix, (1), 502 pages, plus 32 publisher's ads dated June 1859 (Freeman's third state); folding diagram; original green cloth (Freeman's variant 'b') with covers decoratively stamped in blind and spine in gilt, slight discoloration from removed circulating library label on front cover, but no other indication of library usage, corners bumped, cloth lightly chipped at foot of spine, newer black coated endpapers, intermittent light foxing and soiling, few short marginal tears, overall very good, bright copy in quarter brown morocco slipcase and brown cloth chemise; Freeman 373; Grolier/Horblit 23b; PMM 344.   Heritage Book Shop 196-178 1996 $17,500.00

DARWIN, CHARLES ROBERT 1809-1882   On the Origin of Species by Means of Natural Selection, or the Preservation of Favoured Races in the Struggle for Life. London: 1859. 1st edition; 8vo; pages x, 502, folding diagram; original green cloth. some very slight foxing and inner joints tender, binding slightly used.   Wheldon & Wesley 207-23 1996 £6,500.00

DARWIN, CHARLES ROBERT 1809-1882   On the Origin of Species by Means of Natural Selection. London: 1859. 1st edition; 8vo; folding diagram, with half title, but without inserted ads, usually found; late 19th century half green morocco, date tooled at foot of spine (which is faded to brown), little worn and scuffed, signature of John Anderson, later in the collection of Dr. Warren G. Smirl, bought from Quaritch in 1978 for $1700.   Maggs Bros. Ltd. 1190-231 1996 £4,200.00

DARWIN, CHARLES ROBERT 1809-1882   On the Origin of Species by Means of Natural Selection or the Preservation of Favoured Races in the Struggle for Life. London: John Murray, 1860. 2nd edition; 5th thousand; 8vo; x, 502 pages ads; original green cloth, gilt, front inner hinge starting, outer hinges frayed, spine quite bright, stamp and signature of the Earl of Lovelace in 1860. Freeman 376, ads dated Jan. 1860. Binding variant A.   Kenneth Karmiole 1NS-85 1996 $1,000.00

DARWIN, CHARLES ROBERT 1809-1882   The Origin of Species by Means of Natural Selection. London: 1872. 6th edition; 11th thousand; 8vo; name torn from blank upper portion of half title, green cloth, somewhat worn and soiled, recased with chocolate brown free endpapers replaced. Freeman 391.   Maggs Bros. Ltd. 1190-232 1996 £125.00

DARWIN, CHARLES ROBERT 1809-1882   The Variation of Animals and Plants Under Domestication. London: John Murray, 1868. 1st edition; 2nd issue, with two line imprint and one line erratum in volume 1; 8vo; 2 volumes, viii, 411, 32 (ads); viii, 486, (2 ads) pages; 43 figures in text; original cloth, some wear to binding, extremities and along joints, corners bumped, internally very good. Very good set. GM 224.1. Freeman 878; Nomran Lib. 597; Waller 10789; Cushing D55.   Edwin V. Glaser 121-76 1996 $485.00

DARWIN, CHARLES ROBERT 1809-1882   The Variation of Animals and Plants Under Domestication. London: 1868. 1st edition; 2nd issue; 8vo; 2 volumes; original green cloth, bit worn and sciffed and marked, several sections starting, signs of contemporary library use, with inserted integral ads; Freeman 878.   Maggs Bros. Ltd. 1190-233 1996 £90.00

DARWIN, CHARLES ROBERT 1809-1882   The Variation of Animals and Plants Under Domestication. London: 1868. Volume 1 is 1st edition, 1st issue, the 32 pages of ads are not present in this copy; volume 2 is 1st edition, 2nd issue, binding is a first issue with imprint being in one line; 8vo; 2 volumes; pages viii, 141, 43, text illustrations; pages viii, 486, 2 ads; cloth, gilt, volume 2 rebacked preserving spine and endpapers. Freeman 877, 878.   John Henly 27-126 1996 £180.00

DARWIN, CHARLES ROBERT 1809-1882   The Variation of Animals and Plants Under Domestication. London: 1868. 1st edition; 2nd issue; 8vo; 2 volumes; 43 text figures; original green cloth, very small nick on spine of volume 2 which is slightly loose but certainly good copy.   Wheldon & Wesley 207-150 1996 £180.00

DARWIN, CHARLES ROBERT 1809-1882   The Variation of Animals and Plants Under Domestication. London: 1899. 8th impression of the 2nd edition; 8vo; 2 volumes; text figures; original cloth; G.D.H. Carpenter's copy with his signature.   Wheldon & Wesley 207-151 1996 £60.00

DARWIN, ERASMUS 1731-1802   The Botanic Garden; a Poem. London: for J. Johnson, 1791. 1st edition; 4to; 2 volumes bound in one; pages xii, 214 (actually 216), 126 ('Additional Notes'), (ii); (12), v-vii, (i), 184 (actualy 186), directions to the binder on two slips, one inserted between volume I and II, the other laid down below text at end of volume 2; frontispiece in each volume, 15 engraved plates, 1 engraved vignette half title in volume 2 only, as issued; contemporary tree calf, rebacked, old spine laid down, red morocco label, gilt in compartments, corners neatly repaired, marbled endpapers, pale yellow edges, occasional light spotting or staining, two of the four plates of the Portland Vase very slightly cropped at one edge (as often), good copy; the Gell copy, with Gell family ownership inscription. Blake 450A; Nissen 451.   Simon Finch 24-64 1996 £680.00

DARWIN, ERASMUS 1731-1802   The Botanic Garden, a Poem. London: printed for J. Johnson, 1799. 4th edition; 8vo; 2 volumes; all plates as listed, the diagram of coal-mine frayed, torn and mounted, but complete; contemporary sprinkled calf, gilt, nice.   Peter Murray Hill 185-47 1996 £200.00

DARWIN, ERASMUS 1731-1802   The Botanic Garden. London: 1973. Limited edition of 500 copies; 4to; 2 volumes in 1; pages (8), xii, 214, 126, (1); (11), viii, 184; frontispiece, 14 plates; cloth.   Raymond M. Sutton VI-117 1996 $100.00

D'ASSIGNY, MARIUS   A Treatise Useful for All, Especially Such as are to Speak in Publick. London: printed by J. Darby for Andr. Bell, 1706. 3rd edition; 8vo; frontispiece, perforation stamp on title, contemporary sheep, rebacked. Hunter & Macalpine pp. 262-266.   Anthony Laywood 108-48 1996 £175.00

DAUBENY, CHARLES   An Introduction to the Atomic Theory, Comprising a Sketch of the Opinions Entertained by the Most Distinguished Ancient and Modern Philosophers with Respect to the Constitution of Matter. Oxford: 1831. 1st edition; 9 x 5.5 inches; 147, 62 page supplement; full roan half, bookplate, covers rubbed, front outer hinge beginning to crack.   John K. King 77-719 1996 $500.00

D'AULAIRE, INGRI   Buffalo Bill. New York: Doubleday Doran, 1952. 1st edition; 4to; colored lithographed illustrations; cloth backed colored pictorial boards, fine in just chipped pictorial dust jacket; Bader 45.   Barbara Stone 70-67 1996 £55.00

DAULBY, DANIEL   A Descriptive Catalogue of the Works of Rembrandt, and of His Scholars, Bol, Livens and Van Vleit... Liverpool: printed by J. M'Creery, 1796. 1st edition; 8vo; half title, portrait, errata leaf at end; contemporary tree calf, rubbed, hinges cracked, label.   Anthony W. Laywood 109-33 1996 £110.00

DAUNT, ACHILLES   In the Land of the Moose, the Bear and the Beaver. 1885. Engraved plates; original ornate pictorial colored and gilt cloth with moose, bear, beaver motifs, etc; excellent copy.   David Grayling J95Biggame-405 1996 £60.00

DAVENANT, WILLIAM 1606-1668   Gondibert: an Heroick Poem. London: printed by Tho. Newcomb for John Holden, 1651. 1st edition; 4to; woodcut device on title, (2), 88, (4), 322, (8) pages, collating correctly A-3K4 with 3K4 blank present; occasional slight soiling and edge fingermarks, few pencilled reader's emphasis marks; contemporary ruled sheep, sometime neatly rebacked, lettered in gilt; good, crisp copy. From the library of Charles Davenant, author's son, this copy with at least 32 author's ms. corrections. MacDonald & Hargreaves p. 24.   John Drury 82-63 1996 £450.00

DAVENANT, WILLIAM 1606-1668   The Works... London: printed by T. N. for Henry Herringman, 1673. 1st edition; folio; contemporary mottled calf, gilt, spine gilt, some rubbing, completely sound; wholly unrestored binding, text crisp and fresh; inscribed "Mrs. Elizabeth de Greys booke, given her by John Knyvett Esq. ye yeere he was High Sheriff of Norfolke, 1681/2." Wing D320; Greg III 1057-8; CBEL I 1208; Woodward & McManaway 309.   Ximenes 109-97 1996 $2,500.00

DAVENANT, WILLIAM 1606-1668   The Works... London: T. N. for Henry Herringman, 1673. 1st collected edition; folio; (viii), 402, 111, (v), 486 pages; frontispiece; (often absent), separate titlepages to various parts, dated 1672; contemporary calf, rebacked, two corners repaired, spine gilt ruled, lael; little wear on edges, endpapers and titlepage opening a bit dusty, scattered minor foxing and soiling, insignificant worming through margin of a few leaves near end (well clear of text), sound copy. Wing D320.   Robert Clark 38-36 1996 £450.00

DA VENEZIA, ANGELO   Giornale Sacro o Sia Metodo de Invocare Ogni Giorno Della Settimana. Il Gloriosissimo Taumaturgo Antonio Santo. Pádua: Per li Conzatti, n.d. 1762. 4to; printed on fine paper, with eng. title in blue & red, entirely within Baroque cartouche, engraved head & tailpieces, historiated initial letters, portraits, engravings; contemporary mottled sheep with gilt floral leaf border entwined around a rope, there is a single flower in each corner, spine with five raised bands and complex floral decoration within compartments (no title), board edges gilt, somewhat rubbed, but solid, attractive copy with early ownership stamp barely visible in lower margin of title, all edges stained red, highly attractive.   Book Block 32-25 1996 $1,375.00

DAVENPORT, CYRIL   Royal English Bookbindings. London:/New York: Seeley & Co. Ltd.,/Macmillan Co. 1896. 10.5 x 7 inches; 95 pages; frontispiece, 7 color paltes, 27 black and white illustrations; first binding, gilt stamped blue cloth; very good.   Joshua Heller 21-73 1996 $110.00

DAVENPORT, CYRIL   Samuel Mearne. Binder to King Charles II. Chicago: Caxton Club, 1906. 1st edition; one of 250 copies printed on handmade paper; 4to; colored frontispiece, 24 chromolithographic plates, illustrations in text, original cloth backed boards, printed paper label on spine, uncut.   Forest Books 74-58 1996 £295.00

DAVENPORT, GUY   The Bowman of Shu. Newtown: Grenfell Press, 1983. One of 115 copies, signed by author (out of a total of 125); 12 1/4 x 10 inches; frontispiece and 16 illustrations in text, 9 of them full page by Henri Gaudier-Brzeska and Guy Davenport; green morocco backed pictorial paper boards, titled in gilt on spine, edges untrimmed; mint.   Phillip J. Pirages 33-268 1996 $275.00

DAVENPORT, GUY   Father Louie: Photographs of Thomas Merton. New York: Timken Publishers, 1991. One of 100 copies, signed by Davenport with original print tipped in; fine as issued in slipcase.   Bev Chaney, Jr. 23-480 1996 $200.00

DAVENPORT, GUY   Jonah: a Short Story. Nadja, 1986. Of 126 copies, signed and dated by author; this one of 100 numbered copies for sale; large 8vo; printed in black, grey and red in handset Stempel Optima on Whatman; grey St. Armand wrappers. Fine.   Bertram Rota 272-302 1996 £55.00

DAVENPORT, JOHN   Aphrodisiacs and Anti-Aphrodisiacs: Three Essays on the Powers of Reproduction: with Some Account of the Judicial 'Congress' As Practised in France During the 17th Century. London: 1869. 1st edition; 154 pages, plus 7 plates; quarter leather, hinges cracked, two 1 inch pieces missing from spine, contents fine.   W. Bruce Fye 71-500 1996 $150.00

DAVEY, RICHARD   The Pageant of London. London: Methuen & Co., 1906. 1st edition; tall 8vo; 2 volumes; 429, 649 pages; 40 illustrations in color; half red morocco, raised bands, gilt decoration in compartments, top edge gilt, spines bit darkened, otherwise nice.   David Mason 71-47 1996 $200.00

DAVID, ELIZABETH   French Country Cooking. London: 1951. 1st edition; illustrations by John Minton; very good in pictorial Minton dust jacket with one chip at head of lower panel.   Words Etcetera 94-343 1996 £55.00

DAVID, ELIZABETH   French Country Cooking. New York: Horizon Press, n.d., c. 1952. 1st American edition, from English sheets; some light wear to bottom of boards, else about fine in lightly chipped very good dust jacket with some loss at crown, about half inch at deepest point; uncommon, attractive copy.   Between the Covers 42-111 1996 $125.00

DAVID, ROBERT BEEBE   Finn Burnett, Frontiersman: The Life and Adventures of an Indian Fighter, Mail Coach Driver, Miner, Pioneer Cattleman, Participant in the Powder River Expediton, Survivor of the Hay Field Fight... Glendale: Arthur H. Clark, 1937. 1st edition; one of 1000 copies; 378 pages; 8 plates from photos; extremely light rubbing to spine ends, overall fine, clean copy. Adams Herd 646; Clark and Brunet 56.   Argonaut Book Shop 113-170 1996 $175.00

DAVIDSON, JOHN   In a Music Hall and Other Poems. London: Ward and Downey, 1891. 1st edition; buckram covers, top edge dusty, covers dusty and slightly soiled, spine browned, head and tail of spine and corners bumped, endpapers browned, edges of some pages nicked, prelims, edges and endpapers spotted, some internal spotting; good. Presentation copy from author; with bookplate of literary agent John Johnson.   Ulysses 39-137 1996 £650.00

DAVIDSON, MARSHALL B.   The American Heritage History of American Antiques. New York: 1967-69. 4to; 3 volumes; profusely illustrated, partly in color; original cloth, dust jacket, slipcase.   Jens J. Christoffersen SL94-145 1996 $250.00

DAVIDSON, PATRICIA F.   Ancient Greek and Roman Gold Jewelry in the Brooklyn Museum. Brooklyn: Brooklyn Museum, 1984. 4to; xxii, 214 pages; profusely illustrated; original cloth, corner bumped. Archaeologia Luxor-3234 1996 $150.00

DAVIDSON, T.   British Fossil Brachiopoda. London: 1851-86. 4to; 6 volumes, 234 plates; cloth, sound ex-library set, bindings trifle soiled, slight foxing. Complete copy, rare.   Wheldon & Wesley 207-24 1996 £450.00

DAVIE, IAN   Oxford Poetry - 1942-1943. Oxford: Basil Blackwell, 1943. 500 copies printed; wrappers, covers slightly marked, rubbed, creased and dusty, tail of spine and corners slightly bumped, titlepage and edges slightly spotted; very good.   Ulysses 39-344 1996 £175.00

D'AVIEDOR, ELIM H.   Loose Rein. London: Bradbury & Agnew, &c., 1887. 1st edition; 8vo; original 11 parts, with original wrappers printed in black and red with colored vignette illustrations, 22 colored plates, 49 vignettes in text by Georgina Bowers, 33 pages of ads on covers, publisher's slip in part 2; preserved in folding cloth cover with brown morocco slipcase; mint, extremely rare. Not in Schwerdt Cat. Mellon Collection no. 231.   Charles W. Traylen 117-297 1996 £695.00

DAVIES, BLODWEN   A Study of Tom Thomson: The Story of a man Who Looked for Beauty and For Truth in the Wilderness. Toronto: Discus Press, 1935. Limited to 450 numbered copies, signed by author; 8vo; pages (xxii), 133, 4 tipped in color plates, text illustrations; cloth, spine faded, else fine.   Hugh Anson-Cartwright 87-407 1996 $150.00

DAVIES, H.   Welsh Botanology...Native Plants of Anglesey... London: 1813. 1st edition; 8vo; 2 parts in 1 volume; engraved plate; original boards, uncut, bit stained and worn; the Plesch copy with booklabel. Maggs Bros. Ltd. 1190-71 1996 £90.00

DAVIES, H. W.   Devices of the Early Printers - 1457-1560 - Their History and Development... London: Grafton & Co., 1935. 1st edition; numerous black and whtie reproductions of printer's devices; original binding, spine slightly faded, covers slightly marked, head and tail of spine and corners slightly bumped, very good; with pencilled ownership signature of James Hart.   Ulysses 39-483 1996 £95.00

DAVIES, JAMES   Relation of a Voyage to Sagadahoc. Cambridge: John Wilson and Son, 1880. One of a small edition for private distribution; 25.2 cm; 43 pages; three quarter leather, marbled endpapers original front wrapper bound in.   Parmer Books O39Nautica-039362 1996 $250.00

DAVIES, JOHN   The Ancient Rites and Monuments of the Monastical and Cathedral Church of Durham. London: printed for W. Hensman, 1672. 1st edition; 8vo; contemporary sheep; two lower corners torn away, affecting several words which are clear from context, otherwise fine. Wing D392.   Ximenes 108-102 1996 $300.00

DAVIES, JOHN   The Innkeeper's and Butler's Guide, or, a Directory for Making and Managing British Wines with Directions for the Managing, Coloring and Flavoring of Foreign Wines and Spirits.... Leeds: Davies, 1811. 14th edition; 8vo; 199 pages; original boards (some foxed), wear to spine; rare.   Second Life Books 103-65 1996 $235.00

DAVIES, MARGARET   The Miss Margaret Davies Complete Collection of Special Gregynog Bindings. Amsterdam: De Zilverdistel B. V., 1994. 1st edition; limited edition; 4to; 700 pages; 95 colored and 15 black and white photos; original cloth, dust jacket, new.   Forest Books 74-95 1996 £88.00

DAVIES, R.   The Histories of the King's Mannour House at York... York: 1883. Signed by artist in pencil and inscribed "Only 150 of this edition printed"; small folio; 24 pages, including contents leaf, 1 plan, etched titlepage, 10 plates by Buckle; original cloth backed board (covers little dusty).   Marlborough 162-21 1996 £85.00

DAVIES, RHYS   Daisy Matthews and Three Other Tales. Waltham St. Lawrence: Golden Cockerel Press, 1932 1st edition; 118/325 copies; 8vo; pages (iii), 64, (1); printed on Batchelor handmade paper and signed by author; 4 wood engravings by Agnes Miller Parker; original quarter tan morocco, backstrip gilt lettered, patterned pink and orange cloth, very faint browning to free endpapers, top edge gilt, others untrimmed, excellent. Chanticleer 87.   Blackwell's B112-123 1996 £100.00

DAVIES, RHYS   Daisy Matthews and Three Other Tales. Waltham St. Lawrence: Golden Cockerel Press, 1932. 1st edition; number 132 of 325 copies, signed by author; 8vo; pages (4), 64 + colophon; four fine wood engravings by Agnes Miller Parker, printed by Gibbings on Batchelor's handmade paper; original tan morocco backed patterned cloth, top edge gilt, others uncut; Chanticleer 87   Claude Cox 107-63 1996 £110.00

DAVIES, RICHARD   An Account of the Convincement, Exercises, Services and Travels of that Ancient Servant of the Lord. Newtown: Gregynog Press, 1928. Limited edition of 175 numbered copies, printed on handmade paper; 8vo; (2), xxii, 163 pages; original black buckram, gilt, edges uncut, spine faded, back cover little marked, very slight foxing to two or three leaves, otherwise fine copy internally.   Thomas Thorp 489-80 1996 £75.00

DAVIES, ROBERTSON   The Dignity of Literature. Toronto: Harbourfront Reading Series, 1994. Signed, limited edition of only 50 numbered copies; 12mo; 12 pages; printed wrappers; at publication price.   Antic Hay 101-396 1996 $150.00

DAVIES, ROBERTSON   Leaven of Malice. New York: Charles Scribner's, 1955. 1st U.S. edition; 312 pages; bright charteuse cloth, author's scarce second novel; fine, crisp and bright copy in beautiful, equally fine dust jacket.   Orpheus Books 17-123 1996 $185.00

DAVIES, ROBERTSON   Table Talk of Samuel Marchbanks. Toronto: Clarke, Irwin, 1949. 1st Canadian edition; decorations by Clair Stewart, edges of pages slightly browned, otherwise very good, in slightly chipped and browned dust jacket, inscription.   Virgo Books 48-58 1996 £95.00

DAVIES, ROBERTSON   A Voice from the Attic. New York: Knopf, 1960. 1st American edition, apparently precedes the Canadian edition; 8vo; cloth in dust jacket, near fine, moderate edgewear and browning, small v-shaped chip to front panel of jacket; signed presentation from author. Antic Hay 101-397 1996 $175.00

DAVIES, ROBERTSON   World of Wonders. London: W. H. Allen, 1977. 1st British edition; moderate darkening to page edges, else near fine in very good+ dust jacket with minor shelf wear to extremities.   Lame Duck Books 19-157 1996 $125.00

DAVIES, THOMAS   A Genuine Narrative of the Life and Theatrical Transactions of Mr. John Henderson, Commonly Called the Bath Roscius. London: printed for T. Evans and sold by S. Leacroft, 1777. 1st edition; 8vo; wanting half title, otherwise very good, uncommon; recent boards, 7 page prelim 'ad' present; LAR 3022; CBEL II 738.   Ximenes 108-103 1996 $500.00

DAVIES, THOMAS   Memoirs of the Life of David Garrick, Esq. London: for the author, 1780. New edition; 2 volumes; frontispiece; full leather, rebacked, some light wear to tips and ends, morocco labels; contents very good. LAR 2932. Courtney & Smith p. 152.   Dramatis Personae 37-54 1996 $175.00

DAVIES, VALENTINE   Miracle on 34th Street. New York: Harcourt, brace and Co., 1947. 1st edition; small octavo; 120 pages; original brown cloth, stamped in blind on front cover and in silver on spine, fine, lightly chipped dust jacket.   Heritage Book Shop 196-276 1996 $200.00

DAVIES, WALTER   General View of the Agriculture and Domestic Economy of North Wales... London: printed for Richard Phillips, 1810. 1st edition; 8vo; pages xvi, 510, (4 ads), one ad leaf misbound, but complete; folding colored map, 2 plates; contemporary half calf, gilt ruled and lettered spine, very good.   James Fenning 133-81 1996 £165.00

DAVIES, WILLIAM HENRY 1871-1940   Foliage Various Poems. London: Elkin Mathews, 1913. Small 8vo; pages 63, (1); original cloth, lettered in gilt on upper cover and spine, cloth box lettered in gilt, somewhat spotted, otherwise excellent; D. H. Lawrence's copy, presentation copy, inscribed by author to Lawrence and dated 1913, with 2 original sketches by Lawrence on rear free endpaper.   Simon Finch 24-152 1996 £1,250.00

DAVIES, WILLIAM HENRY 1871-1940   The Lovers' Song-Book. Newtown: Gregynog Press, 1933. One of 19 copies specially bound, of a total edition of 250; 9 1/4 x 6 1/4 inches; v, (1), 30 pages, (1) leaf (colophon); printed on Japanese vellum, green initials, ruled in green; printer's device in green on title; bound by the Gregynog Press Bindery (signed in gilt by George Fisher on rear turn-in) in fine Emerald green polished levant morocco, two raised bands, covers, spine and turn-ins tooled in gilt with foliate sprays rising vertically from double line of lozenges, spine titled in gilt, top edge gilt, other edges untrimmed, in custom made folding cloth box with paper labels (somewhat soiled), a choice copy, virtually as bright and clean as when it was produced. Harrop 28.   Phillip J. Pirages 33-261 1996 $4,250.00

DAVIES, WILLIAM HENRY 1871-1940   Selected Poems. Newtown: Gregynog Press, 1928. One of 310 numbered copies; 8vo; frontispiece; printed in Baskerville on japon, rules and device in ochre; quarter black buckram, marbled sides, spine little faded, very nice, largely unopened. Bertram Rota 272-199 1996 £135.00

DAVIES-COLLEY, T. H.   The Family of Colley of Churton Heath in the County of Chester, with Some Pedigrees of Related Families. London: 1931. 4to; folding pedigree in pocket, 42 plates and illustrations, 255 pages; original buckram, gilt top, leather label.   Howes Bookshop 265-169   1996 £75.00

DAVIS, A. C.   A Hundred Years of Portland Cement. 1824-1924. London: Concrete Publications, 1924. 8vo; (ii), xxii, 281, (1) page, including photo plates, frontispiece; publisher's cloth.   Elton Engineering 10-33   1996 £75.00

DAVIS, ANDREW MC FARLAND   The Journey of Moncacht-Ape, an Indian of the Yazoo Tribe, Across the Continent, About the Year 1700. Worcester: printed by Charles Hamilton, 1883. 1st separate edition; 30 pages; printed wrappers, fore-edges of wrappers chipped, some pencil annotations, else fine; presentation copy, signed by author, signed by George Davidson. Howes D103.   Argonaut Book Shop 113-171   1996 $125.00

DAVIS, BRITTON   The Truth About Geronimo. New Haven: Yale University Press, 1929. 1st edition; 253 pages; numerous illustrations; gray cloth; very fine with chipped pictorial dust jacket. Rader 1066. Argonaut Book Shop   113-172   1996 $100.00

DAVIS, C. H.   Narrative of the North Polar Expedition. U. S. Ship Polaris... Washington: GPO, 1876. 1st edition; 10.5 x 7.5 inches; 696 pages, with index; illustrations; gilt pictorial cloth, hinges cracked, scattered foxing, spine darkened, extremities frayed, rear outer hinge with short tear.   John K. King 77-786   1996 $150.00

DAVIS, GWENN   Drama by Women to 1900: a Bibliography of American and British Writers. London: Mansell Pub., 1992. Small 4to; 224 pages; original cloth, new.   Forest Books 74-62   1996 £60.00

DAVIS, GWENN   Personal Writings by Women to 1900: a Bibliography of American and British Writers. London: Mansell Pub., 1989. Small 4to; 320 pages; original cloth, new.   Forest Books 74-60   1996 £60.00

DAVIS, GWENN   Poetry by Women to 1900: a Bibliography of American and British Writers. London: Mansell Pub., 1991. Small 4to; 336 pages; original cloth, new.   Forest Books 74-61   1996 £60.00

DAVIS, H. P.   Gold Rush Days in Nevada City. Nevada City: 1948. 1st edition; xi, 64 pages, frontispiece, photos; cloth, signed, nice. Very scarce.   T. A. Swinford   49-278   1996 $150.00

DAVIS, HENRY GEORGE   The Memorials of the Hamlet of Knightsbridge. London: J. Russell Smith, 1859. 8vo; pages xi, 282, tinted litho frontispiece, 7 tinted litho plates, text illustrations; original mauve cloth, spine faded; Rosebery bookplate.   Marlborough 162-129 1 1996 £80.00

DAVIS, HENRY H.   The Fancies of a Dreamer. London: Simpkin Marshall and Co. and Kirby Lonsdale: A Foster, 1842. 1st edition; 8vo; pages (vi), 112; original blindstamped cloth, paper label on upper board; fine. Rare.   R.F.G. Hollett & Son 78-369   1996 £180.00

DAVIS, HENRY T.   Solitary Places Made Glad, Being Observations and Experience for Thirty-Two Years in Nebraska with Sketches and Incidents. Cincinnati: 1890. 1st edition; 422 pages; frontispiece; cloth, nice; Mattes 772; Howes D114; Mintz 116; Graff 1058;   T. A. Swinford 49-280   1996 $125.00

DAVIS, J. SCARLETT   Fourteen Plates of Bolton Abbey. London: Cock, 1829. Folio; title, 5 pages, 14 litho plates; half calf. Boyne 123. Marlborough   162-20   1996 £550.00

DAVIS, JOHN   Travels of Four Years and a Half in the United States of America; 1798, 1799, 1800, 1801 and 1802, Dedicated by Permission to Thomas Jefferson, Esq. London: 1803. 454 pages; later half leather and wine cloth, small cancelled stamps on titlepage and 1 other page, titlepage has some soiling, map has some tears (old mends and extraneous fold creasing);   Bookworm & Silverfish 276-66 1996 $250.00

DAVIS, JOHN KING   Willis Island: a Storm Warning Station in the Coral Sea. Melbourne: Critchley Parker, 1923. 1st edition; 21.4 cm x 14 cm; 119 pages, frontispiece, 15 plates; blue cloth, blindstamped on front cover, gilt spine titles. Mark from paperclip on front pastedown, free endpaper and recto of frontispiece; this copy inscribed by author for E. F. Carter.   Parmer Books Nat/Hist-039380   1996 $150.00

DAVIS, JOHN KING   Willis Island: a Storm Warning Station in the Coral Sea. Melbourne: Critchley Parker, 1923. 1st edition; 21.4 x 14 cm; 119 pages; frontispiece, 15 plates; blue cloth, blindstamped on front cover, gilt spine titles, mark from paper clip on front pastedown, free endpaper and recto of frontispiece, else light wear; inscribed by author fo E. F. Carter.   Parmer Books O39Nautica-039380   1996 $150.00

DAVIS, JOSEPH BARNARD   Crania Britannica. London: printed for the subscribers, 1865. Folio; 2 volumes bound in 1; frontispiece, numerous text engravings and tables; later rebinding, blue gilt half morocco with marbled boards and raised bands, some text foxing and occasional browning, else, clean, tight copy. Rare.   James Tait Goodrich K40-114 1996 $1,295.00

DAVIS, MATTHEW L.   Memoirs of Aaron Burr with Miscellaneous Selections from His Correspondence. New York: Harper & Bros., 1838. 2 volumes, 436, 449 pages; original cloth, paper labels on spine, covers with some spotting, interior foxing, about good. Tompkins 40. Howes D126.   Blue River Books 9-124   1996 $120.00

DAVIS, NATHAN   Carthage and Her Remains: Being an Account of the Excavations and Researches on the Site of the Phoenician Metropolis in Africa and Other Adjacent Places. London: Richard Bentley, 1861. 1st edition; 8vo; half title, 631 pages, frontispiece, 26 plates, 6 maps & ground plans; full tan calf, double gilt rule border, tiny corner ornaments, portion of upper board sunned, fully gilt panelled spine, red morocco label, marbled edges and endpapers, Eton prize inscription.   Beeleigh Abbey BA56-59   1996 £125.00

DAVIS, NATHAN   Ruined Cities with Numidian and Carthaginian Territories. London: John Murray, 1862. 1st edition; half title, frontispiece, engraved vignette on title, folding map, 7 plates, some slight foxing of text; original cloth.   Anthony W. Laywood 109-34   1996 £85.00

DAVIS, NATHAN   Ruined Cities Within the Numidian and Carthaginian Territories. London: John Murray, 1862. 1st edition; demy 8vo; (xvi), (392), 12 pages; illustrations, plates, folding map; original binding, gilt, by Edmonds & Remnants, with their ticket, expertly restored, cloth repaired, endpapers replaced, good.   Ash Rare Books Zenzybyr-24 1996 £125.00

DAVIS, NATHAN   Ruined Cities within Numidian and Carthaginian Territories By... London: John Murray, 1862. 1st edition; 8vo; 391 pages, 2 vignettes to text, 2 maps, 8 plates; full tan calf, double gilt rule borders, tiny corner ornaments, fully git panelled spine, brown morocco label, marbled edges and endpapers, ink signature to front free endpaper.   Beeleigh Abbey BA56-58   1996 £90.00

DAVIS, NATHAN   Ruined Cities Within Numidian and Carthaginian Territories. London: John Murray, 1862. 8vo; xvi, 391 pages, folding map 8 plates; original cloth.   H. M. Fletcher 121-135   1996 £50.00

DAVIS, NOAH   A Narrative of the Life of Rev. Noah Davis, a Coloured Man, Written by Himself at the Age of Fifty-Four. Baltimore: John S. Weishampel, 1859. 1st edition; frontispiece, foxing to pages of first half of the book, spine ends lightly worn and slight loss to finish on back board, still very good or better, with title lettering clear and readable; attractive copy, uncommon.   Between the Covers 43-406   1996 $850.00

DAVIS, RICHARD HARDING   Cuba in War Time. New York: R. H. Russell, 1897. 1st edition; illustrations by Frederic Remington; fragile paper covered boards, show some rubbing inevitable with use, mainly on spine, where the first letter in title and couple of other leters are partly effaced, and at fore corners, light outer soil, too, but still very collectible copy, for it is tight, with one dirty fingermark on rear flyleaf as an isolate blemish on text. Scarce. BAL 4524.   Magnum Opus 44-31   1996 $100.00

DAVIS, RICHARD HARDING   Three Gringos in Venezuela and Central America. New York: Harper & Bro.s, 1896. 1st edition; ink name on fron free endpaper, light sunning to spine, otherwise fine, bright copy. Hermitage SP95-1098   1996 $125.00

DAVIS, WINFIELD J.   History of Political Conventions in California 1849-1892. Sacramento: California State Library, 1893. 1st edition; 711 pages; light rubbing to spine ends and corners, upper corners jammed, endpapers renewed; very good. Zamorano 80 28.   Argonaut Book Shop   113-174   1996 $100.00

DAVISON, FRANCIS   Davison's Poetical Rhapsody. London: printed at the Chiswick Press for George Bell and Sons, 1890. One of 250 large paper copies; 8 1/2 x 5 1/2 inches; 2 volumes, titles printed in red and black; very attractive dark brown three quarter crushed morocco by Sotheran, linen sides, spine gilt in compartments, feautring turtle dove ornament in center, top edge gilt, other edges rough trimmed, marbled endpapers, one tiny marginal tear in volume 2, the only defect; remarkably fine condition.   Phillip J. Pirages 33-155 1996 $250.00

DAVISON, JEAN M.   Attic Geometric Workshops. New Haven: Yale University Press, 1961. 8vo; xi, 161 pages, 145 illustrations; original cloth. Archaeologia Luxor-3235 1996 $125.00

DAVITT, MICHAEL   Leaves from a Prison Diary; or, Lectures to a Solitary Audience. London: 1885. 1st edition; 8vo; 2 volumes, frontispiece, xv, 251, xi, 256 pages, 32 page publisher's catalog dated Nove. 1884; cloth, very good.   C. P. Hyland 216-144 1996 £75.00

DAVY, HENRY   A Series of Etchings Illustrative of the Architectural Antiquities of Suffolk... Southwold: published for the author, 1827. Folio; title, 1 f., subs. and contents, 10 pages, 70 etched plates by Davy; later half morocco by G. Pulman and sons, uncut.   Marlborough 162-22 1996 £480.00

DAVY, HUMPHRY 1778-1829   Elements of Agricultural Chemistry in a Course of Lectures for the Board of Agriculture. London: W. Bulmer for Longman, Hurst et al, 1813. 1st edition; 4to; viii, 323, lxiii, (4) pages; 10 copper engraved plates, 1 folding; contemporary boards, rebacked in early binders cloth, some wear to boards and top and bottom of spine, several plates bit foxed, in all very nice, wide margined, untrimmed copy; with early 19th century bookplate of Walter Wade, the Dublin physician and botanist. Fullmer p 70. Kress B6111.   Edwin V. Glaser 121-79 1996 $500.00

DAVY, HUMPHRY 1778-1829   Elements of Agricultural Chemistry, in a Course of Lectures for the Board of Agriculture. London: printed by W. Bulmer for Longman...et al, 1813. 1st edition; 4to; frontispiece, 9 plates, viii, 323, lxiii pages, 2 leaves, some offset to title, contemporary full polished calf, unidentified Earl's crest in blind on both covers, front joint tender; very good.   H. M. Fletcher 121-136 1996 £275.00

DAVY, HUMPHRY 1778-1829   Elements of Agricultural Chemistry, In a Course of Lectures for the Board of Agriculture. London: Longman, et al, 1814. 2nd edition; 8vo; pages 479 + index; 9 folding plates; somewhat worn calf backed boards. Fussell III p. 101-103.   Second Life Books 103-67 1996 $225.00

DAVY, HUMPHRY 1778-1829   Elements of Agricultural Chemistry, in a Course of Lectures for the Board of Agriculture. London: printed for A. Constable & Co., Edin.: Longman, Hurst, Rees, Orme... 1814. 2nd edition; 8vo; 10 folding engraved plates; contemporary half calf, slightly rubbed, spine gilt, label; Fullmer 1813.7.   Anthony W. Laywood 109-35 1996 £90.00

DAVY, HUMPHRY 1778-1829   Salmonia: or Days of Fly Fishing. London: John Murray, 1828. 1st edition; 8vo; pages viii, 273, 2 folding plates; uncut in original boards, paper torn off along edge of spine, affecting edge of label, some minor foxing, but excellent tight copy. Second Life Books 103-66 1996 $250.00

DAVY, JOHN   Memoirs of the Life of Sir Humphry Davy, Bart. London: Longman, Rees, et al, 1836. 1st edition; 8vo; 2 volumes, xii, 507; vii, 419, (1) pages; frontispiece, illustrations; title and portrait strengthened at gutter in volume one; new half calf over marbled boards, lather spine labels; neat library stamp in text; very good. Fullmer p. 17.   Edwin V. Glaser 121-80 1996 $375.00

DAWKINS, JOHN   Rogues and Marauders. London: 1967. 1st edition; illustrations; fine in protected dust jacket.   David Grayling J95Biggame-70 1996 £70.00

DAWSON, CHARLES   Finola: an Opera, Chiefly Composed of Moore's Irish Melodies. Dublin: M. H. Gill, 1879. 1st and apparently only edition; large 12mo; 64 pages; original green cloth, gilt, very good; inscribed by author for P. F. O'Carroll.   James Fenning 133-83 1996 £75.00

DAWSON, CHARLES   History of Hastings Castle; the Castle, Rape and Battle of Hastings. London: 1909. Imperial 8vo; pages 600; 2 volumes; 16 plates; original blue cloth, gilt tops.   Howes Bookshop 265-2235 1996 £85.00

DAWSON, CHARLES   Pioneer Tales of the Oregon Trail and Of Jefferson County. Topeka: 1912. xv, 488 pages; frontispiece, plates; pictorial cloth, nice. Rare. Adams 150 45; Graff 1025; 6 Guns 570; Howes D150; Smith 2336.   T. A. Swinford 49-281 1996 $550.00

DAWSON, HENRY   Reminiscences of the Park and its Vicinity. New York: 1855. Limited to 25 copies, signed and dated by authors; 8vo; 64 pages of text; this copy extra illustrated, with 17 tipped in plates; three quarter green morocco and marbled red boards, slightly rubbed at head of joints, spine in 6 panels with raised bands, triple ruled gilt frames and gilt lettered black leather label, top edge gilt; near fine, very attractive; with ALS by Jeffrey Amherst mounted on thick stock.   Blue Mountain SP95-13 1996 $1,250.00

DAWSON, J. W.   Contributions Toward the Improvement of Agriculture in Nova-Scotia... Halifax: Nugent, 1856. 2nd edition; 8vo; 230 pages; black publisher's cloth (cut along the rear hinge), some signatures badly foxed, still very good.   Second Life Books 103-68 1996 $125.00

DAWSON, NICHOLAS   Narrative of Nicholas 'Cheyenne' Dawson (Overland to California in '41 & '49 and Texas in '51). San Francisco: The Grabhorn Press, 1933. One of 500 copies; 8vo; (xi), 100 pages, (6) pages notes, titlepage and chapter head illustrations; cloth backed illustrated paper over boards, with paper spine label, slightest of discoloration on endpapers, else fine. Howes D159; Graff 1027 (1st ed.); Cowan p. 161 (1st); Herd 661.   Andrew Cahan 47-158 1996 $150.00

DAWSON, OSWALD   The Bar Sinister and Licit Love. London: William Reeves, 1895. 1st edition; 4 portraits; printed stiff green wrappers, stamped in black and gold, black cloth backstrip.   Beasley Books 82-364 1996 $200.00

DAWSON, S. J.   Report on the Exploration of the Country Between Lake Superior and Red River Settlement. Toronto: 1859. Folio; pages 45, 3 maps, very scarce individual issue; Streeter 3725; Wagner Camp Becker 322.1.   Stephen Lunsford 45-41 1996 $325.00

DAWSON, SIMON J.   Report of the Exploration of the Country Between Lake Superior and the Red River Settlement, and Between the Latter Place and the Assiniboine and Saskatchewan. Toronto: Legislative Assembly, 1859. Large 4to; pages 45, 3 large folding maps; modern cloth. StTr 3885; Sabin 18958; Peel 171.   Richard Adelson W94/95-183 1996 $385.00

DAWSON, THOMAS   Memoirs of St. George, the English Patron; and of the Most Noble Order of the Garter. London: printed for Henry Clements, 1714. 1st edition; 8vo; pages (18), 336; frontispiece, engraved vignette title in red and black, engraved portrait by Vander Gucht; recent quarter calf with label, gilt; light browning in places, but very good. James Fenning 133-84 1996 £95.00

DAWSON, W. R.   A Leechbook or Collection of Medicinal Recipes of the Fifteenth Century. London: 1934. 8vo; pages 344; cloth, former owner has provided typescript index and glossary 43 pages, loose in plastic cover;   Wheldon & Wesley 207-1903 1996 £60.00

DAWSON, WARREN   Magician and Leech: a Study in the Beginnings of Medicine with Special Reference to Ancient Egypt. London: 1929. 1st edition; 159 pages; original binding. GM 6471.   W. Bruce Fye 71-514 1996 $100.00

DAWSON, WILLIAM   Medicine and Science: a Bibliographical Catalogue of Historical and Rare Books from the 15th to the 20th Century. Catalogue No. 91. London: 1956. 1st edition; 610 pages; wrappers.   W. Bruce Fye 71-515 1996 $200.00

DAWSON, WILLIAM LEON   The Birds of California. San Diego: South Moulton Co., 1923. Large quarto; 3 volumes; xvii, 696; xiii, 597-1432; xiii, 1433-2121; many illustrations, some in color; spines faded, light wear, else very good.   Dumont 28-67 1996 $325.00

DAY, F.   The Fishes of Great Britain and Ireland. London: 1880-84. 1st edition; 4to; 2 volumes; 180 attractive lithograph plates; dark green cloth, bit worn, several splits in joints; minor foxing.   Maggs Bros. Ltd. 1190-192 1996 £320.00

DAY, HORACE B.   The Opium Habit, with Suggestions as to the Remedy. New York: Harper & Bros., 1868. 1st edition; 8vo; (ii), 335, (3) pages; panelled ochre cloth, gilt, edges shelfworn, one signature sprung; good, scarce. (also issued in green silk and purple cloth bindings). Dailey Cat. 13, Phantastica 1979 # 160.   John Gach 150-122 1996 $275.00

DAY, JAMES M.   Texas Almanac: 1857-1873, a Compendium of Texas History. Waco: Texian, 1967. 1st edition; 792 pages; dust jacket, ex-library. Basaic 172S.   Maggie Lambeth 30-132 1996 $125.00

DAY, LEWIS F.   Nature in Ornament. London: B. T. Batsford, 1902. 8vo; frontispiece, xxiii, (i), 260 pages; 123 plates; publisher's green gilt cloth, top edge gilt, front hinge internally strengthened, slight edgewear, else very good.   Bookpress 75-41 1996 $225.00

DAY-LEWIS, CECIL   Posthumous Poems. London: Whittington Press, 1979. Limited to 250 numbered copies, this being one of 25 specially bound copies, signed by editor; 4to; printed on Arches mould made paper; (28) pages; original oasis tan morocco, top edge gilt, others uncut, Senecio Press marbled endpapers, preserved in publisher's cloth trimmed brown board slipcase, virtually mint.   Thomas Thorp 489-191 1996 £125.00

DAY-LEWIS, CECIL 1904-   Collected Poems - 1929-1933 - Transitional Poem. London: Hogarth Press, 1935. 1st edition; original binding, top edge dusty, free endpapers browned, spine and top edge of lower cover slightly darkened, very good in nicked, rubbed and dusty, slightly torn and soiled dust jacket browned at spine and edges and wormed along almost the entire length of the upper flap fold and slightly at lower flap fold; leonard Woolf's copy; from the library of Ian Parsons who inherited Leonard Woolf's library.   Ulysses 39-300 1996 £175.00

DAY-LEWIS, CECIL 1904-   A Penknife in My Heart. New York: Harper & Bros., 1958. 1st edition; fine with publishers blue seal unbroken, wrapping the rest of the book starting on page 123, daring reader to stop reading and return the book for a refund, in near fine dust jacket with light soiling and minor edge wear.   Quill & Brush 102-1070 1996 $100.00

THE DAYS of Old and Days of Gold British Columbia. Victoria: William H. Cullin, 1912. 1st edition; 15 pages; plates; original blue stiff wrappers, title stamped in gold, minor chipping;   Michael D. Heaston 23-79 1996 $225.00

DAYS On the Hill by an Old Stalker. London: Nisbet and Co., 1926. 1st edition; 8vo; pages xv, 262; 8 plates, 4 sketch maps; original cloth, gilt, little spotting in places, but very good.   R.F.G. Hollett 76-227 1996 £75.00

THE DEAD Sea Scrolls. Westerham: Limited Editions Club, 1966. Number 39 of 1500 copies, signed by artist; illustrations by Shraga Weil; fine in slipcase with one side unevenly sun faded.   Hermitage SP95-966 1996 $225.00

DEAN'S Moveable Book of Children's Sports and Pastimes. London: Dean & Son, 11 Ludgate Hill, March, 1859. 250 x 175mm; 8 fine hand colored moveables operated by a tab; pictorial orange boards, light wear to covers and content, 3 moveables professionally repaired, with 3 small parts in facsimile, else very good.   Marjorie James 19-160 1995 £550.00

DEAN, JAMES   An Alphabetical Atlas, or, Gazetteer of Vermont: Affording a Summary Description of the State... Montpelier: S. Goss, Jan. 1808. 21cm; 43, (1) page, errata; removed, little darkened, no wrappers, library stamp on verso of titlepage; Howes D167; Gilman p. 70; S&S 14840; McCorison VT Imprints 984.   Bohling Book Co. 191-848 1996 $150.00

DEAN, MALLETTE   The Duchow Journal: a Voyage from Boston to California, 1852. Fairfax: Mallette Dean, 1959. Limited to 200 copies; illustrations by Mallette Dean; cloth backed decorated boards, paper spine label, spine bit faded, else very fine; Allen Press 21.   Argonaut Book Shop 113-176 1996 $250.00

DEANE, ANN   A Tour through the Upper Provinces of Hindostan; Comprising a Period Between the Years 1804 and 1814. London: printed for C. & J. Rivington, 1823. 1st edition; 8vo; xii, 291, (1 ad) pages, folding engraved map (browned around edges); original blue boards, neatly rebacked, printed label; very uncommon.   James Burmester 29-39 1996 £350.00

DEANE, SAMUEL   The New-England Farmer; or, Georgical Dictionary... Worcester: 1790. 8vo; pages viii, 335; later cloth (front cover detached, backstrip partially perished, perforation stamp on title, title repaired at inner and outer margins, small tear to title, text browned. From the John Crerar Library, Chicago. Sabin 19056.   Raymond M. Sutton VII-7 1996 $500.00

DEANE, SAMUEL   The New-England Farmer; or Georgical Dictionary. Boston: Wells & Lilly, 1822. 3rd edition; 8vo; 532 pages; little worn contemporary full calf, front hinge loose. Imprints 8520; Rink 1268. Second Life Books 103-69 1996 $150.00

DEARBORN, HENRY   Revolutionary War Journals, 1775-1783. Chicago: Caxton Club, 1939. Limited to 350 copies; 8vo; xvi, 264 pages; maps and plates; unopened, boxed; fine.   Edward Morrill 369-88 1996 $125.00

DEARN, THOMAS DOWNES WILMOT   Hints on an Improved Method of Building; Applicable to General Purposes. London: printed for J. Harding, 1821. 8vo; 52 pages, 2 engraved plates, disbound; 2 copies in NUC.   James Burmester 29-40 1996 £175.00

DEBATE on the Evidence of Christianity;...Between Robert Owen, of New Lanark, Scotland and Alexander Campbell, of Bethany, Virginia. Bethany: printed and published by Alexander Campbell, 1829. 1st edition; 2 volumes in 1, 251, 301 pages; full calf, little worn and fragile, some dampstaining to interior, but overall very good.   Blue River Books 9-125 1996 $195.00

DE BAZANCOURT, BARON   Secrets of the Sword. London: & New York: george Bell & Sons, 1900. 1st edition in English; 8vo; viii, 248 pages, few page corners creased; illustrations by F. H. Towsend; three quarter green morocco and cloth with raised bands, titled in gilt on spine, top edge gilt; few page corners creased; near fine.   Blue Mountain SP95-169 1996 $285.00

DE BELLIS, JACK   John Updike: a Bibliography, 1967-1993. Westport: Greenwood, 1994. 1st edition; fine as issued.   Bev Chaney, Jr. 23-748 1996 $125.00

DE BERNIERE, LOUIS   The War of Don Emmanuel's Nether Parts. London: S&W, 1990. 1st edition; fine in dust jacket, signed by author. Lame Duck Books 19-159 1996 $175.00

DE BERNIERES, LOUIS   Captain Corelli's Mandolin. London: Secker & Warburg, 1994. 1st edition; 8vo; signed by author; boards, dust jacket; new.   James S. Jaffe 34-127 1996 $125.00

DE BERNIERES, LOUIS   Captain Corelli's Mandolin. London: S&W, 1994. 1st edition; fine in dust jacket, signed by author.   Lame Duck Books 19-164 1996 $100.00

DE BERNIERES, LOUIS   Senor Vino and the Coca Lord. London: S&W, 1991. 1st edition; fine in dust jacket, signed by author.   Lame Duck Books 19-160 1996 $150.00

DE BURGH, ULICK H. H.   The Landowners of Ireland. Dublin: Hodges, Foster, 1878. 8vo; pages xxviii, 486, errata leaf; strongly bound in recent boards, occasional finger mark, but very good.   James Fenning 133-86 1996 £155.00

DE CAMP, L. SPRAGUE   Demons and Dinosaurs. Sauk City: Arkham House, 1970. One of 500 copies, signed by author on special printed label pasted to flyleaf; front corner tips very slightly bumped, otherwise fine in slightly soiled dust jacket.   Steven C. Bernard 71-407 1996 $300.00

DE CAMP, L. SPRAGUE   Sir Harold and the Gnome King. Wildside Press, 1991. 1st edition; 1/26 lettered copies, signed by author; as new without dust jacket as issued.   Aronovitz 57-321 1996 $175.00

DE CAMP, L. SPRAGUE   Wall of Serpents Avalon, 1960. 1st edition; signed by author; fine in just about fine dust jacket.   Aronovitz 57-319 1996 $125.00

DE CHAIR, SOMERSET STRUBEN 1911-   The First Crusade. Waltham St. Lawrence: Golden Cockerel Press, 1945. Limited to 500 numbered copies; royal 8vo; 93 pages; printed on Arnold's handmade paper, 7 wood engravings by Clifford Webb, including 5 full page; publisher's half vellum with orange buckram sies, gilt decoration on front cover, top edge gilt, others uncut; fine. Cockalorum 168.   Thomas Thorp 489-82 1996 £120.00

DE CHAIR, SOMERSET STRUBEN 1911-   The Silver Crescent. London: Golden Cockerel Press, 1943. 4to; numerous illustrations; linen boards, over blue morocco spine, gilt top; fine, attractive copy.   Appelfeld Gallery 54-108 1996 $200.00

DECHARME, PAUL   Euripides and the Spirit of His Dramas. New York 1906. 1st edition; 378 pages; very good in slipcase; Edward Dahlberg's copy with anntoations by him, and 20 line original poem.   Lyman Books 21-104 1996 $275.00

DE COCK, L.   Ansel Adams. New York Graphic Society, 1972. 1st edition; 117 illustrations; dust jacket.   J. B. Muns 154-13 1996 $100.00

DE COETLOGON, CHARLES EDWARD   The Temple of Truth; or the Best System of Reason, Philosophy, Virtue and Morals, Analytically Arranged. London: printed for J. Mawman, 1806. 1st edition; 8vo; half title; original boards, uncut, rebacked.   Anthony W. Laywood 108-165 1996 £75.00

DECRETALES   Gregorii Papae IX. Venice: s.n. 1600. Large 4to; vignette title, 26 ff. n.n., 2 full page woodcuts, 2 ff., 1388 pages; red morocco elaborately gilt broad outer borders w/arabesque & heraldic tools, sq. corners w/dragons & winged putti, oval centre-piece w/the combined, quartered arms of Caffarelli (lions) & Borghese (dragons rampant & spread eagles), surmounted by a Cardinal's hat, broad spine gilt in 5 panels, single raised bands, middle 3 panels w/dragon, lion & eagle, respectively, flanked by salamanders & arabesques, later labels to first and last panels, all edges gilt & gauffered, plain endpapers, spine skilfully repaired with restoration at head, foot and lower band, corners also sympathetically restored, edges little worn, in half morocco folding case; from the collection of Victor von Stedingks Bokband. A Fine Soresini binding.   Marlborough 160-17 1996 £4,500.00

DEE, ARTHUR   Fasciculus Chemicus; or Chymical Collections. London: 1650. 16mo; 251, 268 pages; frontispiece, later full leather, gilt printed backstrip labels, extra set prepared and laid in by Mr. Lannon, library discard stamp on titlepage, and 2 other leaves, uncancelled library stamp on frontispiece, laid down.   Bookworm & Silverfish 276-40 1996 $7,650.00

THE DEESIDE Guide: Descriptive and Tradtionary... Aberdeen: Lewis Smith & Co., 1885. 12mo; (ii), (122) pages; 8 original mounted photographic plates and folding map at rear; original cloth, very small name on endpaper, some minor rubbing at extremities, otherwise fine. David Mason 71-135 1996 $240.00

DEFEBAUGH, JAMES ELLIOTT   History of the Lumber Industry of America. Chicago: 1906-07. 10 x 7 inches; volumes 1 and 2 of 4 volume set; 559, 655 pages; photos; three quarter leather, top edge gilt, ink name, volume 2 spine sunned, but both with bright lettering, couple of spine chips.   John K. King 77-118 1996 $100.00

DEFENDERS and Offenders. New York: 1885. 1st edition; 124 pages, photos; decorated cloth, nice, rare. 6 Guns 578.   T. A. Swinford 49-251 1996 $750.00

THE DEFENSE of Gracchus Babeuf Before the High Court of Vendome. Northampton: Gehenna Press, 1964. In an edition of 300 copies, this one of 250 with one set of signed etchings, numbered and signed by Leonard Baskin; 12.75 x .75; suite of etchings printed on blue Fabriano by Emiliano Sorini in New York, all signed by artist; unbound signatures in full brown leather cover with title in gilt on spine, clamshell box in light brown buckram with brown leather spine, title in gilt; Fine, prospectus laid in; neat bookplate of previous owner inside box lid. Joshua Heller 21-126 1996 $875.00

DEFOE, DANIEL 1661?-1731   A Brief Reply to the History of Standing Armies in England. London: printed in the year 1698. 1st edition; 4to; pages (vi), 25; later wrappers; very good. Wing D829; Moore 19. Peter Murray Hill 185-48 1996 £150.00

DEFOE, DANIEL 1661?-1731   The History of the Kentish Petition. N.P.: n.d. 1701. quarto; 8 pages, drop-head title; disbound, very nice. Moore 37.   C. R. Johnson 37-55 1996 £125.00

DEFOE, DANIEL 1661?-1731   A Journal of the Plague Year. Oxford: Basil Blackwell, 1928. Limited to just 750 copies; crown 8vo; (viii), 302 pages; bound in smart recent half calf, banded and gilt, marbled sides, top edge gilt, very good.   Ash Rare Books Zenzybyr-25 1996 £85.00

DEFOE, DANIEL 1661?-1731   A Letter from a Gentleman at the Court of St. Germains, to One of His Friends in England. London: printed in the year 1710 and Re-Printed in the year 1715. Small 8vo; later grey wrappers, label, sewn; this ed. not in Lampeter, Lampeter 4730 for 1710 ed.   Freedom Bookshop 14-22 1996 $110.00

DEFOE, DANIEL 1661?-1731   The Life and Strange Surprizing Adventures of Robinson Crusoe, of York, Mariner... London: for W. Taylor, 1719-20. 1st edition; volume 1 has the second state of the titlepage, with semi-colon after 'London' the 3rd state of the preface with the catchword 'apply' on A2r and the first state of Z4, with readings 'Pilate' and 'Portuguese'; volume 2 is second issue with A4v not blank, volume 3 has 12 uncancelled and catchword "the" on S7v; 3 volumes; frontispiece, folding world map and plate, the former torn and laid down, 4 pages, 11 pages, 2 pages of ads at end of volumes I, II & III respectively; modern antique style panelled calf, two rule blind border, roll and cornerpieces on sides, spines richly gilt in compartments with rolls, flowers and leay sprays, red morocco lettering pieces, green morocco numbering pieces, red morocco onlays, blue sprinkled edges, occasional spotting, staining and soiling, mostly light, very good. Moore 412, 417, 436; Hutchins passim; Rothschild 775; PMM 180.   Simon Finch 24-65 1996 £15,000.00

DEFOE, DANIEL 1661?-1731   The Life and Strange Surprizing Adventures of Robinson Crusoe...(and) The Farther Adventures of Robinson Crusoe. London: printed for W. Taylor, 1719. 1st edition of volume 2, 2nd edition of volume 1; 2 volumes, 364; 373 pages, (11) ads, 6 ads; frontispiece in volume 1, folding map in volume 2, in fine full dark green morocco, spines gilt, all edges gilt, some soiling (washed), few minor defects, very good, scarce; PMM 180; Grolier 100 English 41.   19th Century Shop 39- 1996 $3,800.00

DEFOE, DANIEL 1661?-1731   The Life and Strange Surprizing Adventures of Robinson Crusoe. (with) The Farther Adventures of Robinson Crusoe. (with) Serious Relfections During the Life and Surprising Adventures of Robinson Crusoe... London: for W. Taylor, 1719/19/20. 1st editions of 2nd and 3rd parts, 3rd edition of first part, all three are first issues; 8vo; 3 works, volume 1 with frontispiece, volume 2 with folding map at beginning of text (laid down on linen), volume 3 with folding map (laid down on linen); all 3 volumes with final ads; uniformly bound in modern dark blue crushed morocco, sides ruled in blind, spines in comaprtments with raised bands, gilt lettering, edges and inner dentelles gilt, marbled endpapers, by Tout and Son, corners little bumped, some slight spotting, browning or soiling, but very good. PMM 180.   Simon Finch 24-66 1996 £2,350.00

DEFOE, DANIEL 1661?-1731   The Life and Strange Surprising Adventures of Robinson Crusoe. (with) Farther Adventures of Robinson Crusoe. London: J. Buckland, Strahan et al, 1784. 16th edition; small 8vo; 2 volumes; frontispiece in volume 1, folding world map in volume 2, 10 engraved plates; full calf, rebacked, red morocco spine labels, nice set attractively illustrated. Osborne 244; Gumuchian 4812.   Barbara Stone 70-69 1996 £250.00

DEFOE, DANIEL 1661?-1731   Life and Surprizing Adventures of Robinson Crusoe. London: Etchells & Macdonald, 1929. One of 535 copies; small 4to; printed on all rag paper; 8 pochoir illustrations by E. McKnight Kauffer; navy cloth with pictorial design in silver, spine slightly faded, small spot on cover, else fresh in cloth slipcase.   Marilyn Braiterman 15-118 1996 $325.00

DEFOE, DANIEL 1661?-1731   No Queen: or, No General. London: printed and sold by the Booksellers of London and Westminster, 1712. 8vo; 2 leaves, 52 pages, some browning, disbound; the issue with the last 4 pages numbered correctly.   H. M. Fletcher 121-90 1996 £110.00

DEFOE, DANIEL 1661?-1731   The Novels... Edinburgh: by James Ballantyne and Co. for John Ballantyne and Co. and Brown &... 1810. Foolscap 8vo; 12 volumes; woodcut illustrations; contemporary red straight grain half morocco, spines decorated in blind and in gilt and lettered in gilt, green paper sides and endpapers, green sprinkled edges, extremities rubbed, attractive set; bookplates of F. I. Cuthbert.   Simon Finch 24-67 1996 £350.00

DEFOE, DANIEL 1661?-1731   The Novels and Selected Writings of Daniel Defoe. Stratford-upon-Avon: Shakespeare Head Press, 1928. Limited to only 530 sets, this one is the publisher's own copy; tall octavo; 14 volumes; frontispieces, some folding, with tissue guards; large paper edition; linen spines and boards, maroon leather labels, gilt; fine, uncut.   Hartfield 48-A6 1996 $1,095.00

DEFOE, DANIEL 1661?-1731   The Political History of the Devil, as Well Ancient as Modern. London: printed for T. Warner, 1726. 1st edition; 8vo; frontispiece, pages (viii), 408; contemporary panelled calf, rebacked bookplate of Lord Wigtoune. Moore 480.   Peter Murray Hill 185-49 1996 £250.00

DEFOE, DANIEL 1661?-1731   The Secret History of State Intrigues in the Management of the Scepter, in the Late Reign. London: printed and sold by S. Keimer, 1715. Re-issue, the same year, of "The Secret History of the Scepter..." with cancel title and addition of half title; 8vo; 67 pages; disbound; half title lacking.   H. M. Fletcher 121-91 1996 £110.00

DEFOE, DANIEL 1661?-1731   The Storm. London: for G. Sawbridge, 1704. 8vo; 8 leaves, 272 pages; folding plate, release stamp of Yale Library inside rear cover, embrowning to first 8 leaves, otherwise very lightly embrowned, overall good plus copy; original calf in good-minus condition, spine chipped, corners bumped, inner hinges repaired with paper tape.   Roy W. Clare XXIV-69   1996 $375.00

DEFOE, DANIEL 1661?-1731   A Tour through the Island of Great Britain, Divided into Circuits of Journies... London: printed for W. Strahan (and 17 other firms), 1778. 12mo; 4 volumes; original cloth, spines gilt with red and green labels, 2 or 3 gatherings working a trifle loose, spines rubbed, slightly worn at head and foot, all joints sound.   David Bickersteth 133-17   1996 £165.00

DEFOE, DANIEL 1661?-1731   A Tour Thro' the Whole Island of Great Britain. London: Peter Davies, 1927. Limited to 1000 copies; royal 8vo; 2 volumes, pages xxxii, 416; viii, 416-858; maps; original cloth backed marbled boards, top edge gilt, with scarce dust jackets; very nice set.   Sotheran PN32-7   1996 £148.00

DE GRAZIA, TED   Father Junipero Serra. Los Angeles: Ward ritchie Press and Southwest Museum, 1970. Limited to 100 numbered copies; large 8vo; unpaginated, profusely illustrated with sketches and original watercolor signed by DeGrazia on colophon leaf; beige cloth in dust jacket, beige paper covered slipcase; fine.   Kenneth Karmiole 1NS-86   1996 $450.00

DEGREVANT. (ROMANCE)   Sire Degrevaunt. Kelmscott Press, 1896. One of 350 copies on paper, there were also 8 on vellum; 8 1/4 x 6 inches; 2 p.l., 81, (1) pages; frontispiece and first page of text with elaborate borders by Sir Edward Burne-Jones, decorative initials, device on colophon; printed in red and black; original holland backed blue grey paper boards, edges untrimmed; trivial foxing and soiling only to spine, but very fine. Armorial bookplate of Edward Penton.   Phillip J. Pirages 33-322   1996 $1,250.00

DE HASS, WILLS   History of the Early Settlement and Indian Wars of Western Virginia. Wheeling: H. Hoblitzell, 1851. 1st edition; 8vo; frontispiece, 416 pages, 5 plates; publisher's blindstamped cloth, ex-library, appropriate markings, bookplate, several waterstains, binding worn. Howes D223.   The Bookpress 75-407   1996 $285.00

DE HAVEN, TOM   Freaks' Amour. New York: Wm. Morrow, 197. Uncorrected proof of first edition; wrappers, fine with fiant sticker shadow on front wrapper, signed by author.   Revere Books 4-104   1996 $100.00

DEHLI DEVELOPMENT AUTHORITY   Master Plan for Dehli. Dehli: the author, 1962. 1st edition; oblong 4to; 2 volumes, (x), iv, 108, (8) pages, 4 folding maps; (vi), 170 pages; cloth spine, boards, dust jacket, jacket of volume 1 torn, some underlining and note taking, name in ink on front free endpaper of volume 2.   Bookpress 75-174   1996 $110.00

DEIGHTON, LEN   An Expensive Place to Die. New York: Putnam, 1967. 1st edition; fine in near fine jacket.   Janus Books 36-134   1996 $125.00

DEIGHTON, LEN   London Dossier. London: Jonathan Cape, 1967. 1st edition; fine in near fine dust jacket with lightly rubbed edges and back flap lightly creased.   Quill & Brush 102-436   1996 $150.00

DEIGHTON, LEN   Only When I Larf. London: Michael Joseph, 1967. 1st edition; fine in near fine dust jacket with light edge wear.   Quill & Brush 102-437   1996 $200.00

DEIGHTON, LEN   Violent Ward. Bristol: Scorpion Press, 1993. 1/20 deluxe lettered copies, signed by author and H.R.F. Keating who provided author appreciation; quarter bound in goatskin with raised bands; fine.   Quill & Brush 102-444   1996 $450.00

DEIGHTON, LEN   Violent Ward. Bristol: Scorpion Press, 1993. 1/130 copies, signed, numbered and specially bound. Quarter bound in leather, marbled paper boards, textured colored endpapers and colored top edges.   Quill & Brush 102-445   1996 $125.00

DE KAY, JAMES   Sketches of Turkey in 1831 and 1832 by an American. New York: Haraper, 1833. 1st edition; 8vo; pages xii, 527; many woodcut illustrations in text; recent quarter calf, titlepage missing, supplied in facsimile, few smudges, otherwise very good.   Worldwide Antiquarian 151-165   1996 $145.00

DEKKER, THOMAS   The Gull's Hornbook. Bristol: Gutch, 1812. 4to; title printed in red and black, vii pages, 2 ff., 177 pages, 6 ff; calf, covers gilt and blindstamped with single rule and broad roll tool borders spine gilt in seven panels with broad raised bands, all edges gilt, blue silk endpapers, by Thomas Gosden, with his engraved label inside upper cover, joints little weak, preserved in recent cloth slipcase.   Marlborough 160-66   1996 £250.00

DE LA BECHE, HENRY   The Geological Observer. London: 1851. 1st edition; 8vo; pages xxxii, 846, 309 text figures; original cloth, very neatly rebacked. Fine.   John Henly 27-425   1996 £100.00

DELACOUR   Waterfowl of the world. London: 1954-64. 1st edition; 4to; 4 volumes; numerous colored plates by Scott; fine in slightly torn dust jackets.   David A.H. Grayling MY95Orn-27   1996 £320.00

DELACOUR, JEAN   Les Oiseaux de l'Indochine Francaise. Paris: 1931. Imperial 8vo; 4 volumes; 2 maps, 67 plates; original wrappers, uncut; signs of ownership neatly erased from foot of spines and titlepages, otherwise good.   Wheldon & Wesley 207-25   1996 £500.00

DELACOUR, JEAN   The Pheasants of the World. London: 1951. First impression; crown 4to; 347 pages; 16 colored and 16 plain plates, 21 maps and diagrams; cloth, very scarce.   Wheldon & Wesley 207-707   1996 £150.00

DELACOUR, JEAN   Waterfowl of the World. London: 1954-64. 1st edition; 4to; 4 volumes; numerous colored paltes by Scott; fine in slightly torn dust jackets,   David A.H. Grayling 3/95-351   1996 £320.00

DELACOUR, JEAN   The Waterfowl of the World. London: 1954-64. Original printing; crown 4to; 4 volumes; 66 colored plates, numerous distribution maps and text figures; cloth; out of print and scarce, nice set with slightly worn dust jackets.   Wheldon & Wesley 207-708   1996 £250.00

DELACOUR, JEAN   The Waterfowl of the World. London: 1954-64. 1st edition; 8vo; 4 volumes; colored plates; cloth, dust jackets, slight fraying at head of each dust jacket, otherwise very nice set.   Maggs Bros. Ltd. 1190-557   1996 £205.00

DELACOUR, JEAN   Waterfowl of the World. London: 1959. Volume 3 only; colored plates, maps, etc; fine n slightly torn dust jacket.   David A.H. Grayling MY95Orn-23   1996 £70.00

DE LA MARE, WALTER 1873-1956   Ding Dong Bell. London: Selwyn & Blount, 1924. One of 300 numbered copies; signed by author; tiny bump bottom of front board, still fine in dust jacket with slight loss at cornw; exceptional copy.   Between the Covers 42-518   1996 $525.00

DE LA MARE, WALTER 1873-1956   Memoirs of a Midget. London: W. Collins Sons, 1921. 1st edition; one of 210 copies, signed by author; 8vo; cloth backed boards, leather label on spine, faint offsetting on endpapers, edge of back cover bumped, otherwise very good.   James S. Jaffe 34-128   1996 $125.00

DE LA MARE, WALTER 1873-1956   Memoirs of a Midget. London: and elsewhere: W. Collins & Co., 1921. One of 210 copies signed by author; 1st edition; 1st issue; 9 1/4 x 6 incches; 1 p.l., xii, 365, (1) pages; original cloth backed paper boards, morocco spine label, untrimmed and unopened, boards faintly faded at edges, otherwise very fine.   Phillip J. Pirages 33-156   1996 $100.00

DE LA MARE, WALTER 1873-1956   The Sunken Garden and Other Poems. London: Beaumont Press, 1917. 1st edition; one of 6 copies, printed for presentation (of an edition of 276 copies); crown 8vo; printed in black and red on handmade paper; original quarter fawn buckram, printed backstrip and front cover labels, that on backstrip trifle darkened, floral patterned pale grey boards, faint free endpaper browning, untrimmed; good. Presentation copy inscribed by Cyril Beaumont to George Sutcliffe of Sangorski & Sutcliffe. Beaumont 2.   Blackwell's B112-17   1996 £95.00

DELAMAYNE, THOMAS HALLIE   The Patricians; or a Candid Examination into the Merits of the Principal Speakers of the House of Lords. London: printed for G. Kearsly, 1773. 1st edition; 4to; disbound; half title present; very good. Jackson p. 22.   Ximenes 108-104   1996 $100.00

DELAND, CHARLES   The Sioux Wars: in South Dakota. Pierre: 1930/34. 730 pages, 654 pages; frontispiece, photos, map; cloth, nice. Dustin 90; Luther 111.   T. A. Swinford 49-286   1996 $250.00

DELANY, S. The Einstein Intersection. London: Gollancz, 1968. 1st British and 1st hard cover edition; fine in like dust jacket with just a hint of soil. Aronovitz 57-330 1996 $425.00

DELAUNE, THOMAS The Present State of London; or, Memorials Comprehending a Full and Succinct Account of the Ancient and Modern State Thereof. London: G. Larkin, for E. Prosser & J. How, 1681. 1st edition with plates; 12mo; title, 5 ff., 478 pages (i.e. 444 after pagination errors, etc., collated complete against Adams and other copies); frontispiece, 12 engraved plates, text illustrations; (close trimmed, repaired tear); old calf, worn, rebacked. Wing D894; Adams 14. Marlborough 162-131 1996 £450.00

DELAURENCE, L. W. The Great Book of Magical Art, Hindu Magic and Indian Occultism. Chicago: Delaurence Co., 1939. frontispiece, plates, 635 pages; beautiful deco cover and spine, fine. Middle Earth 77-252 1996 $100.00

DE LILLO, DON Americana. Boston: Houghton Mifflin, 1971. 1st edition; 8vo; cloth backed boards, dust jacket, fine, uncommon thus; author's first book. James S. Jaffe 34-129 1996 $275.00

DE LILLO, DON Americana. Boston: Houghton Mifflin Co., 1971. 1st edition; near fine in very good+ dust jacket with two connecting one inch edge tears to rear panel; now quite scarce. Lame Duck Books 19-165 1996 $250.00

DE LILLO, DON Great Jones Street. Boston: Houghton Mifflin, 1973. 1st edition; slith erasure to corner of half title, else fine in very near fine dust jacket, with just a touch of rubbing; signed by author. Between the Covers 42-130 1996 $200.00

DE LINT, CHARLES Paperjack. New Castle: Cheap Street, 1991. 1st edition; one of 121 numbered copies, signed by author and artist; illustrations by Judy King; very fine in Japanese yuzen paper dust jacket laid into traycase. Robert Gavora 61-21 1996 $230.00

DELL, FLOYD Intellectual Vagabondage. New York: George H. Doran, 1926. 1st edition; small 8vo; cloth, dust jacket, with new price sticker; fine. James S. Jaffe 34-136 1996 $125.00

DELL, FLOYD Looking at Life. New York: Knopf, 1924. 1st edition; 8vo; cloth, bookseller's label on front endsheet, otherwise fine in slightly faded and rubbed jacket. James S. Jaffe 34-135 1996 $125.00

DELLA BELLA, STEFANO Recueil de Douze Cartouches. Paris: F. L. D. Ciartres, 1643. Oblong 4to; 12 plates, each with its outer border entirely untrimmed, tipped into an album on handmade sheets; included are two counter proofs, plates 5 and 6; each plate is signed with monogram of Stefano Della Bella; bound in three quarter green morocco over marbled boards. From the collection of John Evelyn. Book Block 32-66 1996 $5,500.00

DELLENBAUGH, FREDERICK S. Breaking the Wilderness. New York: and London: G. P. Putnam's Sons, 1905. 1st edition; 8vo; xxiii, 360 pages, (5) ads; color frontispiece with tissue guard, numerous text and photo illustrations, folding map; cloth, dull on spine, lightly rubbed on extremities, very good. Andrew Cahan 47-63 1996 $150.00

DELLENBAUGH, FREDERICK S. A Canyon Voyage. New Haven: Yale University Press, 1926. 2nd edition; 8vo; xxxviii, 277 pages; color frontispiece with tissue guard, numerous photos illustrations, chapter head and tailpieces (by author), maps, 4 folding; occasional light foxing, else very good; inscribed to Elwood Bonney on endpaper with sketch of a canoe dated March 6th, 1932, New York, with lengthy inscription; with initialled annotations by author and Bonney. Andrew Cahan 47-64 1996 $350.00

DELLOYE, H. L. Chants et Chansons Populaires de la France... Paris: Felix Locquin, imprimeur, Libraririe de Garnier, freres, 1843. 1st edition; super royal 8vo; 3 volumes; steel engraved illustrations, musical notation; late 19th century dark green straight grain full morocco, sides ruled in gilt with triple fillet, spines lettered and decorated in gilt, gilt inner dentelles, spot marbled endpapers, silk bookmarks, gilt edges, by L. Guetant (spines evenly sunned); excellent set. Simon Finch 24-68 1996 £1,500.00

DELOLME, J. L. The History of the Flagellants, or the Advantages of Discipline... London: printed for Fielding and Walker, 1777. 1st edition in English; 4to; half title, pages 9-340, including errata and index; 4 full page copperplate engravings, 3 vignettes to text; old speckled calf boards, decorative gilt bands and tools to spine, dark green label and speckled edges, library shelf reference to front pastedown and owner's ink signature to upper margin of title; some light foxing to plates and some light offsetting to initial and final leaves. Lowndes II p. 625; Brunet I pt. 2 22386. Beeleigh Abbey BA56-136 1996 £800.00

DE LONG, GEORGE The Voyage of the Jeannette. The Ship and the Ice Journals of George W. De Long and Lieutenant-Commander of the Polar Expedition of 1879-1881. Boston: Houghton Mifflin and Co., 1883. 1st edition; 8vo; 2 volumes, pages xii, 440; x, 441-911; 2 steel engraved portraits, numerous maps, text illustrations; original pictorial brown cloth, gilt, image of the Jeannette stamped in black on front and in blind on back, head and tail of spines very slightly bumped, slight tear to rear pocket (repaired), tear along one fold of map in pocket, otherwise very good, clean copy. Arctic Bib. 3839. Sotheran PN32-161 1996 £298.00

DE LONG, GEORGE The Voyage of the Jeannette. The Ship and Ice Journals of... Boston: Houghton Mifflin and Co., Riverside Press, Cambridge, 1884. 1st U.S. edition; demy 8vo; 2 volumes; 911 pages of text, frontispieces,, 13 full page wood engravings, 41 woodcut vignettes to text, 1 uncalled for to face p. 826, volume 2, 23 maps, charts and plans, 1 steel engraving and 1 facsimile letter; final fold of folding map to volume 2 detached and loosely inserted; original publisher's brown cloth, pictorial black/gilt stamped upper boards and spines, blind repeat of upper board to lower boards, bookplates; very good, tight copy. Arctic Bib. 3839. Beeleigh Abbey BA56-60 1996 £450.00

DEL POMAR, FELIPE COSSIO The Art of Ancient Peru. New York: Wittenborn, 1971. 8vo; 228 pages; 37 illustrations, 23 color plates; original cloth, dust jacket. Archaeologia Luxor-4388 1996 $150.00

DE LYRA, NICOLAUS Praeceptorium (divinae legis), Cum Additionibus et Tractatulis Pulcerrimus Multis. Cologne: Retro Minores (Martin von Werden? for Denis Roce 7, May, 1502. Early calf, expertly rebacked with blind decoration; Petersfield Bookshop FH58-45 1996 £1,100.00

DE MARGERIE, PIERRE Eloge de La Typographie. Cranach Press, 1931. One of 115 copies on paper, (there were also 14 on vellum); 11 1/4 x 7 1/4 inches; 12 pages, (1) leaf (colophon); raised historiated initial in blue, orange and gold, engraved by Eric Gil after a drawing by Aristide Maillol, headlines printed in red; fine scarlet crushed morocco by O. Dorfner of Weimar, covers framed with single gilt rule, gilt titling on front cover, raised bands, top edge gilt, other edges untrimmed, fine felt lined folding cloth box with red morocco spine label; especially fine in handsome, unworn binding. Schroder p. 11. Phillip J. Pirages 33-143 1996 $7,800.00

DEMING, ELIZUR An Address, Delivered at the First Annual Exhibition of the Philomathean Society of Wabash College, September 28, 1835. Crawfordsville: 1835. 1st edition; 16mo; 16 pages; original printed wrappers; Byrd & Peckham 574. Rinderknecht 31317. M & S Rare Books 60-347 1996 $125.00

DE MORGAN, AUGUSTUS 1806-1871 Arithmetical Books from the Invention of Printing to the Present Time. London: Taylor and Walton, 1847. 1st edition; 8vo; xxviii, 124 pages; original cloth, uncut; nice. Forest Books 74-187 1996 £95.00

DE MORGAN, AUGUSTUS 1806-1871 An Essay on Probablities, and on Their Application to Life Contingencies and Insurance Offices. London: printed for Longman and John Taylor, 1838. 1st edition; small 8vo; xviii, 306; xl, (2 ad) pages, additional engraved title (waterstained), 12 page publisher's catalog at front; original plum linen, neatly rebacked. James Burmester 29-41 1996 £150.00

DENDY, WALTER COOPER The Philosophy of Mystery. London: Longman, Orme, Brown, Green & Longmans, 1841. 1st edition; 8vo; (iii)-xii, 443, (1) pages; embossed brown cloth. John Gach 150-128 1996 $125.00

DENHAM, MICHAEL AISLABIE The Denham Tracts. London: David Nutt for the Folklore Society, 1892-95. 2 volumes; original brown cloth, very good. Jarndyce 103-82 1996 £65.00

DENMAN, THOMAS An Introduction to the Practice of Midwifery. Brattleborough: Wm. Fessenden, 1807. 8vo; contemporary calf. Austin 651; Waller 2360 (London 1805 ed.). Argosy 810-145 1996 $200.00

DENNIS, GEORGE   The Cities and Cemeteries of Etruria. London: John Murray, 1848. 1st edition; 2 volumes, c, (532); xiv, (558), 16 pages; maps, colored frontispiece to volume 2, 3 tinted litho plates, numerous illustrations; original binding, gilt, little worn and frayed, minor repairs to binding, few faint marks, even so a nice set.   Ash Rare Books Zenzybyr-26 1996 £195.00

DENNIS, GEORGE   The Cities and Cemeteries of Etruria. London: John Murray, 1883. 3rd edition; 8vo; 2 volumes; pages (ii), cxxviii, 501, (ii); (xv), 579, (i), colored frontispiece to volume 2, over 100 text illustrations in each volume 12 plans in volume 1 (1 folding), 11 plans in volume II (1 folding); extremely fine; original green cloth, with Etruscan motifs in gilt and meander pattern in blind on all edges of upper and lower covers, edges uncut;   Sotheran PN32-162 1996 £130.00

DENNIS, JOHN   A Proposal for Putting a Speedy End to the War, by Ruining the Commerce of the French and Spaniards, and Securing Our Own, Without Any Additional Expense to the Nation. London: printed for Daniel Brown and Andrew Bell, 1703. Issue in which the dedication is unsigned; 4to; viii, 5-28 pages; 20th century boards, red morocco spine, fine, clean wide margined copy.   C. R. Johnson 37-56 1996 £180.00

DENNIS, R. W. G.   British Ascomycetes. Vaduz: 1981. 4th edition; 8vo; 585 pages, including 44 colored and 31 plain plates; boards.   Wheldon & Wesley 207-1615 1996 £84.00

DENNISTOUN, JAMES   Memoirs of the Dukes of Urbino, Illustrating the Arms, Arts and Literature of Italy 1440-1630. London: John Lane, 1909. New edition; thick 8vo; 3 volumes; 100 plates and illustrations; original blue cloth, gilt tops.   Howes Bookshop 265-1234 1996 £85.00

DENON, VIVANT   Travels in Upper and Lower Egypt, in Company with Several Divisions of the French Army, During the Campaigns of General Bonaparte in That Country... London: printed for T. N. Longman and O. Rees, 1803. 1st English edition; quarto; 2 volumes; viii, (4), xiii, (3), (17)-343, (1); vii, (1), 320 pages (leaf G1 in volume 2 bound following G3); 61 engraved plates and maps, one text illustration; modern half polished calf, ruled in gilt, over marbled boards, gilt decorated spines with dark green morocco labels, corners lightly bumped, occasional light to moderate foxing, some offsetting from plates; 3 folding plates with short tears (one along fold); very good, extremely rare.   Heritage Book Shop 196-254 1996 $3,000.00

DENSMORE, FRANCIS   Nootka and Quileute Music. Washington: Smithsonian Inst. 1939. 23 cm; xxvi, 358 pages; illustrations, portraits, musical notations, maps, diagrams; gilt stamped blue cloth; fine, scarce. Rockland Books 38-61 1996 $125.00

DENT, J.   Catalogue of the Splendid, Curious & Extensive Library of the Late John Dent, Esq. London: Mr. Evans, 29th Mar. & 8 following days & 25th Apr. & 8 following days 1827. 2 volumes, 1502 and 1474 lots; paper backed, titles darkened, uncut, prices and buyers names marked in ink throughout; De Ricci pp. 99.   Maggs Bros. Ltd. 1191-42 1996 £215.00

DENTON, N.   Catalogue of Short Horn Cattle at Oak Grove Stock Farm, Manchester, Delaware Co., Iowa. Manchester: Democrat Book and Job Print, 1876. 1st edition; 16mo; 13 pages; original printed wrappers. Very scarce.   M & S Rare Books 60-298 1996 $150.00

DE QUINCEY, THOMAS 1785-1859   The Collected Writings. London: A. & C. Black, 1896-97. 2nd issue of the David Masson edition; 8vo; 14 volumes; frontispiece in volume 1; original blue cloth, spines gilt, top edge gilt, extremities rubbed, one board little damp spotted; good set. Robert Clark 38-235 1996 £185.00

DE QUINCEY, THOMAS 1785-1859   Dr. Johnson and Lord Chesterfield. New York: Ben Abramson, 1945. One of 250 copies; cloth backed patterned paper boards, endpaper and page edges slightly browned, cover edges browned and worn, head and tail of spine and corners bumped and rubbed, corners also bruised, good.   Ulysses 39-139 1996 £65.00

DE QUINCEY, THOMAS 1785-1859   Select Essays...Narrative and Imaginative. Edinburgh: Adam and Charles Black, 1888. Small 8vo; 2 volumes, pages x, 347; vii, (i), 329; steel engraved portrait to volume 1, tissue guard, half titles; contemporary half brown calf, rubbed, backstrips with raised bands, dark green and red morocco labels, gilt compartments (rubbed), slight loss at head of volume 1, short splits at head of front joint, marbled boards and endpapers, top edge gilt, good. Blackwell's B112-87 1996 £60.00

DERBY, ELIAS H.   The Overland Route to the Pacific: a Report on the Condition, Capacity and Resources of the Union Pacific and Central Pacific Railways. Boston: Lee and Shepard, 1869. 1st edition; 97 pages; origina printed grey wrappers, very minor chipping; fine copy in half morocco slipcase;   Michael D. Heaston 23-340 1996 $850.00

DERBY, GEORGE HORATIO   Phoenixiana. Chicago: Caxton Club, 1897. 1st 2 volume edition, one of 165 copies; small 8vo; 2 volumes; xxxiii, 123; viii, 119 pages, 2 frontispieces, 12 plates; gilt lettered green cloth, spines somewhat faded, else fine set. BAL 4652.   Argonaut Book Shop 113-191 1996 $125.00

DERBY, GEORGE HORATIO   Report of the Secretary of War...a Reconnoisance of the Gulf of California and the Colorado River by Lieutenant Derby. Washington: Senate Executive Document 81, 1852. 1st edition; 28 pages; 13 illustrations and 2 sketch maps, folding map; half morocco, title in gilt on spine; fine. Farquhar Books of Col. River 15; Wheat MTW III pp. 213-214.   Michael D. Heaston 23-129 1996 $350.00

DERBY, GEORGE HORATIO   The Squibob Papers. New York: Carleton, 1865. 1st edition; 1st state; 247, 6 pages; illustrations by author, with frontispiece, 11 plates, 17 tet illustrations; original green cloth, very light wear to spine ends, corners somewhat jammed, overall fine, internally fine and exceptionally clean. BAL 4651 state A.   Argonaut Book Shop 113-192 1996 $150.00

DERBY, J. C.   Fifty Years Among Author, Books and Publishers. New York: Carleton, 1884. 1st trade edition; quarto; 739 pages; portraits; original purple cloth, gilt, very good, tight copy of very thick book usually found in tatters.   Mac Donnell 12-97 1996 $165.00

DE RINALDIS, ALDO   Neapolitan Painting of the Seicento. Florence: Pantheon and Pegasus Press, Paris. 1929. Large 4to; text set in Monotype Poliphilus and Blado by the Officina Bodoni, collotypes executed by Sinsel, Leipzig; three quarter russet morocco, gilt, corners, edges and raised bands somewhat worn, internally nice, bookplate; scarce.   Bertram Rota 272-340 1996 £150.00

DERLETH, AUGUST WILLIAM 1909-   Dark of the Moon - Poems of Fantasy and the Macabre. Sauk City: Arkham House, 1947. 1st edition; very fine in dust jacket which has small tears to spine.   Bromer Booksellers 87-8 1996 $100.00

DERLETH, AUGUST WILLIAM 1909-   Dark Things. Sauk City: Arkham House, 1971. 1st edition; very fine in dust jacket, which shows discoloration and rubbing at spine edges.   Bromer Booksellers 87-9 1996 $100.00

DERLETH, AUGUST WILLIAM 1909-   Fire and Sleet and Candlelight. Sauk City: Arkham House, 1961. 1st edition; very fine in dust jacket, bookplate.   Bromer Booksellers 87-14 1996 $125.00

DERLETH, AUGUST WILLIAM 1909-   Last Light. Mt. Horeb: Perishable Press, 1978. Limited to 150 copies; large octavo; (28) pages; 3 wood engravings by Frank Utpatel, poems and engravings printed in browns, blues, black, greys, greens and reds on papers in shades of blues, greens, greys and browns; papers used were made for the occasion from 'elapsed clothing of author, artist, editor & printer', bound in vellum backed paste paper boards with vellum, hidden corners and gilt stamped to spine, extremely fine. Hamady 86.   Bromer Booksellers 87-252 1996 $375.00

DERLETH, AUGUST WILLIAM 1909-   Lonesome Places. Sauk City: Arkham House, 1962. 1st edition; signed by author; fine with slight offsetting from original dust jacket.   Bromer Booksellers 87-19 1996 $110.00

DERLETH, AUGUST WILLIAM 1909-   Over the Edge. Sauk City: 1964. 1st edition; very fine in Frank Utpatel dust jacket which is slightly chipped at base of spine.   Bromer Booksellers 87-21 1996 $100.00

DERLETH, AUGUST WILLIAM 1909-   Someone in the Dark. Sauk City: Arkham House, 1941. 1st edition; 1/1115 copies; some foxing, else just about fine in very good+ dust jacket save for some light wear and tear. Aronovitz 57-331 1996 $365.00

DERLETH, AUGUST WILLIAM 1909-   Something Near. Sauk City: Arkham House, 1945. 1st edition; fine in dust jacket, bookplate. Bromer Booksellers 87-24 1996 $150.00

DERMOTT, LAURENCE   The Constitution of Freemasonry; or, Ahiman Rezon: to Which is Added a Selection of Masonic Songs. Dublin: 1804. 1st edition; 8vo; with "A List of Lodges...Ireland. Scotland, America, Indies" often missing; in Dublin (?Mullen) red morocco binding, this copy was originally bound for (Dublin) Lodge 324 and later presented to West Yorkshire G.P. Lodge, who have left their mark (Library stamp) in a few places; firm, clean copy, scarce. Pencil note.   C. P. Hyland 216-154 1996 £300.00

DESANI, G. V.   Hali, a Play. London: Saturn Press, 1950. 1st edition; quarter leather and cloth in dust jacket, touch of rubbing to edges of leather spine, still just about fine in near fine dust jacket, small chip and tear at foot and one other short tear, very uncommon.   Between the Covers 42-131 1996 $150.00

DE SAULCY, F.   Narrative of a Journey Round the Dead Sea and In the Bible Lands; in 1850 and 1851. Philadelphia: Parry & M'Millan, 1854. New edition; 8vo; 2 volumes, 462, 506 pages; original maroon cloth, one signature slightly pulled in volume 1; still very good set.   Chapel Hill 94-278 1996 $125.00

DESAULT, PIERRE J.   A Treatise on Fractures, Luxations and Other Affections of the Bones. Philadelphia: Kimer & Sharpless, et al, 1817. 3rd American edition; 8vo; 398 pages; 3 full page plates; contemporary calf, rebacked, some browning and foxing, very good. Austin 657; GM 5580. Edwin V. Glaser B122-44 1996 $150.00

DE SAUSSURE, L. A.   Travels in Scotland; Descrptive of the State of Manners, Literature and Science. London: Printed for Sir Richard Phillips, 1821. Tall 8vo; viii, 112 pages; recently rebound with calf spine, boards, leather spine label; fine.   David Mason 71-143 1996 $120.00

DE SAUSSURE, L. A.   A Voyage to the Hebrides, Or, Western Isles of Scotland... London: Sir Richard Phillips, 1822. Tall 8vo; 116 pages, 5 plates; recently rebound with calf spine, boards, leather spine label; fine. David Mason 71-142 1996 $180.00

DESBOROUGH, V. R. D'A.   Protogeometric Pottery. Oxford: Clarendon, 1952. 4to; xvi, 330 pages; 38 plates, 1 map; original cloth, dust jacket (corner bumped, bookplate).   Archaeologia Luxor-3249 1996 $650.00

DESCARTES, RENE   Epistolae...in Quibus Omnis Generis Questiones Philosophicae Tractantur... London: Impensis Joh. Dunmore & Octavian Pulleyn, 1668. Small 4to; 2 volumes bound in 1, 4 leaves, 368 pages, 10 folding plates, 2 leaves, 404 pages, 2 leaves; contemporary calf, rebacked, worn; bookplate of Hon. Edward Monckton, Sumerford Hall, Staffs.   H. M. Fletcher 121-61 1996 £400.00

DESCARTES, RENE   Geometria a Renato des Cartes Anno 1637 Gallice Edita: Postea Auatem Una cum Notis florimondi de Beaune...Opera Atque Studio Francisci a Schooten... Amsterdam: Blaeu, 1683. 3rd and final Latin edition; 8vo; 2 volumes (16), 520; (20), 420, 8 pages; fine engraved portrait, printer's device on title, numerous woodcut diagrams; contemporary vellum, joints just starting on volume 1, some very occasional light browning and foxing; near fine. Zeitlinger 7260; Guibert p. 33; sotheran 7260.   Edwin V. Glaser 121-84 1996 $2,850.00

DESCARTES, RENE   De Homine Figuris et Latinitate Donatus a Florentio Schuyl. Leiden: Petrus Leffen & Franciscus Moyardus, 1662. 1st edition; 4to; (36), 121, (1) pages; 10 engraved plates, plus text woodcuts and engravings, lacks engraved overlay for mid-brain plate facing titlepage, but has the 2 overlays for the plate of the heart facing page 9; modern brown gilt calf, light rubbing, else very good. Iowa 468. James Tait Goodrich K40-119 1996 $1,650.00

DE SCHAUENSEE, R. M.   The Birds of Columbia, and Adjacent Areas of south and Central America. U.S.A.: 1964. Many colored and other plates, text illustrations; very fine in protected dust jacket.   David A.H. Grayling MY95Orn-26 1996 £70.00

DE SCHAUENSEE, R. M.   A Guide to the Birds of South of America. London: 1971. Many colored and other plates; mint in very slightly frayed dust jacket.   David A.H. Grayling MY95Orn-125 1996 £75.00

DESCLOZEAUX, ADRIEN   Gabrielle D'estrees. London: Arthur L. Humphreys, 1907. 1st edition in English; 8 1/4 x 6 inches; vi, 330 pages; title printed in red and black; pleasing green smooth calf by Bayntun (Riviere), covers with double gilt rule frame, raised bands, spine densely gilt in compartments featuring many floral stamps, morocco labels of blue and orange, gilt edges, marbled endpapers; very fine.   Phillip J. Pirages 33-157 1996 $195.00

DESCRIPTION Exacte de Tout ce Qui S'est Passe Dans les Guerres Entre le Roy d'Angleterre, Le Roy de France, les Estats des Provinces... Amsterdam: chez Jacques Benjamin, 1688. 1st edition in French; small 4to; engravings; contemporary calf, spine gilt, slight wear to spine; nice copy. Howes K253; cf. Sabin 38246-7 (Dutch printings).   Ximenes 108-275 1996 $1,500.00

A DESCRIPTION of East-Bourne and Its Environs. Eastborne: John Heatherly, 1819. 12mo; pages 44, (1), folding map frontispiece, 3 engraved plates; original boards, worn, backstrip gone.   Marlborough 162-25 1996 £85.00

DESFONTAINES, R.   Flora Atlantica, Sive Historia Plantarum, Quae in Atlante, Agro Tunetano et Algeriensi Crescunt. Paris: 1798-1800. Only 500 copies printed; 4to; 4 volumes in 2; leather spine, marbled covers, hinges tender, otherwise nice set; scarce.   John Johnson 135-194 1996 $1,500.00

DE SHIELDS, JAMES T.   Border Wars of Texas... Tioga: The Herald Co., 1912. 1st edition; 8vo; 400 pages; dozens of plates; original pictorial cloth, very bright; fine. Howes D277; Rader 1125.   M & S Rare Books 60-420 1996 $400.00

DE SHIELDS, JAMES T.   Border Wars of Texas...Conflict Waged Between Savage Indian Tribes and Pioneer Settlers of Texas... Tioga: The Herald Co., 1912. 1st edition; 8vo; 400 pages; illustrations; original pictorial tan cloth with title stamped in black, with red border on front cover and in black on spin; red, blue, black and brown colored Indian and fort in background on front cover very bright; fine, choice copy. Graff 1063; Howes D277.   Michael D. Heaston 23-133 1996 $300.00

DE TABLEY, JOHN BYRNE LEICESTER WARREN, 3RD BARON 1835-1895 Poems Dramatic and Lyrical. London: Elkin Mathews and John Lane, 1893. 1st edition; limited to 600 copies; 8vo; pages xiv, 212, (2); 6 plates; original green cloth, gilt; very good.   Claude Cox 107-138 1996 £55.00

DE TABLEY, JOHN BYRNE LEICESTER WARREN, 3RD BARON 1835-1895 Poems, Dramatic and Lyrical. (with) ...Second Series. London: John Lane, 1895. 1st editions; limited to 600 and 550 copies (for U.K.); 8vo; 2 volumes, pages xiv, 212, (2); viii, 160, 16 page publisher's catalog for 1895; volume 1 inscribed "With the Publisher's Compt."; 6 plates by Charles Ricketts who also designed the famous binding of hearts and petals which was repeated on the second volume; original green cloth, gilt, top edge gilt, others uncut, slight rubbing of extremities, backstrip of volume 2 slightly faded, but good set.   Claude Cox 107-137 1996 £85.00

DETROSIER, ROWLAND   Lecture On the Utility of Political Unions, for the Diffusion of Sound Moral and Political Information Amongst the People. London: John Brooks, 1832. 1st edition; 8vo; 24 pages; recently well bound in linen backed marbled boards lettered, very good, presentation copy, inscribed by author for Joseph Dawson. Kress C3122; Goldsmiths 27698; not in Black or Williams.   John Drury 82-64 1996 £250.00

DETTLAFF, T. A.   Sturgeon Fishes, Devlopmental Biology and Aquaculture. Berlin: 1993. 8vo; 313 pages; 20 plates, 81 figures; hardcover.   Wheldon & Wesley 207-962 1996 £125.00

DEUCER, JOHANNES   Metallicorum Corpus Juris Oder Bergkrecht. Leipzig: H. Grossheirs, 1624. 1st edition; folio; (21) leaves, 272 pages, (11) leaves (without two blanks), fine etching on titlepage, title printed in red and black; modern vellum backed boards; foxing and browning, occasionally heavy because of qualtiy of the paper. Rare.   Jeffrey D. Mancevice 20-23 1996 $950.00

DE VAUX, MARIE DE MAUPEOU FOUQUET, VICOMTESSE   Recueil de Receptes, Ou est Expliquee la Maniere de Guerir a Peu de Frais Toute Forte de Maux Tant Internes... Lyon: Jean Certe, 1676. 2nd edition; 12mo; (22) leaves, 322, (2) leaves; contemporary vellum, with some minor stains and soiling, little soiled, but sound; very good. Bitting 163 (for 1680 ed.). Wellcome III 46; Waller 3150 (1678 ed.).   Second Life Books 103-80 1996 $850.00

DEVENS, SAMUEL ADAMS   Sketches of Martha's Vineyard and Other Reminiscences of Travel at Home, Etc. Boston: James Munroe & Co., 1838. 1st edition; 12mo; 8, 207, (1) pages; original cloth, spine shot, front cover detached; Howes D293; Rinderknecht 50061; Sabin 19809; not in Buck or Clark   M & S Rare Books 60-372 1996 $225.00

DEVENS, SAMUEL ADAMS   Sketches of Martha's Vineyard and Other Reminiscences of Travel at Home, Etc. Boston: 1838. 1st edition; 12mo; viii, 207, (1) pages; paper label (label slightly chipped); original cloth, French circulating library stamp on title. Howes D302.   Edward Morrill 368-543 1996 $125.00

DEVEVOISE, NEILSON C.   Parthian Pottery from Seleucia on the Tigris. Ann Arbor: University of Michigan Press, 1934. 8vo; xiv, 132 pages, 8 figures, 16 plates; original cloth.   Archaeologia Luxor-3239 1996 $200.00

THE DEVILS in London. London: sold by Newman and Co. and W. Harwood, J. Innes, printer, n.d., ca. 1825. 1st edition; 12mo; original drab boards, spine worn; apparently unrecorded; one bookseller's name neatly clipped from imprint on titlepage, otherwise very good.   Ximenes 109-119 1996 $300.00

DE VINNE, THEODORE LOW 1828-1914   The First Editor: Aldus P. Manutius. New York: Targ Editions, 1983. Signed limited edition, one of 250 copies; printed on Rives, designed by Antonio Frasconi, frontispiece printed in five colors; Fabriano cloth, white linen spine, publisher's box, mint; fine.   Priscilla Juvelis 95/1-37 1996 $125.00

DEVOLPI, CHARLES P.   Montreal: a Pictorial Record. Historical Prints and Illustrations of the City of Montreal, Province of Quebec, Canada 1535-1885. Montreal: Dev-Sco Pub., c. 1963. Large 4to; 2 volumes, pages xii, 9; viii, 7; 311 plates, map on endpapers; gilt cloth with paste-on vignette; fine in worn and torn dust jackets.   Hugh Anson-Cartwright 87-294 1996 $250.00

DE VRIES, PETER   The Blood of the Lamb. Boston: Little Brown, 1961. 1st edition; foxing to endpapers and edges of pages, thus ner fine in like dust jacket foxed on flaps and with little tanning to spine; inscribed by author for Berton Rouche and his Wife Kay.   Between the Covers 42-133 1996 $250.00

DE VRIES, PETER   But Who Wakes the Bugler? Boston; Houghton Mifflin, 1940. 1st edition; illustrations by Charles Addams; very slight soiling, faint offsetting on rear board, near fine lacking dust jacket; author's first book; inscribed by author for Faith Baldwin.   Between the Covers 42-132 1996 $550.00

DEWAR, DOUGLAS   Game Birds. London: Chapman & Hall, 1928. 1st edition; crown 4to; (x), (256) pages; plates and illustrations by Eric Fitch-Daglish; original binding, nice, clean copy.   Ash Rare Books Zenzybyr-27 1996 £85.00

DEWEES, WILLIAM POTTS   A Treatise On the Diseases of Females. Philadelphia: Blanchard & Lea, 1831. 3rd edition; 8vo; 590 pages; 12 engraved plates; original sheep, front joint repaired, text with foxing, overall good, clean, tight copy.   James Tait Goodrich K40-206 1996 $115.00

D'EWES, SIMONDS   The Journal...from the Beginning of the Long Parliament to the Opening of the Trial of the Earl of Strafford. (with) The Journal...from the First Recess of the Long Parliament to the Withdrawal of King Charles from London. New Haven: Yale University Press, 1923/42. 8vo; 2 volumes, (xxii), 598, (ii); (xlvi), 459, (i) pages; original buckram, slightly marked, two corners slightly worn, library labels on endpapers, few small marginal stamps. Good, clean copies.   Robert Clark 38-37 1996 £85.00

DE WET, H. OLOFF   The Valley of the Shadow. London: William Blackwood and Sons Ltd., 1949. 1st edition; 4 plates by author; original binding, top edge dusty, head and tail of spine slightly bumped, covers slightly marked and dusty, very good in nicked, chipped and slightly rubbed, marked, torn and dusty dust jacket, which repeats the frontispiece, missing a small piece at the head of spine.   Ulysses 39-140 1996 £55.00

DEWEY, SQUIRE P.   The Bonanza Mines and the Bonanza Kings of California. San Francisco: 1880. 2nd edition; 87 pages; illustrations; this copy has small broadside inserted to back flyleaf: Important Decision. Probate Court, Nov. 10, 1879. Burke's Bonanza Suites. His Opposition to the Distribution of the O'Brien Estate Sustained; also on verso of page (3), a small printed piece inserted: (From Mayor Kalloch's Inaugural, Dec. 2, 1879) concening, the Bonanza Kings; original black pebbled cloth, title in gilt on front cover, some wear to spine and minor bumping; good copy; presentation copy from author. Graff 1074; Cowan p. 168. Paher Nevada 476.   Michael D. Heaston 23-134 1996 $750.00

DEXTER, COLIN   The Dead of Jericho. London: Macmillan, 1981. 1st edition; fine in dust jacket.   Quill & Brush 102-453 1996 $300.00

DEXTER, COLIN   Last Bus to Woodstock. London: Macmillan Ltd., 1975. 1st edition; original binding, pages browned, head and tail of spine and bottom edge of upper cover bumped, top corners of a few pages slightly creased, very good in nicked and slightly rubbed and dusty, very slightly creased dust jacket missing a small piece at head of spine; inscribed by author, ownership inscription above author's inscription. Ulysses 39-142 1996 £950.00

DEXTER, COLIN   Last Bus to Woodstock. New York: St. Martins, 1975. 1st U.S. edition; author's first book; fine in dust jacket.   Quill & Brush 102-449 1996 $350.00

DEXTER, COLIN   Last Seen Wearing. London: Macmillan, 1976. 1st edition; fine in dust jacket, scarce.   Quill & Brush 102-450 1996 $750.00

DEXTER, COLIN   Morse's Greatest Mystery. Bristol: Scorpion Press, 1993. 1/20 deluxe lettered copies, signed by author and J. Thomson who provided author appreciation; quarter bound goatskin with raised bands.   Quill & Brush 102-464 1996 $450.00

DEXTER, COLIN   Neighbourhood Watch. London: Harley Moorhouse, 1993. 1/50 signed, numbered (#37) copies; illustrations by Suzanne Hammond; cream paper wrappers, black paper slipcase.   Quill & Brush 102-466 1996 $150.00

DEXTER, COLIN   The Riddle of the Third Mile. London: Macmillan, 1983. 1st edition; fine in price clipped dust jacket.   Quill & Brush 102-454 1996 $300.00

DEXTER, COLIN   Service of All the Dead. New York: St. Martins, 1979. 1st edition; fine in dust jacket with light edge wear.   Quill & Brush 102-452 1996 $200.00

DEXTER, COLIN   The Silent World of Nicholas Quinn. London: Macmillan 1977. 1st edition; original binding, head and tail of spine and fore edge of upper cover slightly bumped, bottom corners of one page creased, very good, in very slightly creased dust jacket; presentation copy from author.   Ulysses 39-143 1996 £650.00

DEXTER, COLIN   The Silent World of Nicholas Quinn. New York: St. Martins, 1977. 1st edition; fine in lightly soiled dust jacket.   Quill & Brush 102-451 1996 $250.00

DEXTER, COLIN   The Way Through the Woods. Bristol: Scropion Press, 1992. One of 1/20 deluxe lettered copies; signed by author and Jonathan Gash who provided an author appreciation; quarter bound goatskin with raised bands; fine.   Quill & Brush 102-460 1996 $450.00

DEXTER, COLIN   The Way through the Woods. Bristol: Scorpion Press, 1992. One of 150 (of 170 total), signed, numbered copies; marbled paper boards, red leather spine with gold stamping; fine.   Quill & Brush 102-461 1996 $150.00

DEZALLIER D'ARGENVILLE, A. J.   The Theory and Practice of Gardening. London: printed by George James and sold by Maurice Atkins, 1712. 1st English language edition; 4to; (13), 218, (3) pages, 32 plates; contemporary calf, rebacked, tastefully rebacked, corners repaired, bookplate hinges internally strengthened, covers rubbed, light waterstains; Berlin 3463; Hunt 471; Harris 381.   Bookpress 75-175 1996 $2,250.00

DHU, SKENE   The Angler in Northern India. Allahabad: Pioneer Press, 1910. 1st edition; 8vo; xiv, 348, viii pages, (9) pages ads; maps and diagrams; original pictorial blue cloth, spine slightly faded, else near fine. Chapel Hill 94-378 1996 $150.00

A DIALOGUE Between a Member of Parliament a Divine, A Lawyer, a Freeholder, A Shopkeeper and a Country Farmer; or Remarks on the Badness of the Market (etc.). London: printed in the year 1703. 39 pages; disbound. Hanson 256; Kress 2383.   C. R. Johnson 37-9 1996 £120.00

DIALOGUES, Poems, Songs and Ballads by Various Writers in the Westmoreland and Cumberland Dialects, Now First Collected. London: John Russell Smith, 1839. 1st edition; 8vo; 403 pages, 8 page publisher's catalog sewn in at front; original cloth with paper spine label (rather worn), neatly recased.   R.F.G. Hollett & Son 78-500 1996 £85.00

DIALOGUES, Poems, Songs and Ballads, by Various Writers, in the Westmoreland and Cumberland Dialects, Now First Collected. London: John Russell Smith, 1839. 1st edition; 8vo; pages x, 403; all edges and endpapers marbled; old polished calf, gilt, little scratchd and scraped. R.F.G. Hollett & Son 78-499 1996 £95.00

DIALOGUS CREATURARUM   Herball Eleven Dialogues from the 1816 English edition of the Dialogues of Creatures Moralized. Janus Press, 1979. One of 150 pencil numbered copies signed by artist; 11.375 x 8.5 inches; 24 unnumbered pages; 11 woodcut illustrations by helen Siegl, foundry flowers throughout, designed by Claire Van Vliet, titles printed in red and black, text in black, woodcuts printed in black, hand colored with watercolors hand colored by Kaja McGowan, printed on Barcham green DeWint, bound in gold Scholco cloth over boards, author/title label on spine printed in black on Barcham Green deWint used also for endpapers and flyleaves; fine.   Joshua Heller 21-17 1996 $300.00

DIAMANT Classics. New York: Diamant Typographic Service, 1944-53. Limited editions; 7 miniature volumes (No. 2 not present), few autograph and printed ephemera inserted; original boards.   Rostenberg & Stern 150-127 1996 $150.00

DIAZ DEL CASTILLO, BERNAL 1496-1584   The Discovery and Conquest of Mexico. Mexico City: Limited Editions Club, 1942. Copy number 904 from a total edition of 1500 copies; illustrations by Miguel Covarrubias; fine in lightly worn publisher's slipcase.   Hermitage SP95-968 1996 $250.00

DIBBLE, SHELDON   History and General Views of the Sandwich Island's Mission. New York: Taylor & Dodd, 1839. 1st edition; 12mo; 268 pages; original dark brown cloth, top of spine little frayed, some text foxing, overall a very nice copy.   Kenneth Karmiole 1NS-120 1996 $350.00

DIBDIN, CHARLES 1745-1814   The Musical Tour of Mr. Dibdin... Sheffield: printed for the author by J. Gales, 1788. 1st edition; 4to; 19th century tree calf, spine worn, some foxing.   H. M. Fletcher 121-92 1996 £150.00

DIBDIN, CHARLES 1745-1814   The Overture, Songs, &c. in the Quaker. London: Longman & Broderip n.d. 1777. 1st edition; oblong folio; engraved titlepage, 39 pages of engraved music, dusting to fore-edge of titlepage; disbound.   Dramatis Personae 37-57 1996 $150.00

DIBDIN, THOMAS FROGNALL 1776-1847   The Bibliographical Decameron; or, Ten Days Pleasant Discourse Upon Illuminated Manuscripts, and Subjects... London: printed for the author by W. Bulmer and Co., Shakespeare Press... 1817. 1st edition; 4to; 3 volumes, large paper copy;, 410, 535, 484 pages of text, without half titles; 54 plates, numerous vignettes to letterpress, some on India paper, some colored, full diced calf, gilt rule and decorative borders, gilt bands, rule and title to panelled spines, all edges gilt, narrow inner gilt dentelles, marbled endpapers, armorial bookplate, later printed book label of Lloyd Kenyon to volume 1. Lowndes II p. 640.   Beeleigh Abbey BA56-143 1996 £750.00

DIBDIN, THOMAS FROGNALL 1776-1847   Bibliomania; or Book Madness; A Bibliographical Romance in Six Parts. London: ptd. for the author by J. McCreery, Longman, Hurst, Rees, Orme & Brown 1811. 2nd edition; ix, 782 pages, plus errata; frontispiece, title vignette, several plates and illustrations in text, first page of each part with decorated border, calf, gilt and blind tooled inner panel, spine blind tooled in compartments with raised bands, few small scuff marks, volume 2 title bound in case owner wanted to bind in 2 volumes; ownership inscription of one Adelaide Forbes of Dublin; attractive copy. Jackson 18.   Maggs Bros. Ltd. 1191-81 1996 £170.00

DIBDIN, THOMAS FROGNALL 1776-1847   Bibliomania; or, Book-Madness; a Bibliographical Romance Illustrated with Cuts. London: Chatto & Windus, 1876. Appears to be a large paper copy, new edition; tall quarto; later half cloth, boards bit scuffed with slight insect abrasion to glazing, very slight foxing, minor uniform embrowning, half title loose. G. W. Stuart 59-29 1996 $210.00

DIBDIN, THOMAS FROGNALL 1776-1847   Bibliomania; or Book Madness. London: Chatto & Windus, 1876. New edition; large royal 8vo; pages xxviii, 486 and errata leaf; strongly bound recent boards, occasional finger mark, but very good.   James Fenning 133-87 1996 £110.00

DIBDIN, THOMAS FROGNALL 1776-1847   Bibliomania; or Book-Madness; A Bibliographical Romance. London: Chatto & Windus, 1876. New edition; 10 1/4 x 7 inches; xviii, 63, (1), 618, xxxiv pages; frontispiece, 2 plates, engraved vignette on title and several illustrations in text, printed in red and black; fine copy, inside and out of a very well printed large paper edition.   Phillip J. Pirages 33-159 1996 $150.00

DIBDIN, THOMAS FROGNALL 1776-1847   Bibliomania; or Book-Madness; a Bibliographical Romance. London: Chatto & Windus, 1876. New edition; 8vo; pages xviii, 618, xxxiv (indices), plates, vignettes and illustrations, including mounted photographs; original green roan backed cloth, head and tail of backstrip sometime repaired a little crudely with leather strips, otherwise good, large margins.   Claude Cox 107-263 1996 £65.00

DIBDIN, THOMAS FROGNALL 1776-1847   The Bibliomania, or, Book Madness. Boston: Bibliophile Society, 1903. Limited edition o 483 copies after which plates were destroyed; 8vo; 4 volumes; parchment boards, title done in colored gilt and each volume has an engraved frontispiece after Howard Pyle; printed on heavy stock rag paper in handsome format;   James Tait Goodrich K40-120 1996 $295.00

DIBDIN, THOMAS FROGNALL 1776-1847   An Introduction to the Knowledge of Rare and Valuable Editions of the Greek and Latin Classics, Including an Account of the Polyglot Bibles. London: Longman, Hurst, Rees & Orme, 1808. 3rd edition; 2 volumes, 1 folding plate; diced calf, gilt and blind tooled outer borders, inner gilt borders, spine gilt in compartments with raised bands, some scuffing and marking, very small hole at base of joint of volume 1, still an attractive copy, light browning to title of volume 1, dampstain on first few leaves of volume 2 (not affecting text), ownership inscription of F. Reginald Forbes.   Maggs Bros. Ltd. 1191-80 1996 £155.00

DIBDIN, THOMAS FROGNALL 1776-1847   The Library Companion; or, the Young Man's Guide, and the Old Man's Comfort in the Choice of a Library. London: by W. Nicol for Harding, Triphook and Lepard and J. Major, 1824. 1st edition; 1st issue; 8 x 5 1/2 inches; 2 volumes, complete with half titles and with ad leaves at front of volume 1 and back of volume 2; original cloth (Smith's variant form with Roman numeral "I" on spine), very artful minor repairs at top of spines, substantial custom made cloth covered slipcase, as always, spines and edges of covers slightly faded, gilt titling rendered a bit indistinct, because of fading, few trivial imperfections in text, but an extraordinarily fine copy otherwise, with hinges in perfect order, with cloth exceptionally clean and with text showing no significant signs of use; armorial bookplates of Samuel Parker and of Edward Hunter in each volume (an earlier owner, no doubt Parker, has pasted a matching sheet of coated paper over the existing pastedown in the first volume, with opening that frames Parker's bookplate this redecoration presumably intended to obscure other marks of ownership. Eckel p. 108; Sabin 19996; Smith II 8-15.   Phillip J. Pirages 33-161 1996 $1,450.00

DICK, PHILIP K.   The Broken Bubble. N.P.: Ultramarine, 1988. One of 150 copies, signed by Tim Powers and James Blaylock; quarterbound in leather and marbled paper boards, gilt stamped; fine.   Ken Lopez 74-107 1996 $150.00

DICK, PHILIP K.   The Broken Bubble. New York: Ultramarine from Arbor House Sheets, 1988. This is "Author's Copy" #3 of a total edition of 150; signed by both Tim Powers and James Blaylock who provided introduction and afterword. Marbled boards and half leather, fine. Between the Covers 42-514 1996 $650.00

DICK, PHILIP K.   Deus Irae. Newton Abbot: Readers Union, 1978. Reissue; fine in near fine dust jacket; inscribed by Dick.   Ken Lopez 74-105 1996 $250.00

DICK, PHILIP K.   Do Androids Dream of Electric Sheep. New York: Doubleday, 1968. 1st edition; just about fine in very good+ dust jacket with some light wear to dust jacket spine extremities; John Brunner's copy with his personal bookplate, nice association.   Aronovitz 57-338 1996 $1,375.00

DICK, PHILIP K.   The Man Who Japed. London: Eyre Methuen, 1978. 1st British and 1st hardcover edition; fine in dust jacket.   Aronovitz 57-341 1996 $225.00

DICK, PHILIP K.   The Three Stigmata of Palmer Eldritch. New York: Doubleday, 1965. 1st edition; publisher's file copy, so stamped; fine in very good+ dust jacket save for label near base of spine, with words file copy and pub. date written in ink; scarce, desirable copy. Aronovitz 57-337 1996 $675.00

DICK, PHILIP K.   Time Out of Joint. Philadelphia/New York: Lippincott, 1959. 1st edition; tiny spot on fore edge and little rubbing at bottom of spine, else near fine in near fine dust jacket with just a touch of tanning to spine, nice, uncommon.   Between the Covers 42-513 1996 $650.00

DICK, PHILIP K.   The Transmigration of Timothy Archer. New York: Timescape, 1982. Uncorrected proof; wrappers; 2 small ink notations on front cover, otherwise fine.   Ken Lopez 74-106 1996 $125.00

DICK, PHILIP K.   Ubik. New York: Doubleday, 1969. 1st edition; very good+/near fine in dust jacket, very scarce.   Aronovitz 57-339 1996 $525.00

DICK, WILLIAM BRISBANE   The American Card-Player... New York: Dick & Fitzgerald, 1866. 1st edition; 8vo; 154, (20) ads, pages; original color illustrated boards with terra cotta cloth spine, edges of boards worn, couple of gatherings inevitably browned, but very good. Rare. NUC locates 3 copies.   Chapel Hill 94-144 1996 $150.00

DICK, WILLIAM BRISBANE   Dick's Games of Patience: or Solitaire with Cards. New York: Dick & Fitzgerald, 1884/1983. New edition; small square 8vo; 50 explantory tableaux; later stiff aqua wrappers, with original pictorial upper cover, printed in black and red (laid down), very good.   George J. Houle   68-117   1996 $125.00

DICKENS, CHARLES 1812-1870   American Notes for General Circulation. London: Chapman and Hall, 1842. 1st edition; 1st issue (first pagination of "Contents" page in volume I); 8vo; 2 volumes; half titles, ad leaf in volume I, 6 pages ads in volume 2; full gilt bordered morocco, spines gilt, top edge gilt, by Riviere, original cloth covers and spines bound in; fine set, bookplates. Smith 3; Eckel pp. 113-5; Tinker Lib. 821; Sterling 261.   Trebizond 39-6   1996 $850.00

DICKENS, CHARLES 1812-1870   The Battle of Life. London: Bradbury and Evans, 1846. 1st edition; 2nd issue; 6 3/4 x 4 1/2 inches; 4 p.l., 175, (1) pages, (1) leaf (ads); frontispiece, engraved title, 11 illustrations in text; original gilt decorated cloth, front endpapers with bookplates of Thomas Leonard Daniels and Edward Jackson Barron, with latter's signature; very tiny tears at spine ends, just hint of soiling to cloth, in all other ways a fine copy, scarce issue, with undamaged joints and hinges and with very bright gilt.   Phillip J. Pirages 33-162   1996 $500.00

DICKENS, CHARLES 1812-1870   The Battle of Life. London: Bradbury & Evans, 1846. 1st edition; (fourth state); foolscap 8vo; frontispiece and vignette titlepage and 11 illustrations finely bound in half crimson morocco, gilt top, for Hatchards. Brilliant copy. Eckels p. 127-130. Charles W. Traylen 117-98   1996 £150.00

DICKENS, CHARLES 1812-1870   The Battle of Life: a Love Story. London: Bradbury & Evans, 1846. 1st edition; 4th issue; 12mo; original scarlet cloth, gilt, all edges gilt, light edgewear and lower hinge starting, else fine in beautiful binding with gilt strapwork and borders on upper and lower covers, gilt spine, inner dentelles, all edges gilt. Smith II 8. Glenn Books   36-84   1996 $250.00

DICKENS, CHARLES 1812-1870   Bleak House. London: Bradbury & Evans, 1853. 1st issue; 1st edition; 8vo; xvi, 624 pages; half title, frontispiece, additional engraved title and 38 plates by Phiz; contemporary maroon straight grained half morocco, spine gilt in five compartments, marbled edges, slightly rubbed, occassional foxing, mostly fairly light, small piece torn from margin of leaf 2R1 without loss of text, very good. Smith 10.   Thomas Thorp 489-84 9196 £320.00

DICKENS, CHARLES 1812-1870   Bleak House. London: Bradbury and Evans, 1853. 1st edition in book form; 9 x 5 3/4 inches; 2 volumes; xvi, 624 pages (pagination continues in second volume); frontispiece, added engraved title and 38 plates by Phiz, with the majority of wrappers and ads from original parts bound in at back of each volume; bound up from parts (stab holes visible), fine rich brown crushed morocco by Bayntun-Riviere, bound for Charles Sawyer, sides with double gilt rule, spine attractively gilt in compartments with large floral ornament at center, headcaps and board edges decorated in gilt, broad turn-ins with multilpe gilt rules, all edges gilt, marbled endpapers; small portion of corner 3 leaves skillfully renewed, few trivial marks to covers, but extraordinarily fine, with text and plates remarkably clean.   Phillip J. Pirages 33-163   1996 $850.00

DICKENS, CHARLES 1812-1870   Bleak House. London: Bradbury & Sons, 1853. 1st edition in book form; 8vo; 40 etched plates, including 10 'dark plates' by Phiz, frontispiece, illustrated titlepage (lacking half title); contemporary half crimson morocco, gilt lettering to spine, 5 raised bands, top edge gilt.   Charles W. Traylen 117-99   1996 £180.00

DICKENS, CHARLES 1812-1870   Bleak House. London: Bradbury & Evans, 1853. 1st edition in book form; 8 1/2 x 5 3/4 inches; xvi, 624 pages; frontispiece, added engraved title, 38 engraved plates by Phiz; bound up from parts, fine medium brown straight grain morocco gilt, covers with French fillet as well as inner dotted frame in blind, raised bands, spine handsomely gilt in compartments in antique style, complex floral ornament at center and elaborate scrolling stamps in corners, two maroon and one olive colored lettering pieces, turn-ins with densely gilt decoration, all edges gilt, front joint little worn (nothing loose), one small scar on back cover, otherwise binding virtually unworn as well as very bright, clean and attractive, slight mottling and faint darkening to some of the plates, otherwise excellent copy; armorial bookplate of Samuel Augustine Courtauld.   Phillip J. Pirages 33-164   1996 $750.00

DICKENS, CHARLES 1812-1870   The Chimes. London: Chapman and Hall, 1845. 1st edition; 1st issue; 12mo; beautifully bound by Bayntun (Riviere) in full scarlet morocco, gilt strapwork, all edges gilt, gilt inner dentelles; lovely copy. Smith II 6.   Glenn Books 36-85 1996 $400.00

DICKENS, CHARLES 1812-1870   The Chimes. London: & New York: J. M. Dent and E. P. Dutton, 1905. Deluxe edition; small 8vo; color illustrations by Charles Brock; finely bound in full vellum, highly gilt. Glenn Books 36-86 1996 $200.00

DICKENS, CHARLES 1812-1870   The Chimes. London: Hodder & Stoughton, n.d. 1913. 1st edition thus; octavo; v, 137 pages, 7 mounted color plates; original red cloth decoratively stamped in black on front cover and in gilt on spine, pictorial endpapers, occasional light foxing, otherwise fine in original cardboard box with color pictorial label. Gimbel B156.   Heritage Book Shop 196-277   1996 $450.00

DICKENS, CHARLES 1812-1870   The Chimes. London: 1931. Limited editions Club, 1 of 1500 signed copies; illustrations by Arthur Rackham; decorative cloth, very near fine in very good slipcase.   Stephen Lupack 83-   1996 $450.00

DICKENS, CHARLES 1812-1870   The Chimes. New York: printed in London by George W. Jones for Members of the Limited... 1931. Limited to 1500 numbered copies, signed by artist; folio; xxxii, 128 pages; original tan buckram decoratively stamped in gilt and black on front cover and lettered in gilt on spine, bevelled boards, top edge gilt, spine slightly darkened, bookplate, near fine in original publisher's cardboard slipcase. LEC Bib. 27.   Heritage Book Shop 196-278   1996 $850.00

DICKENS, CHARLES 1812-1870   The Chimes. Barbarian Press, 1985. One of 150 numbered copies; 4to; printed in handset English Scotch roman on Zerkall; wood engravings by Colin Paynton; linen boards; fine copy in slipcase.   Bertram Rota 272-27   1996 £60.00

DICKENS, CHARLES 1812-1870   Christmas Books. London: Chapman and Hall, 1852. 1st collected edition; 8vo; original celery cloth blocked in blind and gilt, moderate overall wear to binding, else very good, early issue.   Glenn Books 36-79 1 996 $300.00

DICKENS, CHARLES 1812-1870   Christmas Books. London: Chapman and Hall, 1852. 1st collected edition; 8vo; original olive green cloth blocked in blind and gilt, spine faded to brown and wear at extremities, endleaves foxed, overall nice, later issue.   Glenn Books 36-78 1996 $250.00

DICKENS, CHARLES 1812-1870   A Christmas Carol. London: Chapman & Hall, 1843. 1st edition; 1st impression, 1st issue, with 14-15mm. between closest points of blindstamping and gilt wreath on upper cover, the 'D' of 'Dickens' unbroken on upper cover, text uncorrected; green endpapers, half title printed in blue, title in red and blue, and 'Stave I on page 1; 8vo; pages (viii), 166, (2) ads; hand colored etched frontispiece, 3 plates, illustrations, after Leech; original brown cloth, gilt, spine slightly faded, lower cover little marked, hinges just cracking, excellent copy. Smith Part II 4; Eckel pp. 110-5.   Simon Finch 24-71   1996 £7,500.00

DICKENS, CHARLES 1812-1870   A Christmas Carol. London: Chapman & Hall, 1843. 1st edition; 1st impression, 1st issue, with 14-15mm. between closest points of blindstamping and gilt wreath on upper cover, the "D" of "Dickens" unbroken on upper cover, text uncorrected, yellow e.p.'s, half title printed in blue, title in red & blue, & 'Stave I' on p. 1; 8vo; pages (viii), 166, (2) ads, hand colored etched frontispiece, 3 plates, illustrations after Leech; original brown cloth, gilt, spine and edges of boards slightly faded as usual, spine just nicked at head, title with two trivial marks, very good. Ownership inscription of Mrs. Whitbread dated Jan. 1844 on half title. Smith Part II 4; Eckel pp. 110-5. Simon Finch 24-72 1996 £3,800.00

DICKENS, CHARLES 1812-1870   A Christmas Carol. London: and New York: J. M. Dent and E. P. Dutton, 1905. Deluxe edition; small 8vo; illustrations in color by Charles brock; bound in full vellum, hightly gilt, all edges gilt.   Glenn Books 36-75   1996 $225.00

DICKENS, CHARLES 1812-1870   A Christmas Carol. London: William Heinemann, 1915. Limited to 525 numbered copies, signed by artist; quarto; xv, 147 pages; 12 colored plates mounted on brown paper with descriptive tissue guards, 20 drawings in black and white, by Arthur Rackham; original vellum over boards, decoratively stamped in gilt on front cover and spine, top edge gilt, others uncut, pictorial endpapers; Latimore & Haskell pp. 44-45.   Heritage Book Shop 196-281 1996 $2,500.00

DICKENS, CHARLES 1812-1870   A Christmas Carol. Cleveland & New York: World Pub. Co., 1916. 1st edition; 6 double page illustrations in full color and 22 black and white drawings, by Ronald Searle; fine in near fine dust jacket.   Glenn Books 36-77   1996 $150.00

DICKENS, CHARLES 1812-1870   A Christmas Carol. Boston: The Atlantic Monthly Press, 1920. Facsimile of first edition; 3 color plates, including frontispiece; original red cloth, few minor faults, including light edgewear, faint dampstaining to several rear leaves andd moderate foxing to endpapers; scarlet cloth and gilt on cover and spine strikingly bright; Podeschi B138.   Glenn Books 36-76   1996 $100.00

DICKENS, CHARLES 1812-1870   A Christmas Carol. London: King Penguin Books, 1946. Small octavo; 138 pages; illustrations by John Leech; bound by Bayntun of Bath in full red crushed levant morocco, gilt decorative border on covers, front cover set with vignette, executed in multicolored morocco onlays, gilt spine, tooled in compartments, gilt board edges and turn-ins, all edges gilt, marbled endpapers, fine in red cloth slipcase.   Heritage Book Shop 196-280 1996 $600.00

DICKENS, CHARLES 1812-1870   The Cricket on the Hearth. London: Bradbury & Evans, 1846. 1st edition; 2nd printing; 16mo; original red ribbed cloth, gilt cover vignette and spine, rebacked, retaining original endpapers and majority of spine, all edges gilt; Smith 6.   Glenn Books 36-88 1996 $300.00

DICKENS, CHARLES 1812-1870   The Cricket on the Hearth. London: Bradbury and Evans, 1846. 1st edition; 1st issue; foolscap 8vo; frontispiece and vignette title, 12 plates; with first issue of ad leaf at end; original red cloth, gilt edges, joints finely repaired. Eckels pp. 125-126.   Charles W. Traylen 117-100 1996 £200.00

DICKENS, CHARLES 1812-1870   The Cricket on the Hearth, A Fairy-Tale of Home. London: Golden Cockerel Press for the Limited Editions Club, 1933. Copy number 904 from a total edtlion of 1500 numbered copies; illustrations by Hugh Thompson; full pictorial cloth, fine in slightly worn publisher's slipcase.   Hermitage SP95-971 1996 $150.00

DICKENS, CHARLES 1812-1870   David Copperfield in Copperplates. Berkeley: Gillick Press, 1939. No. 419 of a limited edition of 500 copies, signed by artist; oblong 8vo; 46 oval illustrations in copperplate by William Ross Cameron; cloth backed pictorial boards; fine.   Barbara Stone 70-72 1996 £55.00

DICKENS, CHARLES 1812-1870   Hard Times. For These Times. London: Bradbury & Evans, 1857. 1st edition; original green cloth, spine and part of boards sunned, very good.   19th Century Shop 39- 1996 $1,500.00

DICKENS, CHARLES 1812-1870   The Haunted Man and the Ghost's Bargain. London: Bradbury & Evans, 1848. 1st edition; 1st issue with the fallen "1" in the number "166" at the top of that page; original red embossed cloth with gilt titling and wreath on upper cover, cloth worn through at two points on hinge of spine with upper cover (at head and foot) with similar but less severe wear to hinge with lower panel, overall a most desirable copy with 19th century inscription on flyleaf.   Words Etcetera 94-354 1996 £220.00

DICKENS, CHARLES 1812-1870   The Haunted Man and The Ghost's Bargain. A Fancy for Christmas-Time. London: Bradbury & Evans, 1848. 1st edition; small 8vo; pages (viii), 188; frontispiece and additional title, little spotted, illustrations in text, ad leaf at beginning; original red vertically ribbed cloth, sides with blindstamped borders, upper cover lettered in gilt within gilt wreath, spine lettered and decorated in gilt, gilt edges, little soiling and very slight wear at head and foot of spine, few spots, ownership inscription, but excellent bright copy. Smith II 9; Eckel pp. 124-25.   Simon Finch 24-73 1996 £200.00

DICKENS, CHARLES 1812-1870   The Holly Tree. East Aurora: Roycrofters, 1903. 1st edition; one of 100 numbered copies, signed by Elbert Hubbard; printed on Japan vellum; original three quarter leather with gilt devices on spine, top edge gilt; fine.   Captain's Bookshelf 38-50 1996 $225.00

DICKENS, CHARLES 1812-1870   The Life and Adventures of Martin Chuzzlewit. London: Chapman and Hall, 1844. 1st edition in book form; 8 1/2 x 5 3/4 inches; xiv, (2), (errata leaf), 624 pages; frontispiece, 37 engraved plates by Phiz; fine medium brown straight grained morocco, gilt, covers with French fillet as well as inner dotted frame in blind, raised bands, spine handsomely gilt in compartments in antique style with complex floral ornament at center and elaborate scrolling stamps in corners, 2 maroon and one olive colored lettering pieces, turn-ins with densely gilt decoration, all edges gilt; front joint just beginning to show minor wear, some plates with hint of foxing, otherwise fine.   Phillip J. Pirages 33-167 1996 $650.00

DICKENS, CHARLES 1812-1870   Martin Chuzzlewit. London: Chapman and Hall, 1844. 1st edition; 8vo; frontispiece, engraved titlepage and 38 other plates by Phiz; contemporary half green calf, green boards, gilt spine with 5 raised bands.   Charles W. Traylen 117-102 1996 £150.00

DICKENS, CHARLES 1812-1870   The Life and Adventures of Nicholas Nickleby. London: April 1838-Oct. 1839. 1st edition, in original monthly parts, 1st issue of text of both parts 4 and 5; part 2 lacks Mechi's cat.; part 3 lacks part of the "Nickleby Advertiser", the note to reading clubs, and all ads; part 8 lacks the ad "Heads of the people", as usual; part 9 lacks a two leaf ad; part 11 contains a different Ackermann cat.; part 19/20 lacks the five colored wafer specimens in Hill ad, as usual; otherwise the set collates with Hatton and Cleaver; plates by Hablot Brown; pictorial wrappers, minor edge browning on 2 early plates, skillful restoration of some spine ends, upper corner of one front wrapper repaired, else very attractive set, in cloth folding box (one hinge worn).   Joseph J. Felcone 64-17 1997 $2,200.00

DICKENS, CHARLES 1812-1870   Nicholas Nickleby. London: Chapman and Hall, 1839. 1st edition; bound from parts; frontispiece, illustration by Phiz, with extra illustrations: two series, one by Peter Palette, and also portraits by Onwhyn; bound in period style in three quarter polished calf, marbled boards and endpapers, red and black labels, slight wear, but nice. From the library of Lady Glentworth. Eckel pp. 64-66.   Hartfield 48-L28 1996 $595.00

DICKENS, CHARLES 1812-1870   Little Dorrit. London: Bradbury & Evans, 1855-57. 1st edition; 1st issue with 'Rigaud' for 'Blandois' in part XV and slip correcting errors in part XVI; this copy has all the slips and ads and all but first part have ownership signature of Miss Whittuck on upper wrapper; 8vo; in original 19/20 parts; etched frontispiece, additional title, 38 plates by Phiz; original blue printed wrappers, red cloth folders and morocco pull of cases, spines with raised bands lettered numbered in gilt, few minor repairs to wrappers, backstrip with only very slight wear, small label on upper wrapper of last part, some plates little spotted, but excellent; Hatton and Cleaver pp. 307-30; Eckel p. 82-85.   Simon Finch 24-74 1996 £1,800.00

DICKENS, CHARLES 1812-1870   Little Dorrit. London: Bradbury & Evans, 1857. 1st edition; 1st issue; 8vo; xiv, 625 pages; frontispiece, additional etched title and 38 plates by Phiz; contemporary maroon half morocco, spine ornately gilt in five compartments, marbled edges, plates slightly foxed and spine trifle faded, but very handsome copy. Smith 12.   Thomas Thorp 489-85 1996 £320.00

DICKENS, CHARLES 1812-1870   Little Dorrit. London: Bradbury and Evans, 1857. 1st edition in book form; 8 1/2 x 5 3/4 inches; xiv, 625 pages, without half title; engraved frontispiece, added engraved title and 39 engraved plates by Phiz; fine medium brown straight grain morocco, gilt, covers with French fillet as well as inner dotted frame in blind, raised bands, spine handsomely gilt in compartments in antique style with complex floral ornament at center and elaborate scrolling stamps in corners, two maroon and one olive colored lettering pieces, turn-ins with densely gilt decoration, all edges gilt, short annotation in ink at foot of final page, text and plates a shade less that bright, two plates with small and very faint dampstain, otherwise fine, binding without any significant wear.   Phillip J. Pirages 33-166 1996 $500.00

DICKENS, CHARLES 1812-1870   Little Dorrit. London: Bradbury & Evans, 1857. 1st edition; 40 etched plates by Phiz, including 8 'dark plates', frontispiece and titlepage; contemporary hal fred morocco, marbled boards, gilt lettered spine, 5 raised bands.   Charles W. Traylen 117-101 1996 £180.00

DICKENS, CHARLES 1812-1870   Master Humphrey's Clock. London: Chapman and Hall, 1840-41. 1st edition in book form; 3 volumes; illustrations by George Cattermole and Hablot Browne; original brown cloth, gilt, recased with new endpapers, some wear and fading to binding, occasional foxing and soiling; with an invitation to the second Clock Dinner, mounted at front blank is a fine 1 page letter signed by Dickens dated 27 March 1841. The letter in secretarial hand.   19th Century Shop 39- 1996 $2,500.00

DICKENS, CHARLES 1812-1870   Master Humphrey's Clock. London: Chapman and Hall, 1840-41. 1st edition in book form; 10 x 7 inches; 3 volumes; frontispiece in each volume, numerous illustrations in text by George Cattermole and H. K. Browne; fine medium brown straight grain morocco, gilt, covers with French fillet as well as inner dotted frame in blind, raised bands, spine handsomely gilt compartments in antique style with complex floral ornament at center and elaborate scrolling stamps in corners, two maroon and one olive colored lettering pieces, turn-ins with densely gilt decoration, all edges gilt; top portion of one cover slightly faded, leather with few minor marks, paper stock slightly darkened in some gatherings, one tear well into skillfully repaired (with no loss of legibility), handful of other quite minor repaired tears, otherwise extremely fine.   Phillip J. Pirages 33-168 1996 $850.00

DICKENS, CHARLES 1812-1870   Master Humphrey's Clock. London: Chapman and Hall, 1840-41. 1st edition; royal 8vo; 3 volumes; frontispiece and many illustrations in text; half blue leather, mottled board sides; fine, unusually clean.   Charles W. Traylen 117-103 1996 £150.00

DICKENS, CHARLES 1812-1870   Master Humphrey's Clock. London: Chapman and Hall, 1840/41. 1st edition; 8vo; 3 volumes; illustrations by G. Cattermole, and H. Browne; recently bound as one in half morocco over boards, lacks dedication leaf, else very clean, relatively free of usual foxing. With Dickens centenary stamp laid in. Smith 6; Eckel 66. Glenn Books 36-81 1996 $350.00

DICKENS, CHARLES 1812-1870   The Mystery of Edwin Drood. London: Chapman and Hall, 1870. 1st edition; 12 illustrations by S. L. Fildes and frontispiece; three quarter leather, bookplate, light soiling on pages, unavoidable offset on front and back endpapers and pastedowns, spine and tips lightly rubbed.   Quill & Brush 102-467 1996 $175.00

DICKENS, CHARLES 1812-1870   The Old Curiosity Shop. London: New York: and Toronto: Hodder & Stoughton, n.d. 1913. Deluxe edition, limited to 350 copies, signed by artist; folio; mounted color plates by Frank Reynolds; bound in full vellum with gilt spine and cvoer with silhouette portrait of Little Nell on gilt background; vellum of upper cover and spine foxed, ties lacking and evidence of bookplate removal on upper pastedown, else very good. Podeschi p. 171.   Glenn Books 36-90 1996 $650.00

DICKENS, CHARLES 1812-1870   Oliver Twist; or, The Parish Boy's Progress. London: Richard Bentley, 1838. 1st edition; 1st issue with the Boz titlepages and the 'Fireside' plate facing p. 313 in volume 3, r pages of publisher's ads at end of volume 1 & leaf of ads beginning of volume 3; 8vo; 3 volumes; frontispiece to each volume, 21 etchings by George Cruikshank; half red morocco, lettered in gilt on spine, gilt tops, choicely bound for Hatchards. Exceptionally fine; Eckels p. 52.   Charles W. Traylen 117-104 1996 £1,500.00

DICKENS, CHARLES 1812-1870   Oliver Twist. London: Richard Bentley, 1838. 1st edition; 1st issue printing; 8vo; illustration imprints have been trimmed off although not uncommon, leaves have been trimmed from 20.1 x 12.4 to 18.7 x 11.5; the fireside plate faces p. 312 instead of p. 313; half calf over rubbed, marbled boards, recently rebacked, spine gilt, green morocco labels, lacks half titles and ads, all first issue points, including fireside plate, hinges have been reinforced in all volumes. all in all, very acceptable copy. Eckel p. 51; Podeschi A27; Smith 4.   Glenn Books 36-74 1996 $2,000.00

DICKENS, CHARLES 1812-1870   Oliver Twist... London: Richard Bentley, 1838. 1st edition; this copy with 'Church' plate & Dickens's name on titlepages, but first state of the 'Charles Dickens' issue with 'pilaster' unchanged on page 164, volume 3; 12mo; 3 volumes, half titles in volumes I and II, ad leaf at beginning of volume 3 as called for, 4 pages ads at end of volume 1, etched frontispieces, 21 plates; original fine diaper reddish brown blindstamped cloth, little soiling, spines with raised bands lettered in gilt, slightly faded, little of usual spotting and offetting internally, but in general an unusually clean, excellent copy. Smith 4; Eckel pp. 59-62.   Simon Finch 24-69 1996 £3,200.00

DICKENS, CHARLES 1812-1870   Oliver Twist. London: Richard Bentley, 1838. 1st edition; this would apear to be a later issue because the 'fireside' plate has been replaced by the 'church' plate in volume 3, howeve, leaf containing a list of illustrationss (which Eckel says signifies a later pringing) is not present, 7 3/4 x 5 inches; 3 volumes; 24 plates by George Cruikshank, including frontispiece in each volume; beautiful polished calf by Zaehnsdorf, French fillet on covers, spines very handsomely gilt in compartments with delicate scrolling stamps, dark blue and ochre lettering pieces, gilt edges, marbled endpapers, modern bookplate in each volume; extraordinarily fine.   Phillip J. Pirages 33-170 1996 $1,750.00

DICKENS, CHARLES 1812-1870   Oliver Twist; or, the Parish Boy's Progress. New York: William H. Colyer, 1839. 2nd American edition; 8vo; 4 unsigned full page plates; original boards, rebacked, new spine label; uncommon, light foxing, but very good. Occasional early owner's pencilled signatures. Not in NCBEL.   Trebizond 39-7 1996 $250.00

DICKENS, CHARLES 1812-1870   The Adventures of Oliver Twist. London: pub. for the author by Bradbury and Evans, 1846. New edition; 8vo; 24 illustrations on steel by George Cruikshank; frontispiece, half title; full red morocco by Bayntun-Riviere, single line gilt border with blindstamped bust to upper boards and facsimile signature to back board, full gilt spine with five raised bands. Sadleir 696c.   Charles W. Traylen 117-97 1996 £350.00

DICKENS, CHARLES 1812-1870   Our Mutual Friend. London: Chapman and Hall, 1865. 8 3/4 x 5 3/4 inches; 2 volumes; 40 plates, including frontispiece in each volume, by Marcus Stone; very attractive 19th century half morocco, cloth sides, decorative rules in blind on sides and in blind and gilt on spines, wide raised bands, marbled edges and endpapers; little darkening at edges of text and paltes, otherwise beautiful inside and out, virtually no wear to binding.   Phillip J. Pirages 33-171 1996 $450.00

DICKENS, CHARLES 1812-1870   Our Mutual Friend. London: Chapman and Hall, 1865. 1st edition; octavo; newly bound in navy blue half morocco over marbled boards, 2 volumes bound in one, lacking half titles, nice, with minimal foxing. Smith p. 107.   Glenn Books 36-82 1996 $300.00

DICKENS, CHARLES 1812-1870   Pictures from Italy. London: Bradbury & Evans, 1846. 1st edition; 1st issue; vignette illustrations on wood by Samuel Palmer; original blue cloth; near fine.   Captain's Bookshelf 38-49 1996 $350.00

DICKENS, CHARLES 1812-1870   Pictures from Italy. London: published for the author, by Bradbury and Evans, 1846. 1st edition; small 8vo; original blue cloth, wood engraved vignette illustrations; very fine. Eckel p. 126.   Ximenes 108-105 1996 $300.00

DICKENS, CHARLES 1812-1870   The Posthumous Papers of the Pickwick Club. London: Chapman and Hall, 1837. 1st edition; 43 illustrations by Seymour and Phiz, plus 2 additional cancelled plates by Buss; three quarter crimson polished calf, marbled boards, endpapers, raised bands, leather labels, top edge gilt, silk ribbon marker, most attractive copy. Elegantly bound by Zaehnsdorf. Eckel pp. 17-18. Hartfield 48-L29 1996 $950.00

DICKENS, CHARLES 1812-1870   The Posthumous Papers of the Pickwick Club. London: Chapman and Hall, 1837. 1st edition in book form; 8 1/2 x 5 3/4 inches; 1 p. l., (v)-xiv, (2) (directions to the binder and errata), 609 pages (bound without half title); frontispiece and added engraved title and 41 engraved plates by R. Seymour and Phiz; fine medium brown straight grain morocco, gilt, covers with French fillet as well as inner dotted frame in blind, raised bands, spine handsomely gilt in compartments in antique style with complex floral ornament at center and elaborate scrolling stamps in corners, two maroon and one olive colored lettering pieces, turn-ins with densely gilt decoration, all edges gilt; very fine.   Phillip J. Pirages 33-172 1996 $850.00

DICKENS, CHARLES 1812-1870   The Posthumous Papers of the Pickwick Club. London: Chapman & Hall, 1837. 1st edition in book form; demy 8vo; bound up from original monthly parts, complete with half title; with part i and ii in early states, with no signature E on p. 25, the 'By God' reading on p. 33, etc., and the original Seymour plates (in second state), rather than the replacement plates usually found, part iv has the first two 'Phiz' plates in earliest state, with the 'Nemo' signatures still visible; this copy also has the sought-after 'Veller' title; bound up, complete with half title, in near Victorian calf, banded and gilt, all edges gilt, very slightly rubbed, seom very minor wear, some browning and discoloration of plates, but nice.   Ash Rare Books Zenzybyr-28 1996 £450.00

DICKENS, CHARLES 1812-1870   The Posthumous Papers of the Pickwick Club. London: Chapman and Hall, 1837. 1st edition; 8vo; 43 illustrations by R. Seymour and Phiz, frontispiece, engraved titlepage; contemporary half red morocco, marbled boards, gilt lettered spine, 5 raised bands.   Charles W. Traylen 117-105 1996 £150.00

DICKENS, CHARLES 1812-1870   The Posthumous Papers of the Pickwick Club. London: 1838. 1st edition; 1st issue; thick 8vo; 2 volumes; 43 plates, extra illustrated by some 148 extra plates; full red morocco, gold borders, inside and out, fully gilt spines, gilt top. Charles W. Traylen 117-107 1996 £1,600.00

DICKENS, CHARLES 1812-1870   The Posthumous Papers of the Pickwick Club. Paris: Baudry's European Library, 1839. 1st Foreign edition; 8vo; 2 volumes; contemporary quarter morocco. Scarce. Charles W. Traylen 117-106 1996 £95.00

DICKENS, CHARLES 1812-1870   The Posthumous Papers of the Pickwick Club. London: Chapman and Hall, 1887. Limited to 2000 copies; this one of 500 with plates on India paper; thick royal 8vo; 2 volumes bound in 4; original illustrations; extra illustrated with the insertion of 326 extra illustrations; full green morocco, elaborate gilt corner pieces, gilt spines, gilt tops, gilt leather doublures, silk endpapers; bound by Riviere. Charles W. Traylen 117-108 1996 £3,750.00

DICKENS, CHARLES 1812-1870   The Short Stories of Charles Dickens. New York: Limited Editions Club, 1971. Number 1029 of 1500 copies, signed by artist and Joseph Blumenthal, the designer/printer; illustrations by Edward Ardizzone; fine in slipcase.   Hermitage SP95-970 1996 $150.00

DICKENS, CHARLES 1812-1870 Sketches by Boz. London: Chapman and Hall, 1839. 1st issue of the "Octavo Edition" (First Edition Combined in One Volume); 8 1/2 x 5 3/4 inches; 2 p.l., 526 pages, bound without leaf of contents; frontispiece, added engraved title, 38 engraved plates by George Cruikshank; fine medium brown straight grain morocco gilt, covers with French fillet as well as inner dotted frame in blind, raised bands, spine handsomely gilt in compartments in antique style with complex floral ornament at center and elaborate scrolling stamps in corners, two maroon and one olive colored lettering pieces, turn-ins with densely gilt decoration, all edges gilt; 3 plates with small dampstain at top, minor darkening or discoloration to a few other engravings, few insignificant tears, but very fine otherwise, binding virtually without defects. Phillip J. Pirages 33-173 1996 $350.00

DICKENS, CHARLES 1812-1870 A Tale of Two Cities. London: Chapman and Hall, 1859. 1st edition; 1st issue with page 213 misnumbered, 8vo; in original 7/8 parts; etched frontispiece, additional title and 14 plates, with requisite number of ads and slips, part 3 with 4 page Mosisonian Monument ad as opposed to the British College of health; original blue printed wrappers, cloth folder and slipcase, leather label, backstrips variously repaired, restored and with pieces missing, final leaf of the 'Advertiser' in part 1 torn at corner with loss; excellent copy. Rare. Hatton & Cleaver pp. 331-42. Eckel pp. 86-90. Simon Finch 24-75 1996 £8,500.00

DICKENS, CHARLES 1812-1870 Works. London: Chapman and Hall, 1874-76. Illustrated Library Edition; 8vo; 30 volumes; original illustrations by Phiz; original green cloth, bevelled boards, blocked in black and gilt; with some Dickens centenary stamps and other ephemeral items pasted in; from the collection of mezzotint engraver Thomas Oldham Barlow, with his bookplate in several volumes. Sotheran PN32-8 1996 £998.00

DICKENS, CHARLES 1812-1870 Works. New York: Routledge, ca. 1880. 26 volumes; original illustrations by Phiz; publisher's ads at end; original gilt stamped dark green cloth, dark green endpapers, top edge gilt, rubbing to spine ends; very good. George J. Houle 68-42 1996 $475.00

DICKENS, CHARLES 1812-1870 The Works. London: Chapman and Hall, 1890-96. Of the 17 volumes here, 10 have half titles indicating that this is the 'Crown Edition', but other 7 half titles have no such designation; 8 1/4 x 5 1/2 inches; 17 volumes; plates and illustrations; rose colored contemporary polished half calf, marbled sides and endpapers, raised bands, spines with gilt titling and large centered floral ornaments, top edge gilt, one hinge neatly reinforced with matching paper; corners of five volumes as well as 3 edges slightly bumped, spines faded to a salmon color and few slightly scuffed and discolored, otherwise bindings in fine condition with just trivial defects, joints virtually unworn; very fine internally. Phillip J. Pirages 33-174 1996 $1,250.00

DICKENS, CHARLES 1812-1870 The Nonesuch Dickens. Bloomsbury: Nonesuch Press, 1937-38. 25 volumes; bound in various colors of buckram, all with gilt titled and bordered black morocco spine labels, top edge gilt, includes boxed plate and prospectus; few spines rubbed, that of 'Pickwick Papers' is lightly sunned; usual offsetting of engravings is present, and few of the spine labels exhibit light wear. Near fine. Dreyfus 108. Glenn Books 36-89 1996 $7,000.00

DICKERSON, PHILIP J. History of the Osage Nation. Pawhuska: 1906. 1st edition; 144 pages; illustrations; pictorial wrappers, fine. Graff 1079; Howes D321; Gilcrease-Hargrett p. 313. Michael D. Heaston 23-135 1996 $150.00

DICKEY, JAMES Buckdancer's Choice. Poems. Middletown: Wesylean, 1965. 1st edition; fine in dust jacket with few tiny nicks; inscribed by author to poet Jonathan Williams. Captain's Bookshelf 38-51 1996 $225.00

DICKEY, JAMES The Eye-Beaters, Blood, Victory, Madness, Buckhead and Mercy. Garden City: Doubleday, 1970. 1st trade edition; near fine in little rubbed, near fine dust jacket with couple tiny tears; surprisingly scarce. Between the Covers 42-135 1996 $100.00

DICKEY, JAMES Helmets. Poems. Middletown: Wesleyan, 1964. 1st edition; fine in dust jacket; inscribed by author to poet Jonathan Williams. Captain's Bookshelf 38-51 1996 $225.00

DICKINSON, EMILY ELIAZABETH 1830-1886 Poems of Emily Dickinson. New York: The Limited Editions Club, 1952. 1st edition; one (number 44) of 1500, signed by artist; 4to; 286 pages; illustrations by Helen Sewall; full black morocco, brown slipcase, lacks glassine dust jacket, slight rubbing, label on slipcase frayed, very good. Myerson B12.1.a. BAL 4700. Robert F. Lucas 42-34 1996 $100.00

DICKINSON, EMILY ELIZABETH 1830-1886 Bolts of Melody. New Poems. New York: & London: Harper & Bros., 1945. 1st edition; 8vo; green cloth, dust jacket, fine in slightly edge worn jacket. James S. Jaffe 34-138 1996 $125.00

DICKINSON, EMILY ELIZABETH 1830-1886 The Poems of Emily Dickinson Including Various Readings Critically Compared with All Known Manuscripts. Cambridge: Belknap Press of Harvard Univ. Press, 1955. 1st printing; 8vo; 3 volumes, 378; 379-820; 821-1266 pages; grey cloth, red slipcase, volumes exhibit minor wear, slipcase worn, slipcase label stained and chipped, good to very good. Myerson A10.1.a. BAL 4701. Robert F. Lucas 42-35 1996 $200.00

DICKINSON, EMILY ELIZABETH 1830-1886 The Poems of Emily Dickinon. Cambridge: Belknap Press of Harvard Unversity Press, 1955. 1st edition; 3 volumes; cloth in cardboard slipcase, as issued; fine. Between the Covers 42-134 1996 $100.00

DICKINSON, EMILY ELIZABETH 1830-1886 The Single Hound. Poems of a Lifetime. Boston: Little, Brown and Co., 1915. 1st edition; 2nd printing; 8vo; 151 pages; white cloth spine and white boards, minor soil, corners bumped, very good, clean and very attractive. Myerson A5.1.b. Robert F. Lucas 42-33 1996 $250.00

DICKINSON, J. C. The Origin of the Austin Canons and Their Introduction to England. London: SPCK, 1947. 1st edition; 8vo; 277 pages; modern cloth, gilt, heavily annotated and altered by author, mostly in pencil. R.F.G. Hollett & Son 78-374 1996 £65.00

DICKINSON, R. E. The Geophysiology of Amazonia: Vegetation and Climate Interactions (Climate and the Biosphere). New York: 1986. 8vo; 560 pages; illustrations; cloth. Wheldon & Wesley 207-381 1996 £110.00

DICKINSON, RODOLPHUS A Digest of the Common Law, the Statute Laws of Massachusetts and of the United States, and the Decisions of the Supreme Judicial Court of Massachusetts, Relative to the Powers and duties of Justices of the Peace. Deerfield: Published by John Wilson, 1818. contemporary sheep, very worn and rubbed, usable copy. Meyer Boswell SL27-63 1996 $125.00

DICKINSON, WILLIAM A Glossary of the Words and Phrases of Cumberland. London: John Russell Smith and Whitehaven: Callander & Dixon, 1859. 1st edition; 8vo; pages xiv, 138, (ii); original blindstamped limp cloth gilt, spine little faded and defective at base, paper label. R.F.G. Hollett & Son 78-375 1996 £60.00

DICKSON, ROBERT Annals of Scottish Printing. Cambridge: 1890. Limited to 500 numbered copies, signed by J. P. Edmonds; 4to; 73 facsimiles; original buckram, gilt. Charles W. Traylen 117-14 1996 £85.00

DICTIONARIUM Sacrum seu Religiosum. A Dictionary of All Religions, Antient and Modern. London: printed for James Knapton, 1704. 1st edition; name on title; contemporary panelled calf, hinges partly cracked, new label. Anthony Laywood 108-49 1996 £185.00

DICTIONARY of National Biography. Missing Persons. London: 1993. 8vo; 800 pages; original cloth; new. Howes Bookshop 265-280 1996 £80.00

DICTIONARY of Quotations, in Most Frequent Use. London: G. G. & J. Robinson, 1799. 3rd edition; contemporary speckled calf, green label, very good, booklabel; signature of Selina Gunn on title. Jarndyce 103-105 1996 £85.00

A DICTIONARY of the Chinook Jargon, Or Indian Trade Language of the North Pacific Coast. Victoria: Victoria Standard Print, 1878. 1st of this issue; 26 pages; original orange pictorial wrappers with Hibben Co. ad on back wrapper; fine. Pilling p. 21; Lande Catalog 1227. Michael D. Heaston 23-171 1996 $750.00

A DICTIONARY of the English Language. London: printed for W. Peacock, 1794. 4th edition; 24mo; title slightly trimmed at fore-edge, contemporary tree calf, neatly rebacked retaining original spine strip and red label, gilt borders. Alston V333. Jarndyce 103-106 1996 £140.00

DIDEROT, DENIS Pensees sur l'Interpretation de La Nature. Paris: 1754. 1st complete and earliest available issue; 12mo; pages (vi), 3-206 (irreg. actually 240 pages), (12) index and errata; minimal restoration of binding, fine contemporary calf, spine elaborately gilt tooled, maroon leather label, boards with triple fillets, fine half brown morocco case, very fine; very scarce; Tchemerzine IV p. 442. 19th Century Shop 39- 1996 $4,500.00

DIGBY, EDWARD   Private Memoirs...Written by Himself. London: Saunders and Otley, 1827. 1st edition; 8vo; lxxxviii, 328 pages; frontispiece; three quarter gilt morocco, raised spine panels, gilt, some wear to extremities, very mild dampstaining to upper margins; now quite scarce.   James Tait Goodrich   K40-121   1996 $150.00

DIGBY, KENELM 1603-1665   Two Treatises: in the One of Which, the Nature of Bodies; in the Other the Nature of Mans Soul, Is Looked Into. London: Williams, 1658. 4to; diagrams in text; panelled calf. Wing D1450. Rostenberg & Stern   150-121   1996 $750.00

A DIGEST of Adjudged Cases in the Court of King's Bench from the Revolution to the Present Period...Comprehending...Holt, Parker, Pratt, Raymond, Hardwicke, Lee and Ryder. London: printed by W. Strahan and M. Woodfall, 1775. contemporary calf, rebacked, some embrowning, but good.   Meyer Boswell   SL27-133   1996 $650.00

DIGESTORUM Seu Pandectarum Libri Quinquaginta Ex Florentinis Pandectis Repraesentati. Florence: in Officina Laurentii Torrentini, 1553. 1st edition; folio; 2 volumes (volumes 1 and 2, of 3); large well margined copy, title and half page detailed woodcut vignette, very large detailed illustrative woodcut initial letters, full 18th century blue French morocco (a pencil note suggest by Derome-le-Jeune), boards with triple gilt fillet, spines elaborately gilt in compartments with gilt lettering direct, spines browned, all edges gilt; very fine, clean and fresh copy. Bookplates of the Earl of Cromer and Viscount Mersey, Bignor Park. Ian Wilkinson   95/1-90   1996 £295.00

DIKAIOS, PORPHYRIOS   Sotira. Philadelphia: University of Pennsylvania, 1961. 4to; wrappers, xiii,2 52 pages, 122 plates, 2 tables; wrappers. Archaeologia   Luxor-3253   1996 $150.00

DIKAIOS, PORPHYRIOS   The Stone Age and the Early Bronze Age in Cyprus. Lund: Swedish Cyprus Expedition, 1962. Large 4to; xlv, 401 pages; 105 figures; 156 plates; original cloth.   Archaeologia Luxor-3254   1996 $250.00

DILKE, CHARLES WENTWORTH   Greater Britain: a Record of Travel in English Speaking Countries, 1866 and 1867. London: 1869. 2nd edition; 8vo; 2 volumes, colored frontispiece, plates and maps; original cloth. Charles W. Traylen   117-441   1996 £75.00

DILLARD, ANNIE   Tickets for a Prayer Wheel. Columbia: University of Missouri Press, 1974. 1st edition; author's first book; fine in dust jacket with few tiny nicks and short tear; signed by author.   Captain's Bookshelf   38-53   1996 $600.00

DILLON, GEORGE   Boy in the Wind. New York: Viking, 1927. 1st edition; rubbing to edges of paper spine label, else solid, very good copy, lacking dust jacket; author's first book; Countee Cullen's copy with his large bookplate and signature, and few pencilled notes.   Between the Covers   43-58   1996 $250.00

DILLON, JOHN TALBOT   A Political Survey of the Sacred Roman Empire... London: printed for R. Baldwin, 1782. 1st edition; 8vo; portrait; contemporary calf, rubbed, hinges cracked.   Anthony Laywood   108-50 196 £65.00

DILLON, P.   Narrative and Successful Result of a Voyage in the South Seas, Performed by Order of the Government of British India... Amsterdam: New York: N. Israel/Da Capo Press, 1972. Reprint of London edition of 1829; 8vo; 2 volumes.   Parmer Books   O39Nautica-039364 1996 $135.00

DILLON, RICHARD H.   Images of Chinatown. San Francisco: Book Club of California, 1976. 1st edition; limited to 450 copies; 68 pages; photos by Stellman; cloth backed decorated boards, very fine, original prospectus laid in.   Argonaut Book Shop   113-198   1996 $175.00

DILLON, RICHARD H.   Texas Argonauts: Isaac H. Duval and the California Gold Rush. San Francisco: Book Club of California, 1987. One of 450 copies; xiii, 199 pages; color illustrations, map on endpaper; cloth backed boards, plain dust jacket.   Bohling Book Co.   191-23   1996 $250.00

DILLON, RICHARD H.   Texas Argonauts: Isaac H. Duval and the California Gold Rush. San Francisco; Book Club of California, 1987. One of 450 copies, signed by author; xiii, 164 pages, many illustrations; full brown leather, gilt title; fine in slipcase.   Bohling Book Co.   191-12 1996 $300.00

DIMOCK, A. W.   Wall Street and the Wilds. n 1915. 1st edition; 8vo; 476 pages + numerous full page illustrations; original blue cloth, top edge gilt, some wear and fading, especially at extremities, but generally clean, internally very good; signed presentation copy with long inscription by author, also laid in is an August 1916 two page ALS of the author thanking Mr. and Mrs. Cass for their visit and for sending him a copy of the First Hundred Thousand which he has just finished. Scarce.   Blue River Books   9-126   1996 $135.00

DIMPLED Hands. Pictures and Rhymes for Chubby Pets. Boston: De Wolfe Fiske & Co., n.d., ca. 1890. 4to; 4 full page color illustrations and other black and white illustrations; glazed pictorial boards, corners worn, else very good.   Marjorie James   19-216   1996 £55.00

DINAN, W.   Monumenta Historica Celtica; Notices of...Celts in the Writings of the Greek and Latin Authors... London: 1911. 1st edition; 8vo; volume 1, all published; cloth, ex-library, cover worn, text good. C. P. Hyland   216-169   1996 £55.00

DINESEN, ISAK 1885-1962   The Angelic Avengers. London: Putnam & Co. Ltd., 1946. 1st edition; original binding, head of spine and bottom corners slightly bumped, very good in nicked, browned, marked and dusty, slightly creased dust jacket.   Ulysses   39-144   1996 £55.00

DINESEN, ISAK 1885-1962   Out of Africa. New York: Random House, 1938. 1st edition; fine in dust jacket, darkened at spine.   Sherwood 3-91   1996 $135.00

DINESEN, ISAK 1885-1962   Out of Africa. New York: Random, 1938. 1st edition; discrete bookplate, front pastedown, otherwise near fine in dust jacket with two closed tears and small chip to top of spine, only a slight amount of the usual darkening to dust jacket, nice copy. Anacapa House   5-84   1996 $135.00

DINESEN, ISAK 1885-1962   Out of Africa. New York: 1938. 1st edition; fine/very good+.   Stephen Lupack 83-   1996 $125.00

DINESEN, ISAK 1885-1962   Seven Gothic Tales. S&H, 1934. 1st American edition, of 1010 copies, this is 1/999 copies for sale; illustrations in color by Majeska; black mesh cloth; bright, near fine copy, save for small light stain at base of inner hinge. Author's first book; most uncommon.   Aronovitz   57-345   1996 $250.00

DINESEN, ISAK 1885-1962   Seven Gothic Tales. New York: Harrison Smith & Robert Haas, 1934. 1st American edition; near fine in price clipped dust jacket missing 1 x 2 inch piece from top of front panel (word 'Seven' gone, otherwise chipped and worn, but complete with exceptions noted).   Sherwood 3-90   1996 $125.00

DINGMAN, REED   Surgery of Facial Fractures. Philadelphia: 1964. 1st edition; 380 pages; several hundred illustrations; original binding.   W. Bruce Fye   71-545   1996 $150.00

DINGWALL, ERIC   The Girdle of Chastity: a Medico-Historical Study. London: 1931. 1st edition; 171 pages; photographic plates; original binding, scarce.   W. Bruce Fye   71-546   1996 $200.00

DINKINS, JAMES   1861 to 1865, by an Old Johnnie. Personal Recollections and Experiences in the Confederate Army. Cincinnati: Rober Clark Co., 1897. 1st edition; 280 pages; original cloth, near fine, scarce. General George Gordon's copy with marks delienating references made to him in the book. Harwell In Tall Cotton 44; Howes D346; Nicholson p 241;   McGowan Book Co.   65-25   1996 $650.00

DINSMOOR, WILLIAM BELL   The Archons of Athens. Cambridge: Harvard University Press, 1931. Folio; xviii,5 67 pages; 4 illustrations, 27 tables; original cloth, corners lightly bumped, otherwise fine. Archaeologia   Luxor-3256   1996 $550.00

DINSMOOR, WILLIAM BELL   The Athenian Archon List in the Life of Recent Discoveries. Morningside Heights: Columbia University Press, 1939. Folio; xvi, 274 pages, 1 illustration; original cloth.   Archaeologia Luxor-3257   1996 $125.00

DIO COCCEIANUS, CHRYSOSTOMUS, OF PRUSA   De Regno. Bologna: Franciscs Plato de Benedictus, 1493. Quarto; modern vellum, lightly washed copy with few faint stains remaining, some contemporary marginalia, first leaf with repairs mainly to blank edges, following leaf with inner blank edge repaired, few other leaves have quite minor repair to blank margins here and there. Hain Copinger 6187; GW 8369; Goff D 205.   G. W. Stuart   59-55   1996 $3,750.00

DIODORUS, SICULLUS   The Historical Library of Diodorus the Sicilian... London: printed and are to be sold by W. Taylor, 1721. 2nd edition of this translation; folio; with 1700 titlepage present; 3 engraved maps (two folding, some tears along side); contemporary panelled calf, covers detached as are first few blanks, rubbed, spine worn, title in red and black; some browning and soiling, stitching loose in few places. James Cummins 14-141 1996 $200.00

DIODORUS, SICULUS   Bibliothecae Historicae Libri VI. Venice: Joannis Tacuinis, de Tridino 20 September 1496. Folio; later vellum, inner blank margin of title leaf restored, some smudges, stains, ink imprint of three leaves (two with twigs), some light watermarks and faint stains throughout, neat contemporary marginalia; Goldwater bookplate, very nice. Hain 6191; GW 8377; Goff D 213.   G. W. Stuart 59-56 1996 $3,100.00

DIOGENES LAERTIUS   De Vita, & Moribus, Philosophorum Libri Decem. Basel: Valentinus Curio, 1524. 4to; (10) leaves, 391, (1) pages, woodcut printer's device on last leaf, historiated initials after Holbein, roman type with considerable use of Greek, few early marginalia in Greek and Latin; modern vellum; Adams D481; Hoffmann I 565.   Jeffrey D. Mancevice 20-24 1996 $850.00

DIOGENES LAERTIUS   De Vita et Moribus Philosophorum. Libri X. Lugduni: Appud Seb. Gryphium, 1541. 8vo; 468, 20 pages, printer's mark on title, title with early ms. writing and with just a bit of spotting, and on verso of last leaf, 10 woodcut initials, contents absolutely fine; modern marbled boards, half cloth, original label on spine, very nice. Roy W. Clare XXIV-73 1996 $195.00

DI PESO, CHARLES C.   Casas Grandes: a Fallen Trading Center of the Gran Chichimeca. Dragoon: Amerind Foundation, 1974. 4to; 3 volumes, (xxii), 1104 pages; 781 illustrations, 3 folding plates, original cloth. Archaeologia Luxor-4396 1996 $175.00

DI PESO, CHARLES C.   Casas Grandes - a Fallen Trading Center of the Grand chichimeca. Flagstaff: 1974. 1st edition; 3 volumes, 1076 pages, photos, color illustrations, maps; pictorial cloth, fine.   T. A. Swinford 49-295 1996 $125.00

DI PESO, CHARLES C.   Casas Grandes, a Fallen Trading Center of the Gran Chichimeca. Flagstaff: Amerind Foundation/Northland Press, 1974. 1st edition; 3 volumes; 1104 pages total; foldout pasted in rear of each volume; half bound in tan and black buckram; fine.   Ken Sanders 8-17 1996 $100.00

DI PESO, CHARLES C.   Casas Grandes: a Fallen Trading Center of the Gran Chichimeca. Dragoon: Amerind Foundation, 1974. 4to; 8 volumes; illustrations; original cloth, corner lightly bumped, otherwise fine set. Archaeologia Luxor-4397 1996 $650.00

DIRECTORY of Churches and Religious Organizations in New Mexico 1940. Albuquerque: The New Mexico Historical Records Survey, July, 1940. 1st edition; 385 pages; maps; original pictorial wrappers, printed in black and red; fine.   Michael D. Heaston 23-276 1996 $125.00

DIRINGER, DAVID   The Hand Produced Book. New York: Philosophical Library, 1953. 1st edition; 8vo; 603 pages, many illustrations; cloth, dust jacket, fine in very good jacket.   The Bookpress 75-284 1996 $110.00

DIRINGER, DAVID   The Illuminated Book, Its History and Production. New York: Philosophical Library, 1958. 1st American edition; 8vo; 524 pages, (254) full page plates in monochrome, (6) in full color; cloth, dust jacket slightly chipped, else very good, scarce.   The Bookpress 75-285 1996 $150.00

DISNEY, WALT   Stories from Walt Disney's Fantasia. New York: Random House, 1940. 1st edition; 4to; illustrations in color and black and white from motion picture; cloth backed pictorial boards; fine in chipped pictorial dust jacket.   Barbara Stone 70-73 1996 £65.00

DISNEY, WALT   Three Little Pigs. Blue Ribbon, 1933. 1st edition; color and black and white illustrations; very good in full color pictorial boards, most attractive dust jacket with some light wear and tear and chipping, scarce in dust jacket.   Aronovitz 57-348 1996 $325.00

DISNEY, WALT   Walt Disney's Snow White and the Seven Dwarfs. London: Collins, 1938. 1st British edition; royal 4to; (80) pages; illustrations; original cloth backed pictorial boards, few very light marks and signs fo age and use, but very good and clean copy nonetheless. Ash Rare Books Zenzybyr-30 1996 £195.00

THE DISOBEDIENT Chicken. New York: R. Shugg, ca. 1870-80. Small octavo; 16 pages; 4 full page colored lithographs; original pictorial wrappers; very fine. Hamilton p. 186.   Bromer Booksellers 90-139 1996 $325.00

DISRAELI, BENJAMIN 1804-1881   Endymion. London: 1880. 1st edition; 3 volumes; original cloth, spine faded and little brown spotted, one or two hinges weakening, otherwise very good.   Words Etcetera 94-358 1996 £65.00

DISRAELI, BENJAMIN 1804-1881   Tancred; or, the New Crusade. London: 1847. 1st edition; 3 volumes; binder's roan; very good. Words Etcetera 94-356 1996 £55.00

D'ISRAELI, ISAAC 1776-1848   Amenities of Literature, Consisting of Sketches and Characters of English Literature. London: Edward Moxon, 1841. 1st edition; large 8vo; 3 volumes; later 19th century vellum, gilt, spines gilt, black morocco labels; fine and attractive copy, with half titles; this copy has the ownership inscription and calling card of Samuel Taylor Coleridge's grand-daughter, Edith Coleridge, 1887, who has added the note "from the books of dear Uncle Derwent Coleridge". CBEL III 1278.   James Burmester 29-42 1996 £250.00

D'ISRAELI, ISAAC 1776-1848   Curiosities of Literature. London: printed for John Murray, 1791. 1st edition; 8vo; original blue boards, drab paper backstrip, backstrip time soiled, but very sound. Fine, original condition, very scarce. Roth, Bib. Anglo Judaica B20(55); CBEL III 1277. Ximenes 108-106 1996 $900.00

D'ISRAELI, ISAAC 1776-1848   Curiosities of Literature. Cambridge: privately printed, Riverside Press, 1864. Large 8vo; 4 volumes; pages 447, 468, 466, 447 pages, plus 23 page index; top edge gilt in red and black with fine stipple engraved frontispiece; half brown morocco, gilt marbled boards, top edge gilt, very good set.   Hartfield 48-A7 1996 $295.00

D'ISRAELI, ISAAC 1776-1848   A Second Series of Curiosities of Literature... London: John Murray, 1823. 1st edition; 8vo; 3 volumes; contemporary half lilac calf, spines elegantly gilt, traces of rubbing; very attractive set. Roth Bib. Anglo Judaica B20(56); CBEL III 1278. Ximenes 109-99 1996 $250.00

A DISSERTATION on the Voluntary Eating of Blood. London: printed for M. Cooper, 1745. 1st edition; 8vo; modern wrappers; margins trimmed trifle close, but very good; very rare.   Ximenes 108-341 1996 $600.00

DISTURNELL, JOHN   Across the Continent and Around the World. Distrunell's Railroad and Steamship Guide... Philadelphia: Published by J. Disturnell, 1873. 1st edition; 138, (22) pages, folding map; original pictorial limp cloth, title in gilt on front cover, some wear, very good. Michael D. Heaston 23-136 1996 $250.00

DITCHFIELD, P. H.   The Cottages and Villages of Rural England. London: 1912. Large 4to; 52 mounted color plates by A. R. Quinton, many line illustrations; original pictorial gilt cloth, showing light wear, lacks front endpaper, prelims lightly foxed, otherwise contents excellent. David A.H. Grayling MY95Orn-28 1996 £100.00

DITCHFIELD, P. H.   The Cottages and the Village Life of Rural England. London: Dent, 1912. 1st edition; 4to; pages 198; 52 mounted colored plates, 19 illustrations; original dove grey cloth, gilt, gilt top, nice.   Howes Bookshop 265-284 1996 £75.00

DITTON, HUMPHRY   An Institution of Fluxions; Containing the First principles, the Operations, with Some of the Uses and Applications of that Admirable Method.. London: printed by W. Botham for James Knapton, 1706. 1st edition; blind and cancellation stamps on verso of title, new half calf, label. Wallis, British Mat. 703DIT06.   Anthony W. Laywood 109-36 1996 £125.00

DIURNALE Pataviense. Augsburg: Erhard Ratdolt, 1494. 1st Augsburg edition; 12mo; (8), 56, 176, 20ff; old calf on wooden boards, claps gone, back partly repaired with top of spine chipped, some spotting and insignificant wormholes not affecting text, 10 prelim leaves and last 2 leaves missing, still remarkably well preserved, internally bright with few ms. annotations in ink; Rare. Goff D283.   Chapel Hill 94-232 1996 $450.00

DIX, D. L.   Remarks on Prisons and Prison Discipline in the United States. Boston: Munroe & Francis, 1845. 1st edition; 8vo; 104 pages; original printed wrappers, wrappers little dusty, but excellent copy. With ink signature of Rev. E. S. Gannett, conservative Unitarian minister.   M & S Rare Books 60-319 1996 $750.00

DIX, JOHN A.   · Speech of General John A. Dix, President of the Mississippi and Missouri Railroad Co., at the Celebration at Iowa City, The Capitol of the State of Iowa, On the Completion of the Road to the Latter Point. January 24, 1856. New York: W. C. Bryant & Co., 1856. 8 3/4 x 5 1/2 inches; 19 pages; newly bound in green cloth with gold stamping on spine and front cover, very good, titlepage lightly foxed, small label has been removed from left hand corner of titlepage. William A. Graf 186-97 1996 $100.00

DIXON, C.   The Game Birds and Wild Fowl of the British Islands. Sheffield: 1900. 2nd edition; 4to; pages xxviii, 476; 41 colored plates; pictorial cloth, binding little used.   Wheldon & Wesley 207-710 1996 £180.00

DIXON, F.   The Geology and Fossils of Sussex; or the Geology and Fossils of the Tertiary and Cretaceous Formations of Sussex. London: 1878. 2nd edition; royal 4to; pages xxiv, 1-160, 160*-167*, 161-469, colored frontispiece, folding colored map, section and 63 plates; original buckram, as usual, some slight foxing to few plates and at ends in text. John Henly 27-430 1996 £185.00

DIXON, GEORGE d. 1800   A Voyage Round the World; But More Particularly to the North-West Coast of America: Peformed in 1785, 1786, 1787 and 1788 in King George and Queen Charlotte, Captains Portlock and Dixon. London: Geo. Goulding, 1789. Large 4to; xxxii, 360, 48 pages, complete with large folding map, 21 maps and plates, half title; old calf with spine label over marbled boards, outer hinges starting but quite sound, one plate with partial tear neatly repaired, particularly fresh, wide margined copy. Howes D365.   Kenneth Karmiole 1NS-245 1996 $2,500.00

DIXON, GEORGE d. 1800   A Voyage Round the World: But More Particularly to the North-West Coast of America: Performed in 1785, 1786, 1787 and 1788 in the King George and Queen Charlotte... London: pub. by Geo. Goulding, 1789. 1st edition; 4to; errata leaf, Directions to Binder, 1-360 pages, appendices 1-47 pages, 16 copper plates, 4 folding maps and charts; some light foxing to most plates and charts, offsetting to text, lacks half title; full contemporary tree calf, very neatly rebacked preserving original spine, red morocco label to spine, owner's bookplate and booksellers ticket, hinges cracked; still a good, tight copy. Lada Mocarski 43; Streeter VI 3484; Hill p. 13.   Beeleigh Abbey BA56-36 1996 £1,300.00

DIXON, GEORGE d. 1800   A Voyage Round the World, but More Particularly to the Northwest Coast of America; Performed in 1785, 1786, 1787 and 1788. London: Geo. Goulding, 1789. 1st edition; 8vo; five folding maps, 17 engraved plates, 13 tables; errata/directions to binder leaf, half title; contemporary calf, gilt, handsomely rebacked, later morocco spine label; fine. Howes D365; Wagner, Northwest Coasat p. 732-5; Hill p. 23.   Trebizond 39-94 1996 $1,700.00

DIXON, J. H.   The "Wuthering Heights" Collection at Oatlands, Harrogate. London: privately published, n.d. 1906. 1st edition; 8 1/4 x 5 1/4 inches; 192 pages; illustrations; purple thin card covers over pale pink wrappers; some fading to edges of covers, very slight occasional spotting to contents, very good, scarce.   Ian Hodgkins 78-426 1996 £70.00

DIXON, JOSHUA   The Literary Life of William Brownrigg, M.D., F.R.S...to which are Added An Account of the Coal Mines Near Whiteheaven... London: Longman & Rees etc., and Whitehaven: A. Dunn, 1801. 1st edition; 8vo; pages xiv, 240, (i errata leaf); original blue boards, paper spine lable, very rubbed, very scarce, excellent, uncut, unsophisticated copy.   R.F.G. Hollett & Son 78-610 1996 £375.00

DIXON, SAM H.   The Poets and Poetry of Texas. Austin: Sam H. Dixon & Co., 1885. 1st edition; thick 8vo; 360 pages, portraits of the poets; original cloth, rubbed, front inner hinge broken; very scarce; with Austin Texas 1886 ownership inscription.   M & S Rare Books 60-243 1996 $500.00

DIXON, T.   The Fall of a Nation. New York: Appleton, 1916. 1st edition; bright, very good+ copy in very nice dust jacket with some light chipping; most uncommon in jacket.   Aronovitz 57-349 1996 $100.00

DIXON, WILLIAM HEPWORTH   Free Russia. London: Hurst and Blackett, Publishers, 13 Great Marlborough St., 1870. Mixed editions, 1st edition of volume 1, 2nd edition of volume 2; 8vo; 2 volumes; (v-vi), (vii-viii),, 1-352 pages, 1-344 pages, color litho frontispiece to both volumes, owner's bookplate, booksellers ticket to both volumes, foxing to final leaves of volume 2; half calf and marbled boards, corners worn, joints rubbed, green morocco labels to spine, edges marbled, marbled endpapers, all uniform with boards.   Beeleigh Abbey BA56-61 1996 £150.00

DIXON, WILLIAM HEPWORTH   Free Russia. London: Hurst & Blackett, 1870. 1st edition; 8vo; 2 volumes; 2 colored frontispieces (fine), uncut copy with both half titles; original decorated cloth, gilt, spines gilt; spine extremities worn, bindings sun faded, internally fine. Nerhood 283. Trebizond 39-95 1996 $230.00

DIXON, WILLIAM HEPWORTH   White Conquest. London: 1876. 1st edition; 2 volumes, 356, 376 paes + ads; cloth; nice. 6 Guns 598 rare; Flake 2849.   T. A. Swinford 49-299 1996 $375.00

DOANE, A. SIDNEY   Surgery Illustrated. New York: Harper & Bros., 1836. 1st edition; 4to; 234 pages; lithographs; disbound (sound), original cloth covers present, one plate duplicataed, one other is lacking. Rinderknecht 37153.   M & S Rare Books 60-453 1996 $250.00

DOBIE, BERTHA MC KEE   Growing Up in Texas. Austin: Encino Press, 1972. 1st edition; one of only 44 copies, signed by all the contributors; 153 pages; woodcuts; two-tone cloth; very fine and bright with pictorial dust jacket; presentation inscription signed by William D. Wittliff, owner of the Encino Press on colophon page.   Argonaut Book Shop 113-202 1996 $300.00

DOBIE, JAMES FRANK 1888-1964   Apache Gold and Yaqui Silver. Boston: Little Brown, 1939. 1st limited, signed edition, limited to 265 numbered copies, this being no. 54, signed by author and artist, with the very scarce envelope of color prints of Lea's plates; 366 pages, plus color plates by Tom Lea; cloth backed boards, silver foil label, label slightly chipped, mild rubbing to extremities, one corner just showing, else fine; extra and perfect spine label tipped to inner rear cover. Argonaut Book Shop 113-203 1996 $1,250.00

DOBIE, JAMES FRANK 1888-1964   Bob More, Man and Bird Man. Dallas: Encino Press, 1965. 1 of 550 copies; vii, 27 pages; illustrations, cloth with printed label, slipcase. Fine.   Bohling Book Co. 191-24 1996 $150.00

DOBIE, JAMES FRANK 1888-1964   On the Open Range Dallas: Southwest, 1951. 1st schoolbook issue; inkstains on titlepage, else very good.   Parker Books of the West 30-51 1996 $100.00

DOBIE, JAMES FRANK 1888-1964   A Vaquero of the Brush Country. Dallas: 1929. 1st edition; 1st issue; 314 pages; illustrations; cloth and handbound in the famous 'rattlesnake skin''; fine, lacing dust jacket. Herd 702; 6 Guns 606; Dobie p. 102; BTB 44; Howes D376.   Gene W. Baade 1094-44 1996 $300.00

DOBIE, ROWLAND   The History of the United Parishes of St. Giles in the Fields and St. George, Bloomsbury. London: for the author, 1829. 8vo; pages viii, 432, 3 ff. index, folding map; half calf by Zaehnsdorf, scuffed, spine head damaged; author's complimentary copy, inscribed on titlepage and with few ms. corrections.   Marlborough 162-132 1996 £100.00

DOBSON, AUSTIN 1840-1921   Fielding. London: Macmillan, 1883. 1st edition; octavo; pages 196; extra illutrated with dozens of fine, professionally mounted engravings; bound by Zaehnsdorf in full tan polished calf, raised bands, gilt extra in panels, double labels, triple fillets front and back, gilt inner dentelles, marbled endpapers, all edges gilt, with most unusual period dust jacket.   Hartfield 48-V13 1996 $275.00

DOBSON, AUSTIN 1840-1921   Proverbs in Porcelain: to Which is Added "Au Revoir" a Dramatic Vignette. London: Kegan Paul, Trench, Trubner & Co., 1895. Large paper edition of 175 numbered copies for distribution in England, another 75 copies - in a different binding - were prepared for America; quarto; 25 illustrations by Bernard Partridge; white cloth, good, binding somewhat worn and browned; ALS from Dobson tipped to front endpaper to Mr. Hoe.   Antic Hay 101-453 1996 $125.00

DOBSON, W.   Kunopaedia. A Practical Essay on Breaking on Training the English Spaniel of Pointer. London: 1817. 2nd edition; engraved frontispiece after Bewick; modern half calf; nice.   David A.H. Grayling 3/95-250 1996 £100.00

DOCKRILL, A. W.   Australian Indigenous Orchids. Volume I. Picnic Point: NSW, 1969. Original limited edition; royal 8vo; pages xxiii, 825; 30 colored illustrations on 16 plates, many hundreds of line drawings in text; cloth.   Wheldon & Wesley 207-1794 1996 £65.00

DOCKSTADER, FREDERICK J.   Indian Art in Middle America. Greenwich: New York Graphic Society, 1964. 4to; 221 pages, 180 illustrations, 70 color plates (tipped in); original cloth, faded dust jacket. Archaeologia Luxor-4400 1996 $125.00

DOCKSTADER, FREDERICK J.   Indian Art in South America. Greenwich: New York Graphic Society, 1967. Folio; frontispiece, 222 pages, 200 illustrations and 49 color plates tipped in; original cloth, dust jacket. Archaeologia   Luxor-4401   1996 $125.00

DR. Last, or the Devil Upon Two Sticks. London: Rob't Sayer, 1771. Narrow octavo; single sheet folded perpendicularly into four, each with flaps hinged to head and foot, hand colored engravings illustrate each panel; sewn into brown wrappers, except for some darkening to outside leaves, this is a fine copy of an early fragile piece. Color Illus. p. 4; Muir, English Children's Books pp. 204/9/28.   Bromer Booksellers 90-103   1996 $2,250.00

DOCTOROW, E. L.   American Anthem. New York: Stewart, Tabori & Chang, 1982. One of 1000 copies, signed by Doctorow and Suares; folio; photos. in pictorial cloth box; as new.   Lame Duck Books 19-171 1996 $150.00

DOCTOROW, E. L.   Billy Bathgate. New York: RH, 1989. Uncorrected proof; yellow wrappers; fine.   Lame Duck Books 19-172 1996 $100.00

DOCTOROW, E. L.   Loon Lake. New York: R&H, 1980. One of 350 copies of this signed limited edition; spine bit faded, else fine in near fine publisher's slipcase.   Lame Duck Books 19-170 1996 $125.00

DOCTOROW, E. L.   Loon Lake. New York: Random House, 1980. One of 350 signed and numbered copies; fine in slipcase.   Bev Chaney, Jr. 23-184   1996 $100.00

DOCTOROW, E. L.   The People's Text. Jackson: Nouveau Press, 1992. 1st edition; limited to 240 signed, numbered copies; this copy one of 200; wood engravings by Barry Moser; issued without dust jacket. Revere Books   4-117   1996 $125.00

DOCTOROW, E. L.   Ragtime. New York: Random Hosue, 1975. 1st edition; original binding, head and tail of spine and corners slightly bumped, very good in nicked and slightly rubbed, marked and creased dust jacket; very good.   Ulysses   39-147   1996 £75.00

DOCTOROW, E. L.   Welcome to Hard Times. New York: S&S, 1960. 1st edition; author's first book; darkening to page edges, as almost inevitable with this title, else very good+ in spine tanned dust jacket. Lame Duck Books   19-168   1996 $275.00

DOCUMENTARY History of the Constitution of the United States of America 1786-1870. Washington: Department of State, 1894. 3 volumes; blue cloth, gilt, showing some wear, but quite sound.   Meyer Boswell SL25-52   1996 $250.00

DODD, WILLIAM 1729-1777   The Beauties of History; or, Pictures of Virtue and Vice... London: printed for Vernor and Hood, E. Newboy &c., 1796. 2nd edition; frontispiece, 6 pages ads; contemporary sheep, hinges cracked, slightly worn at head and tail of spine and corners, booklabels. Hugo 88; Roscoe J94 (2).   Jarndyce   103-459   1996 £50.00

DODD, WILLIAM 1729-1777   A New Book of the Dunciad Occasion'd by Mr. Warburton's New Edition of the Dunciad Complete. London: for J. Payne and J. Bocquet (sic), 1750. 1st edition; 4to; pages viii, 27; uncut in contemporary buff wrappers, wrappers little soiled anf frayed, horizontal crease throughout where formerly folded; Foxon D363. Simon Finch   24-76   1996 £350.00

DODD, WILLIAM 1729-1777   The Visitor. London: printed for Edward and Charles Dilly, 1764. 1st edition; 12mo; 2 volumes; frontispiece; contemporary calf, gilt, spines gilt, contrasting red and blue morocco labels, some rubbing, one upper joint slightly cracked; very good, uncommon;   Ximenes   109-101   1996 $900.00

DODDRIDGE, PHILIP 1702-1751   Some Remarkable Passages in the Life of the Honourable Col. James Gardiner, Who Was Salin at the Battle of Preston-Pans, 21st September 1745. London: ...for the Booksellers, 1747. 1st edition; 8vo; pages ix, 10-262; old mottled calf, few sections slightly shaken.   R.F.G. Hollett 76-77   1996 £220.00

DODDS, MADELEINE   The Pilgrimage of Grace 1536-1537 and The Exeter Conspiracy 1538. London: Cambridge University Press, 1915. Original edition; royal 8vo; 2 volumes, 5 folding maps, pages 396, 388; original buckram, printed labels, from the Cambridge University Lbirary with perforated stamp on titles and label and stamp on endpapers. Scarce. Conyers Read 489.   Howes Bookshop 265-286 1996 £75.00

DODGE, RICHARD I.   The Black Hills. New York: 1876. 1st edition; 151 pages; frontispiece; illustrations; folding maps; front hinge starting, decorated cloth, very good. Howes D401; Dustin 382; Jennewein 59. T. A. Swinford   49-303   1996 $200.00

DODGE, RICHARD I.   The Hunting Grounds of the Great West - a Description of the Plains, Game and Indians of the Great North American Desert. London: 1877. 1st edition; lxii, 446 pages, frontispiece, plates, folding color maps; cloth; nice. Dustin 95. Rader 1170; Luther 134; Howes D404.   T. A. Swinford 49-301 1996 $125.00

DODGSON, CAMPBELL   Old French Colour-Prints. London: Halton & Truscott Smith, 1924. Limited to 1250 numbered copies; 4to; viii, 30 pages; 88 plates including 24 tipped in plates in color; original parchment backed cloth gilt, with oval parchment label on front cover, top edge gilt, spine just trifle dust soiled, but nice.   Thomas Thorp   489-88 1996 £65.00

DODGSON, CHARLES LUTWIDGE 1832-1898   Alice's Adventures in Wonderland. Lee & Shepard, 1869. 1st American printing; some wear to corner tips, more so to spine extremities, rear inner hinge starting, else tight, good/very good copy in custom cloth traycase, despite faults, still a most collectable copy.   Aronovitz 57-247 1996 $1,000.00

DODGSON, CHARLES LUTWIDGE 1832-1898   Adventures d'Alice Au Pays des Merveilles. London: Macmillan, 1869. 1st French edition; 42 illustrations by John Tenniel; blue cloth, triple gilt ruled, gilt medallion vignettes to both boards, crease in corner, else unusually fine, bright copy.   Barbara Stone 70-51 1996 £295.00

DODGSON, CHARLES LUTWIDGE 1832-1898   Alice's Adventures in Wonderland. London: Heinemann, 1907. 1st trade edition thus; illustrations by Arthur Rackham; original yellow green cloth lettered in darker green and decorated in gilt, some fraying at spine ends and some shelfwear on bottom edge of covers, small area of cover marked lightly by damp, text foxing, but frontispiece and 12 color plates on coated paper are pleasingly free of that disturbance; front hinge bit shaken, reinforced with short length of archival tape. Latimore & Haskell pp. 28-9.   Magnum Opus 44-88 1996 $175.00

DODGSON, CHARLES LUTWIDGE 1832-1898   Alice's Adventures in Wonderland. London: John Lane, The Bodley Head, n.d. 1907. 1st edition; xv, 152 pages; color frontispiece, title vignette, 7 color plates, 44 text illustrations by W. H. Walker; red cloth, black lettering and pictorial white dust jacket color pictorial; light nicks in spine, dust jacket quite worn. This copy would appear to be Larger Paper than the edition normally found, with dust jacket, wider margins enhance the illustrations. Robin Greer 94A-2 1996 £95.00

DODGSON, CHARLES LUTWIDGE 1832-1898   Alice in Wonderland and through the Looking-Glass and What Alice Found There. Chicago: Rand McNally, 1916. Large octavo; 242 pages; 14 full page color plates by Milo Winter; dark green linen with gilt letters and pictorial label; fine. Bromer Booksellers 90-148 1996 $100.00

DODGSON, CHARLES LUTWIDGE 1832-1898   Alice's Adventures in Wonderland. New York: Limited Editions Club, 1932. Number 832 of 1500 copies, illustrations by John Tenniel, full decoratively gilt brown morocco, fine in slightly darkened slipcase.   Hermitage SP95-951 1996 $300.00

DODGSON, CHARLES LUTWIDGE 1832-1898   Alice's Adventures in Wonderland. (and) Through the Looking Glass and What Alice Saw There. Paris: Edmund S. Wood, 1950. 1st of this edition; 2 x 3 inches; charming miniature set; 2 volumes; 42 illustrations by John Tenniel; half morocco, marbled boards, endpapers, gilt titles, top edge gilt; cased in specially made parchment box, fine.   Hartfield 48-A4 1996 $295.00

DODGSON, CHARLES LUTWIDGE 1832-1898   Alice Au Pays Des Merveilles. Paris: Hachette, 1951. 1st edition thus; large 4to; colored illustrations by Walt Disney; colored pictorial boards; fresh. Lovett 652. Barbara Stone 70-47 1996 £65.00

DODGSON, CHARLES LUTWIDGE 1832-1898   Alice Au Pays Des Merveilles. Paris: Del Duca, 1955. 4to; 24 pages of colored illustrations (unsigned); cloth backed colored pictorial boards, edges little rubbed, else fresh; not in Lovett.   Barbara Stone 70-46 1996 £55.00

DODGSON, CHARLES LUTWIDGE 1832-1898   Alice's Adventures in Wonderland. West Hatfield: Pennyroyal Press, 1982. Limited to 350 copies; folio; with suite of plates, signed by Barry Moser; text bound in purple half morocco over marbled boards, as new in morocco backed clamshell box and mailing carton.   Glenn Books 36-206 1996 $2,200.00

DODGSON, CHARLES LUTWIDGE 1832-1898   Alice's Adventures in Wonderland. (with) Through the Looking Glass and What Alice Found There. West Hatfield: Pennroyal Press, 1982. Each volume one of 50 (of 350) deluxe copies, with extra signed suite of prints in cloth folder; 148 pages, 75 wood engravings by Barry Moser, printed in Bembo on Pulegium, special paper; 2nd title printed in five colors on special Strathmore paper made for Pennyroyal and called Pulegium, 174 pages, 92 wood engravings by Moser; 1st title in full purple morocco with an additional suite of signed prints in a cloth folder, the whole laid in a quarter leather traycase; 2nd title in full maroon morocco, gilt stamped, extra suite laid in matching traycase; on colophon page Moser has drawn a finished drawing in ink of Dee's and Dum's rattle, 2 signed pencil sketches also incuded; fine throughout.   Taurus Books 83-98 1996 $5,000.00

DODGSON, CHARLES LUTWIDGE 1832-1898   Doublets a Word-Puzzle. London: Macmillan and Co., 1879. 1st edition; 16mo; 39 pages; original red cloth, sides ruled in blind, upper cover with publisher's blindstamp and lettered in gilt, in original envelope, preserved in maroon cloth and morocco slipcase lettered and ruled in gilt, title somewhat browned as often the case, cloth little soiled, small stain from cloth to rear pastedown, but an excellent copy. Presentation copy inscribed by author in purple ink to Mrs. Neate. Williams and Madan 130.   Simon Finch 24-31 1996 £3,500.00

DODGSON, CHARLES LUTWIDGE 1832-1898   Feeding the Mind. London: Chatto & Windus, 1906. 1st edition; 12mo; cloth and printed boards, very good. Williams, Madan, Green 290-291.   Antic Hay 101-276 1996 $125.00

DODGSON, CHARLES LUTWIDGE 1832-1898   The Hunting of the Snark an Agony in Eight Fits. London: Macmillan and Co., 1876. 1st edition; one of 100 copies in red cloth; 8vo; pages xiv (including frontispiece), 83, (iii), imprint, ad leaf, wood engraved frontispiece, 9 full page illustrations after Holiday, 'chart'; original red pictorial cloth, densely gilt, gilt edges, spotting to endpapers and half title, little to title, ad and rear free endpaper browned where what was presumably a news cutting was inserted; inscriptions on half title, externally bright copy; bookplate of Rose O'Connor. Williams and Madan 115.   Simon Finch 24-30 1996 £1,500.00

DODGSON, CHARLES LUTWIDGE 1832-1898   The Hunting of the Snark. The Whittington Press, 1975. Limited to 750 copies, numbered and signed by artist; 4to; x, 48 pages; handset in Caslon type and printed on mould made paper; 15 full page illustrations from drawings by Harold Jones; cloth, gilt, top edge gilt, others uncut, hand marbled endpapers, fine in slipcase.   Thomas Thorp 489-54 1996 £120.00

DODGSON, CHARLES LUTWIDGE 1832-1898   The Hunting of the Snark. University of California Press, 1983. 1st edition thus; folio; wood engravings in black and white by Barry Moser; blue wrappers; fine. Barbara Stone 70-49 1996 £55.00

DODGSON, CHARLES LUTWIDGE 1832-1898   Phantasmagoria and Other Poems. London: Macmillan, 1869. 1st edition; 2nd issue; 7 x 4 3/4 inches; viii, 202 pages; device on verso of half title; modern very pleasing and imaginative dark maroon morocco, four blindstamped and four gilt rules running from front to rear cover, two double raised bands, spine with title in gilt, displayed in a descending spiral against a field of small gilt dots, all edges gilt, isolated trivial smudges and faint creases in text, otherwise fine. Williams, Madan and Green 69.   Phillip J. Pirages 33-178 1996 $450.00

DODGSON, CHARLES LUTWIDGE 1832-1898   Rhyme? and Reason? Macmillan, 1883. 1st edition; illustrations; some light cover soil and dulling, but tight, very good copy.   Aronovitz 57-248 1996 $250.00

DODGSON, CHARLES LUTWIDGE 1832-1898   Sylvie and Bruno. (with) Syvlie and Bruno Concluded. London: and New York: Macmillan and Co./London: Macmillan and Co., 1889/93. 1st editions; 8vo; pages xxiii (including frontispiece), (i), blank, 400, (4) ads, wood engraved frontispiece and illustrations in text after Furniss; pages xxxi including frontispiece (i) blank, 423, (1) blank, (6) ads; wood engraved frontispiece and illustrations after Furniss; loosely inserted rare single-leaf ad expressing author's outrage at poor printing of 60th thousand of "Through the Looking Glass"; original red cloth, 1st title triple fillet gilt border and central meadllion to sides, spine lettered and ruled in gilt, gilt edges, little worn, occasional slight soiling, but very good; 2nd title with triple fillet border gilt to sides, sides with medallion portrait gilt at centre, spine ruled, lettered and decorated in gilt, gilt edges, dust jacket torn with some slight loss, '8/6 Net' label on spine, the 2 volumes together in maroon quarter morocco slipcase, ruled and lettered in gilt; excellent copy; Pres. copy of first book inscribed by author for Ruth Martin Woodhouse   Simon Finch 24-32 1996 £1,500.00

DODGSON, CHARLES LUTWIDGE 1832-1898   Sylvie and Bruno Concluded. London: Macmillan, 1893. 1st edition; 1st issue with error in table of contents; small 8vo; loosely inserted is the ad by Carroll requesting that all copies of the 60th thousand impression of "Through the Looking Glass' be returned to the printer due to the poor quality of the illustrations; 46 illustrations by Harry Furniss; gillt red cloth, all edges gilt; near fine. Williams 250.   Antic Hay 101-277 1996 $175.00

DODGSON, CHARLES LUTWIDGE 1832-1898   Sylvie and Bruno Concluded... London: Macmillan and Co., 1893. 1st edition; 8vo; pages xxxi, including frontispiece, (i) blank, 423, (1) blank, (6) ads; frontispiece, illustrations; original red cloth, triple fillet border gilt to sides, sides with medallion portrait gilt at centre, spine ruled, lettered and decorated in gilt, gilt edges, dust jacket with few short tears; loosely inserted author's rare ad leaf expressing his outrage at poor printing of 60th thousand of Through Looking Glass; excellent bright copy, rare in dust jacket, which has an old price label partly removed over the printed price on spine with slight concomitant surface wear; Osborne I p. 336.   Simon Finch 24-33 1996 £300.00

DODGSON, CHARLES LUTWIDGE 1832-1898   Sylvie and Bruno Concluded. London: Macmillan, 1893. 1st British edition, 1st issue with chapter 8 in the table of contents given as at p. 110 instead of p. 113; small 8vo; 46 illustrations by Harry Furniss; gilt red cloth, all edges gilt, near fine, some foxing and scattered spotting to endpapers; Williams 250.   Antic Hay 101-278 1996 $125.00

DODGSON, CHARLES LUTWIDGE 1832-1898   Through the Looking Glass, and What Alice Found There. London: Macmillan, 1872. 1st edition; octavo; pages (8), 224, (2); 50 illustrations by John Tenniel; original red pebbled cloth, gilt rules, pictorial gilt medallions, both covers, all edges gilt, slightly worn red linen box, neat bookticket of former owner, else fine; with the rare original special issue of the Special Advertisment for the Christmas 1893 edition; fine; scarce. Madan 67, 219.   Hartfield 48-V8 1996 $1,650.00

DODGSON, CHARLES LUTWIDGE 1832-1898   Through the Looking Glass and What Alice Found There. New York: and London: Harper, 1902. Octavo; xvi, 211 pages; 40 full page plates and frontispiece portrait of the artist, Peter Newell; decorataions by Robert Murray Wright; deluxe binding in crimson cloth with gold lettering, protected by matching canvas dust jacket repeating lettering; book is very fine, dust jacket has some wear to bottom edge and spine is sunned; owner's inscription. Bromer Booksellers 90-125 1996 $175.00

DODGSON, CHARLES LUTWIDGE 1832-1898   Through the Looking Glass. New York: Harper, 1923. color frontispiece and 39 plates in black and white by Peter Newell; black cloth, gilt with colored pictorial onlay; spine gilt gone, else fresh copy.   Barbara Stone 70-50 1996 £65.00

DODGSON, CHARLES LUTWIDGE 1832-1898   The Two Brothers. Poole Press, 1994. One of 65 signed and numbered copies; patterned brown, green and black velvet over board folder, brown paper title label on front, strap fitting into elastic holder holding two items - 7 x 7.5 Inch booklet set in front cover 6 x 6.5 inches; designed, illustrated, letterpress printed and handbound by Maryline Poole Adams, black wrappers with brown title label; peep-show (tunnel book) 7 x 7.25 inches set in back cover, brown paper cover with title and decoration in black with viewing hole; black and white illustration of two brothers fishing with some color and black string. Fine.   Joshua Heller 21-191 1996 $125.00

DODGSON, CHARLES LUTWIDGE 1832-1898   The Wasp in a Wig. Lewis Carroll Society of North America, 1977. 1/750 numbered copies of this deluxe limited edition; fine, issued without dust jacket.   Aronovitz 57-249 1996 $125.00

DODGSON, CHARLES LUTWIDGE 1832-1898   The "Wonderland" Postage Stamp Case (with) Eight or Nine Wise Words About Letter-Writing by Lewis Carroll. Oxford: 1890. 16mo; 41 pages; postage stamp case with colored renditions of Alice and the Chesire Cat (after Tenniel) opening to contain 12 slots inside for various denominations of stamps, the whole in a pictorial slipcase; printed wrappers, complete in printed evelope (torn).   Charles W. Traylen 117-86 1996 £220.00

DODINGTON, GEORGE BUBB 1691-1762   The Diary of the Late George Bubb Dodington. Salisbury: printed by E. Easton, 1784. 1st edition; 8vo; xv, 502, (1) pages; contemporary full tree calf, raised bands, morocco spine label, gilt tooled spine panels, bookplate, front joint lightly rubbed, else near fine.   Chapel Hill 94-219 1996 $125.00

DODOENS, REMBERT   Medicinalium Observationum Exempla Rara, Recognita & Aucta. Cologne: M. Cholinus, 1581. 1st edition; 8vo; (32), 367 (i.e. 400) pages, woodcut device on title, light uniform toning of paper, contemporary tooled calf, rubbed and worn at head and tail of spine with some cracking to hinges, but sound copy. Bibl. Belgica 1 ser D 122; Durling 1179; Wellcome I 1822;   Jeffrey D. Mancevice 20-25 1996 $1,500.00

DODRIDGE, JOHN   The History of the Ancient and Moderne Estate of the Principality of Wales, Dutchy and Cornwall and Earldome of Chester. London: Tho. Harper, for Godrey Emondson & Thomas Alchorne, 1630. 1st edition; 4to; (xvi), 142, (ii) pages; old calf, neatly rebacked and recornered, spine gilt ruled, old label ladi down, final blank present; some paper browning, uncommon, good copy. STC 6982.   Robert Clark 38-38 1996 £325.00

DODSLEY, ROBERT 1703-1764   Beauty; or the Art of Charming. London: printed for Lawton Gilliver, 1735. 1st edition; folio; modern marbled wrappers; some waterstains in lower margins, otherwise very good, complete with half title and final leaf of ads, uncommon. Foxon D381; CBEL II 788.   Ximenes 108-108 1996 $400.00

DODSLEY, ROBERT 1703-1764   The Chronicle of the Kings of England. London: printed for Lawton Gilliver, 1735. 1st edition; folio; modern marbled wrappers; some waterstains in lower margins, otherwise very good, complete with half title and final leaf of ads; uncommon. Foxon D381; CBEL II 788.   Ximenes 108-108 1996 $400.00

DODSLEY, ROBERT 1703-1764   A Collection of Poems...by Several Hands... London: J. Hughes for R. and J. Dodsley, 1758. 5th edition of volumes 1-3, 2nd edition of volume 4, 1st edition of volumes 5 & 6; 8vo; 6 volumes; (iv), 335, (i); (iv), 336; (iv), 351, (i); (iv), 360; (iv), 336; (iv), 336 pages; vignette on each titlepage, vignette headpieces, leaf of music at end of volume 4; half titles present; contemporary calf, spines gilt ruled; slightly rubbed, few corners little worn, one spine slightly chipped at head, little staining in volume 1; good set.   Robert Clark 38-171 1996 £150.00

DODSLEY, ROBERT 1703-1764   Fugitive Pieces, on Various Subjects. London: for J. Dodsley, 1765. 8vo; 2 volumes, pages (iv), 352; (iv), 357, (ii); contemporary sprinkled tan calf, red morocco labels, spines gilt numbered direct, gilt between raised bands, red sprinkled edges, owner's device (a brazier?) stamped in gilt at centre of both upper covers, upper joint of volume 1 just starting, spine of same volume chipped at head, still pleasant binding, internally excellent good.   Simon Finch 24-77 1996 £150.00

DODSLEY, ROBERT 1703-1764   The Preceptor; Containing a General Course of Education. London: printed for J. Dodsley, 1775. 6th edition; 2 volumes; frontispiece, folding plates, 3 pages ads in volume 1; contemporary calf, hinges splitting, but sound, red labels; from the library of Anne and Fernand Renier. Alston VII.202.   Jarndyce 103-460 1996 £120.00

DODSLEY, ROBERT 1703-1764   Trifles: viz. The Toy Shop. The King and the Miller of Mansfield. The Blind Beggar of Bethnal-Green. Rex & Pontifex. The Chronicle of the Kings of England. The Art of Preaching... London: 1745. 1st collected edition; 8vo; bound without half title, otherwise very good, 10 pages of publisher's ads at end; contemporary half calf, spine gilt, some wear to spine. CBEL II 788.   Ximenes 108-110 1996 $150.00

DODWELL, HENRY   A Treatise Concerning the Lawfulness of Instrumental Musick in Holy Offices. London: printed for William Haws, 1700. 2nd edition; 8vo; pages (2), 84, (2); 143, (1 ads), (1 errata); contemporary panelled calf, recently and neatly rebacked, very good. Wing D1821.   James Fenning 133-91 1996 £275.00

DOERR, HARRIET   Stones for Ibarra. New York: Viking, 1984. 1st edition; author's first book; near fine in dust jacket with inscribed card laid in.   Anacapa House 5-344 1996 $140.00

DOHAN, EDITH HALL   Italic Tomb-Groups in the University Museum. Philadelphia: University of Pennsylvania Press, 1942. Folio; xii, 113 pages, 69 figures, 55 plates; original cloth.   Archaeologia Luxor-3258 1996 $350.00

DOHENY, ESTELLE BETZOLD   The Estelle Doheny Collection from the Edward Laurence Doheny Memorial Library St. John's Seminary, Camarillo, California, sold on Behalf of the Archdiocese of Los Angeles. New York: Christie, Manson & Woods 22 Oct. 1987-19th May 1989. 4to; 7 volumes; colored and black and white plates, illustrations in text; red cloth, prospectus for sale inserted loose.   Maggs Bros. Ltd. 1191-43 1996 £200.00

DOHENY, ESTELLE BETZOLD   The Estelle Doheny Collection of Books and Manuscripts. Christie's Auction Catalogues, 1988-89. 10 x 7 3/4 inches; 7 volumes; illustrations; original cloth, very fine.   Phillip J. Pirages 33-93 1996 $325.00

DOIG, IVAN   This House of Sky. New York: HBJ, 1978. 1st edition; author's first book; signed by author; laid in is TLS dated Oct. 18, 1978 from a White Sulphur Springs, Montana resident which compares one person's remembrance of the area with that presented in the book; fine in very good plus dust jacket with one tiny edge tear and small snag on spine.   Thomas Dorn 9-99 1996 $195.00

DOLBY, J.   Six Views of Eton College... Eton: T. Ingalton and Son, 1838. Folio; tinted litho title and vignette and 6 plates, all on card; loose in original printed wrappers. Not in Abbey. Rare.   Marlborough 162-23 1996 £800.00

DOLCE, LODOVICO   Dialogo Piacevole Nelqvale Messer Pietro Aretino Parla in Difesa d'i Male Aventvrati Mariti. Venice: Curtio Toriano d'i Navo, 1542. 1st edition; small 8vo; ff. 20, italic letter, woodcut printer's lion device on titlepage, repeated at end, 1 woodcut initial; contemporary vellum over boards; little foxing or browning, 18th century armorial library stamp and ms. note "Proibito" on titlepage, generally good. BM STC I. p. 220; Adams 729; Graesse II 418. Brunet II 792.   A. Sokol XXV-27 1996 £1,500.00

DOLE, N. H.   America in Spitsbergen, the Romance of an Arctic Coal-Mine... Boston: 1922. 8vo; 2 volumes; pages xvii, 440; x, 484; 61 plates, 2 double page maps; original gilt stamped cloth, light spotting and wear, dampstaining to lower corner of few pages.   Raymond M. Sutton VI-1101 1996 $165.00

DOLGIN, I. M.   Climate of Antarctica. Rotterdam: 1986. 8vo; 224 pages; illustrations; cloth.   Wheldon & Wesley 207-382 1996 £62.00

DOLLAR, ROBERT   Private Diary of Robert Dollar on His Recent Visits to China. San Francisco: Robert Dollar Co., 1912. Only edition; 8vo; 19 photos, one folding; original cloth, gilt; spine sun faded, else very good.   Trebizond 39-89 1996 $100.00

DOMAT, JEAN   The Civil Law In Its Natural Order. Boston: Little Brown and Co., 1861. 2 volumes; new speckled quarter calf, goog, clean set.   Meyer Boswell SL26-65 1996 $350.00

DOMESTIC Management; or, the Beautiful Cookery-Book. London: B. Crosby & Co., 1810. Small thick 8vo; contemporary three quarter calf, gilt, stamped brown calf over marbled boards, spine with gilt stamped dark brown morocco label, glazed edges, rubbing, light foxing, front free endpaper lacking; very good. Bitting p. 544; Oxford p.1 39.   George J. Houle 68-35 1996 $300.00

DOMESTIC Prospects of the Country Under the New Parliament. London: james Ridgway and Sons, 1837. 1st edition; 8vo; (iv), 47 pages; recent blue boards lettered, very good; Goldsmith 30222; not in Kress or Black, nor Halkett & Laing.   John Drury 82-65 1996 £50.00

DOMESTIC Scenes in Greenland and Iceland. London: 1844. 12mo; pages 114, frontispiece, several fine text engravings; cloth, front hinge worn, but very good.   Stephen Lunsford 45-9 1996 $200.00

DOMINGUIN, LUIS MIGUEL   Pablo Picasso: Toros & Toreros. New York: Abrams, 1961. Folio; 32 pages text with illustrations + numerous plates, some in color; cloth, slipcase.   Brannan 43-515 1996 $165.00

DOMINICETI, BARTHOLOMEW   An Address from Dr. Dominiceti, of Chelsea. London: printed in the year 1782. 1st edition; 8vo; disbound; outer margins trimmed close, touching one letter on titlepage but without other loss.   Ximenes 108-111 1996 $200.00

DOMINICUS DE FLANDRIA   Questinoum Super XII Libros Metaphisice. Venice: Petrus de Quarengiis for Alessandro Calcedonius, 20 August 1499. 1st edition; folio; 19th century red quarter sheep, cloth boards, bit worn and rubbed, lower inner blank gutter with some minor worming just touching letter here and there, with tissue mends which partly obscure text in some cases and should be lifted, few annotations, minor watermarking, lovely woodcut Archagnel device of Calcedonius at beginning and end. Rare. hain 7125; GW 8640; not in British Mus. Goff D306.   G. W. Stuart 59-57 1996 $3,750.00

DOMINICY, MARC ANTOINE   Assertor Gallicvs, Contra Vindicias Hispanicas Ioannes Iacobi Chiffletii. Paris: Typographia Regis, 1616. Large4to; title arms, fine head and tailpieces and 3 full page plates; calf, gilt impressed on both covers the arms of Jacques-Auguste de Thou II; fine. Brunet 24008.   Rostenberg & Stern 150-45 1996 $1,875.00

DON, GEORGE   A General History of the Dichlamydeous Plants, Comprising Complete Descriptions of the Different Orders... London: 1831-38. New edition; 4to; 4 volumes; pages xxviii, 818; viii, 875; viii, 867; viii, 908; recent buckram, name and embossed library stamp on titles, pencilled numbers on verso, few brown stains to text, pages lightly tanned.   Raymond M. Sutton VI-9 1996 $485.00

DONALDSON, ALFRED L.   A History of the Adirondacks. New York: Century Co., 1921. 1st edition; 2 volumes; xii, 383; (viii), 383 pages, plates, maps; cloth, touch of cover wear, one folding map torn, otherwise very good set.   Metacomet Books 54-34 1996 $125.00

DONELLAN, JOHN   The Proceedings at Large on the Trial of John Donellan, Esq. for the Willful Murder (by Poison) of Sir the Edward Allesley Boughton...Tried Before Mr. Justice Buller. London: 1781. 152 pages; half leather.   W. Bruce Fye 71-1707 1996 $250.00

DONELLAN, JOHN   The Trial of John Donellan, Esq. for the Wilful Murder of Sir Theodosius Edward Allesley Boughton... London: sold by George Kearsley...and Martha Gurney, 1781. 2nd edition; contemporary quarter calf, rebacked, embrowning but well preserved; William Roughead's copy with his bookplate and elaborate notes.   Meyer Boswell SL27-229 1996 $650.00

DONI, ANTONIO FRANCESCO   La Zucca. En Spanol. Venice: Francesco Marcolini, 1551. 1st edition thus; 8vo; pages 166, (x), unusual italic letter, full pae woodcut archit. title, 15 over half page woodcuts; contemporary limp vellum, recased, gilt single fillets, corner fleurons and spine, occasional very slight soiling, upper edge of titlepage slightly shaved, 2 leaves partly browned or waterstained, small tear in another, final leaf and small piece in fore edge of titlepage repaired, all without loss; otherwise good.   A. Sokol XXV-28 1996 £1,950.00

DONLEAVY, J. P.   The Ginger Man. London: Neville Spearman, 1956. 1st British edition, signed by author; small name to front free endpaper, else near fine in very good plus lightly soiled dust jacket, scarce signed.   Thomas Dorn 9-103 1996 $250.00

DONLEAVY, J. P.   The Ginger Man. Paris: Olympia Press, 1958. 1st unexpurgated and 1st hardcover edition; small 8vo; author's first book; signed by author; green boards, printed labels, dust jacket; as new.   James S. Jaffe 34-139 1996 $275.00

DONN, JAMES   Hotus Cantabrigiensis; or an Accented Catalogue of Indigeonous and Exotic Plants Cultivated in the Cambridge Botanic Garden. London: Rivington, 1826. 11th edition; 8vo; pages 415; modern buckram with new endpapers and first and last signatures neatly taped; very good, some light foxing.   Second Life Books 103-70 1996 $125.00

DONNE, JOHN 1571-1631   Bianthanatos (in Greek). A Declaration of That Paradox or Thesis, that Self-Homicide Is Not so Naturally Sin, That It may Never Be Otherwise... London: John Dawson, 1644. 1st edition; 4to; (14), 218, (4) pages; contemporary blindstamped calf, very neatly rebacked, front blank not present, lovely fresh, untrimmed copy. Pforzheimer 292; Grolier, W-P 294; Wing D1858.   Kenneth Karmiole 1NS-92 1996 $2,750.00

DONNE, JOHN 1571-1631   The Courtier's Library, or Catalogus Librorum Aulicorum. London: Nonesuch Press, 1930. One of 950 numbered copies; paper covered boards in style of dust jacket affixed by the endpapers, spine sunned with piece (below printed label) lacking, still not unattractive in slightly dusty publisher's slipcase.   Hermitage SP95-1054 1996 $125.00

DONNE, JOHN 1571-1631   Devotions Upon Emergent Occasions and Several Steps in My Sicknes. London: printed by A. M. for Thomas Jones, 1624. 2nd edition; 12mo; contemporary calf, ruled in blind, central floral ornament in gilt on covers, red morocco label (spines little rubbed); one small paper flaw touching a catchword, but fine unsophisticated copy, complete with prelim blank. Keynes 36; STC 7034.   Ximenes 109-102 1996 $7,500.00

DONNE, JOHN 1571-1631   Love Poems. London: Nonesuch Press, 1923. One of 725 numbered copies; 8vo; printed in Garmond on Perusia handmade; 7 engravings on copper by Stephen Gooden; quarter parchment with gold paper boards, somewhat soiled and rubbed, internally nice, name on flyleaf, bookplate (by Reynolds Stone). Bertram Rota 272-315 1996 £650.00

DONNE, JOHN 1571-1631   Poems on Several Occasions... London: printed for Jacob Tonson and sold by William Taylor, 1719. 6th edition; 12mo; 3 pages of ads, contemporary panelled calf, rebacked, label. Keynes 85.   Anthony Laywood 108-51 1996 £125.00

DONNE, JOHN 1571-1631   Poems. London: J. M. Dent, 1931. some fading to cloth on spine, otherwise very good; ownership signature "Philip Larkin - Christmas 1939", later ownership signataure underneath with numerous annotations by Larkin.   R. A. Gekoski 19-89 1996 £650.00

DONNE, JOHN 1571-1631   The Poems. Cambridge: Limited Editions Club, 1968. 1st edition; one of 1500 copies, signed by artist; tall 8vo; wood engravings by Imre Reiner; quarter leather and cloth, glassine dust jacket, slipcase; spine very slightly faded, otherwise fine in jacket with minor tear.   James S. Jaffe 34-412 1996 $175.00

DONNE, JOHN 1571-1631   A Prayer. Banyan Press, 1947. Limited edition of 120 numbered copies; 8vo; 6 leaves, including blanks, title printed in 2 colors; title printed in 2 colors; decorative paper wrappers, 6 leaves, including blanks, fine in publisher's original mailing envelope. Though not called for, this copy inscribed by the printers, Claude Fredericks and Milton Saul to the bookman Paul Standard; laid in is prospectus for the Banyan Press edition of Spender's "Returning to Vienna 1974'.   Blue Mountain SP95-48 1996 $175.00

DOOLITTLE, HILDA 1886-1961   Collected Poems of H.D. New York: Boni & Liveright, 1925. Near fine copy with light spinal wear, very good spine darkened dust jacket with couple of small tears and cracked tear at flap folds, nonetheless a desirable book.   Thomas Dorn 9-139 1996 $200.00

DOOLITTLE, HILDA 1886-1961   Kora and Ka. Vaud: privately printed fo the author, 1930. One of 100 copies; wrappers; head and tail of spine and corners slightly bumped, covers slightly marked and dusty, bottom corners of upper cover slightly creased, single nick in fore-edge of uppe cover, front free endpaper slightly spotted; very good.   Ulysses 39-257 1996 £400.00

DOOLITTLE, HILDA 1886-1961   Red Roses for Bronze. New York: Random House, 1929. One of 475 copies; printed on handmade paper; wrappers, fine.   Ulysses 39-256 1996 £85.00

DORAN, JOHN   "Their Majesties' Servants": Annals of the English Stage from Thomas Betterton to Edmund Kean. London: William H. Mallen & Co., 1864. 1st edition; 8 1/2 x 5 3/4 inches; 2 volumes extended to four; extra illustrated with a total of 252 plates, two of them double page, 42 of them in color, many of them inlaid to size, almost a with tissue guards, titles and dedications printed in red and black; boun by Bayntun in handsome crushed moroccco in dark honey brown color, sides with simple gilt rule frame, central panel in gilt and black in geometric design with pointed ears in corners, raised bands ornamented with gilt disks, spine compartment decoration similar to cover panels, g ruled turn-ins, marbled endpapers, all edges gilt; a number of the plates lightly foxed, isolated cases of more noticeable foxing, adjacent pages sometimes slightly affected, otherwise very fine and attractive set, bright clean bindings virtually unworn.   Phillip J. Pirages 33-179 196 $1,750.00

DORAN, JOHN   Their Majesties' Servants, Annals of the English Stage from Thomas Betterton to Edmund Kean. London: Nimmo, 1888. Numbe 268 of 300 copies; tall thick quarto; fine, large paper edition; 50 copperplate portraits and wood engravings, plates in two states; origina maroon spines and linen boards, printed labels, uncut, some wear, but excellent set. LAR 857.   Hartfield 48-A8 1996 $295.00

DORE, GUSTAVE   The Dore Bible Gallery. Philadelphia: Altemus, n.d., c. 1880. Quarto; over 100 full page illustrations; decorated cloth; very good+.   Stephen Lupack 83- 1996 $100.00

DORSEY, J. O.   The Cegiha Language. Washington: 1890. 1st edition; xviii, 794 pages; cloth, very good+; very scarce.   T. A. Swinford 49-307 1996 $100.00

DORTU, M. G.   Toulouse-Lautrec et Son Oeuvre. Limited to 2450 copies; 4to; 6 volumes, pages 1800; over 6000 illustrations, publisher's cloth. Freitag 9542; Riggs 765.   Rainsford A54-555 1996 £1,250.00

DOS PASSOS, JOHN RODERIGO 1896-1970   The 42nd Parallel. New York: Harper, 1930. 1st edition; fine but for inevitable discoloring of spine label, lightly used dust jacket with tiny chip at head of spine. Beasley Books 82-52 1996 $150.00

DOS PASSOS, JOHN RODERIGO 1896-1970   1919. New York: Harcour Brace, 1932. 1st edition; light wear at spinal extremities, else near fine i very good dust jacket with some chipping at extremities.   Thomas Dorn 9-104 1996 $110.00

DOSSIE, ROBERT   The Elaboratory Laid Open, or, the Secrets of Modern chemistry and Pharmacy Revealed. London: for J. Nourse, 1758 1st edition; 8vo; (2), xi, (3), 375, (9) pages; later antique style calf, red morocco spine label, small library stamp on title, few brown spots here and there, very good, attractive copy. Duveen p. 179; bolton I 405; Kop II 131 & III 244, 306.   Edwin V. Glaser 121-86 1996 $650.00

DOSSIE, ROBERT   The Elaboratory Laid Open; or, the Secrets of Modern Chemistry and Pharmacy Revealed... London: printed for J. Nourse, 1768. 2nd edition; 8vo; xviii, (ii), 456, (viii) pages; original sheep covers rubbed, spine worn at head and foot, joints cracked; signature Philip Gell, of Hopton House, Derbyshire.   David Bickersteth 133-185 1996 £220.00

DOSTOEVSKII, FEDOR MIKHAILOVICH 1821-1881   The Brothers Karamazov. New York: Limited Editions Club, 1949. Number 214 of 1500 signed by artist; 2 volumes; lithographs by Fritz Eichenberg; two toned red cloth stamped in silver, fine in publisher's slipcase.   Hermitage SP95-973   1996 $125.00

DOSTOEVSKII, FEDOR MIKHAILOVICH 1821-1881   Buried Alive or Ten Years of Penal Servitude in Siberia. New York: Holt, 1881. 1st American edition; pictorial cloth, spine cocked and extremities bit frayed, front hinge lightly cracked, very good. Uncommon.   Between the Covers 42-144   1996 $350.00

DOSTOEVSKII, FEDOR MIKHAILOVICH 1821-1881   A Gentle Spirit: a Fantistic Story. Paris: Harrison of Paris, 1931. One of 495 copies on Satanized paper from a total issue of 570; 9 1/4 x 5 3/4 inches;; designed by Monroe Wheeler, hand set in 10 point stempel Baskerville, printed by Vittich in Darmstadt, Germany; frontispiece; black silk, housed in grey paper over boards, slipcase, with green paper label on spine. Priscilla Juvelis 95/1-119   1996 $125.00

DOSTOEVSKII, FEDOR MIKHAILOVICH 1821-1881   The Grand Inquisitor. London: printed by George W. Jones at the Sign of the Dolphin for... 1930. 32/300 copies; 8vo; printed on Kelmscott handmade paper, title printed in black and turquoise, pages xvi, 36, (i); original cream vellum with some minor natural discoloration, backstrip and front cover lettered in black, front cover with period abstract design of turquoise and black morocco onlays, bookplate, untrimmed, board slipcase little rubbed; fine. Blackwell's B112-177   1996 £300.00

DOSTOEVSKII, FEDOR MIKHAILOVICH 1821-1881   Poor Folk. London: Elkin Mathews and John Lane, 1894. 1st edition; titlepage design repeated on front cover by Aubrey Beardsley, original binding, upper hinge partially cracked, spine darkened, head and tail of spine snagged and slightly bumped, corners slightly bumped, covers dusty, good. Ulysses 39-152   1996 £125.00

DOSTOEVSKII, FEDOR MIKHAILOVICH 1821-1881   A Raw Youth. Verona: Limited Editions Club, at the Stamperia Valdonega, 1974. 1st edition thus, number 713 of 2000 copies; 4to; 2 volumes, 514 pages; illustrations by Fritz Eichenberg, signed by artist; original green cloth, couple of corners lightly bumped, but virtually fine in publisher's slipcase. Chapel Hill 94-256   1996 $100.00

DOTY, WILLIAM KAVANAUGH   The Confectionery of Monsieur Giron. Lexington: King Library Press, 1978. Number 90 of 100 numbered copies; 9.25 x 6 inches; 16, (iv) pages; measured line drawings by Jed Porter, printed in black on handmade paper; grey decorated paper boards, matching plain grey dust jacket. very fine.   Joshua Heller 21-149 1996 $100.00

DOUGHTY, CHARLES MONTAGU 1843-1926   Travels in Arabia Deserta. London: Jonathan Cape, 1936. New edition; small 4to; 2 volumes; 674, 696 pages; illustrations, large folding map in rear of each volume; original brown buckram, spines very slightly faded, otherwise fine. David Mason 71-109   1996 $240.00

DOUGHTY, CHARLES MONTAGU 1843-1926   Wanderings in Arabia. London: Duckworth, 1908. 1st edition; 8vo; 2 volumes, prelims in volume 1 slightly foxed; original cloth, slightly soiled, library labels removed from front covers, inscription on each front free endpaper "Philip Tomlinson from H. M. T." (H. M. Tomlinson to his brother).   H. M. Fletcher 121-154   1996 £650.00

DOUGLAS, ALFRED   Hymn to Physical Beauty. Sub Signo Libelli, 1976. One of 30 copies; 8 3/4 x 6 1/4 inches; 12 pages, (2) leaves (blank, colophon); one yellow initial; original paper wrappers, paper label on front cover, yellow vignette on title; very fine.   Phillip J. Pirages 33-473   1996 $500.00

DOUGLAS, C. L.   Cattle Kings of Texas. Dallas: Cecil Baugh, 1939. 2nd printing; xiv, 376 pages; numerous photos; original pictorial cloth, fine with chipped pictorial dust jacket. Scarce. Adams Herd 719; Howes D434; Six Guns 619.   Argonaut Book Shop 113-208   1996 $150.00

DOUGLAS, D.   The Biographical History of Sir William Blackstone, Late One of the Justices of Both Benches... London: printed for the author and sold by J. Bew 1782. 1st edition; 8vo; 3 parts in one, small piece missing from lower blank margin of title, separate title to second and third parts, separate pagination to each part but with continuous signatures; contemporary mottled calf, spine worn, hinges cracked, text fresh and clean. Sweet and Maxwell p. 27, 7.   Anthony Laywood 108-53   1996 £375.00

DOUGLAS, FREDERICK SYLVESTER NORTH   An Essay on Certain Points of Resemblance Between the Ancient and Modern Greeks. London: printed for John Murray, 1813. 1st edition; 8vo; original drab boards, printed papr label, some wear to spine, label rubbed; very good in original condition, scarce. 5 copies in NUC. Not in Blackmer Ximenes 109-103   1996 $750.00

DOUGLAS, HOWARD   Considerations on the Value and Importance of the British North American Provinces, and the Circumstances on Which Depend Their Further Prosperity and Colonial Connection with Great Britain. London: John Murray, 1831. 1st edition; 8vo; 36 pages, couple of leaves slightly soiled; disbound. McCulloch p. 94; Kress C2784 (3rd ed.). James Burmester 29-44   1996 £200.00

DOUGLAS, JAMES   Nenia Britannica; or, a Sepulchral History of Great Britain... London: printed by J. Nichols for B. and J. White, 1793. Folio; 2 titlepages, 36 sepia aquatint plates, 10 smaller aquatints in text, various woodcut head and tailpieces; contemporary half morocco, somewhat worn, uncut, slight foxxing.   H. M. Fletcher 121-93   1996 £480.00

DOUGLAS, JOHN   Pandaemonium; or, a New Infernal Expedition. London: printed for W. Owen, 1750. 1st edition; 4to; full polished marbled calf, gilt, spine gilt, by Zaehnsdorf; very rare; fine; from the library of R. H. Isham. Foxon P28.   Ximenes 108-112   1996 $2,250.00

DOUGLAS, KEITH   Alamein to Zem Zem. London: Editions Poetry 1946. 1st edition; 3 color plates and several black and white drawings in text by author; cloth backed boards, page edges browned, spine and covers faded, head and tail of spine and corners bumped, corners also bruised, covers slightly marked, top edge spotted, endpaper gutters spotted, good in chipped, spotted, soiled, torn, rubbed, marked and dusty dust jacket browned at spine and edges and missing small pieces at head and tail of spine.   Ulysses 39-154   1996 £65.00

DOUGLAS, KEITH   The Collected Poems of Keith Douglas. London: Editions Poetry, 1951. 1st edition; black and white frontispiece; original binding, top edge slightly dusty, prelims, edges and endpapers spotted, free endpapers browned, spine slightly darkened, very good, no dust jacket; bookplate of literary agent John Johnson.   Ulysses 39-155 1996 £80.00

DOUGLAS, M.   Notes of a Journey from Berne to England through France, Made in the Year 1796. London: 1797. 8vo; 2nd part only; 56 pages; contemporary calf, gilt, by C. Kalthoeber, with his binder's ticket, rebacked. This copy fromt he Althorp Library with its label and Spencer bookplate.   Thomas Thorp 489-89   1996 £135.00

DOUGLAS, MARJORY STONEMAN   Road to the Sun. New York: Rinehart, 1952. One of a special limited Florida Edition; light foxing to endpapers and barely cocked, near fine in very good plus dust jacket, with tear on spine and little rubbing at extremities, author's second book; inscribed by author.   Between the Covers 42-145   1996 $350.00

DOUGLAS, NORMAN 1868-1952   The Angel of Manfredonia. San Francisco: Windsor Press, 1929. Limited edition of 225 copies, this number 18; decorations by Howard Simon; signed by author, spine slightly faded, otherwise very good in glassine wrapper in rubbed slipcase, split at top and bottom edges. Woolf A31.   Virgo Books 48-66   1996 $150.00

DOUGLAS, NORMAN 1868-1952   D. H. Lawrence and Maurice Magnus. A Plea for Better Manner. London: privately printed, 1924. 1st edition; unopened, stiff paper wrappers, very good.   Virgo Books 48-84 1996 £55.00

DOUGLAS, NORMAN 1868-1952   London Street Games. London: St. Catherine Press, 1916. 1st edition; limited to 500 copies; some slight foxing, mostly to first and last few pages, uncut, edges dusty, boards little scratched and rubbed; good, lacking dust jacket.   Virgo Books 48-63   1996 £150.00

DOUGLAS, NORMAN 1868-1952   Nerinda. Florence: Orioli, 1929. Limited edition, 112/475 signed; name and address on f.e.p., otherwise fine, unopened in new slipcase with original title laid on; nice. Woolf A28. Virgo Books 48-65   1996 £70.00

DOUGLAS, ROBERT K.   Society in China. London: A. D. Innes, 1894. 1st edition; 8vo; pages xvi, 415; 22 plates; original binding, gilt, spine lightly faded, otherwise nice. James Fenning 133-92   1996 £65.00

DOUGLAS, STEPHEN A.   Remarks of the Hon. Stephen A. Douglas, on Kansas, Utah and the Dred Scott Decision. Chicago: Daily Times Book and Job Office. 1857. 1st edition; 15 pages; tall untrimmed copy, very fine. Flake 2985; Byrd Illinois Imprints 2635.   Michael D. Heaston 23-139   1996 $300.00

DOUGLAS, WILLIAM O.   Go East, Young Man, The Early Years, The Autobiography of William O. Douglas. New York: Random House, 1974. Presentation copy, 4 lines, entirely in the hand of Justice Douglas, signed by him in full.   Meyer Boswell SL27-67 1996 $250.00

DOUGLAS, WILLIAM O.   North from Malaya, Adventure on Five Fronts. Garden City: Doubleday & Co., 1953. Quite good copy, in chipped dust jacket; presentation copy from Justice Douglas to Raymond A. Spruance, then U.S. amabassador to the Philippines.   Meyer Boswell SL27-69 1996 $350.00

DOUGLAS, WILLIAM O.   Of Men and Mountains. New York: Harper and Bros., 1950. 1st edition; very good in chipped dust jacket; inscribed copy.   Meyer Boswell SL27-70 1996 $250.00

DOUGLAS, WILLIAM O.   The Right of the People. Garden City: Doubleday & Co., 1958. Very well preserved copy in slightly embrowned dust jacket; Presentation copy from Justice Douglas to Vern Countryman, one of his earliest law clerks.   Meyer Boswell SL25-72 1996 $250.00

DOVE, RITA   Lady Freedom Among Us. West Burke: Janus Press, 1994. Limited to 110 copies; tall octavo; (12) pages; text printed on white paper that is bound into lower quarter of the book; above text looms the face of 'Lady Freedom', with two profiles and front-view cut out from purple paper; covers of light blue paper, with cut-out overlay depicting the Capitol across both covers; housed in corrugated plastic chemise and blue cloth slipcase with printed paper label to spine, mint. Bromer Booksellers 87-102 1996 $300.00

DOVE, RITA   Lady Freedom Among Us. West Burke: Janus Press, 1994. One in an edition of 100 copies, plus 10 hors commerce signed by artist and author; 10.5 x 6.25 inches; images and design by Claire Van Vliet, handprinted and bound by Van Vliet on various handmade papers of brown, blue and black, text on white card between two cut-out profiles and fold-out face in black with three cut-out brown stars, blue card wrappers with wrap-around white ard relief of the Capitol, black reproduction of "Freedom" on spine where white card relief and blue wrappers meet; opaque plastic chemise, blue cloth slipcase with red, white and blue paper title label on spine.   Joshua Heller 21-38 1996 $300.00

DOVE, RITA   Lady Freedom Among Us. West Burke: Janus Press, 1994. 1st edition; one of 1000 copies, signed by author, artist and Van Vliet; text is Century Schoolbok printed on Mohawk Superfine, handmade papers are Sky blue from MacGregor & Vinzani Gelatin sized white and Mica rose from Twinrocker; designed by Ms. Van Vliet, the book is sculptural and can be folded outward so that the structure, when seen from above, makes two diamonds, that way she stands solidly and can be viewed 360 degrees; slipcases made by Mary Richardson and Judi Conant.   Priscilla Juvelis 95/1-137 1996 $300.00

DOVETON, F. B.   Maggie in Mythica; or, What She Saw in Fairyland. London: Swan Sonnenschein, 1890. 1st edition; illustrations; pictorial cloth; very good in very good very good+ binding; uncommon. Aronovitz 57-353 1996 $125.00

DOW, GEORGE FRANCIS   The Arts and Crafts in New England 1704-1775. Topsfield: Wayside Press, 1927. Limited edition, number 30 of 97 copies, of which 87 are for sale; 39 black and white plates; quarter cloth and decorative boards. near fine.   Blue River Books 9-128 1996 $200.00

DOWDEN, EDWARD   The Life of Percy Bysshe Shelley. London: Kegan Paul, Trench and Co., 1886. 1st edition; 2 volumes; frontispieces in each volume, 6 plates, folding facsimile, errata slip; original maroon cloth, gilt, rubbed, spines little faded, sound set.   Robert Clark 38-259 1996 £65.00

DOWDEN, EDWARD   Robert Southey. New York: Harper & Bros., Publishers, 1880. 1st edition; 197 page study; original binding; top ede dusty, spine slightly faded, head and tail of spine and corners slightly bumped, cover edges slightly rubbed; very good; with bookplate of John Kendrick Bangs on front pastedown; subsequently from the library of James D. Hart who has pencilled at top corner of the recto of the rear free endpaper the name of bookshop he bought the book in, with date & price.   Ulysses 39-157 1996 £55.00

DOWELL, COLEMAN   The Silver Swanne. Grenfell Press, 1983. One of 115 copies, signed by author; 4 x 8 3/4 inches; 3 p.l. (one blank), 7-41, (1) pages, (2) leaves (dedication, colophon); color vignette on title, silver initial, printed in brown and black; original vellum backed pictorial paper boards, spine titled in gilt, edges untrimmed; mint.   Phillip J. Pirages 33-269 1996 $190.00

DOWELL, COLEMAN   The Silver Swanne: a Ghost Story. New York: Grenfell Press, 1983. One of 115 numbered copies, signed by author; small folio; set byMichael Bixler in 16 pt. Centaur and printed in black and deep red, large opening initial in sivler grey, on Barcham Green's Chatham vellum handmade; quarter vellum, boards, titlepage decoration repeated on upper; fine.   Bertram Rota 272-206 1996 £125.00

DOWN Down the Mountain. New York: Nelson, 1934. 1st edition; 4to; lithographed illustrations in blue and brown by Ellis Credle, brown cloth lettered in blue, fresh copy.   Barbara Stone 70-63 1996 £55.00

DOWNES, JOHN   Roscius Anglicanus, or, an Historical Review of the Stage... London: ptd. for the editor, and sold at No. 62, Great Wild Street... 1789. 2nd edition; 8vo; half calf (top of spine worn); uncommc LAR 825-6; CBEL II 725.   Ximenes 108-113 1996 $600.00

DOWNEY, GLANVILLE   A History of Antioch in Syria from Seleucus the Arab Conquest. Princeton: Princeton University Press, 1961. 8vo; xx 754 pages, 21 illustrations; original cloth, dust jacket.   Archaeologia Luxor-3265 1996 $110.00

DOWNING, A. J.   The Fruits and Fruit Trees of America; or, the Culture, Propagation and Management in the Garden and Orchard, of Fruit Trees Generally... New York: 1845. 1st edition; 8vo; pages xiv, 59 (14 page ads); 214 engraved illustrations; original cloth, gilt decorated spine, worn at corners and edges, spine ends partially perished, inch piece missing at head of spine, spot on front cover, small tear to titlepage, some page browning, mostly marginal, missing pages vii-x in preface. Signed presentation from author for Rev. F. D. Huntington. Raymond M. Sutton VII-8 1996 $650.00

DOWNING, A. J.   The Fruits and Fruit Trees of America... New York 1845. 1st edition; 8vo; pages xiv, 594, (14 pages ads); 214 engraved illustrations; original cloth with gilt decorated spine, wear to ends and edges of spine, corners worn, rubbing to boards, bookplate, 3 signatures loose or partially loose, pages tanned; signed in blindstamp Bradley Binder Boston.   Raymond M. Sutton VII-906 1996 $300.00

DOWNING, A. J.   The Horticulturist and Journal of Rural Art and Rur Taste, Devoted to Horticulture, Landscape Gardening, Rural Architectur Botany, Pomology, Entomology, rural Economy Etc. Albany: 1846-48. 8 volumes 1 and 2; pages ix, 576; 576, (i-) iv; lithographic plates and tex engravings; contemporary half calf, some wear and rubbing, minor cracking of leather spines, scattered foxing and some page browning. Raymond M. Sutton VII-905 1996 $350.00

DOWSE, THOMAS STRETCH   The Brain and Its Diseases. London: Bailliere, Tindall and Cox, 1879. 1st edition; 8vo; Part 1, (viii), 144 page 3 original chromolithographs; printed green cloth, joints & edges moderately shelfworn, small stain near lower right front corner, very good with bookplate and stamp of Hartford Retreat; Rare.   John Gac 150-131 1996 $250.00

DOYLE, ARTHUR CONAN 1859-1930   Adventures of Gerard. London: Newnes, 1903. 1st edition; full red box calf, double gilt rule on front ar back panels, spine with five raised bands and gilt tooled with floral vir pattern, title in gilt on blue calf, author in gilt on green calf, gilt dentell marbled endpapers, all edges gilt, cloth slipcase, handsome binding, fir Bound by Bayntun.   Priscilla Juvelis 95/1-311 1996 $450.00

DOYLE, ARTHUR CONAN 1859-1930   The Adventures of Sherlock Holmes. (with) The Memoirs of Sherlock Holmes. London: George Newnes, 1892/94. 1st editions; royal 8vo; 2 volumes; illustrations by Sidney Paget; 1st title in first issue binding, with no name on street si on cover, original light blue cloth, gilt edges, inscription on half title; 2 title in original dark blue cloth, gilt edges, inscription, slight attention t binding, but fine. Green and Gibson A10 and A14.   Charles W. Trayl 117-111 1996 £1,800.00

DOYLE, ARTHUR CONAN 1859-1930   A Duet; with an Occasional Chorus. New York: D. Appleton, 1899. 1st American edition, 1st printir with 19 titles by Doyle listed opposite the titlepage; reportedly, only 1 copies of this printing; small 8vo; decorative maroon cloth, very good bright, with minor fade to spine, all lettering intact, ink name, dated 18 on front blank page; nice.   Antic Hay 101-459 1996 $100.00

DOYLE, ARTHUR CONAN 1859-1930   The Exploits of Brigadier Gerar London: Newnes, 1896. 1st edition; full red box calf, double gilt rule c front and back panels, spine with five raised bands and gilt tooled wit floral vine pattern, title in gilt on blue calf, author in gilt on green calf, gilt dentelles, marbled endpapers, all edges gilt, cloth slipcase, handsome binding; fine.   Priscilla Juvelis 95/1-313 1996 $450.00

DOYLE, ARTHUR CONAN 1859-1930 His Last Bow. London: John Murray, 1917. 1st edition; crown 8vo; original cloth, little dull, worn and faded, minor repairs to binding, endpapers cracked, some foxing and browning, passable copy of a cheaply produced book. Green & Gibson A40. Ash Rare Books Zenzybyr-31 1996 £95.00

DOYLE, ARTHUR CONAN 1859-1930 The Hound of the Baskervilles. M-P, 1902. 1st American edition (later issue with the word 'illustrated' on cancelled titlepage); white spine lettering all but gone, as usual, else bright, very good+/near fine copy with white lettering on front cover virtually unblemished; Aronovitz 57-355 1996 $285.00

DOYLE, ARTHUR CONAN 1859-1930 The Hound of the Baskervilles. London: George Newnes, 1902. 1st edition; 8vo; frontispiece, 15 full page illustrations by Sidney Paget; full dark red calf by Bayntun-Riviere, spine with raised bands and gilt stamped floral designs within gilt ruled compartments, contrasting blue and green gilt stamped morocco labels, covers double ruled in gilt, gilt stamped floral inner dentelles, marbled endpapers, all edges gilt; very good to fine in red cloth slipcase; scarce. George J. Houle 68-43 1996 $1,750.00

DOYLE, ARTHUR CONAN 1859-1930 The Hound of the Baskervilles. San Francisco: Arion Press, 1985. 1st edition; limited to 400 copies signed by Michael Kenna; photos by Kenna; as new in publisher's slipcase. Hermitage SP95-751 1996 $325.00

DOYLE, ARTHUR CONAN 1859-1930 The Last Galley. Garden City: Doubleday, Page, 1911. 1st edition; beautiful color frontispiece by N. C. Wyeth; bookplate, otherwise very good or better. Quill & Brush 102-479 1996 $100.00

DOYLE, ARTHUR CONAN 1859-1930 The Lost World. H&S, 1912. 1st American edition (variant issue?); bound in red cloth, has the title, author and publisher (being Doran only) stamped in gold on spine, has title and author stamped in black on front cover, measures only 1 1/16" across top page edges and contains only 2 photographic plates; just about very good; Aronovitz 57-357 1996 $150.00

DOYLE, ARTHUR CONAN 1859-1930 The Memoirs of Sherlock Holmes. London: George Newnes Ltd., 1894. 1st edition; crown 8vo; original blue cloth, gilt, all edges gilt, covers are slightly edge worn, small ink signature at top of titlepage, a 1/2" x 1" piece missing from bottom of back free endpaper, bright copy. Green and Gibson A14a. Glenn Books 36-96 1996 $1,400.00

DOYLE, ARTHUR CONAN 1859-1930 The Memoirs of Sherlock Holmes. London: George Newnes, 1894. 1st edition; illustrations by Sidney Paget; blue cloth boards stamped in gold and black with all edges gilt, very good with covers slightly worn and lettering bright, pages show light aging and soling with few closed tears, hinges starting, frontispiece intact but worn on edges and contemporary owner's name, etc. on half title, still nice. Quill & Brush 102-478 1996 $750.00

DOYLE, ARTHUR CONAN 1859-1930 My Friend the Murderer (an Other Mysteries and Adventures). New York: Lovell, Coryell, 1893. Piracy; blue cloth, gold gilt lettering on front and spine, uncommon. Bud Schweska 12-941 1996 $125.00

DOYLE, ARTHUR CONAN 1859-1930 Our Second American Adventure. Boston: Little Brown and Co., 1924. 1st American edition; tall 4to; 3 p.l., 150 pages; illustrations; complete; original black cloth with title, author and publisher on spine (very faded), spine and rear cover with some spotting, binding firm, contents excellent. Green B33b. Roy W. Clare XXIV-35 1996 $100.00

DOYLE, ARTHUR CONAN 1859-1930 Rodney Stone. New York: Appleton, 1896. 1st American edition; decorated red cloth, fine, in the rare dust jacket which is just lightly worn and has two neeedless internal mends, housed in custom slipcase. Captain's Bookshelf 38-56 1996 $1,000.00

DOYLE, ARTHUR CONAN 1859-1930 Sherlock Holmes, the Complete Long Stories. London: John Murray, 1929. 1st edition; 8vo; original red cloth with gold lettering, spine slightly faded. Green and Gibson A58a. Glenn Books 36-95 1996 $125.00

DOYLE, ARTHUR CONAN 1859-1930 A Visit to Three Fronts: Glimpses of the British, Italian and French Lines. London: 1916. 1st edition; 4to; wrappers, lower third of spine wrapper torn away, corners little creased, wrappers bit marked, otherwise very good, rare. Inscribed by the author. Words Etcetera 94-368 1996 £850.00

DOYLE, ARTHUR CONAN 1859-1930 The Wanderings of a Spiritualist. New York: Doran, 1921. Tall 4to; xi, (2), 15-299 pages; illustrations; original green cloth with title and author in black on front cover and on spine (top and bottom of spine lightly chipped, corners bumped, slight corner stains to rear cover), otherwise cover is in good condition; contents fine. Roy W. Clare XXIV-34 196 $300.00

DOYLE, ARTHUR CONAN 1859-1930 Collected Works. London: Smith, Elder & Co., 1903. Author's edition, 1st edition thus, signed by author in volume 1, one of 1000 copies; 12 volumes; full green morocco, gilt tooling, red rosettes onlaid, spine panelled, minor wear but generally very good set in lovely binding. Priscilla Juvelis 95/1-312 1996 $5,000.00

DOYLE, ARTHUR CONAN 1859-1930 The Works. Garden City: Dobuleday, Doran and Co., 1930. Number 557 of 760 copies; signed by author; 8vo; 24 volumes, frontispiece, contemporary brown half morocco, marbled boards, sides ruled in gilt, spines in compartments with raised bands, gilt rues, ornament and lettering, top edge gilt, others uncut, marbled endpapers, bookplate, fine. Simon Finch 24-79 1996 £3,800.00

DOYLE, CHARLES WILLIAM The Military Exploits, Etc., Etc. of Don Juan Martin Diez, the Empeciando; Who First Commenced and Then Organized the system of Guerrilla Warfare in Spain. London: printed for Carpenter and Son, 1823. 8vo; frontispiece, viii, 174 pages, folding map; paper over boards, printed label on spine, rubbed, expertly rebacked, occasional foxing, else very good. Andrew Cahan 47-141 1996 $225.00

DOYLE, RICHARD 1824-1883 Scenes from English History. London: Pall Mall Gazette Office, 1886. Oblong 4to; 12 color plates after water color drawings, tan cloth, gilt, pictorially stamped in black, crack at inner hinge, else very nice, bright copy, very scarce. Barbara Stone 70-76 1996 £375.00

DOYLE, RODDY Paddy Clarke Ha Ha Ha. New York: Viking, 1993. 1st edition; fine in fine dust jacket with "e" on Clarke; signed by author. Bella Luna 7-209 1996 $100.00

DOYLE, RODDY The Snapper. London: Secker & Warburg, 1990. 1st edition; fine in dust jacket. Between the Covers 42-146 1996 $175.00

A DOZEN All Told. London: Blackie, 1894. 1st edition; fine; from the collection of John H. Dalton. Harland H. Eastman 10/94-89 1996 $225.00

DRAGO, HARRY SINCLAIR Wild, Woolly and Wicked: the History of the Kansas Cow Towns and the Texas Cattle Trade. New York: Clarkson N. Potter, 1960. 1st deluxe edition, one of 250 numbered copies, signed by author; viii, 354 pages; endpaper map; simulated cowhide, very fine in printed and gilt decorated acetate dust jacket. Six Guns 629. Argonaut Book Shop 113-210 1996 $150.00

DRAKE, JOSEPH RODMAN The Culprit Fray and Other Poems. New York: 1835. 1st edition; 8vo; 84 pages; frontispiece, extra engraved title (foxed); contemporary morocco, elaborately gilt stamped, all edges gilt, rubbed; ownership inscription of Jan. 1, 1836. BAL 4825; Rinderknecht 31416. M & S Rare Books 60-149 1996 $175.00

DRAKE, LEAH BODINE Hornbook for Witches. Sauk City: Arkham House, 1950. 1st edition; 1/500 copies; fine in dust jacket. Aronovitz 57-358 1996 $1,325.00

DRAKE, LEAH BODINE A Hornbook for Witches. Sauk City: Arkham House, 1950. 1st and only edition; small 8vo; only 553 copies printed; rare, house titles, previous owner's signature, otherwise fine in like dust jacket. Glenn Books 36-7 1996 $950.00

DRAKE, MILTON Almanacs of the United States. New York: 1962. 1st edition; 2 volumes, 1397 pages; cloth, light smoke damage. W. M. Morrison 436-61 1996 $125.00

DRAKE, SAMUEL A Systematic Treatise, Historical, Etiological and Practical, on the Principal Diseases of the Interior Valley of North America. Cincinnati: Winthrop B. Smith (1st Series) Phila.: Lippincott, Grambo (2nd Series) 1850/54. 8vo; xvi, 878, including tables, 19 plates; xix, (17)-985 pages, including tables, volume one rebound in cloth, volume 2 in original sheep, worn, joints splitting, internally some foxing and browning, clean tear in title of volume 1. Iowa 1409. GM 1777. James Tait Goodrich K40-122 1996 $695.00

DRAKE, ST. CLAIR   Black Metropolis: a Study of Negro Life in a Northern City. New York: HB&Co., 1945. 1st edition; errata slip tipped in; neat contemporary gift inscription, light wear to base of the spine, else near fine in very good, spine tanned dust jacket with some chipping to crown and with large chip on rear panel.   Between the Covers 43-301 1996 $135.00

DRAKE-BROCKMAN, R. E.   British Somaliland. London: 1912. 8vo; pages xvi, 334, 74 illustrations and map; cloth.   Wheldon & Wesley 207-383 1996 £80.00

DRAKE-BROCKMAN, R. E.   The Mammals of Somaililand. L 1910. illustrations; original pictorial cloth, light rubbing, very light foxing. David Grayling J95Biggame-73 1996 £75.00

DRANNAN, WILLIAM F.   Thirty-One Years on the Plains and in the Mountains; or, the Last Voice from the Plains... Chicago: Rhodes & McClure Pub. Co., 1899. 1st edition; 586, (587-95 ads) pages; illustrations; original blue cloth, title stamped in silver on front cover and spine, minor repairs to spine, fine, bright copy. Graff 1147; Howes D482. Smith 2568; Adams Six Guns 630.   Michael D. Heaston 23-140 1996 $325.00

DRAPER, GEORGE   Beleigh (sic) Abbey, Essex. London: Draper, Colnaghi & Hookham, 1818. 4to; 5 parts in 1 volume, 8 pp., 1 f., 2, 2, 2, 2 ff., 20 aquatint paltes; old half calf (rebacked), original wrappers of part 2 loosely inserted, unevenly foxed and slightly dampstained margins. Rare. Note in Abbey; UCBA p. 445.   Marlborough 162-24 1996 £950.00

DRAPER, JOSHUA   An Essay Upon Friendship... London: printed in the year 1725. 1st edition; 8vo; contemporary panelled calf, spine gilt; fine, rare, errata leaf present at end.   Ximenes 108-114 1996 $500.00

DRAYTON, MICHAEL 1563-1631   Poems... London: printed by W. Stansby for John Methwicke, 1613. 4th edition; 8vo; 19th century black morocco, wide gilt borders, spine and inner dentelles gilt, all edges gilt, by Winstanley of Manchester, joints bit rubbed; titlepage bit dusty, slight scattered foxing and couple of minor wormholes near end, but very good; flyleaf preserved bears the contemporary signature of Charles Brandon, Duke of Suffolk. STC 7221; Pforzheimer 305.   Ximenes 109-104 1996 $850.00

DRAYTON, MICHAEL 1563-1631   Poems. London: by W. Stansby for John Swethwicke (sic), 1619. 1st folio edition, 1st issue, the state with the misprint in imprint, the engraved title on (A)1a, and the engraved portrait of Drayton on verso of printed title; folio: (6), 487 pages, added engraved title, engraved portrait, wooduct initials and headpieces; very skillful period style modern full calf, aside from barely noticeable marginal dampstain on few leaves and very faint spotting on 2C2-3; exceptionally fine, fresh and wide margined copy. Pforzheimer 307; Grolier L-W 90; STC 722.3.   Joseph J. Felcone 64-18 1996 $3,000.00

DREDGE, JAMES   Thames Bridges from the Tower to the Source. London: Offices of 'Engineering', 1897. Oblong 4to; (iv), 255, (1) pages, 77 photo engraved plates numbered 1-75, 1, 44 and some text illustrations; contemporary quarter morocco; from the library of J. G. James.   Elton Engineering 10-39 1996 £550.00

DREER, HERMAN   The Immediate Jewel of His Soul: a Romance. St. Louis: The Saint Louis Argus Pub. Co., 1919. 1st edition; photos; miserable copy of a cheaply produced novel, spine and front endpaper lacking, boards detached but present, couple of editorial blue pencil marks in text, small tear to edges of few pages, probably issued without dust jacket. Rare.   Between the Covers 43-62 1996 $150.00

DREISER, THEODORE 1871-1945   An American Tragedy. Limited Editions Club. 1954. One of 1500 copies; 11 x 7 3/4 inches; 6 p.l., 556 pages, (1) leaf (colophon); many line drawings in text by Reginald Marsh; original cloth, publisher's (slightly soiled and faded) slipcase; very fine.   Phillip J. Pirages 33-356 1996 $100.00

DREISER, THEODORE 1871-1945   Chains. New York: Boni & Liveright, 1927. One of 440 specially bound copies, numbered and signed by author; handsome rice paper covered boards, cloth backstrip and paper label, bit worn box.   Beasley Books 82-53 1996 $250.00

DREISER, THEODORE 1871-1945   Dawn: Autobiography of Early Youth. New York: Liveright, 1931. 1st edition; small bookplate to front pastedown, else near fine in very good dust jacket with some loss at foot of spine 1 inch at its deepest point and little bit of edge wear. Between the Covers 42-147 1996 $185.00

DREISER, THEODORE 1871-1945   Epitaph: a Poem. New York: Heron Press, 1929. Out of a total edition of 1100 copies, this one of 700 printed on handmade Keijyo Kami paper; bound in cloth, and signed by author; decorations by Robert Fawcett; very fine in lightly chipped glassine and fine publisher's blox; uncommon in this condition.   Left Bank Books 2-29 1996 $175.00

DREISER, THEODORE 1871-1945   Epitaph, a Poem. New York: Heron Press, 1929. 1st edition; one of 200 special copies, bound thus (of 1100 total); 12 1/2 x 9 1/4 inches; (60) pages, printed on one side only and unopened at top edge; frontispiece and other decorations by Robert Fawcett; printed by August Gauthier on handmade Keijyo Kami paper; original silk, titled in silver on front and spine, original glassine, dust jacket (bit brittle and frayed at edges, with discreet tape repairs) and publisher's (slightly worn and abraded) slipcase; except for defects mentioned, a very fine copy.   Phillip J. Pirages 33-195 1996 $150.00

DRESSER, CHRISTOPHER   Principles of Decorative Design. London: Cassell, Peter & Galpin, n.d., ca. 1874. 2nd edition; 4to; viii, 167, (1), (4) pages, 2 chromolithgoraphic plates; publisher's cloth, very good. Bookpress 75-43 1996 $475.00

DRESSER, H. E.   A History of the Birds of Europe. London: 1871-96. Royal 4to; 9 volumes, 2 plain and 632 hand colored plates, 89 hand colored plates; half red morocco; complete set, some rather obtrusive foxing of plates in volume 4, some limited slight foxing in volumes 3 and 5, otherwise good set; from the collection of Jan Coldewey.   Wheldon & Wesley 207-26 1996 £8,500.00

DREW, SAMUEL   An Original Essay on the Immateriality and Immortality of the Human Soul, Founded Soley on Physical and Rational Principles. Bristol: printed by and for Richard Edwards, 1803. 2nd edition; 8vo; 306, (2) pages, subscriber's list, blindstamp on first and final few leaves, discreet withdrawal stamp on title; contemporary marbled boards, neatly rebacked, second edition; uncommon.   James Burmester 29-45 1996 £125.00

DREYFUS, JOHN   Eric Gill for Father Desmond. Bain and Williams, 1993. One of 70 copies accompanied by additional proofs and specially bound; 8vo; 12 illustrations; half dark brown morocco, proofs mounted in matching folder, fine in slipcase.   Bertram Rota 272-24 1996 £125.00

DREYFUS, JOHN   Eric Gill for Father Desmond. London: Bain and Williams Ltd., 1993. Deluxe edition, limited to 70 copies; with letterpress proof of the original block on india paper from Gill's Studio and an intaglio proof from an electro of the printing block; leather backed boards, parchment label, two prints similarly bound in display mount, cloth slipcase.   Claude Cox 107-60b 1996 £125.00

DREYFUS, JOHN   Four Lectures by T. J. Cobden-Sanderson. San Francisco: Book Club of California, 1974 1st edition; one of 450 copies; 4to; 11 plates; original cloth backed decorated boards, printed paper label on spine, uncut.   Forest Books 74-72 1996 £85.00

DREYFUS, JOHN   A Typographical Masterpiece: an Account...of Eric Gill's Collaboration with Robert Gibbings in Producing the Golden Cockerel Press edition of "The Four Gospels" in 1931. Bain & Williams, 1991. Of 250 copies, this one of 40 hand bound, and with proof from one of Gill's original blocks printed by hand on handmade Gampi paper by Graham Williams; folio; title and chapter headings set in Golden Cockerel type; hand bound by Clare Skelton, quarter red goatskin, orange cloth sides with triangular inalys of iridescent blue and green Tha silks, fine copy in slipcase.   Bertram Rota 272-23 1996 £285.00

DREYFUS, JOHN   A Typographical Masterpeice: an Account.. of Eric Gill's Collaboration with Robert gibbings... San Francisco: Book Club of California, 1990. One of 450 copies; folio; designed by author, chapter headings set in GoldenCockerel type; profusely illustrated; beige cloth, pictorial device in gilt on upper cover, fine.   Bertram Rota 272-51 1996 £95.00

DREYFUS, JOHN   A Typographical Masterpiece: an Account... Bain & Williams, 1991. One of 250 copies; folio; designed by author, title and chapter headings set in Golden Cockerel type at Rampant Lions Press; burgundy cloth, gilt, fine.   Bertram Rota 272-22 1996 £95.00

DREYFUS, JOHN   A Typographical Masterpiece. London: Bain & Williams, 1993. Deluxe edition, limited to 40 copies; proof from one of the original wood blocks, printed by hand by Graham Williams; hand bound in a design using 3 cloths, leather backed, by Clare Skelton; slipcase.   Claude Cox 107-61B 1996 £285.00

DREYFUS, JOHN   A Typographical Masterpiece. London: Bain and Williams, (prtd. by Meriden Stinehour Press, Vermont), 1993. 1st edition; limited to 200 copies (+499 for the Book Club of California); large 4to; pages 120; 41 illustrations; full red cloth by Judi Conant with Fabriano endpapers.   Claude Cox 107-61A 1996 £95.00

DREYFUS, JOHN   William Caxton and His Quincentenary. San Francisco: Book Club of California, 1976. One of 400 copies, there were also 700 copies for the Typophiles; original binding, one corner slightly bumped, fine, without dust jacket, as issued; presentation copy from author inscribed for James Hart; loosely inserted prospectus for this book, together with first day cover postmarked 12th Nov. 1976, of the William Caxton stamps issued by the British G.P.O.   Ulysses 39-159 1996 £65.00

DREYFUS, JOHN   The Work of Jan Van Krimpen: a Record in Honour of His Sixtieth Birthday. Haarlem: Joh. Enschede en Zonen, 1952. 1st edition; 4to; numerous illustrations, original buckram, title gilt on spine and upper cover; Ruari McLean's copy with bookplate.   Forest Books 74-319 1996 £120.00

DRIGGS, FRANK   Black Beauty, White Heat. A Pictorial History of Classic Jazz. New York: Morrow, 1982. 1st edition; 360 pages; superbly illustrated; original cloth, fine in very close to fine dust jacket.   Beasley Books 82-224 1996 $150.00

DRINKWATER, JOHN 1882-1937   Abraham Lincoln - A Play. London: Sidgwick & Jackson Ltd., 1923. Reprint; original binding, top edge dusty, head and tail of spine and corners bumped, covers marked and slightly soiled, free endpapers browned, good; ownership signature of Ian Fleming; mounted on front free endpaper are remains of label "House Library E. V. Slater's, Esq. D.D." after the letters "D.D." Fleming has written his name.   Ulysses 39-674 1996 £125.00

DRINKWATER, JOHN 1882-1937   Cotswold Characters. New Haven: Yale University Press, 1921. 1st edition; octavo; 54 pages; 5 wood engravings by Nash; brown boards, lightly chipped dust jacket; very fine.   Bromer Booksellers 87-240 1996 $175.00

DRINKWATER, JOHN 1882-1937   Loyalties. London: Beaumont Press, 1918. 1st edition; 125/120 copies (of an edition of 200), foolscap 8vo; printed on handmade paper, pages 41, (1); 10 wood engravings and cover design by Paul Nash; original quarter tan buckram, printed backstrip and front cover labels, backstrip label and corners trifle rubbed, untrimmed; good. Beaumont 5.   Blackwell's B112-18 1996 £60.00

DRINKWATER, JOHN 1882-1937   Peresphone: a Poem. New York: Rudge, 1926. One of 550 copies; large 8vo; printed in Centaur and Arrighi; black and gold medallion, gold initials and ornaments; black cloth, covers somewhat rubbed and marked, but internally very nice; with author's autograph signature.   Bertram Rota 272-413 1996 £60.00

DRINKWATER, JOHN 1882-1937   Swinburne: an Estimate. London: J. M. Dent/New York: E. P. Dutton, 1913. 1st edition; 8vo; decorative blue cloth, top edge gilt; very good; signed by author.   Antic Hay 101-474 1996 $125.00

DROWN, WILLIAM   Compendium of Agriculture or Farmer's Guide, in the Most Essential Parts of Husbandry and Gardening... Providence: Field & Maxcy, 1824. 1st edition; 8vo; 288 pages; uncut and unopened, paper backed original boards, paper label, little worn, fine. Imprints 16006; Rink 1305.   Second Life Books 103-73 1996 $225.00

DRUCE, GEORGE CLARIDGE   The Flora of Oxfordshire: Topographical and Historical Account of the Flowering Plants and Ferns in the County. London: Oxford University Press, 1927. 2nd edition; thick crown 8vo; pages 130, 538; original cloth.   Howes Bookshop 265-924 1996 £55.00

DRUMMOND, JAMES   Ancient Scottish Weapons. Edinburgh & London: 1881. Limited to 500 numbered copies; folio; 54 colored or tinted plates, few textual illustrations; original quarter morocco, sides little spotted.   Charles W. Traylen 117-231 1996 £300.00

DRUMMOND, JAMES   Ancient Scottish Weapons &c. A Series of Drawings... London: George Waterston & Sons, 1881. Limited to 500 copies; folio; pages 26, plus 54 full page colored lithographs; original morocco backed bevelled boards gilt, little marked, neatly recased. R.F.G. Hollett 76-79 1996 £350.00

DRUMMOND, THOMAS   Musci Scotici; or Dried Specimens of the Mosses that Have Been Discovered in Scotland. Volume 1 Only. London: c. 1800. 4to; 99 pages of mounted specimens; original boards with ties, backstrip missing.   Petersfield Bookshop FH58-238 1996 £70.00

DRYDEN, JOHN 1631-1700   Alexander's Feast. London: Essex House Press, 1904. Limited to 140 numbered copies printed on vellum; small 8vo; 14 pages; wood engraved hand colored frontispiece by Reginald Savage, text printed in black and red and initials supplied in red, blue, green and gold; original blindstamped vellum.   Thomas Thorp 489-92 1996 £300.00

DRYDEN, JOHN 1631-1700   All for Love, or the World Well Lost... Stourton Press, 1931, i.e. 1932. One of 8 copies printed on vellum (there were also 158 copies on paper); 11 1/2 x 9 inches; 12 p.l. (the first blank), 99 pages; woodcut headpieces by Eliot Hodgkin and Edward le Bas; printed in red and black; in publisher's special binding of fine russet morocco, gilt, cover panels formed by 3 pairs of double gilt rules, inner frame scalloped at corners to accommodate elegant fleurons as cornerpieces, front cover with pictorial crest representing Cleopatra and Mark Anthony, raised bands, spine with gilt ruled compartments and turn-ins; leather slightly marked with with minor soiling, two leaves with hint of yellowing, otherwise very fine.   Phillip J. Pirages 33-497 1996 $3,250.00

DRYDEN, JOHN 1631-1700   The Comedies, Tragedies and Operas. London: printed for Jacob Tonson, Bennet & Wellington, 1701. 1st edition; issue without frontispiece portrait; bound in present-day; 8 1/4 x 13 3/4 inches; 2 volumes; waterstain on volume 1 cover, otherwise fine. Lyman Books 21-544 1996 $125.00

DRYDEN, JOHN 1631-1700   The Dramatic Works. London: 1735/17 (vol 4) 6 volumes; illustrations; modern boards, leather labels, fine, most attractive set.   Stephen Lupack 83- 1996 $250.00

DRYDEN, JOHN 1631-1700   The Dramatic Works. London: Nonesuch Press, 1931. Number 564 of 750 sets (& 50 specials); large 8vo; 6 volumes; original green buckram backed marbled boards, top edge gilt, on the rough, others uncut and partly unopened, backstrips faded, but very good set, scarce. Dreyfus 80.   Claude Cox 107-105 1996 £165.00

DRYDEN, JOHN 1631-1700   Fables Ancient and Modern. London: Jacob Tonson, 1700. 1st edition; folio; half title present (blank right hand corner torn away with no loss), small tear to lower maring of title, not affecting text, slight staining to prelims, occasional spotting, final 4 leaves damaged with loss of a few letters, otherwise good; full contemporary calf, corners worn, recently rebacked to style, black morocco label. Wing D2278.   Ian Wilkinson 95/1-91 1996 £220.00

DRYDEN, JOHN 1631-1700   Fables Ancient and Modern. (with) Poems on Various Occasions. London: Jacob Tonson, 1700/01. 1st editions; folio; 2 works in 1 volume, (xliii), 646 pages, half title present as well as final leaf, often lacking; (ii), xvi, (iv, 232 pages; contemporary calf, later rebacked, joints and one corner repaired, little wear on edges, one small defect in calf, scattered paper browning, some leaves in "Poems" dampstained. Macdonald 61, 73a; Wing D2278.   Robert Clark 38-40 1996 £450.00

DRYDEN, JOHN 1631-1700   Of Dramatick Poesie, an Essay. London: printed By T. Warren for Henry Herringman, 1693. 4to; upper margins cropped close with loss or partial loss of some headlines, full 19th century calf by C. and C. McLeish; Wing D2329; MacDonald 127c. Jaggard p. 85. Lee, Shekespeareiana 256.   Anthony Laywood 108-7 1996 £125.00

DRYDEN, JOHN 1631-1700   The Poems... Oxford: Clarendon Press, 1958. 8vo; 4 volumes; frontispiece to volume 1; original bue cloth, gilt lettered, dust jackets, fine.   Blackwell's B112-89 1996 £100.00

DRYDEN, JOHN 1631-1700   Songs and Poems. Waltham St. Lawrence: Golden Cockerel Press, 1957. One of 100 special copies hand bound (out of a total edition of 500 copies); 15 x 10 1/4 inches; 64 pages; 8 full page illustrations and several black and white drawings and vignettes by Lavinia Blythe; this copy (no. 36, should have an extra suite of illustrations, but none is present); bound by Sangorski & Sutcliffe in original full morocco, half of each cover dyed russet and half dyed green, large stylized gilt vignettes on covers, gilt spine titling, hint of soil to binding, otherwise very fine.   Phillip J. Pirages 33-250 1996 $375.00

DRYDEN, JOHN 1631-1700   The Works. London: printed for William Miller, by James Ballantyne, Edinburgh, 1808. 8 3/4 x 5 3/4 inches; 18 volumes; frontispiece, one folding plate; very pleasing polished calf from the first third of the 19th century, sides with simple frame of double gilt fillets, spines densely gilt in compartments featuring many floral and foliate stamps, raised bands with oblique gilt hatching, olive and ochre morocco labels, very pretty gilt floral roll on board edges, marbled text block edges and endpapers, most volumes with at least some foxing, occasional gatherings with noticeable spotting, otherwise excellent internally, little wear to some spine ends, and to one corner, labels slightly faded, handful of covers lightly scratched or chafed, few other minor defects, but quite appealing set, nevertheless, with almost no wear to joints. Macdoanld p. 185.   Phillip J. Pirages 33-196 1996 $1,750.00

DUAINE, CARL   Caverns of Oblivion. Packrat: 1971. Number 480 of 500 copies, signed; 4to; 245 pages + index; illustrations;   Maggie Lambeth 30-152 1996 $100.00

DU BELLET, LOUIS P.   Some Prominent Virginia Families. Lynchburg: 1907. 1st edition; 4 volumes, over 1500 pages; unbound; scarce. Bookworm & Silverfish 280-65 1996 $125.00

DUBIN, ARTHUR D.   Some Classic Trains. Milwaukee: 1964. 1st edition; 4to; 434 pages; more than 1300 illutrations; dust jacket, very nice; presentation copy.   Edward Morrill 369-386 1996 $110.00

DU BOCCAGE, MARIE ANNE FIQUET   Letters Concerning England, Holland and Italy. London: printed for E. and C. Dilly, 1770. Small 8vo; 2 volumes; portrait; contemporary calf, rebacked.   Peter Murray Hill 185-52 1996 £135.00

DU BOIS, DOROTHEA   The Lady's Polite Secretary, or New Female Letter Writter. London: printed for J. Coote, 177-? 12mo; pages xxov. 273' contemporary sheep, rebacked.   Peter Murray Hill 185-53 1996 £100.00

DU BOIS, W. E. B.   The Correspondence of W. E. B. Dubois. Amherst: University of Massachusetts Press, 1973/76. 1st edition; 1st two volumes of this series; very slight wear, about fine (few pages bit creased in volume two), in lightly worn about fine dust jackets with little rubbing to volume two and slight discoloration to edge of volume one. Volume 2 is advance reievw copy with slip laid in.   Between the Covers 43-305 1996 $125.00

DU BOIS, W. E. B.   Darkwater. New York: Harcourt Brace, Howe, 1920. 1st edition; owner name on titlepage and name and bookplate under front flap, overall very good in supplied, nearly fine jacket, creased twice, attractive copy.   Ken Lopez 74-110 1996 $1,250.00

DU BOIS, W. E. B.   Encyclopedia of the Negro: Prepatory Volume with Reference Lists and Reports. New York: Phelps-Stokes Fund, 1946. 2nd edition; 8vo; 216, (2) pages, photo; cloth; near fine; the copy of Guy B. Johnson and signed by him.   Andrew Cahan 47-1 1996 $200.00

DU BOIS, W. E. B.   Mansart Builds a School. New York: Mainstream, 1959. 1st edition; light wear, near fine in attractive, very good dust jacket with couple of small internal repairs, signed by author and dated within a couple of months of publication.   Between the Covers 43-63 1996 $500.00

DU BOIS, W. E. B.   The Negro American Family. Atlanta: Atlanta University Press, 1908. 1st edition; faint crease to top corner of front wrapper and first few pages, still near fine with slight loss to foot of wrappers; very nice, fragile.   Between the Covers 43-306 1996 $200.00

DU BOIS, W. E. B.   The Negro. New York: Holt, 1915. 1st edition; slight creasing to a few page corners and bit of soiling, else near fine lacking rare dust jacket, uncommon title.   Between the Covers 43-304 1996 $250.00

DU BOIS, W. E. B.   The Souls of Black Folks. Chicago: McClurg, 1903. 2nd edition; printed a little more than a month after the first; slight tear to edge of one page, rebound in black cloth with black leather spine label gilt, touch of rubbing to label, else fine. Bookplate. Between the Covers 43-302 1996 $185.00

DU BOIS, W. E. B.   The Souls of Black Folks. London: Constable, 1905. 1st English edition from American sheets; frontispiece; crease on free front endpaper, where there is also a small, contemporary owner's name, else very lightly worn, about fine with gilt spine lettering bright, nice copy, scarce.   Between the Covers 43-304 1996 $250.00

DU BOSE, JOHN WITHERSPOON   General Joseph Wheeler and the Army of Tennessee. New York: Neale Pub. Co., 1912. 1st edition; 476 pages; plates; original cloth, minor rubbing to extremities, else near fine. Krick 120; Dornbusch II 3163; Howes D 523; not in Nevins.   McGowar Book Co. 65-27 1996 $450.00

DUBOST, ANTOINE   Hunt and Hope. London: printed for the author b Compton, n.d. 1st edition; 8vo; disbound; wanting half title, bit dusty, but very good copy of an uncommon title; eary pencilled margina notes (cropped) by an owner who seems to have known something about the incident.   Ximenes 108-211 1996 $400.00

DUBOUCHET, JEAN   Histoire Genealogique de la Maison Royale de Courtenay. Paris: J. Du Puis, 1661. Folio; 2 parts in 1, (12) leaves, 400, 262 pages; engraved title vignette, 5 engraved portraits, 2 double page folding engravings, numerous engravings and woodcuts in text; contemporary calf, gilt spine, front hinge cracked; some light foxing. Goldsmith D888; Brunet V 543; Univ. Cat. of Books on Art I 452. Jeffrey D. Mancevice 20-27 1996 $575.00

DUBUS, ANDRE   The Last Worthless Evening. Boston: Godine, 1986. Advance review copy; fine in jacket and signed by author.   Ken Lopez 74-113 1996 $125.00

DUBUS, ANDRE   The Lieutenant. New York: Dial, 1967. 1st edition; author's first book; fine in dust jacket with small tear; warmly inscribed by author.   Captain's Bookshelf 38-57 1996 $200.00

DUBUS, ANDRE   The Lieutenant. New York: Dial, 1967. 1st edition; author's uncommon first book; sticker removal abrasion of front pastedown and foxing to top edge, very good in very good jacket chipped at spine crown and along front spine fold.   Ken Lopez 74-11 1996 $175.00

DUBUS, ANDRE   Lieutenant. New York: Dial, 1967. 1st edition; author's uncommon first book; near fine in very good jacket and with several small chips along upper edge.   Ken Lopez 74-112 1996 $175.00

DUBUS, ANDRE   Selected Stories. Boston: Godine, 1990. Uncorrected proof, this if the full proof, printing the book's entire contents, and is much scarcer than the editions set to most reviewers which contained 10 of the stories; wrappers (marked 'press copy') and signed by author near fine.   Ken Lopez 74-114 1996 $200.00

DUBUS, ANDRE   Separate Flights. Boston: Godine, 1975. 1st edition; very good in dust jacket, signed by author.   Lame Duck Books 19-174 1996 $150.00

DU CAMBOUT DE PONT CHATEAU, SEBASTIAN JOSEPH   The Moral Practice of the Jesuites; Demonstrated by Many Remarkable Histories c Their Actions In All Parts of the World... London: Simon Miller, 1671. probably a reissue of the sheets of first English edition, printe dthe previous year, with new titlepage; 12mo; (xxxiv), 405, (iii) pages; recent quarter calf, marbled boards, gilt lettering; good, clean copy. Wing D2416.   Robert Clark 38-42 1996 £90.00

DUCAREL, ANDREW COLTEE   The History and Antiquities of the Archiepiscopal Palace of Lambeth, from Its Foundation to the Present Time. (with) The History and Antiquities of the Parish of Lambeth, in the County of Surrey... London: printed by and for J. Nichols, 1785/86. 4to; titles in 1 volume, pages x, 132, 72, 10 engraved plates, pages vii, 128, 164, 20 engraved plates; contemporary polished calf, spine very worn. H. M. Fletcher 121-95 1996 £225.00

DUCAREL, ANDREW COLTEE   Some Account of the Town, Church ar Archiepiscopal Palace of Croydon. London: printed by and for J. Nichol 1783. 4to; 3 leaves, 80 pages, 158 pages, 10 engraved plates, lacks ha title; half calf, marbled boards, gilt spine little rubbed. Upcott 1221. X. H. M. Fletcher 121-94 1996 £125.00

DU CHAILLU, PAUL B.   Explorations and Adventures in Equatorial Africa... New York: Harper & Bros., 1861. 1st U.S. edition; large 8vo; 5 pages + 4 pages of ads; 80 engravings, larage folding colored map (w repaired tear); original rust cloth, decoratively gilt spine, spine extremitie and corners slightly rubbed.   Kenneth Karmiole 1NS-1 1996 $150.00

DU CHAILLU, PAUL B.   In African Forest and Jungle. New York: Scribner,, 1903. 1st edition; Octavo; xii, 24 full page plates by Victor Perard; charming publisher's cloth binding of an elephant bathing, with gilt letters, light fading to front cover, else fine.   Bromer Booksellers 90-95 1996 $100.00

DU CHAILLU, PAUL B.   A Journey to Ashango-Land: and Further Penetration Into Equatorial Africa. New York: D. Appleton, 1867. 1st U.S. edition; tall 8vo; xxiv, 501, (2) pages ads; illustrations, large folding map at rear, name on endpaper; original green cloth, pictorial decoration in gilt in center of upper cover, some light rubbing to spine ends, still about fine.   David Mason 71-7 1996 $280.00

DUCHENNE, G. B.   Physiology of Motion Demonstrated by Means of Electrical Stimulation and Clinical Observation and Applied to the Study of Paralysis and Deformities. Philadelphia: 1949. 1st English translation; 612 pages; quarter leather, ex-library; GM 624 (Paris 1867).   W. Bruce Fye 71-577 1996 $175.00

DUCHENNE, G. B.   Selections from the Clinical Works of Dr. Duchenne. London: 1883. 1st edition; 472 pages; original binding dull, waterstain affecting inner margin of portrait, otherwise very good, ex-library. Haymaker 430.   W. Bruce Fye 71-578 1996 $150.00

DU CHESNE, ANDRE   Bibliotheque des Autheurs...de la France. Paris: Sebastien Cramoisy, 1618. 1st edition; 8vo; pages (iv), 236, Roman and Italic letter, printer's woodcut device on title, early 18th century ex-libris in ink at head; contemporary vellum over boards; Goldsmith D1123; Besterman 1064 & 1080.   A. Sokol XXV-29 1996 £985.00

DUCK, ARTHUR   The Thresher's Miscellany; or, Poems on Several Subjects. London: printed for A. Moore, 1731. 3rd edition; 8vo; pages (viii), 24; new half gilt; nice. All editions are scarce.   Peter Murray Hill 185-54 1996 £145.00

DUCK, STEPHEN   Poems on Several Occasions. London: printed for the author, 1736. 1st edition; 4to; contemporary calf, neatly rebacked, very good. Foxon p. 201; CBEL II 545.   Ximenes 108-115 1996 $450.00

DUDEK, LOUIS   East of the City (Poems). Toronto: Ryerson Press, 1946. 1st edition; 51 pages; boards, dust jacket; fine in near fine jacket; author's first book; with ownership signature of Wesley Scott; author's signed presentation to John Metcalf.   Nelson Ball 118-43 1996 $450.00

DUDEK, LOUIS   Patterns of Recent Canadian Poetry (an Essay). Quebec: Culture, 1958. Reprint; printed wrappers; very good, scarce; from the library of John Metcalf, with his ownership signature.   Nelson Ball 118-51 1996 $150.00

DUDLEY, DONALD R.   Urbs Roma: a Source Book of Classical Texts on the City and Its Monuments. London: Phaidon, 1967. 8vo; 339 pages; 110 illustrations; original cloth.   Archaeologia Luxor-3270 1996 $125.00

DUDLEY, JEBB SAMUEL   The Life of Robert Earl of Leicester the Favourite of Queen Elizabeth. London: Woodman and Lyon, 1727. 8vo; frontispiece, title in red and black; calf. Halkett & Laing III 361. Rostenberg & Stern 150-81 1996 $225.00

DUDLEY, ROBERT   Monthly Maxims. Rhymes and Reasons to Suit the Seasons and Pictures New to Suit Them Too. London: Thos. de la Rue & Co., 1882. 1st edition; 4to; pages 64; illustrations in color, with full page finely printed color plates, decorations around borders of verse, each leaf stiff quality card, original blue cloth, elaborately stamped with black, pictorial endpapers, all edges gilt, very fine.   Sotheran PN32-112 1996 £150.00

DUERER, ALBRECHT 1471-1528   Albert Durer's Designs of the Prayer Book. London: Ackermann, 1817. 1st edition; folio; (ii), 8, (2) pages; 43 plates; later half gold morocco, large, if not large paper copy; illustrations are extremely fine, scarce thus. Abbey Life 202; Friedman 120;   Bookpress 75-45 1996 $2,250.00

DUERER, ALBRECHT 1471-1528   Designs of the Prayer Book. London: Ackermann's Lithographic Press, 1817. Folio; title in red and black, full page portrait, reprodution of original 1st page, 43 ltihographed plates; quarter morocco; occasional slight dampstain; Graesse I 453. Rostenberg & Stern 150-102 1996 $675.00

DUFF, ALEXANDER   A Description of the Durga and Kali Festivals, Celebrated in Calcutta, at an Expense of Three Millions of Dollars. Troy: pub. by Caleb Wright, 1846. 1st edition; 8vo; woodcut illustrations; original green printed wrappers, slight wear to tips of spine; rather foxed, otherwise very good. 5 copies in NUC.   Ximenes 109-105 1996 $100.00

DUFFY, CHARLES G.   Young Ireland: a Fragment of Irish History 1840 to 1845 & Young Ireland, Part II: Or Four Years of Irish History, 1845-49. London: 1884/87. 8vo; 2 volumes in 1; xvi, 196; (xiv), 240 pages; illustrations; half calf, very good.   C. P. Hyland 216-187 1996 £52.00

DUFLOT DE MOFRAS, EUGENE b. 1810   Travels on the Pacific Coast. Santa Ana: Fine Arts Press, 1937. 1st edition in English; 2 volumes, pages xxxiv, 273; x, (2), 352; 4 plates and 5 maps; original half brown morocco, gilt lettering on spine, 2 corners slightly jammed, spines lightly rubbed, else fine set. Curtiss 30; Cowan p. 186; Graff 1169; Howes D542; Zamorano 80 30.   Argonaut Book Shop 113-213 1996 $425.00

DUFOUR, PHILIPPE SYLVESTRE   The Manner of Making of Coffee, Tea and Chocolate. London: printed for William Crook, 1685. 1st edition in English; 12mo; contemporary calf, bit worn, morocco slipcase; excellent copy, prelim leaf of ads. Wing D2454; Bitting p. 134; Cagle, A Matter of Taste 654; Sabin 11788.   Ximenes 109-106 1996 $3,000.00

DU FRESNOY, CHARLES ALPHONSE 1611-1665   The Art of Painting. London: printed for Bernard Lintott, 1716. 2nd edition; small 8vo; lxviii, (4), 397, (7) pages; contemporary brown calf, decoratively blind tooled and with spine in 6 compartments, modest external wear, bookplates, else good, internally very clean; with engraved heraldic bookplate and ownership signature of early Virginia historian William Stith. Interesting association.   Chapel Hill 94-53 1996 $500.00

DU FRESNOY, CHARLES ALPHONSE 1611-1665   The Art of Painting, with Remarks. London: for B. L. and sold by William Taylor, 1716. 2nd edition; foolscap 8vo; (16), lxviii, (4), 397, (7) pages; frontispiece and decorative head and tailpieces; contemporary panelled calf, neatly rebacked, retaining original spine, but with new red gilt label; some minor worming to upper margins, neatly repaired on first few leaves, and disappearing to a single hole by p. 25 of the preface.   Ken Spelman 30-3 1996 £120.00

DU FRESNOY, CHARLES ALPHONSE 1611-1665   The Art of Painting... Dublin: ptd. for Messrs. Whitestone, Wilson, Moncrieffe, Walker, Jenkin... 1783. 1st Dublin edition of this translation; contemporary tree calf, rubbed; ownership inscription on half title.   Anthony W. Laywood 109-40 1996 £75.00

DUGDALE, FLORENCE   The Book of Baby Beasts. London: Henry Frowde Hodder and Stoughton, 1911. 1st edition; 4to; pages (viii), 9-119, 19 delicately colored mounted plates; original yellow cloth backed boards with onlaid pictorial label to upper cover, just slightly scuffed at upper cover, otherwise excellent copy, internally fine.   Sotheran PN32-109 1996 £128.00

DUGDALE, WILLIAM 1605-1686   The History of St. Paul's Cathedral in London, From Its Foundation Until These Times... London: T. Warren, 1658. 1st edition; folio; 3 ff., 299 pages (numbering irregularities), 3 ff., 46 text engravings and engraved plates, including portrait, most by Hollar, large folding plate with small hole and old repair; contemporary mottled calf spine gilt, label, upper hinge starting; Very presentable copy. Wing D2482; Adams 8; cf. Pennington.   Marlborough 162-134 1996 £1,000.00

DUHAMEL DU MONCEAU, HENRI LOUIS 1700-1781   The Elements of Agriculture... London: printed for P. Vaillant, & T. Durham; and R. Baldwin, 1764. 1st English edition; 8vo; 2 volumes, perforation and cancellation stamps on blank verso of titles, 14 folding engraved plates (plate VII of volume II slightly offset), contemporary calf, rebacked, labels. Fussell pp. 48-9; Kress S4335.   Anthony W. Laywood 109-41 1996 £395.00

DUHAMEL DU MONCEAU, HENRI LOUIS 1700-1781   A Practical Treatise of Husbandry... London: 1762. 2nd edition; 4to; pages xxiv, 489, (1), (index 6 pages); 6 copperplates, plus folding chart; contemporary full tan calf, 5 raised bands, gilt rules and red leather label, spine chipped, worn at extremities, outer hinges splitting, although the book is solid, top inch of titlepage clipped, flyleaf nearly loose, bookplate, internally clean.   Raymond M. Sutton VII-10 1996 $425.00

DUHEME, JACQUELINE   Birthdays. San Francisco: Determined Productions, 1966. folio; 6 full page water color illustrations by Jacqueline Duheme; printed on glazed purple paper lettered in white on left hand pages with illustrations on facing pages; purple boards pictorially printed in white, edges of boards slightly faded, else very fresh in matching pictorial dust jacket.   Barbara Stone 70-82 1996 £55.00

DUKE, BASIL WILSON   Morgan's Cavalry. New York: Neale Pub. Co., 1906. 1st edition thus; 441 pages; Coleman 1177; Dornbusch III 1230a; Howes D548; Nicholson p. 251.   McGowan Book Co. 65-28 1996 $350.00

DUKE, THOMAS S.   Celebrated Criminal Cases of America. San Francisco: James H. Barry Co., 1910. Brown cloth, gilt, rubbed and worn, sound only.   Meyer Boswell SL25-74 1996 $125.00

DULAC, EDMUND   Edmund Dulac's Fairy-Book. London: Hodder & Stoughton, 1916. 1st edition deluxe, limited to only 350 numbered copies, singed by Dulac; a4to; pages (xii), 169; 15 fine colored plates mounted within gilt borders by Dulac; original white buckram, stamped with blue and gilt, uncut, lower cover and spine cloth little discolored, prelims and endleaves faintly browned, very nice, scarce.   Sotheran PN32-117 1996 £598.00

DULAC, EDMUND   A Fairy Garland Being Fairy Tales from the old French. London: 1928. Limited edition, 626/1000 copies, signed by Dulac; 12 color plates by Dulac; vellum, spine gilt lettering, top edge gilt, uncut, silk ties; contents fine, covers near fine.   Polyanthos 22-450 1996 $250.00

DULAC, EDMUND   Lyrcis Pathetic and Humorous from A to Z. London: Frederick Warne & Co., 1908. 1st edition; 4to; pages 95); large colored plates to every leaf; original cloth backed pictorial boards, stamped in colors, pictorial endpapers, spine lightly dust soiled, little minor wear to bevelled fore-edge, generally an unusually fresh and clean copy.   Sotheran PN32-113 1996 £498.00

DULAC, EDMUND   Picture-Book for the French Red Cross. London: published for the Daily Telegraph, 1915. 1st edition; 4to; pages (viii), 134, (ii), 19 mounted colored plates by Edmund Dulac; original yellow cloth printed in green; extremely fine.   Sotheran PN32-116 1996 £88.00

DULAC, EDMUND   The Sleeping Beauty and Other Fairy Tales. London: n.d., c. 1910. Limited to 1000 copies, signed by artist, this being number 696; large 4to; tipped in color plates by Dulac; full brown morocco, gilt, spine defective rendering the book in need of rebacking at least, possibly rebinding.   Words Etcetera 94-373 1996 £175.00

DUMAS, ALEXANDRE 1825-1895   Camile. Ptd. by the Curwen Press for Members of the Limited Editions Club, 1937. One of 1500 copies, signed by the artist; 11 x 9 inches; xi, (1) (blank) pages, (1) leaf, 213, (1) (blank) pages, (1) leaf (colophon); 12 watercolors by Marie Laurencin, printed in process collotype by Chiswick Press, tissue guards; original white linen, gilt rose on front cover, titled in gilt on spine, in publisher's (slightly soiled but sound) slipcase; very fine; small oval leather bookplate of Arthur Wilmer Lissauer. Quarto Millenary 93.   Phillip J. Pirages 33-357 1996 $350.00

DUMAS, ALEXANDRE 1825-1895   Camille. London: Limited Editions Club, 1937. Copy number 904 from a total edition of 1500 numbered copies, signed by artist; 12 drawings by Marie Laurencin; cloth with slightly chipped paper jacket and slightly sunned, and dusty publisher's slipcase.   Hermitage SP95-976 1996 $600.00

DUMAS, ALEXANDRE 1825-1895   Camille. London: Limited Editions Club, 1937. Limited to 1500 copies, signed by artist; 4to; drawings by Marie Laurencin; original cream buckram, slipcase, fine in lightly worn slipcase.   James S. Jaffe 34-696 1996 $500.00

DU MAURIER, DAPHNE   Rebecca. New York: Doubleday Doran, 1938. 1st American edition; one of an unspecified number of copies issued with page signed by author; couple of tiny, insignificant spots to top edge, else fine in very good dust jacket with triangular chip on front panel, some slight loss at crown and some overall rubbing.   Between the Covers 42-150 1996 $350.00

DU MAURIER, GEORGE 1834-1896   Trilby. London: Osgood, McIlvaine & Co., 1895. One of 250 copies signed by author; 11 x 8 1/4 inches; x pages, (1) leaf, 447 pages; 121 illustrations by author; quarter vellum, buckram sides, top edge gilt, other edges untrimmed and unopened; binding slightly scratched on rear cover, just slightly soiled, but showing almost no wear, internally mint; fine.   Phillip J. Pirages 33-197 1996 $750.00

DU MAURIER, GEORGE 1834-1896   Works. London: 1892-98. 1st uniform edition, 1st edition; 8vo; 3 volumes; illustrations by author; choicely bound in full blue calf, red leather labels, gilt tops by Zaehnsdorf; original cloth covers bound in; superb set.   Charles W. Traylen 117-114 1996 £250.00

DUMMER, JEREMIAH 1681-1739   A Defence of the New-England Charters. Boston: Re-printed by B. Green and Comp. for D. Gookin, 1745. 2nd American edition; 8vo; (4), 44 pages; woodcut decorations; 19th century brown calf over marbled boards, black morocco spine label, extremities lightly rubbed, top margin trimmed rather closely. Howes D554.   Kenneth Karmiole 1NS-11 1996 $300.00

DUNBAR, FLANDERS   Emotions and Bodily Changes: a Survey of the Literature on Psychosomatic Interrelationships. New York: Columbia University Press, 1935. 1st edition; 8vo; (ii), (xviii), 595, (5) pages; blue green buckram, very good in lightly worn dust jacket.   John Gach 150-133 1996 $100.00

DUNBAR, PAUL LAURENCE   Poems of Cabin and Field. New York: Dodd Mead, 1899. 1st edition; photos; slight stain, barely noticeable amongst the decoration of the front board, still fine, handsome copy.   Between the Covers 43-67 1996 $150.00

DUNBAR, PAUL LAURENCE   I Greet the Dawn. New York: Atheneum, 1978. 1st edition; illustrations; fine in near fine dust jacket, slighty faded on spine and with some light soiling, very nicely inscribed by Ashley Bryan who provided introduction.   Between the Covers 43-228 1996 $125.00

DUNBAR, PAUL LAURENCE   Lyrics of Lowly Life. New York: Dodd, 1896. 1st edition; 1st issue; frontispiece guard darkened and has offset onto titlepage as well as small, neat name also on titlepage, still especially ncie copy with virtually none of the wear associated with this book.   Between the Covers 43-66 1996 $450.00

DUNBAR, PAUL LAURENCE   Speaking' O' Christmas New York: Dodd, Mead, 1914. 1st edition; numerous illustrations; 1st issue binding, slight foxing to gutters and boards, neat bookplate and contemporary gift inscription, at least very good, surprisingly scarce collection.   Between the Covers 43-68 1996 $485.00

DUNCAN, ANDREW   The Edinburgh New Dispensatory, Containing I. The Elemtns of Pharmaceutical Chemistry. II. The Materia Medica... III. The Pharmaceutical Preparations and Compositions... Worcester: from the Press of Isaiah Thomas, Jr., 1805. 1st Worcester edition; 8vo; xii, 694 pages; 6 plates; contemporary tree calf, red leather spine label, edges bit rubbed, very nice.   Kenneth Karmiole 1NS-178 1996 $300.00

DUNCAN, DAVID JAMES   The River Why. San Francisco: Sierra Club, 1983. Uncorrected proof; author's first book fine in wrappers.   Ken Lopez 74-116 1996 $100.00

DUNCAN, HARRY   Doors of Perception; Essays in Book Typography. Austin: W. Thomas Taylor, 1983. One of 325 copies, signed by author; 8vo; designed by Carol J. Blinn at Warwick Press and printed in perpetua in black and brown on Frankfurt Cream by Daniel Keleher; hand bound by Sarah Creighton and C. J. Blinn in quarter grey Niger goatskin with boards covered in Blinn's pasted papers. Fine.   Bertram Rota 272-487 1996 £75.00

DUNCAN, HARRY   Doors of Perception: Essays in Book Typography. Austin: W. Thomas Taylor, 1983. One of 325 copies, signed by author; 9 x 6 inches; 99 pages; leather backed paste paper covered boards; fine. Timothy Hawley 115-49 1996 $125.00

DUNCAN, JOHN M.   Travels through Part of the United States and Canada in 1818 and 1819. Glasgow: printed at the University Press, for Hurst, Robinson & Co.... 1823. 1st edition; 8vo; 2 volumes; 14 woodcut maps; contemporary half red straight grained morocco, spines gilt, minor rubbing; fine, attractive copy with half titles; Sabin 21259; Howes D561; TPL 1165.   Ximenes 108-116 1996 $500.00

DUNCAN, LOUIS   Medical Men in the American Revolution. New York: 1970. 1st edition; 414 pages; original binding, very scarce.   W. Bruce Fye 71-582 1996 $100.00

DUNCAN, P. M.   The British Fossil Corals. Second Series. London: 1866-72. 4to; pages vii, iii, 66, 46, 24, 73, 49 plates; cloth, fine.   John Henly 27-758 1996 £90.00

DUNCAN, ROBERT   Notebook Poems: 1953. San Francisco: Press in Tuscany Alley, 1991. One of 90 copies from a total issue of 100; signed and numbered by artist; page size 9 3/4 x 12 1/4 inches; drawings by Jess Collins; terra cotta handmade wrappers by Robert Serpa's Oakland Paper Foundery who made the Tuscany Alley watermark paper for the text.   Priscilla Juvelis 95/1-202 1996 $225.00

DUNCAN, ROBERT   A Paris Visit. Grenfell Press, 1985. One of 115 copies, signed by author and artist (of total edition of 130); 13 3/4 x 9 3/4 inches; (14) leaves; 10 full page drawings by Kitaj, printed partly in red on heavily textured handmade Indian paper; scarlet morocco backed pictorial paper boards, edges untrimmed, mint.   Phillip J. Pirages 33-270 1996 $275.00

DUNCAN, THOMAS D.   Recollections of Thomas D. Duncan, a Confederate Soldier. Nashville: McQuiddy Print Co., 1922. 1st edition; 213 pages; illustrations; original printed stiff brown wrappers, minor chipping, fine. Dornbusch II 2703; Coulter Travels in Conf. States 139.   Michael D. Heaston 23-141 1996 $225.00

DUNCKLEE, WALES & CO.   The Daily Advertiser Directory for the City of Detroit for the Year 1850. Detroit: 1850. 7.5 x 5 inches; 269 pages plus ads; leather backed printed boards, ink name on title, top of spine slightly chipped, worn, but generally nice copy.   John K. King 77-140 1996 $150.00

DUNGLISON, ROBLEY   History of Medicine from the Earliest Ages to the Commencement of the Nineteenth Century. Philadelphia: 1872. 1st edition; 287 pages; original binding.   W. Bruce Fye 71-584 1996 $150.00

DUNGLISON, ROBLEY   Human Physiology. Philadelphia: 1846. 6th edition; large 8vo; 2 volumes, 268 illustrations; contemporary sheep, rubbed.   Argosy 810-157 1996 $175.00

DUNGLISON, ROBLEY   Medical Lexicon. A Dictionary of Medical Science. Philadelphia: 1874. New edition; 1131 pages; full leather.   W. Bruce Fye 71-585 1996 $100.00

DUNKIN, ROBERT   The Impossible Island. 1923. illustrations; fine in frayed/protected dust jacket, scarce and very hard to find with jacket. David Grayling J95Biggame-576 1996 £75.00

DUNKIN, ROBERT   The Roedeer. A Monograph. 1987. Limited to 150 copies, signed by McReddie and Mckelvie; new color frontispiece, other plates; with original pencil sketch of a roe buck by artist on front endpaper; finely bound in half green morocco, gilt emblem on upper cover and housed in buckram slipcase; mint.   David Grayling J95Biggame-317 1996 £150.00

DUNLAP, WILLIAM   The Father of an Only Child, a Comedy. New York: published by David Longworth, 1807. 1st edition thus; 12mo; disbound; some foxing, but very good. BAL 5001. Hill 79; Shaw & Shoemaker 12479.   Ximenes 108-117 1996 $150.00

DUNLAP, WILLIAM   The Father of an Only Child, a Comedy. New York: published by David Longworth, 1807. 1st edition thus; 12mo; disbound; some foxing, but very good. BAL 5001; Hill 79; Shaw and Shoemaker 12479.   Ximenes 108-117 1996 $150.00

DUNLOP, DURHAM   The Philosophy of Bath; or, Air and Water in Health and Disease. Belfast: Simpkin, Marshall, 1868. 1st edition; 8vo; pages xiv, 465; original binding, spine faded and inside hinges weak, still nice.   James Fenning 133-95 1996 £65.00

DUNN, KATHERINE   Truck. New York: Harper, 1971. 1st edition; author's 2nd book; fine in fine dust jacket.   Pettler & Lieberman 28-80 1996 $125.00

DUNNING, JOHN   Booked to Die. New York: Scribners, 1992. 1st edition; perfect copy in dust jacket, signed by author.   Bud Schweska 12-943 1996 $225.00

DUNNING, JOHN   Booked to Die. New York: Scribners, 1992. 1st edition; wrappers with two small spots on back panel; fine, signed. Book Time 2-589 1996 $200.00

DUNNING, JOHN   Booked to Die. New York: Scribners, 1992. 1st edition; fine in fine dust jacket.   Book Time 2-598 1996 $125.00

DUNNING, RICHARD   A Letter Sent to Mr. James Shepheard, Whilst Prisoner in Newgate, Persuading Him to Repent to His Design to Murder the King. London: printed for J. Roberts, 1718. Sole edition; 8vo; half title, 37 pages; disbound, lacking final ad leaf.   David Bickersteth 133-19 1996 £185.00

DUNSANY, EDWARD JOHN MORETON DRAX PLUNKETT 1878-1957   The Sword of Welleran and Other Stories. London: George Allen and Sons, 1907. 1st edition; illustrations by Sime; beautifully bound in contemporary full green coarse grained morocco with double gilt rules on panels and gilt devices in compartments, gilt dentelles, top edge gilt.   Captain's Bookshelf 38-58 1996 $150.00

DUNSTERVILLE, G. C. K.   Venezuelan Orchids Illustrated. London: 1959. 4to; pages 448; 216 illustrations; cloth, dust jacket (chipped and with small tears);   Raymond M. Sutton VI-889 1996 $105.00

DUNTHORNE, GORDON   Flower and Fruit Prints of the 18th and Early 19th Centuries... Washington: 1938. One of 2500 copies from the original edition; tall 4to; pages xiv, 275, (1); 78 illustrations, 71 full page reproductions; buckram, some scuffing to title plate and spine ends, spine darkened, backstrip title chipped, some smudging to front endpaper, slipcase (with edge wear).   Raymond M. Sutton VI-10 1996 $550.00

DUNTON, JOHN   The Athenian Oracle. Being an Entire Collection of All the Valuable Questions and Answers in the Old Athenian Mercuries. London: J. and J. Knapton & 6 others, 1728. 3rd edition; 8vo; 4 volumes, (ii), 532,(xviii); (viii), 554, (xxii); (ii), 562, (xxii); (ii), 487, (xv) pages; contemporary calf, uniformly rebacked in morocco, gilt lettering, library numbers on spines, stamps on titlepage and last leaf of each volume, no other markings, bit rubbed, minor browning. Sound set. Robert Clark 38-172 1996 £175.00

DUPIN, JACQUES   Miro. New York: Abrams, n.d. 4to; 580 pages, 1158 illustrations, including 46 tipped in color plates; cloth, dust jacket. Freitag 6565.   Brannan 43-422 1996 $225.00

DUPIN, JACQUES   Miro Engravings. New York: Rizzoli, 1989. Folio; 2 volumes, 184; 232 pages; 605 color illustrations in catalog, plus illustrations in text and original woodcuts; cloth, dust jackets.   Brannan 43-423 1996 $475.00

DUPIN, JACQUES   Miro Engraver. Volume I, 1928-1960. New York: Rizzoli, 1989. 1st edition; 3 original woodcuts; fine in lightly soiled dust jacket.   Hermitage SP95-774 1996 $150.00

DU PONT, SAMUEL FRANCIS   Samuel Francis Du Pont a Selection from His Civil War Letters. Ithaca: Cornell University Press, 1969. 1st edition; 3 volumes; original cloth, near fine set.   McGowan Book Co. 65-26 1996 $125.00

DUPPA, RICHARD 1770-1831   A Journal of the Most Remarkable Occurrences that Took Place in Rome; Upon the Supervision of the Ecclesiastical Government in 1798. London: for G. G. and J. Robinson, 1799. 8vo; viii, 149, (3) pages, half title and final errata leaf; uncut in contemporary roan backed boards, head of spine neatly repaired, but joints rubbed and corners bumped, new front endpaper.   Ken Spelman 30-24 1996 £85.00

DURAND, EDWARD   Rifle, Rod and Spear in the East. 1911. illustrations; original pictorial gilt buckram, spine faded.   David Grayling J95Biggame-369 1996 £55.00

DURANTE, CASTORE   Herbario Nuovo...con Figure che Rappresentatno le vive Piante che Nascono in Tutta Europa & Nell Indie Orientali & Occidentali... Venice: Presso Michele Hertz, 1718. Folio; 4 leaves, 480 pages, 14 leaves, profusely illustrated with woodcuts, short tear to inner margin of title and small piece missing from blank fore margin; contemporary calf, rubbed.   H. M. Fletcher 121-96 1996 £750.00

DURET, THEODORE   Whistler et son Oeuvre. Paris: Boussod, Valadon, 1888. Limited to 25 copies on Japon, quarto; 16 pages; illustrated with four examples of Whistler's work, including two original etchings; covers show wear, still internally fine. Kennedy, Etched Work of Whistler 1978. Bromer Booksellers 87-277 1996 $1,500.00

D'URFEY, THOMAS 1653-1723   New Opera's, with Comical Stories and Poems on Several Occasions, Never Before Printed... London: printed for William Chetwood, 1721. 8vo; some light staining of upper margins of first 60 pages; contemporary panelled calf, worn, hinges cracked, Foxon p. 208;   Anthony Laywood 108-54 1996 £175.00

D'URFEY, THOMAS 1653-1723   Stories, Moral and Comical. Viz. The Banquet of the Gods. Titus and Gissipus; or the Power of Friendship. London: printed by Fr. Leach and sold by Isaac Cleave, n.d. 1707. 1st edition; no half title, name on title, ad leaf after dedication, ad leaf at end; new half calf, label.   Anthony Laywood 108-55 1996 £245.00

DURHAM, W. E.   Summer Holidays in the Alps. 1898-1914. London: 1916. 1st edition; 49 plates; gilt on green, some light rubbing, inner hinges reinforced, but very good copy; bookplates of Manchester Central Library and Rucksack Club, small label inscribed 'Presented by A. R. Thompson/Jany 1917". Few neat circular stamps of Rucksack Club. Moutaineering Books 8-RD01 1996 £60.00

DURIE, JOHN   Confvtatio Responsionis Gvlielmi VVitakeri. Paris: Brumennius, 1582. Thick 8vo; calf and vellum; Revd. H. Campbell and Bib. Mai. Heythrop booktickets.   Rostenberg & Stern 150-82 1996 $425.00

DURLING, RICHARD   A Catalogue of Sixteenth Century Printed books in the National Library of Medicine. Bethesda: 1967. 1st edition; 698 pages; original binding. GM 6786.9.   W. Bruce Fye 71-590 1996 $150.00

DURNING-LAWRENCE, EDWIN   Bacon is Shakespeare. New York: McBride, 1910. 1st edition; page 95 torn and tape repaired by F. Scott Fitzgerald, a fact acknowledged and apologized for by him in his hand on appropriate page "F Scott Fitzgerald did this and is very sorry"; well worn, hingres cracked, at least one endpaper missing; overall, at best, a good copy.   Ken Lopez 74-138 1996 $1,500.00

DURRELL, LAWRENCE GEORGE 1912-1990   The Alexandria Quartet. London: Faber & Faber, 1962. One of 500 numbered copies, signed by Durrell on tipped in leaf; fine in cardboard slipcase with rubbing to extremities and edges.   Lame Duck Books 19-175 1996 $950.00

DURRELL, LAWRENCE GEORGE 1912-1990   The Alexandria Quartet. London: Faber & Faber, 1962. 1st one volume collection; one of 500 numbered copies, signed by author on tipped in leaf. top edge gilt; near fine in rubbed but near fine slipcase.   Ken Lopez 74-117 1996 $950.00

DURRELL, LAWRENCE GEORGE 1912-1990   The Alexandria Quartet. London: Faber and Faber, 1962. 1st collected edition; number 193 of 500 copies, signed by author; 8vo; 884 pages; original orange buckram with black handprint motif on upper cover, spine blocked in black and gilt, top edge gilt; spine trifle faded as usual, very nice in clear plastic wrapper and slipcase as issued.   Sotheran PN32-10 1996 £498.00

DURRELL, LAWRENCE GEORGE 1912-1990   The Alexandria Quartet. Justine. Balthazar. Mountolive. Clea. London: Faber & Faber, 1962. One of 500 specially bound and numbered copies, signed by author; 1st one volume edition; fine in lightly rubbed slipcase.   Captain's Bookshelf 38-59 1996 $750.00

DURRELL, LAWRENCE GEORGE 1912-1990   Beccafico. La Licorne: 1963. One of 150 copies, signed by author, this copy being marked hors commerce by the translator; wrappers, small mark on upper cover, spine and fore edges of covers browned, very good.   Ulysses 39-163 1996 £150.00

DURRELL, LAWRENCE GEORGE 1912-1990   The Black Book. London: Faber & Faber, 1973. Uncorrected proof copy of the first English edition; 8vo; printed wrappers, uncommon; near fine, moderate sunning to spine. Antic Hay 101-494 1996 $100.00

DURRELL, LAWRENCE GEORGE 1912-1990   Collected Poems. London: 1980. Limited edition of 26 lettered copies, with signed etching by Henry Moore as frontispiece, signed by author; bound in full blue niger morocco, preserved in slipcase; fine.   Words Etcetera 94-960 1996 £450.00

DURRELL, LAWRENCE GEORGE 1912-1990   Collected Poems: 1931-1974. London: Bernard Stone, 1980. 2nd edition, one of 100 copies; this issue contains an original signed etching by Henry Moore bound in as frontispiece; full oasis goatskin stamped in silver, very fine in slipcase, with prospectus laid in; signed by author.   Captain's Bookshelf 38-60 1996 $1,250.00

DURRELL, LAWRENCE GEORGE 1912-1990   Deus Loci, a Poem by Lawrence Durrell. Ischia: Di Maio Vito, 1950. 1st edition; one of 200 copies, signed by author; 12mo; 10 pages; grey printed wrpapers, fine, uncut copy, rare. Thomas A18.   Bromer Booksellers 90-29 1996 $650.00

DURRELL, LAWRENCE GEORGE 1912-1990   Deus Loci. Ischia: privately printed, 1950. Limited edition, one of 200 copies, this not numbered, signed by author; 8 pages; red wrappers, spine slightly faded, otherwise very good. Brigham A18.   Virgo Books 48-68 1996 £250.00

DURRELL, LAWRENCE GEORGE 1912-1990   Deus Loci. A Poem. Ischia: the author, 1950. 1st edition; one of 200 copies, signed by author; small 8vo; printed pale green wrappers, fine.   James S. Jaffe 34-141 1996 $350.00

DURRELL, LAWRENCE GEORGE 1912-1990   Deus Loci. Ischia: 1950. Limited to 200 copies, signed by author; wrappers; fine.   Words Etcetera 94-383 1996 £150.00

DURRELL, LAWRENCE GEORGE 1912-1990   Justine. New York: Dutton, 1957. 1st American edition; fine in dust jacket with very little rubbing to spine, lovely copy.   Between the Covers 42-151 1996 $125.00

DURRELL, LAWRENCE GEORGE 1912-1990   Nurse and Mistress of the Crossroads; Arles and the Alyscamps. London: privately printed, Alyscamps Press, 1993. Limited to 50 copies; mint in dust jacket; signature of Karl Orend who provides introduction.   Virgo Books 48-69 1996 £60.00

DURRELL, LAWRENCE GEORGE 1912-1990   Private Drafts. Nicosia: the author, 1955. 1st edition; one of 100 copies; 12mo; signed by author; pictorial wrappers; fine.   James S. Jaffe 34-142 1996 $450.00

DURRELL, LAWRENCE GEORGE 1912-1990   Spirit of Place: Letters and Essays on Travel. London: Faber & Faber, 1969. Uncorrected proof; 8vo; printed wrappers; near fine, in custom made slipcase.   Antic Hay 101-504 1996 $125.00

DURRELL, LAWRENCE GEORGE 1912-1990   Vega and Other Poems. London: Faber & Faber ltd., 1973. 1st edition original binding, top edge spotted, very good in nicked and slightly rubbed, marked and dusty dust jacket; signed and dated 1974 by author.   Ulysses 39-164 1996 £75.00

DUSSAUCE, H.   A New and Complete Treatise on the Arts of Tanning, Currying, and Leather Dressing... Philadelphia: 1867. 2nd edition; 9.5 x 6 inches; 596 pages; 212 wood engravings; cloth, stamped names of leather manufacturer, some stianing, covers well worn and frayed, scarce.   John K. King 77-720 1996 $100.00

DUTENS, LOUIS   An Inquiry into the Origin of the Discoveries Attributed to the Moderns... London: printed for W. Griffin, 1769. 1st English edition; 8vo; 4 parts in 1; contemporary calf, rebacked, label. Babson 51 (1st ed. 1766).   Anthony Laywood 108-56 1996 £150.00

DUTT, UDAY CHAND   The Materia Medica of the Hindus. Calcutta: 1922. Revised edition; text bit browned, half cloth, soiled.   Maggs Bros. Ltd. 1190-403 1996 £85.00

DUTTON, CLARENCE E.   Tertiary History of the Grand Canyon District. Salt Lake City: Peregrine Smith, 1970's. Reprint, itself, long out of print; 2 volumes; text and atlas, both as new in sipcases and shrinkwrap. Parker Books of the West 30-55 1996 $350.00

DUTTON, HELY   Statistical Survey of the County Clare. London: 1808. 1st edition; map; half calf, very good; ex-library C. Coote, author, of a number of other 'Stat Surveys'.   C. P. Hyland 216-195 1996 £300.00

DUVOISIN, ROGER   The Happy Hunter New York: Lothrop, Lee and Shepard, 1961. 1st edition; small oblong 4to; colored illustrations by Duvoisin; colored pictorial boards; fine in original pictorial dust jacket. Inscribed by Roger Duvoisin to Maria Cimino.   Barbara Stone 70-87 1996 £65.00

DUYCKINCK, EVERET A.   Memorial of John Allan. New York: printed for the Bradford Club, 1864. 1st edition; one of 250 copies; large 8vo; portrait; original grey printed wrappers, edges chipped, some wear to spine; aside from some wear to flimsy wrappers, very good. Sabin 21503.   Ximenes 109-108 1996 $200.00

DUYCKINCK, EVERT A.   National Portrait Gallery of Eminent Americans. New York: Johnson, Fry & Co., 1862. 4to; 2 volumes, 119 full page engravings, some foxing; full red leather, elaborate gilt designs, some scuffing. Howes D606.   Blue River Books 9-130 1996 $300.00

DWIGGINS, W. A.   The Glistening Hill. Athalinthia III. Puterschein-Hingham, 1950. Small octavo; 30 pages; printed in WAD's Winchester type; stiff wrappers with wraparound label; very fine. Agner 50.04.   Bromer Booksellers 90-30 1996 $140.00

DWIGHT, E. W.   Memoir of Henry Obookiah, a Native of the Sandwich Islands, Who Died at Cornwall, Connecticut, Feb. 17, 1818 aged 26. New York: American Tract Society, n.d., c. 1830's. Revised edition; 16mo; (7), 8-124 pages; frontispiece with tissue guard; original leather backed marbled boards, gilt lettered spine, covers somewhat rubbed, foot of spine with bit of wear, some very light internal foxing, overall fine copy of this fragile book. Hill p. 92.   Argonaut Book Shop 113-219 1996 $150.00

DWIGHT, TIMOTHY   Greenfield Hill: a Poem, in Seven Parts. (with) The Triumph of Infidelity: a Poem. New York: 1794/88. 1st edition; 12mo; 183, (1); 40 pages; bound together in later boards (very worn, hinges split), second work is bound in prior to the notes for the first work, but both are complete. BAL 5048, 5041 printin a. Wegelin 130, 129; Evans 26925, 21065.   M & S Rare Books 60-151 1996 $375.00

DWINELLE, JOHN W.   The Colonial History of the City of San Francisco... San Francisco: Towne and Bacon, 1866. 3rd edition; xlv, (1), 34, (2), 106, 391 pages, with pages 363*-(370*) inserted after p. (366); 3 lithographed plates, one single map; with 2 errata slips preceding pages xlv and 365; original three quarter black morocco, gilt lettered spine, marbled boards, very slight rubbing to extremities, corners lightly worn, inner front hinge cracked (cords strong), overall fine; with bookplate of James Phelan (mayor of San Francisco & U.S. Senator); Cowan p. 75-76; Graff 1189; Howes D614; Rocq 7961; Zamorano 80 32.   Argonaut Book Shop 113-220 1 996 $1,500.00

DWINELLE, JOHN W.   The Colonial History of San Francisco. San Diego: City Attorney of San Diego, 1924. Reprint of 1863 1st ed.; 102, 115, ix pages; frontispiece map; original printed wrappers, contemporary owner's name in ink on lower portion of front cover, else fine. for first ed. see Cowan p. 189; Howes D614; Rocq 7959. Zamorano 80 32. Argonaut Book Shop 113-221 1996 $125.00

DWYER, CHARLES P.   The Economy of Church, Parsonage and School Architecture, Adapted to Small Societies and Rural Districts. Buffalo: Phinney & Co., 1856. 1st and only edition; 8vo; vi, (7)-95 pages; 40 plates; publisher's cloth, sporadic foxing, else very good; with A. C. Bicknell's rubber stamp on endpaper.   Bookpress 75-46 1996 $500.00

DWYER, P. W.   The Shield of the United Kingdom of Great Britain and Ireland. London: printed by J. Galton for the author, 1803. 1st edition; 4to; no half title, 23 pages; disbound.   Anthony W. Laywood 109-42 1996 £50.00

DYCHE, THOMAS   A New General English Dictionary... London: printed for Richard Ware, 1744. 4th edition; names and scrawls on endpapers; full contemporary calf, worn at corners and head and tail of spine, splits in hinges, but sound. Alston V 146.   Jarndyce 103-140 1996 £90.00

DYER, JOHN   Poems...Viz. I. Grongar Hill. II. The Ruins of Rome. III. The Fleece. London: printed by John Hughs for Messrs. R. and J. Dodsley, 1761. 1st collected edition; 8vo; 3 engraved plates on integral leaves; pages (i)-v, (iii), 9-188; contemporary sprinkled calf, head and tail of backstrip and front joint skilfully repaired, backstrip with raised bands, chipped label, gilt compartments, rubbed, corners repaired, red polished edges, early ownership signature, later inscription on prelim blank, very good.   Blackwell's B112-90 1996 £150.00

DYER, JOHN   Poems...I. Grongar Hill. II. The Ruins of Rome. III. The Fleece. London: printed for J. Dodsley, 1770. 8vo; 3 plates; half calf antique, old marbled sides.   Peter Murray Hill 185-55 1996 £50.00

DYKES, OSWALD   The Royal Marriage. King Lemuel's Lesson of 1. Chasity. 2. Temperance. 3. Clarity. 4. Justice. 5. Education. 6. Industry. 7. Frugality. 8. Religion. 9. Marriage &c.... London: printed for the Author and sold by P. Meighan etc., 1722. 8vo; pages xxiv, 368; frontispiece; 19th century calf, gilt, lacks label.   Peter Murray Hill 185-44 1996 £200.00

DYKES, W. R.   The Genus Iris. Cambridge: 1913. 1st edition; folio; pages (6), 245; 47 colored drawings by F. H. Round, one colored plate, 30 line drawings; half leather, some rubbing to spine, corners frayed, hinges tender, although solid; occasional light foxing, plates clean. Rare. Raymond M. Sutton VI-11 1996 $1,150.00

DYMOCK, CRESSEY   An Invention of Engines of Motion Lately Brought to Perfection. London: printed by I.C. for Richard Woodnoth next door to the Golden Hear... 1651. the insertion of too large a decorative ornament at head of the first page has resulted in slight trimming to the first few words int he bottom line of text, otherwise very good sized copy with good clear margins.   C. R. Johnson 37-10 1996 £1,250.00

DYSON, ANTHONY   Pictures to Print. London: Farrand Press, 1984. Copy Number 12 from an unstated limited edition (100?); small 4to; (2), xxx, 234 pages; 95 illustrations, hand colored engraving as frontispiece; half brown morocco over brown cloth, gilt, fine.   Kenneth Karmiole 1NS-95 1996 $125.00

E

E., B.　A New Dictionary of the Terms Ancient and Modern of the Canting Crew, in Its Several Tribes of Gypsies, Beggards, Thieves, Cheats, &c. London: printed for W. Hawes, &c., 1699? 4TO; Uncut, original blue boards, cream paper spine and paper label dulled. Jarndyce 103-141　1996 £85.00

EACKER, GEORGE I.　Observations on the National Character of the Americans: an Oration. Delivered Before the Tammany Society on the 12th of May, 1798. New York: William A. Davis, 1798. 1st edition; 12mo; 20 pages; removed. Rare. Evans 33658.　M & S Rare Books 60-321 1996 $125.00

EADON, JOHN　The Arithmetician's Guide... Sheffield: printed for W. Ward, and sold by S. Crowder and J. Wilkie in London ..1766. 1st edition; 12mo; (4), iv, (2), v, 333 pages, p. 1 being on verso of A3, numerous text figures, last leaf torn across, but with no loss, marginal wormhole in title, contemporary panelled sheep, unlettered, very good. John Drury 82-68　1996 £150.00

EARBERY, MATHIAS　An Historical Account of the Advantages that Have Accru'd to England... London: printed in the Year 1722. Crown 8vo; disbound.　H. M. Fletcher 121-97　1996 £110.00

EARHART, AMELIA　20 Hours. 40 Minutes: our Flight in the Friendship. New York: Putnam/Knickerbocker Press, 1928. 1st edition; 8vo; frontispiece, numerous photos; gilt stamped maroon cloth, facsimile ms. endpapers (slight rubbing); very good Signed and inscribed by author for Edith R. Brown.　George J. Houle 68-8　1996 $1,500.00

EARLY Treatises on the Stage viz Northbrooke's Treatise Against Dicing, Dancing, Plays and Interludes, Etc. London: printed for the Shakespeare Society, 1853. 1st edition; 306 pages; moderate wear.　Lyman Books 21-125　1996 $135.00

EARWAKER, J. P.　East Cheshire, Past and Present, or a History of the Hundred of Macclesfield... London: printed for the author, 1877. Thick 4to; 2 volumes, titlepage in red and black, 108 plates and illustrations, including some photos; original cloth, gilt.　Charles W. Traylen 117-357 1996 £85.00

EAST INDIA COMPANY　Report of the Committee of Warehouses, on a Memorial from the Manufacturers of Gunpowder and Other Commodities Made from Saltpetre, Presented to the Right Honourable the Lords of the Committee of Privy Council for Trade. N.P.: ?London, 1793. 1st edition; 4to; 24 pages, including 2 folding tables; disbound. Kress B2494. Goldsmith 15613.　Anthony Laywood 108-57 1996 £85.00

EAST RIDING ANTIQUARIAN SOCIETY　Transactions. London: 1893-1920. 8vo; volumes 1-22, only part 2 of volume XIII present, not part 1; red cloth, gilt lettered, good.　K Books 441-195 1996 £220.00

EASTLAKE, CHARLES L.　Hints On Household Taste in Furniture, Upholstery and Other Details. London: Longmans, Green and Co., 1868. 1st edition; 8vo; xiv, 269 pages; 33 plates; publisher's cloth, minor spotting on early and later leaves, minor coverwear, else very bright, scarce thus.　Bookpress 75-49　1996 $450.00

EASTLAKE, CHARLES L.　Hints on Household Taste... London: Longmans, Green and Co., 1872. 3rd edition; 8vo; xviii, 306 pages; 32 plates, illustrations in text; publisher's cloth; Fine.　Bookpress 75-48 1996 $325.00

EASTLAKE, CHARLES L.　Hints on Household Taste in Furniture Upholstery and Other Details. Boston: James R. Osgood, 1874. 2nd American edition; 8vo; xxxiv, (2), 304 pages, frontispiece, 35 plates; original blindstamped and gilt lettered cloth, covers little marked.　Ken Spelman 30-51　1996 £95.00

EASTLAKE, CHARLES L.　A History of the Gothic Revival. London: Longmans, Green and Co., 1872. 1st edition; 4to; xvi, 427, (3) pages, 35 plates; publisher's blindstamped gilt cloth; minor wear along edges, occasional spotting, rear hinge internally cracked, else very good; Nathaniel Lloyd's copy.　Bookpress 75-47　1996 $350.00

EASTLAKE, CHARLES L.　Materials for a History of Oil Painting. London: Longman, 1847. 1st edition; 8vo; xii, 561, (i) pages, bound without final 32 pages of ads; bound by Riviere in later 19th century polished tree calf, gilt panelled spine, joints expertly repaired; most handsome copy.　Ken Spelman 30-44　1996 £140.00

EASTLAKE, WILLIAM　Go in Beauty. London: Secker & Warburg, 1957. 1st British edition; very good+ in dust jacket, inscribed by author.　Ken Sanders 8-385　1996 $350.00

EASTLAKE, WILLIAM　Go In Beauty. London: Secker & Warburg, 1957. 1st British edition; 279 pages; inscribed by author, very good+ in dust jacket.　Ken Sanders 8-386　1996 $300.00

EASTMAN, GEORGE　Chronicles of an African Trip. Privately printed, 1927. 1st edition; 29 photos; uncut.　J. B. Muns 154-99 196 $125.00

EASTMAN, GEORGE　Chronicles of an African Trip. USA: privately printed for the author, 1927. illustrations, very light damage to lower corner of upper cover, otherwise an excellent copy, cloth backed boards.　David Grayling J95Biggame-76　1996 £60.00

EASTMAN, LUKE　Masonick Melodies a Choice Selection of the Most Approved Masonick Songs, Duets, Glees, etc... Boston: 1818. 208 pages; calf, worn, hinges weak.　William Reeves 309-9467　1996 £102.00

EASTMAN, MARY　Dahcotha; or Life and Legends of the Sioux Around Fort Snelling. New York: John Wiley, 1849. 1st edition; 268 pages; 4 tinted plates; original green embossed cloth, title stamped in gilt on spine, Dahcotha mis-spelled on spine, usual foxing; very good. Field 478; Becker Wagner Camp 167b.　Michael D. Heaston 23-142 1996 $500.00

EASTON, J.　The Salisbury Guide; Giving an Account of the Antiquities of Old Sarum and of the Ancient and Present State of the City of New Sarum. Salisbury: E. Easton, 1777. 4th edition; 12mo; pages viii, 80; comb marbled endpapers, later boards. Anderson p. 301. Marlborough 162-26　1996 £90.00

AN EASY Introduction to the Game of Chess: Containing One Hundred Examples of Games... London: 1806. 1st edition; 7 x 4 inches; 2 volumes, 184, 142 pages, frontispiece, boards, ink inscription, spine mostly gone, covers loose and spotted.　John K. King 77-565 1996 $250.00

EATES, MARGOT　Paul Nash Paintings, Drawings and Illustrations. London: Lund Humphries, 1948. 30 x 24 cms; xii, 80 pages, 132 plates; plates on slightly cockled Ingres paper; original cloth, dust jacket slightly torn;　Rainsford A54-437　1996 £150.00

EATON, ALLEN H.　Handicrafts of the southern Highlands, with an Account of the Rural Handicraft Movement in the United States and Suggestions for the Wider Use of Handicrafts in Adult Education and in Recreation. New York: Russell Sage, 1937. 1st edition; 8vo; pages 370; 112 full page illustrations, including 58 illustrations from photos by Doris Ulmann; fine in little nicked dust jacket.　Second Life Books 103-197 1996 $125.00

EATON, ELON HOWARD　Birds of New York. Albany: New York State Museum, 1910-14. 1st (and only) edition; 4to; 2 volumes, 501, 716 pages; 42 colored plates, black and white photographic illustrations; original green cloth, corners slightly bumped. Nissen IVB 282; Zimmer I p. 190.　Sotheran PN32-84　1996 £155.00

EATON, ELON HOWARD　Birds of New York. Albany: University of the Stte of New York, 1910. 1st edition; 2 volumes, 3 small spots to front boards of volume 2, else fine.　Hermitage SP95-1061　1996 $200.00

EATON, J. C.　70 Years Observations of a Trout Fisherman. Richmond: 1937. original cloth, gilt, fine; presentation copy from author's nephew, inscribed; very scarce.　David A.H. Grayling 3/95-582　1996 £75.00

EBEL, JOHANN GOTTFRIED   An Atlas to Ebel's Traveller's Guide through Switzerland.... London: printed for Samuel Leigh by W. Clowes, c. 1819. 12mo; (iv), 29, (3 ad) pages, 5 engraved plates, engraved "Explanation" laid down on last leaf, very large hand colored folding dissected map; original drab boards, new black calf spine, printed side label. 1 copy in NUC.   James Burmester 29-46 1996 £160.00

EBERHART, RICHARD   Burr Oaks. London: Chatto & Windus, 1947. 1st edition; precedes American edition; 8vo; viii, 68 pages; yellow cloth, soiled, slightly warped, titled in gilt on spine; near fine internally; presentation copy for Royal Murdoch, inscribed by poet with 3 or 4 corrections in poet's hand; tipped in TLS by poet on verso of a first edition of his 1947 broadside 'Ruminations'.   Blue Mountain SP95-97 1996 $250.00

L'ECHO des Bardes ou Le Menestrel. Dedie Aux Dames. Paris: Le Fuel, 1821. 12mo; frontispiece, title, 68 ff. with 14 vignette headpieces, 6 ff., 4 ff. letterpress; gold covered boards with multi colored silk onlays, neo-classical borders around central winged figures, flat spine with matching onlaid backstrip decorated in four compartments, all edges gilt, matching silk covered slipcase (slipcase little darkened), attractive and unusual binding in remarkably fine state of preservation.   Marlborough 160-71 1996 £500.00

THE ECHOES of the Lands and Mountains: or Wonderful Things in the Lake District... London: James Ivison, c. 1870. 1st edition; 8vo; pages viii, 160, (iv), woodcut vignettes; original blindstamped cloth, gilt, extremities trifle rubbed.   R.F.G. Hollett & Son 78-899 1996 £85.00

ECK, C.   Traite de Construction en Poteries et fer, a l'Usages des Batimens Civils, Industriels et Militaires. Paris: J. C. Blosse, 1836. Folio; (vi), 72, 21, (1) pages; 66 engraved plates; contemporary quarter calf, little stained and worn.   Elton Engineering 10-42 1996 £1,450.00

ECK, C.   Traite de l'Application du fer, de la Fonte et de la Tole Dans les Constructions Civiles, Industrielles et Militaires... Paris: Carilian-Goeury et Dalmont, 1841. Folio; (viii), 115, (1), 8, 32 pages, 80 engraved plates; contemporary quarter morocco, little rubbed, but overall lovely copy.   Elton Engineering 10-43 1996 £1,850.00

ECKEL, JOHN   Prime Pickwicks in Parts: a Cenusus, with Complete Collation, Comparison and Comment. New York: Edgar H. Wells; London: Charles J. Sawyer, 1928. Only edition, 1 of 440 numbered copies, signed by Eckel and Newton; 11 photos; original pictorial cloth, original pictorial box; fine. NCBEL III 787.   Trebizond 39-8 1996 $275.00

ECO, UMBERTO   The Aesthetics of Chaosmos: the Middle Ages of James Joyce. Tulsa: Univeristy of Tulsa, 1982. 1st American edition; 96 pages; perfect bound in wrappers as issued; fine, warmly inscribed by author; scarce.   Between the Covers 42-153 1996 $135.00

EDDINGTON, A. S.   Stellar Movements and the Structure of the Universe. London: Macmillan, 1914. 1st edition; 8vo; 266 pages; text figures; blue cloth, endpapers browned, fore-edge lightly foxed, blindstamp on titlepage, good, scarce.   Knollwood Books 70-65 1996 $175.00

EDDISON, E. R.   A Fish Dinner in Memison. New York: Dutton, 1941. 1st edition; 1/998 copies; very good+ in very good dust jacket with some light wear and tear.   Aronovitz 57-367 1996 $150.00

EDDISON, E. R.   The Worm Ouroboros. London: Cape, 1922. 1st edition; tight, very good+/near fine copy; author's first novel.   Aronovitz 57-366 1996 $125.00

EDDY, ARTHUR G.   Two Thousand Miles on an Automobile. Philadelphia & London: J. B. Lippincott Co., 1902. 329 pages; cloth, barely noticeable dampstain on spine, very good. Streeter Sale 3994.   Robert G. Hayman 11/95-34 1996 $250.00

EDEL, LEON   Henry James - the Master - 1901-1916. London: Hart-Davis Ltd., 1972. 1st edition; original binding, top edge faded, head and tail of spine slightly bumped, very good in slightly creased, soiled, rubbed and dusty dust jacket faded at spine; presentation copy from author, inscribed for Trekkie and Ian Parsons.   Ulysses 39-315 1996 £75.00

EDEN, EMILY   The Semi-Attached Couple. London: Richard Bentley, 1860. 1st edition; 8vo; 2 volumes, bound without half titles, pages iv, 266; (ii), 259, (1); 2 volumes, foxed, one gathering in volume 1 starting; contemporary half tan calf by Carss & Co., little rubbed, backstrip with gilt ruled raised bands between black rules, red labels, marbled boards and edges, endpapers foxed, blue silk markers, good. Sadleir 760; Wolff 1982.   Blackwell's B112-91 1996 £350.00

EDEN, EMILY   The Semi-Detached House. London: Richard Bentley, 1859. 1st edition; 12mo; half title discarded, pages (ii), 327; contemporary half tan calf by Carss & Co., backstrip rubbed, raised bands, red labels, marbled boards, hinges split but firm, blue silk marker, good. Sadleir 761; not in Wolff.   Blackwell's B112-92 1996 £250.00

EDGERTON, CLYDE   Raney. Chapel Hill: Algonquin, 1985. Uncorrected proof; author's first book; the last paraagraph of the novel has been typed on plain paper, glued in, and hand corrected (typical of proofs?); light wear and soiling, very good in printed light blue wrappers.   Thomas Dorn 9-105 1996 $575.00

EDGERTON, CYLDE   Walking Across Egypt. Chapel Hill: Algonquin, 1987. Corrected proof; author's second book; printed salmon colored wrappers; fine.   Thomas Dorn 9-106 1996 $125.00

EDGEVILLE, EDWARD   Castine. Southern Field and Fireside Novelette, No. 2. New Series. Raleigh: Wm. B. Smith & Co., 1865. 1st edition; 12mo; 32 pages; original pictorial wrappers; fine. Crandall 3088; P&W 6307; Wright II 835. Harwell Conf. Belles Lett. 27.   M & S Rare Books 60-142 1996 $1,000.00

EDGEWORTH, MARIA 1768-1849   Comic Dramas. Love and Law: The Two Guardians; the Rose, &c. London: printed for R. Hunter, 1817. 1st edition; original boards, uncut, worn, lacking part of spine, small rip on titlepage, otherwise about fine internally, uncommon.   Lyman Books 21-546 1996 $185.00

EDGEWORTH, MARIA 1768-1849   Harry and Lucy Concluded; Being the Last Part of "Early Lessons". London: R. Hunter and Baldwin, Craddock & Joy, 1825. 1st edition; 12mo; 4 volumes; contemporary quarter calf, gilt, boards, bookplates, wanting ads in last volume; despite excision top margin of ten leaves (text unaffected); fine. sadleir 769; Osborne p. 248; Gumuchian 2345.   Trebizond 39-33 1996 $125.00

EDGEWORTH, MARIA 1768-1849   Helen, a Tale. London: Richard Bentley, 1834. 1st edition; 8vo; 3 volumes, pages 336, 336, 322; half titles; original publisher's boards, tan linen spines, paper labels, in modern slipcase, typographic label, spines and labels faded and volume 1 lacks half title, sound set. Scarce in original publisher's issue. CBEL III 367.   Hartfield 48-L31 1996 $395.00

EDGEWORTH, MARIA 1768-1849   Letters for Literary Ladies. London: printed for J. Johnson, 1795. 1st edition; 8vo; author's first book; contemporary tree calf, spine gilt; very fine, rare. Slade 1A; CBEL III 665.   Ximenes 108-119 1996 $6,000.00

EDGEWORTH, MARIA 1768-1849   Letters of Maria Edgeworth and Anna Letitia Barbauld. Waltham St. Lawrence: Golden Cockerel Press, 1953. Of 300 numbered copies, this one of 60 signed by editor and artist; specially bound; tall 8vo; quarter white sheepskin, cloth of gold sides, very nice, bright copy, sides remarkably untarnished.   Bertram Rota 272-190 1996 £120.00

EDGEWORTH, MARIA 1768-1849   Practical Education... London: J. Johnson, 1801. 2nd edition; 8vo; 3 volumes, xiv, (2), 412; (2), 386; (2), 387, (1) pages; 3 engraved plates, outer margins of 2 leaves soiled; contemporary half calf, gilt with labels, very good. Williams II 459.   John Drury 82-69 1996 £350.00

EDGEWORTH, MARIA 1768-1849   Tales and Novels. New York: Harper & Bros., 183/39. Harper's Stereotype edition; 12mo; 10 volumes; decorated cloth, occasional small perforations along spine joint of some volumes, otherwise nice appearing, very good set.   Freedom Bookshop 14-35 1996 $175.00

EDLIN, ABRAHAM   A Treatise on the Art of Bread-Making. London: Vernor and Hood, Poultry, 1805. 1st edition; 8vo; publisher's blue grey boards, over an ivory paper back, with original printed spine label, some minor chipping, but solid copy, preserved in custom case. rare.   Book Block 32-47 1996 $2,450.00

EDMONDS, EMMA   Nurse and Spy in the Union Army... Hartford: 1865. 1st edition; 384 pages; original binding.   W. Bruce Fye 71-606 1996 $125.00

EDMONDSON, JOSEPH   An Historical and Genealogical Account of the Noble Family of Greville... London: printed, 1766. 8vo; pages 108, 11 plates; old calf, somewhat scratched, rebacked.   Peter Murray Hill 185-76 1996 £60.00

EDSON, CARROLL A.   Edson Family History and Genealogy: Descendants of Samuel Edson of Salem and Bridgewater, Mass. Ann Arbor: c. 1965. Thick royal 8vo; 2 volumes; 1540 pages; many illustrations; original cloth.   Howes Bookshop 265-1749 1996 £65.00

EDSON, RUSSELL   The Wounded Breakfast. Madison: Red Ozier Press, 1978. 1st edition; one of 160 signed by author; thin 8vo; illustrations; original wrappers; mint.   James S. Jaffe 34-567 1996 $150.00

EDWARDS, AMELIA B.   Untrodden Peaks and Unfrequented Valleys: a Midsummer Ramble in the Dolomites. London: Longmans, Green and Co., 1873. 1st edition; 9 x 6 1/2 inches; xxvi, 385 pages; frontispiece, 7 plates, 1 colored folding map and 17 illustrations in text; recent oxblood coarse grain morocco, raised bands, original calf label, marbled edges; title and frontispiece somewhat mottled, otherwise very fine.   Phillip J. Pirages 33-198 1996 $250.00

EDWARDS, BRYAN   An Historical Survey of the French Colony in the Island of St. Domingo... London: printed for John Stockdale, Piccadilly, 1797. 1st edition; 4to; (i-xxiii), errata, 1-247 pages, large folding map, slightly foxed, contemporary ink ownership inscription, few pages slightly foxed; modern tan morocco and vellum styled boards, original leather title laid down to spine, new endpapers. Sabin 21894.   Beeleigh Abbey BA56-64 1996 £150.00

EDWARDS, BRYAN   The History Civil and Commercial of the British Colonies in the West Indies. London: 1799. folding map; contemporary quarter calf, marbled sides.   Petersfield Bookshop FH58-426 1996 £100.00

EDWARDS, E. I.   Desert Voices. A Descriptive Bibliography. Los Angeles: Westernlore Press, 1958. 1st edition; limited to 500 copies; xxviii, 215 pages; original gilt decorated and lettered cloth; very fine with pictorial dust jacket. Scarce.   Argonaut Book Shop 113-223 1996 $175.00

EDWARDS, E. I.   Lost Oases Along the Carrizo. Los Angeles: Westernlore Press, 1961. 1st edition; one of 500 copies; xvi, 126 pages; 8 plates after photos; very fine with dust jacket; presentation inscription, signed author for Lulu Rasmussen O'Neal. Edwards p.73; Miller p. 78. Argonaut Book Shop 113-224 1996 $150.00

EDWARDS, EDWIN   Old Inns. First Division - Eastern England. London: privately published, 1873. Limited to 250 numbered copies on large paper, folio; printed and etched titlepages, etched dedication leaf, 18 leaves and 28 etched illustrations, 34 engraved leaves of text (reproduced from manuscript), numerous etched illustrations and decorations, 5 pages of letterpress prospectus and index; contemporary half morocco and cloth, gilt panelled spine and gilt top. Scarce. Charles W. Traylen 117-232 1996 £350.00

EDWARDS, EMORY   Modern American Locomotive Engines; Their Design, Construction and Management. Philadelphia: 1890. 383 pages, 78 engravings; new old style quarter calf, very good.   K Books 442-192 1996 £50.00

EDWARDS, GEORGE   Essays Upon Natural History, and Other Miscellaneous Subjects... London: J. Robson, 1770. 1st edition; 8vo; 231 pages; frontispiece; recent period-style quarter calf and marbled boards, morocco spine label, small marginal inkspot and unobtrusive blindstamp on title, else nice, clean copy.   Chapel Hill 94-299 1996 $250.00

EDWARDS, GEORGE WHARTON   Vanished Towers and Chimes of Flanders. Philadelphia: The Penn Pub. Co., 1916. Special limited edition, one of 35 numbered copies, signed by author and publishers; folio; 211 pages, mounted color titlepage and 30 mounted plates, 21 color, including frontispiece; full vellum over boards stamped in gilt on front cover and spine, top edge gilt, others uncut; fine.   Heritage Book Shop 196-255 1996 $500.00

EDWARDS, H. S.   The Lyrical Drama, Essays on Subjects, Composers and Executants of Modern Opera. 1881. 2 volumes.   William Reeves 309-9735 1996 £63.00

EDWARDS, JOHN N.   Noted Guerillas, or the Warfare of the Border. St. Louis: Chicago and San Francisco: Bryan, Brand and Co., et al, 1877. 1st edition; 8vo; original brick red cloth, previous owner's inscriptions and one small sticker, extremities rubbed and chipped, else very good. Howes E53; Adams 150 #51; Graff 1213; 6 Guns 664; Rader 1283. Glenn Books 36-203 1996 $200.00

EDWARDS, JONATHAN   A Careful and Strict Enquiry Into the Modern Prevailing Notions of that Freedom of Will... Boston: S. Kneeland, 1754. 1st edition; 8vo; (2), vi, (4), 294, (14) pages; including final 9 page list of subscriber's, title little stained, some intermittent foxing, verso of last leaf slightly affected by adhesion, just affecting a few letters; contemporary panelled sheep, gilt, some wear to spine, generaly good. Sabin 21930.   John Drury 82-70 1996 £400.00

EDWARDS, MATILDA BETHAM   Through Spain to the Sahara. London Hurst and Blackett, 1868. 1st edition; tall 8vo; 317, (16) pages ads; original brown cloth decorated in gilt, bevelled edges; upper corners bit bumped, otherwise fine.   David Mason 71-151 1996 $200.00

EDWARDS, RICHARD   The Book! Or, the Proceedings and Correspondence Upon the Subject of the Inquiry Into the Conduct of Her Royal Highness the Princess of Wales, Under a Commission Appointed by the King In the Year 1806. London: printed by and for Richard Edwards, 1813. 1st edition thus; 8vo; 248, 133 pages; early 20th century half mottled calf and marbled boards by Root & Son with morocco spine labels, top edge gilt; signatures of "W. P. Williams, Mar. 19th 1813" and later owner, else very good to near fine.   Chapel Hill 94-220 1996 $150.00

EDWARDS, S.   The New Botanic Garden. London: 1812. 4to; 2 volumes in 1; 61 fine hand colored plates; contemporary half green calf, trifle rubbed, m.e. Very rare.   Wheldon & Wesley 207-27 1996 £2,500.00

EDWARDS, THOMAS   The Canons of Criticism and Glossary; the Trial of the Letter Y(upsilon)), Alias Y, and Sonnets. London: for C. Bathurst, 1765. 1st edition thus; 8vo; pages 351, (xvii), index and ads; contemporary calf, rather worn; good, firm copy. Bookplate of Jonathan Pytts. Jaggard p. 90.   Simon Finch 24-80 1996 £140.00

EDWARDS, W. H.   Voyage Up the River Amazon Including a Residence at Para. New York: & Philadelphia: 1847. 256 pages, 1 plate, figures; original brown cloth, corners and edges of spine worn. scarce. John Johnson 135-29 1996 $100.00

EDWARDS, WILLIAM   Two Health-Seekers in Southern California. Philadelphia: 1897. 1st edition; 144 pages; original binding, library stamp on front endpaper and small number on spine, waterstain affecting top margin of most leaves; overall very good. Scarce.   W. Bruce Fye 71-608 1996 $150.00

EDWARDS, WILLIAM H.   Football Days. New York: Moffat, Yard & Co., 1916. 1st edition; 8vo; 463 pages; photos; original blue cloth, near fine.   Chapel Hill 94-203 1996 $100.00

EDWARDS, WILLIAM J.   Twenty-Five Years in the Black Belt. Boston: Cornhill Co., 1918. 1st edition; rear board bumped at bottom resulting in warp aat the bottom of pages, thus very good with very slight spine wear.   Between the Covers 43-309 1996 $200.00

EDWORDS, C. E.   Campfires of a Naturalist. 1893. Photographic plates; original pictorial gilt cloth, slight discoloration, but generally very good.   David Grayling J95Biggame-409 1996 £65.00

EGAN, PIERCE 1772-1849   Boxiana; or Sketches of Antient & Modern Pugilism. N.P.: n.d., but c. 1840. Imperial 8vo; engraved title, 63 engraved plates, no text save engraved title and captions; 19th century quarter roan, spine lettered in gilt, cloth sides, somewhat rubbed, few plates fox spotted, but majority are not foxed. Hartley 587.   Sotheran PN32-70 1996 £698.00

EGAN, PIERCE 1772-1849   Every Gentleman's Manual. A Lecture on the Art of Self-Defence. London: Flintoff, 1851. 12mo; iv, 199 pages, 6 full page wood engraved illustrations; original blue ribbed cloth, printed paper labels on upper cover and spine, little rubbed and faded, but nice very uncommon book, ownership inscription of J. Rimington Wilson. Magriel 43 (1st ed.); Hartley 597.   James Burmester 29-48 1996 £375.00

EGAN, PIERCE 1772-1849   The Finish to the Adventures of Tom, Jerry and Logic, in Their Pursuits through Life In and Out of London. London: Reeves & Turner, 1889. Royal 8vo; pages xvi, 321, 32 pages ads dated Oct. 1889; 36 attractive hand colored plates by Robert Cruikshank, including frontispiece; original roan backed cloth, top edge gilt, inside joints neatly repaired, otherwise very good to nice.   James Fenning 133-97 1996 £125.00

EGAN, PIERCE 1772-1849   Fistiana; or the Oracle of the Ring from 1780 5o 1840...Scientific Hints on Sparring, Etc. London: Wm. Clement, Junr., 1841. Foolscap 8vo; frontispiece; frontispiece and title foxed; original cloth, gilt edges; rare.   Charles W. Traylen 117-284 1996 £55.00

EGAN, PIERCE 1772-1849   Real Life in London. 1821-22. 1st edition; large paper copy (231 x 139mm trimmed), 2 volumes, pages 656, 668; 33 colored aquatints and etchings reinforced by aquatinting; contemporary tree calf, backstrips gilt, splits in 2 hinges and backstrips but sound, small chip at head of backstrip of volume 1, with two woodcuts on letterpress titles only found on large paper copies. Limestone Hills 41-149 1996 $400.00

EGAN, PIERCE 1772-1849   Real Life in Ireland; or, the Day and Night Scenes, Rovings, Rambles and Sprees, Bulls, Blunders, Bodderation and Blarney of Brian Boru, Esq. and His Elegant Friend Sir Shawn O'Dogherty. London: ptd. by B. Bensley, Bolt Court, Fleet St., Pub. by Jones & Co... 1821. 1st edition; 8vo; 5-296 pages; hand colored aquatint frontispiece, 18 hand colored aquatints by Alken and others, some plates shaved at margins, no watermarks, bound by Zaehnsdorf, handsome copy, full crimson morocco, triple gilt rule borders to boards, gilt tiel to spine and tooling to compartments, raised bands, all edges gilt, marbled endpapers. Tooley 201; Abbey Life 282.   Beeleigh Abbey BA/56-8 1996 £525.00

EGERTON, FRANCIS   Journal of a Tour in the Holy Land, In May and June 1840. London: Harrison & Co., 1841. 1st edition; 8vo; pages (viii), 141, (i); tinted lithograph frontispiece, 3 other plates original green cloth, decorated in blind, gilt lettering, very slight crack in cloth at head of spine, otherwise very good. Abbey 384.   Sotheran PN32-163 1996 £375.00

EGERTON, GEORGE, PSEUD.   Flies in Amber. London: Hutchison & Co., 1905. 1st edition; original cloth, covers little soiled and stained, endpapers somewhat browned as usual, edges foxed; scarce; presentation copy inscribed by author for Annie Russell (who wrote fiction under the name of "Annie Carruthers".   David J. Holmes 52-42 1996 $250.00

EGERTON, THOMAS   The Speech of the Lord Chancellor of England in the Eschequer Chamber, Touching tht Post-nati. London: printed for the Societie of Stationers, 1609. Later black morocco over boards, some foxing and embrowning, sound.   Meyer Boswell SL26-70 1996 $650.00

EGLESFIELD, FRANCIS   Monarachy Revived: Being the Personal History of Charles the Second. London: for Charles Baldwyn, 1822. Reprint of the 1661 edition; demy 8vo; (ii), 262 pages, tipped in list of 14 plates; contemporary calf, neatly rebacked and gilt on broad bands, original covers panelled, fine oak leaf border, little light wear, some browning and spotting, but nice copy   Ash Rare Books Zenzybyr-32 1996 £75.00

EHRLICH, J. W.   Howl of the Censor, The Four Letter Word on Trial. San Carlos: Nourse Pub. Co., 1961. Lawrence Ferlinghetti's copy with his signature on first blank.   Meyer Boswell SL27-74 1996 $150.00

EISELEY, LOREN   Francis Bacon and Modern Dilemma. Lincoln: University of Nebraska Press, 1962. 1st edition; ink name on verso, of front free endpaper, otherwise fine in price clipped dust jacket. Hermitage SP95-1077 1996 $125.00

EISEN, GUSTAVUS A.   Glass: its Origin, History, Chronology, Technic and Classification to the Sixteenth Century. New York: William Rudge, 1927. 8vo; 2 volumes, 768 pages, 284 figures and 198 plates; original boards, spines soiled, light waterstaining at lower margins of both volumes.   Archaeologia Luxor-3280 1996 $375.00

EISSLER, M.   The Metallurgy of Gold. London: 1897. 4th edition; 496 pages; many plates, illustrations; original illustrated cloth, light wear, generally very good, scarce.   Stephen Lunsford 45-53 1996 $100.00

EKINS CHARLES   Naval Battles from 1744 to the Peace in 1814 Critically Reviewed and Illustrated. London: Baldwin, Craddock and Joy, 1824. 1st edition; 4to; xix, 426 pages, 2 page subscribers, folding illustrations; later banded half calf, generally very good.   John Lewcock 30-82 1996 £425.00

ELDREDGE, ZOETH SKINNER   The Beginnings of San Francisco from the Expedition of Anza, 1774 to the City Charter of April 15, 1850. San Francisco: by the author, 1912. 1st edition; 2 volumes, 837 pages; plates, folding map; spines faded as usual, else very fine set. Argonaut Book Shop 113-225 1996 $150.00

ELGOOD, GEORGE S.   Some English Gardens. London: Longmans, 1904. 1st edition; folio; frontispiece, (iii)-xii, 130 pages, 49 color plates; cloth, lower board spotted, otherwise very good.   Bookpress 75-176 1996 $375.00

ELIADE, MIRCEA   No Souvenirs. New York: H&R, 1977. 1st U.S. edition; near fine in price clipped dust jacket with mild tanning to spine and upper portion of front panel. Inscribed by author in year of publication.   Lame Duck Books 19-177 1996 $200.00

ELIAS, LEVITA   Grammatica Hebraica Absolutissima... Basel: Froben, 1525. 8vo; ff. 176; text in Latin and Hebrew on facing pages, printer's device on title and final leaf; contemporary vellum, rebacked in modern vellum, title bit soiled, endpapers lacking, early annotations throughout. Adams E114.   Kenneth Karmiole 1NS-136 1996 $400.00

ELIOT, ANDREW   A Discourse on Natural Religion Delivered in the Chapel of Harvard College in Cambridge, New England May 8, 1771 at the Lecture Founded by the Hon. Paul Dudley. Boston: Daniel Kneeland, 1771. 1st edition; 8vo; xlv, (1) (of 2) pages; sewn and uncut, slight fraying, browned, lacks final leaf with list of Dudleian lecturers after 1764. Scarce. Evans 12033.   M & S Rare Books 60-326 1996 $225.00

ELIOT, CHARLES   Turkey in Europe. London: Edward Arnold, 1908. New edition; 8vo; 2 folding maps; worn; enclosed in attractive black cloth box with blue labels; Rupert Brooke's copy, boldly inscribed less than two months before his death.   Lakin & Marley 3-3 1996 $1,250.00

ELIOT, CHARLES W.   Charles Eliot, Landscape Architect. Boston: 1903. 8vo; (26), 770 pages; folding maps, plates, text illustrations; original cloth, inner front hinge slightly cracked.   Edward Morrill 368-108 1996 $110.00

ELIOT, GEORGE, PSEUD. 1819-1880   Adam Bede. Edinburgh & London: William Blackwood and Sons, 1859. 1st edition; 8vo; 3 volumes;, 16 page publisher's catalog at end of 3rd volume; original orange brown cloth; superb copy of author's first novel. Sadleir 812; Wolff 2056; Grolier Hundred 95.   Ximenes 108-120 1996 $4,500.00

ELIOT, GEORGE, PSEUD. 1819-1880   Daniel Deronda. London: William Blackwood and Sons, 1876. 1st edition; 8vo; 4 volumes; (iv), (368; (iv), 364; (iv), (394); (iv), (368) pages; half titles present, errata slip in each of volumes 2 and 3; contemporary half calf, marbled boards, spines gilt, double labels; scuffed, corners little worn, sound, clean set.   Robert Clark 38-240 1996 £175.00

ELIOT, GEORGE, PSEUD. 1819-1880   Felix Holt the Radical. London: William Blackwood and Sons, 1866. 1st edition; Carter's C binding; 8vo; 3 volumes, without half titles, volume 1's title with small oval inkstamp "Presented by the publisher' between title and author's name; original chocolate brown sand grain cloth, sides stamped in blind, spines lettered and decorated in gold, dark green endpapers, top edges uncut, others cut, as issued, skilfully unobtrusive restoration at head and tail of spines, one or two spots to endpapers, excellent copy; Parrish pp. 20-21; Carter p. 111-12.   Simon Finch 24-82 1996 £300.00

ELIOT, GEORGE, PSEUD. 1819-1880   George Eliot's Life as Related in Her Letters and Journals. Edinburgh and London: William Blackwood and Sons, 1885. 1st edition; 8vo; 3 volumes, errata slip at end of volume 3; original lilac-grey diagonally fine ribbed cloth, sides decorated in black within single black rule, spines numbered and lettered in gilt and ruled and decorated in black, dark brown endpapers, bottom edges trimmed, others uncut, as issued; fine; Mary A. Ewart's copy, with her ownership inscription dated 27 Jan. 1885 on first half title verso and her note "Mr. Cross read the proofs of this book to Barbara Bodichon at Grafse(?) in Feby 1884 when I was with her'. Parrish p. 47; Tinker 1018.   Simon Finch 24-83 1996 £475.00

ELIOT, GEORGE, PSEUD. 1819-1880   The Mill on the Floss. Edinburgh and London: William Blackwood and Sons, 1860. 1st edition; in Carter's A binding, indicating an early issue; 8vo; 3 volumes, 16 page undated publisher's catalog at end of volume 3; original bright brown ripple grain cloth, sides blocked in blind, spine lettered in gold and with gold designs, deep cream endpapers, top and fore-edges uncut, bottom cut as issued, Binder's ticket of Burn at end of volume 1, cloth very slightly cockled on spine of volume 1, tiny area of front joint of volume 3 worn, skilful and minimal restoration not detracting from an excellent set, clean and fresh; Parrish pp. 14-15; Carter pp. 110-11; Sadleir 816.   Simon Finch 24-81 1996 £600.00

ELIOT, GEORGE, PSEUD. 1819-1880   The Mill on the Floss. London: William Blackwood and Sons, 1860. 1st edition; 8vo; 3 volumes; (viii), 362; (viii), (320); (viii), (314) pages, 16 page catalog; original brown blindstamped cloth, spines gilt, Carter's "B" binding with Edmonds & Remnants' ticket, though without the integral ad leaf and blank found in some copies; very slight wear to a couple of corners, cloth marked and bit darkened, stitching of volume 1 little loose, spine of volume 3 faded; good.   Robert Clark 38-239 1996 £270.00

ELIOT, GEORGE, PSEUD. 1819-1880   Romola. Boston: Estes and Lauriat, 1890. One of 250 copies of the edition deluxe; 8 3/4 x 6 1/4 inches; 2 volumes; frontispiece in each volume, 60 other plates, each with printed tissue guard, titles in red and black; very fine olive green onlaid morocco, covers framed with multiple plain and stippled rules and an onlaid strip of ochre morocco, especially pretty large cornerpieces featuring onlaid blue morocco flower amidst delicate gilt stems and leaves, raised bands, spine gilt in compartments with simple floral corner ornaments, butterscotch morocco doublures, elegant gilt cornerpieces similar to those on covers, but larger, patterned flyleaves, gilt edges; faint mark to one cover, otherwise a very fine copy, handsomely bound. Virtually faultless inside and out.   Phillip J. Pirages 33-63 1996 $450.00

ELIOT, GEORGE, PSEUD. 1819-1880   Scenes of Clerical Life. London: Macmillan, 1906. 1st edition thus; 16 colored plates and black and white illustrations by Hugh Thomson; dark blue cloth pictorially stamped on spine and top board with gilt shepherd and sheep grazing in field of daisies. Fine.   Barbara Stone 70-207 1996 £55.00

ELIOT, GEORGE, PSEUD. 1819-1880   Silas Marner; the Weaver of Raveloe. London: William Blackwood, 1861. 1st edition; 8vo; some foxing to prelims, half title guarded, publisher's cat. at end; ink marks on last page of ads; pages (vi), 364, 16; modern half brown morocco, backstrip with bead roll decorated raised bands, compartments gilt panelled, lettered direct in second, single ornament in remainder, green cloth sides, orange endpapers, original ripple grain blindstamped brown cloth covers (Carter A) bound in at end, top edge gilt, excellent. Muir 4; Parrish p. 15; Sadleir 819; Wolff 2063.   Blackwell's B112-93 1996 £220.00

ELIOT, GEORGE, PSEUD. 1819-1880   Silas Marner. London: Macmillan and Co., 1907. 1st edition with these illustrations; illustrations by Hugh Thomson; original pictorial cloth, all edges gilt; covers very slightly worn, unusually nice.   David J. Holmes 52-123 1996 $125.00

ELIOT, GEORGE, PSEUD. 1819-1880   George Eliot's Complete Works. Boston: Aldine Book, n.d. 8vo; 6 volumes; illustrations; tan half calf and marbled boards, marbled edges and endpapers, gilt worked spines with brown and black title labels, very good, paper somewhat brittle resulting in occasional small tears or tiny chips to few pages, titlepage torn and repaired, still, nice set.   Antic Hay 101-515 1996 $250.00

ELIOT, THOMAS STEARNS 1888-1965   An Address to Members of the London Library. London: printed for the London Library by the Queen Anne Press, 1952. 1st edition; one of 500 copies; crown 8vo; pages (8); original printed pale blue sewn card wrappers; fine. Gallup A59a. Blackwell's B112-97 1996 £85.00

ELIOT, THOMAS STEARNS 1888-1965   Animula. London: Faber & Faber Ltd., 1929. One of 400 numbered copies, signed by author; 2 wood engravings by Gertrude Hermes, one of which is colored; printed at Curwen Press on handmade paper; boards, large paper copy, covers dusty and slightly marked, very good.   Ulysses 39-174 1996 £350.00

ELIOT, THOMAS STEARNS 1888-1965   Animula. London: 1929. Limited to 400 numbered copies, signed by author; 8.5 x 5.5 inches; boards, spine badly chipped, covers heavily soiled.   John K. King 77-282 1996 $250.00

ELIOT, THOMAS STEARNS 1888-1965   Ash-Wednesday. New York: Fountains Press: Faber, 1930. 1st edition; 501/600 copies, signed by author; crown 8vo; 28 pages; original mid blue linen, backstrip and front cover lettering and front cover design all gilt blocked, endpapers lightly browned as usual, top edge gilt, others untrimmed, excellent; Blackwell's B112-94 1996 £335.00

ELIOT, THOMAS STEARNS 1888-1965   The Classics and the Man of Letters. London: Oxford University Press, 1942. 1st edition; pale blue wrpapers, spine sunned, else very good. Gallup A40.   Priscilla Juvelis 95/1-86 1996 $100.00

ELIOT, THOMAS STEARNS 1888-1965   The Cocktail Party. London: Faber & Faber, n.d. 1950. 1st edition; octavo; 167, (5) pages, original green cloth, gilt lettered spine, fine in original dust jacket (jacket spine darkened), chipping at upper extremity. Gallup A55.   Heritage Book Shop 196-241 1995 $850.00

ELIOT, THOMAS STEARNS 1888-1965   Collected Poems 1901-1935. London: Faber & Faber, 1936. 1st edition; one of 6000 copies; blue cloth, dust jacket, covers lightly rubbed, otherwise fine in somewhat chipped, rubbed and price clipped jacket with residue from old internal tape mends.   James S. Jaffe 34-145 1996 $150.00

ELIOT, THOMAS STEARNS 1888-1965   Dante. London: Faber and Faber Ltd., 1929. 1st edition decorated boards, pages unopened; head and tail of spine slightly bumped, free endpapers partially browned, rear pastedown slightly spotted, very good in very slightly creased, rubbed and dusty dust jacket browned at spine and edges, dust jacket repeats cover design.   Ulysses 39-176 1996 £95.00

ELIOT, THOMAS STEARNS 1888-1965   Ezra Pound. His Metric and Poetry. New York: Knopf, 1917. 1st edition; crown 8vo; 31 pages; frontispiece; original pink boards, front cover gilt lettred, spine faded, small front cover stain, good. Gallup A2.   Blackwell's B112-95 1996 £325.00

ELIOT, THOMAS STEARNS 1888-1965   Ezra Pound. His Metric and Poetry. New York: Knopf, 1917. 1st edition; 1000 copies printed; small, fragile and uncommon volume; this copy lacking dust jacket, otherwise very good in spine faded boards, two tiny holes at front spine fold. Ken Lopez 74-122 1996 $350.00

ELIOT, THOMAS STEARNS 1888-1965   Ezra Pound - His Metric and Poetry. New York: Alfred A. Knopf, 1917, i.e 1918. Only 1000 copies were printed; original binding, spine and cover edges faded, head and tail of spine and corners bumped, covers slightly marked, very good in quarter morocco custom made slipcase, which is faded at spine and slightly faded. Bookplate of James D. Hart.   Ulysses 39-170 1996 £485.00

ELIOT, THOMAS STEARNS 1888-1965   Four Quartets. New York: Harcourt Brace, 1943. 1st collected edition; 2nd impression, one of 3500 copies; (all but 788 copies of the 1st impression were destroyed by publisher due to poor production values); thin 8vo; black cloth, dust jacket lightly sunned; former owner's neat bookplate, otherwise fine. Gallup A43.   James S. Jaffe 34-146 1996 $225.00

ELIOT, THOMAS STEARNS 1888-1965   Four Quartets. New York: HB Co., 1943. 1st U.S. edition, 1st issue; because of typesetting error which caused the margins to be unacceptably narrow, only 788 copies of the first printing were sent out for review and other purposes, the remainder, some 3300 copies, were destroyed; rust mark from paper clip to titlepage, else near fine in very good dust jacket with few edge tears and with small internal piece missing to spine panel.   Lame Duck Books 19-178 1996 $1,500.00

ELIOT, THOMAS STEARNS 1888-1965   Four Quartets. New York: HB Co., 1943. Corrected 1st edition; some ink notation to several pages, D. I. Ross's bookplate to front pastedown, else near fine in dust jacket with chipping to extremities and couple of tiny, tape repaired edge tears to front panel; scarce.   Lame Duck Books 19-179 1996 $300.00

ELIOT, THOMAS STEARNS 1888-1965   Four Quartets. London: Faber & Faber Ltd., 1944. 1st collected edition; original binding, top edge slightly dusty, lower cover slightly creased, endpapers spotted and partially browned, covers slightly bowed, very good in dusty and slightly torn, creased, rubbed and spotted dust jacket, browned at spine and edges. Ulysses 39-180 1996 £145.00

ELIOT, THOMAS STEARNS 1888-1965   Four Quartets. London: Faber and Faber, 1944. 1st British edition; near fine in near fine, spine darkened dust jacket.   Ken Lopez 74-123 1996 $350.00

ELIOT, THOMAS STEARNS 1888-1965   The Idea of Christian Society. London: Faber & Faber Ltd., 1939. 1st edition original binding, inscription, top edge slightly dusty, head and tail of spine and corners slightly bumped, free endpapers partially browned, lower cover slightly marked, very good in dusty and slightly torn, rubbed and marked dust jacket, faded at spine and edges.   Ulysses 39-179 1996 £75.00

ELIOT, THOMAS STEARNS 1888-1965   From Poe to Valery - A Lecture Delivered at the Library of Congress on friday, November 19, 1948. Washington: 1949. 2nd edition; one of 1000 copies, which were distributed gratis by the Library of Congress Information and Publication Office; offprint; wrappers, covers slightly marked and dusty, cover edges browned and rubbed; very good.   Ulysses 39-181 1996 £55.00

ELIOT, THOMAS STEARNS 1888-1965   The Letters of T. S. Eliot, Volume I 1898-1922. New York: Harcourt Brace, 1989. Limited to 500 copies, signed by editor, Valerie Eliot; numerous photos; very fine, in slipcase.   Bella Luna 7-221 1996 $100.00

ELIOT, THOMAS STEARNS 1888-1965   Old Possum's Book of Practical Cats. London: Faber & Faber, 1939. 1st edition; foolscap 4to; smartly bound in recent half morocco, banded and gilt, preserving original front cover (with Eliot's own caricature design) at the rear, edges little browned, but very good.   Ash Rare Books Zenzybyr-33 1996 £250.00

ELIOT, THOMAS STEARNS 1888-1965   Old Possum's Book of Practical Cats. New York: Harcourt Brace & Co., 1939. 1st American edition; considerable foxing to boards, little to page edges, slight offsetting to free front endpaper, thus very good in very good dust jacket with some light foxing and bit of rubbing to paper, still quite presentable. Between the Covers 42-156 1996 $300.00

ELIOT, THOMAS STEARNS 1888-1965   A Song for Simeon. London: 1928. Large paper edition, limited to 500 numbered copies, signed by author; 8.5 x 5.5 inches; drawing by E. McKnight Kauffer; boards, minor cover staining, soiled copy, couple of bumped corners.   John K. King 77-285 1996 $250.00

ELIOT, THOMAS STEARNS 1888-1965   A Song for Simeon. London: Faber & Gwyer Ltd., n.d. 1928. 1st edition full page color illustrations by E. McKnight Kauffer; wrappers, cover edges slightly darkened; frontispiece and final page of text partially browned, very good in printed envelope, which is dusty and slightly creased, torn, rubbed and marked, as well as browned at join between the envelope flap.   Ulysses 39-173 1996 £85.00

ELIOT, THOMAS STEARNS 1888-1965   Sweeney Agonistes. London: Faber, 1932. 1st edition; crown 8vo; pages 31; original pale blue boards, faintly faded backstrip lettered in red, dust jacket little defective, excellent.   Blackwell's B112-98 1996 £425.00

ELIOT, THOMAS STEARNS 1888-1965   Odermarken og Andre Digte. (The Waste Land and Other Poems). Kobenhavn: Westermann, 1948. 1st Danish edition; CLXVIII/235 copies (of an edition of 885 copies), signed by author and translators, Kai Moller and Tom Kristensen; crown 8vo; pages 87; title printed in black and blue; unbound sheets loosely inserted in original pale blue board folder with printed front cover label, its backstrip faded, matching board slipcase with printed label, fine. Gallup D49.   Blackwell's B112-99 1996 £335.00

ELIZABETH II, QUEEN OF GREAT BRITAIN   The Address of Her Majesty Queen Elizabeth II. Delivered at Westminster Hall and Guildhall on the Occasion of Her Silver Jubilee 1952-1977. Worcester: 1977. Limited to 1000 copies; 2 3/4 x 1 7/8 inches; 24 pages; portrait frontispiece; blue leather with gilt stamped lion on one cover and unicorn on other; very fine, all edges gilt.   Bromer Booksellers 87-222 1996 $110.00

ELKINS, JOHN M.   Indian Fighting on the Texas Frontier. Amarillo: privately printed, ca. 1929. 1st edition; 96 pages; portraits, original pictorial grey wrappers, some minor foxing, very good. Tate, Texas Indians 2366; not in Adams Herd.   Michael D. Heaston 23-143 1996 $125.00

ELKINS, JOHN M.   Indian Fighting on the Texas Frontier. Amarillo: 1929. 96 pages; portrait, 3 plates; grey wrappers with black stamping, very good+.   Bohling Book Co. 191-31 1996 $100.00

ELKO. CHAMBER OF COMMERCE   Elko County the Agricultural Center of Nevada. Elko: Free Press and Independent, ca. 1920's. 1st edition; 23 pages, maps and illustrations; original stiff pictorial wrappers, title stamped in red on front cover; fine. Paher Nevada 547.   Michael D. Heaston 23-254 1996 $125.00

ELKUS, RICHARD J.   Alamos: a Philosophy in Living. San Francisco: Grabhorn Press, 1965. Limited to 487 copies, signed by author and by Edwin and Robert Grabhorn; folio; 64 pages; 24 mounted photographic plates; leather backed decorated cloth; very fine.   Argonaut Book Shop 113-226 1996 $300.00

ELLEN Irving, the Female Victimizer, Who Cruelly Murdered Sixteen Persons in Cool Blood, for Revenge on Her First Love, William Shannon, Who Betrayed Her. Baltimore: Philadelphia: New York and Buffalo: pub. by Arthur R. Orton, 1856. 1st edition; 8vo; 4 wood engraved illustrations, original pink pictorial wrappers (slight wear); very rare;   Ximenes 108-132 1996 $450.00

ELLENBECKER, JOHN G.   The Jayhawkers of Death Valley. Marysville: privately printed for the author, 1938. 1st edition; 130 pages, printed in double columns; illustrations; original stiff brown printed wrappers, minor chipping, very fine. Rocq California Local History 2301 and 2302; Mintz Trail 141.   Michael D. Heaston 23-144 1996 $200.00

ELLENPORT, SAMUEL B.   An Essay on the Development and Usage of Brass Plate Dies... Boston: Harcourt Bindery, 1980. 1st edition; one of 500 copies; large 4to; colored frontispiece, 32 pages of text, 99 plates; original cloth, leather label on spine.   Forest Books 74-75 1996 £55.00

ELLES, G. L.   British Graptolites. London: 1901-18. 4to; pages clxxi, 539, 52 plates, 359 text figures; cloth; University Library copy with stamp on title and edges, otherwise fine.   John Henly 27-759 1996 £120.00

ELLICE, EDWARD C.   Place-Names in Glengarry and Glenquoich and Their Origin. London: Swan Sonnenschein, 1898. 8vo; pages viii, 127; uncut, frontispiece and large folding map; original cloth, gilt, extremities minimally rubbed.   R.F.G. Hollett 76-85 1996 £55.00

ELLICOTT, ANDREW   The Journal of Andrew Ellicott...During Part of the Year 1796, the Years 1797, 1798, 1799 and Part of the Year 1800. Philadelphia: Thomas Dobson, 1803. 1st edition; 4to; viii, 299, 151, (1) pages; 14 folding maps and charts; contemporary calf, joints cracked, some cover wear, lacking blank half of errata leaf, with no loss of text. The Bookpress 75-410 1996 $3,000.00

ELLIOT, DANIEL GIRAUD   The Birds of Daniel Giraud Elliott, a Selection of Pheasants and Peacocks Printed by Joseph Wolf and Taken from the Original Monograph Published in New York in 1872. Ariel Press, 1979. Limited to 1000 copies, this number 319; imperial folio; 12 fine color plates; green cloth, dust jacket, mint.   John Henly 27-11 1996 £75.00

ELLIOT, DANIEL GIRAUD   The Birds of Daniel Giraud Elliot: a Selection of Pheasants and Peacocks... London: Ariel Press, 1979. Limited to 1000 signed and numbered copies; folio; 12 color plates and facsimile titlepage, 11 page introduction, 1 leaf of text facing each plate, cloth, label on upper cover.   Thomas Thorp 489-93 1996 £75.00

ELLIOT, DANIEL GIRAUD   The Life and Habits of Wild Animals. London: 1874. Folio; pages 72, 20 plates; original cloth, neatly refixed in slightly used case.   Wheldon & Wesley 207-486 1996 £100.00

ELLIOT, DANIEL GIRAUD   A Review of the Primates. New York: 1912/13. Imperial 8vo; 3 volumes; 28 colored plates, 140 plain plates; buckram, trifle used. First half of volume 1 somewhat waterstained, otherwise good, few pencil anntoations.   Wheldon & Wesley 207-554 1996 £450.00

ELLIOT, DANIEL GIRAUD   Review of the Primates. New York: 1913. 3 volumes, 28 color plates, 140 black and white plates; buckram, slightly worn, ex-library, internally good.   John Johnson 135-428 1996 $350.00

ELLIOT, JAMES   The Poetical and Miscellaneous Works of James Elliot,, Citizen of Guilford, Vermont and Late a Noncommissioned Officer in the Legion of the United States. Greenfield: Thomas Dickman for the author, 1798. 1st edition; 12mo; 271, (5) pages; contemporary sheep, leather label, hinges starting slightly, still firm; lovely copy, very rare. Howes E97; Streeter Sale 1320; Brinley Sale 6847; Graff 1231.   M & S Rare Books 60-152 1996 $1,850.00

ELLIOT, JOHN   Elements of the Branches of Natural Philosophy Connected with Medicine... London: 1786. 2nd edition; xvi, 338 pages, 2 folding plates; contemporary half calf, joints cracked. Cole 405. Graham Weiner C2-74 1996 £50.00

ELLIOTT, BENJAMIN   The Militia System of South-Carolina. Charleston: A. E. Miller, 1835. 1st edition; 8vo; 84, 211 pages, index; contemporary calf, leather label, front hinge weak, rubbed, some foxing, but good. Very scarce. Rinkderknecht 31480; not in LCP/HSP Afro Amer. Cat.   M & S Rare Books 60-410 1996 $600.00

ELLIOTT, HENRY W.   A Monograph of the Seal Islands of Alaska. Washington: 1882. 4to; pages 176, 2 maps and 29 plates; cloth, trifle worn.   Wheldon & Wesley 207-387 1996 £60.00

ELLIOTT, HENRY W.   Report on the Seal Islands of Alaska. Washington: GPO, 1880. 1st edition; quarto; 188 pages; 29 plates, 2 double page maps, 13 smaller maps, numerous text figures; green cloth, gilt lettered spine, very fine; rare.   Argonaut Book Shop 113-18 1996 $375.00

ELLIOTT, HENRY W.   Report on the Seal Islands of Alaska. Washington: GPO, 1884. 4to; 188 pages; 29 plates + 2 double faced maps; covers unsightly, soiled and worn, interior very good. Arctic Biblio 4546.   Parmer Books Nat/Hist-051485 1996 $165.00

ELLIOTT, ROBERT   Views in India, China and on the Shores of the Red Sea. London: H. Fisher, R. Fisher and P. Jackson, 1835. Quarto; 2 volumes; 68; 64 pages; engraved vignette titles, 62 engraved plates, including color printed frontispiece in volume 1; original quarter burgundy morocco over plum moire cloth boards, spine stamped in gilt, all edges gilt, extremities lightly rubbed, some discoloration to cloth, hinges cracked but sound, occasional light foxing, previous owner's ink signature on front free endpapers; very good.   Heritage Book Shop 196-256 1996 $1,000.00

ELLIOTT, S.   A Sketch of the Botany of South-Carolina and Georgia. Charleston: 1824. 8vo; pages viii, 743; Volume 2 (of 2): 6 copper plates (browned, 2 plates severely); contemporary full sheep, some wear to extremities, piece of leather missing from lower front corner, pages browned or foxed to varying degrees, ink notations to endpapers, institutional bookplate, embossed stamp on title.   Raymond M. Sutton VI-502 1996 $750.00

ELLIOTT, W. R.   Encyclopaedia of Australian Plants Suitable for Cultivation. Volume 6 K-M. Melbourne: 1993. Royal 8vo; 526 pages, several hundred color photos and text figures; hardbound.   Wheldon & Wesley 207-1687 1996 £67.00

ELLIOTT, WILLIAM   Carolina Sports by Land and Water. London: Richard Bentley, 1867. 1st English edition; 12mo; 292 pages; publisher's green cloth, rubberstamp on inside front cover, otherwise very good, bright copy.   The Bookpress 75-464 1996 $275.00

ELLIS, BRET EASTON   Less than Zero. New York: S&S, 1985. 1st edition; near fine in dust jacket; inscribed by author in 1986.   Lame Duck Books 19-180 1996 $150.00

ELLIS, GEORGE   Specimens of the Early English Poets. London: Edwards, 1790. 1st edition; octavo; contemporary dark blue straight grain morocco, gilt, all edges gilt, light wear, nice.   G. W. Stuart 59-32 1996 $295.00

ELLIS, GEORGE   Specimens of Early English Metrical Romances, Chiefly Written During the Early Part of the Fourteenth Century. Edinburgh: ptd. for A. Constable & Co./London: Longman, Hurst, Rees & Orme, 1805. 8vo; 3 volumes; boards covered with marbled paper, uncut. Anthony W. Laywood 108-168 1996 £55.00

ELLIS, HENRY HAVELOCK 1859-1939   Chapman: an Essay with Illustrative Passages. London: Nonesuch Press, 1934. Of 700 numbered copies, this, no. 3, is one of only 75 specially bound; 8vo; printed on Van Gelder in Monotype Centaur and Arrighi; full niger goatskin, spine lavishly gilt, leather very slightly scuffed in places and endpapers discolored, as usual, but very nice, scarce.   Bertram Rota 272-330 1996 £200.00

ELLIS, HENRY HAVELOCK 1859-1939   The Criminal. London: Walter Scott, 1890. 1st edition; 12mo; viii, 337, (7) pages, 16 plates, text illustrations; printed pebbled mauve cloth, spine faded, very good. John Gach 150-136 1996 $100.00

ELLIS, HENRY HAVELOCK 1859-1939   Studies in the Psychology of Sex. Philadelphia: F. A. Davis Co., 1928. Various printings; 8vo; 7 volumes; brown cloth, hinges cracked, else good set with some shelfwear.   John Gach 150-137 1996 $150.00

ELLIS, W. T.   Memories: My Seventy-Two Years in the Romantic County of Yuba, California. Eugene: 1939. 4to; boards with buckrjam spine, spine slightly faded and edges little worn, faint traces of adhesive tape on flyleaf, but nice.   Bertram Rota 272-310 1996 £60.00

ELLIS, WILLIAM CHARLES   A Treatise on the Nature, Symptoms, Causes and Treatment of Insanity with Practical Observations on Lunatic Asylums, and a Description of the Pauper Lunatic Asylum...at Hanwell... London: Samuel Holdsworth, 1838. 1st edition; 8vo; viii, 344 pages plus inserted publisher's catalog; embossed green cloth, expertly rebacked, corners shelfworn, moderate dampstaining to endleaves, lacking folding frontispiece lithograph, otherwise clean, unopened copy; scarce. Wellcome II p. 521; Norman Cat. 705; Hunter & Macalpine p. 870-77. John Gach 150-135 1996 $475.00

ELLIS, WILLIAM CHARLES   A Treatise on the Nature, Symptoms, Causes and Treatment of Insanity, with Practical Observations on Lunatic Asylums... London: 1838. 1st edition; 8vo; modern boards, leather label. Argosy 810-166 1996 $400.00

ELLISON, H.   Love Ain't Nothing But Sex Misspelled. Trident, 1968. 1st edition; signed by author; very good in very good dust jacket. scarce. Aronovitz 57-370 1996 $165.00

ELLISON, JAMES   The American Captive, or the Siege of Tripoli. Boston: published by Joshua Belcher, 1812. 1st edition; 18mo; disbound; scarce, foxed, one lower corner torn, catching a couple of words (essentially clear from context); Hill 100; Quinn p. 153; Shaw & Shoemaker 25330.   Ximenes 108-121 1996 $200.00

ELLISON, RALPH   Invisible Man. New York: Random House, 1952. 1st edition; some rubbing to spine lettering, otherwise about fine in very good dust jacket with little rubbing to extremities and some loss at crown which at its deepest point is 3/8 inch; nice.   Between the Covers 43-72 1996 $650.00

ELLISON, RALPH   Invisible man. New York: Random House, 1952. 1st edition; 8 1/2 x 5 3/4 inches; 4 p.l., 439 pages; original cloth and dust jacket, front endpapers with shadow of previously laid in paper, otherwise fine in very good jacket that is bit frayed at edges and neatly tape repaired on verso in several places; inscribed and signed by author for P. Magarick.   Phillip J. Pirages 33-199 1996 $500.00

ELLWOOD, T.   The Landnama Book of Iceland As It Illustrates the Dialect, Place Names, Folk Lore & Antiquities of Cumberland, Westmorland and North Lancashire. Kendal: T. Wilson, 1894. 1st edition; 8vo; paes xvii, 69; original cloth, gilt.   R.F.G. Hollett & Son 78-379 1996 £85.00

ELLYS, ANTHONY   Tracts on the Liberty, spiritual and Temporal, of Protestants in England. Addressed to J. N. Esq.; at Aix-la-Chapells. Part I (-II). London: /ptd. by Wm. Bowyer & sold by Whiston & White../Ptd. for J. Whiston &.. 1763-65. 1st edition; 4to; 2 parts in 1 volume, pages xi, (iii)-x, 301, (1 errata; vii, 96, 99-286 and 2 leaves of new general title (Whiston & White imprint) for binding as one volume and leaf of contents for part one paged xi-xii, complete in spite of pagination jump; contemporary; paper flaw on corner of one leaf, just touching a catch-word with minor very light foxing in some places, otherwise nice copy.   James Fenning 133-100 1996 £275.00

ELMES, JAMES   Memoirs of the Life and Works of Sir Christopher Wren. London: Priestley and Weale, 1823. 1st edition; 4to; xxxvi, 532, 147, (1), (4 ads) pages, 12 plates, 4 are double page; later 19th century half morocco, frontispiece heavily offset on titlepage, otherwise nice. The Bookpress 75-259 1996 $850.00

ELMES, JAMES   Memoirs of the Life and Works of Sir Christopher Wren with a Brief View of the Progress of Architecture in England from the Beginning of the Reign of Charles the First to the End of the Seventeenth Century. London: Priestly and Weale, 1823. Large 4to; frontispiece, xxxvi, 532, 147; 12 engraved plates; later half linen and marbled boards, uncut, foxing and browning of text, otherwise clean, tight copy.   James Tait Goodrich K40-298 1996 $395.00

ELMORE, STANTON   A Gentleman of the South. New York: Macmillan Co., 1903. 1/100 large paper (unnumbered copy); 8vo; 232 pages; frontispiece, illustrations; original yellow beige silk cloth, spine label worn and spotted; very good.   Robert F. Lucas 42-71 1996 $100.00

ELPHINSTONE, H.   Patterns for Turning: Comprising Elliptical and Other Figures. London: 1872. 1st edition; 8vo; 70 plates, 9 cards of tables in pocket, printed on pink paper; brown cloth, decorated in gilt and black, trifle worn. Abell 77.   Maggs Bros. Ltd. 1190-627 1996 £80.00

ELPHINSTONE, MOUNTSTUART   An Account of the Kingdom of Caubul and Its Depedencies in Persia, Tartary and India. London: printed for Longman, Hurst, Rees, Orme and Brown and J. Murray, 1819. 2nd edition; demy 8vo; 2 volumes in 1; 512, 495 pages, 2 hand colored frontispiece aquatints, 1 hand colored aquatint plate, 1 large folding aquatint, 1 folding map partially colored, some offsetting to title volume 1, foxing to uncolored aquatint, offsetting to map; half red morocco, blind rule to covers, gilt bands and title to panelled spine, marbled boards, edges and endpapers, ink signatures.   Beeleigh Abbey BA56-65 1996 £425.00

ELSBERG, CHARLES   Diagnosis and Treatment of Surgical Diseases of the Spinal Cord and Its Membranes. Philadelphia: 1916. 8vo; 330 pages, illustrations, some colored; original binding, clean, bright copy. GM 4910; Iowa 1172.   James Tait Goodrich K40-125 1996 $295.00

ELSBERG, CHARLES   Tumors of the Spinal Cord and the Symptons of Irritation and Compression of the Spinal Cord and Nerve Roots. New York: Paul Hoeber, 1925. 8vo; 421 pages; 354 illustrations; original binding; J. Lawrence Pool's copy with his signature.   James Tait Goodrich K40-126 1996 $350.00

ELSEN, ALBERT   Paul Jenkins. New York: Abrams, n.d. Square 4to; 284 pages; 171 plates, 56 tipped in and in color; cloth.   Brannan 43-278 1996 $110.00

ELSEN, ALBERT   The Sculpture of Henri Matisse. New York: Abrams, n.d. 4to; 223 pages, 284 illustrations; cloth, dust jacket. Freitag 6212. Brannan 43-398 1996 $275.00

ELSEN, ALBERT   Seymour Lipton. New York: Abrams, n.d. Oblong 4to; 244 pages; 215 illustrations, including 52 tipped in color plates, cloth, dust jacket. Freitag 5687.   Brannan 43-361 1996 $125.00

ELSTOB, ELIZABETH   The Rudiments of Grammar for the English-Saxon Tongue, First Given in English... London: printed by W. Bowyer & Sold by J. Bowyer and C. King, 1715. 4to; title in red and black; contemporary speckled calf, gilt spine and borders, red label, slight rubbing to hinges, very good. Alston III 18.   Jarndyce 103-234 1996 £550.00

ELTON, G.   Voles, Mice and Lemmings: Problems in Population Dynamics. Oxford: 1942. Royal 8vo; 504 pages, text figures; cloth; scarce original issue, nice copy.   Wheldon & Wesley 207-555 1996 £75.00

ELUARD, PAUL   Pablo Picasso. Geneva/Paris: Trois Collines, 1944. 1st edition; many plates; wrappers in paper dust jacket, fine but for owner's inscriptions on blank prelim, in lightly used dust jacket in nice slipcase, with rubbing to one panel   Beasley Books 82-60 1996 $150.00

ELWES, D. G. C.   A History of Castles, Mansions, and Manors of Western Sussex. London: 1876. 4to; illustrations; half red morocco. Petersfield Bookshop FH58-185 1996 £200.00

ELWES, HENRY JOHN   The Trees of Great Britain and Ireland. Edinburgh: 1906-13. 4to; 7 volumes, pages xvi, 1933, (i)-xxiv, (1935-) 2022; 7 colored titlepages, 5 colored frontispieces, portrait, 414 plates; green binder's cloth, some soiling and flecking to covers, some fading around spines, overall solid, nice set. Now very scarce   Raymond M. Sutton VII-11 1996 $1,850.00

ELWORTHY, FREDERICK THOMAS   The Evil Eye: an Account of the Ancient and Widespread Superstition. London: John Murray, 1895. 1st edition; illustrations; bookplates on both front pastedown and front free endpaper, light rubbing to joints, otherwise clean and bright; two autograph letters from author laid in.   Hermitage SP95-746 1996 $200.00

ELY, EZRA STILES   The Journal of the Stated Preacher to the Hospital and Almshouse in the City of New York, for the year of Our Lord 1811. New York: published by Whiting and Watson; J. Seymour, printer, 1812. 1st edition; 12mo; contemporary tree calf, spine gilt, bit rubbed; foxed, but very good, uncommon. Sabin 22384; Austin 726; Shaw & Shoemaker 25332.   Ximenes 108-122 1996 $275.00

EMDEN, WALTER   Picturesque Westminster. London: privately printed, 1902. 7th edition; 15 plates; 64 plates; decorated printed wrpapers, loose in original cloth portfolio; inscribed in pencil at head of front wrappers "From the producer W. Emden, Jany. 1903."   Marlborough 162-135 1996 £90.00

EMERSON, G. E.   A Report on the Trees and Shrubs Growing Naturally in the Forests of Massachusetts. Boston: 1846. 8vo; pages xv, 547, 17 plates; boards, cloth back, uncut, paper label from original binding affixed to endpaper, little minor foxing, scarce.   Wheldon & Wesley 207-1829 1 996 £75.00

EMERSON, RALPH WALDO 1803-1882   An Address Delivered Before the Senior Class in Divinity College. Boston: James Munroe, 1838. 1st edition; 1000 copies printed; three quarter tan calf, raised bands, gilt, by Bayntun; fine. BAL 5184; Myerson A7.1.   Mac Donnell 12-9 1996 $275.00

EMERSON, RALPH WALDO 1803-1882   An Address Delivered in the Court-House in Concord. Boston: James Munroe, 1844. 1st edition; 1st state of wrappers; original brown printed wrappers, very fine, fresh copy, housed in cloth slipcase, leather label. Myerson A17.1.a. BAL 5199. Mac Donnell 12-10 1996 $600.00

EMERSON, RALPH WALDO 1803-1882   The Conduct of Life. Boston: Ticknor & Fields, 1860. 1st edition; 1st printing, Binding B (no priority), sequence 3 (no priority); original brown cloth, gilt, very good, scarce; BAL 5231; Myerson A26.1.a.   Mac Donnell 12-11 1996 $150.00

EMERSON, RALPH WALDO 1803-1882   English Traits. Boston: Phillips, Sampson, 1856, 1st edition; 1st printing; the edition was 3100 copies (or less); original black cloth, gilt, spine ends frayed, otherwise tight, clean copy; BAL 5226; Myerson A24.1.a.   Mac Donnell 12-14 1996 $100.00

EMERSON, RALPH WALDO 1803-1882   English Traits. Boston: Phillips, Sampson, 1856. 1st edition; 1st printing; original black cloth, gilt, fine, tight copy; housed in slightly rubbed half morocco slipcase, gilt, inner cloth wrapper; early owner's inscription dated August 22, 1856; BAL 5226; Myerson A24.1.a.   Mac Donnell 12-15 1996 $200.00

EMERSON, RALPH WALDO 1803-1882   Essays. Boston: 1841. 1st edition; original cloth, rebacked with original spine laid in, occasional light foxing, corners rubbed, otherwise nice, tight copy.   Stephen Lupack 83- 1996 $625.00

EMERSON, RALPH WALDO 1803-1882   Essays. (with) Essays: Second Series. Boston: James Munroe, 1844. 1st editions; 12mo; 2 volumes; 1st title in original cloth with correct first binding, some tiny inoffensive chipping to top and tail of spine, otherwise near fine for this fragile cloth; 2nd title in correct first binding and correct first issue, some fading, some foxing and faint wax mark on upper cover, otherwise very bright and also near fine, enclosed in custom double-compartment quarter morocco slipcase; both volumes are tight with perfect hinges, and are well matched as to light wear.   Lakin & Marley 3-10 1996 $3,500.00

EMERSON, RALPH WALDO 1803-1882   Essays: Second Series. Boston: James Munroe, 1844. 1st edition; 1st printing, 1st state of binding; original olive grey-green cloth, gilt, fine, tight copy of a very scarce book. From the library of John Ware (brother of Henry Ware, whom Emerson replaced as pastaor of Second Church); Rusk Life p. 136; BAL 5198; Myerson A16.1.a.b.   Mac Donnell 12-20 1996 $1,000.00

EMERSON, RALPH WALDO 1803-1882   Essays: Second Series. Boston: James Munroe, 1844. 1st edition; 1st printing, 2nd state of binding; original brown cloth, gilt, spine ends expertly strengthened, otherwise tight copy with mild foxing; Grolier American Hundred 47; BAL 5198; Myerson A16.1.a.b.   Mac Donnell 12-19 1996 $400.00

EMERSON, RALPH WALDO 1803-1882   Essays: Second Series. Boston: james Munroe, 1844. 1st edition; 2nd printing, 2nd state of binding; original dark brown cloth, gilt, spine ends chipped, short split in rear joint, else tight clean copy; Grolier American Hundred 47; BAL 5198; Myerson A16.1.a-b.   Mac Donnell 12-21 1996 $150.00

EMERSON, RALPH WALDO 1803-1882   Essays. Doves Press, 1906. One of 300 copies on paper (there were also 25 on vellum); 9 1/4 x 6 1/2 inches; initials in red, two pages partly printed in red, original flexible vellum, gilt titling on spine, fore edge and tail edge untrimmed, usual variation in color of vellum because of grain, couple of small wrinkles in vellum at bottom of front cover, otherwise very fine. Front pastedown with small ownership cipher and two bookplates. Tomkinson p. 55. Phillip J. Pirages 33-185 1996 $950.00

EMERSON, RALPH WALDO 1803-1882   Essays. London: Macmillan, 1910. Octavo; 538 pages; full crushed dark green morocco, double gilt and blind fillets, raised bands, gilt, inner gilt dentelles, all edges gilt; with skilfully rendered fore-edge painting depicting Christopher Columbus and the Santa Maria on stormy seas; slight wear, old writing on flyleaf, generally an excellent copy.   Hartfield 48-F1 1996 $695.00

EMERSON, RALPH WALDO 1803-1882   Fortune of the Republic. Boston: Houghton, Osgood, 1878. 1st edition; one of 504 copies bound in cloth; original dark brown cloth, gilt; near fine. Myerson A36.1.a. BAL 5278.   Mac Donnell 12-22 1996 $165.00

EMERSON, RALPH WALDO 1803-1882   May-Day and Other Pieces. Boston: Ticknor & Fields, 1867. 1st edition; one of 100 copies, specially bound for presentation purposes; original white cloth, gilt, spine browned, spine ends lightly chafed, covers somewhat aged, else tight, clean copy; housed in cloth folding case, leather labels; inscribed by author for Mrs. Sylvina Jackson. BAL 5250; Myerson A28.1.a.   Mac Donnell 12-28 1996 $1,850.00

EMERSON, RALPH WALDO 1803-1882   May-Day and Other Pieces. Boston: Ticknor & Fields, 1867. 1st edition; original wine cloth, light rubbing at tips, but no fading, as nearly always seen with this color; BAL 5250; Myerson A28.1.a.   Mac Donnell 12-26 1996 $125.00

EMERSON, RALPH WALDO 1803-1882   May Day and Other Pieces. Boston: Ticknor and Fields, 1867. 1st edition; one of 200 copies printed; original terra cotta cloth, gilt, chip at crown, else fine, crisp copy. BAL 5250; Myerson A28.1.a.   Mac Donnell 12-27 1996 $100.00

EMERSON, RALPH WALDO 1803-1882   May-Day and Other Pieces. London: George Routledge, 1867. 1st English edition; original green cloth, gilt, top edge gilt, paper of inner hinges beginning to crack, otherwise an attractive copy of this fragile and elusive printing. BAL 5374.   Mac Donnell 12-29 1996 $125.00

EMERSON, RALPH WALDO 1803-1882   The Method of Nature, an Oration Delivered Before the Society of the Adelphi. Boston: Samuel Simpkins, 1841. 1st edition; one of 500 copies; three quarter tan calf, raised bands, gilt, by Bayntun; fine, rare. BAL 5190; Myerson A11.1.   Mac Donnell 12-30 1996 $350.00

EMERSON, RALPH WALDO 1803-1882   Miscellanies. Boston: Phillips, Sampson, 1856. 1st edition under this title; one of 500 copies; original black cloth, gilt, near fine, scarce. Myerson A21.1.a. BAL 5367.   Mac Donnell 12-31 1996 $150.00

EMERSON, RALPH WALDO 1803-1882   Moments with Emerson. London: Henry Frowde, n.d. 1st edition; 16mo; original binding, top edge gilt, upper cover soiled, head and tail of spine and corners slightly bumped, endpaper gutters browned, front free endpaper and fore-edge slightly soiled; good; ownership signature of Ian Fleming.   Ulysses 39-675 1996 £125.00

EMERSON, RALPH WALDO 1803-1882   Nature. Boston: James Munroe, 1836. 1st edition; 1st state of page 94 (no priority). Original green coral pattern embossed cloth, gilt, minor rubbing and foxing, but fine, from the library of Caroline D. Brooks, who married E. R. Hoar in 1840. Myerson A3.a.a. (frame A cloth 2); BAL 5181.   Mac Donnell 12-35 1996 $3,000.00

EMERSON, RALPH WALDO 1803-1882   Nature. Boston: James Munroe, 1836. 1st edition; 2nd state of page 94 (no priority); original blue green maze pattern embossed cloth, gilt, small nick at crown, light rubbing at foot, some foxing in text, but fine, bright copy; in some copies there are 2 pencil corrections on page 32, either in Emerson's hand or that of his editorial assistant Charles S. Wheeler, the corrections appear to be in Emerson's hand in this copy; Myerson A3.1.a (frame B and cloth 8). BAL 5181.   Mac Donnell 12-34 1996 $2,500.00

EMERSON, RALPH WALDO 1803-1882   Nature. Boston: James Munroe and Co., 1836. 1st edition; 12mo; page 94 is correctly paged (presumed 2nd state); original purple red cloth, traces of rubbing at ends of spine; Myerson's cloth 9, stamping b; very good copy of author's first book; early 19th century oval stamp of the Mercantile Library Assoc. of New York, with a couple of other related markings; BAL 5181; Myerson A3.1.8.   Ximenes 109-109 1996 $2,000.00

EMERSON, RALPH WALDO 1803-1882   Nature: Addresses and Lectures. Boston & Cambridge: James Munroe, 1849. 1st edition; binding variant, undescribed by BAL or Myerson (no priority between various bindings), original black cloth, gilt, covers blindstamped with triple rule border enclosing a floral design with center blank, spine stamped and lettered as in binding A, minor rubbing, else tight, fresh, attractive copy. BAL 5218; Myerson A21.1.a.   Mac Donnell 12-33 1996 $300.00

EMERSON, RALPH WALDO 1803-1882   An Oration Delivered Before the Literary Societies of Dartmouth College. Boston: Charles C. Little and James Brown, 1838. 1st edition; 1000 copies printed; three quarter tan calf, raised bands, gilt, by Zaehnsdorf, very fine. Myerson A8.1. BAL 5185.   Mac Donnell 12-36 1996 $275.00

EMERSON, RALPH WALDO 1803-1882   Poems. London: Chapman, 1847. 1st edition; 12mo; errata slip present, half title discarded, titlepage slightly short; pages vii (vor v), (i), 199, (1); contemporary tan calf, backstrip with raised bands, dark blue polished morocco label in second compartment, remainder filled with gilt scales, gilt double fillet and blind hounds tooth roll border on sides, edges gilt milled, endpapers and edges marbled, dark green silk marker, excellent.   Blackwell's B112-101 1996 £135.00

EMERSON, RALPH WALDO 1803-1882   Representative Men. Boston: Phillips, Sampson, 1850. 1st edition; 1st printing, 1st binding; original black cloth, gilt, fine, front free endpaper neatly excised and brief note pasted in forwarding the book signed by Judge E. R. Hoar. BAL 5219.   Mac Donnell 12-38 1996 $450.00

EMERSON, RALPH WALDO 1803-1882   Representative Men: Seven Lectures. Boston: Phillips, Sampson & Co., 1850. 1st edition; 1st printing, without ads; black cloth, hourglass design on front and back covers, top of spine chipped, otherwise very good. BAL 5219.   Blue River Books 9-133 1996 $125.00

EMERSON, WILLIAM   The Principles of Mechanics. London: printed for G. G. and J. Robinson, 1800. 5th edition; 4to; xii, 287 pages; 43 folding plates, contemporary sprinkled calf, spine chipped at head and foot. H. M. Fletcher 121-137 1996 £230.00

EMMERTON, ISAAC   A Plain and Practical Treatise on the Culture and Management of the Auricula, Polyanthus, Carnation, Pink and the Ranunculus... London: printed for the author, 1819. 2nd edition; large 12mo; hand colored frontispiece, pages xi, 228; contemporary half calf, very good, rather scarce.   James Fenning 133-101 1996 £125.00

EMMONS, E.   Agriculture of New York. Albany: 1843-49. 4to; Volumes I-III (of 5); pages xi, 371; viii, 343, 46; xi, 371; 46 plates, 16 hand colored, 3 colored folding sections, 2 folding maps, 14 colored charts, numerous text drawings; original gilt decorated cloth, worn at corners, spine ends frayed, those of volume 2 partially perished, some scattered foxing, plates mostly clean.   Raymond M. Sutton VII-918 1996 $375.00

EMMONS, E.   Agriculture of New York; Comprising an Account of the Classification, Compsotion and Distribution of the Soils and Rocks and the Natural Waters of Different Geological Formations. London: 1846. 4to; pages xi, 371; additional engraved titlepage and vignette, 22 plates, 4 folding and hand colored sections, 15 folding hand colored sections, 15 plain plates, folding hand colored agricultural map, 7 engravings in text, 38 figures, cloth, gilt, some foxing.   John Henly 27-365 1996 £65.00

EMMONS, E.   Agriculture of North Carolina. Part II... Raleigh: 1860. 8vo; pages 112; half leather, light soiling, backstrip worn and rubbed, outer hinges split but solid, browning to text from offsetting, marginal dampstaining to back pages, original front wrapper retained; rare. Raymond M. Sutton VII-919 1996 $175.00

EMORY, WILLIAM HELMSLEY 1811-1887   Notes of a Military Reconnoissance, from Fort Leavenworth, in Missouri, to San Diego, in California, Including Part of the Arkansas, Del Norte, and Gila Rivers. Washington: Wendell and Van Benthuysen, 1848. 614 pages; 64 plates, 3 plans, 2 maps, plus one large folding map; rebound in three quarter leather, large folding map in separate folder and slipcase, collated complete; rarest issue. Cowan p. 195; Edwards p. 54; Howes E145; Wagner Camp 148.5.   Argonaut Book Shop 113-230 1996 $1,500.00

EMORY, WILLIAM HEMSLEY 1811-1887   United States & Mexican Boundary Survey. Report of... Washington: Nicholson, 1857-59. 2 volumes, bound in 3; 346 plates, 3 mpa; new brown linen bindings with gilt stamped leather spine labels (2 on each volume), new endsheets by Teresa Avini; some foxing. Howes E147; Basic 57; Raines p. 76; Wagner Camp 291.   Maggie Lambeth 30-158 1996 $2,500.00

THE EMPIRE Gold Mining Company Plymouth, Amador County, California. Capital $2,000,000. Philadelphia: McLaughlin Bros., 1879. 1st edition; 23 pages; original printed green wrappers, minor chipping and soiling, very good. Cowan p. 844.   Michael D. Heaston 23-73 1996 $225.00

EMPSON, PATIENCE   The Wood Engravings of Robert Gibbings, with Some Recollections of the Artist. London: 1969. 1st edition; 8vo; with publisher's prospectus; cloth, dust jacket, near fine.   C. P. Hyland 216-267 1996 £135.00

EMPSON, WILLIAM   Letter IV. Cambridge: W. Heffer & Sons Ltd., 1929. 1st edition wrappers, covers slightly dusty and very slightly creased; near fine.   Ulysses 39-189 1996 £85.00

ENAULT, LOUIS   Londres. Paris: Librairie Hachette, 1876. 1st French edition; large 4to; 2ff., 434 pages, 54 wood engraved plates and 120 text illustrations; half blue morocco, very slightly scuffed, original printed wrappers bound in; first French edition; Carteret III 252; Ray French Books 207.   Marlborough 162-133 1996 £500.00

THE ENCYCLOPAEDIA Britannica. London: Encyclopaedia Britannica Co., 1926. 13th edition; large quarto; 32 volumes in 16; original dark green cloth stamped in light green on front cover and in gilt on spine, light wear to extremities of some volumes; near fine.   Heritage Book Shop 196-227 1996 $800.00

ENCYCLOPAEDIA Britannica. A Dictionary of Art, Sciences, Literature and General Information. London: 1910-26. 13th edition (comprises the 11th edition, together with the 3 supplementary volumes of 1992 called 12th edition and further three of 1926 called the thirteenth) 4to; 35 volumes, Cambridge issue on thin paper; original red cloth, one volume little worn at head.   Howes Bookshop 265-330 1996 £225.00

ENCYCLOPAEDIA Britannica; or a Dictionary of Arts, Sciences, and Miscellaneous Literature. Edinburgh: A. Bell and C. Macfarquhar, 1768-71. 1st edition; 4to; 3 volumes; 160 copperplates; some minor spotting, otherwise very good, clean copy, excellently rebound in full speckled calf, spine with bands, gilt rules, red and green labels in appropriate 18th century style; most handsome copy. Alston III 560.   Jarndyce 103-131 1996 £18,500.00

ENDGRAIN: Contemporary Wood Engraving in North America. Barbarian Press, 1995. Of 300 copies, this one of 50 with tipped in signed frontispiece by Rosemary Kilbourn, specially bound; printed in handset Joanna roman and italic on Zerkall mouldmade; full leather, fine copy in slipcase.   Bertram Rota 272-30 1996 $375.00

ENDGRAIN: Contemporary Wood Engraving in North America. Barbarian Press, 1995. One of 300 copies; printed in handset Joanna roman and italic on Zerkall mouldmade; one engraving each, by 121 American and Canadian artists, all printed from wood; patterned boards cloth spine, fine in slipcase. Bertram Rota 272-29 1996 £225.00

ENGEL, MARIAN Bear. New York: Atheneum, 1976. 1st American edition; fine in dust jacket, scarce. Between the Covers 42-158 1996 $100.00

ENGEL, MARIAN Bear. Toronto: McClelland and Stuart, 1976. 1st edition; signed by author in year of publication; fine in near fine dust jacket with two closed edge tears near spine crown; uncommon. Ken Lopez 74-126 1996 $350.00

ENGELBACH, WILLIAM Endocrine Medicine. Springfield: 1932. 4to; 3 volumes plus index, 4 volumes in all; 933 illustrations; Argosy 810-169 1996 $125.00

ENGELBRECHT, MARTIN Elogia Mariana... Augsburg? n.p., 1732. Apparently the sole edition; small 8vo; 59 full page engravings; contemporary full polished mottled calf, covers panelled with brilliant wide gilt roll and border, floral corner stamps, rebacked, very clean, fine. Bennett Gilbert LL29-34 1996 $1,450.00

ENGELS, JOHANN ADOLPH Ueber Papier und Einige Andere Gegenstande der Technologie und Industrie. Duisburg und Essen: Badeker und Kurzel, 1808. 1st edition; octavo; viii, 234 pages, plus (5)ff. samples; lightly rubbed marbled boards; marginal dampstaining to first 3 leaves, light foxing to frontispiece and sample leaves, else near fine, rare; possibly inscribed and dated by author. Bromer Booksellers 87-246 1996 $1,650.00

ENGINEERING RESEARCH ASSOCIATES High-speed Computing Devices. New York: McGraw Hill, 1950. 1st edition; 5th printing; 8vo; xi, 451 pages; illustrations; original cloth, signature neatly clipped from titlepage with no loss; very good. Goldstine p. 315; Sarrazin F2. Edwin V. Glaser 121-68 1996 $150.00

ENGLAND Illustrated, or, a Compendium of the Natural History, Geography, Topography and Antiquities Ecclesiastical and Civil of England and Wales. London: printed for R. and J. Dodsley, 1764. 4to; 2 volumes; 54 maps, 29 engraved views, numerous vignettes in text; contemporary polished calf, backs very worn, but internally good. H. M. Fletcher 121-98 1996 £1,000.00

ENGLAND'S Black Tribunal: Containing the Compleat Tryal of King Charles the First. London: printed for J. Wilford, 1720. 5th edition; modern three quarter speckled calf, quite pretty. Meyer Boswell SL27-42 1996 $250.00

ENGLAND, JOHN The Works of the Rt. Rev. John England. Cleveland: 1908. 1st edition; 8vo; 7 volumes; cloth, ex-library, very good. C. P. Hyland 216-207 1997 $75.00

ENGLEHEART, N. B. A Concise Treatise on Eccentric Turning. London: 1952. 1st edition; 4to; 50 figures on 16 plates, few text figures, slightly soiled copy, contemporary morocco, stained, repaired; inscribed by author in rather tremulous hand, to R. N. Cresswell. Abell 91. Maggs Bros. Ltd. 1190-628 1996 £185.00

ENGLEIELD, HENRY C. A Walk through Southampton... Southampton: T. Baker, 1805. 2nd edition; 8vo; titlepage, pages iv, 3 ff., (+1 errata), extra aquatint titlepage, 8 aquatint plates, 3 engraved plates, text illustrations; later full calf, spine gilt, label, marbled endpapers, part uncut; Abbey Scenery 269 Marlborough 162-269 1996 £165.00

ENGLISH Bijou Almanac for 1836. London: Schloss, 1835. 11/16 x 9/16 inches; (64) pages; stiff paper covers with gilt floral stamp, protected by paper case with matching gilt stamp; ribbon bookmark frayed; bookplate of A. Horodisch. Bondy pp. 165-7; Welh 2654-6. Bromer Booksellers 90-189 1996 $375.00

THE ENGLISH Gardener's New and Complete Kalendar... London: printed for J. Wenman, 144 Fleet St., 1778. 1st edition; 8vo; frontispiece, engraved plate; contemporary calf, very worn, covers off. Maggs Bros. Ltd. 1190-21 1996 £175.00

AN ENGLISH Garner In Gatherings from Our History and Literature. London: 1897. 8vo; 8 volumes; fine initial letter, 150 other ornaments; choicely bound in half red levant morocco, gilt tops; Charles W. Traylen 117-115 1996 £600.00

THE ENGLISH Lakes in the Neighbourhood of Ambleside. London: T. Nelson and Sons, 1870. 8vo; 24 pages, 12 highly finished chromolithographed paltes; original blindstamped cloth, gilt, slight mark on upper cover. R.F.G. Hollett & Son 78-902 1996 £60.00

ENGLISH Lyrcis from Spenser to Milton. London: George Bell & Sons, 1898. 1st edition; limited to 125 on Japanese vellum, this number 105; xv, 222 pages; frontispiece and title with red decorated border, 19 full page and 38 text illustrations, green and yellow binding design from trade edtiion bound in; beige holland cloth, titled in black and red on spine. Robin Greer 94A-35 1996 £250.00

ENGLISH Lyrcis from Spenser to Milton. London: George Bell & Son, 1898. 1st edition; 8vo; xv, 222 pages; frontispiece, and title with red decorated border, 19 full page and 38 text illustrations, white endpaper gilt pictorial; beirge cloth, gilt lettering on spine, red and green decorated, top edge gilt, others uncut, light prelim and fore-edge foxing. Exceptionally bright copy. Robin Greer 94A-8 1996 £75.00

ENGLISH Rustic Pictures Drawn by Frederick Walker and G. J. Pinwell and Engraved by the Brothers dalziel. India Proofs. London: George Routledge and Sons, 1882. Limited to 300 copies; folio; pages (14), 30 plates (15 of each artist), printed on india paper from the original blocks, each with accompanying leaf of letterpress; bound by Burn in original full japon decorated and lettered in gold and browns; inscribed by the Dalziels for Edith Warne. Claude Cox 107-36 1996 £135.00

ENGLISH, THOMAS H. A Memoir of the Yorkshire Esk Fishery Association. London: 1925. Privately printed, it is likely that around 50 copies were produced; 4to; original buckram; this copy has a letter fromthe author to a Miss Yeoman; book is also inscribed to Miss Yeoman by author on dedication leaf. David A.H. Grayling 3/95-433 1996 £350.00

AN ENQUIRY Into the Nataure and Obligation of Legal Rights; With Respect to the Popular Pleas of the Late K. James's Remaining Right to the Crown. London: Printed by Thomas Hodgkin, 1693. Modern marbled boards, quite fresh, clean copy. Meyer Boswell SL26-187 1996 $350.00

ENRIGHT, D. J. Poems of the 1950s an Anthology of New English Verse. Tokyo: Kenkyusha Ltd., 1955, i.e. 1956. 1st edition; original binding, free endpapers partially browned, head and tail of spine and corners slightly bumped, covers slightly bowed, very good in nicked, rubbed, chipped and dusty, slightly torn, creased, spotted and marked dust jacket browned at spine and edges and missing small piece at head of spine. With ownership signataure of Elizabeth Jennings. Ulysses 39-343 1996 £350.00

ENSCHEDE, CHARLES Typefoundries in the Netherlands from the Fifteenth to the Nineteenth Century... Haarlem: Stichting Museum Enschede, 1978. Limited to 1500 numbered copies; folio; pages xxviii, 477; frontispiece, 519 facsimile illustrations; handset in van Krimpen's Romanee and printed letterpress on laid paper; original calf backed decorated boards, as new in card slipcase; Claude Cox 107-222 1996 £220.00

ENSOR, GEORGE The Independent Man; or, an Essay on the Formation and Development of Those Principles and Faculties of the Human Mind Which Constitute Moral and Intellectual Excellence. London: printed by R. Taylor and co. & pub. for the benefit of the Literary... 1806. 1st edition; 8vo; 2 volumes, viii, 563; iv, 480 pages, bound without half title, prelim leaves in both volumes foxed, as are final leaves in volume I, inscription in red crayon on ad leaf in volume I, neat repair to contents leaf in vol. affecting some page numerals on verso; contemporary half roan, spines gilt with contrasting labels, rubbed, corners and joints rather worn. John Drury 82-73 1996 £175.00

ENTICK, JOHN Entick's New Spelling Dictionary... London: printed for Charles Dilly, 1788. New edition; samll 4to; few spots; rebound in half speckled calf, marbled boards, red label; very good. Alston V263. Jarndyce 103-143 1996 £110.00

ENTICK, JOHN Entick's new Spelling Dictioanry... London: printed for J. Mawman... 1801. Small 4to; contemporary sheep, rubbed, hinges splitting, spine slightly defecctive; owners' names. Jarndyce 103-144 1996 £60.00

ENTICK, JOHN Entick's New Spelling Dictionary... London: printed for J. Mawman &c., 1803. Small 4to; contemporary red sheep, hinges splitting, slight worming to leather only, spine chipped at tail. Jarndyce 103-145 1996 £70.00

ENTICK, JOHN   A New and Accurate History and Survey of London, Westmisnter, Southwark... London: for Edward & Charles Dilly, 1766. 1st edition; post 8vo; 4 volumes, frontispiece, portraits, 30 engraved views, folding map; late 18th century tree calf, spines gilt in overall pattern, contrasting labels, number roundels, lemon edges, etc.; little rubbed, lettering labels expertly replaced, few minor splits and repairs, one leaf with small hole, but nice. Adams 44.   Ash Rare Books   Zenzybyr-34   1996 £395.00

ENTWISLE, E. A.   French Scenic Wallpapers 1800-1860. Leigh-On-Sea: E. Lewis, Publishers, Ltd., 1972. 1st edition; limited to 500 copies; 11 1/8 x 8 5/8 inches; numerous black and white plates; fine in original publisher's glassine wrapper. With card laid in from noted historian H. W. Janson reading "From the library of H. W. Janson".   Hermitage   SP95-776   1996 $150.00

EPICTETUS   All the Works of Epictetus Which are Now Extant... London: Rivington, 1768. 3rd edition by Elizabeth Carter; 8vo; 2 volumes; pages xiii, (6), 266 and (2), 340, (14, index, appendix, contents); full early polished calf, gilt, nicely rebacked in period style, original red leather labels, gilt, laid down; sligh marginal worming to volume 2, but pretty set in generally very good condition. CBEL II 842. Lowndes I 354.   Hartfield   48-L22   1996 $385.00

EPICTETUS   Arte di Correrrger la Vita Humana. Venice: Francesco Ziletti, 1583. Small 8vo; title with woodcut vignette, printed throughout in italics, slight worming to fore margin not affecting text, generally fresh copy for a 16th century book; 18th century full calf, joints cracked but sound, spine gilt, no morocco label.   Ian Wilkinson   95/1-94   1996 £95.00

EPICTETUS   Discourses. Berne: Limited Editions Club, 1966. Limited to 1500 copies, signed by artist; 4to; xxx, 310 pages; 6 colored plates by Hans Erni; buckram, gilt, slipcase.   Thomas Thorp   489-94   1996 £60.00

EPICURUS   Epicurus: the Extant Remains of the Greek Text. New York: Limited Editions Club, 1947. Copy number 904 from a total edition of 1500 numbered copies, signed by Bruce Rogers. Fine in publisher's slipcase.   Hermitage   SP95-978   1996 $175.00

THE EPISCOPAL Registers of Carlisle. The Register of Bishop John de Halton, Part I 1293-1300. Kendal: Titus Wilson, 1906. Large 8vo; 128 pages; original wrappers.   R.F.G. Hollett & Son   78-560   1996 £75.00

THE EPISCOPAL Registers of Carlisle. The Register of Bishop John de Halton, Part II: 1003-1309. Kendal: Titus Wilson, 1909. Large 8vo; pages 129-320; original wrappers, rather chipped and rebacked.   R.F.G. Hollett & Son   78-561   1996 £65.00

THE EPISCOPAL Registers of Carlisle. The Register of Bishop John de Halton. Part III 1292-1324. Kendal: Titus Wilson, 1913. Large 8vo; pages xliii, 275, last 3 leaves of index creased and soiled; original wrappers, rather chipped and creased; last 3 leaves of index creased and soiled. R.F.G. Hollett & Son   78-562   1996 £85.00

EPPS, JAMES   The Cacao Plant: a Trip to the West Indies. Croydon: 1897-1903. 8vo; 2 offprints in 1 volume, 6 plates in the first item, extra illustrated with 75 plates, (1 real photo, 74 photographic plates, possibly collotype); contemporary half leather, gilt edges, by Truslove and Bray of West Norwood (bit worn, front joint cracked).   Maggs Bros. Ltd.   1190-236   1996 £400.00

ERASMUS, DESIDERIUS 1466-1536   Enchiridion Militis Christiani. (with) De Conte(m)ptu Mundi Epistola. (with) Liber De Sarcienda Ecclesiae Concordia. Paris: Knobloch, Cervicorn, Wechel, 1525-28-33. 8vo; 3 works in 1; titles of first two works within fine woodcut borders, title device in third work; quarter modern vellum; slight staining at end of third work; ownership signature of 1582 at foot of third titlepage. Small tear at top of last leaf of 1st work affecting 1 letter of text.   Rostenberg & Stern   150-83   1996 $2,500.00

ERASMUS, DESIDERIUS 1466-1536   Moriae Encomium, an Oration spoken by Folly in Praise of Herself. New York: Limited Editions Club, 1943. Copy number 904 from a total edition of 1500 numbered copies, signed by artist; mezzotints by Lynd Ward; full leather, slightly rubbed at crown and heel, else fine in slightly rubbed publisher's slipcase.   Hermitage   SP95-979   1996 $100.00

ERASMUS, DESIDERIUS 1466-1536   Vita...Additi sunt Epistolarum...Libri Duo... Leyden: Basson, 1607. 1st edition; 4to; device on titlepage and circular woodcut of Erasmus on title verso; quarter calf. Vander Haeghen 182.   Rostenberg & Stern   150-84   1996 $475.00

ERBER, CHRISTIAN   A Wealth of Silk and Velvet: Ottoman Fabrics and Embroideries. Bremen: Temmen, n.d. 1990's. Small 4to; 288 pages, profusely illustrated in color; pictorial boards; fine.   J. M. Cohen   35-21   1996 $125.00

ERDRICH, LOUISE   Jacklight. New York: Rinehart and Winston, 1984. 1st edition; author's first book, only issued in wrappers, light rubbing at spine folds and edges, otherwise fine, signed by author.   Anacapa House   5-345   1996 $200.00

ERDRICH, LOUISE   Love Medicine. New York: Holt, Rinehart and Winston, 1st edition; fine in dust jacket.   Anacapa House   5-93   1996 $160.00

ERDRICH, LOUISE   Love Medicine. HRW, 1984. 1st edition; author's first novel; fine in fine dust jacket.   Book Time   2-128   1996 $115.00

ERDRICH, LOUISE   Love Medicine. New York: HR&W, 1984. 1st edition; light rubbing to spinal extremities, otherwise near fine in like dust jacket.   Lame Duck Books   19-182   1996 $175.00

ERDRICH, LOUISE   Love Medicine. New York: Holt, Rinehart & Winston, 1984. 1st edition; fine in dust jacket.   Steven C. Bernard   71-89   1996 $150.00

ERDRICH, LOUISE   Love Medicine. New York: Holt, Rinehart & Winston, 1984. 1st edition; 272 pages; near fine in dust jacket.   Ken Sanders   8-330   1996 $125.00

ERNST, MAX   At Eye Level and Paramyths. Beverley Hills: Copley Galleries, 1949. One of 513 copies; some waterstaining to lower margins of early pages, front hinge rather fragile, but very good; presentation copy from Ernst for Dylan and Caitlin Thomas.   R. A. Gekoski   19-142   1996 £875.00

ERREGED, JOHN   History of Brightelmston or, Brighton As I View It and Others Knew It. Brighton: printed by F. Lewis "Observer" Office, 1862. 1st edition; tall 8vo; viii, 383 pages; original purplish blue cloth; inner hinges cracked, spine faded, small mark from removal of label, but certainly very good.   David Mason   71-19   1996 $100.00

ERSKINE, CHARLES   Twenty Years Before the Mast. Boston: 1890. 1st edition; 7.5 x 5 inches; 311 pages; gilt pictorial cloth, ink inscription, covers moderately worn.   John K. King   77-768   1996 $125.00

ERSKINE, JOHN ELPHINSTONE   Journal of a Cruise Among the Islands of the Western Pacific, Including the Feejees and Others Inhabited by the Polynesian Negro Races, in Her Majesty's Ship Havannah. London: John Murray, 1853. 1st edition; 8vo; folding map, 7 plates, 4 are tinted lithographs; half maroon morocco, gilt, spine gilt, by Period Bookbinders of Bath; fine. Hill p. 98; Abbey Travel 602.   Ximenes   109-110   1996 $500.00

ERSKINE, RALPH   Gospel Sonnets, or Spiritual Songs. Boston: reprinted by Rogers and Fowle for J. Blanchard, 1743. 7th edition; 8vo; contemporary deerskin over paper boards (rubbed but quite sound); titlepage bit soiled, some slight foxing, but excellent copy, complete with final leaf of publishers ads; very uncommon, particularly in good condition. Evans 5174.   Ximenes   108-123   1996 $450.00

ERSKINE, THOMAS   The Speech of the Hon. T. Erskine, at the Court of King's Bench...in the Cause of the King v. Williams, for Publishing Paine's Age of Reason. London: printed for J. Bell, 1797. 23 pages; modern wrappers, last leaf defective, affecting one word.   Meyer Boswell   SL25-78   1996 $350.00

ERSKINE, THOMAS   Two Actions for Criminal Conversation with the Whole of the Evidence; Both Tried Before the Right Hon. Lord Kenyon, In the Court of King's Bench, Westminster Hall, on Wednesday, June 26, 1790... London: printed for M. Smith, 1790. Original(?) publisher's backed marbled boards, very worn, usable.   Meyer Boswell   SL25-79   1996 $450.00

ERTE   Erte Maquettes. Hyattsville: Rebecca Press, 1984. Limited to 2200 copies, signed by Rebecca Bingham, the publisher; 1 1/2 x 2 1/8 inches; 58 pages, 42 color design reproductions; in 1994 designer binding of aqua morocco by Louise Genest, a Canadian binder, on each cover, there are four rectangular onlays of metallic foils in tones of gold, bronze, copper and red, one rectangle on each cover cut out to shape of a fashion plate, leaving silhouette of female form showing through to aqua cover; foil fashion plate is then onlaid to another part of the cover, doublures are of mottled gold foil on paper, housed in box of handmade aqua paper, accented with metallic foil. Mint.   Bromer Booksellers 87-183 1996 $1,200.00

ERWIN, MARIE H.   Wyoming Historical Blue Book - a Legal and Political History of Wyoming 1868-1943. Denver: 1946. 1st edition; 1471 pages, plates; photos; pictorial leather, nice.   T. A. Swinford 49-343 1996 $100.00

ESCHENBACH, WOLFRAM VON   The Romance of Parzival and the Holy Grail. Gwasg Gregynog, 1990. One of 210 numbered copies; large folio; printed double column in Bembo in black and red on Zerkall; 12 wood engravings by Stefan Mrozewski, initial and Press device by Ieuan Rees; half red goatskin, patterned cloth sides; fine.   Bertram Rota 272-211 1996 £240.00

ESCUDERO, JOSE A. DE   Noticias Estadisticas Del Estado De Chihuahua... Mexico: Por Juan Ojeda, 1834. 1st edition; (1)-(260) (pages 256-60 mispaginated 156-60); full calf with gilt in gilt on spine, some foxing, very good. Howes E176; Graff 1258; Streeter Sale 408.   Michael D. Heaston 23-265 1996 $2,000.00

ESDAILE, A.   A List of English Tales and Prose Romances Printed Before 1740. London: Bib. Soc., 1912. 1st edition; small 4to; original cloth backed boards, spine faded with 'before 1740' written in ink, headcaps and corners bumped, bit worn.   Maggs Bros. Ltd. 1191-85 1996 £65.00

ESDAILE, JAMES   Mesmerism in India, and Its Practical Application in Surgery and Medicine. Hartford: Silas Andrus and Son, 1851. 2nd American edition; 12mo; xxvi, (27)-259 pages; original blue stiff printed wrappers; some erosion of spine at top and bottom, very good. Norman Lib. 710; Tinterow p. 49; GM 5650.3 & Crabtree 536 for London 1846 ed. Edwin V. Glaser B122-51 1996 $250.00

ESHLEMAN, CLAYTON   Brother Stones. Kyoto: Catepillar Book, 1968. 1st edition; limited to 250 copies, signed by author and by William Paden; 8vo; original woodcut prints on Japanese mulberry paper by Paden; loose sheets in blue cloth box with Japanese fasteners. Mint. James S. Jaffe 34-148 1996 $150.00

ESMONDE, THOMAS   Hunting Memories of Many Lands. 1925. Many illustrations; spine and upper cover slightly discolored, contents fine. Presentation copy inscribed to William Bland.   David Grayling J95Biggame-512 1996 £55.00

ESMONDE, THOMAS   More Hunting Memories. London: 1930. Many photos plates; near mint in dust jacket. very scarce.   David A.H. Grayling 3/95-435 1996 £75.00

ESMONDE, THOMAS   More Hunting Memories. London: 1930. Phot plates, original pictorial gilt cloth, very light staining to edges of plates, otherwise very good. Very scarce..   David A.H. Grayling 3/95-434 1996 £65.00

ESPIARD DE LA BORDE, FRANCOIS IGNACE   The Spirit of Nations. London: Lockyer Davis and R. Baldwin, 1753. 1st edition in english; 8vo; woodcut device on title, xvi, 406, (2) pages, including final leaf of publishers' ads; contemporary calf gilt, neatly rebacked, very good. John Drury 82-74 1996 £250.00

ESPIE, COMTE D'   The Manner of Securing All Sorts of Buildings from Fire. London: for H. piers, 1756. 8vo; 62 pages; 2 folding engraved plates; quarter calf; Harris & Savage 224.   Elton Engineering 10-46 1996 £680.00

ESPY, JAMES   The Philosophy of Storms. Boston: Little and Brown, 1841. 1st edition; large 8vo; 552 pages; original cloth, some worn, some foxed.   Second Life Books 103-209 1996 $300.00

ESQUIROL, JEAN   Des Maladies Mentales Considerees Sour les Rapports Medical, Hygenique et Modico-Legal...Edition Publiee a Bruxelles en 1838 Entierement Conforme a l'Edition Francaise Paris: J. B. Bailliere & London: H. Bailliere, 1838. 1st edition; 8vo; 3 volumes in 2; 27 fine engraved plates by Tardieu, minor foxing; contemporary half black leather, bit worn and scuffed. GM 4929 & 4798.   Maggs Bros. Ltd. 1190-405 1996 £700.00

ESQUIROL, JEAN   Mental Maladies: a Treatise on Insanity. Philadelphia: Lea and Blanchard, 1845. 1st edition in English; 8vo; 496 pages + inserted ads; modern calf backed marbled boards, leather spine label, attractive copy with slight foxing.   John Gach 150-140 1996 $1,500.00

ESQUIVEL, LAURA   Like Water for Chocolate. New York: Doubleday, 1992. Advance review copy with publisher's material laid in, as new in dust jacket.   Between the Covers 42-161 1996 $200.00

ESQUIVEL, LAURA   Like Water for Chocolate. New York: Doubleday, 1992. Advance reading copy of the first American edition; wrappers, signed by author; fine.   Anacapa House 5-98 1996 $135.00

ESQUIVEL, LAURA   Like Water for Chocolate. New York: Doubleday, 1992. 1st U.S. edition; 246 pages; brown cloth spine, rust paper covered boards; fine in fine dust jacket.   Orpheus Books 17-21 1996 $115.00

ESQUIVEL, LAURA   Like Water for Chocolate. New York: 1992. 1st edition; author's first novel, uncommon. As new.   Stephen Lupack 83-1996 $100.00

AN ESSAY on the Present State of Our Public Records; Shewing the Absolute Necessity of a Total Prohibition of the Use of Narrow Wheels, On All Carriages Drawn by Moret than One Horse Lengthways. London: R. Baldwin, 1756. (2), 28 pages, woodcut illustration; recent marbled wrappers; very nice wide copy. Goldsmiths 9175; Kress 5512; Higgs 1321.   C. R. Johnson 37-11 1996 £150.00

ESSAYS Honoring Lawrence C. Wroth. Portland: N.P., 1951. 1st edition; 4to; xxi, 515 pages; cloth; fine.   The Bookpress 75-288 1996 $100.00

ESSAYS on Various Subjects; Intended to Elucidate the Causes of the Changes Coming Upon all the Earth at This Present Time and the Nature of the Calamities That Are so rapidly Approaching.... New York: Published for the proprietor, 1861. 1st edition; 8vo; 200 pages; original printed wrappers, 2 holes through inner margins.   M & S Rare Books 60-412 1996 $150.00

ESTES, MATTHEW   A Defence of Negro Slavery, As It Exists in the United States. Montgomery: Press of the Alabama Journal, 1846. 1st edition; 18mo; 260 pages; contemporary calf backed boards. LCP/HSP Afro Amer. Cat. 3516; Howes E 200; Sabin 23046.   M & S Rare Books 60-330 1996 $950.00

ESTIENNE, HENRI 1528-1598   Epistolia, Dialogi Breves, Oratiunculae, Poematia... Geneva: Estienne, 1577. 1st collected edition; 12mo; 220 pages; contemporary full vellum, covers soiled, inner hinges starting, bookplates and 3 tipped in clippings; still very good, tight copy with dark, clear impressions of the type, rare.   Chapel Hill 94-194 1996 $500.00

ESTIENNE, HENRI 1528-1598   In M. T. Cicero Quamplurimos Locos Castigationes. N.P.: Geneva: ex officina Henrici Stephani Parisensis Typographi, 1557. 1st edition; 8vo; 18th century calf, gilt, 'toison d'or' device on covers, spine gilt, ends of spine slightly rubbed. Fine. Adams S1778.   Ximenes 109-111 1996 $750.00

ESTIENNE, HENRI 1528-1598   De Latinitate Falso Suspecta...Eivsdem De Plavti Latinitate Dissertatio. Geneva: Henri Estienne, 1576. 1st edition; small 8vo; pages (xvi), 400, Roman letter with occasional italic and Greek, woodcut printer's 'Noli altum' device on titlepage, very slightly dusty, woodcut initials, old autograph on blank portion of title, good copy in contemporary vellum over boards; Not in BM STC Fr. Adams S1763; Renouard p. 144; Buisson p. 266.   A. Sokol XXV-33 1996 £650.00

ESTRACTO de Noticias Del Puerto De Monterey, De La Mission, Y Presido Que Se Han Establecido En El Con La Denominacion De San Carlos, Y Del Sucesso De Las Dos Expediciones De Mar, Y Tierra Que A este Fin Se Despacharon En Al Ano Proxima... Mexico: En la Imprenta del Superior Govierno 16 de Agosto de 1770. Small folio; (5) pages; later marbled wrappers, slight browning, else exceptionally fine, with contemporary note of '31' at top of first leaf, in half morocco slipcase; the Everett Graff copy with his bookplate. Cowan p. 199; Graff 1264; Wagner Spanish Southwest 150.   Michael D. Heaston 23-290 1996 $45,000.00

THE ESTRAY: A Collection of Poems. Boston: Ticknor, 1847. 1st edition; one of 1150 copies; 8vo; cream paper boards, spine chipped three quarter inch at top deleting title from original paper label, horizontal tear across spine, small stain at bottom of boards which are otherwise quite bright as are the contents, spine frayed some along edges, quite uncommon. BAL 12088.   Charles Agvent 4-835 1996 $150.00

ETCHECOPAR, R. D.   The Birds of North Africa. London: 1967. Many colored plates; lovely copy in protected dust jacket. Mint.   David A.H. Grayling MY95Orn-30 1996 £85.00

ETHEREGE, GEORGE   The Works of Sir George Etherege... London: printed for H. H. and sold by J. Tonson and T. Bennet, 704. 1st collected edition; 8vo; contemporary calf, slight wear to spine; very good. CBEL II 741.   Ximenes 108-124 1996 $400.00

ETIQUETTE for the Ladies; Eighty Maxims on Dress, Manners and Accomplishments. London: Charles Tilt, 1837. 16mo; pages 57 (including half title and title), (6 ads); original blind patterned limp purple cloth, gilt roundel title on cover, gilt edges, very good.   Peter Murray Hill 185-58 1996 £105.00

ETIQUETTE of the Dinner Table, with the Art of Carving. London: Frederick Warne, c. 1860. 16mo. contents, text pages (7)-95; frontispiece, additional illustrated title; original blue black stamped cloth, pictorial label on upper cover, gilt edges, slightly used, but good. Peter Murray Hill 185-59 1885 £75.00

ETTLINGER, LEOPOLD L.   Antonio and Pero Pollaiuolo. London: 1978. 4to; 183 pages; 162 illustrations; cloth, dust jacket; fine.   Rainsford A54-466 1996 £60.00

EUCLIDES   Diligentenmente Rassettato, &...Ridotto, per...Nicolo Tartalea...Di Nuouo...Corretto, e Ristampato. Venice: Heredi di Troian Navo, 1585. 6th revised edition; 4to; ff. 316, italic letter, large woodcut printer's device on titlepage, smaller one at end, woodcut initials, many diagrams, occasional light age yellowing, printing surface of 2 lines faint, contemporary limp vellum, lacking ties; very good. BM STC It. p. 239; Thomas Stanford 44; Honeyman 1012.   A. Sokol XXV-34 1996 £1,450.00

EUCLIDES   Elementorum Libri XV. Parisiis: apud Viduam Guilielmi Cavellat, 1598. Small 8vo; printer's device on titlepage and full page device on otherwise blank leaf, numerous woodcut diagrams; contemporary vellum, wanting ties, nice. Thomas Stanford 24; Adams E1002.   James Fenning 133-103 1996 £450.00

EUCLIDES   Elementorum Eluclidis Libri Tredecim. Secundum Vetera Exemplaria Restituti. Ex Versione Latina Federici Commandini. London: Gulielmus Jones, 1620. 1st edition thus; 4to; (2), 250 pages; diagrams, woodcut device on title, woodcut initials and few headpieces, text in parallel columns of Greek and Latin; early calf, title bit browned at edges, crudely rebacked, covers worn along edges, lacks front and rear blanks, good. STC 10559.   Edwin V. Glaser 121-97 1996 $1,200.00

EUCLIDES   Elementorvm Evclidis Libri Tredecim. London: Excudebat Gulielmus Iones, 1620. 1st edition published in England of the original Greek text. Folio in 4's; pages (ii), 250, final blank missing, Greek & roman letter in parallel columns, woodcut vignette on titlepage and initials at beginning of each book, diagrams in text, lightly yellowed, few small light lamp oil spots on last 2 leaves; contemporary calf, rebacked, blindstamped fleurons, covers worn, front hinge beginning to crack; owner's autograph of Thos. Middleton 1668, W. Stanley Jevons 1879 & Robert Honeyman 1963; good copy. STC 10559; Lowndes 755; Graesse II 510; Honeyman 1030.   A. Sokol XXV-35 1996 £985.00

EUCLIDES   Euclid's Elements. London: printed for Christopher Huss and E. P., 1686. 2nd edition in English; 12mo; 14 folding engraved plates; contemporary calf, bit rubbed, slight wear to ends of lower joint; small flaw to margin of one leaf of preface, touching couple of letters which are clear from context; otherwise very nice, very uncommon. Wing E3398B.   Ximenes 108-126 1996 $750.00

EUCLIDES   The Elements of Euclid Explain'd, in a New, but Most Easie Method... Oxford: Printed by L. L. for M. Gillyflower and W. Freeman, 1700. 3rd edition; 8vo; iv, 380 pages; original calf, some light waterstaining, covers slightly buckled and chip at foot of spine; ownership inscription. Wing E3402.   David Bickersteth 133-187 1996 £150.00

EUCLIDES   Euclide's Elements. London: printed for W. and J. Mount and T. Page, et al, 1751. 8vo; (8), 384 pages; copper engraved frontispiece, 9 folding plates; upper blank margin of titlepage trimmed, lacking front free endpaper; contemporary calf, gilt spine label, outer hinges partly cracked, but holding, covers and extremities somewhat rubbed.   Kenneth Karmiole 1NS-168 1996 $125.00

EUCLIDES   The First Six Books of the Elements of Euclid in which Coloured Diagrams and Symbols are Used Instead of Letters for the Greater Ease of Learners. London: William Pickering, 1847. 1st edition; 4to; xxix, 268 pages; numerous diagrams and symbols printed in 4 colors, wood engraved initials; colored diagram on title; contemporary half morocco with morocco grain cloth, red edges, marbled endpapers, small tear at top of leaf ii3, not obscuring text; some scattered foxing as usual, very lightly worn at extremities, very good. Keynes p. 65. Edwin V. Glaser 121-99 1996 $3,500.00

EULOGIUM Historiarum Sive Temporis: Chronicon ab Orbe Conditio Usque ad Annum Domini 1366... London: 1848-63. 8vo; 3 volumes, pages 1650; original cloth. Gross/Graves 2865.   Howes Bookshop 265-1564 1996 £85.00

EURIPDIES   Three Plays of Euripides. Limited Editions Club, 1967. Limited to 1500 copies, signed by artist; folio; illustrations by Michael Ayrton; cloth backed boards, very good in original slipcase (splitting). Words Etcetera 94-74 1996 £95.00

EURIPIDES   The Plays of Euripides. Newtown: Gregynog Press, 1931. Limited to 500 numbered copies; folio; 2 volumes, 32 wood engraved text illustrations by R. A. Maynard and H. W. Bray; xi, 270; 264 pages; original red cloth, gilt, edges uncut; fine. Harrop 18.   Thomas Thorp 489-95 1996 £380.00

EURIPIDES   Tragoediae XIX. Heidelberg: Hieronymi Commelini, 1597. 1st edition thus; small thick 8vo; 2 volumes in 1; 800, 659 pages; contemporary full vellum; few leaves closely trimmed, affecting headings only, else tight, very good copy.   Chapel Hill 94-156 1996 $250.00

EURIPIDES   Tres Tragoediae, Phoenissae, Hippolytvs Coronatvs, atqve Andromacha... Antwerp: Ex officina Christophori Plantini, 1581. 16mo; paes 248, mainly italic letter, woodcut printer's compass device on titlepage, fairly uniform light age browning, paper flaw in 1 leaf with slight loss, later calf, rebacked, gilt triple border fillets, edges, inner dentelles and spine, corners and edges only very slightly worn, vellum endpapers; good copy. 19th French bibliographer Renouard had vellum endpapers in any Classical texts which he had rebound, & this vol. is likely to have come from his own collection. BM Dutch p. 73; Adams E1050; Voet 1145; Buelens/De Backer 224.8.   A. Sokol XXV-37 1996 £385.00

EUSTACE, JOHN CHETWODE   A Classical Tour through Italy. London: printed for J. Mawman, 1815. 3rd edition; 8vo; 4 volumes; large folding engraved map of Italy in volume 1, 10 plans; contemporary half calf, slightly rubbed, five labels (ex 8).   Anthony W. Laywood 108-169 1996 £100.00

EUSTACE, JOHN CHETWODE   An Elegy to the Memory of the Right Honourable Edmund Burke. London: printed for F. and C. Rivington and J. Hatchard, 1798. 1st edition; 4to; 15 pages; original wrappers, stitched as issued, uncut, fine.   Anthony Laywood 108-58 1996 £165.00

EUSTACHIUS, BARTOLOMEO   Anatomii Summi Romanae Archetypae Tabulae Anatomicae Novis Explicationibus Illustratae ab Andrea Maximino Romano in Nosocomio B. M. Consolationis Chirurgo Primario. Rome: Ex Typographia Pauli Junchi, 1783. Tall folio; half title, Ix, 130 (i.e. 128), plus 47 engraved plates, title in red and black with fine engraved anatomical theatre dissection scene; rebound in period style binding, but quite handsome, occasional light foxing, final two leaves skillfully repaired in blank margins. GM 391 (1714 ed.).   James Tait Goodrich K40-127 1996 $1,750.00

EUTHYMIUS ZIGABENUS   Commentarii in Omnes Psalmos. Paris: Charlotte Guillard, for J. de Roigny, 1543. 8vo; (31) leaves (of 32: fol. A5 of index missing, last blank present), 407, (1) leaves (last blank); italic for the text, roman for the commentary, with use of Greek in side notes and occasionally in the commentary, crible initials, ruled in red, 18th century sprinkled calf, flat spine handsomely gilt; on title are 2 early ownership inscriptions, incuding that of Jean Seguier ("Joannis Seguier & amicorum"); 2nd leaf lacking, otherwise fine copy; rare.   Jeffrey D. Mancevice 20-29 1 996 $450.00

EUTROPOIS   Eutropii Historiae Romanae Breviarium... London: printed for C. Hitch, 1744. 4th edition; 8vo; xxiii, 1 leaf, 164 pages, 3 pages index, 1 page catalog of books, 2 leaves partially loose; contemporary calf, very worn, corners bumped, spine cracked and chipped, covers with scratches, evidence of clasps, lacks flyleaves, front and back; overall very good.   Roy W. Clare XXIV-68 1996 $100.00

EUXINE or Black Sea and Sea of Marmora and Azov Containing Full Instructions for Frequenting the Ports of Constantinople, Galatz, Odessa, Sevastopol, Trebizond, &c. London: James Imray, 1853. 1st edition; 8vo; 55 pages, 33 pages ads; original paper, very good.   John Lewcock 30-139 1996 £85.00

EVANS, ABEL   Vertumnus. An Epistle to Mr. Jacob Bobart, Botany Professor to the University of Oxford and Keeper of the Physick-Garden. Oxford: printed by L. L. for Stephen Fletcher, 1713. 1st edition; 8vo; 33 pages; frontispiece, little light foxing of text, short tear in last leaf expertly repaired; modern marabled boards; Sir Sydney Cockerell's copy with inscriptions, with letter to Sir Sydney tipped in, inscribed "B. S. Cron from SCC 31 Jan. 1960". Foxon E530.   Anthony W. Laywood 109-53 1996 £150.00

EVANS, ARTHUR   The Palace of Minos at Knossos. New York: Biblo and Tannen, 1964. Facsimile reprint edition; 8vo; 4 volumes in 7 parts, 3108 pages, 221 page index, 2434 figures, plans, tables, 13 colored and 11 supplementary plates; red gilt embossed cloth, mint set. Archaeologia Luxor-3285 1996 $1,250.00

EVANS, ARTHUR   "The Ring of Nestor". A Glimpse into the Minoan After-World and a Sepulchral Treasure of Gold Signet-Rings and Bead-Seals from the Thisbe, Boeotia. London: Macmillan, 1925. 8vo; 75 pages; 57 figures, 5 plates; original cloth, tattered dust jacket. Archaeologia Luxor-3286 1996 $150.00

EVANS, CERINDA W.   Collis Potter Huntington. Newport News: Mariners' Museum, 1954. 1st edition; 2 volumes, pages 912), 384, (11), 386-775; frontispiece, 127 illustrations from photos and drawings; gilt lettered green cloth, minor spot to front cover of volume 1, else fine set.   Argonaut Book Shop 113-362 1996 $125.00

EVANS, ELIZABETH   The Cults of the Sabine Territory. New York: American Academy in Rome, 1939. 8vo; xiv, 254 pages; 7 plates; original cloth. Inscribed by author.   Archaeologia Luxor-3287 1996 $125.00

EVANS, ELWOOD   Annual Address Before the Western Washington Industrial Association, At Its Fourth Annual Exhibition, Held in Olympia, Washington Territory By...Friday, October 9th, 1874. Olympia: R. H. Hewitt, Printer, Excelsior Job Office, 1875. 1st edition; 32 pages; original printed yellow wrappers, bottom edge slightly stained and chipped; very good. Soliday I 798; Not in Smith; Beard, Washington Imprints 182. Michael D. Heaston 23-350 1996 $500.00

EVANS, J. H.   Ornamental Turning. London: published by the author, 1886. 1st edition; 8vo; 17 folding autotype plates, 192 text illustrations; cloth, trifle worn, but nice. Abell 95.   Maggs Bros. Ltd. 1190-629 1996 £165.00

EVANS, JOHN   The Ancient Stone Implements, Weapons and Ornaments of Great Britain. London: Longmans, Green, Reader and Dyer, 1872. 1st edition; 8vo; xvi, 640 pages; 476 figures, 2 folding plates; original gilt pictorial cloth, spine faded, chipped and torn; from the collection of Heinrich Schliemann, and was acquired by Professor Akerstrom; with facsimile letter about acquisition; inscribed by author for Schliemann, with traces of Schliemann's private paper library label at foot of spine.   Archaeologia Luxor-3984 1996 $650.00

EVANS, JOHN   The Ancient Stone Implements, Weapons and Ornaments of Great Britain. London: 1897. 2nd edition; royal 8vo; xviii, 747 pages, over 470 illustrations, plates; brown cloth, gilt decorated with 'flint' motif; good.   K Books 442-209 1996 £50.00

EVANS, MARIAN   Essays and Leaves from a Note-Book. London: William Blackwood and Sons, 1884. 1st English edition; 8vo; x, 382 pages, ad leaf; original cloth, little spotted and lower cover discolored by damp, contents fine.   David Bickersteth 133-146 1996 £80.00

EVANS, THOMAS   An English and Welsh Vocabulary; or, an Essay Guide to the Ancient British Language... London: Gomerian Press, printed and sold by R. Jones, 1816. 8vo; 3 parts in one volume, 66, 64, 52 pages; original(?) blue wrappers, neatly repaired, uncut and largely unopened; very good.   John Drury 82-75 1996 £150.00

EVANS, THOMAS   Old Ballads, Historical and Narrative, With Some of Modern Date. London: for T. Evans, 1784. 1st collected edition; small octavo; 4 volumes; full tree calf, spine gilt in panels, nice engraved titlepages by Isaac Taylor; slight wear, text excellent. Scarce. Lowndes III 688 for 1810 collection; CBEL II 232 and 237.   Hartfield 48-L32 1996 $495.00

EVANS, WILL F.   Border Skylines, Fifty Years of "Tallying Out" On the Bloys Roundup Ground. A History of the Bloys Cowboy Camp Meeting. Dallas: 1940. 1st edition; 587 pages; frontispiece, photos; dust jacket, signed; Very good+. Herd 777.   T. A. Swinford 49-346 1996 $100.00

EVANS, WILLIAM   The Mammalian Fauna of the Edinburgh District. London: 1892. One of only 200 copies; original cloth, excellent.   David A.H. Grayling MY95Orn-473 1996 £60.00

EVANS-PRITCHARD, E. E.   Witchcraft, Oracles and Magic Among the Azande. Oxford: Clarendon Press, 1937. 1st edition; 8vo; xxvi, 558, (2) pages; 34 photographic plates, 9 text figures, 2 maps; blue gilt cloth, bookplate; first edition is scarce.   Kenneth Karmiole 1NS-2 1996 $100.00

EVARTS, R. C.   Alice's Adventures in Cambridge. Cambridge: Harvard Lampoon, 1913. Black and white drawings by E L. Barron; brown pictorial boards; fine, scarce.   Barbara Stone 70-44 1996 £75.00

EVELEIGH, JOSIAH   An Account of the Reasons Why Many Citizens of Exon Have Withdrawn from the Ministry of Mr. Jos. Hallet and Mr. James Pierce. Exon: printed by Jos. Bliss and sold by the Booksellers of Exon, 1719. 1st edition; 8vo; 16 pages; disbound, small stain in upper outer corner of title.   David Bickersteth 133-74 1996 £60.00

EVELEIGH, JOSIAH   A Defence of the Account, &c. London: printed for John Clark, 1719. 1st edition; 8vo; 24 pages; disbound.   David Bickersteth 133-75 1996 £65.00

EVELYN, JOHN 1620-1706   Directions for the Gardiner at Says-Court But Which May Be of Use for Other Gardens. London: Nonesuch Press, 1932. One of only 800 copies; 8vo; 109 pages; printed on grey Van Gelder paper; uncut, very nice in little worn printed dust jacket. Second Life Books 103-74 1996 $300.00

EVELYN, JOHN 1620-1706   Directions for the Gardiner at Says-Court, But Which May Be of Use of Other Gardens. London: Nonesuch Press, 1932. 1st edition; 214/800 copies; crown 8vo; pages 109, (2); printed on pale grey Van Gelder paper, line block illustration, typographical border to each page of text; marbled mid-green boards and matching endpapers, pale green leather label, backstrip faded and little rubbed at head and tail, top edge gilt on rough, others untrimmed, good. Dreyfus 82.   Blackwell's B112-205 1996 £80.00

EVELYN, JOHN 1620-1706   Memoires for My Grand-Son. Oxford: for the Nonesuch Press, 1926. 1st edition; number 775 of 1250 copies; 8vo; pages xii, (2), 104, colophon; original vellum stamped in blind, lettered in gold, printed in Fell type on Auvergne handmade paper; unopened in original marbled paper slipcase (defective); very good. Nonesuch Century 37.   Claude Cox 107-106 1996 £65.00

EVELYN, JOHN 1620-1706   Memoirs... London: for Henry Colburn and sold by John and Arthur Arch, 1818. 1st edition; 4to; 2 volumes, pages ix, (i) blank (i) list of plates, (i) blank, ix-xiii, (i) blank, 620; viii, (4), 335, (i imprint, each volume with engraved frontispiece, 6 engraved plates, large folding table; uncut in original boards, rebacked to style retaining original printed spine labels, new endpapers; excellent, clean and fresh. Simon Finch 24-84 1996 £450.00

EVELYN, JOHN 1620-1706   Memoirs Illustrative of the Life and Writings of John Evelyn, Esq. F.R.S... (with) Additional Plates &c. to the First Edition of Memoirs of John Evelyn. London: ptd. for Henry Colburn & sold by John and Arthur Arch, 1818/19. 1st edition; 4to; 3 volumes bound in 2; numerous portraits, plates and tables, some folding, some foxing and dustiness, margins of one table dust soiled and reinforced, contemporary calf, rebacked, Signet Library arms on covers.   James Burmester 29-49 1996 £110.00

EVELYN, JOHN 1620-1706   Memoirs, Illustrative of the Life and Writings of John Evelyn, Esq. F.R.S. London: 1819. 2nd edition; 4to; 2 volumes; 12 plates; xxvii, 671; (8), 342, (2), 336 pages; plates foxed; new cloth, ex-library.   Edward Morrill 368-111 1996 $195.00

EVELYN, JOHN 1620-1706   A Philosophical Discourse on Earth, Relating to the Culture and Improvement of It for Vegetation, and the Propagation of Plants, Etc., As It Was Presented to the Royal Society, April 29, 1675. London: printed for John Martyn, 1676. 1st edition; small 8vo; contemporary mottled calf, spine gilt, some rubbing of spine; some of gilt on spine rubbed away, but very fine and fresh; complete with prelim leaf giving order to print from the Royal Society; ownership inscripiton of Nidrie Castel, Tues. 18 Octo. 1681. later Hopetoun bookplate. Keynes 93; wing E3507.   Ximenes 109-112 1996 $3,500.00

EVELYN, JOHN 1620-1706   Sculptura, or the History and Art of Chalcography and Engraving in Copper. London: Payne, 1755. 2nd edition; large 8vo; 3 plates, including frontispiece; calf; Universal Cat. of Books on Art I 520.   Rostenberg & Stern 150-103 1996 $475.00

EVELYN, JOHN 1620-1706   Silva; or, a Discourse of Forest-Trees and the Popagation of timber In His Majesty's Dominions...Pomona...Kalendarium Hortense. London: 1729. 5th edition; folio; pages xxviii, 235, (5); engraved plate, 9 engravings and diagrams in text plus engraed chapter headings, tailpieces and initials; modern calf over white boards, some soiling, rubbing and browning to boards, dampstaining to corner of page, occasional slight marginal foxing, text, clean and bright.   Raymond M. Sutton VII-12 1996 $625.00

EVELYN, JOHN 1620-1706   Silva; or, a Discourse of Forest Trees. York: 1776. 1st of Hunter's editions; 4to; pages (liv), 649, (9); portrait, folding table 40 engraved plates; old calf, binding neatly repaired, bound in at back is a copy of Terra, contents in excellent condition. Wheldon & Wesley 207-29 1996 £300.00

EVELYN, JOHN 1620-1706   Silva: or, a Discourse of Forest-Trees and the Propagation of Timber In His Majesty's Dominions. London: 1786. 2nd Hunter edition; 4to; 2 volumes; (xlvi), 311, (ix); (ii), 343, (x); (viii), 72, (iv); portrait, 42 plates, 3 folding tables; calf, rebacked; bookplate of the Duke of Bedford.   John Henly 27-351 1996 £250.00

EVELYN, JOHN 1620-1706   Sylva, or a Discourse of Forest Trees and the Propagation of Timber. London: Jo. Martyn and Ja. Allestry, 1664. 1st edition; folio; (16), 120 pages; (2), 20, (2), 21-83, (1) pages, 1 f. errata; contemporary calf, expertly rebacked, new red gilt label, corners repaired, some occasional minor dust soiling and browning; very good. errata leaf is scarce.   Ken Spelman 30-71 1996 £950.00

EVELYN, JOHN 1620-1706   Sylva, or a Discourse of Forest-Trees, and the Propagation of Timber in His Majesties Dominions... Together with an Historical Account of the Sacredness and Use of Standing Groves... York: A. Ward for J. Dodsley (& 5 others), 1776. 4to; (lii), 649, (xl) pages; frontispiece, 40 plates, some folding; contemporary tree calf, neatly rebacked, with old decorated gilt spine and label laid down; corners little worn, little browning and foxing; nice.   Robert Clark 38-43 1996 £325.00

EVENINGS At Haddon Hall. London: Henry G. Bohn, 1850. Small octavo; viii, 432 pages; 24 plates by George Cattermole; contemporary tan polished calf by Riviere & Son, gilt double rule border on covers, gilt spine, tooled in compartments with black morocco label, gilt board edges and turn-ins, all edges gilt, marbled endpapers, minor wear to covers, scattered light foxing, near fine. Heritage Book Shop 196-215 1996 $300.00

EVERGREEN Tales. New York: 1949. One of 2500 numbered copies; quarto; 15 volumes; lavishly illustrated in color; glassine wrapper to each volume, in five slipcases, one of which has a chip; very fine; inscribed by editor, Jean Hersholt.   Bromer Booksellers 90-111 1996 $500.00

EVERMANN, B. W.   Lake Maxinkuckee, a Physical and Biological Survey. Indiana Dept. of Conservation, 1920. Royal 8vo; 2 volumes; 1172 pages, 37 plates, 24 text figures; cloth, volume 2 upper outer corner bumped but good.   Wheldon & Wesley 207-314 1996 £75.00

EVERWINE, PETER   Keeping the Night. Lisbon: Penumbra Press, 1977. One of 230 copies, signed by author; tall 8vo; illustration by John Thein; cloth, printed spine label; mint.   James S. Jaffe 34-149 1996 $125.00

EVERY Man Entertained or, Select Histories; Giving an Account of Persons Who Have Been Most Eminently Distinguished by Their Virtues or Vices, Their Perfections or Defects, Either of Body or Mind. London: printed for Thomas Truth and Daniel Daylight, 1756. 1st edition; 2nd issue, 8vo; contemporary calf, gilt, spine gilt, some wear to ends of spine; wanting flyleaf at front, otherwise very good, rare.   Ximenes 108-98 1996 $800.00

EVISON, J.   Compleat Book of Psalmody Containing Variety of Psalm-Tunes, Hymns and Anthems to be Sung in 2, 3 and 4 Parts. 1760. 4th edition; 240 pages; calf, worn binding; inscription on title by Nath. Cooke, composer and organist dated July 28, 1826.   William Reeves 309-9648 1996 £102.00

EWBANK, JANE M.   Antiquary on Horseback. Kendal: Titus Wilson, 1963. 8vo; pages xvi, 163; illustrations; original cloth, gilt, dust jacket (little worn, some loss to top edge). C. Roy Hudleston's copy with autograph postcard signed from author.   R.F.G. Hollett & Son 78-904 1996 £50.00

EWEN, C. L'ESTRANGE   The Families of Ewen of East Anglia and the Fenland. London: privately printed by Mitchell, Hughes and Clarke, 1928. 4to; pages 505; 11 plates, 23 illustrations and maps; original cloth. Howes Bookshop 265-1759 1996 £55.00

EWERS, H. H.   Alraune. Muller, 1911. 1st edition; pictorial cloth with giant lizard on front cover; spine and rear cover with some light dust soil, else tight, very good copy;   Aronovitz 57-381 1996 $750.00

AN EXACT Journal of the Victorious Expediton of the Confederate Fleet, the Last Year, Under the Command of the Right Honourable Admiral Russel... London: for J. Taylor, 1695. 1st edition; 4to; (4), 28 pages, old splash of ink on p. 28; recently bound in linen backed marbled boards, lettered, very good. Apparently very scarce. Wing C 3650.   John Drury 82-76 1996 £125.00

EXAMPLES of San Bernardino of Siena. Gerald Howe, 1926. 8vo; illustrations by Robert Austin; buckram, very nice in slightly marked dust jacket, on prelim blank artist has made a small pen and ink drawing, signed and tipped in his Autograph Letter presenting the book to Martin Hardie.   Bertram Rota 272-61 1996 £70.00

EXERCISES for Ingenuity: Consisting of Queries, Transpositions, Charades Rebuses and Riddles. London: E. Wallis, c. 1825. 2nd edition; 90 x 137mm; pages 36; hand colored frontispiece and 1 other plate; original buff card wrappers, spine expertly repaired, stab sewing renewed, title printed on upper side and ad on lower both within typographic border, very good, early owner's name on upper pastedown (dated 1828), 20th century bookplate tipped in, good. Osborne II p. 847.   Blackwell's B112-67 1996 £145.00

EXLEY, FREDERICK   A Fan's Notes. New York: Harper & Row, 1968. 1st edition; near fine in very good dust jacket with moderate wear at corners and spine extremities, inscribed by author.   Ken Lopez 74-12 1996 $450.00

EXLEY, FREDERICK   A Fan's Notes. New York: H&R, 1968. 1st edition; author's first book; tight, fine copy in bright dust jacket with small unobtrusive closed tear at back of gutter, otherwise fine. Thomas Dorn 9-111 1996 $125.00

EXPANDED METAL & CORRUGATED BAR CO.   Corrugated Bars for Reinforced Concrete. St. Louis: Expanded Metal & Corrugated Bar Co., 1906. Small oblong 8vo; 232 pages; many photo and line illustrations; original stiff embossed wrappers.   Elton Engineering 10-47 1996 £65.00

AN EXPLANATION of the Works of the Thames Tunnel Now Completed from rotherhithe to Wapping. London: Warrington, 1851. 16th edition; 12mo; 1 f., 23 pages, 1 f., folding plan frontispiece, 9 engraved plates; original rust colored printed pictorial wrappers.   Marlborough 162-210 1996 £175.00

EXPOSITIO Officii Missae Sacrique Canonis. Reutlingen: Johann Otmar 1 Sept. 1483. Folio; 125 leaves (of 126, lacking fol. 1 containing one line of title on recto, verso blank), gothic type, double column, initial spaces with guide letters, initials suppled in red and white, capital strokes, underlining and paragraph marks all suppled in red, 10 line note in very early hand on verso of last blank, small piece missing from lower margi of fol. 2 and small spot of wax adhering to text of same page, otherwise good, clean broad margined copy, most leaves still showing deckle edges; bound in early 19th century German (?) decorated paper boards. Goff E168; HCR 6810; BMC II 584.   H. M. Fletcher 121-7 1996 £975.00

EXQUEMELIN, ALEXANDRE OLIVIER   The Buccaneers of America. London: George Allen and Co. Ltd., 1911. Reprinted from the edition of 1684; to which is added reprint of the very scarce 4th part 1685; 23cm; xxxv, 508 pages, frontispiece, folding map, 6 other plates; brown cloth, gilt spine titles and vignette; some modest shelfwear, foxing on edges and prelims, overall nice copy.   Parmer Books, O39Nautica-039295 1996 $175.00

EYLAND, E. S.   Working Drawings and Designs in Architecture and Building... London: A. Fullarton and Co., c. 1863. Large folio; titlepage and 115 ff. (6) page index and description of plates, 55 plates; later half morocco, gilt titled spine; some occasional minor foxing, but good. Ken Spelman 30-72 1996 £300.00

EYLES, DESMOND   George Tinworth, Chronology of Principal Works. Los Angeles: 1982. 4to; 164 colored illustrations; padded binding with colored decorative title to front cover.   Petersfield Bookshop FH58-18 1996 £76.00

EYLES, DESMOND   Royal Doulton ....The Rise and Expansion of the Royal Doulton Potteries. London: Hutchinson, 1965. 4to; colored and other illustrations; dust jacket chipped and repaired with tape, otherwise fine.   Petersfield Bookshop FH58-6 1996 £140.00

EYLOT, THOMAS   The Book Named the Governour. Newcastle-upon-Tyne: 1834. New edition; 8vo; xxxviii, 293, vi pages; new old style quarter calf, very good.   K Books 441-205 1996 £55.00

EYRE, ALAN MONTGOMERY   Saint John's Wood. Its History, Its Houses, Its Haunts and Its Celebrities.Saint London: Chapman and Hall, 1913. 8vo; pages xii, 312; illustrations; original green cloth, gilt. Marlborough 162-136 1996 £50.00

EYRE, ALICE   The Famous Fremonts and Their America. N.P.: 1948. 374 pages; illustrations and maps; nice inscription, laid in is printed book mark card of Western authority and author Harry C. James. Fine in moderately soiled, lightly worn dust jacket.   Gene W. Baade   1094-54 1996 $125.00

EYRE, EDWARD JOHN   Journals of Expeditions of Discovery into Central Australia and Overland from Adelaide to King Georges Sound in the Years 1840-41. London: T. W. Boone, 1845. Primary edition pagination and binding; 2 volumes, (ii), (xx), 448 pages, 4 pages ads, frontispiece, 10 litho plates, 1 loose map in front pocket (lacks 1 loose map); (iv), (vi), 512 pages, 8 pages ads, frontispiece and 10 litho plates; original green ribbed and embossed cloth, spines lettered and decorated in gilt, several folds of the Arrowsmith map strengthened at folds, otherwise crisp, neatly recased with original cloth, gilt slightly faded, otherwise very nice. Presentation copy from author for Rev. Hogg. Wantrup 133a.   Antipodean   28-617   1996 $3,500.00

EYRE, VINCENT   The Military Operations at Cabal, Which Ended in the Retreat and Destruction of the British Army, Jan. 1842 with a Journal of Imprisonment in Afghanistan... London: 1843. 2nd edition; 8vo; xx, 330 pages, folding plan; new old style quarter calf, very good.   K Books 442-255   1996 £90.00

F

FABES, GILBERT H.   Modern First Editions Points and Values. London: W. and G. Foyle/2nd volume by Fabaes and William A. Foyle, 1929-32. 1st editions; one of 750, 1000 and 750 copies; 9 x 6 inches; 3 volumes, (1st, 2nd and 3rd series); original cloth and dust jackets, fore edges and tail edges untrimmed, errata slip in volume 1, fine in fine linen textured jackets.   Phillip J. Pirages 33-94 1996 $150.00

FABLE, LEONARD   The Gingerbread Man. London: George H. Harrap & Co., n.d. 1916. 1st edition; 28 pages; title vignette, 8 double page color plates, each in 3 parts and 6 text illustrations (repeated); brown boards, onlaid extra small color plate, bit loose, light wear, corners worn, scarce.   Robin Greer 94A-70 1996 £75.00

FABRE, JEAN ANTOINE   Essai Sur La Theorie des Torrens et des Rivieres. Paris: Bidault, 1797. 1st edition; large 4to; 318 pages; 8 engraved folding plates; contemporary calf, light scuffing, gilt backstrip. Iowa 204; not in Roberts.   Bennett Gilbert LL29-37 1996 $1,200.00

FABRE, JEAN HENRI   Der Abend Des Nachtpfauenauges. Raamin-Presse, 1988. One of 140 copies, signed by artist, (from a total edition of 185); 11 1/4 x 7 1/2 inches; 39, (1) pages, (5) leaves; small device on first leaf, 14 pages of color illustrations in blues and browns, plus 2 leaves of black paper with illustrations in blind, all by Roswitha Quadflieg; original blind pressed black paper, mauve paper labels on front cover and spine, as new.   Phillip J. Pirages 33-435 1996 $1,450.00

FABRE, JEAN HENRI   Fabre's Book of Insects. London: Hodder & Stoughton Ltd., 1921. 1st edition thus; 4to; pages viii, 184; 12 fine mounted colored plates behind tissue guards by E. J. Detmold; original white cloth gloriously stamped in gilt, preserved in original pictorial wrappers with onlaid plate to upper cover, fine, exceptional copy in excellent and rare wrapper with must minor soiling of jacket which has one or two insignificant tears.   Sotheran PN32-110 1996 £298.00

FABRE, JEAN HENRI   Fabre's Book of Insects. New York: Tudor, 1935. Large 4to; 12 beautiful mounted plates; green cloth pictorially stamped in gilt; lovely fresh copy.   Barbara Stone 70-70 1996 £75.00

FABRICIUS, HIERONYMUS   The Embryological Treatise of Hieronymous Fabricius of Aquapendente. Ithaca: 1942. 1st edition; 883 pages; original binding; GM 465.   W. Bruce Fye 71-634 1996 $175.00

FABRICIUS, HIERONYMUS   The Embryological Treatises of Hieronymous Fabricius of Aquapendente. Ithaca: Cornell University Press, 1967. Reissue of 1942 1st edition in English; 4to; 2 volumes; original cloth, slipcase; fine set. GM 465, 466.   Edwin V. Glaser B122-54 1996 $125.00

FABRICIUS, HIERONYMUS   L'Opere Cirugiche... Padua: Cadorino, 1671. 1st Italian edition; folio; vignette title, 9 engraved plates; first five leaves repaired with slight loss (first two partly backed), worming in inner margin of first few leaves, affecting a few letters, rather waterstained throughout, plates trifle trimmed; late 18th century Italian half red leather, gilt, bit worn and slightly wormed. Very rare. This ed. not in NUC, Wellcome, Waller of Krivatsy.   Maggs Bros. Ltd. 1190-406 1996 £725.00

FABRICIUS, HIERONYMUS   Opera Chirugica. Lugdvni Batavorum: Ex Officina Boutestenian, 1723. 8vo; (12), 744 pages, plus 9 folding surgical plates; full recent vellum, occasional leaf repaired, internally crisp. James Tait Goodrich K40-129 1996 $1,450.00

FACSIMILES of Choice Examples of the Art of Book-Illumination During the Middle Ages/Facsimiles of Choice Examples Selected from Illuminated Manuscripts, Unpublished Drawings and Illustrated Books of Early Date. London: Bernard Quaritch, 1889-92. 4to; 10 parts in one volume; 113 mostly colored chromolithographic plates by William Griggs, including 5 folding plates; original wrappers bound into handsome red morocco by Zaehnsdorf, hinges expertly repaired, gilt ruled raised bands with gilt ruled framed panels, titled in gilt on spine, quadruple gilt ruled frame within single gilt ruled frame on covers, all edges gilt, marbled endpapers; near fine.   Blue Mountain SP95-26 1996 $650.00

FACULTY OF ADVOCATES   Catalogue of the Library of the Faculty of Advocates. Edinburgh: printed by Thomas, Walter and Thomas Ruddiman, 1742. 2 volumes; contemporary mottled calf, neatly rebacked Meyer Boswell SL25-80 1996 $1,500.00

FAHEY, HERBERT   Early Printing in California... San Francisco: Book Club of California, 1956. 1st edition; limited to 400 copies; folio; ix, 142 pages; illustrated with facsimiles, frontispiece; cloth, morocco label, spine label slightly chipped, spine ends and corners slightly rubbed, else fine.   Argonaut Book Shop 113-234 1996 $250.00

FAHIE, J. J.   A History of Wireless Telegraphy 1838-1899, Including Some Bare-Wire Proposals for Subaqueous Telegraphs. Edinburgh: William Blackwood and Sons, 1899. 1st edition; 8vo; xvii, 325, 32 (ads) pages; frontispiece, 66 figures in text; original cloth, bookplate on front pastedown; very good.   Edwin V. Glaser 121-102 1996 $175.00

FAHIE, J. J.   Memorials of Galileo Galilei, 1564-1642. Leamington & London: for the author, 1929. 1st edition; complete with limitation slip stating only 200 copies printed, of which 105 were for sale; tall square 8vo; xxiv, 172 pages; frontispiece, 46 plates; original cloth; fine. Bookplate of James J. Waring.   Edwin V. Glaser 121-121 1996 $285.00

FAIRBAIRN'S Book of Crests of the Families of Great Britain and Ireland. London: T. C. and E. C. Jack, 1905. 4th edition; 4to; 2 volumes, xiv, 613, 148 pages; 314 plates; cloth, gilt, top edge gilt, others uncut, slightly worn.   Thomas Thorp 489-96 1996 £120.00

FAIRBAIRN, THOMAS   Relics of Ancient Architecture and Other Picturesque Scenes in Glasgow. Glasgow: pub. and lithographed in colors by Miller & Buchanan, 1849. Large folio; 4 pages letterpress, litho title with vignette view and 20 plates, all printed in colors and finished by hand; contemporary half calf, head and foot of spine worn. Occasional foxing, mainly marginal.   Marlborough 162-27 1996 £1,750.00

FAIRBAIRN, WILLIAM   On the Application of Cast and Wrought Iron to Building Purposes. London: Weale, 1854. 1st edition; 8vo; viii, 183, (1) pages, handsome folding tinted litho frontispiece (slight staining at lower edge), 2 folding litho plates, 1 foldint table and many text illustrations; publisher's cloth, head and foot of spine bumped.   Elton Engineering 10-49 1996 £280.00

FAIRBANKS, ARTHUR   Catalogue of Greek and Etruscan Vases I: Early Vases, Preceding Athenian Black-Figured Ware. Cambridge: Harvard University Press, 1928. 4to; 235 pages, 100 plates; boards, fine. Archaeologia   Luxor-3316 1996 $125.00

FAIRFIELD, SUMNER LINCOLN   The Last Night of Pompeii: a Poem; and Lays and Legends. New York: Elliot and Palmer, 1832. 1st edition; 8 1/2 x 5 1/2 inches; 309 pages; impressive recent replica binding by Bernard Middleton of black half morocco and marbled sides, spine with broad raised bands and multiple wide decorative gilt rules, as well as centered lyre ornaments; very slight yellowing to text, but very fine, rare Phillip J. Pirages 33-213 1996 $125.00

FAIRFIELD, SUMNER LINCOLN   Lays of Melpomene. Portland Todd and Smith, 1824. 1st edition; 12mo; 72 pages; original two toned plain and marbled boards, lacks front endleaves. Rare. BA 5582, 5583.   M & S Rare Books 60-154 1996 $200.00

FAIRFIELD, SUMNER LINCOLN   The Passage of the Sea; a Poem. With Other Pieces. New York: Folsom & Allen, 1826. 1st edition; 12mo; 48 pages; removed, uncut, upper corners chipped; very scarce. BAL 5585; Shoemakeer 24478.   M & S Rare Books 60-153 1996 $175.00

A FAIRY Garland: Being Fairy Tales from the Old French. New York: Scribner, 1929. 1st American edition; large 8vo; 12 full page color plates by Edmund Dulac; gilt stamped blue cloth, dust jacket (spine slightly faded); very good.   George J. Houle 68-45 1996 $150.00

A FAIRY Garland. London: Cassell & Co., 1928. 1st edition; limited to 1000 numbered copies, signed by artist; large quarto; 251 pages; 12 color plates by Edmund Dulac; original quarter vellum over blue cloth boards, spine stamped in gilt, top edge gilt, others uncut, light wear and soiling to binding, hinges starting, little minor foxing, otherwise near fine. Heritage Book Shop 196-216 1996 $600.00

THE FAIRY Mythology. London: W. H. Ainsworth, 1828. 1st edition; 2 volumes; numerous drawings and etchings by W. H. Brooke; half leather and marbled boards, outer front hinge starting on volume one, else fine good.   Aronovitz 57-21 1996 $175.00

THE FAIRY Shoemaker and Other Fairy Poems. New York: Macmillan, 1928. 1st edition; beautiful drawings in black and white by Boris Artzybasheff; green cloth tripped in yellow, very fresh copy, very scarce. Bader 189.   Barbara Stone 70-22 1996 £150.00

FAITHFULL, EMILY   Three Visits to America. New York: Fowler and Wells, 1884. 8vo; 16 pages of publishers' ads at end; original pictorial cloth; withdrawn from Derby Neck Library. Stern, Heads and Headlines 228-9.   Rostenberg & Stern 150-3 1996 $300.00

FAKHRY, AHMED   The Egyptian Deserts: Siwa Oasis, Its History and Antiquities. Cairo: Government Press, 1944. 4to; xii, 188 pages; 34 plates, 48 text figures; original wrappers, faded, first six leaves of text loose as a result of broken sewing, otherwise good internally.   Thomas Thorp 489-97 1996 £65.00

FALCONER, THOMAS   Letters and Notes on the Texan Santa Fe Expedition 1841-1842. New York: Dauber & Pine Bookshops, 1930. Pages 159, frontispiece; some age browning, else fine, unopened. Howes F14/15; WC90n; BTB 116n.   Dumont 28-125 1996 $135.00

FALCONER, THOMAS   On Surnames and the Rules of Law Affecting Their Change. London: Charles W. Reynell, 1862. Patterned cloth, later?, lalbel, dusty, but still sound and clean; presentation copy with armorial bookplate of Cornelius Walford, the Middle Temple barrister.   Meyer Boswell SL27-78 1996 $150.00

FALCONER, W.   An Account of the Epidemical Catarrahl Fever Commonly called the Influenza, As It Appeared at Bath in the Winter and Spring of the Year 1803. Bath: Cruttwell, 1803. 1st edition; 8vo; pages 46; old brown paper wrappers, inscribed by author, but name of recipient cut from upper blank margin of title, additional ms. note about the spread to Paris on p. 45 apparently in author's hand, later in Phillipps collection, with pressmark.   Maggs Bros. Ltd. 1190-407 1996 £120.00

FALCONER, WILLIAM   The Shipwreck, a Poem. London: printed for William Miller by T. Bensley, 1804. 9 1/4 x 6 1/4 inches; 8 p.l., xiii-xlvi pages, (1) leaf, 220 pages; 5 vignettes and 3 plates engraved by J. Fittler from paintings by N. Pocock; fine contemporary diced russia bound from James Stewart of Killymoon, sides with gilt frame of thick and thin rules, spine with gilt decorated broad raised bands, pretty gilt floral rows at spine ends, top and bottom compartments with intricate blindstamping, gilt titling, marbled edges and endpapers; covers little variegated, but virtually pristine;   Phillip J. Pirages 33-214 1996 $250.00

FALKIRK IRON CO.   Book of Patterns. London: n.d., ca. 1860. Oblong 4to; 350 plates, almost all tinted lithographs, few with tears or defects, 2 with half cut away, many with pencilled annotations or measurements, etc. on verso; contemporary half morocco, rather worn.   Charles W. Traylen 117-251 1996 £600.00

FALKNER, JOHN MEADE   A Bath - Its History and Social Tradition. London: John Murray, 1918. 1st edition 12mo; 86 pages; boards, top edge dusty; free endpapers browned, prelims and edges spotted, title label on spine browned and dusty, covers slightly rubbed, spine rubbed, very good.   Ulysses 39-195 1996 £75.00

FALKNER, JOHN MEADE   A History of Oxfordshire. London: Elliot Stock, 1899. 1st edition original binding, letters BM/BCYR stamped on front free endpaper, top edge dusty; inscription, prelims, edges and endpapers spotted, covers marked, cocked and bowed, head and tail of spine bumped, bottom edges of several pages soiled, good only; Ulysses 39-194 1996 £85.00

FALKNER, WILLIAM   A Vindication of Liturgies, Shewing the Lawfulness, Usefulness and Antiquity of Performing the Publick Worship of God, by Set Forms of Prayer... London: Walter Kettilby, 1680. 1st edition; 8vo; (xvi), 283, (iii) pages; contemporary sheep, ruled in blind, rebacked, label, blank leaf before title, lower corners little worn; good. Wing F336.   Robert Clark 38-44 1996 £60.00

THE FAMOUS History of Kasperl and the Adventures He Meet With on His Travels. London: Egyptian Hall and Joseph Myers, 1857. 12mo; (9)ff.; 6 silhouette illustrations; original printed yellow wrappers; light staining to last few pages, else nice.   Bromer Booksellers 90-96 1996 $250.00

FAMOUS Men of Britain. London: Tilt & Bogue, ca. 1835. 2 15/16 x 2 1/2 inches; 191 pages; 48 wood engravings; half speckled calf by Arthur S. Colley, with gilt tooling, spine in compartments and morocco label, all edges gilt, original cloth cover bound in; Bondy p. 67; Welsh 2772. Bromer Booksellers 90-195 1996 $550.00

FANNING, EDMUND   Voyages Round the World; with Selected Sketches of Voyages to the South Seas, North and South Pacific Oceans, China, etc., Peformed Under the Command and Agency of the Author. New York: Collins and Hannay, 1833. 1st edition; 8vo; frontispiece and 4 lithographed plates; original drab boards, green cloth spine, rebacked, lacks label; fair amount of foxing, but excellent uncut copy, very scarce. Sabin 23780; Howes F28; Hill p. 100-1; Ferguson 1643;   Ximenes 109-113 1996 $2,000.00

FANNING, EDMUND   Voyages and Discoveries in the South Seas 1792-1832. Salem: Marine Research Society, 1924. 15.5 cm; 8vo; 32 plates, 355 pages; gilt titles, decorated endpapers, blue cloth, light wear to corners, some foxing, generally very good.   Parmer Books O39Nautica-047056 1996 $115.00

FANNING, J. T.   A Practical Treatise on Water-Supply Engineering: Relating to the Hydrology, Hydrodynamics and Practical Construction of Water-Works in North America with Numerous Tables and Illustrations. 1877. 1st edition; 619 pages; original binding.   W. Bruce Fye 71-638 1996 $100.00

FANSHAW, RICHARD   Il Pastor Fido; the Faithful Shepherd. London: printed for Henry Herringman, 1676. 4th edition; 8vo; contemporary panelled calf, slight wear to ends of spine, wanting prelim blank, some slight soiling, but generally very good. Wing G2177; Woodward & MManaway 618; Greg 629 (cl); CBEL I 1741.   Ximenes 109-114 1996 $250.00

FANTE, JOHN   Dreams from Bunker Hill. Black Sparrow Press, 1982. Number 29 of 200 copies of the signed limited edition; fine in acetate wrapper.   Book Time 2-137 1996 $125.00

FANTE, JOHN   Full of Life. Boston: Little Brown, 1952. 1st edition; previous owner's name in several places; scarce; very good+ copy in near fine dust jacket.   Book Time 2-138 1996 $100.00

FARADAY, MICHAEL 1791-1867   Experimental Researches in Chemistry and Physics. London: Richard Taylor & William Francis, 1859. 1st collected edition; 8vo; viii, 496 pages, 3 plates, 1 folding and a number of illustrations in text; erratatum slip at p. 445; embossed cloth, spine lightly sunned, bit of wear to top and bottom of spine, front hinge starting, very good, partially unopened copy; armorial bookplate of Sir Andrew Noble. Duveen p. 208; Norman 765.   Edwin V. Glaser 121-104 1996 $600.00

FARADAY, PHILIP MICHAEL   "Amasis", an Egyptian Princess. A Comic Opera in 2 Acts. London: Metzler & Co., 1906. 1st edition; 152 pages, (4) pages ads; contemporary full cream morocco by Zaehnsdorf, with raised bands, gilt turn-ins, red silk endpapers and doublures, all edges gilt, some soiling, else very good. Rare.   Chapel Hill 94-291 1996 $150.00

FARGO, FRANK F.   A True and Minute History of the Assassination of James King of Wm. at San Francisco, Cal. San Francisco: Whitton Towne, 1856. 1st edition; 26 pages; original pictorial blue wrappers, some chipping, very good, laid in half morocco slipcase. Cowan p. 232; Howes F31; Not in McDade.   Michael D. Heaston 23-145 1996 $550.00

FARINA, RICHARD   Been Down So Long It Looks Like Up to Me. New York: RH, 1966. 1st edition; fine in first issue dust jacket, beautiful copy.   Ken Lopez 74-128 1996 $350.00

FARIS, EL-SHIDIAC   A Practical Grammar of the Arabic Language. London: Bernard Quaritch, 1866. 2nd edition; small 8vo; (2), ii, 162 pages; original blind stamped blue cloth, gilt spine, extremities slightly rubbed.   Kenneth Karmiole 1NS-19 1996 $100.00

FARIS, JOHN T.   Old Gardens In and About Philadelphia and Those Who Made Them. Indianapolis: Bobbs Merrill Co., 1932. 1st edition; 8vo; (ii), 311 pages, 53 illustrations on plates; cloth, front hinge internally cracked, occasional foxing, light cover wear, else very good. Bookpress 75-179 1996 $110.00

FARLOW, WILLIAM GILSON   Icones Farlowianae, Illustrations of the Larger Fungi of Eastern North America. Cambridge 1929. Folio; pages x, 120; 103 colored plates; original green buckram, light scuff marks to edges and rear cover, occasional light offsetting from plates. Raymond M. Sutton VII-13 1996 $1,275.00

FARMER, JOHN   Merry Songs and Ballads. London: privately printed for subscribers only, 1897. 8vo; 5 volumes, titles printed in red and black; contemporary dark brown half morocco, spines gilt with an ornate Art Nouveau design of a rose flower on a leafy stem surrounded by a decorative border, top edge gilt, others uncut, by Zaehnsdorf, corners slightly bumped.   Thomas Thorp 489-98 1996 £250.00

FARMER, P., MRS.   The Captives and Other Poems. Laporte: Millikan and Holmes, 1856. 1st edition; 12mo; 6, 236 pages, errata slip; original cloth.   M & S Rare Books 60-179 1996 $175.00

FARMER, PHILIP   The Green Odyssey. Ballantine, 1957. 1st edition; signed by author; scarce first book.   Aronovitz 57-394 1996 $1,250.00

FARMERS' Cyclopeda. Garden City: 1916. 8vo; 7 volumes, over 4700 pages; 400 illustrations; original cloth, some fraying to heel of volume 1, spines slightly dulled, some bowning to volume 6, pages tanned, very good.   Raymond M. Sutton VII-925 1996 $225.00

FARNSWORTH, R. W. C.   A Southern California Paradise, in the Suburbs of Los Angeles: Being a Historic and Descriptive Account of Pasadena, San Gabriel, Sierra Madre and La Canada. Pasadena: R. W. C. Farnsworth, 1883. 2nd edition; 10 1/4 x 7 inches; 142, ix pages; numerous full page and smaller illustrations, map; printed blue wrappers, substantial chipping to wrappers, generally unobtrusive stain to titlepage and lower margin of book, short tear to foremargin of last few leaves. Dawson's Books Shop 528-80 1996 $300.00

FARQUHAR, FRANCIS P.   The Books of the Colorado River and the Grand Canyon: a Selective Bibliography. Los Angeles: Glen Dawson, 1953. 1st edition; xi, 75 pages; frontispiece; red cloth with paper label extending from spine to both covers, fine. Very scarce.   Argonaut Book Shop 113-235 1996 $225.00

FARQUHAR, FRANCIS P.   History of the Sierra Nevada. Berkeley: University of California Press, 1965. 1st edition; 276 pages; frontispiece in color, drawings, photos, maps; original silver decorated blue cloth, spine lettered in gilt, minor offsetting to endpapers from jacket flap, else very fine, with badly torn and repaired pictorial dust jacket; original errata slip laid in.   Argonaut Book Shop 113-236 1996 $100.00

FARRAR, VICTOR   The Annexation of Russian America to the United States. Washington: 1937. Pages viii, 142;   Stephen Lunsford 45-55 1996 $100.00

FARRELL, DAVID   The Stinehours Press - A Bibliographical Checklist of the First Thirty Years. Lunenburg: Meriden-Stinehour Press, 1988. One of 1200 numbered copies; 12 pages of color illustrations; original binding, fine in dust jacket; presentation copy from compiler to James D. Hart; loosely inserted ALS from compiler to presentee.   Ulysses 39-564 1996 £75.00

FARRELL, JAMES T. $1000 a Week. New York: Vanguard, 1941. 1st edition; owner name and date (1942) on front endpaper, otherwise very good in dust jacket with some spine darkening, attractive copy, scarce. Ken Lopez 74-130 1996 $125.00

FARRELL, JAMES T.   Young Lonigan. New York: Vanguard Press, 1932. 2nd issue, with new introduction; near fine in good, fragile jacket, chipped along edges and front flapfold. Quite scarce.   Ken Lopez 74-129 1996 $375.00

FARRELL, JOHN   Harrison High. New York: Rinehart, 1959. 1st edition; author's first novel; cheap paper browning which is typical of this title, dust jacket rubbed in several areas, otherwise fairly bright copy.   Bud Schweska 12-330 1996 $100.00

FARRER, REGINALD   Among the Hills: a Book of Joy in High Places. London: 1911. 1st edition; 8vo; 326 pages, map, 14 colored and 8 plain plates; original cloth, tape marks on endpapers, otherwise nice. Wheldon & Wesley 207-1770 1996 £75.00

FARRER, REGINALD   The English Rock Garden. London: 1919. 2 volumes; numerous illustrations; original cloth, expertly restored, new endpapers.   David A.H. Grayling MY95Orn-31 1996 £95.00

FARRER, REGINALD   The English Rock Garden. London: 1948. Royal 8vo; 2 volumes, 100 plates; original cloth.   Wheldon & Wesley 207-1690 1996 £55.00

FARRER, REGINALD   The English Rock Garden. London: 1955. 8vo; 2 volumes, 107 plates; cloth, dust jackets, dust jackets chipped at head of spines, otherwise fine, clean copy.   John Henly 27-290 1996 £60.00

FARRER, REGINALD   On the Eaves of the World. London: 1917. 1st impression; 8vo; 2 volumes; 64 illustrations and map; original blue cloth, nice, apart from slight foxing and tape marks on endpapers.   Wheldon & Wesley 207-1771 1996 £100.00

FARRER, REGINALD   On the Eaves of the World. London: Edward Arnold & Co., 1926. 2nd impression; 8vo; 2 volumes, xii, 312; viii, 328 pages; 64 plates, folding map; blue gilt cloth; fine set.   Kenneth Karmiole 1NS-246 1996 $125.00

FARRER, REGINALD   The Rainbow Bridge. London: 1926. 3rd impression; 8vo; pages xi, 383, 16; map and 16 plates; cloth; fine. John Henly 27-376 1996 £52.00

FARRER, WILLIAM   Records Relating to the Barony of Kendale. Kendal: Titus Wilson, 1924. Editor's proof copy with mss. corrections for printer, plates before letters with title added in ms; 8vo; Volume 2, pages x, 513; 4 plates, all leaves punching for filing; old boards, handsomely rebacaked in green levant morocco, gilt.   R.F.G. Hollett & Son 78-869 1996 £195.00

FASCH, JOHANN RUDOLF   Anderer Versuch Seiner Architect...Part Four. Nurnburg: Johann Christoph Weigel, 1725. 1st edition; oblong folio; (iii) pages, 25 plates; later quarter morocco; some occasional, minor smudging on margins, not affecting illustrations; else very good, scarce. Berlin 1996.   Bookpress 75-180 1996 $1,250.00

FASS, JOHN S.   Some Oriental Versions of the Turtle. Hammer Creek: Hammer Creek Press, 1952. Small octavo; (18) pages, frenchfold, printed in 3 colors on Japanese paper; bound oriental-style in decorated wrappers, cartouche on title label is a variant design printed in two colors; extremely fine. Cohen 17.   Bromer Booksellers 87-91 1996 $135.00

FASS, JOHN S.   Some Oriental Versions of the Turtle. New York: Hammer Creek Press, 1952. Small octavo; (18) pages, frenchfold; printed in five colors on Japanese paper and bound oriental style in decorated wrappers, titlepage accented with gold; extremely fine, variant title label laid in.   Bromer Booksellers 87-90 1996 $140.00

FASS, JOHN S.   Some Oriental Versions of the Turtle. New York: Hammer Crreek Press, 1952. Small octavo; (18) pages, frenchfold, printed in 3 colors on Japanese paper, bound oriental style in variant binding of green handmade paper, cartouche on title label matches that on titlepages, extremely fine. Bookplate. Cohen 17.   Bromer Booksellers 87-92 1996 $125.00

FASS, JOHN S.   The Work of the Hammer Creek Press 1950-1956. New York: Hammer Creek Press, 1956. Limited to 10 copies; small octavo; (20) pages; variant with 3 titlepages; marbled boards, very fine. Cohen 35.   Bromer Booksellers 87-96 1996 $385.00

FASS, JOHN S.   The Work of the Hammer Creek Press 1950-1956. New York: Hammer Crreek, 1956. Limited to 100 copies; small octavo; (20) pages, the variant with two titlepages; marbled boards, very fine. Bromer Booksellers 87-97 1996 $365.00

FASS, JOHN S.   The Work of the Hammer Creek Press 1950-1956. New York: Hammer Creek Press, 1956. Limited to 100 copies; small octavo; (20) pages, with one titlepage, as issued; marbled boards, very fine. Cohen 35.   Bromer Booksellers 87-98 1996 $350.00

FATIO, LOUISE   The Christmas Forest. New York: Aladdin Books, 1950. 1st edition; colored illustrations to every page by Roger Duvoisin; cloth backed colored pictorial boards, fine in original pictorial dust jacket.   Barbara Stone 70-85 1996 £55.00

FAUJAS DE SAINT-FOND, BARTHELEMY   Description des Experiences de la Machine Aerostatique de M.M. de Montgolfier, et de Celles Auxquelles Cette Decouvert a Donne Lieu. Paris: & se Trouve a Bruxelles Chez B. Le Franq, 1784. Early reprint; 8vo; disbound; fine, very rare; cf. PMM 229.   Ximenes 109-116 1996 $1,500.00

FAULCONER, ALBERT   Foundations of Anesthesiology. Springfield: 1965. 1st edition; 2 volumes, 1337 pages; original binding. GM 5733.2. W. Bruce Fye 71-643 1996 $250.00

FAULKNER, T.   An Historical and Descriptive Account of the Royal Hosptial, and the Royal Military Asylum at Chelsea... London: J. Cundee for T. Faulkner, 1805. 1st edition; 12mo; half title; 115 pages, 3 engraved plates (cropped at one edge); contemporary marbled calf, spine gilt; Anderson p. 102.   Marlborough 162-138 1996 £190.00

FAULKNER, WILLIAM HARRISON 1897-1962   As I Lay Dying. New York: Jonathan Cape & Harrison Smith, 1930. 1st edition; 1st issue; very good/near fine; lacking dust jacket.   Captain's Bookshelf 38-62 1996 $300.00

FAULKNER, WILLIAM HARRISON 1897-1962   As I Lay Dying. New York: Jonathan Cape and Harrison Smith, 1930. 1st edition; later state; 7 1/2 x 5 1/4 inches; 3 p.l., 254 pages; original cloth and dust jacket, portions of the recessed joints little discolored (from binder's glue), rear endpapers sl. darkened because of paper formerly laid in, otherwise fine, extremely clean and bright; jacket with slightly darkened spine, one small spot and with minor fraying at spine ends, but very nearly fine nevertheless, with front and rear panels especially clean and smooth. Phillip J. Pirages 33-215 1996 $500.00

FAULKNER, WILLIAM HARRISON 1897-1962   Big Woods. New York: Random House, 1955. 1st edition of this collection; 9 1/4 x 6 1/4 inches; 5 p.l., 198 pages (7) leaves; vignette on title and several illustrations in text, some in russet and black; original cloth and dust jacket; very fine in fine jacket.   Phillip J. Pirages 33-216 1996 $150.00

FAULKNER, WILLIAM HARRISON 1897-1962   Doctor Martino and Other Stories. New York: Smith and Haas, 1934. One of 360 specially bound copies, numbered and signed by author; original cloth, very good+ to near fine with 1 inch sunned strip at top of front board and slightly sunned spine.   Beasley Books 82-64 1996 $650.00

FAULKNER, WILLIAM HARRISON 1897-1962   Doctor Martino and Other Stories. New York: Harrison Smith and Robert Haas, 1934. 1st edition of this collection; 7 3/4 x 5 1/4 inches; 4 p.l., 371 pages; original cloth and dust jacket, cloth spine slightly faded and with shadow of dust jacket lettering (as usual with this title), otherwise very fine, jacket with small tear on front panel (neatly repaired with tape on verso), spine slightly darkened, three tiny tears along top, otherwise very clean, bright and fine.   Phillip J. Pirages 33-217 1996 $350.00

FAULKNER, WILLIAM HARRISON 1897-1962   A Fable. New York: Random House, 1954. 1st edition; fine in very near fine dust jacket with spine lettering slightly darkened, touch of rubbing and short tear on rear panel.   Between the Covers 42-164 1996 $150.00

FAULKNER, WILLIAM HARRISON 1897-1962   A Fable. New York: Random House, 1954. 1st edition; 8 1/2 x 5 3/4 inches; 5 p.l., 437 pages; original cloth and dust jacket, very fine, in nearly fine jacket (with few faint creases, spine with just hint of fading).   Phillip J. Pirages 33-218 1996 $150.00

FAULKNER, WILLIAM HARRISON 1897-1962   Go Down Moses and Other Stories. New York: Random House, 1942. 1st edition; 1st issue; 8vo; original black cloth, dust jacket; 1st issue price clipped jacket which shows very slight wear. Difficult to find in fine condition.   James S. Jaffe 34-153 1996 $1,000.00

FAULKNER, WILLIAM HARRISON 1897-1962   Go Down, Moses and Other Stories. New York: Random House, 1942. 1st edition; 1st issue; in black cloth binding; near fine in very good price clipped dust jacket that shows moderate edgewear and has one small chip at upper back panel. Ken Lopez 74-131 1996 $650.00

FAULKNER, WILLIAM HARRISON 1897-1962   A Green Bough. New York: Harrison Smith & Robert Haas, 1933. Limited edition; one of 360 copies; signed by author; wood engravings by Lynd Ward; very good+, spine tanned, with medium size chip to fore-edge of one page.   Lame Duck Books 19-184 1996 $950.00

FAULKNER, WILLIAM HARRISON 1897-1962   The Hamlet. New York: Random House, 1940. One of 250 copies, signed by author; 8vo; pictorial titlepage, original cloth and boards, glassine dust jacket; very fine.   James S. Jaffe 34-151 1996 $3,000.00

FAULKNER, WILLIAM HARRISON 1897-1962   The Hamlet. New York: Random House, 1940. 1st edition; 2nd issue jacket; 8 1/4 x 5 3/4 inches; 4 p.l., 421 pages; original cloth and variant price clipped dust jacket featuring reviews of this work, very fine in excellent jacket (rear panel unevenly faded, spine ends creased and frayed, few other small tears, otherwise bright and clean and pleasing.   Phillip J. Pirages 33-219 1996 $450.00

FAULKNER, WILLIAM HARRISON 1897-1962   The Hamlet. New York: Random House, 1940. 1st edition; 8vo; black cloth, dust jacket, former owner's neat booklabel on lower corner of front endsheet, otherwise fine copy in bright, lightly rubbed jacket.   James S. Jaffe 34-152 1996 $1,000.00

FAULKNER, WILLIAM HARRISON 1897-1962   Intruder in the Dust. New York: Random House, 1948. 1st edition; some flaking to spine gilt, a condition that is endemic to this title, otherwise near fine in near fine price clipped dust jacket with very mild rubbing at edges, very nice. Ken Lopez 74-132 1996 $250.00

FAULKNER, WILLIAM HARRISON 1897-1962   Intruder in the Dust. New York: Random House, 1948. 1st edition; 8 1/4 x 5 3/4 inches; 2 p.l., 247 pages; original cloth and dust jacket, title printed in blue and black, one tiny dent in front cover, otherwise nearly mint, in nearly fine jacket with only minor soiling and rubbing.   Phillip J. Pirages 33-220 1 996 $175.00

FAULKNER, WILLIAM HARRISON 1897-1962   Knight's Gambit. New York: Random House, 1949. 1st edition; 8 1/4 x 5 3/4 inches; 3 p.l., 246 pages; title printed in red and black; original cloth and dust jacket, fine, jacket very good (bit creased and frayed at extremities, small loss at top of one joint, panels slightly soiled and marked).   Phillip J. Pirages 33-221 1996 $125.00

FAULKNER, WILLIAM HARRISON 1897-1962   Light in August. New York: Harrison Smith & Robert Haas, 1932. 1st edition; 8 1/4 x 5 3/4 inches; 2 p.l., 480 pages; original cloth and dust jacket, original protective glassine wrapper, with several small chips in edges and one larger chip at bottom of spine, endpapers with shadows of paper formerly laid in, otherwise extremely fine; nearly fine jacket (slightly frayed and wrinkled at spine ends and few other places along edges, otherwise very clean and bright.   Phillip J. Pirages 33-222 1996 $750.00

FAULKNER, WILLIAM HARRISON 1897-1962   The Mansion. New York: Random House, 1959. 1st edition; 8 3/4 x 5 3/4 inches; 6 p.l., 436 pages, title printed in blue and black; original cloth, issued without jacket; virtually mint copy. Petersen A36c.   Phillip J. Pirages 33-224 1996 $550.00

FAULKNER, WILLIAM HARRISON 1897-1962   The Mansion. New York: Random House, 1959. 1st edition; 8 3/4 x 5 3/4 inches; 6 p.l., 436 pages; original cloth and titlepage; extremely fine in very fine jacket. Peterson A36b.   Phillip J. Pirages 33-223 1996 $150.00

FAULKNER, WILLIAM HARRISON 1897-1962   The Mansion. New York: Random House, 1959. 1st edition; fine in bright price clipped dust jacket. Bev Chaney, Jr. 23-202 1996 $125.00

FAULKNER, WILLIAM HARRISON 1897-1962   The Mansion. New York: Random House, 1959. 1st edition; fine in near fine jacket with slight edgewear at spine and extremities and corners.   Ken Lopez 74-133 1996 $100.00

FAULKNER, WILLIAM HARRISON 1897-1962   Mirrors of Chartres Street. Minneapolis: Faulkner Studies, 1953. One of 1000 copies; 8 1/2 x 5 3/4 inches; xv, (1), 93 pages; several full page illustrations by Mary Demopoulos; original cloth and dust jacket; extremely fine in excellent (slightly marked, soiled and frayed) jacket. Petersen A29a.   Phillip J. Pirages 33-225 1996 $300.00

FAULKNER, WILLIAM HARRISON 1897-1962   Mosquitoes. New York: Boni & Liveright, 1927. One of only 3047 copies; light shelfwear to board edges, else very good+ in dust jacket with chipping to extremities, one inch tear to front flap fold, and residue of sticker to front panel, overall nice copy, Scarce, first issue mosquito design dust jacket.   Lame Duck Books 19-183 1996 $2,500.00

FAULKNER, WILLIAM HARRISON 1897-1962   The Portable Faulkner. New York: Viking, 1946. 1st edition; 12mo; fine in dust jacket with few small tears and internal, archival mend to front flap.   Captain's Bookshelf 38-64 1996 $125.00

FAULKNER, WILLIAM HARRISON 1897-1962   Pylon. London: Chatto & Windus, 1935. 1st English edition; crown 8vo; pages vii, 319; 2nd issue pink cloth, backstrip lettered in white, dust jacket trifle frayed and soiled, excellent. Morrow & Lafourcade V p. 123.   Blackwell's B112-107 1996 £200.00

FAULKNER, WILLIAM HARRISON 1897-1962   Pylon. New York: Smith and Haas, 1935. One of 310 copies, numbered and signed by author; bright silver boards, with only slight rubbing and sunned spine in damaged box, missing fore-edge panel.   Beasley Books 82-65 1996 $650.00

FAULKNER, WILLIAM HARRISON 1897-1962   The Reivers: a Reminiscence. New York: Random House, 1962. 1st edition; one of 500 copies, signed by author; 8 1/4 x 5 3/4 inches; 4 p.l., 305 pages; printed on special paper; specially bound, original cloth, acetate jacket; virtually mint. Petersen A37e.   Phillip J. Pirages 33-227 1996 $550.00

FAULKNER, WILLIAM HARRISON 1897-1962   The Reivers. New York: Random House, 1962. 1st edition; fine in price clipped, very near fine dust jacket with little rubbing to edge of spine; nicer copy than usual; the copy of Peter DeVries with his pencil ownership.   Between the Covers 42-166 1996 $250.00

FAULKNER, WILLIAM HARRISON 1897-1962   Requiem for a Nun. New York: Random House, 1951. 1st edition; one of 750 specially bound copies, signed by author, this one out of series; 8vo; cloth backed marbled boards, fine.   James S. Jaffe 34-154 1996 $850.00

FAULKNER, WILLIAM HARRISON 1897-1962   Requiem for a Nun. New York: Random House, 1951. 1st edition; one of 750 specially bound and numbered copies, signed by author; spine slightly sunned, otherwise fine, without dust jacket or slipcase, as issued.   Captain's Bookshelf 38-65 1996 $750.00

FAULKNER, WILLIAM HARRISON 1897-1962   Requiem for a Nun. New York: Random, 1951. 1st edition; 1st issue, with gray top edge and no FIRST PRINTING as required; lower front corner lightly bumped, else near fine in near fine jacket.   Timothy P. Slongo 5-110 1996 $115.00

FAULKNER, WILLIAM HARRISON 1897-1962   Requiem for a Nun. New York: Random House, 1951. 1st edition; 8 1/4 x 5 3/4 inches; 3 p.l., 286 pages; original cloth and dust jacket; two tiny spots of minor discoloration on front and rear endpaper, otherwise virtually mint in very fine jacket, remarkably bright and clean; Petersen A28b.   Phillip J. Pirages 33-228 1996 $175.00

FAULKNER, WILLIAM HARRISON 1897-1962   Sartoris. New York: Harcourt, 1929. One of 1998 copies; original cloth, near fine.   Beasley Books 82-63 1996 $250.00

FAULKNER, WILLIAM HARRISON 1897-1962   The Sound and the Fury. New York: Jonathan Cape and Harrison Smith, 1929. 1st edition; with the generally preferred issue point of 'Humanity Uprooted' priced at $3.00 on the lower panel; 8vo; enclosed in lovely black morocco slipcase; very good or better copy with very good dust jacket, the red quite faded on spine as usual, some chipping at spine ends and at top of upper panel, some light soiling on white of lower panel, but jacket is 100 per cent complete; pleasant copy.   Lakin & Marley 3-11 1996 $4,500.00

FAULKNER, WILLIAM HARRISON 1897-1962   These Thirteen. Stories. New York: Jonathan Cape & Harrison Smith, 1931. 1st edition; very nice, near fine copy, bookplate, dust jacket with few small chips and somewhat darkened spine.   Captain's Bookshelf 38-63 1996 $500.00

FAULKNER, WILLIAM HARRISON 1897-1962   These Thirteen. New York: 1931. 1st edition; near fine in dust jacket with 2 chips at spine top.   Stephen Lupack 83- 1996 $500.00

FAULKNER, WILLIAM HARRISON 1897-1962   These Thirteen. New York: Jonathan Cape & Harrison Smith, 1931. 1st edition; 8 x 5 3/4 inches; 5 p.l., 358 pages; original cloth and dust jacket, few pages at beginning unopened, hint of fading at edges of covers, spine with very faint shadow of dust jacket lettering (as usual), otherwise very fine in an excellent jacket (spine slightly darkened, minor fraying with two tiny chips missing at spine ends, but with both panels quite bright and clean. Petersen A9a or A9c.   Phillip J. Pirages 33-229 1996 $450.00

FAULKNER, WILLIAM HARRISON 1897-1962   Thinking of Home. New York: W. W. Norton, 1922. Limited edition of 100 copies, signed and dated by James Watson; fine in dust jacket.   Bev Chaney, Jr. 23-204 1996 $125.00

FAULKNER, WILLIAM HARRISON 1897-1962   The Town. New York: Random House, 1957. 1st edition; 1st issue; fine in attractive, near fine dust jacket with short tears on edge of spine and at bottom of front flap and touch of rubbing, nicer copy than usual.   Between the Covers 42-165 1996 $175.00

FAULKNER, WILLIAM HARRISON 1897-1962   The Town. New York: Random House, 1957. 1st edition; 8 1/4 x 5 3/4 inches; 4 p.l., 371 pages; original variant deep orange cloth and dust jacket; very fine in like jacket; Petersen A34c.   Phillip J. Pirages 33-230 1996 $125.00

FAULKNER, WILLIAM HARRISON 1897-1962   Uncollected Stories. Franklin Center: Franklin Library, 1979. True 1st edition; signed by Albert Erskine, who provides introduction; full gilt stamped leather, fine.   Lame Duck Books 19-186 1996 $150.00

FAULKNER, WILLIAM HARRISON 1897-1962   The Unvanquished. New York: Random House, 1938. One of 250 copies, specially printed and bound and signed by author; 8vo; drawings by Edward Shenton; cloth backed boards, glassine dust jacket, very fine, virtually as new in rare original glassine dust jacket which is little torn, in custom made cloth folding box.   James S. Jaffe 34-150 1996 $3,500.00

FAULKNER, WILLIAM HARRISON 1897-1962   The Unvanquished. New York: Random House, 1938. One of only 250 copies of the limited edition, signed by author; very slight fading to spine, overall very nice, scarce, issued without dust jacket or slipcase.   Lame Duck Books 19-185 1996 $2,500.00

FAULKNER, WILLIAM HARRISON 1897-1962   The Wild Palms. New York: Random House, 1939. 1st edition; 8 1/4 x 5 3/4 inches; 2 p.l., 339 pages; original cloth and dust jacket; virtually mint in as good a jacket as one could hope to find. Petersen A19b.   Phillip J. Pirages 33-232 1996 $750.00

FAULKNER, WILLIAM HARRISON 1897-1962   The Wishing Tree. New York: Random House, 1964. 1st edition; limited to 500 copies; spine of dust jacket faded, else very fine, bright copy in slipcase.   Bromer Booksellers 87-69 1996 $250.00

FAULKNER, WILLIAM HARRISON 1897-1962   The Wishing Tree. New York: Random House, 1967. 1st edition; one of 500 copies printed on special paper and specially bound; 8 1/4 x 5 1/4 inches; 4 p.l., 81, (1) pages, (2) leaves; title and facing page illustrated in color and several other illustrations in text, all by Don Bolognese; original cloth and dust jacket in publisher's pictorial slipcase; nearly mint, in very fine jacket, just slightly faded, otherwise as new. Petersen A40d.   Phillip J. Pirages 33-233 1996 $150.00

FAUST, BERHARD CHRISTOPH   Catechism of Health, for the Use of Schools, and for Domestic Instruction. Dublin: printed by P. Byrne, 1794. 1st Irish edition; 12mo; disbound; woodcut frontispiece and several illustrations; frontispiece torn, not affecting image, few page numbers shaved, but sound, very scarce. NLM p. 144.   Ximenes 108-128 199 $200.00

FAUST, FREDERICK   Secret Agent Number 1. Philadelphia: Macrae-Smith Co., 1936. 1st edition; scarce, very good with light soiling and unavoidable offset in dust jacket with light rubbing, edge wear and soiling.   Quill & Brush 102-520 1996 $150.00

FAVOUR, ALPHEUS H.   Old Bill Williams, Mountain Man. Chapel Hill: The University of North Carolina Press, 1936. 1st edition; (10), 229 pages; folding map, 19 illustrations, map endpapers; original cloth, slight offsetting to rear endpapers, else fine, with dust jacket from the 1962 reprint edition. Presentation inscription, signed by author.   Argonaut Book Shop 113-239 1996 $150.00

FAWCETT, F. BURLINGTON   Broadside Ballads of the Restoration Period from Jersey Collection Known as the Osterley Park Ballads. London: John Lane, 1930. Limited edition, number 524 of 750 copies; folio; xxvi, (ii), 248 pages; woodcut on titlepage; original buckram backed cloth, gilt lettering, top edge gilt, others untrimmed, good copy in soiled and frayed dust jacket.   Robert Clark 38-3 1996 £115.00

FAWCETT, GRAHAM   Poems for Shakespeare 2. London: Globe Playhouse Trust Publications, 1973. 1st edition; one of 100 copies, printed (hors commerce), signed by 14 contributin poets; 8vo; quarter calf and red cloth, all edges gilt, red cloth slipcase, bound by A. W. Lumsden; fine   James S. Jaffe 34-243 1996 $450.00

FAWKES, F. A.   Horticultural Buildings. London: Batsford, n.d 1881. 1st edition; 8vo; frontispiece, (ii), ii, 255, (i), xvii pages; 123 in text illustrations; publisher's cloth, minor rubbing along spine, inscription in pencil on front free endpaper, else very good.   Bookpress 75-50 1996 $385.00

FAY, ELIZA   Original Letters from India - (1779-1815). London: Hogarth Press, 1925. 1st edition one black and white plate; original binding, top edge dusty, spine and cover edges slightly faded, fore-edge very slightly soiled, very good in chipped, torn, worn and dusty dust jacket browned at spine and edges and missing small piece from centre of spine.   Ulysses 39-209 1996 £155.00

FEARING, F.   Reflex Action: a Study in the History of Physilogical Psychology. Baltimore: 1930. 350 pages; original binding, spine spotted and dull; autographed by Fearing.   W. Bruce Fye 71-644 1996 $125.00

FEARN, JOHN   A Review of the First Principles of Bishop Berkeley, - Dr. Reid and Professor Stewart. London: printed by D. Cock and Co. for Messrs. Longman, Hurst, Rees... 1813. 1st edition; 4to; original boards, uncut, spine frayed, printed paper label on upper cover; nice.   Anthony W. Laywood 108-170 1996 £425.00

FEARNSIDE, W. G.   The History of London: Illustrated by Views in London and Westminster. London: Orr & Co., n.d. ca. 1838. 8vo; engraved frontispiece, extra engraved titlepage, titlepage, 1 f., 203 pages, (1 page index), 23 steel engraved views; publisher's blindstamped and gilt lettered cloth, all edges gilt; fine, with tissue guards.   Marlborough 162-139 1996 £210.00

FEARNSIDE, WILLIAM GRAY   The History of London: Illustrated by Views of London and Westminster... London: Orr & Co., ca. 1838. Royal 8vo; 2 prelim blanks, engraved title, iv, 201, (iii), 2 blanks, 29 engraved plates, all edges marbled; quarter calf over marbled boards, marbled endpapers; binding little worn at extremities, otherwise a handsome copy with bright, clean plates.   Sotheran PN32-183 1996 £298.00

FEARON, HENRY BARDSHAW   Sketches of America; a Narrative of a Journey of Five Thousand Miles Through the Eastern and Western States of America. London: Longman, Hurst, et al, 1818. 1st edition; vii, (1), 462 pages, errata, small map; later three quarter red leather, gilt top, untrimmed pages; nice copy with some foxing.   Buck 98; Thomson, Ohio 406; Graff 1301; Clark, Old South II 22.   Bohling Book Co. 191-352 1996 $200.00

FEATHER, JOHN   English Book Prospectuses: an Illustrated History. Bird & Bull Press & Daedalus Press, 1984. One of 325 copies; 10 x 6 1/2 inches; 109, (1) pages, (1) leaf (colophon); 24 facsimiles of prospectuses, 10 in text and 14 in separate chemise; black quarter morocco, patterned metallic paper boards, spine titled in gilt, fore edge and tail edge untrimmed, separate facsimiles in chemise, the volume and facsimiles housed in publisher's matching paper slipcase. As new.   Phillip J. Pirages 33-79 1996 $300.00

FEATHER, JOHN   English Book Prospectuses. Newtown & Minneapolis: Daedalus Press, 1984. Limited to 325 copies; large octavo; 109 pages; morocco backed 'Dutch Gilt' decorated paper boards, accompanied by a folder with single leaf of text and 14 facsimile prospectuses; the whole housed in matching slipcase; extremely fine.   Bromer Booksellers 87-32 1996 $300.00

FEATHERSTON, JOHN   The Visitation of the County of Cumberland in the Year 1615, Taken by Richard St. George, Norroy King of Arms. London: Harleian Society, 1872. Large 8vo; pages vii,3 8 (ii, plates of arms), (v), 9, 31 shields; original cloth, gilt, spine faded, rare.   R.F.G. Hollett & Son 78-926 1996 £140.00

FEDER, NORMAN   American Indian Art. New York: Abrams, 1969. 1st edition; thick 4to; many color plates tipped in, 59 color, 242 black and white; very good, all plates fine; long owner's inscription.   Parker Books of the West 30-65 1996 $100.00

FEHER, JOSEPH   Hawaii: a Pictorial History. Honolulu: Bishop Museum Press, 1969. 33 cm; 518 pages, many black and white plates, illustrations, photos; gold cloth, design on front cover.   L. Clarice Davis 111-125 1996 $225.00

FEINSTEIN, ELAINE   The Ecstasy of Miriam Garner. London: 1976. 1st edition; presentation copy from author to Angela Carter; small stian on flyleaf, otherwise very good in dust jacket.   Words Etcetera 94-418 1996 £50.00

FELICIANO DA LAZESIO, FRANCESCO   L'Arithmetica et Geometrica Speculativa et Praticale. Venice: Simon Rocca, 1570. New edition; 4to; (4), 79, 1 blank leaves, woodcut on titlepage; woodcuts and diagrams in text, some minor browning to some leaves, slightly affecting one letter, last few leaves little frayed; contemporary annotations on endpapers; contemporary limp vellum. Riccardi II 22. Not in Plimpton collection.   Jeffrey D. Mancevice 20-30 1996 $875.00

FELL, ALFRED   A Furness Military Chronicle. Ulverston: Kitchin & Co., 1937. Tall 8vo; pages (vi), 282, (iii, subscribers), uncut, frontispiece, original cloth, gilt, spine trifle faded; fine, very scarce.   R.F.G. Hollett & Son 78-907 1996 £340.00

FELL, ALFRED   A Furness Military Chronicle. Ulverston: Kitchin & Co., 1937. Tall 8vo; pages (vi), 282, (iii, subscribers), frontispiece, uncut, original cloth, gilt, spine little faded, small mark at head; flyleaves lightly spotted.   R.F.G. Hollett & Son 78-908 1996 £290.00

FELLIG, ARTHUR 1900-   Naked Hollywood. New York: Pellegrini, 1953. 1st edition; 4to; numerous photos; dust jacket, few nicks and creases; very good.   George J. Houle 68-152 1996 $125.00

FELLIG, ARTHUR 1900-   Weegee's People. New York: Essential Books/Duel, Sloan & Pearce, 1946. 1st edition; photo illustrations; very good+ in dust jacket which is slightly worn at spine bottom.   Steven C. Bernard 71-181 1996 $100.00

FELLOWES, ROBERT   The History of Ceylon, from the Earliest Period to the Year MDCCCXV... London: printed for Joseph Mawman, 1817. 4to; 2 parts in one volume, engraved portrait, folding map, 15 plates; half calf, marbled boards, rubbed, top edge gilt, others uncut; bookplate of Baron de Worms.   H. M. Fletcher 121-138 1996 £450.00

FELLOWES, W. D.   A Visit to the Monasatery of La Trappe, In 1817. London: printed for Thomas McLean, 1823. 4th edition; tall 8vo; xii, 188 pages; 12 colored aquatints, 3 uncolored engravings; contemporary full green morocco, raised bands, gilt compartments, gilt borders on covers, all edges gilt, some light wear and rubbing to spine, still very good with very nice colored plates.   David Mason 71-66 1996 $600.00

FELLOWS, CHARLES   Travels and Researches in Asia Minor...Province of Lycia. London: John Murray, 1852. 12mo; pages xvi, 510; 2 maps, 6 plates; gilt pictorial cloth, spine ends worn.   Richard Adelson W94/95-194 1996 $120.00

FELS, CATHARINE   Graphic Work of Louis Monza. Plantin Press, 1973. 4to; cloth, printed labels, spine faded, otherwise very nice. Bertram Rota 272-373 1996 £60.00

THE FEMALE Instructor; or, Young Woman's Companion; Being a Guide to All the Accomplishments Which Adorn the Female Character, Either as a Useful Member of Society... Liverpool: printed by Nuttall, Fisher and Dixon, 1815. 8vo; 560 pages; frontispiece, additional title, 9 plates (lightly browned), later 19th century half morocco, rubbed; uncommon in any edition. Cagle, Matter of Taste 682.   James Burmester 29-36 1996 £200.00

FEMALE Robinson Crusoe, a Tale of the American Wilderness. New York: Printed by Jared W. Bell, 1837. 1st edition; 12mo; 286 pages; original figured cloth, spine faded. Wright I 942; Rinderknecht 44273. M & S Rare Books 60-108 1996 $250.00

FEMALE SOCIETY FOR INSTRUCTING POOR CHILDREN   Constitution. Hagerstown: William D. Bell, 1815. 1st edition; 18mo; 7 pages; sewn, disbound; horizontal tears at old center fold but complete. Rare.   M & S Rare Books 60-438 1996 $250.00

FENELLOSA, MARY   Blossoms from a Japanese Garden. London: Heinemann, 1913. 1st edition; 8vo; 60 pages; 20 tipped in colored plates; decorated boards gilt with square pictorial onlay; rear cover nicked, light foxing, else very good.   Marjorie James 19-132 1996 £75.00

FENELON, FRANCOIS SALIGNAC DE LA MOTHE, ABP. 1651-1715   Treatise on the Education of Daughters. Cheltenham: H. Ruff and sold by Longman, Hurst, 1805. 1st English edition; half title, frontispiece (slightly spotted), excellently rebound in full calf, gilt spine and borders, black label, scarce.   Jarndyce 103-469 1996 £350.00

FENN, G. MANVILLE   George Alfred Henty, the Story of an Active Life. London: Blackie, 1907. 1st edition; frontispiece in facsimile, otherwise very good+ from the collection of John H. Dalton.   Harland H. Eastman 10/94-8 1996 $150.00

FENNING, DANIEL   The British Youth's Instructor; or, a New and Easy Guide to Practical Arithmetic... London: printed for J. Hodges, 1754. 2nd edition; tear in pages 19-20 without loss, repaired; contemporary sheep rubbed and marked, split in leading hinge, lacking leading free endpapers. Jarndyce 103-470 1996 £85.00

FENNING, DANIEL   The Royal English Dictionary. London: printed for L. Hawes & Co., T. Caslon, 1775. 5th edtlion; closed trimmed on fore-edge just touching text, attractive contemporary speckled calf, spine with black stained bands and label, gilt lettered and decorated. Alston V231. Jarndyce 103-147 1996 £220.00

FENOLLOSA, ERNEST F.   Epochs of Chinese and Japanese Art... London: William Heinemann, 1921. New edition; 4to; xxxvii, 204; xiv, 235 pages; 2 volumes; 15 color and 10 monochrome plates; cloth; nice set in slightly worn dust jacket.   Thomas Thorp 489-99 1996 £65.00

FENTON, JAMES   Our Western Furniture. Oxford: Sycamore Press, 1968. 1st edition author's first book; wrappers, signed by author on titlepage; spine and cover edges slightly browned, covers slightly rubbed; very good.   Ulysses 39-198 1996 £250.00

FERDOOSEE   Episodes from the Shah Nameh; or Annals of the Persian Kings; by Ferdoosee. London: printed for the author, 1815. 8vo; frontispiece, ad leaf at end; original boards, uncut; fine; presentation inscription "From the author to Sir H. Strachey Bt.".   Anthony W. Laywood 108-171 1996 £120.00

FERGUS County Argus Pictorial Edition Lewistown, Montana. Lewistown: n.d. 1st edition; 50 unnumbered pages; photos; stiff pictorial wrappers, very good+.   T. A. Swinford 49-797 1996 $125.00

FERGUSON, ADAM   An Essay on the History of Civil Society. Edinburgh: printed for A. Millar and T. Caddel (sic), London: & A. Kincaid &... 1767. 1st edition; 4to; viii, 430 pages; paper somewhat browned and with slight waterstain on extreme edges of margins, one or two tiny wormholes in blank margins at beginning, recently most attractively bound in 18th century style half calf, gilt. Goldsmiths 10264; Higgs 3973; Kress 6432; Jessop p. 122;   John Drury 82-77 1996 £1,500.00

FERGUSON, ADAM   Remarks on Dr. Price's Observations on the Nature of Civil Liberty, Etc. London: G. Kearsley, 1776. (4), 76 pages; contemporary marbled boards, rebacked, nice. Sabin 24090; not in Goldsmiths or Kress.   C. R. Johnson 37-57 1996 £250.00

FERGUSON, CHARLES D.   The Experiences of a Forty-Niner During Thirty-Four Years' Residence in California and Australia. Cleveland: 1888. 1st edition; 9 x 5.5 inches; 507 pages; illustrations; cloth, covers moderately rubbed.   John K. King 77-25 1996 $100.00

FERGUSON, CHARLES J.   A Short Historical and Architectural Account of Lanercost, A Priory of Black Canons, Eight Miles from Carlisle, Upon the North Side of the River Irthing, Close to the Picts Wall. Carlisle: C. Thurnam, n.d. plan measured April 1870. 8vo; pages 56, lithographed title, 1 double page lithographed plan, 2 large photographic plates; binders cloth.   R.F.G. Hollett & Son 78-920 1996 £60.00

FERGUSON, JAMES 1710-1776   Lectures on Select Subjects in Mechanics, Hydrostatics, Pneumatics and Optics. London: printed for W. Strahan (and 9 others), 1770. 2nd quarto edition; 4to; (viii), 252, (iv), 40 pages; 36 folding engraved plates; original calf, morocco spine label, joints cracked, covers little rubbed, binding firm.   David Bickersteth 133-188 1996 £370.00

FERGUSON, JAMES 1710-1776   Select Mechanical Exercises; Shewing How to Construct Different Clocks, Orreries and Sun-Dials, on Plain and Easy Principles... London: W. Strahan and T. Cadell, 1773. 8vo; (12), xliv, 272 pages; 9 folding copper engraved plates; old calf, worn, spine and outer corners recovered with modern pebbled calf, new endpapers. Kenneth Karmiole 1NS-124 1996 $175.00

FERGUSON, LADY   Life of the Right Rev. William Reeves, D.D. 1893. 1st edition; 8vo; portrait; cloth, cover stained, text good.   C. P. Hyland 216-705 1996 £55.00

FERGUSON, MUNGO   Printed Books in the Library of the Hunterian Museum in the University of Glasgow: a Catalogue. Glasgow: 1930. 1st edition; folio; 396 pages; original binding. GM 6772.1. Osler 3024.   W. Bruce Fye 71-651 1996 $150.00

FERGUSON, RICHARD S.   The Boke Off Recorde of Kirkbie Kendall. Kendal: T. Wilson, 1892. 8vo; pages xiv, 437; original cloth, gilt, extremities trifle rubbed, joints cracked.   R.F.G. Hollett & Son 78-910 1996 £110.00

FERGUSON, RICHARD S.   The Boke off Recorde of Kirkbie Kendall. Kendal: T. Wilson, 1892. 8vo; pages xiv, 437; original cloth, gilt, extremities trifle worn, top of spine defective and frayed, blind library stamp on upper board, ex-library with usual labels and stamps, joints cracked, prelims lightly spotted; good, working copy.   R.F.G. Hollett & Son 78-911 1996 £75.00

FERGUSON, RICHARD S.   Cumberland and Westmorland M.P.'s (sic) from the Restoration to the Reform Bill of 1867, (1660-1867). London: J. Bell and Daldy and Carlisle: C. Thurman, 1871. Large paper limited edition (20 copies only); 4to; pages xix, 478; frontispiece; frontispiece; three quarter levant morocco gilt by Riviere, with 5 flattened raised bands and marbled boards, spine trifle mellowed, front flyleaf foxed, some occasional foxing and light spotting elsewhere, but generally very nice, scarce; printed memo affixed to flyleaf lists 15 recipients of the large paper copies, and a further 4 recipients are added in Ferguson's hand, including this Naworth Castle library copy; presentation copy from author for Mr. Howard (Earl of Carlisle).   R.F.G. Hollett & Son 78-152 1996 £275.00

FERGUSON, RICHARD S.   Cumberland and Westmorland M.P.'s (sic) from the Restoration to the Reform Bill of 1867 (1660-1867). London: Bell and Daldy and Carlisle: C. Thurman, 1871. 1st edition; 8vo; pages xix, 478; frontispiece; original cloth, gilt, over bevelled boards, little faded, handsomely rebacked in matching levant morocco with raised bands and contrasting double spine labels; very good, scarce.   R.F.G. Hollett & Son 78-153 1996 £175.00

FERGUSON, RICHARD S.   Cumberland and Westmorland M.P.'s (sic) from the Restoration to the Reform Bill of 1867 (1660-1867). London: Bell and Daldy and Carlisle: C. Thurman, 1871. 1st edition; 8vo; pages xix, 478; frontispiece; modern half green levant morocco gilt, occasional spots, but very good; presentation copy inscribed by author for Miss Esther Robson.   R.F.G. Hollett & Son 78-154 1996 £150.00

FERGUSON, RICHARD S.   Miscellany Accounts of the Diocese of Carlisle, with the Terriers Delivered In to Me at My Primary Visitation... London: George Bell and Carlisle: C. Thurnam & Sons, 1877. 8vo; pages (iv), 274, original brown cloth, gilt, very scarce.   R.F.G. Hollett & Son 78-916 1996 £145.00

FERGUSON, RICHARD S.   A Short Historical and Architectural Account of Lanercost, a Priory of Black Canons... London: Bell and Daldy, Carlisle: C. Thurnam, n.d., before 1868. Large paper copy; 4to; pages 56, 2 lithographed plans and 2 large photographic plates; presentation copy inscribed on title to W. H. St. J. Hope, with author's compliments.   R.F.G. Hollett & Son 78-919 1996 £120.00

FERGUSON, RICHARD S.   A Short Historical and Architectural Account of Lanercost, a Priory of Black Canons, 8 miles from Carlisle... London: Bell and Daldy; Carlisle:....n.d., c. 1870. Square 4to; 56 pages; lithographed title and plan, 2 large photographic plates mounted on card flyleaf and card mounts foxed; full blind ruled tan calf, gilt, edges little rubbed and scaped; presentation copy inscribed by author for George Howard, Lord Carlisle; loosely inserted 6 page ALs from author to Lord Carlisle.   R.F.G. Hollett & Son 78-921 1996 £160.00

FERGUSON, ROBERT   The Northmen in Cumberland and Westmorland. London: Longman & Co. and Carlisle: R. & J. Steel, 1856. 8vo; pages (iv), 228; early 20th century three quarter crushed morocco gilt with marbled boards, spine rather faded.   R.F.G. Hollett & Son 78-925 1996 £85.00

FERGUSSON, WILLIAM   Notes and Recollections of a Professional Life. London: 1846. 248 pages; original binding. Scarce.   W. Bruce Fye 71-652 1996 $250.00

FERLINGHETTI, LAWRENCE   Pictures of the Gone World. San Francisco: City Lights, 1955. 1st edition; author's first book, tiny bump to back cover, else fine in stiff wrappers as issued.   Sherwood 3-12 1996 $450.00

FERLINGHETTI, LAWRENCE   The Sea and Ourselves at Cape Ann. Madison: Red Ozier Press, 1979. 1st edition; one of 200 copies, signed by author, artist and publishers, Steve Miller and Ken Botnick; thin 8vo; illustrations by Janet Morgan; original wrappers, dust jacket; mint. James S. Jaffe 34-569 1996 $150.00

FERLINGHETTI, LAWRENCE   Starting from San Francisco. New York: New Directions, 1961. 1st edition; very good in hard covers, LP recording included at back.   Sherwood 3-128 1996 $150.00

FERNANDEZ, JOHN   An Address to His Majesty's Ministers, Recommending Efficacious Means for the Most Speedy Termination of African Slavery. London: for the author by G. Cox, 1827. 1st and only edition; 8vo; iv, (5)-36, (xxxvii)-xxxviii, (2) pages, including the final errata leaf (bit stained), marbled wrappers; rare. Black 3720; Goldsmiths 25384; Ragatz p. 502.   John Drury 82-78 1996 £125.00

FERNANDEZ, NICHOLAS   Dying Declaration of Nicholas Fernandez, Who with Nine Others Were Executed in front of Cadiz Harbour, Dec. 29, 1829. For Piracy and Murder in the High Seas. N.P.: New York, 1830. 1st edition; 8vo; disbound; little stained, but very good. Nat. Maritime Mus. Cat. 199.   Ximenes 109-117 1996 $650.00

FERRAR, JOHN   A View of the Ancient and Modern Dublin...(and) A Tour to Bellvue, the Sea of Peter La Touche. Dulbin: s.n. 1796. 8vo; eng. dedn., pages iii-viii, 140, 2 engraved frontispieces, 6 engraved plates, limp boards, uncut, spine rubbed. Colvin p. 718.   Marlborough 162-28 1996 £250.00

FERRERS, EDMUND   Illustrations of Hogarth: i.e. Hogarth Illustrated from Passages in Authors He Never Read and Could Not Understand. London: printed by and for Nichols, Son and Bentley, 1816. 1st edition; 8vo; 55 pages, engraved portrait; uncut in original drab wrappers. Not found in NUC.   James Burmester 29-50 1996 £80.00

FERRETTI, MARC ANTONIO   Mirinda Favola Pastorale... Venice: D. Venturati, 1612. 1st edition; 4to; 188 pages; engraved armorial and emblematic title, plus 5 full page engravings, woodcut tailpieces and initials; italic throughout; old limp vellum (stained); rare. Piantinida 4070. Bennett Gilbert LL29-38 1996 $975.00

FERREY, BENJAMIN   Recollections of N. Welby Pugin and His Father Augustus Pugin; with Notices of their Works. London: Edward Stanford, 1861. 1st edition; 8vo; frontispiece, xv, (i), 473, (1) pages, 7 plates; frontispiece; publisher's blue blindstamped cloth; signature in pencil on titlepage, light cover wear, some foxing on early and later leaves, else very good.   Bookpress 75-104 1996 $385.00

FERRIAR, JOHN   Illustrations of Sterne with Other Essays and Verses. Manchester: by George Nicholson for Cadell and Davies, London: 1798. 1st edition; 8vo; pages viii, (ii), 314; uncut in original boards, sometime rebacked with vellum, slightly soiled externally, one or two small areas of browning, good copy.   Simon Finch 24-215 1996 £225.00

FERRIAR, JOHN   Medical Histories and Reflections. Volume 3. London: 1798. 1st edition; 232 pages; marbled boards, detached, with backstrip missing.   W. Bruce Fye 71-655 1996 $125.00

FERRIER, SUSAN EDMONDSTONE 1782-1854   The Inheritance. Edinburgh: William Blackwood and T. Cadell, London, 1824. 1st edition; 8vo; 3 volumes; half titles present; contemporary half rose calf, gilt, spines elaborately gilt. Fine attrative set, from the library of Frances Mary Richardson Currer. Wolff 2235; Block p. 74; CBEL III 720. Ximenes 108-129 1996 $450.00

FERRIS, CORNELIA   The Mormons at Home; with Some Incidents of Travel from Mississippi to California, 1852-53. New York: Dix and Edwards, 1856. 1st edition; 8vo; viii, 299, (4) pages ads; original brown cloth, spine is slightly faded, some minor wear to extremities, still near fine.   David Mason 71-120 1996 $120.00

FERRIS, ROBERT G.   Lewis and Clark. Historic Places Associated with Their Transcontinental Exploration (1804-06). Washington: U. S. Dept. of Interior, 1975. 429 pages; color frontispiece, illustrations from facsimiles, maps and photos, pictorial endpapers; yellow cloth, ink inscription, else fine.   Argonaut Book Shop 113-415 1996 $175.00

FERRIS, WARREN ANGUS   Life in the Rocky Mountains... Denver: the Old West Publishing Co., 1940. 1st book edition; xcv, 365 pages, 5 plates, large folding map; original gilt lettered maroon cloth, very fine, uncut, pictorial dust jacket. Howes F100.   Argonaut Book Shop 113-244 1996 $250.00

FERRISS, HUGH   The Metropolis of Tomorrow. New York: Ives Washburn, 1929. 1st edition; small folio; frontispiece, 140, (4) pages; cloth, minor rubbing on covers, small rubberstamp on front free endpaper and titlepage, else very good.   Bookpress 75-181 1996 $175.00

FESSENDEN, THOMAS GREEN   An Essay on the Law of Patents for New Inventions. Boston: D. Mallory, 1810. 1st edition; 8vo; 229, (1) pages; recent cloth, label, browned. S&S 20110.   M & S Rare Books 60-464 1996 $200.00

FETTES, D. J.   Synthesis of the Caledonian Rocks of Britain. London: 1986. 8vo; 368 pages; illustrations; hardbound.   Wheldon & Wesley 207-1329 1996 £72.75

FEUCHTWANGER, LION   Paris Gazette. New York: Viking, 1940. 1st U.S. edition; shelf wear to board edges and extremities, price in crayon to front pastedown, else very good+ in illustrated boards, lacking dust jacket; inscribed by author.   Lame Duck Books 19-187 1996 $200.00

FEWKES, JESSE WALTER   The Aborigines of Porto Rico and Neighboring Islands. Washington: GPO, 1907. 8vo; 220 pages, 43 figures, 93 plates; worn at extremities, endpaper torn, signature; original cloth. Archaeologia Luxor-4476 1996 $200.00

FFINCH, MICHAEL   The Dame School at Raisbeck. Kendal: Titus Wilson, 1984. Signed limited edition, one of 5 specially bound copies; large square 8vo; page 29; illustrations; full blue levant morocco, boards blind tooled with ovrall diaper pattern, upper board titled in blind in central panel, matching cloth slipcase.   R.F.G. Hollett & Son 78-386 1996 £85.00

FFINCH, MICHAEL   Donald Maxwell 1877-1936. Kendal: Titus Wilson for the Maxwell Estate, 1995. 1st edition; large 4to; pages xv, 245, 369 illustrations in color and monochrome; original cloth, gilt, dust jacket. R.F.G. Hollett & Son 78-54 1996 £125.00

FFOLLIOTT, WILLIAM   Cartmel Parish and Parish Church and Sermons Preached therein. London: Wertheim & Macintosh, 1854. 1st edition; 8vo; pages (iv), 134, (ii), frontispiece, small piece torn from top inner corner and folding tan plan, repaired in fold, one pair of leaves slightly caraelessly opened; scarce; original blindstamped red cloth, gilt, little marked.   R.F.G. Hollett & Son 78-297 1996 £75.00

FICHTE, JOHANN GOTTLIEB   Der Geschlossene Handelsstaat. Tubingen: Gottashcen, 1800. 1st edition; three quarter leather and marbled paper covered boards, with wear to edges, extremities and spine folds; very good+.   Lame Duck Books 19-188 1996 $1,500.00

FIDLER, ISAAC   Observations on Professions, Literature, Manners and Emigration in the United States and Canada Made During a Residence Thre in 1832. New York: J. & J. Harper, 1833. 1st American edition; 247 pages, plus ads; rebacked, original cloth laid down, cloth worn and marked, label stained, but good, serviceable copy.   Hermitage SP95-852 1996 $150.00

FIELD, EUGENE   The Land of Make-Believe. Racine: Whitman Publ., 1931. Tall 4to; 15 full page colored plates and many smaller illustrations in color and black and white drawings by Shay Stone; cloth backed pictorial boards; fresh copy.   Barbara Stone 70-91 1996 £55.00

FIELD, EUGENE   The Mouse and the Moonbeam. New York: William Edwin Rudge, Christmas 1919. Limited to 250 copies; 8vo; 26 pages; frontispiece, decorative headpiece and burgundy decorated initial; violet cloth backed marbled boards, top edge very slightly darkened, title in gilt on spine. Very nice.   Blue Mountain SP95-57 1996 $125.00

FIELD, F. J.   An Armorial for Cumberland. Kendal: Titus Wilson, 1937. 1st edition; 8vo; pages xvi, 343; 18 illustrations; original brown cloth, gilt, little worn, neatly recased.   R.F.G. Hollett & Son 78-155 1996 £75.00

FIELD, F. J.   An Armorial for Cumberland. Kendal: Titus Wilson, 1937.. 1st edition; 8vo; xvi, 343 pages, 18 illustrations; original brown cloth, gilt, extremities little rubbed.   R.F.G. Hollett & Son 78-156 1996 £85.00

FIELD, MICHAEL, PSEUD.   Fair Rosamund. London: Hacon & Ricketts, 1897. 1st edition; one of 210 copies; 8vo; pages lxxv, plus colophon, printed in red and black and Vale type on handmade paper; full page border and initials by Charles Ricketts; original two-paper decorated boards (heart and rose back, bird and arrow sides), paper label (browned); scarce. Tomkinson 10.   Claude Cox 107-174 1996 £135.00

FIELD, MICHAEL, PSEUD.   The Race of Leaves. London: Hacon & Ricketts, 1901. 1st edition; limited to 280 copies on handmade paper; 8vo; pages lxxxv, + colophon; pictorial woodcut border and half border by Charles Ricketts; original boards with Ricketts' green leaf patterned paper, paper label, slight rubbing at corners and head of backstrip, but very good, largely unopened. Tomkinson 31.   Claude Cox 107-175 1996 £135.00

FIELD, MICHAEL, PSEUD.   The World at Auction, A Play... Vale Press, 1898. One of 210 copies on paper; there were also 2 copies on vellum; 9 1/4 x 6 inches; cxvi pages, (1) leaf (colophon); 1st page of text with elaborate woodcut border and historiated initial, 3 pages with half border, all by Charles Ricketts; original paper boards, half grey and half patterned, papaer label on spine, edges untrimmed, unopened; one leaf with diagonal crease at lower corner, otherwise virtually pristine. Tomkinson p. 166.   Phillip J. Pirages 33-491 1996 $500.00

FIELD, MICHAEL, PSEUD.   The World at Auction. London: Vale Press, 1898. 1st edition; one of 210 copies (of an edition of 212 copies); 8vo; pages cxvii; printed on Arnold's handmade paper, large wood engraved decorated border and initial letter to first page of text designed by Charles Ricketts and wood engraved half border on first page of each act; fawn boards with repeated peacock pattern printed in green, free endpapers browned as usual, untrimmed, good.   Blackwell's B112-275 1996 £225.00

FIELD, RICHARD   A Stark Fantasy by Daddy Dumps. South Duxbury: Faulkner & Field, 1949. 1st printing, signed twice by author; 8vo; paper wrappers, covers watermarked and slightly rubbed, else nice, very scarce.   Barbara Stone 70-45 1996 £175.00

FIELD, STEPHEN J.   Personal Reminiscences of Early Days in California, with Other Sketches. N.P.: by the author, 1893. 1st edition; (6), 406 pages; newly bound in three quarter leather; fine. This copy signed by author. Cowan p. 209; Graff 1316; Howes F117; Rocq 9359.   Argonaut Book Shop 113-246 1996 $500.00

FIELDING, H.   The Soul of a People. London: Richard Bentley, 1898. 1st edition; tall 8vo; viii, 363 pages; original blue cloth decorated on upper cover with peacock stamped in gilt surrounded by a read border; inner hinges cracked, small hole in rear spine gutter, still very good, pretty book.   David Mason 71-57 1996 $120.00

FIELDING, HENRY 1707-1754   The Beauties of Fielding... London: printed for G. Kearsley, 1782. 1st edition; 12mo; disbound; scarce; very good. Cross III 330.   Ximenes 108-133 1996 $200.00

FIELDING, HENRY 1707-1754   An Enquiry Into the Causes of the Late Increase of Robbers, &c. With some Proposals for Remedying This Growning Evil. London: for A. Millar, 1751. 2nd edition; 12mo; xxxii, 203 pages, final leaf laid down, wanting half title, else fine, entirely uncut, in original(?) wrappers. Williams II 360; Kress 5113; Higgs 161; Goldsmiths 8658.   John Drury 82-80 1996 £125.00

FIELDING, HENRY 1707-1754   The History of the Adventures of Joseph Andrews and Of His Friend Mr. Abraham Adams. London: A. Millar, 1743. 3rd edition; 12mo; 2 volumes; 12 plates; half titles not called for; contemporary calf, spines gilt, morocco labels, bindings attractive but rather worn, otherwise very good. Cross III p. 306. NCBEL II 929.   Trebizond 39-13 1996 $275.00

FIELDING, HENRY 1707-1754   The History of the Adventures of Joseph Andrews, and Of His Friend Mr. Abraham Adams. London: A. Millar, 1742. 1st edition; octavo; 2 volumes; full red morocco gilt, all edges gilt, by Riviere, bookplate, nice. Rothschild 844.   G. W. Stuart 59-34 1996 $1,750.00

FIELDING, HENRY 1707-1754   The History of the Adventures of Joseph Andrews, and Of His Friend Mr. Abraham Adams. London: A. Millar, 1743. 3rd edition; octavo; 2 volumes; contemporary calf, spine ends chipped, joints cracked, extremities worn, later endpapers, bookplate.   G. W. Stuart 59-35 1996 $295.00

FIELDING, HENRY 1707-1754   The History of the Adventures of Joseph Andrews, and Of His Friend Mr. Abraham Adams. London: printed for A. Millar, 1749. 4th edition; 12mo; 2 volumes; 12 copperplates; contemporary mottled calf, gilt, spines gilt, bit rubbed; fine; early armorial bookplates of the Earl of Northesk. Cross III 306; Beasley 903.   Ximenes 108-134 1996 $800.00

FIELDING, HENRY 1707-1754   The History of Tom Jones. London: A. Millar, 1749. 1st edition; 8vo; 6 volumes; original calf, bit worn, joints cracked, minor chipping, attracctive set, preserved in fine quarter morocco gilt slipcases, this set has all the cancels as per the Rothschild set and volume 6 is true first edition (not the close reprint) and volume 5 has the first issue titlepage; contemporary bookplate of Ambrose Isted; Rothschild 850; Cross Fielding II 122.   G. W. Stuart 59-33 1996 $4,100.00

FIELDING, HENRY 1707-1754   The History of Tom Jones. London: printed for A. Millar, 1749. 1st edition; 8vo; 6 volumes; errata leaf in volume 1 and with all cancels called for by Rothschild, volume V: N8 is unsigned cancel, it contains an additional cancel overlooked in Rothschild; viz, Vol. II:N12; handsomely rebound in three quarter acid calf over boards covered with 18th century marbled paper, the books have hand sewn blue and white matching headbands, spines with five raised bands and black morocco labels, all edges sprinkled.   Book Block 32-54 1996 $2,950.00

FIELDING, HENRY 1707-1754   The Journal of a Voyage to Lisbon. London: A. Millar, 1755. 1st published edition; 8vo; complete with half title; contemporary calf spine with five raised bands and red morocco label, over marbled boards, slight strengthening to spine bardely visible, all edges sprinkled, in protective slipcase with inner chemise, bookplate of Col. R. H. Isham. Rothschild I pp. 207-208; Cross III 84-88.   Book Block 32-55 1996 $700.00

FIELDING, HENRY 1707-1754   The Journal of a Voyage to Lisbon. London: A. Millar, 1755. 1st published edition; 8vo; half title; contemporary calf, spine gilt, original morocco label; in modern pullout slipcase, hinges rather worn but firm, internally fine, crisp copy; early bookplate of George Garnier. Cross III p. 326; Sterling Lib. 363.   Trebizond 39-14 1996 $625.00

FIELDING, HENRY 1707-1754   The Journal of a Voyage to Lisbon. London: pirnted for A. Millar, 1755. 1st published edition; 12mo; contemporary calf, some wear to hinges, but neat, with half title. Rothschild 875; Cross III 84-8 and 326.   Peter Murray Hill 185-60 1996 £185.00

FIELDING, HENRY 1707-1754   Live in Several Masques. London: John Watts, 1728. 1st edition; octavo; disbound, title trifle dusty, bit soiled, lightly wrinkled, some embrowning; uncommon.   G. W. Stuart 59-36 1996 $650.00

FIELDING, HENRY 1707-1754   Pasquin. London: John Watts, 1736. 1s edition; octavo; disbound, title and final leaf of ads slightly dusty; nice. G. W. Stuart 59-37 1996 $295.00

FIELDING, HENRY 1707-1754   A Serious Address to the People of Great Britain. London: printed for M. Cooper, 1745. 1st edition; 8vo; restitched in old style blue wrappers, cloth folding envelope and half red morocco gilt case; fine. Cross III 310; Rothschild 846.   Peter Murray Hill 185-61 1996 £350.00

FIELDING, HENRY 1707-1754   The Wedding-Day. London: printed for A. Millar, 1743. 1st edition; 8vo; 1st impression throughout; disbound; very good, complete with epilogue at end; Cross III 308.   Ximenes 108-135 1996 $1,250.00

FIELDING, HENRY 1707-1754   The Works... London: for A. Millar, 1762. 1st edition; 4to; 4 volumes; frontispiece; contemporary sprinkled calf, single fillet gilt border to sides, spines in compartments, raised bands, top compartments with device of Thomas Conolly, the others with black leather labels and ornaments, with Conolly's bookplate and shelf label, marbled endpapers, rubbed at extremities, hinges reinforced, little slight spotting, but very good. Cross III 328-9.   Simon Finch 24-85 1996 £750.00

FIELDING, HENRY 1707-1754   The Works. London: and Edinburgh: for F. C. and R. Rivington, 1821. 8 3/4 x 5 1/2 inches; 10 volumes; frontispiece in vol. 1, diagram in vol. 8; fine retrospective binding of flamed calf (ca. 1915?), flat spines with wide & narrow gilt bands forming compartments w/lg. gilt sunburst ornament in center, black morocco double labels, gilt hatching on board edges, text block edges gilt, marbled endpapers, lower inch of one joint wormed, two inch abrasion in one cover, otherwise only trivial defects to this very attractively bound set, volume 1 with few minor repaired tears (and one 3 inch tear into text, with slight displacement of letters, but no loss), text with isolated minor discoloration, final two volumes with slightly creased upper corners, otherwise fine, internally quite clean, smooth and fresh. Bookplate of English politician Neil Primrose in each volume, with presentation to him, inscribed and signed by British Prime Minister H. H. Asquith.   Phillip J. Pirages 33-235 1996 $1,250.00

FIELDING, HENRY 1707-1754   The Works... London: at the Chiswick Press, by Charles Whittingham and Co. for ... 1898-99. One of 750 copies only, printed for England and America; 8vo; 12 volumes; frontispieces; contemporary blue half morocco, spines lettered and decorated in gold with date at foot, marbled sides and endpapers, blue silk bookmarks, top edge gilt, others uncut, little light rubbing to some spine ends; excellent set.   Simon Finch 24-86 1996 £1,200.00

FIELDING, SARAH   The Adventures of David Simple: Containing an Account of His Travels. London: A. Millar, 1744. 2nd edition; octavo; 2 volumes; original calf but now a bit worn, yet sound, name on endpapers, quite minor spotting or slight embrowning.   G. W. Stuart 59-39 1996 $450.00

FIELDING, SARAH   Familiar Letters Between the Principal Characters in David Simple and some Others. London: printed for the author, and sold by A. Millar, 1747. 1st edition; a "Royal Paper" copy (i.e. on large and fine paper); large 8vo; 2 volumes; contemporary calf, gilt, spines gilt, slight rubbing, careful restoration to tips of spines; fine set. Beasley 223; Block p. 74.   Ximenes 109-125 1996 $1,750.00

FIELDING, T. H.   Cumberland, Westmorland, and Lancashire. London: Howlett & Brimmer for Thomas M'Lean, 1822. Folio: (no half title), titlepage, 1 f. "Address", 44 ff. letterpress, 1 f. (plates), 44 fine hand colored aquatint views with an additional suite of 44 monochrome india proofs before letters (the majority in the Tooley 'early state'), uncut, modern half green morocco; Abbey Scenery 194-195; Tooley 215. Marlborough 162-29 1996 £4,750.00

FIELDING, WILLIAM RUSSELL   Drawings. London: Collins, 1950. 1st edition; one of 500 copies signed by Flint; 14 1/4 x 10 1/2 inches; 5 p.l., 188 pages; 134 photogravure drawings by Flint (mostly in sepia, some in more than one color) and with extra print signed by Flint in inserted publisher's envelope; original cloth backed patterned paper boards, blue morocco label on spine, in clean publisher's slipcase that is tape repaired along two seams; extremely fine.   Phillip J. Pirages 33-236 1996 $350.00

FIELDS, JAMES T.   Anniversary Poem Delivered Before the Mercantile Library Association of Boston, September 13, 1838. Boston: William D. Ticknor, 1838. 1st edition; 8vo; 18 pages; removed; BAL 5903; Rinderknecht 50322.   M & S Rare Books 60-156 1996 $125.00

FIFTY Years of Robert Frost. Hanover: Dartmouth College, 1944. 1st edition; surface soiling and darkening, otherwise near fine in thin paper covered boards, which are slightly warped with age; fragile item, presumably quite scarce.   Ken Lopez 74-148 1996 $100.00

FIGULUS, BENEDICTUS   A Golden and Blessed Casket of Natures Marvels. London: V. Stuart, 1963. Reprint of 1893 edition, limited to 500 copies; xxxi, 361 pages; cloth, fine/very good-.   Middle Earth 77-268 1996 $195.00

FILIPPI, F. DE   The Ascent of Mount St. Elias (Alaska) by H.R.H. Prince Luigi Amedeo Di Savoia Duke of Abruzzi. London: 1900. 1st English edition; 34 plates, some folding, 4 folding photographic panoramic views, 2 folding colored maps, many small photographic illustrations; some very slight fading of boards, mainly of rear panel, faint mark at top of front panel, repaired 5 mm nick at top of spine, nice above average, very good+ copy, gilt lettering on spine and front board are particularly bright.   Moutaineering Books 8-EF01. £750.00

FILIPPI, F. DE   Karakoram and Western Himalay. 1909. An Account of the Expedition of H.R.H. Prince Lugigi Amedeo of Savoy, Duke of Abruzzi. London: 1912. 1st English edition; 2 volumes, 1st volume contains text, 32 photographic plates including 1 folding, 194 photographic illustrations in text, 2 colored plates; 2nd volume contains list of illustrations and index, 18 folding photographic panoramas and 3 folding colored maps; boards and gilt lettering clean and bright, some occasional light internal foxing; much above average set, in very good/fine condition.   Moutaineering Books 8-EFO2 1996 £1,200.00

FILIPPI, F. DE   Ruwenzori. An Account of the Expedition of H. R. H. Prince Luigi Amedeo of Savoy, Duke of Abruzzi. London: 1908. 1st English edition; 32 plages, 5 photographic panoramas, plus smaller photographic illustrations on nearly every page, 5 folding maps; gilt lettering on red cloth, presentation label of Newport Public Libraries inside rear board, small neat circular stamp on reverse of plates, some marks, mainly on front boards, few missing tissue guards replaced; sound, very good, with gilt lettering hardly rubbed.   Moutaineering Books 8-EF03 1996 £400.00

FILIPPI, ROSINA   Duologues and Scenes from the Novels of Jane Austen. London: Dent, 1895. 1st edition; 6 3/4 x 4 1/2 inches; pages xi, 139; frontispiece, decorated titlepage and 7 illustrations, few text illustrations; pale green cloth, gilt titling and decorated backstrip and front cover, top edge gilt, others uncut, rear free endpaper discolored and dated inscription, 4 inch red stain to fore edge of front cover and tiny snag to rear joint, very good, scarce. Gilson H1; Keynes 170.   Ian Hodgkins 78-79 1995 £55.00

FILIPPINI, ALESSANDRO   The Table: How to Buy Food, How to Cook It, and How to Serve It. New York: 1889. 1st edition; vii, 432 pages; white oil cloth covers.   Bookworm & Silverfish 276-61 1996 $125.00

FINCH, CHRISTOPHER   The Art of Walt Disney. New York: Abrams, 1973. 1st edition; fine in original acetate cover.   Book Time 2-811 1996 $250.00

FINCH, HENRY   Law, or, a Discovrse Thereof, in foure Bookes. London: Societie of Stationers, 1627. 12mo; calf, front cover weak; STC 10871.   Rostenberg & Stern 150-46 1996 $500.00

FINCH, PEARL   The History of Burley-on-the-Hill, Rutland with a Short Account of the Owners and Extracts from Their Correspondence and Catalogue of the Contents of the House. London: John Bale, Sons & Danielsson, Ltd., 1901. Limited to 200 copies, of which this is numbered 33 and initialled by author; 4to; 2 volumes; pages xvi, 360; 76 plates, 5 folding tables, half title, 82, 4 plates; full parchment, occasional light soiling.   Sotheran PN32-184 1996 £250.00

FINCH, WILLIAM COLES   Watermills & Windmills: a Historical Survey of their Rise, Decline and Fall as Portrayed by Those of Kent. London: C. W. Daniel, 1933. Original edition; thick royal 8vo; pages 336; plates, illustrations; original crimson cloth, gilt, spine trifle faded, but very nice, very scarce.   Howes Bookshop 265-2144 1996 £120.00

FINDEN, EDWARD   Great Brtain Illustrated: a Series of Original Views from Drawings by William Westall, A.R.A. London: Charles Tilt, 86 Fleet St., 1830. 4to; 118 steel engraved plates, plus 4 plates and vignette title, few plates heavily foxed; half calf and marbled boards, binding very rubbed and worn, marbled boards also worn, black morocco label to spine, raised bands to spine, marbled endpapers.   Beeleigh Abbey BA56-28 1996 £225.00

FINDEN, WILLIAM   The Ports, Harbours, Watering Places, Fishing Villages and Picturesque Scenery of Great Britain. London: Virtue and Co., n.d., ca. 1845. 4to; 2 volumes, extra engraved title, titlepage, 145 pages, extra engraved title, titlepage, 143 pages, 71 and 71 engraved plates and tissue guards; navy blue morocco, ornate borders roll tooled in gilt and blind with large gilt neo-classical urn at centre of each panel, spines gilt in compartments, raised bands, gilt inner dentelle, all edges gilt; magnificently bound.   Marlborough 162-30 1996 £975.00

FINDLEY, PALMER   Priests of Lucina, the Story of Obstetrics. Boston: 1939. 421 pages; original binding; scarce.   W. Bruce Fye 71-660 1996 $100.00

FINE, ORONCE   Quadratura Circuli, Tandem Inventa & Clarissime Demonstrata. De Circuli Mensura, & Ratione Circumferentiae ad Diametrum... Paris: Simon de Colines, 1544. 1st edition; folio: (12), 107 pages, illustrations, woodcut initials and ornaments, title with woodcut border; 3 leaves scortched at upper edge of outer margin; new limp vellum, titled on spine in calligraphy, very good, wide margined copy. Otto Struve's copy with his neat signature. Norman Lib 795. Mortimer French 16th Cent. Books 229; Adams F479.   Edwin V. Glaser 121-107 1996 $3,000.00

FINE, ORONCE   De Solaribus Holologiis & Quadrantibus Libri Quatuor. Paris: apud Gulielmum Cavellat, 1560. 1st edition thus; 4to; paes (vi), 223, (i) plus large folding diagram, Roman letter; ornamental initials, 56 ornamental woodcut diagrams and figures of sundials; contemporary limp vellum, lacking ties, light foxing, couple of leaves bit browned, short tear in folding diagram without loss, good, well margined copy; near early autograph of Stephani Casellas in blank portion of title; BM STC Fr. p 166; Adams F 473; Hozeau & Lancasater 11351.   A. Sokol XXV-38 1996 £2,250.00

FINE, RUTH   Summer Day/Winter Night. Newark: Janus Press, 1994. One of 150 copies, signed by Fine; 7.25 x 4.125 inches; fold-out illustration in blue, green, yellow and brown with yellow and gold trim along bottom reversing to blue, tan, brown and cream with light brown and gold trim edge along bottom; one side glued into brown card folder, gold paper over card slipcase. Fine.   Joshua Heller 21-37 1996 $175.00

FINGER, C.   The Spreading Stain. New York: Doubleday, 1927. 1st American edition; just about fine in very good dust jacket with some wear and tear, chipping and soil, scarce in dust jacket.   Aronovitz 57-413 1996 $150.00

FINLAY, VIRGIL   The Book of Virgil Finlay. de la Ree, 1971. 1st edition; 1/1950 copies, this copy with full color Finlay print laid in; fine in dust jacket.   Aronovitz 57-416 1996 $120.00

FINLAYSON, W. F.   A Review of the Authorities as to the Repression of Riot or Rebellion, With Special Reference to Criminal or Civil Liability. London: Stevens & Sons and Chapman and Hall, 1868. Sole edition; 8vo; (vi), 224 pages, partly unopened, original cloth, little soiled.   David Bickersteth 133-147 1996 £56.00

FINLAYSON, W. J.   Yacht Racing on the Clyde from 1883 to 1890. Glasgow & London: Maclure, Macdonald & Co., c. 1891. 1st edition; folio; pages (vi), 75 photographic plates; original blue cloth, blocked in gilt, slightly rubbed on spine, but very good.   Sotheran PN32-80 1996 £575.00

FINN, ELIZABETH ANNE   Reminiscences of Mrs. Finn. London: Marshall, Morgan and Scott, n.d. 1929. Thick 8vo; (256) pages; frontispiece, 2 additional plates; burgundy cloth, gilt lettered spine; Roth, Encyclopedia Judaica VI 1300.   Paulette Rose   16-241   1996 $180.00

FINNEY, CHARLES G.   The Circus of Dr. Lao. New York: Viking, 1935. 1st edition; 8vo; drawings by Boris Artzybasheff, illustrated endpapers, cloth, dust jacket; unusually fine.   James S. Jaffe   34-155   1996 $350.00

FINNEY, CHARLES G.   The Circus of Dr. Lao. Limited Editions Club, 1982. One of 2000 numbered copies, signed by artist; 4to; printed in black, orange and brown; Thebes patterned cloth, fine in slipcase. Bertram Rota   272-269   1996 £95.00

FINNEY, CHARLES G.   The Circus of Dr. Lao. New York: Limited Editions Club, 1982. Number 1761 of 2000 copies, signed by artist; illustrations by Claire Van Vliet; fine in lightly soiled slipcase. Hermitage   SP95-981   1996 $125.00

FINNEY, CHARLES G.   The Circus of Doctor Lao. Newark: 1984. Limited to 10 copies, signed by author and artist; thick quarto; 123 pages, 7-16 fold-out to form double panoramas, with illustrations by Claire Van Vliet, the images are a combination of relief etchings and pochoir done in a glossy black and brilliant pastel shades; cloth that was colored on the etching press, with vellum and string spine, and housed in clamshell box covered in a similar material with a different landscape design.   Bromer Booksellers   90-75   1996 $1,500.00

FINNEY, JACK   Good Neighbor Sam. New York: Simon & Schuster, 1963. 1st edition; small stamp front pastedown, corners little bumped, very good plus in dust jacket with light nicking at spine ends as well as some very slight darkening there, uncommon.   Between the Covers 42-170   1996 $100.00

FIRBANK, RONALD 1886-1926   The Flower Beneath the Foot - Being a Record of the Early Life of St. Laura de Nazianzi and the Times in Which She Lived. New York: Brentano's, 1924. 1st American edition, preceded by first U.K. edition; frontispiece by C. R. W. Nevinson, titlepage portrait of author by Wyndham Lewis; original binding, top edge dusty, gilt lettering on spine slightly oxidised, head and tail of spine and one corner slightly bumped, endpapers partially browned, very good in nicked, spotted, rubbed and dusty, slightly chipped and marked dust jacket browned at spine and edges, dust jacket repeats frontispiece.   Ulysses 39-201   1996 £225.00

FIRBANK, RONALD 1886-1926   Odette: a Fairy Tale for Weary People. London: 1916. 1st edition; illustrations by Albert Buhrer; wrappers, lower wrapper little browned, otherwise very good, scarce.   Words Etcetera 94-421   1996 £125.00

FIREBAUGH, ELLEN   The Physician's Wife and the Things that Pertain to Her Life. Philadelphia: 1894. 1st edition; woodcuts; inner hinges cracked, original binding, rubbed.   W. Bruce Fye   71-667   1996 $100.00

THE FIRST Chapter of Tear-em the son of Gore'am, in the Apocripha. London: printed for Timothy Halifax, 1750. 2nd edition; 8vo; disbound, wanting half title, otherwise very good; very uncommon. 5 locations in ESTC.   Ximenes   109-255   1996 $225.00

THE FIRST Fleet. The Record of the Foundation of Australia from Its Conception to the Settlement at Sydney Cove. Waltham St. Lawrence: Golden Cockerel Press, 1937. 1st edition; 204/370 copies (of an edition of 375 copies); small folio; pages 150, (1); printed on Arnold's handmade paper, wood engraved frontispiece, 4 large headpieces by Peter Barker-Mill, 4 full page collotype facsimiles; original mid-blue cloth, backstrip gilt lettered, original large fawn cloth square onlaid to front cover and containing gilt Cockerel device designed by Barker-Mill, untrimmed, excellent. Pertelote 123.   Blackwell's B112-124   1996 £335.00

FIRTH, CHARLES H.   The Last Years of the Protectorate 1656-1658. London: 1909. Original edition; 8vo; 2 volumes, pages 361, 357; original cloth.   Howes Bookshop   265-361   1996 £65.00

FISCHER, MARJORIE   The Dog Cantbark. New York: Random House, 1940. 1st printing; 4to; colored illustrations by Roger Duvoisin; blue cloth lettered in gilt, nice, scarce title.   Barbara Stone   70-86   1996 £55.00

FISCHER, MARTIN   Christian R. Holmes: Man and Physician. Springfield: Thomas, 1937. 1st edition; 4to; illustrations, titlepage printed in red and black, large initials and top borders in text printed in red; gilt stamped dark blue morocco over blue cloth, uncut, partly unopened; dust jacket, very good; signed and inscribed by author.   George J. Houle   68-94   1996 $125.00

FISHBOUGH, WILLIAM   The Macrocosm and Microcosm; or the Universe Without and the Universe Within. New York: Fowler and Wells c. 1852. 2 volumes; original cloth, ends of spines chipped, very good set.   M & S Rare Books   60-414   1996 $150.00

FISHER, A. K.   The Hawks and Owls of the United States in Their Relation to Agriculture. Washington: 1893. 8vo; 26 chromolithographs after J. Ridgway; cloth, trifle worn and shaken.   Maggs Bros. Ltd. 1190-564   1996 £155.00

FISHER, DOROTHEA FRANCES CANFIELD 1879-1958   The Day of Glory. New York: Holt, 1919. 1st edition; fine in very good dust jacket with large chip on rear panel and few smaller chips at extremities, uncommon in jacket.   Between the Covers   42-80   1996 $100.00

FISHER, HARRISON   Bachelor Belles. New York: Dodd, Mead & Co., 1908. 1st edition; illustrations by Harrison Fisher and with decorations Theodore B. Hapgood; gray cloth titled in gilt with pictorial paper onlay on front board stamped in gilt, few light stains, else very good to fine. Hermitage   SP95-898   1996 $150.00

FISHER, JOHN   The Funeral Sermon of Margaret, Countess of Richmond and Derby, Mother to King Henry VII. and Foundress of Christ's and St. John's College in Cambridge... London: printed for A. Bosvile, 1708. 1st edition; 8vo; 2 parts in 1; frontispiece, folding engraved plate, separate title, pagination and signatures to second part contemporary panelled calf, rebacked.   Anthony Laywood 108-59 1996 £50.00

FISHER, LILLIAN ESTELLE   The Intendant System in Spanish America. Berkeley: University of California Press, 1929. 1st edition; x, 385 pages; blue cloth, gilt lettered spine, very fine.   Argonaut Book Shop   113-24 1996 $150.00

FISHER, MARY FRANCES KENNEDY   A Cordiall Water. Boston: Little Brown and Co., 1961. 1st edition; text decorations. decorated orange paper over boards, turquoise cloth spine stamped in gold, lower tips rubbed, decorated orange jacket lightly used showing some rubbing along spine, half inch tear at bottom edge rear panel and tape reinforcement to rear flap's interior, generally very good.   Priscilla Juvelis   95/1-91   1996 $125.00

FISHER, MARY FRANCES KENNEDY   Not Now, But Now. New York: Viking Press, 1947. 1st edition; 8vo; green wove cloth stamped in blind on front cover and lettered in gold on spine, pictorial dust jacket by Leo Manson, book near fine, jacket lightly used with some wear to spine ends.   Priscilla Juvelis   95/1-93   1996 $250.00

FISHER, MARY FRANCES KENNEDY   Serve It Forth. New York: Harper & Bros., 1937. 1st edition; author's first book; very good in very good dust jacket with light uniform dust soiling and modest edgewear, nice.   Ken Lopez   74-136   1996 $450.00

FISHER, MARY FRANCES KENNEDY   Spirits of the Valley. New York: Targ Editions, 1985. One of 250 copies on all rag Fabriano, signed by author; quarto; quarter cloth and paper covered boards and glassine wrapper.   Lame Duck Books   19-189   1996 $150.00

FISHER, MARY FRANCES KENNEDY   With Bold Knife and Fork. New York: Putnam, 1969. 1st edition; price clipped dust jacket, beautiful copy. Captain's Bookshelf   38-67   1996 $100.00

FISHER, O. C.   It Occurs in Kimble. Houston: 1937. 1st edition; limited to 500 copies; 237 pages, frontispiece, photos, illustrations; pictorial cloth, very good+. 6 Guns 722 scarce.   T. A. Swinford   49-369   1996 $185.00

FISHER, O. C.   The Texas Heritage of the Fishers and Clarks. Salan 1963. 1st edition; xx, 241 pages, limited edition in slipcase, frontispiece plates, photos, illustrations, pictorial cloth, nice. 6 Guns 723.   T. A. Swinford   49-368   1996 $175.00

FISHER, R. A. A Digest of the Reported Cases (From 1756 to 1870, Inclusive) Relating to Criminal Law, Criminal Information and Extradition, Founded on Harrison's Analytical Digest. San Francisco: Sumner and Whitney and Co., 1871. Contemporary sheep, rubbed, some staining, but quite nice. Meyer Boswell SL26-81 1996 $125.00

FISHER, ROY Bluebeard's Castle. Surrey: Circle Press, 1972. One of 175 copies all on Kent Hollingsworth paper and all signed by artist/designer Ronald King and poet Roy Fisher; page size 12 3/4 x 7 1/2 inches; 9 pop-up designs screenprinted in 75 printings with typesetting by Walker Taylor at Circle Press, loose in printed plum cardboard box laid into black and clear perspix box, prospectus with pop-up laid in, fine except for hairline crack in perspix box about 1 3/4 inches long at lower left corner. Priscilla Juvelis 95/1-67 1996 $3,500.00

FISHER, SAMUEL The Testimony of Truth Exalted, by the Collected Labours of that Worthy Man... London: printed in the year 1679. Tall folio; 6 printed leaves, 89 (i.e. 86), 91-692, 695-856, 54, i.e. (43) 46-92, 95-98, (16) pages; original or contemporary calf, corners bumped, early 19th century library label on front cover, clear lacquer has been applied to spine, which is chipped at top and bottom, binding is worn, very clean, with excellent margins. Wing F1058; McAlpin 3.801. Roy W. Clare XXIV-77 1996 $200.00

FISHER, THEODRE WILLIS Plain Talk About Insanity: its Causes, Forms, Symptoms and the Treatment of Mental Diseases, with Remarks on Hospitals and Asylums and the Medico-Legal Aspect of Insanity. Boston: Alexander Moore, 1872. 1st edition; 8vo; 98, (2) pages, printed mauve cloth, lightly shelfworn, very good. John Gach 150-148 1996 $125.00

FISHER, THOMAS Monumental Remains and Antiquities in the County of Bedford. Hoxton: Redman, 1828. One of only 50 copies; folio; title, 4 ff., 36 hand colored lithograph plates with MS captions, lithographed throughout; contemporary half russia. Marlborough 162-31 1996 £950.00

FISHER, VARDIS Children of God. An American Epic. New York: 1939. 1st edition; 769 pages; brown and yellow cloth; very good in slightly chipped dust jacket (minor chip). Dykes HS p. 26. Gene W. Baade 1094-57 1996 $125.00

FISHER, VARDIS Passions Spin the Plot. Caldwell/Garden City: Caxton Printers Ltd./Doubleday, Doran & Co., 1934. 1st edition; (approximately 2000 copies); endpapers slightly browned, otherwise very good+ in wonderful color pictorial dust jacket. Steven C. Bernard 71-94 1996 $100.00

FISHER, W. K. Asteroidea of the North Pacific and Adjacent Waters. Washington: 1911-30. 4to; 3 volumes; pages vi, 419, 120 of 122 plates; pages iii, 245, 81 plates; iii, 356, with 94 plates; buckram, wrappers bound in, small library stamps on endpapers and verso of titlepages. John Henly 27-76 1996 £148.00

FISHER, WALTER M. The Californians. London: 1876. 1st edition; 236 pages + ads; cloth, very good+; 6 Guns 726; T. A. Swinford 49-371 1996 $100.00

FISHER, WILLIAM R. The Forest of Essex: It's History, Laws, Administration and Ancient Customs and the Wild Deer Which Lived In It. 1887. Imperial 8vo; maps, frontispiece; original cloth boards, rebacked with calf; excellent copy. David Grayling J95Biggame-252 1996 £85.00

FISHWICK, HENRY The Lancashire Library. A Bibliographical Account of Books on Topography, Biography, History, Science and Miscellaneous Literature Relating to the County Palatine. London: George Routledge and Sons, 1875. 1st edition; small 4to; original cloth, rubbed, small tears to hinges, inner hinges shaken, uncut. Forest Books 74-80 1996 £85.00

FITCH, ELIJAH The Beauties of Religion. Providence: Printed by John Carter, 1789. 1st edition; 8vo; 129 pages; contemporary calf, rubbed, with attractive, although partially damaged, Massachusetts bookplate of 1790. Wegelin 138; Evans 21826. M & S Rare Books 60-157 1996 $250.00

FITZENMEYER, FRIEDA Once Upon a Time. Book Six. Easthampton: Warwick Press, 1992. One of 125 copies, signed by author and artist/printer; 8vo; 13 hand colored drawings by Carol Blinn; Japanese paper over boards, colored labels; fine. Bertram Rota 272-494 1996 £80.00

FITZGERALD, DAVID A Narrative of the Irish Popish Plot, for the Betraying that Kingdom Into the Hands of the French, Massacring all English Protestants There... London: Tho. Cockerill, 1680. 8vo; (iv), 35, (i) pages, imprimatur leaf (detached), minor staining and soiling; Wing F1072. Robert Clark 38-94 1996 £65.00

FITZGERALD, E. A. Climbs in the New Zealand Alps: Being an Account of Travel and Discovery by... 1896. 2nd edition, only 500 copies printed; 59 plates, folding map in pocket at back; few neat circular ink stamps of Rucksack Club, some rubbing and bumping, new front endpapers, but sound, near very good copy. Moutaineering Books 8-RF01 1996 £250.00

FITZGERALD, E. A. Climbs in the New Zealand Alps, being An Account of Travel and Discovery By... London: 1896. 1st edition; only 1000 copies printed; 58 plates, folding map in pocket at back; leather bound boards; some or all of the 3 leather labels with gilt lettering on spine may have been restored or replaced, small neat bookplate, some slight soiling of boards, but sound, very good+ copy. Moutaineering Books 8-EF06 1996 £350.00

FITZGERALD, E. A. The Highest Andes. London: 1899. 1st edition; 45 plates, 7 drawings, 2 folding maps; few faint marks on boards, but clean, bright, above average, very good/fine copy; attractive and interesting bookplate of the Cavalry Club. Moutaineering Books 8-EF07 1996 £185.00

FITZGERALD, EDWARD Polonius: a Collection of Wise Saws and Modern Instances. Portland: Thomas B. Mosher, 1901. Limited to 450 copies on Van Gelder handmade paper; top edge gilt, half leather, Stineman binding, decorated spine, gilt, raised bands, marbled boards, bookplate, some offsetting one f.e.p., fine. Polyanthos 22-346 1996 $150.00

FITZGERALD, FRANCIS SCOTT KEY 1896-1940 All the Sad Young Men. New York: Scribner, 1926. 1st edition; very fine in dust jacket which, though lightly chipped to top edge, is also a fine specimen. Bruccoli A12. Bromer Booksellers 87-70 1996 $1,850.00

FITZGERALD, FRANCIS SCOTT KEY 1896-1940 All the Sad Young Men. New York: Scribner, 1926. 1st edition; near fine copy, spine moderately bright, lacking dust jacket; bookplate. Captain's Bookshelf 38-69 1996 $125.00

FITZGERALD, FRANCIS SCOTT KEY 1896-1940 The Beautiful and the Damned. New York: 1922. 1st edition; 1st issue; without publisher's seal on copyright page; near fine. Stephen Lupack 83- 1996 $175.00

FITZGERALD, FRANCIS SCOTT KEY 1896-1940 The Beautiful and the Damned. New York: Scribner's Sons, 1922. 1st edition; very clean copy, lacking rare dust jacket, in second issue binding with Scribners' seal on copyright page. Left Bank Books 2-34 1996 $125.00

FITZGERALD, FRANCIS SCOTT KEY 1896-1940 The Great Gatsby. New York: Limited Editions Club, 1980. One of 2000 numbered copies, signed by artist; illustrations by Fred Meyer; pictorial cloth by Deborah M. Evetts; fine in publisher's slipcase. Hermitage SP95-982 1996 $125.00

FITZGERALD, FRANCIS SCOTT KEY 1896-1940 The Great Gatsby. San Francisco: Arion Press, 1984. One of 350 copies; signed by artist; page size 10 x 6 1/2 inches; 182 pages, printed on Rives, 97 photo engravings printed in terra-cotta, titling and chapter numbers in blue-green, text composed in Monotype Goudy Light with Piehler capitals and figures for display; blue green cloth spine and corners with printed grey paper over boards, decorated endpapers, matching publisher's slipcase. Priscilla Juvelis 95/1-7 1996 $400.00

FITZGERALD, FRANCIS SCOTT KEY 1896-1940 Tales of the Jazz Age. New York: Charles Scribner's, Sons, 1922. 1st edition; 1st printing with page 232, line 6 uncorrected and very little wear to the type of the six words listed by Bruccoli; 8vo; pages (11), xi, (i) blank, 317; original green cloth, lettered in blind on upper cover and in gilt on spine, spine very slightly faded, little browned internally, nevertheless an excellent, bright copy. Bruccoli A9.1.a. Simon Finch 24-87 1996 £220.00

FITZGERALD, FRANCIS SCOTT KEY 1896-1940 Tales of the Jazz Age. New York: Scribner, 1922. 1st edition; spine dull, but legible, else near fine, lacking dust jacket. Captain's Bookshelf 38-68 1996 $150.00

FITZGERALD, FRANCIS SCOTT KEY 1896-1940 Taps at Reville. New York: Scribner's, 1935. 1st edition; near fine in very good dust jacket with light edgewear; inscribed warmly by author to David O. Selznick in 1939. Ken Lopez 74-137 1996 $25,000.00

FITZGERALD, FRANCIS SCOTT KEY 1896-1940   Tender is the Night.
New York: Scribners, 1934. 1st edition; pen and ink drawings by Edward
Shenton; near fine in lovely, very good+ dust jacket, only slightly sun
faded, few minor chips and tears.   Lame Duck Books   19-192   1996
$4,500.00

FITZGERALD, FRANCIS SCOTT KEY 1896-1940   Tender is the Night.
London: Grey Walls, 1953. 1st English edition; endpapers darkened, from
flap offsetting, else fine in fine dust jacket; attractive edition.   Between
the Covers   42-171   1996 $125.00

FITZGERALD, FRANCIS SCOTT KEY 1896-1940   Tender is the Night.
Limited Editions Club, 1982. One of 2000 copies, signed by artist and by
Charles Scribner III who wrote introduction; 11 1/4 x 9 inches; 10 p.l.,
319, (1) pages, (1) leaf (colophon); frontispiece and 8 color plates by
Fred Meyer, initials and part of titlepage printed in aquamarine; original
very attractive pictorial cloth (showing an elegant lotus pattern in 3
colors, adapted from an oriental jade, original tissue jacket and
publisher's slipcase; mint.   Phillip J. Pirages   33-358   1996 $125.00

FITZGERALD, FRANCIS SCOTT KEY 1896-1940   Tender is the Night.
New York: Limited Editions Club, 1982. One of 1500 numbered copies,
signed by Charles Scribner III and by Fred Meyer; illustrations by Fred
Meyer; pictorial cloth, fine in publisher's slipcase.   Hermitage
SP95-983   1996 $125.00

FITZGERALD, FRANCIS SCOTT KEY 1896-1940   This Side of Paradise.
New York: Charles Scribner's Sons, 1920. 1st edition; 1st printing, with
dedicatee's name misspelled on page (v); original dark green cloth,
better than good copy, slightly discolored and dusty, without much wear,
but without that freshness either; enclosed in lovely black morocco
box with marbled paper sides; presentation inscription from author for
Whitney Darrow.   Lakin & Marley   3-13   1996 $8,000.00

FITZGERALD, FRANCIS SCOTT KEY 1896-1940   The Vegetable, or
From President to Postman. New York: Charles Scribner's, 1923. 1st
edition; 1st printing; octavo; 145 pages; original green cloth stamped in
blind on front cover and in gilt on spine, front hinge cracked after front
endpaper, light browning to margins, very good, in dust jacket with
spine creased and with some tears mended with tape; with ALS by
Fitzgerald to broadway producer and manager, David Wallace, and
playbill for the production of the play at Princeton. The three items
housed together in quarter brown morocco pull off case.   Heritage
Book Shop   196-242   1996 $6,000.00

FITZGERALD, FRANCISC SCOTT KEY   This Side of Paradise. New
York: 1920. 1st edition; author's first book; top spine professionally
mended, new endpapers, corners slightly rubbed, front cover little faded.
Polyanthos   22-347   1996 $250.00

FITZGERALD, PERCY   The Story of the Incumbered Estates Court.
London: 1862. 1st edition; 8vo; vi, 104 pages; cloth, very good.   C. P.
Hyland   216-229   1996 £100.00

FITZGIBBON, GERALD   Ireland in 1868, the Battle-Field for English
Party Strife; Its Grievances, Real and Factious; Remedies, Abortive or
Mischievous. London: Longman, Green, 1868. 2nd edition; 8vo; pages
(4), viii, 366, (2 blank - extreme upper corner torn off), recent quarter
calf, gilt, nice.   James Fenning   133-110   1996 £55.00

FITZHERBERT, ANTHONY   La Novel Natura Breuium du ludge
Tresreuerend Monsieur Anthony Fitzherbert Dernierement Reuieu &
Corrigee per Laueteur... London: printed for the Companie of Stationers,
1616. contemporary calf, neatly rebacked, good.   Meyer Boswell
SL27-82   1996 $750.00

FITZPATRICK, WILLIAM JOHN   The Life of Charles Lever. London:
Chapman and Hall, 1879. 1st edition; large 8vo; 2 volumes; original dark
green cloth, very minor rubbing; fine set. Presentation copy, inscribed on
first titlepage from author for J. M. Doyle. CBEL III 944.   Ximenes
109-126   1996 $250.00

FITZSIMONS, F. W.   The Natural History of South Africa - Mammals.
London: 1919-20. 8vo; 4 volumes; 222 illustrations; cloth.   Wheldon &
Wesley   207-559   1996 £80.00

FITZWILIAM G. W.   The Pleasures of Love; Being Amatory Poems,
Original and Translated from the Asiatic and European Languages.
Boston: Belcher & Armstrong, 1808. Only American edition; 12mo; half
title evidently not called for; disbound, light foxing, two leaves torn (no
loss), but very good, crisp. Shaw & Shoemaker 15018.   Trebizond
39-15   196 $225.00

FITZWILLIAM MUSEUM   Catalouge. An Exhibition of Printing at the
Fitzwilliam Museum, 6 May to 23 June 1940. Cambridge: 1940. Blue
quarter morocco, marbled boards, original wrappers with Reynolds
Stone's red insignia on upper cover bound in, bound for Schuster by his
daughter Renate Hirsch, wife of Paul, with ink inscription "Bound for
Papa, Christmas 1940, Renate Hirsch". Bookplate of Renate Schuster.
Maggs Bros. Ltd.   1191-194   1996 £140.00

FIVE Blind Men. Fremont: Sumac Press, 1969. 1st edition; one of 26
lettered copies, signed by each poet; fine in gilt stamped cloth, without
dust jacket, as issued. Signed by each poet.   Captain's Bookshelf
38-3   1996 $850.00

FLACIUS ILLYRICUS, MATTHIAS   Nona...Decima...Undecima Centuria
Ecclesiasticae Historiae... Basilae: Per loan. Oporinum, 1565/67/67. Folio;
front flyeaf and first title present, but detached, (20), (320) (29) pages
index plus blank, 2 genuine blanks; 6 (358) (38) pages, 2 genuine blanks
14 (376) (44) pages; text in very nice condition, decorated with four
large and four small historiated initials, 2 large flower pictorial initials and
46 small initials; original vellum with owner's initials and date of 1568 on
front cover, over oak boards, one clasp and catch in place, binding very
worn, small parts of vellum missing to front of both covers and spine
completely gone, revealing cords, front board holding by upper cords,
volume firmly bound.   Roy W. Clare   XXIV-2   1996 $325.00

FLACK, MARJORIE   Wait for William. Boston: & New York: Houghton
Mifflin, 1935. 1st edition; small oblong 4to; colored illustrations; colored
pictorial boards; fine in pictorial dust jacket. Bader 63.   Barbara Stone
70-92   1996 £55.00

FLAHERTY, ROBERT J.   My Eskimo Friends "Nanook of the North".
Garden City: 1924. 1st edition; 10 x 7 inches; 170 pages; photos by
author, drawings by Eskimo artists; cloth backed boards, spine spotted,
else good in slightly chipped, slightly stained, and rubbed dust jacket.
John K. King   77-33   1996 $100.00

FLANAGAN, HALLIE   Shifting Scenes of Modern European Theatre.
New York: 1928. 1st edition; 280 pages; illustrations; pasted in
autograph letter by Flanagan to critic John Mason Brown; sunned, very
good.   Lyman Books   21-146   1996 $125.00

FLANNER, JANET   The Cubical City. New York: & London: Putnam's,
1926. 1st edition; small 8vo; cloth, dust jacket; former owner's signature
on front free endpaper, covers bit worn, but very good in somewhat
worn, dust soiled pictorial jacket. Author's rare first book.   James S.
Jaffe   34-156   1996 $1,250.00

FLATMAN, THOMAS   Poems and Songs. London: printed by S. &
B.G. for Benjamin Took & Jonathan Edwin, 1674. 1st edition; 8vo;
contemporary sheep, half morocco slipcase; particularly fine copy,
complete with two original blanks at beginning (one signed "A"), and
two at end. The Greenhill-Borowitz-Slater copy. Wing F1151; Grolier 356;
Hayward 131; CBEL II 473.   Ximenes   109-127   1996 $2,500.00

FLAUBERT, GUSTAVE 1821-1880   Madame Bovary. London: Vizetelly &
Co., 1886. 1st edition in English; crown 8vo; illustrations; original
decorative cloth, gilt, slightly rubbed, slight browning of prelims and
edges, rear endpaper slightly cracked, but still pleasant copy of an
uncommon book.   Ash Rare Books   Zenzybyr-35   1996 £345.00

FLAUBERT, GUSTAVE 1821-1880   Madame Bovary. New York: Limited
Editions Club, 1950. Copy number 904 from a total edition of 1500
numbered copies, signed by artist; illustrations by Pierre Brissaud; fine in
slightly sunned publisher's slipcase.   Hermitage   SP95-984   1996
$125.00

FLAUBERT, GUSTAVE 1821-1880   Salambo; a Story of Ancient
Carthage. New York: Brown House, 1930. One of 800 numbered copies;
illustrations by Alexander King; full leather, stamped in silver on spine,
near fine in slightly faded and chipped publisher's slipcase.   Hermitage
SP95-903 1 996 $250.00

FLAUBERT, GUSTAVE 1821-1880   Salammbo. London: and New York:
Saxon & Co., 1886. 1st edition in English; 8vo; half title; original cloth,
gilt, spine gilt; first owner's name inscribed. Light spotting of covers, but
very good. Mahaffey p. 156.   Trebizond   39-60   1996 $120.00

FLAUBERT, GUSTAVE 1821-1880   Salammbo. Limited Editions Club,
1960. One of 1500 copies, this unnumbered but designated "M.S." and
with publisher's presentation blindstamp; small folio; 8 double page
colored illustrations and 50 drawings in black and white by Edward
Bawden; cream buckram with decorated spine, one corner and foot of
spine just a little bruised, but very nice bright copy in slipcase.
Bertram Rota   272-266   1996 £85.00

FLAUBERT, GUSTAVE 1821-1880   The Temptation of St. Anthony. Harriman, 1910. 1st edition; near fine in very good+ dust jacket save for several small chips, very scarce in dust jacket.   Aronovitz 57-423 1996 $285.00

FLAUBERT, GUSTAVE 1821-1880   The Temptation of St. Anthony. London: Allen Press, 1974. One of 140 copies; 13 1/2 x 9 3/4 inches; illustrations by Odilon Redon, printed in 3 colors in distinctive unical typeface using damp mould-made paper; lovely blue and gold brocaded binding from a 15th century Persian design, hand blocked in Venice, paper spine label, edges untrimmed. Very fine.   Phillip J. Pirages 33-6 1996 $450.00

FLAXMAN, JOHN 1755-1825   Compositions from the Works, Days and Theogony of Hesiod. (with) Compositions from the Tragedies of Aeschylus. pub. for J. Flaxman, Jun. by J. Matthews, Jan 12, 1795. 1st editions; oblong folio; 2 volumes in 1; 37 stipple engraved copperplates, bound in at front is original printed side-label for the book as bound in boards; 31 plates; half tan morocco, gilt, spine gilt, slight rubbing. Some spotting as usual, generally in very good condition. Bentley 456.   Ximenes 108-136   1996 $750.00

FLECKER, JAMES ELROY   Hassan: the Story of Hassan of Bagdad and How He Came to Make the Golden Journey to Samarkand. London: William Heinemann, 1922. 1st edition; original binding, top edge dusty, free endpapers browned, head and tail of spine and corners bumped, top corners of few pages creased, spine darkened, covers rubbed and partially faded, good; ownership signature of Ian Fleming.   Ulysses 39-678   1996 £125.00

FLECKER, JAMES ELROY   Letters to Frank Savery. London: Beaumont Press, 1926. 1st edition; number 84 of 310 copies (of an edition of 390 copies); crown 8vo; printed on handmade paper, color printed title vignette by Randolph Schwabe, pages 125, (1); original quarter white parchment, backstrip gilt lettered, patterned cream boards, designed by Claudia Guercio, untrimmed and partly unopened, tissue jacket, fine. Blackwell's B112-20   1996 £50.00

FLEET, WILLIAM HENRY   How I Came to Be Governor of the Island of Cacona. Arion Press, 1989. One of 325 copies, 8 1/4 x 5 3/4 inches; xiii, (1), 204, pages, (1) leaf (colophon); title printed in green and black; original cloth backed pictorial paper boards, paper label on spine; mint. Phillip J. Pirages 33-22   1996 $200.00

FLEETWOOD, WILLIAM   Chronicon Preciosum; or, an Account of English Money, the Price of Corn, and Other Commodities for the Last 600 Years. London: Charles Harper, 1707. 1st edition; 8vo; (16), 181, (11) pages, complete with final 5 pages of Charles Harper's ads; contemporary cottage panelled calf, gilt label on spine; fine, crisp copy; from the contemporary library of James Earl of Bute, with his armorial bookplate. Kress 2553; Goldsmiths 4403; hanson 823; Hollander 635. McCulloch p192   John Drury 82-82   1996 £250.00

FLEMING, IAN LANCASTER 1908-1964   Casino Royale. London: Jonathan Cape, 1953. 1st edition; 8vo; pages 218; original black cloth, blocked in red, dust jacket, covers slightly marked, otherwise very nice. The dust jacket on this copy is from the second impression.   Sotheran PN32-11 1996 £995.00

FLEMING, IAN LANCASTER 1908-1964   Casino Royale. New York: Macmillan, 1954. 1st edition; near fine with spine ends lighty worn, near fine price clipped dust jacket with light rubbing and very minor edge wear, nice, scarce.   Quill & Brush 102-528   1996 $1,000.00

FLEMING, IAN LANCASTER 1908-1964   Chitty Chitty Bang Bang: The Magical Car. London: Jonathan Cape, 1964. 1st edition; small quarto; 3 volumes; white boards, illustrated with magical car and its owners flying across both covers, light wear to extremities, else fine.   Bromer Booksellers 87-128 1996 $285.00

FLEMING, IAN LANCASTER 1908-1964   The Diamond Smugglers. London: Jonathan Cape, 1957. 1st edition; 8vo; fine in very good dust jacket.   Glenn Books 36-106   1996 $200.00

FLEMING, IAN LANCASTER 1908-1964   Dr. No. London: Joanthan Cape, 1958. 1st edition; some foxing to page top edges, bookseller's sticker on pastedown, otherwise fine in price clipped dust jacket with white lettering on spine slightly darkened, faint soiling on rear panel and touch of very minor edge wear.   Quill & Brush 102-530   1996 $350.00

FLEMING, IAN LANCASTER 1908-1964   From Russia, with Love. London: Jonathan Cape, 1957. 1st edition; covers and page edges show some light soiling, few leaves creased and nicked on top corner, few with minor staining (lower margins), small "Times Library" stamp on rear pastedown, still very good or better in price clipped dust jacket with very faint, flattened creasing at folds, only a touch of minor soiling and edge wear.   Quill & Brush 102-529   1996 $600.00

FLEMING, IAN LANCASTER 1908-1964   The Man with the Golden Gun. London: Jonathan Cape, 1965. 1st edition; gilt stamped black cloth and pictorial dust jacket; extremely fine.   Bromer Booksellers 90-35 1996 $100.00

FLEMING, IAN LANCASTER 1908-1964   Thunderball. London: Jonathan Cape, 1961. 1st edition; fine in price clipped dust jacket with only one tiny chip.   Quill & Brush 102-531   1996 $150.00

FLEMING, IAN LANCASTER 1908-1964   You Only Live Twice. London: Jonathan Cape, 1964. 1st edition; 1st printing; 8vo; fine in stunning dust jacket designed by Richard Chopping.   Glenn Books 36-107 1996 $125.00

FLEMING, IAN LANCASTER 1908-1964   You Only Live Twice. London: Jonathan Cape, 1964. 1st edition; presumed first issue without "March" in published line on copyright page; near fine with small store sticker on lower front endpaper, owner's name on front endpaper, light foxing on page edges, fine dust jacket with very minor edge wear.   Quill & Brush 102-533   1996 $100.00

FLEMING, J. ARNOLD   Flemish Influences in Britain. Glasgow: 1930. 1st edition; 8vo; 2 volumes, pages 422, 442; 35 plates; original blue cloth.   Howes Bookshop 265-367 1996 £65.00

FLEMING, K.   "Can Such Things Be?" Or The Weird of the Beresfords - a Study in Occult Will-Power. London: Routledge, 1890. 1st edition; some wear to head of lightly darkened spine, otherwise very good. Scarce.   Aronovitz 57-424   1996 $125.00

FLETA, Seu Commentarius Juris Anglicani sic Nuncupatus, sub Edwardo Rege Primo, Seu Circa Annos ab Hinc CCCXL. ab Anonymo Conscriptus, Atque e Codice Veteri... London: Typis S.R. Postant apud H. Twyford, T. Bassett, J. Place & S. Keble, 1685. 2nd edition; 4to; name on title, 553 pages; some slight browning, contemporary calf, rebacked, label. Wing F1291.   Anthony Laywood 108-14   1996 £145.00

FLETCHER, ANDRES   A Speech Upon the State of the Nation. N.P.: n.d. Edinburgh? 1701. 1st edition; 4to; 6 pages, (2) blanks), folded, unsewn and uncut as issued, short marginal tear in one edge (no loss of surface); preserved in specially made cloth chemise with morocco spine label lettered in gilt; very fine. Macfie p. 14 and facsimile no. XIII. Not in Kress, Goldsmiths, Hanson.   John Drury 82-83 1996 £500.00

FLETCHER, JOHN   Studies on Slavery, in Easy Lessons. Natchez: published by Jackson Warner, 1852. 8vo; xiv, 637 pages; contemporary calf with morocco spine label, marbled endpapers, light soiling and moderate wear, scattered foxing, very good. the copy of Benjamin Lloyd Beall. Sabin 24729.   Andrew Cahan 47-181 1996 $125.00

FLETCHER, ROBERT SAMUEL   A History of Oberlin College from Its Foundation through the Civil War. Oberlin: Oberlin College, 1943. 1st edition; 2 volumes; fine, signed by author.   Between the Covers 43-313 1996 $175.00

FLETCHER, WILLIAM J.   Philip Hagreen. The Artist and His work. N.P.: Milford: at the sign of the Arrow, 1975. 1st and only edition; one of 200 numbered copies; 4to; 120 pages, 206 illustrations; printed on Curtis Rag Ivory Wove; green linen buckram; fine.   Taurus Books 83-68 196 $125.00

THE FLEURON, a Journal of Typography. Cambridge: University Press, 1928. 1st edition; 11.25 x 8.5 inches; 264 pages; blue cloth boards, title in gilt on spine, pastedowns and endpapers lightly foxed, otherwise fine. Joshua Heller 21-121 1996 $175.00

THE FLEURON. London: 1925. One of a limited edition of 120 numbered copies; 4to; Number IV; x, 164, (18) pages; printed on handmade paper; plates and text illustrations; buckram, top edge gilt, others uncut, covers very slightly scuffed, otherwise nice, fresh copy;   Thomas Thorp 489-102 1996 £80.00

THE FLEURON. Cambridge: University Press, 1926. Limited edition; 4to; illustrations; original decorated cloth.   Forest Books 74-82 1996 £65.00

THE FLEURON. At the Office of the Fleuron, Cambridge University Press, 1929-30. Volume 1 is from the handmade paper issue of 110 copies, remaining volumes from the ordinary issue; 4to; 7 volumes; profusely illustrated with folding plates, insets, type specimens, etc., some in color; original cloth or cloth backed boards, some very slight wear, prelims to volumes 2 and 5 slightly spotted; complete set in good condition.   Thomas Thorp 489-224 1996 £650.00

THE FLEURON. Cambridge University Press, 1930. One of 1000 copies; 4to; Number VII; xiv, 254, (27) pages; numerous plates and text illustrations; cloth; a nice copy in torn dust jacket. Thomas Thorp 489-103 1996 £75.00

FLEXNER, ABRAHAM Medical Education: a Comparative Study. New York: 1925. 1st edition; 334 pages; original binding, GM 1766.504. W. Bruce Fye 71-679 1996 $125.00

FLEXNER, JAMES THOMAS Doctors On Horseback: Pioneeers of American Medicine. New York: Viking Press, 1937. 1st edition; 8vo; xiv, 370 pages; illustrations; full red morocco, with inlaid black morocco rules and staf of Aesculapius on front cover, title is hand stamped in gold in large condensed modern typeface, with additional gold rules; fine in rubbed clamshell case of morocco backed linen. Andrew Cahan 47-127 1996 $285.00

FLINDERS, MATTHEW 1774-1814 Narrative of His Voyage in the Schooner Francis: 1798. Waltham St. Lawrence: Golden Cockerel Press, 1946. Of 750 numbered copies, this one of 100 specially bound; small folio; printed in 16 pt. Bembo with Centaur initials and Lyons capitals in black and green on grey mouldmade; 9 wood engravings by John Buckland Wright; full green morocco, pictorial devices in gilt on upper and lower covers, spine faded, otherwise very nice in slipcase. Bertram Rota 272-183 1996 £450.00

FLINDERS, MATTHEW 1774-1814 A Voyage to Terra Australis. Netley: 1989. Limited to 500 numbered copies; 4to; 2 volumes of text, with colored plate and 9 engravings and atlas of 16 charts, 2 views and 10 plates, together 3 volumes; half leather, lined wooden box. Wheldon & Wesley 207-391 1996 £315.00

FLINT, WILLIAM RUSSELL 1880-1969 Minxes Admonished, or Beauty Reproved. Waltham St. Lawrence: Golden Cockerel Press, 1955. Of 550 numbered copies, this one of 150 signed by author, specially bound and with 8 additional plates; small folio; full scarlet morocco, gilt, upper joint repaired, darkened and tender, but very good in slipcase. Bertram Rota 272-191 1996 £250.00

FLINTOFF, EDDIE Punting to Islip: a Long Narrative Poem. Old School Press, 1994. One of 30 special copies bound thus; oblong 8vo; 2 wood engravings by Simon Brett; printed in handset 10 pt. Gill Sans on Kawanaka ivory paper; bound 'Japanese album stle' (i.e. concertina fashion) betweeen boards in Japanese paper; fine in publisher's cloth box. Bertram Rota 272-358 1996 £64.00

FLITTNER, C. G. Anmuth und Schonheit Aus de Misterien der Natur und Kunst... Berlin: Oehmigke, 1797. 1st edition; 8vo; 322 pages; frontispiece, 3 full page engravings, all hand colored, engraved title; original blue paper wrappers, chipped; fine. Not in NUC, not in Lipperheide; Hayn-Gotendorf 1.87. Bennett Gilbert LL29-75 1996 $1,000.00

FLITTNER, C. G. Die Feyer der Liebe. Aus Einer Handschrift des Oberpriesters zu Paphos... Berlin: Oehmigke the younger, 1795. 1st edition; 8vo; 196, 232 pages; frontispiece, title vignette, both hand colored, both signed by Chodowiecki, engraved title; contemporary vellum, gilt backstrip label, redenned edges; fine. Hayn Gotendorf 2.254-255. NUC 175.474 (2 copies). Bennett Gilbert LL29-76 1996 $1,000.00

FLORES Historiarum. From the Creation to 1326. London: 1890. 8vo; 3 volumes, pages 1850; original cloth. Howes Bookshop 265-1606 1996 £95.00

FLORIO, JOHN Queen Anna's New World of Words, or Dictionarie of the Italian and English Tongues. Menston: Scolar Press, 1968. Facsimile reprint of London 1611 edition; very tall wide folio; pages (15), 690, (30); blue cloth, gilt, ex-library, unobtrusive library markings; very good. STC 11098 for original. Hartfield 48-11F 1996 $185.00

FLORY, H. C. An Essay on the Causes of the Indifference to the Study of Modern Languages and Literature in this Town and Vicinity... Sheffield: printed for the author by J. Pearce & Son, 1834. 1st and probably only edition; 8vo; 16 pages; recently well bound in cloth, lettered in gilt; very good, rare; not in BLC or NUC. John Drury 82-84 1996 £125.00

THE FLOWER-Piece: a Collection of Miscellany Poems. London: printed for J. Walthoe and H. Wlathoe, 1731. 1st edition; 12mo; contemporary panelled calf, rebacked, most of original spine laid down; very good, scarce; early armorial bookplate of John Cator. Case 367; CBEL II 360 and 541. Ximenes 109-229 1996 $900.00

FLUCKIGER, F. Pharmacographia. A History of the Principal Drugs of Vegetable Origin Met with in Great Britain and British India. London: 1874. 1st edition; 704 pages; quarter leather, GM 2032. W. Bruce Fye 71-684 1996 $200.00

FOLKHARD, H. C. The Wildfowler. London: 1859. engraved plates; original pictorial gilt cloth, expertly restored; nice, apart from light foxing, attractive and clean copy. David A.H. Grayling 3/95-356 1996 £155.00

FOLSOM, GEORGE Mexico in 1842...To Which is Added an Account of Texas and Yucatan and of the Santa Fe Expedition. New York: Wiley & Putnam, 1842. 1st edition; 256 pages; folding map, original black embossed cloth with title in gilt on spine, minor repairs to spine, fine copy for this work. Raines p. 83; Rittenhouse Santa Fe Trail 694; Streeter Texas 1413. Michael D. Heaston 23-147 1996 $1,750.00

FONDA, HENRY Fonda: My Life. New York: New American Library, 1981. 1st edition; 8vo; 32 pages of black and white photos; dust jacket (few nicks), very good; signed and inscribed by author. George J. Houle 68-50 1996 $125.00

FONTAINE, JAMES Memoirs of a Huguenot Family. London: c. 1890. 8vo; cloth; very good. C. P. Hyland 216-238 1996 £65.00

FONTELLE, BERNARD LE BOVIER DE A Plurality of Worlds. London: printed for R. Bentley and S. Magnes, 1688. 1st edition of this translation by John Glanvill; 8vo; 2 leaves are cancels (E4 and F1), they appear to have been printed as A7 and A8; contemporary speckled calf, spine gilt, splendid copy. Wing F1416; CBEL II 1513. Ximenes 109-128 1996 $2,500.00

FONTENELLE, BERNARD LE BOVIER DE Conversations on the Plurality of Worlds. London: Albion Press, printed for James Cundee, 1808. 12mo; xviii, 198 pages, engraved portrait; contemporary green calf. Not in NUC. James Burmester 29-51 1996 £50.00

FONTENELLE, BERNARD LE BOVIER DE Fontenelle's Dialogues of the Dead in Three Parts. London: printed for Jacob Tonson, 1708. 1st editio of this translation; 8vo; frontispiece, contemporary panelled calf, hinges cracked, spine gilt, lacks label. Anthony Laywood 108-81 1996 £50.00

FONTENELLE, BERNARD LE BOVIER DE A Plurality of Worlds. London: Nonesuch Press, 1929. One of 1600 numbered copies; 8vo; decorations by T. L. Poulton stencilled in color and gold leaf; printed on Van Gelder, limp vellum, thonged, gilt; nice in worn slipcase. Bertram Rota 272-322 1996 £65.00

FONTENELLE, BERNARD LE BOVIER DE A Plurality of Worlds. London: Nonesuch Press, 1929. Of 1600 numbered copies, this one unnumbered; 8vo; decorations by T. L. Poulton in color and gold leaf; printed on Van Gelder; 'house' binding of patterned boards, plain cloth back, some foxing, especially of prelims, but nice. Bertram Rota 272-323 1996 £50.00

FOORD, A. Catalogue of Fossil Cephalopoda in the British Museum. London: 1888-1934. 8vo; 5 volumes; original cloth, ex-library set, but in good condition. Wheldon & Wesley 207-1330 1996 £80.00

FOOT, JESSE The Life of John Hunter. London: T. Becket, 1794. 287 pages; contemporary tree calf, red label, spine slightly rubbed, otherwise very nice, handsome copy. Thomas Coutts's copy with his bookplate. Wellcome III p. 39. C. R. Johnson 37-79 1996 £350.00

FOOT, MIRJAM M. The Henry Davis Gift: a Collection of Bookbindings. Volume 1, Studies in the History of Bookbinding. London: the British Library, 1978. 1st edition; 4to; 352 pages; illustrations; leather spine, cloth over boards; fine. The Bookpress 75-292 1996 $200.00

FOOTE, HENRY GRANT, MRS. Recollections of Central America and the West coast of Africa. London: T. Cautley Newby, 1869. 1st edition; 8vo; (vi), 221, (17 ad) pages, original blue cloth, gilt; fine; Robinson, Wayward women p. 281. James Burmester 29-52 1996 £300.00

FOOTE, HORTON Harrison Texas, Eight Television Plays. New York: Harcourt Brace, 1956. 1st edition; signed; dust jacket. Maggie Lambeth 30-192 1996 $100.00

FOOTE, SAMUEL   Bon-Mots of Samuel Foote and Theodore Hook. London: J. M. Dent, 1894. 1st edition; very small 8vo; i, 192 pages; vignette on half title, 2 portraits, decorated title, 13 plates and 51 text illustrations by Aubrey Beardsley, brown floral endpapers; cream pictorial cloth gilt, small maroon vignette, top edge gilt, small text tear, browning to endpapers and half title, cloth bit rubbed.   Robin Greer 94A-15 1996 £110.00

FOOTE, SAMUEL   A Treatise on the Passion, so Far as They Regard the Stage... London: printed for C. Corbet, n.d. 1747. 1st edition; 8vo; disbound; very good. LAR 2770. CBEL II 810.   Ximenes 108-137 1996 $750.00

FOOTE, SHELBY   The Civil War: a Narrative. New York: Random House, 1958-74. 1st edition; 3 volumes; each volume near fine in dust jackets, excepting volume 1 which has lightly chipped dust jacket and volume 2 which has an inch and one half scrape on d.j. spine, volumes 1 and 2 have a Civil War motif bookplates, volume 1 signed by author on special tipped in leaf; volume 3 inscribed by author.   Captain's Bookshelf 38-73 1996 $600.00

FOOTE, WILLIAM HENRY   Sketches of Virginia, Historical and Biographical. Philadelphia: William S. Martien, 1850/55. 1st edition; 8vo; v, (iii), 568 pages; frontispiece, xiv, 14-596 pages; 2 volumes; publisher's blindstamped cloth, ex-library with appropriate markings, bookplates, edges worn, spine of volume 1 torn. Howes F241.   The Bookpress 75-412 1996 $225.00

FOR Love of the King. A Burmese Masque in Three Acts and Nine Scenes. N.P.: 1921. 1st edition, preceding the 1922 limited edition by one year; 8vo; drawings by W. T. Benda; vellum spine, paper over boards with gold gilt and sepia woodcut, illustrations in orange, black, pages ruled in orange, fine.   Priscilla Juvelis 95/1-297 1996 $150.00

FOR Shop Use Only: Curwen & Dent Stock Blocks and Devices. Devizes: Garton & Co., 1993. Of 512 numbered copies, this one of 75 accompanied by a suite of twenty engravings printed from the wood; 8vo; printed in Gill's Perpetua on Zerkall; one original wood engraving tipped in, 31 engravings; Ravilious patterned boards, with cloth spine, suite of engravings presented in individual window mounts, preserved together in matching box of cloth and patterned paper with boldly contrasting labels, fine.   Bertram Rota 272-260 1996 £575.00

FORBES, ALEXANDER   California: a History of Upper and Lower California from Their First Discovery to the Present Time... London: Smith, Elder, 1839. 1st edition; octavo; xvi, 352 pages; lithograph frontispiece, 9 lithograph plates, large folding map with original outline coloring; original blind and gilt stamped brown cloth, repaired areas to top blank border of two pages, otherwise beautiful. Barrett 866; Cowan p. 217; Graff 1377; Hill p. 107; Howes F242.   Argonaut Book Shop 113-252 1996 $1,750.00

FORBES, ALEXANDER   California: a History of Upper and Lower California. London: Smith, Elder and Co., 1839. 1st edition; 8 3/4 x 5 1/2 inches; xvi, 352 pages, folding map, frontispiece, 9 other lithographed plates, 32 page publisher's catalouge (dated Jan. 1848) at end; blindstamped plum cloth, tips bumped, some foxing to map and plates (generally confined to margins); bookplate of Carl I. Wheat. Zamorano 80 38.   Dawson's Books Shop 528-84 1996 $1,000.00

FORBES, ALEXANDER   California: a History of Upper and Lower California. San Francisco: John Henry Nash, 1937. Reprint, limited to 650 copies; quarto; 229 pages; plates, large folding map; cloth backed marbled boards, paper label on spine, very fine with elusive printed dust jacket (bit of chipping).   Argonaut Book Shop 113-253 1996 $225.00

FORBES, ALEXANDER   California: a History of Upper and Lower California. San Francisco: 1937. One of 650 copies; 4to; plates and facsimiles, including foldout colored map; marbled boards, cloth spine, edges little rubbed, but very nice in dust jacket.   Bertram Rota 272-308 1996 £75.00

FORBES, ARCHIBALD   My Experiences of the War Between France and Germany. London: Hurst and Blackett, 1871. 1st edition; 8vo; 2 volumes 476, 503 pages; contemporary half red morocco; very good, early owner's signature.   Chapel Hill 94-287 1996 $125.00

FORBES, DUNCAN   A Grammar of the Hindustani Language. London: Wm. H. Allen & Co., 13 Waterloo Place, S.W... 1862. New edition; 8vo; (v-viii), 1-148, vocabulary (1-40 pages), (41-48), 49-56; frontispiece, and 15 plates; ms. ink ownership inscription, some pencil notations to few pages, some light foxing; bound by Sizer, half maroon morocco and maroon embossed cloth, gilt title to spine, raised bands, new endpapers and prelims.   Beeleigh Abbey BA56-67 1996 £125.00

FORBES, E.   A History of British Mollusca With Their Shells. London: 1848-53. Large paper edition, small paper copies were not colored; royal 8vo; 4 volumes, 2 plain and 201 hand colored plates; contemporary half brown morocco; bindings rather used and some joints just beginning to crack, but very reasonable copy.   Wheldon & Wesley 207-30 1996 £650.00

FORBES, HENRY OGG   A Naturalist's Wanderings in the Eastern Archipelago... London: Sampson Low, Marston, Searle & Rivington, 1885. 1st edition; demy 8vo; (xx), 536, 32 pages; colored frontispiece, plates, illustrations, folding maps; original pictorial cloth, gilt, expertly strengthened and refurbished, covers little mottled and discolored, few minor marks and nicks, but good.   Ash Rare Books Zenzybyr-36 1996 £195.00

FORBES, WILLIAM ALEXANDER   In Memoriam. The Collected Scientific Papers of the Late William Alexander Forbes... London: R. H. Porter, 1885. 8vo; pages xvi, 496; frontispiece, 25 lithograph plates, 15 hand colored; contemporary green morocco with double gilt fillet and inner dentelle, spine ruled in gilt, gilt edges, slight rubbing to one corner of binding, otherwise a handsome volume;   Sotheran PN32-85 1996 £450.00

FORCE, PETER   Tracts and Other Papers, Relating Principally to the Origin, Settlement and Progress of the Colonies in North America, from the Discovery of the Country to the Year 1776. Washington: 1838/44/46. 3 volumes; original cloth, untrimmed, overall very good, clean and bright, volume 2 with chipping of hinges, volume 4 spine top chipped. Howes F247; Larned 13.   Bohling Book Co. 191-565 1996 $300.00

FORD, CHARLES HENRI   Secret Haiku. New York: Red Ozier Press, 1982. 1st edition; one of 155 copies, signed by author and artist; 8vo; prospectus laid in; drawings by Isamu Noguchi; cloth; mint.   James S. Jaffe 34-571 1996 $225.00

FORD, EDWARD   Bibliography of Australian Medicine, 1790-1900. Sydney: Sydney University Press, 1976. Square 8vo; xv, 348 pages; original cloth, dust jacket; fine. GM 6604.7.   Edwin V. Glaser B122-58 1996 $100.00

FORD, FORD MADOX 1873-1939   Henry for Hugh. Philadelphia: J. B. Lippincott, 1934. 1st edition 327 pages; original binding, head and tail of spine and bottom corners slightly bumped, endpapers partially and faintly browned, edges slightly spotted, very good in nicked and rubbed, slightly chipped, soiled, creased and dusty dust jacket slightly darkened at spine and edges.   Ulysses 39-206 1996 £225.00

FORD, FORD MADOX 1873-1939   A Man Could Stand Up. London: Duckworth, 1926. 1st edition; slight offsetting to endpapers, otherwise fine in lovely pictorial dust jacket marred only by two internal mends at spinal extremities, nice.   Captain's Bookshelf 38-75 1996 $150.00

FORD, FORD MADOX 1873-1939   The March of Literature. From Confucius' Day to Our Own. New York: Dial, 1938. 1st edition; large thick 8vo; just about fine in lightly chipped dust jacket, uncommon in jacket. Captain's Bookshelf 38-76 1996 $125.00

FORD, FORD MADOX 1873-1939   New York Essays. New York: William Edwin Rudge, 1927. 1st edition; limited to 750 copies; 8vo; cloth backed boards, lacking dust jacket with faint offsetting from clipping on half title, otherwise fine; inscribed by author for Elizabeth Madox Roberts.   James S. Jaffe 34-158 1996 $275.00

FORD, FORD MADOX 1873-1939   Provence. From Minstrels to the Machine. Philadelphia: Lippincott, 1935. 1st edition; 8vo; illustrations, cloth, dust jacket, fine in slightly chipped and torn jacket.   James S. Jaffe 34-159 1996 $250.00

FORD, FORD MADOX 1873-1939   Selected Poems. Cambridge: 1971. Limited to 50 numbered copies, signed by Basil Bunting, this copy being signed, but marked 'Out of Series'; very good in slightly used white dust jacket with two internal repairs.   Words Etcetera 94-251 1996 £125.00

FORD, FORD MADOX 1873-1939   Some Do Not... London: Duckworth, 1924. 1st edition; 8vo; green cloth, pictorial dust jacket; top of spine faded, extremities of spine trifle worn, otherwise very good in rare dust jacket which is chipped and somewhat soiled; inscribed by author for Arthur Spingarn.   James S. Jaffe 34-157 1996 $1,500.00

FORD, H. L.   Shakespeare 1700-1740, a Collation of the Editions and Separate Plays with some Account of T. Johnson and R. Walker. New York: Benjamin Blom, 1968. Reprint of 1935 edition; 7 plates; blue cloth. Maggs Bros. Ltd. 1191-88 1996 £65.00

FORD, HENRY CHAPMAN   An Artist Records the California Missions. San Francisco: Book Club of California, 1989. 1st edition; limited to 450 copies; oblong quarto; xl, 100 pages; 66 illustrations, plus 7 full page color plates; original cloth, decorated in a California Mission wallpaper pattern, very fine.   Argonaut Book Shop 113-254 1996 $225.00

FORD, HENRY CHAPMAN   An Artist Records the California Missions. San Francisco: Book Club of California, 1989. One of 450 copies; oblong 4to; 7 color plates and 66 black and white illustrations; half linen, patterned cloth sides, fine.   Bertram Rota 272-50 9196 £95.00

FORD, HORACE A.   Archery, It's Theory and Practice. London: 1856. illustrations; original pictorial gilt cloth, nice.   David A.H. Grayling 3/95-140 1996 £55.00

FORD, JOHN   The Works... London: Lawrence and Bullen, 1895. 8vo; 3 volumes; (cviii), 320; (viii), 322; (viii), 424 pages; original red cloth, spines gilt, extremities little rubbed; good set.   Robert Clark 38-46 1996 £95.00

FORD, PAUL LEICESTER 1865-1902   Franklin Bibliography. Brooklyn: 1889. Royal 8vo; interleaved copy; original cloth.   Charles W. Traylen 117-21 1996 £70.00

FORD, PAUL LEICESTER 1865-1902   Monographs of the American Revolution: Thomas Jefferson. Cambridge: University Press/Boston: A. W. Elson and Co., 1904. Limited to 500 numbered copies; folio; 37 pages; vignette and 2 plates, additionally laid in is a cancelled strike of each of the 2 plates; natural parchment wrappers, titled in gilt on front cover. Blue Mountain SP95-1 1996 $125.00

FORD, PAUL LEICESTER 1865-1902   The New England Primer. New York: Dodd Mead, 1897. 1st edition; number 328 of 425 copies; xiv, 354 pages; numerous plates, facsimiles, deckle edges; half sheep, covers slightly rubbed, but very good.   Metacomet Books 54-42 1996 $225.00

FORD, RICHARD   A Piece of My Heart. New York: Harper & Row, 1976. Advance reading copy; author's very rare first book; near fine in near fine illustrated special wrappers.   Pettler & Lieberman 28-92 1996 $200.00

FORD, RICHARD   The Sportswriter. New York: Vintage Books, 1986. 1st edition of this paperback original; signed by author; pictorial wrappers; fine.   Captain's Bookshelf 38-77 1996 $100.00

FORD, RICHARD   The Ultimate Good Luck. Boston: Houghton Mifflin, 1981. Uncorrected proof copy; wrappers, slight staining on bottom edge of pages, otherwise fine. Inscribed by author, uncommon proof.   Ken Lopez 74-139 1996 $500.00

FORD, RICHARD   Wildlife. New York: Atlantic Monthly Press, 1990. One of 200 signed and numbered copies; fine in slipcase.   Bev Chaney, Jr. 23-224 1996 $125.00

FORD, ROCHESTER   Tucson, Arizona. Tucson: Tucson Chamber of commerce, ca. 1902. 16 pages; illustrations; original pictorial colored covers on white glazed paper, minor chipping.   Michael D. Heaston 23-19 1996 $125.00

FORD, SIMON   A Discourse Concerning Gods Judgements: Resolving Many Weighty Questions and Cases Relating to Them... London: 1678. 1st edition; 12mo; 2 tracts in 1 volume; full contemporary calf. Wing F1484.   Argosy 810-180 1996 $400.00

FORD, WILLIAM   A Description of Scenery in the Lake District Intended as a Guide to Strangers. Carlisle: 1839. 1st edition; 8vo; pages ix, 175, 3 double page hand colored maps, each with panoramic view and extending table of Distances, little waterstained; original patterned cloth, gilt, engraved paper label with view of waterfall on upper panel, spine and edges faded; Bicknell 118.1.   R.F.G. Hollett & Son 78-929 1996 £135.00

FORDE, H. A.   The Fruit of the Spirit. London: De La More Press, n.d. 1919. Number 7 of 21 copies printed on vellum; 8vo; 23 pages, printed on rectos only, wood engraved frontispiece of George and the Dragon within elaborate Morris-style border as it is facing the titlepage, contemporary morocco backed Cockrell marbled boards, lettered in gold; very good; bookplate of Albert Sperisen. Ridler 26(1).   Claude Cox 107-44 1996 £220.00

FOREEST, PIETER VAN 1522-1597   Observationum et Curationum Medicinalium Libri Quinque; Nempe XI. De Morbis Oculorum & Palpebrarum. XII. De Aurium Morbis. XIII. De Nasi Affectibus. XIV. De Aegritudinibus Labiorum, Gingivarum... Leiden: ex officina Plantiniana, apud Franciscum Raphelengium, 1591. 1st edition; small 8vo; contemporary calf, slight wear; excellent copy, rare. Durling (NLM) 1613 Wellcome I 2363; Adams F766.   Ximenes 108-139 1996 $1,250.00

FOREEST, PIETER VAN 1522-1597   Observationum & Curationum Medicinalium de Febribus Ephemeris et Continuis Libri Duo. (with) Observationum et Curationum Medicinalium Libri Tres... (with) Observataionum & Curationum Medicinalium de Febribus Publice Grassantibus... Leiden: 1593/91/91. 3rd edition of parts I-V, 2nd edition of parts VI-VII; small 8vo; 3 volumes in one; contemporary calf, top of spine slightly defective, some wear to cornerss; very good, occasional underlining, other signs of use by an early owner; Durling 1607 and 1610; Wellcome I 2361 and 2362; Adams F759, 762, 764.   Ximenes 108-138 1996 $750.00

FOREEST, PIETER VAN 1522-1597   Observationum et Curationum Medicinalium Liber Decimus-Octavus, de Ventriculi Affectibus....(with) Observationum & Curationum Medicinalium Liber XIX de Hepatis Malis ac Affectibus... Leiden: ex officina Plantiniana, apud Franciscum Raphelengium, 1594/95. 1st editions; small 8vo; 2 volumes in 1; contemporary calf, slight wear, corners rubbed; in excellent condition, very scarce. Wellcome I 2365-6; Adams F768-9.   Ximenes 108-140 1996 $2,000.00

FOREEST, PIETER VAN 1522-1597   Petri Foresti Alcmariani Observationum et Curationum Chirurgicarum Libri Quinque, de Tumoribus Praeter Naturam. (with) Observationum et Curationum Chirurgicarum Libri Quatuor Posteriores... Leiden: ex officina Plantiniana Raphelengii, 1610/10 1st editions; small 8vo; 2 volumes in one; contemporary calf, slight rubbing; first title bit dusty, generally in excellent condition; very scarce. Wellcome I 2376 and 2378.   Ximenes 108-141 1996 $1,500.00

FOREMAN, CHARLES   A Letter to the Right Honourable Sir Robert Walpole, for Re-Establishing the Woollen Manufactures of Great Britain Upon Their Ancient Footing... London: T. Warner, 1732. 1st edition; 8vo; 70 pages, together with final blank (14), title dusty; marbled wrappers. Kress 4012; Goldsmiths 6931; Hanson 4305; Massie 2870.   John Drury 82-85 1996 £80.00

FOREMAN, GRANT   The Adventures of James Collier: First Collector of the Port of San Francisco. Chicago: printed and published by the Black Cat Press, 1937. 1st edition; one of 250 copies; 61 pages; original silver stamped blue cloth, printed label on front cover, some rubbing to spine ends and edges, else fine. Scarce. Edwards p. 87; Rader 1430; Rocq 9400.   Argonaut Book Shop 113-256 1996 $125.00

FOREPAUGH, ADAM   The Progress of Civilization Thrilling Incidents in Actual Border Life in the Wild West. N.P.: ca. 1887. (32) pages, including wrappers; illustrations; original pictorial wrappers, minor chipping, very good.   Michael D. Heaston 23-365 1996 $225.00

FORESTER, CECIL SCOTT 1899-1966   The Barbary Pirates. New York: Random House, 1953. 1st American edition; 8vo; 187, (i) pages; illustrations in blue and black by Charles Majoujian; red cloth, titled in black and decorated in blue and black in color pictorial dust jacket; near fine.   Blue Mountain SP95-38 1996 $100.00

FORESTER, CECIL SCOTT 1899-1966   The Earthly Paradise. London: Michael Joseph, 1940. Good copy (stained edges) in good dust jacket. Limestone Hills 41-46 1996 $158.00

FORESTER, CECIL SCOTT 1899-1966   Flying Colours. London: Michael Joseph Ltd., 1938. 1st edition original binding, prelims and edges spotted, head and tail of spine slightly bumped and faded, very good in torn, chipped, rubbed, marked, spotted, creased and dusty dust jacket, by Rowland Hilder, defective at head of spine; signed by author. Ulysses 39-208 1996 £300.00

FORESTER, CECIL SCOTT 1899-1966   Flying Colours - Including a Ship of the Line. London: Book Society Ltd. in conjunction with Michael Joseph Ltd., 1938. 1st edition, precedes 1st trade edition by one day; original binding, top edge slightly dusty, prelims and edges slightly spotted, head and tail of spine and corners, very slightly bumped and rubbed, very good in nicked and slightly rubbed, spotted, marked and dusty, internally repaired dust jacket, slightly browned at spine and edges and slightly frayed at head of spine.   Ulysses 39-207 1996 £175.00

FORESTER, CECIL SCOTT 1899-1966   The Hornblower Companion. London: Michael Joseph, 1964. Fine copy in a very good dust jacket. Limestone Hills 41-45 1996 $120.00

FORESTER, CECIL SCOTT 1899-1966   Lord Hornblower. Boston: Little, Brown & Co., 1946. 1st edition; 8vo; 322 pages; teal cloth, bumped, slightly soiled, in color pictorial dust jacket, chipped and creased at edges with small piece out from tail of spine, dust jacket illustration by Andrew Wyeth; near fine in good dust jacket; inscribed by Andrew Wyeth.   Blue Mountain SP95-82 1996 $375.00

FORESTER, CECIL SCOTT 1899-1966   Poo-Poo and the Dragon. Boston: Little brown, 1942. 1st edition; illustrations by Robert Lawson; original cloth, fine but for owner's inscription, in fine dust jacket with just a smattering of wear to spine ends.   Beasley Books 82-37 1996 $175.00

FORESTER, THOMAS   Rambles in the Islands of Corsica and Sardinia. London: Longman, Green, Longman and Roberts, 1861. 2nd edition; tall 8vo; xxxiv, 450, (2) pages ads, 2 chromolithographs, 5 tinted lithographs, map in color, several wood engravings in text; original orange cloth, professionally rebacked with original spine laid down, original spine chipped at ends, dampstaining to upper corner of front cover, dampstaining to frontispiece, title and one tinted lithograph, (not affecting the image), still acceptable copy. Abbey 77 for first edition of 1858. David Mason 71-79 1996 $200.00

FORESTI, JACOPO FILIPPO DA BERGAMO 1434-1520   De Memorabilibvs et Claris Mvlieribvs...Opera.. Paris: Colines, 1521. Folio; Colines device on titlepage; handsome woodcut initials; quarter calf; Renouard, Bib. de Colines 20.   Rostenberg & Stern 150-112 1996 $1,500.00

FORMENI, LORENZO   Indice de' Teatrali Spettacoli... Milan: 1789. 12mo; 330 pages; frontispiece, typographic ornaments; original wrappers; fine. 1 copy in NUC; not in BLC or Soleinne.   Bennett Gilbert LL29-39 1996 $2,000.00

FORNARO, CARLO DE   John Wenger. New York: Joseph Lawren, 1925. Limited to 1000 copies; small 4to; 24 pages, plus 50 plates, including color frontispiece; boards, very good; this copy inscribed by Wenger.   J. M. Cohen 35-112 1996 $125.00

FORREST, EARLE R.   Lone War Trail of Apache Kid. Pasadena: Trail's End Publishing Co., 1947. 1st deluxe edition, one of 250 numbered copies, signed by both authors; 143 pages, photos, full page color plate by Charles Russell, endpaper map by Clarence Ellsworth; original leatherette, fine with slightly worn jacket; very scarce edition. Six Guns 748.   Argonaut Book Shop 113-257 1996 $175.00

FORREST, G.   The Journeys and Plant Introductions of George Forrest. London: 1952. Royal 8vo; pages xi, 252; map, portrait, 105 illustrations; cloth, good, dust jacket.   Wheldon & Wesley 207-1772 1996 £50.00

FORREST, JOHN   Explorations in Australia. London: Sampson Low, Marston, Low & Searle, 1875. (vii), 351 pages, 4 folding maps, frontispiece, 7 illustrations by G. F. Angas; prize leather binding, raised bands, gold gilt, marbled edges and endpapers, endpaper, small tear on hinge restored, good plus condition; the Absolon copy. Ferguson 9681; Wantrup 200.   Antipodean 28-618 1996 $950.00

FORREST, LEON   The Bloodworth Orphans. New York: Random House, 1977. 1st edition; fine in lightly soiled, about fine dust jacket; very warmly inscribed to fellow novelist Barry Beckham and dated 1979. Between the Covers 43-79 1996 $125.00

FORRESTER, ALFRED HENRY 1804-1872   Pictures Picked from the Pickwick Papers. London: 1838. 40 fine hand colored plates; full coarse grained morocco by Riviere with triple gilt rules on panels and with extra gilt floral devices in compartments, gilt dentelles, top edge gilt, original front wrapper bound in at rear.   Captain's Bookshelf 38-48 1996 $375.00

FORRESTER, ALFRED HENRY 1804-1872   The Tutor's Assistant, or Comic Figures of Arithmetic... London: J. and F. Harwood, 1843. frontispiece, illustrations; original dark green cloth, slight rubbing at head of spine, all edges gilt; very good, bright, from the collection of Anne and Fernand Renier with label.   Jarndyce 103-456 1996 £50.00

FORRESTER, JAMES   The Polite Philosopher; or, an Essay On that Art Which Makes a Man Happy in himself, and Agreeable to Others. Dublin: printed by S. Powell, for P. Crampton, 1734. 1st Irish edition; 12mo; old diced calf, gilt, plainly rebacked; some soiling, few headlines bit shaved, but sound, very scarce printing; cf. Newberry, Courtesy Books 600; CBEL II 1936.   Ximenes 108-143 1996 $300.00

FORRESTER, JAMES   The Polite Philosopher; or, an Essay on that Art Which Makes a Man Happy in Himself, and Agreeable to Others. Edinburgh: printed by Robert Freebairn, 1734. 1st edition; 8vo; recent wrappers; titlepage rather dusty, small tear in blank inner margin; uncommon. CBEL II 1936. Newberry, Courtesy Books 600.   Ximenes 108-142 1996 $400.00

FORSHAW, J. M.   Birds of Paradise and Bower Birds. Sydney: 1977. Demy folio; 304 pages; text figures, distribution maps and 60 fine colored plates; cloth, few small library stamps, but good copy with dust jacket and slipcase.   Wheldon & Wesley 207-32 1996 £300.00

FORSHAW, J. M.   Parrots of the World. Melbourne: 1973. Original edition; imperial 4to; pages 584, 158 colored plates by W. Cooper; cloth. Wheldon & Wesley 207-31 1996 £300.00

FORSHAW, J. M.   Parrots of the World. London: 1989. 3rd edition; 4to; 616 pages, including 169 colored plates by W. Cooper, numerous maps; cloth.   Wheldon & Wesley 207-727 1996 £65.00

FORSTER, EDWARD MORGAN 1879-1970   Alexandria: a History and Guide. Alexandria: Whitehead Morris, Ltd., 1938. 2nd edition, one of 250 numbered copies of this edition, signed by author for Royal Archaeological Society of Alexandria; 8vo; pages (vi), xii, 218; large folding plan, numerous other maps and plans; 7 plates; original yellow boards, lettered in black, very good. Kirkpatrick A8b.   Sotheran PN32-12 1996 £425.00

FORSTER, EDWARD MORGAN 1879-1970   Battersea Rise. New York: Harcourt Brace, 1955. Limited edition; printed as a New Year's greeting and signed by author; embossed owner library stamp on titlepage, otherwise near fine, without dust jacket.   Ken Lopez 74-140 1996 $175.00

FORSTER, EDWARD MORGAN 1879-1970   The Eternal Moment and Other Stories. S&J, 1928. 1st edition; very good+/near fine in very good dust jacket with some light chipping to extremities of somewhat darkened dust jacket spine.   Aronovitz 57-425 1996 $275.00

FORSTER, EDWARD MORGAN 1879-1970   Howard's End. London: 1910. 1st edition; flyleaf torn away at top right corner but crudely repaired, 8 pages of ads at end; red cloth gilt, spine little faded, otherwise very good, scarce.   Words Etcetera 94-432 1996 £300.00

FORSTER, EDWARD MORGAN 1879-1970   The Longest Journey. Edinburgh: William Blackwood, 1907. 1st edition; some foxing to prelims and with very small hole to head of spine, otherwise near fine, scarce. Kirkpatrick A2.   Captain's Bookshelf 38-78 1996 $300.00

FORSTER, EDWARD MORGAN 1879-1970   A Passage to India. London: 1924. 1st edition; 3 pages ads at end, spine little soiled, otherwise very good.   Words Etcetera 94-433 1996 £125.00

FORSTER, EDWARD MORGAN 1879-1970   A Passage to India. London: 1924. 1st edition; contemporary inscription on flyleaf, spine hinges little rubbed, spine a touch dull, otherwise good, tight copy with minimal foxing on title.   Words Etcetera 94-434 1996 £125.00

FORSTER, EDWARD MORGAN 1879-1970   A Passage to India. Toronto: Longmans, Green/London: Edward Arnold, 1924. 1st Canadian edition, from English sheets, with title leaf and cancel and 'Longmans' at foot of spine; small manufacturing rumple on edge of front cover cloth, else at least very good, text fresher than that; Connolly Mod. Movement 45.   Magnum Opus 44-43 1996 $135.00

FORSTER, EDWARD MORGAN 1879-1970   A View Without a Room. Albondocani Press, 1973. Limited to 200 copies; patterned wrappers, slight browning to spine area, otherwise fine.   Words Etcetera 94-438 1996 £65.00

FORSTER, EDWARD MORGAN 1879-1970   Where Angels Fear to Tread. New York: Alfred A. Knopf, 1920. 1st U.S. edition; author's first book; orange binding, slightly faded at spine, otherwise very good. Steven C. Bernard 71-98 1996 $100.00

FORSTER, GEORGE   A Voyage Round the World, in His Britannic Majesty's Sloop Resolution, Commanded by Capt. James Cook, During the Years 1772, 3, 4 and 5. London: printed for B. White, Fleet St., J. Robson, Bond St., P. Elmsley... 1777. 1st edition; 4to; 2 volumes, large paper copy; folding map; full contemporary tree calf, corners very neatly restored, very tastefully rebacked, preserving original backstrip, laid down, red and green morocco labels to spines, elegant gilt tooling to spines, gilt greek key roll tooled borders, marbled endpapers; except for one signature, which has some slight foxing, this set is extremely clean and handsome copy. Mitchell 1247; Hill Pac. Voyages p. 108; Sabin 25130; Holmes 23.   Beeleigh Abbey BA56-53 1996 £3,500.00

FORSTER, JOHN   The Life and Adventures of Oliver Goldsmith. London: Chapman and Hall, 1848. 1st edition; illustrations; original pictorial cloth, all edges gilt, in cloth folding box (also little worn); inner hinges cracked as usual on this thick book, covers somewhat faded and worn; presentation copy, inscribed "M. W. Savage (probably the Irish-born novelist and editor, Marmion W. Savage) from his old and attached friend J.F." Bookplate of Estelle Doheny.   David J. Holmes 52-36 1996 $550.00

FORSTER, NATHANIEL   Reflections on the Natural Foundation of the Hight Antiquity of Government, Arts and Sciences in Egypt. Oxford: Printed at the Theatre, 1743. 8vo; pages (iv), 22, (2 ads); later wrappers. Peter Murray Hill 185-64 1996 £55.00

FORSTER, THOMAS I. M.   Researches About Atmospheric Phaenomena. London: for Baldwin, Cradock, and Joy, 1815. 2nd edition; 8vo; xvi, 272 pages, 6 hand colored plates; 19th century calf over pastepaper boards, hinges rubbed.   Kenneth Karmiole 1NS-226 1996 $350.00

FORSYTH, FREDERICK   The Day of the Jackal. London: Hutchinson, 1971. author's first novel; very good plus in very good plus chipped dust jacket.   Limestone Hills 41-47 1996 $160.00

FORSYTH, WILLIAM   A Lay of Lochleven. Glasgow: Robert Forrester, 1887. 1st edition; 8vo; pages 108; top edge gilt, illustrations, portraits; original cloth gilt over bevelled boards.   R.F.G. Hollett 76-92 1996 £85.00

FORSYTH, WILLIAM   Observations on the Diseases, Defects and Injuries in All Kinds of Fruit and Forest Trees. Dublin: printed by Richard White, 1791. 1st Irish edition; 8vo; pages (2), 62, with half title; recent paper wrapper; nice.   James Fenning 133-113 1996 £95.00

FORSYTH, WILLIAM   A Treatise on the Culture and Management of Fruit-Trees... London: Nichols, 1802. 1st edition; 4to; 371 pages 13 folding plates; rebacked contemporary calf, very good. Fussell p. 150. Second Life Books 103-78 1996 $500.00

FORSYTH, WILLIAM   A Treatise on the Culture and Management of Fruit-Trees... Whiting: 1803. 1st U.S. edition; 8vo; pages 280; 13 folding plates; contemporary calf, very good. Imprints 4218; Rink 1644. Second Life Books 103-79 1996 $250.00

FORT SMITH. CHAMBER OF COMMERCE   Fort Smith, Arkansas, Its History, Its Commerce, Its Location, Itself. Fort Smith: Chamber of Commerce, ca. 1892. 1st edition; 27, (1) pages; illustrations; original printed pink wrappers, minor chipping; fine. Howes F276.   Michael D. Heaston 23-29 1996 $225.00

FORT, C.   New Lands. B&L, 1923. 1st edition; very good in attractive dust jacket with some chipping and dust soil, most uncommin in dust jacket.   Aronovitz 57-427 1996 $175.00

FORTEGUERRI, NICOLO   Ricciardetto di Niccolo Carteromaco. Paris (in fact Venice): A spese di Francesco Pitteri, 1738. 1st edition; 4to; portrait, xxxvi, 420 apges, 2 leaves, 412 pages, 1 leaf (errata), historiated initials and finely engraved title vignette and head and tailpieces by F. Zucchi, Cattini, M. Pitteri and P. Monaco... contemporary vellum boards, engraved armorial bookplate of George Philips. Gamba 2241; Brunet I 1604.   H. M. Fletcher 121-99 1996 £550.00

FORTESCUE, HUGH   Public Schools for the Middle Classes. London: Longman, 1864. 1st edition; half title; original brown cloth, very good; inscribed presentation copy to Stafford Northcote, with author's compliments.   Jarndyce 103-474 1996 £75.00

FORTESCUE, J. W.   The Story of a Red-Deer. Newtown: Gregynog Press, 1935. Limited to 250 numbered copies; crown 4to; viii, 125 pages; 11 wood engravings in color by Dorothy Burroughes; original cloth, gilt, covers little dust soiled, 3 or pages slightly spotted. Harrop 35.   Thomas Thorp 489-104 1996 £150.00

A FORTNIGHT'S Ramble Through London; or, a Complete Display of All the Cheats and Frauds Practiced in the Great Metropolis, With the Best Methods for Eluding Them. London: printed and sold by Dean and Munday, c. 1810. 12mo; 66 pages; frontispiece; disbound.   James Burmester 29-91 1996 £175.00

FORTOUL, HIPPOLYTE   La Danse des Morts Dessinee par Hans Holbein, Gravee sur Pierre par Joseph Schlotthauer. Paris: Jules Labitte, n.d. 1842. 8vo; 180 pages; 53 lithographic impressions; plates printed on fine paper; contemporary crushed three quarter dark brown morocco over marbled sides, spine, rebacked much earlier, with 5 raised bands, gilt decoration and gilt titling, top edge gilt. Warthin p. 49 and p. 86. Book Block 32-18 1996 $750.00

THE FORTUNATE Orphan; or, Memoirs of the Countess of Marlou. London: printed for F. Needham, 1745. 1st edition; 12mo; modern calf, gilt, spine gilt, by Bennett, joints rubbed. Margins little marked by damp, bit limp throughout, but sound copy of a rare novel.   Ximenes 109-120 1996 $750.00

FORTUNE, ROBERT   A Residence Among the Chinese Inland, on the Coast and at Sea. London: John Murray, 1857. 1st edition; 8vo; (xvi), 440 pages, frontispiece, 5 plates, 17 text illustrations; contemporary half calf, rebacked.   David Bickersteth 133-148 1996 £145.00

45 Wood-Engravers. Wakefield: Whittington Press, 1982. 88/350 copies; imperial 8vo; pages (xii) + engravings, (i); printed on Zerkall mouldmade paper; original quarter dark green cloth, backstrip gilt lettered, mid green marbled boards, untrimmed, faded board slipcase. Fine.   Blackwell's B112-285 1996 £125.00

FORWARD Into the Past. For May Sarton on Her Eightieth Birthday. Concord: William B. Ewart, 1992. Although the colophon page calls for 150 letterpress copies, it is reported that less than 35 were actually distributed for sale; 2 small creases on verso barely visible; wine-red wrappers stamped in gold, near fine.   Bev Chaney, Jr. 23-597 1996 $100.00

FOSCOLO, NICCOLO UGO   Essays on Petrarch. London: John Murray, 1823. 1st published edition; 8vo; (viii), 325 pages, folding frontispiece; contemporary tree calf, rebacked;   James Burmester 29-53 1996 £125.00

FOSTER, BIRKET   Birket Foster's Pictures of English Landscape. London: Routledge, Warne & Routledge/New York: 56 Walker Street, 1864. New edition; 4to; 30 engraved plates by Dalziel Brothers; full dark green morocco, highly decorative gilt tooled borders, elaborate gilt tooling to panelled spine, gilt title and raised bands to spine, all edges gilt; text and plates all on thick card, joints very tastefully restored, handsome copy.   Beeleigh Abbey BA/56-9 1996 £250.00

FOSTER, BIRKET   Pictures of English Landscape. London: George Routledge & Sons, 1881. Number 671 of 1000 copies; folio; pages (18), + 30 plates, printed by hand on india paper from original wood blocks, each with accompanying leaf of verse (all printed on rectos only); engraved by Brothers Dalziel. original full japon decorated and lettered in gold and browns, lightly soiled, uncut, by Burn and Co.; inscribed by the Brothers Dalziel for Miss Edith Warne.   Claude Cox 107-35 1996 £135.00

FOSTER, CHARLES WILMER   History of the Wilmer Family, Together with Some Account of Its Descendants. Leeds: privately printed, 1888. Crown 4to; folding map, 5 folding pedigrees, 10 plates; original half maroon morocco gilt, gilt top.   Howes Bookshop 265-2095 1996 £75.00

FOSTER, J. W.   Prehistoric Races of the United States of America. Chicago: Griggs & Co., 1873. 1st edition; original decorated cloth, light wear to corners of covers and top and bottom of spine, else very good to fine.   Ken Sanders 8-21 1996 $165.00

FOSTER, JAMES   Discourses On All the Principal Branches of Natural Religion and Social Virtue. London: printed for the author and sold by Mr. Noon in Cheapside... 1749-52. 1st edition; 4to; 2 volumes; viii, 391 and xxxix; (1), 400, (1) pages, including final errata leaf; contemporary polished calf, spines fully gilt with raised bands and labels, red edges; fine; from the contemporary library of John Wilson, M.A., Fellow & Bursar of Trinity College, Cambridge. Lowndes 824; New CBEL II 1675; not in Chuo.   John Drury 82-86 1996 £450.00

FOSTER, JOSEPH   Pedigree of Wilson of High Wray and Kendal, and the Families Connected With Them. London: privately printed, 1871. 4to; pages 148; frontispiece; original cloth, gilt over bevelled boards, little marked, extremities worn and bumped, top edge gilt, joints cracking. R.F.G. Hollett & Son 78-158 1996 £140.00

FOSTER, JOSEPH   Pedigree of Sir Josslyn Pennington, Fifth Baron Muncasater of Muncaster and Ninth Baronet. London: privately printed, Chiswick Press, 1878. Tall 4to; pages v, 73 leaves, uncut, 3 page pedigree; flyleaves rather browned; original cloth, gilt, little scratched, corners repaired and neatly recased; flyleaves rather browned; very scarce. C. Roy Hudleston's copy with his Mss. annotations to the pedigree, 2 letters to him and a typescript copy of a Pennington deed in Manchester Cent. Lib. loosely inserted.   R.F.G. Hollett & Son 78-157 1996 £180.00

FOSTER, MICHAEL   A Report of Some Proceedings on the Commission for the Trial of the Rebels in the Year 1746 in the County of Surry... London: printed for E. and R. Brooke, 1792. 3rd edition; royal 8vo; pages xxxvi, 441, (19); contemporary calf, binding rubbed and worn, but sound and strong, internally fine; with Hodder bookplate. Pargellis & Medley 630.   James Fenning 133-114 1996 £125.00

FOSTER, SANDYS B.   The Pedigres of Crewdson of Crook, Withwell of Kendal, Pease of Hutton and Low Cross. London: privately printed, Christmas 1890. Large 4to; pages (ii), 11-140, interleaved; original cloth, gilt, corners trifle bumped, neatly recased.   R.F.G. Hollett & Son 78-159 1996 £65.00

FOSTER, SANDYS B.   The Pedigrees of Wilson of Rigmaden Park and Low Nook Gibson of Shelprigg, Fox of Grisby Co. Linc and Statham, Cheshire, Braithwaite-Wilson of Plumtree Hall, Argles of Eversley, Westmorland and Moser of Kendal. London: privately printed Christmas, 1890. Large 4to; pages 50, interleaved copy; original cloth; nice. R.F.G. Hollett & Son 78-160 1996 £55.00

FOSTER, SANDYS B.   The Pedigrees of Wilson of Rigmaden Park and Low Nook, gibson of Whelprigg, Fox of Girsby Co. Linc and Statham, Cheshire, Braithwaite-Wilson of Plumtree Hall, Argles of Eversley, Westmorland and Moser of Kendal. London: privately printed, Christmas 1890. Large 4to; pages 50, interleaved; original cloth, gilt, neatly rebacked in matching levant morocco.   R.F.G. Hollett & Son 78-161 1996 £65.00

FOSTER, SANDYS B.   Wilson of High Wray and Kendal, Together with the Families Connected With Them. London: privately printed, Christmas 1890. 2nd edition; 8vo; pages (viii), 238, corrigenda slip, endapeprs and fore edge rather spotted, upper joint cracked; original red cloth, gilt, extremities little worn.   R.F.G. Hollett & Son 78-162 1996 £120.00

FOSTER, WILLIAM Z.   Toward Soviet America. New York: Coward McCann Inc., 1932. 1st edition; original binding, top edge dusty and slightly spotted, head and tail of spine slightly bumped, very good in nicked, chipped and slightly creased price clipped dust jacket; signed by author, the words "Defense (sic) Trial Copy" stamped on titlepage and front free endpaper.   Ulysses 39-544 1996 £85.00

FOTHERGILL, ANTHONY   A New Experimental Inquiry Into the Nature and Qualities of the Cheltenham Water. Bath: ptd. by R. Cruttwell & sold by W. Taylor, R. Baldwin and J. Johnson... 1788. 2nd edition; 8vo; disbound; very good, complete with final leaf of ads; NLM p. 152; Wellcome III 45.   Ximenes 108-144 1996 $150.00

FOUCAULT, MICHEL   Histoire de la Folie a L'Age Classique. Paris: Plon, 1961. 1st edition; near fine, unopened, dust jacket; inscribed by author; quite scarce in first edition, and presentation copies rarely appear on the market.   Lame Duck Books 19-193 1996 $1,500.00

FOUCHET, MAX-POL   Johnny Friedlaender: Oeuvre, 1961-65. New York:. Touchstone, n.d. Limited to 200 copies, each with original color lithograph laid in loose, signed in white ink by Friedlaender; folio; 76 pages; 80 illustrations, including many tipped in color plates; cloth, acetate dust jacket, slipcase.   Brannan 43-219 1996 $100.00

FOUCHET, MAX-POL   Wifredo Lam. New York: Rizzoli, 1976. 1st edition; 266 pages; fine in lightly worn dust jacket with short closed tear to upper front panel.   Hermitage SP95-778 1996 $125.00

FOUGHT, H. W.   The Trail of the Loup-A History of the Loup River Region with Some Chapters on the State. N.P.: 1906. 1st edition; 196 pages, frontispiece, photos, illustrations, maps; decorated cloth, nice. Herd 816; 6 Guns 671.   T. A. Swinford 49-386 1996 $275.00

FOULKE, WILLIAM D.   A Random Record of Travel During Fifty Years. New York: 1925. 1st edition; 241 pages, photos; cloth, fine. Flake 3411. T. A. Swinford 49-387 1996 $100.00

FOULSTON, JOHN   The Public Buildings Erected in the West of England as Designed by John Foulston F.R.I.B.A. London: John Williams for the author. 1838. Folio; litho frontispiece, litho title (top margin cut away, not affecting printed surface), 85, (1) pages; 117 litho plates; publisher's cloth, rebacked.   Elton Engineering 10-52 1996 £750.00

THE FOUR Elements: a Poem for Each. Printed for the Cheltenham Festival by the Whittington Press, 1989. 1st edition; folio; loose leaf in printed original folio folder, fine.   Words Etcetera 94-595 1996 £100.00

FOURCROY, ANTOINE FRANCOIS DE   Elements of Natural History, and of Chemistry... London: printed for G. G. J. and J. Robinson, 1788. 8vo; 4 volumes, 2 folding tables in volume 1 and 8 in volume 4, short clean tear in two leaves (e3 in volume 1, Ff2 in volume 2); original tree calf, red morocco labels for the titles, oval green labels for the volume numbers; rough patch in the calf at foot of upper cover of volume 1, two small similar patches on upper covers of volumes 2 and 3, but very fine, crisp set. Partington III 537; Bolton I 449; Not in Duveen.   David Bickersteth 133-189 1996 £450.00

FOURNIER, ALAIN 1886-1914   The Wanderer. Boston: Houghton Mifflin Co., 1928. 1st American edition and 1st complete edition in English; original binding, covers slightly marked and rubbed, head and tail of spine bumped, bottom edges of covers slightly worn, small stain at bottom edge of prelims, very good in nicked, rubbed, torn, creased, marked and dusty dust jacket slightly browned at spine and edges and with external tape repair; one word inscription; bookplate.   Ulysses 39-5 1996 £350.00

FOURNIER, PIERRE SIMON 1712-1768   Fournier on Typefounding. London: the Fleuron Books, Published by Soncino Press, 1930. Limited to 260 copies; 8vo; pages xxxviii, (4), 323; 16 double page plates; original buckram backstrip faded little marked, but good; inscribed "W. Turner Berry for his indispensable library. J.R." and subsequently in the collection of Walter Tracy with his ownership signature.   Claude Cox 107-268 1996 £75.00

FOURNIER, PIERRE SIMON 1712-1768   Manuel Typographique. Paris: Fournier, 1764-66. 8vo; 2 volumes, 2 frontispieces, portrait of Fournier, 21 folding and double page plates; with half title (usually missing) in volume 1; full brown morocco, gilt edges, detnelle, bound by A. Motte; Robert Hoe bookticket in each volume. Bigmore & Wyman I 228; Updike Printing Types I 260 ff; Brunet II 1359.   Rostenberg & Stern 150-128 1996 $8,500.00

FOWLER, ALFRED   The Woodcut Annual for 1925. Kansas City: Alfred Fowler, 1925. Limited to 600 copies; folio; pages 52, (1) (pub. ads), color frontispiece, illustrations; cloth, covers scuffed and somewhat soiled, endpapers slightly foxed, interior fine.   Hugh Anson-Cartwright 87-349 1996 $250.00

FOWLER, ORSON SQUIRE   A Home for All, or the Gavel Wall and Octagon Mode of Building. New York: Fowlers and Wells, 1854. 12mo; frontispiece, (iii), 192, 11, (1) pages; 32 in text wood engravings; publisher's blue gilt cloth, text foxed, inscription in pencil on front flyleaf, covers lightly rubbed, else very good.   Bookpress 75-52 1 1996 $285.00

FOWLER, ORSON SQUIRE   Prospectus Of the Fowler Colony, Irrigation and Industrial Company. Denver: C. J. Kelly, Printer, ca. 1887. 1st edition; 26 pages; original pictorial wrappers, minor stain to back wrapper; fine, very rare. Not in Wynar.   Michael D. Heaston 23-100 1996 $750.00

FOWLER, RUSSELL   The Operating Room and the Patient. Philadelphia: 1906. 1st edition; 172 pages; 33 photographic illustrations; publisher's copy with notations in text regarding the photographic illustrations, original binding.   W. Bruce Fye 71-697 1996 $300.00

FOWLES, JOHN 1926-   The Aristos: a Self Portrait in Ideas. Boston: Little Brown and Co., 1964. 1st edition; author's second book; fine in near fine dust jacket.   Priscilla Juvelis 95/1-97 1996 $100.00

FOWLES, JOHN 1926-   The Collector. Boston: Little Brown, 1963. 1st American edition; 8vo; pages 305; cloth, dust jacket by Tom Adams (wrapper very slightly worn at extremities), otherwise fine; inscribed by author for Fred Uhlman.   Thomas Thorp 489-105 1996 £180.00

FOWLES, JOHN 1926-   The Collector. Boston: Little Brown and Co., 1963. 1st American edition; author's first book, fine in very good dust jacket.   Priscilla Juvelis 95/1-98 1996 $100.00

FOWLES, JOHN 1926-   The Collector. London: Jonathan Cape, 1963.
1st edition; author's first book; fine in first issue dust jacket with very
small spot on rear panel; signed by author.   Captain's Bookshelf
38-79 1996 $750.00

FOWLES, JOHN 1926-   Daniel Martin. London: Cape, 1977. 1st edition;
fine in dust jacket, signed by author.   Between the Covers 42-177
1996 $150.00

FOWLES, JOHN 1926-   The Ebony Tower. London: Jonathan Cape,
1974. 1st British edition; owner name and date front endpaper, near fine
in like jacket with rubbing at spine extremities and corners.   Ken Lopez
74-142 1996 $175.00

FOWLES, JOHN 1926-   The French Lieutenant's Woman. London:
Jonathan Cape, 1969. 1st British edition; minor end wear; scarce, fine
copy in very good+ dust jacket; signed bookplate.   Book Time 2-147
1996 $250.00

FOWLES, JOHN 1926-   A Maggot. London: Jonathan Cape, 1985.
1/500 copies, signed; handsome patterned boards, back in brown cloth
stamped in gold; fine.   Bev Chaney, Jr. 23-230 1996 $150.00

FOWLES, JOHN 1926-   The Magus. Boston: Little Brown, 1965. 1st
edition; preceding English edition; fine in dust jacket with touch of wear
to crown, much nicer than usually found.   Between the Covers 42-176
1996 $200.00

FOWLES, JOHN 1926-   The Magus. London: Cape, 1966. 1st English
edition; price inked out in red on front endpaper, else fine in near fine
jacket with spots of wear at corners of spine folds.   Ken Lopez
74-141 1996 $125.00

FOWLES, JOHN 1926-   Mantissa. Boston: Little Brown, 1982. Signed
limited edition of 510 numbered copies; 8vo; cloth, in slipcase, mint in
original shrink wrap, unopened.   Antic Hay 101-568 1996 $100.00

FOWLES, JOHN 1926-   Of Memoirs and Magpies. Austin: W. Thomas
Taylor, 1983. 1st edition; one of 174 numbered copies (from a total
edition of 200); blue printed wrappers; very fine.   Captain's Bookshelf
38-82 1996 $150.00

FOX, CHARLES JAMES   A History of the Early Part of the Reign of
James the Second. London: printed for William Miller by William Savage,
1808. 1st edition; 11 x 8 3/4 inches; 2 p.l., li, (1), 277, (1) pages, (1)
leaf, clviii pages, (1) leaf (blank), 8 pages (ads); frontispiece; errata slip
tipped in; fine contemporary marbled calf, sides framed with 4 closely
spaced gilt fillets, raised bands flanked by multiple gilt rules, spine
compartments with large and elegant gilt foliate ornament in center,
black morocco label, marbled edges and endpapers; trivial marks on
covers, offsetting from frontispiece onto titlepage, occasional very minor
foxing in text, but very fine and handsome copy. Armorial bookplate of
T. Thornhill.   Phillip J. Pirages 33-238 1996 $450.00

FOX, CHARLES JAMES   Memorials and Correspondence of Charles
James Fox. London: Richard Bentley, 1853. 1st edition; 8vo; 3 volumes;
original diapered cloth, blocked in blind on covers and spine, lettered gilt
on spine, spines faded but good set.   David Bickersteth 133-149
1996 £68.00

FOX, CHARLES JAMES   The Speech of the Right Honourable Charles
James Fox, at a General Meeting of the Electors of Westminster,
Assembled in Westminster Hall, July 17, 1782... London: printed for J.
Debrett, n.d. 1782. 1st edition; 8vo; disbound; 2 leaves of ads
at end, wanting half title; uncommon, p. 9-24 misbound at end, but very
good. Adams 82-37; Sabin 25337.   Ximenes 108-147 1996 $150.00

FOX, CHARLES JAMES   The Speech of the Right Honourable Charles
James Fox, in the House of Commons, on Tuesday, the 9th Instant, in
Defence of His Resignation. London: printed for Debret and Stockdale,
Kearsly; Bew; and Sewell, 1782. 1st edition; 8vo; disbound; very scarce,
half title present. Sabin 25336. Adams 82-38a.   Ximenes 108-146
1996 $100.00

FOX, W. J.   Finsbury Lectures. Reports of Lectures Delivered at the
Chapel in South Place, Finsbury. No. I. The Morality of Poverty... London:
Charles Fox, 1835-36. 8vo; 7 parts in 1 volume, (4), 32, 36, 36, 35, (1),
32, 36, 32 pages; contemporary half calf, slightly worn; very good.
Goldsmiths 28923 and 29327; not in Williams.   John Drury 82-87
1996 £120.00

FOX-DAVIES, ARTHUR CHARLES   Armorial Families: a Directory of
Gentlemen of Coat-Armour, Showing With Arms in Use at the Moment
are Borne by Legal Authority. London: T. C. & E. C. Jack, 1902. 4th
edition; thick 4to; xxviii, 1412 pages; approximately 2000 illustrations;
buckram, gilt, top edge gilt, others uncut, slightly worn with trace of
foxing in places, but good, clean copy, largely unopened.   Thomas
Thorp 489-106 1996 £80.00

FOXON, D. F.   English Verse 1701-1750. A Catalogue of Separately
Printed Poems with Notes on Contemporary Collected Editions.
Cambridge: Cambridge University Press, 1975. 4to; 2 volumes; brown
cloth, dust jacket, together in slipcase.   Maggs Bros. Ltd. 1191-90
1996 £200.00

FOXTON, THOMAS   Sereino: or the Character of a Fine Gentleman;
With Reference to Religion, Learning and the conduct of Life... London:
sold by T. Tonson, 1725? 12mo; pages 134; contemporary sheep, hinges
worn. Newbery, Courtesy Books 604.   Peter Murray Hill 185-45 1996
£50.00

FRACASTORO, GIROLAMO   Contagion, Contagious Diseases and Their
Treatment. New York: 1930. 1st English translation; 356 pages; original
binding. GM 2528 (Venice 1546).   W. Bruce Fye 71-701 1996 $125.00

FRACASTORO, GIROLAMO   The Sinister Shepherd. Los Angeles: 1934.
1st edition; 88 pages; original binding.   W. Bruce Fye 71-702 1996
$100.00

FRACASTORO, GIROLAMO   Opera Omnia, in vnum Proxime Post Illius
Mortem Collecta. Venetiis: Apud Ivntas, 1555. 1st edition; 4to; 1 full page
woodcut (slightly damaged), several text woodcuts, 6, 281, 32 leaves;
contemporary vellum, spine slightly worn at tail, several leaves
misnumbered as usual, front free endpaper lacking, slight worming of
last leaf and lower hinge, slight marginal waterstaining on first few
leaves; neat contemporary marginalia in Latin, Fracastoro's name in ink
on lower edge and leather ex-libris of Charles L. Dana. Crisp, wide
margined copy; several inscriptions, indicating the volume belonged to
Givoanni Battista Capponi, doctor.   Argosy 810-185 1996 $3,250.00

FRANCE   Plan of the French Constitution and Declaration of Rights;
as Presented to the National Convention of France. London: printed for
J. S. Jordan, No. 166 Fleet St., 1793. Modern full calf, extra gilt, bit
dusty, but quite pretty.   Meyer Boswell SL26-85 1996 $750.00

FRANCE, ANATOLE   Penguin Island. London: John Lane, Bodley Head,
1924. Reprint; original binding, top edge dusty, head and tail of spine
and corners bumped, free endpapers browned, covers marked and
dusty; good; ownership signature of Ian Fleming.   Ulysses 39-679
1996 £125.00

FRANCE, ANATOLE   The Seven Wives of Bluebeard. London: John
Lane, Bodley Head, 1925. Reprint; original binding, top edge dusty, head
and tail of spine and corners bumped, spine darkened, covers marked
and dusty, good; ownership signature of Ian Fleming.   Ulysses 39-680
1996 £125.00

FRANCE, ANATOLE   Stendhal. London: 1926. One of 110 numbered
copies, this copy being additionally inscribed; wrappers, first two pages
and final page partially browned, covers slightly marked and spotted;
very good; inscribed by Holbrook Jackson for E. A. Ratcliffe.   Ulysses
39-134 1996 £85.00

FRANCE, R. S.   Lord Redesdale and the New Railways: a Review of
His Lordship as a Railway Legislator... London: printed for the author by
Witherby & Co., 1867. 1st (?only) edition; 8vo; 24 pages; original
printed paper wrappers. Nice.   James Fenning 133-117 1996 £75.00

FRANCESCO D'ASSISI, SAINT 1182-1226   I Fioretti Del Glorioso
Poverello di Cristo S. Francesco Di Assisi. Ashendene Press, 1922. One
of 200 copies on paper for sale (of 240 printed); 9 x 6 inches; 1 p.l., viii
pages, (1) leaf, 239, (1) pages; printer's device, 53 woodcuts in text by
Charles M. Gere, cut by J. B. Swain, red and blue initials designed by
Graily Hewitt; original gilt titled vellum, green silk ties, in attractive folding
buckram box with paper spine label; binding with usual variation in color
as a result of the grain in the vellum, but very fine, faultless internally.
Hornby 31; Tomkinson p. 7.   ]Phillip J. Pirages 33-26 1996 $1,600.00

FRANCESCO D'ASSISI, SAINT 1182-1226   I Fioretti del Glorioso
Poverello di Cristo S. Francesco di Assisi. Arundel Press, 1922. One of
240 copies; 8vo; printed in Subiaco in black and red with initials in red
and blue; limp vellum, ties, exceptionally fine, fresh and crisp copy.
Bertram Rota 272-17 1996 £700.00

FRANCESCO D'ASSISI, SAINT 1182-1226   The Little Flowers of Saint Francis of Assisi. Hans Mardersteig at the Officina Bodoni for the Limited Editions Club, 1931. Limited to 1500 numbered copies, signed by artist; 4to; xxix, 262 pages; numerous wood engraved text vignettes by Paolo Molnar; patterned silk cloth by fortuny, edges uncut, fine, in repaired dust jacket.   Thomas Thorp 489-107 1996 £120.00

FRANCH, JOSE ALCINA   Pre-Columbian Art. New York: Harry N. Abrams, 1983. Folio; 614 pages, 1052 illustrations; original cloth, dust jacket.   Archaeologia Luxor-4486 1996 $250.00

FRANCIA, LOUIS   A Series of Progressive Lessons, Intended to Elucidate the Art of Flower Painting in Water Colours. London: Whittingham and Rowland for T. Clay, 1815. 1st edition; 4to; 32 pages, 12 engraved plates, comprising 1 aquatint color scheme, 1 plate in 4 states, 7 colored aquatints; contemporary half roan, original red morocco label on upper marbled boards; very good, some occasional foxing and minor browning; presentation inscription. Dunthorne 17; Nissen 2385.   Ken Spelman 30-30 1996 £480.00

FRANCIS, DICK 1920-   Blood Sport. London: Michael Joseph, 1967. 1st edition; fine in near fine price clipped dust jacket with light rubbing and very light wear on spine ends.   Quill & Brush 102-566 1996 $250.00

FRANCIS, DICK 1920-   Blood Sport. New York: Harper, 1967. 1st edition; small stain at base of pages, else fine in fine dust jacket, with one slight wrinkle in lamination.   Between the Covers 42-483 1996 $135.00

FRANCIS, DICK 1920-   Blood Sport. New York: Harper & Row, 1967. 1st edition; top corners lightly bumped, light stain on top corner of rear cover, otherwise fine in lightly soiled dust jacket with touch of minor creasing.   Quill & Brush 102-567 1996 $125.00

FRANCIS, DICK 1920-   Bonecrack. London: Michael Joseph, 1971. 1st edition; fine in dust jacket with very light edge wear.   Quill & Brush 102-570 1996 $125.00

FRANCIS, DICK 1920-   Bonecrack. London: Michael Joseph, 1971. 1st edition; near fine with page edges slightly soiled, in price clipped dust jacket with back flap lightly creased and minor edge wear.   Quill & Brush 102-571 1996 $100.00

FRANCIS, DICK 1920-   Flying Finish. London: Michael Joseph, 1966. 1st edition; exceptionally nice, near fine with light foxing on page edges in fine dust jacket with very light rubbing, very scarce in this condition.   Quill & Brush 102-565 196 $300.00

FRANCIS, DICK 1920-   In the Frame. London: Michael Joseph, 1976. 1st edition; fine in dust jacket with very light rubbing.   Quill & Brush 102-579 1996 $100.00

FRANCIS, DICK 1920-   Knock Down. London: Michael Joseph, 1974. 1st edition; fine in price clipped dust jacket with light rubbing and very minor edge wear; nice contemporary inscription from author.   Quill & Brush 102-576 1996 $150.00

FRANCIS, DICK 1920-   Odds Against. London: Michael Joseph, 1965. 1st edition; fine in price clipped dust jacket with back panel lightly soiled.   Quill & Brush 102-563 1996 $350.00

FRANCIS, DICK 1920-   Odds Against. London: Michael Joseph, 1965. 1st edition; near fine in dust jacket slightly soiled on rear panel with only minor edge rubbing and one short closed tear.   Quill & Brush 102-564 1996 $275.00

FRANCIS, DICK 1920-   Rat Race. London: Michael Joseph, 1970. 1st edition; fine with owner's name and date on front endpaper, in dust jacket with very light rubbing.   Quill & Brush 102-569 1996 $200.00

FRANCIS, DICK 1920-   Slay-Ride. London: Michael Joseph, 1973. 1st edition; fine in price clipped dust jacket with light rubbing.   Quill & Brush 102-575 1996 $125.00

FRANCIS, DICK 1920-   Smokescreen. London: Michael Joseph, 1972. 1st edition; fine in dust jacket with very light rubbing.   Quill & Brush 102-573 1996 $125.00

FRANCIS, DICK 1920-   Smokescreen. London: Michael Joseph, 1972. 1st edition; fine in near fine price clipped dust jacket with light edge wear and back panel lightly soiled.   Quill & Brush 102-574 1996 $100.00

FRANCIS, DICK 1920-   Smokescreen. London: Michael Joseph, 1972. 1st edition; fine in like dust jacket.   Left Bank Books 2-36 1996 $100.00

FRANCIS, DICK 1920-   Twice Shy. London: Michael Joseph, 1981. 1st edition; near fine with light soiling on page edges, in dust jacket with light creasing and one small closed tear.   Quill & Brush 102-589 1996 $100.00

FRANCIS, DICK 1920-   Wild Horses. Bristol: Scorpion Press, 1994. 1/20 deluxe lettered copies, signed by author and H.R.F. Keating who provided an author appreciation; fine in quarter bound goatskin with raised bands.   Quill & Brush 102-607 1996 $450.00

FRANCIS, ROBERT   The Trouble with God. Pennyroyal Press, 1984. One of 100 copies, signed by author and designer; 7 1/2 x 5 inches; 6 p.l. (one blank), 114 pages, (2) leaves; yellow decoration on title, decorative initials printed in reverse; designed and with initials by Barry Moser; original cloth backed patterned paper boards, spine titled in gilt; as new.   Phillip J. Pirages 33-413 1996 $150.00

FRANCKLIN, WILLIAM   The History of the Reign of Shah-Aulum, the Present Emperor of Hindostaun. London: printed for the author, by Cooper & Graham & sold by R. Faulder, J... 1798. 1st edition; 4to; folding map and 4 engraved plates, 12 page list of subscribers; contemporary half calf, spine gilt, upper joint rubbed, but sound; some light foxing, but very good, uncut. CBEL II 1443.   Ximenes 108-148 1996 $600.00

FRANCO, NICCOLO   La Philena. Historia Amorosa Vltimamente Composta. Mantua: Jacomo Ruffinelli, 1547. 1st edition; 8vo; ff. 470, italic leetter, woodcut portrait of author on titlepage, woodcut printer's device and repeated portrait at end, slight foxing in places; faded contemporary ex-libris on titlepage; 19th century straight grained green morocco by C. Smith, gilt fillets and corner fleurons and richly gilt spine, all edges gilt, very good; bookplate of Baron Landau on pastedown.   A. Sokol XXV-40 1996 £1,650.00

FRANK, LARRY   Indian Silver Jewelry of the Southwest, 1868-1930. Boston: National Geographic Society, 1978. 1st edition; 214 pages; very good in price clipped dust jacket, minor rubbing.   Ken Sanders 8-141 1996 $150.00

FRANK, ROBERT   The Americans. Millerton: Aperture, 1978. New edition; photos; fine in fine dust jacket with one wrinkle at spine crown.   Ken Lopez 74-238 1996 $125.00

FRANK, WALDO   America and Alfred Steiglitz. Garden City: Doubleday, Doran, 1934. 1st edition; couple of short tears to foot of spine and wear to cloth of remaining extremities, overall very good in dust jacket with chipping to extremities; this copy belonged to Steiglitz, with his ownership signature and bookplate. Inscribed by Steiglitz for Mildred Wilson.   Lame Duck Books 19-507 1996 $2,500.00

FRANKAU, GILBERT   One Of Us. London: Chatto & Windus, 1917. 1st illustrated edition, number 48 of 110 copies signed by author and artist; small 4to; 173 pages; frontispiece, vignette titlepage and 8 plates by A. H. Fish; original full parchment, top edge gilt, some soiling to cover, else very good, Clementine Waring's copy with her bookplate.   Chapel Hill 94-57 1996 $165.00

FRANKENSTEIN, ALFRED   Karel Appel. New York: Abrams, 1980. Oblong 4to; 191 pages; 162 illustrations; cloth, dust jacket.   Brannan Books 43-11 1996 $110.00

FRANKFORT, H.   The Mural Painting of El-'Amarneh. Egypt Exploration Society, 1929. Folio; xii, 74 pages; 21 plates including 8 in color, 22 text illustrations; publisher's half buckram, gilt, top edge gilt.   Thomas Thorp 489-108 1996 £185.00

FRANKFURTER, FELIX   The Labour Injunction. New York: Macmillan Co., 1930. Olive green cloth, showing wear, but fresh copy. With presentation in author's hand to William G. Thompson, lawyer for Sacco and Vanzetti.   Meyer Boswell SL25-85 1996 $500.00

FRANKLAND, C. COLVILLE   Narrative of a Visit to the Courts of Russia and Sweden, in the Years 1830 and 1831. London: Henry Colburn and Richard Bentley, New Burlington St., 1832. 1st edition; 8vo; 2 volumes; folding sepia aquatint frontispiece to volume 1, lacks plan to volume 2; (iii-vi), (vii-xii), 1-399 pages; (iii-viii), 1-464 pages; full tan calf, gilt ruled border to boards, inner blind tooling duplicating border device to boards, gilt titles to spines, raised bands to spine, marbled endpapers; contemporary ink inscription, joints slightly rubbed. Abbey Travel 27.   Beeleigh Abbey BA56-68 1996 £150.00

FRANKLIN, BENJAMIN 1706-1790   Experiences et Observations Sur L'Electricite Faites a Philadelphie en Amerique par M. Benjamin Franklin... Paris: Durand, 1756. 2nd French edition; 8vo; 2 volumes, (102), 245; 349, (1) pages; 2 plates called for lacking in this copy, there is no evidence of their ever having been bound in; original unprinted drab grey wrappers with title handwritten on spines, some wear at spine ends, front wrapper of first volume separating, but remarkably fine, untrimmed set, very clean internally; excessively rare, particularly in original wrpapers. Chapel Hill 94-350 1996 $800.00

FRANKLIN, BENJAMIN 1706-1790   Experiments and Observations on Electricity, Made at Philadelphia in America. London: for David Henry and sold by Francis Newbery, 1769. 1st collected edition; 4to; (2), iv, (2), 496, (16) pages; 7 engraved plates, half titles present; contemporary mottled calf, skillfully rebacked in period style with original spine label retained, unusually nice with only light occasional foxing and minor soiling of one plate, entirely free from offsetting and heavier foxing so often associated with this book; PMM 199 (1st ed.); Wheeler Gift 367b; Ford 307; Howes F320.   Joseph J. Felcone 64-19 1996 $3,500.00

FRANKLIN, BENJAMIN 1706-1790   Memoires de la Vie Privee de Benjamin Franklin Ecrits par Lui-meme et Adresses a Son Fils... Paris: 1791. 8vo; vi, 363 pages; quarter calf, bit browned, otherwise good, scarce.   K Books 441-238 1996 £250.00

FRANKLIN, BENJAMIN 1706-1790   Memoires de la Vie Privee de Benjamin Franklin. (with) Vie Publique et Privee de Honore-Gabriel Riquetti, Comte de Mirabeau. Paris: Chez Buisson, 1791/92. 1st edition;; (2), vi, 156, 207 (pages 204-207 misnumbered 360-363); (2), 92 pages; later marbled boards, spine gilt, vellum label, very light wear to extremities, faint scattered foxing, very small and discreet library stamp in blank margin of preface leaf; very nice. Grolier American 100 21; Streeter Sale 4171; Howes F323 (b); Ford 383.   Joseph J. Felcone 64-20 1996 $2,500.00

FRANKLIN, BENJAMIN 1706-1790   Political, Miscellaneous and Philosophical Pieces... London: J. Johnson, 1779. 1st edition; xii, 568, (6) pages; one folding table, 4 plates; original calf, neatly rebacked, old spine and label laid down. Sabin 25565; Howes F330; Goldsmith 11784. Kenneth Karmiole 1NS-107 1996 $1,000.00

FRANKLIN, BENJAMIN 1706-1790   La Science du Bonhomme Richard, ou Moyen Facile de Payer les Impots. Philadelphie: et se Trouve a Paris; chez Ruault, 1777. 1st edition in French; 12mo; original blue wrappers, old ms. label (some soiling, some wear to spine); couple of blank corners torn, but fine in original condition, complete with half title and 4 pages of publisher's ads at end; rare in this condition. Ford 113. Ximenes 109-131 1996 $2,000.00

FRANKLIN, BENJAMIN 1706-1790   The Way to Wealth, The Preface to Poor Richard's Almanac for the Year 1758. New York: Random House, 1930. Number 109 of an edition of 390 numbered copies; folio; 25 pages; cloth backed boards, unprinted dust jacket, jacket chipped and torn, else fine in slightly sunned, original slipcase.   Hermitage SP95-842 1996 $250.00

FRANKLIN, BENJAMIN 1706-1790   The Works. Boston: Hilliard Gray and Co., 1840. 1st Sparks edition; 8vo; 10 volumes; three quarter navy blue morocco, raised bands, gilt tops, fine, attractive set in handsome bindings.   Appelfeld Gallery 54-102 1996 $500.00

FRANKLIN, COLIN   A Catalogue of Early Colour Printing from Chiaroscuro to Aquatint. Culham: C. & C. Franklin, 1977. 1st edition; large 4to; colored frontispiece, 15 colored plates; original cloth.   Forest Books 74-83 1996 £95.00

FRANKLIN, COLIN   Emery Walker. Some Light on His Theories of Printing and On His Relations with William Morris and Cobden-Sanderson. Cambridge: 1973. 1st edition; limited to 500 copies; folio; pages x, 36; portrait, 2 facsimile pages plus 3 items in pocket at end, original morocco backed boards, decorated with reduced version of a Morris wallpaper; fine; from the library of Ruari McLean, with his booklabel. Claude Cox 107-28 1996 £130.00

FRANZKE, ANDREAS   Dubuffet. New York: Abrams, 1981. Folio; 282 pages; 376 illustrations, 102 in color; cloth, dust jacket. Freitag 2411. Brannan 43-167 1996 $225.00

FRASER, CLAUD LOVAT 1890-1921   Designs (1890-1921). London: Morland Press, 1922. 1st edition; limited edition, 21/25 copies (of an edition of 32 copies); large 4to; 25 leaves; drawings printed on rectos of 24 leaves and titlepage border, light foxing, mainly to prelims and final few leaves, original quarter fawn linen, bright yellow boards printed in black on front cover, corners trifle rubbed, untrimmed, good. Rare. Blackwell's B112-110 1996 £200.00

FRASER, CLAUD LOVAT 1890-1921   Five New Poems. London: printed by A. T. Stevens for Flying Fame, 1913. drawings by Claud Lovat Fraser, all colored by hand, grey wrappers with hand colored drawings to both covers, strengthened at fold, else very fresh copy. Millard 75.   Barbara Stone 70-96 1996 £55.00

FRASER, CLAUD LOVAT 1890-1921   Sixty-Three Unpublished Designs. London: printed at the Curwen Press for the First Edition Club, 1924. 1st edition; 87/50 copies; foolscap 8vo; pages xii, 63; printed on yellow dyed Ingres handmade paper, 63 drawings, one repeated on titlepage; original quarter black cloth, gilt lettered lightly faded backstrip, white boards with overall purple, orange and black design by Lovat Fraser; untrimmed, good; bookplate of Robert Arundel Hudson and bookticket of Raymond Lister.   Blackwell's B112-111 1996 £70.00

FRASER, DUNCAN   Newton's Interpolation Forumlas. London: 1927. Reprinted from Journal Inst. Actuaries 1918-27. 95 pages; 5 folding facsimiles, digrams; presentation copy to members attending the 8th International Congress of Actuaries. Scarce. Babson 212.   Graham Weiner C2-304 1996 £50.00

FRASER, JAMES   The History of Nadir Shah, Formerly Called Thamas Kuli Khan, the Present Emperor of Persia. London: by W. Strahan and sold by G. Strahan and J. Brotherton... 1742. 1st edition; 8vo; folding frontispiece, folding map; contemporary mottled calf, gilt, spine gilt, slight wear to ends of spine; fine. Blackmer 629.   Ximenes 108-149 1996 $500.00

FRASER, JAMES   The History of Nadir Shah, Formerly Called Thamas Kuli Khan, the Present Emperor of Persia. London: printed for A. Millar, 1742. 2nd edition; 8vo; folding frontispiece, folding map; contemporary mottled calf, gilt, spine gilt, slight rubbing; fine. cf. Blackmer 629. Ximenes 108-150 1996 $250.00

FRASER, JAMES H.   John Anderson and the Pickering Press. Madison: Fairleigh Dickinson University Library, 1980. Limited to 90 copies; quarto; 19 pages; printed in two colors; wood engravings by John De Pol; laid in is greeting from De Pol, limited to 100 copies, with signed wood engraving by him; brown printed wrappers; very fine. Bromer Booksellers 87-53 1996 $150.00

FRASER, JAMES H.   The Paste Papers of the Golden Hind Press. Florham-Madison: Fairleigh Dickinson University Library, 1983. Limited to 70 copies, signed by papermaker, Delight Rushmore Lewis; tall quarto; 17 pages, (10)ff; printed at the Tideline Press on Fabriano paper and illustrated with 17 tipped in samples of the original paste papers used on Golden Hind Press Publications from the 1920's and 30's; cloth backed boards; mint.   Bromer Booksellers 90-48 1996 $350.00

THE FRAUDS and Abuses of Coal-Dealers Detected and Exposed; in a Letter to an Alderman of London. London: M. Cooper, 1747. 3rd edition; 33 pages; recent marbled wrappers; nice. Hanson 5774; Kress 4704 citing first edition of 1744.   C. R. Johnson 37-12 1996 £75.00

FREDERICK, J. L.   Ben Holiday - the Stagecoach King. Glendale: 1940. 1st edition; 334 pages; illustrations, folding map; cloth, nice. 6 Guns 762. T. A. Swinford 49-391 1996 $250.00

FREE, JOHN   Tyrocinium Geographicum Londoninense, or the London Geography, Consisting of Dr. Free's Short Lectures... London: printed for the author, 1789. 1st edition; 12mo; 2 parts in 1; 10 page list of subscribers, diagrams in text, 3 pages ads at end, contemporary half calf, rebacked, label.   Anthony Laywood 108-63 1996 £125.00

FREEDBERG, SYDNEY J.   Parmigianino, His Works in Painting. Cambridge: Harvard University Press, 1950. 1st edition; 8vo; xx, 265, (3) pages, 167 illustrations on plates; signature, else very good.   The Bookpress 75-446 1996 $185.00

FREELAND, ROBERT   The Soap Maker's Private Manual. Philadelphia: 1876. 314 pages; 25 figures, photo tipped in as frontispiece; full leather, wear and rubbing at extremities, rear clasp lacking.   Bookworm & Silverfish 280-77 1996 $225.00

FREEMAN, DOUGLAS SOUTHALL   R. E. Lee A Biography. New York: Charles Scribner's Sons, 1936. 1st printing of the Pulitzer Prize edition; 4 volumes; elaborate gilt on spine not found on later printings, original cloth, very good to ner fine set. Harwell In Tall Cotton 62; Dornbusch II 2930; Howes F350; Nevins II 57   McGowan Book Co.   65-31   1996 $275.00

FREEMAN, DOUGLAS SOUTHALL   Robert E. Lee, a Biography. New York: 1936. 1st state of the Pulitzer edition; 4 volumes, bound in CSA grey w/geometrical gilt and stars enhancing the gilt on red labels, very good set with opaque spot on top of front cvoer volume 1, shelf backs glisten.   Bookworm & Silverfish   280-42   1996 $185.00

FREEMAN, E. A.   Historical Essays. London: Macmillan, 1886-92. Demy 8vo; 4 volumes; original cloth.   Howes Bookshop   265-380   1996   £75.00

FREEMAN, E. A.   The History of the Norman Conquest of England, Its Causes and Its Results. London: Oxford University Press, 1877-75-79. 3rd edition of volumes I-II, 2nd edition of volumes III-IV, sole edition of volumes V-VI. 8vo; 6 volumes; original cloth, withdrawn from library with stamp on titles, ticket inside front covers, press mark on spines, still very good, sound set.   Howes Bookshop   265-381   1996   £150.00

FREEMAN, E. A.   The History of Sicily from the Earliest Times (to the Death of Agathokles, 289 B.C.). London: Oxford University Press, 1891-94. Original edition; large 8vo; 4 volumes; 21 maps and plates, some folding; original maroon cloth; slight chafing of spines, but good set; presentation to Girton College by Mrs. Henry Sidgwick, with college's neat ownership (now deaccessioned), slight chafing of spines, but good set.   Howes Bookshop   265-382   1996   £120.00

FREEMAN, JAMES W.   Prose and Poetry of the Live Stock Industry of the United States. New York: Antiquarian Press, 1959. Reprint of the 1905 edition, limited to 550 copies; thick quarto; 757 pages, numerous illustrations from photos, old prints, etc; half cowhide and gilt stamped buckram, spine lettered in gilt, very fine with publisher's slipcase. Adams herd 844; Howes P636; Six Guns 764; Reese Six Score 41.   Argonaut Book Shop   113-259   1996 $350.00

FREEMAN, SAMUEL   The Probate Auxiliary; or, a Director and Assistant to Probate Courts, Executors, Administrators and Guardians. Portland: Benjamin Titcomb, Jun, 1793. 1st edition; 12mo; 11, (1), 156, 3 pages; old calf, front cover loose, small piece torn from top margin of title leaf. Evans 25511; Noyes 44.   M & S Rare Books   60-360   1996 $175.00

FREEMAN, SARAH   Medals Relating to Medicine and Allied Sciences in the Numismatic Collection of the Johns Hopkins University. Baltimore: 1964. 1st edition; 430 pages, plus 32 plates; original binding.   W. Bruce Fye   71-716   1996 $200.00

FREEMAN, WALTER JACKSON   Psychosurgery: Intelligence, Emotion and Social Behavior Following Prefrontal Lobotomy for Mental Disorder. Springfield: Charles C. Thomas Pub., 1950. 2nd revised edition; tall 8vo; (xxx), 598, (4) pages, 162 text figures, 21 tables; blue cloth.   John Gach   150-160   1996 $200.00

FREIBURG. LAWS, STATUTES, ETC.   (Freiburg im Breisgau). Nuwe Stattrechten und Statuten der Loblichen Statt Fryburg im Pryssgow Gelegen. Colophon: Basel: Adam Petri, 1520. 1st edition; folio; 2 splendid woodcuts by Hans Holbein the younger, large folding genealogical plate (clean tear without loss), early paper boards (bit worn), cloth folding case, fine, fresh copy.   Ximenes   109-158   1996 $6,000.00

FREIND, JOHN   Emmenologia: Written, in Latin...Translated Into English by Thomas Dale, M.D. London: T. Cox, 1729. 1st edition in English; 8vo; (xvi), 216, (viii) pages; contemporary calf, gilt ruled, label, ad leaf before title and another at end, engraved vignette on titlepage, extremities little worn, joints cracked, internally clean.   Robert Clark   38-195   1996   £160.00

FRELINGHUYSEN, ALICE COONEY   Splendid Legacy, the Havemeyer Collection at the Metropolitan Museum of Art, New York. New York: Metropolitan Museum of Art, 1993. 31 x 24 cm; xvi, 415 pages, 800 illustrations, including 176 in full color;   Rainsford   A54-306   1996   £65.00

FREMONT, JOHN CHARLES 1813-1890   Defense of Lieut. Colonel Fremont, Before the Court Martial. N.P.: 1848. 1st edition; cover title, sewn; fine, laid in half morocco slipcase. Howes F365.   Michael D. Heaston   23-148   1996 $500.00

FREMONT, JOHN CHARLES 1813-1890   Memoirs of My Life... Chicago & New York: Belford, Clarke & Co., 1887. 1st edition; thick quarto; xix, (1), 655 pages; frontispiece, 81 plate,s 7 maps; original pictorial cloth, stamped in black, silver, gold and red; very light wear to spine ends, minimal rubbing to extremities; overall fine.   Argonaut Book Shop   113-261   1996 $900.00

FREMONT, JOHN CHARLES 1813-1890   Narrative of the Exploring Expedition to the Rocky Mountains in the Year 1842 and to Oregon and North California in the Years 1843-44. Washington: 1845. 2nd edition; 278 pages; bound in cloth, very good; Reprint Howes F370; Wagner Camp 115; Graff 1436 in Cowan.   T. A. Swinford   49-393   1996 $125.00

FRENCH, A. D. WELD   County Records of the Surnames of Francus, Francis, French, in England 1100-1350. Boston: 1896. Limited to 525 numbered copies; thick 8vo; 610 pages; original cloth.   Howes Bookshop   265-1780   1996   £55.00

FRENCH, JAMES WEIR   Machine Tools Commonly Employed in Modern Engineering Workshops. London: Gresham Pub. Co., 1911. Folio; 2 volumes; pages xxxv, 170; xiv, 222, erratum slip: 10 colored plates, each with moveable colored overlays, 459 text illustrations from photos; original cloth, gilt, slight wear to corners and joints, but bindings and inside joints strong and internally very good to nice.   James Fenning   133-120   1996   £165.00

FRENCH-SHELDON, M., MRS.   Sultan to Sultan. London: 1892, Many photo illustrations and line drawings; ex-library with single stamp on verso title, few blindstamps on prelims, title has slight tear and is bit soiled, rebound in maroon buckram. scarce.   David Grayling   J95Biggame-90   1996   £120.00

FREUD, SIGMUND 1856-1939   The Case of the Wolf-Man: from the History of an Infantile Neurosis. Arion Press, 1993. One of 250 copies, signed by artist; 12 1/4 x 10 inches; 114 pages, (1) leaf (colophon); title vignette, etched frontispiece, 10 other exrpessive etched or woodcut plates, some in color, by Jim Dine; printed on French mould made paper; hard grain black leather spine, pictorial cloth boards, publisher's cloth and paper slipcase.   Phillip J. Pirages   33-18   1996 $1,800.00

FREUD, SIGMUND 1856-1939   Collected Papers. New York: & London: 1924-34. Small 4to; volumes 1-4, cloth, rubbed.   Argosy   810-192   1996 $125.00

FREUD, SIGMUND 1856-1939   Collected Papers. London: Hogarth Press and Inst. of Psychoanalysis, 1953-6. Volumes 1-5;   Argosy   810-191   1996 $150.00

FREUD, SIGMUND 1856-1939   Die Traumdeutung. Leipzig und Wien: Franz Deuticke, 1900, actually issued Nov. 4th, 1899. 1st edition; 8vo; (ii), 371, (5) pages; early pebbled black cloth with marbled endpapers, housed in cloth drop box in morocco backed slipcase, slight staining to front cover, near fine. Grinstein 10614; Norman Cat. F33; Norman Freud Cat. 23; PMM 389.   John Gach   150-163   1996 $12,500.00

FREUD, SIGMUND 1856-1939   The Interpretation of Dreams. New York: Macmillan Co., 1913. 1st edition in English; 1st issue with integral titlepage. 8vo; (xiv), 510, (2) pages; printed straight grained blue cloth, cloth along rear joint bubbled, very good to fine with slight rubbing to edges, scarce.   John Gach   150-161   1996 $750.00

FREUD, SIGMUND 1856-1939   Introductory Lectures on Psycho-Analysis: a Course of Twenty-Eight Lectures Delivered at the University of London. London: Allen & Unwin, 1929. Revised edition; 8vo; frontispiece, 4 pages of publisher's ads at end; three quarter gilt stamped dark blue morocco over matching cloth, spines with raised bands, occasional underlining and margin annotations in pencil; very good.   George J. Houle   68-51   1996 $200.00

FREVILLE, ANNE FRANCOIS JOACHIM DE   Histoire des Nouvelles Decouvertes Faites dans la Mer du Sud en 1767. Paris: De Hansy le Jeune, 1774. 1st edition; 8vo; 2 volumes; large folding engraved chart by Robert de Vaugondy; half titles, errata leaf, 4 pages approbation leaves; contemporary half calf, gilt, morocco labels, vellum covered boards, armorial bookplates; some warping of cvoers, but very fine, scarce. Beddie 720; O'Reilly & Reitman 100; Kropelien 468; Polak 3644.   Trebizond   39-100   1996 $1,200.00

FREYTAG, GUSTAV   Pictures of German Life in the XVth, XVIth and XVIIth Centuries. London: Chapman and Hall, 1862. 8vo; 2 volumes; vii, 311, vii, 388 pages, name on endpaper, spine faded to tan with touch of rubbing at ends, otherwise fine set.   David Mason   71-81   1996 $240.00

FREZIER, AMEDEE FRANCOIS   A Voyage to the South-Sea and Along the Coasts of Chili and Peru in the Years 1712, 1713, and 1714. London: for Jonah Bowyer, 1717. 1st edition in English; 4to; (12), 335, (9) pages; 37 maps and plates; modern marbled boards, white paper covered spine, paper label, one small repair on verso of title; nice in modern binding. European Americana 717/66; Borba de Moraes I 281; Hill p. 115. Joseph J. Felcone 64-21 1996 $1,200.00

FRICKER, KARL   The Antarctic Regions. New York: Swan Sonnenschein/Macmillan, 1900. 1st edition in English; 8vo; xii, folding map, 292 pages; maroon cloth, ex-library with stamps, card pocket, covers badly faded; scarce. Spence 485.   Parmer Books Nat/Hist-061242 1996 $110.00

FRIEDENWALD, HARRY   The Jews and Medicine, Essays. Baltimore: 1944-46. 1st edition; 2 volumes, 817 pages; original binding, very fine; rare.   W. Bruce Fye 71-729 1996 $250.00

FRIEDMAN, I. K.   The Radical. New York: Appleton, 1907. 1st edition; original cloth, fine.   Beasley Books 82-313 1996 $175.00

FRIEDMANN, H.   Birds Collected by the Childs Frick Expedition to Ethiopia and Kenya Colony. U.S.A.: 1930/37. 2 volumes, each volume over 500 pages; colored frontispieces, many photos illustrations; original wrappers, mainly unopened; near fine, scarce.   David A.H. Grayling MY95Orn-134 1996 £55.00

FRIEDRICH II, EMPEROR OF GERMANY 1194-1250   The Art of Falconry. U.S.A.: 1969. Large thick 8vo; numerous plates and text illustrations, some colored; 747 pages; mint in dust jacket.   David A.H. Grayling MY95Orn-33 1996 £75.00

FRIEL, BRIAN   The Gold in the Sea. Stories. London: Victor Gollancz, 1966. 1st edition; small 8vo; boards, dust jacket, fine.   James S. Jaffe 34-164 1996 $150.00

FRIENDLY Advice to Irish Mothers, on Training Their Children. Armagh: John M'Watters, English St. 1842. 1st edition; 12mo; 116 pages; original binding, printed paper, spine label, some minor fingering, label little worn at edges and wanting blank flyleaf, otherwise very good. Neat signature of Anna (?) Hawell, Dec. 1842.   James Fenning 133-96 1996 £225.00

FRIENDS, SOCIETY OF   Transactions of the Central Relief Committee During the Famine in Ireland. 1846 and 1847. 1852. 1st edition; 8vo; xxiii, 481 pages; half leather; presentation copy from Committee to W. E. Forster, bound for him.   C. P. Hyland 216-242 1996 £170.00

FRIES, B.   A History of Scandinavian Fishes. Stockholm: 1892-95. 2nd edition; 4to; 3 volumes; pages 1240, 305 text figures and atlas of 1 plain and 54 colored plates; half morocco, very scarce, slight creasing of text at beginning of volume 1, but good.   Wheldon & Wesley 207-35 1996 £575.00

FRINK, MAURICE W.   When Grass Was King. Boulder: University of Colorado Press, 1956. 1st edition; one of 1500 numbered copies; xv, 465 pages, 35 illustrations, map endpapers; fine in dust jacket; presentation inscription signed by Agnes Wright Spring. Adams 853; Reese Six Score 45; Six Guns 777.   Argonaut Book Shop 113-267 1996 $150.00

FRISCH, MAX   Three Plays. London: Methuen, 1962. 1st British edition; slight bump to head of spine and occasional pencil scoring to text, else near fine in lightly soiled dust jacket; signed by author. Lame Duck Books 19-194 1996 $175.00

FRISCH, MAX   A Wilderness of Mirrors. New York: Random House, 1966. 1st edition; near fine in very good+, mildly spine darkened dust jacket, with short edge tear to rear panel; signed by author, uncommon thus.   Lame Duck Books 19-195 1996 $200.00

FRISCH, TERESA G.   The Excavations at Dura-Europos. Final Report IV. Part IV: The Bronze Objects, Fascicule 1: Pierced Bronzes, Enameled Bronzes and Fibulae. New Haven: Yale University Press, 1949. large 4to; viii, 69 pages, 14 figures, 16 plates; stiff wrappers.   Archaeologia Luxor-3276 1996 $125.00

FRISWOLD, CARROLL   The Killing of Chief Crazy Horse. Glendale: 1976. Limited to 300 copies; 8vo; 152 pages; illustrations; fine. Edward Morrill 369-525 1996 $100.00

FRITH, FRANCIS   Egypt and Palestine. London: James S. Virtue, City Road and Ivy Lane, 1858. 1st edition; folio; 2 volumes; pages (vi) + 37 albumen photograph plates and (iv), + 39 albumen photo plates, page of text with each photograph; contemporary green half morocco, cloth boards with gilt lettering, decorative gilt spine with raised bands, all edges gilt; spine and corners rubbed, upper joints to spine of volume I cracked, spotting throughout, mostly marginal, affecting the photos in only a few cases, otherwise good set. Ibrahim-Hilmy 249; Blackmer 1942.   Sotheran PN32-164 1996 £2,900.00

FRITH, FRANCIS   Photographs of the Holyland... London: Glasgow: and Edinburgh: William Mackenzie 1863. Folio; 4 volumes, 148 albumen photos, each approximately 6 1/2 x 9 inches, mounted, each volume containing 37 photos; most signed in negative and with occasional date 1857; photos are in outstanding bright condition with rich tones; half green morocco gilt, minor wear and spotting to bindings. Gorgeous set. 19th Century Shop 39- 1996 $28,500.00

FRITSCHE, MARCUS   Meteorum, hoc est Impressionum Aerearum et Mirabilium Naturum Operum, Loci Frere Omnes. Nuremberg: J. Montanus & U. Neuber, 1563. 2nd edition; 8vo; 3 works in 1 volume, (27), 180, (130) leaves, several early ownership inscriptions on titlepage, short inner margins, Harvard duplicate with small stamp on verso of titlepage; modern calf in antique style; Adams F1054; BM STC German p. 325; Zinner 2305;   Jeffrey D. Mancevice 20-33 1996 $875.00

FROHLICH-BUME, L.   Ingres. His Life and Art. London: 1926. 4to; viii, 66 pages; frontispiece, 79 photogravure or collotype plates; buckram, gilt, top edge gilt.   Rainsford A54-334 1996 £95.00

FROISSART, JEAN   Historiarum Opus Omne. Paris: ex off. Simonis Colinae, 1537. 1st edition thus; 8vo; ff. (xvi), 115, (i), attractive Roman letter and white on black initials, printer's celebrated 'reaper of time' device on title, slightly dusty, 17th century calf, rebacked, schoalrly pencil notes on blank prelims; good copy. BM STC Fr. p. 189; Adams F1070; Renouard p. 279. Brunet II 1406-7.   A. Sokol XXV-41 1996 £375.00

FROMMER, HARVEY   New York City Baseball. The Last Golden Age: 1947-1957. New York: Macmillan, 1980. 1st edition; fine in near fine dust jacket; book signed by Willie Mays, Yogi Berra, Bobby Richardson, Duke snider, Phil Rizzuto, Cal Abrams, Johnny Mize and Eddie Stanky.   Bud Schweska 12-44 1996 $350.00

FROST, A. B.   Stuff and Nonsense. New York: Scribner, 1884. 1st edition; 4to; author's first book; illustrations; cloth backed pictorial boards somewhat soiled as are a number of interior pages; good, uncommon.   Captain's Bookshelf 38-84 1996 $150.00

FROST, CHARLES   Notices Relative to the Early History of the Town and Port of Hull. London: 1827. 1st edition; 4to; xvi, 150, 58 pages, 7 plates, 2 pedigrees, green paper, uncut, new black buckram, very good, scarce.   K Books 442-231 1996 £150.00

FROST, JOHN   Pictorial History of Mexico and the Mexican War. Philadelphia: Thomas Cowperthwait and Co. for James A. Bill, 1849. 640 pages; 500 engravings and several multi-color lithographic plates; original leather binding little scuffed, some staining and foxing to text, but overall very good.   Blue River Books 9-145 1996 $225.00

FROST, ROBERT LEE 1874-1963   A Boy's Will. New York: Henry Holt, 1915. 1st American edition; owner name to front pastedown, spine gilt faded with slight fraying of cloth at extremities, overall very good, without dust jacket.   Ken Lopez 74-143 1996 $375.00

FROST, ROBERT LEE 1874-1963   Collected Poems. New York: Random House, 1930. 1st edition; limited to 1000 copies, tall 8vo; original buckram, leather label on spine; exceptionally fine.   James S. Jaffe 34-165 1996 $850.00

FROST, ROBERT LEE 1874-1963   The Guardeen. Los Angeles: Ward Ritchie, 1943. 1st edition; limited to 96 copies; quarto; (4) pages; printed wrappers; very fine. Crane B11; Blumenthal Frost & His Printers p. 34. Bromer Booksellers 90-40 1996 $500.00

FROST, ROBERT LEE 1874-1963   The Lovely Shall Be Choosers. New York: Random House, 1929. One of 475 copies; wrappers, very small mark on upper cover, fine.   Ulysses 39-213 1996 £60.00

FROST, ROBERT LEE 1874-1963   A Masque of Reason. New York: Henry Holt, 1945. 1st edition; one of 800 specially bound and numbered copies, signed by author; moderately worn slipcase; fine.   Captain's Bookshelf 38-85 1996 $300.00

FROST, ROBERT LEE 1874-1963   A Masque of Reason. New York: Holt, 1945. 1st edition; blue cloth with slightly chipped dust jacket; nice copy; inscribed by author. Crane A27.1.   Bromer Booksellers 90-41 1996 $525.00

FROST, ROBERT LEE 1874-1963   Mountain Interval. New York: Holt, 1924. 2nd edition; spine gilt largely rubbed away, still about very good without dust jacket; inscribed by author; with attractive bookplate of Leslie Taylor.   Ken Lopez 74-146 1996 $400.00

FROST, ROBERT LEE 1874-1963   New Hampshire. Hanover: New Dresden Press, 1955. 1st separate edition; limited to 750 copies; signed by Frost; cloth backed boards; very fine.   Bromer Booksellers 90-42 1996 $350.00

FROST, ROBERT LEE 1874-1963   North of Boston. New York: Holt, 1915. Later printing of second edition; some rubbing and fraying to spine, overall very good, without dust jacket; remarkable copy; inscribed by author for Mrs. Bruce Taylor, with poem "Reluctance" 24 lines long in author's hand and initilled by him, and Misgining" which consists of 16 lines and is also initialled by author.   Ken Lopez 74-144 1996 $650.00

FROST, ROBERT LEE 1874-1963   North of Boston. New York: Holt, 1926. Later edition; good copy, lacking the dust jacket, but again with lengthy and thoughtful inscription from author to Lesley Taylor in 1927; owner's attractive bookplate and offsetting to the first page of text from an additional Frost poem, on newsprint, laid in. Spine cloth on rear joint sliced for 2 inches from base, and some wear to extremities and corners.   Ken Lopez 74-145 1996 $450.00

FROST, ROBERT LEE 1874-1963   A Witness Tree. New York: printed by the Spiral Press, 1942. Limited edition, 735 numbered copies, signed by author; frontispiece, uncut, patterned boards, gilt spine; fine in near fine box.   Polyanthos 22-353 1996 $250.00

FROST, THOMAS   Circus Life and Circus Celebrities. London: Chatto & Windus, 1881. New edition; original decorataive cloth, dull, spine ends frayed, some marginalia. Toole Stott 295;   Dramatis Personae 37-67 1996 $150.00

FROST, THOMAS   The Old Showman and the Old London Fairs. London: Tinsley, 1875. 2nd edition; 8vo; pages xii, 388; blue pictorial cloth, worn, starting, lacks free endpapers.   Marlborough 162-141 1996 £60.00

FROST, THOMAS   The Secret Societies of the European Revolution, 1776-1876. London: 1876. 1st edition; 8vo; 2 volumes, xv, 300, 338 pages; cloth, spine cloth dried and cracked, partly unopened, very good. C. P. Hyland 216-243 1996 £110.00

FRY, CHRISTOPHER   Venus Observed. London: 1950. 1st edition; programme cast list laid in; very good in torn dust jacket; signed by the entire cast headed by Laurence Olivier and Denholm Elliott & with piece of paper laid in a foot of signed cast page from Christopher Fry. Words Etcetera 94-444 1996 £250.00

FRY, EDMUND   Pantographia: Containing Accurate Copies of all the Known Alaphabets in the World... London: printed by Cooper & Wilson for John & Arthur Arch, &c., 1799. Folio; uncut, with slight dusting of edges and handsomely rebound in half calf, marbled boards, red label, very good. Signed at head of title by John White, perhaps one of the booksellers in imprint. Alston III 862.   Jarndyce 103-245 1996 £350.00

FRY, ROGER ELIOT 1866-1934   A Sampler of Castile. London: Hogarth Press, 1923. One of 550 numbered copies; quarto; 16 black and white plates by author; cloth backed decorated paper boards, covers slightly bowed, free endpapers partially browned, prelim edges and endpapers spotted, very good in torn, creased and chipped, rubbed and dusty, internally repaired dust jacket, which repeats cover design, faded at spine and edges; From the library of Ian Parsons, who worked at Hogarth Press and inherited Leonard Woolf's library.   Ulysses 39-214 1996 £395.00

FRYE, F. L.   Biomedical and Surgical Aspects of Captive Reptile Husbandry. Melbourne: 1991. 2nd edition; royal 8vo; 2 volumes; 712 pages, over 1850 color photos and 180 radiographs; cloth.   Wheldon & Wesley 207-922 1996 £189.00

FRYER, GEORGE   The Poetry of Various Glees, Songs, &c. as Performed at the Harmonists. London: printed at the Philanthropic Reform, 1798. 1st edition; 8vo; frontispiece; contemporary calf, rubbed, Bentley, Blake Books p. 510.   Anthony Laywood 108-64 1996 £60.00

FRYER, JOHN   A New Account of East India and Persia Being Nine Years' Travels. 1672-1681. London: Hakluyt Society, 1909/12/15. 8vo; 3 volumes, xxxviii, 11., 353 pages, 35 pages, 371 pages, viii, 1 l., 271 pages, index, one illustration; blue cloth, paper aged, touch of shelfwear, else very good, unopened set.   Parmer Books O39Nautica-039260 1996 $350.00

FRYER, MARY ANN   John Fryer of the Bounty. Waltham St. Lawrence: Golden Cockerel Press, 1939. 1st edition; 78/300 copies; small folio; pages 53, (1); printed on Arnold's handmade paper, signed by author and artist; 12 wood engravings, 3 full page by Averil Mackenzie-Grieve, included is a greeting card printed at the Golden Cockerel Press, an illustration by Averil Mackenzie-Grieve, signed and inscribed by her; original mid-blue canvas, backstrip lettering and Mackenzie-Grieve design on front cover, all gilt blocked, endpapers lightly foxed, top edge gilt, others untrimmed, original tissue jacket; excellent. Blackwell's B112-125 1996 £300.00

FUENTES, CARLOS   Aura. New York: FSG, 1965. 1st edition; uncommon; fine in very near fine dust jacket, very attractive copy, scarce.   Ken Lopez 74-149 1996 $125.00

FUENTES, CARLOS   Terra Nostra. New York: Farrar Straus Giroux, 1976. 1st U.S. edition; mauve cloth spine, orange paper covered boards, fine in dust jacket with short, creased tear to rear panel, else about fine, inscribed by author.   Orpheus Books 17-23 1996 $125.00

FUGITIVES. An Anthology of Verse. New York: Harcourt, Brace & Co., 1928. 1st edition; 8vo; original cloth backed decorated boards, dust jacket, former owner's stamp on front free endpaper, otherwise fine in jacket which is sunned along spine and very slightly rubbed, with one short half inch closed tear; superior copy of a book seldom seen in jacket.   James S. Jaffe 34-7 1996 $1,500.00

FUJIWARA, KANESUKE   The Lady Who Loved Insects. London: Blackamore Press, 1929. One of 550 numbered copies; 8vo; 4 dryppoints by Hermine David; cream silk over boards, plates faintly offset as usual, but very nice, fresh copy.   Bertram Rota 272-102 1996 £75.00

A FULL and Correct Account of the State Trials, held at the Old Bailey...Containing the Whole of the Evidence...With a Copious and Correct Detail of the Various Arrangements Made to...Effect a Revolution in this Country. London: printed and published by Grove & Co., 1, Leicester Square, 1820. 4th edition; modern quarter black morocco over marbled boards, quite pretty.   Meyer Boswell SL26-40 1996 $250.00

A FULL Relation Concerning the Wonderful and Wholesome Fountain. At First Discovered in Germany, Two Miles from the City of Halberstadt, by a Certain Youth Upon the Fifth of March 1646, as He Was Coming from Schoole. London: printed by T. W. for Joshua Kirton, 1646. 4to: (2), 21, (1) pages; neatly rebound in quarter calf, marbled boards; excellent copy, uncut on fore and lower edges; ex-libris of John Crerar, with neat perforation stamp on titlepage and small neat de-accession stamp on reverse. Wing F2355; Krivatsy 4462.   C. R. Johnson 37-80 1996 £450.00

A FULL Relation Concerning the Wonderfull and Wholsome Fountain At First Discovered in Germany, Two Miles from the City of Halberstadt, by a Certaine Youth Upon the Fifth of March 1646 as He Was Comming from Schoole. London: printed by T. W. for Joshua Kirton, 1646. 1st edition; 4to; title within woodcut border, perforation stamp on title and accession number on lower blank margin of A2, 21 pages; disbound. Wing F2355; Krivatsy 4462.   Anthony Laywood 108-8 1996 £185.00

FULLARTON, WILLIAM   A View of the English Interests in India, and an Account of the Military Operations in the Southern Parts of the Peninsula, During the Campaigns of 1782, 1783, and 1784. London: printed for T. Cadell and W. Creech, Edinburgh, 1787. 1st edition; 8vo; folding plate, contemporary mottled calf, spine gilt, label, nice. Anthony Laywood 108-65 1996 £275.00

FULLER, ANDREW S.   The Grape Culturist... New York: printed for the author by Davies & Kent, 1864. 1st edition; 8vo; 262 pages + ad; illustrations; faded and little soiled brown cloth, otherwise a nice, clean copy.   Second Life Books 103-83 1996 $125.00

FULLER, HENRY CLAY   Adventures of Bill Longley: Captured by Sheriff Milton Mast and Deputy Bill Burrows, near Keatchie, Louisiana in 1877 and Was Executed at Giddings, Texas, 1878. Nacogdoches: n.d. 1st edition; original wrappers, light overall wear, otherwise fine.   Hermitage SP95-704 1996 $150.00

FULLER, HENRY CLAY   "A Texas Sheriff". A Vivid and Accurate Account of Some of the Most Notorious Murder Cases and Feuds in the History of East Texas... Nacogdoches: Baker Printing Co., 1931. 1st edition; illustrations, title printed in black on front cover; stapled as issued, original orange pictorial wrappers; minor chipping; fine copy for this work, usually found very worn. Adams Six Guns 784.   Michael D. Heaston 23-150 1996 $150.00

FULLER, RONALD   The Work of Rex Whistler. London: Batsford, 1960. 1st edition; 600 copies printed; 4to; pages xxiv, 112 illustrations on 68 pages, (ii), 122; 9 of the illustrations are in color, numerous other illustrations in text; original green buckram, decorated in gilt, with dust jacket, lower cover little marked, dust jacket slightly frayed, very good. Loosely inserted autograph letter from Laurence Whistler to artist John Goodall.   Sotheran PN32-66 1996 £498.00

FULLER, SAMUEL   Practical Astronomy, in the Description and Use of Both Globes, Orrery and Telescopes... Dublin: 1732. x, 237, (1) pages, 10 folding plates; old calf very worn; plate IV defective, plate 1 torn at fold without loss, Q3 torn with very slight loss, title grubby, crudely tipped onto dedication leaf and with unsightly erasure of owner's name, endpapers torn and stuck down with heavy contemporary annotation, some other spots and stains, overall rather poor and well used copy of a rare book.   Graham Weiner C2-22 1996 £50.00

FULLER, THOMAS 1608-1661   The Church History of Britain...Until the Year 1648. London: printed for John Williams, 1656. Thick folio; folding plan, 4 engraved plates, with blank leaves Rr4, Hhhh2 and 6C4; strongly bound in recent cloth, light old waterstain throughout, neat repair to tear without loss in title and final leaf (verso blank), remargined and neatly mounted, strongly bound in recent cloth, very good. Wing F2417. James Fenning 133-122 1996 £245.00

FULOP-MILLER, RENE   The Russian Theatre. London: George Harrap & Co., 1930. Small folio; pages 136, 405 plates; top edge gilt, decorative publisher's cloth; good, bright copy.   Sotheran PN32-185 1996 £550.00

FULTON, JOHN F.   Aviation Medicine In its Preventive Aspects, a Historical Survey. London: 1948. 1st edition; original binding. Very scarce. GM 2138.   W. Bruce Fye 71-742 1996 $150.00

FULTON, JOHN F.   A Bibliographical Study of the Galvani and the Aldini Writings on Animal Electricity. 1936. Offprint; 39 pages; wrappers. W. Bruce Fye 71-775 1996 $100.00

FULTON, JOHN F.   A Bibliography of the Honourable Robert Boyle. N.P.: n.d. Early galley copy of the Oxford University Press 1932 edition; 8vo; 172 pages; uncut, bound in plain blue linen, heavily annotated in the hand of Hugh MacDonald Sinclair, significant collector of Boyle; choice association, with TLS from Fulton to Sinclair.   James Tait Goodrich K40-36 1996 $795.00

FULTON, JOHN F.   Selected Readings in the History of Physiology. Springfield: 1930. 1st edition; 317 pages; original binding. GM 1588.3. (Springfield 1966).   W. Bruce Fye 71-753 1996 $100.00

FULTON, JOHN F.   Sir Kenelm Digby. Writer, Bibliophile and Protagonist of William Harvey. New York: Peter & Katharine Olvier, 1937. Limited edition of 300 copies; 8vo; 75 pages; original binding; author's presentation copy with presentation to Hubert Norman, with TLS from Fulton to Norman. Nice association item.   James Tait Goodrich K40-134 1996 $395.00

FUN at the Circus. London: ca. 1893. Octavo; (16) pages; 6 moving pictures of circus performers, bright color lithographs show performers in the midst of action and the reader may move the whole picture from side to side, extremities lightly rubbed, original color printed boards, extremities lightly rubbed, inner hinges repaired, still very bright, near fine, with all movable parts intact and working. Whitton p. 100. Bromer Booksellers 87-155 1996 $575.00

FUN Upon Fun, or the Humours of a Fair. Giving a Description of the Curious Amusements in Early Life; Also an Account of a Mountebank Doctor and His Merry Andrew. Glasgow: J. Lumsden, ca. 1810-15. 32mo 47 pages; 8 leaves of wood engravings printed in red and 3 vignettes ascribed by Hugo to Thomas Bewick; printed wrappers; one corner torn at end of chapbook, not affecting text or cuts, else nice. Roscoe and Brimmell 74; Hugo 318.   Bromer Booksellers 90-86 1996 $385.00

FURHANGE, MAGUY   Carzou: Engraver and Lithographer. Nice: editions d'Art de Francony, 1971. Limited edition; folio; 215 pages; 3 original lithographs, 1 in color, numerous plates and illustrations, mostly in color; cloth, dust jacket.   Brannan 43-110 1996 $195.00

FURNESS, C. E.   Land for Emigrants. Lake Superior & Mississippi Railroad. St. Paul to Duluth, Minn. Saint Paul: Press Printing Co., 1873. 1st edition; 8 pages; folding map; original printed grey wrappers; fine. Michael D. Heaston 23-245 1996 $500.00

FURNESS, WILLIAM   History of Penrith, from the Earliest Record to the Present Time. Penrith: William Furness, 1894. 1st edition; 8vo; pages viii, 376, frontispiece and numerous illustrations; little shaken, but very good; original cloth, gilt, spine lettering dulled, extremities trifle frayed. R.F.G. Hollett & Son 78-931 1996 £120.00

FURNISS, HARRY   Royal Academy Antics. London: 1890. 8vo; pages xi, 111, (5 ads); text illustrations; publisher's cloth backed boards. Marlborough 162-142 1996 £100.00

FURNIVAL, FREDERICK J.   Phillip Stubbe's Anatomy of the Abuses in England in Shakespere's Youth. A.D. 1583. London: for the New Shakespeare Society, 1877-82. 1st edition thus; large 8vo; 2 volumes; engraved plates, some folding, one colored, some text within decorative borders, illustrations in text; cloth, rubbed. LAR 263; Jaggard p. 655. Dramatis Personae 37-68 1996 $100.00

FURTHER Communications from the World of Spirits, on Subjects Highly Important to the Human Family. New York: Published for the Proprietor, 1861. 1st edition; 8vo; (2), 6, (5), 174 pages; original printed wrappers, 2 holes through inner margins, old library labels on title and front wrapper. NUC records 2 copies.   M & S Rare Books 60-413 1996 $150.00

FURTWANGLER, ADOLF   Sammulung Somzee: Antike Kunstdenkmaler. Munchen: F. Bruckman, 1897. Folio; text (ii), 80 pages, 104 illustrations, original cloth, spine taped and 43 plates loose in portfolio as issued, three quarter cloth, tap on flaps of portfolio.   Archaeologia Luxor-3351 1996 $1,500.00

G

GABLE, KATHLEEN   Clark Gable: a Personal Portrait. Englewood Cliffs: Prentice Hall, 1961. 1st edition; frontispiece, black and white photos, dust jacket (few nicks); very good. Signed and inscribed by author to columnist Sidney Skolsky.   George J. Houle 68-52 1996 $150.00

GABRIEL, RICHARD   A History of Military Medicine. Westport: 1992. 1st edition; 2 volumes, 247, 304 pages; original binding.   W. Bruce Fye 71-757 1996 $130.00

GABRIELSON, IRA N.   Birds of Alaska. Harrisburg/Washington: Stackpole Co./Wildlife Management Inst., 1959. Thick heavy 8vo; 922 pages; full color illustrations; very good in worn dust jacket.   Parmer Books Nat/Hist-051497 1996 $350.00

GABRIELSON, IRA N.   Birds of Alaska. Harrisburg/Washington: Stackpole Co./Wildlife Management Inst., 1959. Thick heavy 8vo; 922 pages; full color illustrations; spine faded, tipped in insert (review slip?) removed from front free endpaper, leaving a small residue of paper. Parmer Books Nat/Hist-071544 1996 $295.00

GABRIELSON, IRA N.   Birds of Alaska. Harrisburg/Washington: Stackpole Co./Wildlife Management Inst., 1959. Thick heavy 8vo; 922 pages; full color illustrations; very good in worn dust jacket. William Sheldon's copy.   Parmer Books Nat/Hist-091142 1996 $395.00

GACON, FRANCOIS   Discours Satiriques en Vers. Lyon or Paris: 1696. 1st edition; 12mo; 204 pages; engraved title; woodcut and typographic ornaments; contemporary calf, gilt, very good. Cior. 29963.   Bennett Gilbert LL29-40 1996 $700.00

GADBURY, JOHN   Ephemerides of the Clestial Motions for X Years: Beginning Anno 1672 (Where the industrious Mr. Wings Expired) and Ending An. 1681. London: John Macock for the Co. of Stationers, 1672. 1st edition; 4to; (193) leaves with titlepages for year year; as usual, without the license leaf which appeared beofre main title, which has printed only: "Licensed, Feb. 19. 167 1/2. Roger L'Estrange" (photo copy laid in); contemporary calf, rebacked. Houzeau-Lancaster 15296. Jeffrey D. Mancevice 20-34 1996 $575.00

GADBURY, JOHN   Ephemerides of the Celestial Motions and Aspects, Eclipses of the Luminaries &c. for XX Years. London: J. Macock for the Co. of Stationers, 1680. 1st edition; 4to; (292) leaves with titlepages for each year; main title printed in red and black; later calf, rebacked; fine. Houzeau Lancaster 15296; not in Crawford Lib. or Roller & Goodman. Jeffrey D. Mancevice 20-35 1996 $575.00

GADDIS, WILLIAM   A Frolic of His Own. London: Viking, 1994. 1st U.K. edition; 586 pages; black paper covered boards, signed by author and dated June 1994.   Orpheus Books 17-144 1996 $175.00

GADDIS, WILLIAM   A Frolic of His Own. London: Viking, 1994. 1st British edition; fine in dust jacket, signed by author.   Lame Duck Books 19-200 1 996 $100.00

GADDIS, WILLIAM   A Frolic of His Own. London: Viking, 1994. 1st British edition; fine in fine dust jacket and signed by author.   Ken Lopez 74-151 1996 $100.00

GADDIS, WILLIAM   A Frolic Of His Own. A Novel. New York: Poseidon Press, 1994. Uncorrected proof; 8vo; printed blue wrappers; faint small stain on upper wrapper, otherwise fine.   James S. Jaffe 34-166 1996 $150.00

GADDIS, WILLIAM   A Frolic Of His Own. New York: Poseidon, 1994. Uncorrected proof; blue printed wrappers, publisher's letter and ads laid in; near fine.   Lame Duck Books 19-199 1996 $150.00

GADDIS, WILLIAM   J.R. New York: Knopf, 1975. Uncorrected proof; light creasing to spine, few tiny spots on rear cover, still just about fine in wrappers.   Ken Lopez 74-150 1996 $250.00

GADDIS, WILLIAM   JR. New York: Knopf, 1975. 1st edition; review copy with publisher's prospectus, slip and photo laid in; published simultaneously in paper covers, and thus, rather uncommon in bound issue; fine in near fine dust jacket, signed by author.   Lame Duck Books 19-197 1996 $500.00

GADDIS, WILLIAM   The Recognitions. New York: HB, 1955. 1st edition; near fine in like dust jacket, with few small patches of rubbing and tiny edge tears to spine panel, better than usual copy.   Lame Duck Books 19-196 1996 $450.00

GADDIS, WILLIAM   The Recognitions. New York: Harcourt Brace, 1955. 1st edition; fine copy in very good+ dust jacket, several small tears.   Book Time 2-155 1996 $200.00

GADDIS, WILLIAM   The Recognitions. New York: Harcourt Brace, 1955. 1st edition; author's first book; very good+ in very good price clipped dust jacket with some edge chipping.   Pettler & Lieberman 28-95 1996 $175.00

GAGE, J. D.   Deep-Sea Biology, a Natural History of Organisms at the Deep Sea-Floor. London: 1991. Royal 8vo; 400 pages, 235 illustrations; 8 tables; cloth.   Wheldon & Wesley 207-315 1996 £90.00

GAGE, JOHN   The Christian Sodality, or Catholick Hive of Bees Sucking the Hony of the Churches Prayers from the Blossomes of the Word of God, Blowne Out of the Epistles and Gospels of the Divine Service throughout the Yeare... London: printed in the year of our Lord, 1652. Only edition; 8vo; (lxxii), 268, (xxii), 237, (xxiii), 373, (xxix) pages; errata leaves after prelims and at end of each volume; contemporary calf with gilt centre ornament on each board, plain reback; corners slightly worn, little soiling and staining; good; inscription. Wing G107; Clancy 413.   Robert Clark 38-84 1996 £150.00

GAGE, WILLIAM   Illustrated Guide to the Black Hills and Picturesque Souvenir of Hot Springs, South Dakota. Battle Creek: Gage Printing Co., 1901. 1st edition; 62, (2) pages, illustrations, map; original pictorial blue wrappers with title stamped in white, gold and blue; fine.   Michael D. Heaston 23-303 1996 $150.00

GAIMAR, GEOFFREY   Lestorie des Engles Solum la Translacion Maistre Geffrei Gaimar. London: 1888-89. 8vo; 2 volumes, pages 793. original cloth.   Howes Bookshop 265-1602 1996 £55.00

GAINE, HUGH   The Journals of Hugh Gaine, Printer. New York: Dodd, Mead, 1902. 1st edition; limited to 350 copies; 2 volumes, xii, 240, xii, 235 pages, facsimiles, plates; red cloth, spine labels, spines and labels well rubbed, spine tips somewhat frayed, bookplates removed, hairline crack at front hinge of volume 2, one endpaper loose.   Metacomet Books 54-41 1996 $125.00

GAINES, ERNEST J.   The Autobiography of Miss Jane Pittman. New York: Dial, 1971. 1st edition; touch of wear to base of spine, still fine in very good dust jacket with couple of short tears and very small nicks, as well as some light stains, only barely visible o rear panel, despite flaws an attractive copy; inscribed by author in year of publication. Between the Covers 43-82 1996 $250.00

GAINES, ERNEST J.   Catherine Carmier. New York: Atheneum, 1964. 1st edition; author's rare first book; fine in fine price clipped dust jacket with 1 short closed tear, very scarce (reputedly only 1000 copies). Pettler & Lieberman 28-21 1996 $225.00

GAIRDNER, JAMES   Lollardy and the Reformation in England: an Historical Survey. London: 1908-13. Original edition; thick 8vo; 4 volumes; original cloth, nice set. Gross/Graves 6870.   Howes Bookshop 265-389 1996 £200.00

GALENUS   On the Natural Faculties. London: 1916. 1st edition of the Brock translation; original binding; GM 569.   W. Bruce Fye 71-764 1996 $100.00

GALENUS   Galen on the Usefulness of the Parts of the Body. Ithaca: 1968. 1st English translation; 2 volumes, 802 pages; original binding, slipcase. GM 570.   W. Bruce Fye 71-768 1996 $175.00

GALILEI, GALILEO   Opere. Bologna: Heirs of Dozza, 1655-56. 1st collected edition; quarto; 19 parts in 2 volumes; engraved frontispiece, engraved portrait, one folding engraved plate, numerous text illustrations and diagrams; contemporary vellum over boards, title in gilt on spine, mottled edges, extremities rubbed, boards of volume 1 bit bowed, occasional light foxing and browning, fine and attractive set. Cinti 132; Riccardi I 518.   Heritage Book Shop 196-179 1996 $8,500.00

GALLAUDET, THOMAS H.   · A Discourse, Delivered at the Dedication of the American Asylum, for the Education of Deaf and Dumb Persons, May 22nd, 1821. Hartford: Hudson and Co., 1821. 1st edition; 8vo; 15 pages, removed, library stamp at foot of title; inscribed by author to friend A. M. Fisher. Shoemaker 5419.   M & S Rare Books 60-316 1996 $275.00

GALLAUDET, THOMAS H.   A Sermon Delivered at the Opening of the Connecticut Asylum for the Education and Instruction of Deaf and Dumb Persons. Hartford: Hudson and Co., 1817. 1st edition; 8vo; 15 pages, removed, library stamp at bottom of title leaf; Sabin 26408; S&S 40885. M & S Rare Books 60-317 1996 $125.00

GALLINI, GIOVANNI ANDREA 1728-1805   Critical Observations on the Art of Dancing... London: ptd. for the author & sold by R. Dodsley, T. Becket & P.A. DeHondt... nd1765. 1st edition; 2nd issue, with dedication to the Duchess of Hamilton and Argyll, a joint title to which she had been elevated in 1766; 8vo; disbound; very good. Magriel p. 99; Niels/Leslie p. 183. CBEL II 1566; Moroda 1033.   Ximenes 108-151 1996 $900.00

GALLO, MIGUEL MUJICA   The Gold of Peru: Masterpieces of Goldsmith's Work of Pre-Incan and Incan Time and the Colonial Period. Recklinghausen: Aurel Bongers, 1967. 2nd edition; 8vo; 286 pages; 144 color plates; original cloth, tattered dust jacket.   Archaeologia Luxor-4499 1996 $150.00

GALLOWAY, ARCHIBALD   Observations on the Law and Constitution, and Present Government of India, On the Nature of Landed Tenures and Financial Resources, as Recognized by Moohummudan Law and Moghul Government... London: Parbury, Allen & Co., 1832. 2nd edition; 8vo; original grey boards, printer's paper label (slight wear, foot of spine restored to match, slight chipping of label); fine, sarce. NUC lists 4 copies.   Ximenes 109-132 1996 $375.00

GALLOWAY, JOSEPH   A Reply to the Observations of Lieut. Gen Sir William Howe, on a Pamphlet Entitled Letters to a Nobleman (On the Conduct of the War in the Middle Colonies). London: printed for G. Wilkie, 1780. 1st edition; 8vo; half title, 2 pages of ads at end, 149 pages; disbound; presentation inscription from author for the Earl of Hillsborough.   Anthony Laywood 108-66 1996 £235.00

GALLUP, GEORGE   A Guide to Public Opinion Polls. Princeton: Princeton University, 1944. 1st edition; Princeton University Archive sticker to front pastedown, else near fine in very good+ dust jacket with couple of short edge tears, inscribed by author in year of publication; scarce.   Lame Duck Books 19-498 1996 $350.00

GALLUP, GEORGE   A Guide to Public Opinion Polls. Princeton: Princeton University Press, 1944. 1st edition; 8vo; dust jacket, very good. George J. Houle 68-53 1996 $150.00

GALLUP, JOSEPH   Sketches of Epidemic Diseases in the State of Vermont: from Its First Settlement to the Year 1815. Boston: 1815. 1st edition; 419 pages; original leather, rubbed. Austin 809; Kelly Burrage 445.   W. Bruce Fye 71-771 1996 $300.00

GALLWEY, NONA   Fairy Moonbeams. Pixie Press, 1945. 1st edition; mounted color frontispiece and black and white drawings by Naomi Heather; red boards pictorially stamped in black, backstrip rubbed, else fresh copy; scarce.   Barbara Stone 70-122 1996 £65.00

GALSWORTHY, JOHN 1867-1933   The Inn of Tranquility. London: Heinemann, 1912. 1st edition; only 2000 copies printed; signed by author on small slip of paper tipped to dedication page; 8vo; green buckram cloth, custom made leather and cloth slipcase (spine browned), near fine.   Antic Hay 101-628 1996 $100.00

GALSWORTHY, JOHN 1867-1933   The Plays of John Galsworthy. London: Duckworth, 1929. Limited edition of 1275 numbered copies; signed by author; thick 8vo; printed on handmade paper; green cloth in dust jacket, near fine, little browning and few tears (one external mend) to white dust jacket.   Antic Hay 101-642 1996 $100.00

GALSWORTHY, JOHN 1867-1933   The Silver Spoon. London: Heinemann, 1926. Limited to 265 signed and numbered copies, large paper edition; 8vo; blue buckram cloth in dust jacket, top edge gilt, fine, moderate edgewear and browning to white dust jacket.   Antic Hay 101-647 1996 $125.00

GALT, JOHN   Annals of the Parish; or the Chronicle of Dalmailing... Edinburgh: William Blackwood; London: T. Cadell, 1821. 1st edition; 12mo; half title, ad leaf; contemporary morocco gilt, carefully rebacked ir antique style; small library stamp inside rear cover, very good. Wolff 2387; Block p. 80; NCBEL III 722.   Trebizond 39-16 1996 $250.00

GALTON, FRANCIS 1822-1911   Finger Prints. London: Macmillan and Co., 1892. 1st edition; 8vo; pages xvi, 216, 16 plates; recent half burgundy morocco, spine with raised bands and lined and lettered in gilt, top edge gilt; very good. PMM 376.   Sotheran PN32-13 1996 £350.00

GALTON, FRANCIS 1822-1911   Hereditary Genius: an Inquiry Into its Laws and Consequences. New York: 1870. 1st American edition; 390 pages; recent buckram. GM 226.   W. Bruce Fye 71-773 1996 $200.00

GALTON, FRANCIS 1822-1911   Hereditary Genius: an Inquiry Into Its Laws and Consequences. London: 1892. 2nd edition; 379 pages; original binding; GM 226.   W. Bruce Fye 71-772 1996 $100.00

GALVEZ, BERNARDO DE   Instructions for Governing the Interior Provinces of New Spain. Berkeley: The Quivira Society, 1951. Limited to 500 copies; 150 pages; cloth backed boards, very fine. Wagner, Spanish Southwest 167.   Argonaut Book Shop 113-271 1996 $250.00

GALVIN, JOHN   The Etchings of Edward Borein. San Francisco: John Howell Books, 1971. 1st edition; frontispiece, 318 black and white illustrations; original brown cloth, gilt lettered on spine and front cover, very fine. With printed dust jacket.   Argonaut Book Shop 113-83 1996 $150.00

GALVIN, JOHN   Etchings of Edward Borein, a Catalogue of His Work. San Francisco: John Howell, 1971. Quarto; unnumbered pages, reproductions of 318 etchings, frontispiece; gilt titled cloth, nearly fine in lightly soiled dust jacket, inscription. Dykes 50 Great; Borein 61. Bohling Book Co. 192-148 1996 $100.00

A GAMUT, or Scale of Music. To Which is Added, Blank Lines for Favorite Music. London: Samuel Green, Printer, 1816. Oblong samll 4to; 32 pages of text plus blanks, mostly filled in, contemporary marbled wrappers, worn, lacking a piece; some foxing and waterstaining. S&S 37680. Metcalf Amer. Psalmody p. 24.   M & S Rare Books 60-384 1996 $250.00

GANDHI, MAHATMA   The Story of My Experiments with Truth. Ahmedabad: Navajivan Press, 1927-29. 1st edition; 2 volumes; bound in dyed Khadi, very good in dust jackets with few tears, rare thus. Words Etcetera 94-245 1996 £200.00

GANNON, JACK   Jack of All Trades and Master of One. San Francisco: Arion, 1987. One of 300 copies only; page size 5 x 7 inches; 64 pages; brown paper boards printed in black.   Priscilla Juvelis 95/1-8 1996 $100.00

GANS, C.   Biology of Reptilia. London: New York: 1969-70. Volumes -3, numerous illustrations, 1132 pages; worn dust jackets, bound, ex-library.   John Johnson 135-602 1996 $200.00

GANT, ROLAND   Steps to the River. Lower Marston, Risbury, Herefordshire: Whittington Press, 1995. One of 40 special copies thus, from an edition of 200 copies, numbered and signed by poet and artist; with set of signed artist's proofs of engravings laid in matching green folder; all in dark green slipcase; fine; bound by the Fine Bindery with green cloth spine, paper title label, green plant patterned paper over board sides printed from wood engraving by artist.   Joshua Heller 21-280 1996 $270.00

GANTT, W. H.   A Medical Review of Soviet Russia. London: 1928. 1s edition; 112 pages; original binding, autographed by Gantt. GM 6569. W. Bruce Fye 71-777 1996 $100.00

GARCIA LORCA, FEDERICO   Romance de la Guardia Civil Espanola./The Ballad of the Spanish Civil Guard. Janus Press, 1974. 2nd edition of the 1963 Janus Press publication, with 1 of 9 woodcut illustrations by Jerome Kaplan redrawn and recut by the artist; 1 of 400 signed by artist; 11.375 x 6.75 inches; 24 pages; designed and letterpress printed by Claire Van Vliet, titles handset and printed in black and silver gray, Spanish handset text in black, English handset text interlinear in silver gray on French-folded Mohawk Superfine; handsewn into linen book cloth covered boards; fine. Joshua Heller 21-7 1996 $125.00

GARCIA LORCA, FEDERICO   From Lorca's Theatre. Five Plays. New York: Scribner's, 1941. 1st U.S. edition; near fine in dust jacket with one tiny chip, scarce.   Lame Duck Books 19-202 1996 $150.00

GARCIA LORCA, FEDERICO   The Lieutenant Colonel and the Gypsy. Garden City: Doubleday, 1971. 1st edition; touch of wear at spine base, else fine in fine, price clipped dust jacket, scarce.   Ken Lopez 74-153 1996 $125.00

GARCIA LORCA, FEDERICO   The Poet in New York and Other Poems. New York: W. W. Norton & Co., 1940. 1st edition; 8vo; 209, (ii) pages; orange cloth (soiled), titled in gilt and brown in brown and gilt rectangles on spine, in pictorial cream dust jacket, soiled, chipped and torn at edges, with 2 very small pieces out from bottom, slight offsetting to endpapers, near fine in good dust jacket.   Blue Mountain SP95-107 1996 $250.00

GARCIA LORCA, FEDERICO   Songs of Childhood. Roslyn: The Stone House Press, 1994. In a total edition of 130 copies, this one of 30 deluxe copies, of which 20 are for sale, numbered and signed by translator, William Jay Smith, the artist and printer/publisher; 10 x 5 inches; 27 pages; 5 wood engravings in blue, by John De Pol, printed in black with red on heavyweight Rives; blue goatskin spine with title in gilt on spine, cream cloth boards, cream slipcase, blue and white patterned endpapers designed by John De Pol; mint.   Joshua Heller 21-224 1996 $150.00

GARCIA LORCA, FEDERICO   Three Tragedies. New York: New Directions, 1947. 1st U.S. edition; near fine in price clipped dust jacket. Lame Duck Books 19-204 1996 $150.00

GARCIA LORCA,, FEDERICO   Poems of F. Garcia Lorca. New York: Oxford, 1939. 1st U.S. edition; near fine in very good+ price clipped dust jacket, scarce.   Lame Duck Books 19-201 1996 $250.00

GARCIA MARQUEZ, GABRIEL 1928-   The General in His Labyrinth. 1st American edition, one of 350 specially bound and numbered copies signed by Garcia Marquez; full leather and slipcase; very fine. Captain's Bookshelf 38-87 1996 $300.00

GARCIA MARQUEZ, GABRIEL 1928-   The General in His Labyrinth. New York: Knopf, 1990. 1/350 numbered copies, signed; fine in slipcase. Alice Robbins 15-139 1996 $350.00

GARCIA MARQUEZ, GABRIEL 1928-   The General In His Labyrinth. New York: Knopf, 1990. 1st American edition; fine in fine dust jacket, tiny bump at crown, nicely inscribed by author, very uncommon inscribed.   Between the Covers 42-184 1996 $850.00

GARCIA MARQUEZ, GABRIEL 1928-   La Mala Hora. Madrid: Esso, 1962. 1st edition; illustrated wrappers with surface loss and short edge tear to spine folds; very good or better, inscribed by author to Colombian poet German Espinoza.   Lame Duck Books 19-208 1996 $4,000.00

GARCIA MARQUEZ, GABRIEL 1928-   In Evil Hour. New York: H&R, 1979. 1st U.S. edition; rare 1st issue in variant dust jacket reading "Marquez" instead of "Garcia Marquez" on spine; very near fine in dust jacket.   Lame Duck Books 19-212 1996 $500.00

GARCIA MARQUEZ, GABRIEL 1928-   Leaf Storm and Other Stories. London: Cape, 1972. 1st English edition; fine in very close to fine price clipped dust jacket.   Thomas Dorn 9-250 1996 $125.00

GARCIA MARQUEZ, GABRIEL 1928-   Leaf Storm and other Stories. New York: Harper, 1972. 1st American edition; fine in fine dust jacket. Bud Schweska 12-355 1996 $225.00

GARCIA MARQUEZ, GABRIEL 1928-   Leaf Storm and Other Stories. New York: H&R, 1972. 1st American edition; increasingly uncommon, name, otherwise fine in fine dust jacket.   Thomas Dorn 9-121 1996 $200.00

GARCIA MARQUEZ, GABRIEL 1928-   Leaf Storm and Other Stories. New York: Harper & Row, 1972. Author's third book; jacket has two small tears at head of spine, otherwise fine in jacket.   Neil Cournoyer 4-71 1996 $112.00

GARCIA MARQUEZ, GABRIEL 1928-   Love in the Time of Cholera. New York: Knopf, 1988. Proof copy; in publisher's folding box; fine in near fine box.   Alice Robbins 15-138 1996 $100.00

GARCIA MARQUEZ, GABRIEL 1928-   Love in the Time of Cholera. New York: Knopf, 1988. 1st American edition; one of 350 specially bound copies, signed by author, this copy unnumbered; printed acetate dust jacket and slipcase; very fine.   Captain's Bookshelf 38-86 1996 $400.00

GARCIA MARQUEZ, GABRIEL 1928-   Love in the Time of Cholera. New York: Alfred A. Knopf, 1988. 1st American edition; 1/350 numbered and signed copies by author, this copy, however, is signed but not numbered; very fine in acetate jacket and publisher's box.   Left Bank Books 2-85 1996 $350.00

GARCIA MARQUEZ, GABRIEL 1928-   No One Writes to the Colonel and Other Stories. New York: H&R, 1968. 1st American edition; just a touch of wear at bottom of spine, else fine, tight copy in very bright fine dust jacket with minute rub at spinal extremities, outstanding copy. Thomas Dorn 9-119 1996 $700.00

GARCIA MARQUEZ, GABRIEL 1928-   No One Writes to the Colonel. New York: Harper, 1968. 1st American edition; slight rubbing to base of boards, some foxing to half title, still near fine in very good plus first issue dust jacket with little rubbing, two small, internally mended tears and couple of very small nicks at corners.   Between the Covers 42-182 1996 $650.00

GARCIA MARQUEZ, GABRIEL 1928-   One Hundred Years of Solitude. London: Cape, 1970. 1st British edition, published the same year as the American; fine in near fine dust jacket with slight wear at crown of spine.   Thomas Dorn 9-120 1996 $450.00

GARCIA MARQUEZ, GABRIEL 1928-   One Hundred Years of Solitude. New York: H&R, 1970. 1st U.S. edition; very near fine in bright example of the dust jacket showing just a bit of surface loss to extremities, warmly inscribed by author.   Lame Duck Books 19-209 1996 $3,500.00

GARCIA MARQUEZ, GABRIEL 1928-   One Hundred Years of Solitude. New York: Harper, 1970. 1st edition; small stain on edge of rear board, else fine in near fine dust jacket with very slight rubbing at spinal extremities, visible only under close scrutiny.   Between the Covers 42-183 1996 $650.00

GARCIA, CHRISTINA   Dreaming in Cuban. New York: Knopf, 1992. 1st edition; author's first novel; as new, signed.   Book Time 2-547 1996 $125.00

GARCILASO DE LA VEGA, EL INCA 1539-1616   Histoire des Yncas Rois Du Perou Depuis le Premier Ynca Manco Capac... L'Historie de la Conquete de la Floride. Amsterdam: Chez Jean Frederic Bernard, 1737. 4to; 2 volumes; half titles, frontispiece to volume 1, 3 large folding maps, 14 engraved copperplates, 3 vignettes to letterpress; old calf boards, rebacked, panelled spine, red and green morocco labels, red speckled edges; some sporadic light foxing. Sabin 98752; Hill, Pacifi Voyages p. 121.   Beeleigh Abbey BA/56-125 1996 £650.00

THE GARDEN of the Night - Twenty-six Sufi Poems. Andoversford: Whittington Press, 1979. One of 35 specially bound copies, signed by editor and artist and numbered with Roman numerals, total edition comprised 235 copies; quarto; lacks extra etching by artist; printed on BFV Rives paper; full decorated gilt Nigerian goatskin by Weatherby Woolnough with Whittington marbled endpapers, top edge gilt, spine darkened, covers very slightly marked, very good in slipcase, which is slightly faded at edges and slightly marked and dusty.   Ulysses 39-625 1996 £450.00

GARDENIER, ANDREW   Hand-Book of Ready Reference. Springfield King-Richardson, 1897. Salesman's sample, includes samples of text and colored Manikins of the horse and cow, each manikin has 4 overlays showing skeleton, muscles, etc. as well as internal organs; very good. Second Life Books 103-87 1996 $135.00

GARDINER, ALLEN F.　　Narrative of a Journey to the Zoolu Country, in South Africa. London: William Crofts, 1836. 1st edition; 8vo; 2 folding maps, 26 lithographed plates, two of them h and colored; original grey green cloth, slight wear to top of spine, back inner hinge bit tender; some plates bit foxed, but nice in original condition. Abbey Travel 322. Theal p. 112.　　Ximenes 109-133　1996 $750.00

GARDINER, JAMES T.　　Special Report of the New York State Survey on the Preservation of the Scenery of Niagara Falls. Albany: Charles Van Benthuysen & Sons, 1880. 1st edition; 4to; 42 pages; large folding map, 3 full page plates, 9 mounted heliotype prints, 2 folding plans; original dark red cloth, library bookplate and blindstamps, still tight and very good.　　Chapel Hill 94-316　1996 $150.00

GARDINER, S.　　Letters and Papers Relating to the First Dutch Wars 1652-1654. London: Navy Records Society, 1894-1930. 1st editions; 8vo; 6 volumes; original blue/white cloth, very good; with very scarce corrigenda 34 page booklet.　　John Lewcock 30-84　1996 £150.00

GARDINER, S. R.　　History of England, from the Accession of James I to the Outbreak of the Civil War 1603-1642. London: 1899-1901. Crown 8vo; 10 volumes; original cloth, printed labels; from the lirary of J. Basil Oldham, with bookplate.　　Howes Bookshop 265-393　1996 £200.00

GARDINER, S. R.　　History of the Commonwealth and Protectorate 1649-1656. London: Longman, 1903. New edition; crown 8vo; 4 volumes; folding maps and many battle plans; original cloth, printed labels, neat library stamp on titles.　　Howes Bookshop 265-395　1996 £75.00

GARDINER, S. R.　　History of the Great Civil War 1642-1649. London: Longman, 1894. New edition; crown 8vo; 4 volumes; folding maps and many battle plans; original cloth, printed labels, neat gilt library stamp on spines.　　Howes Bookshop 265-394　1996 £75.00

GARDNER, DANIEL PEREIRA　　The Farmer's Dictionary: a Vocabulary of The Technical Terms Recently Introduced Into Agriculture and Horticulture from Various Sciences, and also a Compendium of Practical Farming... New York: Harper, 1846. 1st edition; 8vo; pages 876, ad; little foxed; well illustrated; bound in publisher's cloth, very good.　　Second Life Books 103-88　1996 $125.00

GARDNER, ERLE STANLEY　　The Case of the Backward Mule. New York: Wm. Morrow & Co., 1946. 1st edition; near fine in lightly soiled and rubbed dust jacket with few small chips and short closed tears and touch of creasing on spine.　　Quill & Brush 102-628　1996 $100.00

GARDNER, ERLE STANLEY　　The D. A. Draws a Circle. New York: Wm. Morrow & Co., 1939. 1st edition; endpapers slightly darkened, still very good in bright but edgeworn dust jacket, only slightly faded on spine.　　Quill & Brush 102-626　1996 $175.00

GARDNER, ERLE STANLEY　　Neighbourhood Frontiers. New York: William Morrow, 1954. 1st edition; near fine in very good+ price clipped jacket. Warm inscription by author.　　Janus Books 36-155　1996 $100.00

GARDNER, ERNEST ARTHUR　　A Catalogue of the Greek Vases in the Fitzwilliam Museum, Cambridge. Cambridge: University Press, 1897. 8vo; xxi, 95 pages; 41 plates; original cloth.　　Archaeologia Luxor-3358 1996 $2,520.00

GARDNER, ISABELLA　　That Was Then. Brockport: Boa Editions, 1979. 1st edition; 8vo; frontispiece; frontispiece by Aaron Siskind; cloth backed marbled boards, signed by author and artist; fine.　　James S. Jaffe 34-168　1996 $125.00

GARDNER, JOHN　　Forms of Fiction. New York: Random House, 1962. 1st edition; issued without dust jacket; clean, tight copy.　　Left Bank Books 2-42　1996 $100.00

GARDNER, JOHN　　Grendel. New York: Knopf, 1971. 1st edition; fine in unfaded dust jacket and most uncommon thus, housed in protective cloth covered slipcase.　　Lame Duck Books 19-215　1996 $250.00

GARDNER, JOHN　　Grendel. New York: Knopf, 1971. 1st edition; fine in dust jacket with virtually no fading to dust jacket spine.　　Aronovitz 57-434　1996 $185.00

GARDNER, JOHN　　Grendel. New York: Knopf, 1971. 1st edition; owner name/date on endpaper, else fine in fine unfaded dust jacket with 1 tiny snag at spine crown.　　Pettler & Lieberman 28-100　1996 $150.00

GARDNER, JOHN　　On Moral Fiction. New York: Basic Books, 1978. 1st edition; advance review copy with publisher's slip; fine in fine dust jacket; inscribed by author to prominent critic, L. Milazzo, thanking him for his kind review of On Moral Fiction. Nice association.　　Thomas Dorn 9-123　1996 $175.00

GARDNER, JOHN　　On Becoming a Novelist.. New York: Harper & Row, 1983. 1st edition; fine in fine dust jacket, signed by Raymond Carver, who provided foreword.　　Revere Books 4-145　1996 $225.00

GARDNER, JOHN　　The Resurrection. New York: New American Library, 1966. 1st edition; author's scarce first novel; near fine in very good price clipped dust jacket which is lightly soiled and internally reinforced with tape at 3 places along top inside edge.　　Steven C. Bernard 71-104　1996 $450.00

GARDNER, JOHN　　Rumplestiltskin. Dallas: New London Press, 1979. One of 250 numbered copies, signed by author; printed cloth, without dust jacket, as published; fine.　　Thomas Dorn 9-124　1996 $100.00

GARDNER, JOHN　　The Temptation Game. N.P.: New London Press, 1980. Out of a total printing of 326, this one of 300 numbered and signed copies; fine, issued without dust jacket.　　Anacapa House 5-115 1996 $100.00

GARDNER, JOHN　·　William Wilson. Dallas: New London Press, 1979. One of 250 numbered copies, signed by author; printed cloth, without dust jacket as issued; fine.　　Thomas Dorn 9-125　1996 $100.00

GARDNER, JOHN　　The Wreckage of Agathon. New York: Harper & Row, et al, 1970. 1st edition; fine in dust jacket.　　Steven C. Bernard 71-105　1996 $150.00

GARDNER, JOHN　　The Wreckage of Agathon. New York: Harper & Row, 1970. 1st edition; fine in fine dust jacket with trace of rubbing on rear white panel; signed by author.　　Revere Books 4-146　1996 $150.00

GARDNER, JOHN　　The Wreckage of Agathon. New York: Harper & Row, 1970. 1st edition; fine in dust jacket.　　Left Bank Books 2-43 1996 $125.00

GARDNER, JOHN　　The Wreckage of Agathon. New York: Harper & Row, 1970. 1st edition; fine copy in fine dust jacket.　　Book Time 2-161　1996 $120.00

GARDNER, KEITH S.　　Sir William Russell Flint 1880-1969. Sir William Flint Galleries, 1986. Limited to 1500 copies, this being one of only 500 deluxe copies, specially bound and containing the catalog of etchings & drypoints not included in the ordinary copies; this copy specially singed by Cecilia Green, the artist's favourtie model; 4to; vi, 450 pages; 106 plates in color, 66 sepia reproductions, several photographic illustrations, publisher's full blue morocco, gilt, gilt edges, cloth slipcase, leather label mint.　　Thomas Thorp 489-110　1996 £650.00

GARGAZ, PIERRE ANDRE　　A Project of Universal and Perpetual Peace. New York: George Simpson Eddy, 1922. One of 1250 copies; 8vo; printed in Monotype Caslon by W.E. Rudge to Bruce Roger's design; full crushed navy blue morocco with series of five gilt borders joined at the corners by an elaborate gilt fleuron, spine with five raised bands and gilt decoration with compartments, except the two that carry the title information, full morocco doublures that more or less repeat the cover design, top edge gilt, other edges untrimmed; fine; handsome copy in very handsome binding. Warde 159.　　Book Block 32-41　1996 $265.00

A GARLAND for Jake Zeitlin. Los Angeles: Grant Dahlstrom and Saul Marks, 1967. One of 800 copies; 8vo; (x), 132 pages; cloth spine, boards, fine.　　The Bookpress 75-372　1996 $135.00

A GARLAND of New Songs. London: J. Marshall, c. 1800. 95 x 150mm; pages 8; woodcut on titlepage, unbound as issued, last 2 leaves unopened; excellent.　　Blackwell's B112-60　1996 £125.00

GARLAND, HAMLIN 1860-1940　　The Book of the American Indian. New York: 1923. 1st edition; 274 pages; color frontispiece, illustrations by Frederic Remington; pictorial cloth, very good+. Howes G66.　　T. A. Swinford 49-402　1996 $175.00

GARLAND, HAMLIN 1860-1940   The Book of the American Indian. New York: Harper & Bros., 1923. 1st edition; small folio; numerous illustrations by Frederic Remington; pictorial boards, black linen spine, renewed, corner tear on one page not affecting text.   Appelfeld Gallery 54-155 1996 $100.00

GARLAND, HAMLIN 1860-1940   The Book of the American Indian. New York: and London: Harper & Bros., 1923. 1st edition; 4to; (xii), 271, ii(ads), 29 illustrations by Frederick Remington, 3 in color; original paper boards with portrait of an American Indian mounted on upper cover, cloth spine with dust jacket and box; box rubbed and cracked along corners, but repaired, dust jacket torn on lower side, portion missing, otherwise extremely clean and bright.   Sotheran PN32-165 1996 £320.00

GARLICK, THEODATUS   A Treatise on the Artificial Propagation of Certain Kinds of Fish, with the Description and Habits of Such Kinds as Are the Most Suitable Kinds for Pisciculture... Cleveland: Tho. Brown, Publisher, Ohio Farmer Office, 1857 142 pages, plus ads; cloth;   Robert G. Hayman 11/95-92 1996 $100.00

GARNER, R. L.   Gorillas and Chimpanzees. London: 1896. illustrations; cloth lightly marked.   David Grayling J95Biggame-92 1996 £50.00

GARNET, J. ROS   Wildflowers of South-Eastern Australia. London: Thomas Nelson, 1974. Limited edtiion of 775 numbered copies, signed by artist and author; folio; 2 volumes, 80 plates in color; publisher's green cloth, gilt, spines slightly faded, otherwise fine, preserved in original cloth slipcase.   Thomas Thorp 489-72 1996 £160.00

GARNETT, DAVID   Aspects of Love. London: Chatto & Windus Ltd., 1955. 1st edition; original binding, edges spotted, spine faded and with offsetting from dust jacket, very good in nicked, spotted and slightly creased, rubbed and dusty dust jacket, by Angelica Garnett, browned at spine and edges; from the library of Ian Parsons.   Ulysses 39-218 1996 £55.00

GARNETT, DAVID   Go She Must! London: Chatto & Windus, 1927. Signed, limited edition of 160 numbered copies; small 8vo; cloth with leather spine label, top edge gilt, very good, some darkening to spine and light soil, With ink name of of George Freedley (and two others) on front endpaper.   Antic Hay 101-673 1996 $125.00

GARNETT, DAVID   Never Be a Bookseller. New York: Alfred A. Knopf, 1929. One of 2000 copies, none of which were for sale; wrappers, patterned paper covers with title label, corners slightly creased, bottom corner of first blank slightly creased, small mark on first blank, near fine.   Ulysses 39-217 1996 £125.00

GARNETT, DAVID   No Love. New York: Alfred A. Knopf, 1929. 1st edition; original binding, corners, edges and several pages dusty, covers also rubbed, marked and slighty soiled, head and tail of spine and corners slightly bumped, spine faded; good; inscribed by author "Corrected copy for the 2nd edition. David Garnett."   Ulysses 39-216 1996 £185.00

GARNETT, FRANK W.   Westmorland Agriculture 1800-1900. Kendal: Titus Wilson, 1912. 1st (only) edition; 4to; pages xvi, 302; 64 illustrations and colored maps; original parchment backed blue boards, endpapers little spotted, extremely scarce.   R.F.G. Hollett & Son 78-612 1996 £345.00

GARNETT, LOUISE AYRES   The Muffin Shop. Chicago: Rand McNally & Co., 1908. Large quarto; 79 pages; illustrations in black and white and color; original color pictorial boards with red cloth backstrip light soiling to boards, minimal rubbing to corners and edges; near fine.   Heritage Book Shop 196-267 1996 $250.00

GARNETT, PORTER   Porter Garnett: Philosophical Writings on the Ideal Book. San Francisco: the Book Club of California, 1994. 1st edition; one of 450 copies; 250 pages; frontispiece, 42 illustrations; original silk cloth, paper spine label; very fine.   Argonaut Book Shop 113-276 1996 $175.00

GARNETT, RICHARD   Iphigenia in Delphi. London: T. Fisher Unwin, 1890. 1/30 copies, signed by publisher; 12mo; frontispiece; full imitation vellum; author's copy with bookplate.   Dramatis Personae 37-69 1996 $200.00

GARRARD, PHILLIS   Running Away with Nebby. Philadelphia: McKay, 1944. 1st edition; small 4to; frontispiece, 6 full page color plates and drawings in black and white by Willy Pogany; blue cloth pictorially stamped in silver, fresh.   Barbara Stone 70-174 1996 £55.00

GARRICK, DAVID 1717-1779   The Fribbleriad. London: printed for J. Coote, 1741 sic for 1761. 1st edition; rare first issue, with date miprinted; 4to; disbound; with acquisition notes of the lending library at Will's Coffee House, Lincoln's Inn, along with names of 3 borrowers, someone has penned several lines of satirical comment across the frontispiece (subsequently lightly crossed out), otherwise very good. Rothschild 898; LAR 2872; CBEL II 803.   Ximenes 108-152 1996 $1,500.00

GARRICK, DAVID 1717-1779   Lethe; a Dramatic Satire...As It is Performed at the Theatre-Royal in Drury Lane, by His Majesty's Servants. London: Paul Vaillant, 1749. 1st authorized edition; 8vo; disbound, half title; staining of edges of some leaves, but very good. Rothschild 894; Ashley Lib. II p. 131; Nicoll p. 329.   Trebizond 39-17 1996 $175.00

GARRICK, DAVID 1717-1779   The Poetical Works... London: For George Kearsley, 1785. 1st edition; 8vo; 2 volumes, pages (iv), lvii, (i), 224; (iv), (225)-540, (iii) ads; contemporary tree calf, flat spines, richly gilt in compartments, red morocco lettering pieces, green morocco labels with red oval numbering pieces onlaid, spines chipped at head, joints cracked but firm, still a pretty set, very clean, fresh internally. Rothschild 901.   Simon Finch 24-90 1996 £185.00

GARRICK, DAVID 1717-1779   The Poetical Works... London: George Kearsley, 1785. 1st edition; 8vo; contemporary calf, spines gilt, morocco labels, half titles, 3 pages ads in volume 2; fine early armorial bookplates of Penry Williams; signatures on flyleaf of early owner. Fine in modern slipcase. Rothschild 901; NCBEL II 801.   Trebizond 39-18 1996 $285.00

GARRICK, T. W.   The Story of Wigton (Cumberland)... Carlisle: Charles Thurnam, 1949. 1st edition; 8vo; pages 304, (vi), illustrations; original cloth, gilt, very good, scarce.   R.F.G. Hollett & Son 78-780 1996 £85.00

GARRIOCH, A. C.   The Correction Line. Winnipeg: Stovel Co. Ltd., 1933. Limited to 400 copies; 24cm; (ix), 414, (vi) pages, portrait frontispiece, illustrations, portraits; fine in near fine dust jacket. Peel 3333.   Rockland Books 38-80 1996 $150.00

GARRISON, FIELDING   An Introduction to the History of Medicine. Philadelphia: 1914. 1st edition; 2nd printing; 763 pages; original binding. GM 6408.   W. Bruce Fye 71-782 1996 $100.00

GARRISON, FIELDING   Introduction to the History of Medicine. Philadelphia: 1929. 4th edition; thick 8vo; illustrations; presentation copy. GM 6408.   Argosy 810-205 1996 $100.00

GARRISON, GEORGE P.   Diplomatic Correspondence of the Republic of Texas. Washington: GPO, 1908/11. 1st edition; 3 volumes, 646; 807; (5), 808-1617 pages; blue cloth, gilt lettered spines, light rubbing to extremities, minor spotting to covers of 3rd volume; overall fine set. Argonaut Book Shop 113-277 1996 $175.00

GARRISON, WILLIAM LLOYD   Sonnets and Other Poems. Boston: 1843. 1st edition; 16mo; 96 pages; original printed wrappers, worn, back wrapper torn. R&B 43-2053; not in LCP HSP Afro Amer. Cat.   M & S Rare Books 60-158 1996 $250.00

GASC, F. E. A.   The Smallest French and English Dictionary in the World. Glasgow: ca. 1896. 1 1/8 x 3/4 inches; 647 pages; flexible gilt stamped red leather, all edges yellow, covers slightly bowed, else fine; bookplate. Spielmann 162; Bondy p. 107.   Bromer Booksellers 87-198 1996 $150.00

GASCOIGNE, MISS   The Handbook of Turning. London: 1846. 2nd edition; small 8vo; portrait, decorative title, 14 plates, printed in sepia (margin of one folding plate slightly frayed), cloth, spine neatly mended. Abell 124.   Maggs Bros. Ltd. 1190-630 1996 £140.00

GASCOIGNE, MISS   The Handbook of Turning. London: 1852. 3rd edition; 8vo; portrait, decorative title, 14 plates printed in sepia; blue cloth, gilt, nice.   Maggs Bros. Ltd. 1190-632 1996 £100.00

GASCOIGNE, MISS   The Handbook of Turning. London: 1859. 4th edition; 8vo; portrait, decorative title, 14 plates, printed in sepia; pink cloth, rebacked, new endpapers, part of original backstrip mounted. Maggs Bros. Ltd. 1190-634 1996 £80.00

GASCOYNE, DAVID　Poems 1937-194. London: Poetry London, 1943. 1st edition; 8vo; pages (vi), 62; illustrated titlepage and 5 other plates by Graham Sutherland, some printed in 3 colors; original orange cloth backed boards with overall designs by Graham Sutherland, repeated on dust jacket, jacket little frayed at head; excellent.　Blackwell's B112-113　1996 £75.00

GASH, JONATHAN　The Lies of Fair Ladies. Bristol: Scorpion Press, 1991. 1/20 deluxe lettered copies, signed by author, and H.R.F. Keating who provided the author appreciation; fine in quarter bound goatskin with raised bands.　Quill & Brush 102-694　1996 $450.00

GASKELL, ELIZABETH CLEGHORN 1810-1865　Cranford. New York: Harpers, 1853. 1st American edition; 8vo; original cloth, gilt, bit worn, trifle soiled, name on title, but better than average example of this uncommon edition.　G. W. Stuart 59-40　1996 $150.00

GASKELL, ELIZABETH CLEGHORN 1810-1865　Cranford. London: Macmillan and Co., 1891. 1st edition thus, large paper copy (no limitation stated); 10 1/4 x 6 7/8 inches; frontispiece and 110 black and white illustrations by Hugh Thomson, pages xxx, 297, printed on handmade paper; crimson buckram, printed paper title label backstrip, uncut, backstrip and edges of covers faded and slightly worn top/bottom, title label worn, endpapers slightly spotted and discolored and partial discolor, verso and recto half title and frontispiece, contents fine.　Ian Hodgkins 78-482　1996 £80.00

GASKELL, ELIZABETH CLEGHORN 1810-1865　The Letters of... Cambridge: Harvard University Press, 1967. 1st American edition; 8 3/4 x 5 1/2 inches; pages xxx, 1010; dark green cloth, gilt titling, fine in slightly worn dust jacket, scarce. Ian Hodgkins 78-499　1996 £95.00

GASKELL, ELIZABETH CLEGHORN 1810-1865　Life of Charlotte Bronte. London: Smith, Elder & Co., 1857. 2nd edition; 7 3/4 x 5 inches; 2 volumes, frontispiece in each volume, pages viii, 352; vii, 327, 16 publisher's ads dated April 1857; dark brown fine diaper grain cloth, blindstamped decorated border on covers, cream endpapers, uncut, some wear top of backstrips, slight foxing of plates, corners bruised, endpapers cracked at hinges, very good, clean copy. Northup 90. Ian Hodgkins 78-491　1996 £150.00

GASKELL, ELIZABETH CLEGHORN 1810-1865　Life of Charlotte Bronte. New York: Appleton & Co., 1857. 1st American edition; 7 1/4 x 4 1/2 inches; 2 volumes; pages viii, 285, 6 pages publisher's ads; viii, 269, 8 pages publisher's ads numbered from p. 7 to p. 14) and ad leaf; bottle green vertical ribbed cloth with blindstamped geometrical design to both covers, gilt titling to backstrip, yellow endpapers, backstrips slightly faded and occasional slight foxing to contents; fine. Northup 91. Ian Hodgkins 78-490　1996 £135.00

GASKELL, ELIZABETH CLEGHORN 1810-1865　The Life of Charlotte Bronte. London: Elder & Co., 1858. 4th edition (1st single volume edition); 7 3/4 x 5 inches; pages xi, 483, 8 pages publisher's ads rear dated August 1858; frontispiece, title vignette; dark green morocco grain cloth with blindstamped borders of both covers, gilt titling backstrip, pale yellow endpapers, corners slightly bruised and very slight wear to front corner of boards, name to endpaper; very good. Northup 98. Ian Hodgkins 78-492　1996 £85.00

GASKELL, ELIZABETH CLEGHORN 1810-1865　Life of Charlotte Bronte. London: Smith, Elder & Co., 1860. 5th edition; 6 3/4 x 4 1/4 inches; with date 1859 on front cover, title vignett, pages viiii, 441, page ads; orange cloth lettered in black on front and backstrip with ads rear cover, yellow endpapers with publisher's ads; backstrip faded and soiled, covers slightly soiled, faded and titling rubbed on front, endpapers repaired at hinges, very good. Northup 116　Ian Hodgkins 78-493　1996 £65.00

GASKELL, ELIZABETH CLEGHORN 1810-1865　Right at Last and Other Tales. New York: Harper & Bros., 1860. 1st American edition; 7 1/4 x 4 5/8 inches; pages (viii), 305, 6 pages publisher's ads at rear; blue cloth, printed paper title label backstrip, brown endpapers, ?rebound, foxing to contents and few small wormholes on joints of covers, very good. Northup 118.　Ian Hodgkins 78-496　1996 £120.00

GASKELL, ELIZABETH CLEGHORN 1810-1865　Ruth. London: Chapman and Hall, 1853. 1st edition; 7 3/4 x 4 7/8 inches; 3 volumes, pages ii, 298; ii, 328; ii, 311; dark purple fine net grain cloth with blindstamped decoration to both covers and backstrip, gilt titling to backstrips, uncut; new endpapers on all volumes, ads can be seen through new endpapers in volumes 1 and 2, front corners of boards on volume 1 bumped, occasional slight mark and slight thumbing to contents, very good, scarce. Northump 52; Sadleir 933.　Ian Hodgkins 78-497　1996 £425.00

GASKELL, J.　Strange Evil. Hutchinson, 1957. 1st edition; author's first book; signed by author; near fine in like dust jacket save for some light soiling to dust jacket spine.　Aronovitz 57-438　1996 $125.00

GASPEY, W.　Tallis's Illustrated London: in Commemoration of the Great Exhibition Of All Nations in 1851... London: J. Tallis, n.d. 1851? 8vo; 2 volumes, pages vii, 320; vii, 304; 2 frontispieces, extra engraved title, 142 engraved plates, calf gilt, all edges gilt. Anderson p. 185. Marlborough 162-143　1996 £400.00

GASS, PATRICK　A Journal of the Voyages and Travels of a Corps of Discovery Under the Command of Captain Lewis and Captain Clarke of the Army of the United States from the Mouth of the River Missouri through the Interior Parts of North America to the Pacific Ocean... Minneapolis: Ross & Haines, 1958. Reprint, limited to 2000 numbered copies; xx, 113 17 pages, 10 plates from photos, one double page facsimile, frontispiece illustration, folded endpaper reproduction; original gilt lettered cloth, fine with lightly soiled pictorial dust jacket; scarce; Argonaut Book Shop 113-416　1996 $145.00

GASS, PATRICK　Voyage des Capitaines Lewis et Clarke. Paris: Arthus-Bertrand 1810. 1st edition in French; 8 x 5 1/4 inches; xviii, 443 pages, half title bound after title, folding engraved map, map with small early patch on verso (perhaps to close tear on recto, but impossible to tell); recent not displeasing unadorned half calf, marbled paper sides, raised bands, bound without fly leaves in front; very slight soiling to a handful of leaves, but very nearly fine, text and map quite fresh and clean, binding unworn. Wagner Camp Becker 6.3. Howes G77; Sabin 26742. Graff Collection 1519.　Phillip J. Pirages 33-344　1996 $1,500.00

GASS, WILLIAM H.　Culp. Grenfell Press, 1985. One of 85 copies, signed by author (of a total edition of 100); 12 1/4 x 8 1/4 inches; 4 p.l. (two blank), 9-46 pages, (2) leaves (blank colophon); frontispiece and several illustrations in text, title in red and black, red initial; original vellum backed patterned paper boards; mint.　Phillip J. Pirages 33-271 1996 $225.00

GASS, WILLIAM H.　Culp. New York: Grenfell Press, 1985. 1st edition; limited to only 85 numbered copies, out of a total edition of 100 copies, signed by author; 4to; frontispiece by Malcolm Morley; quarter vellum and boards; as new.　James S. Jaffe 34-169　1996 $450.00

GASS, WILLIAM H.　The First Winter of My Married Life. Northridge: Lord John Press, 1979. Out of a total printing of 301, this one of 275 numbered and signed copies; fine, issued without dust jacket. Anacapa House 5-117　1996 $100.00

GASS, WILLIAM H.　In the Heart of the Heart of the Country. New York: H&R, 1968. 1st edition; author's second book; very fine in dust jacket; housed in attractive custom case; inscribed by author and somewhat uncommon thus.　Lame Duck Books 19-216　1996 $250.00

GASS, WILLIAM H.　Omensetter's Luck. New York: NAL, 1966. 1st edition; small remainder mark bottom edge, else fine in near fine dust jacket with some rubbing and tiny puncture to front gutter, author's first book, not usually found in such nice condition. Between the Covers 42-187　1997 $150.00

GASS, WILLIAM H.　Omensetter's Luck. London: Collins, 1967. 1st edition; fine in dust jacket; inscribed.　Bev Chaney, Jr. 23-251　1996 $135.00

GASS, WILLIAM H.　The Tunnel. New York: Knopf, 1995. Uncorrected proof; thick 8vo; printed wrappers, fine.　James S. Jaffe 34-170　1996 $100.00

GASS, WILLIAM H.　The Tunnel. New York: Alfred A. Knopf, 1995. Uncorrected proof; 652 pages; 27 illustrations; printed white wrappers, fine.　Bev Chaney, Jr. 23-253　1996 $100.00

GASTIUS, JOANNES　De Virginitatis Custodia, Stupri Vindicta, Uxorum in Viros Pietate & Perfidia, de Scortationis Scelere, & Eius Poena, de Moribus ac Uirtutibus Uariarum Gentium... Basel: R. Winter, 1544. 1st edition; 8vo; 400 pages; woodcut ornaments; 18th century full mottled calf, gilt (title backed); fine, quite rare. NUC 192. 279 (3 copies); BM STC 333; VD16 G 536.　Bennett Gilbert LL29-77　1996 $2,750.00

GATES, R. R.　A Botanist in the Amazon Valley, an Account of the Flora and fauna in the Land of Floods. London: 1927. Crown 8vo; pages 203, map and 10 plates; cloth, trifle worn, signatures on endpaper. Wheldon & Wesley 207-1773　1996 £60.00

GATES, WILLIAM G.　Illustrated History of Portsmouth. Portsmouth: Charpentier & Co., 1900. Hampshire Telegraph Centenary Edition; thick 4to; 734 pages; contemporary half black morocco, upper joint cracked; presentation inscription to Stan Kenton.　Howes Bookshop 265-451 1996 £85.00

GATHORNE-HARDY, GATHORNE   The Diary 1866-1892: Political Selections. London: Oxford University Press, 1981. Thick royal 8vo; 946 pages; portrait; original cloth, dust jacket.   Howes Bookshop 265-402 1996 £60.00

GATHORNE-HARDY, ROBERT   Darian: a Poem. Mill House Press, 1928. One of 25 numbered copies; 12mo; initials in red and blue supplied by hand; half vellum, marbled boards, very nice.   Bertram Rota 272-288 1996 £80.00

GATHORNE-HARDY, ROBERT   A Month of Years: Poems. Mill House Press, 1956. One of only 50 copies; 4to; blue cloth, covers little faded and bubbled, but internally very nice, crisp copy; with author's signed autograph presentation inscription to David Cecil.   Bertram Rota 272-293 1996 £60.00

GATKE, H.   Heligoland as an Ornithological Observatory, the Result of Fifty Years' Experience. Edinburgh: 1895. Royal 8vo; pages x, 599; portrait; original cloth.   Wheldon & Wesley 207-733 1996 £65.00

GATSCHET, ALBERT SAMUEL   The Klamath Indians of Southwestern Oregon. Washington: 1890. 1st edition; 4to; volume II in two equal volumes, 1422 pages, map; ex-library but only library markings are bookplate on front pastedowns, small call number label on lower backstrips and stamped number on blank page, hinges of part 1 professionally reinforced, fraying to top/bottom of backstrips, small spots to cover of part 1, moderate overall cover wear, good plus set; quite scarce. Not in Smith.   Gene W. Baade 1094-60 1996 $250.00

GATTY, MARGARET SCOTT 1809-1873   British Sea Weeds. London: 1872. Royal 8vo; 2 volumes; 80 plates of 384 figures; original cloth, slightly worn.   Wheldon & Wesley 207-1617 1996 £90.00

GAUNT, W.   The Etchings of Frank Brangwyn, R.A.: a Catalogue Raisonne. London: Studio, 1926. 4to; 236 pages, 331 illustrations, 8 Photogravure plates; morocco backed boards, some wear at edges. Freitag 1022.   Brannan Books 43-77 1996 $225.00

GAVIN, G. M.   Royal Yachts. London: Rich and Cowan, 1932. Number 525 of 1000; 4to; 338 pages, 15 color illustrations tipped in, tissue guarded, numerous half tones; gilt leather, top edge gilt, uncut; nice. John Lewcock 30-86 1996 £180.00

GAWAIN AND THE GRENE KNIGHT   Sir Gawain and the Green Knight. Oxford: 1925. 1st edition thus; bright, very good+ copy.   Aronovitz 57-1171 1996 $375.00

GAWAIN AND THE GRENE KNIGHT   Sir Gawain and the Green Knight. New York: Limited Editions Club, 1971. Number 1029 of 1500 copies, signed by artist; illustrations by Cyril Satorsky; fine in slipcase. Hermitage SP95-1038 1996 $175.00

GAWAIN AND THE GRENE KNIGHT   Sir Gawain and the Green Knight, Pearl and Sir Orfeo. Allen & Unwin, 1975. 1st edition; uncorrected proof; wrappers; very good+; scarce.   Aronovitz 57-1180 1996 $250.00

GAY, JOHN 1685-1732   Achilles, an Opera. London: printed for J. Watts, 1733. 1st edition; 12mo; disbound, but well preserved copy, uncommon.   Lyman Books 21-557 1996 $175.00

GAY, JOHN 1685-1732   The Beggar's Opera. London: printed for John Watts, 1742. 5th edition; 8vo; pages (8), 8, 76; unbound.   Peter Murray Hill 185-65 1996 £50.00

GAY, JOHN 1685-1732   The Beggar's Opera. London: Strahan, 1777. 8vo; 96 paes; frontispiece, corner stained, tears in one leaf repaired, half calf, hinges weak.   William Reeves 309-9651 1996 £72.00

GAY, JOHN 1685-1732   The Beggar's Opera. London: Heinemann, 1921. Limited to 430 copies; imperial 8vo; printed on handmade paper; 8 tipped in color plates by Claud Lovat Fraser; minor shelfwear but attractive.   Lyman Books 21-556 1996 $100.00

GAY, JOHN 1685-1732   The Distress'd Wife. London: printed for Thomas Astley, 1743. 1st edition; 8vo; disbound, very good, complete with half title, CBEL II 498.   Ximenes 109-134 1996 $400.00

GAY, JOHN 1685-1732   Fables. London: W. Osborne, 1792. 8vo. in 6's; title with woodcut vignette (slight stain in inner margin only), dozens of woodcuts in text; rebound in half calf marbled boards, original red morocco label laid down.   Ian Wilkinson 95/1-99 1996 £56.00

GAY, JOHN 1685-1732   Fables by John Gay. London: John Stockdale, 1793. 1st of this edition; tall octavo; wide margined copy; pages xi, 225; vii, 187, (1); 2 volumes; titlepage vignettes, 70 fine engraved plates by William Blake, tissue guards and subscriber list present; elegantly bound by Tout in three quarter morocco, marbled boards and endpapers, raised bands, spines elaborately gilt in compartments, all edges gilt, slight wear to covers, spines uniformly sunned, but beautiful set. Lowndes II 772; CBEL II 293.   Hartfield 48-L33 1996 $1,295.00

GAY, JOHN 1685-1732   Fables... London: ptd. for John Stockdale, 1793. 1st edition thus; large 8vo; 2 volumes in one; engraved title to each volume, 68 plates; contemporary tree calf, neatly rebacked, spine gilt; tall set, with margins of engraved titles well clear of ornaments at top and bottom; very good. Bentley 460.   Ximenes 108-153 1996 $450.00

GAY, JOHN 1685-1732   The Fables of Mr. John Gay. London: T. Wilson and R. Spence, 1806. 12mo; 252 pages; titlepage vignette and dozens of woodcuts by Bewick; original burgundy calf over marbled boards, boards and front hinge rubbed.   Kenneth Karmiole 1NS-109 1996 $150.00

GAY, JOHN 1685-1732   The Poems. Chiswick: printed by Chas. Whittingham, College House, n.d., ca. 1820. 8vo; 2 volumes, pages 252, 250; elegantly bound in full striated crimson morocco, elaborate gilt titles and decorations, gilt inner, all edges gilt, cased in specially made linen box; with 2 fine early fore-edge paintings: Volume 1 a split scene showing Gay's portrait in an oval frame and Lincoln's Inn Gate, Chancery Lane, the whole in a surround of grapes and vines; volume II offers a similarly designed painting with a portrait of Richard Steele in an oval frame, & depiction of Covent Garden in 1660 in a surround of masks of comedey & tragedy w/laurel ribbon & decorations. Small bookplate. Hartfield 48-F2 1996 $2,800.00

GAY, JOHN 1685-1732   Polly. London: 1923. Limited to 380 copies, signed by artist; tipped in color plates by William Nicholson; blue cloth, silver gilt, rubbed at head and foot of spine, otherwise very good. Words Etcetera 94-988 1996 £185.00

GAY, JOHN 1685-1732   Trivia; or, the Art of Walking the Streets of London. London: printed for Bernard Lintot, n.d. 1716. 2nd eidtion; 8vo; disbound; very good; signed on titlepage by Anthony Blackwall, the classical scholar and schoolmaster. Foxon G83; CBEL II 498.   Ximenes 108-154 1996 $150.00

GAY, JOHN 1685-1732   Trivia; or, the Art of Walking the Streets of London. London: Bernard Lintott, n.d. 1716. 1st edition; tall octavo; contemporary calf, bit rubbed, joints trifle cracked, spine gilt, fine and thick paper copy. Foxon G82; Rothschild 914; Hayward 142.   G. W. Stuart 59-42 1996 $595.00

GAY, JOHN 1685-1732   Two Epistles; One, to the Right Honourable Richard Earl of Burlington; the Other to a Lady. London: printed for Bernard Lintot, n.d. 1717. 1st edition; 8vo; modern mottled calf, gilt, spine and inner dentelles gilt, top edge gilt, slight rubbing; bound without half title, 2 leaves of ads are present at end; very good, scarce; bookplate of Oliver Brett, Lord Esher. Foxon G88; Rothschild 913 (lacking ads); CBEL II 498.   Ximenes 108-155 1996 $600.00

GAY, JOHN 1685-1732   The What D'Ye Call It: a Tragi-Comi-Pastoral Farce. London: Bernard Lintott, n.d. 1715. 1st edition; octavo; modern boards, cover detached, final leaf rehinged with few letters supplied; very rare; the Gathorne-Hardy copy with bookplate.   G. W. Stuart 59-41 1996 $685.00

GAY, MARY ANN HARRIS   The Pastor's Story and Other Pieces; or Prose and Poetry. Nashville: pub. for the author. 1861. 7th edition; 12mo; 266 pages; original cloth, chipped; Wright II 986-7 for 6th edition and 1858 1st ed.   M & S Rare Books 60-159 1996 $250.00

GAYARRE, CHARLES   Louisiana: Its Colonial History and Romance. New York: Harper & Bros., 1851. Enlarged edition; 546 pages; bound in back is 14 page pamphlet "Historical Sketch of Louisiana"; original black cloth, light edgewear, newspaper clippings pasted down to front free endpaper; Howes G88.   Blue River Books 9-213 1996 $125.00

GAYARRE, CHARLES   Louisiana: Its History as a French Colony. New York: John Wiley, 1852. 1st edition; 380 pages; folding map; original olive cloth, gilt, few chips and spotting, foxing. Howes G87.   Blue River Books 9-212 1996 $150.00

GAYER, ARTHUR EDWARD   The Catholic Layman. Dublin: 1852-58-62. Large 4to; complete file of 7 volumes, together with supplement issued in 1862 containing the general index; strongly bound in cloth, label, nice state.   James Fenning 133-127 1996 £125.00

GEBOW, JOSEPH A.   A Vocabulary of the Snake, Or Sho-Sho-Nay Dialect... Green River City: Freeman and Bros. print, 1868. 2nd edition; 24 pages; original printed front wrapper only bound in three quarter morocco, very good. From the library of Edward Ayer with his booklabel. Graff 1533; Streeter Sale 2232. Pilling 1487;   Michael D. Heaston 23-154 1996 $6,500.00

GEDDES, MICHAEL   The Life of Maria de Jesus of Agreda, a Late Famous Spanish Nun. (with) A Tract Proving the Adoration of Images... London: 1714/14. 2nd edition? 8vo; 2 works in 1; (ii), 59; 52 pages; half black morocco; good.   K Books 442-237 1996 £70.00

GEELHAAR, CHRISTIAN   Paul Klee and the Bauhaus. Greenwich: New York Graphic Society, 1973. Square 4to; 174 pages; 24 tipped in color plates, 108 monochrome illustrations; cloth, dust jacket.   Brannan 43-301 1996 $125.00

GEESTERANUS, R. A. M.   Mycenas of the Northern Hemisphere. Amsterdam: 1992. 8vo; 2 volumes; numerous text figures; art leather. Wheldon & Wesley 207-1618 1996 £60.00

GEIGER, MAYNARD J.   The Life and Times of Fray Junipero Serra, O.F.M., or the Man Who Never Turned Back (1713-1784). Washington: Academy of American Franciscan History, 1959. 1st edition; 2 volumes, x, 448; viii, 508 pages; frontispiece in each volume, 11 plates, 6 maps; gilt lettered blue cloth, very fine set.   Argonaut Book Shop 113-280 1996 $175.00

GEIKIE, ARCHIBALD   Text-Book of Geology. London: Macmillan and Co., 1882. 1st edition; 8vo; xi, 971 pages; folding frontispiece, folding printed sheet, 435 text figures; original cloth, endpapers slit along inner joints, but joints firm, very good copy.   David Bickersteth 133-192 1996 £115.00

GEIKIE, JAMES   Prehistoric Europe, a Geological Sketch. London: Edward Stanford, 1881. 1st edition; 8vo; xviii, 592 pages, 3 ad leaves, text figures, 5 colored plates and maps; original cloth, corner cut from front flyleaf.   David Bickersteth 133-193 1996 £68.00

GEISEL, THEODORE SEUSS 1904-1994   The Cat's Quizzer. New York: Beginner Boosk, Random House, 1976. 1st edition; 4to; colored illustrations by author; yellow pictorial boards, tips just rubbed, else fresh copy.   Barbara Stone 70-79 1996 £65.00

GEISEL, THEODORE SEUSS 1904-1994   Horton Hears a Who! New York: Random House, 1954. 1st edition; quarto; unpaginated; illustrations; original glazed pictorial boards, color pictorial endpapers, top corners lightly bumped, otherwise near fine in lightly chipped dust jacket with faded spine.   Heritage Book Shop 196-273 1996 $300.00

GEISEL, THEODORE SEUSS 1904-1994   The Sneetches and Other Stories. New York: Random House, 1961. 1st edition; 4to; colored illustrations by author; colored pictorial boards, fine in matching pictorial dust jacket.   Barbara Stone 70-78 1996 £150.00

GEKOSKI, R. A.   William Golding. A Bibliography 1934-1993. Deutsch, 1994. 63/100 copies (of an edition of 1026 copies), signed by author; 8vo; pages xiii, 158; 8 color printed plates; quarter dark blue morocco grained sheepskin, backstrip gilt lettered and front cover gilt blocked with a copy of Golding's signature, gilt edges, board slipcase; new. Blackwell's B112-133 1996 £150.00

GEKOSKI, R. A.   William Golding. A Bibliography 1934-1993. Deutsch, 1994. One of 900 numbered copies, unsigned; red cloth and complete with board slipcase as issued.   Blackwell's B112-133a 1996 £75.00

GELDART, ERNEST   The Art of Garnishing Churches at Christmas and Other Times. London: Cox Sons, 1882. 1st edition; 8vo; 70, (34) pages, 25 plates; frontispiece; publisher's cloth; inscription in ink on front free endpaper, paper slightly sunned, else fine.   Bookpress 75-53 1996 $110.00

GELL, WILLIAM 1777-1836   The Geography and Antiquities of Ithaca. London: Longman, Hurst, Rees, and Orme, 1807. 1st edition; 14 engraved plates, large margins, very fresh and free of foxing; full diced calf with leather labels, head and tail of crown expertly restored, attractive copy.   Hermitage SP95-1101 1996 $1,000.00

GELL, WILLIAM 1777-1836   The Topography of Rome and Its Vicinity. London: Henry G. Bonn, 1846. New edition; 8vo; viii, 499 pages, numerous figures, maps; three quarter calf antique and 5 raised bands, bookplate, several pages foxed.   Archaeologia Luxor-3359 1996 $250.00

GELLERT, CHRISTLIEB EHREGOTT   Metallurgic Chymistry. London: for T. Becket, 1776. 1st edition in English; 8vo; (4), iii, xv, 416 pages, folding table, 4 folding plates; original boards, rebacked in manner of the original; untrimmed and partially unopened, one minor tear repaired, unusually fine. Rare. Duveen pp. 242-243 noting only 3 folding plates; Bolton I 473.   Edwin V. Glaser 121-132 1996 $1,500.00

GELLI, GIOVANNI BATISTA   La Circe Di Giovan-Batista Gelli. Firenze: Lorenzo Torrentino, 1549. 1st edition; octavo; late 17th or early 18th century polished grained sheep, gilt spine with contrasting title labels of tan and black morocco gilt; joints slightly rubbed, cracked at head and foot of spine with excellent restoration to top of spine, tiny chip at top back joint, light soiling tot title and final leaf, small collector's stamp at foot of title, very respectable copy of a very rare book; several bookplates, including De Vernaccia and Landau bookplates. Adams G333 Gamba 491.   G. W. Stuart 59-43 1996 $750.00

GELLI, GIOVANNI BATISTA   Circe. London: James Bettenham, 1744. Large octavo; original calf, joints cracked, slight peeling along hinges, light embrowning, nice;   G. W. Stuart 59-44 1996 $320.00

GENARD, FRANCOIS   The School of Man. London: printed for Lockye Davis, 1753. 2nd edition; 12mo; xxiv, 304, (viii) pages; original calf, rebacked.   David Bickersteth 133-20 1996 £65.00

GENAUER, EMILY   Rufino Tamayo. New York: Abrams, n.d. Square 4to; 175 pages; 146 illustrations, including 54 color plates, cloth, dust jacket, signed by Gamayo; Freitag 9261.   Brannan 43-631 1996 $225.00

THE GENEALOGIST. London: 1877-91. 8vo; 14 volumes; volumes 1-7 in original cloth, some spines little worn, 3 volumes repaired; volumes 1-7 new series handsomely bound in contemporary half morocco gilt. Howes Bookshop 265-1791 1996 £150.00

THE GENEALOGIST'S Pocket Library. London: 1908-10. Foolscap 8vo; 8 volumes; original cloth; from the library of art historian G. C. Williamson with his book label in each volume.   Howes Bookshop 265-1792 1996 £65.00

GENERAL Jackson Vetoed; Being a Review of the Veto Message of the Bank of the United States. N.P.: 1832. 1st edition; 8vo; 24 pages; sewn and uncut as issued. Not in Imprints Survey; not in Kress; 3 copies in NUC.   M & S Rare Books 60-281 1996 $150.00

GENERAL Stevenson. Cambridge: Printed by Welch, Bigelow & Go., 1864 1st edition; 12mo; 129 pages; photo of Stevenson pasted in as frontispiece; full brown morocco, lightly scuffed, all edges gilt, published without top edge gilt; presentation copy from Stevenson's parents. Scarce.   M & S Rare Books 60-302 1996 $225.00

GENLIS, STEPHANIE FELICITE DUCREST DE ST. AUBIN, COMTESSE DE 1746-1830   Adelaide and Theodore; or Letters on Education... London T. Cadell, 1788. 3rd edition; 12mo; 3 volumes contemporary tree calf, spines in compartments with raised bands, gilt rules and delicate ornamentation, red and black morocco labels, lettered in gilt; slight spotting to just a few leaves, otherwise fine; bookplate of Count le Pelletier, inscription presenting the book to Mary Pottinger on rear pastedowns, one little chipped.   Simon Finch 24-23 1996 £285.00

GENT, THOMAS   The Life of Mr. Thomas Gent, Printer of York, Written by Himself. London: printed for Thomas Thorpe, 1832. One of 3 copies, large paper copy on thick paper; portrait, several woodcuts; Birmore & Wyman I p. 260.   Maggs Bros. Ltd. 1191-179 1996 £300.00

GENTHE, ARNOLD   As I Remember. New York: Reynal & Hitchcock, 1936. 290 pages; 112 photos by author; near fine.   Hermitage SP95-1064 19964 $125.00

GENTHE, ARNOLD   The Book of the Dance. New York: 1916. 1st edition; limited to 100 numbered, signed copies; Japanese vellum boards, spine darkened, front cover somewhat soiled, inscribed and signed by Genthe.   J. B. Muns 154-120 1996 $600.00

GENTHE, ARNOLD   Isadora Duncan: Twenty Four Studies. New York: 1929. 1st edition; slipcase somewhat worn; laid in U.S. Camera printed portrait of Genthe with note in pencil; uncommon in slipcase. Inscribed and signed by Genthe.   J. B. Muns 154-121 1996 $400.00

GENTHE, ARNOLD   Isadora Duncan: Twenty-Four Studies By... New York: Kennerley, 1929. 1st edition; small folio; 24 black and white photos; gilt stamped black cloth, bevelled edges, top edge gilt; very good in publisher's pictorial white board slipcase.   George J. Houle 68-112 1996 $275.00

GENTHE, ARNOLD   Isadora Duncan. New York: Mitchell Kennerley, 1929. Folio; 914) pages text + 24 leaves of photographic plates and one facsimile plate; black gilt cloth.   Kenneth Karmiole 1NS-207 1996 $150.00

GENTILLET, INNOCENT   Discours, Svr Les Moyens de Bien Govverner et Maintenir en Bonne Paix vn Royaume ou Autre Principaute... Geneva: Stoer?, 1576. 8vo; fine title device, repeated at end; vellum, light marginal dampstain at beginning and marginal worming on 14 leaves. Adams G439.   Rostenberg & Stern 150-47 1996 $1,250.00

THE GENTLEMAN Angler. London: G. Kearsley, 1786. 12mo; 122 pages; frontispiece; beautifully bound in dark green half dark green half morocco with marbled boards and endpapers, gilt flies on panelled spine, few light stains to text, otherwise very clean copy;   Glenn Books 36-100 1996 $650.00

GENTLEMAN OF ELVAS   The Discovery of Florida, Being a True Relation of the Vicissitudes that Attended the Governor Don Hernando de Soto and Some Nobles of Portugal in the Discovery of Florida. San Francisco: printed at the Grabhorn Press, for the Book Club of California, 1946. Limited to 280 copies; folio; (vii), 106 pages, titlepage and decorative initials in colors, designed and cut by Mallette Dean; printed on French handmade paper; decorative paper over boards with cloth spine and paper spine label, in plain paper dust jacket, as issued; fine, as new, with prospectus laid in. Grabhorn Bib. 432.   Andrew Cahan 47-73 1996 $265.00

THE GENTLEMAN'S Recreation. London: 1721. 6th edition; 5 parts in 1; 5 copper plates, name in ink to titlepage and not affecting text, new endpapers; modern half tan calf with marbled sides.   Petersfield Bookshop FH58-322 1996 £320.00

GENTLEMAN, DAVID   Bridges on the Backs; a Series of Drawings. Cambridge University Press, Christmas, 1961. One of 500 copies; oblong 4to; printed in Monotype Times Wide, with plates touched with color; glued into green buckram folder; fine.   Bertram Rota 272-66 1996 £160.00

GENTLEMAN, FRANCIS   The Theatres. London: printed for John Bell and C. Etherington, York, 1772. 1st edition; 4to; disbound; wanting half title and final leaf of ads, otherwise very good. LAR 2325; Jackson p. 16. Ximenes 108-156 1996 $450.00

THE GENUINE Rejected Addresses, Presented to the Committee...for Drury Lane Theatre; Preceded by that Written by Lord Byron and Adopted by the Committee. London: printed and sold by B. McMillan, 1812. 1st edition; 1st issue; 8vo; 19th century full calf, Signet arms on covers, good tall copy. LAR 1382.   Peter Murray Hill 185-25 1996 £225.00

GEOGHEGAN, EDWARD   A Commentary on the Treatment of Ruptures, Particularly in a State of Strangulation. London: for Samuel Highley, 1810. 1st edition; 8vo; 95 pages; original boards, expertly rebacked in style of the original, new printed paper label, marginal dampstaining, boards bit worn at extremities, very good, scarce, fragile. Blocker p. 156. Not in Wellcome, Waller, Osler, Orr, Pybus.   Edwin V. Glaser B122-65 1996 $200.00

GEOPONICA   Constantini Caesaris Selectarum Praeceptionum, de Agricultura Libri Uiginti. Basle: Froben, 1540. 8vo; printer's device on titlepage which is browned, woodcut initials, pages 385, (15); contemporary vellum, gilt lettered red morocco label on spine, very good. Adams C865.   Blackwell's B112-114 1996 £500.00

GEORGE & CO.   Trade Catalogue for George & Co. London: George & Co., 1928. 1st edition; 8vo; 7 pages, 23 samples of leather bindings, only one sample detached, otherwise very good, self wrappers.   The Bookpress 75-275 1996 $125.00

GEORGE and His Hatchet. Greenfield: A. Phelps, 1847. Early edition; page size 2 7/8 x 4 3/8 inches; 28 original woodcuts; original wrappers, some dampstaining, all but completely faded ownership signature in pencil on front free endpaper; very rare.   Priscilla Juvelis 95/1-61 1996 $750.00

GEORGE IV, KING OF GREAT BRITAIN   The Correspondence of George, Prince of Wales 1770-1812. London: Cassell, 1963-71. Standard edition; royal 8vo; 8 volumes, plates and folding pedigrees; buckram, lettering pieces, dust jackets.   Howes Bookshop 265-406 1996 £200.00

GEORGE, ANDREW L.   A Texas Prisoner. Charlotte: Elam & Cooley, Sept., 1895. 1st edition; 32 pages; illustrations; original pictorial grey wrappers with title stamped in black on front, minor stain to several pages and small wormhole in margin not affecting text; very good. Scarce. Adams Six Guns 822.   Michael D. Heaston 23-155 1996 $500.00

GEORGE, DANIEL   The Modern Dunciad, Virgil in London and Other Poems. London: Pickering, 1835. 1st of this edition; octavo; pages 341, original pebbled cloth, facsimile typographic label, uncut; nice, scarce. Keynes p. 62.   Hartfield 48-71 1996 $185.00

GEORGE, ELIZABETH   Missing Joseph. London: Bantam Press, 1992. 1st edition; signed; fine in dust jacket.   Quill & Brush 102-702 1996 $100.00

GEORGE, ELIZABETH   Well-Schooled in Murder. New York: Bantam Books, 1990. 1st edition; signed; fine in dust jacket.   Quill & Brush 102-699 1996 $100.00

GEORGE, ERNEST   Etchings of Old London. Fine Art Society, 1884. Folio; 20 finely etched plates printed in sepia; original pictorial cloth, cloth, gilt edges, corners worn, occasional very marginal finger soiling and few plates loose.   Thomas Thorp 489-112 1996 £200.00

GEORGE, ERNEST   Etchings of Old London. London: Fine Art Society, 1884. Folio; 20 magnificent etched plates; original printed cloth, covers trifle dull.   Charles W. Traylen 117-369 1996 £225.00

GEORGE, ERNEST   Etchings of Old London. London: Fine Art Society, 1884. Folio; pages vi, 20 etchings with letterpress, original pictorial cloth, slightly soiled.   Marlborough 162-144 1996 £200.00

GEORGE, GERTRUDE A.   Eight Months with the Women's Royal Air Force - (Immobile). Heath Cranton Ltd., n.d. 1920. 1st edition; full page drawings by author; cloth backed boards; head and tail of spine and corners bumped and rubbed, prelims, edges and endpapers spotted, covers slightly marked, very good.   Ulysses 39-637 1996 £65.00

GEORGE, H.   The Oberland and Its Glaciers: Explored and Illustrated with Ice-Axe and Camera. London: 1866. 1st edition; 28 hand mounted albumen photos; green boards, gilt lettering and decoration, all edges gilt, light rubbing of spine and corners of boards, some foxing of first plate and titlepage, small repair to half title, new endpapers, good, sound, very good copy.   Moutaineering Books 8-EG01 1996 £400.00

GEORGE, JOHN NIGEL   English Guns and Rifles. Plantersville: Small-Arms Technical Pub. Co., 1947. 1st edition; royal 8vo; (x), (346) pages; plates and illustrations; bound in elegant modern half morocco, banded and gilt with rifles by Bayntun-Riviere, top edge gilt, very good. Ash Rare Books Zenzybyr-37 1996 £250.00

GEORGE, JOHN NIGEL   English Guns and Rifles. U.S.A.: 1947. 1st edition; illustrations; dust jacket thoroughly stuck up with clear adhesive sheeting, otherwise excellent.   David A.H. Grayling 3/95-296 1996 £60.00

GEORGE, JOHN NIGEL   English Pistols and Revolvers. London: 1938. 1st edition; illustrations; dust jacket thoroughly stuck up with adhesive sheeting etc; book itself, apart from small tape marks on endpapers, excellent copy. Very scarce.   David A.H. Grayling 3/95-295 1996 £55.00

GEORGI, CHRISTIAN SIEGISMUND   Wittenbergische Jubel-Geschichte... Wittenberg: J. J. Ahfeld, 1756. Small 4to; 2 ff., xii, 122 pages, 1 f., 7 engraved plates; 19th century marbled boards, small repair to title, text lightly browned. Berlin Kat. 2917; not in Lipperheide or vinet. Marlborough 162-229 1996 £1,450.00

GEORGI, J. P.   Russia: or, A Compleat Historical Account of All the Nations Which Compose that Empire. London: printed for J. Nichols; T. Cadell, H. Payne and N. Conant, 1770. 1st English edition; 8vo; 2 volumes, name on titles, 4 plates; contemporary mottled calf, spines worn, hinges cracked.   Anthony Laywood 108-68 1996 £135.00

GEORGIA. (COLONY). LAWS STATUTES ETC.   Acts Passed by the General Assembly of the Colony of Georgia 1755-1774. Wormsloe: privately printed, 1881. 1st and only edition, limited to 49 copies; large folio; 427 pages; original green patterned cloth, red morocco spine label, minor repairs to spine, some foxing to several pages, otherwise fine, tight copy; presentation copy from Mrs. George De Renne. Quite rare. Michael D. Heaston 23-156 1996 $2,500.00

GEORGIAN SOCIETY   Records of the 18th Century Domestic Architecture & Decoration in Dublin. Volume II. London: 1910. Limited to 400 copies; 8vo; subscribers notice loosely inserted; 115 plates; cloth, marks on cover, otherwise very good.   C. P. Hyland 216-253 1996 £140.00

GEORGIAN SOCIETY   Records of the 18th Century Domestic Architecture & Decoration in Dublin. Volume V. London: 1913. Limited to 600 copies; 8vo; 129 plates; cloth, mark on cover, else very good.   C. P. Hyland 216-254 1996 £75.00

GERARD, FRANCES   Picturesque Dublin, Old and New. London: 1898. 1st edition; 8vo; 91 Rose Barton illustrations; cloth, some damp marking; goodish.   C. P. Hyland 216-255 1996 £95.00

GERARD, JOHN 1545-1612   The Herbal or General History of Plants. 1975. Reprint of 1633 edition; 4to; over 1600 pages, numerous woodcuts; cloth.   Wheldon & Wesley 207-1906 1996 £90.00

GERARD, JOHN 1545-1612   The Herball or General Historie of Plantes. London: Adam Islip, Joice Norton & Richard Whitakers, 1633. Best edition; folio; pages (xxxviii), 1630, (xlvi), first and last blanks missing, Roman letter, splendied engraved titlepage by Payne with figures of Ceres and Pomona, Theophrastus and Discorides and portrait of author at foot, large woodcut illustrations; 19th century old style panelled calf, rebacked, spine remounted, very small paper flaws in two leaves, another torn not touching text or woodcuts, fine, remarkably good and clean in 19th century old style panelled calf, rebacked, spine remounted. STC 11751; Lowndes 879. Rohde pp. 98-119; Bitting 181.   A. Sokol XXV-42 1996 £2,950.00

GERARD, MONTAGU   Leaves from the Diaries of a Soldier and Sportsman, During Twenty Years Service in India, Afghanistan, Egypt and Other Countries. 1865-1885. 1903. Photo plates and drawings by author; finely bound in modern half green morocco, gilt borders; very light foxing on few pages.   David Grayling J95Biggame-372 1996 £120.00

GERARD, MONTAGU   Leaves from the Diaries of a Soldier and Sportsman, During Twenty Years Service in India, Afghanistan, Egypt and Other Countries. 1903. Photo plates and drawings by author; original cloth, expertly restored.   David Grayling J95Biggame-373 1996 £75.00

GERBER, HELMUT E.   Annotated Secondary Bibliography of Thomas Hardy. Northern Illinois University Press, 1973. 1st edition; 2 volumes; near fine in dust jackets.   Words Etcetera 94-576 1996 £55.00

GERE, J. A.   Taddeo Zuccaro. His Development Studies in His Drawings. London: 1969. 28 x 19 cm; 239 pages; 176 plates; original cloth, dust jacket, mint.   Rainsford A54-666 1996 £85.00

GERISH, WILLIAM BLYTH   Sir Henry Chauncey, Kt. London: Waterlow & Sons..., Bishop's Stortford; Boardman & Son, 1907. Large paper edition, limited to only 50 numbered copies, signed by author; octavo; 2 volumes, pages (8), 114, (2) pages; original cloth backed printed boards, spine somewhat frayed and torn and corners bit worn, little spotting at beginning and end, otherwise internally very good;   Thomas Thorp 489-113 1996 £60.00

GERNING, J. J. VON   A Picturesque Tour along the Rhine, from Mentz to Cologne. London: published by R. Ackermann, 1820. 1st English edition, one of 750 copies on Elephant paper, later issue (plates watermarked 1836-1842), with most of the plates having numbers in top right hand corner; large quarto; xiv, (2), 178 pages; large folding map, with color, and 24 highly finished hand colored aquatint plates; list of subscribers; original green blindstamped cloth stamped in gilt on front cover and spine, all edges gilt, extremities lightly rubbed, joints expertly restored, little minor offsetting, overall, unusually clean, bright copy, with brilliant plates, in green cloth slipcsse. Abbey Travel 217; Tooley 234. Heritage Book Shop 196-257 1 996 $3,750.00

GERNSHEIM, H.   Alvin Langdon Coburn, Photographer. London: 1966 1st edition; dust jacket slightly torn.   J. B. Muns 154-75 1996 $100.00

GERNSHEIM, H.   Julia Margaret Cameron, Her Life and Photographic Work. London: 1948. 1st edition; 54 photo illustrations; dust jacket slightly torn.   J. B. Muns 154-58 1996 $125.00

GERRARE, W.   Phantasms. Roxburghe Press, 1985. 1st edition; spine darkened, else just about very good; the copy of Oswald Train, with his bookplate; quite scarce.   Aronovitz 57-445 1996 $295.00

GERSHWIN, GEORGE 1898-1937   George Gershwin's Song Book. New York: 1941. Revised edition; very good.   Lyman Books 21-161 1996 $100.00

GERSHWIN, GEORGE 1898-1937   Porgy and Bess. New York: Gershwin Publ. Corporation, 1935. 1st edition; large quarto; 559 pages; frontispiece photo of composer; stiff printed wrappers with cloth spine; scarce.   Left Bank Books 2-48 1996 $285.00

GERSTAECKER, FRIEDRICH WILHELM CHRISTIAN 1816-1872 Gerstacker's Travels. London: T. Nelson and Sons, 1854. 1st English translation; viii, (1) 10-290 pages, 2 double page lithographed plates; original brown cloth lettered and decorated in gilt on front cover and spine, all edges gilt, expertly rebacked preserving original spine, inner hinges expertly reinforced with Japanese tissue, overall fine. Cowan p. 234; Wheat Calif. Gold Rush 81.   Argonaut Book Shop 113-284 1996 $300.00

GERSTAECKER, FRIEDRICH WILHELM CHRISTIAN 1816-1872   Western Lands and Western Waters. London: S. O. Beeton, 1864. 1st English edition; xii, 388 pages, text engravings; bound by Bickers and Son, London in full dark blue morocco, marbled edges and endleaves, gilt ruling on edges, elaborate gilt tooling on spine; very good/fine light rubbing of edges, in later slipcase; 1st. English ed. of Howes G140. Bohling Book Co. 192-152 1996 $350.00

GESSNER, SOLOMON   New Idylles. London: printed for S. Hooper, 1776. 1st edition thus; 4to; 129 pages; engraved titlepage, 8 full page plates and in text illustrations; contemporary half red morocco and marbled boards, library bookplate and unobtrusive blindstamps, extremities rubbed, but very good.   Chapel Hill 94-60 1996 $300.00

GETLEIN, FRANK   Chaim Gross. New York: Abrams, 1974. Oblong 4to; 235 pages; 251 illustrations, including 56 color plates; cloth, dust jacket.   Brannan 43-250 1996 $125.00

GETLEIN, FRANK   Jack Levine. New York: Abrams, n.d. Square 4to; 26 pages text, 169 plates, 27 tipped in and in color; cloth, plastic dust jacket.   Brannan 43-350 1996 $165.00

GIARRE, GAETANO   Alfabeto di Lettere Iniziali Adorno di Animali e Proseguito da Vaga Serie di Caratteri. Firenze: Giacomo Moro, 1797. 1s edition; folio; each of the 25 copper engraved leaves including title is beautifully decorated with floral garlands, arabesques, birds, animals, vases, trophies and masks; these decorations surround the various calligraphic examples which follow the initial letters; contemporary brown pastepaper covered wrappers, little worn at very edges, preserved in quarter morocco clamshell case; Morison, Early Italian Writing Books...p 146; Bonacini 672.   Book Block 32-75 1996 $5,250.00

GIBBINGS, ROBERT   Samson and Delilah. Waltham St. Lawrence: Golden Cockerel Press, 1925. Limited to 325 numbered copies; wood engravings by Gibbings; white buckram, very good in somewhat foxed dust jacket with small chips to corners, scarce.   Words Etcetera 94-490 1996 £225.00

GIBBINGS, ROBERT   Sweet Cork of Thee. London: 1951. 1st edition; 8vo; woodcuts by author; cloth, dust jacket, very good; signed presentation copy from author.   C. P. Hyland 216-263 1996 £95.00

GIBBON, EDWARD 1737-1794   Histoire de la decadence et de la Chu de l'Empire Romain... Paris: Chez Les Freres Debure; Moutard, 1786. 12mo; 4 parts in 2 volumes; contemporary calf, sides with border toole in blind, spine with ornately gilt tooled compartmetns between raised bands, double contrasing beige and brown morocco labels, blue edges marbled endpapers; fine; contemporary ownership inscription of A. Weilmann in ink on titlepages. Norton 80.   Simon Finch 24-91 1996 £575.00

GIBBON, EDWARD 1737-1794   The History of the Decline and Fall of the Roman Empire. London: Strahan and Cadell, 1787-89. 1st editions of volumes 4-6, early editions of volumes 1-3; quarto; 6 volumes; contemporary tree calf, spines elaborately gilt tooled, contrasting red and green morocco labels, joints invisibly restored, minor foxing; extremely handsome set. PMM 222.   19th Century Shop 39- 1996 $4,250.00

GIBBON, EDWARD 1737-1794   The History of the Decline and Fall of the Roman Empire. London: A. Strahan and T. Cadell Jun. and W. Davies, 1797. 1st London octavo edition; 12 volumes; frontispiece to volume 1, 3 folding maps; contemporary speckled tan calf, minor rubbing, light surface wear to head of joint of volume iv, smooth backstrips, divided into compartments by gilt rules and 'Greek-key' roll, red morocco title label in second compartment, oval volume labels originally in fourth, but all lacking, gilt circular flower head in centre of remainder, gilt rope roll between fillets on joints, roundel and hatching roll on board edges, endpapers lightly stained by turn-ins, early owner's name on front pastedowns, silk markers, polished & speckled edges, very good. Norton 39.   Blackwell's B112-115 1996 £650.00

GIBBON, EDWARD 1737-1794   Miscellaneous Works. London: A. Strahan and T. Cadell Jun. and W. Davies, 1796. 1st edition; 4to; 2 volumes; silhouette portrait frontispiece in volume 1, offset to titlepage, as usual; pages xxv, (i),703; viii, 726, (2), errata and ad; contemporary quarter calf, rubbed and marked, smooth backstrip divided by double gilt rules, gilt lettered red morocco labels, calf tipped marbled boards, contemporary owner's signature (Nicholas Nicholas), contents unpressed and untrimmed, very good. Norton 131 & 136; Rothschild 949. Blackwell's B112-116 1996 £350.00

GIBBON, EDWARD 1737-1794   Miscellaneous Works... London: A. Strahan, T. Cadell Jun. and W. Davies/ (Vol. 3 John Murray), 1796/1815. 1st edition; 4to; 3 volumes; frontispiece in volume 1 and 3, folding pedigree; black binder's cloth, ex-library, little rubbed and marked, occasional foxing; sound, clean set.   Robert Clark 38-309 1996 £150.00

GIBBONS, WILLIAM   A Reply to Sir Lucius O'Brient, Bart. Bristol: Cocking and Rudhall, 1785. Half title, 64 pages; wrappers.   C. R. Johnson 37-13 1996 £120.00

GIBBS-SMITH, C. H.   Balloons. Ariel Press, 1956. Folio; xvi pages text, 12 full page illustrations in color on plates; cloth, dust jacket.   Thomas Thorp 489-115 1996 £55.00

GIBSON, CHARLES DANA   The Education of Mr. Pipp. New York: R. H. Russell, 1899. 1st edition; oblong folio; cloth backed boards, front board slightly bowed, soiling to white spine cloth, otherwise fine in broken publisher's box.   Hermitage SP95-779 1996 $125.00

GIBSON, EDMUND   Observations Upon the Conduct and Behaviour of a Certain Sect, Usually Distinguished by the Name of Methodists. London: ca. 1740. 1st edition; 4to; disbound; very good, very scarce. CBEL II 1624.   Ximenes 108-158 1996 $200.00

GIBSON, FRANK   Charles Conder, His Life and Work. London: John Lane, 1914. 1st edition; 121 illustrations, including 12 color plates; linen backed boards, crown and heel of spine frayed and torn; bookplate on recto of frontispiece and on pastedown endpaper and rear hinge cracked, good, sound and complete copy in newly made slipcase. Hermitage SP95-770 1996 $400.00

GIBSON, J. T.   History of the Seventy-Eighth Pennsylvania Volunteer Infantry. Pittsburgh: 1905. 1st edition; 267 pages, photos; cloth, very good. Donrbusch PA 220.   T. A. Swinford 49-411 1996 $100.00

GIBSON, JAMES   Dr. Bodo Otto and the Medical Background of the American Revolution. Springfield: 1937. 1st edition; 345 pages; original binding, binding and free endpaper spotted.   W. Bruce Fye 71-798 1996 $100.00

GIBSON, R. W.   St. Thomas More: a Preliminary Bibliography of His Works and of Moreana to the Year 1750, with a Bibliography of Utopiana. New Haven and London: Yale University Press, 1961. Numerous illustrations; red cloth, black and gilt on spine, dust jacket mildly defective; inscribed copy from Gibson to Dr. Ettinghausen. Maggs Bros. Ltd. 1191-92 1996 £120.00

GIBSON, THOMAS   Legends and Historical Notes on Places in the East and West Wards, Westmorland. Climate &c. Manchester: John Hewood, 1877. 1st edition; 8vo; pages 95; original cloth, gilt, little worn; scarce.   R.F.G. Hollett & Son 78-938 1996 £75.00

GIBSON, THOMAS   Legends and Historical Notes on Pales of North Westmoreland. London: Unwin Brothers and Appleby; J. Whitehead, 1887. 1st edition; 8vo; pages xv, 308, fine woodcut frontispiece, pictorial title and 4 illustrations; original cloth, gilt, little worn, neatly recased. Scarce.   R.F.G. Hollett & Son 78-937 1996 £75.00

GIBSON, WILLIAM   The Institutes and Practice of Surgery: Being the Outlines of a Course of Lectures. Philadelphia: Carey & Lea, 1832. 3rd edition; 8vo; 2 volumes; xx, (17)-391, (3); viii, (9)-413, (2) pages; 23 plates, some partially hand colored, usual browning and foxing, but good, attractive set. Rutkow GS7; Cordasco 30-0350.   Edwin V. Glaser B122-67 1996 $350.00

GIBSON, WILLIAM SIDNEY   A Descriptive and Historical Guide to Tynemouth:...the Monastery, the Church and the Castle... North Shields: Philipson & Hare, 1849. 1st edition; 8vo; xiii,. 161, viii pages of ads; fine steel engravings, text illustrations; original embossed cloth, neatly and expertly respined, very good. ad tipped in at end.   K Books 442-243 1996 £60.00

GIDE, ANDRE 1869-1951   Montaigne. An Essay in Two Parts. London: New York: Blackamore/Liveright, 1929. One of 800 copies, signed by author; original cloth, fine in close to fine dust jacket but for sunned spine, in somewhat worn box.   Beasley Books 82-69 1996 $200.00

GIDE, ANDRE 1869-1951   Montaigne: an Essay in Two Parts. London: Blackamore Press, 1929. 1st edition; one of 800 numbered copies, signed by Gide; fine in dust jacket darkened and chipped at spine. Captain's Bookshelf 38-90 1996 $100.00

GIDE, ANDRE 1869-1951   Montaigne. London: and New York: Blackamore and Liveright, 1929. One of 800 copies, signed by author; gilt top edge, near fine.   Thomas Dorn 9-127 1996 $100.00

GIEDION-WELCKER, CAROLA   Constantin Brancusi. New York: Braziller, 1959. 4to; 240 pages, 157 plates, 2 in color, cloth, dust jacket. Lucas p. 127; Freitag 1006.   Brannan Books 43-74 1996 $150.00

GIEDION-WELCKER, CAROLA   Jean Arp. New York: Abrams, 1957. 4to; 43 pages of text with illustrations, 101 pages plates and 20 pages plate descriptions, catalog of sculpture and bibliography; cloth, acetate dust jacket. Lucas p. 121; Freitag 245.   Brannan Books 43-19 1996 $275.00

GIES, WILLIAM J.   Dental Education in the United States and Canada. New York: 1926. Large 8vo; illustrations; original stiff wrappers, soiled. Argosy 810-211 1996 $125.00

GIFFORD, BARRY   No Enemy of Horses. Madrugada Press, 1970. One of 50 copies printed as a Christmas keepsake; slim pamphlet; near fine in spine faded stiff stapled wrappers, with xerox of newspaper article on Gifford laid in; scarce.   Lame Duck Books 19-218 1996 $150.00

GIFFORD, JOHN   A History of the Political Life of the Right Honourable William Pitt... London: printed for T. Cadell and W. Davies, 1809. 1st edition; 8vo; 6 volumes; 2 frontispieces; later half morocco, light foxing on couple of flyleaves, else fine.   Chapel Hill 94-221 1996 $160.00

GIFFORD, JOHN   A History of the Political Life of the Right Honourable William Pitt; Including Some Account of the Times In Which He Lived. London: printed for T. Cadell and W. Davies, 1809. 1st edition; 11 1/2 x 10 inches; 3 volumes; frontispiece in volumes 1 and 2; original diced Russia, covers ornately gilt in double frame w/broad outer border of triple fillets & lg. scrolling foliage, spine w/4 pairs of raised bands, gilt rules & attractive floral & foliate ornaments, marbled e.p.'s, front hinge of volume 1 neatly reinforced w/brown cloth, corners somewhat worn, joints cracked (though bds. still secure), 1 cover w/lg. round stain, spine ends little worn, sl. mottling or soiling to covers, not without defects, but a deluxe binding that was once quite impressive & that is still rather nice, endsheets and frontispieces foxed, light offsetting & occas. minor foxing in text, 1 leaaf w/sizable chip in fore margin (but still well away from text), otherwise excellent copy internally, with ample margins; armorial bookplate in each volume.   Phillip J. Pirages 33-424 1996 $125.00

GIFFORD, JOHN   A Residence in France, During the Years 1792, 1793, 1794 and 1795; London: T. N. Longman, 1797. 2nd edition; 8vo; 2 volumes; (ii), xxxvi, 456; (ii), 476 pages; contemporary tree sheep, spines gilt ruled, labels, corners slightly worn, short splits in joints; good set. Robert Clark 38-176 1996 £110.00

GIFFORD, WILLIAM   The Baviad, a Paraphrastic Imitation of the First Satire of Persius. London: printed for R. Faulder, 1791. 1st edition; 8vo; title and 51 pages, disbound, possibly lacking half title.   David Bickersteth 133-21 1996 £60.00

GIFFORD, WILLIAM   The Baviad and Maeviad. London: John Murray, etc., 1811. 8th edition; tall octavo; pages xxi, 191; original full tree calf, gilt, arms of the Writers to the Signet on front and back covers, wear to spine and hinges, page xxi mended, else very good.   Hartfield 48-L35 1996 $225.00

THE GIFT. Philadelphia: Carey & Hart, 1838. 1st edition; steel engravings; gilt decorated morocco, hinge cracked, rubbed, joints worn, good. BAL 19325.   Charles Agvent 4-1072 1996 $200.00

THE GIFT. Philadelphia: Carey & Hart, 1839. 1st edition; 8vo; steel engravings; original gilt maroon morocco; occasional foxing, f.f.e.p. lacking, light edgewear, quite good. BAL 992 and 16130.   Charles Agvent 4-950 1996 $300.00

THE GIFT. Philadelphia: Carey & Hart, 1843. 1st edition; 1st issue; 8vo; with the first appearnace in print of "The Pit and the Pendulum" by Poe; steel engravings; original gilt decorated morocco; this copy lacks front and rear endpapers and 1" piece at base of spine, some rubbing to covers, light to moderate foxing.   Charles Agvent 4-946 1996 $600.00

THE GIFT. Philadelphia: Carey & Hart, 1843. 1st edition; 2nd issue; 8vo; with the first appearance of Poe's "The Pit and the Pendulum"; original gilt decorated red morocco, this copy lacks rear blanks and endpaper, 1 engraving and printed title; the engraved title (2nd issue) is present; leather bookplate, backstrip lacking, moderate to heavy foxing.   Charles Agvent 4-947 1996 $300.00

GILBERT, FRANK T.   Historic Sketches of Walla Walla, Whitman, Columbia and Garfield Counties, Washington Territory and Umatilla County, Oregon. Portland: Printing House of A. g. Walling, 1882. 1st edition; thick quarto; pages 488, (12), (1)-66; frontispiece, plus approximately 150 lithographs; newly bound in maroon cloth with original gilt and black stamped cloth inlaid on front cover, gilt stamped spine, fine, clean and complete; Smith 3547.   Argonaut Book Shop 113-285 1996 $400.00

GILBERT, GEOFFREY   The History and Practice of the High Corut of Chancery. London: printed by Henry Lintot for J. Worral and W. Owen, 1758. 1st edition; 8vo; (x), 347 pages, (xlvii); contemporary tan calf, red morocco label, light browning, joints neatly reinforced, handsome copy in fine half morocco case; from the law library of John Marshall, Chief Justice of the Supreme Court; books from Marshall's Library are extremely rare on the market.   19th Century Shop 39- 1996 $22,500.00

GILBERT, GEOFFREY   The Law and Practice of Ejectments: Being a Compendious Treatise of the Common and Statute Law Relating Thereto... In the Savoy: printed by R. and B. Nutt and F. Gosling..., 1741. 8vo; pages (4), 360, (40), with half title/ad leaf; contemporary calf, label supplied, just very slight wear at headband, still very good to nice. James Fenning 133-130 1996 £125.00

GILBERT, GEOFFREY   The Law of Evidence. London: printed by Catherine Lintot...for W. Owen (etc.), 1760. contemporary calf, rebacked, definite foxing and embrowning, sound.   Meyer Boswell SL25-89 1996 $450.00

GILBERT, GEOFFREY   The Law of Evidence. Philadelphia: Joseph Crukshank, 1788. 1st American edition; 8vo; 286, (76) pages; contemporary tan calf, binding worn, pages lightly browned, bookplate, ownership signature, else good. Evans 21113.   Chapel Hill 94-251 1996 $150.00

GILBERT, GEOFFREY   The Law of Uses and Trusts... London: printed for W. Reed...and P. Phelan, etc., 1811. 3rd edition; contemporary calf, rebacked, worn, some foxing, but good.   Meyer Boswell SL26-88 1996 $250.00

GILBERT, GEOFFREY   A Treatise on the Court of Exchequer (etc.). London: printed by Henry Lintot etc., 1758. contemporary calf, rebacked, definite embrowning, but sound.   Meyer Boswell SL25-90 1996 $450.00

GILBERT, J.   The Dolomite Mountains. London: 1864. 1st (and only) edition; 576 pages, 6 colored plates, 27 wood engravings by Whymper, 2 maps; leather corners and spine (with raised bands and decoration), decorated 1864 at foot of spine, marbled boards with matching endpapers and page edges, some general wear with outer hinges weak and foxing of endpapers, generally very good-.   Moutaineering Books 8-EX01 1996 £200.00

GILBERT, JACK   Poetry Selections from Views of Jeopardy. Storrs: privately printed, 1964. 1st edition; 4to; 5 page mimeograph, stapled; singed by author, fine.   James S. Jaffe 34-171 1996 $400.00

GILBERT, JAMES WILLIAM   Logic for the Million, a Familiar Expositic of the Art of Reasoning by a Fellow of the Royal Society. London: 185 2nd edition; xii, 380 pages; original decorated blindstamped cloth, slight marked.   Graham Weiner C2-305 1996 £50.00

GILBERT, JOHN T.   Register of the Abbey of St. Thomas, Dublin. London: 1889. 1st edition; original quarter cloth; very good.   C. P. Hyland 216-274 1996 £60.00

GILBERT, JUDSON   Disease and Destiny: a Bibliography of Medical References to the Famous. London: 1962. 1st edition; 535 pages; original binding. GM 6742.1.   W. Bruce Fye 71-806 1996 $150.00

GILBERT, MERCEDES   Aunt Sara's Wooden God. Boston: Christophe Publishing House, 1938. 1st edition; fine in attractive, very good dust jacket, bit darkened on spine with faint stain to base of spine and with some slight chipping at crown, rare. Not in Blockson.   Between the Covers 43-83 1996 $750.00

GILBERT, WILLIAM SCHWENCK 1836-1911   Fifty "Bab" Ballads - Muc Sound and Little Sense. London: George Routledge & Sons Ltd., n.d. Reprint; 12mo; full leathetr covers, top edge gilt, cover edges worn, head and tail of spine and corners bumped and worn, good only; ownership signature of Ian Fleming.   Ulysses 39-682 1996 £125.00

GILBERT, WILLIAM SCHWENCK 1836-1911   Sweethearts. London: an New York: Samuel French, n.d. 1875. 1st edition? original printed wrappers, stitched backstrip worn, manuscript cues to text; with ownership inscription of the Boston Museum to upper wrap and cues 1 music, curtains and sound effects to text.   Dramatis Personae 37-76 1996 $100.00

GILCHRIST, ALEXANDER   The Life of William Blake with Selections from His Poems and Other Writings... London: Macmillan and Co., 1880 8vo; 2 volumes; xxi, (iii), 431, (i); ix, (v), 383, (i) pages; frontispiece in each volume, 60 full page plates and facsimiles, many vignettes and illustrations in text; original turquoise cloth, decorated gilt with designs by Blake, little wear to lower corners, half titles browned. Good set. Bentley 1680b.   Robert Clark 38-224 1996 £280.00

GILCHRIST, ELLEN   The Land Surveyor's Daughter. Fayetteville: Lost Roads Pub. Co., 1979. 1st edition; author's first book; decorative wrappers, close to fine, scarce; signed and inscribed by author. Thomas Dorn 9-129 1996 $525.00

GILCHRIST, OCTAVIUS GRAHAM   Rhymes. London: 1805. 1st edition 8vo; contemporary red straight grained morocco, gilt, gilt Lowther monograms on each cover, all edges gilt, spine bit faded, very slight rubbing; elegant copy; presentation copy, inscribed by recipient William Lowther, later 2nd Earl of Lonsdale also from the library of John Sparrow.   Ximenes 108-159 1996 $750.00

GILDAS   Opvs Novvm...de Calamitate Excidio, & Conquestu Britannia Antwerp? C. Ruremond? 1525? 1st edition; small 8vo; ff. (xliv), italic letter, 5 white on black woodcut initials; lightly browned, some light waterstaining at or near edges, little light marginal soiling, otherwise good in 19th century calf, gilt spine. STC 11892- Lowndes 891; Shaabe G315. 4 copies in NUC.   A. Sokol XXV-43 1996 £1,350.00

GILDON, CHARLES   The Life of Mr. Thomas Betterton, the Late Eminent Tragedian. London: printed for Robert Gosling, 1710. 1st editic 8vo; portrait; contemporary panelled calf, spine gilt, slight wear to spin variant without Gildon's name printed at end of epistle dedicatory, wanting flyleaf at front, but nice. LAR 2453; CBEL II 1049.   Ximenes 108-160 1996 $475.00

GILES   Daily and Sunday Express Cartoons. London: Lane Publicatic Ltd., 1946. 1st edition; artist's scarce first book; color pictorial wrappe covers slightly rubbed at edges, very good.   Ulysses 39-222 1996 £325.00

GILES, L. B.   Terry's Texas Rangers. Austin: 1911. 1st edition; 105 pages; original brown cloth, title stamped in gilt on front cover, neatly rebacked, some wear, very good. Howes G168; Jenkins BTB 75; Vandlae 72; Dornbusch 1059.   Michael D. Heaston 23-329 1996 $1,500.00

GILFILLAN, GEORGE   First and Second Galleries of Literary Portraits. Edinburgh: James Hogg, 1851. 3rd edition of volume 1, 2nd edition of volume 2; octavo; 2 volumes, 302, 330 pages; 54 portraits; uniformly bound in original green textured cloth, blind decorations to all covers, gilt titles; very good set. CBEL III 714.   Hartfield 48-V19 196 $195.00

GILL, ERIC 1882-1940   Art and Manufacture. Fanfare Press for the New Handworkers' Gallery, 1929. 7 3/4 x 5 inches; 2 p.l., 43-56 pages, (1) leaf, device on title and 2 illustrations in text; original white paper self wrappers, first and last leaves slightly creased and soiled, otherwise fine. Inscribed presentation copy from Eric Gill to G. Coulton. Gill 19.   Phillip J. Pirages 33-241 1996 $750.00

GILL, ERIC 1882-1940   Engravings 1928-1933. London: Faber & Faber, 1934. 1st edition; of which only 400 copies were pritned; 4to; pages xvi, 102; 133 wood engravings, all but 2 printed from original blocks; original green cloth, spine lettered in gilt, dust jacket, spine of jacket repaired internally, occasional slight foxing, otherwise very nice in original slipcase; this copy inscribed by Eric Gill for A. R. Squire. Evan Gill 27. Sotheran PN32-14 1996 £998.00

GILL, ERIC 1882-1940   The Future of Sculpture. London: ptd. for private distribution in the Office of the Lanston Monotype... 1928. 1st edition; one of 55 copies; foolscap 8vo; pages 18, (1); original black cloth, backstrip gilt lettered, faint waterstaining to tail edges of covers, good.   Blackwell's B112-117 1996 £400.00

GILL, ERIC 1882-1940   Sculpture. An Essay. Ditchling: Saint Dominic's Press, 1918. 1st edition; one of 400 copies; crown 8vo; pages (i), 22, (4) (ads); printed on handmade paper, pagination on page 5 present and misspelling 'frll' on page 10, typographical rule border present on titlepage; original pale brown wrappers, front cvoer printed in black, price is printed "Price One Shilling" and is unaltered, faint edges fading, rear cover, because of brittle nature of paper, is almost detached, untrimmed and almost entirely unopened; good. Superb association copy, given by Gill to his father the Revd. Arthur Tidman Gill and inscribed by Gill. Later in Gill's library with bookplate; Sewell 17; Gill, Eric Gill Bib. 5.   Blackwell's B112-247 1996 £450.00

GILL, ERIC 1882-1940   Sculpture on Machine-Made Buildings - a Lecture Delivered to the Birmingham and Five Counties Architectural Association in the Royal Birmingham Society of Artists Galleries, Nov. 1936. Birmingham: City of Birmingham School of Printing, 1937. 1st edition; wrappers; ownership name on upper cover, covers slightly creased, marked and dusty, yapp edges slightly creased, spine browned, very good.   Ulysses 39-224 1996 £95.00

GILL, ERIC 1882-1940   Songs Without Clothes. S. Dominic's Press, 1921. One of 240 copies; 8vo; light grey boards with linen back, linen little soiled and spotted, otherwise very nice, fresh copy.   Bertram Rota 272-420 1996 £80.00

GILL, ERIC 1882-1940   Twenty-Five Nudes. High Wycombe: J. M. Dent & Sons, Ltd., 1938. 1st edition; original binding, head and tail of spine slightly bumped, near fine in slightly rubbed, chipped, nicked and creased dust jacket darkened at spine.   Ulysses 39-225 1996 £225.00

GILL, WILLIAM   Gems of the Coral Islands; or, Incidents of Contrast Between Savage and Christian Life of the South Sea Islanders. London: Ward and Col, 1856. Presumably a remainder issue with volume one being 'third thousand' and volume two a first edition; 8vo; (xvi), ii, 243, xvii, 320, (4) pages ads; illustrations; original green cloth with blindstamped design; extremities bit rubbed, otherwise fine;   David Mason 71-145 1996 $280.00

GILLES, PIERRE   Antiquities of Constantinople... London: printed for the Benefit of the Translator, John Ball, 1729. 1st edition in English; 8vo; engraaved frontispiece, 11 fine engraved plates, 3 of them folding, engraved title part i; contemporary calf, spine gilt, titlepage torn but without loss; fine; owner's elaborate inscription; Blackmer 688; Weber 679.   Trebizond 39-102 1996 $1,350.00

GILLESPIE, W. M.   A Manual of the Principles and Practice of Road-Making. New York: A.S. Barnes & Co., 1847. 1st edition; 8vo; 336 pages; extensively illustrated; original cloth, fine.   M & S Rare Books 60-457 1996 $325.00

GILLIARD, E. T.   Birds of Paradise and Bower Birds. London: 1969. Royal 8vo; pages xxii, 485, 9 colored and 39 photographic illustrations and distribution maps; cloth.   Wheldon & Wesley 207-737 1996 £60.00

GILLIES, JOHN   A View of the Reign of Frederick II of Prussia; with a Parallel Between That Prince and Philip II of Macedon. London: printed for S. Strahan and T. Cadell, 1789. 1st edition; 8vo; contemporary tree calf, gilt, spine gilt, trifle rubbed, lacks label; half title present, very good.   Ximenes 108-161 1996 $150.00

GILLILAND, MAUDE T.   Rincon, Remote Dwelling Place, a Story of tthe Life on a South Texas Ranch at the Turn of the Century. Brownsville: Springman King, 1964. 1st edition; 105 pages; photos; dust jacket.   Maggie Lambeth 30-213 1996 $100.00

GILLILAND, MAUDE T.   Wilson County Texas Rangers 1837-1977. N.P.: 1977. 1st edition; 134 pages; signed, dust jacket, uncommon.   Maggie Lambeth 30-478 1996 $125.00

GILLING, ISAAC   A Sermon Preach'd at Lyme Regis in the County of Dorset, at a Quarterly lecture... London: 1705. Sole edition; 8vo; 44 pages, including half title, disbound.   David Bickersteth 133-22 1996 £80.00

GILLISPIE, CHARLES COULSTON   Dictionary of Scientific Biography. New York: Charles Scribner's, 1970-76. 4to; 14 volumes, few diagrams in text; cloth, dust jacket.   Thomas Thorp 489-116 1996 £850.00

GILLMOR, FRANCES   Windsinger, an Idyll of the Navajos. New York: Milton, Balch & Co., 1930. 218 pages; near fine in price clipped dust jacket with light soiling and several small nicks.   Ken Sanders 8-392 1996 $100.00

GILMAN, DANIEL   The Launching of a University and Other Papers. New York: 1906. 1st edition; 386 pages; original binding, scarce.   W. Bruce Fye 71-809 1996 $125.00

GILPIN, LAURA   The Enduring Navaho. Austin: University of Texas Press, 1968. 1st edition; 4to; xiii, 263 pages; color and black and white photos; fine in illustrated, price clipped dust jacket.   Andrew Cahan 47-80 1996 $150.00

GILPIN, LAURA   The Rio Grande: River of Destiny. New York: 1949. 1st edition; edge torn dust jacket.   J. B. Muns 154-124 1996 $125.00

GILPIN, SIDNEY   The Songs and Ballads of Cumberland, to which are added Dialect and Other Poems. London: Geo. Routledge & Sons; Edinburgh: John Menzies & Carlisle: G. Coward, 1866. 8vo; pages xiv, 560; frontispiece, front flyleaf removed; old half calf gilt, with raised bands and spine label (few slight chips to spine).   R.F.G. Hollett & Son 78-399 1996 £75.00

GILPIN, WILLIAM 1724-1804   An Essay Upon Prints. London: G. Scott, 1768. 2nd edition; foolscap 8vo; xii, 1f., 246, 6ff index; contemporary tree calf, gilt greek key pattern border, expertly rebacked, with new red gilt label; very good.   Ken Spelman 30-12 1996 £120.00

GILPIN, WILLIAM 1724-1804   The Last Work Published of the Rev. William Gilpin, M.A. Representing the Effect of a Morning, a Noon Tide and an Evening Sun. In Thirty Designs from Nature. London: Edward Orme, 1810/11. 1st edition; slim folio; 8 pages text, 30 tinted aquatint plates, each with additional contemporary hand coloring, uncut in original boards, later morocco spine, original paper label on upper board, dated 1811; very good. Abbey Life 131.   Ken Spelman 30-82 1996 £650.00

GILPIN, WILLIAM 1724-1804   Observations Relative Chiefly to Picturesque Beauty, Made in the Year 1772, on Several Parats of England. London: R. Blamire, 1788. 2nd edition; 8vo; 2 volumes, (2), xvi, 238; (2), 268, xiv pages, 30 aquatint plates; very good, later 19th century half morocco, marbled boards, raised and gilt banded spines; binder's ticket of R. Hynes of Dover.   Ken Spelman 30-83 1996 £260.00

GILPIN, WILLIAM 1724-1804   Remarks on Forest Scenery and Other Woodland Views, Relative Chiefly to Picturesque Beauty Illustrated by the Scenes of New Forest in Hampshire. London: 1808. 3rd edition; 2 volumes; 323 plates; diced calf, gilt and blind decorated, new and neatly rebacked with gilt design to backstrips.   Petersfield Bookshop FH58-186 1996 £200.00

GILPIN, WILLIAM 1724-1804   Three Dialogues on the Amusements of Clergymen. London: printed for B. and J. White, 1796. 1st edition; 8vo; original pale blue wrappers, rebacked to match at an early date; half title present, fine, uncut copy, scarce; booklabel of John Sparrow. CBEL II 1561.   Ximenes 108-162 1996 $300.00

GIMBEL, R.   Thomas Paine: a Bibliographical Check List of Common Sense with an Account of Its Publication. New Haven: Yale University Press, 1956. 19 facsimiles of titles and half titles, blue cloth, dust jacket. Maggs Bros. Ltd.   1191-93   1996 £52.00

GINGER Beer; a Grand Pindaric, in Honour of the Radicals and Whigs; Humbly Dedicated to Those Great Northern Allies. Leeds: printed by Wm. Headley, 1819. Only (?) edition; 8vo; half title; unbound, stitched as issued, uncut; very rare. Fine. Not in NUC or BL Cat.   Trebizond 39-19   1996 $300.00

GINSBERG, ALLEN   Ankor Wat. London: Fulcrum Press, 1968. 1st edition; limited to 100 copies, signed by author; 8vo; boards, dust jacket, fine in price clipped dust jacket.   James S. Jaffe 34-174 1996 $150.00

GINSBERG, ALLEN   Bixby Canyon/ Ocean Path/ Word Breeze. New York: Gotham Book Mart, 1972. 1st edition; limited to 26 copies signed by author; thin 8vo; black and white photos; cloth; mint.   James S. Jaffe 34-178   1996 $150.00

GINSBERG, ALLEN   Careless Love. Madison: Red Ozier Press, 1978. 1st edition; limited to 280 copies; 8vo; signed by author; marbled wrappers; mint.   James S. Jaffe   34-572   1996 $150.00

GINSBERG, ALLEN   The Gates of Wrath. Rhymed Poems. 1948-1952. Bolinas: Grey Fox Press, 1972. 1st edition; limited to 100 copies, signed by author; 8vo; cloth, glassine dust jacket, mint in jacket with one short closed tear at head of spine.   James S. Jaffe 34-179   1996 $125.00

GINSBERG, ALLEN   Iron Horse. Toronto: Coach House Press, 1972. 1st edition; one of 1000 copies; bolong 8vo; pictorial wrappers; fine; inscribed by author for Richard Eberhart.   Captain's Bookshelf 38-91 1996 $100.00

GINSBERG, ALLEN   Kaddish...With Two Other Related Poems: White Shroud and Black Shroud. Arion Press, 1992. One of 200 copies for sale, signed by author and artist; 12 3/4 x 10 1/2 inches; 62 pages; (1) leaf colophon; 2 portrait plates by Kitaj, prospectus laid in; two toned cloth, triangular foldover tab fastening on front cover, fore edge and tail edge untrimmed; as new.   Phillip J. Pirages 33-19   1996 $950.00

GINSBERG, ALLEN   Planet News 1961-1967. California: City Lights Books, 1968. 1st edition; limited to 500 copies, signed by author; small 8vo; cloth, slipcase; mint in slightly rubbed slipcase.   James S. Jaffe 34-175   1996 $125.00

GINSBERG, ALLEN   Scrap Leaves. Tasty Scribbles. New York: Poet's Press, 1968. 1st edition; limited to 150 copies signed by author; thin 8vo; printed wrappers; mint.   James S. Jaffe   34-176   1996 $125.00

GINSBERG, ALLEN   Wales -- a Visitation, July 29th 1967. London: Cape Goliard Press, 1968. 1st edition; limited to 100 copies, signed by author; square 8vo; black and white photos; boards, glassine dust jacket and printed dust jacket, with small vinyl record in pocket at back; fine in slightly rubbed dust jacket.   James S. Jaffe 34-177   1996 $150.00

GIOIA, DANA   Journeys in Sunlight. Ex Ophidia, 1986. One of 90 copies, signed by author and artist; 13 1/4 x 8 1/4 inches; (1) pages, (2) leaves; 3 delicate etchings in text by Fulvio Testa; morocco backed marbled paper boards, fore edge and tail edge untrimmed, in glassine dust jacket, contained in folding cloth box with paper label on front cover.   Phillip J. Pirages   33-212   1996 $425.00

GIOIA, DANA   Summer. Poems. N.P.: Arlia Press, 1983. 1st edition; one of 15 specially bound copies, signed by author; small thin 8vo; inscribed by author; quarter leather and boards; as new.   James S. Jaffe 34-186   1996 $250.00

GIOIA, DANA   Two Poems. N.P.: Bowery Press, 1982. 1st edition; one of 70 copies signed by author; thin 8vo; original wrappers, inscribed by author (ink inscription has bled slightly into titlepage, otherwise fine copy).   James S. Jaffe 34-183   1996 $225.00

GIRALDUS CAMBRENSIS 1146?-1220?   Opera. London: 1861-91. 8vo; 8 volumes; original cloth.   Howes Bookshop 265-1571   1996 £225.00

GIRARD, ALFRED C.   A Sketch of the Official Career of Colonel Edward Perry Vollum, Chief Medical Purveyor, U.S. Army. Fort Sheridan: 1891. 1st edition; 18 pages; original printed pale green wrappers, fine. Very rare.   Michael D. Heaston 23-158   1996 $1,250.00

GIRARDIN, R. L.   An Essay on Landscape; or, On the Means of Improving and Embellishing the country round Our Habitations. London: J. Dodsley, 1783. 1st English edition; foolscap 8vo; (2), lv, (i), 160 pages; frontispiece; contemporary tree calf, expertly rebacked but retaining original red gilt label; very good.   Ken Spelman 30-84 1996 £380.00

GIRAUDOUX, JEAN   Rues et Visages de Berlin. Paris: Editions de la Roseraie, 1930. One of 90 copies on Velin d'Arches (of total edition of 141), with etchings in 2 states, one hand colored and one in black and white; folio; 18 etched plates plus illustrations in text by Charles Laborde; quarter vellum and silver paper covered board portfolio with lettering and bear emblem in red and black, new spine and inner protective flaps, ties intact.   Marilyn Braiterman 15-127 1996 $2,250.00

GIRVIN, BRENDA   Alice and the White Rabbitt. Their Trips Round About London. London: S. W. Partridge, n.d. 1st edition; x, 11-160, 32 pages of ads; frontispiece, 7 full page and 35 text illustrations by E. Stuart Hardy; green cloth, gilt and color pictorial, spine gilt; foxing on endpaper browned, neat split in head of spine.   Robin Greer 94A-1 1996 £65.00

GISBORNE, THOMAS   An Enquiry Into the Duties of the Female Sex. London: T. Cadell & W. Davies, 1801. 5th edition; contemporary half maron morocco, very good signature on title of Catherine Jane Parkenham.   Jarndyce 103-439   1996 £85.00

GISBORNE, THOMAS   A Familiar Survey of the Christian Religion, and of History as Connected with the Introduction of Christianity, and With Progress to the Present Time. London: printed for T. Cadell, Jun. and W. Davies, 1801. 3rd edition; 8vo; xvi, 542, (2) pages; contemporary speckled calf, spine gilt, contrasting morocco labels; fine James Burmester 29-56   1996 £75.00

GISSING, GEORGE ROBERT 1857-1903   New Grub Street, a Novel. London: Smith Elder & Co., 1891. 1st edition; 2nd issue; 3 volumes; (5) 305, ad leaf, (5), 316, (5), 335 pages; original textured dark green cloth spines lettered gilt with blindstamped decoration to head and foot of spines and front covers, little light spotting to endpapers, otherwise very fine. Collie 1xb (variant binding).   Thomas Thorp 489-117 1996 £450.00

GISSING, GEORGE ROBERT 1857-1903   The Private Papers of Henry Ryecroft. Westminster: Archibald Constable and Co., 1903. 1st British edition; 12mo; 3 leaves of ads bound in the rear; decorative green cloth very good, small crack to front hinge, still tight, some darkening to spine.   Antic Hay 101-685   1996 $125.00

GIUSTINIAN, LEONARDO   Strambotte Canzonette D'Amore. Officina Bodoni, 1945. One of 150 copies of a total edition of 160; 7 1/2 x 4 3/ inches; 158, (2) pages; with titlepage woodcut by Piero Ghezzo, title printed in red and black, initials hand drawn in red and blue by Claudio Bonacini; original vellum over stiff boards, gilt fleuron on front cover, g titling on spine, top edge gilt, other edges untrimmed, in tape repaired and slightly soiled slipcase; just a hint of soiling to vellum, but very fine Mardersteig 72.   Phillip J. Pirages 33-404   1996 $1,550.00

GJERSTAD, EINAR   Early Rome. Lund: C. W. K. Gleerup, 1953-73. 4t volumes I-IVI (complete; illustrations; volumes I-IV in uniform three quarter cloth with leather labels, volumes V-VI in original printed wrappers, several corners bumped, otherwise fine. Volumes I and III ar inscribed by author, Mario A. Del Chiaro's signature appears in volumes I, III and IV.   Archaeologia Luxor-3367   1996 $1,500.00

GLADKY, SERGE   Motifs Decoratifs, Six Planches en Couleurs. Paris: Editions des Quatre Chemins, n.d. One of 500 copies, with each plate initialled in pencil by artist; 16mo; 2 volumes (of 3); (8); (8)ff; each volume contains 6 plates, colored brightly by pochoir and protected by tissue guards; unbound as issued, in pochoir illustrated paper folders; fine.   Bromer Booksellers 90-45   1996 $1,250.00

GLADSTONE, HUGH, S.   A Catalogue of the Vertebrate Fauna of Dumfriesshire. Dumfries: J. Maxwell and Son, 1912. Limited edition of 2 copies; 8vo; pages xiv, 80; colored folding map; original cloth, uncut; flyleaves lightly browned, but excellent copy.   R.F.G. Hollett 76-100 1996 £65.00

GLANVILL, JOSEPH 1636-1680   Essays on Several Important Subje in Philosophy and Religion. London: printed by J.D. for John Baker, an Henry Mortlock, 1676. 1st edition; small 4to; (xvi), 66, (ii), 56, (ii), 43, (ii), 28, (ii), 61, (ii), 58 pages, 2 ad leaves; original panelled calf, slight rubbed at top of spine, light waterstain along upper margin of final fou leaves of book, but fresh, crisp copy.   Wing G3809.   David Bickerste 133-23   1996 £585.00

GLANVILL, JOSEPH 1636-1680   Two Choice and Useful Treatises: The One Lux Orientalis: or an Enquiry Into the Opinion of the Eastern Sages Concerning the Praeexistence of Souls...The Other a Discourse of Truth... London: printed for James Collins and Sam. Lowndes, 1682. 8vo; engraved frontispiece, title in red and black, (xlvi), 195, (v); (i), 171, (vi), 173-276 pages, 2 ad leaves; original calf, rebacked, morocco spine labels, original endpapers preserved. Wing G833; Wing M2638.   David Bickersteth 133-24 1996 £245.00

GLASGOW. ROYAL COLLEGE OF SCIENCE & TECHNOLOGY Bibliotheca Chemica. A Catalogue of the Alchemical, Chemical and Pharmaceutical Books in the Collection of the Late James Young of Kelly and Durris. 1954. Reprint of the 1906 edition; 8vo; 2 volumes; original cloth, ex-library, library stamps.   Forest Books 74-79 1996 £95.00

GLASGOW. ROYAL COLLEGE OF SCIENCE & TECHNOLOGY Bibliotheca Chemica: a Bibliography of Books on Alchemy, Chemistry and Pharmaceutics. London: 1954. Facsimile of 1906 edition; 2 volumes, 487, 598 pages; original binding. Osler 7040.   W. Bruce Fye 71-649 1996 $250.00

GLASGOW. ROYAL COLLEGE OF SCIENCE & TECHNOLOGY Bibliotheca Chemica. London: Derek Verschoyle, 1954. Reprint of 1906 edition; 2 volumes; cloth, red spine labels, dust jacket (volume 1 only, bit scruffy).   Maggs Bros. Ltd. 1191-87 1996 £90.00

GLASGOW. ROYAL COLLEGE OF SCIENCE & TECHNOLOGY Bibliotheca Chemica. London: Holland Press, 1954. Facsimile reprint of 1906 edition; royal 8vo; xxiv, 488; vi, 599 pages; 2 volumes; buckram, slightly dust soiled.   Thomas Thorp 489-100 1996 £65.00

GLASS, MARK   Ancient Song. New York: Red Ozier Press, 1980. 1st edition; one of 10 copies with fold-out illustration hand colored by artist, out of a total edition of 100 copies, signed by artist and publisher, Steve Miller; thin 4to; illustrations by Janet Morgan; original wrappers; mint. James S. Jaffe 34-574 1996 $500.00

GLASSE, HANNAH   The Art of Cookery, Made Plain and Easy. London: printed for W. Strahan, J. and F. Rivington, et al, 1770. New edition; 8vo; pages (xxxii), 384, (24); text browned in places; contemporary calf, recently rebacked, spine lined in gilt, leather label; very good.   Sotheran PN32-15 1996 £398.00

GLEANINGS From the Most Celebrated Books on Husbandry, Gardening and Rural affairs. Philadelphia: ptd. and sold by James Humphreys, 1803. 1st American edition; perforation and cancellation stamps on blank verso of title, text slightly browned throughout, ad leaf at end, modern cloth, leather label. Fussell, Old English Farming Books 1793-1893, 111 p. 43. Anthony W. Laywood 109-54 1996 £85.00

GLEDITSCH, JOHANN GOTTLIEB   Methodus Fungorum Exhibens Genera, Species et Varietates cum Charactere, Differentia Specifica... Berlin: 1753. 8vo; pages 162, (36 index), 6 copper engraved plates; hardbound; inscription on endpaper and small cut out of corner, splitting to bottom third of front cover, very rare.   Raymond M. Sutton VII-14 1996 $1,200.00

GLEIG, G. R.   The Chelsea Pensioners. London: 1829. 1st edition; 3 volumes; half contemporary calf, gilt, little rubbed at extremities, but still attractive set.   Words Etcetera 94-485 196 £85.00

GLEIG, G. R.   The Life of Major-General Sir Thomas Munro, Bart. London: Henry Colburn and Richard Bentley, 8 New Burlington St., 1830. 1st edition; 8vo; 3 volumes; (v-xxiii), errata leaf, (xxv-xxvi), errata slip for volume 2 tipped in to volume 1, steel engraved frontispiece, large folding map, frontispiece to volume 2; full polished tan calf, corners very slightly bumped, gilt ruled border, blind tooled inner dentelles, brown morocco label and raised bands to spine, brown morocco volume labels missing from spines, blind tooling to compartments, edges speckled; armorial bookplates, ink ms. initials to titles, handsome set.   Beeleigh Abbey BA56-71 1996 £250.00

GLEIG, G. R.   The Soldier's Help to the Knowledge of Divine Truth. London: J. G. & F. Rivington, 1835. 8vo; full purple crushed morocco with a Scotch-rule gilt fillet border inside of which is a border composed of leafy vines and flower heads, at top of the central panel an oval with a gilt crown beneath which are entwined rustic initials "WR", spine with five raised bands and gilt decoration within compartments, board edges gilt, inner gilt dentelles, all edges gilt, signed at bottom of front turn in: bound by J. Mackenzie Bookbinder to the King, very attractive royal binding. Bound of William IV.   Book Block 32-40 1996 $950.00

GLENN, EDWIN F.   Reports of Explorations in the Territory of Alaska (Cooks Inlet, Sushitna, Copper and Tanana Riers), 1898. Washington: GPO for the War Department, 1899. 23cm; 464 pages; large folding map; modern wrappers with original cover laid down; very good to fine. Arctic 5816 and 5817.   Rockland Books 38-83 1996 $150.00

GLENN, THOMAS ALLEN   Some Colonial Mansions and Those Who Lived in Them. Philadelphia: Henry T. Coates & Co., 1899-1900. 1st edition; 4to; 2 volumes, 503 pages; full page portraits, photographic illustrations; original green cloth, near fine in green cloth protective wrapper.   Chapel Hill 94-164 1996 $125.00

GLIMPSES Along the Canadian Pacific Railway. Indian Series A. N.P.: ca. 1890. 7 x 9 inches; portfolio containing 12 excellent photogravures, printed on tissue and mounted, original printed portfolio, backstrip slightly frayed, else near fine.   Stephen Lunsford 45-25 1996 $450.00

GLOVER, J. W.   St. Patrick at Tara; a National Oratorio. n.d. 8vo; cloth, good; signed presentation copy.   C. P. Hyland 216-275 1996 £55.00

GLOVER, ROBERT   Nobilitas Poltica Vel Civilis. London: William Jaggard, 1608. 1st edition; 4to; 190, (1) pages; 9 full page engravings; contemporary full limp vellum, covers soiled, text leaf R4 wanting, one plate trimmed and mounted, various notices tipped to front endpaper, thus fair only; with ownership signatures of William Bedford and Charles Kirkpatrick Sharpe, with Bedford's bookplate.   Chapel Hill 94-222 1996 $125.00

GNUDI, MARTHA T.   The Life and Times of Gaspare Tagliacozzi, Surgeon of Bologna, 1545-1599. New York: Reichner, 1950. One of 2100 numbered copies; first edition; 4to; xxii, 538 pages; frontispiece, illustrations; original cloth; fine. GM 5734.   Edwin V. Glaser B122-68 1996 $200.00

GOADBY, ROBERT   The King of the Beggars; or, the Surprising Adventures of Bamfylde Moore Carew... London: Hodgson & Co., c. 1825? Color folding frontispiece by Marks of Carew in 11 disguises, marginal tear repaired and reinforced, without wrappers, slightly dusted, spine guarded.   Jarndyce 103-248 1996 £50.00

GOBINEAU, JOSEPH ARTHUR, COMTE DE   Essai sur l''Inegalite des Races Humaines. Paris: Firmin Didot Freres, 1853-55. 1st edition; 8vo; 4 volumes, (4), xi, (1), 492, errata leaf, (4), 512, errata leaf, (4), 423, (1); (4), 359, (1) pages; occasional insignificant foxing in volume 2 and some minor marginal worming, not affecting text, in few leaves in volume 3; otherwise fine in new half calf, spines gilt and lettered, with all original printed wrappers preserved, uncut; rare. PMM 335; Headicar & Fuller I 112.   John Drury 82-90 1996 £3,500.00

GOBIUS, JOHANNES   Scala Coeli. Ulm: Johannes Zainer, 1480. Folio; 19th century blindstamped pigskin, finely rebacked period style with new endpapers, first leaf containing register laid down with few tears neatly mended with no loss, prologue leaf also has few tears neatly mended with no loss and has two small collector's stamps in blank outer margin and with inner blank margin restored, few inner blank margins of next few eleaves restored or repaired, lightly washed throughout, few minor spots, some faint waterstaining, nicely rubricated, really quite decent; rare. Hain 9406; Goff G311.   G. W. Stuart 59-59 1996 $4,850.00

GOBLE, WARWICK   The Book of Fairy Poetry. London: Longmans, Green and co., 1920. 1st edition; royal 8vo; pages x, 180; 16 beautiful delicately colored pprints of fairies by Goble; original grey cloth stamped in blue, pictorial endpapers, one or two leaves little speckled, very ncie, very pretty.   Sotheran PN32-118 1996 £200.00

GODDARD, ROBERT H.   Rocket Development: Liquid-Fuel Rockt Research, 1929-1941. New York: Prentice Hall, 1948. Large 8vo; 291 pages; photo illustrations; blue cloth, very good.   Knollwood Books 70-409 1996 $175.00

GODEFROY, JACQUES   The History of the United Provinces of Achaia. London: printed by Andrew Clark for Jonathan Edwin, 1673. 1st edition in English; small 4to; disbound; very good. Wing G924.   Ximenes 109-136 1996 $200.00

GODEY'S Lady's Book and Magazine. Philadelphia: Louis A. godey, 1851/54. 1st printings; 8vo; 3 volumes; numerous full page engraved plates, many hand colored; early 20th century half red morocco with raised bands, all edges gilt, library bookplate and blindstamp, former owner's inscriptions, else lovely set.   Chapel Hill 94-111 1996 $200.00

GODFREY, M. J.   Monograph and Iconograph of Native British Orchidaceae. Cambridge: 1933. 4to; pages xvi, 259; portrait, 67 plates; cloth, binding trifle rubbed.   Wheldon & Wesley 207-36 1996 £300.00

GODINE, DAVID R.   Lyric Verse, a Printer's Choice. N.P.: Godine Press, 1966. Of 500 copies, one of 280 on Curtis Tweedweave; 10 x 6.5 inches; 75 pages; cream paper spine with title in gilt, brown-tan marbled paper over boards; small tape mark on front pastedown, otherwise fine in publisher's box.   Joshua Heller 21-130 1996 $200.00

GODKIN, G. S.   The Monastery of San Marco. Florence: printed by G. Barbera, 1887. 8vo; 90 pages; 31 original photos tipped in; full vellum with elaborate decoration in gilt on covers and spine;   David Mason 71-101 1996 $200.00

GODMAN, F. DU CANE   A Monograph of the Petrels (Order Tubinares). London: 1907-10. Limited to 225 numbered copies; royal 4to; paes iv, 381, 106 hand colored plates by Keulemans; full brown morocco gilt, uncut; some limited marginal staining, especially towards end, some very slight offsetting, still good copy; from the collection of Jan Coldewey.   Wheldon & Wesley 207-38 1996 £3,500.00

GODOLPHIN, JOHN   Repertorium Carnonicum; or an Abridgment of the Ecclesiasatical Laws of This Realm... London: printed by S. Roycroft, for Christopher Wilkinson, 1680. 2nd edition; 4to; licence leaf before title, with signature of John Evelyn (junior) on title, press mark G54 (deleted) in his father's hand; contemporary mottled calf, hinges slightly rubbed, spine gilt, label; this copy passed from John Evelyn Jr. to his father, after the former's death in 1699. Wing G950.   Anthony Laywood 108-9 1996 £345.00

GODWIN, BENJAMIN   The Substance of a Course of Lectures on British Colonial Slavery, Delivered at Bradford, York and Scarborough. London: published by J. Hatchard and Son, and J. and A. Arch, 1830. 1st edition; 8vo; half title, folding table; original boards, upper hinge cracked, uncut, printed paper label, chipped, nice. Goldsmith 26505; Ragatz p. 560; Williams II p. 441.   Anthony W. Laywood 108-175 1996 £185.00

GODWIN, FRANCIS   Rerum Anglicarum Henrico VIII, Edwardo VI et Maria Regnantibus Annales. London: John Bill, 1628. 2nd edition; 4to; pages (viii), 246, (ii), Roman letter, side notes in italic, printer's woodcut device on title, colophon within typographical border on recto of last leaf, else blank, woodcut initials and headpieces; small light waterstain in extreme upper inner corner of first few leaves; contemporary limp vellum; good, clean copy, contemporary autograph of Thomas Oddys on fly. STC 11946; Lowndes 905; Hazlitt II 697.   A. Sokol XXV-44 1996 £395.00

GODWIN, G. N.   The Geology, Botany and Natural History of the Maltese Islands. Valetta: printed by P. Bonavia, 1880. Small 4to; pages 80, one uncolored plate; cloth, rather stained.   Maggs Bros. Ltd. 1190-241 1996 £135.00

GODWIN, WILLIAM 1756-1836   Considerations on Lord Grenville's and Mr. Pitt's Bills, Concerning Treasonable and Seditious Practices and Unlawful Assemblies. London: printed for J. Johnson, n.d. 1795. 1st edition; 8vo; recent half calf, spine gilt, half title present, just a trifle dusty, fine, very scarce. CBEL II 1250.   Ximenes 108-163 1996 $2,500.00

GODWIN, WILLIAM 1756-1836   An Enquiry Concerning Political Justice, and its Influence on General Virtue and Happiness. Dublin: printed for Luke White, 1793. 1st and only Dublin edition; tall 8vo; 2 volumes; half titles present in each volume, that in volume 1 frayed along outer margin; title leaf with small amount of fraying, clean tear in T5 without any surface damage; original calf, front cover of each volume detached but present, covers show much wear; occasional light staining/foxing in both volumes, but contents generally almost fine. Kress B2528.   Roy W. Clare XXIV-10 1996 $675.00

GODWIN, WILLIAM 1756-1836   The History of the Life of William Pitt, Earl of Chatham. Dublin: printed for Messrs. Potts, Wilson, Walker and Byrne, 1783. 1st Irish edition; xvii, 257 pages; contemporary sheep, red label, very nice.   C. R. Johnson 37-59 1996 £225.00

GODWIN, WILLIAM 1756-1836   The History of the Life of William Pitt, Earl of Chatham. London: printed for the author and sold by G. Kearsley, 1783. 1st edition; 8vo; pages xvi, 302; contemporary calf, slight outer wear to hinges and staining to outer margins of title, but good, tall copy.   Peter Murray Hill 185-67 1996 £1,850.00

GODWIN, WILLIAM 1756-1836   Life of Geoffrey Chaucer, the Early English Poet... London: by T. Davison for Richard Phillips, 1803. 1st edition; 4to; 2 volumes; pages xxxvi, 489; vii, (i), 642, (32); frontispiece; contemporary green straight grain morocco, smooth spines richly decorated and lettered in gilt, sides with gilt border enclosing central panel of marbled paper, red marbled edges; spines rubbed, sides little stripped; attractive copy in unusual Regency binding. Bookplate of Mere Hall.   Simon Finch 24-94 1996 £575.00

GODWIN, WILLIAM 1756-1836   Things As They Are; or, the Adventures of Caleb Williams... London: for G. G. and J. Robinson, 1796. 2nd edition; 12mo; 3 volumes, half titles; contemporary half russia, marbled boards, from the Boulton Library with labels, extremities rubbed, spines in compartments with gilt rules and lettering, one cracked, one with pieces missing, few leaves clumsily opened, but internally very clean, fresh copy.   Simon Finch 24-93 1996 £650.00

GODWYN, THOMAS   Romanae Historiae Anthologia. London: T. J. for Peter Parker, 1668. Small 4to; (6), 270, (10) pages; 19th century full black calf, some minor marginal waterstains. Wing G991.   Kenneth Karmiole 1NS-111 1996 $125.00

GOEDE, C. A. G.   The Stranger in England; or Travels in Great Britain. London: Mathews, 1807. 1st English edition; small 8vo; 3 volumes; full contemporary tree calf, joints cracking, but sound, some wear at extremities, spines gilt with black morocco labels;   Ian Wilkinson 95/1-100 1996 £150.00

GOELL, MILTON J.   The Wall that is My Skin: Poems Inspired by the Negro's Flight for Democratic Rights. New York: Wendell Mailliet, 1945. 1st edition; fine in lightly worn dust jacket, few short splits along spine with some light chipping to thin spine ends, nice, signed by author. Between the Covers 43-86 1996 $150.00

GOETHE, JOHANN WOLFGANG VON 1749-1832   Die Leiden des Jungen Werther. Doves Press, 1911. One of 200 copies on paper; 9 1/2 x 6 3/4 inches; 187, (1) pages; original flexible vellum, gilt titled spine; faint crease at upper corner of prelim leaves, otherwise virtually flawless. Phillip J. Pirages 33-188 1996 $1,250.00

GOETHE, JOHANN WOLFGANG VON 1749-1832   Fancies Bizarreries & Ornamented Grotesques. Eremite Press, 1989. One of 27 copies, from a total of 35; page size 15 3/4 x 10 1/2 inches; 24 etchings by Leonard Baskin; bound by Gray Parrot in half red morocco with marbled paper over boards, title on black morocco label on spine, housed in half morocco black clamshell box.   Priscilla Juvelis 95/1-89 1996 $6,000.00

GOETHE, JOHANN WOLFGANG VON 1749-1832   Faust. A Tragedy. London: Frederick Bruckmann, 1877. Atlas folio; numerous detailed wood engravings to text, 14 fine mounted photographic plates, some margins occasionally little soiled, leaves somewhat loose as usual with this very large and heavy book; magnificently bound in original full morocco, upper board very elaborately embossed and gilt decorated, large central panel surrounded by 20 smaller panels, 8 large and elaborate silver corner pieces to boards, upper board with 6 large silver circular embossed portraits onlaid, little rubbed at extremities, very minor wear to upper joint, all edges gilt. Magnificent example of Victorian bookbinding.   Ian Wilkinson 95/1-102 1996 £490.00

GOETHE, JOHANN WOLFGANG VON 1749-1832   Faust, Eine Tragoedie (Part 1). Doves Press, 1906. One of 300 copies on paper; 9 1/4 x 6 1/2 inches; 260, (1) pages; printed in red and black; original flexible vellum, title on spine in gilt, covers with slightly discolored strip along joints (from glue underneath the vellum), isolated very minor marginal foxing, but very fine otherwise.   Phillip J. Pirages 33-186 1996 $850.00

GOETHE, JOHANN WOLFGANG VON 1749-1832   Faust. London: George G. Harrap & Co. Ltd., 1925. 1st edition deluxe, limited to 1000 copies for the U.K. and 1000 for the U.S. markets of which this is number 404 of the English issue, signed by artist; 4to; (vi), 7-253, (iii), colored frontispiece, 7 full page color plates, 14 monochrome plates on fine paper and 65 dramatic black and white illustrations by Harry Clarke; original quarter vellum backed grey boards, top edge gilt, others uncut, colored pictorial endpapers; deckle edges slightly speckled, otherwise extremely fine.   Sotheran PN32-105 1996 £798.00

GOETHE, JOHANN WOLFGANG VON 1749-1832   Iphigenie auf Tauris: Ein Schauspiel. Doves Press, 1912. One of 32 copies on vellum (12 of which had gold initials, there were 200 copies printed on paper); 9 1/4 6 3/4 inches; 110 pages, (1) leaf (colophon); printed in red and black, with tiny stamped cipher of Ernst Kyriss; bound by Doves Bindery in 1913 in Russet morocco, covers and turn-ins with simple gilt rule borders, raised bands, spine compartments ruled and titled in gilt, all edges gilt, except for inevitable slight discoloration of the vellum flyleaves where they touch the facing leather turn-ins, this is a virtually mint copy in unworn and extremely pleasing Doves binding.   Phillip J. Pirages 33-187 1996 $8,750.00

GOETHE, JOHANN WOLFGANG VON 1749-1832   Italian Journey. London: Collins, 1962. 4to; 67 illustrations, most in color; patterned cloth, fine in dust jacket.   Bertram Rota 272-441 1996 £110.00

GOETHE, JOHANN WOLFGANG VON 1749-1832   The Sorrows of Werter. London: printed for J. Dodsley, 1780. 2nd edition in English; small 8vo; 2 volumes; contemporary calf, spines gilt, spines rubbed; half titles present, very good; CBEL II 1175 and 1538.   Ximenes 108-164 1996 $325.00

GOETHE, JOHANN WOLFGANG VON 1749-1832   The Story of Reynard the Fox. New York: Limited Editions Club, 1954. Limited to 1500 copies; 10 3/4 x 7 3/4 inches; 264 pages; set in linotype Janson on Curtis special ivory paper, wood engravings by Fritz Eichenberg; cloth spine, illustrated paper sides; fine in box. Newsletter laid in.   Taurus Books 83-116 1996 $125.00

GOETHE, JOHANN WOLFGANG VON 1749-1832   The Story of Reynard the Fox. New York: Limited Editions Club, 1954. Limited to 1500 copies; signed by artist; quarto; 248 pages; 24 large wood engravings by Fritz Eichenberg; cloth backed patterned boards with slipcase, spine slightly darkened, else extremely fine.   Bromer Booksellers 90-32 1996 $100.00

GOETHE, JOHANN WOLFGANG VON 1749-1832   Wilhelm Meister's Apprenticeship. Edinburgh: Published by Oliver and Boyd, G. and W. B. Whittaker, London, 1824. 1st edition in English; 8vo; 3 volumes; original drab boards, rebacked, new endpapers, original printed paper labels preserved, small nick in one spine; excellent copy, uncut. Tarr A2; Wolff 1132. Block p. 86; CBEL III 1249.   Ximenes 108-60 1996 $750.00

GOFF, FREDERICK R.   Incunabula in American Libraries. New York: Bibliographical Society of America, 1964. 1st edition; 4to; 978 pages; original cloth.   Forest Books 74-90 1996 £85.00

GOGARTY, OLIVER ST. JOHN 1878-1957   An Offering of Swans. London: 1924. 1st Public edition; 8vo; portrait; cloth, very good. Presentation ALS from Gogarty's son to Sir George Bull.   C. P. Hyland 216-276 1996 £85.00

GOGOL, NIKOLAI   The Overcoat. Officina Bodoni, 1975. One of 150 numbered copies, signed by artist; small folio; 6 etchings by Pietro Annigoni, printed in black and green on handmade Pescia paper in Mardersteig's Dante and in Lazursky's Cyrillic type; half vellum with Fabriano paper boards, fine in slipcase; prospectus laid in.   Bertram Rota 272-353 1996 £600.00

GOLD MINING CO.   Charter and By-Laws of the Gold Mining Company. Washington: Bass & Simms, Book and Job Printers, 1886. 1st edition; 12 pages; original printed grey wrappers; fine.   Michael D. Heaston 23-18 1996 $750.00

GOLDAST AB HAIMINSFELD, MELCHIOR   Suevicarum Rerum Scriptores Aliquot Veteres. Frankfurt: Wolfgang Richter, 1605. 1st edition; 4to; pages 317, (xxxi), Roman letter, printer's woodcut device on title, extensive index and printed side notes; general paper browning, very poor paper, heavy at blank outer edges, small waterstain at lower outer corners, contemporary polished calf, rebaacked, old armorial library label on pastedown; acceptable copy. Brunet II 1649; Graesse II 107.   A. Sokol XXV-45 1996 £295.00

GOLDBERG, NORMAN L.   John Chrome the Elder. New York: 1978. 4to; 16 colored plates and 243 other reproductions; 2 volumes; dust jackets.   Petersfield Bookshop FH58-5 1996 £98.00

THE GOLDEN Gate Bridge. Report of the Chief Engineer to the Board of Directors of the Golden Gate Bridge and Highway District, California. San Francisco: Golden Gate Bridge and Highway District, 1970. 2nd edition; quarto; 246, 53 pages; folding color frontispiece, many illustrations from photos, text maps and diagrams, 15 large tipped in folding plans in back, pictorial endpapers, orange cloth stamped in white, very fine with worn dust jacket.   Argonaut Book Shop 113-287 1996 $125.00

GOLDEN, RICHARD L.   Sir William Osler: An Annotated Bibliography with Illustrations. San Francisco: Norman, 198. 1st edition; 4to; xv, 214 pages; grey cloth, dust jacket; fine.   Jeff Weber 31-155 1996 $100.00

GOLDEN, RICHARD L.   Sir William Osler: an Annotated Bibliography with Illustrations. San Francisco: 1988. 1st edition; 214 pages; original binding, dust jacket.   W. Bruce Fye 71-1583 1996 $125.00

GOLDING, HARRY   The Motor Boy. London: Ward Lock, n.d. 1st edition; 85 pages; color frontispiece and 26 color plates, extra color pictorial endpapers, brown boards, onlaid color plate, little loose; excellent copy, scarce.   Robin Greer 94A-80 1996 £85.00

GOLDING, WILLIAM 1911-1993   The Brass Butterfly - a Play in Three Acts. London: Faber & Faber, 1958. 1st edition; original binding, top edge very slightly dusty, head and tail of spine very slightly bumped, near fine in nicked and slightly rubbed, marked and dusty dust jacket by Anthony Gross, faded at spine and slightly browned at edges.   Ulysses 39-234 1996 £95.00

GOLDING, WILLIAM 1911-1993   The Hot Gates and Other Occasional Pieces. London: Faber & Faber, 1965. 1st edition; original binding, head and tail of spine and corners slightly rubbed and bumped, very good in slightly rubbed and creased dust jacket by Michael Ayrton, slightly faded at spine and with later price sticker on upper flap.   Ulysses 39-235 1996 £95.00

GOLDING, WILLIAM 1911-1993   The Inheritors. London: Faber, 1955. 1st edition; very good+ in like dust jacket with some slight fading to dust jacket spine; formerly Van Cleaver's copy with his ownership signature.   Aronovitz 57-455 1996 $285.00

GOLDING, WILLIAM 1911-1993   Nobel Lecture: 7 December 1983. Leamington Spa: the Sixth Chamber Press, 1984. Signed, limited edition of only 50 numbered copies; another 500 'ordinary' copies in wrappers, unsigned, were issued; 8vo; gilt worked full Oasis Nigerian goatskin leather in marbled slipcase; fine.   Antic Hay 101-704 1996 $575.00

GOLDING, WILLIAM 1911-1993   The Scorpion God - Three Short Novels. London: Faber & Faber Ltd., 1971. 1st edition; original binding, head of spine very slightly bumped, near fine in very slightly creased dust jacket.   Ulysses 39-236 1996 £65.00

GOLDING, WILLIAM 1911-1993   The Spire. London: Faber & Faber, n.d. 1964. Uncorrected proof; wrappers, covers slightly marked, creased and cocked, very good.   Ulysses 39-233 1996 £85.00

GOLDMAN, EMMA   Anarchism and Other Essays. New York: Mother Earth, 1911. 2nd edition; signed by author; frontispiece; beige cloth, spine sunned, else very good.   Blue River Books 9-150 1996 $200.00

GOLDMAN, EMMA   The Psychology of Political Violence. New York: Mother Earth Pub., 1911. 1st edition; wrappers, fine but for rubber stamp and pencilled number, scarce.   Beasley Books 82-315 1996 $150.00

GOLDMAN, HETTY   Excavations at Eutresis in Boestia. Cambridge: Harvard University Press, 1931. Folio; 294 pages, 341 figures and 21 plages, 4 plans; original cloth, spine lighty frayed and faded, corners rubbed.   Archaeologia Luxor-3372 1996 $550.00

GOLDMAN, WILLIAM   The Princess Bride. New York: HBJ, 1973. 1st edition; fine in near fine dust jacket with crease to rear flap and relatively unobtrusive surface scratch to laminate across lower portion of front panel.   Lame Duck Books 19-222 1996 $350.00

GOLDMAN, WILLIAM   The Princess Bride. New York: HBJ, 1973. 1st edition; some sppotting to half title, else fine in ner fine dust jacket.   Ken Lopez 74-155 1996 $250.00

GOLDMAN, WILLIAM   The Season: A Candid Look at Broadway. New York: HBW, 1969. 1st edition; fine in dust jacket.   Between the Covers 42-191 1996 $100.00

GOLDMAN, WILLIAM   Soldier in the Rain. New York: Atheneum, 1960. Advance reading copy; self wrappers, couple of glue shadows under front flap and little rubbing to extremities, else nice, near fine.   Between the Covers 42-190 1996 $250.00

GOLDONI, CARLO   The Gold Humoured Ladies. London: Beaumont Press, 1922. 1st Aldington edition, 36/75 copies (of an edition of 475 copies); crown 8vo; printed on Japanese vellum and signed by Aldington, White and Beaumont; pages xxvi, 76, (1); wood engraved frontispiece, title design, large headpieces and endpaper designs all by Ethelbert White and printed in pale grey; original quarter white vellum, backstrip gilt lettered, gilt patterned orange boards, corners rubbed; untrimmed, good; ownership inscription on half title. Beaumont 15.   Blackwell's B112-22 1996 £65.00

GOLDSCHMIDT, E. P. The Printed Book of the Renaissance: Three Lectures on Type, Illustration, Ornament. Cambridge University Press, 1950. One of 750 copies; 11 1/2 x 9 1/4 inches; vii, (1), 92, (1) pages, (2) leaves; 32 cuts and 8 plates in collotype; original cloth and printed dust jacket, jacket slightly creased and soiled, nevertheless well preserved, excellent copy. Phillip J. Pirages 33-96 1996 $195.00

GOLDSCHMIDT, RICHARD The Mechanism and Physiology of Sex Determination. London: 1923. 1st English translation; 259 pages; original binding, GM 529. W. Bruce Fye 71-822 1996 $100.00

GOLDSMITH, J. The Natural and Artificial Wonders of the United Kingdom. London: 1825. 1st edition; 7 x 4 inches; 3 volumes; 360; 360; 356 pages; engravings; leather, covers rubbed, else nice set. John K. King 77-801 1996 $150.00

GOLDSMITH, JOHN An Almanack for the Year of OUr Lord 1701. London: Mary Clarke, 1701. 16mo; red and black printed title, 23ff.; interleaved with blanks (some excised, pages shaved with some loss of text towards back), 2 woodcuts; contemporary brown morocco gilt a l'eventail, 'wheel' centre-piece surmounted by birds, ruled border, spine with running pattern, ruled head and foot, marbled endpapers, clasps lost, all edges gilt. Marlborough 160-24 1996 £500.00

GOLDSMITH, OLIVER 1730-1774 The Beauties of English Poesy. London: printed for William Griffin, 1767. 1st edition; 12mo; 2 volumes, half titles; contemporary calf, hinges cracked, labels, some faint staining in some blank margins. Temple Scott pp. 199-200. Anthony Laywood 108-69 1996 £145.00

GOLDSMITH, OLIVER 1730-1774 The Citizen of the World. London: printed for J. Newbery, 1762. 1st edition; 12mo; 2 volumes; polished calf, spines and inner dentelles gilt, all edges gilt, by R. de Coverly, traces of rubbing, small worn spot in one lower joint; very nice, clean copy. Rothschild 1021; Iolo Williams pp. 123-4; Roscoe A190; Raven 717. Ximenes 108-165 1996 $800.00

GOLDSMITH, OLIVER 1730-1774 The Citizen of the World... London: R. Whiston et al, 1782. Early edition; 12mo; 2 volumes, 276, 244 pages; original full calf with raised bands, former owner's leather labels at bottom of spines, library bookplate and blindstamp, couple of hinges cracked, still good or better, scarce. Chapel Hill 94-213 1996 $150.00

GOLDSMITH, OLIVER 1730-1774 The Deserted Village. London: W. Griffin, 1770. 4th edition; (one monther after the first); 4to; very fine copperplate vignette by Isaac Taylor on titlepage; later wrappers; fine, complete with half title. NCBEL II 1198. Trebizond 39-20 1996 $150.00

GOLDSMITH, OLIVER 1730-1774 The Deserted Village. Campden: Essex House Press, 1904. Limited to 150 numbered copies; all on vellum; colored frontispiece; pictorial vellum covers slightly soiled; fine. Polyanthos 22-702 1996 $400.00

GOLDSMITH, OLIVER 1730-1774 The Deserted Village. Boston: Bibliophile Society, 1912. One of 469 copies printed on vellum; 6 etchings signed in pencil by W H W Bicknell from drawings by him, engraved titlepage signed in pencil by engraver, A. W. MacDonald; full leather, gilt, very fine in fine slipcase, unusually nice. Freedom Bookshop 14-18 1996 $125.00

GOLDSMITH, OLIVER 1730-1774 A History of the Earth and Animated Nature. London: and New York: n.d. 8vo; 2 volumes in 6; 60 colored plates; original red cloth, gilt spines. Wheldon & Wesley 207-160 1996 £85.00

GOLDSMITH, OLIVER 1730-1774 An History of the Earth, and Animated Nature. London: printed for J. Nourse, 1774. Octavo; 8 volumes; 101 copper engraved plates; contemporary mottled calf, gilt spines, tooled in compartments, red and green morocco labels, edges sprinkled red, corners, spine extremities lightly rubbed; bookplate; fine set, housed in two quarter brown slipcases and brown cloth chemises. Heritage Book Shop 196-180 1996 $1,500.00

GOLDSMITH, OLIVER 1730-1774 History of the Earth and Animated Nature. London: 1853. Volume 2 only (of two); hand colored engraved plates; original pictorial gilt cloth, some fading and light rubbing. David A.H. Grayling MY95Orn-386 1996 £65.00

GOLDSMITH, OLIVER 1730-1774 A History of the Earth and Animated Nature. London: 1855. 2 volumes, approximately 1300 pages; 35 plain plates, approximately 40 hand colored plates; contemporary half calf, marbled boards, some foxing/browning to plates, light rubbing. David A.H. Grayling MY95Orn-385 1996 £75.00

GOLDSMITH, OLIVER 1730-1774 The Poems of Olvier Goldsmith. London: ptd. by T. Bensley, Bolt Court, Fleet St. for F. J. Du Roveray, 1800. New edition; 8vo; large paper copy, half title, (v-xxxiv), (xxxv-xxxvi) 5-129 pages, publisher's ad leaf, 6 steel engraved plates; full straight grain green morocco, double gilt rule border to boards, gilt title to spine, decorative inner gilt dentelles, corners very slightly worn, marble endpapers; 2 previous owner's bookplates, spine slightly sunned, otherwise fine copy. Beeleigh Abbey BA56-145 1996 £350.00

GOLDSMITH, OLIVER 1730-1774 The Poems of Oliver Goldsmith. London: George Routledge and Co., 1859. 1st edition thus; large 8vo; xvi, 160 pages; full green morocco by Omega, sunned along spine and edges, otherwise very nice. Scarce. McLean, Publishers Book Bindings 82. Bookpress 75-27 1996 $325.00

GOLDSMITH, OLIVER 1730-1774 The Poems and Plays. London: Der 1889. 1st of this edition; octavo; 2 volumes, pages xxix, 197, 234; frontispiece, titlepages in red and black, beautifully printed on fine laid paper; white vellum spines, olive linen boards; uncut and largely unopened, some minor flaws but excellent copy. CBEL II 637. Hartfie 48-A9 1996 $195.00

GOLDSMITH, OLIVER 1730-1774 The Poetical and Dramatic Works... London: by H. Goldney, for Messieurs Rivington, T. Carnan and F. Newbery... 1780. 1st London edition? 8vo; 2 volumes, pages viii, lxiv, 106, (iv), 107-120, (ii); (vi), 271, 2 leaves from first unsigned gathering volume 2 are misbound ater H5 in volume 1, frontispiece by Cook in volume 1; contemporary sprinkled calf, flat spines, red and green labels sprinkled edges, spines slightly chipped at head, small area of leather c lower board of volume 2 torn away, lightly rubbed; good firm set; bookplates. I.A. Williams pp. 174-5; Roscoe A196(1). Simon Finch 24-95 1996 £95.00

GOLDSMITH, OLIVER 1730-1774 The Poetical Works. London: printe by Ellerton and Henderson for Suttaby, Evance and Co., 1811. 1st printing of this edition; 11 1/4 x 9 inches; iv, 182 pages, 6 quite pleasin yellow tinted aquatint plates by Samuel Aiken after drawings by R. H. Newell; contemporary smooth calf by E. Paul of Southampton (with his ticket at front), covers framed with blind and gilt foliate borders, raised bands, spine compartments pleasantly gilt, maroon calf label, new endpapers, joints lightly rubbed, tiny cracks just starting at top, covers slightly marked, small loss of leather in bottom spine compartment, bu very good, sturdy original binding, small paper repair below titlepage imprint, minor foxing and offsetting, but excellent internally; bookplate c Merton Russell Cotes. Abbey Scenery 456. Phillip J. Pirages 33-254 1996 $175.00

GOLDSMITH, OLIVER 1730-1774 The Traveller or, a Prospecct of Society. London: printed for J. Newbery, 1765 1st published edition; 4t half title (neat repair to small hole at fore edge), 22 pages text, 2 page publisher's ads; full polished calf, triple gilt rule borders, tiny corner ornaments, fully gilt panelled spine, red morocco label, all edges gilt, inner gilt dentelles, marbled endpapers, brown paper book label of Pau Francis Webster; bound by F. Bedford. Very fine copy. Rothschild 1024 Tinker 1101. Beeleigh Abbey BA56-144 1996 £1,500.00

GOLDSMITH, OLIVER 1730-1774 The Traveller: a Poem. London: T. Carnan and F. Newbury, Jun 1770. 7th edition, half title fine engraving by Charles Grignion on titlepage; signature dated 1829. Slight marginal worming, not touching text, external pages dusty; good. Trebizond 39-21 1996 $150.00

GOLDSMITH, OLIVER 1730-1774 The Vicar of Wakefield. Salisbury: F Collins for F. Newbury, 1766. 1st edition; octavo; 2 volumes, (iv), 214; (ii), 223 pages; Rothschild's variant 2; with final blank; contemporary mottled calf, bindings have been skilfully rebacked with most of the original spines, including morocco labels, laid down; 2 volumes preserved in morocco dropback box. Rothschild 1028; Grolier/English 5 Bromer Booksellers 87-77 1996 $5,000.00

GOLDSMITH, OLIVER 1730-1774 The Vicar of Wakefield. London: George G. Harrap & Co. Ltd. 1929. One of 575 numbered copies, sign by artist; there were also 200 signed deluxe copies of the U.S.A.; quarto; endpapers, 12 color plates and numerous black and white drawings by Arthur Rackham; full vellum, top edge gilt, covers sprung, dusty and slightly soiled, head and tail of spine and bottom corner bumped, fore-edges of few pages slightly creased, very good. Ulysses 39-489 1996 £995.00

GOLDSMITH, OLIVER 1730-1774 The Vicar of Wakefield. Philadelphia David McKay, 1929. 1st Deluxe edition; 1 of 200 numbered copies; 12 full page plates in color, many uncolored full page and text drawings, original endpapers by Arthur Rackham; original vellum, gilt, spine gilt. Very fine. Trebizond 39-46 1996 $900.00

GOLDSMITH, OLIVER 1730-1774   The Miscellaneous Works. Perth: printed by R. Morison Jr. for R. Morison and Son, 1792. 8vo in half sheets; 7 volumes; frontispiece and engraved additional titlepage to volume 1, frontispiece in each volume, these browned; contemporary tree calf, smooth backstrips divided by ball and bolt roll between rules, gilt lettered and red leather title labels in second compartments, dark blue circular volume labels in fourth; contemporary ownership signature of Rb. Auld, Edinb. 1796, sprinkled and polished edges, small chip to head of two backstrips and tail of another, otherwise excellent. Blackwell's B112-134 1996 £250.00

GOLDSMITH, OLIVER 1730-1774   The Works of Oliver Goldsmith. London: John Murray, Albemarle St., 1854. 8vo; 4 volumes; full polished calf, gilt rule dentelles to boards, gilt tooling to compartments, green morocco title and volume labels to spines, all edges gilt, marbled endpapers; bound by Sotheran with binders stamp to front pastedown of all volumes, booksellers ticket to rear endpaper of volume 1; owner's stamp to front f.e.p. of all volumes, some light foxing to prelims and endpapers of all volumes, bookseller's ticket to rear endpaper of volume 1.   Beeleigh Abbey BA56-146 1996 £250.00

GOLDSTEIN, SIDNEY M.   Pre-Roman and Early Roman Glass in the Corning Museum of Glass. Corning: Corning Museum of Glass, 1979. 4to; 312 pages, 12 figures and numerous illustrations, 42 plates; original cloth, dust jacket (fine).   Archaeologia Luxor-3373 1996 $175.00

GOLENBOCK, PETER   BUMS. An Oral History of the Brooklyn Dodgers. 1st edition; fine in fine dust jacket; signed by Leo Durocher, Don Newcombe, Cookie Lavagetto, Gene Hermanski, Billy Herman, Ralph Branca and Carl Erskine.   Bud Schweska 12-49 1996 $250.00

GOLL, CLAIRE   Love Poems. New York: 1947. Limited to 600 numbered copies; 9 x 7 inches; 70 + pages; 8 drawings by Marc Chagall; pictorial wrappers, covers darkened/soiled, spine splitting and rubbed.   John K. King 77-589 1996 $150.00

GOLL, YVAN   Der Neue Orpheus: Eine Dithyrambe, Dazu Sieben Orphische Hymnen. Raamin-Presse, 1989. One of 140 copies, signed by artist, from a total edition of 185; 10 x 8 3/4 inches; 4 p.l. (one blank), (9)-50 pages, (1) leaf (colophon), printed on one side only and unopened at fore edge; printed in black, grey and maroon; original grey paper boards with an all over pattern of stamped black rectangles, titled in black on front cover pattern of stamped black rectangles, titled in black on front cover and spine, matching publisher's papear slipcase; as new. Phillip J. Pirages 33-437 1996 $1,350.00

GOLL, YVAN   Lackawanna Elegy. Fremont: Sumac Press, 1970. 1st edition; one of 26 lettered copies, signed by translator, Galway Kinnel; fine, without dust jacket as issued.   Captain's Bookshelf 38-132 1996 $250.00

GOLTZ, HUBERT   Le Vive Imagini Di Tutti Quasi GlImperatori da C. Iulio Caesare, in sino a carlo. Antwerp: Gilles Coppens, 1557, colphon 1560. 1st Spanish edition; tall 4to; chiaroscuro woodcuts, 176 leaves, unnumbered, carefully restored, including repair of worm tracks and paper loss; contemporary vellum with ties (renewed) and new endleaves, title lettered on spine, notwithstanding the presence of the woodcut titlepage from the Latin edition and one leaf substituted (A6) from the Italian edition, text and collation conforms to Fairfax Murray copy (187); in cloth clamshell case. Rare. Fairfax Murray 187; Adams G840; Palau 103463.   Book Block 32-73 1996 $6,750.00

GOMBROWICZ, WITOLD   Ferdydurke. New York: HBW, 1961. 1st American edition; near fine in very good dust jacket with small surface skinned area bottom of back panel, not affecting any type or color; uncommon.   Thomas Dorn 9-131 1996 $100.00

GONCALEZ DAVILA, GIL   Entrada que Hizo en la Corte del Rey de les Espanas Don Felipe Quatro el Serenissimo Don Carlos Principe de Gales. Madrid: Tomas de Junta, 1623. Folio; 2 unnumbered unsigned leaves, Roman letter, double column, woodcut initials, light waterstain in lower margin just touching last line of text on first leaf, otherwise good, clean copy in modern wrappers; Palau 105287; Goldsmith G254 for another edition.   A. Sokol XXV-46 1996 £875.00

GONCOURT, EDMOND   Les Freres Zemganno. Paris: Charpentier, 1879. 1st edition; starting to front inner hinge, else very good+ in contemporary percaline with leather spine label, with original yellow wrappers bound in; inscribed by author for J. K. Huysmans.   Lame Duck Books 19-224 1996 $3,500.00

GONCOURT, EDMOND   Salon de 1852. Paris: Levy, 1852. One of only 10 copies; original wrappers, chip to rear panel split to length of spine and half of front spine fold; presentation copy from Goncourt Brothers to Ludwig II, King of Bavaria.   Lame Duck Books 19-225 1996 $1,000.00

GOOCH, ELIZABETH SARAH VILLA-REAL   The Contrast: a Novel. Wilmington: Wilson, 1796. 1st American edition; 8vo; calf. Evans 30498. Rostenberg & Stern 150-18 1996 $150.00

GOOD Company for Every Day of the Year. Boston: Ticknor & Fields, 1866. 1st edition; original green cloth, gilt, all edges gilt, very good bright copy.   Mac Donnell 12-89 1996 $100.00

GOOD Health: 1870. Boston: 1870. 1st edition; 576 pages; original binding.   W. Bruce Fye 71-823 1996 $100.00

GOODE, D.   Cyads of Africa. Cape Town: 1989. 4to; 256 pages; 173 fine colored plates, several distribution maps; cloth, dust jacket, slipcase. Raymond M. Sutton VI-719 1996 $115.00

GOODE, GEORGE BROWN   Fisheries and Fishery Industries of the United States, Section 1. Natural History of Useful Aquatic Animals. Washington: 1884. 4to; 2 volumes, pages xxxiv, 895, with atlas of 277 plates; cloth, trifle used, joints of text volume loose.   Wheldon & Wesley 207-966 1996 £150.00

GOODE, GEORGE BROWN   Oceanic Ichthyology. Washington: Smith. Inst. Con., 1895. 1st edition; 4to; 2 volumes; 123 plates; half calf, bit worn, library stamp on flyleaves and general titles (only).   Maggs Bros. Ltd. 1190-199 1996 £75.00

GOODE, GEORGE BROWN   Oceanic Ichthyology. Washington: Smithsonian Inst. Con., 1895. 1st edition; folio; 2 volumes; 123 plates; cloth, bit worn.   Maggs Bros. Ltd. 1190-198 1996 £65.00

GOODE, GEORGE BROWN   The Smithsonian Institution 1846-1946. The History of Its First Half Century. Washington: 1897. 1st edition; 4to; 856 pages; original binding, ex-library.   W. Bruce Fye 71-824 1996 $100.00

GOODING, MEL   Knife Edge Texts. London: Dinosaur Press and Knife Edge Press, 1992. 1st edition; one of 100 copies, each signed and numbered by author and artist; page size 8 7/8 x 8 /18 inches; 8 colored etchings by Bruce McLean; grey boards and black linen spine, red endpapers;   Priscilla Juvelis 95/1-106 1996 $175.00

GOODIS, DAVID   Dark Passage. New York: Messner, 1946. 1st edition; spine gilt faded, wear to cloth and foxing to endpapers, about very good, internally tape repaired dust jacket with considerable edgewear, rubbing and chipping at heel.   Ken Lopez 74-156 1996 $250.00

GOODIS, DAVID   Of Missing Persons. New York: Morrow, 1950. 1st edition; mild offsetting to endpapers and shelfwear to cloth, near fine in very good dust jacket that is spine faded around red title block and has small chip and mild rubbing on front panel; nice.   Ken Lopez 74-157 1996 $550.00

GOODIS, DAVID   Retreat from Oblivion. New York: Dutton, 1939. 1st edition; owner's name, else near fine in bright very good+ dust jacket. Lame Duck Books 19-361 1996 $2,500.00

GOODLAND, ROGER   A Bibliography of Sex Rites and Custom: an Annotated Record of Books, Articles and Illustrations in all Languages. London: George Routledge & Sons, 1931. 4to; vi, 742 pages; buckram, some slight dust soiling.   Thomas Thorp 489-119 1996 £50.00

GOODRICH, LLOYD   Edward Hopper New York: Abrams, 1971. Oblong folio; 306 pages; 88 color and 158 monochrome plates and illustrations; cloth, dust jacket. Freitag 4480.   Brannan 43-269 1996 $150.00

GOODRICH, LLOYD   Reginald Marsh. New York: Abrams, n.d. Oblong folio; 307 pages, 239 illustrations, 85 in color; cloth, dust jacket. Brannan 43-389 1996 $235.00

GOODRICH, LLOYD   Reginald Marsh. New York: Harry N. Abrams, 1972. 1st edition; oblong 4to; 307 pages; lavishly illustrated, 239 illustrations, including 85 plates in full color; near fine in dust jacket. Blue River Books 9-22 1996 $150.00

GOODRICH, SAMUEL GRISWOLD 1793-1860   Manners, Customs and Antiquities of the Indians of North and South America. New York: John Allen, 1844. 1st edition; 12mo; part 1 and 2 bound together; iv, 336 pages, numerous illustrations; cloth with gilt title on spine with original printed wrappers bound in, previous owner's name on wrappers, bookplate on pastedown, contents near fine, binding very good. Andrew Cahan 47-93 1996 $175.00

GOODWIN, ARTHUR   Two Letters of Great Consequence to the House of Commons: the One from Alisbury in Buckinghamshire Dated March 22, 1642... London: printed for Edw. Husbands, 1642. 1st edition; 4to; title within woodcut border, some browning of text, 8 pages; modern calf backed boards; bookplate of Fairfax of Cameron. Wing G1144b. Anthony Laywood 108-10 1996 £135.00

GOODWIN, CHARLES CARROLL   The Comstock Club. Salt Lake City: Tribune Job Printing Co., 1891. 8 3/4 x 5 3/4 inches; (x), 288 pages; black and gold stamped red cloth, 2 gatherings at center partly sprung. Paher 711.   Dawson's Books Shop 528-88 1996 $100.00

GOODWIN, FRANCIS   Domestic Architecture. London: the author, 1833. 1st edition; small folio; 41 plates with accompanying text; some of the plates hand colored; cloth spine, publisher's boards and labels, minor staining to cover, foxing; ex-library from the Glasgow Architectural Society.   Bookpress 75-54 1996 $385.00

GOODWIN, THOMAS   An Account of the Neutral Saline Waters Recently Discovered at Hampstead. London: for the author, 1804. 8vo; pages viii, 118, 1 f., engraved frontispiece, engraved map; later cloth, title, frontispiece, map stained and dusty. Scarce.   Marlborough 162-145 1996 £160.00

GOODYEAR, WATSON ANDREWS   The Coal Mines of the Western Coast of the United States. San Francisco: A. L. Bancroft and Co., 1877. 1st edition; 4, (2), 5-153 pages; illustrations; green cloth with gilt title, very good, rubbed at extremities. Cown p. 243; Smith 3657.   Bohling Book Co. 192-157 1996 $110.00

GORDIMER, NADINE   Burger's Daughter. New York: Viking, 1979. 1st edition; fine in fine dust jacket and signed by author.   Ken Lopez 74-162 1996 $150.00

GORDIMER, NADINE   The Conservationist. New York: Viking, 1975. 1st American edition; fine in fine dust jacket and signed by author.   Ken Lopez 74-160 1996 $300.00

GORDIMER, NADINE   A Correspondence Course and Other Stories. Eurographica: 1986. 1st edition thus, one of 350 copies, signed and dated by author; 8vo; printed on Michelangelo paper from Magnani paper mills in Peschia, printed letterpress by Tipografia Nobili in Pesaro; blue wrappers, fine. Priscilla Juvelis 95/1-107 1996 $150.00

GORDIMER, NADINE   My Son's Story. London: Bloomsbury, 1990. 1st edition; fine in dust jacket, signed by author.   Between the Covers 42-195 1996 $150.00

GORDIMER, NADINE   Occasion for Loving. London: Gollancz, 1963. 1st English edition; offsetting to half title, near fine in very good, spine sunned dust jacket, crisp, attractie copy.   Ken Lopez 74-158 1996 $125.00

GORDIMER, NADINE   On the Mines. Cape Town: Struik, 1973. 1st edition; quarto; photos; fine in fine jacket with touch of rubbing at spine crown and along front spine fold.   Ken Lopez 74-159 1996 $175.00

GORDIMER, NADINE   Selected Stories. New York: Viking, 1976. 1st edition; fine in fine, price clipped dust jacket, signed by author.   Ken Lopez 74-161 1996 $150.00

GORDON, ADAM LINDSAY   Bush Ballads and Galloping Rhymes. Melbourne: Clarson, Massina & Co., 1876. 2nd edition; 8vo; pages (iv), 108; original green publisher's cloth, sides blocked in blind and gilt lettered direct, slightly worn at head and foot of spine, internally clean, good copy.   Simon Finch 24-96 1996 £150.00

GORDON, ALEXANDER   The Lives of Pope Alexander VI and His son Caesar Borgia. London: C. Davis, 1729. 1st edition; folio; 2 parts in 1, 2 fine full page engraved portrait plates, 4 page list of subscribers, faint stain to margin of title; contemporary calf, nicely rebacked to style original red morocco label laid down; very good.   Ian Wilkinson 95/1-104 1996 £175.00

GORDON, CAROLINE   The Forest of the South. New York: Charles Scribner's Sons, 1945. 1st edition; spine bit faded, otherwise very good in dust jacket which is slightly chipped at spine ends and with one short tear at right mid-spine edge, very nice copy, scarce.   Steven C. Bernard 71-109 1996 $175.00

GORDON, CAROLINE   The Garden of Adonis. New York: Scribner's, 1937. 1st edition; very good in very good dust jacket, nice copy.   Ken Lopez 74-164 1996 $250.00

GORDON, CAROLINE   The House of Fiction: an Anthology of the Short Story with Commentary. New York: Scribner, 1950. 1st edition; small stain to fore-edge and front gutter, otherwise near fine in like dust jacket, signed by the following contributors: Andrew Lytle, Peter Taylor, Robert Penn Warren and Eudora Welty.   Captain's Bookshelf 38-4 1996 $600.00

GORDON, CAROLINE   The Strange Children. New York: Charles Scribner's Sons, 1951. 1st edition; name, date and place on flyleaf, otherwise very good+ in dust jacket.   Steven C. Bernard 71-110 1996 $100.00

GORDON, DONALD E.   Ernst Ludwig Kirchner. Cambridge: Harvard University Press, 1968. 4to; 475 pages, 37 tipped in color plates, 113 monochrome illustrations; cloth, dust jacket. Freitag 4817.   Brannan 43-297 1996 $295.00

GORDON, GEORGE   The Annals of Europe for the Year 1739. London printed for George Hawkins, 1740. 8vo; 2 volumes; (ii), xiii, (xiii), 453; (ii) iv, (xiv), 514 pages, final ad leaf in second volume, all uncut; contemporary marbled boards with calf spine, top of spine of volume 1 slightly defective.   David Bickersteth 133-25 1996 £75.00

GORDON, GEORGE BYRON   Examples of Maya Pottery in the Museum and Other Collections. Parts I-III. Philadelphia: University Museum, 1925-43. Large folio; 3 volumes; (ii), plages I-XXV (23 in color); (iv), plates XXVI-L (21 in color); plates LI-LXVI (13 in color); original printed wrappers.   Archaeologia Luxor-4511 1996 $1,500.00

GORDON, JOHN   A Probationary Surgical Essay, on the Dislocations of the Thigh Bone. Edinburgh: Printed by J. Johnstone, 1808. 1st edition; some leaves foxed, modern wrappers; Not in Wellcome.   Anthony W. Laywood 109-55 1996 £45.00

GORDON, JULIEN   Painted Tapestry and Its Application to Interior Decoration. London: Lechertier, Barbe and Co., 1879. 1st English edition; large 8vo; xviii, 89, 26 pages publisher catalog, 6 plates ptinted on ribbed paper in imitation of tapestry; original red gilt cloth, slight wear to upper joint; very good.   Ken Spelman 30-53 1996 £90.00

GORDON, RICHARD   Meta Photographs. Chimaera Press, 1978. Limited to 100 signed and numbered copies, slipcase, laid in original photos, numbered and signed; folio; slipcase.   J. B. Muns 154-128 1996 $175.00

GORDON, W. J.   Round About the North Pole. London: John Murray, 1907. 1st edition; 8vo; xii, 294 pages; 67 plates, 6 maps; cloth, occasional very slight spotting.   Thomas Thorp 489-120 1996 £60.00

GORDON-CUMMING, ROUALEYN GEORGE 1820-1866   Five Years of a Hunter's Life in the Far Interior of Southern Africa. London: 1850. 2nd edition; 8vo; 2 volumes; map, 15 plates; half morocco, joints weak. Wheldon & Wesley 207-377 1996 £140.00

GORE, CATHERINE   The Snow Storm: a Christmas Story. London: Willoughby & Co., n.d. Reissue (first published in 1845); small octavo; 253 pages; 4 etched plates by George Cruikshank, bound by Zaehnsdorf in full red polished calf, gilt triple rule border on covers, gilt spine, tooled in compartments, with burgundy calf labels, gilt board edges and turn-ins, top edge gilt, marbled endpapers, corners, joints lightly rubbed little light foxing, very good. Cohn 356 (first ed.).   Heritage Book Shop 196-282 1996 $150.00

GORE, CATHERINE   Stokeshill Place; or the Man of Business. London: Henry Colburn, 1837. 1st edition; 12mo; 3 volumes; contemporary half calf, spines gilt; bound without half titles (and two leaves of ads at end of volume 3), but attractive copy in excellent condition; very scarce. Sadleir 1035; Wolff 2640 (2nd ed.); CBEL III 727.   Ximenes 109-138 1996 $750.00

GORER, EDGAR   Chinese Porcelain and Hard Stones. London: Bernard Quaritch, 1911. 1st edition; 12 1/4 x 9 1/2 inches; 2 volumes; 254 pages of illustrations; cream linen, gilt, light foxing, mostly to prelims and not affecting plates, spines slightly darkened and overall light wear wear, still fine.   Hermitage SP95-740 1996 $800.00

GOREY, EDWARD   The Bug Book. New York: Looking Glass Library, 1959. True first edition, limited to 600 copies, signed by Gorey; printed wrappers; near fine, bookplate.   Bromer Booksellers 87-78 1996 $450.00

GOREY, EDWARD   The Doubtful Guest. Garden City: Doubleday, 1957. 1st edition; signed by author/artist on titlepage, bound in printed boards, fine in dust jacket, which is lightly soiled.   Bromer Booksellers 87-79 1996 $350.00

GOREY, EDWARD   The Doubtful Guest. Garden City: Doubleday & Co., Inc., 1957. 1st edition; yellow cloth with black and with portrait of 'guest' on cover, price clipped jacket repeats cover illustration, near fine and unusual thus.   Priscilla Juvelis 95/1-108 1996 $200.00

GOREY, EDWARD   A Limerick. Dennis: Salt Works Press, 1973. 1st edition; (4)ff; printed brown wrappers; very fine; this copy signed by Gorey on titlepage.   Bromer Booksellers 90-49 1996 $185.00

GOREY, EDWARD   The Listing Attic. New York: Duell, Sloan, Pierce, 1954. 1st edition; author's second book; illustrations; pictorial boards, faint wear to extremities, else very fine in equally fine dust jacket. Bromer Booksellers 90-50 1996 $250.00

GORGAS, JOSIAH   The Civil War Diary of General Josiah Gorgas. University: University of Ablabama Press, 1947. 1st edition; xi, 208 pages; original cloth, near fine in very good and scarce dust jacket with presentation from the editor, Frank Vandiver. Dornbusch II 2759. McGowan Book Co. 65-32 1996 $175.00

GORHAM MANUFACTURING CO.   Gorham Silver. Trade Catalogue. Providence: n.d. 1930's. 4to; 17 folded sheets with holes in left margins for putting into notebook, each sheet with photographic illustrations, sheets loose in felt wrappers with "Gorham Sterling" imprinted in silver on coer; fine, scarce.   J. M. Cohen 35-91 1996 $100.00

GORHAM, GEORGE CORNELIUS   The History and Antiquities of Eynesbury and St. Neot's in Huntingdonshire and of St. Neot's in the County of Cornwall. London: T. Davison for Lackington, etc. 1820-24. 8vo; 2 volumes in 1; (2), xii, (4), 340; (2), clxxxvii pages, engraved frontispiece, 10 plates, wood engravings in text, slightly later half morocco, gilt, top edge gilt. P. A. Hanrott's copy with his note on flyleaf, probably purchased in his sale in 1830 by Frances Richardson Currer.   Marlborough 162-33 1996 £290.00

GORHAM, MAURICE   The Local Colour. London: 1939. 1st edition; color lithographs by Edward ARdizzone; original printed boards, slightly nicked at head of spine and weakening a little along lower hinge and spine; scarce.   Words Etcetera 94-59 1996 £150.00

GORING, C. R.   Micrographia: Containing Practical Essays, on Reflecting Solar, Oxy-Hydrogen Gas Microscopies... London: 1837. 3 plates; half calf.   Petersfield Bookshop FH58-147 1996 £52.00

GORKI, MAXIM   Reminiscences of Leond Andreyev. New York: Crosby Gaige, 1928. 1st edition of this translation by Katherine Mansfield, one of 400 copies; 8vo; drab boards, black linen gilt stamped spine, edges sunned and worn at tips, generally very good.   Priscilla Juvelis 95/1-161 1996 $150.00

GOSS, HELEN ROCCA   The Life and Death of a Quicksilver Mine. Los Angeles: Historical Society of Southern California, 1958. 1st edition; xv, 150 pages; illustrations, portraits; endpaper map; fine copy with chipped dust jacket; signed by author.   Argonaut Book Shop 113-288 1996 $100.00

GOSSE, EDMUND 1849-1928   Gossip in a Library. London: William Heinemann, 1892. One of 100 copies, numbered and signed by author; large paper edition; buckram backed boards; bookplate, top edge dusty, prelims, edges and endpapers spotted, free endpapers browned, head and tail of spine and corners bumped, head and tail of spine rubbed, corners bruised, covers marked & dusty, good.   Ulysses 39-238 1996 £165.00

GOSSE, EDMUND 1849-1928   Gray. London: Macmillan and Co., 1882. 1st edition; Presentation copy inscribed by author for Robert Louis Stevenson; original cloth, paper spine label; inner hinges cracked, covers glazed (as were many of the books from Stevenson's library), with preservative varnish which has darkened a little with age, little worn, in handsome full morocco solander case.   David J. Holmes 52-114 1996 $1,000.00

GOSSE, PHILIP   Sir John Hawkins. London: John Lane, Bodley Head, 1930. 1st edition; demy 8vo; (xiv), 290 pages; plates; bound in later half blue calf, banded and gilt with ships, by Bayntun, top edge gilt, few faint marks, but very good.   Ash Rare Books Zenzybyr-38 1996 £85.00

GOSSE, PHILIP HENRY   Actinologia Britannica. Van Voorst, 1860. 8vo; xl, 362 pages + ad leaf; 11 chromolithograph plates, 1 uncolored lithograph, original cloth, gilt, extremities slightly worn, but very good. Thomas Thorp 489-121 1996 £100.00

GOSSE, PHILIP HENRY   Actinologia Britannica: a History of the British Sea Anemones and Corals. London: 1860. 12 colored plates; half green morocco, gilt, slight foxing.   Petersfield Bookshop FH58-244 1996 £65.00

GOSSE, PHILIP HENRY   Actinologia Britannica: a History of the British Sea-Anemeones and Corals. London: 1860. 12 colored plates; original cloth, slight foxing.   Petersfield Bookshop FH58-245 1996 £58.00

GOSSE, PHILIP HENRY   Tenby: a Sea-Side Holiday. London: John Van Voorst, 1856. 1st edition; 8vo; 400, (6) pages; frontispiece, 23 chromolithographed paltes; original green cloth, exceptionally fine, bright copy with only minimal traces of foxing;   Chapel Hill 94-301 1996 $200.00

GOSSE, PHILIP HENRY   A Year at the Shore. London: 1865. 3rd thousand; crown 8vo; pages xii, 330, 2, 36 color plates; cloth, gilt. John Henly 27-129 1996 £60.00

GOTCH, J. ALFRED   Early Renaissance Architecture in England. London: Batsford, 1901. 1st edition; 8vo; frontispiece, xxii, 281, (5) pages, 87 plates; cloth, top edge gilt, inscription in ink on half title leaf, minor cvoer wear, front hinge internally cracked, light foxing.   The Bookpress 75-190 1996 $110.00

GOTTLIEB, GERALD   Early Children's Books and Their Illustration. New York: The Pierpont Morgan Library/Toronto: Oxford University Press, 1975. 1st edition; 4to; pages (ii), xxx, 263; frontispiece, 225 illustrations on letterpress; original red cloth, backstrip gilt lettered direct, slightly rubbed blue/grey dust jacket, with colored illustration on upper side, short tears at head of fore-edge, excellent.   Blackwell's B112-70 1996 £190.00

THE GOUDHURST Coronation Book. Turnbridge Wells: 1937. 8vo; 896 pages; plates and illustrations; original lambskin gilt, signed by compiler on flyleaf.   Howes Bookshop 265-2155 1996 £75.00

THE GOUDHURST Jubilee Book. Turnbridge Wells: 1935. 8vo; folding map, many plates and illustrations, 504 pages; original cloth, spine faded as usual.   Howes Bookshop 265-2154 1996 £55.00

GOUDY, FREDERIC WILLIAM 1865-1947   Typologia. Berkeley & Los Angeles: University of California Press, 1940. 1st edition; limited to 300 copies, signed by author; tall 8vo; decorated endsheets, half leather and boards, glassine dust jacket; very fine in torn jacket.   James S. Jaffe 34-663 1996 $250.00

GOULD, A. A.   Report on the Invertebrata of Massachusetts. Cambridge: 1841. 8vo; pages xiii, 373, 15 plates; buckram; scarce; waterstained at beginning and end.   Wheldon & Wesley 207-1161 1996 £90.00

GOULD, A. A.   A System of Natural History... Brattleboro: 1834. frontispiece, 880 pages, first 3 pages blank; wood engravings; original calf, very worn, spine very chipped; contents very nice, with only miniumum of very light staining. 2 gatherings partially loose, still very good.   Roy W. Clare XXIV-63 1996 $115.00

GOULD, E. R. L.   The Gothenburg System of Liquor Traffic. Washington: GPO, 1893. three quarter morocco over marbled boards, bit rubbed, but quite nice.   Meyer Boswell SL26-91 1996 $125.00

GOULD, GEORGE   The American Year-Book of Medicine and Surgery... Philadelphia: 1896-99. 1st editions; 4 volumes, 1183, 1257, 1077, 1102 pages; lithographic and woodcut illustrations; original binding.   W. Bruce Fye   71-837   1996 $200.00

GOULD, JOHN 1804-1881   The Birds of Australia. Melbourne: 1972-75. Facsimile reprint, limited to 1000 copies; imperial folio; 8 volumes; 681 colored plates, art leather. Good.   Wheldon & Wesley   207-37   1996 £800.00

GOULD, JOHN 1804-1881   An Introduction to the Birds of Australia. London: printed for the author, 1848. Printed from the proof sheets of the great folio edition, at end is 6 page prospectus for the folio, with list of subscribers, and note that 250 copies were printed, of which 180 were subscribed; original cloth, spine faded, bit worn, two rather inappropriate leather labels added; presentation copy inscribed by Gould to Alfred Malherbe of Metz.   Maggs Bros. Ltd.   1190-570   1996 £215.00

GOULD, ROBERT   The Twelve of Hearts. Boston: 1982. Limited to just 36 copies; 2 11/16 x 2 1/16 inches; 12 original watercolor designs on soft gray paper by Gould, calligraphy by Colleen; full vellum with exposed bands of red ribbon by David Bourbeau of the Thistle Bindery; title stamped in gold on spine; extremely fine.   Bromer Booksellers 90-178   1996 $350.00

GOULD, WILLIAM   An Account of English Ants; Which Contains. I. their Different Species and Mechanisms. II. Their Manner of Government...III. The Production of Their Eggs...IV. The Incessant Laborus of the Workers of Common Ants. London: printed for A. Millar, 1747. 1st edition; 8vo; ad leaf at end; contemporary calf, gilt, slightly rubbed, nice. Anthony Laywood   108-70   1996 £285.00

GOWANS, WILLIAM   The Phenix; a Collection of Old and Rare Fragments; viz The Morals of Confucius the Chinese Philosopher; the Oracles of Zoroaster... New York: pub. by William Gowan (sic), 1835. 1st edition; 8vo; original black cloth, printed paper label; very light foxing, but fine.   Ximenes   108-168   1996 $400.00

GOWERS, W. R.   Diagnosis of Diseases of the Brain and of the Spinal Cord. New York: William Wood & Co., 1885. 1st American edition; 8vo; viii, 293 pages, blank leaf, (6) pages publisher's ads, final blank, one plate, 32 text figures; original pictorial cloth, covers little rubbed and spotted, but an excellent. GM 4568. GM 4562.   David Bickersteth 133-195   1996 £130.00

GOYEN, WILLIAM   The House of Breath. London: Chatto & Windus Ltd., 1951. 1st edition; author's first book; original binding, free endpapers partially browned, edges and endpapers spotted, bottom edge partially browned, spine faded and with offsetting from dust jacket, very good in spotted and slightly rubbed, creased and dusty dust jacket, browned at spine and edges.   Ulysses   39-239   1996 £55.00

GOYEN, WILLIAM   Precious Door. New York: Red Ozier Press, 1981. 1st edition; one of 115 copies, signed by author and artist; 12mo; wood engravings by John DePol; cloth backed marbled boards; mint.   James S. Jaffe   34-575   1996 $225.00

GRABHORN, ROBERT   A Short Account of the Life and Work of Wynkyn de Worde. With a Leaf from the Golden Legend printed by Him at the Sign of the Sun in Fleet Street, London the Year 1527. San Francisco: The Book Club of California, 1949. Limited to 375 copies; folio; (6), 16 pages; text illustrations, original leaf (with one woodcut), printed in red and black; brown cloth over decorative boards, paper spine and cover labels. Grabhorn press Bib. 486.   Kenneth Karmiole 1NS-114   1996 $350.00

GRACE G. A.   Ornamental Turning Design... Harnhill Rectory, Cirencester, 1923. 1st edition; 8vo; 29 pasted in photos, title and 30 duplicated leaves of text, comprising introduction (pasted inside front cover), 28 leaves of text (12 and 29 on one), index and list of subscribers (pasted inside back cover), original cloth, ringback folder, one or two leaves working loose. Abell 116.   Maggs Bros. Ltd. 1190-635   1996 £245.00

GRACE, FREDERICK R.   Archaic Sculpture in Boeotia. Cambrdige: Cambridge University Press, 1939. Folio; viii, 86 pages, 83 illustrations; original cloth, tattered and stained dust jacket (light staining on top board).   Archaeologia Luxor-3376   1996 $175.00

GRACIAN Y MORALES, BALTASAR 1601-1658   The Courtiers Manual Oracle, or the Art of Prudence. London: M. Flesher for Abel Swalle, 1685. 1st edition in English; 8vo; (xxviii), 272, (iv) pages; contemporary calf, ruled in blind, neatly rebacked and recornered, spine gilt ruled, label, 4 page catalog at end; localised dampstaining on leaves; good. Wing G1468.   Robert Clark   38-50   1996 £160.00

GRAETZ, H.   History of the Jews. Philadelphia: Jewish Publication Society, 1891-92. 1st American edition; thick 8vo; 6 volumes; three quarter black morocco, slight wear at extremities.   Appelfeld Gallery 54-125   1996 $350.00

GRAF, OSKAR MARIA   Ua-Pua! Regensburg: Bei Franz Ludwig Habb 1921. 1st edition; 59, (5) pages, illustrations by Georg Schrimpf; origina tan pictorial boards, cloth spine with title stamped in black on spine ar front cover, some wear and minor bumping, very light dampstain to several pages, very good.   Michael D. Heaston   23-159   1996 $175.0

GRAFER, JOHN   A Descriptive Catalogue of Upwards of Eleven Hundred Species and Varities of Herbaceous or Perenial Plants... Londc printed and sold by J. Smeeton, n.d. 1794. 3rd edition; 8vo; contemporary half calf, spine gilt, some rubbing, blank strip clipped from foot of titlepage, just touching last line of publisher's ads, very good, scarce; inscribed to Mrs. Egerton with Mr. Vanbrugh's respects.   Ximenes   108-169   1996 $600.00

GRAFTON, SUE   "A" is For Alibi. New York: Holt, 1982. 1st edition; fine in jacket with some minor edgewear and creased inside front flap, signed by author.   Janus Books   36-166   1996 $850.00

GRAFTON, SUE   "A" is for Alibi. London: Macmillan, 1986. 1st Engli edition; fine in jacket, signed by author.   Janus Books   36-167   1996 $100.00

GRAFTON, SUE   "B" is for Burglar. New York: Holt, Rinehart, 1985. 1st edition; fine in dust jacket; signed by author.   Quill & Brush 102-729   1996 $600.00

GRAFTON, SUE   "C" is for Corpse. New York: Holt, 1986. 1st editic fine in jacket with just touch of edgewear, signed by Grafton, promotional bookplate laid in.   Janus Books   36-169   1996 $400.00

GRAFTON, SUE   "C" is for Corpse. New York: Henry Holt, 1986. 1s edition; fine in dust jacket; inscribed, bookplate on front endpaper that the publisher included with the book.   Quill & Brush   102-730   1996 $350.00

GRAFTON, SUE   "D" is for Deadbeat. New York: Holt, 1987. 1st edition; fine in jacket, signed by Grafton.   Janus Books   36-170   199 $250.00

GRAFTON, SUE   "D" is for Deadbeat. New York: Henry Holt, 1987. 1st edition; fine in dust jacket; inscribed.   Quill & Brush 102-731   19 $200.00

GRAFTON, SUE   "E" is for Evidence. New York: Holt, 1988. 1st edition; fine in jacket, signed by author.   Janus Books   36-171   1996 $150.00

GRAFTON, SUE   Kinsey and Me. A Collection of Short Stories. Sant Barbara: Bench Press, 1991. One of 300 signed, numbered copies; fine slipcase.   Quill & Brush   102-737   1996 $300.00

GRAFTON, SUE   Mark, I Love You. Los Angeles: Aubrey Co., 1980. Revised final draf, printed on multi-colored sheets with color coded revisions, signed by author; clasp bound, small spots to front cover, else fine. Scarce.   Ken Lopez   74-166   1996 $500.00

GRAFTON, SUE   Sex and the Single Parent. New York: Time-Life Films, 1979. Revised final draft, mimeographed on multi-colored sheets with color coded revisions; signed by author; clasp bound; near fine i card stock covers.   Ken Lopez   74-165   1996 $500.00

GRAGLIA, G.   The New Pocket Dictionary of the Italian and English Languages... London: printed for C. Dilly, Vernor & Hood, &c., 1795. N edition; 4to; few spots; contemporary sheep, slightly scarred, recently neatly rebacked.   Jarndyce   103-150   1996 £60.00

GRAHAM, FREDERIK U.   Notes of a Sporting Expedition in the Far West of Canada, 1847. London: printed for private circulation, 1898. 3: cm; (vii), 120 pages; illustrations and maps in color; uncut, fine in dee blue cloth. Peel 1542.   Rockland Books   38-86   1996 $450.00

GRAHAM, JAMES D.   Report of Lieutenant Colonel Graham on the Subject of the Boundary Line Between the United States and Mexico. August 27, 1852. 1st edition; 250 pages; 3 folding maps; new black linen with gilt stamped spine. Wagner Camp 212; Howes G286; Wheat Trans West III map 717 p. 227.   Maggie Lambeth 30-218   1996 $150.00

GRAHAM, MARIA   Voyage of the H.M.S. Blonde to the Sandwich Islands, in the Years 1824-1825. London: John Murray, 1826. 1st edition; 4to; contemporary red morocco, gilt, spine gilt, all edges gilt, some scuffing, joints and edges rubbed, but sound; very good in rather elaborate early binding. Abbey Travel 597; Hill p. 309.   Ximenes 109-140   1996 $1,750.00

GRAHAM, RIGBY   Holt Mill Papers. Santa Cruz: Donna and Peter Thomas, 1994. 1st edition; one of 50 copies, signed by the author and by the Thomas's; page size 15 x 11 3/8 inches; handset in Centaur types, paper handmade using cotton rag and 'a few other fibers' by Peter Thomas with the help of Joanna Gibson; tipped into each copy of the book are two samples of paper made at the Holt Mill in 1958; Coptic binding with handmade paper boards by John Babcock, by Donna and Peter Thomas.   Priscilla Juvelis 95/1-109   1996 $235.00

GRAHAM, THOMAS   On the Diseases of Females; a Treatise... London: Simpkin, Marshall, 1841. 3rd edition; 8vo; (1, xii, 272 pages, 31); modern blue-grey boards with new title label; with schedule and address of physician tipped in; very nice. 2nd ed. in Wellcome III 143; Sur. Gen. Cat. I. V 546.   Paulette Rose 16-224   1996 $300.00

GRAHAME, KENNETH 1859-1932   The Wind in the Willows. London: Methuen, 1908. 1st edition; original blue cloth decorated in gilt with Pan amongst the reeds and with Mole and Rat at his feet, spine showing toad in his driving gear amidst the willows; fine, bright, fresh copy in half morocco case; rarely seen in this lovely condition.   19th Century Shop 39-   1996 $7,500.00

GRAHAME, KENNETH 1859-1932   The Wind in the Willows. London: Methuen & Co., 1908. 1st edition; 8vo; pages (x), 302; black and white frontispiece by Graham Roberts, head and tail of spine little bruised and rubbed, very short (1 cm.) split to cloth at lower edge of lower joint, new front blank endpaper expertly inserted and all but indistinguishable from the original, very occasional speckling to front prelims; original blue cloth pictorially stamped in gilt to spine and upper cover, top edge gilt, others uncut; attractive copy, increasingly scarce.   Sotheran PN32-119   1996 £1,250.00

GRAHAME, KENNETH 1859-1932   The Wind in the Willows. London: Methuen and Co., 1908. 1st edition; 8vo; pages (ii) blank, (vi0, 302, (ii) blank, imprint; frontispiece by Graham Robertson, some spotting; original pictorial cloth, gilt, top edge gilt, others uncut, little wear, short tears at head and foot of spine, hinges cracked; good copy; bookplate of Mary Grey Bonham Carter.   Simon Finch 24-97   1996 £1,200.00

GRAHAME, KENNETH 1859-1932   The Wind in the Willows. New York: Scribners, 1908. 1st American edition; spine somewhat faded, else very good.   Aronovitz 57-461   1996 $275.00

GRAHAME, KENNETH 1859-1932   The Wind in the Willows. New York: Charles Scribner's Sons, 1913. Probable first American edition; 8vo; illustrations in full color; original blue cloth, pictorial cover panel in colors and gilt, spine and top edge gilt, light edgewear and previous owner's inscription on pictorial endpaper, else fine, lacking Scribner's seal. Glenn Books 36-117   1996 $150.00

GRAHAME, KENNETH 1859-1932   The Wind in the Willows. New York: Limited Editions Club, 1940. Limited to 2020 numbered copies, signed by designer, Bruce Rogers; quarto; 16 mounted color plates by Arthur Rackham; original cloth backed decorative paper boards stamped in gilt on spine, top edge gilt, others uncut, fine in slightly rubbed slipcase. LEC Bib. S7.   Heritage Book Shop 196-268   1996 $1,250.00

GRAHAME, KENNETH 1859-1932   The Wind in the Willows. New York: Limited Editions Club, 1940. 1st edition with these illustrations, limited to 1500 copies, signed by designer, Bruce Rogers; 4to; tipped in color plates by Arthur Rackham; original cloth backed boards, slipcase, spine slightly foxed, otherwise fine in lightly worn slipcase.   James S. Jaffe 34-697   1996 $650.00

GRAHAME, KENNETH 1859-1932   The Wind in the Willows. London: Methuen Children's Books Ltd., 1971. 1st edition thus, one of 250 copies numbered and signed by artist; color endpapers and numerous color illustrations, several full page by E. H. Sehpard; full decorated gilt morocco with raised bands, all edges gilt, fine in very slightly marked slipcase.   Ulysses 39-532   1996 £675.00

GRAINGER, FRANCIS   The Register and Records of Holm Cultram. Kendal: Titus Wilson, 1929. 8vo; pages xiii, 310; original cloth, gilt, partly unopened.   R.F.G. Hollett & Son 78-580   1996 £65.00

GRAINGER, LYDIA   Modern Amours. London: printed by Austin Weddell, 1733. 1st edition; unrecorded first issue; 12mo; old calf covers pitted, later morocco spine; scholarly notes of a collector on front flyleaf, titlepage, just a trifle dust soiled, but very good. McBurney 283.   Ximenes 108-170   1996 $3,000.00

GRAM, HANS   The Massachusetts Compiler of Theoretical and Practical Elements of Sacred Vocal Music... Boston: ptd. by Isaiah Thomas & Ebenezer T. Andrews... 1795. 1st edition; oblong 4to; contemporary half sheep and marbled boards, rubbed but sound; some foxing, but excellent copy, rare. Evans 28848.   Ximenes 108-171   1996 $1,750.00

GRAMMONT, SIEUR DE   Heartsease and Honesty; the Pastimes. Waltham St. Lawrence: Golden Cockerel Press, 1935. Of 300 numbered copies, this is number 2 of 25 on handmade paper signed by the translator and the artist, specially bound; printed in 14 pt. Perpetua and Felicity, borders in red, decorative borders by Tirzah Ravilious; full vellum, gilt, very nice, bookplate;   Bertram Rota 272-177   1996 £250.00

THE GRAND Case of England, So Fiercely Now Disputed by Fire and Sword, Epitomized. London: printed for J. Partridge, 1642 i.e. 1643. 1st and only edition; 4to; woodcut device on title, 8 pages; recently well bound in linen backed marbled boards lettered, very good with good margins. Wing G1487; Thomason I 231.   John Drury 82-91   1996 £150.00

GRAND TRUNK PACIFIC RAILWAY   Bread Book. a Few Terse Stories of Success and Why Failures are Unheard of Along that Line of Railway through the Most Fertile Districts of Western Canada. Winnipeg: 1911. Pages 24, 10 full page photo illustrations; bread-box shaped and illustrated wrappers; near fine. cf. Peel 2396 for later ed.   Stephen Lunsford 45-58   1996 $135.00

GRAND, GORDON   Redmond C. Stewart: Foxhunter and Gentleman of Maryland. New York: Charles Scribner's Sons, 1938. 1st American edition; photos; quarter Japan vellum over cloth, endpapers darkened, fading and darkening along top edge and upper spine panel; despite flaws, a nice copy.   Hermitage SP95-890   1996 $100.00

LES GRANDES Merveilles d'Amour. France? n.d. Limited to 35 copies, signed by artist; 1 3/4 x 1 11/16 inches; (26) pages; printed in blue by Sergent Fulbert, surrounded by dark green engraved border by Francis Righi, who also illustrated the book with 2 full page color images; in unique binding by Michael Wilcox, dated 1994, of full salmon morocco, onlays of purple morocco form two open roses on each cover, which are accented with circular purple onlays and with gilt tooled dots, circles and other geometric shapes, doublures show reverse of covers with rectangular purple onlays silhouetting the salmon colored flowers, circular salmon onlays and corresponding gilt tooling; handsome binding, housed in buckram dropback box with gilt titled spine label in purple morocco, lined w/purple velvet & latched w/thread and buttom.   Bromer Booksellers 87-186   1996 $1,750.00

GRANGE Over Sands. With Excrusions Therefrom. Windermere: J. Garnett, 1884. Oblong small 8vo; pages 30; 12 engraved plates and map, all leaves decorated and bordered in red; original cream boards, gilt, little rubbed, little light spotting, corner of lower flyleaf creased, but very good, scarce.   R.F.G. Hollett & Son 78-933   1996 £65.00

GRANGER, J.   A Biographical History of England, from Egbert the Great to the Revolution... London: William Baynes and Son, 1824. 5th edition; 8vo; 6 volumes; extra illustrated with over 300 engraved portraits; contemporary calf, old morocco rebacks, labels; few with small marginal stamps, but mostly quite clean, spines quite rubbed and frayed at ends, some splits in joints.   Robert Clark 38-310   1996 £200.00

GRANIT, RAGNAR   Receptors and Sensory Perception. New Haven: Yale University Press, 1956. 8vo; dust jacket.   Argosy 810-218   1996 $500.00

GRANT, ANNE MAC VICAR 1755-1838   Essays on the Superstitions of the Highlanders of Scotland: To Which Are Added, Translations from the Gaelic; and Letters Connected With Those Formerly Published. London: Longman, Hurst...and John Anderson, 1811. 1st edition; 12mo; 2 volumes, iv, 304, iv, (366) pages; contemporary half calf, labels, binding quite rubbed along spines, otherwise very good set.   David Mason 71-140   1996 $320.00

GRANT, GEORGE MONRO   Picturesque Canada. Toronto: n.d. 1882-85. Thick 4to; 2 volumes; frontispiece, over 500 full page and other engraved views; contemporary half brown morocco, gilt; scarce Canadian edition, fine.   Charles W. Traylen 117-423   1996 £280.00

GRANT, JAMES   History of the Burgh Schools of Scotland. London: and Glasgow: William Collins, Sons & Co., 1876. 1st edition; royal 8vo; xvi, 571 pages, little spotting here and there and some paper darkening; original maroon cloth, gilt, partially unopened; very good.   John Drury 82-92 1996 £95.00

GRANT, JAMES   The Narrative of a Voyage of Discovery, Performed in His Majesty's Vessel the Lady Nelson, of Sixty Tons Burthen, with Sliding Keels in the Years 1800, 1801 and 1802 to New South Wales. London: printed by C. Roworth, for T. Egerton, 1803. 1st edition; 4to; modern half calf, spine gilt; fine, uncut copy, complete with leaf "list of encouragers of this work" often missing. Ferguson 375; Hill p. 126-7. Ximenes 109-141 1996 $6,500.00

GRANT, JAMES   The Narrative of a Voyage of Discovery, Performed in His Majesty's Vessel the Lady Nelson of Sixty Tons Burthen with Sliding Keels in the Years 1800, 1801 and 1802. to New South Wales. Melbourne: n.d. Fascimile reproduction; 11 x 8.5 inches; (approximately); xxvi, 195 pages; illustrations; red cloth, gilt spine titles, fine in dust jacket. Ferguson 375.   Parmer Books O39Nautica-039035 1996 $150.00

GRANT, KENNETH   Aleister Crowley and the Hidden God. Muller, 1973. 1st edition; 245 pages, plus 20 glossy plates; fine in fine dust jacket.   Middle Earth 77-64 1996 $150.00

GRANT, ROBERT   The Expediency Maintained of Continuing the System by Which the Trade and Government of India are Now Regulated. London: for Black, Parry and Co., 1813. 1st edition; royal 8vo; (4), xix, 404 pages, including two folding tables, complete with half title; original boards, neatly rebacked, original printed label preserved, entirely uncut; excellent. Goldsmiths 20727; Kress B6136.   John Drury 82-93 1996 £200.00

GRANT, ULYSSES S.   Personal Memoirs of U. S. Grant. New York: 1885. 1st edition; volumes 1 and 2; professionally repaired, protective slipcases for each volume added.   Early West 22-334 1996 $130.00

GRANVILLE, A.   The Fallen Race. F. T. Neeley, 1892. 1st edition; illustrations; inner front hinge starting, else very good; quite uncommon. Aronovitz 57-464 1996 $200.00

GRANVILLE, A. B.   Spas of England, and Principal Sea-Bathing Places. Bath: Adams and Dart, 1971. thick 8vo; 2 volumes, pages 423, 639, index; few woodcut illustrations, text and titlepage are in excellent clear facsimile; white vellum paper boards, fine in pictorial jackets.   Hartfield 48-A16 1996 $165.00

GRASS, GUNTER   The Flounder. New York: Limited Editions Club, 1985. Limited to 1000 copies, signed by author/artist; oblong quarto; 3 volumes; 530 pages; reproductions of 28 drawings by author, printed letterpress from relief plates in two colors; natural eelskin cloth, housed together in matching slipcase, prospectus laid in; near mint.   Bromer Booksellers 90-164 1996 $750.00

GRASSUS, BENEVENTIUS   De Oculis Eorumque Egritudinibus et Curis. Stanford: Stanford University Press, 1929. Reprint of the 1474 edition; 8vo; xiv, 104 pages; 5 manuscript facsimiles (each with printed tissue guards); decorative grey and white cloth, publisher's slipcase, bookplate. Kenneth Karmiole 1NS-179 1996 $100.00

GRATIANUS   Decretum Gratiani, Seu Verius Decretorum Canonicorum Collectanea... Paris: Appud Jolandam Bonhomme, Vidua Industrii Viri Thielmani Kerver, 1550. 4to; A-38, F6, a-z, aa-zz, A-X, AA-SS8, TT-UU6 (lacking UU6, ?blank), 46 lls. + folios 1-691, gothic letter, text surrounded by scholia, printed in red and black, decorated woodcut initials mainly white on black, other initials printed in red, Kerver's second device on title (Davies 130a); 3 full page woodcuts, bound in modern brown morocco with remains of the original (?) Parisian calf laid in as doublures; little light waterstaining, corner of last leaf torn affecting last digit of numeral.   H. M. Fletcher 121-22 1996 £550.00

GRATTAN, HENRY   The Speeches of the Rt. Hon. Grattan in the Irish and Imperial Parliament. London: 1822. 1st edition; 8vo; 4 volumes; portrait; half calf, all need rebacking; text good.   C. P. Hyland 216-280 1996 £60.00

GRATTAN, THOMAS COLLEY   The Heiress of Bruges; a Tale of the Year Sixteen Hundred. London: Henry Colburn and Richard Bentley, 1830. 1st edition; 12mo; 4 volumes in 2; contemporary rose calf, covers decorated in blind with gilt borders, spines elaborately gilt, all edges gilt. terminal ads in volumes III-IV, but an exceptionally pretty set, in fine condition; contemporary bookseller's labels of Maccallum's Library, Glasgow. Sadlier 1062; Block p. 93; not in Wolff. CBEL III 728. Ximenes 108-172 1996 $350.00

GRATTEN, J. H. G.   Anglo-Saxon Magic and Medicine. London: 1952. 1st edition; 234 pages; illustrations; original binding. GM 6546.   W. Bruce Fye 71-850 1996 $125.00

GRATULATIO Academiae Cantabrigiensis de Pace Annae Auspiciis Feliciter Constituta Anno 1713. Cantabrigiae: Typis Academicis, 1713. Small folio; (139) pages; quarter calf antique, marbled boards, new endpapers. Case 266.   David Bickersteth 133-27 1996 £85.00

GRATULATIO Solennis Universitatis Oxoniensis ob Celsissimum Georgium Fred. Aug. Walliae principem Georgio II et Charlottae Reginae Auspicatissime Natum. Oxonii: e Typographeo Clarendoniano, 1762. Folio; (173) pages, fine engraved vignette, modern quarter calf antique, marbled boards.   David Bickersteth 133-108 1996 £95.00

GRAVES, GEORGE   British Ornithology: Being the History with a Coloured Representation of Every Known Species of British Birds. London: printed for the author, 1811. 1st edition; 8vo; 2 volumes, (237) pages + plates; 48 hand colored plates in each volume; turn of the century half brown calf and marbled boards, gilt tooled spines and morocco labels, library bookplate, unobtrusive blindstamp on titlepages and plates, else very good.   Chapel Hill 94-302 1996 $550.00

GRAVES, GEORGE   The Naturalist's Companion... London: 1824. 8vo; pages viii, 335, (7), 8 plates; half calf, surface of plate 7 slightly damaged.   Wheldon & Wesley 207-163 1996 £90.00

GRAVES, R. P.   Life of Sir William Rowan Hamilton. London: 1882/85. 8vo; 2 portraits; cloth, very good.   C. P. Hyland 216-311 1996 £70.00

GRAVES, RICHARD   Euphrosyne; or Amusements on the Road of Life. London: printed for J. Dodsley, 1776. 1st edition; 8vo; frontispiece; contemporary calf, spine gilt, slight wear, upper joint cracked; very good. CBEL II 1175.   Ximenes 108-173 1996 $300.00

GRAVES, RICHARD   The Festoon: a Collection of Epigrams, Ancient and Modern. London: for Mess. Robinson and Roberts and W. Frederick, Bath, 1766/65. 1st edition; 12mo; pages xx, 200; full green calf, spine with gilt floral motifs between gilt bands, sides bordered in gilt, with gilt motifs in corners; very attractive Irish binding, ca. 1780. Simon Finch 24-98 1996 £350.00

GRAVES, RICHARD   The Spiritual Quixote; or, the summer's Ramble of Mr. Geoffrey Wildgoose. London: J. Dodsley, 1774. 2nd edition; 12mo; 3 volumes; frontispieces in each volume, half titles present; pages xxiv, 352; viii, 287; xii, 323; contemporary tan calf, backstrips and raised bands, red and green albels in second and third compartments, remainder gilt, but rubbed, expert repairs at head and foot of all joints, board edges gilt hatched, printed book ticker in volume II (D. Gell, Hopton 1776); very good.   Blackwell's B112-135 1996 £180.00

GRAVES, ROBERT 1895-1985   Across the Gulf. Deja, Mallorca: 1992. Limited to 175 copies; signed by editors, printer and binder; printed on handmade paper; bound by Carmen Garcia-Gutierrez, fine in protective wrapper.   Words Etcetera 94-527 1996 £95.00

GRAVES, ROBERT 1895-1985   Across the Gulf; Late Poems. Deya: New Seizin Press, 1992, i.e. 1994. One of 175 numbered copies; signed by all 3 editors, printer and binder; large 8vo; handset 18 pt Bembo by Tomas Graves on paper specially made by Lluis Morera; double title spread in blue and black; decorated boards by Carmen Garcia-Gutierrez; fine.   Bertram Rota 272-313 1996 £80.00

GRAVES, ROBERT 1895-1985   Antigua, Penny, Puce. Majorca & London: Seizin Press/Constable, 1936. 1st edition; 1st issue with misprints on pages 100, 103 and 293; slight offsetting to endpapers, otherwise very nice, bright copy in slightly soiled, rubbed and nicked but very good dust jacket with usual cancel upper fold.   Virgo Books 48-86 1996 £200.00

GRAVES, ROBERT 1895-1985   The Antigua Stamp. New York: Random House, 1937. 1st American edition of Antigua Penny Puce, original binding, top edge slightly dusty, head and tail of spine slightly bumped, cover edges slightly marked, gilt lettering on spine dull, very good in very slightly creased dust jacket by Steinberg.   Ulysses 39-245 1996 £250.00

GRAVES, ROBERT 1895-1985   The Antigua Stamp. New York: Random House, 1937. 1st edition; fine in dust jacket darkened on spine and with several very shallow chips.   Bev Chaney, Jr. 23-270 1996 $125.00

GRAVES, ROBERT 1895-1985   Contemporary Techniques of Poetry. London: Hogarth Press, 1925. 1st edition; some foxing, covers slightly soiled and faded, spine split and chipped at tail, good; wrappers; small label of "Shakespeare and Company, Paris" inside back cover.   Virgo Books 48-102 1996 £50.00

GRAVES, ROBERT 1895-1985   Fairies and Fusiliers. London: William Heinemann, 1917. 1st edition; original binding, top edge dusty, spine and cover edges faded, head and tail of spine and corners bumped, endpaper edges slightly browned, slightly shaken, binding slightly loose, good only, no dust jacket.   Ulysses 39-241 1996 £85.00

GRAVES, ROBERT 1895-1985   Ich, Claudius - Kaiser und Gott. Leipzig: Paul List Verlag, 1934. 1st German edition; decorated cloth gilt, prelims, edges and endpapers slightly spotted, fore edge slightly soiled, cvoers marked and rubbed, tail of spine and fore-edge of lower cvoer slightly bumped; good.   Ulysses 39-243 1996 £135.00

GRAVES, ROBERT 1895-1985   Love Respelt Again. New York: Doubleday, n.d. 1969. 1st edition thus, one of 1000 numbered copies, signed by author; titlepage and several black and white decorations by Ameilia Laracuen; original binding, tail of spine and top corners bumped, tiny stain to fore-edge, stamp of library of the University of California, Berkeley on front pastedown; letters XMAC stamped on verso of titlepage, very good in nicked, rubbed and dusty, slightly soiled dust jacket slightly browned at spine and edges.   Ulysses 39-247 1996 £75.00

GRAVES, ROBERT 1895-1985   Mock Beggar Hall. London: published by Leonard & Virginia Woolf at the Hogarth Press, 1924. 1st edition; 8vo; printed boards, issued without dust jacket, fragile book; near fine, most pages unopened, moderate wear, small nick spine.   Antic Hay 101-726 1996 $375.00

GRAVES, ROBERT 1895-1985   The More Deserving Cases. Marlborough College Press, 1962. 1st edition; limited to 750 numbered copies, this one of 400 copies in leather binding, signed by Graves; pages (viii), 19; frontispiece; original full burgundy lettered in gilt on upper cover, top edge gilt; fine.   Sotheran PN32-16 1996 £225.00

GRAVES, ROBERT 1895-1985   The More Deserving Cases. N.P.: Marlborough College Press, 1962. One of 400 copies, signed by author; full morocco, some light scratching to rear board, otherwise fine. Between the Covers 42-196 1996 $150.00

GRAVES, ROBERT 1895-1985   On English Poetry. London: William Heinemann, 1922. 1st edition; original binding, top edge dusty, endpapers partially browned, head and tail fo spine and corners slightly bumped, cover edges rubbed, very good in remains of dust jacket which have been clumsily sellotaped together, head of spine defective and remnants are chipped, worn and browned; pencilled inscription.   Ulysses 39-242 1996 £150.00

GRAVES, ROBERT 1895-1985   On English Poetry. New York: 1922. 1st edition; 1st issue; top heel spine with few tiny tears, heel of spine with small area stained, near fine, dust jacket professionally repaired, flaps, spine and top edges internally strengthened, 2 inch piece top of spine and half inch heel missing, but most of title present; quite acceptable copy of the scarce first issue book and dust jacket.   Polyanthos 22-403 1996 $100.00

GRAVES, ROBERT 1895-1985   Poems 1914-1927. London: 1927. Limited to 11 copies, signed by author; vellum backed boards, top edge gilt, endpapers lightly foxed, otherwise very good in slightly dust soiled dust jacket, very scarce.   Words Etcetera 94-520 1996 £525.00

GRAVES, ROBERT 1895-1985   Poems 1914-1927. London: 1927. Limited to 115 copies (100 of which wre for sale); this copy unnumbered and unsigned; vellum backed white parchment, gilt, unopened, fine in dust jacket with coffee or tea stain on upper panel and with browned spine.   Words Etcetera 94-519 1996 £275.00

GRAVES, ROBERT 1895-1985   Poems, 1953. London: Cassell & Co., 1953. Limited to 250 numbered and signed copies, small 8vo; cloth backed boards, very slightly rubbed on extremities, very good, issued with plain tissue dust jacket, which is lacking.   Andrew Cahan 47-82 1996 $275.00

GRAVES, ROBERT 1895-1985   The Real David Copperfield. London: 1933. 1st edition; very good in dust jacket with two closed tears to upper panel and with small tear with loss at extreme head of upper panel, generally a most acceptable collector's copy.   Words Etcetera 94-522 1996 £65.00

GRAVES, ROBERT 1895-1985   Sergeant Lamb's America. New York: Random House, 1940. 1st American edition; original binding, top edge slightly dusty, spine slightly faded, head and tail of spine and corners slightly bumped, very good in nicked and slightly creased, rubbed and dusty dust jacket slightly darkened at spine and edges.   Ulysses 39-246 1996 £145.00

GRAVES, ROBERT 1895-1985   The Shout. London: Woburn Books, 1929. Limited to 530 copies, signed by author; boards, very good in dust jacket split down spine, otherwise very good.   Words Etcetera 94-521 1996 £75.00

GRAVES, ROBERT 1895-1985   To Whom Else? Deya, Majorca: Seizin Press, 1931. 1st edition; one of 200 numbered copies; this copy marked 'Out of Series' by Graves and signed by him, as were all copies; imperial 8vo; pages (iii), 19, (1); original quarter tan buckram, silver lettered backstrip, somewhat sunned, board sides with overall Len Lye designs in dark blue, slate grey and silver, the 'silver' oxidised as usual, untrimmed; good. Higginson & Williams A37.   Blackwell's B112-136 1996 £185.00

GRAVES, ROBERT 1895-1985   Treasure Box. London: privately printed for the author at the Chiswick Press, 1919. 1st edition; crown 8vo; 15 pages; titlepage illustration and further illustrations in text by Nancy Nicholson; original pale blue sewn wrappers; fine; presentation inscription from Graves to fellow poet David Posner. Higginson & Williams A4. Blackwell's B112-137 1996 £1,650.00

GRAVES, ROBERT J.   A System of Clinical Medicine. Dublin: Fannin and Co., 1843. 1st edition; 8vo; pages xvi, 637, (1); recent quarter calf, label, gilt; some very light foxing at beginning and end, still very good to nice. GM 2218.   ]James Fenning 133-138 1996 £450.00

GRAY, ASA   Characters of Some New Genera and Species of Plants of the Natural Order Compositae. Boston: Journal Nat. History, 1845. Offprint; 8vo; pages 8; plate; later plain wrappers, staples bit rusted; inscribed by author to Bentham (one great botanist to another). Maggs Bros. Ltd. 1190-9 1996 £75.00

GRAY, ASA   Letters of Asa Gray. Boston: 1893. 1st edition; 8vo; pages (4), 838; 2 volumes, 6 illustrations; original cloth, some corner rubbing and wear to spine ends, piece missing from page margin, light foxing to frontispiece; included are 2 ALS's by Gray, the recipient is E. B. Avery.   Raymond M. Sutton VI-12 1996 $450.00

GRAY, ASA   A Manual of the Botany of the Northern U.S. from New England to Wisconsin, And South to Ohio and Pennsylvania. Boston: 1848. 1st edition; lxxi, 710 pages; rebound in black cloth.   John Johnson 135-219 1996 $175.00

GRAY, ASA   Plantae Wrightianae Texano-Neo-Mexicanae, Account of a Collection of Plants Made by Charles Wright. Washington: 1852-53. Folio; 2 parts in 1 volume, 265 pages, 14 plates; cloth.   John Johnson 135-220 1996 $150.00

GRAY, ASA   Scientific Papers of Asa Gray.. London: 1889. 8vo; 2 volumes; pages viii, 397; iv, 503; pages yellowed, institutional bookplates, small number sticker on spines; original cloth.   Raymond M. Sutton VI-173 1996 $135.00

GRAY, CECIL   Gilles de Rais - a Play. London: Simpkin Marshall, 1941. Limited to 200 numbered copies, out of an edition of 250 copies, signed by author and artist; titlepage and several decorations by Michael Ayrton; wrappers, pages unopened, erratum slip loosely inserted; covers and front free endpaper slightly spotted, small tear at bottom edge of upper flap; near fine.   Ulysses 39-25 1996 £125.00

GRAY, JOHN CHIPMAN   Essays: Agricultural and Literary. Boston: Little Brown, 1856. 1st edition; 8vo; pages 386; morocco backed paper, little worn, top inch of front hinge split; good; inscribed by author. Second Life Books 103-94 1996 $125.00

GRAY, JOHN S.   Centennial Campaign. The Sioux Indian War of 1876. Fort Collins: 1976. 1st edition; 392 pages; maps, endpaper maps; nice in dust jacket.   T. A. Swinford 49-439 1996 $125.00

GRAY, ROBERT   The Birds of the West of Scotland Including the Outer Hebrides. Glasgow: Thomas Murray and Son, 1871. 1st edition; pages x (i), 520; 15 tinted lithograph plates; three quarter sage green mroocco, gilt, raised bands, elegantly gilt spine panels, all edges gilt, few spots to one or two plates, otherwise a handsome copy.   R.F.G. Hollett 76-111 1996 £160.00

GRAY, ROBERT   Observations on the Automaton Chess Player, Now Exhibited in London at 4, Spring Gardens. London: printed for J. Hatchard, 1819. 1st edition; 8vo; 32 pages; half title; disbound; very good, rare.   James Burmester 29-58 1996 £650.00

GRAY, THOMAS   The Value of Life and Charitable Institutions. Boston: printed by Hosea Sprague, 1805. 1st edition; 8vo; 46, (2 blank) pages, half title torn and frayed, browned, uncut; stitched as issued.   James Burmester 29-59 1996 £50.00

GRAY, THOMAS 1716-1771   The Correspondence... Oxford: Clarendon Press, 1971. Reprint; 8vo; 3 volumes; 3 portrait frontispieces, other illustrations and facsimiles; pages lx, 1-453; xxxiv, 455-909; xxxiv, 911-1369; original dark blue cloth, gilt lettered, dust jackets, excellent; J.D. Fleeman's copy with his signature.   Blackwell's B112-138 1996 £150.00

GRAY, THOMAS 1716-1771   An Elegy Written in a Country Churchyard. London: Sampson Low, Son & Co., 1861. 1st edition; 48 pages; title vignette, medallion and 22 illustrations; green cloth decorated gilt, all edges gilt, plain yellow endpapers; very scarce; unattractive inscription, bit loose, cloth rubbed.   Robin Greer 94A-18 1996 £125.00

GRAY, THOMAS 1716-1771   Elegy Written in a Country Churchyard. London: Edward Arnold, 1900. Limited to 125 copies; octavo; 13 pages; printed entirely on vellum, with opening full page hand colored wood engraving by George Thomson; full vellum over boards, blindstamped with rose logo and motto of series "Soul is Form", very fine. Crawford pp. 384-85. Ashbee p. 68.   Bromer Booksellers 87-60 1996 $550.00

GRAY, THOMAS 1716-1771   Elegy Written in a Country Churchyard. London: Essex House Press, 1900. One of 125 numbered copies printed on vellum; 8vo; hand colored woodcut frontispiece by George Thomason, initials and captials hand colored in red, blue and green; vellum boards with decoration in blind on upper cover, very nice, booklabel.   Bertram Rota 272-139 1996 £300.00

GRAY, THOMAS 1716-1771   Elegy Written in a Country Churchyard. London: Limited Editions Club, 1938. Copy number 904 from a total edition of 1500 numbered copies; signed by artist; wood engravings by Agnes Miller Parker; full pictorial cloth stamped in silver, fine in glassine wrapper and slightly marked publishers slipcase.   Hermitage SP95-989 1996 $250.00

GRAY, THOMAS 1716-1771   Elegy Written in a Country Churchyard. Norwalk: Heritage Press, 1951. Small 4to; title vignette and 32 full page wood engravings by Agnes Miller Parker; dark blue cloth, pictorially stamped in silver; fresh.   Barbara Stone 70-168 1996 £85.00

GRAY, THOMAS 1716-1771   Elegy Written in a Country Churchyard. Worcester: 1960. Limited to 1000 copies, 2 5/16 x 1 5/8 inches; 45 pages; 6 illustrations; gilt stamped calf, all edges gilt.   Bromer Booksellers 87-227 1996 $125.00

GRAY, THOMAS 1716-1771   Odes... Strawberry Hill: for R. and J. Dodsley, 1757. 1st edition; 4to; pages (3)-21; rebound without half title, in old style quarter calf, red morocco label, marbled sides, vellum tips, some light waterstaining. Hazen (SH)1.   Simon Finch 24-99 1996 £300.00

GRAY, THOMAS 1716-1771   Poems by Mr. Gray. London: Printed by J. Dodsley, 1768. New edition; 12mo; contemporary calf, skillfully rebacked; very good.   Captain's Bookshelf 38-93 1996 $175.00

GRAY, THOMAS 1716-1771   The Poems of Mr. Gray. London: printed by H. Hughs; and sold by J. Dodsley...and J. Todd 1775. 4to; pages (iv), 416; 109, (1); frontispiece, small waterstains in outer corners, titlepage lightly browned; contemporary marbled tan calf, 20th century tan russia reback, with raised bands, original label laid down, lower corners of boards bumped, corners repaired, extensive ms. note no prelim pages; good; contemporary owner's signature of D. Gell at head.   Blackwell's B112-139 1996 £225.00

GRAY, THOMAS 1716-1771   Poems and Letters. London: printed at th Chiswick Press, 1867. 4to; actual photograph as frontispiece, 3 oval photos; contemporary calf, spine gilt, slightly worn, all edges gilt, by Riviere.   Anthony W. Laywood 108-176 1996 £60.00

GRAY, THOMAS 1716-1771   Stanzas. N.P.: n.d., c. 1790. 1st English edition; 4to; with A1 blank, 12 pages; disbound.   Anthony W. Laywood 109-56 1996 £450.00

GRAYSON, A. J.   Birds of the Pacific Slope. San Francisco: 1986. Limited to 400 sets for sale; 4to; 500 pages of text and atlas volume, large folio, with 156 colored plates in portfolio; text volume in cloth. Wheldon & Wesley 207-40 1996 £3,000.00

THE GREAT Bastard, Protector of the Little One. Cologne: London: Baldwin, 1689. 4to; wrappers. Wing G1663.   Rostenberg & Stern 150-48 1996 $150.00

GREAT BRITAIN. COLONIAL OFFICE - 1863   Vancouver Island..."Copies or Extracts of Correspondence Between Mr. Langford and the Colonial Department, Rleative to Alleged Abuses in the Government of Vancouver's Island... London: Colonial Office, 1863. 33 cm; 52 pages; gilt stamped quarter leather and cloth, bit of scuffing to leather; very good. Bookplate of Robie Reid. Lowther 200.   Rockland Books 38-87 1996 $450.00

GREAT BRITAIN. COURT OF STAR CHAMBER - 1633   A Decree lately Made in the High Court of Starre-Chamber...(13 November 1633, Concerning Grain, Bread Prices, etc.)...And Also a Confirmation of that Decree by His Sacred Maiestie... London: Robert Barker...and...Assignes of Iohn Bill, 1633. 1st edition; small 4to; 15 unnumbered leaves A-D 4. A (signed blank) missing, chiefly Roman letter; full page engraved royal arms on verso of titlepage, engraved ornaments and 1 initial; modern half calf, gilt, mottled boards, STC 7755. Kress 483; Golsmith 648; not original copy in NUC.   A. Sokol XXV-30 1996 £950.00

GREAT BRITAIN. COURT OF STAR CHAMBER - 1884   A Decree of Star Chamber Concerning Printing, Made July 11, 1637. New York: Grolier Club, 1884. One of 150 copies; 9 x 6 inches; (48) leaves, including initial blank; color device on title, full page woodcut coat of arms, decorative headpieces, tailpieces and initials; original printed paper wrappers, apparently original tissue jacket, in cloth chemise and slipcase, tissue little wrinkled (as expected), hint of soiling to wrappers, occasional light foxing to text, surprisingly fine, quite fragile; armorial bookplates of Robert Woods Bliss and Mildred Bliss, both stamped withdrawn. Phillip J. Pirages 33-282 1996 $600.00

GREAT BRITAIN. LAWS, STATUTES, ETC. - 1556   Magna Charta, Cum Statius Quae Antiqua Vocantur... London: Richardum Totelum, 1556. 1st Tottel edition; 12mo; 2 parts in 1, 172, 72ff; contemporary full calf, corners bumped and spine ends chipped, some general wear, but remarkably well preserved; the John Croft copy, with his bookplate. Chapel Hill 94-253 1996 $1,750.00

GREAT BRITAIN. LAWS, STATUTES, ETC. - 1610   Anno Regni Iacobi...at the Fourth Session of Parliament Begun...the IX Day of February...Continued Vntill ...July...1610. London: Robert Barker, 1610. 1st edition; small folio; 84 unnumbered leaves, black letter with Roman titlepage, tables of contents and final imprint, occasional italic, large woodcut border with royal arms on titlepage, repeated in different form and larger size on next leaf, large woodcut initials, including 5 attractive historiated, also ornaments; foot of titlepage and last leaf and corners and edges of some leaves repaired (no loss), occasional ink and waterstains in blank lower margins; uncut in modern quarter calf, marbled boards; very good, wide margined copy. STC 9506; 4 copies in NUC; McKerrow & Ferguson 168 (b).   A. Sokol XXV-54 1996 £485.00

GREAT BRITAIN. LAWS, STATUTES, ETC. - 1643   An Ordinance of the Lords and Commons (on the Scottish Army) Assembled in Parliament Declaring the Cases, Wherefore After the Refusall of Many Remonstrances, Declarations and Treaties Had Been Sent by the Kingdome of Scotland... London: printed for John Wright, Oct. 19 1643. 1st edition; 8vo; pages 8, black letter with typographical border to title, headpiece and initial letter; modern three quarter calf, gilt; excellent copy, scarce. Wing E1835.   R.F.G. Hollett 76-86 1996 £175.00

GREAT BRITAIN. LAWS, STATUTES, ETC. - 1644   An Ordinance of the Lords and Commons Assembled in Parliament, for Providing of Drught-Horses for Carriages of the Traine of Artillery to the Army Under the Command of Sir Thomas Farifax. And for Paying of Coat and Conduct Money. London: for Edward Husbands, 1644. 1st edition; 4to; 5 pages, as folded; title within woodcut border, uncut. Wing E1900. Anthony Laywood 108-1 1996 £135.00

GREAT BRITAIN. LAWS, STATUTES, ETC. - 1760   The Act for Permitting the Free Importation of Cattle from Ireland, Considered with a View to the Interests of Both Kingdoms. London: R. and J. Dodsley, 1760. Half title, 43 pages; disbound; nice. Rare. Kress 5823; Goldsmiths 9550; Higgs 2168.   C. R. Johnson 37-1 1996 £125.00

GREAT BRITAIN. LAWS, STATUTES, ETC. - 1946   Coal Industry Nationalization Act, 1946. London: HMSO, 1946. 1st edition; interleaved throughout with blank leaves; full vellum covers, bound by Hatchards, the words "The Rt. Hon. Emanuel Shinwell M.P." are stamped in gilt on upper cover, top edge gilt, covers bowed and slightly marked and soiled, spine and cover edges darkened, front free endpaper slightly creased, edges slightly browned; very good. Signed by all members of the first National Coal Board.   Ulysses 39-113 1996 £475.00

GREAT BRITAIN. PARLIAMENT - 1753   A Bill, with the Amendments, for the Amendment and Preservation of the Public Roads of This Kingdom; and for the More Effectual Execution of the Laws Relating Thereto. London: 1753. Folio; drop head title, 15 pages, folded, very nice.   C. R. Johnson 37-4 1996 £75.00

GREAT BRITAIN. PARLIAMENT - 1855   Report from the Select Committee on Downing Street Public Offices Extension Bill; Togethr with the Minutes of Evidence, Proceedings of the Committee and Appendix. London: 24th July, 1855. 4to; iv, 10, (2) pages; 3 folding litho plates, hand colored; cloth.   Elton Engineering 10-38 1996 £320.00

GREAT BRITAIN. PARLIAMENT - 1966   Report from the Select (Parliamentary) Committee on Aborigines (British Settlements). Cape Town: 1966. Facsimile reprint; folio; 2 volumes, pages 841, 212; buckram.   Howes Bookshop 265-3 1996 £75.00

GREAT BRITAIN. PARLIAMENT. HOUSE OF COMMONS - 1680   A True Copy of the Journal-Book of the Last Parliament, Begun at Westminster the Sixth Day of march 1678... London: n.p., 1680. 8vo; (8), 316 pages; old calf, rebacked, worming at lower margin of first 12 leaves.   Kenneth Karmiole 1NS-102 1996 $225.00

GREAT BRITAIN. PARLIAMENT. HOUSE OF COMMONS - 1836 Third Report from the Select Committee (of the Commons) Appointed to Inquire Into the State of Agriculture; with the Minutes of Evidence, Appendix and Index. London: 1836. Folio; pages (4), 624, 149; strongly bound in paper boards, label; nice.   James Fenning 133-2 1996 £85.00

GREAT BRITAIN. PARLIAMENT. HOUSE OF COMMONS - 1855 Report from the Select Committee on Metropolitan Communications; Together with the Proceedings of the Committee, Minutes of Evidence and Appendix. London: House of Commons, 1855. 8vo; xii, 204 pages, 36 litho plates, some hand colored and many folding.   Elton Engineering 10-106 1996 £1,150.00

GREAT BRITAIN. ROYAL COMM. FOR METROPOLITAN IMPROVEMENTS First Report of the Commissioners Appointed by Her Majesty to Inquire Into and consider the Most Effectual Means of Improving the Metropolis, and of Provided Increased Facilities of Communication Within the Same. London: 27 January, 1844. 4to; (ii), 261, (1) pages, 60 folding maps and plans; original stiff blue printed wrappers.   Elton Engineering 10-105 1996 £650.00

GREAT BRITAIN. SOVEREIGNS, ETC. - 1642   His Majesties Instructions to His Commissioners of Array, for the Several Counties of England, and the Principality of Wales and to be Observed by All Sheriffs, Maiors, Justices of the Peace, Bayliffs, Head-boroughs, Constables... London: ...Robert Barker, and now reprinted for R. Best, Yorke, 1642. 4to; title within woodcut border, woodcut arms on blank verso of title, Black Letter, 7 pages; disbound. Wing C2350.   Anthony Laywood 108-4 1996 £125.00

GREAT Toronto Illustrated. Toronto: Ernest E. Fligg and Albert E. Hacker, c. 1909. Oblong 8vo; pages (4), (90) (Plates); gilt stamped paper covers, covers chipped, some plates starred in pencil, else fine.   Hugh Anson-Cartwright 87-416 1996 $125.00

GREAVES, EDWIN   Kashi, the City Illustrious, or Benares. Allahabad: 1909. 1st edition; 8vo; pages (12), 153, iv, folding map and 25 plates; original cloth, gilt, four small ink stains on upper cover, otherwise, nice, fresh copy.   James Fenning 133-139 1996 £55.00

GRECOURT, JEAN BAPTISTE JOSEPH   Oeuvres Completes. Paris: Chaignieu, 1796. 8vo; 4 volumes; portrait, 8 engraved plates by Gragonand fils; contemporary vellum gilt by Bozerian Jeune (with his name in gilt on spine), gilt roll tooled borders, flat spine, gilt in compartments, lettered and dated in gilt, turquoise marbled endpapers, all edges gilt; the Pixerecourt copy, with engraved, green label. Marlborough 160-39 1996 £1,500.00

GREEN, BEN K.   Back to Back. Austin: Encino Press, 1970. 1st edition; limited, signed by author; 51 pages; portrait; original red boards, portrait paper label on front cover of Green, title stamped in black on spine, text printed in red and black, slipcase; very fine.   Michael D. Heaston 23-160 1996 $125.00

GREEN, BEN K.   Ben Green Tales. Flagstaff: Northland Press, 1974. 1st edition; 4 volumes; illustrations; slipcase; very fine limited set. Wilson 22.   Michael D. Heaston 23-161 1996 $200.00

GREEN, BEN K.   A Thousand Miles of Mustangin'. Flagstaff: 1972. 1st edition; small 4to; 145 pages; illustrations; pictorial cloth, fine in price clipped dust jacket. Wilson 17; Dykes 50 p. 9.   Gene W. Baade 1094-64 1996 $135.00

GREEN, BEN K.   Wild Cow Tales. New York: Alfred A. Knopf, 1969. 1st and limited edition of 300 copies, signed by Green; 306 pages; illustrations; original tan cloth with black morocco spine label, slipcase; very fine. Dykes Bjorklund 54 & 55; Reese Six Score 50.   Michael D. Heaston 23-162 1996 $225.00

GREEN, D. M.   Amphibian Cytogenetics and Evolution. New York: 1991. 8vo; 429 pages; illustrations; hardbound.   Wheldon & Wesley 207-925 1996 £84.50

GREEN, HENRY   Concluding. London: Hogarth Press, 1948. 1st edition; original binding, top edge dusty, prelims, edges and endpapers slightly spotted, head of spine slightly bumped, very good in nicked, torn, marked and heavily spotted, slightly creased, rubbed and dusty dust jacket, browned at spine and edges; from the library of Ian Parsons.   Ulysses 39-251 1996 £85.00

GREEN, HENRY   Living. London: J. M. Dent & sons, 1929. 1st edition; original binding, top edge dusty, prelims, edges and endpapers spotted, free endpapers partially browned, head and tail of spine slightly bumped and faded, very good in chipped rubbed and spotted, marked, frayed, creased and dusty dust jacket browned at spine and edges and missing small pieces at head of spine.   Ulysses 39-250 1996 £1,600.00

GREEN, HENRY   Nothing. London: Hogarth Press, 1950. 1st edition; original binding, top edge dusty, spine slightly faded, prelims, edges and endpapers spotted, covers slightly cocked, very good in nicked, spotted and slightly rubbed, chipped and soiled dust jacket, browned at spine and edges.   Ulysses 39-252 1996 £75.00

GREEN, HENRY   Nothing. London: Hogarth Press, 1950. 1st edition; fine copy in price clipped dust jacket.   Captain's Bookshelf 38-94 1996 $100.00

GREEN, R.   The Works of John and Charles Wesley. A Bibliography. London: 1896. 1st edition; original blue cloth, slightly rubbed, headcaps and corners mildly bumped, with single leaf extracted from Gooding Catalogue Newcastle 1744 inserted loose entitled Books PUb. by the Rev. Mr. John and Charles Wesley. Besterman 6525.   Maggs Bros. Ltd. 1191-96 1996 £100.00

GREEN, STANLEY   Starring Fred Astaire. New York: Dodd, Mead, 1973. 1st edition; 4to; numerous black and white illustrations; dust jacket, very good; taped down on front free endpaper is ALS from Astaire to actress Lana Wood.   George J. Houle 68-5 1996 $275.00

GREEN, THOMAS   The Case of Capt. Tho. Green, Commander of the Ship Worcester and His Crew, Tried and Condemned for Pyracy & Murther, in the High Court of Admiralty of Scotland. London: printed and are to be sold by John Nutt, 1705. One of 2 edition printed at about the same time, the imprint of the other is simply "printed in the year 1705". Small 4to; modern boards; very good, crisp, uncommon pamphlet; McLeod Scottish Tracts 1701-1714 54.   Ximenes 109-143 1996 $1,500.00

GREEN, THOMAS   Some Cursory Remarks on a Late Printed Paper, Called, the Last Speeches and Dying Words of Capt. Thomas Green, Commander of the Ship Worcester; and of Capt. John Madder, Chief Mate of the Said Ship &c... Edinburgh: printed by James Watson, 1705. 1st edition; folio; half brown morocco, gilt, spine gilt; titlepage bit dusty, otherwise very good, uncut; rare. McLeod, Anglo Scottish Tracts 1701-1714, 414.   Ximenes 109-144 1996 $2,000.00

GREEN, THOMAS J.   Reply of Gen. Thomas J. Green, to the Speech of General Sam Houston, in the Senate of the United States, August 1, 1854. Washington: 1855. 1st edition; 67 pages; original printed wrappers, fine, laid in half morocco slipcase, with chemise. Littell Sale 416; Raines p. 99; Jenkins BTB 80n; Howes G372.   Michael D. Heaston 23-163 1996 $1,500.00

GREEN, WILLIAM   A Description of a Series of Sixty Small Prints, Etched by... ptd. for the author by John Tyler and published by Wm. Green... 1814. 1st edition; oblong small 4to; pages 34, 60 soft ground etchings, corner of title little dusty, small neat repair, occasional spot, few edges trifle darkened, but excellent copy, with few small corrections to text in an early hand, poossibly by author; modern quarter calf, gilt, original label preserved on upper board. Bicknell 67.   R.F.G. Hollett & Son 78-948 1996 £750.00

GREEN, WILLIAM   The Tourist's New Guide Containing a Description of the Lakes, Mountains and Scenery in Cumberland, Westmorland and Lancashire. Kendal: R. Lough and Co., 1819.. 1st edition; 8vo; 2 volumes; pages 461; ix, 507, lv, with 1 half title, folding map and 33 plates, volume 1 lacks folding map, preface (pages v-xii), index (iii-viii) and errata leaf, volume 2 lacks half title, errata leaf and 2 aquatints (Ilse of Windermere and Derwentwater); old half calf, gilt, neatly recased; little spotting in places, small tear neatly repaired, but good sound set, rarely found complete. From the library of Norman Nicholson.   R.F.G. Hollett & Son 78-949 1996 £850.00

GREENAWAY, KATE 1846-1901   Almanack for 1885. London: Routledge, 1884. 1st edition; 24mo; pages (24) (including covers); engraved and printed in black and colors; original cream glazed pictorial boards with yellow, cloth backstrip, plain blue green endpapers, front hinge split; good. Schuster & Engen 5.3.a. Osborne p. 421.   Blackwell's B112-140 1996 £50.00

GREENAWAY, KATE 1846-1901   Almanack for 1887. London: George Routledge & Son, 12mo; original yellow cloth backed pictorial boards, blue green endpapers, yellow edges, preserved in original printed mailing envelope, very good. Schuster & Engen 7 5(a).   Sotheran PN32-121 1996 £200.00

GREENAWAY, KATE 1846-1901   Almanack for 1890. London: George Routledge & Sons, Original deluxe issue; 12mo; bound in pale green cloth stamped with decorative border in blue, gilt vignette to upper cover, blue green endpapers, gilt edges, preserved in original printed mailing envelope; fine. Schuster & Engen 10 8(b).   Sotheran PN32-122 1996 £250.00

GREENAWAY, KATE 1846-1901   Almanack for 1894. London: George Routledge & sons, 12mo; original brown cloth backed pictorial boards, green endpapers and edges, preserved in original mailing envelope which has some edge repair with archival tissue, endpapers marked, very nice. Schuster & Engen 14 12(a).   Sotheran PN32-123 1996 £200.00

GREENAWAY, KATE 1846-1901   A Day in a Child's Life. London: Routledge, 1881. 1st edition; 1st issue; 4to; colored illustrations by Greenaway; light green glazed pictorial boards with cover design of sunflowers,, corners knocked, edges rubbedd, generaly very good, fresh copy; Schuster and Engen 66 1a.   Barbara Stone 70-108 1996 £125.00

GREENAWAY, KATE 1846-1901   The Little Folks Painting Book. London: Paris: and New York: Cassell, Petter and Galpin, 1879. 1st edition; 1st issue; 8vo; pages ix,, 10-96, (ii), 3-4; profusely illustrated with engravings by Greenaway, frontispiece with original hand coloring as issued as a guide for colourists, 34 of the engravings beautifully hand colored by the accompolished previous owner; original yellow paper wrappers printed in black, neatly, expertly and uniformly rebacked with yellow paper; excellent copy, scarce. Schuster & Engen 116 1(a). Sotheran PN32-120 1996 £298.00

GREENAWAY, KATE 1846-1901   Under the Window. London: Routledge, 1879. 1st edition; 4to; colored illustrations, cloth backed pictorial boards corners little knocked, else very nice.   Barbara Stone 70-109 1996 £125.00

GREENE, E. L.   Landmarks of Botanical History. Stanford: 1893. 8vo; nearly 300 portraits and figures; cloth.   Wheldon & Wesley 207-241 1996 £75.00

GREENE, GRAHAM 1904-1991   The Comedians. New York: Viking Press, 1966. Limited to 500 copies; buckram, very good in torn acetate jacket.   Words Etcetera 94-537 1996 £50.00

GREENE, GRAHAM 1904-1991   Doctor Fischer of Geneva or the Bomb Party. London: Bodley Head, 1980. 1st edition; crown 8vo; pages 140; original mid green linen backstrip gilt lettered, dust jacket; fine; superb association copy, inscribed by author for his wife Vivien.   Blackwell's B112-142 1996 £700.00

GREENE, GRAHAM 1904-1991   Doctor Fisher of Geneva of the Bomb Party. New York: Simon & Schuster, 1980. 1/250 copies, signed and numbered, unopened in slipcase.   Bev Chaney, Jr. 23-276 1996 $250.00

GREENE, GRAHAM 1904-1991   It's a Battlefield. London: William Heinemann, 1934. 1st edition; 2nd issue dust jacket (with "3/6 net" on spine); crown 8vo; just a trifle knocked, but very good and clean in worn and split but still near complete dust jacket.   Ash Rare Books Zenzybyr-39 1996 £495.00

GREENE, GRAHAM 1904-1991   The Little Horse Bus. London: Max Parrish, 1952. 1st edition; color and black and white illustrations by Dorothy Craigie; red cloth, pictorially printed in gilt; fine.   Barbara Stone 70-110 1996 £195.00

GREENE, GRAHAM 1904-1991   The Little Horse Bus; The Little Fire Engine; The Little Train; and The Little Steamroller. London: Bodley Head, 1973-74. 1st editions thus; oblong quarto; 4 volumes, 47, 48, 47, 44 pages; pictorial boards, matching dust jackets, very fine set showing only the faintest of rubbing to extremities.   Bromer Booksellers 87-105 1996 $250.00

GREENE, GRAHAM 1904-1991   The Living Room - A Play in Two Acts. London: William Heinemann, 1953. 1st edition; original binding, fore-edge of lower cover bumped, tail of spine slightly bumped, very good in slightly rubbed, creased and dusty dust jacket with one inch tear at top edge of lower panel.   Ulysses 39-254 1996 £55.00

GREENE, GRAHAM 1904-1991   May We Borrow Your Husband? London: Bodley Head, 1967. Signed, limited edition of 500 numbered copies; 8vo; cloth and patterned boards in acetate dust jacket, lacks cardboard slipcase; fine.   Antic Hay 101-745 1996 $250.00

GREENE, GRAHAM 1904-1991   Monsignor Quixote. New York: Simon and Schuster, 1982. 1/250 copies, signed and numbered; fine in slipcase. Bev Chaney, Jr. 23-278 1996 $200.00

GREENE, GRAHAM 1904-1991   The Power and the Glory. London: William Heinemann, Ltd., 1940. Uncorrected proof of the first edition; 8vo; original buff wrappers lettered in red, apart from darkened spine and one tiny cover crease, the proof is in remarkably fine condition; exceedingly rare.   Lakin & Marley 3-16 1996 $7,500.00

GREENE, GRAHAM 1904-1991   The Power and the Glory. London: William Heinemann, 1940. 1st edition; 8vo; pages (vi), 280; original yellow cloth, blocked in red, scarce dust jacket, covers little soiled, slightly rubbed dust jacket that has two internal repairs to top edge and appears to have been trimmed slightly at bottom edge, otherwise very good.   Sotheran PN32-17 1996 £1,998.00

GREENE, GRAHAM 1904-1991   The Quiet American. London: Wm. Heinemann, 1955. 1st edition; base of spine very lightly rubbed, few small spots on page top edges (stained brown), otherwise fine in dust jacket slightly darkened on spine and edges with only minor soiling on rear panel.   Quill & Brush 102-749 1996 $100.00

GREENE, GRAHAM 1904-1991   Reflections on Travels with My Aunt. New York: Firsts and Co., 1989. Limited to 250 copies, signed by author; stiff wrappers with gilt monogram; mint.   Words Etcetera 94-544 1996 £120.00

GREENE, GRAHAM 1904-1991   The Third Man. (and) The Fallen Idol. London: Heinemann, 1950. 1st edition; fine in near fine dust jacket with light rubbing and minor edge wear, still nice.   Quill & Brush 102-748 196 $450.00

GREENE, GRAHAM 1904-1991   The Third Man (and) The Fallen Idol. London: William Heinemann, 1950. 1st edition; original binding, top edge slightly dusty, head and tail of spine and corners slightly bumped, very good in nicked, chipped and rubbed, slightly marked and dusty, very slightly torn dust jacket darkened at spine and edges, and missing a small piece at head of spine.   Ulysses 39-253 1996 £180.00

GREENE, GRAHAM 1904-1991   This Gun for Hire. Garden City: Doubleday, 1936. 1st edition; very good with light wear on spine ends, in bright dust jacket with light soiling and edge wear.   Quill & Brush 102-747 1996 $1,500.00

GREENE, GRAHAM 1904-1991   A Visit to Morin. London: Heinemann, 1959. One of only 250 copies; very good+ in rather soiled dust jacket with ink squiggle to upper front panel; extraordinary association copy, inscribed by author to Ian Fleming.   Lame Duck Books 19-228 1996 $3,750.00

GREENER, W.   The Science of Gunnery, As Applied to the Use and Construction of Fire Arms. London: 1841. 7 engraved plates, many text illustrations; tastefully bound in modern half calf, marbled boards, contents somewhat browned, some pages grubby; engraved half title has been neatly repaired.   David A.H. Grayling 3/95-297 1996 £250.00

GREENEWALT, CRAWFORD   Humming Birds. London: 1960. Folio; brilliantly exected color photos; pencil drawiangs &c; fine in frayed dust jacket.   David A.H. Grayling MY95Orn-35 1996 £200.00

GREENEWALT, CRAWFORD   Humming Birds. New York: 1960. 1st printing; 4to; pages xxi, 250, 70 color photos and numerous illustrations; buckram.   Wheldon & Wesley 207-744 1996 £120.00

GREENFIELD, JEFF   Television: the First Fifty Years. New York: Abrams, 1977. 1st edition; small folio; author's preface, 516 illustrations, including 156 color plates; dust jacket with few nicks, very good. George J. Houle 68-55 1996 $125.00

GREENHILL, ELIZABETH   Elizabeth Greenhill Bookbinder. A Catalogue Raisonne. Foss: K. D. Duval, 1986. 1st edition; limited to 500 copies; 4to; 81 illustrations in color and 22 in black and white, cloth spine gilt; new.   Forest Books 74-94 1996 £60.00

GREENLEAF, ABNER   An Address Delivered at Jefferson-Hall, Portsmouth, N.H. Jan. 8, 1828 Being the 13th Anniversary of Jackson's Victory at New Orleans. Portsmouth: G. Beggs, 1828. 12 pages; wrappers, untrimmed, soiled, edge worn, portion of front wrapper torn away. Not in NUC; AI 33419 cites 3 locations (this copy is one). Bohling Book Co. 192-6 1996 $100.00

GREENWOOD'S Pictures of Hull. Hull & London: published by J. Greenwood, t Bowlalley Lane, Hull; colophon: Driffield: printed by B. Fawcett, 1835. 1st edition; 8vo; viii, 206 pages, 66 of 70 engravings; new old style quarter calf, good. Presentation copy from author to John Andrews.   K Books 441-254 1996 £140.00

GREENWOOD, JAMES   Curiosities of Savage Life. London: S. O. Beeton, 1863. 1st edition; 8 1/2 x 5 3/4 inches; xiv, 418 pages; 9 plates printed in color from watercolor drawings by F. W. Keyl and R. Huttula, 78 illustrations in text engraved by H. Newsom Woods from designs by Harden S. Melville; contemporary green half calf, cloth sides, spine ends and raised bands hatched in gilt, red morocco label, inscription; front cover detached, slight wear to corners, binding little marked, in all other ways a fine copy.   Phillip J. Pirages 33-258 1996 $150.00

GREENWOOD, JAMES   An Essay Towards a Practical English Grammar. London: printed for John Clark, 1722. 2nd edition; 12mo; neatly rebound in half calf, marbled boards, red label, very good. Alston I 53.   Jarndyce 103-252 1996 £200.00

GREENWOOD, JAMES   Legends of a Savage Life. London: John Camden Hotten, 1869. 9 x 7 3/4 inches; 2 p.l., (5)-164 pages, (8) leaves (ads); 24 plates and 12 illustrations by Ernest Griset, engraved by H. Newsom Woods, added engraved title, device on title; original pictorial green cloth, front joint neatly reinforced with matching paper; gilt inscription on title, bit of wear and small tears to joints and corners, spine ends bumped, otherwise binding tight and pleasing; very good internally; quite scarce.   Phillip J. Pirages 33-259 1996 $200.00

GREENWOOD, JAMES   The London Vocabulary, English and Latin... London: for T. Longman, B. Law, et al, 1797. 21st edition; 12mo; viii, 123 pages; woodcut illustrations in text, minor worming at inner corner of first gathering, antique style paper boards.   H. M. Fletcher 121-102 1996 £95.00

GREENWOOD, JAMES   The Purgatory of Peter the Cruel. London: George Routledge, 1868. Crown 4to; 164, 2 ad pages; additional hand colored illustrated title, 35 other hand colored wood engraved illustrations by Ernest Griset; contemporary calf, gilt, neatly rebacked, but retaining gilt morocco labels from previous spine, gilt edges; original green cloth, gilt, covers bound in, sides rubbed, otherwise good. Thomas Thorp 489-123 1996 $150.00

GREENWOOD, THOMAS   Free Public Libraries, Their Organisation, Uses and Management. London: Simpkin, Marshall, 1886. 1st edition; frontispiece, illustrations, ads; original dark green cloth, slightly defective at head of spine; from the collection of Anne and Fernand Renier. Jarndyce 103-483 1996 £75.00

GREER, GEORGEANNA H.   The Meyer Family: Master Potters of Texas. Santonio: Trinity University Press, 1971. 1st edition; small 4to; 97 pages; photos;   Maggie Lambeth 30-229 1996 $100.00

GREG, RICHARD   Memoria Technica; or, a New Method of Artificial memory, Applied to and Exemplified in Chronology, History, Geography, Astronomy. London: printed for Charles King, 1730. 1st edition; 8vo; xviii, (6), 120 pages, title printed in red and black; contemporary panelled calf, top of spine slightly chipped, otherwise very nice.   Kenneth Karmiole 1NS-115 1996 $650.00

GREGER, DEBORA   Blank Country: Twenty Poems. Meadow Press, 1985. One of 130 numbered copies, signed by author and artist; slim 4to; 3 page foldout lithograph; printed in blue, black and green in Monotype Dante and Castellar on Frankfurt Cream Laid, the illustration on Nideggen; quarter cloth, Roma boards, printed label; fine.   Bertram Rota 272-286 1996 £56.00

GREGG, FRANK M.   The Founding of a Nation. Cleveland: 1915. 1st edition; 341 pages; color frontispiece, illustrations, pictorial cloth, very good+; very scarce.   T. A. Swinford 49-448 1996 $100.00

GREGG, JOSIAH   Commerce of the Prairies: or, the Journal of a Santa Fe trader, During Eight Expeditions Across the Great Western Prairie. New York: Henry G. Langley, 1844. 1st edition; 1st issue; 2 volumes, 6 plates, 2 maps; one folding; original black cloth, blind embossed borders on sides, gilt vignettes on front covers, title in gilt on backstrip, professionally rebacked with original spine and overall very good, clean copy. Graff 1559. Bay pp. 367, 371-72; Howes G401; Jones 1087. Michael D. Heaston 23-164 1996 $3,000.00

GREGG, JOSIAH   Commerce of the Prairies; or the Journal of a Santa Fe Trader, During Eight Expeditions across the Great Western Prairies and a Residence of Nearly Nine Years in Northern Mexico. New York: Henry G. Langley, 1844. 1st edition; 1st issue; 12mo; 2 volumes; pages 320; 318; 3 plates in each volume, large folding map in volume 1, small map in volume 2; original blind and gilt stamped brown cloth, gilt vignette on spines and front covers, rear free endpaper lacking in volume 2, light scattered foxing, primarily to frontispiece and titlepage, one plate and one leaf quite spotted, large folding map with 6 inch tear, expertly repaired with acid free document repair tape, covers with light wear to spine ends and corners, light rubbing, overall very good set, collated complete, housed in gilt lettered cloth slipcase. Howes G401; Field 265; Graff 1659; Larned 2040; Rader 1684.   Argonaut Book Shop 113-295 1996 $2,250.00

GREGORGY, THE GREAT, SAINT   Libri Dialogorum. Basel: Michael Furter, 1496. 4to; 58 unnumbered leaves, 2 sizes of Gothic letter 2 line title in larger third, strictly contemporary marginalia to 4 page table, some light age yellowing, one blank outer corner repaired, unimportant waterstain to a few leaves; modern vellum; good, well margined copy. BMC III 784; Hain 7966; Goff G407.   A. Sokol XXV-147 1996 £1,950.00

GREGOROVIUS, FERDINAND   History of the City of Rome in the Middle Ages. London: 1894. Small 8vo; 8 volumes in 13; original cloth, (4 spines little marked). Scarce set.   Charles W. Traylen 117-123 1996 £130.00

GREGOROVIUS, FERDINAND   History of the City of Rome in the Middle Ages. London: 1900. Original edition; thick crown 8vo; 8 volumes in 13; original maroon cloth; ex-library with bookplate and stamp, but good set.   Howes Bookshop 265-431 1996 £200.00

GREGORY, DAVID   A Treatise of Practical Geometry. Edinburgh: printed by W. and T. Ruddimans, for Messrs. Hamilton and Balfour, 1745. 1st edition; 5 folding engraved plates; contemporary calf, neatly rebacked, spine gilt; slight dust soiling, but very good, uncommon. Ximenes 109-146 1996 $450.00

GREGORY, G.   A New and Complete Dictionary of Arts and Sciences... London: Richard Phillips & Thomas Tegg, 1807. 1st edition of volume 1, 2nd edition of volume 2; thick quarto; 2 volumes, pages 960, 624, index, ads; engravings (some uniformly foxed); full calf, original boards, gilt fillets, recently rebacked and relabelled, reasonable set, scarce. Cordell p. 76.   Hartfield 48-11h 1996 $385.00

GREGORY, HORACE   D. H. Lawrence, Pilgrim of the Apocalypse, a Critical Study. New York: 1957. Limited to 100 numbered copies, signed by author; 8 x 5.5 inches; 118 pages; cloth backed boards; very good, specially bound.   John K. King 77-366 1996 $200.00

GREGORY, ISABELLA AUGUSTA PERSE 1859-1932   Gods and Fighting Men. 1904. 1st edition; 8vo; cloth, light marking on cover, else very good.   C. P. Hyland 216-289 1996 £65.00

GREGORY, ISABELLA AUGUSTA PERSE 1859-1932   Kincora, a Drama in Three Acts. New York: John Quinn, 1905. 1st American edition; one of 50 copies, signed by author; light grey printed wrappers; fine.   Bromer Booksellers 90-55 1996 $850.00

GREGORY, JOHN 1607-1646   The Works of the Reverend and Learned Mr. John Gregory, Masater of Arts of Christ's Church, Oxon, in Two Parts... London: printed for Richard Royston and Thomas Williams, 1671. 2nd edition; small 4to; (xxiv), 166, (ii); (xxiv), 330 pages, engraved vignette on title, one text engraving and 4 large text woodcuts; original reverse calf, little rubbed. Wing G1914.   David Bickersteth 133-32 1996 £85.00

GREGORY, LADY   Spreading the New, a Play in One Act. New York: John Quinn, 1904. 1st American edition, limited to 50 copies, signed by author; light grey printed wrappers; fine.   Bromer Booksellers 90-56 1996 $850.00

GRENFELL, WILFRED T.   Labrador Looks at the Orient. Boston: Houghton Mifflin, 1928. 1st edition; small bookplate on front pastedown, otherwise fine in dust jacket with one small chip from upper front panel and small private library numbers on spine; inscribed with drawing by author.   Hermitage SP95-1102 1996 $100.00

GRENFELL, WILFRED T.   Tales of the Labrador. Boston: 1926. 240 pages; original binding. Autographed by Grenfell with full page drawing by him depicting a boat in the Sea.   W. Bruce Fye 71-858 1996 $250.00

GRESSIT, J. L.   Biogeography and Ecology of New Guinea. London: 1981. 8vo; 2 volumes; 1008 pages, 330 figures, 64 tables; cloth. Wheldon & Wesley 207-398 1996 £268.00

GRESWELL, WILLIAM PARR   Annals of Parisian Typography. London: Cadell and Davies, et al, 1818. 1st edition; one of an unspecified number of large paper copies; 8vo; 356 pages; 12 full page plates; 19th century three quarter green morocco and cloth by L. & F. Bumpus with gilt spine and raised bands, spine faded to brown, covers little bowed, else very good, quite nice internally.   Chapel Hill 94-328 1996 $250.00

GREUB, SUZANNE   Authority and Ornament. Art of the Sepik River, Papua, New Guinea. Basel: Edition Greub Base. Jan.-June, 1985-88. 31.5 cm; 217 pages, maps, many color and black and white plates, illustrations; decorated paper over boards.   L. Clarice Davis 111-118 1996 $150.00

GREVILLE, CHARLES CAVENDISH FULKE 1794-1865   The Greville Memoirs: a Journal of the Reigns of King George IV and King William IV. (and) A Journal of the Reign of Queen Victoria. London: Longmans, Green and Co., 1874-87. 1st edition; 8 3/4 x 6 inches; 8 volumes; attractive deep purple crushed three quarter morocco, linen sides, spine compartments with large gilt royal emblems at center, ochre double labels, marbled endpapers, top edge gilt, spines slightly faded to a rich brown, cloth sides with bit of uneven fading, small pen mark on one cover, but only trivial imperfections otherwise, bindings virtually unworn and quite appealing, internally fine.   Phillip J. Pirages 33-275 1996 $650.00

GREVILLE, CHARLES CAVENDISH FULKE 1794-1865   Greville Memoirs. 1814-1860. London: Macmillan, 1938. Limited to 630 copies; royal 8vo; 8 volumes; original red buckram, leather labels, gilt tops, out of print & scarce.   Charles W. Traylen 117-126 1996 £600.00

GREVILLE, CHARLES CAVENDISH FULKE 1794-1865   A Journal of the Reign of Queen Victoria from 1837 to 1852. London: Longmans, Green & Co., 1885. 1st edition; 8vo; 3 volumes; contemporary half black morocco with raised bands, lightly rubbed, former owner's name clipped from top of title, not affecting lettering, else very good.   Chapel Hill 94-112 1996 $100.00

GREVILLE, ROBERT KAYE   Scottish Cryptogamic Flora. Edinburgh: 1823-28. 8vo; 6 volumes; descriptive text unpaginated; 360 hand colored engraved plates; half morocco with marbled boards, gilt decorated spines, some scuffing, mostly to extremities, boards slightly rubbed, light dampstaining to lower outer corners of covers and some pages, affecting text of one page, scattered light foxing, plates mostly clean, all edges gilt.   Raymond M. Sutton VII-15 1996 $1,500.00

GREW, J. C.   Sport and Travel in the Far East. 1910. 264 pages; many photo illustrations; original cloth, rubbed, lacks front endpaper, contents very clean.   David Grayling J95Biggame-520 1996 £55.00

GREW, NEHEMIAH 1628-1711   Museum Regalis Societatis. London: by W. Rawlins for the author, 1681. 1st edition; folio; (12), 386, (2), index, 1 f. blank, (2) titlepage to part II, 43 pages, frontispiece, 31 engraved plates (several folding); contemporary calf, expertly rebacked and with new red gilt label and corners also neatly repaired, some old and faint waterstaining to lower margin, but very good; contemporary note of purchase on front free endpaper, and 19th century bookplate of Edward Lydall. LeFanu III 2; Wing G1952; G&M 297; Babson 406.   Ken Spelman 30-1 1996 £650.00

GREY, EDWARD GREY, 1ST VISCOUNT 1862-1933   Fallodon Papers. London: Constable & Co., 1926. Limited to 100 numbered copies, signed by author and artist; 8vo; vii, 179 pages; 15 woodcut illustrations by Robert Gibbings; original white buckram, gilt, top edge gilt, others uncut; fine, unopened copy.   Thomas Thorp 489-124 1996 £75.00

GREY, GEORGE   Journals of Two Expeditions of Discovery in Northwest and Western Australia During the Years 1837, 1838 and 1839. London: T. & W. Boone, 1841. 2 volumes, 4,, (2), (xiv), 412 pages, 16 pages ads; 4 ads, (viii), 482 pages, 22 plates, 2 large folding, map; original brown cloth, gilt title on spine, decorated at base laid down on new reback, covers little marked and spine sunned, otherwise very good; 3rd crack restored in center of volume 2 spine; Ferguson 3228; Wantrup 131.   Antipodean 28-619 1996 $1,450.00

GREY, JANE   The Literary Remains of Lady Jane Grey, with Memoir of Her Life. London: published by Harding, Triphood an Lepard, 1825. 1st edition; 8vo; (vi), vi, cxlviii, (ii), 61 pages; half title, engraved portrait (spotted), folding letterpress table; 19th century cloth; uncommon. James Burmester 29-60 1996 £85.00

GREY, RICHARD   A System of English Ecclesiastical Law. London: printd by E. and R. Nutt, and R. Gosling, 1735. Modern quarter calf, good, clean copy.   Meyer Boswell SL26-93 1996 $250.00

GREY, ZANE 1872-1939   Desert Gold: a Romance of the Border. New York: Harper, 1913. 1st edition, later printing ("G-P": July 1915); 8vo; 4 black and white illustrations by Douglas Duer; original gilt stamped olive green cloth, color pictorial label, very good. With author's blindstamp. George J. Houle 68-57 1996   George J. Houle 68-57 196 $125.00

GREY, ZANE 1872-1939   Desert Gold: A Romance of the Border. London: Nelson, 1926. Small 8vo; dust jacket with few chips; very good. Boldly signed by author, his son's copy (Romer Grey) with his signature. George J. Houle 68-56 1996 $350.00

GREY, ZANE 1872-1939   The Lost Wagon Train. New York: & London: Harper & Bros., 1936. 1st edition; near fine in very good dust jacket which has quarter size hole in rear panel and moderately chipped at spine ends, still quite attractive pictorial dust jacket.   Steven C. Bernard 71-116 1996 $175.00

GREY, ZANE 1872-1939   Majesty's Rancho. New York: Harper, 1938. 1st edition; 297 pages; gray cloth lettered in black; fine and clean with pictorial dust jacket, housed in later slipcase; signed by author's son, Loren.   Argonaut Book Shop 113-298 1996 $275.00

GREY, ZANE 1872-1939   The Rainbow Trail: a Romance. London: Nelson, ca. 1925. Small 8vo; dust jacket (few nicks); very good; author's copy, boldly signed by him in purple ink, also with his blindstamp. George J. Houle 68-58 1996 $350.00

GREY, ZANE 1872-1939   The Shepherd of Guadalupe. New York: Harper & Bros., 1930. 1st edition; 333 pages; blue cloth lettered in yellow; very fine with pictorial dust jacket (jacket with very minor chipping at lower spine with slight soiling), housed in later slipcase; signed by author.   Argonaut Book Shop 113-299 1996 $650.00

GREY, ZANE 1872-1939   Tales of Fishing Virgin Seas. New York: Harpers 1925. 1st edition; large quarto; 112 full page photos; fine in near fine, price clipped dust jacket with couple of very faint, barely noticeable small stains on front panel, few short tears and little rubbing at extremities; nice copy, very scarce in dust jacket, as well as in this condition.   Between the Covers 42-197 1996 $575.00

GREY, ZANE 1872-1939   Tales of the Angler's Eldorado New Zealand. New York: & London: Harper & Bros., 1926. 1st edition; 4to; 228 pages over 100 full page photos; original dark blue cloth, near fine.   Chapel Hill 94-379 1996 $250.00

GRIBBLE, F.   The Early Mountaineers. London: 1899. 1st edition; 48 plates; gilt lettering and decoration on blue-green cloth; light foxing to titlepage, but fine.   Moutaineering Books 8-EG02 1996 £250.00

GRIESINGER, WILHELM   Die Pathologie und Therapie der Psychischen Krankheiten, fur Arzte und Studirende. Stuttgart: Verlag von Adolf Krabbe 1845. 1st edition; 8vo; viii, 396, (2) pages; original patterned boards, paper spine label, boards rubbed, shelfwear to joints and edges, very nice, pleasing copy in original condition; rare; Jelliffe's copy with his name stamp. Norman Cat. 948; Zilboorg pp. 275-277; GM 4930.   John Gach 150-188 1996 $1,750.00

GRIESINGER, WILHELM   Mental Pathology and Therapeutics. New York: William Wood and Co., 1882. 1st American edition; 8vo; (ii), viii, 375, (3) pages; embossed Victorian cloth, crown chipped, very good. John Gach 150-187 1996 $150.00

GRIEVE, CHRISTOPHER MURRAY 1892-   The Kind of Poetry I Want: a Long Poem. Edinburgh: K. D. Duval, 1961. One of 300 numbered copies, signed by author; 4to; printed 16 and 13 pt. Griffo on Magnani handmade; quarter vellum with patterned paper sides; very nice in slipcase, bookplate discreetly tipped between prelim blanks.   Bertram Rota 272-347 1996 £400.00

GRIEVE, CHRISTOPHER MURRAY 1892-   Selected Lyrics. Vergona: Kulgin D. Duval and Colin H. Hamilton, 1977. One of 135 press numbered copies; 33 pages; frontispiece by Freddy Theys; half vellum titled in gilt, fine in grey paper slipcase.   Hermitage SP95-1058 1996 $750.00

GRIEVE, M., MRS.   A Modern Herbal, the Medicinal, Culinary, Cosmetic and Economic Properties, Cultivation and Folk-Lore of Herbs, Grasses, Fungi, Shrubs and Trees, with All Their Modern Scientific Uses. New York: 1931. 1st edition; 8vo; 2 volumes; pages xvi, 888; 96 plates; cloth, light soiling and spotting, some wear to corners and ends of spine of volume 2, inner hinges cracked or open.   Raymond M. Sutton VI-1061 1996 $235.00

GRIFFIN, JAMES B.   Archeology of Eastern United States. Chicago & London: University of Chicago Press, 1966. Large 4to; frontispiece, x, 394 pages, 205 figures; original cloth.   Archaeologia Luxor-4517 1 996 $175.00

GRIFFIN, L. E.   The Anatomy of Nautilus Pompilius. Washington: 1900. 4to; 95 pages, 17 plates; half morocco, very slightly affected by damp. Wheldon & Wesley 207-1164 1996 £65.00

GRIFFIN, RALPH   A List of Monumental Brasses Remaining in the County of Kent in 1922. Ashford & London: 1923. Original edition; 8vo; 32 plates, 20 other illustrations in text, 244 pages; Very scarce. Howes Bookshop 265-2156 1996 £65.00

GRIFFIN, SUSAN   Let Them Be Said. Oakland: Mama's Press, 1973. 1st edition; printed wrappers; near fine.   Captain's Bookshelf 38-95 1996 $125.00

GRIFFITH, ELIZABETH   The Morality of Shakespeare's Drama Illustrated. London: printed for T. Cadell, 1775. 1st edition; 8vo; frontispiece; contemporary calf, gilt, rebacked. very good. Jaggard p. 124; LAR 2964; CBEL II 835.   Ximenes 108-174 1996 $250.00

GRIFFITH, G.   The Gold-Finder. White, 1898. 1st edition; pictorial cloth, very good/very good+.   Aronovitz 57-469 1996 $125.00

GRIFFITH, GEORGE   The Free Schools and Endowments of Staffordshire, and their Fulfilment. Hill and Halden, Stafford: Whittaker and Co., 1860. 1st edition; 8vo; frontispiece, 2 folding tables, original cloth, upper inner hinge shaken.   Anthony W. Laywood 109-57 1996 £90.00

GRIFFITH, GEORGE   The Free Schools of Worcestershire, and their Fulfilment. London: Charaales Gilpin, 1852. 1st edition in book form; 8vo; engraved vignette on title, large folding table (torn with loss of 2 or 3 letters), (2), xxiv, 464 pages, one plate; contemporary calf, panelled in blind, spine restored with raised bands, label, bevelled sides, red edges, little wear, but good; verey scarce.   John Drury 82-94 1996 £175.00

GRIFFITH, HARRISON PATILLO   Variosa A Collection of Sketches, Essays and Verses. N.P.: 1911. 1st edition; 266 pages, frontispiece, original cloth, ex-libris, yet very good with presentation from author. quite scarce. Dornbusc IV 1200. Not in Nevins.   McGowan Book Co. 65-34 1996 $350.00

GRIFFITH, J. W.   The Micrographic Dictionary, a Guide to the Examination and Investigation of the Structure and Nature of Miscroscopic Objects. London: 1875. 3rd edition; 8vo; 2 volumes; 812 text figures and atlas of 48 plates; modern buckram, name on half title, some slight foxing.   Wheldon & Wesley 207-164 1996 £80.00

GRIFFITH, PEGGY   The New Klondike: a Story of a Southern Baseball Training Camp. New York: Jacobsen-Hodgkinson-Corp., 1926. 1st edition; photos; edges of pages yellowed and faint creases to couple of corners, still near fine in wrappers as issued of this fragile photoplay edition. Between the Covers 42-34 1996 $125.00

GRIFFITH, RICHARD   The Triumvirate; or, the Authentic Memoirs of A.B. and C. London: W. Johnston, 1764. 1st edition; 12mo; pages xxvii, (i), 264, (ii), 5; 338, (1) (errata); bound together in contemporary brown sheep, backstrip faded, lightly rubbed, red morocco label 'D. Gell, Hopton Hall' on front pastedown; owner's name of D. Gell at head of titlepage, F7-F12 opened carelessly with slight damage to fore-edges, excellent.   Blackwell's B112-143 1996 £750.00

GRIGG, E. R. N.   The Trail of the Invisible Light: from X-Strahlen to Radio(bio)logy. Springfield: Thomas, 1965. 4to; 974 pages; original binding, near fine. GM 2702.3.   James Tait Goodrich K40-252 1996 $105.00

GRIMALDI, STACEY   The Toliet. London: Rock Brothers & Payne, n.d. 12mo; full blue crushed morocco du cap with single gilt fillet border, with gilt titling and decoration on spine, board edges gilt, inner gilt dentelles, front cover and spine lightly sunned, all edges gilt, signed on lower turn-in: Sangorski & Sutcliffe; rare in any edition. Not in Abbey. 10 1996 $1,250.00

GRIMBLE, A.   More Leaves from My Game Book. 1917. Limited to 250 copies; illustrations; original half vellum, top of spine slightly frayed, corners lightly rubbed; contents excellent; inscribed by author to Maurice Hill.   David Grayling J95Biggame-260 1996 £80.00

GRIMES, MARTHA   The Anodyne Necklace. Boston: Little, Brown, 1983. Uncorrected proof; gray paper wrappers; fine.   Quill & Brush 102-758 1996 $250.00

GRIMES, MARTHA   The Anodyne Necklace. Boston: Little Brown, 1983. 1st edition; signed, fine in dust jacket with very light edge wear. Quill & Brush 102-759 1996 $175.00

GRIMES, MARTHA   The Deer Leap. Boston: Little Brown, 1985. Uncorrected proof; paper wrappers, fine.   Quill & Brush 102-770 1996 $150.00

GRIMES, MARTHA   The Deer Leap. Boston: Little Brown, 1985. 1st edition; review copy; fine in dust jacket with slip laid in.   Quill & Brush 102-771 1996 $125.00

GRIMES, MARTHA   The Dirty Duck. Boston: Little Brown, 1984. Uncorrected proof; green paper wrappers; fine.   Quill & Brush 102-761 1996 $200.00

GRIMES, MARTHA   The Dirty Duck. Boston: Little Brown, 1984. 1st edition; fine in dust jacket with light edge wear, signed with publisher's note and photo laid in.   Quill & Brush 102-762 1996 $125.00

GRIMES, MARTHA   The Five Bells and Bladebone. Boston: Little Brown, 1987. Uncorrected proof; paper wrappers; fine.   Quill & Brush 102-781 1996 $150.00

GRIMES, MARTHA   Help the Poor Struggler. Boston: Little Brown, 1985. Uncorrected proof; green paper wrappers; fine, signed.   Quill & Brush 102-773 1996 $175.00

GRIMES, MARTHA   Help the Poor Struggler. Boston: Little Brown, 1985. 1st edition; review copy with slip laid in; fine in dust jacket with light edge wear; signed.   Quill & Brush 102-774 1996 $125.00

GRIMES, MARTHA   I Am the Only Running Footman. Boston: Little Brown, 1986. Uncorrected proof; green paper wrpapers; fine.   Quill & Brush 102-776 1996 $125.00

GRIMES, MARTHA   Jerusalem Inn. Boston: Little Brown, 1984. 1st edition; signed review copy with slip laid in; fine in dust jacket.   Quill & Brush 102-767 1996 $125.00

GRIMES, MARTHA   Jerusalem Inn. Boston: Little Brown, 1984. Advance uncorrected proof; signed on titlepage, reviewer's notes handwritten around publisher's publicity on endpaper; paper wrappers; fine.   Quill & Brush 102-765 1996 $200.00

GRIMES, MARTHA   Jerusalem Inn. Boston: Little Brown, 1984. Uncorrected proof; green paper wrpapers; fine.   Quill & Brush 102-766 1996 $150.00

GRIMES, MARTHA   The Man with a Load of Mischief. Boston: Little Brown, 1981. Uncorrected proof; white printed wrappers, very good, some soil and little residue on front cover from former tipped on promotional sheet.   Antic Hay 101-753 1996 $250.00

GRIMES, MARTHA   The Man with a Load of Mishief. Boston: Little
Brown, 1981. 1st edition; author's first book; fine in dust jacket with very
light rubbing.   Quill & Brush 102-755 1996 $250.00

GRIMES, MARTHA   The Man with a Load of Mischief. Boston: Little
Brown, 1981. 1st edition; author's first book; fine in dust jacket with very
light rubbing.   Quill & Brush 102-755 1996 $250.00

GRIMES, MARTHA   The Old Fox Deceiv'd. Boston: Little Brown, 1982.
Uncorrected proof; paper wrappers; fine.   Quill & Brush 102-756 1996
$250.00

GRIMES, MARTHA   The Old Fox Deceiv'd. Boston: Little Brown, 1982.
Uncorrected proof, advance review copy; near fine in mock up dust
jacket, scarce.   Timothy P. Slongo 5-23 1996 $100.00

GRIMES, MARTHA   The Old Fox Deceiv'd. Boston: Little Brown, 1982.
1st edition; fine in dust jacket with very light rubbing.   Quill & Brush
102-757 1996 $150.00

GRIMES, ROY   300 Years in Victoria County. Victoria Advocate, 1968.
1st edition; 649 pages; photos; dust jacket.   Maggie Lambeth 30-230
1996 $150.00

GRIMM, THE BORTHERS   Grimm's Fairy Tales. New York:
Worthington, 1888. 4to; drawings in black and white by Walter Crane
and E. H. Wehnert; colored plates by George Cruikshank; cloth backed
colored pictorial boards, edges rubbed, corners knocked, else fresh
copy.   Barbara Stone 70-111 1996 £65.00

GRIMM, THE BROTHERS   The Fairy Ring. London: John Murray, 1847.
2nd edition; 12 illustrations in black and white by Richard Doyle; three
quarter contemporary tan calf, double gilt ruled, spine in compartments,
binding very slightly rubbed, else very nice, very scarce.   Barbara
Stone 70-77 1996 £125.00

GRIMM, THE BROTHERS   Grimm's Fairy Tales. London: Humphrey
Milford, Oxford University Press, n.d., ca. 1920. 4to; 346 pages;
frontispiece, 22 mounted color plates; cream boards, heavily decorated
in gilt, uncut fine in original slipcase.   Marjorie James 19-178 1996
£150.00

GRIMM, THE BROTHERS   Fairy Tales. London: Peter Lunn Publishers
Ltd., 1943. 1st edition thus; 16 black and white illustrations, double page
color illustration by R. A. Brandt; original binding, head and tail of spine
slightly bumped, very good in torn, creased chipped, rubbed, marked
and dusty, internally repaired and price clipped dust jacket, which
repeats centre spread illustration.   Ulysses 39-65 1996 £65.00

GRIMM, THE BROTHERS   German Popular Stories. London: Pub. by.
C. Baldwyn/ London: James Robins & Co. & Joseph Robins Dublin
1823/26. 1st edition, 1st issue of volume 1, without umlaut in word
"marchen" on titlepage; 12mo; 2 volumes; xii, 240; iv, 256, (2) pages; 22
etched plates by George Cruikshank, including 2 vignette titles, plates in
volume I printed in brown, without publisher's ads called for at end of
volume 1 and at beginning of volume 2, but otherwise complete, with all
first issue points called for by Cohn; full red crushed levant morocco by
Riviere & Son, gilt triple rule border on covers, gilt spines, tooled in
compartments, gilt board edges and turn-ins, all edges gilt; occasional
light soiling, browning or offsetting, few expert marginal repairs in
volume 2, overall very good, handsomely bound in red cloth slipcase.
Cohn 369; Morgan Lib. Early Children's Books 197.   Heritage Book
Shop 196-217 1996 $7,500.00

GRIMM, THE BROTHERS   Grimm's Other Tales. Waltham St.
Lawrence: Golden Cockerel Press, 1956. Number 325 of a limited edition
of 500 copies; wood engraved illustrations by Gwenda Morgan; purple
cloth, pictorially stamped in gilt; fine.   Barbara Stone 70-155 1996
£110.00

GRIMM, THE BROTHERS   Hansel and Gretel. Zurich: 1944. 1st edition;
oblong 4to; title vignette, 16 pages; 7 color plates by Herbert Leupin;
blue cloth spine, blue pictorial boards, spine worn, other light wear,
excellent color plate.   Robin Greer 94A-82 1996 £65.00

GRIMM, THE BROTHERS   Household Stories. London: Macmillan,
1882. Full page drawings, borders, head and tailpieces and capitals by
Walter Crane; olive cloth stamped pictorially in white and terra cotta;
extremities just rubbed, else very nice.   Barbara Stone 70-60 1996
£75.00

GRIMM, THE BROTHERS   The Juniper Tree and Other Tales From
Grimm. New York: Farrar, Straus & Giroux, 1973. 1st trade edition; small
8vo; 2 volumes; pictures by Maurice Sendak; cloth, dust jackets slightly
spine darkened; fine.   James S. Jaffe 34-614 1996 $125.00

GRIMM, THE BROTHERS   Snow White and the Seven Dwarfs. New
York: Coward McCann 1938. 1st edition; illustrations in black and white
by Wanda Gag; green pictorial boards, extremities slightly rubbed,
boards little spotted, else fresh in slightly chipped and spotted pictorial
dust jacket, very scarce.   Barbara Stone 70-98 1996 £275.00

GRIMSLEY, DANIEL AMON   Battles in Culpeper County, Virginia,
1861-1865. Culpeper 1900. 1st edition; 56 pages; original printed
wrappers; near fine. Nevins II 222; Dornbusch II 1220.   McGowan Book
Co. 65-35 1996 $375.00

GRIMSTON, CHARLOTTE   The History of Gorhambury. London:
privately printed, ca. 1821. Folio; lithographed throughout, title, 90 pages,
10 plates; contemporary diced russia gilt, rebacked, edges and corners
rubbed. Harris p. 38; Martin p. 42; Twyman pp. 179-80.   Marlborough
162-35 1996 £750.00

GRIMWOOD, ETHEL ST. CLAIR   My Three Years in Manipur and
Escape from the Recent Mutiny. London: Richard Bentley, 1891. 3rd
edition; tall 8vo; xii, 321 pages; illustrations; full brown morocco, raised
bands, top edge gilt; inner hinges have been reinforced with cloth,
otherwise fine.   David Mason 71-91 1996 $160.00

GRINNELL, GEORGE BIRD   American Duck Shooting. New York:
Forest and Stream, 1901. 1st edition; 58 portraits; original green cloth
with pictorial gilt stamping, fine, bright copy.   Chapel Hill 94-380 1996
$175.00

GRINNELL, JOSEPH   Fur-Bearing Mammals of California: Their Natural
History, Systematic Status and Relations to Man. Berkeley: University of
California Press, 1937. 1st edition; 2 volumes, pages xii; xiv,
3777-777, 2 colored frontispieces, 11 colored plates, 345 text
illustrations; original cloth, gilt lettered spines, very fine set. Scarce.
Argonaut Book Shop 113-301 1996 $225.00

GRISCOM, L.   The Warblers of North America. New York: 1957. Large
4to; 365 pages; 35 full page colored plates; fine in protected dust jacket.
David A.H. Grayling MY95Orn-36 1996 £80.00

GRISCOM, L.   The Warblers of America, a Popular Account of the
Wood Warblers as They Occur in the Western Hemisphere. New York:
1957. 1st issue; royal 8vo; pages xii, 356, 35 colored plates, numerous
distribution maps and line drawings; cloth, good, clean copy, signature
on half title.   Wheldon & Wesley 207-747 1996 £60.00

GRISHAM, JOHN   The Chamber. New York: Doubleday, 1994. 1/350
signed, numbered copies; fine in slipcase.   Bev Chaney, Jr. 23-280
1996 $250.00

GRISHAM, JOHN   The Firm. New York: Doubleday, 1991. 1st edition;
fine in dust jacket; inscribed.   Quill & Brush 102-790 1996 $300.00

GRISHAM, JOHN   The Firm. New York: Doubleday, 1991. 1st edition;
as new in dust jacket.   Between the Covers 42-198 1996 $285.00

GRISWOLD, NORMAN W.   Beauties of California: Including Big Trees,
Yosemite Valley, Geysers, Lake Tahoe, Donner Lake, S.F. '49 and '83,
Etc. San Francisco: H. S. Crocker & Co., 1883. 1st edition; 9 x 5 7/8
inches; (44) pages, 26 fine chromolithographed plates on 13 leaves;
chromolithographed pictorial wrappers, some of original spine chipped
away, but wrappers expertly reattached, green cloth clamshell case with
marbled paper spine label. Variant with inner wrappers of this copy
blank.   Dawson's Books Shop 528-91 1996 $750.00

GRISWOLD, NORMAN W.   Beauties of California. San Francisco: H. S.
Crocker & Co., 1884. 2nd edition; 70 pages, 38 colored lithographic
prints; original colored pictorial lithographed wrappers; minor wear, very
fine, laid in half morocco and chemise slipcase, beautiful and splendid
copy. Cowan p. 251.   Michael D. Heaston 23-59 1996 $1,250.00

GROHMANN, WILL   The Art of Henry Moore. New York: Abrams, n.d.
Square 4to; 279 pages, 293 illustrations, including 12 color plates; cloth,
dust jacket. Freitag 6703.   Brannan 43-450 1996 $125.00

GROHMANN, WILL   The Drawings of Paul Klee. New York: Valentin, 1944. Limited to 700 copies; 4to; wrappers, text and plates loose, as issued, in folding cloth box.   Brannan 43-303 1996 $200.00

GROHMANN, WILL   Paul Klee. New York: Abrams, n.d. 4to; 448 pages, 40 tipped in color plates, monochrome illustrations; cloth, light wear. Lucas p. 159; Freitag 4842.   Brannan 43-304 1996 $135.00

GROHMANN, WILL   Wassily Kandinsky: Life and Work New York: Abrams, n.d. 4to; 428 pages, 920 illustrations, including 41 tipped in color plates; cloth, dust jacket. Lucas p. 159; Freitag 4708.   Brannan 43-286 1996 $200.00

GROHMANN, WILL   Willi Baumeister: Life and Work. New York: Abrams, n.d. 4to; 361 pages, 1143 illustrations, including 53 color plates; cloth, dust jacket. Freitag 468.   Brannan Books 43-41 1996 $295.00

GROLIER CLUB, NEW YORK.   Catalogue of Original and Early Editions of Some of the Poetical and Prose Works of English Writers from Wither to Prior (and, from Langland to Wither). New York: 1963. Reprint of 1905 edition; royal 8vo; 4 volumes; many illustrations of titlepages; original cloth, nice set.   James Fenning 133-142 1996 £75.00

GROLIER CLUB, NEW YORK.   Catalogue of Original and Early Editions of Some of the Poetical and Prose Works of English Writers from Wither to Prior... New York: Grolier Club, 1905. 1st edition; limited to 400 copies; large 8vo; 3 volumes, printed on Holland handmade paper; many frontispiece and titlepage facsimiles; original quarter calf, volume 1 rebacked, little rubbed, uncut.   Forest Books 74-288 1996 £125.00

GROLIER CLUB, NEW YORK.   Catalogue of the Works of Rudyard Kipling. New York: Grolier Club, 1930. One of 325 numbered copies on Fabriano paper; 8vo; original binding, fine in worn slipcase.   Charles Agvent 4-808 1996 $150.00

GROLIER CLUB, NEW YORK.   Fifty-Five Books Printed Before 1525, Representing the Works of England's First Printers. New York: Grolier Club, 1968. One of 1500 copies of a total edition of 1650; 10 1/4 x 7 1/4 inches; xiii, (1), 62 pages, (3) leaves (including colophon); 3 plates, title printed in red and black; as new.   Phillip J. Pirages 33-283 1996 $125.00

GROLIER CLUB, NEW YORK.   The Grolier Club 1884-1984: Its Library, Exhibitions and Publications. New York: Grolier Club, 1984. One of 600 copies; 11 14 x 8 3/4 inches; 5 p.l., (one blank), 11-258 pages, (1) leaf (colophon); 8 plates with illustrations on both sides, prospectus laid in; mint.   Phillip J. Pirages 33-285 1996 $125.00

GROLIER CLUB, NEW YORK.   Grolier 75: A Biographical Retrospective to Celebrate the Seventy-Fifth Anniversary of the Grolier Club in New York. New York: Grolier Club, 1959. One of 1000 copies; 10 3/4 x 7 inches; 8 p.l., 240 pages, (2) leaves (blank, colophon); original tissue jacket, publisher's patterned paper slipcase; very fine.   Phillip J. Pirages 33-284 1996 $125.00

GROLIER CLUB, NEW YORK.   Printers' Choice: a Selection of American Press Books, 1968-1978. Austin: W. Thomas Taylor, 1983. One of 325 numbered copies; 14.5 x 10 inches; 67 pages; photos, tip-ins, printed in black with brown on Rives heavyweight paper, bound in graduated light brown-orange-cream linen paper with paper title label on spine; very fine. Joshua Heller 21-201 1996 $425.00

GRONOVIUS, JOHAN FREDERICK   Flora Orientalis Siv Recensio Plantarum Quas Botanicorum Coryphaeus Leonhardus Rauwolffus, Medicus Augustanus, Annis 1573 1574 and 1575. Leiden: 1755. 8vo; pages (23), 150, errata; contemporary paper covered boards and spine, leather label, some wear to edges, leather label partially perished. Raymond M. Sutton VI-13 1996 $25,000.00

GRONOW, REES HOWELL 1794-1865   Reminiscences of Captain Gronow, Formerly of the Grenadier Guards, and M.P. for Stafford. London: Smith, Elder and Co., 1862. Mixed set; octavo; 4 volumes; bound by Morrell in full red polished calf, gilt double rule border on covers, gilt spines, tooled in compartments, gilt board edges and turn-ins, all edges gilt; handsome set.   Heritage Book Shop 196-188 1996 $500.00

GROOM, C. LAURENCE   The Singing Sword. Lees: The Swan Press, 1927. 1st edition; lightly soiled, very good, with no remarkable flaws, without dust jacket presumably as issued; Countee Cullen's copy with his ownership signature and one pencil notation in text.   Between the Covers 43-59 1996 $175.00

GROOM, WINSTON   Forrest Gump. Garden City: Doubleday, 1986. Unbound proof pages, stamped 'Preliminary (Proofread) Pages" with an indication that remaining errors and alterations will be corrected in succeeding readings; fine.   Ken Lopez 74-169 1996 $650.00

GROOM, WINSTON   Forrest Gump. Garden City: Doubleday, 1986. Uncorrected proof; wrappers; near fine.   Ken Lopez 74-167 1996 $550.00

GROOM, WINSTON   Forrest Gump. Garden City: Doubleday, 1986. Advance reading copy; illustrated wrappers, near fine.   Ken Lopez 74-168 1996 $275.00

GROOM, WINSTON   Forrest Gump. Garden City: 1986. 1st edition; fine in dust jacket.   Between the Covers 42-198a 1996 $350.00

GROOM, WINSTON   Forrest Gump. Garden City: Doubleday, 1986. 1st edition; fine in fine dust jacket, hard to find title.   Pettler & Lieberman 28-119 1996 $250.00

GROOM, WINSTON   Forrest Gump. Garden City: Doubleday, 1986. 1st edition; original cloth, fine in lightly rubbed dust jacket, with few tiny tears.   Beasley Books 82-71 1997 $200.00

GROOM, WINSTON   Forrest Gump. New York: 1986. 1st edition; fine/very near fine.   Stephen Lupack 83- 1996 $350.00

GROOM, WINSTON   Forest Gump. Garden City: Doubleday, 1986. 1st edition; fine in dust jacket with minor wear to extremities.   Lame Duck Books 19-229 1996 $300.00

GROOME, FRANCIS H.   Ordnance Gazetteer of Scotland: A Survey of Scottish Topography, Statistical, Biogrphical and Historical. Edinburgh & Glasgow: c. 1895. New edition; royal 8vo; 6 volumes; many colored maps, some double page and plates; original blue cloth, gilt, gilt tops. Howes Bookshop 265-1101 1996 £65.00

GROPIUS, WALTER   The New Architecture and the Bauhaus. Boston: Charles T. Branford, n.d. 12mo; 112 pages; illustrations; cloth, dust jacket, very small tear on base of front cover of dust jacket, else fine. The Bookpress 75-194 1996 $165.00

GROPIUS, WALTER   Town Plan for the Town of Selb. Cambridge: MIT, 1969. 1st American edition; oblong folio; frontispiece, (viii), 72, (4) pages; 56 plans and map; cloth, very good.   The Bookpress 75-193 1996 $125.00

GROSCH, HENRIK AUGUST   Haandbog til Brodering of Tegning... Copenhagen: Glydendal, 1794. 1st edition; oblong folio; 12 pages, 48 full page hand colored engravings, 1 partially torn away; contemporary calf backed boards. Bib. Danica Suppl. 209; not in NUC, BLC or Berlin Kat. Bennett Gilbert LL29-41 1996 $2,850.00

GROSE, D.   The Flora of Wiltshire. London: 1957-75. Royal 8vo; 2 volumes, including supplement; pages 824, 11 plates and numerous maps in text; pages xvi, 150, portrait, line drawings; cloth, supplement royal 8vo. in boards;   Wheldon & Wesley 207-1476 1996 £60.00

GROSE, FRANCIS 1731-1791   The Antiquities of England and Wales. London: printed for Hooper & Wigstead,... n.d., c. 1783-97. New edition; 4to; 8 volumes; vignette title to all volumes, County Index to all volumes, (iii-iv), preface 1-142 pages, addenda to preface 143-160 pages, text, to the Public (i-iv) to volume VIII, General Index 165-172 pages, Directions to Binder to final leaf volume VIII, engraved frontispiece to all volumes, 589 engraved plates, and 1 extra plate not called for, 88 maps and plans and 1 extra plate not called for, 88 maps and plans and 1 extra plate not called for; full diced calf, gilt rule border to boards, gilt titles and tooling to spines, few joints rubbed, corners slightly bumped, very fine and handsome set; plates in near mint condition with no foxing or offsetting, signature O to volume 1 heavily browned, only light foxing to few other pages, uniformly marbled endpapers & edges, bookplate of Charles Vere Dashwood & E. N. Thornton.   Beeleigh Abbey BA/56-10 1996 £950.00

GROSE, FRANCIS 1731-1791   A Classical Dictionary of the Vulgar Tongue. London: printed for Hooper & Co., 1796. 3rd edition; uncut in original blue boards, brown paper spine chipped, hinges splitting, paper label chipped; from the collection of Fernand & Anne Renier.   Jarndyce 103-153 1996 £130.00

GROSE, FRANCIS 1731-1791 A Classical Dictionary of the Vulgar Tongue. London: printed for Hooper & Wigstead, 1796. 3rd edition; much later half black morocco, hinges & corners rubbed. Reform Club blindstamp. Alston IX 327. Jarndyce 103-152 1996 £100.00

GROSE, FRANCIS 1731-1791 Lexicon Balatronicum. London: printed for C. Chappel &c., 1811. Reprint; uncut in original boards, marked, rubbed, later black leather label and endpapers. Jarndyce 103-155 1996 £90.00

GROSE, FRANCIS 1731-1791 Lexicon Balatronicum. London: printed for C. Happel, 1811. Reprint; half title; contemporary tree sheep, rubbed at corners, hinges splitting, red label; from the collection of Fernand & Anne Renier. Jarndyce 103-154 1996 £85.00

GROSE, FRANCIS 1731-1791 The Olio. London: S. Hooper, 1792. 1st edition; octavo; pages 321, 3 pages ads; original marbled boards, recent calf spine and label; wear to marbled boards, but text fine. Lowndes II 834. Hartfield 48-L37 1996 $295.00

GROSE, FRANCIS 1731-1791 A Provincial Glossary, with a Collection of Local Proverbs and Popular Superstitions London: Printed for S. Hooper, 1787. 1st edition; 2 parts; 19th century half calf, red label, rubbed, leading hinge splitting; from the collection of Fernand & Anne Renier. Alston IX 58. Jarndyce 103-55 1996 £110.00

GROSE, FRANCIS 1731-1791 A Provincial Glossary: with a Collection of Local Proverbs and Popular Superstitions. London: printed for S. Hooper, 1790. 2nd edition; slightly later calf, gilt spine and borders, slight rubbing with splits at head of hinges. Alston IX 59. Jarndyce 103-56 1996 £100.00

GROSE, FRANCIS 1731-1791 A Provincial Glossary; with a Collection of Local Proverbs and Popular Superstitions. London: Edward Jeffrey, 1811. New edition; tall 12mo. (in sixes); pages viii, (142, unpaginated glossary), 143-304; original publisher's boards, paper spine renewed, uncut; text excellent, scarce. Alston 59; Cordell p. 77. Hartfield 48-11i 1996 $285.00

GROSE, FRANCIS 1731-1791 A Provincial Glossary; with a Collection of Local Proverbs and Popular Superstitions. London: printed for Edward Jeffery, 1811. New edition; 4to; spotting in prelims, original boards, neatly rebacked, paper label. Jarndyce 103-57 1996 £85.00

GROSS, SAMUEL D. History of American Medical Literature from 1776 to the Present Time. Philadelphia: 1876. 1st edition; 8vo; limp black cloth, edges worn, neatly rebacked. GM 6761. Maggs Bros. Ltd. 1190-421 1996 £85.00

GROSS, SAMUEL D. A System of Surgery. Philadelphia: 1872. 5th edition; large 8vo; 2 volumes; 1400 engravings; original full sheep, some scuffing, rear boards stained, internally fine. GM 5607; Iowa 1680. James Tait Goodrich K40-138 1996 $145.00

GROSZ, GEORGE Ecce Homo. New York: 1966. 1st edition; 84 drawings and 16 color plates; inserted are 2 supplementary plates for framing; fine, dust jacket little edge sunned. Polyanthos 22-412 1996 $125.00

GROTE, GEORGE A History of Greece; from the Earliest Period to the Close of the Generation Contemporary with Alexander the Great. London: John Murray,, 1862. 8vo; 8 volumes; handsome three quarter tan polished calf, richly gilt panelled spines, raised bands, red leather labels, marbled edges; fine, bright set. Appelfeld Gallery 54-109 1996 $600.00

GROTE, JOHN An Examination of the Utilitarian Philosophy... Cambridge: Deighton, Bell and Co., 1870. 1st edition; 8vo; xxiv, 362, (2) pages, 12 pages publisher's ads at end, occaional oval ink stamp of the Working Men's college (but only a shelf number on title); original cloth; presentation copy inscribed "From the Editor" (Joseph Bickersteth Mayor), with later presentation bookplate donating the copy to the library by F. D. Maurice's daughter-in-law. Sorley p. 365. John Drury 82-96 1996 £100.00

GROVE, RICHARD ANDREW Views of the Principal Seats and Marine and Landscape Scenery, in the Neighbourhood of Lymington (Hampshire). Lymington: for the author, 1832. folio; litho titlepage with vignette, (mounted as usual), 1 f. dedication, 26 ff. letterpress, 1 f. subscribers, 24 litho plates by L. Haghe after Gilbert et al, on laid india paper and bound in a folded broadside with litho vignette, 2 litho plates on laid india paper, all entitled "Proposed Suspension Bridge across the Lymington River...March 1834"; modern half calf, dampstain and little spotting. One of the extra plates inscribed by Benjamin Ferrey in pencil. Marlborough 162-270 1996 £650.00

GROVES, J. P. Sketches of Adventure and Sport. c. 1885. 4to; colored plates; excellent copy in original pictorial cloth. David Grayling J95Biggame-522 1996 £80.00

GRUBB, DAVIS The Night of the Hunter. New York: Harper Bros., 1953. 1st edition; one o 100 copies, specially autographed for presentation to friends; author's first book; ine as issued, without dust jacket. Bev Chaney, Jr. 23-281 1996 $125.00

GRUBB, SARAH Some Account of the Life and Religious Laborus of Sarah Grubb. Dublin: printed for R. Jackson, 1792. 1st edition; 12mo; (vi), 435 pages, contemporary calf, worn, joints cracked, inner joints strengthened, spine defective at top and bottom. David Bickersteth 133-33 1996 £65.00

GRUBE, ERNST, J. Islamic Paintings From the 11th to the 18th Century in the Collection of Hans P. Kraus. New York: H. P. Kraus, n.d. Limited to 750 numbered copies; large 4to; 293 pages; 252 items described, most illustrated in black and white, 54 color plates; cloth, front hinge starting to split, otherwise very good. Scarce. J. M. Cohen 35-34 1996 $350.00

GRUELLE, JOHNNY Raggedy Ann's Magical Wishes. New York: Volland, 1928. 1st edition; tall thin 8vo; numerous color illustrations, pictorial endpapers and cvoers by author; black cloth over color pictorial boards, edges rubbed, corners bumped; very good. George J. Houle 68-29 1996 $150.00

GRUFFYDD, W. J. Caniadau. Newtown: Gregynog Press, 1932. One of 25 specially bound copies, of a total edition of 25; 10 1/4 x 7 1/2 inches; vii, (1), 101, (1) pages, (1) leaf (colophon); printed in russet and black on stone colored handmade paper; 4 full page wood engravings as well as shadow initials by Blair Hughes-Stanton; very handsome brown crushed levant morocco by the Gregynog Press Bindery (signed in gilt by Blair Hughes-Stanton and George Fisher on turn-in), panel of 24 closely spaced gilt lines connecting the covers across the spine with half panels on each cover continuing around board edges onto turn-ins, raised bands, spine titled in gilt, top edge gilt, other edges untrimmed; remarkably fine, especially bright and clean. Harrop 21. Phillip J. Pirages 33-262 1996 $5,500.00

GRUNER, LEWIS The Decorations of the Garden-Pavilion in the Grounds of Buckingham Palace. London: John Murray and others, 1846. 1st edition; large folio; 12 pages, 15 plates, 6 of which are hand colored, remaining 9 are engravings; publisher's cloth, neatly respined, good copy. Bookpress 75-57 1 1996 $2,500.00

GRUNER, LEWIS Decorations and Stuccos of Churches and Palaces in Italy. London: Thomas McLean, 1854. Large folio; (viii) pages, 56 plates; contemporary half red morocco, respined, ex-library from Yale University, with appropriate markings, covers worn, some occasional foxing, scarce, not in NUC. Bookpress 75-58 1996 $1,250.00

GRUNER, O. CAMERON A Treatise on the Canon of Medicine of Avicenna, Incorporating a Translation of the First Book. London: 1930. 1st edition; 612 pages; original binding, GM 45. W. Bruce Fye 71-72 1996 $200.00

GSELL-FELS, THEODOR Switzerland: Its Scenery and People. London: Blackie & Son, 1881. Folio; xvi, 472 pages; frontispiece, additional vignette title, 62 full page engraved plates, 304 engraved text illustrations contemporary dark green half morocco, gilt panelled spine in 6 compartments, gilt edges, slightly rubbed, some slight foxing. Thomas Thorp 489-125 1996 £285.00

GUARE, JOHN Six Degrees of Separation. New York: RH, 1900. 1st edition; fine in dust jacket, signed by author. Lame Duck Books 19-230 1996 $225.00

GUELLETTE, THOMAS SIMON Tartarian Tales; or, a Thousand and One Quarters of Hours. London: printed for J. and R. Tonson, 1759. 1st English edition; 12mo; engraved frontispiece, name on title, modern calf backed decorated boards; labels. Block p. 93. McBurney 391; Conant p. 36. Anthony W. Laywood 108-100 1996 £165.00

GUERBER, HELENE ADELINE Myths of the Norsemen, from the Eddas and Sagas. London: George G. Harrap & Co., 1911. 8 3/4 x 6 inches; xvi, 397 pages; partly unopened, 64 plates, including frontispiece; very pleasing red morocco gilt, by Morrell, covers framed by triple gilt rules, large and graceful impressionistic art nouveau floral ornament in corners, raised bands, spine attractively gilt in compartments with simila art nouveau decoration, gilt inner dentelles, top edge gilt, other edges untrimmed; hint of soiling to covers, but fine in attractive binding. Phillip J. Pirages 33-293 1996 $165.00

GUERINI, V.   A History of Dentistry from the Most Ancient Times Until the End of the Eighteenth Century. Philadelphia: 1909. 1st edition; 8vo; 355 pages; numerous plates and illustrations; bit shaken, cloth lightly worn, else good. Scarce.   James Tait Goodrich K40-118 1996 $150.00

GUERNSEY, ORRIN   History of Rock County, and Transactions of the Rock County Agricultural Society and Mechanics' Inst. Janesville: Wm. M. Doty & Brother, 1856. xii, 350 pages, frontispiece, 4 views; original cloth, extremities frayed, front endpaper removed, light foxing. Howes G454; All Wisc. 161.   Bohling Book Co. 192-300 1996 $175.00

GUERRA, FRANCISCO   American Medical Bibliography 1639-1783. New York: 1962. 885 pages; original binding. GM 6786.4.   W. Bruce Fye 71-867 1996 $125.00

GUEVARA, ANTONIO DE d. 1545?   (Greek title), or, The Diall of Princes... London: by Bernard Alsop, 1619. 1st edition under this title; folio; pages (xlvi), 768, printed in double column within double rules, with side notes; decorated initials; 19th century calf, sides with cathedral arch enclosing armorial and oriel devices in blind, cathedral blind roll-at foot, rebacked to match, gilt lettered direct, marbled endpapers, gilt edges, edges of boards rubbed, bookplates sometime removed from endpapers, occasional trivial spot or stain, very good, clean and firm, marks of an extremely close reading made in early 17th century, margin of almost every page scored with unobtrusive crosses and where words have been omitted from printed text, these have been carefully written in; early ms. note "Amee Skisswith her Booke".   Simon Finch 24-100 1996 £475.00

GUEVARA, ANTONIO DE d. 1545?   The Dial of Princes... London: by Richard Tottill An. Domini, 1582. Small quarto; black letter, fine historiated woodcut border to title (McKerrow & Ferguson 139), first few leaves lightly soiled, occasional early marginal annotations, ownership note on Niii, later half calf, neatly rebacked, stained edges; STC 12429; McKerrow & Ferguson: Title-Page Borders...Bib. Soc. no. 139   H. M. Fletcher 121-23 1996 £850.00

GUEVARA, ANTONIO DE d. 1545?   The Praise and Happinesse of the Countrie-Life. Newtown: Gregynog Press, 1938. Reprinted fromt he edition of 1651; one of 400 numbered copies; foolscap 8vo; 7 wood engravings by Reynolds Stone; half red morocco with floral fillet border blindstamped, green paper sides, engraved label, prelim and endleaves, and some pages within, quite severely spotted, otherwise nice, bright copy in rare dust jacket, inscription.   Bertram Rota 272-201 1996 £200.00

GUGLIELMINI, DOMENICO   Della Natura de'Fiumi Trattato Fisico-Matematico. Bologna: Per gl'Eredi d'Antonio Pisarri, 1697. 1st edition; small 4to; (7) leaves (including engraved frontispiece), 375, (1) pages, 15 folding engraved plates, engraved frontispiece, contemporary vellum backed boards. Riccardi I 643; Gamba 1904; Brunet II 1802. Roller I 492.   Jeffrey D. Mancevice 20-36 1996 $1,550.00

GUIART, JEAN   The Arts of the South Pacific. New York: Golden Press, 1963. 28.1 cm; 468 pages, 417 color and black and white plates, illustrations, photos, maps; cloth, dust jacket (repaired tears)/Bro-dart dust jacket cover.   L. Clarice Davis 111-127 1996 $250.00

GUICCIARDINI, FRANCESCO 1483-1540   The Historie of Guicciardin... London: Richard Field, 1599. 2nd edition; folio; pages (viii), 943, (10); wood engraved device on titlepage, corners of Eee 2 and Yyy1 turned down, creases in fore-edges of first gathering, otherwise internally fine; 17th century motled calf, possibly an example of remboitage, backstrip with raised bands between blind rules, modern green morocco label in second compartment, double blind fillet border to sides, blind central ornaments almost obliterated, early endpapers, hinges strengthened, excellent.   Blackwell's B112-144 1996 £350.00

GUICCIARDINI, FRANCESCO 1483-1540   The Historie of Guicciardin... London: Richard Field, 1618. 3rd edition; folio; (8), 821, (9) pages; contemporary blind paneled calf, worn, rebacked and corners renewed; spine with red morocco label, title somewhat soiled and with few minor marginal repairs, some internal stains, overall decent, sound copy. STC 12460.   Kenneth Karmiole 1NS-118 1996 $350.00

GUIDE to the City and County of Perth. London: ca. 1820. 8vo; engraved plan and titlepage, 142 pages (including pages 45*-48*), 11 engraved plates; contemporary half green roan, old wormhole, slight wear. cf. Anderson p. 406.   Marlborough 162-81 1996 £125.00

A GUIDE to the English Lake District Intended Principally for the Use of Pedestrians. London: Simkin, Marshall and Co. and Windermere: J. Garnett, c. 1865. 2nd edition; 8vo; pages viii, 123, viii (Garnett's ads), with colored frontispiece and 4 folding maps, printed in blue, 2 woodcut plates and several tables; original blindstamped cloth, gilt; label of "The People's Library" and signature of James Payn.   R.F.G. Hollett & Son 78-966 1996 £65.00

GUIDOTT, THOMAS   A Collection of Treatises Relating to the City and Waters of Bath. London: printed for J. Leake, 1725. 1st edition; 8vo; 4 engraved plates, engraved full page illustration in text, separate title for each treatise but continuous pagination and signatures, small tear in Z2 repaired; contemporary half calf, rebacked, albel. Blake p. 189; Wellcome II p. 178.   Anthony Laywood 108-71 1996 £235.00

GUILLERMUS, EPISCOPUS PARISIENSIS   Rhetorica Divina. Basel: Johan Froben, 1492. Octavo; 19th century boards under handsome 18th century vellum antiphonal leaf in red and black, light thumbing, few small waterstains at blank lower edge, quite decent; minor mends to blank portion including repairs to tiny wormholes which also pierce the Tabula with slight loss but disappear before the Beginning of the text proper; the Manuel Cervantes copy with bookplate, title soiled, few early ms. notes on title and small booklabel of former owner. Hain Copinger 8305; Goff G715.   G. W. Stuart 59-60 1996 $2,950.00

GUILLET DE SAINT-GEORGE, GEORGES 1625?-1705   The Gentleman's Dictionary. London: printed for H. Bonwicke; T. Goodwin, M. Wotton, B. Tooke, &c., 1705. 1st English edition; half title, 3 folding plates, illustrations, proposal leaves after parts II and III, slight worming in prelims not affecting text; contemporary panelled calf, brown label, old paper library labels, hinges with slight weakening, but nice copy. Jarndyce 103-156 1996 £380.00

GUILLIE, SEBASTIEN   Essai sur l'Instruction des Aveugles. Paris: Imprime par les Aveugles, 1817. 1st edition; 8 3/4 x 5 1/2 inches; 4 p.l., (9)-224 pages; full page diagram in text, frontispiece, 21 engraved plates; original pink paper boards, spine with gilt rules and black morocco label, edges untrimmed, custom made folding cloth box; corners and spine ends rather worn, covers somewhat chafed, spine uniformly faded, but the original insubstantial binding, quite sound and much less worn than might be expected, light foxing. Heirs of Hippocrates 811; Cushing G462; Waller 3858.   Phillip J. Pirages 33-294 1996 $1,950.00

GUILLIM, JOHN   A Display of Heraldry: Manifesting a More Easie Access to the Knowledge Thereof Than hath Hitherto Been Published by Any... London: T. R. for Jacob Blome, 1660. 4th edition; small folio; (xvi), 402, (iv), 403-432, 435-144 (=444), 36, (vi) pages; woodcut arms throughout; 19th century moocco, old diced calf panels laid on sides, old red morocco gilt spine laid down, label, one corner slightly worn, two leaves M2/3 repeated, Fff2/3 cropped at foot, slightly affecting two woodcuts, scattered foxing, final leaf rather soiled; good. Wing G2219a; Lowndes p. 956.   Robert Clark 38-55 1996 £250.00

GUINN, J. M.   A History of California and an Extended History of Los Angeles and Environs. Los Angeles; Historic Record Co., 1915. 10 7/8 x 8 1/2 inches; 3 volumes, portraits; red cloth boards with brown leather spines and tips, top edge gilt, light edge wear. Unusually nice set. Dawson's Books Shop 528-93 1996 $250.00

GUINNESS, MARY GERALDINE   The Story of the China Indland Mission. London: Morgan and Scott, 1893-4. 1st edition; 8vo; 2 volumes; xvii, (i), 476, (2 ad); xi, (i), 512, (2 contents), (2 ad) pages, large colored folding map, 2 other colored maps, photographic illustrations and maps; original dark blue cloth, traces of rubbing.   James Burmester 29-61 1996 £85.00

GUITRY, SACHA   Deburau. Published by Belasco, 1925. 1st edition; 178 pages; 34 plates with tissue; stiff boards with jacket, fine in board box. Inscribed by David Belasco to Dr. Arthur Hobson Quinn.   Lyman Books 21-493 1996 $100.00

GUNN, JOHN C.   Gunn's Domestic Medicine, or Poorman's friend, in the Hours of Affliction, Pain and Sickness. New York: 1849. 893 pages; portrait; full leather, one spine label lacking; Kaufman 312.   W. Bruce Fye 71-872 1996 $200.00

GUNN, M.   Botanical Exploration of Southern Africa. Rotterdam: 1981. 4to; 416 pages, numerous portraits and other illustrations; boards. Wheldon & Wesley 207-1775 1996 £89.00

GUNN, THOM   Unsought Intimacies: Poems of 1991. Berkeley: 1993. One of 130 numbered copies, signed by author and artist; small folio; 3 etchings by Theophilus Brown; printed in monotype Van Dijck on paper specially made by Robert Serpa; boards, fine in slipcase.   Bertram Rota 272-247 1996 £230.00

GUNN, THOM   The Explorers. Bow Rediton: Richard Gilbertson, 1969. 1st edition; one of 100 copies, signed by author; thin 8vo; wrappers; fine.   James S. Jaffe 34-196 1996 $250.00

GUNN, THOM   Games of Chance. Omaha: Abattoir Editions, 1979. 1st edition; one of 220 copies; small 8vo; etching by John Thein; cloth, printed label; mint.   James S. Jaffe 34-200 1996 $100.00

GUNN, THOM   Mandrakes. London: Rainbow Press, 1973. 1st edition; one of 150 copies signed by author; 4to; quarter vellum and boards, slipcase; mint.   James S. Jaffe 34-197 1996 $375.00

GUNN, THOM   Songbook. New York: Albondocani Press, 1973. 1st edition; limited to 200 numbered copies, signed by poet and artist; 8vo; drawings by Bill S; marbled wrappers; fine.   James S. Jaffe 34-198 1996 $150.00

GUNN, THOMAS   The Missed Beat. Janus Press, 1976. 1st edition; in an edition of 220 unnumbered copies, signed by author, this one of 50 published by the Janus Press, the other 170 copies were issued in wrappers by the Gruffyground Press, the other 170 copies were issued in pages; 1 wood engraving illustration (printed twice) by Simon Brett; designed, set and printed by Claire Van Vliet; titles and text printed in black copyright note and colophon in sap green, wood engraving printed in sap green on titlepage and in black on page 11; printed on French-folded Okawara; bound with grey book cloth spine with Verona Verde Fabriano Miliani Ingress (decorated with sap green stripes pritned from a woodblock cared by Claire Van Vliet) over boards; author/title paper label on spine printed in black housed in slipcase covered with matching patterned paper over boards, with black trim; author title label as above. Fine.   Joshua Heller 21-11 1996 $400.00

GUNTER, ARCHIBALD CLAVERING   My Japanese Prince. New York: Home, 1904. 1st edition; 8vo; yellow wrappers, some chipping to spine, foxing to first two leaves and edges, some soiling to covers, spine slightly cocked, but generlay very good, fragile book never meant to last.   Priscilla Juvelis 95/1-115 1996 $100.00

GUNTER, EDMUND   The Works of... London: printed by A.C. for Francis Eglesfield, 1673. 5th edition; thick small 4to; (24), 309, (3), 224, (168) (2 ads) pages; 3 plates, 2 of which are folding, and the third for the construction of the volvelle at p. 64; with a profusion of large woodcuts in text, complete with 2 half titles, lacking engraved title; later polished calf, red morocco label; very good. Zeitlinger 1717. Wing G2241;   Edwin V. Glaser 121-145 1996 $950.00

GURDIJIAN, E. S.   Mechanisms, Diagnosis and Management of Head Injuries. Boston: 1958. 1st edition; 482 pages; original binding.   W. Bruce Fye 71-874 1996 $100.00

GURNEY, J. H.   The Gannet. London: 1913. Many illustrations, maps, etc; original cloth, spine little faded and strengthened, contents near fine. scarce.   David A.H. Grayling MY95Orn-37 1996 £95.00

GURNEY, JOSEPH JOHN   A Winter in the West Indies, Described in Familiar Letters to Henry Clay of Kentucky. London: John Murray, 1840. 8vo; xv, 282 pages, 15 ads; original cloth, gilt titles; very good in faded edgeworn boards. Sabin 29312.   Parmer Books O39Nautica-039105 1996 $175.00

GURNEY, WILLIAM   The Nosegay. London: printed for the author and sold by Seeley & Son, 1830. 1st edition; 8vo; xi, (i), 154, (2) pages, engraved titlepage, engraved plate, list of subscribers, half title and final author's ad leaf; original salmon moire cloth, gilt edges; very nice. James Burmester 29-62 1996 £85.00

GUTCH, JOHN   Collectanea Curiosa; or Miscellaneous Tracts Realting to the History and Antiquities of England and Ireland... Oxford: 1781. 1st edition; 8vo; 2 volumes; xix, lxiv; 448, (xii), 468 pages; contemporary calf, hinges worn, text very good. Not in Gilbert or Bradshaw.   C. P. Hyland 216-299 1996 £200.00

GUTHE, CARL E.   Pueblo Pottery Making, a Study at the Village of San Ildefonso. Andover: Pub. for Dept. of Arch., Phillips Acad. by Yale Univ. Press New Haven, 1925. 88 pages; 35 plates; green cloth with front interior hinge starting; scarce, very good.   Ken Sanders 8-25 1996 $200.00

GUTHRIE, A. B.   The Big Sky. New York: Wm. Sloane Associates, 1947. 1st edition; fine in very good+ dust jacket which is slightly worn at spine ends, also slight rubbing of edges.   Steven C. Bernard 71-117 1996 $100.00

GUTHRIE, A. B.   The Big Sky. New York: William Sloane, 1947. 1st edition; fine in attractive, near fine dust jacket with one small chip at corner of base of spine and some rubbing, nice.   Between the Covers 42-199 1996 $100.00

GUTHRIE, WOODY   American Folksong. New York: Moe Asch/DISC Co. of America, 1947. 1st edition; drawings; canvas and stiff card cvoers; very near fine, some slight rubbing to extremities. Rare. Between the Covers 42-200 1996 $750.00

GUTY, ROSA   Bird at My Window. Philadelphia: New York: Lippincott, 1966. 1st edition; modest dampstain to top edge, else fine in near fine dust jacket, with slight nicking at crown; author's very uncommon first book.   Between the Covers 43-89 1996 $300.00

GUY, WILLIAM AUGUSTUS   The Factors of the Unsound Mind with Special Reference to the Plea of Insanity in Criminal Cases and the Amendment of the Law. London: Thos. de la Rue & Co., 1881. 1st edition; small 8vo; xx, 232 pages + inserted ads; panelled ochre cloth, spine shellacked, covers scratched and shelfworn, some gouging to right edge of text block, still nearly very good, partly unopened, uncommon. John Gach 150-192 1996 $175.00

GUYER, I. D.   History of Chicago; Its Commercial and Manufacturing Interests and Industry... Chicago: Church, Goodman & Cushing, 1862. 1st edition; 4to; 200 pages; numerous woodcut in text, plus several colored plates; original cloth, some fading, few leaves with short tears, but very good. Howes G468; Chicago Ante-Fire Imprints 628.   M & S Rare Books 60-301 1996 $600.00

GUYTON DE MORVEAU, LOUIS BERNARD   Methode de Nomenclature Chimique... Paris: Cuchet, 1787. 1st edition; 2nd issue, with pages 257-272 mispaginated 241-256, and woodcut ornament of a floral vase on titlepage; 8vo; (4), 314 pages, large folding engraved table, 6 folding plates, woodcut headpiece and woodcut title ornament, complete with half title; original wrappers, ink lettered paper spine label, occasional light foxing, rear wrapper lacking, some erosion to spine, preserved in half cloth clamshell library box with deaccession letter laid in; very good, untrimmed copy. Duveen & Klickstein 130; Partington III 481; Duveen p. 340. PMM 238.   Edwin V. Glaser 121-146 1996 $1,200.00

GWYNN, JOHN   London and Westminster Improved, Illustrated by Plans. London: printed for the author, 1766. 4to; xv, (i), 132 pages, 4 folding engraved plates, hand colored; contemporary full calf, rebacked; fine. Harris & Savage no. 276.   Elton Engineering 10-64 1996 £650.00

GWYNNE, JOHN   An Essay on Design: Including Proposals for Erecting a Public Academy...for Educating the British Youth in Drawing and the Several Arts Depending Thereon. London: printed and sold by Jn. Brindley, etc. 1749. 8vo; pages vi, 92, 2 engraved headpieces and tailpiece; frontispiece, engraved title, dedication leafl; recent half calf. Peter Murray Hill 185-70 1996 £375.00

THE GYPSY. London: Pomegranate Press, 1915-16. 4to; 2 volumes, Volume 1, no. 1 and 2, complete run; many drawings by Allan Odle; first in decorated boards, second in decorated wrappers, linen spines applied;   Book Block 32-23 1996 $500.00

GYSIUS, JOHANNES   Origo & Historia Belgicorum Tumultuum Immanissimaeque Crudelitatis per Cliviam & Westphaliam Patratae... Leiden: Bart. vander Bild, 1619. 1st Latin edition; 8vo; 2 parts in 1 volume, (14), 288; 46 pages; engraved vignette on title, 18 engraved portraits, 3 folding engraved plates; contemporary vellum over boards; Brunet II 1046; Simoni G198.   Jeffrey D. Mancevice 20-37 1996 $1,250.00

H

H & S. Brass, Iron and Composite Bedsteads, Cots &c. Birmingham: H&S, 1895. Oblong 4to; publisher's cloth, (iii) pages; 106 chromolithographic plates; publisher's cloth, slight stain on front cover, else very attractive. Bookpress 75-129 1996 $1,500.00

H. P. M. Harold Patrick McGrath. Easthampton: Cheloniidae Press, 1991. Edition of 210 (100 for sale); 11 x 8 1/2 inches; 96 pages, 35 illustrations; hand bound with hand marbled paper over boards, gilt stamped leather spine label. Taurus Books 83-83 1996 $450.00

HAAS, IRVIN Bibliography of Modern American Presses. Chicago: Black Cat Press, 1935. 1st edition; one of 300 copies; 8vo; xi, 95 pages; glazed linen with printed label on front board, fine. Andrew Cahan 47-31 1996 $100.00

HABBERTON, JOHN Helen's Babies. Boston: Loring, Publishers, 1876. 1st edition; small square 8vo; three quarter blue morocco over marbled boards, floral tooling on spine, raised bands, gilt top; original cloth covers bound in and autograph card by author mounted on front flyleaf. Appelfeld Gallery 54-126 1996 $125.00

HABERLY, LOYD The Antiquary: a Poem Written in Waterperry Church... Long Crendon: Seven Acres Press, 1933. Limited to 100 numbered copies; 4to; 3 full page plates, hand colored by author, 4 smaller decorations; original full brown niger morocco, spine lettered gilt, gilt and blind design on front cover, top edge gilt, others uncut, binding trifle faded. Printed and bound by author, woodcuts by author; with his signature. Thomas Thorp 489-129 1996 £300.00

HABERLY, LOYD The Boy and the Bird. Long Crendon: Seven Acres Press, 1932. Limited to 155 numbered copies; 8vo; (8), 18, (2) pages; 19 hand colored woodcuts by author, text printed in red and black; original full brown niger morocco, spine lettered gilt, top edge gilt, others uncut; from the library of dedicatee, Sir Harry K. Newton, with his bookplate. Thomas Thorp 489-128 1996 £350.00

HABERLY, LOYD The City of the Sainted King and Other Poems. St. Louis: Haberly Press, 1941. One of 1250 copies; 8vo; printed by author on pure rag paper; woodcut decorations; quarter cloth with patterned paper sides; fine. Bertram Rota 272-221 1996 £50.00

HABERLY, LOYD Daneway. Long Crendon: Seven Acres Press, 1929. Limited to only 60 numbered copies, signed and dated by author; 8vo; (8), 45 pages; 6 illustrations by Haberly, titlepage and section dividers printed in red, green and gold; original niger morocco, spine blind tooled and lettered in gilt, blind fillets on covers, gilt edges, very fine. Thomas Thorp 489-127 1996 £480.00

HABERLY, LOYD Mediaeval English Pavingtiles. Oxford: Shakespeare Head Press, 1937. Limited to 425 copies; 4to; 327 pages; printed in red and black, over 260 illustrations by author, these mostly printed in red; original red half niger morocco gilt, top edge gilt, others uncut, sides very lightly dust soiled, as usual and endpapers little foxed, otherwise fine. Thomas Thorp 489-130 1996 £280.00

HABERLY,, LOYD Poems. Seven Acres Press, 1930. One of 120 numbered copies, signed by author; squat 8vo; elaborate woocut initials in red and green; full white pigskin, spine lettered in gilt, sides decorated and lettered in blind, top and fore edges gilt, very nice. Bertram Rota 272-220 1996 £350.00

HACHISUKA, M. The Dodo and Kindred Birds, or the Extinct Birds of the Mascarene Islands. London: 1953. Copy no. 1 of a limited edition of 485 numbered copies; 4to; pages 264, 11 colored, and 11 plain plates; half blue levant morocco gilt, gilt top, trifle faded, trifle marked; nice, clean copy. Author's signature pasted to titlepage and photo of him in Japanese dress on reverse of frontispiece, original prospectus loosely inserted. Wheldon & Wesley 207-41 1996 £800.00

HACHIYA, MICHIHIKO Hiroshima Diary: the Journal of a Japanese Physician, August 6-September 30, 1945. Chapel Hill: 1955. 1st English translation; 238 pages; original binding. W. Bruce Fye 71-881 1996 $100.00

HACKENBROCH, YVONNE English and Other Needlework, Tapestries and Textiles. Cambridge: Metropolitan Museum of Art by Harvard University Press, 1960. Large 4to; 75 full color and 108 monochrome plates and 103 figures; cloth and boards, fine in dust jacket with tears and tape repairs; scarce. Marilyn Braiterman 15-193 1996 $350.00

HACKETT, C. Edible Horticultural Crops. London: 1982. 8vo; 673 pages; cloth. Wheldon & Wesley 207-1876 1996 £87.00

HACKETT, CHARLES WILSON Historical Documents Relating to New Mexico, Nueva Vizcaya and Approaches Thereto to 1773. Washington: Carnegie Inst., 1923/26/37. 1st edition; 3 volumes, pages 502, 497, 532; map, 5 facsimiles; original dark blue cloth, gilt lettered spines, spine lettering bit rubbed, overall a fine set. Presentation inscription in volume 1 from author to his father and mother. Argonaut Book Shop 113-306 1996 $750.00

HACKETT, CHARLES WILSON Revolt of the Pueblo Indians of New Mexico and Otermin's Attempted Reconquest 1680-1682. Albuquerque: The University of New Mexico Press, 1970. 2nd printing; 10 1/2 x 7 inches; 2 volumes; maroon cloth, dust jackets, uncut and unopened. Dawson's Books Shop 528-95 1996 $100.00

HACKETT, MARIA A Brief Account of Cathedral and Collegiate Schools; with an Abstract of their Statautes and Endownments. London: J. Nichols & Son, 1827. 8vo; viii, 60 pages; original printed wrappers, spotted. James Burmester 29-63 1996 £45.00

HACOBIAN, M. P. The Armenian Church - History, Ritual and Communion Service. Sydney: Robert Dey, Son & Co., 1947. 1st edition; 39 pages of text, black and white drawings; wrappers; spine slightly browned, cover edges slightly bumped; very good; presentation copy from author, inscribed for William Saroyan. Ulysses 39-21 1996 £65.00

HADFIELD, JOHN Georgian Love Songs. London: The Cupid Press, 1949. 1st edition; limited to 660 numbered copies; 8vo; pages xx, 147; 6 collotype plates from drawings by Rex Whistler; original buckram backed marbled boards, leather spine label, top edge gilt, others uncut; original prospectus loosely inserted. Sotheran PN32-64 1996 £148.00

HAEMSTEDE, A. C. Historien der Vromer Martelaren. Dordrecht: 1643, colophon to read dated 1644. Folio; 132 woodcut illustrations; full antique style panelled calf covered wooden boards, tastefully rebacked, corners restored, new clasps, new endpapers, lacks half title (?) and contents (?); minor worming to last leaf of Voor-Reden and dedication, with no loss to text, minor dampstaining to upper corners not affecting text, text in good, clean condition with no foxing, browning or offsetting, both text and woodcuts good strong imprints, small burn to leaf 105 with no loss of text. Beeleigh Abbey BA56-147 1996 £850.00

HAFEN, LE ROY R. Broken Hand: The Life of Thomas Fitzpatrick, Mountain Man, Guide and Indian Agent. Denver: the Old West Pub. Co., 1973. One of 200 copies; 8 1/2 x 6 1/2 inches; six, 359 pages, double page map, 9 pages of illustrations; brown cloth with illustration applied to front cover, blue slipcase with applied illustration; signed by author. Dawson's Books Shop 528-96 1996 $125.00

HAFEN, LE ROY R. The Far West and Rockies Historical Series, 1820-1875. Glendale: Arthur H. Clark Co., 1954/60-61. 2nd printing of volumes 1, 2 and 3, others 1st printing; 9 1/2 x 6 1/4 inches; 15 volumes; illustrations; green cloth, some light wear and spotting to bindings. Dawson's Books Shop 528-97 1996 $1,000.00

HAFEN, LE ROY R. Fremont's Fourth Expediton, a Documentary Account of the Disaster of 1848-49 with Diaries, Letters and Reports by Participants in the Tragedy. Glendale: 1960. 1st edition; 319 pages, frontispiece, illustrations, folding map; cloth, fine. T. A. Swinford 49-462 1996 $100.00

HAFEN, LE ROY R. The Mountain Men and the Fur Trade of the Far West: Biographical Sketches of the Participants by Scholars of the Subject and With Introductions by the Editor. Glendale: Arthur H. Clark Co., 1965-72. 1st edition; 9 3/8 x 6 1/4 inches; 10 volumes, maps and illustrations; brown cloth. Dawson's Books Shop 528-98 1996 $900.00

HAFEN, LE ROY R. Old Spanish Trail Sante Fe to Los Angeles...Diaries of Antonio Armijo and Orvell Pratt. Glendale: 1954. 1st edition; 377 pages; illustrations, folding map; cloth. T. A. Swinford 49-461 1996 $125.00

HAFEN, LE ROY R.   The Overland Mail, 1849-1869. Promoter of Settlement, Recursor of Railroads. Cleveland: 1926. 1st edition; 361 pages; foldout map, illustrations; book very good with some wear to binding and its edges, protective slipcase added.   Early West 22-569 1996 $250.00

HAFEN, LE ROY R.   The Overland Mail 1849-1869. Cleveland: 1926. 1st edition; 361 pages; folding map, illustrations; cloth, very good+. Howes H10; Smith 3943; Rittenhouse 267.   T. A. Swinford 49-460 1996 $225.00

HAFEN, MARY ANN   Recollections of a Handcart Pioneer of 1860. Denver: privately printed for her descendants, 1938. 1st edition; 117 pages, frontispiece; plates; original dark green cloth, title in gilt on front cover and spine; fine. Paher Nevada 753; Mintz The Trail 196.   Michael D. Heaston 23-165 1996 $500.00

HAFTMANN, WERNER   Emil Nolde. New York: Abrams, 1959. Folio; 44 pages text + 55 tipped in color plates, 19 monochrome illustrations; cloth, dust jacket. Freitag 7084.   Brannan 43-490 1996 $120.00

HAGELIN, OVE   The Byrth of Mankynde Otherwyse Named the womans booke: Embryology, Obstetrics, Gynaecology, through Four Centuries. Stockholm: 1990. 1st edition; illustrations; original binding. W. Bruce Fye 71-884 1996 $100.00

HAGELIN, OVE   Rare and Important Medical Books in the Library of the Karolinska Institute: an Illustrated and Annotated Catalogue. Stockholm: 1992. 1st edition; 208 pages; illustrations; original binding. W. Bruce Fye 71-885 1996 $125.00

HAGGARD, ELLA   Myra; or the Rose of the East. London: Longman, etc., 1857. 1st edition; 8vo; original orange brown cloth; errata slip, very fine, scarce.   Ximenes 108-175 1996 $175.00

HAGGARD, HENRY RIDER 1856-1925   Allan Quartermain. L-G, 1887. 1st edition; slight wear to corner tips and some minor fading to spine, else tight very good copy.   Aronovitz 57-477 1996 $325.00

HAGGARD, HENRY RIDER 1856-1925   Benita. London: Cassell & Co., Ltd., 1906. 1st edition; 16 black and white illustrations by Gordon Browne; 16 pages publisher's ads at rear; original binding, top edge dusty, head and tail of spine and corners bumped, covers marked and rubbed, bottom edge of upper cover dampstained, prelims and edges spotted, some internal spotting; good.   Ulysses 39-258 1996 £75.00

HAGGARD, HENRY RIDER 1856-1925   Cetywayo andd His White Neighbors. London: Trubner & Co., 1882. One of 750 copies; 1st edition; octavo; original cloth, gilt, inner hinges cracked and repaired, spine ends and corners slightly worn, signataure on blank endpaper and at head of pages 100-101, respectable copy; rare. Scott Haggard 1.   G. W. Stuart 59-45 1996 $750.00

HAGGARD, HENRY RIDER 1856-1925   Cleopatra... London: Longmans, Green and Co., 1889. 1st edition; 8vo; pages xvi, 336, 16 (ads), without slip concerning illustrations, wood engraved frontispiece, 28 plates and initials; original cloth, lettered in gilt, rather worn, rebacked, preserving most of original spine, hinges reinforced, some spotting, good copy. Presentation copy inscribed by author on half title and dated by him 25 June 1889 and with another inscription in another hand.   Simon Finch 24-101 1996 £500.00

HAGGARD, HENRY RIDER 1856-1925   The Days of My Life. London: Longmans, Green, 1926. 1st edition; 2 volumes; photos; near fine set. Aronovitz 57-494 1996 $185.00

HAGGARD, HENRY RIDER 1856-1925   The Ghost Kings. London: Cassell, 1908. 1st edition; half title absent, spine somewhat lightened, else just about very good; most uncommon.   Aronovitz 57-488 1996 $125.00

HAGGARD, HENRY RIDER 1856-1925   Jess. London: Smith, Elder, 1887. 1st edition; spine lightened with some spotting, else tight, very good with unbroken inner hinges; most uncommon.   Aronovitz 57-478 1996 $225.00

HAGGARD, HENRY RIDER 1856-1925   The Mahatma and the Hare. New York: Longmans, Green, 1911. 1st edition; illustrations by W. T. Horton and H. M. Brock, illustrated red cloth covered boards; bright, near fine copy.   Lame Duck Books 19-231 1996 $150.00

HAGGARD, HENRY RIDER 1856-1925   She. London: Longmans, 1887. 1st edition; upper section of front inner hinge weakened, else bright very good/very good+ copy.   Aronovitz 57-479 1996 $475.00

HAGGARD, HENRY RIDER 1856-1925   Swallow. London: Longmans Green, 1899. 1st edition; tight, bright, very good+ copy.   Aronovitz 57-483 1996 $135.00

HAGGARD, HENRY RIDER 1856-1925   The Witch's Head. Leipzig: Tuachnitz, 1887. Early edition; 2 volumes; some staining to front cover of volume 2, else very good+ set bound in later wrappers; uncommon. Aronovitz 57-480 1996 $175.00

HAGUE & GILL LIMITED   Type Designed by Eric Gill and printed by Hague & Gill Ltd. High Wycombe. n.d. 1937/38. 4to; 292 x 225 mm; pages (12), titling in various single colors, well preserved in slightly soiled and rubbed original stiff blue paper wrappers, lettered in red and black.   Claude Cox 107-225 1996 £55.00

HAGUE, RENE   The Death of Hector. Wellingborough: Christopher Skelton, 1973. Limited edition, 118/150 copies (of an edition of 200); tall 8vo; pages 19; printed on Tre Kronor paper, 4 full page line drawings by Peter Campbell on pale grey paper, title printed in orange; original quarter pale grey cloth, printed pale grey boards, glassine jacket; fine. Blackwell's B112-258 1996 £60.00

HAHNEMANN, SAMUEL   Organon of Homoeopapthic Medicine. Allentown: Academical Bookstore, 1836. 1st American edition; 8vo; 23, (9)-212 pages; original cloth, spine worn and cracking at hinges, but very sound, clean and tight. Rare. PMM 265 (1810 ed.); GM 1966. Bradford p. 117; Rinderknecht 37841.   M & S Rare Books 60-458 1996 $750.00

HAILE, BERARD   Beautyway: a Navajo Ceremonial. New York: Pantheon Books, 1957. 1st edition; supplement in rear pocket, numerous reproductions; light spotting to fore and bottom edges, also apparent on f.f.e.p. and inside dust jacket flap, else very good in jacket showing minor wear and faint traces of spotting.   Ken Sanders 8-151 1996 $200.00

HAILE, BERARD   Emergence Myth, Accourind to the Hanelthnayhe or Upward-Reaching Rite. Santa Fe: Museum of Navajo Ceremonial Art, 1949. 186 pages; many line drawings; original plain light blue dust jacket, with sun fading at spine and extremities, several nicks a top edges; near fine.   Ken Sanders 8-149 1996 $350.00

HAILE, BERARD   Learning Navajo. Arizona: St. Michael Press, 1941/42/47. first two volumes are approximately 5 x 7 inches, third volume is 5 x 8 inches and 4th volume is 5 3/4 x 8 1/2 inches; 184, 224, 166, 296 pages; first 3 volumes uniform in tan wrappers; 4th volume in red wrappers; covers show some wear, about very good overall; one is inscribed by author; scarce set.   Ken Sanders 8-150 1 996 $200.00

HAILE, BERARD   Prayer Stick Cuttings in a Five Night Navajo Ceremonial of the Male Branch of Shootingway. Chicago: 1947. 1st edition; 229 pages, color plates, illustrations, stiff printed wrappers, extremely uncommon.   T. A. Swinford 49-465 1996 $150.00

HAILEY, ARTHUR   Flight Into Danger. London: Souvenir Press, 1958. 1st edition; author's first book; page fore edges lightly foxed, otherwise fine in lightly rubbed dust jacket with light soiling on rear panel and few small chips and short closed tears.   Quill & Brush 102-797 1996 $100.00

HAINES, HERBERT   Manual of Monumental Brasses Comprising an Introduction to the Study of These Memorials and a List of Those Remaining in the British Isles. Oxford and London: Parker, 1861. 22.5 x 15 cm; 2 volumes, cclxiii pages + color frontispiece, 200 illustrations; 286 pages (text only), some pencil annotations; original cloth, marked, top edge gilt.   Rainsford A54-301 1996 £55.00

HAINING, PETER   Movable Books. An Illustrated History. New English Library, 1979. 1st edition; oblong 4to; 142 pages; color illustrations; black cloth, gilt, min in similar d.   Marjorie James 19-162 1996 £55.00

HAKE, A. EGMONT   Paris Originals. London: C. Kegan Paul & Co., 1878. 8vo; 192, (32) pages ads; 20 etchings by Leon Richeton; original brown cloth with small vignette in gilt on upper cover, bevelled edges; some light dampstaining affecting some plates, rear cover stained, otherwise very good.   David Mason 71-67 1996 $120.00

HAKE, LUCY   Something New on Men and Manners, a Critique on the Follies and Vices of the Age, Interspersed with Amusing Anecdotes, Biographical Skethces, and Useful Suggestions on various Interesting topics. Hailsham: printed by G. Breads and sold by him for the author, 1828. 1st edition; 8vo; (xvi), 295 pages, brief list of subscribers; contemporary boarads, neatly rebacked in calf; scarce. 2 copies in NUC. James Burmester 29-64 1996 £150.00

HAKLUYT, RICHARD 1552-1616   The Principal Navigations, Voyages, Traffiques & Discoveries of the English Nation. (with) The Voyages, Traffiques & Discoveries of Foreign Voyagers. London: & Toronto: J. M. Dent and Sons Ltd., New York: E. P. Dutton & Co., 1927/28. Dent edition; 8vo; 10 volumes; frontispieces to all volumes, numerous illustrations and maps; original light blue cloth, gilt 'ship' vignettes to front covers and spines, decorative map endpapers, top edges brown. Beeleigh Abbey BA56-74 1996 £250.00

HAKOLA, JOHN W.   Frontier Omnibus. Helena: Historical Society of Montana, 1962. Limited to 298 numbered copies, 436 pages; illustrations by Charles M. Russell, buckskin; book fine, binding beautiful.   Early West 22-574 1996 $125.00

HALE, EDWARD E.   Kansas and Nebraska: the History, Geographical and Physical Characteristics...an Account of the Emigrant Aid Companies. Boston: Phillips, Sampson and Co., 1854. 1st edition; 256, (4) pages, last four pages ad, folding map; original black embossed cloth with title in gilt on spine, minor repairs to spine, fine, bright copy, scarce in fine condition. Graff 1709; Becker Wagner Camp 239a.   Michael D. Heaston 23-166 1996 $450.00

HALE, JOHN PETER   Trans-Allegheny Pioneers. Cincinnati: Graphic Press, 1886. 1st edition; 12mo; 330 pages, 11 plates; publisher's cloth; bookplate, covers soiled, minor foxing, otherwise good. Howes H32. The Bookpress 75-414 1996 $150.00

HALE, JOHN PETER   Trans-Allegheny Pioneers. Cincinnati: Graphic Press, 1886. 1st edition; 330 pages; plates, folding facsimile; blue cloth, gilt, very good plus, bright and attractive. Howes H32; Ayer.   Bohling Book Co. 192-263 1996 $125.00

HALE, KATHLEEN   Orlando and the Water Cats. London: Cape, 1972. 1st edition; 4to; colored lithographed illustrations by author; green pictorial boards; mint, very scarce.   Barbara Stone 70-114 1996 £65.00

HALE, M.   Spring Water, Versus River Water, for Supplying the City of New York. New York: Marsh & Harrison, 1835. 1st edition; 50 pages; 2 plates; grey paper boards, backed in plain brown paper; very good, bound with four short reports of the Boards of Alderman relating to the water issue.   19th Century Shop 39- 1996 $950.00

HALE, MATTHEW   History of the Pleas of the Crown. London: printed for T. Payne, P. Uriel, 1778. New edition; contemporary calf, spine ends chipped, but good, fresh set.   Meyer Boswell SL25-97 1996 $850.00

HALE, MATTHEW   The History of the Common Law. London: printed for G. G. and J. Robinson, 1794. 5th edition; 2 volumes; modern boards, some embrowning, but good crisp set.   Meyer Boswell SL25-96 1996 $650.00

HALE, MATTHEW   The History of the Common Law. London: printed for G. G. and J. Robinson, 1794. 5th edition; 8vo; 2 volumes, pages (8), lxiv, 306; (20), 172; 137, (24) and ad leaf; engraved plate; strongly bound in recent paper boards, labels, very good to nice.   James Fenning 133-146 1996 £75.00

HALE, MATTHEW   Pleas of the Crown; or, a Methodical Summary of the Principal Matters Relating to that Subject. London: printed by the Assigns of Richard Atkyns and Edward Atkyns, 1685. Badly stained and mildewed, ex-library, working copy only.   Meyer Boswell SL27-102 1996 $150.00

HALE, MATTHEW   The Primitive Origination of Mankind, Considered and Examined According to the Light of Nature. London: printed for Mat. Wotton at the Three Daggers etc., 1710. 2nd edition; 26 pages; modern marbled wrappers, embrowned but sound.   Meyer Boswell SL26-97 1996 $450.00

HALE, NATHAN CABOT   Embrace of Life: the Sculpture of Gustave Vigeland. New York: Abrams, 1968. Oblong 4to; 363 pages, 32 tipped in color paltes, 277 monochrome illustrations; cloth, dust jacket.   Brannan 43-656 1996 $225.00

HALE, THOMAS   A Compleat Body of Husbandry. T. Osborne & J. Shipton, J. Hodges, T. Trye, S. Crowder and H.... 1756. Folio; frontispiece, 13 engraved plates, 1 folding, xii, 719 pages; contemporary panelled calf, rubbed, joints cracked, good internally, apart from some slight staining to laste plate; Kress 5528; Perkins 737; Fussell II p. 37-38. Thomas Thorp 489-131 1996 £250.00

HALES, STEPHEN   Statical Essays. London: 1731-33. 1st edition; 2 volumes, 376, 361 pages, plus index; recent quarter leather; Philip Bard's copies with his signature. GM 765.   W. Bruce Fye 71-893 1996 $2,750.00

HALEY, ALEX   Roots. Garden City: Doubleday & Co., 1976. 1st edition; 8vo; cloth backed boards, dust jacket, fine, bright copy. James S. Jaffe 34-202 1996 $100.00

HALEY, JAMES EVETTS 1901-   Charles Goodnight, Cowman and Plainsman. Boston: Houghton Mifflin Co., 1936. 1st edition; xiii, 485 pages; frontispiece, maps, text illustrations by Harold Bugbee; tan cloth lettered in brown on spine and front cover, very small split to top of spine, lower edge of covers very lightly worn, near corners; overall fine copy. Scarce. Adams Herd 960; Dobie p. 104; Dykes Bugbee 74; Dykes Kid 225.   Argonaut Book Shop 113-314 1996 $250.00

HALEY, JAMES EVETTS 1901-   Charles Schreiner, General Merchandise, the Story of a Country Store.. Austin: 1944. xiii, 70 pages; illustrations; cloth, dust jacket; very good+, jacket with plastic protective covering attached. Adams Herd 968; Dykes 50; Great Bugbee 76. Bohling Book Co. 191-57 1996 $125.00

HALEY, JAMES EVETTS 1901-   Earl Vandale on the Trail of Texas Books. Canyon: Paolo Duro, 1965. Limited edition, 500 copies; 44 pages. Lowman 191.   Maggie Lambeth 30-233 1996 $180.00

HALEY, JAMES EVETTS 1901-   Earl Vandale on the Trail of Texas Books. Canyon: Palo Duro Press, 1965. 1st edition; 44 pages; frontispiece, illustrations; original red cloth, title in gilt on front cover and spine, very fine. Lowman 191; Robinson Haley 39.   Michael D. Heaston 23-167 1996 $175.00

HALEY, JAMES EVETTS 1901-   Fort Concho and the Texas Frontier. San Angelo Standard Times, Texas, 1952. 1st edition; 352 pages; absolutely pristine for a 43 year old book; illustrations; BTB 83.   Early West 22-622 1996 $230.00

HALEY, JAMES EVETTS 1901-   Fort Concho and the Texas Frontier. San Angelo: 1952. 1st edition; 352 pages; illustrations by H. D. Bugbee; remarkably fine in fine dust jacket. BTB 83.   Early West 22-272b 1996 $230.00

HALEY, JAMES EVETTS 1901-   Fort Concho and the Texas Frontier. San Angelo: 1952. 1st edition; 352 pages, map, frontispiece, illustrations; signed; very good+. Jenkins BTB 83. Lowman 7BB.   T. A. Swinford 49-471 1996 $200.00

HALEY, JAMES EVETTS 1901-   Fort Concho and the Texas Frontier. San Angelo: Standard Times, 1952. 1st edition; 352 pages; illustrations; dust jacket, very fine. Basic 83; Lowman 79; Robinson 23.   Maggie Lambeth 30-234 1996 $150.00

HALEY, JAMES EVETTS 1901-   Jeff Milton, a Good Man With a Gun. Norman: 1948. 1st edition; 430 pages; photos, illustrations by H. D. Bugbee; book fine, dust jacket chipped, signed by author; Six Guns 892; Adams 150 #64.   Early West 22-10 1996 $150.00

HALEY, JAMES EVETTS 1901-   Jeff Milton, A Good Man With a Gun. Norman: 1948. 1st edition; missing dust jacket, but with slipcase; lovely copy.   Early West 22-11 1996 $120.00

HALEY, JAMES EVETTS 1901-   Jeff Milton, A Good Man with a Gun. Norman: 1948. 1st edition; book very fine, dust jacket with usual amount of wear.   Early West 22-12 1996 $120.00

HALEY, JAMES EVETTS 1901-   The XIT Ranch of Texas and the Early Days of the Llano Estacado. Chicago: 1929. 1st edition; 258 pages; photos, folding map; broken hinges have been professionally repaired, slipcase. Six Guns 894; BTB 92. Reese 120 #54.   Early West 22-7 1996 $400.00

HALFORD, FREDERIC M. Dry Fly Entomology: a Brief Description of Leading Types of Natural Insects Serving as Food for Trout and Grayling with the 100 best Patterns of Floating Flies and the Various Methods of Dressing Them... London: Vinton & Co., 1897. Limited edition, number 11 of only 100 copies of the edition deluxe, signed by author; 4to; 2 volumes, printed on handmade paper; pages 314, ad leaves, 100 original feathered flies window mounted in a separate volume; partially uncut, recent full green morocco, reproducing in full the original binding, titled in gilt on spine and upper covers, top edge gilt; some light spotting to fly mounts, otherwise a superb set, extremely rare.   Sotheran PN32-86 1996 £1,950.00

HALFORD, FREDERIC M. The Dry-Fly Man's Handbook. London: George Routledge, 1913. 1st edition; 8vo; xvi, 416 pages; frontispiece, 43 plates, 62 text figures; cloth, top edge gilt, slightly worn, one or two plates slightly dust soiled on fore-edge as a result of having worked loose at some time, one plate reinserted on guard.   Thomas Thorp 489-134 1996 £135.00

HALFORD, FREDERIC M. Making a Fishery. London: Horace Cox, 1895. One of 150 large paper deluxe copies; 11 1/2 x 7 3/4 inches; 4 p.l., 212 pages; frontispiece, 4 plates, illustrations in text; title printed in red and black, printed on fine textured paper; dark green full morocco, raised bands, simple gilt titling, gilt and blind rules, densely gilt inner dentelles, top edge gilt, other edges untrimmed; spine slightly sunned, front joint rather flaked, covers bit marked, but binding completely tight and generally well preserved; extremely fine itnernally.   Phillip J. Pirages 33-295 1996 $550.00

HALFORD, FREDERIC M. Making a Fishery. London: 1895. 1st edition; illustrations; nice copy.   David A.H. Grayling 3/95-450 1996 £60.00

HALFORD, FREDERIC M. Making a Fishery. Vinton & Co., 1902. 1st edition; 8vo; viii, 212 pages; frontispiece, 4 plates; publisher's dark blue cloth, gilt, extremities trifle worn, two or three minor stains on covers.   Thomas Thorp 489-132 1996 £60.00

HALFORD, FREDERIC M. Making a Fishery. London: 1902. illustrations, light marking to covers.   David A.H. Grayling 3/95-449 1996 £50.00

HALFORD, FREDERIC M. Modern Development of the Dry Fly, the New Dry Fly Patterns, the Manipulation of Dressing Them and Practical Experiences. London: George Routledge and Sons, 1910. 1st edition; 8vo; color and black and white plates; original cloth, repairs to cracked joints, lightly foxed.   Glenn Books 36-102 1996 $200.00

HALFORD, FREDERIC M. Modern Development of the Dry-Fly... London: George Routledge, 1913. 2nd edition; 8vo; viii, 219 pages; 9 colored plates, 18 color charts, 22 text figures and 15 photograuvre plates; publisher's dark blue buckram, spine faded, covers slightly marked, occasional very slight foxing; scarce.   Thomas Thorp 489-135 1996 £80.00

HALIBURTON, THOMAS CHANDLER 1796-1865 The Americans at Home; or, Byeways, Backwoods, and Prairies. London: Hurst and Blackett, 1854. 1st edition; 8vo; 3 volumes; original green cloth, spines evenly faded; fine set. Sabin 29680; TPL 3442.   Ximenes 108-177 1996 $400.00

HALIBURTON, THOMAS CHANDLER 1796-1865 Sam Slick's Wise Saws and Modern Instances; or, What He Said, Did or Invented. London: 1853. 2 volumes; original cloth, backstrips little darkened, head and heel of backstrips trifle worn, generally very good, complete with ads in both volumes, tipped to endpapers are several contemporary newspaper reviews of the book; laid in to volume 1 is carte-de-visite of Haliburton, tipped to front endpaper of volume 2 is a fine letter from Haliburton.   Stephen Lunsford 45-61 1996 $1,000.00

HALIFAX, GEORGE SAVILE, 1ST MARQUIS OF 1633-1695 The Lady's New-Years Gift: or, Advice to a Daughter, Under these Following Heads... London: Matt. Gillyflower & James Partridge, 1688. 3rd edition; 12mo; frontispiece; contemporary speckled calf, very good; signature on title of A. N. Antrim, and neat contemporary handwriting on blank prelims. Wing H305a.   Jarndyce 103-440 1996 £480.00

HALL, BASIL 1788-1844 Extracts from a Journal Written on the Coasts of Chili, Peru and Mexico, in the Years 1820, 1821, 1822. Edinburgh: printed for Archibald Constable and Co., Edinburgh, & Hurst... 1824. 3rd edition; 8vo; 2 volumes, half titles; large folding map frontispiece to volume 1, small tear to map neatly repaired; full contemporary calf, corners slightly bumped, blind rule border to boards, red and green morocco labels to spines, raised bands, owner's bookplate and bookseller's ticket to front pastedown of both volumes, contemporary presentation inscription, ownership inscription to frontispiece volume 2, slight foxing to prelims, otherwise very handsome copy. Sabin 29718; Lownes' II p. 977.   Beeleigh Abbey BA56-237 1996 £300.00

HALL, BASIL 1788-1844 Extracts from a Journal, Written on the Coasts of Chili, Peru and Mexico, in the Years 1820, 1821, 1822. Edinburgh: ptd. for Arch. Constable & Co., & Hurst, Robinson & Co., London, 1824. 1st edition; 8vo; 2 volumes; folding map; contemporary half dark blue calf, spines gilt, binder's tickets of Upham's Library in Bath; fine set in attractive provincial ticketed binding. Sabin 29718.   Ximenes 109-148 1996 $300.00

HALL, BASIL 1788-1844 Forty Etchings from Sketches Made with the Camera Lucida, in North America 1827 and 1828 of Arable and Pasture Grounds. Edinburgh: Simpkin & Marshall, 1829. 1st edition; ii, list of subscribers, 20 pages of descriptive text, engraved and colored map, 40 outline etchings on 20 plates; original boards, very fine, scarce in original boards. Sabin 29721. Howes H46.   Thomas Thorp 489-136 1996 £350.00

HALL, BASIL 1788-1844 The Great Polyglot Bibles, Including a Leaf from the Complutensian of Acala, 1514-17. San Francisco: Book Club of California, 1966. One of 400 copies; 15 x 10 3/4 inches; (33) pages, loose gatherings in cloth folding case, folding case slightly chipped at front outer hinge, otherwise fine. Harlan 124; Allen Press Bib. 180; Olmstead 35a.   Timothy Hawley 115-239 1996 $400.00

HALL, BASIL 1788-1844 Travels in North America, in the Years 1827 and 1828. Edinburgh: 1829. 1st edition; 3 volumes, (10), 421; (6), 432; (8), 436 pages; half titles present; lightly colored folding map, folding financial sheet; three quarter green leather and marbled boards, clean and tight, some scuffing, shellac stains on one portion of each spine, apparently from touching up after removal of labels, personal bookplates, blindstamp on titlepage of volume 3, short tear in map repaired. Howes H47; Larned 1623; Buck 207; Clark, Old South III 48; Hubach p.65   Bohling Book Co. 191-357 1996 $400.00

HALL, BASIL 1788-1844 Travels in North America, in the Years 1827 and 1828. Edinburgh: printed for Robert Cadell, 1830. 3rd edition; 8vo; 3 volumes; xiv 421, vi, 432, vii, 436, 1-9 pages; folding map in color and folding table; map has been backed with linen, probably when book was in this binding, bookplate, corners a touch worn, otherwise attractive copy in contemporary paper boards, leather spines, leather labels. Sabin 29725.   David Mason 71-121 1996 $400.00

HALL, CARROLL D. Bierce and the Poe Hoax. San Francisco: Book Club California, 1934. One of 250 numbered copies; quarto; original binding, title label on spine browned, head and tail of spine and corners slightly rubbed, free endpapers browned, covers slightly marked; very good; from the library of James D. Hart.   Ulysses 39-292 1996 £75.00

HALL, CHARLES B. Military Records of General Officers of the Confederate States of America 1861-1865... Austin: 1963. x, 108 pages, illustrations; cloth; nice. Reprint Howes H52. Dornbusch III 1050.   T. A. Swinford 49-473 1996 $100.00

HALL, CHARLES FRANCIS 1821-1871 Arctic Researches and Life among the Esquimaux... New York: 1866. 9.5 x 6 inches; 595 pages; folding map, illustrations; cloth; map torn; inner hinges broken, loose, covers rubbed, corners bumped; presentation copy, inscribed and signed by author.   John K. King 77-788 1996 $175.00

HALL, DONALD String Too Short to be Saved. New York: Viking, 1960. 1st edition; illustrations by Mimi Korachi; owner's signature and date to pastedown, otherwise very good+ in price clipped dust jacket with staining to verso and some chipping to extremities, signed by author.   Lame Duck Books 19-232 1996 $125.00

HALL, E. R. Mammals of North America. New York: 1981. 2nd edition; large 4to; 2 volumes, 634 text figures, 546 maps, 1361 pages; cloth, dust jacket.   John Johnson 135-442 1996 $150.00

HALL, EDWIN Sweynheym and Pannartz and the Origins of Printing in Italy: German Technology and Italian Humanism in Renaissance Rome. Minnville: printed by the Bird and Bull Press for Phillip J. Pirages, 1991. 1st edition; one of 231 copies (of 239 total); 9 1/4 x 6 1/4 inches; 131 pages; text with 4 nine-line initials in red and blue, two pages of typographic facsimiles; with a large folio Sweynheym and Pannartz leaf from the 1471 printing of Nicholas of Lyra's "Postilla super totam Bibliam"; a Campbell-Logan Co. binding of purple quarter morocco using marbled papers, especially designed for this edition by Iris Nevins, paper label on front cover, two edges untrimmed; the book and leaf (which is secured in mylar envelope behind a hinged cloth mat) contained in impressive 15 1/2 x 11 3/4 inch navy blue folding cloth box constructed of acid-free materials by Nancy Cuthbert.   Phillip J. Pirages 33-341 1996 $450.00

HALL, EMMA SWAN Antiquities from the Collection of Christos G. Bastis. New York: Philipp von Zabern, 1987. 4to; ix, 340 pages; 424 illustrations, original cloth, dust jacket, fine.   Archaeologia Luxor-3403 1996 $150.00

HALL, FRANCIS   Travels in Canada and the United States in 1816 and 1817. Boston: Wells and Lilly, 1818. 1st American edition; 8vo; 332 pages; small woodcuts; later cloth, uncut. Howes H62.   The Bookpress 75-415 1996 $150.00

HALL, FREDERIC   The History of San Jose and Surroundings with Biographical Sketches of Early Settlers. San Francisco: A. L. Bancroft and Co., 1871. 1st edition; xv, 537 pages; frontispiece, 3 lithographed plates, large folding map in rear; gilt letered brown cloth, very light wear to spine ends and corners, else fine; laid in is original signed mortgage between Frederic Hall and F. J. Atherton for a tract of land known as the Northern Third of Rancho Canada de Pala, in the County of Santa Clara. Cowan p. 259; Howes H63.   Argonaut Book Shop 113-315 1996 $500.00

HALL, FREDERICK G.   The Bank of Ireland, 1783-1946. Dublin: 1949. Royal 8vo; pages x, 523; 87 plates and illustrations; original cloth, gilt, fine in worn dust jacket.   James Fenning 133-147 1996 £65.00

HALL, H. B.   The Sportsman and His Dog, or Hints on Sporting. London: 1850. frontispiece; finely bound in modern half calf.   David A.H. Grayling 3/95-19 1996 £55.00

HALL, HARRISON   Hall's Distiller, Containing...Full and Particular Directions for Mashing and Distilling all Kinds of Grain and Imitating Holland Gin and Irish Whiskey... Philadelphia: John Bioren, 1813. 8vo; x, 244 pages, folding copperplate frontispiece, one additional plate, frontispiece in expert facsimile; modern quarter calf and marbled boards, browned and stained, but very good. Lowenstein 63.   Edwin V. Glaser 121-148 1996 $475.00

HALL, J.   Palaeontology of New York. Volume 5. Part 1. Lamellibranchiata. Albany: 1883. Printed slip states that this is an advance issue of 100 copies of the plates so far prepared; 4to; pages 20, plates 1-34, 36-41, 43-80; boards loose.   Wheldon & Wesley 207-1338 1996 £60.00

HALL, J. K.   One Hundred Years of American Psychiatry. New York: 1944. 649 pages; original binding.   W. Bruce Fye 71-897 1996 $125.00

HALL, JOSEPH, BP. OF NORWICH 1574-1656   The Great Mysterie of Godliness, Laid Fort by Way of Affectuous and Feeling Meditation. London: John Place, 1652. 1st edition; 12mo; (xxvi), 365, (v) pages; frontispiece; contemporary plain sheep; worn, spine defective at foot, some soiling and worming of early leaves, latter slightly affecting text, sound. Wing H383.   Robert Clark 38-56 1996 £80.00

HALL, JOSEPH, BP. OF NORWICH 1574-1656   Mundus Alter et Idem, Sive Terra Australis Antchac Semper Incognita... Utrecht: Apud Joannem a Waesberge, Anno 1643. 4th printing; 12mo; 3 works in one volume, plate, folding maps; (xiv), 213; 106; 96 pages; original vellum, blind library stamp on printed title of first work, small round wormhole through middle of text in latter half of the volume, affecting a few letters, some old ink underlining of text, old notes in ink on flyleaves.   David Bickersteth 133-34 1996 £220.00

HALL, MARTIN HARDWICK   The Confederate Army of New Mexico. Austin: 1978. 1st edition; one of the limited edition of 35 numbered copies, bound thus, signed by author; 422 pages; photos, illustrations; leather, slipcase, very nice.   Early West 22-335 1996 $350.00

HALL, ROBERT   The History of Galashiels. Galashiels: Alexander Walker & Son, 1898. Thick small 4to; pages (vii), 601, top edge gilt, uncut, 25 illustrations and folding maps; original cloth, gilt, top edge gilt, uncut.   R.F.G. Hollett 76-115 1996 £120.00

HALL, SAMUEL CARTER 1800-1889   The Baronial Halls, and Ancient Picturesque Edifices of England. London: Willis and Sotheran, 1858. Folio; 2 volumes; 71 tinted lithograph plates, each accompanied by descriptive text leaves, unpaginated; all edges gilt, bottle green quarter morocco, gilt titles to upper boards and spines; nice, clean set.   Sotheran PN32-186 1996 £320.00

HALL, SAMUEL CARTER 1800-1889   The Book of Gems. The Poets and Artists of Great Britain. London: Saunders & Otley, 1836-37. 1st edition; large and tall octavo; 2 volumes; original red morocco gilt, gilt extra, all edges gilt, scuffed and worn, few minor spots, quite decent. G. W. Stuart 59-20 1996 $150.00

HALL, TREVOR H.   Old Conjuring Books. London: Duckworth, 1972. One of 1000 copies; signed; 8vo; xvi, 228 pages; cloth, frontispiece; fine. The Bookpress 75-304 1996 $100.00

HALL, WILLIAM   Irrigation Development, History, Customs, Laws and Adminsitrative Systes...in France, Italy and Spain. Sacramento: 1886. Cloth, gilt, very nice, presented by Hall to his mother.   Meyer Boswell SL26-99 1996 $350.00

HALL, WILLIAM E.   A Treatise on International Law. Oxford: Clarendon Press, 1884. 4th edition; original cloth, rubbed, spine marked, but serviceable.   Meyer Boswell SL26-98 1996 $125.00

HALL, WILLIAM HENRY   The New Encyclopaedia; or Modern Universal Dictionary of Arts and Sciences... printed for C. Cooke, n.d., c. 1802. Folio; 3 volumes; frontispiece, 143 copper engraved plates, 6 folding maps; contemporary reversed calf, red and black double lettering pieces, rubbed, corners worn, slightly browned in places, few short tears, one plate having a longer one.   Thomas Thorp 489-137 1996 £350.00

HALLENBECK, CLEVE   Alvar Nunez Cabeza de Vaca: the Journey and Route of the First European to Cross the Continent of North America 1534-1536. Glendale: Arthur H. Clark Co., 1940. 9 1/4 x 6 1/4 inches; 326 pages; gold stamped dark blue cloth, previous owner's signature, bookplate and small stamp on inside of rear cover.   Dawson's Books Shop 528-101 1996 $125.00

HALLENBECK, CLEVE   Journey of Fray Marcoss De Niza. Dallas: University Press, 1949. Limited edition of 1065 copies; 4to; Cisneros headpiece vignettes for each chapter; dust jacket.   Maggie Lambeth 30-240 1996 $200.00

HALLEY, ANNE   Between Wars and Other Poems. Northampton: Gehenna Press, 1965. 1st edition; one of 500 numbered copies; small thin 4to; illustrations by Leonard Baskin; fine in dust jacket which is somewhat browned at spine and edges.   Captain's Bookshelf 38-89 1996 $125.00

HALLIDAY, BRETT   Blood on the Black Market. New York: Torquil, 1943. 1st edition; very good in dust jacket with chipping, rubbing, light soiling and edge wear.   Quill & Brush 102-800 1996 $125.00

HALLIDAY, BRETT   Bodies Are Where You Find Them. New York: Henry Holt and Co., 1941. 1st edition; very good with light soiling and boards lightly rubbed, in dust jacket with rubbing, few closed tears, one chip on top spine and light soiling.   Quill & Brush 102-799 1996 $100.00

HALLIDAY, BRETT   Michael Shayne's 50th Case. New York: Torquil, 1964. 1st edition; fine with page edges lightly soiled in near fine dust jacket with light rubbing and edge wear; lengthy inscription from author to a close friend.   Quill & Brush 102-838 1996 $150.00

HALLIFAX, CHARLES   Familiar Letters on Various Subjects of Business and Amusement... London: printed for R. Baldwin, 1755. 3rd edition; initial ad leaf; contemporary speckled calf, rubbed at corners and at some time crudely rebacked with morocco, now scarred.   Jarndyce 103-291 1996 £120.00

HALLIWELL-PHILLIPPS, JAMES ORCHARD 1820-1889   A Dictionary of Archaic and Provincial Words... London: William Boone, 1855. 3rd edition; 8vo; 2 volumes, 480, (481)-960 pages; original cloth backed boards, paper spine labels, spine labels chipped, armorial bookplate in each volume, else very good.   Chapel Hill 94-171 1996 $200.00

HALLOWELL, ANNA DAVIS   James and Lucretia Mott. Life and Letters Boston: Houghton Mifflin Co., c. 1884. 1st edition; 8vo; frontispiece with tissue guarad, 5 illustrations; brown cloth, uncut and unopened, fine; inscribed by James Mott Hallowell for Carl Pforzheimer.   James Cummins 14-139 1996 $100.00

HALSEY, HARLAN PAGE   Macon Moore, the Southern Detective. New York: J. S. Ogilvie & Co., 25 Rose Set., 1881. 1st edition; 12mo; 161 pages; 1 plate; original printed wrappers (front wrapper detached). Wright III 2412.   M & S Rare Books 60-161 1996 $375.00

HALSEY, HARLAN PAGE   Phil Scott, the Indian Detective: a Tale of Startling Mysteries. New York: J. s. Ogilvie & Co., 1882. 1st edition; 12mo; pages (17)-136 (complete); original printed wrappers, frayed, small blank portions lacking, foxed, but nice. Wright III 2413.   M & S Rare Books 60-162 1996 $500.00

HALSTEAD, B. W.   Poisonous and Venomous Marine Animals of the World. Washington: 1965-67. Large 4to; volumes 1 and 2, 416 plates, 236 color, 389 figures, 2064 pages; bound, ex-library.   John Johnson 135-609 1996 $200.00

HALSTEAD, B. W.   Poisonous and Venomous Marine Animals of the
World. Washington: 1965-70. 4to; 3 volumes; 611 plates, 18 portraits, 13
maps and numerous text figures; cloth.   Wheldon & Wesley 207-318
1996 £300.00

HALSTED, EDWARD PELLEW   The Navy Unarmed Still. Westminster:
printed by J. B. Nichols, 1865. 1st and only collected edition; 8vo; pages
(2), 86; original printed wrappers, small piece torn from lower blank
corner of lower paper wrapper, otherwise nice, fresh copy; scarce.
James Fenning 133-148 1996 £85.00

HALSTED, WILLIAM   The Employment of Fine Silk in Preference to
Catgut and the Advantages of Transfixing Tissues and Vessels in
Controlling Hemorrhage, also an Account of the Introduction of Gloves,
Gutta-Percha Tissue and Silver Foil. 1913. Offprint; 8 pages; wrappers.
GM 5640.   W. Bruce Fye 71-905 1996 $150.00

HALSTED, WILLIAM   Surgical Papers by William Stewart Halsted.
Baltimore: 1924. 1st edition; 2 volumes, 586, 603 pages; skilfully recased,
white library adhesive label at bottom of each spine; remarkable
association set, presentation from Halsted's sister to Alfred Blalock, with
Blalock's signature in both volumes. GM 863.   W. Bruce Fye 71-906
1996 $600.00

HALSTED, WILLIAM   Surgical Papers by William Stewart Halsted.
Baltimore: 1924. 1st edition; 2 volumes, 586, 603 pages; illustrations by
Max Broedel; original binding, backstrips worn with tears at head and tail
of spine, contents very good, scarce.   W. Bruce Fye 71-907 1996
$400.00

HALSTED, WILLIAM   Surgical Papers. Baltimore: Johns Hopkins, 1952.
1st collected edition, 2nd printing; 4to; 2 volumes, xliii, 586; vii, 603
pages; 2 frontispiece portraits, 103 plates and numerous figures and
tables, small innocuous library stamp at bottom of front free endpaper in
both volumes, original cloth, just a trifle wear to extremities, else near
fine set. GM 86.3.   Edwin V. Glaser B122-73 1996 $275.00

HAM, GEORGE H.   The New West Extending from the Great Lakes
Across the Plain and Moutain to the Golden Shores of the Pacific.
Winnipeg: 1888. Quarto; pages 205, (14), many plates, folding
panoramas, bird's eye views, illustrations, maps (some colored), ads;
original illustrated wrappers, lightly soiled, backstrip quite worn, internally
very good. Peel 1055.   Stephen Lunsford 45-62 1996 $450.00

HAMADY, WALTER   Since Mary: Seventeen New Poems. Springdale:
Perishable Press, 1969. 1st edition; one of 167 copies; square 24mo;
fine in plain wrappers; inscribed by author.   Captain's Bookshelf 38-96
1996 $125.00

HAMADY, WALTER   Voltaire the Hamadeh. Interminable Gabberjabbs.
(with) Hunkering in Wisconsin. (with) Thumbnailing the Hilex. Gabberjabb
Number 3. (with) The Interminable Gabberjabb Volume One (&) Number
Four. Mt. Horeb: Perishable Press, 1973-81. 1st editions, limited to 120,
125 125, 60 and 200 copies respectively; various sizes; 5 volumes,
wrappers and boards; "Thumbnailing the Hilex" is a variant, in which the
half title is printed in a single line at bottom of the page without
ornamental stars, and bound in light brown paper wrappers with an
original collage by Hamady pasted to front wrapper where the printed
tilte appears in other copies; very fine set, extremely difficult to find
complete.   James S. Jaffe 34-539 1996 $3,500.00

HAMBLETON, RONALD   Unit of Five. Toronto: Ryerson, 1944. 1st
edition; (x), 87 pages; cloth, in dust jacket; inscribed by author to John
Metcalf. Near fine.   Nelson Ball 118-62 1996 $500.00

HAMEL, MAURICE   Corot and His Work. Glasgow: 1905. Limited
edition of 200 numbered copies; thick large 4to; 2 volumes; portrait and
100 fine reproductions mounted on cards; original quarter morocco,
endpapers foxed.   Charles W. Traylen 117-11 1996 £95.00

HAMER, F.   Orchids of Nicaragua. Sarasota: 1982-85. 4to; parts 1-6
(complete), 600 plates, distribution maps; unbound.   Raymond M.
Sutton VI-905 1996 $450.00

HAMER, F.   Orchids of Central American, an Illustrated Field Guide.
Selbyana: 1988-91. Royal 8vo; 2 volumes; plates; sewed.   Wheldon &
Wesley 207-1798 1996 £80.00

HAMERTON, PHILIP GILBERT 1834-1894   Etching and Etchers. London:
Macmillan and Co., 1876. Revised edition; royal 8vo; xxxii, 459 pages; 12
etched plates, 2 are originals; publisher's brown cloth, decorated in
black and gilt, top edge gilt, somewhat worn and joints bit shaky,
occasional light spotting.   Thomas Thorp 489-139 1996 £75.00

HAMILTON, ALEXANDER   A New Account of the East Indies. London
printed for C. Hitch, 1744. Apparently 2nd London edition, though not so
designated; 8vo; 2 volumes; 8 folding maps and 11 plates; contemporay
calf, spines gilt; very rare; very fine set; early signatures of Dudley
North. CBEL II 1437.   Ximenes 108-178 1996 $1,500.00

HAMILTON, ALEXANDER   The Works of Alexander Hamilton... New
York: Charles S. Francis & Co., 1851. 7 volumes; original black cloth,
gilt, very light chipping at heads of spine, otherwise very good, foxing.
Blue River Books 9-153 1996 $150.00

HAMILTON, AUGUSTA   Marriage Rites, Customs and Ceremonies of
all the Nations of the Universe. London: printed for Chapple and Son, J.
Bumpus; E. Barrett, Bath, 1822. 1st edition; 8vo; viii, 400 pages,
engraved portrait; occasional light browning, later half calf.   James
Burmester 29-65 1996 £100.00

HAMILTON, AUGUSTUS   The Art Workmanship of the Maori Race in
New Zealand. Dunedin: New Zealand Inst., 1896. 4to; 448 pages; 65
plates, 78 other illustrations; green half morocco, covers slightly
discolored in places; scarce; inked presentation from author for Dr. Ch.
Rock.   Thomas Thorp 489-140 1996 £280.00

HAMILTON, E.   The Haunted Stars. D-M, 1960. 1st edition; fine in
near fine dust jacket.   Aronovitz 57-501 1996 $100.00

HAMILTON, ELIZABETH   Letters on Elementary Principles of Education
Bath: Printed by R. Crutwell; for G. and J. Robinson, London, 1801-02.
2nd edition; 8vo; 2 volumes; contemporary tree calf, spines gilt, slight
crack in one joint, hinges just a trifle rubbed; half title present in volume
2, all required; pretty set. CBEL III 729.   Ximenes 108-179 1996
$450.00

HAMILTON, F.   An Acocunt of the Fishes Found in the River Ganges
and Its Branches. London: 1822. 4to. and oblong royal 4to; 2 volumes,
text and plates; pages vii, 405; plate volume - titlepage and 39 engraved
plates; recent half calf, small piece chipped from titlepage and some
spotting in text volume, plate volume has small piece torn from upper
right hand corner and is creased, offsetting from plate one to verso of
title and occasional spotting elsewhere, otherwise genenraly clean.
John Henly 27-47 1996 £300.00

HAMILTON, IAIN   Variations on an Original Theme for Strings. Op. 1.
London: Schott, 1953. 1st edition; 8vo; 38 pages; stiff grey wrappers;
very good; miniature score, signed and inscribed on titlepage to noted
author and radio broadcaster Carl Haverlin.   George J. Houle 68-60
1996 $200.00

HAMILTON, JAMES   The Gospel of St. John Adapted to the
Hamiltonian System, by an Analytical and Interlineary Translation. London
pritned for and published by the author, 1824. 1st edition; 8vo; vii, (1),
106 pages, early press cutting pasted on to blank facing title,
contemporary red straight grained morocco, gilt fillets on sides, spine
gilt with raised bands, gilt edges, joints bit worn, endpapers renewed,
otherwise very good. Very scarce.   John Drury 82-99 1996 £175.00

HAMILTON, JAMES   Outlines of Midwifery, for the Use of Students.
Edinburgh: printed for Bell and Bradfute, 1826. 1st edition; 8vo; viii, 239
pages; uncut, recent pale brown half morocco with marbled boards,
large old pale library stamp on title. Wellcome III 203.   David
Bickersteth 133-198 1996 £220.00

HAMILTON, JANE   The Book of Ruth. New York: Ticknor & Fields,
1988. 1st edition; 'Network' stamp on top edge, indicating an early copy
sent to booksellers, else fine in dust jacket; uncommon first book.
Between the Covers 42-200a 1996 $350.00

HAMILTON, JOSEPH GREGOIRE DE ROULHAC   Reconstruction in Nort
Carolina. Raleigh: Edwards & Broughton, c. 1906. 1st edition; 264, (1)
pages; original printed wrappers bound in later cloth, both wrappers
bound in, bookplate removed, small library blindstamp, else very good,
presented 'with the cimpliments of the author'; Scarce; Howes H129;
Thornton 5559.   McGowan Book Co. 65-118 1996 $175.00

HAMILTON, PATRICK, of Arizona   The Resources of Arizona. San
Francisco: A. L. Bancroft & Co., 1883. 2nd edition; 275 pages;
illustrations; original black cloth, title in gilt on front cover, scattered ligh
waterstaining to few pages, very good.   Michael D. Heaston 23-21
1996 $350.00

HAMILTON, PATRICK, of Arizona   The Resources of Arizona. San
Francisco: A. L. Bancroft & Co., 1884. 3rd edition; pages 414, xiv;
illustrations, folding map; spine darkened with some wear at ends, liberal
use of initial stamp, otherwise good, tight copy. Howes 134b; Herd 983
Dumont 28-35 1996 $250.00

HAMILTON, PATRICK, or Arizona   The Resources of Arizona. Prescott: n.p., 1881. 1st edition to have author's name; 120 pages; stitched, no wrappers (as issued), crease to bottom corner of front page, light fold down middle, else fine. Howes H133; Herd 983.   Dumont 28-34 1996 $225.00

HAMILTON, RICHARD VESEY   Letters and Papers of Sir Thos. Byam Martin. London: 1903-1898. 8vo; 3 volumes; portrait, 3 lithos, portrait, 2 lithos, portrait, 1 litho; blue/white loth, very good, ex-library. With Sir Courtenay Boyle's bookplate.   John Lewcock 30-90 1996 £90.00

HAMILTON, S. B.   A Qualitative Study of Some Buildings in the London Area. London: HMSO, 1964. 8vo; vi, 165, (1) pages; 18 photo plates, some text illustrations; publisher's cloth.   Elton Engineering 10-65 1996 £65.00

HAMILTON, SINCLAIR   Early American Book Illustrators and Wood Engravers, 1670-1870. Princeton: 1968. 4to; 2 volumes; cloth.   Jens J. Christoffersen SL94-136 1996 $125.00

HAMILTON, SINCLAIR   Early American Book Illustrators and Engravers 1670-1870. Princeton: Princeton University Press, 1970. 3rd printing; 4to; 2 volumes, xlviii, 265; xv, 178 pages; illustrations; original brown cloth, fine.   Chapel Hill 94-61 1996 $100.00

HAMILTON, THOMAS   Men and Manners in America. London: William Blackwood, 1834. 2nd edition; 8vo; 2 volumes, ix, 384, 401 pages; contemporary half calf, raised bands, top edge gilt; front hinges of both volumes tender, boards rubbed, but very good set.   David Mason 71-122 1996 $240.00

HAMILTON, THOMAS   The Youth and Manhood of Cyril Thornton. Edinburgh: William Blackwood, and T. Cadell, London, 1827. 1st edition; 8vo; 3 volumes; contemporary half red morocco, gilt, spines gilt, binder's tickets of John Fox and Son of Pontefract. Spines bit faded and rubbed, nice set, complete with half titles; Ramsden p. 75; Sadleir 1101; Wolff 2948; Block p. 96; CBEL III 730.   Ximenes 109-149 1996 $450.00

HAMILTON, VIRGINIA   W. E. B. DuBois: a Biography. 1st edition; fine in dust jacket, uncommon.   Between the Covers 43-307 1996 $100.00

HAMILTON, W. T.   My Sixth years on the Plains, Trapping, Trading and Indian Fighting. New York: 1905. 1st edition; 244 pages; illustrations by Charles M. Russell, replaced endsheets; book very good but for missing two plates.   Early West 22-575 1996 $110.00

HAMILTON, WALTER   A Hand-Book; or Concise Dictionary of Terms Used in the Arts and Sciences. London: John Murray, 1825. 1st edition; half calf, maroon label, nice.   Jarndyce 103-157 196 £50.00

HAMILTON, WESTON G.   A Compend of Domestic Medicine and Household Remedies with the Treatment of Diseases of Adult and Infant. Greensboro: Phillips & Stout Bros., 1887. 1st edition; 8vo; 250, (1) pages; tipped in errata slip dated 1888; original black cloth, inner hinges cracked but firm, gift inscription dated 1956, still at least very good, rather curdely made volume; rare.   Chapel Hill 94-269 1996 $150.00

HAMILTON, WILLIAM T.   Address on the Importance of Knowledge; Delivered Before the Eroscophic Society of the University of Alabama at Tuscaloosa. Tuscaloosa: printed at the Office of the Independent Monitor, 1841. 1st edition; 8vo; 16 pages, removed. Ellison 427 (incomplete); R&B 41-2356.   M & S Rare Books 60-272 1996 $100.00

HAMMER CREEK PRESS   Type Specimen Book. New York: Hammer Creek Press, 1954. Limited to 100 copies, although Herman Cohen notes that severa copies were 'spoiled'; (44) pages; marbled wrappers, printed paper label to front cover; fine. Cohen 31.   Bromer Booksellers 87-94 1996 $325.00

HAMMER, KENNETH   Biographies of the 7th Cavalry. June 25, 1876. Ft. Collins: 1972. 1st printing; 238 pages; illustrations; gold stamped pictorial cloth, near fine, quite scarce.   Gene W. Baade 1094-69 1996 $200.00

HAMMER, WILLIAM J.   Radium and Other Radio-Active Substances; Pollonium, Actinium and Thorium, with a Consideration of Phosphorescent and Fluorescent Substances the Properties and Applications of Selenium and the Treatment of Disease by the Ultra-Violet Light. New York: 1903. 1st edition; thin 8vo; frontispiece, 7 plates, text illustrations, 86 pages; original cloth.   Argosy 810-224 1996 $450.00

HAMMER, WILLIAM J.   Radium and Other Radio-Active Substances; Polonium, Actinium and Thorium. New York: D. Van Nostrand, 1903. 1st edition; 8vo; viii, 72, (7) pages, frontispiece and numerous illustrations; original cloth, near fine. GM 4002.   Edwin V. Glaser 121-149 1996 $150.00

HAMMETT, DASHIELL   The Battle of the Aleutians. San Francisco: 1944. Blue wrappers, near fine, scarce.   Stephen Lupack 83- 1996 $150.00

HAMMETT, DASHIELL   Dead Yellow Women. New York: 1947. 1st edition; original wrpapers, near fine copy of fragile item.   Stephen Lupack 83- 1996 $125.00

HAMMETT, DASHIELL   Red Harvest. New York: 1929. 1st edition; author's first book; original cloth with skull and bones on cover; very near fine, bright copy, usually quite faded.   Stephen Lupack 83- 1996 $250.00

HAMMETT, DASHIELL   Red Harvest. New York: and London: Alfred A. Knopf, 1929. 1st edition; 7 3/4 x 5 1/2 inches; 4 p.l., 270 pages, (1) leaf; title in orange and black; original cloth, spine uniformly and slightly faded, slightly rolled, trivial rubbing to joints and corners, extremely firm, clean and smooth, fine internally.   Phillip J. Pirages 33-297 1996 $350.00

HAMMETT, DASHIELL   The Thin Man. New York: 1934. 1st edition; some wear to head and foot of spine, cover and spine designs strong, overall very good, uncommon.   Stephen Lupack 83- 1996 $250.00

HAMMETT, DASHIELL   The Thin Man. New York: Alfred A. Knopf, 1934. 1st edition; 7 1/2 x 5 1/4 inches; 4 p.l., 258, (2) pages; original cloth, spine and board edges faded as usual, very slightly rolled, but in all other ways fine, extremely clean and tight copy.   Phillip J. Pirages 33-298 1996 $250.00

HAMMOND, GEORGE P.   Don Juan de Onate: Colonizer of New Mexico 1595-1628. Albuquerque: University of New Mexico Press, 1953. 10 1/4 x 7 inches; 2 volumes; gold stamped red cloth in dust jackets, uncut, unopened.   Dawson's Books Shop 528-103 1996 $250.00

HAMMOND, GEORGE P.   Narratives of the Coronado Expedition 1540-1542. Albuquerque: University of New Mexico Press, 1940. 1st edition; 413 pages; erasure on top of title page with thinning to paper, spine faded, otherwise very good.   Hermitage SP95-708 1996 $125.00

HAMMOND, GEORGE P.   The Treaty of Guadalupe Hidalgo, February Second 1848. Berkeley: Friends of the Bancroft Library, 1949. Facsimile edition, one of 500 copies; 4to; (10), 79 pages, plus large folding map in separate folder (often lacking); original orange and white patterned boards, white linen spine with printed paper label, very fine.   Argonaut Book Shop 113-317 1996 $175.00

HAMMOND, N.   Twentieth Century Wildlife Artists. London: 1986. Royal 8vo; 224 pages, 176 colored plates; cloth.   Wheldon & Wesley 207-242 1996 £60.00

HAMMOND, NATHANIEL   The Elements of Algebra, to Which is Prefixed an Introduction Containing a Succinct History of This Science... London: 1764. 3rd edition; xxiv, 328 pages; waterstained, ex-library with stamps on title, page ix and last page, new quarter calf, marbled boards.   Graham Weiner C2-307 1996 £50.00

HAMMOND, WILLIAM ALEXANDER   Cerebral Hyperaemia the Result of Mental Strain or Emotional Disturbance. New York: G. P. Putnam's Sons, 1878. 1st edition; 12mo; 108, (4) pages, printed mauve cloth, library bookplate to pastedown and stamp to front flyleaf, else very good.   John Gach 150-194 1996 $125.00

HAMMOND, WILLIAM ALEXANDER   Physics and Physiology of Spiritualism. New York: D. Appleton & Co., 1871. 12mo; 86, (2) pages; printed embossed green cloth, right edge of front board gouged, joints rubbed, good to very good, fragile, scarce; presentation copy.   John Gach 150-196 1996 $250.00

HAMMOND, WILLIAM ALEXANDER   A Treatise on Insanity In Its Medical Relations. New York: D. Appleton & Co., 1883. 12mo; 108, (4) pages; printed mauve cloth, library bookplate to pastedown and stamp to front flyleaf, else very good.   John Gach 150-194 1996 $125.00

HAMMOND, WILLIAM ALEXNADER   Sexual Impotence in the Male. New York: Bermingham & Co., 1883. 1st edition; 8vo; (ii), 274, (2) pages; bevelled brown cloth, lightly shelfworn, very good.   John Gach 150-197   996 $175.00

HAMNETT, NINA   Is She a lady. A Problem in Autobiography. London: Wingate, 1955. 1st edition; very nice in soiled and frayed dust jacket, chips from corners and head of spine.   Virgo Books   48-96   1996 £55.00

THE HAMPSTEAD Annual. London: at the Priory Press, Sydney C. Mayle, 1897,1898-1907. Tall 8vo; complete set, 10 volumes; illustrations; cloth, printed paper labels, wrappers preserved, edges untrimmed. Marlborough 162-149   1996 £250.00

HANAFORD, PHOEBE ANN   Our Martyred President. Boston: B. B. Russell and Co., 1865. 1st edition; square 12mo; 22, (2) pages; frontispiece and wrapper portrait; original printed stiff front wrapper, lacks back wrapper, light waterstaining to front and back.   M & S Rare Books   60-194   1996 $125.00

HANCOCK, J.   The Herons of the World. London: 1978. 4to; pages 300, maps, line drawings and 64 colored plates; cloth.   Wheldon & Wesley   207-752   1996 £60.00

HANCOCK, JOHN   A Fasciculous of Eight Drawings on Stone of Groups of Birds. London: 1853. Printed title, half title, one page of text, 8 fine lithographic plates, half title has long expertly repaired tear, some edges have small tears, corners somewhat chipped/torn; housed in new cloth folder. Recently restored by an expert, it has not been restitched, the 12 leaves are therefore loose in folder; reasonable copy, rare. David A.H. Grayling   MY95Orn-38   1996 £250.00

HANCOCK, THOMAS   Essay on Instinct and Its Physical and Moral Relations. London: William Phillips, 1824. 1st edition; 8vo; 551 pages; contemporary half morocco with raised bands; very good.   Chapel Hill 94-325   1996 $135.00

HANDBOOK of Calistoga Springs, or, Little Geysers, Its Mineral Waters, Climate, Amusements, Baths, Drives, Scenery, the Celebrated Great Geysers and Petrified Forest and the Clear Lake Country. San Francisco: 1871. 1st edition; 8vo; 30, (1) pages, plus 2 pages of ads; plates; original limp blue cloth, lettering in gilt; fine, clean copy.   Edward Morrill   368-64   1996 $500.00

HANDFORTH, THOMAS   Faraway Meadow. New York: Doubleday Doran, 1939. 1st edition; oblong 4to; colored illustrations by author; green/blue pictorial cloth, fine in pictorial dust jacket.   Barbara Stone 70-116   1996 £55.00

HANDLER, HANS   The Spanish Riding School. New York: McGraw Hill, 1972. 1st U.S. edition; 4to; original binding, very good in good dust jacket.   October Farm   36-237   1996 $135.00

HANDYSIDE, ANDREW, & CO.   Works in Iron. London: E. & F. N. Spon, 1868. Small oblong 4to; iv, 106, (2) pages,, 10 actual mounted albumen photographic plates and many wood engraved text illustrations; original green cloth, gilt, binding little shaky, but overall lovely copy of a rare trade catalog.   Elton Engineering   10-66   1996 £1,250.00

HANHAM, F.   Natural Illustrations of the British Grasses. Bath: Binns and Goodwin, 1846. Small folio; pages xx, 130, 62 neatly mounted natural specimens; original full red morocco, gilt; rare.   Wheldon & Wesley   207-1477   1996 £250.00

HANKEY, THOMSON   The Principles of Banking... London: Effingham Wilson, 1867. 1st edition; demy 8vo; (iv), (14), (xvi) pages; recently rebound in neat quarter cloth, marbled sides, few small and unobtrusive library blindstamps, some creases, some soiling of text, some pencil annotation, but serviceable copy.   Ash Rare Books   Zenzybyr-40   1996 £85.00

HANKINS, SAMUEL W.   Simple Story of a Soldier. Nashville: 1912. 1st edition; 63 pages, plate; original printed wrpapers, bit of chipping about edges, else very good; housed in custom made clamshell case with leather spine and antique marbled sides; rare; presentation to John W. Morton, Forrest's chief of artillery. Dornbusch II 572; not in Nevins; Nicholson p. 354.   McGowan Book Co.   65-38   1996 $950.00

HANNA, WILLIAM   Memoirs of Thomas Chalmers, D.D., LL.D. Edinburgh: Thomas Constable, 1854. 8vo; 2 volumes, pages viii, 723; viii, 780; steel engraved portrait (little spotted); half calf, gilt, spines with broad raised bands, double labels and panels blind tooled in overall diaper design.   R.F.G. Hollett   76-119   1996 £85.00

HANNAY, JAMES   Satire and Satirists. Six Lectures. London: David Bogue, 1854. 1st edition; 8vo; green cloth, slight wear, spine faded; very good; presentation copy, inscribed "with the author's comps.". CBEL III 1387.   Ximenes   108-180   1996 $125.00

HANNEMAN, AUDRE   A Comprehensive Bibliography. Princeton: Princeton University Press, 1969/75. 2nd printing and 1st edition; 8vo; 2 volumes, xi, (iii), 568 pages; xii, (ii), 393, (1) pages; covers of volume 1 spotted, spine of volume 2 faintly rubbed, else very good.   The Bookpress   75-306   1996 $125.00

HANNIBAL Not at Our Gates; or, an Enquiry into the Grounds of Our Present Fears of Popery and the Pre(ten)der: in a Dialogue Between My Lord Panic and George Steady... London: printed in the year 1714. 8vo; pages 47; stitched as issued, uncut, rather dust soiled.   Peter Murray Hill   185-50   1996 £100.00

HANNINGTON, C. F.   Journal of Mr. C. F. Hanington, from Quesnelle through the Rocky Mountains During the Winter of 1874-75. Ottawa: 1888. Pages cx-cxxii, large folding map; original wrappers, backstrip deteriorated, internally near fine.   Stephen Lunsford   45-63   1996 $125.00

HANOTAUX, GABRIEL   Contemporary France (1870-82). London: 1903-09. Original edition; thick 8vo; 4 volumes; original cloth, gilt tops, nice set.   Howes Bookshop   265-459   1996 £85.00

HANSARD, GEORGE A.   The Book of Archery. London: 1841. pages xxii, 448; frontispiece, half title, 33 other plates; original cloth, top of spine slightly snagged, hinges sprung internally; 20 plates at rear have very light frayig to fore-edges.   David A.H. Grayling   3/95-152   1996 £150.00

HANSBERRY, LORRAINE   A Raisin in the Sun. New York: Random House, 1959. 1st edition; fine, bright, unsoiled white dust jacket with jus a touch of wear at spinal extremities; unusually nice.   Between the Covers   43-90   1996 $300.00

HANSEN, JOSEPH   Fadeout. New York: Harper & Row, 1970. 1st edition; fine in near fine dust jacket with light rubbing and soiling.   Qu & Brush   102-856   1996 $125.00

HANSEN, RON   Desperadoes. New York: Knop, 1979. 1st edition; fin in dust jacket with slightest of wear, signed by author.   Between the Covers   42-201   1996 $125.00

HANSON, ANNE COFFIN   Jacopo Della Quercia's Fonte Gais. Oxford: Clarendon Press, 1965. 28.5 x 22.5 cm; xiv, 123 pages, 97 illustrations; original cloth, in dust jacket, ex-library with several rubber stamps and labels on endpapers.   Rainsford   A54-474   1996 £95.00

HANSON, JOHN ARTHUR   Roman Theater-Temples. Princeton; Princeton University Press, 1959. 4to; 112 pages, 55 illustrations; origina cloth.   Archaeologia   Luxor-3411   1996 $150.00

HANSON, JOSEPH MILLS   The Quest of the Missouri, Being the Story of the Life and Exploits of Captain Grant Marsh. Chicago: 1909. 1st edition; 458 pages; illustrations, map; professionally reinforced; slipcase for protection, pictorial hardcovers bright.   Early West   22-577   1996 $100.00

HANWAY, JONAS   An Historical Account of the British Trade Over th Caspian Sea... London: sold by Mr. Dodsley and others, 1753. 1st edition; 4to; 4 volumes, 9 maps, 19 plates, 13 engraved vignettes and half titles in volumes 3 and 4 as called for; contemporary calf, sides worn, skilfully restored and rebacked with labels gilt, occasional insignificant spots and minor browning, pin prick wormholes in blank outer margin of part of volume IV; complete and very good set. Higgs 481; Kress 5268; Goldsmiths 8801.   John Drury   82-100   1996 £575.0

HANWAY, JONAS   A Journal of Eight Days Journey from Portsmou to Kingston Upon Thames... London: printed by H. Woodfall, 1756. 1st edition; 4to; (vi), 202, (iv), 203-361 pages, 2 engraved plates, original calf, rubbed, small defective patch on lower cover, corners worn, rebacked, preserving original endpapers.   David Bickersteth   133-35   1996 £380.00

HANWAY, JONAS   Soldier's faithful Friend; Being Moral and Religious Advice to Soldiers... London: 1780. 3rd edition; frontispiece, 199 pages; contemporary sheep, joints cracking, still very nice. 3 copies in NUC. C. R. Johnson 37-41 1996 £350.00

HANWAY, MARY ANN   A Journey to the Highlands of Scotland. London: printed for Fielding and Walker, n.d. 1777. 1st edition; small 8vo; contemporary mottled calf, gilt, spine gilt, slight rubbing, fore-edges slightly marked by damp, but attractive copy, very scarce. CBEL II 1153; Courtney p. 120.   Ximenes 108-181 1996 $900.00

HARA, H.   Catalogue of the Works of Dr. Hiroshi Hara. Tokyo: 1991. 8vo; 295 pages; portrait; cloth.   Wheldon & Wesley 207-243 1996 £76.00

HARDAKER, ALFRED   A Brief History of Pawnbroking. London: Jackson, Ruston & Keeson, 1892. 1st edition; crown 8vo; viii, (368) pages; original decorative cloth, gilt, touch shaken, few minor marks, but nice, bright copy.   Ash Rare Books Zenzybyr-41 1996 £75.00

HARDCASTLE, MARY SCARLETT   Life of John Lord Campbell. London: John Murray, Albermarle St., 1881. 2nd edition; 2 volumes; modern quarter calf, bit of foxing, but attractive set.   Meyer Boswell SL25-98 1996 $200.00

HARDEN, DONALD B.   Catalogue of Greek and Roman Glass in the British Musem. Volume I (only): Core and Rod Formed Vessels and Pendants and Mycenaean Cast Objects. London: British Museum, 1981. 4to; 187 pages, 47 plates, 1 map; original cloth.   Archaeologia Luxor-3412 1996 $250.00

HARDIE, JAMES   An Account of the Malignant Fever, Lately Prevalent in the City of New York. New York: 1799. 1st edition of Austin 877; thin 8vo; 139 pages + tables; original boards, rebacked in buckram, tips renewed, tear in title repaired, library stamps.   Argosy 810-226 1996 $500.00

HARDIE, MARTIN   The Etched Work of W. Lee-Hankey, R.E. from 1904-1920. London: L. H. Lefevre, n.d., c. 1920. Limited deluxe edition (no. 61 of 110); 30 x 23 cm; xiv, 97 pages; 187 illustrations, original etching as frontispiece signed by artist (1 of 110); new half morocco (heavy boards), edges uncut.   Rainsford A54-368 1996 £350.00

HARDIE, MARTIN   War Posters Issued by Belligerent and Neutral Nations 1914-1919. London: A. & C. Black, 1920. 1st edition; 80 images in color and black and white; green cloth pictorially stamped in black, red and gilt, corners bumped, spine expertly restored, else very good. Hermitage SP95-782 1996 $200.00

HARDIE, R. P.   The Roads of Mediaeval Lauderdale. London: Oliver and Boyd, 1942. 1st edition; tall 8vo; pages xv, 106; original cloth, gilt, dust jacket, edges darkened, uncut, folding map frontispiece.   R.F.G. Hollett 76-121 1996 £55.00

HARDIN, JOHN WESLEY   The Life of John Wesley Hardin, from the Original Manuscript Written by Himself. Seguin: 1896. 1st edition; 144 pages; illustrations; wrappers, usual foxing, covers fragile, better than most, added wrap slipcase; scarce; BTB 84. Adams 150 66; Six Guns 919.   Early West 22-28 1996 $250.00

HARDIN, JOHN WESLEY   The Life of John Wesley Hardin. Sequin: 1896. 1st edition; 144 pages; illustrations, pictorial wrappers, very good+. 6 Guns 919; Adams 150 66; Rader 1773. Howes H88.   T. A. Swinford 49-485 1996 $125.00

HARDING, CHESTER   My Egoistigraphy. Cambridge: privately printed, John Wilson and Son, 1866. 1st edition; 8vo; 185 pages; original cloth, slight waterstaining in front. Scarce. Sabin 30332.   M & S Rare Books 60-275 1996 $375.00

HARDING, GEORGE L.   Don Agustin V. Zamorano: Statesman, Soldier, Craftsman and California's First Printer. Los Angeles: Zamorano Club, 1934. 1st edition; although not indicated, limited to 325 copies; 308 pages, frontispiece, large folding map, numerous facsimiles; offsetting to 2 blank flyleaves from newspaper articles, otherwise fine with lightly soiled and slightly chipped dust jacket. From the collection of Edward Dean Lyman, with his card laid in.   Argonaut Book Shop 113-323 1996 $275.00

HARDING, GEORGE R.   The Acts and Orders Relating to Joint Stock Companies. Brisbane: Watson, Ferguson and Co., 1887. 1st edition; 8vo; xxviii, 239, (1) pages, final leaf of publisher's ads, occasional ink stamp (on title and elsewhere) of the Law Society; original cloth, paper spine label, label rubbed; presentation inscription by author in ink on titlepage. John Drury 82-101 1996 £75.00

HARDY, CAMPBELL   Sporting Adventures in the New World; or, Days and Nights of Moose Hunting in the Pine Forests of Acadia. London: Hurst and Blackett, 1855. 1st edition; 8 x 5 1/4 inches; 2 volumes; frontispiece in 3 colors in each volume; original cloth, elaborately blocked in blind, gilt stamp of a moose on front covers, gilt titling on spines; slightly cocked, one section of 4 leaves with stitching litle loose, bindings especially well preserved, cloth remarkably clean and smooth and joints and hinges virtually unworn, frontispieces lightly foxed, widely scattered traces of foxing elsewhere, but quite fine copy internally. 19th century armorial bookplate and shelf label in each volume. Schwerdt I 230; Sabin 30350.   Phillip J. Pirages 33-299 1996 $500.00

HARDY, CHARLES FREDERICK   The Hardys of Barbon and some Other Westmorland Statesman; Their Kith, Kin and Childer. London: Constable, 1913. 1st edition; 8vo; paes xv, 176; original green cloth, top edge gilt, map frontispiece and illustrations; original green cloth, gilt. R.F.G. Hollett & Son 78-169 1996 £50.00

HARDY, FLORENCE   All Change Here. The Story of a Seaside Trip. London: Humphrey Milford, n.d., ca. 1915. 1st edition; 50 pages; title in red, title vignette, 24 color plates and 24 text illustrations; light blue boards, extra color pictorial, light foxing on endpaper, boards very light wear. Exceptionally good.   Robin Greer 94A-55 1996 £85.00

HARDY, JOSEPH   A Picturesque and Descriptive Tour in the Mountains of the High Pyrenees...with some Account of the Bathing Establishments... London: Ackermann, 1825. 8vo; vii, 84 pages; engraved map, 24 hand colored aquatint plates mounted as drawings on thick paper; contemporary half roan. Fine copy. Abbey Travel 210; Tooley 245; Prideaux p. 229.   Marlborough 162-271 1996 £2,800.00

HARDY, THOMAS 1840-1928   A Changed Man. London: 1913. 1st edition; frontispiece, green cloth, gilt, very good.   Words Etcetera 94-565 196 £75.00

HARDY, THOMAS 1840-1928   The Dynasts. London: Macmillan and Co., 1904-06-08. 1st edition; volume 1 is second issue with cancel titlepage, the first issue had 1903 titlepage; volume 2 in second state and has a cancel titlepage as well, dated 106; the original was dated 1905; original cloth, dust jackets (somewhat frayed, worn and soiled); books little faded and worn, but generally in very good condition, together in two quarter morocco folding cases, along with good copy of the rare first issue of Volume 1 (lacking dust jacket) with the 1903 titlepage, blindstamped by publishers "Presentation Copy".   David J. Holmes 52-50 1996 $3,000.00

HARDY, THOMAS 1840-1928   The Dynasts. London: Macmillan and Co., 1927. One of 525 copies; printed on large paper, signed by author; large octavo; 3 volumes; frontispiece, signed by Francis Dodd; original quarter vellum over decorative boards, spines lettered in gilt, corners lightly rubbed, little light foxing, bookplate; near fine. Purdy pp. 134-135. Heritage Book Shop 196-189 1996 $750.00

HARDY, THOMAS 1840-1928   The Dynasts. London: Macmillan, 1927. One of 525 copies printed on large paper, signed by author; 11 x 8 inches; 3 volumes; frontispiece, signed in pencil by Francis Dodd, printed in red and black, volume 1 largely unopened; original vellum backed patterned boards, corner tips of two volumes very skillfully refurbished, very fine, spines unusually clean and bright.   Phillip J. Pirages 33-300 1996 $650.00

HARDY, THOMAS 1840-1928   Far From the Madding Crowd. Cambridge: Limited Editions Club, 1958. Limited to 1500 numbered copies, signed by artist; wood engravings by Agnes Miller Parker; brown calf backed patterned boards, very good in printed patterned board slipcase, which is rubbed along one upper edge; scarce.   Words Etcetera 94-944 1996 £135.00

HARDY, THOMAS 1840-1928   Far from the Madding Crowd. Cambridge: Limited Editions Club, 1958. One of 1500 numbered copies, signed by artist and inclues a signed additional plate laid in; engravings by Agnes Miller Parker; fine in publisher's slipcase.   Hermitage SP95-990 1996 $225.00

HARDY, THOMAS 1840-1928   Far from the Madding Crowd. New York: Limited Editions Club, 1958. One of 1500 numbered copies, signed by artist; 18 full page wood engravings and various wood engraved decorations by Agnes Miller Parker; loosely inserted is a copy of the wood engraving on page 5 of the book, signed and dated by artist, as called for; leather backed decorated paper boards; spine rubbed and faded, very good in slightly soiled and dusty matching slipcase, slightly soiled.   Ulysses 39-457 1996 £165.00

HARDY, THOMAS 1840-1928   A Group of Noble Dames. London: 1891. 1st edition; cloth, gilt, spine trifle faded, otherwise very good. Words Etcetera 94-560 1996 £65.00

HARDY, THOMAS 1840-1928   Human Shows Far Phantasies. London: Macmillan, 1925. 1st British edition; small 8vo; cloth in dust jacket; near fine, some foxing to endpapers, many pages unopened, some edgewear to dust jacket.   Antic Hay 101-772 1996 $100.00

HARDY, THOMAS 1840-1928   In Time of "The Breaking of Nations." N.P.: privately printed for Clement Shorter, 1st separate edition, limited to 25 copies; printed purple wrappers with slight fading; fine.   Bromer Booksellers 90-60 1996 $125.00

HARDY, THOMAS 1840-1928   An Indiscretion in the Life of an Heiress. London: privately printed, 1934. 1st book edition, limited to 100 copies (this copy unnumbered); 8vo; pages (vi), 90; original limp vellum, spine lettered in gilt, gilt edges; very nice in original black board slipcase; author's own copy from the library at Max Gate. Purdy pp. 274-76. Sotheran PN32-19 1996 £398.00

HARDY, THOMAS 1840-1928   Jude the Obscure. London: 1896. 1st edition; 1st issue with 'Osgood' on spine and title; green cloth, gilt, very good.   Words Etcetera 94-562 1996 £110.00

HARDY, THOMAS 1840-1928   Life's Little Ironies. London: Osgood, McIlvaine & Co., 1894. 1st edition; crown 8vo; viii, (368) pages; original decorative cloth, little rubbed, spine very slightly marked and sunned, somewhat shaken, few very minor marks, still good copy. Purdy p. 81. Ash Rare Books Zenzybyr-42 1996 £145.00

HARDY, THOMAS 1840-1928   The Mayor of Casterbridge: the Life and Death of a Man of Character. London: Smith, Elder and Co., 1886. 1st edition; of which 758 copies were published; 8vo; 2 volumes, pages (iv), 313, (3) blank, ads; (iv); 312 (4) ads, half titles; original blue cloth, decorated and lettered in black on upper covers, spines decorated in black and lettered in gilt, some wear, label removed from front pastedown of volume 2, very good. Purdy pp. 50-4; Sadleir 1111; Wolff 2983.   Simon Finch 24-102 1996 £2,800.00

HARDY, THOMAS 1840-1928   The Mayor of Casterbridge. New York: Heritage Press, 1964. 1st edition thus; wood engravings by Agnes Miller Parker; very good in slightly rubbed slipcase.   Words Etcetera 94-945 1996 £75.00

HARDY, THOMAS 1840-1928   Moments of Vision - and Miscellaneous Verses. London: Macmillan and Co. ltd., 1917. 1st edition; 254 pages; 4 pages publisher's ads at rear; original binding, head and tail of spine and corners slightly bumped, upper hinge cracked, edges slightly spotted, very good in tron, worn, chipped, frayed, marked and dusty, internally repaired dust jacket browned at spine and edges.   Ulysses 39-266 1996 £75.00

HARDY, THOMAS 1840-1928   Moments of Vision and Miscellaneous Verses. London: 1917. 1st edition; very good in heavily internally repaired dust jacket, inner upper hinge weak, otherwise very good.   Words Etcetera 94-567 1996 £75.00

HARDY, THOMAS 1840-1928   The Return of the Native. London: Macmillan & Co., 1929. One of 1500 copies signed by artist, this copy was one of 500 copies reserved for the U.K.; 13 full page wood engravings and wood engraved headpieces and tailpieces by Clare Leighton, frontispiece wood engraving is tipped in; parchment backed patterned paper boards, top edge gilt, tail of spine and bottom corners slightly bumped, cover edges very slightly faded, spine slightly browned, very good.   Ulysses 39-366 1996 £360.00

HARDY, THOMAS 1840-1928   The Return of the Native. New York: Heritage Press, 1942. 1st edition thus; wood engravings by Agnes Miller Parker; very good in rare dust jacket which is slightly rubbed along upper edges and on corners.   Words Etcetera 94-943 1996 £85.00

HARDY, THOMAS 1840-1928   Selected Poems. Riccardi Press for Philip Lee Warner, pub. to the Medici Society, 1921. One of 1000 paper copies for sale (there were also 14 copies printed on vellum); 9 1/4 x 6 3/4 inches; x, 144 pages, (2) leaves (colophon, device); tinted wood engraved frontispiece portrait and title vignette by William Nicholson, device on final leaf, extra paper labels tipped in at end; original holland backed blue paper boards, paper labels on front cover and spine, top edge gilt, other edges untrimmed, spine darkened (as usual), faint browning at edges of boards, but quite sound, clean copy, very fine internally. Tomkinson p. 153.   Phillip J. Pirages 33-448 1996 $250.00

HARDY, THOMAS 1840-1928   Tess of the D'Urbervilles a Pure Woman. London: James R. Osgood, McIlvaine and Co., 1891. 1st editio 1st issue, with all points listed by Purdy, of which 1000 copies were published; 8vo; 3 volumes; original tan cloth, honeysuckle gilt on upper covers, spine lettered in gilt, cloth folders in dark blue quarter morocco book form box, ruled and lettered in gilt, just a little slight wear, otherwise an excellent copy. Purdy pp. 67-78; Sadleir 1114; Wolff 2993. Simon Finch 24-105 1996 £5,000.00

HARDY, THOMAS 1840-1928   Tess of the D'Urbervilles a Pure Woman... London: James R. Osgood, McIlvaine and Co., 1891. 1st edition; 1st issue, with all points listed by Purdy of which 1000 copies were published; 8vo; 3 volumes; original tan cloth with honeysuckle gilt on upper covers, spines lettered in gilt, quite worn, label removed from two upper covers, spotted at fore-edges and occasionally elsewhere, new endpapers, otherwise very good; Purdy pp. 67-78; Sadleir 1114; Wolff 2993.   Simon Finch 24-106 1996 £2,400.00

HARDY, THOMAS 1840-1928   Tess of the D'Urbervilles. London: James R. Osgood, McIlvaine & Co., 1892. 1st edition; 2nd impression; 3/4 x 5 1/2 inches; 3 volumes; original light brown cloth with gilt design and titling by Charles Rickettes, evidences of bookplate removal in each volume, bindings slightly cocked, as ususal, two corners bit bumped, small stain on one cover, front free endpaper in each volume with faint darkened square, in all other ways an extraordinarily fine copy, remarkably clean inside and out, no wear to joints or hinges. Purdy p. 74.   Phillip J. Pirages 33-301 1996 $1,950.00

HARDY, THOMAS 1840-1928   Tess of the D'Urvervilles. London: James R. Osgood, McIlvaine and Co., 1892. 1st edition; 2nd issue; 8vo 3 volumes, half titles; original tan cloth with honeysuckle gilt on upper covers, spines lettered in gilt, small stain to one upper cover, bookplates removed, excellent fresh copy. Purdy pp. 67-78; Wolff 2993a Simon Finch 24-107 1996 £1,000.00

HARDY, THOMAS 1840-1928   Tess of the D'urbervilles. London: James R. Osgood, McIlvaine & Co., 1892. 1st edition; 2nd issue; 3 volumes; original gilt decorated covers, spine volume 1 slightly sunned, extremities little chipped, covers slightly soiled, otherwise fine set. Polyanthos 22-418 1996 $750.00

HARDY, THOMAS 1840-1928   Tess of the D'Urbervilles. London: James R. Osgood, McIlvaine & Co., 1892. 1st one volume edition, calle 'Fifth' edition; original decorated cloth, designed by Charles Rick!tts, covers little worn, spine trifle faded, else very good in attractive full morocco solander case (just bit worn); inscribed by author for Frederi Greenwood.   David J. Holmes 52-52 1996 $6,500.00

HARDY, THOMAS 1840-1928   Tess of the D'Urbervilles. London: 189 1st edition; 2nd issue dated 1892; 3 volumes, volume 1 appears to be lacking a flyleaf, otherwise this is a handsome set with spines bit dull but gilt on covers, still bright, corners a touch bumped, otherwise very good.   Words Etcetera 94-561 196 £450.00

HARDY, THOMAS 1840-1928   The Three Wayfarers: a Play in One A New York: Fountain Press, London: Cayme Press, 1930. One of 542 numbered copies, of which 500 were for sale; small 4to; pages (viii), 3 + colophon, 4 colored plates by William Cotton; original quarter dark re lambskin, cloth sides, titled in gilt on spine and upper cover, top edge gilt, others uncut; some foxing in text, but very good copy. This the author's copy from library at Max Gate. Purdy pp. 78-80.   Sotheran PN32-18 1996 £250.00

HARDY, THOMAS 1840-1928   The Three Wayfarers. Market Drayton; Tern Press, 1990-92. One of 125 copies; signed by Mary and Nicholas Parry; 9 x 7.75 inches; illustrations by Mary Parry, woodcuts in brown; printed in black in Italian Old Style type on T.H. Saunders papers; floral cloth covered boards.   Joshua Heller 21-248 1996 $105.00

HARDY, THOMAS 1840-1928   The Vineyards and Wine Cellars of California. San Francisco: Book Club of California, 1994. One of 450 copies; quarto; xxiii, (3), 64 pages, 12 high quality duotone reproductio of photos, 12 tipped in color reproductions of trade cards and wine labels; burgandy printed paper over boards, burgandy cloth spine, pap spine label, housed in slipcase of gray paper over light boards, mint. Argonaut Book Shop 113-324 1996 $250.00

HARDY, THOMAS 1840-1928   The Well Beloved. London: 1897. 1st edition; cloth gilt, head of spine neatly repaired, otherwise very good. Words Etcetera 94-564 196 £55.00

HARDY, THOMAS 1840-1928   Wessex Poems and Other Verses. Harper, 1898. 1st edition; crown 8vo; pages xi, 228; frontispiece, 12 other full page illustrations, 18 head and tailpieces by author, frontispie tissue guard, prelims and rear endpapers foxed; original fine ribbed da green cloth, backstrip lettering and Hardy emblem on front cover all g blocked, top edge gilt, others untrimmed excellent. Purdy p. 96 Blackwell's B112-145 1996 £300.00

HARDY, THOMAS 1840-1928 The Woodlanders. London: and New York: Macmillan, 1887. 1st edition; 8vo; 3 volumes, half titles; original dark green pebbled cloth, spines gilt, secondary binding without leaf of ads in volume 1, large bookplate, inner hinges in first volume cracked but excellent copy. Purdy pp. 54-57. Simon Finch 24-104 1996 £1,250.00

HARDY, THOMAS 1840-1928 The Woodlanders. London: and New York: Macmillan and Co., 1887. 1st edition; 8vo; 3 volumes; original dark green buckram grain cloth, ruled in black and blind on upper and lower covers respectively, spines lettered and decorated in gilt, primary binding without leaf of ads in volume 1, some wear, especially at foot of spines, label removed from front pastedown in volume 1, very good. Purdy pp. 54-57; Sadleir 1120; Wolff 3002. Simon Finch 24-103 1996 £1,000.00

HARDY, THOMAS 1840-1928 The Woodlanders. London: Macmillan and Co., 1887. 1st edition; 8vo; 3 volumes; half titles in each volume, ad leaf end of volume 1; original dark green cloth blocked in blind and in black on covers, lettered gilt on spines, dark brown endpapers, signs of library label removal from lower half of each upper cover, some spotting on covers and fore-edges of both upper and lower cover of volume 2 slightly discolored by damp, very slight wear at head and foot of spines. Purdy p. 54. David Bickersteth 133-151 1996 £580.00

HARDY, THOMAS 1840-1928 The Woodlanders. London: Macmillan and Son, 1887. 1st edition; 8vo; 3 volumes, half title to each volume, 2 pages of publisher's ads in volume 1, finely bound in half crimson morocco, two line gilt borders, gilt panelled spines, top edge gilt by Root & Son. Purdy p. 54; Sadlier 1120. Charles W. Traylen 117-128 1996 £485.00

HARE, AUGUSTUS J. C. Life and Letters of Frances Bunsen, Baroness. London: 1879. 1st edition; small 8vo; 2 volumes; choicely bound in three quarter blue levant morocco, gilt panelled spines, gilt tops; from the library of Andrew Carnegie. Charles W. Traylen 117-79 1996 £65.00

HARE, AUGUSTUS J. C. The Story of My Life. London: George Allen, 1896. 1st edition; 8vo; frontispiece in each volume, plates, illustrations in letterpress, half titles; original black buckram, backstrip gilt lettered, red bands at head and tail, continued around head and tail of sides, gilt coat of arms on front cover, occasional small mark, black endpapers, generally very good. Blackwell's B112-146 1996 £75.00

HARE, AUGUSTUS J. C. The Story of Two Noble Lives, Being Memorials of Charlotte, Countess of Canning and Louisa, Marchioness of Waterford. London: George Allen, 1893. 1st edition; 8vo; pages x, 381, (3 blank); (8), 489; viii, 495; 3 volumes; original binding, gilt, very good to nice copy. GM 1604.1. James Fenning 133-48 1996 £145.00

HARE, FRANCIS The Conduct of the Duke of Marlborough During the Present War. London: printed in the Year 1712. 1st edition; 8vo; contemporary calf, rather worn, spine rubbed. Peter Murray Hill 185-69 1996 £50.00

HARFORD, JOHN S. The Life of Michael Angelo Buonarroti: With Translations of Many of His Poems and Letters, also, Memoirs of Savonarola, Raphael and Vittoria Colonna. London: Longman, Brown, Green, Longmans and Roberts, 1857. 1st edition; 8vo; 2 volumes, 342, 24 page publisher's catalog; plates; 367 pages, plates; original green cloth, minor wear, tiny bruise on spine, very good. Robert F. Lucas 42-54 1996 $125.00

HARGRAVE, CATHERINE PERRY A History of Playing Cards and Bibliography of Cards and Gaming. Boston: 1930. 1st edition; 4to; (26), 468 pages; profusely illustrated in color and black and white; original cloth. Edward Morrill 368-531 1996 $185.00

HARGRAVE, FRANCIS A Collection of Tracts Relative to the Law of England, from Manuscripts. Dublin: printed for E. Lynch, G. Burnet, W. Wilson et al, 1787. contemporary calf, rebacked, good, clean copy. Meyer Boswell SL26-101 1996 $450.00

HARGRAVE, FRANCIS A Collection of Tracts Relative to the Law of England, from Manuscripts.. London: printed by T. Wright..., 1787. 1st edition; 4to; pages (6), lii, 578, errata leaf; contemporary calf, gilt, headband and corner of label worn, lower joint cracked, but binding very strong, otherwise nice copy; attractive armorial bookplate of Redmond Barry. James Fenning 133-151 1996 £245.00

HARGROVE, E. Anecdotes of Archery from the Earliest Ages to the Year 1791. London: 1845. Revised edition; 5 plates of 6; original pictorial gilt cloth, slight rubbing and top of spine frayed, inner front hinge sprung, contents excellent. David A.H. Grayling 3/95-153 1996 £150.00

HARGROVE, E. The History of the Castle, Town and Forest of Knaresborough with Harrogate and Its Medicinal Waters. York: printed by W. Blanchard, 1789. 4th edition; 12mo; iv, 330 pages; illustrations, folding map; rebound in 19th century half leather, boards, raised bands, top edge gilt. Cox III p. 212. David Mason 71-21 1996 $260.00

HARINGTON, JOHN The Metamorphosis of Ajax. London: Fanfrolico Press, 1927. Number 409 of 450 copies; large 8vo; pages xxviii, (4), 144; printed in Poliphilus types on handmade paper at Westminster Press; uncut, original decorated boards, backstrip slightly darkened. Very good. Ransom 8. Claude Cox 107-54 1996 £65.00

HARLAN, RICHARD Fauna Americana: Being a Description of the Mammiferous Animals Inhabiting North America. Philadelphia: Finley, 1825. 1st edition; 8vo; pages 318, ii; contemporary calf, cover separate, light foxing, very good. Imprints 20815. Second Life Books 103-101 1996 $350.00

HARLAN, ROBERT D. The Two Hundredth Book. A Bibliography of the Books Published by the Book Club of California 1958-1993. San Francisco: Book Club of California, 1993. 1st edition; limited to 500 copies; folio; x, (2), 62 pages; reproductions in color, one insert; title, initial letters and colophon in red and black, marginal notes, dates, decorations and plate numbers in red; tan, black and yellow green decorated boards, linen back, paper spine label lettered in black; very fine. Argonaut Book Shop 113-326 1996 $250.00

HARLAN, ROBERT J. The Two Hundredth Book: a Bibliography of the Books Published by the Book Club of California 1958-1993. San Francisco: Book Club of California, 1993. One of 500 copies; folio; 6 facsimiles, one insert; patterned boards, half cloth; fine. Bertram Rota 272-53 1996 £150.00

HARLEY, DEE Mean as Hell. Albuquerque: 1948. 1st edition; 224 pages; illustrations; nice in dust jacket. 6 Guns 922; Herd 993; Dykes 386. T. A. Swinford 49-486 1996 $100.00

HARLOW, ALVIN Old Waybills: The Romance of the Express Companies. New York: D. Appleton Century, 1934. 1st edition; xii, (2), 504 pages; profusely illustrated; minor spot to front cover, spine slightly faded, overall fine. scarce. Argonaut Book Shop 113-327 1996 $125.00

HARLOW, NEAL Maps and Surveys of the Pueblo Lands of Los Angeles. Los Angeles: Dawson's, 1976. 1st edition; limited to 375 copies; this copy signed by author; 4to; xviii, 169 pages, 14 plates, (mostly folding, two laid into rear pocket); cloth backed decorated boards, gilt lettered spine, very fine. Argonaut Book Shop 113-328 1996 $350.00

HARMAN, JOHN N. Harman Genealogy (Southern Branch) with Biographical Sketches 1700-1924. Richmond: 1925. 1st edition; 376 pages; 2 volumes; front inner joint reglued, ex-library. Bookworm & Silverfish 280-93 1996 $125.00

HARMETZ, ALJEAN The Making of the Wizard of Oz. New York: Knopf, 1977. 1st edition; 8vo; 18 color and 75 black and white illustrations; very good in dust jacket. George J. Houle 68-12 1996 $100.00

HARNEY, GEORGE E. Stables, Outbuildings and Fences. New York: Geo. E. Woodward, 1870. 1st edition; 4to; (vi), 90 pages; 62 plates; publisher's cloth, front inner hinge strengthened, covers rubbed, some wear along spine, rubberstamp on endpapers and titlepage, still clean, respectable copy, scarce. Bookpress 75-60 1996 $750.00

HAROLD Patrick McGrath. Cheloniidae Press, 1991. One of 100 copies, of a total edition of 210; 11 1/4 x 8 1/4 inches; (48) leaves (including one blank); printed in red and black on different kinds of papers; frontispiece and many woodcut illustrations, color photos of McGrath in sleeve at back; marbled paper boards with leather tips, paper labels on front cover and spine; marbled paper boards with leather tips, paper labels on front cover and spine; mint. Phillip J. Pirages 33-124 1996 $675.00

HARPER, CHARLES G. The Hastings Road and the "Happy Springs of Tunbridge". London: 1906. 1st edition; 8vo; 287 pages; 18 plates and many illustrations; original ochre cloth, blocked and lettered in black; nice. Howes Bookshop 265-2158 1996 £50.00

HARPER, CHARLES G. The Old Inns of Old England. London: Chapman and Hall, 1906. 1st edition; 8vo; 2 volumes, pages xv, 327; xi, 316; 238 full page and other illustrations; original red cloth, top edge gilt, very good to nice. James Fenning 133-152 1996 £115.00

HARPER, CHARLES G.   The Oxford, Gloucester and Milford Haven Road; the Ready Way to South Wales. London: Chapman & Hall, 1905. 1st edition; 8vo; 2 volumes; 38 plates and 89 text illustrations; original blue pictorial cloth.   Howes Bookshop 265-464 1996 £75.00

HARPER, J. R.   Portrait of a Period: a Collection of Notman Photos 1856-1915. Montreal: 1967. 1st edition; large folio; well illustrated, dust jacket slightly rubbed.   J. B. Muns 154-221 1996 $275.00

HARPER, LATHROP   A Selection of Incunabula from Over 150 Presses...Part I (-Part V with index) ... for Sale by Lathrop C. Harper. New York: Lathrop C. Harper, 1927-30. 8vo; 5 parts, frontispieces; original printed wrappers.   Forest Books 74-120 1996 £95.00

HARRING, HARRO   Dolores: a Novel of South America. New York: author: Motevideo: Hernandez; New York: Marrenner, Lockwood, 1846. 4to; 4 parts as issued; front printed wrappers on parts 2-4, browned and stained; extremely rare in original parts; presentation inscription from author to Capt. Robert Griswold. Rostenberg & Stern, Connections 108-9. Rostenberg & Stern 150-20 1996 $875.00

HARRINGTON, CHARLES E.   Summering in Colroado. Denver: Richards & Co., 1874. 1st edition; 158 pages; (4) pages ads, 10 original mounted photographic plates, original brown cloth, title in gilt on front cover, minor wear, fine. Not in Howes or Graff; Allen Col. Imprints 223. Adams Herd 534.   Michael D. Heaston 23-101 1996 $550.00

HARRINGTON, H. NAZEBY   The Engraved Work of Sir Francis Seymour Haden, P.R.E. Liverpool: Henry Young, 1910. Limited edition of 225 copies; 29 x 24 cm; xxiv, 125 pages, 108 plates and frontispiece; original cloth, top edge gilt, foxed.   Rainsford A54-299 1996 £140.00

HARRINGTON, JAMES 1611-1677   The Rota; or, a Model of a Free-State, or Equall Common-Wealth: Once Proposed and Debated in Brief and to be Again More at Larage Proposed To, and Debated by a Free and Open Society of Ingenious Gentlemen. London: for John Starkey, 1660. 1st edition; 4to; (ii), 29, (1) pages, recently well bound in calf backed marbled boards, spine gilt with raised band, slight paper, browning, else very good. Wing H821; Goldsmiths 1558; Kress 1026. John Drury 82-103 1996 £950.00

HARRINGTON, JOHN P.   Exploration of the Burton Mound at Santa Barbara Social and Religious Beliefs and Usages of the Chickasaw Indians, Uses of Plants by the Chippewa Indians. Washington: GPO, 1928. vii, 555 pages; 98 plates, 16 figures; spine faded, else very good. Parmer Books Nat/Hist-073259 1996 $145.00

HARRIS, A. C.   Alaska andd the Klondike Gold Fields... Philadelphia?: J. R. Jones, c. 1897. 21cm; xi, 17-556 pages; frontispiece, illustrations, maps; fine with slight scuff on bottom front cover; Arctic 6683. Rockland Books 38-94 1996 $125.00

HARRIS, ALBERT   The Blood of the Arab. Chicago: 1941. 1st edition; 4to; original binding, shelfwear.   October Farm 36-34 1996 $125.00

HARRIS, C. FISKE   Catalogue of American Poetry, Compriling Duplicates from the Collection of the Late... Providence: 1883. 1st edition; square 16mo; 83 pages; original plain back wrapper, lacking front wrapper, light waterstaining throughout.   M & S Rare Books 60-164 1996 $125.00

HARRIS, HENRY   California's Medical Story. Springfield: 1932. 1st edition; 421 pages; original binding, ex-library.   W. Bruce Fye 71-925 1996 $125.00

HARRIS, JAMES 1709-1780   Hermes or a Philosophical Inquiry Concerning Universal Grammar. London: printed for F. Wingrave, successor to Mr. Nourse, 1794. 5th edition; frontispiece; contemporary tree calf, gilt spine and borders, black label, very good. Alston III.815. Jarndyce 103-256 1996 £75.00

HARRIS, JAMES 1709-1780   Three Treatises. The First Concerning Art. The Second Concerning Music, painting and Poetry. The Third Concerning Happiness... London: H. Woodfall Jun., for J. Nourse and P. Vaillant, 1744. 1st edition; 8vo; (iv), 357, (i) pages; contemporary calf, spine gilt, label, K3, S4 cancels as usual, rubbed, slight wear to corners and joints, spine ends slightly chipped, some foxing, good copy.   Robert Clark 38-177 1996 £120.00

HARRIS, JOEL CHANDLER 1848-1908   Mr. Rabbit at Home. Boston: Houghton Mifflin Co., 1896. Octavo; (4), iv, (5)-304 pages; 25 plates; original tan cloth pictorially stamped in brown and green and lettered in gilt on front cover and stamped in brown on back cover and spine; signed by author.   Heritage Book Shop 196-269 1996 $500.00

HARRIS, JOEL CHANDLER 1848-1908   Uncle Remus His Songs and Sayings. New York: Appleton, 1896. Early edition (first was 1895); 12 illustrations by A. B. Frost; decorated red cloth, top edge gilt; fine, this copy has the rare dust jacket which mirrors the designs on the binding, dust jacket lightly chipped.   Captain's Bookshelf 38-97 1996 $150.00

HARRIS, JOHN   Hofer, The Tyrolese. London: Harris & Son, 1824. 1st edition; xi, 155 pages; frontispiece with 2 illustrations, title vignette, 10 illustrations on 5 plates; quarter red calf, printed boards, offsetting, stain 1 plate, boards worn.   Robin Greer 94A-44 1996 £65.00

HARRIS, MOSES   An Exposition of English Insects, Including Several Classes of Neuroptera, Hymenoptera and Diptera... London: 1782. 2nd edition; 4to; text in English and French; pages viii, 9-166, (iv), engraved titlepage, hand colored frontispiece, one plain and 50 hand colored copper engravings; contemporary calf, rubbed, gilt, rebacked preserving spine.   John Henly 27-58 1996 £600.00

HARRIS, N. SAYRE   Journal of a Tour in the 'Indian Territory', Performed by Order of the Domestic Committee of the Board of Missions of the Protestant Episcopal Church... New York: published for the Domestic Committee of the Board of Missions, 1844. 1st edition; 74 pages, 3 maps; titlepage silked; half calf, marbled boards; very good. Field 806; Becker Wagner Camp 109; Graff 1794; Streeter Sale 555. Michael D. Heaston 23-168 1996 $1,200.00

HARRIS, R. C.   Report to the Civic Transportation Committee on Radial Railway Entrances and Rapid Transit for the City of Toronto. Toronto: 1915. 4to; Volume I (of 2); pages (v), 89, maps and diagrams; stiff paper covers, perfect binding with staples, covers dusty, interior fine.   Hugh Anson-Cartwright 87-418 1996 $100.00

HARRIS, SARAH HOLLISTER   An Unwritten Chapter of Salt Lake 1851-1901. New York: printed privately, 1901. (1) pages; gree cloth with gilt stamping, gilt top; very good overall, light rubbing and etching. Howes H231; Graff 1795; flake 3867; Mintz 213.   Bohling Boo Co. 191-775 1996 $400.00

HARRIS, THADDEUS MASON   Constitutions of the Ancient and Honorable Fraternity of Free and Accepted Masons... Worcester: Isaiah Thomas, 1798. 1st edition; 4to; (8), 288 pages; fine large engraved frontispiece; contemporary calf, leather label, hinges very weark, binding rubbed, frontispiece offset on title, otherwise very clean.   M & S Rare Books 60-368 1996 $650.00

HARRIS, THADDEUS MASON   The Minor Encyclopedia, or Cabinet of General Knowledge. Boston: printed for West & Greenleaf, by Manning Loring, 1803. 1st edition; 12mo; 4 volumes; contemporary tree sheep, neatly rebacked to stype with gilt spines and red morocco labels, edge stained yellow, light foxing and browning; very good. Shaw and Shoemaker 4340.   Heritage Book Shop 196-228 1996 $750.00

HARRIS, W. CORNWALLIS   Adventures in Africa; During a Tour of Two Years through that Country. Philadelphia: T. B. Peterson, n.d. 8vo; xii, (13)-392 pages; brown embossed cloth, gilt spine titles; text foxed, some places heavily so; cloth worn, especially at perimeter of spine. Parmer Books Nat/Hist-065274 1996 $200.00

HARRIS, W. CORNWALLIS   Portraits of the Game and Wild Animals o Southern Africa. Cape Town: 1969. Reprint; large 4to; large folding colored plates, text engravings; near fine in frayed dust jacket.   David Grayling J95Biggame-98 1996 £95.00

THE HARRISON Almanac 1841. New York: J. P. Giffin, c. 1840. Unpaginated, 18 leaves; 13 woodcuts; original sewn wrappers, chipped at edges. Miles 92.   Blue River Books 9-62 1996 $125.00

HARRISON Melodies. Boston: Weeks, Jordan & Co., 1840. 72 pages; original printed wrappers with portrait of Harrison on front cover, lackin back wrapper, foxing; scarce.   Blue River Books 9-63 1996 $125.00

HARRISON, EVELYN   Archaic and Archaistic Sculpture. Princeton: American School of Classical Studies at Athens, 1965. Folio; xx, 194 pages, 68 plates; original cloth; bookplate.   Archaeologia Luxor-3414 1996 $250.00

HARRISON, EVELYN   Portrait Sculpture. Princeton: ASCSA, 1953. 4to; xlv, 114 pages, 49 plates; spine lightly faded.   Archaeologia Luxor-3415   1996 $350.00

HARRISON, FAIRFAX   Landmarks of Old Prince William: a Study of Origins in Northern Virginia... Richmond: 1924. 2 volumes, pocket map not present; ex-library, paper labels worn.   Bookworm & Silverfish 280-264   1996 $125.00

HARRISON, FREDERIC   Annals of an Old Manor-House. Sutton Place, Guildford: Macmillan & Co., 1893. 4to; xviii, 231 pages; 67 plates, wood engraved head and tailpieces; original dark blue buckram, gilt, edges uncut, very slightly worn, spine faded, nice, fresh copy internally. Thomas Thorp   489-295   1996 £95.00

HARRISON, FREDERIC   Annals of an Old Manor-House. Sutton Place, Guildford Surrey. London: Macmillan, 1899. 8vo; pages xi, 2 ff., 248 pages, 1 f., frontispiece and text vignettes; original gilt lettered green cloth, little worn, first gathering loose.   Marlborough 162-38   1996 £65.00

HARRISON, GEORGE   Fifty Years Adrift. London: Genesis Publications, 1984. Limited to 2000 copies, signed by Harrison and Taylor; photos; all edges gilt, half calf, morocco title label, spine very lightly rubbed, otherwise fine in slipcase.   Words Etcetera 94-128   1996 £150.00

HARRISON, H.   Bill, the Galactic Hero. New York: Doubleday, 1965. 1st edition; review copy with accompanying review slip laid in; signed by author; fine in very good+ dust jacket with some slight scraping to dust jacket spine.   Aronovitz 57-505   1996 $125.00

HARRISON, H.   Make Room! Make Room! New York: Doubleday, 1966. 1st edition; signed by author; fine in fine dust jacket.   Aronovitz 57-507   1996 $225.00

HARRISON, J. M.   The Birds of Kent. London: 1953. demy 4to; 2 volumes; many colored and other plates; very fine in dust jackets. David A.H. Grayling   MY95Orn-39   1996 £140.00

HARRISON, JAMES   The Biographical Cabinet. London: printed for Sherwood, Jones and Co., 1823. 1st edition; octavo; 2 volumes; 192 small oval stipple engravings; contemporary polished speckled calf, gilt triple rule border on covers, gilt spine, tooled in compartments, red and green calf labels, gilt board edges and turn-in, all edges gilt, edges stained yellow, marbled endpapers, light wear to extremities, hinges just starting, intermittent light foxing and browning, bookplate, overall near fine.   Heritage Book Shop 196-229   1996 $600.00

HARRISON, JIM   Farmer. New York: Viking, 1976. 1st edition; fine in dust jacket, author's second novel.   Between the Covers 42-202a 1996 $150.00

HARRISON, JIM   Farmer. New York: 1976. 1st edition; signed by Harrison with the disclaimer that he rarely signs books, very fine in dust jacket.   Bev Chaney, Jr.   23-299   1996 $145.00

HARRISON, JIM   Farmer. New York: Viking, 1979. 1st edition; very near fine in dust jacket, signed by author.   Lame Duck Books   19-233 1996 $250.00

HARRISON, JIM   A Good Day to Die. New York: Simon & Schuster, 1973. 1st edition; fine in fine dust jacket and is signed by author, without remainder mark usually found. Scarce.   Ken Lopez   74-178 1996 $500.00

HARRISON, JIM   Julip. Boston: Houghton Mifflin/Lawrence, 1994. 1st edition; limited to 200 signed copies, numbered; fine in slipcase.   Bev Chaney, Jr.   23-301   1996 $100.00

HARRISON, JIM   Just Before Dark. Livingston: Clark City Press, 1991. Uncorrected proof; signed by author and artist; illustrations by Russell Chatham; glossy illustrated wrappers; fine.   Lame Duck Books   19-236 1996 $200.00

HARRISON, JIM   Just Before Dark. Collected Nonfiction. Livingston: Clark City Press, 1991. 1st edition; one of 26 copies, signed by author, containing 2 small original prints, signed by Russell Chatham, out of a total edition of 250 signed copies; 8vo; cloth backed marbled boards, cloth slipcase; new.   James S. Jaffe   34-204   1996 $350.00

HARRISON, JIM   Just Before Dark. Livingston: Clark City Press, 1991. 1/250 copies, signed; fine in slipcase.   Bev Chaney, Jr.   23-302   1996 $150.00

HARRISON, JIM   Just Before Dark. Livingston: Clark City, 1991. 1st edition; illustrations by Russell Chatham; quarterbound in cloth and marbled paper boards, fine in fine slipcase, signed by author.   Ken Lopez   74-180   1996 $150.00

HARRISON, JIM   Just Before Dark. Livingston; Clark City, 1991. One of 26 lettered copies, signed by author, with 2 original numbered etchings by Chatham laid in; half cloth and paper covered boards, acetate protector, publisher's cloth covered slipcase.   Lame Duck Books 19-237   1996 $500.00

HARRISON, JIM   Legends of the Fall. New York: Delacorte Press/Seymour Lawrence, 1979. Uncorrected proof copy, 8vo; red printed wrappers; fine.   James S. Jaffe   34-203   1996 $350.00

HARRISON, JIM   Legends of the Fall. New York: Delacorte, 1979. 1st edition; light foxing to fore-edge, faint remainder mark to bottom edge, else near fine in dust jacket; signed by author.   Lame Duck Books 19-234   1996 $150.00

HARRISON, JIM   New and Selected Poems 1961-1981. New York: Delacorte, 1982. One of 250 specially bound copies, numbered and signed by author; original cloth, fine, slipcase.   Beasley Books 82-74 1996 $200.00

HARRISON, JIM   The Raw and the Cooked. New York: Dim Gray Bar, 1992. Limited edition, of a total edition of 126, this one of 26 lettered copies; quarter bound in leather and handmade paper infused with garlic and herbs, signed by author. Fine.   Ken Lopez   74-181   1996 $350.00

HARRISON, JIM   The Raw and the Cooked. New York: Dim Gray Bar, 1992. One of 100 numbered copies; signed by author; quarter bound in cloth and paper covered boards; fine.   Ken Lopez   74-182   1996 $125.00

HARRISON, JIM   Selected and New Poems. New York: Delacorte, 1982. Uncorrected proof, signed by Harrion, printed grey wrappers; fine. Thomas Dorn   9-134   1996 $195.00

HARRISON, JIM   Selected and New Poems. New York: Delacorte/Seymour Lawrence, 1982. One of 250 numbered copies, signed by author; drawings by Russell Chatham; fine in slipcase.   Between the Covers   42-203   1996 $200.00

HARRISON, JIM   The Theory and Practice of Rivers. Seattle: Winn Books, 1986. Limited first edition, one of 350 copies, signed by author; 53 pages; illustrations by Russell Chatham; green cloth spine, ivory cloth boards in cloth slipcase; beautiful production.   Orpheus Books 17-155 1996 $125.00

HARRISON, JIM   The Theory and Practice of Rivers. Seattle: Winn Books, 1986. True 1st edition; illustrations by Russell Chatham; fine in slipcase, signed by author.   Bella Luna 7-270   1996 $100.00

HARRISON, JIM   Warlock. New York: Delacorte 1981. Uncorrected proof; printed yellow wrappers; fine, signed by author.   Thomas Dorn 9-133   1996 $175.00

HARRISON, JIM   Warlock. New York: Delacorte/Lawrence, 1981. Limited edition, one of 250 numbered copies, signed by author; clothbound, all edges gilt, fine in fine slipcase.   Ken Lopez   74-179 1996 $250.00

HARRISON, JIM   Warlock. New York: Delacorte, 1981. One of 250 specially bound copies, numbered and signed by author; original cloth, fine in slipcase.   Beasley Books   82-73   1996 $150.00

HARRISON, JIM   Warlock. New York: Delacorte, 1981. 1st edition; near fine in price clipped dust jacket, signed by author.   Lame Duck Books   19-235   1996 $150.00

HARRISON, JIM   Wolf. New York: Simon & Schuster, 1971. 1st edition; very fine in fine dust jacket, without ubiquitous remainder line, exceptional copy, scarce.   Ken Lopez   74-177   1996 $400.00

HARRISON, JOHN W., MRS.   A. M. Mackay, Pioneer Missionary of the Church Missionary Society to Uganda. London: Hodder & Stoughton, 1890. 1st edition; post 8vo; viii, 488 pages; original cloth, gilt, few very slight marks and bumps, nonetheless very good.   Ash Rare Books Zenzybyr-43   1996 £95.00

HARRISON, JOSEPH   The Accomplish'd Practiser in the High Court of Chancery... London: printed by A. Strahan and W. Woodfall, etc., 1790. 7th edition; 2 volumes; later cloth, bit dusty, but generally good, clean set.   Meyer Boswell SL26-102   1996 $350.00

HARRISON, TONY   Bo Down. London: Rex Collings, 1977. 1st edition; wrappers; covers marked and slightly soiled, cover edges browned, corners slightly bumped; very good; presentation copy from author, inscribed on titlepage by author.   Ulysses   39-273   1996 £95.00

HARRISON, TONY   Earthworks. Leeds: Northern House Pamphlet Poets, 1964. 1st edition; wrappers; covers slightly marked and dusty and very slightly creased, cover edges very slightly browned, very good copy of author's first book.   Ulysses 39-267 1996 £55.00

HARRISON, TONY   A Kumquat for John Keats. Newcastle-upon-Tyne: Bloodaxe Books, 1981. One of 25 numbered copies, signed by author; original binding, bottom edge of upper cover slightly faded and marked, very good.   Ulysses 39-274 1996 £85.00

HARRISON, TONY   The Loiners. London: London Magazine Editions, 1970. 1st edition; original binding, head and tail of spine and corners slightly bumped, very good in slightly marked and very slightly creased dust jacket rubbed at head of spine; presentation copy from author. Ulysses 39-268 1996 £150.00

HARRISON, TONY   The Loiners. London: London Magazine Editions, 1970. 1st edition; original binding, head of spine slightly bumped, very good in nicked and slightly rubbed and dusty dust jacket slightly torn and creased at head of spine; bookplate of literary agent John Johnson. Ulysses 39-269 1996 £55.00

HARRISON, WALTER   A New and Universal History, Description and Survey of the Cities of London and Westminster. London: Cooke, 1775. Folio; 720 pages; frontispiece, 101 plates; contemporary half calf, very worn. Internally clean and crisp; Adams 57.   Marlborough 162-150 1996 £850.00

HARRISSE, HENRY   Christopher Columbus and the Bank of Saint George: Two Letters Addressed to Samuel L. M. Barlow, Esquire. New York: privately printed, 1888. 1st edition; one of 150 copies; 12 1/2 x 10 inches; quarter leather over boards, front hinges cracked, boards and spine rubbed, bottom of spine torn and crinkled, still not a bad copy, very scarce. This copy inscribed by Samuel Barlow.   Hermitage SP95-1103 1996 $250.00

HARROD, W.   The History of Mansfield. The History of Mansfield and it's (sic) Environs. Mansfield: printed and sold by it's (sic) author, 1801. 4to; title, 2 ff., 64, 53 pages, 1 f., frontispiece and 16 engraved plates or plans, 1 hand colored folding plate; later half green morocco, top edge gilt; scarce.   Marlborough 162-39 1996 £380.00

HART, J. COLEMAN   Designs for Parish Churches, in the Three Styles of English Architecture. New York: Dana and Co., 1857. 1st edition; 4to; 111 pages, 42 plates, publisher's cloth, top edge gilt; scarce, front hinge internally cracked, inscription in ink on titlepage, text foxed.   Bookpress 75-61 1996 $425.00

HART, JAMES D.   Fine Printing in California. Berkeley: Tamalpais Press, 1960. 1st edition; limited to 100 copies; (4), 26 pages, printed in orange and black, numerous text illustrations; cloth backed decorated boards, printed paper label; fine. Very scarce.   Argonaut Book Shop 113-330 1996 $150.00

HART, JAMES D.   An Original Leaf from the First Edition of Alexander Barclay's English Translation of Sebastian Brant's 'Ship of Fools' Printed by Richard Pynson in 1509. San Francisco: David Magee, 1938. An edition of 260, this is one of 115 of the preferred edition, containing an original leaf bearing a woodcut; quarto; (2)ff., 15 pages; color printed facsimiles of woodcut fools in Pynson 1509 edition; buckram backed printed boards, paper label to spine. Very fine. Heller & Magee 300; Harlan 300.   Bromer Booksellers 87-167 1996 $750.00

HART, JAMES D.   An Original leaf from the First Edition of Alexander Barclay's English translation of Sebastian Grant's "Ship of Fools", printed by Richard Pynson in 1509. San Francisco: printed for David Magee by the Grabhorn Press, 1938. One of 260 copies, this copy being one of 115 copies, with an original leaf bearing a woodcut; printed in Deepdene text on heavy American mould made paper; cloth backed decorated paper boards, top edge slightly dusty, covers very slightly marked, cloth spine very slightly soiled, very good; loosely inserted also is the prospectus for this book; Hart's own copy, loosely inserted ALS from Magee to Hart.   Ulysses 39-357 1996 £385.00

HART, JULIA C.   Tonnewonte, or the Adopted son of America. Exeter B. H. Meder, 1831. 16mo; 312 pages; full contemporary calf, rubbed, lacks front endleaves, small hole in one leaf affecting a few letters; B&B 7459. Lande 1824; Sabin 96169.   M & S Rare Books 60-130 1996 $450.00

HART, WILLIAM H.   Historia et Cartularium Monasterii S. Petri Gloucestriae. London: 1863-67. 8vo; 2 volumes; original cloth.   Howes Bookshop 265-1577 1996 £85.00

HART, WILLIAM S.   My Life East and West. Boston: 1929. 1st edition; 362 pages; illustrations; cloth, bookplate, slight fading to backstrip and part of front cover, otherwise fine. Herd 1005; 6 Guns 940 Gene W. Baade 1094-72 1996 $100.00

HART, WILLIAM S.   My Life East and West. New York: 1929. Probably second edition; 363 pages; photos; cloth covers nice and bright; inscribed by author.   Early West 22-37 1996 $350.00

HART, WILLIAM S.   The Order of Chanta Sutas. A Ritual. Hollywood: 1925. 1st edition; 98 pages; illustrations; leather cover worn, book fine. Early West 22-444 1996 $150.00

HART-DAVIS, RUPERT   Edmund Blunden - 1896-1974 - an Address. London: 1974. One of 75 copies; wrappers; very good; inscribed presentation from author, apparently to John Carter.   Ulysses 39-275 1996 £125.00

HARTE, BRET 1836-1902   Fac-Simile of the Original Manuscript of the Heathen Chinee, as Written for the Overland Monthly... San Francisco: John H. Carmany & Co., 1871. 1st facsimile edition; 9 leaves (1 blank), printed and lithographed on one side only; original printed wrappers; very scarce; from the collection of bibliographer Robert Ernest Cowan, with his bookplate. BAL 7248J; Cowan p. 266.   Argonaut Book Shop 113-333 1996 $225.00

HARTE, BRET 1836-1902   The Luck of Roaring Camp and Other Sketches. Boston: James R. Osgood and Co., 1872. 1st illustrated edition; folio; 75 pages, 6 plates, tiny tear to front edge of several leaves; green cloth, bumped, quite rubbed, rebacked with new spine and gilt lettered black leather label, titled with vignettes in gilt within decorative blind frames on front cover, all edges gilt, new endpapers; good; mounted to front pastedown is rare photographic CDV of Bret Harte (torn horizontally, signed in ink by Harte.   Blue Mountain SP95-65 1996 $375.00

HARTE, BRET 1836-1902   A Millionaire of Rough-and-Ready. Kentfield: the L-D Allen Press, 1955. Limited to 220 copies; 110 pages; printed in colors; printed on all-rag paper. bound in two contrasting brown Oriental papers, lettered and decorated in gold; very fine. Allen Press 16. Argonaut Book Shop 113-334 1996 $250.00

HARTE, BRET 1836-1902   Outcroppings: Being Selections of California Verse. San Francisco: and New York: A. Roman and Co., and W. J. Widdleton, 1866. 1st edition; 6 1/2 x 5 inches; 144 pages; gold stamped purple cloth, binding coated with glaze by a later owner. BAL 7238. Dawson's Books Shop 528-104 1996 $250.00

HARTE, BRET 1836-1902   The Queen of Pirate Isle. London: Chatto & Windus, 1866. 1st edition; illustrations by Kate Greenaway; buckram decoratively stamped in colors and gilt, green endpapers, light overall soiling, else near fine and pleasing copy.   Hermitage SP95-899 1996 $200.00

HARTE, BRET 1836-1902   The Queen of the Pirate Isle. London: Chatto & Windus, n.d. 1886. 1st edition; square octavo; 58 pages; 28 colored illustrations; original beige cloth stamped in gilt and black with covers pictorially stamped in colors, all edges gilt, blue endpapers, light shelfwear, near fine. BAL 7337; Osborne I p. 350; Schuster & Engen 16 (1e); Thompson 109b.   Heritage Book Shop 196-270 1996 $250.00

HARTE, BRET 1836-1902   The Wild West. Harrison of Paris, 1930. Of an edition of 876 copies, this one of 36 printed on Japan vellum; octavo; 187 pages; illustrations by Pierre Falke colored stencilled by E. Charpentier; grass cloth with embroidered spine and slipcase; very fine. Bromer Booksellers 90-61 1996 $450.00

HARTE, GLYNN BOYD   Temples of Power, Lithographs... Burford, Oxon: The Cygnet Press, 1979. One of 250 numbered copies, signed by John Betjeman; oblong folio; 16 color lithos and text illustrations; original decorated baords, dust jackets.   Marlborough 162-40 1996 £75.00

HARTE, WALTER 1709-1774   Essays on Husbandry. London: Frederick, et al, 1764. 1st edition; 8vo; pages xxviii, (iv), (214), 232; 5 copperplates, 25 woodcuts; contemporary calf, lacks front flyleaves and free endpaper, some marginal tears around two of the copperplates, very good, rare. Fussell, More Old English Farming Books pp. 38, 45, 46, 71, 72.   Second Life Books 103-103 1996 $475.00

HARTE, WALTER 1709-1774   Essays on Husbandry. London: Frederick et al, 1770. 2nd edition; 8vo; pages (xxvii), (214), 232 + ad leaf, 5 copperplates and 25 woodcuts; rebacked contemporary calf, nicce, clean copy. Rare. Armorial bookplate.   Second Life Books 103-102 1996 $475.00

HARTE, WALTER 1709-1774   The History of the Life of Gustavus Adolphus, King of Sweden, Surnamed the Great. London: J. Hinton, 1767. 2nd edition; 8vo; 2 volumes; pages (ii), xxxiv, 328; (iv), 385, (1), (60), (54); frontispiece to volume i, 3 folding plans, 2 with tipped in explanatory leaf, folding diagram, some creasing to few fore-edges in volume i; contemporary tan calf, backstrips raised bands between double gilt rules, red title label in second compartment, volume number lettered direct in third, darkened, blind roll on board edges, endpapers stained by turn-ins, contemporary; very good; contemporary bookplate of Nic. Heath U.C. Oxon.   Blackwell's B112-147 1996 £115.00

HARTE, WALTER 1709-1774   Poems on Several Occasions. London: printed for Bernard Lintot, 1727. 1st edition; 8vo; frontispiece, xxx, 244 pages, 2 pages ads; original panelled calf, spine gilt, leaf A3, the dedication, is a cancel, as usual; nice.   David Bickersteth 133-36 1996 £140.00

HARTLEY, L. P.   The Collections. London: Hamish Hamilton Ltd., 1972. 1st edition; original binding, tail of spine slightly bumped, very good in dust jacket, slightly browned at spine and edges; inscribed presentation from author.   Ulysses 39-276 1996 £55.00

HARTLIB, SAMUEL   Considerations Tending to the Happy Accomplishment of Englands Reformation in Church and State. Colophon: N.P.: L anno 1647. 1st edition; small 4to; 19th century half red morocco, fine; rare. Wing H981; not in Kress.   Ximenes 109-150 1996 $2,500.00

HARTNOLL, PHYLLIS   The Grecian Enchanted. Waltham St. Lawrence: Golden Cockerel Press, 1952. One of 360 numbered copies; narrow folio; pink and grey cloth, large gilt decoration on upper cover, spine little marked and rubbed, otherwise very nice.   Bertram Rota 272-89 1996 £110.00

HARTSHORNE, ALBERT   Old English Glasses. London: & New York: Edward Arnold, 1897. 1st edition; folio; 490 pages; numerous full page plates (some in color), in text illustrations; original blackstamped half vellum and cloth, top edge gilt, vellum somewhat darkened, else very good.   Chapel Hill 94-14 1996 $165.00

HARTZENBUSCH, JUAN EUGENIO   The Lovers of Teruel. London: Gregynog Press, 1938. Limited to 175 numbered copies; small 4to; xii, 112 pages; printed on batchelor handmade paper, 5 initial letters by Alfred Fairbank, printed in red; publisher's red niger morocco, covers decorated with blindstamped Moorish design of interlaced strapwork, spine lettered gilt, top edge gilt, others uncut; fine. Harrop 38. Thomas Thorp 489-141 1996 £380.00

THE HARVARD Medical School, 1782-1906. Boston: 1906. 1st edition; 212 pages; numerous photographic illustrations; original binding, scarce. W. Bruce Fye 71-932 1996 $100.00

HARVARD UNIVERSITY   Catalogue of Books and Manuscripts. French 16th Century Books. Cambridge: 1964. 1st edition; 8vo; 2 volumes, numerous facsimiles; original cloth.   Forest Books 74-192 1996 £295.00

HARVARD UNIVERSITY   Catalogue of Books and Manuscripts. Italian 16th Century Books. Cambridge: 1964. 1st edition; 8vo; 2 volumes; original cloth, slipcase.   Forest Books 74-191 1996 £295.00

HARVARD UNIVERSITY   Catalogue of Books and Manuscripts. Part I: French 16th Century Books. Cambridge: Belknap Press of Harvard University Press, 1964. 4to; 2 volumes; illustrations and reproductions; blue cloth, spine black and gold.   Maggs Bros. Ltd. 1191-209 1996 £265.00

HARVARD UNIVERSITY   A Catalogue of the Law School of the University at Cambridge for the Academical Year 1853-54. Cambridge: Metcalf and Co. 1854. 28 pages; blue wrappers, bit chipped and foxed, but fresh.   Meyer Boswell SL25-100 1996 $150.00

HARVARD UNIVERSITY   The Houghton Library 1942-1967. A Selection of Books and Manuscripts in Harvard Collections. Cambridge: Harvard College Library, 1967. 1st edition; folio; numerous plates and illustrations, some in color; original buckram, top edge gilt.   Forest Books 74-113 1996 £75.00

HARVEY, ELLWOOD   Valedictory Address to the Graduating Class of the Female Medical College of Pennsylvania... Philadelphia: Register Association, 1854. Slim 8vo; pamphlet, (14, 2 pages); original printed pink wrappers, tied as issued, wear to wrappers, short tear to front; scarce.   Paulette Rose 16-225 1996 $175.00

HARVEY, FRED   First Families of the Southwest. Kansas City: pub. by Fred Harvey, n.d., early 1900's. illustrations in color; original decorated boards, moderate wear at corners, otherwise very good.   Ken Sanders 8-134 1996 $115.00

HARVEY, M.   Newfoundland in 1897 Being Queen Victoria's Diamond Jubilee Year and the Four Hundredth Anniversary of the Discovery of the Island by John Cabot. London: 1897. Small 8vo; folding map, 23 plates; original cloth; small embossed library stamp on title.   Charles W. Traylen 117-402 1996 £60.00

HARVEY, MICHAEL   Reynolds Stone: Engraved Lettering in Wood. London: Fleece Press, 1992. One of 270 copies; folio; printed in black and 3 shades of red, Bembo type set at the Rocket Press; fine in slipcase.   Bertram Rota 272-149 1996 £164.00

HARVEY, W.   Strange Conquest. Lincoln-Williams, 1934. 1st edition; bright very good+ copy, in nice dust jacket.   Aronovitz 57-511 1996 $175.00

HARVEY, WILLIAM 1578-1657   The Anatomical Exercises...De Mortu Cordis. De Circulatione Sanguinis. London: Nonesuch Press, 1928. Limited edition, 763/1450 copies; crown 8vo; pages xvi, 202, (1), printed on Van Gelder handmade paper, folding copper engraved plate by Stephen Gooden; original russet-red niger morocco, backstrip gilt lettered between raised bands, double gilt ruled border to sides, offsetting to endpaper edges, top edge gilt on rough, others untrimmed, excellent. Dreyfus 51.   Blackwell's B112-206 1996 £165.00

HARVEY, WILLIAM 1578-1657   The Anatomical Exercises of Dr. William Harvey. De Motu Cordis 1628: De Circulatione Sanguinis 1649. London: Nonesuch Press, 1953. 1st edition thus, one of 1450 copies; 8vo; illustrations; full morocco, top edge gilt, offsetting along edges of front and back endpapers and covers, very slightly rubbed at extremities, otherwise fine.   James S. Jaffe 34-511 1996 $250.00

HARVEY, WILLIAM 1578-1657   Exercitationes Anatomicae, De Motu Cordis & Sanguinis Circulatione. Roterdami: Ex Officina Arnoldi Leers, 1671. 12mo; 2 works together; engraved and printed titles, (xxviii), 285, (xix); 252, (xxiv) pages, 2 full page engraved plates; original vellum, repaired, wormholes in lower margin in first half of book repaired. Keynes II. Wellcome III 219.   David Bickersteth 133-199 1996 £550.00

HARVEY, WILLIAM 1578-1657   The Works of William Harvey, M.D. London: 1847. 1st edition; 624 pages; original binding, Keynes 48.   W. Bruce Fye 71-952 1996 $300.00

HARVIE-BROWN, J. A.   A Fauna of the Tay Basin and Strathmore. London: 1906. illustrations; original cloth, just slightly faded; nice. David A.H. Grayling MY95Orn-387 1996 £80.00

HARWOOD, J.   Harwood's Views of the Lakes. London: J. & F. Harwood, c. 1852. Oblong 8vo; 24 engraved plates, few trifle spotted, some numbered and dated between 1842 and 1846; original cloth backed color printed boards, blindstamp of James Ivison, bookseller of Keswick on flyleaf.   R.F.G. Hollett & Son 78-974 1996 £85.00

HARWOOD, J.   Illustrations of the Lakes. London: J. & F. Harwood, c. 1852. Oblong 8vo; original ribbed cloth, gilt, upper board little soiled, 30 engraved vignette tissue guarded plates, rather spotted or browned in places, occasionally heavily; Bicknell 127.   R.F.G. Hollett & Son 78-975   1996 £95.00

HARWOOD, THOMAS   History of New Mexico Spanish and English Missions of the Methodist Episcopal Church from 1850 to 1910. Albuquerque: El Abogado Press, 1908/10. 1st edition; 2 volumes; portraits and illustrations; original dark blue cloth with title in gilt on spines, volume one having new endsheets, some wear, but very good for this crudely bound and printed work. Howes H276; Graff 1811. Saunders 68.   Michael D. Heaston 23-267   1996 $750.00

HARZBERG, HILER   Slapstick and Dumbbell. New York: 1924. 4to; 6 tipped in plates and numerous text illustrations; spine edges bumped, but very good, scarce. Toole Stott 345.   Lyman Books 21-193   1996 $100.00

HASELDEN, THOMAS   The Seaman's Daily Assistant, Being a Short, Easy, and Plain Method of Keeping A Journal At Sea... London: printed for J. Mount and T. Page, 1764. 1st edition; 4to; woodcut diagrams in text, age browning of text; contemporary mottled calf, rebacked, label. This edition not in ESTC.   Anthony W. Laywood 109-59   1996 £350.00

HASELDEN, THOMAS   The Seaman's Daily Assistant, Being a Short, Easy and Plain Method of Keeping a Journal at Sea... London: J. Mount, T. Page and W. Mount, 1780. Later edition; 4to; 160 pages; contemporary full sheep, covers worn, hinges weak, thus very good only.   Chapel Hill 94-314   1996 $350.00

HASELER, H.   A Series of Views of Sidmouth and Its Neighbourhood, Drawn from Nature and on Stone. Sidmouth: pub. by H. Haseler, Teacher of Drawing and Painting... 1825. Folio; 6 hand colored lithograph plates on India paper, slightly spotted, original cloth backed printed boards, spine frayed.   Anthony W. Laywood 109-60   1996 £495.00

HASKINS, J.   James Van Der Zee: the Picture-Takin' Man. New York: 1979. 1st edition; illustrations; dust jacket.   J. B. Muns 154-312   1996 $150.00

HASLAM, JOHN   A Letter to the Governors of Bethlem Hospital Containing an Account of Their management of that Insitution for the Last Twenty Years... London: Taylor and Hessey, 1818. 8vo; (2), 58, (2) pages, ads; original boards, paper label; inscribed presentation from author "A. Carlisle, Esq., from his friend the author", first blank leaf has signature also of Robert Wilfred Skeffington Lutwidge dated 1844, Lutwidge was Commissioner for Lunacy 1842-45.   C. R. Johnson 37-82   1996 £350.00

HASLAM, JOHN   Observations on Madness and Melancholy; Including Remarks on Those Diseases...(with) Illustrations of Madness; Exhibiting a Singular Case of Insanity, and a No Less Remarkable Difference in Medical Opinion... London: printed for J. Callow/London: G. Hayden, 1809/1810. 2nd edition; 8vo; vii, (1), 345, (1) pages; xi, (1), 81, (3) pages, half title, ads; 2 items bound together in boards, old reback. C. R. Johnson 37-81   1996 £350.00

HASLEM, JOHN   The Old Derby China Factory and The Workmen and Their Productions. London: George Bell and Sons, 1876. 1st edition; small 4to; xvi, 255 pages; frontispiece, 11 plates; contemporary half morocco, text slightly browned and brittle, occasionally thumbed, wear along spine and edges, front endpapers detached, inscription on front endpaper.   Bookpress 75-62   1996 $250.00

HASLER, P. W.   The House of Commons, 1558-1603. London: 1981. crown 4to; 3 volumes, pages 2000; original cloth, dust jackets. Howes Bookshop 265-468   1996 £100.00

HASLUCK, F. W.   Cyzicus: Being Some Account of the History and Antiquities of that City and of the District Adjacent to It, with the Towns of Apollonia ad Rhyndacum, Miletupolis, Hadrianutherae, Priapus, Zeleia, etc. Cambridge: Cambridge University Press, 1910. 8vo; x, 326 pages, 24 illustrations, 3 folding maps (on 2 sheets) in pocket at rear, minor discoloration at top board.   Archaeologia Luxor-3418   1996 $125.00

HASSALL, A. H.   The Microscopic Anatomy of the Human Body, in Health and Disease. London: 1849. 2 volumes; 69 colored plates, backstrips defective, plate volume loose in binding, name to title, otherwise contents very good.   Petersfield Bookshop FH58-149   1996 £50.00

HASSALL, JOAN   Dearest Sydney: Joan Hassall's Letters to Sydney Cockerell from Italy and France, April-May 1950. London: Fleece Press, 1991. One of 220 copies; 8vo; 5 tipped in plates, including two facsimiles; half cloth, patterned boards; fine.   Bertram Rota 272-147   1996 £56.00

HASSELL, JOHN   Aqua Pictura. London: for the proprietors c. 1818. 2nd edition; oblong folio; title and preface (2ff), (18ff) text and 19 plates (2 on one leaf), each present in four states, etching, aquatint, aquatint with sepia wash and hand colored aquatint; many color specimens in text, plates dated 1818 except for three dated 1811 and 1812; introduction dated March 1, 1812; contemporary grey boards with original printed paper label on upper cover, very neatly rebacked and re-cornered in accurate contemporary style with straight grain red morocco, flat backed spine with gilt bands and stars, and with matching morocco backed slipcase with marbled paper sides; some occasional minor spotting and some slight old and faint waterstaining, but very good. Abbey Life 140 (1813 ed.).   Ken Spelman 30-33   1996 £2,600.00

HASSELL, JOHN   Graphic Delineation. London: printed for W. Simpkin and R. Marshall, 1826. 1st edition; 4to; frontispiece, 8 etched plates; original boards covered in brown paper, uncut, original paper label on upper cover.   Anthony W. Laywood 108-177   1996 £145.00

HASSELL, JOHN   Graphic Delineation. London: M. Hassell, 1827. 2nd edition; slim 4to; 23 pages, 9 plates; original boards, paper label; backstrip neatly repaired; very good.   Ken Spelman 30-39   1996 £240.00

HASSELL, JOHN   Picturesque Rides and Walks with Excursions by Water... London: printed for J. Hassell, 27, Richard Street Islington, 1817-18. Small octavo; 2 volumes, 120 colored aquatints (margins of 1 plate renewed), fine contemporary straight grain green morocco, expertly and unobtrusively rebacked, fully gilt spines, all edges gilt, half red morocco slipcase. Fine.   H. M. Fletcher 121-139   1996 £1,100.00

HASSELL, JOHN   Picturesque Rides and Walks with Excursions by Water, Thirty Miles Round the British Metropolis. London: J. Hassell, 1817/18. 8vo; 2 volumes, pages viii, 249; 272; 6 ff; 120 hand colored aquatints, tissue guards; calf gilt, rebacked using original spines, some slight scattered foxing; scarce large paper edition; Abbey Scenery 218; Tooley 251.   Marlborough 162-151   1996 £1,200.00

HASSRICK, PETER   Frederick Remington. New York: 1973. 1st edition; 218 pages, photos, illustrations; book fine, dust jacket very good. Early West 22-444b   1996 $100.00

HASTINGS, MICHAEL   The Handsomest Young Man in England. London: 1967. 1st edition; 4to; illustrated with photos of Raverat, Cornford and others; very good in dust jacket frayed at head and foot of spine and on one corner, extremely hard book to find.   Words Etcetera 94-208   1996 £50.00

HASTINGS, WARREN   The Means of Guarding Dwelling Houses, by Their Construction, Against Accidents by Fire. London: printed for Carpenter and Son, 1816. Reprint; 8vo; 31, (1) pages, boards; rare. Elton Engineering 10-69   1996 £180.00

HASTINGS, WARREN   A Short Account of the Resignation of Warren Hastings, Esq. Governor General of Bengal in the Year MDCCLXXV, with Remarks. London: printed in the Year, 1781. 1st edition; 4to; 26 pages; disbound.   Anthony W. Laywood 109-62   1996 £110.00

HASWELL, J. F.   The Registers of Cliburn 1565-1812. Penrith: the Herald, 1932. 8vo; pages 99; original printed wrappers.   R.F.G. Hollett & Son 78-563   1996 £85.00

HASWELL, J. F.   The Registers of Newbiggen (Westmorland) 1571-1812. Penrith: Herald Printing Co., 1927. 8vo; 107 pages; original printed wrappers.   R.F.G. Hollett & Son 78-589   1996 £95.00

HATCHER, ROBERT   The Pharmacopoeia and the Physician: a Series of Articles Which Originally Appeared in the Journal of the American Medical Association... Chicago: 1908. 2nd edition; 485 pages; original binding.   W. Bruce Fye 71-953   1996 $100.00

HATZFELD, JOHN CONRAD FRANCIS DE   The Case of the Learned Represented According to the Merit of the Ill Progress Hitherto Made in Arts and Sciences... London: ptd. for the author and only to be had at Thomas Churchill's ... 1724. 1st edition; small 8vo; contemporary calf, gilt, rebacked, original spine laid down, recent red morocco label, some rubbing. Very uncommon, very good; with a number of ms. corrections in text, very probably by author; Babson 73; Wallis 95.1. Ximenes 108-183   1996 $600.00

HAVERFORDWEST UNION SOCIETY   Rules and Orders to be Observed and Kept by an Union Society of Tradesman, Artits, Etc. Held at the House of Mr. Joseph Perkins, at the Black Horse Inn, In Bridge-Street, in the Town and County of Haverfordwest, first Instituted on the 6th March 1772. Carmarthen: printed by J. Ross in Lammas Street, 1786. 16, (4) pages; original blue wrappers, stabbed, as issued.   C. R. Johnson 37-14 1996 £350.00

HAWEIS, MARY ELIZA   The Art of Beauty. New York: Harper & Bros., 1878. 1st American edition; 12mo; xiv, 298, 6 pages; frontispiece; publisher's cloth; pencil and ink inscriptions on front endpapers, minor wear to tips and extremities of spine, else very bright.   Bookpress 75-63 1996 £300.00

HAWES, WILLIAM POST   Sporting Scenes and Sundry Sketches. New York: Gould, Banks, 1842. 1st edition; 8vo; 2 volumes in 1; 3 plates, due to size (uncut) of these sheets there was no need to fold; contemporary (or slightly later) palin boards, green cloth shelf back; very large copy, sheets measuring 8 3/8 x 5 inches, uncut and unopened. Fine. BAL 8068. Wright I 1138; Henderson p. 60.   M & S Rare Books 60-165 1996 $225.00

HAWKER, PETER   The Diary. 1802-1853. London: 1893. vo; 2 portraits and 8 plates; original cloth.   Charles W. Traylen 117-303 1996 £160.00

HAWKER, PETER   Instructions to Young Sportsmen in all that Relates to Guns and Shooting. London: printed for Longman, Hurst, Rees, Orme, Brown and Green, 1824. 3rd edition; royal 8vo; pages xxii, 470, 16 page publisher's catalog, 10 aquatint or engraved plates, 4 of which are hand colored, fine; handsomely bound (for Hatchards) in full green morocco, spine with raised bands, and lettered and ruled in gilt, marbled endpapers, edges uncut; fine. Tooley 256; Abbey Life 389; Schwerdt I p. 235.   Sotheran PN32-75 1996 £850.00

HAWKER, ROBERT STEPHEN   Ecclesia: a Volume Of Poems. Oxford: printed by T. Combe; sold by J. G. and J. Rivington, London... 1840. 1st edition; 8vo; original blue cloth, printed paper label, slight soiling; very good. CBEL III 524.   Ximenes 109-152 1996 $300.00

HAWKES, JOHN   Innocence in Extremis. Grenfell Press, 1985. One of 85 copies signed by author and artist, of a total edition of 118; 11 1/4 x 8 3/4 inches; 3 p.l., (one blank), 7-64 pages, (2) leaves (blank, colophon), mounted frontispiece, title in red and black, red initials; black morocco backed pictorial paper boards, edges untrimmed; mint. Phillip J. Pirages 33-272 1996 $225.00

HAWKES, JOHN   Innocence in Extremis; a Novella. New York: Grenfell Press, 1985. Of 118 copies, signed by author and artist; one of 85 bound thus; large 4to; frontispiece; printed in black and red in Dante with Weiss initials on Saunders Blue Laid; quarter black morocco, lettered in gilt on spine, morocco tips, fine.   Bertram Rota 272-207 196 £150.00

HAWKES, JOHN   Lunar Landscapes. Stories and Short Novels 1949-1963. New York: New Direction, 1969. One of 150 numbered copies, signed by author; fine in near fine slipcase with small sticker ghost top of back; from the collection of Richard Levey with bookplate from Poet's House Library.   Thomas Dorn 9-136 1996 $125.00

HAWKINS, ANTHONY HOPE 1863-   Comedies of Courtship. New York: Charles Scribner's Sons, 1896. spine bumped, otherwise very good; ownership signature of P. G. Wodehouse.   R. A. Gekoski 19-163 1996 £120.00

HAWKINS, ANTHONY HOPE 1863-   The Prisoner of Zenda. New York: Henry Holt, 1894. 1st American edition; 12mo; buckram cloth stamped in red, top edge gilt; very good, small engravings of Hope tipped to front pastedown.   Antic Hay 101-831 1996 $125.00

HAWKINS, BENJAMIN   Letter from the Principal Agent for Indian Affairs, South of the Ohio. Philadelphia: 1801. 1st edition; 11 pages, sewn as issued; very good.   Michael D. Heaston 23-124 1996 $750.00

HAWKINS, FREDERICK   Annals of the French Stage, from Its Origin to the Death of Racine. London: Chapman and Hall, 1884. 1st edition; 8vo; 2 volumes; frontispieces, errata slip; original blue green cloth, blocked in black; fine.   James Burmester 29-66 1996 £90.00

HAWKINS, JOHN   The Life of Samuel Johnson, LL.D. London: for J. Buckland (& 39 others in London), 1787. 1st separate edition; large 8vo; pagaes (ii), 602, (xv) index, final leaf of index pasted onto inside back board, uncut, probably original boards, re-covered sometime during the early 19th century with plain paper, spine with painted gold lines and stars on black paper background cut out and pasted on in imitation of comartments, the whole a pleasing amateur construct, possibly the work of Miss Pigotts of Underdale whose signature is at the head of the titlepage; attractive and unusual copy.   Simon Finch 24-109 1996 £340.00

HAWKINS, RICHARD   The Observations of Sir Richard Hawkins Knight, in His Voiage Into the South Sea. London: printed by I. D. for John Jaggard, 1622. 1st edition; small folio; full red morocco by Sangorski & Sutcliffe; some very pale waterstains in lower margins, but fine, crisp copy. STC 12962; Sabin 30957; Hill p. 140; Borba de Moraes p. 395. Ximenes 109-153 1996 $17,500.00

HAWLES, JOHN   The Englishman's Right: a Dialogue Between a Barrister at Law and a Juryman. London: n.p., 1771. Modern quarter calf, quite attractive.   Meyer Boswell SL25-103 1996 $450.00

HAWLES, JOHN   Remarks Upon the Tryals of Edward Fitzharris, Stephen Colledge, Count Coningsmark, the Lord Russel, Colonel Sidney, Henry Cornish and Charles Bateman. London: Jacob Tonson, 1689. 1st edition; folio; (iv), 104 pages; pasted on errata slip on A2, disbound, outer leaves dusty, good. Wing H 1188.   Robert Clark 38-73 1996 £65.00

HAWORTH, MARTIN E.   Road Scrapings: Coaches and Coaching. London: Tinsley Bros., 1882. 1st and apparently only edition; 8vo; pages viii, 202, (2 ads) and errata slip; with additional decorative title and 11 tinted plates; original red cloth, gilt, some minor foxing, very good to nice.   James Fenning 133-156 1996 £55.00

HAWTHORNE, JULIAN   Hawthorne and His Circle. New York: Harper and Bros., 1903. 1st edition; illustrations; gilt top edge, name on front free endpaper with light wear at extremities; near fine.   Thomas Dorn 9-138 1996 $125.00

HAWTHORNE, JULIAN   Nathaniel Hawthorne and His Wife. Cambridge: Riverside Press, 1884. 1st edition; one of 350 sets printed on large paper; copy number 2; 2 volumes; original boards, labels, uncut, some flaking of paper to spine of first volume, else, tight, clean set, much nicer than usually seen; Clark C47; BAL IV 33.   Mac Donnell 12-112 1996 $300.00

HAWTHORNE, NATHANIEL 1804-1864   The Blithedale Romance. Boston: Ticknor, Reed & Fields, 1852. 1st edition; 1st printing with copyright notice opposite lines 4-6 of preface; (5090 copies); original brown cloth, gilt, fine, fresh copy. Wright I 1134. Clark A20.1.a. BAL 7611.   Mac Donnell 12-52 1996 $400.00

HAWTHORNE, NATHANIEL 1804-1864   The Blithedale Romance. Boston: Ticknor & Fields, 1852. 1st edition; catalog dated April 1855 (not noted by BAL); binding A; lower corners slightly bumped, minor wear to top of spine, fine.   Charles Agvent 4-631 1996 $250.00

HAWTHORNE, NATHANIEL 1804-1864   The Blithedale Romance. Boston: Ticknor, Reed and Fields, 1852. 1st American edition; 12mo; 288 pages; original cloth, top and bottom of spine chipped, edges worn, ads dated April 1852; BAL 7611 binding a; Clark A20.2a. 1st printing.   M & S Rare Books 60-167 1996 $250.00

HAWTHORNE, NATHANIEL 1804-1864   Doctor Grimshawe's Secret. Boston: James R. Osgood, 1883. 1st edition; 1st printing, 1st binding with Osgood's logo at foot; original grey pictorial cloth, gilt, minor bubbling due to quality of binding glue, else fine, fresh copy, unusual thus; BAL 7642.   Mac Donnell 12-56 1996 $125.00

HAWTHORNE, NATHANIEL 1804-1864   Doctor Grimshawe's Secret. Cambridge: Riverside Press, 1883. 1st edition; one of 250 numbered copies on large paper; original boards, labels, uncut, extremely scarce in this format, mild dust soiling on covers, else fine, with no signs of wear; Clark A31.1.d. BAL 7642.   Mac Donnell 12-57 1996 $350.00

HAWTHORNE, NATHANIEL 1804-1864   Grandfather's Chair: a History for Youth. Boston: Tappan & Dennet, 1842. 2nd edition; 2nd binding, original lavender cloth, gilt, front free endpaper excised, else fine. Clark A6.2.a.1.   Mac Donnell 12-58 1996 $100.00

HAWTHORNE, NATHANIEL 1804-1864   The House of the Seven Gables. Boston: Ticknor, Reed & Fields, 1851. 1st edition; 2nd printing (1st and 2nd printing totalling about 3000 copies, were all pub. on April 9, 1851) with perfect type on p. 149 as noted only by Clark; original brown cloth, gilt; minor rubbing, else crisp, tight copy with March catalog; BAL 7604; Clark A17.1.b.   Mac Donnell 12-59 1996 $500.00

HAWTHORNE, NATHANIEL 1804-1864   The House of the Seven Gables. Boston: Ticknor, Reed & Fields, 1851. 1st edition; 2nd printing with perfect type at p. 149 as noted only by Clark; later three quarter tan calf, raised bands, gilt compartments, fine; Clark A17.1.b. BAL 7604. Mac Donnell 12-62 1996 $100.00

HAWTHORNE, NATHANIEL 1804-1864   The House of the Seven Gables. Boston: Ticknor, Reed & Fields, 1851. 1st edition; 3rd printing; original brown cloth with March 1851 catalog at front (formerly accepted as a 'first issue'), mild rubbing, little shaken, but nice copy; bookplate of Byron Price (prominent newspaper editor). Clark A17.1.c. BAL 7604. Mac Donnell 12-61 1996 $450.00

HAWTHORNE, NATHANIEL 1804-1864   The House of the Seven Gables. Boston: Ticknor, Reed & Fields, 1851. 1st edition; 4th printing; original brown cloth, gilt, with March 1851 catalog at front (formerly accepted as '1st issue'), crown slightly chipped and foot of spine frayed, but solid, tight, clean copy. Clark A17.1.d. BAL 7604.   Mac Donnell 12-60 1996 $350.00

HAWTHORNE, NATHANIEL 1804-1864   The House of the Seven Gables. Boston: Ticknor, Reed & Fields, 1851. 1st edition; 4th printing of only 1000 copies; Catalog dated October 1851; binding A, occasional foxing, head of spine chipped to text block, spine significantly cocked, rear outer hinge partly cracked. Clark A17.1.d.   Charles Agvent 4-633 1996 $150.00

HAWTHORNE, NATHANIEL 1804-1864   The House of Seven Gables. Boston & New York: Houghton Mifflin & Co., 1899. Limited to 250 numbered large paper copies; 8vo; 2 volumes, ix, (v), 265 pages; (vi), 277 pages; 20 plates, decorative headpieces and initials; cream parchment covered boards titled in gilt on spines with floral gilt vignettes, covers framed by quadruple gilt rules, title and decorations in gilt on front covers, original light gray linen dust jackets, titled in gilt on spines, top edge gilt. Fine.   Blue Mountain SP95-61 1996 $250.00

HAWTHORNE, NATHANIEL 1804-1864   The House of the Seven Gables. New York: Limited Editions Club, 1935. Limited to 1500 copies; signed by artist; linoleum cuts in color by Valenti Angelo, signed by artist; half polished calf, adhesive remnant from bookplate, near fine in lightly worn case; with montly letter.   Charles Agvent 4-634 1996 $150.00

HAWTHORNE, NATHANIEL 1804-1864   Legends of the Province House. Boston: James R. Osgood, 1877. 1st edition; 1st printing; original green cloth, gilt, fine fresh copy of this rare printing; inscribed by an early owner in June 1877. Cclark A2.17; BAL 7681.   Mac Donnell 12-63 1996 $150.00

HAWTHORNE, NATHANIEL 1804-1864   The Life of Franklin Pierce. Boston: Ticknor, Reed and Fields, 1852. 1st edition; original brown cloth, gilt, spine ends chipped or frayed, else tight, clean copy; Clark A21.a. BAL 7612.   Mac Donnell 12-64 1996 $100.00

HAWTHORNE, NATHANIEL 1804-1864   Life of Franklin Pierce. Boston: Ticknor, Reed & Fields, 1852. 1st edition; original black TR cloth, gilt, spine ends frayed or chipped, faint marginal stain, else good, tight copy. Clark A21.1.a. BAL 7612.   Mac Donnell 12-65 1996 $100.00

HAWTHORNE, NATHANIEL 1804-1864   The Marble Faun. Boston: Ticknor & Fields, 1860. 1st edition; 2nd printing; original brown cloth, gilt, with March 1860 ads at rear; near fine set. With March 1860 ownership inscription on titlepage of each volume. Clark 23.3.b. BAL 7621.   Mac Donnell 12-67 1996 $200.00

HAWTHORNE, NATHANIEL 1804-1864   The Marble Faun. Boston: Ticknor & Fields, 1860. 1st edition; 4th printing with the 'Conclusion' added; 2 volumes; original brown cloth, gilt, minor nicks at crown, else tight fine fresh set; BAL 7624; Clark A23.3.d.   Mac Donnell 12-66 1996 $150.00

HAWTHORNE, NATHANIEL 1804-1864   The Marble Faun. Boston: Ticknor & Fields, 1860. 1st edition; 4th printing with the 'Conclusion' added; 2 volumes; original brown cloth, gilt, spine tips lightly frayed, else nice, tight set; BAL 7624. Clark A23.3.d.   Mac Donnell 12-68 1996 $100.00

HAWTHORNE, NATHANIEL 1804-1864   Mosses from an Old Manse. New York: Wiley & Putnam, 1846. 1st edition; 1st printing with Craighead and Smith imprints below copyright notice in both volumes, state 1 of the front wrappers, state 3 of back wrapper present; 12mo; 2 volumes; original printed wrappers, lacking back wrapper of volume 2, ends o spine chipped (textually complete), bookplate on half title of each volume, some glue show through, light waterstaining in lower corner of first 100 pages of second volume; very good set. Entirely unsophisticated, early pencilled signature in each volume of A. P. Williams of Augusta, Me. BAL 759 state A. Clark A15.1.a1. Bradley Marti Sale 2064.   M & S Rare Books 60-166 1996 $3,500.00

HAWTHORNE, NATHANIEL 1804-1864   Mosses from an Old Manse. New York: Wiley & Putnam, 1846. 1st edition; 1st printing of the first volume and 2nd printing of the second volume, primary binding; original blue green cloth, gilt, fine, seldom found well preserved; housed in quarter leather slipcase that is more sturdy than attractive BAL 7598; Clark A151.a./b.   Mac Donnell 12-69 1996 $850.00

HAWTHORNE, NATHANIEL 1804-1864   Mosses from an Old Manse. New York: Wiley & Putnam, 1846. 1st edition; 1st printing of both parts 2 volumes bound in 1; contemporary (possibly original publisher's) three quarter red morocco, raised bands, gilt, blue-green T cloth sides; fine, uncommon. BAL 7598. Clark A15.1.a.1.   Mac Donnell 12-70 1996 $750.00

HAWTHORNE, NATHANIEL 1804-1864   Mosses from an Old Manse. New York: Wiley & Putnam, 1846. 1st edition; 1st printing of both volumes; 2 volumes bound as one, as issued; original faded slate cloth, gilt, quite rubbed, with splits at joints neatly reglued; from the library of John Milton Cheney, with his signature on titlepage. BAL 7598; Clark A15.1.a.b.   Mac Donnell 12-71 1996 $225.00

HAWTHORNE, NATHANIEL 1804-1864   Our Old Home. Boston: Tickno & Fields, 1863. 1st edition; original binding, corners worn, small nicks along spine, gilt faded, some fraying to tips; tight, clean copy. BAL 7626.   Charles Agvent 4-636 1996 $125.00

HAWTHORNE, NATHANIEL 1804-1864   Our Old Home. Boston: 1863. 1st edition with one page of ads; 7.5 x 4.5 inches; 398 pages; cloth, ex-school library, ink inscription, extremities rather frayed, slight offset from pressed flowers on few pages, still good.   John K. King 77-333 1996 $150.00

HAWTHORNE, NATHANIEL 1804-1864   Our Old Home. Boston: Tickno & Fields, 1863. 1st edition; 2nd state; original binding, gilt bit faded, fraying to spine tips; good+; dedicated to Franklin Pierce, this copy has the pencil signature on front blank of Theo. Pierce.   Charles Agvent 4-637 1996 $125.00

HAWTHORNE, NATHANIEL 1804-1864   Our Old Home: a Series of English Sketches. Boston: Ticknor & Fields, 1863. 1st edition; 2nd printing, variant; original brown cloth, gilt, with variant without the inserted catalog at end, but with 'mysterious' reading still not corrected to 'mysterious'; fine, fresh copy. Clark A24.1.b. BAL 7626.   Mac Donnell 12-72 1996 $125.00

HAWTHORNE, NATHANIEL 1804-1864   Passages from the American Note-Books. Boston: Ticknor & Fields, 1868. 2nd printing of 500 copies with Fields Osgood binding, extra leaf at end of volume 2; 8vo; 2 volumes; original binding, gilt a touch dull on spine of volume 2, otherwise fine, bright set.   Charles Agvent 4-638 1996 $200.00

HAWTHORNE, NATHANIEL 1804-1864   Passages from the American Note-Books. Boston: Ticknor & Fields, 1868. 1st edition; 1st printing, 1s binding, only 1500 sets were printed; 2 volumes; original green cloth, gilt, some fraying at crowns, else bright clean set, scarce. Clark A26.1.a BAL 7632.   Mac Donnell 12-75 1996 $200.00

HAWTHORNE, NATHANIEL 1804-1864   Passages from the English Note-Books. Boston: Fields, Osgood, 1870. 1st edition; 1st printing; only 1000 sets were printed; 2 volumes; original green cloth, gilt, chips at crown and bookplates removed from inside front covers, otherwise very good set. BAL 7634; Clark A27.1.a.   Mac Donnell 12-76 1996 $100.0

HAWTHORNE, NATHANIEL 1804-1864   Passages from the French an Italian Note-Books. Boston: James R. Osgood, 1872. 1st edition; 1st printing, binding A (first of 3 bindings); original green cloth, gilt, fine crisp set. BAL 7636; Clark A28.2.a.   Mac Donnell 12-77 1996 $225.0

HAWTHORNE, NATHANIEL 1804-1864   Passages from the French an Italian Note-Books. Boston: James R. Osgood, 1872. 1st edition; 1st printing, binding A (1st of 3 bindings); 2 volumes; original green cloth, gilt, some fraying at crown, else bright set. BAL 7636; Clark A28.2.a. Mac Donnell 12-78 1996 $150.00

HAWTHORNE, NATHANIEL 1804-1864   The Scarlet Letter. Boston: Ticknor, Reed & Fields, 1850. 2nd edition, 2nd printing; original brown cloth, gilt, minute rubbing at spine tips, else fine, tight crisp copy, with photo (ca. 1890) of the Wayside Inn, Concord, laid in; BAL 7601 (noting only Nov. ads. this copy has May ads); Clark A16.3.a.   Mac Donnell 12-80   1996 $375.00

HAWTHORNE, NATHANIEL 1804-1864   The Scarlet Letter. Boston: Ticknor, Reed & Fields, 1850. 2nd edition, printing 2; brown cloth, rebacked with original spine laid down. BAL 7601.   Blue River Books 9-158   1996 $150.00

HAWTHORNE, NATHANIEL 1804-1864   The Scarlet Letter. New York: Privately printed, 1904. Limited edition, one of only 126 copies; 10 1/2 x 7 1/4 inches; 4 p.l., 333 pages; 15 original plates, each in two states, hand colored and uncolored, for a total of 30 plates in all by A. Robaudi and C. Graham, each plate with printed tissue guard, printed on fine Japanese vellum; sumptuous crimson morocco by MacDonald, heavily gilt in 18th century French design, covers bordered with multiple plain and decorative gilt rules and lavish foliate dentelles, raised bands, spine attractively gilt in compartments, similar ornaments at corners of broad gilt ruled turn-ins, marbled endpapers, top edge gilt, other edges untrimmed; evidence of bookplate removal, perhaps a hint of fading to binding, but extremely fine in handsome binding.   Phillip J. Pirages 33-302   1996 $325.00

HAWTHORNE, NATHANIEL 1804-1864   The Scarlet Letter. New York: 1904. One of 125 copies; 333 pages, printed on Imperial Japanese paper; 15 original illustrations in both colored and uncolored states; vellum paper wrappers as issued, some copies later slipcased with silk folding wrapper (as is this), case very good, wrapper well frayed; fine. Bookworm & Silverfish 276-114   1996 $125.00

HAWTHORNE, NATHANIEL 1804-1864   The Scarlet Letter. New York: Limited Editions Club, 1941. Limited to 1500 copies; signed by artist; octavo; lithographs by Henry Varnum Poor drawn on stone; sheepskin; light scuff marks to spine, near fine in case.   Charles Agvent 4-639 1996 $125.00

HAWTHORNE, NATHANIEL 1804-1864   The Scarlet Letter. West Hatfield: Pennyroyal Editions, 1984. illustrations by Barry Moser, original cloth, paper labels, fine in publisher's slipcase.   Hermitage SP95-907 1996 $125.00

HAWTHORNE, NATHANIEL 1804-1864   Septimius Felton. Berlin: A. Asher & Co., 1872. 1st European copyright edition; contemporary half red calf and marbled boards, gilt, very good, very scarce printing; Clark A29.3. cf. BAL 7638.   Mac Donnell 12-81   1996 $100.00

HAWTHORNE, NATHANIEL 1804-1864   Septimius Felton; or the Elixir of Life. Boston: Osgood, 1872. 1st edition; decorated green cloth; small chip at head of spine, tape repair to front blank; near fine. BAL 7638. Charles Agvent 4-640   1996 $150.00

HAWTHORNE, NATHANIEL 1804-1864   The Snow Image and other Twice-Told Tales. Boston: Ticknor, Reed and Fields, 1852. 1st edition; 273 pages; original brown cloth, gilt, brown stain to back yellow endpapers, otherwise very good; publisher's catalog pp. (1)-4, earliest issue dated Jan. 1852, inserted at front.   Blue River Books 9-159 1996 $150.00

HAWTHORNE, NATHANIEL 1804-1864   The Snow-Image, a Childish Miracle. New York: James G. Gregory, 1864. 1st separate edition; five color illustrations by Marcus Waterman; original blue cloth, gilt, some foxing in text, else near fine with early owner's inscription; rather scarce. Clark A19.4. BAL 7660.   Mac Donnell 12-83   1996 $225.00

HAWTHORNE, NATHANIEL 1804-1864   Tanglewood Tales for Boys and Girls: Being a Second Wonder-Book. Boston: Ticknor, Reed and Fields, 1853. 1st American edition, 1st printing; small octavo; 366 pages; engraved vignette title and six engraved plates, 8 page publisher's Catalog inserted at front in Blanck's A printing, dated July 1853 with 'Tanglewood Tales' listed as "In Press"; full red levant morocco by the Booklover's Bindery, New York, gilt lettered spine with raised bands, gilt board edges and turn-ins, top edge gilt, marbled endpapers, original red cloth bound in at back, original front free endpaper bearing previous owner's ink signature has been preserved by binder, bookplate; occasional foxing and browning to text, otherwise fine.   Heritage Book Shop 196-218   1996 $500.00

HAWTHORNE, NATHANIEL 1804-1864   True Stories from History and Biography. Boston: Ticknor, Reed & Fields, 1851. 1st edition; 3rd printing; original slate cloth, spine elaborately gilt in earlier design that does not match "Tanglewood Tales", rear free endpaper excised, else very good faded copy with very little rubbing, some heavy foxing in last several gatherings due to printer's use of a different paper stock for these gatherings. BAL 7655; Clark A12.3.a.   Mac Donnell 12-84   1996 $150.00

HAWTHORNE, NATHANIEL 1804-1864   True Stories from History and Biography. Boston: Ticknor, Reed & Fields, 1851. 1st edition; 3rd printing; original dark blue cloth, spine elaborately gilt in earlier design that does not match "Tanglewood Tales", faint stain on front cover, but handsome copy with very little rubbing.   Mac Donnell 12-85 1996 $150.00

HAWTHORNE, NATHANIEL 1804-1864   Twice-Told Tales. Boston: American Stationers, 1837. 1st edition; original dark brown cloth, minor wear to joints, foxed, excellent copy in remarkably well preserved and entirely untouched original binding, half morocco case. Grolier 100 American Books 44.   19th Century Shop 39-   1996 $4,500.00

HAWTHORNE, NATHANIEL 1804-1864   Twice-Told Tales. Boston: James Munroe, 1842. 1st edition thus, 1st issue; full green morocco, gilt panels, raised bands, gilt compartments, inner dentelles gilt, silk markers, uncut, signed by Stikeman; fine, fresh set with only the slightest rubbing; from the library of Charles B. Foote; extremely rare book. Dickinson p. 121-2; BAL 7594; Clark A2.3.1.   Mac Donnell 12-86 1996 $850.00

HAWTHORNE, NATHANIEL 1804-1864   Twice-Told Tales. New York: Limited Editions Club, 1966. Limited to 1500 copies; 4to; signed by artist, Valenti Angelo; original binding, fine in partly sunned case.   Charles Agvent 4-643   1996 $125.00

HAWTHORNE, NATHANIEL 1804-1864   A Wonder-Book for Girls and Boys. Boston: Ticknor, Reed & Fields, 1852. 1st edition; 2nd printing; original green cloth, extra gilt with medallions on spine in gilt instead of blind, all edges gilt, front free endpaper excised, else fine, fresh copy of a book seldom found in gift binding. Clark A18.1.b. BAL 7606.   Mac Donnell   12-88   1996 $1,000.00

HAWTHORNE, NATHANIEL 1804-1864   A Wonder-Book for Girls and Boys. Boston: Ticknor, Reed & Fields, 1852. 1st edition; 2nd printing; original blue cloth, gilt, some signature slightly sprung, some general rubbing, vut very good in rarer binding style that matches "Tanglewood Tales (1853)"; Clark A18.1.b. BAL 7606.   Mac Donnell 12-87 1996 $500.00

HAWTHORNE, NATHANIEL 1804-1864   A Wonder-Book for Girls and Boys. Boston: Ticknor, Reed & Fields, 1852. 1st edition; 2nd printing; original brown cloth, gilt, spine ends chipped or frayed, else tight clean copy; Clark A18.1.b. BAL 7606.   Mac Donnell 12-89 1996 $350.00

HAWTHORNE, NATHANIEL 1804-1864   A Wonder Book for Girls and Boys. London: Ogsood MacIlvaine & Co., 1892. 1st edition illustrated by Walter Crane; 8vo; pages x, 210, 19 beautiful color printed plates and color printed titlepage and chapter headings and tailpieces; original pictorial white cloth printed with green, decorated endpapers, stunning copy unusually crisp and clean internally and externally.   Sotheran PN32-107 1996 £150.00

HAWTHORNE, NATHANIEL 1804-1864   A Wonder Book and Tanglewood Tales for Girls and Boys. New York: Duffield, 1910. 1st Parrish edition; small 4to; ix, 358 pages; 10 color plates by Maxfield Parrish; original navy cloth with large pictorial cover label, spine slightly darkened, extremities of front cover lightly rubbed, else near fine. Chapel Hill 94-81 1996 $185.00

HAWTHORNE, NATHANIEL 1804-1864   A Wonder Book. London: Hodder & Stoughton, 1922. 1st Rackham edition, 374/600 copies, signed by artist; imperial 8vo; pages (i), viii, 208; printed on large paper, 16 color printed plates, each tipped to cream card backing and with captioned tissue guard; original cream cloth, gilt blocked lettering and decoration on backstrip and front cover and endpaper designs, all by Rackham, top edge gilt, others untrimmed; fine. Riall p. 146. Blackwell's B112-237 1996 £750.00

HAWTHORNE, NATHANIEL 1804-1864   The Works. Cambridge: Riverside Press, 1883. 1st edition; large paper issue, one of 250 numbered sets; original cream boards, labels, uncut, thin crack in upper joint of first volume, mild aging of spine paper and minor signs of wear, unusually tight, fresh set, far nicer than average for this impossibly delicate binding. BAL 7643. Clark B10.   Mac Donnell 12-90 1996 $475.00

HAWTREY, GEORGE P.   Chester Historical Pageant, July 18th to 23rd, 1910: Book of Words. Chester: Philipson & Golder, 1910. 1st edition; 4to; original cloth, pictorial label on front cover; rather soiled and worn, binding little dampstained but good; author's own copy with his initials on front cover, interleaved and with notes in pen and pencil in his hand, together with five pages of Hawtrey's ms. stage directions, 54 page booklet in which estimates are given for number of character & costumes needed; ALS to Hawtrey from J. C. Bridge.   David J. Holmes 52-121 1996 $150.00

HAY, ALEXANDER   The History of Chichester. Chichester: J. Seagrave, 1804. 8vo; pages xiv (including half title), 605, 14ff., 4 ff. subscribers; contemporary speckled calf, spine little worn, hinges starting. Anderson p. 281.   Marlborough 162-42 1996 £130.00

HAY, D. R.   Original Geometrical Diaper Designs, Accompanied by an Attempt to Develope (sic) and Elucidate the True Principals of Ornamental Design... London: D. Bogue, 1844. 1st edition; oblong folio; (ii), 43, (1) pages, 24 plates; 33 plates; later cloth with original wrapper label to front cover, occasional smudging and thumbing, cover wear, titlepage creased, but good, uncommon.   Bookpress 75-64 1996 $750.00

HAY, GEORGE   The Necronomicon. N. Spearman, 1798. 1st edition; 184 pages; cloth, fine, very good+ dust jacket.   Middle Earth 77-77 1996 $145.00

HAY, WILLIAM   Mount Caburn. A Poem. London: printed for J. Stagg, 1730. 1st edition; folio; pages 24; disbound; slight browning, tall copy, some fore-edges uncut.   Peter Murray Hill 185-73 1996 £225.00

HAYDON, BENJAMIN ROBERT   The Autobiography and Memoirs of Benjamin Robert Haydon (1786-1846). London: Peter Davies, Publisher, 1926. 1st edition thus; 2 volumes, 427, 435 pages, 15 page introduction by Aldous Huxley; original binding, top edge dusty, spines marked and darkened, covers slightly marked and dusty, cover edges slightly rubbed, edges and endpapers slightly spotted, some very slight internal spotting, some page edges nicked, good.   Ulysses 39-278 1996 £85.00

HAYES, HARRY   Anthology of Plastic Surgery. Rockville: 1986. 1st edition; 338 pages; illustrations; original binding.   W. Bruce Fye 71-956 1996 $125.00

HAYES, ISAAC ISRAEL   The Open Polar Sea. London: Sampson Low, Son & Marston, 1867. 1st British edition; demy 8vo; xxiv, (456), 16 pages; plates and colored maps; original cloth, gilt, expertly restored and refurbished, endpapers rejointed, little dull and bumped, few slight marks, but good; bookplate of Herbrand Russell.   Ash Rare Books Zenzybyr-44 1996 £250.00

HAYES, ISAAC ISRAEL   The Open Polar Sea. New York: 1867. Pages xxiv, 454, 9 plates and maps, text illustrations; bit faded and worn, internally near fine.   Stephen Lunsford 45-64 1996 $100.00

HAYES, JOHN W.   Roman and Pre-Roman Glass in the Royal Ontario Museum: a Catalogue. Toronto: Royal Ontario Museum, 1975. Folio; xii, 229 pages, over 600 illustrations; original cloth.   Archaeologia Luxor-3424 1996 $150.00

HAYES, JOHN W.   Roman Pottery in the Royal Ontario Museum: a Catalogue. Toronto: Royal Ontario Museum, 1976. Folio; ix, 69 pages, 40 plates; original cloth.   Archaeologia Luxor-3425 1996 $100.00

HAYES, SAMUEL   Prayer: A (Seatonian-Prize) Poem. Cambridge: ptd. by J. Archdeacon, Printer to the University, 1777. 1st edition; 4to; 28 pages; disbound.   Anthony W. Laywood 109-63 1996 £90.00

HAYLEY, WILLIAM   An Elegy on the Ancient Greek Model. Cambridge: printed by Francis Hodson, sold by T. Payne, London and T. & J. Merril 1779. 1st edition; 4to; disbound; half title present, nice. CBEL II 658.   Ximenes 108-184 1996 $175.00

HAYLEY, WILLIAM   An Essay on History; in Three Epistles to Edward Gibbon, Esq. London: printed for J. Dodsley, 1780. 1st edition; 4to; disbound; very good, complete with half title; Norton p. 235; Rothschild 1123; CBEL II 658.   Ximenes 108-186 1996 $200.00

HAYLEY, WILLIAM   The Life of George Romeny, Esq. Chichester: printed by W. Mason, for T. Payne, London 1809. 1st edition; large 4to; xiv, 416 pages; portrait, 11 engraved plates; contemporary diced calf, rebcked, Signet library arms on covers; CBEL II 659   James Burmester 29-67 1996 £150.00

HAYLEY, WILLIAM   The Triumphs of Temper, a Poem. London: printed for J. Dodsley, 1781. 1st edition; 4to; disbound; very good, complete with half title; CBEL II 658.   Ximenes 108-187 1996 $175.00

HAYNES, CHARLES   A Treatise of Fluxions; or an Introduction to Mathematical Philosophy. London: 1704 1st edition; 13 x 8 inches; diagrams; 315 pages; old panelled calf, bookplate, ink inscription, front cover detached, covers frayed.   John K. King 77-722 1996 $1,250.00

HAYNES, ELIZABETH ROSS   The Black Boy of Atlanta. Boston: Hous of Edinboro, 1952. 1st edition; frontispiece, light rubbing to base of boards, otherwise fine in very good dust jacket with couple of medium sized chips and tears and faint stain on spine; still decent example of the very fragile jacket.   Between the Covers 43-336 1996 $275.00

HAYNES, SYBILLE   Etruscan Bronzes. London: Sotheby, 1985. Folio; 359 pages, over 200 illustrations; original cloth, fine, dust jacket.   Archaeologia Luxor-3429 1996 $150.00

HAYWARD, ABRAHAM   The Art of Dining; Gastronomy and Gastronomers. London: Murray, 1852. 1st edition; 12mo; vi, 137 pages; original half leather and marbled paper over boards, attractive binding with title on spine in gilt, shows only little wear; contents fine, with only slightest of embrowning.   Roy W. Clare XXIV-25 1996 $115.00

HAYWARD, ABRAHAM   Verses of Other Days. London: 1847. 1st edition; slim 12mo; original green cloth, tips of spine little worn; very good. Very scarce. 3 copies in NUC; CBEL III 1387.   Ximenes 108-18 1996 $100.00

HAYWOOD, ELIZA FOWLER 1693-1756   The Husband. In Answer to The Wife. (with) The Wife. London: for T. Gardner, 1756/56. 1st editions 8vo; 2 works in one volume, pages (ii), v, (i) ad, 279, (i) ads; pages (iv), half title and title, v, (i) blank, 282, first leaf of contents of second work torn across with loss of lower half of leaf; contemporary calf, red morocco label, spine gilt in compartments, rubbed, gilt faded, occasion neglible spotting in margins, very good; ownership inscription of Richar Greenham.   Simon Finch 24-115 1996 £580.00

HAYWOOD, ELIZA FOWLER 1693-1756   Memoirs of the Court of Lilliput. London: printed for J. Roberts, 1727. 1st edition; 8vo; disbound fine, rare. Teerink 1221; McBurney 204; Guerinot, Pamphlet Attacks on Pope p. 99.   Ximenes 108-189 1996 $1,750.00

HAYWOOD, FRANCIS   An Analysis of Kant's Critick of Pure Reason. London: William Pickering, 1844. 1st edition; 8vo; vi, 215, (1) pages, shelf numbers on blank verso of title and first page of Preface, few readers' emphasis marks in pencil; original dark green cloth, printed lab on spine, head and tail of spine little worn, else very good. Rand p. 30 John Drury 82-130 1996 $75.00

HAZARD, SAMUEL   Cuba With Pen and Pencil. London: 1873. 584 pages; extensively illustrated with full page and text engravings; original cloth, nice.   Stephen Lunsford 45-65 1996 $135.00

HAZELIUS, ERNEST LEWIS   The Life of John Henry Stilling, Doctor o Medicine and Philosophy. Gettysburg: 1831. 1st edition; 8vo; original ca spine damaged.   Argosy 810-223 1996 $200.00

HAZEN, A. T.   A Bibliography of the Strawberry Hill Press: with a Record of the Prices at Which Copies Have Been Sold... New Haven: Yale University Press, 1942. 1st edition; large 8vo; frontispiece, 84 facsimile pages; cloth.   Thomas Thorp 489-143 1996 £65.00

HAZLITT, WILLIAM 1778-1830   Characters of Shakespear's Plays. London: printed by C. H. Reynell, for R. Hunter and C. and J. Ollier, 1817. 1st edition; 8vo; contemporary calf, gilt, rebacked, spine gilt, old label preserved, edges rubbed; very good. Keynes 17.   Ximenes 108-190 1996 $200.00

HAZLITT, WILLIAM 1778-1830   Literary Remains. London: Saunders Otley, 1836. 1st edition; tall 8vo; 2 volumes; frontispiece; three quarter tan polished calf, expertly rebacked, raised bands, red and black leathe labels; apart of foxing, a sound copy.   Appelfeld Gallery 54-112 199 $125.00

HAZLITT, WILLIAM 1778-1830   The Plain Speaker, Opinions on Book Men and Things. (Essays). London: Henry Colburn, 1826. 1st edition; 8vo; 2 volumes; three quarter brown calf, raised bands, red and black labels, apart from rebacking, good copy.   Appelfeld Gallery 54-113 1996 $100.00

HAZLITT, WILLIAM 1778-1830   Political Essays, with Sketches of Public Characters. London: printed for William Hone, 1819. 1st edition; 8vo; contemporary half calf, spine gilt, bit scuffed, edges rubbed; very good; bookabel of Roger Senhouse. Keynes 49.   Ximenes 108-191 1996 $400.00

HAZLITT, WILLIAM 1778-1830   Political Essays, with Sketches of Public Characters. London: William Hone, 1819. 1st edition; 8vo; three quarter tan calf, expertly rebacked, raised bands, red and black leather labels, gilt top, some signatures browned.   Appelfeld Gallery 54-114 1996 $125.00

HAZLITT, WILLIAM 1778-1830   A Reply to the Essay on Population by the Rev. T. R. Malthus. London: printed for Longman, 1807. 1st edition; 8vo; iv, 3-378 pages, tears in 3 leaves repaired (without loss of text), light marginal dampstaining thereafter, C8 in cancel, as usual; recent half calf; Keynes 4.   James Burmester 29-68 1996 £500.00

HAZLITT, WILLIAM 1778-1830   Table Talk or Original Essays on Men and Manners. London: Henry Colburn, 1824. 2nd edition; tall 8vo; 2 volumes, 400, 401 pages; handsome three quarter black pebbled morocco, raised bands, gilt in panels, marbled boards and endpapers, silk ribbon markers; fine set. Keynes 61.   Hartfield 48-L38 1996 $295.00

HAZLITT, WILLIAM 1778-1830   Winterslow: Essays and Characters Written There. London: David Bogue, 1850. 1st edition; small 8vo; (vi), 314 pages; later olive morocco by Zaehnsdorf, spine gilt, lightly rubbed; Keynes 111; CBEL III 1233.   James Burmester 29-69 1996 £95.00

HDRLICKA, ALES   Physiological and Medical Observations Among the Indians of Southwestern United States and Northern Mexico. Washington: 1908. 1st edition; 450 pages; illustrations; original binding. GM 6455.1.   W. Bruce Fye 71-1052 1996 $100.00

HEACOX, CECIL E.   The Compleat Brown Trout. U.S.A.: 1983. Colour and other plates by W. Trimm; full leather, all edges gilt, silk moire endpapers and silk marker, housed in slipcase; mint.   David A.H. Grayling 3/95-453 1996 £55.00

HEAD, FRANCIS BOND   A Narrative by Sir Francis B. Head, Bart. London: John Murray, 1839. 1st edition; demy 8vo; viii, 488, (40), 8 pages; original cloth gilt, covers faded and discolored, somewhat shaken, few minor marks, nevertheless good, serviceable copy. Staton & Tremaine 2275.   Ash Rare Books Zenzybyr-45 1996 £125.00

HEAD, FRANCIS BOND   A Narrative. London: John Murray, 1839. 2nd edition; 8vo; modern binder's cloth, small library stamp on title. Sabin 31133.   Charles W. Traylen 117-403 1996 £70.00

HEADLAM, CUTHBERT   The Three Northern Counties of England. Gatehead: Northumberland Press, 1939. Limited to 500 copies; small 4to; pages xii, 343, 23 plates, 8 maps and plans; untrimmed, original full dark levant morocco gilt; few faint spots to title, but most attractive copy. R.F.G. Hollett & Son 78-981 1996 £85.00

THE HEALING Art; or, Chapters Upon Medicine, Diseases, Remedies and Physicians, Historical, Biographical and Descriptive. London: 1887. 1st edition; 2 volumes, 316, 377 pages; original binding; rare.   W. Bruce Fye 71-53 1996 $200.00

HEALTH Science Books, 1876-1982. New York: 1982. 1st edition; 4 volumes; 3988 pages; original binding.   W. Bruce Fye 71-961 1996 $200.00

HEALY, JEREMIAH   Blunt Darts. Walker, 1984. 1st edition; fine in fine dust jacket.   Book Time 2-629 1996 $325.00

HEALY, M. A.   Report of the Cruise of the Revenue Marine Steamer Corwin in the Arctic Ocean in the Year 1885. Washington: GPO, 1887. 4to; 3 maps, including 2 folding, 70 illustrations, including 4 in color, 102 pages; cloth, gilt, worn, little staining to top margin of many leaves, few library stamps.   Thomas Thorp 489-144 1996 £65.00

HEANEY, HOWELL J.   Thirty Years of Bird and Bull: a Bibliography 1958-1988. Bird & Bull Press, 1988. One of 300 numbered copies; small 4to; printed in Van Dijck on special Bird & Bull handmade; illustrations; half grey morocco, paste paper sides made at the Press, preserved with larger cloth portfolio, in matching cloth box with morocco label; fine. Bertram Rota 272-39 1996 £220.00

HEANEY, SEAMUS 1939-   After Summer. Old Deerfield: Deerfield Press; Dublin: Gallery Press, 1978. 1st edition; one of 250 copies, signed by author; thin 8vo; boards, dust jacket, head of spine bumped, otherwise fine.   James S. Jaffe 34-219 1996 $250.00

HEANEY, SEAMUS 1939-   A Boy Driving His Father to Confession. Farnham: Sceptre Press, 1970. One of 150 copies; small thin 8vo; wrappers lightly dust soiled, otherwise fine.   James S. Jaffe 34-211 1996 $350.00

HEANEY, SEAMUS 1939-   Death of a Naturalist. London: Faber & Faber, 1966. 1st edition; 8vo; cloth, dust jacket; foot of spine slightly bumped, otherwise fine inf aded and price clipped jacket; fine.   James S. Jaffe 34-208 1996 $375.00

HEANEY, SEAMUS 1939-   Door Into the Dark. London: Faber and Faber, 1969. 1st edition; 8vo; black cloth, dust jacket, fine in price clipped jacket with one small closed tear;   James S. Jaffe 34-209 1996 $250.00

HEANEY, SEAMUS 1939-   Eleven Poems. Belfast: Festival Publications, 1965. 1st edition; 1st issue; small 8vo; author's scarce first book; pictorial printed white wrappers, with red-violet sun symbol on front cover, trifle dusty, otherwise fine. Pearson A1a.   James S. Jaffe 34-205 1996 $1,250.00

HEANEY, SEAMUS 1939-   Eleven Poems. Belfast: Festival Publications, 1965. 1st edition; 2nd issue; small thin 8vo; printed self wrappers, signed by author; mint.   James S. Jaffe 34-206 1996 $450.00

HEANEY, SEAMUS 1939-   Eleven Poems. Belfast: Festival Publications, 1965? 2nd edition; small thin 8vo; light blue green printed self wrappers; mint. Pearson A1c.   James S. Jaffe 34-207 1996 $250.00

HEANEY, SEAMUS 1939-   Field Work. London: Faber & Faber, 1979. Uncorrected proof copy; 8vo; printed wrappers, dust jacket, binding flaw at back of book, otherwise fine in slightly rubbed and edge worn jacket.   James S. Jaffe 34-220 1 996 $250.00

HEANEY, SEAMUS 1939-   Field Work. London: Faber & Faber, 1979. 1st edition; 8vo; boards, dust jacket; mint.   James S. Jaffe 34-221 1996 $150.00

HEANEY, SEAMUS 1939-   Field Work. London: Faber & Faber, 1979. 1st edition; Poetry Book Society brochure laid in; fine in fine dust jacket; inscribed by author.   Revere Books 4-182 1996 $125.00

HEANEY, SEAMUS 1939-   Field Work. London: Faber and Faber Ltd., 1979. 1st edition; original binding; spine slightly faded, head of spine slightly bumped, fine in dust jacket; signed and dated 16th May 1981 by author on titlepage.   Ulysses 39-280 1996 £65.00

HEANEY, SEAMUS 1939-   Field Work. New York: Farrar, Straus, Giroux, 1979. 1st American edition; 8vo; cloth, dust jacket; mint.   James S. Jaffe 34-222 1996 $100.00

HEANEY, SEAMUS 1939-   The Gravel Walks. Hickory: Lenoir Rhyne College, 1992. One of four printer's proofs, inscribed and initialled by printer on colophon; handmade paper; marbled paper covers; near fine. Ulysses 39-281 1996 £135.00

HEANEY, SEAMUS 1939-   Gravities: a Collection of Poems and Drawings. New Castle upon Tyne: Charlotte Press, 1979. 1st edition; oblong 8vo; wrappers, covers lightly rubbed at extremities, otherwise fine.   James S. Jaffe 34-223 1996 $125.00

HEANEY, SEAMUS 1939-   The Haw Lantern. New York: Farrar, Straus & Giroux, 1987. Signed, limited edition of 250 numbered copies; cloth, slipcase; fine.   Antic Hay 101-785 1996 $125.00

HEANEY, SEAMUS 1939-   The Haw Lantern. New York: Farrar, Straus, Giroux, 1987. 1st American edition; one of 250 specially bound copies, signed by author; 8vo; cloth, slipcase, as new.   James S. Jaffe 34-233 1996 $125.00

HEANEY, SEAMUS 1939-   The Haw. New York: 1987. Limited to 250 copies, signed by author; fine in slipcase, as issued.   Words Etcetera 94-593 1996 £65.00

HEANEY, SEAMUS 1939-   Hedge School. Sonnets from Glanmore. Newark: Janus Press, 1979. 1st edition; limited to 285 copies, signed by author and artist; 4to; color woodcuts by Claire Van Vliet; embossed wrappers; fine.   James S. Jaffe 34-224 1996 $450.00

HEANEY, SEAMUS 1939-   In Their Element. A Selection of Poems. Northern Ireland: Arts Council of Northern Ireland, 1977. 1st edition; square 8vo; glossy silver wrappers, light offsetting on inner front cover, otherwise fine.   James S. Jaffe 34-241 1996 $100.00

HEANEY, SEAMUS 1939-   North. London: Faber & Faber, 1975. 1st edition; 8vo; cloth, dust jacket, green wraparound band, front endsheets darkened, otherwise fine, very scarce.   James S. Jaffe 34-216 1996 $500.00

HEANEY, SEAMUS 1939-   Poems and a Memoir. New York: Limited Editions Club, 1982. One of 2000 numbered copies, signed by author, artist Henry Patterson and Thomas Flanagan who provided introduction; folio; full leather, slipcase; fine.   Between the Covers 42-208 1996 $300.00

HEANEY, SEAMUS 1939-   Responses. Great Britain: National Book League, 1971. One of 500 copies; 8vo; red wrappers, fine.   James S. Jaffe 34-213 1996 $100.00

HEANEY, SEAMUS 1939-   Selected Poems 1965-1965. London: Faber & Faber, 1980. 1st edition; 8vo; boards, dust jacket; fine.   James S. Jaffe 34-227 1996 $125.00

HEANEY, SEAMUS 1939-   Selected Poems 1966-1987. New York: 1990. Limited to 200 copies signed by author; fine in slipcase.   Words Etcetera 94-599 1996 £75.00

HEANEY, SEAMUS 1939-   Selected Poems 1966-1987. New York: Farrar, Straus, Giroux, 1990. 1st American edition, one of 200 specially bound copies, signed by author; 8vo; cloth, slipcase, as new.   James S. Jaffe 34-237 1996 $100.00

HEANEY, SEAMUS 1939-   The Sounds of Rain. Atlanta: Emory University, 1988. 1st edition; one of 300 copies; small thin 8vo; wrappers, as new.   James S. Jaffe 34-236 1996 $100.00

HEANEY, SEAMUS 1939-   Stations. Belfast: Ulsterman Publications, 1975. 1st edition; thin 8vo; printed self wrappers, corners very slightly bumped, otherwise mint.   James S. Jaffe 34-217 1996 $150.00

HEANEY, SEAMUS 1939-   Sweeney Astray. Derry: Field Day, 1983. 1st edition; 8vo; boards, dust jacket; fine.   James S. Jaffe 34-229 1996 $100.00

HEANEY, SEAMUS 1939-   Sweeney Astray. New York: Farrar, Straus Giroux, 1984. 1st American edition, one of 350 specially bound copies, signed by author; 8vo; illustrations by Barrie Cooke; cloth, slipcase; mint. James S. Jaffe 34-230 1996 $100.00

HEANEY, SEAMUS 1939-   Sweeney Praises the Trees. New York: Kelly Winterton Press, 1981. 1st edition; limited to 110 copies; thin 8vo; original wrappers; as new.   James S. Jaffe 34-228 1996 $275.00

HEANEY, SEAMUS 1939-   Wintering Out. London: Faber & Faber, 1972. 1st edition; 8vo; boards, dust jacket, mint, very scarce.   James S. Jaffe 34-214 1996 $500.00

HEAP, GWINN H.   Central Route to the Pacific From the Valley of the Mississippi to California: Journal of the Expedition of E. F. Beale, Superintendent of Indian Affairs in Californa, and Gwinn Harris Heap from Missouri to California 1853. Philadelphia: 1854. 1st edition; 136 pages; frontispiece, illustrations; decorated cloth with leather spine with raised bands; nice. Wagner Camp 235; Howes T378 B. Rittenhouse 290; Flake 3943.   T. A. Swinford 49-503 1996 $750.00

HEAP, GWINN HARRIS   Central Route to the Pacific: With Related Material on Railroad Explorations and Indian Affairs by Edward E. Beale, Thomas H. Benton, Kit Carson, and Col. E. A. Hitchcock and In Other Documents 1853-54. Glendale: The Arthur H. Clark Co. 1957. 1st edition; one of 1272 copies; 346 pages; illustrations, maps and portraits; bookplate; green cloth, gilt lettered spine, very fine. Clark and Brunet 104-VII; Howes H 378; Rittenhouse 290.   Argonaut Book Shop 113-343 1996 $150.00

HEARD, JAMES   A Practical Grammar of the Russian Language. St. Petersburg ptd. for the author and sold by Sleunine & by Boosey & Sons, London, 1827. Half title, errata leaf; half calf, excellently rebacked. Jarndyce 103-609 1996 £250.00

HEARN, LAFCADIO 1850-1904   A Drop of Dew. Tokyo: the Hokuseido Press, 1950. Limited to 350 numbered copies on watermarked Japanese vellum, signed by editor; 4to; 12 leaves, including blanks; includes facsimile of ms., speckled tan paper covered boards, split along top of joint, tail of spine slightly chipped, titled in gilt on front cover; internally fine.   Blue Mountain SP95-99 1996 $250.00

HEARN, LAFCADIO 1850-1904   Gleanings in Buddha-Fields: Studies of Hand and Soul in the Far East. Boston: Houghton Mifflin, 1897. 1st edition; small 8vo; gilt stamped blue cloth, top edge gilt, front hinge starting, very good. State A of spine imprint. BAL 7929.   George J. Houle 68-61 1996 $175.00

HEARN, LAFCADIO 1850-1904   Glimpses of Unfamiliar Japan. Boston: Houghton Mifflin & Co., 1894. 1st edition; post 8vo; 2 volumes; original black cloth, patterned in silver, top edge gilt, little very minor wear, few very faint marks, but very good set.   Ash Rare Books Zenzybyr-46 1996 £295.00

HEARN, LAFCADIO 1850-1904   In Ghostly Japan. Boston: Little Brown 1899. 1st edition; 8vo; frontispiece and 3 full page plates, titlepage printed in black and orange; original gilt stamped blue cloth, cherry blossom design stamped in white and dark blue on upper cover, continuing onto spine and lower cover, top edge gilt, uncut, spine slightly faded, with minor wear to ends; very good.   George J. Houle 68-62 1996 $150.00

HEARN, LAFCADIO 1850-1904   Japan: an Attempt at Interpretation. New York: Macmillan Co., 1904. 1st edition; 8vo; color frontispiece; original brown decorated cloth, as issued, gilt top; fine.   Appelfeld Gallery 54-115 1996 $175.00

HEARN, LAFCADIO 1850-1904   A Japanese Miscellany. Boston: Little Brown, 1901. 1st edition; 8vo; frontispiece, 7 full page plates, 5 drawing in text, titlepage printed in black and orange, small decorative label laid down on half titlepage; original gilt stamped light green cloth, floral design stamped in orange, beige and dark green on upper cover, continuing onto spine and lower cover, top edge gilt, uncut, spine slightly soiled and minor wear to ends; very good. BAL 7936: State A o copyright page.   George J. Houle 68-63 1996 $150.00

HEARN, LAFCADIO 1850-1904   Kotto: Being Japanese Curios, with Sundry Cobwebs. New York: Macmillan, 1902. 1st edition; 1st state; decorated olive cloth, little dulled at spine; fine. BAL 7938.   Captain's Bookshelf 38-101 1996 $200.00

HEARN, LAFCADIO 1850-1904   Stray Leaves from Strange Literature. Boston: Osgood, 1884. 1st edition; original binding, backstrip rubbed bu still readable, short tear to f.f.e.p., old glue repair to both hinges, otherwise quite good in rubbed half morocco case.   Charles Agvent 4-646 1996 $450.00

HEARNE, SAMUEL   A Journey from Prince of Wales' Fort in Hudson Bay, to the Northern Ocean. London: printed for A. Strahan and T. Cade and sold by T. Cadell Jun. ... 1795. 1st edition; 4to; large paper copy; (iii-iv), (v-x), (xi-xix), errata leaf, xxi-xliv, 1-458 pages, publisher's ad/directions to binder to rear, 4 folding engraved copperplates, 3 foldin maps and charts; full speckled calf, rebacked, tastefully preserving original spine, small loss to foot of spine, gilt tooled border to baords, similar tooling to board edges, uniform marbled edges and endpapers; only some very slight foxing on minor scale, otherwise very fine. Sabin 31181; Hill Pacific Voyages p. 141; Rich I 390.   Beeleigh Abbey BA56-75 1996 £3,000.00

THE HEART of Man, Either a Temple of God, or a Habitation of Satan. Harrisburg: Printed by Scheffer & Beck, 1853. 16mo; 72 pages, 10 emblematical figures; paper over boards with red cloth spine, binding attractive though worn, corners bumped, full page wood engraving on both covers, contents nice, minimum of foxing.   Roy W. Clare XXIV-2 1996 $150.00

HEARTMAN, CHARLES F.   American Primers, Indian Primers, Royal Primers and Thirty-Seven other Types of Non-New-England Primers Issued Prior to 1830. Highland Park: Harry B. Weiss, 1935. Limited to 500 copies; 8vo; 160 pages; frontispiece, illustrations; brown cloth, paper label.   Kenneth Karmiole 1NS-51 1996 $100.00

THE HEARTY Old Boy, Who Looked Always the Same. London: 1866. Large octavo; 8ff.; hand colored illustrations on each page; original pictorial boards, which shows rubbing to extremities and light soiling, last page of text affixed to rear cover, thus lacking rear free endpaper and pastedown, still bright, near fine copy.   Bromer Booksellers 87-125 1996 $950.00

HEATH, FRANCIS GEORGE   The English Peasantry. London: Frederick Warne, 1874. 1st edition; 8vo; frontispiece, pages x, (2), 271, (4 ads); original cloth, gilt, very good. Hanham 6701.   James Fenning 133-158 1996 £65.00

HEATH, WILLIAM   Pickwickian Illustrations. London: T. McLean, 1837, imprint from first plate. Demy 8vo; numbered plates, without text; original jade green wrappers, black label, lettered and decorated in gilt, much rubbed and worn, front wrapper detached, few plates slightly fingeed and chipped, but in good condition for such fragile production.   Ash Rare Books Zenzybyr-29 1996 £200.00

HEATHCOTE, RALPH   Sylva; or, The Wood; Being a Collection of Anecdotes, Dissertations, Characters, Apophthegms, Original Letters, Bon Mots, and Other Little Things. London: printed for T. Payne and Son, 1786. 1st edition; contemporary ms. notes on half title, name erased from upper blank margin of title, some contemporary marginalia and alterations to text in ink; modern half calf, label.   Anthony W. Laywood 109-65 1996 £175.00

HEATON, CHARLES, MRS.   Masterpieces of Flemish Art Including Examples of the Early German and Dutch Schools. London: Bell & Daldy, 1869. Only edition; 4to; 158 pages, 26 mounted original albumen photos; original ornately gilt decorated green cloth, occasional light foxing, frontispiece and last plate spotted, tissue guard lacking from frontispiece, still very good overall with covers bright and clean. 5 copies in NUC. Chapel Hill 94-327 1996 $250.00

HEBER, REGINALD   The Life of the Right Rev. Jeremy Taylor, D. D. London: printed for James Duncan...and R. Priestly, 1824. 8vo; 2 volumes; portrait; 19th century calf, gilt, nice.   Peter Murray Hill 185-75 1996 £50.00

HEBER, REGINALD   Narrative of a Journey through the Upper Provinces of India... London: John Murray, 1892. 4th edition; demy 8vo; (lxviii), 450, (ii); (viii), 564; (viii), (528), viii pages, plates; bound in neat and functional modern quarter cloth, marbled sides, morocco labels, occasional light spotting, good, sound set.   Ash Rare Books Zenzybyr-47 1996 £75.00

HEBER, RICHARD   Bibliotheca Heberiana. London: 1834-37. 8vo; complete set of English catalogues, together 15 parts in 5 volumes; contemporary cloth, early ms. labels; fine, fresh set.   Ximenes 108-11 1996 $6,750.00

HEBERT, THOMAS   Some Years Travels into Divers Parts of Africa, and Asia the Great. London: printed by R. Everingham for R. Scot, T. Basset, F. Wright and ... 1677. 4th edition; folio; 1 leaf of dedications to author, 1-399 pages, 3 full engraved plates, 48 engraved vignettes, 6 maps; full contemporary panelled calf, corners restored, what appears to be scorch marks to upper boards, rebacked with new spine which is lighter modern style calf, black and maroon morocco labels to spine, marbled endpapers. lacks front f.e.p. and prelim, some occasional pencil markings to margins. Wing H1536; Cox 1248; Sabin 31471. Cox p. 248. Beeleigh Abbey BA56-77 1996 £750.00

HECHT, B.   Fantazius Mallare. Covici McGee, 1922. 1st edition; (2nd state binding), 1/2025 copies; illustrations; fine in very good+/near fine dust jacket.   Aronovitz 57-514 1996 $125.00

HECHT, B.   The Kingdom of Evil. Covici, 1924. 1st edition; 1/2000 copies; illustrations; bright, very good+ copy in very good dust jacket save for thumb-nail size chip missing from front dust jacket panel and some inner reinforcement.   Aronovitz 57-515 1996 $125.00

HECKER, J. F. C.   The Epidemics of the Middle Ages. London: 1846. 1st English translation; 380 pages; original binding.   W. Bruce Fye 71-966 1996 $150.00

HECKETHORN, CHARLES WILLIAM   The Secret Societies of All Ages and Countries. London: Richard Bentley & son, 1875. 1st edition; 8vo; 2 volumes; original green cloth, slightly marked.   James Burmester 29-71 1996 £75.00

HEDGECOE, JOHN   Henry Moore. New York: Simon and Schuster, 1968. Folio; 524 pages; 525 illustrations, some in color; cloth, slipcase. Brannan 43-452 1996 $135.00

HEDGES, ISAAC A.   Sugar Canes and Their Products Culture and Manufacture... St. Louis: Published by the author, 1879. Small 8vo; illustrations, plates, 2 folding, one illustration of litmus papers in colors; original plum cloth, covers blindstamped, spine lettered in gilt, some rubbing, browning, mostly of endpapers, good.   James Cummins 14-199 1996 $150.00

HEDGPETH, J. W.   Treatise of Marine Ecology and Paleoecology. 1957. Royal 8vo; 2 volumes; illustrations; cloth.   Wheldon & Wesley 207-320 1996 £80.00

HEDIN, SVEN   Adventures in Tibet. London: Hurst & Blackett, 1904. 1st edition; demy 8vo; xvi, (488) pages; numerous illustrations, original cloth, pictorial onlay, little rubbed and worn at extremities of spine, little shaken, lacks front fly, but good; bookplate of Hooker's son, Joseph Symonds Hooker.   Ash Rare Books Zenzybyr-48 1996 £185.00

HEDIN, SVEN   Central Asia and Tibet. Towards the Holy City of Lassa. London: Hurst & Blackett Ltd., 1903. 1st edition; royal 8vo; 2 volumes, 5 folding maps and over 420 illustrations; publisher's cloth, gilt, slightly dust stained and faded at fore-edge of both volumes, otherwise good. Tipped into front of volume 1 is holograph note by author on notepaper bearing his arms to Captain Baker-Carr. The recipient was Robert George Teesdale Baker-Carr.   H. M. Fletcher 121-155 1996 £300.00

HEDIN, SVEN   A Conquest of Tibet. New York: E. P. Dutton, 1934. 1st edition; fine in fine dust jacket with small neat bookplate on front pastedown.   Hermitage SP95-1104 1996 $100.00

HEDIN, SVEN   Trans-Himalaya. Discoveries and Adventures in Tibet. New York: Macmillan, 1909-13. 1st edition; 8vo; xxiv, 436, 4, xviii, 439, 4, xvi, 426, 2 pages; numerous plates and illustrations; original cloth, edges rubbed, spines rebacked, otherwise very good ex-library, top edge gilt. Worldwide Antiquarian 162-326 1996 $250.00

HEDIN, THOMAS   The Sculpture of Gaspard and Bathazard Marsy. Art and Patronage in the Early Regin of Louis XIV. Columbia: University of Missouri Press, 1983. 4to; 250 pages; well illustrated; cloth.   Rainsford A54-390 1996 £60.00

HEDRICK, U. P.   The Peaches of New York. Albany: 1917. Thick 4to; pages xiii, 541; 92 colored plates and map; cloth, covers scuffed, inner joint cracked, rear pastedown scraped.   Raymond M. Sutton VII-974 1996 $160.00

HEDRICK, U. P.   The Plums of New York. Albany: 1911. Thick 4to; pages xii, 616; frontispiece, 98 colored plates, 2 small scraps on rear cover, occasional light foxing, mostly marginal, lacks "October" plate as usual.   Raymond M. Sutton VII-975 1996 $160.00

HEDRICK, U. P.   The Vegetables of New York. Albany: 1928-31-34-37. 4to; Volume 1, parts 1-4; 1 volume in 4; pages vi, 132; iii, 110; (3), 111; (3), 131; 136 colored plates; stiff wrappers, some dampstaining around center of backstrips of part 3, light soiling to wrappers, overall very good.   Raymond M. Sutton VII-973 1996 $225.00

HEDWIG, JOHANNES   Theoria Generationis et Fructificationis Plantarum Cryptogammicarum... St. Petersburg: Imperial Academy of Sciences, 1784. Sole edition; large 4to; 166 pages; 37 folding engraved plates, stitched at end; entirely untrimmed, original stiff wrappers, fine. Superb copy in strictly original condition.   Bennett Gilbert LL29-44 1996 $1,500.00

HEFELE, CHARLES JOSEPH   A History of the Christian Councils, from the Original Documents to the Close of the Council of Nicea, A.D. 325...(later volumes to the Close of the Second Council of Nicea, A.D. 787). Edinburgh: T.& T. Clark, 1871-6-83-95-6. 1st edition in English; 8vo; 5 volumes, (xii), 502, (xiv); xvi, 503, (i), 8, (viii); xii, 480, 8; x, 498, (ii), 16; xvi, 472, (viii) pages; original brown cloth, blocked in black and gilt, extremities little rubbed; good set.   Robert Clark 38-241 1996 £100.00

HEHN, VICTOR   The Wanderings Of Plants and Animals from their First Home. London: 1885. contemporary morocco, gilt, top edge gilt; very fine.   David A.H. Grayling MY95Orn-40 1996 £75.00

HEIDEGGER, MARTIN   Zur Sache des Denkens. Tubingen: Niemeyer, 1969. 1st edition; fine, lacking dust jacket; superb association, inscribed by author to great scholar of Gnosticism, Hans Jonas.   Lame Duck Books 19-240 1996 $1,500.00

HEINE, HEINRICH   Poems. New York: Limited Editions Club, 1957. Limited to 1500 copies; 4to; illustrations by Fritz Kredel, signed by artist; half green calf, decorated paper; spine tips rubbed, near fine in like case. With Monthly Letter.   Charles Agvent 4-648 1996 $100.00

HEINEMANN, LARRY   Close Quarters. New York: FSG, 1977. 1st edition; very faint offsetting to front free endpaper, else fine in dust jacket.   Between the Covers 42-209 1996 $150.00

HEINLEIN, ROBERT ANSON 1907-1988   Assignment in Eternity: Four Long Science Fiction Stories. Reading: Fantasy Press, 1953. 1st edition; 1st state, with author's name on spine being 3mm high; bound in unrecorded variant in blue cloth with gilt lettering, fine in dust jacket. Captain's Bookshelf 38-103 1996 $300.00

HEINLEIN, ROBERT ANSON 1907-1988   The Cat Who Walks through Walls. New York: Putnam, 1985. 1st edition; limited to 350 copies, signed by author; frontispiece in full color by Michael Whelan; black cloth, matching slipcase; fine.   Bromer Booksellers 90-62 1996 $185.00

HEINLEIN, ROBERT ANSON 1907-1988   Double Star. Garden City: Doubleday, 1956. 1st edition; stunning copy, extremely scarce, very fine in bright and flawless dust jacket; inscribed and signed by author. Robert Gavora 61-23 1996 $2,000.00

HEINLEIN, ROBERT ANSON 1907-1988   Double Star. New York: Doubleday, 1956. 1st edition; fine in just about fine dust jacket with several tiny tears, wonderful copy.   Aronovitz 57-526 1996 $1,250.00

HEINLEIN, ROBERT ANSON 1907-1988   Double Star. London: M. Joseph, 1958. 1st British edition; very good in dust jacket with some soil to rear dust jacket panel.   Aronovitz 57-527 1996 $150.00

HEINLEIN, ROBERT ANSON 1907-1988   Friday. HRW, 1982. 1st edition; uncorrected proof; wrappers, near fine proof dust jacket, small stain on front cover, else very good+; signed by author; rare thus.   Aronovitz 57-540 1996 $375.00

HEINLEIN, ROBERT ANSON 1907-1988   The Green Hills of Earth. Shasta, 1951. 1st edition; 6 pages exhivit a faint moist stain along the fore edge, else very good+/near fine in very good dust jacket. Aronovitz 57-521 1996 $175.00

HEINLEIN, ROBERT ANSON 1907-1988   Have Space Suit - Will Travel. New York: Charles Scribner's, 1958. 1st edition; bottom front corner tip slightly frayed, otherwise very good+ in dust jacket which is lightly soiled and chipped at top spine edge.   Steven C. Bernard 71-416 1996 $300.00

HEINLEIN, ROBERT ANSON 1907-1988   The Man Who Sold the Moon. Shasta, 1950. 1st edition; insignificant stain to small section of bottom edge of front panel, else fine in very good+/near fine dust jacket; subscriber's issue, signed by author.   Aronovitz 57-518 1996 $495.00

HEINLEIN, ROBERT ANSON 1907-1988   The Man Who Sold the Moon. Malian Press, 1952. 1st separate edition; wrapprs; very good+. Aronovitz 57-519 1996 $125.00

HEINLEIN, ROBERT ANSON 1907-1988   The Menace from Earth. Dobson, 1966. 1st English edition; near fine dust jacket with 2 short closed tears; uncommon edition.   Aronovitz 57-535 1996 $100.00

HEINLEIN, ROBERT ANSON 1907-1988   Methuselah's Children. Gnome, 1958. 1st edition; near fine in bright, very good+ dust jacket with some slight wear and tear.   Aronovitz 57-528 1996 $190.00

HEINLEIN, ROBERT ANSON 1907-1988   Orphans of the Sky. London: Gollancz, 1963. 1st edition; fine in dust jacket with several tiny spots and tears, attractive copy in nice condition.   Robert Gavora 61-24 1996 $650.00

HEINLEIN, ROBERT ANSON 1907-1988   Orphans of the Sky. Putnam, 1964. 1st Ameican edition; fine in dust jacket.   Aronovitz 57-533 1996 $235.00

HEINLEIN, ROBERT ANSON 1907-1988   Sixth Column. Gnome, 1949. 1st edition; fine, in just about fine dust jacket.   Aronovitz 57-517 1996 $285.00

HEINLEIN, ROBERT ANSON 1907-1988   Sixth Column. New York: Gnome, 1949. 1st edition; fine in as new dust jacket.   Robert Gavora 61-25 1996 $350.00

HEINLEIN, ROBERT ANSON 1907-1988   The Star Beast. New York: Scribners, 1954. 1st edition; light brownish stain in gutter near base of approximately half the pages (not affecting text), otherwise very good+ in near fine dust jacket.   Aronovitz 57-524 1996 $135.00

HEINLEIN, ROBERT ANSON 1907-1988   Starman Jones. New York: Scribners, 1953. 1st edition; very good+/near fine in very good dust jacket with some light wear and tear.   Aronovitz 57-523 1996 $165.00

HEINLEIN, ROBERT ANSON 1907-1988   Starship Troopers. Puntam, 1959. 1st edition; fine in dust jacket.   Aronovitz 57-529 1996 $1,200.00

HEINLEIN, ROBERT ANSON 1907-1988   Stranger in a Strange Land. New York: Putnams, 1961. 1st edition; fine in attractive, near fine dust jacket with couple of short tears and some rubbing to extremities, nice copy.   Between the Covers 42-516 1996 $750.00

HEINLEIN, ROBERT ANSON 1907-1988   Stranger in a Strange Land. NEL, 1975. 1st English hardcover edition; fine in dust jacket.   Aronov 57-531 1996 $195.00

HEINLEIN, ROBERT ANSON 1907-1988   Time Enough for Love. Putna 1973. 1st edition; very good in dust jacket with some slight wear and tear; from the library of Poul Anderson with his ownership signature, nice association.   Aronovitz 57-536 1996 $185.00

HEINLEIN, ROBERT ANSON 1907-1988   Tunnel in the Sky. New York: Scribners, 1955. 1st edition; very good in near fine dust jacket save for area near base of dust jacket spine lifted off from sticker removal. Aronovitz 57-526 1996 $125.00

HEINLEIN, ROBERT ANSON 1907-1988   Waldo & Magic, Inc. New York: Doubleday, 1950. 1st edition; very fine in just about fine dust jacket, truly spectacular copy.   Aronovitz 57-520 1996 $285.00

HEISTER, LORENZ 1683-1758   A General System of Surgery, in Three Parts. London: printed for J. Whiston, L. Davis and C. Reymers (& 10 other firms), 1768. 8th edition; 4to; 2 volumes; bound in one; xvi, 456; (ii), 414 pages; 40 folding engraved plates, recased with new old style endpapers in its original plain calf binding, rather rubbed but absolutely sound, with original small morocco spine label, some pages little spott and other lightly browned, and few plates with short slit in fold; two early ink signatures at top of titlepage of volume 1, one dated 1778. GI 5576 for first edition.   David Bickersteth 133-200 1996 £685.00

HEISTER, LORENZ 1683-1758   Institutiones Chirurgicae. Amsterdam: Janssonius Waesberge, 1739. 1st Latin edition; 4to; 2 volumes, (11) leaves, 48 pages, (4) leaves, (8), 715 pages; (1) leaf, pages 715-1249, (24) leaves; engraved portrait, 2 engraved title vignttes, 1 engraved headpiece, 38 folding engraved plates; few marginal dampstains on son leaves, outer edge of some of the large folding plates repaired, and jus barely affecting the image on one or two plates; modern half calf and marbled boards; rare. Wellcome III 236.   Jeffrey D. Mancevice 20-44 1996 $2,650.00

HELD, JULIUS S.   Rubens Selected Drawings. London: Phaidon, 195 31 x 23 cm; 2 volumes, xvi, 186 pages, 61 illustrations, 5 color plates; 178 black and white plates, color frontispiece; original cloth.   Rainsfo A54-509 1996 £65.00

HELLER, JOSEPH   Catch-22: a Dramatization. New York: Delacorte, 1973. 1st edition; photos; near fine in price clipped dust jacket.   Lam Duck Books 19-241 1996 $200.00

HELLER, JOSEPH   Catch-22. New York: Simon & Schuster, 1961. Advance copy; 8vo; printed wrappers, covers somewhat darkened and with minor foxing, otherwise very good copy.   James S. Jaffe 34-24 1996 $750.00

HELLER, JOSEPH   Catch-22. London: Cape, 1962. 1st English edition; small spot to front pastedown, else fine in fine dust jacket, very slightl darkened on rear panel, nice copy, scarce.   Between the Covers 42-210 1996 $450.00

HELLER, JOSEPH   Catch-22: a Dramatization. New York: Delacorte, 1973. Advance Review copy with slip laid in; fine in dust jacket. Between the Covers 42-211 1996 $175.00

HELLER, JOSEPH   Catch-22: a Dramatization. New York: Delacorte, 1973. Fine in near fine dust jacket with just a trace of wear, this copy inscribed by author for George Ball, Under Secretary of State Under Kennedy and Johnson.   Between the Covers 42-212 1996 $450.00

HELLER, JOSEPH   God Knows. New York: Alfred A. Knopf, 1984. First edition, one of 350 copies, signed by author; 9 1/2 x 6 1/2 inches; 6 p.l., 353 pages, (1) leaf; printed on special paper; original cloth backed boards, publisher's slipcase (special binding for the limited printing), virtually mint.   Phillip J. Pirages 33-305 1996 $125.00

HELLINGA, W.   Copy and Print in the Netherlands. An Atlas of Historical Bibliography. Amsterdam: 1962. Folio; numerous plates; cloth, gilt; inscribed to and with booklabel of Ruari McLean.   Maggs Bros. Ltd. 1191-181 1996 £100.00

HELLMAN, LILLIAN   Watch on the Rhine. London: privately published, 1942. Limited to 349 copies, this copy not numbered; 4to; drawings; top of spine cloth frayed, offsetting to top left front and front hinge weak; very acceptable copy, internally clean.   Lyman Books 21-573 1996 $100.00

HELLWIG, CHRISTOPH VON   Der Curieuse und Vernunfftige Zauber-Artzt Welcher Lehret und Zeiget, Wie Man Nich Alleine ex Triplici Regno Curieuse Artzeneyen Verfertigen, Sondern auch per Sympathiam et antipathiam... Franckfurt und Leipzig: Ernst Ludwig Niedt, 1725. 1st edition; small 8vo; (14), 320, (16) pages; frontispiece, title in red and black, lightly browned; contemporary vellum, very good, rare. Blake p. 205; Waller 4278 for later edition of 1737.   Edwin V. Glaser 121-156 1996 $1,500.00

A HELP to Elocution. Containing Three Essays. 1. On Reading and Declamation...II. On the Marks and Characters of the Different Passions...III. On Compostion... London: printed for Field & Walter & James McGowan, 1780. 12mo; half title, slightly chipped at fore edge, neatly rebound in half speckled calf, marbled boards, brown label.   Jarndyce 103-6 1996 £110.00

HELPRIN, MARK   A Dove of the East and Other Stories. New York: 1975. 1st edition; very near fine in like dust jacket, author's first book.   Stephen Lupack 83- 1996 $200.00

HELPRIN, MARK   A Soldier of the Great War. New York: HBJ, 1991. Limited to 250 copies; fine in slipcase, signed by author.   Bella Luna 7-274 1996 $100.00

HELPS, ARTHUR   Casimir Maremma. London: Bell and Daldy, 1870. 1st edition; 8vo; 2 volumes; original orange brown cloth, spines evenly faded; Sadleir 1186; Wolff 3134; CBEL III 1388.   Ximenes 108-192 1996 $325.00

HELPS, ARTHUR   Life and Labours of Mr. Brassey 1805-1870. London: Bell and Daldy, 1872. 1st edition; 8vo; xiv, (2), 386 pages, 2 prelim leaves carelessly opened with edge tears (not affecting text), frontispiece, 7 other plates, including 4 maps; original brown cloth embossed in black and gilt with emblematic device on upper cover, cloth bit cockled on lower cover, else very good. Williams I 139; Ottley 2503.   John Drury 82-29 1 1996 £50.00

HELPS, ARTHUR   Thoughts Upon Government. London: Bell and Daldy, 1872. 1st edition; 8vo; viii, 245 pages, contemporary brown half morocco, gilt, raised bands, marbled edges and endpapers; very fine; from the library of the Earl of Ducie with his signature on title.   John Drury 82-104 1996 £60.00

HELY-HUTCHINSON, JOHN   The Commercial Restraints of Ireland Considered. Dublin: printed by William Hallhead, 1779. 1st edition; 8vo; pages (ii, title), v-xxii, 240, lacks half title, 3 folding tables, author's name supplied in ink on title, which is browned; ownership inscription on following leaf; contemporary calf, recently rebacked, spine lined in gilt, leather label. Kress B203; Goldsmiths' 11826.   Sotheran PN32-20 1996 £550.00

HELY-HUTCHINSON, JOHN   The Commercial Restraints of Ireland Considered in a Series of Letters to a Nobel Lord. Dublin: printed by William Hallhead, 1779. 1st edition; 8vo; xxii, 240 pages, 3 folding tables, complete with half title; contemporary calf, gilt, little wear to extremities, else very good. Kress B203; Goldsmiths 11826; Wagner 348; Black 1056.   John Drury 82-105 1996 £475.00

HEMANS, FELICIA   Works. Edinburgh: Blackwood, 1839. 1st edition; small 8vo; 7 volumes; frontispieces, volume 1 has a date of 1841 on titlepage and may be from a later edition; marbled boards, floral gilt decorations on spine with date stamped at bottom, maroon and burgundy morocco labels, split hinge on 1 volume has been repaired with glue, moderate wear, leather rubbed away at spots, labels bit dry.   Charles Agvent 4-649 1996 $175.00

HEMINGWAY, ERNEST MILLAR 1899-1961   Across the River and Into the Trees. New York: 1950. 1st edition; first dust jacket with yellow spine, near fine in near fine jacket.   Stephen Lupack 83- 1996 $150.00

HEMINGWAY, ERNEST MILLAR 1899-1961   Across the River and Into the Trees. New York: Charles Scribners, 1950. 1st edition; 8vo; black cloth, as issued; fine in slightly nicked wrapper.   Appelfeld Gallery 54-116 1996 $100.00

HEMINGWAY, ERNEST MILLAR 1899-1961   Death in the Afternoon. New York: Charles Scribner's Sons, 1932. 1st edition; color frontispiece of Juan Gris painting; original cloth, some wear and uneven fading, front inner hinge tender; important copy in attractive dust jacket (supplied); superb presentation copy, inscribed by author for John H. Mackey.   19th Century Shop 39- 1996 $12,500.00

HEMINGWAY, ERNEST MILLAR 1899-1961   Death in the Afternoon. New York: Scribner's, 1932. 1st edition; photos; near fine in dust jacket that is uniformly dust soiled and has a number of edge chips, overall about very good.   Ken Lopez 74-185 1996 $750.00

HEMINGWAY, ERNEST MILLAR 1899-1961   Death in the Afternoon. New York: 1932. 1st edition; near fine and bright.   Stephen Lupack 83- 1996 $150.00

HEMINGWAY, ERNEST MILLAR 1899-1961   A Divine Gesture. New York: 1974. Limited to 250 numbered copies; wrappers, fine.   Words Etcetera 94-611 1996 £125.00

HEMINGWAY, ERNEST MILLAR 1899-1961   A Farewell to Arms. New York: Charles Scribner's Sons, 1929. 1st edition; 2nd issue, with legal disclaimer; original blue cloth, paper labels, good plus, labels browned, with complete dust jacket which is chipped at top of spine and boasts quite a few small closed tears; overall effect is not at all unpleasant; enclosed in elegant black cloth box; presentation copy from author for Annie Daivs, wife of his old friend Nathan "Bill" Davis.   Lakin & Marley 3-18 1996 $7,500.00

HEMINGWAY, ERNEST MILLAR 1899-1961   A Farewell to Arms. New York: Scribner's, 1929. 1st edition; 8vo; black cloth, paper labels, worn, apart from wear to labels; good.   Appelfeld Gallery 54-117 1996 $100.00

HEMINGWAY, ERNEST MILLAR 1899-1961   The Fifth Column and the First Forty-Nine Stories. New York: Scribner's, 1938. 1st edition; bright rose cloth has kept is color and lustre on this copy, even on spine (which on many copies fades despite dust jacket), text is also quite fresh, imperfections are niggling (such as slight darkening at tips of free endpapers), dust jacket is hardly worn, some rubbing, not quite chipping at head of backstrip, but its maroon has faded on spine, gold belt and white lettering still stand out; one spot stain on dust jacket backstrip, some lettering in 3 lines of blurb on rear panel either effaced or didn't print. Nice in very good jackets.   Magnum Opus 44-50 1996 $950.00

HEMINGWAY, ERNEST MILLAR 1899-1961   For Whom the Bell Tolls. New York: Scribners, 1940. 1st edition; slight foxing to page edges, else fine in near fine, first issue dust jacket with couple of internal repairs but no chipping, couple of very short tears, considerabley nicer than generally found.   Between the Covers 42-213 1996 $650.00

HEMINGWAY, ERNEST MILLAR 1899-1961   For Whom the Bell Tolls. New York: Chas. Scribner's, 1940. 1st edition; 8vo; beige linen; dust jacket with small tear at head of spine and small nicking.   Appelfeld Gallery 54-118 1996 $150.00

HEMINGWAY, ERNEST MILLAR 1899-1961   For Whom the Bell Tolls. London: Cape, 1941. 1st English edition; crown 8vo; 462 pages; original mid blue cloth, backstrip gilt lettered, 2 tiny stains on covers, usual partial browning to free endpapers, top edge gilt, dust jacket, excellent. Hanneman 42a.   Blackwell's B112-149 1996 £135.00

HEMINGWAY, ERNEST MILLAR 1899-1961   For Whom the Bell Tolls. Limited Editions Club, 1942. One of 1500 copies; 10 1/4 x 7 inches; 6 p.l., 498 pages, (1) leaf (colophon); 24 lithographed plates, plus vignettes, all by Lynd Ward; original cloth and publisher's slipcase (tape reinforced); spine uniformly faded, otherwise very fine.   Phillip J. Pirages 33-359 1996 $125.00

HEMINGWAY, ERNEST MILLAR 1899-1961   The Green Hills of Africa. New York: Charles Scribner's, 1935. 1st edition; original cloth and dust jacket, very good in faded and lightly chipped jacket; signed by author.   19th Century Shop 39- 1996 $6,000.00

HEMINGWAY, ERNEST MILLAR 1899-1961   In Our Time. New York: Boni & Liveright, 1925. Revised from the Paris edition, only 1335 copies printed; author's second book and first trade book and first book published in America; original binding, lacking dust jacket, fine.   Charles Agvent 4-650 1996 $950.00

HEMINGWAY, ERNEST MILLAR 1899-1961   In Our Time. New York: 1925. 1st edition; near fine.   Stephen Lupack 83- 1996 $625.00

HEMINGWAY, ERNEST MILLAR 1899-1961   In Our Time. New York: Scribners, 1930. 2nd American edition; One of 3240 copies; original binding, light wear to spine tips, backstrip of dust jacket darkened, with old stain and chipped, moderate edgewear, tears; still quite good example of uncommon dust jacket.   Charles Agvent 4-651 1996 $600.00

HEMINGWAY, ERNEST MILLAR 1899-1961   The Nick Adams Stories. New York: Scribners, 1972. 1st edition; fine in fine, price clipped dust jacket.   Between the Covers 42-215 1996 $125.00

HEMINGWAY, ERNEST MILLAR 1899-1961   (Yiddish Title): The Old Man and the Sea. London: New York: Der Kval, 1958. 1st edition in Yiddish; illustrations by Leonard Baskin; yellow cloth and original unprinted tissue dust jacket; fine, very uncommon; inscribed by Baskin. Between the Covers 42-214 1996 $275.00

HEMINGWAY, ERNEST MILLAR 1899-1961   Three Stories and Ten Poems. Paris: Contact, 1923. 1st edition; only 300 copies printed, this one of only 2 known copies in original dust jacket; original wrappers, with extremely rare glassine wrapper, spectacular copy, mint, as issued, in half morocco case.   19th Century Shop 39- 1996 $27,000.00

HEMINGWAY, ERNEST MILLAR 1899-1961   To Have and Have Not. New York: Scribner's, 1937. 1st edition; fine in very good dust jacket, creased along spine folds and shows minor edgewear at spinal extremties, still, much nicer than usual.   Ken Lopez 74-186 1996 $850.00

HEMINGWAY, ERNEST MILLAR 1899-1961   To Have and Have Not. New York: Scribner, 1937. 1st edition; fine, nice bookplate, dust jacket with bit of very light edge wear, few tiny tears.   Captain's Bookshelf 38-105 1996 $750.00

HEMINGWAY, ERNEST MILLAR 1899-1961   Today Is Friday. Englewood: As Stable Publications, 1962. 1st edition; one of 300 copies; wrappers with drawing by Jean Cocteau printed to front cvoer; very fine with original envelope printed to a geometric design; in quarto case which displays pamphlet and envelope separately under clear lucite; very fine; this copy signed by author. Hanneman A5a.   Bromer Booksellers 90-63 1996 $4,000.00

HEMINGWAY, ERNEST MILLAR 1899-1961   The Torrents of Spring. Paris: Published by the Black Sun Press for Crosby Continental Editions, 1932. Colophon dated 1931. 1st Continental edition; 6 1/4 x 5 inches; vii, (1), 176 pages, (1) leaf (colophon); tipped in Crosby ad at back; original printed wrappers and (torn) publisher's printed glassine jacket, slightly soiled covers, short tear at top of rear cover, otherwise very fine, quite rare in original glassine. Hanneman A4B.   Phillip J. Pirages 33-306 1996 $300.00

HENDERSON GEORGE WYLIE   Jule. New York: Creative Age Press, 1946. 1st edition; neat owner's name stamp, otherwise fine in dust jacket with touch of rubbing ad tiny tear; author's scarce second novel. Between the Covers 43-97 1996 $450.00

HENDERSON, ARCHIBALD   Old Homes and Gardens of North Carolina. Chapel Hill: UNC Press, 1939. 1st edition; number 450 of 1000 copies, signed by Gov. Clyde R. Hoey at the conclusion of his foreword; 4to; 32 pages, plus 100 black and white photographic plates; original dark green cloth, bookplate, else fine in worn publisher's slipcase, mimeographed errata slip laid in.   Chapel Hill 94-23 1996 $300.00

HENDERSON, DAVID   Felix of the Silent Forest. New York: Poets Press, 1967. 1st edition; crease on rear wrapper and touch of wear to extremities, at least very good in wrappers, as issued; author's first book; inscribed by him.   Between the Covers 43-94 1996 $100.00

HENDERSON, DAVID   De Mayor of Harlem. New York: Dutton, 1970. 1st edition; bookplate, fine in very good plus dust jacket bit darkened on spine, some tears and light wear to extremities; very warm full page inscription from author.   Between the Covers 43-96 1996 $100.00

HENDERSON, EBENEZER   Iceland, or the Journal of a Residence in that Island, During the Years 1814 and 1815. Edinburgh: ptd. for Waugh & Innes, Hunter Square, Edinburgh: & T. Hamilton... 1819. 2nd edition; 8vo; (vii-xiv) pages, directions to binder, 1-36 pages, 37-458 pages, 461-563, 565-576 pages, 1 large folding map, partially colored, 16 copperplates; half black calf and marbled boards, corners bumped and slightly worn, joints rubbed, gilt title to spine, raised bands to spine, edges speckled.   Beeleigh Abbey BA56-76 1996 £225.00

HENDERSON, ELLIOTT BLAINE   The Soliloquy of Satan and Other Poems. Springfield: the author, 1907. 1st edition; portrait; author's second book, original cloth.   Beasley Books 82-193 1996 $150.00

HENDERSON, G.   Lahore to Yarkand. London: 1873. Royal 8vo; page xiv, 370, map, 16 plain and 38 colored plates; original cloth, neatly rebacked; signature of Sir Clements Markham on titlepage, few pencil annotations in text.   Wheldon & Wesley 207-43 1996 £900.00

HENDERSON, GEORGE WYLIE   Ollie Miss. New York: Stokes, 1935. 1st edition; woodblock illustrations by L. Balcom; couple of tiny spots t edge and small contemporary bookstore label on free front endpaper, a well as slight fading to corner of base of spine, still very good or bette in about very good dust jacket with chip at foot and some light dampstaining along spine, author's first novel.   Between the Covers 43-97 1996 $450.00

HENDERSON, PAUL   Landmarks on the Oregon Trail. New York: Published by Peter Decker for the Westerners, 1953. 1st edition; limited to 300 copies, this being a presentation copy from Peter Decker to George Harding; 61 pages; folding map in rear pocket, 32 views and 8 line drawings; original pictorial tan cloth with title stamped in green on spine, slipcases, very fine.   Michael D. Heaston 23-170 1996 $200.00

HENDERSON, W. A.   The Housekeeper's Instructor, or, Universal Family Cook...to which is added The Complete Art of Carving. London: for Thomas Kelly, c. 1850. 17th edition; frontispiece, vignette to title, 10 engraved table settings, contemporary sheep neatly rebacked with red leather, plates slightly foxed and margins soiled, corner rubbed. Petersfield Bookshop FH58-120 1996 £98.00

HENDERSON, WILLIAM   Homoeopathy Fairly Represented. Philadelphia: Lindsay & Blakiston 1854. 1st American edition; 8vo; 302 pages; original cloth, spine faded, otherwise fine. Bardford p. 143.   M & S Rare Books 60-461 1996 $125.00

HENDERSON, WILLIAM   My Life as an Angler. London: W. Satchell, Peyton & Co., 1879. 2nd edition; large paper copy, this being number 1, numbered and signed yb publisher; royal 8vo; xvi, 312 pages; woodburytype portrait, 6 full page wood engraved plates on India paper 59 wood engravings in text engraved by Edmund Evans; contemporary dark green half morocco gilt, gilt edges, rubbed, very slight spotting throughout text; presentation inscription from angling bibliographer Thomas Satchell to John Moore.   Thomas Thorp 489-145 1996 £200.00

HENNELL, THOMAS   Poems. Oxford University Press/Humphrey Milford, 1936. 1st edition; original binding, top edge slightly dusty, edges slightly spotted, head and tail of spine and corners bumped, covers, slightly marked, very good, no dust jacket; with ownership signature of William Rothenstein; bookplate of literary agent John Johnson. Ulysses 39-284 1996 £75.00

HENNELL, THOMAS   Six Poems. Tunbridge Wells: School of Arts and Crafts, 1947. 1st edition; hand printed on crown folio 'Arab' platen machine, 14 pages of text, handmade paper; wrappers, top edge dusty, edges slightly spotted, top edges of covers slightly creased and browned, covers slightly spotted and dusty, very good. Loosely inserted is single leaf with note by headmaster of the school, E. Owen Jennings; bookplate of literary agent John Johnson.   Ulysses 39-285 1996 £125.00

HENNESSY, J. B.   Stephania: a Middle and Late Bronze-Age Cemeter in Cyprus. London: Bernard Quaritch, 1985. Folio; xii, 56 pages, 64 plates; original cloth, corners bumped.   Archaeologia Luxor-3439 1996 $125.00

HENNING, S. F.   The Charaxinae Butterflies of Africa. Johannesburg: 1989. 4to; 472 pages, more than 750 color photos and numerous line drawings; cloth.   Wheldon & Wesley 207-1049 1996 £130.00

HENREY, BLANCHE   British Botanical and Horticultural Literature Before 1800. London: 1975. Royal 8vo; 3 volumes; 1128 pages; 32 colored and many other illustrations; cloth.   Wheldon & Wesley 207-245 1996 £180.00

HENRY VIII, KING OF GREAT BRITIAN   A Necessary Doctrine and Ervidition for any Christen Man, set Furthe by the Kynges Maiestie of Englande &c. London: Thomas Barthelet, 1543. Small 4to; 118 unnumbered leaves, black letter with Roman and italic titlepage, the latter with woodcut architectural border, woodcut initials, contemporary ms. annotations on 3 pages, title and laste page bit dusty, small repairs without loss to edges of titlepage and 5 other leaves, occasional light margina stain; 18th century red morocco richly gilt, rebacked, spine remounted, all edges gilt; good copy; bookplates of Viscount Mersey and Charles Butler of Hatfield. STC 5168.7. Lowndes 1040.   A. Sokol XXV-50 1996 £1,350.00

HENRY, DAVID   An Historical Account of All the Voyages Around the World, Performed by English Navigators... London: printed for F. Newbery, 1774/73. 1st edition; 8vo; 4 volumes; five folding maps and 44 engraved plates; contemporary half calf, spines gilt, rather rubbed, spines worn, but essentially sound; very good set. Sabin 31389; Beddie 655; Hill p. 142; Roscoe A218.   Ximenes 108-193 1996 $1,250.00

HENRY, FREDERICK   Founders' Week Memorial Volume Containing Histories of (Philadelphia's) Principal Scientific Institutions, Medical Colleges, Hospitals, Etc. Philadelphia: 1909. 1st edition; 912 pages; illustrations; half leather.   W. Bruce Fye 71-975 1996 $175.00

HENRY, JAMES   My Book. Dresden: printed by E. G. Teubner, 1853. Only edition; 8vo; pages (220), 313, (1); contemporary German marbled boards, leather label, later ownership siganture and bookplate. Howard S. Mott 227-160 1996 $325.00

HENRY, JAMES   Poems Chiefly Philosophical, in Continuation of My Book and a Half Year's Poems. Dresden: C. C. Meinhold and Sons, 1856. Only edition; 8vo; 1 p.l., pages 285, (1), 15; frontispiece; contemporary German marbled boards, leather label, presentation copy inscribed by author for Professor Fleckeisen, Frankfurt. With later ownership signature and bookplate.   Howard S. Mott 227-161 1996 $275.00

HENRY, JAMES P.   Resources of the State of Arkansas with Description and the Counties, Railroads, Mines and the City of Little Rock. Printed by Price & M'Clure, 1873. 3rd edition; 136, (4) pages; folding map, one untitled map; original orange printed wrappers, minor chipping; very good. Allen Arkansas Imprints 684.   Michael D. Heaston 23-30 1996 $300.00

HENRY, JOHN JOSEPH   An Accurate and Interesting Account of the Hardships and Sufferings of that Band of Heroes, Who Traversed the Wilderness in the Campaign Against Quebec in 1775. Lancaster: Printed by William Greer, 1812. 1st edition; 12mo; 235 pages; decorative bordered copy-right slip pasted to verso of titlepage, full contemporary flamed calf with red morocco spine label, hinges partially cracked, front blank endpaper excised, rear blank endpapers soiled, else very good. Howes H423; Staton & Tremaine 465.   Andrew Cahan 47-14 1996 $375.00

HENRY, WILLIAM CHARLES   Memoirs of the Life and Scientific Researches of John Dalton. London: Cavendish Society, 1854. 8vo; pages xv, 249, (iv, bibliography), (vii, ads, etc.), frontispiece, 3 folding plates; modern half polished calf gilt, spine label and raised bands; A.L. Smyth 480.   R.F.G. Hollett & Son 78-173 1996 £150.00

HENSHALL, J. A.   Book of the Black Bass, Comprising Its Complete and Scientific and Life History...Angling and Fly Fishing...Tools, Tackle and Implements. Cincinnati: 1889. 1st edition; 2nd issue of first volume; 8vo; 2 volumes; numerous illustrations; green cloth, fish blocked in gilt on front covers, first volume with few slight spots, both trifle dusty, generally in good state.   Maggs Bros. Ltd. 1190-200 1996 £90.00

HENSHAW, J. W.   Mountain Wild Flowers of America, a Simple and Popular Guide to the Names and Descriptions of the Flowers That Bloom Above the Clouds. Boston: 1906. 8vo; pages xxi, 384; frontispiece, 99 black and white plates; cloth, small tear to head of spine, name on endpaper.   Raymond M. Sutton VI-531 1996 $165.00

HENSHAW, J. W.   Mountain Wild Flowers of Canada. Toronto: 1906. 8vo; pages xxvii, 384; frontispiece, 99 black and white photos; cloth, corners and spine ends worn, front hinge starting, marginal dampstaining along edges of pates, some signs of sticking, slightly shaken. Raymond M. Sutton VI-728 1996 $125.00

HENTY, GEORGE ALFRED 1832-1902   At the Point of the Bayonet. London: Blackie, 1902. 1st edition; fine; from the collection of John H. Dalton.   Harland H. Eastman 10/94-11 1996 $100.00

HENTY, GEORGE ALFRED 1832-1902   Battles of the 19th Century. London: Cassel & Co., 1896/1902. 3 volumes; red cloth, ex-library with very faint mark at bottom of spine where library label removed, number written in upper corner of front free endpaper, some wear to spine ends, small nick to one spine, binding tight, overall a very good set; from the collection of John H. Dalton.   Harland H. Eastman 10/94-117 1996 $100.00

HENTY, GEORGE ALFRED 1832-1902   Bonnie Prince Charlie. London: Blackie, 1888. 1st edition; edges worn, soiling, front free endpaper out, good plus; from the collection of John H. Dalton.   Harland H. Eastman 10/94-13 1996 $100.00

HENTY, GEORGE ALFRED 1832-1902   The Brahmins' Treasure. Philadelphia: Lippincott, 1900. 1st edition; binding with Brhamin peering from a curtained doorway (one of two bindings for this edition); fine; from the collection of John H. Dalton.   Harland H. Eastman 10/94-84 1996 $175.00

HENTY, GEORGE ALFRED 1832-1902   Brains and Bravery. W. & R. Chambers, 1903. 1st edition; minor rubbing; very good-fine; from the collection of John H. Dalton.   Harland H. Eastman 10/94-85 1996 $250.00

HENTY, GEORGE ALFRED 1832-1902   Bravest of the Brave. London: Blackie, 1887. 1st edition; near fine; from the collection of John H. Dalton.   Harland H. Eastman 10/94-14 1996 $250.00

HENTY, GEORGE ALFRED 1832-1902   Bravest of the Brave. London: Blackie, 1887. 1st edition; spine bit darkened, stain on front cover, otherwise very good+; from the collection of John H. Dalton.   Harland H. Eastman 10/94-15 1996 $200.00

HENTY, GEORGE ALFRED 1832-1902   Bravest of the Brave London: Blackie, 1887. 1st edition; rubbed, spine ends worn, nevertheless very good copy; from the collection of John H. Dalton.   Harland H. Eastman 10/94-16 1996 $150.00

HENTY, GEORGE ALFRED 1832-1902   By England's Aid. London: Blackie, 1891. 1st edition; very slight soiling, nevertheless about fine; from the collection of John H. Dalton.   Harland H. Eastman 10/94-18 1996 $165.00

HENTY, GEORGE ALFRED 1832-1902   By Pike and Dyke. London: Blackie, 1890. 1st edition; top of spine slightly chipped, minor soiling, very good+; from the collection of John H. Dalton.   Harland H. Eastman 10/94-19 1996 $140.00

HENTY, GEORGE ALFRED 1832-1902   By Right of Conquest. London: Blackie, 1891. 1st edition; fine; from the collection of John H. Dalton. Harland H. Eastman 10/94-20 1996 $165.00

HENTY, GEORGE ALFRED 1832-1902   By Sheer Pluck. London: Blackie, 1884. 1st edition; inner hinges somewhat cracked, otherwise fine, absolutely brilliant copy; from the collection of John H. Dalton. Harland H. Eastman 10/94-21 1996 $375.00

HENTY, GEORGE ALFRED 1832-1902   A Chapter of Adventures. London: Blackie, 1891. 1st edition; minor edge wear, very good+; from the collection of John H. Dalton.   Harland H. Eastman 10/94-23 1996 $135.00

HENTY, GEORGE ALFRED 1832-1902   Colonel Thorndyke's Secret. London: Chatto & Windus, 1899. Presentation edition; very good; from the collection of John H. Dalton.   Harland H. Eastman 10/94-118 1996 $100.00

HENTY, GEORGE ALFRED 1832-1902   Condemned as a Nihilist. London: Blackie, 1893. 1st edition; near fine; from the collection of John H. Dalton.   Harland H. Eastman 10/94-24 1996 $100.00

HENTY, GEORGE ALFRED 1832-1902   Curse of Carne's Hold. Spencer Blackett, 1st one volume edition, with Oct. 1890 catalog; very good; from the collection of John H. Dalton.   Harland H. Eastman 10/94-87 1996 $350.00

HENTY, GEORGE ALFRED 1832-1902   Cuthbert Hartington. S. W. Partridge, 1st edition; 6 illustrations; fine, from the collection of John H. Dalton.   Harland H. Eastman 10/94-88 1996 $185.00

HENTY, GEORGE ALFRED 1832-1902   Cuthbert Hartington. S. W. Partridge, fine; from the collection of John H. Dalton.   Harland H. Eastman 10/94-121 1996 $100.00

HENTY, GEORGE ALFRED 1832-1902   The Dragon and the Raven. London: Blackie, 1886. 1st edition; bit rubbed and soiled, nevertheless very good; from the collection of John H. Dalton.   Harland H. Eastman 10/94-25 1996 $175.00

HENTY, GEORGE ALFRED 1832-1902   Facing Death. London: Blackie, 1883. 2nd edition, with 1883 catalog announcing "New Series for Season 1884"; near fine; from the collection of John H. Dalton.   Harland H. Eastman 10/94-26 1996 $300.00

HENTY, GEORGE ALFRED 1832-1902   The Fall of Sebastopol. Charles E. Brown Co., red cloth; fine; from the collection of John H. Dalton. Harland H. Eastman 10/94-128 1996 $125.00

HENTY, GEORGE ALFRED 1832-1902   Fighting the Saracens. Charles E. Brown, 1st edition; bit soiled and rubbed, nevertheless a very good copy; from the collection of John H. Dalton.   Harland H. Eastman 10/94-96 1996 $150.00

HENTY, GEORGE ALFRED 1832-1902   Fighting the Saracens. Charles E. Brown Co., red cloth; fine; from the collection of John H. Dalton. Harland H. Eastman 10/94-129 1996 $125.00

HENTY, GEORGE ALFRED 1832-1902   For Name and Fame. London: Blackie, 1887. 1st edition; fine; from the collection of John H. Dalton. Harland H. Eastman 10/94-28 1996 $300.00

HENTY, GEORGE ALFRED 1832-1902   For the Temple. London: Blackie, 1888. 1st edition; very good+; from the collection of John H. Dalton.   Harland H. Eastman 10/94-29 1996 $200.00

HENTY, GEORGE ALFRED 1832-1902   Friends Though Divided. Griffith & Farran, 1883. 1st edition; 1st issue, with publisher's 32 page catalog dated 9/83; brown cloth, very good, near fine; from the collection of John H. Dalton.   Harland H. Eastman 10/94-96 1996 $350.00

HENTY, GEORGE ALFRED 1832-1902   Friends though Divided. Griffith & Farran, 1883. 1st edition; 1st issue, with publisher's 32 page catalog dated 9/83; green cloth, very good plus; from the collection of John H. Dalton.   Harland H. Eastman 10/94-97 1996 $325.00

HENTY, GEORGE ALFRED 1832-1902   A Girl of the Commune. R. F. Fenno, 1895. 1st edition; very good+; from the collection of John H. Dalton.   Harland H. Eastman 10/94-98 1996 $125.00

HENTY, GEORGE ALFRED 1832-1902   Held Fast for England. London: Blackie, 1892. 1st edition; fine, from the collection of John H. Dalton. Harland H. Eastman 10/94-31 1996 $125.00

HENTY, GEORGE ALFRED 1832-1902   In the Hands of the Cave-Dwellers. New York: Harper & Bros., 1900. 1st edition; small oval stamp on titlepage, indicating former ownership by private library, otherwise very fine; from the collection of John H. Dalton.   Harland H. Eastman 10/94-102 1996 $125.00

HENTY, GEORGE ALFRED 1832-1902   In the Heart of the Rockies. London: Blackie, 1895. 1st edition; fine; from the collection of John H. Dalton.   Harland H. Eastman 10/94-34 1996 $110.00

HENTY, GEORGE ALFRED 1832-1902   In the Reign of Terror. London: Blackie, 1888. 1st edition; near fine; from the collection of John H. Dalton.   Harland H. Eastman 10/94-35 1996 $250.00

HENTY, GEORGE ALFRED 1832-1902   Jack Archer. Roberts Bros., 1884. 1st American edition; minor edge wear, very good; from the collection of John H. Dalton.   Harland H. Eastman 10/94-103 1996 $175.00

HENTY, GEORGE ALFRED 1832-1902   A Knight of the White Cross. London: Blackie, 1896. 1st edition; crown 8vo; pages 392, 32 (publisher's list); frontispiece, 11 other plates by Ralph Peacock and portrait of author, double page diagrammatic plate, prelims lightly foxed, original mid green bevel edged cloth, lettering and design on backstrip and front cover blocked in gilt and colors, grey endpapers; excellent. Dartt p. 91. Blackwell's B112-150 1996 £65.00

HENTY, GEORGE ALFRED 1832-1902   A Knight of the White Cross. London: Blackie, 1896. 1st edition; fine; from the collection of John H. Dalton.   Harland H. Eastman 10/94-38 1996 $100.00

HENTY, GEORGE ALFRED 1832-1902   The Lion of St. Mark. London: Blackie, 1889. 1st edition; near fine, from the collection of John H. Dalton.   Harland H. Eastman 10/94-40 1996 $200.00

HENTY, GEORGE ALFRED 1832-1902   The Lion of the North. London: Blackie, 1886. 1st edition; edge wear, front hinge reglued, rubbed, nevertheless nar very good copy of a difficult title to find; from the collection of John H. Dalton.   Harland H. Eastman 10/94-41 1996 $125.00

HENTY, GEORGE ALFRED 1832-1902   Maori and Settler. London: Blackie, 1891. 1st edition; fine; from the collection of John H. Dalton. Harland H. Eastman 10/94-43 1996 $225.00

HENTY, GEORGE ALFRED 1832-1902   March to Coomassie. London: Tinsley, 1874. 1st edition; spine professionally relaid, very good; from the collection of John H. Dalton.   Harland H. Eastman 10/94-5 1996 $1,000.00

HENTY, GEORGE ALFRED 1832-1902   March to Coomassie. London: Tinsley, 1874. 2nd edition; very good plus, scarce as the first edition; from the collection of John H. Dalton.   Harland H. Eastman 10/94-6 1996 $1,000.00

HENTY, GEORGE ALFRED 1832-1902   March to Magdala. London: Tinsley, 1868. 1st edition; very good; from the collection of John H. Dalton.   Harland H. Eastman 10/94-4 1996 $1,000.00

HENTY, GEORGE ALFRED 1832-1902   On the Irrawaddy. London: Blackie, 1897. 1st edition; crown 8vo; pages 352, 32 (publisher's list); frontispiece, 7 other plates, prelim leaves lightly foxed; original pale blue cloth, backstrip and front cover gilt lettered and decorated in gilt, white, pink and brown, lightly rubbed at backstrip head and tail, grey endpapers, gift inscription; good. Dartt p. 100.   Blackwell's B112-151 1996 £65.00

HENTY, GEORGE ALFRED 1832-1902   Orange and Green. London: Blackie, 1888. 1st edition; minor rubbing at edges, otherwise fine copy of a very difficult title; from the collection of John H. Dalton.   Harland H. Eastman 10/94-48 1996 $250.00

HENTY, GEORGE ALFRED 1832-1902   Out of the Pampas. London: Griffith & Farran, 1871. 1st edition; author's first book for boys; very good; from the collection of John H. Dalton.   Harland H. Eastman 10/94-7 1996 $650.00

HENTY, GEORGE ALFRED 1832-1902   Out with Garibaldi. London: Blackie, 1901. 1st edition; fine, with summary slip laid in; from the collection of John H. Dalton.   Harland H. Eastman 10/94-49 1996 $100.00

HENTY, GEORGE ALFRED 1832-1902   Peril and Prowess. New York: E. P. Dutton, 1st American edition; minor rubbing, near fine; from the collection of John H. Dalton.   Harland H. Eastman 10/94-104 1996 $100.00

HENTY, GEORGE ALFRED 1832-1902   The Queen's Cup. London: Chatto & Windus, 1897. 1st edition; (publisher's records show only 350 copies were printed); 3 volumes; original cloth, some edge wear and soiling, overall very good set; from the collection of John H. Dalton. Harland H. Eastman 10/94-2 1996 $3,000.00

HENTY, GEORGE ALFRED 1832-1902   Redskin and Cowboy. London: Blackie, 1892. 1st edition; near fine copy of a difficult to find title in nice condition; from the collection of John H. Dalton.   Harland H. Eastman 10/94-52 1996 $125.00

HENTY, GEORGE ALFRED 1832-1902   A Roving Commission. London: Blackie, 1900. 1st edition; spine slow slightly faded as to be hardly noticeable (this title is notorious for spine fading); fine; from the collection of John H. Dalton.   Harland H. Eastman 10/94-53 1996 $125.00

HENTY, GEORGE ALFRED 1832-1902   Rujub the Juggler. London: Chatto & Windus, 1893. 1st edition; 3 volumes; original cloth, minor edg wear, very good; from the collection of John H. Dalton.   Harland H. Eastman 10/94-3 1996 $3,000.00

HENTY, GEORGE ALFRED 1832-1902   Rujub the Juggler. London: Chatto & Windus, 1899. Presentation edition; very good+; from the collection of John H. Dalton.   Harland H. Eastman 10/94-142 1996 $100.00

HENTY, GEORGE ALFRED 1832-1902   St. Bartholomew's Eve. London: Blackie, 1894. 1st edition; fine; from the collection of John H. Dalton. Harland H. Eastman 10/94-54 1996 $100.00

HENTY, GEORGE ALFRED 1832-1902   St. George for England. London: Blackie, 1885. 1st edition; first 3 pages once folded, leaving slight creases; otherwise fine copy of early Blackie title; from the collection of John H. Dalton.   Harland H. Eastman 10/94-55 1996 $250.00

HENTY, GEORGE ALFRED 1832-1902   A Search for a Secret, Gall and Inglis. 1st one volume edition; new endpapers, near fine. from the collection of John H. Dalton.   Harland H. Eastman 10/94-106 1996 $115.00

HENTY, GEORGE ALFRED 1832-1902   Seaside Maidens. London: Tinsley, 1880. original dark red cloth, minor spotting, nevertheless a very good, near fine copy.   Harland H. Eastman 10/94-1 1996 $6,500.00

HENTY, GEORGE ALFRED 1832-1902   Steady and Strong. W. & R. Chambers, 1905. 1st edition; bit rubbed, quarter inch tear to top of spine, nevertheless very good; from the collection of John H. Dalton. Harland H. Eastman 10/94-107 1996 $100.00

HENTY, GEORGE ALFRED 1832-1902   A Tale of Waterloo. Worthington, 1st edition; fine copy, scarce; from the collection of John H. Dalton.   Harland H. Eastman 10/94-108 1996 $200.00

HENTY, GEORGE ALFRED 1832-1902   A Tale of Waterloo. Worthington, Later issue, with 2 battle plans and 9 page catalog as in first edition, but not the 8 illustrations called for; binding less ornate than first; near fine; from the collection of John H. Dalton.   Harland H. Eastman 10/94-144 1996 $100.00

HENTY, GEORGE ALFRED 1832-1902   Those Other Animals. Henry & Co., 1st edition; fine, from the collection of John H. Dalton.   Harland H. Eastman 10/94-109 1996 $145.00

HENTY, GEORGE ALFRED 1832-1902   Through the Sikh War. A Tale of the Conquest of the Punjaub. London: Blackie, 1912. New edition; crown 8vo; pages 384, 16 (publisher's list); 8 plates by Hal Hurst, 3 color double page map, prelim and final few leaves lightly foxed; original mid green cloth backstrip and front cover gilt lettered and decorated in black, pin and tan, grey endpapers, bookplate; dust jacket; excellent. Dartt p. 137.   Blackwell's B112-152 1996 £100.00

HENTY, GEORGE ALFRED 1832-1902   The Tiger of Mysore. London: Blackie, 1896. 1st edition; fine copy; from the collection of John H. Dalton.   Harland H. Eastman 10/94-59 1996 $100.00

HENTY, GEORGE ALFRED 1832-1902   True to the Old Flag. London: Blackie, 1885. 1st edition; quarter inch cut in spine, otherwise near fine copy, difficult to find early title; from the collection of John H. Dalton. Harland H. Eastman 10/94-62 1996 $225.00

HENTY, GEORGE ALFRED 1832-1902   Two Sieges. S. W. Partridge, 1st edition; minor soiling, front free endpaper out, otherwise near fine, exceedingly scarce; from the collection of John H. Dalton.   Harland H. Eastman 10/94-110 1996 $150.00

HENTY, GEORGE ALFRED 1832-1902   Under Drake's Flag. London: Blackie, 1883. 1st edition; fine; from the collection of John H. Dalton. Harland H. Eastman 10/94-63 1996 $300.00

HENTY, GEORGE ALFRED 1832-1902   Under Wellington's Command. London: Blackie, 1899. 1st edition; fine, from the collection of John H. Dalton.   Harland H. Eastman 10/94-64 1996 $100.00

HENTY, GEORGE ALFRED 1832-1902   Venture and Valour. London: W. & R. Chambers, 1900. 1st edition; bit soiled, nevertheless very good+; from the collection of John H. Dalton.   Harland H. Eastman 10/94-111 1996 $100.00

HENTY, GEORGE ALFRED 1832-1902   With Clive in India. London: Blackie, 1884. 1st edition; fine, from the collection of John H. Dalton. Harland H. Eastman 10/94-67 1996 $300.00

HENTY, GEORGE ALFRED 1832-1902   With Frederick the Great. London: Blackie, 1898. 1st edition; fine, from the collection of John H. Dalton.   Harland H. Eastman 10/94-70 1996 $100.00

HENTY, GEORGE ALFRED 1832-1902   With Lee in Virginia. London: Blackie, 1890. 1st edition; very good+/near fine, from the collection of John H. Dalton.   Harland H. Eastman 10/94-72 1996 $150.00

HENTY, GEORGE ALFRED 1832-1902   With Moore at Corunna. London: Blackie, 1898. 1st edition; fine, from the collection of John H. Dalton.   Harland H. Eastman 10/94-73 1996 $100.00

HENTY, GEORGE ALFRED 1832-1902   With Wolfe in Canada. London: Blackie, 1887. 1st edition; bit rubbed and soiled, nevertheless very good; from the collection of John H. Dalton.   Harland H. Eastman 10/94-77 1996 $175.00

HENTY, GEORGE ALFRED 1832-1902   A Woman of the Commune. F. W. White & Co., 1895. 1st edition; spine bit faded, endpapers brittle and chipped, otherwise very good+; from the collection of John H. Dalton. Harland H. Eastman 10/94-113 1996 $150.00

HENTY, GEORGE ALFRED 1832-1902   Wulf the Saxon. London: Blackie, 1895. 1st edition; fine; from the collection of John H. Dalton. Harland H. Eastman 10/94-79 1996 $100.00

HENTY, GEORGE ALFRED 1832-1902   Yarns on the Beach. London: Blackie, 1886. 1st edition; minor edge wear, otherwise very good+, near fine, almost impossible to find Blackie first; from the collection of John H. Dalton.   Harland H. Eastman 10/94-83 1996 $300.00

HENTY, GEORGE ALFRED 1832-1902   The Young Carthaginian. London: Blackie, 1887. 1st edition; blue cloth; very good+; from the collection of John H. Dalton.   Harland H. Eastman 10/94-81 1996 $200.00

HENTY, GEORGE ALFRED 1832-1902   The Young Carthaginian. London: Blackie, 1887. 1st edition; rust cloth; very good+, from the collection of John H. Dalton.   Harland H. Eastman 10/94-82 1996 $200.00

HEPBURN, A. BARTON   The Story of an Outing. New York: & London: Harper & Bros., 1913. 1st edition; 8vo; (109) pages; frontispiece, photos plates and in-text photos; original cloth backed boards, top edge gilt, bright, near fine copy; scarce.   Chapel Hill 94-382 1996 $150.00

HEPBURN, H. P.   Reports of Cases Argued and Determined in the Supreme Court of the State of California in the Year 1852. Volume II. Philadelphia: T. & J. W. Johnson, Law Booksellers, 1854. contemporary sheep, quite worn and rubbed, sound copy.   Meyer Boswell SL27-35 1996 $150.00

HEPBURN, KATHARINE   Me. Stories of My Life. New York: Knopf, 1991. 1st edition; 8vo; cloth, dust jacket, as new, scarce.   James S. Jaffe 34-246 1996 $150.00

THE HERALDIC Visitation of Westmorland, Made in the Year 1615, by Sir Richard St. George, Knt., Norroy King at Arms. London: John Gray Bell, 1853. 4to; pages vi, (ii), 57, woodcut vignette on title, title trifle spotted, original blindstamped cloth, gilt, rather damped, spine cracked and repaired, lower board stained at base, title trifle spotted, very scarce, especially in this extremely large form; extra large copy. R.F.G. Hollett & Son 78-174 1996 £225.00

(HERBARIUS Latinus). Speier: Johann and Conrad Hist, 1484. 2nd known edition of the first book printed in Germany to contain solely botanical illustrations. Small 4to; incomplete, but by no means a fragment; of the 150 illustrated leaves, 145 are present and in excellent fresh condition, remainind five provided in facsimile; old calf; Goff H63.   Ximenes 109-154 1996 $5,000.00

HERBERSTAIN, SIGISMUND   Rervm Moscoviticarvm Commentarij. Basle: Oporin, 1571. Folio; 6 full page plates, 3 double page mapps, half page plate, woodcut initials; boards. Adams H302.   Rostenberg & Stern 150-105 1996 $2,500.00

HERBERT, AGNES   Casuals 1912. illustrations, some light foxing, otherwise near fine; very scarce.   David Grayling J95Biggame-529 1996 £150.00

HERBERT, EDWARD   A Short Account of the Authorities in Law, Upon Which Judgement Was Given in Sir Edw. Hales His Case, London: printed for M. Clark, etc., 1688. Modern cloth, title cut close, but sound. Meyer Boswell SL27-110 1996 $350.00

HERBERT, EDWARD HERBERT, BARON 1583-1648   The Life of Edward Lord Herbert of Cherbury. Dublin: printed for H. Saunders, J. Potts, D. Chamberlaine, J. Hoey, Jun... 1771. 1st Dublin edition; 12mo; contemporary marbled calf, top of spine little worn; very good, scarce. cf. Hazen 11.   Ximenes 109-296 1996 $125.00

HERBERT, FRANK   Children of Dune. Putnam, 1976. 1st edition; near fine in very good dust jacket with some wear and tear.   Aronovitz 57-548 1996 $100.00

HERBERT, FRANK   Children of Dune. Putnam, 1976. 1st edition; near fine in very good dust jacket with some wear and tear.   Aronovitz 57-548 1996 $100.00

HERBERT, FRANK   Dune. London: Gollancz, 1966. 1st English edition; just about fine in dust jacket with small chip missing from head of dust jacket spine.   Aronovitz 57-544 1996 $175.00

HERBERT, FRANK   God Emperor of Dune, Heretics of Dune and Chapter House Dune. Putnam, 1981/84/85. Uncorrected proofs; 1st editions; signed by author in last volume; wrappers; fine.   Aronovitz 57-553 1996 $375.00

HERBERT, FRANK   Whipping Star. Putnam, 1970. 1st edition; signed by author; near fine in dust jacket with tiny tear and chip near upper left corner of front dust jacket panel.   Aronovitz 57-545 1996 $135.00

HERBERT, GEORGE   The Temple. Sacred Poems and Private Ejaculations. London: Nonesuch Press, 1927. Number 1175 of 1500 copies; 8vo; pages x, 214, engraved frontispiece, set in Janson type at the Nonesuch Press and printed by the Chiswick Press on Van Gelder paper, each page rubricated; original tapestry cloth binding, top edge gilt on the rough. Nonesuch Century 44.   Claude Cox 107-106 1996 £70.00

HERBERT, GEORGE   Works...in Prose and Verse. London: William Pickering, 1846. 1st edition thus; 8vo; 2 volumes; frontispiece, titlepage printed in red and balck; full black morocco, all edges gilt, minor rubbing and light soiling.   Charles Agvent 4-652 1996 $160.00

HERBERT, GEORGE   The Works in Prose and Verse. London: William Pickering, 1853. 9 x 6 inches; 2 volumes; frontispiece in each volume 2 small woodcut seals, woodcut device on each title, woodcut headpieces, tailpieces and initials; frontispieces and endpapers bit foxed and darkened, barely perceptible wear to leather, but bindings and text almost flawless; fine original black morocco (probably by Hayday), covers with double gilt rule frame and elaborate blind tooled center panel, spines with gilt decorated raised bands and compartments elaborately stamped in blind, board edges and turn-ins densely gilt in an antique floral pattern, all edges gilt; frontispieces and endpapers bit foxed and darkened, barely perceptible wear to leather, but bindings and text are almost flawless. Keynes p. 60.   Phillip J. Pirages 33-420 1996 $375.00

HERBERT, HENRY WILLIAM 1807-1858   The Horse of America. New York: Stringer & Townsend, 1857. 1st edition; 2 volumes; original binding; corners bumped, spine tops frayed.   October Farm 36-199 1996 $325.00

HERBERT, J.   The Spear. NEL, 1978. 1st edition; fine in dust jacket. Aronovitz 57-554 1996 $135.00

HERBERT, W.   Antiquities of the Inns of Court and Chancery (etc.). London: printed for Vernor and Hood, Poultry etc., 1804. Large paper copy; 24 engraved plates, interleaved and extensively extra illustrated, extending work to 2 volumes; early elaborately tooled calf, joints cracking, still handsome.   Meyer Boswell SL26-106 1996 $1,250.00

HERD, RICHARD   Scraps of Poetry. Sedbergh: Miles Turner, n.d., c. 1900. 12mo; pages ix, 95; original cloth, damped and cockled, one leaf worn at edges, some marginal tears and soiling to lasat few leaves, rear endpapers creased and damped, final leaf supplied in facsimile, from the first edition, little shaken, but acceptable copy, extremely scarce. R.F.G. Hollett & Son 78-405 1996 £50.00

HERDMAN, WILLIAM   Picturesque Views in Liverpool. Liverpool: the author, 1864. 1st edition; folio; (4) pages, 28 chromolithographic plates; publisher's half morocco, rebacked; light foxing to few plates, some minor water stains and inscription in pen on verso of titlepage, still respectable copy of a scarce book.   The Bookpress 75-199 1996 $1,200.00

HERE, H.   The Genera of the Mesembryanthemaceae. Cape Town: 1971. 4to; pages (9), 316; cloth, some dampstaining around spine, mostly blending with dark cloth, few spots.   Raymond M. Sutton VI-1007 1996 $125.00

HERGESHEIMER, JOSEPH   Triall by Armes. London: Elkin Mathews & Marrot, 1929. 1st edition; one of 530 copies, numbered and signed by author; 8vo; set in Monotype 12 pt. Caslon Old face and printed by Robert Maclehose at the University Press in Glasgow; grey paper decorated and printed in red over boards, paper used again for dust jacket, book lightly used as is jacket, jacket slightly soiled, ex-libris on front pastedown, very good.   Priscilla Juvelis 95/1-298 1996 $125.00

HERING, CONSTANTINE   The Homoeopathist, or Dometic Physician. Allentown: Academical Bookstore, 1835-38. 1st edition; 18mo; 177, (1), (2); 290 pages; printed slip listing 45 numbered herbs pasted to inside front cover; contemporary calf backed marbled boards, minor wear to binding, slight browning and staining, very good. Rinderknecht 32129. Bradford p. 145.   M & S Rare Books 60-462 1996 $600.00

HERMES, WILLIAM   A Collection of 30 Lithograph Plates of Cottage and Landscape Scenery. Berlin and London? c. 1845. Oblong 8vo; gilt lettered brown cloth, with Newman, 24 Soho Square, ticket on inner pastedown, one corner little bumped.   Ken Spelman 30-85 1996 £65.00

HERNDON, WILLIAM H.   The True Story of a Great Life. The History and Personal Recollections of Abraham Lincoln. Chicago: 1889. 1st edition; 8vo; 3 volumes, 638 pages, original cloth, inner hinges of volume 1 slightly cracked, ends of backstrips minutely frayed, otherwise nice. Howes H429.   Edward Morrill 368-151 1996 $175.00

HERODIAN   Herodian of Alexandria His Imeriall History of Twenty Roman Caesars and Emperours of His Time. London: printed by W. Hun for the author, 1652. 1st edition of this translation; small 4to; contemporary reversed calf, rubbed, rebacked; very good, rare title, uncommon.   Ximenes 108-194 1996 $850.00

HERODIAN   De Romanorum Imperatorum Vita ac Rebus Gestis Libri VIII, Graece & Latine... Basel: per Henricum Petri, 1563. Nice early edition; 8vo; (16), 597 pages + index (lacks last 4 leaves of index); parallel Greek/Latin text; old calf, neatly and expertly respined, small portion of title removed, with no loss of text, some minor staining; K Books 441-115 1996 £150.00

HERODOTUS   Historiae Libri VIIII Musarum Nominibus Inscripti...De Genere Vitaque Homeri Libellus. Lyons: Heirs of Seb. Gryphius, 1558. 16mo; pages (1)-892, 65ff. n.n., 2 ff. blank; stiff vellum, sewn through the vellum in account-book style, yapp edges, sides decorated with cornerpieces of arabesque ornament on a gilt ground and a large centrepiece of interlaced fillets and arabesque flowers also on a gilt ground , the field seme with triple dots, flat spine with three concealed bands marked by lines of gilt tooling, gilt quatrefoil in each compartment, edges handsome gauffered with large foliate ornament and parcel-gilt, pastedown and one endleaf at each end, in very sound unrestored condition; a contemporary Lyonnese binding; the copy of William Bragge, his sale Sotheby's 10 Nov. 1880 lot 457; the copy of Arthur Ram, his sale Sotheby's 25 May 1906, lot 81.   Marlborough 160-3 1996 £2,250.00

HERODOTUS   Historico Delle Guerre de Greci, et de Persi. Venetia: Appresso Lelio Bariletto, 1565. 3rd edition of Boiardo's Italian translation; 8vo; (xvi) pages, folios 1-336; 18th century vellum, gilt device on each board, morocco labels, titlepage little soiled, otherwise very nice. Adams H414.   Robert Clark 38-62 1996 £140.00

HERODOTUS   The Histories of... Haarlem: Limited Editions Club, 1958. Limited to 1500 copies; signed by artist; 4to; illustrations by Edward Bawden; brown buckram; fine in case.   Charles Agvent 4-653 1996 $175.00

HERODOTUS   The Histories of Herodotus of Halicarnassus. Haarlem: Printed by Joh. Enschede en Zonen, 1958. One in an edition of 1500 copies, numbered and signed by artist; 9.75 x 6 inches; 615 pages; illustrations by Edward Bawden, 10 double page color spreads which serve to introduce the volume and each of its nine divisions have been printed separately, numerous pen and ink drawings, printed in monotype spectrum designed by Jan van Krimpen on paper specially made by the Wolvercote Paper Mill; bound in dark brown buckram over boards, with cameo portrait of Herodotus embossed in ivory linen on front cover and an ivory linen label in gold on spine, top edge gilt, slipcase of patterned paper. Spine slightly faded, nevertheless fine.   Joshua Heller 21-153 1996 $125.00

HERODOTUS   The History of Herodotus. London: Nonesuch Press, 1935. Limited to 675 numbered copies; small folio; xxvii, 778 pages; 9 wood engraved illustrations, 9 maps, titlepage printed in red and black; original blue vellum backed cloth, spine gilt, top edge gilt, others uncut, extremities very lightly rubbed.   Thomas Thorp 489-147 1996 £300.00

HERODOTUS   The History of Herodotus of Halicarnassus, to Which is Added a Life of Herodotus and the Behistun Inscription. London: Nonesuch Press, 1935. One of 675 numbered copies; narrow folio; 9 wood engravings by V. Le Campion with maps by T. L. Poulton; half blue vellum, lavishly gilt, spine somewhat faded, less so than on many copies, lower board and fore-edge spotted, little sproadic foxing elsewhere, otherwise nice, clean copy, original prospectus laid in. Bertram Rota 272-331 1996 £280.00

HERODOTUS   History. London: Nonesuch Press, 1935. One of 675 copies; 12 x 7 1/2 inches; xxvi, 778 pages; woodcut title illustration and 9 half page woodcuts by V. Le Campion, 9 maps and plans by T. L. Poulton, title in red and black; original blue vellum backed cloth boards, backstrip lettered and attractively decorated in gilt, top edge gilded on rough, other edges untrimmed, hint of fading to spine (as usual), cloth somewhat soiled, corners ittle bumped, binding completely solid and showing no significant wear; fine internally; bookplate of Merle Armitage. Phillip J. Pirages 33-401 1996 $450.00

HERODOTUS   The History of Herodotus of Halicarnasus. London: Nonesuch Press, 1935. One of 675 copies; small folio; 9 wood engravings by V. Le Campion, maps; blue linen boards over blue gilt stamped vellum spine as issued, gilt top; good copy.   Appelfeld Gallery 54-120 1996 $375.00

HERODOTUS   Pyramids. London: 1995. In an edition of 12 copies, this one of 10 for sale, numbered and signed by the artist; 6.5 x 5 inches; 28 printed pages; set in 14 pt. Centaur and printed letterpress on Fabriano Artistico, together with 6 etchings (some hand colored and viewed through cut-out pyramid shapes) and 4 lino-cuts; hand decorated endpapers of stenciled triangles; prints by Susan Allix; bound in red boatskin and printed terracotta cloth with lacquered brass plate, python skin pyramid; title, blind tooled on goatskin; laid in folder of red cloth with pyramid shapes, trimmed with red leather triangle, brown paper triangle with title and gold color stud to close;   Joshua Heller 21-40 1996 $650.00

HERON, ROBERT   The Comforts of Human Life; or Smiles and Laughter of Charles Chearful and Martin Merryfellow. London: printed for Oddy and Co., 1807. 1st edition; small 8vo; pages xi, 226; folding hand colored frontispiece; 19th century calf backed marbled boards; very good to nice.   James Fenning 133-159 1996 £95.00

HERON-ALLEN, E.   Violin Making, As It Was and Is. London: and Melbourne: Ward, Locke & Co., 1885. 2nd edition; 8vo; original cloth, fine in dust jacket.   Glenn Books 36-279 1996 $120.00

HERONDAS   The Mimiambs of Herondas. London: Fanfrolico Press, n.d. Limited edition of 375 numbered copies; 4to; (72) pages; 19 decorations by Alan Odle; patterned boards, cloth spine, top edge gilt, others uncut, lightly rubbed.   Thomas Thorp 489-148 1996 £85.00

HERRERA, ANTONIO DE   The General History of the Vast Continent and Islands of America, Commonly Call'd the West Indies, from the First Discovery Thereof; with the Best accounts the People Could Give of Their Antiquities. London: printed by Jer. Batley, 1725-26. 1st edition in English; 8vo; 6 volumes; 3 folding maps and 15 engraved plates; contemporary calf, gilt, spines gilt, some rubbing, slight wear to joints, one label renewed, one label missing; excellent set. Sabin 31557; Streeter I 140; Wagner Spanish Southwest 121.   Ximenes 108-195 1996 $3,500.00

HERRESHOFF, L. FRANCIS   The Common Sense of Yacht Design. New York: Rudder Pub., 1948. 1st edition; 4to; 2 volumes, 176 pages, 155, diagrams, plates, cloth, very good.   John Lewcock 30-185 1996 £85.00

HERRICK, JAMES   A Short History of Cardiology. Springfield: 1942. 1st edition; ex-library; original binding.   W. Bruce Fye 71-978 1996 $100.00

HERRICK, ROBERT 1591-1674   Love's Dilemmas. Chicago: Stone, 1898. 1st edition; designed and decorated by Will Bradley; tan cloth, near fine. Charles Agvent 4-654 1996 $150.00

HERRICK, ROBERT 1591-1674   Poetical Works. London: George Bell, 1900. 8vo; 2 volumes; handsome three quarter tan polished calf over marbled boards, richly gilt panelled spines, raised bands, leather labels, gilt tops by Zaehnsdorf. Fine, attractive bindings.   Appelfeld Gallery 54-121 1995 $200.00

HERRICK, ROBERT 1591-1674   Poetical Works. London: Cresset Press, 1928. Limited edition of 750 numbered copies; 4 volumes; printed on mouldmade paper, decorations by Albert Rutherston with frontispieces in color, tailpieces; original parchment, top edge gilt, others uncut, spines very slightly dust soiled, otherwise good set in original harlequin cloth slipcase.   Thomas Thorp 489-149 1996 £95.00

HERRIES, ROBERT   A Letter from a Member of the House of Commons to His Constituents, on the Great Constitutional Questions Lately Agitated in Parliament. London: n.p., n.d. 1784. 39, (1) pages; stabbed pamphlet as issued; fine, letter signed in ms. "Robert Herries" and annotated on titlepage "Sir Rob. Herries M.P. for Dumfries". With loose copy of Herries's engraved bookplate.   C. R. Johnson 37-61 1996 £65.00

HERRING, JAMES   National Portrait Gallery of Distinguished Americans. New York: Monson Bancroft, et al, 1834-39. 1st edition; 4 volumes, three quarter leather and marbled boards, gilt tooled spines, very good, edges scuffed, some offsetting and foxing. Howes H443. Bohling Book Co. 191-580 1996 $150.00

HERRLINGER, ROBERT   History of Medical Illustration from Antiquity to 1600. New York: 1970. 1st English translation; 4to; 178 pages; illustrations; original binding, slipcase. GM 6610.4.   W. Bruce Fye 71-981 1996 $150.00

HERRLINGER, ROBERT   History of Medical Illustration from Antiquity to 1600. New York: Medicina Rara, 1970. 4to; original binding, nice copy in slipcase, last bit sunned in parts.   James Tait Goodrich K40-143 1996 $135.00

HERRMANN, GOTTFRIED   De Metris Poetarum Graecorum et Romanorum Libri III. Leipzig: Fleischer, 1796. 8vo; 461 pages; contemporary vellum, covers panelled with blue double rules, upper cover with full length portrait, flat spine in 6 panels, gilt rules, blue title and imprint lables, all edges gilt, marbled endpapers, preserved in drop side cloth box within morocco backed slipcase, a German binding in the style of Edwards of Halifax; from the libraries of F. Lee Warner, the gift of Dr. Butler and thus inscribed and Ham Court, Upton-on Severn, with bookplate.   Marlborough 160-41 1996 £1,950.00

HERSCHEL, CAROLINE   Memoir and Correspondence of Caroline Herschel. London: John Murray, 1876. 1st edition; 8vo; (xii, 355 pages, 32 pages publisher's ads); maroon cloth with gilt lettered spine, except for fading to spine, this is a fine, unopened copy.   Paulette Rose 16-299 1996 $125.00

HERSCHEL, JOHN FREDERICK WILLIAM   A Preliminary Discourse on the Study of Natural Philosophy. London: Longman, Rees, Orme, Brown, Green & Longman, 1832. 3rd U.K. printing; 4 x 6.5 inches; 372 pages; half leather and marbled boards, gilt bands on spine and speckled edges, engraved titlepage browned; very good.   Knollwood Books 70-293 1996 $125.00

HERSEY, JOHN   Hiroshima. Limited Editions Club, 1983. One of 1000 copies, signed by author, artist and Robert Penn Warren; 12 3/4 x 9 3/4 inches; (58) leaves, including 2 blanks; 8 original grisly silkscreens by Jacob Lawrence; in publisher's slightly soiled and slightly frayed slipcase, upper corners of binding and text slightly bumped, otherwise fine. Phillip J. Pirages 33-360 1996 $450.00

HERTRICH, W.   Camellias in the Huntington Gardens. San Marino: 1954-55-59. 8vo; pages ix 380; vii, (1), 378; xii, 366; 3 volumes; 5 colored plates and hundreds of life size black and white photos; cloth, light scuffing to lower edges, rear hinge cracked in volume 1, dust jackets, with some staining and edge wear; author's signature on each titlepage.   Raymond M. Sutton VII-570 1996 $125.00

HERTRICH, W.   Camellias in the Huntington Gardens. San Marino: 1954-59. Royal 8vo; 3 volumes; 5 colored plates, about 800 photos; good set in slightly worn dust jackets, complete copies are very scarce. Wheldon & Wesley 207-1834 1996 £100.00

HERTY, THOMAS   A Digest of the Laws of the United States of America. Baltimore: printed for the editor by W. Pechin, 1800. contemporary sheep, worn and embrowned, but sound.   Meyer Boswell SL26-107 1996 $450.00

HERVEY, JOHN   Memoirs of the Reign of George the Second... London: John Murray, 1848. 1st edition; 8vo; 2 volumes, lxvi, 520; vii, 593 pages; contemporary three quarter maroon morocco by Hatchards of Picadilly with raised bands, top edge gilt, attractive set.   Chapel Hill 94-223 1996 $175.00

HERVEY, THOMAS KIBBLE   Australia; with Other Poems. London: for Hurst Robinson and Co., 1824. 1st edition; 16mo; pages xxiii, (i), 64, (ii), 65-141, (i); contemporary panelled calf, spine with gilt lyre devices in compartmetns, label gone, triple gilt rules, pink endpapers, gilt inner dentelles, gilt edges, rubbed, joints little tender; good copy; with dedication inscribed on printer's blank "To Mrs. Hervey, from her Son, the author". Ferguson 953.   Simon Finch 24-113 1996 £285.00

HES, LEX   The Leopards of Londolozi. London: 1991. Limited to 150 copies, signed by author; large 4to; profusely illustrated with superb photographic illustrations; finely bound in half brown morocco, in fine quality cloth slipcase with leather trimmings.   David Grayling J95Biggame-102 1996 £150.00

HESIOD   The Works of Hesiod. London: printed by N. Blandford, for T. Green, 1728. 1st edition; 4to; 2 works in 1, frontispiece by Hogarth; contemporary calf, rebacked, original spine laid down, spine gilt; very good. Foxon p. 142; CBEL II 1491. Paulson, Hogarth's Graphic Works 111.   Ximenes 108-197 1996 $650.00

HESS, HANS   Lynoel Feininger. New York: Abrams, 1961. 4to; 355 pages; 30 tipped in color plates, 510 monochrome illustrations; cloth, dust jacket. Lucas p. 143; Freitag 2976.   Brannan 43-203 1996 $495.00

HESS, THOMAS B.   Willem De Kooning Drawings. London: 1972. 4to; 296 pages; 15 color plates, 138 black and white illustrations; original cloth, slightly worn dust jacket, library inkstamp to verso of titlepage, library labels, slight sellotape marks to pastedowns.   Rainsford A54-356 1996 £85.00

HESSE, ALICE, GRAND DUCHESS OF   Biographical Sketch and Letters. London: 1884. 1st edition; portraits; blue cloth, gilt, crown emblem and name ALICE in gilt on upper cover; very good; presentation copy from author's siter, Princess Helena for W. Gostelow.   Words Etcetera 94-15 1996 £75.00

HESSE, HERMAN   Goldmund. London: Peter Owen, 1959. 1st edition; very good in dust jacket slightly rubbed on one or two corners, rare thus.   Words Etcetera 94-618 1996 £75.00

HESSE, HERMANN   Demian. Berlin: Fischer, 1919. True 1st edition in German; 8vo; original illustrated paper covered boards, attractively designed and in remarkably fine condition.   Lakin & Marley 3-19 1996 $1,250.00

HESSE, HERMANN   Eine Stunde Hinter Mitternacht. Leipzig: Eugen Diederichs, 1899. 1st edition; contemporary three quarter cloth and marbled paper covered boards; nice, rare.   Lame Duck Books 19-246 1996 $2,000.00

HESSE, HERMANN   The Officina Bodoni in Montagnola. Verona: Stamperia Voldonega, 1976. One of an edition of 50 copies; octavo; 7 pages; grey wrappers with device in red; extremely fine.   Bromer Booksellers 90-210 1996 $450.00

HESSE, HERMANN   Peter Camenzin...Neundzwanzige Auflage. Berlin: S. Fischer, 1906. 8vo; pages (viii), 260, (i) blank, (iii) ads; original decorated cloth, spine lettered in gilt, slightly darkened, top edge gilt, short tears at extremities, cloth folder, brown morocco pull-off case, spine in compartments with raised bands, rules and lettering gilt, very good. With author's autograph inscription dated August 1906, and signed photo of author tipped in.   Simon Finch 24-114 1996 £1,250.00

HETHERINGTON, A. L.   The Early Ceramic Wares of China. London: Benn Bros., 1922. 4to; xviii, 160 pages; 94 illustrations on 45 plates, cloth, slightly dust soiled.   Thomas Thorp 489-150 1996 £50.00

HETHRINGTON, WILLIAM   Branthwaite Hall, Canto III. Cockermouth: printed for the author by Daniel Fidler, 1850. 1st edition; 8vo; pages xii, 194, complete with half title, errata slip and sugar paper endpapers; original cloth, paper spine label, little drkened, extremites minimally worn. R.F.G. Hollett & Son 78-406 1996 £140.00

HETLEY, THOMAS   Reports and Cases Taken in the Third (-) Seventh Years of the Late King Charles...at the Common Pleas Barre (etc). London: printed by F. L. for Matthew Walbancke and Thomas Firby, etc., 1657. contemporary sheep, front joint cracked, worn and embrowned, usable.   Meyer Boswell SL26-108 1996 $250.00

HEWETT, EDGAR L.   The Fiesta Book. Papers of the School of American Research. Santa Fe: Archaeological Inst. of America, 1925. 1st edition; 8vo; 100 pages; 2 plates; printed stiff wrappers showing light edge wear, else very good.   Andrew Cahan 47-144 1996 $100.00

HEWETT, SARAH   The Peasant Speech of Devon with Other Matters Connected Therewith. London: Elliot Stock, 1892. Half title; uncut in original blue cloth, dulled; with signature of A. L. Hayward and some ms. additions in pencil.   Jarndyce 103-66 1996 £55.00

HEWISON, JAMES KING   The Romance of Bewcastle Cross. Glasgow: John smith, 1923. Small 4to; paes 54, 10 plates; original wrappers, spine faded; scarce.   R.F.G. Hollett 76-128 1996 £65.00

HEWITSON, WILLIAM C.   British Oology. Newcastle-upon-Tyne: 1831-38. 155 fine hand colored plates; contemporary half morocco, light rubbing, contents excellent; nice copy.   David A.H. Grayling MY95Orn-42 1996 £200.00

HEWITT, E. R.   A Trout and Salmon Fisherman for Seventy-Five Years. New York: 1948. Pages xxiv, 338; illustrations; original binding. Stephen Lunsford 45-73 1996 $100.00

HEWITT, GRAILY   The Pen and Type Design. London: First Edition Club, 1928. Limited to 250 copies; royal 8vo; 47 pages; printed in Treyford Type on Barcham Green handmade paper, 10 text figures; publisher's full crimson morocco, gilt geometric 'V' shaped design on both cvoers, top edge gilt, very good.   Thomas Thorp 489-151 1996 £195.00

HEWLETT, MAURICE HENRY 1861-1923   Quattrocentisteria: How Sandro Botticelli Saw Simonetta in the Spring. New York: Grolier Club, 1921. One of 300 copies; small folio; printed on Van Gelder paper with elaborate opening initial in red; marbled boards with cloth spine, corners little worn, faint stain at edge of titlepage and initial lightly offset onto facing page, otherwise nice, enormous bookplate tipped in.   Bertram Rota 272-303 1996 £60.00

HEYDEN, DORIS   Pre-Columbian Architecture of Messoamerica. New York: Harry N. Abrams, 1975. 4to; 336 pages, 363 illustrations; original cloth, dust jacket.   Archaeologia Luxor-4550 1996 $150.00

HEYDEN, HERMAN VAN DER   Speedy Help for Rich and Poor. London: J. Young for O. P(ulleyn), 1653. 1st edition in English; 12mo; lacking front blank endleaves; modern calf in period style with raised bands and blind tooling, tear in blank outer margin of leaf K8. Wing H1661; Wellcome III p. 260; Hirsch III pp. 196-197.   James Tait Goodrich K40-144 1996 $495.00

HEYECK, ROBIN   Marbling at the Heyeck Press. Heyeck Press, 1986. One of 150 numbered copies, signed by author; 4to; printed in handset Centaur and Arrighi in black and grey on Barcham Green's Langley handmade; half grey morocco, marbled boards, fine in slipcase. Bertram Rota 272-232 1996 £260.00

HEYECK, ROBIN   Marbling at the Heyeck Press. California: Heyeck Press, 1986. Limited to only 150 numbered copies; 4to; 68 pages printe on handmade paper; 28 examples of marbled paper tipped in, including frontispiece; publisher's dark grey morocco backed marbled boards, edges uncut, slipcase; mint, bound by Schuberth Bookbindery. Thomas Thorp 489-152 1996 £200.00

HEYERDAHL, THOR   American Indians in the Pacific, the Theory Behind the Kon-Tiki Expedition. London: George Allen & Unwin, 1952. 1s British edition; large 8vo; 90 plates, 11 maps, xv, 821 pages; brown cloth; some soiling and wear to covers, hinges weak, small piece cut from front free endpaper.   Parmer Books O39Nautica-039114 1996 $150.00

HEYERDAHL, THOR   The Art of Easter Island. Garden City: Doubleday & Co., 1975. 4to; 350 pages, 15 colored, 320 black and white plates; bit of soil on base of text block, else near fine in worn dust jacket. Parmer Books O39Nautica-039345 1996 $175.00

HEYERDAHL, THOR   The Art of Easter Island. Garden City: Doubleday & Co., 1975. 4to; 350 pages; 336 color plates; light green linen, dust jacket.   Kenneth Karmiole 1NS-121 1996 $150.00

HEYLYN, PETER 1600-1662   Cosmographie in Four Bookes. London: Henry Seile, 1652. 1st edition; folio; the 4 maps not present; full contemporary calf, rebacked, original spine laid down, new red morocco label. Wing H1689.   Ian Wilkinson 95/1-109 1996 £260.00

HEYMAN, MAX L.   Prudent Soldier, a Biography of Major General E.R.S. Canby 1817-1873. Glendale: 1959. 418 pages; photos; book fine. Early West 22-288 1996 $100.00

HEYWARD, DU BOSE   Jasbo Brown and Selected Poems. New York: Farrar & Rinehart, 1931. 1st edition; fine in lightly soiled, near fine pictorial dust jacket; inscribed by author for Selma Robinson. Captain's Bookshelf 38-108 1996 $375.00

HEYWOOD, JAMES   Illustrations of the Principal English Universities. London: plates dated 1840's/last plate 1863. 8vo; titlepage, 1 f. contents, 44 plates, 10 interior scenes, 1 plan, 5 views, lithographs, aquatints and engravings; original green cloth, gilt lettering, top edge gilt, excellent condition. Abbey Scenery 451.   Marlborough 162-43 1996 £850.00

HEYWOOD, THOMAS   Gunaikeion; or, Nine Bookes of Various History Concerninge Women. London: by Adam Islip, 1624. 1st edition; folio; (8), 466 pages, engraved title, woodcut head and tailpieces; full brown levant morocco, gilt fillets, spine richly gilt in compartments, gilt dentelles, by Sangorski & Sutcliffe, lacking front and rear blanks, couple of tiny rust holes repaired, superb copy, fine and clean in elegant, flawless binding. Grolier L-W 142; STC 13326.   Joseph J. Felcone 64-42 1996 $3,200.00

HEYWOOD, THOMAS   The Life of Merlin, Sirnamed Ambrosius. London: by J. Okes and are to be sold by Jasper Emery, 1641. 1st edition; 4to; (70), 376 pages, frontispiece; early 19th century calf in quasi-period style, blank margin of frontispiece skillfully extended, few neat early marginal repairs, else nice. Wing H1786.   Joseph J. Felcone 64-22 1996 $2,000.00

HEYWOOD, V. H.   The Biology and Chemistry of the Umbelliferae. London: 1972. 4to; pages x, 438; numerous plates and text figures; hardbound.   Raymond M. Sutton VI-198 1996 $163.00

HIAASEN, CARL   A Death in China. New York: Atheneum, 1984. 1st edition; bookplate on front pastedown mostly hidden by the front flap, small spot on fore edge, else near fine in near fine dust jacket, with tiny ter and slightly discolored on rear panel.   Between the Covers 42-488 1996 $200.00

HIAASEN, CARL   Double Whammy. New York: Putnam, 1987. 1st edition; fine in dust jacket, signed by author.   Between the Covers 42-489 1996 $100.00

HIAASEN, CARL   Powder Burn. New York: Atheneum, 1981. Uncorrected proof; very slight soiling to page edges, still easily fine, laid into the finished jacket for the book which, because it is slightly oversized, is a little worn along top edge.   Between the Covers 42-487 1996 $850.00

HIAASEN, CARL   Tourist Season. New York: Putnam's, 1986. 1st edition; light sporadic foxing to top edge, else near fine in dust jacket; signed by author.   Lame Duck Books 19-365 1996 $200.00

HIAASEN, CARL   Tourist Season. New York: Putnam, 1986. 1st edition; fine in very near fine dust jacket.   Ken Lopez 74-190 1996 $150.00

HIAASEN, CARL   Tourist Season. New York: G. P. Putnam's, 1986. 1st edition; fine in near fine dust jacket which is slightly worn at bottom right corner of front panel.   Steven C. Bernard 71-325 1996 $125.00

HIBBERD, SHIRLEY   New and Rare Beautiful Leaved Plants. London: 1870. Royal 8vo; pages viii, 144, 54 colored plates; original cloth, refixed, trifle worn; bookplate of Amos Perry, with inscription from author for Perry.   Wheldon & Wesley 207-1701 196 £120.00

HICKERINGILL, EDMUND   The Test or, Tryal of the Goodness and Value of Spiritual Courts. London: printed by George Larkin, for the Assigns of the author, 1683. Somewhat dusty in attractive modern quarter calf, gilt.   Meyer Boswell SL25-106 1996 $450.00

HICKS, EDWARD   Sir Thomas Malory - His Turbulent Career - a Biography. Cambridge: Harvard University Press, 1928. 1st edition; 8 black and white plates; buckram backed boards, top edge gilt, page and endpaper edges slightly browned, head and tail of spine slightly bumped, covers slightly marked, cover edges faded, very good; with ownership signature of Frederick Pottle.   Ulysses 39-710 1996 £55.00

HICKSON, SYDNEY J.   A Naturalist in North Celebes. London: John Murray, 1889. 1st edition; demy 8vo; (xvi), 392, 28 pages; colored frontispiece, plates, folding colored maps, illustrations; original decorative cloth, gilt, very slightly rubbed, few very minor marks, occasional slight spotting, but good.   Ash Rare Books Zenzybyr-49 1996 £185.00

HIEB, LOUIS A.   Collecting Tony Hillerman. Santa Fe: Vinegar Tom Press, 1992. One of 75 handbound, numbered copies, signed by Hieb and Hillerman; fine.   Quill & Brush 102-919 1996 $175.00

HIEROCLES   Commentarius in Aurea Pythagoreorum Carmina. Paris: ex Typ. Steph. Prevosteau 1583. Editio princeps; 8vo; pages (xxiv), 347 (misnumbered 247), (i), text in Greek letter; armorial woodcut on title of the Abbot Franciscus Rupifucaldius. 17th century ex-libris, ornate headpieces and initials; Parisian vellum over boards, gilt arabesque on covers, spine gilt, all edges gilt; uniform light age yellowing, but very good. Brunet III 154; BM STC Fr. p. 368; Adams P2313. Hoffman II p. 407.   A. Sokol XXV-51 1996 £1,250.00

HIERONYMUS, SAINT   Epistolae Selectae. Paris: Nivel, 1602. 12mo; 417ff. num., 48 ff. n.n.; contemporary brown calf, covers gilt with triple outer rule and seme of fleur-de-lys, corners with crowned H and laurel wreath, flat spine gilt in similar fashion with central Maltese cross, all edges gilt, later endpapers, gilt armos of Henry IV, King of France, corners and covers worn and rubbed, Henry IV bindings are of some rarity in commerce.   Marlborough 160-19 1996 £2,100.00

HIERONYMUS, SAINT   Vitae Sanctorum Patrum, Sive Vitas Patrum. Venice: Octavianus Scotus, 14 Feb. 1483/84. 251 of 252 leaves, lacking initial blank a1; in highly unusual early 19th century Irish binding of dark maroon morocco, spine fully gilt in panels, covers with central arabesque design bound in blind within an ornamental gilt and blind border, gilt edges and turn-ins, cloth endleaves printed with tiny sunburst pattern, yellow and blue silk endbands, signed in gilt along front fore-edge turn (and visible with book closed) "Bibliotheca Conoviana Dublinii. M.D.CCC.XXXIV. James Adams Binder Dublin." Very slightest of rubbing to covers, else fine, clean copy. BMC V 279; Goff H 206; Hain Copinger 8599.   Joseph J. Felcone 64-24 1996 $3,500.00

HIGDEN, RALPH   Polychronicon. London: 1865-86. 8vo; 9 volumes; original cloth.   Howes Bookshop 265-1583 1996 £300.00

HIGGINS, BRYAN   Experiments and Observations with the View of Improving the Art of composing and Applying Calcareous Cements, and of Preparing Quick-Lime... London: T. Cadell, 1780. 8vo; viii, 232 pages; contemporary marbled boards with seemly new calf spine and corners; bookplates of Buddle Atkinson and Gilbert Redgrave. Harris & Savage No. 347.   Elton Engineering 10-73 1996 £450.00

HIGGINS, C. A.   New Guide to the Pacific Coast Santa Fe Route. Chicago and New York: Rand, McNally & Co., 1894. 1st edition; 282 pages, (6) pages ads; illustrations; folding map; original red cloth with title in gilt on front cover and spine, fine, very minor wear. Not in Wynar or Wilcox.   Michael D. Heaston 23-33 1996 $125.00

HIGGINS, F. R.   Progress in Irish Printing. Dublin: Alex. Thom, 1936. Large 4to; 143 pages, plates and illustrations; original stiff colored printed paper wrappers; very good.   James Fenning 133-160 1996 £85.00

HIGGINS, GEORGE   "The King of Counties." Miami County, Her Towns, Villages and Business, Timber, Water, Land Agricultural Resources.... Paola: Western Spirit Print, June 10, 1877. 1st edition; 32 pages; frontispiece; original printed yellow wrappers, small piece from upper left and corner of front where torn away affecting word The; very good. Very rare. Howes H467.   Michael D. Heaston 23-192 1996 $550.00

HIGGINS, GEORGE V.   The Friends of Eddie Coyle. New York: 1972. 1st edition; very good in dust jacket.   Words Etcetera 94-622 1996 £60.00

HIGGINS, GODFREY   The Celtic Druids: an Attempt to Shew, That the Druids Were the Priests of Oriental Colonies Who Emigrated from India. London: R. Hunter, 1829. (Engraved title reads 1827); small folio; lxxxi, 324 pages; frontispiece map, engraved title and 45 plates on India paper, all laid down, 14 wood engravings; modern three quarter dark brown morocco over matching cloth, spines with raised bands and gilt stamped red morocco label, minor foxing; very good. Bookplate of Vincent Lloyd-Russell.   George J. Houle 68-65 1996 $650.00

HIGGINS, R. A.   Catalogue of the Terracottas in the Department of Greek and Roman Antiquities, British Museum. Volume II (only). London: British Museum, 1959. 4to; 74 pages, 43 plates; original cloth, bookplate. Archaeologia   Luxor-3449 1996 $125.00

HIGGINSON, A. HENRY   Try Back, a Huntsman's Reminiscences. New York: Huntington Press, 1931. 1st edition; limited to 401 numbered copies, signed by author; 241 pages; two tone cloth with label, very good in lightly worn and darkened publisher's slipcase.   Hermitage SP95-891 1995 $225.00

HIGGINSON, HENRY H.   Letters from an Old Sportsman to a Young One. Garden City: Doubleday, 1929. 1st edition; limited to 201 copies, numbered and signed by author; octavo; xvii, 248 pages; 10 full page color plates, etching in rear pocket, signed by Lionel Edwards; peach cloth, little faded, else fine.   Bromer Booksellers 90-171 1996 $200.00

HIGGINSON, THOMAS   Oldport Days. Boston; Osgood, 1873. 1st edition; 10 heliotype views; original binding, minor edgewear, hinges cracked but tight; BAL 8282.   Charles Agvent 4-655 1996 $135.00

HIGSON, DANIEL   Seafowl, Shooting sketches. Preston, Lancs.: 1909. 2nd edition; frontispiece, original cloth, excellent copy. Scarce.   David A.H. Grayling 3/95-359 1996 £200.00

HIJUELOS, OSCAR   Mr. Ives' Christmas. New York: Harper Collins, 1995. Special limited edition, not offered for sale; fine, without dust jacket in die-cut slipcase, gold on black cloth.   Oracle Books 1-187 1996 $100.00

HIJUELOS, OSCAR   Our House in the Last World. New York: Persea Books, 1983. Advance uncorrected proofs; wrappers; fine, scarce, with promotional material laid in.   Beasley Books 82-79 1996 $250.00

HIJUELOS, OSCAR   Our House in the Lost World. New York: Persea, 1983. 1st edition; small printing of 5000 copies, signed by author; fine in near fine lightly dust soiled dust jacket;   Thomas Dorn 9-141 1996 $150.00

HILDRETH, RICHARD   The Slave; or Memoirs of ARchy Moore. Boston: Whipple and Damrell, 1840. 2nd edition; 8vo; 123, 115 pages; 2 volumes in 1; original cloth backed boards, front cover nearly detached, binding soiled, light waterstaining. LCP/HSP Afro Amer. Cat. 4800; Wright I 1188.   M & S Rare Books 60-168 1996 $500.00

HILL, BERT HODGE   Corinth. Volume I. Part VI: The springs, Peirene, Sacred Spring, Glauke. Princeton: ASCSA, 1964. Folio; 2 volumes, text, 235 pages with 144 figures; and large folio plate volume: 18 loose plates in portfolio with ties, as issued; fine set.   Archaeologia Luxor-3184 1996 $350.00

HILL, BERT HODGE   The Temple of Zeus at Nemea. Princeton: American School of Classical Studies in Athens, 1966. Folio; xii, 49 pages, 43 figures, 29 plates (loose in portfolio, as issued); cloth backed boards.   Archaeologia Luxor-3457 1996 $150.00

HILL, CONSTANCE   Jane Austen: Her Home and Her Friends. London: Lane, 1902. 1st edition; 8 1/2 x 5 3/4 inches; pages xiv, 279; frontispiece, 61 illustrations; dark blue cloth with decoration in white on front cover and backstrip from design by Jane Austen; contemporary inscription, some rubbing of design on front cover and corners slightly bruised, front endpapers repaired at hinge, very good, scarce. Gilson M251; Keynes 223; Chapman 11.   Ian Hodgkins 78-119 1996 £85.00

HILL, DEAN   Football Thru the Years. New York: Published by Gridiron Pub. Co., 1940. Folio; 114 pages; illustrations; original dark green cloth lettered in gilt on spine, light wear to extremities, otherwise fine, inscribed by author.   Heritage Book Shop 196-202 1996 $175.00

HILL, EDWIN   Principles of Currency. London: Longman, Brown, Green & Longmans, 1856. 1st edition; 8vo; iv, 216 pages, folding table before title, occasional annotations in pencil; original cloth, rubbed and somewhat shaken; good. Masui p. 126; not in Cotton & Little or Einaudi. John Drury 82-106 1996 £95.00

HILL, GEOFFREY   Collected Poems. London: Deutsch, 1985. Limited to 112 special copies, Signed by author; 8vo; quarter blue morocco and marbled boards, marbled board slipcase; spine trifle faded, otherwise fine.   James S. Jaffe 34-252 1996 $250.00

HILL, GEOFFREY   For the Unfallen - Poems 1952-1958. London: Andre Deutsch, 1959. 1st edition; original binding, bookplate, some slight offsetting from upper flap to front free endpapers, front pastedown partially and faintly browned, head and tail of spine and corners slightly bumped, very good in nicked and slightly torn, creased, rubbed, marked and dusty dust jacket browned at spine and edges.   Ulysses 39-290 1996 £145.00

HILL, GEOFFREY   Mercian Hymns. London: Andre Deutsch Ltd., 1976. 1st edition; 2nd impression; wrappers, covers internally slightly spotted, very good. Inscribed by author.   Ulysses 39-291 1996 £75.00

HILL, GEOFFREY   The Mystery of the Charity of Charles Peguy. London: Agenda Editions/Andre Deutsch, 1983. 1st edition; one of 100 special copies, signed by author; 8vo; red cloth, acetate dust jacket; as new.   James S. Jaffe 34-251 1996 $150.00

HILL, GEOFFREY   Preghiere. Leeds: Northern House Pamphlet Poets, 1964. 1st edition; 8vo; white glossy printed wrappers;; fine; presentation copy, inscribed by author to Allen Tate and his wife Isabella Gardner. James S. Jaffe 34-248 1996 $1,000.00

HILL, GEOFFREY   Somewhere Is Such a Kingdom. Boston: Houghton Mifflin, 1975. 1st edition; 8vo; cloth, dust jacket; fine in jacket with one tiny spot of rubbing at one fold, scarce.   James S. Jaffe 34-249 1996 $150.00

HILL, GEORGE   Medals of Renaissance. London: British Museum Publications, 1978. 28 x 22 cm; 230 pages; 32 plates; original cloth, in dust jacket (fine).   Rainsford A54-313 1996 £75.00

HILL, GEORGE FRANCIS   A Corpus of Italian Medals of the Renaissance Before Cellini. London: British Museum, 1930. 40 x 29 cm; 2 volumes; xvii, 371 pages; plates: vii, 201 plates; original cloth, slightly soiled, corners rubbed, slightly foxed and some fingermarks.   Rainsford A54-314 1996 £850.00

HILL, JAMES   The Following is an Authentic Copy of a Letter Sent by James Hill to His Brother in Manchester. N.P.: n.d. Manchester, 1782. Quarto; 4 pages; nice.   C. R. Johnson 37-15 1996 £75.00

HILL, JOHN   A Series of Progressive Lessons, Intended to Elucidate the Art of Flower Painting in Water colours. Philadelphia: M. Thomas, 1818. 1st edition; 4to; 32 pages; 10 fine colored aquatints, plus 2 uncolored aquatints; original red calf backed brown printed boards, some foxing and offsetting, but splendid copy; very rare. S&S 45685; M & S Rare Books 60-276 1996 $4,500.00

HILL, JOHN 1716?-1775   The Actor. London: for R. Griffiths, 1750. 1st edition; 12mo; pages (x), 326; contemporary calf, unlettered, double gilt rules, worn; from the library of Charles Maurice de Talleyrand-Perigord, bookplate of Bibliotheque du Chateau de Valencay.   Simon Finch 24-116 1996 £500.00

HILL, JOHN 1716?-1775   The Actor; a Treatise on the Art of Playing. London: printed for R. Griffiths, 1750. 1st edition; 12mo; early half calf, bit worn, very good. LAR 683; CBEL II 739.   Ximenes 108-199 1996 $450.00

HILL, JOHN 1716?-1775   The British Herbal: an History of Plants and Trees, Natives of Britain, Cultivated for Use, or raised for Beauty. London: 1756 Folio; pages (4), 533, (3), frontispiece, title vignette and 75 plates of figures; contemporary calf, neatly repaired, one corner of binding neatly repaired but very satisfactory.   Wheldon & Wesley 207-44 1996 £750.00

HILL, JOHN 1716?-1775   The History of a Woman of Quality; or, the Adventures of Lady Frail. London: printed for M. Cooper and G. Woodfall, 1751. 1st edition; 12mo; 19th century half calf, spine gilt, joints rubbed; very good, very uncommon. Raven 91; Block p. 103; CBEL II 997.   Ximenes 109-156 1996 $1,500.00

HILL, JOHN 1716?-1775   Lucina Sine Concubitu; a Letter Humbly Address'd to the Royal Society. Waltham St. Lawrence: Golden Cockerel Press, 1930. One of 500 numbered copies, from the text of the 1750 edition; foolscap 8vo; 3 engrvings on copper by Hester Sainsbury; half parchment, patterned boards; nice.   Bertram Rota 272-174 1996 £55.00

HILL, JOHN H.   Princess Malah. Washington: Associated Pub., 1933. 1st edition; two tiny gouges to front gutter, some foxing to endpapers, else about fine in very good dust jacket with moderate chip on rear panel and some light spotting to spine; very uncommon. rare in jacket. Not in Blockson.   Between the Covers 43-100 1996 $575.00

HILL, JOSEPH J.   The History of Warner's Ranch and Its Environs. Los Angeles: privately printed, 1927. Limited to 300 numbered copies; royal 8vo; 221 pages; half cloth and boards, bookplate, 2 etchings; near fine. Howes H486; Herd 1036; Cowan p. 280.   Gene W. Baade 1094-73 1996 $350.00

HILL, JOSEPH J.   The History of Warner's Ranch and Its Environs. Los Angeles: John Treanor, 1927. One of 300 copies; 11 x 7 7/8 inches; xii, 221 pages, 2 etchings by Loren Barton; brown boards with linen spine and tips and paper spine label, small spot to tail of spine; inscribed by Treanor to Sol Lesser.   Dawson's Books Shop 528-108 1996 $100.00

HILL, JOSEPH J.   History of Warner Ranch and Its Environs. Los Angeles: 1927. 1st edition; 221 pages; frontispiece, illustrations; dust jacket, very good+. Farquhar 11; Howes H486; Herd 1036.   T. A. Swinford 49-515 1996 $100.00

HILL, M. O.   Atlas of the Bryophytes of Britain and Ireland. Colchester: 1991-94. Royal 8vo; 3 volumes, maps; boards.   Wheldon & Wesley 207-1624 1996 £85.00

HILL, MATTHEW DAVENPORT   Suggestions for the Repression of Crime, Contained in Charges Delivered to Grand Juries of Birmingham... London: John W. Parker and son, 1857. 1st edition; 8vo; xii, 707, (1) pages, few leaves carelessly opened; original cloth, rebacked, most of original backstrip restored; uncut; good; presented to the library of the Working Men's College, London. With college bookplate and inkstamps. Headicar & Fuller I 613; Williams II 395.   John Drury 82-107 1996 £180.00

HILL, NAPOLEON   The Master-Key to Riches. Los Angeles: Willing Publishing, 1945. 1st edition; 8vo; dust jacket (few chips), very good. Signed by author.   George J. Houle 68-66 1996 $200.00

HILL, NATHANIEL   The Ancient Poem of Guillaume de Guileville Entitled Le Pelerinage de l'Homme... London: Basil Montagu Pickering, 1858. 1st edition; 4to; frontispiece, 14 plates, 7 woodcut illustrations and other decorations; original dark green cloth; fine. CBEL II 878. Ximenes 108-200 1996 $175.00

HILL, OLIVER   The Garden of Adonis. London: 1923. 1st edition; 48 tipped in gravure plates; gilt cover and spine.   J. B. Muns 154-224 1996 $425.00

HILL, REGINALD   Pictures of Perfection. Bristol: Scorpion Press, 1994. 1/20 deluxe lettered copies signed by author and E. Wright who provided author appreciation; quarter bound goatskin with raised bands; fine. Quill & Brush 102-908 1996 $450.00

HILL, REGINALD   Pictures of Perfection. Bristol: Scorpion Press, 1994. 1/75 signed, numbered and specially bound copies; quarter bound in leather, marbled paper boards, textured colored endpapers and colored top edges.   Quill & Brush 102-909 1996 $125.00

HILL, REGINALD   Recalled to Life. Bristol: Scorpion Press, 1992. 1/20 deluxe lettered copies, signed by author and Peter Lovesey who provided an author appreciation. Quarter bound goatskin with raised bands, fine.   Quill & Brush 102-906 1996 $450.00

HILL, REGINALD   Recalled to Life. Bristol: Scorpion Press, 1992. 1/99 signed, numbered and specially bound copies; quarter bound in leather, marbled paper boards, textured colored endpapers and colored top edges.   Quill & Brush 102-907 1996 $125.00

HILL, ROWLAND 1795-1879   Journal through the North of England and Parts of Scotland. (and) Extract of a Journal of a Second Tour from London through the Highlands of Scotland and the Northern Western Parts of England. London: Gillet/London: by A. Paris, 1799/1800. 8vo; pages xii, 182, 1 f; half title, 39 pages; both parts disbound, some light foxing and old blindstamps on title of first part.   Marlborough 162-44 1996 £150.00

HILL, ROWLAND 1795-1879   The Life of Sir Rowland Hill and the History of the Penny Postage. London: Thomas de la Rue, 1880. 8vo; 2 volumes, 6 plates; choicely bound in half red morocco, gilt tops; superb copy from the library of Andrew Carnegie.   Charles W. Traylen 117-50 1996 £190.00

HILL, ROY L.   Booker T.'s Child: the Life and Times of Portia Marshal Washington Pittman. Newark: McDaniel Press, 1974. 1st edition; slight stain to corners of pages, otherwise fine without dust jacket, presumably as issued. Nicely inscribed by author in year of publication.   Between the Covers 43-340 1996 $125.00

HILL, W. C. O.   Primates, Comparative Anatomy and Taxonomy. Edinburgh: 1953-66. Volumes 1-6, 3296 pages; 190 plates, 740 figures; cloth.   John Johnson 135-445 1996 $450.00

HILL, W. C. O.   Primates, Comparative Anatomy and Taxonomy. Edinburgh: 1953-74. 1st edition; 8vo; 8 volumes; plates; cloth, dust jackets.   Maggs Bros. Ltd. 1190-692 1996 £325.00

HILL, WILLIAM HENRY   The Violin-Makers of the Guarneri Family (1626-1762). Their Life and Work. William E. Hill & Sons, Violin Makers, 1931. Limited edition, published for the subscribers; 4to; xl, 181 pages; 17 plates in color, 46 in photogravure, 51 text illustrations; publisher's quarter vellum, cloth sides, top edge gilt, others uncut, covers somewhat soiled, occasional light finger soiling inside.   Thomas Thorp 489-153 1996 £400.00

HILL-TOUT, CHARLES   The Native Races of the British Empire: British North America: The Far West, The Home of the Salish and Dene. London: Archibald Constable & Co., 1907. 22.5 cm; 263 pages; frontispiece, illustrations, portraits, folding map; gilt stamped decorated cloth; fine, ex-private library, 3 small stamps; lovely copy. E&L 1728. Rockland Books 38-96 1996 $125.00

HILLARD, GEORGE STILLMAN   Six Months in Italy. Boston: Ticknor, Reed and Fields, 1854. 3rd edition; 8vo; 2 volumes, 432, 455, 8 pages ads dated 1853; lacking free endpaper in volume two; original brown cloth, some wear to spine ends, still near fine.   David Mason 71-102 1996 $120.00

HILLARY, WILLIAM   An Appeal to the British Nation, on the Humanity and Policy of forming a National Institution for the Preservation of Lives and Property from Shipwreck. London: G. and W. B. Whittaker, 1823. 1st edition; 8vo; (iv), 25 pages, recently well bound in calf backed marbled boards, gilt; very scarce. Williams I 501; Goldsmiths 23810; not in Kress or Black.   John Drury 82-108 1996 £250.00

HILLERMAN, TONY   The Blessing Way. New York: Harper & Row, 1970. 1st edition; near fine in very good+ unfaded dust jacket with light wear to extremities and short edge tear to front panel, in custom made clamshell box.   Lame Duck Books 19-366 1996 $1,750.00

HILLERMAN, TONY   The Blessing Way. New York: H&R, 1970. 1st edition; near fine in dust jacket that is slightly faded on spine, as usual, shows some wear at crown, otherwise near fine, very nice.   Ken Lopez 74-192 1996 $1,250.00

HILLERMAN, TONY   The Boy Who Made Dragonfly. New York: Harper & Row, 1972. 1st edition; 86 pages, illustrations; scarce, near fine in price clipped dust jacket.   Ken Sanders 8-393 1996 $500.00

HILLERMAN, TONY   Coyote Waits. New York: Harper, 1990. 1st edition; 1/500 numbered copies, signed by author; fine in slipcase, issued without jacket.   Janus Books 36-189 1996 $125.00

HILLERMAN, TONY   Dance Hall of the Dead. New York: Harper, 1973. 1st edition; fine in fine dust jacket (wrapped very slightly off center), signed by author; exceptional copy.   Ken Lopez 74-193 1996 $1,500.00

HILLERMAN, TONY   Dance Hall of the Dead. New York: H&R, 1973. 1st edition; near fine in dust jacket.   Lame Duck Books 19-368 1996 $1,250.00

HILLERMAN, TONY   The Dark Wind. New York: H&R, 1982. 1st edition; fine in dust jacket, inscribed by author.   Lame Duck Books 19-369 1996 $275.00

HILLERMAN, TONY   The Dark Wind. New York: Harper & Row, 1982. 1st edition; fine in jacket with tiny chip at bottom of front panel and light creasing on inside rear jacket flap; inscribed by author.   Janus Books 36-186   1996 $135.00

HILLERMAN, TONY   The Dark Wind. New York: Harper and Row, 1982. 1st edition; fine in fine dust jacket, one inch tear to jacket front. Book Time 2-637   1996 $125.00

HILLERMAN, TONY   The Dark Wind. New York: Harper Row, 1982. 1st edition; fine in dust jacket.   Quill & Brush 102-912   1996 $125.00

HILLERMAN, TONY   The Fly on the Wall. New York: Harper, 1971. 1st edition; very good+ or better copy in price clipped, very good dust jacket. Scarce.   Lame Duck Books 19-367   1996 $750.00

HILLERMAN, TONY   Hillerman Country. New York: Harper Collins, 1991. According to publisher, this is one of 150 copies, no limitation, but signed by Hillerman (on half title); photos by Barney Hillerman; large cloth covered boards with silver lettering and design, minor bump in head of spine, otherwise very fine in slipcase.   Quill & Brush 102-918 1996 $200.00

HILLERMAN, TONY   Listening to Woman. New York: Harper & Row, 1978. 1st edition; signed; top corners slightly bumped, very short tear at base of spine, otherwise fine in dust jacket.   Quill & Brush 102-911 1996 $400.00

HILLERMAN, TONY   Listening Woman. New York: Armchair Detective Library, 1994. 1st edition; one of 100 specially bound copies, signed by author; 8vo; cloth, slipcase, new.   James S. Jaffe 34-253 1996 $225.00

HILLERMAN, TONY   New Mexico. Portland: 1974. 1st edition; folio; 186 pages; photos; cloth and boards, first few and last few leaves with slight vertical bend, otherwise in very good price clipped dust jacket (front and back flaps formerly creased).   Gene W. Baade 1094-75 1996 $150.00

HILLERMAN, TONY   Rio Grande. Portland: 1975. 1st edition; folio; 127 pages; color photos; cloth and boards; fine in dust jacket.   Gene W. Baade 1094-77   1996 $150.00

HILLERMAN, TONY   Rio Grande. Portland: Graphic Arts Center, 1975. 1st edition; fine in jacket with publication price present but pre-publication price clipped   Janus Books 36-185   1996 $150.00

HILLERMAN, TONY   Sacred Clowns. New York: Harper Collins, 1993. 1/500 copies, signed; fine in slipcase.   Bev Chaney, Jr. 23-324 1996 $100.00

HILLERMAN, TONY   Sacred Clowns. New York: Harper Collins, 1993. 1st edition; 1/500 numbered copies signed by author; fine in slipcase, issued without jacket.   Janus Books 36-190   1996 $100.00

HILLERMAN, TONY   The Spell of New Mexico. Albuquerque: University of New Mexico Press, 1976. 1st edition; fine in very lightly soiled, price clipped dust jacket with only few tiny nicks on head of spine, one short, closed tear and small pen mark on front panel.   Quill & Brush 102-910 1996 $175.00

HILLERMAN, TONY   Talking God. New York: Harper, 1989. 1st edition; 1/300 numbered copies, signed by author. As new in slipcase, issued without jacket.   Janus Books 36-188   1996 $150.00

HILLERMAN, TONY   A Thief of Time. New York: Harper, 1988. One of 250 numbered copies, signed by author; fine in paper covered boards in paper covered cardboard slipcase, as issued.   Between the Covers 42-491 1996 $250.00

HILLERMAN, TONY   A Thief of Time. New York: Harper & Row, 1988. 1st edition; 1/250 numbered copies, signed by author; fine in slipcase, issued without jacket.   Janus Books 36-187   1996 $150.00

HILLERMAN, TONY   A Thief of Time. New York: Harper & Row, 1988. 1st edition; signed; fine in dust jacket with sticker on lower back panel. Quill & Brush 102-913   1996 $150.00

HILLIAR, ANTHONY   A Brief and Merry History of Great Britain... London: printed for J. Roberts; J. Shuckburgh; J. Jackson; J. Penn, n.d. 1730. 1st edition; 8vo; early 19th century half red morocco, top edge gilt, some rubbing, in red half morocco slipcase; from the library of Charles Lamb, with his signature on titlepage, presented by Lamb to his good friend Henry Crabb Robinson. Outside rather dusty, but uncut and essentially in very good condition.   Ximenes 109-157   1996 $3,500.00

HILLIER, J. H.   Catalogue of the Japanese Paintings and Prints in the Collection of Mr. and mrs. Richard Gale. London: Routledge & Kegan Paul ltd. for the Minneapolis Inst. of Arts, 1970. 1st edition; 4to; 2 volumes; 526 pages; color and black and white plates, many folding; original cloth, near fine in worn and stained publisher's slipcase. Hermitage SP95-765   1996 $150.00

HILLMAN, BRENDA   Coffee, 3 A.M. Poems. Lisbon: Penumbra Press, 1981. 1st edition; one of 125 numbered copies (from a total of 250), signed by author and artist; 4to; illustration on titlepage by Bonnie O'Connell; pictorial wrappers; fine.   Captain's Bookshelf 38-182 1996 $100.00

HILSOP, HERBERT R.   An Englishman's Arizona. Tucson: Overland Press, 1965. 1st edition; limited to 520 copies; 74 pages; original cloth, printed paper label, fine. Reese Six Score 57; Lowman 193.   Michael D. Heaston 23-22   1996 $100.00

HILTON, JAMES   Goodbye, Mr. Chips. Boston: Little Brown, 1934. 1st edition; handsome bookplate, otherwise fine in dust jacket.   Captain's Bookshelf 38-110   1996 $150.00

HILZINGER, J. GEORGE   Treasure Land: a Story. Tucson: Arizona Advancement Co., 1897. 1st edition; 160, (1) pages, profusely illustrated; original green cloth, gilt lettered front cover, very light rubbing to extremities, cover slightly spotted, else fine. Presentation inscription signed by author; scarce. Adams Herd 1069.   Argonaut Book Shop 113-348   1996 $200.00

HIMES, CHESTER   Tout Pour Plaire. (Big Gold Dream). N.P.: Paris: Gallimard, 1959. 1st edition; published in America as Big Gold Dream; slight spotting to fore edge and edges of pages browned, else very good plus in unprinted and presumably original tissue dust jacket. Between the Covers 43-107   1996 $250.00

HIMES, CHESTER   Une Affaire de Viol. (Case of Rape). Paris: Editions Les Yeux Ouverts, 1963. 1st edition; light stmall stain to top of rear wrapper, else fine in tissue dust jacket, this copy signed by author in France, Himes inscriptions are very scarce.   Between the Covers 43-110 1 996 $550.00

HIMES, CHESTER   Une Affaire de Viol. (A Case of Rape). Paris: Editions Les Yeux Ouverts, 1963. 1st edition; fine, lacking unprinted glassine dust jacket; fine.   Between the Covers 43-109   1996 $185.00

HIMES, CHESTER   Cast the First Stone. New York: Coward McCann, 1952. 1st edition; faint insignificant stain to fore edge, else fine in unusually fine dust jacket, author's third novel.   Between the Covers 43-105   1996 $300.00

HIMES, CHESTER   Cast the First Stone. New York: Coward-McCann, 1952. 1st edition; 8vo; cloth backed paper over boards, slightly darkened on top edge, else fine in illustrated dust jacket, which is showing very lightwear at spine ends and bit of darkening on rear at top edge. Andrew Cahan 47-85   1996 $150.00

HIMES, CHESTER   La Croisade De Lee Gordon. Paris: Correa, 1952. 1st French edition of The Lonely Crusade. Page edges browned, chipping to corners of a couple of pages, else near fine with slight wear to extremities in slightly chipped original tissue dust jacket.   Between the Covers 43-104   1996 $250.00

HIMES, CHESTER   The Heat's On. New York: Putnam, 1966. 1st edition; signed by author; very good in somewhat rubbed and spine faded dust jacket; Himes's signature is quite uncommon.   Ken Lopez 74-196   1996 $650.00

HIMES, CHESTER   The Heat's On. New York: Putnam, 1966. 1st edition; fine in near fine, unrubbed dust jacket with small amount of creasing to spine and lower front panel.   Ken Lopez 74-195   1996 $250.00

HIMES, CHESTER   The Heat's On. New York: Putnam, 1966. 1st edition; very faint offsetting to front endpaper,, else fine in about fine lightly rubbed dust jacket with single tiny nick, attractive copy. Between the Covers 43-111 1996 $200.00

HIMES, CHESTER   If He Hollers Let Him go. Garden City: Doubleday Doran, 1945. 1st edition; slight foxing to fore edge and endpapers, else near fine in about very good d with some light loss to spinal extremities affecting no lettering and some general wear to corners, presentable copy, increasingly scarce first book.   Between the Covers 43-101 1996 $375.00

HIMES, CHESTER   Lonely Crusade. New York: Knopf, 1947. 1st edition; fine in attractive near fine dust jacket with small internal repair and little rubbing at extremities; very nice; inscribed by author. Between the Covers 43-102 1996 $1,500.00

HIMES, CHESTER   Lonely Crusade. New York: Knopf, 1947. 1st edition; slight foxing to endpapers, else fine in price clipped, unusually bright, very fine dust jacket.   Between the Covers 43-103 1996 $250.00

HIMES, CHESTER   Mamie Mason, ou Un Exercise de la Bonne Volante. Paris: Plon 1962. 1st edition in French; slight foxing to endpapers, ele near fine in very good dust jacket with some small nicks and tears and some loss of lamination.   Between the Covers 43-108 1996 $200.00

HIMES, CHESTER   Le Manteau du Reve. Paris: Lieu Commun, 1982. 1st edition; wrappers with unprinted acetate dust jacket, presumably not original to book; fine.   Between the Covers 43-114 1996 $135.00

HIMES, CHESTER   The Primitive. New York: Signet/NAL, 1956. 1st edition; pages barely darkened at edges, short tear at edge of spine, otherwise bright, square copy, probably unread.   Between the Covers 43-106 1996 $125.00

HIMES, CHESTER   The Quality of Hurt. Garden City: Doubleday, 1972. 1st edition; fine in lightly rubbed, still fine dust jacket, first book of author's autobiography.   Between the Covers 43-113 196 $125.00

HINCKS, THOMAS   A History of the British Hydroid Zoophytes. London: 1868. 2 volumes, frontispiece, 67 plates.   Petersfield Bookshop FH58-253 1996 £60.00

HIND, ARTHUR M.   Wenceslaus Hollar and His Views of London and Windsor in the 17th Century. London: 1922. 4to; xiv, 92 pages; frontispiece, 64 plates; buckram, slightly foxed.   Rainsford A54-323 1996 £75.00

HIND, C. LEWIS   Authors and I. New York: John Lane, 1921. 1st edition; beautiful copy in like dust jacket; stunning copy.   Between the Covers 42-221 1996 $150.00

HIND, C. LEWIS   More Author's and I. New York: Dodd Mead, 1922. 1st edition; fine in dust jacket.   Between the Covers 42-222 1996 $150.00

HIND, HENRY YOULE   British North America. Reports on Progress. Together with a Preliminary and General Report of the Assinniboine and Saskatchewan Exploring Expedition. London: 1860. Folio; pages 219, 7 hand colored maps, plans and sections; original wrappers, lightly soiled and worn, internally crisp and near fine. Peel 211n. Wagner Camp Becker 330.3. TPL 3913.   Stephen Lunsford 45-74 1996 $450.00

HIND, HENRY YOULE   North-West Territory. Report of Progress...On the Assinboine and Saskatchewan Exploring Expedition. Toronto: John Lovell, 1859. Pages 201, (vi), folding maps and charts; original boards, some wear to extremities, several of the folding maps fully split, but no loss.   Dumont 28-83 1996 $275.00

HIND, W.   A Monograph of the British Carboniferous Lamellibranchiata. London: 1896-1905. 4to; 2 volumes, 79 plates; cloth, ex-library.   Wheldon & Wesley 207-1340 1996 £80.00

HINDERER, ANNA   Seventeen Years in the Yoruba Country. London: Seeley, Jackson, 1873. 2nd edition; crown 8vo; pages xi, (4), 343, (ads); portrait, map and 6 plates; original cloth, gilt, neatly repaired, very good.   James Fenning 133-161 1996 £85.00

HINDLEY, CHARLES   The Life and Times of James Catnach, (Late of Seven Dials), Ballad Monger... London: Reeves and Turner, 1878. One of 6 copies printed on yellow paper; octavo; xvi, 432, 12 pages; 230 woodcuts; with woodcuts on prelim pages hand colored; cloth, printed label, bookplate; light foxing to endpapers and adjacent leaves, otherwise fine.   Bromer Booksellers 90-14 1996 $1,500.00

HINDS, JAMES PITCAIRN   Bibliotheca Jacksoniana. Kendal: Titus Wilson, 1909. Limited edition, number 69; 8vo; pages viii, 199; original cloth, gilt, flyleaves trifle browned, otherwise fine; with original receipt tipped on to pastedown.   R.F.G. Hollett & Son 78-175 1996 £75.00

HINE, E. CURTISS   The Signal; or, the King of the Blue Isle. Boston: F. gleason at the Flag of Our Union Office, 1848. 1st edition; 8vo; 100 pages; disbound, few stains, quite good; Wright I 1196.   M & S Rare Books 60-169 1996 $300.00

HINES, EDWARD   Amateur's Turning Lathes and Accessories of the Workshop. Norwich: Griffin Works, 1892. Offprint; 8vo; pages 45-83, (83 bis), 84-99 (99 bis), 100-104 + two inserted leaves, index and extracts from letters; numerous text illustrations; wrappers bit soiled and worn. Abell 136.   Maggs Bros. Ltd. 1190-639 1996 £100.00

HINES, GORDON   Alfalfa Bill, an Intimate Biography. Oklahoma City: 1932. Limited deluxe edition, number 135 of 325 copies; signed by Hines and William Murray, Governor of Oklahoma, presented to Gover Jim and Ma Ferguson; 308 pages; photos; book fine, cover worn, slipcase added for protection.   Early West 22-638 1996 $250.00

HINGESTON-RANDOLPH, F. C.   Royal and Historical Letters During the Reign of Henry the Fourth, King of England and France, and Lord of Ireland. London: 1965. 8vo; 2 volumes; 1050 pages; original cloth. Howes Bookshop 265-1569 1996 £65.00

HINKSON, KATHARINE TYNAN 1861-1931   Cuckoo Songs. London: Elkin Mathews and John Lane, 1894. 1st edition; limited to 500 copies; titlepage drawing by Laurence Housman; rose colored cloth boards with gilt lettering and flower motif, gilt on front and back panels, bump to tail of spine and spine also faded, but still sharp, fore and bottom edges untrimmed; very good.   Hermitage SP95-636 1996 $150.00

HINKSON, KATHARINE TYNAN 1861-1931   Shamrocks. London: Kegan Paul, Trench & Co., 1st edition; soiled beige cloth with gilt lettering and shamrock design on front panel; overall very good, showing very litte if any wear; bookplate of Richard LaGallienne. Colby College Library bookplate.   Hermitage SP95-637 1996 $150.00

HIPPOCRATES   De Flatibus Liber ab Adriano Alemano...Commentariis Illustratus. Paris: Martin le Jeune, 1557. 1st edition of this version; 8vo; (8), 96 leaves (last blank), some minor foxing and stains; Greek and Latin text; vellum. Celli, Bib. Hipocratica 49; Durling 2406; Osler 187; Wellcome I 3246.   Jeffrey D. Mancevice 20-45 1996 $550.00

HIPPOCRATES   On Intercourse and Pregnancy. New York: 1952. 1st English translation; 128 pages; original binding.   W. Bruce Fye 71-990 1996 $100.00

HIPPOCRATES   Opera Omnia Quae Extant..Oeconomia Hippocratis Alphabeti Serie Distincta... Geneva: Samuel Chouet, 1657-62. Large folio; 2 volumes, lacks frontispiece to volume 1, otherwise complete work; contemporary vellum, joints splitting, spine ends worn, text with usual foxing and browning. GM 6793.   James Tait Goodrich K40-145 1996 $595.00

HIPPOCRATES   The Genuine Works of Hippocrates. London: 1849. 1st edition; 2 volumes, 874 pages, plus paltes; original binding, head and tail of spine chipped as usual, otherwise fine set.   W. Bruce Fye 71-987 1996 $300.00

HIPPOCRATES   The Genuine Works of Hippocrates. London: Sydenham Society, 1849. 8vo; 2 volumes; 8 plates; rebound in new linen, other than some light browning, a nice tight set; GM 14.   James Tait Goodrich K40-147 1996 $125.00

HIRSCH, AUGUST   Handbook of Geographical and Histological Pathology. London: New Sydenham Society, 1883-86. 1st English edition; 8vo; 3 volumes; original binding, each volume rebacked, good tight set. GM 1778.   James Tait Goodrich K40-148 1996 $125.00

HIRSCHFELD, AL   The World of Hirschfeld. New York: Harry N. Abrams, 1969. 1st edition; oblong 4to; 233 pages, 189 illustrations, including 32 plates in color; illustrated white cloth, slight darkening along edges, very good in dust jacket.   Andrew Cahan 47-87 1996 $125.00

HIRST, BARTON COOKE   Human Monstrosities. Philadelphia: Lea Brothers, 1891-93. 1st and only edition; folio; 4 volumes, 220 pages, 39 photographic plates, 123 woodcuts in text; private and institutional bookplate in each volume; original cloth, bit of wear at spine ends, volume 3 rebacked with tape; very good. GM 534.68. Cordasco 90-3520. Edwin V. Glaser B122-79 1996 $1,500.00

HISLOP, HERBERT R.   An Englishman's Arizona the Ranching Letters of Herbert R. Hislop 1876-1878. Tucson: 1965. Limited to 510 copies; 74 pages; illustrations by Hazel Fontana, photos; book very fine.   Early West 22-230 1996 $100.00

HISLOP, HERBERT R.   An Englishman's Arizona, the Ranching Letters Of...1876-1878. Tucson: 1965. 1st edition; limited to 550 copies; frontispiece, photos, illustrations, map endpapers; cloth; fine. 6 Score 57; Lowman 193.   T. A. Swinford 49-524 1996 $125.00

AN HISTORIC Epistle from Omiah to the Queen of Otaheite; being His Remarks on the English Nation. London: printed for T. Evans, 1775. 1st edition; 4to; disbound, some light browning and marginal stains, but very good, uncommon. Kallich, British Poetry & the Amer. Revolution 75-10. Ximenes 109-231 1996 $400.00

HISTORICAL & Descriptive Guide to Carlisle and District. Carlisle: Albert Barnes Moss, 1881. 4th edition, large paper copy; small 4to; pages (viii), 290; original decorated cloth, gilt, over bevelled boards, edges and upper board little rubbed and damped, all edges gilt.   R.F.G. Hollett & Son 78-987 1996 £75.00

HISTORICAL Collections; or, a Brief Account of the Most Remarkable Transactions of the Two Last Parliaments... (with) Historical Collections...or the Continuation...of the Parliament...at Oxford. London: 1681. 2nd edition of part 1, 1st edition of part 2; 8vo; blank leaf, title leaf, 2 leaves, 302 pages, added titlepage; frontispiece, 19th century red half morocco with marbled boards and flyleaves, binding nice except worn along edges and hinges; fine.   Roy W. Clare XXIV-79 1996 $300.00

HISTORICAL Memoranda Relative to the Discovery of Etherization, and to the Connection With It of the Late Dr. William T. G. Morton. Boston: 1871. 1st edition; 16 pages; wrappers (soiled). Fulton & Stanton IV 41. W. Bruce Fye 71-46 1996 $150.00

HISTORICAL SOCIETY OF MONTANA   Contributions to the Historical Society of Montana. Volume 1. Helena: 1902. 311 pages; frontispiece; cloth, nice.   T. A. Swinford 49-798 1996 $125.00

HISTORICAL SOCIETY OF MONTANA   Contributions to the Historical Society of Montana. Volume II. Helena: 1896. 1st edition; 409 pages; frontispiece, photos, illustrations; cloth. Dustin 23 & 53; Luther 50.   T. A. Swinford 49-799 1996 $125.00

HISTORICAL SOCIETY OF MONTANA   Contributions to the Historical Society of Montana. Volume III Helena: 1900. 1st edition; 375 pages; frontispiece, photos, illustrations; cloth.   T. A. Swinford 49-802 1996 $100.00

HISTORICAL SOCIETY OF MONTANA   Contributions to the Historical Society of Montana. Volume IV. Helena: 1903. 1st edition; 326 pages; photos; illustrations; cloth; nice. Luther 75.   T. A. Swinford 49-800 1996 $125.00

HISTORICAL SOCIETY OF MONTANA   Contributions to the Historical Society of Montana. Volume V. Helena: 1904. 1st edition; 467 pages, photos; cloth.   T. A. Swinford 49-801 1996 $100.00

THE HISTORY and Description of Colchester. Colchester: printed and sold by W. Keymer, sold also by Messrs. Robinsons... 1803. 8vo; 2 volumes in 1; 1-276 pages, appendix 1-22, errata leaf to volume 2, 1-232 pages, index 4 pages; frontispiece to both volumes, 7 engraved plates, half calf and cloth boards, red morocco label to spine, gilt rule to compartments, new endpapers and prelims, owner's pen inscriptions. Beeleigh Abbey BA/56-5 1996 £125.00

A HISTORY and Description of the Royal Abbaye of Saint Denis, with an Account of the Tombs of the Kings and Queens of France... London: J. S. Jordan, 1795. 8vo; pages iv, 96; disbound, signature on titlepage. Marlborough 162-256 1996 £110.00

HISTORY of Alameda County, California. Oakland: 1883. 1st edition; 999 pages; frontispiece, illustrations; full leather, tight copy, very good+. 6 Guns 2439.   T. A. Swinford 49-1279 1996 $300.00

HISTORY of Company A and the 22d Regiment N.G.N.Y. New York: Styles & Cash, 1901. 1st edition; 132 pages; illustrations; original stiff printed wrappers, bit of edge chipping, one corner clipped, yet very good or better, scarce. Dornbusch I NY 262; not in Broadfoot, Nevins or Nicholson.   McGowan Book Co. 65-40 1996 $175.00

THE HISTORY of Discoveries and Inventions, Chiefly Intended for the Entertainment and Instruction of Young Persons... London: Tabart and Co., 1808. Sole edition; 12mo. in 6's; pages (i)-viii, (9)-144; original red roan backed marbled boards, smooth spine divided by single gilt rules, gilt lettered direct, lacks upper free endpaper; some foxing, early ownership signature on upper pastedown, very good. Moon 59. Blackwell's B112-68 1996 £125.00

THE HISTORY of Little Dame Crump and Her White Pig. London: J. L. Marks 91 Long Lane, Smithfield, n.d., ca. 1840. Small 8vo; 8 hand colored illustrations; illustrated thin wrappers, covers slightly stained and chipped, else very good.   Marjorie James 19-146 1996 £85.00

THE HISTORY of Little Goody Two-Shoes: Otherwise Called Mrs. Margery Two-shoes. London: printed in the year, 1796. 32mo; pages 128, frontispiece, 32 woodcuts; title and two or three early foremargins made up, without loss of text, gut in general a very good copy; modern full morocco, gilt, top edge gilt, others uncut.   Peter Murray Hill 185-39 1996 £450.00

HISTORY Of Medicine and Surgery and Physicians and Surgeons of Chicago. Chicago: 1922. 1st edition; 928 pages; ex-library, original binding, head and tail of spine worn; scarce.   W. Bruce Fye 71-1001 1996 $175.00

HISTORY of 124th Machine Gun Battalion - 66th Brigade, 33rd Division - A.E.F. N.P.: 1919. 1st edition; frontispiece; wrappers, covers slightly marked, very good.   Ulysses 39-645 1996 £50.00

HISTORY of Southeastern, Its Settlement and Growth, Geological and Physical Features. Sioux City: Western Pub. Co., 1881. 1st edition; 392 pages, plus (10) pages of local ads; original black cloth, title in gilt on spine, minor repairs to spine and some wear, very good. Graff 1907; Howes D14.   Michael D. Heaston 23-130 1996 $550.00

THE HISTORY of the Church of Crosthwaite. Cumberland. London: John Bowyer Nichols and Sons, 1853. 1st edition; 8vo; pages viii, 146, woodcut frontispiece and 8 text illustrations; modern half blue levant morocco, gilt; scarce.   R.F.G. Hollett & Son 78-988 1996 £95.00

THE HISTORY of the Church of Crosthwaite. Cumberland. London: John Bowyer Nichols and sons, 1853. 8vo; pages viii, 146; woodcut frontispiece and 8 text illustrations; original blindstamped cloth, gilt, extremities rubbed, some plates foxed, sarce.   R.F.G. Hollett & Son 78-989 1996 £65.00

HISTORY of the Foundations in Manchester of Christ's College, Chetham's Hospital, and the Free Grammar School. London: Thomas Agnew and Joseph Zentti, 1828-33. 4to; 3 volumes; frontispieces to all volumes, 32 engraved plates, extra plate 'Northwest view of Chetham's College' not called for to volume 3, 2 full page wood engravings, 3 groundplans and several woodcuts to text; old tree calf boards, decorative gilt borders, skilfully rebacked, red and green labels, yellow edges, inner gilt dentelles, marbled endpapers with bookplate to front pasatedowns, some surface damage to upper board of volume 2; bound by Hayday. some sporadic foxing to few pages, dampstain to frontispiece in volume 2. Halkett & Laing III p. 81.   Beeleigh Abbey BA56-26 1996 £375.00

THE HISTORY of the House That Jack Built. London: Grant and Griffith, successors to J. Harris, n.d., ca. 1850. 175 x 106mm; hand colored titlepage and 16 other hand colored illustrations, all printed on untearable linen; pictorial green glazed wrappers, covers very rubbed, surface area at corner and base worn away, else very good.   Marjorie James 19-209 1996 £65.00

THE HISTORY of the Lives and Bloody Exploits of the Most Noted Pirates. Hartford: Published by Silas Andrus and son, 1836. Embossed cloth, worn, some margins defedtive, usable copy.   Meyer Boswell SL26-188 1996 $250.00

HISTORY Of the 127th Regiment Pennsylvania Volunteers Familiarly Known as the "Dauphin County Regiment". Lebanon: Report Publishing Co., 1902. 1st edition; faint, half ring on front board, else fine, tight and bright.   Between the Covers 42-102 1996 $150.00

THE HISTORY of the Rise and Progress of the Judicial or Adawlut System, as Established for the Administration of Justice Under the Presidency of Bengal. London: sold by John booth, 1820. 1st edition; 8vo; 2 parts in 1; name on title; contemporary calf, roughly rebacked. Anthony W. Laywood 109-71 1996 £95.00

THE HISTORY of the Rise and Progress of the Judicial or Adawlut System. Part II. An Inquiry into the Supposed Existence of Trial by Jury in India. London: sold by John Booth, Duke St. Portland Place, 1822. contemporary quarter calf, joints cracked but holding, usable. Meyer Boswell SL26-232 1996 $450.00

THE HISTORY of the Times. London: printed and published at The Times, 1935-52. 1st edition; royal 8vo; 4 volumes in 5; numerous plates, some in color; original buckram, nice, with dust jackets. Appleton 137. Howes Bookshop 265-1212 1996 £120.00

THE HISTORY of the Whiggish-Plot: or, A Brief Historical Account of the Charge and Defence of William Lord Ruffel, Capt. Tho. Walcot, John Rouse, William Hone, Captain Blague, Algernon Sidney, Esq... London: T. B. to be sold by Randal Taylor, 1684. 1st edition; 8vo; (iv), 71, (i) pages; disbound; little dusty and browned, good copy. Wing H2190b. Robert Clark 38-63 1996 £55.00

HITCHCOCK, HENRY RUSSELL   Early Victorian Architecture in Britain. London: Architectural Press, 1954. 1st edition; 4to; 2 volumes, xxi, (i), 635, (1); xxxii, (i) pages, 522 illustrations on plates; cloth, dust jacket, very good in chipped dust jackets.   Bookpress 75-65 1996 $175.00

HITTELL, THEODORE H.   El Triunfo de la Cruz - a Description of the Building by Father Juan Ugarte of the First ship Made in California. San Francisco: 1930. One of 50 copies; titlepage and decorations by Valenti Angelo; loosely inserted woodcut by Angelo, signed and titled by him; boards, front endpapers slightly browned, covers very slightly marked, spine and title label on spine browned; very good. Inscribed by Angelo for James Hart, sometime publisher.   Ulysses 39-14 1996 £175.00

HJORTSBERG, WILLIAM   Gray Matters. New York: Simon & Schuster, 1971. Uncorrected proof; unbound signatures laid into the dust jacket, stain on fore edge, else near fine in like dust jacket with neat name on front panel.   Between the Covers 42-223 1996 $100.00

HOADLY, BENJAMIN   The Original and Institution of Civil Government, Discuss'd. London: James Knapton, 1710. 2nd edition; 8vo; (2), xiv, 200, 204, 11, (1) pages; contemporary panelled calf, recent paper labels on spine, joints cracked, but very good. with contemporary ownership and John Orlebar's bookplate. Sweet & Maxwell I 608(39); not in Goldsmiths. John Drury 82-109 1996 £175.00

HOAGLAND, EDWARD   African Calliope. A Journey to the Sudan. New York: Random House, 1979. Uncorrected proof; wrappers, spine faded, else fine.   Ken Lopez 74-198 1996 $125.00

HOAGLAND, EDWARD   Notes from the Century Before. New York: Random House, 1969. 1st edition; review copy; fine in unlaminated jacket with some surface soiling, otherwise also fine.   Ken Lopez 74-197 1996 $150.00

HOARE, PRINCE   An Inquiry into the Requisite Cultivation and Present State of the Arts of Design in England, London: printed for Richard Phillips, by B. McMillan, 1806. 1st edition; 12mo; frontispiece by William Blake after a painting by Joshua Reynolds; modern polished calf, gilt, spine gilt; few edges trifle dusty, but very good, entirely uncut, uncommon. CBEL II 837.   Ximenes 108-201 1996 $850.00

HOARE, RICHARD COLT   A Classical Tour through Italy and Sicily... London: printed for J. Mawman, 1819. 2nd edition; 8vo; (xvi), 395, 358, (6) pages ads; full contemporary calf, professionally rebacked with new sines and leather labels, some scuffing to covers, otherwise nice set. David Mason 71-103 1996 $280.00

HOARE, RICHARD COLT   A Tour Through the Island of Elba. London: printed by W. Bulmer and Co., 1814. 1st edition; 4to; pages (8), 32; map, 8 three quarter; original boards, uncut, printed paper spine label, upper joint cracked, otherwise nice, fresh copy.   James Fenning 133-162 1996 £385.00

HOBART, HENRY   The Reports...Henry Hobart Knight and Baronet, Lord Chief Justice of His Majesties Court of Common Pleas... London: printed for William Lee, Allen Banks and Charles Harper, 1671. Modern cloth, titlepage defective, working copy.   Meyer Boswell SL25-108 1996 $150.00

HOBBES, R. G.   Reminiscences and Notes of Seventy Years' Life Travel and Adventure: Military and Civil; Scientific and Literary. London: Stock, 1895. 8vo; 1st edition; 2 volumes, pages 558, 571, original red/blue cloth, uncut, very good.   John Lewcock 30-94 1996 £85.00

HOBBES, THOMAS 1588-1679   The Correspondence. London: 1994. 8vo; 2 volumes, pages 592, 414; original cloth.   Howes Bookshop 265-533 1996 £120.00

HOBBES, THOMAS 1588-1679   Decameron Physiologicum; or Ten Dialogues of Natural Philosophy... London: printed by J.C. for W. Crook, 1678. 1st edition; 8vo; pages (viii), 136, (8); folding plate, 3 engravings on letterpress, license leaf before title, small worm hole in bottom margin of last four leaves (ads); contemporary sheep, rebacked, smooth backstrip, divided by black rules, gilt lettered in second compartment, dated at foot, sides with blind border, hinges strengthened, small area of insect damage on front pastedown, generally very good; bookplate of Augustus Hare. Macdonald & Hargreaves 84; Wing 2226.   Blackwell's B112-154 1996 £650.00

HOBBES, THOMAS 1588-1679   Leviathan, or the Matter, Forme and Power of a Common-Wealth Ecclesiasticall and Civill. London: for Andrew Crooke, 1651. 1st edition; often called the first issue, with the 'head' ornament on titlepage; folio; (6), 396 (i.e. 394) pages, added engraved title, folding table; contemporary calf, rebacked in period style retaining original spine label, new endpapers, dampstain at corner of some leaves, tiny hole in 2H4 with loss of a letter or two, engraved title very lightly soiled. PMM 138; Macdonald & Hargreaves 42; Grolier W-P 454; Wing H2246.   Joseph J. Felcone 64-23 1996 $6,000.00

HOBBES, THOMAS 1588-1679   The Treatise on Human Nature and That On Liberty and Necessity. London: printed for J. Johnson and Co. by J. M'Creery, 1812. Limited to 250 copies (so stated); 12mo; iv, (2), 81, (5), 216 pages; moderate pencil underlining and notes; 19th century black calf over marbled boards, gilt morocco spine labels, extremities and covers somewhat rubbed.   Kenneth Karmiole 1NS-122 1996 $100.00

HOBBES, THOMAS 1588-1679   The Treatise on Human Nature and That on Liberty and Necessity. London: printed for J. Johnson and Co., by J. M'Creery, 1812. Limited to 250 copies (so stated); 12mo; iv, (2), 81, (5), 216 pages; moderate pencil underlining and notes; 19th century black calf over boards, gilt morocco spine labels, extremities and covers somewhat rubbed.   Kenneth Karmiole 1NS-122 1996 $100.00

HOBHOUSE, JOHN CAM   A Journey through Albania, and Other Provinces of Turkey in Europe and Asia, to Constantinople, During the Years 1809 and 1810. London: printed for James Cawthorn, 1833. 3rd edition; 11 x 8 3/4 inches; 2 volumes; 24 plates, including 2 folding maps and 18 hand colored aquatints; old probably contemporary half calf, marbled sides, red morocco spine labels, gilt rules and volume numbers, joints and extremities somewhat rubbed (one joint partly cracked, with board just slightly wobbly), sides little chafed and leather bit marked, but early bindings still rather bright and pleasing, despite defects, very faint marginal dampstain on 20 leaves in first volume, slight browning to text, few leaves of volume 2 with small stain at inner margin, plates very clean with pleasing color; front pastedowns with engraved bookplate of Sir George Douglas and paper shelf label of Springwood Park, Kelso. Abbey 202 (1813 ed.). Blackmer Sale Cat. 688. Phillip J. Pirages 33-307 1996 $1,750.00

HOBSON, ROBERT LOCKHART   Chinese Ceramcis in Private Collections. London: Halton & Truscott, 1931. Limited edition of 625 numbered copies; 4to; xvi, 301, xvii-xxii pages; 32 color mounted plates, 361 half tone text figures; buckram, spine little faded.   Thomas Thorp 489-155 1996 £100.00

HOBSON, ROBERT LOCKHART   The George Eumorfopoulos Collection: Catalogue of the Chinese, Corean and Persian Pottery and Porcelain. London: Ernest Benn, 1925. Limited to 725 numbered copies; folip printed on Van Gelder mouldmade paper; volume 1 only; xxviii, 66 pages text; 75 plates containing 517 illustrations, including 52 mounted in color (one torn), cloth, gilt, extremities worn.   Thomas Thorp 489-154 1996 £65.00

HOBSON, ROBERT LOCKHART   The Wares of the Ming Dynasty. London: Benn Brothers, 1923. 1st edition; edtion deluxe, one of 27 printed on Japan vellum, signed by author; 128 illustrations, 11 of which are in color; full vellum, titled in gilt, gilt Oriental motif on center front cover, upper rear joint just starting, otherwise very fine with boards perfectly flat.   Hermitage SP95-741 1996 $500.00

HOCHTS, LUCIUS & BRUNING   Colour Works Trade Catalogue. The Coal Tar Colours. Main: 1896. Large 8vo; 190 pages, text in English, frontispiece, decorative titlepage, 173 plain and decorataive color samples tipped in; original decorative cloth, very good.   Ken Spelman 30-55 1996 £180.00

HOCKLEY, WILLIAM BROWNE   The English in India. And Other Sketches. London: Longman, 1835. Sole edition; 12mo; pages vii (i.e. v.), (i), 358; (ii); 365; bound without half titles, prelim and final leaves foxed; contemporary green calf, minor rubbing and fading, backstrips with wide low raised bands, red and blue gilt lettered labels in second and fourth compartments, remainder gilt, sides with fillet and narrow gilt and blind rolls border, gilt roll on board edges, blind on turn-ins, marbled endpapers, very good.   Blackwell's B112-155 1996 £250.00

HODDER, W. R.   The Daughter of the Dawn. Page, 1903. 1st American edition; illustrations; spine lettering flaked, front inner hinge starting, else tight, bright, very good+; very scarce.   Aronovitz 57-559 1996 $100.00

HODGE, FREDERICK WEBB   History of Hawikuh, New Mexico: One of the So-Called Cities of Cibola. Los Angeles: Southwest Museum, 1937. 1st edition; xviii, 155 pages; numerous plates; original stiff wrappers, lettered on spine, very fine.   Argonaut Book Shop 113-350 1996 $125.00

HODGE, HIRAM C.   Arizona As It is: or, the Coming Country. New York: Hurd and Houghton, 1877. 1st edition; 273 pages, frontispiece, double page map, text illustration; original green cloth stamped in black and gilt, light rubbing to extremities, bit of minor wear to lower front corner, fine.   Argonaut Book Shop 113-351 1996 $225.00

HODGES, NATHANIEL   Loimologia; or, an Historical Account of the Plague in London in 1665... London: E. Bell and J. Osborn, 1720. 1st edition; 8vo; vi, 288 pages; folding table (one area strengthened on back), paper uniformly browned, otherwise good. recent half calf, marbled boards, spine gilt ruled, label;   Robert Clark 38-180 1996 £200.00

HODGKIN, JOHN ELIOT   Rariora London: Sampson Low, n.d. 4t0; 3 volumes; xix, 124; iv; 297; xiv, 161; viii, 92, 11 pages; 65 plates including few in color, numerous text illustrations and tipped in pictorial head and tailpieces; cloth, top edge gilt, others uncut, spines soiled.   Thomas Thorp 489-156 1996 £120.00

HODGKIN, THOMAS   Italy and Her Invaders. Oxford: 1892-99. 2nd edition; 8vo; 9 volumes, over 4000 pages, maps, illustrations; original cloth, good, ex-library copy, good except for library markings; sound set. K Books 441-274 1996 £80.00

HODGKINSON, CLEMENT   Australia, from Port MacQuarie to Moreton Bay.... London: T. and W. Boone, 1845. 8vo; (xi), 244 pages, vi), (8) pages, (last pages colophon), frontispiece and 6 sepia aquatint plates, 1 engraved maps, (iv), and 8 pages ads; oriignal tight grained green coth, extra blind borders and decorations on boards, gilt decoration and titles on spine; with James Edge Partington bookplate. Bright, clean copy. Ferguson 4067; Wangraup 158a.   Antipodean 28-620 1996 $3,000.00

HODGSON, HENRY W.   A Bibliography of the History and Topography of Cumberland and Westmorland. Carlisle: The Record Office, 1968. 1st edition; large 8vo; 301 pages; fine copy in original cloth, dust jacket. R.F.G. Hollett & Son 78-177 1996 £55.00

HODGSON, HENRY W.   A Bibliography of the History and Topography of Cumberland and Westmorland.Bibliography Carlisle: The Record Office, 1968. 1st edition; large 8vo; 301 pages; original cloth, fine.   R.F.G. Hollett & Son 78-176 1996 £50.00

HODGSON, HENRY W.   A Topographical and Historical Description of the County of Westmoreland... London: printed for Sherwood, Neely and Jones and George Cowie & Co., 1820. Reprint; 8vo; pages (ii), 245, (vi, index), untrimmed, complete with folding map and engraved title (both little spotted), 6 engraved plates, bound in at end, some upside down; publisher's cloth, paper spine label, little rubbed. very good.   R.F.G. Hollett & Son 78-993 1996 £120.00

HODGSON, W.   The House on the Borderland. Sauk City: Arkham House, 1946. 1st edition; very good in dust jacket, some wear and tear and chipping with some inner tape reinforcement.   Aronovitz 57-560 1996 $165.00

HODIN, J. P.   John Milne: Sculptor - Life and Work. London: Latimer New Dimensions Ltd., 1977. 1st edition; illustrations in color and black and white; wrappers, slightly soiled, very good, head and tail of spine and corners slightly bumped, free endpapers slightly rubbed, very good in nicked, rubbed and slightly chipped and creased dust jacket; presentation copy from artist to engraved plates. H. Ramsden and Margot Eates.   Ulysses 39-410 1996 £95.00

HODING, SARAH   The Land Logbook. London: 1836. 278 pages + errata slip; newer half leather and wine cloth, small cancelled library stamp on titlepage and one other page.   Bookworm & Silverfish 276-115 1996 $500.00

HODSON, A. W.   Trekking the Great Thirst. London: 1913. 2nd edition; illustrations, folding maps; corners bit bumped and rubbed, some foxing. David Grayling J95Biggame-105 1996 £50.00

HODSON, WILLIAM S. R.   Twelve Years of a Soldier's Life in India. London: 1859. 8vo; xvi, 384 pages; portrait; contemporary calf, trifle rubbed, but good sound copy.   K Books 442-284 1996 £55.00

HOE, ROBERT 1839-1909   Catalogue of the Library of Robert Hoe of York. New York: Anderson Auction Co., 1912. Only edition; 8 volumes; many illustrations; price list for first volume tipped in; original pictorial wrappers; creasing of spine of first volume, but very good.   Trebizond 39-24 1996 $275.00

HOFF, E. C.   A Bibliographical Sourcebook of Compressed Air, Diving and Submarine Medicine. Washington: 1948/56/66. Quarto; 3 volumes; original binding, nice set.   James Tait Goodrich K40-38 1996 $125.00

HOFFMAN, ABBIE   Revolution for the Hell Of It. New York: Dial, 1968. 1st edition; fine in near fine dust jacket.   Sherwood 3-139 1996 $100.00

HOFFMAN, HERBERT   Early Cretan Armorers. Mainz: Philipp von Zabern, 1972. Folio; xv, 69 pages, 7 figures and 57 plates (4 in color); original cloth, minor spotting at bottom edge.   Archaeologia Luxor-3464 1996 $225.00

HOFFMAN, HERBERT   Tarentine Rhyta. Mainz: Philipp von Zabern, 1966. 4to; viii, 167 pages and 62 plates; original cloth.   Archaeologia Luxor-3466 1996 $250.00

HOFFMAN, WERNER   Art in the Nineteenth century. London: Faber & Faber, 1961. 4to; 456 pages; 16 color plates, 218 black and white plates; cloth, dust jacket.   Rainsford A54-319 1996 £60.00

HOFFMANN, ERNST THEODOR AMADEUS 1776-1822   Tales of Hoffman. London: G. G. Harrap, 1932. 1st edition; 207 pages; color title vignette, 10 color plates, 8 color chapter headings and 20 color text illustrations; dark red decorated cloth, top edge red; very good.   Robin Greer 94A-50 1996 £95.00

HOFFMANN, ERNST THEODOR AMADEUS 1776-1822   The Tales. New York: Limited Editions Club, 1943. Limited to 1500 copies, signed by artist; lithographs by Hugo Steiner-Prag drawn on stone; decorated black linen; near fine in like case.   Charles Agvent 4-656 1996 $125.00

HOFFMANN, WERNER   The Sculpture of Henry Laurens. New York: Harry N. Abrams, 1970. 30 x 25 cm; 186 illustrations; original cloth, dust jacket, mint.   Rainsford A54-365 1996 $75.00

HOFFMANN-DONNER, HEINRICH 1809-1894   Slovenly Peter. New York: Limited Editions Club, 1935. 1st edition translated by Mark Twain; limited to 1500 copies; folio; illustrations from the rare first edition by Fritz Kredel; quarter maroon leather and pictorial cloth, felt chemise and slipcase, fine in somewhat soiled and faded slipcase.   James S. Jaffe 34-698 1996 $200.00

HOFLAND, BARBARA WREAKS HOOLE 1770-1844   A Descriptive Account of the Mansion and Gardens of White-Knights... London: printed for His Grace the Duke of Marlborough, by W. Wilson, 1819. folio; (8) 152 pages; 23 engraved plates on india paper (mounted); later half green morocco, little rubbed, some slight foxing in margins; from the library of Frances Mary Richardson Currer, with her armorial ex-libris. Abbey Scenery 425; Tooley 268.   Marlborough 162-45 1996 £1,850.00

HOFLAND, BARBARA WREAKS HOOLE 1770-1844   The Young Cadet; or, Henry Delamere's Voyage to India, His Travels in Hindostan, His Account of the Burmese War, and Wonders of Elora. New York: Orville A. Roorbach, 1828. 12mo; x, 206 pages plus 12 engraved illustrations; original maroon calf over green boards, bit rubbed, leather label of "Josiah Chapin" on front cover, some text foxing. Not in Osborne. Kenneth Karmiole 1NS-70 1996 $100.00

HOFMANN, HANS   Hans Hofmann. New York: Abrams, n.d. 2nd edition; oblong 4to; 227 pages, 168 illustrations; 51 tipped in color plates; cloth, dust jacket. Freitag 4330.   Brannan 43-268 1996 $495.00

HOFMANN, WERNER   The Sculpture of Henri Laurens. New York: Abrams, 1970. 4to; 228 pages, 3 tipped in color and 186 monochrome plates; cloth, dust jacket. Freitag 5203.   Brannan 43-337 1996 $165.00

HOFMANNSTAHL, HUGO VON   Der Tod Des Tizian, Bruchstuck. Cranach Press, 1928. One of 225 copies on paper (there were also 6 copies on vellum); 10 3/4 x 7 inches; 18 pages, (1) leaf (colophon); printed in orange and black, decorative woodcut initials in orange; original vellum backed paper boards, in fine vellum backed folding cloth box, just a hint of soil or discoloration to the binding, otherwise beautiful copy. Schroder p. 9.   Phillip J. Pirages 33-144 1996 $1,950.00

HOGAN, CLIO D.   Index to Stakes Winners 1865-1967. Solvang: Flag Is Up Farms, n.d. 4to; 2 volumes; original binding, very good. October Farm 36-326 1996 $425.00

HOGAN, CLIO D.   Index to Stakes Winners 1865-1967. Solvang: Flag Is Up Farms, n.d. 4to; volume 1 only; original binding, very good. October Farm 36-326 1996 $195.00

HOGARTH, WILLIAM 1697-1764   The Works... London: Jones and Co., 1833. 4to; 2 volumes, pages (2), 116; (4), (117)-225; portrait, 108 engraved plates; contemporary calf, gilt, gilt spines, contrasting labels, pencil scribbling on 1 leaf, some light marginal foxing, but very good, strongly bound.   James Fenning 133-163 1996 £75.00

HOGARTH, WILLIAM 1697-1764   The Works... Philadelphia: George Barrie and Son, 1900. 1st of this edition; number 35 of 1000 sets; quarto; 10 volumes; splendidly printed on fine paper; lavishly illustrated with plates on India paper, mounted, and with double tissue guards; red cloth, uncut, top edge gilt, each volume in fitted cloth slipcase; fresh and bright.   Hartfield 48-A10 1996 $950.00

HOGG, JAMES   A Boys Song. Market Drayton: Tern Press, Autumn, 1994. One of 10 special copies from a total edition of 100; 7 x 9 inches; 23 pages; printed on Goatskin paper with original water color paintings by Nicholas Parry, signed by Parry; bound in pink print on cream paper with orange lettering; fine.   Joshua Heller 21-262 1996 $275.00

HOGG, JAMES   The Private Memoirs and Confessions of a Justified Sinner. London: printed for Longman, Hurst, Rees, Orme, Brown and Green, 1834. 1st edition; 8vo; 390 pages of text, frontispiece (fore-edge margin cropped, offset to title), final leaf blank but not the original; half black straight grain morocco, gilt bands and title to panelled spine, marbled edges and endpapers, bound by Slocombe & Simms, Leeds; armorial bookplate. Block English Novel p. 111; Sadlier 1198.   Beeleigh Abbey BA56-148 1996 £2,500.00

HOGG, JAMES   Songs and Poems of the Ettrick Shepherd. London: T. N. Foulis, 1912. 1st edition; iv, 152, 4 pages of ads; color frontispiece, color pictorial title and 5 color plates all mounted on grey paper; grey cloth spine gilt, grey boards gilt, onlaid color plate, top edge gilt, others uncut; light foxing, light wear. White 93.   Robin Greer 94A-48 1996 £85.00

HOGG, JAMES   Winter Evening Tales, Collected Among the Cottagers in the South of Scotland. Edinburgh: printed for Oliver & Boyd; and G. & W. B. Whittaker, London, 1820. 1st edition; 12mo; 2 volumes; original boards with calf spines and labels, no half titles called for, many pages in voluem 2 very lightly foxed. Not in Sadleir or Wolff; Block p. 111. David Bickersteth 133-152 1996 £160.00

HOHL, REINHOLD   Alberto Giacometti. New York: Abrams, 1971. 4to; 328 pages; 270 illustrations, 4 in color; cloth. Freitag 3448.   Brannan 43-230 1996 $395.00

HOLBEIN, HANS   The Dances of Death, through the Various Stages of Human Life. London: S. Gosnell, 1803. Small 4to; 46 plates; contemporary panelled calf with blind decorated sides and spine, which has been rebacked, much earlier, red morocco label, all edges stained red, occasional foxing, mainly to beginning and end, handsome well printed copy. Large uncut copy, rare.   Book Block 32-17 1996 $575.00

HOLBEIN, HANS   Icones Veteris Testamenti. London: William Pickering, 1830. 1st edition; 8vo; pages 14, 180 unnumbered leaves, 90 woodcuts after Holbein (by John and Mary Byfield) printed by Whittingham on Blaston, laid paper; good, uncut copy; original tan morocco backed boards, backstrip and edges rubbed; scarce and handsome. Buechler 5. Keynes 72*.   Claude Cox 107-195 1996 £85.00

HOLBERG, LUDVIG, BARON   A Journey to the World Under-Ground. London: printed for T. Astley and B. Collins, 1742. 1st edition in English; 12mo; (iv), 324 pages; original calf, rebacked, arms in gilt on centre of each cover, upper outer corner of title defective and repaired, nowhere near printed surface.   David Bickersteth 133-38 1996 £485.00

HOLBURG, LUDWIG, BARON   An Introduction to Universal History. London: printed for A. Millar, J. Ward and A. Linde, 1758. 8vo; xxx, 341 pages, 1 engraved plates, 5 folding maps; original calf, small round wormhole in lower margin in second half of book, slight wear at head and foot of spine, short crack at top of upper joint, but in general a good copy.   David Bickersteth 133-39 1996 £135.00

HOLCROFT, THOMAS   A Narrative of Facts, Relating to a Prosecution for High Treason; Including the Address to the Jury. London: printed for D. Symonds, 1795. 1st edition; 8vo; disbound; small hole in last leaf, but very good, complete in two parts; CBEL II 839.   Ximenes 108-202 1996 $350.00

HOLDEN, EDWARD S.   Catalogue of Earthquakes on the Pacific Coast 1769 to 1897. University of California: Lick Observatory, 1898. 1st separate printing; (4), 253 pages, illustrations, charts and text maps; original cloth wrappers, extremities darkened, else fine.   Argonaut Book Shop 113-352 1996 $125.00

HOLDEN, WILLIAM C.   Rollie Burns or an Account of the Ranching Industry on the South Plains. Dallas: 1932. 1st edition; 243 pages; frontispiece; pictorial cloth, very good+. Herd 1050; 6 Score 60.   T. A. Swinford 49-530 1996 $150.00

HOLDEN, WILLIAM C.   The Spur Ranch a Story of the Enclosed Range Phase of the Cattle Industry in Texas. Boston: 1934. 1st edition; 229 pages; endpaper plates, cloth; nice, rare. Howes H583.   T. A. Swinford 49-531 1996 $250.00

HOLDER, CHARLES FREDERICK   Big Game at Sea. New York: Outing Publishing Co., 1908. 1st edition; 8 1/8 x 5 1/2 inches; xviii, 352 pages + frontispiece, 31 pages of photographic illustrations; pictorial blue green cloth, light wear to extremities.   Dawson's Books Shop 528-111 1996 $125.00

HOLDER, WILLIAM   A Treatise of the Natural Grounds and Principles of Harmony. London: printed by Jeptinstall, and sold by J. Carr, B. Aylmer, W. Hensman ... 1694. 1st edition; 8vo; three are 3 issues of this first edition, with no precedence the present variant adds 3 booksellers to the imprint; woodcut diagrams in text and 2 engraved plates, errata leaf present; contemporary mottled calf, rebacked, some rubbing, corners worn; very good, scarce. Wing H23898.   Ximenes 108-203 1996 $1,250.00

HOLDERLIN, FRIEDRICH   Patmos. Raamin Presse, 1978. One of 100 copies, signed by artist (of a total edition of 105); 12 1/2 x 7 1/2 inches, 2 p.l. (one blank), (v)-xxxii pages, (2) leaves (colophon blank), five full page color initials and several small color initials and decorative line fillers in text by Roswitha Quadflieg, printed in brown; blue-grey paper, vignette on front cover, large geometrical emblem on back cover, titling on spine stamped in blind, fore edge and tail edge untrimmed, in publisher's slipcase; as new.   Phillip J. Pirages 33-438 1996 $1,650.00

HOLE, S. REYNOLDS   Our Gardens. London: Dent, 1901. 4th edition; 8vo; 1 f., titlepage, 3 ff., 304 pages, frontispiece, 8 plates, text illustrations, top edge gilt; a vellucent binding by Cedric Chivers of Bath, signed on lower turn-in; vellum, running "Art Nouveau" motif of stylised roses, thorns and leaves, gilt studded, framing a central hand colored panel of a garden scene, with the pattern repeated on the spine, executed and lettered by hand in colored inks, gilt fillets on turn-ins, top edge gilt, marbled lemon endleaves.   Marlborough 160-82 1996 £650.00

HOLLAND'S Fond Du Lac City Directory, for the Years 1880-84. Chicago: Holland Pub. Co., 1880. 108, (129)-331 pages including many ads, folded map frontispiece; original cloth, gilt stamping, somewhat worn and frayed, inner hinges cracked.   Bohling Book Co. 192-319 1996 $200.00

HOLLAND, HENRY   Resolutions of the Associated Architects... London: 1793. 8vo; (iv), 31, (1) pages; original wrappers, stitched as issued.   Elton Engineering 10-75 1996 £230.00

HOLLAND, HENRY RICHARD VASSALL FOX, 3RD BARON 1773-1840   A Dream. London: printed by Bensley & Sons, 1818. 1st edition; uncut as issued in drab wrappers, slightly creased and chipped at edges, library label; inscribed by Lady Holland for Mde. de Serza.   Jarndyce 103-491 1996 £120.00

HOLLAND, JOHN   The History, Antiquities and Description of the Town and Parish of Worksop. Sheffield: J. Blackwell, 1826. One of 150 copies; 4to; x pages, 1 f., 204 pages, 32 engraved text illustrations; original boards, joints cracked; subscriber's copy with ex-libris of Sir Arnold Knight. Anderson p. 238.   Marlborough 162-46 1996 £220.00

HOLLAND, RAY P.   Bird Dogs. New York: A. S. Barnes, 1948. Limited to 250 copies, signed by author and artist; 8vo; red cloth, gilt, top edge gilt, beautiful copy in slipcase.   Glenn Books 36-247 1996 $125.00

HOLLAND, ROBERT E.   The Song of Tekakwitha: the Lily of the Mohawks. New York: Fordham University Press, 1942. 1st edition; 8vo; (vi), 167 pages, (1); titlepage and numerous text illustrations in color, illustrated endpapers, tips slightly bumped, small tape marks on endpapers; otherwise fine and unopened in dust jacket, prospectus laid in, with another of the same title, which has small tape marks on endpapers and dust jacket, otherwise very good in dust jacket. 3 letters from author to Brother E. ignatius, a reviewer of the book.   Andrew Cahan 47-137 1996 $250.00

HOLLAND, W.   History of West Cork and the Diocese of Ross. London: 1949. 1st edition; 8vo; illustrations, unusual black cloth binding; very good, very scarce.   C. P. Hyland 216-328 1996 £75.00

HOLLINGSHEAD, JOHN   The Story of Leicester Square. London: Simpkin, 1892. 4to; 76 pages; illustrations; red cloth.   Marlborough 162-142 1996 £65.00

HOLLOWAY, W. L.   Wild Life on the Plains an Horrors of Indian Warfare by a Corps of Competent Authors and Artists. St. Louis: 1891. 1st edition; 592 pages; superbly illustrated; decorated covers fine and bright, slipcase. Six Guns 1015.   Early West 22-57 1996 $125.00

HOLLOWY, WILLIAM   The Peasant's Fate: a Rural Poem. Boston: Hosea Sprague, 1802. 1st American edition, same year as London; 12mo; contemporary calf, rebacked; leaf C5 repaired without loss, otherwise fine. Shaw & Shoemaker 2419.   Trebizond 39-25 1996 $125.00

HOLM, E.   Fruit Chafers of Southern Africa (Scarabaeidae: Cetoniini). Hartebeesport: 1992. Imperial 8vo; 326 pages; 32 colored plates, 173 text figures; cloth.   Wheldon & Wesley 207-1052 1996 £90.00

HOLMAN, DAVID   Buckskin and Homespun: Frontier Texas Clothing 1820-1870. Austin: David Holman at Wind River Press, 1979. 1st Limited edition of only 450 copies; 130 pages; color plates tipped in; dust jacket.   Maggie Lambeth 30-262 1996 $130.00

HOLMAN, DAVID   Buckskin and Homespun. Austin: Wind River Press, 1979. Number 91 of 450 copies, signed by Holman; 13.5 x 9.25 inches; drawings by Pat Massey; 130 pages; photos, some in color and illustrations; printed on Curtis Rag, light tan cloth boards with title in brown on spine and illustration in brown on front, unprinted brown dust jacket, prospectus laid in. Fine.   Joshua Heller 21-281 1996 $120.00

HOLMAN, DAVID   Letters of Hard Times in Texas, 1840-1890. Austin: Roger Beacham, publisher, 1974. One of 23 copies, on this size and type of paper, of an edition of 295, numbered and signed by Holman; 56 pages, title vignette; cloth backed boards with printed labels on spine and front cover.   Bohling Book Co. 191-69 1996 $200.00

HOLMBERG, ERIK J.   The Swedish Excavations at Asea in Arcadia. Lund: C. W. K. Gleerup, 1944. 4to; xv, 192 pages; 154 illustrations and 6 plates (3 in color); chipped wrappers, inscription on top wrapper. Archaeologia   Luxor-3473 1996 $150.00

HOLME, C. GEOFFREY   Decorative Art 1930. London: The Studio, 1930. 4to; pages viii, 180, illustrations; cloth; slightly scuffed, spine darkened, else fine; signature of Anne Harris, one of the first professional decorators in Toronto.   Hugh Anson-Cartwright 87-376 1996 $150.00

HOLMES, EUGENIA K.   Adolph Sutro. San Francisco: San Francisco Photo Engraving Co., 1895. 1st edition; 56 pages; frontispiece and illustrations; original brown pictorial cloth with title stamped in gilt on front cover; fine. Paher Nevada 880.   Michael D. Heaston 23-172 1996 $125.00

HOLMES, J. H. H.   A Treatise on the Coal Mines of Durham and Northumberland... London: Baldwin, Cradock and Joy, 1816. 1st edition; 8vo; 7 plages, xxii, (2), 259, (5) pages, including final five pages of ads; original boards, spine and edges somewhat worn, partially unopened and entirely uncut; fine, rare. Williams II 100; Goldsmiths 21415; Kress B6711. John Drury   82-110 1996 £325.00

HOLMES, JOHN   The Art of Rhetoric Made Easy; or, the Elements of Oratory Briefly Stated, and Fitted for the Practice of the Studious Youth of Great Britain and Ireland... London: printed for A. Parker & sold by A. Bettesworth & Hitch &c., 1739. 1st edition; 2 parts; title in red and black, each page separately signed and paged, contemporary speckled sheep, gilt borders, slight rubbing, hinges cracking with chip on front board. Alston VI 167.   Jarndyce 103-260 1996 £85.00

HOLMES, JOHN CLELLON   Go. New York: Scribner's, 1952. 1st edition; very good+ in dust jacket with insignificant surface loss to extremities and spine folds.   Lame Duck Books 19-145 1996 $850.00

HOLMES, JOHN CLELLON   Go. New York: Scribner, 1952. 1st edition; owner name under front flap, very good in unlaminated dust jacket that is rubbed along folds and worn at spine extremities, still very good or better.   Ken Lopez 74-204 1996 $850.00

HOLMES, JOHN CLELLON   Go. New York: Scribners, 1952. 1st edition; covers slightly soiled, otherwise very good, lacking dust jacket; inscribed by author in year of publication.   Ken Lopez 74-205 1996 $650.00

HOLMES, KENNETH L.   Covered Wagon Women Diaries and Letters from the Western Trails 1840-1890. Glendale: Arthur C. Clarke Co., 1983-93. 11 volumes; new as issued, all fine.   Hermitage SP95-709 1996 $350.00

HOLMES, LOUIS A.   Fort McPherson, Nebrasak. Guardian of the Tracks and Trails. Lincoln: 1963. 108 pages, photos; book very fine with bright covers.   Early West 22-290 1996 $100.00

HOLMES, OLIVER WENDELL 1809-1894   Astraea; the Balance of Illusions. A Poem. Boston: Ticknor, Reed and Fields, 1850. 1st edition; 1st printing, state A and binding A; 12mo; 39 pages; original glazed printed boards; fine, early owner's signature (F. Crosby) Oct. 9, 1850. BAL 8757. Tryon & Charvat A189b. Carroll Wilson p. 500.   M & S Rare Books 60-172 1996 $300.00

HOLMES, OLIVER WENDELL 1809-1894   Astraea. Boston: Ticknor, Reed & Fields, 1850. 1st printing, BAL state A, binding A, 2500 copies; 39 pages; original glazed boards, spine, as usual, partly eroded, rubbed, edgeworn, contents partly soiled, foxed; good+.   Charles Agvent 4-658 1996 $200.00

HOLMES, OLIVER WENDELL 1809-1894   The Autocrat of the Breakfast Table. Boston: Phillips, Sampson & Co., 1858. 1st issue according to points in BAL 8781; viii, 373 pages; brown cloth, gilt lettering, one signature loose, else near fine. Grolier American Hundred 69.   Blue River Books 9-164 1996 $300.00

HOLMES, OLIVER WENDELL 1809-1894   The Autocrat of the Breakfast Table. Boston: Phillips, Sampson, 1858. 1st edition; Binding A, all first issue points; 12mo; 8 plates, engraved title; original binding, spine frayed at head and heel with frayed spots on spine edge as well, corners open, internally very clean, very good; former owner's inscription in pencil. Charles Agvent 4-660 1995 $275.00

HOLMES, OLIVER WENDELL 1809-1894   The Autocrat of the Breakfast Table. Boston: Phillips, Sampson, 1858. 1st edition; printing 2, binding C; sheets measure 7 1/2 x 4 3/4"; bound with 6 (of 8) plates; original binding, moderate foxing, later signature on f.f.e.p., near fine.   Charles Agvent 4-661 1996 $125.00

HOLMES, OLIVER WENDELL 1809-1894   The Autocrat of the Breakfast Table. Boston: Phillips, Sampson & Co., 1859. Early edition; 12mo; 8 plates, extra illustrated with tipped in engraved portrait of Holmes and 1 page ALS dated May 26, 1864 donating autographed copies of his poems (not included) to a charity fund-raiser; on verso of letter is pasted a photo of Holmes; original binding, backstrip laid on, edgewear; good+.   Charles Agvent 4-662 1996 $250.00

HOLMES, OLIVER WENDELL 1809-1894   The Autocrat of the Breakfast Table Every Man His Own Boswell. Boston: 1858. 1st edition; 373 pages; original binding, backstrip and corners worn.   W. Bruce Fye 71-1016 1996 $150.00

HOLMES, OLIVER WENDELL 1809-1894   Border Lines of Knowledge in some Provinces of Medical Science. Boston: Ticknor and Fields, 1862. 1st edition; 8vo; (4), 80 pages; final blank excised; original maroon cloth, embossed in blind, spine lettered in gilt, faded; very good.   John Drury 82-111 1996 £150.00

HOLMES, OLIVER WENDELL 1809-1894   Border Lines of Knowledge in Some Provinces of Medical Science. Boston: Ticknor and Fields, 1862. 1st edition; 8vo; 80 pages; original black cloth, binding 1, wear along edges of spine, last signature of pages starting to loosen, good, relatively scarce. BAL 8814.   Robert F. Lucas 42-43 1996 $175.00

HOLMES, OLIVER WENDELL 1809-1894   Border Lines of Knowledge in some Provinces of Medical Science. Boston: 1862. 1st edition; 80 pages; ex-library, original binding. Currier Tilton 105.   W. Bruce Fye 71-1018 1996 $150.00

HOLMES, OLIVER WENDELL 1809-1894   Currents and Counter-Currents in Medical Science with other Addresses and Essays. Boston: 1861. 1st edition; 406 pages; original binding, spine rubbed, head and tail of spine chipped, faint waterstain affecting a few leaves, otherwise very good. GM 6390.   W. Bruce Fye 71-1019 1996 $175.00

HOLMES, OLIVER WENDELL 1809-1894   Currents and Counter Currents in Medical Science with Other Addresses and Essays. Boston: 1861. 1st edition; 406 pages; recent cloth, library stamp on title, otherwise fine. GM 6390.   W. Bruce Fye 71-1020 1996 $125.00

HOLMES, OLIVER WENDELL 1809-1894   Homoeopathy, and Its Kindred Delusions. Boston: 1842. 1st edition; limited to 1000 copies; 12mo; original boards, scattered foxing, spine bit worn, unusual in binding. Iowa 1745.   James Tait Goodrich K40-155 1996 $295.00

HOLMES, OLIVER WENDELL 1809-1894   Mechanism in Thought and Morals. Boston: Osgood, 1871. 1st edition; one of 1500 copies; original binding, old inscription, private library label; fine. BAL 8876.   Charles Agvent 4-664 1996 $200.00

HOLMES, OLIVER WENDELL 1809-1894   Mechanism in Thought and Morals. Boston: 1871. 1st edition; 101 pages; original binding. Tilton 302. W. Bruce Fye 71-1023 1996 $140.00

HOLMES, OLIVER WENDELL 1809-1894   Poems. Boston and New York: 1836. 1st edition; 8vo; 163 pages; top and bottom of spine quite chipped, text foxed, but sound. BAL 8729 cloth C. Rinderknecht 38075.   M & S Rare Books 60-171 1996 $175.00

HOLMES, OLIVER WENDELL 1809-1894   Poems. Boston: Otis, Broaders, 1836. 1st edition; octavo; 163 pages; author's first book; original embossed green cloth, faint rubbing to corners, paper spine label lacking, else unusually fine. Clipped signature "O.W. Holmes" laid in. BAL 8729; Currier p. 24.   Bromer Booksellers 90-66 1996 $575.00

HOLMES, OLIVER WENDELL 1809-1894   Poems. London: O. Rich & sons, 1846. 1st English edition; 12mo; original cloth, quite worn, especially the spine. With Bradley's embossed stamp on front flyleaf; Inscribed by Holmes for Dr. Samuel G. Morton and Holmes' signature on titlepage, inserted ALS; bookplates of William Harris Arnold & Stephen Wakeman. BAL 8743 binding B (Ticknor).   M & S Rare Books 60-173 1996 $550.00

HOLMES, OLIVER WENDELL 1809-1894   The Poet at the Breakfast Table. Boston: 1872. 1st edition; 418 pages; original binding; Currier Tilton 144.   W. Bruce Fye 71-1029 1996 $100.00

HOLMES, OLIVER WENDELL 1809-1894   Songs in Many Keys. Boston: 1862. 1st edition; 308 pages; original binding, scarce. Currier Tilton 109. W. Bruce Fye 71-1031 1996 $100.00

HOLMES, OLIVER WENDELL 1809-1894   Speeches. Boston: Little Brown, 1891. 1st edition; contemporary three quarter morocco, some rubbing along joints, near fine.   Charles Agvent 4-665 1996 $175.00

HOLMES, OLIVER WENDELL 1809-1894   The Writings. Cambridge: Riverside Press, 1891. One of 275 copies printed for America, large paper edition; 9 x 6 1/4 inches; 14 volumes; partly printed in red; five fine engraved frontispiece portraits, few illustrations in text; quite pleasing contemporary green crushed three quarter morocco, linen sides, gilt decorated raised bands, spines very attractively gilt in compartments featuring large and elegant art deco flowers, marbled endpapers, top edge gilt, other edges rough trimmed, two corners bruised, spines faded (as always) to a pleasant tan, 5 volumes with uneven fading of leather on covers, otherwise bindings in very fine condition with only trivial signs of wear, faint stains at inner margin of few leaves, otherwise fine internally, only isolated trivial foxing, very attractive set, handsome printed on good paper.   Phillip J. Pirages 33-308 1996 $950.00

HOLMES, OLIVER WENDELL 1841-1935   The Common Law. Boston: Little Brown and Co., 1881. 1st edition; original russet cloth, gilt, worn and spotted, good.   Meyer Boswell SL26-114 1996 $1,750.00

HOLMES, OLIVER WENDELL 1841-1935   The Common Law. Boston: Little Brown and Co., 1881. 1st edition; 8vo; 16, 422 pages; original brick red cloth, slight soiling and very slight wear on lower spine, inner hinge touch tender, penciling in text, mostly at front, except for latter, an especially nice copy. Grolier American 100 84.   M & S Rare Books 60-340 1996 $1,450.00

HOLMES, RICHARD   Queen Victoria by Richard R. Holmes, Librarian to the Queen. London: Boussod, Valadon & Co... 1897. Proof specimen copy, 4to; large paper copy; title on japan vellum, 4 tipped in letters, penciled specimen of 3 dedication leaves, half title facsimile color portrait frontispiece, additional printed title, (i-ii), 1-195 pages, list of illustrations 199-200, publisher's colophon, 44 full page plates, all tissue guarded, 15 vignettes to letterpress, all tissue guarded, 4 facsimiles and decorative letterpieces; this copy contains a duplicate set of plates and facsimiles on japan vellum; bound by Zaehnsdorf, full red morocco with gilt royal coat of arms to both boards, gilt crown and Tudor rose emblem to all corners of both boards, gilt ruled dentelles to boards, gilt title and crowns to compartments, raised bands to spine, top edge gilt, rest untrimmed, watered silk endpapers; very handsome copy. Beeleigh Abbey BA56-149 1996 £650.00

HOLMES, THOMAS JAMES   Cotton Mather: a Bibliography of His Works. Cambridge: Harvard University Press, 1940. 1st edition; one of 500 copies; 8vo; 3 volumes; original quarter morocco and cloth, near fine.   Chapel Hill 94-258 1996 $225.00

HOLMES, THOMAS JAMES   Increase Mather, His Works. Cleveland: for Private Distribution, 1930. Limited to 250 copies printed on handmade paper; large 8vo; (6), 60 pages; green morocco over marbled boards, edges lightly rubbed, prospectus laid in.   Kenneth Karmiole 1NS-123 1996 $100.00

HOLMES, THOMAS JAMES   Increase Mather: a Bibliography of His Works. Cleveland: William Gwinn Mather, 1931. 1st edition; one of 500 copies; 8vo; 2 volumes, 711 pages; original quarter morocco and cloth, spines uniformly faded to brown, but unopened and near fine.   Chapel Hill 94-259 1996 $200.00

HOLSTEIN, ANNA   Three Years in Field Hospitals of the Army of the Potomac. Philadelphia: 1867. 1st edition; 131 pages; original binding, very rare.   W. Bruce Fye 71-1034 1996 $375.00

HOLTZAPFFEL, C.   Turning and Mechanical Manipulation. London: 1846-1904. Comprises I 2nd thousnad, 1846; II 1875 on title, 1893 on binding; III 1850, 1st ed.; III rev. 1894, 1st ed. thus; IV 2nd thousand, 1881; V 1894 on title, 1904 on binding; 8vo; volumes 1-5 plus the revised volume 3, in 6 volumes; numerous illustrations, some foxing; black cloth, bit marked and slightly worn, volume 1 rather worn, joints splitting, one or two patches of nibbled cloth on turn-ins. Abell 142. Maggs Bros. Ltd. 1190-640 1996 £650.00

HOLWELL, JOHN ZEPHANIAH   A Genuine Narrative of the Deplorable Deaths of the English Gentlemen and Others, Who Were Suffocated in the Black Hole in Fort William, at Calcutta in the Kingdom of Bengal... London: printed for A. Millar, 1758. 1st edition; 8vo; title and last page dusty, modern half calf by Sangorski & Sutcliffe; uncut.   Anthony Laywood 108-72 1996 £275.00

HOLY Songs and Sonnets. Groningen: La Stampa Chiara, 1985. Each one of 50 numbered copies, signed by artist; narrow folio; text in Bembo and ornamental borders printed in 6 color silkscreen on Simili Japon, 2 volumes; etchings by Marjolein Varekamp; fine grey cloth by Phoenix Bindery, Amsterdam; fine in dust jackets.   Bertram Rota 272-439 1996 £130.00

THE HOME of the Emigrant from Everywhere. St. Louis: M. Olshausen & Co., 1876. 1st edition of this issue; 43 blank (2) pages; original printed salmon wrappers, minor chipping, laid in half morocco and chemise slipcase; very good. Adams Herd 2275;   Michael D. Heaston 23-313 1996 $1,500.00

HOME, FRANCIS   The Principles of Agriculture and Vegetation.
Edinburgh: printed for A. Kincaid and J. Bell; and for A. Millar, 1759. 2nd
edition; library accession number on lower blank margin of A2,
contemporary calf, rebacked, label. Fussell pp. 36-7.   Anthony W.
Laywood 109-67 1996 £135.00

HOMER, HENRY SACHEVERELL   An Enquiry Into the Means of
Preserving and Improving the Publick Roads of This Kingdom. Oxford:
Printed for S. Parker, 1767. (4), 87, (1) pages; recent wrpapers, nice.
Higgs 4168; Goldsmiths 10351.   C. R. Johnson 37-16 1996 £125.00

HOMERUS   The Homeric Hymn to Aphrodite. Waltham St. Lawrence:
Golden Cockerel Press, 1948. One of 750 numbered copies; narrow folio;
13 wood engravings by Mark Severin; printed in 13 pt. Poliphilus and 12
pt. New Hellenic in black and terracotta; quarter parchment, green cloth
sides with pictorial decoration in gilt on upper cover, very nice, variant
binding.   Bertram Rota 272-186 1996 £150.00

HOMERUS   The Iliad and Odyssey of Homer. London: for J. Johnson,
1791. 1st edition; 4to; 2 volumes, xvii, (xi), 668; (iv), 583 pages; early
19th century polished tan calf, spines richly gilt in compartments, green
lettering and numbering pieces, sides with triple gilt rules, blindstamped
inner dentelles, marbled endpapers and edges, scattered light spotting
but generally very clean and fresh internally, excellent copy; bookplates
of Philip Lyttelton Gell. Rothschild 684.   Simon Finch 24-117 1996
£350.00

HOMERUS   The Iliad and Odyssey of Homer. London: printed for J.
Johnson, 1791. 1st edition of this translation; 4to; 2 volumes in 1; 8
page list of subscribers, errata leaf, 19th century half morocco, rebacked
with original spine.   Anthony W. Laywood 109-68 1996 £75.00

HOMERUS   The Iliad of Homer Rendered Into English Prose for the
Use of Those Who Cannot Read the Original. London: Longmans, Green
and Co., 1898. 1st issue with last page of ads marked 50,0000 3/98;
original red cloth.   Jarndyce CII-62 1996 £120.00

HOMERUS   Iliad. Munich: Bremer Press, 1923. Limited to 615
numbered copies; folio; text finely printed in Greek in Monachos type;
superbly bound by Jeff Clements in full brown morocco, blind tooled,
geometrically designed inlays in blue, red, grey and black colored
moroccos, black morocco doublures, suede endpapers, gilt edges,
preserved in drop down cloth box. Outstanding copy.   Thomas Thorp
489-157 1996 £1,250.00

HOMERUS   The Iliad and the Odyssey. Haarlem: for the members of
the Limited Editions Club, 1931. Number 1089 of 1500 sets, each signed
by designer, J. van Krimpen; 12.5 x 8.5 inches; 2 volumes, xxxviii, 706,
(4) pages; xiv, 548, (4) pages; volume 1 in red buckram boards, volume
2 in blue buckram boards, original yellow slipcases very worn, spines
sun faded, boards and books fine.   Joshua Heller 21-152 1996
$200.00

HOMERUS   The Odyssey. Glasgow: Excudebant Robertus et Andreas
Foulis, 1758. Folio; 2 volumes, half title in volume 1, small library stamp
on titles, greek letter, verso of 4A2 soiled, slight spotting of text, later
cloth backed boards, uncut, leather labels. Gaskell 319.   Anthony
Laywood 108-61 1996 £145.00

HOMERUS   The Odyssey Rendered Into English Prose for The Use of
Those Who Cannot Read the Original. London: Longmans, Green and
Co., 1900. Map, original light cloth, spine faded. Hoppe 39.   Jarndyce
CII-65 1996 £150.00

HOMERUS   The Odyssey of Homer. London: Medici Society, 1924.
One of 500 copies; 11 1/2 x 9 1/2 inches; xxviii,3 15, (1) pages, (2)
leaves; 20 color collotype plates by William Russell Flint, title printed in
green and black; original cloth and dust jacket, morocco spine labels,
top edge gilt, other edges untrimmed, unopened; bright, clean and
generally fine, especialy impressive because bound in white - with nice,
somewhat loose fitting jacket (spine slightly darkened, some fraying,
spine top bit chipped, verso with neat but extensive reinforcing),
excellent copy, generally very attractive, obviously without any internal
signs of use.   Phillip J. Pirages 33-237 1996 $275.00

HOMERUS   The Odyssey. London: ptd. & published by Sir Emery
Walker, Wilfred Merton & Bruce Rogers, 1932. 1st edition; one of 530
copies; small folio; set in 16 point Monotype Centaur with 2 point
leading, paper specially handmade grey toned paper from J. Barcham
Green Mill with watermark of Greek Galley; 25 black on gold leaf
roundels as title vignette and headpieces designed by Bruce Rogers;
bound by W. H. Smith and Son, black niger morocco, spine gilt, top
edge gilt, others uncut, original publisher's board slipcase (slightly worn),
edges of turn-ins browned as usual, else lovely copy (edge of one page
slight bit ruffled); O'Brien A141.   Priscilla Juvelis 95/1-128 1996
$1,250.00

HOMERUS   The Odyssey. London: Oxford University Press, 1935. 1st
edition translated by T. E. Lawrence; decorated buckram gilt, top edge
gilt, top edge dusty, edges spotted, spine faded, head and tail of spine
and one corner slightly bumped, covers slightly marked, very good, no
dust jacket; bookplate of the literary agent John Johnson.   Ulysses
39-354 1996 £45.00

HOMERUS   The Odyssey. Limited Editions Club, 1981. One of 2000
numbered copies, signed by Wilson and Moser; 4to; 25 wood
engravings by Barry Moser; cloth, fine copy in slipcase.   Bertram Rot
272-268 1996 £75.00

HOMERUS   The Works of Homer. London: Alex Hogg, n.d., ca. 1780
1st edition; very tall wide quarto (signed as folio), pages 659, plus
printer's directions, book announcements and subscribers list; 40
splendid full page copperplates after Fourdrinier, with tissue guards;
bound by Root in full brown polished calf in reptile skin pattern, double
gilt rules and doublures, raised bands, all edes gilt, marbled endpapers,
sillfully rehinted, elegant copy; fine. Lowndes III 1250.   Hartfield 48-L6
1996 $950.00

HOMES in Texas on the Line of the International & Great Northern R.R.
1880-'81. Buffalo: Printing House of Matthews Bros., & Bryant, 1880. 1st
edition of this issue; 135 pages; illustrations, folding map, colored with
insets; minor splitting repaired and slight loss along one fold, original
pictorial wrappers, laid in half morocco and chemise case, very good.
Michael D. Heaston 23-315 1996 $1,200.00

HOMES of American Authors. New York: & London: G. P.
Puntam/Sampson Low, 1853. 1st edition; 2nd printing, with color
illustrations printed directly on text pages, with dual London imprint (no
priority), binding B (no priority); original green cloth, gilt, all edges gilt,
BAL notes only brown and blue cloth, edges plain, spine little dull,
faint damp mark at corner of one cover, fresh and attractive copy.
Bennett, 19th Cent. American Color Plate Books p. 58; BAL 1345 20665.
Mac Donnell 12-139 1996 $250.00

HONE, J. M.   Bishop Berkeley - His Life, Writings and Philosophy.
London: Faber & Faber Ltd., 1931. 1st edition; 4 black and white plates
original binding, inscription, prelims, edges and endpapers slightly, head
and tail of spine and corners slightly bumped, very good in nicked,
spotted, rubbed, marked and dusty, slightly soiled dust jacket browned
at spine and edges.   Ulysses 39-665 1996 £55.00

HONE, JOSEPH   The Love Story of Thomas Davis Told in the Letters
of Annie Hutton. Cuala Press, 1945. 1st edition; limited to 250 copies;
quarter cloth, very good.   C. P. Hyland 216-142 1996 £75.00

HONE, WILLIAM   The Divine Right of the Kings to Govern Wrong.
London: for William Hone, 1821. 1st edition; octavo; pages 60; titlepage
and tailpiece engravings by George Cruikshank; recent marbled paper
wrappers, uncut, slight wear, but excellent copy generally.   Hartfield
48-L39 1996 $165.00

HONE, WILLIAM   The Three Trials of William Hone for Publishing
Three Parodies... London: William Hone, 1818. 1st edition; octavo;
separate pagination, totalling 120 pages; recent marbled wrappers,
typographic label, very good. NCBEL III 1285.   Hartfield 48-L40 1996
$195.00

HONE, WILLIAM   The Three Trials of William Hone, for Publishing
Three Parodies; viz. The Late John Wilkes's Catechism, The Political
Litany and the Sinecurit's Creed. (with) Trial by Jury and Liberty of the
Press, (etc.). London: printed by and for William Hone, 67, Old Bailey,
1818. 17th, 15th, 14th editions stated, respectively, 5th edition stated fo
last tract; contemporary boards, untrimmed, serviceably rebacked,
sound.   Meyer Boswell SL26-115 1996 $125.00

HONE, WILLIAM   The Yearbook of Daily Recreation and Information,
Concerning Remarkable Men and Manners... (with) The Every-Day Book;
or, Everlasting Calendar of Popular Amusements, Sports, Pastimes,
Ceremonies... London: 1832/26/33/33. Large 8vo; 4 volumes; 170, 436,
436 engravings; uniformly bound in full leather (one spine label missing
some very moderate scratching. Very attractive set.   Roy W. Clare
XXIV-16 1996 $275.00

HONIG, LOUIS O.   James Bridger. The Pathfinder of the West. Kansa
City: Brown White Lowell Press, 1951. Subscriber's edition; number 110
of 525 signed by author; portrait frontispiece; original purple fabrikoid
cover.   Glenn Books 36-121 1996 $150.00

HOOD'S CANAL LAND & IMPROVEMENT CO.   Union City, Its
Resources and Prospects. Port Towsend: Morning Leader Steam Print,
1890. 1st edition; 19 pages; folding map; original printed yellow
wrappers; fine. Smith 4608.   Michael D. Heaston 23-351 1996
$500.00

HOOD, JOHN   Australia and the East; Being a Journal Narrative of a Voyage to New South Wales in an Emigrant Ship... London: John Murray, 1843. 1st edition; 8vo; half title, errata slip, 12 pages ads; original cloth, spine gilt, upper portion of spine carefully repaired; very good, later bookplate. Hill collection p. 147.   Trebizond 39-105 1996 $220.00

HOOD, THEODORE EDWARD   Maxwell. London: Henry Colburn and Richard Bentley, 1830. 1st edition; 12mo; 3 volumes, contemporary half blue calf, gilt, spines ornately gilt, traces of rubbing; half titles present in volumes 1 and 2 (all required), 14 line errata slip at end of first volume; occasional foxing, bound without publisher's ads at end of 3rd volume, but a pretty set; from the library of Frances Mary Richardson Currer; Sadleir 1207; Wolff 3256; Block p. 113; CBEL III 732.   Ximenes 108-204 1996 $450.00

HOOD, THOMAS 1799-1845   The Loves of Tom Tucker and Little Bo-Peep. London: Griffith & Farran, 1863. 1st edition; 4to; hand colored titlepage vignette and 8 hand colored full page engravings; original cloth backed colored pictorial boards, extremities worn and other light wear to covers, some thumbing, else very good. Oppenheimer 1295.   Marjorie James 19-124 1996 £95.00

HOOD, THOMAS 1799-1845   Miss Kilmansegg and Her Precious Leg. Chipping Camden: Essex House Press, 1904. Limited edition, 159/200 copies (of an edition of 204); crown 8vo; pages (ii), 94, (1); printed on handmade paper; 3 full page wood engravings by Reginald Savage; original quarter holland, printed backstrip and front cover labels, that on backstrip chipped, mid blue boards, untrimmed, good.   Blackwell's B112-103 1996 £150.00

HOOD, THOMAS 1799-1845   Odes and Addresses to Great People. London: Baldwin, Cradock and Joy, 1825. 1st edition; octavo; later polished tan calf, gilt, top edge gilt, by Bedford, edges untrimmed; very fine; Charles Tennant bookplate.   G. W. Stuart 59-47 1996 $325.00

HOOD, THOMAS 1799-1845   The Poems of Thomas Hood. New York: Cassell, Petter and Galpin, 1870. Folio; 58 pages; headpieces, initials and finials drawn by J. Moyr Smith, 8 full page engravings by Gustave Dore; pebbled cloth with mediaeval design in gold and black, light wear to extremities, otherwise fine, all edges gilt.   Bromer Booksellers 90-28 1996 $150.00

HOOD, THOMAS 1799-1845   Poems by Thomas Hood. London: Moxon, 1871. Large paper edition; quarto; 109 pages; 14 steel engraved plates by Birket Foster, with tissue guards; handsome half green morocco, spine gilt in compartments with all over chain link design and blue morocco label, all edges gilt.   Bromer Booksellers 90-38 1996 $300.00

HOOD, THOMAS 1799-1845   Poems. London: E. Moxon, Son & Co., 1881. 4to; 2 volumes in 1; viii, 180; viii, 109, (1) page ads; 41 steel engravings (of 42), lacking plate 'Sestos and Abydos', probably result of binder's error; contemporary full green morocco over bevelled boards, spine extra gilt in 6 compartments of which 5 compartments contain red morocco rose shaped inlays, sides with elaborate wide gilt borders and with inlaid red morocco panel, red morocco rose corner ornaments, inside dentelles, gilt edges, handsome binding, text slightly foxed in places.   Thomas Thorp 489-158 1996 £150.00

HOOD, THOMAS 1799-1845   Whims and Oddities, in Prose and Verse... (with) Whims and Oddities...(Second Series). London: Lupton Relfe/ London: Hurst, Chance and Co., 1827/29. 2nd edition; 8vo; 2 works; pages xiv, 146, 150, each with 40 humorous illustrations by Hood; uniformly bound in 19th century half green hard grain morocco, spines gilt lettered direct, combe marbled sides and endpapers, gilt edges, rubbed, one or two trivial spots or stains; very good; presentation copies from author to Edward Moxon.   Simon Finch 24-118 1996 £500.00

HOOK, THEODORE EDWARD   The Soldier's Return; or, What Can Beauty Do? London: Longman et al, 1805. 1st edition; octavo; author's first book; modern wrappers, slight wear, minor spots, complete with half title and ads;   G. W. Stuart 59-48 1996 $175.00

HOOKE, ANDREW   An Essay On the National Debt, and National Capital; or, the Account Truly Stated, Debtor and Creditor. London: W. Owen, 1750. half title, 59 pages; disbound, fine, uncut, signed by author in authentification of the edition. Kress 5040; Goldsmiths 8530.   C. R. Johnson 37-17 1996 £125.00

HOOKER, J. D.   A Century of Indian Orchids Selected from Drawings in the Herbarium of the Botanic Garden, Calcuta. Lehre: 1967. Folio; pages (1), v, 68, 101 plates; cloth, some bumping to lower edge of covers, minor yellowing to edges of plates.   Raymond M. Sutton VI-910 1996 $115.00

HOOKER, J. D.   Flora of British India. New Delhi: n.d. Reprint; 8vo; 7 volumes; cloth.   Wheldon & Wesley 207-1550 1996 £120.00

HOOKER, WILLIAM JACKSON 1785-1865   British Jungermanniae: Being a History and Description... London: 1816. 4to; 88 fine hand colored plates; half morocco slightly rubbed, faded stamp and inscription on titlepage, occasional minor soiling, but in general a good copy, rare. Wheldon & Wesley 207-46 1996 £900.00

HOOKER, WILLIAM JACKSON 1785-1865   The British Ferns; or Coloured Figures and Descriptions... London: 1861. Royal 8vo; 66 hand colored plates; original cloth, used; stamps on half title and titlepage, edges of titlepage and text to plate 1 frayed and soiled, otherwise good ex-library.   Wheldon & Wesley 207-1626 1996 £160.00

HOOKER, WILLIAM JACKSON 1785-1865   A Century of Orchidaceous Plants Selected from Curtis's Botanical Magazine. London: 1849. Royal 4to; pages 78, (2), 100 hand colored plates; new half morocco, small blindstamp on titlepage, some plates slightly foxed, plate by rather heavily soiled, but in general a good copy; rare.   Wheldon & Wesley 207-48 1996 £3,000.00

HOOKER, WILLIAM JACKSON 1785-1865   Exotic Flora. Edinburgh: August 1822-Dec. 1824. Royal 8vo; 17 parts in 1 volume; full morocco, uncut, extremely rare.   Wheldon & Wesley 207-47 1996 £1,000.00

HOOKER, WILLIAM JACKSON 1785-1865   Journal of a Tour in Iceland in the Summer of 1809. London: printed for Vernor, Hood, and Sharpe, Poultry; & Wm. Miller,... 1811. 1st edition; 2nd issue; 8vo; half title, title, dedication (3 pages), introduction (v-lxii), 1-301 pages, appendices 305-496, index, errata and directions to binder, hand colored etched plate frontispiece, 7 vignettes to letterpress and 1 plan; modern tree calf boards, tastefully rebacked, gilt tool scrolled border, elaborate gilt tooling to panelled spine, green morocco label to spine, corners very slightly worn, marbled endpapers, hinges cracked, but still good, tight copy, armorial bookplate, edges stained red. Lowndes II p. 107. Beeleigh Abbey BA56-78 1996 £300.00

HOOKER, WILLIAM JACKSON 1785-1865   The Journal of Botany, Being a Second Series of the Botanical Miscellany. London: 1834-42. 1st edition; 8vo; 4 volumes, 5 portraits, 71 (on 65) plates; original green cloth, spines faded, trifle worn, one section becoming loose; scarce. Maggs Bros. Ltd. 1190-99 1996 £220.00

HOOKER, WILLIAM JACKSON 1785-1865   Synopsis Filicum; or a Synopsis of All Known Ferns. London: 1883. 2nd edition; 8vo; pages xiv, 9-559, 9 hand colored plates of 75 figures; cloth, joints loose. Wheldon & Wesley 207-1627 1996 £60.00

HOOLE, CHARLES   An Easie Entrance to the Latine Tongue... London: William Dugard for Joshuah Kirton, 1649. 1st edition; 8vo; (xiv), 429, (1) pages, (although actual number of pages little different owing to printer's misnumbering of several leaves), many running headlines cut close or cropped in first half of book, wanting first leaf A1 (imprint recto and Latin title verso); contemporary calf, neatly rebacked, bit worn. New Wing H 2681.   John Drury 82-112 1996 £150.00

HOOPER, GEORGE   Waterloo: the Downfall of the First Napoleon: a History of the Campaign of 1815. London: Smith, Elder, 1862. Thick 8vo; extra illustrated with 28 folded, full page and in-set engravings, 2 color lithograph views, original small watercolor bust portrait of Louis XVIII, and 5 folding maps; also tipped in signed document: Divison de Paris, 1817, 1 printed note to Marshal Francois Etienne de Kellerman, Duc De Valmy on folded quarto sheet with contemporary hand written note by subordinate, and signed by Duc de Valmy, with orig. red wax seal & postmarked address to Duc de Valmy on verso of second leaf; later full crushed navy mor. gilt by Sangorski & Sutcliffe of Charles J. Sawyer Ltd., alternating motif of crowns & bees, initial 'N' with crowns at corners, crimson morocco at pastedown under bevelled glass with brass frame is a very fine miniature on enamel of Napoleon on the deck of the 'Belelrophon", deck rigging and ropes in background with sea in distance; binding in perfect condition in fleece lined blue cloth box. Marilyn Braiterman 15-151 1996 $3,750.00

HOOTON, CHARLES   St. Louis' Isle, or Texiana; with Additional Observations Made in the United States and in Canada. London: Simmonds and Ward, 1847. 1st edition; 204 pages; frontispiece and plates; original green cloth, title in gilt on spine, very fine, laid in half morocco clamshell case. Raines p. 118; Howes H626; Clark Travels in Old South III 328.   Michael D. Heaston 23-173 1996 $3,500.00

HOOTON, EARNEST ALBERT   The Indians of Pecos Pueblo: a Study of Their Skeletal Remains. New Haven: Yale University Press, 1930. 10 7/ 8 x 8 1/8 inches; xxviii, 391 pages, 15 plates in pocket at end, many pages of illustrations; dark green cloth, mild spotting to lower edges of binding.   Dawson's Books Shop 528-112 1996 $125.00

HOPE, THOMAS CHARLES   Experiments and Observations Upon the Contraction of Water by Heat at Low Temeparatures. Edinburgh: 1805. 4to; 27 pages; disbound.   Graham Weiner C2-725 1996 £50.00

HOPE, WILLIAM H. ST. JOHN   The Abbey of St. Mary in Furness, Lancashire. Kendal: T. Wilson, 1902. Limited to 200 copies; large 4to; pages 82, 18 steel engraved plates on thick paper tipped on to guards, 12 collotypes, etc., 4 maps; prospectus for work loosely inserted; original buckram gilt, little soiled and rubbed; from the library of Daniel Scott of Penrith, with his booklabel.   R.F.G. Hollett & Son 78-998 1996 £180.00

HOPE, WILLIAM H. ST. JOHN   Cowdray and Easebourne Priory in the County of Sussex. London: Country Life, 1919. Limited to 400 numbered copies; folio; pages 158; frontispiece, 53 plates; original half parchment, gilt top, binding trifle dust soiled; armorial bookplate of Charles, 9th Earl of Egmont.   Howes Bookshop 265-2248 1996 £120.00

HOPING, JOHANN A. J.   Chiromantia Harmonica... Jena: J. Gollner, 1673. 1st edition; 8vo; 128 pages; 66 large text woodcuts, 2 double page engravings; modern three quarter calf, gilt, fine. Not in NUC; Sabbatini 280; Guyot 411; not in Caillet, Rosenthal, etc.   Bennett Gilbert LL29-56 1996 $1,800.00

HOPKINS, GERARD MANLEY   Pied Beauty. London: Simon King Press, 1994. Limited to 100 numbered copies; folio; pages (22), four full page linocut illustrations, printed in 18 pt. Baskerville of 176gsm Mohawk paper; with an additional set of the prints, signed and numbered in stiff paper folder; bound by Alan Wood at the Gregynog Bindery in quarter blue morocco lettered in gold, paste paper boards, with an additional set of prints, signed and numbered, in stiff paper folder.   Claude Cox 107-74B 1996 £150.00

HOPKINS, GERARD MANLEY   Pied Beauty. A Selection of Poems. London: Simon King Press, 1994. Limited to 100 numbered copies; folio; pages (22), four full page linocut illustrations, printed in 18 pt. Baskerville of 176 gsm Mohawk paper; blue buckram backed decorated paste paper boards.   Claude Cox 107-74a 1996 £75.00

HOPKINS, GERARD MANLEY   Selected Poems. London: Nonesuch Press, 1954. Limited edition, 271/1100 copies; 16mo; pages vii, 104, (1); wood engraved title vignette by Kenneth Lindley printed in brown; original decorated brown boards with white vellum gilt lettered backstrip, untrimmed, board slipcase; fine. Dreyfus 122.   Blackwell's B112-207 1996 £60.00

HOPKINS, JOSEPH R.   Hamiltoniad; or, the Efects of Discord. Philadelphia: printed for the author, Aug. 3, 1804. 1st edition; 8vo; 40, (1), 34-55 pages; removed. S&S 6948; Wegelin 998.   M & S Rare Books 60-163 1996 $375.00

HOPKINS, KENNETH   She is My Bright and Smiling and Shy Dear. Easthampton: Warwick Press, 1985. Limited to 75 copies, signed by poet and artist/printer; quarto; 63 pages; printed on one side of Japanese handmade paper; 3 full page illustrations and 1 illustration on titlepage, which have been subtly hand watercolored by printer; tan boards, extremely fine.   Bromer Booksellers 90-241 1996 $325.00

HOPKINS, SAMUEL   Historical Memoirs, Relating to the Housatunnuk Indians; or, an Account of the Methods Used and Pains Taken for the Propagation of the Gospel Among the Heathenish-tribe, and the Success Thereof, Under th Ministry of the Late. Rev. Mr. John Sergeant... Boston: printed and sold by S. Kneeland, 1753. 1st edition; small 4to; contemporary calf, covers bowned, some wear to upper joint, cords strong; few minor marginal dampstains, but excellent copy. Sabin 32945; Evans 7023; Howes H632; Vail 460; Church 986;   Ximenes 109-159 1996 $8,500.00

HOPKINSON, TOM   Down the Long Slide. London: Hogarth Press, 1949. 1st edition; original binding, prelims, edges and endpapers spottted, gilt lettering on spine slightly oxidised, covers slightly bowed, very good in nicked and slightly rubbed, torn, marked, spotted and dusty dust jacket, browned at spine and edges.   Ulysses 39-304 1996 £55.00

HOPKINSON, TOM   The Transitory Venus - Nine Stories. London: Horizon, 1948. 1st edition; original binding, top edge dusty, spine and cover edges slightly faded, endpapers slightly spotted and partially browned, very good in nicked, chipped, rubbed and slightly marked and dusty, internally repaired dust jacket, slightly darkened at spine and edges.   Ulysses 39-303 1996 £55.00

HOPPE, A. J.   A Bibliography of the Writings of Samuel Butler... London: the Office of the Bookman's Journal, 1925. Number 297 of 500 copies; brown cloth.   Jarndyce CII-120 1996 £85.00

HOPPE, E. O.   In the Gipsy Camp and Royal Palace, Wanderings in Rumania. New York: 1924. 1st American edition; 9 x 6 inches; 240 pages, with index; photos; cloth backed boards; covers heavily rubbed, soiled; with one page holograph presentation signed by Hoppe laid-in (right edge frayed).   John K. King 77-836 1996 $150.00

HOPPE, E. O.   Picturesque Great Britain: the Architecture and the Landscape Wasmuth. Berlin: 1926. 1st edition; small folio; profusely illustrated with photos; spine little dull, otherwise very good.   Words Etcetera 94-638 1996 £60.00

HOPPIN, JOSEPH CLARK   Euthymides and His Fellows. Cambridge: Harvard University Press, 1917. 8vo; xvi, 186 pages, 36 figures and 48 plates; original cloth.   Archaeologia Luxor-3481 1996 $125.00

HOPPIN, JOSEPH CLARK   A Handbook of Attic Red-Figured Vases Signed or Attributed to the Various Masters of the Sixth and Fifth Centuries B.C. Cambridge: Harvard University Press, 1919. 8vo; 2 volumes, 1072 pages, numerous illustrations, original cloth, top edge gilt foxing to few pages.   Archaeologia Luxor-3482 1996 $300.00

HOPTON, ARTHUR   A Concordancy of Yeares. London: printed by Nicholas Okes for Thomas Adams, 1615. 8vo; title within woodcut decorative border, short tear in blank margin of A5, most of text black letter, 7 pages of 'Kalendar' shaved close, few spots and stains towards end, expertly bound in modern panelled calf, label, generally nice. STC 13779.   Anthony Laywood 108-11 1996 £475.00

HORACE Wells, Dentist, Father of Surgical Anesthesia. Hartford: 1948. 1s edition; 415 pages; original binding, ex-library.   W. Bruce Fye 71-2244 1996 $125.00

HORACE Wells, Dentist. Father of Surgical Anesthesia. N.P.: American Dental Assoc., 1948. 1st edition; 8vo; xiii, 415 pages; illustrations; original cloth. Very good.   Edwin V. Glaser B122-158 1996 $100.00

HORAN, JAMES D.   The McKenney-Hall Portrait Gallery of American Indians. New York: Crown Publishers, 1972. 1st edition; 373 pages; 125 full page color portraits, plus illustrations; original cloth, very fine with pictorial dust jacket. Scarce thus.   Argonaut Book Shop 113-354 1996 $150.00

HORATIUS FLACCUS, QUINTUS 65-8 BC   Carmina Sapphica. Chelsea: Ashendene press, 1903. Limited to 175 copies, this one of 150 on japan vellum; 8vo; pages 46, (i), printed in red and black, first initial in gold, others in red and blue, by Graily Hewitt, woodcut device at end; original limp vellum, spine lettered in gilt, slightly soiled, but excellent copy. Simon Finch 24-119 1996 £600.00

HORATIUS FLACCUS, QUINTUS 65-8 BC   Odes and Epodes. New York: Limited Editions Club, 1961. Limited 50 1500 copies; 8vo. and folio 2 volumes; original Latin with English translations on facing pages; buckram/hand marbled paper; fine in glassine and dual slipcase. Charles Agvent 4-668 1996 $200.00

HORATIUS FLACCUS, QUINTUS 65-8 BC   Opera. Leiden: Elzevier, 1629 12mo; 3 parts in one; 1f., (30), 239; 296 (i.e. 286) pages, 1 blank f; 256 pages, 3 blank ff.; full contemporary vellum with wallet edges and blue silk ties, stamped in gilt on both covers is the Auchinleck Library mark, spine with horizontal gilt bands and brown morocco title label, Lord Auchinleck's library mark is also stamped at the foot of the engraved title, on first blank at end (Q6) there are 8 lines of verse in praise of Horace, believed to be in the hand of Alexander Boswell, Lord Auchinleck; very fine copy with an excellent association. Copinger 2396; Willems 314;   Book Block 32-56 1996 $1,750.00

HORATIUS FLACCUS, QUINTUS 65-8 BC   Opera. Leyden & Rotterdam Ex Officina Hackiana, 1670. 8vo; engraved title, 7 ff., 832 pages, 28ff. n.n.; black calf gilt by Poujade of Millau and with his ticket, ornate rich gilt and red painted neo-gothic central plaque, gilt and blind outer borders, spine with raised gilt bands enclosing blind stamped compartments, red label, all edges gilt; eye catching binding, little marre by inaccurate tool placement.   Marlborough 160-18 1996 £450.00

HORATIUS FLACCUS, QUINTUS 65-8 BC   Opera. Londini: Aeneis Tabulis Incidit, Johannes Pine, 1733-37. 1st edition; 2nd issue with reading 'potest' at p. 108 in volume 2; 8vo; 2 volumes, pages (xxxii), 264; (xxiv), 191, (14, index); finely bound in contemporary red morocco covers with wide gilt floral borders enclosing large ?Dutch crowned armorial, spines gilt in compartments, marbled endpapers, all edges gil Rothschild 1548; Lowndes p. 1113.   Sotheran PN32-21 1996 £1,650.00

HORATIUS FLACCUS, QUINTUS 65-8 BC   The Works of Horace...
London: ptd. for W. Flexney, Mess. Johnson & Co. and T. Caslon, 1767.
1st edition; 8vo; 4 volumes; half title in each volume; contemporary calf,
gilt, rebacked, spines gilt, contrasting morocco labels, edges bit rubbed;
some foxing, but very good set; early armorial bookplates of Francis
Gregg. Mahony & Rizzo 158. CBEL II 591.   Ximenes 108-327 1996
$900.00

HORATIUS FLACCUS, QUINTUS 65-8 BC   Opera. Birmingham: Typis S.
Baskerville, 1777. Octavo; contemporary calf, covers and extremities
scuffed, early armorial bookplate, partly defaced, minor foxing, very nice.
Rare. Not in Gaskell.   G. W. Stuart 59-6 1996 $275.00

HORATIUS FLACCUS, QUINTUS 65-8 BC   (Opera) Quae Supersunt
Recensuit et Notulis Instruxit Gilbertus Wakefield. London: Kearsley, 1794.
Large 8vo; 2 volumes in 1; pages viii, 186, 4 ff., 2 engraved plates, title,
pages 168, 5 ff., errata slip on final blank; large paper copy of this
scarce edition; crimson morocco gilt, relatively plain, covers panelled
with two single fillets, one straight and one indented and looped at
corners, spine with repeated gilt pattern within double raised bands,
binder's ticket "Bound by L. Cordavau".   Marlborough 160-42 1996
£800.00

HORATIUS FLACCUS, QUINTUS 65-8 BC   Opera Omnia. Paris: Printed
by Didot Jeune for A. Sautelet, 1828. 2 15/16 x 1 7/8 inches; 4 p.l., 229
pages; fine contemporary red morocco, covers framed with simple gilt
rule connecting floral corner ornaments, large and attractive arabesque in
blind at center of each board, spine very attractively gilt with wide
decorated raised bands and complex flourished ornaments between
them, turn-ins with very nice gilt decoration, all edges gilt, lower third of
back cover slightly discolored, otherwise only a hint of wear to joints
and corners, virtually faultless internally, very bright and especially
appealing contemporary copy. Bondy pp. 91-92; Bigmore & Wyman I
177.   Phillip J. Pirages 33-389 1996 $950.00

HORDEN, JOHN   A Grammar of the Cree Language, as Spoken by
The Cree Indians of North America. London: 1881. 1st edition; pages viii,
238; original binding, very good, very scarce.   Stephen Lunsford 45-76
1996 $300.00

HORGAN, PAUL 1903-   Great River: the Rio Grande in North American
History. Rinehart, 1954. Limited and signed edition, with extra color
plates by author; 2 volumes, white linen, slipcase.   Maggie Lambeth
30-263 1996 $300.00

HORGAN, PAUL 1903-   Great River: The Rio Grande in North American
History. New York: Rinehart & Co., 1954. 1st edition; 2 volumes, 1020
pages, 1 single page map; original black cloth, gilt
lettered spines, fine set in very lightly worn pictorial slipcase. Very
scarce.   Argonaut Book Shop 113-355 1996 $125.00

HORN, W. F.   The Horn Papers; Early Western Movement on the
Monongahela and Upper Ohio, 1765-1795. Scottdale: 1945. 8vo. and folio;
3 volumes, 900 pages; plates, maps; buckram.   Howes Bookshop
265-1853 1996 £120.00

HORNADAY, WILLIAM   Camp-Fires on Desert and Lava. London: ca.
1910. Color and other plates, light marking/rubbing, spine title has lost
some of the lettering.   David Grayling J95Biggame-416 1996 £65.00

HORNE, HENRY   Essays Concerning Iron and Steel. London: T. Cadell,
1773. 1st edition; 12mo; iii, 223 pages; later polished calf; rebacked
using original spine as overlay; from the library of Matthew Boulton.
The Bookpress 75-418 1996 $2,500.00

HORNE, RICHARD HENGIST   Exposition of the False Medium and
Barriers Excluding Men of Genius from the Public. London: pub. by
Effingham Wilson, 1833. 1st edition; 12mo; frontispiece (small stain in
blank lower margin); contemporary grey wrappers, rebacked, recent
label; very good, scarce. CBEL III 525.   Ximenes 108-205 1996
$450.00

HORNE, T. H.   A Catalogue of the Library of the College of St.
Margaret & St. Bernard, Commonly Called Queen's College in the
University of Cambridge. London: for the Society of Queen's College,
1827. 2 volumes; original cloth backed boards, paper spine labels, worn,
spines partly detached and boards of volume 2 coming loose, mild
spotting to first and last few leaves; ownership inscription of Dawson
Turner with ALS dated 21st Nov. 1827 presenting it to him from Thomas
Clowes of Queen's College.   Maggs Bros. Ltd. 1191-48 1996 £290.00

HORNELL, JAMES   Fishing in Many Waters. Cambridge: University
Press, 1950. 1st edition; 8vo; 67 plates, copies, over 50 text figures; dust jacket
(few nicks), very good.   George J. Houle 68-47 1996 $125.00

HORNER, JOHN   The Linen Trade of Europe During the Spinning
Wheel Period. Belfast: 1920. xiv, 591 pages, plates, tipped in portraits,
numerous illustrations; folding tables; cloth.   Graham Weiner C2-163
1996 £50.00

HORNUNG, CLARENCE P.   Treasury of American Design. New York:
1976. 4to; 2 volumes, 846 pages, 2900 illustrations, 850 are in full color;
original cloth, original plastic jackets; mint.   Jens J. Christoffersen
SL94-154 1996 $195.00

HORNUNG, E. W.   The Camera Fiend. London: T. Fisher Unwin, 1911.
1st edition; crown 8vo; plates by Koekoek; original cloth, little minor
wear, slight splash to spine, but good copy.   Ash Rare Books
Zenzybyr-50 1996 £60.00

HORNYOLD, HENRY   Genealogical Memoirs of the Family of Strickland
of Sizergh. Kendal: Titus Wilson, 1928. Signed limited edition of 250;
small 4to; pages ix, 332, 24 illustrations, 8 tables and pedigrees, some
folding; original black cloth, silver lettering; near fine.   R.F.G. Hollett &
Son 78-179 1996 £225.00

HORR, N. T.   A Bibliography of Card-Games and of the History of the
Playing Card. Cleveland: printed for Charles Orr, 1892. Limited to 250
hand numbered and signed copies (this no. 43); typed addenda of
books and magazine articles on playing cards to 1927 and prospectus
for the book bound in; red morocco, paper spine label, bit rubbed and
worn.   Maggs Bros. Ltd. 1191-101 1996 £90.00

HORSBRUGH, B.   The Game-Birds and Water-Fowl of South Africa.
London: 1912. Crown 4to; xii, 159 pages; 67 colored plates; quarter
morocco, trifle rubbed; very good, plates entirely free from usual foxing,
though text is slightly affected.   Wheldon & Wesley 207-49 1996
£600.00

HORSFALL, T. C.   Proceedings of the Conference on Education Under
Healthy Conditions. Manchester: & London: John Heywood, 1885. 6, 4
pages ads; original brown cloth, very good.   Jarndyce 103-493 1996
£80.00

HORSFIELD, T.   Zoological Researches in Java and the Neighbouring
Islands. London: 1991. Facsimile reprint; 4to; 560 pages, portrait, 71
colored and 13 plain plates; buckram, gilt.   Wheldon & Wesley
207-401 1996 £175.00

HORSLEY, VICTOR   The Structure and Function of the Brain and Spinal
Cord. London: 1892. 8vo; 224 pages; illustrations; original binding,
occasional pencilling in text, signature on title, else very good, clean,
tight copy. McHenry p. 223.   James Tait Goodrich K40-159 1996
$495.00

HORSLEY, VICTOR   The Structure and Functions of the Cerebellum
Examined by a New Method. London: John Bale, 1908. 8vo; 80 pages,
with several text illustrations; original wrappers, newly mounted on soft
wrappers; author's presentation "With Author's Compl" inscribed at top
of front wrapper. GM 4879.1.   James Tait Goodrich K40-158 1996
$995.00

HORSLEY, WILLIAM   A Treatise on Maritime Affairs; or a Comparison
Between the Commerce and Naval Power of England and France.
London: R. Wellington, 1744. 1st edition; 8vo; (2), 94 pages; recently
well bound in linen backed marbled boards; very good. Kress 4711;
Hanson 5782; Goldsmith 8057.   John Drury 82-113 1996 £175.00

HORST, TILEMAN VAN DER   Theatrum Machinarum Universale; of
Keurige Verzameling Van Verscheide Groote en Zeer Fraaie Waterwerken,
Schutsluizen, Waterkeringen, Ophaal-en Draaibruggen. Amsterdam: W.
Holtrop en N. T. Gravius, n.d. & Amsterdam: Petrus Schenk, 1774. Large
folio; 2 parts in 1 volume, half title, title, engraved arms, 2 leaves, text
14 pages, 25 plates on 21 double page sheets; title, text 9 pages, 30
plates on 27 double page sheets; contemporary (original?) calf backed
boards, small split in joints, uncut, fine and clean internally.   H. M.
Fletcher 121-103 1996 £1,200.00

THE HORTICULTURIST and Journal of Rural Art and Rural Taste. New
York: 1858. 8vo; 576 pages; 12 chromolithographic plates, some
offsetting to backgrounds, numerous text engravings; half morocco,
rubbed, front hinge tender, some pages tanned.   Raymond M. Sutton
VII-980 1996 $250.00

HORWOOD, MURRAY   Public Health Surveys: What They Are, How to
Make Them, How to Use Them. New York: 1921. 1st edition; 403 pages;
original binding; autographed by author.   W. Bruce Fye 71-1042 1996
$100.00

HOSKING, WILLIAM   Treatises on Architecture, Building, Masonry, Joinery and Carpentry. Edinburgh: Black, 1846. 7th edition; 4to; (ii), 157, (1) pages, 36 engraved plates (last one browned); publisher's cloth, rebacked. From the library of J. G. James.   Elton Engineering 10-77 1996 £130.00

HOSKINS, G. A.   Travels in Ethiopia. London: Longman, Rees, Orme, Brown, Green, & Longman, 1835. 1st edition; 4to; titlepage with ink inscription "From the Author"; errata, 367 pages of text, frontispiece on india paper, 42 lithographic plates, 2 hand colored, all on india paper, colored illustrations, 7 plans, 35 woodcut illustrations, large folding map; original green cloth covered boards, printed paper label to spine, uncut, joints worn, corners bumped, ink signature, ex-library with ink stamp to corner of front pastedown. Blackmer 833; Brunet III 20815; Lowndes II p. 1121; Gay 2574.   Beeleigh Abbey BA56-80 1996 £750.00

HOSKINS, G. A.   Visit to the Great Oasis of the Libyan Desert... London: Longman, Rees, Orme, Brown, Green and Longman, 1837. 1st edition; 8vo; 338 pages of text, 16 page publisher's catalogue; frontispiece, 19 lithographic plates, 1 folding map; original brown cloth, neatly recased, blind decoration to covers, gilt title to spine, yellow endpapers. Some light foxing to frontispiece and map, otherwise nice, clean copy.   Beeleigh Abbey BA56-79 1996 £225.00

HOST, N. T.   Synopsis Plantarum in Austria. Vienna: 1797. 1st edition; 8vo; few light waterstains, contemporary boards, sometime rebacked with paper, worn, bit defective. Stafleu 3066.   Maggs Bros. Ltd. 1190-100 1996 £100.00

HOTMAN, FRANCOIS   Brutum Fulmen. N.P.: n.p., n.d., Leyden? 1585. 1st edition; 8vo; pages 234, (xi), Roman letter, quotations in italic, woodcut of the seal of Sixtus V; contemporary calf, spine gilt, worn in usual places; light age yellowing, generally good; autograph of Claude de Saumaise. not in BMC STC Fr. or Dutch; Adams H1056; Haag V 537. 1 copy in NUC.   A. Sokol XXV-52 1996 £750.00

HOTMAN, FRANCOIS   Franco-Gallia: or, An Account of the Ancient Free State of France. London: Goodwin, 1711. 1st English edition; 8vo; calf, some browning. Hauser 2215; CBEL II 783.   Rostenberg & Stern 150-49 1996 $475.00

HOTTEN, JOHN CAMDEN 1832-1873   A Dictionary of Modern Slang, Cant and Vulgar Words, Used at the Present Day in the Streets of London... London: John Camden Hotten, 1859. 1st edition; late issue; half title, 2 pages ads; original dull purple cloth by Bone & Son, very good.   Jarndyce 103-160 1996 £120.00

HOUDIN, J. P.   Barbara Hepworth. Boston: Boston Book and Art, 1961. 4to; 172 pages; profusely illustrated; cloth, dust jacket. Freitag 4230.   Brannan 43-262 1996 $175.00

HOUGH, A.   Samoan Phrase Book. Samoa: The London Missionary Society, 1924. 1st edition?; 12mo; 124 pages; cloth spine and printed boards, staples have caused small amount of offset on endpapers, paper turning brownish, very good. Not in NUC.   Robert F. Lucas 42-65 1996 $125.00

HOUGHTON, ARTHUR A.   Collection of Miniature Books Formed by Arthur A. Houghton, Jr. London: Christie's, 1979. Large octavo; 95, (26) pages; illustrations; list of prices realized laid in; light wear to extremities, else fine with notes penned to front free endpaper and price list. Bromer Booksellers 87-182 1996 $100.00

THE HOUSE That Jack Built. London: Dean and Son, ca. 1860. 12mo; (12) pages; wood engraved titlepage and 11 illustrations, all hand colored; pale blue wrappers embossed in red with striking gilt background; in fine state of preservation.   Bromer Booksellers 90-107 1996 $135.00

HOUSEHOLD, GEOFFREY   The Third Hour. Boston: Little Brown, 1938. 1st U.S. edition; advance proof copy; author's first book; yellow, red and black pictorial paper wrappers, cover edges frayed with some light bumping on spine and edges, light soiling and spine very slightly darkened, otherwise good to very good copy of this fragile book. Quill & Brush 102-928 1996 $200.00

HOUSMAN, ALFRED EDWARD 1859-1936   Last Poems. London: Richards, 1922. 1st edition; foolscap 8vo; 79 pages; original dark blue buckram, backstrip and front cvoer gilt lettered, backstrip lightly faded, good; Professor Oliffe Richmond's copy with 2 page letter dated 6th Feb. 1923 from Houseman to Richmond.   Blackwell's B112-157 1996 £500.00

HOUSMAN, ALFRED EDWARD 1859-1936   A Shropshire Lad. New York: Heritage Press, 1935. 1st Heritage Press edition, no limitation stated, initialled by E. A. Wilson; illustrations by E. A. Wilson; full leather, fine in slightly sunned publisher's slipcase.   Hermitage SP95-887 1996 $150.00

HOUSMAN, ALFRED EDWARD 1859-1936   A Shropshire Lad. New York: Heritage Press, 1935. 10 x 5 inches; illustrations in color by E. A. Wilson, with folded frontispiece (creased at corner), initialled by artist in pencil; full blindstamped pigskin with gilt stamped spine in cardboard slipcase (latter sunned); otherwise fine.   Beasley Books 82-81 1996 $100.00

HOUSMAN, JOHN   A Descriptive Tour and Guide to the Lakes, Caves, Mountains and Other Natural Curiosities in Cumberland, Westmoreland, Lancashire... Carlisle: F. Jollie, 1800. 1st edition; 8vo; pages iv, (iii), 226, bound in 4's, complete with engraved frontispiece, large folding map, hand colored in outline, one small old repair on reverse, 2 further folding engraved plates of maps; contemporary full tree calf, gilt, hinges cracked, very good, clean and sound copy. Bicknell 41.1.   R.F.G. Hollett & Son 78-1001 1996 £225.00

HOUSMAN, JOHN   A Descriptive Tour and Guide to the Lakes, Caves, Mountains and Other Natural Curiosities in Cumberland, Westmoreland, Lancashire, and a Part of the West Riding of Yorkshire. Carlisle: F. Jollie, 1812. 5th edition; 8vo; pages v, (iv), 264, 10 engraved maps, plans, plates, several folding; lacks general map, frontispiece little browned and offset on to title; original printed boards, rather worn, backstrip defective at tail.   R.F.G. Hollett & Son 78-1002 1996 £120.00

HOUSMAN, JOHN   A Descriptive Tour and Guide to the Lakes, Caves, Mountains and Other Natural Curiosities in Cumberland, Westmoreland, Lancashire... Carlisle: F. Jollie, 1814. 6th edition; 8vo; pages (vi), 264, folding general map, folding plan, 2 folding sheets of plans, 6 folding engraved plates; very nice, uncut copy in near contemporary paper covered boards, small worm track on upper board, spine rubbed, ms. spine label.   R.F.G. Hollett & Son 78-1003 1996 £185.00

HOUSMAN, LAURENCE 1865-1959   False Premises: Five One-Act Plays. Stratford-upon-Avon: Oxford Basil Blackwell, 1922. Signed, limited edition of 150 numbered copies; 8vo; vellum and boards, issued without dust jacket; fine.   Antic Hay 101-840 1996 $150.00

HOUSMAN, LAURENCE 1865-1959   The Story of the Seven Young Goslings. London: Blackie & Son, n.d. 1899. 1st edition; 4to; 6 color plates and other 3 tone color illustrations by Mabel Dreamer; color pictorial boards, corners worn, pale foxing to prelims, else very good. Marjorie James 19-126 1996 £125.00

HOUSTON, PAM   Cowboys Are My Weakness. New York: & London: W. W. Norton & Co., 1992. 1st edition; author's first book; fine in dust jacket.   Steven C. Bernard 71-128 1996 $150.00

HOUTCHENS, CAROLYN WASHBURN   The English Romantic Poets and Essayists - A Review of Research and Criticism. New York: Modern Language Association of America, 1957. 1st edition; original binding, top edge slightly dusty, head and tail of spine slightly bumped, very good in nicked, chipped, torn, rubbed, frayed and dusty, slightly creased and marked dust jacket browned at spine and edges; pencilled ownership signature of Frederick A. Pottle.   Ulysses 39-696 1996 £75.00

HOUTTUYN, MARTINUS   Hotkunde, Behelzende de Abfeeldingen van Meest Alle Bekund, in-en Uitlandsche Houten. Amsterdam: J. C. Sepp, 1773-91. 4to; titles and text in Dutch, German, French, English and Latin; 100 hand colored engraved plates, 50 leaves describing timbers dealt with on the 100 copperplates; later gilt stamped diced calf, rubbed, all edges gilt; signature of William Forsyth, 1808; Currer bookplate. Raymond M. Sutton VII-16 1996 $8,500.00

HOVEY, CHARLES MASON   The Fruits of America... Boston: 1852-56. Tall octavo; pages xii, 100; iv, 96; 2 volumes; frontispiece in each volume, 96 fine chromolithographic plates by William Sharp; contemporary black half morocco, ruled in gilt, over marbled boards (rebacked with original gilt spine laid down), some rubbing to marbled endpapers, occasional light foxing, browning and offsetting, some page cropping, previous owner's ink signature on half title of volume 2; very good set, housed in modern blue cloth and marbled paper slipcase. Bennett p. 59; BM NH II p. 881; Nissen BB1, 941; Plesch p. 270. Raymond M. Sutton VII-17 1996 $6,000.00

HOVHANESS, ALAN   The Burning House: Opus 185. New York: C. F. Peters, 1960. Manuscript facsimile; 4to; black cloth over stiff brown wrappers, very good; dedication copy, the copy of dedicatee Carl Haverlin; with TLS from Walter Hinrichsen to Haverlin. Extra ms. page laid in loose.   George J. Houle 68-68 1996 $850.00

HOVHANESS, ALAN   Magnificat for Soli, Chorus and Ochestra. New York: C. F. Peters, 1961. 1st edition; 4th printing; small 4to; stiff light green wrappers, very good; signed and inscribed by author for Carl Haverlin.   George J. Houle 68-69 1996 $295.00

HOWARD, CHARLES   Historical Anecdotes of the Howard Family. London: printed by G. Scott for J. Robson, 1769. 8vo; pages (vi), 201, engraved vignette on title; old speckled calf, edges worn and little scraped, sometime rebacked, spine worn at head and tail. signed on flyleaf by Daniel Scott of Penrith. Loosely inserted 4 page ALS from Philip J. C. Howard of Corby Castle, a pres offprint concerning the latter's Golden Wedding and an example of Corby Castle headed notepaper.   R.F.G. Hollett & Son 78-181 1996 £120.00

HOWARD, H. ELIOT   An Introduction to the Study of Bird Behaviour. London: 1929. Folio; fine plates by George Lodge; binding very slightly marked.   David A.H. Grayling MY95Orn-43 1996 £80.00

HOWARD, H. H.   The History of Virgil A. Stewart and His Adventures...and the Execution of Five Professional Gamblers by the Citizens of Vicksburg, on 6th July 1835. New York: Harper & Bros., 1842. Dampstain to fore-edge of first one third of book, more so at beginning, overall moderate soiling and .new spine label, otherwise very good. Howes H700.   Hermitage SP95-710 1996 $200.00

HOWARD, JAMES   Continental Farming and Peasantry. London: William Ridgeway, 1870. 1st edition; 8vo; iv, 104 pages; original gilt lettered green cloth, fine; few pencil notes in margins; although without any marks of provenance, this is the Duke of Bedford's copy.   Ken Spelman 30-86 1996 £75.00

HOWARD, JAMES H. W.   Bond and Free: a True Tale of Slave Times. Harrisburg: Edwin K. Meyers, 1886. 1st edition; 12mo; 280 pages; lacks portrait; original cloth, some spotting, endpapers pasted down, title nearly loose. Wright III 2797. LCP/HSP Afro Amer. Cat. 4998.   M & S Rare Books 60-174 1996 $250.00

HOWARD, JOHN 1726?-1790   The State of the Prisons in England and Wales. (and) Appendix to the State of Prisons, etc. (and) An Acocunt of the Principal Lazarettos in Europe. Warrington: printed by William Eyres and sold by T. Cadell, 1777. 1st edition; 33 full page plates; very fresh presentation copies.   Meyer Boswell SL26-118 1996 $3,500.00

HOWARD, JOSEPH J.   Visitation of England and Wales. London: privately printed, 1903-11. Limited to 500 copies on handmade paper; imperial 8vo; volumes 11-17; many plates and facsimiles, original quarter parchment, gilt tops, other edges untrimmed, one side little stained.   Howes Bookshop 265-1855 1996 £85.00

HOWARD, MRS.   Reminiscences for My Children. London: privately printed, Carlisle: Charles Thurman, 1836. 8vo; pages 216; original cloth, gilt, rather faded and little worn; uncut; extremely scarce; armorial bookplate of William Lowther, some contemporary notes on Howard family pinned to flyleaf, one or two alterations to text in author's hand. R.F.G. Hollett & Son 78-182 1996 £175.00

HOWARD, ROBERT E.   Conan the Conqueror. The Sword of Conan. King Conan. The Coming of Conan. Conan the Barbarian. Tales of Conan. Gnome Press, 1950-55. 1st editions; 6 volumes; all very good+ to fine in like dust jackets; Tales of Conan is inscribed by co-author, L. S. De Camp.   Aronovitz 57-565 1996 $750.00

HOWARD, ROBERT E.   The Dark Man. Sauk City: Arkham House, 1963. 1st edition; illustrations by Frank Utpatel; very fine in dust jacket. Bromer Booksellers 87-7 1996 $175.00

HOWARD, ROBERT E.   The Devil in Iron. West Kingston: Grant, 1976. 1st edition thus; tipped in color illustrations by Dan Green; two corners bumped, otherwise fine in dust jacket with corresponding corners bumped, in scarce publisher's cloth tray case with printed leather labels on spine.   Robert Gavora 61-26 1996 $100.00

HOWARD, ROBERT E.   The Garden of Fear and Other Stories of the Bizarre and Fantastic. Los Angeles: Crawford, 1945. 1st edition; octavo; (2), 80 pages; printed wrappers, small chip to head of spine; fine, bookplate. Bleiler p. 104.   Bromer Booksellers 87-171 1996 $150.00

HOWARD, ROBERT E.   A Gent From Bear Creek. West Kingston: Grant, 1965. 1st U.S. edition, one of 732 copies; fine in price clipped dust jacket with several short tears.   Robert Gavora 61-32 1996 $100.00

HOWARD, ROBERT E.   King Conan. New York: Gnome Press, 1953. 1st edition; fine in dust jacket.   Hermitage SP95-552 1996 $250.00

HOWARD, ROBERT E.   Queen of the Black Coast. West Kingston: Grant, 1978. 1st combined edition; illustrations by Michael Hauge; very fine in dust jacket in scarce publisher's cloth tray case with printed leather labels on spine.   Robert Gavora 61-27 1996 $125.00

HOWARD, ROBERT E.   Red Nails. West Kingston: Grant, 1975. 1st separate edition; illustrations by George Barr; very fine in dust jacket in scarce publisher's cloth tray case with printed leather labels on spine. Robert Gavora 61-28 1996 $125.00

HOWARD, ROBERT E.   Rogues in the House. West Kingston: Grant, 1976. 1st edition thus; illustrations by Marcus Boas; very fine in dust jacket in scarce publisher's cloth gray case with printed leather labels on spine.   Robert Gavora 61-29 1996 $125.00

HOWARD, ROBERT E.   Skull-Face and Others. Sauk City: Arkham House, 1946. 1st edition; fine in Hannes Bok illustrated dust jacket which is lightly chipped to edges.   Bromer Booksellers 87-23 1996 $500.00

HOWARD, ROBERT E.   Skull Face and Others. Sauk City: Arkham House, 1946. 1st edition; very good+ in very good dust jacket with some wear and tear; Doc Smith's copy with his hand printed name and address, and his hand printed pencil notations on contents page and verso.   Aronovitz 57-566 1996 $500.00

HOWARD, ROBERT E.   Skull-Face and Others. Sauk City: Arkham House, 1946. 1st edition; royal 8vo; xxvi, 474, (2) pages; cloth, gilt spine, dust jacket by Hannes Bok (extremities very slightly worn), little fraying to edges of dust jacket, otherwise unusually fine. Scarce thus. Thomas Thorp 489-159 1996 £250.00

HOWARD, ROBERT E.   The Tower of the Elephant. West Kingston: Grant, 1975. 1st edition thus; illustrations by Richard Robertson; very fine in dust jacket in scarce publisher's cloth tray case with printed leather labels on spine.   Robert Gavora 61-30 1996 $150.00

HOWARD, ROBERT E.   A Witch Shall be Born. West Kingston: Grant, 1975. 1st separate edition; color tipped in illustrations by Alicia Austin; very fine in dust jacket with tiny tear and associated crease in scarce publisher's tray case with printed leather labels on spine.   Robert Gavora 61-31 1996 $150.00

HOWARD-BURY, C. K.   Mount Everest. The Reconnaissance, 1922. London: 1921. 1st edition; 33 plates, 3 folding maps; clean and bright copy, slightly bumped at top of spine, otherwise very good+. Moutaineering Books 8-EH02 1996 £150.00

HOWBERT, ABRAHAM R.   Reminiscences of the War. Springfield: 1884. 1st edition; 388 pages; original cloth, extremities scuffed, yet very good; Ryan 371; Dornbusch I Ohio 345; not in Nevins.   McGowan Book Co. 65-42 1996 $125.00

HOWE, ELLIC   A List of London Bookbinders, 1648-1815. London: Bibliographical Society, 1950. 1st edition; 8vo; xxxviii, 105 pages; cloth, paper spine over boards, fine, uncut, unopened.   The Bookpress 75-311 1996 $100.00

HOWE, HENRY   The Travels and Adventures of Celebrated Travelers in the Principal Countries of the Globe. Cincinnati: Henry Howe, published, 1861. Tall square 8vo; 2 leaves, 83 pages; frontispiece, title and 11 plates (one with clear vertical tear at fold), most of the colored illustrations appear to be a combination of hand painting and mezzotint backgrounds, partial separation of colored title leaf from book, still holding firmly; original boards, rubbed and worn, spine rebacked a long time ago, decorations very visible but faded, except for a few leaves with minor staining/foxing, contents are very nice.   Roy W. Clare XXIV-67 1996 $175.00

HOWE, JULIA WARD   Is Polite Society Polite? And Other Essays. Boston/New York: Houghton Mifflin, 1900. 1st edition; paper covered boards, faint dampstaining to corners of pages and to boards, thus only about very good but with only light wear to fragile boards; nicely inscribed by author.   Between the Covers 42-227 1996 $500.00

HOWELL, GEORGE   The Conflicts of Capital and Labour Historically and Economically Considered... London: Chatto & Windus, 1878. 1st edition; 8vo; xxviii, 520 pages, 36 page Chatto & Windus catalog at end (dated March 1878), two leaves carelessly opened with marginal tears; original maroon cloth, lettered in gilt; good copy from the Working Men's College with ownership marks; Headicar & Fuller III 778; Stammhammer I 109.   John Drury 82-114 1996 £70.00

HOWELL, JAMES 1594?-1666   Epistolae Ho-Elianae. Familiar Letters Doemstic and Forren (sic)... London: Humphrey Moseley, 1645. 1st edition; small 4to; (120, 88, 120, 40, 48, 92, (2) pages; several corrections in unknown hand; original full speckled calf, spine quite worn, front cover detached, but very clean internally.. Wing 3071.   Chapel Hill 94-230 1996 $300.00

HOWELL, WILLIAM   Medulla Historiae Anglicanae. London: Timothy Childe, William Taylor and John Osborn, 1719. 7th edition; 8vo; (xiv), 562, (xiv) pages; frontispiece, 12 plates, folding pedigree, few woodcuts in text; contemporary calf, rebacked, gilt lettering, corners worn, minor soiling; sound copy.   Robert Clark 38-64 1996 £55.00

HOWELLS, WILLIAM DEAN 1837-1920   Between the Dark and the Daylight. London: Harper and Brothers, 1907. 1st edition; 8vo; (10), 185 pages, frontispiece and five plates; original flexible red cloth. BAL 9783.   M & S Rare Books 60-175 1996 $150.00

HOWELLS, WILLIAM DEAN 1837-1920   A Boy's Town. New York: Harpers, 1890. 1st edition; 1st state; plates; original binding, 1890 inscription on f.f.e.p. which is partly detached, otherwise bright and fine.   Charles Agvent 4-672 1996 $150.00

HOWELLS, WILLIAM DEAN 1837-1920   Indian Summer. Boston: Ticknor & Co., 1886. 1st edition; decorated brown cloth, minor wear to spine tips, pages bit darkened, near fine; inscribed by author for his sister Joanna M. Shepard. BAL 9624.   Charles Agvent 4-675 1996 $1,200.00

HOWELLS, WILLIAM DEAN 1837-1920   The Lady of the Aroostook. Boston: Houghton Osgood, 1879. 1st edition; with all 1st issue points, but with leafy pattern endpapers; decorated green cloth, some spotting to rear cover, near fine. BAL 9584.   Charles Agvent 4-676 1996 $100.00

HOWELLS, WILLIAM DEAN 1837-1920   Letters Home. New York: Harpers, 1903. 1st edition; Binding B (no sequence determined), private library number on pastedown, faint stain to covers; very good; signed by author.   Charles Agvent 4-677 1996 $350.00

HOWELLS, WILLIAM DEAN 1837-1920   A Little Girl Among the Old Masters. Boston: Osgood, 1884. 1st edition; 54 plates by Author's 10 year old daughter; decorated brown cloth, small tear base of spine, front hinge partly cracked, covers bit darkened, very good; author's signature laid down on f.f.e.p. BAL 9612 Form A.   Charles Agvent 4-679 1996 $125.00

HOWELLS, WILLIAM DEAN 1837-1920   The Mouse-Trap. New York: Harpers, 1889. 1st edition; 8 plates; original binding, slight hinge crack, spine sunned, soiled; very good; inscribed by author for his sister Joanna Shepard.   Charles Agvent 4-687 1996 $1,000.00

HOWELLS, WILLIAM DEAN 1837-1920   Poems. Boston: James Osgood, 1873. 1st edition; binding 2 (no priority); near fine. BAL 9567.   Charles Agvent 4-682 1996 $125.00

HOWELLS, WILLIAM DEAN 1837-1920   The Rise of Silas Lapham. Boston: Ticknor & Co., 1885. 1st edition; 1st state of ads with last word on p. 176 in broken type, similar to the copy Howells inscribed as "First Copy"; decorated blue cloth, little soiled, lower front corner bit chewed, very good. BAL 9619.   Charles Agvent 4-683 1996 $225.00

HOWELLS, WILLIAM DEAN 1837-1920   Suburban Sketches. Boston: Osgood, 1875. Reprint; original binding; near fine; inscribed by Howells to Mrs. W. D. Conway.   Charles Agvent 4-686 1996 $150.00

HOWELLS, WILLIAM DEAN 1837-1920   Their Wedding Journey. Boston: James Osgood, 1872. 1st edition; 8vo; illustrations by Augustus Hoppin; original binding, state A, binding a; near fine. BAL 9558.   Charles Agvent 4-689 1996 $150.00

HOWELLS, WILLIAM DEAN 1837-1920   Their Wedding Journey. Cambridge: Riverside Press, 1895. 1st illustrated edition; one of 250 numbered copies on large paper; 8vo; drawings by Clifford Carleton; vellum over boards, spine of dust jacket sunned with few small chips, slight foxing to spine and endpapers, otherwise fine in rare dust jacket.   Charles Agvent 4-690 1996 $200.00

HOWELLS, WILLIAM DEAN 1837-1920   The Undiscovered Country. Boston: Houghton Mifflin, 1880. 1st edition; 8vo; binding A; light wear; near fine. BAL 9589.   Charles Agvent 4-693 1996 $100.00

HOWELLS, WILLIAM DEAN 1837-1920   Venetian Life. New York: Hurd & Houghton, 1866. 1st American edition; purple cloth; owner stamp obliterated on pastedown, some foxing to prelims, minor wear to spine tips, bit rubbed; BAL 9547.   Charles Agvent 4-694 1996 $150.00

HOWELLS, WILLIAM DEAN 1837-1920   Venetian Life. Cambridge: Riverside Press, 1892. 1st trade edition; 12mo; 2 volumes; 18 color plates; white cloth stamped in gold, near fine in scarce linen dust jacket which are also near fine. BAL 9664.   Charles Agvent 4-695 1996 $200.00

HOWELLS, WILLIAM DEAN 1837-1920   Venetian Life. 1907. Autograph edition, one of 550 numbered copies, signed; 2 volumes; illustrations by Edmund Garrett; cloth backed boards; light wear to spine labels, some soiling, very good.   Charles Agvent 4-696 1996 $200.00

HOWES, WRIGHT   U.S. Howes Iana 1700-1950. New York: 1954. 1st edition; 656 pages; cloth, very good+.   T. A. Swinford 49-558 1996 $100.00

HOWISON, JOHN   Sketches of Upper Canada, Domestic, Local and Characteristic. Edinburgh: Oliver & Boyd, High Street, G. & W. B. Wittaker, Ave Maria Ln. London 1821. 1st edition; 8vo; half title, (v-vii), (ix-xvi), 349 pages, half title; full polished tan calf, gilt tooled borders to boards, maroon morocco labels to spines, gilt tooling to compartments of panelled spine, edges and endpapers marbled; bound by James Condle of Paisley. Sabin 33366; Gagnon 1710; Stanton & Tremaine 1200.   Beeleigh Abbey BA56-81 1996 £295.00

HOWITT, MARY   The Children's Year. London: Longman, Brown, Green and Longman, 1847. 1st edition; 8vo; 254 pages; 4 full page tissue guarded illustrations by John Absolon; blue blindstamped boards with spine lettered in gilt; spine and part of rear cover faded to brown, edges of plates foxed, else very good. Osborne 263.   Marjorie James 19-129 1996 £75.00

HOWITT, MARY   Illustrated Library for the Young. London: W. Kent and Co., 1856. 1st edition; royal 8vo; 13 parts, each 24 pages, bound together; 89 fine full page engravings excellently hand colored, original publisher's red grained cloth decoratively gilt, all edges gilt, joints lightly rubbed and cloth gilt matured but a remarkable copy, internally crisp and fine.   Sotheran PN32-127 1996 £350.00

HOWITT, MARY   Mary Howitt. An Autobiography. London: Wm. Ibister Ltd., 1889. 1st edition; 4to; 2 volumes; pages (xviii), 326, (ix), 360; frontispiece; 33 illustrations; top edge gilt, blue boards lettered in gilt; very good.   Marjorie James 19-127 1998 £125.00

HOWITT, MARY   Tales in Verse for the Young. London: William and Darton Son, n.d. 1836. 1st edition; 160 x 95 mm; 212 pages; frontispiece, 8 other engraved plates; marbled early half boards, spine compartmented and lettered in gilt; light wear to covers, else very good. Osborne 68.   Marjorie James 19-128 1996 £125.00

HOWITT, WILLIAM   The Student Life of Germany. London: Longman, Brown, Green and Longmans, 1841. 1st edition; tall 8vo; xviii, 484 page illustrations; original brown cloth, cloth has some light scattered spotting, otherwise near fine.   David Mason 71-82 1996 $160.00

HOWLAND, RICHARD HUBBARD   The Architecture of Baltimore. Baltimore: Johns Hopkins Press, 1953. 1st edition; signed by both authors; 4to; xx, 149 pages; 108 illustrations; cloth, dust jacket; very good in worn dust jacket.   The Bookpress 75-200 1996 $125.00

HOWLAND, RICHARD HUBBARD   Greek Lamps and their Survivals. Princeton: American School of Classical Studies in Athens, 1958. Folio; ix, 252 pages, 56 plates, 1 folding chart; original cloth, corners bumped. Archaeologia Luxor-3489 1996 $150.00

HOWLETT, BARTHOLOMEW   A Selection of Views in the County of Lincoln... London: Miller, 1805. Large paper copy of the first edition; large 4to; vignette title, engraved dedn., 2 ff. subscribers, 55 ff., 2 ff. index, 53 engraved plates, engraved hand colored map, 23 engraved vignettes; contemporary green morocco gilt, few minor blemishes. Cox III 182; Isaac 274.   Marlborough 162-47 1996 £800.00

HOYER, M. A.   The Tale of a Dog. London: Ernest Nister, n.d., ca. 1890. 1st edition; 12 pages; 4 color plates and 8 sepia text illustrations by E. S. Hardy; dark green cloth spine, extra color pictorial cream boards, light foxing, excellent.   Robin Greer 94A-61 1996 £65.00

HOYER, M. A.   The Tale of a Dog. London: Ernest Nister, n.d., ca. 1890. 1st edition; 12mo; 12 pages; 4 color plates and 8 sepia text illustrations by E. S. Hardy; dark green cloth spine, extra color pictorial cream boards, light foxing, excellent.   Robin Greer 94A-61 1996 £65.00

HOYLAND, FRANCIS   Poems and Translations. London: printed for W. Bristow...and C. Etherington... 1763. 4to; pages (1)-54; title rehinged). recent boards;   Peter Murray Hill 185-80 1996 £80.00

HOYLAND, ROSEMARY   Ethelbert Under the Sea. London: Collins, 1956. 1st edition; oblong folio; 32 pages; pictorial pages, yellow decorated endpapers; color pictorial boards, similar dust jacket.   Robin Greer 94A-46 196 £55.00

HOYLE, EDMOND 1672-1759   Hoyle's Games Improved. London: For J. F. and C. Rivington, T. Payne & Son, 1790. Revised version; crown 12mo; viii, 290, (ii) pages; diagram, folding plate, bound as two plates; contemporary sheep, little rubbed, starting to split at hinges, lacks front free endpaper, few faint marks, small hole in one margin, good, unrestored copy.   Ash Rare Books Zenzybyr-51 1996 £400.00

HOYLE, JOHN   A Complete Dictionary of Music. London: printed for H. D. Symonds &c., 1791. 1st published in 1770; rebound in half calf, raised bands, red label, library stamps.   Jarndyce 103-161 1996 £140.00

HOYLE, WILLIAM   Crime in England and Wales in the Nineteenth Century. London: Effingham Wilson, 1876. 1st edition; 8vo; x, 126, (2) pages; original brown cloth, lettered in gilt; very good. Headicar and Fuller I 615.   John Drury 82-115 1996 £75.00

HOYNINGEN-HUENE, GEORGE   Baalbek Palmyra. New York: Augustin, 1946. 1st edition; ('October 1946'); 4to; 55 black and white photos, 2 plans; dust jacket, rubbed, few nicks, very good. Signed and inscribed by Hoyningen-Huene to George Cukor with Cukor's Paul Landacre bookplate.   George J. Houle 68-113 1996 $225.00

HOZIER, H. M.   The Russo-Turkish War... London: 1877. 2 volumes, bound in 5 parts; numerous steel engraved plates, portraits; original decorative cloth, backstrips just little dull.   Petersfield Bookshop FH58-336 1996 £120.00

HUARTE DE SAN JUAN, JUAN   Examen de Ingenios. The Examination of Mens Wits. London: pritned by Adam Islip, for Richard Watkins, 1594. 1st edition in English; 8vo; (xvi), 333, (3) pages; 19th century panelled morocco, joints and head and foot of spine quite rubbed, front flyleaf and blank excised, internally very good, clean copy, rare. Hunter & Macalpine p. 46; Diamond 11.2, 15.4 and 17.1.   John Gach 150-218 1996 $3,500.00

HUARTE DE SAN JUAN, JUAN   Examen de Ingenios. The Examination of Mens Wits. London: by R(ichard) C(arew) Esq., Adam Islip, 1596. 2nd edition of this translation; 4to; (xvi), 333, (iii) pages; woodcut device on titlepage; 19th century mottled calf, gilt lettering, neatly rebacked with old backstrip laid down, corners slightly worn, paper browned, some staining, cropped at head, affecting a few running titles, minor marginal worming, just touching a few leaves; uncommon, sound. STC 13893.   Robert Clark 38-65 1996 £550.00

HUARTE DE SAN JUAN, JUAN   Examen de Ingenios. The Examination of Mens Wits. London: printed by Adam Islip for Thomas Adams, 1616. 4to; woodcut evice on title which is soiled and laid down, woodcut initials, upper margin cropped close, sometimes shaving headlines, later pigskin label. STC 13895; Krivatsy 6089.   Anthony Laywood 108-12 1996 £220.00

HUBBACK, J. H.   Jane Austen's Sailor Brothers. London: Lane, 1906. 1st edition; 8 3/4 x 5 5/8 inches; pages xv, 294 2 pages ads; frontispiece, 22 illustrations; sage green cloth, gilt titling to front cover and backstrip, top edge gilt, others uncut, covers with some marks and slight wear to top backstrip, bookplate, occasional slight foxing to contents, very good. Gilson M277.   Ian Hodgkins 78-175 1996 £65.00

HUBBARD, L. RON   Dianetics. Hermitage, 1950. 1st edition; just about fine in like dust jacket.   Aronovitz 57-54 1996 $300.00

HUBBARD, L. RON   Final Blackout. Hadley, 1948. 1st edition; very good+ in very good dust jacket with some slight chipping at dust jacket spine extremities.   Aronovitz 57-571 1996 $165.00

HUBBARD, L. RON   Final Blackout. Providence: Hadley, 1948. 1st hardbound edition; fine in very good dust jacket with small hole to spine panel & couple of tiny chips.   Sherwood 3-155 1996 $250.00

HUBBARD, L. RON   Slaves of Sleep. Shasta Press, 1948. 1st edition; fine in dust jacket.   Aronovitz 57-572 1996 $325.00

HUBBARD, L. RON   Triton. F.P.C.I., 1949. 1st edition; just about fine in bright, very good+/near fine dust jacket.   Aronovitz 57-573 1996 $235.00

HUBBELL, ALVIN   The Development of Ophthalmology in America 1800-1870. Chicago: 1908. 1st edition; 197 pages, original binding, ex-library.   W. Bruce Fye 71-1054 1996 $175.00

HUBER, JEAN PIERRE   The Natural History of Ants. London: Longman et al, 1820. 1st edition; 8vo; 398 pages; hand colored frontispiece, one other plate; leather backed boards, worn at extremities of spine, uncut,, some offsetting, but nice, clean copy.   Second Life Books 103-11 1996 $225.00

HUC, EVARISTE REGIS   Christianity in China, Tartary, and Thibet. London: Longman et al, 1857-58. 2nd edition; 8vo; 3 volumes; contemporary half morocco with raised bands, heavily gilt tooled spine panels, and red morocco spine labels; fine.   Chapel Hill 94-149 1996 $350.00

HUC, EVARISTE REGIS   A Journey through the Chinese Empire. New York: Harper & Bros., 1878. 8vo; 2 volumes, xxvi, (27)-421, vi, 422, 10 pages ads; folding map at front of volume 1, name on endpapers, map has been repaired with tape along one fold and there are some small pieces missing in this area, trace of wear at spine ends, still fine set; original green cloth.   David Mason 71-58 1996 $200.00

HUCKELL, JOHN   Avon. A Poem. Birmingham: John Baskerville for R. and J. Dodsley, 1758. 1st edition; quarto; author's first book; later half calf, nice. Gaskell 3; Rothschild 1167.   G. W. Stuart 59-7 1996 $450.00

HUDDESFORD, GEORGE   The Poems of... London: printed for J. Wright...by W. Bulmer, 1801. 8vo; 2 volumes in 1; new quarter calf.   Peter Murray Hill 185-81 1996 £75.00

HUDDESFORD, GEORGE   Salmagundi: a Miscellaneous Combination of Original Poetry...(with) Topsy Turvy; With Anecdotes and Observations Illustrataive of the Leading Characters in the Present Government of France. London: ptd. by E. Hodson for J. Anderson/London: ptd. for the author... 1793/93. 3rd edition of the first title, re-issue of the sheets of the second edition of 1792 with new titlepage; 2nd edition of the 2nd title, reissue of sheets of the 1st edition; 8vo; 2 volumes in one; engraved titlepage and 2 other plates (one in sepia); contemporary blue morocco, gilt, spine gilt, all edges gilt, pink endpapers by Kalthoeber, with his orange ticket (some scuffing of spine); half title present. Presentation copies, inscribed by author for Sir Edward Blackett, Bart. CBEL II 660.   Ximenes 109-160 1996 $275.00

HUDDESFORD, GEORGE   The Wiccamical Chaplet, A Selection of Original Poetry. London: Leigh Sotheby and Sons, 1804. 1st edition; octavo; pages 223; original blue publisher's boards, uncut, typographical label. Moderate wear but very good, not often found in original boards. CBEL II 365.   Hartfield 48-L41 1996 $195.00

HUDLESTON, C. ROY   The Registers of Morland. Part I: 1538-1742. London: 1957. 8vo; 299 pages; original wrappers.   R.F.G. Hollett & Son 78-588 1996 £75.00

HUDSON'S BAY COMPANY   Copy-Book Letters Outward &c Begins 29th May, 1680 Ends 5 July 1687.. London: 1948. Pages xli, 415; fine, unopened copy.   Stephen Lunsford 45-67 1996 $100.00

HUDSON'S BAY COMPANY   Minutes of the Hudson's Bay Company 1671-1674. London: 1942. Pages lxviii,276; fine, unopened copy. Stephen Lunsford 45-70 1996 $150.00

HUDSON'S BAY COMPANY   Minutes of the Hudson's Bay Company 1679-1684. First Part 1679-1682. London: 1945. Pages xlvi, 378; original binding, fine, unopened.   Stephen Lunsford 45-71 1996 $150.00

HUDSON'S BAY COMPANY   Moose Fort Journals 1783-85. London: 1954. Pages xxx, 392, several maps, near fine, unopened copy; Stephen Lunsford 45-72 1996 $125.00

HUDSON, C.   Where There's a Will There's a Way: an Ascent of Mont Blanc. London: 1856. 1st edition; 1 plate, 1 folding colored map; few small neat oval inked stamps of "Assoc. of S.A.C. British member" and stamp of owner, inserted hand written diagram identifying climbers in the frontispiece, slight bumping of ends of spine and edge of front board, but good sound, very good copy, scarce.   Moutaineering Books 8-EH04 1996 £475.00

HUDSON, C. T.   The Rotifera; or Wheel-Animalcules. London: 1886-89. 4to; 3 volumes in 2; 4 plain and 30 colored plates, pages 64, 4 plates; cloth, generally a satisfactory copy but with hint of soot marking on fore-edges binding faded with volume 2 cloth, very slightly bubbled. Wheldon & Wesley 207-50 1996 £325.00

HUDSON, DEREK   Arthur Rackham: His Life and Work. London: William Heinemann, 1960. 1st edition; 4to; colored frontispiece, numerous tipped in colored plates, original cloth, dust jacket torn and repaired with sellotape.   Forest Books 74-115 1996 £60.00

HUDSON, ELIZABETH   A Bibliography of the First Editions of the Works of E. Oe. Soemrville and Martin Ross. New York: The Sporting Gallery, 1942. Limited to 300 copies, of which this is no. 46 signed by Somerville; marbled endpapers uncut and largely unopened, very good+ in original tissue dust jacket.   October Farm 36-219 1996 $195.00

HUDSON, JOHN   Photographs of Killarney with Descriptive Letterpress. Glasgow: London: & Dublin: Simpkin and Smith, 1867. crown 4to; half title, title, 2 ff., 24 ff. letterpress, 1 f. ad, 13 photos by John Hudson, card mounted; with extra photo as frontispiece, not called for in Gernsheim or the book itself; gilt decorated green cloth covered bevelled boards, gilt lettering (employing a different title: Photographs of Irish Scenery, Killarney), all edges gilt; minimal foxing, fine, bright copy. Marlborough 162-48 1996 £275.00

HUDSON, WILLIAM HENRY 1841-1922   Birds in London. London: Longmans, Green and Co., 1898. 1st edition; 8vo; pages xvi, 339, 40 (ads); illustrations, photos; original green cloth, very nice. Mullens & Swann p. 302.   Sotheran PN32-88 1996 £88.00

HUDSON, WILLIAM HENRY 1841-1922   Birds of La Plata. London: 1920. Limited to 3000 copies; royal 8vo; 2 volumes, pages xvii, 244; ix, 240; 22 color plates by H. Gronvold; half buckram.   John Henly 27-19 1996 £100.00

HUDSON, WILLIAM HENRY 1841-1922   Birds of La Plata. London: 1920. Limited to 3000 copies; royal 8vo; 2 volumes; 22 colored plates by H. Gronvold; cloth. Payne A38a.   Wheldon & Wesley 207-770 1996 £100.00

HUDSON, WILLIAM HENRY 1841-1922   Birds of La Plata. London: & Toronto: Dent: New York: Dutton, 1920. 1st edition; one of 3000 copies; 2 volumes, 244, 240 pages; 21 handsome color plates; original two-toned cloth, bright, near fine.   Chapel Hill 94-304 1996 $175.00

HUDSON, WILLIAM HENRY 1841-1922   Far Away and Long Ago: a History of My Early Life. London: J. M. Dent, 1918. 1st edition; 8vo; decorative green cloth; very good, some wear to ends of spine and edges; bookplate of English author, Maurice Hewlett.   Antic Hay 101-852 1996 $135.00

HUDSON, WILLIAM HENRY 1841-1922   Far Away and Long Age, a History of My Early Life. Buenos Aires: Limited Editions Club, 1943. Number 904 from 1500 copies, signed by Alberto Kraft and Raul Rosarivo; illustrations by Rosarivo; cowhide binding, fine in publisher's slipcase.   Hermitage SP95-994 1996 $175.00

HUDSON, WILLIAM HENRY 1841-1922   Green Mansions. London: Duckworth, 1904. 1st edition; 2nd issue, publisher's device stamped in blind on rear panel, rear hinges neatly repaired, otherwise fine, bright copy.   Captain's Bookshelf 38-112 1996 $175.00

HUDSON, WILLIAM HENRY 1841-1922   Green Mansions. New York: Knopf, 1943. 4to; illustrations in color by Horatio Butler; sumptuous full crimson morocco with gilt mitre lines on covers, gilt panelled spine, raised bands, inner wide gilt borders, gilt top; fine in slipcase. Appelfeld Gallery 54-122 1996 $250.00

HUDSON, WILLIAM HENRY 1841-1922   Letters from William Henry Hudson. London: Nonesuch Press, 1923. Limited to 1000 copies; brown buckram, very good in dust jacket creased and snagged at bottom corner of upper panel and with couple of other small tears, scarce in dust jacket.   Words Etcetera 94-996 1996 £75.00

HUDSON, WILLIAM HENRY 1841-1922   W. H. Hudson's Letters to R. B. Cunninghame Graham - with a Few to Cunninghame Graham's Mother Mrs. Bontine. Waltham St. Lawrence: Golden Cockerel Press, 1941. One of 250 numbered copies; black and white drawings; printed on Arnold's mould made paper; half morocco buckram covers, top edge gilt; covers slightly marked and dusty, front free endpaper slightly creased, spine slightly darkened, very good.   Ulysses 39-306 1996 £95.00

HUET, PIERRE DANIEL   Catalogue des Livres de la Bibliotheque de la Maison Professe des ci-devant soi-disans Jesuites. Paris: Pissot, and Gogue, 1763. Sole edition; 8vo; 630 pages; woodcut title ornaments, contemporary full mottled calf, wear to extremities, gilt; fine. Taylor p. 64.   Bennett Gilbert LL29-11 1996 $1,000.00

HUET, PIERRE DANIEL   A Treatise of the Situation of Paradise... London: printed for James Knapton, 1694. 1st edition in English; 12mo; contemporary calf, rebacked, very good, scarce. Wing H3302; CBEL II 1515.   Ximenes 108-206 1996 $200.00

HUFFMAN, EUGENE HENRY   "Now I Am Civilized". Los Angeles: Wetzel Publishing Co., 1930. 1st edition; frontispiece, illustrations by Herbert Rasche; stain to top of pages throughout but mostly visible in front half of book, slight fraying at extremiteis, fair only, but sound copy with remnants of dust jacket laid in; inscription from "the Columinst" that has all the earmarks of an author inscription but can not be conclusively stated to be. Not in Blockson or Work.   Between the Covers 43-117 1996 $250.00

HUGHES, HENRY MARSHALL   A Clinical Introduction to the Practice of Auscultation and Other Modes of Physical Diagnosis... Philadelphia: 1846. 1st American edition; 8vo; illustrations, frontispiece, original cloth. Argosy 810-244 1996 $125.00

HUGHES, HUBERT   The Joyce Book. Sylvan Press and Humphrey Milford, n.d. 1933. One of 500 numbered copies; black and white frontispiece; printed on paper mould made in Holland, frontispiece printed by John Johnson at the University Press, Oxford, covers of hand woven silk from Edinburgh weavers; original binding, top edge silver, remarkable copy, usually found in worn and poor condition; head and tail of spine and corners bumped, covers very slightly marked, free endpapers browned, front free endpaper slightly marked, near fine in rare printed envelope, which is torn, split, creased, rubbed and marked.   Ulysses 39-326 1996 £1,600.00

HUGHES, J. T.   Doniphan's Expedition... Cincinnati: publ. by E. P. James, 1847. 144 pages; frontispiece, 3 plans, text illustrations; original salmon pictorial wrappers with title stamped in black on spine, book ad on verso of front wrapper and inside outside of back wrapper; laid in folding case, very minor chipping and wear; fine. Cowan p. 115; Graff 5(Texas Rarities 32n.   Michael D. Heaston 23-175 1996 $600.00

HUGHES, JOHN   An Itinerary of Provence and the Rhone, Made During the Year 1819.... London: James Cawthorn, 1822. Sole edition; 8vo; frontispiece (offset to title), 12 plates, pages vi, (ii), 293, (3); contemporary half brown morocco, backstrip with wide gilt decorated low raised bands, gilt lettered direct in second compartment, marbled boards, drab endpapers, front hinge split, but excellent.   Blackwell's B112-158 1996 £150.00

HUGHES, JOSIAH   Australia Revisited in 1890. London: Simpkin, Marshall.../Bangor: Nixon & Jarvis, 1891. 1st edition; crown 8vo; xvi, (500, (iv) folding colored map; original cloth, gilt, bevelled board some very light wear, front endpaper slightly strained, edges little spotted, few slight marks, but nice.   Ash Rare Books Zenzybyr-52 1996 £125.00

HUGHES, LANGSTON   The Book of Negro Humor. New York: Dodd, Mead, 1966. 1st edition; somewhat worn, fair only, corners bumped an several tears to cloth spine lacking dust jacket; inscribed by author to author Lindsay Patterson, pleasing association.   Between the Covers 43-21 1996 $450.00

HUGHES, LANGSTON   Famous Negro Music Makers. New York: Dodd, Mead, 1955. 1st edition; some underlining in text, else fine in very good dust jacket with light chipping to extremities; signed by author; uncommon; ownership signature of Edith Dodson, wife of author Owen Dodson.   Between the Covers 43-119 1996 $425.00

HUGHES, LANGSTON   Simple Takes a Wife. New York: Simon & Schuster, 1953. 1st edition; owner name on front fly and another page, usual darkening to edges of pages, else near fine with some of the usual delamination to the glossy boards, without dust jacket as issued; increasingly difficult to find.   Between the Covers 43-118 1996 $200.00

HUGHES, LANGSTON   Simple's Uncle Sam. New York: Hill and Wang, 1965. 1st edition; bookplate, tiny faint stain on front board, else fine in near fine dust jacket, with a series of small stains to edge of front flap, scarce.   Between the Covers 43-120 1996 $200.00

HUGHES, LANGSTON   Tambourines to Glory. London: John Day, 1958. 1st edition; good copy in good dust jacket, spots on page tops, shelf wear, small pieces missing from dust jacket spine and some chipping.   Book Time 2-505 1996 $110.00

HUGHES, MARY   Pleasing and Instructive Stories: for Young Children. London: William Darton, 1821. 1st edition; 140 x 86 mm; 104 pages, 4 page booklist; frontispiece, 5 copperplates dated 1821; contemporary marbled boards, red calf spine and gilt title, cover with light wear, plates with pale waterstain, else very good. Osborne 898.   Marjorie James 19-130 1996 £85.00

HUGHES, RICHARD   The Innocent Voyage. New York: Limited Editions Club, 1944. One of 1500 copies, signed by artist; lithographs in color by Lynd Ward; near fine in decorated cardboard sleeve in publisher's slipcase.   Hermitage SP95-995 1996 $100.00

HUGHES, RICHARD   The Spider's Palace - and Other Stories. London: Chatto & Windus, 1931. One of 110 numbered copies, signed by author; 4 full page color illustrations, 7 full page black and white illustrations and numerous black and white drawings by George Charlton; buckram backed decorated paper boards, top edge gilt, pages unopened, spine slightly faded, head and tail of spine and corners slightly bumped and rubbed, edges spotted, very good.   Ulysses 39-307 1996 £175.00

HUGHES, RICHARD B.   Pioneer Years in the Black Hills. Glendale: 1957. 1st edition; 366 pages, frontispiece, illustrations; cloth; Nice. 6 Guns 1066; Jennewein 99.   T. A. Swinford 49-563 1996 $125.00

HUGHES, T. HAROLD   Towns and Town Planning, Ancient and Modern. Oxford: Clarendon Press, 1923. 1st edition; 4to; frontispiece, xii, 156 pages; cloth spine, boards, covers lightly sunned and rubbed, bookplate, tips worn, else very good.   The Bookpress 75-201 1996 $125.00

HUGHES, TED 1930-   The Burning of the Brothel. London: Turret Books, 1966. 1st edition; one of 300 copies, this one out of series; thin 4to; plain wrappers, dust jacket; mint. Sagar & Tabor A9.   James S. Jaffe 34-260 1996 $150.00

HUGHES, TED 1930-   Chiasmadon. Baltimore: published by Charles Seluzicki, Poetry Bookseller, 1977. One in an edition of 175 pen numbered copies, signed by author and artist; 9.5 x 7.5 inches; 12 unnumbered pages, 1 relief etching illustration by Claire Van Vliet, designed by Claire Van Vliet, titles printed in blue and black, text in black with blue numerals, copyright notice in black, colophon in blue; relief etching printed in black, printed on Rives BFK and handsewn into Newport blue Strathmore covers and endpapers with Adriatic blue Fabriano Miliani Ingres flyleaves; fine.   Joshua Heller 21-14 1996 $200.00

HUGHES, TED 1930-   Chiasmadon. Baltimore: Charles Seluzicki, 1977. One of 175 copies signed by author and artist; thin 8vo; relief print by Claire Van Vliet; original wrappers; fine.   James S. Jaffe 34-275 1996 $150.00

HUGHES, TED 1930-   The Coming of the Kings and Other Plays. London: Faber & Faber, 1970. 1st edition; one of 2000 copies; 8vo; boards, dust jacket, light offsetting to front and back endpapers, otherwise fine.   James S. Jaffe 34-264 1996 $125.00

HUGHES, TED 1930-   Crow. From the Life and Songs of the Crow. London: Faber & Faber, 1970. 1st edition; 8vo; black cloth, dust jacket, light offsetting to front and back endpapers as usual, otherwise fine in price clipped dust jacket.   James S. Jaffe 34-265 1996 $125.00

HUGHES, TED 1930-   Crow: Poems. London: 1970. 1st edition; inscribed by author and with 2 TLS's from Stephen Tabor (one of Hughes' bibliographers) dated 1983 and 1984, book has additional signature, and is little dusty, otherwise very good in dust jacket. Words Etcetera 94-645 1996 £65.00

HUGHES, TED 1930-   Crow Wakes. Essex: Poet & Printer, 1971. 1st edition; One of 200 copies; thin 8vo; boards; fine. Sagar & Tabor A28.   James S. Jaffe 34-272 1996 $150.00

HUGHES, TED 1930-   Crow. From the Life and Songs of the Crow. New York: Harper & Row, 1971. 1st American edition, one of 5000 copies; review copy with slip laid in; 8vo; cloth backed boards, dust jacket; fine. Sagar & Tabor A25b   James S. Jaffe 34-271 1996 $100.00

HUGHES, TED 1930-   The Earth-Owl and Other Moon-People. London: Faber & Faber Ltd., 1963. 1st edition; 11 full page black and white drawings by R. A. Brandt; original binding, top edge dusty, covers very slightly spotted and dusty dust jacket, by R. A. Brandt, slightly darkened at spine and edges.   Ulysses 39-71 1996 £75.00

HUGHES, TED 1930-   A Few Crows. Exeter: Rougemont Press, 1970. 1st edition; one of 150 copies; thin square 8vo; illustrations by Reiner Burger; full leather, dust jacket; foot of spine bumped, otherwise fine in slightly soiled jacket chipped at foot of spine; inscribed by author to poet John Montague.   James S. Jaffe 34-266 1996 $375.00

HUGHES, TED 1930-   The Hawk in the Rain. London: Faber & Faber, 1957. 1st edition; one of 2000 copies; 8vo; cloth, dust jacket, fine in slightly chipped and spine darkened jacket; Sagar & Tabor A1.   James S. Jaffe 34-257 196 $225.00

HUGHES, TED 1930-   The Hawk in the Rain. New York: Harper & Bros., 1957. 1st American edition; 8vo; author's first book, boards, dust jacket, fine.   James S. Jaffe 34-256 1996 $150.00

HUGHES, TED 1930-   Lupercal. London: Faber & Faber, 1960. 1st edition; one of 2250 copies; 8vo; cloth, dust jacket, fine in jacket slightly worn at head of spine. Sagar and Tabor A3.   James S. Jaffe 34-258 1996 $125.00

HUGHES, TED 1930-   The Martyrdom of Bishop Farrar. Bow, Crediton, Devon: The Manuscript Series, 1970. 1st edition; one of 100 copies, numbered and signed by Hughes; 4to; frontispiece, pictorial wrappers; fine; Sagar & Tabor A22.a.2.   James S. Jaffe 34-268 1996 $225.00

HUGHES, TED 1930-   The Martyrdom of Bishop Farrar. Bow, Crediton, Devon: the Manuscript Series, 1970. 1st separate edition; 1st issue, withdrawn owing tot he transposition of two lines of the poem and the poet's disapproval of the wrappers, one of 'probably somewhat more than 100'; 4to; frontispiece, pictorial marbled wrappers, riveted; fine; inscribed by publisher, Richard Gilbertson. Sagar & Tabor A21.   James S. Jaffe 34-269 1996 $150.00

HUGHES, TED 1930-   Meet My Folks! London: Faber & Faber, 1961. 1st edition; one of 5000 copies; 8vo; pictorial boards, pictorial dust jacket, top edge of back cover slightly bumped, small closed tear in front free endpaper, otherwise fine. Sagar and Tabor A4.   James S. Jaffe 34-259 1996 $225.00

HUGHES, TED 1930-   Meet My Folks! London: Faber & Faber, 1961. 1st edition; illustrations by George Adamson; pictorial boards, dust jacket; near fine with slight rubbing to bottom of rear cover.   Bromer Booksellers 87-133 1996 $125.00

HUGHES, TED 1930-   Seneca's Oedipus. Adapted by Ted Hughes. London: Faber & Faber, 1969. 1st published edition, one of 2000 copies printed; 8vo; cloth, dust jacket; fine; Sagar and Tabor A16c.   James S. Jaffe 34-263 1996 $100.00

HUGHES, TED 1930-   Orts. London: Rainbow Press, 1978. 1st edition; one of 200 copies; small 8vo; printed on Italian paper; signed by author; drawing by Leonard Baskin; bound by Zaehnsdorf, decorated endpapers, full black leather, slipcase; fine.   James S. Jaffe 34-278 1996 $175.00

HUGHES, TED 1930-   Poetry Is. Garden City: Doubleday, 1970. 1st American edition, one of 2000 hardbound copies; 8vo; black cloth, dust jacket spine darkened; fine. Sagar & Tabor A14b.   James S. Jaffe 34-270 1996 $150.00

HUGHES, TED 1930-   Rain-Charm for the Dutch: Poems. (with) The Unicorn. London: Faber & Faber, 1992. Limited to 280 copies, signed by author; 1st title in cloth backed boards, fine in slipcase; 2nd title in wrappers.   Words Etcetera 94-651 1996 £60.00

HUGHES, TED 1930-   Spring, Summer, Autumn, Winter. London: Rainbow Press, 1973. 1st edition; one of 140 copies; oblong 8vo; full leather, cork slipcase; fine in very slightly rubbed slipcase.   James S. Jaffe 34-274 1996 $225.00

HUGHES, THOMAS   Mental Furniture; or, the Adaption of Knowledge for Man. London: Hamilton, Adams and Co., 1857. 1st edition; 8vo; original cloth, gilt, slightly soiled.   Anthony W. Laywood 108-178 1996 £50.00

HUGHES, THOMAS 1822-1896   Fifty Years Ago. A Layman's Address to Rugby School, Quinquagesima Sunday, 1891. London: Macmillan: Rugby: A. J. Lawrence, 1891. 12 pages; original pale brown printed wrappers, foxed and slightly dusted.   Jarndyce 103-495 1996 £65.00

HUGHES, THOMAS 1822-1896   The Scouring of the White Horse; or, the Long Vacation Ramble of a London Clerk. Cambridge: Macmillan, 1859. 1st edition; small 8vo; illustrations by richard Doyle; original gilt stamped dark blue pictorial cloth, all edges gilt, some fraying to spine, very good. Houfe p. 288.   George J. Houle 68-44 1996 $150.00

HUGHSON, DAVID   Walks through London. London: Sherwood, 1817. 8vo; 2 volumes, pages xii, 162, 1 f., ii, 163-368, viii, 1 f., 45 + 52 engraved plates; original illustrated boards, rebacked, original spines laid down, uncut, preserved in box.   Marlborough 162-155 1996 £400.00

HUGO, HERMANN   Pia Desideria Emblematis... Antwerp: Henricus Aertssens, 1628. 16mo; pages (39), 456, (2), apparently lacks two prelim (blank?) leaves; title, vignettes and 47 woodcut emblematic figures; plain full vellum; Graesse III 386; Brunet III 366; Landwehr 1046; Funk 338; Praz p. 377.   Family Album Tillers-337 1995 $550.00

HUGO, RICHARD   Death and the Good Life. New York: St. Martin's Press, 1981. 1st edition; 8vo; boards, dust jacket; fine.   James S. Jaffe 34-289 1996 $150.00

HUGO, RICHARD   Sea lanes Out. Langley: Dooryard Press, 1983. 1st edition; one of 100 hardbound copies, out of a total edition of 400 copies; tall 8vo; cloth backed printed boards. Fine.   James S. Jaffe 34-290 1996 $125.00

HUGO, VICTOR 1802-1865   Les Miserables. Bruxelles: A. LaCroix, Verboeckhoven & Cie, 1862. 1st edition; 8vo; five parts in 10 volumes, with half titles, volume and second titles, cumulative contents tables for each part, 32 pages of publisher's ads in volume 10; original printed drab wrappers, spine gilt on volume 1, spines lightly sunned, some occasional spotting in margins, several pages browned, generally as fine a set as one could hope to find. Vicaire IV 328; Talvert & Place IX 59a, cf. IX.59b.   Priscilla Juvelis 95/1-129 1996 $5,000.00

HUGO, VICTOR 1802-1865   Les Miserables. New York: Carleton, 1862. 1st American edition; 5 volumes; original purple cloth, spine extremities of each volume chipped, cloth spotted, good set.   Captain's Bookshelf 38-115 1996 $500.00

HUGO, VICTOR 1802-1865   Notre Dame De Paris. Paris: Limited Editions Club, 1930. One of 1500 copies; 4to; 2 volumes; signed by artist, Frans Masereel; wrappers, fine in torn glassine.   Charles Agvent 4-701 1996 $250.00

HUGO, VICTOR 1802-1865   The Toilers of the Sea. Paris: Limited Editions Club, 1960. One of 1500 copies; 4to; wood engravings by Tranquillo Marangoni, signed by artist and by designer, Giovanni Mardersteig; cloth backed decorated boards; spine sunned, fine in like slipcase.   Charles Agvent 4-702 1996 $125.00

HUGO, VICTOR 1802-1865   Works. Boston: Estes, n.d. Cabinet edition; 8vo; 24 volumes; plates; half green morocco, marbled boards, 5 raised bands, spines with gilt decorated floral motif, each flower with 7 red leather inlay petals, light wear overall, spines darkened, few dry, very good.   Charles Agvent 4-703 1996 $850.00

HUISH, MARCUS B.   The American Pilgrim's Way in England to Homes and Memorials of the Founders of Virginia, the New England States and Pennsylvania... Fine Art Society, 1907. Large paper edition, limited to 500 numbered copies, initialled by publisher; 4to; xxvi, 312 pages; ornamental titlepage and frontispiece printed in red and black, 130 illustrations, publisher's half morocco, top edge gilt, others uncut, slightly rubbed, fine internally.   Thomas Thorp 489-162 1996 £85.00

HUISH, MARCUS B.   The American Pilgrim's Way in England, to Homes and Memorials of the Founders of Virginia, the New England States, Pennsylvania, Harvard & Yale. London: Fine Art Soc., 1907. 1st edition; crown 4to; pages 402; 40 full page plates in color and 20 in black and white from watercolors by Elizabeth Chettle, numerous other monochrome illustrations, map; original decorated cloth, gilt top; ownership inscription of Signet Library.   Howes Bookshop 265-549 1996 £50.00

HUISH, MARCUS B.   British Water-Colour Art in the First Year of the Reign of King Edward the Seventh, and During the Century Covered by the Life of the Royal Society of Painters in Water Colours. Fine Art Society and A. & C. Black, 1904. limited to 500 numbered copies, signed by author; 4to; xvi, 219 pages; 62 plates; publisher's white cloth, spine and front cover decorated in red, green and gilt, top edge gilt, others uncut, slighly worn and soiled, joints sprung, small puncture in spine, occasional spotting and dust soiling.   Thomas Thorp 489-161 1996 £150.00

HUISH, MARCUS B.   Japan and Its Art. London: Fine Art Society, 1889. 1st edition; small 8vo; frontispiece, xii, 254, (2), 4 pages; publisher's cloth, uncommon, covers worn, text very good.   The Bookpress 75-420 1996 $325.00

HUISH, ROBERT   Memoirs of George the Fourth, Descriptive of the Most Interesting Scenes of His Private and Public Life... London: T. Kelly 1830. 8vo; 2 volumes; frontispieces, additional engraved titles, engraved plates; contemporary three quarter brown calf, spines gilt in compartments, little rubbed at base, double red and green morocco labels; very occasional light foxing, very good, very rare.   Ian Wilkinson 95/1-112 1996 £195.00

HULBERT, CHARLES   The History and Description of the County of Salop, Comprising Original Historical and Topographical Notices of the Hundreds, Towns, Parishes and Villages... Providence Grove, near Shrewsbury, 1837. 1st edition; 4to; frontispiece, 4 page list of subscrbers, map, 15 engraved plates (some foxed); 2 extra plates; contemporary half calf, slightly rubbed, spine gilt, label.   Anthony W. Laywood 108-179 1996 £175.00

HULL, WILLIAM   The History of the Glove Trade, with the Customs Connected with the Glove... London: Effingham Wilson, 1834. 1st edition; 8vo; xvi, 144 pages, errata slip tipped in before B1, small marginal defec to one leaf (not touching printed surface); original green cloth, front join worn, new endpapers; good. Goldsmiths 28500; Kress C3752; not in Williams.   John Drury 82-116 1996 £95.00

HULME, F. EDWARD   Principles of Ornamental Art. London: Cassell Petter & Galpin, n.d. 1875. 1st edition; small folio; xiii, (i), 137 pages; 32 plates; publisher's gilt cloth, front hinge internally cracked, occasional light foxing, minor cover wear, else very good. In prize binding from the Birmingham Society of Arts and School of Design.   Bookpress 75-66 1996 $275.00

HULME, F. EDWARD   Suggestions in Floral Design. London: cassell Petter & Galpin, n.d. 1878-79. 1st edition; folio; 52 pages, 52 plates; publisher's cloth.   Bookpress 75-67 1996 $1,400.00

HULSE, ELIZABETH   A Dictionary of Toronto Printers, Publishers, Booksellers and the Allied Trade, 1798-1900. Toronto: Anson-Cartwright Editions, 1982. Limited to 500 numbered copies; large 4to; pages xxii, 311; illustrations; cloth, mint, designed by Glenn Goluska.   Hugh Anson-Cartwright 87-419 1996 $125.00

HULTEN, E.   Flora of Alaska and Neighboring Territories. Stanford: 1968. 1st edition; 4to; xxii, (1), 1008, 8 pages of colored photos, colore endpaper maps, plus drawings and range maps; cloth, dust jacket with tear;   Raymond M. Sutton VI-545 1996 $115.00

HULTEN, PONTUS   Italian Art 1900-1945. New York: Rizzoli, 1989. 1s edition; remainder star stamp on bottom edge, else very fine in dust jacket.   Hermitage SP95-784 1996 $100.00

HULTEN, PONTUS   Jean Tinguely. Boston: New York Graphic Society 1975. Folio; 364 pages; 519 illustrations, 13 in color; cloth, dust jacket. Brannan 43-640 1996 $145.00

HULTEN, PONTUS   The Machine as Seen at the End of the Mechanical Age. New York: Museum of Modern ARt, 1968. 1st edition; illustrations; bound in pictorial aluminum, outer edges sunned and aluminum scratched and rubbed on front panel, else very good. Hermitage SP95-785 1996 $100.00

HULTON, P.   The Work of Jacques Le Moyne de Morgues, a Huguenot Artist in France, Florida and England. London: 1977. Small folio; 2 volumes, pages xii, 241; ix, 144, plates; cloth, in cloth slipcase. Raymond M. Sutton VI-1145 1996 $150.00

HUMANIORA. Essays in Literature, Folklore and Bibliography Honoring Archer Taylor, On His Seventieth Birthday. Locust Valley: J. J. Augustin, 1960. 1st edition; 4to; x, 374 pages; frontispiece; cloth; fine, scarce. The Bookpress 75-289 1996 $200.00

HUMBER, WILLIAM   A Practical Treatise on Cast and Wrought Iron Bridges and Griders, as Applied to Railway Structures, and to Buildings Generally, with Numerous Examples... London: Spon, 1857. Small folio; x, (ii), 106, (2) pages, tinted litho frontispiece, 58 litho plates, numbered 1-57, 36a, of which 2 folding and 33 double page; cloth.   Elton Engineering 10-78 1996 £520.00

HUMBER, WILLIAM   A Record of the Progress of Modern Engineering: Comprising Civil, Mechanical, Marine, Hydraulic, Railway, bridge and Other Engineering Works. London: Spon, 1863. Folio; (ii), (iv), 57 (1) pages, actual mounted photo frontispiece, 37 litho plates; cloth, few plates foxed.   Elton Engineering 10-79 1996 £250.00

THE HUMBLE Petition and Representation of the Gentry, Ministers and Others of the Counties of Cumberland and Westmorland, to His Sacred Majestie; with His Majesties Answer Thereunto. York 5th Julii 1642. London: printed by Robert Barker and the Assignes of John Bill, 1642. 4to; pages 5, title with typographical border, page 1 with decorated initial, last two pages in black letter with decorated initial and typographic headpiece; old half crimson morocco, gilt, marbled boards; attractive copy, with armorial bookplate of Fairfax of Cameron. Wing 3442/3. Thomason Trats: E1541 (46).   R.F.G. Hollett & Son 78-413 1996 £150.00

THE HUMBLE Petition of Many Thousand Citizens and Inhabitants in and About the City of London. London: printed for Livewell Chapman, 1658. Sole edition; 4to; pages 7; foxed and browned, leaves parting; 19th century green wrappers, creased and dog eared. McAlpin III p. 250; Wing H3474.   Blackwell's B112-78 1996 £75.00

THE HUMBLE PETITION of the Right Honourable the Lord Mayor, Aldermen and Commons of the City of London in Common-Council Assembled on 13. January 1680 to the King's Most Excellent Majesty for the Sitting of this Present Parliament Prorogu'd... London: printed by Samuel Roycroft, Printer to the Hon. City of London, 1680. Folio; 8 leaves, woodcut arms on fol. 1v, uncut, disbound; Wing H3577.   H. M. Fletcher 121-46 1996 £85.00

HUMBOLDT, FRIEDIRCH HEINRICH ALEXANDER, BARON VON 1769-1859 Commons: a Sketch of a Physical Description of the Universe. London: 1849-58. Crow 8vo; 5 volumes; portrait; cloth; fine.   John Henly 27-133 1996 £85.00

HUMBOLDT, FRIEDRICH HEINRICH ALEXANDER, BARON VON 1769-1859 Cosmos: a Sketch of a Physical Description of the Universe. London: 1949-68. Crown 8vo; 5 volumes; cloth.   Wheldon & Wesley 207-169 1996 £120.00

HUMBOLDT, FRIEDRICH HEINRICH ALEXANDER, BARON VON 1769-1859 Researches, Concerning the Institutions and Monuments of the Ancient Inhabitants of America. London: Longman, Hurst, 1814. 1st British edition; 2 volumes, 20 plates on 19 sheets, some in color; 19th century tan calf over marbled boards, light foxing scattered throughout, spines expertly restored, all in very handsome set in modern custom slipcase. Volume One has the plate 'Statue of an Azteck Priestess' bound in as frontispiece rather than at page 43 where called for.   Hermitage SP95-1105 1996 $1,000.00

HUME, A. O.   Contributions to Indian Ornithology. No. 1 Cashmere Ladak. Yarkand. London: 1873. Royal 8vo; pages (vi), 152; 32 fine hand colored plates by Keulemans; cloth. Narrow waterstain on margins of plates; from the collection of Jan Coldewey.   Wheldon & Wesley 207-51 1996 £750.00

HUME, A. O.   The Game Birds of India, Burmah and Ceylon. Calcutta: 1879-81. Royal 8vo; 3 volumes, 144 colored plates; original cloth, gilt, somewhat worn and rebacked, some slight foxing and browning of text as usual, library stamp on title and two other pages in volume 3. Wheldon & Wesley 207-772 1996 £275.00

HUME, D. C. H.   Nursairy Rhymes. The "Aeroplane" & General Pub., Co. Ltd., 1919. 1st edition; 34, 1 pages of ads; 46 text illustrations; blue cloth spine, white boards, blue, orange and black pictorial; boards bit worn; previous owner has provided pencilled explanations of some of the slang. Scarce.   Robin Greer 94A-56 1996 £75.00

HUME, DAVID 1711-1776   Dialogues Concerning Natural Religion. London: no publisher's name, 1779. 2nd edition; 8vo; 264 pages, including half title; original calf, rebacked, spine gilt, red morocco label, old endpapers preserved.   David Bickersteth 133-41 1996 £450.00

HUME, DAVID 1711-1776   Dialogues Concerning Natural Religion. London: 1779. 2nd edition; 8vo; complete with half title; contemporary calf, spine gilt; fine, rare; Jessop p. 41; CBEL II 1875.   Ximenes 108-207 1996 $750.00

HUME, DAVID 1711-1776   Essays and Treatises on Several Subjects. London: printed for T. Cadell, 1788. New edition; 2 volumes; contemporary calf, black labels, very handsome set in attractive contemporary binding.   C. R. Johnson 37-72 1996 £350.00

HUME, DAVID 1711-1776   The History of England, from the Invasion of Julius Caesar to the Revolution of 1688. (with) The History of England Under the House of Tudor. (with) The History of Great Britain, Under the House of Stuart; London: printed for A. Millar, 1762/59/59. 2nd edition; 4to; together 6 volumes; uniformly bound in contemporary calf, spines with raised bands, black morocco spine labels, ruled gilt, marbled endpapers, first two volumes lack their half titles, the other volumes either have their half titles, or no half titles, the other volumes either have their half titles, or no half titles are called for, bindings little rubbed, especially the spine labels, but sound, handsome set. Jessop p. 29; Bib. of British History 270.   David Bickersteth 133-40 1996 £980.00

HUME, DAVID 1711-1776   The History of England, from the Invasion of Julius Caesar to the Revolution in 1688. London: T. Cadell, 1788. New edition; 8vo; 8 volumes; frontispiece; old half calf, (one volume quarter calf), uniformly rebacked in morocco; ex-library, rubbed, some staining and foxing.   Robert Clark 38-312 1996 £60.00

HUME, DAVID 1711-1776   The History of England. (With Continuations to 1859). London: Virtue, c. 1860. Thick imperial 8vo; 3 volumes; over 90 steel engraved portraits and plates, 12 double page maps; well bound in contemporary half calf, spines gilt decorated with maroon and black lettering pieces.   Howes Bookshop 265-550 1996 £120.00

HUME, DAVID 1711-1776   The Letters. Oxford: Clarendon Press, 1969. Reprint; 8vo; 2 volumes; 2 frontispieces, 3 plates, pages xxxii, 532; vi, 498; original blue cloth, gilt lettered, excellent; J.D. Fleeman's copy with some marginalia by him.   Blackwell's B112-159 1996 £150.00

HUME, DAVID 1711-1776   Political Discourses. Edinburgh: Printed by R. Fleming for A. Kincaid and A. Donaldson, 1752. 1st edition; 304 pages, 6, 2 ads; contemporary calf, spine in 6 compartments, one with tan leather label, others each bearing gilt crown device, joints and head of spine repaired, very good, fresh, in cloth case.   19th Century Shop 39- 1996 $6,500.00

HUME, DAVID 1711-1776   A Treatise on Human Nature Being an Attempt to Introduce the Experimental method of Reasoning into Moral Subjects and Dialogues Concerning Natural Religion. London: Longmans, Green and Co., 1874. 8vo; 2 volumes, half titles; original cloth, spines faded, uncut; nice set.   Anthony W. Laywood 108-180 1996 £75.00

THE HUMOURIST. London: Nimmo, 1892. One of 70 copies with plates in both their uncolored and colored states; reprint of the first edition; large octavo; 4 volumes; 220, 228, 224, 226 pages; illustrations and caricatures by George Cruikshank, brightly colored by hand; original navy cloth with printed spine labels, extremities show only a minimum of rubbing, with few light scratches to rear cover of volume 1, else fine, bright set.   Bromer Booksellers 87-49 1996 $750.00

HUMPHREY, MAUD   Little Rosebuds. New York: 1898. 11 x 8.5 inches; 6 full page color paltes and drawings; cloth backed pictorial boards, very worn with pencil scribbling on endpapers, pages torn and plates soiled.   John K. King 77-598 1996 $200.00

HUMPHREYS, DAVID   The Miscellaneous Works. New York: Hodge, Allen and Campbell, 1790. 1st edition; 348 pages; old marbled paper sides, later quarter morocco with red spine label, small worming at bottom margin of final few pages. Evans 22578. Wegelin 224.   Taurus Books 83-110 1996 $150.00

HUMPHREYS, DAVID   A Poem on Industry. Philadelphia: printed for Mathew Carey, Oct. 14, 1794. 1st edition; 12mo; 22, (2) pages; recent three quarter calf, crisp copy. Wegelin 225; Evans 27145.   M & S Rare Books 60-178 1996 $250.00

HUMPHREYS, H. D.   An Address Delivered Before the Western Literary Society of Wabash College, July 12, 1836. Crawfordsville: Harland and Holmes, Printers, 1836. 1st edition; 8vo; 16 pages; original printed wrappers; Byrd & Peckham 632 (1 copy); Rinderknecht 38152.   M & S Rare Books 60-348 1996 $150.00

HUMPHREYS, HENRY NOEL 1810-1879   Ancient Coins and Medals: an Historical Sketch of the Origin and Progress of Coining Money in Greece and Her Colonies. London: Grant & Griffith, 1851. 2nd edition; bound into text at regular intervals are heavy board plates numbered 1-10 into which are recessed Gold, Silver & Bronze facsimiles, there is a total of 120 coins offered in 3 dimensional examples (actual foil over pressed paper in full relief), opposite which there are printed identifications; publisher's blind blocked dark brown calf over bevelled boards, spine with five raised bands, contrasting morocco lettering piece, marbled endleaves, all edges stained red, few descrete ex-library markings, which hardly detract from this exceptionally clean and crisp copy; rarely found in such fine condition.   Book Block 32-3 1996 $1,450.00

HUMPHREYS, HENRY NOEL 1810-1879   British Moths and Their Transformations. London: 1843. Large 4to; 2 volumes, 124 hand colored plates; contemporary half morocco, gilt, some light rubbing; slight offsetting on occasional page and little light foxing. Scarce. Lovely set. David A.H. Grayling MY95Orn-44 1996 £600.00

HUMPHREYS, HENRY NOEL 1810-1879   The Coinage of the British Empire. London: David Bogue, 1855. 1st edition; 8vo; 160 pages, 24 plates, 12 are chromographic; publisher's cloth.   Bookpress 75-68 1996 $385.00

HUMPHREYS, HENRY NOEL 1810-1879   The Genera of British Moths. London: T. J. Allman, n.d. 1859-60. 1st edition; royal 8vo; 62 hand colored plates; original cloth, gilt, gilt edges.   Charles W. Traylen 117-309 1996 £270.00

HUMPHREYS, HENRY NOEL 1810-1879   A Record of the Black Prince. London: Longman, Brown, Green and Longmans, 1849. 8vo; (vi), xciv, (ii), ii pages; 6 color printed illustrations from medieval designs, decorative borders and initial letters, text printed in black letter; original black composition binding in high relief with designs adapted from the Black Prince's tomb, all edges gilt, rebacked, old spine relaid, slight loss at one end; minor wear to 3 corners of binding with slight loss, few cracks in composition, some page edges dusty.   Robert Clark 38-243 1996 £140.00

HUMPPHREYS, HENRY NOEL   The Genera and Species of British Butterflies. London: n.d. 1859. 1st edition; royal 8vo; 32 beautiful colored plates, mostly with their original tissues opposite, original highly decorated cloth; unusually fine.   Charles W. Traylen 117-308 1996 £250.00

HUNT, LEIGH 1784-1859   Captain Sword and Captain Pen. London: Charles Knight, 1835. 1st edition; small 8vo; viii, 112 pages + 4 pages of ads; engraved frontispiece and 7 plates; original patterned green cloth, spine extremities lightly chipped.   Kenneth Karmiole 1NS-127 1996 $100.00

HUNT, LEIGH 1784-1859   The Indicator, and the Companion; a Miscellany for the Fields and the Fireside. London: published for Henry Colburn, 1834. Large 12mo; 2 volumes; recent full green morocco, gilt, top edge gilt, others uncut.   Peter Murray Hill 185-82 1996 £120.00

HUNT, LEIGH 1784-1859   A Jar Of Honey from Mount Hybla. London: Smith, Elder and Co., 1848. 1st edition; 8 x 5 1/2 inches; 4 p.l., viii, xxiv, 200 pages, (8) leaves ads; frontispiece, title vignette and 24 vignettes in text by Richard Doyle, with half title; text on acidic paper that has evenly browned, closed tear on one leaf from bottom well into text (no loss), otherwise fine copy; lovely and animated light brown crushed morocco exhibition binding by Zaehnsdorf, dated 1895, and with Zaehnsdorf emblem, normally reserved for the firm's better work, impressed at back, both covers filled with large panel of inlaid black tulips on long gilt foliated stems, flowers within diapered compartments and with a background of gilt dots, flat spine similarly decorated (there are a total of 54 inlaid tulips on sides and spine), fine inner gilt dentelles, silk pastedowns and free endpapers, gilt edges, in fine cloth folder and morocco backed slipcase with gilt stamped spine; virtually no external wear.   Phillip J. Pirages 33-65 1996 $1,250.00

HUNT, LEIGH 1784-1859   A Jar of Honey from Mount Hybla. London: Smith Elder, 1848. 1st edition; 8vo; designed by owen Jones, on glazed yellow paper, printed in gold, blue, green and black and placed over boards, binding is exceptionally bright, some light wear to edges, tips and hinges along spine, very desirable copy, very scarce; with presentation in ink dated "Christmas 1847".   Bookpress 75-72 1996 $550.00

HUNT, LEIGH 1784-1859   Juvenilia; or, a Collection of Poems. London J. Whiting, 1802. 3rd edition; 8vo. in 4's; pages xxiii, (i), 215; engraved oval portrait and plate engraved by Bartolozzi, with tissue guards (all foxed), half title, printer's ornament on titlepage; contemporary dark brown calf, red and dark blue marbling, surface slightly rubbed and cracking, as often, smooth backstrip divided by gilt bands of diamond and roundel on gilt, scallop and pointille rolls, upper joint tender, sides with double fillet and 'Greek-key' roll border, fillet on boards, narrow roll on turn-ins, marbled endpapers and edges. Brewer pp. 9 and 12. Blackwell's B112-160 1996 £95.00

HUNT, LEIGH 1784-1859   The Story of Rimini, a Poem. London: printed by T. Davison for J. Murray, W. Blackwood (Edinburgh) and .... 1816. 1st edition; 8vo; contemporary green straight grained morocco, covers decorated in blind with gilt borders, spine gilt, all edges gilt, spine rubbed; half title present, very good. Brewer pp. 72-77; Hayward 230.   Ximenes 108-210 1996 $350.00

HUNT, LYNN BOGUE   An Artist's Game Bag. New York: Derrydale Press, 1936. 1st edition; one of 1225 numbered copies; illustrations by Lynn Bogue Hunt, 4 full color and 44 black and white illustrations, in very worn dust jacket. Siegel 98; Frazier H20a.   Glenn Books 36-69 1996 $425.00

HUNT, PETER   Muder Among the Nudists. New York: Vanguard, 1934 1st edition; bit cocked, else about near fine in dust jacket that has been trimmed about quarter inch, at top just touching top of lettering and getting deeper near rear flap.   Between the Covers 42-493 1996 $100.00

HUNT, RACHEL MC MASTERS MILLER   Catalogue of Botanical Books in the Collection of Rachel McMasters Miller Hunt. Pittsburgh: 1958-61. Limited to 750 copies; 8vo; 2 volumes in 3; pages lxxxiv, 517; ccxliv; ix, 655; 3 plates; buckram;   Raymond M. Sutton VI-25 1996 $1,450.00

HUNT, ROBERT   Researches on Light In Its Chemical Relations: Embracing a Consideration of all the Photographic Processes. London: Longman, Brown, 1854. 2nd edition; 8vo; pages xx, 396; folding color plate, recent quarter calf, label, nice.   James Fenning 133-169 1996 £165.00

HUNTER, ALEXANDER   Georgical Essays: In Which the Food of Plant Is Particularly Considered. London: printed for T. Durham, 1769. 1st edition; small 8vo; contemporary calf, gilt, spine gilt (minor wear); attractive copy, very scarce.   Ximenes 109-161 1996 $450.00

HUNTER, ALEXANDER   Outlines of Agriculture, Addressed to Sir John Sinclair, Bart, President of the Baord of Agriculture. York: printed by Wilson, Spence & Mawman & sold by Cadell Jun. & Davies... 1797. 2nd edition; 47, (1) pages; plates; contemporary calf, rebacked; good; inscribed presentation copy from author to Fr. Atkison. Goldsmith's 16249.   C. R. Johnson 37-18 196 £150.00

HUNTER, DARD 1883-1966   Laid and Wove. Washington: GPO, 1923. Offprint; octavo; (8)ff; 6 plates; slightly yellowed printed wrappers, with small tear to edges; about fine.   Bromer Booksellers 90-67 1996 $100.00

HUNTER, DARD 1883-1966   My Life with Paper. New York: Knopf, 1958. 1st edition; octavo; xii, 237, vii pages; original cloth, front endpaper lightly browned, else extremely fine in dust jacket which is faded to spine with small chip.   Bromer Booksellers 90-68 1996 $175.00

HUNTER, DARD 1883-1966   My Life with Paper. New York: Knopf, 1958. 1st edition; 8vo; 236, (1), (7), (2) pages; complete with paper samples tipped in at p. 105 and p. 145; original brownish red cloth, near fine in dust jacket.   Chapel Hill 94-322 1996 $125.00

HUNTER, DARD 1883-1966   Papermaking by Hand in India. New York Pynson Printers, 1939. 1st edition; number 22 of 375 copies signed by author and publisher; photos, 27 paper samples at back; leather backed cloth patterned boards, bookplate on front pastedown, few minor scuffs to spine, expertly retouched, otherwise fine in expertly restored original slipcase.   Hermitage SP95-1062 1996 $2,100.00

HUNTER, DARD 1883-1966   Papermaking in Pioneer America. Philadelphia: University of Pennsylvania, 1952. 1st edition; xiv, 178 pages, 11 pages plates; quarter cloth, terra cotta boards, small edge dents and light fading to edge of back cover, otherwise fine.   Bromer Booksellers 90-71 1996 $150.00

HUNTER, DARD 1883-1966   Paper-making in the Classroom. Peoria: Manual Arts Pres, 1931. 1st edition; 80 pages; fully illustrated; light soiling to tan cloth, else near fine; inscribed by Hunter for Robert H. Orchard.   Bromer Booksellers 90-69 1996 $250.00

HUNTER, DARD 1883-1966   Papermaking: The History and Technique of an Ancient Craft. New York: Knopf, 1947. 2nd edition; octavo; xxiv, 611, xxxvii pages; 317 illustrations, folding map; liht wear to extremities, otherwise fine.   Bromer Booksellers 90-70 1996 $175.00

HUNTER, DARD 1883-1966   Papermaking through Eighteen Centuries. New York: Rudge, 1930. 1st edition; octavo; xvii, 358 pages; 214 illustrations; folding frontispiece; linen, morocco spine label; some chipping to label, otherwise fine; with presentation from Dard Hunter Jr. to Robert Orchard. Laid in are TLS from Hunter to Robert Orchard's father, and watermarked portrait specimen of D.H.   Bromer Booksellers 90-73 1996 $350.00

HUNTER, DARD 1883-1966   The Romance of Watermarks, a Discourse on the Origin and Motive of These Mystic Symbols Which First Appeared in Italy Near the End of the 13th Century... Cincinnati: Stratford Press, ca. 1938. One of 210 copies; small octavo; 34 pages; vellum backed brown boards, portrait label; very fine in matching slipcase.   Bromer Booksellers 90-74 1996 $475.00

HUNTER, DARD 1917-   A Specimen of Type. Cambridge: Paper Museum Press, 1940. Limited to 100 copies; folio; (5) ff; with type specimen of a face designed, cut and handcast by Hunter; blue wrappers, paper label; fine.   Bromer Booksellers 87-101 1996 $750.00

HUNTER, JOHN   A Tribute to the Manes of Unfortunate Poets; in Four Cantos. London: printed for T. Cadell, Junior and W. Davies, 1798. 1st edition; small 8vo; original pink boards, drab paper backstrip, very slight wear; fine, very scarce; booklabel of John Sparrow.   Ximenes 108-212 1996 $500.00

HUNTER, JOHN 1728-1793   Essays and Observations on Natural History, Anatomy, Physiology, Psychology and Geology... London: John Van Voorst, 1861. 8vo; 403; 507 pages; 2 volumes; frontispiece; original binding, quite rubbed, still tight. Iowa 976.   James Tait Goodrich K40-162 1996 $125.00

HUNTER, JOHN 1728-1793   A Treatise on the Blood, Inflammation, and Gunshot Wounds to Which is Prefixed a Short Account of the Author's Life... London: Richardson for Nicol, 1794. 1st edition; 4to; lxvii, 575 pages, facsimile portrait on old laid paper, plate one in facsimile on old laid paper, other 8 plates present; 19th century morocco, richly tooled, gilt inner dentelles, rebacked with spine richly tooled in gilt, new endpapers of old laid paper, some minor worming in blank margins of leaves; ad leaf is laid down. GM 2283.   James Tait Goodrich K40-161 1996 $895.00

HUNTER, JOHN 1728-1793   A Treatise on the Blood, Inflammation and Gun-Shot Wounds. London: 1812. 2nd English edition; 8vo; 2 volumes, 8 plates (on 7 leaves), trimmed in places, few pencil annotations; early 20th century half red morocco, public library style binding (though not actually from a library).   Maggs Bros. Ltd. 1190-437 1996 £200.00

HUNTER, JOHN MARVIN   The Album of Gunfighters. Bandera: 1951. 1st edition; 236 pages; illustrations, photos; book fine, protective slipcase,, author's signatures tipped in on titlepage; scarce. Six Guns 1085; Adams 150 #77.   Early West 22-86 1996 $300.00

HUNTER, JOHN MARVIN   The Album of Gunfighters. Bandera: 1976. Later printing; book fine, dust jacket scuffed and chipped.   Early West 22-87 1996 $110.00

HUNTER, JOHN MARVIN   The Trail Drivers of Texas. Nashville: Cokesbury Press, 1925. 2nd edition; thick octavo; 2 volumes in one, xvi, 1044 pages; frontispiece, numerous portraits; original gilt lettered dark blue cloth, light wear to spine ends and corners, corner bit jammed, gutter of two leaves darkened from scotch tape (removed); very good. Adams Herd 1103; Dobie p. 108; Dykes Kid 77, 93, 98; Graff 2020. Argonaut Book Shop 113-361 1996 $200.00

HUNTER, JOHN MARVIN   The Trail Drivers of Texas. Nashville: 1925. 2nd edition; 1044 pages, photos; book fine but for one page has hole which has been skillfully repaired, slipcase.   Early West 22-236 1996 $125.00

HUNTER, JOHN MARVIN   Trail Drivers of Texas. New York: Argosy-Antiquarian Ltd., 1963. One of 97 numbered sets, signed by Harry Sinclair Drago, who provides introduction; 2 volumes, xxviii, 549, vii, - 1070 pages; portraits; half leather and tan boards, gilt spines tiltes and tops, lightly soiled slipcase. Later printing of Howes H816; Graff 2020; Adams Guns 1084; Herd 1103.   Bohling Book Co. 191-72 1996 $300.00

HUNTER, JOHN MARVIN   The Trail Drivers of Texas. New York: 1963. Reprint; one of 97 copies signed by Harry Sinclair Drago; 2 volumes, photos; specially bound in leather, books fine, slipcase near fine. Reese 120 #61. Six Guns 1084; Herd 1103.   Early West 22-234 1996 $300.00

HUNTER, JOHN MARVIN   The Trail Drivers of Texas. New York: 1963. Reprint; 2 volumes; photos; cloth, books near fine.   Early West 22-237 1996 $100.00

HUNTER, KRISTIN   The Landlord. New York: Scribners, 1966. 1st edition; small number on front free endpaper and little fading at extremities of cloth; very good in about very good dust jacket with couple of short tears and small stain at top edge of spine; although there is no tangible evidence, this was Hal Ashby's copy, Ashby directed the film made from this book.   Between the Covers 43-125 1996 $100.00

HUNTER, RICHARD ALFRED   Three Hundred Years of Psychiatry 1535-1860. Hartsdale: Carlisle Pub. Inc., 1982. Correct reprint of 1970 edition; thick 8vo; (xxviii), 1107, (1) pages; blue buckram, fine in dust jacket.   John Gach 150-219 1996 $125.00

HUNTER, SAM   Larry Rivers. New York: Abrams, 1970. Oblogn 4to; 261 pages, 220 illustrations, including 52 tipped in color plates; cloth, dust jacket. Freitag 8235.   Brannan 43-557 1996 $275.00

HUNTER, WILLIAM   Anatomia Uteri Humani Gravidi Tabulis Illustrata. The Anatomy of the Human Gravid Uterus Exhibited in Figures. London: printed for the Sydenham Society, 1851. Folio; (ii), iv, 16 pages, printed slip 'Notice to members' following titlepage, 34 plates, rebound in plain dark red cloth, prelim leaf before titlepage with just the date and name of the Sydenham Society on it, has been torn and neatly repaired, apart from this, a good, clean copy. GM 6157.   David Bickersteth 133-202 1996 £185.00

HUNTER, WILLIAM S.   Chisholm's Panoramic Guide from Niagara Falls to Quebec. Montreal: 1868. Pages 66, colored ads plus long folding panorama; original decorated cloth, upper backstrip worn away, internally near fine. TPL 3664.   Stephen Lunsford 45-77 1996 $100.00

HUNTON, W. GORDON   English Decorative Textiles: Tapestry and Chintz, Their Design and Development from the Earliest Times to the Nineteenth Century. John Tiranti & Co., 1930. 4to; 3 text figures, 181 collotype illustrations; cloth, stain on front cover, slightly worn. Thomas Thorp 489-165 1996 £50.00

HURD, PETER   Peter Hurd Sketch Book. Chicago: Swallow Press, 1971. Number 96 of 250 copies, signed by the artist; 121 pages, some prelim text with black and white sketches, then 40 color reproductions with desriptive text opposite, cloth, dust jacket, slipcase; fine, slipcase with some wear and short split.   Bohling Book Co. 192-173 1996 $125.00

HURD, RICHARD   Dialogues on the Uses of Foreign Travel... London: printed by W.B. for A. Millar...; and W. Thurlbourn and J. Woodyer... 1764. 1st edition; 8vo; title printed in red and black, (4), 201, (1) pages, few inoffensive spots at beginning and end, author's name and shelf number supplied in red ink on title; contemporary quarter calf, neatly rebacked, label on spine; very good, large copy, entirely uncut; late 18th century armorial label of Thomas Llewelyn and early 19th century label of the Bristol Education Society.   John Drury 82-118 1996 £200.00

HURD, RICHARD   Dialogues on the Uses of Foreign Travel...(with) Letters on Chivalry and Romance. London: ptd. by W.B. for A. Millar...London: ptd. for A. Millar and W.... 1764/62. 1st edition; 8vo; 2 volumes in one; contemporary sprinkled calf, spine gilt, joints cracked, lacks label very good. CBEL II 1780.   Ximenes 108-213 1996 $500.00

HURD-MEAD, KATE CAMPBELL   Medical Women of America: a Short History of the Pioneer Medical Women of America and a Few of Their Colleagues in England. 1933. 1st edition; 95 pages, plus portraits; original binding, ex-library. GM 6650.   W. Bruce Fye 71-1064 1996 $150.00

HURDIS, JAMES   The Village Curate, and Other Poems... London: ptd. by C. Whittingham, for Vernor, Hood and Sharpe, Longman, etc... 1810. 1st edition; 8vo; portrait (offsetting onto titlepage), half title present; contemporary full red straight grained morocco, gilt, spine gilt, all edges gilt, slight rubbing; elegant copy in fine condition. Russell, William Cowper 337; CBEL II 660.   Ximenes 108-214 1996 $275.00

HURRY, JAMIESON   Imhotep: the Vizier and Physician of King Zoser and Afterwards the Egyptian God of Medicine. London: 1928. 2nd edition; 211 pages; original binding. GM 6470. Smit 245.   W. Bruce Fye 71-1065 1996 $150.00

HURST, FANNIE   Lummox. New York: Harpers, 1923. 1st edition; fine in near fine dust jacket with some very shallow nicking to crown. Between the Covers 42-229 1996 $200.00

HURST, FANNIE   Mannequin. New York: Knopf, 1926. 1st edition; light wear, near near fine in very near fine dust jacket, touch darkened on rear panel and with single tiny sliver at corner of base of spine and front panel, pretty copy.   Between the Covers 42-230 1996 $150.00

HURST, JOHN F.   Indika the Country and People of India and Ceylon. New York: Harper and Bros., 1891. 1st edition; tall 8vo; (xxii), 794 pages; illustrations, with 6 maps including large folding map in pocket at front; original green cloth decorated in gilt and lettered in red; some minor rubbing at spine ends, else fine.   David Mason 71-92 1996 $225.00

HURSTON, ZORA NEALE   Seraph on the Swanee. New York: Scribner, 1948. 1st edition; fine, lacking dust jacket.   Captain's Bookshelf 38-116 1996 $175.00

HURSTON, ZORA NEALE   Tell My Horse. Philadelpha/New York: Lippincott, 1938. 1st edition; near fine with fading to spine and light rubbing at foot, lacking dust jacket.   Between the Covers 43-126 1996 $200.00

HURSTON, ZORA NEALE   Tell My Horse. Philadelphia: Lippincott, 1938. 1st edition; shelfwear to extremities, else very good+ in bright dust jacket with couple of short edge tears, extraordinarily nice copy, scarce in this condition.   Lame Duck Books 19-16 1996 $1,250.00

HURTLEY, THOMAS   A Concise Account of Some Natural Curiosities in the Environs of Malham, in Craven, Yorkshire. London: Logographic Press, 1786. 1st edition; 8vo; 199, (1) pages; 3 plates, 1 folding; contemporary boards, respined; boards worn, else very nice.   The Bookpress 75-319 1 1996 $350.00

HURWITZ, A.   Milestones in Modern Surgery. New York: 1958. 1st edition; 520 pages; original binding. GM 5813.1.   W. Bruce Fye 71-1066 1996 $100.00

HUSENBETH, F. C.   The History of Sedgley Park School, Staffordshire. London: Richardson and Son, 1856. 1st edition; large 12mo; frontispiece, 4 other plates, xi, (1), 253, (1) pages; frequent underlinings of passages of text in pencil; original pink cloth, embossed in blind and lettered in gilt, very good   John Drury 82-119 1996 £45.00

HUSON, THOMAS   Round About Helvellyn. London: Seeley & Co., 1895. 1st edition; small folio; pages 51, (iv), 24 photogravure plates, title in red and black; original cloth, gilt, rather mottled, corners little worn, lower hinge just fraying, top edge gilt.   R.F.G. Hollett & Son 78-1022 1996 £140.00

HUSSERL, EDMUND   L'Origine de la Geometrie. Paris: Presses Universitaires de France, 1962. 1st edition translated by Jacques Derrida. Wrappers; near fine; exceptional association copy, inscribed by Derrida to American critic and novelist Susan Sontag.   Lame Duck Books 19-460 1996 $1,500.00

HUSSEY, A. M.   Illustrations of British Mycology. London: 1847-55. 4to; Series 1 and 2, 2 volumes, 90 hand colored plates, 50 hand colored plates; contemporary half green roan; nice complete copy, some very limited foxing, especially of endpapers; presentation inscription to Revd. M. J. Berkeley with compliments of author and publisher.   Wheldon & Wesley 207-52 1996 £2,250.00

HUSSEY, A. M.   Illustrations of British Mycology. London: 1847. 4to; text unpaginated; 90 hand colored plates; contemporary green double ruled ornately tooled calf with gilt decorated spine, some rubbing, cracking to front hinge, rear cover detached, slight browning to page edges, beautiful copy, virtually free of foxing; rare.   Raymond M. Sutton VII-18 1996 $3,300.00

HUSTON, JOHN   An Open Book. New York: Knopf, 1980. 1st edition; 8vo; 32 pages of black and white photos; dust jacket, very good; signed by author; with "Autographed at Hunter's" label on upper cover.   George J. Houle 68-71 1996 $150.00

HUTCHESON, FRANCIS 1694-1746   An Essay on the Nature and Conduct of the Passions and Affections. London: printed for A. Ward, J. and P. Knapton, (& 7 others), 1742. 3rd edition; 8vo; contemporary panelled calf, upper hinge cracked. This edition not in Kress or Goldsmith.   Anthony Laywood 108-75 1996 £375.00

HUTCHINS, WELLS A.   Water Rights Laws in the Nineteen Western States. Washington: U.S.D.A. 1971. Maroon buckram, little dull and worn but good, clean set.   Meyer Boswell SL27-120 1996 $350.00

HUTCHINSON, EDWARD   Girder-Making and the Practice of Bridge Building in Wrought Iron. London: Spon, 1879. 8vo; (x), 184 pages, (4) page of the Tees-Side Iron and Engine Works Co., List of Manufactures; frontispiece, 34 wood engraved plates, 2 unnumbered plates, many wood engraved text illustrations, publisher's cloth, excellent copy.   Elton Engineering 10-80 1996 £190.00

HUTCHINSON, HORACE   British Golf Links. London: J. S. Virtue & Co., 1897. 1st edition; folio; viii, 331, v (ads) pages; numerous illustrations and portraits; original olive green cloth decoratively stamped in gilt and black on front cover and spine, some soiling and wear to cloth, hinges restored, repaired tear on one leaf, still very good overall.   Heritage Book Shop 196-199 1996 $1,250.00

HUTCHINSON, J.   A Botanist in Southern Africa. London: 1946. Royal 8vo; pages xii, 686; colored portrait, numerous photos, drawings and maps; cloth, ownership stamps on endpaper.   Wheldon & Wesley 207-1776 1996 £75.00

HUTCHINSON, JOHN   John Hutchinson's Tour through the High Peak of Derbyshire. Macclesfield: printed by J. Wilson 1809. 1st edition; 12mo; frontispiece, 5 plates; contemporary cloth, leather label, uncut.   Anthony W. Laywood 109-69 1996 £90.00

HUTCHINSON, R. C.   Elephant & Castle. London: Cassell, 1949. 1st edition; near fine in like dust jacket; inscribed by author.   Captain's Bookshelf 38-117 1996 $100.00

HUTCHINSON, WILLIAM   An Excursion to the Lakes in Westmoreland and Cumberland, August 1773. London: printed for J. Wilkie and W. Goldsmith, 1774. 1st edition; 8vo; pages 193, engraved vignette on title, few spots on endpapers and prelims, but very nice; old half calf, gilt, marbled boards little rubbed.   R.F.G. Hollett & Son 78-1023 1996 £275.00

HUTCHINSON, WILLIAM   An Excursion to the Lakes in Westmoreland and Cumberland, with a Tour through Parts of the Northern Counties, in the Years 1773 and 1774. London: for J. Wilkie, 1776. 8vo; (2), 382, (4) pages; 19 engraved plates, one plate expertly repaired; contemporary mottled calf, neat repairs to joints and head and tail of gilt spine, original red gilt label; very good. Bicknell 7.   Ken Spelman 30-87 1996 £260.00

HUTCHINSON, WILLIAM   The History of the County of Cumberland. London: E. P. Publishing, 1974. Facsimile edition; small 4to; 2 volumes, pages xxiii, 600, 686; 4 folding maps, over 50 full page illustrations; original cloth, gilt, dust jackets; fine set.   R.F.G. Hollett & Son 78-1024 1996 £120.00

HUTT, HENRY   Rosebuds. N.P.: The Bobbs-Merrill Co., 1912. 1st edition; Innocuous light foxing, else fine.   Hermitage SP95-902 1996 $150.00

HUTTON, CHARLES   A Course of Mathematics... London: for G. G. and J. Robinson, 1799-98. 1st edition of volume 2, 2nd edition of volume 1; 8vo; 2 volumes; iv, 368; iv, 364 pages; numerous figures in text; later marbled boards, cloth spines, very good set.   Edwin V. Glaser 121-163 1996 $150.00

HUTTON, WILLIAM   The Beetham Repository. Kendal: Titus Wilson, 1906. 8vo; pages xi, 199; modern half levant morocco, gilt, original printed wrappers bound in at end, extremely scarce.   R.F.G. Hollett & Son 78-928 1996 £150.00

HUTTON, WILLIAM   A Journey from Birmingham to London. Birmingham: Pearson & Rollason, 1785. 1st edition; post 12mo; (iv), 228 pages, engraved plate; old vellum tipped boards, neatly rebacked (in calf), and re-covered, one leaf torn and neatly repaired, few minor marks,b ut good.   Ash Rare Books Zenzybyr-53 1996 £225.00

HUTTON, WILLIAM   A Journey from Birmingham to London... Birmingham: Pearson and Rollason, 1785. Small 8vo; 1 engraved plates, (iv), 228 pages; contemporary sheep, worn and rubbed; not in Straus and Dent.   Marlborough 162-50 1996 £190.00

HUTYRA, FRANZ   Special Pathology and Therapeutics of the Diseases of Domestic Animals. Chicago: 1926. thick 4to; 3 volumes, 28 color plates, 609 text illustrations; corners rubbed, volumes 1 and 2 shaken. Argosy 810-247 1996 $150.00

HUXLEY, ALDOUS LEONARD 1894-1936   Along the Road. London: Chatto & Windus, 1925. 1st edition; fine in very near fine dust jacket. Ken Lopez 74-211 1996 $175.00

HUXLEY, ALDOUS LEONARD 1894-1936   Antic Hay. London: Chatto & Windus, 1923. 1st edition; very near fine in dust jacket that is very slightly spine sunned and has tiny bit of edgewear at crown, still near fine; exceptionaly copy.   Ken Lopez 74-208 1996 $375.00

HUXLEY, ALDOUS LEONARD 1894-1936   Brave New World. C&W, 1932. 1st edition; tight copy, very good in bright, very good/very good+ dust jacket save for some light chipping to head of dust jacket spine and some other light wear and tear, very nice.   Aronovitz 57-579 1996 $750.00

HUXLEY, ALDOUS LEONARD 1894-1936   Brave New World. London: Chatto & Windus, 1932. 1st edition; 8vo; (vi), 306 pages; original blue cloth, dust jacket just a trifle nicked at extremities and has one tiny chip at head of spine panel, very nice, scarce in this condition.   Sotheran PN32-22 1996 £598.00

HUXLEY, ALDOUS LEONARD 1894-1936   Brave New World. New York: Doubleday Doran, 1932. One of a limited U.S. edition of 250 numbered copies, signed by author; quarter cloth and paper covered boards; ownership signature, else very fine.   Lame Duck Books 19-251 1996 $950.00

HUXLEY, ALDOUS LEONARD 1894-1936   Brave New World. New York: Limited Editions Club, 1974. One of 2000 numbered copies,s igned by artist; gravures by Mara McAfee.   Hermitage SP95-996 1996 $125.00

HUXLEY, ALDOUS LEONARD 1894-1936   The Burning Wheel. Oxford: B. H. Blackwell, 1916. 1st edition; 8vo; original cream wrappers, printed paper labels on spine and front wrapper, in cloth folding case. Fine. Ximenes 108-215 1996 $750.00

HUXLEY, ALDOUS LEONARD 1894-1936   The Burning Wheel. Oxford: 1916. 1st edition; author's first book; wrappers, scarce, near fine. Stephen Lupack 83- 1996 $450.00

HUXLEY, ALDOUS LEONARD 1894-1936   The Defeat of Youth. Oxford: B. H. Blackwell, 1918. 1st edition; 8vo; patterned wrappers; very good, restoration to spine, little wear to lower end spine.   Antic Hay 101-866 1996 $175.00

HUXLEY, ALDOUS LEONARD 1894-1936   The Discovery: a Comedy in Five Acts. London: Chatto & Windus, 1924. Special edition, limited to 210 numbered copies of which 200 were for sale; 8vo; cloth and patterned boards in dust jacket; uncommon; fine, moderate wear to dust jacket with few tears and sunned spine.   Antic Hay 101-867 1996 $200.00

HUXLEY, ALDOUS LEONARD 1894-1936   The Doors of Perception. New York: Harper, 1954. 1st American edition; slight crease on front board, else fine in near fine dust jacket, bit soiled and with one short tear; Alice Longworth's copy with her pencil signature.   Between the Covers 42-233 1996 $125.00

HUXLEY, ALDOUS LEONARD 1894-1936   Heaven and Hell. London: Chatto & Windus, 1956. 1st edition; fine in midly spine faded dust jacket with mild war at corners and spine extremities, overall about near fine. Ken Lopez 74-214 1996 $100.00

HUXLEY, ALDOUS LEONARD 1894-1936   Island. London: Chatto & Windus, 1962. 1st edition; 8vo; cloth in dust jacket; near fine, minor wear and browning (price clipped) dust jacket.   Antic Hay 101-871 1996 $125.00

HUXLEY, ALDOUS LEONARD 1894-1936   Little Mexican and Other Stories. London: Chatto & Windus, 1924. 1st edition; fine in very close to fine dust jacket, beautiful copy.   Ken Lopez 74-209 1996 $250.00

HUXLEY, ALDOUS LEONARD 1894-1936   Mortal Coils. London: Chatto & Windus, 1922. 1st edition; fine in fine, soft paper dust jacket with touch of soiling, lovely copy, uncommon thus.   Between the Covers 42-231 1996 $250.00

HUXLEY, ALDOUS LEONARD 1894-1936   Mortal Coils. London: Chatto & Windus, 1922. 1st edition; very fine in soft paper dust jacket that is just about fine, remarkably nice.   Ken Lopez 74-206 1996 $250.00

HUXLEY, ALDOUS LEONARD 1894-1936   On the Margin. London: Chatto & Windus, 1923. 1st edition; still very near fine in bright, clean, crisp near fine dust jacket; exceptionaly copy.   Ken Lopez 74-207 1996 $250.00

HUXLEY, ALDOUS LEONARD 1894-1936   Point Counter Point. London: Chatto & Windus, 1928. 1st British edition; 8vo; orange cloth in dust jacket; fine, moderate edgewar, some soiling and faint stain to white dust jacket.   Antic Hay 101-880 1996 $225.00

HUXLEY, ALDOUS LEONARD 1894-1936   Selected Poems. Oxford: Basil Blackwell, 1926. 1st edition; although not explicityly stated, this issue was limited to 100 copies; signed by author on half title; decorated boards and with vellum spine, vellum very lightly spotted and tips slightly bumped, still near fine, without dust jacket, as issued.   Ken Lopez 74-212 1996 $375.00

HUXLEY, ALDOUS LEONARD 1894-1936   Themes and Variations. New York: Harper, 1950. 1st American edition; spine decoration bit rubbed, thus a very good copy, lacking dust jacket; this copy inscribed to British artist E. McKnight Kauffer and his wife Marion.   Between the Covers 42-232 1996 $375.00

HUXLEY, ALDOUS LEONARD 1894-1936   Those Barren Leaves. London: Chatto & Windus, 1925. 1st edition; fine in near fine dust jacket with minor wear along upper edge and slightly darkened spine, still very nice.   Ken Lopez 74-210 1996 $200.00

HUXLEY, ALDOUS LEONARD 1894-1936   Two or Three Graces and Other Stories. London: Chatto & Windus, 1926. 1st edition; slight mottling to extremities of cloth and rear gutter, otherwise near fine in dust jacket that is uniformly browned from acidification, otherwise crisp and near fine.   Ken Lopez 74-213 1996 $150.00

HUXLEY, ALDOUS LEONARD 1894-1936   Two or Three Graces. London: Chatto & Windus, 1926. 1st British edition; small 8vo; blue cloth in dust jacket, fine in near fine (little soiled) dust jacket.   Antic Hay 101-877 1996 $125.00

HUXLEY, LEONARD   Life and Letters of Thomas Henry Huxley. London: 1900. 1st edition; 8vo; 2 volumes, 11 plates, text illustrations; cloth; good.   John Henly 27-176 1996 £80.00

HUXLEY, THOMAS HENRY 1825-1895   Critiques and Addresses. London: Macmillan & Co., 1873. 1st edition; demy 8vo; (xvi), (352), 48 pages; original cloth, few very minor marks, some contemporary press cuttings inserted, but very good, bookplate.   Ash Rare Books Zenzybyr-54 1996 £75.00

HUXLEY, THOMAS HENRY 1825-1895   Lectures On the Elements of Comparative Anatomy... London: John Churchill & Sons, 1864. 1st edition; 8vo; 303, 31 pages; full page and in text illustrations; original brown cloth, traces of light foxing, else near fine.   Chapel Hill 94-305 1996 $225.00

HUXLEY, THOMAS HENRY 1825-1895   The Monkey. Northampton: Apiary Press, 1959. Number 34 of 60 copies, signed by artist; 14 x 10 inches; printed under the direction of Leoanrd Baskin, 10 full page and 3 smaller etchings by Thomas Browne Cornell, printed on Arnold's handmade collotype paper, copper and zinc plates etched from Nature and printed by Thomas Browne Cornell; green leather spine and green marbled paper boards, original green paper board slipcase; spine lightly worn, else fine.   Joshua Heller 21-48 1996 $1,000.00

HUXLEY, THOMAS HENRY 1825-1895   On Our Knowledge of the Causes of the Phenomena of Organic Nature. London: 1863. 1st edition; 156 pages; original binding.   W. Bruce Fye 71-1072 1996 $100.00

HUYSMANS, J. K.   Against the Grain. Lieber & Lewis, 1922. 1st American edition; fine in very good dust jacket with some slight wear, very scarce.   Aronovitz 57-582 1996 $250.00

HUYSMANS, J. K.   Down There (La Bas). New York: Albert & Charles Boni, 1924. 1st edition of Wallis's translation; black cloth, jacket edges bumped, hinges tender, jacket split at hinge, some chipping, still good; red dust jacket with cover illustration in red and black;   Priscilla Juvelis 95/1-130 1996 $120.00

HYAMS, E.   The Orchard and Fruit Garden, a New Pomona of Hardy and Sub Tropical Fruits. London: 1961. Tall 4to; pages xv, 208, 80 fine colored plates; cloth, dust jacket, minor edge wear.   Raymond M. Sutton VII-989 1996 $135.00

HYATT, THADDEUS   The Prayer of Thaddeus Hyatt to James Buchanan...in Behalf of Kansas, Asking for a Postponement of All the Land Sales in that Territory... Washington: Henry Polkinhorn Printer, 1860. 1st edition; 65 pages (blank) (67)-70 pages; original plain wrappers with Hyatt's signature on front wrappers, fine. Graff 2035; Dary Kanaza 86. Michael D. Heaston 23-177 1996 $350.00

HYDE, C. W. G.   History of the Great Northwest. Minneapolis: 1901. 1st edition; 592 pages; photos; professionally repaired with added slipcase for protection, lovely condition.   Early West 22-469 1996 $200.00

HYDE, CATHERINE   Secret Memoirs of the Royal Family of France During the Revolution. London: H. S. Nichols, 1895. Later edition, one of 500 copies; 8vo; 2 volumes, 332, 307 pages; contemporary three quarter brown morocco by Stikeman & Co., with gilt tooled spine panels, raised bands, top edges gilt, bookplate, boards little mottled, still very good. Chapel Hill 94-113 1996 $100.00

HYDE, DOUGLAS   The Three Sorrows of Storytelling and Ballads of St. Columkille. 1895. 1st edition; 8vo; ex-library in special cloth binding for Clery & Co. (Dublin Department Store), very good.   C. P. Hyland 216-342 1996 £50.00

HYDE, J. A. LLOYD   Oriental Lowestoft, with Special Reference to the Trade With China and the Porcelain Decorated for the American Market. New York: 1936. Number 330 of a limited edition; 4to; (viii), 162 pages, frontispiece and 30 plates; original cloth.   K Books 441-286 1996 £65.00

HYGINUS   The Poeticon Astronomicon. 1985. One of 140 copies, signed by Lewis and Dorthy Allen; 4to; printed in Garamond Bold and Solemnis in black, blue and Vermilion on Barcham Green handmade; decorated linen boards, fine in slipcase.   Bertram Rota 272-11 1996 £400.00

THE HYMNARY. A Book of Church Song. London: Novello, 1872. 2nd edition; large 8vo; pages xlv, 618; crimson morocco gilt, covers decorated by a seme of VA ciphers, each encircled by four s fernes, the borders carrying a verse between gilt fillets; spine in more restrained style, double gilt and blind ruled compartments, raised bands, all edges gilt, marbled endpapers. Bound by De Coverley.   Marlborough 160-69 1996 £200.00

HYNDMAN, HENRY MAYERS   The Economics of Socialism: Being a Series of Seven Lectures on Political Economy. London: Twentieth Century Press, 1896. 1st edition; 8vo; frontispiece, title printed in red and black; (4), iv, 257 pages, final ad leaf; original red cloth, lettered in black and gilt; very good. New Palgrave II 704. Einaudi (2973) for 3rd edition. John Drury 82-120 1996 £45.00

HYNDMAN, HENRY MAYERS   The Record of an Adventurous Life. (with) Further Reminiscences. London: 1911-12. 1st editions; large 8vo; 2 volumes; pages 470, 545; portrait; original cloth, first volume has library withdrawal stamp and flyleaf pasted down to inside cover, but good set. Howes Bookshop 265-554 1996 £65.00

HYNE, C. C.   The New Eden. L-G, 1892. 1st edition; inner hinges starting, otherwise very good+ copy, scarce.   Aronovitz 57-583 1996 $125.00

I

IBBETSON, J. H.   Specimens in Eccentric Circular Turning... London: 1838. 3rd edition; 8vo; decorative title, pages iv, 5-176, 2 folding engraved plates of apparatus, 27 specimens on 17 leaves, comprising frontispiece and 1-6 engraved, the rest woodcut, numerous text figures and 2 further woodcuts on separate leaves, cloth, stained, repaired. Abell 159.   Maggs Bros. Ltd. 1190-642 1996 £160.00

IBSEN, HENRIK   The Doll's House. New York: D. Appleton & Co., 1889. 1st American edition; octavo; 148, (4 ads) pages; original white cloth over decorative green boards, some soiling to covers and spine, bright, attractive copy, contemporary ownership signature.   Heritage Book Shop 196-244 1996 $275.00

IBSEN, HENRIK   The Doll's House. New York: 1889. 1st U.S. edition; cloth and decorated boards; near fine.   Stephen Lupack 83- 1996 $150.00

IBSEN, HENRIK   Hedda Gabler. Kobenhavn: Gyldendalske, 1890. 1st edition; original printed wrappers, backstrip and lower cover slightly defective, rear wrapper loose. PMM 375.   Dramatis Personae 37-94 1996 $400.00

IBSEN, HENRIK   Peer Gynt. London: George G. Harrap & Co., 1936. One of 450 copies, signed by artist; 10 3/4 x 8 1/4 inches; 255, (1) pages, (1) leaf (colophon); color frontispiece & 11 other color plates by Arthur Rackham, each with printed tissue guard, color vignettes on title and half title, several other illustrations in text, mostly as tailpieces; very handsome cinnamon colored crushed morocco by Bayntun, covers framed with French fillet and featuring ealborate floral cornerpieces, raised bands, spine densely gilt in compartments, marbled endpapers, wide turn-ins decorated like covers, top edge gilt, other edges untrimmed, extremely fine in quite handsome binding.   Phillip J. Pirages 33-443 1996 $1,600.00

IBSEN, HENRIK   Poems. New York: Vincent Fitz Gerald, 1988. 1st edition in English, one of 75 copies; page size 8 1/2 x 11 1/2 inches; 6 etchings by Nell Welliver; printed on handmade Dieu Donne paper by Dan Keleher at the Wild Carrot Letterpress in Perpetua;   Priscilla Juvelis 95/1-259 1996 $4,000.00

IBSEN, HENRIK   Three Plays. Oslo: Limited Editions Club, 1964. One of 1500 copies, signed by artist; 8vo; wood engravings by Frederik Matheson; half leather; fine in case.   Charles Agvent 4-705 1996 $125.00

IBY TUFAYL, MUHAMMUD IBN ABD AL-MALIK   The Improvement of Human Reason, Exhibited in the Life of Hai Ebn Yokdhan: Written in Arabick above 500 Years Ago... London: printed for W. Blay, 1711. 2nd edition; 8vo; 195, (1) pages; frontispiece and 1 plate; contemporary vellum, vellum soiled, scattered foxing and browning; good to very good. 2 copies in NUC.   Robert F. Lucas 42-4 1996 $500.00

ICELANDIC Sagas and Other Historical Documents Relating to the Settlements and Descents of the Northmen on the British Isles. London: 1887-94. 8vo; 4 volumes, facsimiles; original cloth.   Howes Bookshop 265-1601 1996 £125.00

IDES, E. YSBRANDT   Three Years Travels from Moscow Over-Land to China...an Exact and Particular Description of the Extent and Limits of Those Countries and the Customs of the Barbarous Inhabitants... London: W. Freeman et al, 1706. 1st edition in English; 4to; (14), 210 pages, added engraved titlepage (dated 1705), large folding map, 30 engraved plates; contemporary panelled calf, finely rebound, old spine laid down, very nice, fresh copy.   Kenneth Karmiole 1NS-247 1996 $2,000.00

IGNATOW, DAVID   Ten Poems. New York: Silver Hands Press, 1981. 1st edition; one of 129 copies (from a total of 155), signed by author; decorated wrappers; fine.   Captain's Bookshelf 38-119 1996 $125.00

ILLINGWORTH, A. HOLDEN   More Reminiscences. Bradford: privately printed, 1936. Color and other plates; scarce. Lovely.   David A.H. Grayling 3/95-460 1996 £90.00

ILLINGWORTH, CAYLEY   A Topographical Account of the Parish of Scampton in the County of Lincoln and of the Roman Antiquities Lately Discovered There... London: Cadell, 1810. 4to: (8), 64 pages, 2 engraved hand colored maps, 11 engraved plates, one engraved vignette; contemporary russia gilt, some marginal dampstaining, one plate shaved. Anderson p. 172; UCBA p. 903; cf. Martin p. 177.   Marlborough 162-51 1996 £135.00

ILLINGWORTH, W. H.   More Reminiscences. 1936. Colored and other plates; original buckram; one stamp an ownership signataure with label pasted over it on front endpaper, otherwise near fine.   David A.H. Grayling 3/95-461 196 £85.00

ILLINOIS SUNDAY SCHOOL UNION   Proceedings of the Fourth Annual Meeting of the Illinois Sunday School Union, Held at the State House in Vandalia, Dec. 4, 1833. Rock Spring: Ashford Smith, 1834. 1st edition; 8vo; 19, (1) pages; removed, uncut. Byrd 154 (1 copy).   M & S Rare Books 60-345 1996 $150.00

ILLUSTRATED Ditties of the Olden Time. London: Henry G. bohn, 1854. Square 8vo; engraved on (30) leaves; original blue cloth, edges gilt, by Burn, with ticket, casing weak, otherwise clean, very good to nice copy; last leaf signed 'G. Inglis fecit".   James Fenning 133-246 1996 £65.00

ILLUSTRATIONS of Japanese Aquatic Plants and Animals. Tokyo: 1935. Large oblong folio; 2 volumes; 100 large fine colored printed plates; cloth. Lower outer corner of volume 1 bumped.   Wheldon & Wesley 207-53 1996 £400.00

ILLUSTRATIONS Of Northern Antiquities from the Earlier Teutonic and Scandinavian Romances. Edinburgh: Longman, etc., 1848. 1st edition; very tall, wide quarto; large paper copy; pages ix, 522; contemporary full polished calf, gilt rules, blind tooling, raised bands, spine gilt in compartments, all edges marbled, spine skillfully rehinged, else very good, tall copy. Scarce. Lowndes II 996.   Hartfield 48-L42 1996 $495.00

IMITATIO CHRISTI   The Imitation of Christ. London: Chapman and Hall, n.d. 1st edition; 8vo; full calf, beautifully bound by Sangorski & Sutcliffe, inscription, light rubbing, near fine.   Charles Agvent 4-1121 1996 $175.00

IMITATIO CHRISTI   De Imitatione Christi Libri Quatuor. Parma: In Aedibvs Palatinis, Typis Bodonianis, 1793. Limited to 162 copies; folio; pages 7, 311, this copy printed on paper water marked with monstrance and initials "FB" and with a fleur-de-lys and initials "SB", uncut and deckle edged, foxed at edges; contemporary full green morocco gilt, crowned (Imperial?) royal stamp at corners of boards, boards edged with wide floral roll; Brunet III 415; Brooks 484.   Family Album Tillers-619 1996 $1,750.00

IMITATIO CHRISTI   L'Imitation de Jesus-Christ. Paris: Curmer, 1856-58. 4to; 2 volumes, 4 full page plates, ca. 400 pages, all with chromolithographic borders by Lemercier; purple morocco, richly gilt, buff onlays, inner borders gilt and stamped by binder, David, the spines gilt in compartments, raised bands, all edges gilt, watered green silk endpapers.   Marlborough 160-65 1996 £1,250.00

IMMERWAHR, SARA ANDERSON   The Neolithic and Bronze Ages. Princeton: ASCSA, 1971. Large 4to; color frontispiece, xx, 286 pages, 3 figures and 92 plates; original cloth, 2 corners lightly bumped.   Archaeologia Luxor-3499 1996 $250.00

IMMIGRATION AND DEVELOPMENT ASSOCIATION   Harris County Houston, Texas Home Seekers Journal. Houston: A. C. Gray Printer, 1888. 1st edition; elephant folio; 8 pages, maps and illustrations; original pictorial grey wrappers; fine.   Michael D. Heaston 23-174 1996 $1,500.00

AN IMPARTIAL Account, of the Nature and Tendency, of the Late Addresses; in a Letter to a Gentleman in the Countrey. London: printed for R. Baldwin, 1681. Folio; 12 pages; disbound, margins cropped. Wing I 73a.   H. M. Fletcher 121-35 1996 £60.00

IMPORTANT Communication, from the Highest Authortiy, to Those Who Are Embracing Arms in Defence of Their Country; as Well as to All Military Men. London: printed and sold by D. Lewis, sold also by T. Egerton, 1804. 1st edition? 8vo; 16 pages; disbound.   James Burmester 29-128 1996 £85.00

THE IMPRINT. 1913. 4to; complete set, 9 parts; plates and figures; original wrappers, cloth box, many wrappers torn and frayed, pieces missing from some.   Thomas Thorp 489-166 1996 £180.00

THE IMPROVED Reading and Spelling Made Easy. Dublin: printed by C. M. Warren, 21 Upper Ormonde Quay, ca. 1840. 12mo; printed in large type, full page alphabet, many woodcuts; 71 pages; original unlettered orange paper wrappers; nice.   James Fenning 133-282 1996 £65.00

INAN, JALE   Roman and Early Byzantine Portrait Sculpture in Asia Minor. London: British Academy, 1970. 4to; xxv, 244 pages, 187 plates; original cloth, dust jacket.   Archaeologia Luxor-3501 1996 $150.00

INCIDENT on the Bark Columbia. Cummington: Cummington Press, 1941. Limited to 300 copies; octavo; (52) pages; bound in beige linen; very fine.   Bromer Booksellers 87-52 1996 $175.00

INCIDENTS and Sketches Connected with the Early History and Settlement of the West. Cincinnati: U. P. James, ca. 1847. 1st edition; 8vo; numerous illustrations; original printed wrappers, publisher's ads on back wrapper, some light soiling and browning of wrapper, chipping at head of back wrapper and lower edges, some light spotting or browning of text, but very nice. Howes I 19.   James Cummins 14-220 1996 $175.00

INDIAN Basket Weaving by the Navajo School of Indian Basketry. Los Angeles: Whedon & Spreng Co., 1903. 1st and only edition; 103 pages; profusely illustrated, mostly from photos; original woven covers printed in red, tied at spine, minor soiling to covers and front endpapers; fine, extremely scarce.   Argonaut Book Shop 113-363 1996 $250.00

INDIAN Population in the United States and Alaska 1910. Washington: 1915. 1st edition; 285 pages; maps, folding map; cloth, nice, scarce. T. A. Swinford 49-583 1996 $125.00

INDIAN TERRITORY   The Seventh Annual Report of the Superintendent and Agents of the Central Indian Superintendency, with Carefully Revised Statistical Table... Lawrence: Journal Steam Book and Job Printing House, 1876. 1st edition; 79, (1) pages; original grey printed wrappers, several minor holes to front wrpaper, not affecting text, minor chipping, very good. Kansas Imprints Inventory 1564. Not in Gilcrease Hargrett. Michael D. Heaston 23-182 1996 $550.00

INDIAN TERRITORY   The Eighth Annual Report of the Superintendent and Agents of the Central Indian Superintendency... Lawrence: Republican Journal Steam Printing Establishment, 1876. 1st edition; 79 pages; original printed green wrappers, minor stain to margin, very good. Kansas Imprints Inventory 1565; not in Gilcrease Hargrett.   Michael D. Heaston 23-183 1996 $550.00

INDIAN TERRITORY   Journal of the Fifth Annual Session of the General Council of the Indian Territory, Composed of Delegates Duly Elected from the Indian Tribes Legally Resident Therein, Assembled in Council at Okmulgee, Indian Territory, from the 4th to 14th day May 1874. Lawrence: Journal Steam Book and Job Printing House, 1874. 1st edition; 58 pages; original grey printed wrappers; fine. Kansas Imprints Inventory 1222. Gilcrease Hargrett p. 215.   Michael D. Heaston 23-180 1996 $500.00

INDIAN TERRITORY   Journal of the Sixth Annual Session of the General Council of the Indian Territory, Composed of Delegates Duly Elected from the Indian Tribes Legally Resident Therein, Assembled in Council on Okmulgee, Indian Territory from 3rd to 15th May, 1875. Lawrence: Republican Journal Steam Printing Establishment, 1875. 1st edition; 114 pages; original pale green wrappers, spine rebacked, else very good. Kansas Imprints Inventory 1350; Graff 2103; Gilcrease Hargrett p. 215.   Michael D. Heaston 23-181 1996 $500.00

INDIANA. LAWS, STATUTES, ETC.   The Revised Laws of Indiana, in Which are Comprised All Such Acts of a General Nature As Are in Force in Said State; Adopted and Enacted by the General Assembly at their Fifteenth Session. Indianapolis: Printed by Douglas and Maguire, 1831. 8vo; 596 pages; full contemporary calf with morocco spine label, rubbed, notations on front free endpaper, foxing, else very good. Byrd & Peckham Bib. of Indiana Imprints 1804-1853 no. 435.   Andrew Cahan 47-92 1996 $200.00

AN INFALLIBLE Remedy for the High Prices of Provisions. Together with a Scheme for Laying Open the Trade to the East Indies. London: printed for William Bingley, 1768. 1st edition; 8vo; no half title, 40 pages, 7 page publisher catalog at end; modern cloth backed boards; Kress 6562; Higgs 6676; not in Goldsmith.   Anthony W. Laywood 109-151 1996 £120.00

THE INFANT'S Grammar, or a Pic-Nic Party of the Parts of Speech. London: Harris & Son, 1822. 12mo; pages 13, (1) (ads) (i.e. 28); 11 hand colored wood engravings at head of pages with text below, printed on one side of sheet only, single sewn gathering in printed stiff buff card wrappers, title and engraving on uper side, small circular engraving of view surrounded by series title within single line border on lower; excellent. Osborne II p. 715.   Blackwell's B112-69 1996 £225.00

INGE, WILLIAM   Come Back Little Sheba. New York: Random House, 1950. 1st edition; author's first book; fine in dust jacket, laid in is a brie TLS signed Bill dated 1962.   Left Bank Books 2-58 1996 $140.00

INGELEFIELD, JOHN NICHOLSON   Capt. Inglefield's Narrative, Concerning the Loss of H.M.S. the Centaur of Seventy-Four Guns... London: for J. Murray and A. Donaldson, 1783. New edition; 8vo; 36 pages + 2 leaves, half title dust stained, last 2 leaves foxed; disbound. H. M. Fletcher 121-104 1996 £70.00

INGHOLT, HAROLD   Gandharan Art in Pakistan. New York: Panetheon Books, 1957. 1st edition; 203 pages, text and 577 black and white plates; very fine in dust jacket in original publisher's slipcase with few seams just starting.   Hermitage SP95-786 1996 $275.00

INGLIS, JOHN   An Examination of Mr. Dugald Stewart's Pamphlet, Relative to the Late Election of a Mathemataical Professor in the University of Edinburgh. Edinburgh: printed for Peter Hill and for Longman, etc., London, 1805. 1st edition; 8vo; disbound; half title present and an inserted slip containing a last minute correction, old library stamp on titlepage, otherwise very good, very scarce. Jessop p 180.   Ximenes 109-163 1996 $250.00

INGRAHAM, J. H.   The Clipper-Yacht; or Moloch, the Money Lender! Boston: H. L. Williams, 1845. 1st edition; 8vo; 54, (4) pages, removed, lacks wrappers. BAL 9979; Wright I 1276; Singerman 0898.   M & S Rare Books 60-180 1996 $125.00

INGRAHAM, J. h.   The South-West. New York: Harper & Bros., 1835. 1st edition; 12mo; 2 volumes; full contemporary polished leather, gilt decorated spine and edging, marbled endpapers, very likely a publisher's presentation binding; Presentation from the author. BAL 9929; Wright I 349; Howes I 49.   M & S Rare Books 60-181 1996 $4,500.00

INGRAHAM, JOSEPH   Joseph Ingraham's Journal of the Britantine Hope on a Voyage to the Northwest Coast of North America 1790-92. Barre: Imprint Society, 1971. fine in slipcase.   Hermitage SP95-921 1996 $125.00

INGRAM, DALE   Practical Cases and Observations in Surgery with Remarks Highly Proper, Not Only for the Improvement of All Young Surgeons. London: J. Clarke, 1751. 8vo; xxxii, 245, (iii), with two plates; contemporary full calf, skillfully rebacked with original spine laid down, other than some light foxing of text, clean crisp copy.   James Tait Goodrich K40-165 1996 $595.00

INGRAM, JAMES   Memorials of Oxford. Oxford: John Henry Parker, 1837. 1st edition; large paper set; 3 volumes; title vignettes, 99 steel engraved plates and numerous wood engravings; brown morocco with large gilt central cover ornament, other gilt decorations, gilt banded and decorated spine; slight rubbing, but generally fine set, inner hinge of volume 1 cracked.   Marilyn Braiterman 15-133 1996 $650.00

INMAN, HENRY   Buffalo Jones' Forty Years of Adventure. London: 1899. 1st English edition; 469 pages, photos; book in fine condition, front hinge barely starting, with bright pictorial covers and added protective slipcase.   Early West 22-595 1996 $225.00

INMAN, HENRY   The Old Santa Fe Trail: the Story of a Great Highway. New York: 1897. 1st edition; 493 pages; folding map, illustrations by Frederic Remington; book fine with bright binding, protective slipcase added. Rittenhouse 323.   Early West 22-591 1996 $175.00

INNERLEITHEN ALPINE CLUB   Principal Excursions of the Innerleithen Alpine Club During the Years 1889-94. London: 1895. 1st edition; 16 plates; gilt lettering on silver grey boards, edges gilt; fine. Moutaineering Books 8-E101 1996 £80.00

INNES, COSMO   Lectures on Scotch Legal Antiquities. Edinburgh: Edmonston & Douglas, 1872. Modern three quarter brown morocco, quite clean and attractive.   Meyer Boswell SL26-121 1996 $275.00

INNES, HAMMOND   The Conquistadors. London: Collins, 1969. 1st edition; limited to 265 numbered copies, signed by author; crown 4to; (ii), 336 pages, numerous illustrations, many in color; bound by Zaehnsdorf, original full morocco with colored onlay to an Aztec design all edges gilt, few very minor marks, but very good, in original box. Ash Rare Books Zenzybyr-55 1996 £195.00

INNESS, GEORGE   The Works of Geroge Inness: an Illustrated Catalogue Raisonne. Austin: University of Texas Press, 1965. 1st edition; illustrations; light spotting to top and fore-edge, otherwise fine in lightly worn dust jacket.   Hermitage SP95-787 1996 $850.00

INNIS, HAROLD A.   The Fur Trade in Canada; an Introduction to Canadian Economic History. New Haven: Yale University Press, 1930. 24cm; (xiv), 444 pages, illustrations, map; fine in neatly repaired dust jacket; beautiful copy Peel 3190.   Rockland Books 38-99 1996 $125.00

AN INQUIRY Into the Rights of Free Subjects; in Which the Cases of the British Sailors and Common Soldiers are Distinctly Consider'd and Compar'd. London: M. Cooper, 1749. 1st edition; 8vo; iv, (5)-84 pages; recent linen backed marbled boards, lettered; very good; rare. Hansom 6380; not in Goldsmiths or Kress.   John Drury 82-121 1996 £175.00

INQUISITIONS and Assessments Relating to Feudal Aids. London: 1899-1920. Thick royal 8vo; 6 volumes; strongly bound in buckram, from library with bookplate and stamp. Mullins 3.37; Gross/Graves 4341. Howes Bookshop 265-1528 1996 £225.00

INSCRIPTIONS on the Great Picture at Appleby Castle, Painted for the Right Honourable George Clifford, Third Earl of Cumberland. Appleby: J. Whitehead, 1877. Small 4to; pages 27, margins ruled in red; original cloth, spine and edges faded; extremely scarce; from the library of Daniel Scott of Penrith, with his label and pencilled signature.   R.F.G. Hollett & Son 78-57 1996 £175.00

INSTRUCTIONS for Officers and Non-Commissioned Officers On Outpost and Patrol Duty and Troops in Campaign. Washington: GPO, 1863. 1st edition; 8vo; 88 pages; illustrations; printed wrappers; rear wrapper missing, approximately 1 1/2 inch of blank bottom of final leaf torn off, affecting two words 'shall still', front wrapper soiled and stained, oil stain on first few leaves, overall condition fair; scarce. Ink signature of "W.H. Burbank" repeated approximately 8 times scattered through the manual, pencil signature and information of E. B. Holt, of 3rd Regt. N.H. V.   Robert F. Lucas 42-19 1996 $200.00

INSTRUCTIONS For Such Merchants and Others Who Shall Have Commissions, or Letters of Marque, or Commissions for Private Men of War Against Against the French King His Subjects...Given at Our Court at Whitehal the 2d Day of May 1693... No Imprint, 1693. Folio; 7, (i) pages; disbound, outer leaves rather dusty, minor staining and foxing, edges little chipped well clear of text.   Robert Clark 38-66 1996 £450.00

INTERNATIONAL CONGRESS OF CLASSICAL ARCHAEOLOGY   The Proceedings of the Xth International Congress of Classical Archaeology, Ankara - Izmir 23-30/IX/1973. Ankara: Turk Tarih Kurumu, 1978. 8vo; 3 volumes, xxix, 1138 pages, numerous figures and plans, 360 plates; original upper wrappers, mounted to upper buckram boards, some corners lightly bumped.   Archaeologia Luxor-2889 1996 $125.00

THE INTRIGUING Courtiers; or, The Modish Gallants...Wherein the Secret Histories of Several Persons are...Represented. London: printed for W. James, 1732. 8vo; new half calf, corner of title torn away and made up (no text loss), minor stains. Gagey p. 179.   Peter Murray Hill 185-4 1996 £90.00

INTRODUCTION to American Indian Art, to Accompany the First Exhibition of American Indian Art Selected Entirely with Consideration of Esthetic Value. Expostion of Indian Tribunal Arts, 1931. 2 parts, black and white, color plates tipped in, 55 pages; black and white illustrations; original wrappers, part 1 heavily chipped and nicked,, part 2 spine missing, else very good.   Ken Sanders 8-165 1996 $150.00

IONESCO, EUGENE   Journeys Among the Dead. Limited Editions Club, 1987. One of 1000 copies, signed by author; 4 color lithographs; as new in slipcase.   Lyman Books 21-583 1996 $125.00

IONESCO, EUGENE   Story Number 1, 2 and 3 for Children Under Three Years of Age. New York: Harlin Quist, 1968-70. 1st illustrated editions; quarto; 3 volumes; (26), (18), (29) pages; illustrations; each volume bound in cloth with matching pictorial dust jacket, fine set with only lighest rubbing to extremities.   Bromer Booksellers 87-135 1996 $125.00

IQBAL   Iqbal Poet of the East. N.P.: Nisar Art Press, n.d., ca. 1962. Folio; (16), 30, 302 unnumbered pages; 36 tipped in plates, 24 black and white plates, 10 decorative chapter headings in color and numerous other illustrations, printed within decorative borders, all illustrations by Chughtai; original cloth, in dust jacket and in original protective cloth and board slipcase which is lined in silk.   Worldwide Antiquarian 151-320 1996 $350.00

IRBY, L. HOWARD   The Ornithology of the Straits of Gibralter. R. H. Porter, 1895. 4to; viii, 326 pages; 13 plates, 8 chromolithographs, 21 text illustrations, 2 folding maps; contemporary green half morocco, gilt panelled sides, heraldic arms on cover, spine gilt in 6 compartments, top edge gilt, covers very slightly worn, nice.   Thomas Thorp 489-167 1996 £600.00

IRBY, L. HOWARD   The Ornithology of the Straits of Gibraltar... London: 1895. 2nd edition; folio; 2 maps, 8 chromolithographs after Thorburn; marginal waterstain on several plates; red cloth, gilt, new endpapers, else not a bad copy.   Maggs Bros. Ltd. 1190-573 1996 £225.00

IREDALE, T.   Birds of New Guinea. Melbourne: 1956. 4to; 2 volumes, 35 colored plates, map; original quarter morocco.   Wheldon & Wesley 207-776 1996 £330.00

IREDALE, T.   Birds of Paradise. Melbourne: 1950. 4to; xii, 239 pages 33 colored plates, map; original quarter leather.   Wheldon & Wesley 207-775 1996 £220.00

IRELAND, ALEXANDER   The Book-Lover's Enchiridion. London: and New York: Macmillan, 1894. 7 x 5 inches; xviii pages, 1 leaf, 511 pages; largely unopened, title in red and black; very pretty green straight grain half morocco by Hatchards, pale green cloth sides, spine compartments and broad raised bands, ruled in gilt, marbled endpapers, top edge gilt, very fine.   Phillip J. Pirages 33-314 1996 $100.00

IRELAND, ALEXANDER   Emerson: His Life, Genius & Writings. London: Simpkin Marshall, 1882. 2nd edition; original blue cloth, label; scarce; Myerson D123; BAL III 68 col. 1.   Mac Donnell 12-44 1996 $100.00

IRELAND, M. W.   The Medical Department of the U.S. Army in the World War. Washington: 1921-29. 17 volumes; illustrations, colored charts, tables; ex-library, but fine set with minimal markings. GM 2179. W. Bruce Fye 71-1438 1996 $950.00

IRELAND, SAMUEL d. 1800   Picturesque Views on the River Medway. London: Egerton, 1793. Large 8vo; half title, 1 f., title, pages v-xii, 206, 1 f., frontispiece, engraved title, 27 plates, all aquatint, engraved map; tree calf, gilt spine, label. Pleasing copy. Prideaux pp. 270/1.   Marlborough 162-52 1996 £300.00

IRELAND, SAMUEL d. 1800   Picturesque Views on the River Wye... London: Faulder, 1797. 4to; pages xii, 159 engraved map, engraved portrait, 4 woodcut text illustrations, 30 sepia aquatint plates; diced russia gilt, rebacked, corners bumped some margins dusty. Abbey Scenery 544.   Marlborough 162-53 1996 £375.00

IRELAND, SAMUEL d. 1800   Picturesque Views, with an Historical Account of the Inns of Court in London and Westminster. London: C. Clark, 1800. 8vo; xvi, 254, (i errata) pages, 21 aquatint plates, 2 text illustrations; contemporary half calf, slightly scuffed. Inscribed "John Crickett, Esqr. & From the Extors of the late Saml. Ireland". Adams 81; Abbey Scenery 207.   Marlborough 162-156 1996 £360.00

IRELAND, W. H.   The Life of Napoleon Bonaparte. London: Published by John Cumberland, 1828. 1st edition; 1st issue; octavo; 4 volumes; engraved vignette titles, 26 folding aquatint plates, 24 hand colored, 1 folding tinted engraved plate, all by George Cruikshank; contemporary full calf, gilt double rule border on covers, gilt spine, tooled in compartments, gilt board edges, marbled edges, and turn-ins; excellent set.   Heritage Book Shop 196-193 1996 $2,250.00

IRELAND, WILLIAM   Scribbleomania, or the Printer's Devil's Polychronicon, a Sublime Poem. London: Sherwood, 1815. 1st edition; tall 8vo; pages 320; three quarter polished calf, gilt extra, panelled spine, leather label, marbled boards and endpapers, some wear, unobtrusive library markings, attractive copy, scarce. CBEL II 236.   Hartfield 48-L43 1996 $295.00

IRELAND, WILLIAM WOTHERSPOON   The Mental Affections of Children: Idiocy, Imbecility and Insanity. Philadelphia: P. Blakiston's Son & Co., 1900. 1st U.S. edition; 8vo; (xii), 450 pages, 14 pages of ads, 21 plates, 11 text illustrations, panelled thatched blue-green cloth,f ront flyleaf detached; good to very good, with titlepage stamp and spine numbers of Hartford Retreat; with Jelliffe's bookplate. Cordaso 00-1670. John Gach 150-221 1996 $100.00

THE IRISH Compendium or, Rudiments of Honour. 1756. 8vo; 564 pages; 85 plates; contemporary calf (worn), text very good.   C. P. Hyland 216-346 1996 £75.00

IRON BRIDGE ASSOCIATION   General Descriptive Treatise on Iron Bridges Applied to Roads and Railways, Together With a Full Description of the Radiating, Parallel Inclined... London: 1857. 4to; 8 pages, 3 litho plates (1 tinted); some ms. amendments to text; seemly modern wrappers, preserved in pamphlet case.   Elton Engineering 10-81 1996 £450.00

IRVING, C.   Daughter of Egypt. Allan, 1937. 1st edition; near fine in attractive full color pictorial dust jacket, with some wear and tear and chipping, very scarce in dust jacket.   Aronovitz 57-586 1996 $110.00

IRVING, JOHN 1942-   The Cider House Rules. Franklin Center: Franklin Library, 1985. Signed, limited edition with special message from Irving, true first edition; very fine.   Bev Chaney, Jr. 23-334 1996 $125.00

IRVING, JOHN 1942-   The Cider House Rules. Franklin Center: Franklin Library, 1985. Limited edition, signed by author on tipped in leaf; leather bound, all edges gilt, silk ribbon marker; fine.   Ken Lopez 74-226 1996 $125.00

IRVING, JOHN 1942-   The Cider House Rules. Franklin Center: Franklin Library, 1985. Franklin Library signed first edition; decorated full leather; fine.   Lame Duck Books 19-261 1996 $100.00

IRVING, JOHN 1942-   Cider House Rules. New York: Morrow, 1985. Advance Reading copy, issued prior to publication, when the trade jacket was reportedly not ready; fine in near fine tissue paper dust jacket with one small quarter inch closed tear at fold.   Anacapa House 5-163 1996 $125.00

IRVING, JOHN 1942-   The Cider House Rules. New York: William Morrow, 1985. 1/250 numbered signed copies; very fine in massive slipcase.   Bev Chaney, Jr. 23-335 1996 $200.00

IRVING, JOHN 1942-   The Cider House Rules. New York: William Morrow, 1985. 1st edition; signed by author; thick 8vo; cloth backed boards, dust jacket; fine.   James S. Jaffe 34-292 1996 $100.00

IRVING, JOHN 1942-   The Cider House Rules. New York: Morrow, 1985. 1st trade edition; slightly cocked, else near fine in dust jacket; signed by author.   Lame Duck Books 19-262 1996 $100.00

IRVING, JOHN 1942-   The Hotel New Hampshire. London: Cape, 1981. Uncorrected proof of the first British edition; wrappers, near fine.   Ken Lopez 74-224 1996 $100.00

IRVING, JOHN 1942-   Hotel New Hampshire. New York: William Morrow, 1981. 1/550 signed and numbered copies; fine in slipcase. Bev Chaney, Jr. 23-337 1996 $135.00

IRVING, JOHN 1942-   The Hotel New Hampshire. New York: Dutton, 1981. 1st edition; near fine in dust jacket, signed by author.   Lame Duck Books 19-259 1996 $200.00

IRVING, JOHN 1942-   The Hotel New Hampshire. New York: Dutton, 1981. 1st edition; fine in dust jacket; inscribed by author, uncommon thus.   Between the Covers 42-235 1996 $150.00

IRVING, JOHN 1942-   The Hotel New Hampshire. New York: Dutton, 1982. Uncorrected proof, wrappers, publisher's errata slip laid in; fine. Ken Lopez 74-223 1996 $150.00

IRVING, JOHN 1942-   The 158-Pound Marriage. New York: RH, 1974. 1st edition; very near fine in dust jacket with minor crease to front flap, signed by author.   Lame Duck Books 19-254 1996 $400.00

IRVING, JOHN 1942-   The 158-Pound Marriage. New York: Random House, 1974. 1st edition; near fine in near fine dust jacket.   Ken Lopez 74-218 1996 $150.00

IRVING, JOHN 1942-   The 158 Pound Marriage. New York: Random House, 1974. 1st edition; fine in just about fine dust jacket with touch of wear at spine ends.   Between the Covers 42-234 1996 $135.00

IRVING, JOHN 1942-   The 158 Pound Marriage. New York: Random, 1974. 1st edition; near fine in dust jacket with some edge wear, relatively scarce.   Anacapa House 5-162 1996 $125.00

IRVING, JOHN 1942-   The Pension Grillparzer. Logan: Perfection Form Co., 1980. 1st separate appearance; illustrated stapled wrappers; very near fine.   Lame Duck Books 19-258 1996 $150.00

IRVING, JOHN 1942-   A Prayer for Owen Meany. New York: Morrow, 1989. One of a limited edition of 250 copies, numbered and signed by author; fine in cloth covered slipcase.   Lame Duck Books 19-263 1996 $150.00

IRVING, JOHN 1942-   The Water-Method Man. New York: RH, 1972. 1st edition; review copy, near fine in dust jacket with light wear to extremities and with review slips and publicity photo laid in.   Lame Duck Books 19-252 1996 $250.00

IRVING, JOHN 1942-   The Water-Method Man. New York: RH, 1972. 1st edition; slightly spine cocked, else near fine in very good+ dust jacket, signed by author, uncommon thus.   Lame Duck Books 19-253 1996 $450.00

IRVING, JOHN 1942-   The Water-Method Man. New York: Random House, 1972. 1st edition; very slight spine slant, otherwise fine in very near fine dust jacket.   Ken Lopez 74-216 1996 $275.00

IRVING, JOHN 1942-   The Water Method Man. New York: Random House, 1972. 1st edition; (6906 copies); slight mar to upper right corner of flyleaf where price sticker removed, otherwise fine in dust jacket. Steven C. Bernard 71-131 1996 $175.00

IRVING, JOHN 1942-   The Water Method Man. New York: Random House, 1972. 1st edition; 8vo; cloth backed boards dust jacket, fine; signed by author.   James S. Jaffe 34-291 1996 $125.00

IRVING, JOHN 1942-   The World According to Garp. London: Gollancz, 1978. 1st British edition; fine in near fine dust jacket radically different in design from that of the American edition.   Ken Lopez 74-222 1996 $150.00

IRVING, JOHN 1942-   The World According to Garp. New York: Dutton, 1978. Uncorrected proof, reputed first issue proof, in mustard colored wrappers; near fine, inscribed by author.   Ken Lopez 74-219 1996 $850.00

IRVING, JOHN 1942-   The World According to Garp. New York: Dutton, 1978. 1st edition; uncorrected proof; this being the issue in green wrappers; near fine, scarce.   Ken Lopez 74-220 1996 $650.00

IRVING, JOHN 1942-   The World According to Garp. New York: Dutton, 1978. Advance reading copy; printed wrappers, very good. Ken Lopez 74-221 1996 $250.00

IRVING, JOHN 1942-   The World According to Garp. New York: Dutton, 1978. 1st edition; advance reading copy; white printed wrappers with publisher's prospectus and erratum slip laid in; near fine.   Lame Duck Books 19-255 1996 $150.00

IRVING, JOHN 1942-   The World According to Garp. New York: Dutton, 1978. 1st U.S. edition; slightly cocked, else near fine in dust jacket, signed by author.   Lame Duck Books 19-256 1996 $300.00

IRVING, WASHINGTON 1783-1859   Astoria, or Anecdotes of an Enterprise Beyond the Rocky Mountains. Philadelphia: Carey, Lea & Blanchard, 1836. 1st edition; 1st state; 2 volumes; folding map; Binding B; contemporary signature, f.f.e.p. missing small section, light foxing, near fine. BAL 10148.   Charles Agvent 4-708 1996 $600.00

IRVING, WASHINGTON 1783-1859   Astoria; or, Anecdotes of an Enterprise Beyond the Rocky Mountains. New York: Putnam's, 1897. Tacoma edition; 2 volumes; cover and page designs by Margaret Armstrong, photos and illustrations by Rufus Zogbaum and others; purplish red gilt stamped cloth somewhat dulled on spines, mild wear started at spine ends, bright and fresh otherwise, few minimal marks to covers and texts. Howes 181; Wagner Camp Becker 61.   Magnum Opus 44-45 1996 $135.00

IRVING, WASHINGTON 1783-1859   A Chronicle of the Conquest of Granada. London: John Murray, 1829. 1st English edition; 8vo; 2 volumes; beautifully bound by Riviere in three quarter maroon morocco with fine gilt detail on spines, fine. BAL 10126.   Charles Agvent 4-709 1996 $400.00

IRVING, WASHINGTON 1783-1859   The Gentleman in Black and Tales of Other Days. London: printed for Charles Daly, 1840. 8vo; (vi), iv, (ii), 392 pages, frontispiece and title darkened, front hinge starting; extra engraved title, 18 plates and vignettes by George Cruikshank and others; full tan calf, split along front joint, head of spine chipped, spine in 6 panels with raised bands and floral decorations in gilt, gilt rules, gilt lettered leather labels on spine, all edges gilt, original dark brown cloth from covers mounted in, including original spine with Cruikshank vignette in gilt; very good. BAL 10321.   Blue Mountain SP95-62 1996 $125.00

IRVING, WASHINGTON 1783-1859   A History of New York, from the Beginning of the World to the End of the Dutch Dynasty... New York: Inskeep & Bradford, 1809. 1st edition; 12mo; 2 volumes; folding view; contemporary tree sheep, maroon morocco labels, minimal repair to head of spine, cloth case, very nice. Grolier 100 American 28.   19th Century Shop 39- 1996 $2,500.00

IRVING, WASHINGTON 1783-1859   A History of New York... New York: pub. by Inskeep & Bradford; Bradford & Inskeep, Philadelphia... 1809. 1st edition; 12mo; 2 volumes; folding engraved frontispiece (slight wear at folds; fine set in good early binding; text very fresh for this title; contemporary tree sheep, some rubbing of spines, top of one spine bit worn, cloth folding case; BAL 10098; Sabin 34159; Howes I83; Wright I 1408; Grolier 100 Amer. 28   Ximenes 108-216 1996 $1,000.00

IRVING, WASHINGTON 1783-1859   A History of New York, from the Beginning of the World to the End of the Dutch Dynasty. London: John Murray, 1821. New edition; 8vo; pages (vi), (i)-xxxi, (i), (33)-341, (1); (vi), 282; 2 volumes; contemporary red calf, backstrips with gilt ruled raised bands, gilt lettered direct in second and fifth compartments, remainder decorated with gilt lozenge blocked pane, slightly dulled, sides with wide border of 'Celtic' plait roll between fillets, roll on board edges and turn-ins, brown chalked endpapers, blue silk markers, gilt edges, excellent; bookplate of Frances Mary Richardson Currer.   Blackwell's B112-161 1996 £75.00

IRVING, WASHINGTON 1783-1859   Knicerbocker's History of New York: New York: G. P. Putnam's, 1894. Van Twiller edition; 2 volumes, (xviii), 364; (xviii), (380) pages; illustrations by E. W. Kemble; slightly later fine full morocco banded and extra gilt, inner gilt dentelles, top edge gilt, few very minor marks and scuffs, but very good set.   Ash Rare Books Zenzybyr-56 1996 £225.00

IRVING, WASHINGTON 1783-1859   The Legend of Sleepy Hollow. Hyattsville: Rebecca Press, 1983. Limited to 150 copies signed by Rebecca Bingham, publisher; 2 1/4 X 2 7/8 inches; (114) pages; wood engravings by Sarah Chamberlain, includes proof of one of the wood engravings signed by Chamberlain; designer binder by Angela James, signed and dated 1994 by her; full dark purple mor. inlaid on both covers with geometric pieces of white sheepskin, which are speckled with inks either in blue and purple or in yellow, other inlays surrounding these colored sections show black ink drawing on white sheepskin, these pieces laminated with transparent vellum, edges alternately treated w/gold, palladium & blue acrylic, doublures are of white sheepskin, speckled in a range from yellow to purple, and flyleaves are of correspondingly dyed paper, housed in matchbox container consisting of tray and sleeve, tray is of purple mor., lined w/matching suede, while sleeve is of purple speckled sheepskin, w/gilt titled purple mor. label. Bromer Booksellers 87-184 1996 $1,750.00

IRVING, WASHINGTON 1783-1859   Lives of Mahomet and His Successors. London: Murray, 1850. 1st English edition; 8vo; 2 volumes; bound without ads but with portrait; half calf, gilt, matching leather labels; armorial bookplates, moderately rubbed but still attractive, very good.   Charles Agvent 4-713 1996 $125.00

IRVING, WASHINGTON 1783-1859   Old Christmas. London: Macmillan & Co., 1925. 4th edition, reprinted; small octavo; xiv, 165 pages; 106 illustrations designed by Randolph Caldecott; bound by Sangorski & Sutcliffe in full green polished calf, covers decoratively bordered in gilt, gilt spine, tooled in compartments, with red morocco labels, gilt board edges and turn-ins, all edges gilt, decorative endpapers, bookplate; fine. Heritage Book Shop 196-283 1996 $225.00

IRVING, WASHINGTON 1783-1859   Oliver Goldsmith. Philadelphia: Lippincott, 1872. Octavo; pages 427; full page engravings, tissue guards; maroon cloth, gilt, top edge gilt, bevelled boards; spine slightly faded, minor fraying to spine ends, text crisp and unfoxed. Very good. Hartfield 48-L36 1996 $165.00

IRVING, WASHINGTON 1783-1859   Rip Van Winkle. McKay, 1921. 1st edition thus; 8 full page color illustrations by N. C. Wyeth; very good. Aronovitz 57-587 1996 $175.00

IRVING, WASHINGTON 1783-1859   Rip Van Winkle. New York: Limited Editions Club, 1930. Limited to 1500 copies; signed by designer, Frederic Goudy; 8vo; illustrations by F. O. C. Darley; full green sheepskin, spine sunned, still strong, very good in case; with Monthly Letter.   Charles Agvent 4-715 1996 $100.00

IRVING, WASHINGTON 1783-1859   Rip Van Winkle: a Legend of the Katskill Mountains. New York: Putnam, 1970. "Jefferson Edition": tall 8vo; engraved titlepage and 14 illustrations, 4 tipped in carbon photos; 32 pages; full maroon cloth, bevelled edges, pictorial upper cover stamped gilt and black, lower cover stamped black, all edges gilt, brown endpapers (spine losses, fading to upper cover), good to very good. George J. Houle 68-72 1996 $350.00

IRVING, WASHINGTON 1783-1859   Rip Van Winkle and the Legend of Sleepy Hollow. West Hatfield: Pennyroyal Editions, 1985. illustrations by Barry Moser; original cloth, paper labels; fine in publisher's slipcase. Hermitage SP95-906 1996 $125.00

IRVING, WASHINGTON 1783-1859   The Rocky Moutains; or, Scenes, Incidents and Adventures in the Far West. Philadelphia: Carey, Lea & Blanchard, 1837. 1st American edition; 12mo; 2 volumes; 2 folding maps, with 12 page catalog at end of volume 1; cloth, contemporary signature, original paper spine labels darkened and chipped, one signature pulled in volume 2, 3 inch tear into map in volume 1, moderate foxing to text, maps with some offsetting.   Charles Agvent 4-716 1996 $400.00

IRVING, WASHINGTON 1783-1859   The Rocky Mountains: or Scenes, Incidents and Adventures in the Far West. Philadelphia: 1837. 1st edition; 2 volumes, 248, 248 pages; folding maps; cloth, with label, very good. Howes I85; Wagner Camp 67; Graff 2160. Rader 2028. Smith 5046.   T. A. Swinford 49-603 1996 $275.00

IRVING, WASHINGTON 1783-1859   Sketch Book. Philadelphia: Lippincott, 1882. Edition deluxe, one of 500 numbered copies; 4to; many engravings by Darley, Hoppin, et al; original binding, partly unopened, very good.   Charles Agvent 4-718 1996 $100.00

IRVING, WASHINGTON 1783-1859   Tales of a Traveller. London: John Murray, 1824. 1st English edition; 8vo; 2 volumes, xvi, 364; vi, 394, (ii) pages; half titles; original boards, untrimmed; worn, joints cracked but secure, lacks most of one label, little minor foxing; good, unsophisticated set. BAL 10115.   Robert Clark 38-244 1996 £60.00

IRVING, WASHINGTON 1783-1859   A Tour on the Prairies. Philadelphia: Carey, Lea & Blanchard, 1835. 1st edition; 1st state; 5000 copies printed; 12mo; original green muslin, occasional stains, bookplate, very good. Howes I 1401; Wagner Camp 56; BAL 10140.   Charles Agvent 4-720 1996 $300.00

IRVING, WASHINGTON 1783-1859   A Tour on the Prairies. Philadelphia: Carey, Lea and Blanchard, 1835. 1st American edition, 1st state; 12mo; 274 pages, 24 pages ads; original cloth, spine label, spine label rubbed, lettering no longer legible, else nice, tight copy, light foxing, free front endpaper removed. Howes I86; Rader 2029; Wagner Camp 67; Blanck 10140; Sabin 35139.   Bohling Book Co. 192-177 1996 $200.00

IRVING, WASHINGTON 1783-1859   Two Tales: Rip Van Winkle and The Legend of Sleepy Hollow. New York: London: Harcourt, Brace Jovanovich, 1984. 1st edition thus; 8vo; woodengravings by Barry Moser; fine jacket.   Priscilla Juvelis 95/1-131 1996 $100.00

IRVING, WASHINGTON 1783-1859   Wolfert's Roost. New York: Putnam's, 1855. 1st edition; 1st printing; 12mo; frontispiece, engraved title; primary binding; near fine. BAL 10188.   Charles Agvent 4-721 1996 $125.00

IRVING, WASHINGTON 1783-1859   The Works... Garden City: Putnam, 1859-60. Sunnyside Edition; 8vo; 21 volumes; three quarter polished calf and marbled boards with matching marbled endpapers, all edges marbled, four of the six spine panels heavily decorated in gilt while remaining two contain leather labels with gilt lettering, marbled boards are lightly rubbed as are some of the leather labels; near fine.   Charles Agvent 4-722 1996 $1,200.00

IRVINGIANA: a Memorial of Washington Irving. New York: Charles B. Richardson, 1860. Limited to 110 copies; 4to; 2 volumes; more than 180 portraits, engravings, illustrations; three quarter brown cloth backed boards, rubbed, front cover of volume 2 stained, gilt lettered leather labels on spines; minor flaws, else near fine internally.   Blue Mountain SP95-105 1996 $450.00

IRWIN, DAVID   Scottish Painters at Home and Abroad 1700-1900. London: Faber & Faber, 1975. Thick 8vo; 508 pages; color frontispiece, 7 color plates, 208 monochrome plates, 13 text figures; cloth, dust jacket.   Rainsford A54-337 1996 £65.00

IRWIN, WILL   Pictures of Old Chinatown. New York: Moffat Yard, 1908. 1st edition; 2nd printing; 57 pages, plus 56 plates by Arnold Genthe; orange cloth with pictorial photographic pastedown on front cover, very small scratch to front pictorial pastedown, small dent to rear cover, upper rear corner showing, else fine.   Argonaut Book Shop 113-282   1996 $150.00

ISAAC, ISAAC S.   Friday Night. A Selection of Tales Illustrating Hebrew Life. New York: Office of the Jewish Messenger, 1870-5630. 1st edition; 12mo; 162 pages; original cloth, one signature shaken. This copy was presented as an award at the Hebrew Free School in the year of publication. Singerman 2209.   M & S Rare Books 60-187   1996 $175.00

ISAAC, PETER   William Bulmer, 1757-1830. The Fine Printer in Context. London: Bain & Williams, 1993. 1st edition; one of 750 copies; large 4to; c. 200 pages, more than 40 illustrations printed on tinted ground, printed in Monotype Bulmer on Exhibition Cartridge; full cloth.   Claude Cox 107-250   1996 £75.00

ISENBART, HANS HEINRICH   The Imperial Horse. The Saga of the Lipizzaners. New York: Knopf, 1986. 1st U.S. edition; 4to; original binding, fine in like dust jacket.   October Farm 36-239   1996 $125.00

ISHAM, ASA BRAINERD   Prisoners of War and Military Prisons Personal Narratives of Experience in the Prisons at Richmond, Danville, Macon, Andersonville, Savannah, Millen, Charleston and Columbia... Cincinnati: Lyman and Cushing, 1890. 1st edition; xii, 571 pages; original cloth, near fine; Coulter 253; Dornbusch III 599; Nevins I p. 194; Nicholson p. 413.   McGowan Book Co. 65-44   1996 $350.00

ISHAM, JAMES   James Isham's Observations on Hudson's Bay, 1743 and Notes and Observations on a Book Entitled a Voyage to Hudson's Bay in the Dobbs Galley, 1749. London: 1949. Pages cv, 352; fine, unopened copy.   Stephen Lunsford 45-68   1996 $150.00

ISHERWOOD, CHRISTOPHER 1904-   The Berlin Stories. New York: New Directions, 1945. 1st edition; near fine in dust jacket with light edge wear.   Thomas Dorn 9-145   1996 $110.00

ISHERWOOD, CHRISTOPHER 1904-   The Berlin Stories: The Last of Mr. Norris, Goodbye to Berlin. New York: New Directions, 1945. 1st American edition; just about fine in lightly rubbed dust jacket. Captain's Bookshelf 38-121   1996 $100.00

ISHERWOOD, CHRISTOPHER 1904-   The Berlin Stories. New York: New Directions, 1945. 1st U.S. edition; near fine in very good+ dust jacket, unusually nice.   Pettler & Lieberman 28-135   1996 $100.00

ISHERWOOD, CHRISTOPHER 1904-   Sally Bowles. London: Hogarth Press, 1937. 1st edition; 12mo; original binding, top edge dusty, tail of spine slightly bumped, edges and endpapers slightly spotted, very good in nicked, rubbed, spotted, darkened and dusty, slightly creased dust jacket browned at spine and edges.   Ulysses 39-309   1996 £395.00

ISHERWOOD, CHRISTOPHER 1904-   Sally Bowles. London: 1937. 1st edition; spine trifle darkened, otherwise very good.   Words Etcetera 94-656   1996 £65.00

ISHIGURO, KAZUO   An Artist of the Floating World. London: Faber & Faber, 1986. 1st British edition; fine in fine dust jacket, signed bookplate laid in.   Book Time 2-202   1996 $175.00

ISHIGURO, KAZUO   An Artist of the Floating World. London: Faber and Faber, 1986. 1st edition; fine in fine dust jacket.   Lame Duck Books 19-264   1996 $150.00

ISHIGURO, KAZUO   A Pale View of the Hills. New York: Putnam, 1982. 1st American edition; fine in near fine dust jacket with slight crease on front flap and short tear on front panel, author's first book.   Between the Covers 42-237   1996 $185.00

ISHIGURO, KAZUO   A Pale View of Hills. New York: Putnam, 1982. 1st American edition, author's first book; fine in fine dust jacket.   Thomas Dorn 9-146   1996 $175.00

ISHIGURO, KAZUO   The Remains of the Day. London: Faber & Faber, 1989. 1st edition; 8vo; boards, dust jacket; mint; signed by author. James S. Jaffe 34-293   1996 $350.00

ISLE of Wight. In a series of Views Printed in Oil Colours. London: T. Nelson & Sons, n.d., ca. 1860-70. Oblong 8vo; titlepage, 6 pages of text, 27 colored plates; loose in original cloth case, corners worn, title and few margins very slightly spotted.   Charles W. Traylen 117-366   1996 £55.00

ISMAN, FELIX   Weber and Fields: Their Triumphs and Their Associates. New York: Boni & Livewright, 1924. 1st edition; illustrations; spine little dull, but near fine; signed by Joe Weber and Lew Fields. Captain's Bookshelf 38-213   1996 $100.00

ISOCRATES   (Greek title) Isocratis Orationes et Epistole. Geneva: Henr Stephanus, 1593. folio; pages (28), 427, 131, (34), (8), 31, 18, plus blanks; printer's device on title (20); ornamental initials and headpieces, long inscription clipped from titlepage, without text loss; old boards (could use rebacking); ex-librris Harvard/Houghton Library (released). Schreiber 224; Renouard 155.1. Dibdin II 126; Brunet III 467.   Family Album Tillers-343   1996 $540.00

ISOCRATES   Orationes Tres. Venice: Haeredes P. Ravani & Sociis, 1555. 2nd eidtion; 8vo; ff. (i), Roman and Greek letter on opposing pages, printer's woodcut device, schoolboy autograph "Nicolai Jani' colophon rubbed to remove printer's surname, contemporary student marginalia, small waterstain to final leaves, mostly in lower margin, some yellowing; unrestored contemporary Venetian calf, central panel divided diagonally into 4 compartments, each with interlaced strapwork central design, borders with small circular patterns, flowers at corners, 2 original ties, few small holes, worn at 2 corners. Well red but till attractive.   A. Sokol XXV-53   1996 £850.00

ISUMBRAS   Syr Ysambrace. Hammersmith: Kelmscott Press, 1897. 8vo; pages (iv), 41, printed in red and black in Chaucer type, woodcut frontispiece after Burne-Jones, woodcut border to first page of text, initials and printer's device; contemporary vellum, sides with single fillet gilt border, spine ruled and lettered in gilt, inner dentelles and top edge gilt, others uncut, by Wood; bookplate, slight soiling to sides, otherwise excellent copy. Cockerell 48; Peterson A48.   Simon Finch 24-138 1996 £750.00

ISUMBRAS   Syr Isambrace. Hammersmith: Kelmscott Press, 1897. Limited to 350 copies; 8vo; (4), 42 pages, wood engravd frontispiece designed by Edward Burne-Jones, 2 woodcut borders and initial letters, printed in red and black, on handmade paper; linen backed blue printed boards, very nice, small round stain at top corner of front board from removal of label. Peterson A48.   Kenneth Karmiole 1NS-141 1996 $650.00

ITALIAN Furniture, Interiors and Decoration... New York: Architectural Book Pub., n.d. 1st edition; folio; portfolio, 1 page, 58 plates; portfolio is worn, however the plates are very good.   Bookpress 75-182 1996 $235.00

ITOH, TEIJI   The Elegant Japanese House. New York: Walker/Weatherhill, 1969. 1st English language edition; folio; (ii), 218, (2) pages; 129 pages of photos, 25 pages of drawings and plans; cloth, dust jacket, very good in chipped jacket.   The Bookpress 75-202 1996 $185.00

IVES, MARGUERITE   Seventeen Famous Outdoorsmen Known to Marguerite Ives. Chicago: Canterbury Press, 1929. 1st edition; number 336 of 500 copies, signed by author; square 8vo; 192 pages; original decorated green cloth, light wear and fading, internally very good. Blue River Books 9-297   1996 $120.00

IVES, SIDNEY   The Trial of Mrs. Leigh Perrot, Wife of James Leigh Perrot, Esq. Which Came on at Somerset Asizes, Holden on 29th March, 1800, On the Charge of Stealing a Card of Lace... London: printed and bound at the Sinehour Press, 1980. 1st edition; limited to 200 copies; 9 x 6 inches; 1 illustration, pages 37 + colophon; buff paper covered boards, printed paper title label to backstrip; mint. Not in Gilson.   Ian Hodgkins 78-177   1996 £70.00

IYER, K. BHARATHA   Art and Thought. London: Luzac & Co., 1947. 2 x 20 cm; xvi, 259 pages, some pages unopened, 51 plates, text illustrations; original cloth, spine faded, corners slightly bumped. Rainsford A54-339   1996 £75.00

IZENOUR, GEORGE C.   Roofed Theaters of Classical Antiquity. New Haven and London: Yale University Press, 1992. Oblong folio; xxii, 234 pages, 116 illustrations; original cloth, dust jacket.   Archaeologia Luxor-3507   1996 $110.00

J

JAASTAD, BEN   Man of the West, Reminiscences of George Washington Oakes, 1840-1917. Tucson: 1956. One of 400 copies; 65 pages; stiff wrappers; fine, scarce. Six Guns 1118.   Early West 22-101 1996 $125.00

JACK, ROBERT L.   History of the National Association for the Advancement of Colored People. Boston: Meador, 1943. 1st edition; spot of paint on bottom edge of pages, otherwise near fine in very good dust jacket lacking 3/4 inch at base of spine and which is splitting at folds, still very presentable copy, extremely fragile jacket.   Between the Covers 43-342 1996 $125.00

JACKMAN, JOSEPH   The Sham-Robbery, Committed by Elijah Putnam Goodridge, on His Own Person in Newbury, Near Essex Bridge, Dec. 19, 1816, with a History of His Journey to the Place Where He Robbed Himself. Concord: printed for the author, 1819. 1st edition; 12mo; 151, (1) pages; contemporary plain wrappers, text somewhat browned, but nice, crisp copy; S&S 48361. Sabin 27930.   M & S Rare Books 60-312 1996 $425.00

JACKMAN, W. J.   Flying Machines: Construction and Operation. Chicago: Charles C. Thompson, 1910. 1st edition; small 8vo; 221 pages; illustrations and diagrams; original cloth, nice.   Edward Morrill 368-16 1996 $110.00

JACKSON, A. L.   When Shiloh Came. Ogilvie, 1899. 1st edition; illustrations; some soiling to covers and page edges, else just about very good, most uncommon.   Aronovitz 57-589 1996 $125.00

JACKSON, ANDREW   Robert O'Hara Burke and the Australian Exploring Expedition of 1860. London: Smith, Elder & Co., 1862. Small 8vo; (xii), 227 pages, 16 pages ads, folding map; 1900's cloth binding, original endpaper bound in, some discoloration of cloth, otherwise good+. Ferguson 10857. Wantrup 173.   Antipodean 28-621 1996 $550.00

JACKSON, C. E.   Bird Illustrators, Some Artists in Early Lithography. London: 1975. Specially bound edition, limited to 45 copies, signed by author; 4to; 133 pages; 14 colored plates; quarter blue levant morocco. Spine trifle faded, otherwise fine.   Wheldon & Wesley 207-250 1996 £85.00

JACKSON, CATHERINE HANNAH CHARLOTTE   Works (On French History). London: John C. Nimmo, 1899. 8 3/4 x 6 1/4 inches; 14 volumes; 113 plates, printed tissue guards, titles printed in red and black, plates printed on fine Japanese vellum; fine burnt orange straight grain morocco by Hatchards, covers simply panelled in gilt, flat spines titled and attractively decorated in gilt with elongated compartments at top and bottom, featuring antique volutes, marbled endpapers, top edge gilt, other edges untrimmed, spines slightly and uniformly faded, few tiny paint flecks on one cover, bit of wear to corners, small inoffensive dent at top of one spine, little soiling to boards, but all these imperfections minor, the set generally in fine condition, with joints showing scarcely any wear and with the bindings quite handsome.   Phillip J. Pirages 33-315 1996 $1,250.00

JACKSON, DONALD   Johann Amerbach. Iowa City: Prairie Press, 1956. 11 1/4 x 8 1/2 inches, accompanied by a leaf, 13 1/2 x 9 1/2 inches, from the Lectura super V Libris Decretalium of Panormitanus de Tudeschis printed by Amerbach in 1487-88, leaf is contained in 14 x 10 inch folder of matching blue paper; original blue printe dpaper wrpapers; very fine; Goff P51; BMC III 749.   Phillip J. Pirages 33-331 1996 $175.00

JACKSON, EDGAR   Three Rebels Write Home Incuding the Letters of Edgar Allan Jackson (Sept. 7, 1860-April 15, 1863), James Fenton Bryant (June 20, 1861-Dec. 1866), Irvin Cross Wills (April 9, 1862-July 29, 1863) and Miscellaneous Items. Franklin: News Pub. Co., 1955. 1st edition; limited to 150 copies; 103, (2) pages; original printed wrappers with cloth backstrip, very good or better, scarce. Dornbusch III 450. McGowan Book Co. 65-45 1996 $300.00

JACKSON, FREDERICK J.   Notes on the Game Birds of Kenya and Uganda (Including the Sand-Grouse, Pigeons, Snipe, Bustards, Geese and Ducks)... London: Williams & Norgate, 1926. 8vo; pages 258, 13 plates; original green ribbed cloth slightly faded, otherwise good, solid copy. Sotheran PN32-89 1996 £176.00

JACKSON, FREDERICK J.   Notes on the game Birds of Kenya and Uganda. London: 1926. 258 pages; 13 color plates; bound; dust jacket. John Johnson 135-517 1996 $125.00

JACKSON, GEORGE A.   Jackson's Diary of 59'. Idaho Springs: 1929. 1st edition; 19 pages; photos, illustrations; full flexible calf, nice. Rare. T. A. Swinford 49-607 1996 $500.00

JACKSON, HELEN HUNT 1830-1885   Ramona. Los Angeles: Limited Editions Club, 1959. Limited to 1500 copies; 4to; illustrations by Everett Gee Jackson, signed by Jackson; full woven fabric, fine in slipcase. Charles Agvent 4-727 1996 $150.00

JACKSON, HENRY R.   Tallulah and Other Poems. Savannah: Cooper, 1850. 1st edition; 12mo; 23 pages; original cloth, some wear, but very good; with 1851 Macon, Georgia presentation inscription.   M & S Rare Books 60-183 1996 $200.00

JACKSON, HOLBROOK   A Cross-Section of English Printing: the Curwen Press 1918-1934. London: Curwen Press, 1935. One of 60 copies for sale (of a total of 75); 10 1/4 x 7 1/2 inches; 4 p.l., 24 pages; numerous illustrations, some in color; original cloth, publisher's patterned paper slipcase; very fine; bookplate of Earl E. Fisk.   Phillip J. Pirages 33-152 1996 $250.00

JACKSON, HOLBROOK   The Early History of the Double Crown Club - Fiftieth Dinner Address delivered by the President Holbrook Jackson at the Cafe Royal Ninth October Nineteen Thirtyfive. London: 1935. One of 100 copies; printed in Eric Gill's Perpetua and Felicity, 14 page address; cloth backed boards, free endpapers browned, covers slightly marked, bowed and dusty, very good.   Ulysses 39-153 1996 £55.00

JACKSON, HOLBROOK   The Eighteen-Nineties. London: Grant Richards, 1913. 1st edition; plates; decorated red cloth, very good; with 1 page TLS by Jackson.   Charles Agvent 4-728 1996 $125.00

JACKSON, ISAAC R.   The Life of William Henry Harrison, the People's Candidate. Philadelphia: Marshall, 1840. 1st edition; 8vo; 60 pages; original wrappers; text lightly foxed, wrappers worn, corners creased and folded.   The Bookpress 75-416 1996 $150.00

JACKSON, JAMES   Letters to a Young Physician Just Entering Upon Practice. Boston: 1855. 1st edition; 344 pages; original binding, front board and backstrip nearly detached; contents very good. Osler 3062; Kelly Burrage 638.   W. Bruce Fye 71-1085 1996 $100.00

JACKSON, JAMES   A Report on Spasmodic Cholera. Boston: 1832. 1st edition; folding map; original cloth backed boards; ex-library. Kaufman 386.   W. Bruce Fye 71-1084 1996 $200.00

JACKSON, JAMES   A Syllabus of the Lectures Delivered in the Massachusetts Medical College to the Medical Students of Harvard University. Boston: 1816. 1st edition; 108 pages, 76 additional inserted and mostly bound leaves containing student's lecture notes; uncut, contemporary quarter calf, slightly foxed. Austin 1038.   Argosy 810-252 1996 $850.00

JACKSON, JOHN   A Defense of Human Liberty, in Answer to the Principal Arguments Which Have Been Alledged Against It. London: J. Noon, 1725. 1st edition; 8vo; (8), 207, (1) pages, ads on verso of last leaf; contemporary calf, gilt, joints cracked, otherwise very good, crisp copy; the Woburn Abbey copy with contemporary armorial bookplate of Duke of Bedford, blue circular Woburn Abbey shelf label and Bedford arms in gilt on each cover.   John Drury 82-122 1996 £350.00

JACKSON, JOHN   Journey from India Towards England, in the Year 1797. London: printed for T. cadell, 1799. 1st edition; 8vo; original pink boards, drab paper backstrip, spine worn, covers detached. Clean tear across one leaf, without loss, aside from binding, very good, uncut copy, very uncomm; CBEL II 1444.   Ximenes 108-217 1996 $450.00

JACKSON, JOHN   Remarks on the Miscellaneous Poems Published by Thomas Pierson of Stockton in the Year 1786. Stockton: for the author by W. Rawson, 1786. 1st edition; 8vo; pages 25, (i); recent wrappers. Rare.   Simon Finch 24-120 1996 £450.00

JACKSON, JOHN   A Vindication of Humane Liberty; in Answer to a Dissertation on Liberty and Necessity, Written by A. C. Esq. London: for J. Noon, 1730. 1st edition; 8vo; viii, 63, (1) pages; small ink stamp of a private library in one blank margin, but very good, recently well bound in old style quarter calf, gilt; apparently rare.   John Drury 82-123 1996 £225.00

JACKSON, JOHN HUGHLINGS 1835-1911   Selected Writings of John Hughlings Jackson. New York: Basic Books, 1958. 8vo; 2 volumes; original binding, very nice set in dust jackets.   James Tait Goodrich K40-166 1996 $145.00

JACKSON, JON A.   The Diehard. New York: Random House, 1977. 1st edition; author's first book; fine with owner's name and date on front endpaper in dust jacket with light rubbing.   Quill & Brush 102-951 1996 $125.00

JACKSON, JOSEPH HENRY   Bad Company - The Story of California's Legendary and Actual Stage-Robbers, Bandits, Highwaymen and Outlaws from the Fifties to the Eighties. New York: Harcourt, Brace and Co., 1949. 1st edition; original binding, top edge slightly dusty, small tear at head of spine, head and tail of spine, bottom corners slightly bumped, very good in chipped and slightly creased rubbed, marked and dusty dust jacket faded at spine, slightly browned at edges and frayed at tail of spine.   Ulysses 39-310 1996 £55.00

JACKSON, MARY E.   The Life of Nellie C. Bailey or a Romance of the West. Topeka: 1885. 399 pages; illustrations; professionally repaired, slipcase; very scarce; Nellie's photo guled into book.   Early West 22-105 1996 $325.00

JACKSON, R. T.   Phylogeny of the Echini... Boston: 1912. 4to; 2 volumes, 491 pages, 258 text figures and 76 plates; new cloth, first leaves of text volume rather stained, paper of plates volume showing signs of age with some staining at beginning and end.   Wheldon & Wesley 207-1265 1996 £140.00

JACKSON, SHIRLEY   The Bird's Nest. New York: Farrar Straus and Young, 1954. 1st edition; fine in very near fine dust jacket; beautiful copy.   Ken Lopez 74-232 1996 $150.00

JACKSON, SHIRLEY   The Haunting of Hill House. New York: Viking, 1959. 1st edition; near fine with very faint dampstain at base of spine, in very good or better dust jacket, bit rubbed at extremities, some faint damp spots on rear panel, still attractive copy, very scarce.   Between the Covers 42-240 1996 $500.00

JACKSON, SHIRLEY   The Haunting of Hill House. M. Joseph, 1960. 1st British edition; near fine in like dust jacket save for some sunning along 2 of the margins of rear dust jacket panel.   Aronovitz 57-592 1996 $150.00

JACKSON, SHIRLEY   9 Magic Wishes. N.P.: Crowell-Collier, 1963. 1st edition; folio; illustrations by Lorraine Fox, small tape repairs to recto of the rear free endpaper, couple of smudges to a couple of pages, and some general rubbing and wear to bottom of boards, about very good copy, without dust jacket, as issued, fragile, very uncommon.   Between the Covers 42-522 1996 $225.00

JACKSON, SHIRLEY   The Sundial. New York: FSC, 1958. 1st edition; fine in fine dust jacket with just a touch of rubbing, lovely.   Between the Covers 42-239 1996 $150.00

JACKSON, SHIRLEY   We Have Always Lived in the Castle. New York: Viking, 1962. 1st edition; review copy with accompanying review slip laid in; very good+ in very good dust jacket.   Aronovitz 57-593 1996 $125.00

JACKSON, SHIRLEY   The Witchcraft of Salem Village. New York: Random House, 1956. 1st edition; fine in about very good dust jacket with relatively long tear on rear panel and moderate chips at either side of the crown, still nice, presentable copy; uncommon.   Between the Covers 42-521 1996 $175.00

JACKSON, W. H.   The Canons of Colorado from Photographs By... Denver: Frank S. Thayer, n.d., c. 1900. 1st edition; 17 accordion folded panels, 16 full page black and white illustrations from photos, title page lettered in silver; fine copy bound accordion style in gilt lettered padded leatherette folder, as issued; light rubbing to spine, 2 repaired splits along creases, overall fine, very scarce.   Argonaut Book Shop 113-366 1996 $300.00

JACKSON, WILLIAM   Papers and Pedigrees Mainly Relating to Cumberland and Westmorland. London: Bemrose & Sons, 1892. 8vo; Volumes V and VI; pages 370, 69, 20 illustrations and plans; half calf, gilt with raised bands and contrasting spine labels; handsome set.   R.F.G. Hollett & Son 78-196 1996 £140.00

JACKSON, WILLIAM   Papers and Pedigrees Mainly Relating to Cumberland and Westmorland. London: Bemrose & Sons, 1892. 8vo; volumes V and VI, pages 370, 369, 20 illustrations and plans; original cloth, gilt, extremities little rubbed, few spots, some neat annotations.   R.F.G. Hollett & Son 78-195 1996 £85.00

JACOB, GILES   The Compleat Court-Keeper; or, Land-Steard's Assistant. London: ptd. by E. and R. Nutt, & R. Gosling, for Bernard Lintot & Thomas Ward 1724. 3rd edition; 8vo; contemporary calf, upper hinge cracked; Sweet and Maxwell p. 400 26.   Anthony Laywood 108-77 1996 £175.00

JACOB, GILES   The Law-Dictionary: Explaining the Rise, Progress and Present State of the English Law, in Theory and Practice... London: printed by Andrew Strahan, 1797. 4to; 2 volumes, unnumbered; contemporary calf, headbands and joints worn, binding strong, internally fine, complete with half title in second volume and leaf of addenda in both volumes.   James Fenning 133-175 1996 £145.00

JACOB, GILES   The Poetical Register; or, the Lives and Characters of all the English Poets. London: A. Bettesworth, W. Taylor, J.Batley, J. Wyat and C. Rivington... 1723. 8vo; 2 volumes, pages xxvi, (vi), 328, (xxviii); vi, (i) blank, 444; engraved frontispiece to each volume, 12 engraved portraits; contemporary panelled calf, red morocco labels, red sprinkled edges, bookplates to titles verso, labels chipped, spines rubbed and worn at head, internally some occasional light spotting, good, firm set.   Simon Finch 24-121 1996 £300.00

JACOB, S. S.   Jeypore Enamels. London: W. Griggs, 1886. Folio; 16 pages, plus 28 full page chromolithographed color plates illustrating 120 designs; new leather spine, original decorataive boards, all edges gilt, very good, scarce.   J. M. Cohen 35-41 1996 $2,000.00

JACOBI, ABRAHAM   A Treatise on Diphtheria. New York: William Wood, 1880. 1st edition; 8vo; x, (1), 252 pages; original cloth, edges of binding bit rubbed, faint library mark on spine, front hinge cracked; bookplates on endpapers, few annotations in text; author's presentation stamp on title, very good. Abt. Garrison pp. 105-108. Courville 2642; Cordasco 80-3143;   Edwin V. Glaser B122-80 1996 $185.00

JACOBI, ABRAHAM   A Treatise on Diptheria. New York: 1880. 1st edition; 8vo; original cloth. Castiglione p. 863.   Argosy 810-253 1996 $125.00

JACOBS, JOSEPH   Celtic Fairy Tales. London: David Nutt, 1892. 1st edition; limited to 125 copies, 115 for sale, number 2; signed by David Nutt; xv, 267 pages; frontispiece and 7 plates in two states with tissue guards, title in black and red, 38 text illustrations, 26 decorated initials, green binding design for trade edition bound in; modern quarter green morocco gilt, green cloth, top edge gilt; lacks 2 tissue guards, light wear.   Robin Greer 94A-10 1996 £375.00

JACOBS, JOSEPH   English Fairy Tales. London: David Nutt, 1890. 1st edition; limited edition of 80 copies, 75 for sale, number 26 signed by David Nutt; xv, 253, 1 pages of ads; on Japanese vellum, frontispiece in two states, title vignette, 7 plates, 1 full page and 59 text illustrations, black design for binding of trade edition bound in; light brown boards, gilt lettering, top edge gilt. Loosely tipped in 4 page prospectus for this volume.   Robin Greer 94A-11 1996 £450.00

JACOBS, JOSEPH   Indian Fairy Tales. London: David Nutt, 1892. 1st edition; limited edition of 160, 150 for sale, number 16 signed by David Nutt; large 8vo; xv, 255 pages; frontispiece and 7 plates in 2 states with tissue guards, title in black and red, 36 text illustrations, 29 decorated initials, red binding design for trade edition bound in; light brown boards, gilt lettering, top edge gilt. Boards bit worn.   Robin Greer 94A-12 1996 £300.00

JACOBSTHAL, PAUL   Ornamente Griechischer Vasen. Berlin: Frankfurter, 1927. Folio; 2 volumes, text 244 pages, plate volume with 149 plates loose in box as issued; original gilt lettered cloth, text volume with small tear at head of spine, joint of box tape reinforced.   Archaeologia Luxor-3510 1996 $1,500.00

JACOBUS DE VARAGINE 1230-1298   Legenda Aurea, or Golden Legened. London: Wynkyn de Worde, Feb. 30 (sic), 1521 One of about 10 extant copies, all imperfect; folio; this copy more complete than some, lacking 9 leaves out of 438, imperfection in gathering h is apparently the result of expurgation, 84 woodcuts and metal cuts; 17th century panelled calf, rebacked, original spine laid down, slight wear. Marginal defects to first few leaves, few other small imperfections but generally in excellent, unsophisticated condition. STC 24879.5.   Ximenes 108-343 196 $6,000.00

JACOBUS DE VARAGINE 1230-1298   Historiae Plurimorum Sanctorum. Louvain: Johannes de Westfalia, Oct. 1485. 1st separate edition; folio; 296 leaves (of 298, lacking last two blanks), gothic letter, double column, initial spaces, some with guide letters, initials, paragraph marks, capital strokes, all supplied in red, few marginal annotations in very near early hand, small paper flaw in margin of P4, minor wormhole in few leaves, but very clean, crisp copy with very broad margins showing pinhole at outer corners of each leaf, bound in antique blindstamped goat over heavy semi-bevelled wooden boards; very nice, rare edition. Goff J111; Copinger 6441; BMC IX 143; Polain B 2226. IDL 2338.   H. M. Fletcher 121-9 1996 £7,500.00

JACQUIN, NICOLAI JOSEPH VON 1727-1817   Miscellanea Austriaca ad Botanicam, Chemiam, et Historiam Naturalem Spectantia. Vindobonae: 1778-81. Large 8vo; 2 volumes; pages iv, 212; 424; 44 hand colored engraved plates by Jacquin and engraved by Adam; quarter leather, chipped, some foxing; plate 2 of volume 2 with smudge only touching the edge of a figure; rare.   Raymond M. Sutton VII-20 1996 $1,800.00

JAEGER, BENEDICT   The Life of North American Insects... Providence: Sayles, Miller and Simons, 1854. 1st edition; 8vo; pages 204; 6 hand colored plates showing 31 specimens; library stamp on titlepage, lacks front flyleaf; very nice.   Second Life Books 103-111 1996 $350.00

JAFFE, MICHAEL   Van Dyck's Antwerp Sketchbook. London: Macdonald, 1966. 1st edition; 4to; 2 volumes, frontispiece, 316; 290 pages; over 250 illustrations; cloth, top edge gilt, slipcase, front hinge of volume 2 internally cracked, otherwise very good in lightly worn, matching slipcase.   The Bookpress 75-474 1996 $225.00

JAGGARD, W.   Shakespeare Bibliography. A Dictionary of Every Known Issue of the Writings Of Our National Poet and of Recorded Opinion Thereon in the English Language. Stratford: Shakespeare Press, 1911. Limited to 500 copies, this one unnumbered, stout 8vo; 28 illustrations in 23 plates on handmade Japanese vellum, 2 vignettes; original buff buckram.   Maggs Bros. Ltd. 1191-102 1996 £85.00

JAGO, F. W. P.   An English-Cornish Dictionary. London: Simpkin, Marshall, 1887. 1st edition; 4to; frontispiece, final errata leaf and subscription list; original maroon cloth, spine slightly faded, rubbed at head and tail.   Jarndyce 103-163 1996 £75.00

JAGO, RICHARD   Edge-Hill, or, the Rural Prospect Delineated and Moralized. London: printed for J. Dodsley, 1767. 1st edition; 4to; recent half calf, gilt, marbled sides, some foxing of half title; Aubin, Topographical Poetry 91-2.   Peter Murray Hill 185-89 1996 £200.00

JAHSS, BETTY   Inro and Other Miniature Forms of Japanese Lacquer Art. Rutland: Charles E. Tuttle Co., 1971. 1st edition; 488 pages; very fine in dust jacket.   Hermitage SP95-788 1996 $175.00

JAMBLICHUS OF CHALCIS   Iamblichi Chalcidensis Ex Coele-Syria. de Mysteriis Liber. Praemittitur Epistola Porphyrii ad Anebonem Aegyptium, Eodem Argumento. Oxford: Theatro Sheldoniano, 1678. 1st edition thus; 4to; 2 parts in 1 volume, (40), 316, (6) pages plus errata leaf, titlepage lightly browned, little marginal worming, most of it neatly repaired; contemporary panelled calf, expertly rebacked with 5 raised bands and contemporary morocco spine label; very good, crisp copy. Wing I26; Madan 3179.   Edwin V. Glaser 121-166 1996 $1,200.00

JAMES I, KING OF GREAT BRITAIN 1566-1625   Dissertatio Politica, De Ivre Monarchiae Liberae. N.P.: 1615. 8vo; boards; browned; rare. Lindsay & Neu 3533 cite one location only.   Rostenberg & Stern 150-51 1996 $425.00

JAMES I, KING OF GREAT BRITAIN 1566-1625   The Political Works... Harvard University Press, 1918. Reprinted from the edition of 1616; 8vo; cxi, (i), 354, (ii) pages; original maroon cloth, gilt lettering, extremities bit rubbed, few pencilled annotations; good.   Robert Clark 38-67 1996 £50.00

JAMES I, KING OF SCOTLAND   The Kingis Quair. Vale Press, 1903. One of 10 copies on vellum; there were also 260 copies on paper; 9 1/2 x 6 inches; Iv, (1) pages; printed in red and black, decorative woodcut initial; original limp vellum, yap edges, gilt rules and titling on spine, half the gatherings unopened; extremely fine. Tomkinson p. 171.   Phillip J. Pirages 33-492 1996 $4,500.00

JAMES, C. L. R.   The Black Jacobins: Toussaint L'Ouverture and the San Domingo Revolution. New York: Dial, n.d. 1939. 1st American edition from English sheets; corners slightly bumped, still about fine in attractive, very good dust jacket with slight loss at crown and some tiny nicks at corners. Blokson 75.   Between the Covers 43-344 1996 $850.00

JAMES, C. L. R.   Mariners, Renegades, and Castaways - The Story of Herman Melville and the World We Live In. New York: C. L. R. James, 1953. 1st edition; wrappers; production fault creases to some pages, covers rubbed, lower cover slightly soiled resulting in loss of some of the text of the blurb; very good, rare.   Ulysses 39-311 1996 £155.00

JAMES, EDWARD   The Venetian Glass Omnibus - Peace Propaganda for Grown-up Children and Sophisticated Cretins. London: James Press, 1933. 2nd edition; one of 25 copies; quarto; numerous black and white drawings, original binding, covers rubbed, marked and soiled, spine worn and repaired, corners bumped and bruised, free endpapers slightly browned; good.   Ulysses 39-312 1996 £485.00

JAMES, FRANK LINSLY   The Wild Tribes of the Soudan. London: John Murray, 1883. 1st edition; 8vo; 3 maps, 7 etched plates; 29 other illustrations; original maroon pictorial cloth, minor rubbing; fine, scarce. Ximenes 109-164 1996 $475.00

JAMES, FRANK LINSLY   The Wild Tribes of the Soudan. London: 1884. 2nd edition; engraved plates and text illustrations; cloth slightly rubbed and dulled.   David Grayling J95Biggame-111 1996 £70.00

JAMES, GEORGE PAYNE RAINSFORD 1799-1860   De L'Orme. New York: printed by J. & J. Harper, 1830. 1st American edition; published same year as the first English edition; 2 volumes; original linen backed boards, paper spine labels; portions of front and rear endpapers torn away in volume 2, some foxing and binding wear, but nicely preserved set in original condition; former owner's signature in each volume. Scarce.   David J. Holmes 52-61 1996 $125.00

JAMES, GEORGE PAYNE RAINSFORD 1799-1860   The History of Chivalry. London: Henry Colburn and Richard Bentley, National Library No. IV, 1830. 1st edition; large 12mo; pages xx, 348; frontispiece, add. engraved title, series title, original cloth, double spine labels, minor foxing, but very good to nice in original state. Sadleir II 92.   James Fenning 133-176 1996 £55.00

JAMES, GEORGE WHARTON   Arizona, the Wonderland. Boston: The Page Co., 1917. 1st edition; 9 3/8 x 6 1/2 inches; xxiv, 478 pages, folding map, 60 full page photographic illustrations; gold stamped brown cloth with applied color illustration on front cover, bottom tips bumped, front inner hinge getting weak, rear cover bit bowed.   Dawson's Books Shop 528-116 1996 $100.00

JAMES, GEORGE WHARTON   California, Romantic and Beautiful. Boston: Page Co., 1914. 1st edition; 2nd printing; xxv, 433 pages; color frontispiece, 71 plates (7 in color with printed tissue guards), color folding map; three quarter green leather, marbled boards, gilt rules and lettering, spine slightly darkened, fine. Not listed in Cowan or Rocq; Larson 6.   Argonaut Book Shop 113-368 1996 $300.00

JAMES, GEORGE WHARTON   Indian Blankets and Their Makers. New York: Tudor Publishing Co., 1937. New edition; numerous plates, many in color; original box, box dented at corners, scuffed and lightly waterstained on bottom yet retains original bright pictorial label; former owner's inscription, else near fine.   Ken Sanders 8-169 1996 $200.00

JAMES, H. E. M.   Extracts from the Pedigrees of James of Barrock. Containing the Descent of the Following Families: James Beckwith, Hill, Wilkinson, Carr and Dale, Nesham, Farquarharson. Exeter: William Pollard & Co., 1913. 4to; pages 15 plus 8 large folding pedigrees on stiff paper, armorial frontispiece; original cloth backed boards, gilt, trifle marked; obituary laid onto rear pastedown.   R.F.G. Hollett & Son 78-197 1996 £50.00

JAMES, H. E. M.   Extracts from the Pedigrees of James of Barrock. Containing the Descent of the Following Families: James Ashton, Henry Warburton, Royal Descent through Warburton, Brooks, Bostock and Yates, Bright, Heywood and Thompson. Exeter: William Pollard & Co., 1913. 4to; 15 pages, plus 9 large folding pedigrees on stiff paper; uncut, original cloth backed boards, gilt.   R.F.G. Hollett & Son 78-198 1996 £50.00

JAMES, H. E. M. Pedigrees of the Family of James of Culgarth, West Auckland and Barrock and Their Kinsfolk. Exeter: W. Pollard, 1913. Only a very small number printed for private cirulation; thick 4to; 46 pedigrees; original half vellum, gilt, edges untrimmed, binding trifle marked, inner hinges cracked. Howes Bookshop 265-1862 1996 £150.00

JAMES, HENRY 1843-1916 The Ambassadors. New York: Harper & Bros., 1903. 1st American edition, 1st issue; owner name and date, minor foxing to endpapers and wear to edges of boards, overall very good in very good cloth dust jacket, darkened on spine and lightly fraying at edges. Ken Lopez 74-234 1996 $600.00

JAMES, HENRY 1843-1916 The Ambassadors. New York: Harper and Bros., 1903. 1st American edition; 8vo; pages (ii), 431, (1); original boards, top edge gilt, others uncut, original cloth dust jackets slightly worn, spine of boards and dust jacket lettered and ruled in gilt; excellent copy. Edel & Laurence A58b. Simon Finch 24-127 1996 £900.00

JAMES, HENRY 1843-1916 A Bundle of Letters. Boston: Loring, 1880. 1st edition; unauthorized, published Jan. 24, 1880; 16mo; original cream white stiff paper wrappers, cut flush, pattern of vertical bands or 5 rules in red and horizontal bands of 5 rules in blue on front and back, lettered in black on front cover, ads on back and on insides of both wrappers; some wear along spine, erasure marks on upper front cover, spot on back cover 1 x 1/4 inch, although wrappers lightly soiled, this is a remarkably fine copy, rare; ink signature dated 1880 on titlepage, establishing it as a true first edition. Edel A130. Priscilla Juvelis 95/1-132 1996 $2,000.00

JAMES, HENRY 1843-1916 Confidence. New York: Houghton, Osgood, 1880. 1st American edition, one of 1500 copies; with 1st issue imprint of Houghton, Osgood & Co., 8vo; terra cotta cloth, fine, crisp copy, quite scarce thus; BAL 10549. Charles Agvent 4-730 1996 $650.00

JAMES, HENRY 1843-1916 Daisy Miller: a Study. Cambridge: Limited Editions Club, 1969. Number 330 of 1500 copies; signed by artist; illustrations by Gustave Nebel; red morocco, fine in publisher's slipcase. Hermitage SP95-1000 1996 $125.00

JAMES, HENRY 1843-1916 Daisy Miller: a Study. Cambridge: Limited Editions Club, 1969. 1st edition thus, one of 1500 copies signed by artist; illustrations by Gustave Nebel; full red leather and original slipcase; fine. Captain's Bookshelf 38-123 1996 $125.00

JAMES, HENRY 1843-1916 Daisy Miller. Cambridge: Limited Editions Club, 1969. Limited to 1500 copies; signed by artist, Gustave Nebel; full red morocco, fine in slipcase. Charles Agvent 4-731 1996 $100.00

JAMES, HENRY 1843-1916 The Diary of a Man of Fifty and A Bundle of Letters... New York: Harper & Bros., 1880. 1st edition; 32mo; pages 135, (8) page publishers' ads, first 4 pages also comprise ads; original buff wrappers, printed in black and red, upper cover torn across and repaired without loss, spine defective at foot and just chipped at head, good copy, fragile and uncommon publication. Phillips pp. 17-18. Simon Finch 24-124 1996 £200.00

JAMES, HENRY 1843-1916 English Hours. Cambridge: Riverside Press, 1905. 1st American edition; Number 1 in a large paper edition of 400 copies; 8vo; 8, 336 pages; dozens of inserted illustrations by Pennell; original cloth backed boards, printed paper label, uncut, spine and front cover sunstruck, uncut. BAL 10662. M & S Rare Books 60-351 1996 $150.00

JAMES, HENRY 1843-1916 The Europeans. London: Macmillan and Co., 1878. 1st edition; the so-called remainder issue, one of over 750 copies; this copy has pages 171-5 in corrected state, with chapter correctly head 'V' but the suceeding gathering is uncorrected and has "IV" in the heading throughout. 8vo; 2 volumes bound in one; pages (iv), 255, (i) blank; (iv), 272; original dark green blue fine bead grain cloth, spine lettered in gold, two decorative bands blocked in black with two thick gold rules, either side running round from front cover to spine design continued in blind only on back cover, chocolate endpapers, spine slightly creased, hinges cracked, two gatherings loose, very good in scarce one volume binding. Simon Finch 24-123 1996 £650.00

JAMES, HENRY 1843-1916 Hawthorne. New York: Harper, 1880. 1st American edition, 1st printing, 1st binding; original black cloth, stamped in red, nearly fine copy, bit scarcer than the English edition. BAL 10547; Edel & Laurence A12.b. Clark C45. Mac Donnell 12-101 1996 $150.00

JAMES, HENRY 1843-1916 Italian Hours. Boston: Houghton Mifflin, 1909. 1st American edition; 4to; illustrations by Joseph Pennell; decorated cloth, gilt, hinges cracked but tight, spine bit rubbed, quite good. Charles Agvent 4-732 1996 $175.00

JAMES, HENRY 1843-1916 The Ivory Tower. New York: Charles Scribner's Sons, 1917. 1st American edition, one of 1500 copies; 8vo; smooth dull brown sateen cloth, top edge gilt, printed beige dust jacket, jacket darkened at ends, narrow 1 inch piece lacking at back panel; book is fresh and attractive (some offsetting to endpapers from dust jacket flaps); appealling copy in uncommon jacket. Edel A77b; BAL 10697. Priscilla Juvelis 95/1-134 1996 $450.00

JAMES, HENRY 1843-1916 Letters to A. C. Benson and Auguste Monod: Now First Published and Edited... London: Elkin mathews & Marrot/New York: Scribner, 1930. 1st edition; 564/1050 copies; 8vo; pages xi, 118; original decorated pale green cloth, green leather label, backstrip faded, free endpapers lightly browned, untrimmed, excellent. Edel & Laurence C9. Blackwell's B112-162 1996 £50.00

JAMES, HENRY 1843-1916 A Little Tour in France. Cambridge: Riverside Press, 1900. Number 1 in a large paper edition of 400 copies; 8vo; 13, 350 pages; original cloth backed boards, printed paper label, spine sunstruck, uncut. bAL 10642. M & S Rare Books 60-350 1996 $175.00

JAMES, HENRY 1843-1916 A Little Tour in France. Cambridge: Riverside Press, 1900. Number 250 of a limited edition of 250 copies; 8vo; paper paper edition, xiii, 350 pages; well illustrated by Joseph Pennell, new old style quarter calf, uncut, rather nicely bound, good. K Books 441-289 1996 £80.00

JAMES, HENRY 1843-1916 A London Life. New York: 1957. Limited to 10 numbered copies, specially bound; 8 x 5.5 inches; 158 pages; cloth backed boards, extremities slightly discolored, else very good. John K. King 77-350 1996 $100.00

JAMES, HENRY 1843-1916 The Notebooks of Henry James. London: George Brazillier, Inc., 1955. 1st edition; original binding, top edge dusty, head and tail of spine and bottom edge of upper cover slightly bumped, very good in nicked, chipped and dusty, slightly rubbed and torn dust jacket browned at spine and edges. From the library of James Hart. Ulysses 39-314 1996 £55.00

JAMES, HENRY 1843-1916 The Novels and Tales. New York: Scribners, 1907-09. New York Edition, ordinary issue; 1st impression wit all volumes containing monogram water marked paper; 8vo; 24 volumes photogravures by Alvin Langdon Coburn; plum cloth, spines only slightly faded with occasional small tear, few volumes with little rubbing or soiling, partly unopened, near fine set. Charles Agvent 4-738 1996 $4,000.00

JAMES, HENRY 1843-1916 A Passionate Pilgrim and Other Tales. Boston: James R. Osgood and Co., Late Ticknor and Fields & Osgood, 1875. 1st edition; one of 1500 copies of the author's first book 8vo. in 12's; pages ii, 496; original fine cross ribbed purple cloth, sides with double rules in blind, spine lettered and ruled in gold, chocolate brown endpapers, spine little worn at head and tail and slightly faded, some gatherings held by only one cord, still good. Blanck 10529; Edel & Laurence A1. Simon Finch 24-122 1996 £975.00

JAMES, HENRY 1843-1916 The Question of Our Speech/The Lesson of Balzac. Boston and New York: Houghton Mifflin and Co., Riverside Press, 1905. 1st edition; one of 2000 copies; narrow 12mo; designed by Bruce Rogers; blue cloth, wear to edges, else very good. Edel A61; Warde 56. Priscilla Juvelis 95/1-135 1996 $100.00

JAMES, HENRY 1843-1916 The Reverberator. London: Macmillan & Co., 1888. 1st American edition; original decorated cloth, extremities and covers slightly worn, but fine, bright copy. BAL 10583. David J. Holmes 52-62 1996 $375.00

JAMES, HENRY 1843-1916 The Reverberator. London: & New York: Macmillan, 1888. One of 3000 copies, 1st American edition; small 8vo; blue cloth with gilt decoration, spine cocked and covers soiled, but decent. Laurence A31b. James S. Jaffe 34-294 1 996 $100.00

JAMES, HENRY 1843-1916 Stories Revived in Three Volumes. London: Macmillan and Co., 1885. 1st edition; 500 copies printed; 8vo; volumes; original dark blue-green fine bead-grain cloth, sides stamped in blind, spines lettered in gold, dark brown endpapers, unobturisve booksellers' inkstamps at extreme upper outer corner of verso of front free endpapers and discreet ownership initials on half titles in two volumes, joints rubbed in places where ties make the cloth stand little proud, very good, bright and fresh. Phillips pp. 29-31; Brussel, Wst to East pp. 65-6; Sadleir 1290. Simon Finch 24-125 1996 £1,200.00

JAMES, HENRY 1843-1916   Theatricals - Second Series - The Album - The Reprobate. Osgood, McIlvaine & Co., 1895. 1100 copies printed, of which 550 were used for the U. S. edition; original binding, top edge dusty, head and tail of spine and corners bumped, spine browned, covers marked, prelims, edges and endpapers spotted, very good. Ulysses 39-313 1996 £250.00

JAMES, HENRY 1843-1916   Theatricals. Second Series. London: Osgood, McIlvaine, 1895. 1st edition, U.K. issue; one of either 460 or 550 copies; foxing, endpapers and page edges, spine faded cloth, else very good, without dust jacket.   Ken Lopez 74-233 1996 $150.00

JAMES, HENRY 1843-1916   Transatlantic Sketches. Boston: 1875. 1st edition; 7.5 x 5 inches; 401 pages; cloth, extremities rather rubbed, spine ends beginning to fray.   John K. King 77-351 1996 $200.00

JAMES, HENRY 1843-1916   Transatlantic Sketches. New York: Osgood, 1875. 1st edition; 1578 copies; 8vo; terra cotta cloth, spine imprint of J. R. Osgood and Co., hint of wear to spine tips and corners; near fine. BAL 10530; Edel A2.   Charles Agvent 4-739 1996 $500.00

JAMES, HENRY 1843-1916   Transatlantic Sketches. New York: Osgood, 1875. 1st edition; 8vo; this copy with variant publisher's stamp on spine of Houghton, Osgood & Co.; purple cloth, slight cracking of hinges, rear possibly repaired at some date, old stain to rear pastedown and endpaper, very minor wear to spine tips, spine touch sunned, near fine.   Charles Agvent 4-740 1996 $400.00

JAMES, HENRY 1843-1916   Washington Square. New York: Harper & Bros., 1881. 1st edition; small 8vo; frontispiece, five plates; original olive green decorated cloth, ends of spine trifle rubbed; very good. Edel & Laurence A15(a); BAL 10551.   Ximenes 108-218 1996 $400.00

JAMES, HENRY 1843-1916   The Wings of the Dove. New York: Charles Scribner's Sons, 1902. 1st edition; 8vo; 2 volumes; half titles; original smooth satin biscuit cloth, gilt lettering on spines, top edge gilt, others uncut; nice. Edel & Laurence A56; Blanck 10647.   Anthony W. Laywood 108-213 1996 £165.00

JAMES, JASON W.   Memories and Viewpoints. Roswell: privately printed, 1928. Pages 183; very good, inscribed by author. Rare. Dumont 28-102 1996 $395.00

JAMES, M. E.   How to Decorate Our Ceilings, Walls and Floors. London: George Bell & Sons, 1883. 1st edition; 12mo; frontispiece, x, 86, (i) pages; 5 plates; original pink publisher's cloth, rubbed, spine sunned, faint foxing on endpapers, else very good.   Bookpress 75-70 1996 $265.00

JAMES, MONTAGUE RHODES   The Apocalypse in Latin. Ms. 10 in the Collection of Dyson Perrins. Oxford: 1927. Folio; color frontispiece, 42 plates; green half morocco, gilt lettering on spine, pencil ownership inscription and booklabel, both of Lord Kenyon, attractive volume. Maggs Bros. Ltd. 1191-155 1996 £100.00

JAMES, MONTAGUE RHODES   A Descriptive Catalogue of the Manuscripts in the Fitzwilliam Museum. Cambridge: 1895. Plates; blue cloth, gilt, bit worn at extremities, booklabel of Lord Kenyon.   Maggs Bros. Ltd. 1191-152 1996 £100.00

JAMES, MONTAGUE RHODES   A Descriptive Catalogue of the Manuscripts in the Library of Lambeth Palace. Cambridge: 1930-32. 3 volumes, 357 mss. described, original wrappers, spines slightly torn. Lord Kenyon's copy.   Maggs Bros. Ltd. 1191-151 1996 £80.00

JAMES, MONTAGUE RHODES   A Descriptive Catalogue of the Manuscripts in the Library of Sidney Sussex College, Cambridge. Cambridge: 1895. Blue and gilt cloth, few annotations throughout in ink and red crayon; Cambridge bookseller's label of Galloway & Porter. Maggs Bros. Ltd. 1191-154 1996 £80.00

JAMES, MONTAGUE RHODES   A Descriptive Catalouge of the Manuscripts in the Library of Peterhouse... Cambridge: 1899. Blue and gilt cloth, slight mark on upper cover, very occasional annotatiaons in red crayon, Cambridge bookeller's label of Galloway & Porter. Maggs Bros. Ltd. 1191-153 1996 £110.00

JAMES, P. D.   The Black Tower. New York: Scribners, 1975. 1st edition; signed, fine in dust jacket with very light rubbing.   Quill & Brush 102-958 1996 $100.00

JAMES, P. D.   Innocent Blood. London: Faber & Faber, 1980. 1st edition; fine in dust jacket.   Quill & Brush 102-960 1996 $100.00

JAMES, P. D.   The Maul and the Pear Tree. London: Constable, 1971. 1st edition; fine in price clipped dust jacket with light rubbing and minor edge wear; signed by author.   Quill & Brush 102-954 1996 $200.00

JAMES, P. D.   A Mind to Murder. New York: Scribners, 1963. 1st edition; near fine with owner's name and date in ink on front endpaper, in near fine dust jacket with rubbing and light soiling.   Quill & Brush 102-952 1996 $150.00

JAMES, P. D.   Shroud for a Nightingale. New York: Scribners, 1971. 1st edition; fine with spine very slightly cocked, not noticeable, in near fine dust jacket with light rubbing and long crease on back cover. Quill & Brush 102-956 1996 $125.00

JAMES, P. D.   Unnatural Causes. New York: Scribner's Sons, 1967. 1st edition; fine in dust jacket.   Quill & Brush 102-953 1996 $150.00

JAMES, P. D.   An Unsuitable Job for a Woman. London: Faber, 1st edition; very good in dust jacket slighty rubbed and faded on spine with chips from corners and ends of spine   Virgo Books 48-113 1996 £95.00

JAMES, PHILLIP   Henry Moore on Sculpture. London: MacDonald, 1966. 4to; 293 pages, 128 illustrations; cloth, dust jacket damaged. Rainsford A54-422 1996 £75.00

JAMES, S. P.   A Monograph of the Anopheline Mosquitoes of India. Calcutta: 1911. 2nd edition; 4to; pages viii, 128, 15 colored and 21 plain plates and text figures; cloth, some slight worming, lacks half title. Wheldon & Wesley 207-1058 1996 £95.00

JAMES, W. S.   Cow-boy Life In Texas of 27 Years a Maverick: a Realistic and True Recital of Wild Life on the Boundless Plains of Texas. Chicago Donohue, Henneberry & Co., 1893. 1st edition; 1st issue; blue cloth, decoratively stamped in black and gilt, light patchiness to spine otherwise, unsually fine. Adams: Rampaging Herd 1159; Howes J54. Hermitage SP95-711 1996 $175.00

JAMES, W. S.   Cowboy Life in Texas or 27 Years a Mavrick. Chicago: 1893. 2nd printing; 213 pages; illustrations; decorated cloth covers, very good, professionally reinforced hinge, slipcase, overall a remarkably fine copy.   Early West 22-243 1996 $225.00

JAMES, WILLIAM 1842-1910   What Is An Emotion? N.P.: n.d., but 1884. 1st separate printing; 8vo; 18 pages; original stapled wrappers, in fine, fresh condition with just one light vertical crease, as if it were folded once for a brief pocket-journey home; presentation copy, inscribed by author for Charles Renouvier, French philosopher. Rare. Lakin & Marley 3-24 1996 $1,250.00

JAMES, WILLIAM d. 1827   The Naval History of Great Britain From the Declaration of War by France in 1793 to the Accession of George IV. London: bentley, 1837. 8vo; 6 volumes; plates, diagrams, tables; original gilt impressed boards, very good.   John Lewcock 30-99 1996 £125.00

JAMES, WILLIAM F.   History of San Jose. San Jose: San Jose Printing Co., 1933. 170 pages; maps, illustrations; original boards with slight wear; scarce.   Dumont 28-86 1996 $160.00

JAMESON, ANNA BROWNELL MURPHY 1794-1860   Legends of the Monastic Orders as Represented in the Fine Arts Forming the Second Series of Sacred and Legendary Art. London: 1850. 8vo; xlviii, 481 pages; elaborately embossed morocco in complex oval shaped pattern, very good.   K Books 441-291 1996 £85.00

JAMESON, ANNA BROWNELL MURPHY 1794-1860   Memoirs of the Beauties of the Court of Charles II. London: Bohn, 1851. Quarto; 350 pages; 21 splendid stipple engravings in perfect condition, all tissue guards present; full polished calf, raised bands, spine gilt in panels, gilt on black leather title, gilt fillets, marbled endpapers, gauffered edges; with colorful triple portrait fore-edge painting of Charles II, flanked by Nell Gwynne & Catherine of Braganza, each in oval frame, with six cupids supporting the portraits at top and bottom.   Hartfield 48-F4 1996 $1,400.00

JAMESON, ANNA BROWNELL MURPHY 1794-1860   Visits and Sketches at Home and Abroad. London: Saunders and Otley, 1835. 2nd eidtion; 8vo; 3 volumes; half morocco, marbled boards, raised bands, gilt compartments; fine set.   David Mason 71-83 1996 $280.00

JAMIESON, FRANCES THURTLE   Ashford Rectory, or, the Spoiled Child Reformed. London: printed for G. and W. B. Whittaker and N. Hailes, 1820. 3rd edition; narrow 8vo; 216 pages, 8 pages publisher's ads at end, 2 copperplate engravings; quarter calf, marbled baords, with spine compartmented in gilt, bottom of spine worn at edge, one small repaired tear, else very good. Osborne 899.   Marjorie James 19-131 1996 £95.00

JAMIESON, JOHN   An Etymological Dictionary of the Scottish Language; In Which the Words Are Explained in Their Different Senses, Authorised by the Names of the Writers by Whom They are Used... Edinburgh: printed for Arch. Constable & Alexander Jameson, by Abernethy &... 1818. 1st octavo edition; 8vo; x, (434) pages, apparently lacking half title; contemporary marbled boards, neatly reacked.   James Burmester 29-76 1996 £140.00

JAMIESON, JOHN   An Etymological Dictionary of the Scottish Language; in Which the Words are Explained In their Different Senses... Edinburgh: Archibald Constable 1818. 8vo; pages x, unpaginated, 4; contemporary vellum, gilt, flyleaves and half title lightly spotted; armorial bookplate of Hon. Marchioness of Hastings.   R.F.G. Hollett 76-136 1996 £75.00

JANE'S Fighting Ships. London: 1938. Split to backstrip, the corners bumped.   Petersfield Bookshop FH58-365 1996 £100.00

JANE'S Fighting Ships. London: 1944/45. Oblong folio; binding little discolored.   Petersfield Bookshop FH58-366 1996 £100.00

JANE, CECIL   A Spanish Voyage to Vancouver and the North-West Coast of America Being the Narrative of the Voyage Made in the Year 1792 by the Schooners Sutil and Mexicana to Explore the Strait of Fuca. London: Argonaut Press, 1930. One of 525 copies; 25.5 x 20cm; 156 pages, 5 plates and 2 folding maps; some darkening to vellum, slight soiling to covers; decorative bookplate.   Parmer Books 039/Nautica-039354 1996 $500.00

JANE, FRED T.   Balke of the 'Rattlesnake' or the Man who saved England. London: Tower Publishing Co. 1895. 1st edition; 8vo; 269 pages; illustrations; original pictorial cloth, gilt on spine, trifle rubbed, very good; with 1895 presentation inscription signed by Jane.   M & S Rare Books 60-184 1996 $425.00

JANES, THOMAS   The Beauties of the Poets; Being a Collection of Moral and Sacred Poetry, from the Most Eminent Authors. London: printed by R. Noble, for J. Scatcherd and J. Whitaker, n.d. 1800? 8vo; contemporary name on title, piece cut from upper blank margin of leaf following title, not touching text; new quarter calf, label.   Anthony W. Laywood 108-218 1996 £225.00

JANET, PIERRE   The Major Symptoms of Hysteria: Fifteen Lectures Given in the Medical School of Harvard University. New York: Macmillan Co., 1907. 1st edition; 12mo; (xii), 345, (1) pages; blue cloth, slight cover soiling and rubbing to joints, very good, titlepage stamp and spine call numbers of Hartford Retreat, with Jelliffe's bookplate.   John Gach 150-222 1996 $125.00

JANET, PIERRE   Mental State of Hystericals: a Study of Mental Stigmata and Mental Accidents. New York: London: G. P. Putnam's Sons/Knickerbocker Press, 1901. 1st edition in English; thick 8vo; xviii, 535, (7) pages; green cloth, recased, label removed from spine, very good, usually turns up in poor condition; very scarce; with Jelliffe's name stamp.   John Gach 150-223 1996 $200.00

JANET, PIERRE   Psychological Healing: a Historical and Clinical Study. New York: Macmillan Co., 1925. 1st U.S. edition; 8vo; 2 volumes, 698, (701)-1265, (3) pages; straight grained brown cloth, slight goudge to spine of volume 2, endleaves lightly foxed, very good.   John Gach 150-224 1996 $250.00

JANKA, GYULA   Advises (sic) for Collectors of Miniature Books. Budapest: Nyomda, 1971. Limited to 500 copies; 2 3/8 x 1 5/8 inches; 151 pages; many black and white photos; gilt stamped navy morocco with light blue inlaid front panel and spine; fine. Bookplate.   Bromer Booksellers 87-187 1996 $100.00

JANOUCH, GUSTAV   "Heckmeck": Ein Prager Nachstuck. Raamin Presse, 1974. One of 70 copies signed by artist (of a total edition of 110); 9 1/2 x 9 3/4 inches; 1 p.l., (1), 18, (1) pp, (1) leaf (colophon); 17 half page illustrations in several colors, overprinted with etchings, all by Roswitha Quadflieg; original printed pink paper boards, as new.   Phillip J. Pirages 33-439 1996 $1,750.00

JANSON, CHARLES WILLIAM   The Stranger in America: Containing Observations Made During a Long Residence in that Country, on the Genius, Manners and Customs... London: printed for James Cundee, 1807. 1st edition; engraved title, plan of Philadelphia, 9 tinted full page engravings; handsomely bound at Monastery Hill Bindery in one half maroon morocco, spine with raised bands bordered by blindstamp rules tapering on to boards ending a fleur-de-lis, title and date in gilt, light foxing, heavier to prelims. Howes J59;   Hermitage SP95-712 1996 $1,250.00

JANSON: a Definitive Collection. San Francisco: Greenwood Press, 1954. One of 350 copies; oblong 4to; foldout plates; unpaginated; vellum spine boards, one plate with crease in margin, otherwise fine.   The Bookpress 75-301 1996 $235.00

JANSON: a Definitive Collection. San Francisco: Greenwood Press, 1954. One of 350 copies; 6 1/2 x 9 1/2 inches; (61) pages; vellum backed boards; near fine.   Timothy Hawley 115-227 1996 $125.00

JANSSON, TOVE   Who Will comfort Toffle? London: Ernest Benn, printed in Finland, 1960. 4t; color and black and white illustrations by author; red cloth, fine in colored pictorial dust jacket.   Barbara Stone 70-129 1996 £135.00

JAQUET, EUGENE   Technique and History of the Swiss Watch. Olten: Urs Graf, 1953. Large 4to; 278 pages; profusely illustrated, including 190 photos (several in color), text figures; purple cloth, gilt.   Kenneth Karmiole 1NS-132 1996 $150.00

JARDI, ENRIC   Torres Garcia. Barcelona: Poligrafa, 1974. Square 4to; 287 pages, text in English; 385 illustrations, 146 in color; cloth, dust jacket. Freitag 9525.   Brannan 43-648 1996 $135.00

JARDINE, ALEXANDER   Letter from Barbary, France, Spain, Portugal, &c. London: printed for T. Cadell, 1788. 1st edition; 8vo; 2 volumes; contemporary tree calf, spines gilt, contrasting red and green morocco labels, minor rubbing. pencilled comment by a reader, uncommon; fine set. CBEL II 1427.   Ximenes 109-165 1996 $450.00

JARDINE, WILLIAM   British Salmonidae. London: 1979. Limited to 500 copies; large folio; 12 very fine colored plates; descriptive text for each; quarter morocco, leather title label on upper cover, mint in slipcase. David A.H. Grayling MY95Orn-45 1996 £175.00

JARDINE, WILLIAM   The Naturalist's Library. Edinburgh: 1833-43. Original issue; post 8vo; complete set, 40 volumes; 40 portraits, 16 plain and 24 hand colored title vignettes, 42 plain and 1246 hand colored plates; contemporary half green morocco, gilt, emblematically tooled, m.e. Volume 22 newly rebound to match.   Wheldon & Wesley 207-54 1996 £2,750.00

JARMAN, W.   U.S.A. Uncle Sam's Abscess, or Hell Upon Earth for U.S. Uncle Sam. Exeter: 1884. Pages 194; original illustrated printed wrappers, near fine. Graff 2199.   Stephen Lunsford 45-81 1996 $135.00

JARRATT, RIE   Gutierrez de Lara, Mexican-Texan: the story of a Creole Hero. Austin: Creole Texana, 1949. xii, 67 pages; illustrations by Jose Cisernos; green cloth, gilt title, designed by Carl Hertzog; fine in glassine wrapper. Dykes 50; Great, Cisneros 97.   Bohling Book Co. 191-75 1996 $110.00

JARRELL, RANDALL   The Animal Family. New York: Pantheon, 1965. 1st edition; short octavo; 180 pages; decorations by Maurice Sendak; blue buckram stamped in silver to front cover and spine, spine and top edges lightly faded, else fine in original dust jacket, printed with Sendak decoration.   Bromer Booksellers 87-153 1996 $125.00

JARRELL, RANDALL   Blood for a Stranger. New York: Harcourt Brace and Co., 1942. 1st edition; one of 1700 copies; 8vo; fine in fine dust jacket, neatly price clipped and slightly sunned, else lovely copy.   Laki & Marley 3-25 1996 $450.00

JARRELL, RANDALL   Blood for a Stranger. New York: Harcourt, Brace, 1942. 1st edition; one of 1700 copies; 8vo; red cloth, dust jacket, fine in very slightly edge worn jacket; Wright A1.   James S. Jaffe 34-298 1996 $350.00

JARRELL, RANDALL   Blood for a Stranger. New York: Harcourt Brace, 1942. 1st edition; 8 3/4 x 5 3/4 inches; x, 82 pages; original cloth, jacket with just slightly faded spine, and with slight tears or fraying at spine ends and at bottom of front panel, in all other ways, very fine copy of author's first book in clean, smooth, nearly fine jacket; Wright A1, Adams 1.   Phillip J. Pirages 33-317 1996 $400.00

JARRELL, RANDALL   The Gingerbread Rabbit. New York: Macmillan, 1964. 1st edition; 8vo; pictorial boards, dust jacket, boards little rubbed along edges, otherwise fine in slightly rubbed jacket, scarce.   James S. Jaffe 34-308 1996 $150.00

JARRELL, RANDALL   Little Friend, Little Friend. New York: Dial Press, 1945. 1st edition; 8vo; very good and tight copy in well chipped dust jacket; presentation copy inscribed by author for Phillip Rahv, founder of The Partisan Review.   Lakin & Marley 3-26 1996 $750.00

JARRELL, RANDALL   Little Friend, Little Friend. New York: Dial Press, 1945. 1st edition; one of 2000 copies; 8vo; cloth, dust jacket, fine in jacket with few small chips.   James S. Jaffe 34-299 1996 $125.00

JARRELL, RANDALL   Little Friend, Little Friend. New York: Dial Press, 1945. 1st edition; not stated; dark blue boards blindstamped with stars, spine printed in gold and blue, fine in very good dust jacket with several small chips and normal wear, from the library of Robie Macauley, Jarrell's friend and advisor.   Bev Chaney, Jr. 23-338 1996 $250.00

JARRELL, RANDALL   Losses. New York: Harcourt Brace, 1948. 1st edition; one of 1000 copies; 8vo; black cloth, dust jacket, fine in slightly rubbed jacket, small closed tear on back panel.   James S. Jaffe 34-300 1996 $200.00

JARRELL, RANDALL   The Lost World. New York: Macmillan, 1965. 1st edition; 8vo; cloth, dust jacket; inscribed by author, mint.   James S. Jaffe 34-311 1996 $450.00

JARRELL, RANDALL   Pictures from an Institution. New York: Knopf, 1954. 1st edition; 8vo; cloth, dust jacket, fine.   James S. Jaffe 34-303 1996 $225.00

JARRELL, RANDALL   Poetry and the Age. New York: Knopf, 1953. 1st edition; one of 2000 copies; 8vo; black cloth, dust jacket, fine in slightly rubbed jacket. Wright A5a.   James S. Jaffe 34-302 1996 $125.00

JARRELL, RANDALL   Selected Poems. New York: Knopf, 1955. One of 2000 copies; 8vo; cloth, dust jacket, spine lightly mottled, otherwise fine in lightly rubbed and edge worn jacket, very difficult book to find in fine condition.   James S. Jaffe 34-304 1996 $125.00

JARRELL, RANDALL   The Seven-League Crutches. New York: Harcourt Brace, 1951. 1st edition; one of 2000 copies; black cloth, dust jacket, previous owner's neat ink signature on front free endpaper, otherwise fine.   James S. Jaffe 34-301 1996 $125.00

JARRY, ALFRED   Le Moutardier du Pape. 1907. One of only 170 copies of the entire first edition; wrappers; partially removed ownership sticker to front fly, sparse foxing to endpapers and to fore-edges of pages, otherwise near fine.   Lame Duck Books 19-265 1996 $1,500.00

JARVES, JAMES JACKSON 1818-1888   History of the Hawaiian or Sandwich Islands, Embracing Their Antiquities, Mythology, Legends, Discovery by Europeans in the Sixteenth Century... Boston: Tappan and Dennet, 1843. 1st edition; 8vo; xx, (map), 407 pages; 25 illustrations; original brown embossed cloth, gilt titles; expertly rehinged, showing some wear to lower edges and corners. Hill p. 154 for London ed. Sabin 35796.   Parmer Books 039/Nautica-039133 1996 $1,500.00

JARVES, JAMES JACKSON 1818-1888   History of the Hawaiian or Sandwich Islands. Boston: James Munroe and Co., 1844. 2nd edition; 8vo; 407 pages; frontispiece and engraved title and illustrations; three quarter brown morocco and marbled boards, relatively light dampstain, mostly affecting the first few leaves, minor rubbing or binding; good to very good.   Robert F. Lucas 42-42 1996 $250.00

JAYNE, WALTER   The Healing Gods of Ancient Civilizations. New Haven: 1925. 1st edition; 569 pages; original binding; GM 6458.   W. Bruce Fye 71-1096 1996 $150.00

JEAN-AUBRY, G.   Joseph Conrad in the Congo. London: 1926. 1st edition; signed limited edition of 470 copies; very near fine.   Stephen Lupack 83- 1996 $100.00

JEAN-AUBRY, G.   Twenty Letters to Joseph Conrad. First Edition club, 1926. One of 220 sets; various sizes, from 12mo. to small 4to; 12 booklets; wrappers; preserved together in original portfolio of quarter cloth and patterned paper, spine renewed, incorporating original backstrip, contents fine; very scarce.   Bertram Rota 272-98 1996 £200.00

JEANNERET-GRIS, CHARLES EDOUARD 1887-1965   The City of Tomorrow and Its Planning. London: John Rodker, 1929. 1st English language edition; 8vo; xxvii, (i), 301, (2) pages; frontispiece; cloth, 2 short tears on left margin of folding plan, not affecting illustration, spine faintly sunned, mark on rear cover, else very good.   The Bookpress 75-208 1996 $285.00

JEANS, JAMES   Problems of Cosmogony and Stellar Dynamics, Being an Essay to Which the Adams Prize of the University of Cambridge for the Year 1917 was Adjudged. Cambridge: Cambridge University Press, 1919. 4to; 293 pages; blue cloth, bevelled edges, cloth wrinkled on rear board, extremities somewhat worn, 5 plates, text figures. Good copy. Knollwood Books 70-112 1996 $110.00

JEBB, SAMUEL   The Life of Robert Earl of Leicester, the Favourite of Queen Elizabeth. London: printed for Woodman and Lyon and C. Davis, 1727. 1st edition; 8vo; frontispiece; early 19th century full polished tree calf, wide gilt borders enclosing gilt crests, spine elaborately gilt, all edges gilt, by John Clarke; pretty copy; from the handsome library of Rev. Theodore Williams, with his characteristic crest on front cover containing initials "T.W." within an oval.   Ximenes 108-219 1996 $330.00

JEBB, SAMUEL   The Life of robert Earl of Leicester, the Favourite of Queen Elizabeth... London: printed for Woodman and Lyon...and C. Davis, 1727. 8vo; contemporary panelled calf, rebacked.   Peter Murray Hill 185-90 1996 £55.00

JEFFERIES, RICHARD 1848-1887   After London; or, Wild England. London: Cassell & Co., Ltd. 1884. 1st edition; 8vo; half title, 2 pages of ads, original cloth, spine faded.   Anthony W. Laywood 108-183 1996 £75.00

JEFFERIES, RICHARD 1848-1887   Bevis. The Story of a Boy. London: Sampson Low, 1882. 1st edition; crown 8vo; 3 volumes, half titles in all volumes, original diagonal green ribbed coth, blocked in black and gold, blue grey endpapers; Carter's "B" binding with note 'No inserted ads in any copies seen'; original diagonal green ribbed cloth, blocked in black and gold, blue grey endpapers. Sadleir 1305b; Wolff 3615.   Charles W. Traylen 117-133 1996 £600.00

JEFFERIES, RICHARD 1848-1887   Hodge and His Masters. London: Smith, Elder & Co., 1880. 1st edition; 8vo; 2 volumes, half titles, 4 pages of ads at end of volume 2; original cloth, gilt, fine.   Anthony W. Laywood 108-184 1996 £100.00

JEFFERIES, RICHARD 1848-1887   A Rook Book. Shropshire: Tern Press, March, 1988. One of 15 specials in an edition of 125 copies signed by Nicholas and Mary Parry; 9.5 x 6.25 inches; illustrations by Nicholas Parry, titlepage in red and black, first text-page in brown and black, set in 16 pt. Poliphilus, printed on Hardy Ends paper; bound in full pigskin, title stamped in brown and gilt on spine, housed in cloth covered drop back box; fine.   Joshua Heller 21-234 1996 $595.00

JEFFERIES, RICHARD 1848-1887   Round About a Great Estate. London: Smith, Elder & Co., 1880. 1st edition; 8vo; half title, 4 pages of ads at end; original cloth, slightly worn, nice.   Anthony W. Laywood 108-185 1996 £80.00

JEFFERIES, RICHARD 1848-1887   Wild Life in a Southern County. London: Smith, Elder and Co., 1879. 1st edition; 8vo; half title; original cloth, gilt, nice.   Anthony W. Laywood 108-186 1996 £85.00

JEFFERIES, RICHARD 1848-1887   Wood Magic: a Fable. London: Cassell, Petter, Galpin & Co., 1881. 1st edition; 8vo; 2 volumes; with half titles and 8 pages of ads at end of each volume; original dark green cloth blocked in black and lettered in gold, neat repair to inner hinge of volume 1. Sadleir 1317.   Charles W. Traylen 117-134 1996 £180.00

JEFFERS, ROBINSON 1887-1962   Be Angry at the Sun. New York:
Random House, 1941. 1st edition; fine in dust jacket.   Left Bank Books
2-61 1996 $165.00

JEFFERS, ROBINSON 1887-1962   The Beaks of Eagles. San Francisco:
privately printed for Albert M. Bender by Edwin Grabhorn, 1936. 1st
edition; limited to 135 copies; folio; title, tinted portrait, 2 pages of text
printed on one side, 2 facsimiles tipped in within rust ruled frames;
original printed rust paper wrappers (chipped with short tears at edges);
near fine internally, very scarce.   Blue Mountain SP95-54 1996
$350.00

JEFFERS, ROBINSON 1887-1962   Brides of the South Wind: Poems
1917-1922. N.P.: Cayucos Books, 1974. 1st edition; one of 285 copies
signed by William Everson; 8vo; quarter leather and cloth, acetate dust
jacket; mint.   James S. Jaffe 34-338 1996 $125.00

JEFFERS, ROBINSON 1887-1962   Californians. New York: Macmillan,
1916. 1st edition; 8vo; pictorial blue cloth, printed dust jacket, touch of
rubbing at extremities of spine, otherwise fine in rare dust jacket which
is slightly worn and darkened, new price sticker on spine.   James S.
Jaffe 34-322 1996 $1,000.00

JEFFERS, ROBINSON 1887-1962   Cawdor and Other Poems. New
York: Horace Liveright, 1928. One of 375 specially bound copies,
numbered and signed by author; original cloth, fine, in very good+ box.
Beasley Books 82-82 1996 $250.00

JEFFERS, ROBINSON 1887-1962   Cawdor. Yolla Bolly Press, 1983. One
of 225 copies, for sale, signed by Houston and Livingston, 13 1/4 x 10
1/4 inches; 3 p.l., 127, (1) pages; printed in red and black, 2 leaves of
olive-green paper separating sections of text; maroon morocco backed
cloth boards, title stamped in blind on front cover and in gilt on spine;
as new.   Phillip J. Pirages 33-520 1996 $350.00

JEFFERS, ROBINSON 1887-1962   Cawdor. Covelo: the Yolla Bolly
Press, 1983. Number 156 of 240 numbered copies (225 for sale); small
folio; (6), 127, (1) pages; text printed in red and black, 4 full page
woodblock illustrations by Mark Livingston; half leather and cloth, title
blindstamped on front cover, lettered in gilt on spine; very fine with
slipcase, case bit faded, signed by James D. Houston and by the artist
Mark Livingston.   Argonaut Book Shop 113-372 1996 $325.00

JEFFERS, ROBINSON 1887-1962   Descent to the Dead. New York:
Random House, 1931. 1st edition; one of 500 copies, signed by Jeffers;
thin tall 8vo; boards, slipcase; previous owner's neat ink inscription,
otherwise very fine.   James S. Jaffe 34-323 1996 $450.00

JEFFERS, ROBINSON 1887-1962   Descent to the Dead. New York:
Random House, 1931. 1/500 copies numbered and signed by author; fine
copy in publisher's box that has one edge partially splitting,, rest of
slipcase fine.   Left Bank Books 2-62 1996 $275.00

JEFFERS, ROBINSON 1887-1962   Give Your Heart to the Hawks and
other Poems. New York: Random House, 1933. 1st edition; 8vo; cloth,
dust jacket; fine in jacket with small closed tear at back panel   James
S. Jaffe 34-326 1996 $150.00

JEFFERS, ROBINSON 1887-1962   Light and Shadows from the Lantern.
San Francisco: pub. by Gelber Lilienthal Inc. at their Bookshop, San
Francisco, 1926. 1st edition; original dark green on tan wove paper; fine.
Left Bank Books 2-60 1996 $125.00

JEFFERS, ROBINSON 1887-1962   Medea. New York: Random House,
1946. 1st edition; 1st issue; 8vo; cloth backed boards, dust jacket; fine.
James S. Jaffe 34-331 1996 $125.00

JEFFERS, ROBINSON 1887-1962   Poems. San Francisco: The Book
Club of California, 1928. One of 310 copies, signed by author and signed
by photographer; (8), v-xi, (3), 3-49, (3) pages; frontispiece by Ansel
Adams; title and initials in red by Valenti Angelo; green cloth, printed
paper spine label, spine bit faded, else fine.   Argonaut Book Shop
113-373 1996 $1,100.00

JEFFERS, ROBINSON 1887-1962   Return; an Unpublished Poem. San
Francisco: privately printed, 1934. 1/250 copies numbered; printed at the
Grabhorn Press; some minor chipping and 1 inch tear to bottom edge of
paper covered boards, otherwise clean copy of a fragile book.   Left
Bank Books 2-64 1996 $285.00

JEFFERS, ROBINSON 1887-1962   The Selected Poetry. New York:
Random House, 1938. 1st edition; 8vo; cloth, dust jacket price clipped,
faintly darkened along spine; fine.   James S. Jaffe 34-330 1996
$150.00

JEFFERS, ROBINSON 1887-1962   Solstice and Other Poems. New
York: Random House/Grabhorn, 1935. One of 320 copies, signed by
author; original cloth, fine in fine dust jacket.   Beasley Books 82-83
1996 $375.00

JEFFERS, ROBINSON 1887-1962   Solstice and Other Poems. New
York: Random House, 1935. 1st edition; 8vo; cloth, dust jacket, light
offsetting on front endpaper, otherwise fine, slightly rubbed jacket.
James S. Jaffe 34-327 1996 $150.00

JEFFERS, ROBINSON 1887-1962   Songs and Heroes. Los Angeles:
Arundel Press, 1988. Limited to 200 numbered copies; printed on
Frankfurt paper; mint, issued without dust jacket, at publication price.
Polyanthos 22-469 1996 $165.00

JEFFERS, ROBINSON 1887-1962   Songs and Heroes; Previously
Unpublished Poems. Los Angeles: Arundel Press, 1988. Of 250 numbered
copies, this one of 200 on Frankfurt; 4to; printed by Patrick Reagh in
Centaur and Arrighi with Castellar initials in black and red; cloth, printed
labels; fine.   Bertram Rota 272-15 1996 £82.50

JEFFERS, ROBINSON 1887-1962   Such Counsels You Gave to Me and
Other Poems. New York: Random House, 1937. 1st edition; one of 300
specially bound copies, signed by author; 8vo; quarter leather, decorated
boards, glassine dust jacket, slipcase; light offsetting on front and black
endpapers, as usual, otherwise fine in somewhat worn glassine; from the
collection of Jeffers' bibliographer, Sidney Alberts, with his ownership
inscription.   James S. Jaffe 34-328 1996 $350.00

JEFFERS, ROBINSON 1887-1962   Such Counsels You Gave To Me and
Other Poems. New York: Random House, 1937. 1st edition; 8vo; cloth,
dust jacket; fine in jacket slightly chipped at head of spine.   James S.
Jaffe 34-329 1996 $150.00

JEFFERS, ROBINSON 1887-1962   Thurso's Landing and Other Poems.
New York: Liveright Inc., 1932. 1/200 numbered copies of which 185 are
for sale, specially printed and bound and signed by author; cloth very
slightly faded at spine and top of front cover, otherwise fine; scarce.
Left Bank Books 2-63 1996 $265.00

JEFFERS, ROBINSON 1887-1962   Thurso's Landing and Other Poems.
New York: Liveright, 1932. 1st edition; 8vo; cloth backed boards, dust
jacket; fine.   James S. Jaffe 34-324 1996 $150.00

JEFFERS, ROBINSON 1887-1962   Thurso's Landing, Dear Judas and
Other Poems. New York: Liveright, 1932. 1st edition; 8vo; cloth, dust
jacket; fine copy in somewhat worn jacket.   James S. Jaffe 34-325
1996 $100.00

JEFFERSON, GEOFFREY   Selected Papers. London: Pitman Medical,
1960. 8vo; 565 pages; very good, only light soiling of boards, internally
mint except for removed bookplates.   James Tait Goodrich K40-167
1996 $175.00

JEFFERSON, SAMUEL   The History and Antiquities of Allerdale Ward,
Above Derwent in the County of Cumberland. Carlisle: S. Jefferson, 1842.
1st edition; 8vo; pages xiii (2 ads), complete with 7 steel engraved
plates; original blindstamped cloth, gilt, rather faded.   R.F.G. Hollett &
Son 78-1032 1996 £60.00

JEFFERSON, SAMUEL   The History and Antiquities of Allerdale Ward,
Above Derwent in the County of Cumberland... Carlisle: S. Jefferson,
1842. 1st edition; 8vo; pages xiii, (iv, additional subscribers, contents
etc.), 462, 7 steel engraved plates; modern half crushed morocco, gilt,
spine little faded.   R.F.G. Hollett & Son 78-1031 1996 £120.00

JEFFERSON, SAMUEL   The History and Antiquities of Carlisle...
Carlisle: Samuel Jefferson, 1838. 8vo; pages xv, (i), 460, 5 engraved
plates (rather foxed), lithographed plan and 11 woodcut illustrations;
original blindstamped cloth, gilt, neatly recased, lower board little
damped.   R.F.G. Hollett & Son 78-1033 1996 £125.00

JEFFERSON, SAMUEL   The History and Antiquities of Leath Ward, in
the County of Cumberland, with Biographical Notices and Memoirs.
Carlisle: S. Jefferson, 1840. Large 8vo; pages xiii, (iii), 515, 14 engraved
plates, frontispiece offset on to tissue, otherwise fine, bright copy;
original blindstamped cloth, gilt.   R.F.G. Hollett & Son 78-1035 1996
£120.00

JEFFERSON, SAMUEL   The History and Antiquities of Leath Ward, in the County of Cumberland... Carlisle: S. Jefferson, 1840. Large 8vo; pages xiii, (iii), 515; 14 engraved plates (some edges little browned), 7 text illustrations; modern rexine, gilt.   R.F.G. Hollett & Son 78-1034 1996 £60.00

JEFFERSON, SAMUEL   The Trial and Life of Thomas Cappoch, (The Rebel-Bishop of Carlisle). Carlisle: Samuel Jefferson, 1839. 2nd edition; 8vo; pages vi, 31, (i), with facsimile titlepage; original stiff wrappers, paper label, spine trifle chipped.   R.F.G. Hollett & Son 78-200 1996 £50.00

JEFFERSON, THOMAS   Catalouge of the Library of Thomas Jefferson. Washington: Library of Congress, 1952-59. 4to; 5 volumes; xvi, 562; vi, 433; vi, 481; viii, 568; x, 442 pages; portrait, 10 other plates; cloth, decorated gilt, few leaves in lasat volume very slightly creased at one corner, otherwise good set.   Thomas Thorp 489-168 1996 £350.00

JEFFERSON, THOMAS   Observations sur La Virginie. (Notes on Virginia). Paris: Barrois, 1786. 1st published edition; folding map printed on thick paper and in outstanding fresh condition, superb untrimmed copy, rare in this original condition; original half calf, spine gilt, marbled boards from binder's waste, untrimmed, minimal repairs to binding; superb, untrimmed copy, rare in this original condition.   19th Century Shop 39- 1996 $21,500.00

JEFFERSON, THOMAS   Notes on the State of Virginia. London: John Stockdale, 1787. 1st edition in English; large folding map, original hand coloring in outline; map has been carefully mounted to linen; fine modern tree calf, spine gilt, occasional minor defect, but a fine, fresh copy. 19th Century Shop 39- 1996 $10,000.00

JEFFRESS, J. MURRAY   Ritual of the Grand United Order of Moses Incorporated... Charlotte: Grand United Order of Moses, n.d., c. 1930. 1st edition; spine ends worn, some pencil notations on several pages, pages soiled, but sound, good plus copy, laid in are 2 printed receipts on the organization's letterhead dated in 1952; scarce.   Between the Covers 43-346 1996 $100.00

JEFFREYS, GEORGE   Miscellanies in Verse and Prose. London: printed for the author, 1754. 1st edition; 4to; contemporary half sheep quite rubbed; aside from the binding wear, very good, scarce. Foxon p. 387; CBEL II 553.   Ximenes 109-166 1996 $400.00

JEFFREYS, J. G.   British Conchology. London: 1904, 1862-69. 8vo; 5 volumes; 40 plain and 107 hand colored plates; later cloth.   Wheldon & Wesley 207-1169 1996 £500.00

JEFFRIES, EWEL   Short Biography of John Leeth. Cleveland: 1904. Limited to 267 numbered copies; 70 pages; bright binding, book very fine condition, added slipcase. Howes J86.   Early West 22-475 1996 $165.00

JEFFRIES, JOHN   A Narrative of the Two Aerial Voyages of Doctor Jeffries with Mons. Blanchard; with Meterological Observations and Remarks. N.P.: n.d. Facsimile reprint of 1786 first edition; folio; 2, (2), 60; (66)-88 pages; frontispiece, several illustrations in text, one full page; half cloth over boards, paper title label on cover, near fine copy, Library of Congress copy, with their discreet 'surplus duplicate' stamp on front free endpaper. Brockett 6577; Milbank, 1st Cent. Flight in Amer. pp. 10-16/211.   Edwin V. Glaser 121-169 1996 $150.00

JEKYLL, GERTRUDE   Wall and Water Gardens. London: Country Life/George Newnes, n.d. 1901. 1st edition; light foxing, inscribed by author for J. T. Bennett-Poe, horticulturist.   Between the Covers 42-185 1996 $950.00

JEKYLL, GERTRUDE   Wood and Garden. Notes and Thoughts, Practical and Critical, of a Working Amateur. London: 1899. 8vo; 71 illustrations from photos; original buckram.   Charles W. Traylen 117-311 1996 £60.00

JELEN, NICOLETTE   A Dog's Story. New York: Vincent FitzGerald, 1987. One of 25 copies only; page size 9 x 12 inches; 30 original etchings; purple Japanese silk with publisher's slipcase.   Priscilla Juvelis 95/1-80 1996 $2,200.00

JELENSKI, CONSTANTIN   Leonor Fini. New York: Olympia Press, 1968. 11 3/4 x 11 3/4 inches; 171 pages; fine in lightly worn, original publisher's cardboard slipcase.   Hermitage SP95-789 1996 $150.00

JEMMY STRING. New York: McLoughlin, n.d., c. 1880. 12mo; color printed pictorial wrappers; fresh copy, scarce.   Barbara Stone 70-123 1996 £75.00

JENKINS, C. FRANCIS   Vision by Radio, Radio Photographs, Radio Photograms. Washington: by author, 1925. 1st edition; 8vo; 139 pages; illustrations; original cloth; fine. Shiers 1797.   Edwin V. Glaser 121-170 1996 $450.00

JENKINS, DAN   Semi-Tough. New York: Atheneum, 1972. 1st edition; very slight fading at crown, else fine in vrey near fine dust jacket. Between the Covers 42-241 1996 $125.00

JENKINS, DAVID   Eight Centurie of Reports, Or Eight Hundred Cases Solemnly adjudged in the Exchequer-Chamber, or Upon Writs of Error. London: Printed by E. and R. Nutt, and R. Gosling, 1734. 1st edition in English; contemporary calf, worn, embrowned, joints cracked, lacking label.   Meyer Boswell SL25-123 1996 $350.00

JENKINS, JAMES   The Martial Achievements of Great Britain and Her Allies, from1799 to 1815. London: printed for Js. Jenkins by L. Harrison and J. C. Leigh, 1815-16. 1st edition; 4to; hand colored vignette title, engraved title, hand colored dedication with coat-of-arms, 51 other hand colored aquatint plates (watermarked 1812); contemporary red half morocco, spine gilt in 6 compartments, rubbed, light marginal soiling. Tooley 281; Abbey Life 365.   Thomas Thorp 489-169 1996 £1,200.00

JENKINS, JOHN   The Art of Writing, Reduced in Seven Books. Cambrdidge: Printed for the author, 1813. 8vo; book 1 (all), 20, 68, (4) pages; plates, some crudely, albeit attratively, hand colored; contemporary calf backed boards, worn, some foxing and soiling, very good. S&S 28833.   M & S Rare Books 60-394 1996 $200.00

JENKINS, JOHN   Naval Achievements of Great Britain, from the Year 1793 to 1817. London: printed for J. Jenkins, No. 48 Strand, by L. Harrison 373 Strand, 4to; text (unpaginated), 56 hand colored aquatints and 1 uncolored plan, this copy contains the two additional portraits of Lord Nelson that are very often missing, plates watermarked 1812-1816 on J. Whatman paper, all plates in mint condition with no foxing or offsetting, plates all Have good wide margins, text also in fine, clean state with wide margins, altogether a very fine and handsome copy; full contemporary calf, gilt panelled spine, very tastefully rebacked, preserving original spine, marbled endpapers and edges, two armorial bookplates to front pastedown, owner's ink inscription. Abbey Life 337; Tooley 282.   Beeleigh Abbey BA56-151 1996 £7,500.00

JENKINS, JOHN H.   Cracker Barrel Chronicles. Austin: Pemberton Press, 1965. 1st and only edition; 509 pages; original cloth, title stamped in brown on spine and front cover.   Michael D. Heaston 23-43 1996 $250.00

JENKINS, JOHN H.   I'm Frank Hamer, the Life of a Texas Peace Officer. Austin: 1968. Deluxe first edition, limited to 300 numbered copies; slipcase; book very fine, signed by authors.   Early West 22-120 1996 $350.00

JENKINS, JOHN H.   The Papers of the Texas Revolution, 1835-1836. Austin: Presidial Press, 1973. 1st edition; 10 volumes; scarce. BTB 106. Maggie Lambeth 30-289 1996 $600.00

JENKINS, WELLBORN VICTOR   "We Also Serve": The Story of a Colored Boy Who Stood Single-Handed Against the World and Played the Part of a Hero. N.P.: Gate City Free Kindergarten Assoc., n.d., c. 1934. 1st edition; illustrations, frontispiece; printed wrappers, with very slight loss at base of spine; about fine, rare.   Between the Covers 43-132 1996 $475.00

JENKINSON, HENRY IRWIN   Practical Guide to Carlisle, Gilshand, Roman Wall and Neighbourhood. London: Edward Stanford, 1875. 1st edition; 8vo; pages viii, 303, 24, engraved frontispiece, folding map in rear pocket, original pictorial green cloth, gilt; very nice, bright, inscribed "With the Publisher's Compliments".   R.F.G. Hollett & Son 78-1036 1996 £65.00

JENKINSON, HENRY IRWIN   Practical Guide to the English Lake District. London: Edward Stanford, 1876. 5th edition; small 8vo; pages xciii, 352, 44, folding map in front pocket, 10 further maps of which 9 are extending and 1 colored, backs of maps and title lightly spotted, otherwise very nice, tight and clean copy; original green cloth, gilt. R.F.G. Hollett & Son 78-1038 1996 £55.00

JENKS, FRANCIS   Mr. Francis Jenk's (sic) Speech Spoken in a Common Hall, the 24th of June 1679. London: 1679. Folio; 2 pages; disbound; Wing J 627.   H. M. Fletcher 121-37 1996 £60.00

JENNER, CHARLES   The Destruction of Niniveh: a Poem. Cambridge: printed by John Archdeacon, for Thomas & John Merrill & sold... 1768. 1st edition; 4to; disbound, titlepage bit dusty and soiled; Roscoe A260. Ximenes 108-220 1996 $125.00

JENNER, CHARLES   Letters from Altamont in the Capital, to His Friends in the Country. London: printed for T. Becker and P. A. De Hondt, 1767. 1st edition; small 8vo; pages xi, 272; contemporary calf backed marbled boards, name neatly cut from extreme upper blank margin of title, else very good in contemporary calf backed marbled boards, gilt ruled spine, with red label, gilt. Block 123.   James Fenning 133-177 1996 £450.00

JENNER, EDWARD   An Inquiry into the Causes and Effects of the Variolae Vaccinae. N.P.: n.d. Facsimile of London 1798 edition; 4to; iv, 75, (1) pages; 4 plates; original boards, spine bit soiled, very good. GM 5423.   Edwin V. Glaser B122-82 1996 $100.00

JENNER, EDWARD   An Inquiry Into the Causes and Effects of the Variolae Vaccinae...Known by the Name of the Cow Pox. 1923. Facsimile reprint of 1798 edition; limited to 500 copies; 11 x 8 inches; 75 + errata; ink name, spine sunned, extremities worn.   John K. King 77-724 1996 $100.00

JENNINGS, DAVID   An Introduction to the Knowledge of Medals. Birmingham: printed by Sarah Baskerville, sold by Joseph Jackson, 1775. Octavo; contemporary tree calf, neatly rebacked, title quite soiled and washed, light waterstain, lightly and uniformly embrowned, complete with rare errata leaf at end.   G. W. Stuart 59-8 1996 $350.00

JENNINGS, EDITH   The Everlasting Animals and Other Stories. London: Duckworth and Co., 1898. 1st edition; 4to; 87 pages; colored frontispiece, 6 other full page colored illustrations by Stuart Bevan; red pictorial boards, slight wear and soiling to covers, some thumbing, else very good.   Marjorie James 19-135 1996 £75.00

JENNINGS, ELIZABETH   Winter Wind. Janus Press, 1979. One of 50 for the Janus Press in an edition of 220 unnumbered copies; 9.25 x 5.875 inches; 12 unnumbered leaves; one wood engraving by Monica Poole, designed and printed by Claire Van Vliet, titles printed in black and silver, text in black, copyright notice and colophon in silver; titlepage wood engraving printed in black and printed on Barcham Green Charles I; bound in white linen over boards; author/title label on spine printed in silver on Barcham green Charles I, used also for flyleaves, endpapers of Barcham Green Michelle cover; fine.   Joshua Heller 21-19 1996 $150.00

JENNINGS, HENRY CONSTANTINE   Summary and Free Reflections, In Which the Great Outline Only, and Principal Features, of the Following Subjects are Impartially Traced and Candidly Examined. Chelmsford: printed by Clachar, Frost and Gray, for the author, 1783. 8vo; xvii, (1), 115, (1), 31, (1), 64, iv, vi, 82, 6, (4), 7-34, 142-178, iv, 68 pages; few annotations in pencil; bound in modern maroon morocco, raised bands, spine lettered in gilt; contemporary signature of Hary Le Dieu on title and bookplate of John Avery; inscribed by author.   John Drury 82-124 1996 £500.00

JENNINGS, JAMES   The Family Cyclopaedia... London: for Sherwood, Neely and Jones, 1822. 2nd edition; 8vo; pages (2), xlviii, (1), xiii, (3 blank), 681; (1), 681-1376 in 1 volume; near contemporary half morocco by J. Collins of Dublin with ticket, extreme corner of one leaf defective with loss of only a few letters, otherwise nice, fresh copy. Attar 158.2. James Fenning 133-178 1996 £85.00

JENNINGS, JAMES   Observations On Some of the Dialects in the West of England. London: Baldwin, Cradock and Joy, 1825. Half title; original brown cloth, very good.   Jarndyce 103-82 1996 £65.00 *

JENNINGS, JAMES   Observations on Some of the Dialects in the West of England, Particularly Somersetshire. London: John Russell Smith, 1869. 2nd edition; half title; original royal blue cloth, very good. Jarndyce 103-86 1996 £60.00

JENNINGS, JOHN J.   Theatrical and Circus Life... St. Louis: Sun Publishing, 1883. New edition; thick 8vo; 163 engraved illustrations; decorative pictorial cloth, lightly soiled, some shelf wear; upper hinge just starting, otherwise very good, clean copy, very scarce. Toole Stott 13329; Wilmeth 220a (1882 ed.).   Dramatis Personae 37-101 1996 $250.00

JENNINGS, JOHN J.   Theatrical and Circus Life, or, Secrets of the Stage, Green-Room and Sawdust Arena, Embracing a History of the Theatre, Exposition of the Mysteries of the Stage, Origin and Growth of Negro Minstrelsy... Chicago: Laird & Lee, 1893. 1st edition; 688 pages; 175 engravings; original pictorial wrappers bound in; very good. Lyman Books 21-227 1996 $200.00

JENNINGS, O. E.   Wild Flowers of Western Pennsylvania and the Upper Ohio Basin. Pittsburgh: 1953. Folio; pages lxxv, 574, (1); xvi, 200 colored plates and descriptions; cloth, light scuffing and smudging, ink name on front pastedown.   Raymond M. Sutton VI-548 1996 $385.00

JENYNS, R. SOAME   Chinese Art: the Minor Arts. Oldbourne Press, 1963-65. 4to; 2 volumes; 462; 324 pages; 133 tipped in plates in color, 292 in monochrome; cloth, dust jackets very slightly torn.   Thomas Thorp 489-170 1996 £100.00

JENYNS, SOAME   Disquisitions on Several Subjects. London: printed for J. Dodsley, 1782. 1st edition; small 8vo; iv, 182 pages; contemporary calf, spine gilt, label, upper joint cracked, else fine.   John Drury 82-126 1996 £140.00

JENYNS, SOAME   Disquisitions on Several Subjects. London: printed for J. Dodsley, 1782. 1st edition; 8vo; disbound; very good; contemporary signature on titlepage of Dudley North. CBELII 554. Ximenes 108-221 1996 $150.00

JENYNS, SOAME   Miscellaneous Pieces in Verse and Prose. London: printed for J. Dodsley, at Tully's Head, 1770. 3rd edition; 8vo; half title, 3-452 pages, separate half titles to each peom and prose piece, vignette half title to The Nature and Origin of Evil; full tree calf, neatly rebacked preserving original backstrip, gilt tooling to compartments, red morocco label to spine, corners bumped. Halkett & Laing IV p. 87.   Beeleigh Abbey BA56-152 1996 £75.00

JENYNS, SOAME   Poems. London: printed for R. Dodsley, 1752. 1st edition; 8vo; contemporary calf, spine gilt, some rubbing, but sound; very good; from the library of John Drinkwater, with his book label and note of acquisition dated 1923, purchased from Hodgson's sale of the library of Eliza Tollet, this volume signed twice by her nephew George Tollet. Foxon P387; CBEL II 554.   Ximenes 108-222 1996 $250.00

JENYNS, SOAME   Poems. London: for R. Dodsley, 1752. 1st edition; 8vo; pages (ii), 194, engraved vignette on title, fly titles to poems included in pagination and register; signatures H5-6 are cancels, bound without half title in contemporary calf, red morocco label, spine gilt in compartments, marbled endpapers, red edges, lightly rubbed, spine worn at head, corners worn, light sprinkling of worming, chiefly marginal; good. Foxon p. 387.   Simon Finch 24-128 1996 £100.00

JENYNS, SOAME   Thoughts on the Causes and Consequences of the Present High Price of Provisions. London: J. Dodsley, 1767. 1st edition; 8vo; (2), 26 pages, wanting half title, but with the final blank D2, very faint cancelled library stamp on blank foot of title; recently well bound in linen backed marbled boards, lettered. Goldsmiths 10313; Black 654; Williams I 23; Higgs 4050n.   John Drury 82-125 1996 £125.00

JENYNS, SOAME   A View of the Internal Evidence of the Christian Religion. Boston: I. Thomas and E. T. Andrews, 1793. 12mo; pages 162; marbled paper wrappers, ribbon ties; early (1799) owner's signature on flyleaf, some foxing, but reasonable copy.   Hartfield 48-L44 1996 $195.00

JEPHSON, R. H.   Observations on the Outdoor Relief Systems in England and Wales. Dublin: Alex. Thom, 1881. 1st edition thus; 8vo; pages (2 blank), 16, (2 blank); original printed paper wrappers, very good to nice. Not in Black.   James Fenning 133-179 1996 £55.00

JERDAN, WILLIAM   National Portrait Gallery of Illustrious and Eminent Personages of the Nineteenth Century. London: Fisher, Jackson, n.d. 1830's. Tall octavo; separately paginated; splendid engraved portraits; original dark green striated cloth, gilt cover and spine decorations, all edges gilt; nice bookplate, some wear to covers, contents excellent. Hartfield 48-V21 1996 $165.00

JEREMY, HENRY   The Law of Carriers, Inn-Keepers, Warehousemen and Other Depositories of Goods for Hire. New York: reprinted and published by I. Riley, 1816. contemporary quarter calf over marbled boards, worn, embrowned, sound.   Meyer Boswell SL25-125 1996 $275.00

JERMY, A. C.   The Island of Mull, a Survey of Its Flora and Environment by the Dept. of Botany, British Museum. London: 1978. Large 8vo; pages xxvi, 630; numerous photos, maps and text figures; rexine.   Raymond M. Sutton VI-739 1996 $100.00

JERMYN, JAMES   Book of English Epithets, Litera and Figurative, with Elementary Remarks and Minute References to Abudant Authorities. London: Smith, Elder, 1849. Small folio; half title with tear at head repaired; bound in at end 12 page "Prospectus & Specimen of an English Gradus, and Dictionary of Ideas..."; original grey cloth, paper label slightly chipped.   Jarndyce 103-261 1996 £75.00

JEROME, JEROME K.   They and I. London: Hutchinson & Co., 1909. 1st edition; original binding, top edge dusty, prelims, edges and endpapers spotted, covers very slightly marked, tail of spine, top corners and bottom edges rubbed, head and tail of spine slightly bumped, spine darkened, very good in chipped, torn and creased, soiled, marked and dusty dust jacket browned at the spine and edges and missing pices at head and tail of spine.   Ulysses 39-318 1996 £275.00

JEROME, JEROME K.   Three Men in a Boat. Bristol: J. W. Arrowsmith, 1889. 1st edition; 1st issue; illustrations by A. Frederics; decorated light blue cloth, some spotting to cloth, minor crumpling of spine tips, former owner signature dated 1890, bookseller blindstamp; very good. Charles Agvent 4-749 1996 $200.00

JEROME, JEROME K.   Three Men on Wheels. New York: Dodd, Mead, 1900. 1st American edition; offsetting to endpapers from flaps, else fine bright copy in lovely near fine dust jacket with few, mostly tiny chips with small rectangular chip (about 1/2" x 1/4" deep) to top left edge of spine.   Between the Covers 42-242 1996 $350.00

JERRARD, PAUL   Flower Painting in Twelve Progressive Lessons. London: Paul Jerrard, 111 Fleet St., n.d., c. 1852. Royal 8vo; frontispiece and engraved title, both hand colored, 11 other finely hand colored lithograph plates, each with titles engraved in gold, contents leaves and descriptive text to each plate printed in gold, with elaborate decorative gold borders, text and plates, each with titles engraved in gold, contents leaves & descriptive text to each plate printed in gold with elaborate decorative gold borders, text and plates all engraved and printed on card, publisher's ad leaf at end; publisher's red cloth with gilt ornamental design on front cover, repeated in blind on back cover, gilt edges, worn and lacks backstrip, contents loose, few leaves very slightly finger soiled.   Thomas Thorp 489-171 1996 £400.00

JERROLD, BLANCHARD 1826-1884   A Brage-Beaker With the Swedes: or, Notes from the North in 1852. London: Nathaniel Cooke, 1854. 1st edition; 8vo; xii, 251 pages; illustrations; original plum cloth with small pictorial decoration in gilt on upper cover, spine faded to tan which makes lettering difficult to read, some light wear to spine ends, but in fact a near fine copy.   David Mason 71-132 1996 $160.00

JERROLD, BLANCHARD 1826-1884   London, a Pilgrimage. London: Grant & Co., 1872. 1st edition; folio; pages (xii), xii, 191, additional engraved title, frontispiece, 52 wood engraved plates, numerous engravings in text, all from drawings by Gustave Dore; contemporary half morocco, new leather labels, joints repaired at foot, marbled endpapers, very good, clean copy.   Sotheran PN32-9 1996 £598.00

JERROLD, DOUGLAS WILLIAM 1803-1857   A Man Made of Money. London: Punch Office, 1849. 1st edition in book form; demy 12mo; 12 engraved plates; contemporary half calf, little rubbed and used, slightly shaken, plates little spotted and thumbed, still good, scarce. Wolff 3667b.   Ash Rare Books Zenzybyr-57 1996 £85.00

JERROLD, DOUGLAS WILLIAM 1803-1857   The Works of Douglas Jerrold. London: Bradbury, Evans and Co., n.d., c. 1855. 8vo; 4 volumes; half blue calf and marbled boards, gilt tooling to spine, red morocco labels to spine, edges and endpapers uniformly marbled; handsome set. Beeleigh Abbey BA56-153 1996 £250.00

JERROLD, WALTER   The Big Book of Fairy Tales. London: Blackie and Son, n.d., ca. 1938. Later printing; quarto; viii, 344 pages; 12 color and 15 black and red plates, text illustrations; original red cloth decoratively stamped and lettered in blind on front cover and in gilt on spine, foot of spine lightly bumped, bookplate removed from front pastedown, previous owner's ink presentation inscription dated 1938 on front endpapers; near fine.   Heritage Book Shop 196-211 1996 $325.00

JERROLD, WALTER   Bon-Mots of the Eighteenth Century. London: J. M. Dent, 1897. 1st edition; small 8vo; i, 192 pages; vignette on half title, 2 portraits, decorated title; 13 plates and 51 text illustrations, brown floral endpaper, cream pictorial cloth gilt, small maroon vignette, top edge gilt, cloth light wear, very good.   Robin Greer 94A-92 1996 £110.00

JESSE, E.   Gleanings in Natural History. London: 1838. 5th edition; crown 8vo; 2 volumes, engraved titlepages and vignettes, 1 plate, text figures; cloth, small library stamps on verso of titles.   John Henly 27-134 1996 £50.00

JESSE, JOHN HENEAGE   Literary and Historical Memorials of London. London: Bentley, 1847. 8vo; 2 volumes; pages vii, 448; vi, 1 f., 456, 10 engraved plates or maps, titles in black and red; contemporary half calf, joints slightly rubbed. Adams 206.   Marlborough 162-157 1996 £100.00

JESSE, JOHN HENEAGE   London; Its Celebrated Characters and Remarkable Places. London: Richard Bentley, 1871. Crown 8vo; 3 volumes, x, 418; vi, (440); viii, (488) pages; frontispieces; contemporary half calf, banded and gilt, red and green labels, all edges gilt, spines little sunned, but very good and clean set.   Ash Rare Books Zenzybyr-58 1996 £200.00

JET Propulsion: a Reference Text. 1946. 4to; 799 pages; black cloth, good, previous owner's name in ink on page edges, front hinge repaired. Knollwood Books 70-324 1996 $140.00

JEVONS, WILLIAM STANLEY   The Principles of Science: a Treatise on Logic and Scientific Method. London: Macmillan, 1874. 1st edition; 2 volumes; original cloth, some wear and fraying to binding, some browning and staining, hinges tender.   19th Century Shop 39- 1996 $850.00

JEVONS, WILLIAM STANLEY   The Principles of Science; a Treatise on Logic and Scientific Method. London: Macmillan, 1905. Later edition; 8vo; xliv, 786 (2 ads); illustrations; original cloth, edges very lightly rubbed, old library label removed from front pastedown, very good.   Edwin V. Glaser 121-171 1996 $150.00

JEWEL, JOHN   The True Copies of the Letters Betwene the Reverend Father in God John Bishop of Sarum and D. Cole, Upon Occasion of a Sermon that the Said Bishop Preched Before the Quenes Majestie, and hyr Most Honorable Counsayle. 1560. London: John Day, 1560. Small 8vo; A1-Q8, R1-3, A1-H8; woodcut titlepage border, woodcut initial letters, 2 final blank leaves present, blank at R4 removed, old ms. fragments and early printed leaves retained in binding, 2 library stamps on each titlepage, few in margins, some corners bit frayed at end, well clear of text, minor staining, shoulder-notes slightly cropped on two leaves; recent antique style calf, decorated in blind. Very reasonable copy, scarce. STC 14612.   Robert Clark 38-69 1996 £1,450.00

THE JEWELERS' Circular-Keystone, Philadelphia. Sterling Flat-Ware Pattern index. 1958. Revised edition; oblong large 4to; xxix pages, 273 pages of photographic illustrations; leather ring binder, very good.   J. M. Cohen 35-49 1996 $260.00

JEWITT, LLEWELLYN   The Corporation Plate and Insignia of Office of the Cities and Towns of England and Wales. London: Bemrose & Sons, 1895 Large 4to; 2 volumes, pages half title, cxxxv, 367; cxxxv, 367; xiii, 638; each volume illustrated; publisher's cloth.   Sotheran PN32-188 1996 £198.00

JEWKES, JOHN   An Industrial Survey of Cumberland and Furness. Manchester: University Press, 19133. Tall 8vo; pages xii, 176; original wrappers, trifle creased, fore-edge and last leaves little spotted, few marginalia.   R.F.G. Hollett & Son 78-1039 1996 £65.00

JEWS. LITURGY & RITUAL. HAGADAH   Haggadah for Passover. Trianon Press, 1966. Of an edition of 292 copies, this one of 16 with an extra set of color plates on Auvergne handmade paper, and an extra set of uncolored plates, 3 of the original guide sheets and stencils and two proof states of the lithograph frontispiece, double page Menorah frontispiece is an original signed lithograph printed from stones at the Imprimerie Mourlot, with additional colors applied by hand through stencils; unbound, as issued, in stiff printed wrappers, the extra plates are laid into labelled wrappers, housed in linen portfolio, the book and portfolio are housed in vellum covered dropback box with metal clasps; front cover is stamped in gold with Shahn's calligraphy; extremely fine. Bromer Booksellers 90-221 1996 $5,000.00

JEWS. LITURGY & RITUAL. HAGADAH   The Haggadah. Jerusalem: n.d. Folio; profusely illustrated in color by Arthur Szyk; gilt decorated covers, fine in fine gilt decorated box.   Polyanthos 22-460 1996 $150.00

JEZREEL, JAMES J.   Extracts from the Flying Roll: Being a Series of Sermons Compiled for the Gentile Churches of All Sects and Denominations. 1879. 1st edition; 3 volumes, v, 271, xxx, 249, 208 pages; attractive deco covers; near fine set.   Middle Earth 77-87 1996 $145.00

JHABVALA, RUTH PRAWER   Esmond in India. London: Allen & Unwin, 1958. 1st edition; 8vo; very nice in price clipped dust jacket.   Virgo Books 48-117 1996 £80.00

JHABVALA, RUTH PRAWER   The Nature of Passion. London: Geo. Allen & Unwin, 1956. 1st edition; front pastedown slightly scuffed, otherwise near fine in price clipped dust jacket, very nice copy.   Virgo Books 48-116 1996 £50.00

JHABVALA, RUTH PRAWER   To Whom She Will. London: Allen & Unwin, 1955. 1st edition; author's first book; very good in very good dust jacket which is very slightly spotted.   Virgo Books 48-115 1996 £95.00

JOAQUIN Murieta, the Brigand Chief of California. San Francisco: Grabhorn Press, 1932. One of 500 copies; tall 8vo; (10), 116, (4) pages; original decorative boards, cloth back, paper label; Howes M912. Edward Morrill 369-527 1996 $110.00

JOCELYN, STEPHEN PERRY   Mostly Alkali. Caldwell: Caxton Printers ltd., 1953. 1st edition; illustrations; fine in price clipped dust jacket. Hermitage SP95-713 1996 $125.00

JOHANNES DE VERDENA   Sermones Dormi Secure de Tempore. Basel: Johann Amerbach, not after, 1484. 4to; ff. 133 (of 134), lacks first blank (a1); disbound, uncased Hain 15970; Goff J 453; BMC III 747. Family Album Tillers-345 1996 $1,600.00

JOHN Davies; Memories and Apprectiations. Newtown: Gregynog Press, printed for private circulation, 1938. One of 150 copies; small 4to; boards; nice, scarce.   Bertram Rota 272-202 1996 £80.00

JOHN, E. B.   Camp Travis and its Part in the World War. New York: 1919. 1st edition; 337 pages; photos; binding shows some wear, but remarkably good condition.   Early West 22-371 1996 $110.00

JOHN, EDMOND   The Flute of the Sardonyx. Old Stile Press, 1991. One of 260 numbered copies, signed by artist; large 8vo; printed in 12 pt. Spectrum with Centaur and Libra in display; drawings printed by Adrian Lack at Senecio Press; pictorial boards, fine in slipcase. Bertram Rota 272-360 1996 £65.00

JOHN, OF SALISBURY, BP. OF SALISBURY d. 1180   Policaraticus. Leyden: Marie, 1639. Thick 8vo; title in red and black; vellum, upper blank margin of titlepage cut away; Brunet III 547.   Rostenberg & Stern 150-52 1996 $475.00

JOHN, W. D.   Pontypool and Usk Japanned Wares: with the Early History of the Iron and Tinplate Industries at Ponypool. Newport: Ceramic Book Co., 1953. 4to; xii, 88 pages; map and 26 plates, including 4 in color; publisher's scarlet calf, top edge gilt, very slightly rubbed; inscribed presentation copy from author to A. J. B. Kiddell.   Thomas Thorp 489-172 1996 £50.00

JOHN, W. D.   William Gillingsley (1758-1828) the Outstanding Achievements as an Artist and Porcelain Maker. Newport: 1968. 4to; 180 illustrations.   Petersfield Bookshop FH58-11 1996 £120.00

JOHNS, JASPER   Technics and Creativity II: Gemini Gel. New York: MOMA, 1971. 1st edition; 364 illustrations, the box features a 10 1/2 x 8 1/2 inch multiple by Jasper Johns entitled Target 1970, signed in pencil by Johns; fine in white plastic box.   Lame Duck Books 19-40 1996 $200.00

JOHNSON'S New Illustrated (Steel-Plate) Family Atals... New York: 1863. 18 x 15 inches; 97 pages of maps; 104 of text, half leather, gilt decorated cloth; leather extremities fraying, spine ends bumped, minor foxing, staining, soil and discolor else very good.   John K. King 77-8 1996 $850.00

JOHNSON, A. F.   Decorative Initial Letters. London: Cresset Press, printed at the Curwen Press, 1931. Limited to 500 numbered copies; 4to; 122 pages of initial letters, few in red and black; original blue cloth, gilt, some staining, headcaps and corners bumped, spine rubbed.   Maggs Bros. Ltd. 1191-184 1996 £130.00

JOHNSON, A. F.   Type Designs: Their History and Development. London: Grafton & Co., 1934. 1st edition; 58 full page illustrations; original binding, large bookshop label on front pastedown, top edge dusty, prelims and edges slightly spotted, head and tail of spine and corners slightly bumped, covers slightly marked and rubbed, spine darkened; very good.   Ulysses 39-482 1996 £65.00

JOHNSON, CHARLES   British Poisonous Plants. London: 1856. 1st edition; 8vo; pages iv, 59; 28 hand colored plates; cloth.   John Henly 27-218 1996 £125.00

JOHNSON, CHARLES   British Poisonous Plants. London: 1856. thin 8vo; 28 colored plates;   Petersfield Bookshop FH58-256 1996 £56.00

JOHNSON, CHARLES   The Middle Passage. New York: Atheneum, 1990. 1st edition; fine in dust jacket with single small rubbed spot; becoming scarce.   Between the Covers 43-135 1996 $225.00

JOHNSON, CHARLES   The Village Opera. London: printed for J. Watts, 1729. 8vo; unbound. Gagey pp. 85-9.   Peter Murray Hill 185-5 1996 £150.00

JOHNSON, D.   Palms for Human Needs in Asia; Palm Untilization and Conversvation in India, Indonesia, Malaysia and the Philippines. Rotterdam: 1991. 4to; pages 258; illustrations; cloth.   Raymond M. Sutton VII-594 1996 $125.00

JOHNSON, DANIEL   Sketches of Field Sports as Followed By the Natives of India. London: 1822. frontispiece, contents have occasional very light foxing; contemporary half calf, gilt, slightly rubbed. Nice copy, very scarce.   David Grayling J95Biggame-376 1996 £150.00

JOHNSON, FRANKLIN P.   The Farwell Collection. Cambridge: Archaeological Inst. of America, 1953. Folio; viii, 76 pages, 90 figures, original cloth, spine lightly soiled.   Archaeologia Luxor-3520 1996 $150.00

JOHNSON, J.   A View of the Jurisprudence of the Isle of Man... Edinburgh: sold by Thomas Bryce and Co., 1811. 1st edition; 8vo; viii, 234, vi, 15 pages, slightly spotted at beginning; contemporary red half morocco, spine gilt and lettered, marbled edges; fine. Contemporary armorial bookplate of John Pollock, Esq.   John Drury 82-127 1996 £195.00

JOHNSON, JACK   Jack Johnson- In the Ring and Out. Chicago: National Sports Pub. Co., 1927. 1st edition; slight darkeneing to front gutters, else fine copy in near fine dust jacket with small hole on edge of spine.   Between the Covers 43-347 1996 $250.00

JOHNSON, JAMES 1777-1845   Change of Air, or the Philosophy of Travelling... New York: 1831. 1st American edtiion; 326 pages; half leather, outer hinges cracked, head of spine chipped.   W. Bruce Fye 71-1112 1996 $150.00

JOHNSON, JAMES WELDON   God's Trombone. New York: Viking, 1928. 1st edition; illustrations by Aaron Douglas; very slight tarnish to gold foil boards, else fine in clean and attractive near fine dust jacket with some small internal repairs and one small external repair on rear panel; primarily off-white dust jacket seldom found this good; nicely inscribed by author.   Between the Covers 43-137 1996 $1,500.00

JOHNSON, LAURA WINTHROP   Eight Hundred Miles in an Ambulance. Philadelphia: 1889. 1st edition; 131 pages; cloth, leather spine, nice. Graf 2220; Howes J41.   T. A. Swinford 49-625 1996 $450.00

JOHNSON, LYNDON BAINES   The Vantage Point. New York: 1971. 1st edition; 636 pages; illustrations, maps, photos; signed, bookplate, book and dust jacket fine.   Early West 22-663 1996 $200.00

JOHNSON, OVERTON   Route Across the Rocky Mountains, with a Description of Oregon and California; Their Geographical Features, Resources, Soil, Climate, Productions, etc. Lafayette: John B. Seman, 1846. 1st edition; 152 pages; original pale green boards, blue cloth back strip with printed label, minor repairs to spine, some light waterstaining and discoloration to front board, text very clean and tight, very good. Rare. Laid in half morocco and chemise slipcase. Cowan p. 315; Howes J142; Jones 1126; Smith 5279; Bradford 2705.   Michael D. Heaston 23-188 1996 $8,500.00

JOHNSON, PHIL   Life on the Plains. Chicago: Rhodes & McClure, 1888. 1st edition as such, variant of Post's Ten Years a Cowboy, 1886; (viii), 17-358 pages, illustrations on pages (ii-viii); semi-limp red cloth; cloth crimped around spine, covers well weathered, rear endpaper almost loose, about good; rare.   Metacomet Books 54-89 1996 $275.00

JOHNSON, RICHARD   The History of North America. London: E. Newbery, 1789. 1st edition; 12mo; frontispiece; contemporary calf, spine gilt, morocco label; corner of leaf G4 excised with small loss, otherwise very good.   Trebizond 39-34 1996 $425.00

JOHNSON, RICHARD   The History of South America. London: E. Newbery, 1789. 1st edition; 12mo; contemporary calf, spine gilt, morocco label; very good. Roscoe J172; Osborne Collection p. 785. Trebizond 39-35 1996 $375.00

JOHNSON, RICHARD   The History of the Seven Champions of Christendom. London: published by J. Bysh...and sold by C. Penny,...c. 1810. Sole edition? 90 x 95mm; ff. 12; engraved, hand colored frontispiece, titlepage, and 10 plates, short tear in fore-margin of last leaf (15mm), soiled, some corners dog eared; disbound, lacking wrappers (?), later oversewing.   Blackwell's B112-58 1996 £200.00

JOHNSON, ROBERT J.   Specimens of Early French Architecture. Newcastle-upon-Tyne: the author, 1864. 1st edition; folio; (vi) pages, 100 plates; contemporary half sheep, covers, rebacked, binding rubbed, light foxing.   The Bookpress 75-203 1996 $325.00

JOHNSON, ROBERT UNDERWOOD   Battles and Leaders of the Civil War. New York: 1884-88. 10.5 x 7 inches; 4 volumes; numerous illustrations, maps; cloth, covers show some wear, still nice set.   John K. King 77-66 1996 $250.00

JOHNSON, ROBERT UNDERWOOD   Battles and Leaders of the Civil War. New York: 1884. 11.5 x 8 inches; 32 parts; illustrations; wrappers, covers soiled, some detached, chipped, disbound, but most good. John K. King 77-67 1996 $125.00

JOHNSON, RONALD   Sports and Divertissements. Urbana: Finial Press, 1969. 1st edition; 1/171 numbered copies, signed by author and artist; drawings by Tom Kovacs; mustard yellow cloth, without dust jacket, fine.   Captain's Bookshelf 38-127 1996 $100.00

JOHNSON, SAMUEL   The History of the Yorubas. From the Earliest Time to the Beginning of the British Protectorate. London: Routledge, 1921. 1st edition; 8vo; 684 pages; frontispiece, folding map; original green cloth, offsetting to endpapers, edges slightly stained, still very good.   Chapel Hill 94-3 1996 $125.00

JOHNSON, SAMUEL 1709-1784   The Beauties of Johnson: Consisting of Maxims and Observations, Moral, Critical and Miscellaneous, Accurately Extracted from the Works of Dr. Samuel Johnson... London: printed for G. Earsley, 1782. 1st complete edition, 2nd edition of volume 1, rare first edition of volume 2; 12mo; 2 volumes; contemporary calf, spines gilt, some wear to spines, edges rubbed, lacks labels. Aside from binding wear, a very good set. Chapman and Hazen pp. 160-61. Ximenes 108-224 1996 $500.00

JOHNSON, SAMUEL 1709-1784   A Compleat Introduction to the Art of Writing Letters Universally Adapted to All Classes and Conditions of Life. London: printed for Henry Dell; & J. Staples, 1758. 1st edition; 12mo; waterstained; contemporary sheep, worn at corners and some time rebacked and subsequently wormed with few holes in spine and scarring of boards, black label. Alston III 267.   Jarndyce 103-292 1996 £70.00

JOHNSON, SAMUEL 1709-1784   A Dictionary of the English Language. London: printed for J. Knapton, C. Hitch and L. Hawes, &c., 2nd edition; 2 volumes; title of volume 1 slightly stained in inner margin, few ink and pencil notes, 2 volumes in 1, neatly rebound in plain half speckled calf, bands, red label. Alston V194.   Jarndyce 103-170 1996 £200.00

JOHNSON, SAMUEL 1709-1784   A Dictionary of the English Language. London: printed by W. Strahan, for J. & P. Knapton, T. & T. Longman, &c., 1755-56. 2nd edition; folio; 2 volumes; titles in red and black, unpaginated; handsomely rebound in half calf, marbled boards, red and black labels, library stamps on title versos, tiny ink stain on top edge volume 1, slight worming in early leaves volume 2, but very good, clean copy. Inscription of William Snooke, 1758; early bookseller's ticket for John Levery, Poultry, London, with small Gloucester library stamps. Jarndyce 103-164 1996 £2,800.00

JOHNSON, SAMUEL 1709-1784   A Dictionary of the English Language. London: printed by W. Strahan, for J. and P. Knapton, 1755. 1st edition; folio; 2 volumes, unpaginated; text in double columns, titlepages printed in red and black; modern antique style full tree calf, gilt double rule border on covers, spine richly gilt in compartments with red and green lettering pieces, occasional foxing, staining or browning; handsome set. Chapman & Hazen p. 137; Courtney & Nichol Smith p. 54; PMM 201. Heritage Book Shop 196-230 1996 $15,000.00

JOHNSON, SAMUEL 1709-1784   A Dictionary of the English Language. London: 1755. 1st edition; folio; unpaginated, titlepage in red and black, very free from foxing, sheet 19-D in 2nd setting, sheet 24) in 1st setting; early or contemporary calf covers and 6 band backstrip with red above green labels, covers rehinged, original marbled endpapers retained. Bookworm & Silverfish 276-68 1996 $8,250.00

JOHNSON, SAMUEL 1709-1784   A Dictionary of the English Language. London: Knapton et al, 1756. 1st octavo edition; 8vo; 2 volumes in 1; contemporary calf, beautifully rebacked and recornered, handful of contemporary ink annotations, corner of one leaf torn with no loss of text, moderate foxing and browning, name clipped from top of titlepage. Charles Agvent 4-751 1996 $1,500.00

JOHNSON, SAMUEL 1709-1784   A Dictionary of the English Language... London: printed for J. Knapton, C. Hitch and L. Hawes, A. Millar, W. Strahan.. 1760. 2nd octavo edition; 8vo; 2 volumes; contemporary calf, gilt, spines gilt, bit worn, some cracking of joints; very good, early armorial bookplates of Samuel Ashby, Trinity College, Cambridge. Courtney p. 62; Alston V 194.   Ximenes 108-225 1996 $450.00

JOHNSON, SAMUEL 1709-1784   A Dictionary of the English Language. London: printed for J. Knapton, C. Hitch, & L. Hawes, &c., 1760. 2nd edition; 2 volumes in 1; short tears without loss to first few leaves; slightly later calf, blind borders, recently neatly rebacked, gilt bands, retaining 19th century label, armorial bookplate and signature 1845, internally good and clean. Alston V 194.   Jarndyce 103-171 1996 £180.00

JOHNSON, SAMUEL 1709-1784   A Dictionary of the English Language. London: printed for A. Millar, W. Strahan, J. Rivington, &c., 1766. 3rd edition; 2 volumes; little internal staining on titles and in volume 1, handsomely rebound in half calf, marbled boards, brown labels, very good. Alston V 195.   Jarndyce 103-172 1996 £220.00

JOHNSON, SAMUEL 1709-1784   A Dictionary of the English Language. London: printed for W. Strahan, J. & F. Rivington, J. Hinton, &c., 1770. 4th edition; 2 volumes; neatly rebound in half calf, marbled boards, red labels, very good. Alston V 197.   Jarndyce 103-173 1996 £180.00

JOHNSON, SAMUEL 1709-1784   A Dictionary of the English Language. London: W. Strahan, 1773. 5th edition; 4to; 2 volumes, bound in full polished calf, nicely rebacked with corners repaired and new leaves, some marginal soiling, but internally clean, red and black spine labels with gilt tooling on panelled spine. Courtney & Smith p. 62.   Glenn Books 36-149 1996 $850.00

JOHNSON, SAMUEL 1709-1784   A Dictionary of the English Language. Dublin: printed for Thomas Ewing, 1775. 4th edition; 4to; 2 volumes; contemporary speckled calf, neatly rebacked retaining original red and green labels, very good. Signature of Reid, Ralph Boyd and bookplate of John Stafford Reid Byers. Alston V184.   Jarndyce 103-168 1996 £480.00

JOHNSON, SAMUEL 1709-1784   A Dictionary of the English Language. London: printed for J. F. and C. Rivington, L. Davis, T. Payne & Son, 1785. 7th edition; folio; handsomely rebound in half calf, bands, marbled boards, red label, very good, clean copy; bound in this copy is the portrait of Johnson, engraved by Thomas Cook after Reynolds published by Longmans, March 23rd, 1787.   Jarndyce 103-165 1996 £750.00

JOHNSON, SAMUEL 1709-1784   A Dictionary of the English Language. London: printed for J. F. and C. Rivington, L. Davis, T. Payne & Sons, &c., 1785. 7th edition; folio; title slightly creased and spotted at edges; contemporary calf, superbly rebacked retaining spine, rubbed, red label slightly chipped, small lot label on front board; armorial bookplate with signature of Thomas Ogden, 12 July 1787.   Jarndyce 103-166 1996 £620.00

JOHNSON, SAMUEL 1709-1784   A Dictionary of the English Language. London: printed for Harrison & Co., 1786. Folio; frontispiece, title in red and black; contemporary reversed calf, slightly rubbed or scarred at head and tail of spine and boards, red label, sound. Alston V183. Jarndyce 103-167 1996 £560.00

JOHNSON, SAMUEL 1709-1784   A Dictionary of the English Language. London: printed for J. F. and C. Rivington, L. Davis, W. Owen, &c., 1786. 8th edition; 2 volumes in 1; neatly rebound in half calf, marbled boards, red label. Very good. alston V202.   Jarndyce 103-174 1996 £160.00

JOHNSON, SAMUEL 1709-1784   A Dictionary of the English Language. London: printed for J. F. and C. Rivington, &c., 1786. 8th edition; 2 volumes; contemporary speckled calf, rubbed, gilt spines worn at head and tail, red and green labels, one lacking, two chipped, hinges cracking. Alston V 202.   Jarndyce 103-175 1996 £110.00

JOHNSON, SAMUEL 1709-1784   A Dictionary of the English Language. London: ptd. for A. Millar; T. Brown and Silvester Doig, Edinburgh; Mozley... 1792. 8th edition; 2 volumes; 2 volumes in 1; corner torn from title without loss of text; contemporary tree sheep, worn, rebacked and repaired, new endpapers, retaining original spine strip. Alston V205; a piracy.   Jarndyce 103-176 1996 £150.00

JOHNSON, SAMUEL 1709-1784   A Dictionary of the English Language. London: printed for J. Johnson, C. Dilly, G. G. & J. Robinson, &c., 1799. 11th edition; half title; contemporary tree calf, slightly scarred and recently neatly rebacked with red label; Signature of Susan Young 1800. Alston V210, variant on laid paper.   Jarndyce 103-177 1996 £160.00

JOHNSON, SAMUEL 1709-1784   A Dictionary of the English Language... Philadelphia: Jacob Johnson, 1805. 2nd American edition; thick 8vo; (883) pages; contemporary calf, scuffed, very sound; quite scarce. S&S 8705.   M & S Rare Books   60-318   1996 $300.00

JOHNSON, SAMUEL 1709-1784   A Dictionary of the English Language... London: printed for Longman, Hurst, Rees, Orme and Brown, 1818. 1st Todd edition; 4to; 4 volumes; contemporary calf, recently rebacked, spines lined in gilt and with contrasting morocco labels, occasional foxing, but very good. Courtney & Nichol Smith p. 59. Sotheran   PN32-23   1996   £598.00

JOHNSON, SAMUEL 1709-1784   A Dictionary of the English Language... London: Longman, Hurst, Rees, Orme and Brown, 1818. Large 4to; 4 volumes; frontispiece; original brown calf, rebacked, all edges marbled, some rubbing, overall nice set.   Kenneth Karmiole   1NS-133   1996 $400.00

JOHNSON, SAMUEL 1709-1784   A Dictionary of the English Language. London: printed by G. Sidney, for W. Sharpe & J. Bumpus, 1818. New edition; frontispiece; neatly rebound in half calf, marbled boards, red label.   Jarndyce   103-180   1996   £50.00

JOHNSON, SAMUEL 1709-1784   A Dictionary of the English Language. London: Offor and many others, 1822. Early edition; 2 volumes; frontispiece; handsomely rebound in three quarter polished calf and linen boards, some offsetting on titlepage and occasional foxing, but handsome set. Courtney p. 60.   Hartfield   48-11j   1996 $1,650.00

JOHNSON, SAMUEL 1709-1784   Johnson's English Dictionary. Boston: Ewer and Carter, 1828. Very tall thick octavo; pages 1156; frontispiece; full early calf, gilt; light foxing and some wear, but sound; Courtney p. 60.   Hartfield   48-11L   1996 $295.00

JOHNSON, SAMUEL 1709-1784   A Dictionary of the English Language. London: Peacock & Mansfield, 1843. New edition; engraved frontispiece and title only; contemporary sheep, recently plainly rebacked, good. Jarndyce   103-184   1996   £55.00

JOHNSON, SAMUEL 1709-1784   A Dictionary of the English Language. Lebanon: 1978. From the 4th edition of 1773; 15 1/2 x 9 1/2 inches; 2 volumes; brown cloth, blind and gilt decorations; excellently printed and bound, mint in acetate jackets.   Hartfield   48-11k   1996 $495.00

JOHNSON, SAMUEL 1709-1784   The Idler.. London: printed for J. Newbery, 1761. 1st edition; 12mo; contemporary tree calf, gilt, rebacked, spines gilt; margins bit browned at beginning and end of each volume, offset from papsedowns, otherwise very good set. Courtney p. 83; Rothschild 1248.   Ximenes   108-226   1996 $500.00

JOHNSON, SAMUEL 1709-1784   The Idler. London: printed for T. Davies, etc., 1767. 3rd edition; 12mo; 2 volumes; old calf rebacked; armorial bookplates of James Fisher, Corpus Christi Oxford. Courtney pp. 83-4; Chapman & Hazen 142.   Peter Murray Hill   185-91   1996   £140.00

JOHNSON, SAMUEL 1709-1784   A Journey to the Western Islands of Scotland. London: printed for W. Strahan and T. Cadell, 1775. 1st edition; 8vo; 384 pages, complete with errata slip; contemporary quarter calf and marbled boards with vellum corner tips, morocco spine label, bookplate, front board nearly detached, blanks missing, but near very good. Interesting association copy, with signature of Thomas Gisborne, the elder.   Chapel Hill   94-241   1996 $250.00

JOHNSON, SAMUEL 1709-1784   A Journey to the Western Islands of Scotland. London: printed for W. Strahan and T. Cadell, 1775. 1st edition; 1st issue, leaves D8 and U4 are cancels, leaf *&v4 is misnumbered 226 for 296, without final errata leaf; 19th century mottled calf, rebacked, all edges gilt; nice, clean copy. Courtney p. 122; Chapman and Hazen p.151; Rothschild 1256.   Anthony Laywood   108-78   1996   £150.00

JOHNSON, SAMUEL 1709-1784   A Journey to the Western Islands of Scotland. London: Strahan & Cadell, 1785. 1st edition; issue C; 6 line errata bound after title, 16 page catalog bound at end; contemporary calf, joints split but tight, corners worn, spine dry, quite good, leather label lacking.   Charles Agvent   4-752   1996 $475.00

JOHNSON, SAMUEL 1709-1784   A Journey to the Western Highlands of Scotland... Glasgow: Stanhope Press, 1817. 8vo; pages vi, 504; portrait frontispiece (slight foxing and offsetting); contemporary half calf, raised bands, gilt armorial stamp; attractively bound.   Marlborough   162-54   1996   £120.00

JOHNSON, SAMUEL 1709-1784   Know Thyself. Kingston: Locks' Press 1992. One of 85 numbered copies, signed by artist; oblong small 4to; larage titlepage woodcut by Margaret Lock, printed in handset 18 and 1 pt. Bembo on Twinrocker handmade; bound by Margaret Lock in marbled boards, cloth back, printed labels; fine.   Bertram Rota   272-280   1996   £80.00

JOHNSON, SAMUEL 1709-1784   Letters to and From the Late Samuel Johnson, LL.D. London: for A. Strahan, and T. Cadell, 1788. 1st edition; 8vo; 2 volumes; pages (ii), xv, (i) blank, (397); xi, (i) blank, without errata slip found in some copies; contemporary tan calf, skilfully rebacked to style and corners repaired, edges of boards worn, with occasional spot or stain; presentation copy from editor, Hester Lynch Piozzi to her friend Mrs. Lambart, with later Lambart family ownership inscriptions. Rothschild 1270; Courtney & Nichol Smith p. 168; Chapman & Hazen p.165.   Simon Finch   24-185   1996   £850.00

JOHNSON, SAMUEL 1709-1784   The Life of Samuel Johnson, LL.D.... (with) The Poetical Works... London: G. Kearsley, 1785/85. 2nd edition; 12mo; iv, 209, (iii) pages; viii, 196, (iv) pages, 4 pages ads at end, A2-N2-4 cancels as usual; frontispiece; bound together in contemporary tiger striped half calf, marbled boards, spine gilt, corners little worn, spine rather rubbed, internally very good. With John Sparrow's booklabel.   Robert Clark   38-185   1996   £550.00

JOHNSON, SAMUEL 1709-1784   The Lives of the Most Eminent English Poets. London: Bathurst et al, 1781. 1st London edition; 8vo; 4 volumes; portrait; tree calf, leather labels, lacks ad leaf and leaf with paper labels, which Chapman notes has seldom survived, old signatures on pastedowns and endpapers, volumes 1-3 rebacked, volume 1 recently; joints tender on volume 4, spines little dry and flaked, very good.   Charles Agvent   4-753   1996 $500.00

JOHNSON, SAMUEL 1709-1784   The Lives of the Most Eminent English Poets. London: Bathurst et al, 1781. 1st London edition; 8vo; 4 volumes; state of portrait without publisher's imprint, signature of Tho. Bull on f.f.e.p.; sheep, lacks ad leaf and leaf with paper labels, as customary, all but one of the leather labels lacking, joints split but tight except on volume IV where front cover is detached, scattered foxing, some pencil notes.   Charles Agvent   4-754   1996 $400.00

JOHNSON, SAMUEL 1709-1784   The Lives of the Most Eminent English Poets, with Critical Obsesrvations on Their Works. London: Baldwin, Johnson, Robinson, Emsly, et al, 1800-01. Apparently a reprint of 1783 edition; small 8vo; 4 volumes, ca. 300 pages each; frontispiece engravings, full page engravings; three quarter polished calf, marbled boards, raised bands, gilt double labels, gilt on black leather; some ver light foxing and offetting; nice early set in contemporary bindings, very good.   Hartfield   48-L45   1996 $495.00

JOHNSON, SAMUEL 1709-1784   The Lives of the Poets. London: Nichols and Son, et al, 1816. New edition; 8vo; 3 volumes, engraved oval portrait frontispiece to volume i (offset, foxed), pages (iv), 460; (iv) 408; v, (iii) 391; contemporary diced tan calf, smooth backstrips divide by gilt fasces roll, dark blue title and dark red volume labels in second and fifth compartments, remainder with central gilt ornament, sides with gilt double fillet and blind scroll roll border, marbled endpapers, red and blue sprinkled polished edges, green silk markers, excellent. Courtney & Nichol Smith p. 143.   Blackwell's   B112-163   1996   £150.00

JOHNSON, SAMUEL 1709-1784   Lives of the Most Eminent Poets... London: John Murray, 1854. Thick 8vo; 3 volumes; extra illustrated by the insertion of some 260 plates; later polished brown morocco, 2 line gilt border, gilt panelled spine in 6 compartments, gilt tops.   Charles W. Traylen   117-136   1996   £800.00

JOHNSON, SAMUEL 1709-1784   London: a Poem and the Vanity of Human Wishes. London: Etchells & Macdonald, 1930. One of 150 numbered copies of a total edition of 450, signed by T. S. Eliot; 8vo; boards; near fine. Gallup B15.   Charles Agvent   4-755   1996 $500.00

JOHNSON, SAMUEL 1709-1784   Miscellaneous and Fugitive Pieces. London: printed for T. Davies/London: ptd. for T. Davies & Carnan & Newbery, 1774/74. 2nd edition of first two volumes, 1st edition of volume three; 8vo; 3 volumes; contemporary calf, spines gilt, red morocco labels, trifle rubbed; fine set, uncommon. Courtney p. 116; Chapman and Hazen p. 150.   Ximenes   108-227   1996 $750.00

JOHNSON, SAMUEL 1709-1784   Mr. Johnson's Preface to His Edition of Shakespear's Plays. London: ptd. for J. and R. Tonson, H. Woodfall, J. Rivington, R. Baldwin... 1765. 1st separate edition; polished green ca gilt, spine and inner dentelles gilt, all edges gilt, slightly rubbed; very good, complete with half title. Courtney pp. 103-7; Rothschild 1249; Chapman and Hazen p. 148.   Ximenes   108-230   1996 $1,750.00

JOHNSON, SAMUEL 1709-1784   The New London Letter Writer...
Waltham St. Lawrence: Golden Cockerel Press, 1948. Limited edition of
500 copies, this being one of 100 specially bound and signed by artist;
8vo; 64 pages; 12 wood engraved illustrations by Averil
Mackenzie-Grieve including 6 full page; original quarter red morocco, top
edge gilt, extremities very slightly worn, text very lightly browned around
edges; Cockalorum 179.   Thomas Thorp 489-173 1996 £60.00

JOHNSON, SAMUEL 1709-1784   The Poetical Works of Samuel
Johnson, LL.D. Dublin: ptd. for L. White, P. Byrne and R. Marchbank,
1785. 1st Irish edition; large 12mo; pages viii, 196; contemporary calf,
red label, binding rubbed and joints cracked, but cords still strong; very
good, unsophisticated copy.   James Fenning 133-183 1996 £285.00

JOHNSON, SAMUEL 1709-1784   The Poetical Works of Samuel
Johnson, LL.D. Dublin: printed for L. White, P. Byrne and R. Marchbank,
1785. 1st Dublin edition; 12mo; contemporary calf, spine gilt; fine,
scarce; bookplates of the Castle Freke Library and Robert William
Rogers. Courtney p. 157; CBEL II 1126.   Ximenes 108-228 1996
$400.00

JOHNSON, SAMUEL 1709-1784   Political Tracts. Containing, The False
Alarm. Falkland's Islands. The Patriot; and Taxation No Tyranny. London:
for W. Strahan and T. Cadell, 1776. 1st collected edition; 8vo; pages (iv),
264, complete with fly-title to "The False Alarm", often lacking, here
misfolded (as often where present) to form half title to the whole book;
uncut in contemporary boards, somewhat rubbed, sympathetically
rebacked in calf, spine with raised bands, gilt rules and red morocco
label, some spotting to endpapers, occasionally internally, small stain
affecting upper and lower inner corners of first two leaves only, still
good. Courtney & Nichol Smith 127; Chapman & Hazen 152.   Simon
Finch 24-131 1996 £450.00

JOHNSON, SAMUEL 1709-1784   Political Tracts. Containing, The False
Alarm. Falkland's Islands. The Patriot. and Taxation No Tyranny. London:
printed for W. Strahan and T. Cadell, 1776. 1st collected edition; 750
copies printed; 8vo; contemporary calf, spine gilt; as often the case,
binder has not preserved the fly-title to the first tract, otherwise fine and
attractive; contemporary signature of Dudley Long, later North. Courtney
p. 127; Chapman and Hazen p. 152; Sabin 36302; Adams 76-71a.
Ximenes 108-229 1996 $400.00

JOHNSON, SAMUEL 1709-1784   Prayers and Meditations. London:
Cadell, 1785. 1st edition; 8vo; worn morocco, occasional marginal note,
foxed, sometimes heavily so, front joint split but tight, heel of spine
chipped half inch.   Charles Agvent 4-756 1996 $300.00

JOHNSON, SAMUEL 1709-1784   Prayers and Meditataions. London:
Cadell & Davis, 1807. 4th edition; tall octavo; pages 230, 1 page ads;
fine full polished morocco binding, raised bands, blind fillets, gilt in
panels, gilt on red leather label; fine; armorial bookplate of Sir James St.
Aubyn who has made some interesting notes. Courtney p. 160.
Hartfield 48-L46 1996 $295.00

JOHNSON, SAMUEL 1709-1784   The Prince of Abissinia. London: for
R. and J. Dodsley and W. Johnston, 1759. 1st edition; small 8vo; 2
volumes in one; pages viii, 159; viii, 165; bound without final blank M4
(volume 2); in this copy A2, vol. 2 is the second state, reading 'contents
of the second volume', page 45 is unnumbered, p. 97 is numbered
correctly, p. 106 H5 verso is mis-signed D4 as usual and p. 161 1.2 is
the first state, reading 'indiscerpiple'; modern full brown crushed
morocco, spine gilt lettered direct, gilt bands, sides with gilt rules, gilt
inner dentelles, top edge gilt, sometime skilfully washed and resized, but
good copy. Rothschild 1242; Courntey & Nichol Smith p. 87; Chapman &
Hazen p.142.   Simon Finch 24-130 1996 £1,000.00

JOHNSON, SAMUEL 1709-1784   The Prince of Abissinia. London:
Rivington et al, 1790. 8th edition; 8vo; tree calf, leather label, gilt ruled
borders and decorated spine, owner's signature on title, joints with old
repairs, some edgewear, very good.   Charles Agvent 4-757 1996
$150.00

JOHNSON, SAMUEL 1709-1784   The Rambler. London: Dodlsey, Owen,
et al, 1794. Small octavo; 4 volumes; fine recent brown polished calf
and marbled boards, raised bands, blind decorations in panels, gilt on
red and green leather labels; fine. Graham 119; Courtney p. 25ff.
Hartfield 48-L47 1996 $495.00

JOHNSON, SAMUEL 1709-1784   Rasselas. Hartford: O. Cooke, 1803.
Stated "First American Edition" but actually the Second after the very
rare 1768 Philadelphia edition; 8vo; worn sheep, leather label, paper
aged, front joint split but still attached, occasional stain, tear, good.
Charles Agvent 4-758 1996 $250.00

JOHNSON, SAMUEL 1709-1784   Rasselas. London: Hector M'Lean,
1942. 1st edition with these illustrations; 10 3/4 x 8 1/2 inches; 2 p.l., iv,
197 pages; 4 appealing engraved plates and 1 vignette by Abraham
Raimbach from pictures by Robert Smirke, printed on India paper; period
style maroon straight grain morocco for Brentano's, front joint neatly
repaired, gilt sides with plain and decorative rules framing large centered
arabesque, spine gilt in compartments with wide raised bands, and
folaite corner ornaments, three black labels (probably later), gilt inner
dentelles, gilt edges, marbled endpapers, slipcase; rear joint with very sl.
wear, otherwise extremely fine copy, with bright, clean binding and
virtually immacualte text.   Phillip J. Pirages 33-318 1996 $200.00

JOHNSON, SAMUEL 1709-1784   Samuel Johnson's Prologue Spoken at
the Opening of the Theatre in Drury-Lane in 1747, with Garrick's Epilogue.
New York: Dodd, Mead and Co., 1902. 1st edition thus; large 4to;
original blue grey boards, printed paper side label, some wear to spine;
very good; presentation copy inscribed by A. S. W. Rosenbach for
Colonel Ralph Isham.   Ximenes 108-231 1996 $600.00

JOHNSON, SAMUEL 1709-1784   The Works. London: J. Buckland, J.
Rivington (& 39 others) (last 3 vols. John Stockdale), 1787-88. 2nd
edition of volume 1 (Hawkins' Life), others 1st editions; 8vo; 14
volumes; library quarter morocco, gilt lettering, numbers on spines,
labels on endpapers, insignificant blindstamp on each titlepage, no other
library markings, bit rubbed, occasional minor browning, unglamorous
but highly serviceable set. Courtney p. 161-3.   Robert Clark 38-183
1996 £300.00

JOHNSON, SAMUEL 1709-1784   The Works of of Samuel Johnson,
LL.D. Dublin: Luke White, 1793. New edition; 12mo; 6 volumes;
frontispiece; contemporary tree calf, spines gilt, original morocco labels;
bindings expertly repaired, attractive contemporary bindings, internally
very good. Uncommon.   Trebizond 39-29 1996 $675.00

JOHNSON, SAMUEL 1709-1784   The Works... Oxford: Talboys and
Wheeler; and W. Pickering, 1825. 8vo; 11 volumes; frontispiece in volume
3; contemporary black straight grain half morocco, spines in
compartments with raised bands, decorated in blind, lettered in gilt, little
slight wear to extremities, bookplates removed, occasional spotting, but
excellent set. Courtney & Nichol Smith pp. 166-67.   Simon Finch
24-132 1996 £875.00

JOHNSON, SAMUEL 1709-1784   Works. London: Henry G. Bohn, 1850.
New edition; thick 8vo; 2 volumes; contemporary half calf, mottled board
sides, fully gilt spines; fine copy.   Charles W. Traylen 117-135 1996
£95.00

JOHNSON, STEPHEN   The History of Cardiac Surgery 1896-1955.
Baltimore: 1970. 1st edition; 201 pages; dust jacket. GM 3161.2.   W.
Bruce Fye 71-1113 1996 $100.00

JOHNSON, T. B.   The Shooter's Companion. London: 1823. 2nd
edition; engraved plates, 19th century half morocco; excellent copy.
David A.H. Grayling 3/95-167 1996 £85.00

JOHNSON, T. B.   The Shooter's Preceptor...ish Isles. London: 1838.
engraved plates; original cloth, light foxing to few pages; very nice,
scarce, rare to find in such good condition, complete with errata slip.
David A.H. Grayling 3/95-26 1996 £165.00

JOHNSON, UWE   An Absence. London: Cape, 1970. 1st British edition;
althought this copy contains a review slip from Grossman in New York;
fine in dust jacket, signed by author.   Lame Duck Books 19-267 1996
$150.00

JOHNSON, UWE   Anniversaries: from the Life of Gesine Gresspahl.
New York: HBJ, 1975. 1st edition; review copy, with slip and publicity
photo laid in; fine in dust jacket, playfully inscribed by author.   Lame
Duck Books 19-269 1996 $125.00

JOHNSON, W. R.   Anno Domini. Janus Press, 1970. One of 140
copies; 6.75 x 6 inches; designed, set, printed and bound by Claire Van
Vliet, titles and text handset, printed in black with old wood type, star
and half title printed in silver on Rives cuve velin BFK Blue Fabriano half
titles, Rives flyleaf into which star is handcut at center (front and back)
and handsewn into red Fabriano wrapper with silver star printed on
front; fine.   Joshua Heller 21-4 1996 $100.00

JOHNSON, W. R.   Easter. Philadelphia: Christ Church, 1970. One of 30
copies commissioned for Christ Church by Bertha von Moschzisker, out
of a total edition of 250 copies; small 8vo; illustrations in color; green
printed wrappers; fine.   James S. Jaffe 34-296 1996 $275.00

JOHNSON, W. R.   Flowering Time. Janus Press, 1976. 1st edition; 7.5 x 5.75 inches; 12 unnumbered pages; 2 lithograph illustrations by Claire Van Vliet, set and printed by Van Vliet, titles printed in brown and tan, text in brown, colophon in tan, frontispiece lithograph printed in grey, white, rose and 3 shades of yellow, lithograph on page 9 in cream, yellow, green, brown, tan and rose; printed on Arches and Rives BFK with lithographs printed from stone in 1973 on Arches; handsewn into natural Zaan covers and endpapers; wrappers lightly darkened at edges, otherwise very good.   Joshua Heller 21-12 1996 $100.00

JOHNSON, W. R.   Lilac Wind. Janus Press, 1983. One in an edition of 150 copies signed and numbered by artist; 8 unnumbered pages; 1-4 and 6-8 are accordion folded into center to rest on p. 5, when closed 1-4 rest on 6-8 w/verso of 8 acting as both titlepage & colophon; unfolded paperwork is 61 inches wide on 2 sheets of paper joined at mid point; top edge is formed from a curvilinear deckle making the vertical measurement irregular from 2.5 to 11.875 inches; folded paperwork landscape by Claire Van Vliet made with Kathryn Clark; designed, set & ptd. by Van Vliet; titles and text printed damp in deep blue on paper work from colored pulps in white, blues, grays, violets, stencil and relief printed moon in light green, housed in clamshell box of three tones of violet Japanese rayon with pale violet twill or turquoise book cloth, title label on spine ptd. in silver on violet calf, paperwork made at Twinrocker Handmade Paper Mill - published with Twinrocker. Fine.   Joshua Heller 21-22 1996 $400.00

JOHNSON, W. R.   Narcissus. Janus Press, 1990. One of 120 copies signed by artist; 9 x 11.5 inches; 14 unnumbered pages, including covers, in diamond shaped format trimmed at top to accomodate concertina binding structure; 7 laser printed images by Claire Van Vliet, designed, set and printed by Claire Van Vliet; concentric diamonds of MacGregor Vinzni paper in plum, green, blue, periwinkle, purple, rose, red, trimmed at top from 7.25 x 7.75 to 9 x 11.5 inches, title and text handset, titles printed in light and dark violet, text in black, printed damp on binding concertina, spine slips out allowing book to be hung in either direction from vellum strips, housed in modified rectangular clam box covered with abaca deep lavender, medium lavender and pink pigmented pulps, brass type title printed in plum, wooden interior structure of triangular inserts accomodates trimmed diamond format of book, framing inset colophon printed damp in violet on sand abaca-cotton paper, housed in slipcase of tan book cloth & Barcham Green paper over bds. w/titles in brass type ptd. in red-violet on spine; cutting & assembly by Van Vliet & Wray. Fine.   Joshua Heller 21-31 1996 $450.00

JOHNSON, W. R.   Narcissus. Newark; Janus Press, 1990. One of 120 copies only; signed by Van Vliet; printed on handmade papers by MacGregor Vinzani, designed by Van Vliet; pentagon shaped with images laser printed, spine can accordion out and it can hang on wall, or it can stay housed in its handsome wood and paper over boards clamshell box.   Priscilla Juvelis 95/1-140 1996 $450.00

JOHNSTON, ALEXANDER KEITH   Atlas to Alison's History of Europe. Edinburgh & London: Wm. Blackwood, 1848. Small oblong 4to; frontispiece and 98 maps all with colored definitions (map 57 was not issued); contemporary calf, loose in case. Bookplate of Viscount Gage. Charles W. Traylen 117-425 1996 £120.00

JOHNSTON, ALEXANDER KEITH   The Physical Atlas of Natural Phenomena. London: 1850. Imperial 4to; pages iv, 122, 2 publisher's ads, maps; later cloth, all edges gilt, occasional slight foxing.   John Henly 27-808 1996 £100.00

JOHNSTON, G. P.   Catalogue of the Rare and Most Interesting Books and Manuscripts in the Library at Drummond Castle. Edinburgh: privately printed, 1910. Limited to 50 copies; 96 pages, title vignette; black cloth, spine bit torn, uncut.   Maggs Bros. Ltd. 1191-51 1996 £80.00

JOHNSTON, GEORGE   A History of the British Zoophytes. London: 1847. 2nd edition; 2 volumes; 74 plates; half calf, nice.   Petersfield Bookshop FH58-257 1996 £66.00

JOHNSTON, HARRY   Liberia. London: Hutchinson & Co., 1906. Royal 8vo; 2 volumes, xxviii, 520; xvi, 521-1183 pages; 22 maps, 28 plates in color, 426 black and white illustrations; cloth, gilt, faded and slightly worn, one inside joint cracking a little, some foxing, but mainly to folding maps.   Thomas Thorp 489-174 1996 £125.00

JOHNSTON, JAMES F. W.   Lectures on Agricultural Chemistry and Geology. Edinburgh: 1844. 1st complete edition; 8vo; pages 16, (2), (7)-911, (2), 116, xx (index), complete thus, 4 parts and errata slip, appendix in 1 volume; contemporary calf, label supplied, very good.   James Fenning 133-184 1996 £55.00

JOHNSTON, JAMES F. W.   Notes on North America, Agricultural, Economical and Social. Edinburgh and London: William Blackwood and sons, 1851. 1st edition; 8vo; 2 volumes; original grey green cloth, slight rubbing, back inner hinge bit tender; very good set. Sabin 36369; Howes J 165; TPL 3004.   Ximenes 108-232 1996 $500.00

JOHNSTON, JENNIFER   The Christmas Tree. London: Hamish Hamilton, 1981. 1st edition; original binding, head and tail of spine and corners bumped, very good in very slightly marked and dusty dust jacket. Presentation copy from author, inscribed for Isaac Bashevis Singer.   Ulysses 39-321 1996 £75.00

JOHNSTON, NATHANIEL   The Assurance of Abby and Other Church-Lands in England to the Possessors, Cleared from the Doubts... London: printed by Henry Hills, 1687. 8vo; titlepage torn at lower corne affecting 2 letters of imprint; 19th century half calf, 1 hinge cracked; Wing J872.   Peter Murray Hill 185-93 1996 £65.00

JOHNSTON, PRISCILLA   The Mill Book. Ditchling and Hammersmith: 1917. 1st edition; 12mo; 12 woodcuts; handmade paper; wrappers, yap edges slightly rubbed, creased and browned, very good.   Ulysses 39-145 1996 £75.00

JOHNSTON, RICHARD W.   Follow Me! The Story of the Second Marine Division in World War II. New York: Random House, 1948. 305 pages; more than 250 photos, drawings and paintings, 9 maps; very good, light dampstaining to top of first few pages, in dust jacket with few tears and light staining.   Blue River Books 9-333 1996 $110.00

JOHNSTONE, CHARLES 1719?-1800?   Chrysal, or the Adventures of a Guinea, with Curious and Interesting Anecdotes of the Noted Persons c Every rank of Life... London: Becket and DeHondt, 1767-71. Mixed early editions; tall 12mo; 4 volumes; uniformly bound in full calf, raised band spines gilt in panels, some wear, generally nice. Hardy p. 129; NCBEL 999; Block p. 124.   Hartfield 48-L23 1996 $495.00

JOHNSTONE, CHARLES 1719?-1800?   The History of Arsaces, Prince of Betlis. London: printed for T. Becket, 1774. 1st edition; 12mo; 2 volumes; contemporary calf, gilt spines, red and green morocco labels; some wear at head of volume 1, still fine; engraved armorial bookplate of Sir George Strickland, bt.   H. M. Fletcher 121-105 1996 £1,800.0

JOHNSTONE, CHEVALIER DE   Memoirs of the Rebellion in 1745 and 1746. London: Longman, Hurst etc., 1822. 3rd edition; 8vo; pages lxxii, 456, folding plan, 2 engraved portraits (little spotted and stained); old roan backed boards gilt, little rubbed. Woodcut bookplate of Thomas Bell, 1797.   R.F.G. Hollett 76-139 1996 £120.00

JOHNSTONE, G. H.   Asiatic Magnolias in Cultivation. London: 1955. 4to; 160 pages; 14 fine color plates, 20 plain plates, folding map and bookmark; buckram, gilt, binding spotted, slight foxing to endpapers, otherwise fine, scarce.   John Henly 27-356 1996 £190.00

JOHNSTONE, JAMES   Historical and Descriptive Account of George Heriot's Hospital. Edinburgh: Cunningham, 1827. Large paper, with proc copies of plates on India paper; 4to; frontispiece, engraved title, title, engraved dedn., 1 f., 6 engraved plates, 44 pages; half red morocco, some foxing.   Marlborough 162-55 1996 £100.00

JOHNSTONE, JAMES FOWLER KELLAS   Bibliographia Aberdonensis. Aberdeen: printed for the Third Spalding Club, 1929-30. 1st edition; 4to; volumes; portrait in each volume, 56 plates; original cloth.   Forest Books 74-126 1996 £55.00

JOHNSTONE, W. G.   Nature Printed British Sea-Weeds. London: 1859-60. 4 volumes; 1 plain and 221 color plates; original cloth, most pages and plates loose in their bindings.   John Johnson 135-366 1996 $450.00

JOHNSTONE, W. G.   Nature Printed British Sea-Weeds. London: 1859-60. 4 volumes; more than 200 colored plates, 2 volumes loose, otherwise bright and clean.   Petersfield Bookshop FH58-259 1996 £150.00

JOLLIE, F.   Jollie's Cumberland Guide and Directory... Carlisle: F. Jo and Sons, 1811. 8vo; pages viii, 84, xxxix (iv), large folding plan, 1 ma (colored in outline), 1 plan, 1 folding engraved plate, 2 woodcut plates old boards, rather worn and roughly rebacked in calf.   R.F.G. Hollett Son 78-1041 1996 £175.00

THE JOLLY Old Man, Who Sings Down, Derry Down. London: ca. 186 Large octavo; 8ff.; 3 large hand colored illustrations on each page, grease spot surrounding the cut-out area, beginning on pastedown and continuing for first few pages, though not affecting illustrations; still bright, near fine copy, original pictorial boards, which shows rubbing t extremities and light soiling.   Bromer Booksellers 87-126 1996 $950.00

JONES & WILLIS, LTD. A Book of Designs of Ecclesiastaical Art by Jones and Willis Ltd. London: Jones & Willis, c. 1910. 4to; viii, 187 plates, plates interleaved with price lists; original cloth backed boards, very good. Ken Spelman 30-60 1996 £45.00

JONES, BENCE The Life and Letters of Michael Faraday. London: Longmans Green, 1870. 1st edition; 8vo; 2 volumes, vi, (4), 427; (12), 499 pages, frontispiece in each volume, illustrations in text; complete with half titles; modern cloth, some dampstaining to frontispiece and title in volume 1, very good. Edwin V. Glaser 121-105 1996 $225.00

JONES, D. CARADOG The Social Survey of Merseyside. Liverpool: Liverpool University Press, 1934. 8vo; 3 volumes; diagrams, maps; original cloth, trifle chafed, slight foxing, little occasional pencil scoring. Howes Bookshop 265-620 1996 £95.00

JONES, DAN BURNE The Prints of Rockwell Kent: a Catalogue Raisonne. Chicago: Unviersity of Chicago Press, 1975. Folio; 219 pages; profusely illustrated; cloth. Freitag 4794. Brannan 43-293 1996 $110.00

JONES, DAVID In Parenthesis. London: 1937. 1st edition; covers bit dusty, otherwise good in torn and worn dust jacket. Words Etcetera 94-681 1996 £75.00

JONES, DAVID In Parenthesis. New York: 1961. 1st American edition; near fine in dust jacket. Words Etcetera 94-682 1996 £65.00

JONES, DAVID An Introduction to the Rime of the Ancient Mariner. London: Clover Hill Editions, 1972. Number 68 of 115 special copies, signed and dated by author (of a total of 330); large 4to; pages (8), 40 + colophon, copper plate engraving on titlepage; on Hodgkinson tinted paper by Will & Sebastian Carter at the Rampant Lions Press; original parchment backed buckram, marbled paper slipcase, top edge gilt, others uncut, prospectus laid in. Claude Cox 107-84 1996 £250.00

JONES, EVAN ROWLAND The Emigrant's Friend: Containing Information and Advice fro Persons Intending to Emigrate to the United States. London: Hamilton, Adams; P. J. Jackson, Newcastle-upon-Tyne: 1880. 1st edition; 8vo; xiv, (ii), 234, (6 ad) pages, folding map, folding table; original tan limp cloth, very uncommon. James Burmester 29-77 1996 £150.00

JONES, FRED R. An Uneventful Tramp. N.P.: Flexible Flyer Press, 1975. Limited to 41 copies; 12mo; 20 pages; woodcuts by Curt L. Carpenter, who also made the paper from old beach towels; light spot on back cover, else very fine. inscribed and signed by artist "For Fr. Catich April 1977". Bromer Booksellers 90-36 1996 $150.00

JONES, GEORGE HENRY Account of the Murder of the Late Mr. William Weare, of Lyon's Inn, London, Including the Cirumstances Which First Led to the Discovery of the Murder and the Detection of the Murderers, the Depositions Taken Before the Magistrates... London: printed by J. Nichols and Son, for Sherwood, Jones and Co., 1824. Tall 8vo; 8, (4), 344; 4 plates and 2 folding plans; original pink boards, uncut, paper spine label (partially chipped away), spine extremities chipped and rubbed, newspaper clippings pasted to rear endpaper. Kenneth Karmiole 1NS-134 1996 $150.00

JONES, GEORGE W. Catalogue of the Library of George W. Jones at the Sign of the Dolphin next to Dr. Johnson's House in Gough Square. London: printed for private circulation only, 1938. 1st edition; folio; pages xii, 132; illustrations in line and half tone, decorations and borders throughout, including various inserted specimens; original boards little rubbed but sound, uncut; good, scarce. Claude Cox 107-298 1996 £120.00

JONES, GLYN The Story of Heledd. Gwasg Gregynog, 1994. One of 400 numbered copies; small folio; printed in Monotype Baskerville in black and deep red on Hahnemuhle and Zerkall papers; quarter black cloth, boards, boldly lettered and decorated in white; fine. Bertram Rota 272-219 1996 £85.00

JONES, GWYN The Green Island. Waltham St. Lawrence: Golden Cockerel Press, 1946. Limited edition, 58/100 copies, specially bound (of an edition of 500 copies); royal 8vo; pages 84; printed on Arnold's mouldmade paper, 12 wood engravings by John Petts, title printed in green; original grey and green crushed morocco, lettering on faded backstrip and Petts's design on front cover, all gilt blocked, top edge gilt, others untrimmed; excellent. Cockalorum 169. Blackwell's B112-127 1996 £140.00

JONES, GWYN The Green Island. Waltham St. Lawrence: Godlen Cockerel Press, 1946. 1st edition; number 82 of 100 copies specially bound; 8vo; 84 pages; frontispiece, 10 other wood engravings by John Petts; original two tone full morocco blocked in gold, top edge gilt, others uncut, by Sangorski & Sutcliffe; very good. Cockalorum 169. Claude Cox 107-64 1996 £85.00

JONES, GWYN The Green Island: a Novel. Waltham St. Lawrence: Golden Cockerel Press, 1946. One of 500 numbered copies; 8vo; half green cloth, grey buckram sides, spine just a little faded; nice. Bertram Rota 272-182 1996 £50.00

JONES, HENRY FESTING Samuel Butler, author of Erewhon (1835-1902). London: Macmillan and Co., 1919. 2 volumes; origina red cloth, dulled; E. W. Hudson's copy, signed by him, enclosed are 2 letters, one typed, the other in autograph and both signed by Henry Festing Jones to Hudson. Jarndyce CII-126 1996 £110.00

JONES, HENRY FESTING Samuel Butler, Author of Erewhon (1835-1902). London: Macmillan and Co., 1920. 2nd impression; 2 volumes; illustrations; red cloth. Jarndyce CII-127 1996 £85.00

JONES, HENRY FESTING The Samuel Butler Collection at Saint John's College Cambridge: a Catalogue and Commentary. Cambridge: W. Hefer, 1921. Grey paper boards, cloth spine; Hoppe III 7. Jarndyce CII-129 1996 £50.00

JONES, HORACE The Story of Early Rice County. Wichita: 1928. 1st edition; 135 pages; frontispiece, illustrations; cloth. Nice 6 Guns 1192; Herd 1139; Rittenhouse 334. T. A. Swinford 49-631 1996 $225.00

JONES, J. P. Flora Devoniensis. London: 1829. 8vo; 2 parts in 1 volume; original boards. Wheldon & Wesley 207-1484 1996 £75.00

JONES, JAMES 1921- From Here to Eternity. New York: Charles Scribner's Sons, 1941. 1st edition; near fine in near fine jacket. Priscilla Juvelis 95/1-141 1996 $150.00

JONES, JAMES 1921- From Here to Eternity. New York: Scribners, 1951. 1st edition; spine creased but covers clean and lettering bright, dust jacket has 1/2 x 3/4 inch piece missing from head of spine panel, other small chips and stains, still very good in dust jacket, author's first book. Sherwood 3-160 1996 $200.00

JONES, JAMES 1921- From Here to Eternity. New York: Scribners, 1951. 1st edition; author's first book, just short of fine in very good plus dust jacket. Bud Schweska 12-434 1996 $125.00

JONES, JOHN FREDERICK DRAKE A Treatise on the Process Employed by Nature in Suppressing the Hemorrhage from Divided and Punctured Arteries, and on the Use of the Ligature... Philadelphia: 1811. 1st American edition; 8vo; 237 pages; 15 wood engravings, contemporary calf, upper cover detached, some light waterstains and browning, signature starting. Austin 1087; H. Winnett Orr 822. Argosy 810-258 1996 $400.00

JONES, JOHN PAUL The Life and Correspondence of John Paul Jones, Including His Narrative of the Campaign of the Liman. New York: 1830. 1st edition; 555 pages; full calf, some rubbing, near fine. Howes S91. Blue River Books 9-274 1996 $175.00

JONES, JOHN PAUL Life and Correspondence of John Paul Jones, Including His Narrative. New York: 1830. 8vo; 555 pages, frontispiece; expertly rebacked, some dampstains to front free endpaper and first few pages. Howes S91? Parmer Books 039/Nautica-039136 1996 $125.00

JONES, JOHN THOMAS Account of the War in Spain and Portugal, and In the South of France, from 1808 to 1814, Inclusive. London: printed for T. Egerton, 1818. 1st edition; 8 3/4 x 5 3/4 inches; xxvi, 448 pages; 4 folding maps, 3 of them colored in part; contemporary calf, recently and very neatly rebacked (new endpapers), boards panelled with unusual stippled and knotted gilt rules, raised bands, new maroon morocco label, turn-ins with gilt foliate border, marbled edges; corners exposed, original covers slightly discolored, but binding artfully restored, completely solid, and rather pleasing, two leaves (including title), with offsetting from maps, just a little foxing here and there in text; excellent. Phillip J. Pirages 33-319 1996 $250.00

JONES, JOHN WILLIAM Life and Letters of Robert E. Lee Soldier and Man. New York: and Washington: Neale Pub. Co., 1906. 1st edition; 486 pages; original cloth; very good to near fine. Krick 257; Nevins II 68; Nicholson p. 435; Dornbusch II 2937. McGowan Book Co. 65-49 1996 $175.00

JONES, KENNETH   Stone Soup. Portland: Chamberlain Press, 1985. One of 150 copies; signed by artist, both book and laid in prospectus are additionally inscribed by artist; octavo; (26) pages; designed, printed and illustrated by Sarah Chamberlain; bound by Barbara Blumenthal in marbled boards, leather spine label stamped in black; extremely fine. Bromer Booksellers 87-120 1996 $200.00

JONES, LESLIE W.   The Miniatures of the Manuscripts of Terence Prior to the 13th Century. Princeton: 1931. Large folio; 2 volumes, 240 pages, 796 illustrations on plates.   Jens J. Christoffersen SL94-58 1996 $160.00

JONES, OWEN 1809-1874   The Grammar of Ornament. London: Day and Son, 1856. 1st edition; folio; gothic chromolithograph titlepage printed in red and black, 100 chromolithographed plates by Francis Bedford, about 114 pages of text; half red morocco, gilt, neatly rebacked with original spine laid down, gilt, edges gilt.   Charles W. Traylen 117-237 1996 £2,500.00

JONES, OWEN 1809-1874   The Grammar of Ornament. London: Bernard Quaritch, 1910. Small folio; 157 pages; additional decorative chromolithograph titlepage and 111 chromolithograph plates, numerous wood engraved text illustrations; original cloth gilt, gilt edges, spine slightly faded and with tiny nick at head, internally in extremely fresh condition with hardly any spotting; very desirable copy.   Thomas Thorp 489-175 1996 £250.00

JONES, OWEN 1809-1874   Scenes from the Winter's Tale. London: Day and Son, n.d. 1866. 1st edition; 4to; 49 plates; publisher's decorated cloth; inscription in ink on front free endpaper, front hinge internally strengthened, nick on edge of rear cover, occasional spotting in margins, else very good in first issue binding.   Bookpress 75-73 1996 $550.00

JONES, OWEN GLYNNE   Rock-Climbing in the English Lake District. London: Longmans, Green and Co., 1897. 1st edition; large 8vo; pages xxv, 284, (32 ads), 30 collotype plates, 9 lithographed route diagrams; original cloth, gilt, little rubbed, neatly recased, inscaription, old photo on flyleaf, scattered spotting; scarce. Neate J35.   R.F.G. Hollett & Son 78-296 1996 £165.00

JONES, PAUL   Flora Superba. Tryon Gallery, 1971. Limited to 406 copies; this is a 'file copy only, ex series', this copy signed by artist; folio; printed on pure rag paper; 16 plates in color; publisher's buckram, gilt, top edge gilt; fine in slightly worn cloth slipcase.   Thomas Thorp 489-176 1996 £180.00

JONES, RAYMOND F.   This Island Earth. Chicago: Shasta, 1952. 1st edition; fine in dust jacket with several small areas of dampstaining at corners, some slight wear; subscriber's copy, signed by author. Robert Gavora 61-33 1996 $150.00

JONES, RICHARD   An Essay on the Distribution of Wealth, and on the Sources of Taxation. London: John Murray, 1831. 1st edition; 8vo; (ii), xlix, (5), 329, (1), 49, (1) pages, with half title (bound after the prelims), and the errata slip; original drab boards, neatly rebacked, printed label; Kress C2843.   James Burmester 29-78 1996 £800.00

JONES, ROBERT   Orthopedic Surgery. New York: 1923. 1st edition; 4to; over 700 pages; 712 illustrations; cloth, corners lightly dampstained. GM 4391.   Argosy 810-259 1996 $100.00

JONES, SAMUEL A.   Pertaining to Thoreau. Detroit: Edwin B. Hill, 1901. 1st edition; only 200 copies printed; 16mo; original binding, quite scarce, one corner worn, small nick to spine, very good. Not in BAL. Charles Agvent 4-1135 1996 $200.00

JONES, SHERIDAN R.   Black Bass and Bass Craft: tthe Life Habits of the Two Bass and Successful Angling Strategy. New York: Macmillan, 1924. 1st edition; 8vo; photos and drawings by author; gilt stamped dark blue cloth, upper cover with pictorial design of an angled fish, stamped in silver, light blue and black; very good.   George J. Houle 68-48 1996 $125.00

JONES, SHIRLEY   For Gladstone. Red Hen Press, 1988. One of 50 numbered copies, signed by Jones; small folio; 10 mezzotints and mezzotint combined with relief etching by author, text printed in 18 pt. Gill Sans in rose pink on Rives; unboudn leaves laid into paper folder and preserved in cloth portfolio with printed label, ties; fine.   Bertram Rota 272-236 1996 £380.00

JONES, SHIRLEY   For Gladstone. South Croydon: Red Hen Press, 1988. One of 50 copies only, each copy signed and dated by artist/author/printer, Shirley Jones; page size 13 x 9 7/8 inches; printed on Rives paper, set in 18 point Gill Sans type; mezzotint portraits; loose as issued in reddish/pink Japanese paper, grey linen clamsheel box with silhouette portrait of the portly Gladstone.   Priscilla Juvelis 95/1-49 1996 $1,000.00

JONES, SHIRLEY   Impressions; Eight Aquatints to Accompany Eight Poems and Prose Pieces. Red Hen Press, 1984. Of 40 numbered copies signed by artist, this is one of 15 'for fine binding' printed entirely on Barcham Green Waterleaf, text handset 18 pt. Baskerville; folio; unique binding by John Pearson of full calf dyed light and darker blues with stripes and stars, upper board further embellished in blind with title lettering and rules and with outline map of America, stars roughtly marking the locations of five of the texts; fine state.   Bertram Rota 272-234 1996 £1,750.00

JONES, STEPHEN   A Pronouncing Dictionary of the English Language. London: printed by J. W. Myers, 1796. One corner slightly damp marked early sheep covered in contemporary buckram wrappers, stitched in place with thread, slightly soiled. Alston V342.   Jarndyce 103-188 1996 £90.00

JONES, STEPHEN   Sheridan Improved. London: printed for Vernor & Hood, 1804. 9th edition; small 4to; contemporary sheep; slight rubbing, recently neatly rebacked; with ink initials WC.   Jarndyce 103-189 199 £80.00

JONES, STEPHEN   Sheridan Improved. London: Vernor & Hood, 1806. 11th edition; square 12mo; calf, rebacked, label; very good.   Jarndyce 103-190 1996 £75.00

JONES, STEPHEN   Sheridan Improved. London: printed by and for J. W. H. Payne, &c., 1812. Stereotype edition; oblong 8vo; slight rubbing at end of text, contemporary sheep with stain on back board, neatly rebacked; from the collection of Fernand & Anne Renier.   Jarndyce 103-191 1996 £65.00

JONES, STEPHEN   Sheridan Improved. Stereotyped by A. Wilson, Camden Town, for John Harris, &c. 1835. Stereotype edition revised; oblong 8vo; contemporary tree sheep, spine neatly repaired, early bookseller's oval ticket for F. & C. Mason, Stationers, Bromyard; very good.   Jarndyce 103-192 1996 £65.00

JONES, T. GWYNN   Detholiad o Ganiadau. Newtown: Gwasg Gregynog, 1926. 1st edition; no. 147 of 474 copies; 8vo; pages xiii, 93), 169; 9 head and tailpieces by Maynard and large Press device in blue o titlepage, printed in Kennerley type on Dutch handmade paper; peacock blue buckram, fine, uncut; contemporary review laid in. Harrop 4. Claude Cox 107-70 1996 £95.00

JONES, WILLIAM   An Essay on the Law of Bailments. London: 1781. 1st edition; 8vo; pages (4), 130, (2), with half title and errata; contemporary calf, label, gilt, slight wear at corners, but binding strong and otherwise, nice, fresh copy; with W. H. M. Hodder bookplate. James Fenning 133-185 1996 £350.00

JONES, WILLIAM TODD   Authentic Detail of an Affair of Honour, Between William Todd Jones, Esq. and Sir Richard Musgrave. Dublin: 1802. 8vo; (ii), 9, (i) pages; disbound, small paper flaw in lower corner of B1, affecting a few letters; good, clean copy, uncommon; inscribed "For the Countess of Granard".   Robert Clark 38-238 1996 £85.00

JONSON, BEN 1573?-1637   Catiline His Conspiracy. London: printed f A. C. and are to be sold by William Cademan, 1669. 4th edition; 4to; modern half calf; wanting prelim blank, some light foxing, but very good, very uncommon revival. Wing J1008; Greg 296(F), Woodward & McManaway 668.   Ximenes 108-233 1996 $1,250.00

JONSON, BEN 1573?-1637   The Poems of Ben Jonson. Oxford: Basil Blackwood, 1936. One of 150 copies; original binding, top edge slightly dusty, spine slightly faded, head and tail of spine and corners slightly bumped, endpaper edges browned, very good.   Ulysses 39-323 199 £125.00

JONSON, BEN 1573?-1637   Volpone, or the Fox. Oxford: Limited Editions Club, 1952. Limited to 1500 copies; 4to; hand colored through stencils by Maurice Beaufume after Rene ben Sussan who signs; origin binding, spine bit sunned, mostly unopened, near fine in fine case. Charles Agvent 4-766 1996 $125.00

JONSON, BEN 1573?-1637   The Workes... (with) The Second Volume. Containing These Playes, Viz. 1. Bartholomew Fayre. 2 The Staple of Newes. 3 The Divell is an Asse. (and with Walkley's Third Volume, issued without volume title, as always) London: by Richard Bishop.../London: for Richard Meighen; 1640/31-40. 1st Canonical collected edition; folio; 3 volumes bund in 2, volume 1 with frontispiece portrait by robert Vaughan (3rd state, as usual), engraved title by Wiliam Hole; fine binding of red crushed morocco, sides with one-line outer gilt rules, panelled in gilt with an intersecting two-line border and lozenge, semicircles at sides, spines with raised bands, lettered in gilt, other panels with gilt border-and-lozenge pattern to match sides, gilt inner dentelels, marbled endpapers, gilt edges by Zaehnsdorf, titles of volumes I and II with early ownership inscriptions of J. Fairfax at head, endpapers with bookplates of the Fairfax family, Earl of Jersey at Osterley Park, the Shakespearian Library of Marsden J. Perry and STuart Bennett; occasional trivial spot or mark, first A6 of volume 2 extended at inner margin, generally clean and fresh. STC 14753 & 14754; greg III 1073, 1076 & 1079; Pforzheimer 560.   Simon Finch 24-133 1996 £7,500.00

JONSON, BEN 1573?-1637   The Works of Ben Johnson (sic). London: printed for J. Walthoe et al, 1716. Bookseller's edition; 8vo; 6 volumes; engraved frontispiece to volume i, frontispieces to volumes ii-iv, 6 plates, text browned; original dark calf, sometime expertly rebacked in lighter russia, raised bands between gilt double rules, pale tan labels, volum numbers lettered direct, gilt double fillet border on sides, red sprinkled and polished edges; good.   Blackwell's B112-164 1996 £500.00

JOPLING, CHARLES M.   Sketch of Furness and Cartmel... London: Whittaker & Co. and Ulverston: Stephen Soulby, 1843. 1st edition; 8vo; pages viii, 276, complete with 2 hand colored folding maps, 8 woodcut plates, 14 text illustrations and 2 text plans; contemporary half calf, gilt, extra with patterned boards; attractive copy. Bicknell 131.   R.F.G. Hollett & Son 78-1048 1996 £75.00

JOPLING, CHARLES M.   Sketch of Furness and Cartmel, Comprising the Hundred of Lonsdale North of the Sands. London: Whittaker & Co., and Ulverston: Stephen Soulby, 1843. 1st edition; 8vo; pages viii, 276, 2 hand colored folding maps, 8 woodcut plates on india paper, 14 text illustrations and 2 text plans; contemporary half calf, gilt, marbled boards, little rubbed, trifle shaken, some browning or spotting in places, but very good. Bicknell 131.   R.F.G. Hollett & Son 78-1047 1996 £65.00

JORDAN, DAVID STARR   The Days of a Man. Yonkers-on-Hudson: World Book Co., 1922. 1st edition; 2 volumes; xxviii, 710; xxviii, 906 pages; green cloth, dust jackets bit chipped, books fine.   Parmer Books Nat/Hist-033049 1996 $125.00

JORDAN, DAVID STARR   The Genera of Fishes and a Classification of Fishes. Stanford: 1917-23. 8vo; pages xvi, cloth.   Wheldon & Wesley 207-969 1996 £60.00

JORDAN, JIM M.   The Paintings of Arshile Gorky: a Critical Catalogue. New York: New York University Press, 1982. 4to; 576 pages, 10 color plates, nearly 400 monochrome illustrations; cloth, dust jacket. Freitag 3748.   Brannan 43-243 1996 $200.00

JORDAN, JOHN W.   Colonial and Revolutionary Families of Pennsylvania: Genealogical and Personal Mmemoirs. New York: Lewis Pub. Co., 1911. 3 volumes, 1706 pages; red leather and boards.   Blue River Books 9-253 1996 $250.00

JOSEPH BEN DAVID IBN YAHYA   Torah-Or. Bologna: Jewish Silkweavers, 1538. 1st edition; small 4to; 37 ll., double column, Hebrew letter; some contemporary Hebrew marginalia; contemporary quarter morocco, marbled paper boards, paper lacking from lower cover, minor soiling and staining; attractive copy of a very rare book; Not in BM, STC It. or NUC.   19th Century Shop 39- 1996 $8,500.00

JOSEPHINE County As It Is! Climate and Resources. Portland: Lewis & Dryden Print Co., Lith., ca. 1887. 1st and only edition; 16 pages; illustrations and maps; original pictorial blue wrappers; minor chipping, very good. Smith 5345; not in Soliday, Graff or Streeter Sale.   Michael D. Heaston 23-283 1996 $1,200.00

JOSEPHUS, FLAVIUS   The Famous and Memorable Works... London: by Tho(mas) Lodge... J. L. for Andrew Hebb, 1640. 5th edition of Lodge's version; folio; (x), 554, (iv), (555)-812, (xxxii) pages; recent half calf, marbled boards, label, woodcut device on general titlepage, one secondary title, minor soiling and spotting, localised dampstaining on a few leaves. Good copy. STC 14813; Allison 10a.   Robert Clark 38-70 1996 £200.00

JOSEPHUS, FLAVIUS   The Famous and Memorable Workes of Josephus. London: printed by J. Lownes for G. Bishop, S. Waterson and Thomas Adams, 1609. 2nd edition of this translation by Thomas Lodge; folio (in 6s); pages (12), 814, (28), great printer's devices, initials and head and tailpieces; title worn and soiled, some old repairs at end, uncased, remnants of original leather. STC 14810.   Family Album Tillers-346 1996 $350.00

JOSEPHUS, FLAVIUS   The Whole Genuine and Complete Works of Flavius Josephus, the Learned and Authentic Jewish Historian and Celebrated Warrior... New York: Printed and Sold by William Durrell, 1792-94. Folio; 723 pages; plus 60 copperplate engravings and maps, age and dampstained; worn contemporary full leather. Evans 24437. Family Album Tillers-347 1996 $200.00

JOSTES, BARBARA DONOHOE   John Parrott, Consul, 18111-1884. San Francisco: printed for the compiler, 1972. 1st edition; quarto; (10), iv, 236 pages, frontispiece, 67 plates, 3 folding charts, 3 maps; original green cloth, gilt lettering on spine and front cover, very fine; scarce. Argonaut Book Shop 113-379 1996 $275.00

JOUBERT, LAURENT   Paradoxorum decas Prima Atque Altera... Lyon: ad Salamandrae (i.e. Senneton freres), 1566. 1st complete edition; 8vo; (16) leaves, 532 pages, (54) leaves, woodcut portrait; early stiff vellum, some foxing and few faint marginal dampstains; Durling 2630; Wellcome I 3498; Baudrier VII 440; Thorndike VI p. 220-1   Jeffrey D. Mancevice 20-50 1996 $350.00

JOUFFROY, ALAIN   Miro Sculpture. New York: Amiel, 1974. Square 4to; 207 pages; numerous illustrations, some in color, 2 original lithographs; cloth, light wear to spine.   Brannan 43-426 1996 $225.00

JOURNAL of Herpetology. 1968-89. Volumes 1-23 in original numbers. John Johnson 135-620 1996 $325.00

JOURNAL of Korean Plant Taxonomy. Seoul: 1969-90. 8vo; volumes 1-20 (in 2 hardbound volumes, 19 and 20 loose in wrappers), over 2500 pages; illustrations;   Raymond M. Sutton VI-743 1996 $495.00

A JOURNEY Round the World. London: George Routledge & Sons, n.d., ca. 1889. Quarto; (40) pages; illustrations in color; original color pictorial boards with dark green cloth backstrip, light soiling and rubbing to boards, lower spine extremity chipped, previous owner's ink presentation inscription dated 1889, on front free endpaper, very good.   Heritage Book Shop 196-258 1996 $150.00

A JOURNEY through the Head of a Modern Poet, Being the Susbstance of a Dream, Occasioned by Reading the Sixth Book of Virgil. London: W. Owen, 1750. Only edition; 4to; half title evidently not called for; later wrappers, very uncommon, some leaves lightly soiled, occasional small tears with no loss; good copy. Very uncommon.   Trebizond 39-30 1996 $200.00

JOUSSE, MATHURIN   Le Theatre de l'Art de Charpentier, Enrichi de Diverses Figures, avec l'Interpretation d'Icelles. La Fleche: George Griveau, 1650. 2nd edition; large 4to; (iv), 172, 14 pages, many woodcut illustrations; 19th century quarter calf, edges shaved with slight loss of printed surface in some cases; few pages set on new stubs and some browning; rare.   Elton Engineering 10-82 1996 £650.00

JOYCE, JAMES 1882-1941   Anna Livia Plurabelle. New York: Crosby Gaige, 1928. One of 800 copies; touch of fraying to cloth at spine extremtieis, still near fine; signed by Joyce, this copy inscribed by Harry Crosby to Aldous Huxley.   Ken Lopez 74-236 1996 $8,500.00

JOYCE, JAMES 1882-1941   Anna Livia Plurabelle. New York: Crosby Gaige, 1928. 1st edition; limited to 800 copies signed by author; gilt and blindstamped brown buckram, top edge gilt; tiny bump at foot of spine, else extremely fine. Slocum & Cahoon 32.   Bromer Booksellers 90-78 1996 $1,500.00

JOYCE, JAMES 1882-1941   Anna Livia Plurabelle... New York: Grosby Gaige, 1928. 1st edition; number 636 of 800 copies; 8vo; original brown cloth, gilt, gilt; minor discoloration of corner of first endpaper, but fine; not issued in dust jacket; signature of author in ink on limitation page.   Trebizond 39-31 1996 $1,400.00

JOYCE, JAMES 1882-1941   The Cat and the Devil. London: Faber & Faber, 1965. 1st edition; stamped 'Proof Only'; illustrations by Gerald Rose in black and white and color; small stain to one page, not affecting text or illustration, else fine.   Bromer Booksellers 87-138 1996 $185.00

JOYCE, JAMES 1882-1941   Chamber Music. London: Cape, 1927. 1st Cape edition; crown 8vo; original dark blue cloth, backstrip gilt lettered, untrimmed, excellent.   Blackwell's B112-165 1997 £100.00

JOYCE, JAMES 1882-1941   Collected Poems. New York: Black Sun Press, 1936. 1st collected edition; 606/750 copies (of an edition of 800 copies); foolscap 8vo; pages lxvi; printed in blue, brown tinted frontispiece, tissue guard present; original white boards, backstrip lettered in blue and front cover with an overall floral pattern within decorative border, all printed in blue, untrimmed, excellent; Slocum & Cahoon 44; Minkoff A Bib. of Black Sun Press 45.   Blackwell's B112-166 1996 £385.00

JOYCE, JAMES 1882-1941   Collected Poems. New York: Black Sun Press, 1936. 1st edition; one of 750 numbered copies; small 8vo; frontispiece by Augustus John; decorated parchment boards, original tissue dust jacket, very fine lightly worn tissue.   James S. Jaffe 34-339 1996 $500.00

JOYCE, JAMES 1882-1941   Dubliners. London: Egoist Press, 1922. 2nd edition; crown 8vo; pages 288; original mid green cloth, faded backstrip gilt lettered and front cover lettered in blind; excellent; Slocum & Cahoon 10 note.   Blackwell's B112-167 1996 £50.00

JOYCE, JAMES 1882-1941   Epiphanies. New York: Vincent Fitz Gerald, 1988. One of 52 copies only, all on Rives du Gue paper; page size 12 x 14 inches; over 150 plates, original watercolors, collage and hand cutting, Letterpress by Dan Kelher's Wild Carrot Letterpress in 40 colors; bound loose in publisher's wrappers in handmade box by David Bourbeau at the Thistle Bindery in Japanese handmade silk woven for this box, with incised line of Japanese tea paper showing profile of Joyce.   Priscilla Juvelis 95/1-142 1996 $15,000.00

JOYCE, JAMES 1882-1941   Exiles. London: Richards, 1918. 1st English edition; crown 8vo; pages (v), 158; original quarter mid blue cloth, printed labels on backstrip and front cover, that on backstrip defective, blue green boards, endpapers lightly foxed, bookticket; good. Slocum & Cahoon 14.   Blackwell's B112-168 1996 £375.00

JOYCE, JAMES 1882-1941   Exiles. New York: Huebsch, 1918. 1st edition; cloth and boards, fine and bright copy.   Stephen Lupack 83-1996 $300.00

JOYCE, JAMES 1882-1941   Verbannte (Exiles). Schauspiel in Drei Akten. Zurich: Rascher, 1919. 1st German edition; crown 8vo; pages 153, (ii), errata slip tipped to half title verso as usual, margins of poor quality paper browned; original printed lime green wrappers, edges and backstrip faded, untrimmed, unopened, good, fragile.   Blackwell's B112-170 1996 £180.00

JOYCE, JAMES 1882-1941   Exiles. London: Egoist Press, i.e. Cape, 1921. 2nd edition; crown 8vo; pages (v), 154; original second issue black cloth, backstrip gilt lettered, fore-edges foxed; excellent. Slocum & Cahoon 14 note.   Blackwell's B112-169 1996 £125.00

JOYCE, JAMES 1882-1941   Giacomo Joyce. New York: Vincent Fitz Gerald, 1989. One of 50 copies only; page size 10 x 13 1/2 inches; on handmade dieu-donne cotton paper, signed by artist on colophon; printed by Dan Keleher and Bruce Chandler at Wild Carrot Letterpress in Dante type designed by Mardersteig and set by Michael Bixler; hand collaged using specially made papers, some with flower petals in paper, Japanese laces, silver tea paper; bound in grey linen over boards stamped in two colors with specially made papers in grey and lime green.   Priscilla Juvelis 95/1-143 1996 $4,500.00

JOYCE, JAMES 1882-1941   Haveth Childers Everywhere. Paris & New York: Henry Babou & Jack Kahane/Fountains Press, 1930. One of 500 numbered copies, out of an edition of 685 copies; 4to; printed on pure linen Vidallon Royal paper; stiff printed wrappers, lacks glassine but with remnants of original slipcase, near fine, small cracks to head of spine and some scattered browning of spine; Slocum & Cahoon A41.   Antic Hay 101-912 1996 $500.00

JOYCE, JAMES 1882-1941   Haveth Childers Everywhere. Paris: Babou and Kahane, New York: Fountain Press, 1930. 1st edition; wrappers in wax paper, in fine slipcase with just a few minor chips to finish. Beasley Books 82-84 1996 $800.00

JOYCE, JAMES 1882-1941   Letters of James Joyce. New York: Viking Press, 1957-66. 1st edition; 8vo; 3 volumes; profusely illustrated; original cloth, dust jackets; light discoloration on first jacket, otherwise almost mint. NCBEL IV 444.   Trebizond 39-32 1996 $185.00

JOYCE, JAMES 1882-1941   Letters of James Joyce. New York: Viking Press, 1966. 1st edition; fine, boxed set, cloth, dust jacket.   C. P. Hyland 216-361 1996 £150.00

JOYCE, JAMES 1882-1941   Letters. New York: Viking, 1966. New edition of volume 1, 1st editions of volumes 2 and 3; 3 volumes; cloth, dust jacket, slipcase somewhat rubbed, with one edge split; fine. James S. Jaffe 34-340 1996 $250.00

JOYCE, JAMES 1882-1941   Collected Poems of James Joyce. New York: Black Sun Press, 1936. Limited edition of 750 from a total of 800 numbered copies, (50 copies signed by Joyce); 12mo; decorative board stamped in blue in original glassine dust jacket and (supplied) acetate dust jacket, near fine, minor browning base of spine because of small chip to glassine.   Antic Hay 101-911 1996$ $750.00

JOYCE, JAMES 1882-1941   Pomes Penyeach. Paris: Shakespeare & Co., 1927. 1st edition; 16mo; pages (21); original plae green boards, covers printed in dark green, spine sunned, front cover faintly foxed; Slocum & Cahoon 24.   Blackwell's B112-171 1996 £225.00

JOYCE, JAMES 1882-1941   Portrait of the Artist as a Young Man. New York: Huebsch, 1916. 1st American edition, precedes English edition; 8vo; original binding; very good.   Charles Agvent 4-750 1996 $850.00

JOYCE, JAMES 1882-1941   A Portrait of the Artist as a Young Man. New York: B. W. Huebsch, 1916. 1st edition preceding the English; very small hole near head of spine and small dark spot on front panel, the blue cloth shows several small patches of discoloration, still very good, spine lettering bright, lacking, of course, the rare dust jacket. Captain's Bookshelf 38-129 1996 $450.00

JOYCE, JAMES 1882-1941   Two Tales of Shem and Shaun. London: Faber, 1932. 1st English edition; foolscap 8vo; pages 45; original pale blue boards, backstrip lettered in blue, tiny nick in backstrip to dust jacket, good. Slocum & Cahoon 37.   Blackwell's B112-172 1996 £60.00

JOYCE, JAMES 1882-1941   Ulysses. New York: Limited Editions Club, 1935. Number 316 of 1500 copies, signed by artist, this copy being one of approximately 250 also signed by Joyce; illustrations by Henri Matisse; small bookplate on front pastedown, nominal darkening to endpapers, otherwise nearly flawless, housed in maroon leather backed custom clamshell slipcase, slipcase very fine.   Hermitage SP95-1001 1996 $10,000.00

JOYCE, JAMES 1882-1941   Ulysses. New York: Limited Editions Club, 1935. Limited to 1500 copies, signed by artist; large 4to; illustrations by Henri Matisse; original gilt decorated cloth, slipcase; fine in lightly worn slipcase. Slocum & Chaoon 22.   James S. Jaffe 34-699 1996 $3,500.00

JOYCE, JAMES 1882-1941   Ulysses. London: 1937. 1st trade edition; fine, dust jacket spine little sunnged, 2 small edge tears top, few slight edge chips, some edge rubbing.   Polyanthos 22-474 1996 $275.00

JOYCE, JAMES GERALD   The Fairford Windows, a Monograph. London: Arundel Society, 1872. Large folio; 3 plates, view, photograph, plan, photograph, 4 woodcuts, 42 most beautiful colored plates; contemporary half morocco.   Charles W. Traylen 117-238 1996 £150.00

JOYCE, JOHN A.   A Checkered Life. Chicago: 1883. 318 pages; frontispiece; illustrated covers bright, front hinge professionally repaired, slipcase; rare. Six Guns 1203.   Early West 22-134 1996 $300.00

JOYCE, JOHN A.   Jewels of Memory. Washington: Gibson Bros., 1895. 1st edition; original cloth, near fine. Dornbusch II 369; Nicholson p 437; not in Coleman or Nevins.   McGowan Book Co. 65-51 1996 $150.00

JOYCE, STANISLAUS   My Brother's Keeper. New York: Viking, 1958. Limited to 375 copies; 8vo; cloth in acetate dust jacket; near fine. Antic Hay 101-915 1996 $150.00

JUDAH, SAMUEL B. H.   Gotham and the Gothamites, a Medley. New York: by the author, 1823. 1st edition; narrow 16mo; original printed boards, rebacked, uncut; BAL 11020; Rosenbach 242.   M & S Rare Books 60-185 1996 $450.00

JUDD, NEIL M.   The Material Culture of Pueblo Bonito. Washington: Smithsonian Inst., 1954. 101 plates; original wrappers, former owner's name, minor tears and creases on covers, else very good.   Ken Sanders 8-32 1996 $150.00

JUDD, NEIL M.   Pueblo Del Arroyo, Chaco Canyon, New Mexico. Washington: Smithsonian Inst., 1959. 55 plates, original wrappers; minor soiling to covers, else very good.   Ken Sanders 8-33 1996 $125.00

JUDGES, A. V.   The Elizabethan Underworld - a Collection of Tudor and Early Stuart Tracts and Ballads Telling of the Lives and Misdoings of Vagabonds, Thieves, Rogues and Cozeners, and Giving Account of the Operation of the Criminal Law. London: George Routledge & Sons, Ltd., 1930. 1st edition; original binding, top edge slightly marked and dusty, head and tail of spine and corners bumped, covers slightly rubbed and marked, very good. From the library of James Hart.   Ulysses 39-329 1996 £75.00

JUDSON, E. Z. C.   The Mysteries and Miseries of New York: a Story of Real Life. New York: Berford & Co., 1848. 1st edition; 8vo; illustrations; original printed wrappers in 3 parts, as noted, uncut and as issued, two parts without wrappers, but rare in this format; wrappers frayed with some tears, piece lacking from cornr of title of first part not affecting text. Wright I 1527, I 1528, 1528a; Sabin 36862.   M & S Rare Books 60-188 1996 $400.00

JUETTNER, OTTO   Daniel Drake and His Followers. Cincinnati: Harvey Pub., 1909. 1st edition; tall 8vo; 496 pages; illustrations; original cloth, trifle rubbed at spine ends; near fine; With W. L. Necker bookplate. Cordasco 00-1804.   Edwin V. Glaser B122-84 1996 $150.00

JUGAKU, BUNSHO   Paper Making by Hand in Japan. Tokyo: Meiji Shobo Pub. Ltd., 1959. 1st edition; illustrated with photos and with 24 mounted paper samples; very good in worn dust jacket.   Hermitage SP95-843 1996 $500.00

JUKES, J. BEETE   Narrative of the Surveying Voyage of H.M. S. Fly, Commanded by Captain F. P. Blackwood, R.N. in Torres Strait, New Guinea and Other Islands of the Eastern Archipelago, During the Years 1842-1846... London: T. & W. Boone, 1847. 1st edition; 8vo; 2 volumes; engraved frontispiece, 17 engraved plates, folded map and chart, text illustrations some stains and dusting, mostly marginal, careful paper repair to volume 1 title affects 4 letters; newly rebound in gilt lettered cloth, new endpapers. Ferguson 4549. Hill p. 159.   Charles W. Traylen 117-443 1996 £520.00

JUNG, CARL GUSTAV   Psychology and Alchemy. New York: 1953. 1st English translation; 563 pages; original binding.   W. Bruce Fye 71-1134 1996 $100.00

JUNG, CARL GUSTAV   Studies in Word-Association: Experiments in the Diagnosis of Psychopathological Conditions Carried Out at the Psychiatric Clinic of the University of Zurich... London: William Heinemann, 1918. 1st edition in English; large 8vo; (ii), (x), (576) pages, printed purple cloth with gilt spine, slight fading to spine and light shelfwear, very good, scarce. Ress 1918a.   John Gach 150-232 1996 $250.00

JUNGE, CARL S.   Ex Libris. New York: H. L. Lindquist, 1935. 1st edition; number 97 of 500 copies signed by Junge; 4to; (51) leaves, original cloth backed printed boards, fine in very good glassine jacket with few pieces missing; with sardonic pencilled inscription on colophon from Leroy Goble to noted Americana bibliographer Wright Howes. Nice association.   Chapel Hill 94-126 1996 $100.00

JUNGER, ERNST   Copse 125 - a Chronicle from the Trench Warfare of 1918. London: Chatto & Windus, 1930. 1st edition; original binding, top edge dusty, prelims and edges spotted, covers faded as usual, head and tail of spine and corners slightly bumped, free endpapers partially browned, very good in nicked rubbed and dusty, slightly marked and chipped dust jacket browned at spine and edges.   Ulysses 39-650 1996 £185.00

JUNIUS, HADRIANUS   Hadriani Junii Medici Emblemata. (with) Aenigmatum Libellus... Antwerp: Ex officina Christophori Plantini, 1565. 1st edition; small 8vo; pages 149, (3), plus 8 ff. (A6 and d8 in facsimile); 58 woodcut emblems; later full vellum. Voet 1476-7; BT 1662; Laborne & Constantina 274-6; Landwehr 399.   Family Album Tillers-348 1996 $1,000.00

JUNIUS, PSEUD.   Stat Nominus Umbra. London: Vernor and Hood, 1797. 8vo; 2 volumes, over 550 pages; additional engraved titles, portraits, numerous vignettes, engraved on wood by John Bewick; tree calf, title labels inset on red and black morocco, hinges cracked; but firm, tight, mellow set.   K Books 442-309 1996 £65.00

JURIN, JAMES   Geometry No Friend to Infidelity; or a Defence of Sir Isaac Newton and the British Mathematicians... London: printed for T. Cooper, 1734. 1st edition; 8vo; 84 pages; original paper wrappers; Babson 177; Keynes, Berkeley 35.   Anthony W. Laywood 109-72 1996 £235.00

A JUST Narrative of the Hellish New Counter-Plots of the Papists, to Cast the Odium of Their Horrid Treasons Upon the Presbyterians... London: Dorman Newman, 1679. 8vo; (iv), 16 pages, imprimatur leaf; outer leaves dusty, minor staining. Wing J1235.   Robert Clark 38-95 1996 £65.00

THE JUSTICE and Necessity of Taxing the American Colonies, Demonstrated. Together with a Vindication of the Authority of Parliament. London: J. Almon, 1766. 36 pages, half title present, but lacking 4 pages ads, nice, large type; removed, exterior darkened, half title lightly chipped. Howes J279; Adams Amer. Controversy 66-31.   Bohling Book Co. 191-593 1996 $110.00

JUSTICE, DONALD   Sixteen Poems. Iowa City: Stone Wall Press, 1970. One of 250 copies; 11.5 x 7 inches; brown printed wrappers, title printed on front wrapper; fine.   Joshua Heller 21-225 1996 $150.00

JUSTINIAN I, EMPEROR   Codicis D. N. Justiniani Sacratiss... Paris: Carolam Guillard and Gulielmum Desbois, 1548. Small 8vo; pages (78), 473; unusual small woodcut initials; old ms. notes and ownerships; later mottled tan French full leather binding, worn, ex-library.   Family Album Tillers-350 1996 $350.00

JUSTINUS, MARCUS JUNIANUS   Justini Ex Trogi Pompeii Historia Libri XLIII. Antwerp: Joan. Graphei for Joannis Steelsii, 1552. Small 8vo; pages (400, 511, 5 woodcut maps, one leaf replaced with clean early ms. transcription; well read, with early ms. annotations and ownerships; contemporary full leather, fleur-de-lis at corners, original vellum guards and printed Latin broadside binders's board are visible.   Family Album Tillers-351 1996 $275.00

JUSTINUS, MARCUS JUNIANUS   Trogi Pompeii Historiarum Philippicarum Epitoma: Ex manuscriptis codicibus Emenadatior... Paris: Dionysium du Val, 1581. Small 8vo; 2 parts in one, (16), 337, (19); 162, (2) pages; old calf, rebacked, title bit soiled. Dibdin Greek & Latin Classics, 4th ed. volume II p. 138-39.   Kenneth Karmiole 1NS-139 1996 $350.00

JUVENALIS, DECIMUS JUNIUS 55-140   Mores Hominum. London: printed by R. Hodgkinsonne, 1660. Folio; pages (24), 522, (28), (2 blank); 16 fine engraved plates by Hollar; contemporary calf, gilt, binding worn and rubbed, but cords very strong and internally very good, large copy.   James Fenning 133-187 1996 £285.00

JUVENALIS, DECIMUS JUNIUS 55-140   Paraphrasi Nella Sesta Satira di Givvenale. Venice: Curtio Naso e Fratelli, 1538. 1st edition; small 4to; 62 unnumbered leaves, italic letter; 19th century straight grainedd morocco (by Tuckett?), gilt double fillets, corner fleurons, spine and inner dentelles, all edges gilt, marbled endpapers; early ms. page numbers and marginal strokes, very few light spots in margins; very good; 19th century bookplate of Edward Cheyney. BM STC It. p. 365; Adams J 769; Brunet II 792. Fontainin II 117.   A. Sokol XXV-55 1996 £1,450.00

JUVENALIS, DECIMUS JUNIUS 55-140   Satyrae. Venice: Joannes Tacuinus de Tridino, 2 December 1492. Folio; 200 leaves, roman letter (with some greek), larger initials supplied in interlocking red and blue, others in red or blue, paragraph marks supplied in red or blue and capital strokes in yellow, woodcut device on last leaf, some browning and waterstaining, some worming, usually in margins, but occasionally affecting a letter of text in last few gatherings, last leaf cut round and mounted; bound in 19th century vellum boards, calligraphic titling on spine. Goff J662; HC 9709; BMC V 527; IGI 5597.   H. M. Fletcher 121-10 1996 £1,750.00

JUVENALIS, DECIMUS JUNIUS 55-140   Satyrae. Birmingham: Baskerville Press, 1761. 4to; 240 pages; plain calf, flat spine gilt in 7 panels, spine and covers stamped with arms of Pembroke Hall, Cambridge, all edges white, marbled endpapers; from the collection of the Rivers family with their 19th century bookplate and from the collection of J. R. Abbey with his bookplate.   Marlborough 160-44 1996 £450.00

JUVENALIS, DECIMUS JUNIUS 55-140   The Satires of Juvenal. London: Payne and Mackinlay, 1807. Large 4to; (8), xl, 572 pages; contemporary red morocco, ornately gilt, extremities bit rubbed, some old faded waterstaining at top margin, all edges gilt.   Kenneth Karmiole 1NS-140 1996 $175.00

K

KAFKA, FRANZ 1883-1924   Betrachtung. Raamin Presse, 1990. One of 175 copies, signed by artist (of a total edition of 180); 14 3/4 x 9 inches; 5 p.l., (1 blank), 11-32, (1) pages, (1) leaf colophon; 5 full page colored illustrations in text by Roswitha Quadflieg, small device on first leaf; printed on thick grey paper; very fine black morocco artfully titled and decorated in blind, in publisher's slipcase; mint.   Phillip J. Pirages 33-440   1996 $1,750.00

KAFKA, FRANZ 1883-1924   Der Kubelreiter/The Bucket Rider. Janus Press, 1972. In an edition of 100 copies, this one of 90 numbered and signed by artist; 12.75 x 11 inches; relief etchings by Jerome Kaplan, 10 unbound folios; designed, set and letterpress printed by Claire Van Vliet, relief etchings printed on hand etching press by Claire Van Vliet and Jerome Kaplan in Philadelphia; German text handset in Franklin Gothic with English text and colophon handset in Monotype Times New Roman, English text and plates printed in black, German text in dark brown with German folio numbers in silver on Rives cuve velin BFK, with Okawara slip sheets and boxed in blue buckram; fine.   Joshua Heller 21-5 1996 $850.00

KAFKA, FRANZ 1883-1924   Ein Landarzt/A Country Doctor. Printed at the Philadelphia College of Art, 1962. Limited to 250 copies numbered and signed by artist; 12.25 x 8.75 inches; 32 pages; printed in black on Rives cuve velin; 12 relief etchings by Claire Van Vliet; unsatisfactorily bound by a Commercial Binder, William Marley Co., in Philadelphia in 1962; Claire Van Vliet, Nancy Southworth and Stephanie Westnedge have disbound di-acidified, sized and repaired 20 copies, of which 5 only are for sale; the new binding is sewn through alum tawed pigskin spine with wooden boards that have the snow storm of the story scratched and painted on them, boxed.   Joshua Heller 21-2 1996 $850.00

KAFKA, FRANZ 1883-1924   Die Verwandlung. Leipzig: Kurt Wolff, 1916. 1st edition; self wrappers, small patch of unobtrusive darkening to upper right portion of front panel; near fine, appealing copy.   Lame Duck Books 19-271 1996 $7,500.00

KAFKA, FRANZ 1883-1924   In the Penal Colony. Limited Editions Club, 1987. One of 800 copies, signed by artist; 11 x 8 inches; 53 pages, (2) leaves; 4 lithographs by Michael Hafftka; attractive handmade and handsewn paper binding, exposed thongs, publisher's fine fleece lined folding cloth box; mint.   Phillip J. Pirages 33-362 1996 $275.00

KAFKA, FRANZ 1883-1924   Metamorphosis. New York: Limited Editions Club, 1984. Limited to 1500 copies, signed by artist; quarto; xii, 61 pages; five etchings and five line drawings by Jose Luis Cuevas; morocco backed pastepaper boards with slipcase, extremely fine, monthly newsletter laid in.   Bromer Booksellers 87-170 1996 $400.00

KAFKA, FRANZ 1883-1924   Parables and Pieces. New York: Vincent Fitz Gerald, 1990. One of 50 copies; all on BFK Rives paper, all signed by Turner and by translator, Michael Feingold; page size 11 x 13 inches; collaged japanese grey paper over boards, housed in black silk box. Priscilla Juvelis 95/1-243 1996 $5,500.00

KAFKA, FRANZ 1883-1924   The Trial. Avon: Limited Editions Club, 1975. One of 2000 numbered copies signed by Alan Cober; illustrations by Alan Cober; full red leather titled in gilt and blind, fine in publisher's slipcase.   Hermitage SP95-1002 1996 $175.00

KAGAN, SOLOMON   Jewish Contributions to Medicine in America from Colonial Times to the Present. Boston: 1939. 2nd edition; 792 pages; original binding. GM 6500.   W. Bruce Fye 71-1137 1996 $250.00

KAHN, MORITZ   The Design and Construction of Industrial Buildings. London: Technical Journal, 1917. 8vo; xii, 63, (5) pages, 62 photo plates, original boards.   Elton Engineering 10-84 1996 £80.00

KAHN, ROGER   The Boys of Summer. New York: Harper & Row, 1972. 1st edition; fine in fine dust jacket; this copy signed by 13 members of this team.   Bud Schweska 12-59 1996 $550.00

KAHNWEILER, DANIEL HENRY   Juan Gris: His Life and Work. New York: Abrams, 1969. Revised edition; 4to; 347 pages, 184 illustrations, including 24 tipped in color plates; cloth, dust jacket. Lucas p. 152. Freitag 3956.   Brannan 43-247 1996 $225.00

KAHNWEILER, DANIEL HENRY   The Sculptures of Picasso. London: Rodney Phillips & Co., 1948(1949). 1st English edition; 4to; (13) pages, 216 black and white gravure plates; cloth backed glazed paper over boards, printed in colors with black and white photo, boards lightly rubbed, as ususal, previous owner's name on endpaper, else near fine. Andrew Cahan 47-33 1996 $150.00

KAISER, HENRY J.   Twenty-Six Addresses Delivered During the War Years by Henry J. Kaiser. San Francisco: Grabhorn Press, 1945. Folio; (vii), 157 pages, initials by Mallette Dean; half red leather and patterned boards, plain dust jacket. Fine. Heller Magee 415.   Bohling Book Co. 192-578 1996 $250.00

KALASHNIKOV, ANATOLII   War and Peace: a Suite of Wood Engravings. Libanus Press, 1991. Of 300 copies, signed by artist, this is one of 150 for the Society; folio; scarlet cloth; fine.   Bertram Rota 272-256 1996 £80.00

KALM, PEHR 1716-1779   Travels Into North America Containing its Natural History. Warrington: printed by William Eyres, 1770. 1st English edition; 8vo; 3 volumes, xvi, 400, ads, 352, + inserted list of subscriber viii,3 10, index; 6 plates, folding map; contemporary speckled calf, plate cropped little close, not affecting images, texts and plates pleasantly fre of foxing, professionally rebacked in matching speckled calf, all in all a very handsome and complete set with expertly repaired map not found in all copies; very handsome set. Howes K5; Streeter II 823; Cox II 177 Hermitage SP95-714 1996 $4,000.00

KAMES, HENRY HOME, LORD 1696-1782   The Gentleman Farmer. Edinburgh: John Bell, 1779. 2nd edition; 8vo; pages 438; 3 plates; later calf backed boards, contemporary ownership signatures little trimmed, some minor foxing; very good. Fussell p. 108-09; MacDonald p. 215. Second Life Books 103-107 1996 $325.00

KANE, ELISHA KENT   Arctic Explorations: The Second Grinnell Expedition in Search of Sir John Franklin, 1853, '54, '55. Philadelphia: Childs & Peterson, London: Trubner and Co., 1856. 1st edition; 8vo; 2 volumes; vignette titlepages, printed titles, publisher's ad, 464, 467 pages; frontispieces, 18 steel engraved plates, 4 maps, numerous woodcuts to text; half purple morocco, gilt rule borders, gilt rule and 'ship' emblems to panelled spines, black morocco labels, marbled boards, edges and endpapers (upper corners slightly rubbed); Arctic Bi 5373; Sabin 37001; Hill p. 159.   Beeleigh Abbey BA56-82 1996 £295.00

KANE, ELISHA KENT   Arctic Explorations: the Second Grinnell Expedition in Search of Sir John Franklin, 1853, '54, '55. Philadelphia: Childs & Peterson, 1856. Large 8vo; 2 volumes; inserted engraved titles with vignettes after James Hamilton, steel engraved portrait frontispiece after Brady, 18 steel engraved plates after Hamilton and others, 3 lithographed charts, numerous text wood engravings after Hamilton and others; publisher's dark brown grained cloth with elaborate pictorial bli blocked decoration on covers, spine with gilt stamped title information; splendid copy, rarely found in such condition.   Book Block 32-78 1996 $395.00

KANE, ELISHA KENT   Arctic Explorations in the Years 1853, '54, '55. Philadelphia: Childs and Peterson, 1856. 1st edition; 2 volumes; 300+ engravings,, folding map; title and some plates foxed.   Parker Books the West 30-96 1996 $175.00

KANE, ELISHA KENT   Arctic Explorations. The Second Grinnell Expedition in Search of Sir John Franklin. Philadelphia: 1856. 2 volumes; original binding, bit worn, but nice, clean, bright set. Arctic 8373. Stephen Lunsford 45-83 1996 $135.00

KANE, THOMAS LEIPER   Alaska and the Polar Regions. Lecture of...Before the American Geographical Society, in New York City, Thursday Evening May 7, 1868. New York: Journeymen Printers' Co-Operative Association, 1868. Pages 32; original wrappers, few corner bent, else about fine, extremely scarce.   Stephen Lunsford 45-84 1996 $350.00

KANGRA Valley Painting. Calcutta: Publications Division, 1954. 1st editior small folio; frontispiece, (viii), 17, (1) pages; 40 plates; cloth, dust jacke torn, name in ink, margins slightly sunned, else very good.   The Bookpress 75-427 1996 $110.00

KANSAS PACIFIC RAILROAD   Opening Excursion. Kansas Pacific Railway. St. Louis to Denver. August 30-September 10, 1870. Denver: Rocky Mountain News Print, 1870. 1st edition; 4 pages; fine. Allen Colorado Imprints 123;   Michael D. Heaston 23-199 1996 $850.00

KANT, IMMANUEL   Kritik of Judgment. London: Macmillan, 1892. 1st edition in English; 8vo; xlviii, 429 pages; publisher's leaf of ads at end; original maroon cloth, gilt, uncut, fine.   John Drury 82-131 1996 £75.00

KANT, IMMANUEL   Religion Within the Boundary of Pure Reason. Edinburgh: Thomas Clark, 1838. 1st edition in English; 8vo; x, (2), 275, (1) pages; 2 leaves of publisher's ads; original cloth, overall embossed pattern of flowers and fruit, spine faded and chipped at head, bit shaken, uncut.   John Drury 82-128 1996 £150.00

KANT, IMMANUEL   Werke Sorgfaltig Reviderte Gesammtausgabe in Zehn Banden. Leipzig: Moxes und Baumann, 1838-39. 1st collected edition; 8vo; 10 volumes in 5; frontispiece in volume 1, folding facsimile in volume 2, 3 plates in volume 3; some spotting and slight browning, sympathetically rebound recently in quarter calf and cloth boards, labels on spines lettered in gilt, marbled endpapers; very good. Rather scarce. Rand p. 286; not in Warda.   John Drury 82-129 1996 £500.00

KANTOR, HELENE J.   The Aegean and the Orient in the Second Millennium B.C. Bloomington; Archaeological Inst. of America, 1947. 4to; 108 pages, 26 paltes, labe removed from spine, original cloth, inscribed 'Wtih the compliments of the author.'   Archaeologia Luxor-3533 1996 $150.00

KANTOR, MACKINLAY   Diversey. New York: Coward-McCann, 1928. 1st edition; author's first book; red cloth, beige printed dust jacket that is torn and chipped, top half of back missing.   Priscilla Juvelis 95/1-317 1996 $150.00

KARAGEORGHIS, VASSOS   Excavations at Kition. Volume I: The Tombs. Nicosia: Department of Antiquities, 1974. 4to; 2 parts, 178 pages, numerous illustrations, 179 plates; original cloth, torn dust jacket.   Archaeologia Luxor-3540 1996 $125.00

KARLSTRON, PAUL J.   Louis Michel Eilshemius. New York: Harry N. Abrams, 1978. 1st edition; oblong 4to; 263 pages; frontispiece, 228 illustrations, including 50 tipped in color plates; illustrated cloth; near fine and bright in illustrated dust jacket.   Andrew Cahan 47-70 1996 $125.00

KARO, GEORGE   Greek Personality in Archaic Sculpture. Cambridge: Pub. for Oberlin College by Harvard University Press, 1948. 8vo; xviii, 346 pages; 32 plates; original cloth, tattered dust jacket, uncut; inscribed presentation copy signed by author.   Archaeologia Luxor-3542 1996 $150.00

KAROUZOU, SEMNI   The Amasis Painter. Oxford: Clarendon Press, 1956. 4to; xii, 46 pages, 44 plates, original cloth, dust jacket, neat ex-library copy.   Archaeologia Luxor-3543 1996 $250.00

KARPMAN, BENJAMIN   Case Studies in the Psychopathology of Crime: a Reference Source for Research in Criminal Material. Washington: Medical Science Press, 1933/47/47/48. 1st edition; thick 4to; pages (xvi), 1042; viii, 738; (xxxvi), 834, (2), 1 color plate; (xxxvi), 876 pages plus 1 color plate; pebbled black cloth, huge heavy volumes, considering which generally very good, 1 page loose in volume 1 label removed from base of spine to titlepage creased and scotch taped in volume 4.   John Gach 150-235 1996 $350.00

KARPOVICH, PETER   Adventures in Artificial Respiration. New York: 1953. 1st edition; 302 pages; illustrations; original binding.   W. Bruce Fye 71-1146 1996 $125.00

KARSH, YOUSUF   Karsh Portraits. Boston: New York Graphic Society, 1979. 48 gravure illustrations; dust jacket; inscribed, signed and dated 1981.   J. B. Muns 154-165 1996 $250.00

KARSLAKE, FRANK   Notes from Sotheby's, Being a Compilation of 2032 Notes from Catalogues of Book-Sales Which Have Taken Place in the Rooms of Messrs. Sotheby, Wilkinson & Hodge, Between the Years 1895-1909. London: Karslake and Co., 1909. 8.75 x 7 inches; 392 pages; frontispiece; blue cloth with title in gilt on spine, some wear to covers, otherwise very good.   Joshua Heller 21-219 1996 $100.00

KAUFFMAN, C. H.   The Agaricaceae of Michigan. Lansing: 1918. 8vo; Volume 2 (plates) only; 172 plates; original cloth, light soiling and wear, head of spine frayed, small hole punched in edge of front cover, overall very good.   Raymond M. Sutton VII-204 1996 $100.00

KAUFFMAN, C. H.   The Dictionary of Merchandize, and Nomenclature in All Languages... London: printed for the author, sold by T. Boosey, 1803. 8vo; iv, 380 pages, piece torn from upper margin of X1 with loss of one word of text, lightly browned; contemporary half calf, neatly rebacked; from the Kenney collection. Kress B4690; 4 copies in NUC.   James Burmester 29-81 1996 £300.00

KAUFMAN, ALICE   The Navajo Weaving Tradition 1650 to the Present. New York: E. P. Dutton, 1987. 1st edition; 150 pages; fine in dust jacket.   Ken Sanders 8-189 1996 $100.00

KAVANAGH, PATRICK   Self Portrait. Dublin: Dolmen Press, 1964. 1st edition; 7 black and white photos by Liam Miller; original binding, top corners of first few pages slightly thumbed, very good in slightly spotted and dusty dust jacket.   Ulysses 39-331 1996 £75.00

KAWAMURA, S.   Icones of Japanese Fungi. Tokyo: 1954-55. 4to; 8 volumes; 863 pages; 110 colored plates; green buckram, slipcases.   Raymond M. Sutton VII-205 1996 $320.00

KAY, R.   The New Preceptor, or, Young Lady's & Gentleman's True Instructor in the Rudiments of the English Tongue. Newcastle-upon-Tyne: printed by and for M. Angus & Son and for W. Charnley, 1801. 1st edition; 12mo; 104 pages, woodcut title vignette & 9 woodcut text illustrations by Thomas Bewick, rebound in old style half calf. Very scarce; 2 copies in NUC; Hugo 167.   James Burmester 29-82 1996 £350.00

KAY, TERRY   The Year the Lights Came On. Boston Houghton Mifflin, 1976. 1st edition; uncorrected proof; signed by author; fine in printed orange wrappers.   Thomas Dorn 9-151 1996 $250.00

KAY, TERRY   The Year the Lights Came On. Boston: Houghton Mifflin Co., 1976. 1st trade edition; signed by author; fine in fine, unfaded dust jacket, which almost always has sunned spine.   Thomas Dorn 9-152 1996 $100.00

KAY, ULYSSES   Symphony. N.P.: n.p., 1967. Manuscript facsimile; small folio; stiff black wrappers, paper label on upper cover, spiral bound; very good; dedication copy, the copy of Carl Haverlin, inscribed to Haverlin by author.   George J. Houle 68-75 1996 $750.00

KEARTON, A.   Kearton's Nature Pictures. London: 1910. 2 volumes; colored and other plates, text illustrations; original cloth, lightly rubbed, nice.   David A.H. Grayling MY95Orn-172 1996 £50.00

KEATE, GEORGE   An Account of the Pelew Islands...from the Journals and Communications of Captain Henry Wilson... London: G. Nicol, 1788. 2nd edition; small folio; frontispiece, xxvii, (i), 378 pages; 16 plates; uncut, contemporary half calf, binding rubbed, rubberstamp on bottom edge of leaf v, some pencilling and leaves crudely repaired, text foxed. The Chamberlain family copy.   The Bookpress 75-428 1996 $550.00

KEATE, GEORGE   An Account of the Pelew Islands; Situated in the Western Part of the Pacific Ocean. London: printed for Captain Wilson and sold by G. Nicol, 1789. 3rd edition; 4to; 378 pages; frontispiece, 13 engraved plates, 3 maps and plans, plates of Abba Thulle and Ludee misbound, plate to face page 127 has lower margin cropped; full tree calf, gilt rule to panelled spine, red morocco label, ink stain and surface scrape to upper board. Hill, Pacific Voyages p. 160.   Beeleigh Abbey BA56-83 1996 £450.00

KEATE, GEORGE   An Account of the Pelew Islands; Situated in the Western Part of the Pacific Ocean. London: printed for Captain Wilson.. G. Nicol, 1789. 3rd edition; 4to; xxvii, (i), 378 pages; engraved frontispiece, large folding chart, 15 engraved plates; rebound in tan half calf, marbled boards, leather spine labels; some offsetting from plates, touch of foxing in folds of folding view, few plates have some light foxing in margins, otherwise fine. Cox II p. 303. Hill I for 1st edition of 1788.   David Mason 71-147 1996 $600.00

KEATE, GEORGE   An Account of the Pelew Islands, Situated in the Western Part of the Pacific Ocean, Composed from the Journals and Communications of Capt. Henry Wilson... London: printed for Capt. Wilson, 1789. 3rd edition; 4to; xviii, 378 pages; 16 plates, full morocco, rebacked, marbled endpapers, back cover with some stains, edges rubbed, light foxing, otherwise very good ex-library, no markings on outside.   Worldwide Antiquarian 162-394 1996 $425.00

KEATE, GEORGE   The Monument in Arcadia; a Dramatic Poem in Two Acts. London: printed for J. Dodsley, 1773. 1st edition; 4to; disbound; wanting half title, last two leaves strengthened in blank inner margins; Jackson p. 21; CBEL II 665.   Ximenes 108-234 1996 $125.00

KEATING, WILLIAM H. Narrative of an Expedition to the Source of St. Peter's River, Lake Winnepeek, Lake of the Woods &c. Performed in the Year 1823... London: printed for Geo. B. Whittaker, 1825. 1st English edition; 8vo; 2 volumes; (xvi), 458, vi, 248, 156 pages; 8 plates, large folding map; original cloth backed boards, paper spine labels; occasional foxing, spines very lightly faded with some slight rubbing, spine labels have few small nicks at edges, not affecting text, boards very lightly soiled, but this is in fact a stunning example of original boards of the period, as good a copy as one could hope to find. TPL 1284; Sabin 37137. David Mason 71-123 1996 $1,200.00

KEATS, JOHN 1795-1821 Endymion: a Poetic Romance. London: for Taylor and Hesey, 1818. 1st edition; 8vo; pages ix, (x-xii), 207, with half title but without ad leaf sometimes found, with five line errata; this copy has a little additional material bound in: engraved portrait of Keats by Henry Meyer after Severn, on india paper, mounted & bound as frontispiece, & 3 critical notices from the Boston Mercury, another from London Athenaeum, cut down & mounted on p. 5; 19th century red half morocco, gilt rules on sides, spine in compartments with raised bands, gilt rules, lettering and date and leafy ornament, top edge gilt, others uncut, marbled boards, endpapers; bookplate of Beatrice Borland, somewhat spotted, otherwise excellent. Ashley III p. 13; Mac Gillvray 2; Hayward 232; Tinker 1419. Simon Finch 24-135 1996 £3,750.00

KEATS, JOHN 1795-1821 Lamia, Isabella, The Eve of St. Agnes and Other Poems. London: for Taylor and Hessey, 1820. 1st edition; 12mo; pages (vi), 199, (1), without half title and ad leaves sometimes found at end; contemporary brown calf, triple fillet gilt border to sides around elaborate blind roll, triple fillets and cornerpieces, spine in compartments with raised bands, gilt rules, place and date, and blind ornament, red morocco label, little rubbed, just a few spots, excellent copy; at one time the copy of scholar Sidney Colvin, signed notes by him, along with another later inscription; presentation copy, inscribed to poet George Darley from his cousin Maria. Ashley III p. 15-16; MacGillivray 3; Hayward 233; Tinker 1420. Simon Finch 24-136 1996 £5,500.00

KEATS, JOHN 1795-1821 Lamia, Isabella, the Eve of St. Agnes and Other Poems. London: printed for Taylor and Hessey, 1820. 1st edition; 12mo; half title present, 8 page catalog of Taylor and Hessey ads at end; full green morocco, gilt, spine and inner dentelles gilt, by Bedford, few traces of rubbing; uncut, fine. Hayward 233. Ximenes 109-169 1996 $7,500.00

KEATS, JOHN 1795-1821 On the Eve of St. Agnes. London: Edward Arnold, 1901. Limited to 125 copies; octavo; 23 pages; printed entirely on vellum, with opening full page hand colored wood engraving by Reginald Savage; illuminated in gold and rubricated by an anonymous hand; full vellum over boards, blindstamped with rose logo and motto of the series "Soul is Form"; very fine. Bromer Booksellers 87-65 1996 $550.00

KEATS, JOHN 1795-1821 Poems. London: George Bell & Sons, 1897. 1st edition; limited to 125 on Japanese vellum, this number 78; xxiv, 338 pages; frontispiece and title with red decorated border, 28 full page and 50 text illustrations by Robert Anning Bell; green and purple binding design from trade edition bound in, beige holland cloth, titled in black and red on spine, small ink marks to bottom of pages 274/75; light stains on top board. Robin Greer 94A-36 1996 £350.00

KEEBLE, SAMUEL E. Industrial Day-Dreams: Studies in Industrial Ethics and Economics. London: Elliot Stock, 1896. 1st edition; 8vo; xii, (2), 218 pages; few former readers' emphasis marks; original maroon cloth, gilt, slightly shaken, else good, uncut. Uncommon. John Drury 82-132 1996 £50.00

THE KEEPSAKE for 1831, 1832, 1833 & 1835. London: Longman, Rees, Orme, Brown & Green, 1st editions; rebound in same style as the original silk bindings with gold-gilt stamping to spine. Aronovitz 57-1038 1996 $385.00

A KEEPSAKE for Alfred A. Knopf. New York: Serendipity Press, 1965. One of 150 copies; 7 x 4 1/2 inches; fine in worn, browned slipcase. Timothy Hawley 115-115 1996 $200.00

KEILIN, DAVID The History of Cell Respiration and Cytochrome. Cambridge: 1966. 1st edition; 416 apges; original binding. GM 968. W. Bruce Fye 71-1151 1996 $100.00

KEITH, ARTHUR Menders of the Maimed. London: 1919. 1st edition; 335 pages; outer hinges cracked, contents fine. Rare. GM 4479. W. Bruce Fye 71-1155 1996 $200.00

KEITH, ELMER Guns and Ammo for Big Game Hunting. Los Angeles: 1965. 1st edition; 384 pages, 179 photos and illustrations; book and dust jacket fine. Early West 22-410 1996 $100.00

KEITH, ELMER Shotguns by Keith. Harrisburg: 1950. 1st edition; 307 pages, photos, illustrations; inscribed by author. Early West 22-409 1996 $100.00

KELEHER, WILLIAM A. Violence in Lincoln County, 1869-1881. Albuquerque: 1957. 1st edition; 390 pages, index, photos; book fine, dust jacket very good. Adams 150 #88; six Guns 1216. Early West 22-144 1996 $100.00

KELEMEN, PAL Medieval American Art: a Survey in Two Volumes. New York: Macmillan, 1943. 1st edition; 4to; 2 volumes, xiv, 414 pages, 306 plates, 33 pages; original cloth. Archaeologia Luxor-4590 1996 $150.00

KELLER, D. Popular Medicine. H. Gernsback, 1934-35. 1st edition; 7 volumes; wrappers, about very good. Aronovitz 57-606 1996 $125.00

KELLER, GOTTFRIED A Village Romeo and Juliet - a Tale. London: Constable and Co. Ltd., 1915. 1st edition; original binding, top edge dusty, free endpapers partially browned, short tear at top edge of front free endpaper, upper hinge cracked, spine slightly faded, head and tail of spine and corners slightly bumped and rubbed, edges spotted; good. Ulysses 39-618 1996 £65.00

KELLER, HELEN The Song of the Stone Wall. New York: Century, 1910. 1st edition; gray decorated boards, fine in scarce dust jacket with few small chips and lacking 2 inches from spine; inscribed by author. Charles Agvent 4-769 1996 $450.00

KELLERMANN, MICHEL Paintings by Andre Derain. Paris: Galerie Schmit, 1992. One of 1000 copies 1st edition;; page size 29 x 34 cm; 440 paintings catalogued, 39 full color reproductions; cloth over boards; new. Priscilla Juvelis 95/1-10 1996 $1,150.00

KELLEY, CHARLES Old Greenwood - the Story of Caleb Greenwood Trapper, Pathfinder and Early Pioneer of the Old West. Salt Lake City: 1936. 1st edition; copy number 136 of 350; 128 pages; photos; pictorial embossed cloth, nice. Very scarce. T. A. Swinford 49-650 1996 $225.00

KELLEY, J. Thirteen Years in the Oregon Penitentiary. Portland: 1918. 1st edition; 142 pages; illustrations; pictorial wrappers, very good+, 6 Guns 1218. T. A. Swinford 49-649 1996 $125.00

KELLEY, ROBERT L. Gold vs. Grain. Glendale: The Arthur H. Clark Co., 1959. 1st edition; one of 1265 copies; 324 pages; illustrations, original gilt lettered brown cloth; very fine. Becoming quite scarce. Clark and Brunet 137. Argonaut Book Shop 113-383 1996 $150.00

KELLOGG, HARRIET S. Life of Mrs. Emily J. Harwood. Albuquerque: El Abogado Press, 1903. 1st edition; 376, (9) pages, frontispiece, illustrations; original green cloth, title in gilt on spine and front cover; fine. Very scarce. Presentation cpy from author plus original photo of Harwood School for Girls tipped to front endsheet; partial ALS from author laid in. Michael D. Heaston 23-268 1996 $750.00

KELLOGG, LOUISE PHELPS The British Regime in Wisconsin and the Northwest. Madison: State Historical Society of Wisconsin, 1935. 22.5 cm; xvii, 361 pages; illustrations, portraits, maps; fine ex-private library, 2 small stamps; fine. Rockland Books 38-109 1996 $100.00

KELLY'S Directory of Bristol and Suburbs. London: 1937. Thick royal 8vo pages 1415; folding map; original cloth, National Liberal Club stamp. Howes Bookshop 265-89 1996 £50.00

KELLY'S Directory of Cumberland and Westmorland. London: Kelly & Co. 1894. Small 4to; pages xxiv, 430, 205, 72 (ads), 2 folding maps; modern cloth, gilt, gilt arms from original binding laid on to upper board, edges of some endpapers and ad leaves stained or repaired. R.F.G. Hollett & Son 78-1051 1996 £95.00

KELLY'S Directory of Cumberland and Westmorland. London: Kelly's Directories, 1925. Small 4to; pages 11, xvi, 444, 196, 14, 2 folding colored maps; original blindstamped crimson cloth gilt, little cockled, spine faded; joints cracking. R.F.G. Hollett & Son 78-1052 1996 £50.00

KELLY'S Directory of Cumberland and Westmorland. London: Kelly's Directories, 1934. Small 4to; pages xvi, 191 48 (ads); map; modern half calf gilt with spine label, folding map (edges soiled and chipped), some ad leaves stained. R.F.G. Hollett & Son 78-1056 1996 £95.00

KELLY'S Directory of Cumberland. Kelly's Directories, 1897. Small 4to; pages xviii, 430, 48; folding map (little repaired), original blindstamped crimson cloth, gilt, very worn and darkened. R.F.G. Hollett & Son 78-1049 1996 £55.00

KELLY'S Directory of Cumberland. London: Kelly's Directories, 1910. Small 4to; pages xvi, 437, 16; folding colored map; original blindstamped crimson cloth, gilt, rather faded. R.F.G. Hollett & Son 78-1050 1996 £60.00

KELLY'S Directory of Suffolk. London: Kelly's Directories Ltd., 1929. 1st edition; 4to; folding colored map; original cloth. Anthony W. Laywood 108-239 1996 £55.00

KELLY, CELSUS La Australia Del Espiritu Santo. Cambridge: for the Hakluyt Society, 1966. 1st edition thus; 2 volumes; fine in slightly darkened dust jackets. Hermitage SP95-1106 1996 $100.00

KELLY, CHARLES Old Greenwood. The Story of Caleb Greenwood Trapper, Pathfinder and Early Pioneer. Georgetown: Talisman Press, 1965. Limited to 750 copies; 361 pages; folding map; cloth; fine in dust jacket. Rocq 7392; Paher 1019. Gene W. Baade 1094-91 1996 $165.00

KELLY, CHARLES Salt Desert Trails - A History of the Hastings Cutoff and Other Early Trails Which Crossed the Great Salt Desert Seeking a Shorter Road to California. Salt Lake City: 1930. 1st edition; 178 pages; frontispiece; photos, pictorial embossed cloth, map endpapers; nice; inscribed. Howes K59. T. A. Swinford 49-651 1996 $225.00

KELLY, CHARLES Salt Desert Trails. Salt Lake City: Western Printing Co., 1930. 1st edition; 8vo; 178 pages; (5) pages, 34 illustrations, map endpapers; textured cloth with embossed illustration in green and gilt, rubbed along spine, name and occasional pencil notations, residue from small piece of cellophane tape affecting 3 leaves, else very good; prospectus and related clipping laid in. Howes K59. Andrew Cahan 47-200 1995 $135.00

KELLY, FRED One Thing Leads to Another - the Growth of an Industry. Boston and New York: Houghton Mifflin Co., 1936. 1st edition; 17 black and white photos by Margaret Bourke-White; decorated cloth silver, endpapers faintly and partially browned; very good in nicked, rubbed, torn, frayed, creased and dusty, internally repaired and slightly soiled dust jacket. Ulysses 39-61 1996 £125.00

KELLY, HOWARD Snakes of Maryland. Baltimore: 1936. 1st edition; 103 pages; photos, colored plates; wrappers, head and tail of spine chipped. W. Bruce Fye 71-1162 1996 $100.00

KELLY, HOWARD Some American Medical Botanists Commemorated in Our Botanical Nomenclature. Troy: 1914. 1st edition; 216 pages; original binding, water stain affecting cover and margins of some leaves; scarce. W. Bruce Fye 71-1163 1996 $150.00

KELLY, ISABEL The Archaeology of the Autlan-Tuxcacuesco Area of Jalisco I-II. Berkeley and Los Angeles: University of California Press, 1945-49. 8vo; 2 volumes, 390 pages, 73 figures, 29 plates, 8 maps; wrappers, ink stamps. Archaeologia Luxor-4592 1996 $150.00

KELLY, ISABEL The Archaeology of the Autlan-Tuxcacuesco Area of Jalisco. I-II. Berkeley: University of California Press, 1945-49. 8vo; 2 volumes, 390 pages, 73 figures and 29 plates, 8 maps; lightly worn wrpapers, with ink stamp of Bennyhoff. Archaeologia Luxor-4591 1996 $150.00

KELLY, JAMES A Complete Collection of Scotish Proverbs Explained and Made Intelligible to the English Reader. London: printed for Iwlliam and John Innys and John Osborn, 1721. 1st edition; 8vo; contemporary panelled calf, green morocco label, vry slight wear to ends of spine; fine. Alston IX 86. Ximenes 108-235 1996 $350.00

KELLY, LUTHER S. 'Yellowstone Kelly.' The Memoirs of Luther S. Kelly. New Haven: Yale University Press, 1926. 1st edition; xiii, 268 pages; illustrations, folding map; original cloth; very fine with pictorial dust jacket, very small tear to spine of jacket. Argonaut Book Shop 113-384 1996 $175.00

KELLY, MATTHEW Dissertations Chiefly on Irish Church History. Dublin: James Duffy, 1864. 1st collected edition; 8vo; pages xvi, 448; original cloth, gilt, very good. James Fenning 133-190 1996 £55.00

KELLY, MICHAEL Reminiscences of Michael Kelly of the King's Theatre, and Theatre Royal Drury Lane, Includes a Period of Half a Century. London: Henry Colburn, 1826. 1st edition; 2 volumes, xxiii, 354; 404 pages; 2 leaves of music; frontispiece; full polished leather, gilt tooled spines, edges bit scuffed, overall a nice pair. Lyman Books 21-320 1996 $250.00

KELLY, MICHAEL Reminiscences...with Original Anecdotes of Many Distinguished Persons, Political, Literary and Musical. London: Henry Colburn, 1826. 2nd edition; large 12mo; 2 volumes; original boards, new backstrips with original labels, uncut, fresh copy. LAR 3175. Peter Murray Hill 185-94 1996 £75.00

KELLY, PATRICK The Universal Cambist and Commercial Instructor... London: printed for the author, 1821. 2nd edition; 4to; 2 volumes, xl, (2), 376; xxiv, 323, (3) pages, complete with half titles and final ad leaf; original boards, carefully restored, very good. Kress C725; Goldsmiths 23211. John Drury 82-133 1996 £175.00

KELLY, PATRICK The Universal Cambist and Commercial Instructor... London: printed for the author, 1835. 2nd edition; 4to; 2 volumes in one; half titles, 2 maps at end of volume 2; contemporary calf, rebacked with original gilt spine, label. Kress C3976; Goldsmith 29054. Anthony W. Laywood 108-188 1996 £175.00

KELLY, R. TALBOT Burma, Painted and Described. London: Adam and Charles Black, 1905. Limited edition deluxe of 300 numbered copies, signed by artist/author; 4to; xvi, 261 pages; 75 plates in color, sketch map; publisher's white buckram over bevelled boards, elaborate design on spine and front cover in blue, red, green and gilt, top edge gilt, binding slightly soiled, affecting mainly the back cover, occasional light foxing, generally very good, somewhat cleaner than usual. Thomas Thorp 489-177 1996 £250.00

KELLY, ROBERT Armed Descent. New York: Hawk's Well Press, 1961. 1st edition; small 8vo; author's first book; signed by author; glossy wrappers; some neat writing in ink on front and back covers, otherwise fine. James S. Jaffe 34-342 1996 $100.00

KELLY, THOMAS Kelly's Practical Builder's Price Book, or Safe Guide to the Valuation of All Kinds of Artificer's Work... London: Kelly, 1857. Small 4to; 168, 31, (1) pages; frontispiece and 5 engraved plates; quarter cloth. Elton Engineering 10-45 1996 £120.00

KELLY, W. The Glob. New York: Viking, 1952. 1st edition; illustrations; just about fine in near fine dust jacket. Aronovitz 57-612 1996 $150.00

KELSEY, HENRY The Kelsey Papers, Ottawa: Public ARchvies of Canada/Public Records Office of Northern Ireland, 1929. 26.5 cm; lxxxiii, 128 pages; frontispiece, large folding map, in color; printed boards; very good. Peel 2; TPL 162. Rockland Books 38-110 199 $125.00

KELSON, GEORGE M. The Salmon Fly: How to Dress It and How to Use It. London: published by the author, 1895. 1st edition; royal 8vo; xiv, 510, 45 ad pages; frontispiece, 8 chromolithograph plates, 84 text illustrations; publisher's maroon cloth on bevelled boards, decorated gilt, top edge gilt, fadedd, particularly on spine, slightly worn, occasional light spotting internally. Thomas Thorp 489-178 1996 £400.00

KELTIE, JOHN S. A History of the Scottish Highlands, Highland Clans, and Highland Regiments. London: A. Fullarton, & Co., n.d. 4to; 8 volumes; 31 colored plates, 20 engraved plates, double pale colored clan map, 205 text woodcuts; original decorative cloth, gilt, few hinges cracked, but excellent, clean set in original divisions. R.F.G. Hollett 76-141 1996 £220.00

KEMBLE, JOHN HASKELL The Panama Route 1849-1869. Berkeley: & Los Angeles: University of California Press, 1943. 1st edition; frontispiece, 8 plates, lithographs, 2 maps; very fine. Argonaut Book Shop 113-386 1996 $175.00

KEMBLE, JOHN PHILIP Fugitive Pieces. York: printed by W. Blanchard and Co., for the author, 1780. 1st edition; 8vo; 19th century half roan, slightly rubbed, top edge gilt, others uncut. Anthony Laywood 108-79 1996 £135.00

KEMP. DONALD   Happy Valley - A Promoter's Paradise-Being an Historical Sketch of Eldora, Colroado and Its Environs. Denver: 1945. 1st edition; limited, signed by both authors; 60 pages, photos, map; stiff printed wrappers, very good+. Scarce.   T. A. Swinford 49-653 1996 $125.00

KENDALL, GEORGE W.   Narrative of the Texan Santa Fe Expedition. New York: Harper and Bros., 1844. 1st edition; 2 volumes, frontispiece and plates, folding map; original black cloth, pictorial spine, title stamped in gilt on spine, fine, very bright set. Martin & Martin texas Maps plate 34. Howes K75; Jenkins BTB 116.   Michael D. Heaston 23-278 1996 $1,000.00

KENDALL, HENRY EDWARD   Designs for Schools and School Houses, Parochial and National. London: John Williams, 1847. 1st edition; folio; portfolio, (xv) pages; 20 plates; few plates thumbed, original decorated covers, kept as an overlay on later portfolio, else fine.   Bookpress 75-75 1996 $1,500.00

KENDALL, JANE   Pride and Prejudice. A Romantic Comedy in 3 Acts Adapted From the Novel. Chicago: Dramatic Pub. Co., 1942. 1st edition; 7 1/4 x 5 inches; pages 107, 1, xxviii, orange card cvoers lettered in black, ink note on titlepage; very good, scarce. Lacking two half tone plates which are not found in all copies; Ink note on titlepage. Gilson H28.   Ian Hodgkins 78-82 1996 £50.00

KENDALL, P. F.   Geology of Yorkshire. London: privately printed, 1924. 8vo; pages 995; numerous illustrations; cloth, neatly refixed. Wheldon & Wesley 207-1346 1996 £80.00

KENDRICK, A. F.   Hand-Woven Carpets Oriental and European. London: Benn, 1922. Limited to 1000 sets; large 4to; 2 volumes, 198 pages, 3 color plates; 202 plates; original cloth, very nice set in excellent condition. Arntzen P611.   J. M. Cohen 35-50 1996 $600.00

KENEALLY, THOMAS   Schindler's Ark. London: Hodder & Stoughton, 1982. 1st English edition; fine in especially bright, fine, dust jacket without any of the usual fading of red on spine and uncommon thus, with touch of wrinkle at crown of spine.   Thomas Dorn 9-153 1996 $500.00

KENEALLY, THOMAS   Schindler's Ark. London: 1982. 1st edition; very good in dust jacket rubbed at top right corner with minimal loss. Words Etcetera 94-700 1996 £65.00

KENEALLY, THOMAS   Schindler's List. New York: 1982. 1st edition; fine.   Stephen Lupack 83- 1996 $200.00

KENEALLY, THOMAS   Schindler's List. New York: Simon & Schuster, 1982. 1st U.S. edition; fine in fine dust jacket.   Timothy P. Slongo 5-166 1996 $150.00

KENNA, V. E. G.   Cretan Seals, with a Catalogue of the Minoan Gems in the Ashmolean Museum. Oxford: Clarendon Press, 1960. Folio; 163 pages, 72 figures and 23 plates; original cloth, torn dust jacket. With signature of J. L. Benson.   Archaeologia Luxor-3554 1996 $350.00

KENNARD, JOSEPH SPENCER   The Italian Theatre: from its Beginning to the Close of the Seventeenth Century. New York: William Edwin Rudge, 1932. 1st edition; 2 volumes; worn and chipped dust jackets; fine, owner's signature in each volume; inscribed by author.   Captain's Bookshelf 38-209 1996 $100.00

KENNEDY, E. B.   Thirty Seasons in Scandinavia. London: 1908. Photo plates; cloth lightly marked, otherwise very good.   David A.H. Grayling 3/95-466 1996 £55.00

KENNEDY, JOHN   A New Method of Stating and Explaining the Scripture Chronology, Upon Mosaic Astronomical Principles, Mediums and Data, as Laid Down in the Pentateuch. London: printed for the author, 1751. 8vo; viii, (2), 432 pages; 2 folding tables; original calf, red spine label, front hinge cracked, but holding, calf rubbed, still decent. Kenneth Karmiole 1NS-218 1996 $125.00

KENNEDY, JOHN FITZGERALD 1917-1963   The Burden and the Glory. New York: 1964. 1st edition; fine.   Stephen Lupack 83- 1996 $100.00

KENNEDY, JOHN FITZGERALD 1917-1963   Profiles in Courage. New York: Harper, 1956. original cloth and dust jacket, very good. Signed by Kennedy.   19th Century Shop 39- 1996 $2,500.00

KENNEDY, JOHN FITZGERALD 1917-1963   Profiles in Courage. New York: 1956. 1st edition; fine.   Stephen Lupack 83- 1996 $275.00

KENNEDY, JOHN FITZGERALD 1917-1963   Profiles in Courage. New York: Harper, 1956. 1st edition; former owner's name to f.f.e.p., else fine in lightly worn dust jacket.   Sherwood 3-169 1996 $250.00

KENNEDY, JOHN FITZGERALD 1917-1963   Profiles in Courage. New York: Harper and Row, 1964. Memoral edition; a small number were prepared in full blue calf, stamped in gold, brown slipcase; fine condition, although unprotected spine appears to be slightly darker than the midnight blue leather covers.   Bev Chaney, Jr. 23-346 1996 $300.00

KENNEDY, JOHN PENDLETON   The Border States. Their Power and Duty in the Present Disordered Condition of the Country. Baltimore:? 1861? 1st edition; 8vo; 46 pages; issued with half title only, no regular titlepage; original wrappers. Howes K85; BAL 11065.   Edward Morrill 369-186 1996 $200.00

KENNEDY, JOHN PENDLETON   Memoirs of the Life of William Wirt, Attorney General of the United States. Philadelphia: Lea and Blanchard, 1850. New edition; 2 volumes; 368, 391 pages; black cloth, gilt, interior foxing, otherwise near mint. Howes K87; BAL 11057.   Blue River Books 9-197 1996 $185.00

KENNEDY, JOHN PENDLETON   Swallow Barn. Philadelphia: Carey & Lea, 1832. 1st edition; 8vo; 2 volumes, (ii), x, 312; iv, 320 pages; publisher's quarter cloth, paper spine labels; professionally respined, using original spines as overlays, some foxing, as usual, still very deisrable set, rare in original binding.   The Bookpress 75-429 1996 $675.00

KENNEDY, MARGARET   Dewdrops. London: Heinemann, 1928. Signed limited edition of 525 numbered copies; 8vo; cloth and boards, dust jacket, enclosed in custom made blue morocco, leather and cloth slipcase; fine, small tear in dust jacket; bookplate of publisher Crosby Gaige.   Antic Hay 101-929 1996 $135.00

KENNEDY, ROBERT F.   The Pursuit of Justice. New York: Evanston: London: Harper & Row, 1964. 1st edition; signed by author; fine. Steven C. Bernard 71-139 1996 $300.00

KENNEDY, WILLIAM 1928-   Billy Phelan's Greatest Game. New York: Viking Press, 1978. 1st edition; fine in very good+ dust jacket which is slightly worn at edges.   Steven C. Bernard 71-140 1996 $100.00

KENNEDY, WILLIAM 1928-   Billy Phelan's Greatest Game. New York: Viking Press, 1978. 1st edition; fine in near fine dust jacket, lightly rubbed at lower spine and edge.   Bev Chaney, Jr. 23-347 1996 $100.00

KENNEDY, WILLIAM 1928-   Ironweed. New York: Viking Press, 1983. Uncorrected proof; printed wrappers, very slightly faded at spine, otherwise fine, uncommon.   Captain's Bookshelf 38-131 1996 $400.00

KENNEDY, WILLIAM 1928-   Ironweed. New York: Viking, 1983. 1st edition; fine in near fine dust jacket, few creases to front panel and short tear to head of spine.   Lame Duck Books 19-273 1996 $150.00

KENNET, WHITE   Parochial Antiquities Attempted in the History of Ambrosden, Burcester and Other Adjacent Parts in the Counties of Oxford and Bucks... Oxford: at the Theatre, 1695. 4to; vignette title, 7 ff., 703 (recte 701) pages, 15 ff. index, 58 ff. glossary, 9 engraved plates, contemporary calf, rebacked; good copy, form the library of Frances Richardson Currer, with her ex-libris. Wing K302.   Marlborough 162-56 1996 £850.00

KENRCIK, W.   The New American Orchardist; or, an Account of the Most Valuable Varieties of Fruit,... Boston: 1844. 7th edition; 8vo; pages 450; original gilt decorated cloth, light wear and corner bumping, foxing to endpapers, institutional bookplate.   Raymond M. Sutton VII-1019 1996 $115.00

KENRICK, WILLIAM   Poems; Ludicrous, Satirical and Moral. London: printed for J. Fletcher, 1768. 1st edition; 8vo; half title, ms. corrections, alterations and deletions made by author on 17 pages; modern half calf, label.   Anthony W. Laywood 109-73 1996 £300.00

KENT'S Original London Directory. London: printed and sold by Henry Kent Causton, 1814. 82nd edition; 12mo; ad leaf, pages (54), (5)-380, ad leaf, pages (vii), (9)-144, 24; contemporary sheep somewhat worn, occasional thumb soiling, but very fair copy, scarce. Goss P. 100. Peter Murray Hill 185-107 196 £125.00

KENT, CHARLES N. History of the Seventeenth Regiment, New Hampshire Volunteer Infantry. Concord: 1898. 1st edition; 325 pages; frontispiece, photos; cloth, very good+. Dornbusch NH 68. T. A. Swinford 49-654 1996 $125.00

KENT, HENRY Bibliographical Notes on One Hundred Books Famous in English Literature. New York: Grolier Club, 1903. Limited to 305 copies; 8vo; printed on French handmade paper; near fine in very good case. Charles Agvent 4-770 1996 $150.00

KENT, J. P. C. Roman Coins. New York: Harry N. Abrams, 1978. Folio; 368 pages, 1430 illustrations, original cloth, dust jacket, fine. Archaeologia Luxor-3555 1996 $175.00

KENT, JAMES An Introductory Lecture to a Course of Law Lectures, Delivered Nov. 17, 1794. New York: Francis Childs, 1794. 1st edition; 12mo; 23 pages; sewn, removed, crisp copy. Evans 27183. M & S Rare Books 60-356 1996 $1,650.00

KENT, JAMES Lectures on Homoeopathic Philosophy. Lancaster: 1900. 1st edition; 290 pages; original binding. W. Bruce Fye 71-1169 1996 $100.00

KENT, NATHANIEL General View of the Agriculture to the County of Norfolk...(with) General View of the Agriculture of the County of Suffolk... London: printed at the Norfolk Press, by Crouse, Stevenson & Matachett... 1796/97. 8vo; 2 volumes in 1; errata leaf and Directions to Binder, large folding map frontispiece, 3 copperplates, 1 large folding, half title; Directions to binder; large folding colored map frontispiece, 2 large folding plates; full speckled calf, corners bumped, joints rubbed, red morocco label to spine, library label to base of spine, edges speckled; owners bookplate and booksellers ticket. Beeleigh Abbey BA/56-12 1996 £300.00

KENT, ROCKWELL 1882- Architect-Tonics. New York: William J. Comstock Co., 1914. 1st edition; 8vo; lightly foxed dust jacket, fine. Glenn Books 36-163 1996 $275.00

KENT, ROCKWELL 1882- The Bookplates and Marks of Rockwell Kent. New York: Random House, 1929. One of 1250 numbered copies; octavo; 79 pages, frenchfold, printed on special thin paper from Japan by Pynson Printers, signed by artist; 90 designs for bookplates and marks; bound in blue cloth with Kent design stamped in gold, in dust jacket with small chip and light fading, else fine; bookplate. Bromer Booksellers 90-152 1996 $250.00

KENT, ROCKWELL 1882- It's Me O Lord. The Autobiography of Rockwell Kent. New York: Dodd, Mead, 1955. 1st edition; lavishly illustrated in color and black and white; front endpaper starting, else very fine in dust jacket with very light wear to extremities. Bromer Booksellers 90-153 1996 $150.00

KENT, ROCKWELL 1882- Of Men and Mountains, Being an Account of the European Travels of the Author and His Wife, Sally... Ausable Forks: Asgaard Press,, 1959. One of 250 copies; octavo; 46 pages; illustrated and signed by author; very fine and partially unopened, in cloth backed marbled boards, with original glassine dust jacket; inscribed by kent for Robert S. Poehler. Bromer Booksellers 90-154 1996 $450.00

KENT, ROCKWELL 1882- Rockwellkentiana; Few Words and Many Pictures. New York: Harcourt Brace, 1933. 1st edition; quarto; (162) pages; reproductions; white cloth, probably a review copy, contains two dust jackets of orange paper, printed to cover design, very fine with inside dust jacket also very fine and outer dust jacket showing only faint rubbing. Johnson p. 354. Bromer Booksellers 87-161 1996 $475.00

KENT, ROCKWELL 1882- Salamina. New York: Harcourt Brace, 1935. 1st edition; 8vo; 336 pages; 80 illustrations; original blue cloth, nearly fine in dust jacket; inscribed by Kent for Harriet and Herbert Rauch. Chapel Hill 94-64 1996 $150.00

KENT, ROCKWELL 1882- What is an American? Los Angeles: Plantin Press, 1936. 1st edition; original wood engraving; original printed wrappers; extremely fine. Bromer Booksellers 90-155 1996 $285.00

KENT, ROCKWELL 1882- Wilderness: a Journal of Quiet Adventure in Alaska. 1st edition; quarto; 217 pages; illustrations; bound in tan cloth, gilt stamped to spine and front cover, extremities lightly soiled, else fine in dust jacket, which is chipped to edges and is darkened to spine. Bromer Booksellers 87-162 1996 $175.00

KEOWN, ERIC The Tale of an Old Tweed Jacket. London: Moss Bros. & Co., Ltd., n.d., c. 1955. 1st edition; color cover drawings, 3 full page color drawings and several black and white drawings in text by Edward Ardizzone, loosely inserted is a circular letter, presenting the book; wrappers; very bright copy; fore-edge slightly spotted, near fine. Ulysses 39-18 1996 £80.00

KER, N. R. The Parochial Libraries of the Church of England. London: the Faith Press, 1959. Small 4to; 4 plates; maroon and white cloth, gilt, dust jacket (slightly soiled). Maggs Bros. Ltd. 1191-103 1996 £85.00

KERENYI, CHARLES Asklepios: Archetypal Image of the Physician's Existence. London: 1960. 1st English translation; 139 pages; well illustrated; original binding. W. Bruce Fye 71-1170 1996 $125.00

KERKUT, G. A. Comprehensive Insect Physiology, Biochemistry and Pharmacology. London: 1985. 8vo; 13 volumes, hardcover, fine, clean, second hand set with dust jackets. Wheldon & Wesley 207-1060 1996 £500.00

KEROUAC, JACK 1922-1969 Excerpts from Visions of Cody. New York: 1959. 1st edition; limited to 750 numbered copies, signed by author; 8.5 x 5 inches; 128 pages; cloth backed boards, with original New Directions slip present; very good. John K. King 77-357 1996 $650.00

KEROUAC, JACK 1922-1969 The History of Bop. New York: Caliban Press, 1993. 1st edition; limited to 200 copies; thin 8vo; printed letterpress on Nideggen paper and jazz sheet music in handmade St. Armand paper covers; original wrappers, as new. James S. Jaffe 34-343 1996 $100.00

KEROUAC, JACK 1922-1969 Satori in Paris. New York: Grove, 1966. 1st edition; very good+ in not quite very good dust jacket with rather large mostly closed tear to front panel; excellent presentation to author's brother-in-law, Nick Sampas. Lame Duck Books 19-275 1996 $3,850.00

KEROUAC, JACK 1922-1969 Satori in Paris. New York: 1966. 1st edition; fine in dust jacket; with signed presentation inscription from Kerouac's friend, Stanley Twardowicz. Polyanthos 22-488 1996 $125.00

KEROUAC, JACK 1922-1969 Take Care of My Ghost, Ghost. Ghost Press, 1977. Published for friends in an edition of 200 ccopies, signed by Allen Ginsberg; pictorial stapled wrappers; fine, scarce. Polyanthos 22-489 1996 $200.00

KEROUAC, JACK 1922-1969 The Town and the City. New York: Harcourt Brace & Co., 1950. Advance reading copy; very near fine, touch of soiling but square and unfaded thus, considerably nicer than usual; author's first book. Between the Covers 42-248 1996 $675.00

KEROUAC, JACK 1922-1969 The Town and the City. New York: Harcourt Brace, 1950. 1st edition; some fading to top edge of pages, corners very slightly bumped, overall near fine in very good dust jacket with moderate edgewear, small chip at front flap fold and 2" closed edge tear at upper back panel; attractive copy; signed by author. Ken Lopez 74-237 1996 $3,500.00

KERR, J. M. MUNRO Historical Review of British Obstetrics and Gynaecology 1800-1950. Edinburgh: 1954. 1st edition; 420 pages, backstrip faded, original binding, contents fine. GM 6311.1. W. Bruce Fye 71-1171 1996 $125.00

KERR, R. Memoirs of the Life, Writings and Correspondence of William Smellie. Edinburgh: 1811. 1st edition; 8vo; 2 volumes; portrait, plate; calf, rebacked; inscribed by Alexander Smellie (the son) to Sir John Majoribanks, Lord Provost. Maggs Bros. Ltd. 1190-246 1996 £120.00

KERR, WILLIAM J. The Genealogical Tree of the Family of Jarrett of Orange Valley, Jamaica and Camerton Court, Somerset. Southampton: Henry King, 1896. 4to; pages 99; folding pedigree mounted on linen and 2 plates; contemporary half calf. Howes Bookshop 265-1863 1996 £75.00

KERRUISH, J. D.　　Babylonian Nights' Entertainments. Archer, 1934. 1st edition; very good+ in attractive dust jacket with some light wear and tear and chipping, very scarce in dust jacket.　Aronovitz 57-616　1996 $100.00

KERSHAW, ALISTER　　Richard Aldington - an Intimate Portrait. Carbondale & Edwardsville: Southern Illinois University Press, 1965. 1st edition; 8 black and white photos; original binding, top edge slightly dusty, head and tail of spine slightly bumped, near fine in nickel and slightly rubbed, marked and dusty dust jacket slightly browned at edges and slightly faded at spine.　Ulysses 39-6　1996 £95.00

KERY, PATRICIA FRANTZ　　Great Magazine Covers of the World. New York: Abbeville Press, 1982. 1st edition; fine in dust jacket.　Hermitage SP95-790　1996 $125.00

KESEY, KEN 1935-　　Kesey's Garage Sale. New York: Viking, 1973. 1st edition; fine in dust jacket; inscribed by Kesey for Brian Aldiss. Aronovitz 57-617　1996 $275.00

KESEY, KEN 1935-　　Kesey's Garage Sale. New York: Viking Press, 1973. 1st edition; signed by author on special printed label pasted to flylef; very good in dust jacket.　Steven C. Bernard 71-143　1996 $150.00

KESEY, KEN 1935-　　Kesey's Garage Sale. New York: Viking, 1973. Softcover edition; wrappers; not quite very good; Hal Ashby's copy with complimentary slip from publisher laid in.　Ken Lopez 74-242　1996 $150.00

KESEY, KEN 1935-　　One Flew Over the Cuckoo's Nest. London: Methuen, 1962. 1st British edition; fine in near fine dust jacket, signed by author.　Lame Duck Books 19-276　1996 $450.00

KESEY, KEN 1935-　　One Flew Over the Cuckoo's Nest. London: Methuen, 1962. 1st British edition; minor browning to front board, near fine in near fine dust jacket with some darkening to spine and edges. Ken Lopez 74-241　1996 $350.00

KESEY, KEN 1935-　　One Flew Over the Cuckoo's Nest. London: 1962. 1st edition; author's first novel; laid in is an attractive bookplate which is a signed presentation from author; fine, dust jacket with small faint crease.　Polyanthos 22-491　1996 $125.00

KESEY, KEN 1935-　　One Flew Over the Cuckoo's Nest. New York: 1962. 1st edition; endpapers with remains of glue from where the dust jacket was affixed, otherwise very good in chipped, torn, creased and worn dust jacket, very scarce.　Words Etcetera 94-713　1996 £120.00

KESEY, KEN 1935-　　Sometimes a Great Notion. New York: Viking Press, 1964. 1st edition; author's second book; very good+ in very good dust jacket.　Steven C. Bernard 71-144　1996 $150.00

KESEY, KEN 1935-　　Sometimes a Great Notion. London: 1966. 1st English edition; very good in dust jacket, uncommon.　Words Etcetera 94-714　1996 £85.00

KESHAVARZ, FATEME　　A Descriptive and Analytical Catalogue of Persian Manuscripts in the Library of the Wellcome Institute for the History of Medicine. London: 1986. 1st edition; 4to; 707 pages; original binding.　W. Bruce Fye 71-1172　1996 $100.00

KESSEL, JOSEPH　　Kisling. New York: Abrams, 1971. Folio; 323 pages, 656 illustrations, 46 in color; cloth, dust jacket. Freitag 4330.　Brannan 43-298　1996 $195.00

KESTER, JESSE Y.　　The American Shooter's Manual. Philadelphia: Carey, Lea & Carey, 1827. 1st edition; 2nd issue with "Ribbon" spelled correctly on p. 235; octavo; xii, frontispiece, 2 plates; half brown morocco over marbled boards, gilt lettered spine with raised bands, very good, previous owner's ink signatures on endpapers, armorial bokplate; very good. Phillips p. 211.　Heritage Book Shop 196-203　1996 $1,250.00

KETTELL, SAMUEL　　Manual of the Practical Naturalist; or, Directions for Collecting, Preparing and Preserving Subjects of Natural History. Boston: 1831. 1st edition; 8vo; frontispiece, bit browned and foxed; original cloth, worn, covers off; pencil inscription by M. Bethune; the Bradley Martin copy.　Maggs Bros. Ltd. 1190-247　1996 £85.00

KETTELL, SAMUEL　　Specimens of American Poetry. Boston: S. G. Goodrich, 1829. 1st edition; 8vo; 3 volumes; half black morocco, light rubbing, old waterstain to bottom margin of first 10 or so pages of volume 3, except for brief stain, a near fine copy. Sabin 37655; BAL 3251.　Charles Agvent 4-771　1996 $750.00

KETTELL, SAMUEL　　Specimens of American Poetry. Boston: S. G. Goodrich, 1829. 1st edition; 12mo; 3 volumes, 48, 353; 10, 408; 10, 406 pages; contemporary three quarter morocco, marbled boards, cover cracked, slightly loose, still sound. Shoemaker 39194.　M & S Rare Books　60-191　1996 $200.00

KEYES, LORD　　Amphibious Warfare and Combined Operations. Cambridge: 1943. 1st edition; very good in somewhat faded and chipped dust jacket. Presentation copy from author.　Words Etcetera 94-984 1996 £65.00

KEYES, ROGER　　The Art of Surimono. Dublin; 1985. Folio; 2 volumes, 569 pages; illustrations, some colored; original cloth, as new, in cloth slipcase.　James Fenning 133-191　1996 £65.00

KEYNES, GEOFFREY 1887-1982　　A Bibliography of Dr. Robert Hooke. Oxford: Clarendon Press, 1960. 4to; 12 plates; blue cloth, dust jacket. Maggs Bros. Ltd.　1191-107　1996 £95.00

KEYNES, GEOFFREY 1887-1982　　A Bibliography of Sir Thomas Browne. Oxford: 1968. 2nd edition; 293 pages; original binding, dust jacket.　W. Bruce Fye 71-255　1996 $200.00

KEYNES, GEOFFREY 1887-1982　　A Bibliography of Sir Thomas Browne. Oxford: 1968. 2nd edition; 4to; 293 pages; original binding, dust jacket present but torn, ex-library, not abused.　James Tait Goodrich K40-70　1996 $125.00

KEYNES, GEOFFREY 1887-1982　　A Bibliography of Sir Thomas Browne. Oxford: Clarendon Press, 1968. 2nd edition; 8vo; xv, 293, (43) pages; illustrations; red cloth, dust jacket, very good.　Jeff Weber 31-7　1996 $125.00

KEYNES, GEOFFREY 1887-1982　　A Bibliography of Sir William Petty and of Observations on the Bills of Morality by John Graunt. Oxford: Clarendon Press, 1971. 1st edition; 2 portraits, 10 full papge facsimiles of titlepages; green cloth, dust jacket, 2 small tears, errata slip tipped in pages 10-11.　Maggs Bros. Ltd.　1191-104　1996 £65.00

KEYNES, GEOFFREY 1887-1982　　Bibliography of William Hazlitt. London: Nonesuch Press, 1931. One of 750 numbered copies; large 8vo; 4 illustrations in collotype; boards with printed label, one corner little worn, very nice in slightly frayed dust jacket, scarce.　Bertram Rota 272-328　1996 £120.00

KEYNES, GEOFFREY 1887-1982　　Blood Transfusion. Baltimore: 1949. 1st American edition; 574 pages. original binding.　W. Bruce Fye 71-1175　1996 $100.00

KEYNES, GEOFFREY 1887-1982　　Engravings by William Blake, the Separate Plates. A Catalogue Raisonne. Dublin: Emery Walker, 1956. One of 500 copies; small folio; xiv, 89 pages; 45 plates; cloth; fine.　The Bookpress 75-272　1996 $235.00

KEYNES, GEOFFREY 1887-1982　　Jane Austen. A Bibliography. London: Nonesuch Press, 1929. 1st edition; limited to 875 numbered copies; 7 1/2 x 4 1/4 inches; pages xxv, 289, colophon, errata leaf tipped in between pages vi and vii, pale pink paper backed grey boards, printed paper title label backstrip, spare label rear, uncut. Fine in slightly discolored dust jacket. Gilson M508.　Ian Hodgkins 78-130　1996 £120.00

KEYNES, GEOFFREY 1887-1982　　Jane Austen: a Bibliography. London: Nonesuch Press, 1929. One of 875 numbered copies; 8vo; boards, very nice slightly frayed dust jacket.　Bertram Rota 272-325　1996 £110.00

KEYNES, GEOFFREY 1887-1982　　Jane Austen: a Bibliography. London: Nonesuch Press, 1929. 1st edition; one of 875 numbered copies; 8vo; frontispiece, 3 plates, numerous facsimiles of titlepages; original boards head of spine slightly chipped, printed paper label on spine, uncut, dust jacket.　Forest Books 74-129　1996 £75.00

KEYNES, GEOFFREY 1887-1982   John Ray, a Bibliography. London: Faber & Faber, 1951. Limited to 650 copies; frontispiece, 3 plates, 16 reproductions of titlepages, green cloth, dust jacket, mild tears to top edge, printed on blue paper.   Maggs Bros. Ltd. 1191-105 1996 £75.00

KEYNES, GEOFFREY 1887-1982   William Pickering, Publisher. A Memoir and a Hand-List of His Editions. London: at the Office of the Fleuron, 1924. Limited to 350 copies, 1st edition; 37 facsimile reproductions of titlepages; maroon cloth, top edge gilt, paper spine label, extra label on inside lower cover, headcaps mildly bumped, slightly scuffed, slight spotting on first and last few leaves; ALS from author to Col. W. E. Moss, the collector and scholar. Besterman 4863.   Maggs Bros. Ltd. 1191-106 1996 £110.00

KEYNES, GEOFFREY 1887-1982   William Pickering Publisher. A Memoir and a Check-List of His Publications. London: Galahad Press, 1969. Revised edition; small 4to; frontispiece, 37 titlepage facsimiles; original cloth, dust jacket.   Forest Books 74-130 1996 £55.00

KEYNES, JOHN MAYNARD, 1ST BARON 1883-1946   The End of Laissez-Faire. London: Hogarth Press, 1926. 1st edition; 8vo; original cloth, dust jacket slightly dust soiled.   H. M. Fletcher 121-157 1996 £45.00

KEYNES, JOHN MAYNARD, 1ST BARON 1883-1946   Indian Currency and Finance. London: Macmillan, 1913. 1st edition; original rust brown cloth, shelf number on spine, minor wear to spine ends, near fine; presentation copy from author to his sister and her husband M.N. and A. V. Hill, Keynes presentation copies of this significance are extremely scarce.   19th Century Shop 39- 1996 $7,500.00

KHATCHATRIANZ, I.   Armenian Folk Tales. Colonial House, 1946. 1st edition; 4 color plates and numerous black and white illustrations by Martyros Saryan; original binding, head and tail of spine and corners bumped, covers faded and rubbed at extremities, top edge spotted, good in nicked, chipped, worn and marked, slightly creased and soiled dust jacket, browned at spine and edges and missing pieces at head and tail of spine.   Ulysses 39-20 1996 £65.00

KHULLAR, S. P.   An Illustrated Fern Flora of West Himalaya. Dehra Dun: 1994. Large 8vo; volume 1, pages xxxx, 506; 168 plates, 3 maps; cloth, dust jacket.   Raymond M. Sutton VII-210 1 996 $135.00

KIDD, BENJAMIN   Social Evolution. London: Macmillan and Co., 1894. 1st edition; 8vo; vi, 348 pages, 4 pages of ads at end; original maroon cloth lettered in gilt; very good.   John Drury 82-134 1996 £50.00

KIDD, SAMUEL   China, or, Illustrations of the Symbols, Philosophy, Antiquities, Customs, Superstitions, Laws, Government, Education and Literature of the Chinse. London: Taylor & Walton, 8vo; hand colored engraved frontispiece, 13 engraved plates, half title; original green blindstamped cloth, gilt spine, uncut edges.   Charles W. Traylen 117-439 1996 £110.00

KIDDER, ALFRED VINCENT   The Artifacts of the Pecos. New Haven: Pub. for Phillips Academy by the Yale University Press, 1932. 1st edition; 4to; 314 pages; 251 figures; original cloth.   Archaeologia Luxor-4598 1996 $350.00

KIDDER, ALFRED VINCENT   An Introduction to the Study of Southwestern Archaeology with a Preliminary Account of the Excavations at Pecos. New Haven: Yale University Press, 1924. original cloth, rebacked, faint scuffing or staining on cvoers, wear to corners, else good-very good.   Ken Sanders 8-34 1996 $125.00

KIDDER, ALFRED VINCENT   Pecos, New Mexico: Archaeological Notes. Andover: Phillips Academy, 1958. 8vo; xx, 360 pages, 72 figures and 8 tables; wrappers, owner's stamp at top edge.   Archaeologia Luxor-4599 1996 $125.00

KIDDER, DANIEL P.   Sketches of Residence and Travels in Brazil, Embracing Historical and Geographical Notices of the Empire and Its Several Provinces. Philadelphia:London: Sorin & Ball/Wiley & Putnam, 1845. 12mo; 2 volumes, xv, (17)-369 pages; viii, (9)-404 pages, frontispiece to volume 2 supplied in facsimile; embossed cloth, gilt spine titles and cover decorations, spines faded, some wear and spotting to covers, both volumes internally clean and tight. Sabin 37708.   Parmer Books Nat/Hist-073145 1996 $295.00

KILBOURNE, DAVID W.   Strictures, On Dr. I. Galland's Pamphlet, Entitled "Villainy Exposed," with Some Account of His Transactions in Lands of the Sac and Fox Reservation... Fort Madison: printed at the Statesman Office, 1850. 1st edition; 24 pages; sewn as issued, some foxing, very good. Howes K131; Graff 2319; Mort 77; Flake 4610.   Michael D. Heaston 23-184 1996 $350.00

KILBURN, RICHARD   Choice Presidents Upon All Acts of Parliament, Relating to the Office and Duty of a Justice of Peace... London: printed for Mary Tonsen within Grays-Inn Gate, 1694. Last 17th century; contemporary panelled sheep, quite worn, neatly rebacked.   Meyer Boswell SL27-131 1996 $450.00

KILGORE, D. E.   A Texas Ranger. Austin: 1973. One of 200 copies; 104 pages; photos, map on endsheets, book fine, case very good.   Early West 22-673 1996 $195.00

KILLENS, JOHN OLIVER   Youngblood. New York: Dial, 1954. 1st edition; author's first book; very good with some wear to corners in poor, although basically intact dust jacket with some staining on rear panel, internal repairs and chipping to the spinal extremities, signed by author; very uncommon thus.   Between the Covers 43-146 1996 $150.00

KILLINS, JOHN O.   Youngblood. New York: Dial Press, 1954. 1st edition; author's first book; very good in somewhat worn, price clipped dust jacket; inscribed and signed by author.   Pettler & Lieberman 28-26 1996 $100.00

KILLION, TOM   Walls: a Journey Across Three Continents. Santa Cruz: Quail Press, 1990. One of 100 numbered copies, signed by author; folio; printed in 16 pt. Centaur and Arrighi on Japanese Torinoko handmade; 65 illustrations by author; half russet morocco, linen sides, fine in slipcase.   Bertram Rota 272-379 1996 £600.00

KILMER, JOYCE   Trees. New York: Doran, 1914. 1st edition; 8vo; brown paper covered boards (preceded by gray paper issue) in scarce dust jacket which is darkened with few tears and chips, former owner signature, offsetting from old clipping, very good/good+.   Charles Agvent 4-775 1996 $150.00

KILNER, DOROTHY   Letters from a Mother to her Children, on Various Important Subjects. London: by John Marshall and Co., 1780? 1st edition; 24mo; in sixes; 2 volumes, pages 178; 179; with half titles and 3 pages of ads at end of volume 2; contemporary quarter calf, volume numbers in gilt on spines, marbled sides, worn, spines restored, especially at head of volume 1, small area of leather missing on same volume, rustmarks to volume 1 prelims, still good set; contemporary ownership inscriptions of Catherine Archer at beginning of each volume. Osborne I p. 153 has only 2nd edition of 1787.   Simon Finch 24-141 1996 £750.00

KIMBER, ISAAC   The Life of Oliver Cromwell. London: J. Brotherton, 1755. 6th edition; 8vo; frontispiece, title lightly browned; full contemporary calf worn, joints cracking but sound.   Ian Wilkinson 95/1-116 1996 £74.00

KINDERSLEY, DAVID   Mr. Eric Gill - Recollections. San Francisco: Book Club of California, 1967. One of 400 copies; 28 black and white reproductions of Eric Gill's drawings and sculpture; original binding, fine; loosely inserted prospectus for this book and a Christmas card bearing a wood engraving by Eric Gill and printed for Duncan Houx Olmsted by Arlen Philpott, Fairfax in an edition of 250 copies; from the library of James D. Hart.   Ulysses 39-230 1996 £65.00

KINDERSLEY, N. E.   Specimens of Hindoo Literature... London: printed by W. Bulmer and Co. & Sold by F. Wingrave... 1794. 1st edition; 8vo; half title, (ix-xiii), list of plates and errata leaf, 1-49 pages, 53-328 pages, 329-335 pages, 3 large folding engraved plates; quarter modern calf and modern marbled boards, maroon morocco label to spine, new endpapers and prelims.   Beeleigh Abbey BA56-84 1996 £125.00

KING, C.   Geological Exploration of the Fortieth Parallel. Washington: 1877-78. Imperial 8vo; 2 volumes, pages xi, 803, 10 chromolithographs, 16 tinted plates, 12 colored maps, 13 tables; pages xiii, 890, 25 tinted plates; new cloth.   John Henly 27-625 1996 £160.00

KING, CHARLES   The British Merchant; or, Commerce Preserv'd. London: printed by John Darby, 1721. 1st edition in book form; 8vo; volume 1 (of 3), pages xxxviii, 378; 2 folding tables; contemporary calf, worn, internally fine, fresh copy.   James Fenning 133-193 1996 £85.00

KING, DANIEL   The Vale-Royall of England or the County Palatine of Chester Illustrated. London: Streater, 1656. Small folio; title, 4 ff., pages 99, 3 ff., 239, 5 ff., 55 pages, title, 2 ff., 34 pages, extra engraved titlepage, 3 double page maps, 16 engraved plates, 4 engraved text illustrations, later polished calf, rebacked using original spine, one plate tear repaired; very presentable copy. Wing K488.   Marlborough 162-57 1996 £900.00

KING, FRANK M.   Wranglin' the Past. Trails End Pub. Co., 1946. Revised edition; fine, very good dust jacket, presentation copy from author to well known collector, Loring Campbell. Six Guns 1239.   Early West 22-151 1996 $150.00

KING, FRANK M.   Wranglin' the Past. Pasadena: 1946. 1st revised edition, after private limited edition; 284 pages; photos; cloth; upper back corner bumped, otherwise fine in worn dust jacket (1 1/2 inch top backstrip missing); Six Guns 1239; Herd 1277; Dobie p. 109.   Gene W. Baade 1094-94 1996 $100.00

KING, G.   The Orchids of the Sikkim-Himalaya. Lehre: 1967. Folio; paes (7), (i-) iii, (i-) iv, (11), 342, (9); 453 plates; cloth, light wear and bumping, light scratching on back cover.   Raymond M. Sutton VI-914 1996 $350.00

KING, MARTIN LUTHER   Where Do We Go From Here: Chaos or Community? New York: Evanston: and London: Harper & Row, 1967. 1st edition; 8vo; (xii), 209 pages; cloth backed paper over boards, lower corners very slightly bumped, spine slightly faded, light foxing along top edge, very good.   Andrew Cahan 47-104 1996 $350.00

KING, P. P.   Narrative of a Survey of the Intertropical and Western Coasts of Australia Performed Between the Years 1818 and 1822... London: John Murray, 1827. 8vo; 2 volumes; xxvii-xxxix, 451, 637 pages of text, errata leaf to volumes I and II at rear of volume II, 2 aquatint frontispieces, 8 un-colored aquatints, 3 line drawings, 3 maps/charts and 17 woodcuts to text, map of volume 1 watermarked 'W. Wetherby 1825', frontispiece to volume 1 watermarked '1818'. Contemporary speckled calf boards, skilfully rebacked preserving original backstrips, gilt bands and decoration to spines, black morocco labels, booksellers ticket to front pastedown volume 1, pencil signature to front free endpapers; Abbey Travel 573; Hill p. 163; Ferguson 1130.   Beeleigh Abbey BA56-85 1996 £2,500.00

KING, PETER   The Life of John Locke, With Extracts from His Correspondence, Journals and Common-Place Books. London: Henry Colburn and Richard Bentley, 1803. New edition; 8vo; 2 volumes, portrait, half title in volume 2; original cloth backed boards, printed paper labels chipped, uncut.   Anthony W. Laywood 108-190 1996 £75.00

KING, RONALD   The White Alphabet. Surry: Circle Press, 1984. One of 150 copies all on Barcham Green paper, all signed by artist/designer Ronald King; page size 10 5/8 x 4 7/8 inches; white cutout pop-ups in the form of letters on embossed square area (1 per letter) A-M on front half of accordion folds, N-Z on verse of folds; titlepage in blind; inlaid wood boards in sycamore and beech as ends on accordion-style binding, housed in linen slipcase and box, title in gilt on spine of box. Priscilla Juvelis 95/1-68 1996 $2,000.00

KING, STEPHEN 1947-   Carrie. Garden City: Doubleday, 1974. 1st edition; author's first novel; several faint glue marks to both front and back pastedown, otherwise near fine in near fine dust jacket.   Bud Schweska 12-430 1996 $450.00

KING, STEPHEN 1947-   Christine. West Kingston: Grant, 1983. Limited edition, one of 1000 numbered copies signed by author and artist; illustrations by Stephen Gervais; fine in dust jacket and slipcase.   Bud Schweska 12-450 1996 $375.00

KING, STEPHEN 1947-   Dark Tower III: the Waste Lands. Hampton Falls: Grant, 1991. 1st edition; one of 1200 numbered copies, signed by author and artist; illustrations by Ned Dameron; very fine in dust jacket with slipcase.   Robert Gavora 61-34 1996 $450.00

KING, STEPHEN 1947-   Different Seasons. New York: Viking, 1982. Uncorrected proof; wrappers; near fine; inscribed by author.   Ken Lopez 74-245 1996 $850.00

KING, STEPHEN 1947-   The Drawing of the Three. Grant, 1987. 1st edition; author's second book; fine in fine dust jacket.   Bud Schweska 12-456 1996 $135.00

KING, STEPHEN 1947-   Four Past Midnight. New York: Viking, 1990. 1st edition; uncorrected proof; dark blue wrappers, unillustrated; fine. Oracle Books 1-435 1996 $125.00

KING, STEPHEN 1947-   Gerald's Game. New York: Viking, 1992. 1st edition; Special ABA edition offered to attendees of the 1992 ABA fair in Anaheim, California; very fine, issued, without dust jacket, in cardboard slipcase.   Robert Gavora 61-35 1996 $175.00

KING, STEPHEN 1947-   The Gunslinger. Grant, 1982. 1st edition; scarce, as new in dust jacket.   Bud Schweska 12-446 1996 $500.00

KING, STEPHEN 1947-   Insomnia. London: Hodder & Stoughton, 1994. 1st British edition, limited issue, this being copy no. 2 of 200 copies, with numbered bookplate signed by author affixed to half titlepage; full leather, gathered in signatures with head bands and ribbon marker, very fine, issued without dust jacket.   Robert Gavora 61-36 1996 $400.00

KING, STEPHEN 1947-   Insomnia. New York: Viking, 1994. 1st edition; as new in dust jacket, signed by author.   Bud Schweska 12-459 1996 $125.00

KING, STEPHEN 1947-   Insomnia. New York: Viking, 1994. 1st edition; signed by King; 787 pages; very fine in dust jacket.   Bev Chaney, Jr. 23-355 1996 $100.00

KING, STEPHEN 1947-   It. New York: Viking, 1986. Uncorrected proof 1144 pages); red wrappers; minor creasing to paper covers, else as new.   Oracle Books 1-440 1996 $150.00

KING, STEPHEN 1947-   My Pretty Pony. Whitney Museum, 1989. 1st edition; 1/250 copies, signed by author and artist; as new, without dust jacket, as issued.   Aronovitz 57-627 1996 $2,500.00

KING, STEPHEN 1947-   Needful Things. New York: Viking, 1991. 1st edition; fine in fine dust jacket; signed copy.   Oracle Books 1-443 1996 $175.00

KING, STEPHEN 1947-   Salem's Lot. NEL, 1975. 1st English edition; near fine in like dust jacket.   Aronovitz 57-619 1996 $385.00

KING, STEPHEN 1947-   Salem's Lot. Garden City: Doubleday, 1975. 1st edition; author's second book; just short of fine in second state dust jacket, light edgewear, several short closed tears and half inch chip to bottom spine panel; attractive copy.   Bud Schweska 12-441 1996 $475.00

KING, STEPHEN 1947-   The Shining. New York: Doubleday, 1977. 1st edition; near mint in dust jacket with small closed tear.   Bromer Booksellers 90-158 1996 $250.00

KING, STEPHEN 1947-   The Shining. New York: Doubleday, 1977. 1st edition; very good+ in like dust jacket.   Aronovitz 57-620 1996 $165.00

KING, STEPHEN 1947-   Skeleton Crew. Santa Cruz: Scream Press, 1985. Limited edition, one of 1000 numbered copies, signed by author and artist; illustrations by J. K. Potter; folded color Potter print laid in; very fine in dust jacket with slipcase.   Robert Gavora 61-39 1996 $500.00

KING, STEPHEN 1947-   The Stand. New York: Doubleday, 1978. 1st edition; fine in fine dust jacket, inscribed by author.   Bud Schweska 12-442 1996 $400.00

KING, STEPHEN 1947-   The Stand. New York: Doubleday, 1978. 1st edition; very good in very good+ dust jacket.   Aronovitz 57-621 199 $125.00

KING, STEPHEN 1947-   The Stand. New York: Doubleday, 1990. 1st illustrated edition; 1/52 lettered copies, signed by author and artist; full leather, as new in wooden box with metallic label.   Aronovitz 57-629 1996 $2,250.00

KING, STEPHEN 1947-   The Tommyknockers. New York: PPutnam, 1987. 1st edition; very faint circle mark made by ball point pen to green front endpage, otherwise fine first issue copy with "Permissions to Come" as the last line of copyright page; in fine dust jacket, signed and dated on titlepage.   Bud Schweska 12-1368 1996 $125.00

KING, STEPHEN 1947-   Whispers Stephen King Issue. Whispers Press, 1982. 1st edition; 1/26 lettered copies, signed by author; fine. Aronovitz 57-622 1996 $475.00

KING, WILLIAM   The Art of Love. London: printed for Bernard Lintott, n.d. 1709. 1st edition; 8vo; frontispiece, 4 pages ads at end; new quarter calf, label.   Anthony W. Laywood 109-74 1996 £80.00

KING, WILLIAM   The Dreamer. London: printed for W. Owen, 1754. 1st edition; 8vo; pages (4), 240, xxviii, 14 and ad leaf; contemporary unlettered gilt ruled calf, very good to nice. Rothschild 1302.   James Fenning 133-194 1996 £485.00

KING, WILLIAM   Letter from the Secretary of War Transmitting a copy of the Proceedings of a Court Martial, for the Trial of (Col. William King). Washington: May 3, 1820. 1st edition; 128 pages; disbound, wrappers; extensive foxing, but good, sound, eminently readable copy. Probably rare.   Gene W. Baade 1094-93 1996 $200.00

KING, WILLIAM 1685-1723   Poetical and Literary Anecdotes of His Own Times. London: John Murray, 1819. 2nd edition; 8vo; 19th century calf, gilt, minor defects, but pleasant copy.   Peter Murray Hill 185-96 1996 £50.00

KINGDON WARD, FRANCIS 1885-1958   Field Notes of Rhododendrons and other Plants Collected by Kingdom Ward in 1927/28. London: 1929. Small 8vo; pages 34, 34; cloth.   Maggs Bros. Ltd. 1190-56 1996 £60.00

KINGDON WARD, FRANCIS 1885-1958   A Plant Hunter in Tibet. London: 1934. 8vo; 317 pages, map and 16 plates; original cloth. Wheldon & Wesley 207-1777 196 £70.00

KINGLAKE, ALEXANDER WILLIAM 1809-1891   The Invasion of the Crimea; Its Origin and an Account of Its Progress Down to the Death of Lord Raglan. London: 1863. 8vo; 8 volumes; plates and maps; well bound in half red morocco, gilt top, by Riviere, small library numbers on spines.   Charles W. Traylen 117-144 1996 £390.00

KINGSBURY, BENJAMIN   A Treatise of Razors; in Which the Weight, Shape and Temper of a Razor, the Means of Keeping it In order and the Manner of Using It, are Particularly Considered, and in Which It Its Intended to Convey a Knowledge of All that is Necessary on this Subject. London: printed by J. S. Hodson, sold by Thomas Kingsbury, 1830. 11th edition; 8vo; 46, (2) pages, half title, tiny hole in final leaf affecting a couple of letters, stitched as issued; uncommon in any edition;   James Burmester 29-83 1996 £85.00

KINGSLEY, ADRIEL   A Bold Arraignment of the Medical Profession for the Practice of False Theories, False Pretenses, Fraudulent Claims for a False Science and for Their Determined Purpose to Oppose the Cold Bath in All Fevers... Indianapolis: 1890. 8vo; 361 pages; illustrations; contemporary cloth.   Argosy 810-266 1996 $150.00

KINGSLEY, CHARLES 1819-1875   At Last: a Christmas in the West Indies. New York: Macmillan, 1871. 1st edition; 8vo; plates; original binding, rear cover partly dampstained, spine tips frayed, about very good; with 4 page ALS written by Kingsley in 1871 about a trip to the West Indies and mentioning Colorado.   Charles Agvent 4-777 1996 $250.00

KINGSLEY, CHARLES 1819-1875   Charles Kingsley: His Letters and His Life. London: Kegan, Paul, Trench and Co., 1883. 14th edition; 8vo; 2 volumes, pages (xi), 359; (viii), 357; full tree calf with gilt decorative border, spine heavily decorated in gilt, very slight wear to covers, else near fine.   Marjorie James 19-136 1996 £95.00

KINGSLEY, CHARLES 1819-1875   Glaucus; or, the Wonders of the Shore. Cambridge: Macmillan & Co., 1855. 1st edition; half title, frontispiece, 16 page catalog (May 1885); original green ribbed cloth, blocked in black and gilt, spine slightly faded, very good.   Jarndyce 103-504 1996 £75.00

KINGSLEY, CHARLES 1819-1875   Hereward the Wake "Last of the English". London: Macmillan, 1867. 8vo; 2 volumes in 1, pages xii, 365, (1); 402, (2 ads); original blue cloth, by Burn, with ticker, very good. James Fenning 133-195 1996 £65.00

KINGSLEY, CHARLES 1819-1875   The Heroes, or Greek Fairy Tales for My Children. London: Philip Lee Warner for the Medici Society, 1912. 1st edition thus; one of 500 numbered copies; 12 color plates by W. Russell Flint; publisher's full flexible vellum with green silk ties, in printed d.j. and publisher's plain outer wrapper, outer wrapper and first eleven leaves stained by damp in lower right corner, else fine in lightly worn dust jacket and stained and chipped outer wrapper.   Hermitage SP95-1073 1996 $375.00

KINGSLEY, CHARLES 1819-1875   Town Geology. London: Strahan & Co., 1872. 1st edition; crown 8vo; pages (2), lvi, 239, (6 ads); original blue cloth, gilt, by Burn, with his ticket; fine.   James Fenning 133-196 1996 £55.00

KINGSLEY, CHARLES 1819-1875   Two Years Ago. Boston: Ticknor and Fields, 1857. 1st American edition, called the "Author's Edition"; original green cloth shows some soil and fading, with some odd wear at heel of spine and rubbing at other extremities, 2 inch split at top of front joint has been glue repaired, text shows light dampstains and foxing in foremargin almost throughout, though there is no evident correspondent marking of cloth; Clement Clarke Moore's copy with his signature (in rather faded ink) dated June 1857 on front free endpaper and again (bit stronger) on titlepage.   Magnum Opus 44-68 1996 $195.00

KINGSLEY, CHARLES 1819-1875   The Water Babies. London: Macmillan & Co., 1882. 8vo; 388 pages; frontispiece with tissue guard, other black and white illustrations by Sir Noel Paton and Percival Skelton; early red full calf with spine heavily decorated in gilt, upper and lower boards with gilt floral borders and gilt dentelles, marbled edges and endpapers; near fine.   Marjorie James 19-137 1996 £55.00

KINGSLEY, CHARLES 1819-1875   The Water Babies. London: Macmillan and Co., 1885. 1st illustrated edition; square 8vo; pages (ix), 4-371; illustrations in line by Linley Sambourne; original dark blue cloth elaborately and pictorially gilt, top edge gilt, slight rubbing to gilt vignette at spine, otherwise fine in exceptional external and internal condition with gilt sparkling.   Sotheran PN32-128 1996 £125.00

KINGSLEY, CHARLES 1819-1875   The Water-Babies. London: T. C. and E. C. Jack, n.d., ca. 1914. 1st edition; vii, 246 pages; color frontispiece and 7 color plates mounted on light grey paper, title vignette by Katharine Cameron; blue cloth, spine gilt and green decorated, onlaid extra color plate, top edge gilt, light prelim foxing, bit loose, cloth with light wear.   Robin Greer 94A-25 1996 £95.00

KINGSLEY, CHARLES 1819-1875   The Water Babies. New York: Dodd, Mead & Co., 1916. 1st edition; quarto; 362 pages; 12 color plates, green and black line drawings; original green cloth stamped in gilt on front cover and spine, color pictorial label on front cover, green pictorial endpapers, light wear to extremities, just slightly skewed, very good, clean. Nudelman A45.   Heritage Book Shop 196-271 1996 $650.00

KINGSLEY, CHARLES 1819-1875   The Water Babies. London: Hodder & Stoughton for Boots the Chemist, ca. 1935. 4to; pages (xii), 3-240; 12 mounted colored plates guarded by tissue; original green cloth, pictorially gilt, little light foxing of prelims; excellent.   Sotheran PN32-154 1996 £78.00

KINGSLEY, J. STERLING   Nature's Wonderland or Short Talks on Natural History for Young and Old. New York: Niglutsch, 1894. 4to; pages 662, 140; 11 color chromolithographic plates; three quarter calf and moderately soiled cloth, hinge to volume 2 loose, nice, clean set. Second Life Books 103-143 1996 $135.00

KINGSMILL, JOSEPH   Chapters on Prisons and Prisoners. London: Longman, Green, Brown and Longmans, 1852. 2nd edition; original cloth, nice; contemporary inscription, ad leaf at end.   Anthony W. Laywood 108-192 1996 £95.00

KINGSOLVER, BARBARA   The Bean Trees. New York: H&R, 1988. 1st edition; advance review copy with publisher's promotional card laid in; fine in fine dust jacket.   Ken Lopez 74-246 1996 $450.00

KINGSOLVER, BARBARA   The Bean Trees. New York: Harper, 1988. 1st edition; author's first book; signed by author; fine in dust jacket. Between the Covers 42-252a 1996 $300.00

KINGSOLVER, BARBARA   The Bean Trees. New York: Harper and Row, 1988. 1st edition; near fine copy in fine dust jacket, slight soiling; signed.   Book Time 2-230 1996 $160.00

KINGSOLVER, BARBARA   The Bean Trees. London: Virago Press, 1989. 1st U.K. edition (only 1250 copies); new in dust jacket.   Steven C. Bernard 71-145 1996 $100.00

KINGSTON, MAXINE HONG   The Woman Warrior. New York: Knopf, 1976. 1st edition; author's first book, near fine in near fine price clipped dust jacket, quite nice.   Ken Lopez 74-247 1996 $150.00

KINGSTON, MAXINE HONG   The Woman Warrior: Memoirs of a Girlhood Among Ghosts. New York: Knopf, 1976. 1st edition; author's first book; near fine in price clipped dust jacket.   Lame Duck Books 19-279 1996 $100.00

KINLOCH, ALEXANDER A. A.   Large Game Shooting in Thibet, the Himalayas, Northern and Central India. Calcutta: 1892. 3rd edition; 36 illustrations, map; small stain to front cover, very slight foxing to few pages.   Petersfield Bookshop FH58-447 1996 £52.00

KINNE, O.   Marine Ecology: a Comprehensive Integrated Treatise on Life in Oceans and Coastal Waters. New York: 1982-84. 8vo; 4 parts; numerous illustrations; cloth.   Wheldon & Wesley 207-326 1996 £570.00

KINNELL, GALWAY   The Last Hiding Places of Snow. Madison: Red Ozier Press, 1980. 1st edition; limited to 150 copies signed by author and artist; 8vo; illustrations by Barry Moser; cloth backed boards, mint.   James S. Jaffe 34-344 1996 $150.00

KINNELL, GALWAY   Two Poems. Newark: Janus Press, 1979. 1st edition; limited to 185 copies, signed by poet; octavo; illustrations by Claire Van Vliet; brown cloth with pictorial front cover; very fine.   Bromer Booksellers 90-76 1996 $150.00

KINNELL, GALWAY   Two Poems. Newark: Janus Press, 1979. 1st edition; one of 185 numbered copies, signed by author and artist; lithographs by Claire Van Vliet; cloth backed pictorial boards; very fine.   Captain's Bookshelf 38-133 1996 $125.00

KINNELL, GALWAY   Two Poems. New York: Red Ozier Press, 1981. 1st edition; one of 200 copies; inscribed by Wakoski, Moser & publishers, Steve Miller and Ken Botnick; 12mo; wood engravings by Barry Moser; original wrappers; mint.   James S. Jaffe 34-576 1996 $150.00

KINSELLA, THOMAS 1928-   Butcher's Dozen. Dublin: printed at the Elo Press for Peppercanister, 1972. 1st edition; one of 125 numbered copies, signed by Kinsella; decorated boards, fine, without dust jacket, as issued.   Captain's Bookshelf 38-135 1996 $175.00

KINSELLA, W. P.   Born Indian. Canada: Oberon, 1981. Hardcover edition; fine in fine dust jacket, flawless copy. Scarce.   Ken Lopez 74-248 1996 $450.00

KINSELLA, W. P.   The Dixon Cornbelt League. Toronto: Harper Collins, 1993. 1st edition; fine in fine dust jacket and signed by author.   Ken Lopez 74-250 1996 $125.00

KINSELLA, W. P.   Shoeless Joe. Boston: Houghton Mifflin, 1982. 1st edition; fine in near fine dust jacket with slight wrinkling at top edge spine.   Revere Books 4-230 1996 $125.00

KINSELLA, W. P.   The Thrill of the Grass. London: Penguin, 1984. Paperback original; wrappers, fine.   Ken Lopez 74-249 1996 $150.00

KINSKI, KLAUS   All I Need Is Love. New York: Random House, 1988. 1st edition; fine copy in fine dust jacket; rare.   Oracle Books 1-30 1996 $100.00

KIP, L.   Hannibal's Man and Other Tales. Argus Christmas Stories, 1878. 1st edition; some slight soil resulting in a lightening of the green cloth along fore-edge of rear cloth panel, else bright, very good+; from the collection of Oswald Train with bookplate.   Aronovitz 57-632 1996 $125.00

KIPLING, RUDYARD   Captains Courageous. London: Macmillan and Co., 1897. 1st edition; small octavo; viii, 245, (1 blank), (2 ads) pages; 22 full page illustrations by I. W. Taber; original blue cloth decoratively stamped in gilt on front cover and spine, all edges gilt, some light spotting to cloth, just slightly skewed, intermittent light foxing; very good, bright copy, in quarter blue morocco clamshell case. Livingston 137; Martindell 68; Stewart 163.   Heritage Book Shop 196-168 1996 $750.00

KIPLING, RUDYARD 1865-1936   Debits and Credits. London: 1926. 1st edition; fine, dust jacket with tiny edge piece missing, chemise and half leather box, gilt, spine with raised bands, fine.   Polyanthos 22-496 1996 $125.00

KIPLING, RUDYARD 1865-1936   The Five Nations. London: Methuen, 1903. 2nd edition; 8vo; full polished acid calf with an abstract 'tree' design on both covers, within a leafy outer border, spine with five raised bands with elegant gilt tooling, red morocco title label, binder's name, Renouf, stamped in gilt at foot, ticket on front pastedown: Publisher, E.M. Renouf, Montreal; fine. Livingston pp. 265-69.   Book Block 32-39 1996 $225.00

KIPLING, RUDYARD 1865-1936   France at War. Garden City: Doubleday Page, 1915. 1st edition; signed by author; front joint split, else very good, internally tape repaired dust jacket chipped at spine crown and upper front panel, small fragile volume, very scarce.   Ken Lopez 74-251 1996 $650.00

KIPLING, RUDYARD 1865-1936   In Black and White. A. Wheeler and Co., 1888. 1st edition; 8 3/4 x 5 1/2 inches; 4 p.l., 106, ii pages, (4) leaves (including ad leaf at front and four at back as well as the green life insurance ad tipped onto first page of text); original lithographed pictorial wrappers, with designs by J. Lockwood Kipling, contained in cloth folder inside an attractive recent red morocco backed slipcase with raised bands, gilt ruled spine compartments and gilt titling, one inch portion of paper at bottom of spine and tiny portion at top missing, otherwise exceptionally fine, remarkably sound, clean and smooth inside and out; Stewart 37; Martindell 27.   Phillip J. Pirages 33-326 1996 $950.00

KIPLING, RUDYARD 1865-1936   The Irish Guards in the Great War. London: MacMillan, 1923. 1st edition; 8vo; 2 volumes; maps; original binding, bookplates, endpapers foxed, some rubbing, very good. Charles Agvent 4-788 1996 $125.00

KIPLING, RUDYARD 1865-1936   The Jungle Book. New York: Century, 1894. 1st American edition; plates; decorated cloth, some spotting to cloth and few pages, former owner signature; very good.   Charles Agvent 4-789 1996 $125.00

KIPLING, RUDYARD 1865-1936   The Jungle Book. (with) The Second Jungle Book. London: and New York: Macmillan and Co., 1894/95. 1st editions; 8vo; 2 volumes; pages vi, (ii), 212; (vi), 238, (ii) ads; frontispiece, illustrations; original pictorial cloth gilt, upper covers and spine decorated and ruled in gilt, spine lettered in gilt, gilt edges; cloth box; hinges to first volume cracked, some spotting, mostly in first volume, but excellent, bright copies. with signed slip "Very sincerley Rudyard Kipling" pasted in 1st title.   Simon Finch 24-142 1996 £1,200.00

KIPLING, RUDYARD 1865-1936   The Jungle Book. New York: Century, 1897. Early American edition, 35th thousand; plates signed by Kipling on titlepage; decorated cloth; near fine.   Charles Agvent 4-790 1996 $950.00

KIPLING, RUDYARD 1865-1936   The Jungle Book. New York: Century 1913. 1st American edition thus; 16 colored plates by Maurice and Edward Detmold and green pictorial borders to each text page; green pictorial cloth, gilt, lacking front endpaper, else fresh copy, scarce. Barbara Stone 70-71 1996 £75.00

KIPLING, RUDYARD 1865-1936   The Jungle Books. Luxenburg: Limited Editions Club, 1968. Limited to 1500 copies, signed by David Gentleman; quarto; illustrations by David Gentleman; cloth and marbled boards, glassine dust jacket, slipcase; fine.   Antic Hay 101-951 1996125.00

KIPLING, RUDYARD 1865-1936   Just So Stories for Little Children. London: Macmillan and Co., 1902. 1st edition; 1st issue; large octavo; 249 pages; 22 full page illustrations by author; original white cloth decoratively stamped in gilt on front cover and spine, red ribbon ties, top edge gilt, others uncut, pictorial endpapers, cloth bit soiled, otherwise fine. Latimore & Hhaskell pp. 33-34.   Heritage Book Shop 196-220 1996 $1,750.00

KIPLING, RUDYARD 1865-1936   Kim. London: Macmillan, 1901. 1st English edition; 8vo; decorative red cloth, top edge gilt, very good in custom made red leather and cloth slipcase with five raised bands and gilt worked lettering on spine, quite handsome.   Antic Hay 101-953 1996 $275.00

KIPLING, RUDYARD 1865-1936   Kim. Garden City: Doubleday, ca. 1935. 8vo; color frontispiece, 9 full page plates; gilt and blindstamped dark blue cloth, spine with gilt stamped Indian scenes, top edge stained blue, uncut, dust jacket (nicked, rubbed), very good, tipped in on verso of frontispiece is photo of an unidentified female cast member. Signed and inscribed by Errol Flynn and over 60 cast & crew members. George J. Houle   68-77   1996 $2,500.00

KIPLING, RUDYARD 1865-1936   The Light that Failed. London: Macmillan, 1891. 1st edition; original binding, corners bumped, near fine. Charles Agvent 4-793 1996 $200.00

KIPLING, RUDYARD 1865-1936   The Naulahka. London: Heinemann, 1892. 1st edition; original binding, uncommon, somewhat rubbed. Livingstone 85.   Charles Agvent 4-794 1996 $150.00

KIPLING, RUDYARD 1865-1936   Poems 1886-1929. London: Chiswick Press for Macmillan, 1929. 1st edition; one of 500 copies, signed by author (of a total edition of 525); 10 3/4 x 8 inches; 3 volumes; printed in red and black on handmade paper; frontispiece portrait of author in volume 1, signed in pencil by Francis Dodd; fine wine colored publisher's polished morocco, spines with raised bands and simple gilt titling, turn-ins with gilt latticework decoration, marbled endpapers, top edge gilt, other edges untrimmed, original printed dust jackets (thin tissue wrapper also present, apparently as issued), almost entirely unopened, jacket spines slightly and uniformly faded, with little chafing, tiny loses at jacket corners, short pen mark on one cover, otherwise only trivial nicks to binding, volumes in especially fine, unworn condition and books virtually perfect internally. Stewart 574.   Phillip J. Pirages 33-327 1996 $1,500.00

KIPLING, RUDYARD 1865-1936   Puck of Pook's Hill. New York: Doubleday, 1906. 1st edition; 4 color plates by Arthur Rackham; original binding, near fine.   Charles Agvent 4-795 1996 $125.00

KIPLING, RUDYARD 1865-1936   Rewards and Fairies. Macmillan, 1910. 1st edition; fine in like dust jacket save for a thin light brown band along front dust jacket panel which is a minor flaw to this otherwise spectacular copy.   Aronovitz 57-634 1996 $425.00

KIPLING, RUDYARD 1865-1936   Sea Warfare. London: Macmillan and Co., 1916. 1st edition; octavo; v, 222, (4 ads) pages; original blue cloth stamped in gilt and blind on front cover and in gilt on spine, extremities lightly rubbed, some minor spotting to covers, just slightly skewed, occasional light foxing and browning, very good overall. Livingston 408; Martindell 149; Stewart 400.   Heritage Book Shop 196-190 1996 $150.00

KIPLING, RUDYARD 1865-1936   Sea and Sussex. London: Macmillan and Co., 1926. One of 500 large paper copies, signed by author; 4to; pages xvi, 96; 24 mounted colored plates by Donald Maxwell; original vellum backed boards, top edge gilt, others uncut, dust jacket chipped and repaired, otherwise very nice in slipcase, Stewart 524.   Sotheran PN32-24 1996 £425.00

KIPLING, RUDYARD 1865-1936   The Seven Seas. London: Methuen, 1913. 24th edition; limp leather, bit stained, in worn dust jacket; signed by author on titlepage.   Charles Agvent 4-802 1996 $350.00

KIPLING, RUDYARD 1865-1936   A Song of the English. London: Pub. on behalf of the Daily Telegraph National Bands Fund, n.d. 1915. 1st edition; 4to; tipped in color plates by Heath Robinson; white decorated cloth, somewhat darkened and marked, otherwise very good with loose sheet printing Kipling's speech on National Bands loosely inserted; scarce thus.   Words Etcetera 94-763 1996 £75.00

KIPLING, RUDYARD 1865-1936   Two Forewords. Garden City: Doubleday, Doran, 1935. Limited to 950 copies; 8vo; cloth backed marbled boards, near fine in worn slipcase.   Charles Agvent 4-807 1996 $150.00

KIPLING, RUDYARD 1865-1936   The Works. London: Macmillan, 1913-. Bombay Edition; signed by author in volume 1; volumes 1-25 (of 31), 25 volumes; boards, holland back, dust jackets, little chipped and discolored, otherwise fine.   Petersfield Bookshop FH58-55 1996 £420.00

KIPLING, RUDYARD 1865-1936   The Years Between. London: Methuen, 1919. 1st edition; just about fine in like dust jacket with few small nicks and tears.   Captain's Bookshelf 38-136 1996 $100.00

KIPPIS, ANDREW   The Life of Captain James Cook. Basil: printed by J. J. Tourneisen, 1788. 8vo; 2 volumes; contemporary half sheep, spines gilt, some rubbing; uncommon; slight foxing, but fine, complete with leaf of ads at end of volume 1, uncommon. Beddie 33; Holmes 70. Ximenes 109-171 1996 $450.00

KIPPIS, ANDREW 1725-1795   A Narrative of the Voyages Round the World Performed by Captain James Cook with an Account of His Life... London: 1826. 8vo; 2 volumes in one, over 450 pages, additional engraved titles; blue calf, title label inlaid on red morocco, raised bands, very good.   K Books 441-302 1996 £60.00

KIPPIS, ANDREW W. 1725-1795   The Life of Captain James Cook... London: printed for G. Nicol...and G. G. J. and J. Robinson, 1788. 1st edition; 4to; 527 pages; frontispiece; old speckled calf boards, double gilt rule borders, rebacked preserving original backstrip (some gilt restoration), emblematic tools and red morocco label, marbled edges and endpapers, inner gilt dentelles, bookplate; hinges cracked, still good, tight copy; occasional dampstaining to margins on whole fairly minor, but more pronounced to final few leaves. Mitchell 32; Hill 163-64. Lada Mocarski 40; Holmes 69.   Beeleigh Abbey BA56-54 1996 £2,000.00

KIRBY, JOHN   The Suffolk Traveller; or a Journey through Suffolk... Ipswich: Bagnall, 1735. 1st edition; 8vo; 2ff., 206 pages, 1 f., blanks at end, contemporary calf, rubbed, title grubby; with signature of Joshua Kirby, author's son.   Marlborough 162-58 1996 £250.00

KIRBY, JOHN   The Suffolk Traveller, first Published by Mr. John Kirby, Who Took an Actual Survey of the Whole County in the Years 1732, 1733 and 1734. London: Shave, 1764. 2nd edition; 8vo; pages xvi, 340; folding engraved map colored in outline; contemporary calf, rebacked, some light foxing; Anderson p. 26.   Marlborough 162-59 1996 £195.00

KIRBY, M.   Birds of Gay Plumage: Sun-Birds &c. London: 1875. 3 colored plates, including frontispiece; original pictorial gilt cloth, color print of parrots on upper cover, light rubbing to corners.   David A.H. Grayling MY95Orn-176 1996 £75.00

KIRBY, W. F.   European Butterflies and Moths. London: Cassell, Petter, Galpin, 1882. 4to; lvi, 427 pages; 62 lithographed plates, all but one colored by hand; black half morocco, red label, joints split and spine detached, occasional light spotting.   Thomas Thorp 489-179 1996 £300.00

KIRK, T.   The Forest Flora of New Zealand. Wellington: 1889. Small folio; pages xv, 345; 142 plates; original gilt decorated cloth, spine darkened with some splitting to edges, upper edge of rear cover bumped, some wear to extremities and splotchiness to covers, light foxing in front and back, browning to some plates.   Raymond M. Sutton VII-601 1996 $250.00

KIRKBRIDE, THOMAS S.   On the Construction, Orgranization an General Arrangements of Hospitals for the Insane. Philadelphia/London: J. B. Lippincott & Co., 1880. 2nd edtion; 8vo; (ii), (xviii), (15)-320, (2) pages, 23 plates; mauve cloth, front hinge cracked, slight shelfwear, very good, scarce. Inscribed from author to Marietta Public Library, dated Oct. 1881.   John Gach 150-244 1996 $850.00

KIRKLAND, ELIZABETH S.   Six Little Cooks; or Aunt Jane's Cooking Class. Chicago: Jansen McClurg & Co., 1877. 1st edition; square 16mo; 236 pages; frontispiece; original pictorial cloth; very nice. Rare.   M & S Rare Books 60-310 1996 $300.00

KIRKMAN, F. B.   The British Bird Book: an Account of All the Birds. London: T. C. and E. C. Jack, 1911-13. 1st edition; 4to 4 volumes; pages 449, 540, 609, 1602; with 280 colored plates; contemporary green half morocco gilt, by Horace C. Commin; occasional mainly light spotting to beginning and end of volumes, spines slightly faded.   Sotheran PN32-90 1996 £398.00

KIRKPATRICK   Alpine Days and Nights. 1932. 1st edition; 8vo; illustrations; cloth, dust jacket, very good.   C. P. Hyland 216-373 1996 £50.00

KIRKPATRICK B. J.   A Bibliography of E. M. Forster. London: Rupert Hart-Davis, 1968. 2nd edition; 8vo; frontispiece, 205 pages; cloth, dust jacket, very good in lightly handled jacket.   The Bookpress 75-294 1996 $100.00

KIRKWOOD, JAMES   Proposals Made by Rev. James Kirkwood in 1699, to Found PUblic Libraries in Scotland. London: privately printed by William Blades, 1889. Limited edition, number 1 of 100 copies for presentation; small square 4to; pages 9, (15, facsimile, printed on handmade paper); modern half levant morocco gilt, marbled boards, few faint marginal blindstamps; this copy presented to the Wigan Public Library by the historian Henry T. Folkard.   R.F.G. Hollett 76-27 1996 £185.00

KIRSTEIN, LINCOLN   The New York City Ballet. New York: Alfred A. Knopf, 1973. Oblong folio; color and black and white illustrations; black boards stamped in blind on front cover and silver on spine, in pictorial dust jacket (chipped with short tears at edges). inscribed by author to his therapist.   Blue Mountain SP95-42 1996 $175.00

KIRSTEIN, LINCOLN   Walker Evans: American Photographs. New York: MOMA, 1938. 1st edition; dust jacket chipped and stained, scarce in jacket.   J. B. Muns 154-107 1996 $350.00

THE KIT Book For Soldiers, Sailors and Marines. Chicago: Consolidated Book Publishers, 1943. 1st edition; 2nd issue; page margins browned as usual (cheap paper), otherwise bright, near fine pictorial paper covered boards, issued without dust jacket.   Steven C. Bernard 71-196 1996 $100.00

KITCHIN, C. H. B.   Streamers Waving. London: Hogarth Press, 1925. 1st edition; one of 1000 copies; 4 pages publisher's ads at rear; original binding, top edge dusty and slightly soiled, head and tail of spine and corners bumped and rubbed, free endpapers partially browned, very good; presentation copy from author in month of publication, inscribed to his Aunt Susan.   Ulysses 39-339 1996 £95.00

KITCHIN, JOHN   Le Court Leete et Court Baron Collect per Iohn Kitchin de Greies Inne..Ouesque Diuers Nouel Additions, Come Court de Marshalsey, Auncient, Demesne Court de Pipowders, Essoines, Imparlance & Diuers Auter Matters. London: in aedibus Thomae Wight & Bonhami Norton, 1598. Modern sheep, light staining, 4 leaves strengthened, sound.   Meyer Boswell SL26-133 1996 $1,250.00

KITCHIN, JOHN   Jurisdictions: or, the Lawful Authority of Courts Leet, Courts Baron, Court of Marshalseyes, Court of Pypowder, and Ancient Demesne. London: Printed for M.: Walbancke at Grays-Inne Gate etc., 1653. contemporary sheep, titlepage repaired, some embrowning but sound.   Meyer Boswell SL25-133 1996 $650.00

KITCHINER, WILLIAM 1775-1827   The Cook's Oracle; and Housekeeper's Manual. New York: J. & J. Harper, 1830. Early American edition; 12mo; 432 pages; original full calf, cover lightly soiled, few pages creased, else tight, very good. American Imprints 2134.   Chapel Hill 94-166 1996 $175.00

KITCHING, A. L.   On the Backwaters of the Nile, Studies of Some Child Races of Central Africa. London: 1912. 1st edition; 8vo; xxiv, 295 pages, 56 illustrations; black cloth, gilt decorated with an African Tribesma motif;   K Books 442-11 1996 £60.00

KLASNER, LILY   My Girlhood Among Outlaws. Tucson: 1972. 1st edition; 336 pages; photos; book and dust jacket exceptionally fine. Early West 22-157 1996 $200.00

KLAUBER, L. E.   Rattlesnakes: Their Habits, Life Histories and Influence On Mankind. Berkeley: 1956. 4to; 2 volues, 1530 pages; 2 color plates, 243 illustrations; bound, dust jacket.   John Johnson 135-625 1996 $175.00

KLEE, PAUL   Notebooks. London: Lund Humphries, 1973. Square 4to; 2 volumes, 541, 454 pages; 8, 15 tipped in color plates, numerous monochrome illustrations; boards, dust jacket. Freitag 4855 and 4859. Brannan 43-307 1996 $495.00

KLEIN, WILLIAM   Photogrpahs. Aperture, 1981. 1st edition; illustrations; dust jacket, slightly torn at edges;   J. B. Muns 154-172 1996 $125.00

KLEINHOLZ, FRANK   Frank Kleinholz: a Self Portrait. New York: Shorewood Publishers, 1964. 1st edition; one of 1000 copies; small 4to; 95 pages; color and black and white reproductions; additionally, this copy has an original drawing in colors, on colophon, signed by artist; illustrated cloth; very good in moderately worn dust jacket.   Andrew Cahan 47-107 1996 $150.00

KLIMT, GUSTAV   Twenty-Five Drawings Selected and Interpreted by Alice Strobl. Vienna: Akademische Druckpund Averlagsanstalt Graz-Wien, 1964. 1st edition; large folio; 14 pages, 25 plates, reproductions; all loosely contained in original black cloth portfolio with paper label, lightly soiled publisher's slipcase.   Chapel Hill 94-66 1996 $450.00

KLIPPART, JOHN H.   The Wheat Plant: Its Origin, Culture, Growth, Development, Composition, Varities, Diseases, etc. Cincinnati: Moore et al, 1860. 1st edition; 8vo; pages 706 + ad, watermark to front blanks, otherwise nice, clean copy; half calf, stamped: Ohio School Library. Second Life Books 103-118 1996 $150.00

KLIPPART, JOHN H.   The Wheat Plant: Its Origin, Culture, Growth, Development, Composition, Varieties, Diseases... Cincinnati: 1860. 8vo; pages 706, (6 pages ads); 8 plates, 79 text figures; original cloth, faded, soiled, stained, ink inscription on endpaper, some endpaper stianing, pages yellowed.   Raymond M. Sutton VII-1026 1996 $115.00

KLONDIKE & BOSTON GOLD MINING & MANUFACTURING CO.   Placer Gold. Concerning the Klondike & Boston Gold Mining and Manufacturing Company's Rich Palcer Mines in Willow Creek, Southern Alaska. Boston: 1902-03. 1st edition; 20 pages; illustrations, folding map; original red and gold wrpapers with title in black on front cover, minor foxing; very good. Michael D. Heaston 23-7 1996 $250.00

KLOPSTOCK, FRIEDRICH   Memoirs of Frederick and Margaret Klopstock. Bath: printed by Richard Cruttwell... 1808. 8vo; c half calf, lacking label.   Peter Murray Hill 185-97 1996 £50.00

KNAPP, JOHN LEONARD   The Journal of a Naturalist. London: John Murray, 1829. 1st edition; 8vo; 396 pages; folding aquatint plate, 6 full and double page engraved plates; contemporary green half morocco with gilt tooled spine, spine rubbed, but very good; rare.   Chapel Hill 94-307 1996 $125.00

KNIGHT, CHARLES   The Bridal of the Isles; a Mask. London: Effingham Wilson, 1817. 2nd edition; color frontispiece; contemporary half calf, gilt spine, black label; attractive, very good; from the collection of Anne and Fernand Renier, with booklabel.   Jarndyce 103-507 1996 £120.00

KNIGHT, CHARLES   Old England: a Pictorial Museum. London: James Sangster & Co., ca. 1860. 1st edition; folio; 2 volumes, 392, 404 pages; in-text engravings, numerous full page chromolithogrph plates; original publisher's half red morocco with heavily gilt tooled spines, all edges gilt, light offsetting to some plates, else very good to near fine. Chapel Hill 94-224 1996 $150.00

KNIGHT, CHARLES   The Old Printer and the Modern Press. London: John Murray, 1854. 1st edition; 1 page + 32 pages ads (Jane. 1854); original dark brown cloth, small repairs, very good.   Jarndyce 103-510 1996 £75.00

KNIGHT, CLIFFORD   The Affair of the Skiing Clown. New York: Dodd, Mead, 1941. Softbound advance copy, short tear at rear, tight, near fine copy, dust jacket.   Janus Books 36-199 1996 $125.00

KNIGHT, JOSEPH   David Garrick. London: Kegan Paul, 1894. Large paper limited to 100 copies; thick royal 8vo; etched portrait, extra illustrated by about 80 plates; full morocco, joints repaired, inside gilt doublures, gilt top, other edges uncut.   Charles W. Traylen 117-120 1996 £75.00

KNIGHT, SARAH K.   The Journals of Madam Knight and Rev. Mr. Buckingham. New York: Wilder & Campbell, 1825. 1st edition; 12mo; 129 pages; original plain boards, disbound. Foxed. Howes K218.   M & S Rare Books 60-357 1996 $275.00

KNIGHTON, HENRY   Chronicon Henrici Knighton, vel Critthon, Monachi Leycestrensis. London: 1889-95. 8vo; 2 volumes, pages 499, 457; origina cloth.   Howes Bookshop 265-1603 1996 £65.00

KNOLLES, RICHARD   The General Historie of the Turkes, from the First Beginning of that Nation... London: Adam Islip, 1638. 5th edition; thick folio; (8), 1500, (20), 31, (31) pages; engraved titlepage, engraved portraits; contemporary blind tooled calf, rebacked, titlepage clipped and mounted but sound, very good copy. Pollard & Redgrave 15055. Chapel Hill 94-414 1996 $900.00

KNOTT, CARGILL GILSTON   Napier Tercentenary Memorial volume. London: for the Royal Society of Edinburgh by Longmans, Green, 1915. 4to; ix, (1), 441 pages; colored frontispiece, 15 plates; former owner's bookplate; original cream cloth, gilt; fine.   Edwin V. Glaser 121-225 1996 $450.00

KNOTT, FREDERICK   Dial "M" for Murder. New York: Random House, 1953. 1st edition; tan cloth boards with photogrpahic plate from original production of play on front cover, faint offset on rear pastedown, still fine in slightly soiled and darkened dust jacket with shallow chipping and few short closed tears.   Quill & Brush 102-999 1996 $100.00

KNOWLE Estate (Cranleigh, Surrey) Particulars. London: Debenham, 1878. Folio; 8 pages, 1 f., litho frontispiece, folding map, pictorial litho covers, O.S. map on lower cover (some wear to covers).   Marlborough 162-60 1996 £250.00

KNOWLES, E. H.   The Castle of Kenilworth, a Hand-Book for Visitors. Warwick: H. T. Cooke, 1872. Large 4to; 5 ff., pages xxxii, 228, 6 ff. (index), 5 engraved plates, engraved vignettes, 24 mounted photographic plates, contemporary red cloth, all edges gilt, very slight spotting to contents. uncommon in this condition; Gernsheim 545.   Marlborough 162-61 1996 £300.00

KNOWLES, JAMES   A Pronouncing and Explanatory Dictionary of the English Language. London: F. De Porquet & Cooper, 1835. 1st edition; slight spotting in prelims; contemporary calf, gilt spine, gilt borders, dark brown label, very good.   Jarndyce 103-193 1996 £85.00

KNOWLES, JAMES   A Vocabulary of the Greek, Latin and Scripture Proper Names, with Their Classical Pronunciation Correctly Marked. London: G. Berger, 1835. Folio; frontispiece, inital ad leaf inserted; original dark green patterned cloth, black paper label chiped.   Jarndyce 103-263 1996 £65.00

KNOWLES, JAMES SHERIDAN   The Beggar's Daughter of Bethnal Green. London: Basil Stewart and J. Ridgway, 1828. 1st edition; half blue morocco, scuffed at points, marbled boards, spine gilt, untrimmed, inscribed presentation copy from author for Ellen Tree who played Bess. Dramatis Personae 37-108 1996 $200.00

KNOWLES, JOHN   A Separate Peace. New York: Macmillan, 1960. 1st American edition; one corner bumped, spine slightly sunned, thus near fine in like, second issue dust jacket with little wear to spinal extremities; author's first book; inscribed by author on the occasion of the 25th anniversary of the publication.   Between the Covers 42-253 1996 $400.00

KNOX, JOHN   Knox's Investors' Guide, Topeka, Kansas Real Estate Mortgage Loans. Topeka: Geo. W. Crane & Co., 1885. 1st edition; 26, (6) pages; illustrations; original orange printed wrappers, minor dampstaining to bottom of pamphlet; very good.   Michael D. Heaston 23-195 1996 $250.00

KNOX, THOMAS W.   Camp-Fire and Cotton-Field; Southern Adventures in the Time of War. New York: Blelock, 1865. 1st edition; thick 8vo; frontispiece, 11 full page wood engravings; original brown cloth, faded spine gilt, worn at head and tail.   Ian Wilkinson 95/1-11 1996 £65.00

KOBEL, JACOB   Astrolabii Declaratio, Eivsdemqve Usus Mire Iucundus, Non Modo Astrologis, Medicis, Geographis, Caeterisque Literarum Cultoribus Multum Utilis ac Necessarius... Paris: Apud Gulielmum Cavellat, 1550. Small 8vo; 31 leaves; woodcut illustrations and diagrams; broken old vellum wrappers. Not in Adams.   Family Album Tillers-373 1996 $250.00

KOCH, KENETH   When the Sun Tries to Go On. Los Angeles: Black Sparrow, 1969. One of 200 numbered copies signed by author, Koch and artist, Larry Rivers; 7 3/8 x 5 7/16 inches; 3 dimensional collage serving as cover by Larry Rivers; yellow cloth with Rivers' collage in pink, yellow and black on various levels, original acetate jacket; fine. In green cloth slipcase with red morocco labels.   Priscilla Juvelis 95/1-210 1996 $750.00

KOCH, KENNETH   Quinevere, or the Death of the Kangaroo. New York: American Theatre for Poets, 1961. 1st edition; playscript with several holograph corrections and additions; 4to; mimeograph, stapled; fine.   James S. Jaffe 34-357 1996 $125.00

KOENIG, EBERHARD   The 1462 Fust & Schoeffer Bible. Austin: printed by W. Thomas Taylor for Bruce Ferrini and Hamill & Barker, 1993. One of 166 copies (of a total 181); 20 x 14 1/2 inches; 31 pages; 12 monochrome plates, printed offset by Wind River Press, with original leaf from 1462 Fust & Schoeffer Bible; the book and leaf enclosed in handsome protective cloth drop-spine box;   Phillip J. Pirages 33-332 1996 $3,500.00

KOESTER, F.   Under the Desert Stars. Washington Square Publishing, 1923. 1st edition; f.e.p. neatly excised, else near fine in very nice dust jacket chipped along top quarter inch of both the head of the dust jacket spine and along the top of the rear dust jacket panel; most uncommon, rare in dust jacket.   Aronovitz 57-643 1996 $135.00

KOHL, JAHNN G.   Wanderings Round Lake Superior. London: Chapman and Hall, 1860. 1st English edition; 8vo; wood engraved illustrations; new half calf and cloth, gilt panelled spine, red morocco label, gilt top and marbled endpapers, by Bayntun; Sabin 38215. Howes 5798.   Charles W. Traylen 117-418 1996 £270.00

KOKINMEIBUTSU Ruishu. (Collection of Special Products, Ancient and Present Cloths.) Tokyo: Tsugiharaya, 1791. 8vo; 2 volumes; more than 160 color woodblock examples; green wrappers, each with paper label, bound in traditional style (printed one one side of the sheet only), ex-library stamp on verso of title. Bright and excellent condition.   Book Block 32-16 1997 $1,250.00

KOLDEWEY, CAPTAIN   The German Expedition of 1869-70, and Narrative of the Wreck of the 'Hansa' in the Ice. London: 1874. 1st English edition; royal 8vo; 4 chromolithographs, 2 steel engraved portraits, 2 colored maps and numerous woodcuts in text; contemporary half calf, gilt spine, red morocco label, gilt; extremely scarce; bookplate of J. Lamont of Knockddow.   Charles W. Traylen 117-419 1996 £600.00

KOMENSKY, JOHN AMOS   The Labyrinth of the World and the Paradise of the Heart. Waltham St. Lawrence: Golden Cockerel Press, 1950. Limited to 370 numbered copies; royal 8vo; 271 pages; line illustrations in black and brown from pen drawings by Dorothea Braby; publisher's cream buckram, with impressed design in brown on both covers by artist, top edge gilt, edges uncut; fine.   Thomas Thorp 489-180 1996 £75.00

KONDOLEON, HARRY   The Cote d'Azur Triangle. New York: Vincent Fitz Gerald, 1985. One of 119 copies only; page size 12 x 14 inches; printed on BFK Rives, all signed by author and artist, handset in janson, lithographs and etched pulled at the Printmaking Workshop of Bob Blackburn under the artist's supervision; illustrations by Mark Beard; yellow stamped cloth.   Priscilla Juvelis 95/1-22 1996 $6,000.00

KONKLE, BURTON   Standard History of the Medical Profession of Philadelphia. New York: 1977. Reprint; 544 pages, 31 pages, 24 pages; original binding, ex-library.   W. Bruce Fye 71-1200 1996 $100.00

KOONTZ, DEAN R.   Chase. New York: Random House, 1972. 1st edition; fine in fine dust jacket.   Bud Schweska 12-466 1996 $155.00

KOONTZ, DEAN R.   Dragon Tears. New York: Putnam, 1993. 1st edition; one of 700 numbered copies, signed by author; dust jacket illustration by Don Brautigan and interior illustrated by Phil Parks; very fine in dust jacket, in slipcase.   Robert Gavora 61-40 1996 $200.00

KOONTZ, DEAN R.   Dragonfly. New York: Random House, 1975. 1st edition; fine in dust jacket with very light rubbing.   Quill & Brush 102-1001 1996 $175.00

KOONTZ, DEAN R.   Dragonfly. New York: Random House, 1975. 1st edition; fine in about fine dust jacket with small tear near spine panel. Bud Schweska 12-471 1996 $125.00

KOONTZ, DEAN R.   Hanging On. Evans, 1973. 1st edition; just about fine in very good+ dust jacket with some light foxing; author's first hard cover book under his own name.   Aronovitz 57-644 1996 $165.00

KOONTZ, DEAN R.   Hanging On. Evans, 1973. 1st edition; very good+ in very good+ dust jacket.   Book Time 2-237 1996 $125.00

KOONTZ, DEAN R.   Hanging On. New York: M. Evans, 1973. 1st edition; near fine in dust jacket that is very lightly soiled on front cover. Bud Schweska 12-467 1996 $150.00

KOONTZ, DEAN R. The House of Thunder. Dark Harvest, 1988. Deluxe 1st edition, limited to 550 numbered copies, signed by author and artist, Phil Parks; this is copy P/C (publisher's copy); fine in mint dust jacket and mint box. Polyanthos 22-770 1996 $100.00

KOONTZ, DEAN R. The House of Thunder. Arlington Heights: Dark Harvest, 1988. 1st U.S. hardcover edition, one of 500 numbered copies, signed by artist, Phil Parks; very fine in dust jacket with slipcase. Robert Gavora 61-41 1996 $150.00

KOONTZ, DEAN R. The House of Thunder. Arlington: Dark Harvest, 1988. Limited edition, one of 550 numbered and signed copies, signed by author and artist, Phil Parks; very fine in fine dust jacket and case. Bud Schweska 12-483 1996 $100.00

KOONTZ, DEAN R. The Mask. London: Headline, 1980. 1st trade hardcover edition, very fine in dust jacket. Robert Gavora 61-43 1996 $125.00

KOONTZ, DEAN R. Mr. Murder. New York: Putnam, 1993. 1/600 copies, signed, fine in slipcase. Bev Chaney, Jr. 23-363 1996 $125.00

KOONTZ, DEAN R. Night Chills. New York: Atheneum, 1976. 1st edition; fine in near fine dust jacket with very faint 2/19 written on spine panel. Bud Schweska 12-472 1996 $150.00

KOONTZ, DEAN R. Night Chills. New York: Atheneum, 1976. 1st edition; ink owner's name and address on front free endpaper, otherwise fine in dust jacket. Hermitage SP95-553 1996 $125.00

KOONTZ, DEAN R. Nightmare Journey. New York: Berkley, 1975. 1st edition; fine in near fine dust jacket. Bud Schweska 12-469 1996 $125.00

KOONTZ, DEAN R. The Servants of Twilight. Piatkus, 1984. 1st British and 1st hard cover edition; fine in dust jacket. Aronovitz 57-647 1996 $175.00

KOONTZ, DEAN R. The Servants of Twilight. Arlington Heights: Dark Harvest, 1988. 1st U.S. hardcover edition; one of 450 numbered copies, signed by author and artist, Phil Parks; very fine in dust jacket and slipcase. Bud Schweska 12-479 1996 $100.00

KOONTZ, DEAN R. Shattered. New York: Random House, 1973. 1st edition; fine in dust jacket. Quill & Brush 102-1000 1996 $200.00

KOONTZ, DEAN R. The Wall of Masks. Indianapolis: Bobbs Merrill, 1975. 1st edition; fine in near fine dust jacket with small chip to front bottom jacket and slightly rubbed front cover. Bud Schweska 12-470 1996 $150.00

KOONTZ, DEAN R. Winter Moon. London: Headline Publishing, 1994. 1st hardcover edition, only 2500 copies printed; as new in dust jacket. Bud Schweska 12-491 1996 $100.00

KOOP, ALBERT J. Early Chinese Bronzes. London: Ernest Benn, 1924. Folio; viii, 85 pages; 110 plates; cloth. Thomas Thorp 489-181 1996 £100.00

KOOPS, M. Historical Account of the Substances Which Have Been Used to Describe Events. London: Jaques & co., 1801. 2nd edition; one of 510 issues, this issue was printed on de-inked waste paper, the other printed on straw; frontispiece lacking; appendix printed on purpe wood pulp paper; half calf, gilt bands, rebacked, original marbled boards, faint stamp on title. Ownership inscription of Edward Lloyd. Maggs Bros. Ltd. 1191-187 1996 £200.00

KOOY, J. M. J. Ballistics of the Future: With Special Reference to the Dynamical and Physical theory of the Rocket Weapons. New York: McGraw-hill, 1946. Small 4to; 472 pages; well illustrated; black cloth; good. Knollwood Books 70-444 1996 $100.00

KORAN L'Alcoran de Mahomet. Amsterdam: Louis Elzevir, 1649. 2nd edition in French; 12mo; 6 leaves, 686 pages, 3 leaves; contemporary vellum boards, yapp fore-edge, morocco label. Willems 1087; Copinger 2962. H. M. Fletcher 121-63 1996 £450.00

KORAN The Koran: Commonly called the Alcoran of Mahammed. London: printed by C. Ackers, 1st edition of this translation; folding map, 4 plates, 508 pages + tables; speckled calf, handsome rebacked in slightly lighter speckled calf with raised bands, gilt with maroon label, edges marbled, corners rubbed, bump to lower front board, otherwise handsome, clean, wide margined copy. Hermitage SP95-929 1996 $1,350.00

KORESH The Cellular Cosmogony or-Earth a Concave Sphere... Guiding Star Pub. House, 1905. 1st edition; photos, maps and drawings; very good, rare. Aronovitz 57-648 1996 $100.00

KORN, ERIC Lepidoptera Fantastica. Leeds: Gehenna Press, 1993. One of 40 copies, this one of 10 deluxe copies with an extra set of proofs in black painted in watercolor by Baskin and an original copperplate and a watercolor; page size 12 5/8 x 10 5/8 inches; printed on various European and Japanese handmade papers, all copies signed by Baskin and Korn; 16 etchings by Leonard Baskin, text printed letterpress in Centaur & Arrighi by Arthur Larson; bound by Gray Parrot with morocco spine and hand marbled paper over boards, title in gilt on cover, housed in custom clamshell box. Priscilla Juvelis 95/1-103 1996 $10,000.00

KORN, GRANINO A. Electronic Analog Computers (D-c Analog Computers). New York: McGraw Hill, 1952. 8vo; xv, 378 pages; numerous figures in text; original cloth, dust jacket, jacket bit shelfworn, else fine. Sarrazin E2. Edwin V. Glaser 121-175 1996 $150.00

KOSMOPOULOS, LESLIE WALKER The Prehistoric Inhabitation of Corinth. Munich: F. Bruckmann, 1948. Limited to 500 copies; 4to; xxii, 73 pages, 51 figures, 4 color plates; wrappers; with signature of F. H. Stubbings, 1949. Archaeologia Luxor-3575 1996 $150.00

KOSOWER, E. M. Molecular Mechanisms for Sensory Signals, Recognition and Transformation. Princeton: 1991. 8vo; 589 pages, 5 colored illustrations, 188 line drawings and equations, 33 tables; cloth. Wheldon & Wesley 207-498 1996 £62.50

KOTZEBUE, OTTO VON A New Voyage Round the world, in the Years 1823, 24, 25 and 26. Amsterdam/New York: N. Israel/Da Capo Press, 1967. Reprint of 1830 London ed.; 21.5 cm; 2 volumes; (8), 341, 362 pages, frontispiece, 2 folding maps, folding plan; Sabin 38288 for 1st. Howes K259; Hill p. 166. Parmer Books 039/Nautica-039355 1996 $125.00

KRAAY, COLIN M. Greek Coins. New York: Harry N. Abrams, 1966. Folio; 396 pages, 1329 photos and 20 color plates; 4 maps; original cloth, dust jacket. Archaeologia Luxor-3528 1996 $650.00

KRAELING, CARL H. Gerasa, City of the Decapolis: an Account Emboyding the Record of a Joint Excavation conducted by Yale University and the British School of Archaeology in Jerusalem (1928-1930) and Yale University and the American Schools of Oriental Research ... New Haven: American School of Oriental Research, 1938. 4to; frontispiece, xxxii, 616 pages, 47 figures, 143 plates, 47 plans; original cloth, annotation at flyleaf, otherwise fine. Archaeologia Luxor-3580 1996 $500.00

KRAELING, CARL H. Ptolemais, City of the Libyan Pentapolis. Chicago: University of Chicago Press, 1967. 4to; xviii, 288 pages; 74 figures, 64 plates, 22 plans (1 in back pocket); original cloth. Archaeologia Luxor-3579 1996 $175.00

KRAEPELIN, EMIL Clinical Psychiatry: a Text Book for Students and Physicians Abstracted and Adapted from the Seventh German Edition of Kraepelin's "Lehrbuch der Psychiatrie"... New York: Macmillan Co./London: Macmillan & Co., Ltd., 1902. 8vo; (xii), 420 pages + 10 pages of ads; blue cloth, titlepage stamp, rear pocket and whited spine numbers of the Hartford Retreat; with Jelliffe's name stamps. John Gach 150-247 1996 $125.00

KRAEPELIN, EMIL Dementia Praecox and Paraphrenia. Edinburgh: E. S. Livingstone, 1919. 1st edition in English; 8vo; (ii), x, (332) pages; rebound in red library buckram, right edge of titlepage and two ensuing leaves chipped, good, scarce; titlepage stamp and spine label of The Hartford Retreat, rear pocket removed, Jelliffe's copy, signed on titlepage. John Gach 150-248 1996 $250.00

KRAEPELIN, EMIL Lectures on Clinical Psychiatry. New York: William Wood & Co., 1913. 3rd edition in English; 8vo; (xviii), 368 pages; panellbed blue buckram, spine label deftly removed, very good, stamp of Hartford Retreat to title and several other pages, uncommon; Jelliffe's copy, signed on titlepage with his bookplate. John Gach 150-250 1996 $150.00

KRAEPELIN, EMIL   Psychologische Arbeiten. Leipzig: Verlag von Wilhelm Engelmann, 1896-1928. 1st edition; 8vo; 6080 pages, 26 plates, 18 folding; early 20th century maroon cloth, crown to volume 2 shelfworn, otherwise very good, clean copies, rare; with titlepage stamp, rear pocket and spine call numbers of Hartford Retreat; with Jelliffe's name stamp and bookplate in every volume.   John Gach 150-256 1996 $1,250.00

KRAFFT, J. C.   Plans, Coupes et Elevations de Diverses Productions de l'Art de la Charpente Executees Tant en France que Dans les Pays. Paris: Levrault, 1805. Folio; 4 parts in 2 volumes; (iv), 27, (1) pages, engraved dedication leaf, engraved frontispiece, 31 engraved plates; 27, (1), 82 engraved plates; (ii), 18 pages, 63 engraved plates; 9, (1) pages, 28 engraved plates; quarter calf; library stamp of Reading Public Library on title and few plates; fromt he library of J. G. James.   Elton Engineering 10-87 1996 £1,250.00

KRAFFT-EBING, RICHARD, FREIHERR VON   Psychopathia Sexualis with Especial Reference to Contrary Sexual Instinct. Philadelphia: The F. A. Davis Co., 1892. 1st edition in English; 8vo; xiv, 436 pages, plus inserted catalog dated 1892; ruled olive cloth, hinges cracked, shelfworn, small library stamp, good copy.   John Gach 150-259 1996 $125.00

KRAFFT-EBING, RICHARD, FREIHERR VON   Text-Book of Insanity Based on Clinical Observations for Practioners and Students of Medicine. Philadelphia: The F. A. Davis Co., 1904. 1st edition in English; 8vo; xvi, 638, (2) pages; blue cloth, front hinge cracked, covers dull; good. John Gach 150-260 1996 $175.00

KRAFT, WILLIAM   The Dream Tunnel: a Magical Journey through the Music of America: for Narrator and Orchestr. N.P.: n.p., 1976. Folio; 71 page musical score; spiral bound, together with 7 4to. sheets of text by Barbara Kraft; stiff blue wrappers; very good; signed and inscribed by author to Olive Behrendt.   George J. Houle 68-78 1996 $395.00

KRAKEL, DEAN   The Saga of Tom Horn. The Story of a Cattleman's War. Laramie: 1954. 1st unexpurgated edition; 277 pages; book fine, dust jacket near fine, reprinted pages that were changed are laid in; exceptional copy, scarce. Adams 150 #92.   Early West 22-164 1996 $350.00

KRAKEL, DEAN   The Saga of Tom Horn. Laramie: 1954. Expurgated first edition; slipcase, signed by author.   Early West 22-165 1996 $175.00

KRAKEL, DEAN   The Saga of Tom Horn. Laramie: 1954. Expurgated first edition; very good, dust jacket, signed by author.   Early West 22-165b 1996 $175.00

KRAMER, HILTON   Richard Lindner. Boston: New York Graphic Society, 1975. Square 4to; 255 pages; 56 tipped in color and 115 monochrome plates; cloth, dust jacket. Freitag 5643.   Brannan 43-356 1996 $245.00

KRAMRISCH, S.   A Survey of Painting in the Deccan. N.P.: Archaeological Department, 1937. 1st edition; 4to; xiii, (i), 234, (2) pages, 24 plates; more than 24 illustrations; cloth spine, boards; light cover wear, text lightly browned and foxed, rear hinge starting to crack internally, still respectable copy.   The Bookpress 75-430 1996 $200.00

KRAUSS, ROSALIND E.   Terminal Iron Works: The Sculpture of David Smith. Cambridge: MIT Press, 1971. 4to; 200 pages, 148 illustrations; cloth, dust jacket. Freitag 9037.   Brannan 43-602 1996 $135.00

KREHBIEL, HENRY EDWARD   Afro-American Folksongs: a Study in Racial and National Music. New York: and London: G. Schirmer, 1914. 1st edition; 8vo; xii, 176 pages; illustrated with musical scores; gilt decorated cloth, rubbed on extremities, very good.   Andrew Cahan 47-3 1996 $200.00

KRESS LIBRARY   The Kress Library of Business and Economics. Catalogue Covering material Published through 1776. (with) 1777-1817. 1993. Reprint of Boston, 1940-56 edition; limited to 250 copies; 4to; 2 volumes, pages x, 414; x, 397; new cloth binding.   Claude Cox 107-302 1996 £80.00

KRESS, N.   Beggars in Spain. Axolotl Press, 1991. 1st edition; of 375 hardcover copies, this is 1/75 of the deluxe edition, signed by author; red leather, as new.   Aronovitz 57-653 1996 $100.00

KREYMBORG, ALFRED   Funnybone Alley. New York: Macaulay Co., 1927. 1st edition with these illustrations; 4to; 7 mounted color plates and numerous black and white illustrations by Boris Zrtzybasheff; blue linen boards over blue morocco spine, gilt panelled spine, raised bands, leather labels.   Appelfeld Gallery 54-127 1996 $300.00

KRIEGER, ALEX D.   Culture Compleses and Chronology in Northern Texas. Austin: University of Texas, Oct. 22,, 1946. 366 pages; pocket with 3 folding diagrams and 1 large folding map; photos and 35 plates; wrappers.   Maggie Lambeth 30-278 1996 $200.00

KROEBER, A. L.   Archaeological Explorations in Peru. Chicago: Field Museum of Natural History, 1926-30. 4to; 2 volumes, 43 pages, 4 figures and 13 plates, 69 pages, 3 figures, 18 plates, 1 table and 1 map; chipped wrappers.   Archaeologia Luxor-4605 1996 $200.00

KROMER, TOM   Waiting for Nothing. New York: Knopf, 1935. 1st edition; fine in dust jacket with few short tears; Rideout p. 297; Hanna 2059.   Captain's Bookshelf 38-137 1996 $150.00

KRUEGER, M.   Pioneer Life in Texas. N.P.: n.d., San Antonio: ca. 1930. 1st edition; 225 pages; presentation copy from author's family to Harry Landa. Howes K269; Herd 1289.   Maggie Lambeth 30-315 1996 $250.00

KRUEGER, M.   Pioneer Life in Texas and Autobiography. San Antonio: n.d., ca. 1930. 1st edition; 226 pages; frontispiece, photos, leatherette, nice. Howes K269; Rader 2192; Herd 1289.   T. A. Swinford 49-665 1996 $350.00

KRUSENSTERN, IEVAN FEDOROVICH   Voyage Round the World in the Years 1803, 1804, 1805 and 1806, by Order of His Imperial Majesty Alexander the First on Board the Ships Nadeshda and Neva, Under the Comman of Captain A. J. von Krusenstern of the Imperial Navy. London: printed by C. Roworth, for John Murray, 1813. 1st edition in English; 4to; 2 volumes in one, as issued; hand colored frontispiece in each volume, folding map, plate; contemporary half calf, spine gilt ('Newby Hall" lettered in gilt on front cover); fine copy, rare; early armorial bookplate of Grantham. Sabin 38331; Howes K272; Hill p. 167; Lada Mocarski 61-62.   Ximenes 109-172 1996 $8,500.00

KRUSSMANN, G.   Manual of Cultivated Broad Leaved Trees and Shrubs. Portland: 1984-85-86. 4to; 3 volumes; pages 1403, 1199 photos and 990 line illustrations; hardbound.   Raymond M. Sutton VII-607 1996 $195.00

KRUTCH, JOSEPH   Samuel Johnson. New York: Holt, 1944. 1st edition; plates; original binding, very good in worn dust jacket; wonderful association copy, Anita Loos's copy with her bookplate and estate stamp, the book was given her by Aldous Huxley, with inscription. Charles Agvent 4-762 1996 $375.00

KUHN, FRITZ   Compositions of Black and White. Paris: 1959. 1st edition; text in English, French and German; 154 illustrations; decorated wrappers, slight chip on wrappers.   J. B. Muns 154-176 1996 $125.00

KUHNEL, ERNST   Cairene Rugs and Others Technically Related, 15th Century - 17th Century. Washington: National Publishing Co., 1957. 4to; 90 pages plus 50 plates; cloth, fine, scarce.   J. M. Cohen 35-55 1996 $685.00

KUMM, H. K. W.   Khnot-Hon-Nofer. The Lands of Ethiopia. London: 1910. tipped in color frontispiece, many other photo illustrations; slight rubbing, good ex-library copy with four neat stamps, light foxing, scarce. David Grayling J95Biggame-124 1996 £50.00

KUNDERA, MILAN   The Joke. New York: Coward mcCann, 1969. 1st American edition; author's first book; outstanding copy, fine in bright, fine, dust jacket without trace of wear.   Thomas Dorn 9-163 1996 $135.00

KUNDIG, JACOB   Dictionarium Affinitatis. Basel: parcus, 1546. 1st edition; 8vo; 16 pages, woodcut title device; light waterstain to head edge; 19th century three quarter vellum; fine, very rare. Not in NUC; VD 16, BM STC, Adams, etc.   Bennett Gilbert LL29-54 1996 $1,250.00

KUNO, TAKESHI   A Guide to Japanese Sculpture. Tokyo: Mayuyama & Co., 1963. 4to; lxix, 38 pages; 100 monochrome plates, several plans and figures; cloth.   Thomas Thorp 489-182 1996 £60.00

KUNZ, GEORGE FREDERICK   The Curious Lore of Precious Stones. Philadelphia: & London: Lippincott, 1913. 1st edition; 4to; 62 pictorial illustrations, blue gilt stamped cloth, as issued, gilt top; fine.   Appelfeld Gallery 54-106 1997 $125.00

KURTZ, BENJAMIN P.   An Original Leaf from the Polycronicon Printed by William Caxton at Westminster in the Year 1482. San Francisco; Book Club of California, 1938. One of 297 copies, signed by Oscar lewis; quarto; (2)ff., 53 pages; tipped in is a leaf from 'Liber Septimus' of the Polycronicon; buckram backed boards, stamped to both covers to a decorative design; very fine, with leaf detached, signed prospectus laid in. Heller & Magee 292; BCC 54.   Bromer Booksellers 87-168 1996 $1,350.00

KURTZ, DONNA CAROL   The Berlin Painter. Oxford: Clarendon Press, 1983. Oblong 4to; xvi, 123 pages, 62 figures; original cloth, dust jacket. Archaeologia Luxor-3594 1996 $125.00

KURTZ, O. H.   Official Route Book of Ringling Brothers' World's Greatest Railroad Shows. Season of 1892. Buffalo: The Courier Co., 1892. 1st edition; 127 pages; frontispiece and illustrations; original full morocco with title in gilt on front cover, some chipping and bumping; very good. Rare.   Michael D. Heaston 23-201 1996 $350.00

KUYKENDALL, IVAN LEE   Ghost Riders of the Mogollon. San Antonio: 1954. 1st edition; book fine, dust jacket worn; rare. Six Guns 1259. Early West 22-167 1996 $495.00

KYNNERSLEY, T. C.   Pratt's Law of Highways...with an Introduction, Explanatory of the Whole Law Upon the Subject. London: Shaw & Sons, Fetter Lane, Printers and Publishers, 1865. 10th edition; green cloth, label rubbed and re-lettered, clean.   Meyer Boswell SL27-138 1996 $125.00

KYNOCH PRESS   Specimens of Types In Use at the Kynoch Press. Corrected to January 1934. (with) Supplement No. 1...showing Types Added During 1934. Kynoch Press, 1934. 8vo; pages 160; (161)-170; vignette wood engravings, initials; original sand buckram with alphabet blocked in blind on upper cover, lightly soiled;   Claude Cox 107-228 1996 £65.00

L

L., J. Poems... London: James Nisbet and Co., J. L. Johnson, Brighton, 1854. 1st edition; 8vo; pages (viii), 58; original brown blindstamped cloth, title in gold on upper cover, gilt edge, initial blank with inscription "Mrs. Aherne June 1st. 1854 with GB's Xtian love", lower inner joint cracked but firm, still good copy.   Simon Finch 24-143 1996 £45.00

LABORDE, M. LEON DE   Journey through Arabia Petraea, to Mount Sinai and the Excavated City of Petra, the Edom of the Prophecies. London: John Murray, 1836. 1st English edition; 8vo; pages xxviii, 331, (1); lithographed frontispiece, 10 plates, 13 wood engraved plates, folding engraved map, numerous wood engravings, browned; contemporary tan calf, backstrip with low raised bands, gilt lettered green label in second compartment, remainder gilt, double gilt fillet border on sides, gilt roll on board edges, blind on turn-ins, marbled endpapers and edges, very good.   Blackwell's B112-173 1996 £165.00

LABOUCHERE, H.   Diary of the Besieged Resident in Paris. London: Hurst & Blackett, 1871. 2nd edition; tall 8vo; viii, 391, (4) pages ads; 1 volume; original purple cloth, spine faded to tan, otherwise near fine. David Mason 71-68 1996 $160.00

LA CHAMBRE, MARIN CUREAU DE   The Art How to Know Men. London: printed by T. R. for Thomas Dring, 1665. 8vo; (xxx), 330, (14) pages; engraved frontispiece; late 19th century polished calf with gilt spine and gilt dentelles, possibly lacking an extra engraved titlepage, joints chafed, front hinge cracked, margins cropped; good, clean copy; scarce. Wing L128.   John Gach 150-268 1996 $650.00

LACKINGTON, JAMES   The Confessions of J. Lackington, Late Bookseller, at the Temple of the Muses, in a Series of Letters to a Friend. New York: John Wilson and Daniel Hitt, for the Methodist Connection, 1808. 2nd American edition; 12mo; 189, (3) pages, 2 pages ads at back; contemporary calf; very pretty copy. American Imprints 15385.   Kenneth Karmiole 1NS-144 1996 $150.00

LACLOS, PIERRE AMBROISE FRANCOIS CHODERLOS DE 1741-1803   Les Liaisons Dangereuses. Paris: Le Vasseur et Cie, 1934. 4to; pages 1 blank, half title, decorated title, (i), 219, (i blank), 10 finely colored pochoir plates, 1 headpiece, 1 blank, half title, decorated title, 218, (i, imprint), 1 head piece, 10 finely colored pochoir plates; publisher's titled and decorated wrappers, glassine covers and slipcase; fine.   Sotheran PN32-173 1996 £2,500.00

LA CROIX, M. B.   The Married woman's Private Medical Companion. Albany: ca. 1870. 56th edition; 18mo; 300 pages, (4) pages, numerous illustrations; original printed wrappers, very nice. Not in Himes; not in NUC.   M & S Rare Books 60-448 1996 $350.00

LACROIX, PAUL   The Arts in the Middle Ages and the Renaissance. London: ca. 1880. 4to; 464 pages; 12 superb chromolithographic plates by F. Klelrhoven, over 400 excellent wood engravings; red cloth, elaborate gilt decorated, very good.   K Books 442-324 1996 £70.00

LACTANTIUS FIRMIANUS, LUCIUS CAELIUS   Divinaru(m) Institutionu(m). Lyon: Jean de Tournes, 1587. 16mo; pages 785, (45), title set within wide woodcut floral border, slight worming and soiling; all edges gilt and beautifully guaffred with wide interlaced floral design, accentuated with red paint, early full red morocco, tooled in blind, each board with blind ownership stamp of an unidentified Cardinal, old repairs to spine; from the library of Count Henry Chardon de Brialles.   Family Album Tillers-377 1996 $400.00

LACTANTIUS FIRMIANUS, LUCIUS CAELIUS   L. Coelii Lactantii Firmiani Divinarum Institutionum Libri Septem... Venice: In aedibus Haeredum Aldi, et Andreae Soceri, March, 1535. Small 8vo; pages (16), 328, (12), 47, (44), + 3 original blanks, printer's device on title, italic type throughout, numerous old ownerships and annotations; old half vellum over decorative paste paper boards, contemporary ms. shelving title on bottom edge. Adams L22; UCLA IIIa 243a; Brunet III.736. Renouard 113.2. Family Album Tillers-376 1996 $750.00

LACTANTIUS FIRMIANUS, LUCIUS CAELIUS   Opera. Lyons: Soubron, 1594. 16mo; 879 pages, 21ff; contemporary Roman brown calf, covers gilt with outer double rules, enclosing panels at head and foot, centre decorated with large and small gyrate, leafy and other small tools, central panel with arms below a helmet and leafy spray, spine gilt in 4 panels, plain endpapers, all edges gilt, gilt and gauffered, upper cover lettered B. Curtus: R/Acad. Parth, lower cover N. Nucctus/Acad. Parth. Small repairs to tie-holes and spine, corners soft, most unusual Roman binding with some elements of fanfare, coats of arms (each different) are those of B. Curtus and N. Nucctus of the Parthenopean Academy; later the copy of J. R. Abbey, Abbey Sale 22 vi. 1965 lot 426 to E. P. Goldschmidt.   Marlborough 160-4 1996 £2,250.00

LACY, GEORGE   Pictures of Travel, Sport and Adventure. London: Pearson, 1899. 8vo; pages xvi, 420; 30 plates; pictorial cloth, lightly rubbed. Theal p. 169.   Richard Adelson W94/95-235 1996 $130.00

THE LADIES Charity School-House Roll of Highgate; or a Subscription of Many Noble, Well Disposed Ladies for the Easie Carrying Of It On. London: 1670. 8vo; 292, (2) pages, drophead title, wanting the four plates; very attractive contemporary London binding in black morocco, richly gilt with all over gilt tooling of 'drawer-handles', tulips, rosettes, dots, pointed leaves, etc. repeated on lower cover, spine gilt in compartments, with presentation "To MADM SEMENS" in gilt in panel on upper cover, joints little rubbed.   John Drury 82-23 1996 £500.00

LAENNEC, R.   A Treatise On the Diseases of the Chest and On Mediate Auscultation... New York: S. & W. Wood; Philadelphia: Thomas, Cowperwaite & Co., 1838. 4th and final American edition, from the 3rd French edition; 8vo; 2 lithographed plates, rather foxed; recent half calf; signature of Fredk. Peterson on title.   Maggs Bros. Ltd. 1190-444 1996 £220.00

LAFAYETTE, MARIE MADELEINE PLOCHE DE LA VERGNE, COMTESSE DE The Princess of Cleves. London: printed for R. Bentley and M. Mages, 1679. 1st edition in English; 8vo; (359 pages, 6 pages ads); contemporary mottled calf, some overall wear, few small paper flaws, expert minor repair to several pages and back cover, all in all, a very good copy, bound without blanks or flyleaves at beginning and end, but complete with a prelim license leaf and 3 terminal leaves of ads; rare; signature on titlepage of Elizabeth Wroth, dated dec. 24, 1680; 18th century ownership inscription of Elizabeth Oxenham. Rare. Bazin 59; Wing L169.   Paulette Rose 16-200 1996 $4,000.00

LAFAYETTE, MARIE MADELEINE PLOCHE DE LA VERGNE, COMTESSE DE La Princesse de Cleves. Paris: la Compagnie des Libraires Associes, 1741. 8vo; 2 volumes, (204, 209 pages and final approbation leaf); contemporary calf, gilt decorated spine (rubbed), binding wear; still a decent, bright copy. Bazin 68.   Paulette Rose 16-201 1996 $275.00

LA FONTAINE, JEAN DE 1621-1695   The Amours of Cupid and Psyche. London: printed for R. Withy, at the Dunciad in Cornhill, 1749. Crown 8vo; 2 volumes, 31 copper engravings; contemporary sprinkled calf, very fine; armorial bookplate of John Middleton.   H. M. Fletcher 121-100 1996 £2,750.00

LA FONTAINE, JEAN DE 1621-1695   Fables. Paris: A. A. Renouard, 1811. 8vo; 2 volumes; 266 illustrations engraved after Oudry, printed using Duplat's newly patented process for printing; contemporary black straight grained morocco with double gilt border on covers, spine with 3 wide raised bands on which there is gilt decoration and some blind tooling, much earlier nearly invisible rebacking, morocco title and volume number labels, handsome set. Twyman p. 8; Ray no. 175. Book Block 32-4 1996 $2,250.00

LA FONTAINE, JEAN DE 1621-1695   Fables. New York: Limited Editions Club, 1930. Limited to 1500 copies; 8vo; 2 volumes, copper engravings by R. Ruzicka, signed by artist; original binding, spines little sunned; near fine in broken case.   Charles Agvent 4-812 1996 $100.00

LA FONTAINE, JEAN DE 1621-1695   Fables. Paris: Les Heures Claires, 1966. Number 139 of a limited edition of 150 copies on velin de Rives; 4to; 3 volumes; 56 wood engraved illustrations and numerous floral tailpieces by Henri Lemarie all printed in color; with 3 suites of the illustrations, one in color, one in black and one in black with illustration and remarque printed from an etched plate; each volume also has a decomposition of one illustration for which an average of 30 different blocks were made; unsewn in original wrappers, 6 volumes, including the companion set of suites in 6 card folders and slipcases, very fine set. Barbara Stone 70-134 1996 £525.00

LA FONTAINE, JEAN DE 1621-1695   Poeme du Quinquina, et Autres Ourages en Vers. Paris: Chez Denis Thierry...et Claude Barbin.. 1682. 1st edition; 2nd issue; 12mo; 2 leaves + 242 pages, lacking L2 blank, 3 cancels denoting the second issue are at A11, B1 (mis-signed E) and G10, slight browning on some leaves, old speckled vellum, split in lower front joint. Tchermerzine VI p. 403.   H. M. Fletcher 121-64 1996 £350.00

LA FONTAINE, JEAN DE 1621-1695   Tales and Novels and Verse.
London: in the Year, 1735. 1st edition; 8vo; pages (ii), vii, (i), xii, 252,
frontispiece, vignettes and head and tailpieces; contemporary calf, lacks
label, double gilt bands, rules, sides also bordered in blind, joints just
cracked but firm, area of damage at foot of spine, consequent very faint,
unobtrusive browning of extreme lower inner corners, O4 with marginal
tear not affecting text, otherwise very good copy internally, clean and
fresh.   Simon Finch   24-144   1996 £125.00

LA FONTAINE, JEAN DE 1621-1695   Tales and Novels in Verse. Paris:
J. Lemonnyer, 1884. Re-issue of the Fermier Genereaux edition; 8vo; 2
volumes; 85 engravings after drawings by Eisen; three quarter maroon
morocco, gilt emblematic tooling on spines, raised bands, gilt tops by
Riviere; attractive set.   Appelfeld Gallery 54-128   1996 $300.00

LA FONTAINE, JEAN DE 1621-1695   Oeuvres Complettes... Paris: chez
Lefevre, 1814. 8vo; 6 volumes; all half titles present, frontispiece, 23
copperplates; half green straight grain morocco, green cloth sides,
spines attractively decorated in gilt, top edge gilt, marbled endpapers, by
Bickers; very nice.   Sotheran PN32-25   1996 £598.00

LA HIRE, M. DE   L'Art de Charpenterie de Mathurin Jousse, Architects
& Ingenieur de la Ville de la Fleche. Paris: Jombert, 1751. 3rd edition;
folio; (viii), 212 pages, 9 folding engraved plates, 1 unnumbered folding
woodcut plate and many woodcut illustrations; contemporary full mottled
calf, corners and head and foot of spine bumped; library label and
bookplate of Marbury Hall.   Elton Engineering 10-83   1996 £680.00

LAINEZ, MANUEL MUJICA   Cantata De Bomarzo. Plain Wrapper Press,
1981. One of 83 copies, signed by author and artist; 16 1/4 x 11 inches;
(18) leaves of text; 7 color etchings, including 2 plates by Luciano de
Vita, with separate texts in Spanish and English; original black morocco
backed paper boards, gilt titling on spine, edges untrimmed, in
publisher's fine matching morocco and paper slipcase; virtually mint.
Phillip J. Pirages 33-425   1996 $550.00

LAING, S.   Prehistoric Remains of Caithness... London: Williams and
Norgate, 1866. 1st edition; 8vo; pages 160, (1 table, 8 ads); frontispiece,
68 figures; original cloth, gilt, joints splitting, little bumped, front hinge
cracking; rare.   R.F.G. Hollett 76-144   1996 £120.00

LAING, SAMUEL   Observations on the Social and Political State of the
European People in 1848 and 1849. London: Longman, 1850. 1st edition;
8vo; xvi, 534 pages; contemporary blue calf, spine fully gilt with raised
bands and contrasting label, marbled edges; handsome copy.
Goldsmiths 36756; Williams I 234.   John Drury 82-137   1996 £90.00

LAING, SETON   The Great City Frauds of Cole, Davidson and Gordon,
Fully Exposed. London: published by the author, 1856. 4th edition;
modern three quarter morocco, bit rubbed; quite good copy.   Meyer
Boswell SL25-137   1996 $275.00

LAKE, STUART N.   Wyatt Earp, Frontier Marshal. New York: 1931. 1st
edition; 1st issue; 392 pages; photos; covers bright, fine. Six Guns 1270;
Dobie 44 #33.   Early West 22-171   1996 $110.00

LAL, MOHAN   Life of the Amir Dost Mohammed Khan of Kabul; with
His Political Proceedings Towards the English, Russian and Persian
Governments... London: Longman, Brown, Green and Longmans,
Paternoster Row, 1846. 1st edition; 8vo; 2 volumes; 1-399, 1-498 pages;
frontispiece to volume 1, 18 engraved portraits on India paper and 1
large folding map; half calf and marbled boards, rebacked, corners and
joints worn, morocco labels to spines, edges and endpapers uniformly
marbled; ex-libris Arnold Toynbee with his ink signature to prelim of both
volumes, some offsetting to title of volume 1, armorial bookplate to front
pastedown.   Beeleigh Abbey BA56-86   1996 £450.00

LA LIVE D'EPINAY, LOUISE FLORENCE PETRONILLE DE   The
Conversations of Emily. London: printed for Darton, Harvey and Darton;
Darton, Harvey & Co., 1815. 1st edition of this abridgment; 12mo; iv,
270, (2 ad) pages, frontispiece; original quarater roan.   James
Burmester 29-84   1996 £75.00

LA LOUPE, VINCENT DE   In Cornelii Taciti Annalium Libros XVI. Paris:
Robert Stephanus (Estienne), April, 1556. 8vo; pages (7), 96; disbound;
not in Schreiber.   Family Album Tillers-378   1996 $250.00

LAMAR, MIRABEAU B.   Calendar of Lamar Papers. Austin: 1914.
Original wrappers, stapled, worn.   W. M. Morrison 436-128b 1996
$150.00

LAMB, CAROLINE 1785-1828   Glenarvon. London: printed for Henry
Colburn, 1816. 3rd edition; 12mo; 3 volumes; engraved half titles in each
volume; contemporary maroon half calf, spines gilt decorated with floral
frame, contrasting green title labels, marbled boards, with 2 leaves of
engraved music in volume 2 and final ad leaf in volume 3; very nice in
lovely 'lady's binding'; the Joyce Cary copy, (with his? notes on free
endpapers). NCBEL III 740.   Paulette Rose 16-204   1996 $850.00

LAMB, CHARLES 1775-1834   Album Verses, with a Few Others.
London: Edward Moxon, 1830. 1st edition; 8vo; pages vii, (i) blank, 150,
(i) ad; 19th century brown morocco, French fillet gilt border to sides,
spine in compartments, raised bands, gilt rules, lettering and date, 4
compartments with urn with bird perched on top and leafy sprays gilt,
top edge gilt, inner dentelles, gilt, by Bedford, bookplates; excellent
copy. Ashley III p. 52.   Simon Finch 24-147   1996 £420.00

LAMB, CHARLES 1775-1834   Bon-Mots of Charles Lamb and Douglas
Jerrold. London: J. M. Dent, 1893. 1st edition; very small 8vo; vignette
on half title, 2 portraits, decorated title, 9 plates, 60 text illustrations by
Aubrey Beardsley; brown floral endpapers, cream pictorial cloth, gilt,
small maroon vignette, top edge gilt; browning on endpapers, some
bubbling on cloth, light wear.   Robin Greer 94A-14   1996 £120.00

LAMB, CHARLES 1775-1834   Final Memorials...Consisting Chiefly of His
Letters Not Before Published, with Sketches of Some of His
Companions. London: Edward Moxon, 1848. 1st edition; 8vo; 2 volumes,
pages xii, 223, (i); (iv), 239; late 19th century half red crushed morocco,
red cloth sides, spines gilt lettered direct "Lamb's Works" above title
and volume numbers, marbled endpapers, top edge gilt, by Root and
son, joints rubbed; good copy.   Simon Finch 24-148   1996 £85.00

LAMB, CHARLES 1775-1834   The King and Queen of Hearts; with the
Rogueries of the Knavew Who Stole the Queen's Pies. London: c. 1900.
Facsimile reprint of London 1809 edition; 15 fine colored engravings;
original stiff wrappers bound in; fine Osborne Collection p. 100.
Trebizond 39-36   1996 $125.00

LAMB, CHARLES 1775-1834   The Letters of Charles Lamb, with a
Sketch of His Life. London: Edward Moxon, 1837. 1st edition; 8vo; 2
volumes, x, 335; (iv), 338 pages; engraved portraits, contemporary dark
green mottled calf, gilt spines, spines very lightly rubbed and faded; nice
set with ownership inscriptions of L Darwin (possibly Leonard, Charles
Darwin's Son) and E. Catherine Darwin.   James Burmester 29-85
1996 £90.00

LAMB, CHARLES 1775-1834   The Letters of Charles Lamb... Boston:
Bibliophile Society, 1905. Limited to 470 sets; Volume 1 is 15 x 9.5
inches; others 9.5 x 7 inches; 5 volumes; etched portraits, facsimiles,
etc.; boards, uncut, spine very darkened, dust jacket volume 1 stained,
some slipcases present but rubbed and some broken.   John K. King
77-364 1996 $175.00

LAMB, CHARLES 1775-1834   Original Letters &c. of Sir John Falstaff
and His Friends... London: for the author & pub. by Messrs. G. G. and
J. Robinsons, J. Debrett, 1796. 1st edition; 12mo; pages (iii)-ssiv, 123,
engraved frontispiece; modern half calf, gilt edges; good. Thomson III.
Simon Finch 24-145 1996 £650.00

LAMB, CHARLES 1775-1834   Satan in Search of a Wife: With the
Whole Process of His Courtship and Marriage, and Who Danced at the
Wedding. London: Edward Moxon, 1831. 1st edition; 8vo; 2 volumes;
engraved frontispiece, engraved plates, owner's bookplate to front
pastedown of both volumes, binders ticket to front f.e.p. of volume 2,
bound by Carss & Co., Glasgow, half green morocco and green
buckram boards, corners slightly bumped, elaborate gilt tooling to
compartments of panelled spine, raised bands, marbled edges; fine,
handsome copy. Sadlier 1400.   Beeleigh Abbey BA56-156   1996
£65.00

LAMB, CHARLES 1775-1834   Specimens of English Dramatic Poets
Who Lived About the Time of Shakespeare... London: J. M. Dent, 1893.
One of the 150 extra illustrated large paper editions; 2 volumes; partially
unopened, uncut, shelf soil, very good, tight copies.   Lyman Books
21-527 1996 $100.00

LAMB, CHARLES 1775-1834   Tales from Shakespeare. London: T. C.
and E. C. Jack/Toronto: Morgan and Co., 1905. 8vo; pages xii, 324;
frontispiece, 20 color paltes by N. M. Price; decorated endpapers and
gilt and blind stamped covers, covers slightly scuffed, else very good;
signed by artist on half title, with ALS from artist on Carlton Studio
letterhead to Mary M. Hendrie of Hamilton.   Hugh Anson-Cartwright
87-354 1996 $200.00

LAMB, CHARLES 1775-1834   Tales from Shakespeare. London: Dent,
1909. 1st edition thus; this revised edition has 12 color plates as well as
line drawings by Arthur Rackham, the plates in the earlier edition were
not colored; half red morocco, gilt, minor wear to joints and edges, very
good.   Charles Agvent 4-815   1996 $175.00

LAMB, CHARLES 1775-1834 The Works. London: Volume I. by Marchant; Volume II by Renell, for C. and J. Ollier, 1818. 1st collected edition; small 8vo; 2 volumes, pages ix, (iii), 291, (i), (vi), 259, (i), (ii) publisher's ads dated June 1818; later blue crushed morocco, sides ruled in gilt with French fillet, quatrefoils in corners, spines gilt with quatrefoil designs in compartments, gilt lettered direct, date at foot, gilt inner dentiles, marbled endpapers, silk bookmarks, top edge gilt, others uncut, by W. Root & Son; spines slightly sunned, one or two trivial spots; very good copy; bookplate of C. H. Wilkinson. Thomson SLI; Ashley III 49. Simon Finch 24-146 1996 £350.00

LAMB, CHARLES 1775-1834 The Works of Charles Lamb. London: ca. 1900. 6 volumes, over 2500 pages; well illustrated; red cloth, gilt decorated, very good. K Books 441-308 1996 £55.00

LAMB, CHARLES 1775-1834 The Works. London: Methuen & Co., 1903-05. 8vo; 7 volumes; frontispiece to each volume, numerous plates and illustrations; original red cloth, paper labels to spines, top edge gilt, spines sunned and slightly rubbed, paper labels soiled, otherwise very good set with spare labels tipped in at rear of each volume; from the library of Algernon Charles Swinburne, also from the collections of Sir James Stevenson, Sir Winston Churchill and Randolph Churchill, with bookplates. Sotheran PN32-5 1996 £1,995.00

LAMB, CHARLES 1775-1834 The Works. London: Dent, 1903. 8vo; 12 volumes, colored frontispiece portrait to volume 1, frontispieces and illustrations by C. E. Brock; original blue cloth backstrips, oatmeal cloth sides, backstrips gilt blocked with overall art nouveau inspired design, titled at head within frame, author's monogram gilt blocked on front covers, some soiling to sides, top edge gilt, remainder untrimmed, overall very good. Blackwell's B112-174 1996 £95.00

LAMB, CHARLES 1775-1834 Works. London: Macmillan, 1904. Reprint; 8vo; 7 volumes; half green morocco, 5 raised bands, gilt ruled borders and spine panels enclosing gold stamped decorative devices, date stamped at bottom of spine, spines evenly sunned to a pleasing brown; near fine. Charles Agvent 4-814 1996 $350.00

LAMB, CHARLES 1775-1834 The Works... London: J. M. Dent & Sons, Ltd., New York: E. P. Dutton & Co., 1914-16. 8vo; 12 volumes; portraits, illustrations and facsimiles; contemporary half blue crushed morocco, spines gilt, blue cloth sides, marbled endpapers, top edge gilt, others uncut; fine set. cf. Ashley III 55. Simon Finch 24-149 1996 £850.00

LAMB, MARTHA J. History of the City of New York. New York: A. S. Barnes, 1877-80. Presumed 1st edition; 2 volumes, xiv, 11-786; xvi, 11-820 pages; numerous plates; cloth, spine tips somewhat frayed, otherwise solid and very good. Metacomet Books 54-56 1996 $175.00

LAMB, W. The World Ends. London: Dent, 1937. 1st edition; 3 wood engravings by John Farleigh; bright, very good copy in attractive dust jacket with some inner reinforcement and some wear and tear. Aronovitz 57-661 1996 $125.00

LAMBARD, WILLIAM Archion, or, A Commentary Upon the High Courts of Justice in England. London: printed for Daniel Frere, 1635. contemporary calf, neatly rebacked, worn, sound. Meyer Boswell SL26-139 1996 $750.00

LAMBARDE, WILLIAM A Perambulation of Kent: Conteining the Description, Hystorie and Cutomes of that Shyre. London: Edm. Bollisant, 1596. 2nd edition; small 4to; lacks map of kingdoms, folding map of Beacons supplied in excellent facsimile on old paper, title within wide typographic border, lower corner of last 6 leaves torn away, just touching letters on two leaves, some dampstaining throughout, worsening at rear, few leaves with slight worming in outer margin, few contemporary marginal notes; 18th century quarter calf, recent red morocco label; generally good. STC 15176. Ian Wilkinson 95/1-118 1996 £390.00

LAMBERT & GERMAN NAVAL ARCHITECTS Floating Equipment. Montreal: 1932. Quarto; 100 pages; hundreds of photos, deck plans, views; original decorated cloth, very nice. very scarce. Stephen Lunsford 45-88 1996 $275.00

LAMBERT, JOHN Travels through Canada and the United States of North America in the Years 1806, 1807 and 1808. London: printed for Baldwin, Cradock and Joy, W. Blackwood Edinburgh &... 1816. 3rd edition; 8vo; 2 volumes; 544, 532 pages, ink staining to pages 287-8 volume 2, top right hand corner of page 308 volume 1 torn away without loss to text; large folding colored map frontispiece, 16 aquatints, colored map, sepia aquatints, all have some foxing; contemporary half calf, gilt decoration to spines, red morocco labels, marbled boards, red speckled edges, bookseller's ticket to front pastedown of volume 1; Abbey Travel 613; Sabin 38735; Gagnon I 1926. Beeleigh Abbey BA56-87 1996 £650.00

LAMI, EUGENE Voyage en Angleterre. Paris: Firmin Didot & Lami Denozan; London: Colnaghi & Charles Tilt, 1829-30. 1st edition; folio; pages (viii), 25 fine hand colored lithograph plates on 24 leaves by Villain after Lami and Monnier, text leaves foxed and stained, few small closed tears to margins of plates, not affecting image, little marginal dust marking, but plates themselves fresh and clean. Recent half red morocco, spine and all edges gilt. Abbey Scenery 34; Ray 139; Colas 1748. Sotheran PN32-26 1996 £1,650.00

LAMM, CARL JOHAN Cotton in Mediaeval Textiles of the Near East. Paris: Librairie Orientaliste Paul Geuthner, 1937. 4to; 265 pages; 71 illustrations and 24 photographic plates; wrappers; very good. Creswell 1205. J. M. Cohen 35-57 1996 $300.00

LAMOND, H. The Sea-Trout. A Study in Natural History. London: 1916. 4to; pages xi, 219, 9 color and 38 plain plates; cloth, gilt, unopened; 2 short tears in bottom of plate 1. John Henly 27-49 1996 £75.00

LA MOTTE FOUQUE, FRIEDRICH HEINRICH KARL, FREIHERR DE 1777-1843 Undine and Other Tales. Leipzig: 1867. Small 8vo; pages (6), 361; full green crushed morocco (backstrip and edges faded to tan), 6 sections of backstrip lettered and decorated in gold wtih four groups of three 3 pointed leaves connected by intertwined stems within ogee border, in each compartment, edges ruled and turn-in triple-ruled with leaf and dot decoration at corners, signed "The Doves Bindery 1894"; contemporary inscripiton to Cecil Boyle with his bookplate carelessly pasted to endpaper. Claude Cox 107-17 1996 £180.00

LA MOTTE FOUQUE, FRIEDRICH HEINRICH KARL, FREIHERR DE 1777-1843 Undine. London: William Heinemann, 1909. 1st edition deluxe, limited to only 1000 numbered copies, signed by artist; 4to; pages viii, 136; 13 colored plates by Arthur Rackham, mounted at large and protected behind tissue guards, half title and two leaves of text evenly lightly browned, otherwise fine in recent full dark blue morocco, gilt with decorative gilt roll to sides, spine ruled and lettered gilt with raised bands, top edge gilt, others uncut, marbled endpapers. Sotheran PN32-143 1996 £498.00

LA MOTTE FOUQUE, FRIEDRICH HEINRICH KARL, FREIHERR DE 1777-1843 Undine. London: 1909. One of 1000 numbered copies, signed by artist; large 4to; viii, 136 pages, 15 mounted color plates plus text illustrations by Arthur Rackham; full vellum, corner slightly nicked, lacking fragile silk ties, else very good, clean. Joseph J. Felcone 64-32 1996 $600.00

LA MOTTE FOUQUE, FRIEDRICH HEINRICH KARL, FREIHERR DE 1777-1843 Undine. London: William Heinemann, 1909. 1st edition thus; 4to; 15 mounted color plates by Arthur Rackham; modern linen boards over maroon morocco spine, raised bands, leather labels. Appelfeld Gallery 54-153 1996 $250.00

L'AMOUR, LOUIS The Californios. New York: Saturday Review Press/Dutton, 1974. 1st edition; very nice, quite scarce. Ken Lopez 74-253 1996 $200.00

L'AMOUR, LOUIS Hopalong Cassidy and the Rustlers of West Fork. London: Hodder & Stoughton, 1951. 1st English edition; fine in nearly fine dust jacket with small faint stain touching the top corners of flaps; scarce. Between the Covers 42-254 1996 $285.00

L'AMOUR, LOUIS Hopalong Cassidy, Trouble-Shooter. London: Hodder & Sstoughton, 1953. 1st English edition; foxing to fore edge, endpapers and at extremities of some pages, thus very good in price clipped, very good plus dust jacket with couple of short tears, some light wear at crown. Between the Covers 42-255 1996 $250.00

L'AMOUR, LOUIS Over on the Dry Side. New York: Dutton, 1975. 1st edition; good copy in good dust jacket. Book Time 2-242 1996 $100.00

L'AMOUR, LOUIS The Walking Drum. New York: Bantam, 1984. One of 500 numbered copies, signed by author; fine in full leather like substance and slipcase, as issue. Between the Covers 42-256 1996 $300.00

LANCASTER, JOSEPH Improvements in Education, As It Respects the Industrious Classes of the Community... London: Darton & Harvey, 1803. 2nd edition; half title, later blue wrappers, spine strengthened, good, clean copy. Jarndyce 103-518 1996 £200.00

LANCASTER, JOSEPH   Improvements in Education as It Respects the Industrious Classes of the Community... London: Darton & Harvey; W. Hatchard, 1805. 3rd edition; subscriber's list, 4 pages ads; corner margin of title repaired, with Education Department stamps; uncut in boards, label.   Jarndyce 103-519   1996 £180.00

LANCASTER, OSBERT   The Letters of Mercurius. London: John Murray, 1970. Number 24 of 40 copies on handmade paper, signed by author; titlepage designed by author; buckram backed patterned paper boards, top edge gilt, other edges untrimmed; fine in original cellophane dust jacket.   Ulysses 39-342   1996 £250.00

LANCASTER, OSBERT   Sailing to Byzantium - an Architectural Companion. London: John Murray Publishers Ltd., 1969. One of 50 numbered copies signed by author; numerous full page color illustrations and black and white drawings by author; top edge gilt, buckram backed marbled paper boards, spine slightly browned, tail of spine slightly bumped, near fine in matching slipcase.   Ulysses 39-341   1996 £225.00

LANDAU, HORACE DE, BARON   Catalogue of Very Important Manuscripts and Printed Books: Selected from the Renowned Library Formed by Baron Horace de Landau (1824-1903). Sotheby's, 1948. Limited edition, one of 100 special copipes with extra plates and with buyer's names and prices printed in red; 4to; vi, 82 pages, 5 page index; 61 plates, several other illustrations and figures in text; contemporary half calf gilt edges, original wrappers bound in, corners rubbed. Thomas Thorp 489-173   1996 £280.00

LANDEN, JOHN   The Residual Analysis; a New Branch of the Algebraic Art of Very Extensive Use, Both in Pure Mathematics and Natural Philosophy. (with) A Discourse Concerning the Residual Analysis. London: for the author/London: for J. Nourse, 1764/58. 1st editions; 4to; viii, 128 pages, 5 folding plates; 43, (1) pages; contemporary full morocco, rebacked, original spine laid down, very lightly browned, fine copy; 2nd title lightly foxed, very good. Cajori p. 247.   Edwin V. Glaser 121-179   1996 $1,200.00

LANDER, RICHARD   Journal of an Expedition to Explore the Course and Terimination of the Niger; with a Narrative of a Voyage Down that River to Its Termination. London: Thomas Tegg, 1845. 3rd edition; small 8vo; xlvii, 319, vii, 398 pages; 2 volumes; engravings and maps; contemporary half leather, boards, raised bands.   David Mason 71-10   1996 $180.00

LANDER, SAMUEL   Our Own School Arithmetic. Greensboro: Published by Sterling, Cambell & Albright/Richmond: W. Hargrave White, 1863. 12mo; 223, (1) pages; original printed paper over boards chipped along edges; text shows some browning, accession numbers on bottom margin of preface, still good. Crandall 4061; Parrish & Willingham 7761. Andrew Cahan 47-55   1996 $200.00

LANDON, LAETITIA ELIZABETH   The Improvisatrice and Other Poems. London: printed for Hurst, Robinson and Co., Archibald Constable & Co... 1824. 1st edition; 8vo; frontispiece, five plates, half title present; contemporary calf, wide gilt borders, spine and inner dentelles gilt. fine in attractive binding. Jackson p. 503; CBEL III 531.   Ximenes 108-236   1996 $175.00

LANDON, LAETITIA ELIZABETH   Complete Works. Boston: Phillips, Sampson, 1854. Large, very thick 8vo; 2 volumes in 1, pages 1045; full pebbled morocco, elaborate blindstamped covers, raised bands, gilt, all edges gilt, sound. CBEL III 294.   Hartfield 48-L52   1996 $165.00

LANDON, LETITIA ELIZABETH   The Fate of Adelaide, a Swiss Romantic Tale; and Other Poems. London: John Warren, 1821. 1st edition; small 8vo; (iv, 154 pages); contemporary dark blue calf, gilt decorated spine, all edges gilt, very small chip at head of spine, otherwise most attractive copy. Davis & Joyce, Poetry by women to 1900 3162.   Paulette Rose 16-206   1996 $225.00

LANDOR, ARNOLD HENRY SAVAGE 1865-1924   Across Widest Africa. London: Hurst & Blackett, 1907. 8vo; 2 volumes; pages xv, 396, 2 ads; xii, 511, 1 ads; folding map, photos, original blue cloth, rubbed, some light foxing.   Richard Adelson W94/95-100   1996 $260.00

LANDOR, ARNOLD HENRY SAVAGE 1865-1924   Across the Unknown South America. London: Hodder, 1913. 4to; 2 volumes, 2 maps, 8 color plates, 260 illustrations; slight foxing to few pages.   Petersfield Bookshop FH58-428   1996 £65.00

LANDOR, ARNOLD HENRY SAVAGE 1865-1924   China and Allies. London: William Heinemann, 1901. 8vo; 2 volumes; xxiv, 382, 32 ads; xx, 446 pages; 8 maps, 53 plates, text illustrations; modern dark blue cloth, red leather labels.   Richard Adelson W94/95-101   1996 $285.00

LANDOR, ARNOLD HENRY SAVAGE 1865-1924   In the Forbidden Land. New York: Harper & Bros., 1899. 8vo; 2 volumes; pages xviii, 307; xiv, 250; folding map, 8 color plates; original pictorial cloth, lightly rubbed. Richard Adelson W94/95-99   1996 $200.00

LANDOR, WALTER SAVAGE 1775-1864   Epicurus, Leontion and Ternissa. London: Hacon & Ricketts, 1896. Limited to 210 copies; 8vo; pages xcix, printed in red and black on handmade paper with elaborate woodcut initials and borders (in red) by Ricketts, slight rubbing at extremities, but very good, unopened; original boards, paper labels; bookplate of Gwendolen Jefferson. Tomkinson 32.   Claude Cox 107-177   1996 £130.00

LANDOR, WALTER SAVAGE 1775-1864   Gebir, Count Julian, and Other Poems. London: Moxon, 1831. 1st collected edition; 8vo; full green calf, gilt; occasional foxing, catalogue description laid down to f.f.e.p.; near fine. Tipped in is a 2 page ALS by Landor as well as an original 10 line epitaph apparently also in Landor's hand.   Charles Agvent 4-816 1996 $500.00

LANDOR, WALTER SAVAGE 1775-1864   Imaginary Conversations. Verona: Limited Editions Club, 1936. Number 904 from 1500 copies, signed by Hans Mardersteig; full decorative cloth and dust jacket, spine of jacket darkened, else fine in publisher's slipcase.   Hermitage SP95-1004   1996 $150.00

LANDOR, WALTER SAVAGE 1775-1864   Pericles and Aspasia. London: Saunders and Otley, 1836. 1st edition; 8vo; 2 volumes; original green backed boards, uncut, printed paper labels; very good set without major fault and quite tight of case, in lush crimson morocco box; boards and labels show rub and wear which is usual to this period of publisher's binding, still very good; the superior H. Bradley Martin-John Drinkwater copy, originally Edward Fitzgerald's copy with his ownership inscription in each volume.   Lakin & Marley 3-28   1996 $1,000.00

LANDOR, WALTER SAVAGE 1775-1864   Poems from the Arabic and Persian... Warwick: printed by H. Sharpe, High St.; and sold by Messrs Rivington, 1800. 1st edition; one of 100 copies, 1st issue; 4to; pages (vi), 13, (1); disbound, stitched, untrimmed, as issued; very good. Tinker 1467; Wise & Wheeler 6; Wise Landor Lib. pp. 11/12.   Blackwell's B112-175   1996 £950.00

LANDRUM, GRAHAM   An Illustrated History of Grayson County, Texas. Fort Worth: 1960. 1st edition; 180 pages, map, frontispiece, photos, padded cloth; nice, very scarce. 6 Guns 1276.   T. A. Swinford 49-675   1996 $135.00

LANDSCAPE Illustrations of the Waverley Novels. London: Charles Tilt, 1832. 1st edition; large 4to; volume 1 only; 38 fine steel engraved views worn half leather, old marginal stain to lower margin on most views, not affecting image, most tissue guards present.   Charles Agvent 4-989 1996 $150.00

LANDSEER, EDWIN   The Landseer Series of Picture Books Containing Sixteen Coloured illustrations after Sir Edward Landseer. London: Thomas Nelson, n.d. 1882. 4to; an untearable book, with illustrations mounted on linen; original brown buckram with Landseer illustration on upper cover; very rare. Osborne p. 206.   Charles W. Traylen 117-239   1996 £180.00

LANDSEER, JOHN   Lectures on the Art of Engraving, Delivered at the Royal Institution of Great Britain. London: printed for Longman, Hurst, Rees and Orme, 1807. 1st edition; 8vo; original boards, uncut and unopened, hinges cracked, printed paper label; nice.   Anthony W. Laywood 108-193   1996 £175.00

LANDWEHR, JOHN   Studies in Dutch Books with Coloured Plates Published 1662-1875. The Hague: Dr. W. Junk, 1976. 1st edition; 4to; x, 605 pages, 16 full page color plates; cloth, dust jacket, fine.   The Bookpress 75-316   1996 $185.00

LANE, WILLIAM   Poems on the Following Subjects: Abram and Lot...Detached Pieces, Chiefly Wrote on Particular Occasions and to Particular Persons... Reading: for the author, & sold by Snare & Co., Reading; Champan... 1798. 1st and only edition; 8vo; pages 112, 4 page list of subscribers, without errata slip found in some copies; contemporary tree calf, lately rebacked to style, corners worn, little light spotting, most noticeable on title, good. Not in Jackson: Johnson, Provincial Poetry 524.   Simon Finch 24-150   1996 £280.00

LANE, YOTI   African Folk Tales. London: Peter Lunn, 1946. 1st editio 10 full page black and white drawings and 8 chapter headings by Blair Hughes-Stanton; original binding, top edge dusty, head and tail of spine and corners slightly bumped, very good in nicked, rubbed, marked and dusty, slightly torn and creased dust jacket slightly browned at spine and edges, upper panel of dust jacket repeats one full page illustration. Ulysses 39-308   1996 $75.00

LANE-POOLE, STANLEY   Social Life in Egypt, a Description of the Country and Its People. London: n.d. 1884? 13 x 10 inches; 138 pages, numerous illustrations, 5 full page steel engravings, decorated cloth, all edges gilt, extremities frayed, outer hinges torn.   John K. King 77-791 1996 $125.00

LANEHAM, ROBERT   A Letter; Whearin Part of the Entertainment Untoo the Queenz Majesty, at Killingwoorth Castl in Warwick Sheer, in This Sommerz Progress 1575 iz Signified... Warwick: printed by and for J. Sharp and sold by Messrs. Rivington's, 1784. 2nd edition; 8vo; original pale blue wrappers, lacks spine, fine, uncut copy. cf. STC 15191; CBEL I 2071.   Ximenes 109-173 1996 $200.00

LANG, ANDREW   The Blue Fairy Book. London: Longman's Green, 1892. 5th edition; 8vo; 390 pages; black and white illustrations by H. J. Ford and Jacomb Hood; blue pictorial cloth, gilt; scattered pale foxing to few pages, else mint.   Marjorie James 19-139 1996 £75.00

LANG, ANDREW   The Book of Dreams and Ghosts. London: Longmans, Green & Co., 1897. 1st edition; crown 8vo; xviii, (304), 32 pages; original enammeled cloth in striking art nouveau design by Paul Woodroffe, top edge gilt, spine slightly darkened, some browning of prelims and edges, but nice; 1893 bookplate of Alfred Baldwin.   Ash Rare Books Zenzybyr-59 1996 £95.00

LANG, ANDREW   The Brown Fairy Book. New York: Longmans, Green and Co., 1904. 1st edition; small octavo; xiii,3 50 pages; 8 color plates and numerous illustrations by H. J. Ford; original reddish-brown cloth pictorially stamped in gilt on front cover and pictorially stamped and lettered in gilt on spine, all edges gilt, pictorial endpapers, light wear to extremities, little minor soiling, very good.   Heritage Book Shop 196-221 1996 $300.00

LANG, ANDREW   The Green Fairy Book. London: Longman's Green, 1893. 2nd edition; 8vo; 366 pages; black and white illustrations by H. J. Ford; green pictorial cloth, gilt; scattered pale foxing to few pages, else mint.   Marjorie James 19-140 1996 £75.00

LANG, ANDREW   A History of Scotland and from the Roman Occupation. London: Blackwood, 1907. 8vo; 4 volumes; frontispieces, folding tables; original cloth, gilt.   Howes Bookshop 265-641 1996 £60.00

LANG, ANDREW   The Lilac Fairy Book. London: Longmans, Green and Co., 1914. Reprint; numerous black and white illustrations by Henry Ford; original binding, top edge gilt, bottom edges of first few pages soiled, head and tail of spine and corners bumped, covers marked, cover edges rubbed, spine darkened, free endpapers browned, upper hinge partially cracked, good.   Ulysses 39-683 1996 £125.00

LANG, ANDREW   The Orange Fairy Book. London: 1906. 1st edition; 8 color plates; orange cloth with gilt decorative design on upper cover, all edges gilt, inscription, spine little dull, otherwise uncommonly bright. Words Etcetera 94-858 1996 £55.00

LANG, ANDREW   Prince Ricardo of Pantouflia. London: Arrosmwith, n.d. 1893. 1st edition; 8vo; 204 pages; 12 plates and 12 illustrations by Gordon Browne; decorated cloth, gilt. Osborne 365.   Marjorie James 19-138 1996 £75.00

LANG, ANDREW   The Red Fairy Book. London: Longman's Green, 1891. 3rd edition; 8vo; 367 pages; black and white illustrations by H. J. Ford and Lancelot Speed; red pictorial cloth, gilt; spine slightly faded, else mint.   Marjorie James 19-141 1996 £75.00

LANG, ANDREW   St. Andrews. London: Longmans, Green and Co., 1893. Large paper edition, limited to 107 copies; large tall 8vo; original paper backed boards, little soiled and rubbed, lower head band missing from spine. Very scarce, particularly in this edition.   R.F.G. Hollett 76-146 1996 £220.00

LANG, ANDREW   The Yellow Fairy Book. London: 1894. 1st edition; yellow cloth with gilt decorative design, all edges gilt, name on flyleaf, covers little shaken, some foxing to prelims, cloth rubbed through on spine hinge with upper cover at one point, spine darkened, otherwise very good.   Words Etcetera 94-857 1996 £55.00

LANG, H. C.   Rhopalocera Europae Descrita et Delineata. The Butterflies of Europe Described and Figured. London: 1884. 8vo; 2 volumes; pages vii, 396; x, 82 fine color plates; cloth, pictorial gilt, bindings slightly worn, inner hinges strengthened.   John Henly 27-62 1996 £278.00

LANG, JOHN DUNMORE   An Historical and Statistical Account of New South Wales, Both as a Penal Settlement and as a British Colony. London: A. J. Valpy, 1837. 2nd edition; 8vo; 2 volumes; pages xii, 465, ad; iv, 527 pages; folding map; original cloth, paper labels, repair to fold of map, spines faded, ends worn; Ferguson 2289.   Richard Adelson W94/95-102 1996 $285.00

LANGE, FRED W.   History of Baseball in California and Pacific Coast Leagues, 1847-1938. Oakland: by the author, 1938. 1st edition; 231 pages, photos; original pictorial wrpapers; very fine.   Argonaut Book Shop 113-398 1996 $225.00

LANGFORD, NATHANIEL PITT   Diary of the Washburn Expedition to the Yellowstone and Firehole Rivers in the Year 1870. N.P.: 1905. rubberstamped on titlepage "Published only by J.E. Haynes, Selby at Virginia, St. Paul, Minnesota". xxxii, 122 pages; text zi and maps, 23 plates and portraits; dark blue cloth with gilt stamping, gilt top, very good/fine. Graff 2389.   Bohling Book Co. 192-600 1996 $175.00

LANGFORD, R.   An Introduction to Trade and Business... London: John Chappell, n.d. 1830? New edition; 8vo; iv, (5)-128 pages; one gathering rather stained, else good in contemporary sheep, rebacked and lettered in gilt. Kress C2554; Goldsmiths 24413.   John Drury 82-139 1996 £150.00

LANGFORD, T.   Plain and Full Instructions to Raise All Sorts of Fruit Trees that Prosper in England... London: Chiswell, 1696. 2nd edition; 8vo; pages xxix, 1-220, vi; 2 plates; modern three quarter calf, with raised bands and leather label, new endpapers, one marginal paper repair, little foxing and some staining; Henrey 216.   Second Life Books 103-120 1996 $650.00

LANGHAM, WILLIAM   The Garden of Health: Containing the Sundry Rare and Hidden Vertues and Properties of all Kindes of Simples and Plants. London: by Thomas Harper, 1633. 2nd edition; 4to; (8), 702, (66) pages; woodcut initials, black letter and roman; contemporary calf, rebacked, fore-edges of first and last few leaves extended or strengthened, edges of title stained, tear with loss of few letters of running head on E4, various minor marginal tears, some dampstaining. Waller 5596; Wellcome I 3658; STC 15196.   Joseph J. Felcone 64-30 1996 $1,400.00

LANGHORNE, JOHN   Frederic and Pharamond, or the Consolations of Human Life. London: for T. Becket and P. A. de Hodnt, 1769. 1st edition; small 8vo; pages (iv), 157, (2) blank, ad; contemporary reversed calf, spine in compartments with raised bands, red morocco label, ruled and lettered in gilt, chipped, little rubbing, ownership signature, but very good. Block p. 133.   Simon Finch 24-151 1996 £285.00

LANGHORNE, RICHARD   Considerations Touching the Great question of the King's Right in dispensing with the Penal Laws... London: printed by H.H. for the Assigns of R. Langhorne & sold by N... 1687. 1st edition; folio; name on title, 31 pages; disbound. Sweet and Maxwell p. 116, 49; Wing L396.   Anthony W. Laywood 109-76 1996 £145.00

LANGLEY, BATTY 1696-1751   The Builder's Jewel; or, the Youth's Instructor and Workman's Remembrancer. London: printed for R. Ware, 1746. 2nd edition; very small 4to; 34, (2) pages; engraved frontispiece and 99 engraved plates; contemporary full sheep, rebacked. Harris & Savage no. 432.   Elton Engineering 10-90 1996 £580.00

LANGLEY, BATTY 1696-1751   The Builder's Jewel; or, The Youth's Instructor and Workman's Remembrancer. Haddington: G. Miller, 1805. Square 12mo; contemporary calf, recently rebacked; occasional foxing and browning, but remarkably nice. Rare.   Marilyn Braiterman 15-128 1996 $400.00

LANGLEY, BATTY 1696-1751   Gothic Architecture, Improved by Rules and Proportions in Many Grand Designs of Columns, Doors, Windows, Chimney-Pieces... London: I. & J. Taylor, ca. 1797. 3rd edition; large 4to; engraved titlepage, 7, (1) pages; 64 plates; old sheep, recased, small tear in gutter margin of titlepage, very good.   The Bookpress 75-206 1996 $1,350.00

LANGLEY, BATTY 1696-1751   New Principles of Gardening, or, The Laying Out and Planting Parterres, Groves, Wildernesses, Labyrinths, Avenues, Parks, Etc. London: A. Bettesworth and J. Bayley, 1728. 1st edition; quarto; 28 folio engravings; modern full leather in period style, blindstamped, red leather title piece gilt, couple of light scratches to binding, small sliver lost from base of dedication page, else fine, though rebound, a splendid wide margined copy with virtually no foxing and plates in excellent condition.   Between the Covers 42-186 1996 $2,500.00

LANGLEY, BATTY 1696-1751   Practical Geometry Applied to the Useful
Arts of Building, Surveying, Gardening and mensuration... London: W. and
J. Innys, J. Osborn and T. Longman, 1726. Folio; (12), viii, 136 pages, 60
copper engraved plates, most of which are double-page or folding;
original panelled calf, nicely rebacked, gilt; bookplate, folding archival
box.   Kenneth Karmiole 1NS-22 1996 $1,250.00

LANGLEY, HENRY G.   A Map and Street Directory of San Francisco.
San Francisco: Henry G. Langley, 1872. 1st edition; 107, (1) pages;
folding map; original purple cloth, title stamped in gilt on front cover,
minor fading, very good. Not in Rocq.   Michael D. Heaston 23-60
1996 $500.00

LANGLOTZ, ERNST   The Art of Magna Graecia: Greek Art in Southern
Italy and Sicily. London: Thames and Hudson, 1965. 4to; 312 pages, 10
figures and 188 plates (20 in color); original cloth, dust jacket.
Archaeologia Luxor-3602 1996 $150.00

LANGLOTZ, ERNST   The Art of Magna Graecia: Greek Art in Southern
Italy and Sicily. New York: Harry N. Abrams, 1965. 4to; 312 pages, 10
figures, 188 plates (20 in color), torn dust jacket, annotations; original
cloth.   Archaeologia Luxor-3603 1996 $150.00

LANGMAN, I. K.   A Selected Guide to the Literature on the Flowering
Plants of Mexico. Philadelphia: 1964. 4to; 1015 pages; cloth, dust jacket.
Raymond M. Sutton VI-1150 1996 $125.00

LANGSDORFF, GEORGE H. VON   Voyages and Travels in Various
Parts of the World, During the Years 1803, 1804, 1805, 1806 and 1807.
London: Henry Colburn, 1813. 1st English edition; 4to; 2 volumes; pages
xxiv, 362, 6; 8, 386, 6; folding map, 21 plates; contemporary boards,
rubbed, rebacked in tan calf, some light foxing.   Richard Adelson
W94/95-103 1996 $3,585.00

LANGTOFT, PIERRE DE   The Chronicle. London: 1866. 8vo; 2 volumes,
pages 527, 503; original cloth.   Howes Bookshop 265-1585 1996
£50.00

LANGWORTHY, FRANKLIN   Scenery of the Plains, Mountains and
Mines: a Diary Kept Upon the Overland route to California by Way of the
Great Salt Lake. Ogdensburg: 1855. 1st edition; iv, 320 pages; decorated
cloth, very good+. Wagner Camp 288; Graff 2392; Howes C84; Mintz
254; Flake 4752.   T. A. Swinford 49-677 1996 $650.00

LANIER, SIDNEY 1842-1881   Letters: Sidney Lanier to Col. John G.
James. Austin: Miriam Lutcher Stark Library, 1942. 165 copies printed,
this copy no. 00 "printer's sample" signed by Carl Hertzog; double fold
wrappers in original tissue jacket. Lowman 18.   Maggie Lambeth
30-319 1996 $200.00

LANKESTER, E. R.   A Treatise on Zoology. London: 1900-09. 8vo;
parts 1, 2, 4, 7 and 9 in 6 volumes; parts 6 and 8 were never issued;
original cloth and buckram. Formerly the property of Walter Garstang
and Alistair G. Hardy.   Wheldon & Wesley 207-499 1996 £120.00

LANMAN, CHARLES   Adventures of an Angler in Canada, Nova Scotia
and the United States. London: R. Bentley, 1848. frontispiece, 8 vignette
woodcuts to text; original brown cloth slightly rubbed, couple of small
tears to top and bottom of backstrip, 'Swaffham book Club' label.
Petersfield Bookshop FH58-308 1996 £125.00

LANMAN, CHARLES   Farthest North; or, the Life and Explroations of
Lieutenant James Booth Lockwood, of the Greely Arctic Expedition. New
York: 1885. 1st edition; 7 x 4.5 inches; 333 pages; folding map,
illustrations; cloth, stamped name, covers darkened and rubbed, map
torn.   John K. King 77-789 1996 $150.00

LANSDOWNE, HENRY WILLIAM PETTY FITZMAURICE, 6TH MARQUIS OF
1872-   Catalogue of the Celebrated Collection of Ancient Marbles, the
Property of the Most Honourable the Marquess of Lansdowne, M.V.O.,
D.S.O....March 5, 1930. London: Christies, Manson and Woods, 1930.
8vo; frontispiece, 109 pages, 35 plates; original boards, expertly
rebacked.   Archaeologia Luxor-2936 1996 $150.00

LANSDOWNE, HENRY WILLIAM PETTY FITZMAURICE, 6TH MARQUIS OF
1872-   The Queeney Letters. New York: Farrar & Rinehart Inc., 1934.
1st edition; original binding, top edge slightly dusty, head and tail of
spine and corners slightly bumped, free endpapers partially browned,
very good in nicked, chipped, rubbed, marked and dusty slightly torn,
creased and soiled dust jacket darkened at spine and edges.   Ulysses
39-319 1996 £70.00

LANSDOWNE, J. F.   Birds of the West Coast. Toronto: 1976-80. Folio
2 volumes, 87 color plates, 4 large foldout, 101 plates of drawings, 342
pages; fine in dust jacket.   John Johnson 135-523 1996 $100.00

LANYON, ANDREW   Peter Lanyon, 1918-1964. Cornwall, 1990. Limited
signed edition, number 419 of 500, signed by author; 27 x 20 cm; 340
pages; profusley illustrated in color and black and white; original cloth,
dust jacket, slipcase, edges untrimmed;   Rainsford A54-362 1996
£250.00

LAPE, ESTHER   American Medicine: Expert Testimony Out of Court.
New York: 1937. 1st edition; 1435 pages; 2 volumes; original binding.
W. Bruce Fye 71-1234 1996 $100.00

LAPINER, ALAN   Pre-Columbian Art of South America. New York:
Harry N. Abrams, 1976. Folio; color frontispiece, 460 pages, 910
illustrations; original cloth, torn dust jacket.   Archaeologia Luxor-4620
1996 $750.00

LA PRIMAUDAYE, PIERRE DE   The French Academie. London: Thomas
Adams, 1618. Folio; (xxii), 330, (x), 331-634, (iv), 635-643, 646-858, (ii),
861-1031, 1034-1038, (vi) pages; 17th century calf, ruled in blind, spine
gilt, label, woodcut titlepage, 3 secondary titlepages, rubbed, minor wear
at extremities, gilt faded, short splits at head of joints and foot of
backstrip, front endpaper torn and covered with pen-trials, some minor
dampstaining, generally very clean. Uncommon, good copy. STC 15241.
Robert Clark 38-71 1996 £650.00

LARDEN, W.   Recollections of an Old Mountaineer. London: 1910. 1st
edition; 17 plates; gilt on red; bookplates of the Rucksack Club and
Manchester Central Library, no obvious rubber stamps, very good.
Moutaineering Books 8-RL01 1996 £60.00

LARDNER, RING W. 1885-1933   Bib Ballads. Chicago: Vollard & Co.,
1915. 1st edition; one of 500 copies; author's first book; illustrations by
Fontaine Fox; housed in rare publisher's box which is stamped with
design on cover of the book, box missing one edge, else very good,
book fine.   Priscilla Juvelis 95/1-149 1996 $600.00

LARDNER, RING W. 1885-1933   The Big Town. New York: 1925. 1st
edition; spine little sunned, extremities slightly rubbed, near fine, scarce.
Polyanthos 22-507 1996 $100.00

LAREN, A. J. VAN   Cactus. Los Angeles: 1935. Limited to 1500
numbered copies; 4to; pages (8), 100, ad; frontispiece, 133 colored
illustrations tipped in plus several drawings; original cloth, covers
somewhat dingy, some worming to hinges, light foxing or browning to
endpapers.   Raymond M. Sutton VI-1013 1996 $100.00

LARKIN, PHILIP 1922-   All What Jazz - a Record Diary 1961-68.
London: Faber & Faber, 1970. 1st edition; original binding, head and tail
of spine & corners slightly bumped, spine and cover edges slightly
faded, some offsetting to covers from dust jacket, very good in slightly
creased and dusty dust jacket; presentation copy from author to Dudley
Snelgrove, loosely inserted 2 page ALS from author to presentee.
Ulysses 39-350 1996 £985.00

LARKIN, PHILIP 1922-   Aubade. Salem: Charles Seluzicki, 1980. One of
250 copies, initialled by author and printer; fine in original envelope.
A. Gekoski 19-88 1996 £275.00

LARKIN, PHILIP 1922-   Aubade. Salem: Charles Seluzicki, 1980. One of
250 numbered copies, initialled by author and printer; 12mo; printed and
illustrated by Kathleen Gray Schallock, printed on Fabriano, Richard de
Bas and Japanese handmade paper; one black and white illustration by
printer; wrappers, fine in antique silver lined envelope.   Ulysses 39-35
1996 £275.00

LARKIN, PHILIP 1922-   The Fantasy Poets - Number Twenty-One.
Swinford, Eynsham: Fantasy Press, 1954. One of about 300 copies;
wrappers, covers slightly marked and dusty, very good.
Ulysses 39-346 1996 £455.00

LARKIN, PHILIP 1922-   The Less Deceived - Poems. London: Marvell
Press, 1955. 1st edition; with first state text, but with the dreaded
rounded spine; original binding, small stain on fore-edge, head and tail
spine slightly bumped, cover edges very slightly faded, very good in
nicked, and slightly creased, rubbed, darkened dusty dust jacket faded
spine and edges.   Ulysses 39-347 1996 £375.00

LARKIN, PHILIP 1922-   The Whitsun Weddings - Poems. London: Faber & Faber, 1964. Uncorrected proof; wrappers, covers slightly marked, spine slightly darkened, very good.   Ulysses 39-349 1996 £185.00

LARKIN, PHILIP 1922-   The Whitsun Weddings - a Poem. London: Faber & Faber, 1964. 1st edition; signed by author on titlepage; original binding, top edge very slightly dusty, bottom edes very slightly rubbed, bottom corners very slightly bumped, very good in slightly nicked, rubbed, marked and dusty dust jacket slightly darkened at spine and edges and internally reddened at spine panel through contact with spine of book.   Ulysses 39-348 1996 £395.00

LARKIN, PHILIP 1922-   The Whitsun Weddings. London: Faber & Faber, 1964. reviews of book laid in, excellent copy in dust jacket.   R. A. Gekoski 19-87 1996 £120.00

LA ROCHE, F.   En Route to the Klondike. A Practical Guide. Chicago: Press of the Henry O. Shepard Co., 1897. 1st edition; (60) pages; illustrations and maps; original grey printed wrappers, title stamped in gold on front cover, very fine. Not in Smith. Tourville 2626.   Michael D. Heaston 23-8 196 $375.00

LA ROCHE, RENE   Yellow Fever, Considered In its Historical, Pathological, Etiological and Therapeutical Relations. Philadelphia: Blanchard and Lea, 1855. 8vo; 2 volumes; original binding, recently rebacked. GM 5454.2.   James Tait Goodrich K40-171 1996 $225.00

LAROCHEJAQUELEIN, MARCHIONESS DE   Memoirs of the Marchioness De Larochejaquelein. Edinburgh: 1816. 8vo; viii, 535 pages, folding colored map; half calf, new title label inset on red morocco, little browned, otherwise good.   K Books 442-327 1996 £50.00

LARSEN, K.   Tropical Botany, Proceedings of a Symposium Held August 10-12, 1978. 1979. 8vo; 453 pages; illustrations; cloth. Raymond M. Sutton VI-239 1996 $164.00

LARSEN, T.   The Butterflies of Kenya and Their Natural History. London: 1991. Royal 8vo; 512 pages; 64 colored plates, 23 text figures; cloth.   Wheldon & Wesley 207-1063 1996 £85.00

LARSON, ROGER KEITH   Controversial James. An Essay on the Life and Work of George Wharton James. San Francisco: Book Club of California, 1991. 1st edition; one of 400 copies; xii, 98, (2) pages; frontispiece, numerous other plates; maroon cloth covered boards, gilt cover design; very fine in slipcase with printed paper spine label. Original announcement laid in.   Argonaut Book Shop 113-370 1996 $225.00

LARTIGUE, J. H.   Boyhood Photos...the Family Album of a Gilded Age. Guichard, 1966. 1st edition; oblong small 4to; tipped in plates, including cover.   J. B. Muns 154-180 1996 $300.00

LARTIGUE, J. H.   Boyhood Photos of J. H. Lartigue. The Family Album of a Gilded AGe. Lausanne: Ami Guichard, 1966. Oblong 4to; 128 pages; profusely illustrated with dozens of mounted photos; elaborately gilt stamped maroon cloth with mounted illustration on front cover; fine. Kenneth Karmiole 1NS-208 1996 $300.00

LARTRIGUE, J. H.   Diary of a Century. New York: 1970. 1st edition; folio; illustrations; dust jacket.   J. B. Muns 154-181 1996 $300.00

LAS CASES, EMMANUEL, COMTE DE 1766-1842   Journal of the Private Life and Conversations of the Emperor Napoleon at Saint Helena. London: Henry Colburn, 1824. 8vo; 8 volumes; 2 engraved portraits, 4 engraved plates, 2 folding maps, 1 folding chart; three quarter blue morocco over marbled boards, gilt panelled spines, raised bands, gilt tops, good, sound set.   Appelfeld Gallery 54-142 1996 $500.00

LASCELLES, EDWARD, PSEUD.   Scenes from the Life of Edward Lascelles, Gent. Dublin: William Curry, Junr. & Co., 1837. 1st edition; 8vo; 2 volumes in one, (6), 324; (6), 352 pages; both volumes with added engraved titlepage and engraved frontispiece by George Cruikshank; original brown cloth, decoratively gilt, extremites and corners slightly rubbed;   Kenneth Karmiole 1NS-146 1996 $150.00

LASSAIGNE, JACQUES   Chagall. Paris: Maeght Editeur, 1957. One of 6000 copies; 4to; 15 original lithographs of which five are double page, 13 are in color and two are in black and white, also with approximately 120 reproductions, many full page and in color; three quarter burgundy morocco and marbled boards, spine with gilt lettering, marbled endpapers, top edge gilt, original pictorial wrappers and backstrip bound in; fine.   Priscilla Juvelis 95/1-50 1996 $1,500.00

LASSAIGNE, JACQUES   Marc Chagall: Drawings and Water Colors for the Ballet. New York: Tudor, 1969. Folio; 155 pages, 79 illustrations, 68 in color; cloth, dust jacket, slipcase.   Brannan 43-116 1996 $235.00

LATH BURY, THOMAS   A History of the Nonjurors; their Controversies and Writings... London: William Pickering, 1845. 1st edition; 8vo; Aldine device on titlepage; half brown morocco by Zaehnsdorf, early Zaehnsdorf binding.   Charles W. Traylen 117-151 1996 £90.00

LATHAM, PETER M.   The Collected Works of Dr. P. M. Latham. London: 1876-78. 1st edition; 2 volumes, 480, 575 pages; original binding. GM 2227.   W. Bruce Fye 71-1237 1996 $225.00

LATHAM, WILFRID   The States of the River Plate. London: Longmans, Green, 1868. 2nd edition; 8vo; pages x, 381, 2 ads; folding map; new tan cloth, leather label. Sabin 39168.   Richard Adelson W94/95-104 1996 $275.00

LATHROP, GEORGE PARSONS   A Study of Hawthorne. Boston: James R. Osgood, 1876. 1st edition; one of 2000 copies printed; original green cloth, gilt, 2 bookplates, minor rubbing, else bright copy of an uncommon book. Clark C42.   Mac Donnell 12-113 1996 $100.00

LATIMER, JONATHAN   The Search for My Great Uncle's Head. Garden City: Doubleday, Doran, 1937. Uncorrected proof; slightly darkened green printed paper wrappers with a few tiny nicks and small chip in head of spine.   Quill & Brush 102-1011 1996 $200.00

LA TOUR LANDRY, GEOFFREY DE   The Book of the Knight of La Tour Landry. London: Alcuin Press for the Verona Society, 1930. One of 500 copies, this copy not numbered; 10 x 7 3/4 inches; xii, 172 pages; fine large dec. capitals in the style of the 16th century crible initials, printed in red & black; very appealing recent exhibition binding by Alan Tarrant of inlaid and onlaid black oasis mor., front bd. with stylized vignette at lower left showing a flowering tree made up of onlaid mor. in olive & blue, tree emananting from a shadowed ground represented by 8 oval orange mor. inlays and 22 especially imaginative pebble-shaped silver studs, upper left corner of back cover featuring a full moon (represented by a silver disk) & illuminated clouds (inlaid slender ovoids of gray & pink mor.), gray mor. doublures w/similar multicolored oval mor. inlays, free endpapers of gray suede, flat spine w/simple gilt titling, a.e.g., in substantial black folding buckram box, plushed lined, w/gilt lettered mor. label, slight wear to box, otherwise in extremely fine condition.   Phillip J. Pirages 33-75 1996 $950.00

LATROBE, BENJAMIN HENRY   The Virginia Journals of Benjamin Henry Latrobe 1795-1798. New Haven: Yale, 1977. 4to; 2 volumes, lxxx, 293 pages, 24 color illustrations + frontispiece, 31 text illustrations, xii, 575 pages, 63 text illustrations, color frontispiece; cloth, dust jacket. Rainsford A54-363 1996 £60.00

LATROBE, CHARLES JOSEPH   The Rambler in Mexico: 1834. London: Published by R. B. Seeley and W. Burnside and sold by L. & G. Seeley, 1836. 1st edition; 8 x 5 1/4 inches; viii, 309 pages; folding engraved map; contemporary owner's name top of title; light brown half calf by Bayntun, linen sides, simple gilt rules, ornaments and titling on spine, marbled endpapers, top edge gilt, tiny tear in map, leaves a shade less than bright because of inexpensive paper stock, but fine, clean, fresh copy in bright, unworn binding. Sabin 39221.   Phillip J. Pirages 33-329 1996 $250.00

LATROBE, CHARLES JOSEPH   The Solace of Song. London: published by R. B. Seeley and W. Burnside,... 1837. 1st edition; 8vo; pictorial titlepage and 10 plates, all printed on thin paper; contemporary half calf, spine gilt, bit rubbed; very good. Scarce.   Ximenes 108-238 1996 $225.00

LATROBE, CHRISTIAN I.   Journal of a Visit to South Africa in 1815, and 1816. London: L. B. Seeley, 1818. 1st edition; 4to; pages viii, 4 06; folding map, 16 plates (12 hand colored); modern quarter calf, blue label, few light waterstains, library blindstamp on title. Abbey Travel 325; Mendelssohn I p. 866; Theal p. 170.   Richard Adelson W94/95-105 1996 $1,875.00

LATROBE, CHRISTIAN I.   Journal of a Visit to South Africa, With some Account of the Missionary Settlements of the United Brethren, Near the Cape of Good Hope. London: L. B. Seeley, 1821. 2nd edition; 8vo; pages xi, 580; folding map, 4 plates, lacks half title; half calf, gilt, marbled boards, rubbed. Mendelssohn I p.867; Theal p. 170.   Richard Adelson W94/95-106 1996 $285.00

LATROBE, JOHN H. B.   Reminiscences of West Point from September 1818 to March 1882. East Saginaw: Evening News Printers and Binders, 1887. 1st edition; 8vo; 36 pages; printed wrappers, minor chipping of spine, very good; "From the Author" written on front wrapper. 1 copy in NUC, the LC copy.   Robert F. Lucas 42-82 1996 $125.00

LAUBER, PATRICIA   Cowboys and Cattle Ranching Yesterday and Today. New York: 1973. 1st edition; small 4to; 147 pages; 124 photos; cloth, scarce, very good in chipped dust jacket; not in Dykes 50. Gene W. Baade 1094-98 1996 $100.00

LAUDER, THOMAS DICK   The Miscellany of Natural History. Volume I. Parrots. Edinburgh: 1833. 1st edition; 8vo; vignette title, portrait of Audubon, 36 engraved plates, 35 hand colored of parrots and 1 plain of detail, all after Joseph Kidd, minor browning; 22 page miscellany advertiser bound in; pink figured cloth, faded and somewhat worn, joints splitting;   Maggs Bros. Ltd. 1190-581 1996 £340.00

LAUDER, WILLIAM   An Essay on Milton's Use and Imitation of the Moderns, in His Paradise Lost. London: printed for J. Payne and J. Bouquet, 1750. 1st edition; 1st issue; 8vo; contemporary calf, rebacked using part of original gilt spine, corners repaired, new endpapers. Courtney, Johnson pp. 36-8.   Peter Murray Hill 185-92 1996 £475.00

LAUGHLIN, JAMES   Gits and Piths: a Memoir of Ezra Pound. Iowa City: Windhover Press, 1982. 1st edition; one of 25 special copies, with an original postcard from Pound to Laughlin laid in pocket at rear, from a total edition of 250 copies, signed by Laughlin; 8vo; intaglio titlepage portrait of Pound after Henri Gaudier-Brzeska; quarter leather and boards, cloth slipcase; fine.   James S. Jaffe 34-549 1996 $1,750.00

LAUGHLIN, JAMES   The House of Light: Poems. Newtown: Grenfell Press, 1986. One of 200 numbered copies; 4to; signed by author and artist, printed in Monotype Poliphilus; illustrations in several colors on Rives; Dieu Donne wrappers, fine.   Bertram Rota 272-208 1996 £60.00

LAUGHLIN, JAMES   The River. Norfolk: New Directions, 1938. 1st edition; small octavo; green stapled wrappers; very good+.   Lame Duck Books 19-286 1996 $100.00

LAUGHTON, BRUCE   The Euston Road School. Aldershot, 1986. 4to; 373 pages; color frontispiece, 16 color plates, 218 text illustrations; cloth, dust jacket.   Rainsford A54-364 1996 £85.00

LAUGHTON, BRUCE   Philip Wilson Steer 1860-1942. Oxford: Clarendon Press, 1971. Medium 8vo; xix, 167 pages; 216 illustrations; cloth, dust jacket.   Rainsford A54-536 1996 £65.00

LAUHTON, L. G. CARR   Old Ship Figure-Heads and Sterns. London: Halton & Truscott, Limited edition, number 424 of 1000 copies; 4to; 279 pages; 8 color plates, 48 black and whites; gilt bevelled boards, some rubbing, very good.   John Lewcock 30-170 1996 £175.00

LAURA'S Pride. London: Chapman and Hall, 1868. Sole edition; 8vo; half titles, pages viii, 291; (vi), 285; (vi), 290; 3 volumes; stitching of volumes i and iii shaken and strained; original morocco grain red cloth, backstrips faded, divided by double gilt rules, gilt lettered direct, sides with blindstamped panel, endpapers foxed, good; rare. Not traced in NUC, Wolff or Sadleir.   Blackwell's B112-4 1996 £350.00

LAUT, AGNES C.   Cadillac. Indianapolis: 1931. 1st edition; 298 pages; illustrations; gilt stamped cloth, near fine in moderately edgeworn dust jacket, scarce.   Gene W. Baade 1094-99 1996 $125.00

LAUTERBACH, ANN   Book One. New York: Spring Street Press, 1975. 1st edition; one of 100 numbered copies, signed by author; oblong 4to; mimemographed sheets in green paper covers, staped; fine; this copy additionally inscribed by Lauterbach.   James S. Jaffe 34-363 1996 $250.00

LAUTERBACH, ANN   Later That Evening. New York: Jordan Davies, 1981. 1st edition; one of 20 copies printed on Canterbury paper and bound in boards out of a total edition of 210 copies, signed by Laterbach; thin 8vo; cloth backed boards; fine.   James S. Jaffe 34-364 1996 $225.00

LAUTERBACH, ANN   Sacred Weather. New York: Grenfell Press, 1984. 1st edition; limited to 130 copies, signed by poet and artist; tall 8vo; illustrations by Louisa Chase; decorated boards, as new.   James S. Jaffe 34-365 1996 $125.00

LAVATER, JOHANN CASPAR 1741-1801   Essays on Physiognomy; for the Promotion of the Knowledge and the Love of Mankind. London: 1789. 1st English translation; 8vo; 3 volumes; 241, 324, 314 pages; full page engraved plates; full leather, 2 hinges cracked, overall a fine set, contents fine. GM 154 (Leipzig 1772); Osler 3176-3179; Hunter & Macalpine 521.   W. Bruce Fye 71-1243 1996 $950.00

LAVELEYE, EMILE DE   The Elements of Political Economy... London: Chapman and Hall, 1884. 1st edition in English; 8vo; xix, (1), 274 pages, 34 pages of publisher's ads dated Nov. 1883; original brown cloth, gilt, very good.   John Drury 82-140 1996 £50.00

LAVENDER, DAVID   The American Heritage History of the Great American West. New York: 1965. 1st edition; 416 pages, index, photos, illustrations, maps; deluxe slipcased edition, near fine. Six Guns 1290. Early West 22-180 1996 $125.00

LAVIN, IRVING   Studies in Late and Medieval Renaissance Painting in Honour of Millard Meiss. New York: University Press, 1977. 2 volumes; xx, 463 pages; 161 pages of monochrome plates, slipcase.   Rainsford A54-405 1996 £75.00

THE LAW of Commons and Commoners. London: Atkins for J. Walthoe, 1698. 1st edition; octavo; contemporary calf, worn, rebacked, some foxing, 2 leaves of prelims with blank corners torn away, with 3 publisher's ads; inscription "Barth Beale, 1706". Wing L634.   Maggs Bros. Ltd. 1190-3 1996 £200.00

LAW Quibbles: or, a Treatise of the Evasions, Tricks, Turns and Quibbles, Commonly Used in the Profession of the Law...and an Essay on the Amendment and Reduction of the Laws of England...and Regulation of the Practice of the Law... London: printed by Elizabeth and R. Nutt, and R. Gosling, 1736. 4th edition; modern calf, bit embrowned, but quite attractive.   Meyer Boswell SL25-140 1996 $750.00

LAW, ALICE   Emily Jane Bronte and the Authorship of Wuthering Heights. Accrington: Old Parsonage Press, n.d. c. 1928. 1st edition; 5 3/4 x 4 1/2 inches; pages (viii), 50; grey wrappers lettered in black on front, very good, scarce.   Ian Hodgkins 78-336 1996 £80.00

LAW, WILLIAM   A Practical Treatise Upon Christian Perfection. London: William and John Innys, 1728. 2nd edition; 8vo; (viii), 535, (i) pages; contemporary panelled calf, neatly rebacked and recornered, label; good copy.   Robert Clark 38-188 1996 £85.00

LAW, WILLIAM   A Serious Call to a Devout and Holy Life. London: William Innys, 1729. 1st edition; 8vo; (i), vi, 499, (v) pages; contemporary panelled calf rebacked, recornered, spine gilt ruled, label, pages ads at end, library stamp on reverse of titlepage, label on rear endpaper, no other markings, minor foxing at beginning and end, good. Robert Clark 38-187 1996 £200.00

LAW, WILLIAM   The Works. Brockenhurst: Reprinted for G. Moreton, 1892-93. Reprint of 1762 edition; 8vo; 9 volumes; x, (ii), 203, (i); vi, (ii), 184; iv, 250; iv, 272; viii, 181, (i); (ii), 209, (i); (ii), 262; (iv), 251, (i); (iv), 264 pages; type facsimile titlepages; original green cloth, spines gilt; extremities rubbed, short tear in one backstrip, small library stickers on spines, inoffensive blindstamp on corner of titles & some text pages, no other markings. Very serviceable set, uncommon.   Robert Clark 38-189 1996 £200.00

LAWES, W. G.   Grammar and Vocabulary of Language Spoken by Motu Tribe (New Guinea). Sydney: Charles Potter, Government Printer, 1888. 2nd edition; 8vo; original calf, most of spine missing; 'With the Author's Compts." on upper blank margin of title. Ferguson 11486. Anthony W. Laywood 108-194 1996 £65.00

THE LAWFULNESSE Of Our Expedition into England Manifested. Edinburgh: printed...by Robert Bryson, and are to be sold at his Shop... 1640. Small 4to; 4 leaves; 3 corners cropped, titlepage with 'of our' in line 3; disbound;   H. M. Fletcher 121-77 1996 £50.00

LAWRENCE, A. B.   A History of Texas, or the Emigrant's Guide to the New Republic, by a Resident Emigrant, Late from the United States. New York: Hafis & Cornish, 1844. 1st published in 1840, these are the original sheets with cancel titlepage and without dedication as sometimes occur in later editions; 12mo; 275 pages; lithographic frontispiece, old calf, spine damaged, sound. Howes L154; Streeter 13861c. Jenkins 120.   M & S Rare Books 60-421 1996 $500.00

LAWRENCE, DAVID HERBERT 1885-1930   Aaron's Rod. London: Martin Secker, 1922. 1st edition; darkening to free endpapers, ownership blindstamp to titlepage, otherwise very good+, lacking dust jacket, signed by author.   Lame Duck Books 19-287 1996 $550.00

LAWRENCE, DAVID HERBERT 1885-1930   Aaron's Rod. New York: Seltzer, 1922. 1st edition; precedes British; bright, clean, unworn copy, no dust jacket.   Sherwood 3-182 1996 $140.00

LAWRENCE, DAVID HERBERT 1885-1930   Amores. New York: Huebsch, 1916. 1st edition; small owner's name on f.f.e.p., front panel of dust jacket laid in, very good+, no dust jacket.   Sherwood 3-178 196 $100.00

LAWRENCE, DAVID HERBERT 1885-1930   Birds, Beasts and Flowers. London: Cresset Press, Ltd., 1930. Limited edition, number 394 of 500 copies; wood engravings by Blair Hughes-Stanton; vellum backed marbled boards, two small marks from tape residue on front free endpaper, two small bookseller's stamps on rear pastedown, tail of spine lightly bumped, otherwise fine.   Hermitage SP95-864 1996 $650.00

LAWRENCE, DAVID HERBERT 1885-1930   The Collected Letters of... London: Heinemann, 1962. 1st edition thus; 2 volumes; edges of page slightly browned, otherwise very good in slightly soiled and chipped dust jacket faded down spine, nice set.   Virgo Books 48-123 1996 £60.00

LAWRENCE, DAVID HERBERT 1885-1930   David: a Play. New York: Knopf, 1926. 1st American edition; attractive bookplate, mostly under front flap, else fine in nice, very good dust jacket.   Between the Covers 42-258 1996 $125.00

LAWRENCE, DAVID HERBERT 1885-1930   England My England. New York: Seltzer, 1922. 1st edition; blue cloth with near fine dust jacket, which has been neatly repaired on inside; fine. Roberts A23.   Bromer Booksellers 90-163 1996 $650.00

LAWRENCE, DAVID HERBERT 1885-1930   England, My England, and Other Stories. New York: Seltzer, 1922. 1st edition; blue gilt stamped cloth, tan jacket lettered in black, with ad for Women In Love on back, very good in jacket that has some tape repairs but is generally very good. Roberts A23a.   Priscilla Juvelis 95/1-152 1996 $450.00

LAWRENCE, DAVID HERBERT 1885-1930   England, My England. London: Martin Secker Ltd., 1924. 1st edition; original binding, top edge dusty, edges spotted, head and tail of spine slightly bumped, endpapers partially browned, very good in nicked and slightly creased, rubbed, marked and dusty dust jacket slightly darkened at spine and edges. Ulysses 39-353 1996 £250.00

LAWRENCE, DAVID HERBERT 1885-1930   England, My England. London: Martin Secker, 1924. 1st English edition; near fine in near fine jacket. Roberts A23 note.   Priscilla Juvelis 95/1-153 1996 $220.00

LAWRENCE, DAVID HERBERT 1885-1930   Fantasia of the Unconscious. London: Martin Secker, 1923. Front and rear free endpapers offset, scattered foxing to title and half titlepage, outside edge more heavily foxed, otherwise excellent in slightly chipped dust jacket.   R. A. Gekoski 19-92 1996 £225.00

LAWRENCE, DAVID HERBERT 1885-1930   Kangaroo. London: Martin Secker, 1923. 1st edition; very good in lgihtly used jacket which is split at front hinge, but complete. Roberts A26.   Priscilla Juvelis 95/1-154 1996 $250.00

LAWRENCE, DAVID HERBERT 1885-1930   Lady Chatterley's Lover. Florence Privately printed by Tipografia Giuntina, 1928. 1st edition; one of 1000 copies; signed by author; 9 x 6 1/2 inches; 2 p.l., 365 pages; very fine simple but elegant forest green crushed morocco by Bayntun-Riviere, spine with raised bands and gilt titling, broad turn-ins with multiple gilt borders, including an animated floral design, marbled endpapers, top edge gilt, other edges untrimmed, isolated trivial spots internally, but extremely fine in unworn binding. Roberts A42a.   Phillip J. Pirages 33-330 1996 $2,950.00

LAWRENCE, DAVID HERBERT 1885-1930   Lady Chatterley. Paris: Deux Rives, 1946. Copy number XXXXVIIII, one of 100 on Marais, from a total issue of 1025; 100 on Marais (this copy), 1025 ordinary issue; 4to; 24 pochoir plates, plus an extra suite in black and white; three quarter green morocco, pastepaper boards, spine panelled, author and title gilt, top edge gilt, original wrapper bound in matching morocco edge slipcase; fine.   Priscilla Juvelis 95/1-150 1996 $500.00

LAWRENCE, DAVID HERBERT 1885-1930   Love Among the Haystacks and Other Pieces. London: Nonesuch Press, 1930. Number 749 of 1600 copies; 8vo; pages xiv, 96 + colophon, printed at the Curwen Press on Auvergne handmade paper, slight spotting of first and final leaves, but rather better than often found; original canvas backed yellow buckram, morocco label, uncut. Roberts A56; Dreyfus 68.   Claude Cox 107-109 1996 £65.00

LAWRENCE, DAVID HERBERT 1885-1930   The Man Who Died. London: Martin Secker, 1931. 1st English edition (after a Paris, Black Sun edition), limited to 2000 copies; tall 8vo; 97, (i) pages; green cloth, spine and edges faded, pinhole on spine, titled in gilt on spine, with device in gilt on front cover, top edge gilt; near fine internally.   Blue Mountain SP95-106 1996 $125.00

LAWRENCE, DAVID HERBERT 1885-1930   The Man Who Died. London: Heinemann, 1935. 1st illustrated edition; quarto; 64 pages; 11 two color engravings by John Farleigh; near fine with some faint foxing to free endpapers and bumping about corners, in original dust jacket which is slightly darkened and with one small tear, bookplate. Roberts A50d. Bromer Booksellers 87-67 1996 $165.00

LAWRENCE, DAVID HERBERT 1885-1930   New Poems. London: M. Secker, 1918. 1st edition; only 500 copies; modern half leather, paper darkened, lacks original wrappers; good+.   Charles Agvent 4-818 1996 $130.00

LAWRENCE, DAVID HERBERT 1885-1930   The Paintings of D. H. Lawrence. London: Mandrake Press, n.d. 1929. One of 500 numbered copies, of which this is number 27; very slight bumping and rubbing, but nice copy, lacking slipcase.   R. A. Gekoski 19-93 1996 £500.00

LAWRENCE, DAVID HERBERT 1885-1930   Pansies. London: Stephensen, 1929. Limited edition, number 318 of 500 numbered copies, signed and numbered by author; tall thin 8vo; frontispiece; stiff cream wrappers, printed in red and black, glassine dust jacket, very good, publisher's white board slipcase.   George J. Houle 68-80 1996 $750.00

LAWRENCE, DAVID HERBERT 1885-1930   Pansies. London: Privately printed, June, 1929. Signed limited edition, one of 500 copies; stiff white wrappers printed in red and black, very fine in glassine dust jacket. Roberts A47C.   Priscilla Juvelis 95/1-155 1996 $400.00

LAWRENCE, DAVID HERBERT 1885-1930   Pansies. London: Secker, 1929. 1st edition; bright clean copy, lacking dust jacket.   Sherwood 3-189 1996 $150.00

LAWRENCE, DAVID HERBERT 1885-1930   Pansies. London: Martin Secker, 1929. 1st (definitive) edition; blue cloth backed patterned boards; fine.   Captain's Bookshelf 38-138 1996 $125.00

LAWRENCE, DAVID HERBERT 1885-1930   Psychoanalysis and the Unconscious. New York: Thomas Seltzer, 1921. 1st American edition; 8vo; 120 pages; original grey boards lettered in blue, soiled, spine slightly worn, few leaves slightly torn in fore margin. McDonald 17a. Thomas Thorp 489-184 1996 £75.00

LAWRENCE, DAVID HERBERT 1885-1930   The Rainbow. New York: Huebsch, 1916. 1st American edition; former owner's name on f.f.e.p., else very good, no dust jacket.   Sherwood 3-177 1996 $125.00

LAWRENCE, DAVID HERBERT 1885-1930   St. Mawr, Together with the Princess. London: Secker, 1925. 1st edition; 1st issue; very good+, lacking dust jacket.   Sherwood 3-186 1996 $125.00

LAWRENCE, DAVID HERBERT 1885-1930   Sons and Lovers. New York: 1913. 1st U.S. edition; spine with fading, otherwise very near fine. Stephen Lupack 83- 1996 $250.00

LAWRENCE, DAVID HERBERT 1885-1930   Sons and Lovers. New York: Kennerley, 1913. 1st American edition; very good, owner's bookplate on front pastedown, name and address on fly, spine slightly faded and edgeworn.   Sherwood 3-174 1996 $175.00

LAWRENCE, DAVID HERBERT 1885-1930   Sons and Lovers. Avon: Limited Editions Club, 1975. Number 849 of 2000 copies, signed by artist; illustrations by Sheila Robinson; fine in slipcase.   Hermitage SP95-1005 1996 $100.00

LAWRENCE, DAVID HERBERT 1885-1930   The Spirit of Place. London: Toronto: William Heinemann, 1935. 1st edition; 8vo; brown cloth, buff jacket printed in blue and orange, fine in near fine jacket, unusual in this condition. Roberts A72.   Priscilla Juvelis 95/1-151 1996 $375.00

LAWRENCE, DAVID HERBERT 1885-1930   Tortoises. New York: Seltzer, 1921. 1st edition; slight wear to corners, else very good in pictorial boards, lacking dust jacket.   Sherwood 3-181 1996 $125.00

LAWRENCE, DAVID HERBERT 1885-1930   Tortoises. Williamsburg: Chelonidae Press, 1983. One of 90 deluxe copies, with an extra suite in quarter vellum; 200 regular copies; page size 11 x 8 inches; text in Centaur and arrighi.   Priscilla Juvelis 95/1-54 1996 $625.00

LAWRENCE, DAVID HERBERT 1885-1930   The Virgin and the Gipsy. Florence: G. Orioli, 1930. One of 810 numbered copies; rear blank is seamlessly repaired with archival tape, else fine in fine, slightly spine faded dust jacket. Very nice.   Between the Covers 42-259 1996 $475.00

LAWRENCE, DAVID HERBERT 1885-1930   The Virgin and the Gipsy. London: Martin Secker, 1930. 1st English edition, one of 5800 copies, preceded only by a limited edition of 810 copies published in Florence five months' previously; brown cloth stamped in gilt on spine, tan jacket printed in red; extraordinary copy, book fresh and gilt stamping as new, jacket showing only minor traces of use and one small tape reinforcement on interior, discreet ex-libris. Roberts A54.   Priscilla Juvelis 95/1-156 1996 $250.00

LAWRENCE, DAVID HERBERT 1885-1930   The Widowing of Mrs. Holroyd. New York: Kennerley, 1914. 1st edition; bookplate on front pastedown, else very good.   Sherwood 3-175 1996 $100.00

LAWRENCE, DAVID HERBERT 1885-1930   Women in Love. New York: privately printed, 1920. One of 1250 copies; scattered foxing to outside and lower edges, otherwise very fine and bright; Roberts A15a.   R. A. Gekoski 19-91 1996 £800.00

LAWRENCE, DAVID HERBERT 1885-1930   Women in Love. New York: Privately privately printed, 1920. 1st limited edition, not signed, lacking preliminaries & dust jacket, still very good copy. Former owner has pointed out location (p. 368) of erotic passage in ink on titlepage. Sherwood 3-180 1996 $150.00

LAWRENCE, E.   It May Happen Yet: a Tale of Bonaparte's Invasion of England. privately printed, 1899. 1st edition; some silverfish damage to covers, else near very good.   Aronovitz 57-668 1996 $125.00

LAWRENCE, JACOB   The Great Migration: an American Story. New York: Museum of Modern Art/Phillips Collections, 1993. 1st edition; oblong quarto; fine in dust jacket; signed by Lawrence.   Between the Covers 43-461 1996 $150.00

LAWRENCE, JOHN   The History and Delineation of the Horse, in all His Varities, Comprehending the Appropriate Uses... London: Albion Press: printed for James Cundee and John Scott, 1809. 1st edition; 4to; with additional engraved title, engraved dedication leaf, pages 288, (4); 13 fine engraved plates; recent half calf, label, gilt, very good to nice. James Fenning 133-203 1996 £245.00

LAWRENCE, JOHN   The New Farmer's Calendar; or, Monthly Remembrancer, for All Kinds of Country Business... London: printed for H.D. Symonds; Vernor & Hood and J. Wright, 1800. 1st edition; 8vo; 616 pages; perforation and cancellation stamps on blank verso of title, folding engraved frontispiece; contemporary half calf, hinges cracked, label chipped.   Anthony W. Laywood 109-79 1996 £95.00

LAWRENCE, ROBERT   Primitive Psycho-Therapy and Quackery. London: 1910. 1st British edition; 276 pages; original binding; scarce.   W. Bruce Fye 71-1247 1996 $100.00

LAWRENCE, THOMAS EDWARD 1888-1935   A Brief Record of the Advance of the Egyptian Expeditionary Force Under the Command of General Sir Edmund H. H. Allenby, G. C. B., G. C. M. G. July 1917 to October 1918. London: published by His Majesty's Stationery Office, 1919. 2nd edition; medium 4to; portrait, vi, 113 pages, 56 full page maps, original printed boards, cloth spine. O'Brien A012.   David Bickersteth 133-156 1996 £110.00

LAWRENCE, THOMAS EDWARD 1888-1935   Crusader Castles. London: Golden Cockerel Press, 1936. 1st edition; limited to 1000 copies; tall 8vo; 2 volumes; (70), 62 pages, plus folding maps, rust half morocco, cloth (cream) boards, cloth very slightly yellowed (usually badly discolored or stained); as nice a copy as one could hope to find. David Mason 71-112 1996 $2,400.00

LAWRENCE, THOMAS EDWARD 1888-1935   Crusader Castles. Waltham St. Lawrence: Golden Cockerel Press, 1936. Limited to 1000 numbered copies; crown 4to; 2 volumes, printed on mouldmade paper; 56, 62 pages; titles printed in red, plates, maps and text figures, 2 folding maps in separate sleeve as issued, publisher's red half morocco, top edge gilt, others uncut, cloth sides slightly dust soiled, otherwise very good. Chanticleer 112.   Thomas Thorp 489-186 1996 £750.00

LAWRENCE, THOMAS EDWARD 1888-1935   From a Letter of T. E. Lawrence. Officina Bodoni, 1959. 8 x 5 inches; 6 leaves, first and last blank; original pink wrappers, Officina Bodoni pressmark on front cover, very slight wrinkles in paper cover, but virtually mint; very rare.   Phillip J. Pirages 33-405 1996 $950.00

LAWRENCE, THOMAS EDWARD 1888-1935   The Home Letters of T. E Lawrence and His Brothers. Oxford: Basil Blackwell, 1954. 1st edition; 8vo; pages xvi, 731; numerous photographic illustrations; original dark blue cloth, dust jacket, very, rather scarce. O'Brien A246.   Sotheran PN32-31 1996 £168.00

LAWRENCE, THOMAS EDWARD 1888-1935   Men in Print: Essays in Literary Criticism. Waltham St. Lawrence: Golden Cockerel Press, 1940. 1st edition; limited to 500 numbered copies; royal 8vo; 60 paes; original quarter blue niger morocco, white linen sides, top edge gilt, others uncut, spine little faded, front endpapers spotteed, generally very good. O'Brien A229; Pertelote 148.   Sotheran PN32-29 1996 £498.00

LAWRENCE, THOMAS EDWARD 1888-1935   Minorities. London: Bertram Rota & Jonathan Cape, 1971. 1st edition; this being one of 125 numbered copies, signed by C. Day Lewis and J. M. Wilson; 8vo; 272 pages, frontispiece, 24 facsimiles of Lawrence's holograph transcriptions original quarter brown pigskin, grey cloth sides, top edge gilt, fine. O'Brien A257.   Sotheran PN32-33 1996 £325.00

LAWRENCE, THOMAS EDWARD 1888-1935   The Mint. London: Cape, 1955. Limited edition, 1290/2000 copies; top edge gilt, prelims slightly foxed, covers little damp spotted, otherwise very good in soiled slipcase Virgo Books 48-125 1996 £180.00

LAWRENCE, THOMAS EDWARD 1888-1935   The Mint. London: Jonathan Cape, 1955. 1st English edition, limited issue, one of 2000 numbered copies; royal 8vo; pagaes (ii), 206; original quarter dark blue pigskin, blue buckram sides, marbled endpapers, original board slipcase Fine; O'Brien A172.   Sotheran PN32-32 1996 £198.00

LAWRENCE, THOMAS EDWARD 1888-1935   Revolt in the Desert. London: Jonathan Cape, 1927. 1st edition; large paper issue, limited to 315 numbered copies, of which only 300 were for sale; royal 8vo; page (ii), 446; folding map, 19 plates, including portrait, plates with tissue guards; fine; original quarter dark brown pigskin, brown buckram sides, spine lettered in gilt, top edge gilt, others uncut and largely unopened. O'Brien A101.   Sotheran PN32-27 1996 £998.00

LAWRENCE, THOMAS EDWARD 1888-1935   Secret Despatches from Arabia. Waltham St. Lawrence: Golden Cockerel Press, n.d. Number 959 of 1000 copies; bound by Sangorski & Sutcliffe in quarter niger, top edge gilt, endpapers and pages slightly foxed and browned at edges, cream cloth covers soiled and spotted, lower corners bumped, otherwise good.   Virgo Books 48-124 1996 £400.00

LAWRENCE, THOMAS EDWARD 1888-1935   Seven Pillars of Wisdom, a Triumph. London: Jonathan Cape, 1935. 1st published edition; royal 8vo; pages 672; 4 maps, 47 plates; original brown buckram, gilt, dust jacket little torn and chipped, otherwise very good. O'Brien A042. Sotheran PN32-28 1996 £148.00

LAWRENCE, THOMAS EDWARD 1888-1935   Shaw - Ede. T. E. Lawrence's Letters to H. S. Ede 1927-1935. Waltham St. Lawrence: Golden Cockerel Press, 1942. 1st edition; no. 354 of 500 copies; 4to; 6 pages; original dark blue morocco backed cream boards, by Sangorski & Sutcliffe, top edge gilt, others uncut. Pertelote 151.   Claude Cox 107-65 1996 £280.00

LAWRENCE, THOMAS EDWARD 1888-1935   T. E. Lawrence's Letters to H. S. Ede 1927-1935. Waltham St. Lawrence: Golden Cockerel Press, 1942. 1st edition; limited to 500 numbered copies; royal 8vo; 62 pages; complete with notice to purchasers concerning alledged inaccuracies in text; original quarter black niger morocco, buff cloth sides, top edge gilt ohters uncut. O'Brien A234; Pertelote 151.   Sotheran PN32-30 1996 £498.00

LAWRENCE, W.   Lectures on Physiology, Zoology and the Natural History of Man, Delivered at the Royal College of Surgeons. London: 1819. 1st edition; 8vo; pages xxiv, 579, 12 engraved plates; original boards, rebacked in calf; dedication copy, with manuscript inscription to dedicatee, Blumenbach, by Lawrence, in addition Blumenbach's letter of acknowledgement has been loosely inserted.   Wheldon & Wesley 207-56 1996 £950.00

THE LAWS and Constitutions of the Master, Wardens and Commonalt of Watermen and Lightermen of the River Thames. London: printed for the Company, by A. Kirkaldy, etc. 1858. Blind embossed cloth, showing definite wear, usable.   Meyer Boswell SL26-227 1996 $150.00

LAWS and Ordinances Relating to the Baltimore and Ohio Rail Road. Baltimore: John Murphy, 1850. 1st edition thus; very worn old roan covers, spine has perished and is covered by eugly old red cloth tape, front hinge entirely broken, but text is hanging together, old markings and brief notes in text, possibly by the owner John H. B. Latrobe (who was legal counsel for the B & O), Latrobe's name stamped on covers. Magnum Opus 44-89 1996 $100.00

LAWS Concerning the Election of Members of Parliament; with Determinations of the House of Commons Thereon, and All Their Incidents: Contuned...to the Present... London: printed for W. Owen, 1774. New edition; 8vo; pages xx, 80, 67 (bis)-392, (12); contemporary calf, red label, gilt, very good to nice. James Fenning 133-254 1996 £125.00

LAWSON, JOHN PARKER The Book of Perth: an Illustration of the Moral and Ecclesiastical State of Scotland Before and After the Reformation. Edinburgh: Thomas G. Stevenson, 1847. Limited edition (251); 8vo; pages xl, 318, (ii), half title, 3 engraved plates, woodcut; little spotting; original cloth, gilt, rather faded, tear across top of spine repaired. Presentation copy from William Turnbull, to whomt he work is dedicated, to Hugh Jones. R.F.G. Hollett 76-152 1996 £75.00

LAWSON, ROBERT Ben and Me. L-B, 1939. 1st edition; just about fine in dust jacket, uncommon in this condition. Aronovitz 57-669 1996 $185.00

LAWSON, ROBERT Mr. Revere and I. Boston: Little, Brown & Co., 1953. 1st edition; number 27 of a special limited edition of 500 copies, signed by author; fine in clear acetate dust jacket in slipcase which is partially split top rear edge and with one corner bumped. Steven C. Bernard 71-446 1996 $100.00

THE LAWYER'S and Magistrate's Magazine...Volume I for the Year MDCCXC. Dublin: printed for W. Jones, 86 Dame Street and H. Watts, 1792. Modern quarter calf over marbled boards, embrowned but quite sound. Meyer Boswell SL27-141 1996 $650.00

LAXTON, HENRY Examples of Building Construction, Intended as an Aide-Memoire for the Professional Man and the Operative... London: Laxton, 1859-60/61-67. Large folio; 2 volumes, double page title, double page contents page, 78 double page litho plates (ex 80); double page title, double page contents page and 80 double page litho plates; drawings; original quarter morocco, worn. Elton Engineering 10-91 196 £380.00

LAY, WILLIAM A Narrative of the Mutiny, on Board the Ship Globe of Nantucket, in the Pacific Ocean, Jan. 1824. New London: Lay & Hussey, 1828. 1st edition; 12mo; 168 pages; contemporary calf, neatly rebacked, original spine laid down. Shoemaker 33826; Judd 107; Howes L158. M & S Rare Books 60-361 1996 $1,650.00

LAYARD, AUSTEN HENRY 1817-1894 Discoveries In the Ruins of Nineveh and Babylon... New York: Putnam, 1853. 1st American edition; thick 8vo; 686, (1) pages; maps and plans; original dark green cloth, with pictorial gilt stamping; excellent copy. Chapel Hill 94-280 1996 $175.00

LAYARD, AUSTEN HENRY 1817-1894 Nineveh and its Remains; with an Account of a Visit to the Chalaean Christians of Kurdistan and the Yezides, or Devil Worshippers. London: 1849. 2 volumes; plates, plans and illustrations; modern half brown calf, mottled board sides, mottled edges. Charles W. Traylen 117-392 1996 £92.00

LAYARD, AUSTEN HENRY 1817-1894 Nineveh and Its Remains: with an Account of a Visit to the Chaldaea Christians of Kurdistan and the Yezidis or Devil-Worshippers... London: 1849. 3rd edition; 8vo; 2 volumes, over 800 pages, numerous illustrations; original pictorial cloth, spine of volume 2 neatly and expertly relaid, good. K Books 442-328 1996 £90.00

LAYARD, AUSTEN HENRY 1817-1894 Nineveh and Its Remains... New York: George P. Putnam, 1853. 2nd American edition; 8vo; 2 volumes in 1; 326, 373 pages; plates, maps and plans; contemporary half maroon morocco with raised bands, gilt tooled spine panels, all edges gilt, spine sunned, corners worn, otherwise very good; Chapel Hill 94-279 1996 $150.00

LAYARD, E. L. The Birds of South Africa. London: 1875-84. New edition; royal 8vo; pages xxvii, 890, 12 hand colored plates; original half green morocco, spine trifle faded and joints rubbed; very scarce, first 2 plates very slightly stained, but good, from the collection of Jan Coldewey. Wheldon & Wesley 207-57 1996 £650.00

LAYARD, JOHN Stone men of Malekula, athe Small Island of Vao. London: 1942. 1st edition; large 8vo; xxiii, 816 pages, folding frontispiece, 24 plates, 87 text illustrations, 11 tables, 10 maps, 11 songs; original cloth, dust jacket, very good. K Books 442-329 1996 £75.00

LAYCOCK, THOMAS An Essay on Hysteria: Being an Analysis of its Irregular and Aggravated Forms... Philadelphia: Haswell, Barrington and Haswell/New Orleans: John J. Haswell & Co., 1840. 1st American edition (published same year in London); 8vo; 192 pages; modern calf backed marbled boards, leather spine label, very clean, unfoxed. Cordasco 40-0785. John Gach 150-275 1996 $185.00

LAYNE, J. GREGG Annals of Los Angeles from the Arrival of the First White Men to the Civil War, 1769-1861. San Francisco: 1935. 1st edition; 97 pages; frontispiece, color illustrations; pictorial cloth, fine; very scarce. 6 Guns 101; Blumann 1489. T. A. Swinford 49-686 1996 $150.00

LAZARUS, EMMA The Poems. (with) Selections from Her Poetry and Prose. Boston and New York: Houghton Mifflin Co./New York: Cooperative Book League, 1888/1944. Later issue; 8vo; 3 volumes; frontispiece; green cloth with gilt lettered spine, top edge gilt; 2nd title in pictorial wrappers; good only, very fine; scarce. BAL 11503. Paulette Rose 16-193 1996 $250.00

LEA, HENRY CHARLES Materials Toward a History of Witchcraft. Philadelphia: University of Pennsylvania Press, 1939. 8vo; 3 volumes, (ii), xliv, 434; (ii), 435-1038, (2); (ii), 1039-1548 pages; red buckram with gilt spines, corners bumped, attractive and comely set; rare. John Gach 150-277 1996 $350.00

LEA, MUNRO Geography Can Be Fun. Philadelphia: Lippincott, 1951. 1st edition; small 4to; profusely illustrated with black and white drawings by Munro Leaf; yellow cloth, pictorially stamped in black, edges just rubbed, else very fresh copy in slightly chipped pictorial dust jacket. Barbara Stone 70-139 1996 £65.00

LEA, TOM 1907- The Hands of Cantu. Boston and Toronto: Little, Brown and Co., 1964. 1st edition; number 40 of only 100 numbered copies; 244 pages; specially printed on mouldmade Arches paper and signed by author; illustrations by author, including mounted frontispiece in color; bound by Harcourt Bindery in full brown crushed levant morocco, raised bands, gilt lettered spine, marbled endpapers, top edge gilt, mint, uncut, in publisher's cloth slipcase; accompanied by a signed and dated print by Lea, additionally, the print with his copy has a presentation inscription signed by Lea. Rare. Argonaut Book Shop 113-403 1996 $3,000.00

LEA, TOM 1907- The Hands of Cantu. Boston: Little Brown, 1964. One of an unspecified number of copies, signed by author on tipped in leaf; original cloth, bookmark laid in; fine in just about fine dust jacket. Beasley Books 82-93 1996 $100.00

LEA, TOM 1907- In the Crucible of the Sun. Meriden: privately printed for the King Ranch by Meriden Gravure, 1974. 1st edition; folio; 97 pages; color plates; scarce. Maggie Lambeth 30-325 1996 $650.00

LEA, TOM 1907- The King Ranch. 1st edition; 1st state; on page 507 the first sentence of that chapter does not begin with 'For' on the first state; volumes 1 and 2; books fine, slipcase frayed and worn. Early West 22-259 1996 $125.00

LEA, TOM 1907- The King Ranch. Boston: 1957. 838 pages; illustrations; cloth; pictorial slip case, fine. Herd 1318; 6 Score 69. T. A. Swinford 49-687 1996 $125.00

LEA, TOM 1907- The King Ranch. Kingsville: 1957. Limited special edition, none of which wre for sale, bound in 'saddle blanket' crash linen, having a running "W" in the center and printed on all rag-paper made especially for this book and watermarked with the running "W" brand; 6 maps, scattered light foxing to slipcase and bindings, label worn, lower hinge in volume one cracked, otherwise fine. Glenn Books 36-170 1996 $1,500.00

LEA, TOM 1907- A Picture Gallery. Boston: Little Brown, 1968. 1st edition; folio; 2 volumes; 35 color plates, many black and whites; slipcase. Maggie Lambeth 30-328 1996 $150.00

LEA, TOM 1907- Picture Gallery: Paintings and Drawings. Boston: 1968. 1st edition; large folio; 160 pages (book) and accompanying portfolio with 35 plates; publisher's slipcase. W. M. Morrison 436-320 1996 $125.00

LEA, TOM 1907-   A Picture Gallery. Boston: 1968. 1st edition; 161 pages, illustrations, 12 in color, 22 in monochrome; slipcases worn, as usual.   Early West 22-689 1996 $110.00

LEA, TOM 1907-   Selection of Paintings and Drawings from the Nineteen Sixties. 1969. Rio Bravo edition, 1 of 200 copies, signed by Lea, Harry Ransom, Al Lowman and Wm. Wittliff; specially bound, publisher's slipcase, light sunfading to 3 edges.   W. M. Morrison 436-321 1996 $135.00

LEA, TOM 1907-   Western Beef Cattle. Austin: Encino Press, 1967. 1/850 copies; 4to; 34 pages, titlepage illustration in color; cloth, slipcase. W. M. Morrison 436-322 1996 $100.00

LEACH, D. G.   Rhododendrons of the World and How to Grow Them. New York: 1961. 4to; pages 544; endpaper maps, 16 pages of half tone photos, line drawings, foldout phylogenetic chart (colored); cloth, dust jacket, some scuffing and chipping to edges.   Raymond M. Sutton VII-620 1996 $100.00

LEACH, THOMAS   Modern Reports; or, Select Cases Adjudged in the Courts of King's Bench, Chancery, Common Pleas and Exchequer. London: printed for G. G. J. and J. Robinson, 1793. 5th edition; 3 volumes; contemporary calf, rubbed and well worn but sound.   Meyer Boswell SL26-142 1996 $150.00

LEADBEATER, MARY   Cottages Dialogues Among the Irish Peasantry. London: printed for J. Johnson, 1811. 1st edition; 12mo; v, (v), 343 pages; contemporary half calf, very slight crack in upper joint; very nice. James Burmester 29-86 1996 £200.00

LEADBITTER, MIKE   Blues Records 1943-1966. London: and New York: Hanover and Oak, 1968. 1st edition; original cloth, fine but for soiled foot of spine, in lightly soiled and lightly worn dust jacket. Beasley Books 82-235 1996 $125.00

A LEAF From the First Edition of the First Complete Bible in English, the Coverdale Bible, 1535. San Francisco: Book Club of California, 1974. One of 425 copies; 13 3/4 x 10 inches; 45 pages; cloth; fine. Harlan 145; Olmsted 37a.   Timothy Hawley 115-240 1996 $250.00

LEAF, MUNRO   The Story of Ferdinand (The Bull). London: Hamish Hamilton, 1937. 1st U.K. edition; small square 4to; 34 pages of black and white illustrations opposite text, titlepage vignette and illustrated endpapers by Robert Lawson; illustrated pink boards, corners rubbed, else fine in soiled dust jacket with several short tears.   Marjorie James 19-142 1996 £55.00

LEAF, MUNRO   The Story of Ferdinand the Bull. New York: Viking Press, 1938. drawings in black and white by Robert Lawson; red pictorial boards backed in grey cloth, pictorial endpapers, covers little faded, else fresh copy; inscribed by Robert Lawson with small ink drawing of posy of flowers.   Barbara Stone 70-137 1996 £135.00

LEAF, MUNRO   The Story of Simpson and Sampson. New York: Viking Press, 1941. 1st edition; 4to; 30 pages of drawings in black and white by Robert Lawson; red cloth, fine in slightly chipped pictorial dust jacket, scarce; signed in ink by author and artist.   Barbara Stone 70-138 1996 £175.00

LEAF, MUNRO   Wee Gillis. New York: Viking, 1938. Limited edition, one of 525 copies signed by author and artist; drawings in black and white by Robert Lawson; bound in tan canvas with paper titling labels, one repaired marginal tear, otherwise very fresh copy.   Barbara Stone 70-140 1996 £150.00

LEAF, MUNRO   Wee Gillis. New York: Viking, 1938. 1st edition; 4to; 32 full page black and white illustrations by Robert Lawson; tartan patterned boards, fine in chipped dust jacket.   Marjorie James 19-143 1996 £65.00

LEAHY, JOHN   The Art of Swimming in the Eton Style. Nottingham: Shepherd Bros., 1875. frontispiece, folding plate; original mauve cloth, slightly faded, very good; inscribed presentation copy from author to Colonel Higginson.   Jarndyce 103-522 1996 £50.00

LEALAND, JOHN   The Itinerary 1535-1543. S. Illinois University Press and Centaur Press, 1964. New edition; 8vo; 5 volumes; plates, maps; original cloth.   Howes Bookshop 265-655 1996 £85.00

LEAR, EDWARD 1812-1888   A Book of Nonsense. London: Routledge Warne and Routledge, 1862. 5th edition; oblong 8vo; pages (iv), 111, (i[) illustrations by Lear; sometime rebound in full tan calf, stamped in blind[some leaves neatly and skillfully strengthened to the reverse at edges, : leaves with loss at corner or edge, expertly made good, some internally browning, despite the repairs, a neat volume.   Sotheran PN32-130 1996 £188.00

LEAR, EDWARD 1812-1888   The Book of Nonsense. London: Frederic[Warne and Co., 1903. Oblong 4to; original dark green grained cloth, elaborately stamped in black and gilt, decorative endpapers, bold illustrations by Lear; fine in excellent, clean state.   Sotheran PN32-13. 1996 £128.00

LEAR, EDWARD 1812-1888   The Complete Nonsense of Edward Lear. London: Faber & Faber Ltd., 1947. 1st edition thus; illustrations; decorated cloth covers designed by Barnett Freedman; covers rubbed a extremities, prelims, edges and endpapers spotted, very good in crease and slightly rubbed, marked and dusty dust jacket which repeats cover design.   Ulysses 39-358 1996 £65.00

LEAR, EDWARD 1812-1888   Illustrations of the Family of Psittacidae, or Parrots... London: Pion Limited, 1978. Facsimile edition; folio; pages 8, 42 colored plates, with 16 page accompanying booklet, illustrated; original burgundy half morocco, gilt, gilt edges, slipcase.   Sotheran PN32-92 1996 £895.00

LEAR, EDWARD 1812-1888   Illustrations of the Family of Psittacidae, or Parrots. New York: 1978. Exact facsimile made from Linnean Society of London's copy; folio; pages (viii), 42 colored plates, with 16 page illustrated bookplate; half leather, gilt, clean second hand copy; Wheldon & Wesley 207-58 1996 £500.00

LEAR, EDWARD 1812-1888   Journal of a Landscape Painter in Corsic London: Robert John Bush,, 1870. 1st edition; 8vo; xvi, 272 pages[40 wood engraved plates from drawings by author, 40 vignettes; mode[binder's cloth, occasional very slight foxing.   Thomas Thorp 489-189 1996 £140.00

LEAR, EDWARD 1812-1888   Journals of a Landscape Painter. (with) Journals of a Landscape Painter in Albania. London: Richard Bentley... 1852/51. 1st editions; 8vo; half title, (v-viii), (ix-xx), 1-205 pages, half title 209-281 pages, index, 2 pages ads; map, frontispiece, 20 chromolitho plates, 1 map; 1-10, 11-428 pages, map frontispiece, 20 chromo-litho plates, light foxing to map frontispiece, title and occasionally to text, plates all in very good condition; full polished green calf, elaborate gilt tooled borders, joints slightly sunned, red morocco label to spine, gilt tooling to compartments, small scuff mark to upper board, all edges gi marbled endpapers; 2nd title bound uniformly with upper board sunned, affecting top of upper board by about 1 3/4", all edges gilt, marbled endpapers; all in all a handsome set. Abbey Travel 175 & 45.   Beelei[Abbey BA56-88 1996 £1,750.00

LEAR, EDWARD 1812-1888   The Jumblies. N.P.: Wind & Harlot, 1991 One of 74 copies; 3 x 2 1/4 inches; hand colored illustrations by Bonni[Baris; sage boards, spine label; mint.   Bromer Booksellers 90-198 1996 $100.00

LEAR, EDWARD 1812-1888   Later Letters...to Chichester Fortescue (Lord Carlingford), Frances Countess Waldegrave and Others. London: T Fisher Unwin, 1911. 1st edition; 8vo; 392 pages; 2 colored plates, numerous black and white plates and text illustrations; original two colored cloth, gilt, top edges gilt, dust jacket; half title spotted, other light spotting; presentation copy with Lady Strachey's visting card paste to front free endpaper inscribed "With the editors kindest remembrance & thans, Sutton Court".   Sotheran PN32-91 1996 £68.00

LEAR, EDWARD 1812-1888   More Nonsense, Pictures, Rhymes, Botany. London: Robert John Bush, 32, Charing Cross, S.W., 1872. 1st edition; square 8vo; illustrations; newly and finely bound in half crimson calf, spine ruled in gilt with gilt centres, top edge gilt, fine.   Sotheran PN32-131 1996 £168.00

LEAR, EDWARD 1812-1888   The New Vestments. Portland: Chamberlain Press, 1978. Limited to 100 copies, signed by artist, this copy additionally inscribed; octavo; (6) pages, french fold; illustrations Sarah Chamberlain; printed in two colors on beige japanese paper, 2 fu page wood engravings, the two illustrations each signed by Chamberlai printed wrappers, extremely fine.   Bromer Booksellers 87-118 1996 $150.00

LEAR, EDWARD 1812-1888   Nonsense Songs. London: Warne, 1900. 1st edition; 1st issue; small 4to; 14 colored plates and numerous drawings in black and white by Leslie Brooke; brown cloth stamped in gilt and darker brown, spine little darkened, occasional pale spotting, else fresh bright copy, scarce.   Barbara Stone 70-141 1996 £125.00

LEAR, EDWARD 1812-1888   The Story of the Four Little Children who Went Round the World. (and) The History of the Seven Families of the Lake Pipple-Popple; Nonsense Stories. Old Stile Press, 1990. One of 225 numbered copies, signed by artist; 4to; printed on Saunders mouldmade in type computer generated from an alphabet drawn by artist; numerous drawings by Gillian Martin; decorated boards with cloth spine; fine in slipcase.   Bertram Rota 272-359 1996 £65.00

LEAR, EDWARDS   Journals of a Landscape Painter in Albania, &c. London: Richard Bentley, 1851. 1st edition; royal 8vo; iv, 428 pages; 20 tinted lithograph plates; publisher's blind and gilt stamped blue cloth, corners slightly worn, covers little dust soiled, occasional foxing, but good.   Thomas Thorp 489-188 1996 £500.00

LEARNED, WILLIAM LAW   The Fancy Ball; a Letter, Lost from the Portfolio of a Young Lady of Albany. Albany W. C. Little & Co., printed by J. Munsell, 1846. 1st edition; 8vo; 28 pages; later stiff wrappers, foxed. Rare.   M & S Rare Books 60-210 1996 $125.00

LEAVITT, JOHN MC DOWELL   Kings of Capital and Knights of Labor. New York: John S. Wiley, 1885. 1st edition; tan cloth, lavishly stamped in gilt and black; near fine but for wear to spine and fraying to spine ends, quite handsome.   Beasley Books 82-322 1996 $125.00

LEAVITT, JONATHAN   A Summary of the Laws of Massachusetts, Relative to the Settlement, Support, Employment and Removal of Paupers. Greenfield: Printed by John Denio, 1810. 1st edition; 8vo; original sheep backed marbled newsprint boards, text showing through the marbling, printed paper label on upper cover, edges chipped with tears, rubbed, text browned; signatures of William Perry on endpaper and Dr. J. W. Proctor of Malden, Mass. on title, with note at foot of title reading "State Board of Charity, April 1, 1901". Marvin p. 456; S&S 20533; Sabin 39559.   James Cummins 14-152 1996 $200.00

LEBEL, ROBERT   Marcel Duchamp. London: Trianon Press, 1959. 1st British edition; 4to; (vi), 192 pages; color illustration tipped on titlepage, 6 color (tippedin) and 129 monochrome plates, text illustrations; owner's bookplate, marginal notation in pencil, else very good, dust jacket with few short tears at spine.   Andrew Cahan 47-67 1996 $150.00

LE BERTHON, J. L.   An Illustrated Souvenir Directory of Southern California. Los Angeles: Los Angeles Herald, ca. 1903. 12 1/2 x 9 1/4 inches; 144 pages; full page and smaller photographic illustrations; modern wrappers, marginal chipping to first and last leaves; Dawson's Books Shop 528-123 1996 $100.00

LE BLANC, H.   The Art of Tying the Cravat... London: Effingham Wilson and Ingrey & Madeley, 1828. 1st edition in English; 12mo; frontispiece, 4 folding lithographed plates; original pink boards, black pictorial side label, boards bit dusty and slightly rubbed; in fine original condition.   Ximenes 108-239 1996 $300.00

LE BLANC, M.   The Engineer and Machinist's Drawing Book. Glasgow: 1855. Folio; 71 plates and woodcuts in text, vignette to title, half calf, joints cracked but sound on strings.   Petersfield Bookshop FH58-153 1996 £56.00

LEBRUN, RICO   Drawings for Dante's Inferno. N.P.: Kanthos Press, 1963. One of 2000 copies, with four original lithographs signed in plate laid in; 17.25 x 12.75 inches; 35 illustrations with text; designed by Leonard Baskin and printed by the Meriden gravure Company; black cloth boards, title in gilt on spine and front, grey paper board slipcase; fine.   Joshua Heller 21-49 1996 $175.00

LE CARRE, JOHN 1931-   Call for the Dead. London: Gollancz, 1961. 2nd printing in same year as the first; fine with page edges lightly soiled, in very good dust jacket with light chipping and soiling.   Quill & Brush 102-1015 1996 $150.00

LE CARRE, JOHN 1931-   The Clandestine Muse. Portland: Co-published with Charles Seluzicki Fine Books, One of 250 copies, signed by author; 9 x 5 inches; 24 unnumbered pages; unillustrated; a solid triangle decoration printed in silver on front cover, half title and last text page and blind embossed and printed in black, text in black, colophon in silver; book and binding designed and printed by Claire Van Vliet, handsewn into brown Roman endpapers inserted in marble paper covers, paper wrappers marbled by Pam Smith, Santa Fe. Fine.   Joshua Heller 21-23 1996 $250.00

LE CARRE, JOHN 1931-   The Honourable Schoolboy. Franklin Center: Franklin Library, 1977. Limited edition; leatherbound, all edges gilt, silk ribbon marker laid in; fine.   Ken Lopez 74-255 1996 $125.00

LE CARRE, JOHN 1931-   The Little Drummer Girl. New York: Knopf, 1983. One of reportedly, 200 copies, with tipped in, signed leaf. Fine in dust jacket.   Quill & Brush 102-1028 1996 $100.00

LE CARRE, JOHN 1931-   The Looking Glass War. London: Heinemann, 1965. 1st edition; fine in unfaded price clipped dust jacket with store sticker on front flap and very minor edge wear.   Quill & Brush 102-1017 1996 $150.00

LE CARRE, JOHN 1931-   The Naive and Sentimental Lover. London: Hodder & Stoughton, 1971. 1st edition; spine very slightly cocked, otherwise fine in dust jacket with only minor edge wear.   Quill & Brush 102-1020 1996 $100.00

LE CARRE, JOHN 1931-   The Naive and Sentimental Lover. London: Hodder & Stoughton, 1971. 1st edition; top corners lightly bumped, still fine in price clipped dust jacket.   Quill & Brush 102-1021 1996 $100.00

LE CARRE, JOHN 1931-   A Perfect Spy. New York: Knopf, 1986. 1st edition; signed on tipped in sheet; fine in dust jacket.   Quill & Brush 102-1031 1996 $125.00

LE CARRE, JOHN 1931-   The Secret Pilgrim. New York: Knopf, 1991. 1st edition; signed, minor flaw in cloth on front cover, otherwise fine in dust jacket.   Quill & Brush 102-1034 1996 $100.00

LE CARRE, JOHN 1931-   A Small Town in Germany. New York: Coward McCann, 1968. One of 500 numbered presentation copies, signed by LeCarre; laid in this copy are cards from both the president and publisher; as issued in bright orange boards; fine.   Bev Chaney, Jr. 23-368 1996 $300.00

LE CARRE, JOHN 1931-   Smiley's People. New York: Knopf, 1980. 1st edition; with signed leaf tipped in; fine in dust jacket with only minor edge wear.   Quill & Brush 102-1025 1996 $125.00

LE CARRE, JOHN 1931-   The Spy Who Came In From the Cold. London: Victor Gollancz, 1963. 1st edition; 8vo; pages 222; original blue cloth, dust jacket, very nice, dust jacket little soiled on lower panel, but has none of the usual faded to spine.   Sotheran PN32-34 1996 £298.00

LE CARRE, JOHN 1931-   The Spy Who Came In from the Cold. London: Gollancz, 1963. 1st edition; exceptionally nice copy, fine in dust jacket with very light rubbing;   Quill & Brush 102-1016 1996 $500.00

LE CARRE, JOHN 1931-   Tinker, Tailor, Soldier, Spy. New York: Knopf, 1974. Uncorrected proof copy of the 1st American edition; uncommon proof, spine faded, otherwise fine in tall wrappers.   Ken Lopez 74-254 1996 $375.00

LECKENBY, CHARLES H.   The Tread of Pioneers. Steamboat Springs: 1944. 1st edition; 206 pages; photos; book near fine, cloth covers with minor wear, signed by author; scarce. Six Guns 1304.   Early West 22-183 1996 $200.00

LECKENBY, CHARLES H.   The Tread of the Pioneers. Steamboat Springs: Pilot Press, 1945. 1st edition; bookplate to front pastedown, small ink stamp to front free endpaper, diagonal wrinkle to front cover, still very good to fine, signed by author.   Hermitage SP95-716 1996 $125.00

LECKY, WILLIAM   Tentamen Medicum Inaugurale, Quaedam Complectens de Morbis ex Graviditate Pendentibus. Edinburgi: Apud Balfour et Smellie, Academiae Typogaphos, 1787. 8vo; 55 pages, all edges gilt, original full green morocco gilt, spine gilt with red morocco label, inscribed by author to his cousin; very fine.   David Bickersteth 133-204 1996 £125.00

LECKY, WILLIAM EDWARD HARTPOLE   History of European Morals from Augustus to Charlemagne. London: Longmans, Green, 1869. Tall 8vo; 2 volumes; full tan polished calf, richly gilt panelled spines, raised bands, marbled edges; attractive.   Appelfeld Gallery 54-130 1996 $200.00

LECKY, WILLIAM EDWARD HARTPOLE   History of the Rise and Influence of the Spirit of Rationalism in Europe. London: Longmans, & Green, 1872. 5th edition; 2 volumes; xxxi, 408, xv, 430 pages; nicely bound, marbled boards, raised bands, gilt spine, very good+.   Middle Earth 77-309 1996 $125.00

LECKY, WILLIAM EDWARD HARTPOLE   A History of England in the Eighteenth Century. New York: D. Appleton, 1888-90. 8vo; 8 volumes; original cloth. From the library of Horace Annesley Vachell with presentation inscription from his mother.   Howes Bookshop 265-648 1996 £120.00

LECKY, WILLIAM EDWARD HARTPOOLE   History of the Rise and Influence of the Spirit of Rationalism in Europe. London: Longman, Green, 1865. 1st edition; tall 8vo; 2 volumes; full tan polished calf, richly gilt panelled spines, raised bands, marbled edges. Nice   Appelfeld Gallery 54-131 1996 $225.00

LECLERC, FREDERIC   Texas and Its Revolution. Houston: Anson Jones, 1950. Limited edition this number 83; 4to; color folding map, 49 pages, in map faced folder, map quite good. foxing; Howes L171; Rader 2214; Raines p. 137.   Maggie Lambeth 30-330 1996 $125.00

LE CLERC, SEBASTIEN   Practical Geometry: or, a New and Easy Method of Treating that Art. London: printed for T. Bowles and J. Bowles, 1742. 4th edition; crown 8vo; titlepage in red and black, text pages (1)-185, index 3 leaves, 81 (sic) copper engravings in text, worming in blank lower corner of title and next 2 leaves; contemporary calf, joints cracked.   H. M. Fletcher 121-108 1996 £120.00

LE CONTE, MICHEL   Les Trophees de l'Amour Divin au Tres-Sainct Sacrement de l'Autel. Charleville: Raoult et Poncelet, 1645. 8vo; title, pages 3-15, 2ff., 1-364; brown morocco gilt, broad outer border of repeated small tools enclosing a central panel with small tool cornerpeices and a lozenge shaped centre-piece enclosing a simple crowned letter "C", flat spine is gilt in 8 panels, all edges gilt, comb-marbled endpapers, bookplate.   Marlborough 160-21 1996 £750.00

LECOUNT, PETER   A Practical Treatise on Railways, Explaining Their Construction and Management... Edinburgh: Adam and Charles Black, 1839. 1st edition; 12mo; viii, 422, (2) pages, 10 folding engraved plates, including a fine engraving of a locomotive, corner of first two leaves torn away, not affecting text; recent calf backed marbled boards.   James Burmester 29-87 1996 £140.00

LECOUVREUR, FRANK   From East Prussia to the Golden Gate. Letters and Diary of the California Pioneer. New York: Los Angeles: and Leipzig: Angelina Book Concern, 1906. 1st edition; 355 pages; 22 half tone plates; original green pictorial binding with title in gilt on spine; fine. Wheat Books of Calif. Gold Rush 123; Cowan p. 387; Rocq 10175. Michael D. Heaston 23-203 1996 $125.00

LECTIUS, JACOBUS   Poetae Graeci Veteres Carminis Heroici Scriptores Qui Extant, Omnes. Aureliae Allobrogum (i.e. Geneva): sumptibus Caldorianae Societatis, 1606. Folio; pages (vi), (ii) blank, (xvi), 739, (i) blank, 624, (xxii), apparently lacks rT8 (final blank), titlepage in red and black, title in Greek at head of titlepage, parallel Greek and Latin texts; late 19th century tan morocco with embossed relief dec. by Mrs. A. S. Macdonald of the Guild of Women Binders, depicting on the upper cover Hermes descending, surrounded by the sacred fire of Olympus and on the lower cover a portrait of Ben Jonson, (this was his copy) within a surround of his ownership inscription, bookplates, binding, lightly rubbed, titlepage dusty and reinforced on verso at inner margin at time of rebinding, some edges little frayed, occasional marginal worming; Simon Finch 24-134 1996 £2,250.00

LEDGER, HENRY   Dramatic Poems. London: printed for the author, 1843. 1st and only edition; foolscap 8vo; original cloth, gold centre ornament, gold border and gilt edges.   Charles W. Traylen 117-153 1996 £120.00

LEDIARD, THOMAS   The Life of John, Duke of Marlborough, Prince of the Roman Empire... London: J. Wilcox, 1736. 1st edition; in 6's; 3 volumes; pages xxx, 529; (ii) 574; (ii), 464, li, (i); frontispiece in volume 1, 1 folding map, 15 folding plans, 26 plates; contemporary sprinkled tan calf, rebacked, with raised bands, red leather gilt lettered labels, volume numbers lettered direct, sides with double gilt fillet border, endpapers browned, red sprinkled and polished edges; very good.   Blackwell's B112-74 1996 £110.00

LEE, AMY FREEMAN   Hobby Horses. New York: Derrydale, 1940. Limited to 200 copies, of which this is no. 12, signed; very good/good. October Farm 36-6 1996 $275.00

LEE, FREDERICK GEORGE   The Other World, or, Glimpses of the Supernatural. London: Henry S. King and Co., 1875. 8vo; 2 volumes; 72 pages publisher's ads at back of volume 2; original brown cloth by Burn and Co., with their label on lower pastedown, decorated in black, lettered in gilt, some rubbing and soiling; some light browning and spotting, mostly of fore-edges, else very good.   James Cummins 14-200 1996 $325.00

LEE, GEORGE W.   Beale Street: Where the Blues Began. New York: Ballou, 1934. 1st edition; couple pages roughly opened with resulting small nicks and tears, else fine in attractive, very good example of the rare dust jacket with some chipping particularly at crown and on rear panel.   Between the Covers 43-149 1996 $475.00

LEE, JAMES W.   The Romance of Palestine: a History. Atlanta: D. E. Luther Pub. Co., 1897. Square 8vo; xxii, (33)-490 pages, profusely illustrated, including 2 color plates and 4 double page color maps; original grayish green cloth pictorially stamped in black and lettered in gilt on front cover and spine, decorative endpapers, light shelfwear, just slightly skewed, previous owner's ink signature on front pastedown, very good.   Heritage Book Shop 196-259 1996 $150.00

LEE, JOHN D.   A Mormon Chronicle: The Diaries of John D. Lee, 1848-1876. San Marino: Huntington Library, 1955. 1st edition; 2 volumes; 344, 480 pages, 4 illustrations, endpaper maps; very fine set in dust jackets, minor spot to spine of one jacket.   Argonaut Book Shop 113-407 1996 $175.00

LEE, JOHN D.   A Mormon Chronicle. The Diaries of John D. Lee 1848-1876. San Marino: Huntginton Library, 1955. 1st edition; 2 volumes, 343, 480 pages; both volumes slightly shelf worn, very good, clean and bright, scarce.   Orrin Schwab 10-25 1996 $155.00

LEE, L. P.   History of the Spirit Lake Massacre! New Britain: L. P. Lee, Publisher, 1857. 1st edition; 47, (1) pages, text engravings; original pictorial wrappers; fine. Ayer 181; Graff 2442; Hanna Yale Exhibit; Howes L210; Jones 1372.   Michael D. Heaston 23-204 1996 $225.00

LEE, LAURIE 1914-   A Rose for Winter - Travels in Andalusia. London: Hogarth Press, 1955. 1st edition; black and white frontispiece by A. Costa; original binding, top edge slightly dusty, head and tail of spine and corners, very slightly bumped and faded, very good in nicked, spotted, rubbed and dusty, slightly marked and soiled dust jacket faded at spine.   Ulysses 39-360 1996 £95.00

LEEPER, DAVID ROHRER   The Argonauts of 'Forty-Nine. South Bend: J. B. Stoll and Co., 1894. 1st edition; pages 146, xvi; illustrations from drawings by O. Marion Elbel; original gilt lettered brown cloth, light wear to spine ends and corners, else fine; errata slip tipped in to rear, lacking in msot copies. Wheat 124.   Argonaut Book Shop 113-408 1996 $190.00

LEESE, JACOB P.   Historical Outline of Lower California. New York: E. S. Dodge & Co., 1865. 1st edition; 48 pages; original printed brown wrappers, neatly rebacked and minor chipping; very good. Barrett Baja 1460; not in Cowan.   Michael D. Heaston 23-38 1996 $375.00

LE FANU, ALICIA   Memoirs of the Life and Writings of Mrs. Frances Sheridan... London: Whittaker, 1824. 1st edition; octavo; pages 435; recent fine rebinding in brown buckram, gilt on red leather label, ex-library with few inoffensive markings, titlepage professionally repaired, nice, crisp copy. Scarce. CBEL II 458.   Hartfield 48-L79 1996 $225.00

LE FANU, JOSEPH SHERIDAN 1814-1873   The Evil Guest. London: Downey & Co., n.d. 1895. 1st U.K. edition; 30 illustrations by Brinsley Le Fanu; dark green and gold decorated cloth with March 1895 ads in rear, top edge gilt, lower left spine corner expertly repaired, binding extremely bright and attractive, exceptional copy, scarce.   Steven C. Bernard 71-421 1996 $600.00

LE FANU, JOSEPH SHERIDAN 1814-1873   A Stable for Nightmares. New Amsterdam: 1896. 1st edition; illustrations; covers of the first American edition in wrappers of the author's novel "The Bird of Paradise" laid in; slightest of fraying at faded spine extremities, some dust soiling to yellow cloth covers, else about very good. Most uncommon;   Aronovitz 57-670 1996 $175.00

LE FANU, W. R.   Seventy Years of Irish Life Being Anecdotes and Reminiscences. London: Edward Arnold, 1893. 1st edition; tall 8vo; (xii), 306, 16 pages ads dated Nov. 1893; original green cloth, inner hinges cracked, spine slightly cocked, otherwise very good.   David Mason 71-96 1996 $100.00

LEFFINGWELL, WILLIAM B.   Wild Fowl Shooting. Chicago: 1890. engraved plates and vignettes; original pictorial gilt cloth; very nice, near fine. Scarce.   David A.H. Grayling 3/95-368 1996 £75.00

LEFORS, JOE   Wyoming Peace Officer. Laramie: 1953. 1st edition; 20 pages; illustrations; cloth, nice. 6 Guns 1315; Herd 1323.   T. A. Swinford 49-692 1996 $150.00

LE FORS, JOE   Wyoming Peace Officer, the Autobiography. Laramie: 1954. 2nd printing; 200 pages, index, photos; scarce in either printing, book remarkably fine, very good dust jacket.   Early West 22-182 1996 $125.00

LE FRERE, JEAN   La Vraye et Entiere Histoire Des Trovbles et Gverres Civiles, Advenves de Nostre Temps. Paris: Loqueneulx, 1578. Thick 8vo; printer's device on titlepage; vellum (front cover damaged). STC French 260.   Rostenberg & Stern 150-86 1996 $525.00

LEFT to Their Own Devices. New York: Typophiles, 1937. 6 x 3 3/4 inches; xxvi, 325 pages; 150 illustrations; top edge gilt, blue cloth, stamped in gold, blue cloth slipcase; dust jacket, mint.   William A. Graf 186-181 1996 $125.00

A LEGACY of Affection, Advice and Instruction, from a Retired Governess, to the Present Pupils of an Establishment Near London for Female Education, Which She Conducted Upward of 40 Years. London: printed for Poole and Edwards, 1872. 1st edition; 12mo; xii, 312 pages; contemporary green roan, lettered in gilt on upper cover, slight traces of wear; scarce.   James Burmester 29-88 1996 £250.00

LE GALLIENNE, RICHARD 1866-1947   Religion of a Literary Man. London: Mathews and Lane, 1893. One of 250 larage paper copies; 8vo; original binding, very good; inscribed by publisher, John Lane to American poet, Robert Bridges.   Charles Agvent 4-819 1996 $185.00

LE GALLIENNE, RICHARD 1866-1947   The Religion of a Literary Man. London: Elkin Mathews, 1893. 1st edition; uncut and partly unopened; spine sunned, extremities slightly rubbed, bookplate; near fine, with 5 page ALS from author.   Polyanthos 22-516 1996 $150.00

LEGER, ALEXIS SAINT-LEGER 1889-   Anabasis - a Poem. London: Faber & Faber Ltd., 1930. One of 350 numbered copies, signed by translator, T. S. Eliot; parallel French and English texts; handmade paper; original binding, top edge gilt, top two inches of spine darkened, free endpapers partially browned, very good in unprinted cellophane dust jacket, which is torn, dusty and nicotine browned at spine, and in scarce slipcase, which is worn, marked and dusty.   Ulysses 39-177 1996 £485.00

LEGG, LEOPOLD G. WICKHAM   English Coronation Records. London: Constable, 1901. Thick crown 4to; pages 500; colored frontispiece and 15 plates; original cloth backed boards, gilt top, other edges untrimmed. Gross/Graves 1354.   Howes Bookshop 265-1890 1996 £55.00

LEGGE, W. V.   A History of the Birds of Ceylon. London: 1878-80. Royal 4to; 3 volumes; pages xlvi, 1237, colored map, plain outline plate, 34 hand colored plates by Keulemans; recent half red morocco, gilt, top edge gilt, one or two minor stains, but nice; from the collection of Jan Coldewey.   Wheldon & Wesley 207-59 1996 £3,000.00

LEGLER, HENRY   Walt Whitman: Yesterday and Today. Chicago: Brothers of the Book, 1916. Limited to 600 numbered copies; 8vo; original binding, head and heel of spine worn, still a wonderful copy of a fragile book in original and near fine dust jacket.   Charles Agvent 4-1206 1996 $125.00

LE GRAND, ANTOINE   Dissertation de Carentia Sensus & Cognitionis in Brutis. London: apud J. Martyn, 1675. 1st edition; 12mo; contemporary calf; fine, scarce. Wing L947; Wellcome III 480.   Ximenes 108-240 1996 $650.00

LE GRAND, LOUIS   The Military Hand-Book, and Soldier's Manual of Information, the Official Articles of War...Regulations for Camp and Service...Health Department, with Valuable Remedies, Etc... New York: Beadle & Co., 1862. 12mo; 125 pages; printed wrappers, crude 'cardboard' boards sewn on; very good; front wrapper intact, rear wrapper missing; signature of Edward B. Holt 3rd Regt. Co. E. N.H.V., Concord, N.H.   Robert F. Lucas 42-20 1996 $150.00

LE GUIN, URSULA   The Dispossessed. H&R, 1974. 1st edition; fine in near fine dust jacket; the copy of SF writer Joanna Russ, with her namd sticker, and this copy inscribed by author for Russ, fully annotated by Russ.   Aronovitz 57-677 1996 $500.00

LE GUIN, URSULA   Findings. Ox Head Press, 1992. 1st edition; 1/26 lettered hard bound copies; (other copies in wrappers), signed by author; 3 3/8 x 2 1/2 inches; as new, scarce.   Aronovitz 57-681 1996 $225.00

LE GUIN, URSULA   The Tombs of Atuan. Atheneum, 1971. 1st edition; near fine in fine dust jacket.   Aronovitz 57-675 1996 $185.00

LE GUIN, URSULA   A Wizard of Earthsea. Parnassus Press, 1968. 1st edition; 1st issue with die break on titlepage; fine in dust jacket. Aronovitz 57-673 1996 $1,250.00

LEHMANN, HERMAN   Nine Years Among the Indians, 1870-1879. von Boeckmann-Jones, 1927. 235 pages; green cloth, new endpapers; dust jacket; Basic 124 a.   Maggie Lambeth 30-333 1996 $125.00

LEHMANN, JOHN   Down River - Danubian Study. London: Cresset Press, 1939. 1st edition; 19 pages of black and white photos; original binding, top edge slightly faded, prelims, edges and endpapers spotted, tail of spine slightly bumped, bottom edges of covers slightly bumped and dusty, very good in nicked, rubbed, dusty and slightly frayed and spotted dust jacket browned at spine and edges.   Ulysses 39-365 1996 £75.00

LEIBER, FRITZ   The Ghost Light. New York: Berkeley, 1984. 1st edition; one of 350 numbered hardcover copies, signed by author; illustrations; fine, issued, without dust jacket.   Robert Gavora 61-63 1996 $150.00

LEIBER, FRITZ   The Secret Songs. RHD, 1968. 1st edition; fine in dust jacket; inscribed by author.   Aronovitz 57-685 1996 $225.00

LEIBER, FRITZ   Two Sought Adventure. Gnome, 1957. 1st edition; near fine in like dust jacket.   Aronovitz 57-682 1996 $135.00

LEIBER, FRITZ   The Wanderer. Dobson, 1967. 1st English and 1st hard cover edition; fine in near fine dust jacket with some light rubbing to rear dust jacket panel.   Aronovitz 57-684 1996 $185.00

LEIBNITZ, GOTTFRIED WILHELM VON   Opera Omnia... Geneva: Fratres de Tournes, 1768. 1st collected edition; 4to; 6 volumes; contemporary French mottled calf, fully gilt backs, 2 red morocco labels, sprinkled edges, few discreet repairs to joints, fine, handsome set, bookplate of Bib. de Mouchy in each volume. Brunet III col.950; Ravier 473.   H. M. Fletcher 121-110 1996 £3,500.00

LEICESTER, ROBERT DUDLEY, EARL OF 1532?-1588   Secret Memoirs of Robert Dudley, Earl of Leciester. London: 1706. 1st edition; 8vo; (30), 218 pages; contemporary calf, worn. '   C. P. Hyland 216-185 1996 £95.00

LEICHHARDT, LUDWIG   Journal of an Overland Expedition in Australia from Moreton Bay to Port Essington, a Distance of Upwards of 3000 Miles During the Years 1844-45. London: T. W. Boone, 1847. (xx), 544 pages, 15 engraved plates, bound in (loose) 19th century half calf and marbled boards, with parts of the original spine laid over, though badly worn and with binding partially sprung (or springing), lacks free endpaper at rear, internally dusty, light damp markings to edge of some plates, still a good working, complete copy.   Antipodean 28-622 1996 $750.00

LEIGH FERMOR, PATRICK   Mani. London: John Murray, 1958. Spine of dust jacket slightly chipped at top and bottom, otherwise excellent; inscribed by author, underneath a holograph variation on book's cover design.   R. A. Gekoski 19-94 1996 £150.00

LEIGH, CHARLES W. E.   Catalogue of the Christie Collection Comprising the Printed Books and Manuscripts Bequeathed to the Library of the University of Manchester by the Late Richard Copley Christie. Manchester University Press, 1915. 1st edition; 4to; frontispiece; original half buckram, small tear to lower hinge, uncut, partly unopened. Forest Books 74-140 1996 £85.00

LEIGH, M. A.   Leigh's Guide to the Lakes and Mountains of Cumberland, Westmorland, and Lancashire... London: sold by G. Biggs, successor to Leigh & Co., 1843. 4th edition; 8vo; pages ix, (i), 168, large folding hand colored map (little roughly tipped on to front pastedown with red buckram), 4 nicely colored maps; original blindstamped crimson cloth, gilt, spine chipped at head and tail. Bicknell 109.4. variant issue R.F.G. Hollett & Son 78-1074 1996 £140.00

LEIGH, SAMUEL   Leigh's New Pocket Road-book of England and Wales. London: printed for Leigh and Sons, 1835. 5th edition; 12mo; frontispiece, pages vi, 498, hand colored engraved map (repaired at one fold); original green roan, gilt, slightly scored.   Marlborough 162-159 1996 £100.00

LEIGHLY, JOHN   California as an Island. San Francisco: Book Club of California, 1972. 1st edition; limited to 450 copies; folio; 154 pages; 25 plates, all but 2 being double page, 1 foldout, color titlepage map, color decorative initial, numerous illustrations; text handset in Goudy Californian on English handmade paper; lettered brown morocco and tan boards, map of California stamped on front cover; very fine and bright. Original prospectus laid in.   Argonaut Book Shop   113-410   1996 $1,500.00

LEIGHTON, CLARE   Growing New Roots - an Essay with Fourteen Wood Engravings. San Francisco: Book Club of California, 1976. One of 500 numbered copies, signed by author; 14 titled wood engravings; original binding, cover edges browned, title label on spine slightly worn, very good, without dust jacket, as issued; loosely inserted is prospectus for the book, spare title label.   Ulysses   39-368   1996 £95.00

LEIGHTON, CLARE   Tempestuous Petticoat: The Story of an Invincible Edwardian. New York: Rinehart, 1947. 1st edition; tall 8vo; titlepage vignette, color endpapers and color jacket design by author; dust jacket with few nicks, very good.   George J. Houle   68-81   1996 $125.00

LEIGHTON, CLARE   Where Land Meets Sea. New York: Rinehart, 1954. 1st edition; 4to; illustrations on wood by author; beige cloth; couple of small spots to cloth, else very fresh.   Barbara Stone   70-142   1996 £55.00

LEIGHTON, CLARE   Woodcuts: Examples of the Work of Clare Leighton. London: Longmans, Green and Co., 1930. One of 450 numbered copies, signed by Leighton; 4to; pages xviii, 36 pages of mounted woodcuts on India paper; original brown cloth, woodcut mounted on upper contemporary, some neat internal repairs to dust jacket, free endpapers browned, otherwise very nice.   Sotheran PN32-35   1996 £598.00

LEIGHTON, W. A.   The Lichen-Flora of Great Britain, Ireland and the Channel Islands. Shrewsbury: privately printed; 1879. 8vo; pages xvii, 547; quarter leather; good ex-library.   Wheldon & Wesley   207-1635   1996 £75.00

LEINSTER, M.   Operation: Outer Space. Fantasy Press, 1954. 1st edition; 1/300 copies of the signed/plated edition; inscribed to Doc smith; near fine in dust jacket.   Aronovitz   57-691   1996 $750.00

LEIRIS, MICHEL   African Art. New York: Golden Press, 1968. 28.2 cm; xiv, 484 pages, 91 color plates, 359 black and white plates, drawings, maps; cloth, some tears to dust jacket.   L. Clarice Davis   111-60   1996 $275.00

LE JEUNE, J. M.   Prayers Before and After Holy Communion in Several Languages of the Natives of British Columbia, in the Diocese of Vancouver... Liege: printed by H. Dessain, 1925. 18.5 cm; 22 pages; printed wrappers, fine in protective covers; Smith 5843.   Rockland Books   38-126   1996 $100.00

LELAND, CHARLES G.   Hans Breitmann's Ballads. Philadelphia: ca. 1880. 8vo; 2 volumes, over 300 pages; green cloth, gilt decorated and gilt lettered, very good.   K Books   441-311   1996 £55.00

LELAND, CHARLES G.   Pidgin-English Sing-Song, or Songs and Stories in the China-English Dialect. London: Trubner & Co., 1876. 1st edition; half title, 3 page list of books by Leland; original printed yellow cloth, spine slightly darkened; cutting from Observer inserted.   Jarndyce   103-266   1996 £65.00

LELAND, CHARLES G.   Ye Book of Copperheads. Philadelphia: Frederick Leypoldt, 1863. 1st edition; oblong 8vo; (2), 24, (6) pages; fully illustrated, original printed and illustrated front wrapper, reinforced, light foxing, spine crudely rebacked, lacks back wrapper. BAL 11537; Sabin 6356 (misdated); Howes L245; not in Hamilton.   M & S Rare Books   60-137   1996 $225.00

LE LOYER, PIERRE, SIEUR DE LA BROSSE 1550-1634   A Treatise of Specters or Straunge Sights, Visions and Apparitions, Appearing Sensibly Unto Men. London: by Val S(immes) for Mathew Lownes, 1605. 1st edition in English; 4to; (8), 145, (1) leaves; errata leaf in very skilfll pen facsimile on old paper, title soiled, two or three leaves with early paper reinforcement at gutter; 19th century calf, very nice, tight copy, extensive contemporary marginal notes in hand of one Daniel Hughes; leather bookplate of Edward Hailstone. STC 15448.   Joseph J. Felcone   64-25   1996 $1,200.00

LE MAY, ALAN   The Searchers. New York: Harpers, 1954. One of 800 specially signed copies by Lemay; fine in near fine, lightly spine sunned dust jacket.   Thomas Dorn   9-164   1996 $120.00

LEMOINE, H.   History, Origin and Progress of the Art of Printing, From Its First Invention in Germany to the End of the Seventeenth Century. London: 1797. 1st edition; 12mo; 156 pages; later library cloth, some browning throughout, first blank very brittle, title flaking little at edges (not affecting text); ex-John Crerar Library copy with booklabel, perforated stamps on first 3 leaves, with release stams; presentation inscription to Ellis Williams, Printer from Miss H. A. Jones. Bigmore & Wyman p. 431.   Maggs Bros. Ltd.   1191-188   1996 £115.00

LEMON, MARK   The Enchanted Doll. London: Wells Gardner DArton, 1899. 1st edition thus; 75 x 60mm; 146 pages and 4 pages; black and white illustrations by Richard Doyle; beige boards illustrated in rust, covers rubbed and loose in binding, else very good. Bondy 69.   Marjorie James   19-154   1996 £55.00

LEMPRIERE, JOHN   Bibliotheca Classica; or, a Classical Dictionary... Reading: printed for T. Cadell, London, 1788. 1st edition; 8vo; contemporary tree calf, nicely rebacked, spine gilt, original red morocco label preserved; fine, complete with final leaf of errata; PMM 236.   Ximenes   108-241   1996 $2,250.00

LEMPRIERE, JOHN   Bibliotheca Classica; or, a Classical Dictionary,... London: printed for T. Cadell, Junior, & W. Davies, 1797. 3rd edition; full contemporary speckled calf, little rubbed, red label; armorial bookplate, very good.   Jarndyce   103-195   1996 £50.00

LEMPRIERE, JOHN   Univeral Biography. New York: Sargeant, etc., 1810. 1st American edition; tall thick octavo; contemporary full calf, leather labels, some wear to headbands, but very good; Lowndes III 1119; Sabin 40018.   Hartfield   48-11o   1996 $245.00

LE NESTOUR, PATRIK   The Mystery of Things: Evocations of the Japanese Supernatural New York: John Weatherhill, Inc., 1972. 1st edition; deluxe issue, limited to 183 copies; each sopy signed by artist author, with 17 original calligraph paintings, this copy 115; 16 1/2 x 14 inches; 17 natural-dye calligraph paintings by Akeji Sumiyoshi; maroon morocco backed black hemp with wood veneer label, whole enclosed in a veneer lined black folding chemise with bamboo clasps; very fine.   Hermitage   SP95-794   1996 $600.00

L'ENGLE, MADELINE   The Small Rain. New York: Vanguard, 1943. 1st edition; owner name and offsetting on endpapers, still nice.   Ken Lopez   74-257   1996 $175.00

LENGLET DUFRESNOY, NICOLAS   Histoire de la Philosophie Hermetique. Paris: Coustelier, 1742. 1st edition; 12mo; 3 volumes; xxiii, 486, (20); xxxii, 120, 360; (22), 432 pages; 2 woodcuts; contemporary calf, gilt tooled spines with raised bands, marbled endpapers, fine, attractive set. Ferguson II p. 25; Caillet 6496; Wellcome III 490;   Edwin V. Glaser   121-183   1996 $2,400.00

LENIN, VLADIMIR IL'ICH 1870-1924   The Letters of Lenin. London: Chapman and Hall ltd., 1937. 1st edition; 10 black and white photos; original binding, top edge dusty, prelims, edges, endpapers and contents spotted, covers patchily faded, head and tail of spine and corners slightly bumped, good in nicked, rubbed, marked and dusty, slightly torn and creased dust jacket darkened at spine and edges frayed at head of spine.   Ulysses   39-369   1996 £65.00

LENNON, JOHN   Skywriting by Word of Mouth. New York: Harper & Row, 1986. 1/500 copies, signed by Yoko, specially bound and slipcase with framable drawing on acid-free paper; outstanding copy.   Bev Chaney, Jr.   23-369   1996 $250.00

LENNOX, CHARLOTTE RAMSEY 1720-1804   The Female Quixote; or, the Adventures of Arabella. Dublin: printed for W. Whitestone, 1763. 3rd edition; 12mo; 2 volumes; contemporary calf, bit worn, lacks one label; very good, complete with final leaf of ads in volume 1, scarce printing; early armorial bookplates of Mrs. Alice Grace. cf. Hazen pp. 94-98; cf. Courtney p. 38.   Ximenes   108-242   1996 $300.00

LE NORMAND, VICTORINE   The Unerring Fortune-Teller: Containing the Celebrated Oracle of Human Destiny... New York: Dick and Fitzgerald, 1866. 16mo; 146, (27) pages; woodcuts, plus large folding colored frontispiece; original colored pictorial and printed boards, cloth backed; talbe/or chart with short tear (no loss); fine.   M & S Rare Books   60-332   1996 $150.00

LENSKI, LOIS   Indian Captive - the Story of Mary Jemison. New York: Stokes, 1941. illustrations by Lenski, with colored lithographed frontispiece and black and white lithographs; beige cloth pictorially printed in red and green; very nice; inscribed by Lenski to Bella Witzner.   Barbara Stone   70-143   1996 £125.00

LENSKI, LOIS   Songs of Mr. Small. New York: Oxford University Press, 1954. 4to; colored illustrations; red cloth pictorially stamped in black; fine in chipped pictorial dust jacket.   Barbara Stone 70-144 1996 £65.00

LENTULUS, CYRIACUS   Princeps Absolutus....Politicus in Annalium Taciti Commentarius. Herborn: n.p., 1663. 1st and only recorded edition; small 8vo; pages 420; roman and italic letter, woodcut printer's device on titlepage, 2 woodcut initials, ornaments; contemporary vellum over boards stamped with black floral border and corner fleurons, both partly faded on back cover, centre pieces, contemporary ms. title on spine, waterstain to 1 inch of upper cover at head, original clasps. Lightly browned, small waterstain to upper blank margin of a few early leaves, very occasional small ink spots and rust marks in text, early Jesuit ex-libris on titlepage, otherwise good. 1 copy in NUC; not found in any other bibliography.   A. Sokol XXV-56 1996 £285.00

LENZ, T. W.   Reise Nach Saint Louis AM Missippi. Nebstmeinen, Wahrend Eines Vierzehnmonatlichen... Weimar: 1838. 1st edition; 12mo; 252 pages (page 252 misnumbered as 251); contemporary paste paper over boards with cloth tips and spine, slightly rubbed, later label affixed to spine, with previous owner's bookplate showing staining from glue; very good, housed in clamshell box. Buck 307; Howes L256; Streeter Sale 1856.   Andrew Cahan 47-135 1996 $1,250.00

LEON & BROTHER   First Editions of American Authors. New York: Leon & Brother, 1885. 1st edition; stitched as issued, no glue residue is visible to the nekkid eye or under high intensity UV light;   Mac Donnell 12-141 1996 $165.00

LEON, GOTTLIEB VON   Ravvinische Legenden. Ernst Ludwig Presse, 1913. One of 30 copies on Japanese vellum (of a total edition of 100); 8 1/4 x 5 inches; 50 pages, 1 leaf (contents, colophon); fine dark blue morocco, gilt titling on front cover, titlepage, other edges untrimmed, spine faded to light brown, otherwise fine.   Phillip J. Pirages 33-208 1996 $1,950.00

LEONARD, AGNES   The Colorado Blue Book. Denver: James R. Ives and Co., 1892. 237 pages; some shelf wear, generally clean and tight. Dumont 28-56 1996 $175.00

LEONARD, ELMORE   Cat Chaser. New York: Arbor House, 1982. Advance review copy, with review slip and promotional photo laid in; fine in fine dust jacket and signed by author.   Ken Lopez 74-260 1996 $125.00

LEONARD, ELMORE   Dutch Treat. New York: Arbor House, 1977. One of 350 signed, numbered copies; cloth covered boards with gold stamped lettering, plate with sketched portrait of Leonard on front cover, very fine in slipcase.   Quill & Brush 102-1041 1996 $100.00

LEONARD, ELMORE   Fifty-Two Pick Up. London: Secker and Warburg, 1974. 1st edition; fine in dust jacket.   Quill & Brush 102-1038 1996 $150.00

LEONARD, ELMORE   Gold Coast. London: W. H. Allen, 1982. 1st hardcover edition; fine in dust jacket with slight rub.   Robert Gavora 61-399 1996 $250.00

LEONARD, ELMORE   Split Images. New York: Arbor House, 1981. 1st edition; fine in fine dust jacket with one crease on front flap, signed by author.   Ken Lopez 74-259 1996 $100.00

LEONARD, ELMORE   Stick. New York: Arbor House, 1983. 1st edition; fine in fine dust jacket, signed by author.   Ken Lopez 74-261 1996 $100.00

LEONARD, ELMORE   Swag. New York: Delacorte, 1976. 1st edition; review copy; very nice, promotional photo laid in; signed by author; cheaply made 'perfectbound' book, this copy has light shelfwear to bottom boards, otherwise fine in fine dust jacket.   Ken Lopez 74-258 1996 $250.00

LEONARD, ELMORE   Swag. New York: Delacorte Press, 1976. 1st edition; corners lightly rubbed, still fine in dust jacket with only light soiling.   Quill & Brush 102-1040 1996 $125.00

LEONARD, ELMORE   The Switch. London: Secker & Warburg, 1979. 1st hardcover edition; signed; fine in price clipped dust jacket with just a little bumping to corners and spine panel ends.   Robert Gavora 61-400 1996 $350.00

LEONARD, ELMORE   Unknown Man No. 89. London: Secker & Warburg, 1977. 1st edition; spine extremities slightly bumped and endpapers lightly foxed, otherwise fine in dust jacket with rear panel faintly soiled.   Quill & Brush 102-1043 1996 $150.00

LEONARD, WILLIAM   Reports of Cases of Law; Argued and Adjudged in the Courts of Law... London: printed by Tho. Roycroft, for Nath. Ekins, etc., 1658. contemporary calf, rebacked, definite embrowning, usable copy.   Meyer Boswell SL26-144 1996 $250.00

LEONARDO DA VINCI 1452-1519   The Notebooks of Leonardo Da Vinci. New York: Reynal & Hitchcock, 1938. 1st English language edition; small 4to; 2 volumes, frontispiece, 655 pages, 31 plates; frontispiece 640 pages, 31 plates; cloth, dust jacket, slipcase; very faint foxing on prelims, jackets browned, otherwise very good.   The Bookpress 75-406 1996 $125.00

LEONARDO DA VINCI 1452-1519   A Treatise on Painting... London: printed for I. and J. Taylor, 1796. New edition; 8vo; (2), xii, 189, (21) pages; frontispiece and 29 plates; 19th century half vellum, gilt decorated spine and red gilt label, some discoloration to the vellum and linen boards little rubbed, signatures at head of titlepage and some staining to frontispiece; Belt 17; Verga 14.   Ken Spelman 30-21 1996 £95.00

LEONTIEF, ESTELLE   Whatever Happens. Janus Press, 1975. One in an edition of 250 pencil numbered copies, signed by author and artist; one relief cut illustration by Claire Van Vliet, designed by Claire Van Vliet, titles printed in black and dark grey, text in black, copyright notice in light gray, frontispiece relief cut printed in mauve, pale green, light gray, dark grey and white, printed on softwhite Mohawk Superfine, bound in charcoal gray book cloth over boards, author/title label on spine printed in black on Vesuvian grey Fabriano Miliani Ingres, used also for endpapers and flyleaves; fine.   Joshua Heller 21-9 1996 $100.00

LEOPOLD, ALDO   A Sand County Almanac. New York: Oxford University Press, 1949. 1st edition; endpapers and prelims foxed as is dust jacket, hence very good copy in similar dust jacket of quite scarce book.   David Holloway 94D-34 1996 $150.00

LE PLONGEON, AUGUSTUS   Sacred Mysteries Among the Mayas and the Quiches. New York: Macoy Pub. and Masonic Supply, 1909. 8vo; frontispiece, xvi, 163 pages, 29 plates; original cloth, worn at extremities, top end page chipped, bookplate.   Archaeologia Luxor-4623 1996 $125.00

LEPSIUS, C. R.   Standard Alphabet for Reducing Unwritten Languages and Foreign Graphic Systems to a Uniform Orthography in European Letters. London: Williams & Norgate: Berlin: W. Hertz... 1863. 2nd edition; half title; original dull green cloth, very good.   Jarndyce 103-268 1996 £65.00

LEPSIUS, RICHARD   Letters from Egypt, Ethiopia, and the Peninsula of Sinai. London: Henry G. Bohn, 1853. 12mo; pages 578; colored frontispiece, title vignette, 2 folding maps; original cloth, backed in new green morocco.   Richard Adelson W94/95-107 1996 $200.00

LERMONTOV, MIKHAIL YUREVICH 1814-1841   A Song About Tsar Ivan Vasilyevitch, His Young Body-Guard, and the Valiant Merchant Kalashnikov. Kensington: The Aquila Press, 1929. Number 74 of 750 copies set and printed by hand; decorations, binding design and format by Paul Nash, full rust niger with white and black rectangular onlays, spine darkened with joints rubbed, overall light soiling, otherwise nice. Hermitage SP95-745 1996 $500.00

LEROUX, G.   The Phantom of the Opera. G&D, 1925. 1st edition thus, photoplay edition; illustrations; bright, very good+ copy in equally very good full color wrap=around dust jacket with several small chips, most uncommon dust jacket.   Aronovitz 57-695 1996 $475.00

LE SAGE, ALAIN RENE 1668-1747   The Adventures of Gil Blas. London: M'Lean et al, 1819. New edition; 8vo; 3 volumes; 15 hand colored plates; full panelled calf, spines heavily gilt with maroon and green morocco labels, gilt ruled borders enclosing intricate blindstamp device and interesting repeating geometric pattern, lacking half title to volume 2, light wear, pretty set. Tooley 139.   Charles Agvent 4-1020 1996 $400.00

LE SAGE, ALAIN RENE 1668-1747   The Adventures of Gil Blas of Santillana. Edinburgh: William Paterson, 1886. 9 3/4 x 6 1/2 inches; 3 volumes; title vignettes, 21 fine etched plates by Adolphe Lalauze; three quarter vellum over sturdy boards by Tout, textured cloth sides, flat spines heavily gilt in compartments in antique style, brown morocco triple labels, marbled endpapers, gilt top, top corners of volume 1 little bumped, turn-ins little spotted (trivial spots and superficial marks elsewhere to covers and spines), otherwise excellent set, with no significant wear, and with gilt still bright and attractive, slight offsetting from plates, but very fine internally. Large attractive engraved bookplate in each volume.   Phillip J. Pirages 33-343 1996 $450.00

LE SAGE, ALAIN RENE 1668-1747   The Adventures of Gil Blas of Santilana. London: Society for English Bibliophilists, ca. 1910. Small 8vo; 4 volumes; several engravings; handsome three quarter navy blue morocco, gilt raised bands, gilt tops; fine.   Appelfeld Gallery 54-132 1996 $200.00

LE SAGE, ALAIN RENE 1668-1747   The Adventures of Gil Blas de Santiallane. Oxford: Limited Editions Club, 1937. Number 904 from 1500 copies, signed by John Austen; 2 volumes; illustrations by John Austen; fine set in publisher's dust jacket and slipcase.   Hermitage SP95-1006 1996 $150.00

LESCARBOT, MARC   The Theatre of Neptune in New France. Boston: Houghton Mifflin Co., 1927. 1st edition; number 208 of 450 copies; maps and plans; blue/green cloth with paper label; fine.   Hermitage SP95-717 1996 $125.00

LESLIE, JOHN   Narrative of Discovery and Adventures in the Polar Seas with an Account of the Whale Fisheries. New York: J. & J. Harper, 1844. 373 pages; folding map, illustrations; original brown cloth, small marginal dampstain, first few pages, else very good; Arctic Bib. 9945. Parmer Books Nat/Hist-041585 1996 $135.00

LESLIE, JOHN   A Short Account of Experiments and Instruments Depending on the Relations of Air to Heat and Moisture. Edinburgh: ptd. for Wm. Blackwood and J. Ballantyne & Co., 1813. 1st edition; engraved plate as frontispiece, 178 pages; accession number on verso of title, some browning of text towards the end; contemporary half calf, rebacked, label.   Anthony W. Laywood 109-80 1996 £125.00

LESSING, DORIS 1919-   Documents Relating to the Sentimental Agents in Volyen Empire. London: Cape, 1983. 1st edition; fine in fine, price clipped dust jacket, signed by author.   Between the Covers 42-265 1996 $150.00

LESSING, DORIS 1919-   Fourteen Poems. London: Scorpion Press, 1959. Of a total edition of 500 numbered copies, this one of only 50, signed by author; stiff wrappers, dust jacket; fine, scarce.   Between the Covers 42-262 1996 $275.00

LESSING, DORIS 1919-   The Golden Notebook. New York: Simon and Schuster, 1962. 1st American edition; owner name front endpaper, else very good in very good dust jacket, signed by author, uncommon book signed.   Ken Lopez 74-262 1996 $250.00

LESSING, DORIS 1919-   The Story of a Non-Marrying Man and Other Stories. London: Jonathan Cape, 1972. 1st edition; fine in dust jacket, price clipped, with shadow from new price sticker, signed by author. Captain's Bookshelf 38-140 1996 $150.00

LESSING, DORIS 1919-   This Was the Old Chief's Country. New York: Crowell: n.d. 1st American edition, from English sheets; some rubbing to base of spine, still fine in price clipped dust jacket with just a touch of soiling, very nice.   Between the Covers 42-261 1996 $200.00

LESSING, DORIS 1919-   Under My Skin: Volume One of My Autobiography to 1949. New York: Harper Collins, 1994. 1/150 copies, signed by author; as new in slipcase.   Captain's Bookshelf 38-141 1996 $100.00

LESSIUS, LEONARDUS   Hygiasticon; or, the Right Course of Preserving Life and Health unto Extream old Age... Cambridge: R. Daniel & T. Buck, printers to the University, 1634. 2nd English edition; 24mo. in 12's; mainly Roman letter, woodcut titlepage border, initials and ornaments, 1st blank missing, titlepage lightly discolored and bit frayed on fore edge, 18th century library stamp of Sion College on verso, 3 or 4 wormholes with very little loss, small pieces torn from 2 leaves with no loss of consequence, otherwise good; modern blindstamped calf, gilt spine, inner edge stamped with gilt ex-libris of Brent Gration-Maxfield, a.e.r. STC 15521; not in GM.   A. Sokol XXV-57 1996 £475.00

LESTER, JOHN HENRY   Bat v. Ball. The Book of Individual Cricket Records &c. 1864-1900. Boots - Nottingham, 1900. 1st edition; crown 8vo; (1), (362) pages; later half calf, banded and gilt, all edges gilt, spine a touch sunned, a few leaves creased, but pleasant and attractively bound copy. Padwick 118.   Ash Rare Books Zenzybyr-60 1996 £95.00

LESTERMAN, JOHN   The Adventures of a Trafalgar Lad - a Tale of the Sea. London: Jonathan Cape, 1926. 1st edition; color frontispiece, endpapers and 29 black and white drawings by Rowland Hilder; decorated cloth gilt. Inscription, top edge dusty, head and tail of spine & corners bumped, fore-edge browned, prelims slightly spotted, spine and cover edges slightly darkened, very good in nicked, chipped, frayed and torn, rubbed, creased and dusty, slightly soiled dust jacket browned at spine and edges.   Ulysses 39-287 1996 £85.00

L'ESTRANGE, A. G.   The Life of Mary Russell Mitford. London: Richard Bentley, 1870. 2nd edition; 8vo; 3 volumes; half titles; original brick bevelled cloth boards, gilt lettered spines, very pleasing set. NCBEL III 749.   Paulette Rose 16-229 1996 $125.00

L'ESTRANGE, ROGER   A Brief History of the Times, etc. London: Charles Brome, 1687. 1st edition; octavo; pages 345 plus index; full mottled polished calf, boards panelled in blind, handsomely rebacked, raised bands, gilt extra in panels, gilt on red leather label; excellent copy; some old scribbles on blank prelims, 2 fine armorial bookplates. CBEL II 569.   Hartfield 48-L54 1996 $395.00

L'ESTRANGE, ROGER   Interest Mistaken, or the Holy Cheat. London: printed for Henry Brome, 1661. 2nd impression (i.e. second edition); 8vo; contemporary sheep, short cracks in joints, corners worn; sound. Wing L1262; CBEL II 1035.   Ximenes 108-243 1996 $100.00

LETAROUILLY, PAUL   Le Vatican et la Basilique de Saint-Pierre de Rome. Paris: Moret, 1882. Imperial folio; 3 volumes; 264 engraved plates, of which 24 are chromolithographs by Lemercier with plate lists and half titles to each section; contemporary green morocco and boards in very nice condition.   Marilyn Braiterman 15-134 1996 $1,250.00

LETCHIOT, REV.   The Southampton Guide; or an Account of the Antient and Present State of that Town. Southampton: Linden, 1768. 1st edition; 12mo; 60 pages; long folding engraved frontispiece, marbled paper wrappers.   Marlborough 162-62 1996 £100.00

LETCHWORTH, WILLIAM PRYOR   The Insane in Foreign Countries. New York/London: G. P. Putnam's Sons/Knickerbocker Press, 1889. 1st edition; 8vo; (ii), xii, 374, (4) pages; 21 plates; bevel edged green cloth, front hinge cracked, moderately shelfworn, good, very scarce.   John Gach 150-282 1996 $275.00

LETI, GREGORIO   Il Cardinalismo de Santa Chiesa; or the History of the Cardinals of the Roman Church... London: printed for John Starkey...in Fleet St., 1670. Folio; 4 leaves, 330 pages, 1 leaf of ads, last 6 leaves with minimal lower marginal loss at gutter, nowhere coming near text, V3 with clean tear (no surface problems), few leaves with small amounts of clear water staining but contents really in excellent condition; rebacked, original calf, in firm condition, lower portion of rear cover rejoined to upper when rebacking was done, some scratches and rubbing, overall appearance as good only; Wing L1330.   Roy W. Clare XXIV-5 1996 $225.00

A LETTER Concerning Libels, Warrants, and the Seizure of Papers... London: printed for J. Almon opposite Burlington House in Piccadilly, 1764. 2nd edition; quite good, attractive modern quarter calf, gilt. Meyer Boswell SL25-81 1996 $450.00

A LETTER to a Friend in the Country, Concerning the Use of Instrumental Musick in the Worship of God; in Answer to Mr. Newte's Sermon Preach'd at Tiverton in Devon, on the Occasion of an Organ Being Erected in the Parish-Church. London: A. Baldwin, 1698. 1st edition; 4to; (ii), 94 pages; 19th century half sheep, marbled boards, gilt lettering, small paper flaw in L3, affecting a few letters, otherwise very good, clean copy. Wing L1650.   Robert Clark 38-75 1996 £250.00

A LETTER to a Member of Parliament, Relating to the bill for the Opening of a Trade to and From Persia through Russia. London: T. Cooper, 1741. 1st edition; 8vo; (4), (1) pages; slightly dampstained, blank corner torn from corner of one leaf, recently well bound in cloth backed marbled boards, gilt; Kress 4565; Goldsmiths 7836; Hanson 5555.   John Drury 82-146 1996 £75.00

A LETTER to the Merchants of the Portugal Committee, from a Lisbon Trader. London: H. Carpenter, 1754. 1st edition; 8vo; 31, (1) pages; complete with half title, recently well bound in cloth backed marbled boards, gilt; Kress 5370; Goldsmiths 8920; Higgs 760.   John Drury 82-147 1996 £75.00

A LETTER Without Any Superscription, Intercepted in the Way to London. N.P.: printed in the Yeare, 1643. 1st and apparently only edition; 4to; 8 pages; recently well bound in old style quarter calf and marbled boards; fine, large copy. Wing L1757; Thomason I 227. Not in Kress or Goldsmiths. John Drury 82-148 1996 £225.00

A LETTER Written To One of the Members of Parliament, About the State of This Present War. London: printed in the Year 1692. 1st edition; small 4to; disbound; fine, scarce. Wing L1771. Ximenes 109-129 1996 $200.00

LETTERS of Religion and Vertue, to Several Gentlemen and Ladies. London: printed for Henry Bonwicke, 1695. 1st edition; 12mo; imprimatur leaf before title, ad leaf after preface, old boards, rebacked. Wing L1786. Anthony W. Laywood 109-81 1996 £110.00

LETTERS from Several Parts of Europe and the East. Written in the Years 1750 &c. In These are Contained, The Writer's Observations on the productions of Nature, the Monuments of Art, the Manners of the Inhabitants. London: L. Davis, J. Ward and J. Fletcher, 1753. 1st edition; 8vo; 2 volumes; viii, (408); vi, 428 pages; recent panelled calf, gilt lettering; first titlepage dusty, frayed around edges (without loss of text) & mounted, some minor spotting. Sound set. Pine Coffin 750/1. Robert Clark 38-157 1996 £100.00

LETTERS Patent, Establishing a Supreme Court of Judicature, at Fort-William, in Bengal, Bearing the Date the Twenty-Sixth Day of March, in the Fourteenth Year of the Reign of George III. London: printed in the year 1774. 1st edition; 4to; 44 pages; disbound. Anthony W. Laywood 109-82 1996 £150.00

LETTSOM, J. C. The Naturalist's and Traveller's Companion... London: 1799. 3rd edition; 8vo; engraved title with hand colored vignette, hand colored frontispiece, 3 plates; original boards, uncut, worn, front cover nearly off; John Sparrow's copy. Maggs Bros. Ltd. 1190-248 1996 £75.00

LETTY, C. Wild Flowers of the Transvaal. Pretoria: 1962. Imperial 8vo; pages xiii, 362; 175 fine colored plates, numerous text figures; cloth. Wheldon & Wesley 207-1564 1996 £65.00

LEUCHARS, ROBERT B. A Practical Treatise on the Construction, Heating and Ventilation of Hot-Houses... Boston: Jewett, 1851. 1st edition; 8vo; 366 pages; wood engraved frontispiece, wood engraved text illustrations; publisher's scarlet cloth, top of spine bumped. Elton Engineering 10-94 1996 £350.00

LEUCHARS, ROBERT B. A Practical Treatise on the Construction, heating and Ventilation of Hot-Houses... Boston: 1851. 8.5 x 5 inches; 366 pages; illustrations; cloth, minor stain at bottom gutter corner, spine defective, inner hinges loose. John K. King 77-568 1996 $100.00

LEUPOLD, JACOB Theatrum Machinarium, Oder: Schauplatz der Heb-Zeuge. Leipzig: Christoph Zunkel, 1725. Small folio; (xviii), 162, (4) pages, 56 folding engraved plates; contemporary full vellum, recased, new endpapers, some browning. Elton Engineering 10-95 1996 £1,450.00

LEUPOLD, JACOB Theatrum Pontificiale, Oder Schau-Platz der Brucken und Brucken-Baues. Leipzig: Zunkel, 1726. Small folio; xvi, 153, (5) pages, 58 fine folding engraved plates; contemporary quarter calf, top of spine neatly repaired, corners little bumped. Elton Engineering 10-96 1996 £2,500.00

LEURECHON, JEAN Mathematicall Recreations. Or, Collection of Many Problems, Extracted Out of the Ancient and Modern Philosophers, as Secrets and Experiments in Arithmetick, Geometry, Cosmographie, Horologiographie, Astronomie, Navigation, Musick, Opticks... London: for William Leake, 1653. 2nd edition in English; 8vo; (38), 286, (i.e. 287), (1), (16) pages; added folding engraved title, many engravings within text; contemporary calf, neatly rebacked in period style, lacks blank A1, engraved title very slightly shaved at head, small wormhole in first couple of leaves, tiny rust hole in B7. Wing L1790. Joseph J. Felcone 64-26 1996 $2,000.00

LEUTZE, E. Washington Crossing the Delaware. New York: Goupil & Co., 1853. 1st edition; 8vo; 10, 1 pages; original printed wrappers. M & S Rare Books 60-277 1996 $175.00

LEVER, CHARLES JAMES 1806-1872 Arthur O'Leary; His Wandering and Pondering in Many Lands. London: Colburn, 1845. 1st edition thus (in one volume); 8vo; 10 etchings by George Cruikshank; original gilt and blindstamped red cloth, rubbing, corners bumped; very good. Cohn 484. George J. Houle 68-41 1996 $135.00

LEVER, CHARLES JAMES 1806-1872 Barrington. London: Chapman and Hall, 1862-63. 1st edition in original monthly parts; 8vo; 13 parts in 12 numbers; numerous inserted ads; original pink printed wrappers (evenly faded), in full green morocco solander case, by Riviere & Son (slight rubbing); fine set. Brown, Ireland in Fiction 935; CBEL III 943. Ximenes 108-244 1996 $750.00

LEVER, CHARLES JAMES 1806-1872 Davenport Dunn. London: Chapman and Hall, 1857-59. 1st edition in original monthly parts; 8vo; 22 parts in 21 numbers; frontispiece, engraved title, 42 plates by Phiz; original pink printed wrappers, evenly faded, cloth folding case. Few very minor signs of restoration to spines, but fine, fresh set, with numerous inserted ads. Brown, Ireland in Fiction 243; CBEL III 943. Ximenes 108-245 1996 $800.00

LEVER, CHARLES JAMES 1806-1872 Davenport Dunn; or, the Man of the Day. London: Chapman and Hall, 1857-59. 8vo; original 22 parts in 21, etched frontispiece, title vignette and 42 engraved plates by Phiz; original printed wrappers, slightly soiled, housed in modern green cloth slipcase, bit frayed. Kenneth Karmiole 1NS-157 1996 $600.00

LEVER, CHARLES JAMES 1806-1872 The Dodd Family Abroad. London: Chapman and Hall, 1852-54. 1st edition; in original monthly parts; 8vo; 20 parts in 19 numbers; frontispiece, engraved title and 38 plates by Phiz; numerous inserted ads; original pink printed wrappers, cloth folding case; fine, fresh set. Brown, Ireland in Fiction 937; CBEL III 943. Ximenes 108-246 1996 $900.00

LEVER, CHARLES JAMES 1806-1872 The Fortunes of Glencore. London: Chapman and Hall, 1857. 1st edition; 8vo; 3 volumes; original green blindstamped cloth, spines lettered in gilt, cloth box, morocco label, lettered in gilt; just a few spots, but fine, bright copy; inscribed by author on titlepage for the Marchioness of Normanby; the Sadleir copy with his and other booklabels. Sadleir 1405; Wolff 4088. Simon Finch 24-154 1996 £2,000.00

LEVER, CHARLES JAMES 1806-1872 The Fortunes of Glencore. London: Chapman and Hall, 1857. 1st edition; 8vo; 3 volumes; original green blindstamped cloth, spines lettered in gilt, occasional spotting or soiling, ownership signature on front free endpapers, but excellent; bookplate of John Hooper. Sadleir 1405. Simon Finch 24-155 1996 £300.00

LEVER, CHARLES JAMES 1806-1872 The Martin's of Cro' Martin. London: Chapman and Hall, 1854-56. 1st edition; in original monthly parts; 8vo; 20 parts in 19 numbers; numerous inserted ads; original pale yellow or pink printed wrappers, cloth folding case; wrappers evenly faded, but very fine, fresh set. Brown, Ireland in Fiction 925; Ximenes 108-247 1996 $900.00

LEVERTOV, DENISE 1923- The Double Image. London: Cresset Press, 1946. 1st edition; small 8vo; cloth, dust jacket; fine copy of author's first book. James S. Jaffe 34-368 1996 $150.00

LEVERTOV, DENISE 1923- 5 Poems. N.P.: White Rabbit Press, 1958. 1st edition; one of 200 copies; signed by author; thin square 8vo; drawings by Jess; pictorial wrappers; fine, rare. James S. Jaffe 34-371 1996 $500.00

LEVERTOV, DENISE 1923- Here and Now. San Francisco: City Lights Pocket Bookshop, 1957. 1st edition; 12mo; printed wrappers, spine lightly sunned, otherwise fine, very scarce. James S. Jaffe 34-369 1996 $350.00

LEVERTOV, DENISE 1923- In the Night. A Story. New York: Albondocani Press, 1968. 1 one of 150 copies, signed by author; thin 8vo; original marbled wrappers, wrappers slightly rubbed at extremities, otherwise fine. James S. Jaffe 34-380 1996 $150.00

LEVERTOV, DENISE 1923- A Marigold from North Viet Nam. New York: Albondocani Press, 1968. 1st edition; 1st state (no priority) one of 300 copies printed hors commerce, signed by author; 12mo; printed wrappers, fine. Wilson A14. James S. Jaffe 34-381 1996 $100.00

LEVERTOV, DENISE 1923- Mass for the Day of St. Thomas Didymus. Concord: William B. Ewert, 1981. 1st edition; one of 26 lettered copies; signed by author; thin 8vo; decorated boards, printed label; mint. James S. Jaffe 34-397 1996 $100.00

LEVERTOV, DENISE 1923- Modulations for Solo Voice. San Francisco: Five Trees Press, 1977. 1st edition; one of 250 copies; tall thin 8vo; original wrappers; fine. James S. Jaffe 34-392 1996 $100.00

LEVERTOV, DENISE 1923-   Summer Poems/1969. Berkeley: Oyez, 1970. 1st edition; one of 50 copies printed on Tovil paper and bound in boards, numbered and signed by author; thin 8vo; cloth backed boards, printed label on spine; mint.   James S. Jaffe 34-386   1996 $250.00

LEVERTOV, DENISE 1923-   Summer Poems/ 1969. Berkeley: Oyez, 1970. 1st edition; one of 350 copies, although not called for this copy signed by author; thin 8vo; original wrappers; mint.   James S. Jaffe 34-387   1996 $100.00

LEVERTOV, DENISE 1923-   A Tree Telling of Orpheus. Los Angeles: Black Sparrow Press, 1968. 1st edition; one of 75 copies handbound in boards and signed and numbered by author; 8vo; drawings by author; boards, printed spine label; spine label slightly rubbed, otherwise mint copy.   James S. Jaffe 34-382   1996 $125.00

LEVERTOV, DENISE 1923-   Two Poems. Concord: William B. Ewert, 1983. 1st edition; one of 50 deluxe copies; signed by author and artist; thin 8vo; wood engraving by Gillian Tyler; hand bound in cloth over museum boards, printed label; as new.   James S. Jaffe 34-404   1996 $100.00

LEVERTOV, DENISE 1923-   Wanderer's Daysong. N.P.: Copper Canyon Press, 1981. 1st edition; one of 240 copies, signed by author; thin 8vo; cloth backed boards, printed spine label, spine very slightly faded, otherwise mint.   James S. Jaffe 34-398   1996 $100.00

LEVESON, HENRY ASTBURY   The Forest and the Field. London: Saunders, Otley & Co., 1867. 2nd edition; 551, (1) pages, (24) pages ads; mounted original portrait photo of author as frontispiece; original green cloth, some spotting on cover, trace of light foxing, else very good.   Chapel Hill 94-233   1996 $100.00

LEVESQUE, RODRIGUES   History of Micronesia. A Collection of Source Documents. Gatineau: Levesque Publications, c. 1992. 11 x 8.5 inches; 2 massive volumes on quality paper; map endpapers, maps, many illustrations, 702 pages; decorated endpapers, 701 pages, illustrations; paper over boards;   Parmer Books 039/Nautica-039181   1996 $200.00

LEVI, DORO   Antioch Mosaic Pavements. Princeton: Princeton University Press, 1947. Folio; 2 volumes; xxi, 650 pages, 229 illustrations; 4 maps, 183 plates; original cloth, blind embossed stamp at flyleaves, otherwise fine set.   Archaeologia Luxor-3620   1996 $1,500.00

LEVI, LEONE   On Taxation: How It Is Raised and How It Is Expended. London: J. W. Parker, 1860. 1st and apparently only edition; crown 8vo; pages xv, 255, (1); original cloth, fine, fresh copy.   James Fenning 133-210   1996 £95.00

LEVINSON, ABRAHAM   Pioneers of Pediatrics. New York: 1936. 1st edition; 112 pages; original binding, scarce. GM 6357.   W. Bruce Fye 71-1276   1996 $100.00

LEVY, FERDINAND   Flashes from the Dark. Dublin: printed at the sign of the Three Candles, 1941. 1st edition; fine in attractive, near fine dust jacket with some foxing to rear panel and touch of rubbing, uncommon title.   Between the Covers 43-150   1996 $225.00

LEWIS, CHARLES THOMAS COURTNEY   The Story of Picture Printing in England During the XIXth Century. Forty Years of Wood and Stone. London: c. 1930. Large 8vo; 61 plates, thick large 8vo; fine, apart from some faint foxing to fore-edge, repaired dust jacket.   Petersfield Bookshop FH58-12   1996 £160.00

LEWIS, CLIVE STAPLES 1898-1963   Beyond Personality: The Christian Idea of God. London: Bles/Centenary Press, 1944. 1st edition; small 8vo; dust jacket with few nicks and short tears.   George J. Houle 68-83   1996 $175.00

LEWIS, CLIVE STAPLES 1898-1963   Broadcast Talks: Reprinted with Some Alterations From Two Series of Broadcast Talks...Given in 1941 and 1942. London: Bles/Centenary Press, 1942. 1st edition; ('July 1942); small 8vo; dust jacket (slight browning, price clipped, tape repair to lower spine and small chip to upper spine end), very good.   George J. Houle 68-84   1996 $150.00

LEWIS, CLIVE STAPLES 1898-1963   The Horse and His Boy. Macmillan, 1954. 1st American edition; near fine in nice dust jacket with some wear and tear and 2 small chips.   Aronovitz 57-701   1996 $100.00

LEWIS, CLIVE STAPLES 1898-1963   The Last Battle. Macmillan, 1956. 1st American edition; very good+ in very good dust jacket with some slight wear and tear.   Aronovitz 57-702   1996 $145.00

LEWIS, CLIVE STAPLES 1898-1963   The Lion, the Witch and the Wardrobe. London: Geoffrey Bles, 1950. Cloth boards sunned and offset through dust jacket, which has little light marginal waterstaining (which has also affected fore-edge of prelims), otherwise quite fresh and has small chip, not affecting lettering, repaired at top of spine.   R. A. Gekoski 19-95   1996 £900.00

LEWIS, CLIVE STAPLES 1898-1963   The Magician's Nephew. London: 1955. Excellent copy in slightly soiled dust jacket, which is chipped and creased at head of spine.   R. A. Gekoski 19-96   1996 £575.00

LEWIS, CLIVE STAPLES 1898-1963   Perelandra. Lane, 1942. 1st edition; uncorrected proof; some sunning to spine and upper extremities, else tight very good/very good+ copy in wrappers with name, author's name and title written in ink on front cover; rare.   Aronovitz 57-696   1996 $1,000.00

LEWIS, CLIVE STAPLES 1898-1963   Perelandra. Lane, 1943. 1st edition; good to very good in like dust jacket with some inner tape reinforcement.   Aronovitz 57-697   1996 $165.00

LEWIS, CLIVE STAPLES 1898-1963   The Screwtape Letters. Macmillan, 1943. 1st American edition; just about fine in near very good dust jacket save for some light wear and tear and chipping & sunning to dust jacket spine, still a most collectable copy; the copy of Norman Corwin, with his signature.   Aronovitz 57-698   1996 $250.00

LEWIS, CLIVE STAPLES 1898-1963   The Silver Chair. Macmillan, 1953. 1st American edition; fine in near fine dust jacket.   Aronovitz 57-700   1996 $250.00

LEWIS, DAVID   Miscellaneous Poems by Several Hands. London: printed by J. Watts, 1726-30. 1st edition; 8vo; 2 volumes; contemporary calf, rubbed, hinges cracked, spines gilt, not uniform. Griffith 232; Case 337 (1) and (2).   Anthony W. Laywood 108-108   1996 £375.00

LEWIS, DAVID   Miscellaneous Poems, by Several Hands. (with) Miscellaneous Poems, by Several Hands. London: J. Watts, 1726/30. 1st editions; 8vo; 2 volumes, pages (xvi), 320; (xvi), 320; both volumes in contemporary panelled calf, first with spine decorated in gilt, red morocco label, second unlettered, both bindings rubbed, first volume slightly browned in gutter of first few gatherings. Case 337; Teerink 1611   Simon Finch 24-156   1996 £275.00

LEWIS, F. C.   Scenery of the River Dart, Being a Series of Thirty-five Views. London: F. C. Lewis, June, 1821. 1st edition; folio; colored aquatint vignettes to half title and titlepage, dedication, colored aquatint vignette to contemporary ink ms. introductory note (?), 36 hand colored aquatint plates; pencil annotations to introduction, subscribers list and 7 of the plates; plates exceptionally clean and bright, no foxing or oxidization; preserved in red cloth chemise within quarter red morocco slipcase, gilt rule and title to panelled spine. Abbey Scenery 118; Anderson p. 86.   Beeleigh Abbey BA/56-13   1996 £3,500.00

LEWIS, FLORENCE   China Painting. London: Cassell & Co., 1883. 1st edition; 16 handsome chromolithographs; some foxing, not affecting plates, hinges loose, otherwise very good.   Hermitage SP95-791   1996 $150.00

LEWIS, GEORGE CORNEWALL   An Essay On the Influence of Authority in Matters of Opinion. London: John W. Parker, 1849. 1st edition; 8vo; xii, 424 pages; early 20th century half morocco, spine gilt and lettered with raised bands, top edge gilt; very good.   John Drury 82-150   1996 £75.00

LEWIS, HENRY C.   Papers and Notes on the Glacial Geology of G. B and Ireland. 1894. 1st edition; 8vo; lxxxi, 469 pages; maps, cloth, very good; scarce.   C. P. Hyland 216-400   1996 £70.00

LEWIS, JAMES HENRY   The Test of Teachers; or, Questions to Detect Impostors in the Art of Writing. London: printed for the author and sold at the Royal Systematic Writing...n.d. c.1820. 1st edition; 8vo; frontispiece, viii, 48 pages; recently well bound in linen backed marbled boards; very good.   John Drury 82-151   1996 £175.00

LEWIS, JOHN FREDERICK   Lewis's Sketches and Drawings of the Alhambra. London: Hodgson Boys & Graves, n.d. 1835. 1st edition; folio; (iv) pages, 26 plates; contemporary quarter red morocco, rebacked, original satin covers, contemporary bookplates, short marginal tears on few plates appropriately repaired, minor cover wear, still very good copy. Abbey Travel 148.   Bookpress 75-79 1996 $4,500.00

LEWIS, LEON   The Facts Concerning the Eight Condemned Leaders. Greenport: Leon Lewis Pub., 1887. 32 pages; letterpress wrappers, about loose, some chipping at edges.   Blue River Books 9-161 1996 $275.00

LEWIS, M. J. T.   Temples in Roman Britain. Cambridge: Cambridge University Press, 1966. 8vo; xvi, 218 pages; 130 figures, 4 plates; original cloth, dust jacket.   Archaeologia Luxor-3626 1996 $125.00

LEWIS, MATTHEW GREGORY 1775-1818   Journal of a West India Proprietor, Kept During a Residence in the island of Jamaica. London: John Murray, 1834. 1st edition; 408 pages; contemporary full calf, some rubbing to binding, but very good.   Chapel Hill 94-240 1996 $150.00

LEWIS, MATTHEW GREGORY 1775-1818   Tales of Wonder. London: W. Bulmer for the author, 1801. 1st edition; tall 8vo; 2 volumes, pages (iv), 236; (iv), 237-482, (1) ad; contemporary dark green half morocco, marbled boards, slightly rubbed, spines in compartments with gilt rules and lettering, few spots, excellent copy.   Simon Finch 24-157 1996 £320.00

LEWIS, MERIWETHER 1774-1809   History of the Expedition Under the Command of Captains Lewis and Clark, to the Sources of the Missouri, Thence Across the Rocky Mountains and Down the River Columbia to the Pacific Ocean, Performed During the Years 1804-5-6. Philadelphia: Bradford & Inskeep, 1814. 1st edition; one of only 1417 copies issued; 2 volumes; folding map in fine condition; original or contemporary tree calf, expertly rebacked, very attractive set, usually found in fragile condition; fine half calf case with morocco labels; Grolier 100 American Books 30; PMM 272.   19th Century Shop 39- 1996 $22,500.00

LEWIS, N. LAWSON   The Sculpture of Max Kalish. Cleveland: Fine Arts Publishing Co., 1933. Limited edition, number 133 of unspecified limitation, signed by artist; 8vo; (12) pages, plus 32 full page black and white plates; printed stiff wrappers with mounted illustration, lightly worn, else near fine.   Andrew Cahan 47-101 1996 $125.00

LEWIS, OSCAR   The Big Four. The Story of Huntington, Stanford, Hopkins and Crocker and of the Building of the Central Pacific. New York: Knopf, 1938. 1st edition; 418 pages, plus foreword and index; numerous illustrations; light offsetting to front endpaper, else extremely fine and bright with perfect dust jacket; very scarce, especially in this condition; presentation inscription signed by author for George Harding. Argonaut Book Shop 113-411 1996 $150.00

LEWIS, OSCAR   The Origin of the Celebrated Jumping Frog of Calaveras County. San Francisco: the Book Club of California, 1931. Limited to 250 numbered copies; 4to; (vi), 27, (xvi) pages, plus colophon; vignettes, pictorial initials by Valenti Angelo; green cloth backed marbled boards titled in gilt on spine with gilt vignette of a frog at bottom of backstrip; near fine.   Blue Mountain SP95-55 1996 $150.00

LEWIS, R. B.   Light and Truth: Collected from the Bible and Ancient and Modern History... Boston: Published by a Committee of Colored Gentlemen, 1844. 1st edition; 1st and last few leaves foxed, extremities very slightly worn, binders embossed stamp on front free endpaper; unusually lovely, very near fine.   Between the Covers 43-356 1996 $850.00

LEWIS, SAMUEL   Topographical Dictionary of Ireland. London: 1837. 1st edition; 8vo; 2 volumes plus atlas to 1846 edition; Dictionary in modern cloth, atlas in original cloth; very good.   C. P. Hyland 216-401 1996 £300.00

LEWIS, SINCLAIR 1885-1951   Dodsworth. New York: Harcourt Brace, 1929. 1st edition; special edition for the trade, published in advance of publication with page bound in to that effect; orange boards, without dust jacket, as issued, small chop mark and signature of Mimi Scott Dejanikus, granddaughter of Harcourt Brace President S. Spencer Scott, rubbing to black spine lettering, still quite readable, very good plus; scarce.   Between the Covers 42-268 1996 $450.00

LEWIS, SINCLAIR 1885-1951   Dodsworth. New York: Harcourt Brace, 1929. 1st edition; fine in very good dust jacket with one small chip in middle of the back panel and small edge tears at corners and folds, still very nice.   Ken Lopez 74-264 1996 $450.00

LEWIS, SINCLAIR 1885-1951   Dodsworth. New York: 1929. 1st edition; very near fine in scarce dust jacket with small chips to extremities. Stephen Lupack 83- 1996 $250.00

LEWIS, SINCLAIR 1885-1951   It Can't Happen Here. New York: Darmatists Play Service, 1938. New version; wrappers, touch of soiling, scarce in the first edition; fine.   Between the Covers 42-270 1996 $125.00

LEWIS, SINCLAIR 1885-1951   Kingsblood Royal. New York: Random House, 1947. 1st edition; book is very good in dust jacket; inscribed by author in year of publication to Janet Nathan, wife of author Robert Nathan, with two ALS's from Lewis to Janet Nathan; excellent association.   Ken Lopez 74-265 1996 $750.00

LEWIS, SINCLAIR 1885-1951   Main Street: the Story of Carol Kennicott. New York: Harcourt Brace and Howe, 1920. 1st edition; 2nd issue; 7 1/2 x 5 1/4 inches; 4 p.l., 451 pages; original denim blue cloth, stamped in orange; hint of fading to spine, trivial rubbing to spine ends, but very clean, little used copy.   Phillip J. Pirages 33-345 1996 $125.00

LEWIS, SINCLAIR 1885-1951   Our Mr. Wrenn. The Romantic Adventures of a Gentle Man. New York: Harper & Bros., 1914. 1st edition; 8vo; frontispiece; original grey cloth, gilt, rubbed, some browning and spotting of text, very nice association copy, inscribed twice by Lewis to Mary Vorse O'Brien and Joseph O'Brien, the first signed only with initials, the other with inscription.   James Cummins 14-123 1996 $1,250.00

LEWIS, SINCLAIR 1885-1951   The Prodigal Parents. Garden City: Doubleday, Doran, 1938. 1st edition; front and rear free endpapers exhibit slight tape shadows, else fine in fine, unusually bright dust jacket with trace of rubbing, especially nice example of black dust jacket. Between the Covers 42-269 1996 $125.00

LEWIS, WILLIAM   The New Dispensatory: Containing. I. The Theory and Practice of Pharmacy. II. A Distribution of Medicinal simples...III. A Full Translation of the London & Edinburgh Pharmacopoeias... IV. Directions of Extremporaneous Prescription....V. A Collection of ... London: printed for J. Nourse, 1753. 1st edition; thick 8vo; contemporary calf, gilt, spine gilt, joints little cracked; nice. NLM p. 270.   Ximenes 109-175 1996 $250.00

LEWIS, WYNDHAM 1882-1957   The Apes of God. London: The Arthur Press, 1930. One of 750 copies numbered and signed by author, dust jacket little rubbed, marginally chipped at top of spine, some fading to outside edges, otherwise excellent copy.   R. A. Gekoski 19-97 1996 £450.00

LEWIS, WYNDHAM 1882-1957   The Apes of God. London: The Arthur Press, 1930. One of 750 copies, signed by Lewis; 10 x 7 3/4 inches; 2 p.l., 625 pages; illustrations by author; original cloth and dust jacket, extremely clean and solid binding, endpapers slightly foxed, very light foxing on a few other leaves, jacket reinforced with tape on verso, back panel little soiled, spine slightly sunned and frayed, despite flaws, an excellent copy.   Phillip J. Pirages 33-346 1996 $375.00

LEWIS, WYNDHAM 1882-1957   The Apes of God. London: Nash & Grayson, 1931. 1st British edition, some foxing on cloth edges and pastedowns, otherwise fine, in spine darkened very good or better dust jacket, with minor chipping to crown of spine. Morrow & Lafourcade A12b.   Thomas Dorn 9-252 1996 $250.00

LEWIS, WYNDHAM 1882-1957   The Art of Being Ruled. New York: Harper, & Bros., 1926. 1st edition; fine in nice dust jacket, nicked at corners and little tanned and rubbed on spine.   Ian Patterson 9-201 1996 £120.00

LEWIS, WYNDHAM 1882-1957   The Art of Being Ruled. New York: Harper & Bros., 1926. 1st American edition; fine in nice dust jacket, nicked at corners and little tanned and rubbed on spine.   Ian Patterson 9-201 1996 £120.00

LEWIS, WYNDHAM 1882-1957   The Childermass. London: Chatto & windus, 1928. 1st edition; some very light dust soil to yellow covers, else just about fine in very good+ dust jacket save for some slight chipping to head of dust jacket spine and some all around dust soil. Aronovitz 57-704 1996 $225.00

LEWIS, WYNDHAM 1882-1957   The Jews - Are They Human? London: George Allen & Unwin Ltd., 1939. 1st edition; original binding, top edge dusty, prelims and edges spotted, head and tail of spine bumped, covers mottled, very good in nicked, chipped and slightly rubbed, creased and dusty dust jacket browned at spine and with two small holes in flap folds.   Ulysses 39-376 1996 £675.00

LEWIS, WYNDHAM 1882-1957   The Old Gang and the New Gang. London: Desmond Harmsworth, 1933. 1st edition; 1st issue cloth, fine in slightly dusty dust jacket, tanned on spine, otherwise very nice.   Ian Patterson 9-202 1996 £85.00

LEWIS, WYNDHAM 1882-1957   The Red Priest. London: Methuen & Co. Ltd., 1956. 1st edition; original binding, top edge dusty, covers very slightly marked and bowed, very good in slightly marked, rubbed and dusty, very slightly creased dust jacket by Michael Ayrton.   Ulysses 39-378 1996 £55.00

LEWIS, WYNDHAM 1882-1957   Self Condemned. London: Methuen & Co. Ltd., 1954. 1st edition; original binding, top edge dusty, tail of spine slightly bumped, gilt lettering on spine oxidised, very good in nicked, dusty and slightly rubbed and marked dust jacket by Michael Ayrton, slightly browned at spine and edges.   Ulysses 39-377 1996 £75.00

LEWIS, WYNDHAM 1882-1957   Time and Western Man. New York: Harcourt Brace and Co., 1928. One of 1500 copies; original binding, top edge spotted and dusty, top edges of covers spotted, head and tail of spine and one corner slightly bumped, gilt lettering on spine slightly chipped, very good in nicked, chipped, torn, creased and rubbed, slightly spotted, marked and dusty dust jacket browned at spine and edges. Ulysses 39-375 1996 £295.00

LEYBOURE, THOMAS   The Mathematical Questions, Proposed in the Ladies' Diary, and Their Original Answers. Together with Some New Solutions, from Its Commencement in the Year 1704 to 1816. London: J. Mawman, 1817. 1st edition; 8vo; 4 volumes, xi, 415; (4), 416; (4), 400; (4), 440, (2) pages; numerous diagrams in text; very nicely rebacked, complete with alll half titles and appendix, index of contributors and errata leaf in volume 4; original half calf, over marbled boards, spines gilt, raised bands; fine set.   Edwin V. Glaser 121-185 1996 $1,200.00

LEYLAND, FRANCIS   The Bronte Family. London: Hurst & Blackett, 1886. 1st edition; 7 1/2 x 4 3/4 inches; 2 volumes, pages xvi, 312; x, 302, 24 pages publisher's ads rear; brown fine diagonal ribbed cloth, black ruled borders to both covers, gilt titling to backstrip, bevelled boards, black endpapers, occasional slight foxing to contents, very good, scarce. Y&T 344b Wise 1917 p. 192 et seq.   Ian Hodgkins 78-341 1996 £145.00

LEYLAND, JOHN   Contemporary Medical Men and Their Professional Work... Leicester: 1888. 1st edition; 4to; 220 pages; 25 magnificent colored portraits; original binding; scarce.   W. Bruce Fye 71-1283 1996 $300.00

LEYLAND, JOHN   Contemporary Medical Men and Their Professional Work. Leicester: Office of the Provincial Medical Journal, 1888. 4to; 2 volumes; 50 tinted lithograph portraits; cloth, gilt, gilt edges, bit worn and scuffed, the BMA set with stamps, few on versos of plates, though not affecting image, loosely inserted 1822 proof engraving of George Harley.   Maggs Bros. Ltd. 1190-452 1996 £95.00

LEYLAND, R. W.   A Holiday in South Africa. London: 1882. Photo plates, 3 have been removed; original pictorial gilt cloth, light rubbing with slight discoloration on lower cover, very scarce. Cheap copy of a scarce work.   David Grayling J95Biggame-131 1996 £60.00

LEYMARIE, JEAN   Balthus. New York: Rizzoli, 1979. Original edition; folio; unpaginated text, 14 tipped in color and 18 monochrome plates; cloth, tiny ink stamps of former owner on several pages, dust jacket; Freitag 373.   Brannan Books 43-32 1996 $165.00

L'HOPITAL, WINEFRIDE DE   Westminster Cathedral and Its Architect. London: Hutchinson, 1919. 1st edition; crown 4to; 2 volumes; 720 pages; 106 plates, several in color, 54 text illustrations; maroon cloth, gilt tops, very nice, unfaded.   Howes Bookshop 265-706 1996 £120.00

LI, CHUAN-SHIH   All Men Rre Brothers. New York: Limited Editions Club, 1948. Copy number 904 from a total edition of 1500 numbered copies, signed by artist; illustrations by Miguel Covarrubias; stiff wrappers sewn Chinese style, fine in original liner and newly made slipcase.   Hermitage SP95-946 1996 $200.00

LI, CHUAN-SHIH 1895-   All Men are Brothers. Limited Editions Club, 1948. One of 1500 copies; signed by artist; 12 1/4 x 9 1/2 inches; hand colored paltes by Miguel Covarrubias, title printed in red and black; rough textured paper over flexible boards, bound in traditional Chinese style with exposed cords looped through holes in joints, paper label on front cover, in publisher's cloth backed orange paper chemise and matching slipcase (case bit stained and heavily tape repaired), except for problems with slipcase, an extremely fine copy. Quarto Millenary 191. Phillip J. Pirages 33-350 1996 $125.00

LIBBY, O. G.   The Arikara Narrative of the Campaign Against the Hostile Dakotas, June, 1876. Bismark: North Dakota Historical Collections, 1920. 1st edition; 276 pages; illustrated from photos, folding plans; original green cloth lettered in gilt, fine. Dustin 171; Luther 70. Argonaut Book Shop 113-164 1996 $175.00

LIBERACE   Liberace Cooks! Garden City: Doubleday, 1970. 1st edition, 2nd printing; 8vo; 9 color illustrations; dust jacket (nicks), very good; boldly signed and inscribed on half titlepage by Liberace with original ink drawing.   George J. Houle 68-37 1996 $125.00

LIBERMAN, M. M.   Maggot and Worm and Eight Other Stories. West Branch: Cummington Press, 1969. Number 267 of 300 copies; 8.5 x 6.5 inches; 119 pages, printed on Rives paper; 8 illustrations printed through silkscreens by Byron Burford; cream cloth over boards, printed paper label on spine, Japanese (chira) paper dust jacket; uncommon in fragile dust jacket, fine.   Joshua Heller 21-116 1996 $125.00

LIBERTY & CO., LONDON.   Modern Silver Designed and Made by Liberty & Co. Trade Catalogue. London: n.d., ca. 1924-25. Small 4to; 24 pages; illustrations; printed wrappers, some stains on cover and covers nearly detached, still very good, rare.   J. M. Cohen 35-92 1996 $350.00

LIBURNIO, NICCOLO   Le Selvette... Venice: Jacopo de Pencio da Lecco, 1513. 1st edition; 8vo; 108 leaves, printed guide letters, contemporary limp vellum; fine in original condition.   Bennett Gilbert LL29-46 1996 $1,800.00

LIBURNIO, NICCOLO   Le Selvette di Messer Nicolao Lyburnio. Venice: Iacopo de Penci da Lecco, May, 1513. 4to; ff. 4 (of 6), 100, (2), lacks 2 prelim leaves by binder's error (?); old repairs on title, attractive blind tooled later Italian calf binding, ex-library. Not in Adams; BMC/STC It. p. 377; Brunet III 1068.   Family Album Tillers-388 1996 $180.00

LICHT, KJELD DE FINE   The Rotunda in Rome: a Study of Hadrian's Pantheon. Copenhagen: Jutland Archaeological Society, 1968. Large 4to; 344 pages; 386 illustrations; stiff wrappers, dust jacket.   Archaeologia Luxor-3629 1996 $250.00

LIDDIE, BRUCE R.   I Buried Custer, the Diary of Pvt. Thomas W. Coleman, Only Enlisted Man's Account of of the Events Surrounding the Battle of Little Bighorn. Special leatherbound edition; slipcase.   Early West 22-332 1996 $200.00

LIEBIG, JUSTUS VON   Animal Chemistry, or Organic Chemistry in Its Application to Physiology and Pathology. Cambridge: 1842. 1st American edition; 8vo; pages xl, 347, (8); contemporary half calf, very rubbed, boards scuffed, foxing and some page browning; scarce; A. G. Summer's copy (publisher of Southern Agriculturalit).   Raymond M. Sutton VII-1038 1996 $275.00

LIEBIG, JUSTUS VON   Animal Chemistry, or Organic Chemistry In Its Applications of Physiology and Pathology. London: 1842. 1st edition in English; xxiv, 354 pages, (2), 16 pages ads; original binding, rear outer hinge neatly and very unobtrusively reparied, spine slightly faded, former owner's blindstamp; Wellcome III p. 515.   Joseph J. Felcone 64-27 1996 $450.00

LIEBIG, JUSTUS VON   Chemistry in Its Application to Agriculture and Physiology. London: 1843. 3rd edition; 8vo; original cloth.   Charles W. Traylen 117-348 1996 £65.00

LIEBIG, JUSTUS VON   Organic Chemistry in Its Applications to Agriculture and Physiology. Cambridge: Owen, 1841. 1st American edition; 8vo; 435 pages; original cloth, little worn paper label, very nice; some foxing; scarce. PMM 310.   Second Life Books 103-124 1996 $350.00

LIEBIG, JUSTUS VON   Researches on the Motion of the Juices in the Animal body. London: for Taylor and Walton, 1848. 1st edition in English; 8vo; xiv, 109, (3) pages; plus 16 page publisher's catalogue; woodcut illustrations in text; original embossed cloth; fine bright copy; with Marcus Crahan bookplate. Wellcome III 516.   Edwin V. Glaser 121-18 1996 $300.00

LIECHTENSTEIN, MARIA, PRINCESS   Holland House. London: Macmillan, 1874. 2nd edition; 8vo; 2 volumes; engraved titles and frontispieces, 6 ff., 289 pages, 4 ff., pages 259; profusely illustrated, half red morocco, raised bands, gilt ruled, one or two corner and spine chips.   Marlborough 162-161 1996 £100.00

LIESS, B.   Classical Swine Fever and Related Viral Infections. 1987. 8vo; 320 pages; illustrations; hardbound.   Wheldon & Wesley 207-1882 1996 £73.25

THE LIFE, Amours and Secret History of Francelia, Late D----ss if O------h, Favourite Mistress to King Charles II. London: printed for A. Amey, 1734. 1st edition; 8vo; frontispiece; recent half calf; small patch to blank outer margin of titlepage, otherwise very good. McBurney 289.   Ximenes 108-130 1996 $1,250.00

THE LIFE and Adventures of Capt. John Avery, the Famous English Pirate (Rais'd from a Cabbin-Boy, to a King) Now in Possession of Madagascar... Colophon: London: Printed and sold by booksellers, 1709. One of two known printings, this a 16 page chapbook, closely and crudely printed, the other is a 64 page version with a J. Baker imprint; 8vo; half calf, few page numbers cropped, some light waterstains, but good. McBurney 43 (the other printing only).   Ximenes 109-121 1996 $1,250.00

THE LIFE and Adventures of that Most Eccentric Character James Hirst. Knottingley: Pub. by W. S. Hepworth; London: W. M. Clark, ca. 1840. 6 3/4 x 4 1/4 inches; 47, (1) pages; frontispiece; original stitched printed paper wrappers; wrappers bit discolored and soiled, very slight losses of paper at spine ends and corners, otherwise excellent copy of this fragile rarity.   Phillip J. Pirages 33-127 1996 $175.00

THE LIFE and Death of Rich Mrs. Duck, a Notorious Glutton. New York: McLoughlin, 1869. Octavo; (8)ff; verse tale printed on stout paper, printed on one side only, 8 chromolithographs, fine in pictorial self wrappers.   Bromer Booksellers 90-115 1996 $125.00

THE LIFE of Captain James Cook, the Celebrated Circumnavigator. Compiled from the Most Authentic Sources. Dublin: printed by R. Napper, 1831. 12mo; 4 woodcut plates, pages vi, (7)-173; original half roan, binding worn and rubbed, but strong, some light internal fingering; good to very good.   James Fenning 133-70 1996 £65.00

THE LIFE Of Christ. New York: Pellegrini & Cudahy, 1951. 1st edition; limited to 150 copies, signed; 8vo; wood engravings by Bruno Bramanti; fine in lightly soiled slipcase.   Glenn Books 36-49 1996 $100.00

THE LIFE of St. George. London: De La More Press, n.d. 1919. Number 20 of 21 copies printed on vellum; 8vo; pages 18, (2); frontispiece, title border and vignette on half title; contemporary morocco backed Cockerell marbled boards, lettered in gold; very good; Ridler 26(3).   Claude Cox 107-43 1996 £220.00

LIGHT, WILLIAM   Sicilian Scenery. London: Rodwell & Martin, 1823. 1st edition; 11 3/4 x 9 1/2 inches; (64) leaves, including engraved title and half title, 61 fine plates, tissue guards; text in English and French; very handsome cont. rose colored hard grain morocco, extra gilt by C. Smith, covers handsomely framed with 3 sets of parallel fillets enclosing two elegant scrolling floral borders, flat spines beautifully gilt in 2 compartments, top one with titling, elongated lower one composed of central vertical band of urn-like roll-tool flanked by gilt rules and pretty borders of acanthus leaves, board edges with triple gilt fillets, turn-in with four gilt rules and corner of ovals, endpapers of deep green coated stock, all edges gilt, spine evenly sunned to a terra cotta, minor scuffing or rubbing to edges, otherwise binding in excellent condition. Plates especially clean.   Phillip J. Pirages 33-487 1996 $1,250.00

LIGHTBOWN, RONALD   Mantegna. Oxford: Phaidon/Christie's, 1986. 29 x 22 cm; 512 pages; 293 illustrations, 16 in color; original cloth, in dust jacket; fine.   Rainsford A54-387 1996 £140.00

LIGHTON, NORMAN   The Paintings of Norman Lighton for Roberts' Birds of South Africa. Cape Town: 1977. Limited to 300 copies numbered and signed by artist and editor; folio; pages (ix), 52 colored plates of about 800 figures; full leather.   Wheldon & Wesley 207-790 1996 £120.00

LILFORD, THOMAS LITTLETON POWYS, 4TH BARON 1833-1896 Coloured Figures of the Birds of the British Islands. London: 1891-97. 2nd edition; royal 8vo; 7 volumes; portrait, 421 colored plates; contemporary maroon morocco, spines faded, gilt top; exceptionally clean, entirely free from usual foxing; from the collection of Jan Coldewey.   Wheldon & Wesley 207-60 1996 £3,000.00

LILFORD, THOMAS LITTLETON POWYS, 4TH BARON 1833-1896 Coloured Figures of the Birds of the British Islands. London: 1891-97. 2nd edition; royal 8vo; 7 volumes, portrait and 422 fine color plates by Keulemans and Thorburn; this copy has the very rare additional plate of the Marsh-Warbler by Thorburn loosely inserted; 8vo; xxiv, 142 pages with edge gilt; work very prone to foxing, text is foxed in some places around edges, some slight foxing to edges of some plates, spines little faded.   John Henly 27-22 1996 £2,100.00

LILIENTHAL, OTTO   Birdflight as the Basis of Aviation. London: Longmans, Green, 1911. 1st edition in English; 8vo; xxiv, 142 pages with frontispiece, 8 folding lithograph plates, 94 illustrations; one plate strengthened at outer edge, original green cloth, just the slightest shelf wear; near fine.   Edwin V. Glaser 121-192 1996 $850.00

LILIENTHAL, OTTO   Der Vogelflug als Grundlage der Fliegekunst. Berlin: R. Gaertners, 1889. 1st edition; 8vo; viii, 187 pages, colored frontispiece, 8 lithographed folding tables, 80 woodcut illustrations; original decorative cloth, just a trifle wear to spine ends, light marginal stain on top edge of frontispiece, very fresh, near fine copy; early owner's signature on title. Brockett 7557; Norman Lib. 1353.   Edwin V. Glaser 121-191 1996 $2,400.00

LILIUS, ZACHARIAS   Orbis Breviarium... Paris: Jean de Gourmont, 1515. Small 4to; 97 leaves (of 100?), lacks 3 (?) prelim leaves, fine printer's device on titlepage, crible initials, ms. marginal headlines; modern cloth. Extremely rare. BMC STC 267; Sabin 41069.   Family Album Tillers-390 1996 $650.00

LILLINGSTON, LUKE   Reflections On Mr. Burchet's Memoirs...of Captain Wilmot's Expedition to the West Indies. London: 1704. 1st edition; crown 8vo; (xx), (172) pages; collation little irregular, but exactly as the British Library copy; contemporary sheep, expertly rebacked, retaining original label, lower cover scuffed, endpapers replaced, otherwise very good.   Ash Rare Books Zenzybyr-61 1996 £295.00

LILLO, GEORGE   The Works. London: T. Davies, 1775. 1st edition; 8vo; 2 volumes; full red morocco, gilt, all edges gilt, lacks ad leaf, rubbing to joints of volume 1, edgewear; attractive.   Charles Agvent 4-822 1996 $175.00

LILLY, JOHN   A Collection of Modern Entries; or, Select Pleadings in the Court of King's Bench, Common Pleas and Exchequer...(with) a Collection of Writs... London: printed by H. Lintot, 1758. 3rd folio; pages (8), 360, 363-378, 377 (bis)-676, (30), complete thus; contemporary calf, label, gilt, just a little worn at corners, binding strong, still nice, crisp copy.   James Fenning 133-215 1996 £185.00

LIMA, E. DA CRUZ   Mammals of Amazonia, Vol. 1, General Introduction and Primates. Rio de Janeiro: 1945. English language edition limited to 975 copies; crown folio; 274 pages, 42 colored plates by author; original wrappers.   Wheldon & Wesley 207-573 1996 £95.00

LIMA, E. DA CRUZ   Mammals of Amazonia. Rio de Janiero: 1945. Limited to 975 copies; folio; 274 pages; 42 color plates; original wrappers.   John Johnson 135-455 1996 £125.00

LIMBOUR, GEORGES   Andre Beaudin. London: Zwemmer, 1961. 4to; unpaginated text, 157 plates, 12 tipped in and in color and 8 original color lithographs; boards. Freitag 506.   Brannan Books 43-44 1996 $125.00

LIMITED EDITIONS CLUB   Quarto-Millenary: The First 250 Publications and the First 25 Years, 1929-1954... Limited Editions Club, 1959. One of 1500 copies (of a total edition of 2250); 12 1/2 x 9 1/2 inches; 4 p.l. (1 blank), ix-xiii, (1) pages, (2) leaves, 295, (1) pages, (1) leaf (colophon); plates, mostly facsimiles, many in color, some pasted on within printed ruled borders, title printed in red, blue and black, section titles printed on blue paper; prospectus and Limited Editions Club newsletter laid in; original black morocco backed red cloth sides, original tissue jacket; publisher's slightly worn slipcase; tissue jacket brittle, torn, chipped and reinforced with tape, volume itself is virtually mint.   Phillip J. Pirages 33-364 1996 $275.00

LIMITED EDITIONS CLUB   Quarto-Millenary: The First 250 Publications and the First 25 Years 1929-1954 of the Limited Editions Club. New York: Limited Editions Club, 1959. Number 625 of 2250 copies; quarter black morocco over red cloth, very fine in publisher's slipcase.   Hermitage SP95-1027 1996 $300.00

LIN, TSAN-PIAO   Native Orchids of Taiwan. Taiwan: 1975-87. Royal 8vo; volumes 1-3, map, 8 colored plates, 500 color photos; cloth.   Wheldon & Wesley 207-1803 1996 £125.00

LINCK, JOANNES BERNARD   Annales Austrico-Clara-Vallenses. Vienna: Schwendimann, 1723. 1st edition; folio; 2 volumes, 830, 656 pages; woodcut ornaments; contemporary full calf; fine. Not in NUC; BLC 192.351.   Bennett Gilbert LL29-47 1996 $1,750.00

LINCOLN Illustrated and Lincoln's Growth. Lincoln: Journal Co., State Printers, 1887. 1st edition; 63 pages; frontispiece, illustrations; original printed wrappers, chipping to spine, very good.   Michael D. Heaston 23-253 1996 $325.00

LINCOLN, ABRAHAM 1809-1865   The Life and Public Services of General Zachary Taylor. Boston: Houghton, Mifflin, 1922. 1st edition; one of 435 copies; 12mo; pages 55; original marbled boards, cloth back, with printed note laid in; fine, with former owner's name and address on endleaf.   Howard S. Mott 227-84 1996 $150.00

LINCOLN, ABRAHAM 1809-1865   Lincoln's Gettysburg Address. New York: 1950. 12mo; (6) pages; text printed within blue ornamental borders, titlepage accented with gold; marbled boards, backed in gilt stamped black morocco; very fine. Cohen 1.   Bromer Booksellers 87-89 1996 $125.00

LINCOLN, ABRAHAM 1809-1865   Political Debates Between Hon. Abraham Lincoln and Hon. Stephen Douglas, in the Celebrated Campaign of 1858, in Illinois. Columbus: Follett, Foster & Co., 1860. Later issue; 268 pages; original green cloth. Howes L338; Monaghan 69.   Blue River Books 9-207 1996 $120.00

LINCOLN, C. ERIC   The Black Muslims in America. Boston: Beacon Press, 1961. 1st edition; some underlining, mostly in pencil and several pages dog eared thus, very good in like dust jacket with some general wear, internal tape repair and small stain on front flap; very uncommon in first edition; Justice Francis E. Rivers copy with his ownership stamp and presumably his underlining.   Between the Covers 43-357 1996 $125.00

LINCOLN, MARY JOHNSON BAILEY 1844-1921   Carving and Serving. Boston: Roberts Brothers, 1887. 1st edition; there were 2084 copies printed; 12mo; 52, (4) ads; original colored pictorial boards, cloth back; red edges. minor wear and cover soiling, but very good.   Howard S. Mott 227-85 1996 $125.00

LIND, J.   A Treatise on the Scurvy... London: 1772. 3rd edition; 8vo; rather browned, library stamp on first and last pages, tear in Dd6 repaired without loss, recent calf.   Maggs Bros. Ltd. 1190-454 1996 £325.00

LIND, L. R.   Studies in Pre-Vesalian Anatomy. Philadelphia: 1975. 1st edition; 344 pages; original binding. GM 461.2.   W. Bruce Fye 71-1288 1996 $100.00

LINDBERGH, CHARLES AUGUSTUS   "We". New York: Putnam, 1927. 1st edition (July 1927); 8vo; publisher's 8 page ad booklet laid in loose; illustrations; gilt stamped dark blue cloth, light blue pictorial endpapers, top edge stained yellow, dust jacket (few nicks and creases), very good. George J. Houle 68-9 1996 $350.00

LINDER, USHER F.   Reminiscences of the Early Bench and Bar of Illinois. Chicago: Chicago Legal News Co., 1879. 2nd edition; maroon cloth, lower edge stained, sound.   Meyer Boswell SL27-146 1996 $125.00

LINDERMAN, FRANK B.   Blackfeet Indians. St. Paul: 1935. 1st edition; 4to; 65, (3) pages; 49 full page colored plates; original red boards, slight rubbing at corners.   Edward Morrill 368-188 1996 $110.00

LINDLEY   The Lindley Library. Catalogue of Books, Pamphlets, Manuscripts and Drawings. London: Royal Horticultural Society, 1927. blue cloth, gilt lettering on spine, bit rubbed at extremities, ownership inscription of Wilfred Blunt.   Maggs Bros. Ltd. 1191-49 1996 £55.00

LINDSAY, DAVID   The Violet Apple. London: Sidgewick & Jackson, 1978. 1st edition; fine in dust jacket with very small crease to front flap. Between the Covers 42-273 1996 $100.00

LINDSAY, H.   Report of Proceedings on a Voyage to the Northern Ports of China in the Ship Lord Amherst. London: B. Fellows, 1833. 1st edition; 8vo; 296 pages of text; original boards, corners bumped, new buff paper backstrip, original paper label to spine, booksellers ticket to front pastedown, 16 page publisher's cat. bound in prelims. Owner's ink signature.   Beeleigh Abbey BA56-90 1996 £200.00

LINDSAY, IAN G.   Inverary and the Dukes of Argyll. Edinburgh: Unviersity Press, 1973. Tall 4to; pages xvii, 487, 48 plages, 114 text illustrations; original cloth, gilt, dust jacket, edges trifle dusty.   R.F.G. Hollett 76-156 1996 £95.00

LINDSAY, JOAN   Picnic at Hanging Rock. Melbourne: F. W. Chesire, 1967. 1st edition; faint erasure to coated front endpaper, else near fine in near fine dust jacket, with just a touch of fading at spine and some slight rubbing; very uncommon.   Between the Covers 42-274 1996 $185.00

LINDSAY, NICHOLAS VACHEL 1879-1931   The Golden Book of Springfield. New York: Macmillan, 1920. 1st edition; lovely decorated boards, lightly edge worn dust jacket; very small chip from head of spine and some discoloration to the fore-edge, otherwise very fine. Captain's Bookshelf 38-144 1996 $100.00

LINE Etchings. A Trip from the Missouri River to the Rocky Mountains Via the Kansas Pacific Railway. St. Louis: Woodward, Tiernan & Hale, 1875. 1st edition; 69, (3) pages; original pictorial wrappers, map and illustrations; neatly rebacked, minor chipping and soiling, text clean, very good. Laid in half morocco slipcase; Streeter Sale 2186. Wynar 2267. Michael D. Heaston 23-200 1996 $750.00

LING, NICHOLAS   Politeuphuia, Wits Common-Wealth. London: W. S. for I. Smethwicke, n.d. 1602? 12mo; (8), 513, (7) pages; title with woodcut device, soiled and backed; old calf, rubbed, hinges partly cracked but quite sound. STC 15688.   Kenneth Karmiole 1NS-159 1996 $250.00

LINGARD, JOHN   The History of England from the First Invasion by the Romans to the Accession of William and Mary in 1688. Dublin & London: 1878. Crown 8vo; 10 volumes; plates; original cloth.   Howes Bookshop 265-666 1996 £200.00

LINGENFELTER, RICHARD E.   Presses of the Pacific Islands, 1817-1867. Los Angeles: Plantin Press, 1967. 1st edition; limited to 500 copies; 129 pages; woodcuts, map, numerous facsimiles, grey linen with gilt cover vignette, paper spine label, very fine.   Argonaut Book Shop 113-418 1996 $175.00

LINK, MAE   Medical Support of the Army Air Forces in World War II. Washington: 1955. 1st edition; 1027 pages; original binding.   W. Bruce Fye 71-1290 1996 $100.00

LINN, JOHN J.   Reminiscences of Fifty Years in Texas. Austin: State House Press, 1986. Photo reproduction of 1883 original; one of 50 numbered copies; pages (vi), 397, frontispiece; slipcase soiled, else fine. BTB 125; Howes L363.   Dumont 28-128 1996 $125.00

LINNE, CARL VON 1707-1778   Critica Botanica in Qua Nomina Plantarum Generica, Specifica, et Variantia Examin Subjiciuntur. Leiden: 1737. 8vo; pages (xvi), 270, (36), (viii), 24, (8); contemporary calf, very rare, nice. Soulsby 276.   Wheldon & Wesley 207-61 1996 £750.00

LINNE, CARL VON 1707-1778   Genera Plantarum Eorumque Characteres Naturales Secundum Numerum, Figuram, Situm & Proportionem Omnium Fructificationis Partium. Leiden: apud Conradum Wishoff, 1737. 1st edition; 8vo; folding table; contemporary half calf, spine gilt, bit worn, front joint cracked, lacks label; very good, very uncommon. Pritzel 5411; cf. PMM 192; Grolier/Horblit 68a; Dibner 27. Ximenes 108-249 1996 $4,500.00

LINNE, CARL VON 1707-1778   Species Plantarum, Exhibentes Plantas Rite cognitas, ad Genera Relatas, Cum Differentiis Specificis Nominibus Trivialibus... Stockholm: 1762-63. 2nd edition; 8vo; 2 volumes; (16), 1684, (64) pages; without portrait sometimes found; contemporary half calf, minor wear to edges and corners, cracking to outer hinges, but solid, some browning to endpaper, light dampstaining to back pages of volume 1, occasional old marginal notation in ink, head of spine of volume 1 chipped; leather spine labels, titles printed in red and black. With signatures of zoologist and entomologist William Morton Wheeler. Raymond M. Sutton VI-17 1996 $2,500.00

LINNE, S.   Zapotecan Antiquities and the Paulson Collection in the Ethnographical Museum of Sweden. Stockholm: Ethnographical Museum of Sweden, 1938. 4to; 196 pages, 27 figures, 32 plates; wrappers. Archaeologia Luxor-4640 1996 $250.00

LINNE, S.   Mexican Highland Cultures: Archaeological Researches at Teotihuacan, Calpulalpan and Chalchicomula in 1934/35. Stockholm: Ethnographic Museum, 1942. 4to; 223 pages, 333 figures and 6 plates; chipped wrappers; with ink stamp and pencil annotations of Bennyhoff. Archaeologia Luxor-4639 1996 $250.00

LINNEAN SOCIETY OF LONDON   Catalogue of the Printed Books and Pamphlets in the Library. London: 1925. New edition; 8vo; pages 860; cloth.   Wheldon & Wesley 207-258 1996 £50.00

LINNERHJELM, JONAS CARL   Bref under Esor (-nya resor, -Senare Resor) i Sverige. Stockholm: Kumblinska 1797 - Delen 1806 - Gadelius 1816. 4to; 3 volumes bound in 1; etched title vignette, 24 etched text illustrations, 10 etched plates, sepia aquatint title vignette and 26 sepia aquatint plates, soft ground etched title vignette and 16 soft ground etched plates; contemporary half calf. Thieme Becker XXIII 256. Marlborough 162-234 1996 £2,400.00

LINSLEY, JOHN S.   Jersey Cattle in America. New York: Burr, 1885. 1st edition; thick 4to; pages 744; profusely illustrated with engraved illustrations after photos; charts, plans, diagrams; little worn cloth, front spine loose, rear cloth soiled, some scattered foxing. Scarce.   Second Life Books 103-125 1996 $200.00

LINTON, E. LYNN   the lake Country. London: Smith, Elder and Co., 1864. 8vo; 100 illustrations; map; green cloth, gilt, worn, hinges cracked, some spotting.   R.F.G. Hollett & Son 78-1076 1996 £65.00

LINTON, W. J.   The Ferns of the English Lake Country... Windermere: J. Garnett, 1865. 1st edition; small 8vo; pages ii, ii, 124, vii (ads), hand colored frontispiece and title vignette and text illustrations; original green decorative cloth, gilt.   R.F.G. Hollett & Son 78-532 1996 £65.00

LINTON, WILLIAM J.   Poems and Translations. London: John C. Nimmo, 1889. 1st edition; number 96 of 780 copies for England and America; 8vo; pages x, 202, (1); frontispiece; uncut, original boards, sheep back; presented by author to his wife, Elizabeth Lynn Linton. Boards somewhat soiled and spine little rubbed, still very good. Howard S. Mott 227-86 1996 $150.00

LINTON, WILLIAM JAMES   The House That Tweed Built. Cambridge: 1871. 1st edition; 8vo; 23, (1) pages; illustrations by Thomas Nast; sewn, some soiling and chiping, without wrappers.. Hamilton 1148.   M & S Rare Books 60-208 1996 $100.00

LIPMAN, JEAN   Calder's Universe. New York: Viking/Whitney Museum of American Art, 1976. Square 4to; 351 pages; 457 illustrations, 103 in color; cloth, dust jacket. Freitag 1217.   Brannan 43-101 1996 $110.00

LIPPARD, LUCY R.   Ad Reinhardt. New York: Abrams, 1981. Oblong 4to; 216 pages; 155 illustrations, including 40 color plates; cloth, remainder mark on top edge, dust jacket. Freitag 7966.   Brannan 43-553 1996 $195.00

LISCOMB, HARRY F.   The Prince of Washington Square. New York: Stokes, 1925. 1st edition; slight wear to extremities of fragile paper covered boards, else very good in very good plus dust jacket with some faint dampstaining to spine and some slight nicking at extremities, very uncommon, rarely found in jacket.   Between the Covers 43-151 1996 $800.00

THE LISLE Letters 1533-1540. Chicago: Chicago University Press, 1981. Complete edition; royal 8vo; 6 volumes, numerous plates; original cloth. Howes Bookshop 265-668 1996 £200.00

LISTER, A.   Monograph of the Mycetozoa. London: 1925. 3rd edition; 296 pages; 223 illustrations on 112 plates, many colored, 56 woodcuts. John Johnson 135-372 1996 $100.00

LISTER, MARTIN   Novae ac Curiosae Exercitationes & Descriptiones Thermarum ac Fontium Medicatorum Angliae... London: Walter Kettilby, 1686. 12mo; (12), 156 pages, engraved titlepages, folding plate, separate titlepage for the Exercitataio altera, engraved title shaved closed with triflig loss along fore-edge, very lightly browned; later half calf over speckled boards, very good. Duveen p. 363; Krivatsy 7058; Wellcome III 529; Wing L2529.   Edwin V. Glaser 121-193 1996 $450.00

LISTON, ROBERT   Elements of Surgery. Philadelphia: 1846. 4th American from the last London edition; 8vo; numerous engravings; contemporary calf, worn. Old signature on title.   Argosy 810-314 1996 $125.00

LITHGOW, WILLIAM   The Totall Discourse, of the Rare Adventures, and Painefull Peregrinations of Long Nineteene Yeares Travailes from Scotland, to the Most Famous Kingdomes in Europe, Asia and Affrica. London: by I. Okes, 1640. 2nd edition; 4to; (16), 444, 447-514, (8) pages, including frontispiece, woodcut text illustrations, woodcut initials; contemporary calf, very nice, clean and tight copy, entirely original. Blackmer 1021; Tobler p. 93; European Americana 640/116; STC 15714. Joseph J. Felcone 64-28 1996 $2,500.00

LITTLE Ann and her Mamma. London: George Routledge, n.d. 1st edition thus; 4to; inscription dated 1870; 6 color printed plates by Kronheim; yellow decorated wrpapers with ads on rear cover. Front cover creased, resewn, else very good.   Marjorie James 19-214 1996 £50.00

LITTLE Bo-Peep. Philadelphia: Davis, Porter and Coates, ca. 1850. 7 hand colored pictures; hand colored pictorial wrappers, 2 inch tear along hinge;   Bromer Booksellers 90-112 1996 $125.00

THE LITTLE Chimney-Sweep. Dublin: W. Curry, Jun. and Co.; R. M. Tims, 1831. 1st edition; 12mo; original pink glazed wrappers; Fine. Not listed in Block, BM Cat. or NUC.   Ximenes 108-66 1996 $600.00

LITTLE Fables for Little Folks. London: Religious Tract Society, n.d., ca. 1870. 1st edition; 22 pages; 6 color printed plates, all pages linen backed; yellow wrappers, ornately color decorated, spine very worn, other light wear.   Robin Greer 94A-39 1996 £75.00

THE LITTLE Frog's Lecture and Other Stories. New York: McLoughtlin Bors., ca. 1880-90. Octavo; (7)ff; 6 full page wood engraved illustrations; original pictorial self wrappers, ads for McLoughlin games on back; nice with few small tears to extremites of cover.   Bromer Booksellers 90-116 1996 $125.00

LITTLE Hydrogen, or, the Devil on Two Sticks in London. London: printed for J. J. Stockdale, 1819. 1st edition; 12mo; frontispiece and 10 plates, all hand colored, most signed by Charles Williams; contemporary calf, gilt, spine gilt, some rubbing, but sound; titlepage foxed, but very good, very scarce. 3 copies in NUC; not in Block, not in Wolff, not in Abbey.   Ximenes 109-122 1996 $475.00

LITTLE Jack of All Trades, or, Mechanical Arts Described, in Prose and Verse, Suited to the Capacities of Children. London: Harvey & Darton, 1823. 1st edition thus; 175 x 108mm; 45 engravings; marbled boards, red roan spine compartmented and lettered in gilt, covers rubbed, extremities worn, some browning of pages, else very good. Osborne 114; Gumuchian 3819.   Marjorie James 19-215 1996 £275.00

THE LITTLE London Directory of 1677, the Oldest Printed List of Merchants and Bankers of London Repritned... London: C. Whittingham for Hotten, 1863. 12mo; xxii, pages, 65 ff. (facsimile text); cloth, gilt. Marlborough 162-167 1996 £100.00

LITTLE Man's Family. Phoenix: U.S. Office of Indian Affairs, 1940. Small 4to; text in Navajo and English; drawings in black and white by Gerald Nailor; pictorial wrappers, wrappers little marked and rubbed, interior fresh.   Barbara Stone 70-127 1996 £95.00

LITTLE Songs of Long Ago. London: Augener, n.d. Oblong 4to; 64 pages; colored illustrations; beige boards with color pictorial onlay; near fine.   Marjorie James 19-228 1996 £110.00

LITTLETON, THOMAS   Littleton's Tenures in England, Lately Perused and Amended. London: printed for the Companie of Stationers, 1612. contemporary calf, joints cracked, repaired, still clean.   Meyer Boswell SL27-147 1996 $650.00

LIVERMORE, MARY   My Story of the War: a Woman's Narrative of Four Years Personal Experience as a Nurse in the Union Army Portraying the Lights and Shadows of Hospital Life and the Sanitary Service of the War. Hartford: 1890. 700 pages; numerous fine steel engraved plates, chromolithographs; original binding. Scarce.   W. Bruce Fye 71-1299 1996 $150.00

LIVERSIDGE, A.   The Minerals of New South Wales. London: 1888. 8vo; pages viii, 326, 2 ads, folding colored map, 2 charts, 1 plate, text figures; tables; gilt library copy with stamp on titlepage, verso of map and half title, refixed in case.   John Henly 27-677 1996 £75.00

LIVES of Distinguished Shoemakers. Portland: Davis & Southworth, 1849. 1st edition; 8vo; 340 pages; original black cloth, extremities worn, scattered stain from press flowers, good.   Robert F. Lucas 42-70 1996 $125.00

LIVES of Distinguished Shoemakers. Portland: Davis and Southworth, 1849. 1st edition; 8vo; original brown cloth, covers stamped in blind, spine lettered in gilt, head and tail of spine and along edges and corners worn, some discreet repair to spine, browning and spotting of text. Sabin 41590.   James Cummins 14-180 1996 $100.00

THE LIVES of the Ancient Philosophers, Containing an Account of Their Several Sects, Doctrines, Actions and Remarkable Sayings... London: printed for John Nicholson and Tho. Newborough, 1702. 1st edition; 8vo; name on title, 8 engraved plates, contemporary panelled calf, spine worn, hinges cracked.   Anthony W. Laywood 108-107 1996 £60.00

LIVES of the Most Remarkable Criminals Who Have Been Condemned and Executed for Murder, Highway Robberies, Housebreaking, Street Robberies, Coining, or Other Offences, from the Year 1720 to the Year 1735. London: Reeves and Turner, 1873. 2 volumes; three quarter calf, good, attractive set.   Meyer Boswell SL27-198 1996 $350.00

LIVINGSTON, J. F.   Birds of the Northern Forest (Canada). Toronto: 1966. 4to; 56 fine colored plates; cloth, good copy, slightly soiled dust jacket, inscription on flyleaf.   Wheldon & Wesley 207-787 1996 £60.00

LIVINGSTON, JOHN H.   A Dissertation on the Marriage of a Man With His Sister in Law. New Brunsick: Deare & Myer, 1816. contemporary tree sheep, rubbed and ebrowned, yet sound.   Meyer Boswell SL25-117 1996 $275.00

LIVINGSTON, LIDA   Dali a Study of His Art-in-Jewels. Greenwich: New York Graphic Society, 1959. 4to; 67 pages; 23 tipped in color plates; cloth backed boards, slipcase.   Brannan 43-149 1996 $110.00

LIVINGSTON, ROBERT R.   Examination of the Treaty of Amity, Commerce and Navigation, Between the United States and Great Britain in Several Numbers. New York: republished from the Argus by Thomas Greenleaf, 1795. 1st edition; 8vo; 96 pages; sewn; Howes L399. Evans 28980; Sabin 29954; Gaines 86.   M & S Rare Books 60-363 1996 $175.00

LIVINGSTONE, DAVID 1813-1873   The Last Journals of David Livingstone, in Central Africa, from 1865 to his Death. London: John Murray, 1874. 1st edition; 8vo; 2 volumes; pages xvi, 360; viii,3 46, 20 ads; 2 folding maps, 21 plates; original pictorial cloth, rebacked, leather labels. Mendelssohn p. 912; Hoover 3064.   Richard Adelson W94/95-111 1996 $425.00

LIVINGSTONE, DAVID 1813-1873   Livingstone's Travels and Researches in South Africa... Philadelphia: J. W. Bradley, 1860. Later edition; cloth rubbed, some wear to spine ends, some foxing throughout; still very good.   David Mason 71-11 1996 $100.00

LIVINGSTONE, DAVID 1813-1873   Missionary Travels and Researches in South Africa. London: John Murray, 1857. 1st edition; 1st issue, with colored frontispiece; demy 8vo; (x), 688), 8 pages, folding frontispiece, plates, some colored, illustrations, maps; original cloth by Edmonds & Remnants, with their ticket, little light wear, frontispiece slightly worn and spotted, endpapers strained, few minor marks, but very good in original binding.   Ash Rare Books Zenzybyr-62 1996 £350.00

LIVINGSTONE, DAVID 1813-1873   Missionary Travels and Researches in South Africa... London: Murray, 1857. 1st edition; 2nd issue; 8vo; pages x, 687, 8 ads; 2 folding maps, 25 plates; original brown embossed cloth, rubbed. Mendelssohn p. 908; Theal p. 178; Hoover 3068.   Richard Adelson W94/95-109 1996 $425.00

LIVINGSTONE, DAVID 1813-1873   Missionary Travels and Researches in South Africa... London: John Murray, 1857. 1st edition; 8vo; pages ix, (i), 711, (1), 8 (ads dated Nov. 1 1857); folding wood engraved frontispiece, steel engraved portrait with tissue guard; 24 plates, 2 folding maps; original blindstamped cloth, backstrip gilt lettered direct, rear cover dampstained at edge, brown chalked endpapers, hinges split but firm; bookplate of Marshall Laird, early owner's name, and ticket of "Edmond and Remnants'.   Blackwell's B112-178 1996 £120.00

LIVINGSTONE, DAVID 1813-1873   Missionary Travels and Researches in South Africa, Including a Sketch of Sixteen Years' Residence in the Interior of Africa. New York: 1858. 1st American edition; 732 pages, plus folding maps and plates; original binding. GM 5269.   W. Bruce Fye 71-1300 1996 $225.00

LIVINGSTONE, DAVID 1813-1873   Narrative of an Expedition to the Zambesi and its Tributaries; and of the Discovery of the Lakes Shirwa and Nyassa. 1858-1864. London: John Murray, 1865. 1st edition; 8vo; pages xv, 608, 32 ads; folding map, 12 plates; new tan cloth, blue leather label, internally fine. Mendelssohn p. 915. Theal p. 179; Hoover 3069.   Richard Adelson W94/95-110 1996 $425.00

LIVY   Historiae Romanae Decades. Milan: Uldrich Sinzenzeler (sic) for A. Minutianus, 25th May, 1495. 1st edition thus; folio, 311 unnumbered leaves; blank missing, Roman letter, white on black printer's device, guide letters in some initial spaces, many early ms. annotations, ms. pagination for each section, few marginal repairs, small holes on 4 pages slightly affecting type, but not legibility, small wormtrail, light waterstains to some fore edges, occasional minor lamp oil stain; contemporary vellum over boards, spine remounted and repaired; generally a good, clean wide margined copy; modern label of Viscount Mersey. BMC VI 769; Hain Coppinger 10140; Goff L246; Polain 4528; A. Sokol XXV-58 1996 £4,250.00

LIVY   Historiarum Ab Urbe Condita, Libri, Qui Extant, XXX. Cum Universae Historiae Epitomis... Venice: Apud Paulum Manutium, Aldi Filium, 1566. 2nd edition; folio in 8s; 557 leaves (lacks 1 blank), titlepage and index worn at corners, no loss of text; early ownerships scribbled out, printer's device; worn 19th century half vellum Italian binding. Renouard 202: 19; Adams L1344; UCCLA IIIb/559; Brunet III.1106. Family Album Tillers-391 1996 $900.00

LIVY   Historiarum Ab Urbe Condita Libri Qui Supersunt. Oxford: E Theatro Sheldoniano, 1708. 1st edition edited by Thomas Hearne; 8vo; 2 folding engraved plates; one volume soiled and uncased, others in contemporary full leather needing restoration. Dibdin II 168.   Family Album Tillers-394 1996 $165.00

LIVY   The History of Early Rome. Verona: Limited Editions Club, 1970. One of 1500 copies; signed by artist, Raffaele Scorzelli and designer printer, G. Mardersteig; 8vo; quarter tan buckram, fine in glassine and slipcase.   Charles Agvent 4-823 1996 $175.00

LIVY   The History of Rome. Verona: Limited Editions Club, 1970. Number 330 of 1500 copies, signed by Mardersteig and artist, Raffaele Scorzelli; cloth over patterned boards, upper left corner of spine lightly bumped, othewise fine in publisher's slipcase.   Hermitage SP95-1008 1996 $150.00

LLEWELLYN, RICHARD   How Green Was My Valley. London: Michael Joseph, 1939. 1st edition; corners little bumped, else about fine in very good dust jacket with some light chipping to crown and some very shallow chips on rear panel and at foot, signed by author.   Between the Covers 42-275 1996 $285.00

LLOYD, ALBERT B.   Uganda to Khartoum. Life and Adventure on the Upper Nile. London: T. Fisher Unwin, 1907. 8vo; pages xii, 312; folding map, 80 plates; original pictorial red cloth, some light foxing, spine faded and starting.   Richard Adelson W94/95-112 1996 $160.00

LLOYD, C. G.   The Geastrae, the Tylostomeae, The Nidulariaceae, synopsis of the Known Phalloids, synopsis of the Genus Cladoderris... Cincinnati: 1902-19. 8vo; (altogether i monographs), numerous illustrations; original wrappers (with wear and soiling, 1 plate missing, 1 set of wrappers missing, most are ex-library).   Raymond M. Sutton VII-230 1996 $235.00

LLOYD, DAVID   State-Worthies: or the Statesmen and Favourties of England from the Reformation to the Revolution. London: J. Robson, 1766. 2 volumes; (xvi), 571, (vii); (ii), 597, iii pages; contemporary calf, spines gilt, double labels, final ad leaf in volume 1; 3 joints cracked, but firm, few small defects in calf. Good set.   Robert Clark 38-77 1996 £90.00

LLOYD, EVAN   A Plain System of Geography. Edinburgh: printed for the author by Mundell & Son, 1797. 8vo; pages xxiv, 205; 12 folding maps; modern blind ruled calf, gilt, little browning and fingering. R.F.G. Hollett & Son 78-1405 1996 £160.00

LLOYD, HUMPHREY   Elementary Treatise on the Wave-Theory of Light. London: Longmans, Green, 1873. 3rd edition; 8vo; xi, 247 pages; illustrations; contemporary calf, large gilt vignette on front cover and gilt panels on spine, marbled edges, joints started, few rubs and scratches, still attractive.   Edwin V. Glaser 121-196 1996 $135.00

LLOYD, JOHN URI   Etidorhpa or the End of the earth. Cincinnati: 1895 Author's Limited edition; 376 pages; cloth, moderate wear at ends of spine and corners.   Robert G. Hayman 11/95-60 1996 $175.00

LLOYD, SETON   Ancient Architecture: Mesopotamia, Egypt, Crete, Greece. New York: Harry N. Abrams, 1974. 4to; 415 pages; 525 illustrations; original cloth, dust jacket.   Archaeologia Luxor-2392 1996 $125.00

LOBB, THEOPHILUS   A Practical Treatise of Painful Distempers, with Some Effectual Methods of Curing Them, Exemplified in a Great Variety of Suitable Histories. London: printed for James Buckland, 1739. 1st edition; 8vo; (ii), 1-146, 145-320, (xiv) pages; original cloth; Wellcome III 533; not in Osler, Waller or Reynolds cat.   David Bickersteth 133-207 1996 £165.00

LOBSTEIN, J. F. DANIEL   A Treatise Upon the Semeiology of the Eye, for the Use of Physicians. New York: C. S. Francis, 1830. 1st edition; 8vo; 175, (5) pages; original cloth backed boards, printed paper label, minor wear and waterstaining, quite good. Inscribed "David Thayer/bought of a/Poor man in the street Feb. 23 '59". Cooper 2262. M & S Rare Books 60-465 1996 $250.00

LOCHER, J. L.   Escher: with a Complete Catalogue of Graphic Works... London: Thames & Hudson, 1981. 4to; 349 pages; 606 illustrations, including 36 in color; cloth, dust jacket.   Thomas Thorp 489-193 1996 £50.00

LOCK, A. G.   A Practical Treatise on the Manufacture of Sulphuric Acid. London: 1879. viii, 247 pages; plates, numerous illustrations and diagrams; original bevelled cloth, corners and spine edges little worn. Graham Weiner C2-99 1996 £50.00

LOCKE, E. W.   Three Years in Camp and Hospital. Boston: 1870. 1st edition; 408 pages; original binding, scarce.   W. Bruce Fye 71-1304 1996 $225.00

LOCKE, JOHN 1632-1704   Some Thoughts Concerning Education. London: printed for A. and J. Churchill, 1699. 4th edition; 8vo; engraved name on title, some ink marks in margin; contemporary calf, spine gilt, hinges cracked, label. Wing L2734.   Anthony W. Laywood 109-84 1996 £175.00

LOCKE, JOHN 1632-1704   Some Thoughts on the Conduct of the Understanding in the Search of Truth. N.P.: 1741. 1st separate edition; 12mo; contemporary sheep, cracked, some rubbing, and chipping, circular mark on upper cover as if an onlay, endpapers removed, without "Advertisement" leaves at front, dated signature of W. R. S. Dwyer, 1844 on title, browned.   James Cummins 14-124 1996 $150.00

LOCKE, JOHN 1632-1704   Two Treatises of Government: in the Former, the False Principles and Foundation of Sir Robert Filmer, and His Followers are Detailed and Overthrown. London: John Churchill, 1713. 4th edition; 12mo; 379, (3) pages, wanting final lea of ads; recently rebound in half calf, gilt; good. Attig 103.   John Drury 82-153 1996 £150.00

LOCKER-LAMPSON, FREDERICK 1821-1895   London Lyrics. London: Macmillan, 1904. 8vo; full crushed green morocco with all-over design featuring a large central arabesque pattern filled with small tools used in combination; fields of pointelles and small trefoils fill most of the remaining space, spine with five raised bands and matching decoration in all but two of the compartments which carry the title information, spine gilt stamped in the manner of Sarah Prideaux, board edges gilt, inner gilt dentelles, marbled endleaves, all edges gilt, binding unsigned, stamped on blind on titlepage "Presentation Copy" (within circle); fine.   Book Block 32-37 1996 $375.00

LOCKER-LAMPSON, FREDERICK 1821-1895   Rowfant Rhymes. Cleveland: Rowfant Club, 1895. 1st edition; limited to 127 copies, printed on Japon at the DeVinne Press; fine in full limp vellum; bookplate. Bromer Booksellers 87-258 1996 $200.00

LOCKHART, JOHN GIBSON 1794-1854   Ancient Spanish Ballads. London: John Murray, 1841. 1st of this edition; tall thick quarto; unpaginated, with 8 pages of publisher's ads; 4 splendid titlepages by Owen Jones, lavishly gilt in the Morrish style, the first to use 4 color chromolithography, every page with wood engraved illustrations in many colors & color lithographed borders or tailpieces; bound by Leighton (& probably designed by Jones) in red pebbled morocco, elaborate gilt and blind decorations to coers & spine, gilt & black floral endpapers; with forepedge painting: a bright, impressionistic view of Gibraltar, with several sailing ships in foreground, book and fore-edge painting in excellent condition, laid in is a glassine envelope with clippings about this historic instance of fine book-making. VBD 58-59 and 125. Hartfield 48-F7 1996 $1,950.00

LOCKHART, JOHN GIBSON 1794-1854   Ancient Spanish Ballads. London: John Murray, 1842. 2nd printing; 4to; 127 leaves; full decorated morocco, light stain to margin of first few leaves, light rubbing at hinges, else very attractive copy.   Bookpress 75-80 1996 $275.00

LOCKHART, JOHN GIBSON 1794-1854   The History of Matthew Wald. Edinburgh: William Blackwood/London: T. Cadell, 1824. 1st edition; 8vo; half title; contemporary quarter calf, spine label, marbled boards; evidently wanting ad leaf; fine, uncommon. Wolff 4171; Block p. 142-3. Trebizond 39-37 1996 $325.00

LOCKLEY, R. M.   Sea-Birds. London: 1954. Color and other illustrations; mint in protected dust jacket.   David A.H. Grayling MY95Orn-184 1996 £70.00

LOCKLEY, R. M.   Sea-Birds. London: 1954. Color and other illustrations; apart from light foxing to fore-edges and minutre tear to dust jacket, a fine copy.   David A.H. Grayling MY95Orn-183 1996 £60.00

LOCKWOOD, FRANK C.   Arizona Characters. Los Angeles: Times Mirror Press, 1928. 1st edition; limited to 1000 copies; 230 pages; frontispiece, illustrations, plates, portraits; decorated green cloth, bookplate, spine slightly darkened, else fine.   Argonaut Book Shop 113-420 1996 $125.00

LOCKWOOD, FRANK C.   Pioneer Days in Arizona, from the Spanish Occupation to Statehood. New York: 1932. 1st edition; 387 pages; photos, illustrations; book good, worn binding and spine punctures, protective slipcase.   Early West 22-189 1996 $100.00

LOCKWOOD, M. S.   Art Embroidery. A Treatise on the Revived Practice of Decorative Needlework. London: Marcus Ward, 1878. Folio; 19 chromolithograph plates by Thomas Crane, gilt decorated pictorial cloth, gilt decorated spine, worn at spine tips and corners, inner hinges strengthened.   Marilyn Braiterman 15-136 1996 $400.00

LODGE, DAVID   Graham Greene. New York: & London: Columbia University Press, 1966. 1st edition; wrappers; spine browned, very good. Ulysses 39-379 1996 £75.00

LODGE, GEORGE   Memoirs of an Artist Naturalist. London: 1946. Colored and other plates by author, upper cover has been creased from top to base, otherwise excellent copy in protected dust jacket.   David A.H. Grayling MY95Orn-47 196 £80.00

LOEB, THEOPHILUS   A Treatise of the Small Pox. London: printed for T. Woodward and C. Davis, and sold by Mr. Green... 1731. 1st edition; 8vo; short tear on lower part of M2 expertly repaired; contemporary calf, rebacked, label.   Anthony Laywood 108-83 1996 £185.00

LOFTIE, ARTHUR G.   The Rural Deanery of Gosforth, Diocese of Carlisle, Its Churches and Endowments. Kendal: T. Wilson, 1889. 1st edition; 8vo; pages 146, plus errata; original blue cloth.   R.F.G. Hollett & Son 78-1084 1996 £65.00

LOFTIE, W. J.   Kensington, Picturesque and Historical. London: Field and Tuer, 1888. 4to; pages xix, 287, lxiv pages subscribers, 4 ff. ads, numerous text illustrations, frontispiece, 5 plates in color; original blue cloth, gilt.   Marlborough 162-162 1996 £100.00

LOFTING, HUGH   Doctor Doolittle in the Moon. New York: Pub. by Frederick A. Stokes Co., 1928. 1st edition; octavo; x, 307 pages; 72 illustrations by Lofting; original purple cloth stamped in turquoise on front cover and spine, color pictorial label on front cover, pictorial endpapers, light wear to extremities and to pictorial label, previous owner's ink presentation inscription on half title; near fine in dust jacket with some staining and tape repairs, in quarter red morocco clamshell case; with original drawing for the illus. p. 161 archivally preserved in case.   Heritage Book Shop 196-272 1996 $2,000.00

LOFTUS, WILLIAM R.   The Brewer: a Familiar Treatise ont he Art of Brewing... London: William R. Loftus, 1856. 1st edition; 12mo; 4 ad leaves before title, illustrations, soiled.   Anthony W. Laywood 109-85 1996 £75.00

LOGAN, C. A.   Physics of the Infectious Diseases. Chicago: 1878. 1st edition; 212 pages; original binding.   W. Bruce Fye 71-1306 1996 $100.00

LOGAN, JOHN   The Bridge of Change. New York: Boa Editions, 1978. 1st edition; limited to 25 roman numeral copies, signed with poem in holograph by author; thin 8vo; cloth backed marbled boards; fine. James S. Jaffe 34-413 1996 $150.00

LOGAN, JOHN   Poems. London: printed for T. Cadell, 1781. 1st edition; 8vo; half title; some slight spotting in text, original boards, uncut, preserved in green half morocco slipcase; nice.   Anthony W. Laywood 109-86 1996 £75.00

LOGAN, OLIVE   Apropos of Women and Theatres. New York: Carleton; S. Low Son & Co., London, 1869. 1st edition; 12mo; original purple cloth, bit rubbed, some foxing, but very good.   Ximenes 108-250 1996 $250.00

LOGUE, CHRISTOPHER   The Girls. London: Stone, 1969. 1st edition; 8/24 copies (of an edition of 50), signed by author; small folio; (1), 21, (1) leaves, pritned on recto of each leaf only, title printed in red; original quarter dark blue calf, backstrip gilt lettered, psychedelic decorated linen sides, fine.   Blackwell's B112-179 1996 £50.00

LOGUE, CHRISTOPHER   Red Bird. London: Circle Press, 1979. One of 30 copies, marked 'Artist's Proof', signed by artist and author; folio; 10 screenprints by John Chritie, loose leaf in fold over canvas boards and slipcase (little rubbed), otherwise fine.   Words Etcetera 94-303 1996 £220.00

LOGUE, CHRISTOPHER   Wand and Quadrant. Paris: Collection Merlin, 1953. 1st edition; one of 300 copies; (of an edition of 600 copies), of the unnumbered issue; 8vo; 63 pages, title printed in red; original printed pale lightly sunned grey dust jacket, over plain white card; good; author's first book.   Blackwell's B112-180 1996 £50.00

LOHF, KENNETH A.   Season: Seven Poems. Janus Press, 1981. One in an edition of 150 numbered copies, signed by author and artist; 7.25 x 5.25 inches; 24 unnumbered pages; color relief print by Clair Van Vliet; woodtype solid circle on half title, centerfold linoleum cut by Claire Van Vliet, designed by Van Vliet, titles printed in red and black, text in black, woodtype circle in orange; printed dry on Fabriano book; linoleum cuts printed in reds and violets on kozo natural, French-folded to avoid show-through and sewing through the image; quarter bound in red Scholco cloth with dyed Japanese paper over boards, and red Fabriano Miliani Ingres endpapers author/title label on spine; fine.   Joshua Heller 21-21 1996 $150.00

LOHNIS, F.   Studies Upon the Life Cycles of the Bacteria. Part I. Review of the Literature, 1838-1918. Washington: 1921. 1st edition; 4to; 252 pages, plus plates; original binding, ex-library.   W. Bruce Fye 71-1307 1996 $125.00

LOLLIUS, ANTONIUS   Oratio Circumcisionis Dominicae Coram Innocentis VIII Habita. Rome: Stephen Plannck, after 1 Jan. 1485. Quarto; modern green quarter morocco gilt by Bennett, lovely copy. Hain 10180; Goff I 275.   G. W. Stuart 59-64 1996 $2,100.00

LOMBARD, DANIEL   A Succinct History of Ancient and Modern Persecutions. London: printed for S. Birt.. 1747. With paste on label - sold by Edward Score, Bookseller in Exon; 8vo; pages 192; new quarter calf.   Peter Murray Hill 185-100 1996 £75.00

LONDINA Illustrata, Graphic and Historic Memorials of Monasteries, Churches, Chapels, Schools, Charitable Foundations, Palaces, Halls, Courts, Processions, Places of Early Amusement and Modern and Present Theatres in the Citities and Suburbs of London... London: Robt. Wilkinson, 1819-25. Stout large 4to; 2 volumes, engraved vignette titles, 99, 109 engraved plates, pages (ii),180; (ii), 197, (ii); 19th century half maroon morocco, rubbed but sound, top edge gilt. Adams 131. Marlborough 162-217 1996 £900.00

LONDON Almanack for the Year of Christ 1774. London: printed for the Company of Stationers, n.d. 1773. 59 x 33 mm; 12 ff. engraved throughout, folding plate mounted as one leaf; original red morocco, gilt, all edges gilt, gold patterned printed endpapers with sponge applied coloring, covers gilt, ruled in squares, dog-tooth border, pointille saltires interspersed with flower-heads and scrollwork, spine gilt with running pattern, (clasp lost, small loss to foot of spine, edges little worn), within colored and embossed paper covered card pull-off case, with marbled paper interior, worn with some loss to pull-off top; top left corner of first page bears the red partial imprint of the penny 'stamp duty'. Marlborough 160-26 1996 £250.00

LONDON MISSIONARY SOCIETY   A Missionary Voyage to the Southern Pacific Ocean, Performed int eh Years 1796, 1797, 1798 in the Ship Duff, Commanded by Captain James Wilson... London: printed for T. Chapman by T. Gillet, 1799. (12), (c), 396 pages (last blank), 7 pages subscribers list; early half calf and marbled boards, calf rubbed, new endpapers, captions on veral plates trimmed, otherwise pleasant copy. Hill p. 184 cites 1st ed.   Antipodean 28-630 1996 $850.00

LONDON MISSIONARY SOCIETY   A Missionary Voyage to the Southern Pacific Ocean, Performed in the Years 1796, 1797, 1798, in the Ship Duff, Commanded by Captain James Wilson. London: T. Chapman, 1799. 1st edition; 4to; pages 12, c, 420, 12; 7 maps, 6 plates; modern quarter imitation vellum, one corner bruised, some light foxing. Ferguson 301; Cox II p. 307; Sabin 49480; Hill I p. 184.   Richard Adelson W94/95-181 1996 $785.00

LONDON MISSIONARY SOCIETY   A Missionary Voyage to the Southern Pacific Ocean, Performed in the Years 1796, 1797, 1798, in the Ship Duff, Commanded by Captain James Wilson. London: 1799. 1st Gillet edition; 28 cm; 6 p.l., c, 395, (+ list of subscribers), 7 folding maps and 6 plates; full modern leather binding, endpapers renewed, offset from plates, occasional maraginal stain to plates. Hill p. 478; Sabin 49480; Ferguson 301.   Parmer Books 039/Nautica-039268 1996 $750.00

THE LONDON Universal Letter-Writer; or, Whole Art of Polite Correspondence... London: B. Crosby, 1802. New edition; 12mo; frontispiece; uncut, stabbed in original ink wrappers, printed with ads, slight chipping, very good. Not traced in BL, Alston or ESTC.   Jarndyce 103-278 1996 £75.00

LONDON, CHARMIAN   The Log of the Snark. New York: Macmillan, 1925. Reprint; 8vo; photos; decorated cloth, covers darkened, edgewworn, good plus; with approximately 25 word inscription by author.   Charles Agvent 4-825 1996 $100.00

LONDON, JACK 1876-1916   Before Adam. Macmillan, 1907. 1st edition; color and black and white illustrations by C. L. Bull; spine little faded, offsetting to f.e.p.'s, else tight, very good+ copy in pictorial cloth; Aronovitz 57-712 1996 $110.00

LONDON, JACK 1876-1916   The Call of the Wild. New York: Macmillan, 1903. 1st edition; some minor shelf wear, else very good+ to near fine in nice, fresh example of the rare dust jacket with only a few little chips and tears and residue of a discreet (probably removable) shelf label at base of spine.   Lame Duck Books 19-291 1996 $5,500.00

LONDON, JACK 1876-1916   The Cruise of the Snark. New York: Macmillan Co., 1911. 1st edition; octavo; xiv, 340 pages, plus (6) pages ads; color frontispiece, one plate, numerous illustrations; original blue cloth lettered in gilt on front cover and spine, color pictorial label on front cover, titlepage, minor wear to extremities, bookplate, otherwise near fine. BAL 11929; Woodbridge 89.   Heritage Book Shop 196-170 1996 $600.00

LONDON, JACK 1876-1916   The Cruise of the Dazzler. New York: Century Co., 1902. 1st edition; 1st issue, with "Published October, 1902" on copyright page; octavo; vii, 250 pages; frontispiece, 5 plates; original ecru cloth decoratively stamped and lettered in black, green and orange, minor wear and soiling to cloth, just slightly skewed; fine, protected in quarter black morocco clamshell case. BAL 11872; Woodbridge 10. Heritage Book Shop 196-169 1996 $2,750.00

LONDON, JACK 1876-1916   The Iron Heel. London: Macmillan, 1908. 1st edition; pictorial cloth, just about very good.   Aronovitz 57-713 1996 $165.00

LONDON, JACK 1876-1916   The Jacket. Mills & Boon, 1915. 1st edition; frontispiece missing, some light wear to corner tips, else tight, justa bout very good.   Aronovitz 57-714 1996 $225.00

LONDON, JACK 1876-1916   John Barleycorn. New York: Century Co., 1913. 1st edition; 1st printing with one blank leaf following page 343; (6), 3-343 pages, frontispiece, 7 full page illustrations by H. T. Dunn; gilt lettered dark green cloth, contemporary owner's name in ink on inner front cover, upper front corner slightly jammed, overall fine. Laid in is ALS by author to Tom Gregory.   Argonaut Book Shop 113-422 1996 $1,250.00

LONDON, JACK 1876-1916   The Red One. Mills & Boon, 1919. 1st English edition spine faded, else tight, very good copy.   Aronovitz 57-716 1996 $150.00

LONDON, JACK 1876-1916   The Scarlet Plague. Mills & Boon, 1915. 1st English edition; some offsetting to endpapers and foxing to fore edge, else bright, near fine copy.   Aronovitz 57-715 1996 $125.00

LONDON, JACK 1876-1916   Theft. New York: Macmillan, 1910. 1st edition; original cloth, near fine; choice presentation copy, inscribed by author to his mother.   19th Century Shop 39- 1996 $8,500.00

LONDON. CHARTER   The Royal Charter of Confirmation Granted by King Charles II to the City of London. London: printed for Samuel Lee and Benjamin Alsop, 1680. 8vo; (24), 247, (1) pages, paper rather age browned, marginal worming in some fore-corners touching some page numerals; 19th century half calf, spine with raised bands, stamped in blind, with label; good. Old Wing 3604a; Sweet & Maxwell I p. 435 (15); Goss 2035.   John Drury 82-98 1996 £150.00

LONDON. COMMON COUNCIL   An Act of Common Councill of the City of London (Made in the 1st and 2nd Years of the Reign of Philip and Mary) for Retrenching of the Expences of the Lord Mayor & Sheriffs, &c. London: printed for Fr. Smith at the Elephant & Castle in Cornhill, 1680. 8 pages; uncut, disbound. Wing L2857a.   H. M. Fletcher 121-40 1996 £85.00

LONDON. COMMON COUNCIL   An Act of Common Council for Regulating the Election of Sheriffs, and for Repealing the Treasonable and Disloyal Acts and Proceedings of that Court in the Time of the Late Rebellion. London: printed by Samuel Roycroft, Printer to this Honourable City, 1683. Folio: 10 leaves, woodcut arms on title, uncut, disbound. Wing L2858.   H. M. Fletcher 121-39 1996 £60.00

LONDON. COMMON COUNCIL   A Brief Account of What Pass'd at the Common Council Held in London, on Fryday 13, May 1681. London: printed for Walter Davis, 1681. Folio; 2 pages; uncut, disbound. Wing L 2857c.   H. M. Fletcher 121-38 1996 £60.00

LONDON. POLICE   Report from the Committe on the State of the Police of the Metropolis, 1816 (and) First (-third) Report on the State of the Police of the Metropolis, 1817-18. Folio; 3 volumes in 4; uncut, recent buckram, ex-library with stamps and labels.   Marlborough 162-193 1996 £1,000.00

LONG, ESMOND   A History of Pathology. Baltimore: 1928. 1st edition; 291 pages; original binding. GM 2317.   W. Bruce Fye 71-1308 1996 $125.00

LONG, F. B.   The Hounds of Tindalos. Sauk City: Arkam House, 1946. 1st edition; near fine in very good+ dust jacket, inscribed by author. Aronovitz 57-717 1996 $225.00

LONG, J.   Voyages and Travels of an Indian Interpreter and Trader, Describing the Manners and Customs of the North American Indians. London: printed for the author & sold by Robson, Bond St.... 1791. 1st edition; 4to; errata, 1-181 pages, 183-295, 1 large folding map, new endpapers; bookplate removed from front pastedown leaving slight traces of glue, some foxing and offsetting to map, lacks first blank. Half calf and marbled boards, black morocco label to spine, edges speckled, corners slightly bumped; Stanton & Tremaine 597; Sabin 41878; Streeter VI 3651; Howes L443.   Beeleigh Abbey BA56-91 1996 £900.00

LONG, W. H.   Medals of the British Navy and How They Were Won. London: Norie & Wilson, 1895. 1st edition; 8vo; 450 pages; 21 color plates, 11 woodcuts, original gilt cloth; very good.   John Lewcock 30-104 1996 £110.00

LONGAKER, MARK   English Biography in the Eighteenth Century. Philadelphia: University of Pennsylvania Press, 1931. 1st edition; original binding, top edge dusty, head and tail of spine, corners and bottom edges of covers bumped and bruised, covers marked, cover edges rubbed, very good; with pencilled ownership signature of Frederick Pottle.   Ulysses 39-707 1996 £75.00

LONGFELLOW, HENRY WADSWORTH 1807-1882   The Courtship of Miles Standish. Boston: Ticknor & Fields, 1858. 1st printing; 8vo; original binding, brown endpapers, small old bookseller's label, mild rubbing; near fine. BAL 12122.   Charles Agvent 4-832 1996 $350.00

LONGFELLOW, HENRY WADSWORTH 1807-1882   The Courtship of Miles Standish. Boston: Ticknor and Fields, 1858. 1st edition; one of the copies with inserted ad for Waverley Novels; 8vo; original binding, touch of wear to spine tips, light spotting to covers, near fine; 1858 pencil signature.   Charles Agvent 4-833 1996 $350.00

LONGFELLOW, HENRY WADSWORTH 1807-1882   The Courtship of Miles Standish. Boston: Ticknor & Fields, 1858. 1st printing; 8vo; purple endpapers, original binding, front outer hinge cracked, still very tight, top of spine chipped to text block, contents bit darkened.   Charles Agvent 4-834 1996 $150.00

LONGFELLOW, HENRY WADSWORTH 1807-1882   The Divine Tragedy. Boston: James R. Osgood and Co., 1871. 1st edition; the 8vo. format (also published in 12mo); BAL does not give priority; original purple cloth gilt, faded, some rubbing with fraying and losses at head and tail of spine, ownership stamp on title and blank, some marginal browning, generally light; contemporary gift inscription "Miss Sallie K. Bates with the best wishes of her friend Mrs. R. Cambridge Christmas 1871."   James Cummins 14-126 1996 $150.00

LONGFELLOW, HENRY WADSWORTH 1807-1882   The Estray. Boston: William D. Ticknor, 1847. 1st edition; origingal glazed yellow boards, paper label, joints rubbed and ends of spine worn, even to sheets, but tight, clean copy with nice full label; BAL 12088; Myerson G11; Livingston p. 44-5.   Mac Donnell 12-46 1996 $225.00

LONGFELLOW, HENRY WADSWORTH 1807-1882   The Estray. Boston: William Ticknor, 1847. 1st edition; in unrecorded publisher's gift binding, original crimson cloth, gilt extra, all edges gilt, outer joints expertly renewed, spine ornamentation is asymetrical, possibly an experimental binding. BAL 12088; Myerson G11; Costbooks of Ticknor & Fields A99a.   Mac Donnell 12-45 1996 $125.00

LONGFELLOW, HENRY WADSWORTH 1807-1882   The Estray. Boston: William D. Ticknor, 1847. 1st edition; original glazed yellow boards, expertly rebacked in matching paper, otherwise nice, clean copy; Myerson G11; BAL 12088; Livingston p. 44-5.   Mac Donnell 12-47 1996 $125.00

LONGFELLOW, HENRY WADSWORTH 1807-1882   The Golden Legend. Boston: Ticknor, Reed & Fields, 1851. 1st edition, 1st printing; 8vo; Oct. 1851 catalog; original binding, corners, spine tips worn; quite good, owner's signature. BAL 12102.   Charles Agvent 4-837 1996 $100.00

LONGFELLOW, HENRY WADSWORTH 1807-1882   Hyperion, a Romance. New York: Samuel Colman, 1839. 1st edition; 12mo; original tan boards, brown endpapers, printed paper labels, labels slightly rubbed, minimal wear and chipping to these fragile boards, very superior set and most unusual in fine condition. BAL 12064 setting a. Wright I 1707. Rinderknecht 56883;   M & S Rare Books 60-195 1996 $375.00

LONGFELLOW, HENRY WADSWORTH 1807-1882   Hyperion. New York: S. Colman, 1839. 1st edition; 1st printing, 1st published edition; 8vo; purple cloth, spine sunned, little frayed, very good. Longfellow bibliographer Luther Livingston's copy with signed note by him on front blank stating the numerous ms. corrections he made in this copy show the differences between the published edition and the earlier private printing of only 10 copies.   Charles Agvent 4-841 1996 $350.00

LONGFELLOW, HENRY WADSWORTH 1807-1882   Hyperion: a Romance. London: Alfred William Bennett, 1865. 1st edition thus; 4to; 24 mounted albumen prints of views, pages x, (2), 270, (1); original purple cloth, gilt extra, edges gilt, by Westleys with ticket, little wear at joints and headbands, one small section starting, still very good to nice, rarely found in nice state.   James Fenning 133-121 1996 £195.00

LONGFELLOW, HENRY WADSWORTH 1807-1882   The Poetical Works. Boston: Houghton Mifflin, 1881. Later edition; small folio; 2 volumes; xvi, 488; xvi, 489-928 pages; profusely illustrated with engravings, original full red morocco with richly gilt turn-ins, library bookplate and blindstamp, extremities lightly rubbed, but nice, very good; BAL 12601.   Chapel Hill 94-115 1996 $150.00

LONGFELLOW, HENRY WADSWORTH 1807-1882   The Seaside and the Fireside. Boston: Ticknor, Reed and Fields, 1850. 1st edition; 8vo; original boards, spine lacking, some loosening of stitching and wear of edges, faint offprint from publisher's ads dated Dec. 1849 on front endpapers and signature of Elizabeth B. Barrett on blank at front, generally pleasant copy internally. BAL 12099; Caroll A. Wilson Cat. 232.   James Cummins 14-127 1996 $100.00

LONGFELLOW, HENRY WADSWORTH 1807-1882   The Song of Hiawatha. Boston: Ticknor and Fields, 1855. 1st American edition; 8vo; some chipping of spine and slight spotting of text, otherwise light wear and nice copy; from the collection of J. T. Fisher. BAL 12112; Carroll Wilson Cat. p. 239.   James Cummins 14-128 1995 $150.00

LONGFELLOW, HENRY WADSWORTH 1807-1882   Tales of a Wayside Inn. Boston: Ticknor & Fields, 1863. 1st edition; 1st printing; 8vo; catalog B; slate cloth, bookplate removed from pastedown, some aging to paper, spine lighter color than covers but gilt still bright, little wear to upper corners and spine tips, about very good. BAL 12136.   Charles Agvent 4-845 1996 $200.00

LONGFELLOW, HENRY WADSWORTH 1807-1882   Tales of a Wayside Inn. Boston: Ticknor & Fields, 1863. 1st edition; 1st printing; Catalog A; green cloth, library name removed from title, leather bookplate, paper aged, spine tips frayed, hinges slightly cracked.   Charles Agvent 4-846 1996 $100.00

LONGFELLOW, HENRY WADSWORTH 1807-1882   Tales of a Wayside Inn. Boston: Ticknor and Fields, 1863. 1st edition; original blue cloth, very good in blue half morocco case; fine presentation copy inscribed by author for John Owen, who published Longfellow's first books of poetry.   19th Century Shop 39- 1996 $4,500.00

LONGFELLOW, HENRY WADSWORTH 1807-1882   Tales of a Wayside Inn. Boston: Ticknor and Fields, 1863. 1st American edition; 12mo; illustrated titlepage; half purple morocco gilt by Stikeman, some light rubbing, light browning and spotting of some leaves of text, without publisher's ads; attractive copy. BAL 12136.   James Cummins 14-125 1996 $250.00

LONGFELLOW, HENRY WADSWORTH 1807-1882   Tales of a Wayside Inn. Boston: Ticknor & Fields, 1863. 1st edition; 1st printing; small 8vo; original forest green ribbed cloth, gilt spine, hinges cracked, extremities rubbed and some light staining to lower board, else very good with first state of ads. BAL 12136.   Glenn Books 36-173 1996 $200.00

LONGFELLOW, HENRY WADSWORTH 1807-1882   The Wreck of the Hesperus. Boston: Carl Prufer, 1845? 1st edition; 4to; 30 pages; original printed wrappers; foxed. Carroll Wilson I 203.   M & S Rare Books 60-196 1996 $250.00

LONGHURST, M. H.   English Ivories. London: G. P. Putnam's Sons, 1926. 4to; 6 color plates, 50 in black and white, 10 text figures, xviii, 172 pages; buckram gilt, top edge gilt, slightly worn.   Thomas Thorp 489-195 1996 £50.00

LONGINUS   Dyonysius Longinus on the Sublime... London: printed by J. Watts; and sold by W. Innys and R. Manby, 1739. 1st edition of this translation; 8vo; engraved frontispiece, (xvi), xxxiv, 187 pages; original panelled calf, rebacked,old endpapers preserved.   David Bickersteth 133-45 1996 £55.00

LONGINUS   Dionysii Longini de Sublimitate Libellus. Oxford: Wilmot, 1718. Large paper copy; 8vo; pages (13), 163, (32), full leather, from the library of the great book collector, Rev. Theodore Williams, probably bound by Clarke for Williams, with Williams' gilt stamps on each board, gilt dentelles, all edges gilt. Dibdin II 177; Brunet III 1152.   Family Album Tillers-398 1995 $300.00

LONGLEY, MICHAEL   No Continuing City. Dublin: Gill and Macmillan, 1969. 1st edition; 8vo; boards, dust jacket; fine in lightly rubbed jacket, signed by author.   James S. Jaffe 34-416 1996 $125.00

LONGLEY, MICHAEL   Ten Poems. Belfast: Festival Publications, 1965. 1st edition; thin 8vo; with 3 corrections made by the poet; printed self wrappers; fine.   James S. Jaffe 34-415 1996 $375.00

LONGSTAFF, GEORGE B.   Butterfly Hunting in Many Lands. London: 1912. 8vo; pages xx, 729, 16 plates; cloth; some very limited foxing, but good set.   Wheldon & Wesley 207-1067 1996 £75.00

LONGSTAFF, GEORGE B.   The Langstaffs of Teesdale and Weardale; Materials for a History of a Yeoman Family. London: Mitchell, Hughes & Clarke, 1906. 1st edition; thick 4to; pages 190, 380; 5 plates, 67 pedigrees; original cloth, binding slightly stained and chafed.   Howes Bookshop 265-1883 1996 £120.00

LONGUEVILLE, PETER   The Hermit; or, the Unparalleled Sufferings, and Surprizing Adventures of Philip Quarll, an Englishman. London: printed for the Book Sellers, 1790. 5th edition; 12mo; iv, 272 pages; frontispiece; contemporary sheep, neatly rebacked to style, gilt spine with red morocco label, very good, printed on blue paper.   Heritage Book Shop 196-238 1996 $250.00

LONSDALE, HENRY   The Life and Works of Musgrave Lewthwaite Watson, Sculptor. London: George Routledge, 1866. 1st edition; large 8vo; pages xii, 244, 12 photographic plates; original cloth, gilt, very nice. R.F.G. Hollett & Son 78-205 1996 £85.00

LONSDALE, HENRY   The Life of John Heysham, M.D... London: Longmans, Green and Co., 1870. Large square 8vo; pages 173; frontispiece; original cloth, gilt over bevelled boards, extremities minimally frayed; scarce.   R.F.G. Hollett & Son 78-206 1996 £95.00

THE LOOKING-GLASS for the Mind... London: printed for Harris and Son, Scatchard and Letterman, Harvey & Darton.. 1821. 15th edition; small 8vo; 1-271 pages, 74 woodcut illustrations by John Bewick; new endpapers, title and text soiled; full modern antique style calf, green morocco label to spine, gilt date to base of spine.   Beeleigh Abbey BA56-135 1996 £55.00

THE LOOKING-Glass for the Mind; or, Intellectual Mirror. London: J. Crowder, 1794. 12mo; (6), 271 pages; 74 woodcut vignettes by John Bewick; 19th century three quarter red morocco and marbled boards, extremities lightly rubbed, else fine. Roscoe J25(4); Hugo 66.   Bromer Booksellers 87-111 1996 $350.00

LOOMIS, LEANDER V.   A Journal of the Birmingham Emigration Company. Salt Lake City: 1928. 1st edition; 182 pages; photos, charts, folding map; decorated cloth; singed, fine. Flake 4986; Wheat Gold Rush 128; Howes L464; Mintz 302.   T. A. Swinford 49-706 1996 $125.00

LOPEZ, BARRY   Giving Birth to Thunder, Sleeping with His Daughter. New York: Sheed, Andrews & McMeel, 1977. 1st edition; 186 pages; fine in very good price clipped dust jacket, worn and creased at top and bottom extremities.   Ken Sanders 8-396 1996 $350.00

LOPEZ, BARRY   Giving Birth to Thunder Sleeping with His Daughter. Kansas City: Sheed McMeel, 1978. 1st edition; cloth faded at edges, els fine in very good jacket with few creases and short tears, but less rubbing than usual, nice, scarce, signed by author.   Ken Lopez 74-26 1996 $450.00

LOPEZ, BARRY   Of Wolves and Men. New York: Scribners, 1978. 1st edition; owner's name, else fine in price clipped near fine dust jacket. David Holloway 94D-35 1996 $120.00

LOPEZ, BARRY   Winter Count. New York: Charles Scribner's Sons, 1981. 1st edition; 112 paes; black cloth, fine in fine dust jacket, signed by author.   Orpheus Books 17-174 1996 $100.00

LOPEZ, KEN   Robert Stone: a Bibliography. 1/150 numbered and signed copies; special paper and binding, fine in marbled dust jacket. Bev Chaney, Jr. 23-661 1996 $125.00

LOPEZ, KEN   Robert Stone. A Bibliography 1960-1992. Hadley: Numinous Press, 1992. Limited edition, one of 150 numbered copies, signed by Robert Stone, variant issue on different paper and in different binding; marbled paper dust jacket, fine in fine dust jacket.   Ken Lopez 74-428 1996 $125.00

LOPEZ, RAFAEL   Utah's Greatest Man Hunt. Salt Lake City: Bertrand E. Gallagher, 1913. 1st edition; 12mo; 142 pages; titlepage with illustration, repeated on front wrapper, text stapled, original pictorial red wrappers stamped in black, front leaf separating from staples, spine bit faded; fine, scarce. Six Guns 1362.   Argonaut Book Shop 113-424 1996 $150.00

L'ORANGE, H. P.   Likeness and Icon; Selected Studies in Classical and Early Mediaeval Art. Odense: Odense University Press, 1973. 8vo; xxiii, 344 pages, numerous illustrations; original cloth.   Archaeologia Luxor-3595 1996 $125.00

LORD, ELIOT   Comstock Mining and Miners. Washington: U.S. Geological Survey, 1883. 11 1/8 x 8 3/4 inches; xiv, 451 pages, 3 maps; brown cloth boards with leather spine and tips, 4 inch tear to map, fror hinge starting, moderate wear and soiling to binding. Paher 1170. Dawson's Books Shop 528-129 1996 $125.00

LORD, ELIZABETH   Reminiscences of Eastern Oregon. Portland: The Irwin-Hodson Co., 1903. 1st edition; 155 pages; illustrations; original dar olive cloth, very minor wear, fine. Presentation copy from author. Howe L468; Smith 6110; Graff 2543.   Michael D. Heaston 23-205 1996 $500.00

LORD, JAMES   Alberto Giacometti Drawings. Greenwich: New York Graphic Society, 1971. Folio; 266 pages, 11 tipped in color plates, 107 monochrome plates; cloth, dust jacket. Freitag 3452.   Brannan 43-23 1996 $395.00

LORD, JOSEPH   A Defense of Dr. Charles T. Jackson's Claims to the Discovery of Ether. Boston: 1848. 1st separate edition; 37 pages; wrappers, waterstained, rear wrapper detached, ex-library. Fulton & Stanton 71.   W. Bruce Fye 71-1313 1996 $350.00

LORD, JOSEPH   A Defense of Dr. Charles T. Jackson's Claims to the Discovery of Ether. Boston: 1848. 1st separate edition; 37 pages; wrappers, waterstained, rear wrapper detached, ex-library. Fulton & Stanton 71.   W. Bruce Fye 71-1313 1996 $350.00

LORD, LOUIS E.   A History of the American School of Classical Studies at Athens 1882-1942: an Intercollegiate Project. Cambridge: published for the American School of Classical Studies... 1947. 8vo; frontispiece, 417 pages, 44 plates, 2 folding plans, original cloth, torn dust jacket.   Archaeologia Luxor-3636 1996 $250.00

LORENTZ, H. A.   The Theory of Electrons and Its Applications to the Phenomena of Light and Radiant Heat, a Course of Lectures Delivered in Columbia University, New York in 1906. Leipzig: 1909. 332 pages; binder's cloth.   Graham Weiner C2-743 1996 £50.00

LORENZINI, CARLO 1829-1890   Pinnoccio, the Adventures of a Marionette. New York: Limited Editions Club, 1937. Copy number 904 from a total edition of 1500 numbered copies, signed by artist; illustrations by Richard Floethe; fine in decorative cloth, publisher's slipcase slightly scuffed.   Hermitage SP95-955 1996 $135.00

LORENZINI, CARLO 1829-1890   Pinocchio. Philadelphia: Lippincott, 1920. Edition deluxe; small 4to; 14 mounted color plates and pictorial boards in green to each text page by Maria L. Kirk; beige blue cloth pictorially stamped in gilt, fresh copy.   Barbara Stone 70-55 1996 £125.00

LORENZINI, CARLO 1829-1890   The Adventures of Pinocchio. New York: Macmillan Co., 1929. 3rd printing; folio; 405 pages; original tan cloth, pictorially stamped in red, green and black on front cover and lettered in red on spine, pictorial endpapers; near fine.   Heritage Book Shop 196-266 1996 $400.00

LORENZINI, CARLO 1829-1890   Pinocchio. New York: Random House, 1946. 1st edition thus; 4to; lithographed illustrations in color and black and white by Lois Lenski; colored pictorial boards, spine ends slightly knocked, edges little rubbed, else fresh copy in pictorial dust jacket.   Barbara Stone 70-56 1996 £55.00

LORIMER, H. L.   Homer and the Monuments. London: Macmillan, 1950. 8vo; xxiii, 552 pages, 61 figures, 32 plates; original cloth, tattered dust jacket, signature at flyleaf, corner bumped.   Archaeologia Luxor-3637 1996 $125.00

LOS Angeles City Directory, 1891. Los Angeles: W. H. L. Corran, 1891. 9 x 5 7/8 inches; 825 pages, including ads at front and rear; black stamped tan cloth boards backed with red leather, spine lacking but book tight.   Dawson's Books Shop 528-131 1996 $450.00

LOS Angeles City Directory, 1907. Los Angeles: Los Angeles City Directory Co., 1907. 8 7/8 x 6 1/8 inches; 2058 pages + ad leaves; black stamped red cloth, edges printed with ads; excellent condition.   Dawson's Books Shop 528-141 1996 $200.00

LOS Angeles County Woman's Christian Temperance Union Historical Number 1884-1908. Los Angeles: Los Angeles County WCTU, 1908. 12 3/4 x 10 inches; 40 pages, photographs, numerous ads in text; printed grey self wrappers, 1 corner of front wrpaper creased. laid in is a program for the thirty-second annual convention of the Union, held at the First Congregational Church on Hill Street in 1914.   Dawson's Books Shop 528-143 1996 $100.00

LOSSING, BENSON JOHN   Our Country. New York: Johnson Wilson & Co., 1875-77? 10 x 8 inches; 481 parts, 1526 pages, 49 plates, text engravings, illustrations; bound together in 3 volumes, original printed wrappers retained; nice set, some wrappers spotted.   Bohling Book Co. 191-604 1996 $110.00

LOSSING, BENSON JOHN   The Pictorial Field Book of the Civil War in the United States of America. Hertford: Thomas Belknap, 1880. Large 8vo; 3 volumes; over 1000 illustrations in text, numerous full page engraved plates, some foxing; attractively boun in original publisher's bindings of three quarter brown morocco, brown cloth boards with large gilt decorative stamps to upper boards, spines with raised bands and gilt devices, all edges gilt, marbled endpapers.   Ian Wilkinson 95/1-12 1996 £220.00

LOTHROP, SAMUEL KIRKLAND   Metals from the Cenote of Sacrifice Chicken Itza Yucatan. Cambridge: Peabody Museum, 1952. Folio; x, 139 pages, 114 figures, 39 tables; wrappers; signed.   Archaeologia Luxor-4654 1996 $150.00

LOTHROP, SAMUEL KIRKLAND   Treasures of Ancient America. The Arts of the Pre-Columbian Civilizations from Mexico to Peru. Geneva: Skira, 1964. Folio; xiv, 229 pages; profusely illustrated with tipped in color and black and white plates; original cloth.   Archaeologia Luxor-4649 1996 $125.00

LOTT, EMMELINE   The English Governess in Egypt. Harem Life in Egypt and Constantinople. London: R. Bentley, 1866. 1st edition; 8vo; 2 volumes; frontispiece; original publisher's ribbed crimson cloth, gilt lettered spines; light wear to fragile cloth, slight spotting to front, some pencil markings, still very nice, hard to find in original binding.   Paulette Rose 16-324 1996 $750.00

LOUD, GORDON   Khorsabad II: the Citadel and the Town. Chicago: University of Chicago Press, 1938. Large folio; xxi, 115 pages, 12 figures and 91 plates; original cloth.   Archaeologia Luxor-2395 1996 $950.00

LOUD, GORDON   The Megiddo Ivories. Chicago: University of Chicago Press, 1939. Folio; xi, 25 pages, 8 figures, 63 plates; original cloth, corner bumped, very scarce.   Archaeologia Luxor-2394 1996 $750.00

LOUDON, JANE   British Wild Flowers. London: 1846. 1st edition; 4to; pages xvi, 311; 60 hand colored plates; three quarter calf with ribbed spine (some rubbing to extremities, spine faded, front hinge starting, 1 plate with 1 inch tear, occasional light foxing, some offsetting from plates, pages tanned.   Raymond M. Sutton VI-19 1996 $2,000.00

LOUDON, JANE   British Wild Flowers. London: 1859. 3rd edition; 4to; pages xvi, 311, 60 hand colored plates, numerous figures; recent half morocco, gilt panels on spine, m.e., nice, clean copy.   Wheldon & Wesley 207-62 1996 £700.00

LOUDON, JOHN CLAUDIUS 1783-1843   An Encyclopaedia of Gardening. London: Longman, Orme, Brown, Green and Longmans, 1845. 8vo; xl, 1,270, (32) pages; profusely illustrated; publisher's green blindstamped cloth, tastefully rebacked, light edgewear and rubbing on covers, else very good.   Bookpress 75-81 1996 $450.00

LOUDON, JOHN CLAUDIUS 1783-1843   An Encyclopaedia of Gardening.. London: Longman, Hurst, 1824. 2nd edition; large 8vo; xii, 1233, (1) pages, 757 wood engraved illustrations; contemporary calf, gilt banded, spine and original red gilt label; some occasional foxing and browning to text. Good.   Ken Spelman 30-89 1996 £180.00

LOUDON, JOHN CLAUDIUS 1783-1843   An Encyclopaedia of Agriculture. London: 1831. 2nd edition; 8vo; 2 volumes; pages xl, 1282; 1145 wood engravings by Branston; contemporary half calf (some wear to extremities, outer hinges of volume 2 cracked, but solid, edge and part of backstrip to volume 2 perished, endpapers foxed, corners of few pages in volume 2 creased, pages yellowed.   Raymond M. Sutton VII-1044 1996 $250.00

LOUDON, JOHN CLAUDIUS 1783-1843   The Villa Gardener... London: Orr & Co., 1850. 2nd edition; 8vo; xii, 516 pages; 378 in text wood engraving illustrations; later half calf, light spotting on early leaves, else very good.   Bookpress 75-82 1996 $475.00

LOUGHEED, VICTOR   Vehicles of the Air. Chicago: Reilly and Britton, 1910. 2nd edition; 8vo; 514 pages, 270 illustrations in text; original cloth, gilt vignette airplane on front cover, very slight trace of library numbers on spine; very good, bright copy.   Edwin V. Glaser 121-198 1996 $100.00

LOUGHRIDGE, R. M.   English and Muskokee Dictionary Collected from Various Sources and Revised. St. Louis: Printing House of J. T. Smith, 1890. 1st of this edition; 236 pages; original brown cloth with gilt title on front cover and spine, minor chipping to several pages, very good printed on poor paper. Gilcrease-Hargrett Cat. p. 180.   Michael D. Heaston 23-125 1996 $250.00

LOUIS XIV, KING OF FRANCE   Edict...Portant Novvelle Fabrication d'Especes D'Argent, Augmentation du Marc d'Argent. Paris: Cramoisy, 1650. 8vo; royal arms on titlepage, 75 full page plates; folding ms. sheet relating to coinage; vellum, small hole in front cover.   Rostenberg & Stern 150-106 1996 $750.00

LOUTHERBOURG, PHILLIPPE JACQUES DE   The Romantic and Picturesque Scenery of England and Wales. London: printed for Robert Bowery by T. Bensely, 1805, but apparently c. 1808. 1st edition; 18 1/4 x 13 inches; (38) leaves of text, including added title in French; 18 fine hand colored views engraved by William Pickett from drawings by Loutherbourg and colored by John Clark, each accompanied by two leaves of descriptive text, one in English and one in French; printed as a large paper copy; later dark green crushed half morocco, recently rebacked, retaining most of the backstrip, linen sides, raised bands, spine with gilt decoration and titling, marbled endpapers, all edges gilt, in new custom made slipcase; cloth sides bit soiled and flecked, two very short neatly repaired tears in titlepage margins, one plate somewhat offset onto facing text page, few other trivial imperfections internally, but a very attractive copy, plates especially bright and unusually clean, 5 of the engravings with just a hint of offsetting from text, others absolutely free of any transfer. Abbey Scenery 9; Tooley 306.   Phillip J. Pirages 33-368   1996 $5,500.00

LOUVAIN, BELGIUM. UNIVERSITY   Privilegia Academiae sive Studio Generali Lovaniensi... Louvain: Masius, 1644. 4to; 208 pages; title and half page armorial woodcuts, woodcut ornaments; contemporary ivory vellum, yapped edges; fine. Duplicate stamp of the Louvain University Library.   Bennett Gilbert LL29-30   1996 $2,000.00

LOUYS, PIERRE   Aphrodite. London: privately printed, 1926. Limited to 650 numbered copies; 9.5 x 6 inches; 284 pages; 8 plates by Clara Tice; finely bound in three quarter blue leather, with richly gilt stamped spine, top edge gilt, some spotting to text, inner hinges loose, bit worn, otherwise attractive.   John K. King 77-617   1996 $125.00

LOVE, E. K.   History of the First African Baptist Church. Savannah: The Morning News Print, 1888. 1st edition; front hinge tender, boards mottled and lightly stained, near very good in original cloth boards. Between the Covers   43-360   1996 $500.00

LOVE, E. K.   History of the First African Baptist Church, from Its Organization, January 20th, 1788 to July 1st, 1888. Savannah: Morning News Print, 1888. 1st edition; 8vo; frontispiece, v, 360 pages; numerous illustrations; newly bound in blue cloth with gilt title on spine, very good. Rare.   Andrew Cahan 47-4   1996 $275.00

LOVE, JOHN   Geodaesia: or, the Art of Surveying and Measuring of Land Made Easie. London: printed for W. Taylor, 1715. 2nd edition; 12mo; (xx), 196, 19, (37), 8, (16) pages; contemporary calf, expertly respined with original leather label, inscription in ink on front endpaper, light edgewear, some annotations in early hand, occasionally extensive, occasional browning.   The Bookpress 75-432   1996 $650.00

LOVECRAFT, H. P.   Collected Poems. Sauk City: Arkham House, 1963. 1st edition; 1/2000 copies; illustrations; near fine in very good+ dust jacket.   Aronovitz 57-726   1996 $125.00

LOVECRAFT, H. P.   The Haunter of the Dark and other Tales of Terror. London: Gollancz, 1951. 1st edition; spine little lightened, else very good+ in like dust jacket with some slight fading to dust jacket spine;   Aronovitz 57-724   1996 $150.00

LOVECRAFT, H. P.   Lovecraft At Last. (with) Supernatural Horror in Literature as Revised in 1936. Carrollton, Clark, 1975. 1st edition, 1/1000 copies of this, the collector's issue; and 1/2000 copies; fine in dust jacket, and slipcase. Second title fine.   Aronovitz 57-731   1996 $100.00

LOVECRAFT, H. P.   The Lurker at the Threshold. Sauk City: Arkaham House, 1945. 1st edition; very fine in slightly chipped dust jacket. Bromer Booksellers 90-166   1996 $250.00

LOVECRAFT, H. P.   The Lurker at the Threshold. Sauk City: Arkham House, 1945. 1st edition; fine in dust jacket.   Aronovitz 57-723 1996 $125.00

LOVECRAFT, H. P.   The Outsider and Others. Sauk City: Arkham House, 1939. 1st edition; one of 1268 copies; first book from Arkham House; previous owners' names to front pastedown endpaper under front flap, small dampstain to front edges, near very good in fine and bright dust jacket.   Robert Gavora 61-64   1996 $1,600.00

LOVECRAFT, H. P.   The Outsider and Others. Sauk City: Arkham House, 1939. 1st edition; first book from this publisher; near fine in most attractive very good dust jacket with some light wear and tear; laid into this copy is an envelope addressed to Clark Ashton Smith in Lovecraft's hand.   Aronovitz 57-720   1996 $2,250.00

LOVECRAFT, H. P.   Something About Cats. Sauk City: Arkham Hose, 1949. Very good in dust jacket.   R. A. Gekoski 19-98   1996 £115.00

LOVECRAFT, H. P.   The Watchers Out of Time. Sauk City: Arkham House, 1974. 1st edition; very fine, with original Herb Arnold drawing and inscription.   Bromer Booksellers 87-27   1996 $150.00

LOVELASS, PETER   The Will Which the Law makes; or, How It Disposes of a Person's Estate, in Case He Dies Without Will or Testament... London: printed for the author, by W. Strahan and M. Woodfall, 1775. 1st edition; 8vo; contemporary calf, rebacked, label. Sweet and Maxwell p. 492, 20.   Anthony Laywood 108-84 1996 £175.00

A LOVER'S Progress: Seventeenth Century Lyrics. Waltham St. Lawrence: Golden Cockerel Press, 1938. One of 215 numbered copies; small folio; printed in 18 pt. Caslon O.F. in black and red, title blocked in gold on specially watermarked handmade paper; half white morocco, yellow buckram sides, upper corners little bruised, otherwise very nice. Bertram Rota 272-178   1996 £150.00

LOVER, SAMUEL   The Flag is Half-Mast-High. London: Duff & Hodgson, n.d., ca. 1852. 1st edition; folio; original printed wrappers, disbound. Presentation copy, inscribed on front cover "To the Editor of the Observer with the Author's Compliments Samuel Lover". Clean tears in each wrapper, few paper repairs, spine split with resulting loose sheets, cloth folding case, very rare.   David J. Holmes 52-65 1996 $375.00

LOVESEY, PETER   The Last Detective. Bristol: Scorpion Press, 1991. 1/15 deluxe lettered copies, signed by author and Jax (author's wife); fine in quarter goatskin with raised bands.   Quill & Brush 102-1087 1996 $350.00

LOVESEY, PETER   The Last Detective. Bristol: Scorpion Press, 1991. 1/99 signed, numbered and specially bound copies; quarter bound in leather, marbled paper boards, textured colored endpapers and colored top edges.   Quill & Brush 102-1088 1996 $125.00

LOVESEY, PETER   Wobble to Death. New York: Dodd, Mead, 1970. 1st U.S. edition; author's first book; fine in lightly rubbed, price clipped dust jacket with touch of minor soiling on rear panel.   Quill & Brush 102-1078   1996 $100.00

LOW, A. P.   Report on the Dominion Government Expedition to Hudson Bay and the Arctic Islands on Board the D.G.S. Neptune, 1903-04. Ottawa: Government Printing Bur., 1906. 23cm; xvii, 355 pages; frontispiece, illustrations, folding map in rear pocket; gilt stamped and decorated olive cloth; very good ex-library; bookplate and spine label only. Arctic 2717.   Rockland Books 38-130   1996 $125.00

LOW, CHARLES RATHBONE   Her Majesty's Navy Including Its Deeds and Battles. London: J. S. Virtue & Co., n.d. 1890-93. Thick small 4to; 3 volumes; colored titlepages and 40 colored plates of ships and dress; contemporary half morocco, gilt panelled spines, gilt edges.   Charles W. Traylen 117-241   1996 £780.00

LOW, FRANCES H.   Queen Victoria's Dolls. London: George Newnes, 1894. 1st edition; 4to; frontispiece, (86) pages; original quarter black cloth, maroon gilt boards; edges rubbed, text very faintly yellowed, as usual, minor coverwear, else very good.   The Bookpress 75-433 1996 $150.00

LOW, J. G.   Plastic Sketches. Boston: Lea & Shepard/New York: Dillingham, 1887. 1st edition; oblong 4to; ex-library with markings, decorated silk board cover, some wear, leather spine, front hinge starting, holes for ties on 3 sides, very good.   Freedom Bookshop 14-19   1996 $100.00

LOW, R.   Amazon Parrots. London: 1983. Limited to 475 copies; folio pages 178, 28 colored plates; silk binding in cloth book box.   Wheldo & Wesley 207-63   1996 £480.00

LOWE, CONSTANCE   Little Folk's Fun. London: Nister, n.d. ca. 1900. Square 8vo; 6 pretty colored circular illustrations operated by a ribbon; color pictorial boards, one repaired tear, else very good.   Marjorie James 19-158   1996 £375.00

LOWE, E. A.   Palaeographical Papers 1907-1965. Oxford: Clarendon Press, 1972. 2 volumes, frontispiece, 150 plates; blue cloth, dust jacket Maggs Bros. Ltd.   1191-158   1996 £75.00

LOWE, EDWARD JOSEPH   Beautiful Leaves Plants, Being a Descriptio of the Most Beautiful Leaved Plants in Cultivation in this Country. Londo 1891. 3rd edition; 4to; 144 pages; 60 colored plates; green cloth, gilt decorated, very good.   K Books 442-337   1996 £135.00

LOWE, EDWARD JOSEPH   A Natural History of British Grasses. London: 1868. Tall 8vo; pages vi, 245; original cloth, rubbed, corners worn, some soiling to endpapers.   Raymond M. Sutton VI-761 1996 $125.00

LOWE, EDWARD JOSEPH   Natural History of New and Rare Ferns. London: 1862. 8vo; viii, 192 pages; 72 colored plates; new binders cloth, very good, ex-library with a few stamps, otherwise very good.   K Books 442-336 1996 £70.00

LOWE, EDWARD JOSEPH   Our Native Ferns: or A History of the British Species and Their Varieties. London: 1867. 8vo; 2 volumes, pages vii, 348; vii, 492, 79 color plates; cloth, gilt, new endpapers, bindings slightly soiled and worn.   John Henly 27-264 1996 £60.00

LOWE, EDWARD JOSEPH   Our Native Ferns: Or a History of the British Species and Their Varities. London: Groombridge, 1867/69. 1st edition; large 8vo; 2 volumes; 79 color plates, 909 wood engravings; original gilt and blindstamped green cloth, rubbing, corners bumped, foxing; very good.   George J. Houle 68-86 1996 $375.00

LOWE, EDWARD JOSEPH   Our Native Ferns, or a History of the British Species and Their Varities. London: 1874-80. Royal 8vo; 2 volumes; 79 colored plates; contemporary half morocco, trifle rubbed. Charles W. Traylen 117-314 1996 £80.00

LOWE, EDWARD JOSEPH   Our Native Ferns. London: Bell, 1880. Reprint; 4to; pages 348, 492 + ad; 79 full page color plates, 909 wood engravings; gold stamped green cloth, hinges tender, very good. Second Life Books 103-130 1996 $175.00

LOWE, WILLOUGBY P.   The Trail that is Always New. 1932. illustrations; nice.   David Grayling J95Biggame-538 1996 £75.00

LOWELL, ANNA CABOT   Seed-Grain for Thought and Discussion. Boston: Ticknor & Fields, 1856. 1st edition; 8vo; original brown cloth, bit rubbed; very good condition; fine presentation copy, inscribed from author to her brother-in-law, James Russell Lowell.   Ximenes 109-178 1996 $250.00

LOWELL, JAMES RUSSELL 1819-1891   Anti-Slavery Papers of James Russell Lowell. Boston: Houghton Mifflin, 1902. 1st edition; one of 525 numbeed copies; 2 volumes, designed by Bruce Rogers; dark grey boards with paper spine labels (bit darkened), heads of spines very slightly rubbed, else fine.   Captain's Bookshelf 38-145 1996 $150.00

LOWELL, JAMES RUSSELL 1819-1891   Conversations On Some of the Old Poets. Cambridge: John Owen, 1845. 1st edition; lithographed wrappers, D wrapper? Moderate foxing but uncut and unopened, lage page worn, detached, rear wrapper lacking, uncommon. BAL 13049. Charles Agvent 4-851 1996 $150.00

LOWELL, JAMES RUSSELL 1819-1891   The Courtin'. Boston: James R. Osgood and Co., 1874. 1st edition thus; 8vo; 7 heliotypes after drawings by Winslow Homer; green cloth stamped in gold gilt and black reproducing the Homer silhouette of a young girl sitting peeling apples in black on gold with author, title and illustrator in black, gilt stamping and lettering on spine, some foxing, cloth front hinge starting to split about two inches, all edges gilt, generally good+, scarce in any condition. Priscilla Juvelis 95/1-158 1996 $500.00

LOWELL, JAMES RUSSELL 1819-1891   Four Poems: The Ballad Of The Stranger, King Retro, The Royal Pedigree, and a Dream I Had. Village Press, 1906. One of 50 copies; 9 1/4 x 6 inches; 32 pages, (1) leaf colophon; original holland backed blue printed paper boards, edges untrimmed, especially fine, almost faultless copy; prospectus and letter from bookseller dated 1906 laid in. Modern bookplate of Stephen H. Wakeman. Cary 33.   Phillip J. Pirages 33-502 1996 $350.00

LOWELL, JAMES RUSSELL 1819-1891   Poems. Cambridge: John Owen, 1844. 1st edition; royal 8vo; 12, 279 pages; contemporary full black tooled morocco, gilt gone from outside covers, all edges gilt, marbled endpapers with binder's ticket of Macdonald of Cambridge; inner front hinge trifle weak, despite loss of gilding, a very fine copy in handsome binding. Rare large paper copy; BAL 13045. Howe Lib. VIII JRL 22; Wakeman Sale 811.   M & S Rare Books 60-198 1996 $750.00

LOWELL, JAMES RUSSELL 1819-1891   The Vision of Sir Launfal. Boston: Fields, Osgood, 1870. Reprint; 8vo; illustrations by S. Eytinge; original binding, near fine. signed by author with inscription below in another hand, to Miss Kate M. Sellars; books signed by Lowell are not terribly common.   Charles Agvent 4-894 1996 $175.00

LOWELL, JOHN   Peace Without Dishonour, War Without Hope. Boston: Greenough and Stebbins, 1807. 1st edition; 8vo; 43 pages; disbound. Shaw & Shoemaker 12947.   The Bookpress 75-434 1996 $110.00

LOWELL, MARIA   The Poems of Maria Lowell. Cambridge: Riverside Press, 1907. Number 279 of 330 copies; 9.25 x 6 inches; frontispiece, designed by Bruce Rogers; gray paper boards, printed paper label on backstrip, bookplate on front pastedown; extra spine label at rear; bookplate on front pastedown, attractive book label on front free endpaper, otherwise lovely copy of a fragile book.   Joshua Heller 21-203 1996 $300.00

LOWELL, ROBERT 1917-1977   For the Union Dead. New York: Farrar, Straus & Giroux, 1964. 1st edition; 8vo; green cloth, dust jacket, custom made folding box; front cover slightly rubbed along bottom edge, otherwise a fine copy in slightly dust soiled jacket with small closed tear; presentation inscribed by author to his lover, poet Sandra Hochman.   James S. Jaffe 34-429 1996 $1,250.00

LOWELL, ROBERT 1917-1977   Land of Unlikeness. Cummington: Cummington Press, 1944. 1st edition; one of 250 copies; 8vo; original blue cloth lettered in red, virtually unworn, but faded unevenly to light brown along spine and edges, one small scuff to lower cover; in attractive blue cloth box with black labels; presentation copy from Randall Jarrell to his brother Charles.   Lakin & Marley 3-33 1996 $3,500.00

LOWELL, ROBERT 1917-1977   Land of Unlikeness. Poems. Cummington: Cummington Press, 1944. 1st edition; limited to 250 copies (the entire edition); 8vo; blue boards printed in blue; covers faded and worn, but good copy; author's rare first book; unusual association copy, inscribed facetiously by poet Robert Mezey to Philip Levine, with Levine's ownership signature.   James S. Jaffe 34-419 1996 $1,750.00

LOWELL, ROBERT 1917-1977   Life Studies. London: 1959. 1st edition; fine, dust jacket spine sunned, few tiny edge chips, tiny edge tear side spine, price clipped.   Polyanthos 22-531 1996 $125.00

LOWELL, ROBERT 1917-1977   Life Studies. New Poems. New York: FS&C, 1959. 1st edition; signed by author; near fine in price clipped dust jacket with small scrape spot on lower spine.   Captain's Bookshelf 38-147 1996 $300.00

LOWELL, ROBERT 1917-1977   Life Studies. New York: Farrar, Straus & Cudahy, 1959. 1st American edition; 8vo; cloth, dust jacket slightly rubbed; fine.   James S. Jaffe 34-423 1996 $100.00

LOWELL, ROBERT 1917-1977   Lord Weary's Castle. New York: Harcourt, Brace, 1946. 1st edition; 8vo; black cloth, dust jacket, light offsetting on front and back endpapers, otherwise fine in somewhat rubbed jacket which is chipped at head of spine and has few internal tape mends.   James S. Jaffe 34-420 1996 $150.00

LOWELL, ROBERT 1917-1977   The Mills of the Kavanaughs. New York: Harcourt Brace, 1951. 1st edition; 8vo; black cloth, dust jacket, fine in slightly rubbed jacket with some wear at head and foot of spine; fine. James S. Jaffe 34-422 1996 $100.00

LOWELL, ROBERT 1917-1977   Poems 1938-1949. London: Faber & Faber, 1950. 1st edition; 8vo; cloth, dust jacket, light offsetting to front and back endpapers, otherwise fine in somewhat worn and spine darkened jacket, chipped at head and foot of spine, scarce.   James S. Jaffe 34-421 1996 $150.00

LOWES, JOHN LIVINGSTON   The Road to Xanadu: a Study in the Ways of the Imagination. Boston and New York: Printed at the Riverside Press for Houghton Mifflin Co., 1927. 1st edition; one of 300 copies; 9 1/2 x 6 3/4 inches; xviii, 639 pages; vignette on title, headpieces and tailpieces, frontispiece and 9 plates; title in green and black; original cloth backed paper boards, paper labels on front cover and spine, edges untrimmed and unopened; apart from the slipcase, an extremely fine copy.   Phillip J. Pirages 33-369 1996 $200.00

LOWES, JOHN LIVINGSTON   The Road ot Xanadu - a Study in the Ways of the Imagination. Boston and New York: Houghton Mifflin, 1927. 1st edition; signed by author; 432 pages, 153 pages of notes; original binding, top edge dusty, covers slightly marked, spine darkened, head and tail of spine and corners slightly bumped and rubbed, very good; presentation copy from Gale Noyes to James D. Hart.   Ulysses 39-381 1996 £85.00

LOWLSEY, BARZILLAI   A Glossary of Berkshire Words and Phrases. London: Pub. for the English Dialect Society by Trubner & Co., 1888. Half title, interleaved; half dark blue calf, red label, all edges gilt; very good.   Jarndyce 103-59 1996 £70.00

LOWNDES, WILLIAM 1652-1724   A Report Containing an Essay for the Amendment of the Silver Coins. London: printed by Charles Bill, and the executrix of Thomas Newcomb, 1695. 1st edition; 8vo; contemporary black morocco, gilt rules, central gilt panels with floral ornaments at corners, spine gilt in six compartments, all edges gilt; magnificent copy, no doubt bound for presentation (and possibly on fine paper); with 2 ms. corrections (pp. 19 and 22), no doubt authorial; signature of D. Lyddell dated Nov. 21, Wing L3323; Kress 1908.   Ximenes 109-179 1996 $3,500.00

LOWNDES, WILLIAM THOMAS 1798?-1843   The Bibliographer's Manual of English Literature... London: William Pickering, 1834. 1st edition; one of 50 large and thick paper copies; 242 x 157mm max. 4 volumes, pages xii, 2002; paginated as one volume (omitting 335/6 & repeating 1611-18 as usual - text continuous), separate titles in each volume, intermittent light marginal waterstain in volume IV, otherwise good uncut set of the deluxe issue in contemporary cloth backed boards, worn at extremities, 2 hinges split but secure, faded gilt lettering (twice on 1 volume), endpapers sometime renewed.   Claude Cox 107-198 1996 £220.00

LOWRY, MALCOLM 1909-1957   Lunar Caustic. London: Jonathan Cape, 1968. 1st edition; original binding, head and tail of spine slightly bumped, near fine in nicked and slightly rubbed, marked and dusty dust jacket very slightly darkened at spine and edges.   Ulysses 39-384 1996 £55.00

LOWRY, MALCOLM 1909-1957   Under the Volcano. London: Cape, 1947. 1st edition; near fine in dust jacket with number of edge tears and deeply price clipped at lower front flap, not affecting text.   Ken Lopez 74-274 1996 $375.00

LOWRY, MALCOLM 1909-1957   Under the Volcano. New York: Reynal & Hitchcock, 1947. 1st edition; spinal extremities bumped, otherwise very good plus in very good lightly edge worn dust jacket with tear along spinal fold.   Thomas Dorn 9-166 1996 $525.00

LOWRY, MALCOLM 1909-1957   Au-Dessous Du Volcan. Paris: Editions Correa, 1950. 1st French trade edition; touch of browning to page edges and faint crease to one corner of front wrapper, still very near fine; warmly inscribed by author, rare inscribed.   Between the Covers 42-276 1996 $2,500.00

LOWSLEY, BARZILLAI   A Glossary of Berkshire Words and Phrases. London: pub. for the English Dialect Society by Trubner & Co., 1888. Half title; half black roan, rubbed at head of spine.   Jarndyce 103-60 1996 £50.00

LOWTH, ROBERT   The Life of William of Wykeham, Bishop of Winchester. London: printed for A. Millar and R. and J. Dodsley, 1759. 2nd edition; 8vo; frontispiece, engraved vignette on title, one plate, one folding engraved tree at end, xxxiv, 357, liv pages; original calf, rebacked, original endpapers preserved.   David Bickersteth 133-113 1996 £60.00

LOY, MINA   The Last Lunar Baedeker. Highlands: jargon Society, 1982. 1st edition; tall 8vo; illustrations; cloth, dust jacket; as new.   James S. Jaffe 34-452 1996 $100.00

LOY, MINA   Lunar Baedecker. Paris: Contact Publishing Co., 1923. 1st edition; small 8vo; original printed buff wrappers; fragile, poorly produced book, spine somewhat worn, covers lightly soiled and worn, still very good copy. Rare first book.   James S. Jaffe 34-451 1996 $1,500.00

LUARD, HENRY R.   Annales Monastici. London: 1864-69. 8vo; 5 volumes; folding facsimiles; original cloth.   Howes Bookshop 265-1579 1996 £150.00

LUBBOCK, BASIL   The Last of the Windjammers. Glasgow: Brown, Son & Ferguson Ltd., 1954. 4th impression; 2 volumes; xiv, 518; xv, 448 pages; profusely illustrated with photos and folding plans; blue cloth, gilt spine titles.   Parmer Books 039/Nautica-039060 1996 $150.00

LUBBOCK, BASIL   Sail, the Romance of the Clipper Ships. New York: 1972. 4to; 3 volumes; Cloth lightly foxed, near fine in near fine box.   Bookworm & Silverfish 280-164 1996 $150.00

LUBBOCK, JOHN   Pre-Historic Times, as Illustrated by Ancient Remains, and the Manners and Customs of Modern Savages. Williams and Norgate, 1869. 2nd edition; 8vo; xxviii, 619 pages + 8 page publisher's catalog; 4 lithograph plates including one tinted and one printed in color; original red cloth, decorated in black, extremities slightly worn and inside hinges neatly repaired, good.   Thomas Thorp 489-197 1996 £50.00

LUBBOCK, JOSEPH G.   From Garden to Galaxy. London: Bertram Rota, 1980. 1st edition; number 11 of 80 copies, signed; small folio; 50 pages, 12 prints (6 of which are doublepage) from copperplates worked by engraving, etching and aquatint in various colours, some which are added by hand, printed on handmade paper by Will Carter; full morocco decorated in gold by George Percival, in glacine wrapper and matching slipcase, top edge gilt, others uncut, shelf mark on endpaper.   Claude Cox 107-91 1996 £220.00

LUBBOCK, JOSEPH G.   From the Snows to the Seas. 1986. One of 95 numbered copies, signed by author/artist; folio; 3 page foldout combined process illustrations by author; printed on handmade paper in blue and black by Will Carter; bound by George Percival in quarter morocco, silk boards, stamped in gilt with design by artist; fine in slipcase.   Bertram Rota 272-281 1996 £300.00

LUBBOCK, JOSEPH G.   From the Snows to the Seas. London: Bertram Rota, 1986. 1st edition; number 18 of 95 copies, signed by author; 4to; 4 folding color prints, titlepage and text printed blue and black; half dark blue morocco over blue linen cloth, gilt stamped spine and covers, grey endpapers, uncut, top edge gilt, fine in publisher's patterned slipcase.   George J. Houle 68-87 1996 $500.00

LUBBOCK, JOSEPH G.   From the Snows to the Seas. London: Rota, 1986. One of 95 copies only, each copy signed by artist/author; page size 14 x 10 1/2 inches; printed on R.W.S. handmade paper; 4 triple fold-out copperplates worked by etching and aquatint; colors printed in intaglio and relief, and additional color applied to some pages by hand; bound by George Percival in gilt stamped blue silk after a design by the artist, blue morocco spine; mylar jacket and publisher's slipcase.   Priscilla Juvelis 95/1-159 1996 $500.00

LUBBOCK, JOSEPH G.   Landscapes of the Spirit. 1994. One of only 65 numbered copies, signed by author; 4to; printed on handmade paper in black and brown by Sebastian Carter; five full page colored prints, two double page, one vertical foldout and 3 page horizontal foldout by author; hand bound by George Percival in quarter purple morocco, ochre silk sides, design by Lubbock in gilt on upper cover, fine in slipcase.   Bertram Rota 272-283 1996 £210.00

LUBBOCK, JOSEPH G.   Love for Earth. 1990. One of 95 numbered copies, signed by author; 4to; text designed and printed in black and deep rose by Will Carter; 5 double page and 6 full page colored illustrations hand printed by author; hand bound by George Percival in quarter red morocco, silk sides with design by Lubbock in gilt on upper cover, fine in marbled slipcase.   Bertram Rota 272-282 1996 £210.00

LUBBOCK, JOSEPH G.   Love for the Earth. Cambridge: Printed by Will Carter at the Rampant Lions Press for Bertram Rota, 1990. One of 95 copies, signed by author; 11 1/2 x 9 3/4 inches; 52 pages, (2) leaves; 11 expressive colored prints; maroon morocco backed silk over boards by George Percival, gilt stamped with design by artist; original marbled slipcase. Mint.   Phillip J. Pirages 33-370 1996 $550.00

LUBBOCK, R.   Observataions on the Fauna of Norfolk, More Particularly of the District of the Broads. Norwich: 1879. 2nd edition; folding map, 2 plates; nice, light rubbing, scarce.   David A.H. Grayling 3/95-369 1996 £65.00

LUCANUS, MARACUS ANNAEUS 39-68   ...De Bello Civili Libri Decem. Lyon: Seb. Gryphium Lugduni, 1547. Small 16mo; 286 pages; pretty 18th century morocco gilt, front board detached, all edges gilt. early ms. presentation.   Family Album Tillers-403 1996 $245.00

LUCANUS, MARCUS ANNAEUS 39-68   Lucanus. Venice: Apud Aldum, April, 1502. 1st Aldine edition; 8vo; 140 leaves, Italic; 18th century red morocco, spine heavily gilt, joints weak, signed with paper label of binder, Padeloup, all edges gilt. Dibdin II 184; Renouard 33.3. Adams L1557; UCLA I/44; Brunet III 1198.   Family Album Tillers-401 1996 $1,400.00

LUCANUS, MARCUS ANNAEUS 39-68   Lucanus. Venice: In Aedibus Aldi, et Andreae Soceri, 1515. 2nd Aldine edition; 8vo; 140 leaves, Italic; early 18th century full morocco, boards, detached, all edges gilt; engraved armorial Bookplate of William Dondesnell Esq. of Pull Cort. Renouard 72.6. Adams L1564; UCLA II 117; Brunet III 1199.   Family Album Tillers-402 1996 $700.00

LUCANUS, MARCUS ANNAEUS 39-68   Lucan's Pharsalia. Dublin: printed by James Carson, for Joseph Leathley, 1719. 1st Irish edition; 8vo; pages (6), x, xvii-lv, (9), 208, 281-469; 72, complete thus; with 7 page subscriber list, though without blank leaf d8; contemporary calf, small piece lacking from fore-edge of one leaf (no serious loss), little light foxing, yet very good to nice, in original state. Foxon R294. James Fenning   133-219   1996 £145.00

LUCAS, EDWARD VERRALL   All the World Over. London: Grant Richards, 1898. 1st edition; oblong folio; original pictorial boards, edges rubbed, cloth back; with the Frank J. Dearden pencilled note, with comment, "Very rare.".   Howard S. Mott   227-90   1996 $120.00

LUCAS, EDWARD VERRALL   Edwin Austin Abbey, Royal Academician. The Record Of His Life and Work. London: Methuen/New York: Scribners, 1921. 1st edition; large 4to; 2 volumes, xii, 268; ix, 269, 518; 200 illustrations and plates; recent cloth, very good plus.   Taurus Books   83-34   1996 $150.00

LUCAS, EDWARD VERRALL   Playtime and Company. A Book for Children. London: Methuen & Co., 1925. 1st edition; cloth backed boards, one corner slightly rubbed, otherwise fine. With poignant ALS from author tipped in.   James S. Jaffe   34-453   1996 $250.00

LUCAS, F. L.   The Golden Cokcerel Greek Anthology. Waltham St. Lawrence: Golden Cockerel Press, 1937. Limited to 206 numbered copies on handmade paper; small folio; 82 pages; titlepage illustration, tailpiece and 12 plates line engraved on zinc by Lettice Sandford, title printed in carmine; original black morocco backed boards, top edge gilt, others uncut by Sangorski & Sutcliffe, few minor spots on covers.   Thomas Thorp   489-198   1996 £150.00

LUCAS, FRED C.   An Historical Souvenir Diary of the City of Winnipeg, Canada. Winnipeg: 1923. 19.5 cm; 240 pages; plates, illustrations, portraits, four panel panorama; brown cloth; very good. Peel 2856. Rockland Books   38-132   1996 $100.00

LUCAS, S.   In Praise of Toadstools. London: 1992. Limited edition of 150 copies, numbered and signed; royal 4to; reproductions; leather bound, slipcase.   Wheldon & Wesley   207-1637   1996 £375.00

LUCAS, S. E..   The Catalogue of Sassoon Chinese Ivories. London: Country Life, 1950. Limited edition of 250 copies, this unnumbered and unsigned; folio; 3 volumes; x, 414; vi 415-930; vi, 931-1384 pages; color frontispiece, 966 monochrome photographic illustrations, several with transparent overlays; original half vellum, spines lettered gilt, top edge gilt, others uncut, slipcases; fine set.   Thomas Thorp   489-199   1996 £950.00

LUCAS, T. J.   Camp Life and Sport in South Africa, Experiences of Kaffir Warare with the Cape Rifles. London: 1878. 8vo; pages xiii,2 58, 4 colored plates; rebound in plain cloth with original decorated front cover (somewhat rubbed) retained.   Wheldon & Wesley   207-417   1996 £150.00

LUCAS, W. J.   British Dragonflies. (Odonata). London: 1900. 8vo; pages xiv, 356, 27 colored plates, 57 text figures; original decorated buckram, trifle used, trifle loose, but in general a good copy; ownership stamp, bookplates and inscription on endpapers.   Wheldon & Wesley   207-1069   1996 £85.00

LUCIANUS SAMOSATENSIS   Certaine Select Dialogues of Lucian; together With His True Historie. Oxford: printed by William Turner, 1634. 1st edition in English; small 4to; bound in 17th century vellum covered boards, vellum from an old document stained black after binding, joints cracking. Rare. STC 16893. Esdaile p. 93.   H. M. Fletcher   121-65   1996 £1,450.00

LUCIANUS SAMOSATENSIS   Lucian's Dialogues, and Other Greek Extracts, Literally Translated Into English. Albany; D. & A. Abbey, 1816. 1st edition of the first translation by an American; 12mo; 69 pages; original boards, spine chipped. Evans 21927 for Philadelphia reprint of British trans. AI 38110   Howard S. Mott   227-91   1996 $200.00

LUCIANUS SAMOSATENSIS   I Dialoi Piacevoli, le Vere Narrationi, le Facete Epitole... Venice: Giovanni de Farri & Fratelli, 1541. Small 8vo; ff. 224, (some errors in foliation); italic letter, woodcut printer's device on titlepage, 30 woodcuts in text; contemporary limp vellum, bit soiled, ties removed; few light early marginal marks and 1 correction in text; good; autographs of Carlo Albertinelli 1576 & Stefano Pergamasci 1605. BM STC It. p. 396; Adams L1632; Brunet III 1213.   A. Sokol XXV-59 1996 £1,850.00

LUCIANUS SAMOSATENSIS   The True Historie of Lucian the Samosatenian. Waltham St. Lawrence: Golden Cockerel Press, 1927. Limited to 275 copies; quarto; 48 pages; wood engravings by Robert Gibbings; quarter bound in morocco and cloth, small tear to last free endpaper, else fine. Chanticleer 53.   Bromer Booksellers 87-75   1996 $650.00

LUCK, BARBARA   Night Street. Janus Press, 1993. One in an edition of 90 copies, signed by the five participants; 13.5 x 8.5 inches; 18 glued together to form 9 leaves bound accordion fold in gold decorated cut-out card covers; poems in different colored papers collaged onto pages, multi-colored images printed by Lois Johnson on an offset press at the University of the Arts in Philadelphia and silkscreened by her at the Janus Press in West Burke, Vermont, with the assistance of Stephanie Westnedge, who, with Audrey Holden, did the production; papers include various Arches, Fabriano, Miliani Ingres and Torinoko with MacGregor-Vinzani abaca for the concertina and Elephant Hide for the cover, book structure designed (without glue or sewing) by Claire Van Vliet, unglued slipcase of stiff shiny blue plastic over card, the same material set into various pages; fine.   Joshua Heller 21-36   1996 $600.00

LUCKENBEILL, DANIEL DAVID   Ancient Records of Assyria and Baylonia. Chicago: University of Chicago Press, 1926-27. 8vo; 2 volumes, (complete), xxviii, 801 pages; original cloth; with annotations and signataures of Caroline Nestmann (Peck).   Archaeologia Luxor-2396 1996 $275.00

LUCKENBILL, DANIEL DAVID   The Annals of Sennacherib. Chicago: University of Chicago Press, 1924. 4to; frontispiece, xi, 196 pages; boards, light rubbing to spine and corners, bookplate.   Archaeologia Luxor-2397   1996 $150.00

LUCKENBILL, DANIEL DAVID   Inscriptions from Adab. Chicago: University of Chicago Press, 1930. 8vo; x, 8 pages, 87 plates; half cloth; with annotations and signature of Caroline Nestmann (Peck). Archaeologia   Luxor-2398   1996 $125.00

LUCKOCK, JAMES   Hints for Practical Economy, in the Management of Household Affairs, with Tables, Shewing Different Scales of Expences... Birmingham: James Drake; and Longman, London: 1834. 1st edition; 12mo; 27, (1) pages; recent cloth.   James Burmester 29-92 1996 £65.00

LUCRETIUS CARUS, TITUS 99-55 BC   Titus Lucretius Carus, His Six Books of Epicurean Philosophy. London: printed for Anthony Stephens, Bookseller, 1683. 4to; pages 944), 223, 60, (5), extra ms. index; 18th century full leather. Brunet III 1222. Wing L3449a.   Family Album Tillers-412   1996 $230.00

LUCRETIUS CARUS, TITUS 99-55 BC   De Rerum Natura Libri Sex. Paris: J. Benenatus, 1570. 4to; (44), 627, (136) pages, royal printer's basilisk device on title, foliated initials; handsome German handpainted armorial bookplate on inside front cvoer, dated 1663, 18th century calf, back gilt, rubbed. Gordon 102a; Renouard Imprimeurs & Libraires Parisiens III no. 640.   Jeffrey D. Mancevice 20-53   1996 $1,250.00

LUCRETIUS CARUS, TITUS 99-55 BC   De Rerum Natura Sex, ad Optimorum Exemplarium Fidem Recensiti. London: Tonson, 1712. Large folio; (4), 282 pages, engraved frontispiece and 6 plates, head and tailpieces, and initials; contemporary gilt panelled red morocco with triple fillet and cornerpieces, gilt roll tooled inner dentelle, spine gilt in compartments, raised gilt bands, all edges gilt, comb marbled endpapers, skilfully rebacked preserving original spine, corners little soft, elegantly understated binding, from Syston Park library.   Marlborough 160-45   1996 £800.00

LUCRETIUS CARUS, TITUS 99-55 BC   Titi Lucretii Cari De Rerum Natura Libri Sex. Glasgow: Robert and Andrew Foulis, 1759. Small 8vo; pages (16), 269; attractive full contemporary dark green morocco binding, spine gilt; early ms. ownership of G. Dunlop and ms. notes of Lionel B. C. L. Muirhead. Gaskell 370; Brunet III 1220.   Family Album Tillers-413   1996 $260.00

LUCRETIUS CARUS, TITUS 99-55 BC   Titi Lucretii Cari De Rerum Natura... Birmingham: Baskerville, 1772. 4to; pages (2), 280; full contemporary red French morocco binding, spine gilt, all edges gilt, very clean; engraved (Russian?) armorial ex-libris and Russian ownership stamps. Gaskell 43; brunet IIi 1220.   Family Album Tillers-414   1996 $725.00

LUCRETIUS CARUS, TITUS 99-55 BC   Titi Lucretii Cari De Rerum Natura... Birmingham: Baskerville, 1773. 12mo; pages (2), 214, (i.e. 218); worn 19th century full leather, foxed, ms. ownerships of H. Mansfield and J. Woolsten Holme. Gaskell 50.   Family Album Tillers-415   1996 $275.00

LUCRETIUS CARUS, TITUS 99-55 BC   De Rerum Natura Libri Sex.
Ashendene Press, 1913. One of 65 paper copies offered for sale (of 85
printed, there were also 5 vellum copies for sale); 11 1/2 x 8 inches; 4
p.l. (including 3 blanks), 256 pages; 6 hand painted initials by Graily
Hewitt, the first in shimmering gold, the others in blue, hand painted
flourishes at beginning of each book, text printed in red and black;
original vellum backed blue paper boards, gilt titling on spine, few
extremely faint spots on spine and 3 or four leaves of text, but very fine.
Phillip J. Pirages 33-27 1996 $2,750.00

LUCRETIUS CARUS, TITUS 99-55 BC   Of the Nature of Things. Los
Angeles: Limited Editions Club, 1956. Limited to 1500 copies; signed by
artist; 8vo; wood engravings by Paul Landacre; full dark blue morocco,
near fine in near fine case, with Monthly Letter; bookplate.   Charles
Agvent 4-855 1996 $125.00

LUDLOW, EDMUND   The Memoirs, 1625-1672. London: Oxford
University Press, 1894. 8vo; 2 volumes, pages 617, 571; portrait and
facsimiles; original cloth.   Howes Bookshop 265-742 1996 £75.00

LUDLUM, ROBERT   Trevayne. London: Weidenfeld and Nicolson, 1974.
1st edition; fine in very good price clipped dust jacket with light soiling,
few small closed tars, light creases and minor edge wear.   Quill &
Brush 102-1091 1996 $125.00

LUER, C. A.   The Native Orchids of Florida. New York: 1972. 4to;
pages 296, 85 colored plates of 102 species and varieties; buckram, fine
with dust jacket.   Wheldon & Wesley 207-1804 1996 £65.00

LUER, C. A.   The Native Orchids of the United States and Canada.
New York: 1975. 4to; pages 363, 96 colored plates of over 400
illustrations, numerous line drawings, distribution maps; cloth.
Wheldon & Wesley 207-1805 1996 £80.00

LUFF, LORRY, PSEUD.   The Texan Captain and the Female Smuggler.
New York: W. F. Burgess, 1850. 1st edition under this ttile; 8vo; 96
pages; sewn, lacks wrappers, foxed, last leaf worn; Wright I 1738 (1
copy).   M & S Rare Books 60-422 1996 $425.00

LUFFMAN, JOHN   The Charters of London Complete: Also Magna
Charta, and the Bill of Rights, with Explanatory Notes and Remarks.
London: printed for J. Luffman...and T. Evans, 1793. 1st (and only)
edition; 8vo; (vi), ii, 320, (1), 321-431 pages; recently well bound in old
style quarter calf, gilt; excellent, complete with half title, apparently rare.
Sweet and Maxwell I 441(69); not in Goldsmiths.   John Drury 82-155
1996 £250.00

LUGARD, FREDERICK D.   The Rise of Our East African Empire. Early
Efforts in Nyasaland and Uganda. Edinburgh: Wm. Blackwood & Sons,
1893. 1st edition; 8vo; 2 volumes, pages xx, 563, 32 ads; x, 682; 54
plates, 14 maps; original pictorial red cloth, fine set. Conover 1278.
Hoover 328.   Richard Adelson W94/95-113 1996 $585.00

LUHAN, MABEL DODGE   Movers and Shakers. New York: Harcourt,
Brace and Co., 1936. 1st edition; 542 pages; portraits from photos; dark
blue cloth, covers bit spotted and with light wear to corners and spine
ends, very good, scarce.   Argonaut Book Shop 113-427 1996
$100.00

LUHAN, MABEL DODGE   Taos and Its Artists. New York: 1947. 1st
edition; 168 pages; photos, plates, fine in dust jacket; signed, rare.   T.
A. Swinford 49-713 1996 $350.00

LUHAN, MABEL DODGE   Taos and Its Artists. New York: 1947. 2nd
printing; 168 pages, illustrations, photos; scarce; signed by author.
Early West 22-528 1996 $200.00

LUHAN, MABEL DODGE   Winter in Taos. New York: Harcourt Brace,
1935. 1st edition; 237 pages; 16 full page photos; cloth, spine and
fore-edge darkened, else fine.   Argonaut Book Shop 113-429 1996
$125.00

LUIS DE GRANADA 1504-1588   A Memoriall of Christian Life... Rouen:
George L'Oyselet, 1586. 1st edition thus; 8vo; pages 580, 585-609, (xi),
complete, mostly Roman letter, side notes and some quotations in Italic,
jesuit emblematic device on title, 10 woodcuts in text mainly half page,
title within printed line border; contemporary ms. notes on endpapers
and in text, small wormtrail through blank outer margin in final
gatherings, pretty well thumbed, still desirable copy in contemporary limp
vellum, remains of original ties. STC 16903; Lowndes 1351; Allison &
Rogers 472; Palau 107983.   A. Sokol XXV-60 1996 £950.00

LUISINO, ALOYSIO   Aphrodisiacus, Sive de Lue Venera: in Duos
Tomos Bipartitus... Leyden: 1728. Folio; 1366 pages; full leather, skilfully
rebacked, retaining contemporary boards; Hirsch 3.870; Waller 6099.
W. Bruce Fye 71-1320 1996 $1,500.00

LUKIN, J.   The Lathe and its Uses. London: 1868. 1st edition; 8vo; 2
folding plates, 434 text figures; cloth, bit worn, repaired, some foxing.
Abell 175.   Maggs Bros. Ltd. 1190-645 1996 £90.00

LUKIN, J.   The Lathe and Its Uses. London: 1874. 4th edition; 8vo; 2
folding plates, 460 text figures; cloth, spine much faded, some foxing.
Abell 175.   Maggs Bros. Ltd. 1190-646 1996 £76.00

LUKIN, J.   Turning Lathes... Colchester: Britannia Co., 1894. 4th
edition; 8vo; 184 pages; catalog bound at end; numerous illustrations;
blue cloth, worn and scruffy. Abell 185 for first ed. and 6th ed.
Maggs Bros. Ltd. 1190-643 1996 £75.00

LUKIS, PARDEY   Tropical Hygiene for Anglo-Indians and Indians.
Calcutta: 1914. 2nd edition; 270 pages; illustrations, folding charts;
original binding, scarce.   W. Bruce Fye 71-1321 1996 $125.00

LULLIES, REINHARD   Greek Sculpture. New York: Harry N. Abrams,
1960. Revised edition; folio; 115 pages, 323 illustrations; original cloth,
dust jacket.   Archaeologia Luxor-3642 19964 $125.00

LUMHOLTZ, CARL   Unknown Mexico. A Record of Five Years'
Exploration Among the Tribes of the Western Sierra Madre; in the Tierra
Caliente of Tepic and Jalisco... New York: Charles Scribner's, 1902. 1st
edition; 8vo; 2 volumes, frontispieces, xlvii, 1026 pages; 416 illustrations,
15 color plates, 1 folding map; original gilt cloth,, top edge gilt, several
corners lightly bumped; signed.   Archaeologia Luxor-4660 1996
$350.00

LUMHOLTZ, CARL   Unknown Mexico. Glorieta: Rio Grande Press,
1902/73. 4to; 2 volumes; frontispiece, (xxvi), 1, 1026 pages, 416
illustrations, 40 color plates, 1 folding map; original cloth, corners lightly
bumped.   Archaeologia Luxor-4659 1996 $150.00

LUMLEY, BRIAN   The Caller of the Black. Sauk City: Arkham House,
1971. 1st edition; illustrations by Herb Arnold; very fine in dust jacket,
inscribed by Arnold and with original drawing by him.   Bromer
Booksellers 87-2 1996 $150.00

LUMMIS, CHARLES F.   Mesa, Canon and Pueblo. New York: 1925.
1st edition; 517 pages; color frontispiece, photos, folding map; fine, dust
jacket, extremely scarce in dust jacket.   T. A. Swinford 49-715 1996
$125.00

LUMMIS, CHARLES F.   A New Mexico David, and Other Stories and
Sketches of the Southwest. New York: 1891. 1st edition; 217 pages;
frontispiece, pictorial cloth; very good+.   T. A. Swinford 49-714 1996
$100.00

LUMSDEN, HARRY   The Records of the Trades House of Glasgow,
1605-1678. Glasgow: 1910. Only 500 copies printed, signed and
numbered; crown 4to; folding facsimile, pages 601; original buckram, g
Howes Bookshop 265-1114 1996 £75.00

LUND, JOHANNES   Die Alten Judischen Heiligthumer...Des Levitschen
Priesterthums... Hamburg: Christian Wilhelm Brand, 1738. Folio; 5 books
in one, (48), 1236, (144) pages; frontispiece, engraved portrait of Lund,
30 engraved plates and palns, title printed in red and black;
contemporary half pigskin over sprinkled paper boards, black calf spine
label, extremities bit rubbed and text with some light browning as usual
with German books of this period, otherwise very attractive in original
binding.   Kenneth Karmiole 1NS-137 1996 $1,500.00

LUNDY, BENJAMIN   The Origin and True Causes of the Texas
Insurrection Commenced in the Year 1835. Philadelphia: 1836. Reprinted
from the Philadelphia 'National Gazette'; 32 pages; removed, trimmed,
darkened/foxed, lacking original bright yellow wrappers; Streeter's
duplicate copy, with his pencilled notes. Raines p. 141. Streeter TX 121
Bohling Book Co. 191-87 1996 $700.00

LUPOFF, RICHARD A.   Edgar Rice Burroughs: Master of Adventure.
New York: Canaveral Press, 1965. 1st edition; number 89 of 150
numbered copies on Number Seventy paper, signed and numbered by
author; 8vo; 12 black and white illustrations; green cloth, gilt stamped
spine, top edge stained green, dust jacket (nicks), very good.   Georg
J. Houle 68-22 1996 $200.00

LUPOLDUS BAMBERGENSIS   Germanorum Veterum Principum Zelus et Fervor in Christianum Religionem Deique Ministros. Basel: Johann Bergmann de Olpe 15 May 1497. 1st and only edition; folio; old boards, worn, title stained, lower and inner blank margins restored, several monastic ownership inscriptions and an old Royal Library, Berlin (Prussian State Library) stamp on title with later withdrawn stamp, lower blank edges on several leaves restored, some waterstains, primarily in blank margins, most inner blank margins restored, blank lower portion of final leaf backed where paper is weakened by several dampstains. Exceedingly rare. Hain Copinger 2725; Goff L399.   G. W. Stuart 59-65 1996 $3,750.00

LURIE, ALISON   Foreign Affairs. Franklin Center: Franklin Library, 1984. Franklin Library signed limited first eidition; gilt stamped full leather, fine. Lame Duck Books   19-293   1996 $125.00

LUTHER, MARTIN 1483-1546   A Commentarie of M. Doctor Martin Luther Upon the Epistle of S. Paul to the Galatians. (with) A Commentarie Upon the Fifteene Psalmes, Called Pslami Graduum, that is Psalmes of Degrees... London: Richard Field, 1616/15. 4to; 2 works bound together, 4 leaves, 296 leaves, printed in black letter, title with device, x, 318 pages, last 3 leaves with only minor worming, touching only a few letters, repair to blank corner of last leaf, printed in black letter; 18th century calf, nicely rebacked, very nice.   Roy W. Clare XXIV-78   1996 $325.00

LUTHER, MARTIN 1483-1546   An Die Pfarrherrn Wider de Wucher zu Predigen. Wittenberg: Klug, 1540. 4to; fine woodcut title border, boards; some browning; Benzing 3350.   Rostenberg & Stern 150-87   1996 $1,750.00

LUTHER, MARTIN 1483-1546   The Way to Prayer. London: William Pickering, 1846. 1st edition in English; 6 1/4 x 5 1/4 inches; xxvi pages, (1) leaf, 68 pages; frontispiece, device on title, decorative headpieces and initials; quite appealing slightly later dark brown morocco by Riviere for B. M. Pickering, covers panelled in gilt and blind, corner fleurons between raised bands, marbled endpapers, all edges gilt (with Pickering booksellers' ticket at front), slight rubbing to joints, spine bands and extremities, inner margin of frontispiece, skillfully repaired without loss, otherwise fine and attractive copy. Modern bookplates of Charles Ballantyne and H. C. Wace, owner's signature of E. Arnett on flyleaf dated 1861. Rare edition. Keynes p. 65.   Phillip J. Pirages 33-421 1996 $325.00

LUTTIG, JOHN C.   Journal of a Fur Trading Expedition on the Upper Missouri, 1812-1813. St. Louis: 1920. 1st edition; copy number 213 of 365; 192 pages; frontispiece, folded map, plates, cloth and boards, nice, very rare.   T. A. Swinford   49-716   1996 $375.00

LUTTRELL, HENRY   Crockford House, a Rhapsody in Two Cantos. (with) A Rhymer in Rome. London: John Murray, 1827. 1st edition; octavo; pages 147; half title present, uncut; original publisher's boards, nice copy, scarce, not often found in original state; scarce; presentation copy inscribed by author, some war to covers, but contents excellent; CBEL III 238.   Hartfield   48-L56   1996 $225.00

LUTWYCHE, EDWARD   The Reports and Entries of Sir Edward Lutwyche, Kt. Sergeant at Law and Late One of the Judges of the Court of Common Pleas... London: printed by Eliz. Nutt and R. gosling, 1718. Panelled calf, worn and rubbed, joints repaired, usable.   Meyer Boswell SL26-150   1996 $500.00

LUTYENS, EDWIN   Fulbrook - A House You Will Love to Live In. Marlborough: Libanus Press, 1989. Number 195 of 300 sets; 2 volumes; reproductions of drawings, sketchbook, tipped in photos; quarter morocco, fine set in cloth slipcase.   Ulysses   39-386   1996 £150.00

LUTYENS, EDWIN   Fullbrook. A House You Will Love to Live In. The Sketchbook, Letters, Specifications of Works and Accounts for a House by Edwin Lutyens 1896-1899. Marlborough: 1989. Large octavo; 2 volumes, 89, 46 pages; drawings; mint in morocco backed boards, slipcase.   Bromer Booksellers   87-169   1996 $300.00

LUXMOORE, H. E.   Some Views and Opinions of Sparrow on Housetops. Eton College: R. Ingalton Drake, 1885. Sole edition; 4to; pages 42, (1), 4 mounted photos, numerous illustrations, contemporary bubble grain dark green cloth, backstrip gilt lettered direct, endpapers browned, very good.   Blackwell's   B112-181   1996 £95.00

LUYKEN, JAN   Afbeelding der Menschelyke Bezighede, Bestaande in Hondert Onderscheiden Printverbeeldingen, Vertonende Allerhande Stantspersonen, zo van Regeeringe, Konsten, Wetenschappen, als Handwerken... Amsterdam: Reinier & Josua Ottens, ca. 1695. 4to; frontispiece, title vignette, 100 fine copperplate engravings printed on one side only; early marbled boards, rebacked in leather, boards lightly rubbed along extremities. v. Landwehr 10; Van Eeghen & Van der Kellen pp. 262-267.   Edwin V. Glaser   121-200   1996 $4,500.00

LYCOPHRONIS CHALCIDENSIS   Cassandra. Romae: Apud Antonium Fulgonium, 1803. One of 500 copies; 11 1/4 x 8 3/4 inches; xl, 416 pages, (1) leaf, 208 pages; engraved title vignette, frontispiece and one plate, Greek and Latin on facing pages; very fine contemporary diced russia, sides framed with triple gilt fillet, gilt titling on spine, spine ends and wide raised bands elegantly decorated in gilt, scrolling gilt border on turn-ins, marbled edges, minor foxing and browning, handful of leaves stained at top, but text very fresh and clean in general and showing no signs of use. Binding in a remarkable state of preservation. Dibdin II 211; Brunet III 1248; Graesse IV 309.   Phillip J. Pirages 33-371 1996 $350.00

LYCOSTEHENES, CONRADUS   Apophthegmata Ex optimis Utriusque Linguae Scriptoribus... Lyon: Anonium de Harsy, 1574. 1st edition; small 8vo; pages (24), 1322, (12); old Lyonaise full leather, modern plain leather back, ex-library.   Family Album   Tillers-417   1996 $250.00

LYDEKKER, RICHARD   Animal Portraiture. n.d. 2nd issue; folio; 50 mounted color plates; original pictorial buckram, lightly rubbed, light foxing to a few pages, hinges bit loose; nice, scarce.   David Grayling J95Biggame-542   1996 £350.00

LYDEKKER, RICHARD   Animal Portraiture. London: n.d. 2nd impression; folio; 50 mounted colored plates by Wilhelm Kuhnert; original pictorial buckram, lightly rubbed, light foxing to few pages, hinges slightly sprung; nice, scarce.   David A.H. Grayling MY95Orn-49 1996 £320.00

LYDEKKER, RICHARD   Harmsworth Natural History. 1910. 4to; 3 volumes; colored plates, many text illustrations; original cloth; lovely set. David Grayling J95Biggame-540   1996 £75.00

LYDEKKER, RICHARD   The Royal Natural History. London: & New York: 1893-94. 6 volumes; 72 color plates; three quarter morocco, rubbed, library label removed from backstrips, no stamping to plates, backstrip plates bright, plates unfoxed.   Bookworm & Silverfish   280-124 1996 $165.00

LYDEKKER, RICHARD   The Royal Natural History. 1893-96. Imperial 8vo; many colored plates, engraved plates and text illustrations; original orange pictorial gilt and silver cloth; near fine set.   David Grayling J95Biggame-541   1996 £200.00

LYDEKKER, RICHARD   The Royal Natural History. London: 1893-96. Imperial 8vo; 6 volumes, many colored plates, engraved plates and text illustrations by Wilhelm Kunhert and others; near fine set in original ornate pictorial gilt and silver cloth.   David A.H. Grayling MY95Orn-48 1996 £200.00

LYDEKKER, RICHARD   The Royal Natural History. London: 1893-96. Imperial 8vo; 6 volumes; 72 colored plates and 1600 text figures; original half morocco, somewhat worn, spine of volume 1 slightly defective. Wheldon & Wesley   207-502   1996 £85.00

LYDON, A. F.   English Lake Scenery. London: John Walker and Co., 1880. %all 8vo; 48 pages, 24 chromolithographs; original green cloth stamped in black and gilt with recessed inlay binding on upper cover consisting of purple cloth stamped in gilt and lettered in red and green, all edges gilt; inner hinges reinforced, blindstamped on couple ofpages but not any of the plates, touch of wear to spine ends, otherwise fine in attractive elaborately decorated Victorian binding. McLean p. 204. David Mason   71-23   1996 $280.00

LYDON, A. F.   Scottish Loch Scenery. London: John Walker, 1882. Large 8vo; pages 50, 25 tissued guarded chromolithographs by Fawcett of Driffield; original decorative red cloth gilt over bevelled boards, spine slightly faded, extremities slightly worn, all edges gilt; very nice clean copy. McLean, Benjamin Fawcett 119.   R.F.G. Hollett 76-159 1996 £140.00

LYELL, CHARLES 1797-1875   Principles of Geology: Being an Enquiry How Far the Former Changes of the Earth's Surface are Referable to causes Now in Operation. London: 1837. 5th edition; 12mo; 4 volumes, 16 maps and plates, some colored, some folding; calf, skilfully rebacked preserving spines; bookplate of Stafford H. Northcote.   John Henly 27-507   1996 £280.00

LYELL, CHARLES 1797-1875   Principles of Geology... London: 1878-72. 11th edition of volume 1, 10th edition of volume 2; 8vo; 2 volumes; text figures, maps, 8 plates; original green cloth, gilt, trifle used.   Wheldon & Wesley   207-1350   1996 £75.00

LYELL, CHARLES 1797-1875   Travels in North America, Canada and Nova Scotia, with Geological Observations. London: John Murray, 1855. 2nd edition; 12mo; 2 volumes, xiii, 2, 316; viii, errata, 272; color folding map, map, 5 plates; original green cloth, spines faded, ends starting to chip. Howes L575; Sabin 42761.   Richard Adelson W94/95-114 1996 $325.00

LYELL, DENNIS D.   The Hunting and Spoor of Central African Game. Philadelphia: Lippincott, ca. 1920. 1st American edition; 4to; xiv, 234 pages; illustrations; original tan buckram, spine darkened, slight bubbling of cloth on front cover, endpapers foxed, but very good or better. Chapel Hill 94-387 1996 $225.00

LYELL, DENNIS D.   The Hunting and Spoor of Central African Game. London: 1929. illustrations, covers bit discolored, light foxing to first few pages.   David Grayling J95Biggame-133 1996 £225.00

LYMAN, CHESTER S.   Around the Horn to the Sandwich Islands and Californa 1845-1850. New Haven: Yale University Press, 1924. 8vo; 16 plates; gilt decorated black cloth, endpaper maps. Hill p 481.   Parmer Books 039/Nautica-039169 1996 $125.00

LYMAN, GEORGE D.   John Marsh, Pioneer. New York: 1930. 394 pages; illustrations, photos; book very fine; signed by author. Scarce. Six Guns 1376. SFT 500.   Early West 22-201 1996 $200.00

LYMAN, HENRY M.   Artificial Anaesthesia and Anaesthetics. New York: 1881. 1st edition; 338 pages; original binding. Fulton Stanton 25; Keys 185.   W. Bruce Fye 71-1322 1996 $150.00

LYMAN, HENRY M.   Artificial Anaesthesia and Anaesthetics. New York: William Wood, 1881. 1st and only edition; 8vo; vii, 338 pages; illustrations; original embossed cloth, bit shelfworn, very good. Rutkow GS101.1. Reynolds 2531. Blocker p. 250; Courville 1398.   Edwin V. Glaser B122-93 1996 $150.00

LYNCH, JAMES J.   Box, Pit and Gallery - Stage and Society in Johnson's London. University of California Press, 1953. 1st edition; black and white frontispiece and 6 black and white plates; original binding, top edge slightly dusty, head and tail of spine slightly faded, very good in nicked, torn, creased, rubbed and slightly marked, chipped and dusty dust jacket, faded at spine and browned at edges. Presentation copy from author for Josephine Miles.   Ulysses 39-320 1996 £55.00

LYNCH, JAMES K.   With Stevenson to California 1846. N.P.: 1896. 1st edition; limited to 100 copies; 65 pages; original green cloth, title in gilt on front cover, fine, rare in choice condition; presentation card from author laid in. Graff 2564; Cowan p. 401; Howes L583; Tutorow Mex. Amer. War 3472.   Michael D. Heaston 23-206 1996 $750.00

LYNDSAY, DAVID   The Poetical Works of Sir David Lyndsay of the Mount. London: Ptd. for Longman, Hurst, Rees, and Orme, Paternoster-Row, and ... 1806. 1st collected edition; 8vo; 3 volumes; half titles, (v-viii) pages, 181-233 pages, 234-524 pages, 5 vignettes to letterpress, decorative head and tailpieces; full tree calf, gilt Greek key borders to boards, red and green morocco labels to spines, gilt tooling to compartments, joints rubbed and worn, marabled endpapers, owner's bookplates to front f.e.p. & pastedown of all volumes, hinges cracked, but still good, tight copy.   Beeleigh Abbey BA56-157 1996 £150.00

LYNN, SAMUEL   A Short Narrative of the Case of Samuel Lynn, Esq. Late Muster Master General of the Late Marine Forces &c... London: printed in the Year 1720. 1st edition; 4to; few page numerals cropped, 34 pages; disbound; Not in Kress, Goldsmtih or Hanson.   Anthony W. Laywood 109-88 1996 £110.00

LYON, GEORGE FRANCIS   A Brief Narrative of an Unsuccessful Attempt to Reach Repulse Bay, in His Majesty's Ship Griper, in the Year 1824. London: 1825. Pages xvi 198, 7 plates; folding map; contemporary full calf, rebacked, gilt panelled spine, very nice, text bright. Arctic 10530.   Stephen Lunsford 45-98 1996 $275.00

LYON, GEORGE FRANCIS   A Narrative of the Travels in Northern Africa, in the Years 1818, 19 and 20... London: John Murray, 1821. 1st edition; 4to; large folding map, 17 hand colored lithographed plates after drawings by author; contemporary half calf, spine gilt, rubbed, some wear, occasional light soiling and signs of use. Abbey Travel 304; Blackmer 1044.   Ximenes 109-180 1996 $800.00

LYON, GEORGE FRANCIS   The Private Journal of Captain G. F. Lyon of H.M.S. Hecla, During the Recent Voyage of Discovery Under Captain Parry. London: 1824. paes xl, 468; map, plates; contemporary full calf, rebacked with original backstrip laid down, handsome bright copy, text bright and clean. Arctic 10531.   Stephen Lunsford 45-99 1996 $350.00

LYON, GEORGE FRANCIS   The Private Journal of Captian G. F. Lyon of H. M. S. Heda during the Recent Voyage of Discvoery Under Captain Parry 1821-1823. Barre: Imprint Society, 1970. One of 1950 numbered copies; frontispiece, illustrations by James A. Houston, folding map; cloth backed pictorial boards, publisher's slipcase, bookplate on endpaper, else fine.   Hermitage SP95-922 1996 $125.00

LYON, H. M.   Sardonics. Stuyvesant, 1909. 1st edition; pictorial cloth with gold and orange stamping; some light wear to front corner tips an spine extremities, else just about very good.   Aronovitz 57-736 1996 $125.00

LYON, LILLIAN BOWES   Collected Poems. London: Jonathan Cape, 1948. 1st edition; titlepage wood engraving and endpapers by Joan Hassall; original binding, top edge dusty, spine slightly faded, head and tail of spine slightly bumped, covers slightly bowed, very good in nicked rubbed and slightly creased and dusty dust jacket darkened at spine an browned at edges.   Ulysses 39-387 1996 £55.00

LYONS, ARTHUR   The Dead are Discreet. New York: Mason and Lipscomb, 1974. 1st edition; fine in near fine dust jacket with rubbing. Quill & Brush 102-1116 1996 $250.00

LYRA Germanica. London: Longmans, Green, Reader & Dyer, 1868. 1st illustrated edition; royal 8vo; pages xvi, 254, ad leaf; frontispiece, other illustrations; original dark green cloth, gilt, red inlays, gilt, edges gilt, by Edmonds & Remnants with ticket, nice, elaborate signed binding by Leighton.   James Fenning 133-208 1996 £65.00

LYRA Germanica: Hymns for the Sundays and Chief Festivals of the Christian Year. London: Longman, Green, Longman and Roberts, 1861. 1st English Language edition; small 4to; xx, 272 pages; publisher's cloth binding design by John Leighton and is the same as the publisher's deluxe morocco covers; very bright, very good, save for light edge wear.   Bookpress 75-77 1996 $225.00

LYSAGHT, A. M.   The Book of Birds. London: 1975. Folio; numerous full page colored plates, many plain plates and text illustrations; beautifully bound in full brown morocco, gilt borders and spine, all edges gilt.   David A.H. Grayling MY95Orn-50 1996 £150.00

LYSERUS, JOHANNES   Polygamia Triumphatrix, Id est Discursus Politicus de Polygamia... Lund: by the author, 1682. 1st edition; 4to; 610 pages; woodcut ornaments; contemporary full mottled calf, some scuffing, wear to extremities, gilt backstrip, fine. NUC 347.536.   Benne Gilbert LL29-78 1996 $1,850.00

LYSIAS   Eratosthenes, Hoc Est, Brevis Lt Lvcvlenta Defensio Lysiae Praelectionibus Illustrata Andreae Dvnaei... Cambridge: Iohannes Legatus 1593. 1st edition thus; small 8vo; pages (xlvii), 248, mixed Green and Roman letter, woodcut decorations on title, ms. index on verso, nice decorated initials and typographical borders; 19th century quarter calf, marbled boards; some 18th/19th century marginalia to early leaves, light paper browning, quite good. STC 17121; Lowndes 1423.   A. Sokol XXV-61 1996 £750.00

LYSONS, D.   Magna Britannia...Volume IV. London: for T. Cadell & W Davies, 1816. Large paper copy; large 4to; pages ccx, 198, 43 plates, many folding, including map; old quarter calf, spine label, rather defectiv top and bottom of spine, but neat and sound; little spotitng to few plates, but very attractive, clean copy, with extending genealogical tree ms. of the Grahams of Esk, map and 17th century map with contemporary notes, all tipped in at end.   R.F.G. Hollett & Son 78-1086 1996 £195.00

LYSONS, D.   Magna Brittania: Being a Concise Topographical Accour of the Several Counties of Great Britain. Volume IV. London: T. Cadell & W. Davies, 1816. 4to; pages ccx, 198, 43 plates, many folding, including map; old half calf, gilt, marbled boards, rather worn, hinges cracked. R.F.G. Hollett & Son 78-1085 1996 £130.00

LYSONS, D.   Magna Brittania...Volume IV. London: T. Cadell and W. Davies, 1816. 4to; pages ccx, 198, 43 plates; new half morocco gilt wit raised bands, spine label, some plates little spotted, generally very goo R.F.G. Hollett & Son 78-1087 1996 £160.00

LYSONS, SAMUEL   A Collection of Gloucestershire Antiquities. London: Cadell & Davies, 1791-1804. One of 12 copies on large paper, with all but two plates colored by hand within wash borders; large folio engraved title, 1 f., iv, 38 pages, 2 ff., 110 plates, drawn and etched by Lysons, 108 colored by hand, 1 in 2 states; plate 81 uncolored and inlaid to size, plate 84 in 2 states (colored and uncolored), title and following leaf bit foxed, occasional offset onto text but very handsome, contemporary dark blue morocco, gilt inner borders, gilt edges, ex-libris of Sir William Fraser, Lindsay Fleming and W. R. Jeudwine. Lowndes 1425.   Marlborough 162-63 1996 £2,200.00

LYTE, H. C. MAXWELL   A History of Eton College (1440-1910). London: Macmillan and Co. Ltd., 1911. 4th edition; royal 8vo; half title, vignette, 627 pages of text, frontispiece, 9 plates, 63 illustrations to text, one colored folding map; full dark blue morocco, triple gilt rule borders, gilt corner ornaments, gilt stamped arms and motto of Eton College to upper board gilt rule, title, date and ornaments to panelled spine all edges gilt, inner gilt rule borders with engraved bookplate of the Seventh Duke of Newcastle, bound by Bumpus; very fine.   Beeleigh Abbey BA/56-14   1996 £250.00

LYTLE, ANDREW NELSON   At the Moon's Inn. London: Eyre & Spottiswoode, 1943. 1st edition; faint foxing to page edges, else very good+ in just less than very good dust jacket.   Lame Duck Books 19-294   1996 $150.00

LYTLE, ANDREW NELSON   Bedford Forrest and His Critter Company. New York: Minton, Balch & Co., 1931. 1st edition; one of 3000 copies; illustrations; first binding, original black ribbed cloth with printed label on spine, pictorial label on front cover, dust jacket lightly soiled with few faint marginal stains; signed by author; author's rare first book. Wright A1a.   James S. Jaffe   34-454   1996 $750.00

LYTLE, ANDREW NELSON   Bedford Forrest. London: Eyre & Spottiswoode, 1939. 1st British edition; xi, 402 pages; original cloth, near fine in very scarce and very good dust jacket. Nevins li 73; Harwell In Tall Cotton 87; Dornbusch II 1190.   McGowan Book Co.   65-54   1996 $350.00

LYTTELTON, GEORGE LYTTELTON, 1ST BARON 1709-1773   Dialogues of the Dead. London: for W. Sandby, 1760. 1st edition; demy 8vo; 18th century tree calf, prettily gilt with variety of devices, lemon edges, lightly rubbed and worn, faintest of cracks in upper hinge, but most attractive copy; contemporary bookplate of Benjamin Foote.   Ash Rare Books Zenzybyr-63   1996 £200.00

LYTTELTON, GEORGE LYTTELTON, 1ST BARON 1709-1773   Dialogues of the Dead. London: Sandby, 1760. 1st edition; tall octavo; pages xii, 320; numerous engraved illustrations; contemporary full polished calf, raised bands, spine gilt in compartments, leather label, some wear, but nice,. Sale I p. 185; Rothschild 1340 citing only 4th ed.   Hartfield 48-L57   1996 $295.00

LYTTLETON, GEORGE COURTNEY   The History of England, from the Earliest Dawn of Authentic Record to the Commencement of Hostilities in the Year 1803... Stratford: 1808/03. 4to; 3 volumes; 98 plates, 2 folding maps; contemporary tree calf, rebacked in morocco; rubbed, corners and edges worn, some foxing.   Robert Clark 38-313   1996 £55.00

LYTTON, EDWARD GEORGE EARLE LYTTON BULWER-LYTTON, 1ST BARON 1803-1873   The Caxtons. Edinburgh: Wm. Blackwood, 1849. 1st edition; small 8vo; 3 volumes; original cloth.   Charles W. Traylen 117-157   1996 £120.00

LYTTON, EDWARD GEORGE EARLE LYTTON BULWER-LYTTON, 1ST BARON 1803-1873   England and the English. London: Richard Bentley, 1833. 1st edition; large 12mo; xii, 399, (1); and xi, (1), 355, (1) pages, no half titles (not called for?); 2 volumes; contemporary half calf, spines gilt with raised bands and double labels, marbled sides and edges by S. Ratcliffe of Faversham; very good. New CBEL III 918.   John Drury 82-35   1996 £250.00

LYTTON, EDWARD ROBERT BULWER-LYTTON, 1ST EARL OF 1831-1891 Lucile. Boston: Osgood, 1873. 1st edition; light rubbing at extremities, else near fine in publisher's deluxe leather binding; inscribed by Civil War General, Philip Sheridan.   Between the Covers 42-393   1996 $650.00

LYTTON, EDWARD ROBERT BULWER-LYTTON, 1ST EARL OF 1835-1891 Poems. Boston: Houghton Mifflin, 1881. New revised edition; 8vo; 406 pages; numerous full page illustrations; contemporary full tree calf with ornately gilt tooled borders, inner dentelles, and spine panel florets, red and green morocco spine labels, raised bands, all edges gilt, beautiful binding in virtually fine condition.   Chapel Hill   94-107   1996 $120.00

M

MAC ADAM, JOHN LOUDON 1756-1836   Remarks on the Present System of Road Making. London: Longman, Hurst et al, 1820. 3rd edition; 8vo; 196 pages; contemporary boards, rebacked, paper spine label, first few leaves foxed, boards trifle shelfworn, otherwise near fine, untrimmed copy.   Edwin V. Glaser 121-201 1996 $250.00

MAC ALISTER, R. A. STEWART   The Excavation of Gezer 1902-1905 and 1907-1909. London: published for the Committee of the Palestine Exploration Fund by... 1912. 4to; 3 volumes (complete), 889 pages, 535 figures, 226 plates; original cloth, owner's stamp at flyleaf, otherwise fine.   Archaeologia Luxor-2404 1996 $950.00

MC ALMON, ROBERT   Distinguished Air: Grim Fairy Tales. Paris: printed for Contact Editions at the Three Mountains Press, 1925. Designated as an edition of 115 copies, this one is specified, printed in the limitation statement as 'Author's Proof", under which author has written; "His Copy", errata slip tipped in; McAlmon has corrected the proof and while many of the corrections are reflected in the errata, some have not been incorporated; bound in full leather, possibly a presentation binding, but as likely bound specially for McAlmon, his bookplate on front pastedown, edges worn and lightly chipped at spine ends, slight chips to edges of brittle endpapers, binding is else about very good, contents near fine.   Between the Covers 42-292 1996 $4,500.00

MC ALMON, ROBERT   North America. Paris: Contact Editions, 1929. Of a total edition of 310, one of 300 unnumbered copies; etchings by Hilaire Hiler; short edge-tear with attendant creasing to fore-edge of front panel and tip of upper fore-corner clipped, very good in wrappers. Lame Duck Books 19-318 1996 $350.00

MC ARTHUR, HARRIET NESMITH   Recollections of the Rickreall. Portland: privately printed, 1930. 1st edition; 24 pages; frontispiece, plates; original stiff boards, green cloth spine with printed paper label on front cover, minor bumping; presentation copy from McArthur to Francis P. Farquhar; fine. Smith 6177 locating only 3 copies; Soliday Sale II 934. Michael D. Heaston 23-207 1996 $500.00

MAC ASKILL, WALLACE R.   Out of Halifax. New York: Derrydale Press, 1937. One of 950 numbered copies for the U.S., out of a total edition of 1400 copies; folio; photographic frontispiece, 99 photographic plates; original half blue cloth over light blue cloth boards, lettered in gilt, top and bottom edges just slightly browned, otherwise fine in original glassine and pictorial cardboard box (chipped). Siegel, Marschalk and Oelgart 123.   Heritage Book Shop 196-171 1996 $250.00

MAC AVOY, R. A.   Tea With a Black Dragon. Hypatia Press, 1987. 1st hardcover edition, 1/25 copies bound in leather and labelled PC from the 275 leather bound copy edition; signed by Anne McCaffrey, the artist; as new in slipcase. Aronovitz 57-739 1996 $150.00

MC BAIN, ED   The Cop Hater. New York: Armchair Detective Library, 1989. 1st separate hardback edition, number 32 of 100 copies numbered and signed by author; fine in slipcase. Quill & Brush 102-1292 1996 $100.00

MC BAIN, ED   The 8th Squad. New York: Simon & Schuster, 1960. 1st edition; near fine with spine ends lightly worn and light foxing on page fore edge, in very good dust jacket with rubbing, light chipping and one long (approximately 1 1/2") tear on lower back panel.   Quill & Brush 102-1261 1996 $100.00

MC BAIN, ED   The 87th Precinct. New York: Simon & Schuster, 1959. 1st edition; near fine in very good dust jacket with light soiling, few faint creases and minor edge wear.   Quill & Brush 102-1260 1996 $135.00

MC BAIN, ED   Hail to the Chief. New York: Random House, 1973. 1st edition; fine in dust jacket.   Quill & Brush 102-1268 1996 $125.00

MC BAIN, ED   The Heckler. New York: Simon & Schuster, 1960. 1st edition; fine in dust jacket with very light soiling; signed.   Quill & Brush 102-1262 1996 $200.00

MC BAIN, ED   The Heckler. New York: Simon and Schuster, 1960. 1st edition; fine in very good or better price clipped dust jacket with light soiling, spine ends slightly chipped, minor edge wear.   Quill & Brush 102-1263 1996 $100.00

MC BAIN, ED   The Pusher. New York: Armchair Detective Library, 1990. 1st separate hardback edition, number 16 of 100 copies, numbered and signed by author; fine in slipcase.   Quill & Brush 102-1296 1996 $100.00

MC BAIN, ED   See Them Die. New York: Simon & Schuster, 1960. 1st edition; near fine with spine ends lightly worn, very good price clipped dust jacket with soiling and light edge wear.   Quill & Brush 102-1264 1996 $175.00

MC BAIN, ED   Shotgun. Garden City: Doubleday, 1969. 1st edition; near fine with minor wear along edges in dust jacket, with very light soiling and edge wear.   Quill & Brush 102-1267 1996 $100.00

MC BAIN, ED   Ten Plus One. New York: Simon & Schuster, 1963. 1st edition; near fine with small store sticker on front pastedown and light soiling on boards, in very good dust jacket with soiling, few small closed tears and pen marks (few small marks) on front flap.   Quill & Brush 102-1265 1996 $100.00

M'BAIN, J.   The Merrick and the Neighbouring Hills. Ayr: Stephen & Pollock, c. 1910. 1st edition; 8vo; pages 335, 40 plates, large folding colored; original cloth, gilt.   R.F.G. Hollett 76-177 1996 £65.00

MAC BRIDE, DAVID   Experimental Essays on Medical and Philosophical Subjects... London: printed for A. Millar and T. Cadell, 1767. 2nd edition; 8vo; 4 folding engraved plates, 2 folding tables; contemporary calf, hinges cracked, library shelf mark in gilt on spine, label.   Anthony W. Laywood 109-89 1996 £325.00

M'CABE, JOHN COLLINS   Scraps. Richmond: J. C. Walker, 1835. 1st edition; 12mo; 192 pages; original cloth, leather label, cloth faded, some foxing and waterstaining to text. Wright I 1741; Rinderknecht 32701.   M & S Rare Books 60-199 1996 $225.00

MC CAFFREY, A.   Cooking Out of This World. Wildside Press, 1992. 1st hardcover edition, 1/26 lettered copies, signed by editor; as new in full leather binding as issued.   Aronovitz 57-783 1996 $195.00

MC CAFFREY, A.   The Dolphins Bell. Wildside Press, 1993. 1/50 copies, specially bound and signed by author; as new in dark green leather binding with silver pictorial stamping.   Aronovitz 57-785 1996 $125.00

MC CAFFREY, A.   Dragonflight. Walker, 1968. 1st edition; fine in dust jacket, inscribed by author.   Aronovitz 57-773 1996 $275.00

MC CAFFREY, A.   Dragonquest. R. & W./A. Deutsch, 1973. 1st British and 1st hardcoer edition; fine in dust jacket, signed by author; quite scarce.   Aronovitz 57-775 1996 $750.00

MC CALEB, WALTER FLAVIUS   The Aaron Burr Conspiracy. New York: Dodd, Mead and Co., 1903. 1st edition; folding map, 369 pages, plus index; green cloth, paper label, label lightly chipped along one edge, overall light rubbing, very good.   Hermitage SP95-720 1996 $100.00

MC CANN, ANNA MARGUERITE   The Portraits of Septimius Severus (A.D. 193-211).. Roma: American Academy in Rome, 1968. 4to; 222 pages, 2 color figures and 108 plates; original cloth, dust jacket, signature at titlepage.   Archaeologia Luxor-3687 1996 $200.00

MC CARTHY, CHARLOTTE   Justice and Reason, Faithful Guides to Truth. London: printed for the author, 1767. 1st edition; 8vo; contemporary calf, spine and corners rather worn. Very uncommon. Clean tear across 2 leaves in subscriber's list, without loss, some signs of use, but sound copy, complete with leaf at end containing a poem addressed to the Prince of Wales, list of errata bears author's signature. Ximenes 108-251 1996 $650.00

MC CARTHY, CORMAC   All the Pretty Horses. New York: Knopf, 198 1st edition; as new.   Book Time 2-280 1996 $200.00

MC CARTHY, CORMAC   All the Pretty Horses. New York: Knopf, 1992. Uncorrected proof copy; wrappers, with "A Border Trilogy" changed to "The Border Trilogy" by pencil on front wrapper.   Ken Lopez 74-302 1996 $350.00

MC CARTHY, CORMAC   All the Pretty Horses. New York: Knopf, 1992. Uncorrected proof copy; grey wrappers, publisher's ads stapled to verso of front wrapper; fine, title of trilogy corrected in pencil to front wrapper.   Lame Duck Books 19-320 1996 $275.00

MC CARTHY, CORMAC   All the Pretty Horses. New York: Knopf, 1992. Uncorrected proof; 8vo; printed wrappers, as new.   James S. Jaffe 34-467 1996 $175.00

MC CARTHY, CORMAC   All the Pretty Horses. New York: Knopf, 1992. 1st edition; presentation proof copy, signed by author; 8vo; decorated wrappers, folding card box; fine,   James S. Jaffe 34-466 1996 $650.00

MC CARTHY, CORMAC   All the Pretty Horses. New York: Knopf, 1992. Advance reading copy; wrappers, publisher's folding box, fine.   Ken Lopez 74-300 1996 $650.00

MC CARTHY, CORMAC   All the Pretty Horses. New York: Knopf, 1992. Advance reading copy, signed; fine, lacking folding box.   Ken Lopez 74-301 1996 $500.00

MC CARTHY, CORMAC   All the Pretty Horses. New York: Knopf, 1992. 1st U.S. edition; fine in dust jacket.   Lame Duck Books 19-321 1996 $250.00

MC CARTHY, CORMAC   All the Pretty Horses. New York: Knopf, 1992. 1st edition; fine in fine dust jacket.   Ken Lopez 74-298 1996 $250.00

MC CARTHY, CORMAC   All the Pretty Horses. New York: Knopf, 1992. 1st edition; fine in near fine price cliped dust jacket.   Bella Luna 7-365 1996 $200.00

MC CARTHY, CORMAC   All the Pretty Horses. New York: Esquire, 1992. 1st edition of this chapter from the novel, offprint from Esquire; 4to; color illustrations by Marshall Arisman; original self wrappers, stapled; fine.   James S. Jaffe 34-468 1996 $100.00

MC CARTHY, CORMAC   All the Pretty Horses. London: Picador/Pan, 1993. Uncorrected proof copy of the first British edition; slight diagonal crease on front wrapper, else fine.   Ken Lopez 74-303 1996 $375.00

MC CARTHY, CORMAC   All the Pretty Horses. London: 1993. 1st English edition; fine.   Stephen Lupack 83- 1996 $125.00

MC CARTHY, CORMAC   All the Pretty Horses. London: Picador, 1993. 1st British edition; one of 3000 copies; fine in fine dust jacket.   Pettler & Lieberman 28-166 1996 $100.00

MC CARTHY, CORMAC   Blood Meridian or The Evening Redness in the West. New York: Random, 1958. 1st edition; fine in dust jacket with one tiny closed tear at flap fold.   Alice Robbins 15-212 1996 $500.00

MC CARTHY, CORMAC   Blood Meridian. New York: RH, 1985. 1st edition; fine in dust jacket.   Lame Duck Books 19-319 1996 $650.00

MC CARTHY, CORMAC   Child of God. New York: Random House, 1973. 1st edition; small sticker to front pastedown, otherwise fine in jacket that has a horizontal crease in the lamination across the front panel and slight wear at spine extremities, overall about near fine, without remainder mark common to this title.   Ken Lopez 74-297 1996 $650.00

MC CARTHY, CORMAC   The Crossing. London: Picador, 1994. 1st English edition, uncorrected proof; 8vo; pictorial white glossy wrappers; as new.   James S. Jaffe 34-470 1996 $225.00

MC CARTHY, CORMAC   The Crossing. London: Pan Macmillan, 1994. Uncorrected proof of the first British edition; glossy illustrated wrpapers; fine.   Lame Duck Books 19-323 1996 $100.00

MC CARTHY, CORMAC   The Crossing. New York: Knopf, 1994. Uncorrected proof; wrappers, fine.   Ken Lopez 74-305 1996 $350.00

MC CARTHY, CORMAC   The Crossing. New York: Knopf, 1994. Uncorrected proof; 8vo; printed blue wrappers; fine.   James S. Jaffe 34-469 1996 $250.00

MC CARTHY, CORMAC   The Crossing. New York: Knopf, 1994. Advance uncorrected proofs; wrappers; fine.   Beasley Books 82-102 1996 $200.00

MC CARTHY, CORMAC   The Crossing. New York: Knopf, 1994. Uncorrected proof copy, signed; wrappers; fine.   Ken Lopez 74-306 1996 $950.00

MC CARTHY, CORMAC   The Crossing. New York: Knopf, 1994. One of an unspecified number of copies, issued with tipped in page, signed by author; fine in dust jacket.   Between the Covers 42-293 1996 $450.00

MC CARTHY, CORMAC   The Crossing. New York: Knopf, 1994. One of 1000 copies signed by author on tipped in leaf; fine in fine dust jacket.   Ken Lopez 74-304 1996 $450.00

MC CARTHY, CORMAC   The Crossing. New York: Knopf, 1994. One of 1000 copies designated for friends of the publisher and signed by McCarthy; fine in dust jacket.   Lame Duck Books 19-322 1996 $375.00

MC CARTHY, CORMAC   The Crossing. New York: Knopf, 1994. Bound sheets 8 1/2 x 11 inch format, from the earliest state of this book; slight surface soiling, else fine.   Ken Lopez 74-307 1996 $450.00

MC CARTHY, CORMAC   The Orchard Keeper. New York: Random, 1965. 1st edition; unobtrusive former owner's signature, else near fine, white dust jacket has few very short closed tears and scattered soiling but none of the usual yellowing, very attractive copy of author's first book.   Alice Robbins 15-211 1996 $1,750.00

MC CARTHY, CORMAC   Outer Dark. New York: RH, 1968. 1st edition; especially nice, without any of the typical fading of the top edge, spine is rounda nd firm and not spongy, in near fine dust jacket with couple of tiny edge tears.   Thomas Dorn 9-178 1996 $800.00

MC CARTHY, CORMAC   Outer Dark. London: Deutsch, 1970. 1st British edition; author's second book, minor spine slant, else fine in near fine jacket that differs from that of the American edition; scarce.   Ken Lopez 74-296 1996 $750.00

MC CARTHY, CORMAC   The Stone Mason. New York: Ecco, 1994. 1-350 numbered and signed copies; new in slipcase.   Thomas Dorn 9-179 1996 $375.00

MC CARTHY, CORMAC   The Stonemason. Ecco, 1994. 1 of 350 numbered and signed copies; as new in publisher's slipcase.   Book Time 2-282 1996 $350.00

MC CARTHY, CORMAC   The Stonemason. Hopewell: Ecco Press, 1994. One of 350 copies numbered and signed by author; housed in maroon cloth covered box; fine.   Lame Duck Books 19-325 1996 $450.00

MC CARTHY, CORMAC   The Stonemason. Hopewell: Ecco Press, 1994. 1st edition; limited to 350 copies, signed by author; 8vo; cloth, slipcase, as new.   James S. Jaffe 34-471 1996 $350.00

MC CARTHY, CORMAC   The Stonemason. New York: Ecco, 1994. 1/350 numbered and signed copies; fine in slipcase.   Alice Robbins 15-214 1996 $400.00

MC CARTHY, JUSTIN   Charing Cross to St. Paul's. London: Seeley and Co., 1891. Number 58 of 100 large paper copies; folio; half title, title list of illustrations, 59 pages, 12 plates in proof tissue and text illustrations by Joseph Pennell; ex-library in contemporary morocco backed green cloth.   Marlborough 162-173 1996 £150.00

MC CARTHY, JUSTIN   The Grey River. London: Seeley and Co. Ltd., 1889. Limited to 230 copies (30 signed for presentation); Folio; iv, 87 pages, 12 etched plates in sepia signed in pencil by Menpes; uncut in original cloth titled in gilt on upper cover, bit soiled, corners bumped, scattered foxing on edges, and to several margins.   Marlborough 162-174   1996 £500.00

MC CAULEY, KIRBY   Dark Forces. New York: Viking, 1980. 1st edition; this copy signed by Etchison, Wagner, Grant, Gahan Wilson. fine in dust jacket.   Aronovitz 57-36 1996 $150.00

MC CAULEY, KIRBY   Dark Forces. New York: Viking Press, 1980. 1st edition; fine in dust jacket with very slight tear to front panel, inscribed by Charles L. Grant and Joe Haldeman and dated Nov. 1980.   Bud Schweska 12-454 1996 $135.00

MC CLELLAN, GEORGE   Organization of the Army of the Potomac and Of its Campaigns in Virginia and Maryland, from July 26, 1861 to November 7, 1862. Washington: 1864. 1st edition; 242 pages; original binding.   W. Bruce Fye 71-1396 1996 $100.00

M'CLINTOCK, FRANCIS LEOPOLD   A Narrative of the Discovery of the Fate of Sir John Franklin and His Companions. London: John Murray, Albemarle St.... 1859. 1st edition; 8vo; (vii-xxii), (xxvii), 1-351 pages, 352-403 pages, 3 pages ads at rear, frontispiece, 13 plates, 2 large folding maps and 1 facsimile; lacks final map of the Arctic regions usually found in rear pocket; full green straight grain morocco, elaborate gilt tooled border, corners slightly bumped, gilt titles and gilt tooled ships to panelled spines.   Beeleigh Abbey BA56-69 1996 £200.00

MC CLINTOCK, JAMES H.   Mormon Settlement in Arizona. Phoenix: by the author, 1921. 1st edition; xi, 307 pages, numerous illustrations, folding map; green cloth, gilt, covers lightly spotted, bookplate, very good. Flake 5120.   Argonaut Book Shop 113-433 1996 $125.00

MC CLINTOCK, JAMES H.   Phoenix Arizona in the Great Salt River Valley. Phoenix: Phoenix and Maricopa County Board of Trade, September, 1908. 1st edition; 20 pages; illustrations; original printed wrappers, title printed in red on front cover, minor soiling, very good. Michael D. Heaston 23-23 1996 $125.00

MAC CLURE, MAC DONALD & CO.   Yacht Raching on the Clyde and Belfast Lough. Season 1898. Glasgow: c. 1899. 1st edition; oblong folio; pages (iv), 60 photographic plates; original blue cloth, blocked in gilt; very good.   Sotheran PN32-81 1996 £575.00

M'COMBIE, WILLIAM   Memoirs of Alexander Bethune... Aberdeen: George and Robert King, 1845. ?edition; 8vo; (2), vii, (8)-390 pages; final leaf of ads, but without leaf before title (blank on half title); contemporary half calf, gilt, very good.   John Drury 82-22 1996 £50.00

MC CONATHY, DALE   Hollywood Costume: Glamour! Glitter! Romance! New York: Harry N. Abrams, Inc., 1976. 1st edition; silk brocade; very fine in publishers printed mylar dust jacket.   Hermitage SP95-861 1996 $200.00

MC CONKEY, HARRIET E. BISHOP   Dakota War Whoop. St. Paul: Published for the author, 1864. 430 pages; illustrations; original boards and spine, recased, new endpapers; generally very good. Scarce. Howes M58; Field 979.   Dumont 28-92 1996 $175.00

MC CONKIE, BRUCE R.   Mormon Doctrine. Salt Lake City: Bookcraft, 1958. 1st edition; 1st printing; 776 pages; rare pebbled black buckram rather than standard green cloth, some fading to spine and slight shelf wear, else very good, scarce.   Orrin Schwab 10-63 1996 $105.00

MC CONNELL, H. H.   Five Years a Cavalryman; or, Sketches of Regular Army Life on the Texas Frontier, Twenty Odd Years Ago. Jacksboro: Rogers, 1889. 1st edition; 319 pages; pink paper stock, original cloth, minor washed out spots on board edges and one on spine, else nice. Howes M59; Graff 2579; Adams Herd 1380; Guns 1393; Jenkins BTB 131.   Bohling Book Co. 191-93 1996 $350.00

MC CORKLE, JAMES   Incident on the Bark Columbia. Being Letters Received and Sent by Captain McCorkle and the Crew of His Whaler, 1860-1862. Cummington: Cummington Press, 1941. 1st edition; 1/300 copies, printed by hand (#172); 12mo; (32) leaves, beige linen like cloth, near fine.   Robert F. Lucas 42-86 1996 $150.00

MC CORKLE, JILL   The Cheerleader. Chapel Hill: Algonquin, 1984. Unbound galley proofs, consisting of 9 numbered unstitched book signatures; inscribed by author for Dick and Nancy. Fine.   Thomas Dorn 9-181 1996 $600.00

MC CORKLE, JILL   July 7th. Chapel Hill: Algonquin, 1984. Unrevised proof; printed orange wrappers; crease to bottom front corner, else fine. Thomas Dorn 9-182 1996 $500.00

M'CORMAC, HENRY   On the Best Means of Improving the Moral and Physical Condition of the Working Classes Being an Address, Delivered on the Opening of the First Monthly Scientific Meetings of the Belfast Mechanic's Inst. London: Longman, 1830. 1st edition; 8vo; 24 pages; paper somewhat browned and with light dampstain in outer for corners original plain wrappers. Black 4054; Kress C2569; Williams I 550; Goldsmiths 24610.   John Drury 82-158 1996 £85.00

MC CORMICK, RICHARD   Arizona: It's Resources and Prospects. New York: D. Van Nostrand, 1865. 1st separate printing; 22 pages; folding map; original printed wrappers, light wear to spine, else fine. Graff 2583; Howes M65; Wagner Camp 419.   Argonaut Book Shop 113-437 199 $175.00

MC CORMICK, RICHARD   A Visit to the Camp Before Sevastopol. Ne York: D. Appleton, 1855. Only edition; 12mo; folding lithograph map, 2 double page maps, 6 litho plates, all fine, 4 pages ads; owner's name on title; original cloth, spine gilt; light foxing of text, but very good. Trebizond 39-92 1996 $175.00

MC COY, JOSEPH G.   Historic Sketches of the Cattle Trade of the West and Southwest. Kansas City: Ramsey, Millett & Hudson, 1874. 1st edition; 1st printing; thick 8vo; rebound in library style cloth with gilt ruling and titling, numerous repairs to margins with several pages guarded or repaired with linen library tape, three text pages and 8 ad pages supplied in facsimile and laid in, some soiling and edge wear to text, several signatures on recto of frontispiece, cloth worn at extremities, despite faults, an acceptable copy of a rare book. Howes M72; Dary 166; Herd 1385; Graff 2594; Streeter 2366.   Glenn Books 36-180 1996 $550.00

MC CRACKEN, HAROLD   The Frederic Remington Book, a Pictorial History of the West. Garden City: Doubleday, 1966. 1st edition; 1 of 50 numbered and signed copies, small folio; 284 pages, profusely illustrate color frontispiece; preceded by tipped in color illustrations; full brown leather with gilt stamping, all edges gilt, slipcase; very nearly fine, slipcase bumped at corner, split along one edge. Dykes 50 Great; Remington 805.   Bohling Book Co. 192-193 1996 $350.00

MC CRACKEN, HAROLD   The West of Buffalo Bill. New York: 1974. 1st edition; oblong 4to; 290 pages; profusely illustrated; gold stamped cloth; fine in dust jacket.   Gene W. Baade 1094-106 1996 $100.00

MC CREERY, JOHN   The Press, a Poem. Liverpool & London: 1803-27. 4to; (2), vii, (1), 29, 20; vii, (1), 80; 2 parts in 1; frontispiece, several vignettes; recent quarter calf, morocco spine label.   Maggs Bros. Ltd. 1191-191 1996 £270.00

MC CULLERS, CARSON 1917-1967   Sweet As a Pickle and Clean as Pig. Boston: Houghton Mifflin, 1964. 1st edition; illustrations by Rolf Gerard; very fine, crisp copy in dust jacket.   Bromer Booksellers 87-174 1996 $95.00

MC CULLOCH, J.   Urban Renewal: A Study of the City of Toronto. Toronto: Advisory Committee on the Urban Renewal Study, 1956. 4to; 193) pages, illustrations, maps; tables; stiff paper covers; very good. Hugh Anson-Cartwright 87-425 1996 $100.00

MC CULLOCH, JOHN RAMSEY 1789-1864   A Dictionary, Practical, Theoretical and Historical Of Commerce and Commercial Navitation. London: Longmans, 1850. New edition; Half title, folding maps, 32 pag catalog (June 1, 1850); original dark green cloth, spine only slightly fad and rubbed on following hinge, very good.   Jarndyce 103-198 1996 £250.00

MC CULLOCH, JOHN RAMSEY 1789-1864   The Principles of Political Economy... Edinburgh: William Tait, 1843. 3rd edition; 8vo; xxix, 574 pages, without half title; contemporary dark blue half calf, spine fully g with raised bands and label, marbled edges, binding little rubbed, over fine. Goldsmiths 33140; Kress C6108.   John Drury 82-160 1996 £250.00

MC CULLOCH, JOHN RAMSEY 1789-1864   A Statistical Account of the British Empire... London: Charles Knight and Co., 1837. 1st edition; 8vo; 2 volumes, xi, (1), 630; viii, 692 pages; original publisher's brown cloth, little wear to head of spines, otherwise good. Goldsmiths 29789; Kress C4426; Einaudi (3572) has only 2nd ed.   John Drury 82-159 1996 £250.00

MAC CURDY, JOHN T.   War Neuroses. Cambridge: Cambridge University Press, 1918. 1st edition; original binding, covers very slightly marked, cover edges slightly rubbed, corners slightly bumped, very good.   Ulysses 39-644 1996 £55.00

M'DERMOT, MARTIN   A Philosophical Inquiry Into the Source of the Pleasures Derived from Tragic Representations... London: Sherwood, Jones and Co., 1824. 1st edition; 8vo; viii, 405, (3) pages, complete with final leaf of ads, few emphasis marks and underlinings in pencil; recently well bound in old style half calf, gilt, small library stamp on blank verso of title, else very good. Arnott & Robinson 3723.   John Drury 82-161 1996 £175.00

MC DEVITT, ELIZABETH   Octopus. Berkeley: Flying Fish Press, 1992. One of 100 copies; page size 10 3/4 x 13 1/2 inches; printed on Magnani Pescia and Crescent papers, letterpress in cochin bold italic; illustrations by Julie Chen, each page is set into double sided accordion fold that lifts up and moves in a wave like motion, cutout area is of varying shapes on each different page so that looking down into the book one is reminded of a whirlpool with the octopus' tenacles swirling about the bottom; bound in inky blue-green silk over boards, housed in matching clamshell box with paper label on front cover and on spine. Priscilla Juvelis 95/1-94 1996 $350.00

MAC DONALD ROBERT   The Romance of Canadian History. Calgary: the Ballantrae Foundation, 1974/78. 31 cm; volumes II and III; vii, 232 pages; vii, 280 pages, frontispieces, illustrations, many in color; portraits, maps; gilt stamped russet cloth; fine.   Rockland Books 38-135 1996 $100.00

MAC DONALD, ARCHIBALD   Peace River. A Canoe Voyage from Hudson's Bay to Pacific, by the Late George Simpson... in 1828. Journal of the Late Chief Factor, Archibald MacDonald... Ottawa: 1872. 1st printing; pages xix, 119; folding map; original binding, fine, preserved in quarter leather slipcase. Quite scarce. TPL 1496.   Stephen Lunsford 45-101 1996 $1,200.00

MAC DONALD, GEORGE 1824-1905   At the Back of the North Wind. Philadelphia: 1919. 1st edition; 8 full color plates by Jessie Willcox Smith; top edge gilt, extremities of spine and 2 corners min. rubbed; fine.   Polyanthos 22-459 1996 $100.00

MAC DONALD, GEORGE 1824-1905   Cross Purposes. London: Blackie, ca. 1905. 1st separate edition; octavo; 96 pages, plus 12 pages ads; color frontispiece by H. M. Brock; blue cloth, with pictorial label stamped to front cover and spine, spine slightly darkened and corners bumped, else fine.   Bromer Booksellers 87-142 1996 $225.00

MAC DONALD, JOHN D.   April Evil. New York: Dell, 1956. Dell First edition; signed; pictorial paper wrappers with very light wear; near fine with first page slightly torn.   Quill & Brush 102-1182 1996 $100.00

MAC DONALD, JOHN D.   Cinnamon Skin. New York: Harper & Row, 1982. 1st edition; fine in dust jacket; inscribed by author on titlepage.   Quill & Brush 102-1212 1996 $125.00

MAC DONALD, JOHN D.   The Crossroads. New York: Simon & Schuster, 1959. 1st edition; spine ends lightly rubbed, page and cover edges slightly darkened, otherwise near fine in lightly soiled dust jacket slightly rubbed on edges with few short closed tears.   Quill & Brush 102-1189 1996 $125.00

MAC DONALD, JOHN D.   A Deadly Shade of Gold. London: Robert Hale, 1965. 1st hardback edition; near fine with page edges lightly soiled, in very good price clipped dust jacket, with rubbing, light chipping, edge wear and back panel soiled.   Quill & Brush 102-1195 1996 $100.00

MAC DONALD, JOHN D.   A Deadly Shade of Gold. Philadelphia: Lippincott, 1974. 1st edition; fine with owner's signature on front endpaper, in very bright, near fine, pricce clipped dust jacket with minor rubbing, few very light creases and one very small closed tear on top of back panel.   Quill & Brush 102-1205 1996 $200.00

MAC DONALD, JOHN D.   A Deadly Shade of Gold. Philadelphia: Lippincott, 1974. 1st U.S. hardbound edition; name, fine in near fine dust jacket with light edgewear and short closed tear.   Janus Books 36-224 1996 $150.00

MAC DONALD, JOHN D.   Free Fall in Crimson. New York: Harper & Row, 1981. 1st edition; fine in dust jacket with one small closed tear on upper front panel; signed inscription by author.   Quill & Brush 102-1211 1996 $125.00

MAC DONALD, JOHN D.   The Good Old Stuff. New York: Harper & Row, 1982. 1st edition; fine in dust jacket; inscribed by author on titlepage.   Quill & Brush 102-1213 1996 $125.00

MAC DONALD, JOHN D.   The Green Ripper. New York: Lippincott, 1979. 1st edition; short inscription from author; fine with very light soiling on bottom page edges, near fine dust jacket with very light impression on front panel and one very small closed tear on top of back panel, otherwise very nice.   Quill & Brush 102-1207 1996 $150.00

MAC DONALD, JOHN D.   The Long Lavender Look. Philadelphia: J. B. Lippincott, 1972. 1st edition; tips lightly rubbed, titlepage hinge starting, still tight, otherwise very good or better in lightly rubbed dust jacket with touch of soiling on rear panel and only minor edge wear.   Quill & Brush 102-1202 1996 $175.00

MAC DONALD, JOHN D.   Nightmare in Pink. Philadelphia: J. B. Lippincott, 1976. 1st hardback edition; touch of minor shelfwear, otherwise fine in dust jacket, with edges lightly rubbed and one short creased but closed tear, remainder mark on bottom page edges, not immediately noticeable, very close to spine.   Quill & Brush 102-1206 1996 $150.00

MAC DONALD, JOHN D.   The Scarlet Ruse. New York: Lippincott, 1980. 1st edition; fine in price clipped dust jacket with very light crease on top front panel and minor rubbing.   Quill & Brush 102-1210 1996 $125.00

MAC DONALD, JOHN D.   A Tan and Sandy Silence. London: Robert Hale & Co., 1971. 1st hardback edition; very good or better with offset from sticker (removed) on front pastedown, light soiling on page edges and residue on front endpaper from someone attempting to erase ink mark, in dust jacket with light rubbing, two closed tears, minor edge wear and back panel is slightly soiled.   Quill & Brush 102-1200 1996 $100.00

MAC DONALD, R. J.   The History of the Dress of the Royal Regiment of Artillery, 1625-1897. London: Henry Sotheran, 1899. Limited to 1500 copies; 4to; xx, 131 pages, errata leaf; 25 chromolithograph plates by author, numerous monochrome text illustrations; cloth backed printed boards, spine rather soiled, corners worn, rear joint sprung.   Thomas Thorp 489-200 1996 £50.00

MAC DONALD, ROSS   Black Money. New York: Knopf, 1966. 1st edition; fine in dust jacket with very light edge wear and one very small tear on lower back panel   Quill & Brush 102-1221 1996 $200.00

MAC DONALD, ROSS   Blue City. New York: Knopf, 1947. 1st edition; sticker abrasion from pastedown, some spotting to cloth, very good in just about very good jacket with chip at upper back panel and several tiny chips at front flap, apparently an early signature; nice.   Ken Lopez 74-276 1996 $750.00

MAC DONALD, ROSS   The Drowning Pool. New York: Alfred A. Knopf, 1950. 1st edition; very good+ in dust jacket which is slightly worn at edges, desirable copy.   Steven C. Bernard 71-337 1996 $850.00

MAC DONALD, ROSS   On Crime Writing. Santa Barbara: Capra Press, 1973. 1st edition; 1/250 numbered copies, signed by author; fine, issued without jacket.   Janus Books 36-249 1996 $150.00

MAC DONALD, ROSS   Self-Portrait: Ceaselessly Into the Past. Santa Barbara: Capra Press, 1981. One of 250 numbered copies, signed by author and by Eudora Welty who provided introduction; (an additional 26 were issued in slipcase); plain black simulated leather covers with gold spine lettering; fine.   Quill & Brush 102-1227 1996 $150.00

MAC DONALD, ROSS   The Three Roads. New York: Knopf, 1948. 1st edition; fine in near fine dust jacket, very nice.   Ken Lopez 74-277 1996 $750.00

MAC DONALD, ROSS   The Zebra Striped Hearse. New York: Knopf, 1962 1st edition; fine in lightly soiled dust jacket with few short closed tears.   Quill & Brush 102-1220 1996 $225.00

MC DONALD, WILLIAM A.   The Political Meeting Places of the Greeks. Baltimore: Johns Hopkins Press, 1943. 8vo; xix, 308 pages, 31 figures, 19 plates; original cloth.   Archaeologia Luxor-3689   1996 $150.00

M'DONNELL, ALEXANDER GREENFIELD   A Narrative of Transactions in the Red River Country... London: 1819. Pages xix, 85, large folding hand colored map; untrimmed, original printed wrappers; fine, crisp copy; preserved in quarter morocco clamshell box; inscribed by Simon McGillivray on front wrapper. Peel 59; Streeter VI 3682; TPL 1100; Wagner Camp Becker 15c.   Stephen Lunsford 45-100 1996 $4,500.00

MC DONNELL, JOSEPH   Gold-Tooled Bookbindings Commissioned by Trinity College Dublin in the Eighteenth Century. Leixlip: Irish Georgian Society, 1987. Folio; xviii, 340 pages; color frontispiece, 10 text illustrations, 106 full page plates (8 in color, blue cloth, gilt, photo illustrated dust jacket.   Kenneth Karmiole 1NS-49 1996 $100.00

MC DONOGH, JOHN   The Last Will and Testament of John McDonogh, Late of Macdonoghville, State of Louisiana, Alos, His Memoranda of Instructions to His Executors, Relative to the Management of His Estate. New Orleans: printed at the Job Office of The Dailey Delta, 1851. 1st edition; 8vo; disbound, first signature rather browned, slight chipping, very scarce Sabin 43175.   Ximenes 109-181 1996 $150.00

MC DOUGLAS, HENRY C.   Recollections 1844-1909. Kansas City: 1910. 1st edition; 466 pages, frontispiece; cloth; very good+. Scarce. 6 Guns 1401.   T. A. Swinford 49-755 1996 $100.00

MC DOWELL, J. R.   Henry Wallace; or the Victim of Lottery Gambling. New York: Wilson and Swain, 1832. Only edition; 18mo; pages 108; original orange boards, brown cloth back.   Howard S. Mott 227-92 1996 $350.00

MC DOWELL, J. R.   Henry Wallace; or the Victim of Lottery Gambling. New York: Wilson & Swain, 1832. Only edition; 18mo; 108 pages; original orange boards, brown cloth back. Wright I 1748.   Howard S. Mott 227-159 1996 $350.00

MC ELRATH, THOMSON P.   A Press Club Outing. New York: the League, 1893. Quarto; 150 pages; illustrations; original cloth, gilt title; nice; inscribed by Chas. W. Price, a delegate.   Bohling Book Co. 191-368 1996 $200.00

MC ELROY, JOSEPH   Hind's Kidnap. New York: H&R, 1969. 1st edition; very good+ copy in dust jacket; inscribed by author to his parents-in-law at the time, Sala and Lefty.   Lame Duck Books 19-327 1996 $550.00

MC ELROY, JOSEPH   Ship Rock: a Place. Concord: Ewert, 1980. Hors commerce copy in the same format as the 1/26 issue, signed by author; half leather and paper covered boards, some rubbing to boards, else near fine; this was presented to a family member.   Lame Duck Books 19-328 1996 $200.00

MC ELROY, JOSEPH   Ship Rock, a Place from Men and Women: a Novel in Progress. Concord: Ewert, 1980. 1st edition; number 22 of 226 numbered copies, signed by author; thin 8vo; titlepage printed in brown and black; gilt stamped brown cloth over ochre boards, brown endpapers; fine.   George J. Houle 68-88 1996 $125.00

MC ELROY, JOSEPH   A Smuggler's Bible. New York: Harcourt Brace, 1966. Advance reading copy; author's first book; printed tan wrappers, very good; signature of Anne Rice on front panel (perhaps she review it?).   Pettler & Lieberman 28-171 1996 $135.00

MC ELROY, JOSEPH   A Smuggler's Bible. New York: HB&W, 1966. 1st edition; scarce first book, very good+ copy in jacket whose spine, unlike most other copies, is unfaded.   Lame Duck Books 19-326 1996 $250.00

MC ELROY, JOSEPH   Women and Men. New York: Knopf, 1987. 1st edition; review copy; fine in dust jacket with publisher's ads laid in. Lame Duck Books 19-329 1 996 $100.00

MC EWAN, CALVIN W.   Soundings at Tell Fakhariyah. Chicago: University of Chicago Press, 1958. 4to; xvii, 103 pages, 87 plates; original cloth, neat, ex-library copy.   Archaeologia Luxor-2433 1996 $175.00

MAC FALL, HALDANE   The Splendid Wayfaring. London: Simpkin Marshall, 1913. 4to; xiii, 201 pages; frontispiece, decorated titlepage an numerous line drawn text illustrations by Lovat Fraser, Gaudier-Brzeska the author and Edward Gordon-Craig; original decorated red watered si cloth gilt, top edge gilt, very fine in worn slipcase. Presentation copy from author, with his ALS loosely inserted.   Thomas Thorp 489-201 1996 £80.00

MAC FARLAN, ROBERT   A New Alphabetical Vocabulary, Gailic and English... Edinburgh: ptd. for the author by John Moir, 1795. Uncut in original boards, spine slightly defective; nice.   Jarndyce 103-611 19 £200.00

MAC FARLANE, WALTER & CO.   Illustrated Catalogue of MacFarlane Castings. Glasgow: MacFarlane, n.d., c. 1880's. 6th edition; 4to; 2 volumes, continuously paginated, 620 pages, many illustrations, issued without parts I-III (pages 7-82) and complete thus; original lettered clot fine, clean set.   Elton Engineering 10-99 1996 £280.00

MAC FIE, MATHEW   Vancouver Island and British Columbia: Their History, Resources and Prospects. London: Longman, Green, Longman Roberts & Green, 1865. 22.5 cm; xxi, 574, (2) pages; frontispiece, illustrations, 2 folding maps, tables; gilt stamped marbled cloth, rebacked, backstrip laid down, fine, uncut, bright copy. TPL 4423; Smit 6334; Lowther 255.   Rockland Books 38-136 1996 $375.00

MAC GILL, STEVENSON   Remarks on Prisons. Glasgow: printed by Hedderwick & Co., 1810. 1st edition; 8vo; (4), 79, (1) pages, tear in on leaf neatly repaired (no loss of surface), recent cloth, lettered in gilt. Very scarce. Goldsmiths 20158.   John Drury 82-162 1996 £200.00

MC GLASHAN, C. F.   History of the Donner Party. Truckee: Crowley McGlashan, 1879. 1st edition; 193 pages; original blindstamped brown cloth, gilt lettered spine, bookplate, expert repair to lower spine area, minor wear to lower front corner, overall, fine copy. Graff 2610; Howes M102; Zamorano 80 53; Cowan p. 406.   Argonaut Book Shop 113-4 1996 $1,750.00

MC GOWAN, EDWARD   Narrative of Edward McGowan, Including a Full Account of the Author's Adventures and Perils While Persecuted b the San Francisco Vigilance Committee of 1856. San Francisco: Printed by Thomas C. Russell, 1917. Reprint of 1857 edition, one of 200 numbered copies; 12mo; pages viii, 9-250, tinted frontispiece, numerou full page tinted illustrations, title in red and black; original light brown boards, paper spine label, very fine, clean copy; presentation inscriptio from printer, Thomas C. Russell to Herbert I. Priestley.   Argonaut Bo Shop 113-439 1996 $300.00

M'GREGOR, JAMES   Medical Sketches of the Expedition to Egypt fr India. London: 1804. 1st edition; 8vo; folding table, old stamps of Bedford medical library on title and name erased; contemporary tree ca bit worn, possibly lacking a half title, bound at end a 16 page Murray cat. of new mecial books.   Maggs Bros. Ltd. 1190-457 1996 £200.

M'GREGOR, JOHN   British America. Edinburgh: William Blackwood/London: T. Cadell, 1832. 1st edition; 8 1/2 x 5 1/4 inches; 2 volumes; folding maps as frontispiece in each volume, one other foldin map, 6 full page maps, 2 small engravings in text, half title in second (though not first) volume; attractive red half morocco by Bayntun-Riviere, cloth sides, raised bands, spine with gilt ruled compartments and gitl titling, marbled endpapers, top edge gilt; very fi in appealing unworn binding. Sabin 43280.   Phillip J. Pirages 33-372 1996 $450.00

MC GUANE, THOMAS   The Bushwhacked Piano. New York: Simon Schuster, 1971. 1st edition; fine in fine dust jacket.   Ken Lopez 74-3 1996 $375.00

MC GUANE, THOMAS   Keep the Change. Boston: Houghton Mifflin/Seymour Lawrence, 1989. 1st edition; fine in fine dust jacket and signed by author on titlepage, with passage from text quoted in his hand.   Ken Lopez 74-312 1996 $125.00

MC GUANE, THOMAS   Ninety-Two in the Shade. New York: Farrar Straus and Giroux, 1973. 1st edition; turquoise cloth spine, light blue cloth boards, fine in fine dust jacket, signed by author.   Orpheus Books 17-183 1996 $175.00

MC GUANE, THOMAS   Nothing But Blue Skies. Boston: Houghton Mifflin, 1992. 1/200 copies, signed; fine in slipcase.   Bev Chaney, Jr. 23-419 1996 $125.00

MC GUANE, THOMAS   To Skin a Cat. New York: Dutton, 1986. Review copy, fine in dust jacket and signed by author.   Ken Lopez 74-310 1996 $125.00

MC GUANE, THOMAS   To Skin a Cat. London: Secker and Warburg, 1987. 1st British edition; fine in dust jacket and signed by author in 1992.   Ken Lopez 74-311 1996 $125.00

MC GUIRE, J. A.   The Alaska-Yukon Gamelands. 1921. illustrations, apart from some pages roughly opened, near fine copy.   David Grayling J95Biggame-424 1996 £75.00

M'HENRY, JAMES   The Jackson Wreath, or National Souvenir. Philadelphia: Jacob Maas, 1829. 1st edition; 8vo; pages (viii), (9)-88, 3 leaves of music; 7 plates and colored folding map; original green boards, red leather back and corners; Sabin 101164.   Howard S. Mott 227-93 1996 $300.00

MC HENRY, LAWRENCE   Garrison's History of Neurology Revised and Enlarged with a Bibliography of Classical, Original and Standard Works in Neurology. Springfield: 1969. 552 pages; illustrations; original binding, dust jacket; GM 5019.8.   W. Bruce Fye 71-1402 1996 $200.00

MC HENRY, LAWRENCE   Garrison's History of Neurology. Springfield: 1969. 8vo; 552 pages; original binding.   James Tait Goodrich K40-181 1996 $195.00

MC ILVAINE, C..   Toadstools, Mushrooms, Fungi, Edible and Poisonous One Thousand American Fungi. Indianapolis: 1900. Limited to 750 numbered copies, signed by author; thick 4to; 704; 182 illustrations, including many plates; original cloth, covers dirty, spine darkened, front joint cracked, yellowed, institutional bookplate, no sticker on spine.   Raymond M. Sutton VII-248 1996 $125.00

MAC ILWAIN, G.   Memoirs of John Abernethy, F.R.S. London: 1853. 1st edition; 8vo; 2 volumes; portrait; cloth, worn and bit soiled, one section sprung; the BMA copy with stamps.   Maggs Bros. Ltd. 1190-458 1996 £60.00

MC INTOSCH, DAVID GREGG   The Campaign of Chancellorsville. Richmond: Wm. Ellis Jones' Sons, 1915. 1st edition; 59 pages; original printed wrpapers; near fine, signed presentation by author. Dornbusch II 1682; Haynes 11926.   McGowan Book Co. 65-56 1996 $350.00

MAC KANESS, GEORGE   Admiral Arthur Phillip, Founder of New South Wales, 1738-1814. Sydney: Angus & Robertson, 1937. 1st edition; 8vo; xvi, 536 pages; 35 plates, 2 folding; original cloth, very good to nice. James Fenning 133-262 1996 £115.00

MAC KAY, ALEXANDER   The Western World, or Tavels in the United States in 1846-47... London: R. Bentley, 1849. 3 volumes, xix, 340, folded frontispiece map; iv, 321; iv, 374 pages; folded frontispiece map; rebacked, retaining original brown cloth covered boards, new black cloth backstrips, gilt spine labels, new endleaves, some wear, corners chipped, some passages marked with pencil, else very good. Howes M1117 (2nd edition, same year as 1st).   Bohling Book Co. 191-366 1996 $250.00

MAC KAY, ANGUS M.   The Brontes. New York: Dodd Mead, 1897. 1st American edition; 7 1/2 x 5 inches; pages (xiii), 187, 3 pages ads rear; green vertical ribbed cloth, gilt titling to front cover and backstrip, top edge gilt, others uncut; free endpapers discolored, very good.   Ian Hodgkins 78-346 1996 £55.00

MAC KAY, CHARLES   The Scenery and Poetry of the English Lakes. London: Longman, Brown, etc., 1846. 8vo; pages xvi, 235; 8 full page vignettes, 52 text illustrations; full polished calf, gilt, by Riviere, extremities little rubbed; margins faintly browned, flyleaves trifle spotted, but handsome copy. Bicknell 138.1.   R.F.G. Hollett & Son 78-1089 1996 £165.00

MAC KAY, CHARLES   The Scenery and Poetry of the English Lakes. London: Longman Brown, 1846. 8vo; pages xvi, 235, 32 (ads), tinted woodcut frontispiece and title, 8 full page vignettes, 52 text illustrations; few stains to ad leaves, otherwise very nice; original blindstamped green cloth, gilt, neatly recased. Bicknell 138.1.   R.F.G. Hollett & Son 78-1090 1996 £145.00

MAC KAY, CHARLES   The Thames and Its Tributaries; Or Rambles Among the Rivers... London: Richard Bentley, 1840. 1st edition; tall 8vo; 2 volumes; pages xi, 400, vii, 412 pages; small engravings in text; full contemporary green calf, raised bands, gilt compartments, leather labels, hinges tender, binding rubbed, wear at heads of spines, gilt in compartments bit flaked, otherwise good set.   David Mason 71-25 1996 $320.00

MC KAY, CLAUDE   Banjo: a Story without a Plot. New York: Harper, 1929. 1st edition; two small holes in cloth of the front outer joint, otherwise this is fine in the great pictorial dust jacket with four very small chips.   Captain's Bookshelf 38-149 1996 $650.00

MAC KAY, ERNEST   Report on the Excavation of the "A" Cemetery at Kish, Mesopotamia (Part I). (and) A Sumerian Palace and the "A" Cemetery at Kish, Mesopotamia (Part II). Chicago: Field Museum of Natural History, 1925-29. Folio; 2 volumes, 215 pages, 62 plates, 1 map; wrappers, spines tape reinforced at top and bottom.   Archaeologia Luxor-2410 1996 $250.00

MAC KAY, J. T.   Flora Hibernica... Dublin: 1836. 8vo; pages xxxiv, (iii), 354, (ii), 279, (1); half calf.   Wheldon & Wesley 207-1490 1996 £140.00

MAC KAY, JOHN HENRY   The Anarchists. A Picture of Civilization at the Close of the 19th Century. Boston: Benj. R. Tucker, 1891. 1st edition; original cloth, near fine.   Beasley Books 82-324 1996 $200.00

MC KAY, RICHARD C.   Some Famous Sailing Ships andd Their Builder Donald McKay, A Study of the American Sailing Packet and Clipper Eras. New York: 1928. Limited to 250 numbered and signed copies, author's autograph edition, printed on specially made paper; 10 x 6 inches; 395 pages with index; 10 color plates and 48 other illustrations; minor cover wear and soil, signed by publisher.   John K. King 77-772 1996 $125.00

MC KAY, SETH SHEPARD   Debates in the Texas Constitutional Convention of 1875. Austin: University of Texas, 1930. 1st edition; 471 pages;   Maggie Lambeth 30-323 1996 $100.00

M'KEAN, JOSEPH   Catalogue of the Library of the Rev. Joseph M'Kean, D.D., LL.D., Boylston Professor of Rhetoric and Oratory in the University of Cambridge. Boston: printed by John Eliot, 1818. 8vo; disbound, blank fore-edges irregularly trimmed, otherwise very good. McKay 184; Shaw and Shoemaker 44657.   Ximenes 109-15 1996 $500.00

MC KELL, C. M.   The Biology and Utlization of Shrubs. 1988. 8vo; c. 648 pages; illustrations; cloth.   Raymond M. Sutton VII-644 1996 $155.00

MC KELVEY, S. D.   Botanical Exploration of the Trans-Mississippi West 1790-1850. Jamaica Plain: 1955. Larage 8vo; pages xl, 1144; 6 folding maps, 3 full page maps and 2 maps in rear pocket; cloth, some browning to edges of pages, glassine dust jacket.   Raymond M. Sutton VI-1110 1996 $250.00

MC KELVEY, S. D.   The Lilac, a Monograph. London: 1928. 1st edition; London issue, with cancel title; folio; 176 plates (4 of color samples); cloth, trifle marked.   Maggs Bros. Ltd. 1190-36 1996 £200.00

MC KELVEY, S. D.   The Lilac, a Monograph. London: 1928. 4to; pages xvi, 581, 4 color charts and 172 half tone plates; cloth. Wheldon & Wesley 207-1842 1996 £160.00

MAC KENNA, F. SEVERNE   Chelsea Porcelain: The Red Anchor Wares. Leight on Sea: F. Lewis, 1951. Limited to 500 numbered copies; 4to; xvi, 105 pages; frontispiece, 156 illustrations on 78 plates; buckram. Thomas Thorp 489-202 1996 £50.00

M'KENNA, THEOBALD   Thoughts on the Civil Condition and Relations of the Roman Catholic Clergy, Religion and People, in Ireland. London: J. Budd, Feb. 1805. 1st English edition; 8vo; (4), 193 pages, first two leaves rather foxed and intermittent spotting, mostly insignificant, recent cloth, lettered in gilt. Goldsmiths 19155; not in Black or Kress.   John Drury 82-163 1996 £100.00

MAC KENTOSH, JOHN   Receipts for the Cure of Most Diseases Incident to the Human Family. New York: printed for the publisher, 1827. 1st edition; 12 pages; sewn as issued, some minor waterstaining; very good, rare. Gilcrease-Hargrett Cat. pp. 20-21 'rare'; Field 966.   Michael D. Heaston 23-209 1996 $550.00

MAC KENZIE, CECIL W.   Donald MacKenzie "King of the Northwest". Los Angeles: 1937. Limited to 100 numbered signed copies; pages 210; illustrations; original binding, very nice. Peel 3571 not noting this limited edition.   Stephen Lunsford 45-102 1996 $250.00

MAC KENZIE, GEORGE 1636-1691   The Laws and Customs of Scotland, in Matters Criminal. Edinburgh: the Heirs & successors of Andrew Anderson for Mr. Andrew Symson, 1699. 2nd edition; folio; (viii), (292), (vi), 30, (ii), 31-32, (iv), 33-66, (iv), 62 pages; titlepage in red and black, 4 secondary titlepages; contemporary calf, rebacked, corners repaired; edges rubbed, closed tears in titlepage neatly repaired, without loss, paper uniformly browned, some minor soiling. Sound copy, early (1703) bookplate of Earl (later First Duke) of Roxburgh. Wing M168; Aldis 3866.   Robert Clark 38-74 1996 £380.00

MAC KENZIE, GEORGE 1636-1691   Memoirs of the Affairs of Scotland from the Restoration of King Charles II. Edinburgh: 1821. Large paper; 4to; pages xii, 332; old diced calf, gilt, edges very rubbed and scraped, sometime rebacked in matching calf gilt, raised bands, upper joint cracking. Armorial bookplate, signed, of T. Dawson Brodie.   R.F.G. Hollett 76-182 1996 £60.00

MAC KENZIE, GEORGE 1636-1691   Pleadings, In Some Remarkable Cases Before the Supreme Courts of Scotland Since the Year 1661. Edinburgh: printed by the Heirs and Successors of Andrew Anderson, 1704. Later three quarter calf, joints repaired, embrowned, margins close, usable.   Meyer Boswell SL27-152 1996 $650.00

MAC KENZIE, HENRY   The Miscellaneous Works. London: Thomas and Joseph Allman, 1819. 12mo; 3 volumes; frontispiece; contemporary gilt bordered covers, lozenge shaped designs in center, spines gilt, morocco labels; fine set.   Trebizond 39-38 1996 $175.00

MAC KENZIE, JAMES   The Grievances and Oppresion of the Isles of Orkney and Shetland. Edinburgh: reprinted by Neill & Co., Pub. by Laing and Forbes, 1836. 8vo; 2 page list of subscribers; contemporary cloth, printed paper label, uncut, nice.   Anthony W. Laywood 108-196 1996 £85.00

MAC KENZIE, JOHN   Ten Years North of the Orange River. Edinburgh: Edmonston and Douglas, 1871. 1st edition; 8vo; frontispiece and 7 plates, folding map; original green cloth, some rubbing; very good; Theal p. 185.   Ximenes 109-182 1996 $250.00

MAC KENZIE, PETER   The Life of Thomas Muir. Glasgow: W. R. M'Phun, Simpkin & Marshall, London, 1831. 1st edition; 8vo; viii, 160 pages, complete with half title and 2 leaves of ads; original boards, rebacked, uncut. Loosely inserted is a 16 page pamphlet on Muir published as Pamphlet No. 1 in Fight for Freedom Series.   John Drury 82-192 1996 £95.00

MC KILLIP, P.   The Forgotten Beasts of Eld. Atheneum, 1974. 1st edition; fine in dust jacket; inscribed by author.   Aronovitz 57-792 1996 $150.00

MC KINLAY, JOHN   McKinlay's Journal of Exploration in the Interior of Australia (Burke Relief Expedtiion). Melbourne: F. F. Bailliere, 1861. 136 pages, 3 large folding maps; late 19th century plain cloth, with pocket for maps, gold gilt on spine; text lightly browned and little spotted, otherwise good+. Some cracks and failures at some folds in some of the maps; the Absolon copy. Ferguson 12057; Wantrup 177.   Antipodean 28-626 1996 $750.00

MAC KINNON, WILLIAM ALEXANDER   History of Civilisation and Public Opinion. London: Henry Colburn, 1849. 3rd edition; 8vo; 2 volumes; (ii), xxviii, 388; xii, 402 pages, complete with half title in each volume; contemporary morocco, fully gilt with raised bands and silk markers by Holloway of London, little wear to upper joints, else fine; from the library of David Murray, novelist and journalist, presentation copy inscribed by author.   John Drury 82-164 1996 £100.00

MC KINSTRY, ELIZABETH   The Fairy Alphabet: as Used by Merlin. New York: Viking Press, 1933. 1st edition; printed rectos only, each page with full page drawing in black and white; cloth backed colored pictorial boards, edges slightly rubbed, else very fresh, in chipped pictorial dust jacket. Very scarce.   Barbara Stone 70-12 1996 £225.00

MAC KINTOSH, JAMES   A Discourse on the Study of the Law of Nature and Nations... London: T. Cadell Jun. and W. Davies, J. Debrett and W. Clarke, 1799. 2nd edition; 8vo; (2), 68 pages, blank corner torn from one leaf, not touching printed surface, recently bound in cloth, spine lettered in gilt, few early pencillings, else very good. Sweet and Maxwell I 597(65); Lowndes 1442; Rand p. 357.   John Drury 82-165 1996 £125.00

MAC KINTOSH, JAMES   History of the Revolution in England in 1688 Comprising a View of the Reign of James Ii... London: Longmans, Rees, Orme, Brown, Green and Longman, 1834. 4to; clxxvi, 734 pages; contemporary half calf, raised bands, outer hinges rubbed and little tender, otherwise nice.   David Mason 71-24 1996 $200.00

MAC LAINE, ARCHIBALD   A Series of Letters, Addressed to Soame Jenyns, Esq; on Occasion of His View of the Internal Evidence of Christianity. London: for Charles Bathurst, 1777. 1st edition; 8vo; (6), 274 page,s complete with leaf of 'Corrections and Additions' (A3), but possibly wanting a following blank; contemporary calf gilt with raised bands and label; very good, armorial bookplate of Toft Hall.   John Drury 82-166 1996 £125.00

MAC LAREN, ARCHIBALD   The Fairy Family. London: Longmans, Brown, Green, Longmans & roberts, 1857. 1st edition; crown 8vo; (xvi), (284) pages; later half morocco by Tout, top edge gilt, spine tanned, damage to marbled sides neatly restored, endpapers gummed and adhesion damaged, little internal browning, one leaf slightly chipped, but looks better than it sounds.   Ash Rare Books Zenzybyr-65 1996 £195.00

MAC LAREN, ARCHIBALD CAMPBELL   The Perfect Batsman: J. B. Hobbs in Action. London: Cassell & Co., 1926. 1st edition; crown 8vo; (vi), (138) pages; cover lettering dull, touch dusty, one gathering mite proud, but good copy in original binding; in slightly ragged and dusty jacket. Padwick 703.   Ash Rare Books Zenzybyr-66 1996 £50.00

MC LAREN, MORAY   Corsica Boswell - Paoli, Johnson and Freedom. London: Martin Secker & Warburg, 1966. 1st edition; 6 black and white plates; original binding, top edge dusty, front free endpaper slightly browned through contact with TLS (review of this book) clipping; head and tail of spine, corners and bottom edge of lower cover bumped, very good in nicked and slightly creased, rubbed and dusty dust jacket; with pencilled ownerhsip signature of Frederick Pottle.   Ulysses 39-709 1996 £55.00

MC LAUGHLIN, J. FAIRFAX   The American Cyclops, the Hero of New Orleans and Spoiler of Silver Spoons. Baltimore: Kelly and Piet, 1868. 1st edition; 8vo; 27 pages; 12 plates; original cloth, edges worn; Sabin 43499.   M & S Rare Books 60-135 1996 $250.00

MAC LEAN, CHARLES   An Excursion in France, and Other Parts of the Continent of Europe... London: printed for T. N. Longman and C. Rees, 1804. 1st edition; tall 8vo; vii, 304 pages; recently rebound with blue morocco spine, cloth, new endpapers, pages browned with some foxing otherwise nice.   David Mason 71-69 1996 $120.00

MAC LEAN, HECTOR   The Watermillock and Matterdale Parish Registers, The Registers of the Parish of Watermillock in the County of Cumberland, Baptisms, Burials and Marriages (1579-1812); The Registers of Matterdale Church 1634-1720. Kendal: Titus Wilson, 1908. 8vo; xiv 212 vii, 46, 5 illustrations; flyleaves faintly browned, otherwise excellent copy original cloth, gilt.   R.F.G. Hollett & Son 78-596 1996 £95.00

MAC LEAN, JOHN   Parochial and Family History of the Deanery of Trigg Manor, in the County of Cornwall. London: Nichols & Sons, 1873-79. 4to; 3 volumes; numerous colored lithographs, folding pedigrees, coats of arms and other textual illustrations; contemporary half calf, red and black leather labels.   Charles W. Traylen 117-358 1996 £620.00

MAC LEAN, NORMAN   A River Runs through It. Chicago: University of Chicago, 1976. Uncorrected page proofs, quarto sheets in blue, illustrated card stock covers with blue tape spine, rare issue, fine in custom quarter leather clamshell box.   Ken Lopez 74-280 1996 $5,500.00

MAC LEAN, NORMAN   A River Runs Through It. Chicago: University of Chicago, 1976. Advance review copy; fine in near fine dust jacket, internally tape strengthened at spine crown and with slight fading to spine, with author photo laid in.   Ken Lopez 74-279 1996 $1,500.00

MAC LEAN, NORMAN   A River Runs Through It. Chicago: University of Chicago, 1976. 1st edition; lovely copy, jacket just a touch faded along spine; scarce, signed by author.   Lame Duck Books 19-295 1996 $2,500.00

MAC LEAN, NORMAN   A River Runs Through It. Chicago: University of Chicago Press, 1976. fine in lightly used dust jacket with couple of faint pencil line thin creases along top edge, jacket is not price clipped, ($7.95).   Thomas Dorn 9-253 1996 $875.00

MAC LEAN, NORMAN   A River Runs through it. West Hatfield: Pennyroyal Press, 1989. Limited to 200 copies, signed by author and artist; 8vo; wood engravings by Barry Moser; quarter red leather and marbled boards with printed label; as new.   James S. Jaffe 34-455 1996 $750.00

MC LEAN, RUARI   Victorian Book Design. University of California Press, 1972. 2nd edition; large 4to; pages xii, 241; 16 color plates, illustrations in half tone; original cloth; very good.   Claude Cox 107-309   1996 £85.00

MC LEAN, RUARI   Victorian Book Design and Color Printing. London: Faber & Faber, 1972. 2nd edition; 4to; plates; original cloth, dust jacket. Forest Books 74-174   1996 £95.00

MC LEAN, RUARI   Victorian Publishers' Book-Bindings in Paper. London: Gordon Fraser, 1983. 1st edition; 4to; frontispiece, illustrations; original decorated cloth, dust jacket.   Forest Books 74-175 1996 £50.00

MAC LENNAN, MALCOLM   Peasant Life. Sketches of the Villagers and Field Labourers in Glenaldie. London: Strahan and Co., 1871. 3rd edition; 8vo; xxxi, 32, 6 pages ads, 313 pages; inner hinges of volume two cracked, some light wear to extremities, still very good set.   David Mason 71-141 1996 $100.00

M'LEOD, ALEXANDER   Trial of Alexander M'Leod for the Murder of Amos Durfee; and as an Accomplice in the Burning of the Steamer Caroline, in the Niagara River... New York: printed at the Sun Office, 1841. 1st edition; 8vo; 32 pages; sewn as issued, unopened; foxed. R&B 41-3254. McDade 662. Sabin 43531; Staton & Tremaine 2469.   M & S Rare Books 60-295 1996 $750.00

MAC LEOD, IAIN   One Nation: a Tory Approach to Social Problems. London: 1950. 1st edition; signed by Edward Heath, MacLeod, Angus Maude and Robert Carr; wrappers, browned on spine and slightly faded around edges, otherwise very good.   Words Etcetera 94-603 1996 £75.00

M'LEOD, JOHN   Voyage of His Majesty's Ship Alceste, to China, Corea, and the Island of Lewchew, with an Account of Her Shipwreck. London: John Murray, 1820. 3rd edition; 8vo; pages 4, 339; portrait, folding map, 5 hand colored plates, extra illustrated with 2 maps and 4 plates from Perry's Narrative of the expedition to the China Seas; modern quarter brown morocco; Hill I p. 189; De Moraes II p. 1. Richard Adelson W94/95-115 1996 $450.00

MAC LEOD, JOSEPH GORDON   The Ecliptic. London: Faber & Faber, 1930. 1st edition; original binding, top edge dusty, bottom corners bumped, covers slightly marked, creased and dusty, cover edges worn and browned, very good, bookplate of literary agent, John Johnson; loosely inserted is a printed circular letter dated July 25th 1933 from author.   Ulysses 39-391 1996 £85.00

MAC LESIH, ARCHIBALD   Land of the Free. New York: Harcourt, Brace, 1938. 1st edition; 8vo; black and white photos; cloth, dust jacket; spine cocked, otherwise very good in somewhat worn and chipped jacket.   James S. Jaffe 34-541 1996 $150.00

MAC MANUS, SEAMUS   Woman of Seven Sorrows. Dublin: M. H. Gill, 1905. 1st edition; decorated wrappers, few creases and very small chip to yapped edges, fine, signed by author, scarce.   Captain's Bookshelf 38-150 1996 $175.00

MC MICHAEL, JOHN   Circulation: Proceedings of the Harvey Tercentneary Congress. Springfield: 1958. 1st American edition; 503 pages; original binding.   W. Bruce Fye 71-1408 1996 $100.00

MAC MICHAEL, WILLIAM 1784-1839   The Gold-Headed Cane. London: 1827. 1st edition; 179 pages; woodcut illustrations; quarter leather with marbled boards, rebacked, minor rubbing at head and tail of spine; GM 6709.   W. Bruce Fye 71-1333 1996 $600.00

MAC MICHAEL, WILLIAM 1784-1839   The Gold Headed Cane. London: John Murray, 1827. 1st edition; 8vo; pages (vii), 179, vignettes in text; uncut in contemporary half calf, blue paper sides, some foxing, binding worn but firm, with yellow octagonal label of Circulating Library, Colchester, to front pastedown. GM 6709.   Simon Finch 24-160 1996 £100.00

MAC MICHAEL, WILLIAM 1784-1839   The Gold Headed Cane. New York: 1915. 1st edition with introduction by William Osler; 4to; 137 pages, plus 15 plates; original binding, ex-library with small stamp on titlepage and verso of plates; overall fine. GM 6769.   W. Bruce Fye 71-1565 1996 $100.00

MAC MICHAEL, WILLIAM 1784-1839   Lives of British Physicians. London: 1830. 1st edition; 341 pages; several engraved portraits; recent quarter leather.   W. Bruce Fye 71-1336 1996 $100.00

MC MILLAN, TERRY   Disappearing Acts. New York: Viking, 1989. 1st edition; author's second book; near fine in dust jacket; signed by author. Lame Duck Books 19-21 1996 $100.00

MC MILLAN, TERRY   Mama. Boston: Houghton Mifflin Co., 1987. 1st edition; author's first book; unread fine copy in near fine dust jacket with superficial soiling, very nice.   Thomas Dorn 9-183 1996 $200.00

MC MURRAY, MARK   Type Specimens of Caliban Press. On the Occasion of Its Sixth Anniversary. Montclair: Caliban Press, 1991. 1st edition; one of 100 copies only; tall 8vo; all on various handmade papers, signed by writer/designer/printer, Mark McMurray; handset and printed on a Vandercook proofpress; bound by McMurray in paper wrappers with exposed sewing on spine.   Priscilla Juvelis 95/1-247 1996 $200.00

MC MURTRIE, DOUGLAS C.   The Beginnings of Printing in Arizona. Chicago: Black Cat Press, 1937. 1st edition; 44 pages; illustrations; original blue cloth, printed paper label on front cover.   Michael D. Heaston 23-44 1996 $125.00

MC MURTRIE, DOUGLAS C.   Eighteenth Century North Carolina Imprints 1749-1800. Chapel Hill: University of North Carolina Press, 1938. Limited to 200 copies; small 4to; 198 pages, facsimile titlepages, cloth spotted along edges, else very good and unopened.   Andrew Cahan 47-149 1996 $275.00

MC MURTRIE, DOUGLAS C.   The First Printers of Chicago with a Bibliography of the Issues of the Chicago Press 1836-1850. chicago: the Cuneo Press, 1927. Limited to 650 numbered copies; 4to; 42 pages; 9 illustrations; black cloth backed marbled boards, gilt lettering on spine, headcaps and corners very mildly bumped, presentation copy with ink inscription from author to Ella M. Salmonsen; ex-John Crerar Library with booklabel.   Maggs Bros. Ltd. 1191-192 1996 £50.00

MC MURTRIE, DOUGLAS C.   A Forgotten Press of Kansas. Chicago: John Calhoun Club, 1930. 1st edition; limited to 160 numbered copies; 30 pages; map, illustration; original black cloth, title in gilt on spine, fine. Michael D. Heaston 23-45 1996 $100.00

MC MURTRIE, DOUGLAS C.   A History of California Newspapers: Being a Contemporary Chronicle of Early Printing and Publishing on the Pacific Coast. New York: Plandome Press, 1927. 7 1/4 x 5 inches; xiv, 281 pages; boards, cloth spine, paper spine label.   Dawson's Books Shop 528-164 1996 $125.00

MC MURTRIE, DOUGLAS C.   Montana Imprints 1864-1880. Chicago: Black Cat Press, 1937. 1st edition; 82 pages; original blue cloth, title in gilt on spine, very good.   Michael D. Heaston 23-46 1996 $125.00

MC MURTRY, LARRY 1936-   Anything for Billy. New York: Simon & Schuster, 1988. Wrappers; Very good +;   Parker Books of the West 30-118 1996 $275.00

MC MURTRY, LARRY 1936-   Cadillac Jack. New York: Simon & Schuster, 1982. Signed, limited edition; fine in slipcase.   Bev Chaney, Jr. 23-433 1996 $135.00

MC MURTRY, LARRY 1936-   The Desert Rose. New York: Simon & Schuster, 1983. One of a limited edition of 250 copies, signed by author; this is apparently an out of series copy, as the space for the copy number on limitation leaf is blank; fine, issued without dust jacket, in near fine slipcase.   Steven C. Bernard 71-160 1996 $250.00

MC MURTRY, LARRY 1936-   The Evening Star. New York: 1992. Advance uncorrected reader's proof, in publisher's printed wrappers, laid in is 20 word holograph note, signed by author; fine.   Polyanthos 22-563 1996 $100.00

MC MURTRY, LARRY 1936-   Horseman, Pass By. New York: Harper, 1961. 1st edition; light foxing to endpapers, else very good+ in dust jacket, signed by author.   Lame Duck Books 19-332 1996 $1,250.00

MC MURTRY, LARRY 1936-   In a Narrow Grave. Austin: Encino, 1968. One of 250 numbered copies; signed by author; quarter bound in rough leather and paper covered boards; fine in slipcase, scarce.   Ken Lopez 74-314 1996 $1,750.00

MC MURTRY, LARRY 1936-   It's Always We've Rambled: an Essay on Rodeo. New York: Frank Hallman, 1974. One of 300 copies, numbered and signed by author; paper covered boards; near fine.   Lame Duck Books 19-334 1996 $475.00

MC MURTRY, LARRY 1936-   The Last Picture Show. New York: Dial Press, 1966. 1st edition; 280 pages; beige cloth, fine, crisp copy in crisp clean price clipped dust jacket with hint of fading to red spine lettering, very close to fine, signed by author.   Orpheus Books 17-184 1996 $630.00

MC MURTRY, LARRY 1936-   Leaving Cheyenne. New York: Harper, 1963. 1st edition; small erasure to free front endpaper, still easily a fine copy in attractive, near fine dust jacket uniformly faded at spine and with ghost of a light stain evident, just along edge of spine on rear panel, warmly inscribed by author to one of his English professors at Rice. Between the Covers 42-294 1996 $1,250.00

MC MURTRY, LARRY 1936-   Leaving Cheyenne. New York: H&R, 1963. 1st edition; spotting to top edge, otherwise near fine in very good, spine faded jacket with moderate edgewear, including small chips at spine crown and one on back panel.   Ken Lopez 74-313 1996 $750.00

MC MURTRY, LARRY 1936-   Lonesome Dove. New York: S&S, 1985. Uncorrected proof of the first edition; over 800 pages; remarkably fine. Lame Duck Books 19-336 1996 $350.00

MC MURTRY, LARRY 1936-   Lonesome Dove. New York: Simon & Schuster, 1985. Uncorrected proof copy; thick 8vo; printed yellow wrappers, slight crease in front wrapper, otherwise fine.   James S. Jaffe 34-475 1996 $250.00

MC MURTRY, LARRY 1936-   Lonesome Dove. New York: Simon & Schuster, 1985. 1st edition; slight soiling to edges of pages, else fine in dust jacket, very slightly wrinkled at crown, nicer than usual copy. Between the Covers 42-295 1996 $250.00

MC MURTRY, LARRY 1936-   Lonesome Dove. New York: S&S, 1985. 1st edition; fine, unread copy in fine dust jacket.   Thomas Dorn 9-184 1996 $185.00

MC MURTRY, LARRY 1936-   Lonesome Dove. New York: 1985. 1st edition; fine.   Stephen Lupack 83- 1996 $175.00

MC MURTRY, LARRY 1936-   Lonesome Dove. New York: Simon & Schuster, 1985. 1st edition; fine in fine dust jacket, almost imperceptible dot to indicate a remainder on bottom edge pages.   Bud Schweska 12-572 1996 $175.00

MC MURTRY, LARRY 1936-   Moving On. New York: Simon & Schuster, 1970. 1st edition; near fine in similar condition dust jacket. Bud Schweska 12-566 1996 $150.00

MC MURTRY, LARRY 1936-   Moving On. New York: 1970. 1st edition; fine.   Stephen Lupack 83- 1996 $125.00

MC MURTRY, LARRY 1936-   Moving On. New York: Simon and Schuster, 1970. 1st edition; fine in very lightly used dust jacket.   Bev Chaney, Jr. 23-435 1996 $100.00

MC MURTRY, LARRY 1936-   Somebody's Darling. New York: Simon & Schuster, 1978. 1st edition; signed by author; fine in dust jacket. Steven C. Bernard 71-165 1996 $100.00

MC MURTRY, LARRY 1936-   Terms of Endearment. New York: Simon & Schuster, 1975. 1st edition; 410 pages; brown cloth spine, beige paper covered boards, fine but for darkening to top edge, which is common to this title in about fine dust jacket, signed by author.   Orpheus Books 17-185 1996 $175.00

MC MURTRY, LARRY 1936-   Texasville. New York: Simon and Schuster, 1987. Advance Reading copy; yellow wrapper over bound galleys with felt-tip marker noting publication date of April 28, 1987 on front cover and price, agent, etc. on back, laid in is letter from Simon and Schuster, with blurb from Simon and Schuster trade catalog taped inside cover, all as sent out by publisher to reviewers, housed in publisher's slipcase and sleeve with label on spine and reduced photocopy of yellow wrapper on front of case, fine   Priscilla Juvelis 95/1-171 1996 $325.00

M'NAB, W.   A Treatise On the Propagation, Cultivation and General Treatment of Cape Heaths... Edinburgh: 1832. 8vo; pages 43, hand colored plate; original wrappers; rare, nice.   Wheldon & Wesley 207-1724 1996 £150.00

MC NABB, VINCENT   Geoffrey Chaucer: a Study in Genius and Ethics London: St. Dominic's Press, 1934. One of 300 numbered copies; 12mo (24) pages, printed on handmade paper; small wood engraving of Chaucer by Philip Hagreen on titlepage; cloth backed boards with glassine wrapper, covers lightly faded with small stain on front cover, else fine, bookplate.   Bromer Booksellers 90-226 1996 $150.00

MC NABB, VINCENT   God's Book and Other Poems. Ditchling, Susse hand printed and published at St. Dominic's Press, 1930. 1st edition; number 65 of 480 copies; 8vo; pages (6), 39; frontispiece, 3 full page engravings by Thomas Derrick, printed on handmade paper; original clo backed boards, lettered in gold; very good, uncut. Sewell 104.   Claud Cox 107-154 1996 £55.00

MAC NEICE, LOUIS   Springboard: Poems 1941-1944. London: Faber Faber, 1944. 1st edition; demy 8vo; few leaves slightly creased, some browning of endpapers, but nice copy in slightly worn and chipped jacket. Armitage & Clark A20a.   Ash Rare Books Zenzybyr-67 1996 £50.00

MC NEIL, MARION   The Blue Elephant and the Pink Pig. Akron: Saalfield Pub. Co., 1931. 4to; illustrations in color and black and white Francoise; cloth backed colored pictorial boards, extremities slightly worn, small mark on front pastedown, else fresh, scarce title.   Barba Stone 70-95 1996 £75.00

MAC NEILL, HECTOR   Bygane Times, and Late Come Changes; or, a Bridge Street Dialouge, in Scottish Verse. Edinburgh: for William Blackwood, in Edinburgh and John Murray, London, 1811. 1st edition; 12mo; pages (ii), xviii, 77, (iii), with half title and final ad leaf; uncut in original drab paper boards, unlettered, joints just cracking, but still firm excellent, scarce.   Simon Finch 24-161 1996 £65.00

MC NICOLL, DAVID   A Rational Enquiry Concerning the Operation of the Stage on the Morals of Society. Newcastle-upon-Tyne: printed by Edward Walker, and sold by Messrs. Charnley, Finlay... 1823. 1st editio 8vo; disbound, very good, scarce. 7 copies in NUC; LAR 537. Ximenes 109-183 1996 $150.00

MC PHEE, JOHN   Alaska. San Francisco: Sierra Club Books, 1981. 1 edition; deluxe issue, limited to 500 copies, signed by author and Galen Rowell; 4to; photos by Rowell; cloth, cloth slipcase; fine.   James S. Jaffe 34-486 1996 $350.00

MC PHEE, JOHN   Annals of the Former World. New York: FSG, 198 Limited to 450 copies; 2 volumes, both signed by author; fine in pictor slipcase.   Bella Luna 7-376 1996 $175.00

MC PHEE, JOHN   Coming Into the Country. New York: FSG, 1977. Uncorrected proof; wrappers, spine very slight faded, otherwise fine, scarce state.   Ken Lopez 74-318 1996 $200.00

MC PHEE, JOHN   Coming into the Country. New York: FSG, 1977. 1 edition; small sticker shadow front fly, otherwise fine in fine, price clipped dust jacket with little darkening at extremities, signed by author. Between the Covers 42-299 1 1996 $165.00

MC PHEE, JOHN   The Crofter and the Laird. New York: FSG, 1970. 1st edition; minor bump to head of spine, else fine in near fine, spine tanned dust jacket; signed by author.   Lame Duck Books 19-339 1996 $250.00

MC PHEE, JOHN   The Crofter and the Laird. New York: FSG, 1970. 1st edition; fine in dust jacket, scarce, especially in this condition. Between the Covers 42-298 1996 $150.00

MC PHEE, JOHN   The Curve of Blinding Energy. New York: Farrar, Straus, Giroux, 1974. 1st edition; 8vo; cloth, dust jacket; fine.   James S. Jaffe 34-483 1996 $125.00

MC PHEE, JOHN   The Curve of Binding Energy. New York: FSG, 197 1st edition; extraordinary copy, scarce in price clipped dust jacket. Lame Duck Books 19-340 1996 $125.00

MC PHEE, JOHN   The Headmaster: Frank L. Boyden of Deerfield. New York: Farrar, Straus, Giroux, 1966. 1st edition; 8vo; cloth, dust jacket with small closed tear; fine.   James S. Jaffe 34-476 1996 $125.00

MC PHEE, JOHN   The Headmaster. FSG, 1966. 1st edition; very good+ in very good+ dust jacket.   Book Time 2-294 1996 $125.00

MC PHEE, JOHN   The Headmaster. Frank L. Boyden/FSG, 1966. 1st edition; very good+ in very good+ dust jacket.   Book Time 2-295 1996 $125.00

MC PHEE, JOHN   The Headmaster. New York: Farrar, Straus and Giroux, 1966. 1st edition; 148 pages; green cloth, fine in price clipped dust jacket with 1 inch tear at back panel, else fine, signed by author.   Orpheus Books 17-67 1996 $175.00

MC PHEE, JOHN   The Headmaster; Frank L. Boyden of Deerfield. New York: FSG, 1966. 1st edition; author's second book; slight wear at spinal extremities, else fine, copy in perfect bright, white dust jacket.   Thomas Dorn 9-185 1996 $125.00

MC PHEE, JOHN   The Headmaster. New York: FSG, 1966. 1st edition; bump to spine crown, near fine in near fine price clipped dust jacket.   Ken Lopez 74-315 1996 $100.00

MC PHEE, JOHN   Levels of the Game. New York: FSG, 1969. 1st edition; fine in very near fine dust jacket, signed by author.   Lame Duck Books 19-338 1996 $175.00

MC PHEE, JOHN   Pieces of the Frame. New York: FSG, 1975. 1st edition; owner's name, else near fine in price clipped dust jacket, signed by author.   Lame Duck Books 19-341 1996 $250.00

MC PHEE, JOHN   Pieces of the Frame. New York: FSG, 1975. 1st edition; very near fine in like dust jacket, scarce.   Ken Lopez 74-317 1996 $175.00

MC PHEE, JOHN   Pieces Of the Frame. New York: Farrar, Straus, Giroux, 1975. 1st edition; 8vo; cloth, dust jacket; fine.   James S. Jaffe 34-484 1996 $150.00

MC PHEE, JOHN   The Pine Barrens. New York: FSG, 1968. Review copy; fine in fine dust jacket.   Ken Lopez 74-316 1996 $250.00

MC PHEE, JOHN   The Pine Barrens. New York: Farrar, Straus, Giroux, 1968. 1st edition; 8vo; cloth, dust jacket; fine in price clipped dust jacket, uncommon, seldom found inscribed. Presentation copy inscribed by author for Jack Emden.   James S. Jaffe 34-478 1996 $250.00

MC PHEE, JOHN   La Place de la Concorde Suisse. New York: Farrar Straus Giroux, 1984. Signed limited edition; fine in slipcase and original carton.   Bev Chaney, Jr. 23-444 1996 $100.00

MC PHEE, JOHN   A Roomful of Hovings and Other Profiles. New York: FSG, 1968. 1st edition; nice copy in dust jacket without usual fading to spine; inscribed by author.   Lame Duck Books 19-337 1996 $275.00

MC PHEE, JOHN   A Roomful of Hovings. New York: FSG, 1968. 1st edition; fine in dust jacket with none of the usual fading to either cloth or the spine of the jacket, scarce in this condition.   Between the Covers 42-297 1996 $175.00

MC PHEE, JOHN   A Roomful of Hovings. New York: FSG, 1968. 1st edition; fine in dust jacket with none of the usual fading to either cloth or spine of jacket, scarce in this condition.   Between the Covers 42-297 1996 $175.00

MC PHEE, JOHN   The Survival of the Bark Canoe. New York: FSG, 1975. 1st edition; author's first book; paper of dust jacket, being uncoated, is easily worn and torn and very infrequently survives in collectable condition, this is a fine copy in near fine price clipped dust jacket with clean, closed tear at rear spinal gutter.   Thomas Dorn 9-187 1996 $175.00

MC PHEE, JOHN   Table of Contents. New York: Farrar Straus Giroux, 1985. Signed limited edition; fine in slipcase.   Bev Chaney, Jr. 23-451 1996 $100.00

MAC PHERSON, DAVID   Annals of Commerce, Manufacataures, Fisheries and Navigation, With Brief Notices of the Arts and Sciences Connected With Them. London: Nichols and Son (and others), 1805. 1st edition; 4to; 4 volumes; 5 folding tables and folding plate, occasional very minor spotting, contemporary uniform half calf with marbled sides, spines gilt with contrasting labels (one label worn), raised bands, little rubbing or wear to joints and headbands, else very good, crisp set. Kress B4939; Williams I 386; Goldsmiths 19000; Einaudi 3593.   John Drury 82-167 1996 £600.00

MAC PHERSON, H. A.   The Birds of Cumberland Critically Studied, Including Some Notes on the Birds of Westmorland. Carlisle: Chas. Thurnam, 1886. 8vo; pages xx, 206, colored lithograph frontispiece, folding colored map; original cloth, gilt. armorial bookplate of W. H. Mullens; presentation copy to P. Leverhulme, with 4 page ALS from Rev. MacPherson tipped in.   R.F.G. Hollett & Son 78-535 1996 £160.00

MAC PHERSON, H. A.   A History of Fowling. Edinburgh: 1897. 1st edition; 8vo; plates; cloth, bit stained.   Maggs Bros. Ltd. 1190-582 1996 £55.00

MAC PHERSON, H. A.   Vertebrata Fauna of Lakeland Including Cumberland and Westmorland and Lancashire North of the Sands. Edinburgh: David Douglas, 1892. 1st edition; large 8vo; pages civ, 552, (ss ads), folding map, 8 plates, 9 text woodcuts; original ribbed cloth, gilt, spine faded, upper joint trifle tender, but excellent, clean and sound copy; armorial bookplate of Sr. Thomas G. Glen Coats, bart.   R.F.G. Hollett & Son 78-533 1996 £120.00

MAC PHERSON, H. A.   Vertebrata Fauna of Lakeland... Edinburgh: David Douglas, 1892. 1st edition; 8vo; pages civ, 552, (xx ads), folding map, 8 plates, 9 text woodcuts; original ribbed cloth, gilt, spine and edges faded as usual, top edge gilt, excellent, clean and sound copy.   R.F.G. Hollett & Son 78-534 1996 £95.00

MAC PHERSON, J. F.   Tabasco-Land. Cincinnati: 1906. 4to; 95 pages; wrappers, front wrapper torn, creased and soiled.   Bookworm & Silverfish 280-125 1996 $125.00

MAC PHERSON, JAMES 1736-1796   Fingal, an Ancient Epic Poem in Six Books, Together with Several Other Poems Composed by Ossian... London: Becket and De Hondt, 1762. 2nd edition; tall wide quarto; pages xvi, 270, (1), engraved titlepage in red and black; original full polished calf, finely rebacked, raised bands, gilt and blind decorations, gilt on red leather label; nice. Armorial bookplate of the Dankeith. CBEL II 343.   Hartfield 48-L58 1996 $365.00

MAC PHERSON, JAMES 1736-1796   An Original Collection of the Poems of Ossian, Orrann, Ulin and Other Bards... Montrose: for the Editors, 1816. 1st edition; 8vo; pages xci, (93)-241, (1) blank, (1) errata, 59 subscribers, uncut; original boards; 1817 gift inscription on title and bookplate inside front cover, fine.   Howard S. Mott 227-108 1996 $150.00

MAC PHERSON, JAMES 1736-1796   The Works of Ossian... London: 1765. 3rd edition; 8vo; 2 volumes, over 820 pages; new old style quarter calf; very good.   K Books 441-325 1996 £74.00

MC PHERSON, SANDRA   Designating Duet. West Burke: Janus Press, 1989. One of 175 copies, each copy signed by author and Claire Van Vliet; page size 7 5/8 x 7 1/2 inches; on handmade paper by Fabriano and Katie MacGregor; bound concertina style, binding can be slipped out of quilt patterned covers to spread out or be free standing, dark blue cloth with quilt design in royal blue, dark blue and red pink paper spine, housed in rust silk clamshell box lined with purple paper.   Priscilla Juvelis 95/1-139 1996 $280.00

MC PHERSON, SANDRA   Duet. Janus Press, 1989. One in an edition of 175 inscribed and numbered copies, signed by all collaborators; 7.625 x 7.625 inches, irregular, 18 unnumbered pages; printed damp in black and red on orange, purple, tan, yellow Fabriano cover with M-V blue, olive, and rose, printed dry on Spanish Gold Strathmore Grandee cover, glued to geometrically cut M-V pink abaca concertina, spine and front cover in pink abaca slip out to allow book to accordion out for display; cloth clover, printed with quilt design in reds, blues, tans, vary in front and back and from book to book; housed in clamshell box covered in rust cloth, lined in violet Fabriano cover, title on spine printed in black; fine.   Joshua Heller 21-30 1996 $350.00

MAC QUEEN, JOHN FRASER   Chief Points in the Laws of War and Neutrality, Search and Blockade... Richmond: West and Johnston, 1863. 8vo; 2, 102 pages; original blue printed wrappers (somewhat chipped), disbound from a volume of pamphlets. Parrish & Willingham, Conf. Imprints 5592; Crandall 2785.   Kenneth Karmiole 1NS-153 1996 $150.00

MAC QUOID, KATHARINE   In the Adrennes. London: Chatto & Windus, 1881. 1st edition; 8vo; xi, 351 pages; illustrations; original light green cloth pictorially decorated in gilt on upper cover and spine; attractive copy.   David Mason 71-70 1996 $100.00

MAC QUOID, PERCY   A History of English Furniture... London: Lawrence & Bullen Ltd., n.d. Folio; 4 volumes; viii, 243; 247; 271; 260 pages; 60 plates, 935 black and white illustrations, many full page; cloth, very good set in slightly worn dust jackets, minor bumping to c corners of one or two volumes and sewing of the Satinwood volume slightly loose in places.   Thomas Thorp 489-203 1996 £300.00

MC TAGGART, M. F.   From Colonel to Subaltern: Some Keys for Horse Owners. London: Country Life, 1928. Limited to 150 copies, numbered and signed by artist/author; 4to; viii, 248 pages; line illustrations by McTaggart; publisher's unbleached vellum gilt, top edge gilt, others uncut, very slightly dust soiled.   Thomas Thorp 489-214 1996 £150.00

MC VAIL, JOHN   Vaccination Vindicated: Being an Answer to the Leading Anti-Vaccinators. London: 1887. 1st edition; 176 pages; original binding; inscribed by author.   W. Bruce Fye 71-1412 1996 $100.00

MC WHORTER, LUCULLUS VIRGIL   The Border Settlers of Northwestern Virginia from 1768 to 1795... Hamilton: 1915. 509 pages, text illustrations, frontispiece, 2 plates; original cloth, heavy volume with some wear and rubbing, spine top bumped. Howes M192; Haynes 11996; Gephart 55551. Rieger 145.   Bohling Book Co. 192-265 1996 $200.00

MACAULAY, AULAY   Polygraphy; or, Short-Hand Made Easy to the Meanest Capacity... London: printed for the author, 1747. 2nd edition; 8vo; entirely engraved by author who signed a notice on verso of title, designed to frighten off prospective pirates; contemporary crushed burgundy morocco, nicely gilt decorated on covers and spine, worn but sound, all edges gilt.   Book Block 32-5 1996 $675.00

MACAULAY, AULAY   Polygraphy, or Short-Hand Made Easy. London: the author, 1747. 1st edition; 12mo; frontispiece, (2), viii, 119 pages; morocco, hinges cracked, but strong, otherwise very good.   The Bookpress 75-435 1996 $285.00

MACAULAY, CATHERINE   The History of England from the Accession of James I to the Elevation of the House of Hanover... London: printed for the author and sold by I. Nourse, 1766-71. 2nd edition of volumes 1 and 2, 1st editions of 3-5; 4to; 5 volumes; frontispiece in volume 3; contemporary calf, old morocco rebacks; rubbed, corners bit worn, ex-library.   Robert Clark 38-314 1996 £75.00

MACAULAY, THOMAS BABINGTON MACAULAY, 1ST BARON 1800-1859 The History of England from the Accession of James II. Philadelphia: John C. Winston Co., n.d. 8vo; 5 volumes; half blue polished calf, gilt flowers on spines, top edge gilt, near fine.   James Cummins 14-129 1996 $400.00

MACAULAY, THOMAS BABINGTON MACAULAY, 1ST BARON 1800-1859 The History of England from the Accession of James the Second. London: Longman, Brown, Green & Longmans/Longman, Green, Longman & Roberts, 1849-61. Mixed set, volumes i and ii fourth editions (although dating from 1849, the original year of publication), remainder first editions; demy 8vo; 5 volumes; bound in later half polished calf by Riviere & Son, banded and gilt, top edge gilt, little very light wear, few minor marks, but still in very good state.   Ash Rare Books Zenzybyr-64 1996 £245.00

MACAULAY, THOMAS BABINGTON MACAULAY, 1ST BARON 1800-1859 The History of England from the Accession of James the Second. London: Macmillan, 1913. Royal 8vo; 6 volumes; hundreds of plates and illustrations; original cloth.   Charles W. Traylen 117-158 1996 £58.00

MACAULAY, THOMAS BABINGTON MACAULAY, 1ST BARON 1800-1859 The Complete Writings. Boston and New York: Houghton Mifflin, 1899. Large paper edition, one of 500 sets; 8vo; 20 volumes, printed entirely on handmade paper; profusely illustrated with numerous engravings, all neatly hand colored; sumptuous full green morocco decorated with multi-colored floral inlays on covers enclosed within double gilt line mitres, floral inlays on spines, raised bands, contrasting olive green inner leather panels, with inlaid gilt floral motifs at corners, silk doublure endleaves, gilt tops; very fine.   Appelfeld Gallery 54-136 1996 $4,000.00

MACAULEY, ELIZABETH WRIGHT   The Wrongs of Her Royal Highness the Princess Olive of Cumberland... Purkess: 1833. 8vo; 26 pages; old marbled boards, rebacked in modern calf gilt; original lavender printed wrappers (worn and soiled) bound in; some browning in places; very scarce. Circular armorial bookplate of Edward Hailstone.   R.F.G. Hollett & Son 78-421 1996 £95.00

MACAULEY, ROSE   The Writings of E. M. Forster. London: Hogarth Press, 1938. 1st edition; octavo; pages 304, with bibliography and index; original blue cloth; nice. Woolmer 434; Kirkpatrick B12a.   Hartfield 48-V33 1996 $125.00

MACHELL, HUGH W.   Some Records of the Annual Grassmere Sports. Carlisle: Charles Thurnam and Sons, 1911. Limited to 250 copies; 4to; pages 80, (ii); photos; uncut, half morocco, gilt, few spots to upper board.   R.F.G. Hollett & Son 78-645 1996 £140.00

MACHELL, HUGH W.   Some Records of the Annual Grasmere Sports. Carlisle: Charles Thurnam and Sons, 1911. 4to; pages 80; photos; original printed wrappers, spine and upper panel rather faded; particulary nice, fresh copy, scarce wrappered form.   R.F.G. Hollett & Son 78-644 1996 £75.00

MACHEN, ARTHUR 1863-1947   Bridles and Spurs. Cleveland: Rowfant Club, 1951. 1st edition; unnumbered copy of 178 copies; fine in slipcase. Hermitage SP95-879 1996 $300.00

MACHEN, ARTHUR 1863-1947   The Green Round. Sauk City: Arkham House, 1968. 1st American edition, 1/2000 copies; fine in dust jacket, from the collection of Robert Bloch with his signature, below previous owner's bookplate.   Aronovitz 57-744 1996 $100.00

MACHIAVELLI, NICCOLO 1469-1527   The Florentine History in VII Books. London: printed for Charles Harper and John Amery, 1674. 1st edition of this translation; Small 8vo; 654 pages, frontispiece, each book separately paginated; repaired hole in titlepage, rebound, German style full leather; early ms. ownerships of J. Short.   Family Album Tillers-421 1995 $220.00

MACHIAVELLI, NICCOLO 1469-1527   Historiae Florentinae. Strasbourg: Zetzner, 1610. 8vo; portrait; boards, some underscorings in text. Moreni, Toscana li 3.   Rostenberg & Stern 150-88 1996 $450.00

MACHIAVELLI, NICCOLO 1469-1527   Historie. (with) Libro dell'Arte Della Guerra. Venice: Comin da Trino, 1540/41. 8vo; 2 works in 1 volume, titlepage, ff. 2-243, 1 f. blank; titlepage, 1 f., ff 1-108, 9 ff., woodcut diagrams at end of second work, woodcut portrait on titles, ruled in red. Light brown calf over stiff pasteboards, gilt, sides decorated with a plaque of illusionistic three dimensional strapwork, an azured 'stirrup' tool repeated upright and reversed in the centre, original sides laid down on a 19th century binding, edges plain gilt, 19th century marbled endleaves; a Parisian binding of c. 1545-50; early ownership inscription on titlepage scribbled over "Gu. Lyly", at foot of titlepage; H.R.H. Augustus Frederick, Duke of Sussex, sixth son of King George III, his sale, evans pt. IV, 30 Jan. 1845 lot 1016, bought by Payne. Marlborough 160-5 1996 £1,950.00

MACHIAVELLI, NICCOLO 1469-1527   The Works of the Famous Nicholas Machiavel, Citizen and Secretary of Florence. London: by T. W. for A. Churchill, (and 10 others), 1720. 3rd edition in English; folio; (24), 543, (i.e. 545) pages; contemporary panelled calf, hinges cracking slightly but held secure by cords, spine ends bit chipped; fine, clean copy in attractive binding; 18th century signature of John Wilkes.   Joseph J. Felcone 64-29 1996 $650.00

MACHIAVELLI, NICCOLO 1469-1527   The Works of Nicholas Machiavel, Secretary of State of the Republic of Florence. London: ptd. for Messrs. Balfour & Hamilton; Mr. James Hoey...at Dublin... 1762. 1st edition of this translation, 8 folding plans and tables; contemporary calf, worn, hinges cracked, lacks 3 (ex 4) labels.   Anthony W. Laywood 108-85 1996 £285.00

MACHIAVELLI, NICCOLO 1469-1527   The Works of Nicholas Machiavel London: printed for T. Davies, J. Dodsley and Other booksellers, 1775. 2nd of this edition; 8vo; 4 volumes; portrait, numerous plans; nice contemporary full English calf, spine very elaborately gilt, joints weak. Family Album Tillers-423 1996 $500.00

MACK, EBENEZER   The Cat-Fight; a Mock Heroic Poem. New York: 1824. 1st edition; 12mo; 276 pages; 5 full page engravings; 19th century three quarter calf and marbled boards, text foxed, plates clean, fore edge uncut. Johnson 176; Shoemaker 16972.   M & S Rare Books 60-177 1996 $475.00

MACK, EBENEZER   The Cat-Fight; a Mock Heroic Poem. New York: 1824. 1st edition; 7 x 4 inches; 276 pages; plates; new plain cloth, foxed, minor text stains.   John K. King 77-378 1996 $250.00

MACK, EFFIE MONA   The Indian Massacre of 1911 at Little High Rock Canyon Nevada. Sparks, 1968. 1st edition; royal 8vo; 147 pages; illustrations; cloth; fine, quite scarce.   Gene W. Baade 1094-102 1996 $200.00

MACK, EFFIE MONA   Nevada - a History of the State fromt he Earliest Times through the Civil War. Glendale: 1936. 1st edition; 495 pages; frontispiece, plates, illustrations, map, folding map; dust jacket; nice, very rare in original dust jacket.   T. A. Swinford 49-721 1996 $175.00

MACKAIL, JOHN WILLIAM 1859-   William Morris, an Address Delivered the XIth November MDCCCC at Kelmscott House Hammersmith Before the Hammersmith Socialist Society. Doves Press, 1901. One of 300 copies on paper; 9 1/4 x 6 1/2 inches; 2 p.l., 27 pages; original flexible vellum, gilt titling on spine, remarkably fine, binding unusually clean, text pristine. Tomkinson p. 52.   Phillip J. Pirages 33-189 1996 $600.00

MACKLEY, GEORGE   Monica Poole: Wood Engraver. Biddenden, Kent: Florin Press, 1984. Of 300 copies, numbered and signed by artist and printer, this one of 250 bound thus; folio; printed in handset Optima on Basingwerk Parchment; bound in quarter dark brown cloth with rust brown Fabriano Ingres boards; fine.   Bertram Rota 272-152 1996 £85.00

MACKWORTH, DIGBY   Diary of a Tour through Southern India, Egypt and Palestine in the years 1821 and 1822. London: printed for Messrs. J. Hatchard and Son, 1823. 1st edition; 8vo; half title, 2 folding maps; original cloth backed boards, uncut, remains of label on spine. Anthony W. Laywood 108-197 1996 £85.00

MACKWORTH-PRAED, C.   Birds of the Southern Third of Africa. London: 1962. 2 volumes; many colored plates, maps; fine set in protected dust jackets.   David A.H. Grayling MY95Orn-51 1996 £80.00

MACKWORTH-PRAED, C.   Birds of Eastern and North Eastern Africa. London: 1980. 2nd edition; 8vo; 2 volumes, 96 colored plates, 19 plates of photos and numerous marginal distributional maps and drawings; cloth, spines slightly stained, otherwise good.   Wheldon & Wesley 207-794 1996 £60.00

MACKY, JOHN   A Journey through England. 1723-24. Mixed set, volume 1 4th edition, volume 2 2nd edition, volume 3 1st edition; 3 volumes; owner's inscription, scarce.   Limestone Hills 41-150 1996 $410.00

MACKY, JOHN   A Journey through England. London: printed for Robert Gosling and John Pemberton, 1732. 5th edition; 8vo; xx, 329, 34 pages; xxii, 284, xxviii pages, half title to volume two; contemporary calf, corners little worn, very good, rebacked.   Ken Spelman 30-90 1996 £280.00

MACLISE, DANIEL   The Story of the Norman Conquest. London: Art Union of London, 1866. 1st edition; oblong folio; (iv), pages, 42 plates; text handled and lightly foxed, endpapers chipped; publisher's cloth, rebacked, corners bruised.   Bookpress 75-85 1996 $250.00

MACLISE, J.   Surgical Anatomy. London: Churchill, 1851. 1st edition; folio; 35 lithographed plates, partly colored by hand, minor soiling, contemporary half red leather, worn and splitting.   Maggs Bros. Ltd. 1190-459 1996 £425.00

MADAN, M.   Thoughts on Executive Justice, With Respect to Our Criminal Laws, Particularly on the Circuits. London: printed for J. Dodsley, 1775. 2nd edition; 12mo; name on title; contemporary tree calf, rubbed, hinges cracked, lacks label. Sweet and Maxwell p. 364, 49.   Anthony W. Laywood 108-86 1996 £200.00

MADDEN, R. R.   Travels in Turkey, Egypt, Nubia and Palestine, in 1824, 1825, 1826 and 1827. London: Henry Colburn, 1829. 1st edition; 8vo; 2 volumes, xvi, 401, viii, 398 pages; contemporary half calf, cloth, raised bands, leather spine labels; bindings rubbed with some light wear at extremities, otherwise very good.   David Mason 71-113 1996 $280.00

MADDOCK, ALFRED BEAUMONT   Practical Observations on Mental and Nervous Disorders. London: Simpkin, Marshall, 1857. 2nd edition; 8vo; 4, (vi), 236, (4) page; printed embossed red cloth, joints and edges shelfworn, (ink?) staining to front cover, good to very good, scarce; gilt embossed titlepage stamps of the Harcourt Retreat.   John Gach 150-302 1996 $250.00

MADDOCK, JAMES   The Florist's Directory, a Treatise on the Culture of Flowers. London: John Harding, 1810. 1st edition thus; 8vo; 271 pages; 8 plates and descriptive letterpress; very nice, clean copy with wide margins, plates quite extraordinary with shimmering hand coloring. Henrey 1003.   Second Life Books 103-132 1996 $750.00

MADDOW, BEN   Edward Weston: Fifty Years. Aperture, 1973. 1st edition; oblong large 4to; 150 black and white photos; dust jacket slightly chipped and sunned.   J. B. Muns 154-326 1996 $150.00

MADDOX, WILLES   Views of Landsdown Tower, Bath... London: Edmund English and others, 1844. 1st edition; folio; (vi), 10 pages; 12 plates; contemporary half black morocco, satin covers, some cover wear, tips repaired, still respectable copy, scarce; Henry Russell Hitchcock's copy.   Bookpress 75-86 1996 $4,250.00

MADOX, THOMAS   The History and Antiquities of The Exchequer of the Kings of England, in Two Periods... London: printed for William Owen...and Benjamin White, 1769. 2nd edition; modern half calf, good, clean set.   Meyer Boswell SL27-154 1996 $750.00

MAETERLINCK, M.   Hours of Gladness. London: George Allen & Co., 1912. 1st edition; 4to; x, 183 pages; text printed on handmade paper; 20 tipped in color illustrations by Detmold, pictorial titlepage; publisher's cream cloth gilt, binding slightly dust soiled, internally fine.   Thomas Thorp 489-83 1996 £95.00

MAGEE, DAVID   Catalogue of Some Five Hundred Examples of the Printing of Edwin and Robert Grabhorn 1917-1960. Grabhorn Press, 1961. One of 250 copies, 4to; patterned boards with canvas back, printed label, corners just little bruised, but very nice.   Bertram Rota 272-196 1996 £50.00

MAGENDIE, FRANCOIS   Formulary for the Preparation and Mode of Employing Several New Remedies. Philadelphia: 1824. 1st American edition; 12mo; " contemporary mottled calf; waterstained.   Argosy 810-335 1996 $100.00

MAGGS BROS.   Bookbinding in Great Britain, Sixteenth to the Twentieth Century. Catalogue No. 893. London: Maggs Bros., Ltd., 1964. Limited edition; small 4to; 85 plates; half red morocco, spine gilt, nice. Forest Books 74-161 1996 £75.00

MAGGS BROS.   Bookbinding in the British isles. Cat. 1075, Parts I and II. London: 1987. 4to; 2 volumes; pages 259, 285; profusely illustrated in black and white and color; limp pictorial card covers.   Marlborough 160-84 1996 £120.00

MAGGS BROS.   Bookbindings of Great Britain, Sixteenth to the Twentieth Century. Catalogue No. 845. London: Maggs Bros., 1957. Small 4to; frontispiece, 65 plates; half blue morocco, spine gilt; nice.   Forest Books 74-159 1996 £75.00

MAGGS BROS.   Catalogue of a Unique Collection of Early Editions of Ronsard by Seymour De Ricci. London: Maggs Bros. Ltd., 1927. Folio; large paper copies, numerous illustrations; original printed wrappers, uncut.   Forest Books 74-154 1996 £55.00

MAGGS BROS.   A Collection of French XVIIIth Century Illustrated Books with Plates After le Jeune, Boucher, Choffard...etc. London: Maggs Bros., c. 1930. Royal 4to; 144 pages; 150 plates; original printed wrappers, covers slightly dust soiled.   Thomas Thorp 489-204 1996 £50.00

MAGGS BROS.   English Armorial and Decorative Bindings. Catalouge No. 665. London: Maggs Bros. Ltd., 1938. 8vo; frontispiece, 88 plates; original wrappers.   Forest Books 74-165 1996 £50.00

MAGGS BROS.   Old Medicine. No. 485. London: 1926. 276 pages; wrappers, backsrip torn.   W. Bruce Fye 71-1340 1996 $100.00

MAGGS BROS.   A Selection of Books, Manuscripts, Engravings and Autograph Letters Remarkable for Their Interest and Rarity, Being the Five Hundredth Catalogue. London: 1928. Folio; 357 pages, frontispiece, color plate, 122 other plates and text illustrations; original printed wrappers, spine worn, slightly soiled.   Graham Weiner C2-45 1996 £50.00

MAGIC Tales. The Devil's Dice; The Magic Ring!; The Fatal Prediction; The Magic Mirror!; The Ocean Spirit; The Magic Dream!; The Three Witches!, also The Dwarf and Miller's Daughter; the Magic Car!; the Elfin Queen!; The Double Transformation... London: printed and published by G. Cowrie, 312 Strand, ca. 1820. 15 volumes bound as one; pages (iii), 4-248; 8 folding hand colored aquatint frontispieces, where called for (three captions shaved); contemporary sheep, 3 line gilt panel to sides, spine ruled in gilt, marbled endpapers; surface leather rubbed, especially at top and base of spine, corners bruised, some internal browning and marking through handling, but sound and attractive, apparently lacking final leaf of text.   Sotheran PN32-133 1996 £198.00

MAGNA Carta and other Charters of English Liberties. London: Guyon House Press, 1938. Number 181 of 250 copies on Batchelor handmade paper, head and tailpieces by Berthold Wolpe; 4to; full tan morocco by Theodore Besterman; 3 line ink inscription.   Petersfield Bookshop FH58-62 1996 £52.00

MAGRA, JAMES   A Journal of a Voyage Round the World, in His Majesty's Ship Endeavour, in the Years 1768, 1769, 1770 and 1771. London: printed for T. Becket and P. A. DeHondt, 1771. 1st edition; 1st issue, with leaf of dedication signed by publisher and with his phrase 'place this next the title' in small print at bottom; 4to; contemporary calf, gilt, nicely rebacked, spine gilt; bit foxed at beginning and end, but fine. First issue is of the greatest rarity. Holmes 3; Beddie 693; Hill p. 158 (2nd state only); Sabin 16242.   Ximenes 109-184 1996 $27,500.00

MAGUIRE, JOHN FRANCIS   The Industrial Movement in Ireland, as Illustrated by the National Exhibition of 1852. Cork: John O'Brien, 1853. 1st edition; 8vo; vii, (1), vi, (7)-476 pages; original green cloth, embossed in blind, Irish harp in gilt on upper cover, spine lettered, covers faded and bit stained, else very good; Headicar & Fuller II 347. 3 copies in NUC.   John Drury 82-169 1996 £175.00

MAHAN, ALFRED THAYER   The Influence of Sea Power Upon the French Revolution and Empire 1793-1812. London: Sampson Low, 1892. 1st edition; 8vo; 2 volumes, 380, 482 pages; maps and plans; gilt cloth, very good.   John Lewcock 30-106 1996 £80.00

MAHAN, ALFRED THAYER   The Life of Nelson. The Embodiment of the Sea Power of Great Britain. London: Sampson Low, 1897. 1st edition; 8vo; 2 volumes; maps and plans, gilt, cloth, very good.   John Lewcock 30-146 1996 £75.00

MAHAN, ALFRED THAYER   The Life of Nelson, the Embodiment of the Sea Power of Great Britain. London: 1897. Original edition; large 8vo; 2 volumes; plates, maps, plans; original cloth, gilt, gilt tops.   Howes Bookshop 265-766 1996 £50.00

MAHAN, ALFRED THAYER   Naval Strategy Compared and Contrasted with the Principles and Practices of Military Operations on Land. Boston: Little, Brown & Co., 1911. 1st edition; xxii, 475 pages, 13 maps and plans; navy blue cloth, gilt.   Blue River Books 9-215 1996 $100.00

MAHAN, ALFRED THAYER   Sea Power in It's Relation to the War of 1812. London: Sampson Low, 1905. 1st edition; 8vo; 2 volumes, maps and plans; gilt cloth, very good.   John Lewcock 30-107 1996 £80.00

MAHAN, ARTHUR THAYER   Great Commanders. Admiral Farragut. New York: D. Appleton and Co., c. 1892. One of 100 large paper copies; 22 cm; 333 pages; 2 portraits five battle plans and maps; corners bumped, covers lightly soiled, paper label rubbed, two kinds of fold colored cloth, paper spine label.   Parmer Books 039/Nautica-039259 1996 $350.00

MAHAN, ARTHUR THAYER   The Life of Nelson. The Embodiment of the Sea Power of Great Britain. Boston: Little Brown and Co., 1897. 8vo; 2 voumes, xxiii, 21, 454 pages, 10 portraits, 10 maps and battale plans; xvi, 21, 427 pages, 9 portraits, 10 maps and battle plans; blue cloth, gilt titles and cover vignette; covers scuffed, wear to head and heel of spine, some internal spotting.   Parmer Books 039/Nautica-039257 1996 $125.00

MAHOMET II, SULTAN OF TURKEY   Epistolae Magni Turci. Padua: Dominicus Siliprandus, c. 1475. 4to; 24 leaves, a-c8, roman letter, a1 & c1 little soiled, b8 torn in 3 places and neatly mended; 19th century paper boards, rebacked with modern morocco; Goff M58; HCR 10501; BMC VII 914.   H. M. Fletcher 121-11 1996 £2,200.00

MAHONY, FRANCIS   The Reliques of Father Prout. London: James Fraser, 1836. 1st edition; small 8vo; 2 volumes; illustrations by Daniel Maclise; full red calf, spines with raised bands, gilt stamped floral devices within gilt ruled compartments, contrasting red and green gilt stamped labels, blindstamped covers, ruled in gilt, gilt stamped inner dentelles, marbled endpapers, top edge gilt; uncut, bookplates, some light foxing; very good to fine.   George J. Houle 68-89 1996 $250.00

THE MAID of Renmore or Platonic Love; a Mock Heroic Romance, in Verse... London: printed for the author, 1810. 8vo; xv, 216, (8) pages; red morocco, elaborate gilt tooling, spine little rubbed, but good, sound copy. Scarce.   K Books 442-343 1996 £65.00

MAIDEN, J. H.   The Forest Flora of New South Wales. Sydney: 1904-24. Royal 8vo; 77 parts forming 8 volumes; 295 plates and numerous photos, volumes 1-6 and 8; uniform cloth, used ex-library copy with many stamps.   Wheldon & Wesley 207-1844 1996 £300.00

MAIDMENT, JAMES   A Book of Scottish Pasquils 1568-1715. Edinburgh: William Paterson, 1868. 8vo; pages xxviii, 438; uncut, modern half morocco, gilt, raised bands and spine label; few marginal blindstamps, accesson stamp verso of title, edges rather dusty. R.F.G. Hollett 76-185 1996 £85.00

MAIDMENT, JAMES   The Court of Session Garland. Edinburgh: Thomas G. Stevenson, 1839. 1st and 3rd parts limited to 150 copies, 2nd to 50 and 4th to 30; later blue pebble cloth, showing wear but sound.   Meyer Boswell SL26-152 1996 $350.00

MAILER, NORMAN 1923-   Ancient Evenings. Boston: Little Brown, 1963. 1st edition; thick 8vo; cloth, dust jacket; signed by author, mint. James S. Jaffe 34-458 1996 $100.00

MAILER, NORMAN 1923-   The Armies of the Night. New York: NAL, 1968. 1st hardcover edition; fine in near fine dust jacket faintly tanned on spine and with touch of wear at crown.   Between the Covers 42-280 1996 $100.00

MAILER, NORMAN 1923-   Barbary Shore. New York: & Toronto: Rinehart & Co., 1951. 1st edition; author's second book; fine in dust jacket, a superb copy.   Steven C. Bernard 71-148 1996 $250.00

MAILER, NORMAN 1923-   The Faith of Graffiti. New York: Praeger Publishing, 1974. 1/350 numbered copies signed by Mailer; large folio; full color full page photos; bound in brown fabrikoid in matching slipcase stamped in gold, fine as issued.   Bev Chaney, Jr. 23-379 1996 $135.00

MAILER, NORMAN 1923-   The Faith of Graffiti. New York: Praeger Publishers, 1974. One of a limited edition of 350 copies, signed by author; photos illustrations, signed by photographers; new, issued without dust jacket, in slipcase.   Steven C. Bernard 71-149 1996 $100.00

MAILER, NORMAN 1923-   Harlot's Ghost. New York: Random House, 1991. Massive proof; 1334 pages; fine.   Bev Chaney, Jr. 23-381 1996 $100.00

MAILER, NORMAN 1923-   Harlot's Ghost. New York: Random House, 1991. 1/300 signed and numbered; fine in slipcase.   Bev Chaney, Jr. 23-380 1996 $150.00

MAILER, NORMAN 1923-   The Naked and the Dead. New York: Rinehart, 1948. dust jacket little rubbed and chipped, minor blemish to outside edge, some slight wear to edges of cloth, but very good. Ownership signature and bookplate; inscribed by author.   R. A. Gekoski 19-99 1996 £300.00

MAILLET, BENOIT DE   Telliamed; or, the World Explain'd. Baltimore: Pechin for Proter, 1797. 1st American edition; 8vo; original calf, scuffed, hinges weak. Trea in pages 249-250, affecting a few letters of text; Evans 32414; Sabin 43892.   Rostenberg & Stern 150-4 1996 $200.00

MAILS, THOMAS E.   The Mystic Warriors of the Plains. Garden City: Doubleday, 1972. 1st edition; quarto; xvii, (3), 618 pages; profusely illustrated, including 32 plates in color; original gilt lettered and blindstamped cloth, very fine with pictorial dust jacket.   Argonaut Book Shop 113-442 1996 $175.00

MAINE, HENRY SUMNER   Lectures on the Early History of Institutions. London: 1875. full prize calf, bit rubbed, but quite attractive. Meyer Boswell SL26-153 1996 $275.00

MAINE, HENRY SUMNER   Village-Communities in the East and West, Six Lectures Delivered at Oxford. London: John Murray, Albemarle St., 1871. 1st edition; original cloth, quite worn, ex-library?, some pencilling; usable.   Meyer Boswell SL25-150 1996 $150.00

MAINWARING, HENRY   The Life and Works. London: 1920-22. 2 volumes.   Petersfield Bookshop FH58-396 1996 £50.00

MAINWARING, THOMAS   A Defence of Amicia, Daughter of Hugh Cyveliok, Wherein It is Proved That Sir Peter Leicester Baronet... London: Sam. Lowndes, 1673. 1st edition; 8vo; (x), 80, (vi) pages; titlepage in red and black, 3 page catalog at end, final blank leaf; old calf, label; rubbed, boards bit bowed, minor staining; sound; from the Evelyn Library, with modern booklabel indicating provenance. Wing M300. Robert Clark 38-80 1996 £100.00

MAIS, CHARLES   The Surprising Case of Rachel Baker, Who Prays and Preaches in Her Sleep... New York: 1814. 2nd edition; 8vo; 32 pages, pamphlet, lacking wrappers; very scarce. Crabtree 1988 #249. John Gach 150-304 1996 $125.00

MAISTRE, FRANCOIS XAVIER, COMTE DE   The Leper of Aost. Boston: Cummings, Hilliard, 1825. 1st American edition; 12mo; pages 37; original brown boards, printed paper label on front cover, uncut; fine; inscribed by translator for Revd. Dr. W. E. Channing; below this in later hand has pencilled "May have been by Rev. Henry Ware?" Howard S. Mott 227-94 1996 $200.00

MAITLAND, JOHN   Observations on the Impolicy or Permitting the Exploration of British Wool, and of Preventing the Free Importation of Foreign Wool. London: printed and published by William Phillips, 1818. 1st edition; 8vo; original boards, uncut; presentation inscription by author for Revd. Dr. Rees. Kress C116; Goldsmith 22072.   Anthony W. Laywood 109-94 1996 £95.00

MAITLAND, SAMUEL ROFFEY   Eruvin; or, Miscellaneous Essays on Subjects Connected with the Nature, History and Destiny of Man. London: published by James Nisbet, 1831. 1st edition; large 12mo; pages (4), 293, (1 errata), 2 ads; original green cloth, printed paper spine label little chipped, otherwise nice.   James Fenning 133-225 1996 £75.00

MAITLAND, WILLIAM   The History of London, from Its Foundation by the Romans to the Present Time. London: by Samuel Richardson, 1739. 1st edition; folio large paper copy, xviii, (1)-800, 14 pages index and errata, double page general map of London, double page prospect of St. Pauls, 2 engraved plans, 20 engraved plates, 4 engraved plates within letterpress; contemporary diced russia, gilt panelled spine and original gilt label, expert repairs to joints, head and tail of spine and corners. Ken Spelman 30-118 1996 £850.00

MAJOR, RALPH A.   A History of Medicine. Springfield: 1954. 8vo; 2 volumes; original binding, nice set in dust jackets. GM 6451.2.   James Tait Goodrich K40-182 1996 $125.00

MAJOR, RICHARD HENRY   India in the Fifteenth Century: Being a Collection of Narratives... London: printed for the Hakluyt Society, by T. Richards, 1857. 1st edition; 8vo; 8 pages ads at end; original blue cloth, spine and upper cover stamped gilt and blind, blindstamped lower cover, yellow endpapers (slight fading to spine, slight foxing), good to very good; inscribed by author for W. O'Moore Bird.   George J. Houle 68-90 1996 $150.00

MAKEMSON, W. K.   Historical Sketch of First Settlement and Organization of Williamson County. Constitution of Old Settlers Association Organized Aug. 27th, 1904. Georgetown: Sun Print, 1904. 1st edition; 26 pages; minor chipping, wrapper title differs from caption title slightly; very good. Howes M233; Jenkins Cracker Barrel Chronicles 4819. Michael D. Heaston 23-317 1996 $225.00

MAKINS, GEORGE   Surgical Experiences in South Africa 1899-1900. London: 1913. 2nd edition; 504 pages; 105 illustrations; original binding, ex-library.   W. Bruce Fye 71-1354 1996 $175.00

MALAMUD, BERNARD 1914-1986   The Assistant. New York: Farrar Straus, 1957. 1st edition; author's 2nd book; couple of bumped corners, else very good+ in first issue dust jacket that has chip at rear bottom edge.   Pettler & Lieberman 28-159 1996 $100.00

MALAMUD, BERNARD 1914-1986   The Fixer. New York: Farrar, Straus and Giroux, 1966. 1st edition; 8 1/2 x 5 3/4 inches; 5 p.l., 335 pages; original cloth and dust jacket, very fine in excellent jacket that is just slightly soiled and with minor fraying at spine ends; autographed by author.   Phillip J. Pirages 33-375 1996 $125.00

MALAMUD, BERNARD 1914-1986   God's Grace. New York: Farrar Straus Giroux, n.d. Signed, limited edition; unopened, slipcase.   Bev Chaney, Jr. 23-384 1996 $100.00

MALAMUD, BERNARD 1914-1986   The Natural. New York: Harcourt Brace, 1952. 1st edition; author's first book; fine, issue in grey boards in very near fine dust jacket and scarce thus.   Ken Lopez 74-281 1996 $1,750.00

MALAMUD, BERNARD 1914-1986   Rembrandt's Hat. New York: FSG, 1973. 1st edition; fine in near fine dust jacket, this copy inscribed by Malamud and uncommon thus.   Lame Duck Books 19-299 1996 $200.00

MALAMUD, BERNARD 1914-1986   The Tenants. New York: Farrar, Straus and Giroux, 1971. One of 250 copies; with tipped in sheet signed by author; 8 1/2 x 5 1/2 inches; 4 p.l., 230 pages; original cloth and dust jacket, very fine in fine, just slightly wrinkled jacket.   Phillip J. Pirages 33-378 1996 $125.00

MALAMUD, BERNARD 1914-1986   The Tenants. New York: FSG, 1971. 1st edition; fine in very near fine dust jacket, this the issue signed by author on special tipped in sheet.   Lame Duck Books 19-298 1996 $250.00

MALCOLM X   The Autobiogrpahy of Malcom X. New York: Grove, 1964. 1st edition; fine in near fine dust jacket with some light soiling and small scratch at bottom of front panel; first printins is remarkably scarce.   Between the Covers 43-363 1996 $750.00

MALCOLM, ALEXANDER   Malcom's Treatise of Music, Speculative, Practical and Historical. London: printed by J. French, 1776. 8vo; 104 pages; disbound.   Anthony W. Laywood 109-92 1996 £125.00

MALCOLM, ALEXANDER 1687-1763   A New Treatise of Arithmetick and Book-Keeping... Edinburgh: John Mosman and William Brown, 1718. 1st edition; thick 8vo; 2 volumes in one, xxiv, 431; viii, 399, 8 (ads) pages, 341 illustrations, many colored and some folding, plus 3 large folding colored maps in text and two large folding colored maps in rear pocket, complete with errata slip, in volume 2; library stamp on top and bottom edge, library card pocket in back; modern buckram, very good. Zittel p. 281.   Edwin V. Glaser 121-205 1996 $375.00

MALCOLM, JAMES PELLER   Anecdotes of the Manners and Customs of London During the Eighteenth Century... London: printed for Longman, Hurst, Rees, and Orme, 1808. 1st edition; 4to; 490, 8 page index, (1) page ad; 50 engravings, including 12 hand colored plates; rebound in half morocco, cloth, raised bands, gilt compartments, top edge gilt; bookplate, some underlining in blue pencil on some pages of text as well as some markings in blue pencil in margins (affecting aprox. 25 pages), some foxing to some plates, but not to any of the hand colored plates. Very nice copy.   David Mason 71-27 1996 $600.00

MALCOLM, JAMES PELLER   Anecdotes of the Manners and Customs of London During the Eighteenth Century. London: for Longman, Hurst, Rees and Orme, 1810. 2nd edition; 2 volumes; frontispiece to each volume, engraved plates; modern half blue morocco, marbled boards, new endpapers, leather labels; Toole Stott 475 (1811 ed.).   Dramatis Personae 37-121 1996 $300.00

MALCOLM, JOHN   Miscellaneous Poems... Bombay: at the American Mission Press, (not published), 1829. 1st edition; 8vo; pages (iv), 75; contemporary calf, red morocco perpendicular label, spine gilt, sides with central lozenge design and border in blind, outer border in gilt, marbled endpapers, extremities little worn, one are of stripping to upper cover, paper slightly browned, still good; one ink MS correction (perhaps authorial), initials "C.J.E." at head of title bookplate of the Oriental Club Library ex dono J. G. Reddie.   Simon Finch 24-162 1996 £750.00

MALCOLM, JOHN   Sketch of the Sikhs: a Singular Nation, Who Inhabit the Provinces of the Penjab, Situated Between the Rivers Jumna and Indus. London: Printed for John Murray by James Moyes, 1812. 1st separate edition; 9 1/2 x 6 1/4 inches; 2 p.l., 200 pages (including ads at back); contemporary half vellum, marbled paper sides, red morocco, label on spine, spine label chipped, with loss of some letters, binding noticeably rubbed and discolored, though perfectly sound, endpapers bit browned and spotted, very slight foxing in text, otherwise excellent internally.   Phillip J. Pirages 33-379 1996 $175.00

MALCOLM, S. B.   Biology and Conservation of the Monarch Butterfly. London: 1993. Royal 8vo; 428 pages, 139 illustrations; cloth.   Wheldon & Wesley 207-1071 1996 £70.00

MALGAIGNE, J. F.   Surgery and Ambroise Pare. Norman: 1965. 1st English translation; 435 pages; original binding. GM 5790 (Paris 1840). W. Bruce Fye 71-1355 1996 $100.00

MALIPIERO, GIROLAMO   Il Petrarcha Spirituale. Venice: Francesco Marcolini, Sept. 1538. 2nd edition; 8vo; titlepage, ff. 2-153, 10ff. n.n., woodcut portrait on titlepage; red mor. over pasteboards, richly gilt, lacks 4 pairs of ties, sides dec. inside upper cover the title Il PE/TRARCHA/SPIR and originally on lower one the (intended) first owner's name MACRO/ANOTIMO(?), subsequently obliterated (by the original binder) by over-tooling, spine with 3 raised bands alternating with four false bands, compartments dec. w/line-ornament in blind & w/motto CONSTANTIA gilt downwards, edges of bds. scored at right angles w/groups of 3 lines, edges gilt & gauffered w/sm. knotwork tools, pastedown and 2 endleaves (origina?) at each end, no watermark; the copy of Franciscus Gianibellus, 16th century signature on titlepage; William Bateman, F.A.S. of Middleton-by-Yolgrave in the County of Derby, with armorial bookplate. A contemporary Bolognese binding by a man whom the late Dr. Schunke called the "Binder of the Acts of the Cabinetmakers' Guild.   Marlborough 160-6 1996 £7,500.00

MALKIEL, THERESA   Woman and Freedom. New York: Socialist Literature Co., n.d. 1st edition; wrappers; near fine.   Beasley Books 82-325 1996 $100.00

MALL, THOMAS   The History of the Martyrs Epitomised. Boston: Rogers & Fowle, 1747. 1st American edition; 8vo; 2 volumes bound in 1; (16), 267, (5); (4), xii, 292, (4) pages; contemporary calf, front hinge cracked but holding soundly. Evans 5991.   Kenneth Karmiole 1NS-162 1996 $350.00

MALLET DU PAN, JACQUES   Memoirs and Correspondence of Mallet du Pan, Illustrative of the History of the French Revolution. 1st edition in English; 8vo; (xxiv), 472; (x), 522 pages; 2 volumes; original green blindstamped cloth, gilt lettering, largely unopened, gilt faded, spine ends slightly frayed, volume 2 inverted in binding. Sound set.   Robert Clark 38-246 1996 £65.00

MALLET, DAVID   Alfred; a Masque. London: A. Millar, 1751. 2nd edition; 8vo; half title; disbound; half title and last leaf of text dusty, but very good. Rothschild 1362; Tinker 1518.   Trebizond 39-39 1996 $175.00

MALLET, DAVID   The Life of Francis Bacon, Lord Chancellor of England. London: printed for A. Millar, 1740. 1st edition; 8vo; contemporary mottled calf, gilt, spine gilt, traces of rubbing; fine, complete with half title and 3 pages of ads at end; CBEL II 557. Ximenes 108-253 1996 $225.00

MALLET, DAVID   Mustapha. London: printed for A. Millar, 1739. 1st edition; 8vo; disbound; variant with price at foot of titlepage, very good. Stratman 3497; CBEL II 557.   Ximenes 108-254 1996 $100.00

MALLET, PAUL HENRI   Northern Antiquities: or, A Description of the Manners, Customs, Religion and Laws of the Ancient Danes... London: printed for T. Carnan and Co., 1770. 1st edition in English; 2 volumes; original dark blue boards, edges worn, green vellum backs, printed paper labels; excellent set. Graesse IV p. 354.   Howard S. Mott 227-96 1996 $575.00

MALLET, PAUL HENRI   Northern Antiquities; or a Description of the Manners, Customs, Religion and Laws of the Ancient Danes, and Other Northern Nations... London: for T. Carnan, 1770. 1st English edition; 8vo; 2 volumes; pages (x), lvi, 415, (i); (vi), xl, 356; contemporary tree calf, smooth spines with ornately gilt compartments, contrasting double red and black morocco labels, yellow edges, joints cracking but firm, spine worn at ends, extremities rubbed, internally clean, good.   Simon Finch 24-163 1996 £240.00

MALLET, ROBERT   On the Physical Conditions Involved in the Construction of Artillery... London: 1856. 12 x 9.5 inches; 283 pages; 5 plates; half leather, ex-library (minor markings), cover heavily rubbed. John K. King 77-824 1996 $200.00

MALLOCK, W. H.   Property and Progress; or, a Brief Enquiry into Contemporary Social Agitation in England. London: John Murray, 1884. 1st edition; 8vo; xii, 248 pages, 32 page publisher's list, one gathering of prelims loose; original maroon cloth, gilt, stitching shaken, still good; Working Men's College bookplate and occasional stamps.   John Drury 82-170 1996 $50.00

MALLOWAN, M. E. L.   Nimrud and Its Remains. New York: Dodd, Mead, 1966. Folio; 2 volumes, folder of maps and plans, 677 pages, 594 figures and 9 color plates, 8 maps; original cloth, worn slipcase, dust jacket.   Archaeologia Luxor-2414 19965 $475.00

MALLOWMAN, MAX   Furniture from SW.7 Fort Shalmaneser; Commentary, Catalogue and Plates. London: The British School of Archaeology in Iraz, 1974. Folio; (viii), 122 pages, 14 figures and 111 plates; original cloth.   Archaeologia Luxor-2416 1996 $150.00

MALORITIE, C. S. DE   A Treatise on Topography, for Both Civil and Military Purposes. London: printed for T. Egerton, 1815. 1st edition; 8vo; 2 volumes; 14 folding plates; contemporary diced calf, rebacked with original spines, all edges gilt.   Anthony W. Laywood 109-93 1996 £75.00

MALORY, THOMAS d. 1471   The Death of King Arthur, Being the 21st Book of Sir Thomas Malory's Book of King Arthur... London: Macmillan, 1928. Limited to 525 copies; 12 illustrations designed and engraved on wood by Catherine Donaldson; printed on handmade paper; bound in half cloth, blue paper boards.   Barbara Stone 70-20 1996 £135.00

MALTBY, WILLIAM J.   Captain Jeff; or, Frontier Life in Texas with the Texas Rangers. Colorado, Texas: Whipkey Printing Co., 1906. 1st edition with copyright notice printed separately and pasted across from titlepage; 161 pages, 2 illustrations; original orange cloth, title stamped in black on front cover, very good copy for this poorly constructed volume. Howes M243. Doble p. 60; Handbook of Texas III p. 566. Michael D. Heaston 23-211 1996 $300.00

MALTBY, WILLIAM J.   Captain Jeff, or Frontier Life. Colorado: Whipkey Printing Co., 1906. 2nd edition; 204 pages; frontispiece and illustrations; original pictorial red wrappers, chipped to spine, very good; Tyler, Big Bend p. 242; Tate Texas Indians 2398 Noting only 2nd ed. Michael D. Heaston 23-212 1996 $125.00

MALTBY, WILLIAM J.   Captain Jeff or Frontier Life in Texas with the Texas Rangers. Colroado: 1906. 204 pages; plates, illustrations; pictorial wrappers, very good+; scarce. Howes R243; tader 2340.   T. A. Swinford 49-726 1996 $100.00

MALTE-BRUN, CONRAD   Universal Geography, or a Description of all the Parts of the World, on a New Plan... Edinburgh: printed for Adam Black and Longman, Hurst, Rees, Orme and Brown, Lon. 1822-33. 1st English edition; 8vo; 10 volumes in 9; 6 large folding plates to rear of volume 1, library stamp of Middle Temple to front f.e.p., half title and title of all volumes, library withdrawal stamp to final leaf of all volumes; full polished calf, double gilt rule borders to boards, gilt tooling to compartments, red and green morocco label to spines, corners very slightly worn, uniformly marbled endpapers and edges, ex-library. Sabin 44166; Lowndes' III p. 1459.   Beeleigh Abbey BA56-93 1996 £450.00

MALTHUS, THOMAS ROBERT 1766-1834   An Essay on the Principle of Population; or, a View of its Past and Present Effects on Human Happiness... London: J. Johnson, 1806. 3rd edition; 8vo; 2 volumes, xvi, 505, (61); vii, (1), 559, (1) pages, bound without half titles; contemporary calf, flat spine ruled in gilt with labels; fine; contemporary ownership inscription of Donald Maclachlan and his armorial bookplate. Kress B5067; Goldsmiths 19210; Einaudi 3669.   John Drury 82-171 1996 £575.00

MALTHUS, THOMAS ROBERT 1766-1834   An Essay on the Principles of Population; or a View of its Past and Present Effects on Human Happiness. London: printed for J. Johnson, 1807. 4th edition; 8vo; 2 volumes; half titles, contemporary half calf, rubbed, labels. Kress B5219; Goldsmith 19373.   Anthony W. Laywood 108-198 1996 £375.00

MALTHUS, THOMAS ROBERT 1766-1834   Additions to the Fourth and Former editions of an Essay on the Principle of Population. London: John Murray, 1817. 1st edition; 9 x 6 inches, 2 p.l., 327, (1) pages; original blue paper boards, neatly rebacked in buff paper, original printed paper spine label, untrimmed edges, spine label chipped and rubbed, significant loss of lebigility, little soil and wear to original sides (as expected), but boards surprisingly well preserved, and well restored binding absolutely tight, first few leaves and last three gatherings freckled with foxing, minor foxing elsewhere, few trivial spots, but excellent internally, still rather fresh and not at all darkened or browned; 19th century bookplate. Goldsmith 21762; Kress B 6973; Palgrave II 676.   Phillip J. Pirages 33-380 1996 $1,250.00

MALTHUS, THOMAS ROBERT 1766-1834   Principles of Political Economy Considered with a View to Their Practical Application. London: William Pickering, 1836. 2nd edition; 8vo; liv, (2), 446 pages; original maroon cloth, somewhat faded, original printed paper label on spine, rubbed, upper joint and extremities little worn, edges untrimmed; very good. Kres C4188; Goldsmiths 29340; Einaudi 3681; Williams I 191. John Drury 82-172 1996 £500.00

MALTON, JAMES   The Young Painter's Maulstick... London: V. Griffiths, 1800. 1st edition; 4to; (4), ii, xiv, 71 pages; 23 engraved plates; 19th century half calf, marbled boards, some rubbing and slight staining to gutter of front endpaper and prelim blank; scarce first edition with titlepage watermarked 1798. Martin Kemp, Science of Art p. 157.   Ken Spelman 30-27 1996 £320.00

MALVEZZI, VIRGILIO   Il Davide Persequitato. David Persecuted. London: printed for Humphrey, 1647. 12mo; (2), 164 pages; copper engraved frontispiece, 19th century boards, rebacked with plain grey paper, some waterstaining to prelim leaves, title with gouge at top fore-edge, frontispiece slightly defective at fore-edge. Wing M357. Kenneth Karmiole 1NS-163 1996 $125.00

MALVEZZI, VIRGILIO   Il Ritratto del Privato Politico Christiano... Bologna: G. Monti and C. Zenero, 1635. 1st edition; 4to; 148 pages; engraved emblematic title, woodcut initials; contemporary limp white vellum, yapp edges (lacking ties); fine. BM STC 523; Piantinida 400. Bennett Gilbert LL29-48 1996 $850.00

MAMIANI DELLA ROVERE, TERENZIO, COUNT   Rights of Nations or, the New Law of European States Applied to the Affairs of Italy. London: W. Jeffs, 1860. 1st edition in English; 8vo; xl, 377, (3) pages, complete with half title and final leaf of ads; original red cloth, embossed in gilt and blind, very good, short split in upper joint.   John Drury 82-173 1996 £85.00

THE MAN Who... Bristol: Scorpion Press, 1992. Deluxe edition 1/15 copies; signed by all contributors, and includes a hand written page by Julian Symonds; quarter bound goatskin with raised bands; fine.   Quill & Brush 102-1638 1996 $600.00

MAN, JOHN   The History and Antiquities of the Borough of Reading. Reading: Snare & Man, 1816. 4to; half title, title, dedn., errata slip tipped in, pages iv, 430, 1 f., pages xxxvi, 21 engraved plates or plans; half calf, rebacked preserving spine, label chipped. Abbey Travel 293. Marlborough 162-64 1996 £220.00

MANDAVILLE, J. P.   The Flora of Eastern Saudi Arabia. London: 1990. Royal 8vo; 492 pages; 268 colored illustrations, maps; cloth.   Wheldon & Wesley 207-1570 1996 £125.00

MANDER, JAMES   The Derbyshire Miners' Glossary; or an Explantion of the Technical Terms of the Miners, Which are Used in the King's Field, in the Hundred of High Peak... Bakewell: printed at the Minerva Press, for the Author, by Geo. Nall, 1824. frontispiece, uncut in original printed blue boards, spine carefully repaired, very good, scarce. Jarndyce 103-64 1996 £480.00

MANDEVILLE, BERNARD   A Treatise of the Hypochondriack and Hysterick Diseases. London: printed for J. Tonson, 1730. 2nd edition; 8vo; library cancellation stamp on blank verso of title; contemporary calf, rebacked, spine gilt, label; nice.   Anthony W. Laywood 108-88 1996 £465.00

MANDEVILLE, JAMES H.   The Rights of American Inventors. Washington: Gibson Bros., 1879. 50 pages; original printed sewn wrappers, worn but sound.   Meyer Boswell SL27-155 1996 $125.00

MANDEVILLE, JOHN   The Travels of... London: Macmillan, 1900. 1st edition thus; 8vo three quarter blue calf over matching cloth by Bayntun, spine with raised bands, red morocco label and gilt floral tooling withing gilt ruled compartments, marbled endpapers, top edge gilt; fine. George J. Houle 68-91 1996 $150.00

MANDIARGUES, ANDRE PIEYRE DE   Chagall. New York: Amiel, 1974. Square 4to; 213 pages; with original Chagall color lithograph, 152 plates, many in color + original lithograph, cloth, corner clipped from front free endpaper;   Brannan 43-119 1996 $195.00

MANDOWSKY, ERNA   Pirro Ligorio's Roman Antiquities: The Drawings in MS XIII. B. in the National Library in Naples. London: Warburg Inst. 1963. 4to; xvii, 153 pages, 76 plates; original cloth, minor stain at top board, two corners bumped.   Archaeologia Luxor-3659 1996 $125.00

MANI, M. S.   Butterflies of the Himalaya. Amsterdam: 1986. 8vo; 206 pages; numerous photos; hardbound.   Wheldon & Wesley 207-1073 1996 £79.25

MANING, FREDERICK EDWARD   Old New Zealand. London: Smith, Elder & Co., 1863. 1st edition; 8vo; viii, 316 pages; cloth, gilt, little worn, some spotting in text.   Thomas Thorp 489-205 1996 £50.00

MANN, ERIKA   A Gang of Ten. New York: Fischer, 1942. 1st edition; near fine in very good+ dust jacket, scarce.   Lame Duck Books 19-301 1996 $125.00

MANN, JAMES   Wallace Collection. European Arms and Armour. London: 1962. 2 volumes, color frontispiece and 206 plates and 1345 illustrations; original green leather, gilt; fine.   David A.H. Grayling 3/95-330 1996 £55.00

MANN, THOMAS   The Beloved Returns: Lotte in Weimar. New York: Alfred A. Knopf, 1940. 1st American edition, one of 375 copies, signed by author; 10 x 6 1/2 inches; 2 p.l., x, 453, (1) pages, (6) leaves; printed on Rives Liampre all rag paper, title printed in red and black; original cloth backed paper boards in original glassine jacket, slipcase; book and case with hint of fading; very fine.   Phillip J. Pirages 33-381 1996 $375.00

MANN, THOMAS   An Exchange of Letters. Stamford: Overbrook Press, 1938. One of 350 copies; 8vo; printed in black and red on one side only of a delicate laid sheet; wrappers with printed label, wrappers little faded at backstrip, but very nice, scarce.   Bertram Rota 272-363 1996 £50.00

MANN, THOMAS   Joseph und Seine Bruder. Berlin: S. Fischer, 1933-43. 1st edition; 4 volumes; 1st 3 volumes very good+ in appealing pictorial dust jackets, the fourth surprisingly scarce volume a very good or better, slightly spine rolled copy in dust jacket with chipping to head of spine.   Lame Duck Books 19-302 1996 $3,500.00

MANN, THOMAS   Joseph the Provider. New York: Knopf, 1944. 1st U.S. edition; near fine in bright example of the dust jacket with light wear and tiny internal chip to lower front flap-fold tip; signed by Mann. Lame Duck Books 19-305 1996 $750.00

MANN, THOMAS   The Magic Mountain. New York: Knopf, 1927. 1st U.S. edition; 2 volumes; starting to front inner hinge of first volume, gift inscription and ownership signature to front endpapers of both volumes, overall very good+ in scarce, but here less than very good illustrated publisher's cardboard slipcase.   Lame Duck Books 19-303 1996 $175.00

MANN, THOMAS   The Transposed Heads - a Legend of India. New York: Alfred A. Knopf, 1941. 1st edition; decorated cloth, head and tail of spine slightly bumped, very good in nicked, rubbed, marked and dusty, slightly torn, price clipped dust jacket browned at spine and edges. Ulysses 39-392 1996 £75.00

MANNEX, P. J.   History, Gazetteer and Directory of Cumberland. Beverley: printed for the authors by W. B. Johnson, 1847. 8vo; pages xvi, 630, (i); original blindstamped cloth, gilt, spine faded and worn at head and tail; very good.   R.F.G. Hollett & Son 78-1095 1996 £125.00

MANNEX, P. J.   History, Topography and Directory of Westmorland; and Lonsdale North of the Sands, in Lancashire... London: Simpkin, Marshall & Co., 1849. 8vo; pages xvi, 465, (iii), old half calf, marbled boards, nicely rebacked by Bayntun in matching calf gilt with raised bands.   R.F.G. Hollett & Son 78-1093 1996 £120.00

MANNING, ANNE   The Spanish Barber; a Tale. London: James Nisbet and Co., 1869. 1st edition; 8vo; frontispiece; old label stuck to blank portion of half title; original blue decorated cloth, little rubbed; but very good. Sadleir 1556; Wolff 4471; CBEL III 947.   Ximenes 109-185 1996 $125.00

MANNING, FREDERIC   Her Privates We. London: Peter Davies Ltd., 1930. 1st trade, abridged edition; pictorial cloth, free endpapers partially browned, pastedowns browned, fore-edge slightly soiled, head and tail of spine and cover edges slightly browned, tail of spine slightly bumped, very good in glassine dust jacket with printed flaps, which is slightly torn, flaps are crinkled.   Ulysses 39-648 1996 £135.00

MANNING, FREDERIC   Her Privates We. London: Peter Davies Ltd., 1930. 1st trade, abridged edition; pictorial cloth, top edge slightly dusty, rear free endpaper partially browned, pastedowns browned, head fo spine and top corners very slightly bumped, near fine. Loosely inserted are flaps of glassine dust jacket.   Ulysses 39-647 1996 £95.00

MANNING, FREDERIC   The Middle Parts of Fortune. Piazza Press, 1929. 1st (unexpurgated) edition, 348/520 sets; crown 8vo; 2 volumes; printed on handmade paper, title to volume i printed in red; pages (vii), 226; (iii), 227-453; original brown buckram, sunned backstrips gilt lettered within gilt frame, marbled endpapers, maroon silk markers, top edge gilt, others untrimmed, excellent.   Blackwell's B112-183 1996 £200.00

MANNING, FREDERIC   The Middle Parts of Fortune. Somme & Ancre, 1916. N.P.: Piazza Press, 1929. 1st edition; one of 520 copies printed on handmade paper; small 8vo; 2 volumes; marbled endpapers, cloth, top edge gilt, attached fabric ribbon bookmark, cloth slipcase, spines slightly cocked, otherwise fine set in somewhat rubbed and bumped slipcase, scarce in original box.   James S. Jaffe 34-461 1996 $500.00

MANNING, HENRY   Modern Improvements in the Practice of Surgery. (with) Modern Improvements in the Practice of Physic. London: Robinson, 1780. 8vo; 2 volumes, v, (4), 423; (4), 440 pages; volume one in full polished calf, raised bands, volume two in quarter calf and marbled boards, binding rubbed, spine label defective; nice set. James Tait Goodrich K40-183 1996 $595.00

MANNING, OLIVIA   The Levant Trilogy. London: Weidenfeld & Nicolson, n.d., c. 1977/78/80. 1st editions; fine set in dust jackets. Virgo Books 48-133 1996 £60.00

MANNING, OLIVIA   The Remarkable Expedition. London: Heinemann, 1947. 1st edition; slight offsetting and foxing of endpapers, covers very slightly rubbed at edges and corners, otherwise very good, in browned and soiled dust jacket, repaired internally where chipped at corners and ends of spine.   Virgo Books 48-131 1996 £50.00

MANNING, ROBERT   A Plain and Rational Account of the Catholick Faith... (with) The Reform'd Churches Proved Destitute of a Lawful Ministry. Rouen: 1721/22. 3rd edition; 8vo; 2 works in 1 volume, xvi, 182, (vi) pages; xiv, 65 pages; old calf, neatly and expertly respined, some minor browning, but good, clean copy; scarace.   K Books 441-328 1996 £90.00

MANSEL, HENRY LONGUEVILLE   Letters, Lectures and Reviews, Including the Phrontisterion, or, Oxford in the 19th Century... London: John Murray, 1873. 1st edition; 8vo; vii, (1), 408 pages; contemporary polished calf, raised bands fully gilt with inner gilt dentelles by Larkins, handsome. Rand p. 364.   John Drury 82-174 1996 £100.00

MANSERGH, JAMES   The Thirlmere Water Scheme of the Manchester Corporation... London: E. & F. N. Spon, 1878. 1st edition; 8vo; pages 40, 3 extending linen backed lithographed plates (ex 4, lacks plan of Thirlmere), original cloth, gilt, rubbed, hinge splitting and repaired, new endpapers, lower edge of title little dusty, scarce.   R.F.G. Hollett & Son 78-622 1996 £95.00

MANSERGH, JAMES   The Water Supply of the City of Toronto, Canada, by... Westminster: 1896. 8vo; pages 72, including 4 folding tables, 1 folding map, 1 folding diagram; original paper covers; very good.   Hugh Anson-Cartwright 87-422 1996 $100.00

MANSFIELD, JARED   Essays, Mathematical and Physical. New Haven: 1801. 1st edition; 8vo; 10, 274, (42), (5) pages, 13 folding plates; full contemporary calf, rebacked, original spine and label laid down. S&S 866; not in Karpinski.   M & S Rare Books 60-466 1996 $850.00

MANSFIELD, JARED   Essays, Mathematical and Physical... New Haven: printed by William W. Morse, 1801. 1st edition; 8vo; viii, 274, (6) pages, (44) pages of tables; 13 engraved copper engraved plates; original mottled calf, red leather spine label, portion of top of spine chipped away (half inch by half inch), edges rubbed.   Kenneth Karmiole 1NS-170 1996 $200.00

MANSFIELD, JOHN   Interesting Collection of Curious Anecdotes, Scarce Pieces, and Genuine Letters... London: printed for the author and sold by J. Bew and H. Gradner, 1790. 1st edition; 8vo; 174 pages; 19th century black half calf, spine gilt, extremities rubbed, little foxing; sound, uncommon.   Robert Clark 38-193 1996 £85.00

MANSTEIN, C. H. DE   Memoirs of Russia. London: printed for T. Gecket and...de Hondt, 1770. 1st edition; tall square 4to; viii, 424, 8 page index, with required 10 large folding maps and ad leaf by David Hume; original calf in very worn condition, front cover detached but present, front flyleaves and map detached, but in very good condition, corners of boards very badly bumped.   Roy W. Clare XXIV-11 1996 $300.00

MANTELL, G.   The Fossils of the South Downs; or Illustrations of the Geology of Sussex. London: 1822. 4to; pages xvi, 327; 42 plain plates; new cloth, some minor waterstaining of many plates, which are slightly foxed, text clean with crease on frontispiece ironed out.   Wheldon & Wesley 207-1351 1996 £220.00

MANUTIUS, ALDUS 1547-1597   Eleganze Insieme Con La Copia Della Lingua Toscana, E Latina, Scielte Da Aldo Manutio... Venice: Ex Bibliotheca Aldina, 1570. 8vo; 164 leaves, italic, Aldine devices on first and last leaves, titlepage worn and soiled, age stain; broken 18th century full leather. Renouard 208.4; Adams E104; UCLA IIIb 582; Brunet III.1385.   Family Album Tillers-429 1995 $450.00

MANUTIUS, ALDUS 1547-1597   Orthographiae Ratio Ab Aldo. Manutio Pauli. F(ilio). Collecta Ex Libris Antiquis, Grammaticis, Etymolgoia... Venice: Paulus Manutius, 1566. 2nd edition; 8vo; 2 volumes in 1; pages 800; 168, 40 (including blanks), Italic and Roman types, Aldine devices on both titlepages; early limp vellum; early Italian Ducal ownership stamp on the titlepage has created some staining, ms. shelving title on bottom edge. Renouard 201.12; Adams M453; UCLA IIIb/556; Brunet II.1384. Family Album Tillers-430 1996 $500.00

MANUTIUS, ALDUS 1547-1597   Phrases Linguae Latinae...Nunc Primum in Ordinem Abecedarium Adductae, & in Anglicum Sermonem Conversae... London: Excusum pro Societate Stationorum, 1636. Small 8vo; pages (6), 256, (22), printer's device on title crudely colored in gold, text in English and Latin; contemporary full leather with slight old repair, edges stained red, top and bottom edges with ms. lettered ownerships of Edward Osborne and Thomas Osborne.   Family Album Tillers-431 1995 $900.00

MANUZIO, PAOLO 1512-1574   Epistolarum Pauli Manutii Libri V. Venice: Paulus Manutius, 1561. 8vo; 248 leaves, italic; contemporary limp vellum, early ms. ownership of Hieronymi Regii Rodien, interesting and extensive early ms. notes on flyleaves. Renouard 184.19; Adams M485; UCLA IIIb/498.   Family Album Tillers-432 1996 $750.00

MANUZIO, PAOLO 1512-1574   Epistolarum Pauli Manutii Libri XII. London: apud Robertum Dexter, 1603. Early English printing; 16mo; contemporary calf, top edge gilt dust soiled, otherwise very nice in well preserved early binding; rare printing. STC 17289.   Ximenes 108-255 1996 $750.00

MANVILL, P. D., MRS.   Lucinda; or the Mountain Mourner. Ballston Spa: printed and sold by William Child, 1810. 2nd edition; 12mo; 168 pages; contemporary leather backed marbled boards, boards cracked, substanial paper lacking from covers, shaken and becoming disbound; still good. Wright I 1801. S&S 20641.   M & S Rare Books 60-200 1996 $400.00

MANVILL, P. D., MRS.   Lucinda; or, the Mountain Mourner. Ballston Spa: J. Comstock for R. Sears, 1817. 3rd edition; 12mo; 180 pages; original boards, rubbed, calf back; good, sound copy. Wright I 1802.   Howard S. Mott 227-97 1996 $175.00

MANZONI, ALESSANDRO   I Promessi Spossi (The Betrothel). Verona: Limited Editions Club, 1951. Number 904 from 1500 copies, signed by Giovanni Mardersteig and by artist; illustrations by Bruno Bramanti, cloth backed decorative boards, fine, in nicked dust jacket and slightly rubbed publishers slipcase.   Hermitage SP95-1010 1996 $150.00

MANZONI, ALESSANDRO   The Betrothed. (I Promessi Sposi). Verona: Limited Editions Club, 1952. Limited to 1500 copies, signed by artist, Bruno Bramanti and by the printer, Giovanni Mardersteig; tall 8vo; wood engravings; half natural Italian linen; fine in worn slipcase.   Charles Agvent 4-861 1996 $125.00

MAPS and Descriptions of Routes of Exploration in Alaska in 1898. Washington: United States Geological Survey, 1899. 1st edition; 138 pages; 10 large folding maps; original full calf, red, green and black morocco spine labels; very good.   Michael D. Heaston 23-9 1996 $500.00

MARAN, RENE   Batouala. New York: Limited Editions Club, 1932. Limited to 1500 numbered copies, signed by artist; folio; (2), xiv, (2), 117, (3) pages; profusely illustrated with 6 color plates and numerous text drawings by Miguel Covarrubias; full brown morocco, extremities bit rubbed, slipcase, bookplate; this copy inscribed by Covarrubias in 1939 with original sketch by Covarrubias.   Kenneth Karmiole 1NS-158 1996 $250.00

MARAT, JEAN PAUL   Les Chaines de L'Esclavage... Paris: Imprimerie de Marat, an premier, 1792. 1st French edition; 8vo; half early 19th century sheep. Some foxing, margin of one leaf defective; Martin & Walter 22849; Cioranescu 42306.   Rostenberg & Stern 150-57 1996 $2,750.00

MARBLE, MELINDA   Herna. Cambridge: Bow and Arrow Press, 1993. Deluxe edition, limited to 50 copies, signed by author and artist, with 2 original drypoint etchings; prospectus laid in; illustrations by Michael Mazur; handmade decorated paper wrappers, housed in red and gold silk dropback box; mint; at publication price.   Bromer Booksellers 87-173 1996 $495.00

MARBURY, MARY ORVIS   Favorite Flies and Their Histories. Boston: Houghton Mifflin, 1896. 3rd edition; thick 8vo; 32 colored plates, 6 engravings, 8 reproductions of photos; early half morocco, gilt tooled spine and fly decoration; clean, unmarked copy in beautiful binding. Glenn Books 36-253 1996 $350.00

MARCET, JANE   Conversations on Chemistry: in Which the Elements of that Science are farmiliarly Explained and Illustrated by Experiments. London: printed for Longman, Hurst..., 1813. 4th edition; large 12mo; 2 volumes, pages xix, 343, (1); xii,3 56, (10), without half titles; 14 engraved plates; neat contemporary half red calf, fully gilt spines, with labels; some light browning in places, but very good.   James Fenning 133-227 1996 £125.00

MARCET, JANE   Conversations on Political Economy; In Which the Elements of that Science are Familiarly Explained. London: Longman, 1827. 6th edition; 12mo; viii, 494 pages; original green cloth, gilt; fine. Kress C1926; Goldsmiths 25181.   John Drury 82-175 1996 £50.00

MARCET, JANE   Conversations on Vegetable Physiology... Boston: Crocker; New York: Leavitt, 1830. 1st U.S. edition; 8vo; 372 pages; 5 hand colored floral plates; worn full calf, hinge loose, good. Imprints 2390.   Second Life Books 103-135 1996 $100.00

MARCH, JOHN   The Jolly Angler or Waterside Companion &c. London: 1933. 1st edition; frontispiece and title, text illustrations; original cloth backed boards, frontispiece and title foxed, corners rubbed, new spine label.   David A.H. Grayling 3/95-598 1996 £55.00

MARCHINI, G.   Italian Stained Glass Windows. New York: Harry N. Abrams, Inc., 1956. Large 4to; 264 pages, including 93 mounted color plates; blue gilt cloth in illustrations, dust jacket. Beautiful book. Kenneth Karmiole 1NS-164 1996 $100.00

MARCHISI, J. B.   Dr. Marchisi's Uterine Catholicon, Is Hereby Most Respectfully Dedicated to the Mothers and Daughters of Our Country, for Whose Benefit It Is Designed, and Whose Happiness It Will Promote. New York: J. A. Gray, Steam Printer, n.d. 1851. 8vo; original printed yellow wrappers; rare, very good;   Ximenes 109-186 1996 $125.00

MARCK, H. VAN DER   Bibliotheca Marckiana. The Hague: Abrahami de Hondt, 31st Oct., 1712. 8vo; 3 parts in 1; engraved half title; light browning throughout, occasional foxing, later cloth backed boards; some pages dampstained on top margin. Taylor p. 252; Pollard and Ehrman pp. 220-1; Blogie IV. col. 7.   Anthony W. Laywood 108-89 1996 £750.00

MARCK, H. VAN DER   Bibliotheca Marckiana. The Hague: Abrahami de Hondt, 31st Oct. 1712. 3 parts in 1, full engraved half title; pages (1), (16), 192, 250, 284; later cloth backed boards, light browning throughout and occasional foxing, some pages dampstained in top right hand margin. Taylor p. 252; Pollard & Ehrman p. 220-221; Blogie IV col. 7 Maggs Bros. Ltd. 1191-53 1996 £700.00

MARCY, L. J.   The Sciopticon Manual, Explaining Lantern Projections in General and the Sciopticon Apparatus in Particular... Philadelphia: 1877. 6th edition; 200, xxvii, 80, 18 pages; top right 2 inch of backstrip reglued, 2 inch of top front edge gently gnawed, some very light flecking, several pencil notes in the hand of M. L. Fitch of Chesterfield Co., Va., cover gilt bright, backstrip gilt fairly distinct, 54 text illustrations. Bookworm & Silverfish 280-126 1996 $300.00

MARCY, RANDOLPH BARNES 1812-1887   Exploration of the Red River of Louisiana, in the Year 1852... Washington: 1854. 8vo; pages xv, 286; 65 plates; missing separate portfolio containing 2 maps; original cloth, scattered foxing, crack to inner joint.   Raymond M. Sutton VI-1109 1996 $285.00

MARCY, RANDOLPH BARNES 1812-1887   Message of the President of the United States...Communicating...The Report and Maps of Captain Marcy of His Explorations of the Big Witchita and Head Waters of the Brazos Rivers. Washington: Senate Executive Document 60, 1856. 1st edition; 48 pages; folding map; half morocco and marbled boards. Graff 2678; Howes M277; Becker Wagner Camp 278.   Michael D. Heaston 23-240 1996 $500.00

MARCY, RANDOLPH BARNES 1812-1887   The Prairie Traveler. New York: Harper & Bros., 1859. 1st edition; 340 pages; frontispiece, illustrations, folding map; original black cloth, title in gilt on spine, fine, bright copy. Major General Wool's copy with his signature. Choice copy of a fine association. Howes M279; Smith 6509; Graff 2676; Streeter Sale 2123.   Michael D. Heaston 23-241 1996 $1,250.00

MARCY, RANDOLPH BARNES 1812-1887   Route from Fort Smith to Santa Fe. Washington: House Executive Document 45, 1850. 1st edition; 89 pages, 2 plates, large folding map; half dark green morocco, matching marbled boards, title lettered in gilt on spine, fine. Howes S500; Wagner Camp 192; Wheat Map. Trans. West III p. 12.   Argonaut Book Shop 113-448 1996 $600.00

MARDERSTEIG, GIOVANNI 1892-1977   The Making of a Book at the Officina Bodoni. Verona: Officina Bodoni, 1973. Limited to 300 copies, with signed presentation card from Mardersteig laid in; small quarto; (30) pages; wrappers; extremely fine. Mardersteig 183.   Bromer Booksellers 87-242 1996 $375.00

MARDERSTEIG, GIOVANNI 1892-1977   The Officina Bodoni. Verona: Edizioni Valdonega, 1980. Limited edition of 125 special copies of an overall edition of 1500; 4to; lix, 285 pages, 40 leaves; 2 volumes, 40 original leaves from 10 works issued by the press; illustrations; publisher's quarter dark brown morocco, slipcase; fine.   Thomas Thorp 489-206 1996 £380.00

MARDERSTEIG, GIOVANNI 1892-1977   The Officina Bodoni. Verona: Edizioni Valdonega, 1980. 1st edition; limited to 1500 copies; folio; pages lx, 286 + colophon; illustrations and facsimiles; fine in original buckram. Claude Cox 107-119 1996 £110.00

MARES, FREDERICK H.   Photographs of Dublin with Descriptive Letterpress. Glasgow: Andrew Duthie, 1867. 1st edition; 4to; (41) recto only, (1) page ad; 12 original mounted photographs by Mares; original green cloth, decorated in gilt, all edges gilt; name on endpaper, inner front hing starting, wear to corners and spine ends, still very good. David Mason 71-94 1996 $600.00

MARES, FREDERICK H.   Sunny Memories of Ireland's Scenic Beauties: Killarney. Dublin: printed by Browne & Nolan, 1867. small 4to; 12 albumen prints each measuring 78 x 78 mm., mounted one to a leaf, each with title and decorative line border, and each accompanied by a leaf of text printed rectos only, ad leaf at end; publisher's green cloth, elaborately decorated in gilt on front cover, design repeated in blind on back cover, gilt edges; superb copy.   Thomas Thorp 489-207 1996 £280.00

MARGERIE, PIERRE DE   Eloge de la Typographie. Weimar: Cranach Press, for Editions de Cluny, Paris, 1931. One of 115 copies on Monval from a total issue of 129; 115 on Monval (this copy) and 14 on vellum; page size 11 1/8 x 7 inches; initial engraved by Eric Gill, hand gilded by Max Goertz; paper handmade woodcut of Aristide Maillol, hand gilded by Max Goertz; paper handmade by Caspard and Raffael Maillol, type set by Walter Tanz and Hans Schulze and book was printed by Max Kopp under the direction of Kessler and Max Goertz; bound by Otto Dorfner in full red morocco with gilt fillet on front and back cover, fillet on both edges and double fillet repeated on inside covers, spine panelled, top edge gilt, title and author tooled in gilt on front cover, grey paper slipcase, outstanding copy; signed on back turn-in Dorfner-Weimar.   Priscilla Juvelis 95/1-72 1996 $5,000.00

MARGUERITE D'ANGOULEME, QUEEN OF NAVARRE 1492-1549   The Heptameron of the Tales of Margaret, Queen of Navarre. London: Society of English Bibliophilists, 1894. 8vo; 5 volumes; 150 head and tailpieces by Dunker; modern half red morocco, mottled board sides, edges untrimmed.   Charles W. Traylen 117-174 1996 £105.00

MARGUERITE D'ANGOULEME, QUEEN OF NAVARRE 1492-1549   The Heptameron. London: 1922. 1st edition thus; 5 volumes, illustrations by S. Freudenberg, with 73 full page engravings, each with tissue guard; white buckram gilt, very good.   Words Etcetera 94-797 1996 £65.00

MARIANI, PAUL   Timing Divices: Poems. Pennyroyal Press, 1978. One of 175 copies, signed by author and artist; 12 1/2 x 6 1/4 inches; 61, (1) pages, (2) leaves (woodcut, colophon); printed in red and black in Hermann Zapf's Palatino on distinctive textured Ingres paper; original vellum backed grey paper boards, gilt titling on spine, marbled endpapers; mint.   Phillip J. Pirages 33-414 1996 $250.00

MARIE, JANE   The Case of Jane Marie, Exhibiting the Cruelty and Barbarous Conduct of James Ross to a Defenceless Woman. Philadelphia: Sept. 1808. 1st edition; 8vo; 28 pages; removed; browned. Sabin 44560; S&S 15493.   M & S Rare Books 60-437 1996 $175.00

MARIN, JOHN   Drawings and Watercolors. New York: Twin Editions, 1950. 1st edition; number 253 of 300 numbeed copies, signed by Marin, there were an additional 125 copies with an extra etching; 4to; loose plates and text laid into original beige cloth portolio, as issued; cloth little darkened at spine and edges, very faint soiling or foxing to few plates, generally near fine.   Chapel Hill 94-72 1996 $250.00

MARIN, JOHN   Letters of John Marin. New York: privately printed for an American Place, 1931. One of an issue of 350 numbered copies (of a total edition of 400), although only the issue of 50 copies was issued, signed; fine in cloth; this copy inscribed by author for William L. McKim. Between the Covers   42-286   1996 $1,500.00

MARINATOS, SPYRIDON   Crete and Mycenae. London: Thames and Hudson, 1960. Folio; 177 pages, 28 figures, 421 illustrations; original cloth, lightly chipped dust jacket (edge lightly soiled).   Archaeologia Luxor-3665   1996 $150.00

MARINELLI, GIOVANNI   Gli Ornamenti delle Donne. Venice: Giovanni Valgrisio, 1574. 8vo; (8), 376, (35) leaves (without last blank leaf), woodcut printer's device on title and woodcut initials, some minor foxing; 18th century half vellum, front hinge cracked but sound. Adams M591; Gay V 392; Durling 2963; Wellcome 4059.   Jeffrey D. Mancevice 20-54   1996 $950.00

MARION, WILLIAM B.   The House that B--- Built. San Bernardino: William P. Doherty, 1929. 8 1/4 x 11 5/8 inches; 148 pages, numerous full page photographic illustrations; masonite boards with title branded on front cover, bound with screws and string, head of spine chipped. Dawson's Books Shop   528-165   1997 $200.00

MARJORIBANKS, ALEXANDER   Travels in New Zealand. London: Smith, Elder, 1845. 12mo; pages viii, 9-174, 4; hand color map; new half brown crushed levant, outer edge of map trimmed close. Hocken p. 128; Taylor p. 185.   Richard Adelson   W94/95-116   1996 $350.00

MARJORIBANKS, ALEXANDER   Travels in South and North America. London: Simpkin Marshall, 1853. 1st London edition; 8vo; xvi, 480 pages; colored frontispiece; recently rebound in half calf, boards; fine.   David Mason   71-124   1996 $240.00

MARK, JOHN   Genealogy of the Family of Mark or Marke, Cumberland, Pedigree and Arms of the Bowscale Branch of the Family. Manchester: privately printed, 1898. 4to; pages 285; 16 engraved plates; original quarter navy morocco and cloth, gilt, gilt top. Presentation copy, inscribed by author to John Bewley of Stanwix, Carlisle.   Howes Bookshop   265-1908   1996 £75.00

MARKHAM, BERYL   West With the Night. Boston: Houghton Mifflin, 1942. 1st edition; heavy wear to bottom edges, else very good in not quite very good price clipped jacket; uncommon book.   Ken Lopez 74-282   1996 $325.00

MARKHAM, CLEMENTS ROBERT 1830-1916   Ollanta. London: Trubner & Co., 1871. 1st edition; 8vo; original orange-brown cloth, some rubbing; very good. Sabin 57224; field 1011 (with good note).   Ximenes 109-187   1996 $275.00

MARKHAM, CLEMENTS ROBERT 1830-1916   Peruvian Bark: a Popular Account of the Introduction of Chinchona Cultivation into British India. London: 1880. Thick 8vo; 550 pages; 3 illustrations, 3 folding maps; cloth.   Argosy   810-340   1996 $125.00

MARKHAM, EARNEST   10,000 Miles in a Balloon! Saint Louis: Mercantile Pub. Co., 1873. 1st edition; 16mo; 96 pages; frontispiece, half title, removed, lacks wrappers, edges stained brown; very rare; Randers-Pehrson and Renstrom 56.   M & S Rare Books   60-103   1996 $750.00

MARKLOVE, H.   Views of Berkeley Castle, Taken on the spot, and Drawn on Stone. Bristol: Gloucester & Nailsworth: Longman, et al, Dec. 1840. Folio; 1f. (subscribers), 7 ff. letterpress, lithographic frontispiece, 9 lithographic plates; original titled wrappers, some creasing and wear at edges, corners turned; Abbey Scenery 405.   Marlborough   162-65 1996 £550.00

MARKOV, VLADIMIR   Russian Futurism, a History. London: MacGibbon & Kee, 1969. 24 x 16 cm; xi, 467 pages; 32 pages illustrations; original cloth, in dust jacket.   Rainsford A54-389   1996 £55.00

MARKS, MARY   Five-Chimney Farm. London: Sampson Low, Marston, Searle & Rivington, 1877. 1st edition; 8vo; 3 volumes; original dark green cloth, covers stamped in blind, spines lettered in gilt, some rubbing of extremities, half title in volume 2 only, front free endpaper of first volume lacking, some spotting, but nice; rare. Wolff 3272.   James Cummins 14-130   1996 $500.00

MARMELSZADT, WILLARD   Musical Sons of Aesculapius. New York: 1946. 1st edition; 116 pages; original binding, dust jacket; scarce; autographed by author.   W. Bruce Fye   71-1365   1996 $225.00

MARMONTEL, JEAN FRANCOIS 1723-1799   Belisarius. London: E. Harding, 1794. 1st English edition; 8vo. in 6's; 6 engraved plates after Stothard, slight foxing; finely bound in full contemporary red straight grained morocco, boards, outer gilt border enclosing gilt scroll, spine with large gilt flowers and other small devices, green morocco label, inner gilt dentelles, all edges gilt;   Ian Wilkinson 95/1-120   1996 £150.00

MARMONTEL, JEAN FRANCOIS 1723-1799   The Incas; or, the Destruction of the Empire of Peru. London: printed for J. Nourse, P. Elmsly and E. Lyde and G. Kearsly, 1777. 1st edition in English; 12mo; 2 volumes in one; contemporary mottled calf, spine gilt, minor rubbing; fine, complete with half title in volume II (all required). Sabin 44653; not in Block.   Ximenes   108-256   1996 $600.00

MAROT, CLEMENT   Les Oeuvres. Lyon: E. Roussin & J. Ausoult for Guillaume Rouille, 1548-47. 16mo; 3 parts in 1, 2 volumes, (32), 527; 175, (1), 32, 127, (1) pages, Italic type, woodcut initials, publisher's device on both titles; 18th century long grain brown morocco, joints worn. Brunet III 1456; Baudrier IX 129-130 and 146. Rothschild no. 612. Jeffrey D. Mancevice   20-55   1996 $1,250.00

MAROT, CLEMENT   Les Oeuvres. Lyon: E. Roussin & J. Ausoult for Guillaume Rouille, 1548-47. 16mo; 3 parts in one; 2 volumes, (32), 527; 175, (1), 32, 127, (1) pages; Italic type, woodcut initials, publisher's device on both titles; 18th century long grain brown morocco, joints worn. Brunet Iii 1456; Baudrier IX 129-130 & 146. Rothschild no. 612. Jeffrey Mancevice   20-55   1996 $1,250.00

MARQUAND, ERNEST DAVID   Flora of Guernsey and the Lesser Channel Islands; Namely Alderney, Sark, Herm, Jethou and the Adjacent islets. London: Dulau & Co., 1901. 1st edition; 8vo; half title, 5 maps, original cloth, uncut, nice.   Anthony W. Laywood   108-199   1996 £50.00

MARQUAND, JOHN P.   Mr. Moto is So Sorry. Boston: Little, Brown, 1938. 1st edition; gift inscription on endpaper, two small snags in cloth, bottom edge front cover, rear cover soiled, otherwise very good in dust jacket with rear panel faintly dampstained.   Quill & Brush   102-1249 1996 $275.00

MARQUAND, JOHN P.   Think Fast, Mr. Moto. Boston: Little Brown, 1937. 1st edition; prelims and page edges foxed, spine and edges rubbed, otherwise very good in edge rubbed dust jacket soiled on rear panel and with spine ends chipped and rubbed; scarce.   Quill & Brush 102-1248   1996 $275.00

MARQUIS, F. DICKINSON   John Marshall, the Tribute of Massachusetts...in Commemoration of the One Hundredth Anniversary of His Elevation to the Bench as Chief Justice of the Supreme Court of the United States. Boston: Little Brown and Co., 1901. Number 398 of 750 copies; Bit worn and stained, but good.   Meyer Boswell   SL25-151 1996 $125.00

MARQUIS, THOMAS B.   A Warrior Who Fought Custer. Minneapolis: 1934. 1st edition; 1st state; 349 pages; photos, maps; cloth. Dustin 192; Smith 6532. Luther 83.   T. A. Swinford   49-731   1996 $125.00

MARRA, JOHN   Journal of the Resolution's Voyage in 1772, 1773, 1774 and 1775. (with) A Journal of the Adventure's Voyage in the Years 1772, 1773 and 1774. London: F. Newbery, 1775. 1st edition; 8vo; (iii-xiii), errata and directions to binder to verso, 328 pages of text, folding map frontispiece, 5 engraved copperplates; some slight offsetting to letterpress from couple of plates, otherwise fine and clean copy internally; old speckled calf boards, very skillfully and tastefully rebacked and corners restored, gilt rule and brown label ot panelled spine, yellow edges, armorial bookplate. Hill p. 60; Streeter IV 2408; Mitchell 1270; Holmes 16.   Beeleigh Abbey   BA56-55   1996 £3,900.00

MARRIAGE & Home. London: Morgan Scott, c. 1873. half title; original white cloth decorated in red and gilt, all edges gilt, very good to fine. Jarndyce   103-422   1996 £55.00

MARRIOTT, JAMES   Poems Written Chiefly at the University of Cambridge... London: printed by James Bettenham, 1761. 8vo; sole edition; lacks half title, title in red and black, viii, viii, 156 pages; all uncut, frontispiece, 6 tailpieces; late 19th century dark maroon limp morocco with marbled endpapers, little worn at head and foot of spine, some spotting on frontispiece.   David Bickersteth 133-47 1996 £85.0

MARRYAT, FRANK   Borneo and the Indian Archipelago. London: Longman, Brown, Green and Longman, 1848. Large 4to; (viii), 232 pages, lithographic titlepage, frontispiece, 20 attractive lithographic plates, woodcuts in text; original red ribbed and blindstamped cloth, gilt title, rebacked with original spine laid on, covers slightly marked and dusty, corners rubbed and bumped, overall very pleasant, tight. NMMC 534. Antipodean 28-631 1996 $750.00

MARRYAT, FRANK   Mountains and Molehills, or Recollections of a Burnt Journal. London: Longman, Brown, Green and Longmans, 1855. 8 3/4 x 5 1/2 inches; xii, 443 pages, 24 page's publisher's catalog at end, frontispiece, 7 other chromolithographed plates, woodcuts in text; blindstamped salmon cloth, recased preserving original endpapers, rear free endpaper lacking, some light marginal stain, stain unobtrusively touching frontispiece image; Bookplate of Carl Wheat. Zamorano 80 52. Dawson's Books Shop 528-166 1996 $600.00

MARRYAT, FREDERICK 1792-1848   The King's Own. London: Henry Colburn and Richard Bentley, 1830. 1st edition; 12mo; 3 volumes, half titles to volumes i and ii and ads in volume iii discarded, half title in volume 3 with errata on verso present, occasional foxing, small paper fault in blank fore-margin L11 volume 3; pages (ii), 324; (ii), 325; (iv), 327; contemporary half calf, very rubbed, lacks volume label to volume 2, others chipped, backstrips with raised bands between gilt rules, black labels in second and third compartments, marbled sides, drab endpapers, red sprinkled and polished edges, bookseller's ticket. Sadleir 1581 and Excursions p. 83; Wolff 4520.   Blackwell's B112-184 1996 £150.00

MARRYAT, FREDERICK 1792-1848   Mr. Midshipman Easy. London: Saunders and Otley, Conduit ST., 1836. 1st edition; 3 volumes; pages (vii), 291; (vii), 306; (viii), 314 pages; uniformly bound by Hering in marbled boards, half black roan with red gilt titles, extremities rubbed and spines scraped, spine to volume III cracked, some page corners missing, no loss, else very nice; all volumes inscribed by Sir Charles Rowley.   Marjorie James 19-147 1996 £125.00

MARRYAT, FREDERICK 1792-1848   Newton Forster; or, the Merchant Service. London: James Cochrane, 1832. 1st edition; 12mo; lacks half titles and ads, some foxing; pages (ii), 270; (ii), 295; (ii), 252; contemporary half calf, very rubbed, backstrips with raised bands and gilt rules, black labels chipped, marbled boards, drab endpapers, bookseller's ticket in volume i, sound. Inscribed "From the Author". Sadleir 1588; Excursions p. 83; Wolff 4527.   Blackwell's B112-185 1996 £150.00

MARRYAT, FREDERICK 1792-1848   The Novels. London: J. M. Dent, 1896. One of 750 sets printed; 8vo; 24 volumes; blue linen as issued (spines sunned as usual), apart from browning to some pages, good, sound reading set.   Appelfeld Gallery 54-137 1996 $275.00

MARRYAT, FREDERICK 1792-1848   Peter Simple. London: Saunders and Otley, 1834. 1st English edition; with author's calling card (oxidized & with offsetting) tipped in, several penned notations annotating the clippings or inserts, including an inserted portrait & 3 illustrations by R.W. Buss; ALS by author to Edward Ingraham, Ingraham signed 1st vol; contemporary half calf, marbled boards, uncut, some rubbing, generally light, half title in volume 2 only as issued, errata slip to third volume inserted in volume 1 following contents, blank and leaves through the title in volume 1 loose, some offsetting of inserts, some light soiling, browning and spotting, mostly at front and back, few ms. markings, newspaper clippings relating to Marryat on blanks & endpapers, without publisher's ads at back of volume 3; brown morocco folding box. Block 153; Sadleir 1592a; Wolff 517a.   James Cummins 14-131 1996 $1,000.00

MARRYAT, FREDERICK 1792-1848   Peter Simple. London: Saunders & Otley, 1834. 1st English edition (same year as Philadelphia); 12mo; 3 volumes, errata slip in volume 3, wanting half title in volume 2 (others not called for) and ads in volume 3; later Riviere style quarter calf, spines gilt, morocco labels, marbled boards; fine, attractive. Sadleir 1592a; wolff 4531.   Trebizond 39-40 1996 $190.00

MARRYAT, FREDERICK 1792-1848   Peter Simple. London: Sanders and Otley, 1834. 1st English edition; 12mo; 3 volumes; pages vii, (i), 328; viii (for vi), 343; viii, 380; half title to volume 2, never having been issued for volume 3, errata slip and volume 3 ads discarded, very small piece of blank margin B1 (vol. 1) and L9 (volume 3) torn away, otherwise internally excellent; contemporary half calf, rubbed, lacks title labels volumes 1 and 3, others chipped, marbled boards, drab endpapers, red sprinkled and polished edges; good; inscribed "From the Author" at head of titlepage.   Blackwell's B112-186 1996 £95.00

MARRYAT, FREDERICK 1792-1848   The Phantom Ship. London: Henry Colburn, 1839. 1st edition; 12mo; 3 volumes; original boards, printed paper labels, some wear to joints and spine, some spotting and offsetting, mostly at front of first volume where an earlier owner has inserted clippings related to Marryat's litigations over his works; very nice in morocco backed folding box (worn). With ms. dedication leaf inserted in first volume.   James Cummins 14-132 1996 $2,250.00

MARRYAT, FREDERICK 1792-1848   The Phantom Ship. London: Henry Colburn, 1839. 1st edition; 12mo; 3 volumes, half title to volume 1, only single leaf of ads at end of volume 3 (i.e. N2), prelim and final leaves foxed; pages (iv), 300; (ii), 289; (ii), 266, (2); contemporary half calf, rubbed, backstrips with raised bands between gilt rules, black morocco labels in second and third compartments, marbled boards, drab endpapers, good. Sadleir 1593 and Excursions p. 89; Wolff 4532. Blackwell's B112-187 1996 £150.00

MARRYAT, FREDERICK 1792-1848   The Settlers in Canada. London: Longmans, 1844. 1st edition; foolscap 8vo; 2 volumes; frontispieces; bound by Zaehnsdorf in half light blue morocco, gilt tops, trifle faded. Charles W. Traylen 117-159 1996 £60.00

MARSH, E. A.   The Evolution of Automatic Machinery as Applied to the Manufacture of Watches at Waltham, Mass. by the American Waltham Watch Company. Chicago: George K. Hazlitt & Co., 1896. 8vo; 150 pages; 4 portraits, 69 photographic illustrations; original blue cloth, gilt, bit rubbed and faded.   Kenneth Karmiole 1NS-125 1996 $100.00

MARSH, HERBERT   The History of the Politicks of Great Britian and France, fromt he Time of the Conference at Pillnitz (1791). London: printed for John Stockdale, 1800. 8vo; 2 volumes, 376, 396 pages; contemporary full tree calf, gilt spines, green leather spine labels, corners and outer hinges bit rubbed.   Kenneth Karmiole 1NS-165 1996 $150.00

MARSH, HONORIA   Shades from Jane Austen. London: Parry Jackman, 1975. 1st edition; edition deluxe limited to 300 numbered copies; 12 x 9 inches; pages xxxviii, 205, vii, over 100 illustrations, mostly in color; full goat skin moire silk taffeta endpapers, all edges gilt, mint in matching goatskin slipcase. Gilson L42.   Ian Hodgkins 78-138 1996 £50.00

MARSH, J. B. T.   The Story of the Jubilee Singers, with their Songs. London: 1886. Revised edition; original photo as frontispiece, light foxing, decorated gilt cover, front hinge starting, slight rubbing at edges.   J. B. Muns 154-162 1996 $125.00

MARSHALL, ALFRED   Principles of Economics. London: 1895. 3rd edition; 8vo; volume 1, all published, pages xxxi, (1), 823, corrigenda slip; original cloth, spine faintly spotted, very good.   James Fenning 133-228 1996 £125.00

MARSHALL, C. H. T.   A Monograph of the Capitonidae or Scansorial Barbets. London: 1870-71. Royal 4to; pages (x), xlii, (190), 73 hand colored plates by Keulemans; contemporary half morocco; exceptionally fine plates are clean and beautiful.   Wheldon & Wesley 207-64 1996 £4,500.00

MARSHALL, F. H.   Catalogue of the Jewellery, Greek, Etruscan and Roman, in the Departments of Antiquities, British Museum. London: British Museum, 1911. 1st edition; 4to; 8vo; lxii, 400 pages, 97 figures, 73 plates; original cloth.   Archaeologia Luxor-3667 1996 $650.00

MARSHALL, JOHN 1755-1835   Atlas to the Life of George Washington. Philadelphia: J. Crissy, 1832. 8vo; 10 double page maps, engraved titlepage, original boards, cloth back and corners, paper label, ex-library, small library label removed from front cover, backstrip rubbed, maps fine; Howes M316.   Edward Morrill 369-212 1996 $150.00

MARSHALL, JOHN 1755-1835   The Life of George Washington, Commander in Chief of the American Forces, during the War Which Established the Independence of His Country... Philadelphia: C. P. Wayne, 1804-07. 5 volumes 8vo. and atlas 4to; pages xxii, 488, 45; v, 565, 67; vii, 576, 28; viii, 626, 16; vii, 779, 36; portrait in volume 1; atlas uncut with 10 maps, 22 pages of subscribers; text in contemporary American tree calf, red and black labels, rubbed; atlas in half tan calf. Sabin 44788; Howes M317.   Richard Adelson W94/95-117 1996 $785.00

MARSHALL, JOHN 1755-1835   The Life of George Washington. Philadelphia: 1804. 1st edition; 1st printing; 5 volumes plus scarce quarto atlas; original boards, paper labels, some wear and minor restoration to boards, atlas in contemporary marbled boards, rebacked and recornered; quite scarce in original condition; cloth case. Lovely set. 19th Century Shop 39- 1996 $3,500.00

MARSHALL, JOHN 1755-1835   The Life of George Washington... Philadelphia: James Crissy and Thomas Cowperthwait & Co., 1839. 2nd edition; 2 volumes; full calf, red leather labels, some foxing, overall near fine. Howes M317.   Blue River Books 9-315 1996 $100.00

MARSHALL, JOSEPH   Travels through Holland, Flanders, Germany, Denmark, Sweden, Lapland, Russia, the Ukraine and Poland in the Years 1768, 1769 and 1770. London: printed for J. Almon, 1773-76. Mixed editions, volumes 1-3 2nd edition, volume 4 1st edition; 8vo; half title to volumes 1 and 4, titlepages with ink signature, slight worm damage to margins of rear leaves of volume 1 and front pastedowns of volumes 2 and 3; full calf, gilt rule and brown labels to spines, red speckled edges, armorial bookplate to front pastedowns, ink stain to lower board of volume 2. Cox I p. 90-145.   Beeleigh Abbey BA56-92 1996 £425.00

MARSHALL, N. B.   Aspects of Marine Zoology. 1967. 8vo; 280 pages; illustrations; cloth.   Wheldon & Wesley 207-330 1996 £50.00

MARSHALL, PAULE   The Chosen Place, The Timeless People. New York: Harcourt Brace, 1969. 1st edition; author's rare 3rd book; near fine in very good dust jacket.   Pettler & Lieberman 28-28 1996 $125.00

MARSHALL, W. E.   A Phrenologist Amongst the Todas, or the Study of a Primitive Tribe in South India... London: 1873. Photos; original red cloth, very lightly marked, otherwise most excellent copy.   David Grayling J95Biggame-377 1996 £50.00

MARSHALL, WILLIAM 1745-1818   A Review of the Landscape. London: 1795. 8vo; pages xvi, 275; modern boards, antique style. Henrey 1270.   Wheldon & Wesley 207-1726 1996 £65.00

MARSHALL, WILLIAM 1745-1818   The Rural Economy of the Southern Classics... London: for G. Nichol, 1798. 8vo; 2 volumes; pages xxxii, 411, 2 ff., ads; xxxii, 416, 8 ff. (index), 2 double page engraved map frontispieces; contemporary half calf, marbled boards, some wear, joints cracked. Macdonald Agricultural Writers p. 215.   Marlborough 162-66 1996 £225.00

MARSHALL, WILLIAM 1745-1818   The Rural Economy of the West of England. Dublin: 1797. 1st Irish edition; 8vo; pages 9, xxxviii, 489, (19); contemporary half calf, binding little rubbed, fine.   John Henly 27-369 1996 £132.00

MARSHALL, WILLIAM 1745-1818   The Rural Economy of the West of England: Including Devonshire; and Parts of Somersetshire, Dorsetshire and Cornwall. Together with Minutes in Practice. London: printed for G. Nicol, G. G. and J. Robinson and J. Debrett, 1796. 1st edition; 8vo; 2 volumes; folding map frontispiece to volume 1, 332, 358 pages; 3 pages publisher's ad, lacks half title; half calf, blind rule borders, gilt rule to spines, red morocco labels, marbled boards, speckled edges, armorial bookplates. Cox III p. 535.   Beeleigh Abbey BA/56-15 1996 £200.00

MARSILIIS, HIPPOLYTUS DE   Mariana Hippolyti de Marsiliis... Venice: apud Dominicum Lilium, 1559. 8vo; A-F 8 (F7 & F8 blank), ff. 179, printer's device on title; half vellum, attractive boards (Dutch 17th century?); good.   K Books 442-349 1996 £230.00

MARSTON, JOHN   The Metamorphosis of Pigmalions Image. Waltham St. Lawrence: Golden Cockerel Press, 1926. One of 325 numbered copies; 8vo; printed in black and brown on handmade paper, half buckram with batik sides; spine little soiled, but nice.   Bertram Rota 272-167 1996 £75.00

MARTIAL D'AUVERGNE d. 1508   Aresta Amorum, cum Erudita Benedicti Curtii Symphoriani Explanatione... Paris: Carolus Langelier, 1544. Crown 8vo; pritner's device on title and last leaf recto, wormhole through first 6 leaves, mended, affecting few letters; 19th century French tree calf, gilt spine, sound. Adams 686; Brunet III 1483/4; Gay/Lemonnyer I col. 272.   H. M. Fletcher 121-24 1996 £145.00

MARTIALIS, MARCUS VALERIUS   Select Epigrams of Martial Englished. In the Savoy: printed by Edward Jones, for Samuel Lowndes, 1689. 1st edition of this translation; 8vo; frontispiece; contemporary mottled calf, spine gilt, little rubbed, slight wear to spine; very good. Wing M8333; CBEL II 14499.   Ximenes 108-259 1996 $500.00

MARTIN'S Annals of Crime; or, New Newgate Calendar...Comprehending a history of the Most Notorious Murderers...Highwaymen, Pirates, Burglars, Pickpockets, Adulterers, Ravishers, Decoyers, Incendiaries, Poachers, Swindlers, etc. London: William Mark Clark, 19, Warwick Lane, Paternoster Row, 1873-38. 108 weekly parts, each part with its own woodcut and 8 pages of text; sheep backed boards, repaired, embrowned and worn but sound.   Meyer Boswell SL26-178 1996 $850.00

MARTIN, EUSTACE MEREDYTH   A Tour through India in Lord Canning's Time. London: Remington and Co., 1881. 1st edition; 8vo; (iv), 264 pages; original tan pictorial cloth, blocked in blue; fine.   James Burmester 29-93 1996 £55.00

MARTIN, GEORGE R. R.   Dying of the Light. New York: Simon & Schuster, 1977. Uncorrected proof; signed; author's first novel; yellow printed wrpapers, covers lightly soiled, two 1" creases, otherwise fine.   Robert Gavora 61-66 1996 $150.00

MARTIN, GEORGE R. R.   Songs the Dead Men Sing. Niles: Dark Harvest, 1983. 1st edition; one of 500 numbered copies, signed by author; very fine in dust jacket with slipcase which shows some of usual fading.   Robert Gavora 61-67 1996 $275.00

MARTIN, LADY   Our Maoris. London: 1884. (iv), 220 pages, black and white plates in text, 1 color map; blue-grey pictorial cloth, gilt, small split on hinge, slightly faded, otherwise very good; scarce. Bicknel 3402.   Antipodean 28-33 1996 $125.00

MARTIN, MARTIN   A Late Voyage to St. Kilda, the Remotest of the Hebrides, or Western Isles of Scotland. London: printed for D. Brown and T. Goodwin, 1698. 1st edition; 8vo; folding map and one other plate heavily foxed (as often), otherwise sound, complete with half title and final leaf of ads; half calf. Wing M847; CBEL II 1398.   Ximenes 108-260 1996 $350.00

MARTIN, ROBERT MONTGOMERY 1803?-1868   China: Political, Commercial and Social... London: James Madden, 1847. 1st edition; 8vo; 2 volumes, 432; 502, xviii, (10) pages; 6 maps; original embossed blue cloth, library bookplates and clipped front endpapers, early owner's signature on titlepages, front inner hinges cracked, rear free endpaper lacking in volume 1, still a good, readable copy, despite faults.   Chapel Hill 94-151 1996 $100.00

MARTIN, ROBERT MONTGOMERY 1803?-1868   The Indian Empire: History, Topography, Geology, Climate, Population, Chief Cities, and Provinces... London: Printing and Publishing Co., n.d. 4to; 3 volumes; 582, viii; 504, viii; 192 pages; 2 double page maps, hand colored in outline, 120 engraved plates; contemporary maroon half morocco, spine gilt in 5 compartments (slightly rubbed, few small marginal tears, occasional foxing and one or two plates slightly loose).   Thomas Thorp 489-208 1996 £200.00

MARTIN, ROBERT MONTGOMERY 1803?-1868   Statistics of the Colonies of the British Empire in the West Indies, South America, North America, Asia, Austral-Asia, Africa and Europe... London: Wm. H. Allen, 1839. 25 cm; v, (x), 602, 304 pages; folding engraved map, in color, frontispiece, engraved plates, illustrations; quarter leather and cloth, the folding map backed with linen; very good to fine. Sabin 44917; Gagnon 2275; not in TPL.   Rockland Books 38-147 1996 $450.00

MARTIN, SADIE   The Life and Professional Career of Emma Abbott (1850-1891). Minneapolis: L. Kimball, 1891. 1st edition; 189 pages; 28 photos; full morocco, all edges gilt, some rubbing, but handsome in gilt design and lettering.   Lyman Books 21-319 1996 $200.00

MARTINEAU, HARRIET 1802-1876   Complete Guide to the English Lakes. Windermere: John Garnett, 2nd edition; 8vo; (2), iv, ii, iv, 233, (i), xviii, (i) pages; 12 engraved plates, 4 plates of hotels, 6 mountain outlines, folding colored map; original red gilt cloth, rebacked, retaining original backstrip, inner joints repaired, some browning and occasional foxing. Bicknell 155.2.a.   Ken Spelman 30-91 1996 £50.00

MARTINEAU, HARRIET 1802-1876   A Complete Guide to the English Lakes... London: Whittaker & Co. and Windermere: John Garnett, 1858. Small 8vo; pages ii, ii, iv, (xiv), 210, xviii (directory), xvi, xv-xvii (first p. xv with blank verso bound in back to front, which confuses pagination further), half title, frontispiece, engraved title, 12 steel engraved plates as called for, plus 5 additional plates, 6 outlines of mountains, hand colored folding map in rear pocket; original red blindstamped cloth, gilt, hinges and top of spine little worn; plates dampstained or little spotted, otherwise very good. Bicknell 155.2b.   R.F.G. Hollett & Son 78-1105 1996 £140.00

MARTINEAU, HARRIET 1802-1876   Guide to Windermere, with Tours to the Neighbouring Lakes and Other Interesting Places... Windermere: John Garnett, n.d. 1856. 3rd edition; small 8vo; pages iii, 117, folding map, 5 tinted illustrations; original pictorial stiff wrappers, rubbed, rebacked, lower corner of back panel defective. Bicknell 157.3.   R.F.G. Hollett & Son 78-1106 1996 £65.00

MARTINEAU, HARRIET 1802-1876   How to Observe. Morals and Manners. London: Charles Knight and Co., 1838. 1st edition; 8vo; vii, (i), 238 pages, lacking leaf of ads, inner margins of first few leaves lightly soiled; original green cloth, covers affected by damp, top of spine repaired; Sadleir 1640;   James Burmester 29-94 1996 £125.00

MARTINEAU, HARRIET 1802-1876   Retrospect of Western Travel. New York: Harper & Bros., 1838. 1st American edition; 2 volumes, (vi), 13-276, 239 pages, 2 pages of prelim ads in volume 1, 4 pages in rear of volume 2; cloth, paper spine labels, spine labels faded, overall light wear and foxing, otherwise very good.   Metacomet Books 54-66 1996 $135.00

MARTINEAU, HARRIET 1802-1876   Sketches from Life. London: Whittaker & Co. and Windermere: J. Garnett, 1856. 1st edition; 8vo; pages ii, (i), 165; half title; vignette title with vignette and 6 engraved plates; original blue cloth, gilt, extremities little rubbedd, all edges gilt; nice.   R.F.G. Hollett & Son 78-422 1996 £120.00

MARTINEAU, HARRIET 1802-1876   Suggestions Towards the Future Government of India. London: Smith, Elder & Co., 1858. 1st edition; 8vo; viii, 153, (1) pages, complete with half title and 18 pages of publisher's ads at end (dated Feb. 1858); original cloth, label, some wear to spine, else good with contemporary press cuttings pasted on to front endpapers;   John Drury 82-176 1996 £95.00

MARTINET, JOHANNES FLORENTIUS   The Catechism of Nature, for the Use of Children. Boston: printed by Young and Etheridge for D. West and E. Larkin, 1793. 3 3/4 x 6 1/4 inches; 108 pages; calf backed paper over boards, wooden boards showing along edge and cracked horizontally, previous owner's names, else very good. Evans 25759; Rosenbach 178 for 1794 ed.   Andrew Cahan 47-98 1996 $200.00

A MARVEL Among Cities! Spokane Falls a Western Wonder Whose Whole History is Comprised Within Eight Years. Saint Paul: Pioneer Press Co., 1888. 1st edition; 31 pages; illustrations; original printed orange wrappers, map on back wrapper, minor soiling, very good. Not in Smith or Soliday; Streeter Sale 3287.   Michael D. Heaston 23-355 1996 $500.00

MARVELL, ANDREW 1621-1678   Miscellaneous Poems. London: for Robert Boulter, 1681. 1st edition; folio; pages (ii) title, blank, 139, without portrait; 18th century marbled boards, skilfully rebacked with calf, green morocco label lettered in gilt, few spots, one or two trivial tears and repairs, very good. Pforzheimer 671; Ashley Cat. III 121.   Simon Finch 24-164 1996 £850.00

MARVELL, ANDREW 1621-1678   Miscellaneous Poems. London: Nonesuch Press, 1923. Limited edition, number 377 of 850 copies; small folio; pages (iii), 148, (3); printed on Italian handmade paper, collotype frontispiece, tissue guard present, decorative design incorporating author's initials printed in red on titlepage; fawn boards, lettered and patterned in gilt, very faint and occasional edge foxing, untrimmed, dust jacket trifle darkened at backstrip; excellent. Dreyfus 4.   Blackwell's B112-209 1996 £150.00

MARX, KARL   Das Kapital. Hamburg: Otto Meissner, 1890-85. 1st edition of Book II; 4th edition of Book I; 8vo; 2 volumes, xxxii, 739, (1); xxvii, (1), 526, (2) pages; contemporary black quarter morocco, spines lettered in gilt, raised bands, extremities rubbed; fine. Einaudi 3772; Stammhammer I 145.   John Drury 82-178 1996 £750.00

MARY THEODORE, SISTER   Heralds of Christ the King: Missionary Record of the North Pacific: 1837-1878. New York: P. J. Kenedy & Sons, 1939. 24.5 cm; xiv, 273 pages; illustrations; mock leather and boxed; fine. Lowther 1795; Smith 6578.   Rockland Books 38-219 1996 $125.00

MARYLAND   The Report of and Testimony Taken Before the Joint Committee of the Senate and House of Delegates of Maryland To Which was Referred the Memorials of John B. Morris, Reverdy Johnson and Ohters... Annapolis: William M'Neir, 1836. 8vo; 77 pages; sewn; contemporary plain wrappers, frayed. Scarce. Rinderknecht 38812.   M & S Rare Books 60-367 1996 $450.00

MARYLAND. SENATE   Journal of the Proceedings of Senate of Maryland, Jan. Session, 1865. Annapolis: Richard P. Bayly, 1865. contemporary sheep, very worn, covers loose, working copy.   Meyer Boswell SL25-153 1996 $100.00

MASCALL, L.   A Booke of the Arte and Manner How to Plant and Graffe. London: 1592. 6th edition; 8vo; black letter, woodcuts, including one full page of a gardener's tools, lacking title and blank at end, A2 worn, rubbed and margins defective, affecting some letters, other leaves dog eared or with small blank corner missing, early ms. transcription of title on A2 (from 1599 ed., the book must have been imperfect since c. 1700); old binder's cloth, bit worn and soiled. STC 17578 (2 England, 4 USA at least one imperfect), Hunt 166.   Maggs Bros. Ltd. 1190-35 1996 £80.00

MASEFIELD, JOHN 1878-1967   The Battle of the Somme. London: William Heinemann, 1919. One of 250 numbered copies; parchment backed boards, top edge gilt, covers slightly marked, head and tail of spine slightly bumped, corners bumped and bruised, very good.   Ulysses 39-646 1996 £95.00

MASEFIELD, JOHN 1878-1967   The Faithful - a Tragedy in Three Acts. London: William Heinemann, 1915. 1st edition; original binding, pictorial endpapers, top edge dusty, head and tail of spine and corners bumped, spine slightly darkened, first blank torn and repaired with sellotape, prelims, edges and endpapers spotted; good only; loosely inserted ALS from author to presentee, presentation copy inscribed by author to Frank Cochran, producer of the play.   Ulysses 39-393 1996 £75.00

MASEFIELD, JOHN 1878-1967   John M. Synge: a Few Personal Recollections, with Biographical Notes. Churchtown: Cuala Press, 1915. One of 350 numbered copies; linen backed boards, top edge dusty, covers marked and dusty, cover edges slightly darkened, corners also bruised, good.   Ulysses 39-131 1996 £125.00

MASEFIELD, JOHN 1878-1967   Midsummer Night and Other Tales in Verse. London: William Heinemann Ltd., n.d. 1928. 1st edition; number 260 of 275 large paper copies, signed by author (this being one of 25 for presentation); original parchment backed boards, dust jacket, bit soiled and torn; fine. dedication copy, the book is dedicated "To my Wife" with Masefield's inscription; fine. With Masefield's bookplate. NCBEL IV 308.   David J. Holmes 52-71 1996 $750.00

MASERES, FRANCIS 1731-1824   Occasional Essays on Various Subjects, Chiefly Political and Historical... London: printed by Robert Wilks, and sold by John White, 1809. 1st edition; 8vo; xvi, 607 pages, tears in 3 leaves (affecting text but without loss), one gathering foxed; contemporary dark blue half calf, spine gilt;   James Burmester 29-95 1996 £240.00

MASLEN, T. J.   The Friend of Australia; or, a Plan for Exploring the Interior and for Carrying on a Survey of the Whole Continent of Australia. London: Smith Elder & Co., 1836. 2nd edition; (xxiv), 428 pages, (8) pages ads; folding map, 5 folding aquatint plates; original blue cloth, spine rebacked with 1920's plain black cloth, stamped on old endpaper South Aus. Rooms A; Gole & Co.; James Partington bookplate; very nice. The Absolon copy. Ferguson 2145; Wantrup 117b.   Antipodean 28-625 1996 $1,450.00

MASON, A. E. W.   The Witness for the Defence. London: printed by J. Miles & Co., Ltd., 1911. 12mo; pages 76 (interleaves); original printed front board, unprinted back board, both trifle soiled, cloth back;   Howard S. Mott 227-98 1996 $500.00

MASON, BOBBIE ANN   The Girl Sleuth. Old Westbury: Feminist Press, 1975. 1st edition; bottom edge of rear cover waterstained but pages aren't affected, tiny tear to edge of front panel, still very nice, scarce, inscribed.   Alice Robbins 15-208 1996 $125.00

MASON, BOBBIE ANN   Nabokov's Garden. Ann Arbor: Ardis, 1974. 1st edition; faint waterstain on lower front cvoer which is more apparent on front panel of jacket, pages not affected and this is still very presentable copy of her first book; inscribed.   Alice Robbins 15-207 1996 $100.00

MASON, BOBBIE ANN   With Jazz. Monterey: Larkspur, 1994. One of 50 copies; printed on dampened Johannot, signed by author and artist; illustrations by LaNelle Mason; hand bound by Carolyn Whitesel, fine in illustrated boards.   Bella Luna 7-360 1996 $125.00

MASON, HENRY JOSEPH MONCK   Reasons and Authorities and Facts Afforded by the History of the Irish Society, Respecting the Dusty of Employing the Irish Language, as a More General Medium for Conveying Scriptural Instruction to the Native Peasantry of Ireland. Dublin: printed by M. Goodwin and Co., 1835. 3rd edition; 8vo; 32 pages; original plain brown paper wrappers; nice; inscribed (twice) "For Earl Belmore" (?by the author).   James Fenning 133-229 1996 £65.00

MASON, J. A.   A Treatise on the Climate and Meteorology of Madeira... London: John Churchill, Liverpool: Deighton and Laughton, 1850. 1st edition; medium 8vo; large paper copy; 386 pages text, 5 climate graphs on 3 plates; original green cloth, elaborately decorated gilt covers and spine, top edge gilt, inner gilt dentelles, yellow endpapers, bound by Westleys & Co., upper and lower hinges cracked, corners bumped.   Beeleigh Abbey BA56-94 1996 £250.00

MASON, J. ALDEN   Archaeology of Santa Marta Colombia; The Tairona Culture, Part I-II: 2. Chicago: Field Museum, 1931-39. 8vo; 3 volumes, 418 pages, 26 figures, 248 plates, 2 maps; wrappers. With signature of J. A. Bennyhoff.   Archaeologia Luxor-4681 1996 $250.00

MASON, JOHN 1706-1763   An Essay on Elocution, or Pronunciation. London: printed for G. Hett, J. Buckland, J. Waugh, &c., 1751. 3rd edition; 43 pages; disbound. Alston VI 324.   Jarndyce 103-307 1996 £80.00

MASON, JOHN 1706-1763   The Student and Pastor, or Directions How to Attain to Eminence and Usefulness In those Respective Characters. Exeter: from the Press of Thomas Odiorne, 1794. 1st American edition; 12mo; contemporary sheep, spine gilt, rubbed, upper joint cracked; very good; early bookplate of Andrew Mack. Evans 27275.   Ximenes 109-188 1996 $100.00

MASON, JOHN 1901-   Five Papers Hand Made at the Twelve by Eight Mill. Leicester: Twelve by Eight Press, 1954. 16mo; wrappers, very nice, with Mason's autograph signature, dated Dec. 1954 on lower wrapper; very scarce.   Bertram Rota 272-471 1996 £50.00

MASON, JOHN 1901-   Paper Making as an Artistic Craft. Leicester: Twelve by Eight, 1963. Revised edition; 8vo; 96 pages; illustrations by Rigby Graham, this copy contains 10 original mounted specimens of author's own handmade paper, variously decorated, illustrated and printed; most copies contain 2-4 specimens only; original parchment, gilt; with note signed by Mason laid in.   Kenneth Karmiole 1NS-167 1996 $200.00

MASON, JOHN 1901-   Papermaking as an Artistic Craft. Leicester: Twelve by Eight Press, 1963. Octavo; 96 pages; illustrations by Rigby Graham; 8 paper specimens tipped in; limp vellum paper wrappers, gilt stamp to front cover; fine.   Bromer Booksellers 90-168 1996 $175.00

MASON, JOHN 1901-   Paper Making as an Artistic Craft. Leicester: Twelve by Eight, 1963. Illustrations by Rigby Graham; 6 paper specimens tipped in; white stiff paper wrappers; signed by author.   Maggs Bros. Ltd. 1191-190 1996 £50.00

MASON, JOHN 1901-   Papermaking: Notes. Leicester: Orpheus Press, 1959. Of an edition of only 41 copies, this one of 17 on paper handmade by John Mason and Douglas Martin; small folio; quarter parchment, marbled boards, very nice.   Bertram Rota 272-362 1996 £160.00

MASON, JOHN 1901-   Some Papers Hand Made by John Mason. London: Maggs, 1959. 8vo; some 34 pages of handmade papers in various colors and textures, some sheets plain, others bearing illustrations or samples; original parchment backed paper covered boards, fern leaf within paper on each cover, edges uncut, fine copy, preserved in original slightly dust soiled. An additional sample of paper lightly tipped onto inside front cover bears typescript "take care of this little book - it is no ordinary textbook but a private press production in very limited edition on a quite unique subject - each copy made up by hand...", then follows author's signature.   Thomas Thorp 489-211 1996 £105.00

MASON, WILLIAM 1725-1797   The English Garden: a Poem. Dublin: Price et al, 1782. 2nd Dublin edition (first complete); pages ii, 156; rubbed full calf, bound with half title; NCBEL II 670; Henrey 1044. Second Life Books 103-137 1996 $150.00

MASON, WILLIAM 1725-1797   The English Garden: a Poem. London: Chas. Wittingham for M. Jones, 1803. Tall 16mo; pages viii, 130, (2 ad), fine portrait frontispiece, early marbled boards, printed label, uncut, original owner's name on flyleaf, nice copy. CBEL II 371 for first collected ed.   Hartfield 48-L59 1996 $175.00

MASON, WILLIAM 1725-1797   Poems. London: printed for Robert Horsfield; and sold by J. Dodsley and C. Marsh... 1764. 1st edition; 8vo; as in all copies, leaf S5 is a cancel; contemporary calf, gilt, spine gilt, some rubbing. very good; Gaskell 8; CBEL II 669.   Ximenes 108-261 1996 $200.00

A MASQUE of Poets. Boston: Roberts Bros., 1878. 1st edition; red line issue, only 500 copies printed in this format, 1500 printed in regular format; original mauve cloth, gilt, top edge gilt, attractive copy with only the lightest rubbing and becoming rather scarce in this format. Borst C7.a. Myerson C1. BAL 118, 4654 and 20121.   Mac Donnell 12-142 1996 $650.00

A MASQUE of Poets. Boston: Roberts Bros., 1878. 1st edition; regular issue, with 'Publisher's Notice' tipped in before titlepage; one of 1500 copies; original black cloth, stamped in red, some close cracks in hinge cloth, moderate rubbing at spine tips, bright copy; Scarce. Borst C7.a. BAL 118, 4654 and 20121.   Mac Donnell 12-4 1996 $400.00

MASSACHUSETTS HORTICULTURAL SOCIETY   Catalogue of the Library of the Massachusetts Horticultural Society. Mansfield: 1994. Limited to 150 copies; 4to; parts 1 and 2, pages (1), vii, 587; cloth.   Raymond M. Sutton VI-1131 1996 $125.00

MASSACHUSETTS MEDICAL SOCIETY   A Report on Spasmodic Cholera... Boston: 1832. 1st edition; thin 8vo; 3 maps, 190 pages; modern marbled boards, ex-library, foxed. Cushing Collection M193; Reynolds Hist. Lib. 2665.   Argosy 810-342 1996 $125.00

THE MASSACRE of Lieutenant Grattan and His Command by Indians. Glendale: 1983. 1st edition; limited to 280 copies; 74 pages; color plates; dust jacket.   T. A. Swinford 49-504 1996 $135.00

MASSON, ELSIE R.   An Untamed Territory, the Northern Territory of Australia. London: 1915. (xii), 181 pages & 2 pages ads, frontispiece and 3 1 pages illustrations; green cloth; very good; Absolon copy. Antipodean 28-37 1996 $145.00

MAST, P. P., & CO., SPRINGFIELD, OHIO.   Grain Drills and Cider Mills. Buffalo: Gies & Co., n.d. 1880's-90's? 10 x 7 inches; 15, (1) pages; illustrations; very attractive color litho wrappers; very good.   Bohling Book Co. 191-262 1996 $125.00

THE MASTERPIECES of the Centennial International Exhibiton. Philadelphia: Gebbie & Barrie, 1875. 1st edition; 4to; 3 volumes; publisher's cloth, all edges gilt, except for a number on spine of volume 3, the books are in very good condition, which is unusual for this set. Bookpress 75-98 1996 $550.00

MASTERS, EDGAR LEE   Spoon River Anthology. New York: Limited Editions Club, 1942. Limited to 1500 copies, signed by author and artist; 8vo; illustrations by Boardman Robinson; full tan buckram, spines darkened, some spotting to cloth, case worn, very good/good+. Charles Agvent 4-864 1996 $150.00

MASTERS, JAMES E.   Shaftesbury; the Shaston of Thomas Hardy. Shaftesbury: High House Press, 1932. Issued without notice of limitation, a special edition of 60 copies printed on handmade paper were also issued; crown 8vo; 7 full page wood engravings by John R. Biggs, and 5 by James E. Masters; pates (vii), (plates and texts); original quarter tan cloth, printed label on backstrip and front cover, marbled pink and mauve boards, untrimmed and unopened; fine.   Blackwell's B112-153 1996 £60.00

MASTERSON, THOMAS   Masterson's Arithmetick, Shewing the Ingenious Inventions and Figurative Operations, to Calculate the True Solution or Answer of Arithmeticall Questions... London: George Miller, 1634. 8vo; (viii), 28, (ii), 242, 263-271, (v), 23, (iii) pages; 2 secondary titlepages, blank leaves bound in at front, 19th century notes on book; 19th century half calf, spine blindstamped, label; rubbed, titlepage dusty and mounted, text slightly cropped at head and fore-edge, worming in lower margin, slightly affecint text on few leaves, some old worm holes repaired, scattered foxing & minor soiling, reasonable copy; scarce. STC 17649.   Robert Clark 38-81 1996 £650.00

MASTERSON, WILLIAM   The Authentic Confessions of William Masterson, the Cruel Murderer of His Father and Mother. Richmond: M. L. Barclay, 1854. 1st edition; 8vo; 34 pages; illustrations, original printed and pictorial wrappers, in binder.   M & S Rare Books 60-207 1996 $450.00

MASUCCIO   The Novellino of Masuccio. London: Lawrence & Bullen, 1895. 1st edition in English, number 1 of 210 copies; 4to; 2 volumes, printed on Japan vellum; xxxi, 294; x, 352; 20 full page images by E. R. Hughes; original brown boards with white spines, covers lightly rubbed and soiled, else nice, unopened, very good set; translator's (W. G. Waters) own copy with his bookplate.   Chapel Hill 94-364 1996 $275.00

MASUDA, H.   The Fishes of the Japanese Archipelago. Tokyo: 1984. 4to; 2 volumes, edition with text in English; 450 pages, numerous text figures and atlas of 380 plates (mostly colored); cloth.   Wheldon & Wesley 207-978 1996 £200.00

MATHER, COTTON 1662-1727   Essays to Do Good, Addressed to All Christians, Whether in Public or Private Capacities. Johnstown: Asa Child, 1815. 12mo; 196 pages; original calf, black spine label; American Imprints #35227 (one copy).   Kenneth Karmiole 1NS-171 1996 $100.00

MATHER, COTTON 1662-1727 Memoirs of the Life of the Late Reverend Increase Mather, D. D. Who Died August 23, 1723. London: John Clark and Richard Hett, 1725. 8vo; pages 8, 88; portrait; full modern calf, gilt, red label. Sabin 46406. Howes M393. Richard Adelson W94/95-118 1996 $525.00

MATHER, COTTON 1662-1727 Psalterium Americanum. Boston: S. Kneeland for B. Eliot, S. Gerrish, D. Henchman and J. Edwards, 1718. 1st edition; 16mo; 36, 426 pages; full contemporary panelled calf, trifle rubbed, excellent copy, very crisp and clean. Holmes Cotton Mather 314; Evans 1946; rosenbach 14. M & S Rare Books 60-201 1996 $4,000.00

MATHER, COTTON 1662-1727 Wonders of the Invisible World... Bostun: (sic) printed, London: Reprinted for John Dunton, 1693. 1st London edition, 1st issue, with short list of errata on p. 51, this was later replaced by a brief publisher's note; contemporary panelled calf, neatly rebacked; large, large copy with full margins, complete with half title (small piece torn from blank upper corner and final leaf of Dunton's ads; these two leaves seem often to be missing; Holmes 454B Sabin 46604; Howes M399; Wing M1174. Ximenes 109-189 1996 $15,000.00

MATHERS, E. POWYS Procreant Hymn. Waltham St. Lawrence: Golden Cockerel Press, 1926. One of 175 copies for sale (of a total of 200); 9 3/4 x 6 3/4 inches; viii, 24 pages; frontispiece, 5 plates on Eric Gill; original white buckram, gilt titling on spine, dust jacket with just little smudging, tiny tears at corners, top edges bent over, otherwise beautiful copy, in exceptionally fine condition inside and out. Phillip J. Pirages 33-251 1996 $1,100.00

MATHERS, E. POWYS Red Wise. Waltham St. Lawrence: Golden Cockerel Press, 1926. One of 500 numbered copies; 8vo; 8 wood engravings by Robert Gibbins; printed in black and red; half white buckram, red paper boards, very nice in dust jacket. Bertram Rota 272-168 1996 £75.00

MATHES, W. MICHAEL Mexico on Stone: Lithography in Mexico 1826-1900. San Francisco: The Book Club of California, 1984. 1st edition; limited to 550 copies; very fine in lightly soiled plain buff dust jacket. Hermitage SP95-796 1996 $150.00

MATHESON, RICHARD Bid Time Return. New York: Viking, 1975. 1st edition; signed by author; fine in dust jacket, scarce book in superior condition. Robert Gavora 61-70 1996 $900.00

MATHESON, RICHARD Bid Time Return. New York: Viking, 1975. 1st edition; fine in dust jacket. Scarce. Aronovitz 57-764 1996 $395.00

MATHESON, RICHARD Collected Stories. Scream Press, 1989. 1st edition; 1/500 copies, signed by author; fine without dust jacket as issued. Aronovitz 57-766 1996 $125.00

MATHESON, RICHARD Collected Stories. Los Angeles: Dream Press, 1989. One of 500 copies signed by author; very fine, issued without dust jacket. Bud Schweska 12-538 1996 $150.00

MATHESON, RICHARD Hell House. New York: Viking, 1971. 1st edition; fine in dust jacket with some rubbing and light creasing along edges. Robert Gavora 61-71 1996 $250.00

MATHESON, RICHARD Hell House. New York: Viking Press, 1971. 1st edition; name and address on flyleaf, but unobtrusive against black color, otherwise near fine in price clipped dust jacket. Steven C. Bernard 71-424 1996 $175.00

MATHESON, RICHARD Hell House. New York: Viking, 1971. 1st edition; fine in dust jacket. Aronovitz 57-763 1996 $150.00

MATHESON, RICHARD Hell House. New York: Viking Press, 1971. 1st edition; bookplate, fine in near fine jacket. Janus Books 36-243 1996 $150.00

MATHESON, RICHARD Hell House. New York: Viking, 1971. 1st edition; very good+ in very good+ dust jacket. Timothy P. Slongo 5-206 1996 $135.00

MATHEWS, ANNE Tea-Table talk, Ennobled Actresses and Other Miscellanies. London: Thomas Cautley Newby, 1857. 1st edition; 2 volumes; original patterned cloth, spines decorative gilt, sunned, hinges of volume 2 tender, head and tail of spine of volume 2 worn, internally very good, scarce. LAR 3303.1. Dramatis Personae 37-122 1996 $150.00

MATHEWS, C. The Annals of Mont Blanc. London: 1898. 1st edition; 30 plates, folding map; grey cloth, gilt lettering and illustrations, top edge gilt; fine; small attractive bookplate of W. N. McClean. Moutaineering Books 8-EM01 1996 £220.00

MATHEWS, HARRY Singular Pleasures. Grenfell Press, 1988. One of 324 copies (of a total edition of 350), signed by author and artist; 8 1/2 x 5 3/4 inches; (142) leaves; 65 monochrome lithographs by Joe Petruzelli and Maurice Sanchez after watercolors by Francesco Clemente; original black cloth, red label on spine with gilt lettering, text leaves joined at top and printed on one side only; as new. Phillip J. Pirages 33-273 1996 $350.00

MATHEWS, HARRY Tlooth. Garden City: Doubleday/Paris Review, 1966. 1st edition; Couple of small waterstains to top edge of pages, else very good+ in very good spine faded dust jacket with several edge tears to front and spine panels; this copy inscribed by author in French to Jean Fanchette. Lame Duck Books 19-310 1996 $200.00

MATHIAS, THOMAS JAMES The Political Dramatist, in November, 1795. London: printed for J. Parsons, n.d. 1795? 1st edition; 4to; no half title, waterstain on lower inner corner of first 8 pages, 18 pages; disbound. Anthony W. Laywood 109-95 1996 £50.00

MATHIAS, THOMAS JAMES The Pursuits of Literature: a Satirical Poem in Dialogue. London: printed for J. Owen; (part 4) London: ptd. for T. Becket, 1797/97/97/97. 2nd editions of parts 1-3, 1st edition of part 4; 8vo; 4 volumes in 1; contemporary tree calf, spine gilt, minor rubbing; fine, half titles present where required; CBEL II 672. Ximenes 108-262 1996 $200.00

MATHIAS, THOMAS JAMES The Pursuits of Literature. (with) A Translation of the Passages from Greek, Latin, Italian and French Writers, Quoted in the Prefaces and Notes to the Pursuit of Literature... London: for T. Becket, 1799/98. 10th edition, 3rd edition of 2nd title; 8vo; pages (ii), iv, 445, (1); (ii), lxxv, (i) blank, (iv) fly-title, ad, 104, bound without half titles; contemporary diced calf, gilt roll border to sides, spine in compartments with gilt rolls, ornaments and lettering, little sunned and rubbed at head and foot, marbled edges and endpapers, by T. B. Watkins of Hereford, occasional slight spotting, otherwise an excellent copy; bookplate of Richard Hopton. Simon Finch 24-165 1996 £95.00

MATON, WILLIAM GEORGE Observations Relative Chiefly to the Natural History, Picturesque Scenery and Antiquities of the Western Counties of England Made in the Years 1794 and 1796. Salisbury: J. Easton, 1797. 8vo; 2 volumes, title, pages (v)-xi, 336;, title pages 216, 10ff., long folding engraved map, 16 sepia aquatint views by Henry Alken; contemporary half russia, gilt lettered and banded spines, marbled boards (trifle rubbed), corners lightly bumped, slightly foxed, uncut and part unopened. Scarce. Abbey Scenery 25; Lowndes p. 1516; Prideaux p. 344. Marlborough 162-67 1996 £450.00

MATRIX 2. London: Whittington Press, Summer, 1993. 2nd edition; limited to 400 copies; small folio; pages 144, broadsides, illustrations and mounted specimens; new in stiff covers and dust wrapper. Claude Cox 107-96 1996 £75.00

MATRIX V. Whittington Press, Winter, 1985. One of 715 copies; wrappers, mint. Words Etcetera 94-913 1996 £150.00

MATRIX 8. London: Whittington Press, Winter, 1988. Limited to 900 copies; small folio; pages (4), 191, many illustrations, plates tipped in and folding specimens; fine in original pictorial boards and dust jacket. Claude Cox 107-97 1996 £135.00

MATRIX 9. Winter, 1989. Limited to 925 copies; 4to; illustrations; decorated boards, fine in pictorial dust jacket. Barbara Stone 70-209 1996 £85.00

MATRIX 11. N.P.: Whittington Press, 1991. One of 955 copies; large 8vo; (vi), 207 pagesp wrappers; fine. The Bookpress 75-322 1996 $200.00

MATRIX XII. Whittington Press, Winter, 1992. One of 925 copies; wrappers, mint. Words Etcetera 94-914 1996 £120.00

MATRIX 12. Herefordshire: Whittington Press, 1992. 1st edition; number 60 of 100 copies; 4to; frontispiece, (vi), 222 pages, five paper samples; quarter blue calf, portfolio, custom slipcase; fine. The Bookpress 75-323 1996 $412.50

MATRIX 12. London: Whittington Press, Winter, 1992/93. 1st edition; limited to 925 copies; small folio; pages (6), 222, plates, engravings, inserts and other illustrations; new in decorated paper boards and printed wrapper; Claude Cox 107-98 1996 £110.00

MATRIX XIV. Whittington Press, 1994. Large 4to; profusely illustrated; wrappers; mint. Words Etcetera 94-915 1996 £120.00

MATRIX 14. London: Whittington Press, Winter, 1994. 1st edition; limited to 975 copies; 8vo; many tipped in illustrations and inserts including hand colored etching by Joe Lubbock; new in stiff printed pictorial wrappers. Claude Cox 107-99 1996 £120.00

MATRIX 14. Whittington Press, 1994. One of 975 copies; 4to; pictorial boards; fine in dust jacket. Bertram Rota 272-496 1996 £120.00

MATTHAEUS WESTMONASTERIENSIS Flores Historiarum... London: Thomas Marsh, 2 June 1570. Folio; lacking 4Q6, blank, roman letter, title within elaborate woodcut border (McKerrow & Ferguson 132); sprinkled calf, gilt spine, top edge gilt, by Bedford, joints repaired, loosely inserted is second copy of leaf O5 with variant setting of text, tall, uncut at fore-edge and foot and clean (washed?) copy. 19th century armorial bookplate of Richard Brinsley Sheridan??? Perhaps transferred from a previous binding - or a descendant of the dramatist. H. M. Fletcher 121-25 1996 £750.00

MATTHEWS, BRANDER Bookbindings, Old and New. Notes of a Book Lover, with an Account of the Grolier Club, New York. New York: Macmillan and Co., 1895. 1st edition; 8vo; frontispiece, 52 plates, illustrations; slight foxing, original cloth, small tears to head and tail of spine, top edge gilt. Forest Books 74-172 1996 £55.00

MATTHEWS, HENRY The Diary of an Invalid, Being the Journal of a Tour in Pursuit of Health in Portugal, Italy, Switzerland and France in the Years 1817, 1818 and 1819. London: John Murray, 1820. 2nd edition; 8vo; contemporary full calf, elaborate gilt borders on both covers, spine gilt, original morocco label; spine somewhat faded, but very clean and attractive copy; fine armorial bookplate of Bannerman of Elsick. Trebizond 39-108 1996 $175.00

MATTHEWS, HENRY The Diary of an Invalid Being the Journal of a Tour in Pursuit of Health in Portugal, Italy, Switzerland and France in the Years 1817, 1818 and 1819. London: 1820. 2nd edition; 516 pages; recent cloth backed boards, new endpapers. W. Bruce Fye 71-1384 1996 $150.00

MATTHEWS, HENRY The Diary of an Invalid. London: John Murray, 1824. 4th edition; 8vo; 2 volumes, xvi, 296; xi, 307 pages; contemporary cream half calf, marbled boards, gilt decoration on spine, leather labels; bookplates, leather bit discolored, slight wear at spine ends, but in fact near fine set. David Mason 71-104 1996 $280.00

MATTHEWS, THOMAS Advice to the Young Whist Player. London: B.C. Collins (Salisbury): and Messrs. Norton and Son, Bristol, 1806. 2nd edition; 12mo; full dark green morocco, front wrapper reproduced in gilt on front cover, spine and inner dentelles gilt, all edges gilt, by Tout and Sons, very slightly rubbed, original light blue printed wrappers bound in; fine; rare. Jessel 1156. Ximenes 109-190 1996 $300.00

MATTHEWS, WASHINGTON The Night Chant, a Navaho Ceremony. May, 1902. 332 pages, 8 plates; rebound in brown textured buckram and has been retrimmed (probably at time of binding), fine in new binding. Ken Sanders 8-210 1996 $750.00

MATTHIAE, AUGUSTUS A Copious Greek Grammar. London: John Murray, 1832. 5th edition; octavo; 2 volumes, liv, 504; (4), (505)-119, (1, ads) pages; contemporary calf, covers decoratively bordered in gilt and blind, spines richly gilt in compartments, gilt board edges and turn-ins, marbled edges and endpapers, minor rubbing and spotting to covers, otherwise fine set. Heritage Book Shop 196-231 1996 $250.00

MATTHIESSEN, F. O. Translation - an Elizabethan Art. Cambridge: Harvard University Press, 1931. 1st edition; original binding, top edge gilt, head and tail of spine and corners slightly bumped, traces of removal of bookplate on front pastedown, covers slightly marked, cover edges rubbed, very good with pencilled ownership signature of James Hart. Ulysses 39-394 1996 £55.00

MATTHIESSEN, PETER At Play in the Fields of the Lord. New York: Random House, 1965. Advance copy; near fine in printed wrappers. Pettler & Lieberman 28-162 1996 $100.00

MATTHIESSEN, PETER At Play in the Fields of the Lord. New York: Random House, 1965. 1st edition; fine in fine dust jacket; beautiful copy, lacking any of the sunning or dust soiling that is endemic to this title; inscribed by author. Ken Lopez 74-290 1996 $650.00

MATTHIESSEN, PETER At Play in the Fields of the Lord. New York: Random House, 1965. 1st edition; fine in price clipped, near fine dust jacket with some very short unobtrusive tears, trace of soiling and very slightest of darkening at spine, still much superior copy to those usually encountered. Between the Covers 42-288 1996 $250.00

MATTHIESSEN, PETER At Play in the Fields of the Lord. New York: RH, 1965. 1st edition; fine in very good plus dust jacket with slight darkening of spine and tiny chip. Thomas Dorn 9-171 1996 $135.00

MATTHIESSEN, PETER The Cloud Forest. London: Deutsch, 1962. 1st British edition; fine in near fine dust jacket and signed by author. Ken Lopez 74-289 1996 $125.00

MATTHIESSEN, PETER Far Tortuga. New York: RH, 1975. 1st edition; near fine in dust jacket. Lame Duck Books 19-314 1996 $100.00

MATTHIESSEN, PETER In The Spirit of Crazy Horse. New York: Viking, 1983. 1st edition; signed by author; fine in fine dust jacket. Thomas Dorn 9-176 1996 $250.00

MATTHIESSEN, PETER In the Spirit of Crazy Horse. New York: Viking Press, 1983. Supressed first edition; fine in dust jacket. Ken Sanders 8-397 1996 $150.00

MATTHIESSEN, PETER Indian Country. New York: Viking, 1984. 1st edition; fine in bright, fine dust jacket, uncommon. Thomas Dorn 9-177 1996 $100.00

MATTHIESSEN, PETER Men's Lives. New York: Random House, 1986. Uncorrected proof; printed yellow wrappers; near fine. Bev Chaney, Jr. 23-395 1996 $100.00

MATTHIESSEN, PETER Partisans. New York: Viking, 1955. 1st edition; light wear at spinal extremities, else near fine in very good plus or better dust jacket with light wear at extremities and sunning of small orange square on spine. Thomas Dorn 9-169 1996 $200.00

MATTHIESSEN, PETER Race Rock. New York: Harper & Bros., 1954. 1st edition; near fine in dust jacket that is lightly worn at top edge of front panel and top of spine, still attractive, much nicer than usual copy, scarce. Ken Lopez 74-288 1996 $325.00

MATTHIESSEN, PETER Race Rock. New York: Harper & Bros., 1954. 1st edition; author's very scarce first book; good copy in good dust jacket. Book Time 2-276 1996 $200.00

MATTHIESSEN, PETER Race Rock. New York: Harper & Bros., 1954. 1st edition; 8vo; author's first book; blue and black cloth over boards, pictorial dust jacketdust jacket with small chip to front cover resulting in loss of the letter "T" in "Peter" and some minor wear to corners, book near fine except for traces of erasure (half inch x half inch) on front flyleaf. Priscilla Juvelis 95/1-166 1996 $150.00

MATTHIESSEN, PETER The Shorebirds of North America. London: 1967. 1st edition; large folio; 32 fine full page color plates, pencil sketches in text; fine in dust jacket, plates superb. David A.H. Grayling 3/95-371 1996 £120.00

MATTHIESSEN, PETER The Shorebirds of North America. London: 1967. 1st edition; large folio; 32 fine full page color plates; fine in dust jacket. David A.H. Grayling MY95Orn-52 1996 £90.00

MATTHIESSEN, PETER The Shorebirds of North America. New York: Viking, 1967. 1st edition; deluxe issue, one of 350 specially bound copies, signed by author, Gardner Stout and Ralph Palmer; folio; color illustrations; full calf, marbled endpapers, top edge gilt, cloth slipcase, printed label; spine trifle rubbed and darkened, otherwise fine, rare issue, in lightly rubbed and soiled slipcase. James S. Jaffe 34-463 1996 $1,250.00

MATTHIESSEN, PETER   The Shorebirds of North America. London: 1968. 2nd edition; large folio; 32 fine full page color plates, pencil sketches in text by Robert V. Clem; fine in dust jacket.   David A.H. Grayling MY95Orn-190 1996 £70.00

MATTHIESSEN, PETER   The Snow Leopard. Franklin Center: Franklin Library, 1978. One of an unspecified number of copies of the first edition; full leather as issued, fine copy of the true first edition. Between the Covers 42-289 1996 $150.00

MATTHIESSEN, PETER   The Snow Leopard. Franklin Center: Franklin Library, 1978. 1st edition, limited, photocopy signature; very fine as issued.   Bev Chaney, Jr. 23-398 1996 $150.00

MATTHIESSEN, PETER   The Snow Leopard. Franklin Center: Franklin Library, 1978. 1st edition; preceding trade edition; fine.   Revere Books 4-267 1996 $100.00

MATTHIESSEN, PETER   The Snow Leopard. New York: Viking, 1978. 1st edition; some fading to bottom board edges, as usual, but fresh, near fine copy in dust jacket.   Lame Duck Books 19-315 1996 $100.00

MATTHIESSEN, PETER   Under the Mountain Wall: a Chronicle of Two Seasons in the Stone Age. New York: Viking, 1962. 1st edition; with all first issue points noted by Lopez pertaining to tipped in table of contents page and misplaced second photographic section; tight, fine copy in near fine dust jacket with few very small spots of surface abrasion.   Thomas Dorn 9-170 1996 $200.00

MATTHIESSEN, PETER   The Valley (working title). Sagaponack: Peter Matthiessen, 1972. Screenplay (1st draft); 8 1/2 x 11 pages; 3 whole punched with brass pins; 85 pages; very light soiling to front yellow cover, else fine.   Thomas Dorn 9-174 1996 $225.00

MATTIOLI, PIER ANDREA   Commentaries svr les Six Livres de Ped. Dioscor. Anazarbeen de la Matiere Medicinale,... Lyon: Roville, 1579. 2nd edition in French; folio; 852 pages plus contents; title within ornamental woodcut border, rehinged, frayed and fragile, with portrait of Mattioli on verso, some large historiated initials and over 1000 woodcuts; rebound in buckram backed calf, waterstained, especially in first half of volume, lower corners being fragile as a result, lacks one leaf (pages 419/420) which is supplied in photostat facsimile, few leaves torn without loss of text, lower blank corner of pages 269/270 torn off.   Argosy 810-347 1996 $1,250.00

MATURIN, CHARLES ROBERT 1782-1824   Women; or, Pour et Contre. Edinburgh: by James Ballantyne & Co. for Arch. Constable & Co., Edinb., &... 1818. 1st edition; 12mo; 3 volumes; fly-title in each volume; contemporary half polished calf, double black lettering pieces, drab paper sides and endpapers, spines worn, corners rubbed; good, clean set; ink monogram stamp of the Marquess of Conyngham (of Slane Castle, Ireland).   Simon Finch 24-166 1996 £1,000.00

MAUDE, AYLMER   A Peculiar People. The Doukhobors. New York: 1904. Pages xi, 338, 15 photo illustrations, 2 maps; original binding, near fine, laid in is one page TLS from Peter Makaroff of the Society of Independent Doukhobors, dated 1937.   Stephen Lunsford 45-107 1996 $325.00

MAUDSLAY, A. P.   Biologia Centrali-Americana; or, Contributions to the Knowledge of the Fauna and Flora of Mexico and Central America. New York: Milpatron, 1974. Oblong folio and 4to; 6 volumes in 4 parts; illustrations; original cloth.   Archaeologia Luxor-4684 1996 $250.00

MAUDSLEY, HENRY   The Physiology and Pathology of the Mind. New York: D. Appleton and Co., 1867. 1st U.S. edition; 8vo; (xvi), 442, (8) pages; pebbled mauve cloth, faded spine and edges; very good, with titlepage stamp, rear pocket & call numbers of the Hartford Retreat, with Jelliffe's name stamp and bookplate.   John Gach 150-313 1996 $150.00

MAUGHAM, WILLIAM SOMERSET 1874-1965   Ah King. London: William Heinemann, 1933. 1st edition; this being one of 175 numbered copies, signed by author; 8vo; pages (viii), 339; original brown buckram, top edge gilt, others uncut; covers little darkened, otherwise very good. Sotheran PN32-37 1996 £298.00

MAUGHAM, WILLIAM SOMERSET 1874-1965   Ah King. London: William Heinemann, 1933. 1st edition; one of 175 specially bound and numbered copies, signed by author; one corner very slightly bumped, spine slightly darkened, otherwise fine, lacking slipcase.   Captain's Bookshelf 38-152 1996 $175.00

MAUGHAM, WILLIAM SOMERSET 1874-1965   Ashenden; or the British Agent. Garden City: Doubleday Doran, 1928. 1st edition; better than very good in slightly darkened and lightly soiled dust jacket, which is much better than normally seen.   Quill & Brush 102-1255 1996 $750.00

MAUGHAM, WILLIAM SOMERSET 1874-1965   Cakes and Ale or the Skeleton in the Cupboard. London: William Heinemann, 1930. 1st edition; blue cloth, cream printed jacket that is chipped and spine darkened, book fine. Stott A41.   Priscilla Juvelis 95/1-167 1996 $100.00

MAUGHAM, WILLIAM SOMERSET 1874-1965   The Casuarina Tree. London: William Heinemann, 1926. 1st edition; original binding, top edge slightly spotted and dusty, prelims slightly spotted, half titlepage and final blank browned, tail of spine slightly bumped, spine slightly rubbed at extremities, very good in nicked and slightly rubbed, marked, creased and dusty, very slightly soiled dust jacket by Ralph Keene.   Ulysses 39-395 1996 £1,950.00

MAUGHAM, WILLIAM SOMERSET 1874-1965   Christmas Holiday. London: Heinemann, 1939. Spine cocked and slight foxing to outside edge, otherwise excellent in slightly chipped dust jacket; inscribed by author for D. G. Rippingale.   R. A. Gekoski 19-103 1996 £250.00

MAUGHAM, WILLIAM SOMERSET 1874-1965   Here and There. London: Heinemann, 1948. top edge dusty, very good, in nicked, creased and rubbed and dusty dust jacket frayed at head of spine and darkened at spine and edges.   Limestone Hills 41-98 1996 $175.00

MAUGHAM, WILLIAM SOMERSET 1874-1965   The Hero. London: Hutchinson, 1901. With publisher's compliments blindstamp on titlepage and dropped 'g' in 'game' on page 129; red cloth shaken and little marked, front hinge little weak, very good. Scarce.   R. A. Gekoski 19-100 1996 £850.00

MAUGHAM, WILLIAM SOMERSET 1874-1965   Liza of Lambeth. London: 1897. 1st edition; 7.5 x 4.5 inches; 242 pages; cloth, small bookplate, inner hinge crudely repaired, covers heavily rubbed, front cover creased, in special lettered box; author's first book.   John K. King 77-387 1996 $350.00

MAUGHAM, WILLIAM SOMERSET 1874-1965   The Making of a Saint. London: T. Fisher Unwin, 1898. 1st edition; green boards stamped in gold, somewhat soiled, spine cocked.   Bev Chaney, Jr. 23-402 1996 $125.00

MAUGHAM, WILLIAM SOMERSET 1874-1965   Of Human Bondage. New Haven: Limited Editions Club, 1938. Number 904 from 1500 copies, signed by artist; 2 volumes; 16 etchings by John Sloan; fine set in publisher's slipcase.   Hermitage SP95-1012 1996 $600.00

MAUGHAM, WILLIAM SOMERSET 1874-1965   Of Human Bondage. New York: printed for Members of the Limited Editions Club, 1938. Limited to 1500 copies, signed by Sloan; 8vo; 2 volumes; 16 original etchings by John Sloan; patterned linen, leather labels, nice in slightly worn box.   Appelfeld Gallery 54-138 1996 $450.00

MAUGHAM, WILLIAM SOMERSET 1874-1965   Of Human Bondage - With a Digression on the Art of Fiction - an Address Washington: Library of Congress, 1946. One of 500 copies signed by author, out of a total edition of 800 copies; original binding, small dent in upper cover, covers slightly marked and dusty, spine browned, very good.   Ulysses 39-396 1996 £95.00

MAUGHAM, WILLIAM SOMERSET 1874-1965   The Painted Veil. London: Heinemann, 1925. spine cocked and some offsetting to endpapers, otherwise very good copy; inscribed by author for D. Rippingale.   R. A. Gekoski 19-101 1996 £200.00

MAUGHAM, WILLIAM SOMERSET 1874-1965   Theatre. London: Heinemann, 1937. Second free endpaper excised, spine slightly cocked and trifle foxing to outside edge, otherwise very good in slightly chipped and foxed dust jacket; signed by author for D. G. Rippingale.   R. A. Gekoski 19-102 1996 £120.00

MAUPASSANT, GUY DE 1850-1893   Claire de Lune. Leipzig: privately printed for Erik-Ernst Schwabach, 1916. Number 7 of 7 copies; numbered in the press, this 'reserve pour M. Schwabach'; small 4to; full red morocco, gilt, backstrip repaired and darkened and sides somewhat sprung, but internally nice, slightly foxed; presentation from Schwabach presenting this to Gerta Herz, with Schwabach's bookplate.   Bertram Rota 272-130 1996 £110.00

MAURICE, ARTHUR BARTLETT   New York in Fiction. New York: Dodd, Mead, 1901. 1st edition; photographic reproductions; pictorial copy; beautiful copy; inscribed by author.   Captain's Bookshelf 38-153 1996 $100.00

MAURICE, F. D.   Social Morality. Twenty-One Lectures Delivered in the University of Cambridge. London: and Cambridge: Macmillan and Co., 1869. 1st edition; 8vo; 483 pages, half title, 4 pages ad leaves at end; original cloth, uncut; nice; presentation inscription from author. Anthony W. Laywood 108-200 1996 £60.00

MAURICE, THOMAS   The Crisis of the British Muse to the British Minister and Nation. London: printed for the author and sold by R. Faulder, 1798. 1st edition; 4to; no half title, 32 pages; disbound. Anthony W. Laywood 109-97 1996 £60.00

MAURICE, THOMAS   An Elegiac and Historical Poem. London: printed for the author and sold by himself, 1795. 1st edition; 4to; 4 pages of notes and 4 pages of proposals;   Anthony W. Laywood 109-96 1996 £60.00

MAURICE, THOMAS   Indian Antiquities; or, Dissertations, Relative to the Antient Geographical Divisions... London: printed for the author by C. & W. Galabin and sold by John White, 1806/1800/01. Mixed set; 8vo; 7 volumes; 309, (i); 384; 244; 391, (i); (ii), 393-724; xv, (ii), 370, (ii); vii, (i), 379, i pages; frontispiece, 27 plates, half titles in all but volume 5; contemporary half calf, marbled boards, spines gilt ruled, labels; rubbed, few joints cracked but firm, first two leaves in volume 1 frayed and dusty on edges, clear of text apart from one small hole affecting a few letters, occasional minor foxing.   Robert Clark 38-247 1996 £425.00

MAUROIS, ANDRE   Fatty Puffs and Thinifers. New York: Holt, 1940. 1st American edition; 4to; colored illustrations by Jean Bruller; blue cloth pictorially stamped in darker blue, fresh, bright copy, very scarce. Barbara Stone 70-152 1996 £85.00

MAURY, MATTHEW FONTAINE 1806-1873   The Physical Geography of the Sea, and its Meteorology. London: Sampson Low, Marston, Low and Searle, 1874. 15th eedtiion; small octavo; xx, 487 pages, folding plates; bound by Mudie in half calf over marabled boards, gilt spine with raised bands, black morocco label, marbled edges and endpapers, light dampstaining to upper margin of last several leaves; overall, very good, clean copy.   Heritage Book Shop 196-172 1996 $125.00

MAURY, MATTHEW FONTAINE 1806-1873   Physical Survey of Virginia. Her Resources, Climate and Productions. Richmond: N. V. Randolph, 1878. 1st edition; 8vo; 142, (1) pages, 1 folding map; map; original quarter black calf, bookplate, some cover wear, tears on map neatly repaired, text lightly foxed, else good.   The Bookpress 75-478 1996 $175.00

MAVERICK, MARY ANN   Memoirs of Mary A. Maverick. San Antonio: Alamo Printing, 1921. 1st edition; 1st issue; 135 pages; frontispiece, plates; original beige decorated wrappers, title stamped in gold, usual browning to spine; fine. Howes M443. Adams Herd 1460. Jenkins BTB 140.   Michael D. Heaston 23-242 1996 $225.00

MAVOR, WILLIAM   The English Spelling Book. London: George Routledge & Sons, 1885. 1st edition; 12mo; 108 pages; frontispiece, 41 drawings, 26 decorative initials, printed in brown; three quarter blue morocco, gilt, over blue cloth boards, gilt spine with raised bands, original grey printed boards bound in, bookplate; fine. Schuster & Engen 71 (1a); Thomson 133.   Heritage Book Shop 196-232 1996 $300.00

MAVOR, WILLIAM   A Tour in Wales, and through Several Counties of England, Including Both the Universities, Performed in the Summer of 1805. London: for Richard Phillips, 1806. 1st edition; 8vo; (4), 182, (2) pages index, 2 folding aquatint plates; recent half green morocco, gilt spine, red gilt label, very good, scarce.   Ken Spelman 30-92 1996 £120.00

MAWE, JOHN 1764-1829   A Treatise on Precious Stones: Including Their History - Natural and Commercial. London: by the author, 1823. 2nd edition; 4 hand colored plates on 3 pages, two black and white plates; original cloth backed boards, some staining and foxing, more so to the prelims, rebacked with original spine laid down, label mostly missing, still very good. Sinkankas 4286.   Hermitage SP95-1081 1996 $450.00

MAWE, THOMAS   Every Man His Own Gardener. London: Rivington, Longman, Cadell et al, 1787. 11th edition; small thick 8vo; pages 615; later half calf, marbled boards, gilt on leather label, foxing to titlepage and engraved frontispiece, some light foxing, very good. Lowndes III 1243.   Hartfield 48-L60 1996 $195.00

MAWE, THOMAS   The Universal Gardener and Botanist; or, a General Dictionary of Gardening and Botany. London: 1778. 1st edition; 4to; calf, rebacked, two small stamps on titlepage; bookplates of Sir R. I. Murchison and the Museum of Practical Geology stating presented Murchison in May 1862.   John Henly 27-312 1996 £150.00

MAWSON, DOUGLAS   The Home of the Blizzard. London: William Heinemann, 1915. 1st edition; 4to; 2 volumes; half titles, 349, 321 pages, errata leaf to volume 1 bound in rather than slip tipped in; frontispieces, 273 black and white photos, 87 illustrations, 3 large folding maps to rear pocket volume 2, internally good, clean copy. Original dark blue cloth, silver stamped vignette to upper boards, glt title to spines, hinges to volume 1 cracked, spines cracked to both volumes, corners bumped and worn, upper board to volume 1 with what appears to be impression of footprint. Internally good, clean copy.   Beeleigh Abbey BA56-95 1996 £295.00

MAWSON, THOMAS H.   The Art and Craft of Garden Making. London: B. T. Batsford, 1900. 1st edition; large 4to; views, plans, sections, pictorial chapter headings, gilt decorated green cloth, little faded, endpapers foxed, occasional marginal smudge but very good, sound copy.   Marilyn Braiterman 15-139 1996 $225.00

MAWSON, THOMAS H.   The Art and Craft of Garden Making. London: Batsford, 1912. 4th edition; fokio; pages x, 404; 435 illustrations, plans, sections, sketches; original cloth, gilt, little worn and marked, upper hinge cracking at base, top edge gilt, joints cracked; half title soiled, few spots, little bumped at head.   R.F.G. Hollett & Son 78-536 1996 £175.00

MAXWELL, HERBERT   The Chronicle of Lanercost 1272-1346. Glasgow: James Maclehose, 1913. Signed limited edition, number 63 of 100 copies; 4to; pages xxxi, 358, 8 plates and colored arms on title; original vellum backed cloth, gilt, flyleaves rather browned; otherwise very nice.   R.F.G. Hollett & Son 78-1111 1996 £120.00

MAXWELL, JAMES CLERK 1831-1879   An Elementary Treatise on Electricity... Oxford: at the Clarendon Press, 1881. 1st edition; 8vo; xvi, 208, 36 (ads), (8 ads) pages, 6 plates, 53 figures in text; original cloth, scuffed and frayed at spine ends; former owner's stamp on titlepage, very good; personal booklabel of Jake Zeitlin on front pastedown. Wheeler Gift I 2243.   Edwin V. Glaser 121-212 1996 $300.00

MAXWELL, WILLIAM   The Chateau. New York: Knopf, 1961. 1st edition; owner name under front flap, otherwise fine in near fine, price clipped dust jacket, very nice.   Ken Lopez 74-294 1996 $100.00

MAXWELL, WILLIAM   So Long, See You Tomorrow. New York: Knopf, 1980. 1st edition; offsetting to front endpaper, which also has a previous owner's pencil signature and embossed stamp and where the book is signed by author, otherwise fine in fine dust jacket.   Ken Lopez 74-295 1996 $125.00

MAXWELL, WILLIAM   Time Will Darken it. New York: Harper & Bros., 1948. 1st edition; 8vo; cloth, dust jacket, spine somewhat cocked, otherwise fine in price clipped jacket.   James S. Jaffe 34-464 1996 $150.00

MAXWELL-HYSLOP, K. R.   Western Asiatic Jewellery c. 3000-612 B.C. London: Methuen, 1971. 8vo; lxvi, 286 pages, 167 figures and 267 (8 in color) illustrations, 1 map, tattered dust jacket.   Archaeologia Luxor-2423 1996 $150.00

MAXWELL-LYTE, H. C.   A History of Dunster and of the Families of Mohun and Luttrell. London: St. Catherine's Press, 1909. Crown 8vo; 2 volumes, xxi, (ii), 328 pages; (iv), 329-596 pages; text illustrations and plates; original black cloth, gilt, shelf wear and edges bit faded. Francis Mohun's copy.   Marlborough 162-68 1996 £90.00

MAY, J.   Brede's Tale. Starmont House, 1982. 1st separate edition, 1/50 copies currently bound in leather (of a potential scheduled 100 copies), initiall ed by author, designer and artist, Stephen Fabian; 7.4 x 5.7 cm; fine, without dust jacket, as issued.   Aronovitz 57-771 1996 $125.00

MAY, J. B.   The Hawks of North America, Their Field Identification and Feeding Habits. New York: 1935. Royal 8vo; pages xxii, 140, 4 plain plates, 37 colored plates; original cloth.   Wheldon & Wesley 207-809 1996 £60.00

MAY, W.   The Little Book of British Birds. London: C. Tilt, ca. 1835. 2 15/16 x 2 1/2 inches; 191 pages; wood engravings; half speckled calf by Arthur S. Colley, with gilt stamping, spine in five compartmnts and morocco label, original gilt stamped cloth cover and pines bound in all edges gilt; Bondy pp. 66-67; Welsh 4889.   Bromer Booksellers 90-192 1996 $450.00

MAY, W.   The Little Book of British Quadrupeds. London: C. Tilt, ca. 1835. 2 15/16 x 2 1/2 inches; 191 pages, 48 wood engraved illustrations; half speckled calf by Arthur S. Colley, gilt tooling, spine in five compartments, morocco label, all edges gilt, original gilt stamped cloth cover and spine are bound in; Bondy pp. 66-7; Welsh 4890.   Bromer Booksellers, 90-193 1996 $450.00

MAYDON, H. C.   Simen, It's Heights and Abysses. London: 1925. illustrations, very good, ex-library with label and stamps of British Legation at Addis Abada, spine faded, contents fine; cheap copy. David Grayling J95Biggame-136 1996 £65.00

MAYER, ALFRED M.   Sport With Gun and Rod in American Woods and Waters. New York: 1883. Imperial octavo; 2 volumes; 900 pages; profusely illustrated with engraved plates and text drawings, several on Japan proof paper; original pictorial gilt cloth, corners/top and base of spines snagged; contents excellent.   David Grayling J95Biggame-421 1996 £80.00

MAYER, BRANTZ   Baltimore: Past and Present. Baltimore: Richardson and Bennett, 1871. 1st edition; 562 pages, plus 62 albumen photos; fine, full dark brown morocco gilt, minor rubbing of extremities; fine.   19th Century Shop 39- 1996 $500.00

MAYER, BRANTZ   Mexico As It Was and As it Is. New York: London & Paris: 1844. 8vo; half title, vignette title, pages iii-xii, 390, 1 f., frontispiece and 27 woodcut plates, text illustrations; cloth, gilt, some foxing of title and elsewhere.   Marlborough 162-237 1996 £260.00

MAYER, BRANTZ   Mexico, Aztec, Spanish and Republican: a Historical, Geographical, Political...Social Account...from...the Invasion by the Spaniards to the Present... Hartford: S. Drake, 1852. 1st edition published in one volume; 2 volumes in one, 433, 399 pages; illustrations; gilt stamped decorative leather binding, worn, front hinge repaired and tender. Raines p. 148.   Maggie Lambeth 30-365 1996 $100.00

MAYER, J.   The Sportsman's Directory, or Park and Gamekeeper's Companion. London: 1819. 3rd edition; frontispiece, few text woodcuts; original boards, neatly respined with cloth and paper label.   David A.H. Grayling 3/95-185 1996 £60.00

MAYER, J.   The Sportsman's Directory, or Park and Gamekeeper's Companion... London: 1823. 4th edition; frontispiece, few text woodcuts; contemporary half morocco; excellent.   David A.H. Grayling 3/95-186 1996 £60.00

MAYER, L. A.   Eretz-Israel: Archaeological, Historical and Geographical Studies. Jerusalem: Israel Exploration Society, 1964. 8vo; Volume 7 (only), xxvii, 178 pages in English, 189 pages in Hebrew, 84 plates; original cloth, chipped dust jacket.   Archaeologia Luxor-2426 1996 $125.00

MAYHEW, AUGUSTUS   Paved with Gold or The Romance and Reality of the London Streets. London: Chapman and Hall, 1858. 1st edition; 8vo; viii, 408 pages; frontispiece, 24 plates (all slightly spotted, one browned), original green cloth, spine pictorially gilt, hinges little strained. Marlborough 162-172 1996 £200.00

MAYHEW, AUGUSTUS   Paved with Gold. London: Chapman & Hall, 1858. 8vo; viii, 408 pages, added illustrated titlepage, frontispiece and 24 full page illustrations; half brown morocco by Birdsall over marbled boards, original cloth bound in.   Kenneth Karmiole 1NS-172 1996 $125.00

MAYHEW, HENRY   The Comic Almanack. London: 1839-42/45-50. 1st edition; 12mo; 10 volumes in 5; numerous full page and folding illustrations by George Cruikshank and H. G. Hine; late 19th century three quarter blue morocco and cloth by Root and Son, gilt tooled spines, top edge gilt, couple of spine ends worn, else near fine.   Chapel Hill 94-47 1996 $375.00

MAYHEW, HENRY   1851; or, the Adventures of Mr. and Mrs. Sandboys and Family, Who Came Up to London to "Enjoy Themselves", and to See the Great Exhibition. London: David Bogue, n.d. 1851. 1st edition in book form, 1st issue with hiatus between pages 62 and 65; 8vo; folding frontispiece, engraved title, 10 plates by George Cruikshank, folding plates expertly backed with linen, contemporary half calf, hinges slightly rubbed, spine gilt, all edges gilt, by Tout. Cohn 548.   Anthony W. Laywood 108-214 1996 £110.00

MAYHEW, HENRY   The Rhine and Its Picturesque Scenery. London: David Bogue, 1856. 1st edition; octavo; vi, (2), 386, (2 ads) pages, engraved vignette title and 19 engraved plates; original blue cloth decoratively stamped in gilt, all edges gilt, light wear to extremities, slightly shaken, very good, clean copy.   Heritage Book Shop 196-260 1996 $300.00

MAYHEW, THE BROTHERS   The Image of His Father; Or One Boy is More Trouble Than a Dozen Girls... London: Henry G. Bohn, 1851.. 1st edition; small 8vo; additional etched vignette titlepage and 9 plates by Phiz, 288 pages; contemporary half red morocco, spine gilt in 6 compartments, marbled edges; externally fine; ownership signature on titlepage and text, slightly finger soiled.   Thomas Thorp 489-213 1996 £75.00

MAYHEW, THE BROTHERS   Whom to Marry and How to Get Married! London: David Bogue, 1848. 1st edition; 8vo; bound from parts, pages (viii), 271; with stab sewing holes visible throughout; frontispiece, 11 plates by Cruikshank, glyphograph on titlepage, half title, upper corner of first gathering lightly bumped; internally excellent; contemporary half calf, extremities rubbed, smooth backstrip, gilt lettered red leather title label, marbled boards, red sprinkled edges, very good. Cohn 545; not in Sadleir or Wolff.   Blackwell's B112-188 1996 £175.00

MAYNARD, HENRY N.   The Viaduct Works' Handbook; Being a Collection of Examples from Actual Practice of Viaducts, Bridges, Roofs, and Other Structures in Iron... London: Spon, 1868. 8vo; 108 pages, some full page wood engraved plates and many wood engraved text illustrations, folding tinted litho frontispiece (slightly stained), publisher's cloth; presentation inscription from author to civil engineer, H. D. Martin, from the library of J. G. James.   Elton Engineering 10-102 1996 £170.00

MAYNE, R. C.   Four Years in British Columbia and Vancouver Island. London: John Murray, 1862. 23cm; xi, 468, (32) pages; frontispiece, illustrations, folding map outlined in color; gilt stamped and illustrated russet cloth, neatly rebacked; fine. From the collection of Alaskan judge and bibliographer James Wickersham. Lowther 178; TPL 4076. Rockland Books 38-149 1996 $375.00

MEAD, CHARLES   Mississippian Scenery: a Poem. Philadelphia: S. Potter, 1819. 1st edition; 12mo; 113, (6) pages, half title; contemporary calf, leather label, front hinge cracked and crudely repaired, affecting half title which also lacks several blank portions, lacks frontispiece. Very scarce. Wegelin 1063; S&S 48656; Sabin 47218.   M & S Rare Books 60-202 1996 $425.00

MEAD, F.   Leaves of Thought. Cincinnati: 1868. 167 pages; terra cotta cloth with gilt lettering bright, small snag bottom of front cover. Bookworm & Silverfish 276-144 1996 $225.00

MEAD, MARGARET   Childhood in Contemporary Cultures. Chicago: University of Chicago Press, 1955. 8vo; xii, 474 pages; 28 plates; blue cloth; presentation copy inscribed by Mead.   Kenneth Karmiole 1NS-173 1996 $125.00

MEAD, MARGARET   People and Places. Cleveland: World Pub. Co., 1959. 1st edition; 4to; 318, (2) pages; 170 illustrations; illustrated yellow cloth, dust jacket; presentation copy, inscribed by author.   Kenneth Karmiole 1NS-174 1996 $125.00

MEAD, RICHARD   The Medical Works of Richard Mead, M.D. Physician to His Late Majesty King George III. Dublin: Thomas Ewing, 1767. 8vo; recent half calf, marbled boards, spine sunned, overall fresh, clean copy.   James Tait Goodrich K40-188 1996 $350.00

MEAD, RICHARD   The Medical Works. Edinburgh: 1775. New edition; 8vo; calf, rubbed, front hinge cracked at top.   Argosy 810-349 1 996 $300.00

MEADE, HERBERT   A Ride through the Disturbed Districts of New Zealand, Together with Some Account of the South Sea Islands. London: John Murray, 1871. 2nd edition; 8vo; pages xi, 375; frontispiece, 2 folding maps, text engravings; modern cloth, leather label. Hocken p. 269; Taylor p. 185.   Richard Adelson W94/95-119 1996 $360.00

MEAKIN, BUDGETT   The Moors. London: Sean Sonnenschien & Co., 1902. 1st edition; tall 8vo; xxii, 503 pages; illustrations; original blue cloth, elaborate pictorial gilt decoration on upper cover, pictorial gilt decoration on spine, inner front hinge cracked, tiny hole in spine, still near fine, very attractive binding.   David Mason 71-12 1996 $240.00

MEAN Streets: the Second Private Eye Writers of America Anthology. New York: Mysterious Press, 1986. 1 of 250 numbered copies, signed by all contributors; mint in slipcase, plastic shrinkwrap still intact. Pettler & Lieberman 28-76 1996 $100.00

MEANWELL, T.   On Common Swearing. To the Publisher of the Edinburgh Magazine. Edinburgh: 1795? in fact c. 1783. 8vo; 8 pages; disbound.   C. R. Johnson 37-42 1996 £250.00

MEARES, JOHN   Voyages Made in the Years 1788 & 1789, from China to the Northwest Coast of America. London: J. Walter, 1790. 1st edition; 4to; pages xx, xcvi, 372, 108; portrait, 17 plates, 10 maps; full new mottled calf, gilt, light stains and foxing to few leaves. Howes M469; Sabin 47260; Smith 6690; LM 46; Hill I p. 195.   Richard Adelson W94/95-121 1996 $3,875.00

MEASOR, CHARLES PENNELL   Criminal Correction. London: William Macintosh, 1864. 1st edition; 8vo; (2), 60 pages; recent printed blue boards lettered; very good. Headicar & Fuller III 215. Not in NUC. John Drury 82-179 1996 £85.00

MECHNIKOV, IL IA IL'ICH 1845-1916   The Nature of Man, Studies in Optimistic Philosophy. London: 1903. 1st English translation; 309 pages; original binding.   W. Bruce Fye 71-1430 1996 $100.00

MEDHURST, G.   Calculations and Remarks...a Plan for the Rapid Conveyance of Goods and Passangers Upon an Iron Road through a Tube of 30 Feet in Area by the Power and Velocity of Air. London: 1812. 1st edition; 8vo; title, pages 5-18, 1 leaf ad, contemporary wrappers, somewhat worn.   Maggs Bros. Ltd. 1190-343 1996 £85.00

THE MEDICAL and Physical Journal. London: 1801-04. Volumes 5, 9, 10, 11; mixed bindings, some boards detached, some backstrips worn, contents very good; ex-library, rare. Le Fanu 28.   W. Bruce Fye 71-2155 1996 $350.00

MEDICAL Classics. Baltimore: 1936-41. 1st and only edition; Volumes 1-5; half leather; GM 6884.   W. Bruce Fye 71-1414 1996 $900.00

MEDICAL Leaves. Chicago: 1937. 1st edition; 4to; 209 pages; wrappers, scarce.   W. Bruce Fye 71-1416 1996 $150.00

MEDICAL Leaves. Chicago: 1939. 1st edition; 4to; original binding; scarce.   W. Bruce Fye 71-1415 1996 $100.00

MEDICAL Leaves. Chicago: 1943. 1st edition; Volume 5, wrappers.   W. Bruce Fye 71-1417 1996 $150.00

MEDICAL SOCIETY OF THE STATE OF NORTH CAROLINA   Provisional Record of Confederate Medical Officers, Offered by the Confederate Veterans Committee, Medical Society, N.C., for Corrections and Additions. N.P.: n.d. 1st edition; 57 pages; original self wrappers, very good or better. Not in Dornbusch.   McGowan Book Co. 65-57 1996 $150.00

MEDICI, LORENZO   Poesie Volgari, Nuovamente Stampate, di Lorenzo De' Medici Che Su Padre Di Papa Leone... Venice: In Casa de' Figliovli di Aldo, 1554. 1st Aldine edition; 8vo; 208 leaves, italic; this copy includes the rarely found five 'suppressed' canzoni (ff. 107-112), historiated initials, name trimmed from first two leaves; nice English full red morocco, gilt rule on boards, all edges gilt, nicely gauffered, bright copy, rare. Gamba 648; Renouard 162.23; UCLA IIIa/410; Adams M1005; Brunet III1568 Family Album Tillers-436 1996 $2,000.00

MEDICINA Flagellata; or, the Doctor Scarified. London: printed for J. Bateman and J. Nicks, 1721. 1st edition; 8vo; engraved and printed titles, both with perforation stamp and de-accession stamps on blank verso; contemporary panelled calf, rebacked with morocco, rubbed, upper hinge partly cracked; bookplate of Mortimer Frank. Waller 6421; Blake p. 297; Heirs of Hippocrates 948.   Anthony W. Laywood 108-90 1996 £345.00

MEDICINE In Modern Times or Discourses Delivered at a Meeting of the British Medical Association at Oxford. London: 1869. 1st edition; 255 pages; original binding, ex-library, outer hinges torn.   W. Bruce Fye 71-2056 1996 $100.00

MEDWIN, THOMAS 1788-1869   Conversations of Lord Byron: Noted During a Residence with His Lordship at Pisa, in the Years 1821 and 1822. London: Henry Colburn, 1824. New edition; 8vo; folding frontispiece, pages (2), (vii)-xxiii, 351; ciii, (1 ads), complete thus in spit of error of pagination; contemporary half red calf, gilt ruled and lettered spine, very good.   James Fenning 133-45 1996 £95.00

MEDWIN, THOMAS 1788-1869   Conversations of Lord Byron; Noted During a Residence with His Lordship at Pisa...1821 and 1822. London: printed for Henry Colburn, 1824. New edition; 8vo; half title, folding facsimile; recent marbled boards, uncut; some foxing.   Peter Murray Hill 185-26 1996 £75.00

MEE, MARGARET   Flowers of the Brazilian Forests. London: 1968. Number 286 of 506 copies; folio; 32 colored plates, 32 vignettes and double page colored map; half morocco over marbled boards by Zaehnsdorf, top edge gilt, cloth slipcase (light staining, some wear and insect markings to backstrip and edges).   Raymond M. Sutton VI-20 1996 $1,850.00

MEEHAN, THOMAS 1826-1901   The American Handbook of Ornament Trees. Philadelphia: 1853. 12mo; pages xv, (25-), 257 (backstrip partially loose, spine ends perished, corners scuffed, spot on rear cover, slight foxing, name on endpapers).   Raymond M. Sutton VII-647 1996 $125.00

MEEHAN, THOMAS 1826-1901   The Native Flowers and Ferns of the United States in Their Botanical, Horticultural and Popular Aspects. Boston: L. Prang/Philadelphia: 1879/80. Royal 8vo; 4 volumes; 193 colored plates; three quarter green morocco, gilt, gilt panelled spines, top edges gilt, one each of the original front and back wrappers bound in   Charles W. Traylen 117-315 1996 £580.00

MEEK, STEPHEN HALL   The Autobiography of a Mountain Man, 1805-1889. Pasadena: Glen Dawson, 1948. 1st book edition; vi, 17 pages; titlepage portrait; cloth, upper corners jammed, else fine. Argonaut Book Shop 113-461 1996 $150.00

MEEKER, EZRA   Pioneer Reminiscences of Puget Sound: The Tragedy of Leschi... Seattle: Lowman and Hanford, 1905. 1st edition; xx, 554, (1) pages; frontispiece, illustrated from photos; blue cloth, gilt lettered spine, some extremity rubbing, corners and spine ends slightly bumped; near fine. Howes M377; Smith 6708.   Argonaut Book Shop 113-462 1996 $150.00

MEHTA, NANALAL CHAMANLAI   Studies in Indian Painting Bombay: 1926. 4to; x, 127 pages, 17 plates in color and 44 half tone plates; cloth.   Rainsford A54-403 1996 £75.00

MEIER, AUGUST   Negro Thought in America, 1880-1915: Racial Ideoloies in the Age of Booker T. Washington. Ann Arbor: University of Michigan, 1963. 1st edition; offsetting of jacket art onto front board, else fine in very good plus dust jacket, rubbed and with little light wear to extremities, nicely inscribed by author in 1964. Inscriptions by this autho are not particularly common.   Between the Covers 43-367 1996 $100.00

MEIER-GRAEFE, JULIUS   Modern Art. London: 1908. 8vo; 2 volumes; ix, 325; ix, 337 pages; well illustrated; decorated buckram, covers little dark.   Rainsford A54-404 1996 £75.00

MEIGS, ARTHUR J.   An American Country House. The Property of Arthur E. Newbold, Jr., Esq.; Laverock, Pa. New York: Architectural Boo Publishing Co., 1925. Folio; 99 pages of photos, drawings and text; two tone brown and tan cloth, near fine in very nice dust jacket;   Marilyn Braiterman 15-140 1996 $225.00

MEIKLE, JAMES   The Traveller; or, Meditations on Various Subjects. New York: S. Dodge, 1811. 1st American edition; 12mo; xii, 360 pages; original calf, black spine label, extremities bit rubbed.   Kenneth Karmiole 1NS-184 1996 $100.00

MEINERTZHAGEN, RICHARD   The Life of a Boy - Daniel Meinertzhagen 1925-1944. London: Oliver and Boyd, 1947. 1st edition; 6 black and white photos and black and white reproduction of a portrait; original binding, head and tail of spine and corners slightly bumped, covers very slightly marked, prelims, edges and endpapers spotted, ver good in rubbed and slightly marked dust jacket browned at spine and edges.   Ulysses 39-397 1996 £165.00

MEINHOLD, WILLIAM   Mary Schweidler, the Amber Witch. London: Hacon & Ricketts, Vale Press, 1903. Limited to 300 copies; folio; pages clvi + colophon; printed in Vale and Avon types on handmade paper; full page wood engraved border by Charles Ricketts; original holland backed blue boards, paper labels, that on spine defective, very good, largely unopened. Tomkinson 39.   Claude Cox 107-178 1996 £150.00

MEISEL, M.   Bibliography of American Natural History. The Pioneer Century 1769-1865. 1994. Reprint; 3 volumes.   John Johnson 135-61 1996 $195.00

MEISS, MILLARD   Essays in Honor of Erwin Panofsky. New York University Press, 1961. 21 x 23 cm; 2 volumes, xxi, 539 pages; v, 177 plates; original cloth, slipcase.   Rainsford A54-450 1996 £95.00

MELANCHTHON, PHILIPP 1497-1560   Oratio Vber der Leich des Ehrwirdigen Hern Martini Lutheri. Wittenberg: Rhaw, 1546. 4to; woodcut on title; modern manuscript boards; Adams M1184.   Rostenberg & Stern 150-89 1996 $1,250.00

MELENDY, H. B.   The Governors of California: Peter H. Burnett to Edmund G. Brown. Georgetown: The Talisman Press, 1965. 1st edition; limited to 1000 copies; 482 pages; portraits, illustrations; fine with spine darkened dust jacket.   Argonaut Book Shop 113-463 1996 $100.00

MELINE, JAMES F.   Two Thousand Miles on Horseback, Sante Fe and Back. New York: 1867. 1st edition; map frontispiece, dust jacket, slipcase; very good+. Howes M488; Rader 2376; Graff 2743; Rittenhouse 409.   T. A. Swinford 49-770 1996 $125.00

MELINE, JAMES F.   Two Thousand Miles on Horseback. New York: Hurd and Houghton, 1867. 1st edition; pages x, 317, folding map; ex-library, shelfwear, some splits to map, else good. Howes M488; SFT 409.   Dumont 28-95 1996 $100.00

MELLOR Meigs & Howe. New York: Architectural Book Pub. co., 1923. 1st edition; folio; photos; original cloth over boards, light edgewear, else fine, in mdoerately worn dust jacket.   Glenn Books 36-5 1996 $350.00

MELVILLE, E. J.   The Arab's Ride to Cairo. London: Seton & Mackenzie, et al, n.d. 1855. 1st edition; square 8vo; illustrations and wide pictorial borders, illuminated in colors and gold by Mrs. Wolfe Murray; publisher's purple cloth, upper cover bordered in gilt, gilt title and motif of Cairo spires, repeated on lower cover in blind, all edges gilt, printed on heavy card with decorative text printed in red and black, wide borders; upper hinge broken, cover gilt and extremities rubbed, very scarce.   Glenn Books 36-278 1996 $250.00

MELVILLE, F. J.   Postage Stamps in the Making, a General Survey of the Practices and Processes Employed in the Manufacture of Postage Stamps. Volume I. London: 1916. 1st edition; 8vo; all published; numerous illustrations, slightly cockling; half cloth, bit worn.   Maggs Bros. Ltd. 1190-647 1996 £110.00

MELVILLE, HERMAN 1819-1891   Battle-Pieces and Aspects of the War. New York: Harper & Bros., 1866. 1st edition; 12mo; x, (11)-272 pages; original blue cloth with publisher's monogram stamped in blind on covers and spine stamped in gilt, bevelled boards, cloth lightly chipped at head and foot of spine, corners rubbed, back hinge just starting, slightly over opened at few gatherings, paper lightly browned, bookplate; previous owner's ink signature on front flyleaf, still very good, housed in quarter black morocco slipcase and black cloth chemise. BAL 13673.   Heritage Book Shop 196-191 1996 $1,250.00

MELVILLE, HERMAN 1819-1891   Battle Pieces. New York: Harpers, 1866. 1st edition; 8vo; brown cloth, minor stains to covers, most noticeably to lower right front where some of the smoothness of the cloth is lacking, remnants only of the free flyleaves which do not figure into the signature count, trivial foxing, above average copy.   Charles Agvent 4-868 1996 $900.00

MELVILLE, HERMAN 1819-1891   Benito Cereno. London: Nonesuch Press, 1926. Limited to 1650 numbered copies; folio; colored plates by McKnight Kauffer; maroon buckram, very good in scarce dust jacket which is torn and chipped around edges with small portion torn away at foot of spine and upper panel.   Words Etcetera 94-997 1996 £225.00

MELVILLE, HERMAN 1819-1891   Benito Cereno. London: Nonesuch Press, 1926. Limited to 1650 copies; tall quarto; 123 pages; 7 full page and 3 smaller pochoir illustrations by Kauffer; red buckram, chipped dust jacket, spine slightly faded, else very fine.   Bromer Booksellers 90-208 1996 $150.00

MELVILLE, HERMAN 1819-1891   Benito Cereno. London: Nonesuch Press, 1926. Limited to 1650 copies; 4to; illustrations by E. McKnight Kauffer, original binding, near fine.   Charles Agvent 4-870 1996 $125.00

MELVILLE, HERMAN 1819-1891   Billy Budd Sailor. Mount Holly; Married Mettle Press, 1987. One of 5 copies from a total edition of 185; page size 9 1/8 x 6 1/8 inches; set in 13 point Van Dijck and Caslon for the display, headpiece/tailpiece engravings; 9 letterpress and wood engraving broadsides, with extra suite of the wood engravings, each signed by the artist, Deborah Alterman; bound by Benjamin and Deborah Alterman with champleve bronze spine with wooden boards riveted to the spine with handmade hinges and the sections of the book sewn with herringbone stitch onto doubled linen cords laced through, cross laminated teakwood and mahogany boards, title raised in relief by etching away the bronze, which has blue-grey patina, housed in clear hand blown leaded glass drop back box; book, extra suite, catalog and broadsides housed in specially made clamshell box.   Priscilla Juvelis 95/1-172 1996 $5,000.00

MELVILLE, HERMAN 1819-1891   The Confidence Man: His Masquerade. New York: Dix, Edwards & Co., 1857. 1st American edition (may have been published simultaneously in London and New York); 8vo; original purple cloth, faded, rubbed, spine darkened and frayed, olive coated endpapers, some light marginal browning of text, otherwise very clean. BAL 13670.   James Cummins 14-133 1996 $1,000.00

MELVILLE, HERMAN 1819-1891   Israel Potter: His Fifty Years of Exile. New York: Putnam, 1855. 2nd printing, in the first binding with pendants on spine; 8vo; original binding, modern bookplate, moderate edgewear, backstrip frayed at tips and detached along one edge as is front cover, in need of some professional help after which is should be fairly handsome.   Charles Agvent 4-872 1996 $150.00

MELVILLE, HERMAN 1819-1891   Mardi: and A Voyage Thither. New York: Harper & Bros., 1849. 1st American edition; 7 1/2 x 5 1/4 inches; 2 volumes; 4 leaves of ads at back of volume 2; original cloth, usual sprinkled foxing on text and endpapers (persistent but not at all offensive or unsightly, especially since the paper is quite white and crisp), 3 spine ends flush with text block (the fourth a bit frayed), corners somewhat worn, otherwise binding very clean and smooth and with joints and hinges virtually unworn; excellent copy. BAL 1365.   Phillip J. Pirages 33-384 1996 $1,400.00

MELVILLE, HERMAN 1819-1891   Mardi: and a Voyage Thither. New York: Harpers, 1849. 1st edition; 8vo; 2 volumes; original binding, ex-library copies with all the markings, moderate foxing and staining, some edgewear, backstrip lacking from volume 1.   Charles Agvent 4-873 1996 $250.00

MELVILLE, HERMAN 1819-1891   The Whale... London: Richard Bentley, 1851. 1st edition of Moby Dick; 8vo; 3 volumes; half title in volume 1 as called for; modern half calf, marbled sides, spines in compartments, with raised bands, blindstamped ornaments, gilt rules, red morocco labels, volume numbers gilt lettered direct, top edge gilt, few spots; very good, rare. Sadleir 1685.   Simon Finch 24-167 1996 £14,000.00

MELVILLE, HERMAN 1819-1891   Moby Dick or the Whale. Chicago: Lakeside Press, 1930. Limited to 1000 copies; quarto; 3 volumes; extremely fine, partially unopened set with original glassine and paper dust jackets, with none of the fading to spines that is so common due to the black cloth binding, housed in original aluminum slipcase.   Bromer Booksellers 87-164 1996 $3,000.00

MELVILLE, HERMAN 1819-1891   Moby Dick or the Whale. New York: 1975. Limited to 1500 coies, signed by Cousteau and Neiman; folio; xlv, 272 pages; preface by Jacques-Yves Cousteau; reproductions of 13 original paintings by Leroy Neiman, with 12 in text illustrations, frontispiece is an original serigraph; gilt stamped brown morocco, housed in slightly soiled slipcase of morocco and linen; very fine.   Bromer Booksellers 90-207 1996 $1,250.00

MELVILLE, HERMAN 1819-1891   Moby-Dick; or, The Whale. San Francisco: Arion Press, 1979. Limited to 265 copies; folio; xv, 576 pages; 100 woodcut illustrations by Barry Moser; printed on Barcham green handmade paper; bound in full blue morocco lettered in silver on spine; fine in blue cloth slipcase.   Heritage Book Shop 196-173 1996 $5,000.00

MELVILLE, HERMAN 1819-1891   Moby-Dick, or, The Whale. San Francisco: Arion Press, 1979. One of 250 (of 265) copies for sale; 15 1/4 x 10 5/8 inches; 1 page, xv, 576, (1); 100 wood engravings, printed in two colors in handset Goudy Modern on handmade Barcham Green paper, the Leviathan capitals for the title and initial letters in blue; bound in full blue leather with spine stamped in silver; fine in lightly faded slipcase, with original publisher's prospectus (scare).   Taurus Books 83-118 1996 $5,000.00

MELVILLE, HERMAN 1819-1891   Omoo: a Narrative of Adventures in the South Seas. New York: Harper & Bros., 1847. 1st American edition; 12mo; xv, (1, blank), (17)-389, (1, blank), (xv)-xxiii ads), (1, blank), (16, ads) pages; frontispiece, one illustration in text; original slate blindstamped cloth stamped in gilt on front cover and spine, marbled endpapers, extremities lightly rubbed, some discoloration to cloth, spine bit faded, little light foxing, overall very good copy. BAL 13656. Heritage Book Shop 196-174 1996 $3,000.00

MELVILLE, HERMAN 1819-1891   Pierre; or, the Ambiguities. New York: Harper, 1852. 1st edition; green cloth with just touch of wear and old and neat removal of label from spine, front orchid endpaper lacking, removal of labels from both pastedowns, moderate foxing, quite good, scarce.   Charles Agvent 4-876 1996 $1,500.00

MELVILLE, HERMAN 1819-1891   Pierre; or, the Ambiguities. New York: 1852. 1st edition; 7.5 x 5 inches; 495 pages; blindstamped cloth, ink names, four ink numbers on reverse of titlepage, some foxing, spine sunned, head frayed, else good.   John K. King 77-389 1996 $850.00

MELVILLE, HERMAN 1819-1891   Pierre; or, the Ambiguities. New York: Harper, 1855. 2nd edition? 8vo; viii, 495 pages; aside from different date on titlepage and use of much thinner and slightly smaller paper, this appears to be an exact reprint of the 1st edition with all of the marred and broken type; green cloth; slight wear to spine tips; near fine, modern signature.   Charles Agvent 4-877 1996 $350.00

MELVILLE, HERMAN 1819-1891   Redburn. New York: Harper, 1849. 2nd printing (according to BAL 13660 (though Schwartz designates this 1st issue), with extended ads; 8vo; original binding, erased signature on f.f.e.p., heavy spotting of cloth and edgewear, marginal old dampstaining.   Charles Agvent 4-880 1996 $300.00

MELVILLE, HERMAN 1819-1891   Rock Rodondo: Sketches Third and Fourth from "The Encantadas". New York: Red Angel Press, 1981. One of 100 numbered copies, signed by artist; large 4to; printed handset Bembo on Fabriano handmade; screen printed cloth; fine.   Bertram Rota 272-406 1996 £150.00

MELVILLE, HERMAN 1819-1891   Typee: a Peep at Polynesian Life. New York: Wiley & Putnam, 1847. 4th printing of the Revised Edition with the sequel; 8vo; map, terminal ads; purple cloth with light spotting, scattered foxing; very good; inscription.   Charles Agvent 4-885 1996 $300.00

MELVILLE, HERMAN 1819-1891   Typee: a Peep at Polynesian Life... New York: Harper & Bros., 1855. 1st American revised edition; 12mo; black library cloth, library stamps on title and several maragins, ads, browning and staining, some short marginal repairs and blanks lacking, owner's signatures on title and preface.   James Cummins 14-134 1996 $125.00

MELVILLE, HERMAN 1819-1891   Typee. New York: Limited Editions Club, 1935. Limited to 1500 copies, signed by artist; 8vo; illustrations by Miguel Covarrubias; decorated boards, slipcase, fine in lightly worn slipcase.   James S. Jaffe 34-700 1996 $250.00

MELVILLE, HERMAN 1819-1891   Typee. New York: Limited Editions Club, 1935. Limited to 1500 copies, signed by artist; 8vo; illustrations by Miguel Covarrubias; full native tappa, small tear to spine, otherwise fine in near fine case.   Charles Agvent 4-886 1996 $150.00

MELVILLE, HERMAN 1819-1891   Typee, a Romance of the South Seas. New York: Limited Editions Club, 1935. Number 904 from 1500 copies, signed by Miguel Covarrubias; full decorated tappa binding, very good in lightly rubbed publisher's slipcase.   Hermitage SP95-1015 1996 $150.00

MELVILLE, HERMAN 1819-1891   White-Jacket; or the World in a Man-of-War. New York: Harper & Bros., 1850. 1st American edition, 1st printing; original brown cloth, ornately stamped in blind, spine lettered in gilt (BAL first cloth binding), fraying and wearing to joints and spine ends, some repair, rubbed, upper joint cracked, title nearly detached, spotting throughout, staining, mostly at front, ads at back; blue morocco backed case (damaged); with signature of R. D. King 1850 on endpaper. BAL 13662.   James Cummins 14-135 1996 $750.00

MELVILLE, LEWIS   The Life and Letters of Tobias Smollett. Boston and New York: Houghton Mifflin, 1927. 1st edition; 8 black and white plates; cloth backed boards, pages unopened, fore edge of page vii nicked and creased, endpaper gutters browned, tail of spine and bottom corners very slightly bumped, near fine in nicked and creased dust jacket browned at spine and edges and slightly frayed at head of spine. Ulysses 39-543 1996 £65.00

MELVILLE, ROBERT   Henry Moore: Sculpture and Drawings. 1921-1969. New York: Abrams, n.d. 4to; 368 pages; 846 illustrations, 32 in color; cloth, dust jacket. Freitag 6708.   Brannan 43-455 1996 $135.00

MELVILLE, ROBERT   Henry Moore. Sculpture and Drawings 1921-1969. New York: Harry N. Abrams, Inc., n.d., ca. 1970. 4to; 368 pages, index; 846 illustrations, including 32 mounted color plates; brown cloth, gilt, dust jacket.   Kenneth Karmiole 1NS-26 1996 $125.00

MEMOIR of Mr. and Mrs. Wood an Authentic Account...in the Lives of These Vocalists, Including the Marriage of Miss Paton to Lord William Lenox; and the Causes Which Led to Their Divorce: Her Marriage to Joseph Wood. Boston: James Fisher, 1840. 36 pages; frontispiece; newly re-wrapped.   Lyman Books 21-286 1996 $125.00

MEMOIRS of the Literary and Philosophical Society of Manchester. Warrington: printed by W. Eyres, 1785. 8vo; 2 volumes, 5 engraved plates; contemporary tree calf, rubbed, spines gilt, hinges cracked, lacks labels.   Anthony W. Laywood 108-87 1996 £65.00

MEMOIRS of the Public and Private Life of Sir Richd. Phillips, Knight High Sheriff for the City of London and County of Middlesex. London: printed by J. Dean for G. Hughes and H. D. Symonds, 1808. 1st edition; 12mo; viii, 160 pages, lacking half title; later calf backed boards, old paper library label at foot of spine. Uncommon.   James Burmester 29-96 1996 £175.00

MEMORIAL and Genealogical Records of Southwest Texas. Chicago: 1894. 1st edition; small folio; 661 pages; illustrations, maps; full leather, new spine, corners chipped.   W. M. Morrison 436-159 1996 $225.00

A MEMORIAL of the American Patriots Who Fell at the Battle of Bunker Hill, June 17, 1775. Boston: pritned by order of the City Council, 1889. 1st edition; 20 views, maps, plans, etc., some folding; brown cloth, gilt, light overall rubbing, still very nice.   Hermitage SP95-1052 1996 $125.00

MENABONI, ATHOS   Menaboni's Birds. New York: Rinehart, 1950. 1st edition; Number 460 of an unspecified numbered signed by the Menabonis. 4to; 2 volumes; 31 plates; original green cloth, spines faded, else near fine in very good publisher's slipcase. Handsome set. Chapel Hill 94-310 1996 $125.00

MENCKEN, HENRY LOUIS   The American Language. New York: Knopf, 1960/61/61. Volume 1 is the fourth edition; very large thick octavo; 3 volumes, pages 806, 841, 933; black cloth, gilt decorations. Fine in jackets (with minor repair).   Hartfield 48-11p 1996 $195.00

MENCKEN, HENRY LOUIS   The Gist of Nietzsche. Boston: John W. Luce & Co., 1910. 1st edition; 60 pages; cloth; very good, scarce. Robert G. Hayman 11/95-68 1996 $125.00

MENCKEN, HENRY LOUIS   Prejudices, Fourth Series. New York: Knopf, 1924. 1st edition; limited to 110 copies; signed by author; printed on rag paper, cloth backed boards, original slipcase, expertly repaired along top; fine.   Bromer Booksellers 90-170 1996 $525.00

MENDELEEFF, DMITRY I.   The Principles of Chemistry. London: Longmans, Green, 1897. 2nd English edition; 8vo; 2 volumes; xviii, 621; (6), 518, 32 (ads) pages, 97 figures; few tables, one folding; original cloth, light wear at extremities, bit of bubbling on covers of volume 2; very good set.   Edwin V. Glaser 121-213 1996 $450.00

MENDELSSOHN, MOSES   Phaedon; or, the Death of Socrates. London: printed for the author by J. Cooper, 1789. 8vo; pages (6), (40), 212, apparently lacks half title; uncased, but with remains of original binding; early bookplate of Library Company of Baltimore, engraved by Allaradice of Philadelphia; ex-library.   Family Album Tillers-438 1996 $200.00

MENDES, CATULLE   Hesperus. Paris: Societe de Propagation des Livres d'Art, 1904. There were 350 copies of the regular octavo edition and 165 deluxe copies, of which only 125 were in quarto size with an extra suite of proofs, and of these 125, only 12 were on Japan Imperial, of which this is one; 4to; the additional suite printed on China paper and mounted, 12 full page plates, floral half title, titlepage vignette, colophon and part-headings, pictorial chapter headings and culs-de-lampe, all hand colored; floral decorated hand colored wrappers with title in gold, spine extremities worn with little loss, occasional minor finger soiling, but excellent copy.   Marilyn Braiterman 15-184 1996 $3,500.00

MENDES, CATULLE   Petits Poemes Russes Mis en Vers Francais. Paris: Charpentier et Fasquelle, 1893. 1st edition; 77 pages, (1) index; contemporary half brown morocco, spine gilt, original yellow wrappers bound in, upper joint rubbed, printed on poor paper, else very good; presentation copy inscribed and signed by Mendes for Emile Zola. 19th Century Shop 39- 1996 $1,800.00

MENDO, ANDRES   Il Principe Perfetto e Ministri Adatti Documenti Politici e Morali Corredati d'Emblemi... Rome: Presso Vincenzo Poggioli Stampatore della R.C.A., 1816. 1st edition in Italian; 4to; xxiv, 472 pages, 1 full page plate, 80 emblematic engravings by G. Mochetti in the text; contemporary Italian brown morocco (?), single gilt fillet border.   H. M. Fletcher 121-141 1996 £850.00

MENETRIES, E.   Monographie de la Famille des Myiotherinae...Extrait des Memoires de l'Academie Imperiale des Sciences. St. Petersburg: 1836. Author's offprint from the third volume of the sixth series of 'Memoires'. folio (the text 4to. stilted); pages (ii), 102, 16 lithographed plates of which 15 are fine hand colored plates of the birds by F. Davignon, the final plate a diagram; contemporary half vellum, bit worn; inscribed by author to his friend Florent Pierott (?).   Maggs Bros. Ltd. 1190-582 1996 £750.00

MENGS, ANTHONY RAPHAEL   The Works of Anthony Raphael Mengs, First Painter to His Catholic Majesty Charles III. London: printed for R. Faulder and G. G. and J. Robinson, 1796. 1st English edition; 8vo; 2 volumes; engraved titles (foxed), contemporary calf, hinges cracked, spines worn.   Anthony W. Laywood 108-91 1996 £60.00

MENKEN, ADAH ISAACS   Infelicia. London: Paris: New York: Published by the author, 1868. Small 8vo; publisher's green cloth over beveled boards with gilt decoration on cover and spine, cloth slightly bubbled in few spots, all edges gilt, gilt mostly missing along top and lower edges, first gathering bit loose with small piece chipped off the fore-edge of content's page; dedication copy, dedicated to Charles Dickens, with his bookplate; in old cloth chemise (for a slipcase) with two labels. Podeschi pp. 207-208; Wolff 4738; Modern Lib. at Watlington Park p.199 Book Block 32-57 1996 $1,350.00

MENNINGER, KARL A.   Man Against Himself. New York: Harcourt, 1938. 1st edition; 5th printing; 8vo; dust jacket (few nicks and creases, spine faded), very good; signed by author, signed by him again on recipients bookplate.   George J. Houle 68-95 1996 $200.00

MENOCAL, A. G.   Report of the U. S. Nicaragua Surveying Party, 1885. Washington: GPO, 1886. 1st edition; 4to; 55 pages, 12 large folding maps and charts, 56 plates; original gilt titled cloth, missing hole to cloth the size of a dime along spine and rubbed through in few places along front edge, light soiling to endpapers, else very good. Andrew Cahan 47-148 1996 $100.00

MENZBIR, M.   (Russian): Game and Commercial Birds of European Russia and the Caucasus. Moscow: 1898-1902. 1st edition; 2 volumes text (royal 8vo.) and 1 volume atlas (oblong 8vo); 140 chromolithographed plates, with half titles and printed flimseys (except for the last plate, where one may be missing, but the flimsey captions add nothing to the plate captions), text rather browned, the flimseys bit torn, corner of flytitle torn away in volume 2 and pages 417/8 in same volume torn without loss, some foxing, original half leather, bit worn and loose; extremely rare.   Maggs Bros. Ltd. 1190-585 1996 £1,600.00

MENZIES, WILLIAM   Forest Trees and Woodland Scenery, as Described in Ancient and Modern Poets. London: Longmans, Green & Co., 1875. Folio; viii, 151 pages; 20 fine chromolitho plates, mounted on thick paper as issued; publisher's dark green pebble grain cloth, decorated on front cover and spine in gilt and brown, gilt edges, skilfully recased with new endpapers, slightly worn, but fresh copy externally and with only a little foxing to text and plates;   Thomas Thorp 489-215 1996 £295.00

MENZIES, WILLIAM   The History of Windsor Great Park and Windsor Forest. London: 1864. Large folio; 20 large photographic plates, 2 folding maps (loose at end); half leather, worn, little loose, frontispiece margins frayed and mounted. Scarce.   Charles W. Traylen 117-354 1996 £300.00

MERA, H. P.   Pueblo Indian Embroidery. Laboratory of Anthropology, ptd. at the Univ. of New Mexico Press, 1943. 73 pages; near fine in wrappers and dust jacket.   Ken Sanders 8-212 1996 $150.00

THE MERCANTILE Penman, a Series of Commercial Letters to Qualify the Pupil for Mercantile Correspondence. London: Relfe and Fletcher, 150 Aldersgate St., 1851. New edition; 4to; (64) pages printed on rectos only, 30 engraved exmaples of commercial letters; original roan backed marbled boards, printed title label on upper cover, fine.   John Drury 82-239 1996 £95.00

MERCER, A. H. H.   The Late Captain Henry Mercer, of the Royal Artillery, who Was Killed by Undue and Useless Exposure at the Battle of Rangiriri, New Zealand, Nov. 1863... Toronto: Leader and Patriot Steam-Press, 1865. 1st edition? 8vo; 28 pages; removed. Not in Statton & Tremaine.   M & S Rare Books 60-388 1996 $100.00

MERCER, A. S.   The Banditti of the Plains. San Francisco: Grabhorn Press, 1935. Limited to 1000 copies, illustrations by Arvilla Parker; fine in publisher's dust jacket.   Hermitage SP95-881 1996 $165.00

MERCIER, LOUIS SEBASTIEN   Paris In Miniature: Taken from...Tableau de Paris... London: Kearsly, 1782. Tall 8vo; publisher's list at end; quarter calf; armorial bookplate of Archibald Speirs of Elerslee. Halkett & Laing IV 300.   Rostenberg & Stern 150-24 1996 $385.00

MEREDITH, GEORGE 1828-1909   The Letters of George Meredith to Alice Meynell, with Annotations Thereto, 1896-1907. London: Nonesuch Press, 1923. One of 850 numbered copies; 8vo; printed in Garamond types on Ingres; boards with buckram spine, very nice fresh copy in frayed dust jacket.   Bertram Rota 272-316 1996 £55.00

MEREDITH, GEORGE 1828-1909   Lord Ormont and His Aminta. London: Chapman and Hall, 1894. 1st edition; limited to 1500 copies; small 8vo; 3 volumes; half brown morocco, gilt top, by Zaehnsdorf, slight foxing; complete with half titles.   Charles W. Traylen 117-162 1996 £70.00

MEREDITH, GEORGE 1828-1909   Lord Ormont and His Aminta. London: Chapman and Hall, 1894. 1st edition; 8vo; 3 volumes; original grey-green cloth, bit rubbed; very good. Sadlier 1699; CBEL III 891. Ximenes 108-263 1996 $100.00

MEREDITH, GEORGE 1828-1909   Modern Love. Portland: Thos. B. Mosher, 1881. 1st U.S. edition, number 68 of 400 copies; first Mosher Press book issued; dust jacket, very good. Hatch 1.   Hartfield 48-A11 1996 $165.00

MEREDITH, GEORGE 1828-1909   One of Our Conquerors. London: Chapman and Hall, 1891. 1st edition; small 8vo; 3 volumes; half brown morocco, gilt tops, by Zaehnsdorf.   Charles W. Traylen 117-165 1996 £70.00

MEREDITH, GEORGE 1828-1909   Rhoda Fleming. London: Tinsley Bros., 1865. 1st edition; 8vo; 3 volumes; half brown morocco by Zaehnsdorf; very good; rare; Collie VI; Sadlier 1702; not in Wolff; CBEL III 890.   Ximenes 109-191 1996 $600.00

MEREDITH, GRACE E.   Girl Captives of the Cheyennes. Los Angeles: Gem, 1927! Revised; 123 pages; illustrations, map; dust jacket. Maggie Lambeth 30-378 1996 $150.00

MERIGOT, JAMES   A Select Collection of Views and Ruins in Rome and its Vicinity... London: sold by Messrs. Robinsons, Paternoster Row; Mr. White, Fleet St... 1819. 3rd edition; 4to; 2 parts in 1 volume; pages (iv), 62 tinted aquatints, each plate accompanied by a leaf of text in both English and French; contemporary half calf, marbled boards, spine gilt, raised bands, tooled in blind, inner front hinge little cracked, otherwise very attractive. Abbey 178.   Sotheran PN32-166 1996 £890.00

MERIMEE, PROSPER   Carmen and Letters from Spain. Paris: Harrison of Paris, 1931. One of 595 copies on Rives, from a total of 645; page size 8 1/2 x 6 3/4 inches; illustrated by Maurice Barraud with monochrome watercolors in white and various shades of brown; tan paper over boards, with illustration on front panel, housed in brown slipcase.   Priscilla Juvelis 95/1-120 1996 $100.00

MERIMEE, PROSPER   Carmen. New York: Limited Editions Club, 1941. Limited to 1500 copies, signed by artist; quarto; 143 pages; 37 lithographs in two to seven colors, each using separate stone, by Jean Charlot; linen backed boards, covered with hand blocked gipsy silk; extremely fine in slipcase.   Bromer Booksellers 90-15 1996 $350.00

MERIMEE, PROSPER   Carmen. New York: Limited Editions Club, 1941. Number 904 from 1500 copies, signed by artist; color lithographs by Jean Charlot; cloth backed bizarre cloth boards, near fine in lightly worn and soiled publisher's slipcase.   Hermitage SP95-1016 1996 $100.00

MERIMEE, PROSPER   Carmen. New York: Limited Editions Club, 1945. Limited to 1500 copies; 4to; 37 lithographs in color drawn on plates by Jean Charlot who signs the book; bright gypsy silk cloth, some darkening to gutters, spine; near fine in partly split worn case.   Charles Agvent 4-892 1996 $200.00

MERITON, GEORGE   Nomenclatura Clericalis; or, the Young Clerks Vocabulary, in English & Latine. London: printed for Richard Lambert, bookseller in York & are to be sold... 1685. Half calf, later rebacked, slight dampstaining; armorial bookplate, author's own copy, signed by him. Wing M1807.   Jarndyce 103-310 1996 £650.00

MERIWETHER, ELIZABETH AVERY   Facts and Falsehoods. Concerning the War On the South 1861-1865. Memphis: A. R. Taylor and Co., 1904. 1st edition; (10), 271 pages; original printed wrappers; near fine. Howes M535.   McGowan Book Co. 65-58 1996 $125.00

MERMAN, ETHEL   Merman. New York: Simon & Schuster, 1978. 1st edition; 8vo; 16 pages black and white photos; dust jacket; very good; signed by Merman.   George J. Houle 68-96 1996 $125.00

MERRICK, JAMES   The Destruction of Troy, Being a Sequel of the Iliad. Oxford: printed at the Theatre, n.d. 1742? 1st edition; 8vo; contemporary mottled calf, rebacked; very good. Foxon M193; CBEL II 673 (misdated).   Ximenes 108-264 1996 $300.00

MERRICK, JAMES   The Destruction of Troy. Oxford: printed at the Theatre, 1742? 1st edition; 8vo; (xxii), 151 pages, including list of subscribers and (viii), 112 pages; engraved vignette on each titlepage, original panelled calf, joints cracked, lacking spine label, but binding firm; first titlepage little dusty. Foxon M193.   David Bickersteth 133-49 1996 £65.00

MERRILL, JAMES   Bronze. New York: Nadja Press, 1984. In an edition of 176 copies, this number 104 of 150 for sale, signed by author; 8.25 x 5.5 inches; set in spectrum and printed on Hayle paper; blue boards with white leather strip showing, title in blue on front cover; fine. Joshua Heller 21-171 1996 $100.00

MERRILL, JAMES   First Poems. New York: Knopf, 1951. 1st edition; one of 999 numbered copies; spine darkened dust jacket; very good, owner's signature, inscribed by author.   Captain's Bookshelf 38-156 1996 $250.00

MERRILL, JAMES   Marbled Paper. Salem: Charles Seluzicki, 1982. 1st edition; one of 200 copies; signed by author; decorated wrappers, fine. Captain's Bookshelf 38-158 1996 $175.00

MERRILL, JAMES   Overdue Pilgrimage to Nova Scotia. New York: Nadja Press, 1990. One in an edition of 100 numbered copies of which 75 are offered for sale; signed by Merrill; 7.25 x 6 inches; handset in Optima and printed on English Somerset paper; blue wrappers with dark blue title on spine and front cover; fine.   Joshua Heller 21-172 1996 $100.00

MERRILL, JAMES   Yannina. New York: Phoenix Book Shop, 1973. 1st edition; one of 100 numbered copies (from a total of 126), signed by author; oblong 12mo; decorated wrappers; very fine.   Captain's Bookshelf 38-157 1996 $300.00

MERRILL, SAMUEL   The Seventieth Indiana Volunteer Infantry in the War of the Rebellion. Indianapolis: Bowen Merrill, 1900. 1st edition; 372 pages; ex-library, rebound in black library binding with gold lettering on spine, no external library markings. Dornbusch 162. Coulter 322.   Blue River Books 9-175 1996 $150.00

MERRILL, SELAH   East of Jordan. A Record of Travel and Observations in the Countries of Moab, Gilead and Bashan during the Years 1875-1877. New York: Charles Scribner, 1883. 8vo; frontispiece, xvi, 549 pages; 64 illustrations, 3 plates, 1 folding map; original cloth. Archaeologia Luxor-2444 1996 $125.00

MERRITT, A.   The Ship of Ishtar. Putnam, 1926. 1st edition; bright very good+/near fine copy in most attractive near very good dust jacket save for some chipping to dust jacket spine extremities and other light wear and tear.   Aronovitz 57-803 1996 $395.00

MERRITT, BENJAMIN DEAN   The Athenian Calendar in the Fifth Century Based on a Study of the Detailed Accounts of Money Borrowed by the Athenian State. Cambridge: Harvard University Press, 1928. 4to; 324, vii, 138 pages, 6 illustrations, 2 folding plates (in pocket at rear); original cloth; bookplate of Henry Schroder Robinson.   Archaeologia Luxor-3699 1996 $150.00

MERRITT, BENJAMIN DEAN   Athenian Financial Documents of the Fifth Century. Ann Arbor: University of Michigan Press, 1932. 4to; xiv, 179 pages, 17 plates; original cloth, stamp on verso of titlepage, 2 corners lightly bumped.   Archaeologia Luxor-3700 1996 $125.00

MERRITT, PERCIVAL   The True Story of the So-Called Love Letters of Mrs. Piozzi. Cambridge: Harvard University Press, 1928. Limited edition 350 copies; small 8vo; (85) pages; cloth covered patterned boards, gilt lettered spine, mostly unopened, corners bumped, otherwise fine. NCBEL II 1597.   Paulette Rose 16-245 1996 $125.00

MERRY Christmas! New York: Alfred A. Knopf, 1943. Large quarto; 83 pages; original color pictorial boards with red cloth backstrip, color pictorial endpapers, light wear to extremities, otherwise fine.   Heritage Book Shop 196-284 1996 $100.00

MERRYMOUNT PRESS   A Selection of Type Ornaments - the Merrymount Press Collection of Daniel Berkeley Updike Now at the Bancroft Library. Berkeley: Bancroft Library Press, University of California, 1984. One of 25 copies; wrappers; fine; from the library of James D. Hart, director of the Bancroft Library.   Ulysses 39-407 1996 £125.00

MERRYWEATHER, JAMES COMPTON   Fire Protection for Mansions. London: Merritt & Hatcher, 1886. 2nd edition; 8vo; (xvi), (132) pages, (12) pages ads; publisher's cloth.   Elton Engineering 10-104 1996 £110.00

MERTON, THOMAS 1915-1968   The Alaskan Journal of Thomas Merton with Sixteen Letters. Isla Vista: Turkey Press, 1988. One of 140 numbered copies; large 8vo; printed in Spectrum in black and terracotta on Barcham Green's Hayle handmade; frontispiece; black linen boards, off white linen spine lettered in black, black slipcase bearing relief print of photo taken by Merton; fine.   Bertram Rota 272-470 1996 £115.00

MERTON, THOMAS 1915-1968   The Christmas Sermons of Bl. Gueric of Igny. Trappist: Gethsemani, 1959. 1st edition; decorative paper covered boards with original glassine, most beautiful, fine.   Bev Chaney, Jr. 23-474 1996 $125.00

MERTON, THOMAS 1915-1968   A Man in the Divided Sea. New York: New Directions, 1946. 1st edition; author's second book; black cloth with black and grey dust jacket, fine. Dell'Isola A2.   Bromer Booksellers 90-172 1996 $185.00

MERTON, THOMAS 1915-1968   Seeds of Contemplation. Norfolk: New Directions, 1949. 1st edition; burlap covered boards with dust jacket; very fine.   Bromer Booksellers 87-179 1 996 $300.00

MERTON, THOMAS 1915-1968   Seeds of Contemplation. Norfolk: New Directions, 1949. 1st edition; fine, fresh copy in dust jacket with small hole in front panel near spine and with fine tiny edge tears.   Left Bank Books 2-88 996 $185.00

MERTON, THOMAS 1915-1968   The Seven Storey Mountain. New York: Harcourt Brace, 1948. Presumed third state in black cloth with necessary blurbs on jacket, cloth fine, dust jacket has light edge wear and rubbing and few small closed tears, else clean and bright.   Neil Cournoyer 4-73 1996 $150.00

MERTON, THOMAS 1915-1968   Thirty Poems. Norfolk: New Directions 1944. 1st edition; author's first book; fine in dust jacket, very slightly faded at spine and extremities; this hardbound edition is uncommon. Left Bank Books 2-87 1996 $300.00

MERTON, THOMAS 1915-1968   Thirty Poems. Norfolk: New Directions 1944. 1st edition; author's first published book; russet brown wrappers printed in red; fine.   Bev Chaney, Jr. 23-465 1996 $125.00

MERVAULT, PETER   The Last Famous Siege of the city of Roche; Together with the Edict of Nantes. London: Wickins, 1680. 8vo; 2 parts in 1; 3 page publisher's catalog at end; calf; Ilchester-Fox copy with bookplates. Wing M1879. Haag VII 393.   Rostenberg & Stern 150-58 1996 $450.00

MERYMAN, RICHARD   Andrew Wyeth. Boston: Houghton Mifflin, 1968 Oblong folio; 174 pages; 165 color plates; cloth, dust jacket. Freitag 10433.   Brannan 43-678 1996 $250.00

METCALF, THERON   Digest of the Cases Decided in the Supreme Judicial Court of...Massachusetts (etc). Cincinnati: 1884. contemporary blind ruled and decorated sheep, worn but good copy.   Meyer Boswell SL26-163 1996 $350.00

METCALFE, FREDERICK   The Oxonian in Norway; or, Notes of Excursions in that Country. London: Hurst and Blackett, 1857. 2nd edition; 8vo; xx, 387 pages; folding map at front; recently rebound with brown calf spine, boards, raised band, leather label, all edges gilt; fine. David Mason 71-133 1996 $240.00

METCALFE, J.   The Feasting Dead. Sauk City: Arkham House, 1954. 1st edition; 1/1242 copies; fine in near fine dust jacket with some dust soiling to rear dust jacket panel.   Aronovitz 57-807 1996 $110.00

METEYARD, ELIZA   The Life of Josiah Wedgwood from His Private Correspondence and Family Papers in the Possession of Joseph Mayer, F. Wedgwood, C, Darwin, Miss Wedgwood and Other Original Sources. London: Hurst & Blackett, 1865. Royal 8vo; 2 volumes, xxxvi, 504; xxiv, 643 pages; 2 steel engraved portrait frontispieces, 2 chromolithograph plates, 8 wood engraved plates, 273 text illustrations; publisher's violet cloth over bevelled boards, elaborately decorated in gilt, silver and blind (rather faded, as usual, especially on spines, corners sorn, sewing little slack in places and text lightly browned throughout.   Thomas Thorp 489-216 1996 £50.00

METHUEN, H. H.   Life in the Wilderness, or Wanderings in South Africa. London: 1846. 8vo; pages xiii, 363, text figures and 3 plates; original cloth; plates somewhat foxed and binding trifle faded, good. Wheldon & Wesley 207-420 1996 £125.00

METTLER, CECILIA C.   History of Medicine. Philadelphia: 1947. 1st edition; 1215 pages; original binding, scarce. GM 6440.   W. Bruce Fye 71-1431 1996 $150.00

METTLER, CECILIA C.   History of Medicine. Philadelphia: Blakiston, 1947. 8vo; 1215 pages, 16 plates; original binding. GM 6440.   James Tait Goodrich K40-193 1996 $150.00

METTLER, FRED A.   Psychosurgical Problems. The Columbia Greystone Associates Second Group. London: Routledge & Kegan, 1952. 8vo; 357 pages; original binding; scarce.   James Tait Goodrich K40-194 1996 $135.00

METZGAR, JUDSON D.   Adventures in Japanese Prints. Los Angeles: printed at the Grabhorn Press for Dawson's Book Shop, 1943. Limited to 300 copies; folio; (14), 116, (4) pages; 10 color plates; linen backed green decorative boards, paper spine label, front cover bit soiled, still very nice. Grabhorn Press Bib. 390.   Kenneth Karmiole 1NS-130 1996 $300.00

MEW, CHARLOTTE   The Farmer's Bride. London: Poetry Bookshop, 1921. New edition; original pictorial boards, pictorial dust jacket (faded chipped and worn); Louis Untermeyer's copy with his bookplate and 3 autograph letters to him from author, envelopes of which are neatly pasted to front and rear endpapers; book in very good condition, letters fine.   David J. Holmes 52-72 1996 $1,250.00

MEYER DE SCHAUENSEE, R.   The Birds of China. Oxford: 1984. 8vo; 602 pages; 38 colored plates, 39 text figures; cloth.   Wheldon & Wesley 207-804 1996 £60.00

MEYER DE SCHAUENSEE, R.   The Species of Birds of South America and Their Distribution. Philadelphia: 1966. 8vo; pages xvii, 578, endpaper maps; cloth, good ex-library.   Wheldon & Wesley 207-803 1996 £65.00

MEYER, ALFRED   Historical Aspects of Cerebral Anatomy. London: Oxford University Press, 1971. 8vo; 230 pages; illustrations; original binding, nice in worn dust jacket.   James Tait Goodrich K40-195 1996 $125.00

MEYER, FRANZ   Marc Chagall: Life and Work. New York: Abrams, n.d. 4to; 775 pages, over 1250 illustrations, including 53 tipped in color plates, cloth, dust jacket. Lucas p. 133; Freitag 1578.   Brannan 43-121 1996 $195.00

MEYER, FRANZ   Marc Chagall: Life and Work. New York: Harry N. Abrams, Inc., n.d., ca. 1964. 775 pages; over 1250 illustrations, including 53 tipped in color plates; fine in dust jacket.   Hermitage SP95-797 1997 $175.00

MEYER, FRANZ   Marc Chagall. New York: Abrams, ca. 1964. 1st edition; 53 mounted color plates; pictorial cloth, small stain at foot of rear cover and odd manufacturing crease at head of spine, little waterstain on fore edge of final pages, not even visible in the text; in all, near fine with price clipped dust jacket only lightly worn but showing a line of paper adhesions on its front panel. Lucas p. 133; Freitag 1578. Magnum Opus 44-10 1996 $125.00

MEYER, RUDOLF   Die Menschliche Sterblichkeit under dem Titel Todten Tanz in LXI Original Kupfern, von Rudolf und Conrad Meyern Beruhmten Kunstmahlern in Zurich abermal Herausgegben... Hamburg und Leipzig: 1759. Small 4to; plates; recent full sombre morocco with blind decoration & gilt titling, 1st edition;; handsome and scarce. Graesse IV p. 513; Brunet III 1690; Faber du Faur 454.   Book Block 32-19 1996 $1,975.00

MEYER, THOMAS   Monotypes and Tracings: German Romantics. London: Enitharmon Press, 1994. 1st edition; one of 50 numbered copies (from a total of 200) signed by Meyer, Fisher and John Ashbery; quarto; monotypes by Sandra Fisher, this issue accompanied by an original etching by Fisher; very fine in slipcase.   Captain's Bookshelf 38-162 1996 $300.00

MEYER, THOMAS   The Umbrella of Aesculapius. Highlands: Jargon Society, 1975. 1st edition; one of 50 (actually 44) copies numbered I-L, this being XXXVIII, drawings by Paul Sinodhinos, bound in handwoven cloth prepared expressly for this edition; very fine, rare.   Captain's Bookshelf 38-160 1996 $250.00

MEYERS, ERIC M.   Excavations at Ancient Merion, Upper Galilee, Israel 1971-72, 1974-75, 1977. Cambridge: ASOR, 1981. Folio; xxii, 276 pages, 75 figures and 68 illustrations, 61 plates, 17 tables; original cloth. Archaeologia Luxor-2455 1996 $125.00

MEYNELL, ALICE   The Children. London: John Lane, 1897. 1st edition; 12mo; decorations by Will Bradley, initials hand illuminated by Mrs. Carrie Way who adds her name to colophon; decorated cloth, cloth very faded and spotted, contents clean. Bookplate.   Charles Agvent 4-893 1996 $135.00

MEYNELL, FRANCIS   The Poetry of Alice Meynell... Cambridge University Press, 1971. One of a small number of copies; tall 8vo; Japanese paper wrappers; very nice, scarce.   Bertram Rota 272-71 1996 £65.00

MEYNELL, FRANCIS   Typography, the Written Word and the Printed Word... London: prepared, printed and published by the Pelican Press, 1923. 1st edition; 500 copies printed; 8vo; pages lxv, 30 leaves of type specimens and titlepages french folded and printed on one side only, large folding title and plate of Pelican devices; printed in black and colors; original blue boards, paper label, good, uncut copy. ownership signature of Walter Tracy. Appleton 19; Meynell My Lives p. 144. Clark Cox 107-231 1996 $85.00

MEYNELL, KATHARINE   Eat Book. London: Gefn Press/New York: Janus Press, 1990. One of 150 copies; page size 9 1/2 x 13 3/8 inches; printed on BFK Rives paper, each signed by Meynell and Johanknecht; 6 duo-tones of photos, 8 relief prints, text printed in letterpress by Johanknecht; bound in archival board painted in south of Thames Plaster mixed with acrylic, wrapperd in rumpled linen dinner napkin.   Priscilla Juvelis 95/1-138 1996 $350.00

MEYNELL, KATHARINE   Eat Book. Co-publication of Gefn Press and Janus Press, 1991. One in an edition of 150 signed copies; 9 x 13 inches; 26 pages; 6 duotones of poet's photos, text lettered by Susan Johanknecht who made the 8 relief prints of eating utensils; Susan Johanknecht designed the binding - sewn through a vellum spine that is attached to acrylic plastered split boards and wrapped in a rumpled linen dinner napkin; fine.   Joshua Heller 21-33 1996 $350.00

MEYNERT, THEODOR HERMANN   Psychiatry: a Clinical Treatise on Diseases of the Fore-Brain Based Upon a Study of Its Structure, Functions and Nutrition. New York/London: G. P. Putnam's Sons/Knickerbocker Press, 1885. 1st edition in English; 8vo; (xii), 285, (7) pages, 1 color lithograph, 64 text illustrations; green cloth, binding lightly stained (as usual), good to very good, scarce; bookplate and gold titlepage stamp of Hartford Retreat.   John Gach 150-325 1996 $150.00

MEYRICK, EDWIN   The Texian Grand March for the Piano Forte. Respectfully Dedicated to Genl. Houston and His Grave Companions in Arms. New York: Firth and Hall, 1836. Folio; 7 pages; very good, laid in half morocco slipcase. Streeter Texas 1171b. Streeter Sale 349; Texana Rev. 13.   Michael D. Heaston 23-320 1996 $550.00

MEYRINK, G.   The Golem. H-M, 1928. 1st American edition, with first issue English sheets; very good in attractive dust jacket with some chipping to dust jacket spine extremities.   Aronovitz 57-809 1996 $185.00

MEZERAY, FRANCOIS   A General Chronological History of France... London: Thomas Basset, 1683. 1st English edition; thick folio; 3 parts in 1; fine additional engraved title, laid down with slight loss, printed title laid down with signature of George Buckley dated 1698, first couple of leaves of prelims little soiled, full contemporary panelled calf, old rebacked with red morocco label;   Ian Wilkinson 95/1-121 1996 £220.00

MICHEAUX, OSCAR   The Masquerade. New York: Book Supply Co., 1947. 1st edition; tiny stain along edge of few pages, tiny nick at base of spine, lacking dust jacket.   Between the Covers 43-161 1996 $125.00

MICHEAUX, OSCAR   The Story of Dorothy Stansfield. New York: Book Supply Co., 1946. 1st edition; slight foxing to base of spine resulting in slight fraying, small crayon price on front fly that is not too intrusive, else very good, lacking dust jacket.   Between the Covers 43-160 1996 $250.00

MICHEAUX, OSCAR   The Story of Dorothy Stanfield. New York: Book Supply Co., 1946. 1st edition; tips very lightly bumped, nick in cloth at base of rear cover, otherwise fine in lightly soiled dust jacket, rubbed on spine, spine ends nicked and rubbed.   Quill & Brush 102-1326 1996 $100.00

MICHEAUX, OSCAR   The Story of Dorothy Stansfield. New York: Book Supply Co., 1946. 1st edition; slight wear to base of spine resulting in slight fraying, small crayon price on front fly that is not too intrusive, else very good, lacking the dust jacket.   Between the Covers 43-159 1996 $100.00

MICHEAUX, OSCAR   The Wind from Nowhere. New York: Book Supply Co., 1943. Stated 5th edition; Label at top front flap indicates this is a "Special Deluxe Edition", which presumably accounts for the presentation bookplate on front pastedown that has been signed by author; slightly cocked and some minor scratching to front fly, very good in not quite very good dust jacket chipped at crown, couple of ther scattered small chips and some internal repairs; books signed by Micheau, even on bookplate, are scarce.   Between the Covers 43-157 1996 $350.00

MICHEL, WALTER   Wyndham Lewis: Paintings and Drawings. Berkeley: University of California Press, 1971. Square 4to; 455 pages, 781 illustrations, including 16 tipped in color plates; cloth, dust jacket. Freitag 5593.   Brannan 43-351 1996 $175.00

MICHELET, JULES   The People. London: Longman, Brown, Green and Longmans, 1846. 1st edition in English; 8vo; xii, 267 pages; original cloth, neatly rebacked and lettered, good copy; Working Men's College bookplate.   John Drury 82-181 1996 £120.00

MICHELET, JULES   The People. London: Longman, Brown, Green and Longmans, 1846. xii, 267 pages; lilac cloth blocked in blind, lettered in gilt on spine, cloth faded, edges of spine beginning to fray, front hinge tender, very good.   Ian Patterson 9-218 1996 £50.00

MICHENER, JAMES ALBERT 1907-   Caravans. London: Secker & Warburg, 1964. 1st English edition; about fine in lightly rubbed and price clipped near fine dust jacket, with single neat internal repair.   Between the Covers 42-305 1996 $125.00

MICHENER, JAMES ALBERT 1907-   Caribbean. New York: 1989. 1st edition; limited to 1000 numbered copies, signed by author; 9.5 x 6 inches; 672 pages; cloth, spine slightly rubbed, else good in slipcase. John K. King 77-391 1996 $150.00

MICHENER, JAMES ALBERT 1907-   The Covenant. New York: Random House, 1/500 copies, signed and numbered; unopened, slipcase.   Bev Chaney, Jr. 23-489 1996 $125.00

MICHENER, JAMES ALBERT 1907-   Literary Reflections. Austin: State House Press, 1993. Limited to 200 copies; fine in slipcase, signed by author.   Bella Luna 7-383 1996 $150.00

MICHENER, JAMES ALBERT 1907-   Literary Reflections. Houston: State House Press, 1993. 1/200 copies, signed; slipcase, fine.   Bev Chaney, Jr. 23-490 1996 $145.00

MICHENER, JAMES ALBERT 1907-   My Lost Mexico. Austin: State House Press, 1992. Limited to 350 copies; drawings and photos by Michener; fine in slipcase, signed by author.   Bella Luna 7-385 1996 $150.00

MICHENER, JAMES ALBERT 1907-   Poland. New York: Random House, 1983. 1st edition; limited to 500 specially bound copies, signed by author; 8vo; decorated endpapers, cloth, slipcase; mint.   James S. Jaffe 34-496 1996 $175.00

MICHENER, JAMES ALBERT 1907-   Poland. New York: Random House, 1983. 1/500 copies, signed and numbered, unopened in slipcase. Bev Chaney, Jr. 23-491 1996 $125.00

MICHENER, JAMES ALBERT 1907-   Rascals. London: Secker & Warburg, 1957. 1st English edition; fine in near fine dust jacket with some foxing on rear panel and a barely visible stain on spine, nice copy of an uncommon edition.   Between the Covers 42-303 1996 $175.00

MICHENER, JAMES ALBERT 1907-   Rascals in Paradise: True Tales of High Adventure in the South Pacific. New York: Random House, 1957. 1st edition; slight soiling to free front endpaper, still fine in attractive very good plus dust jacket, with shallow chip at base of front panel and small chip on rear panel.   Between the Covers 42-302 1996 $150.00

MICHENER, JAMES ALBERT 1907-   Space. New York: Random House, 1982. 1st edition; limited to 500 specially bound copies, signed by author; 8vo; decorated endsheets, cloth, lightly faded slipcse; mint. James S. Jaffe 34-494 1996 $175.00

MICHENER, JAMES ALBERT 1907-   Space. New York: Random House, 1982. 1/500 copies, signed and numbered; unopened in slipcase.   Bev Chaney, Jr. 23-492 1996 $125.00

MICHENER, JAMES ALBERT 1907-   Texas. Austin: March 1, 1986. 1st illustrated edition; quarto; 2 volumes, 940 pages; 250+ pencil drawings by Charles Shaw; two color printing throughout on cream color acid free paper; bound in buckram, slipcase, as new.   Bohling Book Co. 191-100 1996 $100.00

MICKLE, WILLIAM ENGLISH   Well Know Confederate Veterans and their War Records. New Orleans: Wm. E. Mickle, 1907. 74, xxxix pages; original cloth, minor cover speckling, rear flyleaf lacking, yet very good, rare portrait album. Dornbusch III 33; not in Nevins or Nicholson. McGowan Book Co. 65-61 1996 $500.00

MICKLE, WILLIAM JULIUS   General Paralysis of the Insane. London: H. K. Lewis, 1880. 1st edition; 8vo; (viii), 246, (2) pages + 24 page inserted catalog dated Jan. 1880; panelled mauve cloth, spine faded, corners bumped, hinges cracked, good, scarce; titlepage stamp and bookplate of Hartford Retreat.   John Gach 150-327 1996 $150.00

THE MICROCOSM. London: Charles Knight, 1825. 5th edition; 8vo; 2 or 3 leaves with insignificant spotting, otherwise fine; beautfiully bound in full contemporary red straight grained morocco, boards with blind and gilt borders enclosing a gilt panel with foliate corners, spine elaborately gilt, gilt lettering direct, gilt dentelles, all edges gilt.   Ian Wilkinson 95/1-50 1996 £65.00

MIDDLEBROOK, LOUIS F.   History of Maritime Connecticut During the American Revolution, 1775-1783. Salem: Essex Inst., 1925. 1st edition; limited to 1250 copies; 2 volumes, xiv, 272; viii, 359 pages; numerous plates and maps; cloth, dust jacket, fine in very good dust jacket (with trivial stain).   Metacomet Books 54-69 1996 $125.00

MIDDLETON, J. HENRY   The Engraved Gems of Classical Times with a Catalogue of the Gems in the Fitzwilliam Museum. Cambridge: Cambridge University Press, 1891. 4to; xvi, 157 pages, 2 plates, xxxvi; original cloth, top edge gilt, bookplate.   Archaeologia Luxor-3710 1996 $125.00

MIDDLETON, JOHN   View of the Agriculture of Middlesex; with Observations on the Means of Its Improvement and Several Essays on Agriculture in General... London: printed by B. MacMillan, 1798. 1st edition; 8vo; half title; colored folding map, errata leaf, folding colored plan, folding chart; contemporary sprinkled calf, rebacked, label. Anthony W. Laywood 109-98 1996 £140.00

MIDDLETON, JOHN   View of the Agriculture of Middlesex. London: Richard Phillips, 1807. 2nd edition; 8vo; xvi, 704, (4) pages ads; (2) catalogu, folding hand colored mpa; contemporary half calf, retaining original gilt spine, label; very good.   Ken Spelman 30-93 1996 £120.00

MIDDLETON, THOMAS   A Tragi-Coomodie Called the Witch Long Since
...cted by His Ma(jes)ties Servants at the Black Friers. London: J.
Nichols, 1778. 1st edition; approximately 100 copies printed; 8vo; 111
...ages; full calf, raised bands on spine, leather labels, professionally
...ebacked, ms. notes on flyleaf, very good.   Robert F. Lucas 42-69
...996 $900.00

MIDDLETON, THOMAS   A Tragi-Coomodie, called The Witch... London:
...rivately printed by John Nichols for Isaac Reed, 1778. 1st edition; 8vo;
...ages 111, (i) colophon, early MS not on blank facing title; full red
...rushed morocco, spine richly gilt between raised bands, sides ruled in
...ilt with a french fillet, gilt inner dentelles, all edges gilt, by Sangorski &
...utcliffe; fine copy; the Heber - Chalmers - Holgate - Bridgewater -
Huntington - Clawson - Spiegelberg copy, with most bookplates;
...imon Finch 24-168 1996 £1,000.00

MIDDLETON, THOMAS   Works. London: Edward Lumley, Chancery
...ane, 1840. 8vo; 5 volumes; beautifully bound in full morocco, 3 line gilt
...order, fully gilt spines, gilt edges, by Francis Bedford. Superb set.
...harles W. Traylen 117-168 1996 £350.00

THE MIDLAND Counties' Railway Companion, with Topographical
Descriptions of the Country through Which the Line Passes. Nottingham:
...ublished by the Proprietors, R. Allen; and E. Allen, Leicester, 1840. 8vo;
...60 pages of ads at end; engraved and printed titles, folding map, 4
...lates, numerous illustrations; original printed upper board, new spine
...nd lower board.   Anthony W. Laywood 108-224 1996 £110.00

MIEGE, GUY   A Relation of Three Embassies from...Charales II to the
Great Duke of Muscovie, The King of Sweden, and the King of Denmark.
Performed by the...Earle of Carlisle in the Years 1663 and 1664. London:
...tarkey, 1669. 8vo; full page portrait, publisher's list at end; calf,
...ebacked, scuffed, hinged; extremely rare English version; ownership
...ignature of John Savile on titlepage. Wing M 2025.   Rostenberg &
...tern 150-59 1996 $385.00

MIERS, HENRY A.   Yukon. A Visit to the Yukon Gold-Fields. N.P.:
...ugust, 1901. 1st edition; 32 pages; original printed white glazed paper
...rinted in red, blue and gold, minor chipping repaired; fine. Tourville
...100.   Michael D. Heaston 23-10 1996 $250.00

MILDMAY, WILLIAM   An Account of the Southern Maritime Provinces
...f France... London: printed for Thomas Harrison, 1764. (4), 133, (1)
...ages, plates, maps; disbound, very nice. Higgs 3322.   C. R. Johnson
...7-22 1996 £350.00

MILES, NELSON A.   Personal Recollections and
Observations...Embracing A Brief View of the Civil War. Chicago: Werner
...o., 1897. 2nd edition; 591 pages; brown pictorial cloth, near fine.
Howes M595; Graff 2789; Rader 2397; Saunders 3051.   Blue River
Books 9-221 1996 $175.00

MILES, W. J.   Modern Practical Farriery, a Complete Ssytem of the
Veterinary Art... London: n.d., ca. 1880. Thick 4to; 20 full page colored
...lates, 28 black and white plates and text illustrations; contemporary half
morocco.   Charles W. Traylen 117-316 1996 £140.00

MILES, WILLIAM   General Remarks on Stables and Examples of
Stable Fittings. London: Longman and Others, 1864. 2nd edition; 4to;
frontispiece, vii, (i), 89 pages, 12 plates; publisher's cloth, some cover
...wear, else good.   The Bookpress 75-214 1996 $585.00

MILL, HUGH ROBERT   The English Lakes. London: George Philip &
Son, 1895. 1st separate edition; 8vo; 64 pages, 8 folding colored maps,
20 illustrations; later cloth, typed label, little damped; original wrappers
bound in, some corners trifle creased, scarce.   R.F.G. Hollett & Son
78-1119 1996 £65.00

MILL, JAMES 1773-1836   Elements of Political Economy. London:
printed for Baldwin, Cradock and Joy, 1821. 1st edition; 8vo; viii, 235, (1)
pages, without 4 pages of publisher's ads found in some copies;
contemporary half calf, neatly rebacked, spine lettered in gilt, new
endpapers; very good. Amex 313; Einaudi 3892; Goldsmiths 23118; Kress
C739. Hollander 2428.   John Drury 82-182 1996 £650.00

MILL, JOHN STUART 1806-1873   Autobiography. London: Longmans,
Green, Reader, and Dyer, 1873. Small 4to; list of Mill's works at end;
cloth. CBEL III 871.   Rostenberg & Stern 150-123 1996 $425.00

MILL, JOHN STUART 1806-1873   Considerations on Representative
Government. London: Longman, Green, Longman, Roberts & Green,
1865. 3rd edition; 8vo; half title, name and address, contemporary notes
on last 2 leaves, ad leaf at end; original cloth, uncut, nice.   Anthony
W. Laywood 108-203 1996 £65.00

MILL, JOHN STUART 1806-1873   England and Ireland. London:
Longmans, 1868. 1st edition; 8vo; 44 pages; disbound. Ownership
inscription of Francis Warre Cornish, teacher, classicist & writer on
education.   James Burmester 29-97 1996 £200.00

MILL, JOHN STUART 1806-1873   Essays on Some Unsettled Questions
of Political Economy. London: John W. Parker, 1844. 1st edition; 8vo; vi,
(ii), 164, 4 pages, complete with half title, 2 final ad leaves; original cloth
backed boards with paper spine label, bit worn, dust soiled, else very
good. Sir Arthur Helps' copy with his signature. Einaudi 3899; Goldsmiths
33591; Kress C6398. MacMinn et al p. 57.   John Drury 82-183 1996
£700.00

MILL, JOHN STUART 1806-1873   Inaugural Address Delivered to the
University of St. Andrews Feb. 1st 1867. London: Longmans, 1867. 1st
edition; 8vo; 99, (1) pages; original maroon cloth, lettered in gilt on
upper cover, neatly rebacked. From the library of William Rathbone
(1787-1868) the Liverpool educationist and philanthropist.   John Drury
82-186 1996 £125.00

MILL, JOHN STUART 1806-1873   Inaugural Address Delivered to the
University of St. Andrews Feb. 1st 1867. London: Longmans, Green,
Reader and Dyer, 1867. 2nd edition; 8vo; 99, (1) pages; early ownership
signature on title; original maroon cloth lettered in gilt on upper cover,
spine bit frayed at head and short split on upper joint, else good.
John Drury 82-185 1996 £50.00

MILL, JOHN STUART 1806-1873   Principles of Political Economy With
Some of Their Applications to Social Philosophy. London: John W.
Parker, 1848. 1st edition; 2 volumes; original cloth, paper labels, minor
ink underlining at beginning, labels very slightly chipped, cloth case, fine,
much better than usually encountered.   19th Century Shop 39- 1996
$4,200.00

MILL, JOHN STUART 1806-1873   Principles of Political Economy with
Some of Their Applications to Social Philosophy... London: John W.
Parker and Son, 1852. 3rd edition; 8vo; 2 volumes, xx, 604; xv, (1), 571,
(1) pages, complete with 4 pages of ads in volume 2; original green
cloth, printed paper labels, slightly rubbed, but overall very good, largely
unopened; from the contemporary library of Sir William Molesworth with
his armorial bookplate. Hollander 2818.   John Drury 82-184 1996
£275.00

MILL, JOHN STUART 1806-1873   The Subjection of Women. London:
Longmans, Green, Reader and Dyer, 1869. 1st edition; 8vo; (2), 188
pages, wanting half title, very few insignificant spots or dust marks, here
and there, neat signature in ink at head of title; recent full panelled calf
gilt, handsome copy. Headicar & Fuller III 1208; CBEL III 871. Hollander
2836 (2nd ed.)   John Drury 82-187 1996 £400.00

MILL, JOHN STUART 1806-1873   The Subjection of Women. New
York: Appleton, 1869. 1st American edition; 8vo; original cloth, Joseph
Albree 1869 bookticket.   Rostenberg & Stern 150-117 1996 $750.00

MILLAIS, JOHN GUILLE 1865-1931   A Breath from the Veldt. London:
1899. New edition; large 4to; numerous plates, some little foxed, text
illustrations by author, frontispiece by J. E. Millais; original cloth.
Charles W. Traylen 117-317 1996 £140.00

MILLAIS, JOHN GUILLE 1865-1931   Game Birds and Shooting
Sketches: Illustrating the Habits, Modes of Capture, Stages of Plumage
and the Hybrids and Varieties Which Occur Amongst Them. London:
Henry Sotheran, 1892. 1st edition; royal 4to; portrait, 15 color printed
lithographic plates, 19 plates, numerous text illustrations (little marginal
spotting), publisher's gilt lettered straight grain morocco and cloth, gilt
tops, trifle rubbed. Schwerdt II p. 27.   Charles W. Traylen 117-318
1996 £350.00

MILLAIS, JOHN GUILLE 1865-1931   The Mammals of Great Britain and
Ireland. London: Longmans, Green & Co., 1904-06. Large 4to; 3 volumes,
xx, 365; xi, 299; xii, 384 pages; 18 photogravure plates by author, 31
colored plates, 63 uncolored plates; cloth, buckram spines, top edge gilt,
binding rather worn and stained as usual, some slight foxing in places.
Thomas Thorp 489-217 1996 £220.00

MILLAIS, JOHN GUILLE 1865-1931   Rhododendrons: in Which is Set
Forth an Account of All species of the Genus Rhododendron (Including
Azaleas) and Various Hybirds (First Series). London: 1917. One of 550
copies only; folio; 2 volumes; 17 colored and 14 collotype plates and 30
illustrations from photos; original cloth; very scarce; binding somewhat
used but good copy internally.   Wheldon & Wesley 207-66 1996
£500.00

MILLAIS, JOHN GUILLE 1865-1931   The Wildfowler in Scotland.
London: 1901. 4to; pages xv, 167, 2 color and 19 photogravure and
plain plates; 40 text illustrations from photos and drawings; half vellum,
gilt, binding slightly soiled and small nick in upper hinge, otherwise good
copy.   John Henly 27-25 1996 £120.00

MILLAR, OLIVER   Later Georgian Pictures in the Collection of Her
majesty the Queen. London: Phaidon, 1969. 30 x 23 cm; 2 volumes; lvi,
174 pages, 92 black and white illustrations; x pages, 302 plates; original
cloth, dust jackets slightly soiled.   Rainsford A54-413 1996 £65.00

MILLAY, EDNA ST. VINCENT 1892-1950   The Ballad of the
Harp-Weaver. New York: Frank Shay, 1922. 1st edition; plain tan
wrappers and pictorial orange dust jacket; fine, oversized dust jacket
has shallow chip from lower front panel, housed in handsome morocco
slipcase; inscribed by author, uncommon thus.   Captain's Bookshelf
38-163 1996 $450.00

MILLAY, EDNA ST. VINCENT 1892-1950   Fatal Interview (Sonnets).
New York: Harper bros., 1931. 1st edition; one of 479 copies; tall 8vo;
printed on handmade paper and signed by author; blue boards over
linen spine, paper label, fine, clean copy in slipcase.   Appelfeld Gallery
54-139 1996 $200.00

MILLAY, EDNA ST. VINCENT 1892-1950   Fatal Interviews. Sonnets by
Edna St. Vincent Millay. New York: Harper & Brothers, 1931. Of a total
edition of 515 copies, this is 1/479 numbered and signed by author on
Arches handmade paper; fine in somewhat torn glassine jacket enclosed
in fine numbered slipcase.   Left Bank Books 2-92 1996 $175.00

MILLAY, EDNA ST. VINCENT 1892-1950   The King's Henchman. New
York: Harper, 1927. Artist's Edition, limited to 500 copies, signed by
author with facsimile copy from the opera score, signed by Deems
Taylor, the composer; octavo; (12), 132 pages; 3 proof etchings of
Urban's set designs; buckram backed boards, fine, unopened copy,
slipcase, bookplate.   Bromer Booksellers 87-274 1996 $225.00

MILLER,   Tricks and Diversions with Cards. New York: Hurst & Co.,
da. 1885. 12mo; 90 pages plus ads; original color pictorial wrappers,
slightly chipped, poor quality paper, but quite good, although broken into
signatures at spine.   M & S Rare Books 60-364 1996 $175.00

MILLER, A. E.   Military Drawings and Paintings. London: Phaidon,
1969/70. 30 23 cm; 2 volumes, 221 pages, 478 plates; 279 pages, 23
illustrations; cloth, dust jackets.   Rainsford A54-592 1996 £60.00

MILLER, ARTHUR   After the Fall. New York: Viking Press, 1964. 1/500
specially bound copies, signed by author; advance copy with
compliments slip laid in; fine in glassine dust jacket in publisher's box.
Left Bank Books 2-97 1996 $165.00

MILLER, ARTHUR   Death of a Salesman. London: 1949. 1st edition;
tiny bookshop stamp; fine in dust jacket (spine sunned, extremities little
edge chipped); this copy specially signed by author.   Polyanthos
22-594 1996 $100.00

MILLER, ARTHUR   Death of a Salesman. New York: Viking, 1949. 1st
edition; small neat name and faint stain on rear board, visible only with
great difficulty, and correspondingly, on inside of the dust jacket, else
near fine in like jacket with bit of rubbing at crown; uncommon.
Between the Covers 42-308 1996 $300.00

MILLER, ARTHUR   Death of a Salesman. New York: Viking Press,
1981. 1/500 signed copies; first illustrated edition; unopened, slipcase.
Bev Chaney, Jr. 23-495 1996 $150.00

MILLER, ARTHUR   Focus. New York: Reynal & Hitchcock, 1947. 1st
edition; fine crisp copy in dust jacket with some very light wear at head
and tail of spine; author's second book.   Left Bank Books 2-95 1996
$100.00

MILLER, ARTHUR   Situation Normal. New York: Reynal & Hitchcock,
1944. 1st edition; author's first book; very good in dust jacket lightly
chipped at head and foot of spine panel.   Sherwood 3-200 1996
$275.00

MILLER, BENJAMIN S.   Ranching in the Southwest: Ranch Life in
Southern Kansas and the Indian Territory. New York: Fless & Ridge
Printing Co., 1896. 1st edition; 163 pages; portrait; original pictorial
wrappers, title stamped in blue on spine and front cvoer, minor chipping
laid in folding slipcase; fine; the Thomas Streeter copy with his
bookplate and several pencil notes. Choice copy, rare; Streeter Sale
2387; Graff 2795; Howes M602; Adams Herd 1485.   Michael D.
Heaston 23-90 1996 $2,000.00

MILLER, E.   The City of Delight. B-M, 1908. 1st edition; illustrations in
color and black and white; bright, very good+ copy in very good dust
jacket save for three short tears and piece missing from head of dust
jacket spine; very scarce in dust jacket.   Aronovitz 57-813 1996
$100.00

MILLER, FRANCIS TREVELYAN   The World in the Air, the Story of
Flying in Pictures. New York: 1930. 1st edition; 11 x 8 inches; 2
volumes, 320, 336 pages, with index; profusely illustrated; cloth; minor
fade to spine ends, else very good in badly chipped dust jackets.
John K. King 77-759 1996 $125.00

MILLER, FRED   The Training of a Craftsman. London: H. Virtue & Co.
1901. 1st edition; 12mo; x, 249, (10) pages; publisher's cloth, very good.
Bookpress 75-89 1996 $185.00

MILLER, GEORGE   Syllabus of Lectures on Modern History Delivered
in Trinity College, Dublin, Part the First. Dublin: printed by R. E. Mercier,
1801. 1st and apparently only edition; 8vo; pages (2), 22; recent
wrapper, very good.   James Fenning 133-232 1996 £85.00

MILLER, HENRY 1891-1980   Black Spring. Paris: The Obelisk Press,
1936. 1st edition; one of 1000 copies; decorated wrappers; very good in
buckram slipcase. Shifteen & Jackson A12.   Priscilla Juvelis 95/1-175
1996 $1,250.00

MILLER, HENRY 1891-1980   Blaise Cendrars. Paris: DeNoel, 1951. 1st
edition; one of 950 copies on Johannot, with two original lithographs;
8vo; three quarter brown morocco with author and title in gilt on
panelled spine, brown marbled paper, original lithographic wrappers
bound in, top edge gilt, near fine with bit of scuffing to tips.   Priscilla
Juvelis 95/1-176 1996 $250.00

MILLER, HENRY 1891-1980   Tropic of Capricorn. Paris: Obelisk Press,
1939. 1st edition; errata slip tipped onto titlepage and price in francs
stamped on spine; pictorial wrappers; fragile book, rarely seen in such
unblemished condition; very fine. Campbell A50.   Bromer Booksellers
90-174 1996 $1,750.00

MILLER, HENRY 1891-1980   Tropique du Capricorne. Les Editions du
Chene, 1950. 1st edition thus; small splits at head and tail of spine,
otherwise very good; wrappers.   Virgo Books 48-138 1996 £85.00

MILLER, J.   Botanicum Officinale... London: 1722. 8vo; pages (vi), 466
(22); full morocco, light waterstain throughout mainly in upper margin,
some slight marginal worming.   Wheldon & Wesley 207-1914 1996
£85.00

MILLER, JAMES   How to Get a Farm and Where to Find One. New
York: James Miller, 1864. 1st edition; 8vo; 345 pages + ad; little worn
publisher's cloth, very good; not in Howes.   Second Life Books
103-139 1996 $125.00

MILLER, JEFFREY   Paul Bowles: a Descriptive Bibliography. Santa
Barbara: Black Sparrow, 1986. One of 26 lettered copies; fine in
unprinted glassine as issued; handbound by Earle Gray; signed by author
and by Bowles; uncommon issue.   Between the Covers 42-63 1996
$450.00

MILLER, JOAQUIN 1841-1913   True Bear Stories. Yolla Bolly Press,
1985. One of 230 copies for sale, signed by Everson and Perez. 10 x 7
inches; 5 p.l. (one blank), xi-xvii, (1) pages, (1) leaf, 80 pages, (2) leaves
(blank colophon); frontispiece and five other woodblock plates by Perez
device in colophon; bound in lined flexible dark brown rawhide, blind
pressed image of a bear on front cover, fore-edge untrimmed,
publisher's slipcase with calf label on spine, mint.   Phillip J. Pirages
33-521 1996 $375.00

MILLER, JOE   Joe Miller's Jests; or, the Wits Vade-Mecum... London:
Printed and sold by T. Read, 1739. Reprint (almost certainly a 19th
century reprint, possibly the 1861 reprint by Bellars); 8vo; 70 pages,
printed on blue paper; quarter calf, spine little rubbed, but good sound
copy.   K Books 442-353 1996 £50.00

MILLER, KARL   Poetry from Cambridge 1952-54. Swinford: Fantasy
Press, 1955. One of 100 copies; thin small 8vo; 1st edition of Ted
Hughes' first appearance in print; wrappers, dust jacket; fine. Sagar &
Tabor B1.   James S. Jaffe 34-255 1996 $350.00

MILLER, KELLY   The Everlasting Stain. Washington: Associated Pub.,
1924. 1st edition; name, slight fading to corner of crown, near fine in
rear very good dust jacket with couple of Internal repairs, some uniform
darkening and with several very small chips. Scarce in jacket.
Between the Covers 43-369 1996 $250.00

MILLER, P. S.   The Titan. Fantasy Press, 1952. 1st edition; 1/350
copies of the subscribers/plated edition; fine in near fine full color
Hannes Bok dust jacket; inscribed by author.   Aronovitz 57-814 1996
$120.00

MILLER, PATRICK   Woman in Detail: a Scientific Survey. Waltham St.
Lawrence: Golden Cockerel Press, 1947. Of 550 numbered copies, this
one of 100 specially bound; small folio; printed in 16 pt. Bembo with
Centaur initials and Lyons captials in black and green on grey
Houldmade; full green morocco, pictorial devices in gilt on upper and
lower covers, spine faded, otherwise very nice in slipcase.   Bertram
Rota 272-184 1996 £150.00

MILLER, PHILIP   The Gardener's Dictionary... London: printed for the
author, sold by Rivington, Millar, White, Hawkins.. 1759. 7th edition; folio;
880 pages; engraved frontispiece, 19 engraved plates; contemporary
calf, stoutly rebacked with brown morocco, old gilt back laid down,
corners renewed, cloth joints, new endpapers, repairs not elegant but
sound and servicable. Henrey 1111.   H. M. Fletcher 121-113 1996
$325.00

MILLER, PHILIP   The Gardener's and Botanist's Dictionary. London:
1795-1807. Folio; 2 volumes in 4; 18 engraved plates plus 3 repeated
plates; unpaginated; contemporary calf over marbled boards, rubbed and
with some loss of surface to the marbled boards, worn at edges, outer
hinges tender, front endpaper to volume 3 loose, several plates foxed,
marginal tear to two plates repaired, some offsetting and light foxing to
text.   Raymond M. Sutton VI-21 1996 $875.00

MILLER, RICHARD L.   Travels Abroad: Embracing Holland, England,
Belgium, France, Sandwich Islands, New Zealand, Australia &c...
Lynchburg: J. P. Bell Co., Stationers and Printers, 1891. 1st edition; 8vo;
221 pages; author's only book; original full brown pebbled calf with gilt
title and inner dentelles, all edges gilt, some edgewear, front outer joint
starting at bottom, but very good; rare; with pencilled ALS from author
presenting the book to Cornelia Jordan. Haynes 12265.   Chapel Hill
34-412 1996 $150.00

MILLER, SAMUEL   A Sermon Delivered January 19, 1812 at the
Request of a Number of Young Gentlemen of the City of New-York. New
York: Whiting & Watson, 1812. 1st edition; 42 pages; 488 pages; original
boards and leather, some foxing, very good.   Lyman Books 21-290
1996 $225.00

MILLER, SLOSS & SCOTT   Tools, Brass Goods, Sporting Goods,
Cutlery, Iron, Steel, Pipe, Etc. Illustrated Catalogue No. 7. San Francisco:
c. 1890's. Very thick 4to; xlii, (1), 1236 pages; illustrations; three quarter
straight grain sheep over cloth, marbled endpapers; some stianing to
front cover, very good. Romaine p. 172.   Edwin V. Glaser 121-313
1996 $850.00

MILLER, STEVE   Hurricane Lake. Madison: Red Ozier Press, 1979. 1st
edition; one of 80 copies bound thus out of a total edition of 138
printed; small 8vo; original wrappers, dust jacket, mint.   James S. Jaffe
34-578 1996 $175.00

MILLER, STEVE   Hurricane Lake. Madison: Red Ozier Press, 1979. 1st
edition; one of 28 specially bound copies, out of a total edition of 138
copies, signed by Miller; small 8vo; illustrations by Marta Anderson;
quarter leather and boards, mint.   James S. Jaffe 34-577 1996
$450.00

MILLER, THOMAS   Common Wayside Flowers. London: and New
York: Routledge, 1860. Square 8vo; 23 color printed floral plates by
Birket Foster; full blindstamped publisher's green morocco, all edges gilt,
with guaffering. Ray, Illustrator & the Book in England 239.   Marilyn
Braiterman 15-143 1996 $275.00

MILLER, WALTER   A Canticle for Leibowitz. Lippincott, 1960. 1st
edition; just about fine in dust jacket.   Aronovitz 57-815 1996
$775.00

MILLER, WALTER   A Canticle for Leibowitz. Philadelphia: Lippincott,
1960. 1st edition; very near fine in bright very good dust jacket worn at
spine crown and chipped at upper edge of rear panel; very scarce book,
particularly in nice condition, and rare signed.   Ken Lopez 74-321
1996 $1,850.00

MILLER, WALTER   A Canticle for Leibowitz. Philadelphia: Lippincott,
1960. 1st edition; fine in lightly soiled dust jacket with just a hint of wear
at corners and spine panel ends.   Robert Gavora 61-80 1996
$1,000.00

MILLER, WALTER   A View from the Stars. London: Gollancz, 1965.
1st hardcover edition; neat name and date, otherwise fine in dust jacket
with one tiny closed tear.   Robert Gavora 61-82 1996 $300.00

MILLINGEN, JOHN GIDEON   The Passions; or Mind and Matter.
London: John and Daniel A. Darling, 1848. 2nd edition; 8vo; (x), 464
pages; embossed green cloth, slight splitting to front joint, very good.
John Gach 150-328 1996 $250.00

MILLIS, WALTER   Road to War - America 1914-1917. London: Faber
& Faber, 1935. 1st edition; 13 pages of black and white photos; original
binding, top edge dusty, edges slightly spotted, head and tail of spine
and corners slightly bumped, endpapers browned, very good in nicked,
rubbed, frayed and dusty, slightly marked and creased dust jacket,
browned at spine and edges.   Ulysses 39-651 1996 £65.00

MILLON, RENE   The Teotihuacan Map. Parts 1-2. Austin & London:
University of Texas Press, 1973. 4to; xvi, 154 pages, 60 illustrations, 3
maps; xlii, 147 plates, 3 lrge folding maps in rear pocket; original cloth,
dust jacket.   Archaeologia Luxor-4709 1996 $300.00

MILLS, ALFRED   Pictures of Roman History, in Miniature. London:
Darton, Harvey and Darton, 1812. 2 5/8 x 2 1/2 inches; 96 pages; 48
delicate engravings; imprint date effaced, otherwise near fine; original
blindstamped green cloth. Moon 547; Bondy p. 63.   Bromer
Booksellers 90-186 1996 $300.00

MILLS, CHARLES   Tumors of the Cerebellum. New York: Elliot, 1905.
8vo; 179 pages; original binding, rubbed, ex-library; interesting
association, bookplate notes 'a gift of Charles K Mills" at the time a
professor in Philadelphia.   James Tait Goodrich K40-196 1996
$150.00

MILLS, CHARLES   Tumors of the Cerebrum. Their Focus Diagnosis
and Surgical Treatment. Philadelphia: 1906. 8vo; original binding,
ex-library, note on bookplate that this was a gift to the library of senior
author C.K. Mills.   James Tait Goodrich K40-197 1996 $150.00

MILLS, JOHN   The Flyers of the Hunt. London: The Field and Ward
and Lock, 1859. 1st edition; 7 1/4 x 5 inches; 5 p.l., 114, (1) pages; 6
etched plates (including frontispiece) by John Leech; fine honey colored
polished calf by Riviere, spine attractively gilt in compartments featuring
equestrian ornaments, red and green morocco labels, board edges
attractively hatched in gilt, densely gilt inner dentelles, marbled
endpapers, top edge gilt, original cloth bound in at back; top of back
cover faintly faded, otherwise binding extremely bright entirely free of
wear and very pleasing, fine internally. Modern signed engraved
bookplate of David M. Ritchie. Podeschi 196.   Phillip J. Pirages 33-386
1996 $225.00

MILLS, JOHN   Stable Secrets; or, Puffy Doddles, His Sayings and
Sympathies. London: Ward and Lock, 1863. 1st edition; 7 1/2 x 5 1/4
inches; 112, (1) pages; vignette on title, 3 etched plates, including
frontispiece; fine honey colored polished calf by Riviere, spine attractively
gilt on compartments featuring equestrian ornaments, red and green
morocco labels, board edges attractively hatched in gilt, densely gilt
inner dentelles, marbled endpapers, top edge gilt, original cloth bound in
at rear, text little darkened (because of inferior paper stock) and slightly
soiled, otherwise excellent internally, one small spot on front cover, but
handsome binding in fine, unworn condition, very attractive. Bookplate of
David M. Ritchie. Podeschi 203.   Phillip J. Pirages 33-387 1996
$200.00

MILLS, LESTER   A Sagebrush Saga. Springville: 1956. 1st edition; x,
112 pages, photos, letter from author on rear flap, signed, maps; stiff
pictorial wrappers; nice, very scarce. 6 Guns 1503.   T. A. Swinford
49-784 1996 $100.00

MILNE, ALAN ALEXANDER 1882-1956   A Gallery of Children. London:
Stanley Paul & Co., 1925. 1st edition; quarto; 12 color plates by H.
Willebeek Le mair; decorated cloth gilt, color plate mounted on upper
cover; covers marked, rubbed, spotted, soiled and dusty, head and tail
of spine and corners bumped; good.   Ulysses 39-356 1996 £225.00

MILNE, ALAN ALEXANDER 1882-1956   The House at Pooh Corner. London: Methuen, 1926. 1st edition; 8vo; decorations by E. H. Shepard; cloth, dust jacket, fine in very slightly rubbed jacket.   James S. Jaffe 34-499 1996 $850.00

MILNE, ALAN ALEXANDER 1882-1956   The House at Pooh Corner. London: Methuen, 1927. 1st edition; 8vo; pages (x), 103; black and white illustrations by Ernest Shepard; custom deluxe full vellum with oval calf onlay within gilt decorated border with original vignette, all edges gilt; very attractive binding; fine.   Marjorie James 19-149 1996 £325.00

MILNE, ALAN ALEXANDER 1882-1956   The House at Pooh Corner. London: Methuen, 1928. 1st edition; deluxe issue; crown 8vo; pages xi, 180; endpaper desgins and drawings by Ernest Shepard; original pale blue leatherette, backstrip lettering and Shepard designs on covers, all gilt blocked, backstrip little faded and lightly chipped at head and tail, blue silk marker, good.   Blackwell's B112-189 1996 £250.00

MILNE, ALAN ALEXANDER 1882-1956   More 'Very Young' Songs from "When We Were Very Young" and "Now We Are Six". London: Methuen, 1928. 1st edition; large 4to; pages (v), 42; decorations throughout by E. H. Shepard; original quarter fawn cloth, dark brown boards, printed front cover label, dust jacket with short tears, excellent.   Blackwell's B112-190 1996 £65.00

MILNE, ALAN ALEXANDER 1882-1956   Now We Are Six. London: Methuen, 1927. 1st edition; crown octavo; full blue gilt stamped leather, all edges gilt, bookseller's embossed stamp front endpaper, light spine fading, otherwise fine in publisher's original cardboard box.   Ken Lopez 74-324 1996 $1,500.00

MILNE, ALAN ALEXANDER 1882-1956   Now We Are Six. London: Methuen, 1927. 1st edition; deluxe issue; crown 8vo; pages xi, 104; endpaper designs and decorations by E. H. Shepard; browning to initiaL and final page as usual; original red leatherette, backstrip lettering and Shepard design on covers, all gilt blocked, backstrip darkened and little rubbed at head, green silk marker, gilt edges. Excellent.   Blackwell's B112-191 1996 £375.00

MILNE, ALAN ALEXANDER 1882-1956   Songs From Now We Are Six. London: Methuen, 1927. 1st edition; folio; illustrations by E. H. Shepard; brown boards with pastedown label, corners bumped, else near fine in chipped dust jacket.   Marjorie James 19-151 1996 £75.00

MILNE, ALAN ALEXANDER 1882-1956   Teddy Bear and Other Songs from When We Were Very Young. London: Methuen, 1926. 1st edition; folio; illustrations by E. H. Shepard brown boards with pastedown label, corners bumped, else near fine in chipped dust jacket.   Marjorie James 19-150 1996 £95.00

MILNE, ALAN ALEXANDER 1882-1956   When We Were Very Young. New York: Dutton, 1924. 1st American edition; number 64 of 100 numbered copies, signed by author; 8vo; illustrations; dark green cloth over pictorial boards, dust jacket with tape repairs to verso, chips, very good.   George J. Houle 68-97 1996 $1,750.00

MILNE-EDWARDS, A.   Notice Sur Quelques Especes d'Oiseaux Actuellement Eteintes Qui se Trouvent Representees dans les Collections du Museum d'Histoire Naturelle. Paris: 1893. Reprint; 4to; pages 68, 5 hand colored plates; half cloth, one inner plate margin cracked, library stamps removed from verso of plates; some (mostly slight) foxing of text and plates, last 2 plates rather browned; from the collection of Jan Coldewey.   Wheldon & Wesley 207-66 1996 £500.00

MILNE-EDWARDS, H.   British Fossil Corals. London: 1850-54. 4to; pages lxxxv, 322, 71 of 72 plates, missing plate 52 supplied in xerox; cloth.   John Henly 27-775 1996 £100.00

MILNER, JOHN   The Cruise of the H.M.S. Galatea, Capt. HRH the Duke of Edinburgh in 1867-1868. London: William H. Allen, 1869. 8vo; pages xii, 488; 6 plates; original pictorial cloth, all edges gilt, lightly rubbed. Mendelssohn II p. 20. Ferguson 12627.   Richard Adelson W94/95-120 1996 $200.00

MILNER, JOHN   The History Civil and Ecclesiasatical and Survey of the Antiquities of Winchester. Winchester printed and sold by Jas. Robbins, 1809. 2nd edition; 4to; 2 volumes; engraved titles (foxed), folding plan, 12 engraved plates, some browned, contemporary mottled calf, slightly rubbed, lower hinge of volume 1 cracked and broken, spines gilt, labels. Upcott 1 pp. 184-85.   Anthony W. Laywood 108-206 1996 £160.00

MILNER, JOSEPH   Gibbon's Account of Christianity Considered; Together with some Strictures on Hume's Dialogues Concerning Natural Religion. York: ptd. by A. Ward & sold by G. Robinson & T. Cadell, London... 1781. 8vo; xiii, (1), 82, *83-*108, 83-262 pages; contemporary tree calf, red label; very nice.   C. R. Johnson 37-73 1996 £550.00

MILTON, JOHN 1608-1674   Accedence Commenc't Grammar, Supply'd with Suffcient Rules, for the Use of Such (Younger or Elder) as Are Desirous, Without More Trouble than Needs to Attain the Latin Tongue. London: printed for S. S. and are to be sold by John Starkey, 1669. 1st edition; issue with Milton's name on titlepage (a cancel), another issue has only his initials, and omits the name of the bookseller Starkey); 12mo; contemporary mottled calf, neatly rebacked; fine, rare. Wing M2088.   Ximenes 109-193 1996 $18,500.00

MILTON, JOHN 1608-1674   L'Allegro & Il Penseroso. New York: Limited Editions Club, 1954. Of a total edition of 1780 copies, this is one of 280 specially designated for fellows of the Pierpont Morgan Library, with TLS from director of the library, F. B. Adams, laid in; large 12mo; 12 reproductions of watercolors by Blake; designed by Bruce Rogers and printed dos-a-dos; original binding; fine in near fine case.   Charles Agvent 4-897 1996 $150.00

MILTON, JOHN 1608-1674   Areopagitica. London: 1664. 1st edition; small 4to; bound without final blank, bound with other pamphlets by Milton, in 18th century panelled calf, maroon morocco label, as always, some croping to sidenotes, attractive, fresh copy, rarely seen in early binding.   19th Century Shop 39- 1996 $37,500.00

MILTON, JOHN 1608-1674   Areopagitica. Hammersmith: Eragny Press, 1903. Although colophon indicates a limitation of 226 copies, only 41 copies survived a fire at the bindery; quarto; 37 pages; original printed boards, with beige paper spine, light rubbing to extremities, faint offsetting to covers and free endpapers, still fine, rare, housed in protective drop back box of morocco backed marbled boards, bookplates. Franklin p. 100; Tomkinson p. 64.   Bromer Booksellers 87-57 1996 $3,000.00

MILTON, JOHN 1608-1674   Areopagitica. Cambrdige: Rampant Lions Press, 1973. Limited edition, 310/400 copies (of an edition of 500 copies); folio; pages (xiv), 49, (1); printed on Barcham Green mouldmad paper, partly printed in double column with large initial letters printed in brown; original black buckram, orange leather label, top edge gilt, other untrimmed; fine.   Blackwell's B112-240 1996 £60.00

MILTON, JOHN 1608-1674   Comus, a Mask. London: Edward Arnold, 1901. Limited to 150 copies; octavo; 47 pages, printed in two colors entirely on vellum, with opening full page hand colored wood engraving by Reginald Savage, elegantly illuminated in colors and gold by Florence Kingsford; full vellum over boards, blindstamped with rose logo and motto of the series "Soul is Form"; very fine.   Bromer Booksellers 87-59 1996 $550.00

MILTON, JOHN 1608-1674   Comus. New York: and London: 1921. 1st deluxe edition with Rackham plates, one of 575 numbered copies, signed by Rackham; 24 full page illustrations in color, each mounted, 37 black and white illustrations, endpapers designed by Rackham; original vellum backed boards, spine gilt, light waterstains on front cover, internally fine Trebizond 39-47 1996 $575.00

MILTON, JOHN 1608-1674   Comus: a Mask. printed by the Cambridge Univ. Press for Ernest Benn Ltd., 1926. Limited to 300 copies; 4to; printed on handmade paper, 8 plates; original buckram gilt, covers with borders of type ornaments, very slightly rubbed, uncut, top edge gilt. Bookplates of Ruari McLean and D. G. Bridson.   Forest Books 74-34 1996 £65.00

MILTON, JOHN 1608-1674   Comus, a Mask. London: pub. for the Julian Editions by Ernest Benn Ltd., 1926. One of 300 copies; quarto; 8 black and white illustrations by William Blake; decorated gilt buckram covers, top edge gilt, bookshop label on rear pastedown, front free endpaper partially browned, cover edges slightly rubbed, very good in nicked, rubbed, marked, browned and dusty slightly chipped dust jacket and in worn slipcse.   Ulysses 39-54 1996 £145.00

MILTON, JOHN 1608-1674   A Defence of the People of England...In Answer to Salmasius's Defence of the King. N.P. (perhaps Amsterdam): printed in the year 1692. 1st edition in English; 8vo; initial blank A1 as front free endpaper, pages (vi), xxii, (ii) blank, 246, (i); contemporary sheep, sides ruled in blind with two line roll with one-line dotted roll either side, lately rebacked, corners repaired, inner hinges reinforced, light soiling to a few margins, one or two trivial marks, very good. Grolier WP 590; Wing M2104; Pforzheimer 726.   Simon Finch 24-172 1996 £475.00

MILTON, JOHN 1608-1674   Latin and Italian Poems of Milton. London: printed by Seagrave, Chichester for J. Johnson and R. H. Evans, 1808. 4to; pages (27), 328, 3 line engravings after Flaxman; uncut, deckle edged, almost uncased. Very scarce in uncut state. Brunet III 1732. Family Album Tillers-440 1996 $350.00

MILTON, JOHN 1608-1674   Latin and Italian Poems of Milton. London: printed by Seagrave, Chichester for J. Johnson and R. H. Evans, 1808. 4to; pages (27), 328, 3 line engravings after Flaxman; worn contemporary full leather, spine gilt. Family Album Tillers-441 1996 $300.00

MILTON, JOHN 1608-1674   The Mask of Comus. The Poem. London: Nonesuch Press, 1937. 169/950 copies; folio; pages xxiv, 44, (1); printed in Fell and Walpergen typefaces on Pannekoek mouldmade paper; 5 colored lino-cut plates by M.R.H. Farrar; original fawn boards with yapped fore-edges, sunned backstrip gilt lettered, covers decorated in blind, untrimmed, excellent. Dreyfus 109. Blackwell's B112-210 1996 £100.00

MILTON, JOHN 1608-1674   The Minor Poems of John Milton. London: George Bell & Sons, 1898. 1st edition; limited to 100 on Japanese vellum, this number 78; xiv, 206 pages; frontispiece and title with red decorated borders, 28 full page and 34 text illustrations by Garth Jones; blue and maroon binding design from trade edition bound in, blue decorated endpaper, beige holland cloth, titled in black and red on spine. Very good. Robin Greer 94A-38 1996 £250.00

MILTON, JOHN 1608-1674   Paradise Lost. London: by S. Simmons and are to be sold by H. Helder, 1669. 1st edition; small 4to; collates complete as issued; modern brown calf by Sangorski & Sutcliffe, paper flaw on title just affecting lower bar of 'L' in Milton's name, quite closed trimmed, occasionally affecting upper frame and once or twice the headline, some browning, occasional stains, good. Amory 4; Wing M2143. Simon Finch 24-169 1996 £3,800.00

MILTON, JOHN 1608-1674   Paradise Lost. London: printed by S. Simmons, 1678. 3rd edition; 8vo; portrait, (viii), 331 pages, 2 final blank leaves present; original panelled calf, rebacked, original endpapers preserved, upper margin trimmed close, occasionally shaving tops of letters in running headline, very little spotting on a few pages, very lightly browned throughout. Wing M2145; Coleridge 92. David Bickersteth 133-50 1996 £350.00

MILTON, JOHN 1608-1674   Paradise Lost. London: by Miles Flesher for Jacob Tonson, 1688. 4th edition; folio; pages (iv), 343, (i) blank, (vi) list of subscribers, frontispiece, 12 engraved plates; Regency diced russia, sides panelled in gilt and blind, spine with double raised bands, decorated in gilt and in blind, inner dentelles with blind border between double gilt rules, drab green endpapers, joints restored, frontispiece skilfully laid down, few trivial spots or stains, chiefly marginal, small repair to blank recto of plate illustrating book IV; very good, large paper copy with bunch of grapes watermark and ample margins, both around text and plates; Leigh bookplate. Coleridge 93b; Wing M2147; Grolier W-P 607. Simon Finch 24-171 1996 £1,750.00

MILTON, JOHN 1608-1674   Paradise Lost...Paradise Regain'd...Samson...Poems. Birmingham: John Baskerville, 1758. 1st Baskerville edition; octavo; 2 volumes; original calf, now worn, joints and extremities rubbed and chipped, joints cracked and near breaking; signature of William Sandys dated March 1, 1759. Gaskell 4(a) and 5(a). G. W. Stuart 59-9 1996 $350.00

MILTON, JOHN 1608-1674   Paradise Lost. Birmingham: John Baskerville for J. and R. Tonson, 1759. 4to; (8), lxxii, 416 pages; frontispiece; nicely rebound in tan calf over marbled boards, old gilt red morocco label laid down, some occasional text foxing; Gaskell Bib. of John Baskerville 6. Kenneth Karmiole 1NS-185 1996 $400.00

MILTON, JOHN 1608-1674   Paradise Lost...Paradise Regain'd...Samson..Poems. Birmingham: John Baskerville, 1759. 2nd Baskerville edition; tall octavo; 2 volumes; contemporary russia gilt, hinges cracked, few pages loose, joints restored, usual foxing, first volume quite waterstained at beginning, all edges gilt. Gaskell 6 and 7. G. W. Stuart 59-10 1996 $295.00

MILTON, JOHN 1608-1674   Paradise Lost...Paradise Regain'd...Samson...Poems. Birmingham: John Baskerville, 1760. 3rd and final Baskerville edition; tall octavo; 2 volumes; contemporary russia finely gilt, joints cracked, spine ends chipped, all edges gilt; contemporary bookplate of Michael Tyson. Gaskell 9 and 10. G. W. Stuart 59-11 1996 $285.00

MILTON, JOHN 1608-1674   Paradise Lost. London: J. & R. tonson, 1763. 6th edition; 8vo; 2 volumes; frontispiece, 12 fine engraved plates; contemporary calf, spines richly gilt, original morocco labels; minor worming of lower margin of leaves in second volume, not touching text, very atttactive. NCBEL II 1777. Trebizond 39-41 1996 $375.00

MILTON, JOHN 1608-1674   Paradise Lost, a Poem. Glasgow: Robert and Andrew Foulis, 1770. 8vo; (xii), 466, (x) pages; vignette on titlepage, 2 page subscriber list; contemporary calf, spine gilt, label, little rubbed, front joint reapired, short split in rear joint, slight wear to corners, minor worming at edge of lower margin, well clear of text; good, large copy. Gaskell 510.   Robert Clark 38-174 1996 £280.00

MILTON, JOHN 1608-1674   Le Paradis Perdu. Paris: Chez Defer de Maisonneuve, 1792. Small folio; 2 volumes, viii,3 91; 377 pages; 12 color stipple engravings by Clement, Colibert, Demonchy and Gautier after paintings by Schall; most of the plates before letters; original marbled boards with leather spine labels, spines show light wear, still remarkable set. All edges speckled. Cohen-de Ricci 708.   Bromer Booksellers 87-181 1996 $4,500.00

MILTON, JOHN 1608-1674   The Paradise Lost of Milton. London: printed for Henry Washbourne, 1849. 4to; pages (viii), 374, (1); 24 full page mezzotint plates by John Martin, all with protective tissues, just two or three plates little spotted in borders, otherwise clean and attractive copy; contemporary black morocco, gilt border to sides, enclosing a centre ornament in blind, fully gilt spine with raised bands, all edges gilt. Sotheran PN32-38 1996 £675.00

MILTON, JOHN 1608-1674   The (sic) Paradise Lost. New York: Baker & Scribner, 1850. 1st edition; 8vo; original purple cloth, decorated in gilt, all edges gilt, spine evenly faded, very slight rubbing; some foxing, but fine, in what appears to be publisher's gift binding. Ximenes 108-266 1996 $125.00

MILTON, JOHN 1608-1674   Paradise Lost. London: Paris: & New York: Cassell, Petter and Galpin, ca. 1873. 15 1/4 x 12 inches; lxii, 329 pages, (2) leaves (ads); device on title, 50 full page plates by Gustave Dore; title in red and black; sumptuously decorated contemporary red morocco, heavily gilt and with onlays, covers framed with French fillet and elegant foliate border, central panel defined by very wide gilt dentelles as well as large neo-classical scrolling ornaments and complex cornerpieces containing onlaid dark green disks with gilt sunburst collars and large fleurons, spine wit raised bands and six compartments (three densely), gilt with green onlays and many foliate stamps and three with gilt titling, fine broad inner gilt dentelles, gilt edges, marbled endpapers; few trivial marks to binding, endpapers, lightly foxed, otherwise only isolated trivial imperfections, extremely fine in most impressive binding. Phillip J. Pirages 33-180 1996 $1,250.00

MILTON, JOHN 1608-1674   Paradise Lost. Philadelphia: Altemus, c. 1880. Quarto; decorated cloth, near fine.   Stephen Lupack 83- 1996 $125.00

MILTON, JOHN 1608-1674   Paradise Lost and Paradise Regain'd. San Francisco: for the Limited Editions Club, New York: 1936. Limited to 1500 copies; folio; 441 pages plus illustrations by Carlotta Petrina; cloth backed decorated paper boards.   Family Album Tillers-443 1996 $100.00

MILTON, JOHN 1608-1674   Paradise Lost and Paradise Regain'd. San Francisco: Limited Editions Club, 1936. Number 904 from 1500 copies, signed by artist; illustrations by Carlotta Petrina; cloth backed decorative boards, paper label, fine in cracked and worn publisher's slipcase. Hermitage SP95-1017 1996 $100.00

MILTON, JOHN 1608-1674   Paradise Regain'd. A Poem in IV Books. To Which is Added Samson Agonistes. London: printed by J.M. for John Starkey, 1671. 1st edition; 8vo; license leaf facing title, errata leaf at end, internally fine; pages (iv), 101, (2); contemporary dark brown calf, rubbed and with surface wear, smooth backstrip divided by blind rules, sympathetic modern gilt lettered red morocco label, sides with blind fillet border and half line, hinges strengthened, very good. Hayward 73; Turnbull Library 168; Wing M2152.   Blackwell's B112-192 1996 £1,650.00

MILTON, JOHN 1608-1674   Paradise Regained...Together with, Poems Upon Several Occasions in English and Latin. (with) A Small Tractae... London: J. Tonson and M. Poulson, 1725. 6th edition; small 8vo; frontispiece; contemporary panelled calf, scuffed, recently rebacked, retaining original endleaves. Glenn Books 36-184 1996 $300.00

MILTON, JOHN 1608-1674   Paradise Regained...Samson Agonistes...Poems... London: Thompson et al, 1761. Later edition; 12mo; frontispiece of Milton laid down to verso of endpaper and causing split between portrait and title; calf, paper uniformly browned, rubbed, label lacking; decent copy, contemporary owner signature.   Charles Agvent 4-899 1996 $100.00

MILTON, JOHN 1608-1674   Poems &c., Upon Several Occasions...Both English and Latin... London: for Tho. Dring at the Blue Anchor, 1673. 2nd edition; 8vo; pages (viii), 165, (1) blank, 117, (5) ads, lacking title, supplied in early ms. facsimile, with conjugate initial blank and early ms. copies of Milton's four political sonnets on 2 extra leaves inserted at end; 19th century divinity calf, extremties little rubbed, trivial tear to D8, some page numbers shaved, little soiling, very good; Isaac Watt's copy, inscribed by Watts. Fine association copy. Wing M2161; Turnbull 85. Simon Finch 24-170 1996 £1,000.00

MILTON, JOHN 1608-1674   Poems. London: Nonesuch Press, 1926. One of 1450 numbered copies on Van Gelder rag paper; 8vo; 2 volumes; illustrations by William Blake; vellum backed boards, minor edgewear, endpapers foxed, vellum darkened, very good.   Charles Agvent 4-900 1996 $250.00

MILTON, JOHN 1608-1674   Poems in English...Miscellaneous Poems, Paradise Regain'd & Sampson Agonistes. London: Nonesuch Press, 1926. Limited edition, number 343 of a limited edition; tall 8vo; (vi), 283 pages; illustrations, title printed in red and black; quarter vellum, spine darkened, otherwise good.   K Books 441-338 1996 £50.00

MILTON, JOHN 1608-1674   The Poetical Works of John Milton. London: printed by W. Bulmer & Co. for John and Josiah Boydell and George ... 1749-97. Folio; 3 volumes; stipple engraved portraits and fine plates, some plates foxed, text offsetting; though it requires some restoration, elaborate straight grained full red morocco gilt binding by Riley is notable; fine paper, wide margins; engraved ex-libris of Francis Frederick Fox.   Family Album Tillers-442 1996 $450.00

MILTON, JOHN 1608-1674   The Poetical Works, with the Life of the Author by William Hayley. London: John and Josiah Boydell and George Nicol, 1794/95/97. 1st edition; folio; 3 volumes; matching red straight grained morocco, hinges have been expertly repaired and there is some offsetting from back of plates, otherwise very good with all tissue guards in place, in nice, contemporary bindings.   The Bookpress 75-440 1996 $1,750.00

MILTON, JOHN 1608-1674   Poetical Works. Guildford: Astolat Press, 1904. 4to; x, 194 pages; 15 plates, several wood engraved head and tailpieces and ornamental initials, text printed in double columns; cloth, gilt, top edge gilt, others uncut, covers very slightly dust soiled, trace of light foxing in places.   Thomas Thorp 489-218 1996 £50.00

MILTON, JOHN 1608-1674   Pro Populo anglicano Defensio, Contra Claudii Anonymi, Alias Almasii, Defensionem Regiam. London: Du Gardianis, 1652. 12mo; 192 pages; old panelled calf, rebacked, outer corners of boards worn down, wormhole at lower blank margin. Wing M2169; Madan 12.   Kenneth Karmiole 1NS-186 1996 $150.00

MILTON, JOHN 1608-1674   Samson Agonistes, a Dramatic Poem. New Rochelle: Elston Press, 1904. 9 x 6 inches; 65 pages; decorations from designs by H. M. O'Kane; printed in red and black; quarter cloth and paper boards, printed paper label on spine; attractive copy. Unopened. Joshua Heller 21-119 1996 $250.00

MILTON, JOHN 1608-1674   Samson Agonistes. Raven Press, 1931. One of 275 numbered copies; small folio; printed in Bembo on handmade paper; 11 wood engravings by Robert Ashwin Maynard; half vellum, gilt, 2 leaes foxed and upper corners little bruised, but exceptionally nice, fresh copy in slipcase, neat inscription.   Bertram Rota 272-405 1996 £210.00

MILTON, JOHN 1608-1674   The Shorter Poems. London: Seeley and Co., 1889. 1st edition; folio; 12 fine plates; original blue cloth, minor rubbing; fine, not especially common. Gordon Ray, Illus. and the Book 223.   Ximenes 108-267 1996 $250.00

MILTON, JOHN 1608-1674   The Sonnets. London: printed by Ballantyne, Hanson & Co. for Kegan, Paul Trench & Co., 1883. One of 50 large paper copies, signed by printer; 8 x 5 1/4 inches; 1 p.l., 222, (1) pages, (1) leaf; frontispiece, vignette on title, title printed in red and black; very attractive contemporary olive brown morocco by Cuzin, covers with French fillet frame, gilt rose in each corner, raised bands, spine compartments handsomely gilt with similar rose in center and with floral sprays in corners, fine beige morocco doublures bordered with multiple plain and decorative gilt rules and featuring large and elegant gilt floral designs at center and each corner, marbled flyleaves, all edges gilt, slight variation in color to one cover, hint of rubbing to joints, otherwise very fine, handsomely bound and virtually pristine internally.   Phillip J. Pirages 33-388 1996 $650.00

MINCHIN, JAMES G. C.   The Growth of Freedom in the Balkan Peninsula. London: John Murray, 1886. 1st (?only) edition; 8vo; pages xvi, 415, (1); folding map; original cloth, gilt, very good.   James Fenning 133-234 1996 £85.00

MINER, DOROTHY   Studies in Art and Literature for Belle Da Costa Greene. Princeton: Princeton University Press, 1954. 1st edition; large 4to; xviii, 502 pages; cloth; fine.   The Bookpress 75-290 1996 $350.00

MINER, H. S.   Orchids, the Royal Family of Plants. Boston: 1885. Folio; pages 90; 24 chromolithographs, later buckram, some stainging and scuffing to covers, endpapers renewed, joint of first signature cracked, light chipping to fore edge of 1 plate, some offsetting from plates, all edges gilt.   Raymond M. Sutton VI-22 1996 $600.00

MINER, H. S.   Orchids, the Royal Family of Platns, with Illustrations from Nature. London: 1885. Small folio; pages 90, 24 colored plates; original cloth, gilt, trifle sued, neatly revised; rare, some slight offsetting of plates on text, but good.   Wheldon & Wesley 207-67 1996 £450.00

MINER, H. S.   Orchids, the Royal family of Plants. London: 1885. Small folio; pages 90, 24 colored plates; original cloth, binding somewh used but good copy internally; very scarce.   Wheldon & Wesley 207-65 1996 £330.00

THE MINES of New Mexico. Inexhaustible Deposits of Gold and Silver Copper, Lead, Iron and Coal. Santa Fe: New Mexican Printing Co., 1896 1st edition; 80 pages; folding map; original pictorial marbled wrappers, fine.   Michael D. Heaston 23-270 1996 $225.00

MINOTAURE. Revue Artistique et Litteraire. Paris: 1933-39. Complete run of 11 issues; profusely illustrated; remarkably fine set (few spines scuffed).   Marilyn Braiterman 15-144 1996 $5,000.00

MINSHULL, JOHN   A Comic Opera. Entitled Rural Felicity; with the Humour of Patrick and Marriage of Shelty. New York: printed for the author, 1801. 1st edition; 8vo; 68, (1), (5) pages; removed, some soilin Hill 188; S&S 934; Wegelin p. 71.   M & S Rare Books 60-150 1996 $350.00

MINTO, GILBERT ELLIOT, 1ST EARL OF   The Speech of Lord Minto i the House of Peers, April 11, 1799 on a Motion...Respecting an Union Between Great Britain and Ireland. (with) The Speech of Lord Minto in the House of Peers, June 6th, 1803 on Certain Resolutions of Censure on the Conduct... London: 1799/1803. 1st edition; 8vo; 2 works bound 1; 155, 3 pages; 199 pages; calf, some staining, otherwise good.   K Books 441-204 1996 £50.00

MINUCIUS FELIX, MARCUS   Minucius Felix, His Dialogne (sic) Called Octavius. Containing a Defence of Christian Religion. Oxford: printed by Leoanrd Lichfield for Thomas Huggins, 1636. 1st English translation; small 12mo; pages (7), 165, (11), worn contemporary leather. STC 17953; Madan Oxford Books 3175.   Family Album Tillers-444 1996 $350.00

MINUCIUS FELIX, MARCUS   Those Two Excellent Monuments of Anicent Learning and Pietry, Minucius Felix's Octavius, and Tertullian's Apology for the Primitive Christians... London: B. Barker, 1708. 8vo. 6), xxii, 250 pages; frontispiece; original mottled calf, maroon spine label, hinges rubbed, early bookplate.   Kenneth Karmiole 1NS-187 1996 $150.00

MINUTES of the Proceedings at a Court-Martial, Assembled to Inquire Into the Cause of the Loss of His Majesty's Late ship Ardent. Taken by George Jackson, Esq. Judge-Advocate of His Majesty's Fleet... London: printed for W. Strahan and T. Cadell, 1780. 4to; some foxing of first 12 pages; disbound.   Anthony W. Laywood 109-29 1996 £65.00

MIRABEAU, HONORE GABRIEL RIQUETTI, COMTE DE 1749-1791   Avis Aux Hessois et Autres Peuples de L'Allemagne Vendus par Leurs Prince a l'Angleterre. Cleves: Bertol, 1777. 1st edition; 8vo; boards; excessively rare edition; Sabin 49392; Martin & Walter 24428 citing reprint of 1782. Rostenberg & Stern 150-5 1996 $1,500.00

MIRABEAU, HONORE GABRIEL RIQUETTI, COMTE DE 1749-1791 Mirabeau's Letters During His Residence in England, with Anecdotes, Maxims, &c. London: E. Wilton, 1832. 1st edition; 8vo; 2 volumes, mounted litho portrait, later half morocco, gilt, hinges repaired. Marlborough 162-69 1996 £250.00

MIRO, JOAN   Lithographs. Volume II. New York: Leon Amiel, 1975. Limited edition; 4to; lithographs by Miro; full white linen; as new with dust jacket and box.   Appelfeld Gallery 54-140 1996 $325.00

MISERDINE Estate. Particulars. London: Driver, 1874. 2nd edition of this estate sale catalogue; folio; 19 pages; hand colored folding map, tinted litho frontispiece, folding map, plan, large folding O.S. map; wrappers, little frayed.   Marlborough 162-70 1996 £250.00

MISHIMA, YUKIO   Confessions of a Mask. Norfolk: New Directions, 1958. 1st edition; slight wear to the crown, else fine in fine dust jacket, with spine slightly tanned, nice.   Between the Covers 42-310 1996 $150.00

MISHIMA, YUKIO   The Sailor Who Fell from Grace with the Sea. New York: Knopf, 1965. 1st American edition; fine in near fine dust jacket with one internally repaired and couple of other short tears.   Between the Covers 42-312 1996 $125.00

MISHIMA, YUKIO   The Sound of Waves. New York: Knopf, 1956. 1st edition; shelf wear to board edges and extremities, short tear to head of spine, thus very good or better in dust jacket with shallow chipping to extremities, inscribed by author, scarce thus.   Lame Duck Books 19-346 1996 $950.00

MISHIMA, YUKIO   The Temple of the Golden Pavilion. New York: Knopf, 1959. 1st American edition; fine in near fine dust jacket with little foxing and rubbing, nicer than usual.   Between the Covers 42-311 1996 $100.00

THE MISSIONARY'S Daughter: a Memoir of Lucy Goodale Thurston, of the Sandwich Islands. New York: 1842. 16mo; 219 pages; missing front free endpaper, old internal dampstains, backstrip gilt quite legible, library stamp on titlepage. Judd 172.   Bookworm & Silverfish 276-112 1996 $150.00

MITCHELL, DONALD GRANT 1822-1908   American Lands and Letters. New York: Scribner's, 1901. Later edition; 8vo; 402 pages; this copy contains 40 extra plates bound in, in addition to the 94 illustrations called for; contemporary three quarter morocco by Hyman Zucker, top edge gilt, very slight rubbing to spine ends and edges, bookplate, else fine and bright. BAL 13980.   Chapel Hill 94-174 1996 $225.00

MITCHELL, FREDERICK SHAW   The Birds of Lancashire... London: Gurney & Jackson, 1892. 2nd edition; 8vo; pages 261, ads; wood engraved illustrations, maps; original green cloth, very fine, uncut and unopened. Mullens & Swann p. 408.   Sotheran PN32-93 1996 £128.00

MITCHELL, ISAAC   A Short Account of the Courtship of Alonzo and Melissa. Plattsburgh: printed for the Proprietor, 1811. 2nd edition; 8vo; 218 pages; contemporary calf backed boards, quite worn, text browned and somewhat shaken, but quite good. Wright I 1887; S&S 23406.   M & S Rare Books 60-203 1996 $500.00

MITCHELL, JAMES   First Lines of Science. London: Tegg, 1827. 1st edition; 8vo; pages 347; 218 plates; cloth backed boards, uncut and partially unopened, nice.   Second Life Books 103-140 1996 $125.00

MITCHELL, JAMES   The Portable Encyclopaedia: or, a Dictionary of the Arts and Sciences... London: printed for Thomas Tegg, 1828. Royal 8vo; pages iv, 710; frontispiece, 51 engraved plates; contemporary half calf, very good to nice.   James Fenning 133-235 1996 £85.00

MITCHELL, JOHN   Notes from Over Sea, Consisting of Observations Mad in Europe in the Years 1843 and 1844. New York: 1845. 8vo; 2 volumes, pages 331, 358; cloth, titles dusty with old stamps. Marlborough 162-238 1996 £90.00

MITCHELL, JOHN   Organized Labor. Philadelphia: American Book and Bible House, 1903. 1st edition; 436 pages; photos; original cloth, very good+; nice association, the copy of Joe Giganti.   Beasley Books 82-331 1996 $100.00

MITCHELL, JOSEPH   The Bottom of the Harbor. Boston: Little Brown, 1959. 1st edition; fine in bright, just about fine price clipped dust jacket. Bev Chaney, Jr. 23-500 1996 $100.00

MITCHELL, JOSEPH   Old Mr. Flood. New York: Duell, Sloan and Pearce, 1948. 1st edition; near fine in lightly used dust jacket (price clipped) with shallow chip from head of spine; signed by author. Captain's Bookshelf 38-164 1996 $100.00

MITCHELL, JOSEPH   Practical Suggestions for Relieving the Over-Crowded Throroughfares of London... London: Stanford, 1857. 8vo; 26 pages, 4 tinted litho plates, 1 large folding litho map; original printed wrappers, joints little weak.   Elton Engineering 10-107 1996 £650.00

MITCHELL, JOSEPH   Up in the Old Hotel. New York: Pantheon, 1992. Uncorrected proof; signed; fine.   Bev Chaney, Jr. 23-503 1996 $100.00

MITCHELL, MARGARET 1900-1949   Gone With the Wind. New York: Macmillan, 1936. 1st edition; 1st issue dust jacket; 8 3/4 x 6 inches; 4 p.l., 3-1037 pages; original grey cloth, dust jacket, signed "Margaret Mitchell (in what may or may not be author's hand) and with signed black and white photos of Clark Gable, Vivien Leigh and David O. Selznick pasted in at front; small stain at top of front cover, joints and extremities showing a little wear (one tiny tear at top and bottom of each joint), otherwise binding in excellent shape with hinges in fine condition, front free endpaper with 5 x 1 1/4 inch pasted on piece of paper reading "Autographed First Edition" (this piece of paper covering some other writing that has been inked over), otherwise fine internally, jacket in fine condition, remarkably clean and showing no significant signs of wear.   Phillip J. Pirages 33-390 1996 $2,500.00

MITCHELL, MARGARET 1900-1949   Gone with the Wind. New York: Macmillan, 1936. 1st edition; 1st printing; very good with vertical crease, the length of spine, pieces of dust jacket laid in.   Captain's Bookshelf 38-165 1996 $450.00

MITCHELL, SAMUEL AUGUSTUS 1792-1868   A New Map of Texas Oregon and California with the Regions Adjoining. Philadelphia: S. A. Mitchell, 1846. 1st printing; 46 pages, lithographic pocket map, with original full coloring, ornate borders; folded into original green roan folder with title in gilt on front cover, minor splitting repaired; fine. Graff 2841; Howes M685; Martin & Martin 36; Becker Wagner Camp 122b. Michael D. Heaston 23-250 1996 $6,000.00

MITCHELL, SILAS WEIR 1829-1914   The Comfort of the Hills and Other Poems. New York: Century, 1911. 2nd edition; 8vo; 98 pages; original binding, bit worn; inscribed by author, also signed by Mitchell, tipped in and pasted to front blank "The Christ of the Snow. A Norwegian Legend" a 4 pp. leaflet.   James Tait Goodrich K40-200 1996 $395.00

MITCHELL, SILAS WEIR 1829-1914   Fat and Blood: an Essay on the Treatment of Certain Forms of Neurasthenia and Hysteria. Philadelphia: J. B. Lippincott Co., 1884. 3rd edition; 12mo; (ii), 164, (2) pages; printed bevel edged green cloth. Cordasco 90-5605.   John Gach 150-329 1996 $100.00

MITCHELL, SILAS WEIR 1829-1914   Lectures on Diseases of the Nervous System, Especially in Women. Philadelphia: 1885. 2nd edition; 8vo; 288 pages + inserted catalog + 5 plates; blind embossed green cloth, owner's signature on titlepage, attractive, near fine copy, scaracer than the first edition.   John Gach 150-330 1996 $475.00

MITCHELL, SILAS WEIR 1829-1914   Some Recently Discovered Letters of William Harvey With Other Miscellanea with a Bibliography of Harvey's Works by Charles Perry Fisher. Philadelphia: 1912. 1st edition; 59 pages; wrappers.   W. Bruce Fye 71-950 1996 $100.00

MITCHELL, T. L.   Three Expeditions into the Interior of Eastern Australia. London: T. & W. Boone, 1838. 2 volumes, (xxii), 352 pages, 16 pages ads & (viii), (ii), 406 pages, 50 plates, large folding hand colored map; engraved folding map loose in volume 1, otherwise good+ condition; original embossed and decorated cloth, rebacked, o laid down; Absolon copy. Ferguson 2553; Wantrup 124a.   Antipodean 28-88 1996 $1,750.00

MITFORD, MARY RUSSELL 1787-1855   Christina, the Maid of the South Seas; Narrative Poems on the Female Character...; Our Village... London: 1811/13/24. 1st editions; 8vo; 3 volumes; uniformly bound in gilt tooled green calf, minor edgewear, front endpapers from poetry volumes lacking; very good; with 2 page AMS, a 56 line poem inscribed to James Webb, the Narrative Poems has a presentation inscription from author to the Miss Webbs.   Charles Agvent 4-901 1996 $475.00

MITFORD, MARY RUSSELL 1787-1855   The Friendships of Mary Russell Mitford As Recorded in Letters from Her Literary Correspondents. London: Hurst and Blackett, 1882. 1st edition; 8vo; 2 volumes; original dark brown cloth; very fine. CBEL III 749.   Ximenes 108-268 1996 $225.00

MITFORD, MARY RUSSELL 1787-1855   Recollections of a Literary Life. London: Richard Bentley, 1852. 1st edition; crown 8vo; 3 volumes; original cloth, gilt by Remnant & Edmonds, with their ticket, some very minor external wear, but very good; pleasing literary association, each volume bards contemporary ownership signatures of John James Ruskin, wine merchant and father of the Victorian sage.   Ash Rare Books Zenzybyr-68   1996 £195.00

MITFORD, MARY RUSSELL 1787-1855   Recollections of a Literary Life; or, Books, Places and People. London: Richard Bentley, 1852. 1st edition; 8vo; 3 volumes; original blue cloth, ends of spine little rubbed; very good set. Wolff 4821; CBEL III 749.   Ximenes 109-194 1996 $250.00

MITFORD, MARY RUSSELL 1787-1855   Recollections of Literary Life; or, Books, Places and People. New York: Harper, 1852. 1st American edition; original green cloth, gilt, very good.   Mac Donnell 12-115 1996 $150.00

MITFORD, MARY RUSSELL 1787-1855   Recollections of a Literary Life. London: Bentley, 1853. 2nd edition; 8vo; 2 volumes; frontispiece; cloth, hinge partly cracked but tight, otherwise fine; with presentation inscription.   Charles Agvent 4-902 1996 $175.00

MITFORD, NANCY 1904-1973   The Pursuit of Love. London: Hamish Hamilton, 1945. 1st edition; original binding, top edge dusty, covers marked, head and tail of spine and corners slightly bumped, cover edges rubbed, very good in nicked, torn, rubbed, marked, creased and dusty dust jacket frayed at head of spine; inscription.   Ulysses 39-411 1996 £55.00

MITFORD, WILLIAM   The History of Greece, from the Earliest Period to the Death of Agesilaus. London: C. Whittingham, Chiswick Press for Tegg & Son, 1835. 8 volumes; some spines taped, ex-library.   Family Album Tillers-446 1996 $100.00

MITTEN, DAVID GORDON   Classical Bronzes. Providence: Museum of Art, Rhode Island School of Design, 1975. 4to; 211 pages, numerous illustrations; stiff wrappers.   Archaeologia Luxor-3719 1996 $125.00

MIVART, ST. G.   Dogs, Jackals, Wolves and Foxes. London: 1890. 4to; pages xxvi, 216, text figures, 45 hand colored plates by Keulemans; recent fullb rown morocco; fine, clean copy; from the collection of Jan Coldewey.   Wheldon & Wesley 207-68 1996 £1,600.00

MIVART, ST. G.   A Monograph of the Lories, or Brush-Tongued Parrots, Comprising the Family Loriidae. London: 1896. Original issue; royal 8vo; pages liii, 193, 4 maps, hand colored plates; original brown cloth, bevelled edges; good copy; formerly the copy of W. E. Oates, from the collection of Jan Coldewey, with bookplate.   Wheldon & Wesley 207-69 1996 £3,950.00

MIVART, ST. G.   A Monograph of the Lories, or Brush-Tongued Parrots, Composing the Family Loriidae. Seibersbach: 1992. 4to; pages liii, 193, 4 maps, 61 colored plates; bound.   Wheldon & Wesley 207-807 1996 £125.00

MIZNER, ADDISON   Florida Architecture of Addison Mizner. New York: William Helburn, 1928. Folio; 185 photos; plain gilt lettered brown cloth, library stamp on all 3 bulked edges, stamp on front pastedown, but plates and text are bright and clean.   Marilyn Braiterman 15-145 1996 $475.00

MOBERLY, WALTER   Early History of Canadian Pacific Railway. Vancouver: 1909. Pages 15; portrait; self wrappers, signed, numerous ms. corrections and annotations.   Stephen Lunsford 45-115 1996 $150.00

MOCKET, RICHARD   God and the King: or, a Dialogue, Shewing, That our Soveraign Lord the King...Doth Rightly Claim Whatsoever Is Required by the Oath of Allegiance. London: imprinted by His Majesties Special Priviledge and Command, 1663. 4to; (4), 40 pages; woodcut frontispiece; old calf, worn, hinges cracked, but still holding. Wing M2302.   Kenneth Karmiole 1NS-188 1996 $200.00

THE MODERN Story-Teller; Being a Collection of Merry, Polite, Grave, Moral, Entertaining and Improving Tales. Poughkeepsie: pub. by Paraclete Potter, P. & S. Potter, printers, 1816. Apparently 3rd recorded edition; 16mo; contemporary paper boards, calf spine (worn); some foxing and soiling, one marginal tear affecting a couple of letters which are clear from context, otherwise very good, rare. Welch 868.2. Shaw & Shoemaker 38275.   Ximenes 108-65 1996 $300.00

THE MODERN Traveller. London: printed for James Duncan, Oliver and Boyd, 1826. Small 8vo; iv, 367 pages; 3 plates, folding map; recently rebound with dark brown calf spine, boards, raised bands, leather label; fine.   David Mason 71-52 1996 $160.00

MOFFAT, A. S.   The Secrets of Angling. Edinburgh: Adam & Charles Black, 1865. 1st edition; post 8vo; (xii), 326 pages, key printed in gold on front paper; original cloth, gilt, tiny ink mark on upper cover, otherwise very good, bookplate.   Ash Rare Books Zenzybyr-69 1996 £75.00

MOFFAT, ALFRED   Little Songs of Long Ago. Philadelphia: London: David McKay, Augener Ltd., n.d. 1912. Probable first American edition; oblong quarto; original cloth with oval pictorial cover pastedown, some soiling to cvoers and light wear to corners and spine extremities, else very good.   Glenn Books 36-166 1996 $150.00

MOFFAT, ALFRED   Our Od Nursery Rhymes. Philadelphia: London: David McKay, Augener Ltd., n.d. 1912. Presumed first American edition; oblong quarto; original cloth, with oval pictorial cover pastedown, upper hinge starting and some light marginal and cvoer soil, else very good. Glenn Books 36-169 1996 $150.00

MOFFAT, JOHN S.   The Lives of Robert and Mary Moffat. New York: A. C. Armstrong & Son, 1886. 8vo; pages xix, 484; 2 folding maps, 2 mounted photos, 4 plates; original green cloth, top edge gilt, spine ends starting. Mendelssohn II p. 31; Theal p. 201.   Richard Adelson W94/95-122 1996 $250.00

MOFFIT, A.   A Manual of Instruction for Attendants on Sick and Wounded in War. London: Charles Griffin, 1870. 8vo; 136 pages; illustrations; original boards, quite rubbed and worn, armorial crest of the Red Cross on front board, boards stained, internally good.   James Tait Goodrich K40-198 1996 $135.00

MOGGRIDGE, J. T.   Contributions to the Flora of Mentone, and to a Winter Flora of the Riviera. London: 1871. 2nd edition; royal 8vo; 99 fine hand colored plates; original cloth, neatly refixed.   Wheldon & Wesley 207-70 1996 £350.00

MOGGRIDGE, J. T.   Harvesting Ants and Trap-Door Spiders, with Supplement. London: 1873-74. 8vo; 2 volumes in 1; pages xi, 304; 20 plates; original cloth.   Wheldon & Wesley 207-1082 1996 £60.00

MOHANTY, BIJOY CHANDRA   Block Printing and Dyeing of Bagru, Rajasthan. Ahmedabad: Calico Museum of Textiles, 1983. 1st edition; 4to; 107 pages with 51 black and white photographic illustrations; 79 woodblock illustrations, 148 actual samples; cloth; fine.   J. M. Cohen 35-69 1996 $300.00

MOHANTY, BIJOY CHANDRA   Natural Dyeing Processes of India. Ahmedabad: Calico Museum of Textiles, Studies in Cont. Textile Crafts o India, 1987. Oblong 4to; 284 pages; profusely illustrated, including numerous tipped in color illustrations; pictorial boards, very good.   J. M. Cohen 35-70 1996 $125.00

MOHOLY, LUCIA   A Hundred Years of Photography. Middlesex: Penguin, 1939. 1st edition; 35 illustrations; wrappers as issued; scarce. J. B. Muns 154-202 1996 $100.00

MOHOLY-NAGY, LASZLO   The New Vision...and Abstract of an Artist. New York: Wittenborn, Schultz, 1947. 2nd English language edition; 4to; 92, (3) pages; wrappers, bookplate; very good.   The Bookpress 75-217 1996 $250.00

MOHOLY-NAGY, LASZLO   Portrait of Eton. London: 1949. Revised edition; dust jacket slightly chipped.   J. B. Muns 154-203 1996 $125.00

MOHOLY-NAGY, LASZLO   Vision in Motion. Chicago: Paul Theobald, 1947. 1st edition; 4to; 371 pages; 439 illustrations; cloth, slightly worn and dust soiled, one corner bumped.   Thomas Thorp 489-219 1996 £85.00

MOIR, DAVID MAC BETH   Domestic Verses. Edinburgh: Blackwood, 1871. Small octavo; pages 174; full black crushed morocco, fillets decorated in blind, raised bands, gilt titles, guaffered edges gilt, doublures, all edges gilt; patterned gilt striped endpapers, echo the unusual honeycomb and floral needlework pattern of the fore-edge painting, which is signed with the initials "A.N."; name on flyleaf, else very pretty copy. CBEL III 410.   Hartfield 48-F5 1996 $895.00

MOKLER, ALFRED J.   History of Natrona County, Wyoming 1888-1922. Chicago: 1923. 1st edition; xiv, 477 pages, frontispiece, photos, maps; cloth; nice. Campbell 68; 6 Guns 1524. Herd 1669.   T. A. Swinford 49-793 1996 $350.00

MOLDENKE, CHARLES   The New York Obelisk, Cleopatra's Needle, with a Preliminary Sketch of the History, Erection, Uses and Signification of Obelisks. New York: Randolph, 1891. Number 35 of limited large paper edition of 150; 4to; (ii), viii, 202 pages, many illustrations; publisher's cloth, rather worn and shaky.   Elton Engineering 10-108 1996 £135.00

MOLEVILLE, F. A. BERTRAND DE   Annals of the French Revolution; or a Chronological Account Of its Principal Events, with a Variety of Anecdotes and Character Hitherto Unpublished. London: J. Harris, 1813. 8vo; 5 volumes; frontispiece; contemporary half calf, rebacked in morocco; ex-library.   Robert Clark 38-315 1996 £60.00

MOLIERE, JEAN BAPTISTE POQUELIN DE 1622-1673   The Dramatic Works. Edinburgh: Wm. Patterson, 1875. Tall 8vo; 6 volumes; engravings by Lalauze; three quarter maroon morocco, emblemataic tooling on spines, raised bands, gilt tops.   Appelfeld Gallery 54-141 1996 $275.00

MOLIERE, JEAN BAPTISTE POQUELIN DE 1622-1673   The Misanthrope. London: Rex Collings Ltd., 1973. 1st edition; wrappers, covers slightly marked and rubbed, very good; bookplate of literary agent John Johnson.   Ulysses 39-270 1996 £65.00

MOLIERE, JEAN BAPTISTE POQUELIN DE 1622-1673   Select Comedies...in French and English. London: printed for John Watts, 1732. 1st edition; 12mo; 8 volumes; contemporary calf, gilt, spines gilt, contrasting morocco labels, slight wear. Very good; early armorial bookplates of Samuel Strode. Paulson Hogarth's Graphic Works 222-3. Ximenes 108-269 1996 $900.00

MOLIERE, JEAN BAPTISTE POQUELIN DE 1622-1673   Tartuffe or the Hypocrite. Leipzig: printed by Poeschel & Trepte at Leipzig for the Members of the LEC, 1930. Limited to 1500 copies; signed by artist; folio; lithograph illustrations by Hugo Stiner-Prag; cloth backed embossed boards, slipcase; covers somewhat foxed, otherwise fine in partially split, edge worn and faded slipcase; very scarce.   James S. Jaffe 34-701 1996 $175.00

MOLIERE, JEAN BAPTISTE POQUELIN DE 1622-1673   Tartuffe, or the Hypocrite. Leipzig: Limited Editions Club, 1930. Limited to 1500 copies; signed by artist; folio; lithographs drawn on stone by Hugo Steiner-Prag; half linen/Japanese paper; fine in lightly worn dust jacket and rather worn case.   Charles Agvent 4-903 1996 $150.00

MOLIERE, JEAN BAPTISTE POQUELIN DE 1622-1673   Tartuffe: or, the French Puritan. London: Richard Wellington, 1707. 2nd appearance in English; small 4to; (6), 66 pages; bound c. 1900 in gilt calf over marbled boards, spine bit rubbed, some foxing of text, overall very clean. Kenneth Karmiole 1NS-189 1996 $375.00

MOLINA, GIOVANNI I.   The Geographical, Natural and Civil History of Chili. Middletown: I. Reilly, 1808. 8vo; 2 volumes, pages 8, xii, 271, errata; 2, viii, 306, 68; folding map; original tree calf, rubbed and worn, repair to map. Sabin 49893.   Richard Adelson W94/95-123 1996 $275.00

MOLLHAUSEN, BALDWIN   Diary of a Journey from the Mississippi to the Coasts of the Pacific... London: 1858. 1st English edition; 2 volumes, 32, 352, 12, 397 pages; plates, some in color, map; cloth/leather; nice, beautiful set. Howes M713; Wagner Camp 305; Graff 2849; Rader 2418. T. A. Swinford 49-794 1996 $2,250.00

MOLLHAUSEN, BALDWIN   Diary Of a Journey from the Mississippi to the Coasts of the Pacific. London: Longman, Brown, 1858. 1st edition in English; 2 volumes; folding map, 19 plates in both chromolithography and tint; ad leaf; original red cloth stamped in blind and gilt, effaced name on front pastedown to volume one and bookplate with effaced name on front pastedown to volume two, minor restoration to spine, otherwise remarkably bright in modern custom slipcase. Howes M713. Hermitage SP95-721 1996 $1,600.00

MOLLIEN, GASPAR THEODORE, COMTE DE   Travels in the Interior of Africa, to the Sources of the Sengal and Gambia; Performed by Command of the French Government, in the Year 1818. London: printed for Henry Colburn & Co., 1820. 1st edition in English; 4to; frontispiece, large folding map, 6 uncolored aquatints, blank portions of frontispiece lightly waterstained, but generally an excellent copy in original condition; original dark green moire cloth, black glazed spine label, printed in gold (top of spine and corners bit worn, label slightly chipped); Abbey Travel 273.   Ximenes 109-196 1996 $750.00

MOLLIEN, GASPARD T.   Travels in Africa, to the Sources of the Senegal and Gambia, in 1818. London: Richard Phillips, 1820. 8vo; pages ix, 128; folding map, 4 plates; modern red buckram, uncut. Hoover 7427. Richard Adelson W94/95-124 1996 $285.00

MOLNAR, FERENC   The Plays of Ferenc Molnar. New York: Vanguard Press, 1929. Special edition, limited to 400 copies, signed by author; thick 4to; 824 pages; frontispiece; blue cloth, elaborately gilt spine, top edge gilt, very good.   Lyman Books 21-611 1996 $200.00

MOLNAR, FERENC   The Plays of Ferenc Molnar. New York: Macy Masius, the Vanguard Press, 1929. Special limited edition of 400 copies, signed by author; thick 4to; xxii, 824 pages; frontispiece; blue cloth, elaborately gilt spine, top edge gilt.   Kenneth Karmiole 1NS-238 1996 $125.00

MOLYNEUX, WILLIAM   The Case of Ireland's Being Bound by Acts of Parliament in England, State. Dublin: printed by and for J. R. and are to be sold by Rob. Clavel... 1698. 1st edition; London issue; copies for sale in Ireland had a titlepage with only the name of printer Jospeh Ray in imprint; 8vo; contemporary sheep, spine and corners bit worn; very good, crisp copy. Wing M2403.   Ximenes 109-197 1996 $850.00

MOMADAY, NATACHEE SCOTT   House Made of Dawn. New York: Harper and Row, 1968. 1st edition; 8vo; cloth backed boards, dust jacket; fine in jacket with one closed tear.   James S. Jaffe 34-501 1996 $250.00

MOMADAY, NATACHEE SCOTT   In the Presence of the Sun: a Gathering of Shields. Santa Fe: Rydal Press, 1992. 1 of a numbered edition of 114, signed by Momaday; (48) pages; illustrations; new in slipcase.   Dumont 28-26 1996 $350.00

MOMADAY, NATACHEE SCOTT   In the Presence of the Sun. Santa Fe: Rydal, 1992. Limited to 114 copies; fine in slipcase, signed by author. Bella Luna 7-392 1996 $300.00

MOMUS; or, the Fall of Britain. London: printed for T. Cadell, 1789. 1st edition; 4to; no half title, 20 pages; disbound. Adams 79-79.   Anthony W. Laywood 109-99 1996 £165.00

MONARDES, NICHOLAS   Joyfull News Out of the New Founde Worlde... London: 1925. 2 volumes, 177, 188 pages; original binding. GM 1817 (Seville 1565).   W. Bruce Fye 71-1455 1996 $225.00

MONCK, CHARLES ATTICUS   An Address to the Agricultural Classes of Great Britain, on the Evils Which are the consequence of Restricting the Importation of Foreign Corn. London: James Ridgway, 1833. 1st edition; 8vo; (iv), 60 pages, few leaves dust soiled, disbound; apparently scarce; not in Kress or BM Cat.   James Burmester 29-98 1996 £175.00

MONDOR, HENRI   Doctors and Medicine in the Works of Daumier: Notes and Catalogue by Jean Adhemar. Boston: 1960. 1st English translation; 4to; 135 pages; lithographs; original binding, dust jacket; W. Bruce Fye 71-498 1996 $100.00

MONNETT, HOWARD N.   Action Before Westport, 1864. Kansas City: Westport Historical Soc., 1964. 1st edition; subscriber's edition, signed by author, #415/525 copies; 8vo; paintings and maps by George Barnett; fine in lightly sunned dust jacket.   Glenn Books 36-56 1996 $150.00

MONRO, DONALD   An Account of the Diseases Which Were Most Frequent in the British Military Hospitals in Germany, from January 1716 to the Return of the Troops to England in March 1763. London: 1764. 1st edition; 408 pages; hlaf leather, marbled boards.   W. Bruce Fye 71-1456 1996 $500.00

MONRO, DONALD   Praelectiones Medicae Ex Cronii Instituto, Annis 1774 et 1775, et Oratio Anniversaria ex Harveii Instituto die Octobris 18 anni 1775. London: Gul Hay, 1776. 1st edition; 8vo; (iv), 199, (1), (4) pages, errata and ad leaf; newly rebound in full English panel style morocco, uncut, fine. Scarce.   James Tait Goodrich K40-201 1996 $795.00

MONRO, DONALD   A Treatise on Medical and Pharmaceutical Chemistry, and the Materia Medica... London: T. Cadell, 1788. 1st edition; 8vo; 3 volumes, folding plate torn, contemporary mottled calf, some hinges reinforced. Blake 309.   Argosy 810-358 1996 $350.00

MONRO, ROBERT   His Expedition with the Worthy Scots Regiment. London: William Jones, 1637. 1st edition; folio; pages (xvi), 89, (xxiii), 224, (xviii), 3 parts in 1; paginated as two; Roman letter, attractive woodcut initials and head and tailpieces; general light age yellowing, faintest waterstain to inner upper corner of early leaves, good clean copy; 17th century panelled calf, spine gilt; armorial bookplate, 1705 of Henry, Duke of Beaufort. STC 18022. Lowndes 1585.   A. Sokol XXV-66 1996 £750.00

MONROE, HAROLD   Collected Poems. London: Cobden-Sanderson, 1933. 1st edition; 8vo; pages xx, 217; frontispiece, faint foxing to prelims and final endpapers; original first issue mid-blue cloth, backstrip gilt lettered, top edges blue, others untrimmed; excellent. Gallup B22. Blackwell's B112-100 1996 £50.00

MONROE, PAUL   A Cyclopedia of Education. New York: Macmillan Co., 1911-13. 4to; 5 volumes; 86 full page plates, several in color; original red cloth stamped in gold and black.   Kenneth Karmiole 1NS-96 1996 $175.00

MONTAGU, EDWARD WORTLEY 1713-1776   Reflections on the Rise and Fall of the Ancient Republicks. London: printed for J. Rivington and Sons, T. Longman, S. Crowder, T. Cadell.. 1778. 4th edition; 8vo; half title; contemporary sheep, rubbed, label, bookplate of George Stephens, signed by him.   Anthony W. Laywood 109-100 1996 £55.00

MONTAGU, ELIZABETH ROBINSON 1720-1800   An Essay On the Writings and Genius of Shakespear, Compared with the Greek and French Dramatic Poets. Dublin: printed for H. Saunders, 1769. 1st Irish edition; 12mo; pages (4), 242, without half title; half calf, gilt ruled spine, with label, very good.   James Fenning 133-309 1996 £115.00

MONTAGU, MARY PIERREPONE WORTLEY, LADY 1689-1762   Letters of the Right Honourable Lady M--y W-----y M------e... London: T. Becket and P. A. de Hondt, 1763. 1st edition; small 8vo; 3 volumes; half titles and blanks present, monogram "PG" on titlepage volume 3 (i.e. P. Gell); pages xii, (iv), 165; (iv), 167; (iv), 134; contemporary sprinkled tan calf, minor rubbing, backstrips with raised bands between gilt rules, green labels (that for volume 3 chipped), double gilt fillet border on sides, endpapers stained by turn-ins, generally excellent. Cox I p. 229; Rothschild 1452.   Blackwell's B112-195 1996 £300.00

MONTAGU, MARY PIERREPONE WORTLEY, LADY 1689-1762   Letters of the Right Honourable Lady... London: M. Cooper, 1777. 12mo; complete in one volume, viii, 280 pages; full 18th century calf with leather label, minor rubbing at extremities, few spots at baords, several 18th century signatures.   Archaeologia Luxor-3724 1996 $350.00

MONTAGU, MARY PIERREPONE WORTLEY, LADY 1689-1762   The Works... London: Richard Phillips, 1803. 1st collected edition; 12mo; 5 volumes; frontispiece in volume i, offset to title, 9 facsimile letters, portrait plate; contemporary half dark blue roan, joints lightly rubbed, smooth backstrips divided into compartments by single gilt rules, gilt lettered direct, marbled boards and endpapers, excellent.   Blackwell's B112-194 1996 £300.00

MONTAGU, MARY PIERREPONE WORTLEY, LADY 1689-1762   The Works. London: R. Phillips, 1803. 1st edition; octavo; numerous finely engraved holograph letters tipped in; frontispiece; three quarter calf and linen boards, top edge gilt, bookplate, some wear to spines, contents excellent; good set. CBEL II 835.   Hartfield 48-A12 1996 $295.00

MONTAGU, WALTER   Miscellanea Spiritualia; or Devout Essaies. London: printed for W. Lee, D. Pakeman and G. Bedell/John Crook & Gabriel... 1648-54. 4to; 2 volumes, (30), 405, (9); 20, 264 pages; lacking frontispiece; 1st part in 20th century calf, gilt spine, 2nd part in contemporary calf. Wing M2473 and M2474.   Kenneth Karmiole 1NS-190 1996 $125.00

MONTAIGNE, MICHEL DE 1533-1592   Essays of Michael, Seigneur de Montaigne... London: printed for Mathew Gillyflower, W. Hensman, Richard Wellington... 1700. 16mo; 3 volumes; fine engraved portrait; later 19th century half leather. Wing M 2481.   Family Album Tillers-448 1996 $250.00

MONTAIGNE, MICHEL DE 1533-1592   Essays. London: Nonesuch Press, 1931. Limited to 1475 numbered copies; 8vo; xxxviii, 724; vi, 708 pages; original full niger morocco, green morocco lettering pieces and oval green morocco labels on upper covers, top edge gilt, others uncut, slipcase, spines darkened and labels faded, as usual;   Thomas Thorp 489-220 1996 £180.00

MONTANA   First Annual Report of the Bureau of Agriculture, Labor and Industry of Montana for the Year Ended Nov. 30, 1893. Helena: 1893. 1st edition; 341 pages; wrappers, extensive edge chipping to opening pages, back cover gone and most of backstrip, browning to page edges, but text still naturally flexible. Very scarce. Not in Adams Herd.   Gene W. Baade 1094-112 1996 $225.00

MONTAUT, H. DE   Vertus & Qualites. Paris: Arnauld de Vresse, ca. 1850. Oblong folio; ornamental lithograph titlepage and 12 splendid color lithograph plates; original navy blue pebbled cloth, blindstamped and gilt lettered within gilt floral border, front free endpaper creased and foxed, else fine. Not in Gumuchian or Osborne.   Marilyn Braiterman 15-146 1996 $1,950.00

MONTECINO, MARCEL   The Crosskiller. New York: Arbor House, William Morrow, 1988. 1st edition; fine in jacket with faint wrinkling at foot of spine.   Janus Books 36-256 1996 $100.00

MONTEIRO, JOACHIM JOHN   Angola and the River congo. London: Macmillan and Co., 1875. 1st edition; 8vo; 2 volumes; folding map and 16 wood engraved plates; original bright green cloth, one upper joint neatly restored; fine set.   Ximenes 109-199 1996 $450.00

MONTESQUIEU, CHARLES LOUIS DE SECONDAT, BARON DE LA BREDE 1689-1755   The Spirit of Laws. Worcester: Isaiah Thomas, Jun. 1802. 1st American edition; tall 8vo; 2 volumes; quarter calf, first two signatures misbound; Shaw & Shoemaker 2682.   Rostenberg & Stern 150-61 1996 $750.00

MONTFERRAND, A. RICARD DE   Eglise Cathedrale de Saint-Isaac. St. Petersburg: F. Bellizard, 1845. Folio; half title, title, chromolitho and gold portrait frontispiece of St. Isaac, 2 page dedication inscr. in dec. gold and chromolitho borders, 61 pages (2 on 1 leaf) of whcih 20 tinted litho views (2 on india paper), 11 litho and tinted litho vignette views, 20 engraved ground plans and sectional elevations, 5 chromolithos and 5 lithos, contemporary quarter morocco,, rejointed, some browning.   Elton Engineering 10-111 1996 £4,800.00

MONTFORT, EUGENE   La Belle Enfant Ou L'Amour a Quarante Ans. Paris: A. Vollard, 1930. Limited to 340 copies, this one of 244 on Arches; 4to; (iv), 252, (iv), 77 etchings and suite of 16 etchings hors texte, illustrated table of etchings; unsewn as issued, publisher's folder and slipcase, decorative covers designed by Dufy; fine. Artist and the Book 93; Manet to Hockney 85.   Sotheran PN32-182 1996 £4,750.00

MONTGOMERY OF ALAMEIN, BERNARD LAW MONTGOMERY, 1ST VISCOUNT 1887-   Normandy to the Baltic. London: privately printed for private circulation... 1946. 1st edition; 279 pages, 46 folding maps, 3 diagrams; original binding, page edges browned, spine browned, worn and chipped, tail of spine and bottom edge of upper cover dampstained, covers slightly marked, good. presentation copy to the Secretary of State for War, Manny Shinwell.   Ulysses 39-416 1996 £600.00

MONTGOMERY, BRIAN   The Montgomery Manuscripts. Belfast: 1830. 1st edition; 8vo; vi, 335 pages; half calf, rebacked, good.   C. P. Hyland 216-509 1996 £180.00

MONTGOMERY, GEORGE WASHINGTON   Bernardo del Carpio. New York: Harper & Bros., 1834. 1st edition in English; 12mo; original rose cloth, faded and trifle soiled, printed paper label; some light foxing, but very good, uncommon. AI 25805.   Ximenes 109-200 1996 $200.00

MONTGOMERY, JAMES   The Chimney-Sweeper's Friend, and Climbing-Boy's Album. London: Longman, eta ia, 1824. 12mo; xvi, 428 pages, 3 engraved plates by Cruikshank; recent paper boards done in contemporary style, library stamps on title.   James Tait Goodrich K40-91 1996 $495.00

MONTGOMERY, JAMES   Journal of Voyages and Travels by Rev. Daniel Tyerman & George Bennet, Esq. Deputed fromt he London Missionary Society... London: Westley & Davis, 1831. 1st U.K. edition; 8vo; 2 volumes; (xxiv), 566 pages; (viii), 568 pages, 7 plates; handsomely rebound in brown morocco and marbled boards, gilt title library stamp on title and verso of illustrations, some slight foxing on plates, otherwise nice.   Antipodean 28-93 1996 $375.00

MONTGOMERY, L M.   Rilla of Ingleside. New York: Frederick Stokes, 1921. 1st edition; frontispiece in color; near fine with fine pictorial label on front cover.   Captain's Bookshelf 38-167 1996 $100.00

MONTGOMERY, RUTHERFORD G.   High Country. New York: Derrydale Press, 1938. 1st edition; number 239 of 950 copies; 8vo; 248 pages; frontispiece, plates; original rust cloth with morocco labels, spine little sunned, otherwise near fine.   Chapel Hill 94-388 1996 $150.00

MONTHAN, GUY   Art and Indian Individualists, The Art of Seventeen Contemporary Southwestern Artists and Craftsmen. Flagstaff: Northland Press, 1975. 1st edition; 197 pages; fine in dust jacket.   Ken Sanders 8-217 1996 $125.00

THE MONTHLY Chronicle of North-Country Lore and Legend. London: 1888-91. 4to; 4 volumes, over 2000 pages, over 400 illustrations; decorated pictorial cloth, good.   K Books 441-339 1996 £70.00

MONTSTRELET, ENGUERRAND DE   The Chronicles of... N.P.: James Henderson at the Hafod Press, 1809. Folio; 5 volumes bound in 4; engravings; contemporary russia boards by J. Wright, rebacked in brown morocco, spines with raised bands, gilt tooling and dark brown gilt stamped labels, covers triple ruled in gilt with decorative floral corner devices, gilt stamped floral inner dentelles, marbled endpapers, edges extra gilt; very good.   George J. Houle 68-103 1996 $1,250.00

MOODY, WALTER D.   Wacker's Manual of the Plan of Chicago, Municipal Economy. Chicago: the author, 1915. 1st edition; 8vo; frontispiece, (vi), 147 pages; cloth, very good.   The Bookpress 75-218 1996 $135.00

MOON, ANNA MARIA   In Memoriam. The Rev. W. Leeves, Author of the Air of 'Audi Robin Gray". N.P.: printed for private circulation, 1873. 8vo; pages xvi, (ii), 185, viii, 11, (12), frontispiece, plate, half title; contemporary dark blue morocco, double and single fillet borders to sides, enclosing ornaments and lettered on upper cover, spine in compartments with raised bands, gilt rules and lettering, gilt edges and inner dentelles, white silk endpapers; few ms. corrections in pencil, extremities rubbed, but very good; booklabel of John Sparrow; presentation copy inscribed by author.   Simon Finch 24-174 1996 £90.00

MOON, GRACE P.   Indian Legends in Rhyme. New York: 1907. 1st edition; iv, 54 pages, color plates, illustrations by Karl Moon; pictorial cloth, nice. rare. Dykes Moon 10.   T. A. Swinford 49-804 1996 $100.00

MOONEY, BOOTH   The Lyndon Johnson Story. New York: FS&C, 1956. 1st edition; book very good in dust jacket has numerous small tears; nice inscription from Johnson to Karl Wyler (El Paso publisher). Parker Books of the West 30-128 1996 $350.00

MOORAT, S. A. J.   Catalogue of Western Manuscripts on Medicine and Science in the Wellcome Historical Medical Library. Wellcome Historical Medical Library, 1962-73. 1st edition; 4to; 3 volumes; hand colored frontispiece, original buckram; from the library of W. R. Le Fanu with few notes on endpapers.   Forest Books 74-185 1996 £110.00

MOORE FRANCIS   Travels into the Indland Parts of Africa... London: printed by Edward Cave, for the author and sold by J. Stagg, 1738. 1st edition; 8vo; large folding map and 11 other engraved plates and charts; contemporary calf, gilt, rebacked; slight foxing, but fine, CBEL II 1449. Ximenes 109-201 1996 $1,750.00

MOORE, BRIAN   An Answer from Limbo. Boston: Atlantic Little Brown, 1962. 1st edition; slight bump to foreedge, else fine in very near fine dust jacket, with touch of rubbing; briefly inscribed by author. Between the Covers 42-315 1996 $175.00

MOORE, C.   Handbook of the Flora of New South Wales. Syndey: 1893. 8vo; xxxix, 582 pages; original blue cloth, ex-library, stamps and press-mark on spine, binding rather used but sound.   Wheldon & Wesley 207-1575 1996 £80.00

MOORE, C. L.   Black God's Shadow. Grant, 1977. 1st edition; 1/150 copies, signed by author and artist; fine in dust jacket and slipcase. Aronovitz 57-830 1996 $150.00

MOORE, C. L.   Shambleau and Others. New York: Gnome, 1953. 1st edition; some offsetting to endpapers, else fine in dust jacket with some foxing.   Robert Gavora 61-99 1996 $190.00

MOORE, CLEMENT C.   The Night Before Christmas. Philadelphia: J. B. Lippincott Co., n.d. 1931. One of 275 copies for America, out of a total edition of 550 numbered copies, signed by artist; small quarto; 4 color pltes and 17 drawings in black and white by Arthur Rackham; full limp vellum lettered in gilt on front cover, top edge gilt, others uncut, pictorial endpapers in red and white, vellum lightly soiled, very good.   Heritage Book Shop 196-285 1996 $850.00

MOORE, CLEMENT C.   The Night Before Christmas; or, Account of a Visit from St. Nicholas. Los Angeles: Arundel Press, 1984. 1st edition thus, copy "M" of 26 lettered copies printed for George Houle (of a total edition of 150); signed by artist; small folio; linoleum prints by Clark Henley; dark red cloth, printed paper spine label, uncut, fine.   George J. Houle 68-104 1996 $150.00

MOORE, CLEMENT C.   Observations Upon Certain Passages in Mr. Jefferson's Notes on Virginia, Which Appear to Have a Tendency to Subvert Religion and Establish a False Philosophy. New York: 1804. 1st edition; 8vo; 32 pages; sewn, contemporary plain wrappers, uncut. BAL 14334; S&S 68122. Gaines 342.   M & S Rare Books 60-379 1996 $275.00

MOORE, CLEMENT C.   A Plain Statement Addressed to the Proprietors of Real Estate, in the City and County of New York. New York: 1818. 1st edition; 8vo; 62 pages; removed, foxed. BAL 14340; S&S 44880.   M & S Rare Books 60-380 1996 $200.00

MOORE, EDWARD   The World. London: Dodsley, 1782. 8vo; 4 volumes; stencilled tree calf covers with narrow leafy small tool border, a central oval of plain calf with large urn and stand in stencilled outline, flat spines gilt with four panels and two lettering pieces, all between red and green or blue onlay, gilt flowers in each corner, all edges yellow, marbled endpapers, some corners soft, occasional small abrasions on covers, overall an excellent set; from the collection of Ficasoli Firidolfi with his label.   Marlborough 160-48 1996 £2,200.00

MOORE, F. F.   The Secret of the Court. London: Hutchinson, 1895. 1st edition; previous owner's embossed stamp at base of titlepage with faint numbers near base of spine, else tight, bright, very good+ copy in wonderful pictorial cloth; very scarce.   Aronovitz 57-831 1996 $125.00

MOORE, FRANK   The Portrait Gallery of the Ar, Civil, Military and Naval: a Biographical Record. 1865. 1st edition; 10 x 6.5 inches; 353 pages; 60 engraved portraits; cloth, spine chipped, outer hinges crudely taped.   John K. King 77-84 1996 $150.00

MOORE, FRANK   Women of the War; Their Heroism and Self-Sacrifice. Hartford: 1867. 1st edition; 596 pages; original binding.   W. Bruce Fye 71-1460 1996 $100.00

MOORE, GEORGE 1852-1933   Aphrodite in Aulis. 1930. Limited to 1825 copies, signed; 8vo; full vellum, ownership inscription, else fine.   C. P. Hyland 216-520 1996 £56.00

MOORE, GEORGE 1852-1933   Aphrodite in Aulis. London: 1930. Limited to 1825 copies; signed; 8vo; full vellum, fine in original slipcase.   C. P. Hyland 216-521 1996 £75.00

MOORE, GEORGE 1852-1933   The Brook Kerith. New York: Macmillan, 1929. One of 500 numbered copies, signed by author and artist; 8vo; illustrations by Stephen Gooden; parchment backed boards, light foxing to spine, near fine.   Charles Agvent 4-905 1996 $125.00

MOORE, GEORGE 1852-1933   Flowers of Passion. London: Provost and Co., 1878. 1st edition; 8vo; author's first book; errata slip; decorated cloth, housed in cloth clamshell box, mild bubbling and rubbing to covers, lovely copy, scarce.   Charles Agvent 4-906 1996 $500.00

MOORE, GEORGE 1852-1933   Hail and Farewell. 1911-14. 1st edition; 8vo; 3 volumes, errata slip, Vale has tipped in replacement half title; cloth; good.   C. P. Hyland 216-511 1996 £60.00

MOORE, GEORGE 1852-1933   Heloise and Abelard. New York: 1921. Limited to 1500 copies; 8vo; 2 volumes; quarter parchment, lacks 1 spine label, very good.   C. P. Hyland 216-513 1996 £50.00

MOORE, GEORGE 1852-1933   Memoirs of My Dead Life. London: Wilson Heinemann, 1906. 1st edition; 8vo; pages vii, (i), 335, (i); original dark blue cloth, spine gilt lettered, sides panelled in blind, lower edges uncut, joints very lightly rubbed, otherwise fine, protected in quarter grey morocco slipcase; author's presentation inscription to Carroll Cartstairs. Simon Finch 24-175 1996 £250.00

MOORE, GEORGE 1852-1933   Ulick and Soracha. London: 1926. 1st edition; limited to 1250 signed copies; 8vo; cloth, near fine in dust jacket.   C. P. Hyland 216-519 1996 £50.00

MOORE, HENRY   Poems, Lyrical and Miscellaneous. London: printed for J. Johnson by J. Crowder and E. Hemsted, 1803. 1st edition; 4to; contemporary calf, spine gilt; fine. Jackson p. 273.   Ximenes 109-202 1996 $250.00

MOORE, HENRY   Poems, Lyrical and Miscellaneous. London: for J. Johnson by J. Crowder and E. Hemsted, 1803. 1st edition; 4to; pages vi, (ii), 153, (i); contemporary half calf, green morocco label, smooth spine with gilt harp motifs between double gilt bands, marbled sides; pleasant copy.   Simon Finch 24-176 1996 £100.00

MOORE, HENRY SPENCER 1898-   Heads, Figures and Ideas. London: George Rainbird, 1958. Folio; printed on handmade paper; 59 full page plates, many printed in sepia or colors; cloth backed designed boards, dust jacket.   Thomas Thorp 489-221 1996 £285.00

MOORE, HENRY SPENCER 1898-   Shelter Sketch Book. London: Wittenborn/Editions Poetry, ca. 1940. 1st American edition; square 8vo; full page color and black and white drawings by Moore; top-bound gilt stamped beige linen, upper cover stamped in gilt and black, slight fading, hinges starting, very good.   George J. Houle 68-105 1996 $175.00

MOORE, J. HAMILTON   The Young Gentleman and Lady's Monitor and English Teacher's Assistant. New York: William Durrell, 1792. 12mo; vi, 406, (8) pages, 4 engraved plates; contemporary calf, red calf spine label, top front outer hinge slightly cracked. Evans 46510.   Kenneth Karmiole 1NS-192 1996 $125.00

MOORE, JAMES   Kilpatrick and Our Cavalry: Comprising a Sketch of the Life of General Kilpatrick, With an Account of the Cavalry Raids, Engagements, and Operations Under His Command... New York: W. J. Widdleton, 1865. 1st edition; 245, (4) pages; plates; original cloth, rubbed, yet very good. Dornbusch PA 76; Howes M 774; Nicholson p. 522.   McGowan Book Co. 65-63 1996 $150.00

MOORE, JAMES CARRICK   A Narrative of the Campaign of the British Army in Spain, Commanded by His Excellency Lieut.-General Sir John Moore. London: printed for J. Johnson, 1809. 3rd edition; 8 1/2 x 5 1/2 inches; (iii)-xix (1), 388, 136 pages; 2 large folding maps colored in part; pleasing recent smooth calf raised bands, red morocco label on spine, maps with minor creasing and offsetting, one of the maps with short tear at inner margin, otherwise quite excellent, in sympatheic binding that shows no significant wear.   Phillip J. Pirages 33-391 1996 $150.00

MOORE, JOHN 1729-1802   A Journal During a Residence in France...to the Middle of December 1792. London: for G. G. J. & J. Robinson/ G.G. & J. Robinson, 1793. 1st edition; demy 8vo; 2 volumes; (iv), 502; (vi), (618) pages; folding colored map; contemporary half calf, numbers in roundels, lemon edges, some wear, slight chipping, few marks, little tender, but good set, contemporary bookplates of Benjamin Dickinson. Ash Rare Books Zenzybyr-70 1996 £200.00

MOORE, JOHN 1729-1802   A Journal During a Residence in France, from the Beginning of August, to the Middle of December, 1792. London: printed for G. and J. Robinson, Paternoster Row, 1794. New edition; 8vo; 2 volumes; 1-502, 1-617 pages; half calf and marbled boards, corners bumped, red and green morocco labels to spines; map to rear volume 2, large folding colored map to volume 1.   Beeleigh Abbey BA/56-98 1996 £125.00

MOORE, JOHN 1729-1802   Mordaunt. Sketches of Life, Characters, and Manners in Various Countries... London: printed for G. G. and J. Robinson, 1800. 1st edition; 3 volumes; original boards, uncut; some minor imperfections, but fine.   Howard S. Mott 227-99 1996 $450.00

MOORE, JOHN 1729-1802   Mordaunt Sketches of Life, Characters and Manners in Various Countries; Including the Memoirs of a French Lady of Quality. London: printed for G. G. and J. Robinson, Paternoster Row, S. Hamilton, ... 1800. 1st edition; 8vo; 3 volumes; half calf, marbled boards, corners bumped, red and green morocco labels to spines, gilt tooling to spines, slight loss of upper joint of volume 1, hinges cracked to all volumes, volume 1 hinges slightly tender.   Beeleigh Abbey BA/56-96 1996 £200.00

MOORE, JOHN 1729-1802   A View of Society and Manners in France, Switzerland, and Germany... London: printed for W. Strahan and T. Cadell in the Strand, 1780. 3rd edition; 8vo; 2 volumes; (i-iii), 1-451, 1-440 pages; top right hand corners of both titles cut away and then restored with new paper, some foxing to title volume 2, sporadic foxing to text, nothing heavy. Cox I p. 150.   Beeleigh Abbey BA/56-99 1996 £75.00

MOORE, JOHN 1729-1802   A View of Society and Manners in Italy... Boston: West and Larkin, 1792. Large thick 8vo; pages 512; fine rebinding in full polished calf, blind fillets, raised bands, gilt, gilt on dark green leather title; titlepage repaired, unobtrusive library stamp; excellent copy. Lowndes III 1291 for first London ed.   Hartfield 48-L62 1996 $245.00

MOORE, JOHN WHEELER   Roster of North Carolina Troops in the War Between the States. Raleigh: 1882. 1st edition; 4 volumes; original cloth, rubbed with staining on front board of volume one, recased with professional repairs to spine ends; good set. Nevins II 233; Dornbusch II 23; Nicholson p. 523; Thornton 8943.   McGowan Book Co. 65-64 1996 $1,500.00

MOORE, JOSEPH   Eighteen Views Taken at and Near Rangoon. (with) Views in the Birman Empire. London: Clay, n.d., plates dated 1825-26. Early issue; folio; 2 series in 1 volume, folding engraved map, 48 pages quarto text on stubs, 24 hand colored aquatint plates; recent half calf, very rare. Abbey Travel 404.   Marlborough 162-239 1996 £7,500.00

MOORE, JOSHUA   A Discourse, Delivered at the Council-House, Detroit, Before the Legislative Council of Michigan Territory, June 21, 1824. Detroit: Sheldon & Reed, 1824. 1st edition; 8vo; 27 pages; removed; foxed, piece clipped from lower margin of title leaf. Ink presentation inscription from author (clipped); Michigan Imprints 77; McMurtrie 93; Shoemaker 17209.   M & S Rare Books 60-376 1996 $150.00

MOORE, M. B., MRS.   Primary Geography, Arranged as a Reading Book, with Questions and Answers Attached. Raleigh: Branson & Farrar, 1864. 2nd edition; 47, (1) pages; maps, some coloring; original pictorial printed boards, cloth backstrip with minor chipping, neatly rebacked, fine, slipcase. Crandall 4071; Parrish & Willingham 7807.   Michael D. Heaston 23-115 1996 $1,750.00

MOORE, MARIANNE 1887-1972   O to Be A Dragon. New York: Viking, 1959. 1st edition; original cloth, fine in near fine dust jacket; signed by author.   Thomas Dorn 9-190 1996 $100.00

MOORE, NORMAN   The History of the Study of Medicine In the British Isles. Oxford: 1908. 1st edition; 202 pages; original binding.   W. Bruce Fye 71-1464 1996 $100.00

MOORE, ROBIN   The French Connection. Boston: Little Brown, 1969. 1st edition; fine in near fine dust jacket with some general rubbing, scarce.   Between the Covers 42-317 1996 $100.00

MOORE, THOMAS   The Life and Death of Lord Edward Fitzgerald. London: Longman, Rees, Orme, Brown, Green & Longmans, 1832. 3rd edition; 8vo; 2 volumes, (viii), 307, 308 pages; frontispiece in volume one, folding map in volume 2; offsetting from portrait on title, portrait and folding map bit foxed, otherwise fine; contemporary half leather, raised bands.   David Mason 71-97 1996 $280.00

MOORE, THOMAS   The Life of Lord Byron, with His Letters and Journals. London: John Murray, 1847. New edition in one volume; large octavo; 735 pages; frontispiece and five pportraits, engraved titlepage with vignette; green pebbled morocco, triple gilt and blind fillets, raised bands, gilt extra in panels, all edges gilt; appropriately elegant fore-edge painting with portrait of Byron and a view of the Acropolis in Athens; some wear and slight foxing, but nice copy, handsome, with finely detailed fore-edge painting under gilt.   Hartfield 48-F6 1996 $950.00

MOORE, THOMAS   Tom Crib's Memorial to Congress. London: printed for Longman, etc., 1819. 1st edition; 8vo; original drab boards, printed paper label (slight wear to spine); fine, not uncommon title, scarce in this state. Hartley 1398; Magriel 25; Jackson p. 449; CBEL III 265. Ximenes 108-270 1996 $250.00

MOORE, THOMAS 1779-1852   M.P. or the Blue-Stocking, a Comic Opera, in Three Acts, first Performed at the English Opera, Theatre Royal, Lyceum, on Monday Sept. 8, 1811. London: Printed by W. Clowes, for J. Power, 1811. 1st edition; 4to; later roan backed marbled boards, some wear to head and tail of spine, some staining of front section of text, not affecting legibility. NCBEL 3.265.   James Cummins 14-137 1996 $125.00

MOORE, THOMAS 1779-1852   Memoirs of Captain Rock, the Celebrated Irish Chieftain, with Some Account of His Ancestors. New York: J. M'Loughlin, 1824. 1st American edition; 12mo; 223 pages; uncut original boards, small splits in spine, printed paper label; AI 17212; Block p. 165.   Howard S. Mott 227-101 1996 $150.00

MOORE, THOMAS 1779-1852   Memoirs of the Life of the Right Honourable Richard Brinsley Sheridan. London: Longman, 1825. 1st edition; 4to; xii, 719 pages; portrait, facsimile manuscript, lacking half title; contemporary calf, rebacked. Signet Library arms on covers, Lowe Arnott & Robinson 3499. CBEL III 236.   James Burmester 29-99 1996 £100.00

MOORE, THOMAS 1821-1887   Nature Printed British Ferns: Being Figures and Descriptions of the Species and Varities of Ferns Found in the United Kingdom. London: 1859-60. 1st octavo edition; royal 8vo; 2 volumes, engraved titlepages with colored fern vignettes, 114 colored plates; original red basket weave cloth, neatly rebacked with original spines laid down.   Charles W. Traylen 117-319 1996 £225.00

MOORE, THOMAS 1821-1887   Nature Printed British Ferns. London: 1863. 8vo; 2 volumes; 122 colored paltes; original cloth, gilt, neatly repaired.   Wheldon & Wesley 207-1640 1996 £160.00

MOORE, THOMAS STURGE 1870-1944   Danae. London: Hacon & Ricketts, 1903. Limited to 230 copies; 8vo; pages xlv + colophon leaf, printed in black and red in King's fount on handmade paper; 3 full page illustrations by Charles Ricketts; original holland backed blue boards, paper label, small chip from blue paper at one corner; very good. Tomkinson 43.   Claude Cox 107-179 1996 £130.00

MOOREHEAD, WARREN K.   Prehistoric Implements: a Reference Book. Cincinnati: Robert Clarke, 1900. 1st edition; limited to 2050 copies; 431 pages + ads, 621 text figures, few folding plates; cloth, covers well worn and soiled, hairline cracks at hinges, endpapers loose.   Metacomet Books 54-72 1996 $100.00

MOORMAN, JOHN JENNINGS   A Guide to the Virginia Springs: Giving, in addition to the Routes and Distances, a Description of the Springs and Also of the Natural Curiosities of the State. Staunton: Robert Cowan & Philadelphia: Cowperthwait & Co., 1851. (2), (xi)-xii, (13)-141 pages, 11 pages ads, folding frontispiece, map; original cloth, title in gilt on front cover, nice copy with receipt laid in for restoration work. Haynes 12565.   Bohling Book Co. 191-993 1996 $200.00

MOORMAN, JOHN JENNINGS   Mineral Springs of North America: How to Reach and How to Use Them. Philadelphia: Lippincott, 1873. 1st edition; 8vo; 294, (22 ad) pages; folding frontispiece, map, folding colored map and several full page illustrations; original terra cotta cloth; very light binding wear along edges, near fine. Cordasco 70-2495; Edwin V. Glaser B122-100 1996 $150.00

MOORMAN, MARY   William Wordsworth - a Biography. The Early Years 1770-1803. Oxford: 1957. 1st edition; 8vo; pages xvi, 632; 4 plates; original cloth, gilt, dust jacket, price clipped.   R.F.G. Hollett & Son 78-221 1996 £50.00

MOORMAN, MARY   William Wordsworth - a Biography. The Later Years 1803-1850. Oxford: Clarendon Press, 1965. 1st edition; 8vo; pages xvi, 632, 4 plates; original cloth, gilt, dust jacket (price clipped).   R.F.G. Hollett & Son 78-222 1996 £50.00

MOORTGAT, ANTON   The Art of Ancient Mesopotamia: the Classical Art of the Near East. London: Phaidon, 1969. 4to; x, 356 pages, 117 figures, 291 illustrations, 15 plates; dust jacket.   Archaeologia Luxor-2468 1996 $125.00

MORAES, D.   Green is the Grass. Bombay & Calcutta: Asia Publishing House, 1951. small 8vo; illustrations, green cloth, dust jacket; fine in price clipped jacket; inscribed by author.   James S. Jaffe 34-503 1996 $450.00

MORAN, JAMES   The Double Crown Club: a History of Fifty Years. London: Westerham Press, 1974. 1st edition; one of 500 numbered copies, signed by author, 4to; illustrations; original cloth, slipcase. Forest Books 74-186 1996 £55.00

MORAND, PAUL   Earth Girdled. New York: Alfred A. Knopf, 1928. 1st edition; 6 full page woodcuts, one headpiece and one tailpiece by Hester Sainsbury; cloth backed marbled paper boards; head and tail of spine slightly bumped, corners bumped and bruised; endpapers partially browned, covers slightly dusty, traces of a crudely removed price sticker on rear pastedown, very good in nicked, rubbed, marked, chipped and dusty, slightly torn and soiled dust jacket.   Ulysses 39-518 1996 £65.00

MORAVIA, ALBERTO   The Conformist. London: Secker & Warburg, 1952. 1st British edition; starting to rear inner hinge, else very good+, lacking dust jacket, inscribed by author.   Lame Duck Books 19-347 1996 $250.00

MORE Plots Found Out, and Plotters Apprehended. A True Relation of the Discovery of a Most Desparate and Dangerous Plot, for the Delivering Up... London: printed for Henry Overton, 1643. 1st edition; 4to; 8 pages; disbound. Wing M2714.   Anthony Laywood 108-13 1996 £145.00

MORE, ALEXANDER G.   Contributions Towards a Cybele Hibernica...Outlines of Geographical Distribution of Plants in Ireland. London: 1898. 1st edition; map, cloth, very good.   C. P. Hyland 216-528 1996 £75.00

MORE, CRESACRE   The Life of Sir Thomas More, Kt. Lord High Chancellour of England Under K. Henry the Eighth... London: Woodman and Lyon, 1726. 8vo; finey engraved frontispiece, title in red and black, publisher's list at end; calf, rebacaked; Lister Holte armorial bookplate. Gibson 108.   Rostenberg & Stern 150-90 1996 $375.00

MORE, HANNAH 1745-1833   Florio; a Tale, for Fine Gentlemen and Fine Ladies; and, The Bas Bleu; or, Conversation; Two Poems. London: printed for T. Cadell, 1786. 1st edition; 4to; final ad leaf, 89 pages; disbound.   Anthony W. Laywood 109-102 1996 £50.00

MORE, HANNAH 1745-1833   Hints Towards Forming the Character of a Young Princess. London: T. Cadell and W. Davies, 1819. 5th edition; 2 volumes bound as 1, half titles; contemporary maroon calf heavily blocked in blind and gilt, all edges gilt.   Jarndyce 103-450 1996 £78.00

MORE, HANNAH 1745-1833   Strictures on the Modern System of Female Education. Dublin: printed by William Porter, for P. Wogan & W. Porter, 1797. 1st Dublin edition, 4th edition; 12mo; without half title; contemporary half calf, slight rubbing to hinges.   Jarndyce 103-540 1996 £120.00

MORE, HANNAH 1745-1833   Strictures on the Modern System of Female Education. Philadelphia: Thomas Dobson, 1800. 1st American edition; 8vo; 216, 227 pages; 2 volumes; contemporary full tree sheep with morocco spine labels, hinges cracked but holding, light wear to bindings, else very good, quite clean internally. Evans 37996.   Chapel Hill 94-422 1996 $180.00

MORE, HANNAH 1745-1833   Strictures On the Modern System of Female Education. London: T. Cadell, 1826. 13th edtion; 8vo; 2 volumes, pages (xvii), 336; 355; original half calf, marbled boards, spine compartmented and decorated in gilt, covers rubbed, endpapers spotted, other very occasional spotting, else very good.   Marjorie James 19-155 1996 £125.00

MORE, THOMAS 1478-1535   De Optimo Reip. Statu Deque Nova Insula Utopia Libellus... Basel: Johann Froben, March 1518. 3rd edition, 1st Froben edition; small quarto; 3 parts in 1 volume, roman types with occasional greek, title within fine woodcut border by Ambrosius Holbein, dedication & divisional titles within fine woodcut borders by Hans Holbein, full page woodcut view of Utopia on b2 verso and woodcut historiated headpiece on d1 recto, both by A. Holbein, woodcut initials by A. and H. Holbein, Froben's device at end of each part; full crimson morocco, gilt and blind fillets, floral centerpieces, edges gilt, by Francis Bedford; superb, tall, clean copy. PMM 47 note; Gibson 3; Adams M1756.   H. M. Fletcher 121-26 1996 £16,000.00

MORE, THOMAS 1478-1535   Utopia. New York: Limited Editions Club, 1934. Limited to 1500 copies; signed by Bruce Rogers; octavo; (x), 165 pages; printed in brown and black; early 16th century woodcuts, titlepage, headpieces and initial letters decorated with type ornaments printed in brown, spine lightly darkened, else fine, unopened, vellum backed pastepaper boards, housed in original slipcase which is lightly rubbed at extremities, top edge gilt.   Bromer Booksellers 87-257 1996 $135.00

MOREAU, JULIAN   The Black Commandos. Atlanta: Cultural Inst. Press, 1967. 1st edition; black cloth stamped in gilt, without dust jacket, almost certainly as issued, slight tarnish to a couple of the gilt letters still fine.   Between the Covers 43-165 1996 $250.00

MOREAU, P.   Description of the Rail Road from Liverpool to Manchester. Boston: Hilliard, Gray and Co., 1833. 12mo; 2 folding plates, from the numbering of the plates it would appear that several plates are lacking, some spotting and light browning, else very good; contemporary green cloth, rubbed, label lacking, folding chart facing page 48, S&S 20476.   James Cummins 14-161 1995 $200.00

MORELY, JOHN   The Life of William Ewart Gladstone. New York: & London: Macmillan Co., 1903. 1st edition; tall 8vo; 3 volumes; 3 engraved portraits; three quarter maroon morocco, gilt floral tooling on spines, raised bands, gilt tops.   Appelfeld Gallery 54-107 1996 $115.00

MORES, EDWARD ROWE   A Dissertation Upon English Typographical Founders and Founderies. New York: Grolier Club, 1924. Tall 8vo; numerous full and half page plates; French marbled boards; handsome Grolier Club reprint; Bigmore & Wyman II 50.   Rostenberg & Stern 150-136 1996 $375.00

MORESBY, JOHN   Discoveries and Surveys in New Guinea and the D'Entrecasteaux Islands. London: J. Murray, 1876. 328 pages, ads, 4 plates, 3 maps; blue gilt stamped cloth, very slightly marked, otherwise very nice, scarce;   Antipodean 28-100 1 996 $950.00

MORETON, C. O.   Old Carnations and Pinks. London: 1955. Folio; pages xi, 51, 8 color plates, illustrations on endpapers; pictorial cloth backed boards, dust jacket torn and repaired.   John Henly 27-316 1996 £60.00

MORGAN, CHARLES   The Flashing Stream. London: Macmillan & Co., 1938. Limited to 15 copies, signed by author and specially bound, this being a presentation copy from author; 8vo; xxii, 264, 2 ad pages; full niger morocco, gilt panelled sides, gilt edges, spine slightly rubbed and faded; this is copy number 3, inscribed for Leo Genn; loosely inserted is 4 page ALS to Genn from author.   Thomas Thorp 489-222 1996 £125.00

MORGAN, CHARLES   Six Philosophical Dissertations on The Mechanical Powers. Elastic Bodies. Falling Bodies. The Cycloid. The Parabola. The Rain-Bow. Cambridge: printed by Fletcher and Hodson, 1770. 1st edition; 4to; library stamp on upper blank margin on title, 3 page list of subscribers, 3 folding engraved plates at end, 19th century cloth backed boards.   Anthony W. Laywood 108-94 1996 £225.00

MORGAN, CHARLES H.   Corinth. Volume XI: The Byzantine Pottery. Cambridge: ASCSA, 1942. 4to; color frontispiece, xv, 373 pages, 226 illustrations, 53 plates; original cloth, titlepage and flyleaves foxed, spine slightly faded.   Archaeologia Luxor-3188 1996 $450.00

MORGAN, DALE   Jedediah Smith and the Opening of the West. Indianapolis: 1953. 1st edition; 458 pages; cloth; near very good in mdoerately worn dust jacket (lower spine chipped); SFT 425; Campbell p. 56.   Gene W. Baade 1094-115 1996 $115.00

MORGAN, DALE   The West of William H. Ashley... Denver: Fred A. Rosenstock, The Old West Publishing Co., 1964. 1st edition of the limited edition; 314 pages; frontispiece and illustrations, large folding map; original three quarter calf with red morocco spine label, slipcase, very fine.   Michael D. Heaston 23-151 1996 $500.00

MORGAN, J.   A Complete History of Algiers. London: printed by J. Bettenham, for A. Bettesworth and C. Hitch, 1731. 1st edition; re-issue of sheets sold by subscription in 1728-9 and bound in 2 volumes so dated; 4to; contemporary panelled calf, joints cracked by holding, lacks label; very good. CBEL II 1448.   Ximenes 108-271 1996 $450.00

MORGAN, JOHN   The Life and Adventures of William Buckley; Thirty-Two Years a Wanderer Amongst the Aborigines of the Then Unexplored Country Round Port Phillip, Now the Province of Victoria. Tasmania: Archibald MacDougall, 1852. (xiv), (ii), 208 pages; frontispiece little foxed, couple of marks; original cloth boards, rebacked, original spine laid down, chipped paper title piece; fully signed presentation copy dated June 11, 1852. Edge-Partington bookplate. Ferguson 12813. Antipodean 28-102 1996 $750.00

MORGAN, LEWIS H.   The American Beaver and His Works. Philadelphia: J. B. Lippincott & Co., 1868. 1st edition; xv, (17)-330 pages, folding map, 23 plates; inscribed from author; original embossed cloth, gilt spine titles, spine faded to an even tan, some fading to covers as well, interior very good. Howes M802.   Parmer Books Nat/Hist-043554 1996 $250.00

MORGAN, LEWIS H.   League of the Ho-De-No-Sau-Nee or Iroquois. New York: Dodd, Mead & Co., 1901. One of 300 sets printed; 8vo; 2 volumes; pages xx, 2, 338; xii, 2, 332, 2 folding maps, 33 plates; original red pictorial cloth. Howes H804; Larned 668.   Richard Adelson W94/95-125 1995 $385.00

MORGAN, M. D.   The Ecology of Mysidacea. The Hague: 1982. 8vo; 232 pages; cloth.   Wheldon & Wesley 207-1275 1996 £74.75

MORGAN, OWEN   The Light of Britannia. Cardiff: Daniel Owen & Co., London: Whittaker & Co., New York: J.W. Boulton, c. 1893. 8vo; (vi), v, (v), 430, (i) pages; frontispiece, text illustrations, folding plate; red cloth, bumped and stained, cloth split at top and bottom of front joint, titled in gilt on spine, gilt vignette on front cover; very scarce.   Blue Mountain SP95-32 1996 $150.00

MORGAN, ROBERT   Zirconia Poems. Northwood Narrows: Lillabulero Press, 1969. 1st edition; pictorial wrappers; poet's first book, fine; with ALS from Russell Banks to Jim Harrison recommending this book. Captain's Bookshelf 38-168 1996 $100.00

MORGAN, SYDNEY OWENSON, LADY 1783?-1859   France in 1829-30. London: Saunders & Otley, 1830. 1st edition; tall 8vo; 2 volumes; xii, 527, iv, 559 pages; contemporary half calf, raised bands, leather labels, binding rubbed, otherwise very good.   David Mason 71-72 1996 $280.00

MORGAN, SYDNEY OWENSON, LADY 1783?-1859   Italy. London: Henry Colburn, 1821. New edition; 8vo; 3 volumes, (xii), 516, vii, 486, viii 433 pages, with half titles; recently rebound in tan cloth, leather spine labels; fine set.   David Mason 71-105 196 $200.00

MORGAN, T. H.   The Physical Basis of Heredity. Philadelphia & London: 1919. 8vo; 305 pages; 117 illustrations; cloth; good copy. Wheldon & Wesley 207-177 1996 £80.00

MORGAN, T. H.   The Theory of the Gene. New Haven: 1926. 8vo; pages xvi,3 43, 156 illustrations; cloth; sound ex-library. GM 251. Wheldon & Wesley 207-178 1996 £95.00

MORGAN, THOMAS CHARLES   Sketches of the Philosophy of Morals. London: for Henry Colburn and Co., 1822. 1st edition; 8vo; xxix, (i), 369 pages, complete with half title, some pencil annotations erased from titlepage, still apparent, otherwise very good; uncut in original boards, neatly rebacked, contemporary Dublin bookseller Milliken's label on upper cover;   John Drury 82-190 1996 £150.00

MORGENSTERN, CHRISTIAN   Das Mittagsmahl (Il Pranzo): Paraodie Auf Gabriele d'Annunzio (and other works). Raamin-Presse, 1991. One of 145 copies (of a total edition of 190) signed by artist; 10 1/4 x 8 inches 3 p.l. (one blank), 55, (1) pages, (2) leaves (one blank), printed on one side only and unopened at fore edge; five double page illustrations in 3 colors by Roswitha Quadflieg; cloth backed decorative flexible paper boards printed in 3 colors, in matching chemise and publisher's cloth slipcase, as new.   Phillip J. Pirages 33-441 1996 $1,600.00

MORHOUS, HENRY C.   Reminiscences of the 123rd Regiment N.Y.S.U. Greenwich: 1870. 1st edition; 220 pages; cloth, very good+. Dornbusch NY 510.   T. A. Swinford 49-812 1996 $150.00

MORIARTY, H. M.   Fifty Plates of Green-House Plants... London: 1807 2nd edition; crown 8vo; pages xii, (104), 50 hand colored plates; original boards, modern calf back, new endpapers; piece cut from plate 26, neatly repaired and missing part painted in; signature on titlepage and small tear in upper margin, otherwise generally good clean copy. Wheldon & Wesley 207-72 1996 £350.00

MORIER, JAMES JUSTINIAN 1780?-1849   The Mirza. London: R. Bentley, 1841. 1st edition; small 8vo; half titles, 3 volumes, copies with half titles are scarce; contemporary half calf, leather labels.   Charles W. Traylen 117-172 1996 £105.00

MORIER, JAMES JUSTINIAN 1780?-1849   An Oriental Tale... Brighton: Printed (not published) by W. Leppard, 1839. 1st edition; 8vo; half morocco, worn, upper cover detached, spine defective, without frontispiece described in Sadleir, some browning, mostly light and to endpapers; inscribed by author for Sir Woodbine Parish (1796-1882). Sadleir 1800; Wolff 4931.   James Cummins 14-138 1996 $250.00

MORIGI, PAOLO   Histori dell' Origine di Tutte le Religioni. Venice: Fioravante Prati, 1590. 12mo; pages (xxiv), 560, Roman letter, printer's small device on title, occasional woodcut text ornament or initial, lower outer corner of second leaf repaired, affecting only catchword, otherwise a good, clean copy in French 17th century morocco, spine gilt, all edges gilt; 19th century label "Pichard Librairie, Quai Voltaire no. 21" on pastedown. Adams M1789. Not in BM STC, Graesse or Brunet; 1 copy in NUC.   A. Sokol XXV-67 1996 £550.00

MORISON, DOUGLAS   Views of Haddon Hall. London: C. Hullmandel for H. Graves & Co., 1842. Large folio; pictorial lithographic title, litho dedication and contents, 1 f. letterpress subscribers, 25 tinted litho plates; contemporary half morocco, rubbed, bumped. Abbey Scenery 419;   Marlborough 162-272 1996 £1,250.00

MORISON, ROBERT   Plantarum Umbelliferarum Distributio Nova, Per Tabulas Cognationis et Affinitatis ex Libro Naturae Observata & Detecta. Oxford: e Theatro Sheldoniano, 1672. 1st edition; folio; contemporary calf, gilt, spine gilt, some wear to spine and corners, joints cracked; very good, seldom seen in contemporary binding. Wing M2773; Henrey 262.   Ximenes 108-272 1996 $800.00

MORISON, SAMUEL ELIOT   Journals and Other Documents on the Life and Voyages of Christopher Columbus. New York: Limited Editions club, 1963. One of 1500 numbered copies, signed by artist; illustrations by Lima de Freitas; fine in lightly rubbed publisher's slipcase.   Hermitage SP95-1018 1996 $150.00

MORISON, SAMUEL ELIOT   Journals and Other Documents on the Life and Voyages of Christopher Columbus. New York: Limited Editions Club, 1965. One of 1500 numbered coies, signed by artist; large 4to; five double page colored and 65 black and white illustrations, maps on endpapers and in text; buckram, portrait medallion embossed on upper cover, leather lettering piece on spine slightly scratched, but essentially fine in slipcase.   Bertram Rota 272-267 1996 £95.00

MORISON, STANLEY 1889-1967   American Copybooks. An Outline of Their History from Colonial to Modern Times. Philadelphia: Wm. F. Fell Co., 1951. This copy number 238 (total copies printed unknown); Small 8vo; 13 illustrations; printed paper boards, bit rubbed at extremities, inscribed by author to his secretary Miriam Gasking, booklabel of Ruari Mclean, pencil note saying the book was bought from Tony Appleton in 1978.   Maggs Bros. Ltd. 1191-160 1996 £88.00

MORISON, STANLEY 1889-1967   'Black Letter' Text. Cambridge: University Press, 1942. Limited to 100 copies; folio; iv, 40 pages; frontispiece, illustrations on title, 43 illustrations in text; original printed wrappers, headcaps bit worn, edges slightly faded; bookplate of Ruari McLean. Appleton 162.   Maggs Bros. Ltd. 1191-196 1996 £220.00

MORISON, STANLEY 1889-1967   A Fifteenth Century Modus Scribendi from the Abbey of Melk. Cambridge: at the University Press, 1940. Limited to 50 copies; 16 pages of facsimile, title vignette, introduction, transcription and translation; original black cloth, headcaps and corners tiny bit bumped; booklabel of Ruari McLean. Appleton 155.   Maggs Bros. Ltd. 1191-161 1996 £100.00

MORISON, STANLEY 1889-1967   Four Centuries of Printing. London: Ernest Benn, 1924. Limited to 390 copies for sale (in addition there were 13 special copies and 100 copies in German); folio; 641 illustrations; half canvas, black cloth boards bit grubby, headcaps slightly bumped, uncut, shelf number on spine; booklabel and perforated stamp on title, ex-John Crerar Library copy. Appleton 35. Fleuron III p. 107-116.   Maggs Bros. Ltd. 1191-199 1996 £285.00

MORISON, STANLEY 1889-1967   Fra Luca de Pacioli of Borgo S. Sepolcro. New York: Grolier Club, 1933. One of 390 printed on handmade paper with hammer and anvil watermark; slim 4to; designed by Bruce Rogers; with prospectus; frontispiece, titlepage border and decorative initials in red, reproductions of Pacioli's Roman letters; gilt lettered vellum and patterned boards printed in brown; fine.   Marilyn Braiterman 15-177 1996 $1,950.00

MORISON, STANLEY 1889-1967   Fra Luca de Pacioli of Borgo S. Sepolcro. New York: Grolier Club, 1933. Limited to 390 copies, initialled by Morison; quarto; 100 pages, designed and printed by Bruce Rogers; frontispiece, large reproductions of Pacioli's roman letters; vellum backed pastepaper boards, housed in defective slipcase, prospectus laid in; bookplate; very fine. AIGA 384; Haas 162.   Bromer Booksellers 87-256 1996 $1,500.00

MORISON, STANLEY 1889-1967   German Incunabula in the British Museum. London: Victor Gollancz Ltd., 1928. 1st edition; limited to 398 copies; folio; 152 plates (many printed in red and black); titlepage slightly foxed; original decorated cloth, fraying to lower corners, head and tail of spine and lower corners worn.   Forest Books 74-188 1996 £75.00

MORISON, STANLEY 1889-1967   German Incunabula in the British Museum. New York: Hacker Art Books, 1975. Reprint of 1928 English edition with reduction in papge size; folio; 152 collotype plates printed in red and black, pictorial cloth. Appleton 72.   Maggs Bros. Ltd. 1191-200 1996 £95.00

MORISON, STANLEY 1889-1967   The History of the Times. London: Printing House Square, 1935-52. Deluxe edition, limited to 125 numbered copies; small folio; 5 volumes, 5 frontispieces, 161 plates; numerous headpieces and illustrations in text; green quarter morocco, green cloth boards, spines in compartments with raised bands and gilt lettering, top edge gilt, slipcses, bit worn, boards bit rubbed, volumes 1 and 2, generally good copy. Rare. Extra illustrated presentation edition. Appleton 137a.   Maggs Bros. Ltd. 1191-111 1996 £1,500.00

MORISON, STANLEY 1889-1967   Ichabod Dawks and His News-Letter, with An Account of the Dawks Family of Booksellers and Stationers, 1635-1731. Cambridge: at the University Press, 1931. Limited to 500 copies; small folio; 4 page letterpress facsimile of 3 Aug. 1699 News Letter, 5 tipped in collotype illustrations, illustrations in text; brown cloth, faded round edges, in original dust jacket (slightly defective). Appleton 113.   Maggs Bros. Ltd. 1191-201 1996 £340.00

MORISON, STANLEY 1889-1967   John Bell, 1745-1831. Bookseller, Printer, Publisher, Typefounder, Journalist &c. Cambridge: printed for the author at the University Press, 1930. 1st edition; one of 100 special copies, bound for members of the First Edition Club, from a total of 300 copies; hand colored frontispiece, 17 plates and insets, illustrations in text; blue buckram, gilt borders and spine, leather spine label, spine bit faded, a 12mo. 4 page address to the First Edition Club on John Bell bound in. Barker, Morison p. 304-305; Appleton 94.   Maggs Bros. Ltd. 1191-112 1996 £300.00

MORISON, STANLEY 1889-1967   Modern Fine Printing. London: Ernest Benn Ltd., 1925. 1st edition; large folio, one of 650 numbered English language copies; 8vo; 328 collotype plates; original buckram, uncut, nice. Appleton 46.   Forest Books 74-189 1996 £225.00

MORISON, STANLEY 1889-1967   Notes on the Development of Latin Script from Early to Modern Times. Cambridge: 1949. Limited to 50 copies; folio; 2 plates; original wrappers, ink inscription from Morison to James Wardrop dated 16 Aug. 1949. Appleton 178.   Maggs Bros. Ltd. 1191-204 1996 £345.00

MORISON, STANLEY 1889-1967   Notes Towards a Specimen of the Ancient Typographical Materials Principally Collected and Bequeated to the Unviersity of Oxford by Dr. John Fell d. 1686. Oxford: privately printed, 1953-57. One of 50 copies; 4to; 3 volumes, 15 pages of specimens; blue wrappers, crease on upper cover of volume 1, extra set of the text of volume 1 on loose pages inserted. Ruari McLean's copy with booklabels.   Maggs Bros. Ltd. 1191-205 1996 £235.00

MORISON, STANLEY 1889-1967   Politics and Script. Aspects of Authority and Freedom in the Development of Graeco-Latin Script from the Sixth Century B.C. to the Twentieth Century. Oxford: Clarendon Press, 1972. Tall 8vo; 186 illustrations; blue cloth, dust jacket; booklabel of Ruari Mclean. Appleton 205a.   Maggs Bros. Ltd. 1191-206 1996 £60.00

MORISON, STANLEY 1889-1967   Printing "The Times" Since 1785. London: Printing House Square, 1953. 1st edition; limited to 250 copies; large folio; 52 plates, numerous line engravings; original cloth, dust jacket slightly soiled; with McLean's signature and bookplate. Appleton 187.   Forest Books 74-346 1996 £175.00

MORISON, STANLEY 1889-1967   Printing "The Times" Since 1785. London: Printing House Square, 1953. 2nd edition; limited to 500 copies; large folio, over 50 plates, numerous line engravings; original cloth, dust jacket slightly soiled. Appleton 188.   Forest Books 74-347 1996 £145.00

MORISON, STANLEY 1889-1967   The Typographic Book 1450-1935. London: Ernest Benn, 1963. 4to; xiii, 99 pages; ornamental title and half title, both printed in red, 378 plates; cloth.   Thomas Thorp 489-223 1996 £85.00

MORISON, STANLEY 1889-1967   The Typographic Book 1450-1935: a Study of Fine Typography Through Five Centuries. Chicago: University of Chicago Press, 1963. 1st American edition; 12 x 9 1/2 inches; 377 plates; small tape stain to front and rear dust jacket flaps and pastedowns, otherwise very fine in dust jacket and slipcase.   Hermitage SP95-841 1996 $225.00

MORISON, STANLEY 1889-1967   Typographic Design in Relation to Photographic Composition. San Francisco: Ptd. at the Black Vine Press for the Book Club of California, 1959. 1st edition; one of 400 copies; 8vo; original parchment backed marbled (Cockerell boards, title gilt on spine, preserved in wrapper; Ruari McLean's copy with bookplate and critical pencilled annotations.   Forest Books 74-349 1996 £95.00

MORISOT, BERTHE   The Correspondence of Berthe Morisot with Her Family and Her Friends... London: Lund, Humphries, 1959. 1st edition; 4to; (149 pages, pages 42-50 repeated); color and black and white illustrations; cloth, matching slipcase, box stained, otherwise fine.   Paulette Rose 16-232 1996 $250.00

MORLEY, CHRISTOPHER DARLINGTON 1890-1957   Don't Open Until Christmas. New York: Doubleday, Doran & Co., 1931. 1st edition; small octavo; 26 pages; decorations by Howard Willard; original red, green and buff decorative paper boards with red cloth backstrip, board edges lightly faded, minor wear to corners, otherwise fine. Lee 102.   Heritage Book Shop 196-287 1996 $100.00

MORLEY, CHRISTOPHER DARLINGTON 1890-1957   Parnassus on Wheels. Garden City: Doubleday, 1917. 1st edition; 1st issue; 8vo; original binding, covers worn and soiled, no dust jacket; scarce; inscribed to a collector in 1935 with his leather bookplate.   Charles Agvent 4-908 1996 $225.00

MORLEY, CHRISTOPHER DARLINGTON 1890-1957   Swiss Family Manhattan. Garden City: Doubleday, Doran & Co., 1932. Limited to 250 copies, 1st edition, signed by author on endpaper; 8vo; 208 pages; gilt decorated green boards, cover label states "This edition is limited to 250 copies before publication.."; original glassine jacket very frayed, bookplate, good to very good. Autographed by author.   Robert F. Lucas 42-57 1996 $150.00

MORLEY, HENRY   Memoirs of Bartholomew Fair. London: Chatto & Windus, 1880. 8vo; pages xvi, 404, 32 page catalog, text illustrations; olive pictorial cloth.   Marlborough 162-176 1996 £75.00

MORLEY, HENRY   Oberon's Horn. London: Chapman & Hall, 1861. 1st edition; engravings in black and white by Charles Bennett; ribbed blue cloth stamped in gilt and blind, covers rubbed, little spotting to prelims, else nice, very scarce.   Barbara Stone 70-25 1996 £95.00

MORLEY, JOHN   The Life of William Ewart Gladstone. London: Macmillan, 1903. Reprint; tall 8vo; 661, 666, 648 pages; contemporary crimson half morocco, cloth, raised bands, gilt decoration in compartments, top edge gilt; fine in very attractive binding.   David Mason 71-29 1996 $390.00

MORLEY, SYLVANUS G.   Guide Book to the Ruins of Quirigua. Washington: Carnegie Inst. of Washington, 1935/47. 8vo; ix, 205 pages; 48 illustrations, 1 plate; original cloth.   Archaeologia Luxor-4718 1996 $125.00

MORLEYANA; A Collection of Writings In Memoriam, Sylvanus Griswold Morley 1883-1948. Santa Fe: School of American Research and Museum of New Mexico, 1950. Limited to 500 copies; 8vo; original cloth. Archaeologia Luxor-4722 1996 $125.00

MORRELL, BENJAMIN   A Narrative of Four Voyages, to the South Sea, North and South Pacific Ocean, Chinese Sea, Ethiopic and Southern Atlantic Ocean, Indian and Antarctic Ocean, from the Year 1822-1831. New York: J. & J. Harper, 1832. 8vo; pages xxvii, 29-492; portrait; original boards, modern cloth back, light foxing. Howes M818; Cowan p. 442; Hill I p. 204; Spence 814.   Richard Adelson W94/95-126 1996 $650.00

MORRELL, JOHN REYNELL   Algeria: The Topography and History, Political, Social and Natural, of French Africa. London: Nathaniel Cooke, 1854. 1st edition; 8vo; 490 pages; numerous full page and in text illustrations; contemporary prize binding of full niger morocco with gilt tooled spine, morocco spine label, double ruled gilt border on covers and gilt fillets on edges; prize award inscription (to Gf. Egerton-Warburton, July 1861), few traces of foxing, but handsome, very good copy.   Chapel Hill 94-4 1996 $150.00

MORRELL, Z. N.   Flowers and Fruits from the Wilderness. Boston: 1872. 1st edition; 386, (28) pages; terra cotta cloth with modest age soil, top quarter inch of backstrip is chipping, inner front hinge reglued, two small cancelled library stamps on titlepage and secret page, no other marks.   Bookworm & Silverfish 276-194 1996 $525.00

MORRIS, ANN   Word Dreams I. Leicestershire: Libra Press, 1979. Limited to 45 copies, with each sheet signed by Morris; folio; (11)ff., unbound as issued, printed entirely by silkscreen by author and artist; text is printed in white, many illustrations heightened with silver or gold, in some cases, sand was mixed with the pigment to produce a rough textured surface. Extremely fine in grey suede portfolio.   Bromer Booksellers 87-238 1996 $500.00

MORRIS, BEVERLEY R.   British Game Birds and Wildfowl. London: 1855. 1st edition; large 4to; 60 fine hand colored plates, apart from light foxing to title and frontispiece, tissue guard, a lovely copy; scarce; original green cloth, gilt, finely rebacked in dark green morocco gilt. David A.H. Grayling 3/95-38 1996 £900.00

MORRIS, CORBYN   A Letter to the Mayor of ------ Wherein the Discouragement of the Seamen Employed in His Majesty's Navy and the Merits of the Bill Brought into Parliament in the Last Session... London: R. Baldwin, 1758. 63 pages; disbound; nice. Kress 5721.   C. R. Johnson 37-23 1996 £85.00

MORRIS, FRANCIS ORPEN 1810-1893   A History of British Birds. London: 1903. 5th edition; imperial 8vo; 6 volumes; 400 hand colored plates; orignal pictorial gilt cloth, some slight discoling to some volumes, contents are excellent.   David A.H. Grayling MY95Orn-59 1996 £500.00

MORRIS, FRANCIS ORPEN 1810-1893   A History of British Moths. London: 1896. 5th edition; imperial 8vo; 4 volumes, 132 hand colored plates; cloth, pictorial gilt.   John Henly 27-65 1996 £132.00

MORRIS, FRANCIS ORPEN 1810-1893   A History of British Moths. London: John C. Nimmo, 1903. 6th edition; large 8vo; 4 volumes; 132 plates colored by hand; original green cloth, gilt, very nice, bright set. Kenneth Karmiole 1NS-196 1996 $375.00

MORRIS, FRANCIS ORPEN 1810-1893   A Natural History of British Moths, Accurately Delineating Every Known Species. Edinburgh: 1871. 1st edition; royal 8vo; 4 volumes; titles in red and black, 132 hand colored plates, some 1933 figures; beautiful set in half brown straight grained morocco, mottled sides, gilt spines, ornaments, gilt tops, bound by Andy Grieve.   Charles W. Traylen 117-322 1996 £300.00

MORRIS, FRANCIS ORPEN 1810-1893   A Natural History of British Moths. London: Bell and Daldy, 1872. 3rd edition; 8vo; 4 volumes; 132 hand colored plates; green cloth gilt, dust jackets, very rare survival, the dust jackets have few slight tears and small holes, but are generally in sound condition; ownership inscriptions of Florence Acton, 3 Dean's Yard, Westminster, dated August 1878, booklabel of Ruari McLean. Maggs Bros. Ltd. 1190-169 1996 £350.00

MORRIS, FRANCIS ORPEN 1810-1893   Natural History of the Nests and Eggs of British Birds. London: 1875. 3 volumes; numerous colored plates; nicely bound in brown crushed morocco gilt, attractive set. David A.H. Grayling MY95Orn-198 1996 £85.00

MORRIS, GEORGE P.   The Deserted Bride; and Other Poems. New York: 1838. 1st edition; 8vo; original blue cloth, fine, two part half morocco slipcase; earliest known copy, presentation copy to President Martin Van Burne, inscribed in ink by Morris. Rinderknecht 51776; BAL 14355.   M & S Rare Books 60-248 1996 $1,750.00

MORRIS, GEORGE P.   The Little Frenchman and His Water Lots, with Other Sketches of the Times. Philadelphia: Lea & Blanchard, 1839. 1st edition; 8vo; 155 pages, 22 text etchings by D. C. Johnston; original cloth, spine faded, slight wear, but very good. BAL 14356; Wright I 1921; Rinderknecht 57363; not in Johnson.   M & S Rare Books 60-205 1996 $225.00

MORRIS, GOUVERNEUR   The Diary and Letters of Gouverneur Morris.. Da Capo, 1970. Reprint of 1888 edition; large 8vo; 2 volumes; portraits; original cloth.   Howes Bookshop 265-854 1996 $50.00

MORRIS, HARRISON, & CO.   Commercial Directory and Gazetteer of the County of Cumberland. Nottingham: Stafford & Co., 1861. 8vo; subscriber's copy; pages (vi), 324, (74 ads); modern half levant morocco, gilt.   R.F.G. Hollett & Son 78-1122 1996 £85.00

MORRIS, HENRY 1925-   Bird and Bull Pepper Pot. Bird & Bull Press, 1977. One of 250 copies, signed by Morris; 11 1/2 x 9 1/4 inches; 86 pages, (2) leaves (blank, colophon); 89 illustrations in text, many full page, and partly in color, paper samples; errata slip laid in; original half morocco and patterned paper boards, gilt titling on spine, two edges untrimmed; very fine. Taylor & Morris A19.   Phillip J. Pirages 33-81 1996 $300.00

MORRIS, HENRY 1925-   The Private Press-Man's Tale. Newtown: Bird and Bull Press, 1990. One of 230 copies on Arches paper; page size 9 x 12 inches; printed on Arches paper; illustrations by Lili Wronker; maroon cloth and handmade paper over boards.   Priscilla Juvelis 95/1-31 1996 $200.00

MORRIS, J. P.   A Glossary of the Words and Phrases of Furness (North Lancashire). London: J. Russell Smith, 1869. 1st edition; small 8vo; pages xvi, 114, (vi); original wrappers, printed label, small crease in upper board; scarce.   R.F.G. Hollett & Son 78-426 1996 £60.00

MORRIS, THOMAS HOLLINGSWORTH   A.D. 1862, or The volunteer Zouave in Baltimore, by an Officer of the "Guards". Baltimore: J. Davis, 1862. 1st edition; 12mo; 7 pages; sewn, thread broken.   M & S Rare Books 60-206 1996 $125.00

MORRIS, W. P.   The Records of Patterdale. Kendal: T. Wilson, 1903. 1st edition; 8vo; pages 161, 8 plates; original cloth, gilt, extremities little rubbed, partly unopened, scarce; C. Roy Huddleston's copy, with some marginal notes and annotations in places.   R.F.G. Hollett & Son 78-1125 1996 £120.00

MORRIS, WILLIAM 1834-1896   The Art and Craft of Printing. New Rochelle: Elston Press, 1902. Limited to 210 copies; large 8vo; 45 leaves, deckle edged, printed in black and red, frontispiece and first page of text printed within elaborate decorated border, ornate decorated initials, ornaments and decorative tailpiece; plain buckram backed light grayish blue paper covered boards, stained, printed paper label on spine, label slightly chipped; internally near fine, partially unopened.   Blue Mountain SP95-51 1996 $295.00

MORRIS, WILLIAM 1834-1896 The Defence of Guenevere and Other Poems. London: and New York: John Lane and Bodley Head, 1904. 1st edition with these illustrations; 7 3/4 x 5 1/2 inches; 310 pages; half title and title, elaborate headpieces and tailpieces, 29 plates, all by Jessie M. King; original pictorial cloth, covers and spine with gilt titling, decoration and large vignette, top edge gilt, other edges untrimmed; spine bit dulled, slight soiling to cloth, but excellent in all respects, sound and very pleasing. Phillip J. Pirages 33-392 1996 $350.00

MORRIS, WILLIAM 1834-1896 Gothic Architecture: a Lecture for the Arts and Crafts Exhibition Society. Hammersmith: Kelmscott Press, 1893. Limited to 1500 copies; 6 x 4 inches; 68 pages; woodcut initials, linen backed handprinted boards, corners worn, mild darkening, slightly loose. John K. King 77-547 1996 $325.00

MORRIS, WILLIAM 1834-1896 Love is Enough. London: Ellis & White, 1873 but 1872. 1st edition; imperial 16mo; original decorative cloth, gilt in a delightful Morris willow-and-myrtle design by Burn & Co., with their ticket, few minor marks, front endpaper very slightly cracked, few tiny nicks, but very attractive copy still. Forman 37. Ash Rare Books Zenzybyr-71 1996 £195.00

MORRIS, WILLIAM 1834-1896 Love Is Enough, or the Freeing of Pharamond: a Morality. Kelmscott Press, 1897. One of 300 copies on paper (there were also 8 on vellum); 11 1/2 x 8 1/2 inches; 2 p.l., 90 pages; 2 full page woodcut illustrations designed by Edward Burne-Jones & engraved by W.H. Hooper, 1 as frontispiece, other at end, woodcut initials in black or blue, elaborate woodcut full border on 1st page of text, smaller borders on many other pages; ptd. in red, blue & black; fine cont. med. brown mor., handsomely gilt by Douglas Cockerell (signed "19 DC 01" on rear turn-in), covers w/broad frame of linked rectangles & stylized interlaced floral ornaments in corners (front cover w/central panel giving author, title & pub. in lg. letters), spine in very attractive compartments filled w/twining tendrils & many broadleaf stamps, gilt dec. turn-ins w/clusters of sm. inlaid green leaves at corners, edges gilded on rough; covers w/hint of soiling & few marks (one 3/4" superficial scratch on front board), otherwise very fine inside and out, especially appealing binding. Armorial bookplate of Baker Tristram. Sparling 52; Tomkinson p. 121. Phillip J. Pirages 33-320 1996 $6,500.00

MORRIS, WILLIAM 1834-1896 Love is Enough, or the Freeing of Pharamond: a Morality. Hammersmith: Kelmscott Press, 1897/98. Limited to 308 copies, this one of 300; folio; pages (iv), 90, (1), printed in Troy and Chaucer types in red and black, woodcut initials in blue and black, first page of text in wise woodcut border, numerous partial borders, frontispiece and another full page woodcut at end by W. H. Hooper after Burne-Jones; light brown morocco, spine and sides decorated in dark brown with flowers on long stems, spine lettered in brown, wise inner dentelles with border of small circles gilt, top edge gilt, others uncut, marbled endpapers by the Guild of Women Binders, some soiling, extremities bumped, internally an excellent copy. Cockerell 52. Simon Finch 24-139 1996 £1,750.00

MORRIS, WILLIAM 1834-1896 News from Nowhere. Kelmscott Press, 1892. One of 300 copies on paper; 8 1/4 x 6 inches; 3 p.l., 305, (1) pages; woodcut initials, elaborate woodcut frontispiece and full border on first page of text, woodcut device in colophon, printed in red and black; original vellum, yap edges, gilt titling on spine, edges untrimmed, original silk ties intact, quire 'f' and one other binding lightly foxed, otherwise very fine, binding unusually clean and bright. Tomkinson p. 110; Sparling 12. Phillip J. Pirages 33-321 1996 $1,650.00

MORRIS, WILLIAM 1834-1896 The Pilgrims of Hope: a Poem in Thirteen Books. London: brought together from the Commonweal, 1886. 1st collected edition; 7 1/2 x 5 3/4 inches; 69 pages; original printed paper wrappers, in cloth chemise and morocco backed slipcase with raised bands and gilt spine titling, wrapper beginning to come away from text block at top, slight fading to wrapper, two integral leaves creased during printing, otherwise very fine copy of a fragile item; with neat signature of John Caldwell. Phillip J. Pirages 33-393 1996 $450.00

MORRIS, WILLIAM 1834-1896 Signs of Change: Seven Lectures Delivered On Various Occasions. London: Reeves and Turner, 1888. 1st edition; 7 1/2 x 5 1/3 inches; viii, (2), 202 pages; very pleasing apple green crushed morocco, handsomely gilt by the Doves Bindery (signed and dated 1903 on rear turn-in), covers with ususal single gilt rule frame accompanied by spaced gilt dots, spine handsomely gilt in compartments densely occupied by large and small oak leaves and circlets, wide turn-ins with triple gilt fillet and gilt foliate ornament at corners, edges gilt and gauffered, spine just slightly and evenly sunned, free endpapers with shadow from turn-ins (as always), otherwise fine in extremely attractive binding; scarce; with slip laid in reading "61. Signs of Change by William Morris. London, 1888...Lent by Mrs. George M. Millard". Forman 104; Tidcombe 555 (for binding). Phillip J. Pirages 33-61 1996 $1,500.00

MORRIS, WILLIAM 1834-1896 Socialist Diary. Windhover Press, 1981. One of 200 copies; 8 x 6 inches; 2 p.l., ix, (1) pages, (1) leaf, 35, (3) pages; one red initial, title in red and black; original cloth and paper over boards, spine and back board in cloth, front board covered with paper, paper label on spine, edges untrimmed; as new; Berger 61. Phillip J. Pirages 33-515 1996 $125.00

MORRIS, WILLIAM 1834-1896 Under an Elm-Tree; or, Thoughts in the Countryside. Aberdeen: James Leatham, 1891. 1st edition; wrappers, two sheets, folded and stitched to make 16 pages, upper outer panel being titlepage, lower outer panel being the final page of text, on verso of titlepage there is a list of publisher's "Penny Pamphlets', covers dusty, cover edges browned and slightly rubbed and spotted; very good; from the library of James D. Hart. Ulysses 39-418 1996 £155.00

MORRIS, WILLIAM 1834-1896 The World of Romance. London: J. Thomson, 1906. 1st edition; 12mo; original binding, top edge dusty, head and tail of spine and corners slightly bumped, title label on spine chipped and browned, spine slightly faded, endpaper edges browned and slightly nicked, page edges slightly browned, upper hinge partially cracked, good. Ulysses 39-419 1996 £110.00

MORRIS, WILLIAM O'CONNOR Letters on the Land Question of Ireland. London: 1870. 1st collected edition; 8vo; folding map, pages (2 ads), xvii, 348; original cloth, inside hinges cracked, small snag at tail of spine, internally very good to nice. James Fenning 133-241 1996 £85.00

MORRIS, WILLIAM, & CO. Metal Casements, Stained Glass & Decorative Ironwork. Westminster: Ruskin House, Rochester Row, c. 1922. Folio; 200 pages, printed on brown, grey and white papers, profusely illustrated, mainly in line, but with 4 blueprints, 23 tipped in color illustrations of stained glass and color illustration; publisher's coarse brown linen, front cover elaborately decorated in black (back cover slightly dust soiled and few pages little foxed, otherwise nice). Thomas Thorp 489-225 1996 £220.00

MORRIS, WRIGHT 1910- The Inhabitants. New York: London: 1946. 1st edition; illustrations; dust jacket slightly rubbed at edges. J. B. Muns 154-206 1996 $150.00

MORRISON, ALFRED Catalogue of the Collection of Autograph Letters and Historical Documents Formed Between 1865 and 1882 by Alfred Morrison. London: printed for Private Circulation, 1883-92. 1st edition; limited to 200 copies; large folio; pages (4), 265, (3); (4), 273; (4), 337; (4), 336; (4), 442; 5 volumes of 6, lacking volume 2; 166 tinted litho plates, some folding, many facsimiles in text; original holland backed boards, paper labels, little rubbed and soiled, volume 1 in paper backed boards, backstrip worn, but sides secure, internally fine, uncut and partly unopened. Claude Cox 107-321 1996 £80.00

MORRISON, ARTHUR R. The Painters of Japan. New York: Stokes, 1911. 1st U.S. edition; folio; 2 volumes; 122 plates, black and white collotypes and color half tones; scarlet cloth with gilt devices and lettering, brilliant set with scarce printed dust jackets (some tears and chips); Marilyn Braiterman 15-148 1996 $400.00

MORRISON, HENRIETTA My Summer in the Kitchen. Indianapolis: Douglas & Carlon, Pritners, 1878. 1st and only edition; 12mo; (137) pages; original blindstamped cloth, gilt lettered front, minor wear to extremities, otherwise fine, scarce. Banta, Indiana Authors, p. 213; 1 copy in NUC. Paulette Rose 16-234 1996 $225.00

MORRISON, JAMES The Journal of James Morrison Boatswain's Mate of the Bounty. London: Golden Cockerel Press, 1935. Limited to 325 copies; quarto; 243 pages; in 'sail type' binding of navy blue and white cloth, extremely fine in original glassine wrapper. Chanticleer 102. Bromer Booksellers 87-74 1996 $750.00

MORRISON, MABEL The Quest of Joy - Fragments from Manuscripts. London: privately printed for lady Gatty, n.d. 1935. 1st edition; 14 black and white plates, on titlepage there is a black and white woodcut by W. Hughes after a drawing by T. Higham, typography by Faber and Faber, printed on laid paper; top edge gilt, pages unopened, original binding, head of spine very slightly bumped, covers slightly bowed, free endpapers partially browned, upper hinge partially cracked, very good. Ulysses 39-450 1996 £145.00

MORRISON, ROBERT Horae Sinicae: Translations from the Popular Literature of the Chinese. London: printed for Black and Parry; J. Black; T. Williams and Josiah Conder.. 1812. 1st edition; 8vo; original tan boards, neatly rebacked; very good, uncut, very scarce. Cordier 1683. Ximenes 109-203 1996 $400.00

MORRISON, TONI Beloved. New York: Knopf, 1987. Uncorrected proof; wrappers; near fine. Ken Lopez 74-329 1996 $175.00

MORRISON, TONI Jazz. New York: knopf, 1992. 1st edition; signed by author; very fine in dust jacket. Captain's Bookshelf 38-169 1996 $125.00

MORRISON, TONI   Sula. New York: Knopf, 1974. 1st edition; this copy has a vertical crease to the cloth on rear cover, minor binder's flaw, but still at least near fine in near fine dust jacket; quite scarce.   Ken Lopez 74-328 1996 $1,000.00

MORSE, EDWARD S.   Japanese Homes and their Surroundings. New York: Harper, 1895. 1st edition; small 4to; vivid gilt, silver and red pictorial blue cloth; fine, bright copy. Hitchcock 803.   Marilyn Braiterman 15-149 1996 $250.00

MORSE, PETER   Jean Charlot's Prints. A Catalogue Raisonne. Honolulu: University Press of Hawaii and the Jean Charlot Foundation, 1976. Limited to 200 copies (this copy not numbered); square folio; xviii, 450 pages; frontispiece, 16 color plates, 714 black and white illustrations; with original etching signed by Charlot laid in rear pocket; blue calf over yellow cloth, slipcase.   Kenneth Karmiole 1NS-193 1996 $300.00

MORTIMER, FAVELL LEE, MRS.   The Peep of Day, Translated Into Tamil. Madras: The Tract and Book Society, American Mission Press, 1852. 8vo; vi, (228) pages, text printed wholly in Tamil; recently bound in half calf with marbled sides, spine gilt and lettered; very good. Not in NUC.   John Drury 82-191 1996 £75.00

MORTIMER, J. R.   Forty Years' Researches in British & Saxon Burial Mounds of East Yorkshire Including Romano-British Discoveries and a Description of the Ancient Entrenchments on a Section of the Yorkshire Wolds. London: & Hull: 1905. 4to; lxxxvi, 452 pages; colored map, folding table, 125 plates, over 1000 illustrations, lacks plate 80 because unfortunately plate 82 has been bound in twice; half green calf, back board spotted, otherwise very good.   K Books 441-345 1996 £130.00

MORTIMER, JOHN   Answer Yes or No. London: Bodley Head, 1950. 1st edition; very good in very good dust jacket.   Limestone Hills 41-104 1996 $115.00

MORTIMER, JOHN   Answer Yes or No. London: Bodley Head, 1950. 1st edition; very good with edges lightly worn and unavoidable offset, in dust jacket with rubbing, edge wear and light soiling.   Quill & Brush 102-1338 1996 $100.00

MORTIMER, JOHN   Charade. London: Bodley Head, 1947. 1st edition; author's first book; fine in near fine dust jacket, with edges lightly rubbed.   Quill & Brush 102-1336 1996 $250.00

MORTIMER, JOHN   Like Men Betrayed. London: Collins, 1953. 1st edition; very good with spine ends and tips lightly bumped and light soiling on page edges, very good dust jacket with tips nicked, few closed tears and back panel soiled; with two ALS's included discussing an invitation to join P.E.N.   Quill & Brush 102-1339 1996 $150.00

MORTIMER, JOHN   Rumming Park. London: Bodley Head, 1948. 1st edition; author's second book; very good with spine slightly cocked and light foxing on page edges, in dust jacket with several chips, few small closed tears and soiling.   Quill & Brush 102-1337 1996 $200.00

MORTIMER, JOHN   Will Shakespare. London: Hodder and Stoughton, 1977. 1st edition; signed on frontispiece, fine in dust jacket with light rubbing around edges.   Quill & Brush 102-1348 1996 $100.00

MORTIMER, W. GOLDEN   Peru, History of Coca: "The Divine Plant" of the Incas. New York: 1901. 1st edition; 576 pages; original binding. GM 2040.1.   W. Bruce Fye 71-1476 1996 $350.00

MORTIMER, WILLIAM WILLIAMS   The History of the Hundred of Wirral with a Sketch of the City and County of Chester. London: Birkenhead and Chester, 1847. 4to; half title, title, pages xvii, 3 ff. subscribers, 440, 36 pages, 2 folding maps, 10 litho plates, printed table; half calf, rubbed; scarce.   Marlborough 162-71 1996 £150.00

MORTON, A. C.   Report on the St. Lawrence and Atlantic Railroad, Its Influence on the Trade of the St. Lawrence and Statistics of the Cost and Traffic of the New York and Massachusetts Rail-Roads. Montreal: 1849. Pages 47; large folding map; TPL 8028 incomplete copy of later reprint.   Stephen Lunsford 45-122 1996 $250.00

MORTON, A. S.   Beyond the Palaeocrystic Sea or the Legend of Halfjord. Chicago: 1895. 1st edition; f.e.p. gone, slight wear at spine extremities, otherwise solid very good; inscribed by author.   Aronovitz 57-835 1996 $275.00

MORTON, DESMOND   Telegrams of the North-West Campaign, 1885. Toronto: Champlain Society, 1972. 1st edition; limited to 1000 copies; ciii, 431 pages; portrait, 5 maps; original gilt lettered red cloth; fine.   Argonaut Book Shop 113-124 1996 $150.00

MORTON, PETER   Fire Across the Desert; Woomera and the Anglo-Australian Joint Project 1946-1980. Canberra: AGPS Press for the Department of Defence, 1989. 4to; 575 pages; photos, some in color, diagrams and drawings; fine in fine dust jacket.   Knollwood Books 70-463 1996 $135.00

MORTON, RICHARD   Phthisiologia Seu Exercitationes de Phthisi Tribus Libris Comprehendae. Londini: Impensis Sam. Smith, 1689. 1st edition; 8vo; license leaf, fine engraved portrait, (xxii), 411 pages, errata leaf and final blank leaf, original speckled panelled calf, spine gilt, red morocco label, tip of lower outer corner of title torn off, nowhere near text, upper joint cracked at head and foot, small defectve spot in calf on spine at top of upper joint, but fine. Wing M2381; GM 3216.   David Bickersteth 133-211 1996 £675.00

MORTON, THOMAS 1575-1646   New English Canaan,, or New Canaan. London: printed for Charles Greene and sold in Pauls Church-yard, 1632? 1st edition; 8vo; 188, (3) pages; full recent calf, five raised bands on spine, unlettered, uncut, with title a distinguishable but close facsimile, otherwise and excellent copy of a great rarity. Sabin 51028. Streeter II 616.   M & S Rare Books 60-382 1996 $5,250.00

MORTON, THOMAS G.   The History of the Pennsylvania Hospital 1751-1895. Philadelphia: 1895. 1st edition; 573 pages; original binding. W. Bruce Fye 71-1478 1996 $150.00

MORTON, THOMAS, BP. OF COVENTRY & LICHFIELD   Of the Institution of the Sacrament of the Blessed Bodie and Blood of Christ. London: by W. Stansby for Robert Mylbourne, 1631. Folio; 10 leaves + 255 pages, 143 pages, 16 pages; contemporary sprinkled calf, 5 raised bands, double fillet border in blind on each cover, upper cover with coat of arms painted in heraldic colors in centre; bookplate of Hickman Barrt (sic). Joints rubbed, head of spine tape renewed. Painted arms on English bindings are rare. STC 18189.   H. M. Fletcher 121-67 1996 £850.00

MORTON, WILLIAM T. G.   Sulphuric Ether. Thirtieth Congress - Second Session. Report No. 114. Washington: 1949. 1st edition; 8vo; disbound. Osler 1407.   Argosy 810-363 1996 $125.00

MOSCATI, SABATINO   The Phoenicians. Milan: Bompiani, 1988. 4to; 765 pages; over 1000 illustrations (many in color); stiff wrappers. Archaeologia Luxor-2475 1996 $250.00

MOSELEY, HENRY N.   Notes by a Naturalist. London: John Murray, 1892. 8vo; pages xxiv, 540, 4 ads; portrait, folding map, text illustrations; new quarter tan morocco, some light foxing. Ferguson 12883b; Snow 721; Spence 820.   Richard Adelson W94/95-127 1996 $225.00

MOSELEY, HENRY N.   Notes by a Naturalist. New York/London: G. P. Putnam's/John Murray, 1892. 8vo; frontispiece, xxiv, folding map, 540 pages, plus 4 pages ads; illustrations; cloth is very age darkened, wear at corners and head and heel of spine. Spence 820.   Parmer Books Nat/Hist-081306 1996 $125.00

MOSELEY, HENRY N.   Notes by a Naturalist, an Account of Observations Made During the Voyage of the H.M.S. "Challenger" Round the World in the Yars 1872-1876. New York: London: G. P. Putnam's/John Murray, 1892. 8vo; 540 pages, plus 4 pages ads, illustrations; tan cloth, spine label; spine and boards darkened, library blindstamp on titlepage, decorative bookplate of James Clark White, small signature of Chas. L. Camp Dec. 1919, else very good.   Parmer Books Nat/Hist-077042 1996 $195.00

MOSELEY, SYDNEY A.   Television To-Day and Tomorrow. New York: Pitman, 1930. 1st American edition; 8vo; xxiii, 130 pages; frontispiece, 46 plates, 38 figures in text; original cloth, gilt, slight wear to extremities, else near fine.   Edwin V. Glaser 121-218 1996 $200.00

MOSER, BARRY   An Alphabet. Northampton: Pennyroyal Press, 1986. Limited to 150 copies; signed by Moser; octavo; (56) pages; each letter printed from calligraphy of Yvette Rutledge, presented in a different color followed by full page wood engraving by Moser; full gray morocco, blindstamped with Rutledges's alphabet; mint, at publication price. Bromer Booksellers 87-251 1996 $600.00

MOSER, J. F.   The Salmon and Salmon Fisheries of Alaska... Washington: 1902. 1st edition; 4to; 47 maps and plates; dark blue cloth, bit soiled.   Maggs Bros. Ltd. 1190-209 1996 £90.00

MOSLEY, OSWALD   The Natural History of Tutbury, Together with the Fauna and Flora of the District Surrounding Turbury and Hurton on Trent. London: 1863. Royal 8vo; appendix, 7 tinted and colored and 2 plain plates; original cloth; rare.   Charles W. Traylen 117-321   1996 £50.00

MOSLEY, WALTER   Devil in a Blue Dress. New York: Norton, 1990. Advance reading copy; wrappers, fine.   Between the Covers 43-169 1996 $150.00

MOSLEY, WALTER   Devil in a Blue Dress. New York: Norton, 1990. 1st edition; fine in dust jacket, signed by author.   Lame Duck Books 19-371   1996 $150.00

MOSLEY, WALTER   Devil in a Blue Dress. New York: Norton, 1990. 1st edition; fine in dust jacket, signed by author.   Between the Covers 43-168   1996 $125.00

MOSLEY, WALTER   Devil in a Blue Dress. New York: Norton, 1990. 1st edition; fine in dust jacket.   Lame Duck Books 19-372   1996 $100.00

MOSLEY, WALTER   Devil in a Blue Dress. New York: Norton, 1990. 1st edition; fine in dust jacket and signed by author.   Anacapa House 5-234   1996 $100.00

MOSLEY, WALTER   A Red Death. New York: Norton, 1991. Uncorrected proofs; red wrappers; fine.   Between the Covers 43-171 1996 $200.00

MOSLEY, WALTER   A Red Death. New York: Norton, 1991. 1st edition; fine in dust jacket, signed by author.   Lame Duck Books 19-373   1996 $125.00

MOSLEY, WALTER   A Red Death. New York: Norton, 1991. 1st edition; fine in dust jacket; signed by author.   Between the Covers 43-170   1996 $100.00

MOSLEY, WALTER   White Butterfly. New York: Norton, 1922. 1st edition; fine in dust jacket; signed by author.   Between the Covers 43-172   1996 $100.00

MOSLEY, WALTER   White Butterfly. New York: Norton, 1992. Uncorrected proof copy, (advance reading copy); with laminated wrappers similar to finished jacket art; fine, signed by author; very scarce.   Between the Covers 43-173   1996 $250.00

MOSLEY, WALTER   White Butterfly. New York: Norton, 1992. 1st edition; fine in dust jacket, signed by author.   Lame Duck Books 19-375   1996 $175.00

MOSLEY, WALTER   White Butterfly. New York: Norton, 1992. 1st edition; fine in fine dust jacket, scarce, signed.   Alice Robbins 15-246 196 $125.00

MOSS, JAMES A.   Memories of the Campaign of Santiago. San Francisco: Mysell Rollins for the author, 1899. 1st edition; quarto; 68 pages; photos, folding map; leatherette covers skinned on boards along edges of spine which has perished and been professionally restored with burgundy cloth spine sound, about very good copy, rare.   Between the Covers 43-411 1996 $350.00

MOSS, ROSALIND   The Life After Death in Oceania and the Malay Archipelago. Oxford: Oxford University Press, 1925. 247 pages & 2 maps; original green gilt cloth, spine slightly faded, otherwise very good. Very scarce.   Antipodean 28-106   1996 $225.00

MOTELAMBERT, COUNT DE   The Monks of the West from St. Benedict to St. Bernard. 1861-79. 8vo; 7 volumes; cloth drying and flaking, needs rebinding, text good.   C. P. Hyland 216-506   1996 £55.00

MOTHER GOOSE   Denslow's Mother Goose A.B.C. Book. New York: Dillingham, 1904. 4to; colored illustrations by W. W. Denslow; stiff colored pictorial wrappers, wrappers little dusty, else fresh; scarce. Barbara Stone 70-10   1996 £195.00

MOTHER GOOSE   Mother Goose Nursery Tales. London: J. Coker, n.d. Large 4to; 74 pages; 16 color plates, numerous two tone and black and white illustrations; colored pictorial boards; light wear to covers, else very good.   Marjorie James 19-156   1996 £65.00

MOTHER GOOSE   Mother Goose. London: William Heinemann, 1913. 1st edition deluxe, limited to only 1130 numbered copies, signed by artist; 4to; pages (xiv), 3-159, 13 beautiful mounted colored plates on brown stock, by Arthur Rackham, tissue guards; original white buckram, gilt, top edge gilt, others uncut, spine browned, otherwise fine. Sotheran PN32-145   1996 £1,250.00

MOTHER GOOSE   Mother Goose in Washington. Harrisburg: Telegraph Press, 1936. 1st edition; 4to; illustrations by Will H. Chandlee and Alden Turner; blue checked pictorial cloth; spine ends worn, else nice in chipped pictorial dust jacket; very scarce.   Barbara Stone 70-156 1996 £75.00

MOTHER GOOSE   Mother Goose. New York: Heritage Club, 1938. Folio; over 140 pages of lithographed illustrations in color and black and white by roger Duvoisin; colored pictorial cloth, very fresh, very scarce. Barbara Stone   70-84   1996 £135.00

MOTHER GOOSE   Mother Goose. Portland: Chamberlain Press, 1987. Of an edition of 200 signed by artist, this one of 20 deluxe copies with an extra suite of prints, each signed by artist and with a pencil drawing by artist to colophon; this copy also has a special dedication printed to the colophon page; small quarto; (28) pages; designed, printed and illustrated by Sarah Chamberlain; each page printed within decorated border, also included are 18 proofs of illustrations and borders, including two which were not used in the book, each numbered 'Proof 1' and inscribed by Chamberlain; clotth backed blue boards, with blindstamped leather label to spine, extra suite of prints enclosed in blue cloth chemise, the whole housed in blue cloth dropback box, mint;   Bromer Booksellers   87-117   1996 $1,000.00

MOTHER Hubbard's Grand Party. London: Dean & Son, n.d. 1873? 11.5 x 9.5 inches; (6) pages; 5 color plates; wrappers, covers worn and slightly chipped, some soil, spine resilked.   John K. King 77-668   1996 $125.00

MOTT IRON WORKS   Mott's Stable Fittings. New York: Mott Iron Works, 1910. 9 1/4 x 11 3/4 inches; 251 pages; paper bound, last few pages insect damaged on outer edges only, otherwise clean, complete; good+.   October Farm 36-85   1996 $265.00

MOTT, VALENTINE   Eulogy on the Late John W. Francis, Being a Discourse on His Life and Character. New York: 1861. 1st edition; 33 pages, 2 portraits, original flexible cloth, worn, front cover detached, ex-library.   Argosy 810-364   1996 $100.00

MOTT, VALENTINE   Narrative of Privations and Sufferings of United States Officers and Soldiers While Prisoners of War in the Hands of the Rebel Authorities. Philadelphia: 1864. 1st edition; 283 pages; original binding, rare.   W. Bruce Fye 71-364   1996 $500.00

MOTTELAY, PAUL FLEURY   Bibliographical History of Electricity and Magnetism...Researches into the Domain of the Early Sciences... New York: Martino, 1992. Reprint of London 1922 edition; one of only 300 copies; 8vo; xx, 673 pages; illustrations; original cloth; as new.   Edwin V. Glaser   121-219   1996 $100.00

MOTTRAM, RALPH HALE   Journey to the Western Front - Twenty Years After. London: G. Bell & Sons, Ltd., 1936. 1st edition; maps on endpapers; original binding, top edge dusty, edges slightly spotted, upper cover slightly bubbled, covers slightly cocked, head and tail of spine and corners slightly bumped, free endpapers browned, very good in chipped, frayed, rubbed, torn, creased and dusty dust jacket darkened at spine and edges and missing pieces at head of spine and top edge of upper panel.   Ulysses 39-652   1996 £55.00

MOUBRAY, BONINGTON   A Practical Treatise on Breeding, Rearing and Fattening All Kinds of Domestic Poultry, Pheasants and Rabbits... London: Sherwood, Neely and Jones, 1816. 2nd edition; 12mo; pages xii, 256; contemporary half calf, smooth backstrip divided into compartments by gilt rules and hound's tooth rolls, lettered direct in second, remainder with large central ornament, small area of leather loss at head of front joint, marbled boards, small piece of paper missing from fore-edge of front cover, otherwise excellent. Perkins 987 for 1822 ed.   Blackwell's B112-196   1996 £90.00

MOUNSEY, GEORGE GILL   Authentic Account of the Occupation in 1745, by Prince Charles Edward Stuart. London: Longman and Co., and Carlisle: James Steel, 1846. 8vo; pages x, 270, engraved title, folding plan, 2 woodcut plates, few spots to titles; mss. index and notes on rear endpapers; original cloth, gilt, little faaded and neatly recased; postcard portrait of Duke of Cumberland loosely inserted.   R.F.G. Hollett & Son   78-1127   1996 £85.00

MOUNT EDGCUMBE, RICHARD EDGCUMBE, EARL OF   Muscial Reminiscences, Containing an Account of the Italian Opera in England, from 1773. London: John Andrews; and F. H. Wall, 1834. 4th edition; 12mo; contemporary half morocco, gilt, spine gilt, rather rubbed, but sound; bound without half title, but very good; LAR 2076.   Ximenes 108-118   1996 $250.00

MOUNTAGU, RICHARD   Appello Caesarem. A Just Appeale from Two Unjust Informers. London: H. L. for Mathew Lownes, 1625. 1st edition; one of 3 issues; 4to; (xxvi), 322 pages; contemporary sheep, spine gilt, label, rubbed, spine chafed, label chipped, little soiling of outer leaves; good. STC 18031.   Robert Clark   38-82   1996 £90.00

MOUNTAINE, WILLIAM   The Seaman's Vade-Mecum and Defensive War by Sea... London: printed for W. and J. Mount, T. and T. Page, 1757. 12mo; 2 part folding plate, 2 other folding plates (one tear repaired, without loss), early signatures on front flyeaves of various seamen, beginning with Samuel Brenton of Portsmouth; contemporary unlettered calf, spine gilt; some foxing and few minor stains, but fine; all early edtions are exceedingly uncommon.   Ximenes   108-273 1996 $1,500.00

MOUNTENEY-JEPHSON, A. J.   Emin Pasha and the Rebellion at the Equator...Nine Months' Experiences in the Last of the Soudan Provinces. London: 1890. 1st edition; 8vo; xxiv, 490 pages, folding map, folding plate, illustrations; red pictorial cloth, gilt lettered, cloth slightly marked, some minor staining, otherwise good.   K Books   441-12   1996 £70.00

MOUNTENEY-JEPHSON, A. J.   Emin Pasha and the Rebellion at the Equator. New York: Charles Scribner's Sons, 1890. 8vo; pages xxiv, 490, 2 ads; 22 plates, folding map; original pictorial cloth lightly rubbed, bottom of spine starting. Hoover 1468.   Richard Adelson   W94/95-128 1996 $185.00

MOUNTFORD, CHARLES P.   Ayers Rock: Its People, Their Beliefs and Their Art. Sydney: 1965. 208 pages; illustrations; hardboard, ruffled pictorial dust jacket, good + copy.   Antipodean   28-110 1 996 $125.00

MOUNTFORD, CHARLES P.   Nomads of the Australian Desert. Rigby: 1976. 628 pages, frontispiece, 737 plates in text, 12 color paltes, 33 figures, 1 color fold-out; hardboard, pictorial dust jacket covered in glassine, spine sun faded, otherwise excellent.   Antipodean   28-113 1996 $600.00

MOUNTFORD, CHARLES P.   The Tiwi Their Art, Myth and Ceremony. London: 1958. 1st U.K. edition; 185 pages; 64 plates, 15 drawings, 1 map; tan orange cloth, ex-library, fine.   Antipodean   28-114   1996 $225.00

MOURELLE, DON FRANCISCO ANTONIO   Voyage of the Sonora in the Second Bucareli Expedition to Explore the Northwest Coast, survey the Port of San Francisco, and Found Franciscan Missions and a Presidio and Pueblo at that Port. San Francisco: private press of Thomas C. Russell, 1920. One of 230 copies; 29cm; xii, 120 pages; frontispiece, 2 maps, tables; light blue cloth spine, decorated light blue paper over boards, just a bit of wear and very light soil, near fine, signed by Russell. Hill p. 504-505.   Parmer Books   039/Nautica-039157   1996 $300.00

MOWAT, FARLEY   Never Cry Wolf. Toronto: McClelland & Stewart, 1963. 1st edition; near fine copy of the true first edition, in two radically different dust jackets, one near fine and one very good; scarce.   Ken Lopez   74-330   1996 $150.00

MOWAT, FARLEY   Wake of the Great Sealers. Toronto: McClelland and Stewart, c. 1973. Square 4to; pages 157; illustrations; cloth, dust jacket, slightly worn at corners, else fine.   Hugh Anson-Cartwright 87-300   1996 $100.00

MOWAT, FARLEY   A Whale for the Killing. Toronto: McClelland and Stewart, 1972. Advance review copy of the true first edition; fine in dust jacket with minor edgewear, else near fine.   Ken Lopez   74-331 1996 $125.00

MOWER, ARTHUR   Zulneida: a Tale of Sicily. London: John Macrone, 1837. 1st edition; 12mo.; 3 volumes; original grey boards, purple cloth backtrips, rubbed and faded, printed paper labels, some chipping. very good set, rare. Block p. 168; not in Wolff.   Ximenes   108-274 1996 $350.00

MOXON, JOSEPH   Mechanick Exercises on the Whole Art of Pritning (1683-84). Oxford: 1958. 1st edition; 8vo; pages lxiv, 480; 58 pages, plates, 17 figures in text; original cloth; fine. Booklabel of CUP designer and founder of the Vine Press, John Peters.   Claude Cox   107-323 1996 £85.00

MOYLLUS, DAMIANUS   A Newly Discovered Treatise on Classic Letter Design Printed at Parma by Damianus Moyllus Circa 1480. Officina Bodoni, 1923. One of 222 copies; 11 1/2 x 8 inches; 38 pages, (1) leaf (colophon); device in colophon, printed in blue-gray and black; original vellum over stiff boards, titled in gilt on spine, gitl device on front cover, edges untrimmed and unopened, hint of soil and discoloration to binding, very slightl browning of leaves right at edges, but these defects quite minor and an extremely fine copy in general; bookplates of Paul Hyde Bonner and of Colton Storm, compiler of the catalog of the Graff collection.   Phillip J. Pirages   33-407   1996 $1,250.00

MRABET, MOHAMMED   The Beach Cafe and the Voice. Santa Barbara: Black Sparrow Press, 1980. 1st edition; limited to 200 copies signed by author and translator, Paul Bowles; 8vo; cloth backed decorated boards, acetate dust jacket; as new.   James S. Jaffe   34-81 1996 $100.00

MRABET, MOHAMMED   Harmless Poisons, Blameless sins. Santa Barbara: Black Sparrow, 1976. 1st edition; copy number 5 of 200 numbered copies; fine in unprinted glassine as issued, signed by author and by translator, Paul Bowles.   Between the Covers   42-61   1996 $325.00

MUDIE, ROBERT 1777-1842   The Feathered Tribes of the British Islands. London: Henry G. Bohn, 1853. 4th edition; 8vo; 2 volumes; 422; ii, 440 pages, publisher's ads at end of each volume; hand colored frontispieces and vignettes titles to each volume, 17 hand colored plates, 7 additional hand colored plates, several text illustrations; publisher's dark green cloth, spines gilt, prelims slightly foxed and small neat blindstamp of title of each volume.   Thomas Thorp   489-226   1996 £75.00

MUDIE, ROBERT 1777-1842   The Feathered Tribes of the British Islands. London: 1853. 4th edition; 12mo; 2 volumes, 2 colored vignette titlepages and 26 colored plates; original cloth, trifle used.   Wheldon & Wesley   207-812   1996 £65.00

MUENSCHER, W. C.   Garden Spice and Wild Pot-Herbs. Ithaca: 1954. Limited to 90 copies; 4to; pages ix 211, hand printed and on handmade Japanese Kochi paper; 56 woodcut plates, 1 fold-out plate; half cloth over paper with some stianing to 14 pages, mostly not touching corners and maragins.   Raymond M. Sutton   VI-1083   1996 $165.00

MUENSTER, SEBASTIAN 1489-1552   Der Horologien, Oder Sonnen Uhren, Kunstliche Beschreibung... Basel: Henricpetri, 1579. 2nd edition, but first appearance under this title and first and only with Schmid additions; folio; 2 parts in 1 volume, (8), clvii, (4), cciii-cclxi, (2) pages, woodcut on first title, printer's device on last leaves of each part and on second title, large double page woodcut attributed to Hans Holbein the Younger, and 94 large woodcuts in text; each part with separate titlepage; modern full calf, antique style, some light browning, last few leaves with few stains, some minor expert paper repairs, tap in pagination, as originally issued, book is absolutely complete; very good; with early (probaby 18th century) engraved bookplate. Zeitlinger/Sotheran 4156; Burmeister 53; BM German Books 633.   Edwin V. Glaser 121-221   1996 $6,000.00

MUENTZ, J. H.   Encaustic; or Count Caylus's Method of Painting in the Manner of the Ancients. London: For the author and A. Webley, 1760. 1st edition; foolscap 8vo; viii, 139, ad, (3) page contents, titlepage vignette by H.M. and one plate; complete with half title; full contemporary calf with red gilt label, slight wear to upper joint and head and tail of spine; scarce.   Ken Spelman   30-9   1996 £450.00

MUIR, EDWIN   First Poems. London: 1925. 1st edition; marbled boards, slightly foxed, otherwise very good.   Words Etcetera   94-634 1996 £65.00

MUIR, EDWIN   The Three Brothers. London: William Heinemann, 1951. 1st edition; original binding, top edge dusty, head and tail of spine and one corner slightly bumped, spine and endpaper edges slightly browned, very good in nicked, rubbed, chipped and dusty dust jacket browned at spine and edges and missing a few small pieces at head of spine. Ulysses   39-424   1996 £550.00

MUIR, JOHN 1838-1914   Catalogue of Books in the Library of the Faculty of Procurators in Glasgow. (and) Supplement to the Catalogue of Books. Glasgow: Robert Maclehose and Co., 1903/23. 2 volumes. Meyer Boswell SL26-146 1996 $275.00

MUIR, JOHN 1838-1914   The Cruise of the Corwin. Boston: Houghton Mifflin, 1917. 1st edition; 8vo; pictorial cloth; tape repair to margin of 1 page, splash stain to spine; very good.   Charles Agvent 4-912 1996 $175.00

MUIR, P. H.   Catnachery. San Francisco: Book Club of California, 1955. One of 325 copies; quarto; five folded reproductions of broadsheets; numerous illustrations; original binding, cover edges slightly rubbed and browned, very good.   Ulysses 39-425 1996 £95.00

MUIR, PERCY   English Children's Books. London: 1954. 1st edition; 4to; color and black and white illustrations; very good in dust jacket nicked at extreme head and foot of spine.   Words Etcetera 94-972 1996 £60.00

MUIR, THOMAS   The Theory of Determinants in the Historical Order of Its Development, Part I. London: 1906. 2nd edition; xi, 491 pages, 2 folding charts, top and bottom blank half inch of title cut away, otherwise very good.   Graham Weiner C2-321 1996 £50.00

MUIR, THOMAS   The Theory of Determinants in the Historical Order of Its Development. Volume II 1841-1860. London: 1911. xvi, 475; cloth; good ex-library.   Graham Weiner C2-322 1996 £50.00

MUIRHEAD, ARNOLD   Grace Revere Osler. A Brief Memoir. printed for private circulation at the Oxford University Press, 1931. Limited to 500 copies; 4to; 56 pages; in vellum backed boards.   James Tait Goodrich K40-219 1996 $150.00

MUIRHEAD, ARNOLD   Grace Revere Osler, a Brief Memoir. London: printed for private circulation at Oxford University Press, 1931. 1st edition; 8vo; 35 pages, frontispiece, 2 plates; original vellum backed grey baords; fine, rare; bookplate of Elmer Belt.   Jeff Weber 31-101 1996 $150.00

MUIRHEAD, GEORGE   The Birds of Berwickshire with Remarks on Their Local Distribution, Migration and Habits and Also on the Folk Lore, Proverbs, Popular Rhymes an Sayings Connected With Them. Edinburgh: David Douglasa, 1889. Large paper edition, limited to 100 copies; 8vo; 2 volumes, pages xxvi, 334; xii, 390; uncut, printed on handmade paper; original etching, numerous text illustrations, large folding map; original buckram, gilt, spines rather darkened.   R.F.G. Hollett 76-211 1996 £180.00

MUIRHEAD, GEORGE   The Birds of Berwickshire With Remarks On Their Local Distribution, Migration and Habits and Also on the Folk-Lore, Proverbs, Popular Rhymes and Sayings Connected with Them. Edinburgh: David Douglas, 1889. 8vo; 2 volumes; pages xxvi, 334; xii, 390; numerous text illustrations, large folding map; original cream cloth, gilt, spines rather spotted; presentation set, inscribed by author,   R.F.G. Hollett 76-212 1996 £120.00

MUKERJI, DHAN GOPAL   Gay-Neck; the Story of a Pigeon. New York: Dutton, 1928. Limited to 1000 copies; octavo; xi, 197 pages; signed by author and artist; illustrations by Boris Artzybasheff; three quarter white paper and decorated boards, cover lightly soiled and faded with some slight rubbing to extremities, else near fine. Kerlan p. 12.   Bromer Booksellers 87-106 1996 $150.00

MULBACH, LOUISA   Historical Romances. New York: and London: 1898. Hohenzollen edition limited to 1000 sets; 8vo; plates, 20 volumes; original cloth, gilt tops.   Charles W. Traylen 117-173 1996 £175.00

MULFORD, CLARENCE E.   Hopalong Cassidy. Chicago: 1910. 1st edition; 8vo; 392 pages; five illustrations in color; original colored pictorial boards, cloth back, slightly rubbed at corners.   Edward Morrill 368-547 1996 $150.00

MULGRAVE, CONSTANTINE JOHN PHIPPS, 2ND BARON 1744-1792   A Voyage Towards the North Pole Undertaken by His Majesty's Command 1773. London: printed by W. Bowyer and J. Nichols, for J. Nourse... 1774. 1st edition; 4to; half title, (iii-viii), (1-15), 19-76, 79-253 pages, directions to binder leaf, ink signature to front f.e.p., slight browning to one chart and one plate, otherwise fine, crisp, clean copy internally. Hill Pacific Voyages p. 207. Cox II p. 19.   Beeleigh Abbey BA/56-105 1996 £1,000.00

MULJI, KARSANDAS   History of the Sect of Maha-ra'jas, or Vallabha 'Cha'ryas in Western India. London: Trubner & Co., 1865. 8vo; 2 parts in 1; xvi, 182; (2), 184 pages; frontispiece, few text figures; finely rebound in early 20th century, half maroon morocco over red cloth, cloth lightly rubbed.   Kenneth Karmiole 1NS-128 1996 $200.00

MULLEN, S.   Kinsmen of the Dragon. Shasta Press, 1951. 1st edition; just about fine in spectacular full wrap around color dust jacket. Aronovitz 57-837 1996 $110.00

MULLENS, W. H.   A Bibliography of British Ornithology, from the Earliest Times to the End of 1912. London: 1916-17. Original edition; 8vo; pages xx, 691; original cloth; library bookplate, few small stamps. Rare. Wheldon & Wesley 207-263 1996 £130.00

MULLER, JOSEPH EMILE   Petite Encyclopedie de L'Art. Klee (Picasso, Bonnard, Matisse). Paris: Hazan, 1956-71. 6 x 4 inches; 4 volumes; in different designer bookbindings by Arthur Johnson after the styles of four of the most important artists of the late 19th and 20th century, all with multi-color onlays and blind tooling on covers, spines with the artists' name elegantly stamped in gilt, housed in quarter morocco clamshell case with its own striking design employing onlays and gilt tooling, each signed with binder's initials on lower rear turn-in, dated 1983; absolutely fine.   Book Block 32-32 1996 $2,250.00

MUMEY, NOLE   The Teton Mountains: Their History and Tradition with Any Account of the Early Fur Trade, Trappers... Denver: Artcraft Press, 1947. 1st edition; number 30 of 700 signed copies; etchings, photos; spine slightly skewed and paper spine label stained along one edge, otherwise fine.   Hermitage SP95-723 1996 $150.00

MUMEY, NOLIE   John Williams Gunnison (1812-1853): The Last of the Western Explorers. Denver: Artcraft Press, 1955. 1st edition; number 50 of 500 numbered and signed copies; lightly sunned along top edge, else fine.   Hermitage SP95-724 1996 $150.00

MUMEY, NOLIE   March of the Dragoons: Ford Diary 1835. Denver: Eames, 1957. 1st edition; limited, 298/350 signed copies; 4to; tipped in frontispiece, tipped in errata slip on limitation page, 3 illustrations, folding map (very good+) tipped in on rear endpaper; hinge starting, bookplate, else very good.   Parker Books of the West 30-133 1996 $125.00

MUMEY, NOLIE   Poker Alice - Alice Ivers, Duffield, Tubbs, Hucker... Denver: 1951. 1st edition; copy 499 of 500, signed; 47 pages; photos, folding map; stiff printed wrpaeprs; nice. 6 Guns 1568.   T. A. Swinford 49-821 1996 $150.00

MUMFORD, ERASMUS   A Letter to the Club at White's. London: for W. Owen, 1750. 1st edition; 8vo; 40 pages; wanting half title, recently well bound in linen backed marbled boards, lettered; very good; Kress 5059; not in Goldsmiths, Hanson or Black.   John Drury 82-193 1996 £250.00

MUMMERY, A. F.   My Climbs in the Alps and Caucasus. London: 1895. 3rd edition, same year and format as the 1st; 11 plates; original binding, gilt lettering on black leather labels on cream linen; little soiled and with base of spine rubbed, some foxing of first 3 pages, very good, sound copy.   Moutaineering Books 8-EM02 1996 £160.00

MUNARI, BRUNO   Circus in the Mist. New York: World Pub. Co., 1969. 1st American edition; small 4to; semi translucent pages illustrated in silhouette, pages of different hues and textures, with cut out shapes create brilliant surprises on every page, white glazed boards, pictorially stamped in colors, fine in original pictorial dust jacket.   Barbara Stone 70-157 1996 £150.00

MUNARI, BRUNO   Tic, Tac and Toc. New York: World Publishing Co., 1957. 1st edition; tall 4to; moveable, with pages cut to different sizes, peepholes and lift up flaps; colored illustrations; cloth backed pictorial boards, fresh, scarce.   Barbara Stone 70-158 1996 £125.00

MUNBY, A. N. L.   British Book Sale Catalogues 1676-1800: a Union List. London: Mansell, 1977. 1st edition; 4to; frontispiece; original cloth. Forest Books 74-194 1996 £75.00

MUNBY, A. N. L.   Some Caricatures of Book-Collectors, an Essay. London: William H. Robinson, 1948. 1st edition; 8vo; 32 pages; wrappers; very scarce, covers handled, still nice.   The Bookpress 75-330 1996 $110.00

MUNCASTER, MARTIN   The Wind in the Oak. Robin Garton, 1978. Limited to 100 numbered copies, signed by author; 315 x 230mm; 2 volumes; 120 pages, 37 illustrations; with portfolio of 12 separate original etchings by artist; uniformly bound, publisher's quarter blue morocco, cloth slipcase.   Thomas Thorp 489-227 1996 £165.00

MUNDY, GODFREY CHARLES   Our Antipodes: or, Residence and Rambles in the Australasian Colones with a Glimpse of the Gold Fields. London: Richard Bentley, 1852. 2nd edition; 8vo; 3 volumes; xii, 410; viii, 405; viii, 431 pages; original gilt decorated blue cloth, good with wear to all edges, spotting and soil.   Parmer Books 039/Nautica-039202 1996 $700.00

MUNDY, TALBOT   King of the Khyber Rifles. Indianapolis: Bobbs Merrill, 1916. 1st edition; slight scuffing to edges of cloth, overall very good in very worn jacket, missing a number of sizable pieces, still very scarce in any jacket.   Ken Lopez 74-332 1996 $475.00

MUNDY, TALBOT   Queen Cleopatra. B-M, 1929. 1st edition; 1/265 copies, specially bound and signed by author; fine.   Aronovitz 57-840 1996 $375.00

MUNFORD, WILLIAM   Poems, and Compositions in Prose on Several Occasions. Richmond: printed by Samuel Pleasants, Jun., 1798. Only edition despite the fact that p. 7 contains "To the Reader of the Second Edition"; 8vo; pages (2), 189, (1); contemporary calf backed boards; mildly foxed, front joint repaired at inner fold Evans 34159; Sabin 51317; Hill 194; Wegelin 279; Quinn p. 427.   Howard S. Mott 227-102 1996 $350.00

MUNILLA, MARTIN DE   His Journal and Other Documents Relating to the Voyages of Pedro Fernandez de Quiros to the south Sea (1605-1606) and the Franciscan Missnary Plan (1617-1627). Cambridge: Cambridge University Press, 1966. 1st edition; octavo; 2 volumes, pages 270, 273 (32 page bibliography), 31 page index); 15 early maps and plates; blue cloth, gilt decorations to covers; fine set in acetate jackets.   Hartfield 48-V20 1996 $135.00

MUNK, WILLIAM   The Roll of the Royal College of Physicians of London; Comprising Biographical Sketches. London: 1878-1968. 2nd edition; 5 volumes; original binding. GM 6715.   W. Bruce Fye 71-1491 1996 $200.00

MUNN, HENRY TOKE   Prairie Trails and Arctic By-Ways. London: Hurst and Blackett, 1932. 8vo; 288 pages; illustrations; gilt cloth, covers rubbed and slightly stained, else very good.   Hugh Anson-Cartwright 87-301 1996 $150.00

MUNNINGS, A. J.   Pictures of Horses and English Life. London: Eyre & Spottiswoode, 1939. 2nd edition; 4to; original binding, very good.   October Farm 36-50 1996 $425.00

MUNNINGS, ALFRED   The Autobiography. London: Museum Press, 1950/51/52. 1st editions; 3 volumes; some corners slightly bruised, gilt on spine of volumes 1 and 2 slightly rubbed, otherwise very good set in slightly chipped and rubbed dust jackets.   Virgo Books 48-140 1996 £110.00

MUNRO, ALICE   Dance of the Happy Shades. Stories. Toronto: Ryerson Press, 1958. 1st edition; author's first book; fine in dust jacket; signed by author.   Captain's Bookshelf 38-170 1996 $375.00

MUNRO, ALICE   Lives of Girls and Women. Toronto: McGraw Hill Ryerson, 1971. 1st edition; front pastedown scuffed, otherwise near fine in very good dust jacket.   Ken Lopez 74-333 1996 $125.00

MUNRO, ALICE   The Progress of Love. Toronto: McClelland and Stewart, 1986. 1st edition; fine in fine dust jacket.   Ken Lopez 74-334 1996 $100.00

MUNRO, H. H.   Beasts and Super Beasts. London: John Lane, 1914. 1st edition; very good.   Robert Gavora 61-102 1996 $125.00

MUNRO, ROBERT   Ancient Scottish Lake-Dwellings or Crannogs... Edinburgh: David Douglas, 1882. 1st edition; 8vo; pages xx, 326; 4 plates and 264 text illustrations; original cloth, gilt, slightly worn.   R.F.G. Hollett 76-213 1996 £85.00

MUNSON, D.   Foundations of American Grape Culture. New York: Orange Judd, 1909. 1st edition; 252 pages, index, list of illustrations.   Maggie Lambeth 30-388 1996 $200.00

MURAKAMI, HARUKI   The Elephant Vanishes. New York: Knopf, 1993. Uncorrected proof; bottom corners of several pages bent, otherwise fine in wrappers.   Between the Covers 42-320 1996 $100.00

MURATOFF, PAUL   Thirty-Five Russian Primitives. Paris: A La Vielle Russie, 1931. 4to; 116 pages, 20 plates; paper wrappers, damaged at head and tail.   Rainsford A54-435 1996 £65.00

MURCHISON, R. I.   Outline of the Geology of the Neighbourhood of Cheltenham. London: 1845. 2nd edition; 8vo; 109 pages, folding map, section, both hand colored, 13 plates; cloth, small piece missing from top of spine; scarce.   John Henly 27-525 1996 £90.00

MURCHISON, R. I.   The Silurian System, Founded on Geological Researches in the Counties of Salop, Hereford, Radnor, Montgomery, Caermarthen, Brecon, Pembroke, Monmouth, Gloucester, Worcester and Stafford. London: 1839. royal 4to; 2 parts in one volume; pages xxxii, 768, 14 lithographic plates, 3 are hand colored and 2 folding, 31 plates, 9 horizontal sections, hand colored and folding, 3 plain maps, 112 woodcut text figures; in separate slipcase is the large hand colored geological map in 3 sections, linen backed; recent half calf.   John Henly 27-526 1996 £1,980.00

MURDOCH, IRIS   The Bell. London: Chatto & Windus, 1958. 1st edition; very good copy in near fine dust jacket, shadow on f.e.p., slight dust jacket wear. Nov. 1958 Book Soc. Choice ribbon.   Book Time 2-308 1996 $160.00

MURDOCH, IRIS   The Bell. London: Chatto & Windus Ltd., 1958. 1st edition; original binding, top edge dusty, free endpapers partially browned, edges spotted, very good in nicked, spotted, rubbed and dusty, slightly marked dust jacket, browned at spine and edges; from the library of Ian Parsons, publisher of this book.   Ulysses 39-429 1996 £85.00

MURDOCH, IRIS   The Flight from the Enchanter. London: Chatto & Windus, 1956. 1st edition; original binding, top edge dusty, head and tail of spine and corners slightly bumped, bottom edge partially browned, fore-edge spotted, very good in nicked, spotted and slightly rubbed, soiled, marked and dusty dust jacket by Edward Bawden, browned at spine and edges; with pencilled ownership signature of publisher of this book, Ian Parsons.   Ulysses 39-428 1996 £355.00

MURDOCH, IRIS   The Flight from the Enchanter. London: Chatto & Windus Ltd., 1956. 1st edition; original binding, top edge dusty, head and tail of spine and corners slightly bumped, bottom edge partially browned, fore-edge spotted, very good in nicked, spotted and slightly rubbed, soiled, marked and dusty dust jacket, by Edward Bawden, browned at spine and edges, with pencilled ownership signature of publisher of this book, Ian Parsons.   Ulysses 39-428 1996 £355.00

MURDOCH, IRIS   Under the Net. London: Chatto & Windus, 1954. 1st edition; original binding, top edge slightly dusty, head of spine slightly bumped, edges spotted, rear free endpaper slightly creased, very good in nicked, spotted and dusty, slightly creased dust jacket faded at spine and slightly darkened at edges; fomr the library of Ian Parsons, publisher of this book.   Ulysses 39-427 1996 £375.00

MURDOCH, IRIS   A Year of Birds. Poems. Tisbury, Wiltshire: Compton Press, 1978. 1st edition; 1857/350 copies; crown 8vo; pages (29); printed on Zerkall mouldmade paper and signed by author and artist; wood engraved title design and 12 other wood engravings by Reynolds Stone; original quarter tan cloth, backstrip gilt lettered blue, brown and yellow marbled boards; fine.   Blackwell's B112-197 1996 £95.00

MURDOCH, JOHN   The Dictionary of Distinctions, in Three Alphabets. London: printed for C. Law; Longman, Hurst..., Lackington, Allen... 1811. 2 pages ads, uncut in original drab boards, well executed spine repairs, paper label chipped, very good.   Jarndyce 103-200 1996 £140.00

MURPHY, ARTHUR   The Desert Island. London: printed for P. Vaillant, 1760. 1st edition; 8vo; A-H4, engraved frontispiece, A2 cropped, portion of last leaf replaced affecting headline, disbound.   H. M. Fletcher 121-116 1996 £40.00

MURPHY, DENIS   The Annals of Clonmacnoise. London: 1896. 1st edition; 8vo; cloth, ex-library, but very good.   C. P. Hyland 216-537 1996 £110.00

MURPHY, DERVIA   Muddling through in Madagascar. London: John Murray, 1985. 1st edition; 16 pages of black and white photos, one map; original binding, head and tail of spine slightly bumped, edges slightly marked and dusty, very good in slightly creased dust jacket; presentation copy from author, inscribed.   Ulysses 39-430 1996 £55.00

MURPHY, J. MORTIMER   Sporting Adventures in the Far West. New York: Harper & Bros., 1880. 1st American edition; engravings; very good. Parker Books of the West 30-134 1996 $125.00

MURPHY, JAMES   Travels in Portugal...Consisting of Observations on the Manners, Customs, Tade, Public Buildings, Arts, Antiquities &c. London: Strachan, Cadell and Davies. 1795. 4to; xii, 311 pages, 24 engraved plates; new half calf, few small library stamps on verso of plates. Cox I p. 165.   Marlborough 162-240 1996 £550.00

MURPHY, JOHN MORTIMER   Sporting Adventures in the Far West. London: Sampson Low, Marston, Searle and Rivington, 1879. 1st edition; original cloth lightly soiled, half inch split in top front joint, but barely worn, text unopened; coated front free endpaper has old scotch tape reinforcement. Riling (1951 ed.) 1051.   Magnum Opus 44-55 1996 $100.00

MURPHY, R. C.   Oceanic Birds of South America. New York: Macmillan, 1948. 4to; 2 volumes; 16 colored and 72 plain plates and 80 text figures; original buckram.   Wheldon & Wesley 207-814 1996 £140.00

MURRAY, A.   Botanical Expedition to Oregon... Edinburgh: 1853. 4to; drophead title, 2 leaves of text, 5 lithographed plates by Lizars after Grenville; old wrappers, bit worn.   Maggs Bros. Ltd. 1190-119 1996 £120.00

MURRAY, A.   The Geographical Distribution of Mammals. London: 1866. 4to; pages xvi, 420, 2 colored plates, 103 colored maps on 61 leaves; original cloth. Blindstamps on titlepage and plates.   Wheldon & Wesley 207-590 1996 £170.00

MURRAY, A.   Geographical Distribution of Mammals. London: 1866. large 4to; 420 pages, 2 color plates, 103 color maps;   John Johnson 135-473 1996 $200.00

MURRAY, A. S.   Terracotta Sarcophagi: Greek and Etruscan in the British Museum. London: British Museum, 1898. Folio; 25 pages, 5 figures, 11 plates; three quarter calf, joint on top board borken, rubbed, interior fine.   Archaeologia Luxor-3734 1996 $150.00

MURRAY, A. W.   Missions in Western Polynesia: Being Historical Sketches of These Missions, from Their Commencement in 1839 to the Present Time. London: John Snow, 1863. 1st edition; tall 8vo; (xii), 489, 16 pages ads; illustrations; original blue cloth, cloth rubbed, with wear to extremities, otherwise very good. Hill I p. 207.   David Mason 71-146 1996 $200.00

MURRAY, AMELIA   Letters from the United States, Cuba and Canada. New York: G. P. Putnam's, 1856. 1st U.S. edition; 8vo; 410 pages; original tan cloth, spine faded which makes gilt lettering difficult to read, some light wear to spine ends, otherwise near fine.   David Mason 71-125 1996 $120.00

MURRAY, CHARLES AUGUSTUS 1806-1895   The Prairie Bird. London: Richard Bentley, 1844. 1st edition; 8vo; 3 volumes; original boards, minor shelf wear, paper labels; with "Escrick Park" labels on front, covers and ownership signature "Wenlock". Graf 2939; Sabin 51489; Wagner Camp 112.1. Wolff 5022; Sadleir 1818.   Howard S. Mott 227-103 1996 $300.00

MURRAY, CHARLES AUGUSTUS 1806-1895   Travels in North America During the Years 1834, 1835 and 1836. London: Richard Bentley, 1839. 1st edition; 8vo; 2 volumes, frontispiece in each volume, tissue guard in volume 1, prelim and final leaves lightly foxed, early ownership signature at head of each titlepage, pages xvi, 473; xi, (i), 372; original horizontal grain purple cloth, backstrips very faded, gilt lettered direct, blindstamped border on all sides, yellow chalked endpapers, contemporary owner's name and crest stamped on front pastedowns; good. Sabin C51490; Wagner Camp 77.1.   Blackwell's B112-198 1996 £150.00

MURRAY, EUSTACE GRENVILLE   Six Months in the Ranks; or the Gentleman Private. London: Smith, Elder, 1881. 1st edition; 8vo; iv, 362 pages; library stamps on title and several text leaves, original maroon cloth, inner hinges cracked.   James Burmester 29-100 1996 £50.00

MURRAY, FLORENCE   The Negro Handbook 1944. New York: Current Reference Pub., 1944. 2nd issue; extremities worn, hinges tender, but sound, good copy lacking dust jacket; this is Pauli Murray's copy with her contemporary ownership stamp. Nice Association.   Between the Covers 43-376 1996 $150.00

MURRAY, HUGH   An Historical and Descriptive Account of China. Edinburgh: Oliver & Boyd, 1843. 3rd edition; 12mo; 3 volumes; folding map, full page and in-text illustrations; contemporary full calf by Neil, with blind tooled arabesque centerpieces, gilt tooled fillets and spines and raised bands, lightly scuffed in spots, still very good or better. Chapel Hill 94-153 1996 $200.00

MURRAY, HUGH   An Historical and Descriptive Account of China; Its Ancient and Modern History, Language, Literature...Manners...Geology... Edinburgh: Oliver and Boyd, 1843. 3rd edition; 8vo; 3 volumes, 368, 498, 462 pages; folding map; original red cloth, spine bit faded, otherwise fine set.   David Mason 71-59 1996 $160.00

MURRAY, JAMES A.   The Avifauna of British India. London: 1890. Volume 2 only; 7 hand colored plates, plain plates and text illustrations; original cloth, nice.   David A.H. Grayling MY95Orn-201 1996 £85.00

MURRAY, JOHN   Elements of Materia Medica and Pharmacy. Edinburgh: A. Neill and Co., 1804. 1st edition; 8vo; 2 volumes; half titles, original boards, uncut, spines worn, hinges partly cracked.   Anthony W. Laywood 108-208 1996 £125.00

MURRAY, JOHN 1786?-1851   Practical Remarks on Modern Paper. North Hills: Bird and Bull Press, 1981. Limited to 300 copies; octavo; 120 pages; quarter leather and decorated boards, prospectus laid in; extremely fine. Heany A30.   Bromer Booksellers 87-35 1996 $265.00

MURRAY, JOHN FISHER   A Picturesque Tour of the River Thames in Its Western Course... London: Henry G. Bohn, 1845. 1st edition; tall 8vo; xii, 356 pages; numerous wood engravings; contemporary half leather, gilt decoration on spine; bookplate, binding rubbed at extremities, otherwise nice.   David Mason 71-30 1996 $240.00

MURRAY, JOHN OGDEN   The Immortal Six Hundred a Story of Cruelty to Confederate Prisoners of War. Winchester: Eddy Press Corp., 1905. 1st edition; 274 pages; original cloth, slightly cocked, else very good to near fine. Nevins I 198; Dornbusch II 1226; not in Haynes or Nicholson. McGowan Book Co. 65-65 1996 $250.00

MURRAY, LINDLEY   An English Grammar; Comprehending the Principles and Rules of the Language... York: printed by Thomas Wilson & Son for Longmans, &c. London, 1809. 2nd edition; 2 volumes, 517, 527 pages; slight spotting, contemporary tree calf, hinges cracking, green labels slightly chipped.   Jarndyce 103-317 1996 £60.00

MURRAY, LINDLEY   Some Account of the Life and Religious Labours of Sarah Grubb. Trenton: Isaac Collins, 1795. 12mo; vi, 418 pages; original brown calf with red leather spine label; nice. Evans 28776. Kenneth Karmiole 1NS-194 1996 $150.00

MURRAY, PAULI   Dark Testament and Other Poems. Norwalk: Silvermine, 1970. 1st edition; fine in about fine dust jacket, lightly rubbed, with tiny tear on rear panel, signed by author.   Between the Covers 43-174 1996 $175.00

MUSAEUS   The Loves of Hero and Leander. London: printed for and sold by T. Osborne, et al, 1747. 1st edition; quarto; modern quarter cloth over boards, housed in lovely quarter morocco slipcase with elaborate floral motifs in red, green and gilt in compartments; John Drinkwater's copy with his small, distinctive leather bookplate and ownership signature.   Captain's Bookshelf 38-171 1996 $350.00

MUSCARELLA, OSCAR WHITE   Ancient Art: The Norbert Schimmel Collection. Mainz: Philipp von Zabern, 1974. Small 4to; 340 pages; profusely illustrated, many in color; original cloth.   Archaeologia Luxor-3736 1996 $150.00

MUSCATINE, CHARLES   The Book of Geoffrey Chaucer: an Account of the Publication of Geoffrey Chaucer's Works from the Fifteenth Century to Modern Times. Book Club of California, 1963. One of 450 copies; 14 1/4 x 10 1/4 inches; 6 p.l., (2 blank), 64 pages; tipped on frontispiece, 2 vignettes and 19 full page reproductions of pages from early and modern printings of Chaucer editions, tipped in leaf with one large woodcut initial, designed and printed in red and black by Lawton Kennedy, Book Club of California prospectus and ad post card laid in; with original leaf from undated edition of Chaucer's Works, ca. 1551, tipped in; original orange cloth, gilt vignette on cover, gilt titling on spine, fore edge and tail edge untrimmed; the Chaucer leaf slightly smudged, still crisp and rather nice, the volume very fine.   Phillip J. Pirages 33-336 1996 $350.00

MUSES, C. A.   Aspects of the Theory of Artificial Intelligence. New York: Plenum Press, 1962. 1st edition; 8vo; x, 283 pages; numerous figures in text, some full page; fine.   Edwin V. Glaser 121-222 1996 $100.00

MUSGRAVE, PERCY   Notes on the Ancient Family of Musgrave of Musgrave, Westmorland and Its Various Branches in Cumberland, Yorkshire, Northumberland, Somerset &c. Leeds: privately printed, 1911. 4to; xvi, 351 pages; 22 plates, numerous pedigrees; original parchment backed blue cloth, leather spine label, lettering a little dulled, top edge gilt, uncut; very good, extremtley scarce.   R.F.G. Hollett & Son   78-223   1996 £350.00

MUSGRAVE, RICHARD   Memoirs of the Different Rebellions in Ireland, from the Arrival of the English... Dublin: printed by Robert Marchbank for John Milliken, 1801. 1st edition; 4to; (xii), 636, 166, (8) page insex, (1) errata; 10 plates and maps; foxing, sometimes considerable and staining to plates and maps and leaves facing and following them, tear in folding map at front has been repaired with archival tape, repairs where a name has been excised from title, still nice copy; recently rebound in tan half calf, cloth, raised bands, leather label.   David Mason   71-98   1996 $400.00

MUSICAL Travels through England by the Late Joel Collier, Licentiate in Music. London: printed for J. Kearsly, 1776. 4th edition; 8vo; (viii), 102, 28 pages; disbound.   David Bickersteth   133-51   1996 £65.00

MUTCH, NATHAN   Cocaine - Being a Paper Read Before Ye Sette of Odd Volumes - On April 24th, 1923, at Oddenino's Imperial Restaurant, by Nathan Mutch, M.D., F.R.C.P., Pessimist to Ye Sette. London: privately printed Opuscula Issued to Members of Ye Sette of Odd Vols. 1924. One of 165 numbered copies; double page black and white plate, drawing by John Hassall of Machu Picchu; wrappers, yapp edges rubbed and creased, covers slightly marked and dusty, small tear at top edge of lower cover, very good.   Ulysses   39-116   1996 £125.00

MUTINELLI, FABIO   Dell'Avvenimento di S.M.I.R.A. Ferdinando I d'Austria in Venezia e delle Civiche Solennita d'allora. Venice: Co Tipi del Gondoliere, 1838. Oblong 4to; title, 43 pages, 1 f., 9 litho plates; contemporary wrappers, text rather foxed, but plates clean. Scarace. Lipperheide Si 61; not in Berlin Kat. or Vinet.   Marlborough   162-241   1996 £600.00

MYERS, F. W. H.   Human Personality and Its Survival of Bodily Death. London: Longmans, Green, 1920. New impression; 2 volumes, xvi, 700; xx, 660 pages; very nice set, original binding in chipped, U.S. issue, dust jackets.   Ian Patterson   9-222   1996 £75.00

MYERS, J. ARTHUR   Fighters of Fate: a Story of men and Women Who Have Achieved Greatly. Baltimore: 1927. 1st edition; 318 pages; original binding.   W. Bruce Fye   71-1497   1996 $100.00

MYERS, VIRGINIA   The Letters and Correspondence of Mrs. Virginia Myers... Philadelphia: n.p., 1847 1st edition; 8vo; 63 pages; original wrappers worn, text water damaged.   The Bookpress   75-441   1996 $110.00

MYLNE, ROBERT SCOTT   The Master Masons to the Crown of Scotland and Their Works. Edinburgh: Scott & Ferguson and Burness & Co., 1893. Folio; pages xviii, 308; colored frontispiece, numerous photographic and tinted plates, text illustrations; original buckram gilt over bevelled boards, little rubbed and faded, light crease to lower board, top edge gilt, joints cracking, but very nice.   R.F.G. Hollett   76-215   1996 £125.00

MYLONAS, GEORGE E.   Aghios Kosmas: an Early Bronze Age Settlement and Cemetery in Attica. Princeton: Princeton University Press, 1959. 4to; xviii, 191 pages, 182 illustrations, 64 diagrams; original cloth, bookplate.   Archaeologia   Luxor-3749   1996 $250.00

MYRES, JOHN L.   Handbook of the Cesnola Collection of Antiquites from Cyprus. New York: Metropolitan Museum of Art, 1914. Limited to 1000 copies; 8vo; lv, 596 pages; profusely illustrated, wrappers, spine tape reinforced, several marginal ink marks.   Archaeologia   Luxor-3752   1996 $125.00

N

NABOKOV, VLADIMIR 1899-1977   Chambre Obscure. Paris: Editions Bernard Grasset, 1934. 1st edition; original binding, pages unopened, top edge spotted and dusty, price on spine altered in ink, covers slightly rubbed, creased and dusty, very good.   Ulysses 39-431 1996 £250.00

NABOKOV, VLADIMIR 1899-1977   Conclusive Evidence. New York: Harper, 1951. 1st edition; near fine in price clipped and lightly spine faded dust jacket.   Lame Duck Books 19-383 1996 $300.00

NABOKOV, VLADIMIR 1899-1977   Despair. London: Weidenfeld & Nicolson, 1966. 1st British edition; very near fine in dust jacket with light wear to extremities.   Lame Duck Books 19-391 1996 $100.00

NABOKOV, VLADIMIR 1899-1977   Despair. New York: Putnam's 1966. 1st U.S. edition; near fine in dust jacket.   Lame Duck Books 19-392 1996 $125.00

NABOKOV, VLADIMIR 1899-1977   The Eye. New York: Phaedra, 1965. 1st edition; advance copy; unprinted wrappers, stiff dust jacket, fine. Lame Duck Books 19-390 1996 $150.00

NABOKOV, VLADIMIR 1899-1977   The Eye. New York: Phaedra, 1965. 1st edition; very minor shelf wear to extremities, else near fine in dust jacket with short edge tear to front panel.   Lame Duck Books 19-389 1996 $100.00

NABOKOV, VLADIMIR 1899-1977   Invitation to a Beheading. New York: Putnam's, 1959. 1st edition; very near fine in dust jacket.   Lame Duck Books 19-385 1996 $125.00

NABOKOV, VLADIMIR 1899-1977   Invitation to a Beheading. New York: G. P. Putnam's Sons, 1959. 1st American edition; 8 1/2 x 5 3/4 inches; 223 pages; original cloth backed paper boards, upper corners bumped, otherwise very fine in very fine jacket.   Phillip J. Pirages 33-394 1996 $125.00

NABOKOV, VLADIMIR 1899-1977   Lolita. Paris: Olympia Press, 1955. 1st issue with printed price of 900 francs on back cover; near fine in original wrappers with small nick on fore edge of volume 1 (1/8") and small pinhead dot on front cover of Volume 1, some blind scratches to front cover of volume 2; unusually nice set.   Priscilla Juvelis 95/1-183 1996 $2,500.00

NABOKOV, VLADIMIR 1899-1977   Lolita. London: Weidenfeld & Nicolson, 1959. 1st British edition; lovely copy in dust jacket with darkening to verso of spine unobtrusive from exterior.   Lame Duck Books 19-386 1996 $300.00

NABOKOV, VLADIMIR 1899-1977   Lolita. London: Weidenfeld and Nicolson, 1959. 1st edition; original binding, head and tail of spine and corners slightly bumped, edges spotted, very good in nicked, rubbed and dusty, slightly torn and creased dust jacket frayed at head and tail of spine and missing very small piece at tail of spine.   Ulysses 39-432 1996 £75.00

NABOKOV, VLADIMIR 1899-1977   Lolita. Rowohlt Verlag, 1960. 1st German edition; near fine in dust jacket.   Words Etcetera 94-976 1996 £55.00

NABOKOV, VLADIMIR 1899-1977   Lolita: a Screenplay. New York: McGraw Hill, 1974. 1st edition; near fine in dust jacket.   Lame Duck Books 19-395 1996 $100.00

NABOKOV, VLADIMIR 1899-1977   Nikolai Gogol. Norfolk: n.d. 1944. 1st edition; small quarto; fine in dust jacket.   Lame Duck Books 19-382 1996 $350.00

NABOKOV, VLADIMIR 1899-1977   Pnin. Garden City: Doubleday, 1957. 1st edition; near fine in very good+, price clipped, lightly spine soiled dust jacket.   Lame Duck Books 19-384 1996 $200.00

NABOKOV, VLADIMIR 1899-1977   Pnin. Garden City: Doubleday, 1957. 1st edition; five colors used for the dust jacket and spine and they all shine; stunning copy in almost perfect dust jacket.   Bev Chaney, Jr. 23-524 1996 $165.00

NADAILLAC, THE MARQUIS DE   Manners and Monuments New York: & London: Putnam's, 1892. 1st American edition; original pictorial cloth, former owner's name on f.f.e.p., light shelf wear to cloth, else bright, very good.   Ken Sanders 8-44 1996 $165.00

NAHUM, PETER   Monograms of Victorian and Edwardian Artists. Victoria Square Press, 1976. 24.5 x 19 cm; 325 pages; over 4000 monograms shown, includes errata slip; original cloth, dust jacket. Rainsford A54-436 1996 £90.00

NAIL, LESLIE   Resurrection Ball. Tuscaloos: University of Alabama, 1982. 1st edition; one of 60 copies, signed by author; thin 8vo; wood engraving by John DePol; original wrappers; mint. Peich 38.   James S. Jaffe 34-581 1996 $250.00

NAIPAUL, VIDIADHAR SURAJPRSAD   A House for Mr. Miswas. London: Andre Deutsch, 1961. 1st edition; thick 8vo; boards, dust jacket, page edges foxed, bottom of spine bit darkened, otherwise a fine, bright copy, scarce;   James S. Jaffe 34-508 1996 $650.00

NAIPAUL, VIDIADHAR SURAJPRSAD   The Mystic Masseur. New York: 1957. 1st American edition; 8 x 5 inches; 215 pages; cloth, good in moderately worn and slightly chipped dust jacket; author's first book. John K. King 77-407 1996 $100.00

NAIPAUL, VIDIADHAR SURAJPRSAD   The Suffrage of Elvira. London: Deutsch, 1958. 1st edition; fading to spinal extremities and faint ownership signature, else near fine in dust jacket, author's scarcest title. Lame Duck Books 19-404 1996 $1,250.00

NAIPAUL, VIDIADHAR SURAJPRSAD   The Suffrage of Elvira. London: Andre Deutsch, 1958. 1st edition; small 8vo; boards, dust jacket, previous bookseller's label on front endsheet, previous owner's signature on front free endpaper, otherwise fine in price clipped dust jacket. Scarce.   James S. Jaffe 34-507 1996 $850.00

NAIPAUL, VIDIADHAR SURAJPRSAD   A Turn in the South. Franklin Center: Franklin Library, 1989. 1st U.S. edition; fine in full decorated leather, signed by author.   Lame Duck Books 19-405 1996 $100.00

NAIPAUL, VIDIADHAR SURAJPRSAD   A Way in the World. London: Heinemann, 1994. 1st edition; 369 pages; signed by author; green paper covered boards, fine in fine dust jacket;   Orpheus Books 17-77 1996 $125.00

NAIPUAL, SHIVA   The Chip Chip Gatherers. London: Deutsch, 1973. 1st edition; very nice in very good dust jacket slightly browned along top edge and with one small closed tear at base of spine.   Virgo Books 48-142 1996 £70.00

NAISMITH, JOHN   General View of the Agriculture of the county of Clydesdale. Edinburgh: printed for Mundell and Son, & J. Mundell, Glasgow, 1798. 1st edition; folding map (browned), mounted on linen; library cancellation stamp on blank verso of title, modern cloth backed boards.   Anthony W. Laywood 109-103 1996 £85.00

NAISMITH, JOHN   General View of the Agriculture of the County of Clydesdale; with Observations on the Means of Its Improvement. London: Richard Phillips, 1806. 8vo; xix, (i)(, 252, (4) pages ads, folding hand colored map; original boards, very good, uncut, pirnted paper label. Ken Spelman 30-94 1996 £150.00

NALDRET, PERCY   Collected Magic Series. Numbers 1-8. Portsmouth: 1920-27. Numbers 1-8; numerous text figures; 8 volumes; wrappers (slightly worn); all but the first number inscribed by Naldret for Jimmy Findlay.   Thomas Thorp 489-229 1996 £120.00

NALL, G. H.   The Life of the Sea Trout, Especially in Scottish Waters... London: 1930. Many illustrations; original buckram; near fine. David A.H. Grayling 3/95-485 1996 £55.00

NAMIER, LEWIS B.　　The House of Commons 1754-1790. London: HMSO, 1964. Original edition; crown 4to; 3 volumes; buckram, gilt, dust jackets.　　Howes Bookshop　265-866　1996 £85.00

NANCE, R. MORTON　　Sailing-Ship Models: a Selection from European and American Collections. London: Halton & Truscott Smith, 1924. Limited to 1750 numbered copies; 4to; 328 pages; frontispiece in color, 124 plates and several text figures; cloth, gilt, top edge gilt, corners rubbed.　　Thomas Thorp　489-230　1996 £75.00

NANKING Memorial Hall of Taiping Tienkuo. The Arts of Taiping Tienkuo. N.P.: The Kiangsu Peoples Publishing House, 1959. 1st and only edition; folio; 114, (3) pages, with accompanying plates; goldstamped yellow satin cloth, dust jacket, original protective slipcase, jacket worn, else very good.　　The Bookpress　75-442　1996 $850.00

NANSEN, FRIDTJOF 1861-1930　　In Northern Mists. London: William Heinemann, 1911. 1st English edition; royal 8vo; 2 volumes; xi, 384; (8), 416 pages; mounted color frontispieces, numerous text illustrations; original cloth, gilt vignettes on upper covers; fine. 1st volume inscribed by author for Mrs. G. Lewis.　　Thomas Thorp　489-231　1996 £350.00

NANSEN, FRIDTJOF 1861-1930　　The Norwegian North Polar Expedition 1893-1896. Scientific Results. New York: Greenwood Press, 1969. 6 volumes; brown cloth, fine.　　Hermitage　SP95-1107　1996 $275.00

NANSON, W.　　Some Municipal Records of the City of Carlisle, viz, the Elizabethan Constitutions, Orders, Provisions, Articles and Rules from the Dormont Book, and Rules and Orders of the Eight Trading Guilds, Prefaced by Chapters on the Corp. Charters & Guilds... Carlisle: 1887. 8vo; pages 340; extending frontispiece facsimile, 2 colored lithographs and 9 illustrations; lacks front flyleaf, otherwise very good; original cloth, gilt, extremities minimally rubbed.　R.F.G. Hollett & Son　78-922　1996 £75.00

NAPIER, FRANCIS　　Notes of a Voyage from New South Wales to the North Coast of Australia. Glasgow: Bell & Bain, 41 Mietchell St., 1876. 96 pages; photograps, frontispiece, 8 lithograph plates, 5 folding maps; early marron buckram rebind, gilt title, original endpapers bound in, text lightly dusty, some plates little foxed, one map tear restored on back, otherwise very good. Proof copy, inscribed "Jas. R. Napier proof copy". Antipodean　28-627　1996 $750.00

NAPIER, MARK　　Memoirs of John Napier of Merchiston, His Lineage, Life and Times with a History of the Invention of Logarithms. Edinburgh: William Blackwood and London: Thomas Cadell, 1834. 1st edition; 4to; xvi, 534 pages; frontispiece, 13 other plates; contemporary calf, rebacked, raised bands, speckled edges; near fine.　　Edwin V. Glaser　121-224　1996 $450.00

NAPIER, MARK　　Memorials and Letters Illustrative of the Life and Times of John Graham of Claverhouse, Viscount Dundee. Edinburgh: Thomas G. Stevenson, 22 Frederick St., London: Hamilton, Adams & Co., 1859. 1st edition; 8vo; 2 volumes; 1-388; 1-430 pages; frontispiece to both volumes, 3 engraved plates, 2 chromolithos, 3 facsimiles; binder's tamp, bound by Leighton of Brewer Street; half green morocco and green buckram boards, elaborate gilt tooling to compartments with Scottish thistles enclosed within gilt scrolling, gilt titles to spines, owenr's name in gilt to foot of spines, endpapers and edges uniformly marbled; some foxing to couple of plates and few pages, owner's inscription to titles, this copy appears to have been specially bound for the owner as the name on the titles is the same as the name gilt stamped to spine, owner's bookplate.　Beeleigh Abbey　BA56-159　1996 £125.00

NAPIER, WILLIAM FRANCIS PATRICK　　History of the War in the Peninsula and In the South of France from the Year 1807 to the Year 1814. London: John Murray (vol. 1), Thomas & William Boone (vols. 2-6), 1828-40. 1st edition; 9 x 5 3/4 inches; 6 volumes; 55 plates; very attractive 19th century smooth calf by Henderson & Bisset, covers framed with rule of blind dots inside double gilt fillet, handsomely gilt spine compartments occupied by 10 plain and decorative rules & central field of stippled scales, raised bands ornamented with twining roll, red calf and green morocco labels, marbled endpapers and edges, variable foxing to perhaps half the maps with offsetting onto facing pages, flyleaves little spotted, isolated small stains or nicks to two or three covers, slightest talking to few joints but text generally clean and bindings both extremely pleasing and very well preserved, contemporaneous presentation inscription at front in first 3 volumes, ownership inscription;　　Phillip J. Pirages　33-395　1996 $1,500.00

NAPIER, WILLIAM FRANCIS PATRICK　　History of the War in the Peninsula and in the South of France from 1807 to 1814. Warne: Chandos Classics, c. .1900. Crown 8vo; 6 volumes; 55 maps and plans; original navy cloth, gilt tops, some bindings with trifle damp mark not affecting text.　　Howes Bookshop　265-867　1996 £55.00

NAPOLEON, JOSEPH CHARLES PAUL, PRINCE　　On the Conduct of the War in the East. London: W. Jeffs, Foreign Bookselelr, 1855. 1st edition; 77 pages; disbound.　　Anthony W. Laywood　109-104　1996 £50.00

NAPTON, WILLIAM B.　　Over the Santa Fe Trail 1857. Santa Fe: 1964. Wagonmaster Edition, limited to 99 copies; 73 pages; reproductions of the 10 original illustrations, done on Linweave Early American paper; cloth. Fine in dust jacket.　　Gene W. Baade　1094-117　1996 $125.00

NARAYAN, R. K.　　The English Teacher. London: Eyre & Spottiwode, 1945. 1st edition; name on f.e.p., crease on half title, otherwise very good in slightly soiled and nicked dust jacket faded on spine.　　Virgo Books　48-144　1996 £75.00

NARDI, JACOPO　　Le Historie Della Citta Di Fiorenze. Lyons: Ancelin, 1582. 1st edition; 4to; title within delicate arabesque woodcut border; calf, gilt arms on both covers; corner of i2 repaired, some browning; contemporary marginal annotations. Moreni, Toscana II 109; Adams N39. Rostenberg & Stern　150-91　1996 $550.00

NARES, EDWARD　　Heraldic Anomalies; or Rank confusion in Our Orders of Precedence. London: Whittaker, 1832. 1st edition; small octavo; 2 volumes, pages xxii, 334, 372; red and black titlepages; contemporary three quarter calf, marbled boards, double leather labels, pleasant set. Scarce.　　Hartfield　48-L63　1996 $265.00

NARES, ROBERT　　Illustrations of Difficult Words and Phrases Occurring in the English Writers of the Age of Elizabeth.. London: printed by Bensley & Son for Robert Triphook, 1818. 4to; 10, 2 pages ads; disbound and slighty cropped at fore-edge and tail affecting text on first two leaves.　　Jarndyce　103-201　1996 £110.00

NARES, ROBERT　　Principles of Government Deduced from Reason, Supported by English Experience and Opposed to French Errors. London: for John Stockdale, 1792. 1st edition; 8vo; xviii, (2), 160 pages, together with 16 pages of Stockdale's ads, title bit soiled, otherwise good, recently rebound in half calf, gilt. Goldsmiths 15476; Not in Kress. John Drury　82-194　1996 £150.00

A NARRATIVE Of the Grand Festival, Given by the Inhabitants of King's Lynn, on Friday the 22nd of July, 1814. Lyn Regis: printed by W. Whittingham, and pub. by F. Goodwin, n.d. 1814. 1st edition; 8vo; 74 pages folding plan; contemporary cloth; nice.　　Anthony W. Laywood　108-191　1996 £145.00

NARRATIVE of the Surveying Voyages of His Majesty's Ships Adventure and Beagle, Between the Years 1826 and 1836... London: Henry Colburn, 1839. 1st edition; 24cm; 3 volumes + appendix; xxviii, directions to binder, errata et corrigenda, 598 pages, frontispiece, 15 plates, folding map and 2 maps loose in pocket; xiv, directions to binder, 694 pages, addenda, frontispiece, 24 plates, 2 loose maps in pocket; viii, 352 pages, 16 pages of Mr. Colburn's list of new publications, 8 pages "Companion to the Waverly Novels" bound in; xiv, 630, 8 page index, 2 maps in pocket. original embossed blue cloth, gilt spine titles, some shelfwear, volumes 1 and 2 professionally rebacked with original spines laid down, bookplates. Hill p. 104-105; Ferguson 2708; Sabin 18647 for later ed. Freeman 10.　　Parmer Books　Nat/Hist-067430　1996 $12,500.00

NARRIEN, JOHN　　An Historical Account of the Origin and Progress of Astronomy... London: Baldwin & Cradock, n.d., but ads at end dated 1850(1833). 8vo; 520 pages; 3 folding plates; original blindstamped cloth, corners bumped and worn, top and bottom edges of spine chipped and frayed, black spots to front board, top of spine wrinkled, moisture stains to plates.　　Knollwood Books　70-159　1996 $145.00

NASATIR, A. P.　　Before Lewis and Clark - Documents Illustrating the History of the Missouri, 1785-1804. St. Louis: 1952. 1st edition; 2 volumes, 771 pages, frontispiece; dust jacket, fine except some underlining of text in ink. Very scarce. Rittenhouse 42.　　T. A. Swinford　49-834　1996 $150.00

NASH, FREDERICK　　Picturesque Views of the City of Paris and Its Environs. London: printed by James Moyes for Longman, et al, 1823. 11 3/4 x 9 1/2 inches; 2 volumes in 1, without titlepage to volume 2; 57 fine engraved plates, tissue guards, text in English and French; very handsome cont. rose colored hard grain morocco, extra gilt by C. Smith, covers handsomely framed with 3 sets of parallel fillets enclosing two elegant scrolling floral borders, flat spines beautifully gilt in 2 compartments, top one with titling, elongated lower one composed of central vertical band of urn-like roll-tool flanked by gilt rules and pretty borders of acanthus leaves, board edges with triple gilt filelts, turn-ins with four gilt rules and corner ovals, endpapers of deep green coated stock, all edges gilt, spine evenly sunned to terra cotta color, minor scuffing or rubbing to edges, otherwise binding in excellent condition; plates especially clean.　　Phillip J. Pirages　33-488　1996 $950.00

NASH, JOHN   Twenty One Wood Engravings. London: Fleece Press, 1993. Limited to 100 copies; quarter vellum backed flecked boards, mint in cloth foldover box; beautiful production.   Words Etcetera 94-978 1996 £145.00

NASH, JOSEPH   The Mansions of England in the Olden Time. (with) Views of the Interior and Exterior of Windsor Castle. London: Thomas Mclean, 1839-52. Folio; bound together as two volumes; pictorial lithographed title and 25 lithographed plates; handsome later 19th century green half morocco and cloth, gilt panelled spines, with elaborate floral emblems in compartments (some text spotting, but mainly marginal). Abbey Scenery 402 and 360; tooley 337 and 339.   Charles W. Traylen 117-370 1996 £1,100.00

NASH, PAUL   Dear Mercia: Paul Nash Letters to Mercia Oakley 1909-18. London: Fleece Press, 1909-18. One of 300 copies; 4to; printed in Baskerville in black and ochre; tipped in plates and numerous facsimiles; half buckram, Maziarczyk paste paper sides; fine in slipcase. Bertram Rota 272-148 1996 £92.00

NASH, PAUL   Engravings on Wood 1919-1928. London: Redfern Gallery Ltd., 1928. 1st edition; 12mo; wrappers, patterned Curwen Press paper covers, designed by Nash; covers slightly spotted and very slightly soiled, corners slightly dog eared; very good; artist's own copy. Ulysses 39-436 1996 £375.00

NASH, PAUL   Monster Field - a Discovery Recorded by Paul Nash. Oxford: Counterpoint Publications, 1946. One of 1000 numbered copies; quarto; wrappers, color plate tipped in on upper cover slightly creased, cover edges browned, corners slightly creased, brown mark on titlepage from glue used on upper cover, very good.   Ulysses 39-440 1996 £925.00

NASH, PAUL   Paul Nash - a Portfolio of Colour Plates. London: Soho Gallery Ltd., 1937. 1st edition; folio; 10 mounted color plates, one of which is one upper cover, 2 black and white reproductions in text; wrappers, covers soiled and dusty, cover edges rubbed, creased and darkened, head and tail of spine and corners bumped and worn, prelims spotted, good; presentation copy from artist to art critic and companion of Margot Eates, E. H. Ramsden, inscribed.   Ulysses 39-438 1996 £950.00

NASH, PAUL   Paul Nash. Harmondsworth: Penguin Books Ltd., 1944. 1st edition; 16 color and 16 black and white plates; landscape format, wrappers; covers dusty, slightly soiled and creased and internally spotted, cover edges rubbed, staples rusted away; good; presentation copy from author to the art critic and companion of Margot Eates, E. H. Ramsden.   Ulysses 39-439 1996 £750.00

NASH, PAUL   Room and Book. London: Soncino Press, Ltd., 1932. 1st edition; 18 black and white plates and one color illustration; Curwen Press patterned papers tipped in on page 73; top edge dusty, head and tail of spine slightly bumped, free endpapers partially browned, cover edges slightly spotted, very good in nicked and slightly torn, creased and rubbed, slightly spotted, marked and dusty, internally repaired dust jacket browned at spine and edges.   Ulysses 39-437 1996 £95.00

NASH, R.   Calligraphy and Printing in the Sixteenth Century. Antwerp: Plantin-Moretus Museum, 1964. 2nd edition, limited to 500 copies; small 8vo; 39 pages; cloth backed pictorial boards, dust jacket, booklabel of Ruari McLean & inscription to him from Rocky Stinehour.   Maggs Bros. Ltd. 1191-210 1996 £40.00

NASR, SEYYED HOSSEIN   Persia. Bridge of Turquoise. Boston: New York Graphic Society, 1975. 4to; 367 pages; magnificently illustrated, mainly in color;   Worldwide Antiquarian 151-486 1996 $145.00

NAST, THOMAS   The Fight at Dame Europa's School. New York: Felt, 1871. 1st edition; 8vo; illustrations by author; original binding, some fading and spotting; signature; quite good, uncommon.   Charles Agvent 4-915 1996 $125.00

NAST, THOMAS   The Fight at Dame Europa's School. New York: Felt, 1871. 1st edition; 8vo; illustrations by author; original binding, spine tips worn, f.f.e.p. detached, good+.   Charles Agvent 4-916 1996 $100.00

NATHAN, LEONARD   The Matchmaker's Lament and Other Astonishments: Poems. Northampton: Gehenna Press, 1967. Number 179 of 400 copies; 11.25 x 8.25 inches; printed on Arches; brown paper covered boards, paper label on spine; corners and head and foot of backstrip bumped, small dent in upper hinge, otherwise very good. Gehenna Press, Work of 50 Years 54.   Joshua Heller 21-127 1996 $100.00

NATHAN, ROBERT   Autumn. New York: Robert M. McBride & Co., 1921. Only 1000 copies printed; fine in bright, fresh dust jacket missing few small chips, not affecting lettering, author's second book; scarce in jacket.   Left Bank Books 2-105 1996 $125.00

NATIONAL GALLERY, LONDON.   Report of the National Gallery Site Commission, Together with Minutes, Evidence, Appendix and Index. London: 1857. 4to; xvi, (ii), 188 pages, 3 folding litho plates, hand colored; cloth.   Elton Engineering 10-112 1996 £380.00

NATIONAL MARITIME MUSEUM   Catalogue of the Library. London: HMSO, 1st edition; 4to; 5 volumes, some paltes; all but volume 4 in dust jacket, very good.   John Lewcock 30-149 1996 £100.00

THE NATIVE Tribes of South Australia. Adelaide: F. S. Wigg & Son, 1879. (xlii), 316 pages, 8 sepia toned lithographs; publisher's half calf and buckram boards, raised bands, title piece on spine, all edges marbled, corners rubbed, otherwise good+. Ferguson 13095; Greenway 10162.   Antipodean 28-131 1996 $650.00

NATTA, MARCO ANTONIO   Marci Antonii Nattae Astensis De Deo Libri XV. Venice: Apud Paulum Manutium, 1560. Folio; 170 leaves, printer's devices; 18th century full sprinkled calf, rubbed; despite some slight staining, an attractive later Aldine folio; early engraved English Rolle family armorial bookplate. Renouard 177.1. Adams N67; UCLA IIIb/481. Family Album Tillers-455 1996 $750.00

NATTER, LAURENT   Traite de la Methode Antique de Graver en Pierres Fines, Comparee avec la methode Moderne... London: Haberkorn for the author, 1754. Small folio; pages xxxix, 1 f., eng. dedn., 37 engraved plates (one extra plate of Sirius, from another work, tipped in); contemporary dark green morocco, triple fillet gilt, spine gilt in compartments with floral device and dog tooth and fillet borders, gilt inner dentelle, comb marbled endpapers, all edges gilt, bound by Antoine Michel Padeloup, called "Le Jeune"; from the De Bure library, with the MS shelf mark of Madame Guillaume, possibly part of the small collection formed by De Bure for her, from the collection of J. J. de Bure, from the collection of Arthur Hamilton Smith, with his bookplate with long letter (presumably to him) from de Bure. Fine, scarce. Marlborough 160-49 1996 £2,500.00

NATTES, JOHN CLAUDE   Bath Illustrated by a Series of Views from the Drawings of John Claude Nattes... London: published by William Miller, Albemarle St. and Wm. Sheppard, Bristol, 1806. 1st edition; later issue; folio; half title, tissue guarded hand colored aquatint frontispiece, title with hand colored vignette, (l-iii), 56 leaves of text, 27 hand colored aquatint plates and 1 hand colored vignette, large paper copy; half red straight grained morocco and marbled boards, edges scuffed, slight damage to top right hand corner of upper marbled board, red morocco label to upper board, raised bands to spine, gilt tooling to compartments, gilt title to second compartment, all edges gilt, new marbled endpapers and new prelims; ink inscription removed from verso front f.e.p. leaving slight mark, very minor oxidisaton to first plates, rest in excellent condition, very minor occasional offset to text only; bound by Bayntun; bookplates of Boies Penrose, another armorial bookplate. Beeleigh Abbey BA56-17 1996 £7,000.00

NATTES, JOHN CLAUDE   Bath, Illustrated by a Series of Views... London: W. Bulmer for W. Miller and W. Sheppard, Bristol, 1806. Folio; title, iv, 56 pages, large color aquatint vignette on title and another on lasata page, 28 color aquatint plates; dark blue morocco, gilt, covers and spine tooled to a geometrical design, gilt inner borders, gilt edges, by Bayntun of Bath for E. H. Wells & Co., New York: original morocco label pasted onto rear endleaf; handsome copy. Ex-libris Francis Palmer, James Comerford and Mildred Davey.   Marlborough 162-72 1996 £5,750.00

NATTES, JOHN CLAUDE   A Graphic and Descriptive Tour of the University of Oxford. London: Cundee, 1805. Large folio; 2 parts, 16 pages, engraved title with sepia vignette, 4 sepia aquatint plates and 1 text illustrations; sewn in original printed wrappers (defective), preserved in fitted cloth box. Very rare. Abbey Scenery 274-75; Prideaux p. 274. Marlborough 162-73 1996 £2,000.00

NAUMANN, J. F.   Iconographie d'Oiseaux d'Europe et de Leurs Oeufs. Paris: 1910. 4to; 4 volumes; pages 24, 409 colored and 5 plain plates; quarter leather; good copy; from the collection of Jan Coldewey. Wheldon & Wesley 207-74 1996 £3,000.00

NAYLOR, G.   Bloomsbury: the Artists, Authors and Designers by Themselves. London: Octopus, 1990. 1st edition; 12 1/2 x 10 inches; many colored plates, profusely illustrated; fine in dust jacket.   Virgo Books 48-35a 1996 £70.00

NAYLOR, GLORIA   Women of Brewster Place. New York: Viking, 1982. 1st edition; author's first book; as new except for a 1 inch closed tear at bottom edge of back of the dust jacket.   Oracle Books 1-12 1996 $375.00

NAYLOR, GLORIA   The Women of Brewster Place. New York: Viking, 1982. 1st edition; bit of fading to top edge of cover, else near fine in jacket with tiny closd tear and crinkle to rear panel; handsome copy of her first book.   Alice Robbins 15-250 1996 $300.00

NEAGOE, PETER   Storm. Paris: New Review Publications, 1932. 1st edition; small stain to front cover, else very good in original wrappers; uncommon.   David Holloway 94D-56 1996 $125.00

NEAL, MARIE C.   In Honolulu Gardens. Honolulu: Bernice P. Bishop Museum, 1928. 8vo; iv, 327 pages, index, 27 plates, 68 text figures; green cloth, gilt spine and cover titles, bit of wear, very good.   Parmer Books Nat/Hist-067413 1996 $125.00

NEALE, JOHN   The Elizabethan House of Commons. 1949. Elizabeth I and Her Parliaments 1559-1581. Elizabeth I and Her Parliaments 1584-1601. London: 1949-57. 1st editions; 8vo; 3 volumes; plates; original cloth, dust jackets. Professor J. S. Bromley's set with ownership. Howes Bookshop 265-878 1996 £65.00

NEANDER, MICHAEL   Opus Aureum et Scholasticum... Leipzig: Steinman, 1577. 1st edition of this collection; 4to; 1,268 pages; printer's device; original full pigskin over wooden boards, dated, with fine, well preserved panels representing medicine, astronomy, theology and jurisprudence, signed by Wittenberg binder, Mathias Juncker; fine. Adams P2311; BM STC 646. NUC 409.55.   Bennett Gilbert LL29-52 1996 $1,850.00

NEARING, SCOTT   Free Born. An Unpublishable Novel. New York: Urquhart Press, 1932. 1st edition; wrappers; very good with cover creasing, signed by author, very uncommon.   Beasley Books 82-332 1996 $275.00

NEBRIJA, ELIO ANTONIO DE   Rerum a Fernando et Elisabe Hispania & Felicissimis Regibus Gestarum Decades Duae, Necnon Belli Navariensis Libri Duo, Nunc Secundo Editi & Exactiore Vigilantia ad Prototypi Fidem Recogniti & Emendati. Granada: Sancho de Nebrija, 1550. 8vo; (18), 213 (misnumbered 113), (1) leaves; woodcut double eagle with arms of Philip II on title, printer's mark of the authors son on last leaf; early inscription on title and owners name stamped in inner blank margin; some faint dampstains. Palau 189344; BL/STC Spanish p. 12; Brunet IV 31.   Jeffrey Mancevice 20-62 1996 $1,900.00

NEED, THOMAS   Six Years in the Bush; or extracts from the Journal of a Settler in Upper Canada, 1832-1838. London: Simpkin, Marshall & Co., Charles Tilt and Robert Edis, 1838. Small 8vo; pages vii, 126; original gilt and blindstamped cloth, names on front endpapers, cvoers worn and somewhat soiled, interior crisp and clean. TPL 2195.   Hugh Anson-Cartwright 87-314 1996 $1,500.00

NEEDHAM, PAUL   Twelve Centuries of Bookbindings 400-1600. New York: London: 1979. Larage 4to; pages xxvii, 338 pages, 1 f., 6 color illustrations (mounted), numerous black and white, many full page, red cloth, dust jacket (chipped and dusty).   Marlborough 160-85 1996 £85.00

THE NEGRO Problem. New York: James Pott 1903. 1st edition; very slight rubbing to boards, still fine, bright copy; bookplate of William Henry Baldwin on front pastedown, Baldwin was a railroad executive, very scarce and nice association.   Between the Covers 43-253 1996 $650.00

NEILL, EDWARD   History of Washington County and the St. Croix Valley, Including the Explorers and Pioneers of Minnesota. Minneapolis: 1881. 1st edition; iv, 636 pages, three quarter leather; nice.   T. A. Swinford 49-840 1996 $200.00

NEILSON, GEORGE   Annals of the Solway Until A.D. 1307. Glasgow: James Maclehose, 1899. Large square 8vo; pages 74, (ii), 5 maps, modern half levant morocco gilt, first few leaves in excellent facsimile, virtually indistinguishable from original, several corners repaired, 1 map repaired, little fingering in places, library stamp on final leaf of text, still very acceptable copy. Scarce.   R.F.G. Hollett & Son 78-1130 1996 £85.00

NEILSON, WILLIAM   Mesmerism in Its Relation to Health and Disease and the Present State of Medicine. Edinburgh: 1855. 250 pages; cloth, shaken, one gathering sprung.   Graham Weiner C2-580 1996 £50.00

NEIMAN, LE ROY   Horses. New York: Abrams, 1979. 1st edition; square folio; original binding; very good in very good dust jacket. October Farm 36-52 1996 $495.00

NELSON, B.   The Sulidae, Gannets and Boobies. Oxford University Press, 1978. 1020 pages; numerous color and other illustrations; mint in dust jacket.   David A.H. Grayling MY95Orn-203 1996 £50.00

NELSON, C.   The Trees of Ireland, Native and Naturalized. London: 1993. Limited to 150 signed and numbered copies; 4to; pages vii, 248, 31 colored plates; quarter morocco, slipcase.   Wheldon & Wesley 207-1846 1996 £205.00

NELSON, EDWARD W.   Report Upon Natural History Collection Made in Alaska Between the Years 1877 and 1881. Washington: GPO, 1887. 337 pages, index, 2 color plates, 9 black and white plates, this copy lacks 10 plates; black cloth; label "Compliments of A. W. Greely, Chief Signal Officer", bookplate of St. Bernard's Seminary Library. Arctic Bib. 12171.   Parmer Books Nat/Hist-081186 1996 $125.00

NELSON, HENRY LOOMIS   The Army of the United States. New York: Whitlock, 1895. 1st edition; limited, 172/1500 copies; large folio; each printed on thick cardstock; 44 plates from water colors by H. A. Ogden; hinges repaired, some damage to f.f.e.p. else very good, all plates very good.   Parker Books of the West 30-135 1996 $1,250.00

NELSON, THOMAS H.   The Birds of Yorkshire. London: Hull: and York: A. Brown & Sons, 1907. 1st edition; large paper copy; 4to; 2 volumes, pages xlv, 1-374; xii, 375-843; colored titles and frontispieces, profusely illustrated with photos; almost pristine copy, original green cloth, Mullens & Swann p. 433.   Sotheran PN32-94 1996 £268.00

NELSON, W.   The Office and Authority of a Justice of Peace... London: printed by E. and R. Nutt, and R. Gosling, 1724. 10th edition; contemporary calf, joints cracked, ex-school library, clean copy. Meyer Boswell SL27-173 1996 $275.00

NELSON, WILLIAM   Fishing in Eden. London: Witherby, 1922. 1st edition; pages 209, colored frontispiece, 12 plates, map; original cloth, gilt, corners trifle frayed.   R.F.G. Hollett & Son 78-647 1996 £60.00

NELSON, WILLIAM   The Laws Concerning Game, Of Hunting, Hawking, Fishing and Fowling &c. London: T. Waller, 1751. 4th edition; 12mo; publisher's ads at front and rear; full contemporary sheep, upper joint cracked but firm.   Ian Wilkinson 95/1-130 1996 £165.00

NEMEROV, HOWARD   Journal of the Fictive Life. New Brunswick: Rutgers University Press, 1963. 1st edition; fine in near fine dust jacket with touch of rubbing, signed by author.   Between the Covers 42-323 1996 $125.00

NERI, ANTONIO   L'Arte Vetratia Distinta in Libri Sette...Impressione Seconda, Ricorretta, ed Espurgata da Vari Errori. Florence: M. Rabbuiati, 1661. 2nd edition; 8vo; (14), 192 pages, woodcut printer's device on titlepage; 19th century boards, rubbed. Ferguson II 135; Partington II 386; Singer Hist. of Tech III 217-9.   Jeffrey Mancevice 20-63 1996 $550.00

NERUDA, PABLO   The Elementary Odes of Pablo Neruda. New York: Cypress, 1961. 1st U.S. edition; small column of numbers on each of th two prelim blanks, else very good+ in dust jacket lacking several small piecies and with few tears.   Lame Duck Books 19-408 1996 $125.00

NERUDA, PABLO   The Heights of Macchu Picchu. New York: FSG, 1967. 1st U.S. edition; review copy with publisher's slip laid in; near fine in price clipped dust jacket.   Lame Duck Books 19-409 1996 $100.00

NERUDA, PABLO   Selected Poems. Boston: Beacon, 1971. 1st edition; fine in dust jacket, signed by one of the Translators, James Wright, uncommon thus.   Lame Duck Books 19-425 1996 $125.00

NERUDA, PABLO   Selected Poems. New York: Delacorte, 1972. 1st edition; review copy with slip and photo laid in. fine in slightly spine tanned dust jacket, scarce; inscribed by one of the translators, W. S. Merwin.   Lame Duck Books 19-414 1996 $100.00

NERUDA, PABLO   We Are Many. London: Cape Goliard, 1967. One of 1400 copies of the first edition of this work in wrappers (there was also a bound signed limited issue of 100 copies); review copy with slip laid in; front wrapper is a Jim Dine cut out of a hammer through which the poet's portrait can be seen; inscribed by author, scarce thus; very near fine in publisher's glassine with few small stains to front panel.   Lame Duck Books 19-410 1996 $950.00

NERUDA, PABLO   We Are Many. London: Cape Goliard, 1967. 1/100 numbered copies; boards, signed by author and translator, Alistair Reid; fine in dust jacket.   Left Bank Books 2-106 1996 $375.00

NERUDA, PABLO   We Are Many. New York: Grossman, 1968. 1st U.S. edition of the hardcover issue (1/500), near fine in spine tanned dust jacket.   Lame Duck Books 19-411 1996 $125.00

NESBITT, PAUL H.   The Ancient Mimbrenos. Beloit: Logan Museum, 1931. original wrappers, spine chipped with old tape repairs, otherwise very good. Saunders NM 591.   Ken Sanders 8-45 1996 $125.00

NESFIELD, W. EDEN   Specimens of Mediaeval Architecture Chiefly Selected from Examples of the 12th and 13th Centuries in France and Italy. London: Day & Son, 1862. Folio; 100 plates; new calf gilt, slight stain to bottom margin off title, preface discolored, plates bright and clean.   Petersfield Bookshop FH58-15 1996 £120.00

NESFIELD, W. EDEN   Specimens of Medieval Architecture Chiefly Selected from Examples of the 12th and 13th Centuries in France and Italy. London: Day & Son, 1862. Folio; decorative titlepage, (12) pages text, 100 lithographe plates (one colored); original cloth backed decorative boards, expertly respined retaining original gilt lettered backstrip; very good.   Ken Spelman 30-96 1996 £85.00

NETTLEFOLD, F. J.   The Collection of Bronzes and Castings in Brass and Ormolu Formed by Mr. F. J. Nettlefold. London: privately printed for the owner by Waterlow & Sons, 1934. Folio; 214 pages; 66 collotype plates; cloth, top edge gilt.   Rainsford A54-439 1996 £135.00

NEUE Thierbilder. Meggendorfer, n.d. ca. 1890. 6th edition; folio; 8 movables operated by a tab; color pictorial boards, light wear to covers, spine repaired, some repair to movements, else very good with original rivets present.   Marjorie James 19-157 1996 £850.00

NEUFELD, E.   The Hittite Laws. London: Luzac, 1951. 8vo; xii, 214 pages; 50 plates, original cloth, lightly chipped dust jacket. Archaeologia Luxor-2506 1996 $150.00

NEUGEBAUER, O.   Astronomical Cuneiform Texts. Princeton: Institute for Advanced Study, n.d. 4to; 3 volumes (complete), 511 pages, 255 plates; original cloth.   Archaeologia Luxor-2510 19964 $250.00

NEUGEBAUER, O.   Mathematical Cuneiform Texts. New Haven: American Oriental Society, 1945. 8vo; x, 177 pages, 49 plates; original cloth.   Archaeologia Luxor-2509 1996 $125.00

NEUMANN, CASPAR   The Chemical Works of Caspar Neumann, M.D., Professor of Chemistry at Berlin... London: printed for W. Johnston, G. Keith (& 6 others), 1759. 1st English edition; 4to; small library stamp on first 4 leaves, single wormhole in lower blank margin; contemporary calf, rubbed, hinges cracked. Duveen 430 (2nd ed. 1773 only); Ferguson 11, 137; Poggendorff II, 273.   Anthony W. Laywood 108-96 1996 £225.00

NEVILL, RALPH   Old English Sporting Books. London: The Studio, 1924. Limited to 1500 numbered copies; 4to; xii, 36 pages text; 107 plates; buckram, gilt, top edge gilt, slightly faded as usual, some very slight foxing.   Thomas Thorp 489-233 1996 £100.00

NEVILL, RALPH   Old English Sporting Prints and Their History. London: The Studio, 1923. Limited numbered edition of 1500 copies; 4to; xvi, 23 pages, 103 plates, including 47 in color; buckram gilt, top edge gilt, faded.   Thomas Thorp 489-232 1996 £75.00

NEVILL, RALPH   Old French Line Engravings. London: Halton & Truscott Smith, Number 26 of a limited edition of 100 copies; 4to; viii, 22 pages; 86 plates, 16 photogravures; publisher's padded blue leather over bevelled boards (slightly rubbed).   Thomas Thorp 489-234 1996 £50.00

NEVILL, A. W.   The History of Lamar County. Paris: North Texas, 1937. Signed card pasted in f.e.p., very good-, scattered foxing. Parker Books of the West 30-136 1996 $200.00

NEVILLE, HENRY   Plato Redivivus; or, a Dialogue Concerning Government... London: for S.I., 1681. 1st edition; small 8vo; (14), 272 pages; contemporary calf, rebacked, retaining portions of original backstrip, red morocco label. Wing N513.   Kenneth Karmiole 1NS-197 1996 $500.00

NEVILLE, HENRY   Plato Redivivus; or, a Dialogue Concerning Government, Wherein, by Observations Drawn from Other Kingdoms and States Both Ancient and Modern... London: printed for S.I. and sold by R. Dow, 1681. 2nd edition; 8vo; (16), 293, (1) pages; contemporary sheep, sides ruled in blind, spine gilt, but bit worn, joints splitting at head, otherwise very good, crisp copy. Lowndes 1661. Wing N515; Sweet & Maxwell I 610; not in Goldsmiths   John Drury 82-197 1996 £250.00

A NEW and General Biographical Dictionary Containing an Historical and Critical Account of the Lives and Writings of the Most Emminent (sic) Persons in Every Nation... London: Robinson, Johnson, Nichols and many others, 1798. New edition; tall octavo; 15 volumes; three quarter calf, marbled boards, raised bands, gilt, some wear, but text excellent. Lowndes I 195.   Hartfield 48-IIR 1996 $750.00

A NEW and General Biographical Dictionary... London: T. Osborne, J. Whiston & B. White, 1761-67. 12 volumes, licence leaf in volume 1; contemporary sprinkled calf, brown and green labels, some slight rubbing, handsome set; armorial booklabels of George de Ligne Gregory. Jarndyce 103-109 1996 £450.00

THE NEW Cambridge Modern History. Cambridge University Press, 1957-79. Large 8vo; 14 volumes; original buckram, neat ownership signature.   Howes Bookshop 265-127 1996 £400.00

A NEW Child's Play. London: Sampson, Low, Marston, Searle and Rivington, 1877. 1st edition; 4to; 16 full page drawings in black and white by Eleanor Boyle; green cloth stamped in gilt and blind, all edges gilt, fine, very scarce; Osborne 91.   Barbara Stone 70-34 1996 £195.00

NEW Clerk's Magazine, Containing All the Most Useful Forms, Which Occur in Business Transactions Between Man and Man. Boston: Lilly, Wait and Co., 1833. 2nd edition; contemporary speckled sheep, showing wear, but quite sound.   Meyer Boswell SL26-75 1996 $150.00

NEW Complete Guide to all Persons Who Have Any Trade or Concern with the City of London and Parts Adjacent... London: printed for T. Longman, etc. 1777. 15th edition; 12mo; title, pages 293, 1 leaf ads; 19th century half roan, marbled sides. Goss London Directories p. 59. Peter Murray Hill 185-104 1996 £185.00

THE NEW Encyclopaedia Britannica. London: 1974. Styled 15th edition; 4to; 30 volumes; original padded leatherette bindings with gilt tops, as new.   Howes Bookshop 265-331 1996 £425.00

A NEW English Dictionary of Historical Principles...(Together with) Introduction, Supplement and Bibliography. Oxford: Clarendon Press, 1888-1933. 4to; 15 volumes; 8 volumes in original half dark maroon morocco, backstrips gilt lettered, 7 volumes in red buckram, gilt lettered; all volumes excellent.   Blackwell's B112-218 1996 £175.00

A NEW General Collection of Voyages and Travels; Consisting of the Most Esteemed Relations, Which Have Been Hitherto Published in any Language.. London: printed for Thomas Astley, 1745-47. 1st edition; 4to; 4 volumes; frontispiece in each volume and full complement of 227 maps and plates; contemporary calf, gilt, spines gilt, contrasting red and blue morocco labels (some wear to spines, joints cracked by cords holding; aside from bining wear, an excellent unsophisticated copy. Sabin 28539; Hill p. 210; Lust 241; CBEL II 1392.   Ximenes 109-14 1996 $3,000.00

THE NEW Hampshire Book: Being Specimens of the Literature of the Granite State. Nashua: David Marsahll, 1842. 1st edition; 391 pages; original gift binding, full brown morocco, some rubbing and foxing; attractive American binding; fine association copy, inscribed by Franklin Pierce for Mrs. B. B. French.   19th Century Shop 39- 1996 $3,200.00

A NEW History of the Holy Bible. Ipswich: printed and sold by Charles Punchard sold also by Messrs. Rivington... n.d. not later than 1783; apparently the first and only edition; 8vo; vi, 229 pages, errata slip pasted on to blank verso of final leaf, occasional very light spotting, contemporary calf, gilt, recently rebacked, spine gilt with label, good; from the contemporary library of I. K. Lowndes with his armorial bookplate and signature.   John Drury 82-198 1996 £150.00

NEW YORK ACADEMY OF MEDICINE   The New York Academy of Medicine Catalogue of an Exhibition of Early and Later medical Americana. New York: 1927. 1st edition; wrappers.   W. Bruce Fye 71-1511 1996 $100.00

NEW YORK STATE CONFERENCE OF CHARITIES & CORRECTION Proceedings. 2nd, 6th, 8th, 9th. For the Years 1901, 1905, 1907, 1908. 1902/06/06/10. 8vo; 4 volumes; printed blue cloth, library bookpates and volume numbers on spines.   John Gach 150-349 1996 $100.00

NEW YORK. (STATE). Report of the Commissioners...to Revise the Laws for the Assessment and Collection of Taxes. Albany: the Argus Co., Printers, 1871. 154 pages; original printed wrappers, somewhat dusty, but sound. Meyer Boswell SL26-177 1996 $175.00

NEW YORK. (STATE). FOREST, FISH & GAME COMMISSION Annual Reports of the Forest, Fish and Game Commissioner for New York State. 1904/05/06. Larage 4to; 415 pages; nice colored plates, many other plates and photo illustrations; original buckram, lower cover slightly discolored; excellent copy. David A.H. Grayling 3/95-625 1996 £75.00

NEW YORK. (STATE). FOREST, FISH & GAME COMMISSION Forest, Fish and Game Commission of the State of New York. Seventh Report. Albany: 1902. 4to; pages 534; 35 full page colored plates; drawings and photos; cloth, extremities scuffed, hinges skillfully reinforced with cloth tape, inner joint cracked, some light foxing, mostly on title and preface pages. Raymond M. Sutton VII-537 1996 $165.00

NEW YORK. (STATE). STATE BOTANIST Annual Report of the State Botanist of the State of New York. Albany: 1897. 2nd edition; 4to; 241 pages; 1 plain and 43 colored plates; original gilt decorated green cloth, rubbed at corners and edges, some soiling to covers, nick to edge of rear cover, some staining to page fore edges. Raymond M. Sutton VII-288 1996 $135.00

NEW YORK. (STATE). STATE BOTANIST Report of the State Botanist on Edible Fungi of New York 1895-99. Albanh: 1900. 4to; (2), (132-234), original boards, some scuffing to edges, spine chipped and faded, dampstain on rear cover. Raymond M. Sutton VII-290 1996 $125.00

NEW YORK. (STATE). STATE BOTANIST Report of the State Botanist. New York for the Years 1900-12. Albany: 1901-13. 8vo; 13 numbers; 94 colored plates; original wrappers, some wear, soiled, some pages browned, unobtrusive library, stamps on plates, ex-library, also included is the portfolio of plates from U.S.N.Y. 48th State Mus. Report 1894, with 44 folded plates; cloth, paper pouch is loose, embossed library stmap on plates, ex-library. Raymond M. Sutton VII-289 1996 $300.00

NEWBERRY LIBRARY A Bibliographical Checklist of North and Middle American Indian Linguistics in the Edward E. Ayer Collection. Chicago: 1941. 1st edition; large 8vo; unpaginated, cloth, leather spine labels; scarce, spines sunned, else very good. The Bookpress 75-332 1996 $185.00

NEWBERY, JOHN Letters on the Most Common, as Well as Important Occasions in Life... London: printed for J. Newbery, 1758. 4th edition; 12mo; contemporary calf, hinges weakening. Roscoe J266(4); ESTC 5053412. Jarndyce 103-293 1996 £140.00

NEWBY, ERIC The Last Grain Race. London: Secker & Warburg, 1956. 1st edition; 25 pages of black and white photos, folding map at rear, maps on endpapers; original binding, top ege dusty, fore-edge slightly spotted, head and tail of spine slightly bumped, very good in chipped, torn, creased, rubbed and dusty dust jacket slightly darkened at spine and edges. Ulysses 39-444 1996 £55.00

NEWCASTLE UNION GAS LIGHT COMPANY Deeds, Rules and Regulations, for the Settlement and Government of the Newcastle Upon Tyne and Gateshead Union Gas Light Company. Newcastle; printed at the Courant office by J. Blackwell and Co., 1839. Apparently 1st edition; 8vo; 84 pages; contemporary (?original) roan backed marbled boards with vellum corners, unlettered; very good. John Drury 82-199 1996 £75.00

NEWCASTLE, 7TH DUKE OF The Clumber Library. Catalogue of the Magnificent Library...Removed from Clumber, Worksop. London: Sotheby & Co., 1937-38. 8vo; 4 parts, 3 colored frontispieces, 110 plates; original printed boards or wrappers (little soiled). Forest Books 74-197 1996 £75.00

NEWCASTLE, THOMAS PELHAM HOLLES, 1ST DUKE OF 1693-1768 The Duke of Newcastle's Letter by His Majesty's Order to Monsieur Michell, the King of Prussia's Scretary of the Embassy, in Answer to the Memorial and Other Papers... London: printed by Edward Owen, 1753. 1st edition; 4to; 46 pages; title partly foxed, 2 folding tables; disbound. Anthony W. Laywood 109-66 1996 £50.00

NEWCOMB, FRANC JOHNSON Navajo Omens and Taboos. Santa Fe: Rydal Press, 1940. 1st edition; one of 1000 copies; 79 pages, review and front portion of dust jacket pasted in rear on endpapers; prepublication ad for volume loose in rear; red cloth, very good+; Saunders NM 1176. Ken Sanders 8-223 1996 $250.00

NEWCOMB, REXFORD The Spanish House for America: its Design, Furnishing and Garden. Philadelphia: J. B. Lippincott Co., 1927. 10 1/8 x 6 3/4 inches; 164 pages + frontispiece, numerous full page and smaller photographic illustrations in pagination; pictorial tan cloth. Dawson's Books Shop 528-179 1996 $125.00

NEWELL, PETER The Hole Book. New York: Harper & Bros., 1928. 1st edition; 4to; 3 tone illustrations, each illustration has a hole in it to illustrate the effects of Tom shooting a gun; pictorial boards, some smal repaired tears, f.e.p. stamped, else very good. Marjorie James 19-166 1996 £125.00

NEWELL, R. H. Letterwriters on the Scenery of Wales... London: for Baldwin Cradock and Joy, 1821. 8vo; xiv, (2), 192 pages, half title, vignette titlepage, 10 aquatint plates; contemporary half calf; very good; bookplate of C. W. H. Sotheby. Ken Spelman 30-97 1996 £160.00

NEWFELD, E. The Hittite Laws. London: Luzac, 1951. 8vo; xi, 209 pages, 50 photographic plates; original cloth. Archaeologia Luxor-2512 1996 $125.00

NEWHALL, FREDERIC CUSHMAN With General Sheridan in Lee's Last Campaign. Philadelphia: J. B. Lippincott, 1866. 1st edition; 235 pages; frontispiece, folding map; original cloth, extremities scuffed, else very good; Dornbusch I PA 54; Howes N116. McGowan Book Co. 65-67 1996 $150.00

NEWHALL, N. The Daybooks of Edward Weston. Aperture, 1973. 2 volumes, dust jackets. J. B. Muns 154-328 1996 $150.00

NEWHALL, N. P. H. Emerson: the Fight for Photography. Aperture, 1972. 1st edition; oblong 8vo; illustrations; dust jacket. J. B. Muns 154-103 1996 $100.00

NEWLANDS, DAVID L. Early Ontario Potters: Their Craft and Trade. Toronto: McGraw-Hill Ryerson, c. 1979. 4to; pages (viii), 245, richly illustrated, maps, cloth; fine in chipped dust jacket. Hugh Anson-Cartwright 87-317 1996 $100.00

NEWLANDS, JAMES The Carpenter and Joiner's Assistant. Glasgow: etc., Blackie, 1860. Folio; engraved title, 110 plates plus 3 "A" plates; contemporary half calf, rubbed. Charles W. Traylen 117-349 1996 £90.00

NEWLANDS, JAMES The Carpenter and Jointer's Assistant. Glasgow: Blackie, 1862. Probably the second edition; 4to; xiii, (i), 291, (1) pages, engraved title and 115 engraved plates, irregularly bound; contemporary quarter morocco, spine rejointed. Elton Engineering 10-114 1996 £180.00

NEWLANDS, JAMES The Carpenter and Joiner's Assistant... London: Blackie & Son, 1880. Folio; xiv, 254 pages; 100 plates, several hundred text figures; contemporary black half calf, brown morocco label, rubbed and worn, endpaper crudely repaired with sellotape, minor marginal repair to fore-edge of titlepage, occasional very slight dust soiling in text, but on the whole a clean copy. Thomas Thorp 489-235 1996 £85.00

NEWLOVE, JOHN Moving in Alone. Toronto: Contact Press, c. 1965. 1st edition; issued in printed wrappers, autographed by author, dated 12 May, 1965; about fine; from the library of John Metcalf, with his ownership signature. Nelson Ball 118-80 1996 $300.00

NEWMAN, FRANCIS WILLIAM Lectures on Political Economy. London: John Chapman, 1851. 1st edition; 8vo; original purple cloth, spine evenly faded, minor rubbing; very good. Ximenes 108-276 1996 $200.00

NEWMAN, JOHN HENRY, CARDINAL 1801-1890 Apologia Pro Vita Sua... London: Longman, Green, 1864. 1st edition; 8vo; blue cloth, page iv misnumbered v, housed in chemise and modern morocco backed cloth slipcase with leather labels, raised cross and gilt, small shelf label on pastedown, light fraying along spine edge, very good in scarce cloth; Newman's bookplate laid in loosely. Charles Agvent 4-917 1996 $600.00

NEWMAN, JOHN HENRY, CARDINAL 1801-1890 Apologia Pro Vita Sua... London: Longman, Green, 1864. 1st edition; 8vo; three quarter morocco by Bayntun, margins trimmed in rebinding, owner name faded from title, gilt decorated spine, all edges gilt, rubbing to joints and edges, near fine. Charles Agvent 4-918 1996 $325.00

NEWMAN, JOHN HENRY, CARDINAL 1801-1890   The Dream of Gerontius... London: Longmans, Green and Co., 1909. Number 32 of and edition of 525 copies; 4to; 44, (ii) pages letterpress, (xxxviii) pages photo facsimile plates; original cloth backed boards, top edge gilt, gilt lettering; good.   Robert Clark 38-251 1996 £55.00

NEWNHAM, WILLIAM   Essay on Superstition; Being an Inquiry Into the Effects of Physical Influence on the Mind in the Production of Dreams, Visions, Ghosts and Other Supernatural Appearances. London: J. Hatchard and Son, 1st edition; 8vo; xvi, 430, (2) pages; contemporary leather backed marbled boards, rear hinge broken, spine taped, fair to good copy. Crabtree 1988 #346.   John Gach 150-350 1996 $150.00

NEWPORT, MARUCIE   Sereniss Principi Carolo Secundo Mag. Brit. Fran. et Hib. Regi Votum Candidum Vivat Rex. Editio Altera Emendatior. Londini: Typis Neucomianis, 1669. 2nd edition; 8vo; (viii), 164 pages, wormhole at edge of lower margin on four leaves in middle of book; contemporary calf. Wing N939A.   David Bickersteth 133-52 1996 £50.00

NEWS from Prince Rupert. Whose Forces Being Discovered by the Earle of Denbigh. The Earle with His Forces Marched Against Them; and How Captaine Pinkney Left Prince Rupert, and Came in to the Earle of Denbigh with 100 Welchmen... London: printed by F. L. May 25, 1644. 4to; (2), 6 pages; choice copy, uncut and unopened. Wing N991.   C. R. Johnson 37-63 1996 £350.00

NEWS from Purgatory. Or, the Jesuits Legacy to all Countries. London: 1679? Folio; 4 pages; disbound. Wing N993.   C. R. Johnson 37-64 1996 £65.00

NEWTE, THOMAS   Prospects and Observations: On a Tour in England and Scotland: Natural, Economical and Literary. London: printed for G. G. J. and J. Robinson, 1791. 2nd edition; 4to; iv, (4), 440 pages; 23 engraved plates, large folding map expertly rebacked and repaired, otherwise fine; recently rebound in blue half calf, marbled boards. Cox III p. 34.   David Mason 71-31 1996 $480.00

NEWTE, THOMAS   A Tour in England and Scotland in 1785. London: Robinson, 1788. 1st edition; octavo; pages 367; 6 fine engraved views, nice later binding in full tan calf, gilt fillets, gilt on red leather label. Very good. Lowndes III 1333.   Hartfield 48-L64 1996 $350.00

NEWTON, A.   President's Address to the Norfolk and Norwich Naturalist's Society. Norwich: 1888. Offprint; 8vo; 8 leaves; contemporary half leather, inscribed by author to Theodore Sauzier and with his annotations.   Maggs Bros. Ltd. 1190-589 1996 £55.00

NEWTON, ALFRED EDWARD   Derby Day and Other Adventures. Boston: Little Brown, 1934. 1st edition; large paper copy, limited to 1129 signed and numbered copies; 9 3/4 x 6 1/2 inches; xii, 389 pages; colored frontispiece and 25 black and white plates; canvas backed green boards, uncut, unopened; very good. In pocket on rear board is 20 page facsimile booklet of original manuscript measuring 4 1/2 x 3 3/4 inches; Y&T 408b.   Ian Hodgkins 78-357 1996 £65.00

NEWTON, ALFRED EDWARD   Mr. Strahan's Dinner Party. printed for the Book Club of California by John Henry Nash 1930. Number 322 of 335 copies, signed by author; folio; pages 43; splendid Nash printing on heavy laid paper, uncut; tan buckram spine, blue boards; fine. Hartfield 48-V37 1996 $195.00

NEWTON, C. T.   Travels and Discoveries in the Levant. London: Day & Son, 1865. 8vo; 2 volumes, xxviii, 635 pages; 38 woodcut illustrations, 41 plates; full 19th century morocco with 5 raised bands, top edge gilt, minor rubbing at extremities, still attractive set.   Archaeologia Luxor-3762 1996 $650.00

NEWTON, HELMUT   Sleepless Nights. New York: 1978. 1st edition; illustrations; dust jacket.   J. B. Muns 154-218 1996 $100.00

NEWTON, HELMUT   White Women. New York: 1976. 1st printing, dust jacket, illustrations, some color.   J. B. Muns 154-219 1996 $125.00

NEWTON, HENRY   Report of the Geology of the Black Hills of Dakota. Washington: 1880. 1st edition; 566 pages; frontispiece, plates, several in color, illustrations; cloth, nice, rare. Jennewin 58.   T. A. Swinford 49-846 1996 $275.00

NEWTON, ISAAC 1642-1727   Opticks; or, a Treatise of the Reflections, Refractins, Inflections and Colours of Light. London: printed for William and John Innys, 1721. 3rd edition; 8vo; (viii), 382 pages, 8 page publisher's list at end, 12 folding engraved plates; original panelled calf, rebacked, new endpapers, title little dusty and early pages rather spotted.   David Bickersteth 133-212 1996 £975.00

NEWTON, ISAAC 1642-1727   Philosophiae Naturalis Principia Mathematica. London: Gull. & Joh. Innys, 1726. 3rd edition, 1st issue; 4to; (36), 530, (8) pages, title in red and black, numerous text diagrams, engraved plate on page 506, complete with half title, frontispiece and imprimatur and ad leaf, some or all of which are often missing; contemporary panelled calf, red morocco spine label; rebacked, some restoration to corners, small stain on portrait and title, last two leaves remargined, not affecting text; very good; 18th century ownership signature on front blank. Babson 13; Gray 9; Wallis 9.   Edwin V. Glaser 121-229 1996 $4,500.00

NEWTON, ISAAC 1642-1727   A Treatise on the System of the World. London: printed for F. Fayram, 1728. 8vo; xxiv, 154, (1) pages, complete with 3 full page plates, illustrations in text; modern quarter calf over marbled boards, spine gilt with five gilt ruled bands, red speckled edges; very good. Babson 18; Gray 30.   Edwin V. Glaser 121-230 1996 $3,000.00

NEWTON, RICHARD   Pluralities Indefensible. A Treatise Humbly Offered to the Consideration of the Parliament of Great Britain. London: printed for J. Osborn, 1745. 3rd edition; 8vo; ; half title, single wormhole in lower blank margin of first 220 pages; contemporary calf, worn, spine gilt, hinges cracked. Inscription "A present from Dr. Newton 1747".   Anthony W. Laywood 108-97 1996 £85.00

NICHOLAS, JOHN L.   Narrative of a Voyage to New Zealand, Performed in the Years 1814 and 1815, in Company with the Rev. Samuel Marsden... London: James Black, 1817. 8vo; 2 volumes; pages xx, 431; xii, 398; 2 maps, 4 plates; modern quarter imitation calf, marbled boards. Hocken p. 37; Taylor p. 191; Ferguson 690.   Richard Adelson W94/95-129 1996 $750.00

NICHOLASON, WILLIAM   The English Historical Library London: Timothy Childe, 1714. 2nd edition; folio; full contemporary panelled calf, joints cracking but firm, red morocco labels.   Ian Wilkinson 95/1-132 1996 £150.00

NICHOLL, JOHN   Some Account of the Worshipful Company of Ironmongers. London: Privately printed, 1866-1916. 2nd edition; very thick 4to; (2), xii, (2), 621, (4), 8, (2), 4, (2), 6, (2), 3, (2), 11, (2), 7, (2), 52, 10, xlviii (623)-657, (1) pages; numerous illustrations, some as folding plates, some in color; photographic illustrations mounted on heavy paper; additional materials realting to Ironmongers bound in; three quarter morocco, top edge gilt, marbled endpapers, binding rubbed, joints tender, very good; with ms. presentation from E. H. Nicholl, Honorary Librarian to the Company laid in.   Edwin V. Glaser 121-234 1996 $475.00

NICHOLLS, W.   The History and Traditions of Ravenstonedale, Westmorland. Manchester: 1877. 2nd edition, identical to first, but over printed 'second edition' on titlepage.   R.F.G. Hollett & Son 78-1134 1996 £85.00

NICHOLLS, W.   The History and Traditions of Ravenstonedale, Westmorland. Manchester: published by request, 1877. 8vo; pages 128; original cloth, gilt, nice.   R.F.G. Hollett & Son 78-1133 1996 £65.00

NICHOLLS, W.   The History and Traditions of Ravenstonedale, Westmorland. Manchester: Abey Hewywood and Son, n.d., c. 1910. 1st edition; 8vo; Volume II; pages 184; illustrations; original cloth, gilt, excellent copy.   R.F.G. Hollett & Son 78-1135 1996 £85.00

NICHOLLS, W. H.   Orchids of Australia. Melbourne: 1969. Folio; pages xxii, 141; 476 colored plates, map; cloth, dust jacket with some tears. Raymond M. Sutton VI-925 1996 $275.00

NICHOLS, GEORGE WARD   Art Education Applied to Industry. New York: Harper and Bros., 1877. 1st edition; royal 8vo; 122 illustrations, 211 pages; original red cloth, gilt, edges gilt, very good to nice. James Fenning 133-244 1996 £55.00

NICHOLS, GEORGE WARD   Pottery, How it is Made, its Shape and Decoration. London: Sampson, Low and others, 1878. 1st edition; 8vo; vi, (ii), 142 pages; frontispiece; original printed boards, some cover wear, front hinge internally cracked, bookplate, else very good. Bookpress 75-92 1996 $110.00

NICHOLS, J.   The History of the Royal Hospital and Collegiate Church of St. Katharine, Near the Tower of London, From Its Foundation in the Year 1273 to the Present Time. London: Nichols, 1782. 4to; frontispiece, title, pages iii-viii, 46, 16 engraved plates, 1 engraved text illustration, 74/5 bis, 112; later half red morocco, upper joint cracked but holding. Marlborough 162-178 1996 £75.00

NICHOLS, J. B.   Account of the Royal Hosptial and Collegiate Church of Saint Katharine Near the Tower of London. London: Nichols, 1824. 4to; title, 1 f., 61 pages, folding engraved frontispiece, 5 plates; original patterned green cloth, small tear to bottom of spine.   Marlborough 162-179 1996 £85.00

NICHOLS, JOHN   Miscellaneous Tracts by the Late William Bowyer, Printer, F.S.A. and Several of His Learned Friends... Edinburgh: printed by and for the editor, 1775. 1st edition; 4to; vignette on title; contemporary "Etruscan" calf by Edwards of Halifax bindery, with central tree calf panel, surrounded by a border of stained classical palmette, and gilt Greek-key pattern roll, rebacked, spine gilt, label, all edges gilt, nice. Anthony W. Laywood 108-98 1996 £175.00

NICHOLS, JOHN GOUGH   Examples of Decorative Tiles, Sometimes Called Encaustic. London: J. B. Nichols & Sons, 1845. 1st edition; 4to; (ii), 22 pages, 101 illustrations on 96 plates; entirely printed in dark orange ink on orange paper; contemporary half calf, very good to fine, scarce.   Bookpress 75-93 1996 $1,250.00

NICHOLS, R.   The Smile of the Sphinx. Beaumont Press, 1920. 1st edition; 1/295 copies; near fine.   Aronovitz 57-849 1 996 $125.00

NICHOLS, T. L.   Supramundane Facts: In the Life of Rev. Jesse Babcock Ferguson: Including 20 Years Observation of Preternatural Phenomena. London: 1865. 1st edition; 264 pages; cloth, very good. Middle Earth 77-122 1996 $145.00

NICHOLSON, A. ASENATH   Ireland's Welcome to the Stranger. New York: Baker and Scribner, 1847. 1st edition; 8vo; viii, 456, 20 pages ads, new endpapers; recently rebound with tan calf spine, marbled boards, raised bands, leather spine label; lengthy inscription, otherwise fine. David Mason 71-99 1996 $200.00

NICHOLSON, CORNELIUS   The Annals of Kendal: Being a Historical and Descriptive Account of Kendal and the Neighbourhood: with Biographical Sketches of Many Eminent Personages Connected with the Town. London: Whitaker & Co., 1861. 2nd edition; 8vo; pages xii, 412, engraved portrait frontispiece, engraved folding map, illustrations; original blindstamped cloth, gilt, hinges just cracking.   R.F.G. Hollett & Son 78-1136 1996 £95.00

NICHOLSON, GEORGE   The Illustrated Dictionary of Gardening. New York: & London: Penman, 1890. 1st edition; 4to; 4 volumes, pages 544, 544, 537, 608; engraved illustrations, 19 colored plates; all edges gilt, green cloth, very good, loose hinges, nice set.   Second Life Books 103-146 1996 $150.00

NICHOLSON, J.   The History and Antiquities of the Counties of Westmorland and Cumberland. London: W. Strahan and T. Cadell, 1777. 1st edition; 4to; 2 volumes, pages cxxxiv, 630; 615, (8 index), 2 large folding maps, excellent, clean and sound set; modern half calf, gilt, marbled boards.   R.F.G. Hollett & Son 78-1142 1996 £475.00

NICHOLSON, J.   The History and Antiquities of the Counties of Westmorland and Cumberland. London: W. Strahan and T. Cadell, 1777. 1st edition; 4to; 2 volumes; pages cxxxiv, 630; 615, (8 index), 2 large folding maps, both relaid on stiff paper, modern full blind ruled soft calf gilt, raised bands; few spots in places, but very good, clean, sound set. R.F.G. Hollett & Son 78-1141 1996 £450.00

NICHOLSON, J.   The History and Antiquities of the Counties of Westmorland and Cumberland. London: printed for W. Strahan and T. Cadell, 1777. 1st edition; 4to; 2 volumes; pages cxxxiv, 630; 615, (8 index), complete with 2 large folding maps; old half morocco gilt, spines faded, rather rubbed; very good, sound set.   R.F.G. Hollett & Son 78-1140 1 996 £385.00

NICHOLSON, JAMES B.   A Manual of the Art of Bookbinding... Philadelphia: Henry Carey Baird, 1856. 1st edition; frontispiece, 12 plates of binding designs, 7 full page samples of marbled paper, illustrations in text; brown half morocco, marbled boards, spine in compartments with raised bands, marbled edges, slightly worn at extremities, upper hinge split, some offset from plates. Brenni 39; Meyer 1950.   Maggs Bros. Ltd. 1191-18 1996 £550.00

NICHOLSON, JAMES B.   A Manual of the Art of Bookbinding... Philadelphia: Henry Carey Baird, 1871. 2nd edition; 8vo; 318 pages, illustrations and 6 tipped in specimens of marbled paper and 24 pages of publisher's catalog; original black cloth, very minor wear, very good. Robert F. Lucas 42-9 1996 $600.00

NICHOLSON, JAMES B.   A Manual of the Art of Bookbinding: Containing Full Instructions in the Different Branches of Forwarding, Gilding and Finishing... Philadelphia: Henry Carey Baird, 1878. 7 marbled leaves, 12 plates, 13 text illustrations, ads at end; new endpapers, original cloth, rebacked preserving original spine.   Forest Books 74-199 1996 £295.00

NICHOLSON, JOSEPH WALKER   Crosby Garrett, Westmorland. Kirkby Stephen: J. W. Braithwaite & Sons, 1914. 1st (only) edition; 8vo; pages xv, 136; 18 illustrations; original blue pictorial cloth.   R.F.G. Hollett & Son 78-1143 1996 £60.00

NICHOLSON, MR.   The Trial at Full Length of Maj. Gen. Sir Robt. Thomas Wilson, Michael Bruce, Esq. and Captain John Hely Hutchinson...for Aiding...the Escape of General Lavalette. c. 1816. 8vo; xxiv, 105 pages; portrait; full calf, needs rebacking.   C. P. Hyland 216-340 1996 £75.00

NICHOLSON, NORMAN   The Fire of the Lord. London: Nicholson and Watson, 1944. 1st edition; 8vo; pages 222; original cloth, spine faded as usual; presentation copy, inscribed by author for Rev. S. Taylor. R.F.G. Hollett & Son 78-430 1996 £65.00

NICHOLSON, NORMAN   A Match for the Devil. London: Faber, 1955. 1st edition; 8vo; pages 83; original cloth, gilt, dust jacket, fine, scarace. R.F.G. Hollett & Son 78-437 1996 £75.00

NICHOLSON, NORMAN   Prophesy to the Wind. London: Faber, 1950. 1st edition; 8vo; pages 80; original cloth, gilt, dust jacket (spine little faded), few light spots on flyleaf, scarce.   R.F.G. Hollett & Son 78-44 1996 £65.00

NICHOLSON, NORMAN   Wednesday Early Closing. London: Faber, 1975. 1st edition; pages 202; original cloth, gilt, dust jacket, price clipped, small mark on upper panel; signed by author. Rather scarce. R.F.G. Hollett & Son 78-226 1996 £50.00

NICHOLSON, PETER   The Builder's and Workman's New Director. London: A. Fullarton and Co., 1864. New edition; 4to; (10), 472 pages, 157 plates; contemporary half morocco, neat repairs to foot of spine; some browning and light spotting to plates, as usual, but very good. Ken Spelman 30-98 1996 £130.00

NICHOLSON, PETER   The Practical Cabinet-Maker, Upholsterer, and Complete Decorator. London: H. Fisher & Son 1843.. 4to; frontispiece, title, 152, 12 pages; 96 engraved plates, some hand colored; contemporary quarter calf.   Sotheran PN32-190 1996 £498.00

NICHOLSON, PETER   The Student's Instructor in Drawing and Working the Five Orders of Architecture. London: J. Taylor at the Architectural Library, 1810. 3rd edition; 41 plates, 2 pages + 2 pages ads, smaller format 12 page catalog of Taylor's publications; some staining to text and plates; excellently rebound in half maroon morocco.   Jarndyce 103-542 1996 £120.00

NICHOLSON, S.   Twenty-Six Lithographic Drawings in the Vicinity of Liverpool. Liverpool: for the authors, 1821. Folio; title, 2 ff., frontispiece, 26 pen litho plates; later half morocco, dusty, some foxing; not in Abbey.   Marlborough 162-74 1996 £675.00

NICHOLSON, WILLIAM   A Collection of Papers Scatter'd Lately About the Town in the Daily-Fourant, St. James's Post, &c... London: printed for B. Barker and C. King, both in Westminster Hall, 1717. Small 8vo; half leather, marbled boards, front cover separated, collector blindstamp on title, very good. Bookplate of Robert Pitcairn. Lampeter 6191. Freedom Bookshop 14-24 1996 $115.00

NICHOLSON, WILLIAM   A Dictionary of Practical and Theoretical Chemistry with Its Application to the Arts and Manufactures... London: printed for Richard Phillips, 1808. 8vo; 12 engraved plates, 13 printed folding tables; original tree calf, rebacked, old spine preserved. Partington IV 19.   David Bickersteth 133-214 1996 £98.00

NICHOLSON, WILLIAM 1872-1949   An Alphabet. London: William Heinemann, 1898. Edition deluxe on handmade paper; large 4to; plates loosely mounted on large brown sheets, colored vignette on titlepage and 26 full page colored plates; original decorated cloth, covers little stained and joints worn, gilt edges.   Charles W. Traylen 117-242 1996 £480.00

NICHOLSON, WILLIAM 1872-1949   Clever Bill. London: Heinemann, 1929. 1st American edition; oblong 8vo; 24 pages of captioned illustrations by Nicholson; colored pictorial boards, covers slightly marked, tips just rubbed, else fresh copy, very scarce.   Barbara Stone 70-161 1996 £325.00

NICHOLSON, WILLIAM 1872-1949   The Square Book of Animals. London: Heinemann, 1900. square folio; 14 pages; 12 plates; cloth boards with vignette, front cover with darkened bottom corner, rear cover slightly dampsstained, else very good, very nice, tight copy. Marjorie James 19-167 1996 £250.00

NICKALLS, JAMES   The Statutes of the Province of Upper Canada; together with Such British Statutes, Ordinances of Quebec and Proclamations.... Kingston: 1831. 12 x 8.5 inches; 692 pages; three quarter leather, marbled baords, ink stamped names, covers heavily rubbed, some ink notes and foxing. Also 13 Page act for Petty Trespasses (1834) present.   John K. King 77-36 1996 $250.00

NICKSON, G.   A Portrait of Salmon Fishing. London: 1976. Limited to 1500 numbered copies; 37 full page color plates; quality cloth binding, housed in pictorial slipcase, bit bumped.   David A.H. Grayling 3/95-488 1996 £75.00

NICOL, WALTER   The Gardener's Kalendar; or, Monthly Directory of Operations in Every Branch of Horticulture. London: 1812. 2nd edition; 8vo; pages xxi, 646, 2 ads; straight grained half morocco, gilt, lightly browned, some slight marginal waterstaining.   John Henly 27-318 1996 £120.00

NICOL, WALTER   The Practical Planter; or, a Treatise on Forest Planting... London: for J. Scatcherd and H. D. Symonds, 1803. 2nd edition; 8vo; vi, pages (7)-306, 11 leaves, some light waterstains, contemporary half calf, marbled boards, joints cracked.   H. M. Fletcher 121-143 1996 £85.00

NICOLAS, HARRIS   A Treatise on the Law of Adulterine Bastardy, with a Report of the Banbury Case, and All Other Cases Bearing Upon the Subject. London: William Pickering, 1836. 1st edition; 8vo; half title, 588 pages, 9 pages ads at end, original cloth, leather label; presentation inscription for Revd. R. H. Barham.   Anthony W. Laywood 109-106 1996 £135.00

NICOLAUS DE AUXIMO   Supplementum. Venice: Franciscus Renner de Heilbron & Nicolaus de Frankfordia, 1474. Folio; 336 leaves, first and last blank (latter largely cut away), gothic letter, large red penwork initial on fol. 2, initials supplied in red, many with vigorous flourishes extending into margins, paragraph marks, initial strokes and underlinings supplied in red, traces of original ms. quiring still visible at lower corner of many leaves; contemporary blindstamped leather (calf?) over wooden boards, sewn on double cords, sewing guards to each gathering of vellum from old Hebrew manuscript, elaborately chased brass bosses at centre and corners of both boards, chased brass clasps and catches, remains of shackle at top of lower board where this binding was formerly chained, spine and top board worn and very discolored commensurate with having lain chained for centuries; tall, clean, crisp copy. Goff N60; HC 2153; BMC V (.B. 19842); IGI 6870.   H. M. Fletcher 121-12 1996 £5,650.00

NICOLAY, C. G.   Notes on the Aborigines of Western Australia. London: William Clowes & Sons, The Colonial & Indian Exhibition, 1886. 18 page pamphlet; original printed wrappers, bound in papered boards, leather spine label; fine, scarace; Edge-Partington bookplate, the Absolon copy. Ferguson 13373; Greenway 7213.   Antipodean 28-147 1996 $350.00

NICOLAYSEN, N.   The Viking-Ship Discovered at Gokstad in Norway. Christiana: 1882. Large 4to; (10), 78 pages; very free from foxing, 13 plates; very good.   Bookworm & Silverfish 280-171 1996 $225.00

NICOLSON, BENEDICT   Joseph Wright of Derby, Painter of Light. London: The Paul Mellon Foundation for British Art, 1968. 32 x 26 cm; 2 volumes; xvi, 300 pages, frontispiece, 140 text figures; xiii, 221 pages, frontispiece, 355 plates; original cloth, dust jackets.   Rainsford A54-605 1996 £75.00

NIDER, JOHANNES   Formicarius. Augsburg: Anton Sorg, c. 1484. Folio; 192 leaves (first and last blank), signatures, gothic letter, initial spaces with guide letters, some marginal annotations in 16th century hand, minor soiling; few wormholes mainly in last few leaves; modern blindstamped brown morocco by Sangorski & Sutcliffe, morocco edged slipcase. Good, tall, clean copy. Goff N 176; HC 11832; BMC II 351. H. M. Fletcher 121-13 1996 £5,000.00

NIEBAUER, ABBY   Three Windows; Poems. Woodside: Heyeck Press, 1980. One of 100 numbered copies, signed by author; 4to; printed in handset Centaur and Arrighi in black and sepia on Barcham Green handmade; half brown cloth, marbled boards, by the Schuberth Bookbindery; fine.   Bertram Rota 272-230 1996 £55.00

NIEBUHR, KARSTEN   Descriptio de l'Arabie d'Apres les Observations et Recherches faites dans le Pays Meme. Copenhague: Nicholas Moller, 1773. 1st edition; small 4to; title vignette, xlvi, 372 pages, 25 plates; three quarter green calf antique with 5 raised bands and leather label, and marbled boards, 19th century signatures, some browning. Archaeologia Luxor-2514 1996 $1,250.00

NIEDECKER, LORINE   From This Condensery: the Complete Writing of Lorine Niedecker. Highlands: Jargon Society, 1985. 1st edition; limited to 100 copies; tall 8vo; full leather, printed labels; as new, signed by editor, Robert J. Bertholf and by Jonthan Williams, publisher.   James S. Jaffe 34-509 1996 $150.00

NIELSON, HARRY B.   An Animal ABC. London: Blackie and Son Ltd., n.d. 1901. 1st edition; tinted frontispiece, title vignette, 22 tinted full page illustrations, 24 pages of text with 4 or 5 images around borders, blue cloth spine, color pictorial board; light wear.   Robin Greer 94A-4 1996 £65.00

NIEMEYER, A. H   Travels on the Continent and In England. London: printed for Sir Richard Phillips, 1823. Tall 8vo; viii, 104 pages; recently rebound with calf spine, boards, leather label; fine.   David Mason 71-32 1996 $140.00

NIEMEYER, A. H.   Travels on the Continent and in England. London: printed for Sir Richard Phillips and Co. Bridge Court, Bridge St., 1823. 8vo; (iii-viii), 1-104 pages; quarter calf and cloth boards, gilt title stamped to backstrip, corners bumped; new endpapers and prelims, owner's bookplate to front pastedown.   Beeleigh Abbey BA/56-100 1996 £75.00

NIEMEYER, WILHELM   Nicola Tuldo und Santa Catarina Im Kerker Zu Siena. Rupprecht-Presse, 1918-19. One of 200 copies; 9 3/4 x 7 1/2 inches; 2 p.l., (1 blank), xxxvi pages, (4) leaves; device on colophon; expressive inlaid black morocco by P. Kersten, covers framed with multiple plain and decorative gilt rules, large round complex sunburst ornament at center of each board featuring 8 inlaid purple tulips, flat spine titled and decorated in gilt, batik endpapers, fanciful flyleaves in colorful and jagged pattern, top edge gilt, very fine.   Phillip J. Pirages 33-452 1996 $2,800.00

NIERENDORF, KARL   Paul Klee: Paintings, Watercolors, 1913 to 1939. New York: Oxford University Press, 1941. 4to; 35 pages text + 2 tipped in color serigraphs and 65 monochrome plates; spiral bound flexible boards, cover browning, some backstrip wear. Lucas p. 159.   Brannan 43-309 1996 $110.00

NIES, JAMES B.   Ur Dynasty Tablets: Texts Chiefly from Tello and Drehem Written During the Reigns of Dungi, Bur-Sin, Gimil-Sin and Ibi-Sin. Leipzig: J. C. Hinrich, 1920. 4to; 224 pages and 64 plates, 27 line drawings; original cloth, corners lightly bumped, small stain at lower board, owner's stamp at titlepage.   Archaeologia Luxor-2516 1996 $275.00

A NIGHT in Venice Belvedere California. N.P.: September Sixteenth, 1899. 1st edition; (84) pages, including wrappers, illustrations; original red pictorial wrappers, minor stain to first few pages, very good. Not in Cowan or Rocq.   Michael D. Heaston 23-62 1996 $200.00

NIGHTINGALE, B.   The Ejected of 1662 in Cumberland and Westmorland. Manchester: 1911. 1st edition; thick 8vo; 2 volumes; pages xxiv, 777; 780-1490 (25 ads); original cloth, gilt, neatly recased, excellent, clean sound set.   R.F.G. Hollett & Son 78-1153 1996 £185.00

NIMMO, WILLIAM   History of Stirlingshire, Corrected and Brought Down to the Present Time by Rev. William M. Stirling. London: printed by John Fraser for Andrew Bean etc., 1817. 2nd edition; 8vo; 2 volumes, pages (viii), 385; 386-772, uncut, complete with folding hand colored map, 1 plan and 1 plate, map with short repaired tear slightly offset on to title, but very nice set; late 19th century half morocco, gilt, raised bands and decorative rolls. Armorial bookplate of Sir Charles Cayzer, Bart, in each volume; ms. notes relating to Garvarton Castle, 14 page article on Merchiston Castle tipped in.   R.F.G. Hollett 76-221 1996 £160.00

NIN, ANAIS   D. H. Lawrence. An Unprofessional Study. Paris: Edward Titus at the Sign of the Black Manikin, 1932. 1st edition; one of 550 copies; very good in faded dust jacket.   Priscilla Juvelis 95/1-184 1996 $400.00

NIN, ANAIS   House of Incest. London: Edwards Bros., 1958. 1st edition; wrappers, very good; presentation copy from author for Elizabeth Moore.   Words Etcetera 94-992 1996 £55.00

NIN, ANAIS   Ladders to Fire. New York: Dutton, 1946. 1st edition; near fine in near fine lightly dust soiled dust jacket. Signed by author. Thomas Dorn 9-196 1996 $200.00

NIN, ANAIS   Solar Barque. London: Edwards Bros., 1958. 1st edition; wrappers; very good; presentation copy from author for Elizabeth Moore.   Words Etcetera 94-991 1996 £55.00

NISBET, ALEXANDER   An Essay on the Ancient and Modern Use of Armories. Edinburgh: Printed by Wm. Adams, 1718. 1st edition; small 4to 7 folding engraved plates; old vellum, wear to one corner, ink stain on cover.   Appelfeld Gallery 54-119 1996 $150.00

NISTER'S Holiday Annual for 1907. London: Nister, 1907. 4to; 6 color plates and black and white illustrations; red pictorial boards, light wear to covers, pages browned, else very good.   Marjorie James 19-168 1996 £85.00

NIVEN, LARRY   A Gift from Earth. MacDonald, 1969. 1st British and 1st hardcover edition, review copy with accompanying review slip laid in; fine in near fine dust jacket; nice association, from the collection of John Brunner with his bookplate.   Aronovitz 57-852 1996 $375.00

NIVEN, LARRY   The Mote in God's Eye. S&S, 1974. 1st edition; fine in dust jacket.   Aronovitz 57-854 1996 $175.00

NIVEN, LARRY   Neutron Star. MacDonald, 1969. 1st British and 1st hardcover edition; review copy with accompanying review slip laid in; fine in near fine dust jacket; from the collection of John Brunner, with his bookplate.   Aronovitz 57-853 1996 $185.00

NIVEN, LARRY   World of Ptavvs. MacDonald, 1969. 1st British and 1st hard cover edition, review copy with accompanying review slip laid in; fine in near fine dust jacket; nice association, the copy of John Brunner with his bookplate.   Aronovitz 57-852 1996 $375.00

NIXON, HOWARD MILLAR 1909-   British Bookbindings Presented by Kenneth H. Oldaker to the Chapter Library of Westminster Abbey. London: Maggs Bros., 1982. 1st edition; small 4to; 71 plates, some colored; original cloth.   Forest Books 74-201 1996 £55.00

NIXON, HOWARD MILLAR 1909-   Sixteenth-Century Gold-Tooled Bookbindings in the Pierpont Morgan Library. New York: Pierpont Morgan Library, 1971. Small folio; 68 bindings; wrappers; with signature of Nixon in ink on half title. Brenni 240.   Maggs Bros. Ltd. 1191-19 1996 £100.00

NIXON, HOWARD MILLAR 1909-   Twelve Books in Fine Bindings from the Library of J. W. Hely-Hutchinson. Oxford: for the Roxburghe Club, 1953. Folio; color frontispiece, 14 plates; quarter red morocco, gilt lettering on spine, ex-Printer's Library copy with booklabel and stamp on verso of title, 2 slight marks on f.f.e.p. Schmidt Kunsemuller 1300. Maggs Bros. Ltd. 1191-20 1996 £1,100.00

NIXON, PAT IRELAND   The Early Nixons of Texas. El Paso: Carl Hertzog, 1956. 1st edition; 172 pages; signed; photos; scarce. Lowman 96.   Maggie Lambeth 30-395 1996 $100.00

NIXON, RICHARD MILHOUS 1913-1994   1999: Victory Without War. New York: Simon & Schuster, 1988. 1st edition; 2nd printing; 8vo; dust jacket; very good to fine. Signed and inscribed by Nixon to actor John Severino.   George J. Houle 68-106 1996 $350.00

NIXON, RICHARD MILHOUS 1913-1994   No More Vietnams. New York Arbor House, 1985. 1st edition; signed by Nixon; fine in matching blue slipcase.   Bev Chaney, Jr. 23-530 1996 $135.00

NIXON, RICHARD MILHOUS 1913-1994   Six Crises. Garden City: Doubleday, 1962. 1st edition; large 8vo; dust jacket (few nicks), very good; boldly signed and inscribed by author.   George J. Houle 68-10? 1996 $450.00

NIXON, ROBERT   The Original Predictions or Prophecies of Robert Nixon, the Cheshire Prophet... London: J. Bailey, c. 1810. 12mo; 28 pages; etched frontispiece, light foxing, padded at end with 12 blank leaves foxed; modern half dark tan mottled sheep by Bayntun, lightly rubbed, backstrip with dark red longitudinal label, gilt lettered, small gilt tools, marbled boards and endpapers, thin paper guard supplied for frontispiece, excellent.   Blackwell's B112-201 1996 £60.00

NIZAMI   The Poems of Nizami. London: Studio Limited, 1928. One of 55 numbered sets; 16 full page reproductions; full yellow vellum with raised bands, lettered in gilt, included is a matching vellum portfolio containing a second set of the 16 plates mounted on heavier paper, original vellum slightly dusty, else fine set in lightly rubbed publisher's slipcase.   Hermitage SP95-757 1996 $500.00

NO Appeal. A Novel. London: Longmans, 1870. 1st edition; 8vo; 3 volumes; some light foxing, contemporary half roan, rubbed; Not in Wolff.   James Burmester 29-150 1996 £90.00

NOBBES, ROBERT   The Compleat Troller, or, the Art of Trolling. London: printed by T. James for Tho. Helder, 1682. 1st edition; small 8vo; contemporary sheep; superb copy, rare. Wing N1193; Westwood and Satchell p. 156; CBEL II 1557.   Ximenes 109-205 1996 $6,500.00

NOBBS, PERCY ERSKINE   Design: a Treatise on the Discovery of Form. London: Oxford University Press, 1937. 8vo; pages ix, 412; illustrations, as issued in four parts; each in yellow paper wrappers, perfect binding and staples, the four parts in one dark blue decorated dust jacket, spine of jacket slightly torn, exterior dusty, else very good, scarce in this form.   Hugh Anson-Cartwright 87-319 1996 $100.00

NOBILI, FLAMINIO   De Rebvs Gestis Stephani I Regis Poloniae... Rome: Haeredes Antonij Blado, 1582. 1st edition; 4to; 24 unnumbered leaves, mainly roman letter, large woodcut Polish Royal Arms on titlepage (old in inscription in upper corner), repeated on separate titlepage; large woodcut of printer's device and landscape on last leaf, woodcut initials and ornaments, somewhat browned, titlepage lightly ink spotted; modern vellum over boards. Very rare.   A. Sokol XXV-69 1996 £950.00

NOBLE, JOHN   Descriptive Handbook of the Cape Colony: its Condition and Resources. Cape Town: J. C. Juta, London: E. Stanford, 55 Charing Cross, 1875. 1st edition; 8vo; errata leaf, 1-315 pages text; folding panoramic lithographic view to frontispiece, 1 litho plate, 1 large folding colored map, map reinforced at margin by small portion of cellotape, panoramic view slightly chipped and worn at margins, not affecting imprint, hinges cracked, still good, tight copy, bound in clear polythene protective wrapper. Original publisher's green cloth, corners bumped, gilt titles to spine, edges speckled, yellow endpapers; Mendelssohn II p. 106.   Beeleigh Abbey BA56-238 1996 £250.00

NOBLE, JOSEPH VEACH   The Techniques of Painted Attic Pottery. New York: Thames & Hudson, 1988. Revised edition; 4to; 216 pages; 278 illustrations; original cloth, dust jacket; fine.   Archaeologia Luxor-3770 1996 $125.00

NOBLE, MARK   Memoirs of the Protectorate-House of Cromwell. Birmingham: printed by Pearson and Rollasaton, 1784. 1st edition; 8vo; 2 volumes; pages xiv, (vi), 480; viii, 544; 2 engraved portrait frontispieces, folding plate of armorial bearings; modern half russet calf, smooth backstrips divided by gilt rules, lettered direct, marbled boards, original endpapers re-used, excellent.   Blackwell's B112-83 1996 £120.00

NOBLE, MARY E.   A History of the Parish of Bampton. Kendal: T. Wilson, 1901. 1st (only) edition; 8vo; pages vi, (i), 268, numerous illustrations and large folding map, hand colored in outline; numerous illustrations, large folding map, hand colored in outline; excellent copy, very scarce.   R.F.G. Hollett & Son 78-1154 196 £240.00

NOLLET, JANE ANTOINE   Lectures in Experimental Philosophy. London: printed for J. Wren, 1752. 1st edition in English; 8vo; engraved plates; early 19th century calf, gilt, spine gilt; titlepage bit foxed, bound without final leaf of ads; very good, uncommon. Wheeler Gift 319a (1748 issue).   Ximenes 109-206 1996 $900.00

NOONAN, D. A.   Alaska, the Land of Now. Seattle: 1923. 1st edition; small octavo; 146 pages; frontispiece; green cloth with map of Alaska stamped in gold, some wear to gold lettering else fine.   Bromer Booksellers 90-126 1996 $125.00

NOORTHOUCK, JOHN   A New History of London, Including Westminster and Southwark. London: printed for R. Baldwin, 1773. 4to; title, dedication, pages i-viii, contents 4 pages, pages 1-902, index and errata and list of plates, 42 pages, 42 maps and plates; contemporary calf, rebacked. Adams 51.   Marlborough 162-180 1996 £750.00

NOORTHOUCK, JOHN   A New History of London, Including Westminster and Southwark. London: for R. Baldwin, 1773. 1st edition; demy 4to; (viii), viii, 902, (xlii) pages; folding maps, some colored, maps and plates; later half calf, banded and gilt, all edges gilt, little rubbed, few margins torn or repaired, one map little creased, but attractive copy still. Adams 51.   Ash Rare Books Zenzybyr-72 1996 £500.00

NORDAN, LEWIS   Welome to the Arrow-Catcher Fair. Baton Rouge: Louisiana State University Press, 1983. 1st edition; author's first book; scarce hardcover issue, fine in fine dust jacket.   Ken Lopez 74-339 1996 $100.00

NORDEN, FREDERICK LEWIS   Travels in Egypt and Nubia. London: Lockyer Davis, Charles Reymers, 1757. 1st one volume edition; small 8vo; 2 volumes in 1; xl, 154, 232 pages; contemporary calf, edges rubbed, hinges tender, bottom spine chipped, slight scuffing, otherwise very good.   Worldwide Antiquarian 151-829 1996 $350.00

NORDEN, MARIKA   The Gentle Men. Paris: Obelisk Press, 1935. 1st edition; gold and black decorative wrappers, very good, scarce. Words Etcetera 94-1005 1996 £75.00

NORDHOFF, CHARLES BERNARD 1887-1947   The Bounty Trilogy. Boston: Little Brown, 1940. 1st edition thus; near fine, bookplate, somewhat rubbed and darkened dust jacket.   Captain's Bookshelf 38-174 1996 $125.00

NORDHOFF, CHARLES BERNARD 1887-1947   California for Health, Pleasure and Residence - a Book for Travelers and Settlers. New York: 1872. 1st edition; 16, 255 pages, frontispiece map, illustrations; leather/boards, raised bands on spine; nice. Flake 5861 (1873 ed.); Herd 1676.   T. A. Swinford 49-850 1996 $275.00

NORDHOFF, CHARLES BERNARD 1887-1947   Mutiny On the Bounty. Boston: Little Brown and Co., 1932. 1st edition; 1st issue with plain endpapers; near fine with some offsetting to front endpaper and pastedown in crisp dust jacket that has some minor edgewear affecting spine edges, still attractive copy of a difficult book.   Left Bank Books 2-108 1996 $325.00

NORMAN, CHARLES BERNARD 1887-1947   Mr. Oddity - Samuel Johnson LL.D. Drexel Hill: Bell Pub. 1951. 1st edition; advance review slip loosely inserted; original binding, top edge dusty, head and tail of spine slightly bumped, very good in nicked, chipped and dusty, slightly rubbed, torn and creased dust jacket slightly faded at spine and slightly browned at edges; with pencilled ownership signature of Frederick Pottle. Ulysses 39-705 1996 £55.00

NORMAN, HOWARD   The Bird Artist. New York: FSG, 1994. 1st edition; fine in dust jacket, signed by author.   Lame Duck Books 19-426 1996 $150.00

NORMAN, HOWARD   Kiss in the Hotel Joseph Conrad. New York: Summit Books, 1989. 1st edition; author's second edition; very fine in very fine, dust jacket.   Bud Schweska 12-615 1996 $125.00

NORMAN, HOWARD   The Northern Lights. New York: Summit, 1987. 1st edition; faint remainder mark bottom edge and crease to corner of first two pages, else fine in fine dust jacket with touch of rubbing at crown;   Between the Covers 42-325 1996 $125.00

NORMAN, HOWARD   The Old Scatterer. Boston: Atlantic Monthly, 1986. 1st edition; oblong quarto; wood engravings by Michael mcCurdy; fine in fine dust jacket.   Ken Lopez 74-340 1996 $125.00

NORMAN, W. M.   A Popular Guide to the Geology of the Isle of Wight, With a Note On its Relation to That of the isle of Purbeck. Published for the author at Ventnar, 1887. 8vo; pages viii, 240, plain geological map, 15 plates, 4 sections and 3 views; cloth, gilt, new front endpaper.   John Henly 27-528 1996 £68.00

NORMAN-NERUDA, L.   The Climbs of Norman-Neruda. London: 1899. 1st edition; 30 plates; gilt lettering on red cloth, engraved plates, some small marks on boards, but clean, bright, near fine copy. Moutainng Books 8-EN01 1996 £165.00

NORMAN-NERUDA, L.   The Climbs of Norman-Neruda. London: 1899. 1st edition; 30 plates; gilt lettering on red cloth, top edge gilt, bookplates of the Rucksack Club and Manchester Central Library, neat circular rubber stamps of the Rucksack Club on 3 pages, some moderate rubbing, marking and bumping of boards, so not quite very good.   Moutainng Books 8-RN01 1996 £90.00

NORMANBY, CONSTANTINE HENRY PHIPPS, 1ST MARQUIS OF 1744-1792   A Voyage Towards the North Pole Undertaken by His Majesty's Command, 1773. London: 1774. Quarto; pages viii, 253, 15 plates and maps, folding tables; original full calf, backstrip and hinges worn, internally very nice, clean and handsome copy. Hill p. 207; Sabin 62572. Stephen Lunsford 45-130 1996 $950.00

NORRIS, FRANK 1870-1902   Collected Letters. San Francisco: Book Club of California, 1986. 1/500 copies; cloth and boards, plain dust jacket.   W. M. Morrison 436-339 1996 $150.00

NORRIS, FRANK 1870-1902   Moran of the Lady Letty, a Story of the Adventure off the California Coast. New York: 1898. 1st edition; decorated cloth, near fine, rather scarce.   Stephen Lupack 83- 1996 $100.00

NORRIS, FRANK 1870-1902   The Octopus. New York: Doubleday, Page & Co., 1901. 1st printing; 8vo; original claret cloth, lettered and decorated in gilt, soiled and rubbed, slightly shaken with upper inner hinge cracking, some light browning of endpapers; rare. BAL 15036. James Cummins 14-143 1996 $200.00

NORRIS, JOAN   Banquet. Lincoln: Penmaen Press, 1978. 1/200 numbered copies, signed by all contributors; fine in slipcase.   Alice Robbins 15-11 1996 $125.00

NORRIS, LESLIE   A Tree Sequence. Seattle: Sean Pen Press & Paper Mill, 1984. 1st edition; number 61 of 125 copies, signed by author and artist; 6.5 x 8.5 inches; (22) pages, printed on various handmade papers in several colors; wood engravings by Gretchen Daiber; cream boards with four color paper design by Judith Johnson in non-traditional case binding, using a single fold concertina to which the text was pamphlet stitched; prospectus laid in indicating the edition size; fine.   Joshua Heller 21-210 1996 $150.00

NORTH, OLIVER   Rambles After Sport: or Travels and Adventures in the Americans and at Home. London: 1874. 1st edition; iv, 268 pages, boards; nice, very scarce.   T. A. Swinford 49-851 1996 $100.00

NORTH-WESTERN RAILROAD   Hot Springs South Dakota. N.P.: ca. 1891. 1st edition; 40 pages; illustrations and map; original grey printed wrappers with title on front cover, center crease, otherwise very good copy for this fragile piece.   Michael D. Heaston 23-304 1996 $225.00

NORTHCOTT, W. H.   A Treatise on Lathes and Turning. London: 1876. 2nd edition; 8vo; 338 figures; cloth, spine very faded.   Maggs Bros. Ltd. 1190-648 1996 £85.00

NORTHERN PACIFIC RAILRAOD   The Yellowstone National Park. Chicago: Rand McNally, 1883. 40 pages; illustrations, map, ads; pictorial wrappers; little soiled, light vertical crease; folding map from Corps of Engineers Annual Report 1899 laid in.   Bohling Book Co. 192-602 1996 $250.00

THE NORTHERN Traveller; Containing the Hudson River Guide, and Tour to the Springs... New York: published by J. Disturnell, 1844. 1st edition; small 8vo; frontispiece plate, 2 maps; original purple cloth, faded, slight worming to spine; light foxing. Howes D353.   Ximenes 108-107 1996 $175.00

NORTON, ANDRE   Gryphon in Glory. Atheneum, 1981. 1st edition; fine in dust jacket; inscribed by author to fellow writer, Robert Adams, laid in is holograph letter to Adams from artist (for this dust jacket) Jack Gaughan.   Aronovitz 57-891 1996 $125.00

NORTON, ANDRE   Merlin's Mirror. S&J, 1976. 1st hardcover edition, fine in dust jacket; inscribed by author to fellow writer Robert Adams. Uncommon.   Aronovitz 57-881 1996 $125.00

NORTON, ANDRE   Octagon Magic. World, 1967. 1st edition; fine in dust jacket, inscribed by author to fellow writer Robert Adams. Aronovitz 57-873 1996 $150.00

NORTON, ANDRE   Ordeal in Otherwhere. World, 1964 1st edition; fine in very good+/near fine dust jacket save for some light rubbing to the dust jacket spine and rear panel; inscribed by author to fellow writer Robert Adams.   Aronovitz 57-870 1996 $150.00

NORTON, ANDRE   Shadow Hawk. New York: Harcourt, Brace & Co., 1960. 1st edition; signed by author on special printed label pasted to flyleaf, some spotting on spine, otherwise near fine in dust jacket which is lightly soiled in rear panel.   Steven C. Bernard 71-428 1996 $100.00

NORTON, ANDRE   Star Man's Son 2250 A.D. Staples, 1953. 1st British edition; near fine in like dust jacket, very scarce.   Aronovitz 57-863 1996 $150.00

NORTON, ANDRE   Wolfshead. Hale, 1977. 1st hard cover edition; fine in dust jacket, inscribed by author to fellow writer Robert Adams; quite scarce.   Aronovitz 57-887 1996 $150.00

NORTON, ANDRE   The X Factor. H-B, 1965. 1st edition; near fine in very good+ dust jacket with some light wear to head of dust jacket spine, inscribed by author for fellow writer Robert Adams.   Aronovitz 57-871 1996 $150.00

NORTON, E.   The Flight for Everest: 1924. London: 1925. 1st edition; 32 plates, some colored; drawings, folding map; small neat bookplate, clean, bright very good/fine copy.   Mountaineering Books 8-EN02 1996 £160.00

NORTON, F. J.   A Descriptive Catalogue of Printing in Spain and Portugal 1501-1520. Cambridge University Press, 1978. 1st edition; 4to; 560 pages; original cloth, dust jacket.   Forest Books 74-202 1996 £125.00

NORTON, FRANK H.   Frank Leslie's Historical Register of the United States Centennial Exposition, 1876. New York: Frank Leslie's Pub., 1877. Folio; 324 pages; 4 colored plates; large folding view, text illustrations; original cloth, ends of spine and 1 corner minutely frayed, occasional light foxing, otherwise very nice;   Edward Morrill 369-351 1996 $200.00

NORTON, JOHN   The Journal of Major John Norton, 1816. Toronto: Champlain Society, 1970. Limited to 900 numbered copies; 8vo; pages cxxiv, 391, xix, color frontispiece; top edge gilt, gilt cloth, crested edition, unopened, mint.   Hugh Anson-Cartwright 87-321 1996 $125.00

NORWOOD, C. W.   Sholes Georgia State Gazetteer and Business Directory. For 1879 & 1880. Atlanta: A. E. Sholes & Co., Publishers, 1879. 1st edition; 934 pages, ads on pink endsheets and flyleafs; folding map; original stiff printed boards with red cloth spine with title in gilt on spine, fine. Quite scarce.   Michael D. Heaston 23-157 1996 $550.00

NORWOOD, RICHARD   Norwood's Epitome: Being the Application of the Doctrine of Triangles...The Use of the Plain Sea Chart, and Meractor's Chart... London: William Fisher, Sarah Passinger and Elizabeth Smith, 1690. Small 8vo; (ii), 34, (3)-94, (72) pages; contemporary sheep, headband chipped, hinges beginning to crack; with bookplate of Hugh Cecil, Earl of Lonsdale and label of Harrison D. Horblit.   The Bookpress 75-443 1996 $1,250.00

THE NOT-Browne Mayd. London: Treherne, 1905. 2 3/4 x 2 1/16 inches; 65 pages; blindstamped red leather, slight darkening to covers, last signature starting, else near fine. Bookplate.   Bromer Booksellers 87-217 1996 $175.00

NOTABLE Lawyers of the West Including Members of the United States Supreme Court, Supreme Courts of Several States and Prominent Lawyers in the Western States. Chicago: 1902. 186 pages; photos; cover with minor wear, professionally reinforced hinge, book good.   Early West 22-509 1996 $100.00

NOTICES and Voyages of the Famed Quebec Mission to the Pacific Northwest: Being the Correspondence, Notices, Etc. of Fathers Blanchet and Demers... Portland: Oregon Historical Society, 1956. Limited to 1000 copies; 243 pages; illustrations, folding map; pictorial cloth; fine. Wagner Camp 80 and 127.   Argonaut Book Shop 113-395 1996 $125.00

NOTMAN, WILLIAM   Portrait of a Period: a Collection of Notman Photographs, 1856 to 1915. Montreal: McGill University Press, 1967. Folio; unpaginated, 174 full and double page plates, 20 page illustrated supplement; frontispiece, decorated endpapers; gilt cloth boards, dust jacket shows some wear, otherwise fine.   Hugh Anson-Cartwright 87-322 1996 $200.00

NOTT, STANLEY CHARLES   Voices from the Flowery Kingdom: Being an Illustrated Descriptive Record of the Beginnings of Chinese Cultural Existence Incorporating a Complete Survey of the Numerous Emblematic Forces Selected from Nature by the Ritualistic Leaders... New York: Chinese Culture Study Group of America, 1947. 1st edition; limited to 500 copies, numbered and signed by author (this volume being out-of-series and neither signed nor numbered); 278 pages; 24 full page color plates, 103 half tones, 79 line engravings; fine in chipped and worn dust jacket with one large piece missing from bottom front and rear panels. Hermitage SP95-1059 1996 $125.00

NOTTAGE, CHARLES G.   In Search of a Climate. London: Sampson Low, et al, 1894. (xvi), 351 pages, (ii), frontispiece, map, 29 printed photo illustrations; blue buckram, gold gilt and decorated in color, rebacked with original spine laid down, corners rubbed, otherwise good condition. Ferguson 13496 cites 1 copy only.   Antipodean 28-148 1996 $225.00

NOVA SCOTIA. VICE-ADMIRALTY COURT, HALIFAX   Reports of Cases Argued and Determined in the Court of Vice-Admiralty, at Halifax in Nova-Scotia, from the Commencement of the War, in 1803, to the End of the Year 1813, in the Time of Alexander Croke, LL.D.... London: printed for J. Butterworth and Son, 1814. 8vo; pages (xvi), 596, xxx, (10, 14, (3) (errata), cloth, labels on spine, covers slightly dusty, else clean crisp copy. Rare addenda and errata not recorded in TPL 6948.   Hugh Anson-Cartwright 87-323 1996 $2,500.00

NOVA, CRAIG   The Geek. New York: Harper, 1975. 1st edition; fine in dust jacket, almost imperceptibly darkened on spine, briefly inscribed by author.   Between the Covers 42-328 1996 $100.00

NOWELL, THOMAS S.   Art Work of Seattle and Alaska. Racine: W. d. Harney Photogravure Co., 1907. Folio; 9 parts with 26 pages text; 80 plates with photographic views, most full page, some leaves with two images; purple wrappers with gilt stamping; overall excellent set, some fading of wrappers, quite scarce and in exceptionally nice condition. Smith 305 notes only 8 parts.   Bohling Book Co. 192-28 1996 $550.00

NOWLAN, ALDEN   A Darkness in the Earth. Eureka: Hearse Press, n.d. 1st edition; (16) pages; printed wrappers; rare, author's second book; from the library of John Metcalf, with his ownership signature.   Nelson Ball 118-96 1996 $1,500.00

NOWLAN, ALDEN   The Rose and the Puritan. Fredericton: Fiddlehead Poetry Books, 1958. 1st edition; 16 pages; printed wrappers; fine copy of author's first book; from the library of John Metcalf, with his ownership signature.   Nelson Ball 118-105 1996 $150.00

NOWLAN, ALDEN   The Things Which Are. Toronto: Contact Press, c. 1962. 1st edition; 1st issue; 71 pages; printed wrappers, printed card covers in printed jacket; fine, very scarce; from the library of John Metcalf, with his ownership signature.   Nelson Ball 118-107 1996 $200.00

NOWLAN, ALDEN   Wind in a Rocky Country. Toronto: Emblem Book, 1960/61. 1st edition; (23) pages; designed, illustrated and printed by Robert Rosewarne at his Blue R Press, Ottawa; printed wrappers; fine, very scarce. from the library of John Metcalf, with his ownership signature.   Nelson Ball 118-110 1996 $450.00

NOWROJEE, JEHANGEER   Journal of a Residence of Two Years and a Half in Great Britain. London: Wm. H. Allen, 1841. 1st edition; 8vo; xxiv, 492 pages; lithographed portrait; contemporary calf, neatly rebacked; excellent copy, very uncommon.   James Burmester 29-102 1996 £450.00

NOYES, JOHN H.   The Berean: a Manual for the help of Those Who Seek the Faith of the Primitive Church. Putney: published at the Office of the Spiritual Magazine, 1847. 1st edition; 8vo; 504 pages; some dampstaining and dust soiling, mostly at beginning and end, disbound, preserved in fine maroon cloth book box, spine lettered in gilt. Very scarce.   John Drury 82-201 1996 £250.00

NOYES, JOHN HUMPHREY   History of American Socialisms. Philadelphia: J. B. Lippincott & Co./London: Trubner & Co., 1870. 1st edition; 8vo; vi, 678 pages, title bit spotted, original brown cloth, litle wear to spine, else very good.   John Drury 82-202 1996 £175.00

NOYES, ROBERT GALE   Ben Jonson on the English Stage 1660-1776. Cambridge: Harvard University Press, 1935. 1st edition; original binding, top edge gilt, endpaper edges slightly browned, covers slightly marked and dusty, very good; presentation copy from author inscribed for James Hart; loosely inserted Christmas card from author, newspaper article on author, programme for a performance of Bartholomew Fair in 1933;   Ulysses 39-324 1996 £75.00

NUCLEAR Explosions and Their Effects. Delhi: The Publications Division, Ministry of Information & Broadcasting... 1958. Revised edtiion; large 8vo; xvi, 276, 64 pages; 4 folding charts, folding map, numerous tables; orange cloth with blue printed paper label on cover, dust jacket (slightly chipped); this copy signed by Nehru.   Kenneth Karmiole 1NS-199 1996 $300.00

NUGENT, THOMAS   The New Pocket Dictionary of the French and English Languages. London: printed for T. Longman, &c. 1793 Oblong 12mo; contemporary speckled calf, gilt spine, red label, very good. Alston XII 721.   Jarndyce 103-203 1996 £60.00

NURA'S Children Go Visiting. New York: Studio Publications, 1943. 4to; 16 full page illustrations in color and black and white; yellow cloth, fresh in slightly chipped pictorial dust jacket.   Barbara Stone 70-164 1996 £55.00

A NURSERY Rhyme Picture Book. London: Warne, n.d., c. 1910. 4to; 14 color plates and drawings in black and white by Leslie Brooke; cloth backed colored pictorial boards, paper chipped at edges of front board, 1 short marginal tear, otherwise very fresh copy, very scarce.   Barbara Stone 70-39 1996 £110.00

NYE, I. W. B.   The Generic Names of Moths of the World. London: British Museum, 1975-91. 4to; 6 volumes; cloth.   Wheldon & Wesley 207-1088 1996 £170.00

NYLANDER, CARL   Ionians in Pasargadae: Studies in Old Persian Architecture. Uppsala: University of Uppsala, 1970. 8vo; 176 pages; 48 illustrations, 1 table; original cloth, torn dust jacket.   Archaeologia Luxor-3772 1996 $125.00

O

O. HENRY Memorial Award Prize Stories 1932. Garden City: Doubleday, Doran, 1932. 1st edition; slight tarnish to gold spine lettering and little fading to small sliver of the spine, else about fine in very good dust jacket with few shallow chips.   Between the Covers 42-13 1996 $125.00

OATES, FRANK   Matabele Land and the Victoria Falls, a Naturalist's Wanderings in the Interior of South Africa. London: 1889. 2nd edition; 8vo; pages xlix, 433, 4 maps, portrait, 20 colored plates, text illustrations; original cloth; nice.   Wheldon & Wesley 207-75 1996 £350.00

OATES, FRANK   Matabele Land and the Victoria Falls. London: Kegan, Paul, Trench & Co., 1889. 2nd edition; thick 8vo; original grey-green pictorial cloth, spine dull, slight restoration; very good, presentation copy inscribed by editor C.G. Oates to Miss Lambert. Theal p. 219. Ximenes 109-207 1996 $450.00

OATES, JOYCE CAROL 1938-   The Assignation. New York: Ecco, 1988. 1st edition; fine in dust jacket; inscribed by author.   Between the Covers 42-330 1996 $100.00

OATES, JOYCE CAROL 1938-   The Assignation. New York: Ecco, 1988. 1st edition; fine in dust jacket, inscribed by author.   Between the Covers 42-330 1996 $100.00

OATES, JOYCE CAROL 1938-   By the North Gate. Vanguard, 1963. 1st edition; author's first book; fine copy in very good dust jacket.   Book Time 2-323 1996 $185.00

OATES, JOYCE CAROL 1938-   By the North Gate. New York: Vanguard, 1963. 1st edition; fine in very near fine slightly spine faded dust jacket, signed by author, scarce.   Lame Duck Books 19-439 1996 $500.00

OATES, JOYCE CAROL 1938-   By the North Gate. New York: Vanguard, 1963. 1st edition; near mint in dust jacket, author's first book. Bromer Booksellers 90-209 1996 $350.00

OATES, JOYCE CAROL 1938-   By the North Gate. New York: Vanguard Press Inc., 1963. 1st edition; author's first book; fine in dust jacket. Priscilla Juvelis 95/1-185 1996 $250.00

OATES, JOYCE CAROL 1938-   By the North Gate. New York: Vanguard Press, 1963. 1st edition; 8vo; author's first book; cloth, dust jacket; fine in lightly edge worn jacket. Dickinson A1.   James S. Jaffe 34-513 1996 $175.00

OATES, JOYCE CAROL 1938-   The Goddess and Other Women. New York: Vanguard, 1974. Review copy; near fine in like dust jacket with publisher's ephemera laid in; inscribed by author.   Lame Duck Books 19-441 1996 $125.00

OATES, JOYCE CAROL 1938-   Nemesis. New York: Dutton, 1990. Advance review copy with publisher's material laid in, signed by author both as Oates and Rosamond; fine in dust jacket.   Between the Covers 42-333 1996 $125.00

OATES, JOYCE CAROL 1938-   Unholy Loves. New York: Vanguard, 1979. Signed by author stating that this is copy Number 45 of 'no more than 100 copies that I have authorized for distribution by Signed editions Limited''; fine in dust jacket.   Between the Covers 42-329 1996 $250.00

OATES, JOYCE CAROL 1938-   Will You Always Love Me? Huntington Beach: Cahill, 1994. One of an unspecified number of 'proof' copies; in the binding of the numbered issue and marked "PC" on colophon. Ken Lopez 74-344 1996 $125.00

OATES, JOYCE CAROL 1938-   Will You Always Love Me? Huntington Beach: Cahill, 1994. One of 26 lettered copies, signed by author; leather spine and marbled paper covered boards, fine.   Between the Covers 42-334 1996 $250.00

OATES, JOYCE CAROL 1938-   Will You Always Love Me? Huntington Beach: Cahill, 1994. 1st edition; of a total of 101 copies, this one of 26 lettered copies, signed by author; without dust jacket, as issued.   Ken Lopez 74-342 1996 $200.00

O'BANLON, NANCE   Domestic Science: Pop-Up Icons. Domestic Science: Idioms. Berkeley: Flying Fish Press, 1990. One of 150 copies from a total edition of 165; page size 6 1/8 x 12 inches; printed on Fabriano Rosaspina paper, each copy signed and numbered by artist; at least 58 linoleum cuts, five of which are pop-ups, many in color; text was handset in 12 point Gill Sans; bound by Julie Chen with the assistance of many hands, black and white linoleum cut paper, Sandy Tilcock produced the boxes of black and white checked linoleum cut paper with gold label, title printed in black on front cover and spine; the book structure is accordion fold front-to-back and back-to-front. Priscilla Juvelis 95/1-95 1996 $575.00

O'BEIRNE, H. F.   Leaders and Leading Men of Indian Territory with Interesting Biographical Sketches... Chicago: American Publisher's Association, 1891. 1st edition; 318, (2), (i)-vi pages; portraits, original brown cloth, title in gilt on spine and front cvoer, minor wear; fine. Not in Graff or Adams; Howes O3.   Michael D. Heaston 23-280 1996 $350.00

OBERTH, HERMANN   The Moon Car... New York: Harper & Bros., 1959. 1st edition in English; 8vo; 98 pages; frontispiece, 24 figures in text, 9 of which are full page; original two toned cloth, dust jacket; near fine.   Edwin V. Glaser 121-236 1996 $250.00

O'BRADLEY, ARTHUR   The Gretna-Green Bolt-a, or, Young Ladies' Man-ual. Paris: Galignani & Co./London: Rudolph Ackermann, n.d. 1853. Oblong 8vo; 70 pages; colored lithograph frontispiece (foxed), text printed on pink paper; original roan backed cloth, spine worn, reproduction of frontispiece on front cover. Abbey Life 408.   Anthony W. Laywood 108-215 1996 £110.00

O'BRIAN, PATRICK   A Book of Voyages. London: Home & Van Thal, 1947. 1st edition; numerous decorations by Joan Burton; original binding top edge dusty, head and tail of spine slightly bumped, spine and cover slightly marked, rear endpaper gutter slightly wormed, very good in nicked, rubbed, darkened and dusty, slightly soiled, marked and torn, price clipped dust jacket browned at spine and edges.   Ulysses 39-445 1996 £195.00

O'BRIAN, PATRICK   The Commodore. Haprer Collins, 1994. 1st edition signed on titlepage, fine in dust jacket.   Virgo Books 48-147 1996 £50.00

O'BRIAN, PATRICK   Desolation Island. New York: Stein & Day, 1979. 1st American edition; fine in very near fine, price clipped dust jacket with tiny, barely noticeable tear on edge of front flap and short tear at crown.   Between the Covers 42-335 1996 $250.00

O'BRIAN, PATRICK   The Road to Samarcand. London: Rupert Hart-Davis, 1954. 1st edition; original binding, small bookseller's label on front pastedown, edges spotted, head and tail of spine bumped and slightly faded, very good in rubbed, chipped, slightly torn and internally repaired dust jacket.   Ulysses 39-446 1996 £275.00

O'BRIEN, FLANN   At Swim-Two-Birds. London: Longmans, 1909. 2nd issue; bound in grey-green cloth with price on dust jacket of 3/6, small bookseller's stamp on front pastedown, but very good in rre dust jacket which is slightly chipped at head and base of spine and somewhat sunned, exceedingly scarce in dust jacket, which carries a pre-publicatio blurb by Graham Greene.   R. A. Gekoski 19-104 1996 £3,500.00

O'BRIEN, FLANN   An Beal Boct. Baile ata Cliat: Naisiunta, 1941. 1st edition; discreet contemporary gift inscription, wear along outer spine joints, else very good or better, rare.   Lame Duck Books 19-217 1996 $1,250.00

O'BRIEN, FLANN   The Dalkey Archive. London: Macgibbon & Kee, 1964. 1st edition; crown 8vo; pages 222, original mid green boards, backstrip gilt lettered, dust jacket, fine.   Blackwell's B112-214 1996 £70.00

O'BRIEN, TIM   Going After Cacciato. London: Cape, 1978. 1st English edition; fine in fine dust jacket, signed by author.   Ken Lopez 74-351 1996 $125.00

O'BRIEN, TIM   Going After Cacciato. New York: Delacorte, 1978.
Uncorrected proof; tall wrappers; near fine, signed by author.   Ken
Lopez 74-349 1996 $650.00

O'BRIEN, TIM   Going After Cacciato. New York: Delacorte, 1978. 1st
trade edition; fine in fine dust jacket, signed by author; fine copies quite
scarce.   Ken Lopez 74-350 1996 $350.00

O'BRIEN, TIM   If I Die in a Combat Zone. London: Calder & Boyars,
1973. 1st British edition; fine in fine dust jacket and signed by author.
Ken Lopez 74-346 1996 $250.00

O'BRIEN, TIM   If I Die in a Combat Zone. New York: Delacorte, 1973.
1st edition; fine in fine dust jacket; exceptional copy, signed and
additionally inscribed by author.   Ken Lopez 74-345 1996 $2,000.00

O'BRIEN, TIM   If I Die in a Combat Zone. New York: Delacorte, 1973.
1st edition; author's first book; very scarce; very good+ spine cocked
copy in very good dust jacket; better than average copy; inscribed by
author to mother of a schoolmate.   Lame Duck Books 19-430 1996
$950.00

O'BRIEN, TIM   In the Lake of the Woods. Boston/New York: HM/SL,
1994. Advance reading copy, laid in photocopy of several pages slated
to serve as replacement for the last chapter; wrappers, covers played,
near fine.   Ken Lopez 74-357 1996 $100.00

O'BRIEN, TIM   Northern Lights. New York: Delacorte, 1975. 1st
edition; light foxing to top and fore edges and minor fading to baord
edges, else very good+ in near fine dust jacket.   Lame Duck Books
19-431 1996 $450.00

O'BRIEN, TIM   Northern Lights. London: Marion Boyars, 1976. 1st
English edition, one of only 900 hardcover copies; fine in price clipped
dust jacket, signed by author.   Lame Duck Books 19-432 1996
$300.00

O'BRIEN, TIM   Northern Lights. London: Marion Boyars, 1976. 1st
English edition; of a total of 2000 copies, only 900 were bound up in
hardcover, the rest being issued in soft cover a year later; fine in fine
dust jacket and signed by author.   Ken Lopez 74-347 1996 $300.00

O'BRIEN, TIM   Northern Lights. London: Marion Boyars, 1976. 1st
English edition; fine in price clipped dust jacket.   Lame Duck Books
19-433 1996 $125.00

O'BRIEN, TIM   Northern Lights. London: Marion Boyars, 1976. 1st
English edition; fine in fine price clipped dust jacket; unsigned.   Ken
Lopez 74-348 1996 $125.00

O'BRIEN, TIM   The Nuclear Age. Portland: Press 22, 1981. Limited
edition, of a total of 151 copies, this one of 25 lettered copies, signed
by author; very fine in very fine dust jacket and now quite scarce.
Ken Lopez 74-353 1996 $450.00

O'BRIEN, TIM   The Nuclear Age. Portland: Press 22, 1981. One of 125
copies, signed by author; wrappers; fine.   Ken Lopez 74-354 1996
$125.00

O'BRIEN, TIM   Speaking of Courage. Santa Barbara: Neville, 1980. One
of 300 numbered copies, signed by author; fine in cloth, as issued.
Between the Covers 42-337 1996 $125.00

O'BRIEN, TIM   Speaking of Courage. Santa Barbara: Neville, 1980. 1st
limited edition, one of 300 numbered copies, signed by author, of a total
edition of 326; fine.   Ken Lopez 74-352 1996 $150.00

O'BRIEN, TIM   Speaking of Courage. Santa Barbra: Neville, 1980. One
of 300 signed and numbered copies; fine in cloth covered boards with
paper labels as issued.   Lame Duck Books 19-434 1996 $150.00

O'BRIEN, TIM   The Things they Carried. Boston: Houghton Mifflin,
1990. 1st edition; fine in dust jacket and inscribed by author.   Ken
Lopez 74-355 1996 $150.00

O'BRIEN, TIM   The Things They Carried. Boston: Houghton Mifflin,
1990. 1st edition; fine, in cloth, as issued, signed by author.   Between
the Covers 42-337a 1996 $150.00

OBSERVATIONS On Mr. Gladstones Denunciation of Certain Millowners of
Lancashire, Contained in a Speech Delivered by Him at Newcastle, on
the 7th of October, 1862. London: James Ridgway, 1862. 1st edition;
8vo: (2), 37, (1) pages, complete with half title; recent printed blue
boards lettered; very good; rare.   John Drury 82-180 1996 £85.00

OBSERVATIONS On the Conduct of Great Britain, with Regard to the
Negociations and Other Transactions Abroad. Edinburgh: printed by
Baskett and Co., 1729. 1st Edinburgh edition; 8vo; 61 pages; disbound.
Kress 3819; Goldsmith 6660. Hanson 3950; Sabin 56514.   Anthony W.
Laywood 109-28 1996 £90.00

OBSERVATIONS Upon the Administration of Justice in Bengal; Occasioned
by Some Late Proceedings at Dacca. N.P.: London: n.d. 1778. 1st
edition; 4to; 2 parts, 52, 68 pages; disbound.   Anthony Laywood
108-27 1996 £110.00

OBSESSIONS. Arlington Heights: Dark Harvest, 1991. Limited to 500
individually signed and numbered coies of which this is number 212;
signed by contributors; very fine in slipcase.   Bud Schweska 12-693
1996 $150.00

OBSOLETE Ideas. In Six Letters, Addressed to Maria by a Friend.
Sherborne: printed for the author, by James Lagndon, 1805. Half title,
excellently rebound in half sheep, very good.   Jarndyce 103-426 1996
£90.00

THE OBSTETRICAL Journal of Great Britain and Ireland Including
Midwifery and the Diseases of Women and Children. London: 1873-79.
Volumes 1-7; one backstrip missing, spine broken on that volume, other
volumes very good.   W. Bruce Fye 71-1532 1996 $300.00

O'CALLAGHAN, E. B.   The Documentary History of the State of New
York. Albany: 1850-51. 2nd printing; quarto; 4 volumes; 78 maps and
plates; original cloth, ex-library, corners rubbed, some tears on
backstrips to varying degrees, sound and clean inside. Howes O17.
Edward Morrill 368-550 1996 $225.00

O'CALLAGHAN, E. B.   The Documentary History of the State of New
York. Albany: 1850. 4to; 4 volumes; quarto; plates, maps, no library
stamps on any maps or plates; very free from foxing; ex-library, formerly
in the Reed Fulton inventory with his industrial size price on front
pastedown.   Bookworm & Silverfish 280-183 1996 $240.00

O'CASEY, SEAN   The Story of the Irish Citizen Army. Dublin: Maunsel
& Co. Ld., 1919. 1st edition; 12mo; original printed wrappers; extremities
of spine slightly chipped, otherwise very good, few pencil notes at
beginning by previous owner; NCBEL IV 881.   David J. Holmes 52-76
1996 $225.00

O'CASEY, SEAN   Windfalls. London: Macmillan and Co., 1934. 1st
edition; fine, crisp copy in dust jacket.   Left Bank Books 2-109 1996
$125.00

OCHSE, J. J.   Tropical and Subtropical Agriculture. New York: 1961.
8vo; 2 volumes; pages liv, 1446; 285 text figures, including 2 colored
plates; cloth, heels of spine frayed, endpapers browned, brown staining
to 2 pages, with signs of dampness or dampstaining along lower edges
of pages; bookplates.   Raymond M. Sutton VII-1095 1996 $125.00

OCHSNER, ALBERT   The Organization, Construction and Management
of Hospitals with Numerous Plans and Details. Chicago: 1907. 1st
edition; 600 pages; 399 illustrations; original binding.   W. Bruce Fye
71-1534 1996 $250.00

O'CIANAIN, TADHG   The Flight of the Earls. 1916. 8vo; xx, 268 pages;
frontispiece, maps, cover faded, else very good.   C. P. Hyland
216-888 1996 £65.00

O'CONNOR, EDWIN   The Edge of Sadness. Boston: Little Brown, 1961.
1st edition; owner name and address on front fly, some darkening to
page edges, but very good copy in spine darkened, about very good
dust jacket with couple of tiny tears, inscribed by author, very scarce.
Between the Covers 42-339 1996 $350.00

O'CONNOR, FLANNERY 1925-1964   The Complete Stories. New York: Farrar, 1971. 1st edition; original cloth, fine but for bookplate, with attendant warping, in fine dust jacket with usual browning to spine. Beasley Books 82-122 1996 $125.00

O'CONNOR, FLANNERY 1925-1964   Every Thing that Rises Must Converge. New York: FSG, 1965. 1st edition; very good in price clipped near fine, bright white dust jacket with wrinkle to back panel.   Thomas Dorn 9-200 1996 $100.00

O'CONNOR, FLANNERY 1925-1964   Mystery and Manners. New York: FS&G, 1969. Advance review copy with slip laid in (slip has small piece of tape at top); fine in dust jacket.   Between the Covers 42-340 1996 $100.00

O'CONNOR, FRANK 1903-1966   The Complete Stories. New York: Farrar Straus, 1971. 1st edition; gift inscription, else fine in near fine dust jacket.   Pettler & Lieberman 28-194 1996 $100.00

O'CONNOR, FRANK 1903-1966   The Saint and Mary Kate. London: Macmillan, 1932. Advance reading copy with slip tipped in; corners slightly bumped, spine little faded and small tape remnant on front pastedown from an old booksellers description, sound, very good copy, lacking the dust jacket; inscribed by author to Irish novelist L.A.G. Strong.   Between the Covers 42-342 1996 $450.00

O'CONOR, CHARLES   An Historical Address on the Calamities Occasioned by Foreign Influence in the Nomintation of Bishops to Irish Seers. 1810-12. 8vo; bound in 1 volume, half calf, worn, serious dampmarking, scarce, tall, untrimmed copy. Bradshaw 6089 and 6095. C. P. Hyland 216-582 1996 £70.00

ODENBERG, CLAES   Store Days: Documents from the Store (1961) and The Ray Gun Theater (1962). New York: Something Else Press, Inc., 1967. 1st edition; with "The Store" business card in glassine envelope on front free endpaper, fine in lightly rubbed dust jacket.   Hermitage SP95-800 1996 $100.00

ODETS, CLIFFORD   Waiting for Lefty and Till the Day I Die. New York: 1935. 1st edition; fine in near fine dust jacket, spine sunned and several nicks on top edge, very scarce.   Lyman Books 21-618 1996 $125.00

ODOM, MARY MC CALEB   Lenare; a Story of the Southern Revolution, and Other Poems. New Orleans: Bouvain & Lewis, 1866. 1st edition; 12mo; 107 pages; original cloth, slight wear and soiling, very good.   M & S Rare Books 60-211 1996 $200.00

O'DONNELL, ELLIOTT   Famous Curses. London: Skeffington & Son Ltd., 1929. 1st edition; 12 black and white plates by Vere Campbell; original binding, bookplate, prelims, edges and endpapers spotted, head and tail of spine and corners slightly bumped, head of spine nicked, front free endpaper creased, cover edges slightly rubbed, very good in nicked worn, torn and soiled, chipped, creased and dusty, internally and externally repaired dust jacket darkened at spine and edges.   Ulysses 39-447 1996 £55.00

OE, KEZABURO   A Personal Matter. New York: Grove Press, 1968. 1st edition; original binding, top edge dusty, very good in slightly darkened dust jacket; presentation copy from author, inscribed for Mrs. Madeleine Agnini.   Ulysses 39-449 1996 £325.00

OELSSNER, GOTTLIEB   Philosophisch-Moralische und Medizinische Betrachtung, Ueber mancherley zur Hoffart und Schonheit Hervorgesuchte... Breslau & Leipzig: D. Piersch, 1754. 1st edition; 8vo; 80 pages; woodcut ornaments (stains to title), contemporary boards; fine. Not in NUC or Blake; Hayn Gotendorf 5.97.   Bennett Gilbert LL29-79 1996 $1,450.00

OERKE, ANDREW   Black Christ and Other Poems. N.P.: the author, 1970. 1st edition; mimeographed pages glued into hand painted boards, desingated as not for sale and for private distribution, few corrections to text, almost certainly in hand of author, tape stains to one page where a new stanza has been taped into text, again, presumably by author, else near fine, fragile.   Between the Covers 43-176 1996 $175.00

OFFCUTS: The Campbell-Logan Bindery's Suggestions for Successful Book Binding. Minneapolis: Bieler Press, 1985. One of 250 numbered copies, signed by Don Campbell; tall 8vo; printed in Centaur and Arrighi, prints in brown; 6 wood engravings by Gaylord Schanilec; half morocco; fine.   Bertram Rota 272-31 1996 £70.00

O'FLAHERTY, LIAM 1897-1984   The House of Gold. 1929. 8vo; fine in dust jacket, cloth, signed by author.   C. P. Hyland 216-605 1996 £95.00

O'FLAHERTY, LIAM 1897-1984   The Informer. London: Cape, 1925. 1st edition; original green cloth, very good in dust jacket, few small chips on top of spine and flap folds, lightly sunned on spine, else bright and solid; scarce.   Left Bank Books 2-111 1996 $450.00

O'FLAHERTY, LIAM 1897-1984   A Tourist's Guide to Ireland. Mandrake Press, 1929. 1st edition; 8vo; cloth, dust jacket, very good.   C. P. Hyland 216-607 1996 £55.00

OGDEN Utah. N.P.: ca. 1910. 1st edition; 34, (2) pages; oiginal pictorial red wrappers, title stamped in black on front cover, very good. Michael D. Heaston 23-344 1996 $300.00

OGILVIE, JOHN   The Imperial Dictionary. Glasgow: Blackie & Son, 1851. 4to; 2 volumes; illustrations; full contemporary calf, gilt borders, signs of label removed on spine, all edges gilt, very good.   Jarndyce 103-204 1996 £90.00

OGILVIE, JOHN   The Imperial Dictionary. London: Blackie & Son, 1851. 2 volumes in 8 parts; half titles, illustrations; original grey printed wrappers, brown cloth spine, slight dusting, top wrapper of part 1 slightly marked, very good.   Jarndyce 103-205 1996 £110.00

OGILVIE, JOHN   The Imperial Dictionary. London: Blackie & Son, 1876. 2 volumes, half titles, plates, illustrations, little spotting; contemporary half calf, little rubbed, maroon labels, small splits at head of spine of volume 1.   Jarndyce 103-206 1996 £65.00

OGILVIE-GRANT, W. R.   A Hand-book to the Game-Birds. London: 1895-97. 8vo; 2 volumes; 48 colored plates; cloth.   Wheldon & Wesley 207-821 1996 £60.00

O'GRADY, DESMOND   Stations. Cairo: American University in Cairo Press, 1976. One of 250 numbered copies, signed by author; 8 black and white drawings by Margo Veillon; errata slip mounted at rear; wrappers; inscription, covers very slightly rubbed and creased, very good.   Ulysses 39-448 1996 £85.00

O'HANDLON, REDMOND   In Trouble Again. London: Hamish Hamilton, 1988. 1st edition; fine in fine dust jacket; inscribed by author, books signed by O'Hanlon are quite uncommon.   Ken Lopez 74-360 1996 $275.00

O'HANLON, REDMOND   Joseph Conrad and Charles Darwin. Atlantic Highlands: Humanitites, 1984. 1st American edition; author's first book; near fine in very good, lightly frayed dust jacket, uncommon first book. Ken Lopez 74-359 1996 $200.00

O'HARA, FRANK   In Memory of My Feelings. New York: Museum of Modern Art, 1967. 1st edition; limited to 2500 copies; 4to; illustrations; loose sheets in portfolio, slipcase; fine.   James S. Jaffe 34-517 1996 $250.00

OHTAISHI, N.   Deer of China - Biology and Management. Amsterdam: 1993. 8vo; 432 pages; illustrations; hardbound.   Wheldon & Wesley 207-593 1996 £116.00

O'KEEFE, ADELAIDE   National Characters Exhibited in Forty Geographical Poems. London: Darton, Harvey & Darton, 1818. 1st edition; 130 x 85 mm; pages (iv), 139; frontispiece, 7 full page engravings; marbled boards, red roan spine compartmented and lettered in gilt, top and bottom of spine, worn, extremities rubbed, else very good. Osborne 73; Lilly Lib. Darton Cat. 42.   Marjorie James 19-170 1996 £150.00

O'KEEFE, GEORGIA   Georgia O'Keefe. New York: Viking Press, 1976. 1st edition; folio; 108 plates with accompanying text; 108 color plates; cloth, dust jacket; fine.   The Bookpress 75-444 1996 $325.00

O'KEEFE, GEORGIA   Georgia O'Keefe. New York: Viking Press, 1976. 1st edition; folio; 108 color plates; white linen as issued, fine with dust jacket.   Appelfeld Gallery 54-146 1996 $125.00

O'KEEFFE, GEORGIA   Georgia O'Keeffe. New York: Viking, 1976. Original edition; folio; unpagianted, 108 color plates; cloth, dust jacket; Freitag 7111.   Brannan 43-495 1996 $290.00

O'KELLY, PATRICK   The Hippocrene: a Collection of Poems. Dublin: 1831. 8vo; portrait, 132 pages, 4 leaves subscriber list, original boards, needs rebinding.   C. P. Hyland 216-623 1996 £50.00

OKUDAIRA, HIEDO   Emaki: Japanese Picture Scrolls. Japan: 1962. 4to; 241 pages; illustrations, cloth, dust jacket.   Rainsford A54-444 1996 £60.00

O'LAVERTY, JAMES   An Historical Account of the Dioceses of Down and Connor: Ancient and Modern. 1878-95. 8vo; 5 volumes; cloth, very good, complete sets are very scarce.   C. P. Hyland 216-625 1996 £350.00

THE OLD Flag. New York: Wm. H. May, 1864. 1st edition in printed form; (18) pages; illustrations in text, text printed in triple columns; original pictorial stiff boards, neatly rebacked, minor soiling and bumping, fine, laid in half morocco clamshell case. Nevins Civil War Books I 199. Michael D. Heaston 23-330 1996 $1,750.00

OLD Villita. San Antonio: City of San Antonio, 1939. 13 1/4 x 10 1/8 inches; 22, (2) pages + glassine leaves at front and rear, double page map and illustrations in text; pictorial beige wrappers, fore margin of book slightly bent.   Dawson's Books Shop 528-239 1996 $100.00

THE OLD Woman and Her Pig. London: Grant and Griffith, Successors to J. Harris, ca. 1845. 7 x 4 1/4 inches; 16, (1) leaves, including ad leaf at back; 15 hand colored woodcuts; original printed self wrappers; covers noticeably soiled from use, but still very much intact, one tear (into image) very neatly repaired, without loss, on verso, leaves bit thumbed and lightly spotted, but actually rather nice internally. cf. Gumuchian 4333.   Phillip J. Pirages 33-129 1996 $225.00

OLDEN, THOMAS   Holy Scriptures in Ireland 1000 Years Ago. 1888. 1st edition; 8vo; frontispiece, xl, 135 pages; cloth, cover damp marked, text very good.   C. P. Hyland 216-628 1996 £55.00

OLDHAM, J. BASIL   English Blind-Stamped Bindings and Blind Panels of English Binders. Cambridge: 1952-58. Folio; 2 volumes, several plates; blue cloth, red leather spine labels, ownership inscription of Lord Kenyon, offprint of Festschrift for Ernst Kyriss, Oldham's English Fifteenth Century Binding, inscribed from author presumably to Kenyon inserted loose, along with few notes on loose leaf & bill for second volume from Quaritch;   Maggs Bros. Ltd. 1191-21 1996 £340.00

OLDHAM, J. BASIL   English Blind-Stamped Bindings. Cambridge University Press, 1952. 1st edition; one of 750 copies; folio; 61 plates; original buckram, leather label on spine, dust jacket torn.   Forest Books 74-205 1996 £155.00

OLDHAM, J. BASIL   Shrewsbury School Library Bindings. Catalogue Raisonne. Oxford: 1943. Limited to 200 copies; folio; colored frontispiece, 62 plates; maroon and white cloth, some slight soiling to spine, mild scuffing. Breslauer p. 24.   Maggs Bros. Ltd. 1191-22 1996 £650.00

OLDHAM, T.   On the Geological Structure of Part of the Khasi Hills, with Observations on the Meteorology and Ethnology of the District. Calcutta: Bengal Military Orphan Press, 1854. 1st edition; 4to; 4 folding hand colored maps, apparently printed on linen, folding table, 11 lithographic plates, some faintly tinted in blue, printed by the Asiatic lithographic Press, T. Black, lithographer; somewhat obtrusive stain at beginning and end, cloth bit worn and stained.   Maggs Bros. Ltd. 1190-306 1996 £90.00

OLDREY, J.   The Devil's Henchmen. London: Methuen, 1926. 1st edition; foxing to bottom and fore edge sheets, else very good= in bright very good pictorial dust jacket with some light wear and tear, very scarce in dust jacket.   Aronovitz 57-908 1996 $175.00

OLDROYD, IDA SHEPARD   Marine Shells of the West Coast of North America. Stanford: Stanford University Press, 1924-27. 4to; 2 volumes in 4, c. 1200 pages; 108 plates; original cloth.   Edwin V. Glaser 121-237 1996 $200.00

OLIPHANT, LAURENCE 1829-1888   The Land of Gilead, with Excursions in Lebanon. New York: D. Appleton, 1881. 1st U.S. edition; 8vo; 430 pages; illustrations, folding map at rear; original brown cloth; fine. Wolff 5210 for 1st English edition.   David Mason 71-114 1996 $140.00

OLIPHANT, LAURENCE 1829-1888   Narrative of the Earl of Elgin's Mission to China and Japan in the Years 1857, 58, '59. Edinburgh: Wm. Blackwood, 1859. 1st edition; tall 8vo; 2 volumes; with half titles; 20 colored and tinted lithographs, five folding maps, many text wood engravings; three quarter red crushed morocco over marbled sides, spines with five raised bands and elaborate gilt tooling, top edge gilt, by J. Larkins; particularly fine set.   Book Block 32-79 1996 $750.00

OLIPHANT, LAURENCE 1829-1888   Narrative of the Earl of Elgin's Mission to China and Japan in the Years 1857, 58, 59. Edinburgh: William Blackwood, 1859. 1st edition; 8vo; 2 volumes; pages xiv, 492, 16 ads; xi, 496; 5 maps, 20 color plates; original blue pictorial cloth, rubbed, some light foxing. Cordier p. 546.   Richard Adelson W94/95-130 1996 $425.00

OLIVER, C.   The Winds of Time. New York: Doubleday, 1957. 1st edition; fine in very good+/near fine dust jacket with some slight wear at extremities of dust jacket spine.   Aronovitz 57-910 1996 $110.00

OLIVER, D.   Flora of Tropical Africa. Ashford: 1868-1917. 8vo; 8 volumes in 10; cloth, fine set, unused and in mint condition. Wheldon & Wesley 207-1582 1996 £200.00

OLIVER, MARY   Provincetown. Lewisburg: Bucknell University/The Press of Appletree Alley, 1987. 1st edition; one of 145 copies, signed by author; 8vo; cloth backed boards; as new.   James S. Jaffe 34-521 1996 $150.00

OLIVER, STEPHEN   Scenes and Recollections of Fly Fishing, in Northumberland, Cumberland and Westmorland. London: Chapman and Hall, 1834. 1st edition; small 8vo; pages (ii), 212, vignette on title and engraved head and tailpieces; original patterned cloth, gilt, spine rather chipped in places.   R.F.G. Hollett & Son 78-648 1996 £120.00

OLIVIER, J.   A Continuation of the Life and Adventures of Signor Rozelli, Late of the Hague. London: printed for Will. Taylor and Tho. Butler, 1724. 1st English edition; engraved frontispiece, 9 engraved plates, text little age browned, contemporary calf, rebacked, label. Esdaile p.280; McBurney 168.   Anthony W. Laywood 109-107 1996 £165.00

OLLE'S Ski Trip. New York: Harper, n.d. Folio; full page colored illustrations by Elsa Beskow, cloth backed colored pictorial boards, extremities little rubbed, light dusting, else very nice. Inscription dated 1930.   Barbara Stone 70-26 1996 £135.00

OLMSTED, DENISON   Outlines of Lectures on Meteorology, Delivered at Yale College for the Use of the Students. New Haven: B. L. Hamlen, 1837. 1st edition; 8vo; 16 pages; removed. Pencilled notes throughout,. Rinderknecht 46077.   M & S Rare Books 60-468 1996 $125.00

OLMSTED, DUNCAN H.   Bartolomeus Zanni, Printer at Venice 1486-1518 and at Portese 1489-90. Berkeley: Tamalpais Press, 1962. One of 135 copies; folio; (8) pages, (1) leaf; wrappers; fine; the leaf is from Zanni's 1503 edition of 'De Sancto Gervaso.'   The Bookpress 75-334 1996 $185.00

OLMSTED, FREDERICK LAW 1822-1903   A Journey through Texas; or, a Saddle Trip on the Southwestern Frontier, with Statistical Appendix. New York: Dix, Edwards, 1857. 1st edition; (ii), xxxiv, 516 pages; folding map, plate; cloth; very good, pleasing copy.   Metacomet Books 54-81 1996 $250.00

OLMSTED, FREDERICK LAW 1822-1903   Yosemite and the Mariposa Grove: a Preliminary Report, 1865. Berkeley: One Heart Press, 1993. 1st edition thus; one of 100 copies signed by Wayne Tiebaud and Victoria Post Ranney; page size 5 x 9 inches; on Rives Heavyweight paper; 3 drawings by Thiebaud; drab paper over boards, green linen spine, author and title on white label on spine, lovely book.   Priscilla Juvelis 95/1-188 1996 $250.00

OLSON, CHARLES   Apollonius of Tyana. A Dance, With Some Words, for Two Actors. Black Mountain: Black Mountain College, 1951. 1st edition; one of only 50 copies printed, of which 30 were bound in wrappers and 20 in boards; 8vo; silk screen map by Stanley Vanderbeek; original decorated wrappers very slightly soiled, otherwise fine; rare. Excellent association copy, the copy of Olson's fellow Black Mountain College colleague, M. C. Richards, with her signature.   James S. Jaffe 34-523 1996 $3,500.00

OLSON, CHARLES   Call Me Ishmael. New York: Reynal & Hitchcock, 1947. 1st edition; very good in good jacket that is edgeworn and spine faded, with several small closed triangular tears along spine; the copy of William Saroyan.   Ken Lopez 74-361 1996 $400.00

OLSON, CHARLES   Projective Verse. New York: Totem, 1959. 1st edition; 8vo; cover drawing by Matsumi Kanemitsu; original wrappers, lightly sunned along spine, otherwise fine, with errata slip; presentation copy, inscribed by author for MC (Richards).   James S. Jaffe 34-525 1996 $650.00

OLSON, CHARLES   'West'. London: Goliard Press, 1966. 1st edition; one of only 25 copies, specially bound and signed by author; 8vo; original boards, dust jacket; creased slightly, otherwise fine.   James S. Jaffe 34-526 1996 $850.00

OLSON, RUTH   Naum Gabo and Antoine Pevner. New York: Museum of Modern Art, 1948. 1st edition; wrappers; covers worn and creased, some corners slightly creased; good. Presentation copy from Herbert Reed for E. H. Ramsden and Margot Eates.   Ulysses 39-495 1996 £95.00

OMAR KHAYYAM   The Rubaiyat of Omar Khayyam. Edinburgh & London: W. P. Nimmo, Hay & Mitchell Ltd., n.d. 1st edition; color frontispiece and color endpapers by Alice Ross, decorated leather wrappers, top edge dusty, spine and cover edges darkened, frayed and chipped; good only; ownership signature of Ian Fleming.   Ulysses 39-677 1996 £125.00

OMAR KHAYYAM   The Rubaiyat of Omar Khayyam. Boston: Riverside Press/London: Bernard Quaritch, n.d. 1884. Folio; illustrated titlepage, frontispiece and 50 full page plates, from drawings by Elihu Vedder (some very sight foxing); superbly bound in full crimson morocco, elaborate gilt design on both covers of the tree of life surrounded by an archway of two pillars with 12 oval ornaments rising and meeting at a peak, outer margins are four and one line with wide leafy border, spine similarly decorated, wide inside morocco doublures, silk endpapers, bound by Fazakerley of Liverpool, enclosed in silk lined box case.   Charles W. Traylen 117-175 1996 £1,800.00

OMAR KHAYYAM   The Rubaiyat of Omar Khayyam. Boston: Houghton Mifflin, 1884. 1st edition thus; folio; (63)ff; original gilt stamped pictorial brown cloth, bookplate, very good with light soiling and rubbing.   Chapel Hill 94-95 1996 $250.00

OMAR KHAYYAM   Rubaiyat of Omar Khayyam. Boston: Houghton, Mifflin and Co., 1894. 1st edition illustrated thus; small 4to; illustrations in monochrome by Elihu Vedder; original grey pictorial cloth over bevelled boards, stamped in black and gilt to a dramatic American art nouveau design, top edge gilt, binding lightly rubbed, but very bright copy with stunning upper cover.   Sotheran PN32-149 1996 £98.00

OMAR KHAYYAM   Rubaiyat of Omar Khayyam. London: Vale Press, 1901. Limited to 310 copies; 8vo; printed in red and black Vale type on handmade paper, pages xxx, (2), frontispiece, borders and initials by Ricketts, faint browning in bottom margin of first opening, otherwise very good; uncommon; original holland backed boards, paper label, uncut; from the library of Will Ransom with his label. Bookplate of J. H. Hanson. Tomkinson 32.   Claude Cox 107-176 1996 £150.00

OMAR KHAYYAM   Rubaiyat of Omar Khayyam. London: Hodder & Stoughton, 1913. 1st edition thus, deluxe, limited to only 250 numbered copies, signed by artist; 4to; pages (80); printed on one side of the paper only; illustrations in blue line and with 19 mounted vignettes in full color set within borders and 10 stunning full page colored plates mounted in gilt frames, by Rene Bull; original full vellum elaborately stamped in gilt and blue to spine and upper cover, top edge gilt, others uncut, new satin ribbon ties; little light mottling and rubbing of covers, fron blank endpaper creased once across, all plates fine and fresh and internally text clean, very attractive book in very nice condition; scarce. Sotheran PN32-150 1996 £450.00

OMAR KHAYYAM   Rubaiyat of Omar Khayyam. London: George G. Harrap & Co., ca. 1915. Early edition; 4to; borders, decorations and calligraphy in colors and 24 mounted colored plates by Willy Pogany; original full green buckram, top edge gilt, uncut, pictorial endpapers; fine. Sotheran PN32-136 1996 £138.00

OMAR KHAYYAM   The Rubaiyat. London: Macmillan, 1920. 6 x 4 1/4 inches; 3 p.l., 111 pages; title printed in red and black; quite pretty deep blue morocco by Zaehnsdorf, covers dominated by a large and intricate gilt arabesque (with unusual onlaid oval of marbled calf at center), raised bands, spine with gilt floral ornaments, rules and titling, very pretty elaborate gilt inner dentelles, all edges gilt, top of spine with tiny chip, backstrip very slightly sunned, otherwise fine in charming binding. Bookplate.   Phillip J. Pirages 33-66 1996 $125.00

OMAR KHAYYAM   Penillion. (Rubaiyat in Welsh). Newtown: Gregynog Press, 1928. One of 25 copies specially bound, out of a total edition of 210; 10 x 7 1/4 inches; xvi, 30 pages; printer's device on title, 10 wood engravings in text by R. A. Maynard, printed in blue and black; bound by Gregynog Press Bindery in fine deep blue polished levant morocco (signed by George Fisher in gilt on rear turn-in), raised bands, spine with gilt titling, two gilt rules on turn-ins, top edge gilt, other edges untrimmed; perhaps very slight variation in color of leather, but an extremely fine copy, virtually pristine internally. Harrop 13.   Phillip J. Pirages 33-263 1996 $3,750.00

OMAR KHAYYAM   Penillion Omar Khayya, Wedi eu Cyfieithu o'r Berseg... (Rubaiyat in Welsh). Newtown: Gregynog Press, 1928. Limited edition of 310 copies; 4to; xvi, 30 pages; printed on batchelor handmade paper, titlepage and text printed in blue and black, 10 wood engravings by R. A. Maynard; publisher's cream buckram, with yellow glazed buckram spine and fore-edge strip, edges uncut, with just a trace of dust soiling to covers, but unusually fresh.   Thomas Thorp 489-237 1996 £180.00

OMAR KHAYYAM   The Original Rubaiyat of Omar Khayyam. Garden City: Doubleday, 1968. 1st edition; one of 500 specially bound and numbered copies, signed by Robert Graves and Omar Ali-Shah; fine in slipcase.   Captain's Bookshelf 38-92 1996 $175.00

O'MEARA, JAMES   Broderick and Gwin. The Most Extraordinary Contest for a Seat in the Senate of the United States Ever Known. San Francisco: Bacon & Co., 1881. 5 3/4 x 3 7/8 inches; x, 254 pages; gold stamped green cloth.   Dawson's Books Shop 528-180 1996 $250.00

OMNIA Comesta A Belo or, an Answer Out of the West to a Question Out of the North. London?: printed in the year, 1667. 1st edition; 4to; 16 (i.e. 15), (1) pages; recently bound in old style quarter calf and marbled boards, gilt, very good, entirely unopened. Kress 1199; Goldsmiths 1857; Wing O 290; Amex 338.   John Drury 82-203 1996 £175.00

OMWAKE, JOHN   The Conestoga Six-Horses Bell Teams of Eastern Pennsylvania 1750-1850. Cincinnati: 1930. 1st edition; 4to; original binding, very good.   October Farm 36-152 1996 $195.00

ON the Ambitious Projects of Russia in Regard to North West America, with Particular Reference to New Albion & New California. San Francisco: Book Club of California, 1955. One of 350 copies; 79 pages, facsimile map; half paper vellum and printed boards, spine lettered in red; very fine. Allen 17.   Argonaut Book Shop 113-318 1996 $200.00

ONDAATJE, MICHAEL   Aardvark. Toronto: Ganglia, n.d., c. 1967. 1st Canadian edition; 3 1/4 x 4 1/4 inch single sheet of blue paper folded once, signed by author; fine; uncommon.   Thomas Dorn 9-202 1996 $200.00

ONDAATJE, MICHAEL   The Collected Works of Billy the Kid. New York: W. W. Norton, 1970. 1st American edition; errata slip present; fine in price clipped dust jacket, signed by author.   Captain's Bookshelf 38-176 1996 $150.00

ONDAATJE, MICHAEL   The Collected Works of Billy the Kid. Toronto: Anansi, 1970. 1st Canadian edition; fine in very bright, fine dust jacket. Thomas Dorn 9-208 1996 $300.00

ONDAATJE, MICHAEL   Coming Through Slaughter. New York: Norton, 1976. 1st U.S. edition; near fine in price clipped dust jacket; inscribed by author to poet Mike Mouton with ALS to him laid in.   Lame Duck Books 19-444 1996 $375.00

ONDAATJE, MICHAEL   Coming through Slaughter. Toronto: Anansi, 1976. 1st edition; fine in dust jacket, signed by author.   Lame Duck Books 19-443 1996 $500.00

ONDAATJE, MICHAEL   The Dainty Monsters. Toronto: Coach House Press, 1967. 1st Canadian edition; 1-500 numbered copies; fine copy in fine dust jacket with one miniscule edge tear; author's first book; fine, scarce, though not called for, signed by author.   Thomas Dorn 9-201 1996 $1,000.00

ONDAATJE, MICHAEL   The English Patient. Knopf, 1992. Advance uncorrected proofs; wrappers; fine.   Beasley Books 82-124 1996 $175.00

ONDAATJE, MICHAEL   The English Patient. London: Bloomsbury, 1992. True 1st edition; fine in fine dust jacket with silk ribbon marker bound in Ken Lopez 74-363 1996 $125.00

ONDAATJE, MICHAEL   The English Patient. Toronto: McClelland & Stewart, 1992. 1st Canadian edition; fine in dust jacket, signed by Ondaatje.   Lame Duck Books 19-448 1996 $150.00

ONDAATJE, MICHAEL   The English Patient. Toronto: McClelland & Stewart, 1992. 1st Canadian edition; fine in fine dust jacket.   Bella Luna 7-434 1996 $100.00

ONDAATJE, MICHAEL   In the Skin of a Lion. Toronto: McClelland & Stewart, 1987. 1st edition; fine in dust jacket, signed by author.   Lame Duck Books 19-447 1996 $150.00

ONDAATJE, MICHAEL   The Man with Seven Toes. Toronto: Coach House, 1969. 1st Canadian edition, there were 300 numbered copies, numbers 1-50 were signed by author, this is copy #8; fine in bright, fine dust jacket.   Thomas Dorn 9-203 1996 $1,600.00

ONDAATJE, MICHAEL   Running in the Family. London: Gollancz, 1983. 1st British edition; fine in dust jacket, signed by author.   Lame Duck Books 19-446 1996 $125.00

ONE Hundred Merrie and Delightsome Stories. Carbonnek: privately printed for subscribers only, 1925. Signed, limited edition of 1250 numbered copies, signed by Arthur Machen who provided introduction; 8vo; 16 full page etchings-engravings by Clara Tice; gilt worked and embossed green cloth, very good or better, nice set.   Antic Hay 101-58 1996 $125.00

O'NEALL, JOHN BELTON   The Annals of Newberry in Two Parts... Newberry: Aull & Houseal, 1892. 2nd edition; 816, vii pages; original cloth, wear to extremities, yet very good. Howes O93. Turnbull IV p.3 10.   McGowan Book Co. 65-120 1996 $285.00

O'NEILL, EUGENE GLADSTONE 1888-1953   Ah, Wilderness. New York: Limited Editions Club, 1972. One of 1500 numbered copies, signed by Shannon Stirnweis; illustrations by Stirnweis; fine in dusty publisher's slipcase.   Hermitage SP95-1019 1996 $100.00

O'NEILL, EUGENE GLADSTONE 1888-1953   Before Breakfast. New York: Frank Shay, 1916. One of 500 copies; wrappers, slight shadow from bookplate removed inside front wrapper and tiny stain at base, still very near fine copy, extremely fragile, in folding tray and custom quarter morocco slipcase, very uncommon.   Between the Covers 42-345 1996 $485.00

O'NEILL, EUGENE GLADSTONE 1888-1953   Desire Under the Elms. New York: 1925. 1st separate edition; very fine in scarce dust jacket with 1 small chip at top of rear panel and tiny chip at spine top.   Stephen Lupack 83- 1996 $300.00

O'NEILL, EUGENE GLADSTONE 1888-1953   Gold. New York: Boni & Liveright, 1920. 1st edition; octavo; 120 pages; signed by author; original green cloth over grey boards, spine extremities slightly rubbed, otherwise fine copy in scarce original dust jacket (minimal soiling and chipping, repaired with tape at foot of spine); Atkinson A16-I-i.   Heritage Book Shop 196-245 1996 $950.00

O'NEILL, EUGENE GLADSTONE 1888-1953   Gold. New York: Boni & Liveright, 1920. 1st edition; fore-edge foxed and little soiling to top edge, else fine in fine example of the dust jacket, little shorter than the book; lovely copy.   Between the Covers 42-346 1996 $850.00

O'NEILL, EUGENE GLADSTONE 1888-1953   The Iceman Cometh. New York: Limited Editions Club, 1982. 2000 copies signed by Baskin who has also specially signed the lithograph; 11 1/4 x 7 inches; 208 pages, 9 drawings, lithograph printed in sanguine on Arches, French handmade paper; Gray Curtis paper over boards, Torino paper labels; mint in slipcase, signed by Baskin who has also specially signed the lithograph, newsletter laid in.   Taurus Books 83-115 1996 $150.00

O'NEILL, EUGENE GLADSTONE 1888-1953   Lazarus Laughed. New York: 1927. Limited edition, 369/775 copies, signed by author; uncut, vellum, spine sunned, fine.   Polyanthos 22-660 1996 $175.00

O'NEILL, EUGENE GLADSTONE 1888-1953   Long Day's Journey into Night. New Haven: Yale University Press, 1956. 1st edition; tall 8vo; very good in chipped and worn dust jacket. Evidence of bookplate removal on endpaper;   Glenn Books 36-199 1996 $110.00

O'NEILL, EUGENE GLADSTONE 1888-1953   Mourning Becomes Electra. New York: Liveright, 1931. 1st edition; near fine in lightly chipped dust jacket with damaged front flap; signed by 17 members of the original cast.   Lame Duck Books 19-438 1996 $1,000.00

O'NEILL, EUGENE GLADSTONE 1888-1953   Mourning Becomes Electra. New York: Liveright, 1931. 1st edition; couple of barely visible tears on rear of dust jacket, otherwise nearly peft copy, fragile, remarkable survivor.   Between the Covers 42-347 1996 $450.00

O'NEILL, EUGENE GLADSTONE 1888-1953   Mourning Becomes Electra. New York: 1931. 1st edition; 8.5 x 5.5. inches; 256 pages, ink inscription, clippings plus 2 Theatre Guild ticket stubs affixed to endpapers, else very good in chipped, edge torn and rubbed dust jacket.   John K. King 77-420 1996 $100.00

O'NEILL, EUGENE GLADSTONE 1888-1953   Strange Interlude. New York: Boni & Liveright 1928. 1st edition; advance copy; stiff wrappers, possibly an earlier and unused dust jacket design, title and author appear to be hand lettered to front cover, mounted pictorial design of a seated woman rendered in Art Deco style and is apparently hand painted in green silver and black, some light wear to extremities and wrappers split at front hinge, else near fine, extremely rare variant; inscribed by author.   Bromer Booksellers 87-243 1996 $650.00

O'NEILL, EUGENE GLADSTONE 1888-1953   Thirst and Other One Act Plays. Boston: Gorham Press, 1914. 1st edition; one of 1000 printed; 8vo; in very good dust jacket which is slightly soiled (two small closed tears on upper panel, and about 18" chipping at top and bottom of jacket spine, not affecting text); nice copy.   Lakin & Marley 3-42 1996 $1,750.00

O'NEILL, EUGENE GLADSTONE 1888-1953   Thirst-Five One Act Plays. Boston: Gorham, 1914. 1st edition; tiny rub at base of front board, still easily fine in near fine white dust jacket with some foxing and price neatly excised from spine but with no appreciable chips or tears; author's first book, very scarce in jacket.   Between the Covers 42-344 1996 $2,000.00

O'NEILL, EUGENE GLADSTONE 1888-1953   Thirst. Boston: Gorham Press, 1914. 1st edition; 8vo; author's first book; original binding, owner stamp; good. Atkinson AI-1-I.   Charles Agvent 4-919 1996 $250.00

O'NEILL, THOMAS   A Concise and Accurate Account of the Proceedings of the Squadron Under the Command of Rear Admiral Sir Sydney Smith, K.S. &c. in Effecting the Escape of the Royal Family of Portugal to the Brazil, on Nov. 29, 1807... London: J. Barfield, for the author, 1810. 2nd edition; 8vo; frontispiece, vi, 189 pages; uncut, original boards, new paper spine; tipped in errata slip; little paper has been chipped of the boards, else very fine. Not in Sabin.   Howard S. Mott 227-106 1996 $350.00

ONIONS, OLIVER   The Compleat Bachelor. London: John Murray, 1900. Reprint; original binding, top edge dusty, free endpapers browned, covers marked and slightly soiled, cover edges rubbed, spine browned, head and tail of spine and corners bumped, remains of labels on upper cover and front free endpaper, good; top edge gilt; ownership signature of Ian Fleming.   Ulysses 39-686 1996 £125.00

OORT, E. D. VAN   Ornithologia Neerlandica, De Vogels van Nederland. The Hague: 1918-22-35. Imperial 4to; 5 volumes; 407 colored plates; half dark green morocco, spines faded. From the collection of Jan Coldewey.   Wheldon & Wesley 207-76 1996 £1,300.00

OPIE, JOHN NEWTON   A Rebel Cavalryman with Lee Stuart and Jackson. Chicago: W. B. Conkey Co., 1899. 1st edition; 336 pages; original cloth, very good to near fine. Coulter 353; Dornbusch II 1224; Haynes 13461; Howes O101.   McGowan Book Co. 65-69 1996 $450.00

OPPEN, GEORGE   Seascape: Needle's Eye. Fremont: Sumac Press, 1972. 1st edition; one of 26 lettered copies, signed by author; fine in dust jacket.   Captain's Bookshelf 38-179 1996 $175.00

OPPENHEIM, MAX VON   Tel Halaf. A New Culture in Oldest Mesopotamia. London: and New York: G. P. Putnam, ca. 1931. 8vo; xvi, 337 pages, 23 figures and 68 plates; original cloth, bookplate removed.   Archaeologia Luxor-2537 1996 $150.00

OPPENHEIMER, JOEL   The Dutiful Son. N.P.: Jonathan Williams, 1956. 1st edition; one of 200 copies; 8vo; lithograph frontispiece by Joe Fiore, original printed buff wrappers, scarce; wrappers somewhat soiled; presentation copy inscribed by author for M. C.(Richards).   James S. Jaffe 34-527 1996 $500.00

OPPENHEIMER, JOEL   New Hampshire Journal: Poems. Mt. Horeb: Perishable Press, 1994. One of 125 numbered copies; illustrations by Margaret Sunday; plain wrappers; fine.   Bertram Rota 272-370 1996 £250.00

OPPENHEIMER, LEHMANN J.   The Heart of Lakeland. Manchester: Sherratt & Hughes, 1908. 1st (only) edition; tall 8vo; pages (x), 196; 39 plates; original cloth, gilt, little faded and marked, top edge trifle frayed in places, flyleaves slightly browned, but very good, sound copy; scarce. Neate O14.   R.F.G. Hollett & Son   78-300 1996 £120.00

OPPRESSION. A Poem. London: printed for the author, 1765. 1st edition; 4to; half title, title, pages 34; contemporary marbled boards, calf back, rebacked; scarce, 1 inch tear in blank inner margin of half title; Adams, American Controversy 65-19; Wegelin 703; Sabin 57416.   Howard S. Mott 227-107 1996 $850.00

OPUSCULA Romana. Volume IV. Lund: C. W. K. Gleerup, 1962. 4to; frontisportrait, 248 pages, numerous illustrations; three quarter green calf with 4 raised bands, original wrappers bound in; the first copy, inscribed by the publisher, specially bound for Gjerstad.   Archaeologia Luxor-3780 1996 $200.00

O'RAHILLY, T. F.   Gadelica: a Journal of Modern-Irish Studies. London: 1912/13. 8vo; volume 1 (all published); original wrapper (worn), text very good.   C. P. Hyland 216-247 1996 £90.00

ORANGE County and the Santa Ana Valley. Santa Ana: Santa Ana Chamber of Commerce, ca. 1900. 5 3/4 x 9 inches; (48) pages; photographic illustrations, except for 7 pages of text and map; pictorial self wrappers.   Dawson's Books Shop 528-182 1996 $200.00

ORATORUM Veterum Orationes... Geneva: Henri Stephanus Estienne, 1575. 2nd edition; folio; pages (12), 208 (misnumbered); 191; 178; printer's device on title (10); ornamental initials and headpieces; 18th century English full leather, joints weak, clean and wide margined copy. Schreiber 192; Renouard 141-42.3.   Family Album Tillers-459 1995 $800.00

THE ORCHID Album. London: 1882-83. 4to; Volumes 1 and 2, 96 hand colored plates; half morocco, scarce early volumes.   Wheldon & Wesley 207-77 1996 £1,500.00

ORCHIDS from the Botanical Register, 1815-1847. Boston: 1991. Tall 4to; 2 volumes, pages 322, 326; 440 full color illustrations, portrait, several text figures; hardbound, slipcase.   Raymond M. Sutton VI-23 1996 $350.00

ORDINAIRE, CLAUDE NICHOLAS   The Natural History of Volcanoes: Including Submarine, Volcanoes and Other Analogous Phenomena. London: T. Cadell, Jun. and W. Davies, 1801. 1st edition; 8vo; xxiv, 328 pages; contemporary calf, rehinged, few marginal notes in 19th century hand, very good. Poggendorff II 331; Sabin 57506.   Edwin V. Glaser 121-238 1996 $450.00

OREGON RAILWAY & NAVIGATION CO.   East Washington Territory and Oregon... Portland: A. Anderson & Co., ca. 1884. 1st edition; 31 (1) pages; folding maps; original printed blue wrappers, minor splitting repaired, fine. Not in Soliday, Streeter Sale, Decker or Eberstadt. Michael D. Heaston 23-359 1996 $500.00

O'REILLY, BERNARD   Greenland and the Adjacent Seas, and the North-West Passage to the Pacific Ocean, Illustrated in a Voyage to Davis's Strait, During the Summer of 1817. London: printed for Baldwin, Cradock and Joy, 1818. 1st edition; 4to; contemporary red straight grained moroccco, covers elaborately decorated in blind and gilt, all edges gilt, slight wear, but sound; attractive copy; from the library of Sir. Thomas Phillipps, with his shelfmark; armorial bookplate of Nicholas Garry. Sabin 57576; Hill p. 219 (American reprint); Abbey, Travel 633. Ximenes 109-208 1996 $1,500.00

O'REILLY, EDWARD   An Irish-English Dictionary. n.d. New edition; 8vo; cloth, ex-library, but very good.   C. P. Hyland 216-647 1996 £56.00

ORIBASIUS   Synopseos ad Eustathium Filium Lib. Novem: Quibus Tota Medicina in Compendium Redacta Contrinetur... Paris: Maurice Menier for Oudin Petit, 1554. 2nd edition; small 8vo; 528 pages; printer's device on title, decorative initials, typographic ornaments; contemporary limp vellum, with 3 or 4 ties, hand lettered backstrip; fine. Not in NUC; Dorling 3410; Hoffmann 3.175.   Bennett Gilbert LL29-50 1996 $600.00

ORIGINAL Compositions in Prose and Verse, Illustrated With Lithographic Drawings; to Which is Added some vocal and Instrumental Music. London: Edmund Lloyd, 1833. 1st edition; oblong 4to; frontispiece, 3 other plates, all lithographs on mounted india paper; original green cloth, black paper side label printed in gold, couple of very small rubbed spots; some foxing, but fine, very rare. 1 copy in NUC.   Ximenes 109-262 1996 $1,250.00

ORIGINAL Papers Relative to Tanjore; Containing All the Letters Which Passed, and the Conferences Which Passed, and the conferences Which Were Held between His Highness the Nabob of Arcot and Lord Pigiot, on the Subject of the Restoration of Tanjore. London: printed for T. Cadell, 1777. 1st edition; 4to; 134 pages; disbound.   Anthony W. Laywood 108-130 1996 £95.00

ORIOLI, G.   Adventures of a Bookseller. Florence: n.d. Limited edition of 300 copies, signed by author, this being copy number 80; orange printed wrappers, trifle shaken and torn at foot of spine, otherwise very good; warmly inscribed by author.   Words Etcetera 94-1010 1996 £185.00

ORLEANS, M. LOUISE PHILIP JOSEPH, DUC D'   The Memoire of...accused of High Treason, Before the Tribunal of the Chatelet in Paris with the Very Interesting Advice of His Counsel as to the Punishment of His Accusers in which is Contained an Authentick Detail of Many Curious Facts... Dublin: P. Wogan, etc., 1791. 58 pages, rebound in boards. C. R. Johnson 37-65 1996 £75.00

ORMOND, JOHN   Cathedral Builders and Other Poems. Gwasg Gregynog, 1991. One of 250 numbered copies; small folio; printed in Monotype Gramond on Mohawk superfine, half black cloth, ochre boards; fine.   Bertram Rota 272-214 1996 £65.00

ORMOND, RICHARD   John Sargent Singer. London: Phaidon, 1970. 31 x 23 cm; over 200 illustrations, including 32 color plates; cloth, dust jacket.   Rainsford A54-517 1996 £140.00

ORMSBY, WATERMAN LILLY.   Ormsby's Pentographic Illustrations of the Holy Scriptures; Being Accurate Copies of Sir Edward Thomason's Celebrated Medals with a Condensed History of the Bible. New York: Ormsby's Pentographic Establishment, 1835. 1st edition; 8vo; 4 engraved plates, each with two medals, descriptive text opposite; original printed front wrapper, becoming loose, red waterstaining throughout, but complete and very adequate for study. Rinderknecht 33529.   M & S Rare Books 60-329 1996 $200.00

ORPEN, ADELA   The Chronicles of Sid, London: Religious Tract Society, 1893. 1st edition; 8vo; 413, (3) pages ads; numerous illustrations; original light green cloth pictorially decorated in gilt; fine. David Mason 71-115 1996 $160.00

ORPEN, CHARLES EDWARD HERBERT   Anecdotes and Annals of the Deaf and Dumb. London: Robert H. C. Tims, 1836. 2nd edition; half title, 2 plates; original dark green cloth, paper spine label, very good. Jarndyce 103-544 1996 £220.00

ORRERY, ROGER BOYLE, 1ST EARL OF 1621-1679   English Adventures. London: printed by T. Newcomb, for H. Herringman, 1676. 1st edition; 8vo; contemporary tree calf, nicely rebacked, spine gilt; occasional light stains, otherwise very good; the copy of Rev. Philip Bliss (1787-1857); Also the copy of David Garrick. Wing O476; Esdaile p. 167; Mish p. 51; CBEL II 770.   Ximenes 109-50 1996 $6,000.00

ORRERY, ROGER BOYLE, 1ST EARL OF 1621-1679   Two New Tragedies. The Black Prince, and Tryphon. London: printed for H. Herringman, 1672. 2nd edition; small folio; contemporary mottled calf, spine gilt, joints and tips of spine bit rubbed; exceptionally nice, uncommon survival thus. Wing O502; Woodward and McManaway 123. Ximenes 109-51 1996 $900.00

ORS, EUGENIO D'   Pablo Picasso. New York: Weyhe, 1930. Limited to 1200 copies; 4to; 62 pages, 4 color plates, many + 48 monochrome plates; wrappers, in cloth backed board portfolio. Freitag 7476. Brannan 43-528 1996 $135.00

ORTA, GARCIA DE   Aromatum, et Simplicium Aliquot Medicamentorum Apud Indos Nascentium Historia... Antwerp: Ex officina Christophori Plantini, Arachitypographi Regii, 1579. 3rd Plantin edition; small 8vo; pages 217, (6), 28 woodcuts by Peter van der Borcht and Arnold Nicolai old paper faults, repaired, with slight loss, title soiled, later full vellum; numerous old ownerships including presentation to William Reynaud from Leonard Gillespie, Fort Royal Naval Hospital, Martinique, 1802.   Family Album Tillers-460 1996 $750.00

ORTIGUE, PIERRE D' The Art of Pleasing in Conversation. London: Richard Wellington, 1708. 12mo; contemporary calf gilt, prior owner's signature; uncommon; binding rather worn, but good copy.   Trebizond 39-65 1996 $225.00

ORTIZ, GEORGE In Pursuit of the Absolute Art of the Ancient World from the George Oritz Collection. London: Royal Academy of Arts, 1994. 4to; over 500 pages; profusely illustrated in color; stiff wrappers. Archaeologia Luxor-3300 1996 $250.00

ORTON, RICHARD H. Records of California Men in the War of the Rebellion, 1861-1867. Sacramento: State Office, 1890. 9 x 6 inches; 887 pages; blind ruled black cloth.   Dawson's Books Shop 528-186 1996 $200.00

ORWELL, GEORGE 1903-1950 Animal Farm. New York: HB & Co. 1946. 1st American edition; fine in dust jacket with little rubbed crease at bottom of front panel and some slight rubbing at extremities of spine, despite the small flaws, this is one of the nicest copies we have seen. Between the Covers 42-348 1996 $200.00

ORWELL, GEORGE 1903-1950 The Clergyman's Daughter. New York: Harper, 1936. 1st American edition; dust jacket internally strengthened and covers lightly soiled, small amount of paper residue on rear cover, still very good in mildly rubbed dust jacket that is about very good, very scarce, particularly in any dust jacket.   Ken Lopez 74-364 1996 $850.00

ORWELL, GEORGE 1903-1950 James Burnham and the Managerial Revolution. London: Socialist Book Centre, 1946. 1st edition; 19 pages; wrappers little discolored at edges, pages browning, otherwise nice. Ian Patterson 9-226 1996 £85.00

ORWELL, GEORGE 1903-1950 Keep the Aspidistra Flying. London: Gollancz, 1936. Boards rubbed, but excellent copy in sunned, soiled and restored dust jacket.   R. A. Gekoski 19-105 1996 £400.00

ORWELL, GEORGE 1903-1950 Nineteen Eighty-Four. H-B, 1949. 1st American edition; very good+/near fine in red issue dust jacket; author's photo laid in.   Aronovitz 57-916 1996 $135.00

ORWELL, GEORGE 1903-1950 Nineteen Eighty-Four. London: Secker and Warburg, 1949. Green cloth somewhat faded, front hinge of (green) dust jacket split, chipping to top of spinea nd cornes, other signs of wear; altogether not a very good copy.   R. A. Gekoski 19-106 1996 £150.00

ORWELL, GEORGE 1903-1950 The Road to Wigan Pier. Abbreviated: Part One Only. London: Gollancz, LBC, 1937. Abbreviated edition; 150 pages, plates; orange limp cloth, light foxing; superb copy, near fine, rare.   Ian Patterson 9-192 1996 £250.00

ORWELL, GEORGE 1903-1950 Talking to India - a Selection of English Language Broadcasts to India. London: George Allen & Unwin, 1943. 1st edition; 5 black and white photos; original binding, top edge spotted and dusty, head and tail of spine and corners slightly bumped, very good in nicked, rubbed and dusty, slightly creased dust jacket, slightly darkened at spine and edges.   Ulysses 39-451 1996 £295.00

OSBALDISTON, WILLIAM A. The British Sportsman, or Nobleman, Gentleman and Farmer's Dictionary of Recreation and Amusement... London: 1792. Large 4to; 35 fine engraved plates, of 42; half cloth, marbled boards, leather spine label; surprisingly good and tasteful binding.   David A.H. Grayling 3/95-190 1996 £160.00

OSBORN, FRANCIS The Works...Divine, Moral, Historical, Political. London: R. D. to be sold by Allen Banks, 1682. 8th edition; 8vo; (xii), 628 pages; recent half calf, marbled boards, label; minor staining, single wormhole through margin, clear of text, good. Wing O506.   Robert Clark 38-83 1996 £85.00

OSBORNE, JOHN Epitaph for George Dillon. London: Faber & Faber, 1958. 1st edition; 8vo; cloth, dust jacket; fine.   James S. Jaffe 34-529 1 996 $100.00

OSGOOD, ERNEST STAPLES The Field Notes of Captain William Clark 1803-1805. New Haven: Yale University Press, 1964. 1st edition; 14 x 9 3/4 inches; reproductions of 67 manuscript documents; fine in rubbed and chipped, though intact dust jacket.   Hermitage SP95-727 1996 $325.00

OSGOOD, FRANCES S. The Poetry of Flowers and Flowers of Poetry. New York: J. C. Riker, 1841. 1st edition; octavo; 276 pages; hand colored title and 12 hand colored full page floral plates; pictorial boards, all edges gilt, light foxing and rebacking to soiled boards. Inscribed in pencil to H. D. Thoreau's sister Helen from a member of Prudence Ward's family.   Bromer Booksellers 90-211 1996 $450.00

OSLER, WILLIAM 1849-1919 Aequanimitas and Other Addresses. Philadelphia: 1905. 1st edition; 2nd printing; 389 pages; original binding. W. Bruce Fye 71-1551 1996 $150.00

OSLER, WILLIAM 1849-1919 An Alabama Student and Other Biographical Essays. New York: Oxford University Press, London: Henry Frowde, 1908. 1st edition; 8vo; (iv), 334 pages; frontispiece, illustrations; red cloth; very good; signed by S. Hamilton Jr. Nov. 1908, bookplate of Dr. Elmer Belt.   Jeff Weber 31-29 1996 $175.00

OSLER, WILLIAM 1849-1919 An Alabama Student and Other Biographical Addresses. London: 1909. 1st edition; 2nd printing; 334 pages; original binding, scarce.   W. Bruce Fye 71-1554 1996 $125.00

OSLER, WILLIAM 1849-1919 An Alabama Student and Other Biographical Essays. New York: Oxford University Press American Branch/London: Henry Frowde, 1909. 1st edition; 2nd impression; 8vo; (iv), 334, ads (16) pages; frontispiece, illustrations; red cloth; very good; booklabel of Joe Webb, Johns Hopkins University.   Jeff Weber 31-30 1996 $100.00

OSLER, WILLIAM 1849-1919 An Alabama Student and Other Biographical Essays. London: Humphrey Milford, 1929. 1st edition; 2nd impression; 8vo; (iii), 334 pages, frontispiece, illustrations; red cloth, spine soiled; inscribed to Willard E. Goodwin from Howard A. Kelly and Goodwin's signature and bookplate.   Jeff Weber 31-31 1996 $100.00

OSLER, WILLIAM 1849-1919 An Annotated Bibliography with Illustrations. San Francisco: 1988. 4to; 105 illustrations; original cloth, dust jacket.   Charles W. Traylen 117-34 1996 £76.00

OSLER, WILLIAM 1849-1919 Bibliotheca Osleriana. A Catalogue of Books Illustrating the History of Medicine and Science...Bequeathed to McGill University. Oxford: Clarendon Press, 1929. 1st edition; limited to 761 copies; 4to; xxxv, 785 pages; navy blue cloth, hinges and spine repaired; bookplate of Elmer Belt. GM 6772; Golden & Roland 1073. Jeff Weber 31-33 1996 $700.00

OSLER, WILLIAM 1849-1919 Bibliotheca Osleriana. Oxford: 1929. 1st edition; 786 pages; recent cloth, ink stains on fore edges. GM 6772. W. Bruce Fye 71-1555 1996 $500.00

OSLER, WILLIAM 1849-1919 Cancer of the Stomach. Philadelphia: P. Blakiston's Son, 1900. 1st American edition; 8vo; iv, 157, ads, 40, (8) pages, 25 figures; dark blue blind stamped cloth, inner hinge cracked signature of Arthur Henry Morse who inscribed the book to Arthur Bliss Dayton, 1921. Bookplate of Elmer Belt. Abbott p. 72; Golden & roland 727.   Jeff Weber 31-36 1996 $325.00

OSLER, WILLIAM 1849-1919 The Collected Essays of Sir William Osler. Birmingham: 1985. 1st edition; 3 volumes, 497, 454, 642 pages; full leather. GR 1485.   W. Bruce Fye 71-1585 1996 $200.00

OSLER, WILLIAM 1849-1919 The Evolution of Modern Medicine. New York: 1921. 1st edition; 243 pages; original binding, inner hinges cracked, shaken, binding rubbed; contents very good.   W. Bruce Fye 71-1560 1996 $125.00

OSLER, WILLIAM 1849-1919 The Growth of Truth as Illustrated in the Discovery of the Circulation of the Blood. London: 1906. 1st edition; 44 pages; original boards. Osler 773 (3rd impression of 1907). GR 974. W. Bruce Fye 71-1564 1996 $250.00

OSLER, WILLIAM 1849-1919 The Growth of Truth, As Illustrated in the Discovery of the Blood. London: Henry Frowde, Oxford University Press, 1906. 1st separate printing; 8vo; 44 pages; grey printed wrappers, blue cloth slipcase, red leather spine label; scarce; occasional pencil notes in margin, otherwise very good; bookplate of Elmer Belt.   Jeff Weber 31-47 1996 $145.00

OSLER, WILLIAM 1849-1919 Incunabula Medica: a Study of the Earliest Printed Medical Books, 1467-1480. Oxford: 1923. 1st edition; 4to; 137 pages, plus 15 plates, ex-library with small stamp on titlepage and verso of plates, overall fine. GM 6769.   W. Bruce Fye 71-1565 1996 $500.00

OSLER, WILLIAM 1849-1919   Lectures on Angina Pectoris and Allied
States. New York: D. Appleton, 1897. 2nd edition; 8vo; vi, 160, ads (8)
pages; dark green embossed cloth; very scarce; bookplate of Elmer
Belt. Bedford 627; Golden & Roland 669.   Jeff Weber 31-50 1996
$300.00

OSLER, WILLIAM 1849-1919   Lectures on Angina Pectoris and Allied
States. New York: D. Appleton, 1897. 2nd edition; 8vo; vi, 160, ads (8)
pages; brown embossed cloth, signature of C. H. Bunting and bookplate
of Elmer Belt. Golden & Roland 669.   Jeff Weber 31-51 1996 $200.00

OSLER, WILLIAM 1849-1919   Lectures on Diagnosis of Abdominal
Tumors. New York: D. Appleton, 1898. Reprinted from NY Medical
Journal 1894; 8vo; (6), 192, ads (dated April 1899), (2), 8 pages; 43
illustrations; dark green cloth, front inner hinge split, back starting, spine
ends frayed, rather ugly label pasted over early signature on front flyleaf,
title leaf loose; good; signature of Melvin Hershkowitz.   Jeff Weber
31-54 1996 $150.00

OSLER, WILLIAM 1849-1919   Lectures on the Diagnosis of Abdominal
Tumors. New York: D. Appleton, 1895. 2nd American edition; 8vo; (iii),
192 ads (2) pages; 43 figures; brown cloth, fine; bookplate and stamps
of Elmer Belt. Golden & Roland 643.   Jeff Weber 31-52 1996 $250.00

OSLER, WILLIAM 1849-1919   Men and Books. Pasadena: 1959. 1st
edition; limited to 200 copies; 675 pages; original binding; autographed
by Earl Nation who provided introduction.   W. Bruce Fye 71-1568
1996 $150.00

OSLER, WILLIAM 1849-1919   The Old Humanities and the New
Science. Boston: 1920. 64 pages; original binding.   W. Bruce Fye
71-1570 1996 $100.00

OSLER, WILLIAM 1849-1919   The Principles and Practice of Medicine.
Edinburgh & London: Young J. Pentland, 1892. 1st British edition, 1st
issue, with famous reading 'Georgias' in the Platonic inscription; 8vo; xvi,
1079, ads (39) pages, figures; navy blue embossed cloth, corners and
text bumped, spine neatly repaired; rare; much pencil underlining. GM
2231; Golden & Roland 1439.   Jeff Weber 31-69 1996 $2,375.00

OSLER, WILLIAM 1849-1919   The Principles and Practice of Medicine.
Edinburgh & London: Young J. Pentland, 1892. 1st English edition; thick
8vo; original cloth, recased.   Charles W. Traylen 117-350 1996
£500.00

OSLER, WILLIAM 1849-1919   The Principles and Practice of Medicine...
New York: D. Appleton, 1892. 1st edition; 1st state with the misspelling
'Georgias' in the quotation from Plato on leaf preceding table of contents
and with second sequence of ads dated Nov. 1891; tall thick 8vo; xvi,
(2), 1079, (6 ads), 8 (ads) pages, with charts and illustrations; original
half morocco, spine ends bit scuffed and frayed, corners trifle bumped,
front joint just starting, few small ink spots on fore edge, very good.
GM 2231; Golden-Roland 1375; Osler 3543; Heirs of Hippocrates 2121.
Edwin V. Glaser B122-113 1996 $2,400.00

OSLER, WILLIAM 1849-1919   The Principles and Practice of Medicine.
New York: D. Appleton, 1892. 1st edition; 1st issue; 8vo; xvi, 1079, ads
(6), 8 pages; figures, index, ads (dated 1891); original sheep, black spine
morocco label, rebound with original sheep mounted on all sides, new
endleaves; rare. GM 2231; Golden & Roland 1375.   Jeff Weber 31-68
1996 $2,250.00

OSLER, WILLIAM 1849-1919   The Principles and Practice of Medicine.
New York: 1892. 1st edition; 2nd printing; original binding, very good.
GM 2231; Bib. Osleriana 3544.   W. Bruce Fye 71-1574 1996
$1,250.00

OSLER, WILLIAM 1849-1919   The Principles and Practice of Medicine.
New York: D. Appleton, 1892. 1st edition; 2nd state, "Georgias"
corrected to read "Gorgias" and other internal corrections. 8vo; xvi,
1079, ads (vi), 8 page index, ads dated March 1892; modern quarter
brown morocco and marbled boards, new endleaves, fine, bookplate of
Elmer Belt. GM 2231; Golden & Roland 1378.   Jeff Weber 31-70 1996
$750.00

OSLER, WILLIAM 1849-1919   The Principles and Practice of Medicine.
New York: D. Appleton, 1896. 2nd edition; 8vo; xvi 1143, ads, (4), 8
pages, 19 charts, 11 figures, ads dated June 1896; later quarter black
leather, green cloth, leather corners; very good; signature of Albert E.
Brown, 1896; bookplate of Elmer Belt.   Jeff Weber 31-73 1996
$275.00

OSLER, WILLIAM 1849-1919   The Principles and Practice of Medicine.
New York: and London: D. Appleton, 1907. 6th edition, 2nd state; 8vo;
xvii, 1143, ads, 11 figures, 22 charts; red blindstamped cloth; very good,
bookplate of Elmer Belt, signature of C. W. Hutchison. GM 2231; Golden
& Roland 1400.   Jeff Weber 31-74 1996 $125.00

OSLER, WILLIAM 1849-1919   The Principles and Practice of Medicine.
Birmingham: Classics of Medicine Library, 1978. 8vo; xvi, 1079, ads
(dated Nov. 1891), (6), 8 pages; accompanied by 31 page brochure
"Notes from the Editors"; blue calf, gilt; fine. GM 2231; Golden & Roland
1376.   Jeff Weber 31-77 1996 $150.00

OSLER, WILLIAM 1849-1919   Science and Immortality. Boston: 1904.
1st edition; 1st printing; 54 pages; original binding. Cushing I.638.   W.
Bruce Fye 71-1575 1996 $125.00

OSLER, WILLIAM 1849-1919   Studies in Typhoid Fever. Nos. I, II, and
III. Baltimore: Johns Hopkins Press, 1901. 1st edition; tall 8vo; 3 parts in
1, iv, 167; 155-552 pages; 4 charts and illustrations, pages 1-2
mutilated; blue cloth, covers soiled, spine ends frayed or worn, covers
badly shaken, front inner hinge pulled and torn, in need or repair; Golden
& Roland 1354.   Jeff Weber 31-84 1996 $250.00

OSLER, WILLIAM 1849-1919   Thomas Linacre. Cambridge: University
Press, 1908. 1st edition; 8vo; 64 pages, frontispiece, 10 plates; variant
binding of light brown boards, upper cover and spine stamped in black;
bookplate of Herbert McLean Evans. Golden & Roland 981.   Jeff
Weber 31-57 1996 $125.00

OSSOLI, SARAH MARGARET FULLER, MARCHESA D' 1810-1850
Memoirs of Margaret Fuller Ossoli. Boston: Phillips, Sampson, 1852. 1st
edition; 2 volumes; original black cloth, gilt, spine ends chipped, else
tight, bright set. BAL 6501; Myerson 17.1.a. F4.   Mac Donnell 12-50
1996 $100.00

OSSOLI, SARAH MARGARET FULLER, MARCHESA D' 1810-1850
Memoirs of Margaret Fuller Ossoli. London: Richard Bentley, 1852. 1st
English edition; 3 volumes; original cream cloth, gilt, some dampstains to
endpapers of third volume, minor soiling of cloth, few nicks and cracks,
but very good, tight and attractive set, very rare printing. BAL 6501;
Myerson F4.   Mac Donnell 12-51 1996 $300.00

OSWALD, FELIX   Index of Figure-Types on Terra Sigillata. University
Press of Liverpool, 1936-37. Imperial 4to; 4 volumes, 325 pages; 89
plates; printed wrappers, some pages spotted, scarce.   Thomas Thorp
489-238 1996 £150.00

OTERO, L. S.   Butterflies: Beauty and Behaviour of Brazilian Species.
Rio de Janeiro: 1990. Small 8vo; pages xv, 270; portrait and numerous
text figures; original cloth; good.   Wheldon & Wesley 207-1090 1996
£65.00

OTES, TITUS   The Tryals, Convictions and Sentence of Titus Otes,
Upon Two Indictments for Willful, Malicious and Corrupt Perjury; at the
Kings-Bench-Bar at Westminster, Before the Right Hon. George Lord
Jeffreys...Lord Chief Justice of His Majesties Court of Kings... London: R.
Sare, 1685. 8vo; (iv), 94, 60 pages; imprimatur leaf; outer leaves dusty.
Wing T2249.   Robert Clark 38-117 1996 £75.00

OTIS, F. N.   History of the Panama Railroad and of the Pacific Mail
Steamship Company. Together with A Traveller's Guide and Buisness
Man's Hand-Book for the Panama Railroad. New York: Harper & Bros.,
1867. 1st edition; 317 pages; 2 maps, numerous woodcuts; cloth, bit of
wear at spine tip, otherwise very good.   Metacomet Books 54-83
1996 $110.00

OTIS, GEORGE ALEXANDER   A Report on the Excisions of the Head
of the Femur for Gunshot Injury. Washington: Jan. 2, 1869. 1st edition;
4to; 71 text figures, 3 full page engraved plates; full calf.   Argosy
810-382 1996 $350.00

OTIS, JAMES   Toby Tyler or Ten Weeks with a Circus. New York:
Harper & Bros., 1881. 1st edition; author's first book; illustrations;
pictorial light brown cloth, light dampstain upper margin of a number of
pages, name, otherwise very good in bright, attractive binding and
custom slipcase.   Steven C. Bernard 71-452 1996 $175.00

OTLEY, JONATHAN   A Concise Description of the English Lakes, and
Adjacent Mountains... Keswick: privately pub. & Kirkby Lonsdale: Arthur
Foster, 1825. 2nd edition; 8vo; 141 pages; folding map, hand colored in
outline; original boards, rebacked in later cloth, tear in flyleaf and upper
joint repaired with tape, old label of High Legh Library on pastedown.
Bicknell 102.2.   R.F.G. Hollett & Son 78-1165 1996 £95.00

OTLEY, JONATHAN   A Concise Description of the English Lakes and Adjacent Mountains... Keswick: privately pub. and Kirkby Lonsdale: Arthur Foster, 1834. 5th edition; 8vo; pages viii, 184, folding map; modern cloth, original paper spine label (rubbed). Bicknell 102.5.   R.F.G. Hollett & Son 78-1166 1996 £75.00

OTLEY, JONATHAN   A Descriptive Guide to the English Lakes, and Adjacent Mountains... Keswick: pub. by the author, 1842. 7th edition; 8vo; pages viii, 220, folding map, hand colored in outline, 13 outlines of mountains and 33 woodcuts in text; original blindstamped cloth, gilt, spine and edges faded. From the library of the late Norman Nicholson. Bicknell 102.6.   R.F.G. Hollett & Son 78-1167 1996 £125.00

OTLEY, JONATHAN   A Descriptive Guide to the English Lakes, and Adjacent Mountains... Keswick: published by the author, 1850. 8th edition; 8vo; pages viii, 216, (iv), 13 outlines of mountains (some rather foxed), 33 woodcuts in text, lacks map; near contemporary blindstamped cloth, gilt. Bicknell 102.8.   R.F.G. Hollett & Son 78-1168 1996 £95.00

OTTO, WHITNEY   How to Make an American Quilt. N.P.: Villard, n.d. Uncorrected proof; this is the earliest state of the proof, consisting of xeroxed 8 1/2 x 11 inch pages of typescript, perfect bound with clear acetate cover; near fine.   Thomas Dorn 9-212 1996 $150.00

OTWAY, SILVESTER   Poems; to Which is added, the Humours of John Bull, an Operatical farce, in Two Acts. London: printed by MacRae, for J. Murray, 1789. 1st edition; 12mo; contemporary name on title, 4 page list of subscribers; contemporary sheep, hinges rubbed.   Anthony W. Laywood 108-102 1996 £475.00

OTWAY, THOMAS 1652-1685   The Atheist; or, the Second Part of the Souldiers Fortune. London: printed for R. Bentley and J. Tonson, 1684. 1st edition; 4to; later wrappers, the 'F' gathering not used with pagination jumping from page 32 to 41 as usual, leaf 12 torn with loss of few words on either page, most of the words have been written into the margins, browning, some staining, else good copy contemporary signature and markings of Thomas Nicoll on final leaf, nice black morocco backed case; Wing O541; W&M 872.   James Cummins 14-147 1996 $200.00

OTWAY, THOMAS 1652-1685   Friendship in Fashion. London: printed by E. F. for Richard Tonson, 1678. 1st edition; 1st state; 4to; red morocco, some light rubbing and darkening, Prologue leaf (K4) bound following the dedication (leaf slightly shorter), publisher's ads on verso of Epilogue, careful marginal repairs to title and few other leaves; Pforzheimer 776; Wing O548; W&M 877.   James Cummins 14-146 1996 $250.00

OTWAY, THOMAS 1652-1685   The Orphan; or, the Unhappy Marriage, a Tragedy. London: printed for R. Bentley and M. Magnes, 1680. 1st edition; 4to; half brown morocco, some rubbing to corners, ends of spine, very good; Nicoll p. 153; Wing O552; Woodward and McManaway 886; CBEL II 748.   Ximenes 109-209 1996 £750.00

OTWAY, THOMAS 1652-1685   Complete Works. London: Nonesuch Press, 1926. One of 1250 numbered sets; 4to; publisher's brown buckram backed boards, paper labels, edges uncut, largely unopened (back cover of volume 1 slightly grazed), short tear on one leaf. Thomas Thorp 489-239 1996 £65.00

OTWAY, THOMAS 1652-1685   The Complete Works. London: Nonesuch Press, 1926. 1st edition; 4to; 3 volumes; pages cvi, 234; (4), 329; (4), 370; original buckram backed boards, paper labels (one lightly rubbed and chiped), uncut and partly unopened, good set. Dreyfus 38; d'Arch Smith B9.   Claude Cox 107-112 1996 £75.00

OUR Exagmination Round His Factification For Incamination of Work in Progress. 1936. 1st English edition; cloth, very good in dust jacket.   C. P. Hyland 216-26 1996 £125.00

OUR Old Nursery Rhymes. London: Augener, 1911. 1st edition; oblong 4to; 68 pages, color plates; pale blue boards with oval color pictorial onlay; rear endpaper creased, else very good.   Marjorie James 19-230 1996 £125.00

OUT of This World. London: 1960-70. 8 volumes; very good in dust jackets, except for volume 1 which has indentation to top edge of upper cover, but otherwise very good in dust jacket.   Words Etcetera 94-30 1996 £75.00

OUTERBRIDGE, PAUL   A Singular Aesthetic: Photos and Drawings 1921-1941. Santa Barbara: 1981. 1st edition; limited; cover 3D with mounted hinged mat framing one of his prints, heavy acetate dust jacket silk screened in 3 colors.   J. B. Muns 154-227 1996 $285.00

OUVRY, HENRY AIME   Stein and His Reforms in Prussia, with Reference to the land Question in England... London: Kerby and Endean, 1873. 1st edition; 8vo; xii, 195, (1) pages; contemporary blue half calf, gilt, spine gilt with raised bands and label, marbled edges; fine. Laine 1378; Headicar and Fuller II 490.   John Drury 82-204 1996 £60.00

THE OVERLAND Alphabet, from Sketches Taken "En Route" by Isabel D... London: William Tegg, n.d. 1853. 1st edition; tall 4to; each of the 28 lithographic illustrations on 9 plates (not counting title and half title), begins with large lettered colored red; publisher's lithographic pictorial boards with the Sphinx and Great Pyramids on upper cover and ad for first translation of Heinrich Hoffmann's "King Nut Cracker, or, the Dream of Poor Reinhold" on lower cover, covers little rubbed, some soiling, endpapers slightly foxed, with new matching paper spine, albeit a rather nice copy, very scarce. Ownership inscription dated Oct. 23, 1853. Book Block 32-11 1996 $1,750.00

OVERTON, CHARLES   The History of Cottingham. Hull: Pub. by J. W. Leng 1861. 1st edition; 8vo; 119 pages; 2 engravings, old vellum, neatly respined at some time, very good, very scarce.   K Books 442-368 1996 £95.00

OVERTON, F.   The Health Officer. Philadelphia: 1919. 1st edition; 512 pages; original binding.   W. Bruce Fye 71-1595 1996 $100.00

OVIDIUS NASO, PUBLIUS 43 BC - AD 17   The Amores. Waltham St. Lawrence: Golden Cockerel Press, 1932. One of 350 numbered copies; royal 8vo; 5 engravings on copper by J. E. Laboureur; half russet morocco, spine just a little spotted and marked and plates lightly offset as usual, otherwise nice, bright copy.   Bertram Rota 272-176 1996 £130.00

OVIDIUS NASO, PUBLIUS 43 BC - AD 17   The Art of Love. New York: Limited Editions Club, 1971. One of 1500 copies; signed by artist; 8vo; illustrations by Eric Fraser, signed by artist; full gold stamped vellum, near fine in fine case.   Charles Agvent 4-921 1995 $125.00

OVIDIUS NASO, PUBLIUS 43 BC - AD 17   Heroides. Milan: Hoepli, 1953. One of 166 numbered copies, signed by artist; large folio; printed in Stempel Garamond with Zeno capitals on Fabriano handmade; unbound sheets in stiff paper folder, laid into box with printed labels, box somewhat bumped, but contents fresh and fine.   Bertram Rota 272-346 1996 £850.00

OVIDIUS NASO, PUBLIUS 43 BC - AD 17   The Heroycall Epistles of the Learnet Poet... London: Cresset Press, 1928. One of 375 numbered copies; 10 full page black and white illustrations by Hester Sainsbury; buckram backed cloth covers, top edge gilt, head and tail of spine and corners bumped, spine faded and slightly rubbed, covers slightly marked and spotted, free endpapers partially browned, very good.   Ulysses 39-519 1996 £95.00

OVIDIUS NASO, PUBLIUS 43 BC - AD 17   The XV Bookes of P. Ovidius Naso, Entituled, Metamorphosis. London: Imprinted by W. White, 1603. 8vo; ff. 10, 191; woodcut printer's device on title, corners and edges of some leaves worn and soiled; remains of original limp vellum. STC 18961.   Family Album Tillers-461 1996 $350.00

OVIDIUS NASO, PUBLIUS 43 BC - AD 17   P. Ovidii Nasonis Metamorphoseon Libri X. Philadelphia: William Spotswood, 1790. 1st American edition; small 8vo; pages (32), 328; old American leather backed boards; ms. ownership of John K. Robbins. Evans 22753. Family Album Tillers-465 1996 $260.00

OVIDIUS NASO, PUBLIUS 43 BC - AD 17   Metamorphoseon Libri X. Philadelphia: William Spotswood, 1790. 1st edition of Ovid's work published in America; 12mo; contemporary calf, worn and stained, early owner's signatures on endpapers, lacking final flyleaf, text leaves age browned, good. Shipton & Mooney 22753.   Trebizond 39-66 1996 $200.00

OVIDIUS NASO, PUBLIUS 43 BC - AD 17   Hys Booke of Methamorphose. Books X-XV. Stratford-upon-Avon: for Houghton Mifflin Co., 1924. One of 375 copies; small folio; printed on Kelmscott handmade paper; green boards over linen spine, paper label, fine, mostly unopened copy;   Appelfeld Gallery 54-164 1996 $250.00

OVIDIUS NASO, PUBLIUS 43 BC - AD 17   Ovid's Metamorphoses. New York: Limited Editions Club, 1958. Copy 417 f 500 printed, signed by artist and by Giovanni Mardersteig; engravings by Hans Erni; as new in dust jacket and publisher's slipcase.   Hermitage SP95-1020 1996 $275.00

OVIDIUS NASO, PUBLIUS 43 BC - AD 17   The Metamorphoses. Verona: Limited Editions Club, 1958. Limited to 1500 copies, signed by artist and by designer/printer, Giovanni Mardersteig; 4to; etchings by Hans Erni; original binding,, fine in dust jacket and case; with Montly Letter.   Charles Agvent 4-922 1996 $425.00

OVIDIUS NASO, PUBLIUS 43 BC - AD 17   De Rimedi Contra L'Amore Ridotti in Ottava Rima... Avignon: P. Roux, 1576. 1st edition of this Italian translation; 4to; 62 leaves; woodcut title device and initials, washed; 19th century red morocco, covers gilt with large armorial stamp within elaborate cartouche, all edges gilt; fine. NUC 435.666; Rep. Bibl. 1.266 no. 4; Pansier 2.159-160, no. 38.   Bennett Gilbert LL29-53 1996 $2,250.00

OVIDIUS NASO, PUBLIUS 43 BC - AD 17   Publii Ovidii Nasonis Opera Omnia. Amsterdam: Changuion, 1727. 4to; 4 volumes; pages (24), 863; 1102, (4); 900; 263, (144), 582, engraved plates, vignettes; title in red and black, foxed; full red straight grained morocco in the Syston Park style, all edges gilt; engraved ex-libris of William Herick. Fine copy. Dibdin II 268-9. Brunet IV 273.   Family Album Tillers-462 1995 $1,400.00

OVIDO Y VALDES, GONZALO FERNANDEZ DE   The Conquest and Settlement of the Island of Boriquen or Puerto Rico. Avon: Limited Editions Club, 1975. Limited to 2000 copies, signed by both artists; folio; xxviii, 143 pages, 8 full page color serigraphs, head, tail and shoulder decorations, rubricated capitals; half vellum and cloth with gilt stamping and titling, fine, as new copy in publisher's cloth slipcase.   Andrew Cahan 47-172 1996 $125.00

OVIEDO Y VALDES, GONZALO FERNANDEZ DE   The Conquest and Settlement of the island of Boriquen or Puerto Rico. Avon: Limited Editions Club, 1975. Copy number 417 of 2000 printed, signed by Jack and Irene Delano; illustrations; fine in slipcse.   Hermitage SP95-980 1996 $100.00

OWEN, ANEURIN   Ancient Laws and Institutes of Wales... London: Commissioners on the Public Records of the Kingdom, 1841. 2nd printed edition; patterned green cloth, paper label, quite sound and attractive. Meyer Boswell SL25-229 1996 $650.00

OWEN, DAVID DALE 1807-1860   Report of a Geological Survey of Wisconsin, Iowa, and Minnesota... Philadelphia: Lippincott, Grambo & Co., 1852. Large 4to; 638, (2) pages, profusely illustrated with woodcuts and engravings on copper, steel and stone, including 30 plates and 18 folding maps and plans; original burgundy cloth, gilt.   Kenneth Karmiole 1NS-14 1996 $300.00

OWEN, HUGH   A History of Shrewsbury. London: Pub. by Harding, Lepard and Co., 1825. 1st edition; 4to; 2 volumes; engraved frontispieces (foxed), half titles in pictorial borders, 48 engraved and lithograph plates (some foxed), contemporary half calf, slightly rubbed, spines gilt. Bookplates of Lord Kenyon.   Anthony W. Laywood 108-216 1996 £395.00

OWEN, R.   Description of the Fossil Reptilia of South Africa in the Collection of the British Museum. London: 1876. 4to; pages xii, 88; 70 plates, many folding; cloth; nice.   Wheldon & Wesley 207-79 1996 £450.00

OWEN, RICHARD   Essays on the Conario-Hypophysial Tract and On the Aspects of the Body in Vertebrate and Invertebrate Animals. London: 1883. 48 pages; illustrations; front wrapper detached, lacking back wrapper, disbound, loose; printed presentation slip "from the author". Graham Weiner C2-498 1996 £50.00

OWEN, ROBERT 1771-1858   Essays on the Formation of the Human Character... London: B. D. Cousins, 1840. 12mo; (ii), 85, (i) pages; original printed yellow wrappers, wrappers dusty, spotted and little frayed at corners, overall pretty good.   Robert Clark 38-253 1996 £160.00

OWEN, ROBERT DALE 1801-1877   Footfalls on the Boundary of Another World. Philadelphia: Lippincott & Co., 1860. 1st edition; 8vo; 528 pages; illustrations; original black cloth, decorative borders on both covers, spine faded and chipped, top and bottom, corners bumped, very slight marginal gouge on front cover, contents fine.   Roy W. Clare XXIV-40 1996 $185.00

OWEN, ROBERT DALE 1801-1877   Threading My Way: 27 Years of Autobiography. New York: G. W. Carleton & Co., 1874. 1st edition; 360 pages; orange cloth; inscribed presentation copy from author dated Nov. 1873.   Blue River Books 9-183 1996 $250.00

OWEN, ROBERT DALE 1801-8177   Hints On Public Architecture. New York: Putnam, 1849. 1st edition; small folio; xvii, (iii), 119 pages; 15 plates; publisher's cloth, front hinge internally strengthened, some cover wear, as usual, else very good. Hitchcock 885.   Bookpress 75-94 1996 $750.00

OWEN, WILFRED   The Seared Conscience: Nine Poems. London: Tern Press, 1993. Limited to 95 copies; 4to; etchings by Nicholas Parry; fine in dust jacket.   Words Etcetera 94-1016 1996 £50.00

OXBERRY, WILLIAM   The Actor's Budget of Wit and Merriment... London: Simpkin, & Marshall, n.d. 1820. 1st of this edition; morocco spine, gilt, by Morrell.   Hartfield 48-L65 1996 $195.00

OXBERRY, WILLIAM   The Actress of All Work; or, My Country Cousin. London: pub. by W. Simpkin and R. Marshall and C. Chapple, n.d. 1819. 1st edition; 8vo; disbound; scarce, very good. 4 copies in NUC. Ximenes 109-210 1996 $100.00

THE OXFORD English Dictionary. Oxford: At the Clarendon Press, 1933. Large quarto; 13 volumes; original red buckram lettered in gilt on spine, light dampstaining to lower edge of few volumes, very good, in lightly chipped dust jacket.   Heritage Book Shop 196-233 1996 $1,500.00

THE OXFORD University and City Guide... Oxford: c. 1870. New edition; 12mo; pages vi, (ii), 278, (2); frontispiece, and engraved additional titlepage (waterstain in gutter margin), folding map (little frayed at fore-edge), 7 plates; original morocco grain dark green cloth, backstrip gilt titled direct, sides with blindstamped border, gilt vignette of University Museum on front cover, yellow chalked endpapers, front free endpaper removed; modern bookplate of Clement Du Pontet and entry clipped from bookseller's catalog on front pastedown, generally very good   Blackwell's B112-216 1996 £40.00

THE OXFORD Visitor; or Picturesque Views of all the Colleges and Halls of the University: Public Buildings of the City; and Representations of Curious Works of Art,... London: Sherwood, Neely and Jones, 1822. 12mo; pages vi, 114, (6); engraved frontispiece, 55 plates, one with small amateur repair to verso of margin, foxed, tissue guards; original 'Cathedral' binding in green morocco, extremities little rubbed, backstrip with wide raised bands, gilt lettered direct in second and fourth compartments, remainder with Gothic tracery decoration, gilt dulled, sides panelled with border of wide gilt diamond pattern roll, diamonds filled with tracery, centre of sides blindstamped with Gothic window of complicated design, green endpapers, large modern bookplate of Clement du Pontet, entry clipped from booksellers catalog, gilt edges, very good.   Blackwell's B112-217 1996 £150.00

OXLEY, JOHN   Journals of Two Expeditions Into the Interior of New South Wales, Under-Taken by Order of the British Government in the Years 1817-1818. London: John Murray, 1820. Quarto; (xv), 408 pages, 6 aquatint engravings, 3 folding maps, 2 folding tables (the two large folding maps have long ago been expertly mounted on folding linen; finely rebound (signed Morrell, London) in half morocco and linen boards, gilt decorated spine, all edges gilt, text is quite clean and bright; very pretty copy; old pen signature in titlepage partially removed with some staining, otherwise very good+; from the Edge-Partington collection, the Absolon copy. Ferguson 796; Wantrup 107.   Antipodean 28-160 1996 $5,500.00

P

PACCHONI, ANTIONI   Dissertatones Physico-Anatomicae de Dura meninge Humana Novis Experimentis, & Lucubrationibus Auctae, & Illustratae. Rome: Antonio de'Rossi, 1721. 8vo; (24), 270, (28) pages, 1 folding engraved plate; contemporary (original?) full vellum, remarkably fresh, crisp copy; author's presentation note on half title, written in author's hand. GM 1380; McHenry p. 64; Neuberger/Clarke pp. 79-80; 347.   James Tait Goodrich K40-223 1996 $4,500.00

PACKARD, A. S.   Monograph of the Bombycine Moths of North America. London: 1875-1914. 4to; 3 volumes; 10 maps, 87 colored and 136 plain plates; new uniform cloth.   Wheldon & Wesley 207-80 1996 £350.00

PACKARD, FRANCIS   The History of Medicine in the United States: a Collection of Facts and Documents Relating to the History of Medical Science in this Country... Philadelphia: 1901. 1st edition; 542 pages; original binding. GM 6590.   W. Bruce Fye 71-1597 1996 $200.00

PACKER, JAMES E.   The Insulae of Imperial Ostia. Rome: American Academy in Rome, 1971. 4to; xxviii, 217 pages, 115 plates; 75 plans; original cloth, corner bumped.   Archaeologia Luxor-3790 1996 $175.00

PACKER, LONA MOSK   The Rossetti-MacMillan Letters... Berkeley & Los Angeles: University of California Press, 1963. 1st edition; original binding, top edge dusty, head and tail of spine slightly bumped and rubbed, very good in nicked, rubbed and dusty, slightly torn and creased price clipped dust jacket, slightly browned at spine and edges. Ulysses 39-512 1996 £55.00

PADILLA, VICTORIA   Southern California Gardens: an Illustrated History. Berkeley & Los Angeles: University of California Press, 1961. 10 1/2 x 6 3/4 inches; xviii, 359 pages, 8 pages of color photographic illustrations, numerous full page and smaller black and white photographic illustrations; black cloth in slightly edgeworn dust jacket. Dawson's Books Shop 528-187 1996 $175.00

PADMORE, GEORGE   How Russia Transformed Her Colonial Empire. London: Dennis Dobson, 1946. 1st edition; xx, 178 pages; cloth, nice in nicked red and black dust jacket; inscribed by author for Peter (Abrahams).   Ian Patterson 9-230 1996 £50.00

PAGAN, WILLIAM   Road Reform: a Plan for Abolishing Turnpike Tolls and Statute Labour Assessments, and for Providing the Funds Necessary for the Public Roads by an Annual Rate on Homes. Edinburgh: William Blackwood and Sons, 1846. 2nd edition; 8vo; (2), ii, 123 pages; HMSO ink stamp on title and two Patent Office Stamps on verso, contemporary green half calf gilt, spine and corners worn, else good;   John Drury 82-205 1996 £85.00

PAGE, FRANCIS   The Charge of J---- P---- to the Grand Jury of M--x, on Saturday May 22, 1736. London: 1737. Modern quarter calf over marbled boards, attractive.   Meyer Boswell SL26-143 1996 $650.00

PAGE, FREDERICK B.   Prairiedom: Rambles and Scrambles in Texas or New Estremadura. New York: Paine & Burgess, 1846. 2nd edition; 166 pages; map; original full calf with morocco spine label, repairs to spine and usual rubbing and minor foxing; very good. Streeter Texas 1604 note; Clark Old Smith III.221.   Michael D. Heaston 23-286 1996 $850.00

PAGE, LEITCH   Philby: The Spy Who Betrayed and Generation. London: Andrew Deutsch, 1968. Signed by author's on half title, though Leitch's is printed; fine in torn dust jacket; Kim Philby's own copy with his annotations, altogether there are marks by Philby on 37 pages.   R. A. Gekoski 19-111 1996 £2,000.00

PAGE, THOMAS NELSON   Two Little Confederates. New York: Charles Scribner's Sons, 1889. 1st edition; 2nd printing with pages 157-8 blank; 8vo; grey pictorial cloth, gilt lettering, bookplate, small unobtrusive inked library stamp on p. 156, aside from only some minor shelf wear, very bright copy; inscribed by author for Mrs. Frederic Taylor, laid in are two TLS's, one to Charles Henry Hart and one to Frederic W. Speirs. BAL 15364.   James Cummins 14-149 1996 $200.00

PAGE, WILLIAM   Victoria County History. Hertfordshire. London: 1902-23. Original edition; but index volume is 1971 reissue; imperial 8vo; 5 volumes; plates, maps, plans; original red cloth, gilt, gilt tops. Howes Bookshop 265-512 1996 £220.00

THE PAGEANT. London: Henry & Co., 1896-97. 1st edition; 10 1/2 x 7 3/4 inches; 2 volumes (all published); woodcut title vignette, dec. woodcut initials, 27 illustrations, 40 plates, including the colored woodcut by Pissarro, not infrequently lacking; orig. purple brown cloth with gilt titling and designs by Charles Ricketts, patterned endpapers designed by Lucien Pissarro, fore edges & tail edges untrimmed, few leaves in first vol. unopened (short portion at top of front joint of first vol. apparently repaired), cloth of first vol. rather soiled, front hinge partly cracked (but no looseness), rear cover of volume 2 spotted, but second volume otherwise entirely sound and quite clean, one plate with closed marginal tear not reaching image, intermittent light foxing but quite good internally. Phillip J. Pirages 33-409 1996 $450.00

PAGES of Glory and History. The 91st Division in Argonne and Flanders. Paris: New York: & San Francisco: printed by Buffet & Leclerc, Paris. 1919. folio; 15 paes text and maps, 26 plates, mostly etchings, interleaved with guard sheets with explanatory letterpress; printed wrappers, cloth library binding added; from Bancroft Library copy, with markins, including perforated blindstamps within images of plates. Bohling Book Co. 192-540 1996 $150.00

PAGET, VIOLET 1856-1935   Proteus - or the Future of Intelligence. London: Kegan Paul Trench, Trubner & Co. Ltd., 1925. 1st edition; 12mo; 22 pages of publisher's ads at rear, top edge dusty, prelims, edges and endpapers slightly spotted, free endpapers faintly and partially browned, cover edges rubbed, very good in nicked, rubbed and dusty, slightly marked and dusty dust jacket browned at spine and edges.   Ulysses 39-362 1996 £55.00

PAIN, WILLIAM   Pain's British Palladio; or, the Builder's General Assistant. London: the authors, 1786. 1st edition; folio; (ii), 14 pages, 42 plates; later half calf, marbled boards; small neatly repaired tear in one plate, else very good.   The Bookpress 75-220 1996 $1,750.00

PAINE   Catalogue of Artistic Furniture... Boston: n.d., ca. 1880's. 12mo; 48 pages; pictorial wrappers, covers slightly soiled, else very good.   Bookpress 75-130 1996 $225.00

PAINE, ALBERT BIGELOW   Captain Bill McDonald. New York: 1909. 1st edition; 454 pages; illustrations; blue covers very bright. BTB 158; Six Guns 1669.   Early West 22-704 1996 $195.00

PAINE, ALBERT BIGELOW   Dwellers in Arcady. New York: Harpers, 1919. 1st edition; illustrations by Thomas Fogarty; original binding, near fine in scarce dust jacket with wear at spine head and short tear on rear; with ownership signature and address of Mildred Clemens; Charles Agvent 4-925 1996 $125.00

PAINE, ALBERT BIGELOW   The Tent Dwellers. New York: Harpers, 1908. 1st edition; 8vo; illustrations by H. Watson; decorated cloth, near fine in very good, lightly chipped and quite early dust jacket. Signed by author.   Charles Agvent 4-928 1995 $125.00

PAINE, ALBERT BIGELOW   Thomas Nast His Period and His Pictures. New York: Harper & Bros., 1904. 1st edition; one ink inscription, some offsetting to front endpapers; otherwise fine.   Hermitage SP95-801 1996 $100.00

PAINE, D. P.   Aerial Photography and Image Interpretation for Resource Management. New York: 1981. Royal 8vo; 571 pages; illustrations; cloth.   Wheldon & Wesley 207-182 1996 £86.00

PAINE, MARTYN   Letters on the Cholera Asphyxia, As It Has Appeared in the City of New York. New York: 1832. 1st edition; 160 pages; original binding. Kelly Burrage 931.   W. Bruce Fye 71-1603 1996 $150.00

PAINE, THOMAS 1737-1809   Agrarian Justice, Opposed to Agrarian
Law and to Agrarian Monopoly... London: printed and sold by J. Adlard
and J. Parsons, n.d. 179-. Reprint of Paris edition; 8vo; 38, (2) pages,
complete with half title; recently well bound in linen backed marbled
boards, lettered; very good. Gimbell II p. 38; Thetford 66.1. Williams Ii
541.   John Drury 82-206 1996 £150.00

PAINE, THOMAS 1737-1809   A Letter to Mr. Secretary Dundas, also
Two Letters to Lord Onslow. London: D. Jordan, 1792. 1st edition; 8vo;
(2), 16, 9 pages; initial and final blanks, recent linen backed marbled
boards, lettered; Gimbel p. 80; not in Thetford collection, Goldsmiths or
Kress.   John Drury 82-209 1996 £125.00

PAINE, THOMAS 1737-1809   The Rights of Man. New York: Limited
Editions Club, 1961. One of 1500 numbered copies, signed by artist;
illustrations by Lynd Ward; fine in publisher's slipcase.   Hermitage
SP95-1021 1 996 $165.00

PAINE, THOMAS 1737-1809   The Writings. Albany: Charles R. and
George Webster, 1794. 8vo; contemporary calf, back cover detached;
Howes P 34 for 1792 editions; Evans 24658, 27466, 46536 & 47149.
M & S Rare Books 60-392 1996 $375.00

PAINE, THOMAS 1737-1809   The Writings... New York: G. P. Putnam's
Sons, Knickerbocker Press, 1894-96. 1st complete collected edition; 8vo;
4 volumes; original maroon cloth, gilt, top edge gilt, others uncut; very
good. Gimbel p. 3.   John Drury 82-207 1996 £250.00

PAKENHAM-WALSH, R. P.   History of the Corps of Royal Engineers.
Chatham, 1958. Volumes 8 and 9; fine in dust jackets.   Petersfield
Bookshop FH58-339 1996 £72.00

PALARDDY, JEAN   The Early Furniture of French Canada. New York:
St. Martin's Press, 1965. 1st edition in English; 4to; 413 pages; 11 color
plates, 585 black and whtie photos; gilt titled red cloth; near fine.
Andrew Cahan 47-75 1996 $165.00

PALATINO, GIOVANNI BATTISTA   Compendio del Gran Volvme Dell'arte
del Bene Leggiadramente Scrivere... Venice: Gio. Antonio Rampazetto for
Aluise Sessa, 1588. Small 4to; 62 ff., A-G8; H6; recent full vellum over
stiff boards with decorative gilt frame border (acorns and leaves), four
corner fleurons and larger central gilt device, square spine with gilt
bands, acorns and leaves in compartments in the manner of
contemporary binding, professional repairs to titlepage with loss of few
letters and the last part of the date, which have been supplied in ms.
facsimile, lower corner of A2 and small piece of border has been skilfully
replaced, occasional soiling and light water staining to lower portion of
leaves in last 3 signatures, few marginal notes. Bonacini 1343; Brunet IV
314; Morison/marzoli 3.   Book Block 32-77 1996 $2,950.00

PALAU I FABRE, JOSEP   Picasso: The Early Years, 1881-907. New
York: Rizzoli, 1981. Square folio; 559 pages, 1587 illustrations, 361 in
color; dust jacket. Freitag 7479.   Brannan 43-529 1996 $125.00

PALESTINE EXPLORATION FUND   Annual I-V. London: PEF, 1911-27.
4to; 5 volumes; illustrations, plates; original printed boards.
Archaeologia Luxor-2552 1996 $950.00

PALESTINE EXPLORATION FUND   Annual 1927. No. V. London:
Palestine Exploration Fund, 1929. 4to; very good, xi, 135 pages, 21
figures, 22 plates; original printed boards, corners lightly bumped;
Archaeologia Luxor-2551 1996 $150.00

PALESTINE EXPLORATION FUND   The Survey of Eastern Palestine.
(and) The Survey of Western Palestine. London: Palestine Exploration
Fund, 1881-99. Large 4to; 9 volumes in 11 parts; original gilt lettered
cloth and atlas folio of maps and plans in original three quarter calf
backed portfolio.   Archaeologia Luxor-2554 1996 $4,500.00

PALEY, GRACE   The Collected Stories. New York: Farrar, Straus and
Giroux, 1994. 1st edition; limited to 150 numbered copies, signed by
author; 8vo; cloth, slipcase, new.   James S. Jaffe 34-531 1996
$125.00

PALEY, GRACE   Enormous Changes at the Last Minute. New York:
FSG, 1973. Uncorrected proof copy; scarce proof; very good in tall
wrappers; the copy of novelist Herb Gold.   Ken Lopez 74-366 1996
$275.00

PALEY, WILLIAM 1743-1805   A View of the Evidences of Christianity.
London: Rivington (and 14 others), 1829. Reprint; 8vo; pages 439;
cathedral style embossed calf, flat spine lettered gilt, all edges marbled,
brown endpapers, bound by Rowley.   Marlborough 160-73 1996
£300.00

PALEY, WILLIAM 1743-1805   The Works... Derby: Henry Mozley and
Sons, 1826. New edition; 8vo; (lviii), (640); x, (624) pages; frontispiece,
slightly rubbed, very small hole at head of one spine; contemporary calf,
gilt ruled, double labels; minor foxing; good set.   Robert Clark 38-254
1996 £55.00

PALGRAVE, FRANCIS TURNER 1824-1897   Gems of English Art.
London: George Routledge, 1869. 1st edition; 4to; viii, 144 pages, 24
plates; publisher's cloth, all edges gilt, light rubbing to binding, else
nice. Binding by Leighton, Sons and Hodge.   Bookpress 75-95 1996
$325.00

PALGRAVE, FRANCIS TURNER 1824-1897   The Golden Treasury
Selected fromt he Best Songs and Lyrical Poems in the English
Language... London: Macmillan and Co. Ltd., New York: The Macmillan
Co., 1900. Revised; small 8vo; pages (x), 381, (1); fine green morocco,
elaborately and densely gilt, with large variety of ornaments, forming a
large central wheel on sides surrounded by a seme of dots and
numerous other tools, borders of a single filelt and two rolls, spine in
compartments with raised bands, also densely gilt, gilt lettering, inner
dentelles, richly gilt with series of roll borders, edges gilt, white silk
endpapers, little spotted, otherwise fine. Delightful example of the work
of John Ramage.   Simon Finch 24-177 1996 £550.00

PALGRAVE, FRANCIS TURNER 1824-1897   A Golden Treasury of
Songs and Lyrics. New York: Duffield & Co., 1921. 8vo; 8 illustrations
after paintings by Maxfield Parrish; original navy blue cloth, gilt bordered
pictorial pastedown, beautiful copy in chipped and soiled pictorial dust
jacket.   Glenn Books 36-204 1996 $125.00

PALGRAVE, W. G.   Dutch Guiana. London: Macmillan, 1876. 1st
edition; 8vo; viii, 264 pages; folding map, folding plan; original cloth,
some light foxing.   Thomas Thorp 489-240 1996 £50.00

PALKE, WILLIAM   The Divinity of Jesus Christ Prov'd from the Words
of Thomas, My Lord and My God. A Sermon Preach'd at Exon, Sept. 9,
1719. London: printed for John Clark, 1719. Sole edition; 8vo; 34 pages,
but lacking pages (1)-(2), the half title; disbound.   David Bickersteth
133-76 1996 £58.00

PALLADIO, ANDREA   The Architecture of A. Palladio, in Four Books.
London: A. Ward and others, 1742. 3rd edition; large folio; frontispiece
and portrait, viii, 104, 100 pages, 230 plates, some folding; contemporary
reversed sheep, rebacked; respined, moderate cover wear and very light,
sporadic foxing.   The Bookpress 75-221 1996 $2,850.00

PALLADIO, ANDREA   I Quattro Libri dell'Architettura. Venice:
Bartolomeo Carampello, 1581. 2nd edition; small folio; 158 full page & 62
smaller illustrations and pictorial woodcut initials; titlepage neatly repaired
from verso, pages crinkled as from old dampstain, with few small rust
marks; final blank missing (as in the Fowler copy) and several plates are
misnumbered, late 18th century pastepaper boards and modern half calf
spine with tooled bands and leather labels, trimmed at upper margin, in
places into running title; an appealing copy PMM 92 (1st ed. of 1570);
Cicognara 595; Fowler 213.   Marilyn Braiterman 15-157 1996
$2,500.00

PALLAS, PETER SIMON   Flora Rossica Seu Stirpium Imperii Rossici
per Europam et Asiam Indigenarum Descriptiones et Icones. St.
Petersburg: 1784-88. 1st edition; folio; 2 parts in 1 volume; pages (3),
(i-) viii, 80; (1), 114; hand colored engraved frontispiece, 101 hand
colored engraved plates; 19th century morocco backed marbled boards,
spine edges rubbed, worn at extremities, front hinge tender, perforation
stamp on one title and one text leaf, ink stamp on verso of both titles
and each plate, oaccession number on bottom right hand corner of
dedication leaf, some soiling to plate 37; near marginal repair to D1 and
verso of plate 13, all edges gilt; fromt he John Crerar Library, Chicago.
Raymond M. Sutton VI-24 1996 $8,500.00

PALLAS, PETER SIMON   Travels through the Southern Provinces of
the Russian Empire in the Years 1793 and 1794. London: John Stockdale,
1812. 2nd edition; 4to; xxiv, 552; xxxii, 510, (14) pages; 52 plates, mostly
hand colored, 24 colored text vignette views and 3 folding maps; later
polished brown calf over older marbled boards, some light soiling and
one plate with repair at fold.   Kenneth Karmiole 1NS-249 1996
$1,250.00

PALLISER, CHARLES   The Quincunx. Edinburgh: Canongate, 1989. 1st
edition; uncommon; fine in fine dust jacket.   Ken Lopez 74-367 1996
$100.00

PALLISER, FANNY MARRYAT 1805-1878   A History of Lace. London: Sampson, Low, Son and Marston, 1869. 2nd edition; 9 x 6 inches; viii, 442 pages; frontispiece, decorative title frame, 18 plates, many illustrations in text; gift inscription dated 1901 on front flyleaf; very fine handsomely gilt and onlaid tan crushed morocco by Zaehnsdorf, covers and spine compartments outlined with onlaid maroon morocco, covers with very board densely gilt dentelles (composed of many complex antique fleurons), spine compartments similarly decorated, elegant inner gilt dentelles, silk pastedowns and flyleaves, all edges gilt, extremely fine inside and out, in splendid binding.   Phillip J. Pirages 33-67 1996 $850.00

PALLISER, JOHN   The Papers of the Palliser Expedition 1857-1860. Toronto: Champlain Society, 1968. Limited to 825 numbered copies; 8vo; pages cxxxviii, 694, xix; frontispiece, folding map; top edge gilt, crested cloth; fine.   Hugh Anson-Cartwright 87-338 1996 $200.00

PALMER,   Four Months Tour through France. Dublin: Printed for Messrs. S. Price, W. Whitestone...and C. Talbot, 1776. 1st edition; 12mo; 2 volumes bound in one; iv, (5)-128, (129)-261 pages; full contemporary calf, raised bands, leather spine label; bookplate, brown staining to lower corners of first 59 pages (not affecting text), stain on pages 60-64 larger, but text still quite legible, stain on titlepage of volume two affecting publisher's imprint, still very good.   David Mason 71-73 1996 $280.00

PALMER, ARNOLD   Recording Britain. London: Oxford Univ. Press in Assocation with The Pilgrim Trust, 1946-49. Royal 8vo; 4 volumes; over 400 plates in sepia or color; original buckram, dust jackets on 3 volumes; bookplate (partly defaced) in each.   Howes Bookshop 265-1018 1996 £65.00

PALMER, JOHN   Papers Relative to the Agreement Made by Government with Mr. Palmer, for the Reform and Improvement of the Posts. London: printed for T. Cadell, Jun. and W. Davies,... 1797. 1st edition; 4to; modern paper wrappers. Kress B3482; Goldsmith 17087. Anthony W. Laywood 108-113 1996 £225.00

PALMER, S.   A General History of Printing; from the First Invention of It In the City of Mentz, to Its Propagation and Progress... London: printed for A. Bettesworth, C.Hitch & C. Davis 1733. 2nd printing; 4to; xii, 400 pages (pages after p.312 beginning a new pagination at pp. 121-144, then they are counted in and pagination made continuous by taking it up at pp. 337); brown cloth, headcaps and corners bumped, bit scuffed and grubby, lettering and shelf mark on spine in gilt, title in red and black, some browning between Rr and Ss, otherwise, clean, crisp copy; ex-John Crerar Library copy with booklabel and perforated stamps. Maggs Bros. Ltd. 1191-211 1996 £200.00

PALMER, SAMUEL   St. Pancras; Being Antiquarian, Topographical and Biographical Memoranda, Relating to the Extensive Metropolitan Parish... London: Samuel Palmer...and Field and Tuer, 1870. 4to; title in red and black, dedn., 2 ff., pages 13-322, 5 f ads, frontispiece and 2 paltes, half morocco, top edge gilt.   Marlborough 162-181 1996 £100.00

PALMER, T. S.   Place Names of the Death Valley Region in California and Nevada. N.P.: 1948. 1st edition; 80 pages; original printed wrappers, spine bit darkened, fine. Edwards p. 188; Rocq 2330.   Argonaut Book Shop 113-177 1996 $175.00

PALMER, W. T.   The English Lakes. London: A. & C. Black, 1905. 1st edition; large 8vo; pages ix, 232, iv; 75 colored plates; original decorative cloth, gilt, spine little rubbed and dulled, top edge gilt, endpapers little spotted or browned, joints tender.   R.F.G. Hollett & Son 78-812 1996 £60.00

PALMER, W. T.   The English Lakes. London: A. & C. Black, 1908. 2nd edition; large 8vo; pages ix, 232; 75 colored plates; original decorative cloth, gilt, spine rather faded, fore edge and endpapers lghtly spotted. R.F.G. Hollett & Son 78-813 1996 £55.00

PALOU, FRANCISCO   The Expedition Into California of the Venerable Padre Fray Junipero Serra... San Francisco: Nueva California Press, 1934. 1st edition; number 315 of 400 copies signed by translator, Douglas Watson; portrait, letter facsimiles and map; vellum backed butterscotch boards, bookplate and promotional sheet tipped onto front pastedown, boards slightly bowed, some overall light soiling, otherwise very good. Hermitage SP95-735 1996 $175.00

PALOU, FRANCISCO   Historical Memoirs of New California. Berkeley: 1926. 1st edition in English; 4 volumes, plates, maps, portraits; cloth, very nice, bright set. Howes P55; Wanger SP SWEST 168a.   W. M. Morrison 436-175 1996 $275.00

PANASSIE, HUGUES   Hot Jazz. New York: M. Witmark, 1934. 1st edition; original cloth, near fine with tiny tear to bit sunned spine, somewhat worn dust jacket with chip at spine head; scarce.   Beasley Books 82-245 1996 $250.00

PANCOAST, JOSEPH   A Treatise on Operative Surgery; Comprising a Description of the Various Processes of the Art... Philadelphia: Carey and Hart, 1844. 4to; 380 pages; 486 illustrations; original binding, spine worn with hinges splitting, covers rubbed, internally fresh, without usual heavy foxing that is so common to this work, some light foxing and outer marginal browning, otherwise plates are quite clean. GM 5598; Rutkow GS22.   James Tait Goodrich K40-225 1996 $1,750.00

PANCOAST, JOSEPH   A Treatise on Operative Surgery; Comprising a Description of the Various Processes of the Art, Including All the New Operations. Philadelphia: Carey & Hart, 1844. 1st edition; 4to; 380 pages plus ads; contemporary cloth, rebacked, slight foxing, ink on top of pages 131-170 not affecting text. GM 5598; Cushing p. 38; Waller 7083. Argosy 810-383 1996 $1,500.00

PANCOAST, JOSEPH   A Treatise on Operative Surgery; Comprising a Description of the Various Processes of the Art... Philadelphia: Carey & Hart, 1844. 4to; 380 pages; 80 plates and 486 text illustrations, contemporary cloth, rebacked, slight foxing, ink on top of pages 131-170 not affecting text. Cushing p. 38; Waller 7083.   Argosy 810-383 1996 $1,500.00

PANCRATIA, or a History of Pugilism. London: printed by W. Hildyard, pub. and sold by W. Oxberry, also by... 1812. 1st edition; 8vo; frontispiece; contemporary calf, gilt, rebacked, original spine laid down, spine gilt, bit rubbed; very good, scarce. 4 copies in NUC; Hartaley 1522; Magriel 19.   Ximenes 109-45 1996 $750.00

PANGHORN, J. G.   The New Rocky Moutain Tourist Arkansas Valley and San Juan Guide. The Tour... Chicago: Knight & Leonard, 1878. 3rd edition; 64 pages; illustrations, folding map; original pictorial wrappers, some chipping, laid in half morocco and chemise slipcase; very good. Wynar 2274; Adams Herd 1753 'Rare'.   Michael D. Heaston 23-109 1996 $550.00

PANOFSKY, ERWIN   Problems in Titian. Mostly Iconographic. London: Phaidon, 1969. 27 x 21 cm; xv, 208 pages; 200 illustrations; ex-library, original cloth, dust jacket.   Rainsford A54-553 1996 £55.00

PANOFSKY, ERWIN   Tomb Sculpture, Its Changing Aspects from Ancient Egypt to Bernini. London: Thames & Hudson, 1964. 29 x 25 cm; 319 pages; 471 black and white illustrations; original cloth, dust jacket, ex-library, rubber stamps on reverse titlepage and label and tape marks on f.e.p.   Rainsford A54-451 1996 £60.00

PANSHIN, A.   Rite of Passage. S&J, 1969. 1st British edition, 1st hardcover edition; author's first book; fine in very good+ dust jacket. Aronovitz 57-924 1996 $250.00

PANVINO, ONOFRIO   Antiquitatum Veronensium, Libri Octo. Padua: P. Frambotti, 1647. 1st and only edition; folio; (xii), 236, (8) pages, 33 plates; contemporary gilt vellum, lacking ties; fine; rare. Bookplate of Miss Richardson Currer, later sold to Sir Mathew Wilson, with his bookplate. Cicognara 4059.   The Bookpress 75-222 1996 $5,800.00

PAPERMAKING in Seventeenth Century England. Santa Cruz: Peter & Donna Thomas, 1990. One of 200 copies; 12mo; unpaginated, calf, slipcase, fresh and bright copy.   The Bookpress 75-336 1996 $165.00

PAPERS Relating to the Treaty of Washington. Volume I-(V). Washington: 1872. original binding, some wear and soil to binding, internally very good; former ownership signatures of a prominent NW historian. Very rare set. Lowther 406.   Stephen Lunsford 45-159 1996 $1,250.00

PAPP, D.   Creation's Doom. Jarrolds, 1934. 1st edition; illustrations; very good in attractive pictorial dust jacket with some light chipping, very scarce in dust jacket.   Aronovitz 57-925 1996 $125.00

PAPWORTH, JOHN BUONAROTTI 1775-1847   Poetical Sketches of Scarborough. London: Rudolph Ackermann, 1813. Tall 8vo; 21 hand colored plates; full olive green morocco with gilt rolled tooled borders, gilt panelled spine, sprinkled edges. Nice.   Appelfeld Gallery 54-157 1996 $650.00

PAPWORTH, JOHN BUONAROTTI 1775-1847   Select Views of London, with Historical and Descriptive Sketches...of Its Public Buildings... London: J. Diggens for R. Ackermann, 1816. Large 8vo; 4 ff., 159 pages, 79 hand colored aquatint or engraved plates; full red morocco, gilt, gilt inner borders, top edge gilt, others uncut by Sangorski; Adams 177; Abbey Scenery 21.   Marlborough 162-184 1996 £2,500.00

PAPWORTH, JOHN W.   An Alphabetical Dictionary of Coats of Arms Belonging to Families in Great Britain and Ireland... London: 1874. Royal 8vo; full black morocco, backstrip slightly worn.   Petersfield Bookshop FH58-123 1996 £52.00

PARACELSUS 1493-1541   Four Treatises of Theophrastus Von Hohenheim Called Paracelsus. Baltimore: 1941. 1st edition; 256 pages; original binding. GM 57.   W. Bruce Fye 71-1607 1996 $100.00

PARACELSUS 1493-1541   Of the Chymical Transmutation, Genealogy and Generation of Metals & Minerals. London: 1657. 164 (of 166) pages, lacks 2 leaves of prelims (including title), disbound. soiled and stained, few headlines cropped, other small defects, but apart from the missing endleaves a complete copy. Rare.   Graham Weiner C2-120 1996 £50.00

PARACELSUS 1493-1541   Selected Writings. New York: 1941. 1st English translation; 347 pages; original binding, dust jacket. GM 57.   W. Bruce Fye 71-1088 1996 $100.00

PARACELSUS 1493-1541   Selected Writings. New York: 1951. 1st English translation; 347 pages; original binding. GM 57.   W. Bruce Fye 71-1608 1996 $100.00

PARBURT, GEORGE R.   Anselmo: a Poem. San Francisco: H. H. Bancroft, 1865. 1st edition; 12mo; 148 pages, errata slip; original cloth; inscribed presentation copy dated 1866.   M & S Rare Books 60-213 1996 $125.00

PARDAL, JOSE   Elephant Hunting in Portuguese East Africa. London: 1990. Limited to 1000 copies, signed by author; many photographic illustrations; full bonded leather binding, gilt titles and elephant designs, silk marker, housed in slipcase.   David Grayling J95Biggame-153 1996 £50.00

PARDOE, JULIA   The Beauties of the Bosphorus. London: George Virtue, 1839. Thick 4to; portrait, engraved titlepage, 78 plates and map; lovely Victorian binding of full red morocco, elaborate gilt panels on each cover, gilt spine, gilt edges (recased); unusually nice, clean copy, plates are invariably foxed.   Charles W. Traylen 117-435 1996 £750.00

PARDOE, JULIA   Louis the Fourteenth and the Court of France in the Seventeenth Century. London: Richard Bentley, 1847. 8vo; 3 volumes extended to 6, by the insertion of hundreds of engraved plates, many mounted and inlaid to size of page; also autographed signed documents by Louis XIV & Colbert, Anne of England, Queen; Louis Duc de Vendome; three quarter citron morocco, spines trifle darkened, gilt panelled spines, raised bands, gilt tops, unusual set.   Appelfeld Gallery 54-103 1996 $1,800.00

PARDON, GEORGE FREDERICK   Beeton's Hand Book of Games. London: S. O. Beeton, 1863? 8vo; xii, 563, (1) pages; illustrations; contemporary green cloth, spine faded.   James Burmester 29-108 1996 £85.00

PARDON, GEORGE FREDERICK   Boldheart the Warrior and His Adventures in the Haunted Wood: A Tale of the Times of Good King Arthur. Blackwood, 1859. 1st edition; 4to; 10 engraved plates by Gustave Dore and decorative initials and tailpieces; maroon morocco cloth, pictorially stamped in blind and gilt, cloth marked, little fingering else nice; extremely scarce.   Barbara Stone 70-74 1996 £150.00

PARE, AMBROISE   The Apologie and Treatise of Amboise Pare... London: Falcon Educational Books, 1951. 1st edition; 4 black and white contemporary portraits of Pare, illustrations; original binding, free endpapers partially browned, tail of spine slightly bumped, bottom edge of upper cover slightly faded, very good in nicked, slightly dusty and very slightly soiled dust jacket slightly browned at spine and edges. Ulysses 39-336 1996 £75.00

PARE, RICHARD   Photography and Architecture, 1839-1939. Montreal: Canadian Centre for Architecture, 1982. 1st edition; oblong thick 4to; 282 pages; frontispiece, 147 full page photo plates, fine in illustrated price clipped dust jacket.   Andrew Cahan 47-20 1996 $125.00

THE PARENTS' High Commission. London: Hatchard, 1843. Half title, 2 pages ads; original purple cloth, small ink marks, otherwise very good. Jarndyce 103-427 1996 £55.00

PARET, J. PARMLY   Methods and Players of Modern Lawn Tennis. New York: American Lawn Tennis, 1915. 1st edition; octavo; xxii, 295 pages; frontispiece, 24 photographic plates, diagrams; original red cloth ruled in blind and decoratively stamped and lettered in gilt on front cover and spine, top edge gilt, lower corners lightly bumped, otherwise near fine.   Heritage Book Shop 196-204 1996 $200.00

PARETSKY, SARA   Deadlock. New York: Dial, 1984. 1st edition; original cloth, fine but for bookplate and without remainder spray-in close to fine dust jacket with few tears at head of spine and top edge of rear panel.   Beasley Books 82-283 1996 $150.00

PARETSKY, SARA   Guardian Angel. Bristol: Scorpion Press, 1992. 1/20 deluxe lettered copies, signed by author and Frances Fyfield who provided an author appreciation; fine in quarter bound goatskin with raised bands.   Quill & Brush 102-1381 1996 $450.00

PARETSKY, SARA   Guardian Angel. Bristol: Scorpion, 1992. One of 99 (of 119 total), signed, numbered and specially bound copies with an appreciation by Frances Fyfield; marbled paper boards, white leather spine, gilt lettering, fine.   Quill & Brush 102-1382 1996 $175.00

PARETSKY, SARA   Killing Orders. New York: Morrow, 1985. 1st edition; original cloth, fine in fine dust jacket but for tiny chip on rear panel.   Beasley Books 82-284 1996 $100.00

PARIS DE MEYZIEU, J. B.   Bibliotheca Parisiana. London: 1791. 8vo; pages viii, 164; uncut, original boards, trifle rubbed. De Ricci p. 217. Howard S. Mott 227-110 1996 $400.00

PARIS, JOHN AYRTON   The Life of Sir Humphry Davy, Bart. LL.D. London: Henry Colburn and Richard Bentley, 1831. 1st edition; 4to; xv, (i), 547 pages, engraved portrait, folding facsimile; contemporary calf, rebacked, Signet Library arms on covers.   James Burmester 29-109 1996 £150.00

PARIS, JOHN AYRTON   Pharmacologia. New York: 1825. 8vo; 2 volumes; sheep, joints broken; GM 2073; Waring 78.   Argosy 810-384 1996 $125.00

PARIS, JOHN AYRTON   Pharmacologia. New York: E. Duyckinek, Collins and Co.; Collins & Hannay, O.A. Roorbach... 1828. 3rd American edition; 8vo; 544 pages; original full sheep with leather label, spine ends chipped, front outer joint cracked, normal foxing, owner's signature on free endpaper, still very good. American Imprints 34638.   Chapel Hill 94-272 1996 $200.00

THE PARISH Registers of Dalston, Cumberland. Baptisms, 1570-1678; Marriages, 1570-1678; Burials 1570-1678. Dalston: William R. Beck, 1893. 8vo; pages xxxi, 236; contemporary half calf, gilt, little scraped, flyleaves spotted and browned, occasional marginal corrections.   R.F.G. Hollett & Son 78-568 1996 £95.00

THE PARISH Registers of Dalton, Cumberland. Baptsims, 1679-1812; Marriages 1679-1812, Burials 1678-1812. Dalston: William R. Beck, 1895. 8vo; pages xxv, 350; modern half calf, gilt, raised bands and contrasting label; additional ms. notes on endpapers, few marginal notes.   R.F.G. Hollett & Son 78-569 1996 £95.00

PARISH, W. D.   A Dictionary of the Sussex Dialecct and Collection of Provincialisms in Use in the County of Sussex. Lewes: Farncombe & Co. 1875. 2nd edition; half title, ads & Report of the English Dialect Society, 1875 bound in; original brown cloth, very good.   Jarndyce 103-89 1996 £75.00

PARK, JOHN JAMES   The Topography and Natural History of Hampstead, in the county of Middlesex. London: White Cochrane, 1814. 4to; pages xxi, 359, xxxix, large paper copy, folding map, 2 printed tables, frontispiece, 8 (ex 9) plates; contemporary half calf, spine worn. Lacks portrait of Sir W. Waad at p. 143.   Marlborough 162-185 1996 £120.00

PARK, MUNGO   Travels in the Interior Districts of Africa; Performed Under the Direction and Patronage of the African Association in the Years 1795, 1796 and 1797. London: printed by W. Bulmer & Co., for the author & sold by G. & W. Nicol, 1799. 3rd edition, same year as the first, possibly 1st edition sheets, re-issued with new titlepage; 4to; contemporary tree calf, ruled in gilt, spine gilt, rebacked, original spine laid down, plates foxed, some very light browning, but very good. cf. PMM 253; CBEL II 1452.   Ximenes 109-213 1996 $400.00

PARK, MUNGO   Travels in the Interior of Africa, in the Years 1795, 1796 and 1797. London: printed by J. W. Myers for Crosby and Letterman, 1799. 1st abridged edition (same year as the regular first); 218 pages; original full sheep nicely rebacked, but covers worn on edges, few pitted spots and slight tape abrasions, archival paper tape used to reinforce inner hinges, front free endpaper out and text has occasional light foxing and small stains, both plates are foxed. PMM 253.   Magnum Opus 44-104 1996 $165.00

PARK, MUNGO   Travels in the Interior of Africa... London: Crosby and Letterman, 1800. 2nd edition; 8vo; half title, title, dedn., pages vii-xvi, 218, 3 ff. ads, engraved frontispiece; later quarter calf, paper aged, frontispiece stained.   Marlborough 162-249 1996 £250.00

PARK, MUNGO   Travels in the Interior Districts of Africa, Performed Under the Direction and Patronage of the African Association, in the Yearss 1795, 1796, and 1797...To Which is added the Life of Mr. Park. London: G. & W. Nicol/London: John Murray, 1800/1816. 8vo; 2 volumes; pages xx, 551; ccviii, xxvii, 2, 301, 2 ads, 2 large folding maps, 6 plates; contemporary cloth, leather labels, rubbed. Cox I p.3 94; Hoover 5655.   Richard Adelson W94/95-131 1996 $425.00

PARK, MUNGO   Travels in the Interior of Africa...Including Both Expeditions... London: A. K. Newman, 1817. 12mo; pages 254, 2 ads; frontispiece; quarter calf, red label. Cox I p. 394.   Richard Adelson W94/95-239 1996 $125.00

PARK, ROSWELL   Selected Papers, Surgical and Scientific. Buffalo: 1914. 1st edition; 383 pages; original binding, scarce. Kelly Burrage 936.   W. Bruce Fye 71-1619 1996 $150.00

PARK, T.   Heliconia. London: from the private Press of Longman Hurst, Rees, Orme & Brown... 1815. 1st edition; according to Lowndes only 200 sets were printed; 4to; 3 volumes, varied pagination; 19th century calf with gilt tooled borders and armorial centerpieces, all edges gilt, nicely rebacked in period style, corners bit rubbed, large 19th century bookplate and small label, still quite nice set.   Chapel Hill 94-188 1996 $450.00

PARKER, B.   The History of the Hoppers. Edinburgh: W. and R. Chambers, n.d. Folio; 12 marvellous 3tone color plates, colored pictorial boards, professionally rebacked with new spine, corners worn, else very good; scarce.   Marjorie James 19-174 1996 £295.00

PARKER, CHARLES ARUNDEL   The Ancient Crosses at Gosforth, Cumberland. London: Elliot Stock, 1896. 1st edition; 8vo; pages 85, text illustrations; original cloth, gilt, trifle scratched, rebacked in matching brown levant morocco, gilt.   R.F.G. Hollett & Son 78-1175 1996 £85.00

PARKER, CHARLES ARUNDEL   The Ancient Crosses at Gosforth, Cumberland. London: Elliot Stock, 1896. 1st edition; 8vo; pages 85; text illustrations; original cloth, gilt, extremities rubbed, lower board damped.   R.F.G. Hollett & Son 78-1176 1996 £55.00

PARKER, CHARLES ARUNDEL   The Runic Crosses at Gosforth, Cumberland. London: Williams and Norgate, 1882. 1st edition; 8vo; pages 22; folding frontispiece; original stiff wrappers, neatly rebacked, original contemporary photo of 3 Gosforth crosses laid on to back of title. Scarce.   R.F.G. Hollett & Son 78-1179 1996 £55.00

PARKER, F. H. M.   The Pipe Rolls of Cumberland and Westmorland 1222-1260. Kendal: Titus Wilson, 1905. 8vo; pages xliii, 229, 2 maps; plain wrappers, scarce.   R.F.G. Hollett & Son 78-1180 1996 £75.00

PARKER, G. H.   The Elementary Nervous System. Philadelphia & London: J. B. Lippincott, 1919. 1st edition; 8vo; 229 pages; 53 text figures; original cloth. GM 528.   David Bickersteth 133-216 1996 £50.00

PARKER, JAMES   The Old Army Memories. Philadelphia: 1929. 1st edition; 454 pages, frontispiece, photos; cloth; very good+. Scarce. Graff 3186; 6 Guns 1680.   T. A. Swinford 49-875 1996 $225.00

PARKER, JOHN HENRY   A Glossary of Terms Used in Grecian, Roman, Italian and Gothic Architecture. Oxford: John Henry Parker, 1845. 4th edition; royal 8vo; 2 volumes; (x), 416, (16); (ii), (24) pages; frontispieces, 166 plates; Victorian half morocco, banded and gilt, very slightly rubbed but nice set.   Ash Rare Books Zenzybyr-73 1996 £100.00

PARKER, JOHN HENRY   A Hand-Book for Visitors to Oxford. Oxford: John Henry Parker, 1847. 1st edition; 8vo; (ii), xx, 187 pages; 20 steel engraved plates, numerous fine text illustrations, folding map; original red cloth, blocked in blind and in gilt on upper cover and in blind on lower cover, lettered gilt on spine, little light spotting on some pages, and two sections of text trifle losoe, but very good.   David Bickersteth 133-120 1996 £45.00

PARKER, K. LANGLOH   The Eutahlayi Tribe. London: 1905. 156 pages; 5 plates, prelims slightly foxed; original navy gilt cloth, very slightly bumped and marked, otherwise very good; scarce.   Antipodean 28-174 1996 $250.00

PARKER, RICHARD DUNSCOMBE   Birds of Ireland. 1983. 1st edition; limited to 250 copies, signed by editor, Martyn Angelsea and Wendy Dunbar, designer; 8vo; 40 mounted color plates; calf, original slipcases, fine, near mint condition.   C. P. Hyland 216-656 1996 £300.00

PARKER, ROBERT B.   A Catskill Eagle. New York: Delacorte, 1985. One of 500 signed, numbered copies (although this one says 400, some say 500 copies); uncorrected proof; blue paper wrappers; fine.   Quill & Brush 102-1415 1996 $125.00

PARKER, ROBERT B.   Ceremony. New York: Delacorte Press, 1982. 1st edition; signed; fine in dust jacket with light rubbing.   Quill & Brush 102-1403 1996 $100.00

PARKER, ROBERT B.   God Save the Child. Boston: Houghton Mifflin Co., 1974. 1st edition; fine in dust jacket with two extremely small tears, barely worthy of mention, especially nice.   Between the Covers 42-501 1996 $375.00

PARKER, ROBERT B.   God Save the Child. Boston: Houghton Mifflin, 1974. 1st edition; fine in near fine dust jacket with light soiling and rubbing.   Quill & Brush 102-1386 1996 $250.00

PARKER, ROBERT B.   God Save the Child. Boston: Houghton Mifflin, 1974. 1st edition; fine in near fine price clipped dust jacket whose spine is faded just a touch; signed by author.   Lame Duck Books 19-376 1996 $200.00

PARKER, ROBERT B.   God Save the Child. Boston: Houghton Mifflin, 1974. 1st edition; fine in price clipped dust jacket.   Quill & Brush 102-1385 1996 $300.00

PARKER, ROBERT B.   God Save the Child. London: Andre Deutsch, 1975. 1st edition; near fine in lightly chipped dust jacket.   Quill & Brush 102-1391 1996 $125.00

PARKER, ROBERT B.   The Godwulf Manuscript. Boston: Houghton Mifflin, 1974. 1st edition; fine in especially bright, white dust jacket.   Between the Covers 42-500 1996 $400.00

PARKER, ROBERT B.   The Godwulf Manuscript. Boston: Houghton Mifflin, 1974. 1st edition; rear cover rubbed (appears to be a flaw in cloth), otherwise near fine in faintly soiled dust jacket with only minor edge wear; inscribed by author.   Quill & Brush 102-1388 1996 $350.00

PARKER, ROBERT B.   The Godwulf Manuscript. Boston: Houghton Mifflin, 1974. 1st edition; author's first book; fine in very good-near fine white dust jacket with light soiling and few very small closed tears, otherwise very nice.   Quill & Brush 102-1389 1996 $200.00

PARKER, ROBERT B.   The Godwulf Manuscript. London: Andre Deutsch, 1974. 1st edition; author's first book; corners lightly bumped, "S" on corner of pastedown (under dust jacket flap), minor skinning on top corner of endpaper, otherwise fine in dust jacket with only minor creasing in top corners and price flap inked over.   Quill & Brush 102-1390 1996 $150.00

PARKER, ROBERT B.   Looking for Rachel Wallace. New York: Delacorte Press, 1980. 1st edition; fine in price clipped dust jacket.   Quill & Brush 102-1399 1996 $100.00

PARKER, ROBERT B.   Mortal Stakes. Boston: Houghton Mifflin, 1975. 1st edition; fine in dust jacket lightly rubbed at tips; signed.   Quill & Brush 102-1392 1996 $225.00

PARKER, ROBERT B.   Mortal Stakes. Boston: Houghton Mifflin, 1975. 1st edition; very fine in dust jacket with few short, closed tears and oly touch of minor edge creasing.   Quill & Brush 102-1393 1996 $175.00

PARKER, ROBERT B.   Mortal Stakes. Boston: Houghton Mifflin Co., 1975. 1st edition; small, neat gift inscription, else fine in near fine dust jacket with some rubbing to embossed gold lettering and little to spinal extremities.   Between the Covers 42-502 1996 $165.00

PARKER, ROBERT B.   Mortal Stakes. London: Andre Deutsch, 1976. 1st edition; scarce, without endpaper, as issued, minor rubbing at base of spine, still fine in dust jacket with touch of offset at bottom of front flap.   Quill & Brush 102-1394 1996 $125.00

PARKER, ROBERT B.   Parker on Writing. Northridge: Lord John Press, 1985. One of 75 signed copies in the deluxe edition; fine.   Quill & Brush 102-1418 1996 $150.00

PARKER, ROBERT B.   Pastime. New York: Putnam's Sons, 1991. One of 150 signed, numbered and specially bound copies; fine in slipcase. Quill & Brush 102-1435 1996 $125.00

PARKER, ROBERT B.   Playmates. New York: Putnam's Sons, 1989. One of 250 signed, numbered copies; cloth covered boards with gilt stamped lettering, all edges gilt; fine in slipcase.   Quill & Brush 102-1427 1996 $125.00

PARKER, ROBERT B.   Poodle Springs. London: Macdonald, 1989. One of 250 copies, signed by Parker on numbered limitation plate (affixed to half title); slipcase.   Quill & Brush 102-1430 1996 $100.00

PARKER, ROBERT B.   Promised Land. Boston: Houghton Mifflin, 1976. 1st edition; fine in dust jacket with very light soiling.   Quill & Brush 102-1395 1996 $125.00

PARKER, ROBERT B.   Stardust. New York: Puntam's Sons, 1990. One of 200 signed, numbered copies; small limitation, over subscribed at publication. fine in lightly marked slipcase.   Quill & Brush 102-1432 1996 $125.00

PARKER, ROBERT B.   Surrogate. Northridge: Lord John Press, 1982. One of 300 (of 350 total) signed, numbered copies, in small tan paper boards, purple cloth spine lettered in gold, fine in dust jacket.   Quill & Brush 102-1406 196 $200.00

PARKER, ROBERT B.   Surrogate. Northridge: Lord John Press, 1982. 1/300 numbered copies (of a total edition of 350); 12mo; signed by author; scarce. fine in dust jacket.   Between the Covers 42-503 1996 $185.00

PARKER, ROBERT B.   Walking Shadow. New York: Putnam, 1994. One of 100 copies, signed by author and numbered; fine in slipcase.   Quill & Brush 102-1437 1996 $125.00

PARKER, THOMAS LISTER   Description of Browsholme Hall. London: privately printed, 1815. One of 100 copies; 4to; 130 pages, large folding table, facsimile plate, 19 etched plates; later half morocco, frontispiece repaired, margins dusty. Martin p. 223; Colvin p. 621. Marlborough 162-78 1996 £425.00

PARKER, WILLIAM B.   Notes Taken During the Expedition Commanded by Capt. R. B. Marcy, U.S.A. Through Unexplored Texas, in the Summer and Fall of 1854. Philadelphia: Hayes & Zell, 1856. 1st edition; 242, (1)-6 ads; original brown cloth, publisher's names on sides in blind, title in gilt on backstrip, minor repair to extremities of spine, fine. Bradford 4186; Howes P91; Graff 3195; Becker Wagner Camp 279.   Michael D. Heaston 23-287 1996 $750.00

PARKINSON, JOHN   Paradisi in Sole Paradisus Terrestris. London: Humfrey Lownes and Robert Young, 1629. 1st edition; folio; pages (xii), 612, (16), engraved titlepage, portrait and 110 full page woodcuts, modern full calf, few scattered marginal stains, otherwise nice, clean copy with wide margins. Henrey 282; Pollard & Redgrave 19300. Second Life Books 103-150 1996 $4,500.00

PARKINSON, RICHARD   The Experienced Farmer. Philadelphia: C. Cist, 1799. 1st edition; 8vo; 2 volumes, pages xx, 275 (276), (ii), 292; contemporary English half calf, somewhat worn and scraped, bookplate removed from first volume.   Maggs Bros. Ltd. 1190-39 1996 £300.00

PARKINSON, SYDNEY   A Journal of a Voyage to the South Seas, in His Majesty's Ship, the Endeavour. London: printed for Standfield Parkinson, the editor... 1773. 1st edition; 4to; (iii-iv), (v-xxiii), 1-212 pages, errata leaf, directions to the binder, frontispiece, 26 engraved copperplates and 1 map; only very occasional slight offsetting to text; full contemporary calf, very neatly rebacked, preserving original spine, gilt tooling to compartments, red morocco label to spine, corners slightly bumped; handsome copy. Holmes 7; Mitchell 712; Sabin 18787; Hill p. 224.   Beeleigh Abbey BA56-56 1996 £3,500.00

PARKINSON, SYDNEY   A Journal of a Voyage to the South Seas, in H.M.S. Endeavour. London: Stanfield Parkinson, 1773. 1st edition; 4to; pages xxiv, 212, errata leaf, map, 27 plates; modern full panelled calf with red label in box, some light plate transfer. Mitchell 712; Hocken p. 12; Hill I p. 223.   Richard Adelson W94/95-132 1996 $4,985.00

PARKINSON, THOMAS   Hart Crane and Yvor Winters - Their Literary Correspondence. Berkeley: Los Angeles: & London: University of California Press, 1978. 1st edition; original binding, tail of spine very slightly rubbed, covers very slightly rubbed at extremities in very slightly creased original dust jacket; dedication copy, inscribed by author for James D. Hart; loosely inserted are clippings of two reviews of the book and an offprint of an article by author on Hart Crane.   Ulysses 39-125 1996 £95.00

PARKMAN, FRANCIS   The Journals. New York: Harper & Bros., 1947. 8vo; 2 volumes, pages xxv, 381; vii, 385-718; illustrations, maps, cloth, covers slightly bumped and dusty, interiors fine. BAL 15491.   Hugh Anson-Cartwright 87-339 1996 $150.00

PARKMAN, FRANCIS   The Journals of Francis Parkman. New York: London: Harper & Brothers Pub., 1947. 24.5 cm; 2 volumes; xxv, 381; vii, (382)-718 pages; frontispieces, illustrations, portraits, maps; fine set in dust jackets. Smith 7910.   Rockland Books 38-170 1996 $125.00

PARKMAN, FRANCIS   Vassall Morton. Boston: Phillips, Sampson and Co., 1856. 1st edition; 8vo; 414 pages, plus 6 pages of ads; contemporary calf backed marbled boards, hinges cracked and rubbed, sound very, clean copy.   M & S Rare Books 60-214 1996 $100.00

PARKMAN, FRANCIS   Complete Works. London: Macmillan (Boston printed), 1899-1913. New Library edition; 8vo; 12 volumes; original sage green cloth, gilt tops.   Howes Bookshop 265-947 1996 £120.00

PARKMAN, FRANCIS   Works. Boston: Little, Brown and Co., 1910. 12 volumes, illustrations, maps; half calf, gilt spines, marbled boards and endpapers, top edge gilt, edges show slight wear, else clean, attractive set.   Hugh Anson-Cartwright 87-340 1996 $400.00

PARKMAN, FRANCIS   Works. Boston: Little Brown, 1919. New Library edition; 8vo; 13 volumes; maps, plates; half deep green morocco, 5 raised bands, gilt ruled borders and spine panels, rubbed, corners worn, few spine tips with loss, very good.   Charles Agvent 4-930 1995 $550.00

PARKS, JOSEPH H.   General Kiry Smith, CSA. Baton Rouge: 1954. 1st edition; 537 pages; frontispiece; nice in dust jacket. Dornbusch 3097. T. A. Swinford 49-877 1996 $125.00

PARKS, JOSEPH HOWARD   General Leonidas Polk C.S.A. the Fighting Bishop. Baton Rouge: Louisiana State Univ. Press, 1962. 1st edition; 408 pages; original cloth, near fine, in near fine dust jacket. Harwell In Tall Cotton 141; Dornbusch II 3059; Nevins II 80.   McGowan Book Co. 65-70 1996 $125.00

PARKS, WILLIAM A.   Report on the Building and Ornamental Stones o' Canada. Ottawa: Department of Mines, Mines Branch, 1912-17. 8vo; 5 volumes, pages xiii, 376, vi; xii, 264, x; xiv, 304, xii; xiv, 333, xxiii; xiii, 236; richly illustrated in color and black and white, maps; stiff paper covers, spines slightly frayed, else fine set. Scarce.   Hugh Anson-Cartwright 87-341 1996 $600.00

PARLBY, SAMUEL   Desultory Thoughts on the National Drama Past and Present. London: pub. by Onwhyn, 1850. 2nd edition; 8vo; disbound; very good, scarce; 3 copies in NUC; LAR 931.   Ximenes 109-214 1996 $150.00

PARNELL, THOMAS   Poems on Several Occasions. London: Lintot, 1737. 8vo; contemporary calf, blind panelled on side, gilt tooled spine, very good.   C. P. Hyland 216-661 1996 £60.00

PARNELL, THOMAS   Poems on Several Occasions...With the Life of Zoilus and His Remarks on Homer's Battle of the Frogs and Mice... Dublin: Thomas Ewing, 1773. 4to; engraved portrait headpiece, some waterstaining to upper portion of text, mostly of front and back, else light browning; contemporary mottled calf gilt, with crest of Thomas Hutton on a morocco label, joints worn, rubbed; pleasant edition. James Cummins 14-150 1996 $150.00

PARNELL, WILLIAM   An Enquiry into the Causes of Popular Discontents in Ireland. London: J. Wallis, 1805. 2nd edition; 8vo; (4), 71 pages; recently bound in cloth, lettered in gilt; very good, complete with half title. Goldsmiths 18805 and Black 2447 for first edition.   John Drury 82-212 1996 £100.00

PARR, BARTHOLOMEW   The London Medical Dictionary... London: 1809. 1st edition; 4to; 3 volumes; pages xxii, (2 blank), 786; (2), 744; (8), 156, (14 index), 1 errata); 3 volumes; strongly bound in recent boards; some browning in places, but good, sound copy.   James Fenning 133-255 1996 £195.00

PARROT, ANDRE   The Arts of Assyria. New York: Golden Press, 1961. 4to; xviii, 380 pages; 491 illustrations, original cloth, dust jacket. Archaeologia Luxor-2562 1996 $125.00

PARROT, ANDRE   Sumer: the Dawn of Art. New York: Golden Press, 1960. 4to; 1, 396 pages, 557 illustrations, original cloth, dust jacket; fine. Archaeologia Luxor-2565 1996 $150.00

PARROTT, WILLIAM   Paris & the Environs Done on Stone from Nature, with Tinted Grounds. Paris: F. Sinnet, n.d., ca. 1843. Oblong folio; title in English and French within border, 12 tinted litho plates; contemporary half roan; excellent. Benezit VIII 140.   Marlborough 162-250 1996 £3,600.00

PARRY, A. N., & CO.   A. N. Parry & Co. Builders of Carriages of the Best Class. Amesbury: ca. 1885-90. Small 4to; (6), 44 pages; 44 drawings; original flexible cloth. Romaine p. 88.   M & S Rare Books 60-481 1996 $250.00

PARRY, D.   The Scarlett Empire. B-M, 1906. 1st edition; color illustrations by Herman Wall; near fine; inscribed presentation copy by author.   Aronovitz 57-926 1996 $125.00

PARRY, H.   The Art of Bookbinding: Containing a Description of the Tools, forwarding, Gilding and Finishing &c. Cambridge: ptd. by Thomas Wayte in Burton-upon-Trent, London: Baldwin, Cradock... 1818. frontispiece, title vignette; half calf, spine gilt in compartments, green morocco spine label, marbled boards, bit worn and rubbed at edges; booklabel of Renate Schuster (daughter of Paul Hirsch), bookseller's label of W. Heffer of Cambridge.   Maggs Bros. Ltd. 1191-24 1996 £850.00

PARRY, NICHOLAS   In Valleys of Springs of Rivers. Shropshire: Tern Press, 1981. One of 8 specials in an edition of 50 copies, signed by Nicholas Parry; 15.75 x 13 inches; 24 leaves; printed from steel plates and handpainted on Zerkall handmade paper; bound in full brown morocco blocked in gilt on front cover, marbled endpapers; fine. Joshua Heller 21-233 1996 $150.00

PARRY, NICHOLAS   A Rook Book. Shropshire: Tern Press, March 1988. One in an edition of 125 copies, signed by Nicholas and Mary Parry; 9.5 x 6.25 inches; illustrations in mixed media by Nicholas Parry; bound by Mary Parry in cloth over boards, illustration on front cover, paper title label on spine; fine.   Joshua Heller 21-235 1996 $125.00

PARRY, WILLIAM EDWARD 1790-1855   Journal of a Voyage for the Discovery of a North-West Passage from the Atlantic to the Pacific, Performed in the Years 1819-20 in His Majesty's Ship Heda and Griper. London: John Murray, 1821. 1st edition; large 4to; (8), xxxii,3 10, (2), clxxx pages, errata tipped in, 20 plates; mid 19th century calf over boards, later spine label, some occasional text soiling, overall nice, uncut copy.   Kenneth Karmiole 1NS-248 1996 $850.00

PARRY, WILLIAM EDWARD 1790-1855   Journal of a Second Voyage for the Discovery of a North West Passage...Performed in the Years 1821-22-23 in His Majesty's Ships Fury and Hecla... London: John Murray, 1824. 1st edition; 4to; 37 plates, maps, plans, occasional very light foxing on few plates, contemporary diced calf, narrow gilt border, centre of each cover carries the Earl of Lonsdale's gilt ex-libris stamp, a monogrammed 'Lowther' within an oak leaf wreath surmounted by an Earl's coronet, fine; Lonsdale bookplate. The Lowther Castle copy.   H. M. Fletcher 121-144 1996 £400.00

PARSON, WILLIAM   History, Directory and Gazetteer of the Counties of Cumberland and Westmorland... Leeds: printed for W. White & Co. by Edward Baines & Son, 1829. 1st edition; thick small 8vo; pages 732; xxiv, (ii); modern full calf, gilt.   R.F.G. Hollett & Son 78-1181 1996 £160.00

THE PARSONIAD; a Satyr. London: printed for Charles Corbet, 1733. 1st edition; folio; disbound, persistent hole in the blank lower inner margins, growing larger towards the end, but touching only 2 letters of the last page of ads; uncommon. Foxon P88.   Ximenes 109-232 1996 $250.00

PARSONS, CLERE   Poems. London: Faber & Faber Ltd., 1932. 1st edition; wrappers, top edge dusty, covers marked, dusty, rubbed and slightly soiled, cover edges nicked and very slightly chipped, corners bumped, spine browned and split at head and tail, very good. Ulysses 39-458 1996 £165.00

PARSONS, THOMAS WILLIAM   The Shadow of the Obelisk and Other Poems. London: Hatchards, 1872. 1st edition; sqare 12mo; 8, 115 pages; original pictorial cloth; with Oct. 20, 1872 ink presentation inscription from author; BAL 15536.   M & S Rare Books 60-215 1996 $125.00

PARSONS, USHER   Directions for Making Anatomical Preparations, Formed on the Basis of Pole, Marjolin and Breschet and Including the New Method of Mr. Swan. Philadelphia: Carey & Lea, 1831. 1st edition; 8vo; xxiv, 316 pages, 4 plates, rebound in calf over boards.   Kenneth Karmiole 1NS-181 1996 $150.00

PARTINGTON, C. F.   National History and Views of London. London: Simpkin, 1834. 8vo; 2 volumes, pages viii, 208; viii, 216, frontispiece, additional engraved titles, 58, 53 plates on laid india paper, large folding vignette bordered hand colored map (one or two map repairs); contemporary elaborately blindstamped half plum morocco, rebacked retaining original spines, hinges strengthened. Adams 177; Howgego (map) 343.   Marlborough 162-186 1996 £500.00

PARTON, JAMES   Eminent Women of the Age: Being Narratives of the Lives and Deeds of the Most Prominent Women of the Past Generation. Hartford: 1871. 1st edition; 628 pages; engraved portraits; original binding.   W. Bruce Fye 71-1624 1996 $100.00

PARTRIDGE, ERIC   The Spectator - the Story of Addison & Steele's Famous Paper. San Francisco: Book Club of California, 1939. One of 455 copies; quarto; cloth backed marbled paper boards; tipped in is an original issue of The Spectator for 12th Dec. 1711 (no. 246); top corners slightly bumped and bruised, near fine; from the collection of James D. Hart.   Ulysses 39-459 1996 $250.00

PARTRIDGE, WILLIAM   A Practical Treatise on Dying of Woolen, Cotton and Skein Silk... New York: Wallis & Co., for the author, 1823. 1st edition; 8vo; pages 288; folding table and ad; bound in chipped full calf, front cover loose, some gnawing to lower foredge of titlepage, but good copy.   Second Life Books 103-152 1996 $250.00

PASADENA, California, Illustrated and Described, Showing Its Advantages as a Place for Desirable Homes. Pasadena: Theodore Parker Lukens, 1886. 9 1/4 x 6 inches; 45 pages, 3 pages of ads for Pasadena businesses at end, 16 pages of lithograph illustrations, lithographed pictorial wrappers, chipping to head and tail of spine.   Dawson's Books Shop 528-188 1996 $450.00

PASCAL, BLAISE   Les Provinciales; or the Mysterie of Jesuitisme, Discover'd in Certain Letters, Written Upon Occasion of the Present Differences at Sorbonne... London: printed by J.G. for R. Royston at the Angel in Ivie Lane, 1657. 1st edition in English; 12mo; contemporary calf, very skilfully rebacked with old back laid down, gilt titling added at later date, very crisp and fresh. Wing P643.   H. M. Fletcher 121-68 1996 £1,100.00

PASCAL, BLAISE   Les Provinciales, or, the Mystery of Jesuitisme. London: printed for Rich. Royston, and are to be sold by Robt. Clavel, 1658. 2nd edition; 12mo; corner torn from G5 affecting few words of ad leaf; contemporary sheep, ms. paper label on spine, bound at end, with separate title is "Additionals to the Mystery of Jesuitisme". Wing P644. H. M. Fletcher 121-69 1996 £350.00

PASCAL, BLAISE   Tratiez de L'Eqvilibre des Liqvevrs. Paris: Desprez, 1664. 2nd edition; 12mo; 2 folding plates and diagram in text; calf; Tchemerzine IX 64; Brunet IV 400; Maire & Webster Silvain I 180. Rostenberg & Stern 150-125 1996 $675.00

PASQUIER, ESTIENNE   Des Recherches de La France, Livres Premier et Second. Paris: Pierre l'Huillier, 1570. 3rd combined edition; small 8vo; ff. 239 (xvii), roman & italic letter, woodcut titlepage border, initials and ornaments; age yellowed, upper edge of titlepage torn without loss, occasional headline shaved, 1 leaf loosening; 19th century calf by Wagner, richly gilt spine, gilt fillets and inner dentiles, marbled endpapers; This ed. not in BM STC Fr., Adams, Brunet, Tchemerzine, NUC.   A. Sokol XXV-71 1996 £550.00

PASSAVANT, G.   Verrocchio Sculpture, Paintings and Drawings. London: Phaidon, 1969. Complete edition; 4to; 220 pages; 216 illustrations, cloth, dust jacket, edges splashed, otherwise very good. Rainsford A54-567 1996 £120.00

PASSE, CRISPIJN VAN DE 1593 or 4-1667   Hortus Floridus. London: Cresset Press, 1928. 1st edition thus, one of 500 copies; oblong 4to; 52, 76 ff; full page plates; original marbled boards, very good in edgeworn dust jackets.   Chapel Hill 94-136 1996 $150.00

PASSE, CRISPJIN VAN DE 1593 or 4-1667   Hortus Floriolus. London: Cresset Press, 1928/29. Limited to 500 copies; oblong 4to; 2 volumes; with a total of 103 full page engraved plates; leather and marbled boards, both volumes with spine ends somewhat rubbed, corners bumped, both in dust jackets with defects; pretty set.   Marilyn Braiterman 15-158 1996 $500.00

PASSE, CRISPIJN VAN DE 1593 or 4-1667   XII Sibyllarum Icones Elegantissimi... N.P.: 1601. 8vo; wuite of 16 plates, brilliant impressions; simply (yet elegantly) bound in green pastepaper over flexible boards with single gilt fillet on both covers and title gilt within oval cartouche, spine with spare gilt decoration & red morocco title label, top edge gilt, preserved in half morocco clamshell case, also preserved are the leather bookplates of 3 previous owners: Beverly Chew, John Camp Williams and Robert Hoe; pencil note indicating that this had also been the copy of William Beckford.   Book Block 32-68 1996 $7,250.00

PASSERAT, JEAN   Recveil des Oevvres Poetiqves. Paris: Claude Morel, 1606. 1st complete edition; 8vo; 2 parts in 1 volume, pages (viii), 464, (viii); (xvi), 248, (vi), 8 pages misnumbered, mainly italic letter, woodcut printer's device on each titlepage, 2 identical engraved potraits by Thos. de Leu, woodcut initials & ornaments, blank corner of 1st titlepage repaired, tiny rust holes touching one letter of one headline; crushed red morocco by De Samblanx & J. Weckesser richly gilt dentelle borders and dentelle fan motif at corners, gilt spine and turn-ins, all edges gilt, marbled endpapers; from the library of Hecotr de Backer, with modern bookplates of Alfred Clericeau and Henri Burton. BM STC Fr. 17th 631; Tchemerzine V113; Cioranesco 17247 & 17259.   A. Sokol XXV-72 1996 £1,650.00

THE PASSPORTS Printed by Benjamin Franklin at His Passy Press. Ann Arbor: William L. Clements Library, 1925. One of 505 copies; 12.5 x 9.25 inches; 10 pages; blue cloth spine with paper title label, marbled paper boards, faint residue from removal of bookplate, otherwise very good. Joshua Heller 21-204 1996 $100.00

PASSY, HIPPOLYTE PHILIBERT   On Large and Small Farms, and Their Influence on the Social Economy. (with) Aristocracy, Considered in its Relations with the Progress of Civilization... London: Arthur Hall and Co., 1848/48. 1st edition in English; 12mo; 94; 173, (3) pages; xii, 252 pages; bound together; contemporary cloth lettered in gilt; fine.   John Drury 82-213 1996 £150.00

PASTERNAK, BORIS 1890-1960   Doctor Zhivago. London: Harvill Press and Collins, 1958. Uncorrected proof of the first English edition; 8vo; original brown wrappers, paper cover label, some editorial markings on upper cover, else quite fine, very scarce.   Lakin & Marley 3-44 1996 $350.00

PASTERNAK, BORIS 1890-1960   Bliznets V Tuchakh (Twin in the Clouds). Moscow: Lyrica, 1914. 1st edition; one of 150 copies; small 8vo; original light brown wrappers, lettered in dark brown; remarkably fine, of extreme rarity, fragile, but physically very attractive item, housed in lovely morocco slipcase.   Lakin & Marley 3-43 1996 $9,000.00

PASTERNAK, BORIS 1890-1960   Bliznets v Tuchakh. (Twin in the Clouds). Moscow: Lyrica, 1914. 1st edition; small, nearly octavo; wrappers; fresh, near fine copy, rare; early gift inscription from another Russian writer to a friend.   Lame Duck Books 19-450 1996 $11,500.00

PASTEUR, LOUIS   Studies on Fermentation. The Diseases of Beer; Their Causes and the Means of Preserving Them... London: Macmillan, 1879. 1st edition in English; 8vo; xv, (1), 418, (2 ads) pages, 12 plates, 85 figures in text; original cloth, skillfully rebaked with original spine laid down, light wear to extremities; very good. GMM 2485 for first French ed. 1876. Waller 10974.   Edwin V. Glaser 121-247 1996 $485.00

PATCHEN, KENNETH   Before the Brave. New York: Random House, 1936. 1st edition; author's first book; original cloth, fine but for sunned spots, bit worn and lightly chipped dust jacket.   Beasley Books 82-125 1996 $175.00

PATER, WALTER 1839-1894   Appreciations: With an Essay on Style. London: and New York: Macmillan, 1901. One of 775 copies; 9 x 6 1/4 inches; 2 p.l., 261, (1) pages; one volume, only (of 8) of an edition of the Works of Walter Pater; half title and title printed in red and black; handsome onlaid black morocco by Sangorski & Sutcliffe, sides framed with parallel gilt rules, two of them enclosing spaced onlaid red circlets, very fine corner decoration of onlaid green leaves and red berries on gilt stems, front cover with beautiful circular onlaid cluster of the same elements, along with gilt leaves and dots, spine with raised bands and gilt ruled compartments, featuring gilt and onlaid red disks, gilt ruled turn ins, all edges gilt, very slight wear at spine top, shadow on free endpaper, opposite leather turn-ins, otherwise very fine in lovely binding. Phillip J. Pirages 33-70 1996 $450.00

PATER, WALTER 1839-1894   Imaginary Portraits. London: Macmillan, 1887. 1st edition; 8vo; original binding, bookplates of Sidney Ball and Morse Peckham, rear endpaper foxed, near fine.   Charles Agvent 4-932 1996 $125.00

PATER, WALTER 1839-1894   Imaginary Portraits and Gaston De La Tour: an Unfinished Romance. London: and New York: Macmillan, 1900. One of 775 copies; 9 x 6 1/4 inches; 2 p.l., 321, (1) pages, one volume (of 8 fromt he Works); half title and title printed in red and black; especially attractive elaborately gilt and onlaid dark brown morocco by Sangorski & Sutcliffe, covers framed by parallel rules with broad gilt leaves in corners, rules on front cover enclosing the author's name and titles of the works as well as gilt clusters of leaves and berries, linked squares and rectangles surrounding a very beautiful central panel with many onlaid green leaves and large and small red flowers, massed on twining gilt stems and with gilt berries, spine with raised bands, compartments gilt ruled and divided into smaller rectangles with gilt disks and red onlaid circlets, gilt ruled turn-ins, gilt edges; spine uniformly faded to pleasing light brown, otherwise in very fine condition. Phillip J. Pirages 33-71 1996 $500.00

PATER, WALTER 1839-1894   Studies in the History of the Renaissance. London: Macmillan, 1873. 1st edition; 8vo; author's first book; old crease on rear board, front inner hinge partly cracked, but tight, very nice.   Charles Agvent 4-933 1996 $200.00

PATER, WALTER 1839-1894   Studies in the History of the Renaissance. London: 1873. 1st edition; 8vo; xiv, 213 pages, ads; original buckram, slightly worn and marked.   Rainsford A54-453 1996 £65.00

PATERSON, DANIEL   Paterson's British Itinerary. London: printed for and sold by the proprietor Carrington Bowles...Jan 3, 1785. 1st edition; 8vo; 2 volumes; contemporary tree calf, gilt, spines gilt, contrasting red and blue morocco labels; very fine, attractive set.   Ximenes 109-216 1996 $900.00

PATERSON, JAMES   The Games Laws of the United Kingdom Comprising the Whole of the Law on the Subject... London: Shaw & Sons, 1861. Blue cloth, paper label, worn and rubbed, nice.   Meyer Boswell SL27-183 1996 $225.00

PATERSON, JAMES   Pietas Londinensis; or, the Present Ecclesiasatica State of London. London: Joseph Downig...and William Taylor, 1714. Small 8vo; title, 5 ff., 308 pages, 2 ff. ads; early 19th century half calf, slightly grazed at extremities.   Marlborough 162-187 1996 £100.00

PATERSON, WILLIAM   A Narrative of Four Journeys into the Country of the Hottentots, and Caffraria. London: J. Johnson, 1789. 1st edition; folio; pages xii, 171, iv, folding map, 17 copperplates; modern full brown calf, some light plate transfer; Mendelssohn II p. 143; Theal p. 229. Richard Adelson W94/95-133 1996 $1,285.00

PATERSON, WILLIAM   Twelve Etchings of Views in Edinburgh. Edinburgh: Macintosh, 1816. 4to; 1 f., 12 etched views, with letterpress, boards, paper torn, spine damaged.   Marlborough 162-79 1996 £175.00

PATMORE, COVENTRY   The Angel in the House. The Bethroal. London: John W. Parker and Son, 1854. 1st edition; 8vo; pages viii, 191; fine binding of aquamarine crushed morocco, spine divided in six panels by raised bands, gilt lettered direct in second, others with red heart shaped onlays within floral borders, place and date in gilt at foot, sides ruled around with dog tooth roll and double fillet enclosing deep border built up from leaf sprays, floral motifs, dosts, etc. and 6 red onlays of fans, inner dentelles rulled all round in gilt, cream watered silk doublures and endpapers, gilt borders, gilt edges by Sangorski & Sutcliffe, folding cloth box, lea. label; from the lib. of Maharajah Jam Sahib.   Simon Finch 24-178 1996 £380.00

PATMORE, COVENTRY   Florilegium Amantis. London: George Bell & Sons, n.d. 1879. 1st edition; 12mo; printed presentation slip from author tipped in at front and Robert Louis Stevenson's "Sherryvore" bookplate on front pastedown; original cloth, paper spine label (partially worn away); covers glazed (as was the case with many of Stevenson's books), inner hinges cracked, else good in half morocco slipcase (spine little rubbed); also bookplate of noted collector, Charles Dexter Allen. David J. Holmes 52-115 1996 $850.00

PATON, ALAN   Cry the Beloved Country. New York: Charles Scribners, 1948. 1st edition; just about fine in near fine dust jacket lightly rubbed on verso and bright on spine and recto, minor edge fraying.   Bev Chaney, Jr. 23-549 1996 $135.00

PATON, E. RICHMOND   The Birds of Ayrshire. London: Witherby, 1929. 1st edition; 8vo; pages xxi, 228, colored frontispiece, 24 plates, numerous text illustrations, folding map; original cloth, gilt.   R.F.G. Hollett 76-233 1996 £65.00

PATON, JAMES   British History and Papal Claims 1066-1892. 1893. 1st edition; 8vo; 2 volumes; cloth, ex-library, but very good.   C. P. Hyland 216-662 1996 £60.00

PATON, JAMES   Missioanry to the New Hebrides. London: Hodder & Stoughton, 1890. 6th edition; 2 volumes, 376 pages, frontispiece; 382 pages, frontispiece; blue gilt buckram, very bright set. ALS loosely inserted from John G. Paton to Miss Clementine Butler.   Antipodean 28-176 1996 $195.00

PATON, JAMES   Scottish History and Life. Glasgow: James Maclehose & Sons, 1902. 1st edition; number 15 of 20 large paper copies; folio; 343 pages, printed entirely on Japanese vellum; numerous in text illustrations and 24 full page plates; original publisher's fll red morocco with gilt tooled borders and armorial centerpeice, ornamental spine panels, raised bands, top edge gilt, bookplate with light wear to edges, corners and spine ends, else handsome, near fine copy. Chapel Hill 94-357 1996 $375.00

PATRICK, SIMON   The Christian Sacrifice. London: printed by R.N. for R. Royston, 1671. 1st edition; 8vo; pages (xiv), 509; frontispiece, additional titlepage; contemporary polished black morocco, backstrip faded, raised bands, unlettered, compartments gilt panelled with single central ornament in each, sides panelled with inner and outer double fillet borders, with poppy-head and arabesque gilt ornaments at corners of central panel, marbled pastedowns; presentation inscription; excellent; from the Gell family library. Wing P760.   Blackwell's B112-220 1996 £85.00

PATRICK, VINCENT   The Pope of Greenwich Village. New York: Seaview, 1979. 1st edition; slight stain to front board, near fine in fine dust jacket; inscribed by author.   Between the Covers 42-350 1996 $100.00

PATRIOTIC Competition Against Self-Interested Combination, Recommended; By a Union Between the Nobility, the Landed and Independent Interest, the Clergy and Consumer... London: James Ridgway, 1800. 1st edition; 8vo; 40 pages; recently bound in calf backed marbled boards, gilt; very good; presentation copy, inscribed "From the Author" in ink on title; Kress B4251; Goldsmiths 17943; Black 2253; not in Halkett & Laing.   John Drury 82-214 1996 £175.00

PATTEN, C. J.   The Aquatic Birds of Great Britain and Ireland. London: 1906. 600 pages; plates and numerous text illustrations; original cloth, light rubbing and inner hinge sprung.   David A.H. Grayling MY95Orn-214 1996 £60.00

PATTERSON, J. B.   Autobiography of Ma-Ka-Tai-Me-She-Kia-Kiak or Black Hawk...Together with a History of the Black Hawk War. Oquawka: 1882. 1st edition; 208 pages, 3 plates; cloth; very good; Howes P120. Metacomet Books 54-86 1996 $165.00

PATTERSON, R.   The Natural History of the Insects Mentioned in Shakespeare's Plays. London: 1841. Small 8vo; pages xv, 270, portrait and numerous text figures; original cloth.   Wheldon & Wesley 207-1093 1996 £65.00

THE PAUL Hounds Will Meet. London: 1905. Oblong folio; 12 hand colored plates; pictorial boards, plates and cover signed H.V., endpapers loose, cvoers rather rubbed, plates fine.   Petersfield Bookshop FH58-326 1996 £100.00

PAUL, ELLIOT   Springtime in Paris. New York: Random House, n.d., c. 1950. 1st American edition; attractive pictorial endpapers, very good in soiled and browned dust jacket nicked and chipped at edges, some staining internally.   Virgo Books 48-152 1996 £50.00

PAUL, ELLIOT   With a Hays Nonny Nonny. New York: Random House, 1942. 1st printing; 8vo; 65 drawings by Quintanila; dust jacket (few nicks); very good, scarce.   George J. Houle 68-108 1996 $125.00

PAUL, HIRAM V.   History of the Town of Durham, North Carolina... Raleigh: Edwards, Broughton & Co., Steam Printers and Binders, 1884. 1st edition; 8vo; (15) pages ads, 257 pages, 7 (of 8 listed) engraved portraits, one of which is bound upside down, several text illustrations, folding map; expert restoration of binding, dampstain affecting a number of leaves, occasional foxing; good. Thornton 10513.   Andrew Cahan 47-151 1996 $200.00

PAUL, JAMES BALFOUR   An Ordinary of Arms Contained in the Public Register of All Arms and Bearings in Scotland. Edinburgh: William Green and Sons, 1893. 8vo; paes xvii, 263; top edge gilt, original quarter morocco gilt, handsomely rebacked in matching levant morocco, flyleaves faintly spotted.   R.F.G. Hollett 76-234 1996 £120.00

PAUL, JOHN   Every Landlord or Tenant His Own Lawyer; or, the Whole Law Respecting Landlords, Tenants and Lodgers... London: printed by Strahan and Woodfall for Richardson and Urquhart, 1776. 3rd edition; 8vo; no free endpapers, name on title which is creased; contemporary calf, rubbed, hole in label.   Anthony W. Laywood 108-103 1996 £100.00

PAUL, JOHN   The Law of Tythes. London: ptd. by W. Strahan and M. Woodfall for W. Richardson and L. Urquhart, 1781. 1st edition; stain on inner blank margin of first 16 pages, ad leaf at end, modern boards. Anthony W. Laywood 108-104 1996 £90.00

PAUL, JOHN DEAN   Journal of a Party of Pleasure to Paris, in the Month of August 1802. London: printed by A. Strahan for T. Cadell jun. and W. Davies, 1802. 1st edition; 8vo; viii, 102 pages, half title, 13 aquatint plates; uncut, nicely rebound in contemporary style boards, printed label; Abbey Travel 101.   James Burmester 29-110 1996 £300.00

PAUL, RODMAN W.   The California Gold Discovery: Sources, Accounts, Documents and Memoirs Relating to the Discovery of Gold at Sutter's Mill. Georgetown: Talisman Press, 1966. One of 100 copies, signed by author; 10 3/4 x 7 3/4 inches; 237 pages + colophon, folding panorama, page of portraits and facsimile letter sheet, 12 pages of photographic illustrations included in pagination; marbled boards, black fabricoid spine, double slipcase, spotting to slipcase and stain to one edge of case.   Dawson's Books Shop 528-192 1996 $150.00

PAUL, W.   The Rose Garden. London: 1848. 1st edition; royal 8vo; pages iv, 151, 177, (3), 15 hand colored paltes; newly bound in half morocco.   Wheldon & Wesley 207-82 1996 £550.00

PAULDEN, THOMAS   An Account of the Taking and Surrendering of Pontefract Castle, and of the Surprisal of General Rainsborough in His Quarters at Doncaster, anno. 1648. Oxford: printed at the Theatre and sold by R. Clements and S. Parker, and... 1747. 3rd edition; 8vo; disbound, very good, complete with half title, scarce.   Ximenes 109-217 1996 $100.00

PAULDING, JAMES KIRKE 1778-1860   The Backwoodsman. Philadelphia: 1818. 1st edition; 12mo; 12, (4), 198 pages; recent boards and paper label, uncut; BAL 15694 state B with pages 177-80 excised. M & S Rare Books 60-216 1996 $200.00

PAULDING, JAMES KIRKE 1778-1860   The Dutchman's Fireside. London: Henry Colburn and Richard Bentley, 1831. 1st English edition; 12mo; 2 volumes; contemporary half red morocco, spines gilt, bit rubbed, spines little dull; scarce; possibly bound without half titles, but very good. 5 copies in NUC; cf BAL 15714; cf. Wright I 2004. Ximenes 109-218 1996 $300.00

PAULDING, JAMES KIRKE 1778-1860 Koningsmarke, the Long Finne, a Story of the New World. New York: Charles Wiley, 1823. 1st edition; 12mo; 2 volumes; contemporary mottled sheep, red morocco labels, some rubbing, especially of joints; very attractive copy; with signature of Jacob W. Bartol on each, final blank in second volume, some spotting and offsetting, generally light; scarce. BAL 15697; Wright Fiction I.2012. James Cummins 14-151 1996 $425.00

PAULDING, JAMES KIRKE 1778-1860 Salmagundi...First Series, Volumes I and II, Second Series, Volumes I and II. New York: Harper and Bros., 1835. 8vo; 4 volumes; publisher's cloth, spines sunned, First Series volumes are slightly cocked, some foxing, but nice set, nevertheless. The Bookpress 75-447 1996 $175.00

PAULDING, JAMES KIRKE 1778-1860 A Sketch of Old England. London: repubished by Sir Richard Phillips, 1822. Tall 8vo; 128 pages; recently rebound with calf spine, boards, leather spine label; fine. David Mason 71-34 1996 $148.00

PAULUS AEGINETA Opera a Ioanne Guinterio Andernaco... Strassburg: W. Rihelius, 1542. Folio; 2 parts in 1 volume, woodcut device on title, minor browning, but good copy with two blank leaves; contemporary limp green vellum, bit worn, ties missing; 17th century inscription 'di Calvina Peri de Roppa, later in the Dr. O. Fisher medical collection, sold at Swann 5 April 1978 lot 744 ($520.00). Durling 3554. Maggs Bros. Ltd. 1190-478 1996 £1,800.00

PAUSANIAS The Description of Greece. London: Richard Priestley, 1824. 2nd edition in English; 8vo; 3 volumes; 2 folding maps, 4 folding plates; contemporary green half morocco and marabled boards, raised bands, gilt tooled spine panels, top edge gilt, library bookplate and unobtrusive blindstamps, one hinge cracked internally; still very good, handsome. Chapel Hill 94-158 1996 $375.00

PAVLOV, IVAN PETROVICH Conditioned Reflexes: an Investigation of the Physiological Activity of the Cerebral Cortex. London: Oxford University Press/Humphrey Milford, 1927. 1st edition in English; large 8vo; (xvi), 430, (2) pages; pebbled black cloth, crisp, tight copy with spine numbers artfully removed, titlepage stamp of Hartford Retreat; with Jelliffe's name stamp and bookplate. John Gach 150-357 1996 $200.00

PAVLOV, IVAN PETROVICH Die Arbeit der Verdauungsdrusen. Wiesbaden: J. F. Bergmann, 1898. 1st translation out of Russian; 8vo; xii, 199 pages; original binding; very good. Iowa 2129; Horblit 83; PMM 385. James Tait Goodrich K40-231 1996 $1,500.00

PAXTON'S Flower Garden. London: 1882-84. 2nd edition; 4to; 3 volumes; 108 color printed plates; half leather, rubbed, slightly foxed, slightly trimmed by binder. Wheldon & Wesley 207-83 1996 £600.00

PAXTON, JAMES Illustrations of Paley's Natural Theology. Boston: Hilliard, Gray, Little and Wilkins, 1827. 1st American edition; 8vo; 36 plates, paper label, front cover loose, worn copy, but plates and text in clean and decent condition, very uncommon. Freedom Bookshop 14-13 1996 $350.00

PAYER, JULIUS New Lands Within the Arctic Circle. Narrative of the Discoveries of the Austrian Ship 'Tegetthoff in the Years 1872-1874. New York: D. Appleton & Co., 1877. 1st American edition; 23cm; xxiv, 399, (6) pages; color frontispiece, illustrations, plates, portraits; gilt and black stamped illustrated deep green cloth; fine. Exceptional copy. Rockland Books 38-172 1996 $150.00

PAYNE, HUMFRY Archaic Marble Sculpture from the Acropolis. New York: William Morrow, 1950. 2nd edition; folio; xiii 75 pages; 140 plates; original cloth, spine lightly faded. Archaeologia Luxor-3806 1996 $125.00

PAYNE, JOHN HOWARD Therese, the Orphan of Geneva, a Drama in Three Acts... New York: published by Murden & Thomson, May 1821. 1st American edition? 12mo; recent wrappers, very uncommon, complete with final leaf of ads for other plays; rather foxed, titlepage bit creased, blank corner trimmed away at top. BAL 15776; Hill 232; Shoemaker 6399. Ximenes 108-286 1996 $225.00

PAYNE, WILLIAM Maxims for Playing the Game of Whist; With all Necessary Calculations and Laws of the Game. London: printed for R. Rayn and Son, 1778. New edition; 8vo; outer upper corner of last leaf missing, with loss of page numeral; 19th century cloth backed marbled boards. Anthony W. Laywood 109-109 1996 £75.00

PAYNE, WYNDHAM Town & Country. London: Beaumont, 1926. 1st edition; 40/60 copies (of an edition of 310 copies); large 4to; printed on handmade paper and signed by author and Cyril Beaumont; pages (viii) (letterpress), 14 (plates), (1), (4) (plates), (1); 14 large hand colored plates, each tipped to recto of single leaf and 30 other smaller hand colored plates, tipped to rectos of single leaf and 30 smaller hand colored plates tipped to rectos of 4 leaves; quarter white parchment, backstrip gilt lettered, pink and cream batik boards, covers little soiled, corners rubbed, untrimmed, good. Prospectus for book loosely inserted. Blackwell's B112-25 1996 £75.00

PAYNE-GALLWEY, RALPH The Fowler in Ireland. London: 1882. 1st edition; illustrations; original cloth, spine repaired, corners bumped. David A.H. Grayling 3/95-380 1996 £100.00

PAZ, OCTAVIO Air Born. Hijos Del Aire. Mexico: Leonardo de Vinci, 1979. Limited to 75 copies, signed by Paz and Charles Tomlinson, 1st bi-lingual edition; small 8vo; quarter vellum and boards, fine. James S. Jaffe 34-532 1996 $350.00

PAZ, OCTAVIO Tres Poemas/Three Poems. Limited Editions Club, 1987. One of 750 copies, signed by poet and artist; 22 x 18 1/2 inches; 26 mounted lithographs by Robert Motherwell on various colors of papers; bound in linen with lithograph inlaid on front board, folding box; mint. Phillip J. Pirages 33-363 1996 $3,500.00

PCIKFORD, MARY Why Not Try God? New York: Kinsey, 1934. 13th printing; small 8vo; dust jacket (nicks, small tears); very good; signed and inscribed by author. George J. Houle 68-115 1996 $125.00

PEABODY, ELIZABETH Sabbath Lessons, or an Abstract of Sacred History... Salem: Thomas C. Cushing, 1810. 1st edition; 12mo; 123 pages; contemporary calf backed boards. S&S 21004. M & S Rare Books 60-325 1996 $200.00

PEACOCK, JAMES Oikidia, or Nutshells... London: for the author, 1785. 1st edition; 8vo; (4), 89 pages, 2, + 25 engraved plates; rebacked original boards, some marking to covers, contemporary signature at head of titlepage cracked. Ken Spelman 30-99 1996 £420.00

PEACOCK, ROBERT BACKHOUSE A Glossary of the Dialect of the Hundred of Lonsdale, North and South of the Sands, in the County of Lancashire. London: Asher & Co. for the Philological Society, 1869. Original purple cloth, spine faded, titlepage ssems to be a cancel. Jarndyce 103-78 1996 £65.00

PEACOCK, THOMAS LOVE The Genius of the Thames: a Lyrical Poet in Two Parts. London: printed by T. Bensley for T. Hookham Jun. and E. T. Hookham... 1810. 1st edition; 8vo; attractive brown morocco, gilt, uncut, half title, minor soiling, very nice, from the library of C. H. Wilkinson with his bookplate. NCBEL 3.701. James Cummins 14-154 1996 $325.00

PEACOCK, THOMAS LOVE Headlong Hall. London: T. Hookham Jun. and Co. and Baldwin, Cradock and Joy, 1816. 2nd edition; 12mo; (iv), 217, (iii) pages; half title, final ad leaf; contemporary maroon half morocco, marbled boards, spine gilt; extremities little rubbed, little foxing. Nice copy. Robert Clark 38-255 1996 £225.00

PEACOCK, THOMAS LOVE Maid Marian. London: printed for T. Hookham and Longman, etc., 1822. 1st edition; 12mo; half red morocco, top edge gilt, very good, scarce; bookplate of C. H. Wilkinson. Block p. 181; CBEL III 701. Ximenes 109-220 1996 $650.00

PEACOCK, THOMAS LOVE Maid Marian. London: Printed for T. Hookham, and Longman, Hurst, Rees, Orme and Brown, 1822. 1st edition; 12mo; with leaf stating that the work was written in the autumn of 1818 following the title; attractive simple half red morocco; minor spotting and browning, attractive copy; from the C. H. Wilkinson library with his bookplate. NCBEL 3.701. James Cummins 14-153 1996 $325.00

PEACOCK, THOMAS LOVE The Misfortunes of Elphin. London: Thomas Hookham, 1829. 1st edition; 12mo; pages (viii), 240, half title; original drab boards, uncut, largely unopened; cloth box, upper joint starting at foot, head of spine very slightly damaged, otherwise fine; rare uncut in original boards; the Doheny copy with her morocco booklabel. Sadlier 1957; Wolff 5481. Simon Finch 24-179 1996 £900.00

PEACOCK, THOMAS LOVE   The Misfortunes of Elphin. Newtown: Gregynog Press, 1928. One of 25 specially bound copies of a total edition of 250; 9 3/4 x 6 1/2 inches; 2 p.l., 119, (1) pages; 21 wood engravings as headpieces and tailpieces, by H. W. Bray, device in colophon; lovely crimson morocco by Gregynog (signed in gilt by Horace Bray and George Fisher on rear turn-in); covers with single gilt rule frame, upper cover with gilt design of two hand-held goblets with wine pouring from one to the other (though with considerable gilt spillage), gilt ruled spine compartments between raised bands, one compartment with gilt titling, turn-ins with double gilt rule, top edge gilt, other edges untrimmed; a faultless copy. Harrop 12.   Phillip J. Pirages 33-264 1996 $4,500.00

PEACOCK, THOMAS LOVE   The Misfortunes of Elphin. Newtown: Gregynog Press, 1928. Limited to 250 numbered copies; 8vo; iv, 120 pages; 21 wood engraved head and tailpieces by H. W. Bray; publisher's patterned blue and black cloth sides, purple buckram spine, edges uncut, spine and covers very slightly worn, internally almost mint, unopened. Harrop 12.   Thomas Thorp 489-241 1996 £150.00

PEACOCK, W. F.   The Adventures of St. George After His Famous Encounter with the Dragon. Blackwood, 1858. 1st edition; small 4to; 10 engraved plates by Gustave Dore, all colored by hand; blue cloth stamped in gilt and blind, spine ends very slightly worn, little pale spotting, else nice; very scarce.   Barbara Stone 70-75 1996 £225.00

PEAKE, MERVYN 1911-1968   Gormenghast. E&S, 1950. 1st edition; very good+ in very good dust jacket with some light wear and tear and chipping to head of dust jacket spine.   Aronovitz 57-930 1996 $100.00

PEAKE, MERVYN 1911-1968   Mr. Pye. London: William Heinemann, 1953. 1st edition; 278 pages; chapter headings by author; original binding, top edge dusty, head and tail of spine and corners slightly bumped, prelims, edges and endpapers spotted, very good in nicked, chipped, rubbed, marked and dusty, slightly torn, creased and soiled dust jacket, darkened at spine and edges.   Ulysses 39-462 1996 £85.00

PEAKE, MERVYN 1911-1968   Shapes and Sounds. London: Chatto & Windus, 1941. 1st edition; near fine in chipped and worn dust jacket. Captain's Bookshelf 38-180 1996 $100.00

PEAKE, ORA BROOKS   The Colorado Range Cattle Industry. Glendale: Arthur H. Clark Co., 1937. 1st edition; 8vo; 357 pages; frontispiece, illustrations, 2 folding maps; top edge gilt, cloth bleached along edge of rear board, text dull on spine, else near fine and unopened; inscribed by author. Herd 1771; Arthur Clark Bib. 181.   Andrew Cahan 47-54 1996 $125.00

PEARCE, F. B.   Zanzibar: the Island Metropolis of Eastern Africa. New York: Dutton, 1920. Small 4to; xii, 431 pages; 31 plates and 3 maps; original cloth, edges little rubbed, top and bottom of spine rubbed and frayed, otherwise very good ex-library, library label on spine and markings on front endpaper.   Worldwide Antiquarian 151-520 1996 $125.00

PEARCH, GEORGE   A Collection of Poems in Two Volumes by Several Hands. London: G. Pearch, 1768. 1st edition; 8vo; pages (iv), 323, (1); (iv), 320; oval engraving on each titlepage, engraved headpieces at beginning of text in each volume, gutter margin at p. 1 in volume 1 slightly soiled; contemporary sprinkled half calf, backstrips with low raised bands, gilt lettered red leather labels, modern volume numbers lettered direct, marbled boards, early owner's name on front pastedown of volume 2, red sprinkled edges; excellent. Seemingly scarce. Blackwell's B112-222 1996 £350.00

PEARL of Great Price. Salt Lake City: LDS Printing and Publishing Establishment, 1878. 1st American edition; 71 pages; foldout woodcut and 2 other woodcut illustrations; gilt faded from cover, some foxing on pastedowns and endsheets, internally very clean and tight.   Orrin Schwab 10-77 1996 $350.00

PEARL, RAYMOND   The Biology of Death. Philadelphia: Lippincott, 1922. 1st edition; 8vo; 275 pages; illustrations; original red cloth, near fine. GM 137.   Edwin V. Glaser B122-115 1996 $100.00

PEARSON, ALEXANDER   Annals of Kirkby Lonsdale and Lunesdale in Bygone Days. Kendal: Titus Wilson, 1930. Signed limited edition, number 28 of 50 copies only); small 4to; pages xvi, 272; 37 illustrations and map on front endpapers; original full brown morocco gilt, few tiny holes at bottom corner of upper board. Near fine, extremely scarce.   R.F.G. Hollett & Son 78-1184 1996 £395.00

PEARSON, ALEXANDER   The Doings of a Country Solicitor. Kendal: Titus Wilson, 1947. Signed limited edition, number 50 of 500 signed copies; tall 8vo; pages xvii, 198, 32 illustrations; original cloth, gilt, dust jacket, rather worn and repaired; presentation copy inscribed to Oswald and Phyllis Brown of Grange-over Sands), loosely inserted 2 sm. original photos of author, P.c.s. and ALS, both from author to Browns.   R.F.G. Hollett & Son 78-230 1996 £55.00

PEARSON, ANTHONY   The Great Gase of Tithes Truly Stated, Clearly Open'd and Fully Resolv'd... Dublin: by and for Isaac Jackson, 1756. 8vo; xvi, 130, (i) pages; old calf, gilt, by J. Tate, Belfast, rather rubbed; label of Friends' Library, Belfast.   R.F.G. Hollett & Son 78-453 1996 £85.00

PEARSON, KARL   The Grammar of Science. London: 1892. 1st edition; 493 pages; original binding.   W. Bruce Fye 71-1641 1996 $100.00

PEARSON, L.   Diseases and Enemies of Poultry. Harrisburg: 1897. 8vo; pages 116; xxiv, 750; 2 volumes in 1; 95 colored and 8 black and white plates plust 39 text figures; three quarter leather (with edge and corner wear, some scuffing; few plates show signs of page sticking, all edges gilt.   Raymond M. Sutton VII-1104 1996 $165.00

PEARSON, T. R.   A Short History of a Small Place. New York: Linden Press, 1985. Advance uncorrected proof; tan printed wrappers; fine. Lame Duck Books 19-452 1996 $150.00

PEARY, ROBERT E.   Northward Over the 'Great Ice'. A Narrative of Life and Work Along the Shores and Upon the Interior Ice-Cap of Northern Greenland in the Years 1886 and 1891-97. London: Methuen & Co., 1898. 1st edition; tall 8vo; 2 volumes; 521, 625 pages; frontispiece portraits, 19 maps and plans, numerous black and white photos to text; original blue cloth, gilt title and sivler stamped vignettes to upper covers, gilt titles to spines, top edge gilt, armorial bookplate to front pastedowns, upper hinge to volume 1 cracked and very slight dampstaing to lower board. Arctic Bib. 13231.   Beeleigh Abbey BA/56-101 1996 £325.00

PEATTIE, DONALD CULROSS   Immortal Village. Chicago: University of Chicago Press, 1945. Limited to 500 numbered copies; signed by author and artist; small 8vo; pages xxiv, 202; printed on all rag paper; woodblocks by Paul Landacre; color dust jacket, original slipcase and woodblock label (rubbed).   Kenneth Karmiole 1NS-145 1996 $175.00

PECHEY, JOHN   Promptuarium Praxeos Medicae. London: imprensis Henrici Bonwicke, 1700. 2nd edition; 12mo; contemporary mottled calf, clasps (slight wear to spine), very scarce; this copy bound with a substantial quantity of blank paper at beginning and end, on which a contemporary hand has written a good many other receipts, prescriptions, notes on dosages, etc. Wing P1029.   Ximenes 108-287 1996 $300.00

PECK, GEORGE W.   Melbourne, and the Chincha Islands; with Sketches of Lima, and a Voyage Round the World. New York: Charles Scribner, 1854. 12mo; pages 2, v, 13, 294; frontispiece, map, text illustrations; original cloth, rubbed, bottom of spine chipped. Sabin 59473; Ferguson 13987.   Richard Adelson W94/95-134 1996 $200.00

PECKHAM, JOHN   Registrum Epistoalrum (1279-92). London: 1882-85. 8vo; 3 volumes; 2 folding facsimiles; original cloth.   Howes Bookshop 265-1597 1996 £85.00

PECKITT, WILLIAM   The Wonderful Love of God to Men, or Heaven Opened in Earth. York: printed by L. Lund for the author, 1794. 8vo; viii, 190, (2) pages; contemporary calf, greek key pattern gilt borders, expertly rebacked with new red gilt label; rare, very good.   Ken Spelman 30-20 1996 £120.00

PECOCK, REGINALD   The Repressor of Over Much Blaming of the Clergy. London: 1860. 8vo; 2 volumes; pages 800; original cloth. Howes Bookshop 265-1570 1996 £50.00

PEDANTIVS. Comoedia, Olim Cantabrig. Acta in Coll. Trin. London: William Stansby (?) Impensis Robert Mylbourn, 1631. 1st edition; 12mo; pages 168; Roman letter, woodcut titlepage border, double page engraved printed on verso of titlepage and recto of following leaf, 1 woodcut initial; 19th century red half morocco, a.e.r.; early ms. annotations or autographs above title (deleted) and on following leaf (pasted over), autograph of Henry White "Lichfield (sic) Octob.. 27 1807". STC 19524; Greg L9; Lowndes 1814.   A. Sokol XXV-73 1996 £485.00

PEEK, HEDLEY   The Encyclopaedia of Sport. London: Lawrence & Bullen, 1897. 1st edition; 4to; 2 volumes, x, 632; v, 655 pages; profusely illustrated; original three quarter maroon morocco and cloth, spines bit faded and one corner slightly chewed, still near fine.   Chapel Hill 94-390 1996 $250.00

A PEEP At the World. London: Thos. Dean and Co., Threadneedle St., n.d., ca. 1850. 4 3/4 x 6 1/4 inches; hand colored illustrations; decorative wrappers with boookseller's ticket, lightly worn and faded around edges, wrappers have short split along spine, else very good.   Andrew Cahan 47-99 1996 $100.00

PEET, STEPHEN DENISON   The Cliff Dwellers and Pueblos. Chicago: American Antiquarian, 1899. 8vo; frontispiece, xviii, 398 pages, 174 illustrations and 95 plates; original gilt embossed cloth, owner's signature at flyleaf and edges, corner lightly bumped.   Archaeologia Luxor-4766 1996 $125.00

PEGGE, SAMUEL   The Roman Roads, Ikenild - Street and Bath - Way Discovered and Investigated through the Country of the Cortiani, or the County of Derby. London: printed by and for J. Nichols, 1784. 1st edition; 4to; 59 pages, stitched as issued, uncut; Upcott I p. 141. Anthony W. Laywood 109-110 1996 £65.00

PEGGE, SAMUEL   Sketch of the History of Bolsover and Peak Castles in the County of Derby. London: printed and for J. Nichols, 1785. 1st edition; 4to; 30 pages, ad leaf at end, 7 engraved plates; disbound. Upcott I p. 140.   Anthony W. Laywood 108-105 1996 £75.00

PEIRCE, JAMES   The Security of Truth, Without the Assistance of Persecution or Scurrility... London: John Clark, 1721. 1st edition; 8vo; 136 pages, errata slip pasted to blank verso of title, modern old style calf backed marbled boards, spine lettered in gilt; nice.   John Drury 82-215 1996 £100.00

PEIXOTTO, DANIEL L. M.   Anniversary Discourse, Pronounced before the Society for the Education of Orphan Children and the Relief of Indigent Persons of the Jewish Persuasion. New York: J. Seymour, 1830. 1st edition; 8vo; 47 pages; original printed wrappers, sewn, uncut; very nice, ink presentation inscription from 'the author' to Francis Jenks, editor of the Christian Examiner.   M & S Rare Books 60-355 1996 $3,500.00

PELICAN PRESS   The Types Borders, Ornaments, Initial Letters, Flowers and Decorations of the Pelican Press. London: 1921. 380 x 250 mm, unfolding to 1000 x 760mm; 16 pages; broadside specimen in red and black incorporating 16 specimen pages with decorative borders, lightly soiled and darkened along horizontal fold but generally well preserved. Scarce. Appleton 7.   Claude Cox 107-230 1996 £55.00

PELTIER, JOHN   The Trial of John Peltier, Esq. for a Libel against Napoleon Buonaparte (etc.). London: 1803. Modern three quarter calf, some embrowning but quite good.   Meyer Boswell SL26-175 1996 $275.00

PEMBERTON, ELIZABETH G.   Corinth. Volume XVIII. Part I: The Sanctuary of Demeter and Kore, the Greek Pottery. Princeton: American School of Classical Studies in Athens, 1989. Folio; xvii, 233 pages, 38 figures, 16 plates; 2 plans; original cloth.   Archaeologia Luxor-3191 1996 $125.00

PEMBERTON, HENRY   A View of Sir Henry Newton's Philosophy. London: S. Palmer, 1728. 1st edition; 4to; pages (1), 407; engraving on titlepage, other engraved head and tailpieces on letterpress, 12 folding plates, waterstain in top outer corner of gatherings (1), a-c, d(singleton), *A-*B, and B-E, getting progressively fainter, other minor soiling, contemporary dark brown calf, well rebacked, raised bands, poor mdoern red label, surface of sides pitted, recornered, hinges strengthened, dated engraved bookplate "The gift of Wm. Mountaine Esqr., F.R.S. to Burnt-Yates School, Parh. of Ripley, W. Riding, Ebor within a Chippendale frame.   Blackwell's B112-200 1996 £350.00

PEMBERTON, THOMAS   Lord Kingsdowon's Recollection of His Life at the Bar and in Parliament. London: printed for Perusal by Private Friends only, 1868. Modern cloth, last leaf defective, else sound.   Meyer Boswell SL27-186 1996 $225.00

PENDERGAST, DAVID M.   Excavations at Altun Ha, Belize 1964-1970. Toronto: Royal Ontario Museum, 1979-82. Folio; Volumes I-II only, xi, 201 pages, 78 figures, 44 plates, 2 maps, 6 tables; xii, 265 pages, 122 figures, 53 plates, 2 tables; text in wrappers, figures loose in box as issued.   Archaeologia Luxor-4768 1996 $150.00

PENE DU BOIS, H. P.   Four Private Libraries of New York. New York: 1892. One of 1000 numbered copies and one of 800 on Holland paper; 12 plates; cloth, spine defective, uncut.   Maggs Bros. Ltd. 1191-116 1996 £55.00

PENGELLY, H.   A Memoir of William Pengelly, of Torquay. London: 1897. 8vo; pages xi, 341; portrait, 10 plates; cloth, slight foxing at ends; inscribed by Hester Pengally.   John Henly 27-180 1996 £65.00

PENN, GRANVILLE   Memorials of the Professional Life and Times of Sir William Penn, Knt. Admiral and General of the Fleet, During the Interregnum... London: 1833. 1st edition; 8vo; 2 volumes, errata leaf, 2 engraved plates, 1 facsimile letter; full polished calf, blind ruled dentelles, gilt tooling to compartments, green morocco labels to spine, joints rubbed, edges marbled; hinges cracked, armorial bookplate to front pastedown of both volumes, review of book loosely inserted, binders ticket to front pastedown of both volumes; Abbott 1740.   Beeleigh Abbey BA56-160 1996 £200.00

PENN, GRANVILLE   The Policy and Interest of Great Britain, with Respect to Malta, Summarily Considered. London: printed for J. Hatchard, 1805. 1st edition; 8vo; pages (4), 156, including half title, colored map; recent boards, label, 3 small neat stamps on title, otherwise very good to nice, uncut.   James Fenning 133-260 1996 £145.00

PENN, IRVING   Moments Preserved: Eight Essays in Photographs and Words. New York: Simon & Schuster, 1960. 1st edition; small folio; numerous photos by Penn, many in color; dust jacket (small chips on upper edges), very good, publisher's board slipcase, with color pictorial upper side.   George J. Houle 68-114 1996 $395.00

PENNANT, THOMAS 1726-1798   Arctic Zoology. London: 1784-85. 1st edition; 4to; 2 volumes, 24 paltes and 2 title vignettes; calf; good copy, without supplement; plates 10, 12, 14, 16 and 21 present in xerox only. Wheldon & Wesley 207-433 1996 £300.00

PENNANT, THOMAS 1726-1798   British Zoology. Warrington and London: 1776-77. 4th edition; 4to; 4 volumes; engraved titlepages, folding plate, 280 engraved plates; polished calf.   Wheldon & Wesley 207-432 1996 £250.00

PENNANT, THOMAS 1726-1798   History of London, Westminster and Southwark... London: Edward Jeffery, 1814. 4to; 2 volumes, title, second title, 2 ff., 144 pages, title, pages 145-381, frontispiece and 120 + 108 plates; extra illustrated copy, extended to 2 volumes, contemporary dark blue morocco, all edges gilt, lower cover to volume 2 detached. Marlborough 162-190 1996 £450.00

PENNANT, THOMAS 1726-1798   The History of the Parishes of Whiteford and Holywell. London: printed for B. & J. White, 1796. 4to; 2 engraved titlepages, 22 engraved plates, some foxing and slight offset from some plates; antique style half calf, marbled boards.   H. M. Fletcher 121-117 1996 £250.00

PENNANT, THOMAS 1726-1798   The Journey from Chester to London...With Notes. London: printed for Wilkie and Robinson...and J. Johnson & Co., 1811. Later edition; tall 8vo; viii, 622 pages; name on title; contemporary half leather, raised bands, boards slightly rubbed, otherwise near fine. Cox II p. 30 citing first ed.   David Mason 71-35 1996 $200.00

PENNANT, THOMAS 1726-1798   The Journey to Snowdon. London: printed by Henry Hughes, 1781. 1st edition; 4to; engraved vignette titlepage with ink inscription "A gift of my worthy Friend the Author", 197 pages of text (p. 173 misnumbered 137), 2 vignettes to letterpress, 11 engraved copperplates, plates in excellent condition; old speckled calf boards, slight surface wear in places, double gilt rule borders, gilt bands, tools and armorial device to panelled spine, red morocco label, speckled edges, marbled endpapers; armorial bookplate of Sir John Saunders Sebright.   Beeleigh Abbey BA56-18 1996 £250.00

PENNANT, THOMAS 1726-1798   The Literary Life of the Late Thomas Pennant, Esq. By Himself. London: sold by Benjamin and John White and Robert Faulder, 1793. 1st edition; 4to; 4 engraved plates, (xiii), 144 pages, ad leaf and contents leaf transposed in binding, but prelims complete with blank leaf (A2); 20th century half morocco, spine fully gilt with raised bands and contrasting labels; very good.   John Drury 82-216 1996 £200.00

PENNANT, THOMAS 1726-1798   Of London. London: Robert Faulder, 1790. 4to; pages vi, 439, 4 ff. index, frontispiece, 11 plates; engraved very good title, later cloth.   Marlborough 162-191 1996 £75.00

PENNANT, THOMAS 1726-1798   Some Account of London, Westminster, and Southark. London: Printed for the illustrator by B. McMillan, 1814. 1st edition thus; 4to; extra illustrated, 272 engraved plates, 3 duotone engraved plates, 20 color plates, titlepages in brown and black, publisher's ad at end; full gilt and blindstamped 19th century green straight grained morocco, spine with raised bands, gilt stamped decorations, gilt stamped inner dentelles, red endpapers, all edges gilt, some foxing to several plates, light rubbing at joints, very good. Allibor II 1553-54.   George J. Houle 68-109 1996 $2,000.00

PENNANT, THOMAS 1726-1798   A Tour from Downing to Alston-Moor. London: printed at the Oriental Press by Wilson & Co., for Edward Harding, 1801. Large paper copy; large 4to; viii, 195, (i), 27 copper engraved plates; modern half levant morocco, gilt with raised bands and spine label; occasional spot and offsetting, but very nice.   R.F.G. Hollett & Son 78-1186 1996 £240.00

PENNANT, THOMAS 1726-1798   A Tour From Downing to Alston-Moor. London: printed at the Oriental Press, by Wilson & Co., for Ed. Harding, 1801. Large 4to; pages viii, 130, complete; 27 engraved plates, some little offset or spotted; recent quarater calf with raised bands and spine label.   R.F.G. Hollett & Son 78-1187 1996 £220.00

PENNANT, THOMAS 1726-1798   A Tour in Scotland 1769. Chester: John Monk, 1771. 1st edition; 8vo; 316 pages; 18 full page engraved plates, one in text engraving; contemporary full calf with raised bands, very good.   Chapel Hill 94-358 1996 $200.00

PENNANT, THOMAS 1726-1798   A Tour in Scotland. London: printed for B. White, 1772. 2nd edition; 8vo; pages viii, 331, (i), complete; 18 engraved plates; contemporary calf, nicely rebacked in matching calf gilt. R.F.G. Hollett 76-235 1996 £160.00

PENNANT, THOMAS 1726-1798   A Tour in Scotland: MDCCLXIX. (with) A Tour in Scotland and Voyage to the Hebrides, MDCCLXXII. Warrington: W. Eyres/Chester: John Monk, 1774/74. 3rd edition, 1st edition of second title; 4to; engraved titlepage, with vignette, pages iii-xiii, 1, 338, 1 f. ad, folding engraved map, 21 fine engraved plates, one vignette; engraved titlepage, with vignette, pages viii, 379, 1 page ad, 44 engraved plates; 1st title in speckled calf, rebacked, 2nd title in calf, little scuffed, rebackedd uniformly with 1st title.   Marlborough 162-80 1996 £280.00

PENNELL, JOSEPH 1857-1926   The Adventures of an Illustrator: Mostly in Following His Authors in America and Europe. Boston: Little, Brown & Co., 1925. 1st trade edition; xxii, 372 pages; fine in original dust jacket and slipcase.   Blue River Books 9-252 1996 $150.00

PENNELL, T. L.   Among the Wild Tribes of the Afghan Frontier. London: Seeley & Co., Ltd., 1909. 3rd edition; frontispiece, 23 plates, 2 maps; original cloth, spine faded, top edge gilt, others uncut.   Anthony W. Laywood 109-111 1996 £75.00

PENNEY, NORMAN   The Household Account Book of Sarah Fell of Swarthmore Hall. Cambridge: University Press, 1920. 1st edition; large 8vo; pages xxxii, 597; original canvas backed boards, spine label (little defective), uncut, flyleaves browned and spotted, few spots elsewhere, but very good, scarce.   R.F.G. Hollett & Son 78-233 1996 £120.00

PENNINGTON, ISAAC   Light or Darkness, Displaying or Hiding It Self, As It Pleases. London: John Macock, 1650. 1st edition; 4to; (viii), 31, (i) pages; disbound, some paper browning; Wing P1177.   Robert Clark 38-87 1996 £65.00

PENNINGTON, RICHARD   A Descriptive Catalogue of the Etched Work of Wenceslaus Hollar, 1607-1677. Cambridge: University Press, 1982. 8vo; 452 pages; frontispiece; cloth.   Rainsford A54-324 1996 £105.00

PENNSYLVANIA. ADJUTANT GENERAL   Report of the Adjutant General of Pennsylvania, for the Year 1877. Harrisburg: lane S. Hart, State Printer, 1878. 221 pages; green cloth.   Blue River Books 9-255 1996 $275.00

PEPLER, HILARY DOUGLAS CLARK d. 1951   The Hand Press - an Essay Written and Printed by Hand for the Society of Typographic Arts, Chicago... Ditchling: 1934. One of 250 numbered copies, signed by author; hand pritned by author and Mark Pepler on a Stanhope Press, Joseph Batchelor & Son handmade paper; wrappers, spine and cover edges browned, cover edges slightly rubbed and creased, tail of spine split, covers slightly marked and dusty, small tear to bottom edges of lower cover; very good; from the library of James D. Hart.   Ulysses 39-146 1996 £275.00

PEPYS, SAMUEL 1633-1703   Diary and Correspondence... London: Swan Sonnenschein, 1890. Verbatim reprint of 1848-49 edition; 8vo; 4 volumes; half titles present, pages viii-551; (iv), 471; (iv), 499; (iv), 567; contemporary half red morocco, one corner little bumped, backstrips with raised bands, gilt lettered direct in second and third compartments, gilt ornament in centre of remainder, marbled boards, which are lightly rubbed and endpapers, top edge gilt; excellent.   Blackwell's B112-223 1996 £125.00

PEPYS, SAMUEL 1633-1703   The Diary of Samuel Pepys... London: 1904. Reissue; 8vo; 8 volumes; blue cloth, bit darkened, otherwise good. K Books 442-374 1996 £70.00

PEPYS, SAMUEL 1633-1703   The Diary... London: G. Bell and Sons ltd., New York: Harcourt, Brace and Co., 1938. 8vo. in half sheets; 8 volumes in 3; india paper, frontispiece; green half morocco, buckram boards, spines in compartments, raised bands, lettered in gilt, top edge gilt, silk bookmarks, spines and head of one cover faded, otherwise excellent copy.   Simon Finch 24-181 1996 £175.00

PEPYS, SAMUEL 1633-1703   The Diary of... London: G. Bell and Sons, 1971-83. 8vo; 11 volumes, 74 plates and maps; buckram, gilt, dust jacket.   Thomas Thorp 489-242 1996 £180.00

PEPYS, SAMUEL 1633-1703   The Life, Journals and Correspondence of Samuel Pepys, Esq. London: Richard Bentley, 1841. 1st edition; 2 volumes; original binding, top edges dusty, heads and tails of spines and corners bumped and bruised, prelims and contents sporadically spotted, covers marked and rubbed, spines browned, spine of volume 2 slightly worn, lower hinge of volume 1 cracked; good; 3 bookplates in each volume, one belonging to Robert Washington Oates.   Ulysses 39-463 1996 £375.00

PEPYS, SAMUEL 1633-1703   Memoirs of Samuel Pepys, Esq. London: 1825. 1st edition; large 4to; 2 volumes, xlii, (2), 498, (2), xlix, (2) pages; (4), 348, vii, (1), 311 pages; engraved plates, half titles and ad leaf, uncut; later half calf, spines gilt, red and green labels by Sangorski & Sutcliffe; beautiful set, fine and fresh, with just the lightest rubbing at extremities, in fleece lined cloth slipcase; Otto Orren Fisher bookplate. Superb condition.   Joseph J. Felcone 64-31 1996 $1,800.00

PEPYS, SAMUEL 1633-1703   Memoirs of Samuel Pepys, Esq. F.R.S. London: Henry Colburn, 1825. 1st published edition; thick quarto; 2 volumes; contemporary three quarter leather and marbled paper boards, very good.   Ken Lopez 74-369 1996 $3,000.00

PERCIVAL, A. B.   A Game Ranger's Note Book. A Game Ranger on Safari. USA: Pub. by the National Sporting Fraternity, Limited to 1000 signed copies; 2 volumes; illustrations; full leather, silk moire endpapers, ribbon markers, all edges gilt; new; housed in double slipcase.   David Grayling J95Biggame-156 1996 £120.00

PERCIVAL, DON   Maynard Dixon Sketchbook. Flagstaff: 1967. 1st edition; 91 unnumbered pages; illustrations; fine in dust jacket.   T. A. Swinford 49-894 1996 $125.00

PERCIVAL, ROBERT   An Account of the Island of Ceylon, Containing Its History, Geography, Natural History, with the Manners and Customs Of Its Various Inhabitants... London: C. & R. Baldwin, 1803. 4to; pages x, 420; 4 folding maps; new half cloth, marbled boards, some light foxing to maps.   Richard Adelson W94/95-135 1996 $425.00

PERCIVAL, THOMAS   The Works, Literary, Moral and Philosophical of Thomas Percival... Bath: printed by Richard Cruttwell, London: J. Johnson, 1807. 2nd collected edition; 8vo; 2 volumes; 14, (2), cclxii, 377, (1); 6, ix, (1), 461, (1) pages; original boards, rebacked, partially unopened and entirely uncut; very good, complete with half titles. John Drury 82-217 1996 £150.00

PERCY, THOMAS, BP. OF DROMORE 1729-1811   Reliques of Ancient English Poetry... London: printed for J. Dodsley, 1767. 2nd edition; 8vo; 3 volumes; contemporary calf, worn, half titles, frontispiece, engraved vignettes, unsigned, but probably after Wale, E6 torn (volume 1), some short marginal tears, engraved leaf of music at end of volume 2, leaf of publisher's ads at back of volume 3; some browning and staining, well red copy; signatures of Nathaniel Bristed, gift inscriptions from Miss Bristed to George Arden dated 1830; Courtney-Nichol Smith p. 111; Chapman & Hazen p. 148; Rothschild 1521. (all for 1st ed.).   James Cummins 14-155 1996 $150.00

PERCY, THOMAS, BP. OF DROMORE 1729-1811   Reliques of Ancient English Poetry. London: Lewis, 1839. Tall octavo; 3 volumes, pages cx, 376, 423, glossary each volume; black leather spines, pebbled cloth boards, gilt, titlepages in red and black, nice engraved head and tailpieces, top edges gilt, uncut, light wear, but very good, bright set. Rothschild 1521 for first ed. CBEL II 223.   Hartfield 48-L67 1996 $395.00

PERCY, WALKER 1916-1990   Bourbon. Winston Salem: Palaemon Press, 1979. 1st edition; one of 200 copies, signed by author; small thin 8vo; marbled wrappers, printed label, mint.   James S. Jaffe 34-533 1996 $150.00

PERCY, WALKER 1916-1990   Bourbon. Winston-Salem: Palaemon Press, 1981. 2nd limited edition; one of 150 copies, signed by Percy; tall thin 8vo; cloth backed decorated boards, printed spine label; mint. Hobson A.1.8.a.   James S. Jaffe 34-535 1996 $125.00

PERCY, WALKER 1916-1990   Lancelot. New York: FSG, 1977. 1st edition; signed by author; fine in dust jacket.   Thomas Dorn 9-213 1996 $100.00

PERCY, WALKER 1916-1990   Lost in the Cosmos. New York: FSG, 1983. 1st edition; fine in near fine dust jacket; singed by author and additionally inscribed by him.   Ken Lopez 74-370 1996 $200.00

PERCY, WALKER 1916-1990   Love in the Ruins. New York: Farrar, Straus & Giroux, 1971. 1st edition; 8vo; signed by author, black cloth, printed jacket, fine in near fine jacket.   Priscilla Juvelis 95/1-192 1996 $150.00

PERCY, WALKER 1916-1990   Love in the Ruins. New York: Farrar Straus and Giroux, 1971. 1st edition; author's third book, couple of tiny water spots to top page edges, else near fine in price clipped dust jacket.   Sherwood 3-223 1996 $125.00

PERCY, WALKER 1916-1990   Love in the Ruins. New York: FSG, 1971. 1st edition; fine in near fine dust jacket.   Lame Duck Books 19-454 1996 $100.00

PERCY, WALKER 1916-1990   Novel Writing in an Apocalyptic Time. New Orleans: Faust Pub., 1986. 1st edition; one of 300 cloth bound copies, each signed by Welty and percy;   Priscilla Juvelis 95/1-260 1996 $250.00

PERCY, WALKER 1916-1990   Questions they Never Asked Me. Northridge: Lord John Press, 1979. One of 50 deluxe numbered copies (from a total of 350), bound thus and signed by Percy; leather, slight rubbing to gilt spine letters, otherwise very fine.   Captain's Bookshelf 38-183 1996 $275.00

PERCY, WALKER 1916-1990   Questions They Never Asked Me. Northridge: Lord John Press, 1979. 1st edition; one of 350 copies signed by author; small 8vo; cloth backed decorated boards, mint.   James S. Jaffe 34-534 1996 $150.00

PERCY, WALKER 1916-1990   The Second Coming. New York: FSG, 1980. One of 450 copies of the first trade edition, numbered and signed by Percy; fine in publisher's slipcase.   Lame Duck Books 19-455 1996 $200.00

PERCY, WALKER 1916-1990   The Second Coming. New York: Farrar, Straus & Giroux, 1980. 1st edition; one of 450 copies, signed by author; as new, in blue cloth and blue publisher's box, shrink wrap untouched. Priscilla Juvelis 95/1-193 1996 $200.00

PERCY, WALKER 1916-1990   The State of the Novel: Dying Art or New Science? New Orleans: Faust Publishing, 1987. 1st edition; one of 75 deluxe copies signed by author; thin 8vo; quarter leather and decorated boards; mint.   James S. Jaffe 34-536 1996 $150.00

PERCY, WALKER 1916-1990   Symbol as Need. New York: Fordham University, 1954. 1st edition; one of no more than 25-50 copies; 8vo; signed by author; cream wrappers.   Priscilla Juvelis 95/1-194 1996 $1,000.00

PERCY, WALKER 1916-1990   The Thanatos Syndrome. Franklin Center: Franklin Library, 1987. 1st edition; signed; very fine.   Bev Chaney, Jr. 23-555 1996 $150.00

PERCY, WALKER 1916-1990   The Thanatos Syndrome. New York: Farrar Straus Giroux, 1987. Signed, limited edition; mint in slipcase. Bev Chaney, Jr. 23-554 1996 $175.00

PERCY, WILLIAM ALEXANDER   The Collected Poems of William Alexander Percy. New York: Knopf, 1943. 1st edition; fine in dust jacket with few very small chips, tipped in is one page TLS from Percy to Edwin Bechtel; with recipient's attractive bookplate and ink notation. Captain's Bookshelf 38-184 1996 $250.00

PERCYVALL, RICHARD   A Dictionary in Spanish and English... London: John Haveland for Matthew Lownes, 1623. Folio; 3 parts in one, (12), 392; (8), 84; (4), 68 pages; rebound in full tan calf (early 20th century?), antique style tooling on both covers, front hinge bit rubbed, titlepage and prelims somewhat soiled, leaf R2 with small section torn away at lower outer margin affecting 2 lines of letterpress.   Kenneth Karmiole 1NS-90 1996 $650.00

PERELMAN, S. J.   Acres and Plains. New York: Simon & Schuster, 1972. Later edition; excellent in dust jacket; inscribed by author for Eric Lister.   R. A. Gekoski 19-108 1996 £100.00

PERELMAN, S. J.   Eastward Ha!. London: Eyre Methuen, 1977. Excellent copy in dust jacket; inscribed by author for Eric Lister.   R. A. Gekoski 19-109 1996 £100.00

PERELMAN, S. J.   Strictly from Hunger. New York: Random House, 1937. Some soiling to cloth on front panel, else excellent; inscribed by author for Eric Lister, owner of Portal Gallery.   R. A. Gekoski 19-107 1996 £100.00

PERHAM, JOSIAH   Descriptive and Historical View of the Seven Mile Mirror of the Lakes, Niagara, St. Lawrence and Saguenay Rivers... New York: 1854. Pages 48; map; original printed wrappers, light wear, else very good.   Stephen Lunsford 45-127 1996 $275.00

PERKINS, CHARLES C.   Tuscan Sculptors: Their Lives, Works and Times with Illustrations... London: 1864. 2 volumes, lvi, 267 pages, 38 etchings, 23 woodcuts; 267 pages, 7 etchings, 5 woodcuts; cloth, spines and endpapers slightly worn, ex-library.   Rainsford A54-455 1996 £75.00

PERKINS, EEDWARD T.   Na Motu; or, Reef Rovings in the South Seas. Pudney & Russell, 1854. (xvi), 456 pages, lithographed titlepage, 11 litho plates, 2 maps; brown cloth covers, blind and gilt stamped, covers sunned, corners little rubbed and bumped, otherwise nice. Taylor p. 116; not in Hill.   Antipodean 28-181 1996 $550.00

PERKINS, JOHN   A Profitable Booke of Master John Perkins, Fellowe of the Inner Temple Treating of the Lawes of England. London: Richarde Tottell, 1581. contemporary calf, rebacked, joints rubbed, one margin torn, sound.   Meyer Boswell SL27-187 1996 $1,250.00

PERKINS, JOHN   A Profitable Book...Treating of the Laws of England. London: printed for Matthew Walbanck, 1657. Penultimate edition; crown 8vo; 16 leaves, 333 pages, early marginal annotations in first part of the book, possibly by John Peck, who has signed rear flyleaf, some browning; old sheep, recently rebacked. Wing P1544.   H. M. Fletcher 121-70 1996 £120.00

PERKINS, SIMEON   The Diary of Simeon Perkins, 1766-1780. Toronto: Champlain Society, 1948. Limited to 550 copies; xxxiv, 298 pages; original gilt lettered red cloth; fine.   Argonaut Book Shop 113-122 1996 $200.00

PERKINS, SIMEON   The Diary of Simeon Perkins, 1780-1812. Toronto: Champlain Society, 1958/61/67/78. Limited editions, limited to 600, 650, 775, 1400 copies respectively; 4 volumes, pages lviii, 531; xliv, 477; lxxii, 550; liii, 520; 5 illustrations, 3 maps; original gilt lettered red cloth, frontispiece leaves in second volume with tape stains at gutter, repaired, else fine set. Scarce as set.   Argonaut Book Shop 113-123 1996 $350.00

PERKINS, WILLIAM   The Workes of that Famous and Worthy Minister of Christ, in the University of Cambridge, M. William Perkins. London: John Legatt, 1613. Tall folio; 2nd volume (only); original calf, gilt medallion in center of both covers, binding worn and scuffed, small holges where clasps and catches were placed, front board separating from leather, but holding; several 'Table' leaves wrinkled in corners, otherwise excellent.   Roy W. Clare XXIV-8 1996 $300.00

PERKINS, WILLIAM   Opera Theologica. Geneva: Pierre et Jacques Chouet, 1611. 1st Latin edition; folio; ff. 488 in double columns, Roman and italic letter, large woodcut printer's device on titlepage, woodcut initials and ornaments, tables and 1 small diagram; very lightly yellowed in parts, very good in contemporary richly blindstamped pigskin over boards, very unusual deeply gauffred edges; this edition not in Lowndes or Shaaber.   A. Sokol XXV-74 1996 £950.00

PERLZWEIG, JUDITH   Lamps of the Roman Period, First to Seventh Century after Christ. Princeton: ASCSA, 1961. 4to; frontispiece, xv, 240 pages, 53 plages; original cloth.   Archaeologia Luxor-3817 1996 $150.00

PERNETY, ANTOINE JOSEPH   The History of a Voyage to the Malouine (or Falkland) Islands Made in 1763 and 1764. London: printed for T. Jefferys in the Strand, 1771. 1st English edition; 4to; (i-vi), (vii-xvii), 1-294 pages, frontispiece, 6 maps, 9 engraved copperplates; owner's ink inscription to front f.e.p. and title, tear to leaf 165/6 with no loss to text, small tear to map of Falkland Island p. 177 without affecting map; full contemporary calf, rebacked skilfully, red morocco label to spine, gilt devices to compartments, corners worn and restored. Hill Pacific Voyages p. 229; Cox Ii p. 282.   Beeleigh Abbey BA/56-102 1996 £850.00

PERNETY, ROBERT   The History of a Voyage to the Malouine (or Falkland) Islands, Made in 1763 and 1764, Under the Command of M. de Bougainville, in Order to Form a Settlement There... London: Thomas Jeffreys, 1771. 1st English edition; 4to; pages 4, xvii, 294; 7 maps, 9 plates; modern full tan morocco, gilt, small library stamps verso title and plates. Sabin 6870; De Moraes II p. 141.   Richard Adelson W94/95-136 1996 $1,185.00

PERON, FRANCOIS   Voyage de Decouvertes Aux Terres Australes. Paris: 1807-16-24. 1st edition; 2nd edition of plates; 2 volumes text 4to. and atlas royal 4to., 2 volume bound in 1 as issued; (iv), xvi, 496 pages, (ii), (&) (xxxii), 472 pages, 3 plates, atlas, 6 pages, 41 plates; original green mroocco and green boards, raised bands and compartments, gilt title and decoration, all edges marbled, marbled endpapers, original owner's bookplate, covers slightly rubbed at edges, otherwise handsome copy. This copy is enhanced by the inclusion of the titlepage & plates from the 2nd ed. atlas (bound in at rear of volume 1 of atlas); Hill p. 229-230; Wantrup 78a and 79a.   Antipodean 28-632 1996 $15,000.00

PEROTTUS, NICCOLAUS   In Hoc Volumine Habentur Haec - Cornucopiae, Sive Linguae Latinae Com(m)entarii Diligentissime Recogniti... Venice: In Aedibus Aldi, et Andreae Soceri, 1513/17. Folio in 8s; 439 (of 440) leaves, lacks last leaf, blank except for device on verso, Aldine device appears on titlepage and on K8v, italic text in double column, last signatures with some marginal dampstaining; 2nd issue of November 1513 edition; modern sprinkled calf by Period Bindery, Bath. Renouard 81.10. Adams P721; UCLA II 132.   Family Album Tillers-476 1996 $1,750.00

PERRAULT, CHARLES 1628-1703   Histoire de Peau d'Ane. Hammersmith: Eragny Press, 1902. One of 230 copies; page size 5 1/8 x 8 inches; printed on Arches paper watermarked for the Press; 3 original wood engravings by T. Sturge Moore and borders, frontispiece and initial letters by Lucien & Esther Pissarro; this copy in unique binding by Jill Tarlau, pale rose and bordeaux iridescent trellis patterned cloth with daisy-shaped rondel on upper panel of bordeaux onlays with lighter pink box calf onlaid on silver box calf to form center of flower, rose/lime green lizard, bordeaux suede surrounding rose/lime green rhinestone in center of rondel, matching chemise and etui edged in pale rose box calf, gilt lettering.   Priscilla Juvelis 95/1-88 1996 $2,000.00

PERRAULT, CHARLES 1628-1703   A New History of Blue Beard, Written by Black Beard, for the Amusement of Little Lack Beard and His Pretty sisters. Philadelphia: John Adams, 1804. 32 mo; 31 pages; 7 rather crude woodcuts; buff wrappers, very fine. Rosenbach 298; Welch 986.4.   Bromer Booksellers 90-129 1996 $200.00

PERRAULT, CLAUDE   The Natural History of Animals... London: printed for R. Smith, 1702. 4th issue of the 1st English edition of 1687; folio; engraved title (cut close, mounted), 35 engraved plates; calf, antique, bit worn.   Maggs Bros. Ltd. 1190-711 1996 £320.00

PERRAULT, J.   Lower Canada Agriculturalist: Manufacturing, Commercial, and Colonization Intelligencer. 1861-1862. Montreal: 1863. pages viii, 316; 41 engravings; original binding, nice. Not in TPL.   Stephen Lunsford 45-128 1996 $350.00

PERRENS, F. T.   The History of Florence Under the Domination of Cosimo, Piero, Lorenzo De' Medicis, 1434-1492. London: 1892. Thick 8vo; pages 475; original cloth.   Howes Bookshop 265-958 1996 £50.00

PERRIN, RENE   Album du Nouveau-Bellevue. Paris: J. F. Ostervald, 1826. Folio; title with aquatint vignette, 9 pages, 6 aquataint plates, printed in color and finished by hand; original paper wrappers, in fitted cloth case.   Marlborough 162-252 1996 £2,000.00

PERRINCHIEF, RICHARD   The Royal Martyr; or the Life and Death of King Charles I. (with) The Sicilian Tyrant; or, The Life of Agathocles. London: R. Royston, 1684/76. 3rd edition, 1st edition; 8vo; frontispiece in 1st title, lacking in second; two works bound in one, full contemporary etched panelled calf, spine gilt, double morocco labels; good, clean copy. Wing P1601 & 1607.   Ian Wilkinson 95/1-134 1996 £110.00

PERRINCHIEF, RICHARD   The Sicilian Tyrant; or, The Life of Agathocles. London: printed for J. Grover and R. Royston, 1676. 1st edition; 8vo; engraved pportrait, engraved vignette on title, small hole in E1-E5 repaired, with loss of a few letters; 19th century calf, spine gilt, label, all edges gilt, bound by F. Bedford; nice copy. Wing P1607.   Anthony W. Laywood 109-112 1996 £225.00

PERRING, F. H.   Atlas of the British Flora. London: 1962. 1st edition; royal 4to; pages xxiv, 432, 1623 distribtuion maps, 6 overlays in pocket; cloth, dust jacket, fine.   John Henly 27-234 1996 £50.00

PERRINS, C. W. DYSON   Italian Book-Illustrations and Early Printing. Austin: W. Thomas Taylor, 1994. New reprint of 1914 Oxford: Quaritch edition; limited to 250 copies; 4to; xiv, 92), 256 pages; profusely illustrated; grey cloth, spine label.   Kenneth Karmiole 1NS-204 1996 $185.00

PERROT, GEORGES   Histor of Art in Phrygia, Lydia, Caria and Lycia. London: Chapman and Hall, 1892. 8vo; xii, 405 pages; 280 figures; original cloth, fine.   Archaeologia Luxor-3819 1996 $175.00

PERROT, GEORGES   A History of Art in Chaldaea and Assyria. London: Chapman and Hall, 1884. 8vo; 2 volumes, 818 pages, 452 engravings and 15 color plates; gilt pictorial cloth, top edge gilt, corner bumped, scattered foxing.   Archaeologia Luxor-2579 1996 $175.00

PERROT, GEORGES   History of Art in Persia. London: Chapman and Hall, 1892. Small 4to; xii, 508 pages, 254 figures, 12 color plates; original pictorial cloth, minor shelfwear, signature at flyleaf.   Archaeologia Luxor-2581 1996 $200.00

PERROT, GEORGES   History of Art in Phoenicia and Its Dependencies. London: Chapman and Hall, 1885. Small 4to; 2 volumes, pages 870, 644 illustrations, 10 plates, original cloth, small tears at spines and volume lightly chipped, stamp at half titles.   Archaeologia Luxor-2582 1996 $150.00

PERROT, GEORGES   History of Art in Phrygia Lydia, Caria and Lycia. London: Chapman and Hall, 1892. 8vo; xii, 405 pages, 280 figures; original cloth, head of spine chipped, corners bumped, covers lightly soiled, bookplate.   Archaeologia Luxor-3820 1996 $125.00

PERROT, GEORGES   History of Art in Sardinia, Judaea, Syria and Asia Minor. London: Chapman and Hall, 1890. Small 4to; 2 volumes, 664 pages, 653 figures, 8 plates; original cloth, top edge gilt.   Archaeologia Luxor-2587 1996 $175.00

PERROTT, C. L. E.   A Selection of British Birds. Publishing Partnership, 1979. Facsimile limited edition of 250 numbered copies; folio; 5 plates in color; publisher's brown half morocco, marbled board sides, printed paper label, matching solander case in cloth and morocco; fine.   Thomas Thorp 489-244 1996 £85.00

PERROUIS, LOUIS   Ancestral Art of Gabon from the Collections of the Barbier-Mueller Museum (Geneva). 1986/87. English edition; 30.9 cm; 238 pages photos, maps and many color and black and white plates, illustrations; cloth, dust jacket.   L. Clarice Davis 111-79 1996 $125.00

PERRY, JAMES   The Electricc Eel; (with) Reply to the Electric Eel. (with) The Old Sperent's Reply to the Electric Eel. (with) The Torpedo... London: printed by J. Bew/printed for M. Smith/printed for Fielding & Walker, 1777/77/77. 1st edition; small 8vo and 4to; half title, title, iii, 19 pages; half title, title and 2 pages; half title, title with engraving and (iv), 17 pages, final leaf of text being reversed by binder; 3 works bound in modern speckled half calf with marbled boards, lettered up the spine in gilt, fine.   David Bickersteth 133-54 1996 £550.00

PERRY, JOHN   An Account of the Stopping of Daggenham Breach; with the Accidents That Have Attended the Same fromt he First Undertaking... London: printed for Benj. Tooke by Peele, 1721. 1st edition; 8vo; folding engraved plan by H. Moll (short tear repaired), some browning of text in places; contemporary calf, rubbed, hinges partly cracked, albels.   Anthony W. Laywood 108-106 1996 £150.00

PERRY, KATE   Reminiscences of a London Drawing Room. Chesham Place, 1849. N.P.: London:? n.d. 1863? 8vo; original dark blue printed wrappers, bit worn. Very good, rare. 4 copies in NUC.   Ximenes 109-221 1996 $375.00

PERRY, THOMAS   Metzger's Dog. New York: Scribner's, 1983. 1st edition; author's second book; fine in dust jacket, signed by author.   Quill & Brush 102-1453 1996 $100.00

PERTELOTE; a Bibliography...October 1936 - April 1943. Waltham St. Lawrence: Golden Cockerel Press, 1943. One of 200 numbered copies on mouldmade paper, signed by partners and specially bound; tall 8vo; numerous illustrations; half red morocco, patterned cloth sides; very good.   Bertram Rota 272-180 1996 £75.00

PERUCCI, FRANCESCO   Pompe Funebri di Tutte Le Nationi Del Mondo. Verona: Francesco Rossi, 1639. Folio; pages 97, (90, engraved title; 30 engravings, numerous woodcut devices and illustrations; worn 18th century French full leather, each board stamped in gilt with large and impressive arms of the notorious Louis Francois Armand du Plessis, Duc de Richelieu; early engraved armorial ex-libris of a French Bishop, B. H. De Fourey, 18th century ms. ownership of John Carter. Brunet IV 524; Michel & Michel V. 6, p. 102.   Family Album Tillers-477 1996 $800.00

PERUCHIO   La Chiromance, La Physionomie et La Geomance Avec la Signification des Nombres & l'Usage de La Roue de Pytagore. Paris: Billaine, 1663. 2nd edition; 4to; 360 pages; 2 folding and 5 full page engravings, dozens of woodcuts, woodcut ornaments; contemporary mottled calf, covers scuffed, gilt backstrip; fine. NUC 452.241; BM STC P 847; Sabattini 428; Caillet 8555.   Bennett Gilbert LL29-57 1996 $1,800.00

PERVIGILIUM VENERIS   The Vigil of Venus. London: Frederick Muller Ltd., n.d. 1st edition thus; quarto; 22 wood engravings by George Buday; parallel Latin and English texts; cloth backed black and white marbled paper boards; spine slightly marked and very slightly dusty, top edge slightly spotted, very good.   Ulysses 39-81 1996 £65.00

PETER MARTYR ANGELERIUS   De Rebus Oceanicis et Novo Orbe, Decades Tres... Cologne: 1574. pages (48), 655, (30); early half vellum, marginal worming in first signatures, not affecting text; some contemporary ms. marginalia, early German and English ownerships including Lord Eliock. Sabin 1558; Brunet I.293; Alden I 574/1; Medina 235.   Family Album Tillers-478 1995 $1,200.00

PETER'S Enquiries After Knowledge, with the Strange Things He Heard and Saw. London: Thos. Dean and Co., Threadneedle St., n.d., ca. 1850. 4 3/4 x 6 1/4 inches; hand colored illustrations; decorative wrappers with bookseller's ticket, creases, owner's name, else very good.   Andrew Cahan 47-100 1996 $100.00

PETER, SARAH   Ate Eight. New York: by the artist, 1994. One of 35 copies only, signed and numbered by artist; page size 2 5/8 x 2 1/2 inches; on whatman paper; 7 color etchings; accordion style binding with varnished museum board at ends, title blindstamped on front, housed in grey 'bakery' box tied with white baker's string;   Priscilla Juvelis 95/1-177 1996 $325.00

PETER, SARAH   Thirty-Six Drawings. Iceland: Oddi, 1994. One of 500 copies, each signed and numbered by artist; page size 8 x 12 inches; all on Simpson Starwhite Vicksburg paper, 36 offset prints of colored pencil drawings of sweets, pastries, breads and crackers from 16 countries; tan cloth over boards, author and title stamped on spine.   Priscilla Juvelis 95/1-100 1996 $175.00

PETERKIN, JULIA   Roll, Jordan, Roll. New York: Robert O. Ballou, 1933. 1st trade edition; 8vo; illustrations; cloth, dust jacket, aside from a touch of wear to jacket at extremities of spine, a very fine copy. James S. Jaffe 34-540 1996 $1,000.00

PETERS, ELLIS   Black is the Colour of My True Love's Heart. New York: Morrow & Co., 1967. 1st edition; fine in dust jacket; inscribed and signed by author and Edith Pargeter.   Quill & Brush 102-1459 1996 $150.00

PETERS, ELLIS   Death Mask. London: Collins, 1959. 1st edition; original binding, top edge slightly dusty, head and tail of spine slightly bumped, very good in nicked, dusty and slightly torn, rubbed and creased dust jacket slightly darkened at spine and edges and with later, cheap price sticker on upper flap.   Ulysses 39-464 1996 £125.00

PETERS, ELLIS   The Devil's Novice. London: Macmillan, 1983. 1st edition; fine in dust jacket.   Quill & Brush 102-1461 1996 $150.00

PETERS, ELLIS   The Devil's Novice. London: Macmillan, 1983. 1st edition; near fine in dust jacket.   Virgo Books 48-154 1996 £65.00

PETERS, ELLIS   The Pilgrim of Hate. London: Macmillan, 1984. 1st edition; fine in dust jacket.   Quill & Brush 102-1462 1996 $125.00

PETERS, ELLIS   The Virgin in the Ice. London: Macmillan, 1982. 1st edition; fine in dust jacket.   Quill & Brush 102-1460 1996 $175.00

PETERS, HARRY T.   California on Stone. Garden City; Doubleday, Doran & Co., 1935. One of 501 copies, 1st edition; 12 x 9 inches; (vi), 227 pages + colophon and 105 plates; black printed glazed linen in dust jacket and slipcase. Beautiful copy.   Dawson's Books Shop 528-193 1996 $600.00

PETERS, HARRY T.   Currier & Ives, Printmakers to the American People. New York: 1929-31. 4to; 2 volumes; reproductions of over 300 prints, many in full color; original tan cloth, both volumes signed by author.   Jens J. Christoffersen SL94-130 1996 $250.00

PETERS, HERMANN   Pictorial History of Ancient Pharmacy: with Sketches of Early Medical Practice. Chicago: 1889. 1st English translation; 184 pages; numerous woodcuts; original binding.   W. Bruce Fye 71-1651 1996 $100.00

PETERS, HERMANN   Pictorial History of Ancient Pharmacy, with Sketches of Early Medical Practice. Chicago: 1902. 3rd edition; 83 illustrations; pictorial cloth. GM 2036.   Argosy 810-393 1996 $150.00

PETERS, HERMANN   Pictorial History of Ancient Pharmacy: with Sketches of Early Medical Practice. Chicago: G. P. Engelhard, 1906. 3rd edition; 8vo; xiv, 210, (2) pages; 83 illustrations; original pictorial cloth; very good. GM 2036; Duveen p. 467.   Edwin V. Glaser B122-118 1996 $125.00

PETERS, JOHN P.   Painted Tombs in the Necropolis of Marissa (Mareshah). London: Palestine Exploration Fund, 1905. 4to; frontispiece, xvii, 100 pages, 24 figures and 22 paltes; original cloth.   Archaeologia Luxor-2588 1996 $250.00

PETERSON, SUSAN   The Living Tradition of Maria Martinez. Tokyo: Kodansha, 1978. 2nd edition; fine in dust jacket; signed by Adam and Santana Martinez, Maria Poveka, Clara Montoya and Anita Martinez; gorgeous book.   Parker Books of the West 30-145 1996 $225.00

PETERSON, WILLIAM S.   The Kelmscott Press "Golden Legend": a Documentary History of Its Production, Together with a leaf from the Kelmscott Edition. Yellow Barn Press and University of Maryland Press, 1990. One of 170 copies; 12 x 9 inches; vi pages, (2) leaves, 32 pages, (1) leaf (colophon); erratum slip and prospectus with woodcut portrait laid in; wood engraved frontispiece, 4 pages of facsimiles; with original leaf from the Kelmscott Golden Legend containing one large and 3 small woodcut initials; original cloth, black morocco label, edges untrimmed, publisher's slipcase. As new.   Phillip J. Pirages 33-340 1996 $275.00

PETIT, J. L.   Remarks on Church Architecture. London: John Petheram, 1841. 1st edition; 8vo; 2 volumes; large number of full page and textual lithographs; contemporary morocco, gilt extra, gilt edges by Hayday; extremely scarce. Not in Abbey Cat.   Charles W. Traylen 117-243 1996 £150.00

THE PETITION of Divers Eminent Citizens of London, Presented to the Lord Mayor and Court of Aldermen the 28th of April 1681. London: printed for B.A. and published by Richard Janaway in Queens-Head... 1681. Folio; 2 pages, uncut, disbound; Wing P 1762.   H. M. Fletcher 121-47 1996 £55.00

PETITION of the Inhabitants of Istleworth in the County of Middlesex, Against William Grant, Minister of the Said Parish; Whereunto Is Added One and Twenty Articles Against the Said Minister by His Parishioners, Presented to the Hon. House of Commons. London: printed, 1641. Only edition; 4to; (ii), (6) pages; disbound, bit browned, slightly cropped at head, affecting one page number; Wing P1802.   Robert Clark 38-88 1996 £95.00

PETO, GLADYS   Gladys Peto's Bedtime Stories. London: John F. Shaw, 1928. 1st edition; 4to; 8 color plates and black and white illustrations; colored pictorial boards, extremities rubbed, else very good. Marjorie James 19-176 1996 £55.00

PETO, MORTON   The Resources and Prospects of America Ascertained During a Visit to the States in the Autumn of 1865. London: A. Strahan, 1866. 1st edition; 8vo; 2 tinted lithograph plates of San Francisco in 1848 and Chicago in 1831 (foxed and margin repaired); cloth, buckram spine, library stamp on spine. Sabin 61289.   Charles W Traylen 117-421 1996 £40.00

PETRARCA, FRANCESCO 1304-1374   The Ascent of Mount Ventoux. A Letter from Petrarch. New York: Petrarch Press, 1989. Signed, limited edition, one of 10 on vellum, from a total issue of 180; page size 9 1/4 x 6 1/4 inches; handset and printed by Peter Bishop in Centaur and Arrighi type on sheepskin parchment; full page wood engraving by John DePol; blue cloth.   Priscilla Juvelis 95/1-195 1996 $750.00

PETRARCA, FRANCESCO 1304-1374   Il Canzoniere. Venice: Giovanni Antonio dei Nicolini da Sabbio and Brothers, 1541. 4to; 23ff. n.n. (with the blank leaf C8), ff. I-CCCLXXXIV, 80 ff.; recased in binding of brown morocco over pasteboards, lacks 4 pair of ties, richly gilt with narrow border of a lacework tool and large centre arabesque plaque, blindfold Cupid with bow and arrows, in centre of upper cover and Fortune with her sail in same position on lower one, spine with 3 double bands alternating with four false bands, compartments cross hatched in blind, edges gilt and gauffered with small knotwork tools, new pastedowns and endleaves; a Bolognese binding of c. 1550, the plaque is akin to one owned by the "Binder of the Acts of the Cabinetmakers' Guild". Marlborough 160-8 1996 £1,500.00

PETRARCA, FRANCESCO 1304-1374   Il Petrarcha. Venice: Aldus, August, 1514. 2nd Aldine edition; 8vo; 208 leaves; 19th century quarter calf over marbled boards, gilt spine; owner's name trimmed from two leaves, some old staining; bookplate of Luigi Fortunato Pieri, with armorial stamps. Renouard 68.6. Adams P790; UCLA I 107; Brunet IV 545.   Family Album Tillers-479 1996 $850.00

PETRARCA, FRANCESCO 1304-1374   Il Petrarcha. (Sonetti et Cazoni). Venice: Bernardino Bindoni, March, 1542. Small 8vo; ff. 180, 16, woodcut portrait, 5 full page woodcuts, Italian Italic text; old Italian leather backed marbled boards, signatures f and g reversed by binder's error. Only 2 copies in NUC; not in Fiske.   Family Album Tillers-480 1996 $750.00

PETRARCA, FRANCESCO 1304-1374   The Sonnets of... Verona: Limited Editions Club, 1965. Limited to 1500 copies; signed by artist; tall 8vo; illustrations by Aldo Salvadori and printer, Giovanni Mardersteig; half blue leather, fine in dust jacket and slipcase.   Charles Agvent 4-936 1996 $200.00

PETRIE, ADAM   Rules of Good Deportment, or of Good Breeding. Edinburgh: n.p., 1835. One of 45 copies; 4to; (iv), iii, (9), 136 pages; full calf, all edges gilt; bookplate of Philip Shirley.   The Bookpress 75-448 1996 $1,200.00

PETRIE, GEORGE   The Ecclesiastical Architecture of Ireland Anterior to the Anglo-Norman Invasion. London: 1845. 2nd edition; 8vo; xxi, 525 pages; illustrations; cloth, very good.   C. P. Hyland 216-675 1996 £120.00

PETRIE, WILLIAM MATTHEW FLINDERS 1853-1942   Decorative Patterns of the Ancient World. London: BSAE, 1930. Folio; 17 pages, 88 plates; three quarter cloth, signature, bookplate.   Archaeologia Luxor-2590 1996 $150.00

PETRIE, WILLIAM MATTHEW FLINDERS 1853-1942   Roman Portraits and Memphis (IV). London: British School of Archaeology in Egypt, 1911. Folio; vii, 26 pages; 35 plates; boards; signature.   Archaeologia Luxor-3821 1996 $200.00

PETRONIO, ALESSANDRO TRAJANO d. 1585   De Victu Romanorum et de Sanitate Tuenda Libri Quinque. Rome: In Aedibus Populi Romani, 1581 (1582). 1st edition; folio; 340 pages (12) leaves, engraved device on titlepage and woodcut device on last leaf, dampstaining at beginning and end of text, brown stain on titlepage and through about a third of the volume (mostly marginal), library stamp in blank margins; contemporary limp vellum gilt tooled; Crahan copy with his bookplate. Adams P858; Bitting 368; Simon 1158; Bibl. Bacchia 498. Brunet IV 577.   Jeffrey Mancevice 20-67 1996 $1,850.00

PETRUS CHRYSOLOGUS, SAINT   Sermones... Bologna: G. B. de Faelli, 1534. 1st edition; 8vo; 326 leaves, woodcut initials; 17th or 18th century full vellum, scattered foxing, some marginalia; fine. Nuc 453.568 (1 copy). Bennett Gilbert LL29-55 1996 $800.00

PETTIGREW, J. B.   Design in Nature. London: 1908. 1st edition; 4to; 3 volumes; numerous illustrations; cloth, bit worn and shabby, tear in top of spine.   Maggs Bros. Ltd. 1190-255 1996 £65.00

PETTIT, EDWARD   The Visions of Government, etc.... London: printed by B. W. for Edward Vize, 1686. 2nd edition; 8vo; (48), 248 pages, collation including frontispiece, tiny burn hole in one leaf affecting single letter of text; contemporary ruled calf with label, some slight evidence of wear, but very good. Wing P1893.   John Drury 82-219 1996 £175.00

PEURBACH, GEORG VON   Novae Theoreticae Planetarum...Locis Compluribus Conspurcatae a Petro Apiano. Venice: Melchior Sessa, 1534. Small 4to; ff. 40, italic letter, many diagrams of differen sizes, many contemporary marginalia and 4 ms. diagrams, general light age yellowing, some light waterstains and damp spotting; contemporary limp vellum, soiled in places, top corners repaired. BM STC It. p. 296; Adams P2273; Houzeau & Lancaster 2252 infra.   A. Sokol XXV-75 1996 £650.00

PEURBACH, GEORG VON   Tabulae Eclypsiu(m)... Vienna: Ioannis Winterburger, Impe(n)sis Leonardi & Lucae Alantse Fratru(m), 1514. 1st edition; folio; (268) pages; with the rare two unsigned leaves of "Tabella manualis" bound in; 2 woodcuts, large woodcut, diagram, woodcut arms of Maximilian I at end, numerous decorative woodcut initials; half vellum over drab boards, ms. title on spine in red and black, corners rubbed, occasional soiling and dampstaining, small wormholes affecting few characters; very good, crisp copy. Adams P2271; Honeyman 2465; Houzeau & Lancaster 2253; Zinner 1013.   Heritage Book Shop 196-181 1996 $5,500.00

PEZZI, LORENZO   Vinea Domini. Cum Brevi Descriptione Sacramentorum et Paradisi, Limbi Purgatorij, Atque Inferni a Catechismo Catholicisque Patribus Excerpta. Venice: Girolamo Porro, 1588. 1st edition; Porro issue, with large plate partly unshaded; portrait in second state; 8vo; 12ff., n.n., pages 1-186, engraved titlepage, portrait, double page plate, 12 large engraved illustrations; ruled in mauve throughout; brown mor. over stiff pasteboards, lacks two pairs of ties, sides & spine richly gilt, border of leafy tendrils issuing from corners, centre dec. with 6 rows each of five oval frames outlined by leafy tendrils, each frame containing 1 of 4 monograms, flat spine with continuous ornament of leafy tendrils, edges plain gilt, rebacked with old spine laid down and very skilfully restored, new pastedowns and endleaves; a Parisian binding of c. 1590-1600; the copy of G. Garcia sale Paris 27 April 1868, lot 118; the copy of Ricardo Heredia, the poet, his sale, Paris 22 May 1891, lot 165 with illustration in sale catalog, the copy of Lord Amherst of Hackney, sale Sotheby's 24 March 1909 lot 679. It was suggested in the Heredia cat. that the initials on binding indicate joint ownership of Francois de Coligny, & his wife Marguerite d'Ailly;   Marlborough 160-9 1996 £6,800.00

PFANNSTIEL, ARTHUR   Modigliani. Paris: Seheur, 1929. 4to; 135 pages text + 64 page catalog, numerous plates, 6 in color; wrappers, some wear, dust jacket. Lucas p 171; Freitag 6609.   Brannan 43-436 1996 $150.00

PFEFFER, P. E.   Nuclear Magnetic Resonance in Agriculture. Boca Raton: 1989. 8vo; pages (8), 441; text figures and tables; cloth, library stamp or sticker on pastedown.   Raymond M. Sutton VII-1106 1996 $125.00

PFEIFFER, ROBERT H.   The Archives of Shilwateshub, son of the King. Cambridge: Harvard University Press, 1932. 8vo; xxv, 90 plates. original cloth.   Archaeologia Luxor-2597 1996 $125.00

PFISTER, R.   The Excavations at Dura-Europos. Final Report IV. Part II: The Textiles. New Haven: Yale University Press, 1945. Large 4to; color frontispiece, vi, 64 pages, 8 figures, 33 plates; original cloth, fine. With signature of N. Toll.   Archaeologia Luxor-3273 1996 $175.00

THE PHARMACOPOEIA of the United States of America. Boston: 1820. 8vo; 272 pages; contemporary calf, foxed. GM 1845; Austin 1500. Argosy 810-395 1996 $1,000.00

THE PHARMACOPOEIA of the United States of America. Boston: 1828. 2nd edition; 272 pages; original boards, paper label, minor waterstain affecting lower margin of some leaves, two library stamps, untrimmed and uncut. GM 1845.   W. Bruce Fye 71-1657 1996 $150.00

THE PHARMACOPOEIA of the United States of America. Philadelphia: 1864. 1st edition; 2nd printing; original binding.   W. Bruce Fye 71-73 1996 $300.00

PHELAN, WILLIAM   A Digest of the Evidence Taken Before the Select Committee of the Two Houses of Parliament, Appointed to Inquire into the State of Ireland; 1824-25. 1826. 8vo; 2 volumes, xvi, 523; viii, 303 pages; modern cloth, volume 2 in half calf, both very good; scarce. C. P. Hyland 216-678 1996 £145.00

PHELAN, WILLIAM   The Remains of William Phelan, D.D. with a Biographical Memoir by John Bishop of Limerick. 1832. 1st edition; 8vo; 2 volumes, (xxvii), 96, 320; 364 pages; partly unopened, cloth; very good.   C. P. Hyland 216-679 1996 £75.00

PHELPS, H. P.   Players of a Century a Record of the Albany Stage, Including Notices of Prominent Actors Who Have Appeared in America. Albany: 1880. Subscriber's Edition, 1 of 250 copies; very good.   Lyman Books 21-332 1996 $125.00

PHILBY, H. ST. JOHN BRIDGER   Arabian Days. London: Hale, 1948. 2nd printing; 8vo; xvi, 336 pages; 49 plates; original cloth, slightly rubbed, very slight foxing, otherwise very good.   Worldwide Antiquarian 151-531 1996 $120.00

PHILBY, KIM　A Handbook of Marxism. London: Gollancz, 1935. Spine faded and soiled, but very good in sunned dust jacket; Bearing ownership signature "Anthony Blunt September 1935"; from the library of Philby, though without indication of his ownership of the book.　R. A. Gekoski　19-110　1996　£800.00

PHILELFUS, FRANCISCUS　Orationes. Paris: Petit, 1515.. Small 4to; fine Petit device on titlepage, ms. on lasat leaf verso in red and black ink; vellum (slightly warped); marginal annotations, slight worming. Rostenberg & Stern　150-92　1996　$575.00

PHILIP, ROBERT KEMP　The Gardener's and Farmer's Reason Why. London: Houlston & Wright, Philadelphia: Lippincott, 1860. 1st U.S. edition; 8vo; pages 330; scarce.　Second Life Books　103-153　1996　$125.00

PHILIPS, JOHN 1676-1709　Cyder. London: for Jacob Tonson, 1708. 1st edition; ordinary paper (i.e. first) issue; 8vo; pages (iv), 89; frontispiece; contemporary panelled calf, red morocco label, red sprinkled edges, front joint cracked, endpapers browned, otherwise very clean, fresh copy; from the library of Thomas Cartwright at Aynho, with his bookplate Hayward 143; I.A. Williams p. 92; Rothschild 1535; Foxon p. 237.　Simon Finch　24-182　1996　£120.00

PHILLIMORE, W. P. W.　Cumberland Parish Registers. Marriages. Volume 1. London: Philimore & Co., 1910. Limited to 150 copies, signed; 8vo; pages (iv), 192; front flyleaf little spotted, original cloth, gilt, spine trifle dulled.　R.F.G. Hollett & Son　78-565　1996　£120.00

PHILLIP, ARTHUR　The Voyage of Governor Phillip to Botany Bay; with an Account of the Establishment of the Colonies of Port Jackson and Norfolk Island... London: printed for John Stockdale, 1789. 1st edition; 2nd issue; 4to; 3-6, errata leaf, (i-iii), (iv), (v), (vi-viii), (i-x), 1-298, i-liii, lv-lxxiv, 2 pages, stipple engraved frontispiece, 46 engraved copperplates, 7 maps and charts, half modern calf and marbled boards, corners worn, maroon morocco label to spine, marbled edges and endpapers, foxing to portrait frontispiece and title, library blindstamp to upper right corner of title and library identification number, blindstamp to one other plate, red ink date to final leaf of appendix, occasional light foxing. Ferguson 47; Hill p. 233.　Beeleigh Abbey　BA/56-104　1996　£1,500.00

PHILLIPPS, E. M.　The Gardens of Italy. London: 1909. 2nd edition; folio; colored frontispiece, numerous illustrations; cloth, bit stained and worn, corners stubbed.　Maggs Bros. Ltd.　1190-41　1996　£75.00

PHILLIPPS-WOOLEY, C.　Big Game Shooting. 1913/01. 2 volumes; many illustrations; original cloth, covers of volume 1 lightly marked/faded, volume 2 very good.　David Grayling　J95Biggame-556　1996　£60.00

PHILLIPS, C. J.　The New Forest Handbook: Historical and Descriptive. Lyndhurst: Short, n.d., 1876. 8vo; titlepage, 2 ff., pages 7-106, 1 f. ads; 10 card mounted albumen photographic prints, large folding litho map, latter with dusty edge and one or two short tears, elaborate gilt and black decorated green cloth, all edges gilt; excellent condition.　Marlborough　162-82　1996　£375.00

PHILLIPS, CHARLES　Recollections of Curran and some of His Contemporaries. London: printed for T. Hookham, Jun.; Baldwin & Co.; & Milliken, Dublin, 1818. 1st edition; 8vo; portrait; half title; contemporary tree calf, spine gilt, slight rubbing; fine.　Ximenes　109-222　1996　$225.00

PHILLIPS, COLES　A Young Man's Fancy. N.P.: Bobbs Merrill Company, 1912. 1st edition; mild foxing to endpapers, else fine. Hermitage　SP95-908　1996　$175.00

PHILLIPS, EDWARD　The New World of Words. London: W.R. for Robert Harford, 1678. 4th edition; folio; frontispiece, no ad leaves at end; contemporary calf, rebacked and recornered, label; minor soiling and staining, sound copy. Wing P2072A; Alston V58.　Robert Clark　38-89　1996　£280.00

PHILLIPS, EDWARD　The New World of Words; or, Universal English Dictionary. London: for J. Phillips, H. Rhodes, J. Taylor, 1706. 6th edition; folio; fine frontispiece, some browning towards end of text; contemporary calf, old reback, hinges slightly weakened, red label, good, sound copy; Granard booklabel. Alston V61.　Jarndyce　103-607　1996　£550.00

PHILLIPS, HENRY　Pomarium Britannicum: an Historical and Botanical Account of Fruits Known in Great Britain. London: 1823. 3rd edition; 8vo; pages ix, 372, 3 hand colored paltes; straight grained morocco, slightly rubbed, plates slightly foxed; Plesch copy with bookplate.　John Henly　27-321　1996　£120.00

PHILLIPS, HENRY　Sylva Florifera; the Shrubbery Historically and Botanically Treated... London: Longman, 1823. 1st edition; 8vo; 2 volumes, vi, 1f., 336 pages, (2), 333 pages; contemporary half calf, gilt spine just slightly chipped at head, good, some slight foxing.　Ken Spelman　30-100　1　996　£180.00

PHILLIPS, J. ARTHUR　The Mining and Metallurgy of Gold and Silver. London: E. & F. N. Spon, 1847. 9 1/2 x 6 1/2 inches; xviii, 532 pages, 8 full page illustrations; dark blue leather with elaborately gold stamped spine all edges gilt, some rubbing. Miner's Association Prize label. Dawson's Books Shop　528-194　1996　$175.00

PHILLIPS, JAYNE ANNE　Black Tickets. New York: Dell, 1979. Uncorrected proof; wrappers; fine.　Ken Lopez　74-373　1996　$225.00

PHILLIPS, JAYNE ANNE　Black Tickets. New York: Delacorte, 1979. 1st edition; page edges slightly darkened as usual, else very near fine in dust jacket; inscribed by author.　Lame Duck Books　19-458　1996　$300.00

PHILLIPS, JAYNE ANNE　Counting. New York: Vehilce, 1978. Of a total edition of 500 copies, this one of 474 copies in wrappers; fine; inscribed by author.　Ken Lopez　74-372　1996　$250.00

PHILLIPS, JAYNE ANNE　Fast Lanes. New York: Vehicle, 1984. Issued in an edition of 2000 copies in wrappers, and 26 hardcover copies, this is one of a handful of unbound copies, issued in lieu of bound proofs; illustrations by Yvonne Jacquette; unbound signatures; fine in self wrappers.　Ken Lopez　74-374　1996　$200.00

PHILLIPS, JAYNE ANNE　Sweethearts. Carrboro: Truck Press, 1976. One of 400 copies in wrappers, from a total edition of 410; some darkening to covers and upper corners bumped, otherwise near fine. Ken Lopez　74-371　1996　$250.00

PHILLIPS, JOHN 1800-1874　The Geology of Oxford and the Valley of the Thames. Oxford: 1871. 8vo; pages xxiv, 523, 2 publishers ads, 2 geological maps, 2 sections, all hand colored, 2 plain sections, 11 plates, 210 text figures; cloth, rebacked preserving spine; presentation copy from author for Rev. P. B. Brodie, pencilled marginal notes by Brodie.　John Henly　27-537　1996　£110.00

PHILLIPS, JOHN 1800-1874　Geology of Oxford and the Valley of the Thames. Oxford: 1871. 1st edition; 8vo; xxiv, 523 pages, 6 maps and sections, 201 other illustrations; brown cloth, slightly frayed and rubbed, but good sound copy.　K Books　441-369　1996　£80.00

PHILLIPS, JOHN 1800-1874　Illustrations of the Geology of Yorkshire: or, a Description of the Strata and organic Remains of the Coast of Yorkshire. London: 1829-36. 1st editions; 4to; pages xvi, 192, hand colored map, 14 plates; pages xx, 253, 22 plates of fossils, 2 plates of sections, 1 folding, folding map; new quarter calf, gilt, as usual, some spotting to some plates.　John Henly　27-536　1996　£420.00

PHILLIPS, JOHN 1800-1874　Illustrations of the Geology of Yorkshire, Part I. The Yorkshire Coast. Part 2. The Mountain Limestone District. London: 1836-75. 3rd edition; 4to; pages xii,3 54, folding colored map, 28 plates; pages xx, 253, 25 plates; uniform cloth, very good ex-library. Wheldon & Wesley　207-84　1996　£350.00

PHILLIPS, JOHN 1800-1874　The Rivers, Mountains and Sea-Coast of Yorkshire. London: 1853. Subscriber's edition; 8vo; pages xvi, (vi), 302; 36 (1-35, 27a) plates; original cloth, does not include half title, plate 30 colored; as usual somewhat foxed.　Wheldon & Wesley　207-1357　1996　£65.00

PHILLIPS, JOHN 1800-1874　The Rivers, Mountains and Sea-Coast of Yorkshire with Essays on the Climate, Scenery and Ancient Inhabitants o the County. London: 1855. 2nd Subscriber's edition; 8vo; xv, 301 pages geology map, litho plates, plates waterstained, otherwise good; new vellum type binding.　K Books　441-370　1996　£55.00

PHILLIPS, MARGARET　English Women in Life and Letters. Oxford: Oxford University Press, 1926. 1st edition; 8vo; (xviii, 408 pages); frontispiece, dozens of illustrations; blue cloth, gilt lettered spine; fine. Paulette Rose　16-244　1996　$200.00

PHILLIPS, PAUL CHRISLER　The Fur Trade. Norman: 1961. 1st editio 1382 pages, 2 volumes; illustrations; cloth; former owner's signature, fi in original labelled slipcase. SFT 464.　Gene W. Baade　1094-125　19 $185.00

PHILLIPS, PAUL CHRISLER   The Fur Trade. Norman: University of Oklahoma Press, 1961. 1st edition; 2 volumes; very good+.   Parker Books of the West 30-146   1996 $150.00

PHILLIPS, PHILIP   Archaeological Survey in the Lower Mississippi Alluvial Valley 1940-1947. Cambridge: Peabody Museum, 1951. 8vo; xii, 472 pages, 113 figures, 17 tables; stiff wrappers.   Archaeologia Luxor-4782   1996 $125.00

PHILLIPS, PHILIP   Archaeological Survey in the Lower Yazoo Basin, Mississippi, 1949-1955. Cambridge: Peabody Museum, 1970. 8vo; 2 volumes, xxix, 999 pages, 450 illustrations and 1 map (in back pocket), 18 tables; wrappers, ink notation along spine.   Archaeologia Luxor-4779   1996 $150.00

PHILLIPS, PHILIP   Pre-Columbian Shell Engraving from the Craig Mound at Spiro, Oklahoma. Cambridge: Peabody Museum of Archaeology and Ethnology, 1975. 1st edition; large folio; 6 volumes; frontispiece, 584 pages, 271 figures, 360 plates; pictorial cloth.   Archaeologia Luxor-4780   1996 $450.00

PHILLIPS, RICHARD   A Letter to the Schoolmasters and Governesses of England and Wales, on the New Theories of Education, and on the Plans Under Legislative Consideration, for Reforming or Altering the Systems of Public Schools. Sherwood: Giblert & Piper, 1835. 48 pages, 16 page catalog; disbound, crease in first 3 leaves, slight marking. Jarndyce 103-547   1996 £50.00

PHILLIPS, THOMAS   The History of the Life of Reginald Pole... London: T. Payne (& 4 others), 1767. 8vo; (xxxii), (496), xii, 340 pages; 2 volumes; folding engraved portrait, half titles, folding pedigree; contemporary half calf, speckled boards, spines gilt, rubbed, slight wear to corners and head of one spine, little marginal staining; good set. Robert Clark 38-198   1996 £85.00

PHILLIPS, W. S.   Indian Tales for Little Folks. New York: Platt & Munk, 1928. quarto; 80 pages; color and black and white borders of Indians, 11 full page colored plates reproduced from watercolor paintings by author; boards with all over color illustration on front cover, front cover of original dust jacket remains; owner's inscription.   Bromer Booksellers 90-130   1996 $125.00

PHILLIPS, WILLARD   The Inventor's Guide. Boston and New York: 1837. 1st edition; 12mo; 8, 385 pages; recent calf backed marbled boards, raised bands. Kress C4460.   M & S Rare Books 60-471   1996 $225.00

PHILLIPS, WILLIAM   Remarks on the Chalk Cliffs Near Dover... London: 1818. 4to; 39, 8 pages; folding plate with hand colored sections; new buckram.   Graham Weiner C2-256   1996 £50.00

PHILOPONUS, JOHANNES   In Primos Quatuor Aristotelis de Naturali Auscultatione Libros Comentaria. Venice: B. Zanetti, 1535. 1st edition; folio; (320) pages, apart from prelims, text in Greek, leaf printed in red and black on recto, with woodcut initial on verso, 2 additional woodcut initials and headpieces in text, large woodcut device on title and final leaf, some very light marginal dampstaining, some annotations in an early hand on front blanks; recent purple quarter morocco, with raised bands, black leather spine label, maroon cloth slipcase; fine; Sarton I pp. 421-22; Adams P1085; Stanitz Sale 340.   Edwin V. Glaser 121-251 1996 $3,500.00

PHILPOT, CHARLES   An Introduction to the Literary History of the Fourteenth and Fifteenth Centuries.. London: printed for T. Cadell Jun. and W. Davies, 1798. 1st edition; 8vo; 19th century half red morocco, gilt, spine gilt, spine and edges rubbed, very good, outer edges uncut. CBEL II 1789.   Ximenes 108-289   1996 $300.00

PHIPPS, HOWARD   Further Interiors... Whittington Press, 1992. One of 300 numbered copies; small 4to; printed in Cochin type and from original blocks; 15 wood engravings; Japanese style wrappers; fine in slipcase. Bertram Rota 272-495   1996 £65.00

PIACENZA, FRANCESCO   I Campeggiamenti Degli Sacchi...che nel Nuove Arcischacchiere... Turin: Antonio Beltrandi, 1683. 1st edition; small 4to; 19th century quarter green calf over marbled sides, 2 leaves in facsimile, ex-Harvard College Library with release stamp. Bright copy. Book Block 32-81   1996 $650.00

PIAGET, HENRY F.   The Watch: its Construction, Its Merits and Defects. New York: for the author, 1860. 1st edition; 12mo; 59 pages; diagrams; original brown cloth, gilt stamped watch centerpiece, foxing, slight rubbing to edges and spine ends, else very good;   Chapel Hill 94-420   1996 $125.00

PIASSETSKY, P.   Russian Travellers in Mongolia and China. London: Chapman and Hall ltd., 1884. 1st English edition; 8vo; 2 volumes, half titles (ink inscription and shelf numbers to margins); 52 wood engraved plates and 23 woodcuts to text; original green cloth, black stamped floral design to upper covers with gilt title, gilt title to spines, volume 1 hinge cracked, volume 2 spine cracked and slightly shaken, brown endpapers with bookplate, ex-library with blindstamp to front free endpaper of volume 1;   Beeleigh Abbey BA/56-103   1996 £250.00

PIAZZA, VINCENZO   Bona Espugnata Poema. Parma: Stampa di Corte di S. A. S., 1694. 1st edition; 8vo; 320 pages; frontispiece, 12 full page engravings; contemporary full mottled calf, richly gilt; fine, handsome copy. NUC 456.685 (3 copies); BM STC 681; Piantinida 2834.   Bennett Gilbert LL29-59   1996 $1,450.00

PICASSO, PABLO 1881-1973   Picasso. New York: Harry N. Abrams, Inc., 1955. 1st edition; 606 reproductions, 38 full page plates, dust jacket, decorated cloth, fine in dust jacket designed by Picasso. Hermitage SP95-802   1996 $125.00

PICASSO, PABLO 1881-1973   Shakespeare. New York: Abrams, 1965. Limited to 1000 copies; folio; 125 pages, 12 gravure plates + titlepage illustration; boards.   Brannan 43-531   1996 $195.00

PICCIONE, ANTHONY   Anchor Dragging. New York: Boa Editions, 1977. 1st edition; one of 10 roman numeralled copies, signed by author and artist; thin 8vo; with poem in holograph by author; cloth backed marbled boards; fine.   James S. Jaffe 34-456   1996 $100.00

PICCOLOMINI, ALESSANDRO   Della Grandezza della Terra et Dell-Acqua. Venice: Giodano Ziletti, 1558. 1st edition; small 4to; (4), 41, (1) leaves, woodcut device on titlepage and last leaf, woodcut historiated initials, 2 text diagrams, faint tide lines in blank margins of few leaves; otherwise fine, wide margined copy; modern boards. Riccardi II 273; BM STC Italian p. 513; Thorndike VI pp. 27-28.   Jeffrey Mancevice 20-68   1996 $1,250.00

PICCOLOMINI, ALESSANDRO   La Seconda Parte de la Filosofia Naturale... Venice: Vincenzo Valgrisio, 1554. small square 8vo; pages (16), 450, (29), woodcut diagrams and figures, early worn limp vellum with ms. title; Adams P1117.   Family Album Tillers-488   1996 $300.00

PICCOLPASSO, CIPRIANO   The Three Books of the Potter's Art. London: 1980. Small folio; 2 volumes; original quarter cloth, printed paper labels, as new in original cloth slipcase.   James Fenning 133-265   1996 £65.00

PICKERING, C.   Chronological History of Plants... Dehra Dun: 1986. 4to; 1238 apges; portrait; art leather.   Wheldon & Wesley 207-270 1996 £75.00

PICKERING, HENRY   The Ruins of Paestum; and Other Compositions in Verse. (with) Athens: and Other Poems. Salem: 1822/24. 1st editions; 4to; 128, 84 pages; old three quarter calf worn, spine very chipped. Each title inscribed to same recipient (first name partially trimmed by binder) on prelim blank.   M & S Rare Books 60-217   1996 $225.00

PICKERING, JOHN   A Vocabulary, or Collection of Words and Phrases Which Have Been Supposed to be Peculiar to the United States of America. Boston: 1816. 1st edition; 8vo; 206 pages, plus errata leaf; original plain boards, rebacked, uncut, very nice. S&S 38631; Sabin 62638.   M & S Rare Books 60-396   1996 $400.00

PICKETT, ALBERT JAMES   History of Alabama and Incidentally of Georgia and Mississippi from the Earliest Period. Sheffield: Robert C. Randolph, 1896. Reprint of 1851 edition; 8vo; frontispiece; original drab cloth, some wear; Howes P346   Glenn Books 36-236   196 $175.00

PICKETT, WILLIAM   Studies for Landscape. London: T. Clay, 1812. Large oblong folio; 96 charming illustrations on 24 aquatint plates, issued without any accompanying text; contemporary half red roan and marbled boards, large red gilt label on upper cover, corners very neatly repaired and some foxing; very good, rare, with good dark impressions.   Ken Spelman 30-31   1996 £240.00

PICO DELLA MIRANDOLA, GIOVANNI FRANCESCO   De Rervm Praenotione Libri Novem. Strasbourg: Knobloch for Schurer, 1507. Folio; contemporary blind panelled calf over boards, rebacked; 19th century bookplate and contemporary 16th century ownership inscription on title margin, inner margins of first leaves rehinged, top edge of 1st leaf repaired, with autograph annotations in several contemporary hands. Rostenberg & Stern 150-93   1996 $4,500.00

THE PICTURE of London for 1816. London: Longman, 1816. 17th edition; 12mo; title, pages xii, 4 ff., 340 pages, 12 page catalogue, 6 engraved maps or plans; sheep, rebacked. Marlborough 162-169 1996 £100.00

PICTURE Story of Preparing Tea. N.P.: n.d., ca. 1900. 8vo; accordion fold, bound in brown silk, paper label. Appelfeld Gallery 54-175 1996 $250.00

PICTURESQUE Europe. London: Cassell, Petter and Galpin, c. 1870. 4to; 5 volumes; half calf, volume 5 has front cover loose and slightly rubbed. Petersfield Bookshop FH58-435 1996 £170.00

THE PICTURESQUE Mediterranean. London: Paris & Melbourne: Cassell & Co., ca. 1890. Special edition, for subscribers only; 4to; 4 volumes; full page and in-text illustrations; original red cloth, all edges gilt, bright, very good to near fine set. Chapel Hill 94-85 1996 $175.00

PIDSLEY, WILLIAM E. H. The Birds of Devonshire. London: W. W. Gibbings and J. G. Commin, 1891. 1st edition; 8vo; pages xxxii, 194; hand colored lithograph frontispiece, large folding map at rear; original green cloth, gilt vignette of bird of prey on upper cover; fine. Mullens & Swann p. 471. Sotheran PN32-96 1996 £298.00

PIERCE, W. E., & CO. Boise Idaho. Topeka: Hall Litho. Co., ca. 1898. 1st edition; 38, (1) pages; illustrations; original printed cream wrappers stamped in green; very fine. Michael D. Heaston 23-178 1996 $225.00

PIERPONT, JOHN The Anti-Slavery Poems. Boston: Oliver Johnson, 1843. 1st edition; 16mo; 64 pages, illustration; original printed wrappers, lower portion of back wrapper lacking. LCP/HSP Afro Americana Cat. 8202; R&B 43-4089. M & S Rare Books 60-218 1996 $125.00

PIERS PLOWMAN The Vision and the Creed of Piers Ploughman. London: William Pickering, 1842. 2 volumes, pages xlix, (3), 272; (4), (273-) 629, title and folding frontispiece printed in red and black; original cloth, rubbed and little worn at extremities, paper labels (browned); good set; Bookplate of Col. Sir Charles J. Hamilton. Claude Cox 107-201 1996 £85.00

PIERSON, JOSIAH Millennium, a Poem in five Books. Rochester: Pub. by Tyler & Chipman, 1831. 1st edition; 8vo; 81, (2) pages; sewn, lacking covers, lower edge uncut. Rare printing. B&B 8762; Gaustad p. 236. M & S Rare Books 60-102 1996 $375.00

PIERSON, THOMAS Roseberry-Toppin; or the Prospect of a Summer's day. Stokesley: for the author, by N. Taylerson, 1783. 1st edition; 8vo; pages (ii), 28; recent wrappers, very good. Not in Aubin, Jackson or NUC. Simon Finch 24-183 1996 £650.00

PIETERSE, A. H. Aquatic Weeds: the Ecology and Management of Nuisance Aquatic Vegetation. London: 1990. 8vo; 500 pages; illustrations; hardback. Wheldon & Wesley 207-1442 1996 £75.00

PIGAULT-LEBRUN, CHARLES ANTOINE GUILLAUME PIGAULT DE L'EPONY My Uncle Thomas. A Romance. New York: printed by Isaac Riley for John Brannan, 1810. 1st American edition and apparently 1st edition in English; 12mo; 2 volumes; original boards, minor spine chipping, printed paper labels (1 label chipped); uncut as issued. Some inconsequential browning and foxing, but fine, totally untouched copy; early bookplates in each volume. Bowe F723; AI 21087. Howard S. Mott 227-113 1996 $700.00

PIGGOTT BROTHERS & CO. Marquees, Tents and Folding Furniture for Abroad. London: Doulton, ca. 1910-20. Octavo; 50 paes wood engravings and photos; printed grey wrappers with light wear to extremities. Fine. Bromer Booksellers 90-237 1996 $185.00

PIGOT, RICHARD The Life of Man, Symbolised by the Months of the Year. London: Longmans, Gree, Reader and Dyer, 1866. 1st edition; 4to; xii, 240 pages, unnumbered plates; each page bears some illumiantion, many leaves are in two colors; publisher's full morocco binding, all edges gilt fine, scarce book. Bookpress 75-78 1996 $385.00

PIGOTT, CHARLES The Jockey Club; or a Sketch of the Manners of the Age. New York: Re-printed by Thomas Greenleaf, 1793. 1st American edition; 8vo; 205 pages; old calf, spine shot. M & S Rare Books 60-415 1996 $200.00

PIKE, ZEBULON MONTGOMERY 1779-1813 An Account of Expeditions to the Sources of the Mississippi, and through the Western Parts of Louisiana, to the Sources of the Arkansaw, Kans, La Platte and Pierre Jaun Rivers; Peformed by Order of the Government of the U.S.... Philadelphia: 1810. 1st edition; 278, (4), 66, 53, 87 pages; lacking all maps and portraits; Wagner Camp Becker 9; Streeter Texas 1047; Graff 3290; Field 1217. Blue River Books 9-257 1996 $500.00

PIKE, ZEBULON MONTGOMERY 1779-1813 Th Expeditions of Zebulon Montgomery Pike. Minneapolis: Ross & Haines, 1965. Facsimile reproduction of 1895 Coues edition; 3 volumes in 2; pages cxiii, 356; vi, 357-955, 6 folding maps in rear pocket; slipcase somewhat worn, volumes fine. Dumont 28-62 1996 $120.00

PILCHER, LEWIS STEPHEN A List of Books by Some of the Old Masters of Medicine and Surgery Together with Books on the History of Medicine and on Medical Biography in the Possession of Lewis Stephen Pilcher... Brooklyn: 1918. Limited to 250 copies; 201 pages; original binding. W. Bruce Fye 71-1667 1996 $250.00

PILCHER, LEWIS STEPHEN A List of Books by some of the Old Masters of Medicine and Surgery Together With Books on the History of Medicine and on Medical Biography in the Possession of Lewis Stephen Pilcher. Brooklyn: 1918. Limited to 250 copies; 8vo; 201 pages; original linen backed boards, light wear. James Tait Goodrich K40-43 1996 $165.00

PILE, GRAFT M. An Address on Intellectual Development. Delivered...Illinois State University. Springfield: Richards & Smith, 1856. 1st edition; 8vo; 20 pages; original printed wrappers. Byrd 2519. M & S Rare Books 60-343 1996 $125.00

PILGRIM, THOMAS Live Boys; or, Charley and Nasho in Texas. Boston & New York: 1878. 12mo; 308 pages, frontispiece, 5 plates, 10 pages ads; mustard cloth with black and gilt stamping; nice, lightly soiled, presentation on endpaper. Howes M790; Adams Herd 1572; Graff 3294; Raines p. 165. Bohling Book Co. 191-119 1996 $300.00

PILLSBURY, ARTHUR C. Picturing Miracles of Plant and Animal Life. Philadelphia: 1937. 1st edition; 66 illustrations; dust jacket slightly torn and edge worn; uncommon with jacket; inscribed, signed. J. B. Muns 154-234 1996 $100.00

PIM, BEDFORD The Gate of the Pacific. London: Lovell Reeve & Co., 1863. 1st edition; demy 8vo; (xiv), 432 pages; maps, some folding, chromolitho plates; neat recent half morocco, banded and gilt, contrasting labels, few minor marks and spots, but very good. Ash Rare Books Zenzybyr-74 1996 £195.00

PINDAR Pindar's Odes of Victory: The Olympian and Pythian Odes. Stratford-upon-Avon: Shakespeare Head Press, 1929. Limited to 100 copies; quarto; xxii, 300 pages; wood engravings by John Farleigh; in cloth backed, gilt speckled boards that have some fading about the extremities and bumping at corners, near fine, slightly worn slipcase with printed label on front. Bromer Booksellers 87-68 1996 $375.00

PINDAR (Greek Title) Olympia. Glasgow: R. & A. Foulis, 1754. Miniature 8vo; pages (1), 158, Greek text; lovely copy, bound in contemporary full morocco gilt with classical bird tool on spine. Gaskell 274. Family Album Tillers-490 1996 $235.00

PINE, GEORGE W. Beyond the West. Utica: 1870. 1st edition; 444 pages, illustrations; decorated cloth, spine sunned, otherwise very good+, scarce. Herd 1803. Howes P381. T. A. Swinford 49-904 1996 $250.00

PINEL, PHILLIPE Traite medico-Philosophique sur l'Alienation Mentale, ou la Manie. Pairs: Chez Richard, Caille et Ravier Libraires, 1801. 1st edition; 8vo; lvi, 318 pages, 2 copperplates; contemporary leather backed marbled boards, rare. GM 4922. John Gach 150-364 1996 $2,250.00

PINERO, ARTHUR The Enchanted Cottage. London: William Heinemann, 1922. 1st published edition; 8vo; original printed wrappers, some creasing, tear repaired on upper cover, upper cover detached, ligt marginal browning, else very good; inscribed by author for Louis Evan Shipman, tipped in TLS sending the volume to Shipman. James Cummins 14-156 1996 $350.00

PINKERTON, JOHN The Medallic History of England. London: E. Harding, 1802. Folio; 112 pages + 40 copper engraved plates, each witl many illustrations; uncut, nicely bound ca. 1900 in brown polished calf. Kenneth Karmiole 1NS-201 1996 $375.00

PINKERTON, JOHN   Rimes. London: for Charles Dilly, 1782. 2nd edition; 8vo; (xxx), 226; frontispiece, spotted and stained, title vignette; 19th century mottled calf, gilt roll border to sides, spine in compartments with raised bands, gilt rules, floral and other ornaments, red and green morocco labels, very slight wear at extremities, marbled endpapers, bookplates, few trivial repairs internally, but excellent copy. Simon Finch 24-184 1996 £50.00

PINKHAM, DANIEL   Symphony No. 1 for Orchestra. New York: Peters, 1961. 1st edition; small 4to; 72 pages; stiff cream wrappers, very good, publisher's complimentary copy (stamped on upper cover); signed and inscribed on titlepage by Pinkham to dedicatee Carl Haverlin.   George J. Houle 68-116 1996 $375.00

PINKS, WILLIAM J.   The History of Clerkenwell. London: by the Proprietor, J. T. Pickburn, 1865. Large 8vo; pages xx, 800, 2 ff., folding map, numerous text and full page illustrations; modern full red morocco, top edge gilt.   Marlborough 162-192 1996 £110.00

PINTER, HAROLD 1930-   The French Lieutenant's Woman. Boston: Little Brown, 1981. 1st edition; signed by Pinter and Fowles. unopened, original acetate, spectacular copy.   Bev Chaney, Jr. 23-228 1996 $165.00

PIOZZI, HESTER LYNCH SALUSBURY THRALE 1741-1821   Anecdotes of the Late Samuel Johnson During the Last Twenty Years f His Life. London: Cadell, 1786. 2nd edition; small octavo; pages 307; fine recent rebinding in full polished morocco, raised bands, blind fillets, gilt in panels, gilt title; fine. Courtney 161.   Hartfield 48-L49 1996 $425.00

PIOZZI, HESTER LYNCH SALUSBURY THRALE 1741-1821   Anecdotes of the Late Samuel Johnson... London: T. Cadell, 1786. 2nd edition; 8vo; half title present, pages viii, 306, (1); contemporary marbled calf, some surface wear, smooth backstrip with wavy, pointille, foliate rolls, gilt dulled, red label with rope roll border, 'hound's tooth' roll border on sides, board edges gilt hatched, marbled endpapers, very good; half title present, signature of early owner D. Gell.   Blackwell's B112-226 1996 £175.00

PIOZZI, HESTER LYNCH SALUSBURY THRALE 1741-1821   Autobiography, Letters and Literary Remains. London: Longman, 1861. 1st edition; revised issue; octavo; pages 358 and 407; 2 volumes, 24 page Longman catalog at back of volume 1 and printed ads on each pastedown; frontispiece, errata sheet, half titles, half blindstamped cloth; very good. CBEL II 137.   Hartfield 48-A14 1996 $295.00

PIOZZI, HESTER LYNCH SALUSBURY THRALE 1741-1821   British Synonymy; or, an Attempt at Regulating the Choice of Words in Familiar Conversation... Dublin: William Porter for P. Byrne & W. Jones, 1794. 1st Dublin edition; contemporary speckled calf, spine with double bands in gilt, red label, handsome copy. Alston III. 535.   Granard booklabel. Jarndyce 103-Jarndyce 103-323 1996 £380.00

PIOZZI, HESTER LYNCH SALUSBURY THRALE 1741-1821   Retrospection or a Review of the Most Striking and Important Events, Characters, Situations and Their Consequences, Which the Last Eighteen Hundred Years Have Presented to the View of Mankind. London: printed for John Stockdale, 1801. 1st edition; 4to; half titles, 2 volumes, engraved portrait by M. Bovi, 3 page list of subscribers, 1 page of ads; contemporary tree calf, upper hinges partly cracked, spines gilt, labels. Rothschild 1553.   Anthony W. Laywood 108-217 1996 £220.00

PIPER, EVELYN   Bunny Lake Is Missing. New York: Harper, 1957. 1st edition; fine in fine dust jacket with tiny tear and little darkening to edges of rear panel; scarce.   Between the Covers 42-504 1996 $150.00

PIPER, H. B.   Junkyard Planet. Putnam, 1963. 1st edition; fine in near fine dust jacket with some slight dust soil to rear dust jacket panel; inscribed by author, rare thus;   Aronovitz 57-940 1996 $675.00

PIPER, W.   The Little Engine That Could. P&M, 1930. 1st edition thus; full color illustrations by L. L. Lenski; one page chipped at corners with no loss of text, else relatively bright, very good/very good+ copy. Aronovitz 57-941 1996 $125.00

PIPPET, GABRIEL   A Little Rosary. Flansham: Pear Tree Press, 1930. Limited edition, 5/20 copies, initialled by printer "JG"; 16mo; pages (25), 15 wood engravings printed in blue, frontispiece in green, engraved titlepage and press-device in mauve, all by Gabriel Pippet, letterpress printed in mauve and green; original silver boards overprinted overall with design in gilt, printed front cover label which includes engraving by Pippet printed in blue, front hinge cracked, bookticket, untrimmed, good. Blackwell's B112-221 1996 £100.00

PIROGOV, NIKOLAI IVANOVICH   Nicol Pirogoff's Chirurgische Anatomie der Arterienstamme und Fascien. Leizpig: and Heidelberg, 1860. Revised edition; 8vo; 2 volumes, including atlas with 50 partly colored lithographic plates; contemporary boards, worn, backstrip of atlas damaged, some foxing, especially of plates. Waller 7463; Hirsch IV 614.   Argosy 810-399 1996 $1,500.00

PIRSIG, ROBERT M.   Zen and the Art of Motorcyle Maintenance. New York: Morrow, 1974. 1st edition; very good+ copy in very good+ dust jacket.   Book Time 2-826 1996 $180.00

PIRSIG, ROBERT M.   Zen and the Art of Motorcylce Maintenance. New York: Morrow, 1974. 1st edition; perfectbound, some slight spotting to top edge of pages, otherwise near fine in near fine jacket with one very small gouge on front panel.   Ken Lopez 74-375 1996 $125.00

PISSARRO, LUCIEN   The Gentle Art - A Collection of Books and Wood Engravings by Lucien Pissarro. Zurich: L'Art Ancien S.A., 1974. One of 350 copies; illustrations in black and white; boards, spine slightly faded, head and tail of spine and top edge of upper cover slightly bumped, very good; loosely inserted is a price list for the exhibits; from the library of James D. Hart.   Ulysses 39-466 1996 £65.00

PISSARRO, LUCIEN   Notes on the Eragny Press and a Letter to J. B. Manson. Cambridge University Press, 1957. Limited to 500 copies; small 8vo; 11 illustrations by Pissaro, 2 text figures, viii, 16, (22), 39-52 pages; original patterned boards, fine.   Thomas Thorp 489-245 1996 £185.00

PITCAIRN, W. D.   Two Years Among the Savages of New Guinea. London: 1891. 286 pages, 4 page appendix; original red gilt cloth, ex-library, uniform light browning, otherwise tight; Ferguson 14178. Antipodean 28-193 196 $120.00

PITISCUS, BARTHOLOMAEUS   Canon Manvel des Sinvs, Tovchantaes et Covppantes... Parais: Abraham Picard, 1619. Much corrected edition; small 8vo; ff. (130), Roman letter with italic dedication and introduction, engraved printer's device on title, woodcut initials and ornaments, 182 pages of tables, many diagrams, old ms. diagram on pastedown, ms. note in margin of 1 page, 2 inconspicuous repairs at edges of leaves, top corner of 1 leaf soiled, very light waterstaining along upper blank edges; contemporary vellum. Not in BM STC Fr. 1601-1700 or Honeyman. This edition not in NUC.   A. Sokol XXV-76 1996 £750.00

PITKIN, TIMOTHY   A Statistical View of the Commerce of the United States of America... Hartford: printed by Charles Hosmer, 1816. 1st edition; 8vo; xii, 407, (1), xix, (1) pages, errata on verso of final leaf; contemporary calf, gilt, rather worn, head and foot of spine chipped, joints cracked; 19th century armorial bookplate of Robert Hyde Greg (1795-1875), the economist and politician.   John Drury 82-220 1996 £150.00

PITTENGER, PEGGY   Morgan Horses. S. Brunswick: Barnes, 1967. 1st edition; original binding, very good copy in good+ dust jacket; signed presentation copy.   October Farm 36-258 1996 $125.00

PITTER, RUTH   Poems 1926-1966. London: Barrie & Rockliff/The Cresset Press Ltd., 1968. 1st edition; original binding, small marks on front pastedown and contents page, fore-edge slightly spotted, head and tail of spine slightly bumped, very good in nicked, spotted and slightly rubbed, and creased dust jacket faded at spine and edges; signed and dated by author.   Ulysses 39-467 1996 £55.00

PITTILOCH, ROBERT   Oppression Under the Colour of the Law, or, My Lord Hrarse His New Practicks As a Way-Marke for Peaceable Subjects to Be Ware of Pleying with a Hot Spirited Lord of the Session... Edinburgh: 1827. 4to; pages iv, 32; old boards, spine defective edges little worn; very scarce. Wing P2311.   R.F.G. Hollett 76-240 1996 £220.00

PITY'S GIFT: a Collection of Interesting Tales to Excite the Compassion of Youth for the Animal Creation. London: Newbery, 1798. 12mo; viii, 147 pages; woodcut vignettes by John Bewick; 19th century three quarter red morocco and marbled boards, extremities lightly rubbed, else fine. Bromer Booksellers 87-112 1996 $300.00

PIUS II, POPE 1405-1464   Epistolae Familiares. Nuremberg: Anton Koberger 17 July, 1486. Quarto; 246 leaves (first blank), gothic letter, initials spaces, initials supplied in alternate blue and red, paragraph marks in red, corner torn from first blank leaf and patched, insignificant wormhole in gutter of few leaves but generally good, clean copy; 19th century half sheep, marbled boards; from the collection of George Kloss, with his bookplate and ink note of the Panzer no. and Manhattan College, New York with bookplate.   H. M. Fletcher 121-15 1996 £2,300.00

PLACCAET Ende Ordinantie Ons Heeren des Coninks, Daerby Wordt Geboden...Dat Die Placcaten Hiervoormaels Gepubliceert Opt Stuck Vande Calmynen wel...Worden Onderhouden (etc). Brussels: Rutgheert Velplus, 1590. 4to; 4 unnumbered, unsigned leaves, Gothic letter, woodcut of royal arms on titlepage, printer's splendid device on verso of last; untrimmed copy in marbled boards; very good. BM STC Dutch p. 152; Bockx-Indestege, Belg. Typogr 3589.   A. Sokol XXV-77 1996 £450.00

PLAIN Reasons Addressed to the People of Great Britain, Against the (intended) Petittion to Parliament from the Owners and Occupiers of Land in the County of Lincoln, for Leave to Export Wool. Leeds: printed by Wright and Son, 1782. 1st edition; 8vo; woodcut vignette of a sheep on title, 45 pages, with final blank C8; disbound. Kress B496; Goldsmith 12289; Black 1212.   Anthony W. Laywood 109-114 1996 £275.00

PLANTE, DAVID   The Ghost of Henry James. Boston: Gambit, 1970. 1st edition; fine in dust jacket with some insignificant rubbing, beautiful copy, author's uncommon first book.   Between the Covers 42-354 1996 $125.00

PLATH, SYLVIA 1932-1963   Ariel. London: Faber and Faber, 1965. 1st edition; 8vo; fine in fine dust jacket; Presentation copy "The brown stains on top edge and cover are thatch-drip from leaking roof of Court Green (where SP had lived) in the winter of 1965/6. Ted Hughes". Lakin & Marley 3-47 1996 $650.00

PLATH, SYLVIA 1932-1963   The Bell Jar. London: Heinemann, 1963. 1st edition; 8vo; fine, in near fine dust jacket (just lightly soiled on white and vulnerable lower panel, with one or two tiny creases at spine ends and top edge of upper panel;   Lakin & Marley 3-45 1996 $2,750.00

PLATH, SYLVIA 1932-1963   Crossing the Water. London: Faber and Faber Ltd., 1971. 1st edition; original binding, endpapers partially browned, head and tail of spine and corners slightly rubbed and very slightly bumped, covers slightly bowed, very good in slightly marked and dusty dust jacket.   Ulysses 39-468 1996 £85.00

PLATH, SYLVIA 1932-1963   Fiesta Melons. Exeter: Rougemont Press, 1971. Limited edition, 150 copies, this no. 29 of 75 copies, signed by Ted Hughes who provides introduction; 8 1/2 x 10 3/4 inches; drawings by Sylvia Plath; fine in dust jacket with one tiny chip at head of spine, prospectus laid in.   Virgo Books 48-156 4996 £200.00

PLATINA, BARTOLOMEO 1421-1481   The Lives of the Popes. London: 1685. 1st edition; folio; pages (28), 416; 394, (18); foxed; modern binding.   Family Album Tillers-492 1996 $260.00

PLATO   Crito, a Socratic Dialogue. Paris: Pleiad, 1926. Number 361 of 475 copies; 9.5 x 6.5 inches; xxxvi, (1) pages; brown marbled paper boards with title label on spine, vellum trip at top and bottom of spine; particularly fine, box slightly bumped at extremities.   Joshua Heller 21-174 1996 $600.00

PLATO   Crito; a Socratic Dialogue. Paris: Pleiad, 1926. One of 475 numbered copies; large 8vo; printed in Arrighi Vincenza italic; marbled boards with printed label on spine, corners and head of backstrip little worn, otherwise very nice, bookplate (by Reynolds Stone).   Bertram Rota 272-338 1996 £280.00

PLATO   Crito. Paris: printed at the Officina Bodoni, Montagnola for, Pleiad, 1926. Number 64 of 470 copies; 8vo; printed on Binda handmade paper (5 on Japanese vellum); pages xxxvi, (2); original marbled boards, paper label, vellum caps at head and tail of backstrip, uncut, hinges rubbed and corners just bumped, generally well preserved. From the library of Ruari McLean. Mardersteig 16.   Claude Cox 107-120 1996 £180.00

PLATO   Crito. Paris: the Pleiad, 1929. Limited edition, number 139 of 475 copies; slim oblong 8vo; original marbled covered boards in worn slipcase, one small bump along joint of upper board, else fine.   Glenn Books 36-207 1996 $225.00

PLATO   The Dialogues of Plato. Oxford: at the Clarendon Press, 1875. 2nd edition; 8vo; 5 volumes in 11; half brown calf and marbled sides, matching endpapers, gilt flowers on spine, black morocco spine labels, spine ends chipped, spines and extremities little rubbed, some light marginal notations (some in ink), but still very good.   James Cummins 14-157 1995 $1,000.00

PLATO   Lysis, or Friendship: the Symposium & Phaedrus. New York: Limited Editions Club, 1968. One of 1500 numbered copies, signed by artist; illustrations by Eugene Karlin; fine in publisher's slipcase. Hermitage SP95-1023 1996 $125.00

PLATO   Phaedon; or, a Dialogue on the Immortality of the Soul. New York: Gowan, 1833. 1st American edition from the rare London edition; 12mo; 209 pages plus ads; original cloth backed boards, worn; foxed, partially uncut. AI 20742.   Family Album Tillers-494 1996 $100.00

PLATO   Opera... Paris: Badius, 1518. Folio; 398 leaves, woodcut printer's device and title border, large crible initials, printed shoulder notes, marginal repairs, 18th century boards, scuffed, backstrip worn, many early marginalia, very good. NUC 466.122 (3 copies); Renouard 2.168 no. 389; Moreau 2.498 no. 1922.   Bennett Gilbert LL29-62 1996 $3,250.00

PLATO   (Greek title) Divini Platonis Opera Omnia Qua Extant. Frankfurt: Marnium & Aubrii, 1602. Large folio; pages 36, 1355, 25, Greek and Latin text; first and last leaves with old repairs; early full leather, should be rebacked, very scarce. Brunet IV 695.   Family Album Tillers-493 1996 $850.00

PLATT, A. E.   The History of the Parish and Grammar School of Sedbergh. London: Longmans, Green & Co., 1876. 1st (only) edition. 8vo; pages 197; original cloth, gilt; scarce.   R.F.G. Hollett & Son 78-1191 1996 £150.00

PLATT, A. E.   The History of the Parish and Grammar School of Sedbergh. London: Longmans, Green and Co., 1876. 1st (only) edition; 8vo; 197 pages;   R.F.G. Hollett & Son 78-1192 1996 £120.00

PLATT, CHARLES A.   Monograph of the Work of Charles A. Platt. New York: Architectural Book Publishing Co., 1925. Large heavy folio; photos, plans and drawings; cloth, fine in nice dust jacket with few closed tears;   Marilyn Braiterman 15-162 1996 $300.00

PLATT, HUGH   The Jewel House of Art and Nature... London: Bernard Alsop, 1653. 2nd edition; 4to; contemporary sheep, spine chipped, morocco label, chipped, hinges reinforced with cloth tape, woodcut border to titlepage, text woodcuts. Wing P2390. Toole Stott (Conjuring) 571; Hall 230; Bitting p. 373.   Dramatis Personae 37-140 1996 $950.00

PLATT, P. L.   Travelers' Guide Across the Plains Upon the Overland Route to California. John Howell, 1963. Reprinted from the 1852 edition; limited edition; facsimile of original map tipped in. Howes P417. Maggie Lambeth 30-418 1996 $200.00

PLATT, T. P.   A Catalogue of the Ethiopic Biblical Manuscripts in the Royal Library of Paris, and in the Library of the British and Foreign Bible Society, Also some Account of Those in the Vatican Library at Rome. London: Richard Watts, 1823. 4to; folding frontispiece, 1 plate; original boards, worn, spine torn with small section missing, starting.   Maggs Bros. Ltd. 1191-163 1996 £115.00

PLATTES, GABRIEL   Practical Husbandry Improved; or, a Discovery of Infinite Treasure, Hidden since the Worlds Beginning. London: printed for Edward Thomas & to be sold at his House in Green Arbor, 1656. 4to; (28), 92 pages; disbound, very good. Wing P2413; Goldsmiths 1368; Kress 941.   C. R. Johnson 37-24 1996 £1,350.00

PLAUTUS, TITUS MACCIUS   M. Plauti Comodiae XX, ex Antiquis, Recentiorbusque Exemplaribus Inucicem Collatis... Paris: Robert Stephani, 1530. Folio; (10), 256 leaves; all edges gilt, bound in handsome 18th century olive morocco with wide gilt dentelles on boards, richly decorated spine; attractive copy. Schreiber 43; Renouard 34/11. Family Album Tillers-497 1996 $1,400.00

PLAY Hours Story Book. London: Nister, n.d. 4to; inscription dated 1912; 6 color plates, many black and white illustrations; glazed pictorial boards, extremities rubbed and front corner worn, rear cover soiled, else very good.   Marjorie James 19-169 1996 £65.00

PLAYFAIR, JOHN   The Works of John Playfair... Edinburgh: 1822. 8vo; 4 volumes, half calf, rather worn and repaired, spines varnished; half calf, rather worn and repaired, spines varnished, few ex-library marks but no obtrusive stamps, joints cracked; rare; portrait and obituary of Playfair pasted in front of volume 1.   Wheldon & Wesley 207-85 1996 £600.00

PLAYFAIR, WILLIAM   Thoughts On the Present State of French Politics and the Necessity and Policy of Diminishing France. London: John Stockdale, 1793. 1st edition; 8vo; viii, (90-187, (1) pages; 2 folding hand colored maps; some browning and spotting; contemporary half calf, rebacked and restored, spine gilt with label; good copy, attractively bound. Goldsmiths 15559; not in Kress or Einaudi.   John Drury 82-221 1996 £250.00

PLEASANTS, J. E., MRS.   History of Orange County, California. Los Angeles: J. R. Finnell & Sons, 1931. 10 1/8 x 6 1/2 inches; 3 volumes, numerous full page and text photographic illustrations; black fabricoid, front inner hinge of volume 2 weak, little mild wear and spotting. Dawson's Books Shop 528-197 1997 $300.00

PLEY, ARTHUR F. E.   St. Paul's Cathedral. London: For the author, 1927. Folio; pages xvi, 29, viii appendices, 22 numbered plates, including frontispiece; bound by Zaehnsdorf in half morocco over cloth boards, gilt stamped design to centre of upper board showing the west elevation of the cathedral, top edge gilt, marbled endpapers. Good, clean copy. Sotheran PN32-191 1996 £298.00

PLEYNET, MARCELIN   Robert Motherwell. Paris: Papierski, 1989. Folio; 243 pages, numerous plates, many in color; cloth, dust jacket, slipcase. Brannan 43-461 1996 $165.00

THE PLIMPTON Press Year Book: an Exhibit of Versatility. Norwood: 1911. 1st edition; 8vo; 254, 83 pages, including samples of bookbindings and other illustrations; cloth; very good.   The Bookpress 75-338 1996 $150.00

PLINIUS CAECILIUS SECUNDUS, C. 61-112   Epistolarum Libri X and Panegyricus. Leiden: Ex Officina Elseviriorum Lugd. Batavorum, 1640. Small 24mo; pages (24), 414, (14), with lacunae, Solitaire printer's mark; lovely full polished French calf, gilt cipher of the Dukes of Orleans(?), spine handsomely gilt, all edges gilt, old marginalia. Dibdin II 331; Willems 506; Brunet IV 722.   Family Album Tillers-507 1996 $325.00

PLINIUS CAECILIUS SECUNDUS, C. 61-112   Novocomensis Epistolarum Libri Deceum... Venice: November, 1508. 1st Aldine edition; 8vo; italic, Aldine device on laste leaf; rubbed full 19th century morocco with nice foliated gilt roll around boards, marbled edges, early ms. ownerships, some old dampstain and spotting that apparently came when the edges were marbled; Fletcher 112-115; Renouard 53.3. Admas P1536; UCLA I/82.   Family Album Tillers-506 1996 $2,000.00

PLINIUS SECUNDUS, C. 23-79   Historie de la Peinture Ancienne... London: William Bowyer, 1725. Folio; pages (18), 308, 8; fine frontispiece, another plate and devices; contemporary French full mottled calf, joints broken; handsome copy; Cloisters Ex-libris. Brunet IV 719. Family Album Tillers-505 1996 $250.00

PLINIUS SECUNDUS, C. 23-79   Historia Naturale... Venice: Alessandro Griffo, 1580. 4to; 55, 1188 pages; woodcut printer's device on titlepage with ornamental title border and woodcut initials; contemporary limp vellum; fine. BM STC Italian p. 527; not in Adams.   Jeffrey Mancevice 20-69 1996 $850.00

PLINIUS SECUNDUS, C. 23-79   Historia Mundi Naturalis. Frankfurt am Main: Ex. Off. Martinus Lechlerus, Impensis Sigismundi Feyerabendij, 1582. Folio; pages (32), 528, (50); (188);, Index lacks 8 leaves, main text apparenly lacks only one blank, titlepage backed, slight worming; magnificently illustrated, 54 woodcuts; late half calf, boards detached. Dibdin II 323.   Family Album Tillers-504 1996 $1,250.00

PLINIUS SECUNDUS, C. 23-79   The Historie of the World: Commonly called, the Natural Historie of C. Plinius Secundus. London: 1634-35. 2nd edition; folio; 2 volumes in 1; pages (lviii), 614, (xxxii); (xii), 632, (lxxxiv), ad; contemporary calf, rebacked preserving most of spine, wormhole from T2 to Y2, blank corner of titlepage torn away and repaired, otherwise better than average copy.   John Henly 27-142 1996 £420.00

PLOMER, HENRY R.   English Printers' Ornaments. London: Grafton & Co., 1924. 1st edition; one of 500 copies; 4to; frontispiece, facsimiles; original cloth backed boards, corners bumped, uncut, top edge gilt; Ruari McLean's copy with signature and bookplate.   Forest Books 74-356 1996 £95.00

PLOMER, WILLIAM   The Case is Altered. London: Hogarth Press, 1932. 1st edition; original binding, top edge dusty, prelims, edges and endpapers spotted, spine and cover edges darkened and slightly rubbed, very good in nicked, creased, rubbed, spotted, marked and dusty, slightly torn dust jacket by John Banting, browned at spine and edges. Ulysses 39-469 1996 £75.00

PLOMER, WILLIAM   Turbot Wolfe. London: 1925. 1st edition; 1000 copies printed; author's first book; signed by Leonard Woolf; original binding, top edge dusty, tail of spine slightly bumped, cover edges slightly rubbed, endpapers slightly spotted, very good in nicked, torn, rubbed and dusty, slightly creased and soiled dust jacket browned at spine and edges, and missing a small piece at head of spine.   Ulysses 39-294 1996 £375.00

PLOSS, HERMANN   Woman: an Historical, Gynaecological and Anthropological Compendium. London: 1935. 1st English translation; 3 volumes, 655, 822, 543 pages; more than 1000 illustrations; original binding; scarce. GM 179.   W. Bruce Fye 71-1672 1996 $600.00

PLOT, ROBERT   The Natural History of Oxford-Shire, Being an Essay Toward the Natural History of England. at the theater in Oxford, 1677. 1st edition; folio; (10), 358, 1 f. errata, (10) page index, prelim imprimatur leaf, vignette titlepage, folding map and 16 engraved plates; contemporary calf, blind ruled panel, expertly rebacked with new gilt label; near contemporary ms. insdex on prelim blank and chapter numbers added by hand to the upper margin of each leaf; contemporary signature of Taylor Russell to front endpaper and Henry Blake to titlepage; good copy.   Ken Spelman 30-101 1996 £580.00

PLUMB, CHARLES S.   Little Sketches of Famous Beef Cattle. Columbus: 1904. 1st edition; 99 pages; cloth, very good+, very scarce. T. A. Swinford 49-910 1996 $125.00

PLUMPTRE, C. E.   Giordano Bruno: a Tale of the Sixteenth Century. London: Chapman and Hall, 1884. 1st edition; 8vo; pages xvii, 278, 292; 2 volumes; brown cloth, gilt and black, unopened; very good, bright copy, scarce. 6 copies in NUC; Wolff 5574.   Hartfield 48-V39 1996 $295.00

PLUTARCHUS   Plutarch's Lives. Philadelphia: William Brown for Hickman and Hazzard, 1822. New edition; 8vo; 4 volumes; frontispiece; contemporary roll mottled roan, spine gilt, morocco labels, some joints weak; ms. ownerships of John P. Bigelow and Prescott Bigelow. Family Album Tillers-511 1996 $140.00

PLUTARCHUS 45-125   Libellus...Quomodo ab Adulatore Discernatur Amicus. Rome: Jacopo Mazochius, 1514. 1st edition; 4to; (34) leaves; beautiful black on white, architectural woodcut title border and woodcut printer's device at end, Roman type with sections in Greek; some light marginal foxing; later vellum over boards; rare. Sander 5774; Hoffmann III 202;   Jeffrey Mancevice 20-70 1996 $1,850.00

PLUTARCHUS 45-125   The Lives of the Noble Grecians and Romanes, Compared Together... London: by Thomas Vautroullier and for John Wight, 1579. 1st edition in English; there is another state of the imprint in which Wight's name is omitted; priority between the two, if any, is not known; folio in sixes; pages (xiv), 1175; Vautrollier's woodcut printer's device on title (McK. 170) and at colophon, woodcut medallion portraits within ornamental borders at beginning of each Life, woodcut initials, head and tailpieces; 17th century panelled calf, neatly rebacked with old spine laid down, later red morocco label, rather browned, scattered tears without loss, small rusthole in 4G5 affecting five letters, good; with ownership inscriptions of Thomas Belasyse, Earl Fauconberg, Oliver Cromwell's son-in-law, dated 1677 on titlepage; Richard Man, 1724 on recto of *2; Josa. Jacques 1731 on title; T. Crowe on title, James Hunter Jr., the Bradley Martin copy with his sale booklabel. STC 20066; Bartlett 226; Pforzheimer 801; PMM 48.   Simon Finch 24-187 1996 £7,800.00

PLUTARCHUS 45-125   The Lives of the Noble Grecians and Romans. London: Abraham Miller, 1657. Folio; rare 'Explanation of the Frontispiece' leaf present but frayed in margin, additional engraved title (lower right-hand corner torn away with loss), printed in title in red and black, tip of top right hand corner, little worn (not affecting text), 2 divisional titles, numerous woodcut portraits to text, some copper plate engraved portraits at rear, 2 or 3 old library stamps to prelims of Royal Inst. of South Wales; modern quarter brown morocco; Wing P2633. Ian Wilkinson 95/1-135 1996 £220.00

PLUTARCHUS 45-125   Plutarach's Lives. London: Dilly, 1770. 1st edition; tall octavo; 6 volumes; full early polished calf, professionally rebacked with original spines laid down, gilt on red leather labels, engraved frontispiece in each volume; very nice. CBEL II 763; Lowndes II 1469.   Hartfield 48-L69 1996 $450.00

PLUTARCHUS 45-125   Lives. London: Lackington, Allen & Co., 1803. 8th edition; 12mo; 6 frontispieces, contemporary marbled calf, smooth backstrips, divided by gilt diamond rolls between plain and rope rules, morocco title and volume labels in second and fifth compartments, small ornament in centre of remainder, board edges gilt hatched, endpapers stained by turn-ins, excellent.   Blackwell's B112-229 1996 £85.00

PLUTARCHUS 45-125   Lives (of the Noble Grecians and Romans). London: printed for J. Mawman et al, 1810. New edition; 7 x 4 1/2 inches; 8 volumes; very attractive contemporary speckled calf, flat spines with curious small gilt agricultural ornament between multiple plain and decorative gilt rules, red and black morocco labels, light rubbing to joints, but never seriously worn, very slight wear to extremities, but still quite handsome and very well preserved set, frequent light foxing, occasionally more noteicable, and isolated stains, minor tears without loss, but generally satisfactory internally, without any serious defect. Bruggemann p. 322 (earlier editions); Brunet IV 742.   Phillip J. Pirages 33-430 1996 $400.00

PLUTARCHUS 45-125   The Lives of the Nobel Grecians and Romanes.
London: Nonesuch Press, 1929-30. Number 48 of 1550 sets; Folio; 5
volumes; original brown buckram, bevelled edges, top edge gilt, others
untrimmed, paper labels (spare labels tipped in), little very minor fading
of cloth; excellent set.   Robert Clark 38-90 1996 £250.00

PLUTARCHUS 45-125   Vitae Illustrium Virorum. Venice: Bartholomaeus
de Zanis, 8 June, 1496. Folio; 290 leaves, roman letter, 62 lines and
headline, woodcut capitals, woodcut border on a2r; later vellum, old
paper repairs at lower corners of a1, marginal worming to last four
leaves, touching one letter only, slight dampstain at head and beginning
of second part, fol. 23. evenly browned, still good, fresh copy; library
stamps of Alexandri Seritecolo on recto of first and verso of last leaf,
inscription erased at foot of a24; HC 13130*; Proctor 5335; BMC V 432
(IB 23719); Goff P 834.   Simon Finch 24-186 1996 £3,500.00

A POCKET Companion for Oxford; or Guide through the University.
Oxford: Prince, 1762. Large 12mo; pages iv, 132, folding engraved map;
8 engraved plates; calf, rebacked.   Marlborough 162-75 1996 £275.00

POCKLINGTON, JOHN   Altare Christianum; or, the Dead Vicar Plea.
London: printed by Richard Badger, 1637. 2nd edition; 4to; limp
parchment, uncut; light dampstain on outer margin. STC 20076.
Anthony W. Laywood 109-115 1996 £100.00

POCOCK, ISAAC   Rob Roy MacGregor; or, Auld Lang Syne. London:
W. Simpkin, R. Marshall and C. Chapple, 1820. 3rd edition; 19th century
sheep, worn and dry, backstrip perished, interleaved with blank leaves,
covers nearly loose, notes to text.   Dramatis Personae 37-141 1996
$250.00

POCOCK, W. F.   Designs for Churches and Chapel... London: M.
Taylor, 1835. 3rd edition; 4to; 28 pages; 44 plates; publisher's
blindstamped cloth, binding worn, spine sunned, else very good.
Bookpress 75-101 1996 $650.00

POE, EDGAR ALAN 1809-1849   Al Aaraff. Phoenix: D'Ambrosio, 1995.
One of 50 copies; 12 x 4 3/4 x 7 inches high, including book stand; 5
p.l., 45, (1) pages, (1) leaf (colophon); illustrated and decorated in
various ways, including some paste-ons, illustrations printed from
handmade paper plates made by D'Ambrosio, letterpress printed from
magnesium plates in blue and black in distinctive "Black Chancery" face,
with separate 16 page booklet of notes, contained in pocket inside back
cover; imaginative trapezoidal design of blue niger-backed boards,
plexiglas mirror mounted on each cover and framed with blue Japanese
paper, book set down into grooved platform and retained by matching
lid (of Japanese papaer and 7 plexiglas mirros) latched into the platform,
this cover with two open sides, revealing the mirrored sides of the
book, the whole forming a truncated reflecting pyramid (with spine of
book at top, under cover).   Phillip J. Pirages 33-153 1996 $800.00

POE, EDGAR ALLAN 1809-1849   The Bells and Other Poems. H&S,
1912. 1st edition thus, one of 750 copies; specially bound in full vellum
with gold-gilt decorative stamping, signed by artist; fine.   Aronovitz
57-942 1996 $1,250.00

POE, EDGAR ALLAN 1809-1849   The Bells and Other Poems. London:
Hodder & Stoughton, 1912. 1st edition deluxe, limited to 750 numbered
copies signed by Dulac; 4to; with 28 fine mounted colored plates behind
tissue guards, by Edmund Dulac; original full vellum decoratively gilt, top
edge gilt, uncut, new gold silk ties supplied, two minute holes at lower
joint of spine, very minor surface marks to vellum, free endpapers
browned, uncut, edges dusted, very clean and unusually bright.
Sotheran PN32-115 1996 £550.00

POE, EDGAR ALLAN 1809-1849   Eureka, a Prose Poem... Arion Press,
1991. One of 250 copies, signed by artist; 13 3/4 x 10 inches, ix, (1),
107, (1) pages, (1) leaf (colophon); 8 photo engravings by Arakawa;
original printed cloth; as new.   Phillip J. Pirages 33-20 1996 $550.00

POE, EDGAR ALLAN 1809-1849   The Fall of the House of Usher. New
York: Limited Editions Club, 1985. One of 1500 copies; folio; illustrated
after paintings and sketches by the late American artist Alice Neel, and
signed by Neel and Raphael Soyer, who has written an appreciation of
the artist for this edition; quarter leather and marbled paper covered
boards, in slightly warped publisher's clamshell box. Fine.   Lame Duck
Books 19-464 1996 $1,500.00

POE, EDGAR ALLAN 1809-1849   Histoires Extraordinaires...(with)
Nouvelles Histoires Extraordinaires... Paris: Levy Freres, 1856-57. 1st
editions; thick 8vo; 2 volumes in one; morocco and 19th century boards;
extremely rare. Vicaire I 339.   Rostenberg & Stern 150-26 1996
$850.00

POE, EDGAR ALLAN 1809-1849   The Mask of the Red Death.
Baltimore: Aquarius, 1969. One of 525 copies; folio; 16 lithographs by
Frederico Castellon and signed by him; original binding, fine in very good
case.   Charles Agvent 4-940 1996 $275.00

POE, EDGAR ALLAN 1809-1849   The Murders in the Rue Morgue.
Antibes: Allen Press, 1958. One of 150 copies, 8vo; with publicity
materials laid in; illustrations by Dorothy & Lewis Allen; boards, acetate
dust jacket; former owner's neat bookplate, otherwise fine, very scarce.
James S. Jaffe 34-3 1996 $750.00

POE, EDGAR ALLAN 1809-1849   The Narrative of Arthur Gordon Pym.
New York: Harper & Bros., 1838. 1st edition; 12mo; 201 pages, plus 14
pages publisher's ads, complete with 2 pages of ads at front dated May
1838; handsomely bound by Stikeman and Co. in full brown morocco,
covers decoratively panelled in gilt, gilt spine, tooled in compartments,
gilt board edges and turn-ins, top edge gilt, marbled endpapers, light
wear to extremities, text exceptionally bright, fine. BAL 16128.   Heritage
Book Shop 196-239 1996 $1,500.00

POE, EDGAR ALLAN 1809-1849   Poems. London: George Bell & Sons,
1900. 1st edition; limited edition; xxxvii, 225 pages; printed on Japanese
vellum; frontispiece, title vignette, 27 plates and 76 text illustrations by
W. Heath Robinson; green and red binding design for trade edition
bound in, beige holland cloth, titled in red and black on spine, beige
holland cloth, titled in red and black on spine; cloth very lightly browned.
Robin Greer 94A-33 1996 £450.00

POE, EDGAR ALLAN 1809-1849   The Poems of Edgar Allan Poe. New
York: Limited Editions Club, 1943. Number 904 of 1500 copies, signed
by artist; lithographs by Hugo Steiner-Prag; full leather, near fine in lightly
worn publisher's slipcase.   Hermitage SP95-1024 1996 $175.00

POE, EDGAR ALLAN 1809-1849   The Poetical Works. New York:
Redfield, 1858. Reprint; 8vo; illustrations; gilt decorated cloth, cloth very
spotted and rubbed, contents quite clean. BAL 16211.   Charles Agvent
4-942 1996 $150.00

POE, EDGAR ALLAN 1809-1849   The Raven. London: Gay and Bird,
1901. 1st edition; limited to 50 copies printed on Japanese vellum,
number 31; 42 pages; decorated title, 2 full page deocrations and 18
pages of handlettered text with red decorated initials and decorated
borders, full white vellum, gilt lettering, white silk ties, one silk tie
defective.   Robin Greer 94A-71 1996 £175.00

POE, EDGAR ALLAN 1809-1849   Le Scarabee d'Or. Paris: F. Ferroud,
1926. Of a total edition of 650, this one of 53 on Japan imperial with
plates in four states (three in color) and illustrations in text; 4to; color
pictorial wrappers; fine.   Marilyn Braiterman 15-175 1996 $500.00

POE, EDGAR ALLAN 1809-1849   The Tales and Poems of... New York:
Brampton Society, 1902. New Tamerlane Edition limited to 500 copies;
8vo; 10 volumes; paltes; cloth; very good.   Charles Agvent 4-944
1996 $175.00

POE, EDGAR ALLAN 1809-1849   Tales of Mystery and Imagination.
London: George G. Harrap & Co., Ltd., 1919. 1st edition de luxe, limited
to only 170 numbered copies, signed by artist; 4to; (iv), 5-381 pages, 24
fine tissue guarded black and white plates by Harry Clarke; original full
vellum with gilt panel and vignette to upper cover, gilt lettered spine, top
edge gilt, others uncut, original polytherne wrapper; very minor dusting
of top edge, otherwise spectacular copy in extremely fine condition.
Sotheran PN32-104 1996 £3,950.00

POE, EDGAR ALLAN 1809-1849   Tales of Mystery and Imagination.
New York: Brentano's, c. 1919. 4to; 412, (i) pages, (short tear at top
edge of half title), title and tailpiece vignettes, 8 color plates and 24
black and white plates by Harry Clarke, corner of frontispiece and of
page 272 creased; black cloth, bumped and rubbed, title with vignette in
gilt on spine, pictorial paper label on front cover, label soiled with small
chip at left edge. Very good.   Blue Mountain SP95-60 1996 $150.00

POE, EDGAR ALLAN 1809-1849   The Complete Works. New York:
Knickerbocker Press (for) G. P. Putnam's Sons, 1902. Tamerlane edition,
number 236 of 300 sets; large 8vo; 10 volumes; printed on Ruisdael
handmae paper; all engravings and illustrations bound in duplicate, with
printed tissue guards, many of the plates in different states;
contemporary dark green crushed half morocco, spines decorated in gilt
with floral devices and lettered in gilt, raised bands, marbled sides and
endpapers, top edge gilt, others uncut, 3 joints skilfully repaired, little
light rubbing; excellent set.   Simon Finch 24-188 1996 £1,800.00

POEMS, Moral, Elegant and Pathetic. London: printed for E. Newbery, and Vernor and Hood, 1796. 1st edition; 12mo; frontispiece, 5 other plates; contemporary tree calf, spine gilt (labelled "Williams's Poems"); uncommon; early armorial bookplate and signature of Benjamin Dickinson, of Tiverton. Roscoe A411(1); CBEL III 423 and 693. Ximenes 108-291 1996 $450.00

THE POET of the Month 1942. New York: New Directions, 1942. Complete set of 12 volumes; printed wrappers, fine in publisher's slipcase. Left Bank Books 2-107 1996 $275.00

POET'S CLUB The Second Book of the Poet's Club. London: 1911. 1st edition; boards, top edge dusty and slightly soiled, head and tail of spine and corners bumped, spine rubbed and slightly darkened, covers very slightly marked, cover edges slightly rubbed; good. Ulysses 39-470 1996 £65.00

THE POET'S of Today IV. New York: Scribner's, 1957. 1st edition; fine in very good dust jacket, with some wear along spine and fore edge; signed by contributor, George Garrett, his first book. Thomas Dorn 9-126 1996 $125.00

THE POETICAL Register and Repository of Fugitive Poetry. London: ptd. for F. & C. Rivington, by Lye and Law, London: R. & C. Rivington, 1802/02. 1st edition; 8vo; original light blue boards, drab paper backstrip, printed paper label, spine partly defective, label rubbed; slight foxing, but aside from spine, a fresh, fine copy in original condition; very scarce. Brewer p. 15; CBEL III 1873. Ximenes 108-292 1996 $300.00

POGSON, NORMAN ROBERT Popular Description of the Total Eclipse of the sun, on August 18th, 1868, Prepared at the Madras Observatory for the Asylum Press Almanac. Madras: printed at the Asylum Press by William Thomas 1867 (sic). 1st edition; 8vo; 3 paltes; original limp maroon morocco, gilt; nice, scarce. Ximenes 109-234 1996 $250.00

POHL, F. The Reefs of Space. Dobson, 1965. 1st British and 1st hard cover edition; some offsetting to front cover, else fine in dust jacket with small hole, signed by authors. Aronovitz 57-950 1996 $110.00

POHL, F. Search the Sky. Ballantine, 1954. 1st edition; signed by author; very good+/near fine in very good+dust jacket. Aronovitz 57-943 1996 $250.00

POHL, F. A Town is Drowning. Ballantine, 1955. 1st edition; fine in near fine dust jacket with some light rubbing, quite scarce, signed by author. Aronovitz 57-945 1996 $500.00

POHL, F. Wolfbane. London: Gollancz, 1960. 1st British and 1st hard cover edition; very good+ in like dust jacket; inscribed by author, most uncommon. Aronovitz 57-948 1996 $150.00

POINTER, JOHN An Account of a Roman Pavement, Lately Found at Stunsfield in Oxfordshire, Prov'd to be 1400 Years Old. Oxford: ptd. by Leonard Lichfield, for Anth. Peisley, 1713. 1st edition; frontispiece (slightly shaved on outer edge), modern cloth. Anthony W. Laywood 109-117 1996 £75.00

POINTER, JOHN Miscellanea in Usum Juventutis Academicae... Oxford: printed at the Theater for Ant. Peisley, 1718. 1st ed.; 8vo; (16), 215, (5) pages; contemporary cottage panelled calf, neatly rebacked to match, raised bands, label, gilt; very good. John Drury 82-222 1996 £100.00

POINTZ, ROBERT Testimonies for the Real Presence of Christes Body and Blood in the Blessed Scarament of the Aultar. Louvain: Jean Fouler, 1566. 8vo; title, 7 ff., n.n., ff. 1-200 (lacking ff. 155-158); sides of original binding laid down on a new binding in 1885, they are of brown goatskin decorated with gilt with border formed by repeated impressions of lacework took, a plaque of arabesque foliate ornament blocked in centre between the name GLASCOK/MARI (the words reversed on lower cover), lacks two slit ties, upper edge dark green, others show traces of guilding; this binding may be Roman, of about the same date as the book; the book was bound for Mary Glascock; the copy of Bartholomew Wicker with early scribblings in margins. Marlborough 160-10 1996 £1,750.00

POITIER, SIDNEY This Life. New York: Knopf, 1980. 1st edition; 8vo; 24 pages of black and white photos; dust jacket, very good; signed by author. George J. Houle 68-119 1996 $125.00

POLACK, JOEL S. Manners and Customs of the New Zealanders; with Notes Corroborative of Their Habits, Usages, Etc. and Remarks to Intending Emigrants. London: James Madden, 1840. 8vo; 2 volumes, pages xxxiv, 288; xviii, 304; folding map, 3 plates; original cloth, rebacked, leather labels. Hocken p. 85. Richard Adelson W94/95-137 1996 $585.00

POLIDORI, JOHN WILLIAM 1795-1802 Vampyren of Lord Byron. Helsingfors: tryckt hos J. Simelius, 1824. 1st edition in Swedish; 8vo; marbled boards, dark green cloth, spine, original pale blue wrappers bound in; some foxing, but nice. Ximenes 109-235 1996 $750.00

THE POLITICAL History of England. London: 1906-10. Thick small 8vo; 12 volumes; maps, original cloth, booklabel of Malcolm MacDonald. Howes Bookshop 265-983 1996 £75.00

POLIZIANO, ANGELO 1454-1494 Illustrium Virorum Epistole ab Angelo Politiano... Paris: Jean Petit and Josse Badius, May 8, 1526. Square 8vo; ff. 4, 184 leaves, large Petit printer's device, wodcut illustration, woodcut initials, early ms. ownerships (cancelled in ink); nice modern full leather. Family Album Tillers-515 1996 $800.00

POLLACK, P. Picture History of Photography, from the Earliest Beginnings to the Present Day. New York: 1969. Revised edition; dust jacket. J. B. Muns 154-235 1996 $100.00

POLLARD, ALFRED WILLIAM 1859-1944 Last Words on the History of the Title Page. N.P.: 1968. One of 260 numbered copies, 8vo; (v), 39 pages; 27 plates; included is facsimile leaf from the Mazarin Bible; cloth, cover worn. The Bookpress 75-343 1996 $135.00

POLLARD, EDWARD A. The First Year of the War. Richmond: 1862. Corrected and improved edition; 9.5 x 5.5 inches; 368 pages; portraits, ink inscription; cloth, minor staining, covers worn and spotted. John K. King 77-89 1996 $150.00

POLLARD, H. B. C. Game Birds, Rearing, Preservation and Shooting. London: 1929. With the quarter vellum binding which was for the limited edition of 99 copies; Large 4to; 12 mounted colored plates by Philip Rickman, with pencil sketch vignettes; original quarter vellum, very slightly marked, contents excellent. David A.H. Grayling 3/95-42 1996 £130.00

POLLARD, PERCIVAL Posters in Miniature. New York: R. H. Russell, 1896. 1st edition; small 8vo; unpaginated, iv, plus 246 black and white illustrations; decorated yellow cloth, very good, some soil, name on flyleaf. Taurus Books 83-82 1996 $150.00

POLLOCK, FREDERICK The History of English Law, Before the Time of Edward I. Cambridge: Cambridge University Press, 1911. 2nd edition; 2 volumes; 2 joints badly cracked and repaired, working set. Meyer Boswell SL27-190 1996 $150.00

POLLOCK, H. E. D. Round Structures of Aboriginal Middle America. Washington: Carnegie Inst., 1936. 4to; vii, 182 pages, 44 illustrations, 1 map; original cloth. Archaeologia Luxor-4787 1996 $250.00

POLO, MARCO 1254-1323? The Book of Ser Marco Polo, the Venetian Concerning the Kingdoms and Marvels of the east. London: Murray, 1875. 2nd edition; tall 8vo; xliii, 444, xxii, 606 pages; 2 volumes; numerous plates and maps; numerous illustrations in text; original cloth, slightly rubbed, front cover of volume 2 soiled due to dampness, otherwise very good. Worldwide Antiquarian 162-741 1996 $250.00

POLWHELE, RICHARD 1760-1838 Traditions and Recollections; Domestic, Clerical and Literary. London: John Nichols and Son, 1826. 1st edition; 8vo; 2 volumes bound in 1; vi, 820 pages; frontispiece, 5 plates; recent black half calf, spine gilt, marbled boards; minor foxing and staining; good copy; bookplate of Richard G. Polwhele. Robert Clark 38-256 1996 £75.00

POLYBIUS Historiarum Libri Priores Quinque, Nicolao Perotto Sipontino Interprete. Eptime Sequentium Librorum.. Lugduni: Apud Seb. Gryphium, 1554. 16mo; printer's device on title, 983 pages; new half calf, label. Adams II 1807. Anthony W. Laywood 109-118 1996 £95.00

POLYBIUS Polybii Megalopolitani Historiarum. Lyon: Sebastian Gryphanus, 1554. Small 4to; pages 790, (52), Griffin printer's device on first and last leaves, Latin text, Italic; old limp vellum. Not in Brunet; Adams P 1807. Family Album Tillers-518 1996 $300.00

POLYBIUS   Histoire de Polybe, Depuis la Seconde Guerre Punique Jusqu'a Celle de Macedoine. Paris: Lamesle for Gandouin (& others), 1727-30. 4to; 6 volumes; over 125 engraved plates, maps and plans, hundreds of woodcut typographic ornaments; fine contemporary French full leather gilt, some joints cracked, red edges; on boards of each volume are the gilt arms of Jean Jacques IV, Comte de Mesmes. Brunet IV 791; Jahns 1461-2; Olivier 1328.   Family Album Tillers-519 1996 $2,000.00

POLYBIUS   Histoire de Polybe, Nouvellement Traduite du Grec Par Dom Vincent Thuillier, Benedictin de la Congregation de Saint maur... Paris: Charles Antoine Jombert, 1753. 1st of this illustrated edition; 7 volumes including supplement; pictorial headpieces, ornamental tailpieces, 3 folding maps and 123 plates, mostly folding; contemporary leather, gilt ornamented spines, bindings worn; old signature in each volume of John Godwin, 46 Regiment, a modern bookplate and a blindstamp on each titlepage.   Marilyn Braiterman 15-163 1996 $1,950.00

POMERANZ, HERMAN   Medicine in the Shakespearean Plays and Dickens's Doctors. New York: 1936. 1st edition; 416 pages; original binding.   W. Bruce Fye 71-1676 1996 $100.00

POMEROY, JOHN NORTON   An Introduction to Municipal Law. New York: D. Appleton and Co., 1865. contemporary sheep, spotted, covers loose, usable copy.   Meyer Boswell SL25-176 1996 $150.00

POMPADOUR, JEANNE ANTOINETTE POISSON, MARQUISE DE   Lettres. London: Owen and Cadell, 1776-78. 8vo; 3 parts in one; title portrait of Pompadour; quarter calf, scuffed.   Rostenberg & Stern 150-27 1996 $175.00

PONGE, FRANCIS   Braque Lithographs. Monte Carlo: Sauret, 1963. Folio; 189 pages; 146 color plates + original lithographs; wrappers, slipcase. Freitag 1044.   Brannan 43-86 1996 $550.00

PONGE, FRANCIS   G. Braque. New York: Abrams, 1971. Square 4to; 261 pages; numerous illustrations, including many color plates; cloth, dust jacket. Freitag 1043.   Brannan 43-87 1996 $150.00

PONICSAN, DARYL   The Last Detail. New York: Dial Press, 1970. 1st printing; fine in fine dust jacket.   Sherwood 3-225 1996 $125.00

PONTING, HERBERT G.   In Lotus-Land Japan. London: Macmillan and Co., 1910. 1st edition; 8vo; pages xvi, 396; 8 color plates, 96 monochrome photographic illustrations; original red cloth, gilt lettering with vignette, head and foot of spine trifle bumped, otherwise good. Sotheran PN32-167 1996 £95.00

PONTING, HERBERT G.   Japanese Studies. Yokohama: kelly Walsh, Ltd., 1906. Photos; Oblong pictorial boards, stab sewn, light rubbing and some foxing, still attractive.   Hermitage SP95-1110 1996 $100.00

POOL, EUGENE   Surgery at the New York Hospital One Hundred Years Ago. New York: 1929. Limited edition, signed by both authors; original binding.   W. Bruce Fye 71-1678 1996 $125.00

POOLE, FRANCIS   Queen Charlotte Islands, a Narrative of Discovery and Adventure in the North Pacific. London: 1872. 1st edition; 9 x 5.5. inches; 347 pages; maps, illustrations; 347 pages; cloth, front hinner hinge detached, covers worn, disbound.   John K. King 77-38 1996 $150.00

POOLE, JACOB   A Glossary, with some Pieces of Verse, of the Old Dialect of the English Colony in the Baronies of Forth and Bargy, County of Wexford, Ireland. London: J. Russell Smith, 1867. Half title; original green cloth, slightly rubbed; bookplates of Charles Doble & John Sparrow.   Jarndyce 103-92 1996 £110.00

POOR, HENRY V.   Poor's Manual of the Railroads. New York: n.p., 1886. pages 76, cxxxvii, 1022, 69; 14 maps in color; hinges cracked, some shelfwear, else good.   Dumont 28-118 1996 $175.00

POPE, ALEXANDER 1688-1744   The Corresondence of Alexander Pope. Oxford: at the Clarendon Press, 1910. 1st edition; later issue, with green lettering; very small chip from head of fragile boards, else near fine. Captain's Bookshelf 38-187 1997 $150.00

POPE, ALEXANDER 1688-1744   An Epistle from Mr. Pope to Dr. Arbuthnot. London: printed by J. Wright for Lawton Gilliver, 1734. 1st edition; folio; disbound; very good. Foxon P802; Griffith 352; Rothschild 1623.   Ximenes 109-236 1996 $600.00

POPE, ALEXANDER 1688-1744   Essai sur l'Homme. N.P.: 1736. Small 8vo; contemporary calf, spine gilt, trifle worn; Rochedieu p. 253. Ximenes 109-237 1996 $225.00

POPE, ALEXANDER 1688-1744   Essay on Man. London: Knapton, 1745. Early edition; 8vo; portrait, frontispiece; bound in what appears to be the original boards backed in calf with red morocco label, minor staining, edgewear; Griffith 608, Edition B.   Charles Agvent 4-958 1996 $175.00

POPE, ALEXANDER 1688-1744   A Key to the Lock. London: printed for J. Roberts, 1715. 1st edition; 8vo; stitched as issued, in cloth slipcase; splendid copy, entirely uncut, rare. From the collection of H. Bradley Martin with his booklabel. Griffith 37; not in Rothschild.   Ximenes 108-297 1996 $2,500.00

POPE, ALEXANDER 1688-1744   Letters of Mr. Alexander Pope and Several of His Friends. London: printed by J. Wright for J. Knapton, L. Gilliver, J. Brindley &... 1737. Reprint of the 1735 collection with important additions; 4to; contemporary calf, spine gilt, spine rubbed, joints bit cracked; very good; Griffith 454.   Ximenes 108-295 1996 $500.00

POPE, ALEXANDER 1688-1744   Of The Characters of Women: an Epistle to a Lady. London: J. Wright for Lawton Gilliver, 1735. 1st edition; folio; pages (ii), 16 (4), half title lacking; modern marbled boards, typographic label, titlepage was unfortunately cropped by first binder, taking part of the lower imprint, but not affecting any text; generally nice, scarce. Foxon P917; Rothschild 1625; Ashley IV 51. Hartfield 48-L70 1996 $395.00

POPE, ALEXANDER 1688-1744   Pope's Poetical Works. Princeton: D. A. Borrestein, Pub., Princeton Press, 1828. 12mo; 3 volumes; frontispiece; original tan cloth backed boards, printed paper labels (chipped), rubbed, some fraying and water staining of spines, half titles, engravd titles, browning and spotting, staining at back of volume 2; library label of F. F. Gaines.   James Cummins 14-158 1996 $150.00

POPE, ALEXANDER 1688-1744   The Poetical Works. London: William Pickering, 1831. 6 1/2 x 4 1/4 inches; 3 volumes; frontispiece in volume 1, device on title of each volume; dark green morocco, covers with triple blind rule border, small blindstamped flower in each corner, gilt titling and small oval ornaments on spine between bands (that are flanked by triple blind rules), attractive animated gilt roll on broad edges, densely gilt floral border on turn-ins, marbled endpapers, all edges gilt, tip of lower corner of one leaf neatly renewed (before printing?), but exceptionally fine, text and especially bindings remarkably clean and bright and with virtually no signs of wear; Prize inscription dated 1867 from Queen Mary's Grammar School at Ripon to John Albert Burton, on front fly leaf in first volume, faint ownership inscription dated 1832 on first page of third volume. Keynes p. 38.   Phillip J. Pirages 33-422 1996 $600.00

POPE, ALEXANDER 1688-1744   The Poetical Works. London: William Pickering, 1835. Small 8vo; 3 volumes; pages clxiii, (i), 168; viii, 311; vii, (i), 363; steel engraved portrait frontispiece in volume i, tissue guard and half titles present, titlepage to volume i lightly browned; dark green morocco by Hayday, backstrips with raised bands, gilt lettered direct, blind triple fillet border on sides, yellow chalked endpapers (slight foxing), green silk markers, gilt edges, excellent.   Blackwell's B112-230 1996 £50.00

POPE, ALEXANDER 1688-1744   The Rape of the Lock. London: printed for Bernard Lintott, 1714. 1st edition; 8vo; frontispiece, five other plates; original pale blue wrappers, in green cloth folding case; superb copy, stitched as issued; from the collection of H. Bradley Martin with his booklabel; Griffith 29; Foxon P9491; Rothschild 1570.   Ximenes 108-296 1996 $10,000.00

POPE, ALEXANDER 1688-1744   The Works. London: Bernard Lintot, 1717. 1st edition; 1st issue; half title, titlepage in red and black, numerous finely engraved head and tail pieces and large initial letters by Gribelin, lacks frontispiece; finely bound in full contemporary red morocco, boards with several gilt panels, floral devices at corners and sides, enclosing different gilt rolls and more floral devices, outer gilt fillet border with small gilt leaves in corners, upper joint cracking but firm, spine elaborately gilt in compartments, all edges gilt, attractive early 18th century English binding; with signature of Joseph Sanford (or Sandford) dated 1717, the scholar & book collector; bookplates of John Sparrow & H.R. Pakenham.   Ian Wilkinson 95/1-136 1996 £450.00

POPE, ALEXANDER 1688-1744   The Works. London: for J. and P. Knapton, H. Lintot, J. and R. Tonson and S. Draper, 1751. 8vo; 9 volumes; frontispiece, 23 engraved plates (one as frontispiece, plate VII detached from volume and loosely inserted), titlepages in red and black; contemporary sprinkled calf, double gilt rules, spines numbered in gilt, red morocco labels, sometime added to style, red sprinkled edges, very slight rubbing, little faint spotting; excellent set. Griffith 653.   Simon Finch 24-190 1996 £450.00

POPE, ALEXANDER 1688-1744   The Works of Alexander Pope, Esq. London: printed for A. Millar, J. and R. Tonson, C. Bathurst, H. Woodfall... 1766. 8vo; 9 volumes; frontispiece to volumes 1 and 5, 22 engraved copperplates and 1 vignette; ink ownership inscription to title of volume 1, armorial bookplate to front pastedown of all volumes; full speckled calf, corners slightly bumped, red morocco label to spine, raised bands to spines, edges speckled, upper hinge of volume 1 tender, small scorch mark to lower board of volume 4.   Beeleigh Abbey BA56-161 1996 £750.00

POPE, ALEXANDER 1688-1744   The Works. Edinburgh: A. Donaldson, 1767. 12mo in half sheets; 6 volumes; titles within typographic borders, 10 engraved plates, 2 as frontispieces; contemporary sprinkled calf, spines with raised bands, double gilt rules and ornaments, numbered in gilt, red morocco labels, red sprinkled edges; lightly rubbed in places, occasional very light spotting, 2 leaves loose in prelims of volume IV, generally an excellent, bright set; armorial bookplate of Carmichael of Eastend.   Simon Finch 24-191 1996 £350.00

POPE, JOHN ALEXANDER   Chinese Porcelains from the Ardebil Shrine. Washington: Smithsonian Inst., Freer Gallery, 1956. 4to; xvi, 194 pages; map, plan, 140 other plates; cloth, corners very slightly worn.   Thomas Thorp 489-247 1996 £100.00

POPE-HENNESSY, JOHN   Catalogue of Italian Sculpture in the Victoria and Albert Museum. London: HMSO, 1964. 28 x 22 cm; 3 volumes; xvi, 395; 396-767; 426 pages, 736 plates; original cloth, top edge gilt, dust jackets (slightly torn), labels on dust jacket spines, ex-library copies with few library marks front and back.   Rainsford A54-467 1996 £200.00

POPE-HENNESSY, JOHN   Drawings of Domenichino. London: 1948. 30 x 23 cm; 187 pages; 69 black and white plates, 73 black and white illustrations; cloth.   Rainsford A54-597 1996 £70.00

POPE-HENNESSY, UNA   Early Chinese Jades. London: Ernest Benn, 1923. 4to; xx, 149 pages; 8 plates in color, 56 in half tone and 13 text illustrations. Cloth.   Thomas Thorp 489-249 1996 £85.00

POPHAM, A. E.   Italian Drawings on the XV and XVI Centuries. London: 1949. 30 x 23 cm; 390 pages; 176 black and white plates, 226 black and white illustrations; cloth.   Rainsford A54-598 1996 £70.00

POPHAM, M. R.   Lefkandi I: The Iron Age. The Settlement the Demeteries. London: British School of Archaeology at Athens, 1980-79. 8vo; 2 volumes, text 464 pages with numerous figures; plate volume: x, 284 palges and pages 309-333; original cloth, dust jacket; signature. Archaeologla Luxor-3847 1996 $250.00

POPPLE, WILLIAM   A Rational Catechism... London: printed for the Widow of J. J. Schipper, 1712. 1st edition; 12mo; contemporary calf, rebacked, label.   Anthony W. Laywood 108-112 1996 £145.00

POPULAR Encyclopaedia, or Conversations Lexicon. A General Dictionary of Arts, Sciences, Literature, Biography, History and Politics. London: Blackie, n.d. 1890-93. Royal 8vo; 14 volumes; folding maps, large number of plates; original cloth.   Charles W. Traylen 117-180 1996 £85.00

PORCACCHI, THOMASO b. 1530   Lettre Di XIII Duomini Illustri... Venice: Heredi di Glovan Maria Bonelli, 1571. Small 8vo; 482 leaves, title mounted, woodcut printer's device on first and last leaves; quite scarce; apparntly not in Adams; BMC STC nor NUC; Gamba 1465; Haym 412.10. Family Album Tillers-521 1996 $300.00

PORSON, RICHARD 1759-1808   Letters to Mr. Archdeacon Travis, in Answer to His Defence of the Three Heavenly Witnesses. London: T. and J. Egerton, 1790. 8vo; (ii), xxxix, (i), 406, pages; 11th century morocco backed boards, spine gilt, rubbed, little foxing; tipped in to this copy is leaf inscribed "To Henry Lord Brougham and Vaux...from Edward Chichester (=Maltby), A.D. 1833"; Brougham's gilt coronet and monogram on spine.   Robert Clark 38-199 1996 £150.00

PORT TOWNSEND. CHAMBER OF COMMERCE   Reports on the Naval Station Site, Relations with Canada, and the North Pacific Fisheries. Port Townsend: Call Printing and Publishing, 1889. 1st edition; 28 pages; original printed grey wrappers, back wrapper illustrated with railroad and steamship, stapled as issued; fine. Not in Smith, Soliday, Eberstadt, Decker, Graff, Howes, etc.   Michael D. Heaston 23-352 1996 $750.00

PORTA, GIOVANNI BATTISTA 1535-1615   La Physionomie Humaine... Rouen: J. & D. Berthelin, 1655. 1st edition in French; 8vo; 616 pages; 97 one third page woodcuts, each with two images, woodcut ornaments, mottled calf, old gilt rebacking, new endpapers. Rare. Caillet 8860; Krivatsy 9185 (1660 edition only); NUC 466.91.   Bennett Gilbert LL29-58 1996 $2,500.00

PORTER, ANNA MARIA   Don Sebastian; or, the House of Braganza. London: Longman, Hurst, Rees and Orme, 1809. 1st edition; 12mo; 4 volumes; half titles present (paper fault in that of volume 3), some foxing, lower corner of N7 volume 3 torn away affecting two words in last line of text on verso; pages (xvi), 278; (iv), 314; (iv), 303; (iv), 320; contemporary crushed dark blue morocco, light rubbing, smooth backstrip divided by gilt rules, gilt lettered direct, marbled boards and endpapers, very good. Wolff 5596.   Blackwell's B112-231 1996 £225.00

PORTER, DAVID D.   The Naval History of the Civil War. New York: Sherman Pub. Co., 1886. 1st edition; 4to; 843 pages; illustrations; plctorial mustard/gold cloth, cloth lightly rubbed, inner hinges beginning to crack, good to very good.   Robert F. Lucas 42-17 1996 $135.00

PORTER, EDWIN H.   The Fall River Tragedy. Fall River: Press of J. D. Munroe, 1893. 1st edition; 8vo; 312 pages; illustrations; original green cloth, rebacked with original spine laid down over new backing, recased with new endpapers, paper browning slightly, minor dampstain in margin at end of book, good. McDade 117.   Robert F. Lucas 42-29 1996 $400.00

PORTER, ELIOT   Galapagos: the Flow of Wildness. San Francisco: Sierra Club, 1967/68. 1st edition; folio; 2 volumes; illustrations; dust jackets slightly torn, slipcase slightly rubbed.   J. B. Muns 154-237 1996 $225.00

PORTER, ELIOT   Intimate Landscapes. New York: 1979. 1st edition; folio; color plates, one tipped on front cover, as issued.   J. B. Muns 154-239 1996 $185.00

PORTER, GENE STRATTON 1863-1924   Birds of the Bible. Cincinnati: 1909. 467 pages; 81 photos; bound, slight wear on back cover, hinge taped.   John Johnson 135-546 1996 $125.00

PORTER, GENE STRATTON 1863-1924   The White Flag. Garden City: Doubleday Page, 1923. 1st edition; slight bend to first several pages, else fine in attractive near fine dust jacket, little spine faded and with some small nicks and tears.   Between the Covers 42-356 1996 $325.00

PORTER, JANE   Sir Edward Seward's Narrative of His Shipwreck and Consequent Discovery of Certain Islands in the Caribbean Sea... London: Longman, Rees, Orme, Brown and Green, 1831. 1st edition; 8vo; 3 volumes; three quarter green morocco and marbled boards, ex-library and early ownership signature in each volume, some wear to bindings, volume 2 front cover with bend in center, volume 3 front joint starting, lacking half titles, still very nice set. Sabin 64323; Wolff 5612.   Priscilla Juvelis 95/1-200 1996 $350.00

PORTER, JOHN GREY V.   Some Agricultural and Political Irish Questions Calmly Discussed. London: J. Ridgway & Sons..., 1843. 1st (?only) edition; 8vo; pages x, (2), 128 and errata slip; original brown printed paper wrappers, spine worn and lower wrapper almost off, but very good in original state. Black 5632.   James Fenning 133-273 1996 £75.00

PORTER, KATHERINE ANNE 1890-1980   A Christmas Story. New York: Delacorte, 1967. 1st edition; drawings; gold stamped boards and dust jacket by Ben Shahn; very fine; review copy with letter to reviewer laid in.   Bromer Booksellers 90-215 1996 $250.00

PORTER, KATHERINE ANNE 1890-1980   French Song Book. N.P.: Harrison of Paris, 1933. 1-595 copies, numbered and signed by Porter; printed on Van Gelder pure rag by J. Enschede en Zonen; laid in are two letterpress printed prospectuses for this book as well as one for Hacienda; book fine, top edge bright gold, in bright dust jacket with small tear to top of front panel and few spots to rear panel, otherwise near fine.   Thomas Dorn 9-216 1996 $350.00

PORTER, KATHERINE ANNE 1890-1980   French Song Book. Paris: Harrison of Paris, 1933. 1st edition; one of 595 copies, signed; printed on Van gelder; fine in blue boards and maroon cloth spine, top edge gilt, printed dust jacket chipped at top, half inch piece missing from bottom edge; bookplate, fine copy in good+ dust jacket.   Priscilla Juvelis 95/1-122 1996 $250.00

PORTER, KATHERINE ANNE 1890-1980   Ship of Fools. Boston: Little Brown, 1962. 1st edition; thick 8vo; decorated endpapers, yellow cloth, dust jacket, signed by author; fine.   James S. Jaffe 34-543 1996 $250.00

PORTER, LAVINIA HONEYMAN   By Ox Team to California. A Narrative Crossing the Plains in 1860. Oakland: Oakland Enquirer, 1910. 1st edition; copy number 25 of 50 copies; 139 pages; original olive buckram, title printed in apple green on front cover and spine, some wear, very good. Graff 3325; Cowan p. 496; Howes P488; Decker 36 330.   Michael D. Heaston 23-289 1996 $2,500.00

PORTER, ROBERT KER 1777-1842   A Narrative of the Campaign in Russia, During the Year 1812. London: printed for Longman, Hurst, Rees, Orme and Brown, n.d. 1813. 1st edition; quarto; (iii)-vii, (1 errata), 282 pages; frontispiece, 2 folding engraved maps; 19th century half calf over marabled boards, neatly rebacked to style, marbled edges, corners and board edges worn, hinges reinforced, occasional light to moderate foxing, few tears to folding maps, expertly repaired, generally very good, clean copy.   Heritage Book Shop 196-194 1996 $450.00

PORTER, ROBERT KER 1777-1842   A Series of Engravings, After Drawings...from the Celebrated Odes of Anacreon. London: pub. by John P. Thompson, June 4, 1805. Small folio; suite of 26 soft ground etched plates; original drab boards, printed paper side label, slightly later cloth spine and corners; some slight marginal spotting at beginning and end, generally very good, scarce.   Ximenes 108-298 1996 $750.00

PORTER, RUFUS   A Choice Selection of Valuable and Curious Arts and Interesting Experiments... Concord: John W. Moore and Co., 1832. Improved edition; 16mo; 107 pages; original printed wrappers, soiled, half title.   M & S Rare Books 60-478 1996 $275.00

PORTER, RUFUS   A New Collection of Genuine Receipts, for the Preparation and Execution of Curious Arts and Interesting Experiments... Concord: Fisk & Chase, 1831. 1st edition; 16mo; 102, 6 pages; contemporary marbled boards, rebacked, leather, last several leaves soiled. Lincoln Lowenstein 123. B&B 8392.   M & S Rare Books 60-479 1996 $350.00

PORTER, RUFUS   A Select Collection of Valuable Curious Arts and Interesting Experiments. Concord: published by Rufus Porter, 1826. 1st edition; 16mo; (2), 132 pages; frontispiece and illustrations at p. 122; contemporary two-toned paper covered boards, uncut, half title. Not in Rink or Imprints Survey.   M & S Rare Books 60-474 1996 $750.00

PORTER, RUFUS   A Select Collection of Valuable and Curious Arts, and Interesting Experiments. Concord: Published by Rufus Porter, J. B. Moore, Printer, 1826. 2nd edition; 16mo; (2), 132 pages; frontispiece and illustrations at p. 122; contemporary two toned paper covered boards, uncut, spine shot, front cover detached, half title. Rink 206.   M & S Rare Books 60-473 1996 $425.00

PORTER, RUFUS   A Select Collection of Valuable and Curious Arts and Interesting Experiments. Concord: pub. by Rufus Porter, J. B. Moore, Printer, 1826. 3rd edition; 16mo; (2), 132 pages, frontispiece and illustrations at p. 122; contemporary two toned paper covered boards, uncut, spine shot, front hinge very weak, half title, few leaves disbound. Rink 207.   M & S Rare Books 60-472 1996 $400.00

PORTER, WILLIAM SYDNEY 1862-1910   The Voice of the City and Other Stories. New York: Limited Editions Club, 1935. Number 904 from 1500 copies, signed by artist; illustrations by George Groscz; fine in tissue wrapper and publisher's slipcase.   Hermitage SP95-991 1996 $350.00

PORTER, WILLIAM WARREN   Engravings from Drawings of the Late Rev. William Warren Porter, fellow of St. John's College, Oxford. London: published by Subscription, 1806. 1st edition; large oblong folio; (9) pages of text, (6) full page plates; original unprinted wrappers, some wear to wrappers, but extremely nice, with excellent impressions of the plates.   The Bookpress 75-451 1996 $485.00

PORTEUS, STANLEY   The Psychology of a Primitive People. London: 1931. 1st edition; 438 pages, many plates; original pink gilt buckram, good+ copy.   Antipodean 28-202 1996 $125.00

PORTIS, CHARLES   Norwood. New York: Simon & Schuster, 1966. 1st edition; fine in near fine dust jacket with couple of faint orange spots that seem to indicate a remainder copy; very scarce.   Between the Covers 42-357 1996 $150.00

PORTLOCK, NATHANIEL   A Voyage Round the World, but More Particularly to the North-West Coast of America, Performed in 1785, 1786, 1787, 1788 in the King George and Queen Charlotte, Captains Portlock and Dixon. London: John Stockdale, 1789. 1st edition; 4to; pages xii, 384, xl, portrait, 6 folding maps; 13 plates; half modern brown calf, blue label, library stamps on 2 maps and 1 plate. Sabin 64389; Howes P497; Hill I p. 239; Smith 8304.   Richard Adelson W94/95-138 1996 $1,785.00

PORTRAITS Of William Harvey. London: 1913. 1st edition; 4to; 50 pages; original binding, margins of a few leaves stained.   W. Bruce Fye 71-951 1996 $100.00

PORTUS, AEMYLIUS   Dictionarium Doricum Graecolatinum, Quod Totius Theocriti, Moschi Syracusani, Bionis, Smyrnaie & Simmiae Rhodii... Frankfurt: ex officina Paltheniana, 1603. 1st edition; 8vo; title with woodcut printer's vignette, Greek and Latin text; full 18th century red morocco boards, elaborate wide gilt floral border, expertly rebacked to style, spine elaborately gilt in compartments; some browning, else good. Ian Wilkinson 95/1-137 1996 £160.00

POSEY, WILLIAM   The Wills Hospital of Philaldelphia: the Influence of European and British Ophthalmology Upon It, and the Part if Played in the Last 100 Years in Developing Ophthalmology in America. Philadelphia: 1931. 1st edition; 340 pages; original binding.   W. Bruce Fye 71-1684 1996 $125.00

POSNER, DAVID   A Rake's Progress; a Poem in Five Sections. Limited Editions Club, 1967. One of 400 copies; folio; printed in black, grey and terracotta; reproductions of 16 etchings by David Hockney; boards, unusually nice, loose errata leaf frayed at lower edge.   Bertram Rota 272-275 1996 £130.00

POST Office Directory for 1829. London: printed for the propriestors, by S. & R. Bentley, 1829. 30th edition; 12mo; pages xi, 564 (at end; pages x, 146); later cloth, institutional copy with "Withdrawn" stamp. Scarce. Peter Murray Hill 185-106 1996 £120.00

THE POST Office London Directory for 1823. London: printed by T. Maiden for the Proprietors, 1823. 24th edition; 12mo; pages xii, 412, lxxii, viii, 136; old sheep, rebacked.   Peter Murray Hill 185-105 1996 £100.00

POST, AUSTIN   Glacier Ice. Toronto: University of Toronto Press, 1971. Oblong folio; pages (xiv), 110, 131 photos; cloth, fine in scuffed dust jacket.   Hugh Anson-Cartwright 87-352 1996 $100.00

POSTELLO, GULIELMO   Cosmographicae... Basel: Johan Oporinum, 1561. 1st edition; small 4to; pages (20), 79, several small woodcut maps, titlepage repaired, with some loss, 2 leaves (K1 K4) from another copy or perhaps in excellent facsimile; early full vellum. Not in Church, Adams, nor OCLOC. Brunet IV.841.   Family Album Tillers-522 1996 $700.00

POSTLEHWAYT, JAMES   The History of the Public Revenue, from the Revolution in 1688 to Christmas 1758. London: printed for the author and sold by J. Knapton, 1759. 1st edition; oblong folio; paes (4), 352; original calf backed marbled boards, rubbed, leather label; few leaves lightly creased, else fine. Kress 5806; McCulloch p. 331; Goldsmith's Lib. 9503. Higgs 2010.   Howard S. Mott 227-114 1996 $950.00

POSTLETHWAITE, JOHN   The Geology of the English Lake District... Keswick: T. Bakewell, 1897. 1st edition; small 8vo; pages iv, 78, (xv), folding map, 2 folding plates, and 2 section; original decorated boards, rebacked in matching cloth, gilt.   R.F.G. Hollett & Son 78-542 1996 £75.00

POSTON, CHARLES D.   The Parsees. N.P.: n.d. 100 pages; decorated cloth; inscribed/signed, very good+.   T. A. Swinford 49-914 1996 $150.00

POSTON, CHARLES D.   Speech of Hon. Charles D. Poston, of Arizona, on Indian Affairs. New York: Edmund Jones & Co., 1865. 1st edition; 20 pages; original printed blue wrappers, minor dampstaining, very good, laid in half morocco slipcase. Graff 3332. Munk Alliot p. 180; Becker Wagner Camp 422. Field 1234.   Michael D. Heaston 23-25 1996 $2,000.00

POTANUS, JOANNES JOVIANUS   Opera Omnia. Venice: Aldus & Asulanus, June 1518 - April 1519 - September 1519. 4to; 3 volumes; Aldine Anchor on titlepage of first volume and at end of 3rd volume; vellum; owner's stamp cut out o title leaf of volume 3 affecting few letters of text on verso; Di Veroli & Paolino Gerli booktickets in all volumes, ownership stamps in title margins of volumes 2 and 3; ownership inscription of Magnoccavalli in volume II. Renouard 82.3, 87.6 and 7; Adams P1860; Brunet IV 808.   Rostenberg & Stern 150-76 $2,750.00

POTOK, CHAIM   The Chosen. New York: Knopf, 1992. Special 25th Anniversary Limited Edition, signed by author; 8vo; black cloth, slipcase. James S. Jaffe 34-544 1996 $100.00

POTT, PERCIVALL   The Chirurgical Works. London: Hawes, W. Clarke and R. Collins, 1775. Quarto; half title, (3), 802 pages; 12 engraved plates, contemporary calf, rebacked, some wear, otherwise tight copy. James Tait Goodrich   K40-238   1996 $1,975.00

POTT, PERCIVALL   Some Few General Remarks on Fractures and Disclocations. London: L. Hawes, et al, 1769. 8vo; (2), 126 pages, 2 engraved plates; recent quarter calf and marbled boards done in contemporary style; text bit foxed and browned, overall quite pleasing copy. GM 4408.   James Tait Goodrich   K40-239   1996 $1,500.00

POTTER, AMBROSE GEORGE   A Bibliography of the Rubaiyat of Omar Khayyam Together with Kindred Matter in Prose and Verse Pertaining Thereto. London: Ingpen and Grant, 1929. 1st edition; number 69 of a limited edition of 300 copies; 8vo; xvi, 314 pages; original boards with cloth spine, rebacked, or spine laid down, edges bumped, otherwise very good.   Worldwide Antiquarian   151-541   1996 $350.00

POTTER, BEATRIX 1866-1943   The Story of Miss Moppet. New York: Frederick Warne and Co., 1906. 1st edition; American issue; wallet format concertina' of color printed text and illustrations (leaf size 110 x 90mm); original decorative cloth, color onlay, some wear, lacks wallet tab, some creasing to some leaves, but good state.   Ash Rare Books   Zenzybyr-75   1996   £195.00

POTTER, BEATRIX 1866-1943   The Tailor of Gloucester. London: F. Warne and Co., 1803. 1st edition; small 8vo; pages 85; original maroon boards, shaped pictorial inlay, extremities minimally rubbed, extremely nice.   R.F.G. Hollett & Son   78-447   1996   £350.00

POTTER, BEATRIX 1866-1943   The Tale of Benjamin Bunny. London: Frederick Warne and Co., 1904. 1st edition; 12mo; pages (vii), 8-84; illustrations in color; original grey boards, lettered in green with onlaid pictorial vignette to upper cover, pictorial endpapers, 2 cm split to paper at upper edge of inner hinge, otherwise fine, both internally and externally of a very scarce and popular book in exceptional condition. Sotheran   PN32-137   1996   £498.00

POTTER, BEATRIX 1866-1943   The Tale of Jemima Puddle-Duck. London: F. Warne & Co., 1908. 1st edition; small 8vo; pages 86; color illustrations; original pictorial green boards, neatly rebacked, in matching levant morocco gilt. Quinby 14.   R.F.G. Hollett & Son   78-448   1996   £250.00

POTTER, BEATRIX 1866-1943   The Tale of Jemima Puddle-Duck. London: F. Warne & Co., 1908. 1st edition; small 8vo; pages 86; color illustrations; original pictorial boards, neatly rebacked in matching calf, gilt; occasional finger mark, but nice. Quinby 14.   R.F.G. Hollett & Son   78-449   1996   £225.00

POTTER, BEATRIX 1866-1943   The Tale of Jemima Puddle-Duck. London: 1908. 1st edition; 16mo; colored plates; colored print to front cover, green boards, backstrip very slightly discolored; contemporary inscription.   Petersfield Bookshop   FH58-66   1996   £160.00

POTTER, BEATRIX 1866-1943   The Tale of Johnny Town-Mouse. London: Frederick Warne and Co., 1919. 1st edition; 12mo; with the "N" present in London of the imprint, so presumably a later printing, despite having the quotes before the first line on page 39 as the first printing; illustrations in color; original pale green boards lettered in dark green with onlaid pictorial vignette to upper cover, pictorial endpapers, spine little darkened and very lightly rubbed, very good.   Sotheran   PN32-142   1996   £368.00

POTTER, BEATRIX 1866-1943   The Tale of Little Pig Robinson. London: Frederick Warne & Co. Ltd., 1930. Early reprint; illustrations by author; original pictorial cloth, dust jacket (extremities and corners somewhat frayed, bit worn and soiled); very nice; presentation, inscribed by author for Mrs. Rogerson. Very nice.   David J. Holmes   52-88   1996 $2,950.00

POTTER, BEATRIX 1866-1943   The Tale of Mr. Jeremy Fisher. London: Frederick Warne & Co., 1906. 1st edition; 8vo; pages 86; illustrations in color; original pictorial boards, neatly rebacked in matching calf gilt, few light finger marks, but very good.   R.F.G. Hollett & Son   78-451   1996   £225.00

POTTER, BEATRIX 1866-1943   The Tale of Mr. Tod. London: Warne, 1912. 1st edition; 12mo; grey boards with oblong pictorial onlay, very top of spine professionally repaired, spine darkened, little worn, else very good. Quinby 21.   Marjorie James   19-179   1996   £275.00

POTTER, BEATRIX 1866-1943   The Tale of Mrs. Tiggy-Winkle. London: Frederick Warne and Co., 1905. 1st edition; 8vo; pages 85; illustrations in color; original pictorial boards, lower board with slight binding fault crease; almost invisibly recased, but very nice.   R.F.G. Hollett & Son   78-452   1996   £275.00

POTTER, BEATRIX 1866-1943   The Tale of Mrs. Tittlemouse. London: Frederick Warne & Co., 1910. 1st edition; 16mo; 86 pages; illustrations in color; original blue paper covered boards with hexagonal color illustration on upper cover, lettered in white, very slightly worn, but unusually fine inside and out.   Thomas Thorp   489-250   1996   £250.00

POTTER, BEATRIX 1866-1943   The Tale of Peter Rabbit. Philadelphia: henry Altemus, 1904. Early American edition; 12mo; 63 pages; 31 full page plates; cloth backed purple boards, printed paper label to front cover, extremities lightly rubbed, else fine.   Bromer Booksellers   87-152   1996 $250.00

POTTER, BEATRIX 1866-1943   The Tale of Pigling Bland. London: Frederick Warne and Co., 1913. 1st edition; 12mo; pages (vi), 7-93; illustrations in color and line; original green boards letttered in brown, with onlaid pictorial vignette to upper cover, pictorial endpapers, very light surface rubbing, very good, crisp.   Sotheran   PN32-141   1996   £368.00

POTTER, BEATRIX 1866-1943   The Tale of the Flopsy Bunnies. London: Frederick Warne and Co., 1909. 1st edition; 12mo; pages (vii), 8-84; illustrations in color; original greyish brown boards, lettered in white with onlaid pictorial vignette to upper cover, pictorial endpapers, cm. split to paper at upper joint, light soiling of spine and covers, tiny prick to centre spine edges dusted, generally very nice, internally very clean.   Sotheran   PN32-139   1996   £148.00

POTTER, BEATRIX 1866-1943   The Tale of Timmy Tiptoes. London: Frederick Warne and Co., 1911. 1st edition; 12mo; pages (vii), 8-84; illustrations in color; original grey boards lettered in white with onlaid pictorial vignette to upper cover, pictorial endpapers, one very minor indentation to lower board, otherwise excellent with very minor rubbing. Sotheran   PN32-140   1996   £368.00

POTTER, BEATRIX 1866-1943   The Tale of Timmy Tiptoes. London: Frederick Warne and Co., 1911. 1st edition; 16mo; 86 pages; illustrations in color; original dark green paper covered boards with color illustration on front cover, lettered in white, ink signature on half title, some slight finger soiling in text, but very good.   Thomas Thorp   489-251   1996   £220.00

POTTER, BEATRIX 1866-1943   The Tale of Two Bad Mice. London: Warne, 1904. 1st edition; 12mo; color illustrations; red boards with colored pictorial onlay, rebacked with original spine laid down, else very good, endpapers and contents near fine; inscription Xmas 1904. Marjorie James   19-180   1996   £250.00

POTTER, FRANCIS   An Interpretation of the Number 666. Oxford: Leonard Lichfield, 1642. 4to; (18), 214 pages; engraved symbolic title by W. Marshall, woodcut illustration and several diagrams in text, woodcut headpiece and initials; contemporary calf, front joint broken, some leather repairs to back cover, some mold staining at lower margins; good copy. Thorndike VI 464; Zeitlinger 3726; Wing P 3028; Caillet 8921. Edwin V. Glaser   121-256   1996 $950.00

POTTER, ISRAEL R.   Life and Remarkable Adventures of Israel R. Potter. Providence: printed by Henry Trumbull, 1824. 1st edition; 12mo; 108 pages; frontispiece, old calf backed boards, rubbed, one leaf with marginal burn, affecting a few letters. Howes T371.   Kenneth Karmiole   1NS-213   1996 $150.00

POTTER, SIDNEY PELL   A History of Wymeswold (Leicestershire). London: J. Miles and Co., Ltd. 1915. 1st edition; 8vo; half title, frontispiece, 16 plates, errata slip, original cloth nice.   Anthony W. Laywood   108-222   1996   £60.00

POTTINGER, DAVID T.   The French Book Trade in the Ancient Regime 1500-1791. Cambridge: Harvard University Press, 1958. 1st edition; 8vo; xiv, 363 pages; cloth, dust jacket; excellent, surprisingly scarce, fine in lightly chipped jacket.   The Bookpress   75-344   1996 $110.00

POUCHER, W. A.   A Camera in the Cairngorms. London: Chapman and Hall, 1947. 1st edition; small 4to; pages 144; 93 photos by author; original cloth, dust jacket, top edge trifle rubbed.   R.F.G. Hollett   76-240   1996   £220.00

POUCHER, W. A.   The Magic of Skye. London: Chapman and Hall, 1949. 1st edition; 4to; 148 photos, pages 223; original cloth, dust jacket, top edge very slightly worn, small nick, lower panel trifle spotted; scarce.   R.F.G. Hollett 76-352 1996 £85.00

POULSEN, FREDERIK   Greek and Roman Portraits in English Country Houses. Oxford: Clarendon Press, 1923. Large 4to; frontispiece, xiv, 112 pages, 57 figures, 112 plates; gilt embossed cloth, small tears at spine, minor shelfwear at extremities, otherwise fine.   Archaeologia Luxor-3853 1996 $350.00

POUND, EZRA LOOMIS 1885-1972   ABC of Reading. London: Routledge, 1934. Front board bowed and dust jacket little rubbed, else excellent.   R. A. Gekoski 19-115 1996 £150.00

POUND, EZRA LOOMIS 1885-1972   The Cantos of Ezra Pound. London: Faber & Faber, 1954. 1st edition; original binding, top edge dusty, head and tail of spine slightly bumped, edges faintly spotted, free endpapers partially browned, very good in nicked, rubbed, chipped and dusty dust jacket browned at spine and edges and frayed at head and tail of spine.   Ulysses 39-475 1996 £95.00

POUND, EZRA LOOMIS 1885-1972   The Exile. Dijon & Chicago: 1927-28. 1st edition; 8vo; wrappers, very decent set, chips on spine ends, noticeably on #1 which also has a tear, very good. Increasingly rare. With pencil change's in Pound's hand.   Charles Agvent 4-961 1996 $650.00

POUND, EZRA LOOMIS 1885-1972   Forked Branches. Windhover Press, 1985. One of 200 copies; 11 1/4 x 7 inches; 3 p.l., xvi, 85, (1) pages, (1) leaf (colophon); mounted wood engraved color frontispiece by Dellas Henke; mint.   Phillip J. Pirages 33-516 1996 $325.00

POUND, EZRA LOOMIS 1885-1972   Imaginary Letters. Paris: Black Sun Press, 1930. Limited to 300 copies on Navarre Paper; 8vo; wrappers, tissue outer wrapper, slipcase, fine in slightly rubbed slipcase..   James S. Jaffe 34-546 1996 $500.00

POUND, EZRA LOOMIS 1885-1972   The Letters of Ezra Pound 1907-1941. London: Faber, 1941. 1st English edition, 1st issue, one of 2990 copies; 8vo; red cloth, dust jacket; fine; Gallup A64b.   James S. Jaffe 34-547 1996 $150.00

POUND, EZRA LOOMIS 1885-1972   Literary Essays. London: Faber, 1954. 1st edition; 8vo; cloth, dust jacket, very fine.   James S. Jaffe 34-548 1996 $150.00

POUND, EZRA LOOMIS 1885-1972   Lustra, with Earlier Poems. New York: 1917. 1st American edition, number 38 of 60 copies printed "For Private Circulation" and distributed gratis; covers slightly soiled, lettering piece browned and rubbed, very good, half title excised, as in most copies, and left as a stub.   R. A. Gekoski 19-113 1996 £500.00

POUND, EZRA LOOMIS 1885-1972   Passages from the Letters of John Butler Yeats. Churchtown, Dundrum: Cuala Press, 1917. Some offsetting to endpapers, otherwise excellent in tissue dust jacket; owner's bookplate designed by Jack B. Yeats.   R. A. Gekoski 19-114 1996 £250.00

POUND, EZRA LOOMIS 1885-1972   Personae. The Collected Poems of Ezra Pound. New York: Boni & Liveright, 1926. 1st edition; 8vo; blue cloth, dust jacket, front free endpaper creased, otherwise exceptionally fine copy, virtually as new.   James S. Jaffe 34-545 1996 $1,250.00

POUND, EZRA LOOMIS 1885-1972   Poems 1918-1921. New York: Boni & Liveright, 1921. 1st edition; 8vo; original quarter vellum and boards, spine cracking, boards slightly worn, not unattractive, but good copy only, in handsome quarter morocco slipcase; Delmore Schwartz's copy, complete with extensive annotations and one original Schwartz poem.   Lakin & Marley 3-48 1996 $1,250.00

POUND, EZRA LOOMIS 1885-1972   Poems 1918-21. New York: 1921. 1st edition; 9.5 x 6 inches; 90 pages; imitation vellum backed boards, covers bit darkened with chipped extremities.   John K. King 77-427 1996 $195.00

POUND, EZRA LOOMIS 1885-1972   Provenca. Boston: Small, Maynard, 1910. One of 200 copies; dust jacket restored where a piece on front panel (without lettering) was missing, else nice, distincly uncommon in jacket.   R. A. Gekoski 19-112 1996 £1,200.00

POUND, EZRA LOOMIS 1885-1972   Translations by Ezra Pound. London: Elkin Mathews, 1915. 1st edition; decorated wrappers, bit of scattered light foxing, otherwise very fine.   Captain's Bookshelf 38-188 1996 $375.00

POUND, ROSCOE   An Introduction to the Philosophy of Law. New Haven: Yale University Press, 1922. 1st edition; bit rubbed, quite good, fresh copy.   Meyer Boswell SL27-192 1996 $125.00

POWELL, ANTHONY DYMOKE 1905-   A Dance to the Music of Time. London: Heinemann, 1951-75. 1st editions; 12 volumes; staining to boards of volume two and wear and minor loss to jackets of first two volumes, overall nice set, most volumes near fine in dust jackets.   Lame Duck Books 19-465 1996 $2,500.00

POWELL, ANTHONY DYMOKE 1905-   John Aubrey and His Friends. London: Eyre & Spottiswoode, 1948. 1st edition; 9 black and white plates, 2 extending charts; original binding, top edge slightly dusty, head and tail of spine and one corner slightly bumped, very good in nicked, rubbed and dusty, slightly torn and creased, internally repaired dust jacket browned at spine and edges.   Ulysses 39-477 1996 £125.00

POWELL, ANTHONY DYMOKE 1905-   A Question of Upbringing. New York: Scribners, 1951. 1st American edition; fore edges slightly tanned, else fine in near fine dust jacket with small nicks and tears at extremities and touch of darkening to extremities, still nice. Author Peter DeVries's copy with his pencil ownership.   Between the Covers 42-358 1996 $375.00

POWELL, ANTHONY DYMOKE 1905-   A Reference for Mellors. London: Moorhouse & Sorensen, 1994. 1st separate edition; of a total edition of 326, one of 100 numbered copies; printed by letterpress at the Libanus Press on velin Arches and signed by Powell; fine in green cloth.   Lame Duck Books 19-466 1996 $150.00

POWELL, ANTHONY DYMOKE 1905-   A Reference for Mellors. London: printed at the Libanus Press for Moorhouse & Sorensen, 1994. 1st edition; 13/100 copies (of an edition of 326); crown 8vo; printed on velin arches mouldmade paper and signed by author; pages 19, (1); quarter black linen, backstrip gilt lettered, mid green linen sides, new copy.   Blackwell's B112-232 1996 £75.00

POWELL, ANTHONY DYMOKE 1905-   A Reference for Mellors. London: Moorhouse & Sorensen, 1994. 1st separate edition; of a total edition of 326, one of 26 lettered copies printed by letterpress on Velin Arches and signed by Powell; fine in attractive quarter goatskin and marbled paper covered boards and cloth covered slipcase.   Lame Duck Books 19-467 1996 $375.00

POWELL, CHARLES   Bound Feet. Boston: 1938. 1st edition; 339 pages; autographed by author; original binding.   W. Bruce Fye 71-1687 1996 $100.00

POWELL, J. W.   Introduction to the Study of Indian Languages. Washington: GPO, 1880. 2nd edition; 2 folding charts in pocket, head and tail of spine worn, rear joint starting, overall little loose, still good.   Hermitage SP95-728 1996 $150.00

POWELL, JOHN J.   Nevada: The Land of Silver. San Francisco: Bacon & Co., 1876. 1st edition; 305, (7) pages, ads; illustrations; original brown cloth, title in gilt on spine and front cover; fine. Howes P526; Paher Nevada 1577; not in Graff.   Michael D. Heaston 23-255 1996 $750.00

POWELL, LAWRENCE CLARK   Musical Blood Brothers: Wolfgang Amadeus Mozart, Franz Josef, Haydn. Malibu: Press of the Prevailing Westerly, 1966. 1st edition; one of approximately 150 copies; small 8vo; 28 pages; stiff light green wrappers, paper label on upper cover, very good.   George J. Houle 68-121 1996 $125.00

POWELL, ROBERT HUTCHINSON   A Medical Topography of Tunbridge Wells; Illustrating the Beneficial Influence of Its Mineral Waters, Climate, Soil, etc... London: John Churchill; John Colbran, Tunbridge Wells, 1846. 1st edition; 12mo; folding colored map, 3 plates (one foxed), 5 page list of subscribers; original cloth, uncut, nice.   Anthony W. Laywood 108-223 1996 £65.00

POWELL, WILFRED   Wanderings in a Wild Country; or, Three Years Amongst the Cannibals of New Britain. London: 1884. (viii), 283 pages, black and white illustrations in text; pictorial blue green cloth loose, rubbed and marked, 1 signature loose, otherwise good.   Antipodean 28-208 1996 $325.00

POWER, TYRONE   Impressions of America, During the Years 1833, 1834 and 1835. London: R. Bentley, 1836. 1st edition; 2 volumes, xv, 440; vi, 408 pages; frontispiece in each volume, ads in front of volume 1; simply rebound in full leather, very good, partially unopened. Howes P533; Clark, Old South III 286.   Bohling Book Co. 191-378 1996 $150.00

POWER, TYRONE   Sketches in New Zealand, with Pen and Pencil. London: Longman, Brown, Etc., 1849. 8vo; pages xlviii, 290; 8 tinted plates, 2 woodcuts; new half calf, red label, marbled boards, library stamp on title.   Richard Adelson W94/95-139 1995 $385.00

THE POWERS and Duties of the Town Officer, as Contained in the Statutes of Maine. Hallowell: pub. by Calvin Spaulding, 1824. 2nd edition; 324 pages; original gilt stamped calf, some aging, light rubbin, slight stain on first few leaves.   Rockland Books 38-177 1996 $125.00

POWERS, ALAN   The Marches: a Picturesque Tour. Merivale Editions, 1989. One of 75 sets, signed by artist and author, each print numbered and signed; folio; 8 lithographs, 7 colored; texts printed on Arches by Sebastian Carter, prints on Rivoli; unbound folded leaves, prints laid to face poems, preserved in stout folding box with red cloth, corners, sides covered in striking green paste paper made by artist; fine.   Bertram Rota 272-287 1996 £400.00

POWERS, RICHARD   The Gold Bug Variations. New York: Morrow, 1991. 1st edition; fine in fine dust jacket.   Ken Lopez 74-377 1996 $175.00

POWERS, RICHARD   Three Farmers on their Way to a Dance. New York: Morrow, 1985. 1st edition; author's first book. Fine in fine dust jacket.   Alice Robbins 15-270 1996 $175.00

POWERS, TIM   The Anubis Gates. London: Chatto & Windus, 1985. 1st hardcover edition; very fine in dust jacket with slight bumping to head of spine panel; inscribed and dated by author.   Robert Gavora 61-106 1996 $375.00

POWERS, TIM   On Stranger Tides. Ultramarine Press, 1987. 1st edition; 1/150 copies, signed by author; specially bound in half leather and spotted boards. as new, without dust jacket, as issued. Aronovitz 57-963 1996 $200.00

POWERS, TIM   The Stress of Her Regard. Lynbrook: Charnel House, 1989. 1st edition; limited to 500 numbered copies, signed by author, by Dean Koontz who provided introduction and by James Blaylock who provided afterword; illustrations by author; crushed blue denim, very fine, issued without dust jacket in denim slipcase.   Robert Gavora 61-110 1996 $175.00

POWICKE, F. M.   King Henry III and the Lord Edward: the Community of the Realm in the Thirteenth Century. London: Oxford University Press, 1947. Original edition; royal 8vo; 2 volumes; 2 folding maps; original buckram, dust jackets. Gross/Graves 4062.   Howes Bookshop 265-989 1996 £75.00

POWYS, THEODORE FRANCIS 1875-1953   The White Paternoster and Other Stories. London: Chatto & Windus, 1930. One of 310 numbered copies, signed by author; buckram backed decorated boards, top edge gilt, spine faded and spotted, covers dusty and slightly marked, cover edges slightly rubbed, endpaper edges slightly browned, very good. Ulysses 39-479 1996 £60.00

POYNTER, F. N. L.   A Catalouge of Incunabula in the Wellcome Historical Medical Library. London: Oxford University Press, 1954. 1st edition; 4to; 12 plates; original cloth, dust jacket little foxed; presentation copy from author to W. R. Le Fanu.   Forest Books 74-221 1996 £80.00

POYNTING, F.   Eggs of British Birds with an Acount of Their Breeding Habits: Limicolae. London: 1895-96. 4to; 2 plain and 55 fine colored plates; new buckram, unique copy, the copy of H. E. Dresser, there are 3 extra plates and few cuttings inserted; one plate is inscribed "With kind regards from H. E. Dresser." The owner has noted "Given to me by Mr. Dresser on Saturday June 5th 1909 - before this plate appeared in his work on Palearctic Eggs." Little foxed, heavily on few leaves. Wheldon & Wesley 207-86 1996 £500.00

POZZO, ANDREA   Rules and Examples of Perspective Proper for Painters and Architects... London: Benjamin Motte, 1707. 1st English language edition; folio; frontispiece, (xx), 130 pages, 103 plates; contemporary calf; spine darkened, hinges beginning to crack, otherwise exceptionally nice; subscriber's copy, belonging to Earl of Coningsby whose arms are stamped on binding.   The Bookpress 75-224 1996 $3,500.00

PRAED, WINTHROP MACKWORTH   The Poems. London: Edward Moxon & Co., 1864. 2nd edition; small 8vo; 2 volumes; half red morocco, spines decorated in compartments to an art nouveau design, gilt lettered direct in second and third compartments and with date in gilt at foot, pink cloth sides, marbled endpapers, top edges gilt, others uncut; for Hatchards.   Simon Finch 24-192 1996 £110.00

PRAEGER, ROBERT L.   The Way That I Went. London: 1937. Imperial 8vo; illustrations, folding map at rear; original cloth, rather rubbed, contents very good.   David A.H. Grayling MY95Orn-427 1996 £60.00

PRAMBHOFER, JOHANNES   Wunderseltsame, Wahrhaffte, Beynabens Lacherliche Traum-Gesichter... Augsburg: Schulter and Happach, 1712. 1st edition; 4to; 424 pages; 12 full page allegorical engravings, woodcut and typographic ornaments, usual browning; three quarter vellum; very good, very rare. Faber du faur 1140; Jantz 2024; Hayn-Gotendorf 6.272. Bennett Gilbert LL29-65 1996 $1,100.00

PRATCHETT, TERRY   Strata. Gerrards Cross: Colin Smythe Ltd., 1981. 1st edition; original binding, head and tail of spine and corners bumped, covers bowed, very good in slightly creased dust jacket.   Ulysses 39-480 1996 £295.00

PRATO, DANIELLO DA   Trattato Della Preservantia Intitolato Corona di Serui D'Iddio... Venice: Comin da Trino, 1544. 1st edition; 8vo; 400 pages; woodcut title vignette, printed shoulder notes, contemporary full limp vellum, hand lettered backstrip, fine. Not in NUC or BM STC. Bennett Gilbert LL29-66 1996 $1,250.00

PRATT, A. E.   To the Snows of Tibet through China. London: Longmans, 1892. 1st edition; 8vo; xviii,2 68 pages; folding lithographed map, portrait, plates; original blue pictorial cloth, gilt, few light marks, corners rubbed; fine, bright copy.   James Burmester 29-111 1996 £300.00

PRATT, A. E.   Two Years Among New Guinea Cannibals... London: Seeley & Co., 1906. 360 pages, black and white plates, folding map; rebound in attractive black half gilt morocco, nice; Mervyn Meggitt's copy.   Antipodean 28-209 1996 $175.00

PRATT, ANNE   The Flowering Plants, Grasses, Sedges and Ferns of Great Britain, and Their Allies the Club Mosses, Pepperworts and Horsetails. London: Warne & Co., n.d. 1874. Royal 8vo; 1 plain and 317 colored plates; fine, clean state, 6 volumes; original cloth, gilt, gilt edges. Charles W. Traylen 117-325 1996 £380.00

PRATT, ANNE   Things of the Sea Coast. London: Society for Promoting Christian Knowledge, 1853. 1st edition; 8vo; original cloth, somewhat worn; enclosed in brown cloth box with matching labels; Gerard Manley Hopkins' copy, inscribed by him to his Aunt Maria. Lakin & Marley 3-20 1996 £750.00

PRATT, DANIEL   Autobiography of Daniel Pratt, Jr., A.A.S. of Boston, formerly of Prattville, Chelsea, Mass. Boston: printed by a Cosmopolitan for the author, from the Original Ms., 1855. 1st edition; 8vo; 32 pages; extensively illustrated, portrait; original printed wrappers, uncut, very nice. Not in Sabin; 2 copies in NUC.   M & S Rare Books 60-398 1996 $750.00

PRATT, FLETCHER   Land of Unreason. New York: Holt, 1942. 1st edition; fine in dust jacket.   Robert Gavora 61-112 1996 $190.00

PRATT, FLETCHER   Land of Unreason. New York: Holt, 1942. 1st edition; signed by De Camp; fine in dust jacket with some wear to extremities and some fading to yellows and oranges of spine panel. Robert Gavora 61-113 1996 $150.00

PRATT, PARLEY PARKER 1807-1857   A Voice of Warning and Instruction to All People... New York: W. Sandford, 1837. 1st edition; 18mo; 216 pages; original cloth, soiled, very sound, clean and cirsp inside. Flake 6627; Crawley & Flake, Notable Mormon Books 6.   M & S Rare Books 60-399 1996 $3,250.00

PRATT, PETER PARLEY   A Voice of Warning and Instruction to All People, Containing a Declaration of the Faith and Doctrine of the Church of the Latter Day Saints, Commonly Called Mormons. New York: W. Sandford, 1837. 1st edition; 18mo; 216 pages, covers lightly dampstained, occasional light foxing, lacks pages 181-204; original cloth, very scarce, pages 181-204 lacking and 145-168 are repeated, binder's error.   Edward Morrill 369-248 1996 $500.00

PRAVAL, CHARLES   The Idioms of the French Language, Compared with Those of English, In a Series of Polite and Instructive Conversations. Dublin: printed by George Burnett, 1794. Stained at tail, early repair to tear in pages 139-140, few ink marks; contemporary tree sheep, slight worming to leather only at head and tail, hinges splitting, black label chipped. Not in Alston; ESTC t153831.   Jarndyce 103-325 1996 £65.00

PRENDERGAST, MAURICE   A Sketchbook of Maurice Prendergast. Erie: Hammermill Papers Group, 1974. 1st edition; small 8vo; pictorial dust jacket, boards; fine copy.   James S. Jaffe 34-11 1996 $125.00

PRENTICE, E. PARMALEE   The Influence of Hunger on Human History. Williamstown: 1938. 1st edition; photographic illustrations; original binding; autographed by author.   W. Bruce Fye 71-1701 1996 $100.00

PRENTICE, H.   Captured by Apes; or, How Philip Garland Became King of Apeland. Burt, 1888. 1st edition; tight, very good copy with unborken inner hinges.   Aronovitz 57-966 1996 $125.00

PRENTIS, NOBLE L.   Kansas Miscellanies. Topeka: Kansas Publishing House, 1889. 7 1/8 x 5 inches; vi, 199 pages; black and gold stamped green cloth, some light soiling to front cover.   Dawson's Books Shop 528-199 1996 $100.00

PRENTISS, CHARLES   The Life of the Late Gen. William Eaton...Principally Collected from His Correspondence and Other Manuscripts. Brookfield: printed by E. Merriam & Co., 1813. 1st edition; viii, 448 pages; original calf, worn, lacking portrait. Howes P570; Burr 77. Blue River Books 9-261 1996 $150.00

PRESCOTT, GEORGE B.   History, Theory and Practice of the Electric Telegraph. Boston: Ticknor & Fields, 1860. 1st edition; 8vo; xii, 468 pages; frontispiece, 98 illustrations in text; original pebbled cloth, binding faded and dull, library card pocket removed from rear pastedown, good, sound copy.   Edwin V. Glaser 121-257 1996 $100.00

PRESCOTT, J. E.   The Register of the Priory of Wetheral. London: Elliot Stock, 1897. 1st edition; 8vo; pages xliii, 552, (iv), frontispiece (cutting laid on to recto), prelims little spotted; original cloth, gilt. R.F.G. Hollett & Son 78-597 1996 £150.00

PRESCOTT, J. E.   The Statutes of the Cathedral Church of Carlisle. London: Elliot Stock, 1903. 2nd edition; 8vo; pages x, 128; 5 plates; original cloth, gilt, notes on rear endpapers, front flyleaf removed. R.F.G. Hollett & Son 78-1206 1996 £65.00

PRESCOTT, WILLIAM HICKLING 1796-1859   History of the Conquest of Mexico with a Preliminary View of the Ancient Mexican Civilization and the Life of the Conqueror, Hernando Cortes. New York: Harper & Bros., 1843. 1st edition; 9 1/2 x 6 1/2 inches; 3 volumes; frontispiece with tissue in each volume, double page map in volumes 1 and 2, one facsimile plate; original slate green cloth, blocked in blind and titled in gilt, few leaves unopened, slight foxing and browning, especially on endleaves, otherwise excellent internally, few scratches on one cover, one volume with two or three tiny white paint flecks, otherwise bindings in beautiful condition, extremely clean and bright and unworn. Fine set. Phillip J. Pirages 33-432 1996 $500.00

PRESCOTT, WILLIAM HICKLING 1796-1859   History of the Conquest of Mexico. London: 1843. 1st edition; 3 volumes; contemporary half calf, light wear, nice set, textually clean and bright.   Stephen Lunsford 45-132 1996 $100.00

PRESCOTT, WILLIAM HICKLING 1796-1859   History of the Conquest of Peru, 1524-1550. Mexico City: Imprenta Nuevo Mundo, 1957. Limited edition, number 1397 of 1500 copies, signed by printer and illustrator; folio; xxxvi, 252 pages, numerous illustrations; full calf, leather labels, slightly worn, slipcase.   Archaeologia Luxor-4795 1996 $150.00

PRESCOTT, WILLIAM HICKLING 1796-1859   The Works. Philadelphia and London: J. B. Lippincott Co., 1904. One of 1000 copies of the Montezuma Edition; 8 1/2 x 5 3/4 inches; 22 volumes; 122 attractive plates by Goupil of Paris, titles in red and black; excellent green three quarter crushed morocco signed by Brentano's, cloth sides, spines attractively gilt in four smaller and one larger compartment featuring elegant stems, leaves and flowers, the larger compartment with prominent inlaid red morocco tulip, marbled endpapers, gilt top, spines faded (as is inevitable with green morocco) to a pleasing tan (3 spines a bit darker than the rest), some corners bit worn, 3 tiny snags in headcaps, otherwise spine ends and joints unworn, finely bound set still bright and quite attractive on the shelf, 3 leaves carelessly opened, 6 volumes with one or more leaves loose or detached because of defective sewing (all leaves still present), otherwise fine internally. Phillip J. Pirages 33-433 1996 $750.00

PRESCOTT, WILLIAM HICKLING 1796-1859   Complete Works. London: Routledge, c. 1900. Library edition; large 8vo; 12 volumes; fs; original brown cloth, gilt.   Howes Bookshop 265-994 1996 £150.00

THE PRESENT Judiciary System of South Carolina; Its Defects Reviewed and Modes Suggested for Its Improvement. Charleston: Walker and James, 1850. 1st edition; 8vo; 24 pages; disbound. Sabin 87918.   M & S Rare Books 60-409 1996 $100.00

THE PRESENT State of the Game Law, and the Question of Property, Considered. Edinburgh: printed by Fleming and Neill, 1772. Modern quarter calf over marbled boards, bit of foxing, attractive.   Meyer Boswell SL27-88 1996 $350.00

PRESENTATION of a Timepiece to Alexander Hamilton and W. A. Blackwell by Ten Fellow Sportsmen and True Friends on the Occasion of the 1947 Quail Hunt on the Delightful Ranch of Alexander Hamilton. Cuero: Texas, January 10, 1947. 1st and only edition; (20) pages; 16 photos on stiff paper boards; original stiff red boards with title on front cover, spiral bound; fine.   Michael D. Heaston 23-176 1996 $200.00

THE PRESENTMENT of the Grand Jury for the City of London, at the Sessions of Peace and Gaol Delivery at Justice-Hall in the Old Baily, on thursday 19th April 1683. London: printed by Samuel Roycroft... 1683. Folio; 4 leaves, uncut, disbound. Wing P3282.   H. M. Fletcher 121-48 1996 £65.00

PRESS, C. A. M.   Westmorland Lives Social and Political. London: Gaskill, Jones & Co., c. 1900. 4to; unpaginated, 19 portraits; original blue cloth, gilt, trifle darkened and marked, all edges gilt.   R.F.G. Hollett & Son 78-235 1996 £85.00

PRESTON, THOMAS   The Life and Opinions of Thomas Preston, Patriot and Shoemaker... London: printed for the author, 1817. 1st edition; 8vo; disbound; very good; rare. 1 copy in NUC.   Ximenes 108-299 1996 $150.00

PRESTWICH, EDMUND   The Hectors; or the False Challenge. London: printed for G. Bedel and T. Collins, 1656. 1st edition; small 4to; disbound, trimmed bit close at bottom, affecting some catchwords and signature marks, otherwise very good. Rare. Wing P3315; Greg 762; Woodward & McManaway 946; CBEL II 1759.   Ximenes 109-239 1996 $750.00

PRESTWICH, JOSEPH   Geology Chemicla, Physical and Stratigraphical. Oxford: 1886. 2 volumes, maps, plates, text illustrations; backstrips rubbed, but sound.   Petersfield Bookshop FH58-163 1996 £52.00

PRETTY Peggy and other Ballads. London: Sampson Low, Marston, Searle and Rivington, n.d., ca. 1890. 4to; 64 pages; colored illustrations by Rosina Emmet; glazed color pictorial boards, extremities rubbed, inner hinge cracked, else very good.   Marjorie James 19-217 1996 £55.00

PRETTY Polly. London: Nister, ca. 1899. Small quarto; (28) pages; 4 colorful pop-ups; original color pictorial boards, first signature starting, light rubbing to extremities, else near fine with bright and fine pop-ups, gift inscription dated 1899.   Bromer Booksellers 87-145 1996 $750.00

PREVOST, ANTOINE FRANCOIS, CALLED PREVOST D'EXILES 1697-1763 Manon Lescaut. London: Geoffrey Bles, 1928. One of 500 copies, pringed and signed by artist; large 4to; 12 full page color lithographs by John Austen; blue linen boards over vellum spine, as issued; nice. Appelfeld Gallery 54-150 1996 $150.00

PRICE, EDWARD   Norway and its Scenery. London: 1853. 21 fine engraved plates; 19th century half calf, light rubbing, contents excellent; scarce.   David A.H. Grayling 3/95-497 1996 £110.00

PRICE, FREDERIC NEWLIN   The Etchings and Lithographs of Arthur B. DAvies. New York: Kennerley, 1929. Folio; 23 pages text, 265 paltes; cloth. Inscribed by author; Lucas p. 138; Freitag 2131.   Brannan 43-152 1996 $325.00

PRICE, J.   The Buyers' Manual and Business Guide... San Francisco: Francis & Valentine, 1872. 1st edition; 8vo; v, (7), 192, 15 pages, first and final leaves pasted onto endpapers, numerous woodcuts in text, 4 leaves of ads; original brown cloth, title in gilt on upper cover.   John Drury 82-225 1996 £250.00

PRICE, JOHN FREDERICK   Ootacamund. A History. Madras: Government Press, 1908. 1st edition; large 8vo; pages xi, (5), 281; 26 maps, plans and plates; original half morocco, gilt, binding little worn, but sound and strong, cloth sides lightly discolored, yet very good; with signed inscription by author.   James Fenning 133-274 1996 £185.00

PRICE, JULIUS M.   From the Arctic Ocean to the Yellow Sea (Across Siberia-Mongolia). New York: Scribners, 1892. 8vo; pages 384, folding map, 42 plates; original pictorial cloth, lightly rubbed.   Richard Adelson W94/95-205 1996 $125.00

PRICE, LANGFORD LOVELL   Economic Science and Practice. London: Methuen & Co., 1896. 1st edition; 8vo; viii, 325, (1) pages, 39 pages of publishers' ads after text; original olive cloth lettered in gilt, bookplate and inkstamp of Working Men's College; uncut, very good. Not in Einaudi or Masui.   John Drury 82-226 1996 £90.00

PRICE, R. N.   Holston Methodism. Nashville: 1904-14. 5 volumes, almost 2500 pages; extremely difficult to find as a set, extra nice looking.   Bookworm & Silverfish 276-167 1996 $275.00

PRICE, REYNOLDS 1933-   A Final Letter: Robinson Mayfield in Essex, North Carolina to Huchins Mayfield, England, June 15 to November 27, 1955. Los Angeles: Sylvester & Orphanos, 1980. 1st edition; number 62 of 330 numbered copies, signed by author; thin 8vo; titlepage printed in tan and black; brown textured cloth, spine with gilt and black printed label, upper cover with large gilt and black monogram, right edge uncut, very good to fine.   George J. Houle 68-122 1996 $125.00

PRICE, REYNOLDS 1933-   The Honest Account of a Memorable Life. North Carolina Wesleyan: College Press, 1994. One of only 100 copies, specially signed by Price; patterned boards backed in wine colored cloth; fine.   Bev Chaney, Jr. 23-568 1996 $125.00

PRICE, REYNOLDS 1933-   A Long and Happy Life. New York: 1962. 1st edition; advance review copy, with slip; author's first book, fine.   Stephen Lupack 83- 1996 $225.00

PRICE, REYNOLDS 1933-   A Long and Happy Life. New York: Atheneum, 1963. 1st edition; 1st issue dust jacket; fine in near fine dust jacket tanned at spine and extremities, author's first book.   Between the Covers 42-359 1996 $125.00

PRICE, REYNOLDS 1933-   Things Themselves. New York: Atheneum, 1972. 1st edition; fine in dust jacket with tiny tear at crown; uncommon.   Between the Covers 42-361 1996 $125.00

PRICE, RICHARD 1723-1791   Ladies' Man. Boston: Houghton Mifflin, 1978. Uncorrected proof; reviewer's comments and small tear on first leaf (half title), otherwise fine; wrappers; uncommon.   Ken Lopez 74-379 1996 $150.00

PRICE, RICHARD 1723-1791   Observations on the Nature of Civil Liberty, the Principles of Government and the Justice and Policy of the War With America.... (with) Additional Observations on the Nature and Value of Civil Liberty, and the War with America... London: printed for T. Cadell, 1776/77. 7th edition, 1st edition respectively; 8vo; 2 volumes in 1; pages (viii), 134; xvi, 176; recent quarter calf, utilizing contemporary marbled boards, little rubbed, red leather label, very good; with armorial bookplate of John Williams. Kress B71.   Sotheran PN32-39 1996 £498.00

PRICE, RICHARD 1723-1791   Observations on Reversionary Payments; on Schemes for Providing Annuities for Widows and for Persons in Old Age... London: printed for T. Cadell, 1792. 5th edition; 8vo; 2 volumes; half titles; contemporary tree calf, slightly rubbed, spines ruled in gilt, labels; nice. Kress B2391; Goldsmith 15317.   Anthony W. Laywood 108-114 1996 £345.00

PRICE, ROSE LAMBART   The Two Americas: an Account of Sport and Travel. London: Sampson, Low, Marston, Searle and Rivington, 1877. 2nd edition; tall 8vo; 368 pages; contemporary red half morocco, raised bands, each compartment has gilt stamped deocrataion of fish or fly, top edge gilt; fine.   David Mason 71-126 1996 $240.00

PRICE, SARAH   Illustrations of the Fungi of Our Fields and Woods Drawn from Natural Specimens. London: 1864-65. Large 4to; 20 hand lithographed plates; original gilt decorated cloth, nice set; scarce with fine plates.   Raymond M. Sutton VII-26 1996 $1,200.00

PRICE, UVEDALE   Essays on the Picturesque, as Compared with the Sublime and the Beautiful; and, on the Use of Sudying Pictures for the Purpose of improving Real Landscape. London: 1810. 1st edition; 8vo; 3 volumes; mid 19th century half purple calf, faded and bit worn and scraped, by (William) Manderson of Brighton, with his ticket; some foxing.   Maggs Bros. Ltd. 1190-43 1996 £300.00

PRICE, UVEDALE   Thoughts on the Defence of Property. Addressed to the County of Hereford. Heredord: sold by J. Allen and all other booksellers, 1797. 8vo; (2), 28 pages; with half title; recent wrappers, very nice; signature of Dudley North (1748-1829), a prominent Whig and close associate of Fox.   C. R. Johnson 37-68 1996 £250.00

PRICE, VINCENT   The Vincent Price Treasury of American Art. Waukesha: Country Beautiful Corp. 1972. 1st edition; 4to; 150 plates in color, over 300 black and white illustrations; dust jacket (few chips and tears), good to very good. Signed by Price and inscribed to Olive Behrendt.   George J. Houle 68-123 1996 $125.00

PRICE, WILLIAM   Clement Falconer; or, the Memoirs of a Young Whig. Baltimore: N. Hickman, 1838. 1st edition; 12mo; 2 volumes in 1; later half red morocco, very worn, some spotting of text, identification of author written on title; the copy of Bruce Price, with signature, great-grandson of author, on title. Wright Fiction 2072.   James Cummins 14-159 1996 $150.00

PRICHARD, JAMES COWLES 1786-1848   The Natural History of Man. London: & 1855. 4th edition; 2 volumes, (xxiv), 343; (vii), 720 pages, 17 litho plates, 43 aquatint plates, mostly hand colored, some tipped in; maroon cloth, gilt decorated, volume 1 rebacked with original spine volume 2 rebacked in maroon cloth, waterstain on frontispiece in volume 1, internally bright and clean copy.   Antipodean 28-211 1996 $450.00

PRICHARD, JAMES COWLES 1786-1848   A Treatise on Insanity and Other Disorders Affecting the Mind. London: Sherwod, Gilbert and Piper, 1835. 8vo; xvi, 483, (1) pages, 20 pages of inserted ads; contemporary mauve cloth, rebacked, new paper spine label, corners bumped and shelfworn, small puncture to titlepage, very good. GM 5 4928; Norman Cat. 1747.   John Gach 150-374 1996 $575.00

PRIDEAUX, SARA T.   Bookbinders and Their Craft. New York: 1903. One of 500 signed and numbered copies, nicely bound; 4to, (4), 298, (2) pages; illustrations; attractively bound in full brown morocco, covers, spine and turn-ins stamped in blind with geometric rosette design, spine lettered in gilt, pastedowns of marbled paper, all edges gilt, by "A.P." and dated 1904 on rear turn-in, tiny three quarter inch crack at top of front hinge, tiny scuff marks on bottom edge, endpapers discolored from turn-ins, very attractive, in practically fine condition.   Joseph J. Felcone 64-5 1996 $1,000.00

PRIDEAUX, SARA T.   Bookbinders and Their Craft. New York: Charles Scribner's Sons, 1903. One of 500 copies; large 8vo; xii, 200 pages; well illustrated; vellum spine, boards, slightly shaken.   The Bookpress 75-345 1996 $325.00

PRIEST, JOSIAH   American Antiquities and Discoveries in the West. Albany: pritned by Packard, Hoffman and White, 1833. 1st edition; 8 1/2 x 5 1/2 inches; viii, (9)-400 pages; large folding frontispiece depicting various early artifacts; original marbled paper sides, rather rudely rebacked with black cloth, original red morocco spine label with gilt titling glued inside front cover, corners exposed, paper sides rather worn, but volume tight and perfectly usable, 2 leaves with small (wax?) stain, vertical tear in top half of one leaf (just touching text, but no loss), lightly dampstaining throughout, occasional pencil marks. Sabin 65484; Howes P 592.   Phillip J. Pirages 33-434 1996 $250.00

PRIEST, JOSIAH   American Antiquities and Discoveries in the West... Albany: Hoffman and White, 1833. 2nd edition; 400 pages; folding map, plate, text illustrations, lacking folding frontispiece; full contemporary calf; now scarce. Field 1245; Howes P592; Pilling 3132; Sabin 65484; S&S 20818.   Blue River Books 9-265 1996 $120.00

PRIESTLEY, ERIC J.   Flame and Smoke! Los Angeles: Watts 13 Foundation/Turnaround Printers, 1974. 1st edition; 157 pages; near fine in very good dust jacket, tape repaired on rear panel; inscribed by author. Between the Covers 43-390 1996 $125.00

PRIESTLEY, ERIC J.   Flame and Smoke! Los Angeles: Watts 13 Foundation/Turnaround Printers, 1974. 157 pages; scrape to edge of spine, else very good, lacking dust jacket, inscribed by author to a noted Black editor and critic.   Between the Covers 43-391 1996 $100.00

PRIESTLEY, JOHN BOYNTON 1894-   Angel Pavement. London: William Heinemann, 1930. Limited to 1025 copies, numbered and signed by author; royal 8vo; frontispiece, xiv, 613 pages; buckram, top edge gilt, others uncut, faint trace of foxing in places, but nice, partly unopened. Thomas Thorp 489-254 1996 £50.00

PRIESTLEY, JOSEPH 1733-1804   An Appeal to the Public, On the Subject of the Riots in Birmingham. Birmingham: printed by J. Thompson, sold by J. Johnson...London, 1791. 1st edition; 8vo; xxxix, (1), 181 pages, wanting half title, but with errata pasted on to blank verso of pages xxxix, small library stamp on blank verso of title; recently bound in calf backed marbled boards, gilt, entirely uncut; very good. Crook 283. John Drury 82-231 1996 £200.00

PRIESTLEY, JOSEPH 1733-1804   An Appeal to the Public, on the Subject of the Riots in Birmingham. Birmingham: printed by J. Thompson, sold by J. Johnson, London, 1792. 2nd edition; 8vo; xxxix, (1), 184 pages, wanting leaf before title (presumably a half title), numerous ms. annotations in pencil, mostly in margins, some of these notes cropped by binder; contemporary calf backed marbled boards, neatly rebacked, spine lettered in gilt, very good; ownership inscription of 'Osborne Wight 1792" on title.   John Drury 82-233 1996 £150.00

PRIESTLEY, JOSEPH 1733-1804   Dr. Priestley's Letter to the Inhabitants of Birmingham... London: Johnson, 1791. Apparently the first edition; 8vo; 16 pages; outer margin of title dusty, small library stamp on blank verso of title and on blank outer margin of p. 15; recently bound in calf backed marbled boards, gilt, entirely uncut; good copy. John Drury 82-232 1996 £150.00

PRIESTLEY, JOSEPH 1733-1804   Experiments and Observations on Different Kinds of Air. London: 1774. xvi, 324 pages, 2 folding plates, 2 leaves contents misbound, hole to margin of page 179; half calf marbled boards worn, library number on spine. Graham Weiner C2-126 1996 £50.00

PRIESTLEY, JOSEPH 1733-1804   Lectures On History, and General Policy; to Which is Prefixed, an Essay on a Course of Liberal Education for Civil and Active Life. Birmingham: printed by Pearson and Rollason for J. Johnson,...London, 1788. 1st edition; 4to; xxii, 548, (12), (4) pages; 2 engraved plates; contemporary calf, neatly rebacked to match, spine with gilt lines and label very good; foxing on titlepage and few other leaves, few ms. corrections in ink; Crook 401; Kress B1470; Goldsmiths 13534; Williams II 524.   John Drury 82-228 1996 £375.00

PRIESTLEY, JOSEPH 1733-1804   Letters to a Philosophical Unbeliever. Part I (with) Part II. Birmingham: Pearson & Rollason, 1787/87. 2nd edition; 304; 231, 8 ads; 2 parts bound in 1, rebound in quarter calf, red label; nice copies. Crook TR 171/174/ Jessop p. 55; Norton p. 240.   C. R. Johnson 37-75 1996 £450.00

PRIESTLEY, JOSEPH 1733-1804   Letters to the Right Honourable Edmund Burke Occasioned by His Reflections on the Revolution in France &c. Birmingham: printed by Thomas Pearson, and sold by J. Johnson...London: 1791. 1st edition; 8vo; xiii, (3), 152 pages; recently bound in calf backed marbled boards, gilt, very good. Crooke 304. John Drury 82-229 1996 £250.00

PRIESTLEY, JOSEPH 1733-1804   Letters to the Right Honourable Edmund Burke, Occasioned by His Reflections on the Revolution in France &c. London: 1791. 2nd edition; 8vo; xiii, (3), 155, (1) pages, perforated stamp on margin of title and another leaf, small marginal tear on leaf M1 (not touching printed surface), title bit soiled; old half cloth, rather worn, label on spine, uncut. From the library of Sir James Mackintosh (1765-1832) the philosopher, with his bookplate. Crook 305. John Drury 82-230 1996 £175.00

PRIME Evil. West Kingston; Donald Grant, 1988. Limited edition, 795/1000 copies, illustrated 1st edition; full leather, gilt, fine in fine folding box. Polyanthos 22-776 1996 $175.00

THE PRINCE Of Peace. Christmas Canticles. Flemington: St. Teresa's Press, 1965. Limited to 150 copies; small quarto; 31 pages; 21 canticles beautifully printed in brown, each with initial capital illuminated with 23 karat gold; paper backed marbled boards, printed in green to spine, near fine.   Bromer Booksellers 90-227 1996 $450.00

PRINCE, JOHN D.   Materials for a Sumerian Lexicon with Grammatical Introduction. Leipzig: J. C. Hinrichs, 1908. 4to; xxxv, 414 pages; original cloth.   Archaeologia Luxor-2619 1996 $250.00

PRINCE, L. BRADFORD   New Mexico A Defence of the People and Country... Santa Fe: Feb. 20, 1882. 1st edition in this form; 4 pages; fine.   Michael D. Heaston 23-271 1996 $250.00

PRINCE, L. BRADFORD   The Present and Future of New Mexico A Land of Prosperity and Happiness. Santa Fe: Bureau of Immigration, 1891. 1st edition; 15 pages; sewn as issued, two minor holes affecting several letters.   Michael D. Heaston 23-272 1996 $175.00

PRINCE, THOMAS   Extraordinary Events the Doings of God, and Maravellous in Pious Eyes. Boston: printed, London: reprinted and sold by J. Lewis, 1746. 3rd London edition; 8vo; disbound, half title present; very good. Sabin 65596.   Ximenes 109-240 1996 $200.00

PRINCE, THOMAS   The Vade Mecum for America; or, a Companion for Traders and Travellers... Boston: S. Kneeland and T. Green for D. Henchman and T. Hancock, 1732. 1st edition; narrow 12mo; 92), 6, (2), 220 pages; contemporary calf, hinges cracked, inner front hinge with old repair, spine chipped, very good. Very scarce, especially so in nice condition. Evans 3598; Kress S3413 (this ed.).   M & S Rare Books 60-400 1996 $2,250.00

THE PRINCESS Elizabeth Gift Book. H. & S., 1933. 1st edition; many full color illustrations; some light soil near fore edge of covers, else bright very good+ in very good dust jacket with some light wear and tear. Aronovitz 57-25 1996 $125.00

THE PRINCIPAL Events in the History of Ireland, in the Form of Stories. London: E. Lloyd & Co., 1829. 1st (?only) edition; 12mo; pages viii, 230 and leaf of imprint; light fingering, in very good recent boards; dedication is to Augusta & Frederic Ponsonby, inscribed "Kathleen Ponsonby March 1851 - from Frederick Ponsonby."   James Fenning 133-188 1996 £55.00

PRINGLE, JOHN   Observations on the Diseases of the Army. London: 1753. 2nd edition; 8vo; buckram. GM 2150; Cushing P 399.   Argosy 810-404 1996 $350.00

PRINGLE, JOHN   Observations on the Nature and Cure of Hospital and Jayl-Fevers. London: for A. Millar and D. Wilson, 1750. 1st edition; small 8vo; (1), 52 pages; titlepage stained and strengthened, tear in upper corner of final two leaves repaired with minor loss; foxed; modern cloth; good; stamp of the Surgeon-General's Office and their withdrawn stamp. GM 5374; Waller 7644; Blake p. 364; Blocker p. 322.   Edwin V. Glaser B122-122 1996 $400.00

A PRINTER'S DOZEN: Eleven Spreads from Unrealised Books... Rampant Lions Press, 1993. One of 200 numbered copies; large 4to; printed on ARches and Fabriano Ingres; marbled boards, cloth spine, fine in slipcase.   Bertram Rota 272-404 1996 £155.00

THE PRINTER. The Guide to Trade. London: Charles Knight & Co., 1845. 1st edition; 12mo; pages 87; 3 folding wood engraved plates and other illustrations; original printed wrappers, lightly soiled and worn along fold, but generally well preserved.   Claude Cox 107-251 1996 £55.00

PRINZING, FRIEDRICH   Epidemics Resulting from Wars. Oxford: 1916. 340 pages; original binding, ex-library. GM 1682.   W. Bruce Fye 71-1705 1996 $150.00

PRIOR, MATTHEW 1664-1721   The Hind and the Panther Transvers'd to the Story of the City Mouse and the Country Mouse. London: printed for W. Davis, 1687. 1st edition; small 4to; disbound; very good, complete with prelim blank; Wing P3511; Grolier 688; Macdonald 241a. Ximenes 109-241 1996 $300.00

PRIOR, MATTHEW 1664-1721   Poems on Several Occasions. London: Jacob Tonson, 1709. 1st Authorized edition; octavo; pages xxiv, (iv), 328; frontispiece; original full chestnut polished calf, elegantly panelled in blind, rebacked in period style, with morocco and gilt label; attractive copy. Rothschild 1676. Ashely IV p. 74; Grolier 682.   Hartfield 48-L72 1996 $395.00

PRIOR, MATTHEW 1664-1721   Poems on Several Occasions. London: Jacob Tonson, 1718. Folio; large paper copy, (xl), 506, (vi) pages; Superfine paper issue, with fleur-de-lys on shield watermark; frontispiece, titlepage vignette, head and tailpieces; contemporary panelled calf, neatly rebacked in brown morocco and recornered, gilt lettering; rubbed, some wear to edges, little foxing. Good copy. Foxon p. 641.   Robert Clark 38-200 1996 £150.00

PRIOR, R. C. A.   On the Popular Names of British Plants, an Explanation of the Origin and meaning of the Names of the Indigenous and Most Commonly Cultivated Species. London: 1879. 3rd edition; small 8vo; original cloth, little faded; presentation copy with inscription; with 4 page letter from W. J. Hooker.   Charles W. Traylen 117-327 1996 £100.00

PRISCIANUS CAESARIENSIS   Prisciani Grammatici Caesariensis Libri Omnes... Venice: May, 1527. 4to; 316 leaves, italic, Aldine devices on first and last leaves; light stai margin of first gathering; nice later French vellum, gilt spine and morocco label, appealing copy. Renouard 103.2. Adams P2113; UCLA II 211; Brunet IV 883.   Family Album Tillers-523 1996 $695.00

PRITCHARD, ANDREW   A History of Infusoria, Living and Fossil... London: 1842. 1st edition; 8vo; 12 hand colored lithographed plates, small abrasion on title; cloth bit worn, one section sprung, rear joint split.   Maggs Bros. Ltd. 1190-259 1996 £90.00

PRITCHARD, ANDREW   A History of Infusoria Animalcules, Living and Fossil. London: 1852. New edition; thick 8vo;   Petersfield Bookshop FH58-274 1996 £65.00

PRITCHARD, ANDREW   A History of Infusoria, Including the Desmidiaceae and Diatomaceae, British and Foreign. London: 1861. 4th edition; thick 8vo; 40 plates, half calf, one joint neatly repaired. Petersfield Bookshop FH58-275 1996 £65.00

PRITCHARD, ERIC, MRS.   The Cult of Chiffon. London: Grant Richards, 1902. Small 8vo; 212 pages, numerous line illustrations; rebound into half cloth on marbled boards, few very minor library markings, very good, scarce.   J. M. Cohen 35-81 1996 $185.00

PRITCHARD, JAMES B.   The Ancient Near East in Pictures Relating to the Old Testament. (and) Ancient Near Eastern Texts Relating to the Old Testament. Princeton: Princeton University Press, 1969/74. 3rd edition; 8vo; 2 volumes, xxvi, 710 pages; original cloth, inscription, signatures, slightly shelfworn dust jackets.   Archaeologia Luxor-2620 1996 $200.00

PRITCHETT, V. S.   When My Girl Comes Home. New York: Alfred A. Knopf, 1961. 1st edition; original binding, spine slightly faded, tail of spine bumped, very good in nicked and slightly rubbed, very slightly creased dust jacket browned at spine and edges; presentation copy from author inscribed for Jane and Gordon McKenzie.   Ulysses 39-487 1996 £75.00

PRIVATE Letter from an American in England to His Friends in America. London: printed for J. Almon, 1769. 1 8vo; later half calf, edges rubbed; very good with outer edges uncut, contemporary reader has added a number of splenetic notes in margins; rare. Sabin 65275; Adams 69-29; Raven 1288; Black, Epist. Novel 279.   Ximenes 109-123 1996 $4,500.00

THE PRIVILEDGES Of the Citizens of London: Contained in the Charters, Granted to Them by Several Kings Of This Realm... London: ptd. for the translator of it and published by Langley Curtiss, 1682. 1st edition; 8vo; later quarter calf, slight soiling of text, spine gilt. Kress 1566; Goldsmith 2497; Wing P3537.   Anthony Laywood 108-15 1996 £145.00

THE PRIVILEGES and Practiace of Parliaments in England: Collected Out of the Common Laws of This Land. London: printed for Robert Harford, 1680. 4to; frontispiece, pages (4), 26, 37-44, signed A-E4, complete thus; recent wrapper, nice. Wing P3535.   James Fenning 133-253 1996 £65.00

PRIVILEGGI e Statuti Della Venerabile Archiconfraternita dell'Anime Piu' Bisognose del Purgatorio eretta in Roma Sotto il Patrocino di Gesu Maria, e S. Giuseppe dal Venerabile Servo di Dio Papa Innocenzo XI. Rome: 1734. 4to; 46 pages, 1 f., woodcut device on titlepage; slightly later brown morocco, ornate ruled borders with swags, gathers and floral festoons; floral cornerpieces, central panel with arms of a cardinal (very similar to Belmas, Chauvelin, cf. Guigard Amateurs Ecclesiastqie), a snake climbing a tree, surmounted by a Maltese Cross, cardinals hat, rope and tassle borders, etc., spine flat, gilt a la repetition panels, alternated with urns in ruled compartments (one or two wormholes to head of spine, slight rubbing to extremities), old all edges gilt, later endpapers; bookplate of Sir Ross O'Connell, 1897, and his marks. Marlborough 160-51 1996 £650.00

THE PROCEEDINGS at the Guild-Hall in London on Thursday July 29th, 1680. London: 1680. Folio; 4 pages; uncut, disbound. Wing P3559.   H. M. Fletcher 121-49 1996 £65.00

THE PROCEEDINGS of the Grand-Jury of Middlesex, in Easter Term. 1681. London: printed for T. Baldwyn in the Old Bayly, 1681. Folio; 2 pages; uncut, disbound; Wing P 3586.   H. M. Fletcher 121-50 1996 £60.00

THE PROCEEDINGS of the Present Parliament Justified by the Opinion of the Most Judicious and Learned Hugo Grotius; with Considerations Thereupon. London: Randal Taylor, 1689. 1st edition; 4to; 20 pages, wanting the half title, slight dust soiling, one or two page numerals just shaved, short tear to inner margin of title (no loss); recently well bound in linen backed marbled boards, lettered; good, crisp copy. Wing G2124; Meulen and Diermanse 631.   John Drury 82-97 1996 £100.00

PROCEEDINGS of the Tribunal of Arbitration, Convened at Paris...for the Determination of Questions...in the Waters of the Bering Sea. Washington: 1895. volumes 1-4, original cloth, nice.   Stephen Lunsford 45-56 1996 $225.00

PROCTER, ELLEN A.   A Brief Memoir of Christina G. Rossetti. London: S.P.C.K., 1895. 1st edition; 12mo; (84) pages; frontispiece; original darak blue cloth, front lettered in white; some offsetting to endpapers, still very nice. NCBEL III 498.   Paulette Rose 16-269 1996 $125.00

PROCTOR, L. B.   Lives of Eminent Lawyers and Statesmen of the State of New York, and Notes of Cases Tried by Them... New York: S. S. Peloubet and Co., 1892. 2 volumes; embossed cloth, chipped and rubbed, but clean set.   Meyer Boswell SL25-178 1996 $175.00

PROKOSCH, FREDERIC   The Red Sea. Privately printed for the author at the Cambridge University Press, 1935. 1st edition; a/5 copies (of an edition of 22 copies); 16mo; pages 8; printed on Japanese rice paper and signed in pen by author, original sewn black wrappers, gold printed label on front cover (spare label tipped in), author's bookplate, untrimmed; fine. With author's pencilled annotation, pencilled copy of poem in author's hand loosely inserted.   Blackwell's B112-235 1996 £150.00

PROKOSCH, FREDERIC   The Stranger. New Haven: Summer, 1931. 1st edition; 2/2 copies typescript copy, typed on recto of each leaf; crown 8vo; 25 leaves, 4 hand colored, pen and ink tipped in drawings by author, tissue guards present; original quarter black cloth, printed label with faded lettering, silver boards, corners rubbed, untrimmed, excellent. Blackwell's B112-236 1996 £200.00

PRONY, MARC ANTOINE, PSEUD.   Models of Letters in French and English... London: G. G. and J. Robinson, F. Wingrave, successor to Mr. Nourse, 1797. 4th edition; half title; contemporary sheep, worn on corners, hinges weakening.   Jarndyce 103-295 1996 £110.00

PRONZINI, BILL   Cat's Paw. Richmond: Waves Press, 1983. 1st edition; 1/50 hardbound copies, of 150 copies (100 in wrappers); cloth covered boards; fine, issued without jacket, signed by author and binder. Janus Books 36-279 1 996 $125.00

PRONZINI, BILL   A Killing in Xanadu. Richmond: Waves Press, 1980. 1st edition; 1/150 numbered copies, signed by Pronzini, signed by publisher; wrappers; fine.   Janus Books 36-278 1996 $100.00

PROPERT, W. A.   The Russian Ballet in Western Europe 1909-1920. New York: & London: John Lane, 1921. One of 450 copies for the U. S. Chapter; folio; 63 illustrations from original drawings, including 56 mounted plates, many in color; cloth and marbled boards, little worn and soiled, spine little frayed at tips;   Marilyn Braiterman 15-169 1996 $600.00

PROSCH, CHARLES   Reminiscences of Washington Territory. Seattle: 1904. 8vo; 128 pages, including frontispiece, 2 plates; brown cloth stamped in black; extremities rubbed, very good; pencilled inscription from author. Howes P633; Graff 3367; Smith 8383; Tweney 89 #62. Bohling Book Co. 192-53 1996 $150.00

PROSI e Versi per Onorare la Memoria de Livia Doria Caraffa... Parma: Stamperia Reale, 1784. 4to; 4 ff., 407 pages, 2 ff. (colophon and errata), 2 engraved portraits, 6 engraved plates, 168 vignettes and initials; contemporary crimson morocco, triple gilt fillet, simple fleuron corner pieces, gilt raised bands, spine gilt in 6 compartments, using only a few tools, including poppy beads (and - on the turn ins - strawberries), black morocco label, gilt lettered, all edges gilt, skly-blue silk endpapers, but lacking f.f.e.p., somewhat restrained binding, but, given the contents, exactly what is called for. Excellent copy. Brooks 250; Geering 39; Updike II 172.   Marlborough 160-52 1996 £3,300.00

PROSKOURIAKOFF, TATIANA   An Album of Maya Architecture. Washington: Carnegie Inst., 1946. 1st edition; oblong folio; (10) pages, 36 plates with letterpress; half cloth, worn at extremities, faded along spine, bottom board stained.   Archaeologia Luxor-4798 1996 $150.00

PROSKOURIAKOFF, TATIANA   Jades from the Cenote of Sacrifice
Chichen Itza, Yucatan. Cambridge: Peabody Museum of Archaeology and
Ethnology, Harvard University, 1974. Folio; frontispiece, xv, 217 pages, 15
figures, 90 plates; stiff wrappers, lightly worn.   Archaeologia
Luxor-4799 1996 $175.00

PROSPECCTUS of Mr. Sheldrake's Undertaking to Cure Distortion of the
Spine and Distortions of the Legs and Feet of Children, at His Residence
No. 10, Adams Street, Adelphia, London at Richmond and at Bath.
London: Stereotyped and printed by Andrew Wilson, n.d. 1816. 8vo; 8
pages; illustrations in text; uncut, fine.   Anthony W. Laywood 108-201
1996 £75.00

THE PROTESTANT Antidote. N.P.: n.d. ?London: Aug. 1680. Folio; 2
pages; uncut, disbound. Wing P3822.   H. M. Fletcher 121-51 1996
£60.00

THE PROTESTANT Petition and Addresse. London April 30, 1681. Upon
Thursday Last There Was Presented to the Lord Mayor and Court of
Aldermen... London: printed for Subscribers April 30 1681. Folio; 1 page,
disbound. Wing P 3839.   H. M. Fletcher 121-52 1996 £60.00

PROTHERO, D. R.   Eocene-Oligocene Climatic and Biotic Evolution.
Princeton: 1992. 8vo; 568 pages; 200 illustrations; cloth.   Wheldon &
Wesley 207-1359 1996 £75.00

PROUDHON, PIERRE JOSEPH   Advertissement aux Proprietaires...
Paris: Librairie de Prevot, 1841. 1st edition; original paper wrappers with
wear to spine and piece missing from lower fore corner of rear panel;
very good, rare.   Lame Duck Books 19-470 1996 $1,500.00

PROULX, E. ANNIE   The Fine Art of Salad Gardening. Emmaus: Rodale
Press, 1985. 1st edition; remainder mark, top page edges, otherwise fine
in near fine dust jacket with slight edge wear, signed by author.
Anacapa House 5-262 1996 $225.00

PROULX, E. ANNIE   Heart Songs. New York: Scribner's, 1988.
Advance review copy with publisher's slip laid in; fine in fine dust jacket.
Thomas Dorn 9-218 1996 $400.00

PROULX, E. ANNIE   Heart Songs. New York: Scribners, 1988. 1st
edition; fine in dust jacket, signed by author; author's first book of
fiction; lovely copy.   Between the Covers 42-363 1996 $500.00

PROULX, E. ANNIE   Heartsongs and Other Stories. New York:
Scribners, 1988. 1st edition; fine in fine dust jacket, signed.   Book
Time 2-353 1996 $350.00

PROULX, E. ANNIE   Postcards. New York: Scribner's, 1992.
Uncorrected proof copy; wrappers; fine, signed by author.   Ken Lopez
74-381 1996 $450.00

PROULX, E. ANNIE   Postcards. New York: Scribners, 1992. 1st
edition; author's second book; fine in fine dust jacket.   Book Time
2-354 1996 $200.00

PROULX, E. ANNIE   The Shipping News. New York: scribner's, 1993.
Uncorrected proof; blue wrappers, fine, signed by author.   Lame Duck
Books 19-472 1996 $375.00

PROULX, E. ANNIE   The Shipping News. New York: Scribners, 1993.
Uncorrected proof; couple of light creases to wrappers, some general
wear, very good in wrappers, as issued.   Between the Covers 42-364
1996 $250.00

PROULX, E. ANNIE   The Shipping News. New York: Scribner, 1993.
1st edition; fine in fine dust jacket and signed by author.   Ken Lopez
74-382 1996 $250.00

PROULX, E. ANNIE `The Shipping News. New York: Charles Scribner's
Sons, 1993. 1st edition; fine in dust jacket.   Steven C. Bernard 71-185
1996 $200.00

PROULX, E. ANNIE   The Shipping News. New York: Scribners, 1993.
1st edition; fine in dust jacket.   Between the Covers 42-363a 1996
$175.00

PROULX, E. ANNIE   The Shipping News. New York: Scribner's, 1993.
1st edition; fine in like dust jacket, signed by author.   Lame Duck
Books 19-471 1996 $175.00

PROULX, E. ANNIE   The Shipping News. New York: Scribners, 1993.
1st edition; as new, signed, scarce.   Book Time 2-355 1996 $165.00

PROUST, MARCEL 1871-1922   A Vision of Paris. New York: 1963. 1st
edition; 120 sepia toned photogravures; dust jacket.   J. B. Muns
154-23 1996 $225.00

PROUT, W.   On the Nature and Treatment of Stomach and Renal
Diseases... London: 1848. 5th edition; 8vo; 7 plates; original black cloth,
bit worn, rear joint splitting, 1849 Churchill Cat. bound at end,
contemporary stamp of Bedford Medical Library.   Maggs Bros. Ltd.
1190-487 1996 £75.00

PROVERBS Exemplified, and Illustrated by Pictures from Real Life.
London: J. Trusler, 1790. 12mo; viii, 196 pages; 50 woodcuts by John
Bewick; 19th century full mottled calf with richly gilt spine and turn-ins,
light rubbing to extremities, else fine. Bookplates. Hugo 43.   Bromer
Booksellers 87-113 1996 $850.00

PROWN, JULES DAVID   John Singleton Copley. Cambridge: Harvard
University Press, 1966. 1st edition; 2 volumes; fine in publisher's
slipcase.   Hermitage SP95-805 1996 $125.00

PROWSE, DANIEL WOODLEY   The Newfoundland Guide Book, 1904,
Including Labrador and St. Pierre. London: Bradbury, Agnew & Co., 1905.
8vo; pages vii, 182, illustrations, large folding map; original cloth, inner
hinges reinforced, covers soiled, else very good. O'Dea 1341a; Morley
pp. 55-56.   Hugh Anson-Cartwright 87-316 1996 $125.00

PRUDENTIUS, AURELIUS PRUDENTIUS CLEMENS   Opera. Amsterdam:
(Blaeu for) Jansson, 1631. Small 24mo; 261 pages, engraved title, slight
loss at corner plus extensive ms. notes in Latin and English; early full
red morocco.   Family Album Tillers-527 1997 $200.00

PRY, PAUL, PSEUD.   Oddities of London Life. London: Richard Bentley,
1838. 8vo; 2 volumes, 316, 234 pages; 22 engraved plates; 19th century
three quarter morocco by F. P. Hathaway, Boston, with original green
cloth covers and spine titles tipped to pastedowns, near fine, with
bookplate of Lucius Poole, Boston.   Chapel Hill 94-49 1996 $200.00

PRYCE, F. N.   Catalogue of Sculpture in the Department of Greek and
Roman Antiquities of the British Museum. London: British Museum, 1928.
8vo; Volume I, part 1 (only), pages viii, 214; 246 figures and 43 plates;
original cloth.   Archaeologia Luxor-3861 1996 $125.00

PRYME, GEORGE   Ode to Trinity College, Cambridge. London: printed
by J. M'Creery & sold by J. Mawman &c., 1812. Uncut, stabbed as
issued, stain at fore-edge, dusted, BM duplicate stamps on title verso
and last page.   Jarndyce 103-550 1996 £65.00

PSALMANAZAR, GEORGE 1679?-1763   An Historical and Geographical
Description of Formosa, An Island Subject to the Emperor of Japan.
London: Robert Holden & Co. Ltd., 1926. Limited Reprint, number 356 of
750 copies; spine faded, one light scrape to front board, otherwise fine.
Hermitage SP95-1111 1996 $125.00

PTLOMAEUS, CLAUDIUS   Geographia Universalis, vetus et Nova. Basil:
Henrich Petrum, 1545. Folio; ff. 26, 98; excellent woodcut devices,
initials, illustrations, diagrams, without all maps; uncut.   Family Album
Tillers-529 1996 $500.00

PUCKLE, JAMES   The Club; in a Dialogue Between Father and Son.
London: printed for the proprietor by John Johnson and sold by
Longman... 1817. One of 500 copies; from a total edition of 735; royal
8vo; pages (2), x, (8), 96, frontispiece, extra illustrated title and 24 wood
engravings, and c. 24 initials and tailpieces; uncut in original printed
boards, rubbed and worn at extremities, neatly rebacked, slip at end
recording a gift of 675 books from H. W. Clemenston of Chepstow to
Newport Library with several faint and small circular stamps of the latter
on blanks and margins; occasional spotting, largely marginal, but good,
large copy.   Claude Cox 107-131 1996 £65.00

PUCKLE, JAMES   England's Path to Wealth and Honour; In a Dialogue
Between an Englishman and a Dutchman. London: printed for F. Cogan,
1750. 8vo; title, 9-53 pages, complete; disbound. Kress S3866; Goldsmith
8493; McCulloch p. 232.   David Bickersteth 133-55 1996 £65.00

PUCKLER-MUSKAU, PRINCE VON Hints on Landscape Gardening. Boston: Houghton Mifflin, 1917. 8vo; cloth and boards, very good with little wear to spine tips and corners, damaged box. Marilyn Braiterman 15-171 1996 $275.00

PUFFENDORF, SAMUEL, FREIHERR VON 1632-1694 De Officio Hominis et Civis Juxta Legem Naturalem Libri Duo. London: 1715. contemporary unlettered calf, worn, joints cracked but clean. Meyer Boswell SL26-193 1996 $250.00

PUGH, DAVID London: Being an Accurate History and Description of the British Metropolis and Its Neighbourhood, to Thirty Miles Extent, from an Actual Perambulation. London: printed by W. Stratford, Crown Court, Temple Bar, for J. Stratford... 1805-09. New edition; 8vo; 6 volumes; steel engraved vignettes half titles to all volumes; steel engraved frontispiece to volume 1, 165 steel engraved plates, 111 woodcut vignettes to letterpress, 6 large folding maps and plans, all linen backed; half blue morocco and marbled boards, gilt tooling to panelled spines, gilt titles and volume numbers to spines, joints rubbed, top edge gilt, marbled endpapers, binder's ticket of Frank Murray of Nottingham. Upcott 659. Beeleigh Abbey BA/56-11 1996 £650.00

PUGH, EDWARD Cambria Depicta; a Tour through North Wales, Illustrated with Picturesque Views. London: printed by W. Clowes...for E. Williams, 1816. 1st edition; 4to; pages xvi, 476; 71 fine hand colored aquatint plates, offsetting from plates, though plates are mostly in good, clean state, marginal browning affecting just a few plates, also a couple of small marginal tears to text leaves and one neat repair, handsome copy, without 2 ad leaves at end; contemporary red straight grain morocco, gilt and blind roll tooled borders and panels to sides, fully gilt spine, gilt edges; Abbey Scenery 521; Tooley 386; Prideaux pp. 278-9. Sotheran PN32-44 1996 £998.00

PUGH, JOHN A Treatise on the Science of Muscular Action. London: 1794. 1st edition; 8vo; engraved title, 15 engraved plates by Kirk, each with key plate, minor browning, ruled border of several plates cut into, several plates mounted and with tears repaired (in case of plate 1 just touching the figure), few other minor repairs, 5 plates with duplicate descriptions mounted on versos (cut from second copy of prelims), contemporary half calf, bit worn; 19th century bookplate of James Brougham. Maggs Bros. Ltd. 1190-488 1996 £345.00

PUGIN, AUGUSTUS CHARLES 1762-1832 Paris and It's Environs: Displayed in A Series of Picturesque Views... London: Robert Jennings, Paris: Truettel & Wurtz, 1829. 1st edition; 4to; text in English and French; 168 engraved plates; three quarter gilt stamped dark green morocco over tan marbled boards, all edges gilt, very good. George J. Houle 68-4 1996 $800.00

PUGIN, AUGUSTUS CHARLES 1762-1832 Paris and Its Environs Displayed in a Series of Two Hundred Picturesque Views from Original Drawings, Taken Under the Direction of A. Pugin. London: Jennings and Chaplin, 62, Cheapside, 1831. 4to; 2 volumes; 200 steel engravings, half calf and cloth backed boards, gilt titles to spines, maroon morocco labels to spines, raised bands to spine, marbled edges, previous owner's inscriptions to rear pastedown of both volumes, two in pencil, one in ink, some occasional light foxing to text, engravings, all in good, clean state. Beeleigh Abbey BA/56-106 1996 £250.00

PUGIN, AUGUSTUS CHARLES 1762-1832 Paris and It's Environs, Displayed in a Series of Two Hundred Picturesque Views... London: Jennings and Chaplin, 1833. Probably one of the 2 large paper India proof issues and measures 13 3/4 x 10 1/2 inches; 2 volumes; (2), 11, 100, (2), (101)-202 pages; volume 1 contains 104 views on 52 leaves, volume 2 contains 100 views on 50 leaves, engraved title in each volume; double views are mounted on pages and are identified on spine as "Proofs"; some offsetting from plates, few plates foxed; full contemporary morocco, elaborate gilt compartments, gilt borders on covers, inner gilt dentelles, gilt, all edges gilt; binding bit rubbed, generally fine, clean copy. David Mason 71-74 1996 $1,200.00

PUGIN, AUGUSTUS WELBY NORTHMORE 1812-1852 Details of Antient Timber Houses of the 15th and 16th Centuries. London: Ackermann, 1836. 1st edition; 4to; engraved title leaf, 21 engraved plates, 1 page (ad); publisher's cloth; cover worn, plates lightly foxed. Bookpress 75-106 1996 $250.00

PUGIN, AUGUSTUS WELBY NORTHMORE 1812-1852 Glossary of Ecclesiastical Ornament and Costume... London: Bohn, 1846. 2nd edition; 4to; xvi, 245, (1) pages, 74 chromolithographic plates; original quarter red morocco, gilt stamp, spine expertly rehinged; Abbey Life 429; Victorian Bibliomania 42. Bookpress 75-107 1996 $750.00

PUGIN, AUGUSTUS WELBY NORTHMORE 1812-1852 Gothic Furniture: Consisting of Twenty-Seven Coloured Engravings from Designs By A. Pugin. London: R. Ackermann, 1828. 1st edition; 4to; iv, 26, (1) ages, additional hand colored aquatint title and 26 hand colored aquatint plates; contemporary half calf, morocco title patch on front board and marbled paper over boards; neatly respine, otherwise very good with excellent impressions of the plates; the copy of Pratt & Sons Ltd. with their name stamped in gold on front cover. Bookpress 75-105 1996 $4,200.00

PUGIN, AUGUSTUS WELBY NORTHMORE 1812-1852 A Treatise on Chancel Screens and Rood Lofts. London: Charles Dolman, 1851. 1st edition, only edition; viii, 1242 pages; 14 plates; publisher's cloth, very good. Bookpress 75-102 1996 $225.00

PUGIN, AUGUSTUS WELBY NORTHMORE 1812-1852 A Treatise on Chancel Screens and Rood Lofts, Their Antiquity, Use and Symbolic Signification. London: Charles Dolman, 1851. 4to; viii, 124 pages, 14 plates' original morocco backed gilt cloth, some foxing to frontispiece and plates; very good; presentation inscription from author on front endpaper and additional letter from Pugin loosely inserted. Ken Spelman 30-103 1996 £120.00

PUGIN, AUGUSTUS WELBY NORTHMORE 1812-1852 The True Principles of Pointed or Christian Architecture. London: John Weale, 1841. 1st edition; 4to; (iv), 67, (1), 40 pages; frontispiece' cloth, cover wear, sporadic foxing. Bookpress 75-108 1996 $325.00

PUGSLEY, ALFRED The Works of Isambard Kingdom Brunel. An Engineering Appreciation. London: Inst. C. E., 1976. 8vo; (x), 222 pages; text illustrations; publisher's cloth. Elton Engineering 10-18 1996 £65.00

PULGAR, HERNANDO DEL Cronica de Los Senores Reyes Cataolicos Don Fernando y Dona Isabel de Castilla y de Aragon... Valencia: Benito Monfort, 1780. 14 1/4 x 10 inches; contemporary full mottled calf with series of gilt outer borders, spine with four raised bands and gilt decoration within compartments, t, inner gilt dentelles, fore and lower edges untrimmed; in cloth clamshell case. fine, tall copy. Palau 242130; Potthasat 946. Book Block 32-74 1996 $2,950.00

PULIGA, COMTESSE DE Madame Sevigne De, Her Correspondents and Contemporaries. London: Tinsley Bros., 1873. 1st edition; thick 8vo; 2 volumes; extra illustrated with 64 engraved portraits and views; three quarter blue morocco, raised bands, gilt tops; occasional foxing, but good, sound copy. Appelfeld Gallery 54-162 1996 $300.00

PULLE, A. An Enumeration of the Vascular Plants Known from Surinam... Leiden: 1906. Royal 8vo; pages 555, map and 17 plates; wrappers. Wheldon & Wesley 207-1588 1996 £60.00

PULLEN-BURRY, B. In a German Colony or Four Weeks in New Britain. London: 1909. 1st U.K. edition; (xi), 238 pages, 8 black and white illustrations, 2 maps; red cloth, ex-library in rough binding, internally very good, very scarce. Antipodean 28-213 1996 $235.00

PULLER, TIMOTHY The Moderation of the Church of England, Considered as Useful for Allaying the Present Distempers Which the Indisposition of the Time Hath Contracted... London: J. M. for Richard Chiswell, 1679. 1st edition; 8vo; (1), 543, (i) pages; frontispiece, faintish dampstaining on a few leaves, paper flaw on b5, affecting a few letters; contemporary calf, rebacked, recornered, spine gilt ruled, label; good. Wing P4197.]118 1996 £60.00

PULTON, FARDINANDO An Abstract of all the Penal Statutes Which Be General, in Force and Use, Wherein Is Conteyned the Effect of All Those Statutes, Which do Threaten to the Offendors, Thereof the Losse of Life, Member, Lands, Goods Or Other Punishments. London: imprinted...by Christopher Barker, etc. 1586. Later panelled calf, rubbed, some dustiness, but still quite sound. Meyer Boswell SL26-194 1996 $1,750.00

PULTON, FARDINANDO A Collection of Sundry Statutes, Frequent in Use: with Notes in the Margent and References to the Book Cases and Books of Entries and Registers, Where They be Treated of... London: printed by M. Flesher, and R. Young; Assignes of Im More, Esquire, 1640. Full calf, rebacked, repairs to some margins. Meyer Boswell SL26-195 1996 $1,250.00

PUMA, RICHARD DANIEL Etruscan Tomb-Groups: Ancient Pottery and Bronzes in Chicago's Field Museum of Natural History. Mainz am Rhein: Philipp von Zabern, 1986. 4to; frontispiece, xiv, 129 pages, 37 illustrations; 48 plates; original cloth. Archaeologia Luxor-3238 1996 $125.00

PUMPELLY, RAPHAEL Across America and Asia. New York: Leypoldt & Holt, 1870. 3rd edition; tall 8vo; xvi, 454 pages; illustrations and maps, including one folding map; original green cloth with globe in gilt on upper cover, some minor wear at foot of spine and corners, else near fine, bright copy. David Mason 71-60 1996 $120.00

PUMPHREY, STANLEY   Indian Civilization: a Lecture. Philadelphia: Bible & Tract Dist. Soc., 1877. 1st edition; 8vo; plates; original binding, light wear, old dampstain to bottom margin of all pages; signed and dated by Whittier though date is hard to make out; signature of Ann Wendell on title & pencil note dated 1883 on verso of leaf Whittier has signed which is a lighter paper but does not appear to have been tipped in; laid in 64 line poem in another hand.   Charles Agvent   4-1222   1996 $375.00

PUNIN, NATAN   N. Pamiatnik III Internatsionaia. Petrograd: Izogiz. 1920. 4to; 8 page pamphlet with decorative title to upper cover incoporating 4 pages of explanatory text and an elevation of the tower to the recto of the final page, preserved in scarlet cloth flap case with ties.   Sotheran   PN32-196   1996   £1,800.00

PUNKIN, JONATHAN, PSEUD.   Downfall of Freemasonry Being an Authentic History of the Rise, Progress, and Triumph of Anti-Masony... Harrisonburg: published for the editor, near the Council Chambers, Unction Room, 1838. 1st edition; 8vo; pages 48, (2), v, (13)-159; (26) plates; original boards, edges trifle worn, cloth back, paper label; foxing is light, rare, especially in nearly fine, original condition. Wright I 2084a.   Howard S. Mott   227-115   1996 $450.00

PURCHAS, SAMUEL 1575?-1695   His Pilgrimes. (with) His Pilgrimage. London: William Stansby for Henrie Fetherstone, 1625-26. 1st edition of first work and best edition of the second work; folio; together 5 volumes; roman letter, printed side notes, titles within printed line border, autograph of Moses Bathurst 1661 at head, innumerable fine engraved maps and plates; contemporary calf, rebacked; few marginal tears not affecting text, else good. STC 20509 and 20508.5. Lowndes 2010-11; Sabin 6683-6 & 66682.   A. Sokol   XXV-78   1996   £10,000.00

PURCHAS, SAMUEL 1575?-1695   Purchas His Pilgrimes. (with) Purchase His Pilgrimage. London: ptd. by William Stansby for Henry Fetherstone, 1625/26. 1st edition of the 1st four volumes and 4th edition of volume 5; folio; 5 volumes; engraved title in volume 1, 7 folding maps, 81 smaller maps, numerous engraved and woodcut illustrations; text maps in volume 1 have been delicately hand colored at an early date; engraved title is in its very rare first state, dated 1624 (most are 1625), map of Virginia in Volume IV is in Tooley's 10th state, last volume is the usual second issue, with title beginning with 'Purchas'; late 18th century russia, panelled in gilt, beautifully rebacked, spines gilt in compartments, all edges gilt; engraved title skilfully remargined, not touching the engraved surface, volume 1 lacks a blank R4 and has one blank lower margin restored; from the library of Boies Penrose; earlier bookplates of Henry Perkins and Lucy Wharton Drexel. STC 20508.5 & 20509; Sabin 66682-6. Church 401a.   Ximenes   109-242   1996 $52,500.00

PURCHON, R. D.   The Biology of the Mollusca. Oxford: 1977. 2nd eidtion; 8vo; pages xxv, 560, 185 tesst figures; cloth.   Wheldon & Wesley   207-1197   1996   £68.00

PURDY, AL   The Blur in Between: Poems 1960-61. Toronto: Emblem Books, 1962. 1st edition; limited to 300 copies; (iv), 21, (ii) pages; printed wrappers; very good; inscribed by author to John Newlove, with Newlove's ownership signature.   Nelson Ball   118-114   1996 $350.00

PURDY, AL   Morning and it's Summer: a Memoir. Dunvegan: Quadrant Editions, 1983. 1st edition; issue in unbound sheets laid into boards, one of 50 copies so housed, numbered and signed by author; in board slipcase with paper label; fine; from the library of John Metcalf, with his ownership signature.   Nelson Ball   118-122   1996 $250.00

PURDY, AL   Morning and it's Summer: a Memoir. Dunvegan: Quadrant Edtiions, 1983. 1st edition; one of 300 copies of the cloth issue, numbered and signed by author; mounted photos; fine in dust jacket; from the library of John Metcalf, with his ownership signature.   Nelson Ball   118-123   1996 $100.00

PURDY, AL   No Second Spring. Coatsworth: Black Moss Press, 1977. 1st edition; one of 100 copies, numbered and signed by author; quarto; (8) pages; cloth and boards, paper label; fine; from the library of John Metcalf, with his ownership signature.   Nelson Ball   118-127   1996 $100.00

PURDY, AL   On the Bearpaw Sea. Burnaby: Blackfish Press, 1973. 1st edition; one of 25 numbered and signed copies; unpaginated; signed by author and artist; this copy number 4; bound in full calfskin, board slipcase; fine; from the library of John Metcalf, with his ownership signature.   Nelson Ball   118-130   1996 $250.00

PURDY, AL   On the Bearpaw Sea. Burnaby: Blackfish Press, 1973. One of 100 numbered and signed copies, bound thus, signed by author, this number 74; Japanese binding and Mulberry covers; fine; inscribed by author for John Newlove, with his ownership signature dated 1973; from the library of John Metcalf, with his ownership signature.   Nelson Ball   118-131   1996   £125.00

PURDY, AL   Pressed on Sand. Toronto: Ryerson, c. 1955. 1st edition; one of 250 copies; 16 pages; boards; fine; inscribed by author; from the library of John Metcalf, with his ownership signature.   Nelson Ball   118-135   1996 $125.00

PURDY, JAMES   Are You In the Wintertree. Sug Signo Libelli, 1987. One of 35 copies, of a total edtiion of 65; 8 1/4 x 5 1/4 inches; 28 pages, (2) leaves (copyright, colophon); original lithograph frontispiece in color by Chris Buursen and signed in pencil by him, printed in purple and black; vellum backed paper boards, title in gilt on spine, fore edge and tail edge untrimmed, virtually mint.   Phillip J. Pirages   33-474   1996 $450.00

PURDY, JAMES   Don't Call Me by My Right Name and Other Stories. New York: William Frederick Press, 1956. 1st edition; author's first book; wrappers, some faint creasing to covers, otherwise fine. Inscribed by author for David O. Selznick, laid in is a TLS from Purdy to Selznick presenting the book.   Left Bank Books   2-125   1996 $250.00

PURDY, JAMES   Proud Flesh: Four Short Plays. Northridge: Lord John Press, 1980. Number 25 of 250 numbered copies, signed by author; tall thin 8vo; pictorial titlepage and headpieces; gilt stamped dark blue cloth, light blue endpapers, fine in dust jacket.   George J. Houle   68-124   1996 $125.00

PURVIS, ROBERT   A Tribute to the Memory of Thomas Shipley, the Pilanthropist. Philadelphia: 1836. 1st edition; 8vo; 20 pages; original printed wrappers; embossed library stamp on title and some soiling to wrappers, but very good. Very scarce. LCP/HSP Afro Americana Cat. 8559. Rinderknecht 39805.   M & S Rare Books   60-219   1996 $750.00

PUSHKIN, ALEKSANDR SERGEEVICH 1799-1837   Il Cavaliere di Bronzo. Officina Bodoni, 1968. One of 165 numbered copies, signed by Wadim Lazursky and by Mardersteig; 4to; printed in Lazursky's Pushkin cyrillic and in Dante in black and red on Magnani handmade; half vellum, patterned boards, fine in slipcase, prospectus laid in.   Bertram Rota   272-351   1996   £500.00

PUSHKIN, ALEKSANDR SERGEEVICH 1799-1837   Eugene Onegin. New York: Limited Editions Club, 1943. Limited to 1500 copies, signed by artist; 8vo; illustrations by Fritz Eichenberg; three quarter black leather, fine in slighty worn glassine, chemise and case.   Charles Agvent   4-964   1996 $125.00

PUSHKIN, ALEKSANDR SERGEEVICH 1799-1837   Eugene Onegin. New York: Bollingen, 1964. 1st edition thus, 2nd issue without ribbon page markers; 4 volumes, very lightly spine sunned in spine tanned dust jackets, else near fine in publisher's cardboard slipcase.   Lame Duck Books   19-403   1996 $200.00

PUSHKIN, ALEKSANDR SERGEEVICH 1799-1837   The Golden Cockerel. New York: Limited Editions Club, 1950. Limited to 1500 copies; folio; color plates by Edmund Dulac, signed by Dulac; paper with set brass design, fine in near fine glassine, chemise and slipcase.   Charles Agvent   4-966   1996 $300.00

PUSHKIN, ALEKSANDR SERGEEVICH 1799-1837   The Golden Cockerel. New York: Limited Editions Club, 1950. Number 1385 of 1500 copies, signed by artist; illustrations by Edmund Dulac; fine in lightly edge sunned slipcase.   Hermitage   SP95-1026   1996 $225.00

PUSHKIN, ALEKSANDR SERGEEVICH 1799-1837   The Talisman. St. Petersburg: printed by Schulz and Beneze, 1835. 1st edition in English, one of only 100 copies printed; 14 pages; later grey paper boards, light foxing, fine, untrimmed copy.   19th Century Shop   39-   1996 $2,250.00

PUTNAM'S Library of Choice Stories. Sea Stories. Now First Collected and Forming, the Fifth Volume... New York: G. P. Puntam, 1858. 1st edition; 12mo; 276 pages; original cloth, foxed. Wright II 2170 (2 copies); M & S Rare Books   60-209   1996 $100.00

PUTNAM, ALLEN   Witchcraft of New England Explained by Modern Spiritualism. Boston: Colby and Rich., 1888. 3rd edition; 8vo; 482 pages; original brown cloth, light fraying, top and bottom of spine, corners bumped, fine, very clean copy.   Roy W. Clare   XXIV-30   1996 $100.00

PUXLEY, F. L.   In African Game Tracks. London: 1929. illustrations, original cloth, rubbed, one leaf frayed, marginal tears, plate removed "A West African Beauty Chorus"; working copy only.   David Grayling   J95Biggame-159   1996   £70.00

PYE, CHARLES   The Stranger's Guide to Modern Birmingham, With an Account of Its Public Buildings and Institutions, Its Show Rooms and Manufactories. Birmingham: Published by R. Wrightson, 1825. Revised edition; 8vo; 194 pages, new endpapers; 5 engraved plates; original paper boards which have been professionally rebacked with new cloth spine, new paper spine label; archival tape repairs to front of one plate, otherwise near fine.   David Mason 71-36 1996 $180.00

PYLE, HOWARD   Howard Pyle's Book of the American Spirit: The Romance of American History Pictured by Howard Pyle. New York: Harper, 1923. 1st edition; with B-X on copyright page, 12 1/2 x 9 1/4 inches; xii, 344, (iv) pages; 101 illustrations of which 22 are full page color plates, paper over boards, black cloth spine, mounted color plate on front cover, very good.   William A. Graf 186-157 1996 $200.00

PYLE, HOWARD   Pepper and Salt or Seasonings for Young Folks. New York: Harper's, 1886. 1st edition; folio; illustrations by author; decorated cloth, covers quite rubbed and faded, contents clean. Charles Agvent 4-967 1996 $175.00

PYLE, HOWARD   The Ruby of Kishmoor. New York: 1908. 1st edition; 10 color plates by Pyle; pictorial covers, gilt, top edge gilt, uncut; bookplate, fine.   Polyanthos 22-457 1996 $125.00

PYM, BARBARA 1913-1980   Jane and Prudence. London: Jonathan cape, 1953. 1st edition; 8vo; (222) pages; wine cloth covered boards with blue-grey print, fine in near fine dust jacket.   Paulette Rose 16-249 1996 $325.00

PYM, BARBARA 1913-1980   Less Than Angels. London: Jonathan Cape, 1955. 1st edition; 8vo; (256) pages; brown cloth covered boards, gilt lettering on spine and front; fine in near fine yellow dust jacket, scarce.   Paulette Rose 16-250 1996 $275.00

PYNCHON, THOMAS 1937-   The Crying of Lot 49. Philadelphia: Lippincott, 1966. 1st edition; owner name on verso of front endpaper, fine in fine dust jacket.   Ken Lopez 74-385 1996 $250.00

PYNCHON, THOMAS 1937-   The Crying of Lot 49. London: Cape, 1967. 1st British edition; near fine in very good or better dust jacket with couple of short edge tears to front panel.   Lame Duck Books 19-473 1996 $250.00

PYNCHON, THOMAS 1937-   Gravity's Rainbow. New York: Viking, 1973. 1st edition; fine in fine dust jacket with tiny tear at bottom of front panel; difficult to find in acceptable condition.   Between the Covers 42-366 1996 $750.00

PYNCHON, THOMAS 1937-   Gravity's Rainbow. New York: 1973. 1st edition; fine in dust jacket.   Polyanthos 22-710 1996 $400.00

PYNCHON, THOMAS 1937-   El Arco Iris de Gravedad (Gravity's Rainbow). Bar: Grijalbo, 1978. 1st Spanish edition; 2 volumes; near fine in dust jackets with small internal chip to front flap fold of volume one, from author's own library.   Lame Duck Books 19-474 1996 $375.00

PYNCHON, THOMAS 1937-   Slow Learner. Boston: Little Brown, 1984. 1st edition; slight spine slant, else fine in fine dust jacket; inscribed by author, rare inscribed.   Ken Lopez 74-386 1996 $3,500.00

PYNCHON, THOMAS 1937-   Slow Learner. London: Cape, 1984. Uncorrected proof of the first British edition; red printed wrappers, some surface loss to spinal extremities, otherwise fine.   Lame Duck Books 19-475 1996 $150.00

PYNCHON, THOMAS 1937-   V. Philadelphia: Lippincott, 1963. 1st edition; small owner label on front pastedown, but near fine in near fine, very slightly faded and rubbed dust jacket with light wear at corners, very nice.   Ken Lopez 74-384 1996 $850.00

PYNE, JAMES BAKER 1800-1870   The First Series of the Mountain, River, Lake and Landscape Scenery of Great Britain... Leeds: D. Banks, 11 Queent St., c. 1877-79. Large format ediiton; folio; 3 volumes, frontispiece to volume one, titlepage and 15 fine chromolithograph paltes in each volume, with contents pages, leaves of descriptive text; original gilt blocked green cloth, gilt blocking on upper covers is identical to that on two volume Leeds printed edition of English Lake Scenery; some slight discoloration to one board.   Ken Spelman 30-102 1996 £850.00

PYNE, JAMES BAKER 1800-1870   Lake Scenery of England. London: Day & Sons, 1859. 1st edition; tall 4to; pages vii, plus 25 chromolithographed plates, each with accompanying leaf of text, woodcuts in text; original blindstamped cloth, gilt, neatly recased, all edges gilt; Abbey Scenery 196; Bicknell 154c.   R.F.G. Hollett & Son 78-1210 1996 £240.00

PYNE, WILLIAM HENRY 1769-1843   The History of the Royal Residences. London: 1819. 4to; 3 volumes, titlepage, 1 f. dedication, caption title, 21 pages (vignette); title, 1 f., half title, 80 pages; half title 92 pages, 13 page list of portraits, 2 page list of plates; title 1 f., half title, 88 pages, half title, 28 pages, half title, 88 pages; 100 hand colored aquatint plates, some heightened with gum arabic; half brown morocco, rebacked. Rare large paper edition; Abbey Scenery 396; Tooley 389. Marlborough 162-85 1996 £7,500.00

Q

QUAMMEN, DAVID   To Walk the Line. New York: Knopf, 1970. Limited to 225 copies; fine in fine dust jacket; signed on bookplate which reads "This Edition of My Book "To Walk the Line" is copy number 160 of no more than 225 copies which I have authorized for distribution by Signed Editions Limited David Quammen".   Bella Luna 7-478 1996 $100.00

QUARLES, BENJAMIN   Frederick Douglass. Washington: Associated Pub., 1948. 1st edition; fine in near fine price clipped dust jacket with few very small nicks and tears at extremities; scarce in dust jacket. Between the Covers 43-342 1996 $185.00

QUARLES, FRANCIS   Boanerges and Barnabas; Judgment and Mercy, or, Wine and Oil for Wounded and Afflicted Souls. London: R. Royston, 1664. 6th edition; 12mo; (xvi), 120, (ii), 121-240, (ii) pages; frontispiece, secondary titlepage to second part, colophon leaf, early ms. notes on prayer on front endpaper; contemporary sheep, ruled in blind, later hand written label; edges worn, internally very good. Good copy of uncommon edition. Wing Q56.   Robert Clark 38-120 1996 £160.00

QUARLES, FRANCIS   Divine Poems, Containing the History of Jonah, Ester, Job, Sampson. Together with Sions Sonnets, Elegies. London: Benj. Tooke, and Tho. Sawbridge, 1674. Variant issue; 8vo; (xvi), 471, (i) pages; old sheep,s pine decorated gilt, label, rubbed, upper joint cracked but firm, minor adhesion at inner margin of engraved title, scattered foxing. Good copy, ownership signature of Samuel Wilberforce. Wing Qu4a.   Robert Clark 38-119 1996 £200.00

QUARLES, FRANCIS   Emblems, Divine and Moral. London: 1839. New edition; 12mo; over 240 pages; 80 engravings; new old style quarter calf; good.   K Books 442-403 1996 £75.00

QUARLES, FRANCIS   Quarles' Emblems. London: James Nisbet, 1861. 1st edition thus; royal 8vo; pages (10), 321; 80 full page illustrations; original blue cloth, gilt, edges gilt, signed "W.H.L."; very good to nice. McLean VPB 83.   James Fenning 133-278 1996 £55.00

QUARTICH, BERNARD   A Catalogue of Illuminated and Other Manuscripts Together with Some Works on Palaeography. London: Bernard Quaritch, 1931. 4to; color frontispiece, 65 plates; original boards, extremities slightly worn, ownership inscription of Lord Kenyon, few annotations in pencil, copy of letter to Maggs offering 3 items for sale, with their descriptions, bill of sale of 3 items to Bernard Quaritch from Kenyon and letter from Geoffrey Hobson to Kenyon about a ms. sold at Sothebys in 1913 inserted loose.   Maggs Bros. Ltd. 1191-35 1996 £65.00

QUASIMODO, SALVATORE   The Tall Schooner. New York: Red Ozier Press, 1980. 1st edition; one of 150 copies signed by artist and publishers; thin 12mo; illustrations by Janet Morgan; original wrappers, mint.   James S. Jaffe 34-582 1996 $100.00

QUEEN Victoria's Jubilee, The Great Procession of June 22, 1897 in the Queen's Honor, Reported Both in the Light of History and as a Spectacle. N.P.: privately printed for private distribution only, n.d. 1st edition; limited to 195 numbered copies; 9 x 6 inches; 22 pages; illustrations; cloth backed pictorial boards, minor stain at top edge affecting margins slightly, front fly repaired, covers soiled, with some staining and wear.   John K. King 77-489 1996 $325.00

QUEEN, ELLERY, PSEUD.   The Adventures of Ellery Queen: Problems in Deduction. New York: Stokes, 1934. 1st edition; no dust jacket, but striking black on bright yellow cover design comes through nicely, even the spine isn't really sunned, book cocked, though, and hinges aren't the tightest, slight soil on rear cover, overall a bright copy, but very good, scarce. Queen's Quorum 90.   Magnum Opus 44-74 1996 $100.00

QUEEN, ELLERY, PSEUD.   The Brown Fox Mystery. Boston: little Brown and Co., 1948. 1st edition; fine in very good, bright dust jacket with light chipping, few small closed tears and back panel lightly soiled. Quill & Brush 102-1483 1996 $250.00

QUEEN, ELLERY, PSEUD.   The Dragon's Teeth. New York: Frederick Stokes, 1939. 1st edition; endpapers slightly darkened, spine and top edge of rear cover lightly foxed, otherwise very good in edge rubbed dust jacket slightly faded on spine, with shallow chipping along top edges and faint '14' on spine.   Quill & Brush 102-1478 1996 $225.00

QUEENY, EDGAR M.   Prairie Wings. New York: Ducks Unlimited Inc., 1946. 1st edition, 1st printing; 4to; fine in beige linen cloth with brown lettering.   Glenn Books 36-261 1996 $275.00

QUEENY, EDGAR M.   Prairie Wings. Pen and Camera Flight Studies. Philadelphia & New York: Lippincott, 1947. 2nd edition; small folio; xiv, 256 pages, color plate plus profuse gravure illustrations; cloth.   Taurus Books 83-80 1996 $125.00

QUEER Stories About Queer Animals, Told in Rhymes and Jingles. Philadelphia: National Pub. Co., ca. 1905. Octavo; (48)ff; illustrations printed in blue or red on every page by Palmer Cox; faintly soiled green cloth illustrated in red and yellow; nice, bright copy.   Bromer Booksellers 90-91 1996 $135.00

QUEKETT, J.   Lectures on Histology. London: 1852-54. 8vo; 2 volumes in 1; 423 woodcuts, original cloth, neatly repaired; very scarce, copy has been neatly refixed in its case, with new endpapers, inner margin of titlepage to volume 2 strengthened.   Wheldon & Wesley 207-187 1996 £120.00

QUEKETT, J.   A Practical Treatise on the Use of the Microscope... London: 1852. 2nd edition; 8vo; pages xxii, 515, 11 (of 12) plates; original cloth, neatly repaired, very scarce; trifle loose, few pages refixed with document tape, lacks plate 10, plates waterstained.   Wheldon & Wesley 207-188 1996 £65.00

QUEVEDO, FRANCESCO   Visions. London: printed in the year 1766. 12mo; engraved frontispiece, iv, 221 pages; original calf, slight wear at head and foot of spines, joints beginning to crack, but nice.   David Bickersteth 133-56 1996 £65.00

QUINCY, JOHN   Pharmacopoeia Officinalis & Extemporanea; or, a Compleat English Dispensatory, in Two Parts, Theoretic and Practical. London: printed for T. Longman, 1749. 12th edition; thick 8vo; contemporary calf, spine gilt, slight rubbing; fine copy; NLM p. 369.   Ximenes 108-304 1996 $250.00

QUINCY, JOSIAH 1772-1864   Remarks on Some of the Provisions of the Laws of Massachusetts, Affecting Poverty, Vice and Crime. Cambride: University Press, 1822. 1st edition; 8vo; 28 pages; removed. Presentation inscription in ink from author, recipient's name clipped. Shoemaker 10058.   ] & S Rare Books 60-313 1996 $150.00

QUINN, EDWARD   Max Ernst. Paris: Cercle d'Art, 1976. Square folio; 442 pages; profusely illustrated, much in color, original lithograph; cloth, dust jacket. Freitag 2739.   Brannan 43-191 1996 $200.00

QUINTIANUS STOA, JOHANNES F.   De Syllabarum Quantitate Epographiae Sex... Venice: Guglielmo da Monteferrato, 1519. 4to; 160 leaves; woodcut portrait; old boards in 13th century vellum manuscript fragment, rubricated and with illuminated initial; fine. Adams Q21; Sander 6076 & 7088; Essling 2036; not in NUC or BM STC.   Bennett Gilbert LL29-68 1996 $4,500.00

R

RABELAIS, FRANCOIS 1494?-1553   Pantagruel. Dijon: Henri Pasquinelly, 1946. 1st edition thus, number 23 of 500 copies; 11 x 9 inches; 537 pages; 2 volumes; profusely illustrated with lithographs and text drawings by Shem; wrappers, enclosed in folding board folder, lower front corner of front wrapper to volume one clipped, otherwise fine in moderately worn board folder.   Hermitage SP95-910 1996 $500.00

RABELAIS, FRANCOIS 1494?-1553   Les Oeuvres. Antwerp: Jean Fuet, 1605-8. 2nd of the 3 (or possibly 4) editions of the works which pruport to have been printed at Antwerp by Jean Fuet; 12mo; pages 347, (vii), 469 (recte 465) (ix), 166 (xvi), some pages misnumbered, final blank missing, separate titlepage to Book V, roman and Italic letter, 1 full page woodcut of the Bottle, woodcut initials and ornaments, light age yellowing, 3 small rust holes affecting the odd letter, early owner's autograph, neatly erased on titlepage, 19th century orange morocco by Claessens, gilt fillets, inner dentelles and spine, all edges gilt, marbled endpapers, good copy; 19th century bookplate. BM STC Fr. 17th R56; Low Countries 1601-21 R1; Tchemerzine V 315.   A. Sokol XXV-79 1996 £950.00

RABELAIS, FRANCOIS 1494?-1553   The Works. London: Gibbings, 1901. Small 8vo; 5 volumes; numerous illustrations; three quarter red crimson straight grain morocco, floral tooling on spines, raised bands, gilt tops; fine, attractive set.   Appelfeld Gallery 54-151 1996 $300.00

RABLEY, CHARLES A.   Devonshire Trout Fishing. London: 1912. Small 8vo; 54 pages; 2 color plates, photo to titlepage, illustrations to text; limp printed wrappers.   Petersfield Bookshop FH58-309 1996 £50.00

RACHFORD, BENJAMIN KNOX   Neurotic Disorders of Childhood Including a study of Auto and Intestinal Intoxications, Chronic Anaemia, Fever, Eclampsia, Epilepsy, Migraine, Chorea, Hysteria, Asthma, etc. New York: E. B. Treat & Co., 1905. 8vo; 440, (8) pages; olive cloth with gilt spine, gold titlepage stamp and spine call numbers of the Hartford Retreat; with Jelliffe's name stamp and bookplate.   John Gach 150-376 1996 $150.00

RACINE, JEAN   Phaedra Britannica. London: Rex Collings Ltd., 1975. 1st edition; wrappers, covers slightly marked, spotted and dusty, spine browned, small stain at fore-edge of half titlepage, very good; bookplate of literary agent John Johnson.   Ulysses 39-271 1996 £65.00

RACINET, ALBERT CHARLES AUGUSTE   L'Ornement Polychrome. Cent Planches en Couleurs or et Argent Contenant Environ 2000 Motifs de Tous les Styles Art Ancient et Asiatique/Moyen Age/Renaissance, XVIIe et XVIIIe Siecles. (and) Deuxieme Serie: Cent Vingt Planches... Paris: Firmin Didot, ca. 1875. 2nd edition; folio; 2 volumes; 220 chromolithograph plates; maroon half morocco and rose moire boards, occasional spotting to first pages of text and to plate explanations of volume 1, but plates clean, volume 2 without blemish.   Marilyn Braiterman 15-172 1996 $1,750.00

RACINET, ALBERT CHARLES AUGUSTE   L'Ornement Polychrome. Paris: Firmin Didot, 1875. 2nd edition; folio; 2 volumes, (iv), 60 pages, 100 plates, with accompanying leaves of text; publisher's half morocco, bindings show some wear at extremities of spine and tips, else very nice set, devoid of foxing, but with occasional waterstains in margins of a few leaves, not affecting text or plates.   Bookpress 75-109 1996 $1,500.00

RACKHAM, ARTHUR   Arthur Rackham's Book of Pictures. New York: Century Co., n.d. 1913. 1st American edition; quarto; 44 mounted color plates, each with captioned tissue guard; original tan cloth, gilt cover and spine, top edge gilt; fine. Latimore & Haskell p. 41.   Glenn Books 36-220 1996 $300.00

RACKHAM, ARTHUR   The Land of Enchantment. London: Cassell, 1907. 1st edition; large folio; color frontispiece, title vignette, 11 color plates, 23 text illustrations, all printed on Japanese vellum; tastefully bound in quarter calf, compartmented spine, lettered and decorated in gilt; beautiful copy.   Marjorie James 19-182 1996 £150.00

RACKHAM, ARTHUR   Some British Ballads. New York: DM, n.d. Early printing; 4to; decorated cloth, 16 tipped in color plates, black and white engravings, some spotting to cloth, very good.   Charles Agvent 4-969 1996 $125.00

RACKHAM, BERNARD   The Ancient Glass of Canterbury Cathedral. London: Lun Humprhies, 1949. Large 4to; 21 full page plates in color, 80 in monochrome, original buckram, gilt top, slipcase.   Howes Bookshop 265-2202 1996 £200.00

RACKHAM, BERNARD   The Ancient Glass of Canterbury Cathedral. London: Humphries and Co., for Friends of Canterbury Cathedral, 1949. 1st edition; 194 pages, plus 25 color and 80 monochrome plates; top edge gilt, original blue cloth; fine.   Hermitage SP95-739 1996 $200.00

RADAU, HUGO   Early Babylonian History Down to the End of the Fourth Dynasty of Ur, to Which is Appended an Account of the E. A. Hoffman Collection of Babylonian Tablets in the General Theological Seminary, New York, U.S.A. New York: Oxford University Press, 1900. 8vo; xx, 452 pages; numerous figures, 2 folding tables.   Archaeologia Luxor-2629 1996 $150.00

RADAU, HUGO   Letters to Cassite Kings from the Temple Arachives of Nippur. Philadelphia: Dept. of Archaeology, University of Pennsylvania, 1908. Folio; xv, 174 pages and 80 plates; tattered wrappers.   Archaeologia Luxor-2620 1996 $125.00

RADCLIFFE, ANN WARD 1764-1823   The Mysteries of Udolpho, a Romance... London: for G. G. and J. Robinson, 1794. 1st edition; large 12mo; 4 volumes, with half titles, but without final blank in volume 2; contemporary Swedish calf, spines with raised bands, pale tan morocco labels, oval black numbering-pieces, extremities little worn, sides rubbed, one or two trivial stains, nice contemporary set. From the library of Swedish Count Nils Gyldenstolpe with his initials and coronet blindstamped on endpapers of 2 volumes, and his large monogram inkstamp on each title, also with later oval lib. inkstamp of C. Fr. Wernher on e.p.'s. Rothschild 1710; Summers p. 434.   Simon Finch 24-193 1996 £950.00

RADCLIFFE, FREDERICK PETER DELME 1804-1875   The Noble Science; a few General Ideas on Fox-Hunting. London: Rudolph Ackermann, 1839. 1st edition; royal 8vo; xii, (328) pages; frontispiece, extra title and 8 plates, wood engravings in text, original red decorative cloth, gilt, spine mite chipped and worn, few marks and slight nicks, one leaf slightly creased, but very good.   Ash Rare Books Zenzybyr-76 1996 £195.00

RADCLYFFE, C. W.   The Palace of Blenheim. Oxford: James Wyatt & Son, 1842. Large folio; tinted lithographic title, litho dedication, 18 tinted litho plates on 16 ff., rebacked with green morocco, original cloth covered boards, original green morocco label on upper cover. Excellent copy, rare. Inscribed by the Duchess of Marlborough.   Marlborough 162-275 1996 £2,500.00

RADDATZ, FRITZ J.   Lithographies 1959-1973. Paris: Editions Vilo, 1974. Limited to 60 copies, with an extra suite of five original lithographs, each one signed and numbered by artist; folio; 157 pages; illustrations by Paul Wunderlich; cloth, dust jacket, extra suite housed in cloth chemise. Mint.   Bromer Booksellers 87-281 1996 $3,250.00

THE RADICAL Programme. London: 1885. 1st edition; crown 8vo; pages xviii, 328; original cloth. Hanham 725.   Howes Bookshop 265-1003 1996 £75.00

RADIN, PAUL   African Folktales and Sculpture. New York: Pantheon Books, 1952. 31.3 cm; xxi, 355 pages + 165 pages of black and white photos, map; black cloth, spine with tan linen over boards.   L. Clarice Davis 111-84 1996 $100.00

RADIO CORPORATION OF AMERICA   Exhibition Catalog for Radio Corportation of America, April 25, 1927. New York: 1927. (8) pages, with 30 news clippings and 5 actual photos, all laid down; extremely bright.   Bookworm & Silverfish 280-192 1996 $175.00

RADLOV, NICHOLAS   The Cautious Carp and Other Fables in Pictures. New York: Coward McCann, 1938. Oblong 4to; color illustrations; colored pictorial boards, backstrip slightly marked, else fresh copy in chipped pictorial dust jacket.   Barbara Stone 70-178 1996 £125.00

RADZINOWICZ, LEON   A History of English Criminal Law and Its Administration from 1750. London: Stevens and Sons Ltd., 1948-56. 3 volumes.   Meyer Boswell SL26-197 1996 $225.00

RAFFLES, SOPHIA   Memoir of the Life and Public Services of Sir Thomas Stamford Raffles. London: John Murray, 1830. 1st U.K. edition; 4to; (xvi), 724 pages, 100 page appendix; frontispiece, 7 aquatint plates, large aquatint, 2 folding maps, all edges marbled; early full calf boards, gilt title and some decoration, rubbed at extremities, slightly marked, nice.   Antipodean 28-219 1996 $1,750.00

RAHEB, BARBARA   A Dark, Dark Tale. Agoura Hills: Pennyweight Press, 1995. 1 1/4 x 7/8 inches; (9)ff; charming miniature pop-up book, pop-up vignette; gilt stamped black morocco. Mint.   Bromer Booksellers 87-218 1996 $110.00

RAIKES, RICHARD   Considerations on the Alliance Between Christianity and Commerce, Applied to the Present State of this Country. London: Cadell and Davies, 1806. 1st edition; 8vo; vi, (3)-81 pages, very slight spotting, mainly marginal, recently well bound in cloth, spine lettered in gilt, very good, with half title. Kress B5098; Goldsmiths 19170; Williams II 542.   John Drury 82-235 1996 £125.00

RAINE, CRAIG   A Free Translation. Edinburgh: Salamander Press, 1981. One of 200 clothbound copies out of a total edition of 1000; on Glastonbury Book Antique Laid paper; covers slightly marked, head and tail of spine very slightly bumped, very good in very slightly marked and creased dust jacket.   Ulysses 39-490 1996 £55.00

RAINE, KATHLEEN   The Written Word. A Speech Delivered at the Annual Luncheon of the Poetry Society 1963. London: Enitharmon Press, 1967. 1st edition; limited to 45 specially bound copies, signed by author; thin 8vo; cockerell paper wrappers, printed label; very fine.   James S. Jaffe 34-554 1996 $125.00

RAINOLDS, JOHN   The Overthrow of Stage-Playes, by the Way of Controversie Betwixt D. Gager and D. Rainoldes... Oxford: printed by John Lichfield for E. Forrest and W. Webbe, 1629. 2nd edition; small 4to; early 19th century panelled calf, rebacked, original spine laid down; titlepage bit foxed, but nice copy with good margins. STC 20618; LAR 267.   Ximenes 108-305 1996 $1,500.00

RAITHBY, JOHN   The Study and Practice of the Law, Considered in Their Various Relations to Society, etc. Portland: Printed by Thomas B. Wait and Co., 1806. 1st and only American edition; contemporary sheep, front joint cracking, some repairs, but crisp.   Meyer Boswell SL25-182 1996 $450.00

RALEIGH, WALTER 1552-1618   The Discoverie of the Large, Rich and Bewtiful Empyre of Guiana, with a Relation of the Great and Golden Citie of Manoa... London: by Robert Robinson, 1595. 1st edition; 3rd issue; 4to; (16), 112 pages; full polished calf, spine richly gilt in compartments by Riviere, upper edge of title very skillfully extended, with 3 letters and parts of 10 other letters in almost imperceptible pen facsimile, two or three repairs to blank margins, else fine; with Boies Penrose bookplates. Church 254; JCB III I.349; Sabin 67554; STC 20636.   Joseph J. Felcone 64-33 1996 $5,500.00

RALEIGH, WALTER 1552-1618   The Discovery of the Large, Rich and Beautiful Empire of Guiana, with a Relation of the Great and Golden City of Manoa... London: printed for the Hakluyt Society, 1848. 2nd edition; 23cm; lxxv, xv, 240 pages; engraved folding map as frontispiece, errata; gilt stamped and decorated blue cloth, bit of wear to spine; very good. NMM 289.   Rockland Books 38-179 1996 $300.00

RALEIGH, WALTER 1552-1618   The Discovery of the Large, Rich and Beautiful Empire of Guiana, with a Relation of the Great and Golden City of Manoa... London: 1848. 2nd edition; pages lxxv, 204; map; original binding, nice copy, scarce.   Stephen Lunsford 45-133 1996 $200.00

RALEIGH, WALTER 1552-1618   The History of the World. London: printed for G. Conyers, J. and J. Knapton, D. Midwinter... 1736. 11th edtiion; folio; 2 volumes; titlepages in black and red, iii-ccxxxii, 817 pages of continuous text, note to reader, chromological table and index to rear volume 2; frontispiece to volume I, 8 double page maps and plans, 2 genealogical trees, woodcut head and tailpieces and initials; old calf, some small surface scrapes to boards, panelled spines with brown morocco labels, speckled edges, armorial bookplate, both hinges of volume 1 cracked, upper hinge volume 2 cracked, corners bumped and worn.   Beeleigh Abbey BA/56-107 1996 £450.00

RALEIGH, WALTER 1552-1618   The History of the World, in Five Books. London: printed for G. Conyers, etc., 1736. Folio; 2 volumes; 6 folding maps, 2 folding charts, 2 diagrams in text; old brown calf, expertly rebacked, emblematic tooling on spines, raised bands, red and green leather labels; fine.   Appelfeld Gallery 54-154 1996 $500.00

RALEIGH, WALTER 1552-1618   An Introduction to a Breviart of the History of England, with the Reign of King William the I. London: Sam Keble, 1693. 1st edition; 16mo; (vi), 77, (3) pages; contemporary half calf, rebacked; scarce; lacking portrait, worn. Wing R169.   The Bookpress 75-452 1996 $150.00

RALEIGH, WALTER 1552-1618   Judicious and Select Essayes and Observations. London: printed by T. W. for Humphrey Mosele, 1650. 1st collected edition; 8vo; frontispiece, title printed within border of typographical fleur-de-lys, (1), 42, (2), 4, (72), (2), 46, (2), 69, (1) pages; mid 19th century calf, gilt, tear at foot of spine, otherwise very good; from the library of the Earl of Yarborough with his bookplate.   John Drury 82-236 1996 £600.00

RALEIGH, WALTER 1552-1618   Judicious and Select Essayes and Observations, by...Upon the First Invention of Shipping. London: by T. W. for Humphrey Molseley, 1650. 1st edition; crown 8vo; title, engraved portrait of Raleigh by R. Vaughan, contemporary sprinkled calf, spine gilt, head and foot of spine unobtrusively repaired. Sabin calls for 4 leaves of ads at end, not present in this copy. Wing R170; Sabin67561.   H. M. Fletcher 121-71 1996 £475.00

RALEIGH, WALTER 1552-1618   The Marrow of History or, an Epitome of all Historical Passages... London: John Place and William Place, 1662. 2nd edition; 16mo; (xxiv), 574 pages; contemporary calf, bookplate, edges rubbed, head of spine chipped, inscriptions in ink on front endpapers and rear endpaper, small wormholes on some leaves. Sabin 67599.   The Bookpress 75-453 1996 $225.00

RALEIGH, WALTER 1552-1618   The Poems of Sir Walter Raleigh, Now First Collected. Lee Priory Press, 1813, i.e. 1814. One of 100 copies; 4to; printed in black and red; modern quarter leather and marbled boards, all edges marbled, some staining and spotting of leaves, generally nice, clean copy.   Bertram Rota 272-249 1996 £100.00

RALEIGH, WALTER 1552-1618   The Prerogative of Parliaments in England: Proued in a Dialogue (Pro & Contra) Betweene a Councellour of State and a Iustice of Peace (etc.). London: 1628. Modern calf, quite embrowned, titlepage very dusty, sound.   Meyer Boswell SL25-183 1996 $650.00

RALPH, JAMES   The Fashionable Lady; or, Harlequin's Opera. London: printed for J. Watts, 1730. 1st edition; 8vo; new half calf, marbled sides; Gagey, Ballad Opera 154-7 and 241; Nicol 267.   Peter Murray Hill 185-6 1996 £175.00

THE RAMBLES and Surprising Adventures of Captain Bolio. London: ptd. for Thomas Tegg; Tegg & Co. Dublin, R. Griffin & Co. Glasgow... 1839. 1st edition; 12mo; half blue morocco, gilt, spine gilt, top edge gilt, by Tout (traces or rubbing); fine, scarce. Not in block; not in Wolff.   Ximenes 108-131 1996 $250.00

RAMHOFFSKY, JOHANN HEINRICH   Drey Beschreibungen, Erstens: Des Koniglichen Einzugs, Welchen Ihre Konigliche Majestat...Maria Theresia, zu Hungarn und boheim Konigin... Prague: C. F. Rosenmuller, 1743. Folio; 3 parts in 1; engraved frontispiece, 3 ff., 21 pages, title, 12 pages, title, 70 pages, 15 engraved plates; contemporary calf, gilt stam of the Bohemian arms on both covers, blind tooled spine, head and foot neatly repaired, later label; handsome copy in original binding, ex-libris Franz, Graf lamberg. Berlin Kat 2135; vinet 684.   Marlborough 162-254 1996 £5,500.00

RAMIE, GEORGES   Picasso's Ceramics. New York: Chartwell, n.d. Square 4to; 292 pages; 759 illustrations, 340 in color; boards, dust jacket. Freitag 7488.   Brannan 43-532 1996 $150.00

RAMON Y CAJAL, S.   Degeneration and Regeneration of the Nervous System. New York: Hafner, 1959. Facsimile reprint of original edition of 1928; 8vo; 2 volumes; original binding, clean set.   James Tait Goodric K40-243 1996 $145.00

RAMON Y CAJAL, S.   Precepts and Councils on Scientific Investigation: Stimulants of the Spirit. Mountain View: 1951. Limited to 230 copies, 1st English translation; 180 pages; original binding.   W. Bruce Fye 71-1726 1996 $100.00

RAMON Y CAJAL, S.   Recollections of My Life. Philadelphia: 1937. 1s English edition; 2 volumes; original printed wrappers, some discoloratior of front wrpaper, otherwise near fine.   James Tait Goodrich K40-244 1996 $165.00

RAMPART Mining Company, Rampart, Alaska. Worcester: Burbank & Co ca. 1901. 1st edition; (8) pages, including titlepage; original brown stiff wrappers with title in gilt on front cover; fine.   Michael D. Heaston 23-11 1996 $150.00

RAMSAY, ALLAN   The Gentle Shepherd, a Pastoral Comedy. Edinburgh: printed by James Ballantyne & Co. for Watt and Baillie, 1808. 8vo; pages xxx, 121, hand colored mezzotint portrait (repaired at fore-edge), 12 hand colored engraved plates, title a trifle creased and spotted, little soiling and fingering in places; contemporary full morocco gilt, panelled boards, edges rather worn, handsomely rebacked in matching levant morocco, gilt.   R.F.G. Hollett 76-249 1996 £375.00

RAMSAY, ANDREW MICHAEL   An Essay Upon Civil Government...with Observations on the Ancient Government of Rome and England (etc.). London: printed for Randal Minshull, 1722. contemporary sheep, quite rubbed, joints cracked, usable.   Meyer Boswell SL25-184 1996 $250.00

RAMSAY, ANDREW MICHAEL   The Life of Francis de Salignac de la Motte Fenelon, Arch-bishop and Duke of Cambray. London: printed for Paul Vaillant, and James Woodman, 1723. 1st edition in English; 12mo; contemporary panelled calf, rebacked; some light soiling, marks in ink by an early reader, but good. CBEL II 1527.   Ximenes 109-243 1996 $225.00

RAMSAY, EDWARD BANNERMAN   Two Lectures on Some Changes in Social Life and Habits. Edinburgh: Edmonston & Douglas, 1857. 1st edition; 8vo; (vi), 108 pages; original maroon cloth, simple spine lettering, faded, very good. Rare. Only 2 locations in NUC.   John Drury 82-237 1996 £95.00

RAMSAY, JAMES   Examination of the Rev. Mr. Harris's Scriptual Researches on the Licitness of the Slave Trade. London: printed by James Phillips, 1788. 1st edition; 8vo; 3 pages of ads at end, 29 pages; disbound. Sabin 6714; Ragatz p.5 42; Goldsmith 13713.   Anthony W. Laywood 109-120 1996 £175.00

RAMSAY, JAMES   Objections to the Abolition of the Slave Trade, with Answers. London: printed and sold by James Phillips, 1788. 1st edition; 8vo; half title, 60 pages; disbound; Sabin 67717; Ragatz p. 542; Goldsmith 13714.   Anthony W. Laywood 109-121 1996 £250.00

RAMSAY, W. M.   Studies in the History and Art of the Eastern Provinces in the Roman Empire. Aberdeen: 1906. 4to; xiii, 391 pages, 11 plates, text figures, 3 maps.   Rainsford A54-475 1996 £65.00

RAND, A. L.   Handbook of New Guinea Birds. London: 1967. Royal 8vo; x, 612 pages, 5 colored and 76 plain illustrations on 24 plates; cloth, scarce and very difficult to obtain; 16 page index, issued separately, is present loose.   Wheldon & Wesley 207-833 1996 £175.00

RAND, AYN   Atlas Shrugged. New York: Random House, 1957. 1st edition; fine in dust jacket with few touches of rubbing.   Captain's Bookshelf 38-191 1996 $400.00

RAND, AYN   Atlas Shrugged. New York: Random House, 1957. 1st edition; some light staining to front cloth board, else very good+ in very good price clipped dust jacket.   Pettler & Lieberman 28-207 1996 $150.00

RAND, AYN   For the New Intellectual: the Philosophy of Ayn Rand. New York: Random House, 1961. 1st edition; fine in dust jacket with few small tears, signed by Rand on half title, scarce thus.   Captain's Bookshelf 38-192 1996 $950.00

RANDALL, DAVID   Thirteen Author Collections of the Nineteenth Century and Five Centuries of Familiar Quotations. New York: privately printed, 1950. 1st edition; one of 375 copies; 2 volumes; original blue cloth, gilt, top edge gilt, uncut; very fine set.   Mac Donnell 12-148 1996 $250.00

RANDALL, JOHN   Our Coal and Iron Industries and the Men Who Have Wrought in Connection with Them - The Wilkinsons... Barrow-in-Furness: News & mail, 1917. 2nd edition; 8vo; pages xxv, 57, 14; portrait, 4 plates, new endpapers; original cloth, gilt, spine and edges faded, head of spine little rucked, new endpapers.   R.F.G. Hollett & Son 78-625 1996 £65.00

RANDALL, THOMAS E.   History of the Chippewa Valley, a Faithful Record of All Important Events, Incidents and Circumstances that Have Transpired in the Valley of the Chippewa from Its Earliest Settlement by White People, Indian Treaties... Eau Claire: Free Press Print, 1875. 207 pages, 4 pages ads; brown cloth, gilt title on front cover, rubbed, extremities frayed, pencil underlining in early pages; good.   Bohling Book Co. 192-365 1996 $200.00

RANDALL-MAC IVER, DAVID   The Iron Age in Italy: a Study of Those Aspects of the Early Civilization Which are Neither Villanovan nor Etruscan. Oxford: Clarendon Press, 1927. 4to; frontispiece, xv, 243 pages; 90 figures, 47 plates; original cloth, small tear at head of spine, corner lightly bumped.   Archaeologia Luxor-3868 1996 $250.00

RANDISI, ROBERT J.   Mean Streets. New York: Mysterious Press, 1986. Number 233 of 250 copies, numbered and signed by editor and by all twelve contributors; fine in slipcase.   Quill & Brush 102-1378 1996 $125.00

RANDOLPH, JOHN   To the Freeholders of Charlotte, Buckingham, Prince Edward and Cumberland. N.P.: n.p., 1812. 1st edition; small 8vo; (i), 14 pages; text lightly browned, as usual, bookplate, else very good. Shaw & Shoemaker 26566/   The Bookpress 75-454 1996 $285.00

RANDOLPH, MARY   The Virginia Housewife; or, Methodical Cook. Baltimore: Plaskitt, 1836. Stereotype edition; 8vo; pages 180; contemporary calf, somewhat foxed; Lowenstein 152. Bitting p. 388.   Second Life Books 103-159 1996 $350.00

RANKE, LEOPOLD   The Ottoman and the Spanish Empires, in the Sixteenth and Seventeenth Centuries. Philadelphia: Lea & Blanchard, 1845. Small 4to; 138 pages; recently rebound in quarter calf, marbled boards, slight foxing, otherwise very good.   Worldwide Antiquarian 151-559 1996 $135.00

RANSOM, JOHN CROWE   Selected Poems. New York: Knopf, 1952. 2nd printing; ink stains to edges of several pages and on back board; only fair copy, lacking dust jacket; inscribed by Langston Hughes.   Between the Covers 43-122 1996 $200.00

RANSOM, WILL d. 1955   Kelmscott, Doves and Ashendene - the Private Press Credos. New York: The Typophiles, 1952. One of 400 copies for Typophile subscribers and contributors, there were a further 300 copies for the Book Club of California, San Francisco; loosely inserted prospectus for this book and related material; spine slightly faded, head and tail of spine slightly bumped, endpaper gutters slightly browned; very good; from the library of James D. Hart, loosely inserted is an APS from Humphrey Stone to Hart.   Ulysses 39-494 1996 £75.00

RAPELJE, GEORGE   Narrative of Excursions, Voyages and Travels... New York: West & Trow, 1834. 8vo; pages 416; portrait; original gilt pictorial cloth, spine faded. Howes R65.   Richard Adelson W94/95-242 1996 $125.00

RAPP, GEORGE   Excavations at Nichoria in Southwest Greece. Minneapolis: University of Minnesota Press, 1978/92. 4to; volumes I and II, xxviii, 339 pages, 80 figures, 15 plates, 4 maps (in pocket at rear), 15 tables; xxvi 993 pages, 331 figures and 181 plates, 77 plates; original cloth, 1st volume with one corner bumped.   Archaeologia Luxor-3869 1996 $175.00

RASHDALL, HASTINGS   The Universities of Europe in the Middle Ages. London: Oxford University Press, 1936. New edition; 8vo; 3 volumes; folding maps, 2 plates; original buckram.   Howes Bookshop 265-1014 1996 £150.00

RASMUSSEN, W. D.   Agriculture in the United States, a Documentary History. New York: 1975. 8vo; 4 volumes; pages xxii, 3652; text figures; cloth, light soiling.   Raymond M. Sutton VII-1121 1996 $200.00

RASTELL, JOHN   Les Termes de la Ley; or, Certain Difficult and Obscure Words and Terms of the Common and Statute Laws of This Realm, Now in Use, Expounded and Explained. London: printed by Eliz. Nutt and R. Gosling, etc., contemporary unlettered calf, showing wear, but fresh copy.   Meyer Boswell SL25-185 1996 $450.00

RATCH, JERRY   Chaucer Marginalia. Berkeley: Sombre Reptiles in Association with Tombouctou Press, 1979. Of 250 copies, this one of 25 in special edition containing copies of Ratch's chapbook, Rose, in pocket on rear pastedown, the pamphlet is one of 47 copies; 8 x 6 inches; printed in black with some color illustration; cream cloth boards, gray fabriano paper wrap-around. Fine.   Joshua Heller 21-215 1996 $100.00

RATCHFORD, FANNY   The Brontes Web of Childhood. New York: Columbia University Press, 1941. 1st edition; 9 x 6 inches; pages xix, 293 including index, frontispiece and 8 illustrations; blue/grey buckram, fine in slightly worn dust jacket, scarce. Y&T 453.   Ian Hodgkins 78-359 1996 £85.00

RATHBONE, HANNAH MARY   The Poetry of Birds, Selected from Various Authors... Liverpool: George Smith...and Ackermann & Co., London, 1833. 4to; 21 hand colored lithographs, vi, (i +) 136 pages; contemporary green morocco, panelled and lettered in gilt, very slightly scuffed; extremely rare.   Marlborough 160-74 1996 £1,500.00

RATHBONE, PERRY T.   Westward the Way. The Character and Development of the Louisiana Territory as Seen by Artists and Writers of the Nineteenth Century. St. Louis: 1954. 1st edition; royal 8vo; 280 pages; 220 plates in black and white and 4 in color; gilt stamped cloth; very attractive, rather scarce, near fine in slightly edgeworn, price clipped dust jacket. Dykes HS p. 56; Dyke 50 p. 318.   Gene W. Baade 1094-132 1996 $100.00

RATTIGAN, TERENCE   The Collected Plays. London: 1953. 1st edition; very good in dust jacket darkened on spine and chipped at head and two corners; inscribed by author.   Words Etcetera 94-1063 1996 £90.00

RATTRAY, DAVID   A Red-Framed Print of the Summer Palace. New York: Vincent Fitz Gerald & Co., 1983. One of 150 copies; page size 6 x 8 1/2 inches; signed by author and artist; titlepage calligraphy by Jerry Kelly; drawings by Peter Thompson; red linen over boards.   Priscilla Juvelis 95/1-204 1996 $300.00

RAUCOURT DE CHARLEVILLE, A.   A Manual of Lithography; Clearly Explaining the Whole Art and the Accidents That May Happen in Printing, with the Different Methods of Avoiding Them. London: Longman, Rees and others, 1832. 3rd edition; 8vo; xix, (1), 117, (1) blank, ad leaf, 2 double page plates (dated 1833); later 19th century half red morocco, neatly rebacked; little occasional minor spotting; very good, large copy. Ken Spelman 30-41 1996 £480.00

RAUMER, FREDERICK VON   America and the American People. New York: Langley, 1846. 512 pages, folding table; very good, faded, spine ends frayed, foxing. Howes R73; Flake 6822. Clark, Old South 227; Buck 389; Larned 1951.   Bohling Book Co. 191-631 1996 $110.00

RAUNICK, SELMA   Koethmanns of Texas 1845-1931. Austin: 1931. 1st edition; color plate, photo illustrations; cloth, dust jacket, little wear. W. M. Morrison 436-344 1996 $110.00

RAUTHMEL, RICHARD   The Roman Antiquities of Overborough. London: printed by Henry Woodfall, 1746. 1st edition; large paper copy; 8vo; pages xv, 111, complete with title, little soiled, 5 engraved plates, 3 folding, some short tears repaired, little spotting in places, but very good wide margined, untrimmed copy; modern half levant morocco with raised bands and spine label.   R.F.G. Hollett & Son 78-39 1996 £245.00

RAUTHMEL, RICHARD   The Roman Antiquities of Overborough. Kirkby Lonsdale: Arthur Foster, 1824. Reprinted from the original edition of 1746, with additions; 8vo; pages vi, 138; frontispiece, 5 plans and plates, 2 folding; contemporary full panelled calf, gilt, contrasting spine label, neatly recased, all edges gilt, little spotting or offsetting of plates, but attractive copy.   R.F.G. Hollett & Son 78-40 1996 £95.00

RAVEN, H. C.   Anatomy of the Gorilla. New York: 1950. Folio; 259 pages; portrait, 116 plates, 41 illustrations;   John Johnson 135-478 1996 $125.00

RAVEN, SIMON   Brother Cain. London: Blond, 1959. 1st edition; with erratum slip; signed by author; very good in very good dust jacket only very slightly soiled on back panel, 1 inch closed tear at back fold. Virgo Books 48-163 1996 £75.00

RAVISIUS TEXTOR, JEAN   Officinae Historicis Poeticis Referrae Disciplinis (etc.). (with) Cornucopia (etc.). Venice: Lucantonio Giunta, 1541. 2nd Giunta edition; small 8vo; 2 volumes, ff. (viii), 296, 312, 76 pages, roman letter, printer's devices on titlepages and at ends, wooduct initials, owner's note on each main titlepage deleted, occasional contemporary ms. annotations, upper edges and corners of 4 leaes gnawed (?) with some loss, few corners or fore edges oil-stained, otherwise good; contemporary limp vellum, rather worn.   A. Sokol XXV-80 1996 £350.00

RAVITCH, MARK M.   A Century of Surgery 1880-1980. Philadelphia: Lippincott, 1981. One of 2000 signed copies; thick 4to; 2 volumes, illustrations; boxed.   Argosy 810-410 1996 $200.00

RAWLING, C. G.   The Land of the New Guinea Pygimes. London: Seeley, Service & Co., 1913. (xvi), 360 pages, 48 black and white illustrations, 1 map; black and green pictorial cloth, corners little rubbed, otherwise good+.   Antipodean 28-223 1996 $195.00

RAWLINGS, MARJORIE KINNAN   The Secret River. New York: Charles Scribner's Sons, 1955. 1st edition; illustrations by Leonard Weisgard; scarce, one corner tip slightly bumped, otherwise near fine in price clipped dust jacket which is slightly rubbed at spine ends.   Steven C. Bernard 71-454 1996 $250.00

RAWLINGS, MARJORIE KINNAN   When the Whipporwill. New York: Charles Scribners, 1940. True first edition, with both publisher's seal and "A" on copyright page; fine in near fine dust jacket, somewhat scuffed at edges and with several small chips.   Bev Chaney, Jr. 23-579 1996 $250.00

RAWLINSON, RICHARD   The English Topographer. London: T. Jauncy, 1720. 1st edition; 8vo; (viii), xliv, 275, (13) pages; contemporary calf, nice, light chipping at extremities of spine, hinges strong but starting. With bookplate of Charles Bruce of Ampthill and later bookplate of G. H. Wyatt.   The Bookpress 75-347 1996 $600.00

RAWLINSON, ROBERT   Designs for Factory, Furnace and Other Tall Chimney Shafts. London: Weale, 1858. 1st edition; folio; (ii), 8, (2) pages, 25 plates; publisher's cloth, rebacked, original spine label laid on, both hinges internally strengthened, covers slightly sunned and rubbed, as usual, faint foxing on early leaves, not affecting illustrations. Bookpress 75-110 1996 $5,500.00

RAWNSLEY, HARDWICKE DRUMMOND   Five Addresses of the Lives and Work of St. Kentigern and St. Herbert, Delivered in St. Kentigern's Church, Crosthwaite. Carlisle: Chas. Thurnam and Sons, 1888. 1st edition; small 4to; pages viii, 54, (i), uncut, 3 plates; original printed wrappers, edges trifle creased, some spotting in places. Single sheet 'Hymn for St. Kentigen's Day' by author laid on to verso of title.   R.F.G. Hollett & Son 78-1214 1996 £55.00

RAWNSLEY, HARDWICKE DRUMMOND   Five Addresses on the Lives and Work of St. Kentigern and St. Herbert. Carlisle: Chas. Turnam and Sons, 1889. 2nd edition; small 4to; pages viii, 54, (i), 3 plates; original coarse weave cloth, title finely woven in blue and black calligraphic script on upper board, cloth produced by Ruskin's Linen industry. R.F.G. Hollett & Son 78-1216 1996 £95.00

RAWNSLEY, HARDWICKE DRUMMOND   Five Addresses on the Lives and Work of St. Kentigern and St. Herbert, Delivered in St. Kentigern's Church, Crosthwaite. Carlisle: Chas. Thurnam and Sons, 1889. 2nd edition; small 4to; pages viii, 54, (i), 3 plates, errata slip; contemporary plain coarse weave cloth; contemporary note reads "the cover of this book is a product of Ruskin's Linen Industry. From Keswick".   R.F.G. Hollett & Son 78-1215 1996 £75.00

RAWNSLEY, HARDWICKE DRUMMOND   Henry Whitehead 1825-1896. Glasgow: James Maclehose, 1898. 1st edition; 8vo; pages ix, 250; untrimmed, portrait frontispiece; flyleaves little browned; original cloth, gilt, spine faded.   R.F.G. Hollett & Son 78-238 1996 £55.00

RAWNSLEY, HARDWICKE DRUMMOND   The Resurrection of Oldest Egypt. Staines: Beaver Press, 1904. 8vo; pages (x), 124; 24 illustrations, blue decorations to prelim pages; original green cloth, few light spots to spine, very scarce; signed by Noel Rawnsley.   R.F.G. Hollett & Son 78-41 1996 £85.00

RAWSON, MRS.   Notes of Eastern Travel: Being Selections from the Diary of a Lady. Manchester: Johnson and Rowson, printed in aid of the Bazaar for the Blackley... 1864. 1st edition; small 4to; (viii), 107 pages, original red cloth, blocked in gilt and blind, fine. inscribed to Ernest C. Harding, from author. Not found in NUC.   James Burmester 29-112 1996 £100.00

RAWSTORNE, LAWRENCE   Gamonia; or, The Art of Preserving Game, and an Improved Method of Making Plantations and Covers, Explained and Illustrated. London: for the Proprietor, by Rudolph Ackermann, Eclipse Sporting Gallery, 1837. 8vo; pages 208, 15 quite superb hand colored aquatint plates, finished with gum arabic, tissue guards; original green morocco with elaborated roll tool borders to covers, titled in gilt on spine, very light rubbing to several extremities and light offsetting to title, but generally a superb copy. Schwerdt Ii p. 127; Abbey Life 392; Tooley 393.   Sotheran PN32-97 1996 £1,950.00

RAWSTORNE, LAWRENCE   Gamonia; or, the Art of Preserving Game and an Improved Method of Making Plantations and Covers. London: Rudolph Ackermann, 1837. 1st edition; 8vo; errata slip; 16 hand colored engravings by J. T. Rawlins taken on spot, each plate with its original tissue, original olive green morocco, wide gilt borders, gilt edges, small scag on upper cover; Tooley 393   Charles W. Traylen 117-328 1996 £800.00

RAWSTORNE, LAWRENCE   Gamonia; or, the Art of Preserving Game. London: 1929. Edition deluxe, limited to 125 copies; 4to; 15 colored plates; green morocco, gilt, gilt top, endpapers renewed.   K Books 442-409 1996 £95.00

RAY, GORDON N.   Books as a Way of Life. New York: Grolier Club and the Pierpont Morgan Library, 1988. One of 750 copies; 9 1/2 x 6 1/2 inches; xxxiii, (1), 432 pages; frontispiece; prospectus laid in; fine in fine original dust jacket.   Phillip J. Pirages 33-289 1996 $150.00

RAY, ISAAC   Contributions to Mental Pathology. Boston: Little Brown and Co., 1873. 1st edition; 8vo; (ii), (viii), 558, (2) pages; printed pebbled green cloth, spine varnished, corners frayed, first several leaves creased and somewhat soiled, very good, usually found in worn condition. John Gach 150-382 1996 $385.00

RAY, ISAAC   A Treatise on the Medical Jurisprudence of Insanity. Boston: Charles C. Little and James Brown, 1853. 3rd edition; 8vo; xvi, (522) pages; modern grey cloth with leather spine label, edges of first leaves to first and last gathering reinforced, else very good, clean copy. John Gach 150-381 1996 $450.00

RAY, JOHN   Catalogus Plantarum Angliae, et Insularum Adjacentium... Londini: Typis E. C. and A. C. Impensis J. Martin, 1670. 1st edition; small 8vo; lacking prelim blank leaf, (xxii), 358 pages and errata leaf at end; original panelled calf, rebacked, old style endpapers, small engraved 18th century bookplate, modern bookplate dated 1934; very good. Wing R381; Henrey 309; Keynes 7;   David Bickersteth 133-217 1996 £385.00

RAY, JOHN   A Collection of Curious Travels and Voyages. London: printed for S. Smith and B. Walford, 1693. 1st edition; third issue; 8vo; (xxxii), 396, (iv), 45 pages, including imprimatur leaf; lacking final blank, original panelled calf, rebacked, new endpapers, blank upper outer corner torn from title, just touching ruled border, many pages lightly browned. Keynes 94.   David Bickersteth 133-57 1996 £150.00

RAY, JOHN   A Collection of English Words Not Generally Used with Their Significations and Origina, in Two Alphabetical Catalogues... London: printed for Christopher Wilkinson, 1691. 2nd edition; 12mo; lacking A1 (blank?), 5 pages ads; contemporary spotted calf, hinges reparied, retaining original blue spine strip. Ink inscription recording a gift from publisher "Dona D. Ch. Wilkinson Bibliopolae Londinensis A.D. 1691". Alston IX.2. Wing R389; Keynes 24.   Jarndyce 103-208 1996 £280.00

RAY, JOHN   Joannis Raii Synopsis Methodica Avium & Piscium: Opus Postumum... London: for William Innys, 1713. 1st edition; octavo; plates; antique style calf backed marbled boards; good copy. Keynes 105; Casey Wood p. 529.   H. M. Fletcher 121-118 1996 £360.00

RAY, JOHN   Synopsis Methodica Stirpium ritannicarum... London: 1724. 3rd edition; 1st issue; 8vo; 2 volumes in 1; pages (16), 482, (30); later full calf, professionally rebacked, name on title margin, light browning to few plates. Keynes 56.   Raymond M. Sutton VI-26 1996 $650.00

RAY, JOHN   Travels through the Low-Countries, Germany, Italy and France... London: printed for J. Walthoe, (and 16 other booksellers), 1738. 2nd edition; 8vo; 2 volumes; half titles and titles printed in red and black, 3 engraved plates in volume 1; original mottled calf, both volumes rebacked, original endpapers preserved; nice 18th century bookplate of Fettiplace Nott inside front cover of each volume. Keynes 22, 96. David Bickersteth 133-58 1996 £320.00

RAY, MAN   Man Ray: Photographs 1920-1934 Paris. Hartford: Soby, 1934. 2nd edition; spiral bound with color illustration on cover. The copy of translator, Joyce Reeves, signed by her.   J. B. Muns 154-247 1996 $1,650.00

RAY, MAN   Self Portrait. Boston: 1963. 1st edition; dust jacket, signed.   J. B. Muns 154-246 1996 $250.00

RAY, MAN   Self Portrait. Boston: 1963. 1st edition; dust jacket.   J. B. Muns 154-245 1996 $125.00

RAY, MILTON S.   The Farallones, the Painted World and Other Poems of California. San Francisco: 1934. One of 2000 numbered copies; small folio; 2 colored portraits and 51 plates; quarter parchment, boards, very nice.   Bertram Rota 272-306 1996 £90.00

RAYLEIGH, JOHN WILLIAM STRUTT, BARON 1842-1919   Argon, a New Constituent of the Atmosphere. Washington: Smithsonian Inst., 1896. 1st edition; folio; (4), 43 pages, figures in text; original green cloth, fine. Dibner 50.   Edwin V. Glaser 121-301 1996 $225.00

RAYLEIGHT, JOHN WILLIAM STRUTT, BARON 1842-1919   The Theory of Sound. London: 1926. 2nd edition; 2 volumes, xiv, 480; xvi, 504 pages; cloth, very good, dust jacket.   Graham Weiner C2-765 1996 £50.00

RAYNAL, MAURICE   Picasso. Munchen: 1921. 1st edition; 23 x 18 cm; 140 pages text, 103 illustrations; decorated buckram, slightly discolored, corners bumped, endpaper joints cracked.   Rainsford A54-459 1996 £75.00

RAYNE, H.   The Ivory Raiders. London: 1923. illustrations, original cloth, slightly discolored and faded, some foxing; scarce.   David Grayling J95Biggame-161 1996 £50.00

RAYNER, ARTHUR E.   Accuracy in the X-Ray Diagnosis of Urinary Stone. Preston: C. W. Whitehead, 1909. 8vo; 40 pages, 49 mounted photos; original binding boards; rare.   James Tait Goodrich K40-285 1996 $395.00

RAZZI, GIROLAMO   Vite di Qvattro Huomini Illustri. Florence: Giunti, 1580. 1st edition; 8vo; medici title device; half vellum; Adams R231; Moreni, Toscana II 23.   Rostenberg & Stern 150-94 1996 $375.00

REA, JOHN   Flora; seu de Florum Cultura. Or, a Complete Florilege, Furnished with all Requisites Belonging to a Florist. London: by J. G. for Richard Marriott, 1665. 1st edition; folio; (24), 239, (4) pages, including "Mind of the front" leaf, added engraved title, 8 engraved plates, woodcut initials and headpieces, title printed in red and black; calf, spine gilt by Thomas Fowler, with his printed label "Bound for the library/of the/ right Honorable Lord Rolle/ at Stevenstone/, by Thomas Fowler, printer & bookbinder,/ Great Torrington. Anno Domini 1834". Absolutely pristine, wide margined copy in very good, very slightly rubbed, ticketed binding. Hunt 301; Wing R421.   Joseph J. Felcone 64-35 1996 $2,800.00

REACH, ANGUS B.   Clement Lorimer, or the Book with the Iron Clasps. London: David Bogue, 1849. 1st edition in book form; 8vo; frontispiece and 11 plates by George Cruikshank; original blue cloth, covers stamped in blind with gilt urn on upper cover, spine decorated and lettered in gilt, variant binding from the usual green or maroon cloths, yellow endpapers, some soiling and rubbing of cloth, light browning and spotting of text, few pages with letter loss onto adjoining leaves, but very good, green cloth case. Block p. 194; Cohn 687; Hubin p. 339; Sadleir 1995. Wolff 5698.   James Cummins 14-162 1996 $500.00

REACH, ANGUS B.   Clement Lorimer; or, the Book with the Iron Clasps. London: David Bogue, 1849. 1st edition; 8vo; frontispiece and 11 etched plates by George Cruikshank; all signed in full; 19th century morocco backed cloth, gilt lettering on spine; nice. Cohn 687. Anthony W. Laywood 109-108 1996 £80.00

READ, HERBERT   Lord Byron at the Opera - a Play for Broadcasting. North Harrow: Philip Ward, 1963. 1st edition; wrappers, covers spotted and slightly soiled and creased, cvoer edges faded, some slight internal spotting; good. Presentation copy from author to E. H. Ramsden and Margot Eates.   Ulysses 39-496 1996 £80.00

READ, HERBERT   Marino Marini: The Complete Works. New York: Tudor, 1970. Folio; 506 pages, about 1000 illustrations, 80 in color; cloth, dust jacket.   Brannan 43-384 1996 $475.00

READ, HERBERT   The Parliament of Women; a Drama in Three Acts. Vine Press, 1960. One of 100 numbered copies; small folio; printed in Centaur in black and terracotta on handmade paper; half morocco, marbled boards; fine, scarce.   Bertram Rota 272-482 1996 £350.00

READE, ALEYN LYELL   Johnsonian Gleanings. New York: Octagon Books, 1968. Facsimile reprint of the 11 volumes issued between 1909-1952; large octavo; 11 volumes in 10; original red cloth; fine set. Hartfield 48-V28 1996 $395.00

READE, ALEYN LYELL   The Mellards and Their Descendants Including the Bibbys of Liverpool. London: 1915. Only 200 copies printed; 4to; pages 260; 26 plates, 4 folding pedigrees; original buckram.   Howes Bookshop 265-1915 1996 £65.00

READE, CHARLES 1814-1884   White Lies. London: Trubner & Co., 1857. 1st English edition; 8vo; 3 volumes; contemporary half calf, brown and black morocco labels on gilt spines, marbled boards, some rubbing and minor discoloration, some knocking of a few corners; bookplates of Andrew K. Hichens, dated 1888, with his small initial blindstamp on titles, some spotting at front and back, else quite clean, pleasant copies. Parrish p. 197; not in Sadleir or Wolff.   James Cummins 14-163 1996 $425.00

READE, CHARLES 1814-1884　　The Works. London: Grolier Society, ca. 1910. One of only 5 copies of L'Edition des Aquarelles; 8 1/2 x 6 inches; 25 volumes; few illustrations in text and 114 plates by F.T. Merrill each in colored & uncolored states (for a total of 228 plates, 6 left uncolored), printed tissue overlays, titles printed in red and black; 4 page ALS by Reade tipped in; elaborately inlaid & gilt dec. lavender crushed mor., each cover framed by double gilt fillet, gilt foliate cornerpieces w/heart-shaped inlays of red calf, lg. & beautiful gilt & onlaid floral centerpiece featuring 2 lilies in white calf & 5 buds in green mor., raised bands, spine compartments dec. in gilt w/2 of the compartments featuring sm. onlaid flower of red calf, morocco doublures, w/multiple plain & stippled rules as well as antique fleuron cornerpieces framing a central panel of green mor. featuring lg. architectural ornament composed of elaborate gilt leaves & ribbons & scrolling inlaid red calf, green silk e.p.'s, mor. hinges, marbled flyleaves, a.e.g., handful of plates bit darkened, spines rather faded to grayish lilac color, some covers bit faded, else remarkably fine.　　Phillip J. Pirages 33-68　1996 $6,500.00

READER, E. E.　　Priestess and Queen. London: Longmans-Green, 1899. 1st edition; some slight discoloration to covers, few pages opened little roughly, else tight, very good+ copy.　　Aronovitz 57-975　1996 $125.00

READY, OLIVER　　Life and Sport in China. 1904. 2nd edition; photo illustrations; original cloth slightly rubbed, contents lightly browned. Very scarce.　　David Grayling J95Biggame-561　1996 £85.00

REAL Life in Dolly Land. Chicago: Stanton and Van Vliet Co., 1913. 1st edition; oblong folio; unpaginated, wrappres, covers foxed and torn, text browned, else good.　　The Bookpress 75-445　1996 $125.00

REAL Life. Pages from the Portfolio fo a Chronicler. Edinburgh: Waugh and Innes, M. Ogle, Glasgow: R. M. Tims, and W. Curry, Dublin.. 1832. 1st edition? 12mo; (viii), 326 pages; original green patterned cloth, recased, lacking spine label. Uncommon.　　James Burmester 29-158 1996 £58.00

REANEY, PERCY H.　　Records of Queen Elizabeth Grammar School, Penrith. Kendal: Titus Wilson, 1915. 1st edition; 8vo; 141 pages, 2 plates; original wrappers, fine, unopened copy.　　R.F.G. Hollett & Son　78-1232 1996 £60.00

REASONS Against a Registry for Lands, Etc. Shewing Briefly the Great Disadvantages, Charges and Inconveniences that May Accrue to the Whole Nation in General Thereby, Much Overbalancing the Particular Advantages That are Imagined... London: C. Wilkinson, and T. Burrel at their shops in Fleetstreet, 1678. Quarto; 22 pages; disbound. Wing R466; Kress 1469; Goldsmiths 2237.　　C. R. Johnson　37-26　1996 £150.00

REASONS for a Registry: Shewing briefly the Great Benefits and Advantages that May Accrue to this Nation Thereby. London: Charles Harper at the Fower-de-Luce over Against St. Dunstan's Church 1678. Quarto; 22 pages, final blank leaf; disbound. Wing R486; Kress 1470; Goldsmiths 2238.　　C. R. Johnson　37-27　1996 £150.00

REASONS Humbly Offer'd to the Honourable House of Commons, Against Dividing the Ancient Parish of St. James Clerkenwell. N.P.: n.d. London: c. 1723. Folio; 2 pages, uncut, left edge slightly frayed.　　H. M. Fletcher 121-119　1996 £110.00

RECAPITULATION of All Masonry; or a Description...of the Universal Heiroglyph... Dublin: for the Sovereign Sanctuary, 1883. 8vo; 3 plates; 32 pages; cloth, ex-Wigan Library, very good.　　C. P. Hyland　216-703 1996 £60.00

RECLUS, ELISEE　　The Earth and Its Inhabitants. New York: D. Appleton & Co., 1886-95. 4to; 19 volumes; numerous engravings and maps; contemporary green pebbled calf over green buckram, gilt, bit rubbed, edges marbled.　　Kenneth Karmiole　1NS-227　1996 $750.00

RECLUS, ELISEE　　The Earth and Its Inhabitants: Oceanica. New York: 1890. 4to; 512 pages; woodcut illustrations; rubbed half morocco, otherwise good+; the Meggitt copy.　　Antipodean　28-232　1996 $145.00

RECORDS of the Lives of Ellen Free Pickton and Featherstone Lake Osler. Oxford: 1915. 4to; 257 pages; portraits; original binding; from the printer's library, rare. Cushing 2.489. Osler 3594.　　W. Bruce Fye 71-1588　1996 $1,250.00

RECORDS of the Royal Military Academy. Woolwich: Parker Furnival & Parker, 1851. Tall folio; lithograph title, chipped and frayed at edges, first prelim leaf little creased, 152 pages + list of plates, 2 fine full page chromolithograph plates and 2 fine full page chromo plates with 12 illustrations of soliders in different military uniform, plus 5 full page uncolored lithographs; original red cloth, somewhat soiled and worn, corners and spine skillfully repaired, little spotting to margins of some plates.　　Ian Wilkinson　95/1-122　1996 £75.00

RECREATIONS in Natural History, or Popular Sketches of British Quadrupeds: Describing Their Nature, Habits and Dispositions...Original Anecdotes. London: 1815. 24 fine engraved plates and numerous engraved vignettes after L. Clennel; full modern panelled calf, blind and gilt tooled; few page tears at rear neatly repaired, otherwise most attractive copy, scarce.　　David A.H. Grayling　MY95Orn-2　1996 £180.00

RECREATIONS in Shooting. London: 1846. Tinted engraved plates, text engravings; original pictorial cloth, top and base of spine slightly snagged, otherwise excellent.　　David A.H. Grayling　3/95-127　1996 £65.00

RECTOR, HENRY M.　　Inaugural Address of Henry M. Rector, Delivered Before the General Assembly of Arkansas, 15th November, 1860. 1st edition; 8 pages; sewn, some foxing, very good.　　Michael D. Heaston 23-31　1996 $200.00

RECUEIL d'Estampes Representant Les Differents Envenements de la Guerre Qui a Procure l'Independance Aux Etats Unis de l'Amerique. Paris: Ponce et Godefroy, 1784? Oblong 4to; engraved title and 13 engraved plates, all in beautiful contemporary color, plus 2 engraved maps; handsome 19th century gilt morocco, spine richly gilt, dentelles and edges gilt, neat repairs at spine ends, some light foxing, else very attractive, with tissue guards intact. Howes C576.　　Joseph J. Felcone 64-43　1996 $6,500.00

RED Riding Hood. New York: Mcloughlin, copyright 1891. 4to; 6 chromolithographed scenes; colored pictorial card wrappers shaped as a theatre, edges of covers chipped, else very good.　　Marjorie James 19-161　1996 £325.00

RED River Insurrection. Hon. Wm. McDougall's Condut Reviewed. Montreal: 1870. Pages 69; original wrappers, edges chipped, small piece broken from upper margin of front wrapper, textually very good. Peel 289.　　Stephen Lunsford　45-134　1996 $400.00

RED, White and Blue Socks. New York: Leavitt & Allen, 1864. Small octavo; 117 pages; 3 full page plates; dark blue cloth, blindstamped to front and rear covers with title gilt stamped to spine, head and tail of spine lightly worn, else fine.　　Bromer Booksellers　87-107　1996 $125.00

REDDING, CYRUS　　A History and Description of Modern Wines. London: Henry G. Bohn, 1851. 3rd edition; frontispiece, wood engraved illustrations; contemporary half black morocco, spine gilt, all edges gilt, bit rubbed; very good. Gabler, Wine in Words p. 221.　　Ximenes 109-244　1996 $225.00

REDDING, J. SAUNDERS　　To Make a Poet Black. Chapel Hill: Unviersity of North Carolina Press, 1939. 8vo; x, 142 pages; cloth; very good, presentation from author to Guy Johnson. Thornton 11607. Andrew Cahan　47-5　1996 $150.00

REDFIELD, AMASA A.　　A Hand-book of the U.S. Tax Law, (Approved July 1, 1862), with All the Amendments, to March 4, 1863: Comprising the Decisions of the Commissioner of Internal Revenue... New York: John S. Voorhies, 1863. 1st edition; 8vo; 312 pages; green cloth, endpapers dust soiled/smudged, good to very good.　　Robert F. Lucas　42-21 1996 $100.00

REDFIELD, H. V.　　Homicide, North and South, Being a Comparative View of Crime Against the Person in Several Parts of the United States. Philadelphia: J. B. Lippincott & Co., 1880. Green cloth, gilt, quite well preserved.　　Meyer Boswell　SL26-198　1996 $150.00

REDGRAVE, MICHAEL　　The Mountebank's Tale. London: William Heinemann Ltd., 1959. 1st edition; author's first novel; original binding, top edge dusty, head and tail of spine bumped, small puncture to lower gutter, very good in nicked and slightly rubbed, torn, creased and dusty dust jacket, slightly browned at spine and edges and frayed at head of spine.　　Ulysses　39-497　1996 £65.00

REDMAYNE, J. S.   Fruit Farming On the "Dry Belt" of British Columbia; The Why and Wherefore. London: Times Book Club/British Columbia Dev. Assoc., 1910. 28cm; 125, (xxxii) pages; frontispiece, illustrations, folding maps, portraits; lightly soiled printed boards, bit of mild wrinkling; very good, very scarce. E&L 2974.   Rockland Books 38-185 1996 $150.00

REDOUTE, P. J.   Beautiful Flowers and Fruits. New York: 1985. Folio; 144 full page colored engravings; cloth, dust jacket.   Raymond M. Sutton VII-1122 1996 $125.00

REED, ISAAC   Bibliotheca Reediana. London: J. Barker, printer, 1807. 8vo; frontispiece; full polished calf, gilt, spine gilt, marbled edges, by Pratt, slight rubbing; fine copy on large paper; tipped in is letter May 2 1808 from auctioneer Thomas King, pres. this copy to noted antiquarian bookseller George Nicol; neatly priced and ruled throughout; fine. LAR 124; De Ricci p. 63.   Ximenes 108-12 1996 $1,250.00

REED, ISAAC   The Repository: a Select Collection of Furitive Pieces of Wit and Humour... London: for C. Dilly, 1790. 8vo; 4 volumes, 19th century half tan morocco, green cloth sides, spines richly gilt in compartments, dark green double lettering-pieces, sides with double gilt rules, green endpapers, top edge gilt, others uncut, second letterin piece on volume 4 defective, a most attractive set. with Carlingford engraved bookplates.   Simon Finch 24-194 1996 £180.00

REED, JOHN   Ten Days that Shook the World. New York: Boni & Liveright, 1919. 1st edition; 8vo; illustrations; pictorial endpapers; cloth, trifle rubbed and bumped, unusually fine.   James S. Jaffe 34-591 1996 $500.00

REED, JOHN   Ten Days That Shook the World. New York: 1919. 1st edition; 8 x 5 inches; 371 pages; illustrations; cloth, inner hinges badly cracked, covers moderately rubbed.   John K. King 77-838 1996 $175.00

REED, JOSEPH   Tom Jones, a Comic Opera: as it is Performed at the Theatre Royal in Covent Garden. London: Becket, De Hondt, et al, 1769. 1st edition; small 8vo; pages 62, later marbled paper wrappers; Gross III 353.   Hartfield 48-L73 1996 $125.00

REED, MYRTLE   The Master Violin. New York: G. P. Putnam's Sons, 1904. 1st edition; 8vo; (315 pages, 2 publisher's ads); mauve and gold on pale grey vertically ribbed cloth with printer's ornament of a gladiolus, designed by Margaret Armstrong, except for short marginal tear on page 303, that has been skillfully repaired, this is a beautiful copy free of bookplates and signatures, in original publisher's decorated box; Paulette Rose 16-255 1996 $100.00

REED, REBECCA T.   Six Months In a Convent, or, the Narrative of Rebecca Teresa Reed who was Under the Influence of the Roman Catholics About Two Years, and an Inmate of the Ursuline Convent on Mount Benedict, Charlestown, Mass... Boston: Russell Odiorne & Metcalf, 1835. 1st edition; original olive cloth, covers decorated in blind, spine lettered with decoration in gilt, rubbed, some fading and soiling, some spotting and staining of text, front free endpaper removed.   James Cummins 14-164 1996 $150.00

REED, WALT   John Clymer: an Artist's Rendezvous with the Frontier West. Flagstaff: Northland Press, 1976. 1st edition; very fine in dust jacket.   Hermitage SP95-806 1996 $125.00

REED, WALTER   The Propagation of Yellow Fever Based on Recent Researches. Baltimore: 1901. 1st edition; 31 pages; wrappers; scarce. GM 5457.   W. Bruce Fye 71-1743 1996 $125.00

REED, WALTER   Yellow Fever. A Compilation of Various Publications. Results of the Work of Maj. Walter Reed, Medical Corps, United States Army, and the Yellow Fever Commission. Washington: GPO, 1911. 8vo; frontispiece, 220 pages, plus several other photos of figures; original binding, library bookplate.   James Tait Goodrich K40-246 1996 $125.00

REEDER, ELLEN D.   Hellenistic Art in the Walters Art Gallery. Baltimore: Walters Art Gallery, 1988. 4to; 260 pages; 152 illustrations; original cloth.   Archaeologia Luxor-3873 1996 $125.00

REEMELIN, CHARLES   The Vine-Dressers Manual, an Illustrated Treatise on Vineyards and Wine-Making. New York: Moore, 1858. 8vo; 103 pages + ad; some text illustrations; publisher's cloth; nice, clean copy.   Second Life Books 103-161 1996 $150.00

REES, ABRAHAM   Ree's Manufacturing Industry (1819-20). David and Charles Reprints, 1972. 4to; 5 volumes; illustrations; xxii, 457; x, 411; viii, 499; viii, 499; viii, 511 pages; cloth, dust jacket, slipcase.   Thomas Thorp 489-258 1996 £100.00

REES, ENNIS   More of Brer Rabbit's Tricks. New York: Scott Young Books, 1968. 1st edition; small oblong 8vo; drawings in color to every page by Edward Gorey; colored pictorial cloth, fine in pictorial dust jacket. Signed by Gorey on titlepage. Bader 556.   Barbara Stone 70-106 1996 £65.00

REEVE, CLARA   The Old English Baron: a Gothic Story. London: printed by T. Gillet, Bartholomew-Close, for Charles Dilly, 1794. 5th edition; 12mo; (xi, 1, 263) pages; frontispiece, one additional plate; contemporary red straight grain morocco, gilt lettered spine, gilt ruled front and back, inner decorated gilt border, all edges gilt, very pretty, fine.   Paulette Rose 16-257 1996 $300.00

REEVE, JOHN   A Transcendent Spiritual Treatise Upon Several Heavenly Doctrines, from the Holy Spirit of the Man Jesus... London: printed for the authors & are to be sold by them... 1st edition; 4to; 48 pages; titlepage mounted and quite dusty, lower inner corner of D2 torn, affecting four or five letters, but no loss of sense, text generally dusty; 19th century calf, label, slightly rubbed; reasonable copy, scarce. Wing R683.   Robert Clark 38-121 1996 £385.00

REEVES, DIANNE L.   From Fiber to Paper. Houston: designed & ptd. by W. Thomas Taylor in Austin, One in an edition of 200 copies; 9.5 x 7.25 inches printed in Monotype Bembo on Nideggan mould made paper, titlepage calligraphy by Jeff Jeffries; stab-sewn binding made from Ogura natural Japanese handmade paper by BookLabe in Austin; fine. Joshua Heller 21-178 1996 $175.00

REEVES, JAMES   The Closed Door. Janus Press, 1977. In an edition of 240 unnumbered copies, this one of 75 unsigned copies; 9.25 x 6 inches; 12 unnumbered pages, 1 wood engraved illustration by Richard Shirley Smith, designed by Claire Van Vliet, titlepage wood engraving printed in black, titles printed in black and gold, text in black, copyright notice and colophon in gold; bound in marbled Fabriano book over boards with natural calf spine, title label on front cover printed in black with gold framing line on Twinrocker Sweetbutter used also for endpapers and flyleaves; fine.   Joshua Heller 21-13 1996 $150.00

REEVES, RICHARD STONE   Classic Lines. Birmingham: Oxmoor House, 1975. Oblong folio; original binding, signed by Robinson; very good in good dust jacket.   October Farm 36-53 1996 $375.00

REEVES, RICHARD STONE   Decade of Champions. New York: Fine Arts/Oxmoor, 1980. Oblong folio; original binding; very good copy in good+ dust jacket.   October Farm 36-54 1996 $150.00

REEVES, RICHARD STONE   Legends. The Art of Richard Stone Reeves. Birmingham: Oxmoor, 1989. Stated 1st edition; oblong folio; original binding, very good in very good dust jacket.   October Farm 36-55 1996 $125.00

REFLECTIONS on Our Common Failings. London: printed by G. Groom, for R. Smith and John Chantry, 1701. 1st Edition in English; 12mo; contemporary mottled calf, spine gilt, little rubbed, slight wear to top of upper joint; excellent copy, scarce. CBEL II 1938.   Ximenes 108-88 1996 $450.00

REGIMEN SANTITATIS SALERNITATM   Regimen Sanitatis Salerni; or, the Schoole of Salernes Regiment of Health. London: B. Alsop, 1649. 1st edition of this translation; small 4to; (iv), 220, (3) pages; later quarter morocco, marbled paper boards; rubber stamps on titlepage and second leaf.   The Bookpress 75-455 1996 $785.00

REGINALD, R.   Science Fiction and Fantasy Literature. A Checklist 1700-1974. (with) Contemporary Science Fiction Authors II. Detroit: Gale, 1979. 1st edition; 2 volumes; original cloth, about fine.   Beasley Books 82-139 1996 $125.00

THE REGISTERS of Middleton-in-Lonsdale, Westmorland. 1670-1812. Penrith: The Herald Co., 1925. 8vo; pages 103; original printed wrappers. R.F.G. Hollett & Son 78-585 1996 £95.00

THE REGISTERS Of Millom, Cumberland, 1591-1812. Kendal: Titus Wilson, 1925. 8vo; pages viii, 300; original wrappers, rather faded and little torn.   R.F.G. Hollett & Son 78-587 1996 £75.00

THE REGISTERS of St. Michael's, Pennington in Furness 1612-1702; The Registers of Urswick in Furness 1608-1695. Cambridge: for Lancashire Parish Record Society, 1907. 8vo; pages 66, 84, 2 plates; original cloth, gilt.　R.F.G. Hollett & Son　78-573　1996 £85.00

THE REGISTERS of the Parish Church of Torver 1599-1792; the Registers of the Parish Chruch of Kirkby Ireleth 1681-1812. Rochdale: Lancashire Parish Register Society, 1911. 8vo; pages 118, 144, 2 plates; unopened; original cloth, gilt.　R.F.G. Hollett & Son　78-572　1996 £85.00

THE REGISTERS of Warcop Westmorland 1597-1744. Kendal: Titus Wilson, 1914. 8vo; pages 174; original wrappers, frontispiece; very scarce.　R.F.G. Hollett & Son　78-595　1996 £95.00

REGISTRUM Malmesburiense. London: 1879-80. 8vo; 2 volume,s pages 537, 585; original cloth.　Howes Bookshop　265-1594　1996 £60.00

REGULATIONS and Instructions for the Cavalry Sword Exercise. London: Clowes, 1819. Tall 8vo; 2 plates, including on large folding plate, 4 page publisher's list of military books at end; calf, front hinge weak, slight foxing; armorial bookplate of Richard Shuttleworth Stretfeild & ownership inscription of Lt. John Watson on p. 3.　Rostenberg & Stern　150-108　1996 $140.00

REGULATIONS for Governing the Province of the Californias...1781. San Francisco: Grabhorn Press, 1929. 1st edition of the English translation; 2 volumes (English and Spanish), 60; 55 pages; tan paper boards, printed titles on spines, spines slightly darkened, final 2 endleaves of one volume slightly foxed, else fine, fragile.　Argonaut Book Shop　113-376　1996 $175.00

REHDER, A.　Bibliography of Cultivated Trees and Shrubs Hardy in the Cooler Temperate Regions of the Northern Hemisphere. Jamaica Plain: 1949. 4to; xl, 825 pages; cloth, some scuffing, piece of tap at top of spine, note and owner's name on endpapers; marking on page xxxv; Raymond M. Sutton　VII-707　1996 $250.00

REICH, SHELDON　John Marin: a Stylistic Analysis and Catalogue Raisonne. Tucson: University of Arizona Press, 1970. 4to; 2 volumes, 891 pages; 209 illustrations + profusely illustrated catalog; cloth, dust jacket. Freitag 6069.　Brannan　43-382　1996 $225.00

REICH, WILHELM　The Function of the Orgasm: Sex-Economic Problems of Biological Energy. New York: Orgone Inst. Press, 1942. 1st edition; 8vo; (ii), xxvi, 368 pages; pale green cloth, very good in edgeworn dust jacket, scarce.　John Gach　150-386　1996 $200.00

REICH, WILHELM　Psychischer Kontakt und Vegetative Stromung. Copenhagen: Sex-Pol, 1935. 1st edition; printed wrappers; very good+, minor loss to spine around staples; inscribed by author and extraordinarly uncommon thus.　Lame Duck Books　19-476　1996 $2,500.00

REICH, WILHELM　The Sexual Revolution: Toward a Self-Governing Character Structure. New York: Orgone Inst. Press, 1945. 1st edition in English; 8vo; (xxviii), (274) pages; printed cream cloth, near fine in slightly defective (but rare) dust jacket, owner's inked signature on front pastedown.　John Gach　150-389　1996 $200.00

REICHARD, GLADYS A.　Navajo Medicine Man, Sandpaintings and Legends of Miguelito. New York: J. J. Augustin, Publisher, 1939. Limited to 500 copies; 83 pages, 24 color plates; maroon buckram, half bound with light leather, some light scuffing, owner's signature on f.f.e.p., in slipcase of matching buckram with applied titles on front and spine. Ken Sanders　8-244　1996 $1,500.00

REICHERT, MADELEINE NEUMANN　Wonderful World. San Francisco: 1961. One of 75 copies; 10.25 x 6.5 inches; 47 pages; vellum spine with title in gilt, decorated paper boards, edges uncut; fine.　Joshua Heller　21-132　1996 $150.00

REID, HIRAM A.　History of Pasadena: Comprising an Account of the Native Indian, the early Spanish, the Mexican, the American, the Colony and the Incorporated City. Pasadena: Pasadena History Co., 1895. 9 1/4 x 6 3/8 inches; 675 pages + photographic frontispiece, folding stree map, errata slip, 10 pages of photographic illustrations; gold stamped black cloth, rebacked with original spine laid down, tips and bottom edges renewed, stree map backed, tear to bird's eye expertly repaired. Dawson's Books Shop　528-200　1996 $500.00

REID, HUGO　The Indians of Los Angeles County. Los Angeles: Arthur M. Ellis, 1926. One of 200 copies; 9 1/2 x 6 1/4 inches; (viii), 70 pages; patterned grey baords with paper spine label, chipping to spine ends and label, paper over front joint cracked. Inscription from Ellis to a San Francisco publisher of Limited Edition reprints of rare California, Thomas Russell.　Dawson's Books Shop　528-201　1996 $135.00

REID, JAMES SEATON　The History of the Presbyterian Church in Ireland... Edinburgh: Waugh & Innes; W. Curry Jun. & Co. Dublin; W. M'Comb, Belfast... 1834. 1st edition; 8vo; 2 volumes; (iii-vii), (ix-xv), errata leaf, 1-411 pages, 413-456 pages; (ii-iv), (v-xiv), errata slip tipped in, 1-480 pages, 481-520 pages; newspaper obituary of Reid pasted in to front free endpaper of volume 1, owners label to front pastedown of both volumes, booksellers ticket to front pastedown of volume 1; full strawberry calf, upper board of volume 2 faded, corners bumped and worn, gilt tooled border to boards, elaborate gilt tooled spines, joints slightly worn, marbled endpapers, all edges gilt.　Beeleigh Abbey BA56-19　1996 £90.00

REID, JOHN　Essays on Hypochondriasis, and Other Nervous Affections. London: Longman, Hurst, Rees, Orme, and Brown, 1816. 8vo; (iv), 272 pages; cloth, disbound, internally clean, very scarce. Hunter & Macalpine pp. 722-25/　John Gach　150-392　1996 $200.00

REID, MAYNE 1818-1883　The Quadroon; or, a Lover's Adventures in Louisiana. London: George W. Hyde, 1856. 1st edition; 8vo; 3 volumes; original orange cloth, spines evenly faded; fine set. Wolff 5753; CBEL III 959.　Ximenes　109-246　1996 $750.00

REID, THOMAS 1710-1796　Essays on the Active Powers of Man. Edinburgh: printed for John Bell, 1788. 1st edition; 4to; vii, 493, (3) pages; bound without half title and ad leaf; near contemporary full green morocco by Hering with his ticket, some very minor scuffing and scratching, but a handsome copy; the Kimbolton Library copy with bookplate. Jessop p. 165.　C. R. Johnson　37-76　1996 £900.00

REID, THOMAS 1710-1796　An Inquiry Into the Human Mind, On the Principles of Common Sense... London: T. Cadell (& 3 others), 1769. 3rd edition; xvi, 383, (i) pages; contemporary gree calf, label, rubbed, upper joint cracked and tender, little foxing. Good.　Robert Clark　38-202　1996 £85.00

REIGART, J. FRANKLIN　The Life of Robert Fulton... Philadelphia: C. Henderson, 1856. 1st edition; 8vo; xxvii, (29)-297 pages, 26 plates, 8 of which are hand colored, many of the others tinted, complete with tissue guards; modern cloth, some offsetting from frontispiece to titlepage, fresh, crisp copy. Howes R178;　Edwin V. Glaser　121-117　1996 $150.00

REILLY, CATHERINE W.　Lake Victorian Peotry 1880-1899. London: Mansell Publishing, 1994. 1st edition; small 4to; 672 pages; original cloth new.　Forest Books　74-226　1996 £70.00

REINECK, REINERUS　Chronicon Hierosolymitanvm, Id est, De Bello Sacro Historia. Helmstadt: Jacobus Lucius, 1584-85. 1st edition; 4to; 2 volumes; ff (xx), 268, (lx), (xvi), 48, (xxiv), 211, Lxxxvii), final blank missing, roman and italic letter, woodcut printer's device on titlepage of volume 1, woodcut initials and ornaments, tables; fairly lightly browned, small repair to corner of title with couple or so letters on verso possibly perfected, early armorial library stamp in blank, otherwise good in contemporary richly blindstamped pigskin over wooden boards, imperial arms on front covers, arms of Augustus I, elector of Saxony on back, spines slightly darkened, original clasps. Not in BM STC Ger. Adams R318-319; Brunet IV 1199; Graesse VI 72.　A. Sokol　XXV-81　1996 £1,450.00

REISNER, GEORGE ANDREW　Harvard Excavations at Samaria 1908-1910. Cambridge: Harvard University Press, 1924. Folio; 2 volumes, xxxi, 417 pages, 247 figures, xxii, 90 plates, 16 plans; owner's stamp at flyleaf.　Archaeologia　Luxor-2641　1996 $1,250.00

RELAND, ADRIAAN　Palaestina ex Monumentis Veteribus Illustrata. Utrecht: Willem Broedelet, 1714. 1st edition; small 4to; 2 volumes, 4 leaves, pages 1-512, pages 513-1068, 47 leaves, titles printed in red and black, engraved title in volume 1, folding portrait, 3 large folding maps, folding plate, 6 small maps, 1 folding engraved pedigree, 1 folding letterpress table, 1 plate, engraved headpieces and 8 engravings of coin in text; contemporary French (?) brown morocco, 3 line fillet borders in gilt, spines fully gilt, red morocco labels, edges gilt over marbling, slight blemish on cover of volume 1, otherwise very fine. Blackmer 1406.　H M. Fletcher　121-120 1 996 £950.00

RELIQUES of Ancient English Poetry. London: printed by John Nichols fo F. and C. Rivington, 1794. Octavo; 3 volumes; engraved vignettes; contemporary calf, gilt double rule border on covers, gilt spines, tooled in compartments, red and balck morocco labels, glt board edges and turn-ins, marbled edges and endpapers, extremities lightly rubbed, scattered light foxing, few neat repairs; armorial bookplate; very good set.　Heritage Book Shop　196-160　1996 $500.00

RELY, JEHAN DE   L'Ordre Tenv et Garde en L'Assemblee des Trois Estats.. Paris: Galliot du Pre, 1558. 8vo; fine large Galliot du Pre device at end; vellum; extremely rare, few blank margins wormed and repaired. Charles V. D. Elst bookticket. Adams R342.   Rostenberg & Stern 150-95   1996 $625.00

REMARKS by a Junior to His Senior, On an Article in the Edinburgh Review of January, 1844 on the State of Ireland, and the Measures for Its Improvement. London: James Ridgway, 1844. 1st edition; 8vo; 83 pages, few contemporary annotations in pencil; recent printed blue boards lettered, very good; from the contemporary library of Lord William Russell with his signature. Black 5761; Goldsmiths 33602; not in Kress.   John Drury 82-240   1994 £95.00

REMARKS on the Morality of Dramatic Compositions with Particular Reference to "La Traviata", etc. London: John Chapman, 1856. 1st edition; 8vo; disbound; rare. LAR 607.   Ximenes 109-286 1996 $150.00

REMARKS On the Rights of Inventors and the Influence of Their Studies in Promoting the Enjoyments of Life and Public Prosperity. Boston: E. Lincoln, 1807. 1st edition; 8vo; 16 pages; removed; disbound, title browned.   M & S Rare Books 60-463 1996 $200.00

REMARQUE, ERICH MARIA   The Road Back. Boston: Little Brown and Co., 1931. 1st edition; original binding, top edge slightly dusty, spine and cover edges browned, head and tail of spine and corners slightly bumped, endpaper edges slightly browned, very good in nicked creased and slightly soiled, rubbed, spotted, chipped and dusty dust jacket, slightly browned at edges; signed and inscribed by author.   Ulysses 39-500   1996 £350.00

REMINGTON, FREDERIC 1861-1909   Frontier Sketches. Chicago: the Werner Co., 1898. 1st edition; 15 plates; publisher's pictorial paper covered beveled boards titled in black; slightly soiled, joints splitting at top and bottom and corners showing, but presentable and sound copy. Hermitage SP95-807 1996 $375.00

REMISE, JAC   The Golden Age of Toys. Edita Lausanne, 1967. 1st American edition; very fine in dust jacket.   Hermitage SP95-742 1996 $100.00

REMY, NICHOLAS   Demonolatry. London: John Rodker, 1930. Limited to 1275 copies, this being #302 of 1275 copies; xlii, 188 pages; cloth; near fine.   Middle Earth 77-374 1996 $199.00

RENAULT, MARY   The Middle Mist. New York: Morrow, 1945. 1st edition; fine in dust jacket with tiny nick at foot and single short tear on rear panel; scarce in this condition.   Between the Covers 42-368 1996 $125.00

RENDELL, RUTH   The Crocodile Bird. London: Hutchinson, 1993. One of 150 signed, numbered copies; specially bound for London Limited Editions; marbled paper boards, light brown cloth, spine lettered in gold, fine in original glassine dust jacket.   Quill & Brush 102-1518 1996 $150.00

RENDELL, RUTH   A Demon In My View. London: Hutchinson, 1976. 1st edition; fine in dust jacket; inscribed by author.   Quill & Brush 102-1499   1996 $250.00

RENDELL, RUTH   The Face of Trespass. London: Hutchinson, 1974. 1st edition; near fine with page edges lightly soiled; near fine in near fine dust jacket with light rubbing and minor edge wear.   Quill & Brush 102-1497 1996 $200.00

RENDELL, RUTH   The Fallen Curtain and Other Stories. London: Hutchinson, 1976. 1st edition; fine in dust jacket.   Quill & Brush 102-1500 1996 $300.00

RENDELL, RUTH   A Judgement in Stone. London: Hutchinson, 1977. 1st edition; fine in price clipped dust jacket.   Quill & Brush 102-1501 1996 $200.00

RENDELL, RUTH   The Lake of Darkness. Garden City: Doubleday, 1980. 1st edition; fine in near fine dust jacket with very light rubbing; inscribed by author.   Quill & Brush 102-1502 1996 $100.00

RENDELL, RUTH   Master of the Moor. London: Hutchinson, 1982. 1st edition; fine in dust jacket; inscribed on titlepage.   Quill & Brush 102-1505 1996 $200.00

RENDELL, RUTH   Put Out by Cunning. London: Hutchinson, 1981. 1st edition; inscribed on titlepage fine in dust jacket.   Quill & Brush 102-1503   1996 $225.00

RENDELL, RUTH   Shake Hands For Ever. London: Hutchinson, 1975. 1st edition; fine in dust jacket with publisher's original wrap around band; inscribed by author.   Quill & Brush 102-1498 1996 $275.00

RENDELL, RUTH   Some Lie and Some Die. London: Hutchinson, 1973. 1st edition; fine in dust jacket; inscribed by author.   Quill & Brush 102-1496 1996 $300.00

RENDELL, RUTH   The Tree of Hands. London: Hutchinson, 1984. 1st edition; fine in dust jacket; inscribed on titlepage.   Quill & Brush 102-1507 1996 $200.00

RENDELL, RUTH   Wolf to the Slaughter. Garden City: Doubleday, 1968. 1st edition; near fine with spine ends lightly rubbed and inside hinge slightly discolored, in very good, near fine dust jacket with back panel very lightly soiled, light rubbing, few very small closed tears. Quill & Brush 102-1495 1996 $175.00

RENDLE, B. J.   World Timbers. London: 1969-69-70. 4to; 3 volumes; pages 191; 150; 175; 73 colored plates; cloth, light wear, pages yellowed, dust jackets, jacket on volume 1 worn.   Raymond M. Sutton VII-710 1996 $225.00

RENNERT, JACK   Alphonse Mucha: The Complete Posters and Panels. Boston: Hall, 1984. Folio; 405 pages, 172 color and 103 monochrome illustrations; cloth, dust jacket.   Brannan 43-463 1996 $135.00

RENNIE, HILL   The Theory, Formation and Construction of British and Foreign Harbours. London: John Weale, 1854. Atlas folio; 2 volumes; 133 steel engraved plates; contemporary half green morocco, gilt, top edge gilt, loose in covers.   Charles W. Traylen 117-52 1996 £1,100.00

RENNIE, R.   Essays on the Natural History and Origin of Peat Moss: the Peculiar Qualities of that Substance... Edinburgh: for Archibald Constable and Co., and John Murray, 1807. 8vo; pages viii, 233, (i), prelims little damped in lower margins, but excellent copy; original cloth, gilt, little marked, initialled note in an early hand on title states that the Rev. Rennie of Kilsyth, was the proprietor of part of Fanny Side Moss in Cumbermauld parish.   R.F.G. Hollett 76-253 1996 £120.00

A REPLY to a Pamphlet, Entitled the Case of the Duke of Portland, Respecting Two Leases Granted by the Lords of the Treasury to Sir James Lowther, Bart. London: printed for G. Kearsly and F. Newbery; and Richardson & Urquhart, 1768. 1st edition; 8vo; half title present; disbound; very good. Roscoe A439.   Ximenes 109-174 1996 $100.00

REPORT of the Cruise of the U.S. Revenue Cutter Bear and the Overland Expedition for the Relief of the Whalers in the Arctic Ocean, from November 27, 1897 to September 13, 1898. Washington: GPO, 1899. 8vo; iv, 3-144 pages, 48 plates; hinges weak, covers scuffed, blue cloth. Ricks 241; Arctic Biblio 18402.   Parmer Books Nat/Hist-071534 1996 $120.00

REPORT of the State Trials, Before a General Court Martial Held at Montreal in 1838-9; Exhibiting a Complete History of the Late Rebellion in Lower Canada. Montreal: 1839. 2 volumes, pages 376; 565, iii; contemporary half leather and boards, overall moderate binding wear, else very good, rare. TPL 2305; Sabin 10588.   Stephen Lunsford 45-135 1996 $1,200.00

REPORT of the Trial of the Students on the Charge of Mobbing, Rioting and Assault, at the College (i.e. University of Edinburgh) on Jan. 11 & 12, 1838. Edinburgh: printed by Andrew Shortrede, 1838. 1st edition; 8vo; 100 pages; uncut, disbound.   Anthony W. Laywood 108-238 1996 £75.00

REPORTS of the United States Commissioners to the Paris Universal Exposition, 1878. Washington: GPO, 1880. 1st editions; 8vo; 5 volumes; illustrations; publisher's cloth, very good.   Bookpress 75-96 1996 $350.00

REPTON, HUMPHRY 1752-1818   Variety; or a Collection of Essays Written in the Year 1787. London: T. Cadell, 1788. 1st edition; 8vo; viii, (4), 297, (1) pages, + errata leaf; complete with half title; early 19th century calf, gilt, blind tooled spine, head of spine very neatly repaired, some rubbing to board edges, very scarce.   Ken Spelman 30-105 1996 £550.00

REPTON, HUMPHRY 1752-1818   Variety; or a Collection of Essays Written in the Year 1787. London: T. Cadell, 1788. 1st edition; 8vo; vii, (4), 297, (1) pages, errata leaf; complete with half title; early 19th century calf, gilt and blind tooled spine; head of spine very neatly repaired, some rubbing to board edges; very good, very scarce.   Ken Spelman 30-105 1996 £550.00

REQUA, RICHARD S.   Architectural Details, Spain and the Mediterranean. Cleveland: J. H. Jansen, 1927. 1st edition; small folio; (x) pages, 144 plates; cloth; ex-library, with appropriate markings, occasional smudging, binding rubbed, else very good.   The Bookpress 75-227 1996 $235.00

RESEWITZ, FRIEDRICH   Die Erziehung des Burgers zum Gebrauch des Gesunden Verstandes... Copenhagen: Heinecke and Faber, 1773. 1st edition; 8vo; 220 pages; two diagrams, woodcut and typographic ornaments; moderate text browning, untrimmed in original wrappers; fine, rare.   Bennett Gilbert LL29-32 1996 $1,750.00

RESTATEMENT of the Law, Second, Torts 2d. St. Paul: American Law Inst. Publishers, 1965. Original buckram; gilt; good, clean set.   Meyer Boswell SL25-179 1996 $150.00

RETURNS from the Several Chartered Banks, Stating the Name and Place of Residence of Each Stockholder, with the Number and Nominal Value of the Shares Held by Them. Quebec: 1860. Pages 70; original wrappers, near fine.   Stephen Lunsford 45-136 1996 $150.00

REVERE, JOSEPH WARREN 1812-1880   A Tour of Duty in California... New York: C. S. Francis & Co., 1849. 1st edition; 305 pages; 6 lithograph plates and large folding map (4" tear along inner hinge) of the "Harbour of San Francisco"; original cloth, light wear at spinal extremities, but overall very good. Field 1294; Cowan p. 530; Graff 3474; Howes R222; Wheat Gold 165.   Blue River Books 9-60 1996 $450.00

REXROTH, KENNETH   The Elastic Retort. New York: Seabury, 1973. 1st edition; near fine in very good+ dust jacket, signed by author. Lame Duck Books 19-477 1996 $125.00

REY ROSA, RODRIGO   The Path Doubles Back. New York: Red Ozier Press, 1982. 1st edition; limited to 185 copies, signed by author and artist and by translator, Paul Bowles; thin 8vo; illustrations by David Craven; cloth backed printed boards; fine.   James S. Jaffe 34-82 1996 $150.00

REY, G.   The Matterhorn. London: 1907. 2nd English edition, issued two months after the first; 35 plates; beige cloth with gilt lettering; few faint patches on spine and foxing of first and last pages, but generally nice, very good+ copy.   Moutaineering Books 8-ER02 1996 £80.00

REY, G.   Peaks and Precipices: Scrambles in the Dalomites and Savoy. London: for T. Fisher Unwin, 1914. 1st English edition; royal 8vo; 238 pages; 76 photographic illustrations on 48 plates; buckram gilt, top edge gilt, faded, text foxed;   Thomas Thorp 489-259 1996 £150.00

REY, H. A.   Elizabite Adventures of a Carnivorous Plant. New York: Harper & Row, c. 1950. colored illustrations by Rey, some spotting to prelims, light dusting to boards, else very nice in chipped, marked pictorial dust jacket, laid in is color lithographed Christmas card from H. A. and Maragret Rey, with handwritten message from Rey.   Barbara Stone 70-179 1996 £125.00

REYNOLDS, GEORGE   The Mormon Metropolis. An Illustrated Guide to Salt Lake and Its Environs. Salt Lake City: J. H. Parry, 1883. 1st edition; 48 pages plus (24) pages ads; folding bird's-eye-view; illustrations and text illustrations; original printed grey wrappers with ads on verso of front wrapper, back wrapper and verso of back wrapper; very fine, laid in half morocco chemise slipcase. Flake 7101.   Michael D. Heaston 23-345 1996 $1,200.00

REYNOLDS, JOHN   Friendship's Offering: a Sketch of the Life of Dr. John Mason Peck. Belleville: Advocate Book and Job Office, Print, 1858. 1st edition; 34 pages; original glazed yellow binding, minor chipping; fine, slipcase; Graff copy with his bookplate. Eberstadt Cat. 168 231. Michael D. Heaston 23-288 1996 $2,250.00

REYNOLDS, JOSHUA 1723-1792   Johnson and Garrick. London: Nichols, Son and Bentley, 1816. 1st edition; one of 250 copies; 8 x 5 1/4 inches; 15 pages; fine modern speckled calf, covers with twining gilt rule, spine heavily gilt in compartments, using sympathetic floral and foliate decoration, maroon double morocco labels, gilt top, inner gilt dentelles; early owner's intials at top of title, slight foxing in few places, but fine, rare. Rothschild 1741.   Phillip J. Pirages 33-447 1996 $1,500.00

REZAC, J.   96 Photographs. Artia, 1964. 1st edition; English, French and German; dust jacket, rare. From the collection of Dutch photographer, Cas Oorthuys, signed by him.   J. B. Muns 154-298 1996 $650.00

RHEAD, G. WOOLLISCOFT   History of the Fan. London: Kegan Paul, Trench, Trubner & Co., 1910. Limited to 450 copies; small thick folio; xix, 311 pages; 127 full page plates, numerous line illustrations; gilt stamped cloth, top edge gilt, ex-library with number on spine, otherwise minimal markings, hinges weak due to size and weight of volume, head of spine torn, overall very nice.   J. M. Cohen 35-83 1996 $500.00

RHEES, WILLIAM   The Smithsonian Institution Documents Relative to Its Orign and History. 1835-1899. Washington: 1901. 1st edition; 1983 pages; 2 volumes; original binding.   W. Bruce Fye 71-1755 1996 $100.00

RHEIMS, MAURICE   Bernard Buffet: Graveur, 1948-1980. Nice: Fracony, n.d. Folio; 244 pages; 370 illustrations; cloth, slipace. Brannan 43-91 1996 $120.00

RHEIMS, MAURICE   The Flowering of Art Nouveau. New York: Harry N. Abrams, 1966. 1st edition; 450 pages; many illustrations; fine in publisher's Mylar jacket.   Hermitage SP95-777 1996 $100.00

RHIND, W.   A History of the Vegetable Kingdom. London: 1868. Revised edition; royal 8vo; pages xvi, 744, portrait, colored titlepage, 23 steel engraved plates, 22 hand colored plates of figures; half calf. Wheldon & Wesley 207-1888 1996 £70.00

RHODE ISLAND SOLDIERS' & SAILORS' HISTORICAL SOCIETY   Personal Narratives of Events in the War of the Rebellion, Being Papers Read Before the Rhode Island Soldiers' and Sailors Historical Society. Sixth Series. Nos. 1-10. Providence: 1903-05. 1st edition; limited to 250 copies; Numbers 1-10, original issues, bound together in period half leather with marbled paper sides; near fine.   McGowan Book Co. 65-75 1996 $350.00

RHODE ISLAND. (COLONY). LAWS, STATUTES, ETC.   Acts and Laws of His Majesty's Colony of Rhode Island and Providence Plantations in New England, in america. Newport: James Franklin, 1752. 1st edition; small folio; (8), 110 pages; contemporary marbled wrappers, label removed from front wrapper; very scarce. Fine, crisp copy. Evans 6919. M & S Rare Books 60-403 1996 $950.00

RHODE ISLAND. (STATE). GENERAL ASSEMBLY   Report of the Important Hearing on the Memorial of the New England Mining Company for Encouragement from the State...Before the Select Special Committee of the General Assembly of Rhode Island N.P.: 1838. 1st edition; viii, 148 pages; lilac cloth, covers faded, scattered foxing; old "Franklin Society" rubber stamp on title.   Metacomet Books 54-77 1996 $125.00

RHODE, CHRISTIAN DETLEV   Cimbrisch-Hollsteinische Antiquitaten-Remarques... Hamburg: J. G. Piscator, 1720. 1st and only edition; 8vo; 460 pages; 10 large text engravings, 39 large text woodcuts, title in red and black, text browning, modern boards, printed backstrip label; very good. NUC 491-497 (1 copy).   Bennett Gilbert LL29-70 1996 $1,950.00

RHODE, JOHN   The Last Suspect. New York: Dodd, Mead and Co., 1952. Advance review copy of the first edition, with review slip, stating that this is an editorial copy and asking for a copy of the review to be written; 8vo; red cloth printed in black, red and black pictorial dust jacket stating this is a "Dr. Priestley Detective Story"; near fine in near fine jacket that has one tiny chip and two tiny (half inch) tears. Priscilla Juvelis 95/1-319 1996 $150.00

RHODES, EUGENE MANLOVE   Say Now Shibboleth. Chicago: The Bookfellow (printed by the Torch Press, Cedar Rapids), 1921. 1st edition; one of 400 copies; 12mo; pages 55; original cloth backed boards, paper labels.   Howard S. Mott 227-117 1996 $150.00

RHODES, GODFREY   Tents and Tent-Life, from the Earliest Ages to the Present Time. London: William Clowes & Sons, Silver & Co., 1859. 2nd edition, with new supplement; 8vo; 27 full page engraved plates and plates, one folding, half title; original cloth, spine gilt, binding bit worn; but good copy; scarce.   Trebizond 39-86 1996 $250.00

RHODES, W. H.   Caxton's Book. Bancroft, 1876. 1st edition; good/very good copy.   Aronovitz 57-982 1996 $125.00

RHYS, JEAN   Voyage in the Dark. London: Andre Deutsch, 1967. 1st edition; near fine in dust jacket; presentation copy from author to her publisher, Andre Deutsch.   Words Etcetera 94-1086 1996 £250.00

RHYS, JEAN   Wide Sargasso Sea. London: Andre Deutsch, 1966. 1st edition; 7 3/4 x 5 inches; pages 190; red linson; very good in dust jacket, scarce.   Ian Hodgkins 78-365 1996 £85.00

RIBADENEIRA, PETER   The Lives of the Saints, with Other Feasts of the Year, According to the Roman Calendar. London: B. s., 1730. 2nd edition; folio; (xvi), 456; (ii), 588, (ii) pages; frontispiece; contemporary blue calf, spines gilt; little rubbed and scuffed, minor foxing. Handsome set.   Robert Clark 38-203 1996 £110.00

RIBOT, THEODULE A.   Diseases of Memory: an Essay in the Positive Psychology... New York: D. Appleton, 1882. 1st U.S. edition of the English translation; 8vo; pages 4 (ads), 209, (14 ads); original cloth, nice.   James Fenning 133-284 1996 £85.00

RICARDO, DAVID 1772-1823   On the Principles of Political Economy and Taxation. London: John Murray, 1817. 1st edition; one of only 750 copies; contemporary tree calf, rebacked, bound without half title and ads; clean and wide margined copy in very good condition, half morocco case, very scarce. PMM 277.   19th Century Shop 39- 1996 $18,500.00

RICCI, ELISA   Old Italian Lace. London: Heinemann/Philadelphia: Lippincott, 1913. Limited to 300 copies; folio; 2 volumes, pages 426, 277; 760 photographic illustrations of lace, many tipped in; some bubbling to covers, small stain at edge of first few pages of each volume, else nice set in original gilt stamped cloth, top edge gilt. Bromer Booksellers 90-217 1996 $850.00

RICCI, JAMES   The Development of Gynaecological Surgery and Instruments... Philadelphia: 1949. 1st edition; 594 pages; more than 100 illustrations; original binding. GM 6310.   W. Bruce Fye 71-1756 1996 $300.00

RICCI, JAMES   The Geneaology of Gynaecology, History of the Development of Gynaecology throughout the Ages 2000 BC-1800 AD.... Philadelphia: 1950. 2nd edition; 494 pages; original binding, scarce. GM 6305.   W. Bruce Fye 71-1757 1996 $200.00

RICCI, SEYMOUR DE 1881-1942   A Census of Caxtons. Oxford: Bibliographical Society, 1909. 1st edition; 4to; frontispiece, 10 plates of facsimile types, title in red and black; original cloth backed boards, upper cover waterstained, lower hinge torn, unopened, uncut, ex-library, library stamps.   Forest Books 74-66 1996 £75.00

RICCI, SEYMOUR DE 1881-1942   English Collectors of Books and Manuscripts (1530-1930) and Their Marks of Ownership. New York: 1930. 1st edition; American issue; 203 pages, 8 plates, 4 figures in text; blue cloth, paper spine label, dust jacket, booklabel of Comerford.   Maggs Bros. Ltd. 1191-79 1996 £80.00

RICCI, SEYMOUR DE 1881-1942   A Hand List of a Collection of Books and Manuscripts Belonging to the Rt. Hon. Lord Amherst of Hackney at Didlington Hall, Norfolk. Cambridge: privately printed, 1906. 4to; frontispiece, 4 plates; cloth backed boards, spine missing, edges bit bumped, printed on rectos only; Lord Kenyon's booklabel and ownership inscription, few pencil annotations in his hand, compliments slip from Lord Amherst tipped in.   Maggs Bros. Ltd. 1191-4 1996 £60.00

RICCOBONI, LEWIS   A General History of the Stage, from Its Origin. London: for W. Owen and Lockyer Davis, 1754. 2nd edition; period gilt ruled calf, joints cracked, erosion to spine, contents very good. LAR 8333. Jaggard p. 261.   Dramatis Personae 37-147 1996 $120.00

RICCOBONI, MARIE JEANNE LABORAS DE MEZIERES, MME.   Letters from Sophia de Valiere to Her Friend Louisa Hortensia de Canteleu. London: printed for T. Becket and P. A. DeHondt, 1772. 1st edition in English; 12mo; 2 volumes, with half titles, errata leaf at end of volume 2, followed by 2 pages of ads; contemporary calf, spines gilt decorated, contrasting title labels, very slight rubbing, otherwise quite lovely; scarce. 4 copies in NUC. Block, English Novel p. 197; NCBEL II 1529.   Paulette Rose 16-259 1996 $750.00

RICE, ANNE   Beauty's Release. New York: Dutton, 1985. 1st edition; rare hardback issue; very fine in very fine dust jacket.   Pettler & Lieberman 28-213 1996 $150.00

RICE, ANNE   Belinda. New York: Arbor House, 1986. Advance review copy with slip and publisher's material laid in; fine in dust jacket, signed by author.   Between the Covers 42-371 1996 $100.00

RICE, ANNE   Cry to Heaven. New York: Knopf, 1982. 1st edition; fine in price clipped dust jacket, signed by author.   Lame Duck Books 19-479 1996 $150.00

RICE, ANNE   Exit to Eden. New York: Arbour House, 1985. 1st edition; slight bmp to corners, else fine in dust jacket.   Between the Covers 42-370 1996 $100.00

RICE, ANNE   The Feast of All Saints. New York: S&S, 1979. 1st edition; remainder mark to bottom edge, else near fine in dust jacket; signed by author.   Lame Duck Books 19-478 1996 $175.00

RICE, ANNE   Interview With the Vampire. New York: Knopf, 1976. Avance reading copy; slight darkening at extremities, still fine in glossy wrappers.   Between the Covers 42-369 1996 $850.00

RICE, ANNE   Interview with the Vampire. New York: Knopf, 1976. Advance reading copy; pictorial wrappers, blue marker along bottom edge; otherwise very good.   Robert Gavora 61-117 1996 $500.00

RICE, ANNE   Interview with the Vampire. New York: Knopf, 1976. 1st edition; fine in very near fine dust jacket and is signed by author; scarce, particularly in nice condition, as the gold foil dust jacket is notoriously prone to wear.   Ken Lopez 74-388 1996 $975.00

RICE, ANNE   Interview with the Vampire. New York: Knopf, 1976. 1st edition; fine in near fine dust jacket. Author's first book.   Aronovitz 57-983 1996 $495.00

RICE, ANNE   Interview With a Vampire. New York: Alfred A. Knopf, 1976. 1st edition; fine in lightly creased and rubbed dust jacket, very nice.   Hermitage SP95-555 1996 $475.00

RICE, ANNE   Interview with the Vampire. New York: Knopf, 1976. 1st edition; signed by author; glue marks to both front and back end pages where dust jacket was separated, some wear to bottom corner edges, very attractive dust jacket although somewhat trimmed, slight lean, overall very clean.   Bud Schweska 12-1379 1996 $150.00

RICE, ANNE   Interview with a Vampire. New York: Knopf, 1986. 1st edition; fine copy in near fine dust jacket, front jacket flap creased top to bottom, minor dings, 3/8" closed tear spine top.   Book Time 2-785 1996 $650.00

RICE, ANNE   Lasher. New York: Knopf, 1993. Uncorrected proof; dark mustard wrappers, as new.   Oracle Books 1-450 1996 $100.00

RICE, ANNE   The Queen of the Damned. Ultramarine and Knopf, 1988. 1st edition; #14/150 copies, specially bound and signed by author and with a signed and numbered print by Walotsky bound in as frontispiece; as new in half leather and textured boards.   Aronovitz 57-985 1996 $350.00

RICE, ANNE   The Queen of the Damned. New York: Knopf, 1988. 1st edition; fine in fine dust jacket and signed by author.   Ken Lopez 74-390 1996 $150.00

RICE, ANNE   The Vampire Lestat. New York: Knopf, 1985. 1st edition; fine in fine dust jacket, signed by author.   Ken Lopez 74-389 1996 $300.00

RICE, ANNE   The Witching Hour. New York: Knopf, 1990. Uncorrected proof; blue wrappers; fine; signed by author.   Lame Duck Books 19-480 1996 $250.00

RICE, DAVID   The Church of Haghia Sophia at Trebizond. Edinburgh: Edinburgh University Press, 1968. 4to; xxii, 275 pages; color frontispiece, 12 color plates, 80 black and white plates, 136 text illustrations, plan in pocket; cloth, dust jacket.   Rainsford A54-492 1996 £55.00

RICH, ADRIENNE   A Change of World. New Haven: Yale University Press, 1951. 1st edition; fine in near fine dust jacket; beautiful copy of author's first book as an adult; signed.   Alice Robbins 15-295 1996 $500.00

RICH, ADRIENNE   Leaflets: Poems 1965-1968. New York: W. W. Norton, 1969. 1st edition; 8vo; cloth, fine, dust jacket.   James S. Jaffe 34-594 1996 $100.00

RICH, CHARLES H.   Specimens of the Art of Ornamental Turning, In Eccentric and Concentric Patterns... Southampton: E. Skelton, c. 1825. 2nd edition; 4to; half title, title, pages (iii), iv-v (vi), (7), 8-33 (34), 6 engraved plates, 4 folding; boards, uncut, somewhat worn and spotted; inscription, C. Hines, Norwich 1841 on front pastedown. Very rare.   Maggs Bros. Ltd. 1190-650 1996 £420.00

RICH, E. E.   The History of the Hudson's Bay Company 1670-1870. London: 1958-59. 2 volumes, over 1700 pages, illustrations, maps; original binding; about fine.   Stephen Lunsford 45-137 1996 $350.00

RICH, E. E.   The History of the Hudson's Bay Company 1670-1870. London: Hudson's Bay Record Society, 1958-59. Royal 8vo; 2 volumes, 6 plates, 2 folding maps; original cloth, top edge gilt, others uncut, author's presentation inscription on half title.   H. M. Fletcher 121-160 1996 £75.00

RICHARD, HENRY   Letters On the Social and Political Condition of the Principality of Wales. London: Jackson, Walford and Hodder, n.d. 1866? 1st edition in book form; 8vo; iv, 112 pages; original lilac cloth, embossed in blind, spine lettered in gilt; very good.   John Drury 82-241 1996 £80.00

RICHARD, of Cirencester   Speculum Historiale de gestis Regum Angliae. London: 1863-69. 8vo; 2 volumes; 3 colored facsimiles;; original cloth.   Howes Bookshop 265-1576 1996 £55.00

RICHARDS, ANTHONY   From a Satyric Country. London: I. M. Imprimit, 1971. Number 25 of 100 copies; folio; pages 61 + colophon; 10 full page woodcuts; original unsewn folded sheets as issued in buckram backed box folder, paper label with shelf mark;   Claude Cox 107-100 1996 £55.00

RICHARDS, EDWARD A.   Shadows-Selected Poems. Saint Thomas: The Reflector, 1933. Small octavo; 20 pages; cloth and paper covered boards, paper label to front board, near fine, little darkening ata edges of boards; nice, rear. Not in NUC or most other standard references.   Between the Covers 43-185 1996 $275.00

RICHARDS, EUGENE   Few Comforts or Surprises: the Arkanasa Delta. Cambridge: and London: MIT Press, 1973. 1st edition; oblong 4to; 123 pages, numerous black and white photos; pictorial paper over boards, near fine in matching dust jacket.   Andrew Cahan 47-175 1996 $200.00

RICHARDS, FRANK   Old-Soldier Sahib. London: Faber & Faber, Ltd., 1936. 1st edition; original binding, top edge dusty, tail of spine bumped, corners very slightly bumped, cover edges slightly rubbed, very good in nicked, rubbed and dusty, slightly marked dust jacket frayed and slightly chipped at head of spine and browned at spine and edges; bookplate of John Gere, who was keeper of books & drawings at the British Museum.   Ulysses 39-244 1996 £450.00

RICHARDS, J. M.   High Street. London: Country Life, 1938. 8vo; 102 pages, including 24 colored lithographs by Eric Ravilious, original printed boards, original glassine wrapper, apar from slight warp in boards due to natural shrinkage of the glassine, this copy is as new.   H. M. Fletcher 121-161 1996 £595.00

RICHARDS, J. M.   High Street. London: Country Life, 1938. 1st edition; 8vo; pages 100, (1); 24 full page illustrations printed in colors and large wood engraved titlepage design incorporating title lettering, all by Eric Ravilious; original flat backed dark green boards, with overall design incoporating the lettering by Ravilious; top 10mm. of backstrip defective and joints and corners rubbed; good.   Blackwell's B112-241 1996 £550.00

RICHARDS, MARIA T.   Life in Israel; or Portraitures of Hebrew Character. New York: and Chicago: 1857. 1st edition; 12mo; 389 pages; original cloth; Wright II 2029; Singerman 1510.   M & S Rare Books 60-220 1996 $100.00

RICHARDS, P. F.   Old Soldier. London: Faber, 1936. 1st edition; very good in dusty yellow dust jacket somewhat browned on spine and with few chips to corners; scarce. Higginson A44.   Words Etcetera 94-523 1996 £100.00

RICHARDS, WALTER   Her Majesty's Army. A Descriptive Account of the Various Regiments Now Comprising the Queen's Forces... London: John Ptheram, 1841. 1st edition; 4to; 3 volumes; colored pictorial and printed titles and 44 colored lithographed plates; contemporary red half morocco and cloth, gilt decorated covers and gilt panelled spines, gilt edges; Army Museum Ogilby Trust 752.   Charles W. Traylen 117-244 1996 £350.00

RICHARDSON, CHARLES   A New Dictionary of the English Language. London: William Pickering, 1836-37. 1st edition; 4to; 2 volumes, half titles, 19th century dark blue binder's cloth, inner hinges cracking, decent copy. Rather scarce.   Jarndyce 103-210 1996 £140.00

RICHARDSON, HAROLD   The Poet and Other Animals. London: Ernet Nister E. C. 2272, 1909. 1st edition; royal 8vo; pages 954), 24 fine color printed plates of animals; original green cloth with onlaid pictorial label to upper cover, pictorial endpapers; neat ownership signature to inner cover, otherwise extremely fine.   Sotheran PN32-135 1996 £128.00

RICHARDSON, JAMES   Narrative of a Mission to Central Africa Performed in the Years 1850-51, Under the Orders and Expense of Her Majesty's Government. London: Chapman and Hall, 1853. 8vo; 2 volumes, pages xxviii, 343; viii, 359; folding map; original cloth, tops of spines chipped. Hoover 5679.   Richard Adelson W94/95-140 1995 $325.00

RICHARDSON, JAMES   Report on the Coal Fields of Vancouver Island, with Map of Their Distribtuion. Ottawa: Geological Survey of Canada, 1872. 24.5 cm; (27) pages, folding map; fine in later wrappers.   Rockland Books 38-187 1996 $100.00

RICHARDSON, JAMES   Travels in the Great Desert of Sahara, in the years 1845 and 1846. London: Richard bentley, New Burlington St... 1848. 1st edition; 8vo; 2 volumes, text pages 1-440, 1-482; steel engraved frontispieces; 1 steel engraved plate, 23 woodcut illustrations to text, 1 large folding map; full polished tan calf, double gilt rule border to boards, tiny gilt ornamental cornerpieces, corners bumped, elaborate gilt tooling to panelled spines, red and green morocco labels to spines, marbled edges; contemporary ink presentation inscription to prelim of volume 1, ownership inscriptions, upper right hand corner of rear endpaper to volume 1 cut away, handsome set.   Beeleigh Abbey BA56-239 1996 £1,000.00

RICHARDSON, JOHN   Fauna Boreali-Americana; or the Zoology of the Northern Parts of British America. Part First Quadrupeds. London: 1829. 1st edition; 8vo; 28 etched plates, 2 leaves misbound, tiny wormhole in blank margin of first four leaves; recent half calf.   Maggs Bros. Ltd. 1190-716 1996 £95.00

RICHARDSON, JOHN   The Museum of Natural History. London: William Mackenzie, ca. 1870. 1st edition; 4to; 2 volumes, 446, 405, 38 pages; chromolithographed titlepages, hand colored title, 137 full page plates, numerous in text illustrations; contemporary dark blue half morocco with gilt tooled spines, very good.   Chapel Hill 94-311 1996 £285.00

RICHARDSON, JOHN   The War of 1812. Toronto: Musson Book Co., 1902. Limited edition, number 22 of 100 copies; 8vo; pages lviii, 14, 320; 15 portraits, 9 plates, 2 maps, 4 plans, 2 facsimiles; half black morocco; StTr 1008; Larned 1749.   Richard Adelson W94/95-141 1996 $285.00

RICHARDSON, JONATHAN 1665-1745   The Works, Containing I. The Theory of Painting. II. Essay on the Art of Criticism. III. The Science of the Conoisseur. London: ptd. at Strawberry Hill, sold by B. White & Son, T. & J. Egerton... 1792. New edition; small 4to; title with engraved vigentte of Strawberry Hill; vi, 287 pages; 12 engraved portraits, original calf, rebacked, modern endpapers. Hazen p. 65.   David Bickersteth 133-59 1996 £160.00

RICHARDSON, JONATHAN 1665-1745   The Works. Strawberry Hill: sold by B. White and Son & others, 1792. 1st edition; 4to; pages vii, 287, 12 etched, stipple and line engraved plates printed on pink washed paper; titlepage in first state described by Hazen p. 65; large copy in contemporary speckled calf, upper hinge cracked but side securely held; very good; bookplate and ownership signature of Earl of Stradbroke, 1827. Hazen p. 83, p. 65.   Claude Cox 107-163 1996 £165.00

RICHARDSON, JOSEPH   Jekyll: a Political Eclogue. London: printed for J. Debrett, 1788. 1st edition; 4to; disbound; very good, complete with half title, outer edges uncut; Jackson p. 140.   Ximenes 108-308 1996 $150.00

RICHARDSON, LEANDER   The Dark City, or Cutoms of the Cockneys. Boston: Doyle and Whittle, 1886. 1st edition; 8vo; iv, 223 pages; original green cloth, pages browned and brittle, otherwise fine.   David Mason 71-49   1996 $100.00

RICHARDSON, RUPERT   Comanche Barrier to South Plains Settlement. Abilene: 1991. 1/225 copies; 260 pages; quarter morocco with maroon colored cloth and brown morocco label.   W. M. Morrison 436-195 1996 $285.00

RICHARDSON, SAMUEL 1689-1761   Clarissa. London: printed for Richardson, sold by Hitch and Hawes, A. Millar et al, 1759. 4th edition; small 8vo; 8 volumes; full original polished calf, raised bands, gilt in panels, double labels gilt on brown; some wear, few spine ends slightly chipped, labels to volume 1 replaced; nice, early set. CBEL II 515. Hartfield 48-L74   1996 $695.00

RICHARDSON, SAMUEL 1689-1761   Clarissa, or the History of a Young Lady. London: S. Richardson, et al, 1759. 4th edition; 12mo; 8 volumes; contemporary speckled calf, 19th century owner's signature to front blanks in all volumes, spines rather dry, occasionally chipped; good, sound set.   Charles Agvent 4-970   1996 $400.00

RICHARDSON, SAMUEL 1689-1761   The History of Sir Charles Grandison. In A Series of Letters Published from the Originals. London: printed for S. Richardson, and sold by C. Hitch and L. Hawes... 1754. 1st edition; 12mo; 7 volumes; (viii), 316; (ii), 358; (ii), (376); (ii), 294; (ii), 372; (ii), 442 pages; final ad leaf in volume 4, cancels all present, second state of volume VI, with catchword "Well" on p. 279; contemporary plain calf, gilt ruled, rubbed, some corners little worn, volume 4 rebacked, with old spine laid down, small burnhole at head of C8-C11 in volume 1, just affecting a few letters of text; G10 in volume 2 torn across, without loss; scattered minor staining, very reasonable set. Sale 39.   Robert Clark   38-204   1996 £240.00

RICHARDSON, SAMUEL 1689-1761   The History of Sir Charles Grandison. (with) Clarissa. Suffield: printed by Havila & Oliver Farnsworth, for Oliver D. & I. Cooke... 1798. 12mo; 2 volumes in one, 143, 138, (1) pages; full contemporary calf, original leather label on spine reading "Novels for Youth"; fine copy, with gilt stamped red leather label of Frank Hogan. Splendid copy. Welch 1104.5. Evans 34465 & 34463.   M & S Rare Books 60-189   1996 $450.00

RICHARDSON, SAMUEL 1689-1761   Letters from Sir Charles Grandison. London: Macmillan, 1896. 8vo; 2 volumes; pages 303, 319; illustrations by Chris. Hammond; black linen, gilt, gilt illustrations to front covers, all edges gilt; attractive set.   Hartfield 48-V40 1 1996 $155.00

RICHARDSON, SAMUEL 1689-1761   The Novels of Samuel Richardson. London: Hurst, Robinson, 1824. Royal 8vo; 3 volumes; pages xxv, (i), xlviii, 728; xix, (i), 786; xxii, 791; contemporary half dark calf, corners and extremities rubbed, backstrips with double gilt ruled raised bands, dark red labels in second and fifth compartments, remainder gilt panelled, watered purple silk sides (faded), red sprinkled and polished edges; good.   Blackwell's B112-242 1996 £185.00

RICHARDSON, SAMUEL 1689-1761   The Novels. New York: Croscup and Sterling, 1901. Founder's Edition, strictly limited to 15 numbered sets, with frontispieces in 2 states (colored and uncolored) and plates in 3 states; 8vo; 20 volumes; half dark blue morocco, gilt panelled spines, top edge gilt, by Riviere.   Charles W. Traylen 117-184   1996 £400.00

RICHARDSON, SAMUEL 1689-1761   Pamela, ou la Vertue Recompensee. Londres: i.e. Paris?: chez Jean Osborne,, 1742. 1st complete edition in French; 8vo; 4 volumes; contemporary French mottled calf, spines gilt, small blemish to one spine; half titles present, one letter punched out on first titlepage, some light waterstains, generally fine and attractive. Sale p. 29; Rochedieu pp. 279-80; CBEL II 918 (wrongly listed 1742-3).   Ximenes 108-309 1996 $2,500.00

RICHARDSON, SAMUEL 1689-1761   Pamela. London: Harrison, 1785. Thick 8vo; 4 volumes in 1; pages 634; 12 nice full page engraved illustrations by Edward Burney; original black leather spine and marbled boards, gilt, old book label, uniform light foxing and minor spotting, hinges rubbed, text in double columns; pleasant copy. CHEL X 5-6. Hartfield 48-L75   1996 $295.00

RICHARDSON, SAMUEL 1689-1761   The Works. Edinburgh and London: at the Ballantyne Press, for Henry Sotheran & Co., London &... 1883. Number 70 of 750 copies only; 8vo; 12 volumes; frontispiece; contemporary dark green crushed half morocco, spines with five raised bands, lettered and panelled in gilt, green cloth sides and endpapers, top edge gilt, slight wear to extremities of first volume, excellent set. Simon Finch 24-196   1996 £650.00

RICHARDSON, T. C.   East Texas Its History and Its Makers. New York: 1940. Folio; volumes 1, 3 and 4 (of 4); illustrations; cloth, spine spotting.   W. M. Morrison 436-196   1996 $180.00

RICHARDSON, W.   Dr. Zell and the Princess Charlotte. L. Kabis & Co., 1892. 1st edition; just about fine, very scarce.   Aronovitz 57-989 1996 $250.00

RICHARDSON, WILLIAM 1743-1814   Anecdotes of the Russian Empire. London: printed for W. Strahan and T. Cadell, 1784. 1st edition; 8vo; 478 pages, errata leaf at end; contemporary tree calf, spine worn, hinges cracked, lacks label, text fresh and clean.   Anthony W. Laywood 108-115   1996 £80.00

RICHELIEU & ONTARIO NAVIGATION CO.   From Niagara to the Sea: the Finest Inland Water Trip in the World. Office Guide, 1902. Montreal; Desbarats & Co., Engravers and Printers, 1902. 8vo; pages 146; illustrations, folding map, paper covers, cvoers dusty, else fine.   Hugh Anson-Cartwright 87-368   1996 $125.00

RICHIE, WARD   John Gutenberg - A Fanciful Story of the Fifteenth Century. Los Angeles: Ward Ritchie Press, 1940. One of 300 copies; wrappers, fore-edge of one page very slightly torn, spine slightly browned, tail of spine slightly split, head and tail of spine and corners slightly bumped, very good.   Ulysses 39-503 1996 £75.00

RICHMOND, IAN A.   The City Wall of Imperial Rome: an Account of its Architectural Development from Aurelian to Narses. Oxford: Clarendon Press, 1930. 8vo; frontispiece, xiv, 279 pages; 45 figures, 21 plates; original cloth.   Archaeologia Luxor-3884   1996 $175.00

RICHMOND, JAMES C..   A Midsummer's Day-Dream: Libellous; or a Little Book of the vision of Shawmut. Boston: Jordan & Wiley; New York: Burgess, Striner & Co., Aug. 1847. 1st edition; 8vo; 24 pages; frontispiece; original printed wrappers, some wrinkling and siling of wrappers. Inscribed presentation "by the writer" on title and dated Aug. 6, 1847.   M & S Rare Books 60-221 1996 $125.00

RICHTER, CONRAD   The Town. New York: Knopf, 1950. 1st edition; fine in slightly spine faded and rubbed, near fine dust jacket, nice. Between the Covers 42-372 1996 $150.00

RICHTER, GISELA M. A.   The Archaic Gravestones of Attica. London: Phaidon Press, 1961. 31 x 23 cm; viii, 184 pages, 216 illustrations; original buckram.   Rainsford A54-496   1996 £55.00

RICHTER, GISELA M. A.   Catalogue of Engraved Gems: Greek, Etruscan and Roman. Roma: L'Erma di Bretschneider, 1956. 4to; xiiii, 143 pages, 75 plates; half calf with marbled boards, spine faded and rubbed; scarce. Daux's copy.   Archaeologia Luxor-3887 1996 $450.00

RICHTER, GISELA M. A.   Catalogue of Greek Sculptures. Cambridge: Harvard University Press, 1954. 4to; xviii, 123 pages; 164 plates; original cloth, tattered dust jacket.   Archaeologia Luxor-3890 1996 $750.00

RICHTER, GISELA M. A.   Engraved Gems of the Greeks, Etruscans and Romans. London: Phaidon, 1968-71. Folio; 2 volumes; 646 pages, 1560 illustrations; original cloth, dust jacket, volume 2 top board stained, minor marginal dampstaining to few pages.   Archaeologia Luxor-3891 1996 $450.00

RICHTER, GISELA M. A.   Kouroi Archaic Greek Youths: a Study of the Development of the Kouros Type in Greek Sculpture. London: Phaidon, 1970. 3rd edition; folio; xvi, 157 pages, 656 illustrations; original cloth, dust jacket.   Archaeologia Luxor-3897 1996 $450.00

RICHTER, GISELA M. A.   The Portraits of the Greeks. London: Phaidon, 1965-72. Folio; 3 volumes + supplement; xiii, 156 pages and figures 1-881; pages 157-251 with 20 illustrations and figures 882-1704; map, pages 252-337 and figures 1705-2059; supplement: 24 pages and 46 figures; original cloth, dust jackets with very light shelf wear, supplement in original printed wrappers.   Archaeologia Luxor-3899 1996 $1,250.00

RICHTER, GISELA M. A.   The Portraits of the Greeks. London: Phaidon Press, 1965. 31 x 22.5 cm; 3 volumes; pages xiii, 156; 157-251; 252-337; 2100 illustrations; original cloth, dust jackets, ex-library with rubber stamps in fronts, dust jacket slightly damaged by sellotape. Rainsford A54-495   1996 £240.00

RICHTER, GISELA M. A.   Red-Figured Athenian Vases in the Metropolitan Museum of Art. New Haven: Yale University Press, 1936. Limited to 500 sets; folio; 2 volumes; 249 pages, 34 figures, 181 plates; original cloth, corner lightly bumped, otherwise fine.   Archaeologia Luxor-3901 1996 $1,750.00

RICHTER, GISELA M. A.   The Sculpture and Sculptors of the Greeks. New Haven: Yale University Press, 1967. New revised edition; 8vo; xxxvi, 337 pages; 775 illustrations; original cloth, dust jacket, fine. Archaeologia Luxor-3903 1996 $100.00

RICHTER, J.   Flower, Fruit and Thorn Pieces. Leipzig: Tauchnitz, 1871. 1st edition thus (?); 2 volumes bound in 1; original binding, front hinge cracked, old tape repair; good; both titlepages signed by Nathaniel Hawthorne, with addditional note 'from his Wife/Jan. 5th, 1874/Dresden"; f.f.e.p. also signed by Hawthorne.   Charles Agvent 4-630 1996 $150.00

RICHTER, JEAN PAUL   The Golden Age of Classic Christian Art. London: 1904. Thick large 4to; xviii,4 28 pages; 52 plates (22 col., 124 black and white illustrations); buckram, top edge gilt.   Rainsford A54-497 1996 £150.00

RICKARDS, CONSTANTINE GEORGE   The Ruins of Mexico. London: H. E. Shrimpton, 1910. Folio; volume 1 (only); frontispiece, viii, 163 pages, 259 illustrations tipped in; original cloth, one corner bumped, worming, foxing.   Archaeologia Luxor-4816 1996 $100.00

RICKETSON, OLIVER G.   Uaxactun, Guatemala. Group E --- 1926-1931. Washington: Carnegie Inst. of Washington, 1937. 8vo; xiii, 314 pages, 198 figures, 88 plates, 1 folding map in pocket at rear; original printed wrappers, scarce; with stamp of J. A. Bennyhoff at foot of spine. Archaeologia Luxor-4817 1996 $275.00

RICKETSON, SHADRACH   Means of Preserving Health, and Preventing Diseases... New York: 1806. 1st edition; 12mo; 298 pages + ads; contemporary sheep, joints weak;   Argosy 810-415 1996 $400.00

RICKETT, HAROLD WILLIAM   Wild Flowers of the United States. Volume 1: the Northeastern States. New York: 1966. 1st edition; tall 4to; pages x, 559; 180 plates (with several colored photos) and many drawings; cloth, light soiling, slipcase (light soiling, minor dampstaining). Raymond M. Sutton VI-609 1996 $150.00

RICKETT, HAROLD WILLIAM   Wild Flowers of the United States: Volume Four - the Southwestern States. New York: McGraw Hill, n.d. 1970. Folio; 3 volumes; pages xii, 241; v, 242-519; v, 520-801, map endpapers, illustrations; ink note on titlepage, box slightly worn, books fine.   Dumont 28-119 1996 $325.00

RICKETTS, CHARLES 1866-1931   A Defence of the Revival of Printing. Vale Press, 1899. One fo 250 copies; 7 3/4 x 5 1/4 inches; 37, (1) pages, (1) leaf; prospectus for book laid in, very elaborate white on black woodcut border occupying most of first page of text, woodcut initial and evice at end; original paper boards, paper labels on front cover and spine, usual browning to endpapers, otherwise especially fine. Large woodcut bookplate of John Morgan, designed by Charles Ricketts. Phillip J. Pirages 33-493 1996 $750.00

RICKETTS, CHARLES 1866-1931   Dell'Arte della Stampa. Verona: Officina Bodoni, 1926. One of 125 copies; 8vo; vellum and marbled boards, spine slightly darkened, light scattered foxing, otherwise fine. Mardersteig 19.   Marilyn Braiterman 15-156 1996 $1,250.00

RICKETTS, CHARLES 1866-1931   Oscar Wilde, Recollections. Bloomsbury: Nonesuch Press, 1932. One of 800 numbered copies; typography by Francis Meynell; full pictorial cloth; fine.   Hermitage SP95-1056 1996 $225.00

RICKETTS, CHARLES 1866-1931   Oscar Wilde: Recollections by Jean Paul Raymond and Charles Ricketts. London: Nonesuch Press, 1932. One of 800 copies; 10 1/4 x 6 1/2 inches; 59, (1) pages, (2) leaves (blank, colophon); large woodcut device on title, original white cloth, covers with elaborate stylized decoration in gilt, including historiated panels, after designs by Ricketts, just a hint of fading to edges of cloth and very slight browning of endpapers, otherwise remarkably fine.   Phillip J. Pirages 33-402 1996 $400.00

RICKETTS, CHARLES 1866-1931   Pages from a Diary in Greece. Edinburgh: The Tragara Press, 1978. 1st edition; limited, number 36 of 150 copies; 8vo; blue cloth; as new.   Priscilla Juvelis 95/1-206 1996 $125.00

RICKETTS, CHARLES 1866-1931   Unrecorded Histories. London: Martin Secker, 1933. 1st edition; Limited to 950 copies; 8vo; pages 139; 6 full page silhouette illustrations in sepia; original sand buckram blocked in gold to Rickett's design, top edge gilt, others uncut, corners slightly bumped; very good.   Claude Cox 107-135 1996 £55.00

RICKMAN, PHILIP   Bird Sketches and some Field Observations. London: 1938. Limited to 250 copies, this number 122; large 4to; 2 colored plates, frontispiece mount has an original pencil sketch; pencil sketch plates, text illustrations; original quarter vellum, very light foxing to odd page, otherwise excellent.   David A.H. Grayling MY95Orn-63 1996 £350.00

RICKMAN, PHILIP   A Selection of Bird Paintings and Sketches and Nature and at the Same Time That It Agreeaby Entertains... 1979. Limited to 500 numbered copies, signed by artist; folio; 142 pages; color photographic portrait, 32 mounted color plates, 37 black and white pencil sketches; publisher's dark green half morocco gilt, spine gilt in 6 compartments, two of which are lettered, remaining 4 containing bird emblems, gilt edges, fine, preserved in original green cloth slipcase. Thomas Thorp 489-261 1996 £450.00

RICKMAN, PHILIP   A Selection of Bird Paintings and Sketches. London: 1979. Limited to 500 copies, signed by Rickman; this is number 116; folio; 32 fine tipped in color plates, approximately 60 pencil sketches; superbly bound in half oasis morocco, gilt motifs on spine, gilt borders, all edges gilt, cloth slipcase; mint.   David A.H. Grayling MY95Orn-62 1996 £650.00

RICORD, PHILIPPE   Practical Treatise On Venereal Diseases; or, Critical and Experimental Researches On Inoculation... New York: 1842. 1st American edition; tall 8vo; original embossed cloth, ex-library worn. GM 2381, 5202.   Argosy 810-416 1996 $200.00

RICORD, PHILIPPE   Traite complet des Maldies Veneriennes. Clinique Iconographique de l'Hopital des Veneriens. London: J. Rouvier, 1851. 1st edition; folio; vignette title, 66 hand colored lithographed plates, text somewhat foxed and bit browned and plates generally in good state; half black leather, bit scuffed and worn, flyleaf chipped, faint inscription of Dr. Wahlenberg on half title.   Maggs Bros. Ltd. 1190-492 1996 £1,100.00

RIDGEWAY, WILLIAM   The Early Age of Greece. Cambridge: Cambridge University Press, 1931. 2nd impression; 8vo; 2 volumes, frontispiece, xxviii, 1431 pages, 312 figures, lightly shelfworn dust jackets. Scarce.   Archaeologia Luxor-3905 1996 $200.00

RIDGWAY, BRUNILDE SISMONDO   The Severe Style in Greek Sculpture. Princeton: Princeton Universtiy Press, 1970. 4to; xviii, 155 pages, 189 illustrations; original cloth, torn dust jacket.   Archaeologia Luxor-3908 1996 $150.00

RIDING, LAURA 1901-   Collected Poems. London: Cassell and Co. Ltd., 1938. 1st edition; original binding, spine darkened, covers marked and rubbed, head and tail of spine and corners slightly bumped, top edge dusty and slightly soiled, prelims, edges and endpapers spotted, good; no dust jacket; obituary of author in Daily Telegraph and review of "First Awakenings" in Sunday Telegraph tipped in.   Ulysses 39-501 1996 £55.00

RIDLER, ANNE   Dies Natalis. Poems of Birth and Infancy. Oxford: Perpetua Press, 1980. 1st edition; 96/100 copies, signed by author and Vivian Ridler; 16mo; pages 21, (1); original fawn boards, front cover lettered in blue within blue and red borders, untrimmed, fine. Blackwell's B112-224 1996 £50.00

RIDLEY, MARK   A Short Treatise of Magneticall Bodies and Motions. London: Printed by Nicholas Okes, 1613. 1st edition; 2nd issue with errata on recto of leaf X3; small quarto; (14), 157, (1) pages; without initial and final blanks, engraved title by R. Elstrak, engraved portrait, 21 engravings, 2 maps, without volvelle on T1; bound by Elizabeth Greenhill in full red morocco, gilt single rule border on covers, gilt spine with raised bands, gilt board edges and turn-ins, all edges gilt, closely trimmed, cutting into a few lines of text, some headlines and catchwords, shaving a few platemarks, few leaves with very skillful paper restoration, overall very good. Very rare. Honeyman 2649; Sabin 71297; STC 21045.5. Wheeler Gift 86.   Heritage Book Shop 196-182 1996 $6,000.00

RIEFENSTAHL, LENI   Coral Gardens. London: 1978. 1st English edition; folio; color illustrations; dust jacket,   J. B. Muns 154-255 1996 $100.00

RIEFENSTAHL, LENI   Vanishing Africa. New York: 1982. 1st edition; folio; color illustrations, dust jacket.   J. B. Muns 154-257 1996 $125.00

RIGBY, ELIZABETH   A Residence on the Shores of the Baltic. London: John Murray, 1841. 1st edition; roayl 12mo; 2 volumes; viii, (294); vi, 286, (ii) pates, etched frontispieces; original cloth, some very slight wear, few faint marks, little turned, but nice set.   Ash Rare Books Zenzybyr-77 1996 £195.00

RIGGS, LYNN   Green Grow the Lilacs. New York: Limited Editions Club, 1954. Limited to 1500 copies, designed by Will Ransom and signed by the artist; quarto; 144 pages; 8 full page black and white lithographs by Thomas Hart Benton; blind embossed buckram with defective glassine dust jacket and slipcase; extremely fine.   Bromer Booksellers 90-5 1996 $250.00

RIGGS, STEPHEN R.   A Dakota-English Dictionary. Washington: 1890. x, 665 pages; decorated cloth, leather label, nice.   T. A. Swinford 49-971 1996 $100.00

RIGGS, STEPHEN R.   Model First Reader Wayawa Tokeheya, Prepared in English-Dakota. Chicago: Geo. Sherwood & Co., 1873. 1st edition; 12mo; 112 pages; illustrations; pictorial printed boards with black cloth spine, spine cloth worn, good to very good. 4 copies in NUC.   Robert F. Lucas 42-30 1996 $200.00

RIGGS, T. C.   Home Seekers Should Purchase Homes in the Northern Portion of San Joaquin County, California. Stockton: Daily Independent Print, 1887. 1st edition; 31, (1) pages; illustrations; original pink printed wrappers, bound into cloth covers with morocco spine label, fine. Rocq 13012.   Michael D. Heaston 23-65 1996 $300.00

THE RIGHT Of Electing Sheriffs of London and Middlesex, Briefly Stated and Declared. London: printed for R. Dew, 1682. Folio; 4 pages; uncut, disbound. Wing P3839.   H. M. Fletcher 121-53 1996 £65.00

RIGHTON, HENRY   Lord Leclerg, and Other Poems. London: 1865. 1st edition; 8vo; pages viii, 256; original green cloth, very good.   James Fenning 133-287 1996 £85.00

RILEY & SARGENT   Price Ten Cents. Multum In Paro, or, the Travelers' Companion, Containing Distance Tables To All Parts of the United States. Philadelphia: Riley & Sargent, ca. 1869-70. 1st edition; (3) pages; original printed yellow wrappers.   Michael D. Heaston 23-291 1996 $250.00

RILEY, E. BAXTER   Among Pauan Headhunters. Philadelphia: Lippincott, 1925. 1st U.S. edition; 316 pages, 50 black and white illustrations, 2 maps; grey pictorial cloth lightly marked and soiled; good+.   Antipodean 28-250 1996 $150.00

RILEY, ELIHU SAMUEL   "Stonewall Jackson" a Thesaurus of Anecdotes and Incidents in the Life of Lieut. General Thomas Jonathan Jackson, C.S.A. Annapolis: 1920. 1st edition; 203 pages; frontispiece; original cloth; near fine, scarce. Haynes 15717; not in Dornbusch or Nevins.   McGowan Book Co. 65-74 1996 $450.00

RILEY, JAMES WHITCOMB 1849-1916   Old-Fashioned Roses. London: Longmans, Green, 1888. 1st edition; 8vo; vellum backed cloth, very good in cloth slipcase; inscribed by author to Robert Carey in 1891 with 15 line poem.   Charles Agvent 4-971 1996 $325.00

RILEY, JAMES WHITCOMB 1849-1916   Old Fashioned Roses. London: Longmans, Green and Co., 1896. 16th edition; 12mo; frontispiece; original parchment backed blue cloth, blue label lettered in gilt, some light soiling and rubbing, endpapers and pages 82-3 are browned from offsetting from inserts (removed). Inscribed to Miss Marabel Rorison with two pleasant quatrains of verse in Hoosier dialect from author.   James Cummins 14-167 1996 $100.00

RILEY, JAMES WHITCOMB 1849-1916   An Old Sweetheart of Mine. Philadelphia: Bobbs Merrill Co., 1903. Reprint of 1902 edition; in variant binding not noted in Russo; bound in red cloth - as the first edition binding - with the colored halftone inlaid within oval border, but without white and orange stamping, spine has the title, author and publisher in white on spine, book fine, but there is some flaking of white lettering on spine, original glassine and box printed in red and green with Christy reproduction present and near fine, box showing bit of wear to edges. Priscilla Juvelis 95/1-208 1996 $150.00

RILING, RAY   The Powder Flask Book. New York: 1953. Large 4to; numerous illustrations; fine in protected dust jacket.   David A.H. Grayling 3/95-202 1996 £120.00

RILKE, RAINER MARIA 1875-1926   Duineser Elegien. Leipzig: Im Insel Verlag, 1923. True first edition, one of 100 copies only, from a total issue of 300, this one of 100 bound in leather; 8vo; full green morocco by publisher, gilt tooling in shape of lozenges, spine panelled, author and title in gilt on red morocco, red silk guards; spine trifle sunned, else fine.   Priscilla Juvelis 95/1-209 1996 $4,500.00

RILKE, RAINER MARIA 1875-1926   Duineser Elegien: Elegies from the Castle of Duino. Cranach Press, 1931. One of 230 copies on paper, signed by the translators, Vita and Edward Sackville West, (there were also 8 vellum copies); 10 x 6 1/2 inches; 132 pages, (1) leaf (colophon), with English and German on facing pages; decorative woodcut initials by Eric Gill; printed in red and black; original vellum backed paper boards, titled in gilt on spine, top edge gilt, other edges untrimmed, in fine folding cloth box with black morocco spine label, slight fading along top and bottom of covers, virtually pristine otherwise. Schroder p. 11.   Phillip J. Pirages 33-146 1996 $3,250.00

RILKE, RAINER MARIA 1875-1926   The Lay of the Love and Death of Cornet Christoph Rilke. Arion Press, 1983. One of 315 copies; 12 1/4 x 10 inches; (34) leaves, with English and German on facing pages; numerous illustrations by Warren Chappell, red initials; original brown cloth, paper label on front cover and spine, fore edge and tail edge untrimmed, mint.   Phillip J. Pirages 33-21 1996 $275.00

RIMBAUD, ARTHUR   Drunken Boat. Reading: Whiteknights Press, 1976. Limited to 300 copies, of which 100 were signed by Beckett, this one of 200 unsigned; 4to; cloth; near fine.   Antic Hay 101-146 1996 $100.00

RIMBAUD, ARTHUR   A Season in Hell. New York: Limited Editions Club, 1986. Limited Edition; quarto; 8 photogravures by Robert Mapplethorpe; full crushed red morocco in calf lined cloth slipcase; signed by translator, Paul Schmidt and by Mapplethorpe; fine.   Lame Duck Books 19-308 1996 $2,500.00

RIMMER, ALFRED   Ancient Stone Crosses of England. London: 1875. 1st edition; 159 pages; 75 illustrations on wood; attractive gilt cover with gold cross on dark green, small spine nick, otherwise very good+.   Middle Earth 77-378 1996 $135.00

RIMMER, ROBERT H.   The Harrad Experiment. Los Angeles: Sherbourne, 1966. 1st edition; corners slightly bumped, else fine in dust jacket, with very light wear.   Between the Covers 42-373 1996 $150.00

RIMMER, W.   Elements of Design. Book First. Boston: printed by John Wilson and Son, 1864. 1st edition; 8vo; 39 pages; author's first book; 36 inserted lithograph plates; paper boards, paper on front cover torn and chipped, cloth, worn.   Freedom Bookshop 14-15 1996 $125.00

RINEHART, MARY ROBERTS   The Bat. New York: Doran, 1926. 1st edition; fine in near fine dust jacket, bit soiled at top of spine. Striking copy.   Between the Covers 42-505 1996 $225.00

RING O'Roses. A Nursery Rhyme Picture Book. London: Warne, c. 1921. 4to; 32 color plates and black and white drawings by L Leslie Brooke; blue cloth, pictorially printed in red; fresh copy, scarce.   Barbara Stone 70-38 1996 £75.00

RINHART, FLOYD   American Daguerreian Art. New York: 1967. 1st edition; illustrations; dust jacket.   J. B. Muns 154-258 1996 $125.00

RINHART, FLOYD   American Miniature Case Art. South Brunswick & New York: A. S. Barnes and Co., 1969. 1st edition; 4to; 205 pages; 229 plates in color and black and white, very good illustrated dust jacket with few closed short tears, fine.   Andrew Cahan 47-43 1996 $200.00

RIPLEY, MARY CHURCHILL   The Oriental Rug Book. New York: Stokes, 1904. 1st edition; 8vo; (18), 310 pages; color frontispiece, full page plates, in text illustrations; original decorated red cloth, small spot at top of rear cover, otherwise tight, near fine.   Chapel Hill 94-19 1996 $100.00

RIPLEY, R. L.   Believe it or Not! Paul, 1928. 1st English edition; very good+/near fine in very good dust jacket chipped at dust jacket spine extremities, very scarce in dust jacket.   Aronovitz 57-991 1996 $150.00

RIPLEY, S. DILLON   Rails of the World. U.S.A.: 1977. Limited to 400 copies, signed by artist and author at rear; folio; 41 fine colored plates, distribution maps; half scarlet morocco, gilt, housed in morocco trimmed cloth sipcse. Fine.   David A.H. Grayling MY95Orn-64 1996 £400.00

RISK, R. T.　　Erhard Ratdolt, Master Printer. Francestown: Typographeum Francestown, 1982. One of 100 copies, signed by author; 9 3/4 x 6 1/2 inches; 55, (1) pages; woodcut device and narrow border on title, 4 facsimile plates (including frontispiece) printed on coated stock, decorative initials, title printed in red and black; original cloth backed paper boards, apper spine label, edges untrimmed; mint. Phillip J. Pirages　33-101　1996 $165.00

RISS, JACOB A.　　How the Other Half Lives. New York: Charles Scribner's Sons, 1891. 1st edition; 8vo; original blue cloth and illustrated boards, browned, some fraying of cloth and rubbing of boards, shaken, inner hinges started, lower portion of pages 13-16 torn out but laid in, slight soiling and browning.　James Cummins　14-166　1996 $175.00

RISTER, C. C.　　Border Captives, the Traffic in Prisoners by Southern Plains Indians 1835-1875. Norman: 1940. 1st edition; 220 pages; folded maps, very good+ in dust jacket.　T. A. Swinford　49-972　1996 $125.00

RISTER, C. C.　　The Southwestern Frontier 1865-1881. Cleveland: 1928. 1st edition; 336 pages, photos, maps; cloth; fine. Howes R317; Rader 2790; 6 Guns 2865.; Herd 1909.　T. A. Swinford　49-973　1996 $225.00

RITCH, WILLIAM G.　　Illustrated New Mexico. Santa Fe: New Mexican Printing and Publishing Co., 1883. 4th edition; 140, (1) pages; frontispiece, plates; original printed tan wrappers; neatly rebacked, some chipping, very good; scarce; Graff 3513; Adams Herd 1910 for 3rd ed. Michael D. Heaston　23-273　1996 $300.00

RITCHIE, JAMES　　The Influence of Man on Animal Life in Scotland. Cambridge: University Press, 1920. 1st edition; 8vo; pages xvi, 550, 90 illustrations, 8 maps; original cloth, gilt.　R.F.G. Hollett　76-256　1996 £85.00

RITCHIE, LEITCH　　Scott and Scotland. London: Longman, Rees, etc., 1835. 8vo; pages viii, 256, 21 engraved plates; full panelled scarlet morocco gilt, little rubbed, some browning, front free endpaper lacking, all edges gilt.　R.F.G. Hollett　76-257　1996 £85.00

RITCHIE, THOMAS EDWARD　　An Account of the Life and Writings of David Hume, Esq. London: printed for T. Cadell and W. Davies, 1807. 1st edition; 8vo; 520 pages; contemporary half calf, rubbed, label. Anthony W. Laywood　108-225　1996 £245.00

RITNER, WILLIAM D.　　Juan, the White Slave; and the Rebel Planter's Daughter. Philadelphia: Barclay, 1865. 2nd edition; 8vo; 97, (1) pages, extensively illustrated; front wrapper illustrations repeated in black and original colored pictorial front wrapper, some fraying and browning. Wright II 2051, note, recording 1 copy of 1857 ed. under variant title M & S Rare Books　60-222　1996 $275.00

RITSON, JOSEPH　　Ancient Popular Poetry from Authentic Manuscripts and Old Printed Copies. Edinburgh: privately printed by Goldschmid, 1884. One of 275 copies; 12mo; 2 volumes, pages 73, 71, glossary; titlepage in red and black; vellum ppaper covers, fine laid watermarked Whatman paper, uncut; nice set. CBEL II 958.　Hartfield　48-V41　1996 $165.00

RITSON, JOSEPH　　Gammer Gurton's Garland, or, the Nursery Parnassus. Edinburgh: printed by R. Clark, Glasgow: Hugh Hopkins, 1866. One of 12 large paper copies, with 100 small paper copies published at the same time; 4to; 61 pages; each of the four parts with decorative headings and tailpieces, decorative initials; early half calf, marbled boards, gilt lettering to spine, extremities worn, endpapers foxed, else very good.　Marjorie James　19-186　1996 £175.00

RITSON, JOSEPH　　The Office of Bailiff of a Liberty. London: printed by A. Strahan..for J. Butterworth, etc., 1811. 80 pages; later(?) defective wrappers, otherwise very fresh and uncut.　Meyer Boswell　SL26-200　1996 $350.00

RITSON, JOSEPH　　Pieces of Ancient Popular Poetry. London: printed by C. Clarke for T. and J. Egerton, 1791. 1st edition; 186 x 123mm; pages (xiv), 135, 16; 15 woodcuts; brown cloth gilt boards, black roan half calf with spine highly decorated in gilt, all edges gilt, spine and corners rubbed, else near fine. Grant Collection 1231; Hugo 58. Marjorie James　19-187　1996 £275.00

RITSOS, YANNIS　　Return and other Poems. Alabama: Parallel Editions, 1983. 1st bi-lingual edition, one of 90 copies signed by author and artist; thin 4to; woodcuts by Sidney Chafetz; quarter leather, boards; as new. James S. Jaffe　34-598　1996 $150.00

RITTENHOUSE, JACK D.　　The Santa Fe Trail, a Historical Bibliography. Albuqerque: 1971. 1st edition; 271 pages; cloth; near fine in slightly worn, very slightly chipped, price clipped dust jacket.　Gene W. Baade 1094-134　1996 $135.00

RITTENHOUSE, JACK D.　　The Santa Fe Trail - a Historical Bibliography. Albuquerque: 1971. 1st edition; 271 pages; nice indust jacket.　T. A. Swinford　49-974　1996 $125.00

RITTENHOUSE, JACK D.　　The Santa Fe Trail: a Historical Bibliography. Albuquerque: University of New Mexico, 1971. 1st edition; fine in dust jacket.　Parker Books of the West 30-155　1996 $100.00

RIVERS, GEORGE PITT, 1ST BARON　　Letters to a Young Nobelman, Upon Various Subjects, Particularly on Government and Civil Liberty. London: J. Robson, 1784. (2), lxii, (2), 364 pages, lacks half title; contemporary calf, red label; nice.　C. R. Johnson　37-66　1996 £550.00

RIVES, JUDITH PAGE WALKER　　Tales and Souvenirs of a Residence in Europe. Philadelphia: Lea and Blanchard, 1842. 1st edition; 12mo; 301, (15) pages; publisher's green gilt cloth; text foxed, few signatures detached, bookplate.　The Bookpress　75-456　1996 $150.00

RIVIERE, LAZARE 1589-1655　　The Practice of Physick. London: F. Streater, 1678. 8vo; portraits, complete copy, despite erratic pagination; new quarter calf with raised bands and marbled boards, quite nice. James Tait Goodrich　K40-249　1996 $995.00

RIVIERE, R. B.　　A History of the Birds of Norfolk. London: 1930-32. 8vo; pages xlviii, 296, large folding colored map and plates; this copy contains the extra page 58a issued in Jan. 1932; original cloth, spine faded under dust jacket.　Wheldon & Wesley　207-839　1996 £70.00

RIVOIRA, G. T.　　Lombardic Architecture, its Origin, Development and Derivatives. London: William Heinemann, 1910. 1st edition; folio; 2 volumes; frontispiece, x, (ii), 250, (1); frontispiece, (viii), 368 pages; over 800 illustrations; cloth, bookplates, lightly rubbed, else very good.　The Bookpress　75-229 1　1996 $225.00

RIVOIRA, G. T.　　Roman Architecture and Its Principles of Construction Under the Empire. Oxford: Clarendon Press, 1925. 4to; frontispiece, xxvi, 310 pages; 358 illustrations; original cloth.　Archaeologia　Luxor-3911 1996 $250.00

ROACH, ALVA C.　　The Prisoner of War, and How Treated. Indianapolis: Railroad City Pub. House, 1865. 1st edition; 220 pages; original cloth, rubbed, scuffing to extremities, neatly rebacked and recased, good, scarce. Coulter 394; Dornbusch I, Indiana 138; Howes R334; Nevins I 200.　McGowan Book Co.　65-79　1996 $225.00

ROBACK, C. W.　　The Mysteries of Astrology, and the Wonders of Magic. Boston: Author, 1854. 1st edition; 238 pages; illustrations; nicely rebound, cloth, very good.　Middle Earth　77-137　1996 $245.00

ROBB, JOHN S.　　Streaks of Squatter Life, and Far-West Scenes. Philadelphia: Carey and Hart, 1847. 1st edition; 12mo; 187 pages; 8 plates by Darley, lacks binding, but sound. Howes R335; Wright I 2126; Hamilton 594 (calling for 8 plates).　M & S Rare Books　60-223　1996 $250.00

ROBBINS, GUY　　The Breast. Austin: 1984. 1st edition; 4to; 357 pages; original binding, dust jacket.　W. Bruce Fye　71-1780　1996 $100.00

ROBBINS, TOM　　Another Roadside Attraction. Garden City: Doubleday, 1971. 1st edition; author's first book; fine in very good dust jacket with minor creasing and soiling, very tiny chips to front corners.　Bella Luna 7-488　1996 $600.00

ROBBINS, TOM　　Another Roadside Attraction. Garden City: Doubleday & Co., 1971. 1st edition; fine in near fine dust jacket, minor rubbing and creasing of jacket at top and bottom of spine, otherwise truly fine specimen of author's first book.　Oracle Books　1-271　1996 $450.00

ROBBINS, TOM　　Skinny Legs and All. New York: Bantam, 1990. 1st edition; fine in fine dust jacket and signed by author.　Ken Lopez 74-301　1996 $100.00

ROBBINS, TOM   Still Life with Woodpecker. New York: Bantam Books, 1980. 1st edition; x, 277 pages; tan cloth, fine in fine dust jacket, signed by author.   Orpheus Books   17-211   1996 $140.00

ROBBINS, TOM   Still Life with Woodpecker. New York: Bantam, 1980. 1st edition; fine in fine dust jacket, signed by author.   Bella Luna 7-493   1996 $125.00

ROBERT LA DIABLE   Robert the Devil. Iowa City: Windhover Press, 1981. One of 310 copies, this one of 260; 13 x 8.75 inches; black and white wood engravings by Roxanne Sexauer; title on titlepage in red, printed in black on handmade Windhover; cream cloth boards, printed title label on spine; erratum laid in, fine.   Joshua Heller   21-285   1996 $125.00

ROBERT, of Gloucester fl. 1260-1300   Robert of Gloucester's Chronicle. Oxford: printed at the Theater, 1724. 8vo; 2 volumes; xciv, (ii), 364; (365)-800 pages; contemporary panelled calf, spines decorated gilt, labels; lightly rubbed, spines slightly chipped at head, little dampstaining in volume 1, insignificant marginal worming; nice set, according to old note on front endpaper "The Beckford copy".   Robert Clark   38-59   1996 £120.00

ROBERT, of Gloucester fl. 1260-1300   Metrical Chronicle of Robert of Gloucester. London: 1887. 8vo; 2 volumes; pages 1060; original cloth.   Howes Bookshop   265-1600   1996 £60.00

ROBERT, the Hermit   Life and Adventures of Robert; the Hermit of Massachusetts, Who Has Lived Fourteen Years in a Cave... Providence: H. Trumbell, 1829. 1st edition; unprinted blue wrappers, as issued, neatly colored frontispiece, several very small tears and nicks at extremities and some splitting along saddle stitched spine, still nice, very good plus, uncommon.   Between the Covers   43-407   1996 $550.00

ROBERTS, AUSTIN   The Mammals of South Africa. London: 1951. Large thick 4to; many colored plates, charts, maps; fine in new green buckram.   David Grayling   J95Biggame-163   1996 £75.00

ROBERTS, B. H.   The Missouri Persecutions. Salt Lake city: George Q. Cannon Publishers, 1900. Presumed 1st edition; 333 pages; cloth, very good.   Metacomet Books   54-92   1996 $165.00

ROBERTS, B. H.   The Rise and Fall of Nauvoo. Salt Lake City: Deseret News, 1900. Presumed 1st edition; 457 pages; cloth, owner's name on endpaper, touch of wear on spine, otherwise very good.   Metacomet Books   54-93   1996 $165.00

ROBERTS, DAVID   The Holy Land. Paris & New York: Cassell, Petter, Galpin, 1879-84. Small folio; 11 pages, 120 lithographic plates; three quarter morocco, 5 raised bands and marbled endpapers, top edge gilt, rubbed, light scattered foxing to first few pages.   Archaeologia Luxor-2647   1996 $1,250.00

ROBERTS, EMMA   Hindostan Its Landscapes, Palaces, Temples, Tombs, The Shores of the Red Sea and the Sublime and Romantic Scenery of the Himalaya Mountains Illustrated in a Series of Views Drawn by Turner, Stanfield, Prout, Cattermole, Roberts, Allom, etc... London: Peter Jackson, Late Fisher Son & Co., the Caxton Press...n.d. ca. 1840's. 4to; 2 volumes in 1; frontispiece to both volumes, 96 steel engraved plates, text 5-104 pages and 5-128 pages; previous owner's ink signature on front f.e.p., booksellers ticket to front pastedown; full blue morocco, gilt tooling to panelled spine, red morocco label to spine, gilt tool scrolled borders, corners bumped and worn, joints tender, previous owner's ink signature booksellers ticket to front pastedown, hinges cracked, plates all in good condition with no offsetting or foxing, some slight offsetting of frontispiece to vignette title.   Beeleigh Abbey BA/56-109   1996 £250.00

ROBERTS, KATE   Two Old Men and Other Stories. Newtown: Gwasg Gregynog, 1981. Part of a printing of 265 copies (15 on handmade paper by Wookey Hole Mill with frontispiece hand colored, 250 on Zerkall mould made paper); out of series copy, specially signed by artist; 10 1/2 x 7 inches; xi, (1), 80 pages, (1) leaf (colophon); frontispiece in 2 colors, each of the six stories with plate in two colors, title vignettes, headpieces, other illustrations, all by Kyffin Williams; title partly printed in blue-grey; a flamboyant expressionistic inlaid binding of gray morocco by Paul Delrue, front cover with long worm shaped orange inlays, back cover with large black onlaid irregularly shaped patches (themselves decorated with several light brown onlaid slivers), front cover highlighted with very many thin black onlays, top edge of text block delightfully painted in complementary colors (giving the impression of a landscape), other edges untrimmed, in very fine folding cloth box, partly lined with matching morocco, similar onlaid morocco spine label; very fine.   Phillip J. Pirages   33-265   1996 $1,950.00

ROBERTS, KATE   Two Old Men and Other Stories. Newtown: Gwasg Gregynog, 1981. One of 250 numbered copies on Zkerall; tall 8vo; printed in 14 pt. Monotype Bembo in black and grey; half black morocco, grey cloth sides with pictorial decoration set into upper cover, linocut endpapers; fine.   Bertram Rota   272-209   1996 £100.00

ROBERTS, KENNETH   Boon Island. Garden City: Doubleday, 1956. Special presentation edition, signed on tipped in page; green boards and beige cloth, fine as issued.   Bev Chaney, Jr.   23-584   1996 $100.00

ROBERTS, KENNETH   Henry Gross and His Dowsing Rod. 1951. 1st edition; (8), 310, (3) pages; very good; 2 news clippings tipped in; with TLS by Roberts discussing dowsing.   Bookworm & Silverfish   276-180   1996 $125.00

ROBERTS, KENNETH   March to Quebec: Journals of the Members of Arnold's Expedition. Garden City: Doubleday Doran, 1938. 1st edition; tiny tear at top of titlepage, else fine in near fine dust jacket with two neat internal repairs and little soiling, nice.   Between the Covers   42-376   1996 $125.00

ROBERTS, KENNETH   Northwest Passage. Garden City: Doubleday, 1937. 1st edition; fine in just about fine dust jacket with two tiny chips; inscribed by author.   Bev Chaney, Jr.   23-584   1996 $165.00

ROBERTS, KENNETH   Northwest Passage. New York: Doubleday, Doran and Co., 1937. 1/1050 copies, numbered and signed by author; 2 volumes; top edge gilt, dust jackets very lightly sunned on spines, housed in fine slipcase; very fine copies.   Left Bank Books   2-126   1996 $275.00

ROBERTS, LORD   Forty-One Years in India. From Subaltern to Commander-in-Chief. London: Richard Bentley & Son, 1897. Later edition, issued same year as the first; 8vo; 2 volumes, 511, 522 pages; frontispieces, plates, maps, 3 folding battle plans; original blue cloth, spine ends worn, corners bumped, else very good.   Chapel Hill   94-234   1996 $100.00

ROBERTS, MICHAEL   New Country - Prose and Poetry by the Authors of New Signatures. London: 1933. One of 1200 copies; original binding, top edge slightly dusty, free endpapers partially browned, head and tail of spine slightly bumped, edges and endpapers spotted, very good in nicked, rubbed, spotted and dusty dust jacket darkened at spine and edges.   Ulysses   39-299   1 996 £150.00

ROBERTS, ROBERT   The House Servant's Directory, or a Monitor for Private Families. New York: Charles S. Francis, 1827. 1st edition; 12mo; 180 pages; original muslin backed marbled boards, printed paper label (chipped), fine, uncut, very rare thus. Lincoln Lowenstein 95; Rink 212; Shoemaker 30585.   M & S Rare Books   60-311   1996 $3,500.00

ROBERTS, S. C.   The Evolution of Cambridge Publishing. Cambridge: Cambridge University Press, 1956. 1st edition; 14 black and white plates; decorated cloth gilt, fine in slightly marked and dusty, price clipped dust jacket browned at spine and edges; loosely inserted publisher's compliments slip; fromt he library of James Hart.   Ulysses   39-504   1996 £55.00

ROBERTS, W.   Catalogue of the Collection of Pictures Formed by John H. McFadden, Esq. of Philadelphia, Pa. London: Chiswick Press, 1917. Limited editon, number 37 of 100 copies signed by McFadden; 32 x 26 cm; x, 90 pages, frontispiece, 43 plates; half terracotta morocco, top edge gilt, 2 line panel and centres by Riviere, cloth sides slightly marked, joints slightly weak.   Rainsford   A54-400   1996 £150.00

ROBERTS, WILLIAM   Memoirs of the Life and Correspondence of Mrs. Hannah More. London: 1835. 3rd edition; 8vo; 4 volumes; portrait; choicely bound in half polished red morocco, gilt tops, gilt spine.   Charles W. Traylen   117-170   1996 £250.00

ROBERTSON, BYRAN   Jackson Pollock. New York: Abrams, 1960. Square 4to; 215 pages, 169 illustrations, many tipped in, 36 in color; cloth, dust jacket. Freitag 7657.   Brannan   43-543   1996 $450.00

ROBERTSON, HENRY   A General View of the Natural History of the Atmosphere an Of Its Connection with the Sciences of Medicine and Agriculture. Edinburgh: Laing, et al, 1808. 1st edition; 8vo; 2 volumes; xvi, 403; vii, 406 pages; later three quarter calf over marbled boards, red morocco spine labels, fine. Blocker p. 339.   Edwin V. Glaser   121-265   1996 $400.00

ROBERTSON, J. C.   Materials for the History of Thomas Becket. London: 1876-85. 8vo; volumes II-VII (of 7 volumes); original cloth. Howes Bookshop   265-1592   1996 £145.00

ROBERTSON, JAMES   General View of the Agriculture in the County of Perth; with Observations on the Means of Its Improvement. Perth: printed by order of the Board of Agriculture,, 1799. 1st edition; 8vo; perforation and cancellation stamp on blank verso of title; contemporary half calf, rubbed, hinges cracked, library shelf mark on spine, label. Goldsmith 17575.   Anthony W. Laywood   109-123   1996 £90.00

ROBERTSON, JOHN W.   Francis Drake and Other Early Explorers Along the Pacific Coast. San Francisco: Grabhorn Press, 1927. One of 1000 copies; 26 x 17.5 cm; 290 pages; 28 maps, vellum spine, paper over boards, bit of darkening to spine, slipcase worn; this copy with warm inscription by author for Owen D. Young Jr.   Parmer Books 039/Nautica-039148   1996 $450.00

ROBERTSON, JOSEPH   An Essay on Punctuation. London: printed for J. Walter, 1786. 2nd edition; 12mo; contemporary half calf, gilt spine, bookplate, very good. Alston III 574.   Jarndyce   103-330   1996 £85.00

ROBERTSON, MANNING   Dun Laoghaire: the History, Scenery and Developemtn of the District. 1936. 1st edition; 8vo; maps, photos; cloth, very good; signed presentation copy to Eleanor Butler, loose insert, 3 page ALS to her husband from a friend discussing architectural education.   C. P. Hyland   216-724   1996 £100.00

ROBERTSON, MERLE GREENE   The Sculpture of Palenque. Princeton: Princeton University Press, 1983-91. Large 4to; volumes I-IV; xxix, 115 pages, 349 illustrations, 3 maps; xiii, 84 pages, 296 illustrations; xvii, 131 pages, 435 illustrations; xv, 90 pages, 286 illustrations, 3 maps; original cloth, dust jackets. Inscribed by author.   Archaeologia Luxor-4837 1996 $1,250.00

ROBERTSON, W. GRAHAM   Gold, Frankincense and Myrrh and Other Pageants for a Baby Girl. London: Bodley Head, 1908. 1st edition; 4to; 12 colored woodcut plates by author; blue pictorial cloth, fresh copy. Barbara Stone   70-180   1996 £75.00

ROBERTSON, WILLIAM 1721-1793   An Historical Disquisition Concerning the Knowledge Which the Ancients Had of India... Philadelphia: printed by Wm. Young, 1792. 8vo; pages viii, 13-420; new quarter calf, red label. Evans 24752. Cox I p. 304.   Richard Adelson W94/95-142   1996 $185.00

ROBERTSON, WILLIAM 1721-1793   The Works... Chiswick: printed by C. Whittingham for Thomas Tegg, 1824. 12mo; additional titlepages, with wood engraved illustrations; contemporary green calf by R. Storr, Grantham, with his ticket on each rear pastedown, smooth backstrips, divided into compartments by narrow gilt rolls, polished morocco title label in third compartment, volume label in fifth, square foliage and flower ornaments in first and seventh, second, fourth and sixth with rope rolls and trellis pointille rolls, marbled boards lightly rubbed, endapers and edges, blank endleaves foxed, excellent.   Blackwell's B112-243 1996 £250.00

ROBERTSON, WILLIAM d. 1686   (Hebrew title) A Gate or Door to the Holy Tongue, Opened in English. London: Flesher for Cranford, 1653. 1st edition; 8vo; Hebrew and English; calf, front cover detached but present; ownership signatures on titlepage, one dated 1653. Wing R1612 cites variant; CBEL I 376 cites 1654 ed.   Rostenberg & Stern 150-28 1996 $450.00

ROBICSEK, FRANCIS   The May Book of the Dead; the Ceramic Codex. The Corpus of Codex Style Ceramics of the Late Classic Period. Norman: University of Oklahoma Press, 1981. Folio; xxi, 257 pages, 90 figures, 161 illustrations, 27 tables; original cloth.   Archaeologia Luxor-4842 1996 $200.00

ROBICSEK, FRANCIS   The Smoking Gods: Tobacco in Maya Art, History and Religion. Norman: University of Oklahoma Press, 1978. 4to; xxv, 233 pages, 234 figures, 265 color plates; original cloth, torn dust jacket.   Archaeologia Luxor-4843 1996 $150.00

ROBIN HOOD   Five Ballads about Robin Hood. Birmingham: The Vincent Press, 1899. Limited to 210 copies; octavo; 39 pages; calligraphic lettering, five black and white illustrations; limp vellum with green ribbon ties, very faint offsetting from ribbon ties, else fine. Tomkinson 175.   Bromer Booksellers 87-275   1996 $450.00

ROBIN HOOD   Robin Hood's Garland: Being a Complete History of All the Notable and Merry Exploits Performed by Him and His Men on Many Occasions. Kidderminster: printed at the Office of G. Gower, 17--? 12mo; 96 pages light marginal pencil marks, 31 fine woodcuts; original printed self wrappers bound into green calf backed marbled boards, with 2 raised bands, title vertically in gilt along a burgundy leather label on spine, original wrappers soiled and darkened, slightly chipped along front edge, 1 1/2 inch vertical tear along bottom of inner edge affecting 1 word. Armorial bookplate of James Wyllie Guild. Rare.   Blue Mountain SP95-40   1996 $750.00

ROBIN HOOD   Robin Hood. A Collection of all the Antient Poems, Songs, and Ballads, Now Extant Relative to that Celebrated English Outlaw... London: T. Egerton and J. Johnson, 1795. 1st edition; 8vo; 2 volumes, half titles present, wood engraved head and tailpieces, by Thomas and John Bewick, K1 volume 2 torn with loss of text, first gathering of volume 2 starting; pages (iv), cxviii, (ii), 167; (viii), 220, (4); contemporary quarter blue roan, slight loss at head of backstrip of volume i, joints rubbed, smooth backstrips divided by gilt rules and open twist rolls, gilt lettered direct in second and fourth compartments, vellum tipped marbled boards, crest and name of 'P. Gell' printed on front pastedowns, with ms. note below 'given by my Brother Dec. 2nd 1795' in both volumes, endpapers and binder's blanks lightly foxed, blue speckled edges, very good. Hugo 86.   Blackwell's B112-244 1996 £450.00

ROBINSON Jeffers. Ave, 1887; Vale, 1962. San Francisco: Printed by the Grabhorn Press, 1962. 1st edition; one of 250 copies; quarto; 30, (2) pages, printed in red and black; original cream wrappers, lettered on front cover, two minor staple rust marks on front cover, else fine. Grabhorn 637.   Argonaut Book Shop   113-374   1996 $150.00

ROBINSON, ALAN JAMES   Cheloniidae Sea Turtles. Easthampton: Cheloniidae Press, 1987. 1st edition; one of 15 copies only, with 2 original watercolors (not called for), from a total issue of 41 copies; with an extra suite of etchings & wood engravings hand watercolored by Robinson in special binding (this copy) and 26 regular copies; page size 14 7/8 x 11 inches; on Rives BFK and Japanes Moriki paper, 7 etchings pulled by Greta Lintvedt on green Jap. Moriki w/Moriki tissue guards; bound by Daniel Kelm, green morocco and beige linen with sculpture of a sea turtle after a wax sculpture by Robinson and cast in paper by Sara Krohn of the Paper Route mounted on front panel on green morocco panel, green morocco spine, endpapers of Japanese green moriki paper; cloth portfolio to house extra suite by Claudia Cohen, matching clamshell box in green paper and linen by Peter Geraty and Linda Lembke;   Priscilla Juvelis   95/1-211 1996 $3,000.00

ROBINSON, ALAN JAMES   An Odd Bestiary. Easthampton: Cheloniidae Press, 1982. One of 6 copies only, the Artist's Proof edition, from a total of 306 copies; page size 13 1/2 x 9 3/4 inches; printed in Centaur and Arrighi, text set monotype by Mackenzie-Harris with some handsetting by Arthur Larson; 26 initial linecuts and 26 woodengravings; with extra suites and original calligraphy plus alphabet hand lettered in red around colophon; full red morocco with title title blindstamped on smooth spine and Cheloniidae logo and "ABC" in blind enclosed in blind rule with another blind rule along outside edge on upper panel and "XYZ" and three blind rules on lower panel, pastepaper guards in brown/red; suites housed in two matching morocco backed portfolios, all housed in morocco and cloth clamshell box.   Priscilla Juvelis 95/1-55 1996 $3,500.00

ROBINSON, ALAN JAMES   Roadkills. Easthampton: Cheloniidae Press, 1981. Signed, limited edition, one of 250 copies each signed and numbered by the artist from a total edition of 300; 4to; printed on handmade Japanese paper; etching and 11 wood engravings by Robinson, text handset in 18pt. Arrighi and Centaur letterpress; bound by Gray Parrot in quarter grey Moroccan goat and Japanese paper in custom quarter leather clamshell box.   Priscilla Juvelis 95/1-56 1996 $750.00

ROBINSON, BERT   The Basket Weavers of Arizona. Albuquerque: University of New Mexico, 1954. 1st edition; 73 black and white and 14 color plates; very good in good+ dust jacket.   Parker Books of the West 30-156   1996 $175.00

ROBINSON, CHARLES N.   Old Naval Prints/Their Artists and Engravers. London: The Studio Ltd. 1924. One of 1500 copies; 12 x 9.5 inches; 36 pages, text plus 96 plates, 24 tipped in color plates with tissue guards; gilt decorated blue cloth, very good with occasional light foxing. Parmer Books 039/Nautica-047064 1996 $650.00

ROBINSON, DANIEL   Practical Suggestions for the Reclamation of Waste Lands, and Improvement in the condition of the Agricultural Population of Ireland. London: Darling and son, n.d. 1846. 1st edition; 8vo; 16 pages; disbound.   Anthony W. Laywood 109-124 1996 £100.00

ROBINSON, DAVID M.   Excavations at Olynthus. Part IV: The Terracottas of Olynthus Found in 1928. Baltimore: Johns Hopkins Press, 1936. 4to; frontispiece, xii, 105 pages, 62 plates; later buckram, marginal soiling to 3 plates, otherwise fine.   Archaeologia Luxor-3776 1996 $250.00

ROBINSON, DAVID M.   Excavations at Olynthus, Part VIII: The Hellenic House. Baltimore: Johns Hopkins Press, 1938. 4to; frontispiece, xxi, 370 pages, 33 figures, 110 plates; later buckram.   Archaeologia Luxor-3777 1996 $450.00

ROBINSON, DAVID M.   Excavations at Olynthus, Part X: Metal and Minor Miscellaneous Finds... Baltimore: Johns Hopkins Press, 1941. 4to; xxvii, 593 pages; 172 plates; later buckram.   Archaeologia Luxor-3778 1996 $450.00

ROBINSON, DOANE   South Dakota Stressing the Unique and Dramatic in South Dakota History. Chicago: 1930. 1st edition; 3 volumes, 651, 524, 524 pages; frontispiece, illustrations, photos; cloth, nice, scarce.   T. A. Swinford 49-980 1996 $275.00

ROBINSON, DR.   Magistrate's Pocket-Book; or an Epitome of the Duties and Practice of a Justice of the Peace, Out of Sessions. London: 1837. 2nd edition; 8vo; xviii, 466, (40) pages; old mellow calf, title label inset on red morocco; very good; with bookplate of A. & F. Renier and lettered in gilt on front board J. Hussey.   K Books 442-417 1996 £60.00

ROBINSON, EDWIN ARLINGTON 1869-1935   Dionysus in Doubt. New York: Macmillan, 1925. 1st edition; fine in dust jacket;   Between the Covers 42-378 1996 $125.00

ROBINSON, EDWIN ARLINGTON 1869-1935   Merlin. New York: Macmillan, 1917. 1st edition; 1st issue; fine in unprinted fragile brown paper dust jacket, splitting along front flap, otherwise near fine. Between the Covers 42-377 1996 $125.00

ROBINSON, F.   The War of the Worlds. Robinson, 1914. 1st edition; wrappers, small chip to head of spine and 2 small chips to fore edge of upper rear cover, otherwise very good. Very scarce.   Aronovitz 57-994 1996 $175.00

ROBINSON, FRANCIS KILDALE   A Glossary of Yorkshire Words and Phrases, Collected in Whitby and the Neighbourhood. London: John Russell Smith, 1855. Half title, 2 pages ads; original brown cloth, spine slightly rubbed at head, very good; bookplate of Signet Library. Jarndyce 103-101 1996 £60.00

ROBINSON, FRANCIS KILDALE   A Glossary of Yorkshire Words and Phrases. London: John Russell Smith, 1855. 1st edition; post 12mo; (2), x, 204, 16 pages; original cloth, just slightly worn and sunned, good copy nonetheless, with booklabel of Edwin Turnbull, also of Whitby. Ash Rare Books Zenzybyr-78 1996 £65.00

ROBINSON, HENRY CRABB   Diary, Reminiscences and Correspondence... London: Macmillan and Co., 1869. 2nd edition; 8vo; 3 volumes; portrait; original green cloth, inner hinges tender; very good set. Bentley Blake Books 2535; CBEL III 1301.   Ximenes 109-248 1996 $100.00

ROBINSON, JACOB   Wrestling and Wrestlers: Biographical Sketches of Celebrated Atheletes of the Northern Ring. London: Bemrose & Sons, 1893. 8vo; pages xlvii, 251, 2 woodcut headpieces; little scattered foxing, but excellent copy; inscribed by F. Nicholson for R. W. Thompson. R.F.G. Hollett & Son 78-649 1996 £120.00

ROBINSON, JOHN   An Account of Sueden: Together with an Extract of the History of that Kingdom. London: printed for Tim. Goodwin, 1711. 2nd edition; small 8vo; pages (8), 85, (3 ads), including half title; recent paper wrpaper; very good, including half title.   James Fenning 133-289 1996 £85.00

ROBINSON, JOHN   Elements of Mechanical Philosophy, Being the Substance of a Course of Lectures on that Science. Edinburgh: Archibald Constable & Co., 1804. 8vo; 696 pages; 22 folding plates; full leather, rebacked original leather spine and raised bands laid down, corners worn to boards, bookplate, light stains to fore-edge margin of some plates and plates, very occasional foxing, interior joints strengthened with tape, otherwise good, clean solid copy.   Knollwood Books 70-171 1996 $140.00

ROBINSON, JOHN   A Guide to the Lakes, in Cumberland, Westmorland and Lancashire. London: printed for Lackington, Hughes, Harding, Mavor and Jones, 1819. 1st edition; 8vo; pages x, 328, folding map frontispiece, hand colored in outline, 20 uncolored aquatints; contemporary half calf, gilt with marbled boards, little scraped; new endpapers, otherwise very good.   R.F.G. Hollett & Son 78-1245 1996 £160.00

ROBINSON, JOHN   A Guide to the Lakes, in Cumberland, Westmorland and Lancashire... London: printed for Lackington, Hughes, Harding, Mavor and Jones, 1819. 1st edition; 8vo; pages x, 328, folding map frontispiece, hand colored in outline, 20 uncolored aquatints, map little offset on to title, few scattered spots; contemporary full calf, gilt, boards scraped, spine rather chipped. Bicknell 89.1.   R.F.G. Hollett & Son 78-1246 1996 £160.00

ROBINSON, P. F.   Designs fro Ornamental Villas. London: Henry G. Bohn, 1836. 3rd edition; 4to; 43 pages + plates; lithographed and printed titlepages, 96 lithographed and engraved plates; original gilt stamped green cloth, front free endpaepr lacking, some foxing, else very good. Chapel Hill 94-27 1966 $200.00

ROBINSON, PERCY J.   Toronto During the French Regime: the History of Toronto Region from Brule to Simcoe, 1615-1793. Toronto: Ryerson Press and Chicago: Unviersty of Chicago Press, 1933. Limited to 500 numbered copies; 8vo; pages xx, 254, illustrations, maps; original gilt cloth; signed by author, fine in soiled and scuffed dust jacket.   Hugh Anson-Cartwright 87-430 1996 $150.00

ROBINSON, ROBERT   Bremers and Their Kin in Germany and Texas. Wichita Falls: 1977. 1st edition; 4to; 2 volumes; 1630 pages, over 2000 photos; inscribed and signed.   W. M. Morrison 436-346 1996 $350.00

ROBINSON, ROBERT   Thomas Bewick, His Life and Times. Newcasatle: printed for R. Robinson, 1887. 1st edition; 4to; xl, 328 pages; 27 plates, numerous wood engraved text illustrations; publisher's green cloth, paper label, edges uncut, binding soiled and somewhat worn, internally good, just a trace of foxing and few thumb marks, some neat pencil annotation.   Thomas Thorp 489-29 1996 £80.00

ROBINSON, S.   Facts for Farmers; Also for the Family Circle. New York: 1864. 8vo; pages 1034; 22 steel engraved plates (dampstain ring to plates); gilt decorated half morocco, worn and soiled, inch split to outer hinge, some dampstaining, especially to rear cover, some light dampstaining in text.   Raymond M. Sutton VII-1132 1996 $115.00

ROBINSON, THOMAS   An Essay Towards a Natural History of Westmorland and Cumberland. London: printed by J. L. for W. Freeman, 1709. 1st edition; 8vo; pages (xiv), 95, 118, (ii ads), trifle used; contemporary paneled calf, very rubbed and worn, spine defective at tail; very scarce. Inscribed "Ex Dono Thomae Robinson"; from the library of Norman Nicholson, Lake District poet and author.   R.F.G. Hollett & Son 78-547 1996 £195.00

ROBINSON, THOMAS   An Essay Towards a Natural History of Westmorland and Cumberland. London: printed by J. L. for W. Freeman, 1709. 1st edition; 8vo; pages (xiv), 95, 118, lacking flyleaves and rear ad leaf; contemporary panelled calf, very rubbed and scraped, hinges cracking at head and tail.   R.F.G. Hollett & Son 78-548 1996 £165.00

ROBINSON, VICTOR   Encyclopaedia Sexualis: A Comprehensive Encyclopedia-Dictionary of the Sexual Sciences. New York: 1936. 1st edition; 819 pages; illustrations; original binding.   W. Bruce Fye 71-1783 1996 $100.00

ROBINSON, WILL W.   Ranchos Become Cities. Pasadena: San Pasqual Press, 1939. 8 3/4 x 5 3/4 inches; 243 pages; vignettes by Irene Robinson; red stamped brown cloth in dust jacket, 3 small chips; inscribed by W. W. and Irene Robinson to another noted California historian.   Dawson's Books Shop 528-205 1996 $150.00

ROBINSON, WILLIAM 1777-1848   The Parks and Gardens of Paris. London: 1878. 2nd edition; 7th thousand; 8vo; xxiv, 548 pages, frontispiece, 7 plates and numerous text illustrations; morocco, somewhat rubbed.   Wheldon & Wesley 207-1740 1996 £65.00

ROBINSON: Some Account of the Family of Robinson of the White House, Appleby, Westmoreland. London: privately printed, Nichols and Sons, 1874. 8vo; pages 101; lithographed plate; contemporary half roan, gilt with raised bands, little rubbed, flyleaves rather spotted, some marginal notes in hand of C. Roy Hudleston to a few leaves, extremely scarce.   R.F.G. Hollett & Son 78-242 1996 £185.00

ROBSJOHN-GIBBINGS, T. H.   Furniture of Classical Greece. New York: Alfred A. Knopf, 1963. Folio; 123 pages; 94 illustrations; original cloth, torn dust jacket.   Archaeologia Luxor-3921 1996 $125.00

ROBSON, GEORGE FENNELL   Scenery of the Grampian Mountains. London: Published by the author, 1814. Oblong folio; title, errata slip tipped in, 41 etched plates, folding map; modern quarter calf, gilt, leather lettering piece on upper board, original printed wrappers bound in (edges little chipped), uncut, edges little dusty in places, but an excellent and sound, clean copy.   R.F.G. Hollett 76-259 1996 £380.00

ROCKWELL, JOHN A.   A Compilation of Spanish and Mexican Law, in Relation to Mines, and Titles to Real Estate, in Force in California, Texas and New Mexico (etc.). New York: John S. Voorhies, 1851. contemporary sheep, showing wear, but well preserved.   Meyer Boswell SL26-203 1996 $850.00

ROCKWELL, MOLLY   Willie Was Different: the Tale of an Ugy Thrushling. New York: Funk & Wagnalls, 1969. 1st edition; pictures by Norman Rockwell; fine in lightly rubbed, price clipped dust jacket; inscribed by the Rockwells.   Hermitage SP95-808 1996 $125.00

ROCKWELL, NORMAN   Willie Was Different. The Tale of an Ugly Thurshling. New York: Funk and Wagnalls, 1969. 1st edition; octavo; 41 pages; illustrations in color; near mint in dust jacket; signed by Norman and Molly Rockwell.   Bromer Booksellers 90-136 1996 $225.00

ROCKY Mountain Scenery...Along the Line of the Denver and Rio Grande Railroad. New York: American Bank Note Co., ca. 1888. 1st edition; 80 pages, 12 tinted photogravures, maps and over 50 text and ad illustrations; original black cloth with title stamped in gilt on front cover and spine, neatly rebacked, new endsheets, minor ex-library markings on title of Library of Congress and Interstate Commerce Library, overall very good, clean copy; photogravures excellent. Wynar 2246; not in Flake or Flake Supp.   Michael D. Heaston 23-132 1996 $500.00

ROCQUE, JOHN   A Plan of the Cities of London and Westminster and Borough of Southwark with the Continuous Buildings, from an Actual Survey Taken by John Rocque... 4to; xi, 46 pages, 1 f., later half calf, slightly rubbed, index volume bound to match.   Marlborough 162-195 1996 £4,000.00

RODD, RENNELL   Rose Leaf and Apple Leaf. Philadelphia: J. M. Stoddart & Co., 1882. 1st edition under this title, the edition deluxe issue of which the publisher recalled the total number of copies printed was 'not over 250'; 12mo; illustrations; original printed full parchment, text printed in brown ink (rectos only) on thin transparent handmade paper, with deckled edges, interleaved with thin leaves of green tissue, top edge gilt, white moire endpapers, covers little soiled and worn, as usual, but very good, in slightly rubbed half morocco slipcase; laid in is ALS from Rodd to Oscar Wilde.   David J. Holmes 52-127 1996 $2,250.00

RODDENBERRY, G.   Star Trek. S&S, 1979. 1st edition; 1500 copies, specially bound and signed by author. Fine, without dust jacket, as issued and in slipcase.   Aronovitz 57-1002 1996 $250.00

RODDIS, LOUIS   A Short History of Nautical Medicine. New York: 1941. 359 pages; original binding; GM 2187.   W. Bruce Fye 71-1792 1996 $100.00

RODITI, EDOUARD   Orphic Love. New York: Hydra Group, 1986. 1st edition; one of 100 copies, signed by author; small thin 8vo; fold-out illustration by Don Gene Bell; original wrappers; mint. Peich 73.   James S. Jaffe 34-584 1996 $250.00

RODMAN, SELDEN   Horace Pippin: a Negro Painter in America. New York: Quadrangle Press, 1947. 1st edition; folio; frontispiece, 48 plates, 4 in color; light rubbing to silver spring lettering and little wear to extremities, otherwise about fine, lacking fragile uncommon dust jacket. Nice.   Between the Covers 43-463 1996 $350.00

RODMAN, SELDEN   The Poetry of Flight: an Anthology. New York: Duell, 1941. 1st edition; 8vo; dust jacket, nicks and small creases; very good.   George J. Houle 68-10 1996 $150.00

RODWELL, GEORGE HERBERT   The Memoirs of an Umbrella. London: E. Mackenzie, ca. 1845. 4to; 68 engravings by Phiz; rebound in full maroon morocco with numerous gilt borders on covers, gilt panelled spine, raised bands, inner gilt lether panels, edges gilt; apart from rebacking and wear at corners and sound copy.   Appelfeld Gallery 54-149 1996 $150.00

RODWELL, GEORGE HERBERT   Old London Bridge, a Romance of the Sixteenth Century. London: Henry Lea, n.d., ca. 1860. 8vo; large folding frontispiece torn at folds, backed with canvas, engraved title, 24 plates, text illustrations; contemporary half calf, rubbed at extremities. Marlborough 162-197 1996 £150.00

ROE, FRANCIS M. A.   Army Letters from an Officer's Wife, 1871-1888. New York: 1909. 1st edition; 387 pages; frontispiece, illustrations; pictorial cloth, very good+. Howes R403; rader 2815.   T. A. Swinford 49-887 1996 $125.00

ROE, FRANK GILBERT   The North American Buffalo. Toronto: University of Toronto Press, 1951. 1st edition; original cloth, inscription of former owner, another inscription and inkstamp on inside rear cover; bookplate and two pictorial stickers affixed to inside cover and f.f.e.p., and large buffalo postcard taped behind titlepage; minor shelf wear, else very good.   Ken Sanders 8-85 1996 $150.00

ROE, THOMAS   Sir Thomas Rowe His Speech at the Councell-Table Touching Brasse-Money, or Against Brasse Money... London: printed Anno, 1641. 1st edition; 4to; (2), 351-358 pages, i.e. a total of 6 leaves including the blank before title, occasional light soiling, woodcut device on title; handsomely bound in late 19th century mottled calf, fully gilt, inner gilt dentelles, by Worsfold, blindstamp on title, in most respects a fine copy. Wing R1778a. Massie 575; Goldsmiths 760; Kress S708. John Drury 82-244 1996 £350.00

ROEBUCK, CARL   Ionian Trade and Colonization. New York: Archaeological Institue of America, 1959. Large 4to; ix, 148 pages, 4 maps; original cloth, spine lightly faded.   Archaeologia Luxor-3927 1996 $150.00

ROESSLE, THEOPHILUS   Roessle's Gardener's Hand-Books. No. 1. How to Cultivate and Preserve Celery. Albany: Theophilus Roessle, 1860. 1st edition; 8vo; 100 pages; illustrations, with 2 (of 3) colored plates; original cloth, rebacked.   M & S Rare Books 60-440 1996 $125.00

ROETHKE, THEODORE   Open House. New York: Alfred A. Knopf, 1941. One of 1000 numbered copies; 8vo; 70 pages; cloth, fair to good only; signed by author, owned by one of author's students at Bennington; fore-edge of covers stained and owner has pasted in review of book from the New Yorker and newspaper account of Roethke.   The Bookpress 75-457 1996 $175.00

ROETHKE, THEODORE   Praise to the End! New York: 1951. 1st edition; fine, dust jacket extremities of spine min. rubbed.   Polyanthos 22-715 1996 $200.00

ROETHKE, THEODORE   Praise To The End! New York: Doubleday, 1951. 1st edition; 8vo; 89 pages; cloth, dust jacket worn, paper slightly browned, as usual.   The Bookpress 75-458 1996 $100.00

ROETHKE, THEODORE   The Waking. New York: Doubleday and Co., 1953. 1st edition; 8vo; near fine in bright, but lightly creased dust jacket, more so at extremities; inscribed presentation copy for John Malcolm Brinnin.   Lakin & Marley 3-51 1996 $1,000.00

ROETHLISBERGER, BIANCO   Cavalier Pietro Tempesta and His Time. University of Delaware Press, 1970. 8vo; 143 pages; 456 illustrations on plates; cloth.   Rainsford A54-551 1996 £75.00

ROGER, of Hoveden   Chronica. London: 1868-71. 8vo; 4 volumes; original cloth.   Howes Bookshop 265-1586 1996 £120.00

ROGER, of Wendover   The Flowers of History, from 1154; Flores Historarium (1154-1235). London: 1886-89. 8vo; 3 volumes; original cloth. Howes Bookshop 265-1599 1996 £75.00

ROGER-MARX, CLAUDE   Variations. Drawings, Water-Colors, Etchings and Lithographs. Greenwich: New York Graphic Society, 1961. 1st edition; number 97 of 100 copies, with an original color lithograph signed in pencil by Vertes laid in, out of a total edition of 1000; 4to; 150, (1) pages; illustrations; original white cloth, near fine in price clipped dust jacket.   Chapel Hill 94-96 1996 $350.00

ROGERS, FRANCIS NEWMAN   The Law and Practice of Elections with Analytical Tables... London: printed for J. & W. T. Clarke, 1820. 1st edition; 8vo; xx, 309, (3), 35, (13) pages; contemporary calf, rebacked. James Burmester 29-113 1996 £50.00

ROGERS, J. B.   War Pictures. Experiences and Observataions of a Chaplain in the U.S. Army in the War of the Southern Rebellion. Chicago: 1863. 1st edition; 7.5 x 4.5 inches; 258 pages; illustrations; cloth, outer hinges torn and crudely taped.   John K. King 77-93 1996 $100.00

ROGERS, JAMES EDWIN THOROLD 1823-1890   Cobden and Modern Political Opinion. London: Macmillan and Co., 1873. 1st edition; 8vo; xvi, (4), 382 pages; rather later brown half morocco, spine gilt, raised bands, top edge gilt, fine; from the library of Andrew Carnegie. Williams I 145. John Drury 82-246 1996 £125.00

ROGERS, JAMES EDWIN THOROLD 1823-1890   Six Centuries of Work and Wages. London: W. Swan Sonnenschein, 1884. 1st edition; demy 8vo; 2 volumes, 304, (ii), 305-(59) pages; original cloth, gilt, spine of volume 2 snagged, some slight discoloration and brittleness from exposure to damp, but reasonable set.   Ash Rare Books Zenzybyr-79 1996 £95.00

ROGERS, JASPER W.   Letter to the Landlords and Ratepayers of Ireland, Detailing means for the Permanent and Profitble Employment of the Peasantry, Without Ultimate Cost to the Land or the Nation... London: James Ridgway, 1846. 1st edition; 8vo; 77, (3) pages including the final 3 pages of ads, early annotations in pencil; recently well bound in cloth, lettered in gilt; very good. Rare. Black 607. Goldsmiths 34854; Not in Kress or Williams.   John Drury 82-245 1996 £150.00

ROGERS, JOHN GODFREY   Sport in Vancouver and Newfoundland. Toronto: Musson Book Co., 1912. 8vo; 275 pages; illustrations, maps; original cloth, covers dusty, spine faded, else very good. Edwards & Lort 3039; O'Dea 1550.   Hugh Anson-Cartwright 87-374 1996 $150.00

ROGERS, JOHN WILLIAM   Finding Literature on the Texas Plains. Dallas: Southwest Press, 1931. 12mo; 57 pages, frontispiece; cloth backed boards, title in gilt on spine and front cover; very good+ with pencilled marginalia by Fred Rosenstock. Dobie 10; McVicker, Dobie B14; Jenkins BTB 167.   Bohling Book Co. 191-127 1996 $125.00

ROGERS, MEYRIC R.   Carl Milles: an Interpretation of His Work. New Haven: Yale University Press, 1940. Limited to 2000 copies; folio; 73 pages text plus 163 plates; cloth. Lucas p. 170; Freitag 6530.. Brannan 43-418 1996 $110.00

ROGERS, ROBERT   Journals of Major Robert Rogers: Containing an Account of the Several Excursions He Made Under the Generals Who Commanded Upon the Continent of North America, During the Late War. London: printed for the author and sold by J. Millan, 1765. 1st edition; viii, 236, (4) pages; modern full calf, spine gilt, period style, very fine fresh copy with half title and ad leaves. Streeter Sale 1029. Howes R419; Vail 563.   Joseph J. Felcone 64-36 1996 $3,200.00

ROGERS, SAMUEL   Italy, a Poem. London: Edward Moxon, 1844. 8vo; illustrations, vignettes; 8 pages of publisher's ads dated Oct. 1, 1844 at back following single leaf ad, stain on fore-edge; brown morocco gilt, slight rubbing and soiling; very attractive copy; presentation copy from author to Margaret Eliza Johnstone.   James Cummins 14-169 1996 $150.00

ROGERS, SAMUEL   Poems. (with) Italy, a Poem. London: Edward Moxon, 1839/40. 8vo; 2 volumes; contemporary maroon morocco, covers decorated in blind and gilt, spine gilt, all edges gilt, slight rubbing of upper joint; fine in attractive early Victorian binding. CBEL III 181. Ximenes 109-249 1996 $125.00

ROGERS, WOODES   A Cruising voyage Round the World; First to the South-Seas, Thence to the East-Indies, and Homewards by the Cape of Good Hope. London: printed for A. Bell and B. Lintot, 1712. 1st edition; 8vo; folding world map, 4 other folding maps, one map mounted and slightly restored at fold, obscuring a few letters which are clear from the context; modern calf, gilt, spine gilt; very good. Sabin 72753. Howes R421; Cowan p. 194; Hill p. 258; CBEL II 1478.   Ximenes 109-250 1996 $2,000.00

ROGERSON, IAN   Agnes Miller Parker, Wood Engraver and Book Illustrator, 1895-1980. Fleece Press, 1990. One of 300 copies; oblong 4to; printed in Garmond in blue and black on Zerkall; illustrations, including 34 engravings; half cloth, boards covered in Claire Maziarczyk's paste paper; fine in slipcase, bookplate;   Bertram Rota 272-146 1996 £200.00

ROH, F.   Foto Auge/Oeil Et Photo/Photo Eye. Stuttgart: Wedekind, 1929. 1st edition; 76 illustrations; illustrated wrappers, rare.   J. B. Muns 154-260 1996 $1,000.00

ROHDE, E. S.   The Old English Gardening Books. London: 1924. Royal 8vo; pages xii, 144, 16 plates and 8 plans; original boards, linen back. Wheldon & Wesley 207-271 1996 £75.00

ROHDE, E. S.   Old English Herbals. London: 1922. 1st edition; royal 8vo; xii, 243 pages, colored frontispiece, 17 other illustrations; original buckram, good, scarce original printing.   K Books 441-435 1996 £58.00

ROHEIM, GEZA   Animism, Magic and the Divine King. New York: 1930. 390 pages; dark brown cloth, dust jacket chipped, rubbed, torn, in protective sheet, good condition; owner's signature.   Antipodean 28-264 1996 $125.00

ROHEIM, GEZA   Australian Totemism. London: 1925. 488 pages, 11 folding maps, 2 in text, black and white frontispieces; green buckram discolored, but covered by near complete original dust jacket; very good, scarce.   Antipodean 28-265 1996 $345.00

ROHEIM, GEZA   The Eternal Ones of the Dream. New York: International University Press, 1945. 270 pages; 4 plates; navy and gilt cloth with chipped dust jacket, otherwise very nice, scarce. Antipodean 28-267 1996 $175.00

ROHLEDER, H.   Test Tube Babies. Panurge Press, 1934. 1st edition; some minor spotting to page edges, else just about fine in very good dust jacket with some light damage to dust jacket spine.   Aronovitz 57-1003 1996 $125.00

ROHLFS, ANNA KATHARINE GREEN   Marked "Personal". New York: G. P. Putnam's Sons, 1893. 1st edition; 12mo; 415 pages; original printed and pictorial wrappers, tear in back wrapper but very good. Wright III 4856.   M & S Rare Books 60-224 1996 $200.00

ROHMER, SAX   The Return of Dr. Fu-Manchu. New York: Robert M. McBride & Co., 1916. 1st edition; spine ends and corners lightly rubbed, otherwie better than very good.   Quill & Brush 102-1523 1996 $200.00

ROHR, JULIUS BERNHARD   ...Neuer Moralischer Tractat Von der Liebe Gegen die Personen Andern Geschlechts, Darinnent so Wohl Uberhaupt Die Regeln der Klugheit so Bey Liebes-Affairen Vorzukommen Pflegen, Vorgestellet Werden... Leipzig: Johan Christian Martini, 1717. 1st and only edition; 8vo; 886 pages; frontispiece, 8 full page engravings, woodcut and typographic ornaments, contemporary vellum over paper boards, hand lettered gilt stamped backstrip, fine, fine contemporary engraved emblematic bookplate, with charming emblem of J.B. Nack and of entomologist J. C. Gerning. not in NUC; Gay-Lemmonyer 3.328; Hayn Gotendorf 1.669.   Bennett Gilbert LL29-80 1996 $3,600.00

ROLEWINCK, WERNER   Fasciculus Temporum. Strassburg: Johann Pruss, not before 1490. Folio; ff. (vi), 90; gothic letter, full page woodcut on verso of title, 24 smaller woodcuts in text, numerous printed diagrams; extensive rubrication, initials in red or blue, intermittent neat contemporary marginalia, 17th century ex-liris and 18th century library stamp, some outer margins bit frayed (nowhere near text), some waterstaining, generally light, 1 leaf loose, overall most attractive in richly blindstamped vellum over paste boards, very sl. wormed, panelled and ruled in blind, various decorative roll toolings, imperial arms in lozenges incoporated in upper cover, probably Bohemian c. 1500; entirely unosphisticated or restored. Not in BMC; Goff R276; Polain B 3362; Hain 6916; Schreiber 5119.   A. Sokol XXV-84 1996 £3,650.00

ROLFE, FREDERICK WILLIAM 1860-1913   Chronicles of the House of Borgia. London: Grant Richards/New York: E. P. Dutton, 1901. 1st American edition; large 8vo; decorative red cloth, top edge gilt, near fine, minor wear.   Antic Hay 101-356 1996 $285.00

ROLFE, FREDERICK WILLIAM 1860-1913   Don Renato: an Ideal Content. London: Chatto & Windus, 1963. 1st edition; fine in dust jacket. Captain's Bookshelf 38-194 1996 $150.00

ROLFE, FREDERICK WILLIAM 1860-1913   Letters to C. H. C. Pirie Gordon...to Leonard Moore...to R.M. Dawkins. Nicholas Vane, 1959-62. Each volume limited edition of between 290 and 330 copies, these being out of series copies; 8vo; 3 volumes; vi, 7-146; vi, 7-76; vi, 7-180 pages; original two-tone cloth, top edge gilt, others uncut, spine of volume 2 very slightly dust soiled, otherwise very good.   Thomas Thorp 489-263 1996 £250.00

ROLLAND, R.   The Revolt of the Machines or Invention Run Wild. Dragon Press, 1932. 1st edition; 1/500 copies; woodcuts by Masereel; spine label somewhat sunned, else very good+.   Aronovitz 57-1005 1996 $150.00

ROLLESTON, HUMPHRY   Cardio-Vascular Diseases Since Harvey's Discvoery. Cambridge: 1928. 1st edition; 149 pages; original binding; inscribed by author to Warfield Longcope. Later inscribed by Emmett Horine to Carleton Chapman. GM 3156   W. Bruce Fye 71-1801 1996 $100.00

ROLLESTON, HUMPHRY   Some Medical Aspects of Old Age. London: 1922. 1st edition; 170 pages; original binding, ex-library.   W. Bruce Fye 71-1807 1996 $100.00

ROLLEY, CLAUDE   Greek Bronzes. London: Sotheby's, 1986. Folio; 267 pages; 302 illustrations, 3 maps; original cloth, dust jacket. Archaeologia Luxor-3930 1996 $125.00

ROLLIN, CHARLES M.   The Method of Teaching and Studying the Belles Lettres; or, an Introduction to Languages, Poetry, Rheotric, History, Moral, Philosophy, Physics... Dublin: printed for J. Beatty, 1778. 11th edition in English, but first Dublin edition; 12mo; 4 volumes; contemporary sprinkled calf, red morocco labels, green morocco number labels (some variation in colors), some rubbing and wear, generally light, small chip missing from heads of volumes 3 and 4, publisher's ads at back of volume 2; very attractive.   James Cummins 14-170 1996 $350.00

ROLLOCK, ROBERT   Lectures Upon the Epistle of Paul to the Colossians. London: Felix Kyngston, 1603. 1st edition of the English translation, by Henry Holland; 4to; pages (xvi), 442, Roman letter, side notes in italic, printer's caduceus and cornucopia device on title, woodcut headpieces, running title cropped on two leaves, otherwise a good, clean copy in contemporary limp vellum covers, gilt line border and panels, central arabesque and corner decorations interposed, initials "M.W." on both, gilt somewhat rubbed. STC 21282. Lowndes 2122; 5 copies in NUC.   A. Sokol XXV-85 1996 £395.00

ROMER, ISABELLA FRANCES   A Pilgrimage to the Temples and Tombs of Egypt, Nubia and Palestine in 1845-46. London: Richard Bentley, 1846. 1st edition; tall 8vo; 2 volumes bound in 1; (xvi), 376, (x), 390 pages; 5 lithographs including hand colored frontispiece in volume two; bookplate, binding rubbed at extremities, some minor wear at head of spine, otherwise very good copy. Robinson p. 191.   David Mason 71-116 1996 $360.00

ROMILLY, HUGH   From My Verandall in New Guinea. London: David Nutt, 1889. (xxviii), 277 pages, 2 pages ads, 1 map; dark turquoise gilt binding, very slightly rubbed, gilt library number on spine and some stamps.   Antipodean 28-271 1996 $250.00

ROMILLY, HUGH   The Western Pacific and New Guinea. London: John Murray, 1886. (viii), 242 pages, 32 pages ads, folding map; red and gilt buckram, chipped at head of spine, front hinge bit tender, ex-library with some stamps but nothing on spine; Overall a pleasant copy of a scarce book. Ferguson 15062.   Antipodean 28-272 1996 $125.00

ROMILLY, SAMUEL   Observations on a Late Publication, Intituled, Thoughts on Executive Justice... London: sold by T. Cadell and R. Faulder, 1786. 1st edition; small 8vo; contemporary tree calf, spine gilt, spine rubbed and worn at top and bottom; aside from wear to spine, very good, complete with half title; very uncommon.   Ximenes 109-251 1996 $650.00

ROMINE, WILLIAM BETHEL   A Story of the Original Ku Klux Klan. Pulaski: Pulaski Citizen, 1934. 2nd edition; original printed wrappers, near fine. Quite scarce. Smith p. 148; Davis, Sims-Wood 118; Work p. 378. McGowan Book Co. 65-116 1996 $250.00

RONALDS, ALFRED   The Fly-Fisher's Entomology. London: Longmans, Green, 1868. Later edition; 8vo; 132 pages, 24 pages ads; hand colored frontispiece and 19 full page hand colored plates; original green cloth, library bookplate, small blindstamp on each plate, hinges cracked internally, top of spine chipped, good plus.   Chapel Hill 94-392 1996 $100.00

RONALDS, ALFRED   The Fly-Fisher's Entomology...Trout and Grayling Fishing... London: 1877. 8th edition; 8vo; 20 hand colored plates; recent quarter morocco; minor soiling, small marginal stain and tiny wormhole in blank margin at end.   Maggs Bros. Ltd. 1190-212 1996 £90.00

RONALDS, ALFRED   The Fly-Fisher's Entomology. London: 1913. Limited to 270 copies, of which 250 were for sale; crown 4to; 2 volumes; 13 hand colored plates, 8 plain plates, printed on handmade paper; volume 2 has thick board pages with 48 actual flies in sunken mounts; original green cloth with fly medallion motifs on upper covers, ornate gilt morocco spine, with fly designs in compartments; excellent copy, very light rubb, volume 1 contents fine, volume 2 contents have light foxing, mainly to prelims.   David A.H. Grayling 3/95-504 1996 £950.00

ROOD, STANDISH   The Silver Districts of Nevada, and Prospectus of the Pan-ranagat Valley Silver Mining Co. New York: Livesey Bros., 1866. 1st edition; 28 pages, folding maps; original printed wrappers, minor chipping, very good.   Michael D. Heaston 23-257 1996 $750.00

ROOKMAAKER, L. C.   The Zoological Exploration of Southern Africa. Rotterdam: 1989. 8vo; 392 pages; 16 colored plates, 165 photos; cloth. Wheldon & Wesley 207-441 1996 £99.00

ROOME, THOMAS   The Self Instructed Philosopher, or Memoirs of the Late Joseph Whitehead, of Sutton in Ashfield, Notts. Mansfield: printed and sold by G. langley, sold also by Longman, London... 1817. 1st edition; 12mo; 130 pages; clean tear in one leaf, original blue printed boards, ends of spine worn, remains of small label on upper cover; scarce.   James Burmester 29-115 1996 £85.00

ROOSEVELT, THEODORE 1858-1919   Inaugural Addresses of Franklin D Roosevelt: President of the United States. Worcester: 1945. Limited to 2000 copies; 3 1/8 x 2 1/8 inches; 88 pages; gilt stamped cloth; very fine.   Bromer Booksellers 87-230 1996 $100.00

ROOSEVELT, THEODORE 1858-1919   Outdoor Pastimes of an American Hunter. 1905. 1st edition; illustrations; very small tear in upper spine, otherwise very good.   David Grayling J95Biggame-434 1996 £65.00

ROOSEVELT, THEODORE 1858-1919   Ranch Life and the Hunting Trail. New York: Century Co., 1888. 1st edition; 186 pages, frontispiece, numerous illustrations by Remington; original brown pictorial cloth, gilt, title stamped in gilt on spine and brown on front cover, all edges gilt, slipcase, minor repairs to cloth, fine. Adams Herd 1951; Dykes Remington 956; Reese Six Score 93. Howes R432.   Michael D. Heaston 23-292 1996 $750.00

ROOSEVELT, THEODORE 1858-1919   The Winning of the West. New York: Putnam, 1900. Alleghany edition; large 8vo; 4 volumes, maps and plates, former owner's inscription on title of volume 1, otherwise very nice; original cloth. Howes R433.   Edward Morrill 368-409 1 996 $150.00

ROOT, FRANK A.   The Overland Stage to California. Topeka: 1901. 1st edition; 630 pages; frontispiece, illustrations, folded maps, pictorial cloth; very good+. Howes R434; 6 Guns 1897; Graff 3562.   T. A. Swinford 49-993 1996 $250.00

ROQUES, JOSEPH   Phytographie Medicale, Histoire des Substances Herioques Dea Poison Tires du Regne Vegetal. Paris & Lyon: 1835. Nouvelle edition; 4 volumes - 3 volumes of text 8vo. and large 4to. atlas of 150 hand colored plates; text volumes of 1740 pages in half red leather, edges rubbed, hinges tender, atlas volume in half leather, covers detached, 2 1/2 inch piece off bottom of spine; scarce.   John Johnson 135-286 1996 $1,200.00

RORSCHACK, HERMANN   Psychodiagnostics: a Diagnostic Test Based on Perception. New York: 1942. 1st English translation; 2 volumes, 226 pages, plus volume of colored tables; original binding.   W. Bruce Fye 71-1814 1996 $125.00

ROSCOE, HENRY   A Digest of the Law of Evidence in Criminal Cases. Philadelphia: T. & J. W. Johnson, 1840. 2nd edition; contemporary sheep very worn and embrowned, usable copy only.   Meyer Boswell SL25-189 1996 $125.00

ROSCOE, HENRY E.   Spectrum Analysis - Six Lectures - Delivered in 1868, Before the Society of Apothecaries of London. London: Macmillan, 1869. 1st edition; 2 double page black and white illustrations, as well as 72 black and white illustrations in text; decorated cloth gilt, monted on upper cover is a multi colored silk ribbon, extending chromolithograph frontispiece; head and tail of spine and corners slightly bumped, covers slightly marked, cover edges slightly rubbed, prelims, edges and endpapers spotted, some very slight internal spotting; very good. Ulysses 39-546 1996 £145.00

ROSCOE, JOHN   The Baganda, an Account of Their Native Customs and Beliefs. London: 1911. 1st edition; 8vo; xix, 547 pages, folding plans 81 illustrations; new old style quarter calf, very good.   K Books 441-15 1996 £80.00

ROSCOE, THOMAS   Wanderings and Excursions in North Wales. (with Wanderings and Excursions in South Wales, with the Scenery of the River Wye. London: Henry G. Bohn, 1853. 8vo; xx, 360, xi, 336 pages; engraved titles and 98 engraved plates and with folding map in each volume; original green cloth with gilt decoration on spines; spines slightly faded, some minor wear at foot of spines, otherwise attractive set. David Mason 71-155 1996 $280.00

ROSCOE, WILLIAM   Catalogue of the Very Select and Valuable Library of William Roscoe, Esq. Which Will Be Sold by Auction... London: J. McCreery, Printer, 1816. 8vo; without portrait and 4 leaves of "books omitted"; 19th century boards, uncut. De Ricci pp. 93-94.   Forest Books 74-232 1996 £165.00

ROSCOE, WILLIAM   The Life of Lorenzo De' Medici, Called the Magnificent. Philadelphia: W. F. M'Laughlin for Bronson & Chauncey, 1803. 1st American from the 4th London edition; 8vo; 3 volumes, pages 426, 427, 435 plus subscriber's list; frontispiece, engraved medallions and devices; nice contemporary full American flame calf binding, joints cracked, spines decorated in gilt with bird and lyre device, edges colored yellow, scarce. AI 4994.   Family Album Tillers-540 1996 $350.00

ROSCOE, WILLIAM   Occasional Tracts Relative to the War Between Great Britain and France... London: printed for T. Cadell and W. Davies, 1810. 1st edition; 8vo; contemporary half calf, slightly rubbed, label. Goldsmith 20188.   Anthony W. Laywood 108-227 1996 £75.00

ROSCOMMON, WENTWORTH DILLON, EARL OF   An Essay On Translated Verse. London: 1709. 8vo; 16 pages; marbled wrappers, very good.   C. P. Hyland 216-168 1996 £70.00

ROSE, A.   Napoleon's Campaign in Russia Anno 1812, Medico-Historical. New York: 1913. 1st edition; 212 pages; original binding; Louis Roddis's copy with his bookplate.   W. Bruce Fye 71-1815 1996 $125.00

ROSE, BARBARA   Frankenthaler. New York: Abrams, n.d. Oblong 4to; 274 pages; 205 illustrations, 54 tipped in color plates; cloth, plastic dust jacket. Freitag 3122.   Brannan 43-215 1996 $325.00

ROSE, COWPER   Four Years in Southern Africa. London: Henry Colburn and Richard Bentley, New Burlington Street, 1829. 1st edition; (v-vii), (ix-xii), 1-308 pages; sepia tinted aquatint frontispiece, ink ms. dedication to preface, some foxing to frontispiece; half calf and marbled boards, scuffed and worn, gilt tooling to compartments, brown morocco label to spine, edges speckled. Mendelssohn II p. 249; Abbey Travel 331. Beeleigh Abbey BA/56-110 1996 £200.00

ROSE, D. MURRAY   Historical Notes and Essays on the '15 and '145. Edinburgh: William Brown, 1897. Limited edition (150); 8vo; pages xii, 198, 2 portraits and 10 facsimiles; original buckram, gilt; armorial bookplate of Walter Leonard Bell.   R.F.G. Hollett 76-260 1996 £65.00

ROSE, FREDRICK G. G.   The Wind of Change in Central Australia: the Aborigines of Angas Downs, 1962. Berlin: 1965. Paperback; 382 pages; illustrations, spine slightly chipped, otherwise very good. The Meggitt copy.   Antipodean 28-273 1996 $300.00

ROSE, H.   The Elements of Botany... London: 1775. 8vo; pages xii, 472, 14 engraved plates; contemporary calf, rubbed. Good, clean copy. Wheldon & Wesley 207-1444 1996 £250.00

ROSE, HUGH JAMES   A New General Biographical Dictionary... B. Fellowes...and others, 1853. 8vo; 12 volumes; contemporary red half morocco, gilt sides, spines fully gilt in 6 compartments, raised bands, marbled edges, extremities very slightly rubbed, but most attractive. Thomas Thorp 489-264 1996 £300.00

ROSE, JOSHUA   Modern Machine-Shop Practice. London: J. S. Virtue and Co. Ltd., 1886-87. 1st edition; folio; 2 volumes, 40 plates, 3077 text figures; clean copy in contemporary half green morocco, gilt, bit worn and scraped.   Maggs Bros. Ltd. 1190-651 1996 £120.00

ROSEN, ERIC VON   Popular Account of Archaeological Research During the Swedish Chaco-Cordillera-Expedition 1901-02. Stockholm: C. E. Fritze, 1924. 4to; xiv, 168 pages, 237 figures, 24 plates (3 in color), 1 map; wrappers.   Archaeologia Luxor-4849 1996 $175.00

ROSENBACH, ABRAHAM SIMON WOLF 1876-1952   Book Hunter's Holiday: Adventures with Books and Manuscripts. Boston & New York: Houghton Mifflin Co./Cambridge: Riverside Press, 1936. 1st edition; one of 760 copies, signed by author; 10 x 6 3/4 inches, 1 p.l., xv, (1) pages, 91) leaf, 259 pages; frontispiece, 73 plates; title in red and black; original cloth, untrimmed edges, in original (slightly darkened and slightly chipped), glassine jacket and publisher's somewhat battered slipcase; except for defects noted, a nearly mint copy.   Phillip J. Pirages 33-102 1996 $150.00

ROSENBACH, ABRAHAM SIMON WOLF 1876-1952   Books and Bidders. Boston: Little Brown, 1927. 1st edition; one of 785 numbered large paper copies, signed by author; 311 pages; illustrations; original boards, cloth spine, paper label; near fine; inscribed by author.   19th Century Shop 39- 1996 $240.00

ROSENBACH, ABRAHAM SIMON WOLF 1876-1952   Books and Bidders: The Adventures of a Bibliophile. Boston: Little Brown, 1927. 1st edition; one of 760 large paper copies for sale, signed by author; 9 3/4 x 6 3/4 inches; 1 p.l., xv, (1), 311 pages; frontispiece and 47 plates and many illustrations in text, title in red and black; original cloth backed boards, top edge gilt, other edges rough trimmed, in original slightly frayed glassine dust jacket and publisher's slipcase, one seam partly cracked, extremely fine.   Phillip J. Pirages 33-103 1996 $125.00

ROSENBACH, ABRAHAM SIMON WOLF 1876-1952   The Earliest Christmas Books. Philadelphia: privately printed, 1927. One of 150 copies; quarto; (10) pages; mounted frontispiece and mounted text illustration; original grey-green wrappers, with printed paper label on front cover, spine starting to split, circular stain on front cover, otherwise fine. Heritage Book Shop 196-288 1996 $150.00

ROSENBACH, ABRAHAM SIMON WOLF 1876-1952   The Libraries of the Presidents of the United States. Worcester: Antiquarian Society, 1935. 1st edition; 5 black and white plates; wrappers; covers slightly marked, cover edges slightly browned, top corners slightly bumped, very good. Ulysses 39-507 1996 £55.00

ROSENBAUM, ELISABETH   A Catalogue of Cyrenaican Portrait Scultpure. London: Oxford University Press, 1960. 4to; xvii, 140 pages, 108 plates; original cloth, dust jacket. Archaeologia Luxor-3932 1996 $150.00

ROSENBERG, ISAAC   Poems. London: William Heinemann, 1922. 1st edition; crown 8vo; original cloth, paper label, label worn, browned and very slightly chipped, few faint marks, one leaf slightly nicked at fore edge, but reasonable copy.   Ash Rare Books Zenzybyr-80 1996 £85.00

ROSENBERG, ISAAC   The Collected Works of Isaac Rosenberg - Poetry - Prose - Letters - and Some Drawings. London: Chatto & Windus, 1937. 1st edition; 8 black and white plates; original binding, top edge dusty, prelims, edges and endpapers slightly spotted, spine faded, covers slightly marked and dusty, free endpapers faintly browned, tail of spine and corners very slightly bumped, top corners of last few pages slightly creased, very good, no dust jacket. Bookplate of library agent John Johnson.   Ulysses 39-508 1996 £75.00

ROSENBLATT, JOE   Dream Craters. Erin: Press Porcepic, 1974. 1st edition; 1st issue with editor's name printed on front cover; 86 pages; fine; inscribed by author to editor, John Newlove; from the library of John Metcalf, with his ownership signature.   Nelson Ball 118-151 1996 $100.00

ROSENSTEIN, I. G.   Theory and Practice of Homoeopathy. First Part. Louisville: 1840. 1st edition; 12mo; 288 pages; marbled boards, rebacked. Bradford 247.   Argosy 810-422 1996 $450.00

ROSETTI, GIOANVENTURA   The Plictho...Instructions in the Art of the Dyers Which Teaches the Dyeing of Woolen Cloths, Linens, Cottons and Silk by the Great Art as Well as by the Common. Cambridge: MIT Press, 1969. 1st edition in English; 4to; xxxvi, (4), 199 pages, facsimile reproductions of titlepages of several early editions, as well as facsimile of the text and woodcuts of the 1548 edition; original cloth, pictorial slipcase, pictorial endpapers; near fine. Kraus/Duveen 326 for Venice 1672 edition; not in Ferguson.   Edwin V. Glaser 121-267 1996 $200.00

ROSIS, ANGELO   A New Book of Ornaments, Consisting of Compartment Decorations of Theatres, Ceilings, Chimney Pieces, Doors, Windows and Other Beautyful Forms Usefull to Painters, Carvers, Engravers, &c. London: F. Vivares, 1753. 1st British edition; folio; engraved title leaf, 23 plates; disbound in later cloth, clamshell box; Rare, 2 leaves show light spotting, few marginal repairs; Berlin Kat. 589. The Bookpress 75-230 1996 $4,850.00

ROSS, ALEXANDER 1590-1654   Pansebeia (in Greek letter); or, a View of all Religions in the World... London: printed for John Williams, 1675. 5th edition; frontispiece, 17 illustrations; contemporary calf, head of spine worn, hinges partly cracked. Wing R1976; Sabin 73316.   Anthony W. Laywood 109-127 1996 £110.00

ROSS, ALEXANDER 1590-1654   The Red River Settlement: its Rise, Progress and Present State, with some Account of the Native Races and its General History to the Present Day. London: 1856. 20.5 cm; xvi, 416 pages; frontispiece; fine in gilt stamped pink cloth. Peel 174; TPL 3304; Sabin 73328.   Rockland Books 38-192 1996 $750.00

ROSS, ALEXANDER 1590-1654   View of All Religions in the World...
London: T.C. for John Saywell, 1655. 2nd edition; 8vo; 2 parts, (32), 544,
(10); (22), 78, (2) pages; frontispiece, engraving on title and part two
with 17 engraved portraits; old calf (18th century?) over marbled boards,
extremities rubbed and front outer hinge cracked, but still quite sound.
Wing R1972.   Kenneth Karmiole 1NS-219   1996 $375.00

ROSS, CHARLES H.   The Book of Cats. London: Griffith and Farran,
1868. 1st edition; viii, 296, 32 pages of ads; frontispiece, pictorial title, 6
plates, 13 text illustrations, plain yellow endpapers; green cloth, gilt
pictorial, lacks flyleaf, foxing on tissue guard and ads, cloth with light
wear.   Robin Greer 94A-27   1996 £110.00

ROSS, JOHN   Joanni Rossi Antiquarii Warwicensis Historia Regum
Angliae. E Codice in Bibliotheca Bodlejana... Oxonii: E Theatro
Sheldoniano, 1716. From a total edition of 60 copies, this one of 12
large paper copies; 2l, 236 pages; 2 folding plates; contemporary red
morocco, gilt panelled, spine gilt, some wear to joints and extremities,
front board almost detached, internally very good.   Robert Clark 38-60
1996 £95.00

ROSS, JOHN   The Book of the Red Deer and Empire Big Game.
London: Simpkin, Marshall, Hamilton, Kent and Co., 1925. Limited edition,
number 442 of 500 copies only; 4to; pages 339, 21, 8; copiously
illustrated with full page portraits and photos; original cream cloth, titled
in gilt on upper cover with onlaid color vignette of a stag standing in
glen; some very light dust marking to covers and very occasional
spotting internally, very attractive.   Sotheran PN32-77   1996 £240.00

ROSS, JOHN 1777-1856   Letter from John Ross, the Principal Chief of
the Cherokee Nation to a Gentleman at Philadelphia. Philadelphia: 1837.
1st edition; 40 pages, cover title; half morocco and marbled boards, title
in gilt on spine, very good, minor foxing.   Field 1324; Howes R461;
Gilcrease-Hargrett Cat. p. 33.   Michael D. Heaston 23-93   1996
$500.00

ROSS, JOHN 1777-1856   Narrative of a Second Voyage in Search of a
North-West Passage and of a Residence in the Arctic Regions During the
Years 1829, 1830, 1831, 1832, 1833... London: A. W. Webster, 1835. 1st
edition; 2 volumes, 1st volume 12.75 x 10 inches, (6), errata, (1), xxxiii,
plate list, 740 pages, 31 plates including 9 colored plates and 5 charts;
large folding chart bound at front, marginal tear at head in plate area; 2nd
volume 11.6 x 9.25 inches, xii, 120, cxliv, cii, (1), 20 pages including 12
colored (2 plates and one text leaf bound out of order; blue cloth,
rebacked, corners lightly bumped, some foxing, endpapers renewed. Hill
p. 181; Sabin 73381, 73384; Arctic Bib. 14866.   Parmer Books
Nat/Hist-071196   1996 $1,450.00

ROSS, JOHNNY   The Biggin Hill Frescoes. Limited Editions Club, 1975.
One of 100 numbered copies, signed by author; large folio; 15
illustrations by author; cloth; fine, scarce.   Bertram Rota 272-279
1996 £65.00

ROSS, MARGERY   Robert Ross - Friend of Friends. London: Jonathan
Cape, 1952. 1st edition; 12 black and white plates, one with printed
tissue guard; buckram covers, top edge slightly dusted, edges and
endpapers spotted, top corners slightly bumped, spine slightly faded,
very good in nicked and slightly rubbed, marked and dusty dust jacket
slightly browned at spine and edges.   Ulysses 39-511   1996 £95.00

ROSS, MARVIN C.   Russian Porcelains...the Collections of Marjorie
Merriweather Post, Hillwood, Washington, D.C. Norman: University of
Oklahoma, 1968. 1st edition; 4to; 427 pages, 144 black and white
illustrations; 87 color plates; cloth, top edge gilt, fine in dust jacket,
scarce.   J. M. Cohen 35-87   1996 $200.00

ROSS,, EDMUND G.   History of the Impeachment of Andrew Johnson.
Santa Fe: New Mexican Printing Co., 1896. (iv), 180; label taped to
spine, else good. Scarce. Howes R453.   Dumont 28-104   1996
$175.00

ROSSETTI, CHRISTINA 1830-1894   Goblin Market. London: George G.
Harrap, 1933. Limited to 410 numbered copies, signed by artist; octavo;
42 pages; 4 color plates and 19 drawings in black and white by Arthur
Rackham; original full limp vellum lettered in gilt on front cover, top edge
gilt, others uncut, pictorial endpapers, fine in original publisher's
cardboard slipcase. Latimore & Haskell p. 69.   Heritage Book Shop
196-222   1996 $1,500.00

ROSSETTI, CHRISTINA 1830-1894   Goblin Market. London: Harrap,
1933. Limited to 410 copies, signed by artist; 8vo; illustrations by Arthur
Rackham; vellum, old stain on backstrip and bottom edge apparently
from glue used in binding, very good without case.   Charles Agvent
4-973 1996 $525.00

ROSSETTI, CHRISTINA 1830-1894   New Poems... Hiethereto Unpublished
or Uncollected. London: Macmillan and Co., 1896. 8vo; (xxiv, 397 pages);
etched frontispiece, original dark blue cloth gilt lettered spine and gilt
design on front cover by D. G. Rossetti, uncut, very nice. Fredeman
44.12.   Paulette Rose 16-267   1996 $250.00

ROSSETTI, CHRISTINA 1830-1894   A Pageant and other Poems.
London: Macmillan and Co., 1881. 1st edition; 8vo; (198) pages; dark
green cloth with gilt interlocking and circle design on front by D. G.
Rossetti, gilt lettered spine; the poem "Birchington Churchyard" written
out in lovely contemporary hand on rear page facing final poem,
otherwise near fine. Schlueter & Schlueter p. 3940; Fredeman 44.9.
Paulette Rose 16-268   1996 $325.00

ROSSETTI, CHRISTINA 1830-1894   A Pageant and Other Poems.
London: Macmillan and Co., 1881. 1st edition; decorated cloth, gilt,
inscription, covers marked, rubbed and slightly soiled, head and tail of
spine and corners bumped, splits at each side of spine at head,
endpapers dusty and slightly spotted, good only.   Ulysses 39-513
1996 £75.00

ROSSETTI, CHRISTINA 1830-1894   Poems. London: Blackie and Son,
n.d. 1st trade edition; quarto; xxiv, 369 pages; 36 color plates mounted
on gray paper, with descriptive tissue guards, 34 full page black and
white illustrations, numerous black and white drawings in text; original
white cloth decoratively stamped and lettered in gilt on front cover and
spine, top edge gilt, others uncut, pictorial endpapers; little minor foxing,
very good.   Heritage Book Shop 196-161   1996 $350.00

ROSSETTI, CHRISTINA 1830-1894   Poems. Boston: Roberts Bros.,
1888. 8vo; pages xi, (i), 231; collotype portrait frontispiece with small
waterstain in blank fore margin, tissue guard, wood engraved illustration
on titlepage, 3 plates, all by D. G. Rossetti, few marginalia in 'Contents'
and on blanks at end, otherwise contents fine; original fine diagonal
grain leaf green cloth, backstrip with title at head and imprint at tail
within gilt panels, between blocked pattern of passion flowers and
tendrils in background green on black, intertwined wavy line roll above
and star roll below, design is carried continued onto front cover, titled
within gilt circular sunburst towrds head of front cover, floral endpapers,
gilt edges, excellent.   Blackwell's B112-245   1996 £70.00

ROSSETTI, CHRISTINA 1830-1894   Poems. London: Macmillan and Co.
and New York, 1891. New edition; 8vo; pages xiv, (2), 450, (2) ads,
frontispiece and 3 plates after D. G. Rossetti; original blue cloth, gilt
rules and small circles on sides and spine to a geometric design after
D. G. Rossetti, spine lettered in gilt, uncut; excellent copy; Aubrey
Beardsley's copy, signed by him.   Simon Finch 24-197   1996
£1,500.00

ROSSETTI, CHRISTINA 1830-1894   Poems Chosen By Walter De La
Mare. Newtown: Gregynog Press, 1930. One of 25 copies, specially
bound, of a total edition of 300; 9 1/4 x 6 1/2 inches; (1), 107, (1)
pages; initial openings and frontispiece portrait by Maynard after
drawings by Dante Gabriel Rossetti, shoulder notes printed in red; fine
very animated scarlet morocco by Gregynog Press Bindery (signed by R.
Ashwin Maynard and George Fisher on rear turn-in), covers tooled in gilt
with 2 large cruciform foliate ornaments elaborated with diagonal blind
and gilt decoration (something like evergreen leaves), ornaments on field
of gold dots, covers framed by gilt and blind rules, fomr which emanate
a series of similar gilt and blind evergreen decorations, spine with raised
bands, panels outlined in blind and gilt ttling, board edges ruled in gilt,
turn-ins with double gilt rule, top edge gilt, other edges untrimmed, in
substantial and attractive morocco backed folding cloth box, fleece lined,
spine with raised bands; extremely fine. Harrop 15.   Phillip J. Pirages
33-266   1996 $5,500.00

ROSSETTI, CHRISTINA 1830-1894   Sing Song. A Nursery Rhyme Book.
Boston: Roberts Bros., 1872. 1st American edition; 8vo; drawings by
Arthur Hughes; decorated purple cloth, touch of wear to spine tips, fine,
bright copy.   Charles Agvent 4-975   1996 $275.00

ROSSETTI, CHRISTINA 1830-1894   Sing-Song. A Nursery Rhyme Book.
London: Routledge, 1872. 1st edition; 8vo; drawings by Arthur Hughes;
decorated blue cloth, spine with large chips, corners worn, hinges
repaired rather crudely, good only; but a great association copy, with
bookplate of photographer Frederick H. Evans.   Charles Agvent 4-974
1996 $175.00

ROSSETTI, DANTE GABRIEL 1828-1882   Ballads and Narrative Poems.
Hammersmith: Kelmscott Press, 1893. One of 310 paper copies; octavo;
227 pages; printed in red and black in Golden type; decorative woodcut
borders and initials; full limp vellum with reddish brown silk ties, spine
lettered in gilt, edges lightly foxed, near fine; bookplate of Alfred Sutro.
Clark Lib. Kelmscott & Doves p. 29; Peterson A20; Sparling 20.
Heritage Book Shop 196-162   1996 $1,750.00

ROSSETTI, DANTE GABRIEL 1828-1882   Ballads and Narrative Poems. London: printed by William Morris at the Kelmscott Press, 1893. One of 310 copies; 206 x 145mm; pages (4), 227, printed in red and black Golden type with two full page borders and six and ten line initials by Morris; printed on Kelmscott flower handmade paper; original limp vellum, little warped, silk ties (2 detached), lettered in gold; very good, uncut, preserved in buckram slipcase; contemporary pen and ink presentation drawing tipped onto flyleaf. Peterson A20.   Claude Cox 107-85   1996 £600.00

ROSSETTI, DANTE GABRIEL 1828-1882   Ballads and Sonnets. Portland: Thomas B. Mosher, 1903. One of 450 copies printed; small 4to; printed on special handmade paper; blue boards over vellum spine, paper label; fine, bright copy.   Appelfeld Gallery 54-158   1996 $100.00

ROSSETTI, DANTE GABRIEL 1828-1882   The Blessed Damozel: a Poem. Vale Press, 1898. One of 210 copies; oblong 16mo; woodcut initials by Charles Ricketts; printed in black and red in Vale type; patterned boards, printed label on spine, nice bright copy; bookplate of Fr. John Gray partially removed.   Bertram Rota 272-481   1996 £200.00

ROSSETTI, DANTE GABRIEL 1828-1882   Hand and Soul. Colophon: London: Strangeways and Walden, printers, n.d. 1869. 1st edition; 8vo; original buff printed wrappers (slight wear); very scarce, very good; with monogram "C.A.H." (most surely Charles Augustus Howell) and "T.H.T. B."? Fredeman 23.6; Tinker 1813; CBEL III 491.   Ximenes 109-252   1996 $2,750.00

ROSSETTI, DANTE GABRIEL 1828-1882   Hand and Soul. London: privately printed by Strangeways and Walden, 1869. 1st separate edition; 12mo; pages 24, title (manuscript coat-of-arms on verso), text (pages (3)-22, imprint at foot of last page), final blank; original drab wrappers, letterpress title on upper cover within one line ms. border, slightly soiled, backstrip slightly split; monograms " C.A.H.(owell)? and T.H.T.B? in same hand dated 23 July 1872 on upper cover, ink inscription on inside upper cover 'Bought of Sotheran 10 dec. 1886...', probably the copy of Charles Augustus Howell. Ashley IV 122.   Simon Finch 24-198   1996 £1,000.00

ROSSETTI, DANTE GABRIEL 1828-1882   Hand and Soul. Hammersmith: Kelmscott Press, 1895. One of 525 copies; 16mo; printed in black and orange-red in Golden type on handmade paper, this copy being one of the American issue printed for Way and Williams, Chicago; woodcut double page title within vine and floral border and many decorated initials; bound in maroon morocco, covers set with panels of red and gold persian floral William Morris silk brocade, fine; from the library of John Saks with his bookplate and ink note.   Marilyn Braiterman 15-120   1996 $950.00

ROSSETTI, DANTE GABRIEL 1828-1882   Sonnets and Lyrical Poems. Hammersmith: Kelmscott Press, 1894. One of 310 paper copies; octavo; x, 197 pages, printed in red and black in Golden type, decorative woodcut borders and initials; full limp vellum with green silk ties, spine lettered in gilt, slight discoloration to spine, near fine. Clark Lib. Kelmscott & Doves p. 29-30; Peterson A20a; Sparling 20a.   Heritage Book Shop 196-163   1996 $1,750.00

ROSSETTI, DOMENICO   Il Sepolcro di Winckelmann in Trieste. Venezia: Alvisopolis for the author, 1823. 4to; (12), 343, (1) pages, 9 plates; original paper wrappers, boxed, clean, fresh, untrimmed copy. Archaeologia Luxor-3933   1996 $1,250.00

ROSSI, FILIPPO   Italian Jeweled Arts. London: Thames and Hudson, 1957. 1st edition; tipped in color plates; very fine copy of a magnificent book in dust jacket and publisher's slipcase.   Hermitage SP95-810   1996 $100.00

ROSSIG, CARL G.   Die Nelken nach Ihren Arten, Besonders Nach der J. C. Etlers in Schneeberg und Andem Beruhmten Sammlungen, in Blattern Nach der natur Gezeichnet und Ausgemahlt... Leipzig: im Industrie Domptoir, 1800-08. 1st edition; small 4to; folding hand colored chart, 30 hand colored plates; contemporary marbled boards, some slight soil and wear.   Marilyn Braiterman 15-179   1996 $1,500.00

ROST, J. L.   Die Wohlangelerichtete Neuerfundene Tugendschule in Welcher Vier und Zwantzig Anmuthige Historien zu Erlaubter Gemuths-Ergotzung der Jugend. Frankfurt & Leipzig: G. N. Raspe, 1743? 2nd edition; 8vo; 598 pages; 2 engraved frontispieces and 24 full page engravings, woodcut ornaments; contemporary three quarter mottled calf and paste paper (scuffed); fine in original condition.   Bennett Gilbert LL29-23   1996 $3,250.00

ROSTEN, LEO   People I Have Loved, Known or Admired. New York: McGraw Hill, 1970. 1st edition; 8vo; dust jacket, very good; signed and inscribed by author to Groucho Marx.   George J. Houle 68-93   1996 $150.00

ROSTOVTZEFF, M.   Iranians and Greeks in South Russia. Oxford: Clarendon Press, 1922. Large 4to; frontispiece, (xvi), 260 pages, 23 figures, 11 plates; original cloth, signature, corners lightly bumped. Archaeologia Luxor-3935   1996 $650.00

ROT, DIETER   246 Little Clouds. New York: Cologne: Paris: Something Else Press, 1968. 9.25 x 6.25 inches; facsimile in shaded grey paper of a hand-written and hand-drawn collaged manuscript; dark grey dust jacket lettered in white on spine, dark grey dust jacket illustrated in white; fine. Joshua Heller 21-207   1996 $100.00

ROTH, H. LING   The Aborigines of Tasmania. Hobart: n.d. Facsimile of 1899 2nd edition; map, 228 pages, ciii vocabulary and appendix; original green cloth and yellow dust jacket, good+ copy. Mervyn Meggitt's copy.   Antipodean 28-279   1996 $125.00

ROTH, H. LING   The Natives of Sarawak and British North Boreno. London: Truslove & Hanson, 1896. 1st U.K. edition; limited to 700 copies; 4to; 2 volumes; (xxxii), 464 pages, map at end; black and white illustrations and maps in text and (ix), 302, ccxl pages appendix; black and white illustrations in text; original green buckram covers, top edge gilt, slightly marked and rubbed at extremities, otherwise very good. Very scarce.   Antipodean 28-280   1996 $1,200.00

ROTH, HENRY   Nature's First Green. New York: Targ Editions, 1979. 1/350 signed and numbered copies; fine in plain yellow dust jacket. Bev Chaney, Jr. 23-589   1996 $100.00

ROTH, PHILIP   The Anatomy Lesson. New York: Farrar Straus, Signed, limited edition; fine in unopened slipcase.   Bev Chaney, Jr. 23-590   1996 $125.00

ROTH, PHILIP   The Anatomy Lesson. Franklin Center: Franklin Library, 1983. Franklin Library edition; fine in gilt stamped full leather with frontispiece portrait of author; signed.   Lame Duck Books 19-484 1996 $125.00

ROTH, PHILIP   Goodbye, Columbus and Five Short Stories. Boston: Houghton Mifflin Co., 1959. 1st pringing; author's first book, tape offsetting to endpapers and pastedowns, otherwise very good, lacking dust jacket.   Sherwood 3-247   1996 $135.00

ROTH, PHILIP   His Mistress's Voice. Lewisburg: Press of Appletree Alley, 1995. One in an edition of 185 copies, signed by author; printed on Arches Cream Text; bound in quarter leather and paper over boards, marbled endpapers, slipcase;   Joshua Heller 21-208   1996 $245.00

ROTH, PHILIP   On the Air. A Long Story. New York: New American Library 10, 1970. 1st edition; one of 500 copies; white wrappers; near fine.   Priscilla Juvelis 95/1-213   1996 $100.00

ROTH, PHILIP   Portnoy's Complaint. New York: Random House, 1969. 1st edition; limited to 600 copies signed by author; extremely fine in dust jacket and slipcase.   Bromer Booksellers 90-218   1996 $250.00

ROTH, PHILIP   Zuckerman Unbound. New York: Farrar Straus Giroux, 1981. Signed and numbered; fine in unopened slipcase.   Bev Chaney, Jr. 23-591   1996 $125.00

ROTH, WALTER E.   Ethnological Studies Among the North-West Central Queensland Aborigines. Brisbane: 1897. viii), 199 pages, 24 pages plates, some in color; blue cloth, fine, owner's signature; Ferguson 15115; Grennway 8141.   Antipodean 28-281   1996 $495.00

ROTHERHAM, JOHN   An Essay on Human Liberty. Newcastle-upon-Tyne: printed by T. Saint for J. Robson, 1782. 1st edition; 8vo; half title; modern cloth backed paper wrappers.   Anthony W. Laywood 109-128   1996 £265.00

ROTHERY, MARY C. HUME   The Bridesmaid, Count Stephen and other Poems. London: John Chapman, 1853. 1st edition; large 12mo; pages v, (2), 362, (2 blank) and 10, (2 ads) dated June 1853; original blue cloth, by Westleys with ticket, very good to nice; inscribed by author for her cousin Mrs. Mary Dudgeon.   James Fenning 133-168   1996 £65.00

THE ROTHSCHILD Miscellany. Jerusalem: the Israel Museum, London: Facsimile Editions, 1989. One of 500 copies; 8 3/4 x 7 inches, 9 1/2 x 7 inches; 2 volumes; 812 pages illuminated with lovely and charming scenes from Jewish history and renaissance life; handsome dark brown very elaborately blindstamped fine grain morocco, silver catches and clasps on leather thongs, (companion volume without clasps or catches), each volume in its own protective slipcase with calf lip; Phillip J. Pirages 33-303 1996 $6,950.00

ROTHSCHILD, MIRIAM Dear Lord Rothschild. Birds, Butterflies and History. London: 1983. 8vo; 426 pages; 18 colored and 152 plain illustrations, 2 family trees and several text figures; cloth; signed on titlepage by Miriam Rothschild and inscribed by her to Alistair and Sylvia Hardy, whose copy it was; inserted is a photo of Ashton Mill. Wheldon & Wesley 207-272 1996 £75.00

ROUQUET, ANDRE L'Art Nouveau de la Peinture en Fromage ou en Ramequin Inventree Pour Suivre Le Louable Projet de Trouver Graduellement des Facons de Peindre Inferieures a Celles Qui Existent. A Marolles (i.e. Paris): 1755. 1st edition; 12mo; 20 pages; recent marbled boards with leather title label on spine; few early underlining to text, very good. Ken Spelman 30-8 1996 £650.00

ROUS AND MANN Toronto: The Capital of Ontario. Eleven Reproductions of Etchings Made in the Art Department of Rous and Mann. Toronto: Rous & Mann, Designers and Printers, 1921. 8vo; 13 leaves; 11 plates tipped in; decorated paper wrapper over boards, wrappers scuffed with stain on front cover, else very good. Very scarce; signed by William Colgate. Hugh Anson-Cartwright 87-431 1996 $125.00

ROUSE, WILLIAM The Doctrine of Chances, or, The Theory of Gaming Made Easy to Every Person... London: for the author, n.d. 1814. 1st edition; engraved titlepage, pictorial vignette, 4 folding plates, errata leaf at end; contemporary calf, rubbed, rebacked, gilt to compartments, morocco label; Jessel 1454; Toole Stott (Conjuring) 1308; Horr 1124. Dramatis Personae 37-152 1996 $500.00

ROUSSEAU DE LA VALETTE, MICHEL The Life of Count Ulfeld, Great Master of Denmark and of the Countess of Eleonora His Wife. London: printed in the year 1695. 1st edition in English; 8vo; contemporary panelled calf, slight wear to upper joint; fine, scarce. Wing R2052. Ximenes 108-312 1996 $350.00

ROUSSEAU, JEAN JACQUES 1712-1778 Letters on the Elements of Botany. London: 1791. 3rd edition; 8vo; pages xxiv, (vi), 503, (28 index), 2 ads, 38 engraved plates, folding table; recent half calf, original label. Fine. John Henly 27-240 1996 £60.00

ROUSSEAU, SAMUEL Punctuation; or, an Attempt to Facilitate the Art of Painting, on the Principles of Grammar and Reason. London: printed by the editor, for Longman, 1813. Half title; uncut, blue boards, cream cloth spine, slightly dulled, paper label slightly rubbed. Jarndyce 103-334 1996 £60.00

ROUSSEAU, V. The Messiah of the Cylinder. McClurg, 1917. 1st edition; negligible stain to rear panel, else bright very good+ copy in very good dust jacket save for small chip missing from top of front dust jacket panel and some light stianing to rear dust jacket panel and spine, rare in dust jacket. Aronovitz 57-1006 1996 $850.00

ROWAN, ARCHIBALD HAMILTON Report of the Trial of Archibald Hamilton Rowan, Esq. New York: reprinted by Tiebout and O'Brien, 1794. 8vo; 92), 152, (2) pages, frontispiece disbound, some occasional internal stains. Evans 27643. Kenneth Karmiole 1NS-154 1996 $150.00

ROWAN, JOHN J. The Emigrant and Sportsman in Canada. London: Edward Stanford, 1876. 1st edition; 8vo; pages vii, 440, 32 (publisher's ads); color folding map; original black and gilt stamped cloth, covers soiled and scuffed, small tear in map, titlepage and preface page torn at hinge with no loss, some pages slightly dusty, else good. Hugh Anson-Cartwright 87-375 1996 $250.00

ROWELL, MARGIT Miro. New York: Abrams, 1970. Square folio; 46 pages, text and 184 plates, 75 in color; cloth, dust jacket. Freitag 6580. Brannan 43-430 1996 $110.00

ROWLANDS, JOHN Historical Notes of the Counties of Glamorgan, Carmarthen & Cardigan and List of the Members of Parliament for South Wales from Henry VIII to Charles II. Cardiff: printed by Hugh Bird, 1866. 1st edition; 8vo; 135 pages; original cloth. Anthony W. Laywood 108-228 1996 £50.00

ROWLANDSON, THOMAS The World in Miniature. London: published by R. Ackermann, 101 Strand, sold by all Respectable Book .. 1817. Tall 8vo; lacks title, 40 hand colored etched plates, no text and not titles to plates; full polished calf, ruled gilt dentelles, decorative gilt tooling to spine, raised bands to spine, red morocco label to spine, all edges gilt, marbled endpapers, armorial bookplate to front pastedown and one other loosely inserted, binders stamp to front free endpaper; margins slightly cropped with occasional partial loss of imprint, plates all in fine, clean state, coloring bright, plates watermarked J. Whatman 1816; preserved in red cloth chemise, within quarter red morocco & cloth box, gilt title to spine, bound by Bedford. Tooley 437. Beeleigh Abbey BA56-162 1996 £2,000.00

ROWLEY, G. D. Ornithological Miscellany. London: 1876-78. Royal 4to; 3 volumes, 3 colored frontispieces, colored maps and 132 plates of which 102 are colored; recent half morocco; good. Wheldon & Wesley 207-88 1996 £3,750.00

ROWLEY, WILLIAM Schola Medicinae, or, the New Universal History and School of Medicine. London: printed for the author and sold at his House, 1803. 4to; cxii, 216 pages, plus 60 plates (numbered) and 8 (unnumbered) plates; leaf 213-214 torn with some loss of text, plates 32 333 and 36 have been repaired with no loss of text; early half calf, recently rebacked, text has foxing and some browning, otherwise overall nice, rare. James Tait Goodrich K40-258 1996 $595.00

ROWSON, CHARLOTTE Charlotte. A Tale of Truth. Philadelphia: printed for Mathew Carey, Oct. 9 1794. 2nd Philadelphia edition; 12mo; 169, (1) pages; full contemporary calf, leather label, spot below label on spine chipped, outer front hinge cracked above this spot; browning and handsoiling throughout to varying degrees, one leaf torn through horizontally without loss; with Clifton Waller Barrett bookplate. Wright I 2160; Evans 276550. M & S Rare Books 60-225 1996 $2,500.00

ROWSON, SUSANNA HASWELL 1762-1824 A Spelling Dictionary, Divided into Short Lessons for the Easier Committing to Memory of Children and Young Persons... Boston: John West, 1807. 1st edition; square 12mo; pages iv, 132; original paper covered boards, leather back (nicked); light stain on paes 99-104, but very good. BAL 17011. Howard S. Mott 227-118 1996 $400.00

ROY, ANDREW A History of the Coal Miners of the United States - from the Development of the Mines to the Close of the Anthracite Strike of 1902... Columbus: n.d., ca. 1904. Presumed 1st edition; viii, 454 pages; illustrations; cloth, child's picture on back flyleaf, cover faded and lightly soiled, otherwise very good. Metacomet Books 54-94 1996 $175.00

THE ROYAL Canadian Air Force Overseas: The Sixth year. Toronto: Oxford University Press, 1949. 8vo; pages xi, 537; illustrations, cloth, slightly bumped, otherwise very good. Hugh Anson-Cartwright 87-287 1996 $150.00

ROYAL HORTICULTURAL SOCIETY The Fruit Yearbook. London: 1947-58. Royal 8vo; volumes 1-10, 10 color and numerous plain plates; cloth. John Henly 27-323 1996 £95.00

ROYAL INSTITUTE OF BRITISH ARCHTIECTS Papers Read at the Royal Institute of British Architects. London: 1859-65. 1st edition; 4to; 4 volumes; full page, in text and folding illustrations (some in color). original flexible green cloth with gilt insignia centerpieces and gilt borders, some general wear to bindings, but very good set. Chapel Hill 94-26 1996 $125.00

ROYAL INSTITUTION Notices of the Proceedings at their Meetings of the Members of the Royal Institution, With Abstracts of the Discourse Delivered at the Evening Meetings. London: W. Nicol and Later William Clowes, 1854-1918. 8vo; volumes 1-21; many illustrations, including folding plates; contemporary half calf, leather labels; extremely rare. Charles W. Traylen 117-53 1996 £400.00

ROYAL INSTITUTION OF CORNWALL Twenty-Seventh-Thirty Fourth Annual Report. Truro: 1846-53. 8 volumes bound in one, approximately 500 pages, 45 plages, illustrations, tables; occasional light spotting, sewing and binding defective. Graham Weiner C2-261 1996 £50.00

ROYAL IRISH ACADEMY Transactions. Volume I/II. 1787/88. 8vo; half calf/boards (worn); good. C. P. Hyland 216-735 1996 £75.00

THE ROYAL Punch and Judy. London: Dean and Son, n.d., c. 1870. Tall 8vo 8 color movable pages, closed tear to one page, neatly repaired, hand colored, moveable figures to each page, all tabs infine working condition; color pictorial boards, cloth spine, rear cover rubbed, closed tear to head of cover, outside of some light wear and soiling, very good. Dramatis Personae 37-143 1996 $1,000.00

ROYALL, ANNE   The Tennessean: a Novel. New Haven: printed for the Author, 1827. 1st edition; 12mo; 372 pages; later cloth (soiled), 2 short tears on title mended. BAL 17068 pagination D; Wright I 2257; Shoemaker 30489.   M & S Rare Books   60-226   1996 $600.00

ROYLE, JOHN FORBES   An Essay on the Antiquity of Hindoo Medicine, Including an Introductory Lecture to the Course of Materia Medica and Therapeutics, Delivered at King's College. London: Wm. H. Allen & Co., and J. Churchill, 1837. 1st edition; 8vo; contemporary half morocco, hinges cracked; presentation inscription "To the editor of the Atlas from the Author", with signature and stamp of William Schroeder. Osler 109.   Anthony W. Laywood   108-229   1996 £175.00

ROYLE, JOHN FORBES   On the Culture and Commerce of Cotton in India and Elsewhere... London: Smith, Elder & Co., 1851. 1st edition; 8vo; xvi, 607, (1) pages; 5 plates, one large folding table, text woodcut; contemporary green calf, neatly rebacked, spine gilt with label; very good.   John Drury   82-247   1996 £120.00

ROYS, RALPH L.   The Book of Chilam Balam of Chumayel. Washington: Carnegie Inst., 1933. 4to; viii, 229 pages, 48 figures and 1 plate, 1 map; wrappers.   Archaeologia   Luxor-4852   1996 $125.00

RUBEUS, THEODOSIUS   Discursus Circa Literas Apostolicas in Forma Brevis S.D.M. Urvani Papae VIII. Rome: Typis Vaticanis, 1639. Folio; title in red and black with woodcut device, pages 3-56; Roman limp vellum, covers panelled gilt with double inner and outer rules, flat spine lettered in ink, gilt arms of Cardinal Maffeo Barberini, later Pope Urban VIII, with Barberini bee at each corner of the central panel.   Marlborough   160-23   1996 £1,250.00

RUBIN, R.   Rubin: My Life, My Art: an Autobiography and Selected Paintings. New York: Funk & Wagnalls, ca. 1970. 1st edition; 4to; 43 plates in color, over 50 black and white illustrations, pictorial endpapers; dust jacket (few nicks and creases); very good; signed and inscribed by Rubin, with large original drawing.   George J. Houle   68-102   1996 $2,500.00

RUBIN, WILLIAM S.   Dada and Surrealist Art. New York: n.d. Thick 4to; 525 pages, tipped in color frontispiece, 805 illustrations, including 59 color tipped in; cloth, dust jacket lightly faded at spine, ex-library with ink stamp on reverse titlepage and sellotape marks on pastedowns.   Rainsford   A54-510   1996 £110.00

RUBIONE, GUGLIELMUS   Disputatorum In Quatuor Libros Magisri Sententiarum. Paris: Josse Bade for Michel Conrad, Simon Vincent, & Himself, 1st edition; folio; 2 volumes, 412, 272 leaves; woodcut device, initials, ornaments; early limp vellum, clean and fine, beautifully preserved. Not in NUC; Moreau 2.1840; renouard 2.167; Palau 280457-8.   Bennett Gilbert   LL29-63   1996 $2,150.00

RUCKER, MAUDE A.   The Oregon Trail and Some Of It's Makers. New York: 1930. 1st edition; 293 pages; photos; nice in dust jacket. Herd 1960; Smith 5337.   T. A. Swinford   49-1001   1996 $200.00

RUCKER, WILBUR   A History of the Opthalmoscope. Rochester: 1971. 1st edition; 127 pages; well illustrated; original binding; autographed by author.   W. Bruce Fye   71-1846   1996 $100.00

RUDGE, THOMAS   The History of the County of Gloucester; Compressed and brought Down to the Year 1803. Gloucester: printed for the author by G. F. Harris, 1803. 1st edition; 8vo; 2 volumes; half titles; folding map, 2 plates; contemporary calf, rebacked, labels. Upcott p. 259.   Anthony W. Laywood   109-129   1996 £165.00

RUDKIN, DAVID   Will's Way. Halford: printed at the Rocket Press for the Celandine Press, 1993. 1st edition; 13/20 specially bound copies (of an edition of 150), printed on Zerkall mouldmade paper and signed by author, title and pagination printed in pale blue; 8vo; pages 41, (1); quarter dark blue morocco, backstrip lettered in silver, marbled yellow and pale and dark grey boards, top edge silver, others untrimmed, board slipcase, new copy.   Blackwell's   B112-246   1996 £56.00

RUDOLF, CROWN PRINCE OF AUSTRIA 1858-1889   Notes on Sport and Ornithology. London: 1889. 640 pages; frontispiece; original cloth discolored, hinges frayed.   David A.H. Grayling   MY95Orn-236   1996 £55.00

RUDOLF, CROWN PRINCE OF AUSTRIA 1858-1889   Notes on Sport and Ornithology. London: 1889. frontispiece; original cloth, discolored, hinges rubbed/frayed.   David A.H. Grayling   3/95-205   1996 £55.00

RUFFHEAD, OWEN   The Life of Alexander Pope, Esq. London: printed for C. Bathurst, H. Woodfall, W. Strahan, etc. 1769. 1st edition; 8vo; frontispiece; contemporary calf, slight cracking of joints, very good. CBEL II 512.   Ximenes   108-313   1996 $250.00

RUFFIN, EDMUND   Anticipiations of the Future, to Serve as Lessons for the Present Time. Richmond: J. W. Randolph, 1860. 1st edition; 12mo; 9, (1), 416 pages, plus 14 page publisher's list; original cloth, library bookplate and slip on front endpapers, but very nice. Howes R493. Right II 2132a; LCP/HSP Afro Amer. Cat. 9003.   M & S Rare Books   60-227   1996 $1,500.00

RUFFNER, E. H.   Lines of Communication Between Colorado and New Mexico. Washington: GPO, 1878. 3 folding maps, 37 pages; rebound in leather, some wear and browning, else good.   Dumont   28-121   1996 $275.00

RUFFNER, W. H.   A Report on Washington Territory. New York: Seattle, Lake Shore and Eastern Railroad, 1889. 242 pages, illustrations, maps; slight wear, otherwise very good, library bookplate, no other marks. Smith 8839; Soliday I-1481.   Dumont   28-122   1996 $185.00

RUFUS FESTUS, SEXTUS   Le Dignita de Consoli, e de gl'Imperadori, e i Fatti de' Romani.... Venice: Gabriel Giolito de; Ferrari, 1561. Small 4to; pages (xxxvi), 766, chiefly italic letter, woodcut printer's device occupying two-thirds of titlepage, woodcut initials of different sizes and ornaments, old ms. note on title and another, dated 1609; blank fore edge of titlepage repaired, light age browning, occasionally heavier - in early part of volume, few spots and splashes, otherwise good in well preserved contemporary vellum. BM STC It. p. 592; Adams R886; Graesse VI 190.   A. Sokol   XXV-87   1996 £475.00

RUGGIERI, CLAUDE   Precis Historique sur les Fetes, les Spectacles et les Rejouissances Publiques. Paris: Chez l'Auteur, 1830. 8vo; 2ff., pages viii, 380; contemporary green calf, triple gilt fillet, elaborate scrolling leaf-work, blindstamped covers, central blank panel with blindstamped egg and dart border, flat spine, 2 ornate fleuron gilt panels and central gilt lettered black calf label, all edges gilt, crease marbled endpapers. Most attractive.   Marlborough   160-75   1996 £650.00

RUHEMANN, HELMUT   The Cleaning of Paintings, Problems and Potentialities. London: 1968. 4to; 508 pages, 6 color and 95 monochrome plates. Cloth.   Rainsford   A54-511   1996 £85.00

RUHRAH, JOHN   Pediatrics of the Past. New York: 1925. 1st edition; 592 pages; original binding, backstrip dull; very scarce. GM 6354.   W. Bruce Fye   71-1847   1996 $300.00

RULE, BOB   Champions Golf Club 1957-1976. Houston: Graphics Unlimited, 1976. 1st edition; 4to; color frontispiece, numerous illustrations; dust jacket (some rubbing); very good, signed and inscribed by Jack Burke and Jimmy Demaret to bandleader Les Brown.   George J. Houle   68-54   1996 $125.00

RUNDALL, L. B.   The Ibex of Sha-ping and Other Himalayan Studies. 4to; 15 tipped in colored plates; expertly rebound in green buckram, original spine and upper cover title and ibex motif laid down.   David Grayling   J95Biggame-567   1996 £60.00

RUNDLE, MARIA ELIZA   A New System of Domestic Cookery; Formed Upon Principles of Economy: and Adapted to the Use of Private Families. London: John Murray, 1813. Small 8vo; frontispiece, 9 full page engraved plates, 7 pages of publisher's ads at end; three quarter brown calf over marbled boards, spine with gilt stamped raised bands and gilt stamped red morocco label, chip to lower spine, rubbing, light foxing; very good. Bitting p. 410; Oxford p. 135.   George J. Houle   68-38   1996 $300.00

RUNDLE, T.   A Sermon Preached at St. George's Church, Hanover Square, On Sunday Feb. 17, 1733-34. To Recommend the Charity for Establishing the New Colony of Georgia. London: printed for T. Woodward...J. Brindley, 1734. 24 pages; half morocco; bookplate of William Clements.   Blue River Books   9-149   1996 $850.00

RUNNINGTON, CHARLES   A Treatise on the Action of Ejectment. Dublin: printed for James Moore, 45, College-Green, 1792. contemporary calf, rebacked, some embrowning, usable.   Meyer Boswell   SL25-192   1996 $250.00

RUNYON, DAMON   Runyon A La Carte. Philadelphia: J. B. Lippincott Co., 1944. 1st edition; fine in price clipped dust jacket.   Left Bank Books   2-130   1996 $160.00

THE RUPERT Book. The Daily Express Annual, 1948. 1st edition; royal 8vo; pages 9v); 6-119; illustrations in color; original pictorial wrappers, excellent copy, just slightly rubbed at spine.   Sotheran PN32-151 1996 £98.00

RUPPERT, KARL   The Caracol at Chichen Itza, Yucatan, Mexico. Washington: Carnegie Inst. of Washington, 1935. 4to; frontispiece, xii, 294 pages, 350 figures; original printed wrappers, owner's stamp at flyleaf, spine lightly soiled.   Archaeologia Luxor-4857 1996 $450.00

RUPPERT, KARL   The Mercado, Chichen Itza, Yucatan. Washington: Carnegie Inst. of Washington, 1943. 4to; pages 225-260, 35 figures; original printed wrappers.   Archaeologia Luxor-4858 1996 $125.00

RUSBY, HENRY HURD   Morphology and Histology of Plants Designed Especially as a Guide to Plant-Analysis and Classification... New York: Pub. by the authors, 1899. 1st edition; 8vo; (xii), 378, (4) pages; leather backed marbled boards with leather spine labels, spine detaching, leather very dry and worn, rare.   John Gach 150-404 1996 $150.00

RUSCELLI, GIROLAMO d. 1566   Epistres des Princes, Lesqvelles, ov sont Addresses Avx Princes, ov Traittent les Affaires des Princes... Paris: Iean Ruelle, 1572. 1st edition of the first French translation; small 4to; ff. (iv), 209, (vii), Roman letter with italic dedication, woodcut printer's device on titlepage, woodcut and engraved initials, early ms. ex-library note above title; contemporary limp vellum, some light browning or waterstaining. BM STC Fr. p. 387; not in Adams; 3 copies in NUC.   A. Sokol XXV-88 1996 £475.00

RUSCELLI, GIROLAMO d. 1566   De Secretis Libri, Mira Quadam Rerum Varietate Utilitateq Referti, Longe Castigatiores and Ampliores Quam Priore Editione. Basel: P. Perna, 1560. 1st complete edition of Wecker's translation; 8vo; (14), 354, (29) pages; 2 early ownership inscriptions on ttile; modern boards made from an incunable leaf. Duveen p. 15; Ferguson I p. 22; Durling III; Wellcome I 180.   Jeffrey Mancevice 20-74 1996 $850.00

RUSCHENBERGER, WILLIAM   Three Years in the Pacific, Containing Notes of Brazil, Chile, Bolivia, Peru &c. in 1831, 1832, 1833, 1834. London: Richard Bentley, 1835. 8vo; 2 volumes, pages x, 403, vi, 440; new green cloth, leather labels. Hill I p. 263; Sabin 74196; De Moraes II p. 221.   Richard Adelson W94/95-143 1996 $425.00

RUSH, BENJAMIN 1745-1813   Essays, Literary, Moral and Philosophical. Philadelphia: printed by Thomas and Samuel F. Bradford, 1798. 1st edition; 8vo; (ii), (viii), 378 pages; modern tooled calf with raised bands and leather spine label, fine, untrimmed copy; inscribed by author for Miss Elisa Gibson, rare thus. Norman Cat. 1863.   John Gach 150-405 1996 $2,500.00

RUSH, BENJAMIN 1745-1813   An Eulogium, Intended to Perpetuate the Memory of David Rittenhouse, Late President of the American Philosophical Society, Delivered Before the Society in the First Presbyterian Church in High Street, Philadelphia on the 17th Dec. 1796. Philadelphia: J. Ormrod, 1796. 1st edition; 8vo; 46 pages; uncut and unopened, few slight tears to wrappers, but remarkably fine; Blake p. 393.   Edwin V. Glaser 121-264 1996 $300.00

RUSH, BENJAMIN 1745-1813   Letters of Benjamin Rush, 1761-1813. Princeton: Princeton University Press, 1951. 1st edition; 2 volumes; lxxxviii, 684, (iv), 625-1295 pages; cloth; fine in fine dust jacket.   Metacomet Books 54-95 1996 $100.00

RUSH, BENJAMIN 1745-1813   Medical Inquiries and Observations Upon the Diseases of the Mind. Philadelphia: Kimber & Richardson, 1812. 1st edition; 2nd issue (actually printing) with signature H reset so that Section VIII begins on page 62; 8vo; (368), (4) pages; original calf, rebacked with new endpapers, boards scraped, exceptionally clean, pretty copy, usually heavily foxed and browned. Austin 1961 #1670.   John Gach 150-406 1996 $1,250.00

RUSH, BENJAMIN 1745-1813   Medical Inquiries and Observataions Upon the Diseases of the Mind. Philadelphia: John Richardson, 1818. 2nd edition; 8vo; 367 pages; original full tree sheep, morocco spine label, text somewhat browned, but very good. Scarce. Sabin 74241; American Imprints 45601; GM 4924.   Chapel Hill 94-273 1996 $450.00

RUSH, BENJAMIN 1745-1813   Medical Inquiries and Observations Upon the Diseases of the Mind. Philadelphia: John Grigg, 1830. 4th edition; 8vo; 365, (3) pages; contemporary sheep, lacking leather spine label, signature cut from titlepage, rear board detached, internally very clean and nearly unfoxed.   John Gach 150-407 1996 $250.00

RUSH, BENJAMIN 1745-1813   Medical Inquiries and Observations Upon the Diseases of the Mind. Philadelphia: 1835. 5th edition; 8vo; 365 pages + ads; full sheep, rubbed at edges, foxing, else fine. GM 4924 (1st ed.); Hunter-Macalpine pp. 662-71.   Argosy 810-426 1996 $500.00

RUSH, BENJAMIN 1745-1813   Medical Inquiries and Observations Upon the Diseases of the Mind. Philadelphia: pub. by Grigg and Elliot, 1835. 5th edition; 8vo; (ii), 365, (5) pages + rear catalog; rebound in modern leatherette, text foxed, several leaves in rear ads defective, good, usable copy.   John Gach 150-408 1996 $250.00

RUSH, JAMES   The Philosophy of the Human Voice. Philadelphia: 1855. 4th edition; 8vo; 559 pages; contemporary sheep, signature clipped form top of title;   M & S Rare Books 60-404 1996 $100.00

RUSH, NORMAN   Whites. New York: Knopf, 1986. Uncorrected proof; fine in wrappers, publisher's note laid in.   Book Time 2-368 1996 $130.00

RUSH, NORMAN   Whites. New York: Knopf, 1986. 1st edition; near fine copy in fine dust jacket, minor fading to top edges (common to this book); author's first book.   Book Time 2-367 1996 $100.00

RUSH, RICHARD   Memoranda of a Residence at the Court of London, Comprising Incidents Official and Personal from 1819 to 1825. Philadelphia: Lea & Blanchard, 1845. 1st edition; xii, 640 pages; original black cloth, 1 inch chip at head of spine, otherwise near fine with bright lettering on spine. Howes R523.   Blue River Books 9-273 1996 $125.00

RUSH, RICHARD   A Residence at the Court of London. London: Richard Bentley, 1833. 1st edition; large 8vo; 16 (ads), xviii, 420 pages; original boards, spine darkened. Howes R522.   The Bookpress 75-459 1996 $250.00

RUSHBY, G. G.   No More the Tusker. London: 1965. illustrations; nice in dust jacket.   David Grayling J95Biggame-171 1996 £70.00

RUSHDIE, SALMAN   Grimus. London: Gollancz, 1975. 1st edition; fine in fine dust jacket.   Ken Lopez 74-392 1996 $650.00

RUSHDIE, SALMAN   Grimus. London: Gollancz, 1975. 1st edition; author's first book; fine in dust jacket with barely noticeable scrape at base of dust jacket spine.   Aronovitz 57-1008 1996 $250.00

RUSHDIE, SALMAN   Grimus. London: Victor Gollancz, 1975. 1st edition; near fine in bright dust jacket, tipped in on front endpaper is author's signature; author's first book.   Left Bank Books 2-133 1996 $225.00

RUSHDIE, SALMAN   Haroun and the Sea of Stories. London: Granata, 1990. 1st edition; very fine in dust jacket, signed by author.   Left Bank Books 2-132 1996 $150.00

RUSHDIE, SALMAN   Midnight's Children. New York: Knopf, 1980. 1st U.s. edition; author's 2nd book; ink name, else near fine in near fine price clipped dust jacket.   Pettler & Lieberman 28-221 1996 $150.00

RUSHDIE, SALMAN   Midnight's Children. London: Cape, 1981. 1st British edition; fine in near fine dust jacket, very slightly faded on spine.   Ken Lopez 74-394 1996 $400.00

RUSHDIE, SALMAN   Midnight's Children. New York: Knopf, 1981. 1st edition; slight spine slant, causing pages to be flush with edges of boards, thus only near fine in fine jacket, without spine fading so common to this title.   Ken Lopez 74-393 1996 $200.00

RUSHDIE, SALMAN   The Satanic Verses. London: Viking, 1988. True 1st edition; fine in fine dust jacket.   Ken Lopez 74-395 1996 $250.00

RUSKIN, ARTHUR   Classics in Arterial Hypertension. Springfield: 1956. 1st edition; 358 pages; original binding.   W. Bruce Fye 71-1855 1996 $125.00

RUSKIN, JOHN 1819-1900   Lectures on Art. New York: Wiley & Son, 1870. 1st American edition; 12mo; (viii), 202 pages; publisher's cloth, rubberstamp on front free endpaper, bottom edge of titlepage shaved, minor wear to extremities of spine, else bright, desirable copy. Bookpress 75-111 1996 $150.00

RUSKIN, JOHN 1819-1900   Letters On Art and Literature by John Ruskin. London: privately printed, 1894. 1st edition; one of 33 copies; 8vo; (xi), (i), 98 pages, printed on Whatman paper; spine faded and dull with minor rubbing to edges, owner's neat signature on front pastedown, else very good.   Andrew Cahan 47-178 1996 $200.00

RUSKIN, JOHN 1819-1900   Modern Painters. (and) The Stones of Venice. New York: Wiley, 1880. 1st edition; 8 volumes; engravings and 141 plates, few in color; half black morocco, marbled boards, 5 raised bands, gilt ruled borders and spine panels with date stamped at bottom; some edgewear and scuffing, corners with wear, very good.   Charles Agvent 4-976 1996 $500.00

RUSKIN, JOHN 1819-1900   Notes by Mr. Ruskin on Samuel Prout and William Hunt... London: Fine Art Society, 1880. 1st edition; 4to; 95 pages, 20 plates; spine worn and rubbed.   Bookpress 75-112 1996 $225.00

RUSKIN, JOHN 1819-1900   Praeterita. Outlines of Scenes and Thoughts Perhaps Worthy of Memory in My Past Life. Sunnyside, Orpington, Kent: George Allen, 1886-89. 1st edition; one of 600 large paper copies, with extra plate not found in ordinary copies, and with all 3 of the plates printed on India paper; 4to; 3 volumes; bound from original parts, including all four of the original titles to parts I-IV of volume 3, which was never completed; this set with extra engraved portrait of Ruskin; three quarter morocco, gilt spines in compartments, marbled endpapers, top edge gilt; extremities and edges bit scuffed and worn, otherwise good set. Presentation copy inscribed by author for John Brown. Wise 258.   David J. Holmes 52-95 1996 $1,250.00

RUSKIN, JOHN 1819-1900   The Seven Lamps of Architecture. London: Smith, Elder & Co., 1849. 1st edition; 8vo; viii, (iv), 205, (1), 16 pages; 14 plates; publisher's cloth, respined professionally, using original as overlay, occasional spotting, bookplate, tips worn, hinges internally cracked.   Bookpress 75-113 1996 $300.00

RUSKIN, JOHN 1819-1900   The Seven Lamps of Architecture. Orpington: George Allen, 1889. Large paper edition; 4to; 14 lithographed plates by Ruskin; full brown tree calf, expertly rebacked, gilt panelled spine, raised bands, edges gilt.   Appelfeld Gallery 54-159 1996 $135.00

RUSKIN, JOHN 1819-1900   The Stones of Venice. London: Smith, Elder and Co., 1873-74. Autograph edition limited to 1500 sets, first volume of each signed by author; 8vo; pages xxi, (i), 400, 21 plates; vi, (ii blank), 394, 20 plates; (iv), 362, 12 plates; publisher's gilt and blindstamped cloth, head and tails of spines little tender, otherwise sound set. Wise 297.   Sotheran PN32-193 1996 £350.00

RUSKIN, JOHN 1819-1900   Works. Boston: Dana Estes, 1900. 8vo; 26 volumes; hundreds of I, many in color; green cloth, as issued, gilt decorations on spines, gilt tops; very fine and bright.   Appelfeld Gallery 54-160 1996 $400.00

RUSKIN, JOHN 1819-1900   Complete Works of... London: George Allen, 1903-12. Library Edition, limited to 2062 copies; 4to; 39 volumes; frontispieces, photogravure plates, other illustrations; publisher's cloth, edges uncut, spines faded, some volumes little worn, internally a reasonably clean set with only occasional light foxing, although volumes 27 and 38 have been supplied from an ex-library set and consequently have a few rubber stamps inside and library numbers on their spines, volume 31 has a small stab-hole in spine and few of the leaves are slightly torn in upper margin. Still very good working set.   Thomas Thorp 489-265 1996 £800.00

RUSSEL, JAMES   Letters from a Young Painter Abroad to His Friends in England. London: printed for W. Russel, 1750. 2nd edition of volume 1, 1st edition of volume 2; large 8vo; 2 volumes; 13 plates, occasional light spotting, but very good set on large paper; contemporary calf, gilt, rebacked, edges and corners restored; early note identifies this as the Fonthill copy. Pine-Coffin 740.1. CBEL ii 1419.   Ximenes 108-315 1996 $450.00

RUSSEL, JAMES   Letters from a Young Painter Abroad to His Friends in England. London: printed for W. Russel, 1750. 2nd edition of volume 1, 1st edition of volume 2; 8vo; 2 volumes; printed on ordinary paper; 13 plates; occasional light spotting, contemporary calf, gilt, reacked, very good set; early engraved bookplates of Mrs. Tichborne. Pine Coffin 740.1. CBEL II 1419.   Ximenes 108-316 1996 $300.00

RUSSEL, JOHN   Letters from a Young Painter Abroad to His Friends in England. London: printed for W. Russel, 1748. 8vo; viii, 283, (5) pages; 5 plates; in this copy all but one of the plates have contemporary hand coloring; contemporary calf, expertly rebacked with new red gilt label; very good. Pine Coffin 7401.   Ken Spelman 30-5 1996 £260.00

RUSSEL, M.   Polynesia: or, an Historical Account of the Principal Islands in the South Sea, Including New Zealand... Edinburgh: Oliver & Boyd, 1865. 1st edition; small 8vo; 440 pages, folding map; original red cloth, some wear to foot of spine, otherwise near fine. Hill p. 558. David Mason 71-148 1996 $100.00

RUSSELL, BENJAMIN   An Address Delivered Before the Massachusetts Charitable Mechanics Assocaition, December 21, 1809... Boston: pub. by order of the Association, from the Press of John Eliot, Jun. 1810. Small 4to; self wrappers, lacks front cover, very good; scarce.   Freedom Bookshop 14-40 1996 $250.00

RUSSELL, BERTRAND   The Principles of Mathematics. Cambridge: at the University Press, 1903. 1st edition; 8vo; xxix, 534 pages; original navy cloth, top and bottom of backstrip lightly frayed, remnant of paper label at bottom of spine, bookplate and contemporary inscription on endpapers; very good.   Edwin V. Glaser 121-271 1996 $1,200.00

RUSSELL, BERTRAND 1872-1970   A Critical Exposition of the Philosophy of Leibniz, with an Appendix. Cambridge University Press, 1900. 1st edition; 8vo; xvi, (ii), 311, (i) pages; original blue cloth, spine gilt, little rubbed and marked, minor foxing; very good, uncommon. Robert Clark 38-283 1996 £100.00

RUSSELL, C. E. M.   Bullet and Shot in Indian Forest, Plain and Hill. 1900. illustrations, spine slightly faded, very light sporadic foxing; inscribed by author for John Upfold.   David Grayling J95Biggame-383 1996 $80.00

RUSSELL, CHARLES MARION 1864-1926   More Rawhides. Great Falls: 1925. 1st edition; royal 8vo; illustrations in pen and ink; pictorial wrappers, published with overlapping covers, latter are generally frayed at overlap, otherwise very good. Very scarce. Herd 1969; Y&R p. 19; Howes R528;   Gene W. Baade 1094-140 1996 $375.00

RUSSELL, CHARLES MARION 1864-1926   More Rawhides. Great Falls: 1925. 1st edition; iv, 66 pages; illustrations; stiff repaired pictorial wrappers; very good+. YR 39; Herd 1969.   T. A. Swinford 49-1004 1996 $375.00

RUSSELL, CHARLES MARION 1864-1926   Rawhide Rawlins Stories. Great Falls: 1921. 2nd printing; royal 8vo; illustrations in pen and ink; pictorial wrappers, stains to back cover, some spotting to front, cover corners with small chips, upper back corner of book has been slightly bent/creased, small printed number upper corner of titlepage, good copy; very scarce. YR p. 18; Dykes HS p. 191; Howes R530; Herd 1972.   Gene W. Baade 1094-141 1996 $200.00

RUSSELL, CHARLES MARION 1864-1926   Rawhide Rawlins Stories. Great Falls: 1921. 4th printing; 40 pages; illustrations by author; pictorial wrappers, some soiling, very good+. Herd 1972.   T. A. Swinford 49-1007 1996 $150.00

RUSSELL, CHARLES MARION 1864-1926   Trails Plowed Under. Garden City: Doubleday, 1927. 1st edition; small 4to; 5 plates in color, 5 black and white plates, 46 black and white illustrations; dust jacket with few chips, very good to fine; boldly signed and inscribed by Will Rogers. George J. Houle 68-130 1996 $1,250.00

RUSSELL, E. F.   Dark Tides. Dobson, 1962. 1st edition; very good+/near fine in near fine dust jacket.   Aronovitz 57-1013 1996 $150.00

RUSSELL, FREDERIC WILLIAM   Kett's Rebellion in Norfolk; Being a History of the Great Civil Commotion that Occurred at the Time of the Reformation, in the Right of Edward VI. London: Longman, et al, 1859. 1st edition; 4to; pages xiii, (iii), 240; frontispiece, 9 plates, foxed; contemporary morocco grain brown cloth, rebacked and original faded backstrip relaid, backstrip gilt lettered, sides with blindstamped border, gilt title within foliage frame on front cover, extremities rubbed, chalked terracotta endpapers, label (?) removed, good.   Blackwell's B112-213 1996 £75.00

RUSSELL, GEORGE WILLIAM 1867-1935   By Still Waters, Lyrical Poems Old and New. Dundrum: Dun Emer Press, 1906. One of 200 copies; 8vo; pages (viii), 33, text printed in black and red; original linen backed boards, lettered in dark blue on upper cover, edges uncut and unopened; this may have been W. B. Yeats's copy, as it has his signature on verso of half title.   Sotheran PN32-47   1996 £450.00

RUSSELL, GEORGE WILLIAM 1867-1935   Some Passages from the Letters to A. E. to W. B. Yeats. Dublin: Cuala Press, 1936. 1st edition; limited to 300 copies; fine.   Hermitage SP95-865   1996 $225.00

RUSSELL, GEORGE WILLIAM 1867-1935   Thoughts for a Convention...Memorandum on the State of Ireland. Dublin and London: Maunsel and Co., 1917. 1st edition; wrappers; cover and pages browned, lower cover slightly spotted and dusty, very good.   Ulysses 39-1   1996 £75.00

RUSSELL, HENRY PATRICK   Biarritz and the Basque Countries. London: Edward Stanford, 1873. 1st edition; 8vo; viii, 192 pages; folding map in color; original cloth, spine faded to tan, otherwise fine.   David Mason 71-154   1996 $100.00

RUSSELL, JOHN   Instructions fro the Drill and the Method of Performing the Eighteen Manoeuvres. Philadelphia: M. Thomas, Sept. 21, 1814. 1st American edition, from the 4th London; 8vo; 239, (1) pages; 33 plates; original printed boards, uncut, light foxing of text, covers somewhat waterstained, spine chipped, appealing copy; Scarce. S&S 32691.   M & S Rare Books 60-377   1996 $325.00

RUSSELL, OSBORNE   Journal of a Trapper: Nine Years in the Rocky Mountains 1834-1843. Boise: Syms-York Co., Inc., 1921. 2nd edition; bookplate, else very good.   Hermitage SP95-730   1996 $175.00

RUSSELL, RACHEL WRIOTHESLEY VAUGHAN 1636-1723   Letters of Rachel, Lady Russell. London: Longman, Brown, Green and Longman, 1853. New edition; 8vo; 2 volumes; xii, 289, viii, 231 pages; original blindstamped cloth; fine, bright copy.   David Mason 71-37 1996 $120.00

RUSSELL, RACHEL, LADY   Letters of Lady Rachel Russell...and the Trial of Lord William Russell for High Treason. London: Printed for J. Mawman, in the Poultry, 1801. 6th edition; contemporary calf, rebacked, title repaired, sound.   Meyer Boswell SL26-234   1996 $150.00

RUSSELL, ROSS   Bird Lives! The High Life and Hard Times of Charlie (Yardbird) Parker. New York: Charterhouse, 1973. 1st edition; original cloth, close to fine in close to fine dust jacket with just a trace of wrinkling to the bit sunned spine.   Beasley Books 82-247   1996 $100.00

RUSSELL, WILLIAM CLARK   "Fra" Angelo: a Tragedy. London: for the author; John Camden Hotten, 1865. 1st edition; 8vo; original green cloth, bit rubbed, old library blindstamp on covers, front inner hinge weak; exceedingly rare first book; with fine inscription by Walter Montgomery to member of the original cast. not in CBEL or BM Cat. Wolff 6016.   Ximenes 108-317   1996 $1,500.00

RUSSELL, WILLIAM HOWARD   My Diary, North and South. London: Bradbury & Evans, 1863. 1st edition; 8vo; 2 volumes; large folding map (torn without loss), very occasional light spotting; original blue cloth, spines gilt, little soiled and worn at head and tail of spines.   Ian Wilkinson 95/1-16   1996 £65.00

RUSSOM, J.   A Word to the Working Classes on Their Improvement and Elevation (with Other Pieces). London: Joulston and Stoneman, 1850. 1st edition; 12mo; (4), 138, (6) pages, including 2 page list of subscribers and 4 pages of publishers' ads at end, marginal tear in B1 (no loss); old cloth, rebacked with label, good, but not attractive copy. Not in Goldsmiths and not in NUC.   John Drury 82-248   1996 £60.00

RUST, BRIAN   Jazz Records 1897-1942. London: Storyville, 1970. Revised edition; 2 volumes; red cloth stamped in gilt, very good to near fine.   Beasley Books 82-249   1996 $175.00

RUTGERS, A.   Birds of Europe. Birds of Australia. Birds of Asia. Birds of New Guinea. Birds of South America. London: 1966-72. royal 8vo; 5 volumes in 6, 160 colored plates from lithographs of John Bould; cloth. Wheldon & Wesley 207-741   1996 £160.00

RUTGERS, A.   Encyclopaedia of Aviculture. London: 1970-77. 4to; 3 volumes; colored plates, numerous figures; cloth.   Wheldon & Wesley 207-844   1996 £70.00

RUTHERFOORD, SAMUEL   Joshua Redivivus: Or, Three Hundred and Fifty-Two Letters. Glasgow: printed by John Bryce, 1765. 9th edtilon; 8vo xxxii, 526 pages, ad leaf; original sheep, head and foot of spine little worn, covers scratched, joints cracked, small round wormhole near the foot of the page in the final quarter of the book, affecting letters, slightly larger in final signature.   David Bickersteth 133-60   1996 £55.00

RUTILIUS LUPUS, PUBLIUS   De Figuris Sententiarum Ac Verborum... Lyon: Apud Seb. Gryphium, Luguduni, 1542. 8vo; pages 119, (5), woodcut griffin on title and last leaf, name excised from foot of title, last index leaf with slight text loss, some notes shaved from fore-edges; old (1564) monastic manuscript ownerships on plain vellum binding, slightly wormed. Baudrier VIII 69.   Family Album Tillers-544   1996 $240.00

RUTKOW, IRA   The History of Surgery in the United States 1775-1900. Volume I: Textbooks, Monographs and Treatises. San Francisco: 1988. 1st edition; original binding; GM 6596.62.   W. Bruce Fye 71-1864 1996 $125.00

RUTLAND, JOHN HENRY, DUKE OF   A Tour through Part of Belgium and the Rhenish Provinces. London: Rodwell and Martin, 1822. 4to; 2 ff., 131 pages, 131 pages, 13 litho plates; near contemporary cloth, partly faded.   Marlborough 162-255   1996 £600.00

RUTLEDGE, SARAH   House and Home: or, the Carolina Housewife. Charleston: John Russell, 1855. 3rd edition; 8vo; 172 pages; original brown cloth, cloth soiled, usual light foxing, but good to very good. Lowenstein American Cookery Books 654.   Chapel Hill 94-167 1996 $250.00

RUTT, JOHN TOWILL   Diary of Thomas Burton, Esq. Member in the Parliaments of Oliver and Richard Cromwell from 1656 to 1659... London: Henry Colburn, New Burlington St., 1828. 8vo; 4 volumes; errata leaf, 2 page publisher's ad, frontispiece to volume 1, facsimile autograph frontispieces to volumes 2 and 3; half titles, errata leaf, frontispiece; full olive calf, some scoring to binding, elaborate gilt tooling to compartments, red morocco labels to spines, gilt ruled borders to spines, joints slightly rubbed, armorial bookplate to front pastedown of all volumes, some light foxing to few pages, otherwise a good set. Abbott 1694.   Beeleigh Abbey BA56-137   1996 £350.00

RUTTLEDGE, H.   Attack on Everest. 1935. 1st U.S. edition; stereoscopic picture plus viewing glasses, not in original; very slight fading of boards, but very good in not quite very good wrapper with slight browning of spine and some restoration.   Moutaineering Books 8-R30   1996 £50.00

RUTTLEDGE, H.   Everest 1933. London: 1934. 1st edition; 59 sepia plates, 4 maps, 3 diagrams; very good/fine; inscribed by Frank Smythe. Moutaineering Books 8-R32   1996 £100.00

RUTTLEDGE, H.   Everest 1933. London: 1934. 1st edition; 59 sepia plates, 4 maps, 3 diagrams; edges and first few pages little foxed, generally fine in above average dust jacket with slight browning of spine and some chipping repaired.   Moutaineering Books 8-R31   1996 £80.00

RUTTLEDGE, H.   Everest Unfinished Adventure. London: 1937. 1st edition; 63 plates, 2 folding maps, 13 pencil portrait sketches by P. R. Oliver; very faint mark on front board, still fine in cream colored pictorial dust jacket, in above average, very good+ condition.   Moutaineering Books 8-R37   1996 £110.00

RUTTLEDGE, H.   Everest Unfinished Adventure. London: 1937. 1st edition; 63 plates, 2 folding maps, 13 pencil portrait sketches, corner slightly bumped, otherwise clean, bright, very good+ copy; presentation bookplate and signature of Lord Dawson.   Moutaineering Books 8-R38 1996 £65.00

RUTTLEDGE, H.   Everest: the Unfinished Adventure. London: 1937. 1st edition; 63 plates, 2 folding maps, 13 pencil portrait sketches, some faint marks on boards, generally bright, very good+ copy.   Moutaineering Books 8-R39 1996 £50.00

RUZICKA, RUDOLPH   Speaking Reminiscently... New York: Grolier Club, 1986. One of 750 copies; 8 3/4 x 5 3/4 inches; 150 pages, (15) leaves; frontispiece, 14 pages with illustrations at end; title in grey and black, very fine.   Phillip J. Pirages 33-290   1996 $125.00

RYAN, ABRAM J.   Father Ryan's Poems. Mobile: 1879. 1st edition; 8vo; 262, (1) pages; frontispiece; original cloth, very good; two part slipcase; bookplate of Estelle Doheny. BAL 17107.   M & S Rare Books 60-228   1996 $250.00

RYAN, J. G.   Life and Adventures of Gen. W. A. C. Ryan, the Cuban Martyr... New York: and Chicago: 1876. 1st and only edition; 256 pages; frontispiece, mounted albumen portrait; contemporary three quarter morocco, minor foxing; fine copy overall. Graff 3625; Howes R557. Michael D. Heaston   23-293   1996 $3,750.00

RYAN, KATHRYN WHITE   Golden Pheasant - Poems. New York: & London: G. P. Puntam's Sons, 1925. 1st edition; original binding, top edge dusty, head and tail of spine and corners bumped, spine darkened, covers marked, endpaper edges browned, top corners of few pages slightly creased, good; ownership signature of Ian Fleming.   Ulysses 39-687   1996 £180.00

RYAN, PETER   Encyclopedia of Papua New Guinea. Melbourne: 1972. Thick small 4to; 3 volumes; illustrations; very good.   Antipodean 28-296   1996 $175.00

RYBERG, INEZ SCOTT   Panel Reliefs of Marcus Aurelius. New York: Archaeological Inst. of America, 1967. Folio; xii, 102 pages, 62 plates; original cloth, spine faded, corners lightly rubbed and bumped. Archaeologia Luxor-3945   1996 $125.00

RYDEN, STIG   Archaeological Researches in the Department of La Candelaria. Goteborg: Elanders Boktryckeri Aktiebolag, 1936. 8vo; 327 pages, 150 illustrations; wrappers; inscribed presentation copy, with scholarly annotations and underlining in pencil.   Archaeologia Luxor-4861   1996 $125.00

RYDER, JOHN   Intimate Leaves from a Designer's Notebook: Essays. Gwasg Gregynog, 1993. One of 80 copies bound thus; quarter goatskin. Bertram Rota   272-218   1996 £160.00

RYDER, JOHN   Intimate Leaves from a Designer's Notebook: Essays. Gwasg Gregynog, 1993. One of 300 numbered copies; designed by author and printed in monotype Baskerville; patterned boards with cloth spine.   Bertram Rota   272-217   1996 £85.00

RYLANDS, GEORGE   Poems. London: 1931. One of 350 numbered copies, signed by author; 12mo; hand printed by Leonard and Virginia Woolf; decorated paper boards, pages and endpaper edges whitened, spine faded, head and tail of spine and corners slightly bumped, covers slightly rubbed, very good.   Ulysses 39-295   1996 £95.00

RYMER, THOMAS 1641-1713   A Short View of Tragedy; its Original, Excellency and Corruption with some Reflections on Shakespear, and Other Practitioners for the Stage. London: Richard Baldwin, 1693. 1st edition; 8vo; (xiv), 182, (ii) pages; contemporary (or slightly later) sheep, spine gilt, label, final ad leaf, no initial blank; rubbed, corners and edges worn, titlepage frayed on outer edge, not affecting text, some dampstaining & slight weakening of paper edges at beginning & end, with no loss of text. Reasonable copy. Wing R2429; A. & R. 3705. Robert Clark   38-123   1996 £275.00

S

S., E.   The Godmother's Tales. London: Harris, 1813. 3rd edition; 12mo; 172 pages; frontispiece; quarter calf marbled boards; covers worn, else very good. Moon 744 (3). Osborne 296.   Marjorie James 19-189 1996 £95.00

SABARTES, JAIME   Picasso: Toreros. New York: Monte Carlo: Braziller/Sauret, 1961. Oblong folio; 153 pages; original lithgoraphs plus 103 plates, some in color; cloth, some discoloration and light wear to cover. Freitag 7495.   Brannan 43-536 1996 $175.00

SABATINI, RAFAEL   The Nuptials of Corbal. Boston: Houghton Mifflin, 1927. 1st edition; 8vo; illustrations by Harold Brett; pictorial endpapers, cloth, dust jacket, covers somewhat rubbed at edges, otherwise fine in chipped and slightly rubbed dust jacket.   James S. Jaffe 34-604 1996 $100.00

SABATINI, RAFAEL   The Writings of... Boston: Houghton Mifflin, 1924-30. One of 750 numbered sets, signed by author; 8vo; 24 volumes; numerous plates; quarter burgundy buckram with paper covered boards, paper spine labels, uncut; fine.   James Cummins 14-171 1996 $750.00

SABIN, JOSEPH 1821-1881   A Dictionary of Books Relating to America, from its Discovery to the Present Time. New York: 1967. Mini-Print Edition; oblong 4to; 29 volumes in 2; original cloth.   Forest Books 74-235 1996 £345.00

SABINE, LORENZO   Notes on Duels and Duelling, Alphabetically Arranged... Boston: Crosby, Nichols, 1855. 1st edition; viii, 394 pages; cloth, light cover wear, otherwise very good. Howes S4.   Metacomet Books 54-96 1996 $125.00

SABINE, W. H. W.   Historical Memoris from 16 March 1763 to 9 July 1776; 12 July, 1776 to 25 July, 1778, of William Smith, Historian of the Province of New York... New York: 1956. 1st edition; 4to; 2 volumes; xvi, 300; xxviii, 459 pages; several maps and facsimiles; cloth bindings with spine rivets, mimeograph format; very good.   Metacomet Books 54-97 1996 $125.00

SACKVILLE-WEST, VICTORIA MARY 1892-1962   All Passion Spent. London: Hogarth Press, 1931. Spine cocked, free endpapers offset, dust jacket slightly creased and chipped at extremities of spine, otherwise very good.   R. A. Gekoski 19-120 1996 £250.00

SACKVILLE-WEST, VICTORIA MARY 1892-1962   Aphra Behn. London: Gerald Howe Ltd., 1927. 1st edition; slim 8vo; (92) pages; frontispiece; blue cloth, gilt lettered spine; very fine in near fine decorated dust jacket slightly chipped at head of backstrip.   Paulette Rose 16-272 1996 $175.00

SACKVILLE-WEST, VICTORIA MARY 1892-1962   Constantinople: Eight Poems. London: Complete Press, 1915. Author's second book; wrappers; excellent copy.   R. A. Gekoski 19-117 1996 £375.00

SACKVILLE-WEST, VICTORIA MARY 1892-1962   The Dark Island. London: Hogarth Press, 1934. dust jacket and endpapers with drawings by Ben Nicolson; endpapers offset with scattered foxing to outside edges, otherwise very good in slighly chipped dust jacket.   R. A. Gekoski 19-121 1996 £250.00

SACKVILLE-WEST, VICTORIA MARY 1892-1962   Devil at Westease - The Story as Related by Roger Liddiard. New York: Doubleday & Co., 1947. 1st edition; original binding, head and tail of spine bumped, endpapers partially browned, fore-edge slightly spotted, very good in nicked, chipped, rubbed, creased, torn, marked and dusty dust jacket faded at spine.   Ulysses 39-514 1996 £185.00

SACKVILLE-WEST, VICTORIA MARY 1892-1962   The Eagle and the Dove - a Study in Contrasts - St. Teresa of Avila - St. Therese of Lisieux. London: Michael Joseph Ltd., 1943. 1st edition; 5 black and white photos; original binding, titlepage slightly creased, some pages slightly crinkled, top edge dusty, head and tail of spine and corners slightly bumped, very good in nicked, spotted and slightly rubbed, marked and dusty, very slightly torn dust jacket browned at spine and edges and slightly chipped at head of spine.   Ulysses 39-515 1996 £55.00

SACKVILLE-WEST, VICTORIA MARY 1892-1962   The Edwardians. London: Hogarth Press, 1930. 1st edition; 8vo; (349) pages; orange cloth, gilt lettered spine; fine with slight browning on free endpaper as usual in very slightly chipped pictorial dust jacket.   Paulette Rose 16-274 1996 $375.00

SACKVILLE-WEST, VICTORIA MARY 1892-1962   The Garden. London: Michael Joseph Ltd., 1946. Limited edition of 750 numbered copies; 8vo 135 pages; wood engraved decorations by Broom Lynne, original buckram gilt, top edge gilt, others uncut, spine slightly faded.   Thomas Thorp 489-266 1996 £200.00

SACKVILLE-WEST, VICTORIA MARY 1892-1962   Orchard and Vineyard. London: John Lane, Bodley Head, 1921. Boards slightly bowed and some wear to title plate on spine, otherwise excellent; bookplate of Edward Sackville-West, inscribed to him from author.   R. A. Gekoski 19-119 1996 £800.00

SACKVILLE-WEST, VICTORIA MARY 1892-1962   Poems of West and East. London: John Lane, Bodley Head, 1917. Spine slightly worn and boards rubbed, otherwise very good;   R. A. Gekoski 19-118 1997 £175.00

SACROBOSCO, JOHANNES DE d. 1244   Opusculu Johannis de Sacrobusto Spericum cu Figuris Optimis et Novis Textu in se Sine Ambiguitate declarantibus. Leipzig: Martin Landsberg, about 1494. Quarte modern quarter vellum, boards, minor spots, minor light embrowning or soiling, numerous contemporary annotations in wide margins provided fo this purpose, in the wide spaces between the lines of text, leaf E1 has inner blank margin reinforced, very nice; Not in Hain (cf. Hain 14118); not in Goff (cf. Goff J413).   G. W. Stuart 59-62 1996 $4,500.00

SACRORUM Rituum Congreagtione...Beatificationis et Canonizationis...Roberti Bellarmini Societatis Iesu. Rome: Typis Reverendae Camerae Apostolicae, 1712. Folio; 2 volumes; portrait, 18 sections variously paginated; later polished brown calf, covers gilt with broad double border of acanthus and vine leaves, central panel with IHS corner-pieces, flat spine gilt with green and red labels, all edges gilt, green endpapers, gilt arms of Pope Leo XII, unobtrusively rebacked preserving spine. From the collection of R. M. Beverley with his ex-libris Marlborough 160-53 1996 £650.00

SADE, DONATIEN ALPHONSE FRANCOIS, COMTE, CALLED MARQUIS DE 1740-1814   Histoire de Justine ou Les Malheurs de la Vertu... (with) Histoire de Juliette ou les Prosperites du Vice... En Hollande: 1797. Both works actually probably Amsterdam, late 19th century; 16mo; 10 volumes, fine engraved plates of an explicitly erotic nature, 4 as frontispiece to each volume of Justine; text printed on laid paper; uniformly bound in half citron morocco, spines lettered in gilt, marbled sides, top edge gilt, excellent set. Rose 4085.   Simon Finch 24-199 1996 £1,500.00

SADLEIR, MICHAEL   XIX Century Fiction. 1992. Reprint; 4to; 2 volumes, plates; original binding, fine.   Charles Agvent 4-979 1996 $200.00

SADLEIR, RICHARD   The Aborigines of Australia. Sydney: Thomas Richards, 1883. 4to; 69 pages, 5 full page plates, 2 color illustrations; red pictorial cloth, covers stamped in gilt and black some marking to front cover, otherwise good + condition; the Absolon copy; Charlotte Fabris copy with her signature. Ferguson 15343; Greenway 8227. Antipodean 28-301 1996 $550.00

SADLER, HENRY   Masonic Facts and Fictions. London: 1887. 1st edition; 8vo; cloth, ex-library, very good.   C. P. Hyland 216-753 1996 £60.00

SADOLETO, JACOPO, CARDINAL 1477-1547   De Liberis Recte Insituendis, Liber. Paris: Simon de Colines, 1534. 8vo; 52 leaves; device on title; vellum; Renouard, Colines 236; Moreau IV no. 1137; Buisson 580; Adams S55.   Jeffrey Mancevice 20-75 1996 $1,550.00

SADOLETO, JACOPO, CARDINAL 1477-1547   De Liberis Recte Instituendis Liber. Paris: Simon de Colines, 1534. 8vo; 52 leavaes, Colones's "Tempus" device on title; vellum. Renouard, Colines 236; Moreau IV no. 1137; Buisson 580; Adams S55.   Jeffrey Mancevice 20-75 1996 $1,550.00

SAFRONI-MIDDLETON, A.   Gabrielle of the Lagoon - a Romance of the South Seas. London: Grant Richards Ltd., 1919. 1st edition; original binding, top edge dusty, head and tail of spine and corners bumped, spine faded, covers marked and slightly soiled, cover edges rubbed, endpapers browned, upper hinge partially cracked, bottom corners of few pages slightly creased; good; ownership signature of Ian Fleming. Ulysses 39-688 1996 £125.00

SAGE, KAY   Mordicus. Paris: Ales PAB, 1962. One of 259 copies only; page size 8 1/16 x 6 15/16 inches; 10 full page drawings after Jean Dubuffet; bound by Jill Tarlau, full royal blue ostrich with onlays of red bordeaux, black and blue calf, silver and iridescent snakeskin, blue on blue striped plastic, blue and black dotted plastic, paste paper guards, blue suede lined chemise with blue ostrich spine, paste paper, author, title, artist and date on spine in lower case red letters, matching blue calf edge etui, original wrappers bound in, top edge gilt, signed on lower front turn-in.   Priscilla Juvelis 95/1-81 1996 $1,250.00

SAGE, RUFUS B.   Rufus B. Sage: His Letters and Papers 1836-1847. Glendale: 1956. 1st edition; 2 volumes, 353, 361 pages; photos, illustrations, maps; cloth, nice.   T. A. Swinford 49-1016 1996 $250.00

SAHAGUN, FRAY BERNADINO DE   Historia General de las Cosas de Nueva Espana. Mexico: Fomento Cultural Benemex, 1982. Limited to 500 copies; large quarto; 2 volumes, xxii, 745 pages, numbered consecutively; 80 full page colorplates reproduced from original ms.; morocco backed red silk covered boards by the Harcourt Bindery, housed in original slipcases. Mint.   Bromer Booksellers 87-259 1996 $2,500.00

SAINT GERMAIN, CHRISTOPHER   The Exact Abridgement of that Excellent Treatise Called Doctor and Student. London: printed by the Assignes of John More Esquire, etc., 1630. contemporary sheep, rebacked in morocco; good.   Meyer Boswell SL27-215 1996 $750.00

SAINT JOHN, BAYLE   The Subalpine Kingdom; or, Experiences and Studies in Savoy, Piedmont, and Genoa. London: Chapman and Hall, 1856. 1st edition; 8vo; 2 volumes; original rose cloth; fine set. Pine Coffin 854.6.   Ximenes 108-318 1996 $350.00

SAINT JOHN, CHARLES   Natural History and Sport in Moray. 1863. 1st edition; frontispiece, text drawings; finely bound in modern quarter calf, marbled boards and endpapers; very light foxing, otherwise lovely. David Grayling J95Biggame-323 1996 £85.00

SAINT JOHN, CHARLES   Natural History and Sport in Moray. London: 1863. 1st edition; Line drawings; original cloth, spine slightly frayed, frontispiece creased on the corner and small section cut from top of titlepage, not affecting text.   David Grayling J95Biggame-322 1996 £50.00

SAINT JOHN, CHARLES   Wild Sports and Natural History of the Highlands. London: 1878. 1st illustrated edition; frontispiece, vignettes; modern quarter calf, apart from light foxing to prelims, a near fine copy. David Grayling J95Biggame-324 1996 £65.00

SAINT MARTHE, SCEVOLE DE   Paedotrophia; or, the Art of Rearing Children. London: printed for the Author, by John Nichols, 1797. 8vo; perforation stamp on title, 16 page list of subscribers, some foxing of text in places; new half calf, label.   Anthony W. Laywood 108-116 1996 £185.00

SAINT PALAYE, JEAN BAPTISTE DE LA CURNE DE   Literary History of the Troubadours. London: Vernor, Hood & Sharpe, 1807. 1st edition; 12mo; 223 pages, (1) ad; contemporary full calf, hinges cracked but holding, else very good.   Chapel Hill 94-413 1996 $145.00

SAINT PIERRE, JACQUES HENRI BERNARDIN DE 1737-1814   Paul and Virginia. London: J. Dodsley, 1789. 8vo; 2 volumes in one, half titles; contemporary calf, rebacked, label. Block p. 204.   Anthony W. Laywood 108-101 1996 £450.00

SAINT PIERRE, JACQUES HENRI BERNARDIN DE 1737-1814   Paul and Virginia. London: 1888. Limited to 800 numbered copies; 11 x 7.5 inches; 208 pages; 12 full page engravings and 120 illustrations by Maurice Leloir; finely bound in three quarter blue morocco, top edge gilt, minor scuffing to extremities.   John K. King 77-601 1996 $150.00

SAINT PIERRE, JACQUES HENRI BERNARDIN DE 1737-1814   Studies of Nature... London: C. Dilly, 1796-99. 1st edition in English; 8vo; 6 volumes; xiv, (ii), lxxx, 350; (vi), 397, (i); xv, (i), 428; (vi), 406; (vi), lxxix, (i), 435, (i); (ii), 366 pages; frontispiece, 4 folding plates, half titles in volumes 1-5; contemporary calf, old rebacks, spines gilt ruled, labels; rubbed, corners and edges worn, small library stickers on spines, inoffensive blindstamp on corner of titles and many text pages, no other markings, some foxing, serviceable set.   Robert Clark 38-205 1996 £180.00

SAINT PIERRE, JACQUES HENRI BERNARDIN DE 1737-1814   Studies of Nature... London: 1796. 1st English translation; 5 volumes; illustrations; polished calf, bit rubbed, but sound, acceptable set.   K Books 442-45 1996 £175.00

SAINT PRIEST, FRANCOIS EMMANUEL GUIGNARD, COMTE DE   Malte, Par Un Voyageur Francois. Valetta: 1791. Small 8vo; 2 volumes in 1, title, dedication, 5-60 pages, 2 ff. blank; title, 1 f., 5-115 pages, engraved dedication, 2 folding engraved maps, 24 engraved plates; contemporary half calf. Scarce and in superb condition.   Marlborough 162-257 1996 $1,350.00

SAINT REAL, CAESAR VISCHARD DE   The Memoirs of the Dutchess Mazarine. London: printed and are to be sold by William Cademan, 1676. 1st edition; 18th century sheep, skillfully repaired, some rubbing and wear to joints and corners, some marginal browning from turn-ins, license leaf and final leaf of errata. Wing S355.   James Cummins 14-172 1996 $250.00

SAINTE-CROIX, GUILLAUME EMMANUEL JOSEPH   History of the Rise and Progress of the Naval Power of England, Interspersed with Various Important Notices, Relative to the French Marine... London: printed by J. S. Barr for J. S. Jordan, 1802. 1st edition in English; 8vo; (x), 412 pages, some foxing and browning, uncut, original blue boards, new drab paper spine, printed label.   James Burmester 29-118 1996 £75.00

SAKEL, MANFRED JOSHUA   The Pharmacological Shock Treatment of Schizophrenia. New York/Washington: Nervous and Mental Disease Pub. Co., 1938. 1st edition in English; 8vo; (xx), 136, (4) pages; printed red cloth, ownership stamp to front and rear pastedowns, otherwise fine. . John Gach 150-411 1996 $150.00

SALA, GEORGE AUGUSTUS   The Seven Sons of Mammon: a Story. London: Tinsley Bros., 1862. 1st edition; 8vo; 3 volumes; original green cloth, little rubbed, couple of inner hinges tender; very good; with W. H. smith subscription library labels on front pastedown; Wolff 6130; not in Sadleir; CBEL III 963.   Ximenes 109-253 1996 $600.00

SALAMAN, MALCOLM C.   The Etchings of Sir Francis Seymour Haden, P.R.E. London: 1923. Number 91 of 200 copies, with an extra suite of 16 etchings on Japon paper; folio; 35 pages text, 96 plates; original half brown calf, cloth sides, top edge gilt, other edges uncut. Jens J. Christoffersen SL94-135 1996 $150.00

SALAMAN, MALCOLM C.   The Etchings of James McBey. London: Halton & Truscott Smith, 1929. 8vo; vii, 32 pages, 97 plates; original cloth, bevelled edges, top edge gilt, dust jacket.   Rainsford A54-398 1996 £75.00

SALAMAN, MALCOLM C.   French Colour Prints of the XVIII Century. London: William Heinemann, 1913. 1st edition; 4to; 49 mounted colored plates; original gilt decorated cloth, top edge gilt, inner hinges sightly shaken; Ruari McLean's copy with bookplate, with ALS from David McKitterick to McLean.   Forest Books 74-364 1996 £95.00

SALAZAR YLARREGUI, JOSE   Datos de los Trabaios Astronomicos y Topograficos...Durante El Ano de 1849 y Principios de 1850 por la Comision de Limites Mexicana en la Linea Que Divide este Republica de las de los Estados-Unidos... Mexico: Navarro, 1850. 1st edition; 123 pages; maps; contemporary black calf with title in gilt on spine over black boards, wear to corners, overall very good; Barrett 2191; Graff 3652; Palau 286944; Becker Wagner Camp 190.   Michael D. Heaston 23-294 1996 $2,500.00

SALES, EDITH TUNIS   Interiors of Virginia Houses of Colonial Times: From the Beginnings of Virginia to the Revolution. Richmond: William Byrd Press, 1927. 1st edition; 4to; xxiii, 501 pages, including 371 photos, measured drawings and other illustrations; lettering on spine rubbed, previous owner's names on endpapers, else fine in printed dust jacket which is chipped and torn. Howes S49.   Andrew Cahan 47-204 1996 $125.00

SALINGER, JEROME DAVID 1919-   The Catcher in the Rye. Boston: Little Brown, 1951. 1st edition; good copy, lettering worn off of spine, in good dust jacket, with quarter inch piece mising from head of spine panel, other chips and light dampstain.   Sherwood 3-265 1996 $550.00

SALINGER, JEROME DAVID 1919- The Catcher in the Rye. London: Hamish Hamilton, 1951. 1st British edition; some fading to spine cloth, tear on page 123, not affecting text, overall very good in good, internally tape repaired jacket with several chips. Ken Lopez 74-396 1996 $475.00

SALINGER, JEROME DAVID 1919- The Complete Uncollected Stories of J. D. Salinger. N.P.: n.d. 1974. 1st issue of this pirated collection; volume 1 in stapled wrappers and volume 2 perfect bound; fine in bright, clean wrappers, outstanding copies. Alice Robbins 15-297 1996 $700.00

SALINGER, JEROME DAVID 1919- Franny and Zooey. Boston: Little Brown Co., 1961. 1st edition; fine in price clipped dust jacket showing only slight touches of wear. Sherwood 3-269 1996 $100.00

SALINGER, JEROME DAVID 1919- Nine Stories. Boston: Little Brown & Co., 1953. 1st edition; (4995 copies); near fine in very good or better dust jacket which is slightly worn at spine ends and lightly foxed on flaps, also foxed on inside of dust jacket, still quite attractive copy. Steven C. Bernard 71-194 1996 $850.00

SALINGER, JEROME DAVID 1919- Nine Stories. Boston: Little Brown, 1953. 1st edition; fine in very good dust jacket with slight spine faded and crinkling to upper back panel, author's very scarce second book. Sherwood 3-266 1996 $800.00

SALINGER, JEROME DAVID 1919- Nine Stories. Boston: Little Brown Co., 1953. 1st edition; spine lettering worn off, else very good, lacking dust jacket. Sherwood 3-267 1996 $250.00

SALISBURY, STEPHEN Troy and Homer. Remarks on the Discovers of Dr. Heinrich Schliemann in the Troad. Worcester: privately printed by Charles Hamilton, 1875. 8vo; 52 pages; original gilt lettered cloth, light shelfwear at spine; from the collection of Heinrich Schliemann, and was acquired by Professor Akerstrom; with facsimile letter about acquisition; with traces of Schliemann's paper private library stamp at foot of spine; inscribed by Scliemann by author. Archaeologia Luxor-3986 1996 $650.00

SALK, JONAS Man Unfolding. New York: Harper, 1972. 1st edition; 8vo; dust jacket with few nicks, slightly rubbed, very good; signed by author. George J. Houle 68-132 1996 $150.00

SALKELD, WILLIAM Reports of Cases Adjudged in the Court of King's Bench; Together with Several Special Cases. In the Savoy: printed by E. and R. Nutt, 1724. 1st edition; folio; pages (8), 400, (38); contemporary calf, just little worn, label chipped, binding strong, else nice. James Fenning 133-296 1996 £65.00

SALLER, SYLVESTER J. Excavations at Bethany (1949-1953). Jerusalem: Franciscan, 1957. 4to; frontispiece, xiv, 397 pages, 69 figures and 134 plates; wrappers. Archaeologia Luxor-2667 1996 $150.00

SALLER, SYLVESTER J. The Excavations at Dominus Flevit (Mount Olivet, Jerusalem). Jerusalem: Franciscan, 1964. 8vo; Part II only; xv, 197 pages, 64 figures, 38 plates; wrappers. Archaeologia Luxor-2668 1996 $125.00

SALLUSTIUS CRISPIUS, C. C. Crispi Sallustii Belli Catilinarii et Jugurthini Historiae. Edinburgh: Guielmus Ged, Aurifaber Edinensis, on typis mobilibus, ut vulgo... 1739. 12mo; contemporary calf, spine gilt, front cover loose, lower joint cracked, in cloth folding case; booklabel of F.S. Ferguson; aside from worn binding, an excellent copy. Ximenes 109-135 1996 $2,500.00

SALLUSTIUS CRISPUS, C. De Conivratione Catilinae. Venice: In Aedibus Aldi, et Andreae Soceri Torresano, 1521. 8vo; 152 leaves, italic, title and terminal devices are different; 18th century full vellum with marbled endpapers; etched ex-libris. Fine. Dibdin II p. 383; Renouard 93.16; Adams S147; UCLA II/170. Brunet V84. Family Album Tillers-545 1996 $800.00

SALLUSTIUS CRISPUS, C. The Two Most Worthy and Notable Histories... London: W. Jaggard for J. Jaggard, 1608-09. Apparently the first edition of Thomas Heywood's translation; 4to; pages (22), 60, (5), 110 plus errata and blanks, printer's device on title, historiated initials; later full leather, front board detached, ms. ownership and engraved armorial ex-libris of Henry H(ucks) Gibbs, Lord Aldenham, book collector. STC 21625. Family Album Tillers-546 1996 $500.00

SALLY Miller. N.P.: n.d., ca. 1840. 8vo; pages (1)-24; sewn; very scarce. 1 copy in NUC. Edward Morrill 369-197 1996 $200.00

SALMON, THOMAS The Modern Gazetteer; or, a Short View of the Several Nations of the World... London: printed for S. and E. Ballard, J. and P. Knapton (and 10 others), 1747. 2nd edition; 8vo; contemporary mottled calf, hinges cracked. Anthony W. Laywood 108-117 1996 £50.00

SALMON, THOMAS A New Historical Account of St. George for England and the Original of the most Noble Order of the Garter. London: R. Janeway for Nath. Dancer, 1704. 8vo; title, 3ff., 109 pages, 2 ff (contents to part II), 113 pages, 2 portraits and 1 view; slight browning, pencil underlinings, later morocco; with Baden-Powell bookplate. Lowndes p. 2179. Marlborough 162-198 1996 £125.00

SALMON, THOMAS A New Geographical and Historical Grammar: Wherein the Geographical Part is Truly Modern... London: 1758. 6th edition; 8 x 5 inches; 23 folding maps, 640 pages plus index; old speckled calf, hinges cracked, covers worn, some maps slightly frayed from being improperly folded, 1st map torn. John K. King 77-708 1996 $195.00

SALMON, WILLIAM Iatrica: seu Praxis Medendi. The Practice of Curing: Being a medicinal History of Many Famous Observations. London: printed for Th. Dawks, also are sold by T. Passinger, 1684. 2nd edition; 4to; (xviii), 1-64, 37-52, 73-762, (xiv) pages, but complete; later full calf with marbled endpapers, rubbed at edges, light waterstain along upper margin and on upper half of inner margin in first 40 pages. Wing S432a. David Bickersteth 133-219 1996 £285.00

SALMON, WILLIAM Polygraphice; or the Art of Drawing, Engraving, Etching, Limning, Painting, Washing, Varnishing, Gilding, Colouring, Dying, Beautifying and perfuming... London: E. T. and R. H. for John Crumpe, 1673. 2nd edition; 8vo; 15 engraved plates; modern panelled calf, one page with marginal notes on making ink, small hole in angel's face in engraved title; Marilyn Braiterman 15-181 1996 $1,200.00

SALOMONSEN, F. The Birds of Greenland. Copenhagen: 1950-51. Small folio; 608 pages, 52 colored plates, map; original half cloth; map loose in original wrappers. Wheldon & Wesley 207-89 1996 £350.00

SALPETER, HOWARD Dr. Johnson and Mr. Boswell. New York: Coward McCann, 1929. 1st edition; 16 black and white plates; original binding, top edge dusty, spine darkened, head and tail of spine and corners slightly bumped, covers slightly marked and rubbed; very good; pencilled ownership signature of Frederick Pottle. Ulysses 39-704 1996 £65.00

SALT, HENRY A Voyage to Abyssinia, and Travels into the Interior of that Country...in 1809 and 1810. London: for F. C. and J. Rivington, 1814. 1st edition; large 4to; printed on thick paper, 34 plates and charts, lower margin of first leaf leaf of text repaired; contemporary half russia, with decorated paper boards, joints very skilfully repaired; inscribed "To the Lady Hester Stanhope from the Author" below in another hand 'purchased at sale of Lady Hester Stanhope's books by E. Kilby(?) at Beirout in 1840" followed by notes signed by "John Maconchy, surgeon HMS Hecate" & Robert Maunsell, Capt. HMS Rodney" H. M. Fletcher 121-146 1996 £2,500.00

SALT, T. J. Trentham Hymnal. Newcastle-under-Lyme: n.d. 1894. 4to; 64 pages; sumptuously bound, perhaps for presentation, by Bagguley, full brown morocco, covers panelled in blind and gilt, upper cover gilt lettered, spine ruled in blind and gilt, gilt lettered, raised bands, wide gilt rolled inner dentelle, brown satin doublures and endpapers, binder's stamp on lower doublure, all edges gilt; Marlborough 160-80 1996 £350.00

SALTEN, FELIX Bambi. New York: Simon & Schuster, 1928. 1st U.S. edition; 8vo; pages (xii), 13-293, (i); 15 black and white illustrations by Kurst Wiese; original green ribbed cloth, gilt, pictorial dust jacket, pictorial endpapers, cloth little damp spotted, wrapper lightly soiled and with one or two small chips at head and tail of spine and corners, still unusually good copy. Sotheran PN32-152 1996 £198.00

SALTEN, FELIX Bambi. New York: Simon & Schuster, 1928. Stated 1st edition; 8vo; 293 pages; 26 black and white illustrations by Kurt Wiese, illustrated endpapers; green boards, gilt, gilt vignette, gilt dull, top and base of spine rubbed, else near fine. Marjorie James 19-190 1996 £75.00

SALTER, H. E. A Cartulary of the Hospital of St. John the Baptist. London: 1914-17. Thick 8vo; 3 volumes; plates, maps and facsimiles; original cloth. Howes Bookshop 265-933 1996 £65.00

SALTER, JAMES The Arm of Flesh. New York: Harper, 1961. 1st edition; neat name, else fine in nice, very good plus dust jacket with two small chips and little rubbing at spinal extremities; author's very scarce. Between the Covers 42-382 1996 $450.00

SALTER, JAMES   The Arm of Flesh. New York: Harper, 1961. 1st edition; scarce second book; very good in moderately rubbed dust jacket, worn at spine extremities, with tape shadow on upper front panel, still about very good; signed by author.   Ken Lopez 74-399 1996 $125.00

SALTER, JAMES   The Hunters. New York: Harper, 1956. 1st edition; very bright copy, extremely scarce, minor creasing to spine, jacket with couple of tiny edge tears and light rubbing at spine extremities and front flap fold, overall very near fine.   Ken Lopez 74-397 1996 $750.00

SALTER, JAMES   Light Years. New York: Random House, 1974. Uncorrected proof; slight wear to spine and very faint crease on front flap.   Between the Covers 42-386 1996 $250.00

SALTER, JAMES   Light Years. New York: Random House, 1975. 1st edition; very light spotting to upper page edges, otherwise fine in fine dust jacket and signed by author.   Ken Lopez 74-399 1996 $125.00

SALTER, JAMES   Solo Faces. Boston: Little Brown, 1979. Uncorrected proof; faint, barely visible crease to corner of front wrapper, else fine.   Between the Covers 42-388 1996 $100.00

SALTER, JAMES   Solo Faces. New York: Random House, 1994. 1st edition; near fine in edge rubbed, almost near fine dust jacket, signed by author.   Ken Lopez 74-402 1996 $125.00

SALTER, JAMES   A Sport and a Pastime. Garden City: Doubleday/Paris Review Editions, 1967. 1st edition; very faint offsetting to pale blue front free endpaper, else about fine in price clipped, near fine dust jacket with bit of rubbing along edges of spine and one small nick.   Between the Covers 42-383 1996 $185.00

SALTER, JAMES   A Sport and a Pastime. London: Cape, 1987. Uncorrected proof copy of first British edition; wrappers; near fine, signed by author.   Ken Lopez 74-400 1996 $150.00

SALVIATI, LEONARDO   Lo' nfarinato Secondo Ovvero dello' nfarinato Accademico della Crusca, Risposta al Libro Intitolato Replica di Camillo Pellegrino ec. Florence: A. Padovani, 1588. 1st edition; 8vo; (8) leaves, 398 pages, (25) leaves (last leaf blank), woodcut printer's device on title, outer blank margins of last few leaves repaired, occasional browning and foxing, modern calf. BM STC Italian p. 339; Gamba 583.   Jeffrey Mancevice 20-76 1996 $275.00

SALVIN, O.   Biologia Centrali-Americana: Aves. London: 1879-1904. Royal 8vo; 3 volumes, with atlas of 84 hand colored plates, together 4 volumes; red buckram; good, clean, sound copy in functional binding.   Wheldon & Wesley 207-10 1996 £5,500.00

SALZMAN, MARK   Iron and Silk. New York: Random House, 1986. 1st edition; fine in fine dust jacket and inscribed by author in 1987, uncommon.   Ken Lopez 74-403 1996 $200.00

SAMPSON, JOHN   XXI Welsh Gypsy Folk-Tales. Newtown: Gregynog Press, 1933. Limited to 250 numbered copies; 4to; pages xiv, 110; printed on Portal's handmade paper, vignette title and 7 wood engravings by Agnes Miller Parker, text hand set in Bembo type; publisher's full mustard yellow Welsh sheepskin gilt, edges uncut, spine and extremities rubbed, endpapers very slightly spotted, otherwise fine copy internally.   Thomas Thorp 489-267 1 996 £280.00

SAMS, S.   A Complete and Universal System of Stenography, or Short-Hand, Rendered Easy and Familiar... London: sold by Hamilton, Harchard, LLoyd and (6 others), 1812. 1st edition; 8vo; half title, 3 folding plates; original wrappers, stitched as issued, uncut, printed paper label, fine.   Anthony W. Laywood 108-230 1996 £60.00

SAN DIEGO. CHAMBER OF COMMERCE   Sunny San Diego: an Illustrated Souvenir. San Diego: N.P., 1896. 1st edition; oblong 4to; numerous black and white illustrations and ads; original stapled stiff color pictorial wrappers, few rear pages becoming detached, very good.   George J. Houle 68-133 1996 $150.00

THE SAN Francisco Directory for the Year Commencing December, 1869. San Francisco: Henry G. Langley, 1869. 8 7/8 x 6 1/8 inches; cxii, 852, 67 pages; folding map lacking; printed boards, new black leather spine.   Dawson's Books Shop 528-214 1996 $400.00

THE SAN Francisco Directory for the Year Commencing October 1868. San Francisco: Henry G. Langley, 1868. 9 x 6 inches; cxii, 788, 95 pages, folding map; printed boards with new black leather spine.   Dawson's Books Shop 528-213 1996 $450.00

SANCHEZ, GASPAR   Conciones, in Dominicis, et Feriis Qvadragesimae... Brescia: Compagnia Bresciana, 1599. 2nd edition; 4to; pages (xx), 628, roman letter, italic dedication, index and side notes, large woodcut printer's device on titlepage, woodcut initials; Early jesuit owner's autograph on titlepage, stamp of Tullabg Collage on fly & title, general age browning and foxing, mostly light, small faint waterstain at head of few leaves, otherwise good; contemporary limp vellum, covers creased, head of spine repaired. BM STC It. Suppl. p. 72; not in Adams. this ed. not in NUC.   A. Sokol XXV-89 1996 £295.00

SAND, GEORGE, PSEUD. OF MME. DUDEVANT 1804-1876   The Devil's Pool. New York: George H. Richmond & Co., 1894. Limited and numbered, one of 250 copies; 8vo; (196) pages; frontispiece, with ornamented headpieces; green gilt decorated cloth, gilt lettered spine, top edge gilt, others uncut; near fine in lovely publisher's binding.   Paulette Rose 16-281 1996 $100.00

SAND, GEORGE, PSEUD. OF MME. DUDEVANT 1804-1876   Francis the Waif. London: George Routledge and Sons, 1889. One of 1000 numbered copies; tall 8vo; illustrations by Eugene Burand; three quarter morocco and marbled boards, raised gilt bands.   Paulette Rose 16-283 1996 $100.00

SAND, GEORGE, PSEUD. OF MME. DUDEVANT 1804-1876   Germain's Marriage, a Tale of Peasant Life in France. New York: Richmond, Croscup & Co., 1892. 1st edition thus; One of 285 copies signed by publishers; 8vo; (iv, 171) pages; printed on Van Gelder handmade paper; frontispiece, 13 etchings by E. Rudaux, each with lettered tissue guard; white linen backed grey boards, gilt lettered spine, top edge gilt, others uncut; spine lightly spotted, endpapers slightly discolored, otherwise fine, quite scarce.   Paulette Rose 16-284 1996 $100.00

SANDBURG, CARL 1878-1967   Address of Carl Sandburg Before a Joint Session of Congress Feb. 12, 1959. New York: Harcourt Brace, 1959. 1st edition; one of 750 copies, although not called for, this copy signed by author; thin 8vo; cloth, glassine dust jacket, covers slightly faded, otherwise very good in slightly chipped glassine.   James S. Jaffe 34-606 1996 $150.00

SANDBURG, CARL 1878-1967   The American Songbag. New York: Harcourt Brace & Co., 1927. 1st edition; 4to; illustrations; near fine in very good+ price clipped dust jacket which is slightly chipped at top spine edge, very attractive.   Steven C. Bernard 71-199 1996 $125.00

SANDBURG, CARL 1878-1967   Remembrance Rock. New York: Harcourt Brace, 1948. 1st edition; limited to 1000 copies; thick 8vo; 2 volumes; printed on rag paper and signed by author; blue cloth and printed spine labels, lacks glassine jackets and slipcase, fine set.   James S. Jaffe 34-605 1996 $100.00

SANDBURG, CARL 1878-1967   Seven Poems. New York: Assoc. American Artists, 1970. Limited to 190 numbered copies signed by artist, this being one of only 20 copies on Auvergne handmade rag paper; 8vo; 7 pages text; 7 original etchings by Gregory Masurovsky and an additional suite of 8 etchings on japon nacre signed in pencil; unsewn as issued, with edges uncut, original wrappers in cloth porfolio and slipcase.   Thomas Thorp 489-268 1996 £150.00

SANDBURG, CARL 1878-1967   Slabs of the Sunburnt West. New York: HB, 1922. 1st edition; 8vo; original binding, portion of dust jacket tipped to rear endpaper and pastedown, some soiling, especially to spine, owner label on pastedown, very good; inscribed by poet to original owner.   Charles Agvent 4-980 1996 $175.00

SANDERS, ALVIN   The Story of the Herefords. Chicago: Breeder's Gazette, 1914. 1st edition; half leather, front edges of first few pages stained, otherwise clean, tight, scarce.   October Farm 36-375 1996 $135.00

SANDERS, DANIEL CLARKE   Tales of the Revolution and Thrilling Stories, Founded on Facts. Methuen: James Jasper Henderson, 1837. 1st edition; 18mo; 64 pages; sewn as issued, fine. Wright I 2536; Sabin 94252.   M & S Rare Books 60-230 1996 $500.00

SANDERS, G. D.   Elizabeth Cleghorn, with a Bibliography by Clark S. Northup. New Haven: Yale University Press, 1929. 1st edition; 8 1/2 x 5 3/4 inches; pages xix, 267; dark green cloth, gilt titling to backstrip; fine, scarce. Y & T 480.   Ian Hodgkins 78-515 1996 £65.00

SANDERS, HENRY A.   The Minor Prophets in the Freer Collection and the Berlin Fragment of Genesis. New York: 1927. 4to; xiii, 436 pages; 7 collotype plates; buckram.   Rainsford A54-514 1996 £65.00

SANDERSON, ALFRED   Historical Sketch of the Union Fire Company, No. 1, of the City of Lancaster, Pennsylvania. Lancaster: published by the company, 1879. 1st edition; 153 pages; illustrations; cloth, bit of wear at spine tips, otherwise very good.   Metacomet Books 54-99 1996 $100.00

SANDERSON, GEORGE P.   Thirteen Years Among the Wild Beasts of India... London: William Allen, 1879. 2nd edition; 8vo; xviii, 387 pages; color frontispiece, 23 plates; original pictorial green cloth, rubbed. Riling 1036.   Richard Adelson W94/95-144 1996 $285.00

SANDERSON, ROBERT   Nine Cases of Conscience: Occasionally Determined... (with) Episcopacy (As Established by Law in England) Not Prejudicial to Regal Power. London: C. Wilkinson and C. Brome,/London: Blanch Palwet for George West, 1685/83. 3rd edition; 8vo; bound together, (vi), 192 pages; (xiv), 103, (ix) pages; frontispiece to each title; 6 pages ads and blank leaf at end; contemporary panelled calf, rebacked, gilt lettering; corners little worn, titlepage of second work cropped at foot with loss of date, otherwise good, clean copies. Wing S619; S602.   Robert Clark 38-126 1996 £65.00

SANDFORD, ELIZABETH   Female Improvement. London: printed for Longman, and J. Hatchard, 1836. 1st edition; 12mo; 2 volumes, viii, 205; (iv), 234, (2) pages; original brown moire cloth, printed labels; very nice James Burmester 29-119 1996 £200.00

SANDFORD, FRANCIS   A Genealogical History of the Kings and Queens of England. London: Nicholson, 1707. One of 25 large paper copies; folio; on large paper, title in red and black, 3 ff., 878 pages, (pages 372, 495-8 exfoliated; pages 84-95 foliated), 13 ff. index, 1 f. errata; 71 full page or folding engraved plates; cont. red mor. gilt, elaborate gilt tooled covers arranged in panels, outer gilt triple fillet, wide border w/semi-circles & fleurons, middle border w/floral compartments of massed sm. tools, urns, roll-tools & lg. & sm. crowned cypher AR used 30 times on each cover, at centre, the Royal Arms, spine gilt in compartments, raised gilt bands, each compartments w/royal cypher (1 lg. & 4 sm.), gilt ruled, gilt inner dentelle, marbled endpapers, all edges gilt, rubbed, some scuff marks, rebacked preserving original compartments, corners sympathetically strengthened, large and impressive binding by Robert Steel, fine.   Marlborough 160-54 1996 £2,500.00

SANDFORD, K. S.   Paleolithic Man and the Nile Valley. Chicago: University of Chicago Press, 1933. 8vo; xvii, 92 pages illustrations and 43 black and white paltes, map; ink inscription by author; buckram. Rainsford A54-515 1996 £60.00

SANDHAM, ALFRED   Coins, Tokens and Medals of the Dominion of Canada. Montreal: Daniel Rose, 1869. 1st edition; 72 pages; illustrations; green pebble cloth; bookplate of Woburn Public Library on front pastedown, head and tail of spine and lower corers worn, otherwise very good.   Hermitage SP95-1057 1996 $350.00

SANDHAM, ELIZABETH   More Trifles! London: printed for J. Harris, 1804. 1st edition; 12mo; (iv), 187 pages; frontispiece, slight worming in lower margins of last few leaves; contemporary calf, oval prize label, 1813, on endpaper; Osborne p. 932. 3 copies in NUC.   James Burmester 29-120 1996 £125.00

SANDS, ROBERT CHARLES   The Bridal of Vaumond; a Metrical Romance. New York: Pub. by James Eastburn and Co.; Abraham Paul, printer, 1817. 1st edition; 12mo; 19th century half calf, spine gilt, bit rubbed, but sound, very good, scarce. Wegelin 1123; Sabin 76441; Shaw & Shoemaker 42050.   Ximenes 109-254 1996 $225.00

SANDYS, WILLIAM   Christmas Carols, Ancient and Modern. London: Richard Beckley, 1833. 1st edition; octavo; cxliv, 188, (4, ads) pages, plus 12 leaves of music, printed on rectos only; contemporary red polished calf, covers decoratively bordered in gilt, gilt spine, with green and brown morocco labels, gilt board edges and turn-ins, top edge gilt, marbled endpapers, little minor soiling, previous owner's ink signature on half title, armorial bookplate, mounted on front pastedown is nicely hand colored engraving of city square; near fine.   Heritage Book Shop 196-289 1996 $750.00

SANDYS, WILLIAM   Christmastide: its History, Festivities and Carols. London: John Russell Smith, n.d. ca. 1852. Octavo; 327 pages; 9 tinted lithographed plates, plus numerous woodcut vignettes, music; contemporary full polished red calf, covers bordered in gilt, gilt spine with raised bands and green and brown morocco labels, gilt board edges and turn-ins, all edges gilt, marbled endpapers, front hinge cracked between half title and frontispiece, little light foxing; otherwise fine.   Heritage Book Shop 196-290 1996 $300.00

SANGER, WILLIAM   The History of Prostitution: Its Extent, Causes and Effects Throughout the World. New York: 1858. 1st edition; 708 pages; original binding, outer hinges cracked, head and tail of spine chipped, otherwise very good.   W. Bruce Fye 71-1872 1996 $150.00

THE SANITARY Commission of the United States Army: a Succinct Narrative Of Its Works and Purposes. New York: 1864. 1st edition; 318 pages; half leather, library stamp on title, otherwise fine; scarce.   W. Bruce Fye 71-1873 1996 $350.00

SANITARY Economy: Its Principles and Practice; and Its Moral Influence On the Progress of Civilization. Edinburgh: 1850. 1st edition; 320 pages; original binding.   W. Bruce Fye 71-1874 1996 $100.00

SANNAZARO, JACOPO 1458-1530   Arcadia Del Sannazaro. (wtih) Sonetti, E Canzoni del Sannazaro. Venice: Paulum Manutium et Andrea Socero (Torresano), July 1534. 8vo; ff. 92; 52 leaves; Aldine devices on first and last leaves; early 18th century blindstamped vellum with complex central florette shield on each cover, framed in line fillets and corner stamps; ms. ownership signature of "Wm. Agnew Paton 1899", old ownership stamp on title obscured, ancient signature clipped from tail of A2. Renouard 112.5 and 6; Adams S320 & S338; UCLA IIIa/236/237.   Family Album Tillers-560 1996 $1,200.00

SANSOM, WILLIAM   The Equilibriad. London: Hogarth Press ltd., 1948. One of 750 numbered copies signed by author; five full page black and white drawings by Lucien Freud; buckram backed marbled paper wrappers, head and tail of spine slightly rubbed, bottom corners bumped and bruised, free endpapers browned, prelims, edges and endpapers spotted, some internal spotting, very good in tissue dust jacket, which is printed only on upper flap, dust jacket is nicked, torn, chipped and creased, slight dusty dust jacket browned at spine and edges. Ulysses 39-211 1996 £155.00

SANTA Cruz County: a Faithful Reproduction in Print and Photography of its Climate, Capabilities and Beauties. N.P.: M. E. Gilbert, 1896. 9 1/4 x 12 1/4 inches; 200 pages, including numerous full page and smaller photographic illustrations; printed white wrappers, cloth tape spine, spotting to wrappers and creases on front cover.   Dawson's Books Shop 528-221 1996 $100.00

SANTA Catalina Island, California. Los Angeles: Newman Post Card Co., ca. 1900? 5 3/8 x 7 /78 inches; (28) pages, including 24 full page chromolithographic illustrations; maroon wrappers printed in gold, mild marginal sunning to wrappers.   Dawson's Books Shop 528-52 1996 $100.00

SANTAYANA, GEORGE 1863-1952   Sonnets and Other Verses. Cambridge: Stone and Kimball, 1894. One of 450 copies printed on small paper; 8vo; original binding, former owner signature; near fine.   Charles Agvent 4-981 1996 $150.00

SANTAYANA, GEORGE 1863-1952   The Works of... New York: Charles Scribner's Sons, 1936-50. Triton edition, number 197 of 940 sets, signed by author; 8vo; 15 volumes; original cloth backed boards, paper spine labels, gilt emblems on upper boards, top edge gilt, uncut and unopened, spines and labels little age darkened, one volume with some white rub marks on upper board, otherwise fine set.   James Cummins 14-173 1996 $750.00

SANTEE, ROSS   Men and Horses. New York: 1926. 1st edition; 268 pages, illustrations by author; pictorial cloth, very good+. Herd 2010; Dykes Hight Spot 47.   T. A. Swinford 49-1024 1996 $125.00

SANTORIO, SANTORIO 1561-1636   (Opera Omnia)...Commentaria in Prima Fen Primi Libri Canonis Avicennae.../...Methodi Vitandorum.../...Commentaria in Artem Medicinalem Galeni... Venice: Franciscum Brogiollum, 1660. Small 4to; 5 works in 3 volumes, pages (20), 1120; (16), 336; (36); (52), 464; (38), 763; fine woodcut medical illustrations plus engraved portrait; old vellum; engraved armorial bookplate of Corn. Henr. A'Roy. Rare. GM 2668; 2 copies in NUC. Family Album Tillers-561 1996 $750.00

SANTUCCI, LUIGI   La Donna Con La Bocca Aperta. (The Woman With Her Mouth Open). Plain Wrapper Press, 1980. One of 110 copies, signed by author and artist; 12 1/2 x 9 inches; 5 p.l. (one blank), 11-45, (1) pages, (1) leaf (colophon); 3 page folding color serigraph by Emilio Tadini; printed in orange and black on very beautiful paper; full limp vellum, leather ties, gilt titling on spine, golden cloth endpapers, edges untrimmed in vellum backed paper chemise inside matching slipcase, spine on chemise little darkened because of natural grain of vellum, but virtually mint.   Phillip J. Pirages 33-426 1996 $350.00

SAPHIRE, LAWRENCE   Fernand Leger: The Complete Graphic Work. New York: Blue Moon, 1978. Limited to 1750 copies in English; folio; 319 pages, 142 plates, many in color, illustrations; cloth, dust jacket. Freitag 5342.   Brannan 43-348 1996 $225.00

SAPHIRE, LAWRENCE   Fernand Leger L'Ouevre Grave. New York: 1978. French edition, 1000 copies; large 8vo; 319 pages; illustrations in color and monochrome; cloth, dust jacket, boxed.   Rainsford A54-369 1996 £175.00

SAPPHO   Fragments from Sappho. Limited Editions Club, 1973. One of only 20 numbered copies, signed by artist/printer; folio; text and prints in shades of brownish-purple; 6 prints by Eileen Hogan; canvas boards, print repeated in black on upper cover, fine, very scarce.   Bertram Rota 272-277 1996 £75.00

SAPPHO   Sappho. London: Coracle, 1982. 1st edition translated by Thomas Meyer, one of 50 copies (from a total edition of 500), signed by artist and translator; 12mo; 9 pictures by Sandra Fisher; yellow wrappers, pictorial label; fine.   Captain's Bookshelf 38-161 1996 $200.00

SAPPHO   (Greek Title) Songs of Sappho. Brmer Presse, 1922. From an edition of 14 copies printed on vellum; 11 1/4 x 7 1/4 inches; (16) pages (i.e. 6 unbound vellum bifolia, 2 of them blank); title beautifully hand painted in gold by Anna Simons; unbound sheets contained in folding board case (slightly faded and worn); leaves with only slight discoloration of the sort normal for vellum.   Phillip J. Pirages 33-112 1996 $8,000.00

SARAYNA, TORELLUS   Le Histoire E Fatti de Veronesi Nelli Tempi d'il Popolo et Signori Scaligeri. Verona: Portese, 1542. 1st edition; 4to; title device; quarter vellum; Adams S394; Lozzi 6322.   Rostenberg & Stern 150-96 1996 $750.00

SARBAN,   Ringstones and Other Curious Tales. London: Peter Davies, 1951. 1st edition; fine in dust jacket with minor wear at corners and spine panel ends with two tiny closed tears with associated crease; very attractive copy.   Robert Gavora 61-126 1996 $250.00

SARDA, DANIEL   Conte de Maitre Espapidour. New York: printed for Mrs. Fern L. Bedaux, 1927. One of 500 copies "imprimes par Vincent Brooks Day & Son sous la direction de la Nonesuch Press a Londres"; 8vo; full limp vellum with leather thongs, title within flourished cartouche in gilt on upper cover; fine, very scarce.   Bertram Rota 272-320 1996 £90.00

SARDI, PIETRO   Corona Imperiale dell'Architettura Militare Divisa in Due Trattati. Il Primo Contienne la Teorica. Il Secondo Contiene la Pratica. Venice: Barezzo Barezzi (at the author's expense), 1618. 1st edition; folio; (14) leaves, 299, 83 pages, engraved titlepage by Gaspar Grispoldi, with prtrait of author at age 58, 2 engraved part titlepages, 40 engraved plates, 4 engraved plates; few small marginal repairs to titlepage, one just touching a line of engraving and neatly drawn in, small worm hole in blank margin of some leaves; vellum backed decorated boards; scarce.   Jeffrey Mancevice 20-77 1996 $1,650.00

SARGANT, JANE ALICE   Two Letters to the Queen, and an Address to the Females of Britain. Maidenhead: G. W. Wetton, 1820. 8th edition; 8vo; 32 pages; original purple calf over marbled boards, gilt spine, spine bit rubbed, rare.   Kenneth Karmiole 1NS-259 1996 $150.00

SARGANT, WILLIAM LUCAS   Recent Political Economy. London: Norgate and Williams, 1867. 1st edition; 8vo; x, (2), 213, (1) pages, ink stamp on verso of title, one gathering coming loose; original cloth, lettered in gilt, rubbed; good; inscribed "From the Author" on titlepage. Headcavr & Fuller I 744; Masui p. 140; not in Einaudi or Hollander. John Drury 82-249 1996 £125.00

SARGANT, WILLIAM LUCAS   Robert Owen and His Social Philosophy. London: Smith, Elder, 1860. 1st edition; 8vo; xxiv, 446, 2 (ad) pages; original plum cloth, neatly rebacked;   James Burmester 29-121 1996 £75.00

SAROYAN, WILLIAM   The Daring Young Man on the Flying Trapeze and other Stories. Yolla Bolly Press, 1984. One of 200 copies for sale, signed by Gold and Prochnow, of a total edition of 220; 10 1/4 x 8 inches; 4 p.l. (one blank), ix-xv, (1), (2) leaves (blank, colophon); vignette on title, several full page color woodblocks in text by Bill Prochnow; original brown cloth, gilt vignette on front cover, author's name in gitl on spine, fore edges untrimmed; mint.   Phillip J. Pirages 33-522 1996 $225.00

SARPI, PAOLO 1552-1623   The Letters of the Renowned Father Paul, Counsellor of State. London: Chiswell, 1693. 8vo; publisher's list at end; gilt morocco; Wing S608.   Rostenberg & Stern 150-68 1996 $385.00

SARPI, PAOLO 1552-1623   The Letters of the Renowned Father Paul Counsellor of State to the Most Serene Republick of Venice. London: Richard Chiswell, 1693. 1st edition in English; 8vo; (iii)cxvii, (iii), 431, (i) pages; frontispiece; contemporary panelled calf; label; rubbed, head of spine slightly worn, localised worming in lower margin, slightly affecting text on some leaves, sound copy. Wing S698.   Robert Clark 38-127 1996 £55.00

SARPI, PAOLO 1552-1623   The Rights of Sovereigns and Subjects... London: Graves, 1722. 1st English edition; 8vo; 2 parts in 1; frontispiece; gilt calf CBEL I 813.   Rostenberg & Stern 150-69 1996 $450.00

SARTON, GEORGE   Introduction to the History of Science. Baltimore: Williams and Wilkins, 1931. 8vo; 2 volumes; very good in dust jackets (bit worn), original binding. Scarce.   James Tait Goodrich K40-262 1996 $150.00

SARTON, MAY   Coming Into Eighty. Concord: William B. Ewart, 1992. One of only 26 lettered copies, signed; fine as issued.   Bev Chaney, Jr. 23-596 1996 $165.00

SARTRE, JEAN PAUL   Les Mains Sales. Paris: Gallimard, 1948. 1st trade edition, review copy; wrappers; very good+; inscribed by author. Lame Duck Books 19-488 1996 $1,000.00

SARTRE, JEAN PAUL   The Wall and Other Stories. N.P.: New Directions, 1949. Limited edition (limitation number not stated) which precedes first trade edition; patterned boards and quarter bound in black slipcase, some surface chipping at extremities.   Thomas Dorn 9-222 1996 $125.00

SASSOON, SIEGFRIED LORRAINE 1886-1967   Counter-Attack and Other Poems. London: William Heinemann, 1918. 1st edition; just 1500 copies printed; crown 8vo; original wrappers, little worn and split, little browned, but good copy of a fragile publication. Keynes A17.   Ash Rare Books Zenzybyr-81 1996 £145.00

SASSOON, SIEGFRIED LORRAINE 1886-1967   Counter-Attack - and Other Poems. London: William Heinemann, 1918. 1st edition; wrappers; top edge dusty, prelims, edges and endpapers spotted, spine cracked and worn, covers marked and dusty, cover edges rubbed and darkened, good in custom made cloth slipcase, which is faded at spine panel. Ulysses 39-522 1996 £95.00

SASSOON, SIEGFRIED LORRAINE 1886-1967   The Daffodil Murderer. London: John Richmond Ltd., 1913. One of 1000 copies; wrappers little rubbed, otherwise excellent; presentation copy from author for E. M. Forster, with Forster's bookplate.   R. A. Gekoski 19-123 1996 £1,000.00

SASSOON, SIEGFRIED LORRAINE 1886-1967   The Heart's Journey. New York: Crosby Gaige, London: Heinemann, 1927. Limited 1st edition, 590 copies signed by author; pages slightly browned around edges, some offsetting to endpapers head of spine browned where piece torn from dust jacket, otherwise very good in original paper dust jacket with 2 inch piece torn from head of spine.   Virgo Books 48-173 1996 £200.00

SASSOON, SIEGFRIED LORRAINE 1886-1967   The Heart's Journey. New York: Crosby Gaige, 1927. One of 590 copies; printed on rag paper, typography by Bruce Rogers; cloth backed paper covered boards, unprinted dust jacket, jacket slightly chipped, else fine.   Hermitage SP95-845 1996 $325.00

SASSOON, SIEGFRIED LORRAINE 1886-1967   The Heart's Journey. New York: Crosby Gaige, 1927. 1st edition; signed, limited to 590 copies on rag, from an edition of 599 (9 copies on green handmade paper); teal blue paper over boards, linen backed spine, paper label, title gilt stamped, tan dust jacket with design of stylized trees; fine in dust jacket, unusual in this condition.   Priscilla Juvelis 95/1-216 1996 $250.00

SASSOON, SIEGFRIED LORRAINE 1886-1967   Memoirs of a Fox-Hunting Man. London: Faber, 1920. 1st illustrated edition; illustrations by William Nicholson, edges spotted, endpapers slightly foxed, with some offsetting, covers slightly faded at top edge, otherwise very good in rather worn and foxed dust jacket.   Virgo Books 48-174 1996 £85.00

SASSOON, SIEGFRIED LORRAINE 1886-1967   Memoirs of a Fox-Hunting Man. London: Faber & Gwyer, 1928. One of 260 numbered copies, signed by author; spine slightly cocked, rear free endpaper offset, corners little bumped, otherwise excellent copy.   R. A. Gekoski 19-122 1996 £170.00

SASSOON, SIEGFRIED LORRAINE 1886-1967   Memoirs of an Infantry Officer. London: Faber & Faber Ltd., 1930. 1st edition; number 298 of 750 copies, printed on handmade paper and signed by author; 8vo; pages 334, (1); original blue buckram, spine lettered in gilt slightly faded, top edge gilt, others uncut and partly unopened, spine and lower cover little marked, otherwise excellent; in this copy author has drawn the lower half of five legs appearing to protrude from text on half title with autograph inscription "Footnote by the Author" and his monogram. Simon Finch 24-200 1996 £750.00

SASSOON, SIEGFRIED LORRAINE 1886-1967   The Path to Peace. Worcester: Stanbrook Abbey Press, 1960. Limited to 500 copies, this no. 335; printed on handmade paper; hand lettered initials; fine in glassine wrapper, as issued.   Virgo Books 48-177 1996 £250.00

SASSOON, SIEGFRIED LORRAINE 1886-1967   Sherston's Progress. London: Faber, 1936. 1st limited edition, number 178 of 300 copies, signed by author, printed on handmade paper, top edge gilt, uncut, blue buckram cover, spine slighty faded, otherwise very good, no dust jacket. Virgo Books 48-175 1996 $200.00

SASSOON, SIEGFRIED LORRAINE 1886-1967   Sherston's Progress. London: Faber, 1936. fine in dust jacket, lovely copy.   Neil Cournoyer 4-88 1996 $150.00

SATTERLEE, MARION P.   The Massacre at the Redwood Indian Agenccy, on Monday, August 18, 1862. Minneapolis: 1916. 1st edition; 10 pages; fine.   Michael D. Heaston 23-299 1996 $225.00

SAUDEK, JAN   The World of Jan Saudek. Aperture, 1983. illustrations, mostly color; dust jacket.   J. B. Muns 154-267 1996 $150.00

SAUGRAIN, CLAUDE MARIN   Code de la Librairie et Imprimerie de Paris. Paris: Aux Depens de la Communaute, 1744. 8vo; title in red and black; calf; Bigmore & Wyman II 296.   Rostenberg & Stern 150-145 1996 $1,250.00

SAUNDERS, D.   Australian Ecosystems: 200 Years of Utilization, Degradation and Reconstruction. Chipping Norton: 1990. Royal 8vo; 600 pages, illustrations, graphs, maps, tables; paper.   Wheldon & Wesley 207-445 1996 £69.00

SAUNDERS, FREDERICK   The Author's Printing and Publishing Assistant, Comprising Explanations of the Process of Printing, Preparation and Calculation of Manuscripts... London: Saunders and Otley, 1839. 1st edition; small 8vo; (viii), 60, (32 ad) pages; original brown embossed cloth, lower part of front cover very slightly damp marked;   James Burmester 29-122 1996 £225.00

SAUNDERS, J. B. DE C. M.   The Illustrations from the Works of Andreas Vesalius of Brussels, with Annotations and Translations, A Discussion of the Plates and Their Background, Authorship and Influence... Cleveland: 1950. 1st edition; 4to; 248 pages; original binding. W. Bruce Fye 71-2169 1996 $100.00

SAUNDERS, JAMES E.   Early Settlers of Alabama... New Orleans: L. Graham & son, 1899. 1st edition; 530, (24) pages; illustrations; original red cloth; Howes S119.   Blue River Books 9-6 1996 $250.00

SAUNDERS, RICHARD   Poor Richard: the Almanacks for the Years 1733-1758. Philadelphia: Limited Editions Club, 1964. Number 304 of 1500 copies; signed by artist; illustrations by Norman Rockwell; quarter suede over marbled boards, very fine in publisher's slipcase.   Hermitage SP95-1030 1996 $350.00

SAUNDERSON, FRANCIS   The Case Stated of Education As It Was and Ought to Be Restored; and As It Now and Ought to be Discontinued. Dublin: George Herbert, 1862 1st (?only) edition; large 12mo; 103 pages; original cloth, large printed paper label on upper cover, nice/fine copy with 6 line inscription by author to Earl of Belmore. Remarkably scarce.   James Fenning 133-298 1996 £85.00

SAVAGE, C. R.   The Reflex or Salt Lake City and Vicinity. Salt Lake City: C. R. Savage, ca. 1890. Early issue, if not first edition; 35, (1) pages; 15 foldout Panels of plates; original red cloth covers with title stamped in gilt on front cover; very fine. Not in Flake Supplement. Michael D. Heaston 23-346 1996 $125.00

SAVAGE, RICHARD   The Works of Richard Savage, Esq. London: T. Evans, 1777. New eidtion; octavo; 2 volumes; pages cxvi, 185, (2); vi, 279, (3), engraved titlepage vignettes and half titles; contemporary flame calf, gilt, leather labels, inscription flyleaf, hinges worn but holding; attractive set of this scarce early collection. CBEL II 326.   Hartfield 48-L77 1996 $295.00

SAVILE, ALBANY   Thirty-Six Hints to Sportsmen. Okehampton; Simmons, Printer, n.d., c. 1825. 1st edition; 12mo; title within ornamental border, original marbled wrappers; fine. Schwerdt 11 p. 148.   Anthony W. Laywood 108-231 1996 £100.00

SAVILE, F.   Beyond the Great South Wall: The Secret of the Antarctic. New Amsterdam: 1901. 1st American edition; good/very good. Aronovitz 57-1017 1996 $135.00

SAVONAROLA, GIROLAMO   Trattato Della Reuelatione della Reformatione della Chiesa Diuninitus. Venice: Bernardino Stagnino, 1536. 2nd recorded edition; small 8vo; ff. 54 in double columns, Gothic letter, almost full page woodcut printer's device on titlepage, monogram within border at end, 2 woodcut initials; some leaves age yellowed, 17th century ex-Ibris on last leaf; modern half vellum; good. BM STC It. p. 611. Not in Adams or Gamba; Brunet V 19; Graesse VI 283.   A. Sokol XXV-90 1996 £950.00

SAVORY, H. S.   Geometric Turning: Comprising a Description of the New Geometric Chuck Constructed by Mr. Plant of Birmingham. London: 1873. 1st edition; 8vo; 3 plates, 570 patterns on 110 leaves; brown cloth, gilt, scuffed. Abell 253.   Maggs Bros. Ltd. 1190-652 1996 £180.00

THE SAVOY. No. 1. London: Leonard Smithers, Jan. 1896. 4to; original pictorial pink paper over boards, soiled and worn, endleaves browned and foxed, many illustrations and cover design by Aubrey Beardsley, wear to covers primarily confined to spine and extremities, laid in are Beardsley's Christmas card and prospectus for the Savory, including subscriber's form, Chistmas card has light soiling, prospectus folded in middle and is also soiled. Reade 414-426.   Glenn Books 36-13 1996 $150.00

SAVVA, MONK 1659-1725   The Book of Wisdom and Lies. Hammersmith: Kelmscott Press, 1894. One of 250 copies; 8vo; woodcut titlepage and facing page of text enclosed by vine leaf borders, printed in Golden type in black and red with numerous six line decorative initials, chapter headings and shoulder notes printed in red; full limp vellum, pale green silk ties (one missing), bright and crisp.   Marilyn Braiterman 15-119 1996 $900.00

SAWARD, BLANCHE C.   Decorataive Painting. London: L. Upcott Gill, n.d. 1883. 1st edition; 8vo; xx, 214, (2) pages; publisher's cloth, previous owner has illuminated a few of the initial letters; very good. Bookpress 75-114 1996 $165.00

SAWYER, ELBERT HENRY   The National Military Park, Established by the Government to Commemorate the Gallant Deeds of the Federal and Confederate Armies in the Four Major Battles, Fredericksburg, Chancellorsville, Wilderness & Spotsylvania, Va. No imprint: (according to NUC: Chickasha, 1932.) 73 pages; printed wrappers, very good, lightly soiled.   Bohling Book Co. 191-1008 1996 $110.00

SAXBY, HENRY L.   The Birds of Shetland with Observations on Their Habits, Migration and Occasional Appearance. Edinburgh: Maclachlan and Stewart, 1874. 1st edition; 8vo; pages xv, (ii), 398, 8 tinted lithographs; original pictorial cloth, few light spots to backs of some plates, otherwise fine, scarce. Mullens & Swann p. 510-11.   R.F.G. Hollett 76-267 1996 £275.00

SAY, THOMAS 1787-1834   American Conchology, or Descriptions of the Shells of North America. New Harmony: Printed at the School Press, 1830. Pages (36), 10 colored engravings of shells; stitched as issued, mostly unopened, titlepage soiled.   Stephen Lunsford 45-143 1996 $250.00

SAY, THOMAS 1787-1834   American Entomology, or Descriptions of the Insects of North America. Philadelphia: Samuel Agustus Mitchell, 1824-25/28. 1st edition; tall 8vo; 3 volumes, (2), viii, 18 hand colored engraved plates with unpaginated explanatory text (3 index); (2), 18 hand colored engraved plates with unpaginated explantory text, (3 index); (2), 18 hand colored engraved plates with unpaginated explantory text (3 index) pages; tissue guards intact; original green pictorial label on front cover of volume 1, original pink spine label on volume 2, with extra engraved title in volume 1; some moderte foxing and occasional spotting; lovely fresh set, entirely untrimmed and uncut in nearly original condition; 19th century bookplate of S. P. Mitchell. Nissen ZBI 3612; Bennett Amer. Colo Books p. 95; Sabin 77370.   Edwin V: Glaser 121-275 1996 $3,000.00

SAYERS, DOROTHY L.   Busman's Honeymoon. London: Gollancz, 1937. 1st edition; 12mo; grey wrappers, some soiling to spine, generally very good.   Priscilla Juvelis 95/1-321 1996 $250.00

SAYERS, DOROTHY L.   Busman's Honeymoon. New York: Harcourt, Brace & Co., 1937. 1st U.S. edition; very good+ in very good dust jacket which is a bit faded at spine and mdoerately worn at edges and folds. Steven C. Bernard 71-353 1996 $250.00

SAYERS, DOROTHY L.   The Nine Tailors. New York: Harcourt Brace and Co., 1934. 1st American edition; spine cocked and somewhat dimmer dust jacket with several interal tape repairs.   Priscilla Juvelis 95/1-322 1996 $175.00

SAYERS, DOROTHY L.   Strong Poison. New York: Brewer & Warren, 1930. 1st U.S. edition, published the same year as the U.K.; better than very good in lgithly soiled yellow dust jacket, very slightly darkened on spine and edges, with only shallow chipping and few short closed tears; nice copy.   Quill & Brush 102-1552 196 $650.00

SAYERS, DOROTHY L.   Strong Poison. New York: Brewer & Warren, 1930. 1st U.S. edition, published same year as the U.K.: contemporary owner's name on endpaper, pages slightly darkened with few small stains on page edges, otherwise about very good with spine very slightly faded, lettering still bright, lacking dust jacket.   Quill & Brush 102-1553 1996 $125.00

SAYLES, JOHN   Annotated Statutes of the State of Texas. St. Louis: 1898. 2 volumes, 2126, 2126 pages; full shaky calf.   W. M. Morrison 436-204 1996 $100.00

SAYLES, JOHN   Pride of the Bimbos. Boston: Little Brown, 1975. 1st edition; fine in very near fine jacket and signed by author. Scarce. Ken Lopez 74-404 1996 $375.00

SAYLES, JOHN   Pride of the Bimbos. Boston: Little Brown, 1975. 1st edition; near fine in dust jacket.   Lame Duck Books 19-491 1996 $150.00

SAYRE, LEWIS ALBERT   Partial Paralysis from Reflex Irritation, Caused By Congenital Phimosis and Adherent Prepuce. Philadelphia: Collins, Printer, 1870. 1st separate printing; 8vo; 9, (3) pages; printed grey wrappers, slight edge chipping and darkening to edges, very good, very scarce. Inscribed copy. Cordasco 70-3200.   John Gach 150-415 1996 $135.00

SCADDING, HENRY   Toronto of Old: Collections and Recollections Illustrative of the Early Settlement and Social Life of the Capital of Ontario. Toronto: Adam, Stevenson & Co., 1873. 1st edition; 8vo; pages xii, 594, 2 portraits, vignettes; all edges gilt, newly rebound in half calf, spine labels, attractive copy.   Hugh Anson-Cartwright 87-433 1996 $200.00

SCADDING, HENRY   Toronto of Old: Collections and Recollections. Toronto: Willing and Williamson, 1878. Reissue of the 1873 first edition; 8vo; pages xii, 594; frontispiece, 14 plates, folding map; original black and gold stamped brown cloth; with ALS and inscription from author to W. S. MacDonald.   Hugh Anson-Cartwright 87-432 1996 $300.00

SCADDING, HENRY   Toronto: Past and Present, Historical and Descriptive: a Memorial Volume for the Semi-Centennial of 1884. Toronto: Hunter, Rose and Co., 1884. Limited to 1025 numbered copies; 4to; pages 330; frontispiece, illustrations, with original tissues; all edges gilt, original gilt cloth, hinges strengthened, covers somewhat scuffed and slightly soiled, interior fine.   Hugh Anson-Cartwright 87-434 1996 $200.00

SCALIGER, JOSEPH JUSTUS   Notitia Galliae. Amsterdam: Ex Musaeo Pauli Terhaarii, 1697. Thick 8vo; pages 501-862, (50), 224, plus engraved folding map, engraved portrait plate, edges colored brown; early full vellum, decorated with small, bold pen drawings of ships sailing below a seven line motto in Latin, painted under fore-edge, and visible only when fanned is the following text "Tullium M. C. Julius Caesar/ Ciceronem ob E Grecias Ejus/ Domitum Salvum et Incolumem/ Esse Jobemus C. Jaboienus/ Nostris Armis Virtuteque". Later ms. vellum spine label "Incerta" (Meaning uncertain or doubtful);   Family Album Tillers-562 1996 $650.00

SCAMOZZI, VINCENT   The Mirror of Architecture; or the Ground-Rules of the Art of Building... London: printed for J. and B. Spring, 1721. Small 4to; engraved title, (vi), 111 pages, 1 page of ads, 1 full page engraved text figure, 1 narrow folding plate, 51 engraved plates; original speckled calf, rebacked, new endpapers.   David Bickersteth 133-61 1996 £260.00

SCAMUZZI, ERNESTO   Egyptian Art in the Egyptian Museum of Turin. New York: Harry N. Abrams, Inc., 1965. 1st edition; 115 mounted plates; fine in dust jacket.   Hermitage SP95-775 1996 $150.00

SCARFE, FRANCIS   Inscapes - Poems. London: Fortune Press, 1940. 1st edition; author's first book; original binding, covers slightly dusty, head and tail of spine and corners slightly bumped, prelims, edges and endpapers spotted, some internal spotting, very good in nicked, rubbed, marked and dusty, slightly soiled dust jacket browned at spine and edges.   Ulysses 39-523 1996 £75.00

SCARPA, ANTOINE   Traite Pratique des Hernies, ou Memoires Anatomiques et Chirirgicaux sur ces Maladies. Paris: 1823. Thin folio; 21 fine copperplates and 14 in outline; cloth backed marbled boards; light foxing. Choulant/Frank 298099; Heirs of Hippocrates 690; Waller 8544. Argosy 810-431 1996 $1,800.00

SCENERY of the East India Islands, Etc. London: n.d. plated dated 1811-13. Oblong 8vo; (iv); title and index, 26 copper engraved plates; stiff paper lettered wrappers, decorative border, original cloth spine, plates now loose inside, covers little browned and rubbed at edges, some plates with light fox spots and marginal tears, generally very good. Antipodean 28-616 1996 $4,500.00

SCHAEFFER, JACOB CHRISTIAN   Fungorum Qui in Baaria et Palatinatu Circa Ratisbonam Nascuntur... Erlangae: 1800. Folio; 4 volumes, pages viii, 136, (8); frontispiece, 2 engraaved titlepages, 330 uncolored paltes; unbound and uncut, fine; exceedingly rare.   Raymond M. Sutton VII-31 196 $3,600.00

SCHAEFFER, SAMUEL BERNARD   Morning Noon Night. New York: Knight Publishers, 1937. 1st edition; photographs; marvelous copy sprial bound in matching cardboard box that is fine and unworn; scarce. Left Bank Books 2-123 1996 $185.00

SCHAFFER, JACOB CHRISTIAN   Vorlaufige Beobachtungen der Schwamme um Regensburg. Regensburg: 1759. 8vo; pages viii, 59, (2); 4 hand colored plates; blut cloth, fine. Rare.   Raymond M. Sutton VII-32 1996 $1,000.00

SCHALDACH, WILLIAM J.   Coverts and Casts. Field Sports and Angling in Words and Pictures. New York: A. S. Barnes, 1943. 1st edition; quarto; illustrations; brick red buckram, gilt, fine, in lightly chipped dust jacket.   Glenn Books 36-255 1996 $125.00

SCHALDACH, WILLIAM J.   Fish by Schaldach. London: Hutchinson & Co., 1937. Limited edition of 1560 numbered copies; 4to; 60 reproductions; cloth, decorated gilt; fine, in original rather worn box. Thomas Thorp 489-269 1996 £75.00

SCHALDACH, WILLIAM J.   Upland Gunning. New York: A. S. Barnes, 1946. 1st edition; quarto; 56 plates, many in full color; russet cloth, gilt, fine in chipped dust jacket;   Glenn Books 36-256 1996 $150.00

SCHARFT, GEORGE   A Descriptive and Historical Catalogue of the Collection of Pictures at Woburn Abbey. Privately printed for Hastings Ninth Duke of Bedford... 1890. Limited to 200 copies; 29.5 x 23 cm; cloth, small cut in back board, slight foxing at front and back pages, otherwise good.   Rainsford A54-602 1996 £85.00

SCHAU, MICHAEL   J. C. Leyendecker. New York: Watson-Guptill Publications, 1974. 1st edition; fine in dust jacket.   Hermitage SP95-812 1996 $250.00

SCHEFFER, JOHN   The History of Lapland Wherein Are Shewed the Original Manners, Habits, Marriages, Conjurations, &c. of that People. Oxford: 1674. 1st English edition; small folio; (i-ii), 1-147 pages, contents to final leaf, 1 folding map, 25 woodcut illustrations to text, fore edge of half title cropped, but not affecting engraving, otherwise text in near mint condition; very handsome copy, uncommon. Full modern speckled calf, double gilt ruled borders, gilt title and tooling to spine, raised bands to spine, new endpapers. Wing S851; Cox I p. 178.   Beeleigh Abbey BA/56-111 1996 £750.00

SCHEURL, CHRISTOPH   Libellus: de Sacerdotum...Prestantia... Nuremberg: Weyssenburger, 1513. 4to; modern wrappers. Adams S659. Rostenberg & Stern 150-97 1996 $675.00

SCHIFF, S.   Whispers. Schiff, 1973-87. 1st editions; 24 issues, complete run; wrappers; fine.   Aronovitz 57-1018 1996 $150.00

SCHILLER, JOHANN CHRISTOPH FRIEDRICH VON 1759-1805 History of the Rise and Progress of the Belgian Republic, Until the Revoltuion Under Philip II. London: printed for K. Coxhead, by J. and W. Smith, 1807. 1st English translation; 12mo; iv, 238 pages; author's first book; contemporary half russia; fine copy of an uncommon book. Morgan 8098; 2 copies in NUC. James Burmester 29-123 1996 £150.00

SCHILLER, JOHANN CHRISTOPH FRIEDRICH VON 1759-1805 The Piccolomini, or the First Part of Wallenstein, a Drama in Five Acts. London: T. N. Longman and O. Rees, 1800. 1st edition; 8vo; (iv), ii, (ii), 214, (ii) pages; half title and final ad leaf present; contemporary half calf, marbled boards, spine gilt ruled, label; edges of boards bit rubbed, head of spine chipped, localised worming at foot of one joint (not penetrating into book), endpapers spotted, good copy. Wise 16. Robert Clark 38-230 1996 £325.00

SCHILLER, JOHANN CHRISTOPH FRIEDRICH VON 1759-1805 The Robbers. London: ptd. by C. Whittingham for H.D. Symonds, W. & J. Richardson... 1799. 1st edition of this translation; 8vo; frontispiece; contemporary half calf, gilt, corners rubbed; very good, complete with five pages of ads at end, uncommon. CBEL II 1540. Ximenes 108-319 1996 $200.00

SCHLECHTER, R. The Orchidaceae of German New Guinea. Melbourne: 1982. Large 8vo; pages (9), 1180; 372 plates, 2 folding mpas; hardbound, embossed owner's stamp on endpaper. Raymond M. Sutton VI-959 1996 $175.00

SCHLEGEL, H. Traite de Fauconnerie. New York: Johnson Reprint, 1980. Large portolio; unbound as issued in original cloth portfolio, with ties, 17 plates; fine copy, with 8 page boonklet on the authors. Sotheran PN32-100 1996 £598.00

SCHLEICHER, GUSTAV Memorial Addresses Life and Character of... Washington: 1879. 86 pages; fine engraving; laid in is ALS; W. M. Morrison 436-347 1996 $125.00

SCHLIEMANN, HEINRICH Ilios: the City and Country of the Trojans: The Results of Researches and Discoveries on the Site of Troy and throughout the Troad in the Years 1871-72-73-78-79. London: John Murray, 1880. 1st British edition; 8vo; frontispiece, xvi, 800 pages; approximately 1800 illustrations, 6 folding plans, 1 folding map; original gilt pictorial cloth, top edge gilt, small tear at top board, otherwise fine. Archaeologia Luxor-3990 1996 $650.00

SCHLIEMANN, HEINRICH Mycenae: a Narrative of Researaches and Discoveries at Mycenae and Tiryns. New York: Scribner, Armstrong, 1878. 1st U.S. edition; 8vo; lxviii, 384 pages; 549 figures, 25 plates, 8 plans; original blue gilt pictorial cloth, top edge gilt, few small tears at spine, few small marginal tears to several pages, contemporary signature on titlepage. Archaeologia Luxor-3991 1996 $300.00

SCHLIEMANN, HEINRICH Mycenae: a Narrative of Researches and Discoveries at Mycenae and Tiryns. New York: Charles Scribner's, 1880. Revised edtlion; 8vo; lxviii, 404 pages; 551 figures, 25 plates, 8 plans; original blue gilt pictorial cloth, top edge gilt, trivial amount of foxing to few pages, otherwise fine. Archaeologia Luxor-3992 1996 $450.00

SCHLIEMANN, HEINRICH Tiryns: the Prehistoric Palace of the Kings of Tiryns. London: John Murray, 1886. 8vo; lxiv, 385 pages; 188 illustrations, 24 chromolithographic plates, 1 map, 4 plans; gilt pictorial cloth, titlepage, worn at extremites, spine soiled and chipped, bookplate removed; with signature of W.H.D. Rouse. Archaeologia Luxor-3994 1996 $250.00

SCHLIEMANN, HEINRICH Trojanischer Alterthumer. Bericht uber Die Ausgrabungen in Troja. Leipzig: F. A. Brockhaus, 1874. 1st edition; 8vo; lx, 320 pages, 1 plate; 19th century half calf with 4 raised bands, gilt lettered spine, initials "S.S." (for Sophia Schliemann at foot, original wrappers bound in (light rubbing at etremities), remnants of Schliemann's paper private label label at foot of spine; from the library of Ake Akerstrom. Archaeologia Luxor-3981 1996 $15,000.00

SCHLOSS, DAVID FREDERICK Methods of Industrial Remuneration. London: Williams and Norgate, 1892. 1st edition; 8vo; xx, 287 pages, 8 pages of publisher's ads at end; original green cloth, spine lettered, few pencil annotations on final blank; very good. Headicar & Fuller III 1135; Masui 635 for French 1902 ed. John Drury 82-251 1996 £60.00

SCHMALENBACH, WERNER Kurt Schwitters. New York: Abrams, 1970. Folio; 401 pages; 54 tipped in color plates, 366 monochrome illustrations; cloth, dust jacket. Lucas p. 191; Freitag 8792. Brannan 43-583 1996 $245.00

SCHMIDT, DOREY Larry McMurtry: Unredeemed Dreams: a Collection of Bibliography, Essays and Interview. Edinburgh: Pan American University, 1978. 1st edition; stapled wrappers, fine; signed, scarce. Between the Covers 42-296 1996 $150.00

SCHMIDT, ERICH F. Excavations at Tepe Hissar Damghan with an Additional Chapter on the Sasanian Building at Tepe Hissar by Fiske Kimball. Philadelphia: University Museum, 1937. Folio; xxi, 478 pages, 177 figures; calf, top edge gilt, corner bumped. Archaeologia Luxor-2694 1996 $150.00

SCHMIDT, GEORG Ten Reproductions in Facsimile of Paintings by Paul Klee. New York: Wittenborn, 1946. Folio; 9 pages text + 10 tipped in color plates, text and plates laid in loose in board portfolio, as issued. Brannan 43-311 1996 $120.00

SCHMITZ, CARL Oceanic Sculpture. New York Graphic Society, 1962. Folio; (xv) (last blank), frontispiece, 32 plates; pictorial hardboard covers, very minor rubbing at edges, otherwise very good+; fine photos. Hanson 4455. Antipodean 28-321 1996 $165.00

SCHMITZ, JAMES H. The Witches of Karres. Philadelphia: Chilton, 1966. 1st edition; fine in dust jacket with just a few very tiny tears and faded spine panel; attractive copy. Robert Gavora 61-135 1996 $450.00

SCHMOLLER, HANS Mr. Gladstone's Washi: a Survey of Reports on the Manufacture of Paper in Japan. Newtown: Bird & Bull Press, 1984. 1st edition; number 454 of 500 copies; lithographic reproductions on Mohawk vellum, accompanied by an extra set of the lithographic plates in paper folder; morocco backed decorative boards, slipcase lightly scuffed, otherwise fine. Hermitage SP95-1063 1996 $300.00

SCHNEIDER, G. The Book of Choice Ferns for the Garden, Conservatory and Stove. London: 1892-94. 4to; 3 volumes; 88 plates, 398 text figures; original decorated cloth, volumes 1 and 2 neatly refixed; contents good, bindings trifle used, but sound. Wheldon & Wesley 207-1748 1996 £300.00

SCHNEIDER, PIERRE Matisse. London: 1984. 33 x 24.0cm; 752 pages; 930 illustrations, 140 in color; cloth, dust jacket. Rainsford A54-395 1996 £160.00

SCHOBERL, FREDERIC Excursions in Normandy, Illustrated of the Character, Manners, Customs and Traditions of the People; or the State of Society in General... London: Henry Colburn, 1841. tall 8vo; 2 volumes; xi, 337, (10) pages ads dated "May 1841", vii, 341, 6 pages ads; name stamped on endpapers; original medium blue cloth, spines faded, otherwise fine set. David Mason 71-75 1996 $280.00

SCHOENHOF, JACOB The Economy of High Wages. New York: G. P. Putnam's Son, 1892. 1st edition; 8vo; xvii, (3), 414 pages; original cloth, very good. Headicar & Fuller III 1136; not in Masui or Einaudi. John Drury 82-252 1996 £50.00

SCHOENRICH, OTTO The Legacy of Christopher Columbus. Glendale: Arthur H. Clark Co., 1949-50. Number 20 of 25 specially bound sets of the 'Commemorative edition', signed by publisher; 2 volumes, 349, 320 pages, illustrations, folding pocket plates; original cloth; fine. Bohling Book Co. 191-474 1996 $200.00

SCHOFIELD, LILY Billy Ruddylox, an Ancient British Boy. London: Swan Sonnenschein, n.d., ca. 1904. 1st edition; 12mo; 89 pages, printed on one side only; 21 color plates; pictorial boards, boards slightly soiled, else very good. Quayle 178. Marjorie James 19-171 1996 £65.00

SCHONFIELD, H. J. The New Hebrew Typography. London: Denis Archer, 1932. 4to; 17 plates; white cloth backed black baords, gilt lettering, some slight soiling to cloth, booklabel and ownership inscription of Ruari McLean. Appleton 125. Maggs Bros. Ltd. 1191-214 1996 £135.00

SCHOOL OF ST. AFRA, MEISSEN, GERMANY. Statuta et Leges... Meissen: Schulze, 1764. 8vo; 96 pages; 2 folding printed charts, woodcut and typographic headpieces; old boards in paste paper; fine, very rare. Bennett Gilbert LL29-31 1996 $1,000.00

SCHOOLCRAFT, HENRY ROWE 1793-1864 Journal of a Tour in the Interior of Missouri and Arkansas. London: printed for Sir Richard Phillips, 1821. 1st edition; 102 pages; folding map; original black patterned cloth, minor wear to extremities of spine, fine. Howes S185; Matthews p. 236. Michael D. Heaston 23-295 1996 $750.00

SCHOOLCRAFT, HENRY ROWE 1793-1864 Journal of a Tour into the Interior of Missouri and Arkansaw, from Potosoi, or Mine a Burton, in Missouri Territory, in a Southwest Direction, Toward Rocky Mountains, Performed in the Years 1818 and 1819. London: Richard Phillips, 1821. 8vo; pages 102; folding map; modern boards, paper label. Howes S185; Sabin 77858; WC 21a. Richard Adelson W94/95-146 1996 $425.00

SCHOOLCRAFT, HENRY ROWE 1793-1864 Letter from Secretary of War, Transmitting Report of Schoolcraft's Expedition Among the Northwestern Indians. Washington: House of Reps. March 2, 1833. 8vo; modern cloth. Howes S187. Richard Adelson W94/95-244 1996 $150.00

SCHOOLCRAFT, HENRY ROWE 1793-1864 Narrative Journal of Travels through the Northwestern Regions of the United States Extending from Detroit through the Great Chain of American Lakes to the Sources of the Mississippi River. Albany: E. & E. Hosford, 1821. 8vo; pages xvi, 17-419, 4, errata; engraved title, folding map, 7 plates; original quarter calf, marbled boards, rebacked, rubbed, some light foxing. Howes S186; Sabin 77862. Richard Adelson W94/95-145 1996 $685.00

SCHOOLCRAFT, HENRY ROWE 1793-1864 Narrative of an Expedition through the Upper Mississippi to Itasca Lake, the Acutal Source of This River... New York: Harper & Bros., 1834. 1st edition; 8vo; pages vi, 7-308, 5 maps; modern cloth, leather label, Long Island Historical Society duplicate. Howes S187; Sabin 77863; Graff 3698. Richard Adelson W94/95-147 1996 $425.00

SCHOOLCRAFT, HENRY ROWE 1793-1864 Notes on the Iroquois; or Contributions to American History, Antiquities and General Ethnology. Albany: Erastus H. Pease and Co., 1847. 8vo; pages xv, 498, 2, 12 ads, 2 color plates, text illustrations; original brown pictorial cloth, spine ends starting to chip. Howes S191; Sabin 77865. Hodge p. 615-620. Larned 676. Richard Adelson W94/95-149 1996 $425.00

SCHOOLCRAFT, HENRY ROWE 1793-1864 Report of the Sec. of Interior Communicating a Report by H. R. Schoolcraft on the State of Indian Statistics. Washington: 1854. 8vo; pages 11; modern cloth. Richard Adelson W94/95-245 1996 $100.00

SCHORER, MARK Sinclair Lewis - an American Life. New York: McGraw Hill Book Co., 1961. 1st edition; 16 pages of black and white photos; original binding, head and tail of spine slightly bumped, near fine in nicked and slightly rubbed, marked and creased dust jacket slightly darkened at spine and edges; presentation copy inscribed by author for James D. Hart. Ulysses 39-374 1996 £55.00

SCHOTT, GASPAR Mechanica Hydraulico-Pneumatica... Wurzburg: Sumptu Heredum Joannis Godefridi Schonwetteri...Excudebat Henricus... 1657. 1st edition; 1st issue; quarto; (32), 488, (16) pages; engraved title, letterpess title, woodcut arms on verso; corners extended on Dd1, Dd2, Eel and Ee2, small hole on Hh4, obscuring one word, short tears at folds on some plates; few other insignificant defects; 46 engraved plates, many trimmed at the neat mark; numerous woodcuts, printed music; contemporary vellum with yapp fore-edges, edges stained green; fine copy. DeBacker-Sommervogel VII col. 904 no.2; Graesse VI p.315. Heritage Book Shop 196-183 1996 $5,000.00

SCHREINER, OLIVE 1855-1920 Trooper Peter Halket of Mashonaland. Boston: Roberts Bros., 1897. 1st American edition; 8vo; (133, 6 publisher's ads); frontispiece; mustard green cloth, gilt lettered front and spine, some negligible foxing, otherwise near fine. Schleuter & Schleuter p. 402. Paulette Rose 16-297 1996 $100.00

SCHRENCK, P. L. VON Vogel des Amur-Landes. St. Petersberg: 1860. 1st edition; small folio; 7 hand colored lithographs by W. Pape, some browning; half leather, repaired; Paul Leverkuhn's copy with his signature, later in Bradley Martin collection. Very rare. Maggs Bros. Ltd. 1190-597 1996 £650.00

SCHROEDER VAN DER KOLK, JACOB L. C. On the Minute Structure and Functions of the Spinal Cord and Medulla Oblongata, and on the Proximate Cause and Rational Treatment of Epilepsy. London: New Sydenham Society, 1859. 1st edition in English; 8vo; (xiv), 292 pages, 10 plates; embossed brown cloth, expertly rebacked, corners worn, otherwise very good, clean copy. GM 4815. John Gach 150-425 1996 $175.00

SCHROEDER, HENRY The Annals of Yorkshire. Leeds: Crosby & Co., 1851/52. Tall 8vo; 2 volumes, (426, (20) pages ads; (407), (26) pages ads; original blue cloth with gilt decoration on upper covers and spines, all edges gilt; spines slightly darkened, very light rubbing at extremities, in fact a nice, near fine set. David Mason 71-38 1996 $160.00

SCHROETER, JOHANN HIERONYMUS Selenotopographische Fragmente zur Gernauern Kenntniss der Mondflache, ihrer Erlittenen Veranderungen und Atmosphare... Lilienthal: Carl Gottfr. Fleckeisen, 1791. 4to; (12), xx, 676, (1) pages, 43 copperplate engravings, some folding, titlepage vignette; new three quarter calf over marbled boards, original morocco spine label, raised bands, red edges; some characteristic light foxing, very good, rare. Poggendorff II 846-847. Zeitlinger 4281. Edwin V. Glaser 121-281 1996 $3,250.00

SCHULZ, H. C. A French Miniature Book of Hours Leaf, with an Essay Entitled 'French Illuminated Manuscripts''. Grabhorn Press, 1958. One of 200 copies; 8 x 6 inches; the minieature leaf, 3 1/4 x 2 3/8 inches, produced in Paris during the first half of the 15th century, cotaiins one two-line and 16 fine one line initials in burnished gold, magenta and blue, the larger initial enclosing a charming orange flower, recto with lovely quarter border of many burnished gold ivy leaves on hairline stems as well as delicate flowers painted in colors; 30 pages text; decorative paper boards, imitation vellum spine with gold titling, edges of elaves untrimmed, leaves of text with couple of tiny spots, but book and leaf both in fine condition. BMC Private Presses p. 94. Phillip J. Pirages 33-334 1996 $550.00

SCHULZ, H. C. A Monograph on the Italian Choir Book. San Francisco: The Grabhorn Press for David Magee, 1941. Limited to 75 copies; folio; (18) pages plus original vellum ms. initial inserted at back, 1 large and 13 smaller initials by Valenti Angelo hand illuminated in red, gold and blue; tan and red linen. Scarce. Grabhorn Bib. 363. Kenneth Karmiole 1NS-224 1996 $1,200.00

SCHUMANN Album of Children's Pieces for Piano; London: Augener, n.d. 1915. 1st edition; Folio; colored illustrations; grey boards with oblong onlay, light wear to coers, else near fine in dust jacket which is torn at spine. Marjorie James 19-229 1996 £125.00

SCHURER, EMIL A History of the Jewish People in the Time of Jesus Christ. Edinburgh & New York: T. & T. Clark, Charles Scribner's, 1908. 8vo; 2 volumes in 5 parts plus index, xxxvi, 2066 pages; signature; original cloth. Archaeologia Luxor-2702 1996 $250.00

SCHURIG, MARTIN Spermatologia Historico-Medica. h. e. Seminis Humani Consideratio Physico-Medico-Legalis... Frankfurt: J. Beck, 1720. 1st and only edition; 4to; 806 pages; woodcut ornaments; contemporary three quarter vellum; fine. Bennett Gilbert LL29-81 1996 $1,500.00

SCHUSTER, THOMAS E. Printed Kate Greenaway: a Catalogue Raisonne. London: T. E. Schuster, 1987. 1st edition; 8vo; 150 illustrations; original cloth, dust jacket, new. Forest Books 74-239 1996 £55.00

SCHUYLER, EUGENE Turkistan, Notes of a Journey in Russian Turkistan, Khokand, Bukhara and Kuldja. New York: 1876. 1st American edition; 9.5 x 5.5 inches; 2 volumes, 411; 463 pages, with index; 3 maps, illustrations; cloth, small paper label on each spine, minor wear, else nice set. John K. King 77-839 1996 $150.00

SCHWARTZ, DELMORE In Dreams Beging Responsibilities. Norfolk: New Directions, 1938. 1st edition; only 1000 copies printed; 8vo; good copy, somewhat marked and faded, married, with bright dust jacket, just lightly chipped at extremities; presentation copy from author for Francis Fergusson, with Fergusson's pencilled notes. Lakin & Marley 3-54 1996 $2,750.00

SCHWARTZ, DELMORE Successful Love and Other Stories. New York: Corinth Books, 1961. 1st edition; 8vo; cloth, dust jacket edge worn; fine copy. James S. Jaffe 34-609 1996 $100.00

SCHWARTZ, DELMORE The World is a Wedding. Norfolk: New Directions, 1948. Uncorrected proof, string tied signatures in unprinted wrappers, light stain and slight crease to one corner of the front wrapper, little darkening to extremities of wrappers, very good; Van Wyck Brooks's copy with his ownership signature, titled in his hand and with some of his notes on front wrap and few in text. Between the Covers 42-389 1996 $750.00

SCHWARTZ, JOZUA MARIUS WILLEM 1858-1915 God's Fool: a Koopstad Story. London: Richard Bentley, 1892. 1st edition; 8vo; half titles present; 3 volumes; pages vi (for viii), 279; vi, 290; vi, 289, (1), 4; original olive green cloth, extremities rubbed, backstrip gilt lettered, Mudie's Select Library labels at head of all front covers, ink mark on front cover of volume i, Bentley's repeated monogram design on endpapers, edges printed with black filigree design on pale green; good. Sadlier 1466; Wolff 4242. Blackwell's B112-182 1996 £95.00

SCHWARZ, ARTURO Marcel Duchamp: Notes and Projects for the Large Glass. New York: Abrams, n.d. Folio; 217 pages, cloth, ink signature on titlepage, front panel of glassine dust jacket present. Brannan 43-171 1996 $395.00

SCHWARZ, H.   David Octavius Hill, Master of Photographer. New York: 1931. 1st American edition; photo illustrations, slipcase as issued, illustrations.   J. B. Muns 154-142 1996 $185.00

SCHWARZ, TED   Arnold Friberg, the Passion of a Modern Master. Flagstaff: Northland Press, 1985. Number 39 of 200 copies; 12.5 x 10 inches; (iii), 175 pages; illustrations; signed by artist, Arnold Friberg on limitation page, accompanied by a red cloth portfolio with color print of Friberg's "Geronimo" 26 x 20 inches, signed in pencil; half leather and red cloth, laid in much larger clamshell box with mounted color illustrations; very good+ overall, though upper corners of portfolio bumped, (incl. dented corners on print) and with narrow strip of dampstaining on lower edge of front board.   Bohling Book Co. 192-214 1996 $700.00

SCHWEINFURTH, C.   Orchids of Peru. Chicago: 1958-61. 8vo; map and 194 pages of line drawings; original wrappers, spines faded, paper residue on lower corner of front wrapper owner's namestamp on wrappers, blanks and edge of pages of parts 3 and 4.   Raymond M. Sutton VI-962 1996 $100.00

SCHWEINFURTH, GEORG   The Heart of Africa. Three Years' Travels and Adventures in the Unexplored Regions of Central Africa from 1868 to 1871. New York: Harper & Bros., 1874. 1st U.S. edition; 8vo; 2 volumes; frontispiece to both volumes, 24 full page illustrations, 98 illustrations to text, 3 maps and plans; brown embossed cloth, gilt illustration to upper boards, corners slightly worn, gilt title to spines, owner's stamp to prelim of both volumes, hinges cracked, but still good, tight copy. Beeleigh Abbey BA/56-112 1996 £250.00

SCHWERDT, C. F. G. R.   Hunting, Hawking, Shooting. London: privately ptd. for the author by Waterlow & Sons, 1928-37. Limited to 300 copies, numbered and signed by author; large 4to; 4 volumes, xxiv, 324; xvi, 359; x, 256; xx, 260 pages; 380 plates; original dark green half morocco gilt, top edge gilt, others uncut, by Kelly & Sons (volumes 1 and 2 neatly rebacked), original backstrips relaid, extremities slightly rubbed, tiny piece chipped from head of volume 3, occasional light dust soiling in upper margin of few leaves.   Thomas Thorp 489-270 1996 £2,000.00

SCLATER, P. L.   The Book of Antelopes. London: 1894-1900. 4to; 4 volumes; 100 fine hand colored plates by Wolf and Smit, 121 illustrations in text; blue buckram; good, rare, well rebound to match spines of original binding, some very limited slight foxing and obituary of G. Rosenboom in Dutch pasted on flyleaf volume 1, from the collection of Jan Coldewey.   Wheldon & Wesley 207-92 1996 £5,000.00

SCLATER, P. L.   A Monograph of the Jacamars and Puff Birds, or Families Galbulidae and Bucconidae. London: 1879-82. Limited to 250 copies; royal 4to; pages liii, 171, 55 hand colored plates; contemporary half morocco. bind trifle rubbed and some extremely limited slight staining; from the collection of Jan Coldewey.   Wheldon & Wesley 207-91 1996 £3,800.00

SCLATER, W. L.   Systema Avium Ethiopicarum... London: 1924-30. 8vo; 2 volumes; interleaved; cloth, worn; from the library of Dr. W. Serle, with numerous notes.   Wheldon & Wesley 207-853 1996 £85.00

SCLATER, WILLIAM   An Exposition with Notes Upon the First and Second Epistles to the Thessalonians. London: printed by John Haviland, and are sold by Richard Thrale, 1630. 4to; 2 parts in one, title dusty, short tear in B2, separate title, signatures and pagination to second part; old marbled boards, rebacked.   Anthony Laywood 108-16 1996 £165.00

SCOLES, IGNATIUS   Sketches of African and Indian Life in British Guiana. Demerara: Argosy Press, 1885. 2nd edition; 8vo; (viii), 109 pages; 4 illustrations, some marginal worming, otherwise good; blue buckram; uncommon.   K Books 442-432 1996 £65.00

SCORESBY, WILLIAM 1760-1829   Journal of a Voyage to the Northern Whale-Fishery... Edinburgh: printed for Archibald Constable and Co., Edinburgh and Hurst, ... 1823. 1st edition; 8vo; 2 large folding maps, neat repair to small tear of inner margin of large general map to face p. 1, some offsetting to text, few illustrations to letterpress, ms. library location to front pastedown; modern half tan calf and marbled boards, red morocco label to spine, edges marbled. Hill Pacific Voyages p. 270; Arctic Bib. 15164.   Beeleigh Abbey BA/56-114 1996 £325.00

SCORESBY, WILLIAM 1760-1829   Journal of a Voyage to Australia and the Round the World, for Magnetical Research. London: Longman, Green, Longman and Roberts, 1859. 1st edition; 8vo; errata slip tipped in, 96 pages, 315 pages; frontispiece, 6 woodcut illustrations, 1 large folding map colored in outline, publisher's catalog to rear, pages 17/18 and 55/56 have very neat repairs to tears with no loss, page 31/32 of Narrative very skilfully supplied in facsimile; modern half calf, gilt rule to panelled spine, red and black morocco labels, marbled boards, yellow edges, new endpapers. Ferguson VII 15510; Spence 780.   Beeleigh Abbey BA/56-113 1996 £300.00

SCORESBY, WILLIAM 1760-1829   Journal of a Voyage to Australia and Round the World, for Magnetical Research. London: Longman, Green, etc., 1859. 8vo; pages xlviii, 315; portrait, folding map, errata; half tan calf, marbled boards, portrait waterstained, map lightly foxed.   Richard Adelson W94/95-151 1996 $285.00

SCOT, REGINALD   The Discoverie of Witchcraft, Wherein the Lewde dealing of Witches and Witchmongers is Notablie detected... London: by William Brome, 1584. 1st edition; 4to; (28), 560, (16) pages, 2 unpagiated leaves signed * between 2C8 and 2D1 and between 2D5 and 2D6, 4 full page woodcuts of magical apparatus, diagrams, large woodcut initials and other woodcuts, Black letter; full red crushed levant morocco, covers with gilt fillets and cornerpieces, spine richly gilt in compartments, inner dentelles gilt, gilt edges by Riviere, absolutely flawless and beautiful copy, with excellent margins, measuring 18.8 x 13.8 cm; STC 21864. Hall, Old Conjuring Books pp. 47-62.   Joseph J. Felcone 64-37 1996 $12,000.00

SCOT, REGINALD   The Discoverie of Witchcraft. John Rodker Pub., 1930. Limited to 1275 copies, this being # 1003/1275; xxxvii, 283 pages; illustrations, 2 bookplates, pencil drawing on endpage of magical seals; very good+.   Middle Earth 77-150 1996 $295.00

SCOT, REYNOLDE REGINALD   A Perfite Platform of a Hop Garden. London: Henrie Denham at the Signe of the Starre, 1574. 1st edition; 4to; pages xvi, 54 (of 56), (lacking last leaf of epilogue (photocopy laid in), decorated initials and 15 woodcuts; very tall, bound with first blank leaf with ornament, marbled boards, modern rebacking in calf, some interior soiling, especially to final leaf; circular indistinct pencil rubbings of coins on front flyleaf, still quite attractive. Bookplate of Earl Fitzwilliam, early ownership signatures of Robert and Tho. Glover. STC 21865; Hunt 128; Henrey 337;   Second Life Books 103-168 1996 $2,200.00

SCOTLAND: Her Sons and Scenery, as Sung by Her Bards, and Seen in the Camera. London: A. W. Bennett, 1868. 1st edition; 8vo; (viii), 192 pages; 14 original mounted albumen photos; full navy blue morocco gilt, with four raised bands to spine and gilt medallion on front and rear covers surrounding an inlay of salmon morocco, gilt, covers have floral designs in blind, fine and bright in fine binding of the period, with bevelled edges, all edges gilt, front hinge shows slight wear, else fine, binding signed by R. & A. Suttaby, London.   Andrew Cahan 47-180 1996 $485.00

SCOTT, DANIEL   The Stricklands of Sizergh Castle. Kendal: Titus Wilson, 1908. 1st edition; 8vo; pages viii, 293, (iv), illustrations, folding pedigrees; original cloth, gilt, rather bumped and creased.   R.F.G. Hollett & Son 78-248 1996 £110.00

SCOTT, EVELYN   The Wave. New York: Cape & Smith, 1929. 1st edition; mild foxing to fore-edge, otherwise fine in fine, mildly spine darkened dust jacket, very nice.   Ken Lopez 74-405 1996 $100.00

SCOTT, GEORGE GILBERT   Gleanings from Westminster Abbey. London: J. H. and Jas. Parker, 1861. 1st edition; 8vo; frontispiece, xvi, 92, 49, 8 pages, 5 plates; publisher's cloth, top edge gilt; covers sunned, signature sprung, sporadic foxing.   Bookpress 75-115 1996 $125.00

SCOTT, JOB   Journal of the Life, Travels and Gospel Labours of that Faithful Servant and Minister of Christ, Job Scott. New York: printed and sold by Isaac Collins, 1797. 1st edition; 12mo; xiv, 360 pages; full leather, outer hinges split, inner hinges reinforced, boards edge worn, paper darkened and foxed, good. Howes S228; Clark Old South II 122. Bohling Book Co. 191-392 1996 $100.00

SCOTT, JOHN   Poetical Works. London: printed for J. Buckland, 1782. 1st edition; 8vo; illustrations; contemporary tree calf, nicely rebacked; very good; from the library of Richard Senhouse with his booklabel. Bentley 494; CBEL II 681.   Ximenes 108-320 1996 $600.00

SCOTT, JOHN F.   The Danzantes of Monte Alban. Washington: Dumbarton Oaks, 1978. 8vo; 2 volumes, text: 79 pages, 30 figures; plate volume: frontispiece, 152 plates; stiff wrappers.   Archaeologia Luxor-4876 1996 $125.00

SCOTT, KENNET   Homage - a Book of Sculptures. London: Geoffrey Bles, 1938. 1st edition; quarto; 40 black and white reproductions; original binding, top edge gilt, covers slightly bowed and dusty, tail of spine and bottom corners slightly bumped, endpapers slightly marked, and partially and faintly browned, very good in nicked, chipped, rubbed and dusty, slightly marked, creased, torn and soiled dust jacket darkened at spine and edges, with remains of later price sticker on spine and frayed at head of spine.   Ulysses 39-355   1996 £155.00

SCOTT, MICHAEL   Tom Cringle's Log. Edinburgh: William Blackwood and T. Cadell, London, 1833. 1st edition in book form; 8vo; 2 volumes; original green cloth, some rubbing and wear, generally light, tear on half title of volume 1 repaired; very nice, worn morocco backed slipcase. Sadleir 3040; Wolff 6228b.   James Cummins 14-174   1996 $400.00

SCOTT, PAUL   After the Funeral. London: Whittington Press & William Heinemann, 1979. Limited to 200 numbered copies; 4to; xvi, 24 pages; 7 full page illustrations by Sally Scott; printed on Zerkall mouldmade paper, signed by Sally Scott and Roland Gant; publisher's quarter cloth with Whittington marbled boards, top edge gilt, others uncut, very fine. Thomas Thorp 489-274   1996 £50.00

SCOTT, PAUL   The Corrida at San Feliu. London: Martin Secker & Warburg Ltd., 1964. 1st edition; original binding, top edge slightly dusty, head and tail of spine and bottom corners slightly bumped, covers slightly cocked, very good in nicked, chipped, rubbed and dusty, slightly creased and marked dust jacket browned at spine and edges and missing small piece at bottom edge of lower panel.   Ulysses 39-528   1996 £75.00

SCOTT, PAUL   The Day of the Scorpion. London: Heinemann, 1968. 1st edition; edges spotted, very slight offsetting to endpapers, small name on front pastedown, otherwise very good in soiled and chipped dust jacket with several closed and internally repaired tears to corners and edges.   Virgo Books 48-181   1996 £55.00

SCOTT, PAUL   A Male Child. London: Eyre & Spottiswoode, 1956. 1st edition; original binding, top edge browned, prelims and edges spotted, last two pages opened clumsily, head and tail of spine bumped, spine slightly darkened, bottom edge of upper cover slightly marked, bookshop stamp on front free endpaper, good in nicked, rubbed, spotted and dusty, slightly torn and frayed dust jacket, by Stein, browned at spine and edges.   Ulysses 39-527   1996 £65.00

SCOTT, PAUL   The Mark of the Warrior. London: Eyre & Spottiswoode, 1958. 1st English edition; near fine in beautiful dust jacket which is in fine condition; warmly inscribed by author who has also signed book's titlepage.   Thomas Dorn 9-224   1996 $200.00

SCOTT, PETER   Morning Flight. London: Country Life, 1935. Limited edition of 750 copies numbered and signed by author/artist; 4to; xiv, 138 pages; woodcut on titlepage, few other woodcuts in text, 16 mounted color paltes, 48 black and white plates; original quarter black buckram, brown cloth sides, gilt, top edge gilt, others uncut, sides little dust soiled.   Thomas Thorp 489-272   1996 £250.00

SCOTT, PETER   Wild Chorus. London: Country Life, 1938. Limited to 1200 copies, numbered and signed by author/artist; 4to; xii, 120 pages; 24 mounted color plates and 64 black and white illustrations; blue buckram, decorated gilt, top edge gilt, others uncut, spine faded. Thomas Thorp 489-273   1996 £235.00

SCOTT, ROBERT N.   The War of the Rebellion: a Compilation of the Union and Confederate Armies. Series I - Volumes I & II. Washington: GPO, 1880. 1st edition; 8vo; v, 752 pages, v, 1101 pages; tears to spine cloth repaired, bottom edge of volume 1 rubbed, marginal dampstain to volume 2, else good; the copies of Lieut. Col. Alexander Robert Chisholm, with his ownership signature. Very fine association.   Andrew Cahan 47-49   1996 $500.00

SCOTT, S. H.   A Westmorland Village, The Story of the Old Homesteads and "Statesman" Families of Troutbeck by Windermere. London: Constable & Co., 1904. 1st edition; 8vo; pages (iv), 269, 8 illustrations; original green cloth, gilt, spine trifle faded and marked. R.F.G. Hollett & Son 78-1267   1996 £65.00

SCOTT, TEMPLE   The Silver Age and Other Dramatic Memories. New York: Scott & Seltzer, 1919. 1st edition; 8vo; crushed dark burgundy morocco du cap with two gilt fillet borders and elaborate corner pieces made up of groupings of individual floral tools, spine with five raised bands and similar floral decoration within compartments, board edges gilt, inner dentelles, top edge gilt, stamped with name of binder on lower front turn in: The Atelier Bindery; the dedication copy, with presentation inscription to dedicatee D. George Derry, Esq. dated Christmas 1919; laid in is one page ALS from Scott to Derry.   Book Block 32-44   1996 $395.00

SCOTT, WALTER 1771-1832   The Ancient British Drama. (with) The Modern British Drama. London: printed for William Miller, 1810. Quarto; 8 volumes; contemporary calf, gilt spines with red and green morocco labels, blind tooled edges, ink signature on half titles, old catalog description pasted to front endpaper of volume 1; very good. Heritage Book Shop 196-246   1996 $1,250.00

SCOTT, WALTER 1771-1832   Halidon Hill: a Dramatic Sketch. Edinburgh: printed for Archibald Constable & Co., and Hurst, Robinson & Co.,... 1822. 1st edition; 8vo; original grey brown printed wrappers, uncut, rubbed, some chipping and tearing along spine, inner hinges strengthened, discreet reinforcement of upper cover, pastedown on lower cover is a page of text from a report on smallpox epidemic in Wicks in early 1822, some light browning or soiling of text, else very good in royal blue cloth box; bookplate of Frank Fletcher.   James Cummins 14-175   1996 $300.00

SCOTT, WALTER 1771-1832   Ivanhoe. New York: Limited Editions Club, 1940. Limited to 1500 copies; 8vo; 2 volumes; linoleum cuts by Allen Lewis who also designed the book, signed by Lewis; embossed silver cloth made to resemble chain mail, fine in soiled, lightly worn case.   Charles Agvent 4-984   1996 $125.00

SCOTT, WALTER 1771-1832   Ivanhoe. New York: Limited Editions Club, 1951. Limited to 1500 copies; 8vo; 2 volumes; hand colored through stencils, signed by the artist, Edward Wilson; decorated linen, fine in partly split slipcase.   Charles Agvent 4-985   1996 $125.00

SCOTT, WALTER 1771-1832   The Lady of the Lake. Edinburgh: Ballantyne/London: Longman, 1810. 8th edition; 8vo; full calf, elaborately bordered in gilt, of Saint Paul's School, London, spine richly gilt, all edges gilt, inner dentelles gilt, ca. 1820; amrorial bookplate, slip dated 1934 awarding the Valpey Prize; fine.   Trebizond 39-49   1996 $125.00

SCOTT, WALTER 1771-1832   The Lady of the Lake, a Poem. Edinburgh: Printed by James Ballantyne and Co. for Longman, 1814. 10th edition; 8 1/2 x 5 1/2 inches; 5 p.l., 433 pages; excellent contemporary sprinkled calf, flat spine with simple gilt rules and delicate centered gilt floral ornaments, red morocco label, marbled endpapers, one cover slightly faded, one leaf with printing fault (few letters displaced but not lost), otherwise only trivial defects, remarkably fine copy, especially clean and fresh internally, virtually unworn contemporary binding.   Phillip J. Pirages 33-455   1996 $125.00

SCOTT, WALTER 1771-1832   The Lady of the Lake. B-M, 1910. 1st edition thus; profusely illustrated in color and black and white and blue by H. C. Christy; near fine.   Aronovitz 57-1024   1996 $125.00

SCOTT, WALTER 1771-1832   The Lay of the Last Minstrel. London: Longman, 1807. 6th edition; lg. 8vo; 340 pages; 3 contemporary ink and wash drawings by Sophia Merrick Hoare bound in; dark blue morocco gilt by Comte Caumont, with his label, gilt & blind roll tooled borders, single fillet panel with small fleuron cornerpieces, spine gilt in compartments, lettered and dated, double raised bands, turn-ins, olive silk doublures and endpapers with gilt roll tooled borders, all edges gilt, exemplary binding.   Marlborough 160-77   1996 £450.00

SCOTT, WALTER 1771-1832   The Lay of the Last Minstrel. Edinburgh: Adam and Charles Black, 1854. 8vo; pages 354; steel engraved frontispiece, titlepage, 100 text woodcuts by Birket Foster and John Giblert; full brown morocco, gilt, gilt ruled panelled boards, raised bands, heavily gilt spine panels, upper panel trifle marked, extremities very slighty rubbed, all edges gilt; fine, clean copy.   R.F.G. Hollett 76-268 1996 £75.00

SCOTT, WALTER 1771-1832   Letters On Demonology and Witchcraft: Addressed to J. G. Lockhart. London: Murray, 1830. 402 pages; rebound; very good+.   Middle Earth 77-387   1996 £145.00

SCOTT, WALTER 1771-1832   Letters on Demonology and Witchcraft, Addressed to J. G. Lockhart. London: John Murray, 1830. 1st edition; 24mo; frontispiece, 16 pages ads at rear; rebound in functional, early 20th century cloth; near fine.   Captain's Bookshelf 38-196   1996 $100.00

SCOTT, WALTER 1771-1832   Letters on Demonology and Witchcraft, Addressed to J. G. Lockhart. London: John Murray, 1831. 2nd edition; small 8vo; pages ix, 396, (ii), frontispiece (lightly browned); full black calf, gilt, boards blind ruled, central basekt weave patterned panel, little rubbed, nicely rebacked to match.   R.F.G. Hollett 76-269   1996 £50.00

SCOTT, WALTER 1771-1832   The Life of Napoleon Buonaparte, Emperor of the French... Edinburgh: printed by Ballantyne and Co. for Longman et al, 1827. 2nd edition; 7 1/4 x 4 3/4 inches; 9 volumes; especially appealing contemporary fawn colored polished half calf in regency style, marbled paper sides, raised bands, spine panels attractively decorated with blind and gilt rules and centered blind floral ornament, elegant gilt latticework at spine ends, red morocco double labels, paper sides bit chafed, 3 or 4 corners with slight wear, binding exceptionally fine, very bright and virtually without wear, first and last few leaves of most volumes freckled with foxing, isolated light foxing or minor stains, otherwise excellent internally quite clean and fresh, extremely pretty set; bookplate of Jane Yates, Irwell House in each volume.   Phillip J. Pirages   33-456   1996 $750.00

SCOTT, WALTER 1771-1832   Minstrelsy of the Scottish Border. Kelso: printed by James Ballantyne, 1802. 1st edition; 8vo; 2 volumes bound in 1; frontispiece, stain on borders of pages 157-170 not affecting text, neatly and expertly respined, original cloth, good.   K Books   442-433 1996 £85.00

SCOTT, WALTER 1771-1832   Minstrelsy of the Scottish Border: Consisting of Historical and Romantic Ballads. Edinburgh: Longman & Rees, 1803. 2nd edition; 8vo; 3 volumes; contemporary full green morocco with gilt border, all edges gilt, lbirary bookplate and blindstamps, couple of spine ends worn, still nice set.   Chapel Hill 94-359   1996 $225.00

SCOTT, WALTER 1771-1832   The Monastery. Longman, Hurst, Rees, Orme and Brown, 1820. 1st edition; 3 volumes; quarter leather with gold gilt tooling to raised bands, plain boards with marbled page edges; good/very good.   Aronovitz   57-1023   1996 $175.00

SCOTT, WALTER 1771-1832   The Poetical Works of Sir Walter Scott. London: Frederick Warne, 1893. Thick 8vo; full blue polished calf, armorial coat of arms and head of man in gilt on front and rear cover respectively, richly gilt paneled spine, raised bands, edges gilt, by Bayntun; with fine quality painting on fore-edge of volume depicting harvesters in a field with landscape in background, fine, bright example. Appelfeld Gallery   54-98   1996 $650.00

SCOTT, WALTER 1771-1832   Rokeby: a Poem. Edinburgh: John Ballantyne, 1813. 1st edition; 4to; handsome full blue morocco with gilt heraldic emblem on front cover, gilt emblematic tooling on spine, gilt top; fine, untrimmed, with half title.   Appelfeld Gallery   54-161   1996 $175.00

SCOTT, WALTER 1771-1832   Rokeby. Edinburgh: Charles and Adam Black, 1869. 16mo; delightful Mauchline binding of Stuart tartan over wooden boards, backed in forest green morocco, gilt, all edges gilt, with the exception of a few light scratches, this is a fine exmaple of a uniquely Scottish bookbinding technique.   Glenn Books   36-27   1996 $225.00

SCOTT, WALTER 1771-1832   The Waverley Novels. Edinburgh: Robert Cadell, 1842. 17 volumes; hundreds of steel plate and wood engravings; elegantly bound by Bickers and Son in full crushed green morocco with raised bands forming 6 compartments; two compartments contain title and volume labels of tan morocco with simple gilt double border and cornerpieces, other compartments elaborately gilt with same double rule but surrounding very ornate floral corner and center pieces on background of circles and stars, boards panelled with both simple rule and decorative roll and elaborate floral pattern surrounding open panel just inside last double rule, fancy gilt dentelles. Beautiful condition. Hermitage   SP95-557   1996 $3,500.00

SCOTT, WALTER 1771-1832   Waverley Novels. Edinburgh: Adam and Charles Black, 1852-53. 8 3/4 x 6 inches; 25 volumes; frontispiece and engraved title in each volume; well bound in contemporary red half morocco by C. S. Smith of Edinburgh, buckram sides, spines with raised bands and gilt rules, ornaments and titling, marbled edges and endpapers, only the slightest signs of wear to bindings, which are especially bright and elegant; faint dampstain in 1 vol. at top and 1st four leaves, another vol. w/dark brown acidic stain (size of quarter) evident on 4 leaves, otherwise no significant faults internally, text especially smooth & clean, very fine and attractive set.   Phillip J. Pirages   33-458   1996 $1,650.00

SCOTT, WALTER 1771-1832   Waverley Novels. Edinburgh: A. & C. Black, 1877. Small 8vo; 48 volumes; frontispieces, vignette titles and numerous engravings on steel and wood; contemporary half red morocco, mottled board sides, mottled edges.   Charles W. Traylen 117-188   1996   £900.00

SCOTT, WILLIAM   Picturesque Scenery in the County of Sussex, sketched from Nature, Drawn on Stone... London: Rodwell and Martin, 1821. Oblong 4to; 6 lithographic plates; stitched as issued, original buff colored paper wrappers. Pristine copy; presentation, inscribed to Miss Radford.   Marlborough   162-87   1996   £650.00

SCOTT, WILLIAM BELL 1811-1890   Antiquarian Gleanings in the North of England, Being Examples of Antique Furniture, Church Decoration, Objects of Historical Interest, etc. London: George Bell, 1850. Large 4to; pages 18, plus 38 hand colored lithographed plates; original blindstamped cloth, gilt, recased; few edges little chipped, occasional spotting, but very good. Scarce.   R.F.G. Hollett & Son   78-58   1996 £350.00

SCOTT, WILLIAM BELL 1811-1890   The Ornamentist, or Artisan's Manual in the Various Branches of Ornamental Art... London: A. Fullerton and Co., 1853. Folio; with added litho title, 86 litho plates, 21 text illustrations, 21 pages; original blue cloth, very slight wear at headbands, boards lightly discolored, some light browning and marginal staining of plates, but binding strong, ticket of C. W. Laird, Montrose, otherwise very good copy.   James Fenning   133-303   1996   £225.00

THE SCOUNDREL'S Dictionary, or an Explantion of the Cant Words Used by the Thieves, Horse-Breeders, Street-Robbers and Pick-Pockets About Town. London: printed for J. Brownell, 1754. pages 32; small corner tear from margin of pages 15-16; original boards, marked, recently neatly rebacked. Small stamp of Williams's Library Cheltenham, bookplate of Asa French (1912). Alston IX 322.   Jarndyce   103-5   1996   £1,250.00

SCRANTON, ROBERT LORENTZ   Corinth. Volume I. Part III: Monuments in the Lower Agora and North of the Archaid Temple. Princeton: ASCSA, 1951. Folio; xiv, 200 pages, 83 figures, 91 plates; original cloth, corners bumped, spine faded.   Archaeologia   Luxor-3181   1996 $450.00

SCRANTON, ROBERT LORENTZ   Corinth. Volume XVI: Mediaeval Architecture in the Central Area of Corinth. Princeton: ASCSA, 1957. Folio; xvi, 147 pages, 15 figures, 36 plates; 7 plans; corner lightly bumped.   Archaeologia   Luxor-3190   1996 $225.00

SCRANTON, ROBERT LORENTZ   Greek Walls. Cambridge: Harvard University Press, 1941. 8vo; xvi, 194 pages; 24 illustrations; later three quarter calf, erasure on verso of titlepage, otherwise fine. Archaeologia   Luxor-4012   1996 $450.00

SCRATCHLEY, J.   The London Dissector; or System of Dissection Practised in the Hospitals and Lecture Rooms of the Metropolis. London: 1816. 1st edition; 8vo; boards, uncut, worn, joints cracked and printed label defective, 24 page publisher catalog of J. Callow, medical books bound at end; signataure of Danl. Owen Davies, surgeon, on title. Maggs Bros. Ltd.   1190-503   1996   £65.00

SCROPE, G. P.   The Geology and Extinct Volcanos of Central France. London: 1858. 2nd edition; 8vo; xvii, 258 pages, 17 plates, 8 folding, one colored, 2 colored folding geological maps in pockets; cloth, library stamp on half title and at end, inner joints repaired.   John Henly 27-550   1996   £90.00

SCROPE, G. P.   The Geology and Extinct Volcanos of Central France. London: 1858. 2nd edition; 8vo; pages xvii, 258; 17 plates, some folding, some colored, 2 folding colored maps; calf, rebacked, binding worn at extremities, library stamp on recot and verso of title.   John Henly 27-551   1996   £72.00

SCRUTON, WILLIAM   Thornton & the Brontes. Bradford, John Dale & Co., 1898. 1st edition; 7 3/8 x 5 inches; frontispiece, 21 illustrations, pages xix, 146; green morocco grain cloth with inset illustrations and gilt titling to front cvoer, gilt titling to backstrip, bevelled boards, top edge gilt, others uncut, name heavily crossed out on front pastedown, very good, scarce. Y&T 485b.   Ian Hodgkins   78-418   1996   £75.00

THE SEA, The Ship and the Sailor. Tales of Adventure from Log Books and Original Narratives. Salem: 1925. Pages xviii, 353, illustrations, maps; near fine.   Stephen Lunsford   45-125   1996 $125.00

SEABROOK, WILLIAM BUEHLER   Diary of Section VIII American Ambulance Field Service. Boston: printed only for private distribution, 1917. 1st edition; 8vo; pages (7), 71; original grey boards, minor rubbing, paper label; NUC locates 4 copies.   Howard S. Mott   227-122 1996 $200.00

THE SEAFARER. Bangor: Tatlin Books, 1991. One of 85 copies; page size 11 1/2 x 4 inches; on handmade Kumoi, Uwa, Saint Gilles & Twinrocker papers, signed by Karl Young, the translator and Walter Tisdale, the printer/publisher and Nancy Leavitt the designer/calligrapher; in accordion fold, grey paper and blue cloth over boards, housed in buff paper over boards, grosgrain tie, by Dan Kelm at the Wide-Awake Garage.   Priscilla Juvelis   95/1-235   1996 $375.00

SEAGER, JOHN   A Supplement to Dr. Johnson's Dictionary of the English Language... London: printed by A. J. Valpy, 1819. 1st edition; 4to; uncut in original blue boards, marked and worn at corners, spine recently neatly rebacked; inscribed as a gift from Captain Brissac to John Budd, 1821.   Jarndyce 103-187   1996 £220.00

SEALSFIELD, CHARLES   The Cabin Book; or, National Characteristics. London: Ingram, Cooke, 1852. 8vo; 8 plates and ads at end; original cloth; Brian B. Barttelot ownership inscription of 1852.   Rostenberg & Stern 150-8   1996 $250.00

SEALY, HENRY NICHOLAS   A Treatise on Coins, Currency and Banking, with Observations on the Bank Act of 1844 and on the Reports of the Committees of the House of Lords and of the House of Commons on the Bank Acts. London: Longman, 1858-67. 1st edition; 8vo; 2 volumes; original brown cloth, neatly repaired; presentation copy, inscribed in each volume by author for Richard Poole King Esq. Very good, uncommon.   James Burmester 29-124   1996 £400.00

SEARIGHT, FRANK THOMPSON   The Doomed City. Chicago: Laird and Lee, 1906. 1st edition; 12mo; 186 pages; extensively illustrated; original pictorial wrappers, spine chipped, but quite good. Rare.   M & S Rare Books 60-229   1996 $125.00

SEARLES, MICHAEL   The Land Steward's and Farmer's Assistant... London: printed for the author, by F. Blyth, 1779. 1st edition; 8vo; 72 pages; contemporary calf backed marbled boards, some wear to spine and corners; 19th century ownership signature, blank 3/8 inch piece trimmed from bottom of title; rare. Taylor, Hanoverian 536.   Howard S. Mott 227-123   1996 $200.00

A SEASONABLE Address to the Right Honurable the Lord Mayor, Court of Aldermen and Commoners of the City of London, Upon Their Present Electing of Sherifs. ?London: 1680. Folio; 4 pages; uncut, disbound. Wing S2205.   H. M. Fletcher 121-29   1996 £65.00

SECCOMBE, JOSEPH   Some Occasional Thoughts on the Influence of the Spirit. Boston: S. Kneeland, and T. Green, 1742. 1st edition; 8vo; (2), 2, 16 pages; modern plain wrappers, lacks half title, foxed. With oxidized signature of Bartholomew Kneeland, presumably a relative of the printer. M & S Rare Books 60-405   1996 $300.00

SECRET Anecdotes of the Revolution of the 18th Fructidor: (September 4th, 1797) and New Memoirs of the Persons Deported to Guiana, Written by Themselves... London: printed for J. Wright, 1799. 1st English edition; 8vo; little spotting of text; 19th century marbled boards, leather label; bookplate of Viscount Birkenhead. Sabin 67633.   Anthony W. Laywood 109-58   1996 £95.00

SECRETAN, LOUIS   Mycographie Suisse, ou Description des Champignons qui Croissent en Suisse... Geneve: 1833. 8vo; 3 volumes, pages lv, 522; iii, 576; viii, 759, (1) (95 page index); cloth backed marbled boards; good, ex-library set.   Raymond M. Sutton VII-33   1996 $1,100.00

THE SECRETARY of the Scots Army, His Relation to the Commissioners Concerning the King, How His Majesty Came Within Two Miles of London: the Garrisons He Marched Through, and His Coming to the Scots. London: printed by Elizabeth Puslow, 1646. 1st edition; 4to; title within woodcut border, 6 pages; disbound.. Wing S2353.   Anthony Laywood 108-17   1996 £135.00

SECUNDUS, JOANNES NICOLAI 1511-1536   Kisses. London: for T. Davies, 1775. 1st edition; crown 8vo; frontispiece, contemporary mottled calf, neatly rebacked, banded, gilt with flowers, lemon edges, little minor wear, endpapers rejointed, some slight browning, but pleasant, bookplate.   Ash Rare Books Zenzybyr-82   1996 £195.00

SEDGWICK, THEODORE   Thoughts on the Proposed Annexation of Texas to the United States. New York: 1844. 1st edition thus; 55 pages; appears to be bound in later stiff wrappers, but with possibly the original label or printed title affixed. very good, very scarce, possibly rare.   Gene W. Baade 1094-148   1996 $150.00

SEDLEY, CHARLES   The Miscellaneous Works of the Honourable Charles Sedley. London: Capt. Ayloffe, 1702. 8vo; pages 213, 24, 64 pages; contemporary panelled full speckled calf, with raised bands, library bookplate and blindstamp, front hinge cracked but holding, endpapers lacking, thus good copy only.   Chapel Hill 94-363   1996 $150.00

SEEBOHM, HENRY   The Birds of Siberia. London: 1901. 8vo; pages xx, 512, map and text figures; deocrated cloth, little minor foxing. Wheldon & Wesley 207-856   1996 £85.00

SEEBOHM, HENRY   Coloured Firgures of the Eggs of British Birds. London: 1896. Imperial 8vo; frontispiece and 59 colored plates, apart from foxing to prelims, a nice copy.   David A.H. Grayling MY95Orn-65   1996 £75.00

SEEBOHM, HENRY   A History of British Birds. London: 1883-85. 1st edition; royal 8vo; 4 volumes; 68 colored plates, half dark green morocco, gilt, top edge gilt.   Charles W. Traylen 117-332   1996 £130.00

SEEBOHM, HENRY   A History of British Birds with Coloured Illustrations of Their Eggs. London: 1885. 1st edition; 8vo; 4 volumes; 68 chromolithograph plates, old repair to small portion of blank margin of few plates, 2 leaves with blank margins soiled and trifle frayed; contemporary half roan, bit worn.   Maggs Bros. Ltd. 1190-600   1996 £145.00

SEELEY, ROBERT BENTON   Remedies Suggested for Some of the Evils Which Constitute "The Perils of the Nation". London: Seeley, Burnside and Seeley, 1844. 2nd edition revised; 8vo; xx, 484 pages, title printed within woodcut border, original black cloth, gilt, untrimmed, fine, complete with half title. Goldsmiths 33956; Williams II 180; Kress (C6457) first ed. only.   John Drury 82-253   1996 £85.00

SEELY, JOHN   A Voice from India, in Answer to the Reformers of England. London: printed for G.B. Whittaker, 1824. 1st edition; 8vo; original grey boards, printed paper label, spine bit rubbed; fine, scarce. 5 copies in NUC; not in McCoy.   Ximenes 109-256   1996 $350.00

SEEMAN, BERTHOLD   Viti: an Account of a Government Mission to the Vitian or Fijian Islands in the Years 1860-61. Cambridge: Macmillan and Co., 1862. 8vo; pages xv, 447, 24 ads; map, 4 tinted plates; original green cloth, rubbed, light foxing, half inch library perforation stamp on title. Snow 783; Taylor p. 376; Hill I p. 271.   Richard Adelson W94/95-152   1996 $250.00

THE SEERLESS of Prevorst. (Justinus Kerner, Chief Physician at Weinsberg). London: J. C. Moore, 1845. 1st edition; xii, large foldout, 338 pages; cloth, cover wear, very good.   Middle Earth 77-248   1996 $170.00

SEGER, JOHN H.   Early Days Among the Cheyenne and Arapaho Indians. Norman: University of Oklahoma Series No. 281, 1924. 1st edition; 91 pages; original grey printed wrappers; very good. Very scarce. Howes S277.   Michael D. Heaston 23-296   1996 $250.00

SEIDENFADEN, G.   The Orchids of Thailand, a Preliminary List. Bangkok: 1959-65. 8vo; 4 parts in 1; 41 colored plates and 623 text figures; hardbound, light corner wear.   Raymond M. Sutton VI-963   1996 $140.00

SEITZ, A.   Les Macrolepidopteres du Globe. Stuttgart: 1906-21. 4to; 4 volumes in 8; 245 colored plates of numerous figures; half morocco, joints trifle rubbed and two have begun to break but on the whole a nice set.   Wheldon & Wesley 207-93   1996 £1,250.00

SELBY, HUBERT   Last Exit to Brooklyn. New York: Grove, 1964. 1st printing, 1st book, fine in dust jacket with several chips off front panel, otherwise very good.   Sherwood 3-276   1996 $100.00

SELBY, P. J.   A History of British Forest Trees Indigenous and Introduced. London: 1842. 8vo; pages xx, 540, 184 engraved head and tailpieces, text figures; cloth, new endpapers.   John Henly 27-360   1996 £65.00

SELBY, P. J.   Illustrations of British Ornithology. Edinburgh: 1833. 2nd edition of 1st volume, 1st edition of 2nd volume; 8vo; boards, uncut, printed labels little defective and bindings considerably repaired, with one back board supplied, waterstain on boards, just affects titles.   Maggs Bros. Ltd. 1190-601   1996 £75.00

SELDEN, JOHN   The Table-Talk. London: John Russell Smith, 1856. Full crushed brown morocco, all edges gilt, very pretty.   Meyer Boswell SL27-206   1996 $250.00

SELDEN, JOHN 1584-1654   Joannis Seldeni I. C. de Dis Syris Syntagmata. London: Excudebat Gulielmus Stansbeius, 1617. 1st edition; 8vo; contemporary calf; fine; contemporary signatures of R. Legard and Joshua Meen. STC 22167; CBEL I 2331.   Ximenes 108-321   1996 $750.00

SELECT Emblems, and Other Short Poems: Religious and Moral. Banbury: printed by R. Rusher, 1820. 6 x 4 1/4 inches; 2 p.l., 32 pages; original paper wrappers, now unstitched, gatherings in loose stack, edges untrimmed, rear wrapper partly torn way at bottom, final leaf with small chip in lower margin, text slightly yellowed and with edges untrimmed, rear wrapper partly torn away at bottom, final leaf with small chip in lower margin, text slightly yellowed and with trivial soiling. Phillip J. Pirages 33-431 1996 $125.00

SELECT Portions of the Psalms of David, According to the Version of Dr. Brady and Mr. Tate...Hymns for..Church Holy-Days and Festivals. Sydney: printed by R. Howe, Government Printer, 1828. 12mo. (but signed in 4's); contemporary sheep, blind tooled borders, head of spine chipped, but nce; inscribed by Lt. General Sir Ralph Darling, Governor of New South Wales for Mrs. Dumaresq. Peter Murray Hill 185-2 1996 £450.00

SELECT Psalms and Hymns for the Use of the Parish Church of Cardington, in the County of Bedford. London: J. W. Galabin, 1786. 1st edition; 8vo; (iv), 100, (iv), 101-131, (i) pages; recent boards; good copy. Robert Clark 38-182 1996 £120.00

A SELECTION from the Harleian Miscellany of Tracts, Which Principally Regard the English History... London: printed for C. and G. Kearsley, 1794. 1st edition; 4to; contemporary red morocco, elaborately ruled in gilt, Lowther arms in gilt on each cover, spine and inner dentelles gilt, all edges gilt, bit rubbed; sumptuously bound and extra illustrated with more than 50 portraits and other engravings; good, early example of a 'grangerized' book in excellent condition; later armorial bookplate of Hugh Cecil (Lowther), Earl of Lonsdale. Ximenes 108-182 1996 $500.00

A SELECTION of Sacred Harmony: Containing Lessons Explaining the Gamut, Keys and Characters Used in Vocal Music... Philadelphia: printed for W. Young, Mills & Son...by John McCulloch, 1797. Oblong narrow 4to; (2), 132 pages; contemporary calf backed plain boards, very good. Evans 32818. M & S Rare Books 60-383 1996 $450.00

SELF, WILL The Quantity of Insanity. London: Bloomsbury, 1991. Correct first edition; author's first book; illustrated wrappers; fine, signed by author. Lame Duck Books 19-492 1996 $150.00

SELFRIDGE, THOMAS O. Trial of Thomas O. Selfridge, Attorny at Law, Before the Hon. Isaac Parker, Esquire, for Killing Charles Austin, on the Public Exchange in Boston, August 4th 1806. Boston: Russell & Cutler, 1806. 1st edition; 8vo; 168 pages, 4 leaves, including plan, uncut; original boards, spine worn, printed spine; rare in boards. AI 11474; McDade 861. Howard S. Mott 227-124 1996 $375.00

SELFRIDGE, THOMAS OLIVER Reports of Explorations and Surveys to Ascertain the Practicability of a ship Canal Between the Atlantic and Pacific oceans by Way of the Isthumus of Darien. Washington: GPO, 1874. Tall 4to; 268 pages; 14 full page inserted photo lithographs, 17 very large folding survey maps; cloth, some spine wear, exterior very good plus, interior near fine. Freedom Bookshop 14-31 1996 $375.00

SELIGMAN, GERMAIN The Drawings of Georges Seurat. New York: Curt Valentin, 1947. Limited to 1000 copies; 30.5 x 23.5 cm; 160 pages; 46 plates + 5 diagrams; original cloth backed boards in dust jacket (grubby). Rainsford A54-527 1996 £75.00

SELKIRK, THOMAS DOUGLAS, 5TH EARL OF Observations on the Present State of the Highlands of Scotland. London: 1805. Pages vii, 233, lvi; original boards, expertly rebacked, original spine label; fine, uncut, preserved in quarter morocco slipcase. Peel 30; TPL 736; Streeter VI 3655. Stephen Lunsford 45-144 1996 $850.00

SELKIRK, THOMAS DOUGLAS, 5TH EARL OF A Sketch of the British Fur Trade in North America; with Observations Relative to the North-West Company of Montreal... London: 1816. 2nd edition; pages 130, ads; superb copy, uncut in original boards, appropriately rebacked, preserved in quarter morocco slipcase; Peel 44; cf. Streeter VI 3667; TPL 1104. Stephen Lunsford 45-145 1996 $2,500.00

SELLERS, WILLIAM, & CO. A Treatise on Machine-Tools... Philadelphia: 1877. 4th edition; 8vo; frontispiece, numerous text figures; green cloth, gilt, nice. Maggs Bros. Ltd. 1190-653 1996 £50.00

SELOUS, FREDERICK COURTENEY 1851-1917 African Nature Notes and Reminiscences. London: Macmillan, 1908. 1st edition; 2nd issue; 8vo; pages xxx, 356; 13 plates; original cloth, light wear to spine ends. Riling 1660; Mendelssohn II p. 303. Richard Adelson W94/95-155 1996 $285.00

SELOUS, FREDERICK COURTENEY 1851-1917 African Nature Notes and Reminiscences. London: 1908. 1st edition; illustrations; original buckram, excellent copy, publisher's presentation copy with blindstamp on title. David Grayling J95Biggame-182 1996 £175.00

SELOUS, FREDERICK COURTENEY 1851-1917 The Gun at Home and Abroad: The Big Game of Africa & Europe. London: The London and Counties Press Association Ltd., 1914. Limited to 750 numbered copies; subscriber's edition; 4to; pages xx, 410, 82 plates, including 10 in color and 3 in photogravure, initials printed in red, occasional slight spotting, but very good. original publisher's full morocco, gilt, top edge gilt. Sotheran PN32-76 1996 £498.00

SELOUS, FREDERICK COURTENEY 1851-1917 A Hunter's Wanderings in Africa. London: 1893. 3rd edition; folding map, engraved plates, text illustrations; contents very lightly marked, otherwise excellent copy, finely bound in modern half dark green morocco, gilt. David Grayling J95Biggame-181 1996 £200.00

SELOUS, FREDERICK COURTENEY 1851-1917 A Hunter's Wanderings in Africa, Being a Narrative of Nine Years Spent Amongst the Game of the Far Interior of South Africa... London: Macmillan and Co., 1919. 5th edition; 8vo; pages xix, 3, 504; folding map, 17 plates; original cloth, lightly rubbed. Mendelssohn II p. 299; Riling 1093. Richard Adelson W94/95-156 1996 $185.00

SELOUS, FREDERICK COURTENEY 1851-1917 Recent Hunting Trips in British North America. 1907. illustrations; very light foxing. David Grayling J95Biggame-440 1996 £130.00

SELOUS, FREDERICK COURTENEY 1851-1917 Recent Hunting Trips in British North America. London: Witherby & Co., 1907. 8vo; pages 400; 65 plates; original green cloth; Riling 1642. Richard Adelson W94/95-154 1996 $425.00

SELOUS, FREDERICK COURTENEY 1851-1917 Sunshine and Storm in Rhodesia. London: Rowland Ward, 1896. 2nd edition; 8vo; pages xxvii, 2, 290, 10 ads; folding map, 9 plates, text illustrations; original tan cloth, rubbed, spine darkened; Theal p. 269; Mendelssohn II p. 302; Riling 1352. Richard Adelson W94/95-153 1996 $315.00

SELOUS, FREDERICK COURTENEY 1851-1917 Sunshine and Storm in Rhodesia. London: 1896. Small format second edition; illustrations; original red cloth, restored, retaining Rowland Ward endpapers; scarce. David Grayling J95Biggame-183 1996 £85.00

SEMON, RICHARD In the Australian Bush and on the Coast of the Coreal Sea. London: 1899. (xvi), 552 pages, 4 folding maps; original green gilt ribbed cloth, slightly shaken, small split side of spine, good+ overall. The Meggitt copy. Ferguson 15574. Antipodean 28-331 1996 $350.00

SEMPLE, EUGENE Report of the Governor of Washington Territory to the Secretary of the Interior. Olympia: 1888. 87 pages; original printed wrappers, little staining, few edge repairs, else very good. Stephen Lunsford 45-146 1996 $135.00

SENAC, JEAN Treatise On the Hidden Nature and Treatment of Intermitting and Remitting Fevers. Philadelphia: Kimber, Conrad, 1805. 1st edition in English; half calf, hinges mended. Austin 1731. Argosy 810-435 1996 $350.00

SENAULT, LOUIS Hevres Nouvelles Dediees A Madame La Davphine. Paris: the author, Versailles: Duval, 1680. 1st edition; 8vo; illustrated with vignettes, borders, initials, head and tailpieces; contemporary black sharkskin with silver clasps and studs intact. Henry Le Court bookticket. Univ. Cat. of Books on Art III 56. Rostenberg & Stern 150-110 1996 $1,750.00

SENDAK, MAURICE Very Far Away. New York: Harper, 1957. 1st edition; original cloth, fine in very good dust jacket with tiny chips at spine ends; Beasley Books 82-38 1996 $150.00

SENDIVOGIUS, MICHAEL Philsophical Account of Nature in General and the Generation of the Three Principles of Nature, Viz. Mercury, Sulphur, Salt, Out of the Four Elements. London: 1722. 3 p., 1, 348 pages;, later red cloth with gilt on black labels, small library discard stamp on inner margin of titlepage and one other leaf. Bookworm & Silverfish 276-137 1996 $265.00

SENECA, LUCIUS ANNAEUS   Cinco Libros de Seneca. Seville: Meynardus Ungut & Stanislaus Polonus, 28 May 1491. 1st edition in Spanish; folio; 129 leaves (of 132, lacking 3 blanks), gothic letter, text surrounded by commentary, 5 lines of title and decorated woodcut initial on a2 printed in red, smaller woodcut initials, printer's device at end, blind impressions of lines of barer type at foot of title and last leaf, 6 leaves neatly remargined, g8 (blank) present but not genuine, few light stains, early inscription on titlepage deleted; modern spanish vellum by Brugalla, 1946; Goff S374; HC 14596; BMC X38; Davies Printers Devices no. 10a.   H. M. Fletcher 121-16 1996 £13,500.00

SENECA, LUCIUS ANNAEUS   The Workes of Lucius Annaeus Seneca. London: printed by Willi Stansby, 1620. Early English edition; folio in 6s; pages 928), 921, (22), engraved title, 2 divisional titles; fine woodcut initials and devices, apparently lacks 3 prelim leaves, but includes Lipsius' "Life of ...Seneca". Original boards, detached, but decorated with central arabesque medallion stamp painted(?) in gilt, requires rebacking, ex-libris of Charles F. Cox, New York.   Family Album Tillers-568 1996 $360.00

SENEFLEDER, ALOIS 1771-1834   A Complete Course of Lithography: Containing Clear and Explicit Instructions in all the Different Branches and Manners of that Art... London: printed for R. Ackermann, 1819. 4to; 14 lithographic plates, some very mild browning to a few of the plates, 2 small dampstains on 2 of them, but not with usual heavy foxing, found on plates in this work, text clean and crisp; contemporary half calf, spine gilt in compartments with raised bands, Cassidy arms in top compartment, marbled boards (bit torn and rubbed), headcaps chipped, corners bumped; remarkably good, clean copy; booklabel of Robert Cassidy. Bigmore & Wyman II p. 340; Bridson & Wakeman D13. Maggs Bros. Ltd. 1191-215 1996 £850.00

SENNERT, DANIEL   Epitome Naturalis Scientiae. Oxford: By W. Hall for G. West, 1664. 12mo; 6 leaves, 560 pages, 9 leaves (index), 1 leaf (t.p.), 76 pages, 1 folding plate; contemporary calf, sound; Wing S2533.   H. M. Fletcher 121-72 1996 £240.00

SENTENTIAE et proverbia ex Poetis Latinis. His Adiecimus. Leosthenis Colvandri Sententias Prophanas... Venice: Ioannes Patauinus, c. 1550. 8vo; pages 216, italic letter, woodcut printer's device on title, frequent contemporary underlining and few ms. annotations in first half of volume, light age yellow, good contemporary vellum; bookplate of Henry Philip Langdon. Not in BM STC. This ed. not in Adams.   A. Sokol XXV-91 1996 £425.00

A SEQUEL to the Endless Amusement, Containing Nearly 400 Interesting Experiments in Various Branches of Science... London: Thomas Boys and Throp and Burch, 1826. 12mo; large folding frontispiece; uncut in original drab printed boards, spine rubbed and little defective at tail.   Jarndyce 103-369 1996 £60.00

THE SERAPHICAL Young Shepherd. London: printed in the year 1762. 1st edition; 12mo; 2 parts in 1; general title and separate titles to parts 1 and 2, some spotting and staining, contemporary calf, rebacked, label. Anthony W. Laywood 108-119 1996 £60.00

SERRES, JEAN DE 1540?-1598   La Vie de Messire Gaspar de Colligny, Seigneur de Chastillon, Admiral de France. Leiden: Chez Bonaventure & Abraham Elzevier, 1643. 1st edition in French; 12mo; 2 parts in 1 volume, title to each part with printer's device; contemporary vellum boards, title in ink on spine. Willems 564; Copinger 2418.   H. M. Fletcher 121-73 1996 £450.00

SERVICE Afloat Comprising the Personal Narrative of a Naval Officer Employed During the Late War and the Journal of an Officer Engaged in the Late Surveying Expedition Under the Command of Captain Owen on the Western Coast of Africa. London: 1933. 1st edition; 8vo; 2 volumes, over 600 pages; original boards, good.   K Books 441-449 1996 £150.00

SERVICE, ROBERT WILLIAM 1874-1958   Rhymes of a Red Cross Man. Toronto: William Briggs, 1916. 1st edition; ink dates on titlepage, pencil name and address on front pastedown, otherwise slightly dulled but fine. Hermitage SP95-560 1996 $125.00

SESSIONS, ROGER   Quintet (for 2 Violins, 2 Violas and Cello). New York: Marks, 1959. 1st printing; tall octavo; stapled wrappers, near fine. This is the dedication copy, inscribed to Berkeley Music professor Albert Elkus from Sessions.   Lame Duck Books 19-350 1996 $275.00

SETON, ERNEST THOMPSON 1860-1946   The Forester's Manual. Garden City: Doubleday, Page & Co., 1912. 1st edition; spine faded, overall light soiling, otherwise very good, titlepage is a cancel. Hermitage SP95-1053 1996 $150.00

SETTLE, MARY LEE   The Kiss of Kin. New York: Harper & Bros., 1955. 1st edition; code 'G-E'; author's second book; very good+ in very good price clipped dust jacket which is a bit worn at edges and with one tiny chip at top edge of front panel.   Steven C. Bernard 71-209 1996 $125.00

SETTLE, MARY LEE   The Love Eaters. New York: Harper, 1954. Review copy with slip laid in, frontispiece; author's first book; bookplate, else near fine in lightly used dust jacket. Signed.   Alice Robbins 15-301 1996 $250.00

SEUPHOR, MICHEL   Piet Mondrian: Life and Work. New York: Abrams, 1956. 4to; 443 pages; 600 illustrations, including 34 tipped in color plates, cloth, dust jacket. Lucas p. 171; Freitag 6651.   Brannan 43-444 1996 $195.00

SEVEN SAGES   The Sayings of the Seven Sages of Greece. Officina Bodoni, 1976. One of 150 numbered copies; 8vo; printed in Griffo and in Greek characters cut by Charles Maling after Garamond on Magnani handmade paper; half vellum with patterned paper sides, fine in slipcase, original prospectus laid in.   Bertram Rota 272-354 1996 £350.00

SEVERINO, MARCO AURELIO   Il Filosofia Overo il Perche Degli Scacchi...(with) Dell'Antica Pettia Overo che Palamede non e Stato L'Inentor Degli Sacchi... Napoli: Antonio Bulifon, 1690. 1st editions; 4to; 2 volumes in 1; (6), 120, (6), 82 (i.e. 64), 2 portraits, illustrations; later vellum backed boards, bookplate, two small and unobtrusive library blindstamps and release stamps, first signature slightly browned, otherwise very attractive copy; from the library of chess collector Adrien Gambet, with his signature.   Joseph J. Felcone 64-10 1996 $700.00

SEVERN, WALTER   The Golden Calendar. London: Day & Son, n.d. 1865. 1st edition; folio; (28) leaves, publisher's cloth, few pieces of overlay missing and book has been neatly rebacked using original spine as an overlay, internally fine.   Bookpress 75-116 1996 $450.00

SEVIGNE, MARIE DE RABUTIN-CHANTAL, MARQUISE DE 1626-1696 The Letters. Philadlephia: J. P. Horn, 1927. Revised edition; 8vo; 7 volumes; three quarter maroon morocco, wear at extremities, gilt paneled spines, raised bands, gilt tops.   Appelfeld Gallery 54-163 1996 $375.00

SEWARD, A. C.   Catalogue of the Mesozoic Plants. London: British Museum, 1894-1915. 8vo; 6 volumes; 99 plates; original cloth, sound ex-library.   Wheldon & Wesley 207-1366 1996 £100.00

SEWARD, A. C.   Darwin and Modern Science: Essays in Commemoration of the Centenary of the Birth of Charles Darwin and of the 50th Anniversary of the Publication of the Origin of the Species. Cambridge: 1909. 1st edition; original binding.   W. Bruce Fye 71-495 1996 $100.00

SEWARD, ANNA   Letters...Written Between the Years 1784 and 1807. Edinburgh: Constable, 1811. 1st edition; octavo; 6 volumes; portrait and facsimile of one of the author's letters; contemporary diced calf, slight wear, but nice set. CBEL II 380.   Hartfield 48-L78 1996 $795.00

SEWEL, WILLIAM 1653-1720   A Large Dictionary English and Dutch, in Two Parts... Amsterdam: Jacob ter Beek, 1735. 3rd edition; 4to; 2 volumes in one; frontispiece, titles printed in red and black, contemporary vellum, new endpapers at end, leather label.   Anthony W. Laywood 108-118 1996 £145.00

SEWELL, ANNA   Black Beauty Told in Short Form Pictures by Paul Brown. New York: Scribner, 1952. 1st (A) edition; oblong 4to; original binding, scarce good+.   October Farm 36-74 1996 $185.00

SEXBY, EDWARD   Killing no Murder. Edinburgh: Ker, and sold at the Highlander, a Snuff Shop in Cecil Court, London, 1749. Title in red and black; quarter calf.   Rostenberg & Stern 150-70 1996 $150.00

SEXBY, EDWARD   Killing No Murder: Briefly Discoursed in Three Questions. London: Ridgway, 1792. Reprint; tall 8vo; half title missing; disbound.   Rostenberg & Stern 150-71 1996 $125.00

SEXBY, EDWARD   Traicte Politique...(Killing No Murder). Paris 1793. 16mo; gilt calf, lower front joint cracking. Brunet I 190; Querard I 271. Rostenberg & Stern 150-72 1996 $175.00

SEXTON, ANNE   The Death Notebooks. Boston: Houghton Mifflin, 1974. 1st edition; 8vo; fine in near fine dust jacket, pre-publication presentation from author to one of her intimate friends. Text has many penciled notataions in the poet's hand and two black ink notations by author.   Lakin & Marley 3-56 1996 $500.00

SEXTON, ANNE   To Bedlam and Part Way Back. Boston: Houghton, Mifflin Co., 1960. 1st edition; 8vo; fine presentation copy to Nolan Miller of The Antioch review.   Lakin & Marley 3-55 1996 $1,250.00

SEXTON, ANNE   To Bedlam and Part Way Back. Boston: Houghton Mifflin, 1960. 1st edition; near fine in near fine price clipped dust jacket bumped at spine crown.   Ken Lopez 74-406 1996 $250.00

SEXTON, ERIC H. L.   A Descriptive and Bibliographical List of Irish Figure Sculptures of the Early Christian Period. Portland: 1946. Limited to 450 copies; 8vo; 300 pages; 55 photos; cloth; very good.   C. P. Hyland 216-761 1996 £105.00

SEYMOUR ROBERT   Comic Readings of Byron and Shakespeare. London: n.d., c. 1830's. 1st edition; 50 engraved plates; recently rebound in red calf backed marbled paper, boards.   Words Etcetera 94-819 1996 £60.00

SEYMOUR, R.   Humorous Sketches. London: 1878. 86 engraved plates, all by Crowquill; original cloth, showing light rubbing and spine faded; attractive copy.   David A.H. Grayling 3/95-211 1996 £75.00

SHACKLETON, ERNEST HENRY 1874-1922   The Heart of the Antarctic. London: William Heinemann, 1909. 1st edition; 4to; 2 volumes; half titles, 371, 414 pages, errata slip tipped in to volume 2; frontispiece portraits, 12 colored plates, 257 black and white photogravure plates, 49 illustrations to text and 3 folding maps, double folding panoramic view to rear pocket of volume 2. original dark blue cloth, silver stamped vignettes to upper boards, gilt title to spines, spines faded, top edge gilt, spines cracked, some occasional light foxing to volume 2, pencil inscription.   Beeleigh Abbey BA/56-118 1996 £250.00

SHADBOLT, JACK   In Search of Form. Toronto: McClelland and Stewart, c. 1968. 4to; pages 239; profusely illustrated, loose errata slip; cloth, dust jacket, covers and dust jacket soiled, else fine.   Hugh Anson-Cartwright 87-383 1996 $150.00

SHADWELL, THOMAS   Bury-Fair. London: for James Knapton, 1689. 1st edition; small 4to; title and final leaf slightly dusty, small piece torn from inner margin of ad leaf, not affecting text; Dramatis Personae.   37-156 1996 $350.00

SHADWELL, THOMAS   The Complete Works. London: Fortune Press, 1927. Out of series copy from an edition of 1200 ordinary paper sets; large 8vo; 5 volumes; frontispiece, 3 hand colored plates, folding pedigree; original blue cloth, gilt lettering, spines irregularly faded, sound set.   Robert Clark 38-128 1996 £170.00

SHAFFER, ELLEN   The Garden of Health: an Account of two Herbals, the "Gart Der Gesundheir" and the "Hortus Sanitatis". Book Club of California, 1957. One of 300 copies; 13 1/4 x 9 1/4 inches; 6 p.l. (two blank), 41 pages; frontispiece, vignette on title and many woodcuts in text, some of them full page, prospectus laid in; with original leaf from the Hortus Sanitatis of ca. 1499, tipped in; original burlap backed paper boards, titled in black on spine, fore edge and tail edge untrimmed, in original plain dust jacket, jacket somewhat unevenly faded, leaf with faint dampstain at top edge, otherwise in extremely fine condition. Goff H489; Klebs 509A.   Phillip J. Pirages 33-338 1996 $450.00

SHAFFER, PETER   Five Finger Exercise; a Play. London: 1958. 1st edition; very good in trifle creased and scuffed dust jacket; inscribed by author to American playwright Langord Wilson.   Words Etcetera 94-1119 1996 £65.00

SHAFTESBURY, ANTHONY ASHLEY COOPER, 3RD EARL OF 1671-1713 Characteristics of Men, Manners, Opinions and Times. Birmingham: printed by John Baskerville, 1783. 5th edition, 1st Baskerville printing; 3 volumes; contemporary pebbled calf, double gilt rules on panels and gilt floral patterns in compartments with red and black morocco spine labels, gilt dentelles, top edge gilt, occasional rubbing on each volume, but very good set.   Captain's Bookshelf 38-198 1996 $375.00

SHAH, IDRIES   Tale of the Sands. Del Mar: Ettan Press, 1980. One of 55 copies; page size 12 x 11 inches; on Rives paper, each copy numbered and the three etchings signed and numbered in pencil by the artist; loos in original wrappers.   Priscilla Juvelis 95/1-174 1996 $500.00

SHAHN, BEN   The Alphabet of Creation. An Ancient Legend from the Zohar. New York: Pantheon, 1954. One of the deluxe issue of 50 copies (total edition of 550) on Umbria handmade paper with an original drawing in brush and ink of one of the letters, signed and numbered by Shahn, as is the colophon; tall 8vo; full linen with inset calligraphic panel on front cover.   Marilyn Braiterman 15-185 1996 $1,500.00

SHAHN, BEN   The Complete Graphic Works. New York: Quandrangle/New York Times Book Co., 1973. 1st edition; oblong 4to; very good in dust jacket.   Hermitage SP95-814 1996 $125.00

SHAHN, BEN   Love and Joy About Letters. New York: Grossman, 1963. Deluxe edition of 100 numbered copies; oblong folio; signed by Shahn beneath mounted limitation statement on last leaf of text; color and black and white art and calligraphy (much in Hebrew); color striped cloth covered boards, fine.   Marilyn Braiterman 15-187 1996 $575.00

SHAHN, BEN   Sweet Was the Song. New York: Odyssey Press, 1965. 1st edition; oblong 32mo; illustrations in color by Shahn; fine in dust jacket, inscribed by Shahn.   Captain's Bookshelf 38-199 1996 $175.00

SHAHN, BERNARDA BRYSON   Ben Shahn. New York: Abrams, n.d. Square folio; 373 pages; 345 illustrations, 154 in color, including some tipped in color plates; cloth, dust jacket. Freitag 8934.   Brannan 43-592 1996 $245.00

SHAHN, BERNARDA BRYSON   Ben Shahn. New York: Harry N. Abrams, 1972. 1st edition; square folio; front free endpaper slightly soiled and creased, otherwise fine in dust jacket.   Hermitage SP95-813 1996 $275.00

SHAKESPEARE, WILLIAM 1564-1616   Anthony and Cleopatra. Paris: Societe des Beaux Arts, Limited to 550 copies; Salon edition; large 8vo; 2 volumes; illustrations by Paul Avril; three quarter morocco, hinges going; clean; signed by cast of the 1947 Cornell production.   Lyman Books 21-632 1996 $150.00

SHAKESPEARE, WILLIAM 1564-1616   The Tragedie of Anthony and Cleopatra. London: Doves Press, 1912. One of 200 copies; small 4to; printed in black and red on handmade paper; limp vellum; nice; inscribed by Thomas James Cobden-Sanderson to Madeline Whyte.   Bertram Rota 272-129 1996 £400.00

SHAKESPEARE, WILLIAM 1564-1616   As You Like It. Hammersmith: Pub. by W. Bromely, 1799. 4to; engraved title and 7 engraved plates by T. Sothard; age browned, engraved leaf of text, unbound.   Anthony W. Laywood 109-137 1996 £110.00

SHAKESPEARE, WILLIAM 1564-1616   Comedies, Histories, and Tragedies... London: printed by Tho. Cotes for Robert Allot, 1632. 2nd edition, 1st issue of the second folio; 12 3/4 x 8 3/8 inches; titlepage with engraved portrait; finely bound in full blue morocco gilt by Riviere, minor restoration, affecting only a few leaves, occasional stains and minor flaws, significantly better than other copies appearing for sale in the past few years, this copy does not have the extensive facsimile work and remargined and inlaid leaves present in almost all copies which have recently appeared, very good and attractive copy.   19th Century Shop 39- 1996 $90,000.00

SHAKESPEARE, WILLIAM 1564-1616   Mr. William Shakespear's Comedies, Histories and Tragedies. London: for H. Herringman, E. Brewster and R. Bentley, 1685. 4th folio edition, this copy with the variant setting of the title omitting Chiswell's name from the imprint; folio in sixes, printed in double columns within ruled borders, pages (xii), 96, 99-160, 163-254, (253)-(273), (i), 328, 303; without frontispiece and final leaf of text (Cccc2) and with titlepage, C2-5, Qq3-4 and Eee8 supplied in excellent facsimile; contemporary calf, some wear, rebacked in 19th century, spine in compartments with raised bands, gilt rules and label lettered in gilt, small piece cut from 9 leaves at blank margin, tear to H2 without loss, small hole affecting 3 letters to Ddd3, occasional rustmarks, but very good, clean copy; signature of Robert Synge on front free endpaper and Markree Library label on pastedown. Wing S2915; Bartlett 123A; greg III p. 1119; Pforzheimer 910.   Simon Finch 24-201 1996 £7,200.00

SHAKESPEARE, WILLIAM 1564-1616   The Comedies. New York: Harper & Bros., 1899. One of 750 sets; 4to; 4 volumes; hundreds of drawings by Edwin A. Abbey; contemporary three quarter dark blue morocco, gilt panelled spines, raised bands, gilt tops.   Appelfeld Gallery 54-165 1996 $375.00

SHAKESPEARE, WILLIAM 1564-1616   The Comedies, Histories and Tragedies. New York: Limited Editions Club, 1939-40. One of 1950 sets; folio; 37 volumes; wood engravings and lithographs, with some hand coloring; half natural buckram, gold stamped, gilt top, paper sides printed in four colors; slight darkening to some spines, fine with many unopened pages.   Charles Agvent 4-991 1996 $950.00

SHAKESPEARE, WILLIAM 1564-1616   The Comedies, Histories and Tragedies of... (with the Two volumes of Poems). New York: Limited Editions Club, at the Press of A. Colish, 1939-40/41. Number 904 from 1500 numbered sets; 39 volumes; illustrations, typography and printing by Bruce Rogers; bound uniformly in gilt stamped buckram backed decorative boards designed from a pattern after a wall painting known to be familiar to the bard, slipcase for the 2 volumes of poems slightly rubbed, else very fine with tissue wrappers torn but present on most volumes.   Hermitage SP95-1032 1996 $1,750.00

SHAKESPEARE, WILLIAM 1564-1616   The Comedy of Errors. London: J. M. Dent & Sons, 1909. Reprint; 12mo; full leather, cover edges worn, head and tail of spine and corners bumped and worn, upper cover creased, good only; ownership signature of Ian Fleming.   Ulysses 39-689 1996 £125.00

SHAKESPEARE, WILLIAM 1564-1616   The Tragedie of Cymbeline. London: Ernest Benn, 1923. One of 500 numbered copies on rag paper; folio; boards, canvas spine lettered in black, edges of leaves little darkened and spotted and boards somewhat soiled, but nice, bookplate. Bertram Rota 272-423 1996 £80.00

SHAKESPEARE, WILLIAM 1564-1616   Dramatic Works. Boston: Phillips, Sampson, 1850-51. Early American edition; 8vo; 8 volumes; 57 steel engravings; volume 7 lacks title; half chocolate brown morocco/marbled boards, gilt lettering, scattered stains and foxing, some plates especially so, rubbed, still very good.   Charles Agvent 4-990 1996 $375.00

SHAKESPEARE, WILLIAM 1564-1616   Dramatic Works. London: Chatto & Windus, 1885. Limited to 250 copies; 8vo; 8 volumes; portrait; beautifully bound in half brown levant morocco, all edges gilt, contents lettered.   Charles W. Traylen 117-191 1996 £120.00

SHAKESPEARE, WILLIAM 1564-1616   Excerpts from The Sonnets. Amsterdam and Paris: International Laboratory for Interdisciplinary Art Studies, 1993. One of 100 copies only; page size 39 x 12 1/2 inches; on Japanese paper, 12 woodcuts in black and with text letterpress iridescent orange on 18 leaves; blue Japanese paper with black plastic spine.   Priscilla Juvelis 95/1-218 1996 $200.00

SHAKESPEARE, WILLIAM 1564-1616   The Family Shakespeare. London: 1825. 4th edition; 12mo; 10 volumes; contemporary half dark brown morocco, spines gilt with raised bands.   David Bickersteth 133-166 1996 £220.00

SHAKESPEARE, WILLIAM 1564-1616   Hamlet. Prinz von Danemark. Leipzig: 1907. 2 x 1 3/8 inches; 598 pages; gilt stamped red morocco, all edges gilt, spine faded, else fine. Bondy pp. 124-125.   Bromer Booksellers 87-219 1996 $100.00

SHAKESPEARE, WILLIAM 1564-1616   The Tragicall Historie of Hamlet Prince of Denmarke. Hammersmith: Doves Press, 1909. Small quarto; 158, (2), 23, (1) pages, printed in red and black, with opening initial flourished in green by Edward Johnson; full dark blue morocco elaborately stamped in gilt, gilt board edges and inner dentelles, all edges gilt and gauffered with dotted fillet, dentelles offsetting to endpapers, fine; beautiful unsigned binding, appears to be the product of the Doves Bindery. Inscribed by Thomas James Cobden-Sanderson for Edmond Holmes.   Heritage Book Shop 196-247 1996 $3,500.00

SHAKESPEARE, WILLIAM 1564-1616   The Handy Volume Shakespeare. London: Bradbury, Agnew, c. 1900. 16mo; 13 volumes; original red morocco, gilt lettered direct, chocolate brown endpapers, gilt edges, contained in red morocco covered box, rehinged, gilt titled within gilt and blind fillet frame on lid, gilt dulled, black and red printed label with list of contents and ads pasted inside lid, overall very good, volumes excellent. Blackwell's B112-253 1996 £250.00

SHAKESPEARE, WILLIAM 1564-1616   Julius Caesar. Dublin: A. Rhames, 1726. Apparently only the second Irish edition; 12mo; disbound. Dramatis Personae 37-157 1996 $200.00

SHAKESPEARE, WILLIAM 1564-1616   The Tragedy of Julius Caesar. London: Vale Press, 1900. One of 310 copies; 9.375 x 6 inches; 88 pages, printed on handmade paper; decorated by Charles Ricketts; green cloth boards with blindstamped design, title in gilt on backstrip. Fine, unopened.   Joshua Heller 21-273 1996 $100.00

SHAKESPEARE, WILLIAM 1564-1616   The Tragedie of King Lear. Printed at the Shakespeare Head Press...for...Benn, 1927. One of 450 copies (of an edition of 600), this unnumbered; large 4to; pages xcix, (136); printed on pure rag paper, 14 designs for a production of the play, by Paul Nash, including 5 color printed plates and 3 other full page illustrations by him; series title printed in black and red; original quarter tan linen, backstrip lettered in black, pale grey boards, little browned at edges, untrimmed, dust jacket, good.   Blackwell's B112-251 1996 £75.00

SHAKESPEARE, WILLIAM 1564-1616   The Tragedie of King Lear. Bangor: Theodore Press/Newark: Janus Press, 1986. One in an edition of 160 copies, signed by Claire Van Vliet; 14.5 x 11 inches; 39 woodcuts, 12 full page and one double page in black and white by Claire Van Vliet, text printed by Michael Alpert at the Theodore Press on grey handmade paper specially made for the edition by Katie MacGregor & Bernie Vinzani; alum-tawed pigskin spine, exposed cords, birch boards decorated by the artist with black and white rain striations; wrapped in black cloth chemise, housed in slipcase of linen-finish grey buckram, grey paper spine label in black; fine.   Joshua Heller 21-24 1996 $1,350.00

SHAKESPEARE, WILLIAM 1564-1616   The Life of King Henry V. New York: Limited Editions Club, 1951. Number 904 from 1500 copies; paintings by Fritz Zkredel; fine in slightly dusty publisher's slipcase. Hermitage SP95-1033 1996 $100.00

SHAKESPEARE, WILLIAM 1564-1616   Love's Labour's Lost. London: Ernest Benn, 1924. One of 500 numbered copies on rag paper; folio; 5 color plates and 3 pages of black and white designs by Norman Wilkinson; boards, canvas spine lettered in black; spine and edges of leaves somewhat darkened, but nice, bookplate.   Bertram Rota 272-424 1996 £60.00

SHAKESPEARE, WILLIAM 1564-1616   Macbeth. London: Circle Press Publications, 1970. Number 26 of 150 copies, large folio; pages (6), 44, colophon; 10 full page screen prints in gold, silver and colors, each titled and signed by artist; hand set in 14 pt. Plantin by Walter Taylor and printed letterpress by the artist on Barcham Green 246lb mould made paper at the Circle Press; fine set in original state of untrimmed, unsewn sheets in cloth bound folder and slipcase.   Claude Cox 107-30 1996 £250.00

SHAKESPEARE, WILLIAM 1564-1616   A Midsummer Night's Dream. London: Constable & Co., 1914. 1st edition with these illustrations; 4to; (xvi), 185, (iii) pages; 12 fine mounted colored plates and 64 startling black and white drawings by Heath Robinson; original blue pictorial cloth, preserved in original brown pictorial dust jacket, uncut; few brown spots to edge of book block, otherwise fine in exceptional wrapper with only a couple of tiny nicks to head of spine.   Sotheran PN32-148 1996 £468.00

SHAKESPEARE, WILLIAM 1564-1616   A Midsommer Nights Dreame. Shakespeare Head Press,...for Benn, 1924. Limited edition, 257/450 copies (of an edition of 600); large 4to; pages liii, (i), 71, (95); printed on pure rag paper, 14 designs for a production of the play by Paul Nash, including 5 color printed plates, series title printed in black and red; original quarter tan linen, backstrip lettered in black, covers faintly soiled and rubbed at corners of pale grey boards, owner's signature, free endpapers lightly browned in part, bookticket, untrimmed, good. Blackwell's B112-252 1996 £60.00

SHAKESPEARE, WILLIAM 1564-1616   A Midsommer Nights Dreame. London: Ernest Benn, 1924. One of 500 copies on rag paper, this unnumbered; folio; five color plates and 9 black and white illustrations by Paul Nash; boards, canvas spine lettered in black, edges of leaves little darkened but very nice, bookplate.   Bertram Rota 272-425 1996 £120.00

SHAKESPEARE, WILLIAM 1564-1616   Othello, the Moor of Venice. London: printed for R. Bentley in Russell St. near Covent Garden 1695. Small 4to; 2 leaves, pages 1-76, poor quality paper and as a result very browned throughout, inner margin of title repaired, modern full red morocco, gilt, relatively tall copy, bottom edge uncut. Wing S2942. Jaggard: Shakespeare Bib. p. 422.   H. M. Fletcher 121-74 1996 £850.00

SHAKESPEARE, WILLIAM 1564-1616   The Passionate Pilgrim and the Songs in Shakespeare's Plays. Vale Press, 1896. One of 310 copies; 8 x 5 1/2 inches; 79 pages (plus 4 blanks at each end); woodcut border, vignette, initials by Charles Ricketts; gray inlaid and onlaid morocco signed by the Swiss binder Hugo Peller, front cover with thin white morocco onlays forming an abstract design suggesting three sinewy trees (three onlays in orange or maroon represent perhaps animals perched in trees), gilt leaves at base of tree and gilt disk above no doubt representing sun, spine lettered in blind capitals, top edge gilt and gauffered, in very nice matching fleece lined morocco backed folding box, virtually flawless copy.   Phillip J. Pirages 33-495 1996 $2,250.00

SHAKESPEARE, WILLIAM 1564-1616   The Passionate Pilgrim and the Songs in Shakespeare's Plays. Vale Press, 1896. One of 310 copies; 8 x 5 1/2 inches; 79 pages (plus 4 blanks at each end); woodcut border, vignette and initials, all by Charles Ricketts, prospectus/order form for book laid in; original paper covered boards, printed paper labels on spine and front cover, two edges untrimmed, tail of spine slightly bumped, endpapers little browned (from laid in sheet?), otherwise nearly mint.   Phillip J. Pirages 33-494 1996 $450.00

SHAKESPEARE, WILLIAM 1564-1616   The Passionate Pilgrim and the Songs in Shakespeare's Plays. Vale Press, 1896. One of 310 copies; 8vo; printed in Vale type, woodcut illustrations, border and initials by Charles Ricketts; original boards with printed labels, backstrip darkened and worn at head and foot, corners bruised, internally nice fresh copy; from the library of John Buckland-Wright with his neat pencilled initials and notes on endpaper; warm signed autograph presentation inscription from T. J. Cobden-Sanderson.   Bertram Rota 272-479 1996 £150.00

SHAKESPEARE, WILLIAM 1564-1616   The Passionate Pilgrim and the Songs in Shakespeare's Plays. London: Vale Press, 1896. One of 310 copies; 12mo; full olive-green levant morocco, ribbed spine in 6 compartments, all tooled in gilt, covers with elaborate gilt tooled borders composed of large foliate quadrilobe centerpieces with similar designs in gilt along all edges with gilt birds, torches and flower urns, all within border of gilt solid and dotted rules with outer border of repeated C-shaped devices, red morocco doublures similarly bordered in gilt with hightly decorative gilt panel, floral silk endpapers, binding signed "Thierry & De Petit-Simies", tiny scuffs to spine ribs, else very fine.   Marilyn Braiterman 15-188 1995 $1,750.00

SHAKESPEARE, WILLIAM 1564-1616   The Plays. London: for C. Bathurst, J. Rivington and Sons (& 28 others in London), 1785. 3rd edition; 8vo; 10 volumes; portraits; contemporary pale tan sprinkled calf, red morocco labels, spines rule and numbered in gilt, five volumes with few thread-like wormholes, generally affecting the front inside boards and little of it going through to contents, only as a tiny single wormhole, never touching the text, joint on volume 7 just starting at head; excellent set.   Simon Finch 24-202 1996 £3,500.00

SHAKESPEARE, WILLIAM 1564-1616   The Tragedy of Richard the Third. Grabhorn Press, 1953. One of 180 copies; 10 1/2 x 7 3/4 inches; 3 p.l., (1) pages; printed in red and black; 6 original colored woodcuts in text, including vignette on title by Mary Grabhorn, original limp vellum, linen ties, edges untrimmed, spine with gilt lettering; only the most trivial imperfections, extremely fine, especially clean inside and out. Signed, dated (1958 and inscribed by Jane Grabhorn to Elaine(?) Goodwin.   Phillip J. Pirages 33-255 1996 $550.00

SHAKESPEARE, WILLIAM 1564-1616   Tales from Shakespeare. London: Dent, 1909. 1st edition thus; 4to; 12 colored plates, drawings in black and white, pictorial endpapers by Arthur Rackham; blue cloth pictorially stamped in gilt, top edge gilt, fore edge little marked, else fresh. Barbara Stone 70-177 1996 £110.00

SHAKESPEARE, WILLIAM 1564-1616   The Taming of the Shrew. London: J. M. Dent and Sons, 1909. Reprint; 12mo; full leather covers, edges rubbed, head and tail of spine and corners bumped and worn, very good; ownership signature of Ian Fleming.   Ulysses 39-690 1996 £125.00

SHAKESPEARE, WILLIAM 1564-1616   The Tempest. London: n.d. 1908. Limited to 500 numbered copies, signed by artist; 11.5 x 8.5 inches; 144 pages; 40 tipped in color plates by Edmund Dulac, on green art paper, with lettered tissue guards; full vellum, top edge gilt, covers slightly rubbed and spotted, spine heavily spotted, slightly warped covers, lacking original ties, text tight and clean; bookplate of Christine Alexander Graham.   John K. King 77-594 1996 $950.00

SHAKESPEARE, WILLIAM 1564-1616   The Tempest. London: Hodder and Stoughton, 1908. 1st edition illustrated by Dulac; 4to; 40 fine mounted color plates behind tissue guards; original green cloth, gilt, preserved in buff printed dust jacket, lower corner bumped, otherwise fine in excellent dust jacket which is remarkably scarce.   Sotheran PN32-114 1996 £450.00

SHAKESPEARE, WILLIAM 1564-1616   The Tempest. London: Hodder & Stoughton, 1908. 1st trade edition thus; 4to; xxv, 143 pages; 40 tipped in color plates by Edmund Dulac; original gilt stamped green cloth, extremities lightly rubbed and spine slightly faded, else very good. White, Edmund Dulac p. 200.   Chapel Hill 94-54 1996 $225.00

SHAKESPEARE, WILLIAM 1564-1616   Titus Andronicus, or the Rape of Lavinia. London: printed by J. B. for J. Hindmarsh, 1687. 1st edition thus; 4to; disbound; uncommon; from the library of Philip Bliss. Wing S2949; Bartlett (1922) 178; CBEL II 771.   Ximenes 109-259 1996 $1,500.00

SHAKESPEARE, WILLIAM 1564-1616   With Fairest Flowers While Summer Lasts. Poems from Shakespeare. Garden City: Doubleday, 1971. 1st edition; with "M9" in lower corner of p. 140, in rare unrecorded library issue in reinforced binding; 8vo; pictorial boards, dust jacket; fine in slightly dust soiled and sunned jacket, signed by Ted Hughes, the editor.   James S. Jaffe 34-285 1996 $250.00

SHAKESPEARE, WILLIAM 1564-1616   The Works... London: for Jacob Tonson, 1709/10 (vo. 7) 1st collected edition; 8vo; 7 volumes; engravings; fine polished calf, spines gilt, some restoration of bindings, attrative set.   19th Century Shop 39- 1996 $7,500.00

SHAKESPEARE, WILLIAM 1564-1616   The Works. London: C. Bathurst (& 31 others), 1773. 12mo; 8 volumes; (iii)-xii, (lvi), 395, (i); 431, (i); 430; 478; 399, (i); 488; 458; 370, (lxxviii) pages; 36 frontispieces; contemporary calf, spines gilt, double labels; rubbed, minor wear at extremities, several joints cracked, scattered foxing, few page edges dusty, serviceable set. Jaggard p. 500.   Robert Clark 38-131 1996 £110.00

SHAKESPEARE, WILLIAM 1564-1616   Works. London: 1866. 2nd edition by Alexander Dyce; 8vo; 9 volumes; portrait; original cloth; fine set.   Charles W. Traylen 117-189 1996 £130.00

SHAKESPEARE, WILLIAM 1564-1616   The Works. London: Chapman and Hall, 1875-76. 3rd edtiion; 8vo; 9 volumes; 2 engraved portraits, plate of facsimile signatures; contemporary red hard grain morocco, spines divided in six panels by raised bands, gilt lettered in 3 panels, double blind rules, green silk markers, comb marbled endpapers, inner dentelles and edges gilt, little trivial rubbing, excellent set; John Ruskin's copy with his booklabel, 4 line ms. pencilled note in his hand on p. 363 vol. V.   Simon Finch 24-203 1996 £1,200.00

SHAKESPEARE, WILLIAM 1564-1616   Complete Works...With Life, Compendium and Concordance. Philadelphia: Gebbie, 1896. Dr. Johnson Edition; 8vo; 7 volumes; 50 photogravures; half calf, gilt spines, maroon and black leather labels, fine set, attractively bound.   Charles Agvent 4-993 1996 $425.00

SHAKESPEARE, WILLIAM 1564-1616   Works. New York: J. F. Taylor, 1902. Irving edition, Limited to 21 sets; 8vo; 100 volumes; extra illustrated by upwards of 2500 engravings, many printed in color and hand colored; full blue levant morocco with intricate gilt stamped tooling on covers, gilt panelled spines, raised bands, inner gilt leather panels, silk doublure endleaves, edges gilt. Fine.   Appelfeld Gallery 54-166 1996 $15,000.00

SHAKESPEARE, WILLIAM 1564-1616   The Works of Shakespeare. New York: Random House, 1929-33. Limited edition of 1050 sets for Great Britain and Ireland, 550 sets for America, this number 1031; 7 volumes; full tan morocco with slight edgewear, three of the spines uniformly darkened somewhat. Bound by A. W. Bain. Dreyfus 58.   Glenn Books 36-198 1996 $1,500.00

SHAKESPEARE, WILLIAM 1564-1616   The Works of William Shakespeare. New York: Nonesuch Press, 1929-33. Limited edition of 1050 copies for sale in Great Britain and Ireland and 550 copies for sale in the USA. This copy number 1076. 8vo; 7 volumes; errata leaf to volume 7; full tan morocco, double gilt rule borders, gilt titles to panelled spines, top edge gilt, uncut, inner gilt rule borders, covers rubbed and worn in places, unevenly sunned; nice set bound by A. W. Bain.   Beeleigh Abbey BA56-163 1996 £750.00

SHAKESPEARE, WILLIAM 1564-1616   The Complete Works. New York: Limited Editions Club, 1940-44. Limited edition of 1950 numbered sets; folio; 40 volumes; illustrations; publisher's cloth backed designed boards, top edge gilt, others uncut; fine set.   Thomas Thorp 489-275 1996 £525.00

SHAKESPEARE, WILLIAM 1564-1616   Complete Works. London: Nonesuch Press, 1953. 8vo; 4 volumes, printed on India paper with titles printed in black and brown, original quarter dark brown cloth, backstrips gilt lettered, brown marbled cloth sides, speckled edges, original tissue jackets, board slipcase, fine. Dreyfus 119.   Blackwell's B112-212 1996 £200.00

SHAKESPEARE, WILLIAM 1564-1616   The Complete Works. London: Nonesuch Press, 1953. Crown 8vo; 4 volumes; headpieces and dedication page from wood engravings by Reynolds Stone; quarter brown buckram, marbled cloth sides, just a little external wear, but nice, name on endpapers.   Bertram Rota 272-335 1996 £140.00

SHALER, N. S.   American Highways. New York: Century, 1896. 1st edition; original binding, very good.   October Farm 36-186 1996 $125.00

SHANNON, C. HAZELWOOD   The Pageant. London: Henry and Co., 1897. 4to; 266 pages, plus ads; numerous illustrations including original color woodblock; cloth, illustrations on front and spine, very slightly rubbed, very good.   Andrew Cahan 47-160 1996 $175.00

SHANNON, C. HAZELWOOD   The Pageant. London: Henry and Co., 1897/98. 1st edition; 4to; 2 volumes; pages (16), 243, (10) ads; (8), 206, (8) ads; illustrations; uncut, volume 2 largely unopened; original cloth, decorated in gold to Ricketts' design, volume 1 little bumped & cockled; very good. McLean VBD p. 233.   Claude Cox 107-159 1996 £175.00

SHAPIRO, KARL JAY   Auden (1907-1973). Davis, Putah Creek Press, 1974. 1st edition; one of 175 copies signed by poet and artist; portrait; tan wrappers, back cover has a wrinkle, else fine.   Bromer Booksellers 90-223 1996 $150.00

SHAPIRO, KARL JAY   Poems. Baltimore: Waverly Press, 1935. Limited edition, 37/200 copies only, signed by author; author's first book; gold lettering on spine faded, extremities little rubbed, small tear and tiny edge tear at 2 lower edges, not affecting text, burgundy covers with some soiling, contents fine; scarce. Included is typed poem by author signed by him.   Polyanthos 22-791 1996 $500.00

SHAPLEIGH, JOHN   Highways: a Treatise Shewing the Hardships and Inconveniences of Presenting, or Indicting Parishes, Towns, Etc. for Not Repairing the Highways. London: printed by S. Birt, in Ave Maria Lane and Aaron Tozer, Bookseller... 1750. 2nd edition; 64 pages; recent wrappers, very nice, clean copy. Hanson 6336; Goldsmiths 8440.   C. R. Johnson 37-29 1996 £125.00

SHAPLEY, FERN RUSK   Paintings from the Samuel H. Kress Collection Italian Schools XVI-XVIII Century. London: Phaidon Press, 1973. 30 x 22.5 cm; 470 pages; 340 illustrations, including 9 color plates; original cloth, in dust jacket.   Rainsford A54-357 1996 £140.00

SHARP, GRANVILLE 1734-1813   The Law of Retribution; or a Serious Warning to Great Britain and Her Colonies... London: White and Dilly, 1776. 8vo; pages 2, 357, 2 ads; modern quarter calf, red label. Richard Adelson W94/95-157 1996 $285.00

SHARP, GRANVILLE 1734-1813   A Short Treatise on the English Tongue. London: printed for R. Horsfield, & I. Allix, 1767. Parallel text in English and French; slight worming in inner margin of prelims; contemporary speckled calf, slightly worn with early repairs, gilt borders, very good, attractive copy. Alston VI 489.   Jarndyce 103-337 1996 £160.00

SHARP, WILLIAM 1855-1905   Vistas. Derby: printed by Frank Murray at the Moray Press, Jan. 1894. 1st edition; number 25 of 75 large paper copies, signed by author; 8vo; frontispiece; original vellum boards, uncut, lightly soiled, else very good. NCBEL III p. 1065.   Howard S. Mott 227-127 1996 $200.00

SHARPE, CHARLES KIRKPATRICK   A Ballad Book, or Popular and Romantic Ballads and songs Current in Annandale and Other Parts of Scotland. Edinburgh: 1883. 1st of this edition; limited to 275 copies; 12mo; 2 volumes; finely printed on laid Whatman paper, uncut; titlepage in red and black; vellum wrappers, covers evenly browned, small piece missing from spine of volume 1, but very good set, very scarce. Lowndes I 101.   Hartfield 48-V43 1996 $145.00

SHARPE, GREGORY   A Short Dissertation Upon that Species of Misgovernment, Called an Oligarchy. London: J. Freeman, 1748. 1st edition; 8vo; 58 pages; slight marginal browning of first few leaves, recently well bound in linen backed marbled boards, lettered; very good. John Drury 82-254 1996 £70.00

SHARPE, REGINALD R.   Calendar of Letter-Books Preserved Among the Archives of the City of London at the Guildhall. From A.D. 1275-(Henry VI). London: 1899-1911. Royal 8vo; Volumes I-X; original cloth, library stamps.   Howes Bookshop 265-705 1996 £200.00

SHARPE, RICHARD BOWLDER   A Handbook to the Birds of Great Britain. London: 1896-97. 8vo; 4 volumes; 128 colored plates; original cloth.   Wheldon & Wesley 207-858 1996 £75.00

SHARPE, RICHARD BOWLDER   Matabele Land and the Victoria Falls, from the Letters and Journals of the Late Frank Oates, F.R.G.S. London: 1882. Original offprint from the book; 8vo; 2 fine hand colored plates, folding hand colored map, grey printed wrappers, signature (bit indistinct) of Edward Hargitt (1835-95, ornithologist).   Maggs Bros. Ltd. 1190-605 1996 £125.00

SHARPE, RICHARD BOWLDER   A Monograph of the Hirundinidae, or Family of the Swallows. London: 1885-94. Royal 4to; 2 volumes; 111 hand colored plates, 26 maps; half red morocco, trifle rubbed; exceptional copy, few plates with minor marginal stains or foxing, one slightly creased and 3 with slight marginal tears, but in general a good, clean copy.   Wheldon & Wesley 207-97 1996 £6,500.00

SHARPE, RICHARD BOWLDER   Monograph of the Paradiseidae, or Birds of Paradise, and Ptilonorhynchidae, or Bower-Birds. London: 1891-98. Imperial folio; 2 volumes; 79 fine hand colored plates; contemporary full green morocco, gilt, gilt edges; binding tifle rubbed and inside covers trifle marked, still very fine, contents excellent; from the collection of Jan Coldewey.   Wheldon & Wesley 207-96 1996 £28,000.00

SHARPE, RICHARD BOWLDER   On a Collection of Birds Made by Dr. A. Donaldson Smith During His Recent Expedition in Western Somali-Land. London: 1895. Offprint; 8vo; 2 hand colored plates by Keulemans; wrappers, very slightly worn.   Maggs Bros. Ltd. 1190-607 1996 £55.00

SHARPE, RICHARD BOWLDER   On the Birds Collected by Professor J. B. Steere in the Philippine Archipealgo. London: 1877. 4to; 49 pages, 9 hand colored plates; modern cloth, from the collection of Jan Coldewey. Wheldon & Wesley 207-94 1996 £675.00

SHARPE, RICHARD BOWLDER   On the Birds of Zululand... London: 1897. Offprint; 8vo; hand colored lithograph; wrappers.   Maggs Bros. Ltd. 1190-610 1996 £55.00

SHARROCK, ROBERT   An Improvement to the Art of Gardening... London: printed by Nathanael Sackett, 1694. 3rd edition; 8vo; engraved plate, facing leaf of explanation, errata leaf at end; contemporary mottled calf, some wear to spine, front cover detached; aside from binding, very good, scarce edition. Wing S3012. Henrey 342. Ximenes 109-260 1996 $750.00

SHAW, B.   The Palace of Eternity. London: Gollancz, 1970. 1st edition; near fine in dust jacket, scarce.   Aronovitz 57-1030 1996 $150.00

SHAW, EDWARD   Civil Architecture; or a Complete Theoretical and Practical System of Building. Boston: Marsh, Capen & Lyon, 1834. 3rd edition; 4to; 208 pages + plates; contemporary full flame calf with morocco spine label; little edgeworn, lightly foxed, else very good. Scarce. American Imprints 26746.   Chapel Hill 94-28 1996 $375.00

SHAW, GEORGE BERNARD 1856-1950   The Apple Cart: a Political Extravaganza. London: Constable, 1930. 1st edition; stained along lower portion of covers, otherwise very good in dust jacket that is darkened and spotted on spine and which has been internally strengthened there with archival tape, also splitting along flap folds and with triangular chip missing from lower rear corner at flap fold, still a fragile, coarse paper dust jacket that is remarkable for surviving at all.   Ken Lopez 74-407 1996 $1,500.00

SHAW, GEORGE BERNARD 1856-1950   The Doctor's Dilemma: Getting Married, the Shewing-Up of Blanco Posnet. London: Constable, 1911. 1st edition; original pale green cloth; near fine, fine half morocco case; presentation copy inscribed by author for Sir L. Clifford Albert.   19th Century Shop 39- 1996 $2,800.00

SHAW, GEORGE BERNARD 1856-1950   Fabian Essays in Socialism. New York: Humboldt, 1891. 1st American edition; 8vo; printed wrappers, housed in cloth clamshell box with label removed from inner cover, owner signature on front wrapper, some wear to spine, old crease to text, occasional pencil notations, library stamp on half title and contents page, no other markings, very good overall.   Charles Agvent 4-1001 1996 $150.00

SHAW, GEORGE BERNARD 1856-1950   Flyleaves. Austin: W. Thomas Taylor, 1977. One of 350 copies; 4to; printed in black, brown and red, 2 foldout facsimiles; russet cloth, special paste paper endpapers; fine; Bertram Rota 272-32 1996 £60.00

SHAW, GEORGE BERNARD 1856-1950   Geneva: a Fancied Page of History in Three Acts. London: Constable & Co., 1939. 1st edition; 8vo; vii, 9i), 111, (iv) pages; profusely illustrated with plates and vignettes by Topolski; light blue cloth titled in gilt on spine in peach dust jacket printed in blue and black; fine.   Blue Mountain SP95-80 1996 $125.00

SHAW, GEORGE BERNARD 1856-1950   Misalliance, The Dark Lady of the Sonnets and Fanny's First Play. London: Constable and Co., 1914. 1st edition; fine in near fine dust jacket.   Hermitage SP95-566 1996 $150.00

SHAW, GEORGE BERNARD 1856-1950   Passion Play, a Dramatic
Fragment 1878. London: Bertram Rota Ltd., 1971. 1st edition; of 350
copies, one of 100 for Bertram Rota Ltd. (no. 302); 13 x 8.25 inches;
printed by hand in black with red, grey and blue at the Windhover Press
on Italian Umbria; cream cloth spine with paper title label, blue patterned
paste paper boards, blue slipcase with cream cloth trim; bookplate,
otherwise fine.   Joshua Heller 21-283 1996 $200.00

SHAW, GEORGE BERNARD 1856-1950   The Sanity of Art. New York:
Benj. R. Tucker, 1908. 1st American edition, 12mo; 113 pages; cloth,
slightly darkened, otherwise near fine. Laurence A86b.   Freedom
Bookshop 14- 1996 $150.00

SHAW, HENRY 1800-1873   The Decorative Arts, Ecclesiastical and
Civil, of the Middle Ages. London: William Pickering, 1851. 1st edition;
folio; unpaginated, 41 plates; contemporary half morocco, light edge
wear to cover, else very good, scarce.   Bookpress 75-117 1996
$750.00

SHAW, HENRY 1800-1873   Dresses and Decorations of the Middle
Ages from the Seventh to the Seventeenth Centuries. London: Henry G.
Bohn, 1858. Later edition; 4to; 2 volumes; 86 full page hand tinted stone
lithographes, plus 2 double page, 86 chromolithographic initial letters,
hand coloring richly and carefully done, red half crushed morocco over
marbled boards, scuffing and wear to edges and corners, as well as
small wormhole in lower endpaper of volume 2, else very good. McLean
VBD p. 66.   Glenn Books 36-234 1996 $500.00

SHAW, HENRY 1800-1873   The Encyclopedia of Ornament. London:
William Pickering, 1842. 1st edition; 4to; 6 pages, 60 plates; bookplate,
contemporary half calf; front hinge internally cracked, edgewear,
occasional foxing, else very good.   Bookpress 75-118 1996 $475.00

SHAW, HENRY 1800-1873   A Handbook of the Art of Illumination as
Practised during the Middle Ages. London: Bell and Daldy, 1866. 1st
edition; small 4to; viii, 66 pages, 16 plates; pubisher's cloth, some minor
sporadic foxing, light chipping at base of spine and lower tips, else very
nice.   Bookpress 75-119 1996 $265.00

SHAW, HENRY 1800-1873   Handbook of the Art of Illumination, as
Practised During the Middle Ages. London: Bell & Daldy, 1866. Royal
8vo; numerous illustrations in text and 16 full page plates, all printed in
sepia; original cloth, gilt extra, gilt edges, few pages little 'sprung' as
usual   Charles W. Traylen 117-247 1996 £125.00

SHAW, HENRY 1800-1873   Specimens of Ancient Furniture. London:
William Pickering, 1836. 1st edition; 4to; iv, 57, (1) pages, 71 of 74
plates; contemporary half morocco, lacking 3 plates; binding rubbed.
Abbey Life 70.   Bookpress 75-120 1996 $275.00

SHAW, JOSEPH T.   Danger Ahead. New York: Mohawk Press, 1932.
1st edition; slight soiling to fore-edge, else fine in near fine dust jacket
with one very small chip and old label on spine, scarce.   Between the
Covers 42-392 1996 $350.00

SHAW, RICHARD NORMAN   Architectural Sketches From the
Continent. London: 1858. Folio; lithograph with view within decorative
border, 100 plates; recent half calf, gilt.   Petersfield Bookshop
FH58-17 1996 £195.00

SHAW, RICHARD NORMAN   Architectural Sketches from the Continent.
London: for the Proprietors, 1872. Folio; decorative titlepage, (12) pages
text and 100 lithograph plates; quarter morocco, gilt decorated cloth
boards; very good.   Ken Spelman 30-106 1996 £120.00

SHAW, RICHARD NORMAN   Architectural Sketches from the Continent.
London: for the Proprietors, 1872. Folio; decorative titlepage, (12) pages
text and 100 lithograph plates; quarter morocco with gilt decorated cloth
boards.   Ken Spelman 30-106 1996 £120.00

SHAW, S.   A Tour to the West of England in 1788... London: printed
for Robson and Clarke and J. Walker, 1789. 1st edition; 8vo; 602 pages
of text; old half calf, gilt bands, red morocco label to spine, joints
rubbed, small split to rear joint, slight surface loss to base of spine,
original marbled boards, armorial bookplate to front pastedown, ink
signature to front free endpaper; Cox III p. 36.   Beeleigh Abbey
BA56-20 1996 £175.00

SHAW, T. E.   More Letters from T. E. Shaw to Bruce Rogers. N.P.:
privately printed, 1936. One of 300 copies, signed by Bruce Rogers; 16
leaves; flexible cloth; fine.   Hermitage SP95-846 1996 $500.00

SHAW, THOMAS   Travels, or Observations Relating to Several Parts
of Barbary and the Levant. London: for A. Millar and W. Sandby, 1757.
2nd edition; quarto; xviii pages, 1 leaf, 5136 pages, 38 maps and plates;
contemporary calf, rebacked in brown morocco, gilt, new endpapers,
sound copy. Bookplate of Howard Vyse.   H. M. Fletcher 121-121
1996 £420.00

SHAWN, TED   Gods Who Dance. New York: 1929. 1st edition; 205
pages; over 100 illustrations; boards, slight corner bumped, else fine.
Laid in is program of St. Denis & Shawn at the Waldorf-Astoria.
Lyman Books 21-379 1996 $125.00

SHEA, MICHAEL   Nifft the Lean. Woodinville: Darkside Press, 1994.
Proof for the forthcoming limited hardcover edition, one of only 9 copies
in ring binders with paper covers; one tiny ink mark, else very fine.
Robert Gavora 61-138 1996 $250.00

SHEBBEARE, JOHN   Letters on the English Nation. London: printed in
the year 1755. 1st edition; 8vo; 2 volumes; (iii-xlvi), (xlvii-lx), 1-288 pages,
1-296 pages, errata leaf to volume 2, owner's bookplates, full speckled
calf, corners bumped and worn, joints cracked and rubbed, double gilt
rule border to boards, raised bands to spines, upper hinge of volume 1
tender, edges speckled. Halkett & Laing III p. 336; Lowndes' IV 2373.
Beeleigh Abbey BA56-21 1996 £95.00

SHEBBEARE, JOHN   Letters to the People of England: I-V. London:
N.P., 1756/57/57. 4th edition of volumes I-IV, 2nd edition of volume V;
8vo; volumes I-V, bound in one; half calf, marbled boards and
endpapers, fine.   Hugh Anson-Cartwright 87-384 1996 $450.00

SHECKLEY, R.   Citizen in Space. Ballantine, 1955. 1st edition; signed
by author; slight wear to one corner tip, else fine in ner fine dust jacket
with some light dust soil to rear dust jacket panel, quite scarce.
Aronovitz 57-1033 1996 $395.00

SHECKLEY, R.   Journey Beyond Tomorrow. London: Gollancz, 1964.
1st British and 1st hard cover edition; small chip at head of dust jacket
spine, else very good+/near fine in dust jacket; uncommon; signed by
author.   Aronovitz 57-1034 1996 $125.00

SHEFFIELD, JOHN BAKER HOLYROYD, 1ST EARL OF 1735-1821
Strictures on the Necessity of Inviolably Maintaining the Navigation and
Colonial System of Great Britain. London: J. Debrett, 1804. 1st edition;
8vo; iv, 65 (3) pages, including final leaf of ads, with few ms notes
added in ink, in contemporary hand; recently well bound in cloth backed
marbled boards gilt, very good; presentation copy from author to Lord
Auckland. Williams I 407; Kress B4849l Goldsmiths 18858; not in Einaudi.
John Drury 82-255 1996 £95.00

SHELDON, CHARLES   The Wilderness of Denali. New York: Scribner's,
1930. 1st edition; 8vo; 412 pages, folding map; original green
cloth, bright, near fine copy.   Chapel Hill 94-396 1996 $200.00

SHELDON, CHARLES   The Wilderness of the North Pacific Coast
Islands. New York: Charles Scribner's Sons, 1912. 1st edition; 8vo; xvi,
246 pages; 45 plates, 5 maps; bright, dark green cloth, gilt spine and
cover titles, gilt bear on cover; small mark or two on cover, else near
fine. Arctic Bib. 15872. Ricks p. 198; Wickerhsam 4225.   Parmer Books
Nat/Hist-071539 1996 $250.00

SHELDON, CHARLES   The Wilderness of the North Pacific Coast
Islands. New York: Scribner's, 1912. 1st edition; 8vo; 246 pages; 5
photogravure plates, numerous full page photos; original gilt stamped
green cloth, bright and nearly fine.   Chapel Hill 94-395 1996 $175.00

SHELDON, CHARLES   The Wilderness of the Upper Yukon...The Pacific
Coast Islands....The Denali. 1983. One of 1000 signed copies; 3 volumes;
photographic illustrations, maps, drawings by Carl Rungius; full leather,
raised bands, gilt edges, silk moire endpapers, silk marker, in single
slipcase; fine.   David Grayling J95Biggame-442 1996 £200.00

SHELDON, FREDERICK   The Minstrelsy of the English Border. London:
Longman, Brown et al, 1847. 1st edition; 432 pages; handsomely bound
in gilt stamped brown leather and marbled paper covered boards, top
edge gilt, spine bit worn, otherwise near fine.   Beasley Books 82-17 1
997 $125.00

SHELDON, H. HORTON   Television. Present Methods of Picture
Transmission. New York: D. Van Nostrand, 1930. 1st edition; 2nd
printing; 8vo; x, 194, (1 ads) pages; 1 color plate, 129 figures in text;
cloth bit soiled and worn; very good.   Edwin V. Glaser 121-284 1996
$150.00

SHELDON, WILLIAM HERBERT   Atlas of Men: a Guide for Somatotyping the Adult Male at All Ages. New York: Harper & Bros., 1954. 1st edition; folio; (xvi), 357, (3) pages; cloth backed russet boards, corners bumped, very good.   John Gach 150-430 1996 $150.00

SHELLEY, G. E.   A Monograph of the Nectariniidae or Family of Sun Birds. London: 1876-80. Only 250 copies printed; royal 4to; cviii, 393 pages, 121 fine hand colored plates; contemporary full brown morocco, gilt, gilt inside borders by Porter, gilt top; rare. Fine, clean copy, beautifully colored, with author's bookplate, from the collection of Jan Coldewey.   Wheldon & Wesley 207-98 1996 £10,000.00

SHELLEY, MARY WOLLSTONECRAFT GODWIN 1797-1851 Frankenstein; or, the Modern Prometheus. Boston and Cambridge: Sever, Francis & Co., 1869. 2nd American edition; 8vo; original maroon cloth, ends of spine and corners rubbed; rare.   Ximenes 109-261 1996 $400.00

SHELLEY, MARY WOLLSTONECRAFT GODWIN 1797-1851 Frankenstein. New York: Limited Editions Club, 1934. Number 904 from 1500 copies, signed by artist; illustrations by Everett Henry; half leather and decorative cloth; fine in publisher's slipcase.   Hermitage SP95-1035 1996 $250.00

SHELLEY, MARY WOLLSTONECRAFT GODWIN 1797-1851 Frankenstein. D-M, 1983. 1st edition thus, 1/500 copies, signed by artist and by Stephen King who provides introduction; illustrations by Bernie Wrightson; fine in tissue dust jacket and slipcase.   Aronovitz 57-1040 1996 $350.00

SHELLEY, MARY WOLLSTONECRAFT GODWIN 1797-1851   Frankenstein or, The Modern Prometheus. West Hatfield: Pennyroyal Press, 1984. One of 300 copies; 13 3/4 x 10 inches; 255 pages, 52 wood engravings by Barry Moser, printed in several colors in Poliphilus and Wilhelm Klingsporschrift on Strathmore Pulegium, specially made for the Press; specially bound by Sarah Creighton in full grey niger goatskin with white and rust leather onlays, blind and palladium tooling, graphite head edge, sewn rust silk endbands with silver teachest flyleaves; one of four so bound, with additional suite of prints in quarter leather traycase, 36 x 36 cm.   Taurus Books 83-125 1996 $3,000.00

SHELLEY, MARY WOLLSTONECRAFT GODWIN 1797-1851   Frankenstein or the Modern Prometheus. West Hatfield: Pennyroyal Press, 1984. Limited to 300 copies; 13 3/4 x 10 inches; 255 pages; 52 wood engravings by Barry Moser; printed in several colors in Poliphilus and Wilhelm Klingsporschirft on Strahmore Pulegium, specially made for the Press; 52 wood engravings by Barry Moser; half leather; extra suite of signed prints, all in slipcase. Fine.   Taurus Books 83-124 1996 $1,600.00

SHELLEY, MARY WOLLSTONECRAFT GODWIN 1797-1851   Valperga; or, the Life and Adventures of Castruccio, Prince of Lucca. London: for G. and W. B. Whittaker, 1823. 1st edition; 12mo; 3 volumes; initial and final blanks in volume 3, but without final blank in volume 1; contemporary calf, rebacked, spine in compartments with gilt rules and morocco labels, some rubbing and stripping, especially to volume 1, bookplate, very light, even browning, good copy in maroon cloth folding box. Wise pp. 17-18.   Simon Finch 24-204 1996 £1,200.00

SHELLEY, PERCY BYSSHE 1792-1822   Adonais. London: printed at the Essex House Press, the Guild of Handicraft, 1900. Number 25 of 50 copies; 8vo; printed on vellum, pages 30 + colophon, frontispiece, hand colored with initials and rubrication by hand; original blindstamped vellum, lettered in gold, vellum chipped along top edge and corners, 7mm piece chipped from foot of backstrip, otherwise well preserved and internally fine. Tomkinson 6; Crawford 6.   Claude Cox 107-53 1996 £220.00

SHELLEY, PERCY BYSSHE 1792-1822   Essays, Letters from Abroad. London: Moxon, 1840. 1st edition; 8vo; 2 volumes; original binding, hinges slightly cracked on volume 2, spines sunned, chipped, gilt still bright, edgewear, near very good. Owner signature.   Charles Agvent 4-1005 1996 $300.00

SHELLEY, PERCY BYSSHE 1792-1822   Harriet & Mary... Waltham St. Lawrence: Golden Cockerel Press, 1944. Limited to 500 numbered and signed copies, this being one of 50 copies specially bound; crown 4to; portrait, collotype reproductions; original full niger morocco, top edge gilt, some slight spotting on cover.   Thomas Thorp 489-277 1996 £95.00

SHELLEY, PERCY BYSSHE 1792-1822   (Laon and Cythna). The Revolt of Islam.. London: for John Brooks, 1829. Re-issue with original sheets; 8vo; pages (ii), v-xxxii, (ii), fly-title to dedication and list of errata, 270, without initial and final blanks; 19th century green calf, sides with double fillet gilt border with roundels at corners, spine in compartments, with raised bands, gilt rules, rolls and floral ornaments, morocco labels, inner dentelles gilt, marbled endpapers, top edge gilt, others uncut, by Riviere & Son, joints cracked, spine with burn mark, rubbed in places and discolored, still very good. Forman 50; Granniss 45; Wise p. 50.   Simon Finch 24-207 1996 £750.00

SHELLEY, PERCY BYSSHE 1792-1822   The Masque of Anarchy: a Poem. London: Edward Moxon, 1832. 1st edition; 6 3/4 x 4 1/4 inches; xxx, 47 pages, (1) leaf ads; original buff paper boards, paper spine label, edges of leaves untrimmed, contained in folding box lined with watered silk and plush velvet and covered in full red levant morocco, French fillets on sides, spine with raised bands, gilt ruled compartments and gilt titling, part of box little worn, part of paper spine label missing (with all the printed letters affected but none of them completely lost), but only very minor smudging or wear to binding, two leaves faintly creased (apparently during binding), otherwise fine, fragile, exceptionally clean internally. Leather bookplate of Estelle Doheny. Granniss 80; Wise p. 71.   Phillip J. Pirages 33-461 1996 $2,500.00

SHELLEY, PERCY BYSSHE 1792-1822   A Philosophical View of Reform. London: Humphrey Milford, Oxford University Press, 1920. 1st edition; 4to; pages xi, 94, 1 plate; frontispiece, original boards, cloth back. Fine in little chipped and stained dust jacket, inscribed "John Quinn from T. W. Rolleston Sept. 23 1920". Bookplate of Great American collector Gordon Craig.   Howard S. Mott 227-128 1996 $135.00

SHELLEY, PERCY BYSSHE 1792-1822   Poems. London: Doves Press, 1914. One of 212 copies, one of 200 on paper. 4to; pages 181; printed in red and black, original limp vellum, spine lettered in gilt, by the Doves Bindery, uncut, excellent.   Simon Finch 24-78 1996 £550.00

SHELLEY, PERCY BYSSHE 1792-1822   The Poems of Percy Bysshe Shelley Cambridge: Limited Editions Club, 1971. One of 1500 numbered copies, signed by artist; wood engravings by Richard Shirley Smith; fine in publisher's slipcase.   Hermitage SP95-1036 1996 $100.00

SHELLEY, PERCY BYSSHE 1792-1822   The Poetical Works... London: Edward Moxon, 1839. 1st edition; small 8vo; 4 volumes; frontispiece in volume 1 (foxed, as often); contemporary vellum, green morocco labels, marbled endpapers, red edges; excellent set; bookplate of Christopher Teesdale. Wise p. 87; Granniss 88; Dunbar, Shelley Studies 345.   Simon Finch 24-208 1996 £580.00

SHELLEY, PERCY BYSSHE 1792-1822   The Poetical Works. London: Moxon, 1839. 1st Collected edition; 8vo; 4 volumes; portrait; half leather; covers moderately rubbed and worn, contents clean.   Charles Agvent 4-1006 1996 $400.00

SHELLEY, PERCY BYSSHE 1792-1822   The Poetical Works. Hammersmith: Kelmscott Press, 1895. One of 250 paper copies; octavo; 3 volumes, printed in red and black in Golden type; decorative borders and initials; full limp vellum lettered in gilt on spines, some light soiling and rubbing to vellum; bookplate, otherwise fine, chemise in 3 grey cloth slipcases. Peterson A29; Ransom Private Presses p. 328 no. 29; Sparling 29.   Heritage Book Shop 196-164 1996 $2,750.00

SHELLEY, PERCY BYSSHE 1792-1822   The Poetical Works of Percy Bysshe Shelley. Hammersmith: Kelmscott Press, 1895. Limited to 250 copies; octavo; 3 volumes, 399; 412; 421 pages; heavily engraved double page title in volume 1 and engraved initials and borders; limp vellum, without ties, as issued; extremely fine.   Bromer Booksellers 87-160 1996 $2,750.00

SHELLEY, PERCY BYSSHE 1792-1822   Prometheus Unbound, a Lyrical Drama in Four Acts With Other Poems. London: C. and J. Ollier, 1820. 1st edition; genuinely scarce first issue with misprint 'Misellaneous' in the 'Contents' list; this leaf (A3) was cancelled and a corrected leaf substituted in the second issue; 8vo; pages (i)-xv, (i) (blank), (17)-222, (2); half title and final (integral) leaf of ads present, half title, title and margins lightly browned; late 19th century polished blue morocco by Riviere, front joint slightly tender, backstrip with raised bands and gilt compartments, dulled, lettered direct in second, triple gilt fillet borders on sides, abrasion on upper side, double fillet on board edges, wide gilt dentelle decoration turn-ins, burgundy chalked endpapers, top edge gilt, overall excellent. Tal copy. Granniss p. 54; Tinker 1898; Wise p. 55/56.   Blackwell's B112-254 1996 £2,750.00

SHELLEY, PERCY BYSSHE 1792-1822   Prometheus Unbound. The Hague: De Zilverdistel Press, 1917. One of 125 copies; 9 3/4 x 7 inches; 143, (3) pages; printer's device on colophon, printed in red and black; original flexible vellum, spine title and press' emblem on front cover in gilt, 3 or 4 leaves with sprinkled foxing, vellum cover just little yellowed, but fine otherwise, text fresh and smooth, binding without any wear.   Phillip J. Pirages 33-525 1996 $1,250.00

SHELLEY, PERCY BYSSHE 1792-1822   Queen Mab. London: by W. Clark, 1821. 1st 'Published' edition, pirated by Clark, much to Shelley's chagrin; 8vo; pages 182, (ii), uncut in original brown boards, neatly rebacked, occasional marginal spotting. Forman 22; Granniss 19. This edition not in Wise.   Simon Finch   24-205   1996 £800.00

SHELLEY, PERCY BYSSHE 1792-1822   Relics of Shelley. London: Edward Moxon & Co., 1862. 1st edition; 8 pages ads dated July 1862; original cloth, purple half leather box and matching cloth wrapper, uncommon, especially in this very near fine condition.   Stephen Lupack   83-   1996 $475.00

SHELLEY, PERCY BYSSHE 1792-1822   The Revolt of Islam: a Poem. London: for C. and J. Ollier, 1818. 1st edition with this title, 2nd issue with correct date on titlepage; 8vo; pages xxxii, (ii), fly title, 270, (iv), errata, blank, with initial blank; uncut in contemporary boards, slightly soiled, corners bumped, new endpapers, front pastedown with portion cut away to reveal inscription of the Ross and William Booksellers Circulating Library, similar inscriptions on title and first pages of preface and text, somewhat spotted; very good. Forman 50; Grannis 44; Wise p. 49.   Simon Finch   24-206   1996 £1,150.00

SHELLEY, PERCY BYSSHE 1792-1822   Rosalind and Helen, a Modern Eclogue; with Other Poems. London: printed for C. and J. Ollier, 1819. 8vo; full brown crushed levant, gilt, spine and inner dentelles gilt, top edge gilt, by Tout; fine, outer edges uncut, complete with half title and 2 leaves of ads at end; Granniss 49.   Ximenes   108-322   1996 $1,750.00

SHELLEY, PERCY BYSSHE 1792-1822   Shelley Memorials: from Authentic Sources. London: Smith, Elder and Co., 1859. 2nd edition; 8vo; pages x, (2), 290, (i) errata, frontispiece; contemporary half vellum, spine gilt, red morocco labels, red sides, endpapers and edges; inscribed by Lady Shelley for Charles Kegan Paul   Simon Finch   24-209   1996 £150.00

SHELLEY, PERCY BYSSHE 1792-1822   Shelley Memorials from Authentic Sources. London: Henry S. King and Company, 1875. 3rd edition; 8vo; original dark green cloth, small damp mark on lower cover, nice copy. Granniss pp. 86-7; CBEL III 315.   Ximenes   108-323   1996 $500.00

SHELLEY, PERCY BYSSHE 1792-1822   Verse and Prose from the Manuscripts of Percy Bysshe Shelley. London: privately printed at the Curwen Press for distribution by... 1934. Limited to 100 copies; buckram covers, top edge gilt, other edges untrimmed, free endpapers partially and faintly browned, fine in nicked, torn, slightly chipped and nicked, partially and faintly darkened dust jacket.   Ulysses   39-530   1996 £125.00

SHELLEY, PERCY BYSSHE 1792-1822   The Works. London: Chas. Daly, 1836. Unauthorized edtiion; 16mo. in 8s; iv, 572 pages; frontispiece; original diamond grained green cloth, spine gilt, all edges gilt, neatly rebacked, original backstrip laid down; corners slightly worn, engravings little foxed; Good.   Robert Clark   38-257   1996 £110.00

SHELLEY, PERCY BYSSHE 1792-1822   Works in Verse and Prose. London: Reeves and Turner, 1876. 8vo; 8 volumes; portrait; finely bound in half blue levant morocco, mottled board sides, 5 raised bands, gilt tops, bound by Riviere, choice set.   Charles W. Traylen   117-194   1996 £850.00

SHELLEY, PERCY BYSSHE 1792-1822   Zastrozzi. Waltham St. Lawrence: Golden Cockerel Press, 1955. Limited edition, 93/140 copies (of an edition of 200); 8vo; printed on Japanese vellum, 8 full page wood engravings by Cecil Keeling; original quarter black morocco, backstrip lettered and decorated in gilt, marbled red and black boards, endpaper faintly foxed, top edge gilt, board slipcase; excellent. Cock-a-Hoop 201.   Blackwell's   B112-129   1996 £120.00

SHELTON, CAROLINE   King William Street, San Antonio, Texas. King William Assn., 1977. Limited edition, number 879 of 1000 copies, signed; water color paintings; 2 accordion style volumes, wrappers in linen slipcase.   Maggie Lambeth   30-466   1996 $375.00

SHELTON, CAROLYN   King William Street: 2 Folios. 1977. Limited edition, 1/1000 copies, signed; 2 folios of water colors by Sheldon, each 9 inches x 16 feet folded accordion style, linen slipcase.   W. M. Morrison   436-351   1996 $250.00

SHELTON, FREDERICK W.   The Trollopiad; or, Traveling Gentlemen in America. Providence: Shepard, Tingley & Co., 1837. 1st edition; 12mo; 151 pages; original figured cloth, faded; Howes S381. Rinderknecht 46750.   M & S Rare Books   60-232   1996 $225.00

SHENSTONE, WILLIAM 1714-1763   The Works in Verse and Prose of William Shenstone. London: J. Dodsley, 1777. 5th edition; 8vo; 3 volumes; original full calf with raised bands and morocco spine labels, former owner's personalized morocco labels at bottom of spines, library bookplate and blindstamp, else very good.   Chapel Hill   94-366   1996 $165.00

SHEPARD, GERALD F.   The Shepard Families of New England. New Haven Colony Historical Society, 1971-73. Royal 8vo; 3 volumes, pages 1750; buckram.   Howes Bookshop   265-2014   1996 £85.00

SHEPARD, LUCIUS   The Jaguar Hunter. U.K.: Kerosina, 1988. 1st British edition, one of 250 numbered copies, signed by author; very fine in dust jacket with slipcase.   Robert Gavora   61-143   1996 $110.00

SHEPARD, LUCIUS   Nantucket Slayrides. Nantucket: Eel Grass, 1989. 1st edition; one of 250 hardcover copies, numbered and signed by authors; pocket mas laid in; very fine in dust jacket.   Robert Gavora   61-149   1996 $100.00

SHEPARD, RUPERT   Passing Scene: Eighteen Images of Southern Africa. London: Stourton Press, 1966. One of 200 numbered copies, signed by artist; folio; brightly colored plates; orange buckram, two color pictorial design on upper cover, fine, laid in is a slip bearing signed autograph presentation inscription of Fairfax Hall.   Bertram Rota   272-456   1996 £90.00

SHEPARD, SAM   Hawk Moon. Los Angeles: Black Sparrow Press, 1973. 1st edition; one of 26 lettered copies, signed by author; 8vo; cloth backed boards; mint.   James S. Jaffe   34-615   1996 $175.00

SHEPHERD, THOMAS H.   Metropolitan Improvements. London: Jones & Co., 1830. 1st edition in book form; demy 4to; vi, 172, ii, (ii) pages, extra title, plan and 158 plates, complete with rare final leaf giving detailed binding instructions, spare label and notes of other Jones (1829) publications; publisher's half roan, with jade green paper label and engraved pictorial glazed boards, some wear, engraved title washed, some minor spotting and browning, one leaf slightly torn at margin, but very attractive, unusual and interesting copy in seldom seen original binding. Adams 154.   Ash Rare Books   Zenzybyr-83   1996 £295.00

SHEPHERD, W.   Systematic Education; or Elementary Instruction in the Various Departments of Literature and Science... London: Longman, Hurst, Rees, Orme and Brown, 1815. 8vo; 2 volumes, viii, 540; iv, 576 pages, 8 plates; original brown diced calf, black spine labels, edges marbled, outer hinges cracked, but holding soundly.   Kenneth Karmiole   1NS-97   1996 $275.00

SHEPHERD, W.   Systematic Education; or Elementary Instruction in Various Departments of Literature and Science... London: Longman, 1817. 2nd edition; 2 volumes; contemporary calf, gilt borders, recently rebacked, red label, very good.   Jarndyce   103-565   1996 £180.00

SHEPPARD, ERIC WILLIAM   Bedford Forrest, the Confederacy's Greatest Cavalryman. New York: 1930. 9 x 5.5. icnhes; 320 pages; cloth, bit worn with soiled half title, spine slightly discolored, remnants of dust jacket present.   John K. King   77-51   1996 $150.00

SHEPPARD, WILLIAM   The Touch-Stone of Common Assurances; or, a Plain and Familiar Treatise, Opening the Learning of the Common Assuraces, or Conveyances of the Kingdom. London: printed by W. Strahan, and M. Woodfall, for P. Uriel, E. Brooke... 1780. 4th edition; folio; contemporary calf, trifle rubbed, very slight cracking of joints; attractive copy.   Ximenes   108-324   1996 $500.00

SHERATON, THOMAS   The Cabinet Makers Dictionary. London: W. Smith, 1803. 1st edition; tall 8vo; pages viii, (8), 440, contains 81 of 88 plates called for; cased in dark blue linen, red leather label, gilt; scattered foxing but plates unaffected; generally good copy, scarce. Hartfield 48-11s   1996 $650.00

SHERBURNE, HENRY   The Oriental Philanthropist, or True Republican. Portsmouth: printed for Wm. Treadwell, 1800. 1st edition; 12mo; 215, (1) pages; full contemporary calf, leather label, front outer hinge cracking, very nice. Wright I 2382; Sabin 80332; Evans 38495.   M & S Rare Books   60-233   1996 $325.00

SHERIDAN'S and Henderson's Practical Method of Reading and Reciting English Poetry. London: E. Newbery and J. Scatchard, 1796. 1st edition; 180 x 105mm; pages (xii), 264; early full calf with spine compartmented and lettered in gilt, gilt dentelles, top hinge cracked, but firm, light wear to spine, else very good. Roscoe A537.   Marjorie James   19-164   1996 £195.00

SHERIDAN, RICHARD BRINSLEY BUTLER 1751-1816   The Critic or a Tragedy Rehearsed. London: printed for T. Becket, 1781. 1st edition; 1st issue; 8vo; engraved illustrated titlepage; half blue morocco, gilt, some rubbing, lacking half title and final leaf of ads, some browning and spotting to few pages; good. NCBEL 2.819; Rothschild 1846.   James Cummins 14-177 1996 $250.00

SHERIDAN, RICHARD BRINSLEY BUTLER 1751-1816   The Letters... Oxford: Clarendon Press, 1966. 8vo; 3 portrait frontispieces; pages lix,(i), 271, (1); (vi), 311, (1); (vi), 417, (1); original blue cloth, gilt lettered, excellent; J. D. Fleeman's copy with his signature in each volume. Blackwell's B112-255 1996 £150.00

SHERIDAN, RICHARD BRINSLEY BUTLER 1751-1816   The School for Scandal, a Comedy. Dublin: printed in the year 1781. One of 6 Irish piracies of 1781; 12mo; (4), 78, (2) pages; full brown morocco gilt, spine gilt, slight rubbing; small repair to margin of second leaf, not affecting text, but very good.   Ximenes 108-325 1996 $1,500.00

SHERIDAN, RICHARD BRINSLEY BUTLER 1751-1816   The School for Scandal, a Comedy. Oxford: Limited Editions Club, 1934. Number 904 from 1500 copies, signed by artist; illustrations by Rene Ben Sussan; full decorative paper covered boards with card liner, fine in publisher's slipcase.   Hermitage SP95-1037 1996 $125.00

SHERIDAN, RICHARD BRINSLEY BUTLER 1751-1816   The Works. London: John Murray, 1821. 1st collected edition; tall octavo; 2 volumes, pages xiii, 398; 408; original publisher's boards, spine renewed, uncut, name on half title, else handsome bright set. CBEL II 454.   Hartfield 48-A15 1996 $225.00

SHERIDAN, THOMAS   British Education: or, the Source of the Disorders of Great Britain. London: printed for R. and J. Dodsley, 1756. 1st edition; 8vo; pages (2), xl, 536, with half title; recent, if undistinguished, calf, very good to nice. Alston X221.   James Fenning 133-311 1996 £350.00

SHERIDAN, THOMAS   A Complete Dictionary of the English Language Both with Regard to Sound and Meaning... London: printed for Charles Dilly, 1789. 4to; half title; frontispiece (slightly stained in margins), contemporary tree calf, excellent repair to head and tail of spine. signature of Mary Woodward. Alston V315.   Jarndyce 103-215 1996 £280.00

SHERIDAN, THOMAS   A Course of Lectures on Elocution; Together with Two Dissertations on Language, and Some Other Tracts relative to Those Subjects. London: printed by W. Strahan, for A. Millar, R. and J. Dodsley, T. Davies... 1762. 1st edition; 4to; xviii, (10), 262 pages, complete with 10 page list of subscribers; occasional emphasis marks in pencil and other insignificant blemishes; later quarter calf, marbled boards, good copy.   John Drury 82-256 1996 £150.00

SHERIDAN, THOMAS   A Course of Lectures on Elocution; Together with Two Dissertations on Language; and Some Other Tracts Relative to those Subjects. London: printed for J. Dodsley, 1781. Uncut in 19th century half calf by Edmondson & Co., Skipton, brown label, very good. Alston VI 359.5.   Jarndyce 103-338 1996 £80.00

SHERIDAN, THOMAS   The Life of Dr. Jonathan Swift, Dean of St. Patrick's Dublin. London: Rivington, etc., 1787. 2nd edition; octavo; pages 488; frontispiece; full polished morocco, gilt fillets, new gilt on red leather label, marbled endpapers; wear to binding, front hinge weakening, text very good. CBEL II 593.   Hartfield 48-L80 1996 $225.00

SHERLOCK, W. P.   Drawing Book of Landscapes, Shipping and Animals, from Designs by Westall, Girtin, Smith, Marlow, Wheatly, Ibbotson, Hill, Anderson. London: by Jon. Watson, 7 Verse St., June 24th, 1819. oblong folio; No's. 1-3, each with 4 large etched plates; original brown sugar paper wrappers, grey paper backstrips and printed paper label on each upper cover, backstrips worn, one rear cover missing, otherwise in very good condition; scarce.   Ken Spelman 30-34 1996 £160.00

SHERLOCK, WILLIAM   The Notes of the Church, As Laid Down by Cardinal Bellarmin; Examined and Confuted. London: Richard Chiswell, 1688. 1st edition; 4to; (vi), 399, (iii), 69, (iii), 22, (xxxii) pages; 3 secondary titlepages, 4 pages ads at end; contemporary panelled calf, label; rubbed, extremities and joints little worn; good. Wing N1392, incorporating B3266, S3374; T3236.   Robert Clark 38-133 1996 £70.00

SHERMAN, WILLIAM TECUMSEH   Memoirs of Gen. William T. Sherman, Written by Himself... New York: Charles L. Webster, 1891. 4th edition; 2 volumes; original green cloth, shoulder strap insignia on spine; very good to near fine set. Union Bookshelf 83; Nevins II 8; Dornbusch II 2431.   McGowan Book Co. 65-80 1996 $150.00

SHERRINGTON, CHARLES   Man On His Nature. New York: 1941. 1st edition; 413 pages; original binding.   W. Bruce Fye 71-1917 1996 $100.00

SHERRINGTON, CHARLES   Selected Writings of Sir Charles Sherrington. New York: 1940. 1st American edition; 532 pages; original binding, scarce.   W. Bruce Fye 71-1918 1996 $250.00

SHERRINGTON, CHARLES   Selected Writings. New York: 1940. 1st edition; 4to; 532 pages; 85 text illustrations; frontispiece; cloth, spine rubbed.   Argosy 810-440 1996 $150.00

SHERWELL, JOHN W.   A Descriptive and Historical Account of the Guild of Saddlers of the City of London. London: printed...for private circulation, 1889. 8vo; xxiv, 240 pages, text printed with red ruled borders, 16 plates, text printed within red ruled borders, contemporary full red morocco, gilt panelled sides and spine, with arms of the Guild on the front cover, gilt dentelles, gilt edges, slightly rubbed, some very minor foxing in places. Presentation copy to Charles Horsey.   Thomas Thorp 489-279 1996 £150.00

SHERWOOD, MARGARET   Undercurrents of Influence in English Romantic Poetry. Cambridge: Harvard University Press, 1934. 1st edition; original binding, bottom corners slightly bumped, free endpapers partially browned, upper cover very slightly soiled, very good; with pencilled ownership signature of Frederick Pottle.   Ulysses 39-714 1996 £85.00

SHERWOOD, MARY MARTHA BUTT 1775-1851   The Lady of the Manor. London: F. Houlston, 1825. 2nd edition; 8vo; 7 volumes; 5 frontispieces; half calf, marbled boards, spines compartmented and lettered in gilt, covers rubbed, endpapers browned; otherwise very good. Marjorie James 19-198 1996 £150.00

SHERWOOD, MARY MARTHA BUTT 1775-1851   The Life of Mrs. Sherwood, Chiefly Autobiographical. London: Darton & Co., 1857. 1st edition; thick 8vo; pages (ix), 573; frontispiece, titlepage engraving; half calf with compartmented spine, heavily decorated in gilt, all edges gilt; minor spotting to preliminary pages, very light wear to covers, else very good.   Marjorie James 19-197 1996 £125.00

SHERWOOD, ROBERT   The Petrified Forest. New York: Scribners, 1935. 1st edition; fine in attractive, very good or better price clipped dust jacket, with couple of negligible nicks and little rubbing at extremities.   Between the Covers 42-394 1996 $250.00

SHEW, JOEL   Hydropathy; or, the Water-Cure; Its Principles, Modes of Treatment &c. New York: 1845. Small 8vo; frontispiece, 6 vignettes; original embossed cloth.   Argosy 810-441 1996 $125.00

SHEW, M. L., MRS.   Water-Cure for Ladies: a Popular Work on the Health, Diet and Regimen of Females and Children, and the Prevention and Cure of Diseases... New York: Wiley and Putnam, 1844. 1st edition; 8vo; 156 pages; 2 full page lithographs by Endicott; maroon cloth, heavily stained, spine faded, printed paper label, rubbed from spine, minor occasional foxing; very nice internally. Not in Lowenstein.   Blue Mountain SP95-126 1996 $125.00

SHIELDS, G. O.   The Big Game of North America. London: 1890. Many plates and text illustrations; 581 pages; apart from some discoloration to the ad leaves at the rear, very nice in original pictorial gilt cloth, new endpapers;   David Grayling J95Biggame-443 1996 £120.00

SHILLABER, BENJAMIN   Knitting-Work: a Web of Many Textures, Wrought by Ruth Partington. Boston: Brown, etc., 1859. 1st edition; 8vo; frontispiece, 7 plates; brown cloth, binding A, minor wear, small loss of cloth on rear cover, about very good; owner inscription dated Sept. 25, two days after Library of Congress copy was deposited.   Charles Agvent 4-1008 1996 $150.00

SHILLABER, BENJAMIN   Knitting-Work: a Web of Many Textures Wrought by Ruth Partington. Boston: Brown, 1859. 1st edition; blue cloth, binding A, minor wear to spine tips, rear cover with small bruise, about very good. Bookplate of Lt. Col. Walter Merriam Pratt.   Charles Agvent 4-1009 1996 $125.00

SHILLABER, BENJAMIN   Life and Sayings of Mrs. Partington and Others of the Family. New York: J. C. Derby; Boston: Phillips, Sampson & Co.; Cincinnati: H. W. Derby, 1854. 1st edition; 8vo; illustrations; original brown cloth, covers stamped in blind, spine in gilt, light rubbing, mostly of corners, some spotting and browning, but attractive copy. Wright 2.2208.   James Cummins 14-178 1996 $200.00

SHILLABER, BENJAMIN   Life and Sayings of Mrs. Partington. New York: Derby, 1854. 1st edition; 8 plates and text engravings, brown cloth; bit worn, some marginal dampstaining; good+. BAL17540: State 1, Imprint A; Wright li 2208.   Charles Agvent 4-1010 1996 $125.00

SHILLABER, BENJAMIN   Partingtonian Patchwork. Boston: Lee and Shepard, 1873. 2nd edition; 8vo; frontispiece, 7 plates; decorated blue cloth, light wear to spine tips, front hinge partly cracked; inserted loosely is a carte-de-visite of the author's daughter, to whom he refers in the letter. Laid down on pastedown and f.f.e.p. is an ALS from author to inventor Samuel Morse. BAL 17578.   Charles Agvent 4-1011 1996 $150.00

SHILLIBEER, JOHN   A Narrative of the Briton's Voyage, to Pitcairn's Island. Taunton: printed for the author by J. W. Marriott and pub. by Law & Whittaker, 1817. 1st edition; 8vo; with final leaf of errata, 12 etched plates; original grey board, printed paper label, spine rather worn, front cover detached, half morocco folding case; Sabin 80484; Hill p. 274; Ferguson 696; Borba de Moraes p. 796.   Ximenes 109-264 1996 $2,750.00

SHILLITO, CHARLES   The Country Book-Club. A Poem. London: for the author, 1788. 1st edition; 4to; in half sheets, pages (3)-39, etched title vignette by T. Rowlandson after James Dunthorne, bound without half title; modern wrappers, some spotting, few minor paper flaws at blank margins; very good; inscribed "Hampshire Library Society from J.P.R." Jackson p. 138.   Simon Finch 24-210 1996 £575.00

SHILOH BATTLEFIELD COMMISSION   Illinois at Shiloh. Chicago: printed by M. A. Donohue & Co., 1905? 1st edition; 9 1/4 x 6 1/2 inches; 187 pages; 2 folding maps in pocket, with army positions marked in red and blue, 12 plates and few smaller illustrations in text, printed slip laid in "Compliments of Capt. Timothy Slatery, commissioner Shiloh Battlefield". original cloth, cloth slightly soiled, but fine copy otherwise.   Phillip J. Pirages 33-132 1996 $175.00

SHINWELL, EMANUEL   Conflict Without Malice. London: Oldhams Press Ltd., 1955. 1st edition; 21 pages of black and white photos; original binding, edges and free endpapers browned, spine faded, head and tail of spine and corners bumped, covers slightly marked, cover edges rubbed; good; Presentation copy from author, inscribed. Ulysses 39-533 1996 £55.00

SHINWELL, EMANUEL   Lead with the Left. London: Cassell Ltd., 1981. 1st edition; numerous black and white photos; original binding, top edge slightly dusty, head and tail of spine slightly bumped, edges slightly browned and soiled, very good in nicked, marked and slightly torn, creased and dusty dust jacket slightly browned at edges; presentation copy inscribed by author.   Ulysses 39-534 1996 £75.00

SHINWELL, EMANUEL   Shinwell Talking - a Conversational Biography to Celebrate His Hundredth Birthday. London: Quiller Press, 1984. 1st edition; original binding, top edge slightly dusty, corners slightly bumped, very good in slightly creased marked and dusty dust jacket faded at spine; presentation copy inscribed by author.   Ulysses 39-535 1996 £65.00

THE SHIP'S Bell. Baltimore: privately printed for Van-Lear Black, 1927. One of 100 numbered copies, signed by Black; folio; printed in black and red on handmade paper; white cloth, gilt, faint stain across centre of spine, otherwise very nice.   Bertram Rota 272-99 1996 £65.00

SHIPP, JOHN   the Military Bijou; or the Contents of a Soldier's Knapsack; Being the Gleanings of Thirty-Three Years' Active Service. London: published by Whittaker, Treacher and Co., 1831. 1st edition; 12mo; 2 volumes, 4 pages ads, rebound in contemporary style boards, one spine lettered upside down; uncommon.   James Burmester 29-125 1996 £75.00

SHIRAS, GEORGE   Hunting Wild Life with Camera and Flashlight. U.S.A.: 1936. Imperial 8vo; 2 volumes; numerous photos; original buckram; near fine.   David A.H. Grayling MY95Orn-433 1996 £60.00

SHIRLEY, JAMES   Six New Plays, viz. The Brothers; The Sisters; The Doubtful Heir; The Imposture; The Cardinal; The Court Secret. London: printed for Humphrey Robinson and Humphrey Moseley, 1652-53. 1st edition of this collection; 8vo; 6 volumes; similarly bound in 19th century dark green morocco backed marbled and mottled boards, rubbed, some wear to heads of spines, marginal browning, some browning and offsetting; W&M 1134.   James Cummins 14-179 1996 $250.00

SHIRLEY, W. W.   Royal and Historical Letters Illustrative of the Reign of Henry III 1216-1272. London: 1862-66. 8vo; 2 folding facsimiles; pages 1146; original cloth.   Howes Bookshop 265-1574 1996 £50.00

SHIROKOGOROFF, S. M.   Psychomental Complex of the Tungus. London: Kegan Paul, Trench, Trubner, & Co., Ltd., 1935. Folio; xvi, 470 pages; several text diagrams and tables; tan cloth stamped in brown, library pocket at rear removed.   Kenneth Karmiole 1NS-17 1996 $150.00

SHOBERL, FREDERIC 1775-1853   The World in Miniature. London: Printed for R. Ackermann, n.d. 1822. 12mo; 6 volumes; 103 colored plates; contemporary green half calf, marbled boards, raised bands, leather labels; binding rubbed, spine labels of volume 6 chipped, otherwise nice set, very attractive colored plates. Tooley 515.   David Mason 71-93 1996 $680.00

SHOBERL, FREDERIC 1775-1853   The World in Miniature: Austria. London: R. Ackermann, 1823. 12mo; 2 volumes; 32 charming hand colored plates; contemporary full tan calf, gilt decorated spine, worn at joints and spine extremities. Colas 2728; Abbey Travel 6.   Marilyn Braiterman 15-189 1996 $250.00

SHOBERL, FREDERIC 1775-1853   The World in Miniature: Illryia and Dalmatia. London: R. Ackermann, c. 1821. 12mo; 2 volumes; xviii, 144; ii, 166 + 18 page publisher's catalog at end; publisher's blue boards (worn, volume 1 lacks backstrip, spin of volume 2 defective at head and foot, few leaves detached or shaky, little finger soiling in text.   Thomas Thorp 489-280 1996 £60.00

SHOCK, NATHAN   A Classified Bibliography of Gerontology and Geriatrics. Stanford: 1951. 1st edition; 599 pages; original binding, dust jacket.   W. Bruce Fye 71-1921 1996 $125.00

SHONE, RICHARD   Bloomsbury Portraits. London: Phaidon, 1976. 1st edition; many illustrations; near fine in dust jacket.   Virgo Books 48-34 1996 £50.00

SHOOK, EDWIN M.   Mound E-III-3, Kaminaljuyu, Guatemala. Washington: Carnegie Inst. 1952. 4to; pages 35-127, 81 figures; original printed wrappers.   Archaeologia Luxor-4888 1996 $150.00

SHOOK, EDWIN M.   Tikal Reports Numbers 1-11 in 3 Parts. Philadelphia: University Museum, 1958-61. Small 4to; 2 volumes of text and 1 volume of maps loose in portfolio; 344 pages, 99 figures; iv, 26 pages, 1 figure, 3 tables, 9 large folding maps loose in portfolio; wrappers. Ink stamps of Bennyhoff.   Archaeologia Luxor-4890 1996 $125.00

SHORT, L.   Woodpeckers of the World. Delaware: 1982. Royal 8vo; 694 pages, 101 colored paltes by G. Sandstrom; hardbound.   Wheldon & Wesley 207-860 1996 £70.00

SHORT, THOMAS   The Natural, Experimental and Medicinal History of the Mineral Waters of Derbyshire, Lincolnshire and Yorkshire... (with) An Essay Towards a Natural, Experimental and Medicinal History of the Principle Mineral Waters of Cumberland, Northumberland... London: ptd. for the author & sold by F. Gayles/Sheffield: ptd. for the author ..1734/40. 1st editions; 4to; 2 volumes in one; five engraved plates; contemporary mottled calf, slight rubbing, fine. NLM p. 417.   Ximenes 108-326 1996 $900.00

A SHORT-HAND Dictionary, To Which is Prefixed All the Rules or Principles of that Useful and Pleasing Art... London: engraved for the author & sold by Mr. Dodsley, Mr. Nourse, &c. 1777? 16mo; engraved plates; uncut as issued, with some dusting and tears in fore-edges of few leaves; recently rebound in plain half calf. Alston VIII 254. Jarndyce 103-111 1996 £220.00

SHORTEN, MONICA   Squirrels. London: 1954. illustrations; dust jacket, fore-edges and prelims have some foxing, dust jacket also lightly frayed. David A.H. Grayling MY95Orn-513 1996 £50.00

SHORTRIDGE, G. C.   The Mammals of South West Africa. 1934. 4to; 2 volumes; 12 maps, 35 plates; cloth, gilt, occasional slight foxing, spines faded.   John Henly 27-44 1996 £68.00

SHORTRIDGE, G. C.   The Mammals of South-West Africa, A Biological Account. London: 1934. Royal 8vo; 2 volumes; numerous illustrations and maps; cloth, covers spotted.   Wheldon & Wesley 207-606 1996 £80.00

SHOW Window Backgrounds. London: Blandford Press, 1934. Reprinted; oblong octavo; 96 pages, new illustrations, tan linen; nice.   Bromer Booksellers 90-224 1996 $250.00

SHOWER, JOHN   Practical Reflections on the Late Earthquakes in Jamaica, England, Sicily, Malta &c. Anno 1692. London: printed for John Salusbury...and Abraham Chandler, 1693. 1st edition; 8vo; titlepage printed within double ruled border, final blank present, pages xvi, 206, (2); modern dark brown stained calf, backstrip with raised bands between gilt rules and pointille rolls, red labels in second and third compartments, gilt flower in centre of remainder, narrow blind roll and fillet border on sides, gilt lettered on turn-in at tail of rear cover "Ex Libris Brent Gration-Maxfield", excellent. Sabin 80740; Wing S3680. Blackwell's B112-256 1996 £650.00

SHULMAN, NEIL   Finally....I'm a Doctor. New York: Scribner's, 1976. 1st edition; fine in fine dust jacket and signed by Shulman.   Ken Lopez 74-187 1996 $250.00

SHULMAN, NEIL   What Dead Again? Baton Rouge: Legacy, 1979. 1st edition; fine in fine dust jacket, signed by author.   Ken Lopez 74-189 1996 $250.00

SHUTE, NEVIL   Most Secret. London: William Heinemann Ltd., 1945. 1st edition; original binding, top edge dusty and slightly soiled, tail of spine slightly bumped, very good in nicked and slightly creased, soiled and frayed dust jacket slightly darkened at spine and edges.   Ulysses 39-536 1996 £75.00

SIBLEY, C. G.   Distribution and Taxonomy of Birds of the World. London: 1991-93. Royal 8vo; 2 volumes, 1136 pages, 24 maps and supplement 112 pages; cloth and limp boards.   Wheldon & Wesley 207-861 1996 £100.00

SIBSON, FRANCIS   Medical Anatomy. London: 1869. 1st edition; folio; text illustrations, 21 hand colored lithographed plates; minor soiling and slight creases, but sound copy; half calf, rebacked, by J. Edmond of Aberdeen, with his ticket, flyleaves creased.   Maggs Bros. Ltd. 1190-507 1996 £1,400.00

SICHEL, JULES   Spectacles: Their Uses and Abuses in Long and Short Sightedness; and the Pathological Conditions Resulting from their Irrational Employment. Boston: 1850. 8vo; cloth; spine chipped, foxed. Argosy 810-444 1996 $175.00

SICK, H.   Birds in Brazil, a Natural History. Princeton: 1993. Royal 8vo; 46 colored plates, 826 pages, 10 plain plates, 327 text figures; cloth.   Wheldon & Wesley 207-862 1996 £90.00

SIDGWICK, HENRY   The Elements of Politics. London: Macmillan and Co., 1891. 1st edition; 8vo; xxxii, 632 pages, complete with errata slip, 55 page publisher's list (dated may 1891), few pencilled annotations; original cloth, gilt, very good.   John Drury 82-257 1996 £95.00

SIDIS, BORIS   Psychopathological Researches: Studies in Mental Dissociation. New York: G. E. Stechert & Co., 1902. 1st edition; tall 8vo; (xxii), (330) pages; 10 folding plates, each with explantory leaf; bevelled ochre buckram, front flyleaf creased, else very good. Crabtree 1988 #1513.   John Gach 150-433 1996 $125.00

SIDNEY, ALGERNON   Discourses Concerning Government. London: printed by J. Darby in Bartholomew-Close, 1704. 2nd edition; modern quarter calf, little dusty, generally good and usable.   Meyer Boswell SL25-199 1996 $450.00

SIDNEY, JOHN APSLEY   A Scheme For Improving Small Sums of Money... Rochester: printed by W. Epps, Troy-Town, 1801. 1st and probably only edition; 8vo; (ii), 45, (1) pages, complete with half title; original boards, gilt morocco lettering on upper cover, fine; from the library of the Rt. Hon. the Earl of Granard at Castle Forbes. Goldsmiths 18292; Not in Kress, Black, Williams, NUC or BLC.   John Drury 82-258 1996 £250.00

SIDNEY, PHILIP 1554-1586   The Countess of Pembroke's Arcadia. London: for George Calvert, 1674. 13th edition; folio; (32), 624, (26) pages; portrait; full brown polished calf, covers panelled, spine richly gilt in compartments, dentelles gilt, by Riviere; some page numbers cropped, front hinge just beginning to crack, else fine, Dartrey bookplate. Wing S3770.   Joseph J. Felcone 64-38 1996 $450.00

SIDNEY, PHILIP 1554-1586   The Lad Philisides: Being a Selection of Songs, Pastoral Eclogues & Elegies from the Countess of Pembroke's Arcadia. Llandogo, nr Monmouth: Old Stile Press, 1988. Limited to 251 copies, signed by artist; this being one of only 26 special copies which include a portfolio of proofs of each of the wood engravings, plus one additional engraving that does not appear in the book; tall 8vo; 54 pages; original quarter red morocco, red and blue designed boards, top edge gilt, others uncut, portfolio being of identical size and materials, preserved in publisher's cloth slipcase; mint.   Thomas Thorp 489-281 1996 £135.00

SIDNEY, RICHARD CHASE   A Brief Memoir of the Life of...Algernon Sidney, with a short Account of His Trial etc. London: James Bohn 12, King William St., 1835. Brown cloth, quite worn, joints repaired, usable only.   Meyer Boswell SL26-214 1996 $125.00

SIEGL, HELEN   A Little Bestiary. A Portfolio of Eight Wood Blocks Cut by Helen Siegl. Philadelphia: Print Club, 1961. 1st edition; limited to 200 numbered copies, printed by Claire Van Vliet, whose wood engraving of Janus decorates the colophon page; this copy no. 1, signed by Siegl; 4to; loose sheets in portfolio, some discoloration to paper as usual, otherwise fine.   James S. Jaffe 34-297 1996 $450.00

SIEMIENOWICZ, CASIMIR   Artis Magnae Artilleriae. Amsterdam: J. Jansoon, 1650. 1st edition; tall 4to; (16), 284, (4) pages, complete with half title, engraved titlepage, 22 full page copperplate engravings, 1 double page depicting 229 figures; modern panelled calf, morocco spine label, occasional marginal notes in contemporary hand, extreme outer edges of first four leaves strengthened, some marginal browning, particularly to the last few leaves; with shelfmark and engraved armorial bookplate of the Hirsel Library; very good copy. Graesse VI 401; Partington Hist. of Greek fire & Gunpowder p. 168.   Edwin V. Glaser 121-286 1996 $3,800.00

SIEVWRIGHT, WILLIAM   Historical Sketch of the Perth Cricket Club (The Premier Club of Scotland) from Its Origin in 1826-27 till 1879. London: James Barlas, 1880. 1st edition; original binding, head and tail of spine and corners bumped and rubbed, covers marked and rubbed, lower cover soiled, prelims, edges and endpapers slightly spotted, pastedowns slightly bubbled, free endpapers slightly marked, good. Inscription.   Ulysses 39-127 1996 £95.00

SIGERIST, HENRY   The Great Doctors. New York: 1933. 1st English translation; 436 pages; original binding. GM 6735.   W. Bruce Fye 71-1943 1996 $100.00

SIGONIO, CARLO   Caroli Sigonii de Antiquo Iure Civium Romanorum Libri Duo. (with) Orationes Caroli Sigonii. Paris: apud Allardum Iulianum, 1573/73. 8vo; 2 works in one; 17th century calf, gilt, spine gilt, bit worn, lacks label; very good, uncommon. 2 copies in NUC; Adams S1098 (1st title only).   Ximenes 109-265 1996 $300.00

SIGSBY, WILLIAM   Life and Adventures of Timothy Murphy...from the Commencement of the Revolution. Schoharie: W. H. Gallup, Jan. 1839. 1st edition; 32 pages; titlepage has been trimmed; overall tall copy. Howes S453; Littel Sale 939; Jones 226.   Michael D. Heaston 23-297 1996 $2,500.00

SILFORD, WILLIAM   The Court Register and Statesman's Remembrancer... London: ptd. for G. Robinson, J. Walter, R. Faulder, J. Nichols, and J. Sewell 1782. 8vo; both cancellans and cancellandum for pp.3 17-318 are present in this copy; contemporary sprinkled calf, rubbed, hinges cracked, lacks label.   Anthony W. Laywood 108-122 1996 £50.00

SILICATE PAINT CO.   A Handbook on Paint. London: Silicate Paint Co.-J. B. Orr & Co. Ltd., 1939. 1st edition; 5 full color illustrations; boards; covers slightly marked, rubby and dusty, head and tail of spine and corners slightly bumped, edges and endpapers spotted, very good. Ulysses 39-51 1996 £250.00

SILIUS ITALICUS, GAIUS   De Bello Punico Secundo XVII Libri Nuper Diligentissime Castigati. Venice: In Aedibvs Aldi, et Andreae Auslani Soceri (Andrea Torresano), July 1523. 1st Aldine edition; 8vo; 212 leaves; Italic Aldine devices on first and last leaves, blank portion of titlepage with old repair, otherwise really clean and tight; attractive half calf, gilt, marbled boards; engraved armorial Ex-libris of R. E. Duncombe Shafto; Dibdin II 405; Renouard 98.6. Adams S1134; UCLA II/194. Brunet V383. Family Album Tillers-571 1996 $1,250.00

SILIUS ITALICUS, GAIUS   De Bello Punico Libri Septemdecim... Paris: Colines, 1531. 8vo; title with device, ff. 2-223, (repair with text loss to f. 7), red stained edges; brown morocco, borders ruled in blind, gilt tooling and the Apollo and Pegasus plaquette added by Villa in the late 19th century; spine little worn, few wormholes; a fake 'Canevari' binding by Vittorio Villa.   Marlborough 160-78 1996 £1,500.00

SILKO, LESLIE MARMON　　Almanac of the Dead. New York: Viking, 1977. 1st edition; 262 pages; very good+ in dust jacket with usual sun faded spine.　Ken Sanders　8-364　1996 $300.00

SILKO, LESLIE MARMON　　Laguna Woman. Greenfield Center: Greenfield Reivew Press, 1974. 1st edition; 35 pages; original wrappers, light stain on back cover, but does not detract; near fine.　Ken Sanders　8-365　1996 $1,500.00

SILKO, LESLIE MARMON　　Storyteller. New York: Seaver Books, 1981. 1st edition; 277 pages; 3 marks at bottom edge, near fine in dust jacket. Ken Sanders　8-366　1996 $250.00

SILKO, LESLIE MARMON　　Storyteller. New York: Seaver, 1981. 1st edition; cloth; uncommon edition; fine in fine dust jacket, signed by author.　Thomas Dorn　9-227　1996 $200.00

SILKO, LESLIE MARMON　　Storyteller. New York: 1981. 1st edition; near fine, in near fine dust jacket.　Polyanthos　22-793　1996 $125.00

SILKO, LESLIE MARON　　Laguna Woman. Greenfield Center: Greenfield Review, 1974. 1st edition; stapled wrappers; fine, elusive first book. Ken Lopez　74-408　1996 $1,500.00

SILLAR, DAVID　　Poems. Kilmarnock: by John Wilson, 1789. 1st edition; 8vo; 247 pages; printed on blueish paper; fine binding of full green straight grain morocco, sides with triple gilt rules, spine lettered in gilt, double gilt rules, purple coated endpapers, top edge gilt, others uncut; protected in modern green morocco backed folding case; the Hoe copy with Robert Hoe's leather booklabel, later label of Herschel V. Jones. Egerer 14; Johnson Provincial Poetry 832.　Simon Finch　24-211 1996 £1,000.00

SILLAR, DAVID　　Poems. Kilmarnock: printed by John Wilson, 1789. 1st edition; 8vo; pages (i)-viii, (9)-247; titlepage and prelim leaves lightly browned, title within typographic border; early 20th century half tan calf by Bayntun, joints rubbed, short splits at head, very firm, gilt milled low bands, green morocco label in second compartment, remainder gilt panelled, fawn glazed cotton boards, marbled endpapers, top edge gilt, generally excellent; bookplates of Robert Woods Bliss and Mildred Bliss. Egerer 14; ECSB 400; Johnson, Provincial Poetry 832.　Blackwell's B112-257　1996 £350.00

SILLIMAN, BENJAMIN　　Remarks Made On a Short Tour Between Hartford and Quebec, in the Autumn of 1819. New Haven: S. Converse, 1824. 2nd edition; 12mo; 444 pages; added engraved title, 9 engraved plates, each with tissue guard; old calf, neatly rebacked. Howes S459. Kenneth Karmiole　1NS-15　1996 $125.00

SILVA, ERCOLE　　Dell'Arte Dei Giardini Inglesi. Milan: Genio Typografico, 1801. 4to; 36 handsome copper engravings; contemporary half calf, gilt Roman style banded spine, green calf label, other compartments with gilt urn device; fine. Berlin Cat. 3498.　Marilyn Braiterman　15-190　1996 $2,500.00

SILVER CITY MINING AND MILLING CO.　　Silver City Mining and Milling Company. Organized January 25th, 1882. New York: Mining Record Press, 1882. 1st edition; 14 pages; folding map; original printed wrappers, splitting neatly repaired, very good, laid in half morocco folding slipcase.　Michael D. Heaston　23-274　1996 $750.00

SILVER, GEORGE　　A Practical Treatise on the Prevention and Cure of Smoky Chimneys. Glasgow: Blackie & Son, 1836. 1st edition; 12mo; 114 pages; original blue cloth with paper cover label, light soiling to cover, else very good; rare.　Chapel Hill　94-173　1996 $150.00

SILVERBERG, ROBERT　　Hawksbill Station. Garden City: Doubleday, 1968. 1st edition; fine in dust jacket.　Robert Gavora　61-157　1996 $125.00

SILVERBERG, ROBERT　　Revolt on Alpha C. Crowell, 1955. 1st edition; fine in very good dust jacket with chip at head of dust jacket spine, author's first book; inscribed by author.　Aronovitz　57-1044　1996 $125.00

SILVERBERG, ROBERT　　Revolt on Alpha C. New York: Crowell, 1955. 1st edition; author's first book; signed, one corner bumped, else near fine in price clipped dust jacket with wear and bit of loss to spine panel ends.　Robert Gavora　61-161　1996 $125.00

SILVERSMITH, JULIUS　　The Miner's Companion and Guide... San Francisco: Pub. by J. Silversmith, "Mining and Scientific Press" Office, 1861. 1st edition; 232, (22) pages, illustrations, folding plate; original printed boards, neatly rebacked in calf, some wear, very good. Cowan p 431. Greenwood Calif. Imprints 1557.　Michael D. Heaston　23-76　199 $550.00

SIMAK, CLIFFORD　　City. Gnome Press, 1952. 1st edition; fine in like dust jacket with some slight dust soiling to rear dust jacket panel. Aronovitz　57-1056　1996 $395.00

SIMAK, CLIFFORD　　Destiny Doll. Putnam, 1971. 1st edition; review copy with accompanying review slip laid in; as new in dust jacket. Aronovitz　57-1059　1996 $150.00

SIMAK, CLIFFORD　　They Walked Like Men. New York: Doubleday, 1962. 1st edition; review copy with accompanying review slip laid in; fine in dust jacket, uncommon.　Aronovitz　57-1058　1996 $175.00

SIMAK, CLIFFORD　　Why Call Them Back from Heaven? Garden City: Doubleday, 1967. 1st edition; fine in dust jacket with slight browning to edges and spine panel.　Robert Gavora　61-166　1996 $125.00

SIMAK, CLIFFORD　　The Worlds of Clifford Simak. S&S, 1960. 1st edition; fine in dust jacket, quite scarce thus.　Aronovitz　57-1057 1996 $110.00

SIMEONI, GABRIELE　　Epitome de l'Origine et Svccession de la Dvche de Ferrare. Paris: Corrozet, 1553. 8vo; woodcut portrait of Simeoni on titlepage, gilt calf, bookpate of Collection Lucien d'Ursin. STC French 402 Rostenberg & Stern　150-98　1996 $1,200.00

SIMIC, CHARLES　　Biography and a Lament Poems 1961-1967. Hartford: Bartholomew's Cobble, 1976. 1st edition; one of 50 numbered copies (from a total of 250), signed by author; pictorial wrappers; fine. Captain's Bookshelf　38-201　1996 $125.00

SIMIC, CHARLES　　White. London: New Rivers Press, 1972. 1st editior one of 30 numbered copies, from a total of 300 cloth bound, numbered and signed by Simic; very fine in dust jacket.　Captain's Bookshelf 38-200　1996 $150.00

SIMINGTON, ROBERT C.　　The Civil Survey, AD 1654-56, County of Tipperary. 1931/34. 8vo; 2 volumes; cloth, cover of volume 1 marked, else very good.　C. P. Hyland　216-789　1996 £100.00

SIMMONS, C. F.　　Home, Sweet Home. A Home in Sunny South Texa for a Song. San Antonio: 1906. 1st edition; 48 pages; illustrations; original printed wrappers; fine.　Michael D. Heaston　23-323　1996 $300.00

SIMMONS, DAN　　Carrion Comfort. Arlington Heights: Dark Harvest, 1989. 1st edition; one of 450 numbered copies signed by author and artist, Kathleen McNeil Sherman; very fine in dust jacket with slipcase. Robert Gavora　61-167　1996 $275.00

SIMMONS, DAN　　Carrion Comfort. Arlington Heights: Dark Harvest, 1989. 1st edition; signed; very fine in dust jacket.　Robert Gavora 61-168　1996 $125.00

SIMMONS, DAN　　Carrion Comfort. Arlington Heights: Dark Harvest, 1989. 1st edition; very fine in dust jacket.　Robert Gavora　61-169 1996 $100.00

SIMMONS, DAN　　Children of the Night. Northridge: Lord John, 1992. 1st edition; one of 500 numbered copies, signed by author; very fine, issued without dust jacket, with slipcase.　Robert Gavora　61-170 1996 $175.00

SIMMONS, DAN　　The Hollow Man. Bantam, 1992. Uncorrected proof in manuscript state; white wrappers; fine, with proof dust jacket. Aronovitz　57-1065　1996 $100.00

SIMMONS, DAN　　Hyperion. New York: Doubleday, 1989. 1st edition; signed, very fine in dust jacket.　Robert Gavora　61-175　1996 $180.0

SIMMONS, DAN   Phases of Gravity. London: Headline, 1990. 1st hardcover edition, one of 250 numbered copies, signed by author; full leather, very fine, issued without dust jacket, slipcase.   Robert Gavora 61-177 1996 $190.00

SIMMONS, DAN   Prayers to Broken Stones. Arlington Heights: Dark Harvest, 1990. 1st edition; one of 550 numbered copies, signed by author and artist; illustrations by Val Lindahm and Ron Lindahm; very fine in dust jacket with slipcase.   Robert Gavora 61-179 1996 $125.00

SIMMONS, DAN   Song of Kali. Bluejay, 1985. 1st edition; author's first book; fine; signed by author; publisher Jim Frenkel's copy with business card laid in.   Aronovitz 57-1062 1996 $425.00

SIMMONS, DAN   Song of Kali. New York: Bluejay Books, 1985. 1st edition; author's first book; fine in fine dust jacket.   Bud Schweska 12-692 1996 $175.00

SIMMONS, JOHN   An Account of a Simple, Easy and Effectual Method for Preserving His Majesty's Navy, From Its Present Great Decays. London: printed in the year, 1774. 4to; (2), ii, 9, (1) pages; original marbled wrappers, very nice.   C. R. Johnson 37-30 1996 £250.00

SIMMONS, NOAH   Heroes and Heroines of the Fort Dearborn Massacre. Lawrence: Journal Publishing Co., 1896. 1st edition; 8vo; 75 pages, 2 plates; original printed wrappers; Howes S465.   M & S Rare Books 60-408 1996 $175.00

SIMMONS, SAMUEL   Elements of Anatomy and the Animal Economy. London: Willie, 1775. 1st edition; 8vo; xii, 396 pages, errata leaf; 3 engraved plates; old quarter calf, worn, with weak joints, early marginal annotations in ink with occasional light penciling.   James Tait Goodrich K40-269 1996 $125.00

SIMMS, WILLIAM GILMORE 1806-1870   The Life of Nathanael Greene, Major-General in the Army of the Revolution. New York: George F. Cooledge & Brother, 1849. 1st edition; 393 pages; black cloth, gilt lettering and design on spine, front hinge little loose, light chipping to extremities, overall very nice. BAL 18118, printing A.   Blue River Books 9-14 1996 $175.00

SIMMS, WILLIAM GILMORE 1806-1870   The Wigwam and the Cabin. First (and Second) Series. New York: Wiley and Putnam, 1845. 1st edition; 8vo; 2 parts in one volume; contemporary half black morocco, marbled boards, quite rubbed, discoloring from leather, short crack at top of upper joint, some browning and staining of endpapers, else light browning, half titles without ad leaves which determine printings, partial image of an ad leaf offset on blank at front; signatures of Rebecca Berger and E. E. Knapp on endpapers. BAL 18093, 18094; Barzun & Taylor Cat. of Crime 3461.   James Cummins 14-181 1996 $750.00

SIMMS, WILLIAM GILMORE 1806-1870   The Wigwam and the Cabin. First Series. New York: Wiley & Putnam, 1845. 1st edition; 12mo; half leather, rubbed and worn at ends, cloth, very good, uncommon. BAL 18093; Salley p. 68.   Freedom Bookshop 14-36 1996 $325.00

SIMON, JOHN   English Sanitary Institutions, Reviewed In Their Course of Development and In Some of Their Political and Social Relations. London: 1897. 2nd edition; 516 pages; original binding. GM 1650.   W. Bruce Fye 71-1968 1996 $275.00

SIMON, JOHN   General Pathology as Conducive to the Establishment of Rational principles for the Diagnosis and Treatment of Disease. Philadelphia: 1852. 1st American edition; 8vo; boards; inscribed to Joseph Henry Green. Osler 3978 (London ed. 1850).   Argosy 810-446 1 1996 $200.00

SIMON, NEIL   The Odd Couple. New York: Random House, 1966. 1st edition; fine in dust jacket, with little rubbing along bottom of front panel; scarce first edition.   Between the Covers 42-395 1996 $185.00

SIMON, OLIVER   Printing of To-Day. London: Peter Davies Ltd., 1928. 1st edition; folio; xix, (i), 15, (1) pages, 122 illustrations on plates; cloth spine, boards; light wear along edges and tips, spine slightly sunned, else very good.   The Bookpress 75-352 1996 $110.00

SIMON, OLIVER   Printing of To-Day - an Illustrated Survey of Post-War Typography in Europe and the United States. London: Peter Davies and New York: Harper, 1928. Large 4to; profusely illustrated; cloth backed marbled boards, lettered in blue, fresh copy in chipped dust jacket.   Barbara Stone 70-201 1996 £55.00

SIMOND, LOUIS 1767-1831   Journal of a Tour and Residence in Great Britain, During the Years 1810 and 1811 by a French Traveller. Edinburgh: George Ramsay and Co., 1815. 1st edition; 8vo; 2 volumes; xiii, (3), 382 pages; (2), 360 pages, 21 tinted aquatints and 2 folding tables; contemporary calf, gilt banded spines with red and black gilt labels. Very good. Bicknell 82.1.   Ken Spelman 30-107 1996 £300.00

SIMONDE DE SISMONDI, JEAN CHARLES LEONARD 1773-1842 Historical View of the Literature of the South of Europe... London: Henry Colburn and Co., 1823. 1st edition in English; 8vo; 4 volumes; contemporary green half morocco, spines gilt, rubbed, small library stickers on spines, inoffensive blindstamp on corner of titles and many text pages, no other markings; sound set.   Robert Clark 38-260 1996 £65.00

SIMONDE DE SISMONDI, JEAN CHARLES LEONARD 1773-1842 Political Economy, and the Philosophy of Government... London: John Cpaman, 1847. 1st edition in English; 8vo; (8), 459, (1) pages, 16 page publishers' list; original embossed brown cloth, sometime rebacked, spine lettered, corners bit worn; good. Kress C7209; Goldsmiths 34978; Einaudi 5308.   John Drury 82-260 1996 £300.00

SIMONS, J.   Jerusalem in the Old Testament; Researches and Theories. Leiden: E. J. Brill, 1952. 4to; xvi, 517 pages; 64 figures and 33 plates; original cloth, 1 corner lightly bumped.   Archaeologia Luxor-2721 1996 $350.00

SIMPSON, GEORGE   Narrative of a Journey Round the World, During the Years 1841 and 1842. London: Henry Colburn, 1847. 1st edition; 8vo; 2 volumes; original grey purple cloth, spines quite faded, some spotting; bookplates removed, but a fine set, despite faded bindings, scarce in cloth; presentation copy inscribed by author for Col. Sir Augustus D'Este. Sabin 81343; Howes S495; Wagner Camp 140.1. TPL 2548; Hill p. 274. Ximenes 109-267 1996 $1,250.00

SIMPSON, GEORGE   Narrative of a Journey Around the World During the Years 1841 and 1842. London: Henry Colburn, 1847. 1st edition; royal 8vo; 2 volumes; frontispiece, folding map, 24 page publisher's catalog; original embossed cloth, spines faded, uncut edges. Sabin 81343; Staton & Tremaine 2548.   Charles W. Traylen 117-445 1996 £400.00

SIMPSON, JAMES YOUNG   Acupressure, a New Method of Arresting Surgical Haemorrahge and of Accelerating the Healing of Wounds. Edinburgh: 1864. 1st edition; 8vo; 42 text illustrations, light waterstain on lower portion of book throughout, becoming more noticeable towards end; green cloth by Burn, with their ticket, binding little worn and stained, front joint beginning to split; inscribed "Mr. Brittain with author's kind regards". Russel & Forster p. 50.   Maggs Bros. Ltd. 1190-508 1996 £225.00

SIMPSON, JAMES YOUNG   Clinical Lectures on Diseases of Women. Philadelphia: Blanchard and Lea, 1863. 1st collected U.S. edition; 8vo; pages xii, (17)-510, apparently complete thus; 102 illustrations; original dark green cloth; light foxing at beginning and end, otherwise nice. Signed by author.   James Fenning 133-314 1996 £165.00

SIMPSON, LESLEY BIRD   The Encomienda in New Spain: Forced Native Labour in the Spanish Colonies, 1492-1550. Berkeley: UCA Publications in History, Vol. XIX, 1929. 1st edition; wrappers; good+, rare.   Parker Books of the West 30-164 1996 $100.00

SIMPSON, LOUIS   Armidale. Brockport: Boa Editions, 1979. 1st edition; limited to 25 roman numeralled copies, signed and with holograph poem by Simpson; thin 8vo; cloth backed marbled boards; fine.   James S. Jaffe 34-616 1996 $100.00

SIMPSON, MONA   The Lost Father. New York: Knopf, 1992. 1st edition; fine in dust jacket, signed by author; complimentary card laid in from Sonny Mehta.   Between the Covers 42-396 1996 $100.00

SIMPSON, N. DOUGLAS   A Bibliographical Index of the British Flora... Bournemouth: 1960. Limited to 750 copies; 4to; full dark blue calf, gilt borders and rules, marbled endpapers and edges, silk marker.   David A.H. Grayling MY95Orn-348 1996 £150.00

SIMPSON, RICHARD, CO., LTD.   Largest Dealers in Baby Carriages, Baby Vehicles and Reed Furniture in Canada. Toronto: 1902. 12mo; pages 128; richly illustrated, paper, stapled, covers worn, slight waterstains, else very good, crisp copy.   Hugh Anson-Cartwright 87-366 1996 $125.00

SIMPSON, THOMAS   Select Exercises for Young Proficients in the Mathematicks. London: printed for J. Nourse, 1752. 1st edition; 8vo; perforation and cancellation stamps on blank verso of title, diagrams in text; new half calf, label.   Anthony W. Laywood 109-140 1996 £145.00

SIMPSON, WILLIAM   Picturesque People. London: W. M. Thompson, 1876. 1st edition; folio; unpaginated, 18 chromolithographic plates; publisher's cloth; very uncommon, spine sunned.   Bookpress 75-122 1996 $425.00

SIMS, GEORGE   An Illustrated design Book of Cabinet Furniture, Manufactured in the Best Seasoned Materials and the Most Approved Styles. London: by the author, 1868. Large 4to; lithographed title, 112 lithograph plates, (ii), 19 page price list (in code) and index; original publisher's cloth, marginal light soiling to some plates.   Sotheran PN32-194 1996 £675.00

SIMS, GEORGE   Sleep No More. London: Victor Gollancz, 1966. 1st edition; small 8vo; boards, dust jacket, top of spine very slightly bumped, otherwise fine in slightly torn dust jacket.   James S. Jaffe 34-618 1996 $100.00

SINCLAIR, GEORGE   Hortus Gramineus Woburnensis: or, an Account of the Results of Experiments on the Produce and Nutritive Qualities of Different Grasses and Other Plants Used as the Food of the More Valuable Domestic Animals. London: printed for James Ridgway, 1825. 2nd octavo edition; 8vo; 438 pages, (6) pages ads; 60 hand colored plates; contemporary full calf with binder's ticket of Lindridge of Maidstone, featuring gilt borders and gilt tooled spine with morocco label, library bookplate and unobtrusive blindstamp on titlepage and plates; otherwise very good.   Chapel Hill 94-7 1996 $200.00

SINCLAIR, JOHN   The Night the Bear Came Off the Mountain. Santa Fe: Rydal Press, 1991. 1 of a numbered edition of 125 copies, signed by Sinclair; pages (vi), 108; frontispiece; new in slipcase.   Dumont 28-27 1996 $100.00

SINCLAIR, JOHN 1754-1835   An Account of the Systems of Husbandry Adopted in the More Improved Districts of Scotland. Edinburgh: printed for Arch. Constable and Co... G. Nicol, 1812. 1st edition; 8vo; pages xii, 432, 152, 77, 16 (ad leaves), uncut, 13 engraved plates and plans; original boards, spine and edges little chipped and worn, very good in original state. From the library of Dr. Arthur Raistrick with his bookplate. Rothamsted p. 135.   R.F.G. Hollett 76-279 1996 £275.00

SINCLAIR, JOHN 1754-1835   Address to the Society for the Improvement of British Wool; Constituted at Edinburgh on Monday, Jan. 31, 1791. London: T. Cadell, 1791. 2nd edition; iv, 46, (2) pages ads; recent marbled wrappers; fine, clean copy. Goldsmiths 14668.   C. R. Johnson 37-31 1996 £75.00

SINCLAIR, MAY   Feminism. London: Women Writers' Suffrage League, n.d. 1st edition; 12mo; wrappers, top edge dusty, prelims and edges spotted, top and bottom corners of upper cover defective, covers slightly marked, torn and creased; good; loosely inserted ALS from author.   Ulysses 39-537 1996 £85.00

SINCLAIR, UPTON 1878-1968   Between Two Worlds. New York: Viking Press, 1941. 1st edition; slight bump to base of spine (of both book and jacket), owner name stamp, else near fine in very good plus dust jacket.   Between the Covers 42-397 1996 $150.00

SINCLAIR, UPTON 1878-1968   The Book of Life Mind and Body. Pasadena: Published by the author, 1921. 1st edition; 8vo; brick red cloth, spine ends and corners with slight wear, else about fine. Inscribed by author.   James Cummins 14-183 1996 $500.00

SINCLAIR, UPTON 1878-1968   Cliff Faraday in Command or the Fight of His Life by Ensign Clarke Fitch, U.S.N. New York: Street & Smith Pub., Feb. 4, 1899. 1st edition; 12mo; original wrappers, some dampstaining to lower edges of front cover, still very good, fragile. Priscilla Juvelis 95/1-221 1996 $300.00

SINCLAIR, UPTON 1878-1968   The Millennium. Laurie, 1929. 1st British and 1st hard cover edition; bright, very good+ copy in very good dust jacket with some light wear and some darkening to dust jacket spine. Aronovitz 57-1070 1996 $125.00

SINCLAIR, UPTON 1878-1968   100%. The Story of a Patriot. Pasadena: Published by author, 1920. 1st edition; 8vo; brick red cloth, spine ends and corners with slight wear, else about fine. inscribed by author for Harry J. Salzberg.   James Cummins 14-182 1996 $500.00

SINCLAIR, UPTON 1878-1968   One Clear Call. New York: Viking, 1948. 1st edition; tiny crimp to edges of few pages, still fine in lightly rubbed, near fine dust jacket, very slightly faded on spine, nice copy.   Between the Covers 42-399 1996 $100.00

SINCLAIR, UPTON 1878-1978   Presidential Agent. New York: Viking, 1944. 1st edition; fine in dust jacket, very nice.   Between the Covers 42-398 1996 $125.00

SINDERMANN, C. J.   Principal Diseases of Marine Fish and Shellfish. New York: 1990. 2nd edition; 8vo; 1036 pages, illustrations; cloth. Wheldon & Wesley 207-338 1 996 £185.00

SINEL, JOSEPH   A Book of American Trademarks and Devices. New York: Alfred A. Knopf, 1924. 1st edition; number 848 of 2050 copies; folio; pages 64 (french-folded printed on one side only), c. 200 marks, some in color; original cloth backed decorated boards and repaired and lightly soiled dust jacket; very good, uncommon.   Claude Cox 107-333 1995 £95.00

SINGER, CHARLES   The Evolution of Anatomy: a Short History of Anatomical and Physiological Discovery to Harvey. New York: 1925. 1st edition; 209 pages; original binding; GM 454.   W. Bruce Fye 71-1975 1996 $100.00

SINGER, CHARLES   From Magic to Science: Essays on the Scientific Twilight. London: 1928. 1st edition; 253 pages; illustrations; original binding.   W. Bruce Fye 71-1976 1996 $125.00

SINGER, CHARLES   A Prelude to Modern Science. London: 1946. 8vo; 59 text figures and 6 plates; some light spotting to boards, else very good. Presentation copy from the Wellcome Librarian.   James Tait Goodrich K40-287 1996 $295.00

SINGER, CHARLES   A Prelude to Modern Science, Being a Discussion of the History, Sources and Cirumstances of the Tabulae Anatomica Sex of Vesalius. Cambridge: 1946. 1st edition; 4to; 144 pages, plus 6 folding plates; original binding; GM 372;   W. Bruce Fye 71-2172 1996 $275.00

SINGER, CHARLES   A Short History of Medicine. Oxford: 1928. 1st edition; 368 pages; half leather with raised bands; very fine. GM 6421. W. Bruce Fye 71-1978 1996 $100.00

SINGER, CHARLES   Studies in the History and Method of Science. Oxford: at the Clarendon Press, 1917-21. Royal 8vo.; colored frontispiece 40 plates (titlepage colored; colored frontispiece, plus 54 plates (6 colored); original binding, spines sunned, bit worn, good nevertheless; ex-library from the Bodleian Library, Oxford with their withdrawal stamp. GM 6411 1996   James Tait Goodrich K40-270 1996 $325.00

SINGER, ISAAC BASHEVIS   The Fearsome Inn. New York: Charles Scribner's Sons, 1967. 4to; illustrations by Nonny Hogrogian; original purple cloth, decorated in black, some light fading, illustrated dust jacket some light browning and offsetting and wear to spine; very good; inscribed by author to Marchette and Joy Chute.   James Cummins 14-184 1996 $100.00

SINGER, ISAAC BASHEVIS   The Golem. New York: Farrar Straus Giroux, 1/450 signed and numbered copies; fine in unopened slipcase. Bev Chaney, Jr. 23-613 1996 $100.00

SINGER, ISAAC BASHEVIS   National Book Award Acceptance Speech, April 18, 1974. New York: n.p., (FSG), 1974. Quarto; mimeographed sheets; fine; housed in sleeve inside custom cloth clamshell box with leather spine label; signed by author; scarce.   Between the Covers 42-400 1996 $450.00

SINGER, ISAAC BASHEVIS   One Day of Happiness. New York: Red Ozier Press, 1982. 1st edition; one of 155 copies, signed by author and artist; tall 8vo; lithographs by Richard Callner; quarter leather, boards, slipcase; spine slightly faded as usual, otherwise fine.   James S. Jaffe 34-585 1996 $450.00

SINGER, ISAAC BASHEVIS   One Day of Happiness. New York: Red Ozier Press, 1982. 1st edition; one of 155 copies, signed by author and artist; tall thin 8vo; lithographs by Richard Callner; quarter leather, boards, slipcase; spine lightly faded, otherwise fine.   James S. Jaffe 34-623 1996 $450.00

SINGER, ISAAC BASHEVIS   The Penitent. Franklin Center: Franklin Library, 1983. Franklin Library signed first edition; full gilt stamped leather; fine. Signed by author.   Lame Duck Books   19-495   196 $100.00

SINGER, ISAAC BASHEVIS   Satan in Goray. New York: Noonday Press, 1955. 1st edition; fine in dust jacket.   Hermitage SP95-574 1996 $200.00

SINGER, ISAAC BASHEVIS   A Tale of Three Wishes. New York: FSG, 1976. 1st edition; pictures by Irene Lieblich; fine in dust jacket with trace of soiling, nice copy, inscribed by author.   Between the Covers 42-526   1996 $200.00

SINGER, ISAAC BASHEVIS   A Young Man in Search of Love. Garden City: Doubleday, 1978. 1st edition; one of 300 copies, signed by author, with numbered color print signed by artist; 8vo; pictorial endpapers, paintings and drawings by Raphael Soyer; cloth, slipcase, light offsetting to left margin of print, otherwise very fine.   James S. Jaffe   34-621 1996 $350.00

SINGER, ISAACH BASHEVIS   Zlateh the Goat and Other Stories. New York: Harper & Row, 1966. 1st edition; one of 500 specially bound copies, signed by author and artist; 8vo; black and white illustrations tipped in, by Maurice Sendak; cloth, top edge gilt, slipcase. Mint. James S. Jaffe   34-619   1996 $750.00

SINGER, KURT   Diseases of the Musical Profession: a Systematic Presentation of Their Causes, Symptoms and Methods of Treatment. New York: 1932. 1st English translation; 253 pages; original binding; scarce.   W. Bruce Fye   71-1980   1996 $250.00

SINGH, CHANDRAMANI   Textile and Costumes from the Maharaja Sawai Man Singh II Museum. Jaipur: City Palace, 1979. 4to; 189 pages; 64 black and white plates; cloth, very good in dust jacket.   J. M. Cohen   35-94   1996 $125.00

SINKIEWICZ, HENRYK   Quo Vadis? Verona: Limited Editions Club, 1959. Limited to 350 numbered and signed copies, signed by artist and by printer; tall 4to; illustrations by Salvatore Fiume; decorated natural linen, fine in dust jacket and case.   Charles Agvent   4-1013   1996 $175.00

SIR Harry Herald's Graphical Representation of the Dignitaries of England... London: J. Harris and Son, 1820. 2nd edition; 12mo; (17) pages; 17 hand colored engravings; printed stiff wrappers, corners slightly bumped, else fine. Osborne p. 139; Moon 800(2).   Bromer Booksellers   87-132   1996 $475.00

SIREN, OSVALD   Early Chinese Paintings from A. W. Bahr Collection. London: Chiswick Press, 1938. Limited to 750 numbered copies; folio; 116 pages; 27 tipped in plates, including 13 in color; buckram, gilt, top edge gilt, others uncut, covers very slightly dust soiled. Inscribed by A. W. Bahr to A. J. Kiddell.   Thomas Thorp   489-282   1996   £125.00

SIREN, OSVALD   The Walls and Gates of Peking London: John Lane, 1924. One of an edition of 800; folio; frontispiece, xvii, 239, 109 plates; cloth spine, paste paper boards; binding lightly soiled, binding lightly soiled, otherwise very good.   The Bookpress   75-461   1996 $950.00

SIRINGO, CHARLES ANGELO 1855-1928   A Lone Star Cowboy. Santa Fe: n.p., 1919. Pages (viii), 291; illustrations; boards spotted, else very good. BTB 185; Howes S518; 6 Guns 2029; Herd 2074.   Dumont 28-131   1996 $125.00

SITWELL, EDITH 1887-1964   Alexander Pope. London: Faber, 1930. Limited edition of 220 copies; signed by author; xvi, 316 pages; on handmade paper; frontispiece and 8 plates, original yellow buckram, top edge gilt, others uncut, some pages unopened, spine very slightly dust soiled, worn slipcase.   Thomas Thorp   489-283   1996   £50.00

SITWELL, EDITH 1887-1964   The Collected Poems of Edith Sitwell. London: Gerald Duckworth and Co. Ltd., 1930. One of 320 numbered copies, signed by author; 272 pages of poems, black and white frontispiece, printed on handmade paper; original binding, top edge dusty, head and tail of spine and corners slightly bumped, very good. Ulysses   39-538   1996   £185.00

SITWELL, EDITH 1887-1964   The Death of Venus. New York: Vincent Fitz Gerald & Co., 1983. One of 50 copies only on BFK Rives, signed by artist, Mark Beard; 6 color lithographs, plus one five page black and white lithgoraph pulled on Arches, each copy signed and numbered by artist; loose in original wrappers, as issued, in publisher's clamshell box of green cloth and silver kid spine.   Priscilla Juvelis   95/1-222   1996 $2,200.00

SITWELL, EDITH 1887-1964   The English Eccentrics. London: Faber & Faber Ltd., 1933. 1st edition; black and white frontispiece, 16 black and white plates; original binding, top edge gilt, top edge dusty, head and tail of spine and bottom corners slightly bumped, free endpapers slightly sellotape marked, spine and cover edges very slightly darkened, very good in nicked and slightly creased, chipped and rubbed, price clipped dust jacket faded at spine and frayed and slightly defective at head of spine, both panels of dust jacket repeats frontispiece.   Ulysses 39-539   1996   £95.00

SITWELL, EDITH 1887-1964   Wheels 1917. Oxford: B. H. Blackwell, 1917. Pastedowns and endpapers offset, boards rubbed, top edge rather dusty, otherwise very good; inscribed by author for John Gawsworth. R. A. Gekoski   19-125   1996   £120.00

SITWELL, H. D. W.   The Crown Jewels and Other Regalia in the Tower of London. London: pub. by the Viscount Kemsley at the Dropmore Press, 1953. One of 99 numbered copies of the specially bound edition, signed by author; 4to; pages xii, 116, 40 plates (8 in color); original three quarter red morocco, spine with raised bands and lettered in gilt, crown blocked in gilt on upper cover, all edges gilt, fine in original slipcase.   Sotheran   PN32-48   1996   £298.00

SITWELL, OSBERT 1892-1969   Who Killed Cock-Robin? London: C. W. Daniel, 1921. 1st edition; 2nd issue binding, with erratum slip; original boards, printed in black and red, some wear to spine, rubbing and light soiling of boards. NCBEL 4.347.   James Cummins   14-185   1996 $150.00

SITWELL, SACHEVERELL 1897-   Fine Bird Books 1700-1900. London: Collins and Van Nostrand, 1953. Limited edition of 295 special copies, signed by authors, from an edition of 2295; folio; viii, 120 pages; 16 color and 22 monochrome plates, decorative half title and headpiece; half crimson morocco, marbled boards, dust jacket, slipcase by Mansell (dust jacket little browned in places); fine.   Thomas Thorp   489-284 1996   £600.00

SITWELL, SACHEVERELL 1897-   Fine Bird Books, 1700-1900. London: 1953. Original edition; folio; pages 104, 16 colored, 24 collotype plates; half buckram, trifle used. Scarce.   Wheldon & Wesley   207-100   1996 £330.00

SITWELL, SACHEVERELL 1897-   Fine Bird Books 1700-1900. London: 1990. New edition; 4to; pages xi, 180, 52 colored plates; cloth. Wheldon & Wesley   207-277   1996   £60.00

SITWELL, SACHEVERELL 1897-   Great Flower Books 1700-1900. London: 1956. Royal folio; 104 pages, 20 colored and 16 plain plates; original half cloth, nice, edges of dust jacket trifle frayed.   Wheldon & Wesley   207-99   1996   £360.00

SIVARAMAMURTI, C.   Nataraja in Art, Thought and Literature. New Delhi: 1974. Small folio; xxxxv, 417 pages, frontispiece and tipped in illustrations, many in color; pictorial cloth, good+.   Antipodean   28-357 1996 $100.00

SIVLERBERG, R.   Lion Time in Timbuctoo. Axolotl Press, 1990. 1st edition; 1/75 copies, signed by author; full leather, as new, without dust jacket as issued.   Aronovitz   57-1051   1996 $125.00

SIX Poems of Mutabilitie by Divers Writers. Shaker Heights: Wind Harlot, 1992. One of 44 copies, signed by printer; 2 1/8 x 1 3/4 inches; (12)ff; finely printed on handmade papers, boards, printed label; mint. Bromer Booksellers   90-197   1996 $100.00

SIX Views of the Scenery at Nesscliff. London: Hullmandel, 1824. Folio; 6 uncolored lithographic plates, 44 x 34 cm. sheet size; original wrappers; Lord Kenyon's copy. Not in Abbey.   Marlborough   162-49   1996 £700.00

SIXTEEN Contemporary Wood Engravers. Newcastle: David Esslemont, 1982. Limited edition, 116/250 copies; royal 8vo; pages (v), 16 (engravings), (1); printed on Zerkall mouldmade paper, original printed tan wrappers, fine.   Blackwell's   B112-104   1996   £75.00

SKEAD, C. J.   The Canaries, Seedeaters and Buntings of Southern Africa. Cape Town: 1960. Royal 8vo; pages xiv, 152, 18 maps, 19 colored plates and 50 photos; cloth, corner bumped.   Wheldon & Wesley 207-865 1996 £60.00

SKEAD, C. J.   The Sunbirds of Southern Africa, Also the Sugarbirds, The White Eyes and the Spotted Creeper. Cape Town: 1967. Royal 8vo; 351 pages, 10 colored plates and numerous photos and line drawings; cloth.   Wheldon & Wesley 207-866 1996 £60.00

SKEAT, WALTER W.   An Etymological Dictionary of the English Language. Oxford: Clarendon Press, 1888. 2nd edition; 4to; half title; original brown cloth, slight rubbing to hinges, very good.   Jarndyce 103-216 1996 £80.00

SKEET, FRANCIS JOHN ANGUS   The Life of the Right Honourable James Radcliffe, Third Earl of Derwentwater (Co. Cumberland), Viscount Radcliffe and Langley & Baron Tynedale (co. Cumberland) Viscount Radcliffe and Langley & Baron Tynedale... London: Hutchinson, 1929. Signed limited edition of 250 copies; 8vo; pages 192, printed on laid paper, 2 pedigrees, 9 portraits, 1 view and 4 text engravings; original publisher's half crimson morocco gilt, spine trifle faded, top edge gilt, uncut; 20th century mss. copy of Lord Derwentwater's last letter dated 1746, tipped in at front.   R.F.G. Hollett & Son 78-253 1996 £120.00

SKEET, FRANCIS JOHN ANGUS   Stuart Papers, Pictures, Relics, Medals and Books. Leeds: John Whitehead & Son, 1930. Signed limited edition of 375 copies; large 8vo; pages xi, 98; 6 tissue guarded plates; original cloth, gilt, top edge gilt, uncut;   R.F.G. Hollett 76-280 1996 £60.00

SKELTON, JOHN   Charles I. London: Paris: & Edinburgh: Goupil & Co., et al, 1898. 1st edition; 12 3/4 x 10 inches; 4 p.l., v, (1), 185, (1) pages, (1) leaf (colophon), device on title, decorative initials, handsomely hand colored frontispiece and 41 engravings, 23 plates; each with printed tissue overlay; appealing contemporary red morocco by Blackwell for Brentano's, covers with double gilt rule borders and floral cornerpieces, front cover with very large central arabesque enclosing coat-of-arms, raised bands, spine gilt in compartments containing large floral ornaments as well as leaves, stars and circlets, turn-ins decorated with gilt tendril, unusual pastedowns and free endpapers of brown and orange brocaded cloth, morocco hinges, all edges gilt, rubbing to spine ends (very shallow chip across top of spine), joints slightly eroded (and growing tender in two places, though boards still snugly attached), covers sightly marked and slightly soiled, frontispiece partly offset onto title, otherwise fine internally.   Phillip J. Pirages 33-121 1996 $150.00

SKELTON, JOHN   A Sculptor's Work 1950-1975. Wellingborough: Christopher Skelton, 1977. One of 22 numbered copies, bound thus and signed by the sculptor and has a slate panel incised ("JS") by him set into front cover, there were a further 200 copies; 2 drawings, one double page and one mounted, endpaper designs by sculptor, 26 mounted black and white photos; leather backed cloth, fine in cellophane dust jacket and slightly bumped and stained slipcase.   Ulysses 39-541 1996 £250.00

SKELTON, JOSEPH   Engraved Illustrations of the Principal Antiquities of Oxfordshire... Oxford: Skelton, 1823, plates dated 1823-27. Large paper, probably a subscriber's copy; large folio; engraved title, 4 ff., 140 pages, variously paginated, 2 ff. index, engraved frontispiece, map, 48 engraved illustrations on India paper, numerous lower text engravings; green morocco gilt with single fillet cathedral pattern on covers and flat spine, all edges gilt, purple silk liners (spine darkened), most unusual, cathedral bindings were normally embossed from a single block, here the unknown binder has used small tools and single rules to create a similar effect. Marlborough 160-79 1996 £850.00

SKETCH, WALTER   The Down-Trodden; or, Black Blood and White. New York: Jonathan Miller, 1853. 1st edition; 8vo; 89 pages; removed, last leaf loose, one leaf slightly defective affecting several words; some stains and library stamps on title; very rare. Not in LCP/HSP Afro Amer. Cat. or Blockson. Wright II 2236.   M & S Rare Books 60-234 1996 $425.00

SKETCHES from "Nine Sharp". London: Samuel French Ltd., 1938. 1st edition; wrappers, spine browned and slightly split, cover edges slightly browned and slightly split, cover edges slightly browned, vestiges of later price sticker on upper cover; good.   Ulysses 39-620 1996 £125.00

SKETCHLEY, ARTHUR   Mrs. Brown On the Alabama Claims. London: George Routledge, 1872. 1st edition; small 8vo; pages 152; original colored pictorial boards, spine chipped; although board edges are rubbed, this is a good copy of a fragile book. Sadleir 3631 (17); Wolff 6363.   Howard S. Mott 227-129 1996 $150.00

SKINNER, HENRY   The Origin of Medical Terms. Baltimore: 1949. 1st edition; 379 pages; original binding, underlining on a few leaves, otherwise fine.   W. Bruce Fye 71-1985 1996 $125.00

SKINNER, JOSEPH   The Present State of Peru: Comprising Its Geography, Topography, Natural History, Mineralogy, Commerce, the Customs and Manners of Its Inhabitants... London: Richard Phillips, 1805. 1st edition; 4to; pages xiv, 488; 20 hand colored plates; modern quarter brown calf, some light plate transfer and foxing to few pages. Sabin 81615; Abbey Travel 723.   Richard Adelson W94/95-158 1996 $875.00

SKIPP, JOHN   Book of the Dead. Shingletown: Ziesing, 1989. 1st hardcover edition, one of 500 numbered copies, signed by editors and contributors; very fine in dust jacket with slipcase.   Robert Gavora 61-186 1996 $190.00

SKIPWITH, P.   The Great Bird Illustrators and Their Art 1730-1930. London: 1979. 4to; 176 pages; 13 portraits in text, title vignette, 70 colored plates; cloth.   Wheldon & Wesley 207-278 1996 £60.00

SKOLSKY, SIDNEY   Don't Get me Wrong - I Love Hollywood. New York: Putnam, 1975. 16 pages of black and white illustrations; dust jacket, few small chips and tears, very good. Laid in loose is publisher's invitation to a reception for the book to be given at Schwab's drugstore with "Dress: old or New Hollywood". Signed and inscribed by author for his wife, Estelle, the dedicatee.   George J. Houle 68-135 1996 $350.00

SKUTCH, ALEXANDER F.   The Life of the Woodpecker. California: 1985. Small folio; many colored plates and illustrations; full leather, housed in cloth slipcase; signed by author and artist; mint.   David A.H Grayling MY95Orn-67 1996 £120.00

SLADE, ADOLPHUS   Travels in Germany and Russia: Including a Steam Voyage by the Danube and the Euxine from Vienna to Constantinople in 1838-39. London: 1840. 1st edition; 8vo; pages viii, 516, 16 (ads); recent paper boards, label, uncut, very good; inscribed "From the author" on title.   James Fenning 133-316 1996 £85.00

SLADEN, F. L. W.   The Humble-Bee, Its Life History and How to Domesticate It, with Descriptions of All the British Species ob Bombus and Psithyrus. London: 1912. 8vo; pages xiii, 283, 2 plain and 5 colored plates and 34 text figures; original cloth, some underlining.   Wheldon & Wesley 207-1109 1996 £75.00

SLATIN, RUDOLPH CARL, FREIHERR VON 1857-1932   Fire and Sword in the Sudan. London: New York: Edward Arnold, 1896. 1st English edition; 8vo; half title, 630 pages, 32 page publisher's catalog, frontispiece, 21 black and white plates, 2 large folding maps, foxing to titlepage; original maroon cloth, gilt vignette to upper board, gilt title to spine, top edge gilt, green endpapers, contemporary ink signature. Beeleigh Abbey BA/56-119 1996 £150.00

SLEDD, JAMES H.   Dr. Johnson's Dictionary, Essays in the Biography of a Book. Chicago: University of Chicago Press, 1955. 1st edition; octavo; 256 pages; frontispiece; tan cloth, black and gilt decorations; now quite scarce.   Hartfield 48-11n 1996 $185.00

SLEEMAN, J. L.   Tales of a Shikari. Big Game Shooting in India. c. 1919. illustrations; 154 pages; original printed boards, new spine; remarkably scarce.   David Grayling J95Biggame-387 1996 £85.00

SLEIGH, W. CAMPBELL   A Handy Book of Criminal Law, Applicable Chiefly to Commercial Transactions. London: G. Routledge and Co., 185? Embossed cloth, gilt, spine faded, but sound.   Meyer Boswell SL25-202 1996 $275.00

SLOANE, H.   An Account of a Most Efficacious Medicine for Soreness, Weakness and Several Other Distempers of the Eyes. London 1745. 1st edition; 8vo; pages vi, 17 (18), bit foxed, small hole in half title patched without loss, issue with half title price (no priority established); modern boards.   Maggs Bros. Ltd. 1190-509 1996 £300.00

SMAIL, DAVID CAMERON   Prestwick Golf Club. Birthplace of the Open The Club, the Members and the Championships 1851 to 1989. Prestwick the Club, 1989. Limited edition of 250 copies; large 4to; pages 238; illustrations; original full green crushed morocco, gilt, pictorial onlay on upper board, glassine wrapper and cloth slipcase. Fine.   R.F.G. Holle? 76-282 1996 £250.00

A SMALL Garden of Flora. Oxford: Alembic Press, 1990. Limited to 10? copies; 2 1/16 x 1 1/2 inches; 46 pages; floral printer's ornaments in red, green and blue; engraved border to titlepage; cloth backed marble boards; mint.   Bromer Booksellers 90-175 1996 $85.00

SMALL World Alphabet. Seattle: Grey Spider Press, 1992. One of 75 copies signed by artist, Michael Dal Cerro; 8.25 x 10 inches; woodcuts by Michael Dal Cerro, printed from the blocks on Mohawk Letterpress paper, printed and bound by Christ Stern, decorated endpapers, green cloth boards, paper title label on spine, larger title label with illustration on front cover; fine.   Joshua Heller 21-44 1996 $125.00

SMALL, ANDREW   Interesting Roman Antiquites Recently Discovered in Fife... Edinburgh: printed for the Author, 1823. 1st edition; 8vo; 297, 20 pages; folding map; original boards, spine ends bit rubbed and corners slightly bumped, else very good, rare in original boards. Chapel Hill 94-360 1996 $200.00

SMALL, GEORGE G.   Fred Douglass and His Mule: a Story of the War. New York: M. J. Ivers and Co., c. 1886. 8vo; 95 pages; wonderful illustrations; staped, original back wrapper, brittle. Wright II 2245 for two copies of an 1873 ed. by another publisher.   M & S Rare Books 60-235 1996 $100.00

SMALL, HAROLD A.   Adventures of Joseph Alexandre de Chabrier de Peloubet at the Time of the French Revolution. San Francisco: Grabhorn Press, 1953. One of 185 copies; fine in publisher's dust jacket. Hermitage SP95-884 1996 $125.00

SMART, CHRISTOPHER 1722-1771   Poems on Several Occasions. London: for the author, by W. Strahan, and sold by J. Newbery, 1752. 1st edition; 4to; pages (xvi), 203, engraved f by Grignion after Hayman, 1 engraved plate; contemporary quarter calf, raised bands, lacks label, marbled sides, front joint cracked, but holding firm, some stripping and rubbing of sides, first four leaves very lightly spotted; good; William Mason's copy with his engraved booklabel. Tinker 1919.   Simon Finch 24-212 1996 £900.00

SMART, CHRISTOPHER 1722-1771   The Poems of the Late Christopher Smart. Reading: printed & sold by Smart & Cowslade; & sold by F. Power & Co. London, 1791. 1st edition; small 8vo; 2 volumes; frontispiece in first volume, 2 leaves of ads at end of volume 2; contemporary tree calf, rebacked; very good. Mahony & Rizzo 178; Roscoe A563; CBEL II 589.   Ximenes 109-268 1996 $500.00

SMART, JOHN   Tables of Time. London: for the author, 1710. 12mo; vignette title, engraved throughout, 17 unnumbered leaves; contemporary black morocco, double gilt fillet, spine gilt in compartments, double ruled, raised bands, comb marbled endpapers, all edges gilt, elegant. Marlborough 160-55 1996 £450.00

SMEATON, JOHN   John Smeaton's Diary of His Journey to the Low Countires 1755 From the Original MS in the Library of Trinity House. Leamington Spa: for the Newcomen Society, 1938. 1st edition; 8vo; (6), ix, 68 pages; frontispiece, folding map and facsimile plate, original half vellum over linen boards, top edge gilt. fine.   Edwin V. Glaser 121-287 1996 $100.00

SMEATON, JOHN   The Report...Concerning the Drainage of the North Level of the Fens, and the OUtfall of the Wisbeach River. Austhorpe: 22 Aug. 1768. 4to; 24 pages; folding plan; paper wrappers. Skempton 1318. Marlborough 162-90 1996 £150.00

SMEE, ALFRED   My Garden Its Plan and Culture, Together with General Description of Its Geology, Botany and Natural History. London: Bell and Daldy and New York: Scribner, 1872. 1st edition; large 8vo; pages 650; 1250 engravings; green cloth stamped in gold, little dust rubbed and foxed, very good.   Second Life Books 103-173 1996 $165.00

SMELLIE, WILLIAM   The Philosophy of Natural History. Edinburgh: Heirs of Charles Elliot, et al, 1790-99. 1st edition; 4to; 2 volumes, xiii, 547; xii, 515 pages; contemporary calf, few leaves marginally stained, bindings somewhat worn, volume one lacking spine label; very good. Freeman 3437; Blake p. 241 cites volume one only.   Edwin V. Glaser 121-288 1996 $485.00

SMETHAN, HENRY   Rambles Round Churches (in the Vicinity of Maidstone, Rochester and Chatham). Chatham: 1925-28. 8vo; 3 volumes; drawings; original cloth, gilt. Complete sets are rare.   Howes Bookshop 265-2210 1996 £75.00

SMILES, SAMUEL   Duty: with Illustrations of Courage, Patience and Endurance. London: John Murray, 1880. 1st edition; 8vo; xv, (1), 430 pages, complete with half title, final leaf of ads; original green cloth, embossed in black and lettered in gilt, largely unopened; fine.   John Drury 82-261 1996 £60.00

SMILES, SAMUEL   George Moore, Merchant and Philanthropist. London: George Routledge and Sons, 1878. 2nd edition; thick 8vo; pages xv, 530, 6, etched portrait; original cloth,, gilt, over bevelled boards, spine little faded, little scattered spotting, but very good sound copy. R.F.G. Hollett & Son 78-255 1996 £55.00

SMILES, SAMUEL   Thrift. London: John Murray, 1875. 1st edition; half title, 12 pages ads; original green decorated cloth, slight rubbing to head and tail of spine.   Jarndyce 103-568 1996 £75.00

SMILEY, JANE   The Age of Grief. New York: Knopf, 1987. Uncorrected proof; light soiling to wrappers, otherwise near fine. Anacapa House 5-280 1996 $150.00

SMILEY, JANE   The Age of Grief. New York: Knopf, 1987. 1st edition; original cloth, fine in fine dust jacket; signed by author.   Beasley Books 82-141 1996 $150.00

SMILEY, JANE   At Paradise Gate. New York: S&S, 1981. 1st edition; fine in price clipped dust jacket with two tiny edge tears; signed by author.   Lame Duck Books 19-497 1996 $450.00

SMILEY, JANE   Barn Blind. New York: Harper & Row, 1980. 1st edition; light spotting to upper edge of pages, otherwise fine in price clipped dust jacket, quite uncommon now.   Ken Lopez 74-409 1996 $450.00

SMILEY, JANE   Duplciate Keys. New York: Knopf, 1984. 1st edition; fine in fine dust jacket.   Thomas Dorn 9-231 1996 $120.00

SMILEY, JANE   A Thousand Acres. New York: Knopf, 1991. Uncorrected proof; faint sticker shadow and small light stain on front panel, thus very good in wrappers.   Between the Covers 42-403 1996 $125.00

SMILEY, JANE   A Thousand Acres. New York: Knopf, 1991. Advance uncorrected proofs; wrappers, close to fine with hint of light crease on rear wrapper.   Beasley Books 82-144 1996 $100.00

SMITH, A. C.   Guide to British and Roman Antiquities of the North Wiltshire Downs in a Hundred Square Miles Round Abury. Wiltshire Archaeological & Natural History Society, 1885. 2nd edition; folio; xviii, 248 pages, 4 page list of subscribers; 20 colored maps, 7 plates; cloth, gilt, covers dampstained and some internal waterstaining also, slight foxing, new endpapers.   Thomas Thorp 489-285 1996 £85.00

SMITH, A. DUNCAN   Trial of Maedleine Smith. London: Sweet and Maxwell, 1905. Original edition; green cloth, gilt, worn but sound. Meyer Boswell SL27-211 1996 $125.00

SMITH, A. H.   A Catalogue of Engraved Gems in the British Museum. London: British Museum, 1888. 1st edition; 12mo; ix, 244 pages, 9 plates; original gilt lettered cloth, 2 corners bumped; inscribed by co author A.S. Murray for R. C. Jebb.   Archaeologia Luxor-4032 1996 $450.00

SMITH, A. H.   Marbles and Bronzes: Fifty Plates from Selected Subjects in the Department of Greek and Roman Antiquities. London: British Museum, 1914. 4to; 8 paes, 6 figures and 50 plates; original cloth.   Archaeologia Luxor-4033 1996 $250.00

SMITH, A. LEDYARD   Explorations in the Motagua Valley, Guatemala. Washington: Carnegie Inst. of Washington, 1943. 4to; pages 101-182, 64 plates; wrappers.   Archaeologia Luxor-4892 1996 $150.00

SMITH, A. LEDYARD   Uaxactun, Guatemala: Excavations of 1931-1937. Washington: Carnegie Inst. of Washington, 1950. 4to; frontispiece, xii, 108 pages, 141 plates, 2 folding maps in pocket at rear; original printed wrappers.   Archaeologia Luxor-4896 1996 $350.00

SMITH, A. MURRAY, MRS.   Westminster Abbey. London: A. & C. Black, 1904. Limited edition of 250 numbered copies, signed by publisher; 4to; viii, 147 pages; 21 full page color illustrations from paintings by John Fulleylove; publisher's white cloth decorated in green and gilt, top edge gilt, others uncut, slightly worn and dust soiled, occasional light foxing.   Thomas Thorp 489-286 1996 £180.00

SMITH, ADAM 1723-1790   Essays on Philosophical Subjects. London: T. Cadell and W. Davies, 1795. 1st edition; 4to; xcv, (1), 244 pages; modern half calf and marbled boards, green morocco label, minor offsetting as usual, fine; bookplate of Leo Olschki. Rothschild 1902. Vanderblue p. 43.   19th Century Shop 39- 1996 $6,500.00

SMITH, ADAM 1723-1790   Essays on Philosophical Subjects...To Which is Prefixed, an Account of the Life and Writings of the author by Dugald Stewart. London: printed for J. Cadell Jun. and W. Davies and W. Creech, Edinburgh, 1795. 1st edition; 4to; contemporary half calf, marbled boards, skilfully rebacked, gilt spine in compartments, leather label, good wide margined copy. Einaudi 326; Goldsmiths 16218; Jessop p 172; Kress B3038.   C. R. Johnson 37-32 1996 £3,500.00

SMITH, ADAM 1723-1790   An Inquiry into the Nature and Causes of the Wealth of Nations. Philadelphia: Dobson, 1789-96-89. 1st American editions of volumes I and 3; 8vo; 3 volumes; original uniform calf, scuffed; ownership signatures of Francis Lasher in volume 1 and Jacob Lasher 1798 in volume 2.   Rostenberg & Stern 150-9 1996 $1,400.00

SMITH, ADAM 1723-1790   An Inquiry Into the Nature and Causes of the Wealth of Nations. London: T. Cadell and W. Davies, 1805. 11th edition; 8vo; 3 volumes; later uniform half calf, spines gilt, raised bands, lettered direct on spine; most attractive; Kress B4976; Goldsmiths 19009. Vanderblue p. 4.   John Drury 82-262 1996 £475.00

SMITH, ADAM 1723-1790   An Inquiry into the Nature and Causes of the Wealth of Nations. Edinburgh and London: printed for Silvester Doig et al, 1817. 8 1/2 X 5 1/2 inches; 3 volumes; excellent contemporary polished calf, sides framed with double gilt fillets and pleasing blindstamped border of linked botanical ornaments, raised bands, spine panels filled with delicate scrolling foliate decoration in blind and gilt, elegant band of leafy gilt stamps at spine ends, dark blue morocco double labels, marbled endpapers, covers just slightly marked, just hint of wear to joints and extremities, but bright, clean, very attractive set in really excellent condition, darkening of endpapers because of binder's glue, consistent offsetting in text, two minor tears neatly repaired without loss, but fresh, smooth and generally very nice internally.   Phillip J. Pirages 33-463 1996 $950.00

SMITH, ADAM 1723-1790   An Inquiry Into the Nature and Causes of the Wealth of Nations. Oxford: at the Clarendon Press, 1869. 1st Thorold Rogers edition; 8vo; frontispiece, lii, 423; viii, 594 pages, 32 page publisher's list in volume 2 dated Dec. 1879; minimal signs of being ex-library (shelf numbers), otherwise very good, uncut in original brown cloth gilt. fine.   John Drury 82-263 1996 £95.00

SMITH, ALBERT   Sketches of London Life and Character. London: n.d., ca. 1870. Small 8vo; title, 2 ff., pages 188, (+4 pages ads), frontispiece, illustrations; gilt and blindstamped cloth.   Marlborough 162-201 1996 £75.00

SMITH, ALEXANDER   Dreamthorp. London: 1863. 1st edition; crown 8vo; pages (8), 296; original cloth, gilt, 3 tiny spots of wear on one joint, else nice and fresh. Rather scarce.   James Fenning 133-317 1996 £65.00

SMITH, ALEXANDER   Dreamthorp. London: Strahan & Co., 1863. 1st edition; 8vo; viii, 296 pages, publisher's catalog at end; original green ribbed cloth, blocked in blind and gilt, lettered gilt on spine.   David Bickersteth 133-167 1996 £55.00

SMITH, ALFRED E.   Progressive Democracy, Addresses and State Papers of Alfred E. Smith. New York: 1928. 2nd printing; 8.5 x 5.5 inches; 392 pages with index; cloth, minor wear; presentation copy inscribed and signed by Smith on dedication page, also tipped in is a TLS by Smith regarding this book.   John K. King 77-170 1996 $125.00

SMITH, AMANDA   An Autobiography: the Story of the Lord's Dealings with Mrs. Amanda Smith, the Colored Evangelist. Chicago: Meyer & Brother, 1893. 1st edition; frontispiece; fine, bright copy.   Between the Covers 43-408 1996 $350.00

SMITH, ANNE   Anthology of Love. London: Acorn Press, 1985. Number 22 of 100 copies; small 4to; pages (43); printed on Zerkall Ingres Terra pale grey paper; 15 full page wood engravings by Hellmuth Weissenborn printed in blue and brown, title printed in brown; original cream cloth, printed front cover label, untrimmed fine.   Blackwell's B112-1 1996 £60.00

SMITH, ASHBEL   A Brief Description of the Climate, Soil and Productions of Texas. Philadelphia: T. Cowperthwait & Co., 1841. 1st edition; separate printing of the appendix which preceded book publication; 16mo; pages 375-388, with specially printed frontispiece; plain green wrappers, light foxing, still excellent, laid in custom made folding cloth case with leather label; rare. Jenkins BTB p. 493-5. Bohling Book Co. 191-135 1996 $2,750.00

SMITH, CECIL   The Birds of Somersetshire. London: John Van Voorst, 1869. 1st edition; 8vo; pages 643; original green cloth, some staing to spine, otherwise extremely sound; scarce. Mullens & Swann p. 545. Sotheran PN32-98 1996 £98.00

SMITH, CECIL H.   Collection of J. Pierpont Morgan. Bronzes, Antique Greek, Roman, etc... Paris: Librairie Centrale des Beaux-Arts, 1913. Large folio; xvi, 55 pages; 38 illustrations, 46 plates; full black morocco with 5 raised bands, gilt extra, top edge gilt, very slight rubbing to few bands, couple of insignificant knocks at two edges, otherwise fine. Archaeologia Luxor-4034 1996 $4,500.00

SMITH, CHARLES   Elegiac Sonnets. London: Printed by R. Noble, for T. Cadell, 1792. 6th edition; 12mo; author's first book; 5 engraved plates, contemporary tree calf, gilt, red morocco initial label centered on covers, some rubbing, upper joint cracked; bookplate, initial label for the Duke of Hamilton (Brandon); very attractive.   James Cummins 14-186 1996 $150.00

SMITH, CHARLES A.   A Comprehensive History of Minnehaha County, South Dakota. Mitchell: 1949. 1st edition; 504 pages, frontispiece, plates; signed; cloth; nice, sarce. 6 Guns 2045.   T. A. Swinford 49-1072 1996 $100.00

SMITH, CHARLES J.   Historical and Literary Curiosities. London: Bohn, 1840. 1st edition; large 4to; numerous autograph facsimiles, steel engraved views and other plates including 9 in color, tissue guards present; three quarter leather, rubbed, minor foxing.   Charles Agvent 4-1015 1996 $225.00

SMITH, CLARK ASHTON   The Abominations of Yondo. Sauk City: Arkham House, 1960. 1st edition; 1/2000 copies; fine in very good+ dust jacket.   Aronovitz 57-1078 1996 $150.00

SMITH, CLARK ASHTON   The Dark Chateau. Sauk City: Arkham House, 1951. 1st edition; 1/563 copies; fine in near fine dust jacket. Aronovitz 57-1077 1996 $550.00

SMITH, CLARK ASHTON   The Double Shadow and Other Fantasies. Auburn Press Journal, 1933. 1st edition; 1/1000 copies; some staining to front cover, else very good in wrappers; inscribed by author to fellow writer Carl Jacobi.   Aronovitz 57-1074 1996 $875.00

SMITH, CLARK ASHTON   Genius Loci and Other Tales. Sauk City: Arkham House, 1948. One of 3047 copies; near fine in lightly soiled dust jacket.   Steven C. Bernard 71-430 1996 $150.00

SMITH, CLARK ASHTON   Lost Worlds. Sauk City: Arkham House, 1944. 1st edition; near fine in very good+/near fine dust jacket with sligh wear to dust jacket spine extremities; very nice.   Aronovitz 57-1076 1996 $375.00

SMITH, CLARK ASHTON   The Star-Treader and other Poems. Robertson, 1912. 1st edition; author's first book; very good, author's holograph addressed envelope laid in.   Aronovitz 57-1073 1996 $185.00

SMITH, DAVID EUGENE   Rara Arithmetica; a Catalogue of the Arithmetics Written Before the Year MDCI with a Description of Those in the Library of George Arthur Plimpton of New York. Boston: Ginn and Co., 1908. 1st edition; 8vo; xiii, 507 pages; 9 plates; 246 illustrations in text; original cloth, paper label; very good.   Edwin V. Glaser 121-291 1996 $200.00

SMITH, EDMUND WARE   The One-Eyed Poacher of Privilege. New York: Derrydale Press, 1941. 1st edition; one of 750 numbered copies; 8vo; very good, bit of browning along lue line on pastedowns and som sligh spine fading; Siegel 166; Frazier S10a.   Glenn Books 36-71 199 $175.00

SMITH, EDMUND WARE   Tall Tales and Short. New York: Derrydale Press, 1938. 1st edition; one of 950 numbered copies; 8vo; near fine. Siegel 142; Frazier S9a.   Glenn Books 36-70 1996 $200.00

SMITH, EDWARD C.   A History of Lewis County, West Virginia. Weston: 1920. 427 pages; endpapers foxed.   Bookworm & Silverfish 276-184 1996 $125.00

SMITH, EDWARD E.   Second Stage Lensmen. Fantasy Press, 1953. 1st edition; 1/500 copies of the plated edition; couple of lightened areas to rear cover, else very good+ in very good/very good+ bright dust jacket with small chip and light wear to head of dust jacket spine. Inscribed by author.   Aronovitz 57-1090 1996 $165.00

SMITH, EDWARD E.   The Skylark of Space. Providence: Buffalo Book co., 1946. 1st edition; 1000 copies printed; author's first book; fine in dust jacket with 2 1" tears.   Robert Gavora 61-194 1996 $225.00

SMITH, EDWARD E.   The Skylark of Space. Hadley, 1947. 2nd edition; 1/1000 copies; very good+ in dust jacket with small piece missing from lower right corner of front dust jacket; inscribed by author to Julius Unger.   Aronovitz 57-1085 1996 $135.00

SMITH, EDWARD E.   The Skylark of Valeron. Fantasy Press, 1949. 1st edition; fine in near fine dust jacket; inscribed by author to Julius Unger.   Aronovitz 57-1088 1996 $135.00

SMITH, EDWARD E.   Spacehounds of IPC. Fantasy Press, 1947. 1st edition; 1t issue dust jacket, 1/300 copies; very good+ in near very good jacket with some slight creasing to front dust jacket panel; first book from the press; inscribed by author.   Aronovitz 57-1084 1996 $225.00

SMITH, EDWARD E.   The Skylark of Space. Buffalo Co., 1946. 1st edition; 1/500 copies, this one specially signed by author; author's first book; bright, near fine copy in like dust jacket with some slight wear and tear.   Aronovitz 57-1083 1996 $475.00

SMITH, EDWARD E.   Triplanetary. Fantasy Press, 1948. 1st edition; some minor spotting to rear cover, else very good/very good+ in like dust jacket; inscribed by author in 1949 to well known fan.   Aronovitz 57-1087 1996 $125.00

SMITH, EDWARD E.   The Vortex Blasater. Fantasy Press, 1960. 1st edition; 1/341 copies; fine in dust jacket.   Aronovitz 57-1096 1996 $450.00

SMITH, EDWIN   Cuts. Previous Parrot Press, 1992. Of 206 numbered copies, signed by Cook, this one of only 28 with an additional suite of 4 engravings printed from the blocks at the Rocket Press; 8vo; printed in black and red on Zerkall; fine in slipcase.   Bertram Rota 272-377 1996 £58.00

SMITH, ELIZABETH OAKES   The Newsboy. Amsterdam: M. H. Binger & Sons, 1856. 8vo; (250) pages; green silk ribbed cloth, spine gilt lettered, lightly rubbed, otherwise very nice; uncommon.   Paulette Rose 16-302 1996 $150.00

SMITH, ERNEST BRAMAH   Kai Lung's Golden Hours. London: Riverside Press, Number 143 of 250 copies; signed by author. Very good.   Limestone Hills 41-15 1996 $120.00

SMITH, ERNEST BRAMAH   The Mirror of Kong Ho. London: Chapman and Hall, 1905. 1st edition; good or better with hinge starting, light soiling and foxing on pages, tips bumped, rubbing and spine ends lightly frayed.   Quill & Brush 102-85 1996 $150.00

SMITH, ERNEST BRAMAH   The Wallet of Kai Lung. London: Grant Richards, 1923. Limited to 200 numbered copies, signed by author; royal 8vo; pages xi, 299; original holland backed boards, label; very good to nice.   James Fenning 133-31 1996 £75.00

SMITH, FREDERICK   The Early History of Veterinary Literature and Its British Development. London: J. A. Allen & Co., 1976. 8vo; 4 volumes, plates, illustrations; original cloth.   Forest Books 74-247 1996 £75.00

SMITH, G.   The Highflyers Guide, or How to Breed and Train Tipplers, Tumblers, Rollers, Cumulets and Cross-Breds. Nottingham: printed by Geo. Richards, 1890. 1st edition; slim 12mo; 72 pages; original crimson cloth, lightly marked; not found in BM Cat.   James Burmester 29-127 1996 £75.00

SMITH, GEOFFREY   A Naturalist in Tasmania. Oxford: 1909. 151 pages, 16 pages ads, frontiespiece and 20 pages illustrations and illustrations in text, folding map; original deocrated cloth, some light rubbing to spine of dust jacket, otherwise fine copy; the Absolon copy.   Antipodean 28-360 1996 $110.00

SMITH, GEORGE   Assyrian Discoveries; an Account of Exlproations and Discoveries on the Site of Nineveh, During 1873 and 1874. London: Sampson Low, 1875. 8vo; xvi, 461 pages, (12 pages ads), folding map, 8 plates, text illustrations; original pictorial cloth.   H. M. Fletcher 121-147 1996 £100.00

SMITH, GEORGE ALBERT   Correspondence of Palestine Tourists; Comprising a Series of Letters. Salt Lake City: Deseret News Ssteam Printing Establishment, 1875. 1st edition; 386 pages; full black leather, some shelf wear to covers and spine, one signature loosening, else near very good.   Orrin Schwab 10-90 1996 $135.00

SMITH, GEORGE BARNETT   Shelley. A Critical Biography. Edinburgh: David Douglas, 1877. 1st edition; 8vo; original dark green cloth, minor rubbing; fine. CBEL III 320.   Ximenes 109-269 1996 $125.00

SMITH, GOLDWIN   The United Kingdom: a Political History. London: Macmillan, 1899. 1st edition; 8vo; 2 volumes; choicely bound in half red levant morocco, gilt tops, panelled spines; from the library of Andrew Carnegie.   Charles W. Traylen 117-197 1996 £65.00

SMITH, HENRY   Observations on the Prevailing Practice of Supplying Medical Assistance to the Poor, Commonly called the Farming of Parishes; with Suggestions for the Establishment of Parochial Medical Chests... London: 1819. 1st edition; 20, 32 pages, plus 2 folding charts; recent cloth backed boards. Rare.   W. Bruce Fye 71-1993 1996 $100.00

SMITH, HORATIO   Amarynthus, the Hympholept. London: Longman, 1821. 1st (only) edition; 8vo; half title, 12 pages dated publisher's ads; modern calf antique, morocco label, marbled boards, uncut; original paper label affixed to final flyleaf. Inner margin of half title soiled, very fine.   Trebizond 39-50 1996 $125.00

SMITH, J. C.   Tempest an Opera. Walsh, 1756. pages 2-6, 47-84, title very badly stained.   William Reeves 309-9688 1996 £103.00

SMITH, J. S.   Anthems Composed for the Choir Service of the Church of England. London: printed for the author, c. 1793. 167 pages, list of subscribers, title and last leaf damaged, some dog ears, no covers.   William Reeves 309-9689 1996 £69.00

SMITH, JAMES EDWARD 1759-1828   Exotic Botany. London: 1804-05. Royal 8vo; 2 volumes; 120 hand colored plates; modern buckram, uncut, complete, rare. Certain amount of foxing and signs of use but in general a good copy.   Wheldon & Wesley 207-101 1996 £1,200.00

SMITH, JAMES EDWARD 1759-1828   An Introduction to Physiological and Systematical Botany. London: 1826. 5th edition; 8vo; xxi, 435, 15 hand colored plates; half calf, fine.   John Henly 27-242 1996 £60.00

SMITH, JAMES, MRS.   The Booandik Tribe of South Austrlian Aborigines. Adelaide: E. spiller, 1880. Small 8vo; (xi), 139 pages, 6 illustrations; leather spine and printed wrapper boards, leather spine rubbed, corners bumped, browning affects lower fore edge of text for first 30 od pages, otherwise good+; presentation copy from Rev. F. H. Robinson to his brother. James Edge Partington bookplate; Ferguson 15823; Greenway 8565.   Antipodean 28-364 1996 $225.00

SMITH, JOHN   The Printer's Grammar... London: printed by L. Wayland and sold by T. Evans, 1787. 8vo; pages (4), 369 (of which pages 272-316 are occupied by Fry specimen), prelim leaves browned, light waterstain across final 60 pages, but generally good survival of scarce book; contemporary half calf, marbled sides, rebacked, morocco label; Birrell & Garnett 92 & 223; Bigmore & Wyman II 365.   Claude Cox 107-334 1996 £350.00

SMITH, JOHN 1580-1631   Travels and Works of Captain John Smith, President of Virginia and Admiral of New England. Edinburgh: John Grant, 1910. 8vo; 2 volumes; 12, xviii, *xix-*xxx, xix-cxxxvi, 382 pages; 4, 383-984 pages; 2 portraits, 6 folded maps and plates; dark burgundy cloth with gilt spine titles, near fine, partially unopened set. Sabin 82857.   Parmer Books 039/Nautica-039220 1996 $250.00

SMITH, JOHN 1580-1631   Travels and Works of Captain John Smith, President of Virginia and Admiral of New England. Edinburgh: John Grant, 1910. New edition; 8vo; 2 volumes; cxxxvi, 382 pages; (383)-984 pages; 12 illustrations, 4 folding maps; half cloth, spines faded, bit of wear to boards.   Parmer Books 039/Nautica-039382 1996 $150.00

SMITH, JOHN 1580-1631   Works. 1608-1631. Birmingham: Unwin, 1884. cxxxvi, 984 pages; illustrations; three quarter leather, marbled paper over boards, marbled endpapers, top edge gilt, boards rubbed and some wear to corners.   Parmer Books 039/Nautica-039051 1996 $125.00

SMITH, JOHN 1630-1679   The Pourtract of Old Age. London: printed by J. Macock, for Walter Kettilby, 1666. 2nd corrected edition; 8vo; imprimatur leaf, (xiv), 266, (6) pages; contemporary calf boards, rebacked, boards quite rubbed, first gathering loose, good copy. Freeman 1979 p. 74.   John Gach 150-435 1996 $575.00

SMITH, JOHN fl. 1747   Chronicon Rusticum - Commerciale; or, Memoirs of Wool, &c. London: printed for T. Osborne, 1747. 1st edition; 8vo; perforation and cancellation stamps on blank verso of titles; new half calf, gilt, labels, generally very nice. Kress 4871; Goldsmith 8283; Hanson 6056.   Anthony W. Laywood 109-141 1996 £450.00

SMITH, JOHN TALBOT   A Woman of Culture. New York: Catholic Pub. Society Co., 1883. 1st edition; tall 8vo; 281 pages; original cloth, some soiling, blindstamp on title, inner front hinge cracked; rare.   M & S Rare Books 60-236 1996 $100.00

SMITH, JOHN THOMAS   Ancient Topography of London... London: J. M'Creery...for John Thomas Smith, 1815. Large 4to; colored engraved title dated 1810, printed title, 1 f., 82 pages, 33 etched/engraved plates; contemporary diced calf, early reback, slightly rubbed; Adams 115. Marlborough 162-202 1996 £150.00

SMITH, JOHN THOMAS   Antiquities of Westminster. London: Bensley, 1807-09. Large 4to; half title, title, dedn., xv, 276 pages, 38 plates, 14 hand colored plates and 62 additional plates, 16 pages, engraved titlepage and 62 plates; later half morocco; large paper. Abbey Scenery 210.; Twyman pp. 29/30; Adams 98.   Marlborough 162-203 1996 £800.00

SMITH, JOHN THOMAS   Remarks on Rural Scenery. London: Nathaniel Smith, 1797. 1st edition; 4to; 27, (1) pages, subscribers leaf, 20 etche dplates, fine decorative titlepage comprising wide ornamental borders enclosing black panelling and white title lettering, additionally hand colored in green and pink; later pebble grain cloth with large red gilt morocco label on upper board; some slight foxing to blank margin of plates; very good.   Ken Spelman 30-108 1996 £620.00

SMITH, JUSTIN HARVEY   Annexation of Texas. New York: Barnes & Noble, 1941. Correccted edition; ix, 496 pages; cloth, lightly soiled dust jacket; very good+. Jenkins BTB 188c; Howes S634 mention.   Bohling Book Co. 191-137 1996 $125.00

SMITH, LEE   Something in the Wind. New York: H&R, 1971. 1st edition; author's second book; fine in very bright, fine dust jacket. Thomas Dorn 9-232 1996 $150.00

SMITH, LUCY MACK   Biographical Sketches of Joseph Smith, the Prophet, and His Progenitors for Many Generations. Liverpool: & London: S. W. Richards, & Latter Day Saints Book Depot, 1853. 1st edition; 297 pages; full black leather, shelf wear and rubbing to extremities, corners rubbed through to board, front free endpaper missing, text block cracking in middle, but nothing loose, binding tight and contents complete, several pages have few pencil written names, notations from a 19th century owner, but these are unobtrusive. Rare.   Orrin Schwab 10-93 1996 $1,200.00

SMITH, MADELEINE   Full Report, of the Extraordinary and Interesting Trial of Miss Madeleine Smith. London: Read and Co. and Clayton & Son, 1857. three quarter morocco, over marbled boards; pretty. Meyer Boswell SL26-216 1996 $225.00

SMITH, MADELEINE   The Story of Minie l'Angelier or Madeleine Hamilton Smith. Edinburgh: Myles Pacphail, 11 South St. David St. 1857. Later three quarter calf over marbled boards, rubbed, but quite pretty. Meyer Boswell SL25-203 1996 $225.00

SMITH, MARY   An Affecting Narrative of the Captivity and Sufferings of Mrs. Mary Smith, Who With Her Husband and Three Daughters, Was Taken Prisoner by the Indians, in August, 1814, and After Enduring the Most Cruel Hardships and Torture of Mind for Sixty Days... N.P.: n.d., ca. 1818. 24 pages; woodcut vignette on titlepage, contemporary plain wrappers sewn, very minor foxing, fine, laid in half morocco and chemise slipcase; exceedingly rare edition; Howes S638; Shea Sale 583. Not in Gilcrease-Hargrett.   Michael D. Heaston 23-300 1996 $6,500.0

SMITH, MISS   Studies of Flowers from Nature... printed for...Miss Smith, Adwick Hall, near Doncaster, c. 1820. Small folio; engraved title with aquatinted and hand colored floral decoration, 19 of 20 hand colored aquatint practice plates (lacking plate 20 Strelitza Regina) and without any of the 20 fine master plates, 20 ll. of text, 2 ll. list of subscribers; contemporary half black straight grained morocco, spine gi in 6 compartments, rebacked relaying original backstrip, gilt edges, worn some finger soiling, occasional light spotting; rare. Dunthorne 283; Nissen 1855.   Thomas Thorp 489-287 1996 £500.00

SMITH, NATHAN   A Practical Essay on Typhous Fever. New York: E. Bliss & E. White, 1824. 1st edition; 8vo; 86 pages; original half speckled calf and boards, front hinge professionally repaired, boards somewhat worn, dampstaining, else very good. GM 5022; American Imprints 18013 Chapel Hill 94-274 1996 $375.00

SMITH, O. H.   Early Indiana Trials and Sketches. Cincinatti: Moore, Wilstach, Keys & Co., 1858. Original embossed cloth, faded, some foxing, but quite sound.   Meyer Boswell SL25-206 1996 $175.00

SMITH, R. D.   Citadel. Cairo: the British Inst., 1942. 1st edition the issue for Oct. 1942. Wrappers, page edges browned, covers slightly marked and dusty, staple rusted; very good.   Ulysses 39-162 1996 £95.00

SMITH, R. R. R.   Hellenistic Royal Portraits. Oxford: Clarendon Press, 1988. 4to; xii, 196 pages; 80 plates; original cloth, dust jacket. Archaeologia Luxor-4038 1996 $200.00

SMITH, RICHARD SHIRLEY   The Wood Engravings of Richard Shirley Smith. Cambridge: Silent Books, 1994. One of 100 special copies, numbered and signed by Richard Shirley Smith and with numbered and signed limited editions of two prints loosely inserted; 4to; 72 pages; 120 engravings; original boards with design composed of a montage of engravings, cloth spine; fine in original board slipcase.   Sotheran PN32-50 1996 £75.00

SMITH, ROBERT 1689-1768   A Compleat System of Opticks in Four Books. Cambridge: for the author, 1738. 1st edition; thick 4to; 2 volume in 1, (6), vi, (8), 455, 171, (9), (2), (1), (1) pages; 83 plates; with errata and instructions to the binder; original calf with gilt rules, expertly rebacked, five raised bands, original red morocco spine label laid down, last few leaves lightly dampstainedd, very good, crisp copy.   Edwin V. Glaser 121-295 1996 $3,000.00

SMITH, ROBERT ANGUS   Loch Etive and the Songs of Uisnach. London: Macmillan and Co., 1879. 8vo; pages xiv, 376; 19 plates; origin. cloth, gilt, little scattered spotting, nice copy.   R.F.G. Hollett 76-285 1996 £65.00

SMITH, ROBERT HOUSTON   Pella of the Decapolis. Wooster: College of Wooster, 1973-89. Folio; Volumes I and II; xxix, 250 pages, 69 illustrations, 94 plates; xxiii, 168 pages, 47 illustrations and 63 plates; with Smith's signature; original cloth.   Archaeologia Luxor-4040 1996 $250.00

SMITH, ROBERT HOUSTON   Pella of the Decapolis. Volume I. The 1967 Season of the College of Wooster Expedtion to Pella. Wooster: College of Wooster, 1973. Folio; xxix, 250 pages; 69 illustrations, 94 plates; original cloth.   Archaeologia Luxor-4039 1996 $150.00

SMITH, S. COMPTON   Chile Con Carne or the Camp and the Field. New York: 1887. 1st edition; 404 pages + ads, frontispiece, plates; pictorial cloth, spine rebacked, very good+.   T. A. Swinford 49-1078 1996 $275.00

SMITH, SAMUEL B.   The Wonderful Adventures of a Lady of French Nobility, and the Intrigues of a Popish Priest, Her Confessor, to Seduce and Murder Her. New York: Office of the Downfall of Babylon, 1836. Probable first edition; 12mo; woodcut frontispiece; very attractive contemporary American red sheep gilt binding, rubbed along edges, small worm holes on front cover and along lower inner cover, blue coated endpapers, some spotting of text; with contemporary signature Harriet Elizabeth Sears of Troy, with her stamp. Not in Shaw or Shoemaker.   James Cummins 14-187 1996 $275.00

SMITH, SEBA   John Smith's Letters, with 'Picters' to Match. New York: Samuel Colman, 1839. 1st edition; 8vo; 139 pages, 7 (of 9) inserted plates; original cloth backed drab boards, printed paper label on front cover; BAL 18382 1st printing; Hamilton 944.   M & S Rare Books 60-176   1996 $325.00

SMITH, SOLOMAN   Theatrical Management in the West and South for Thirty Years. New York: Harper & Bros., 1868. 1st edition; 8vo; 275 pages, 4 pages ads; portrait, in-text engravings; original cloth, superb copy, housed in custom cloth chemise and quarter morocco slipcase. Scarce. Clark III 415; Howes S672.   Chapel Hill 94-408   1996 $250.00

SMITH, SOLOMAN   Theatrical Management in the West and South for Thirty Years. New York: Harper & Bros., 1868. 1st edition; illustrations; original cloth, sunned, text in double column; Howes S672. Hamilton 1625.   Dramatis Personae 37-165   1996 $100.00

SMITH, STEVIE   A Good Time Was Had by All. London: Jonathan Cape Ltd., 1937. 1st edition; original binding, top edge dusty and partially faded, prelims, edges, endpapers and contents spotted, covers slightly marked, spine and cover edges darkened, head and tail of spine and corners bumped, very good, no dust jacket. Presentation copy from author for novelist Alice Ritchie.   Ulysses 39-542   1996 £185.00

SMITH, STEVIE   Novel on Yellow Paper or Work It Out for Yourself. London: Jonathan Cape, 1936. 1st edition; spotting to front and rear boards, top edges slightly dusty, but very good in dust jacket missing the word 'novel' on spine, otherwise showing normal wear.   Hermitage SP95-584   1996 $300.00

SMITH, THOMAS   Extracts from the Diary of a Huntsman. London: Whittaker & Co., 1838. 1st edition; demy 8vo; viii, (232) pages, litho f, 2 plates, 3 plans and 5 litho vignettes by author; bound with half title and final blank, but without ads and errata slip sometimes found; contemporary half straight grain morocco, neatly gilt, little light wear, few faint marks, but pleasant copy. Podeschi 159.   Ash Rare Books Zenzybyr-84   1996 £195.00

SMITH, THOMAS 1513-1577   De Republica Anglorum Libri Tres. Lug. Batavorum: Ex Officina Elzeviriana, 1630. 24mo; x, 404, (xii) pages; engraved title, contemporary vellum; bookplate, very good. Willems 337.   K Books 442-203   1996 £85.00

SMITH, THOMAS SHARPE   On the Economy of Nations. London: James Carpenter, 1842. 1st edition; 8vo; xii, 130 pages, complete with half title; recently well bound in linen backed marbled boards; very good. Black 5531; Goldsmiths 32581; Williams I 201; not in Kress.   John Drury 82-264   1996 £175.00

SMITH, W.   Synopsis of the British Diatomaceae with Remarks on Their Structure, Functions and Distribution. London: 1853-56. 2 volumes, 200 pages, 74 plates, 12 in color by T. West; cloth, edges worn. John Johnson 135-392   1996 $200.00

SMITH, W.   A Synopsis of the British Diatomaceae. London: 1853. 2 volumes in 1, 69 plates; half morocco, trifle rubbed, somewhat foxed, as usual; from the library of S. H. Meakin with a number of insertions, including a small correction to Sowerby English Botany.   Wheldon & Wesley 207-1658   1996 £200.00

SMITH, W. RAMSAY   Myths and Legends of the Australian Aboriginals. London: Geo. Harrap, 1930. 356 pages; many plates in black and white and 16 in color; original pictorial grey stamped and gilt cloth, spine very slightly faded, otherwise pristine; Mervyn Meggitt's copy, signed on endpaper.   Antipodean 28-365   1996 $125.00

SMITH, W. RAMSAY   Myths and Legends of the Australian Aboriginals. New York: Farrar & Rinehart, 1930. 1st U.S. edition; large 8vo; 356 pages; frontispiece and 20 pages and 15 color illustrations and illustrations in text; green cloth, paper title labels, attractive art deco dust jacket, little dusty, otherwise very good. Greenway 8586.   Antipodean 28-366   1996 $135.00

SMITH, WALTER   Art Education, Schoalstic and Industrial. Boston: James R. Osgood, 1872. 1st edition; 8vo; 40 full page, inserted illustrations; cloth, gilt, very good; copy of the Boston and Gloucester artist, Walter Dean, with his signature.   Freedom Bookshop 14-16 1996 $125.00

SMITH, WALTER E.   Charles Dickens in the Original Cloth. A Bibliographical Catalogue of the First Appearance of His Writings in Book Form in England... Los Angeles: 1982-83. 1st edition; 8vo; 2 volumes; 75 plates; original cloth, dust jacket.   Forest Books 74-248   1996 £70.00

SMITH, WILLIAM   History of Canada, from Its First Discovery to the Peace of 1763... Quebec: printed for the author by John Neilson, 1815. 1st edition; 8vo; 2 volumes; errata leaf, 333, 235 pages of text, 72 pages, 1 folding table, edges untrimmed, several unopened; original boards, paper backstrip to spines, printed paper labels, spines cracked and browned, booksellers ticket to front pastedown of volume 1, preserved in hessian backed slipcase with brown label, uncommon, in very good condition. Sabin 84701. GAgnon I 3337; Streeter VI 3554. Beeleigh Abbey BA/56-120   1996 £1,500.00

SMITH, WILLIAM   The History of the Post Office in British North America, 1639-1870. Cambridge: Cambridge University Press, 1920. 25 cm; ix, 358 pages; portraits, very good to fine in gilt stamped green cloth.   Rockland Books 38-203   1996 $250.00

SMITH, WILLIAM   Memoirs of William Smith. London: 1844. 8vo; pages ix, 150, 5 portraits and 13 illustrations; original cloth, neatly repaired, very rare; ex-library.   Wheldon & Wesley 207-279   1996 £75.00

SMITH, WILLIAM 1813-1893   A Dictionary of Christian Antiquites. (with) A Dictionary of Christian biography, Literature. Sects and Doctrines. London: 1875-80/75-87. Original edition; thick royal 8vo; together 2 works in 6 volumes; numerous illustrations; original cloth, gilt, joints little chafed.   Howes Bookshop 265-1132   1996 £150.00

SMITH, WILLIAM B.   Incidents of a Journey from Pennsylvania to Wisconsin Territory in 1837, Being the Journal of... Chicago: 1927. Limited edition, 18 out of 115 copies; 82 pages; cloth, fine, very scarce. Howes S720.   T. A. Swinford 49-1075   1996 $100.00

SMITH, WILLIAM B.   On Wheels and How I Came There. New York: Hunt and Eaton, 1893. 2nd edition; 338 pages; original cloth, rubbed, very good; Nevins I 202; Coulter 425; Dornbusch I Illinois 116. Nicholson p. 789.   McGowan Book Co. 65-83   1996 $200.00

SMITHS' CASH STORE, SAN FRANCISCO.   On the Klondike How to Go When to Go Where to Go What to Take Where To Get It. San Francisco: Valleau & Peterson, Printers, ca. 1897. 1st edition; (16) pages, including wrappers; illustrations within text; original pictorial wrappers with title on front cover; fine. Tourville 4208; not in Smith, Soliday or Streeter Sale.   Michael D. Heaston 23-13   1996 $1,200.00

SMOLLETT, TOBIAS GEORGE 1721-1771   The Adventures of Peregrine Pickle London: Wilson, 1751. 1st edition; octavo; 4 volumes, ix, 288; x, 322; v, 205; vii, 315 pages; contemporary dark calf with red and green lettering panels on spines, slight dampstaining to rear board of volume 1, light rubbing to extremities, still fine set with only light occasional foxing, housed in dropback box of morocco and cloth. Rothschild 1910. Bromer Booksellers   90-225   1996 $2,500.00

SMOLLETT, TOBIAS GEORGE 1721-1771   The Adventures of Peregrine Pickle. London: printed for the author, 1751. 1st edition; 12mo; 4 volumes; pages ix, (i), 288; x, 322; v, (i), 205; vii, (i), 315; titlepages stained by turn-ins, L12 (pp. 227/28) in volume ii cancelled (as often); contemporary tan calf, rebacked, raised bands between double gilt rules, gilt lettered red leather labels, double gilt fillet border on sides, some corners repaired, endpapers stained by turn-ins, hinges strengthened, generally very good; early owner's name 'P. Gell', Hopton stamped at tail of titlepage. Ashley Lib. V p. 185/86; Rothschild 1910; Tinker 1927. Blackwell's B112-259   1996 £550.00

SMOLLETT, TOBIAS GEORGE 1721-1771   The Adventures of Peregrine Pickle. London: Strahan, Rivington, etc., 1784. 7th edition; small 8vo; 4 volumes, pages (xii), 268, 298, 282, 304; frontispiece to each volume; full contemporary calf, gilt; attractive early set. CBEL II 524.   Hartfield 48-L81   1996 $395.00

SMOLLETT, TOBIAS GEORGE 1721-1771   The Expedition of Humphry Clinker. London: Johnston, Collins, 1771. 1st edition; octavo; 3 volumes; xv, 250; 249; 275 pages; full speckled calf with spines gilt in 6 compartments and housed in cloth slipcase; extremities show faint rubbing, top outer hinge of volume 1, just starting, slight offsetting to endleaves, still remarkably clean and tight, near fine set; bookplates. Rothschild 1925; Grolier/English 56.   Bromer Booksellers 87-260   1996 $1,850.00

SMOLLETT, TOBIAS GEORGE 1721-1771   The Expedition of Humphry Clinker. London: printed for W. Johnston...and B. Collins, 1771. 2nd edition; 12mo; 3 volumes; half titles present, hinges strengthened, pages xv, (i0, 250; (iv), 249; (iv), 275; contemporary sprinkled calf, edges darkened, rebacked with raised bands between gilt bands, gilt lettered red labels, endpapers browned, early owner's name "D. Gell" on cut out scrap bouquet of holly within wreath, surmounted by cut out eagle crest. Blackwell's B112-260   1996 £250.00

SMOLLETT, TOBIAS GEORGE 1721-1771   The Expedition of Humphry Clinker. London: printed for J. Sibbald, 1793. Early illustrated edition; 8vo; 2 volumes in one; 10 engraved plates by Thomas Rowlandson; contemporary tree calf, lightly chipped at head of spine, very good, attractive and uncommon.   Captain's Bookshelf 38-203 1996 $250.00

SMOLLETT, TOBIAS GEORGE 1721-1771   A Complete History of England... (with) A Continuation of the Complete History. London: James Rivington and James Fletcher/Richard Baldwin, 1757/60/60/61. 2nd/3rd edition; 15 volumes; many plates; contemporary calf, double labels, worn, 3 boards detached, most joints tender, one folding map torn, some foxing, ex-library.   Robert Clark 38-323 1996 £125.00

SMOLLETT, TOBIAS GEORGE 1721-1771   The History of England, from the Revolution to the Death of George the Second. London: printed for T. Cadell and R. Baldwin, 1796. Later edition; 8vo; 5 volumes, 515, 574, 548, 510; 390 pages, (122) page index; later flame calf bindings with gilt spines in 6 compartments and red morocco spine labels; bookplates in all volumes, extremities rubbed, foxing, couple of volumes spines chipped and outer joints cracked, still very good, complete set. Chapel Hill 94-228 1996 $150.00

SMOLLETT, TOBIAS GEORGE 1721-1771   The Novels. Boston: Houghton Mifflin, 1926. 1st of this edition; number 196 of only 500 large paper copies; tall octavo; printed on fine paper; 11 volumes, plus the very scarce Salesman's prospectus with binding and illustration samples; titlepage in red and black; linen spines, blue boards, gilt on black leather labels, uncut, largely unopened; very handsome set. Ransom II no. 36. Hartfield 48-A17 1996 $895.00

SMOLLETT, TOBIAS GEORGE 1721-1771   Select Essays On Commerce, Agriculture, Mines, Fisheries and Other Useful Subjects. London: printed for D. Wilson & T. Durham, 1754. 1st edition; 8vo; mottled calf antique, spine gilt; light browning, small library stamp on verso of titlepage, but nice, attractive binding; Kress 5401; Higgs 740; CBEL II 964.   Ximenes 109-270 1996 $1,750.00

SMOLLETT, TOBIAS GEORGE 1721-1771   The Works. London: Gibbings & Co., ca. 1910. Limited edition; small 8vo; 12 volumes; handsome three quarter brown levant morocco, gilt panelled spines with floral inlays, raised bands, gilt top, by Zaehnsdorf. Fine, attractive set. Appelfeld Gallery 54-167 1996 $600.00

SMYTH, H. WARINGTON   Mast and Sail in Europe and Asia. London: Murray, 1906. 1st edition; 8vo; 448 pages, diagrams, plates; cloth, very good. Very scarce   John Lewcock 30-158 1996 £50.00

SMYTH, HENRY DE WOLF   Atomic Energy for Military Purposes. Princeton: Princeton University Press, 1945. 1st public edition; fine in dust jacket with small, neat private library numbers on spine; bookplate of James J. Waring.   Hermitage SP95-1083 1996 $150.00

SMYTH, HENRY DE WOLF   Atomic Enery for Military Purposes a General Account of the Scientific Research and Technical Development That Went into the Making of Atomic Bombs. Princeton: Princeton University Press, 1945. 1st edition; signed by Dr. Edward Teller; good/very good in like dust jacket.   Aronovitz 57-1105 1996 $150.00

SMYTH, HENRY DE WOLF   A General Account of the Development of Methods of Using Atomic Energy for Military PUrposes. N.P.: August 1945. 1st issue of advance distribution to the press; large 8vo; mimeographed format; very good; this copy has the rubber stamp of Allen V. Hazeltine, Lt. Colonel of the General Staff Corps.   Metacomet Books 54-101 1996 $1,750.00

SMYTH, R. BROUGH   The Aborigines of Victoria: with Notes Relating to the Habits of the Natives of Other Parts of Australia and Tasmania. London: 1878. Volume 1 only, (lxxii), 483 pages, illustrations, large map; pictorial gilt blue buckram, hinges loose, otherwise good+. The Absolon copy. Ferguson 15882.   Antipodean 28-367 1996 $250.00

SMYTH, W. H.   The Cycle of Celestial Objects Continued at the Hartwell Observatory to 1859. London: printed for private circulation by John Bowyer Nichols & Sons, 1860. 4to; 480 pages; 6 plates; many engravings; rebound in black cloth, boards scuffed, white stain to front board, corners of 2 pages cut, some pencil notes in margins, otherwise good; Walter Scott Houston's copy with his bookplate.   Knollwood Books 70-181 1996 $500.00

SMYTH, WILLIAM   English Lyricks. Liverpool: printed by J. M'Creery and sold by Cadell and Davies, 1797. 8vo; contemporary calf, gilt ruled borders, spine decorated in gilt, rubbed; very attractive; with inscription "M. M. White. The gift of Mr. C. Peers."   James Cummins 14-188 1996 $225.00

SMYTHE, F.   Camp Six. 1937. 1st edition; 36 plates, some slight foxing of pages; generlaly very good to fine.   Moutaineering Books 8-S40 1996 £55.00

SMYTHE, F.   Camp Six. London: 1937. 1st edition; 36 plates; fine in very good dust jacket with slight soiling and minor repairs. Moutaineering Books 8-R39 1996 £110.00

SMYTHE, F.   Edward Whymper. 1940. 1st edition; 24 plates, 2 folding maps; some browning of endpapers, otherwise bright, fine copy in cream colored above average very good dust jacket, little foxed and browned.   Moutaineering Books 8-S45 1996 £90.00

SMYTHE, F.   Kamet Conquered. 1932. 1st edition; 50 plates, folding map; some foxing mainly of page edges, boards slightly bumped at head of spine, but clean and bright, so very good+, scarce white dust jacket has usual light soiling and repair to head of spine.   Moutaineering Books 8-S46 1996 £70.00

SMYTHE, F.   Kamet Conquered. London: 1932. 1st edition; 50 plates, plus folding map; fine in dust jacket, which is, as usual, slightly soiled and has neat repairs to front panel, but is in above average condition. Moutaineering Books 8-S45 1996 £80.00

SMYTHE, HENRY   Historical Sketch of Parker County and Weatherford, Texas. St. Louis: Louis C. Lavat, 1877. 1st edition; (16), (7) 476 pages; later cloth, original morocco backstrip laid down; very good. Graff 3873; Raines p. 191-92. Howes S734; Vandale 162.   Michael D. Heaston 23-301 1996 $1,500.00

SMYTHE, ROBERT   Historical Account of Charter House. London: printed for the editor by C. spilsbury, Angle Court, Snowhill... 1808. 1st edition; 4to; (2), (i-iv), (4), 1-298 pages, appendix 1-84 pages; frontispiece, 3 engraved plates, vignette to letterpress; new endpapers, modern paper backed boards, paper label to spine, slight marking to boards, others untrimmed. Good copy. Upcott 772.   Beeleigh Abbey BA56-22 1996 £95.00

SMYTHE, SARAH M.   Ten Months in the Fiji Islands. Oxford: John Henry & James Parker, 1864. 8vo; pages xviii, 282, 4 maps, 10 plates (4 colored); quarter green morocco, small half inch library perforation stamp on title. Taylor p. 373; Snow 789; Hocken p. 233.   Richard Adelson W94/95-160 1996 $385.00

SMYTHE, WILLIAM   Narrative of a Journey from Lima to Para, Across the Andes and Down the Amazon. London: 1836. vii, (1), 305, (ii), (4 ad) pages, 10 plates, 3 maps, 1 map separated at fold; later half navy leather, with an unneeded 'e' at end of 1st author's name; cancelled library stamp on back of frontispiece and 1 internal page.   Bookworm & Silverfish 280-221 1996 $295.00

SMYTHIES, BERTRAM E.   The Birds of Burma. London: Oliver & Boyd, 1953. 2nd edition; royal 8vo; xliiii, 668 pages; 31 color plates by A. M. Hughes; cloth, dust jacket, very nice.   Thomas Thorp 489-288 1996 £100.00

SMYTHIES, BETRAM E.   The Birds of Burma. London: 1953. 2nd edition; 31 colored plates; good in very frayed dust jacket, light discoloration to covers.   David A.H. Grayling MY95Orn-68 1996 £90.00

SNELL, CHARLES   The Art of Writing. In its Theory and Practice By... London: Henry Overton, 1712. Oblong folio; engraved title (1), portrait, 1? pages letterpress, engraved calligraphic title and plates (2)-28; 19th century half brown roan slightly rubbed.   Jarndyce 103-344 1996 £350.00

SNELLING, THOMAS   Snellings Seventy-One Plates of Gold and Silver Coin, with Their Weight, Fineness and Value. London: printed for H. Chapman, W. Collins and T. King, ca. 1788-92. 8vo; title leaf, 71 plates, 24 leaves; 19th century calf backed boards.   Howard S. Mott 227-13? 1996 $250.00

SNIDER, DENTON J.   A Walk in Hellas, or the Old in the New. St. Louis: privately printed, 1881. 8vo; 350 pages; original publisher's gilt lettered cloth, spine with light shelfwear and tears, label no longer present; from the collection of Heinrich Schliemann, and was acquired b? Professor Akerstrom; with facsimile letter about acquisition; inscribed b? Charles Parsons for Schliemann.   Archaeologia Luxor-3988 1996 $450.00

SNODGRASS, JOHN JAMES   Narrative of the Burmese War... London: John Murray, 1827. 1st edition; 8vo; pages xii, 319, (8) ads, 1 plate and large folding map, small fold tear with no loss, uncut; original boards, hinges starting, but firm, paper label; some rubbing to edges, excellent copy, seldom found in original condition; bookplate of John, 1st Baron Crewe.   Howard S. Mott 227-158 1996 $450.00

SNODGRASS, W. D.   Traditional Hungarian Songs. Baltimore: Published by Charles Seluzicki, Poetry Bookseller, 1978. In an edition of 300 copies, this one of 285 pencil numbered copies, signed by translator; 11.5 x 8.75 inches; 24 pages; 8 masonite relief cuts by Dorian McGowan variously combined for 17 decorations, relief decorations printed in rose, designed and set by Claire Van Vliet, printed on Softwhite Mohawk Superfine, handset titles printed in black and spruce blue, text machine set in spruce blue, musical staves, copyright notice, colophon and afterword in brown, handsewn into Natural Zaan covers with Tampico brown Strathmore endpaper, Masonite relief decoration printed in rose on front cover; fine.   Joshua Heller 21-16 1996 $150.00

SNOW, JACK   The Shaggy Man of Oz. Chicago: Reilly & Lee, 1949. 1st edition; small 4to; 254 pages; illustrations by Frank Kramer; original light green cloth, large pictorial cover label, bookplate, spine faded, else near fine.   Chapel Hill 94-243 1996 $125.00

SNOW, PHILIP   The People from the Horizon. Oxford: Phaidon/New York: Dutton, 1979. 29 cm; 296 pages, color and black and white plates, illustrations; photos; cloth, dust jacket, cardboard slipcase.   L. Clarice Davis 111-139 1996 $150.00

SNYDER, GARY   North Pacific Lands and Waters. A Further Six Sections. Waldron Island: Brooding Heron, 1993. Of a total edition of 300 copies, this one of 274 signed by author; prints by Bill Holm; fine, without dust jacket, as issued.   Ken Lopez 74-413 1996 $275.00

SOBY, JAMES THRALL   Tchelitchew - Paintings - Drawings. New York: Museum of Modern Art, 1942. 1st edition; 2 color plates and 72 black and white reproductions; wrappers, top edge slightly dusty, spine faded, covers slightly marked, very good; from the library of James Hart.   Ulysses 39-584 1996 £55.00

SOCIETY FOR PURE ENGLISH   Tracts I-XL. Oxford: Clarendon Press, 1919-34. 8vo; 2 volumes; facsimile plates; maroon half morocco, spines gilt, labels, untrimmed; with Tract XX (Index) loosely inserted, in original wrappers.   Robert Clark 38-285 1996 £250.00

SOCIETY FOR THE IMPROVEMENT OF NAVAL ARCHITECTURE   An Address to the Public, from the Society for the Improvement of Naval Architecture. N.P.: London: n.d. 1791. 8vo; disbound; very scarce.   Ximenes 109-204 1996 $100.00

SOCIETY OF ANTIQUARIES OF LONDON   The Antiquaries Journal Being the Journal of... Oxford University Press, 1973-89. Royal 8vo; 17 volumes (volumes 53-69); with 3 general index volumes, XI-XX, XLI_L, LI-LX. original paperbound parts as issued;   Howes Bookshop 265-27 1996 £150.00

SOCIETY OF ARTISTS OF GREAT BRITAIN   A Catalogue of the Pictures, Sculptures, Models, Drawings, Prints, &c. Exhibited by the Society of Artists of Great Britain, at the Great Room in Spring-Garden, Charing-Cross, May the 9th, 1761. London: 1761. 4to; illustrations, incuding 2 plates by Hogarth; sewn as issued; somewhat dusty at beginning and end, bit dog eared and creased throughout, but essentially in very good condition, entirely uncut.   Ximenes 108-329 1996 $1,250.00

SOCIETY OF FRIENDS   An Epistle from Our General Spring Meeting of Ministers. N.P.: n.p., 1755. Folio slipcase and 4to. text; 4 pages; original wrappers, and gray slipcase; paper browned, short tears along creases, otherwise very good. Rare.   The Bookpress 75-462 1996 $125.00

THE SOLDIER'S Hymn Book. Chicago: Chicago Young Men's Christian Association, ca. 1863. 39th thousand; 24mo; 62, (2) pages; original cloth backed colored pictorial boards. fine; pencil signature of Edwin A. Gallup, Co. H, 9th Vt. Volunteers.   M & S Rare Books 60-303 1996 $250.00

SOLE, W.   Menthae Britannicae; Being a New Botanical Arrangement of All the British Mints Hietherto Discovered. Bath: 1798. Folio; pages viii, 55, (1), 24 colored engraved plates; half morocco; rare, especially colored. Henrey 1362.   Wheldon & Wesley 207-102 1996 £1,500.00

SOLIS Y RIBADENEYRA, ANTONIO DE 1610-1686   Historia de la Conquista de Mexico, Poblacion, y Progresos de la America Septentrional, Conocida por el Nuenra Espana. Barcelona: Joseph Llopis (sic), 1691. 2nd edition; folio; half title; decorative title printed in red and black; contemporary limp vellum, front free endpaper defective; very good, black cloth slipcase. Palau 318603; sabin 86447.   George J. Houle 68-137 1996 $1,500.00

SOLIS Y RIBADENEYRA, ANTONIO DE 1610-1686   The History of the Conquest of Mexico by the Spaniards. London: T. Woodward, etc., 1724. 1st edition in English, folio; 9 ff., 163, 252, 152 pages; portrait, 6 plates, 2 maps; contemporary caf, gilt, slightly worn. Tall and handsome copy. Inscribed "Frances Clerk July ye 22 1724,..." Sabin 86487.   Marlborough 162-259 1996 £750.00

SOLL, IVAN   Tryangulations. Madison: Tirmamisu, 1991. One of 90 copies only; page size 11 1/2 x 9 1/2 x 6 3/4 inches, triangular book nested in rectangular box so as to divide the rectangle into four triangular shapes; cover of the box folds around the box twice ending in triangular tongue that divides the outer rectangular surface visually into three triangles; the form of the book and box are appropriate to the text images.   Priscilla Juvelis 95/1-241 1996 $450.00

SOLON, L. M.   The Art of the Old English Potter. London: Bemrose & sons, 1885. Large paper edition, limited to only 250 numbered copies, signed by publisher; imperial 8vo; pages xxiv, 269; 55 illustrations by author on India paper; publisher's morocco backed cloth, edges uncut, spine slightly rubbed, corners and edges to cloth sides little worn;   Thomas Thorp 489-289 1996 £60.00

SOLT, MARY ELLEN   Flowers in Concrete. Bloomington: Design Program Fine Arts Dept. Indiana University, 1966. 1st edition; one of 100 copies; square 8vo; illustrations; original decorated Fabriano wrappers, fine.   James S. Jaffe 34-118 1996 $150.00

SOLT, MARY ELLEN   Flowers in Concrete. Bloomington: Fine Arts Department, Indiana University, 1969. Portfolio edition, limited to 40 copies, with each of the prints signed by Solt; elephant folio; 11 loose sheets in portfolio; fine.   James S. Jaffe 34-119 1996 $650.00

SOLZHENITSYN, ALEXANDER   One Day in the Life of Ivan Denisovich. London: Gollancz, 1963. 1st British edition; near fine in very good dust jacket.   Timothy P. Slongo 5-238 1996 $100.00

SOLZHENITSYN, ALEXANDER   Stories and Prose Poems. New York: FSG, 1971. 1st U.S. edition; near fine in like dust jacket with faint yellowing to both flaps; inscribed by author, quite uncommon thus.   Lame Duck Books 19-503 1996 $750.00

SOLZHENITSYN, ALEXANDER   Stories and Prose Poems. New York: FSG, 1971. 1st American edition; fine in very near fine jacket, inscribed by author, books signed by Solzhenitsyn are quite uncommon.   Ken Lopez 74-415 1996 $750.00

SOLZHENITSYN, ALEXANDER   We Never Make Mistakes. Columbia: University of South Carolina Press, 1963. 1st edition; good, unlaminated dust jacket that is spine faded, much rubbed, couple of very tiny edge chips; fine, extremely scarce.   Ken Lopez 74-414 1996 $125.00

SOME Account of the English Stage, from the Restoration in 1660 to 1830. Bath: printed by H. E. Carrington, 1832. Octavo; 10 volumes, with 377 extra illustrations, 192 of which are hand painted; bound by Bayntun in full red morocco, covers decoratively stamped in gilt, gilt spine with raised bands tooled in compartments, gilt board edges and inner dentelles, all edges gilt, marbled endpapers, small stains to some covers, armorial bookplate, handsome set.   Heritage Book Shop 196-248 1996 $3,000.00

SOME British Ballads. London: Constable, 1919. Limited to 575 numbered copies, signed by Rackham; quarto; 170 pages; 16 full page color illustrations mounted on white paper and 24 black and white drawings by Arthur Rackham; cream boards, quarter vellum, pictorial stamping in gold on cover and spine; fine.   Bromer Booksellers 87-255 1996 $2,000.00

SOME British Ballads. London: Constable & Co., Ltd., 1919. 1st edition illustrated by Rackham; 4to; pages 8, (ii), 170; 16 colored plates mounted on grey stock behind tissue guards, fore-edge little speckled; original mid blue cloth, gilt, uncut, pictorial endpapers; excellent, bright and smart copy.   Sotheran PN32-146 1996 £198.00

SOME Fragments for C.R.H. Lexington: Stamperia del Santuccio, 1967. Number 70 of 125 copies; 8.25 x 5.25 inches; 91 pages; printed in black with red on handmade paper; brown Japanese Omni paper boards, wrap-around printed label, fragile Japanese paper dust jacket; fine. Joshua Heller 21-140 1996 $250.00

SOME Remarks on a Pamphlet Intituled, Reflections on the Expediency of Opening the Trade with Turkey. London: printed in the Year, 1753. 24 pages, with half title; light brown stain in lower inner margin only, otherwise very good, rebound in boards, paper label. Higgs 467; Kress 5305; Goldsmiths 8808.   C. R. Johnson 37-34 1996 £150.00

SOME Southwestern Trails. El Paso: Carl Hertzog, 1948. Limited 1st edition; one of 750 copies; oblong 4to; illustrations; lacks paper slipcase, cover faded. Lowman 54C; Robinson 13c.   Maggie Lambeth 30-238 1996 $200.00

SOME Trout. Poetry on Trout and Angling by Various Authors. North Humberside: Chevington Press, 1989. One of 75 copies; each signed by printer and artist, D. R. Wakefield; page size 20 1/2 x 15 inches; 13 etchings printed in color; bound loose in green cloth clamshell box; Priscilla Juvelis 95/1-4 1996 $2,500.00

SOMERS, JOHN, LORD   Iura Populi Anglicani; or, the Subject's Right of Petitioning Set Forth... London: printed in the year 1701 and reprinted for J. Almon, 1772. Definite foxing, and embrowning, but nice in new speckled calf.   Meyer Boswell SL27-200 1996 $450.00

SOMERVELL, JOHN   Some Westmorland Wills 1686-1738. Kendal: Titus Wilson, 1928. 1st edition; 8vo; pages 119; uncut, 9 plates; original cloth, gilt.   R.F.G. Hollett & Son 78-1294 1996 £65.00

SOMERVELL, JOHN   Water-Power Mills of South Westmorland, on the Kent, Bela and Gilpin and Their Tributaries. Kendal: Titus Wilson, 1930. 1st edition; 8vo; 4 plates; original cloth, gilt, very nice, scarce.   R.F.G. Hollett & Son 78-626 1996 £80.00

SOMERVELL, JOHN   Water-Power Mills of South Westmorland, on the Kent, Bela and Gilpin and Their Tributaries. Kendal: Titus Wilson, 1930. 1st edition; 8vo; 4 plates; cloth gilt, remainder binding; very nice. R.F.G. Hollett & Son 78-627 1996 £60.00

SOMERVILLE,   An Incorruptible Irishman: Being an Account of Chief Justice Charles Kendal Bushe... 1932. 1st edition; 8vo; portrait, illustrations, cloth, dust jacket repaired; signed by author, very good. C. P. Hyland 216-794 1996 £75.00

SOMERVILLE, ALEXANDER   The Autobiography of a Working Man. London: Charles Gilpin, 1848. 1st edition; large 12mo; iv, 511, (1) pages, 12 pages of publisher's ads; original brown ribbed cloth, patterned in blind, spine lettered in gilt, little wear to joints, else good, uncut copy. Stammhammer III 316; Kress C7588; Goldsmiths 35899.1.   John Drury 82-265 1996 £125.00

SOMERVILLE, EDITH   The States through Irish Eyes. Boston: Houghton Mifflin, 1930. Limited 1st edition of only 375 copies, signed by author; very good+ in slipcase.   October Farm 36-222 1996 $185.00

SOMERVILLE, WILLIAM 1675-1742   The Chase, A Poem; to which is added Hobbinol. Birmingham: printed by Robert Martin, sold by A. Donaldson, 1767. Quarto; original calf, joints cracked, ends of spine chipped, bookplate, name on endpaper, some foxing throughout as usual. Gaskell, Baskerville Add. 3.   G. W. Stuart 59-13 1996 $250.00

SOMERVILLE, WILLIAM 1675-1742   The Chace. Garden City: Doubleday, Doran & Co., Inc., 1929. In an edition of 375 numbered copies, this is one of 325 for America; 12 x 8 inches; 118 pages; 16 reproductions of woodcuts by John Bewick, designed and printed by Richard W. Ellis; green cloth over board with title label on spine; spine slightly darkened and edges of pages slightly browned, else very good. Joshua Heller 21-51 1996 $185.00

SOMNER, WILLIAM   The Antiquities of Canterbury in Two Parts. London: printed for R. Knaplock, 1703. 2nd edition; folio; 2 volumes in 1, large paper copy; 192 pages of text, 80 page appendix, 4 page table to part 1, 178 pages of text, 70 page appendix, 3 page table to part 2, with errata to both parts on verso of last leaf; frontispiece, 13 engraved plates, 6 maps, city plans, ground plans; full red morocco, triple gilt rule borders enclosing central gilt rule rectangle with ornate cornerpieces to both covers, fully gilt panelled spine, top edge gilt, inner gilt dentelles, marbled endpapers, bound by F. Bedford. Cox III p. 187; Upcott pp. 388-90; Lowndes V2442.   Beeleigh Abbey BA56-23 1996 £900.00

SONDEHEIM, STEPHEN   Sweeney Todd: the Demon Barber of Fleet Street. New York: Dodd Mead, 1979. 1st edition; fine in dust jacket. Between the Covers 42-405 1996 $125.00

SONDHEIM, STEPHEN   Sunday in the Park. New York: Dodd, Mead, 1986. 1/250 numbered copies, signed by Sondheim and James Lapine; mint in handsome matching forest-green slipcase.   Bev Chaney, Jr. 23-620 1996 $175.00

SONDHEIM, STEPHEN   Sunday in the Park with George. New York: Dodd Mead, 1986. 1st edition; top corners bumped, else fine in dust jacket.   Between the Covers 42-406 1996 $175.00

SONDLEY, F. A.   A History of Buncombe County, North Carolina. Asheville: Advocate Printing Co., 1930. 1st edition; 8vo; 2 volumes, (x), 455; 456-916 pages; illustrations; black morocco, gilt title on spines, bible corners, rubbed on extremities, inner hinges reinforced with tape, light foxing on endpapers of volume 1, owner's name in volume 2, else very good. Thornton 12904.   Andrew Cahan 47-152 1996 $200.00

A SONG in Favour of Bundling Leicester: printed at the Orpheus Press for the Twelve by Eight Press, 1963. 64/200 copies; 21 pages; printed in red and black on grey, green, pink and blue papers handmade by John Mason and signed by him, 5 wood engravings by Rigby Graham; original quarter cream linson vellum, backstrip gilt lettered, white boards with overall closely linked pattern of maroon, untrimmed, glassine jacket, white card chemise; fine.   Blackwell's B112-273 1996 £60.00

SONNICHSEN, C. L.   Pass of the North: Four Centuries on the Rio Grande. El Paso: Texas Western, 1968. 1st edition; 2 volumes; signed by Cisneros and Sonnichsen; illustrations; very good+ in good dust jacket. Parker Books of the West 30-168 1996 $250.00

SONNINI, C. S.   Travels in Upper and Lower Egypt: Untertaken by Order of the Old Government of France... London: printed for J. Debrett, 1800. 1st 4to. edition; xl, 730, 14 pages; frontispiece, folded map, 27 plates; recent morocco, lacking half title, 3 plates with minor tears and repairs, slightly foxing, otherwise very good.   Worldwide Antiquarian 151-850 1996 $850.00

SOPHOCLES 496-406 BC   (Greek title) Sophoclis Tragoediae VII. Ex officina Christophori Plantini, Archtypographi Regii, 1579-80. 16mo; pages 431, (18), text in small Greek script, small printer's device on title, woodcut initials, all edges gilt, fine straight grained red morocco binding; Brunet V447; Dibdin II 411-12; Adams S449.   Family Album Tillers-575 1996 $680.00

SOPPE, JOAN M.   Living Room. 1994. Punched on metal strip on back cover is "Case Number 4/10 February 1994 J. M. Soppe". 9.5 x 6.5 inches; 12 leaves of handmade paper from linen in cream, flecked rust and tan, minimal letterpress by Soppe; cut-outs, punched holes, thread, onlays, photos, illustrations, with tiny beads contained in opaque packet sewn to page, metal insert, glass slide of living room bordered in black inset into front cover board, decorative metal design on spine incorporating small beads in narrow glass tube, opaque paper over board punched with tiny holes, metal rings and threads visible under paper, fine in cream cloth drop-back box.   Joshua Heller 21-218 1996 $400.00

SOPPE, JOAN M.   Trespasses. An Artist's Book. Cedar Rapids: 1993. One in an edition of 25 copies, stamped on copperplate; 5.25 x 4.5 x 0.75 inches; minimal letterpress text, handmade paper from flax, etched copperplate and small copperplates and threads, gauze, torn printed page, negative, onlays and inlays, hand sewing, in dos-a-dos binding, one side of cream board with central cut out to show page below, the other side with glass slide showing house plan design inset; cream cloth and green paper trim drop=back box.   Joshua Heller 21-217 1996 $295.00

SOREDD, CURTIUS   One Hundred and Thirty Quatrains by Curtius Soredd. Pasadena: Grey Bow Press, 1928. One of 75 copies numbered and signed by translator; 8 1/2 x 5 3/4 inches; (viii), 44 pages + colophon, marginal notes printed in blue; marbled boards with cloth spine and paper spine label, label chipped, replacement label tipped in at rear, uncut.   Dawson's Books Shop 528-49 1996 $250.00

SORIA, MARTIN S.   The Paintings of Zurbaran. London: 1953. Medium 8vo; x, 200 pages, 280 illustrations; buckram, dust jacket.   Rainsford A54-614 1996 £55.00

SORLEY, CHARLES HAMILTON   Marlborough and Other Poems. Cambridge: Cambridge University Press, 1916. 1st edition; black and white frontispiece photo of author; titlepage, buckram, top edge dusty, prelims, edges and endpapers spotted, covers slightly marked and rubbed, free endpapers browned, head and tail of spine and corners slightly bumped, very good; Cambridge University Press's onw copy, bookplate of literary agent John Johnson.   Ulysses 39-643 1996 £250.00

SORLIER, CHARLES   Chagall's Posters: a Catalogue Raisonne. New York: Crown, 1975. folio; 159 pages; profusely illustrated, mostly in color; cloth, dust jacket. Freitag 1582.   Brannan 43-126 1996 $245.00

SORRENTINO, GILBERT   A Beehive Arranged on Humane Principles. Grenfell Press, 1986. One of 70 copies signed by author and artist (of total edition of 85); 10 3/4 x 8 3/4 inches; (28) leaves, joined at top and printed on one side only, 4 full page color linocuts by David Storey; erratum slip laid in, title and first page of text partly printed in red; Original black morocco backed pictorial paper boards, edges untrimmed; mint.   Phillip J. Pirages 33-274 1996 $225.00

SOSEKI, MUSO   Sun at Midnight: 23 Poems. Nadja, 1985. Of 226 numbered copies, signed by translator and artist, this one of 200 in wrappers; 8vo; printed in black, red and blue in handset Stempel Optima on cream Arches; woodcuts by Antonio Frasconi; fine.   Bertram Rota 272-301 1996 £50.00

SOTEROPOULOS, S.   The Brigands of the Morea. London: Saunders, Otley and Co., 1868. 1st edition in English; thick 8vo; 2 volumes in one; xvi, 294; (iv), 326 pages; engraved frontispiece, original blue cloth, gilt, gilt edges, inner hinges cracked (but firm); apparently rather scarce, not in NUC or BM Cat.   James Burmester 29-130 1996 £200.00

SOTHEBY, WILLIAM   Constance de Castile, a Poem in Ten Cantos. London: 1810. 1st edition: 4to; (vi), 191 pages; original grey boards, bit rubbed, small patch of 'extinct' worm affecting the first 9 leaves, but with no loss, good;   K Books 441-457 1996 £70.00

SOTO, HERNANDO DE   The Discovery of Florida. San Francisco: Book Club of California, 1946. Limited to 280 copies; folio; 115 pages, coat-of-arms on title, 47 initials and special printer's device, all in red, yellow and black, designed and cut by Mallette Dean; cloth backed decorated boards, bottom corners lightly bumped, rear cover with uniform soiling, else fine.   Argonaut Book Shop 113-194 1996 $225.00

SOUDER, CASPER   The Mysteries and Miseries of Philadelphia, as Exhibited and Illustrated by a late Presentment of the Grand Jury and by a Sketch of the Condition of the Most Degraded Classes of the City. Philadelphia: 1853. 1st edition; 8vo; 20 pages; rebacked with paper. Sabin 51653.   M & S Rare Books 60-395 1996 $275.00

SOULE, FRANK   The Annals of San Francisco.. New York: San Francisco: & London: Appleton, 1855. 1st edition; 824 pages, frontispiece, plates, portraits and maps, folding map; original full black morocco, title in gilt on spine, all edges gilt, minor wear and repairs to spine, overall fine. Cowan p. 601; Graff 3901. Howes S769; Wheat Gold 193. Zamorano 80 70.   Michael D. Heaston 23-68 1996 $350.00

SOUSTER, RAYMOND   As Is. Toronto: Oxford University Press, 1967. 1st edition; of the last 75 copies, one of 62 each with a different unpublished poem written on front flyleaf, signed and dated August 1971 on back flyleaf; cloth, dust jacket; fine; with John Newlove's ownership signature, from the library of John Metcalf, with his ownership signature. Nelson Ball 118-155 1996 $150.00

SOUSTER, RAYMOND   City Hall Street. Toronto: Ryerson, c. 1951. 1st edition; near fine; author's copy with his pencilled notations and revisions; from the library of John Metcalf, with his ownership signature. Nelson Ball 118-157 1996 $200.00

SOUSTER, RAYMOND   The Colour of the Times: the Colleccted Poems. Toronto: Ryerson Press, c. 1964. 1st edition; 121 pages; cloth, dust jacket; about fine, autographed by author; from the library of John Metcalf, with his ownership signature.   Nelson Ball 118-158 1996 $100.00

SOUSTER, RAYMOND   Go to Sleep, World. Toronto: Ryerson, 1947. 1st edition; vii 59 pages; boards; fine in dust jacket; from the library of John Metcalf, with his ownership signature.   Nelson Ball 118-160 1996 $400.00

SOUSTER, RAYMOND   A Local Pride. Toronto: Contact Press, 1962. 1st edition; 131 pages; issued in printed card covers, printed dust jacket; fine; from the library of John Metcalf, with his ownership signature.   Nelson Ball 118-163 1996 $250.00

SOUSTER, RAYMOND   A Local Pride. Toronto: Contact Press, 1962. wrappers, dust jacket has light edge wear, including several tiny tears, otherwise fine.   Neil Cournoyer 4-93 1996 $109.00

SOUSTER, RAYMOND   Shake Hands with the Hangman: Poems 1940-1952. Toronto: Contact Press, 1953. 1st edition; mimeographed; one of 100 copies; (i), 24 pages, mimeographed cover; internally fine, covers good; with Henry Moscovitch's ownership signature; from the library of John Metcalf, with his ownership signature.   Nelson Ball 118-165 1996 $1,000.00

SOUSTER, RAYMOND   When We Are Young. Montreal: First Statement, 1946. 1st edition; unpaginated; plain card covers in printed jacket, edges of front cover time darkened, one short closed tear, about very good copy of author's first book; inscribed by author for Wesley Scott, from the library of John Metcalf, with his ownership signature. Nelson Ball 118-167 1996 $1,250.00

SOUTH Carolina Deed Abstracts 1791-1772. Easley: 1983. 4 volumes. As new.   Bookworm & Silverfish 280-212 1996 $150.00

SOUTHARD, ELMER ERNEST   Neurosyphilis: Modern Systematic Diagnosis and Treatment Presented in One Hundred and Thirty-Seven Case Histories. Boston: W. M. Leonard, Pub., 1917. 1st edition; 8vo; 496 pages + 25 halftones; panelled green cloth with painted spine labels, lightly shelfworn, with stamp of Hartford Retreat to titlepage and several over leaves; with one page TLS from publisher to W. H. Thompson presenting the book.   John Gach 150-440 1996 $125.00

SOUTHARD, ELMER ERNEST   Shell-Shock and Other Neuropsychiatric Problems Presented in 589 Histories from the War Literature 1914-1918. Boston: W. M. Leonard, 1919. 1st edition; 8vo; (viii), (xxviii), 982, 21, (5) pages; + 3 half tones; brown buckram with painted spine labels, good used copy with some shelfwear, with titlepage stamp and spine call numbers of Hartford Retreat; inscribed by author for Jelliffe, with Jelliffe's bookplate.   John Gach 150-439 1996 $175.00

A SOUTHERN HARVEST: Short Stories by Southern Writers. Boston: Houghton Mifflin, 1937. 1st edition; foxing to endpapers and edges, not affecting text block, boards slightly faded, else very good in intact but worn dust jacket, not bad, all flaws considered.   Hermitage SP95-657 1996 $175.00

SOUTHERN IMMIGRATION CO.   Texas, Her Resources and Capabilities... New York: E. D. Slater, General Book and Jobbing Printer, 1881. 1st edition; 255 pages; frontispiece and plates, folding map; original brown cloth with title in gilt on front cover, splitting neatly repaired and several loss areas, overall very good. Adams Herd 2274; Howes L73 and 74.   Michael D. Heaston 23-325 1996 $1,500.00

SOUTHERNE, THOMAS   The Fate of Capua. A Tragedy. London: printed for Benjamin Tooke, 1700. 1st edition; 4to; half red morocco, marbled boards, some light rubbing, some browning and staining of text, generally light, half title and final leaf of publisher's ads; very good. Pforzheimer 956; Wing S4757; W&M 1162.   James Cummins 14-190 1996 $200.00

SOUTHERNE, THOMAS   The Fate of Capua. London: for Benjamin Tooke, 1700. 1st edition; small 4to; wanting half title, titlepage foxed and fore-edge chipped, darkening to contents, few small closed marginal tears, all edges gilt, modern three quarter red morocco and cloth, gilt lettered spine, raised bands, in slipcase. Wing S4757; Stratman 5913. Dramatis Personae 37-166 1996 $200.00

SOUTHERNE, THOMAS   The Maids Last Prayer: or, Any, Rather Than Fail. London: R. Bentley and J. Tonson, 1693. 1st edition; issue with 'upon' on page l line 3; 4to; half calf, marbled boards, joints rubbed, text browned; the Robert Hoe copy with his bookplate, contemporary signature of "M. Adye" on title. Wing S4760; W&M 1166; Pforzheimer 958.   James Cummins 14-191 1995 $300.00

SOUTHEY, ROBERT 1774-1843   The Doctor, &c. London: Longman, Rees, Orme, Brown, Green and Longman, 1834-47. 1st edition; 8vo; 7 volumes, titles printed in red with pyramid motif printed in black, with half titles; contemporary half pink polished calf, spines decorated in compartments with intersecting circles in blind, double black morocco lettering pieces, marbled edges and endpapers, top edge gilt, spines slightly soiled and rubbed, sides rubbed, endpapers spotted, early marginalia in volume I, correctly identifying the author, good set; contemporary bookplates of George Meek.   Simon Finch 24-213 1996 £750.00

SOUTHEY, ROBERT 1774-1843   The Life of Nelson. London: John
Murray, 1813. 1st edition; 8vo; 2 volumes; printed on large paper;
portrait, 1 plate; full brown straight grain morocco expertly rebacked, gilt
panelled spines, raised bands, leather labels, edges gilt.   Appelfeld
Gallery 54-168 1996 $300.00

SOUTHEY, ROBERT 1774-1843   The Life of the Rev. Andrew Bell.
London: John Murray, 1844. 1st edition; 3 volumes; frontispiece volume
1; original brown cloth paper labels, very good.   Jarndyce 103-399
1996 £480.00

SOUTHEY, ROBERT 1774-1843   Sir Thomas More... London: John
Murray, 1831. 2nd edition; 8vo; 2 volumes, xiv, (2), 389, (1); (4), 460
pages, leaf of ads at end of volume 1; 7 plates; original green cloth,
printed paper labels, volume 1 bit warped and with short split in upper
joint, otherwise very good, edges uncut. Goldsmiths 26691; Williams II
549; Kress C2970.   John Drury 82-266 1996 £125.00

SOUTHGATE, FRANK   Wildfowl and Waders. London: 1928. Limited to
950 copies, of which this is number 675; folio; 16 mounted color plates
by Frank Southgate, 48 black and white illustrations; original vellum
backed boards; excellent copy.   David A.H. Grayling MY95Orn-72
1996 £150.00

THE SOUTHWARK Address. London: printed for Benj. Tooke, 1681.
Folio; 2 pages, uncut, disbound.   H. M. Fletcher 121-54 1996
£100.00

SOUVENIR of Scotland, Its Cities, Lakes and Mountains. London: T.
Nelson and Sons, 1890. 8vo; 120 chromolithographs; original decorative
cloth, gilt, extremities trifle rubbed; very nice.   R.F.G. Hollett 76-288
1996 £250.00

SOUVENIR of the Klondyke. Dawson: H. J. Goetzman, 1901. 1st edition;
(90) pages, including title; profusely illustrated; original pictorial red
wrappers, minor crease to text; very good. Not in Tourville, Smith,
Soliday, Eberstadt, nor Decker.   Michael D. Heaston 23-4 1996
$300.00

SOUVENIR of the West Highlands and the Caledonian Canal. London: T.
Nelson & Sons, 1892. 8vo; pages iv, 48, text illustrations, maps, 24
glazed chromolithographs; original blue decorated cloth, gilt.   R.F.G.
Hollett 76-289 1996 £75.00

SOUVESTRE, EMILE   Translations from the French of Emile Souvestre.
N.P.: privately printed, 1856. Small 4to; 2 volumes; full dark blue crushed
morocco over beveled boards, spine & covers heavily ornamented with
gilt & blind relief decoration, far too elaborate to describe, at top &
bottom (on edges of outer gilt fillet borders) are two gilt lines "To the
Memory of Elizabeth Strachey and Coelum Non Animum; board edges
gilt, inner gilt dentelels, all edges gilt, on inside rear pastedown is
binder's ticket of Leighton, Son & Hodge, on front flyleaf is inscription
"Constance Strachey from E. S. 1 June, 1887". Fine.   Book Block
32-45 1996 $1,250.00

SOWERBY, G. B.   A Selection o 150 Plates from Sowerby's Thesaurus
Conchyliarum or Genera of Shells. London: 1847-87. Royal 8vo; 150 plain
plates, without text; publisher's cloth.   Wheldon & Wesley 207-1211
1996 £150.00

SOWERBY, JAMES 1757-1822   Coloured Figures of English Fungi or
Mushrooms. London: 1797-103-15. Folio; 3 volumes and supplement in 2
volumes; 440 hand colored plates (some brown splotchiness to a few
plate backgrounds); half morocco, some rubbing, scattered foxing,
mostly in text, several plates after 152 appear to be later issues).
Raymond M. Sutton VII-35 1996 $4,300.00

SOWERBY, JAMES 1757-1822   English Botany; or, Coloured Figures of
British Plants. London: 1902. 3rd edtion; Royal 8vo; 12 volumes and
supplement, together 13 volumes, 1938 hand colored plates; 2 plain and
13 hand colored plates; quarter morocco, except for very slight foxing a
nice copy of the special Re-issue.   Wheldon & Wesley 207-104 1996
£800.00

SOWERBY, JAMES 1757-1822   A New Elucidation of Colours, Original
Prismatic and Material... London: 1809. 4to; pages (iv), 51, 1 plain and 6
colored plates; original boards, uncut, spine worn, contents good;
bookplate of W. Sowerby.   Wheldon & Wesley 207-103 1996 £600.00

SOWERBY, JOHN EDWARD 1825-1870   British Wild Flowers. London:
1863. Reissue to which is added a supplement; 8vo; pages liii, 186,
colored frontispiece, 2 plain and 89 colored plates of 1780 figures; neatly
refixed.   Wheldon & Wesley 207-1504 1996 £75.00

SOWERBY, R. R.   Historical Kirkby Stephen and North Westmorland.
Kendal: Titus Wilson, 1950. 2nd edition; 8vo; pages 116, 5 maps, 65
illustrations; modern half levant morocco gilt, corner torn off one plate
(repaired), few old tape marks, but good.   R.F.G. Hollett & Son
78-1298 1996 £65.00

SOYER, RAPHAEL   Self-Revealment: a Memoir. New York: Maecenas
Press/Random House, 1969. 1st edition; 4to; (viii), 117 pages;
frontispiece, over 40 black and white color reproductions; very good in
illustrated dust jacket, which has few creases and closed tears along
edges. Inscribed by artist with sketch.   Andrew Cahan 47-188 1996
$175.00

SOZINSKEY, THOMAS   Medical Symbolism in Connection with
Historical Studies in the Arts of Healing and Hygiene. Philadelphia: 1891.
1st edition; 171 pages; illustrations; original binding; scarce.   W. Bruce
Fye 71-2019 1996 $150.00

SPALDING, LYMAN   An Inaugural Dissertation on the Production of
Animal Heat Read and Defended at a Public Examination. Walpole:
Carlisle, 1797. 8vo; 30 pages; rebound in recent quarter paper backed
boards, text foxed and browned, title leaf frayed at outer edge but with
no loss of text, two shelf numbers pasted to title in blank portions;
author's presentation copy with presentation note. Rare.   James Tait
Goodrich K40-273 1996 $295.00

SPALDING, WILLIAM   Italy and the Italian Islands, from the Earliest
Ages to the Present Time. Edinburgh: Oliver & Boyd, 1845. 3rd edition;
12mo; 3 volumes; 400, 416, 414 pages; maps at front of each volume;
original red cloth with gilt decoration on spines, lacking front free
endpapers, some minor wear at tops of spines, otherwise nice, very
good set.   David Mason 71-106 1996 $120.00

SPANDUGINO, THEODORO   I Commentari di Theodoro Spandugino
Cantacuscino Gentilhumomo Costantinopolitano, Dell'Origine de Principi
Turchi... Florence: Lorenzo Torrentino, Impressor Ducale, Aug. 1551.
Octavo; 8 leaves, 202 pages, 1 leaf, foremargin of first gathering stained
and frayed; bound in contemporary red morocco with, on each cover, a
panelled design of stylised leaves and flowers, and the Appollo and
Pegasus palcquette at centre, added about 1890, this is one of the
celebrated fake 'Canevari' bindings made by Vittorio Villa at end of the
last century. Inscription at lower margin of title torn away (perhaps by
the forger?). Adams S1531;   H. M. Fletcher 121-27 1996 £1,500.00

SPARKE, MICHAEL   Truth Brought to Light; or, the History of the First
14 Years of King James I. London: Baldwin, 1692. 4 parts in 1;
emblematical titlepage and portrait of Overbury; disbound. wING s4818 c;
Rostenberg, Pub...in England I 200-1 and 201 n. 45.   Rostenberg &
Stern 150-73 1996 $200.00

SPARKMAN, ROBERT S.   Day in the Life of Lon Tinkle. Dallas: 1981.
1/500 copies; folio; color photographic illustrations tipped into place.
W. M. Morrison 436-355 1996 $100.00

SPARKS, JARED 1789-1866   The Library of American Biography.
Boston: Charles C. Litte & James Brown, 1844. 1st edition; volumes 1-3
(incomplete); purple cloth, paper spine labels, 2nd series in purple
pebbled cloth, spines faded, but tight, attractive set.   Metacomet
Books 54-102 1996 $175.00

SPARKS, JARED 1789-1866   The Life of Gouverneur Morris, with
Selections from His Correspondence and Papers... Boston: Gray &
Brown, 1832. 1st edition; 3 volumes, (1571 pages); original cloth backed
boards, printed paper labels, 1 1/2 inch tear to top of spine of volume
one, some spotting to covers, foxing, very good set. Howes S817.
Blue River Books 9-226 1996 $175.00

SPARLING, H. HALLIDAY   The Kelmsoctt Press and William Morris
Master-Craftsman. London: Macmillan and Co., 1924. 1st edition; 16
black and white plates; linen backed boards, top edge dusty, covers
slightly marked, spine browned, head and tail of spine and corners
slightly bumped, pastedown edges browned, some page edges nicked,
very good. From the library of James Hart.   Ulysses 39-334 1996
£185.00

SPARRMANN, ANDERS   Voyage Round the World With Captain James
Cook in H.M.S. Resolution. London: Golden Cockerel Press, 1944. Limited
to 350 numbered copies; tall 4to; 218, (2) pages, illustrated with
numerous wood engravings and one large folding map; original green
cloth, decoratively gilt, calf spine label.   Kenneth Karmiole 1NS-112
1996 $650.00

SPARROW, ANTHONY   A Collection of Articles, Injunctions, Canons, Orders, Ordinances and Constitutions Ecclesiastical... London: printed for Robert Cutler and Joseph Clarke, 1671. 2nd edition; 8vo; frontispiece, 1 folding table; early full dark brown calf, skillfully rebacked, gilt stamped dark red morocco spine label, slight rubbing, annotations, good to very good.   George J. Houle 68-138 1996 $550.00

SPATE, VIRGINIA   Orphism. The Evolution of Non-Figurative Painting in Paris 1910-1914. Oxford University Press, 1979. 25.5 x 19 cm; 409 pages, 8 color plates, 254 monochrome plates; original cloth, dust jacket. Rainsford A54-534 1996 £85.00

SPEAR, ELSA   Bozeman Trail Scrapbook. Sheridan: 1967. 1st edition; number 90 of 500 signed copies; 68 pages; photos; stiff printed wrappers; nice.   T. A. Swinford 49-1089 1996 $100.00

THE SPECTATOR. Oxford: Clarendon Press, 1987. Reissue; 8ov; 5 volumes; frontispiece in each volume; original dark blue cloth, backstrips gilt lettered, glassine jackets, excellent.   Blackwell's B112-262 1996 £200.00

SPECTORSKY, A. C.   The Book of the Sea. New York: Appleton-Century-Crofts, 1954. 1st edition; half tones, gravures and line drawings; very good+ in clear acetate dust jacket.   Steven C. Bernard 71-223 1996 $125.00

A SPEECH Made by a True Protestant English Gentleman, to Incourage the City of London to Petition for the Sitting of the Parliament. N.P.: n.d. 1679. Folio; 2 pages; uncut, disbound. Wing S4854.   H. M. Fletcher 121-30 1996 £65.00

SPEECHLY, WILLIAM   A Treatise on the Culture of the Vine; with New Hints on the Formation of Vineyards in England...A Treatise on the Culture of the Pine Apple... London: 1821. 3rd edition; 8vo; pages 352; 10 plates; contemporary full calf with gilt tooled spine and morocco spine label (worn and scuffed; front hinge tender, light foxing to plates, tear o plate, light marginal dampstaining to prelim pages).   Raymond M. Sutton VII-36 1996 $375.00

SPEEDY, THOM   Craigmillar and Its Environs. Selkirk: George Lewis and Son, 1892. Square 8vo; pages xv, 248, (ii), numerous illustrations; original cloth, gilt, edges, trifle darkened.   R.F.G. Hollett 76-290 1996 £55.00

SPEEDY, TOM   The Natural History of Sport in Scotland with Rod and Gun. 1920. Small 4to; plates by J. G. Millais; finely bound in modern quarter calf; lovely copy.   David Grayling J95Biggame-319 1996 £75.00

SPEEDY, TOM   The Natural History of Sport in Scotland with Rod and Gun. London: William Blackwood & Sons, 1920. 1st edition; small 4to; page xxviii, 440, portrait frontispiece, numerous illustrations by J. G. Millais; original cloth, gilt; presentation copy inscribed.   R.F.G. Hollett 76-291 1996 £75.00

SPEISER, E. A.   Excavations at Tepe Gawra, Levels I-XX. Philadelphia: ASOR & University Museum, 1935-50. 4to; Volumes I and II (complete), 480 pages; 270 plates; original cloth, volume 1 with light stain at top board, volume 2 lower margin of text waterstained (not affecting plates), some yellow highlighting to 9 pages of text, minor staining to boards, signature.   Archaeologia Luxor-2732 1996 $275.00

SPEISER, E. A.   Excavations at Tepe Gawra. Philadelphia: ASOR, 1935. 4to; volume I (only): Levels I-VIII; frontispiece, xvi, 220 pages; 86 plates; original cloth; R. M. Engberg copy with his scholarly annotations in pencil.   Archaeologia Luxor-2731 1996 $150.00

SPEKE, JOHN HANNING   Journal of the Discovery of the Source of the Nile. Edinburgh: William Blackwood & Sons, 1863. 1st edition; 8vo; pages xxxi, 658, 2 maps, 26 plates, numerous text illustrations; modern half brown calf. Hoover 417.   Richard Adelson W94/95-161 1996 $695.00

SPEKE, JOHN HANNING   Journal of the Discovery of the Source of the Nile. London: 1864. New edition; 8vo; 2 volumes; protraits, map; original cloth; fine.   Charles W. Traylen 117-395 1996 £290.00

SPELLMAN, A. B.   The Beautiful Days. New York: Poets Press, 1965. 1st edition; white stapled wrappers, slight crease to bottom corner of front wrapper, else near fine; inscribed by author to fellow poet Joel Oppenheimer. Nice association.   Between the Covers 43-191 1996 $135.00

SPELMAN, HENRY   Glossarium Archaiologicum: Continens Latino-Barbara...Scholiis and Commentariis Illustrata. London: Alice Warren, 1664. Folio in 4's; pages (xii), 576; imprimatur leaf, titlepage printed in black and red within double ruled frame; mid 19th century half tan russia, backstrip darkened, front joint weak, slight wear to head, raised bands, gilt compartments, morocco grain maroon cloth sides, marbled endpapers; early ownership signature, lengthy 19th century ms. note on verso, owner's name "B. Chadwick" stamped on head margin of titlepage. Ex-libris of John Henry Johnson; good. Cordell p. 158; Wing S4925.   Blackwell's B112-263 1996 £200.00

SPENCE, JOSEPH 1699-1768   A Parallel: in the Manner of Plutarch: Between a Most Celebrated Man of Florence, and One, Scarce Ever Heard of, In England. Strawberry Hill: Robinson, 1758. 1st edition; one of 700 copies; 8vo; vignette; ad at end; gilt calf, joints weak; contemporary engraved armorial bookplate of Pitt family. Hazen 44.6.   Rostenberg & Stern 150-148 1996 $450.00

SPENCE, JOSEPH 1699-1768   Polymetis: or, an Enquiry Concerning the Agreement Between the Works of the Roman Poets and the Remains of the Antient Artists. London: J. Dodsley, 1774. 3rd edition; folio; frontispiece, vi, 362 pages; 41 plates and engraved tailpieces; contemporary calf, worn binding, with hinges holding but deeply cracked; internally very good, bookplates.   The Bookpress 75-463 1996 $300.00

SPENCE, ROBERT TRAILL   Minstrelsey of Edmund the Wanderer. New York: D. & G. Bruce, 1810. 1st edition; 8vo; 340 pages; portraits; contemporary calf backed boards, boards worn, lacks flyleaves, blank portion above title clipped; rare. Wegelin 1154; S&S 21398.   M & S Rare Books 60-252 1996 $150.00

SPENCE, RUTH ELIZABETH   Prohibition in Canda: a Memorial to Francis Stephens Spence. Toronto: Ontario Branch of the Dominion Alliance, c. 1919. 23.5 cm; xvi, 624 pages; frontispiece portrait tipped in, illustrations, maps, tables; gilt stamped wine cloth; very good to fine. Rockland Books 38-206 1 996 $100.00

SPENCE, S. A.   Antarctica Its Books and Papers from the Earliest to the Present Time. London: 1966. Limited to 130 copies only, 1st edition; wrappers, faded around edges.   Maggs Bros. Ltd. 1191-119 1996 £90.00

SPENCE, THOMAS   Manitoba, and the North-West of the Dominion, Its Resources and Advantages to the Emigrant and Captialist. Quebec: S. Marcotte, 1876. Pages 36, folding map (dated 1874), spine of wrappers taped, else very nice. Peel 336 note.   Stephen Lunsford 45-152 1996 $100.00

SPENCER, BALDWIN   Across Australia. London: Macmillan, 1912. 1st edition; 2 volumes, (xiv), 254 pages, 105 illustrations and 5 color, folding map; (xvii), 255-525 pages, 2 pages ads, illustrations, folding map, 2 color, 1 folding map, red gilt buckram with gilt title and stamped decoration, light spotting on lower boards, corners slightly bumped, else very good; the Absolon copy.   Antipodean 28-377 1996 $650.00

SPENCER, BALDWIN   Across Australia. London: Macmillan, 1912. 2nd edition; 2 volumes (xiv), 254 pages, 105 illustrations, 5 color, folding map; xvii), 255-515 pages, 2 pages ads, 106-365 plates, some color, folding map, illustrations in text, 2 pages ads; secondary red cloth without gilt decoration; very good+.   Antipodean 28-576 1996 $600.00

SPENCER, BALDWIN   The Arunta. A Study of a Stone Age People. London: Macmillan, 1927. Large 8vo; 2 volumes, 390 pages and black and white illustrations; 256 pages, 4 color plates and black and white illustrations; original green cloth, gilt; pristine in original printed dust jackets; Mervyn Meggitt's copy.   Antipodean 28-386 1996 $750.00

SPENCER, BALDWIN   The Horn Expedition. II: Zoology. London: Dulau & Co., 1896. Small 4to; (iv), 431 pages, 29 litho plates, 8 are fine color; original blue cloth, good + original condition. Ferguson 16071. Antipodean 28-383 1996 $450.00

SPENCER, BALDWIN   The Native Tribes of Central Australia. London: Macmillan, 1899. 1st edition; 670 pages; 135 plates, 2 maps; original brown and gilt stamped buckram, slightly chipped top and base of spine, otherwise very good.   Antipodean 28-378 1996 $550.00

SPENCER, BALDWIN   The Native Tribes of Central Australia. London: Macmillan, 1938. Reprint; (xxiv), 670 pages; illustrations and folding map in text; very good.   Antipodean 28-379 1996 $275.00

SPENCER, BALDWIN   Native Tribes of the Northern Territory of Australia. London: Macmillan, 1914. 1st edition; (xx), 516 pages, 2 pages ads, 92 illustrations, 36 plates, 1 folding map; original green gilt cloth, slightly marked on lower boards, bright gilt decoration and title with original dust jacket. Very nice.   Antipodean 28-385 1996 $675.00

SPENCER, BALDWIN   Native Tribes of the Northern Territory of Australia. London: Macmillan, 1914. 1st edition; (xx), 516 pages, 2 pages ads; 92 illustrations, 36 plates, 1 folding map; original green gilt cloth, few small marks, very crisp.   Antipodean 28-384 1996 $595.00

SPENCER, BALDWIN   The Northern Tribes of Central Australia. London: Macmillan, 1904. (xxxvi), 784 pages, 315 figures, mostly in text, 2 color folding plates, folding map, folding chart; original green gilt decorated cloth, covers dusty, lightly rubbed at edges, some browning in text; good+.   Antipodean 28-380 1996 $550.00

SPENCER, BALDWIN   The Northern Tribes of Central Australia. London: Macmillan, 1904. (xxxvi), 784 pages, 315 black and white illustrations in text, 2 color plates, 1 map and 1 foldout chart; original green gilt decorated cloth, rubbed on all extremities to the point of small separations on hinges, bit marked, scattered foxing; good working copy. Antipodean 28-381 1996 $400.00

SPENCER, BALDWIN   Notes on Certain of the Initiation Ceremonies of the Arunta Tribe, Central Australia. Melbourne: 1898. Offprint from the Proceedings of the Royal society of Victoria; original printed wrappers bound in attractive linen and boards binding, very good; presentation copy from author to J. Edge Partington. Greenway 8678; Ferguson 16073.   Antipodean 28-382 1996 $175.00

SPENCER, BERNARD   Agean Islands and Other Poems. London: Editions Poetry/Nicholson and Watson, 1946. 1st edition; original binding, top edge dusty and slightly spotted, covers dusty, head and tail of spine and corners bumped and worn as usual, covers cocked, very good in nicked and slightly rubbed, marked and dusty dust jacket, by Nicols Engonopoulos, darkened at spine and edges; bookplate of literary agent John Johnson.   Ulysses 39-547 1996 £75.00

SPENCER, ELIZABETH   The Crooked Way. New York: Dodd, Mead & Co., 1952. 1st edition; author's second book; name and date on flyleaf, otherwise near fine in dust jacket which has one very tiny chip at bottom edge of front panel, rear panel lightly soiled.   Steven C. Bernard 71-213 1996 $125.00

SPENCER, GEORGE   Private Papers. London: 1913-24. 4 volumes; little faint foxing.   Petersfield Bookshop FH58-406 1996 £95.00

SPENCER, J. A.   History of the United States from the Earliest Period to the Administration of James Buchanan. New York: Johnson, Fry & Co., 1858. 4to; 3 volumes; numerous steel engravings; bound in full purple leather with gilt designs, nice set.   Blue River Books 9-282 1996 $180.00

SPENCER, JESSE AMES   The East: Sketches of Travel in Egypt and the Holy Land. New York: Putnam/London: John Murray, 1850. 1st edition; 8vo; 9 sepia tonted lithographs, 6 text wood engravings, folding plan, 4 pages ads; original pictorial cloth, gilt, spine gilt, prevasive foxing, binding worn. Smith S127.   Trebizond 39-104 1996 $150.00

SPENCER, SPENCE   The Scenery of Ithaca and the Head Waters of the Cayuga Lake... Ithaca: Spence Spencer, 1866. 1st edition; 12mo; 150, (1), errata, 20 mounted albumen photos, numerous wood engravings; publisher's diced purple cloth with light wear to spine ends and slight chipping to front endpapers, else very good.   Andrew Cahan 47-95 1996 $650.00

SPENCER, THEODORE   A Garland for John Donne - 1631-1931. Cambridge: Harvard University Press, 1931. One of 769 copies; original binding, top edge gilt, inscription, head and tail of spine and corners bumped, spine slightly faded, covers slightly marked, endpaper gutters browned, some page edges nicked, very good in later issue dust jacket, which is chipped, torn, spotted and rubbed, marked, frayed and dusty as well browned at spine and edges and missing several small pieces, upper panel of dust jacket is dated 1932 rather than 1931.   Ulysses 39-151 1996 £125.00

SPENCER-CHURCHILL, E. G.   Catalogue of Antiquites from the Northwick Park Collection, the Property of the Late Captain E. G. Spencer-Churchill, M.D.....June 21, 1965 and the Two Following Days... London: Christie's, 1965. 8vo; frontisportrait, 143 pages, 83 plates; original printed wrappers.   Archaeologia Luxor-2929 1996 $250.00

SPENDER, HAROLD   Through the High Pyrenees. London: 1898. 1st edition; 8vo; xii,3 65 pages; text figures, 31 plates, 5 maps; original cloth, cloth on lower joint slit. Neate S152.   David Bickersteth 133-168 1996 £60.00

SPENDER, STEPHEN 1909-   China Diary. London: Thames & Hudson, 1982. One of 1000 copies signed by author and artist, with folder containing an original lithograph signed by Hockney laid in; fine in bumped slipcase.   R. A. Gekoski 19-126 1996 £750.00

SPENDER, STEPHEN 1909-   The Generous Days. Boston: David R. Godine, 1969. One of 250 numbered copies, cloth backed marbled paper boards, bottom corners slightly bumped, near fine; presentation copy, signed and inscribed by author "(printer's copy) Stephen Spender"; inscribed by author for Jim and Ruth Hart. Loosely inserted are two newspaper cuttings and top panel of envelope in which this book had been posted from author to Hart.   Ulysses 39-550 1996 £100.00

SPENDER, STEPHEN 1909-   Poems. London: Faber & Faber Ltd., 1934. 2nd edition; original binding, top edge dusty, head and tail of spine slightly bumped, head of spine slightly split, prelims, edges and endpaper spotted, covers slightly marked and dusty, good, no dust jacket; signed by author; loosely inserted ALS from author to literary John Johnson, with Johnson bookplate.   Ulysses 39-549 1996 £75.00

SPENDER, STEPHEN 1909-   Recent Poems. London: Anvil Press Poetry, 1978. One of 400 numbered copies, signed by author; original binding, spine faded, bottom corner of upper cover slightly creased, very good; presentation copy inscribed by author for James Hart.   Ulysses 39-551 1996 £75.00

SPENDER, STEPHEN 1909-   Returning to Vienna 1947. Banyan Press, 1947. Limited to 500 numbered copies, signed by Stephen Spender; small 4to; 13 leaves, including blanks, titlepage printed in green and black, green initial letters; color decorated paper over wrappers with printed paper label on front cover, near fine.   Blue Mountain SP95-49 1996 $125.00

SPENDLOVE, F. ST. GEORGE   The Face of Early Canada: Pictures of Canada Which Have Helped to Make History. Toronto: Ryerson Press, 1958. 4to; pages xxi, 162, 128 plates (6 in color); cloth, with scarce errata slip in facsimile; very good in torn dust jacket.   Hugh Anson-Cartwright 87-388 1996 $100.00

SPENSER, EDMUND 1552-1599   Epithalamion. London: Edward Arnold, 1901. Limited to 150 copies; octavo; 22 pages, printed in two colors entirely on vellum, with opening full page hand colored wood engraving by Reginald Savage; full vellum over boards, blindstamped with rose logo and the motto of series, "Soul is Form", very fine.   Bromer Booksellers 87-61 1996 $550.00

SPENSER, EDMUND 1552-1599   The Fairie Queen: The Shepheards Calendar: Together with the Other Works of England's Arch Poet. London: H. L. for Mathew Lownes, 1611-09-12. 1st collected edition; folio; woodcut illustrations, head and tailpieces, decorated title; 18th century mottled calf with armorial crest on covers of lion rampant loading a cannon, rebacked, new lower endpapers and corners, joints worn, some chipping, especially along lower edges, final blanks Ii4 and F4 present, upper corner torn A2, minor worming in blank upper margins, underlinings on one leaf, loss of lower outer corners of last gathering, some staining, browning and soiling, mostly light; good. From the library of Charles Viscount Bruce of Ampthill and Baron Bruce of Whorleton, with his dated bookplate of 1712.   James Cummins 14-193 1996 $1,500.00

SPENSER, EDMUND 1552-1599   The Faerie Queen; The Shepherds Calendar; Together with the Other Works. H. L. for Mathew Lownes, 1611. 1st collected edition, variant issue; folio; paes (iv), 363, (xix), (x), 56, (ii), (iv), 5-16, (cxxxvi), double column, roman letter, general title within elaborate woodcut border incoporating an Arcadian shepherd and Amazon (McKerrow & Ferguson 212); 12 separate title with devices in text, extensive woodcut head and tailpieces and other ornaments, 12 large cuts; 18th century calf, rebacked; uniform paper yellowing, some minor inoffensive old stains and thumb marks, overall good; fine 18th century armorial bookplate on pastedown of Richard Warner of Woodford Row, Essex, the celebrated Shakespearean scholar. STC 23084; Lowndes 2477; Grolier, Langland to Wither 239.   A. Sokol XXV-92 1996 £1,150.00

SPENSER, EDMUND 1552-1599   The Faerie Queen: The Shepheards Calendar: Together with the Other Works of England's Arch-Poet, Edm. Spenser.. London: printed by H. L. for Mathew Lownes 1611, actually closer to 1615. 1st collected edition (essentially); folio; contemporary calf, large gilt lozenge ornament on each cover, spine gilt, red morocco label, bit rubbed but quite sound; in half morocco folding case, upper hinge of case broken; fine, fresh unsophisticated copy in attractive and well preserved binding. STC 23084, 23077.3, 23086.2, 23087 and 23093.5. Ximenes 109-271 1996 $2,500.00

SPENSER, EDMUND 1552-1599   Spenser's Faerie Queen. London: George Allen, 1894-97. 4to; 6 volumes; over 80 full page illustrations by Walter Crane; white cloth, gilt, with red lettering, wrappers of the original 19 parts bound in, top edge gilt, prospectus laid in; fine. Masse p. 47. Glenn Books 36-237 1996 $1,200.00

SPENSER, EDMUND 1552-1599   The Faerie Queene. Oxford: Limited Editions Club, 1953. Limited to 1500 copies; samll folio; pen decorations by John Austen/wood engravings by Agnes M. Parker, signed by Parker; original binding, fine in near fine dust jackets and slipcase.   Charles Agvent 4-1025 1996 $200.00

SPENSER, EDMUND 1552-1599   Spenser's Minor Poems... Ashendene Press, 1925. One of 200 copies, 175 of them for sale; there were also 15 copies on vellum, 12 of them for sale; 17 1/4 x 12 inches; 2 p.l., 216 pages; device in blue on final page, printed in black, red and blue, numerous large and small roman style intials; original calf backed thick vellum boards, raised bands, gilt spine titling, hint of splaying, vellum somewhat speckled, mainly as a manifestation of grain, otherwise the binding in superb condition, with leather backstrip bright and virtually unworn, especially fine internally. Hornby 35; Franklin pp. 240-41. Phillip J. Pirages 33-28 1996 $2,400.00

SPENSER, EDMUND 1552-1599   The Shepheard's Calender. London: Harper & Bros., 1898. 1st edition illustrated by Walter Crane; small 4to; pages xxiii, (ii), 3-118; border decorations and illustrations by Crane; original green pictorial cloth, gilt, pictorial endpapers; minor surface rubbing of cloth, but excellent, bright, clean example.   Sotheran PN32-108 1996 £98.00

SPENSER, EDMUND 1552-1599   Thalamos or the Brydall Boure Being the Epithalamion and Prothalamion... At the sign of the Boar's Head, Manaton, Devon, 1932. Number 2 of 200 copies; octavo; pages 36; 4 full page wood engravings and tailpiece by Lettice Sandford, printed in Baskerville on Millbourn handmade paper; original sheepskin backed Cockerell marbled boards, top edge gilt, others uncut; inscribed at some length to Edwin & Margery Cox, from Christopher and Lettice Sandford. Claude Cox 107-23 1996 £85.00

SPERONI, SPERONE   Dialoghi... Venice: Heirs of Aldus Manutius, 1550. 8vo; 144 leaves, italic; full 19th century morocco, tooled in blind with fine Aldine device stamped in gilt on both boards, all edges gilt, slight spotting to title, otherwise clean and handsome copy. Renouard 149.13; Adams S1569; UCLA IIIa/352.   Family Album Tillers-581 1996 $750.00

SPEWACK, SAMUEL   Kiss Me Kate. New York: Alfred A. Knopf, 1953. 1st edition; fine in dust jacket.   Hermitage SP95-589 1996 $125.00

SPICER, JACK   A Lost Poem. Verona: Plain Wrapper Press, 1974. 1st edition; limited to 114 numbered copies; 4to; hand printed on Fabriano roma and signed by artist; 2 etchings by Ariel; decorated cloth; mint. James S. Jaffe 34-625 1996 $225.00

SPICER, JOHN L.   Correlation Methods of Comparing Idiolects in a Transition Area. N.P.: Language, 1952. 1st edition; 8vo; 12 page offprint; self wrappers, stapled, this copy signed by Spicer and Reed; marginal sunning to outer pages, some random stains to 3 plates, otherwise very good. Rare.   James S. Jaffe 34-626 1996 $1,650.00

SPIES, AUGUST   Auto-Biography. Chicago: Nina van Zandt, 1887. Portrait frontispiece; orange wrappers.   Blue River Books 9-162 1996 $750.00

SPIES, WERNER   Sculpture by Picasso with Catalogue of the Works. New York: Abrams, 1971. Folio; 331 pages, 670 illustrations; cloth, dust jacket. Freitag 7501.   Brannan 43-537 1996 $350.00

SPIES, WERNER   Victor Vasarely. New York: Abrams, 1971. Square folio; 206 pages, 187 illustrations; 68 color plates; cloth, dust jacket. Freitag 9768.   Brannan 43-655 1996 $175.00

SPIKES, NELLIE W.   Through the Years: a History of Crosby County Texas. San Antonio: 1952. 1st edition; xxiv, 493 pages, photos, brands, dust jacket, very good+. Scarce. Herd 2133.   T. A. Swinford 49-1092 1996 $100.00

SPILLANE, MICKEY   I, the Jury. New York: E. P. Dutton, 1947. 1st edition; author's first book; name and street address on flyleaf, rear pastedown and endpaper foxed, one corner tip bumped, otherwise very good in very good dust jacket which is chipped at top of spine corners and moderately worn at edges, very presentable copy, scarce.   Steven C. Bernard 71-359 1996 $375.00

SPILLER, BURTON L.   Thoroughbred. New York: Derrydale Press, 1936. 1st edition; one of 950 numbered copies; 4to; illustrations by Lynn Bogue Hunt; very good, light wear to spine. Siegel 106; Frazier S16a. Glenn Books 36-72 1996 $185.00

SPINDEN, HERBERT J.   A Study of Maya Art; its Subject Matter and Historical Development. Cambridge: Peabody Museum, 1913. Folio; xxiii, 285 pages, 286 illustrations, 30 plates; original cloth.   Archaeologia Luxor-4910 1996 $250.00

SPINDLER, WILL   Rim of the Sandhills. Mitchell: 1941. 1st edition; 346 pages; photos; cloth; fine. Herd 2135; 6 Guns 2079.   T. A. Swinford 49-1093 1996 $125.00

SPINNIKER, ADRIAAN   Leerzaame Zinnebeelden. Haarlem: Izaak Vander Vinne, 1714. 1st edition; 8vo; 222 pages; 50 engravings; original full vellum, bookplate, expected soiling to covers, internally bright and generally very good to near fine.   Chapel Hill 94-184 1996 $1,200.00

SPINOZA, BENEDICT DE   Tractatus Theologico-Politicus Continens Dissertationes Aliquot... Hamburg: apud Henricum Kunrath (actually Amsterdam: Jan Rieuwertsz, 1670. Small 4to; pages (xii), 233, (i, blank); contemporary calf, spine gilt; generally very good but with some slight worming affecting inner margins throughout, some neat marginal annotation in early hand and pencil annotation and scoring in more recent hand. Bamberger T5; PMM 153.   Sotheran PN32-51 1996 £1,250.00

SPITTA, PHILIPP   John Sebastian Bach. His Work and Influence on the Music of Germany, 1685-1750. London: Novello, Ewer & Co., 1884-85. 1st edition in English; thick 8vo; 3 volumes; portrait in volume 1; original dark green cloth, edge of one cover slightly marked by damp; fine, largely unopened, scarce thus.   Ximenes 109-272 1996 $500.00

SPIVEY, RICHARD L.   Maria. Flagstaff: Northland, 1979. 1st edition; many beautiful color plates; near fine in dust jacket, signed by Maria Poveka.   Parker Books of the West 30-171 1996 $295.00

SPOERRI, JAMES FULLER   Finnegans Wake a Check List - Including Publications of Portions Under the Title Work in Progress. Evanston: Northwestern University Library, 1953. 1st edition; wrappers; fine. Ulysses 39-326 1996 £55.00

SPOFFORD, HARRIET ELIZABETH PRESCOTT 1835-1921   Art Decoration Applied to Furniture. New York: Harper & Bros., 1878. 1st edition; 8vo; frontispiece, 237, (3) pages; publisher's cloth, gilt, all edges gilt, spine and edges worn, front hinge internally cracked, portions of text loose. Bookpress 75-123 1996 $225.00

SPON, ISAAC   The History of the City and State of Geneva, From Its First Foundation to This Present Time. London: Bernard White, 1687. 1st English edition; folio; frontispiece, engraved town plan, engraved plate of seals, lacks third plate and map, worming to inner margin of prelims, not affecting text, occasional faint spotting and light stains; full contemporary calf, worn, joints cracked and weak; scarce. Wing S5017.   Ian Wilkinson 95/1-142 1996 £190.00

SPORTING Sketches: Home and Abroad. London: 1866. Original photo frontispiece; light scuffing and fading.   David A.H. Grayling 3/95-390 1996 £55.00

SPORTSMAN'S Dictionary, or the Gentleman's Companion for Town and Country. London: Robinson, 1792. 4th edition; tall thick quarto; unpaginated; frontispiece, 12 other full page engravings; recent fine rebinding in three quarter polished morocco, raised bands, gilt and blind decorations, gilt on black leather title, marbled boards; light uniform foxing, but handsome copy. Lowndes IV 1725.   Hartfield 48-11t 1996 $495.00

SPRAT, THOMAS 1635-1713   The History of the Royal Society of London. London: Scot, Chiswell, Chapman and Sawbridge, 1702. 2nd edition; 4to; device of Royal Society, and 2 folding plates; cloth; CBEL II 286; Lyons Royal Soc. VII.   Rostenberg & Stern 150-126 1996 $425.00

SPRAT, THOMAS 1635-1713   The History of the Royal Society of London, for the Improving of Natural Knowledge... London: J. Knapton, J. Walthoe (& 7 others), 1722. 3rd edition; 4to; (xvi), 438 pages; frontispiece, 2 folding plates; contemporary panelled calf, rebacked and recornered, lettered in blind; little foxing, one page edge dusty; good. Robert Clark 38-135 1996 £175.00

SPRENGEL, K. An Introduction to the Stury of Cryptogamous Plants in Letters. London: 1807. 8vo; pages viii, 411; 10 folding hand colored plates; contemporary boards, backstrip replaced, with cloth tape, covers worn and soiled, occasional foxing, plates clean. Raymond M. Sutton VII-353 1996 $350.00

SPRENGELL, CONRAD The Aphorisms of Hippocrates and the Sentences of Celsus; with Explantations and References to the Most Considerable Writers in Physick and Philosophy. London: R. Wilkins, F. and F. Bonwich, 1735. 2nd edition; 8vo; frontispiece, title in red and black, (6), 435, (28) pages; full contemporary calf, skillfully rebacked, clean, crisp copy. James Tait Goodrich K40-146 1996 $350.00

SPRENGLING, MARTIN Barhebraeus' Scholia on the Old Testament. Chicago: University of Chicago Press, 1931. 4to; Part I (all Published): Genesis II Samuel; xvi, 393 pages; numerous plates, original cloth, torn dust jacket. Archaeologia Luxor-2734 1996 $125.00

SPRIGGS, A. O. Champion Restorative Art. Springfield & Toronto: Champion Co., 1934. 1st edition; 8vo; 125 pages; photos and drawings; original red cloth, very nice, with meadllion, title and author name on top board; fine. Roy W. Clare XXIV-5 1996 $110.00

SPRIGGS, A. O. Textbook on Embalming. Springfield and Toronto: Champion Co., 1933. 1st of this edition; large 8vo; 261 pages; diagrams and photos; original blue cloth with medallion title and author name on top board, very nice. Roy W. Clare XXIV-57 1996 $110.00

SPRIGGS,, A. O. Champion Anatomy for Embalmers. Springfield and Toronto: Champion Co., 1934. 1st edition; large 8vo; 199 pages, color and black and white illustrations; original blue cloth, 2 inch frayed edge of top board, with medallion, title and author name in gilt on top board, very good. Roy W. Clare XXIV-56 1996 $100.00

SPROTT, THOMAS Thomae Sprotti Chronica. E Codice Antiquo... Oxonii: E Theatro Sheldoniano, 1719. 1st printing; 8vo; lxxx, 334, (ii) pages; folding plate, final ad leaf, 10 pages subscribers list; recent half calf, marbled boards, spine gilt; minor browning, otherwise very good. Robert Clark 38-61 1996 £50.00

SPRY, W. The British Coleoptera Delineated... London: 1861. 8vo; pages vii, 83, 94 hand colored plates of 638 figures; original cloth, binding neatly repaired, inscription inside front cover, lacks front free endpaper. Wheldon & Wesley 207-1115 1996 £220.00

SPRY, W. The Cruise of Her Majesty's Ship "Challenger". Voyages over Many Seas, Scenes in Many Lands. Toronto: Belford Brothers, 1877. 8vo; pages xviii, 388, (28); illustrations, folding map, original decorated cloth, covers dusty and slightly scuffed, else very attractive. Hugh Anson-Cartwright 87-389 1996 $125.00

SPURR, GEORGE G. A Fight with a Grizzly Bear. A Story of Thrilling Interest. Boston: George G. Spurr, 1886. 1st edition; 26 pages; original pictorial yellow green wrappers; fine. Cowan p. 606. Michael D. Heaston 23-305 1996 $250.00

SPURZHEIM, JOHANN GASPAR 1776-1832 Observations on the Deranged Manifestations of the Mind or, Insanity. Boston: Marsh, Capen & Lyon, 1833. 1st American edition; 8vo; viii, 260 pages, 4 lithographs; modern cloth backed marbled boards, paper spine label, front and rear gatherings smudged and bit mildewed, good. faint old library stamp to titlepage. John Gach 150-444 1996 $250.00

SQUIER, EPHRAIM GEORGE 1821-1888 Notes on Central America; Particularly the States of Honduras and San Salvador... New York: Harper & Bros., 1855. 1st edition; 8vo; pages xvi, 17-397, 4 folding maps, folding plan, 9 plates; original brown cloth, lightly rubbed. Sabin 89981. Richard Adelson W94/95-163 1996 $185.00

SQUIER, EPHRAIM GEORGE 1821-1888 Peru. Incidents of Travel and Exploration in the Land of the Incas. New York: Harper & Bros., 1877. 8vo; pages xx, 599; map, 14 plates, numerous text illustrations; original pictorial cloth, rubbed, ex-library. Sabin 89987. Richard Adelson W94/95-162 1996 $185.00

STACEY, C. P. The Canadian Army 1939-1945 - an Official Historical Summary. Ottawa: Pub. by authority of the Minister of National Defence, 1948. 1st edition; pasted in afater first blank in specially inscribed, tissue guarded sheet, signed by Minister of National Defence; 12 color plates, 3 black and white maps; original binding, gilt lettering on spine dull, head and tail of spine and corners bumped and rubbed, covers slightly marked, spine slightly faded, fore-edge very slightly soiled, top edge dusty, good. Ulysses 39-658 1996 £95.00

STACKHOUSE, J. Nereis Britannica... Bath: 1795-1801. Folio; xl, 112, 7 pages; portrait, 2 title vignettes and 17 hand colored or color printed plates; original boards, rebacked with paper, in leather backed cloth book box. Internally good, clean, uncut copy. Boards show signs of age. Wheldon & Wesley 207-105 1996 £1,100.00

STAEL-HOLSTEIN, ANNE LOUISE GERMAINE NECKER, BARONNE DE 1766-1817 Corinne, or Italy. London: J. M. Dent, 1894. One of 100 numbered copies, large paper edition; 8vo; frontispiece, decorated titlepage and 2 additional illustrations in each volume by H. S. Greig; frontispiece, decorated titlepage, 2 additional illustrations in each volume; contemporary tan calf, gilt decorated spine with contrasing labels, raised bands, top edge gilt; fine and extremely handsome copy, bound by Root & Son. Paulette Rose 16-304 1996 $300.00

STAFFORD, JEAN The Collected Stories of Jean Stafford. New York: FSG, 1969. 1st edition; slight fading to edge of boards, still fine in like dust jacket with just a little darkening at extremities, nice. Between the Covers 42-410 1996 $100.00

STAFFORD, JEAN A Mother in History. New York: FSG, 1966. 1st edition; fine in dust jacket with tiny tear and faint spot on rear panel; inscribed by author for Peter DeVries and his wife. Between the Covers 42-409 1996 $275.00

STAFFORD, WILLIAM William Stafford; Eleven Untitled Poems. Perishable Press, 1968. One in an edition of 250 numbered copies; 8 x 6 inches; 32 page surfaces, 26 printed; handset in Palatino printed in black and red on Medway and Shadwell paper, single signature bound into a blue Fabriano cover wrapper with silk screened diagram, title printed in red letterpress by printer, uncut; fine. Hamady 16. Joshua Heller 21-184 1996 $150.00

STAFFORD, WILLIAM Wymoning Circuit. N.P.: Tideline Press, 1980. 1st edition; one of 125 copies; 8vo; printed on Barcham Green handmade paper and signed by author; accordion fold embossed two-tone boards, as new. James S. Jaffe 34-627 1996 $150.00

STAGG, JOHN The Cumbrian Minstrel. Manchester: T. Wilkinson, 1821. 1st edition; 8vo; pages vii, 289, (iii); 292, (iv); 2 volumes in 1; old half calf gilt with broad gilt raised bands and marbled boards, little rubbed and scraped, small piece torn from top of second title. R.F.G. Hollett & Son 78-469 1996 £175.00

STAMMA, PHILLIP The Noble Game of Chess; or a New and Easy Method to Learn to Play Well in a Short Time. London: printed for James Brindley, 1745. 1st edition in English; 16mo; xxiv, 115 pages, 1 folding diagram; 5mm strip cut from head of title without loss, little light foxing, 19th century half calf, worn. H. M. Fletcher 121-122 1996 £500.00

STANDLEY, P. C. Trees and Shrubs of Mexico. Washington: 1920-26. 8vo; 5 volumes; pages 1721, (i-) cxxii; wrappers, some soiling or fading, small tears to some wrappers; pages of part 1 tanned, minor scratching to rear wrapper and last 3 leaves of part 4, embossed stamp on title of part 5. Raymond M. Sutton VII-748 1996 $400.00

STANESBY, SAMUEL The Wisdom of Solomon. London: Griffith & Farran, 1861. 1st edition; 8vo; (ii), 25, (1) pages; frontispiece; gold and blindstamped cloth over heavy bevelled boards, all edges gilt, spine and cvoers faded and rubbed, else very good. Bookpress 75-124 1996 $175.00

STANFIELD, CLARKSON Stanfield's Coast Scenery. London: Smith, Elder & Co., 1836. 1st edition; royal 8vo; viii, 128 pages; 40 plates; original publisher's morocco gilt, blocked in an elaborate paattern of dolphins, anchors and shells, expertly restored and refurbished, few minor marks, some foxing and browning to plates, but still handsome copy. Ash Rare Books Zenzybyr-85 1996 £200.00

STANHOPE, PHILIP HENRY STANHOPE, 5TH EARL OF 1805-1875 History of England from the Peace of Utrecht to the Peace of Versailles 1713-1783. London: John Murray, 1853. 3rd edition; small 8vo; 7 volumes; contemporary half leather, raised bands, gilt compartments, top edge gilt, extremities slightly rubbed, otherwise nice in pretty binding; David Mason 71-26 1996 $280.00

STANLEY, ARTHUR PENRYHYN Sinai and Palestine in Connection with Their History. London: John Murray, 1858. 8vo; colored folding frontispiece, lviii, 550 pages; 10 maps, full green calf, 5 raised bands, leather label, marbled endpapers and edges, gilt tooled spine, contemporary bookplate, signature, 1 page chipped. Archaeologia Luxor-2738 1996 $125.00

STANLEY, CHARLES HENRY   The Chess Player's Instructor; or, Guide to Beginners... New York: Robert M. De Witt, 1859. 12mo; 72 pages, chess diagrams, limp green cloth, rubbed and soiled, titled in gilt with illustration of chess board in gilt within blindstamped decorations on front cover; hinges cracked, few page corners creased, very scarce; Not in RLIN.   Blue Mountain SP95-32 1996 $125.00

STANLEY, CHARLES HENRY   Paul Morphy's Match Games. New York: Robert M. DeWitt, 1859. 1st edition; 12mo; 108 pages; semi-limp green cloth; very good.   Metacomet Books 54-103 1996 $100.00

STANLEY, E. J.   Life of Rev. L. B. Stateler or Sixty-Five Years in the Frontier. Nashville: 1907. 1st edition; 356 pages; photos, illustrations, pictorial cloth, very good+. Quite scarce. Howes S879; 6 Guns 2090; Smith 9807.   T. A. Swinford 49-1100 1996 $150.00

STANLEY, E. J.   Rambles in Wonderland. New York: D. Appleton and Co., 1878. 1st edition; 179 pages, ads pages (181-90); original green embossed cloth with title in gilt on front cover and spine, very good; Howes S880; Graff 3944; Streeter Sale 2250.   Michael D. Heaston 23-306 1996 $225.00

STANLEY, F.   The Apache of New Mexico, 1540-1940. Pampa: 1962. 1st edition; v, 449 pages; nice in dust jacket, scarce, signed.   T. A. Swinford 49-1101 1996 $125.00

STANLEY, HENRY MORTON 1841-1904   The Congo and the Founding of Its Free State. New York: Harper & Bros., 1885. 8vo; 2 volumes, pages xxvii, 528; x, 483, 12 ads, 5 maps, 44 plates, text illustrations; original pictorial cloth, rubbed. Hoover 4274.   Richard Adelson W94/95-164 1996 $285.00

STANLEY, HENRY MORTON 1841-1904   How I Found Livingstone; Travels, Adventures and Discoveries in Central Africa... Montreal: Dawson Brothers, 1872. 1st Canadian edition; tall 8vo; xxiii, 736 pages; illustrations and maps, 4 folding maps; original photograph frontispiece; recently rebound with brown calf spine, boards, leather spine label, some wormhole in first xxxii pages and last 100 pages not affecting text, archival tape repairs to rear of large folding map, otherwise nice. David Mason 71-14 1996 $280.00

STANLEY, HENRY MORTON 1841-1904   In Darkest Africa. London: Sampson Low, Marston, Searle and Rivington, Ltd., St. Dunstan's... 1890. 1st edition; 8vo; 2 volumes; frontispiece to volume 1, photogravure portrait frontispiece to volume 2, 39 full page illustrations, 85 illustrations to text, 21 maps; bound by Roger de Coverly & Sons, half crimson morocco and buckram boards, corners slightly worn, gilt titles, raised bands to spines, top edge gilt, marbled endpapers, owner's bookplate to front pastedown of both volumes, new endpapers and prelims; fine, handsome copy in excellent condition.   Beeleigh Abbey BA/56-121 1996 £275.00

STANLEY, HENRY MORTON 1841-1904   In Darkest Africa. New York: Scribners, 1890. 1st edition; 8vo; 2 volumes, pages xiv, 547; xvi, 540; 3 folding maps, 46 plates, many text illustrations; original green pictorial cloth, lightly rubbed. Hoover 155.   Richard Adelson W94/95-165 1996 $200.00

STANLEY, HENRY MORTON 1841-1904   In Darkest Africa. New York: Scribner's, 1890. 1st American edition; 8vo; 2 volumes, 547, 540 pages; frontispiece in each volume, 3 folding maps in pockets at rear. original green cloth with embossed outline of the African continent, gilt facsimile of Stanley's signature, rear inner hinge cracked in volume 1, but very nice, very good set.   Chapel Hill 94-6 1996 $150.00

STANLEY, HENRY MORTON 1841-1904   In Darkest Africa or the Quest, Rescue and Retreat of Emin, Governor of Euitoria. New York: 1890. 1st American edition; 9 x 5.5 inches; 2 volumes, 547, 540 pages; 3 folding maps; illustrations; cloth, inner front hinge of volume 2 cracked, covers rubbed, one map in pocket splitting.   John K. King 77-783 1996 $125.00

STANLEY, THOMAS 1625-1678   The History of Philosophy... London: printed by Ralph Holt for Thomas Bassett and Thomas Cockerill, 1687. 2nd edition; folio; pages (26), 1091, bookseller's ad, titlepage in red and black; fine portrait of Stanley by Lilly, engraved by Faithorne; 25 large engraved text portraits, 7 of these engraved by an early hand; contemporary full calf, spine gilt, front board detached.   Family Album Tillers-582 1996 $450.00

STANLEY, THOMAS 1625-1678   The History of Philosophy... London: A. Millar (7 8 others), 1743. 4to; (xxxvi), 828 pages; contemporary calf, spine gilt, label, rubbed, some wear at extremities, joints cracked, wormhole through lower margin, just touching text on a few leaves, scattered foxing. Sound.   Robert Clark 38-136 1996 £85.00

STANSBURY, HOWARD 1806-1863   Exploration and Survey of the Valley of the Great Salt Lake of Utah... Philadelphia: 1852. 8vo; 2 volumes; pages 487; 57 plates, 3 folding maps; original gilt decorated cloth, light wear to head of spine of portfolio; contemporary inscription, mild browning to 2 plates, 2 institutional bookplates, stamped released; near fine.   Raymond M. Sutton VI-29 1996 $600.00

STAPLEDON, O.   Last and First Men. Cape and Smith, 1931. 1st American edition; some light dust soil, but tight, very good copy in attractive dust jacket with some wear and tear and chipping. Aronovitz 57-1115 1996 $135.00

STAR Science Fiction Stories. Boardman, 1954. 1st English edition; very good+/near fine in dust jacket with some slight wear to base of dust jacket spine; signed by F. Pohl.   Aronovitz 57-31 1996 $100.00

STAR Short Novels. Ballantine, 1954. 1st edition; signed by editor; very good+/near fine in dust jacket with some soil along upper quarter inch of rear dust jacket panel, very nice.   Aronovitz 57-32 1996 $165.00

STARBACK, EDITH   Crossing the Plains. Nashville: 1922. 1st edition; 224 pages; frontispiece, plates; pictorial cloth; very good+. Mintz 434; Smith 7820.   T. A. Swinford 49-1105 1996 $100.00

STARBUCK, ALEXANDER   History of the American Whale Fishery From Its Earliest Inception to the Year 1876. Waltham: 1878. Pages 767, 6 plates, extra pencil drawing of a whale; original binding, backstrip repaired, some shelf wear, some pencilling; fully signed by W. F. Williams with three quarter page ms. note by him. Arctic 16698. Stephen Lunsford 45-153 1996 $950.00

STARK BROS.   Cenennial Fruits, the Products of a Hundred Years Successful Tree Growning 1816-1916. Louisiana: 1916. Salesman's edition; tall 4to; pages 49, (1); 25 colored plates, plus numerous photos; original stiff wrappers.   Raymond M. Sutton VII-1184 1996 $135.00

STARK, ARTHUR   The Fauna of South Africa. London: 1900-01. Royal 8vo; 5 volumes; large folding map in volume 2 (often missing), portrait (foxed) and 450 textual illustrations; original cloth. Extremely scarce. Charles W. Traylen 117-334 1996 £880.00

STARK, FREYA   Baghdad Sketches. Baghdad: Times Press, 1932. 1st edition; 12 black and white drawings by E. N. Prescott, endpapers, prelims and edges browned and very slightly spotted, covers slightly soiled, corners very slightly rubbed, spine faded, title label on spine chipped and browned, nevertheless very good, scarce.   Virgo Books 48-190 1996 £350.00

STARK, FREYA   Letters. 1914-80. Salisbury: Compton and Michael Russell, 1974-82. 1st edition; 8vo; 8 volumes; black cloth, fine set in like dust jackets. Robinson p. 30.   Paulette Rose 16-327 1996 $140.00

STARK, JAMES   Scenery of the Rivers of Norfolk, Comprising the Yare, the Waveney and the Bure. Norwich & London: 1834. Large paper copy with india paper proofs; imperial quarto; 24 full page and 12 vignette steel engravings, all on india paper; bound in at end are original printed paper wrappers for the four parts, an "Address to Subscribers" dated 1830 and another dated 1831, two prospectuses containing various states of the "List of Subscribers", the latter carefully inlaid to size, full hard grain red morocco, narrow gilt border, fully gilt spine, inner dentelles gilt, top edge gilt, others uncut, by F. Bedford, very fine, uncommon; the copy of Thomas Basil Duguid with engraved armorial bookplate.   H. M. Fletcher 121-148 1996 £500.00

STARR, F. RATCHFORD   Farm Echoes. New York: Orange Judd, 1881. 1st edition; 8vo; pages 108, 16 illustrations; soiled and chipped publisher's cloth, good.   Second Life Books 103-177 1996 $125.00

STARRETT, VINCENT   Penny Wise and Book Foolish. New York: Covici Friede, 1929. 1st edition; one of 275 copies for sale, signed by author; 9 3/4 x 6 3/4 inches; 199, (1) pages; frontispiece, 15 plates; elaborately gilt decorated paper covered boards, top edge gilt, other edges untrimmed, largely unopened, in original (torn and repaired) glassine dust jacket and publisher's slipcase, worn but sound, except for defects to jacket and sipcase, an extremely fine copy.   Phillip J. Pirages 33-106 1996 $150.00

STATISTICAL Account of the Shetland Isles by the Ministers of the Respective Parishes. London: Blackwood and Sons, 1841. 1st edition; pages (iv), 179, colored map; original cloth, slightly faded and worn, paper label; little neat underlining; scarce.   R.F.G. Hollett 76-292 1996 £120.00

STATIUS, PUBLIUS PAPINIUS   Statii Sylvarum Libri V/ Achilleidos Libri XII./ Thebaidos Libri II./ Orthographia et Flexus Dictionum Graecarum Omnium... Venice: In aedibvs Aldi et Andreae Soceri (Andrea Torresano), November, 1502. 1st Aldine edition; small 8vo; 296 leaves, Italic and Greek, Aldine device on last leaf; French vellum gilt binding. Brunet V512; Renouard 35.7; Adams S 1670; STC IT 646; UCLA I 49.   Family Album Tillers-584 1996 $1,600.00

STATIUS, PUBLIUS PAPINIUS   Statii Sylvarum Libri V./ Achilleidos Libri XII./ Thebaidos Libri II./ Orthographia et Flexus Dictionum Graecarum Omnium... Venice: In Aedibvs Aldi, et Andreae Soceri (Andrea Torresano), 1502. Small 8vo; last 20 leaves with slight dampstains, otherwise quite clean, worn 18th century calf; the copy of historian Winthrop Sargent. Renouard 35.7; Adams S1670; STC IT 646; UCLA I/49.   Family Album Tillers-585 1996 $1,000.00

STATIUS, PUBLIUS PAPINIUS   Statii Sylvarum Libri V./ Achilleidos Libri XII./ Thebaidos Libri II./ Orthographia et Flexus Dictionum Graecarum Omnium... Venice: in aedibvs Aldi, et Andreae Soceri (Andrea Torresano), 1502. Small 8vo;; light age stain, all edges gilt, full black morocco by Mackenzie, with repaired spine.   Family Album Tillers-586 1996 $1,000.00

STATIUS, PUBLIUS PAPINIUS   Statii Sylvarum Libri V./ Achilleidos Libri XII./ Thebaidos Libri II./ Orthographia et Flexus Dictionum Graecarum Omnium... Venice: In aedibvs Aldi, et Andreae Soceri (Andrea Torresano), 1519. 1st Aldine edition; 8vo; 296 leaves, italic, Aldine devices on first and last leaves; red morocco binding by Bozerian le jeune, with gilt arms of Edward George Geoffrey Smith Stanley, 14th Earl of Derby, statesman and Greek scholar, silk doublures, tooled in gilt, all edges gilt, very clean and handsome copy. Renouard 88/12; Adams S1672; UCLA II/153; Brunet V512.   Family Album Tillers-587 1996 $1,600.00

STATON, FRANCES   A Bibliography of Canadiana. (with) First and Second Supplement. Toronto: The Public Library, 1934-85. Small 4to; 3 volumes, numerous facsimiles; original cloth, volume 1 in contemporary cloth.   Forest Books 74-255 1996 £145.00

THE STATUTES at Large Made for the Preservation of the Game. London: printed by J. Baskett and sold by R. Gosling, 1734. 8vo; text mostly Black Letter; contemporary sheep, rubbed, hinges cracked. Anthony Laywood 108-67 1996 £135.00

STAUFFACHER, JACK   Porter Garrett: Philosophical Writings on the Ideal Book. San Francisco: Book Club of California, 1994. One of 450 copies; 8vo; printed in Cycles types on Mohawk Superfine; 43 pages of illustrations; cloth; fine.   Bertram Rota 272-54 1996 £95.00

STAUFFER, DAVID M.   American Engravers Upon Copper and Steel. c. 1960. Reprint of New York 1907 edition; 2 volumes; cloth, very rare. Jens J. Christoffersen SL94-138 1996 $200.00

STAUNFORDE, WILLIAM   An Exposition of the Kinges Prerogative Collected Out of the Great Abridgement of Iustice Fitzherbert and Other Olde Writers of the Lawes of England. London: by Richarde Tottle, 1573. Modern three quarter calf, joints rubbed, title repaired and backed, usable.   Meyer Boswell SL27-217 1996 $1,250.00

STAUNTON, GEORGE   An Authentic Account of an Embassy from the King of Great Britain to the Emperor of China... London: W. Bulmer and Co., for G. Nichol, 1798. 2nd edition; 4to; 2 volumes, plus atlas; 518, 614 pages of text, 1 full page plate (misbound at p. 435 rather than p. 466) and 26 engraved illustrations to text; text volumes bound in diced russia boards, skilfully rebacked with calf backstrip, gilt rule borders, inner decorative gilt borders to boards, gilt bands, tools and title to panelled spines, slight surface damage to front cover of volume 2; atlas 12 maps and plans, 32 engraved plates; modern half calf, side strips and corners diced, gilt bands and tools to panelled spine, marbled boards and endpapers with binders ticket to rear pastedown. Cordier 2382; Lust 545; Morrison I 696; Hill pp. 280-81.   Beeleigh Abbey BA/56-122 1996 £3,500.00

STAUNTON, HOWARD   The Chess-Player's Text Book: a Concise and Easy Introduction to the Game. London: Jaques and Son, 1849. 1st edition; small 8vo; (viii), 128, (8 ad) pages; original green printed stiff wrappers, rubbed; uncommon. Not found in BM Cat.   James Burmester 29-131 1996 £85.00

STAWELL, MAUD MARGARET KEY   My Days with Fairies. New York: Hodder & Stoughton, n.d. 1913. 1st edition; square octavo; 169 pages; 8 color plates mounted on tan paper, by Edmund Dulac, with descriptive tissue gaurds; original mauve cloth decoratively stamped and lettered in gilt, minor shelfwear, previous owner's ink presentation inscription; near fine, very scarce.   Heritage Book Shop 196-223 1996 $450.00

STEALINGWORTH, SLIM   Tom Wesselmann. New York: Abbeville, 1980. Square folio; 321 pages, 215 illustrations, 123 in color; cloth, dust jacket.   Brannan 43-572 1996 $120.00

STEARN, WILLIAM T.   The Australian Flower Paintings of Ferdinand Bauer. Basilisk Press, 1976. Limited edition of 500 numbered copies; folio; 128 pages; 25 mounted color plates, double page map; publisher's green quarter calf, spine lettered in blind, with Swedish marbled paper sides and vellum tipped corners, by A. W. Lumsden, cloth box with paper label, publisher's prospectus containing 'proof' plate; fine. Thomas Thorp 489-22 1996 £450.00

STEARNS, E.   Notes on Uncle Tom's Cabin... Philadelphia: Lippincott, Grambo, 1853. 1st edition; 8vo; brown cloth, near fine.   Charles Agvent 4-1073 1996 $250.00

STEARNS, JOSIAH   A Sermon Preached at Epping, in New Hampshire on Lord's Day, September 19, 1779. Exeter: 1780. 1st edition; 12mo; 40 pages; sewn, becoming loose. Evans 16998.   M & S Rare Books 60-417 1996 $100.00

STEARNS, JOSIAH   A Sermon Preached at the Ordination of the Rev. Mr. Nicolas Dudley. Newbury-port: John Mycall, 1778. 1st edition; 12mo; 31 pages; sewn and uncut, as issued. Presentation copy, inscribed in ink by author. Evans 16079.   M & S Rare Books 60-416 1996 $125.00

STEDMAN, JOHN   Laelius and Hortensia; or, Thoughts on the Nature and Objects of Taste and Genius, in a Series of Letters to Two Friends. Edinburgh: ptd. for J. Balfour and T. Cadell, London, 1782. 8vo; xiv, 536 pages, with errata slip bound in at end; contemporary tree calf, neatly rebacked, fine; from the library of Ripley castle.   C. R. Johnson 37-77 1996 £450.00

STEDMAN, JOHN GABRIEL   Narrative of a Five Years' Expedition Against the Revolted Negroes of Surinam, in Guiana, on the Wild Coast of South America, from the Year 1772 to 1777. London: J. Johnson, 1806-13. 2nd edition; 4to; 2 volumes, xviii, 423, (4); iv, 419, (5) pages; 2 hand colored engraved titlepages and 8 hand colored engraved plates, 16 of which are engraved by William Blake; contemporary full diced morocco, gilt tooled spines and borders, slight discoloration of covers near spine, spine ends worn, couple of hinges little weak, shallow vertical crack in spine leather of volume 1, still nice, very clean internally. Field 1494; Sabin 91075.   Chapel Hill 94-367 1996 $2,000.00

STEDMAN, JOHN GABRIEL   Narrative of a Five Years' Expedition Against the Revolted Negores of Surinam, in Guiana, on the Wild Coast of South America, from the Year 1772 to 1777. London: printed for J. Johnson, St. Paul's Church Yard & Th. Payne, Pall Mall 1813. 3rd edition; 4to; 2 volumes; text 1-423, 1-419 pages; hand colored aquatint frontispiece to both volumes, 71 hand colored aquatints, 8 maps and plans, text watermarked 1805, plates watermarked J. Whatman 1812; half modern tan morocco and marbled boards, corners bumped, gilt tooling to panelled spines, red and blue morocco labels to spines, plates all in good condition with no foxing or offsetting, new endpapers, owenr's bookplate, hinges cracked, still very good, tight copy.   Beeleigh Abbey BA56-240 1996 £3,500.00

STEDMAN, JOHN GABRIEL   Narrative of Five Years' Expedition Against the Revolted Negroes of Surinam. Barre: Imprint Society, 1971. Number 107 from a total edition of 1950 numbered copies; 2 volumes; illustrated from author's original aquatint and copperplate engravings, including 3 folding maps and folding plate; cloth backed French marbled paper covered boards with paper labels, fine set in publisher's slipcase; signed by Rudolf van Lier, who contributed a new introduction. Hermitage SP95-924 1996 $150.00

STEEDMAN, A.   Wanderings and Adventures in the Interior of Southern Africa. Cape Town: 1966. Reprint, limited to 750 numbered copies; 2 volumes, plates and text illustrations; fine in dust jackets. David Grayling J95Biggame-191 1996 £65.00

STEEL, DAVID   Seamanship, Both in Theory and Practice. London: printed for David Steel, 1795. 1st separate edition; 8vo; pages viii, 227, (1), 3 folding dust jacket, in text diagrams; original marbled boards, rebacked, printed paper label, 2 bookplates. Excellent copy.   Howard S. Mott 227-132 1996 $525.00

STEEL, DAVID   Steel's Elements of Mastmaking, Sailmaking and rigging. London: 1932. Large 4to; xv, 300 pages; 59 folding and other plates.   Bookworm & Silverfish 280-143 1996 $200.00

STEELE'S Book of Niagara Falls. Buffalo: Oliver G. Steele, 1840. 7th edition; 24mo; 109 pages; folding double map frontispiece, 6 lithographic illustrations; full contemporary red calf, gilt title with interlocking rules in gilt on borders and rosettes on spine, lightly rubbed on extremities, scattered foxing, owner's name, very good. Fine American binding. Sabin 91137; American Imprints 40-5262.   Andrew Cahan 47-147 1996 $350.00

STEELE, J. W.   Guide to the Pacific Coast, Sante Fe Route. Chicago: 1893. illustrations, folded maps, decorated cloth, very good+.   T. A. Swinford 49-1107 1996 $150.00

STEELE, JAMES   A Golden Era. The New Gold Fields of the United States. Chicago: Chicago, Milwaukee & St. Paul Railway, Dec. 1897. 1st edition; 60, (1) pages; illustrations, folding map; original green printed wrappers, title embossed on front cover, fine.   Michael D. Heaston 23-307 1996 $250.00

STEELE, RICHARD 1672-1729   An Essay Upon Gardening, Containing a Catalogue of Exotic Plants for the Stoves and Green-Houses of the British Gardens... York: printed for the author by G. Peacock, 1793. 1st edition; 4to; pages xx, (1), (2), p. xxii, pages (2), 126, (1), (127)-159, 102, (2), 3 folding engraved plates; uncut, contemporary marbled boards, rebacked with green cloth, new label on front cover; two leaves and one plate are misbound, but present; fine, large copy. Henrey 1384; Pritzel 8912.   Howard S. Mott 227-156 1996 $1,000.00

STEELE, RICHARD 1672-1729   Essays. London: Macmillan, 1914. 6 1/4 x 4 1/4 inches; xv, (1), 358 pages, (1) leaf (colophon); frontispiece; bookplate; very appealing dark green crushed morocco by Bayntun (for Brentano's), spine with raised bands and gilt titling, turn-ins ruled and ornamented in gilt, marbled endpapers, all edges gilt; hint of sunning to spine, but extremely clean, binding very bright and showing virtually no wear.   Phillip J. Pirages 33-74 1996 $100.00

STEELE, RICHARD 1672-1729   The Theatre...To Which are added, the Anti-Theatre; The Character of Sir John Steel's Case with the Lord Chamberlain the Crisis of Property, with the Sequel, Two Pasquins &c. &c. London: printed by and for the editor, 1791. 8vo; 2 volumes, pages vii, (i), (1)-314; iv, 315-615, (1); additional engraved portrait vignette titlepage volume i, early owner's name at head of titlepages; modern half russet calf with contemporary marbled boards, smooth backstrips divided by gilt rules, contemporary red morocco labels, early ownership name on front pastedown "D. Gell - Hopton-Hall", excellent. Arnott & Robinson 4069; Lowe pp. 321/22.   Blackwell's B112-264 1996 £200.00

STEELE, WILLIAM   Beauties of Gilsland. London: George Routledge and Carlisle: C. Thurnam, 1836. 8vo; pages iv, (ii), 144; original cloth, gilt, old paper label on spine, rather faded, edges little bumped, very good.   R.F.G. Hollett & Son 78-1303 1996 £95.00

STEEN, MARGUERITE   Oakfield Plays Including the Inglemere Christmas Play. London: Ivor Nicholson & Watson, 1932. 1st edition; 4to; pages 155, 12 fine full page colored plates by author.   R.F.G. Hollett & Son 78-470 1996 £85.00

STEENTOFT, M.   Flowering Plants in West Africa. London: 1988. 8vo; 350 pages; 86 illustrations; cloth.   Wheldon & Wesley 207-1590 1996 £60.00

STEFANSON, VIHJALMUR   Hunters of the Great North. New York: Harcourt Brace, 1922. 1st edition; 8vo; 26 black and white illustrations, 2 black and white folding maps at end, dust jacket (small chips to spine, nicks), very good. Signed and inscribed by author to Mrs. S. F. Cottle.   George J. Houle 68-140 1996 $150.00

STEFANSSON, VIHJALMUR   The Friendly Arctic: The Story of Five Years in Polar Regions. New York: Macmillan, 1921. 1st edition; ("November 1921"); thick 8vo; 103 black and white illustrations, 7 text maps, 2 folding maps in pocket at end; full dark blue cloth, gilt stamped spine and upper cover; very good; acetate dust jacket. Signed and inscribed by Stefansson to Dr. C. E. Pitkin on front free endpaper.   George J. Houle 68-139 1996 $175.00

STEGNER, WALLACE   Angel of Repose. Garden City: Doubleday, 1971. 1st edition; about fine in very good dust jacket, little tanned on spine and slightly worn at extremities, sticker indicating that the novel won the Pulitzer Prize.   Between the Covers 42-413 1996 $100.00

STEGNER, WALLACE   Beyond the Hundredth Meridian: John Wesley Powell and the Second Opening of the West. Boston: Houghton Mifflin, 1954. 1st edition; illustrations, fine in near fine dust jacket with light rubbing and small nicks at spinal extremities, nicer than usual copy, scarce.   Between the Covers 42-412 1996 $350.00

STEGNER, WALLACE   The Big Rock Candy Mountain. New York: Duell, Sloane and Peace, 1943. 1st edition; browning, or acidification, to endpapers and some slight foxing to page edges, there are two small holes in gutter, otherwise at least a very good copy in dust jacket that is moderately spine faded with some mild chipping at extremities of spine, overall attractive, scarce.   Ken Lopez 74-418 1996 $550.00

STEGNER, WALLACE   The Big Rock Candy Mountain. Franklin Center: Franklin Library, 1978. Limited edition; 9 1/8 x 6 1/4 inches; xii, 733 pages, including full page color illustrations; gold stamped tan leather; signed by Stegner.   Dawson's Books Shop 528-234 1996 $125.00

STEGNER, WALLACE   The Collected Stories of Wallace Stegner. New York: Random House, 1990. 1st edition; fine in fine dust jacket and inscribed by author in month of publication.   Ken Lopez 74-419 1996 $150.00

STEGNER, WALLACE   Crossing to Safety. Franklin Center: Franklin Library, 1987. Signed limited edition; true first edition; unopened, slipcase.   Bev Chaney, Jr. 23-624 1996 $125.00

STEGNER, WALLACE   Fire and Ice. New York: Duell Sloan Pearce, 1941. 1st and only printing of 2500 copies; good copy only, with embossed ownership stamp on front endpaper and lacking dust jacket and with fraying to cloth at extremities of spine; inscribed by author and dated in year of publication.   Ken Lopez 74-417 1996 $400.00

STEICHEN, EDWARD   A Life in Photography. Garden City: 1963. 1st edition; square 4to; illustrations; dust jacket.   J. B. Muns 154-282 1996 $125.00

STEIN, AUREL   Wall Paintings from Ancient Shrines in Central Asia. London: Oxford University Press, 1948. Large porfolio, large 4to, cloth and slim 4to. wrappers; portfolio of plates with small split at top of spine, waterstain at lower part of front cover near joint, original ties, gilt lettering bright, inner edge of titlepage stained, with 32 large plates of which 12 are in color; text volume cloth and boards with some spine wear, inner hinges broken, endpapers discolored and some scattered foxing, with 128 pages and 4 plates, including folding map.   Marilyn Braiterman 15-191 1995 $1,000.00

STEIN, ELIZABETH P.   David Garrick, Dramatist. New York: Modern Language Assoc. of America, 1938. 1st edition; 271 pages; 12 black and white plates; original binding, top edge slightly dusty, head and tail of spine and corners bumped, covers marked, tail of spine faded, endpaper edges slightly browned and spotted; very good; presentation copy from author, inscribed in 1938.   Ulysses 39-219 1 996 £75.00

STEIN, GERTRUDE 1874-1946   The Autobiography of Alice B. Toklas. New York: Harcourt Brace and Co., 1933. 1st edition; illustrations; blue cloth with silver encircled 'rose is a rose' motif on front panel; traces of water stain to front and back panel, same to dust jacket, but very good in handsome dust jacket, creased with small chip from upper front corner.   Hermitage SP95-590 1996 $150.00

STEIN, GERTRUDE 1874-1946   The Autobiography of Alice B. Toklas. New York: Harcourt, Brace and Co., 1933. 1st edition; light foxing to prelims, quarter inch spot on front cover, spine slightly frayed at head and foot, otherwise very good, no dust jacket.   Sherwood 3-297 1996 $100.00

STEIN, GERTRUDE 1874-1946   Blood on the Dining-Room Floor. Banyan Press, 1948. 1st edition; limited to 626 numbered copies; 8 x 6.5 inches; 80 pages; cloth backed marbled boards, minor wear in slightly used slipcase.   John K. King 77-466 1996 $175.00

STEIN, GERTRUDE 1874-1946   Geography and Plays. Boston: Four Seas and Co., 1922. 2nd binding; 7 3/4 x 5 1/2 inches; 419 pages; original cloth and dust jacket, largely unopened, few minor tears and little discoloration internally, otherwise extremely fine, binding virtually immaculate, in neatly repaired jacket (jacket spine renewed at top and bottom, darkened and marked, tiny losses at corners, otherwise very clean and pleasing), signed "Paul Miner(?)/Gertrude Stein/December(?) '34", this inscription with thin red 'x' drawn across it. Wilson A5b. Phillip J. Pirages 33-466 1996 $850.00

STEIN, GERTRUDE 1874-1946   Geography and Plays. Boston: Four Seas Co., 1922. 1st edition; 1st binding; 7 3/4 x 5 1/2 inches; 419 pages; device on title; original cloth backed paper boards, about half opened, boards little marked, otherwise fine, in scarce first binding. Wilson A5a.   Phillip J. Pirages 33-465 1996 $100.00

STEIN, GERTRUDE 1874-1946   Lucretia Borgia - a Play. New York: Albondocani Press, 1968. one of 150 numbered copies, out of a total edition of 176 copies; wrappers, Italian Fabriano paper; title label on upper cover slightly dusty, fine.   Ulysses 39-557 1996 £75.00

STEIN, GERTRUDE 1874-1946   Picasso. London: Batsford/Scribners, 1939. 1st edition; rose boards stamped in light blue, lightly faded on spine, in very good dust jacket with several small chips at spine tips; near fine.   Bev Chaney, Jr. 23-632 1996 $165.00

STEIN, GERTRUDE 1874-1946   Portraits and Prayers. New York: Random House, 1934. 1st edition; 8 1/4 x 6 1/4 inches; 264 pages; original cloth (front cover with portrait of Stein by Carl Van Vechten), clear double layer cellophane dust jacket printed in red and with grey paper flaps (one of which folds partly over onto the front board, cellophane portion of the jacket not being quite wide enough to cover spine and boards completely, fragile original cellophane slightly chipped at spine top and at one other place along top edge, one long closed tear in one layer of cellophane on back panel, but not the other layer, otherwise mint, very fine, with rare and delicate jacket still in excellent condition; signed and inscribed by Stein. Wilson A22.   Phillip J. Pirages 33-468 1996 $850.00

STEIN, GERTRUDE 1874-1946   Three Lives. New York: Grafton, 1909. Author's first book; spine bumped at extremities and soiling to outside edge, otherwise very good; inscription.   R. A. Gekoski 19-127 1996 £175.00

STEIN, GERTRUDE 1874-1946   Useful Knowledge. London: Bodley Head, n.d. 1928. 1st edition; extraordinary copy, fine in very near fine dust jacket and with full page inscription by author; very nice.   Ken Lopez 74-421 1996 $1,500.00

STEIN, GERTRUDE 1874-1946   Wars I Have Seen. London: B. T. Batsford, 1945. 1st edition; 4 black and white photos of author by Cecil Beaton; original binding, top edge partially faded, corners slightly bumped, spine slightly faded, prelim edges and endpapers spotted, very good in nicked and slightly rubbed, marked and dusty dust jacket by Cecil Beaton, slightly browned at spine and edges.   Ulysses 39-555 1996 £55.00

STEIN, GERTRUDE 1874-1946   What Are Masterpieces. Los Angeles: Conference Press, 1940. 1st edition; 2 full page line drawings by Francis Picabia; original binding, top edge dusty, endpapers partially browned, very good in nicked, rubbed, faded and dusty, slightly marked dust jacket; loosely inserted prospectus for this book, folded twice; from the library of James D. Hart.   Ulysses 39-556 1996 £125.00

STEIN, GERTRUDE 1874-1946   The World is Round. New York: Scott, 1939. 1st edition; 4to; printed on rose colored paper, illustrations in blue and white by Clement Hurd; cloth backed blue boards, boards slightly rubbed at lower edges, else very fresh in rubbed colored pictorial dust jacket; very scarce.   Barbara Stone 70-203 1996 £190.00

STEIN, HEINRICH F. KARL, BARON   Life and Times of Stein, or Germany and Prussia in the Napoleonic Age. London: Cambridge University Press, 1878. Large 8vo; 3 volumes; 3 portraits, and 5 maps; original cloth.   Howes Bookshop 265-1152 1996 £55.00

STEIN, JOSEPH   Fiddler on the Roof. New York: 1965. 1st edition; review slip laid in; fine.   Lyman Books 21-638 1996 $125.00

STEINBECK, JOHN ERNST 1902-1968   Bombs Away: the Story of a Bomber Team. New York: Viking Press, 1942. 1st edition; photos by John Swope; very good in color illustrated dust jacket, which is worn on extremities.   Andrew Cahan 47-192 1996 $135.00

STEINBECK, JOHN ERNST 1902-1968   Burning Bright. New York: Viking Press, 1950. 1st edition; near fine in very good dust jacket which is lightly soiled and with one very tiny chip at top right spine corner.   Steven C. Bernard 71-216 1996 $100.00

STEINBECK, JOHN ERNST 1902-1968   East of Eden. New York: Viking Press, 1952. Limited to 1500 copies, signed; bright green boards, stamped in gold, all edges stained, fine in near fine slipcase that is only slightly rubbed at edges.   Bev Chaney, Jr. 23-636 1996 $960.00

STEINBECK, JOHN ERNST 1902-1968   Flight. Yolla Bolly Press, 1984. One of 250 copies for sale, signed by artist and Wallace Stegner who provided afterword; 12 1/4 x 10 1/2 inches; 4 p.l. (one blank), 52 pages, (1) leaf (illustration, colophon), 6 full page mounted colored illustrations by Karin Wikstrom, few small colored illustrations, in text; original patterned tan cloth, paper label on spine, fore edge untrimmed, in publisher's slipcase; mint.   Phillip J. Pirages 33-523 1996 $325.00

STEINBECK, JOHN ERNST 1902-1968   The Grapes of Wrath. New York: Viking, 1939. 1st edition; original cloth and dust jacket, very fine.   19th Century Shop 39- 1996 $2,000.00

STEINBECK, JOHN ERNST 1902-1968   The Grapes of Wrath. New York: Viking, 1939. 1st edition; ("April 1939"); 8vo; pictorial endpapers, top edge stained yellow, dust jacket with few nicks, very good to fine.   Goldstone & Payne A12a.   George J. Houle 68-141 1996 $1,250.00

STEINBECK, JOHN ERNST 1902-1968   The Grapes of Wrath. New York: Viking Press, 1939. 1st edition; 8vo; original cloth, dust jacket chipped with 4 small portions lacking, generally little worn, upper corner of p. 615-6 creased, binding still very good.   James Cummins 14-194 1996 $500.00

STEINBECK, JOHN ERNST 1902-1968   John Emery. New York: 1964. One of 200 privately printed copies, none of which was for sale; light wear to upper fore-corners, else fine in attractive quarter leather and paper covered boards; Rare.   Lame Duck Books 19-508 1996 $1,250.00

STEINBECK, JOHN ERNST 1902-1968   Journal of a Novel: The East of Eden Letters. New York: Viking Press, 1969. One of 600 copies; color frontispiece, 7 facsimile pages from the manuscript; top corner tips slightly frayed, red line on bottom page edges, otherwise very good+, but lacking original glassine dust jacket and slipcase.   Steven C. Bernard 71-217 1996 $175.00

STEINBECK, JOHN ERNST 1902-1968   The Log from the Sea of Cortez. New York: Viking, 1951. 1st edition; fine in dust jacket with two small tears and slightly faded spine.   Captain's Bookshelf 38-204 1996 $200.00

STEINBECK, JOHN ERNST 1902-1968   The Long Valley. New York: 1938. 1st edition; 1 of only 8000 copies; very near fine, tight copy in near fine dust jacket.   Stephen Lupack 83- 1996 $450.00

STEINBECK, JOHN ERNST 1902-1968   Of Mice and Men. London: Heinemann, 1937. 1st English edition; spine gilt dull, some offsetting to pink endpapers, otherwise nice in nicked dust jacket, with some foxing.   R. A. Gekoski 19-128 1996 £200.00

STEINBECK, JOHN ERNST 1902-1968   Of Mice and Men. New York: Covici Friede, 1937. 1st edition, 1st issue; near fine in very good dust jacket which is uniformly darkened on spine; inscribed by author, very uncommon signed.   Ken Lopez 74-423 1996 $5,500.00

STEINBECK, JOHN ERNST 1902-1968   Of Mice and Men. New York: Limited Editions Club, 1970. Number 330 of 1500 copies; signed by artist; illustrations by Fletcher Martin; fine in publisher's slipcase.   Hermitage SP95-1040 1996 $175.00

STEINBECK, JOHN ERNST 1902-1968   The Pearl. New York: Viking, 1947. 1st edition; 8vo; drawings by Jose Clemente; cloth, lightly edgeworn dust jacket; fine.   James S. Jaffe 34-628 1996 $125.00

STEINBECK, JOHN ERNST 1902-1968   The Red Pony. New York: Covici Friede, 1937. 1st edition; one of 699 copies, signed by Steinbeck; 10 1/4 x 7 inches; 81, (1) pages; color vignette on title, nicely printed on handmade paper; original pictorial cloth, fore edge and tail edge untrimmed, in publisher's slightly rubbed and chafed slipcase with penned number on spine, extremely fine.   Phillip J. Pirages 33-469 1996 $800.00

STEINBECK, JOHN ERNST 1902-1968   Sea of Cortez. New York: Viking, 1941. Salesman's promotional dummy; printing 2 pages from introduction, 4 pages from chapter two, and minor excerpts from appendix, which were altered prior to publication, with all other pages blank; blue cloth stamped in silver on front cover only, top edge stained green, fine in uniformly age toned, else fine dust jacket with blank flaps and rear panel, in specially made quarter leather slipcase; exceedingly rare.   Between the Covers 42-414 1996 $3,500.00

STEINBECK, JOHN ERNST 1902-1968   Sea of Cortez: a Leisurely Journal of Travel with Research. New York: Viking Press, 1941. Advance proof copy; octavo; x, 277 pages; original plain brown wrappers with publisher's yellow label on front cover, label stained, edges of wrappers lightly chipped, very slightly skewed, very good, housed in quarter black morocco slipcase, black cloth chemise; Goldstone & Payne A15a.   Heritage Book Shop 196-175 1996 $3,000.00

STEINBECK, JOHN ERNST 1902-1968   The Short Novels of John Steinbeck. New York: Viking, 1953. 1st edition; fine in dust jacket with tiny tear on rear panel, exceptional copy.   Between the Covers 42-415 1996 $250.00

STEINBECK, JOHN ERNST 1902-1968   Tortilla Flat. New York: Covici Friede, 1935. 1st edition of only 4000 copies; minor foxing to page edges, else fine in dust jacket that is mildly spine darkened with some wear at crown and light vertical pencil markings through title and author's name; attractive copy, scarce.   Ken Lopez 74-422 1996 $4,750.00

STEINBECK, JOHN ERNST 1902-1968   Viva Zapata! Viking Compass, 1975. 1st edition; wrappers, diagonal crase on back cover, slight shelf wear; very good.   Book Time 2-424 1996 $100.00

STEINBOCK, R. TED   Paleopathological Daignosis and interpretation: Bone Diseases in Ancient Human Populations. Springfield: 1976. 423 pages; original binding. GM 2312.7.   W. Bruce Fye 71-2038 1996 $150.00

STEJNEGER, L.   Herpetology of Japan and Adjacent Territory. Washington: 1907. 8vo; pages xx, 577, 35 plates and 409 text figures; new cloth.   Wheldon & Wesley 207-939 1996 £100.00

STELL, J.   The Hastings Guide. London: Barry, 1815. 4th edition; 8vo; pages iv, 83, (1), frontispiece and folding map; original boards, printed label, spine and joints worn, cracked. Anderson p. 282.   Marlborough 162-91 1996 £50.00

STELLA, BENEDETTO   Il Tabacco. Opera...Nealla Quale si Tratta dell'Origine, Historia, Coltura, Preparatione, Qualita, Natura, Virtu & Uso in Fumo in Polvere, in Foglia, in Lambitivo et in Medicina. rome: Filippo Maria Mancini, 1669. 1st edition; small 8vo; (32), 480 pages; 6 full page woodcuts, contemporary vellum; some browning and dampstaining, lacks rear free endpaper, very good. Waring II 711. Arents 309; Krivatsy 11425; Sabin 91215.   Edwin V. Glaser 121-298 1996 $1,000.00

STEPHEN, GEORGE   The Adventures of a Gentleman in Search of a Horse. Philadelphia: John W. Moore, 1857. 1st American edition, from the 6th edition; 8vo; illustrations; original red cloth, decorated and lettered in gilt and blind, some rubbing and soiling; some spotting, offsetting and browning, generally light; from the John Schiff collection with his bookplate.   James Cummins 14-195 1996 $150.00

STEPHEN, JAMES FITZJAMES   A Digest of the Law of Evidence. St. Louis: F. H. Thomas and Co., 1879. 2nd edition; new quarter calf, morocco label, pocket book sized.   Meyer Boswell SL26-220 1996 $150.00

STEPHEN, JAMES FITZJAMES   The Story of Nuncomar and the Impeachment of Sir Elijah Impey. London: 1885. 1st edition; 8vo; 2 volumes, over 500 pages; half calf, title labels inset on brown and maroon morocco, good.   K Books 442-451 1996 £65.00

STEPHEN, LESLIE   Hours in a Library. (First Series-Third). London: Smith, Elder & Co., 1874-79. 1st edition; 8vo; 3 volumes, half titles; half morocco by Bayntun of Bath, volume 3 slightly faded, uncut, top edge gilt.   Forest Books 74-257 1996 £75.00

STEPHEN, LESLIE   Hours in a Library. New York: & London: 1894. New edition; 8vo; 3 volumes extended to 6, extra illustrated by the insertion of 235 extra plates, mainly portraits; beautifully bound in 1948 in three quarter brown levant morocco, gilt panelled spines, gilt tops; choice copy from the library of Louise Whitefield Carnegie with her bookplate.   Charles W. Traylen 117-199 1996 £650.00

STEPHEN, LESLIE   The Science of Ethics. London: Smith, Elder & Co., 1882. 1st edition; 8vo; original brown cloth; occasional intelligent marginal notes by an early reader, but fine. CBEL III 1405.   Ximenes 108-330 1996 $250.00

STEPHEN, LESLIE   Sketches from Cambridge. London: Macmillan, 1865. 1st edition; 28 page catalog; original red cloth, bevelled boards, dulled.   Jarndyce 103-574 1996 £60.00

STEPHENS, ANN S.   Malaeska: the Indian Wife of the White Hunter. New York: Irwin P. Beadle and Co., 1860. 12mo; 128 pages; frontispiece; disbound, sound. American Grolier 70; Johannsen, Dime Novels 1.   M & S Rare Books 60-237 1996 $750.00

STEPHENS, ANN S.   The Portland Sketch Book. Portland: Colman and Chisholm, 1836. 1st edition; engraved title; original binding, some loss of cloth along spine edges, light to moderate foxing, name on pastedown scratched out; inscribed twice by Stephens in 1840 to R. Ralph Hinman, in addition the author has changed two words in one of her works. Charles Agvent 4-1026 1996 $350.00

STEPHENS, EDWARD   Reflections Upon the Occurrences of the Last Year. From 5 Nov. 1688 to 5 Nov. 1689. London: printed in the year 1689. 1st edition; small 4to; disbound; fine; Wing S5437.   Ximenes 109-273 1996 $150.00

STEPHENS, FERRIS J.   Votive and Historical Texts from Babylonia and Assyria. New Haven: Yale University Press, 1937. 4to; xvii, 45 pages; 35 autographic plates and 11 photographic plates; boards, minor wear at head of spine.   Archaeologia Luxor-2741 1996 $150.00

STEPHENS, FREDERIC G.   Flemish Relics; Architectural, Legendary and Pictorial, as Connected with Public Buildings in Belgium. London: Alfred W. Bennett, 1866. 1st edition; tall 8vo; (179), (4) ads; 15 original mounted photos; original red cloth.   David Mason 71-17 1996 $520.00

STEPHENS, GEORGE   Incidents of Travel in Egypt, Arabia, Petraea and the Holy Land. London: Richard Bentley, New Burlington St... 1838. New edition; 2 volumes; text 1-317; 1-359 pages, note 360-363 pages; full speckled calf, very tastefully rebacked, elaborate gilt tooling to panelled spine, brown and green morocco labels to spine, raised bands, corners slightly bumped, single gilt rule border to boards, upper hinge to volume 1 cracked, prelims slightly foxed, otherwise good.   Beeleigh Abbey BA56-241 1996 £300.00

STEPHENS, H.   The Book of the Farm, Detailing the Labours of Farmer, Farm-Steward, Ploughman, Shepherd, Hedger, Cattle-Man, Field-Worker and Dairy-Maid. London: 1844. 1st edition; 8vo; 3 volumes; pages xix, 670; iii, 728; vi, 729-1407, 33 engraved plates, 608 text figures; original boards, new half calf, plates in volume 1 waterstained. John Henly 27-372 1996 £180.00

STEPHENS, JAMES 1882-1950   The Crock of Gold. London: Macmillan, 1912. "Presentation Copy" stamped in blind on titlepage; apart from little light foxing to pastedowns, small area of dampstaining on upper board, nice in very good dust jacket somewhat sunned at spine and missing two tiny chips, quarter leather drop back case, little faded at spine. R. A. Gekoski 19-129 1996 £300.00

STEPHENS, JAMES 1882-1950   The Crock of Gold. London: Macmillan, 1926. One of a limited edition of 525 printed on handmade paper and signed by author; large 4to; 228 pages; 12 mounted color plates, decorative headings and tailpieces, all by Thomas Mackenzie; blue boards with vellum spine; pictorial bookplate of Eleanor, Countess of Castle Stewart.   Marjorie James 19-145 1996 £225.00

STEPHENS, JAMES 1882-1950   Hunger. Dublin: Candle Press, 1918. 1st edition; 8vo; wrappers; scarce, near fine.   Charles Agvent 4-1027 1996 $150.00

STEPHENS, JAMES 1882-1950   Hunger. Dublin: Candle Press: 1918. 1st edition; small 8vo; pages 29 and ad leaf; original printed wrapper, nice.   James Fenning 133-324 1996 £55.00

STEPHENS, JAMES 1882-1950   The Insurrection in Dublin. Dublin and London: Maunsel & Co. Ltd., 1916. 1st edition; 16 pages publisher's ads dated Sept. 1916 at rear; original binding, bottom edges of covers slightly rubbed, head and tail of spine slightly bumped, very good in torn, rubbed, marked and dusty dust jacket browned at spine and edges, price on spine has been altered in ink; preserved in custom made quarter morocco slipcase, spine of slipcase rubbed and browned; bookplate of H. Bradley Martin.   Ulysses 39-558 1996 £195.00

STEPHENS, JAMES 1882-1950   Insurrections. Dublin: Maunsel, 1909. 1st edition; 8vo; author's first book; original binding, foxing of endpapers, primarily rear, spine bit sunned, minor fraying.   Charles Agvent 4-1028 1996 $125.00

STEPHENS, JAMES 1882-1950   Julia Elizabeth: a Comedy in One Act. New York: Crosby Gaige, 1929. 1st edition; limited issue, one of 600 copies for American distribution out of a total print run of 861, numbered and signed by author. quarter cloth over decorative boards, fine in torn and chipped publisher's tissue wrapper.   Hermitage SP95-595 1996 $125.00

STEPHENS, JAMES 1882-1950   Theme and Variations. New York: Fountain Press, 1930. Number 356 of 892 copies, signed by author; very fine in publisher's slipcase.   Hermitage SP95-594 1996 $125.00

STEPHENS, JAMES WILSON   An Historical and Geographical Account of Algiers; Containing a Circumstantial and Interesting Detail of Events Relative to the American Captives, Taken From Their Own Testimony. Brooklyn: printed by Thomas Kirk, 1800. 2nd edition; without frontispiece and lacking two (of three) of the leaves of the list of subscribers; contemporary? sheep, new? spine, very worn, working copy.   Meyer Boswell   SL25-210   1996 $225.00

STEPHENS, JOHN LLOYD 1805-1852   Incidents of Travel in Central America, Chiapas and Yucatan. New York: Harper and Bros., 1841. 1st edition; 8vo; 2 volumes, viii, 9-424 pages, folding map; vii, (2 page list of engravings), 7-474 pages; frontispieces, numerous engravings; gilt decorated cloth, chipped on spine ends, lightly rubbed, scattered foxing, very good set.   Andrew Cahan   47-193   1996 $350.00

STEPHENS, JOHN LLOYD 1805-1852   Incidents of Travel in Central America, Chiapas and Yucatan. London: Arthur Hall, Virtue & Co., 1854. 1st British one volume edition; demy 8vo; xvi, 548 pages; plates, some folding, map, illustrations; Victorian full calf, banded and heavily gilt, marbled edges, little rubbed, few minor marks, but nice.   Ash Rare Books   Zenzybyr-86   1996 £145.00

STEPHENS, JOHN LLOYD 1805-1852   Incidents of Travel in Central America, Chiapas, and Yucatan. London: John Murray, 1846. 8vo; 2 volumes, pages ix, 10-424; vii, 2, 8-474; folding map, 65 plates, 4 plans; full contemporary calf, black labels. Sabin 91297; Larned 4020.   Richard Adelson   W94/95-166   1996 $385.00

STEPHENS, JOHN LLOYD 1805-1852   Incidents of Travel in Greece, Turkey, Russia and Poland. New York: Harper and Bros., 1838. 1st edition; 8vo; 2 volumes; xi, (13)-268, v, (7)-275 pages; illustration and folding map; original green cloth, blindstamped pattern; foxing throughout, some wear to spine ends, chip in spine of volume 1,, still better than very good set.   David Mason   71-88   1996 $180.00

STEPHENS, JOHN LLOYD 1805-1852   Incidents of Travel in the Yucatan. New York: Harper & Bros., 1843. 1st edition; 8vo; 2 volumes; 937 pages, 124 illustrations, 1 folding map; original gilt pictorial cloth, light chipping and small tears at spines, scattered foxing and browning; inscribed by author for President Martin Van Buren.   Archaeologia Luxor-4914   1996 $2,500.00

STEPHENS, JOHN LLOYD 1805-1852   Incidents of Travel in Yucatan. London: John Murray, 1843. 1st edition; 8vo; 2 volumes, pages xii, 9-459; xvi, 9-478; 64 plates, 2 plans, 2 maps; full contemporary calf, black labels. Sabin 91299; Larned 590.   Richard Adelson   W94/95-167   1996 $400.00

STEPHENS, JOHN LLOYD 1805-1852   Incidents of Travel in Yucatan. New York: Harper & Bros., 1843. 1st edition; 8vo; 2 volumes; folding frontispiece, folding map, 65 plates, numerous wood engraved illustrations; original grey purple cloth, decorated in gilt, signs of white shelf numbers removed from spines; some foxing, old library marks, release stamps on titlepages, but generally in very good condition. Sabin 91299; Smith, Amer. Travelelrs Abroad S149.   Ximenes 108-331   1996 $450.00

STEPHENS, WALTER   Notes on the Mineralogy of Part of the Vicinity of Dublin. 1812. 1st edition; 8vo; 3 folding plates; original boards, spine worn, else very good, very scarce.   C. P. Hyland   216-803   1996 £200.00

STEPHENS, WALTER   Notes on the Mineralogy of the Part of the Vicinity of Dublin, Taken Principally from Papers of the Late... London: 1812. 57 pages, 2 plates, folding panorama; lacking map; old blank paper covered boards.   Graham Weiner   C2-592   1996 £50.00

STEPHENSON, ALAN M. G.   The Victorian Archbishops of Canterbury. Rocket Press, 1991. Of 525 numbered copies, this one of 75 specially bound; 4to; printed in Baskerville in black and purple on Zerkall mouldmade; full purple morocco, vellum label on spine, fine in slipcase.   Bertram Rota   272-411   1996 £96.00

STEPHENSON, BLAKE & CO.   Lining Type Borders, Brass Rule, &c. Material and Machinery. London: Stephenson Blake & Co. ltd., 1915/19. 2nd issue; 4to; pages xviii, 144, 72 (machinery) + 8 inserted pages; original cloth, gilt, dated 1915 but with new price list and inserted slips dated 1919; very good; contemporary ownership signature of H. Langley Jones, subsequently in the library of Walter Tracy, with few pencilled marginal notes by him.   Claude Cox   107-237   1996 £65.00

STEPHENSON, BLAKE & CO.   Specimens of Printing Types, Borders, Ornamnts, Plain and Fancy Rules, &c. Sheffield: Stephenson, Blake & Co., 1895. Thick 8vo; 40 pages, 236 leaves, mostly printed on one side only, 1 small text illustrations having been cut; original decorated cloth, gilt, fine.   Forest Books   74-258   1996 £275.00

STEPHENSON, T. A.   The British Sea Anemones. London: Ray Society, 1928-35. 8vo; 2 volumes; cloth, good.   Wheldon & Wesley 207-1294   1996 £90.00

STERLING, GEORGE   The Testimony of the Suns. San Francisco: Robertson, 1907. 3rd edition; one of 1000 copies; 8vo; decorated cloth, near fine; inscribed across title from author to his mistress, Vera Connolly, with 2 sonnets to Vera in Sterling's hand and signed by him. Charles Agvent   4-1030   1996 $375.00

STERLING, Kansas. The Actual Advantages and Resources of a Grand Young Town Carefully and Candidly Discussed. Sterling: Sterling Land and Investment Co.?, 1887. 1st edition; 46, (2) pages, illustrations; original brown pictorial wrpapers with ranch featured on back wrapper, little staining to few pages at end, overall very good; rare and attractive publication.   Michael D. Heaston   23-193   1996 $775.00

STERLING, LOUIS   The Sterling Library. A Catalogue of Printed Books and Literary Manuscripts Collected by...and Presented by Him to the University of London. privately printed, Cambridge University Press, 1954. 1st edition; one of 300 copies; 4to; frontispiece, 7 plates, prospectus tipped in; original cloth, top edge gilt.   Forest Books   74-259   1996 £75.00

STERLING, WILLIAM   Annals of the Artists of Spain. London: John Ollivier, 1848. 1st edition;one of 25 extra illustrated sets; thick octavo; 2 volumes; pages 1480 in all; 52 illustrations, plus an additonal 6 noted by Stirling on holograph slips; bound by Leighton in red striated morocco, raised bands, all edges gilt, 7 coats of arms in gilt on front covers, gilt monograms on backs, marbled endpapers, bound for Duke of Somerset, with his fine armorial bookplate in volume 1.   Hartfield 48-L81   1996 $850.00

STERN, F. C.   A Study of the Genus Paeonia. London: 1946. Folio; pages viii, 155; colored plates by L. Snelling plus drawings; cloth. Raymond M. Sutton   VI-30   1996 $575.00

STERNBERG, THOMAS   The Dialect and Folk-lore of Northamptonshire. London: John Russell Smith, 1851. 1st edition; original red cloth, spine slightly dulled, very good; with signature of Algernon Gissing, 1887, with few pencil notes and cutting about author inserted. Jarndyce   103-80   1996 £65.00

STERNE, HENRY   A Statement of Facts, Submitted to the Right Hon. Lord Gleneig, His Majesty's Principal Secretary of State for the Colonies, Prepatory to an Appeal About to Be made by the Author... London: printed by J. C. Chappell, 1837. 1st edition; 8vo; xii, 282, vii, (1) pages, folding table; contemporary drab cloth, gilt lettering piece on spine, bit rubbed; very good. Kress C4505; Sabin 91339; Goldsmiths 30192. John Drury   82-268   1996 £150.00

STERNE, LAURENCE 1713-1768   The Beauties of Sterne... London: ptd. for T. Davies, J. Ridley, W. Flexney, and G. Kearsley, 1782. 1st edition; 12mo; contemporary half calf, spine gilt, little rubbed; first printing is very scarce, fine, complete with half title and final leaf of ads. CBEL II 949.   Ximenes 108-332   1996 $300.00

STERNE, LAURENCE 1713-1768   The Life and Letters of Laurence Sterne. London: Stanley Paul & Co., n.d. 1st edition; 2 volumes; color frontispieces, 24 black and white plates; original binding, top edges dusty, heads and tails of spines bumped, free endpapers partially browned, production fault to prelims of volume two, small hole in spine of volume 2, very good in nicked, chipped, frayed and dusty, slightly torn, creased and marked dust jackets browned at spine and edges. Ulysses 39-560   1996 £125.00

STERNE, LAURENCE 1713-1768   The Life and Opinions of Tristram Shandy, Gentleman. York & London: for R. and J. Dodsley, & for T. Becket and P. A. DeHondt, 1760-69. 1st edition; small 8vo; 9 volumes bound in 5; volumes IV, V, VI and IX with half titles, as called for, volume III with frontispiece; Sterne's signature in ink, as usual, inscribed at head of chapter one in volumes V, VII and IX; uncut, contemporary quarter calf, marbled sides, green morocco spine labels, remains of paper library spine labels, binding on volume IX slightly variant, scarce and desirable in uncut state; spines worn, few trivial tears not affecting text, very good copy, protected in folding polished calf backed book-form. The Gell copy, with contemporary ownership stamps of P. Gell, Hopton on titles of first work in each volume except last. Rothschild 1970.   Simon Finch 24-214   1996 £9,500.00

STERNE, LAURENCE 1713-1768   The Life of Opinions of Tristram Shandy, Gentleman. London: J. C. Nimmo and Bain, 1883. Large paper edition, one of 150 numbered copies, printed on laid paper, with proof etchings on Japanese paper, 8 etchings by Danmman from original designs by Harry Furniss; original binding, top edges dusty, heads and tails of spines and corners bumped, covers slightly marked, spines darkened, title labels on spines browned and chipped, free endpapers browned, very good.   Ulysses 39-559   1996 £155.00

STERNE, LAURENCE 1713-1768   The Life and Opinions of Tristram Shandy. New York: Limited Editions Club, 1935. Number 904 from 1500 copies, signed by artist; illustrations by T. M. Clelland, cloth backed decorative boards, fine set in publisher's slipcase.   Hermitage SP95-1042 1996 $125.00

STERNE, LAURENCE 1713-1768   The Life and Opinions of Tristram Shandy. New York: Limited Editions Club, 1935. Limited to 1500 copies; 8vo; 2 volumes; illustrations by T. M. Cleland, signed by Cleland; half blue linen; fine in broken case.   Charles Agvent 4-1032 1996 $100.00

STERNE, LAURENCE 1713-1768   A Sentimental Journey through France and Italy. London: printed for T. Becker and P. A. de Hondt, 1768. 1st edition; small octavo; 2 volumes, xx, 203, (1, blank); (4), 208 pages; with the following variants: Vol. I, p. 150, line 12 reads 'vous' and in Vol. 2 p. 133 the last line reads 'who have', complete with half titles and list of subscribers; contemporary speckled calf, gilt double rule border on covers, gilt spines with five raised bands, edges sprinkled red, extremities lightly rubbed, some minor browning to text, early ink signatures on front free endpaper and half title, near fine, in brown cloth folding case. Ashley Lib. V p. 206-207; Grolier 100 English 54; Rothschild 1971-72.   Heritage Book Shop 196-261 1996 $3,000.00

STERNE, LAURENCE 1713-1768   A Sentimental Journey through France and Italy. London: Becket & De Hondt, 1768. 2nd edition; 12mo; contemporary calf, gilt, list of subscribers, except for occasional stain, contents clean and bright, half titles not present, leather title label present, volume label absent, front joint split, holding by one cord. Charles Agvent 4-1033 1996 $500.00

STERNE, LAURENCE 1713-1768   A Sentimental Journey through France and Italy. New York: 1885. Facsimile of first edition, one of 100 numbered copies; 7 x 4 inches; 2 volumes, 203, 208 pages; boards, spine labels defective, covers heavily worn and chipped, hinges splitting. John K. King 77-468 1996 $100.00

STERNE, LAURENCE 1713-1768   A Sentimental Journey through France and Italy. Waltham St. Lawrence: Golden Cockerel Press, 1928. One of 500 copies; 9 1/4 x 6 inches; 151, (1) pages, (1) leaf; 6 copper engraved plates by J. E. Laboureur, one woodcut in text; original gilt titled buckram, top edge gilt, other edges untrimmed, original printed dust jacket, spine of dust jacket evenly faded, minor chipping and fraying at top, otherwise extremely fine, book virtually mint and jacket unusually well preserved; bookplate reading "Exhibition copy of a Golden Cockerel Press Book: Waltham Saint Lawrence, Berkshire". Chanticleer 59. Phillip J. Pirages 33-253 1996 $325.00

STERNE, LAURENCE 1713-1768   A Sentimental Journey through France and Italy. High Wycombe: Limited Editions Club, 1936. Limited to 1500 copies; small folio; hand set in Bunyan type, etchings by Denis Tegetmeier, signed by Tegetmeier and by designer, Eric Gill; decorated buckram, backstrip slightly darkened, near fine in near fine case. Charles Agvent 4-1034 1996 $200.00

STERNE, LAURENCE 1713-1768   A Sentimental Journey through France and Italy. High Wycombe: printed for the Limited Editions Club, by Hague & Gill, 1936. Limited to 1500 copies, this unnumbered but signed by Gill & Tegtmeier; larage 4to; pages (4), vi, (6), 135, (3); 5 full page and 2 vignette etchings, designed by Gill and printed in 14pt Bunyan created by him expressly for this book; printed by Hague & Gill on Barcham Green handmade paper; original decorated sand buckram, little marked, backstrip darkened, top edge gilt, others uncut.   Claude Cox 107-160 1996 £85.00

STERNE, LAURENCE 1713-1768   The Works of... London: 1819. 8vo; 4 volumes; portrait; half calf, raised bands, gilt tooled spines, title labels inset on red morocco; good set.   K Books 441-471 1996 £100.00

STEUART, HENRY   The Planter's Guide; or a Practical Essay on the Best Method of Giving Immediate Effect to Wood, by the Removal of Large Trees and Underwood. Edinburgh: 1828. 2nd edition; 8vo; (6), xxxvii, (i), 527 pages; 6 lithograph plates; original linen backed boards, paper spine label, some marginal dustiness and boards evenly soiled. Ken Spelman 30-109 1996 £120.00

STEUART, HENRY   The Planter's Guide; or, a Practical Essay on the Best method of Giving Immediate Effect to Wood, by the Removal of Large Trees and Underwood... Edinburgh: John Murray, 1828. 2nd edition; 8vo; frontispiece, ad slip before title; 5 engraved plates, original boards, uncut, hinges cracked, printed paper label, contained in cloth box, leather label on spine.   Anthony W. Laywood 108-235 1996 £100.00

STEVENS, GEORGE THOMAS   Three Years in the Sixth Corps. New York: D. Van Nostrand, 1867. 2nd edition; 8vo; original cloth, minor wear to extremities, else very good. Nevins I 162. Dornbusch I NY 396; Coulter 431; Union Bookshelf 237.   McGowan Book Co. 65-87 1996 $150.00

STEVENS, HENRY   An Account of the Proceedings at the Dinner Given by Mr. George Peabody to the Americans Connected with the Great Exhibition. London: Pickering, 1851. 8vo; 114 pages, 1 f., blue cloth, top of spine chipped; presentation copy from Mrs. Henry Stevens. Marlborough 162-205 1996 £135.00

STEVENS, HENRY   Historical Nuggets Bibliotheca Americana... London: Whittingham and Wilkins, 1862. 1st edition; 2 volumes; half morocco and cloth, title in gilt on spine, mostly unopened, very good. Michael D. Heaston 23-47 1996 $250.00

STEVENS, HENRY   Rare Americana: a Catalogue of Historical and Geographical Books, Pamphlets and Manuscripts Relating to America. London: Henry Stevens, Son & Stiles, 1926. 24.5 cm; vii, 578, (10) pages, frontispiece, illustrations, illustrated wrappers; very good. Rockland Books 38-209 1996 $150.00

STEVENS, ISAAC I.   Campaigns of the Rio Grande and of Mexico. New York: D. Appleton and Co., 1851. 1st edition; 108, (8) pages; original printed wrappers chipped; very good; formerly in the New Jersey Historical Society Library. Howes L962; Raines p. 195; Hakerkorn p. 19. Michael D. Heaston 23-308 1996 $500.00

STEVENS, JOHN   The Royal Treasury of England; or, an Historical Account of all Taxes, Under What Denomination Soever, fromthe Conquest to This Present Year... London: printed for T. Tebb and J. Wilcox, 1725. 1st edition; 8vo; library perforation stamp on title and accession number on blank margin of following leaf; 19th century buckram; Kress 3619; Goldsmith 6395; Hanson 3319.   Anthony W. Laywood 109-142 1996 £165.00

STEVENS, SAMUEL   A Wilding Posy. London: Selwyn & Blount Ltd., 1925. 1st edition; original binding, top edge dusty, head and tail of spine and corners bumped, covers marked, cover edges darkened, spine faded, title label on spine worn and browned, edges spotted, endpaper edges browned; good; ownership signature of Ian Fleming.   Ulysses 39-691 1996 £275.00

STEVENS, WALLACE 1879-1955   The Auroras of Autumn. New York: Knopf, 1950. 1st edition; 8vo; cloth, dust jacket, fine in price clipped jacket which is faintly spotted at base of spine.   James S. Jaffe 34-631 1996 $350.00

STEVENS, WALLACE 1879-1955   The Auroras of Autumn. New York: Alfred A. Knopf, 1950. 1st edition; very fine in original dust jacket which is lightly browned at extremities; Edelstein A14.a.1.   Bromer Booksellers 90-228 1996 $350.00

STEVENS, WALLACE 1879-1955   The Auroras of Autumn. New York: Alfred A. Knopf, 1950. 1st edition; original binding, head and tail of spine very slightly bumped, very good in nicked, rubbed and dusty, slightly marked, price clipped dust jacket browned at spine and edges. Ulysses 39-563 1996 £195.00

STEVENS, WALLACE 1879-1955   The Collected Poems. New York: Knopf, 1954. 1st edition; one of 2500 copies; thick 8vo; cloth, dust jacket, previous owner's name on front free endpaper, otherwise fine in lightly rubbed jacket with some fading to spine.   James S. Jaffe 34-632 1996 $350.00

STEVENS, WALLACE 1879-1955   Esthetique du Mal. Cummington: Cummington Press, 1945. One of 300 copies; illustrations by Wightman Williams; quarter bound in black morocco with green "Natsume" straw paper covered boards, marginal wear to top and bottom of spine and slight offsetting to front and rear pastedowns and free endpapers, otherwise excellent in collector's solander box.   R. A. Gekoski 19-132 1996 £975.00

STEVENS, WALLACE 1879-1955   Harmonium. New York: Alfred A. Knopf, 1931. 1st edition; third binding with blue boards backed in black cloth, fine unfaded copy sans dust jacket.   Bev Chaney, Jr. 23-648 1996 $175.00

STEVENS, WALLACE 1879-1955   Letters of Wallace Stevens. New York: Knopf, 1966. 1st edition; thick 8vo; decorated endpapers; cloth, dust jacket slightly edge worn; fine, scarce.   James S. Jaffe 34-633 1996 $200.00

STEVENS, WALLACE 1879-1955   Notes Toward a Supreme Fiction. Cummington: Cummington Press, 1942. One of 80 copies, on Worthy Hand and Arrows paper, signed by author; there were also 190 unsigned copies on Dutch charcoal paper; very slight sunning to spine, otherwise excellent copy in handsome collector's box.   R. A. Gekoski 19-131 1996 £3,500.00

STEVENS, WALLACE 1879-1955   Notes Toward a Supreme Fiction. Cummington: Cummington Press, 1942. One of 190 copies; top of spine bumped, slight soiling to top edges of boards, otherwise excellent in collector's solander box.   R. A. Gekoski 19-130 1996 £1,000.00

STEVENS, WALLACE 1879-1955   Notes Toward a Supreme Fiction. Cummington: Cummington Press, 1942. 2nd edition, scarce itself, as only 330 copies were printed; near fine in glassine dust jacket lacking a significant portion of rear panel.   Lame Duck Books 19-509 1996 $275.00

STEVENS, WALLACE 1879-1955   Opus Posthumous, Poems, Plays, Prose. New York: Alfred A. Knopf, 1957. 1st edition; fine in near fine jacket.   Hermitage SP95-596 1996 $100.00

STEVENS, WALLACE 1879-1955   A Primitive Like an Orb. New York: Banyan Press, 1948. 1st edition; limited to 500 copies; 8vo; drawings by Kurt Seligmann; original green paper wrappers; fine. Edelstein A13. James S. Jaffe 34-630 1996 $250.00

STEVENS, WALLACE 1879-1955   A Primitive Like an Orb - a Poem. New York: Gotham Book Mart, 1948. One of 500 copies; text pages on Etruria paper, 4 drawings by Kurt Seligmann, on Zebu paper; wrappers, spine and cover edges browned, covers slightly marked, bottom corner of upper cover creased and slightly torn, very good; from the library of James D. Hart.   Ulysses 39-562 1996 £125.00

STEVENS, WALLACE 1879-1955   Transport to Summer. New York: Alfred A. Knopf, 1947. 1st edition; review copy with presentation slip to reviewer laid in; fine in dust jacket with small chip and light browning to spine. Edelstein A11.a.1.   Bromer Booksellers 90-229 $450.00

STEVENS, WALLACE 1879-1955   Transport to Summer. New York: Knopf, 1947. 1st edition; one of 1750 copies; small 8vo; cloth backed boards, printed spine label, dust jacket, light offsetting on front and back endsheets, otherwise fine in jacket with usual faded spine. Edelstein A11. James S. Jaffe 34-629 1996 $500.00

STEVENS, WILLIAM BAGSHAW   Poems. London: ptd. for Ab. Portal; R. Faulder, and G. Kearsley, 1782. 1st edition; 4to; no half title, engraved vignette on title, 39 pages; disbound.   Anthony W. Laywood 109-143 1996 £135.00

STEVENSON, J.   Two Centuries of Life in County Down, 1600-1800. Belfast: 1920. 1st edition; 8vo; illustrations; cloth, good.   C. P. Hyland 216-804 1996 £50.00

STEVENSON, MATILDA COXE   Ethnobotany of the Zuni Indians. Washington: GPO, 1915. 4to; 453 pages, 7 plates, 6 figures; original olive cloth, gilt titles;   Parmer Books Nat/Hist-073256 1996 £115.00

STEVENSON, MERRITT R.   Marine Atlas of the Pacific Coastal Waters of south America. Berkeley/Los Angeles: University of California Press, 1970. folio; issued without dust jacket, 23 pages of text in English and Spanish, over 50 charts; blue cloth over boards, brads, gilt cover title. Parmer Books 039/Nautica-039180 1996 $125.00

STEVENSON, ROBERT LOUIS BALFOUR 1850-1894   Aes Triplex. N.P.: printed for the American Subscribers to the Stevenson memorial, 1898. 1st edition; one of 160 copies; printed tissue guard for portrait frontispiece foxed, otherwise very good in French fold, gilt printed wrappers which are somewhat browned and rubbed.   Captain's Bookshelf 38-205 1996 $125.00

STEVENSON, ROBERT LOUIS BALFOUR 1850-1894   The Best Thing in Edinburgh: an Address... San Francisco: John Howell, 1923. 1st edition; number 48 of 250 copies on handmade paper; linen backed boards with paper label, light overall soiling, end of paper label chipped, otherwise very good; inscribed by John Howell to W. Hannah.   Hermitage SP95-885 1996 $150.00

STEVENSON, ROBERT LOUIS BALFOUR 1850-1894   A Child's Garden of Verses. London: John Lane Bodley Head, n.d. 1st edition; color endpapers and top edge gilt, cover designs, 6 color plates and numerous black and white drawings, some full page by Charles Robinson; decorated cloth, gilt, covers dusty and slightly soiled, spine darkened, head and tail of spine and corners bumped and rubbed, some page edges nicked; good.   Ulysses 39-505 1996 £55.00

STEVENSON, ROBERT LOUIS BALFOUR 1850-1894   A Child's Garden of Verses. London: John Lane, The Bodley Head, 1896. 1st illustrated edition; 8vo; illustrations in line and silhouette by Charles Robinson, lacking front blank leaf; original dark green ribbed cloth beautifully and finely stamped in gilt to spine and covers, uncut edges, fine. Untrimmed and thus a larage paper copy.   Sotheran PN32-155 1996 £198.00

STEVENSON, ROBERT LOUIS BALFOUR 1850-1894   A Child's Garden of Verses. New York: Limited Editions Club, 1944. Limited to 1100 copies; signed by artist; 4to; hand colored in the studio of Charlize Brakeley; illustrations by Roger Duvoisin; half blue leather, fine in lightly worn glassine and box.   Charles Agvent 4-1038 1996 $150.00

STEVENSON, ROBERT LOUIS BALFOUR 1850-1894   The Jolly Jump-Ups Child's Garden of Verses. Springfield: McLouglin Bros., 1946. 1st edition thus; 8vo; 6 enchanting pop-up illustrations by Geraldine Clyne; glazed pictorial boards, edgewear and light soiling, else very good.   Glenn Books 36-210 1996 $125.00

STEVENSON, ROBERT LOUIS BALFOUR 1850-1894   A Child's Garden of Verses. San Francisco: Press in Tuscany Alley, 1978. 1st edition; limited to 500 copies, signed by author, and by printer, Adrian Wilson; 8vo; illustrations by Joyce Lancaster Wilson; cloth backed decorated boards, very fine.   James S. Jaffe 34-550 1996 $450.00

STEVENSON, ROBERT LOUIS BALFOUR 1850-1894   Diogenes at the Savile Club. Chicago: Grabhorn Press, 1921. One of 150 copies printed; minor soiling and binding crease to paper covered boards, else quite nice.   David Holloway 94D-150 1996 $150.00

STEVENSON, ROBERT LOUIS BALFOUR 1850-1894   Fables. New York: Charles Scribner's Sons, 1914. 4to; 83 pages, pictorial initials, tailpieces and 20 black and white plates; red cloth, bumped and soiled, titled and decorated in gilt on front cover and spine, top edge gilt, hinge starting; very good.   Blue Mountain SP95-66 1996 $150.00

STEVENSON, ROBERT LOUIS BALFOUR 1850-1894   A Footnote to History. London: Cassell & Co., 1892. 1st edition; published simultaneously with the American edition; 8vo; ads dated May 1892; original binding, slight foxing of endpapers, very mild edgewear, near fine. Hugh Walpole's bookplate.   Charles Agvent 4-1039 1996 $125.00

STEVENSON, ROBERT LOUIS BALFOUR 1850-1894   An Inland Voyage. London: C. Kegan Paul & Co., 1878. 1st edition; 8vo; author's first book; bound by Stikeman in three quarter black morocco and marbled boards with original sky blue covers and spine bound in rear, binding rubbed along edges, especailly spine, with head of spine peeling back; very good.   Charles Agvent 4-1040 1996 $350.00

STEVENSON, ROBERT LOUIS BALFOUR 1850-1894   Island Night's Entertainments. London: Cassell & Co., 1893. 1st edition; 1st issue; illustrations; decorated cloth; moderate edgewear, very good; price corrected in ink, ads dated March 1893; bookplate of Robert Peel Sheldon dated Sept. 1893; moderate edgewear, very good.   Charles Agvent 4-1041 1996 $185.00

STEVENSON, ROBERT LOUIS BALFOUR 1850-1894   Kidnapped. London: Cassell & Co., 1886. 1st edition; 1st issue; crown 8vo; text 1-311 pages, publisher's ad, 16 page publisher's catalog to rear, half title; large folding colored map frontispiece; rebound in half crimson morocco and red cloth boards, gilt panelled spine, gilt titles to compartments, top edge gilt, marbled endpapers, new prelims, original crimson cloth spine and board bound in rear; fine and handsome copy, blue crayon/pencil ownership inscription of J. S. Masterman.   Beeleigh Abbey BA56-164 1996 £350.00

STEVENSON, ROBERT LOUIS BALFOUR 1850-1894   Kidnapped. London: Cassell & Co. Ltd. 1886. 1st edition; 2nd issue; 7 1/2 x 5 inches; viii, 311, (17) pages, including ads at back; colored folding map as frontispiece; pleasing slate blue crushed levant three quarter morocco by Sangorski & Sutcliffe, blue cloth sides, raised spine bands with stippled rule and flanked by plain gilt rules, spine panels with gilt titling or lage centered ornament, marbled endpapers, top edge gilt, spine evenly faded to light blue green, minor tear in map, otherwise very fine. Phillip J. Pirages 33-470 1996 $375.00

STEVENSON, ROBERT LOUIS BALFOUR 1850-1894   Kidnapped. (with) Catriona: a Sequel to Kidnapped. London: Cassell & Co., 1886/93. 1st editions; 8vo; 2 volumes; pages viii, 311, (9 ads); (ii), x, 372, (18 ads); folding map frontispiece to first title; original red and dark blue cloth respectively, spines lettered in gilt, spine of 1st title just a little dull, inner hinges of 2nd title strengthened and its spine leaning, overall very good, housed together in cloth slipcase. Prideaux 18 and 39.   Sotheran PN32-52 1996 £498.00

STEVENSON, ROBERT LOUIS BALFOUR 1850-1894   Kidnapped. New York: Limited Editions Club, 1938. Limited to 1500 copies; 4to; signed by the artist, Hans Alexander Mueller; brick linen, fine in slightly darkened case.   Charles Agvent 4-1042 1996 $100.00

STEVENSON, ROBERT LOUIS BALFOUR 1850-1894   The Letters to His Family and Friends. London: Methuen, 1900. 1st edition; large 8vo; 2 volumes, pages xliv, 375; xiii, 384; 2 portraits; original cloth, gilt, little rubbed and scratched, paper spine labels, top edge gilt, uncut. from Sir John Usher's library.   R.F.G. Hollett 76-357 1996 £65.00

STEVENSON, ROBERT LOUIS BALFOUR 1850-1894   The Merry Men and Other Tales and Fables. London: Chatto & Windus, 1887. 1st edition; 8vo; 32 pages ads dated Sept. 1886; original blue cloth, upper cover decorated with five silver stars and a group of flowers, spine lettered in gilt, decorated in black with flowers, lower cover with publisher's insignia in black, some rubbing and soiling, mostly light, upper inner hinge starting, discreet pencilled notations in contents leaf gutter, minor browning of endpapers, generally marginal; very nice in green morocco backed case (some rubbing and fading). Beinecke 411.   James Cummins 14-197 1996 $150.00

STEVENSON, ROBERT LOUIS BALFOUR 1850-1894   More New Arabian Nights. The Dynamiter. London: Longmans, Green and Co., 1885. 1st edition; 8vo; half title; original pictorial wrappers bound in; excellent copy in quality three quarter red crushed morocco, spine attractively gilt.   Ian Wilkinson 95/1-143 1996 £65.00

STEVENSON, ROBERT LOUIS BALFOUR 1850-1894   Prayers Written at Vailima. London: Chatto & Windus, 1910. 4to; illuminations by Alberto Sangorski; full citron morocco, gilt borders on covers, corner fleurons, 2 raised bands, gilt top by Sangorski & Sutcliffe.   Appelfeld Gallery 54-172 1996 $250.00

STEVENSON, ROBERT LOUIS BALFOUR 1850-1894   A Stevenson Medley. London: Chatto & Windus, 1899. One of 300 copies of the first edition; 8vo; portrait, with facing tissue reading "Yours ever affectionately R. L. Stevenson", printer's mark on title, facsimiles of the Davos-Platz booklets, many printed from original blocks, some marginal browning and soiling, generally light. navy morocco backed cloth, head and tail of spine repaired, rubbed, half title with limitation on verso. NCBEL 3 1008.   James Cummins 14-196 1996 $175.00

STEVENSON, ROBERT LOUIS BALFOUR 1850-1894   Strange Case of Dr. Jekyll and Mr. Hyde. London: Longmans, Green and Co., 1886. 1st English edition; small 8vo; pages (viii), 141, (i) blank, (i) publisher's ads; original paper wrappers, printed and decorated in blue and red, ads printed on inside covers, spine skilfully restored, wrappers very slightly soiled and rubbed; contemporary ownership inscription at head of front cover, faint bookseller's inkstamp at foot, very good, protected in red morocco backed slipcase. Prideaux 17; Beinecke I.349.   Simon Finch 24-216 1996 £1,200.00

STEVENSON, ROBERT LOUIS BALFOUR 1850-1894   Travels with a Donkey. New York: Limited Editions Club, 1957. Limited to 1500 copies; 8vo; lithos by Rober Duvoisin, hand colored through stencils, signed by artist; aqua basket weave linen, fine in glassine and case.   Charles Agvent 4-1046 1996 $100.00

STEVENSON, ROBERT LOUIS BALFOUR 1850-1894   Treasure Island. London: Cassell and Co., 1883. 1st edition; 1st printing; with all the early issue ppoints uncorrected, one of 2000 copies only; with 'preferred' October ads, based on the premise that the July ads were actually inserted last, once the October ads had run out; original brown cloth, slightly foxed, otherwise bright and perfect, remarkably unrubbed, very fine. In beautiful quarter morocco slipcase.   Lakin & Marley 3-58 1996 $13,500.00

STEVENSON, ROBERT LOUIS BALFOUR 1850-1894   Treasure Island. London: Cassell and Co., Ltd., 1883. 1st edition; 8vo; viii, 292 pages, map facing title, 8 pages of ads at end dated 5R-1083; original blue cloth, lettered in gilt on spine, black endpapers, page 83 lacks its numeral 83, page 127 has 7 from a different font of type, 'dead man's chest' on pages 2 and 7 are without capitals, 'a' is lacking on line 6 page 63, 'worse' instead of 'worst' appears on line 3 of page 197; cloth on spine darkened, spotted and marked (though not broken) on covers, with very small holes in cloth in both joints, and at head and foot of spine.   David Bickersteth 133-169 1996 £385.00

STEVENSON, ROBERT LOUIS BALFOUR 1850-1894   Treasure Island. Humphrey Milford at Oxford University Press, 1920. 1st edition thus; 12 mounted color plates, covers, endpapers and chapter headings by Rowland Hilder; decorated cloth gilt, top edge gilt, edges slightly spotted, spine slightly spotted and with some offsetting from the dust jacket, very good in nicked and slightly dusty dust jacket browned at spine and edges and rubbed at spine and in matching slipcase, which is worn, dusty and slightly soiled and split.   Ulysses 39-289 1996 £185.00

STEVENSON, ROBERT LOUIS BALFOUR 1850-1894   Treasure Island. London: Frederick Muller, 1934. 1st edition thus; 8vo; 252 pages; 10 color plates by Monro Orr; red cloth gilt with vignette, covers slightly soiled, else near fine.   Marjorie James 19-201 1 1996 £55.00

STEVENSON, ROBERT LOUIS BALFOUR 1850-1894   Treasure Island. London: Paul Elek, 1947. 1st edition; endpapers illustrated in color by John Minton, black and white plates and illustrations in text, also by Minto; very good in heavily price clipped dust jacket with few tears and creases around edges.   Words Etcetera 94-951 1996 £70.00

STEVENSON, ROBERT LOUIS BALFOUR 1850-1894   The Waif Woman. London: Chatto & Windus, 1916. 1st edition; 24mo; drab boards, purple cloth spine, some wear to edges, but generally very good copy of this fragile book; ex-libris of Clement Shorter with his bookplate. Prideaux 74.   Priscilla Juvelis 95/1-226 1996 $150.00

STEVENSON, ROGER   Military Instructions for Officers Detached in the Field: Containing a Scheme for Forming a Corps of a Partisan. Philadelphia: R. Aitken, 1775. 1st edition; (8), vii, (1), 232, (4) pages; 12 engraved plates; contemporary sheep, hinges very skilfully restored, other than small piece torn from upper blank corner of one plate, this is a remarkably fine, fresh copy, completely free of foxing and in handsome original binding, signed "Josiah Bartlett's Book 1776"; beneath is are 3 other signatures of later 18th and 19th century members of Bartlett's family; bookplate of William S. Greenough. In attractive cloth clamshell box with leather label. Howes S981; Evans 14475.   Joseph J. Felcone 64-39 1996 $4,000.00

STEWARD, RICHARD   An Answer to a Letter Writen at Oxford, and Superscribed to Dr. Samuel Turner, Concerning the Church and the Revenues Thereof. N.P.: London: printed in the Yeere, 1647. 1st edition; 2nd issue, with 'plus aitra' on p. 1 (for 'plus ultra'); 4to; (2), 53, (1) pages, A1 being a cancel title, p. 11 beginning 'blood, because they'; recently well bound in old style quarter calf; very good. Kress S921; Thomason I 505 (26 April); not in Goldsmiths or Massie.   John Drury 82-269 1996 £150.00

STEWARD, RICHARD   Catholique Divinity; or, the Most Solid and Sententious Expressions of the Primitive Doctors of the Church. London: H. M. to bee sold by Timo. Smart, 1657. 1st edition; (iv), 274, (x) pages; later half calf, gilt lettering, rubbed, corners slightly worn, few early marginalia; good. Wing S5518.   Robert Clark 38-137 1996 £58.00

STEWARD, WILLIAM   The First Edition of Steward's Healing Art, Corrected and Improved by the Original Hand. Saco: Putnam & Blake, 1827. 1st revised edition; 8vo; pages (1)-126, 46, 22; contemporary calf, some foxing, but very good; Imprints 30710.   Second Life Books 103-178 1996 $425.00

STEWART, BASIL   Subjects Portrayed in Japanese Colour-Prints. London: Kegan Paul, Trench, Trubner & Co., Ltd., 1922. 1st edition; folio; xvi, 382 pages, profusely illustrated; tan linen over blue boards, gilt black morocco spine label, lower spine lightly soiled, very nice copy for this book.   Kenneth Karmiole 1NS-131 1996 $450.00

STEWART, CHARLES JAMES   Two Sermons on Family Prayer, with Extracts from Various Authors; and a Collection of Prayers, Selected and Compiled by the Hon. and Rev. Charles Stewart, A. M. Minister of St. Armand, Lower Canada and Chaplain to the Lord Bishop of Quebec. Montreal: printed by Nahum Mower, 1814. 8vo; pages viii, (1) (errata), (9)-394, duplicate pages vii-viii and duplicate errata leaf removed, pages 393-4 wanting (TPL copy also lacking these two pages), pages 251-256 mended, with paper strips, missing words supplied in ink; original tree calf worn at extremities and along spine, small wormhole affecting first few leaves. Inscribed by author on titlepage. TPL 1010.   Hugh Anson-Cartwright 87-392 1996 $350.00

STEWART, CHARLES S.   Journal of a Residence in the Sandwich Islands, During the Years 1823, 1824 and 1825. London: Fisher & Jackson, 1828. 2nd edition; 12mo; pages xxiv, 25-407, ads, folding map, 3 plates; new cloth, red leather label. Sabin 91665; Taylor p. 144.   Richard Adelson W94/95-168 1996 $375.00

STEWART, CHARLES S.   A Visit to the South Seas in U.S. Ship Vincennes, During the Years 1829 and 1830. New York: John P. Haven, 1833. Small 8vo; 2 volumes; (v), 312 pages; slight foxing throughout; original green embossed cloth, gilt title on spine, bit faded, rubbed and bit bumped on extremities, but quite pleasant overall; inscribed by John Gay for W. Gay, St. Louis Sept. 1843.   Antipodean 28-401 1996 $400.00

STEWART, DUGALD 1753-1828   Elements of the Philosofhy of the Human Mind. Edinburgh: ptd. for W. Creech; London: T. Cadell & W. Daiess & Edin. Archibald... 1814-16. 5th edition of volume 1, 2nd edition of volume 2; 8vo; 2 volumes; half titles; contemporary half calf, slightly rubbed, labels; nice.   Anthony W. Laywood 109-144 1996 £110.00

STEWART, EDGAR I. Custer's Luck. Norman: 1955. 1st edition; 522 pages; photos, maps; dust jacket, signed; nice. Luther 108. T. A. Swinford 49-1115 1996 $100.00

STEWART, GEORGE R. Earth Abides. New York: Random House, 1949. fine in very good dust jacket heavily worn at head of spine panel with several tears and tape mends to reverse, front and rear panels are bright and clean, attractive copy. Robert Gavora 61-209 1996 $160.00

STEWART, JAMES Jimmy Stewart and His Poems. New York: Crown, 1989. 1st edition; 5th printing; thin 8vo; 9 duotone illustrations and color jacket design by Cheryl Gross, fine in dust jacket. Signed by author. George J. Houle 68-142 1996 $125.00

STEWART, JOHN An Account of Jamaica, and Its Inhabitants. London: Longman, Rees, Hurst and Orme, 1808. 1st edition; 8vo; pages xii, 305, (2) ads; uncut, original boards, spine repaired, printed label (rubbed); small stamp of author's name on title and early 20th century ownership signature from Spanish Honduras. Sabin 35557. Howard S. Mott 227-134 1996 $425.00

STEWART, JOHN A View of the Past and Present State of the Island of Jamaica... Edinburgh: Oliver and Boyd, 1823. 1st edition; 8vo; pages xiii, (3), 363, (1), uncut; original boards, top and bottom of spine chipped, printed paper label, mostly gone; with the exception of the spine wear and bumped corners, an excellent copy. Sabin 91692. Howard S. Mott 227-135 1996 $275.00

STEWART, ROBERT The American Farmer's Horse Book... Cincinnati: Vent, 1867. 1st edition; 8vo; 600 pages; many illustrations; gold stamped calf. Second Life Books 103-180 1996 $150.00

STEWART, WILLIAM M. The Mineral Resources of the Pacific States and Territories. New York: D. Van Nostrand, 1865. 1st edition; 32 pages; original printed wrappers with ad on back wrapper, small portion missing from front wrapper not affecting text; very good. Michael D. Heaston 23-309 1996 $200.00

STEWART, WILLIAM M. Reminiscences of Senator William W. Stewart of Nevada. New York: Neale Pub. Co., 1908. 1st edition; 8 1/2 x 5 3/4 inches; 358 pages, frontispiece, black and gold stamped red cloth in dust jacket, stain to spine and inner margin of book (most noticeable between front endpaper and titlepage), head and tail of jacket spine chipped, rear flap detached. Paher 1883. Dawson's Books Shop 528-235 1996 $100.00

STEWART, WILLIAM M. Reminiscences of Senator William M. Stewart of Nevada. New York: and Washington: Neale Pub. Co., 1908. 1st edition; 358 pages; original cloth, near fine in slightly chipped and very scarce dust jacket; Krick 482; Howes S994; Adams Guns 295; Cowan p. 616. McGowan Book Co. 65-91 1996 $250.00

STICKLEY, GUSTAV Craftsman Homes. New York: Craftsman Publishing Co., 1909. 2nd edition; coarse grained linen stamped in brown, hinges cracked, corners bumped, light overall soiling, still pleasing. Hermitage SP95-749 1996 $225.00

STIFF, EDWARD The Texan Emigrant: Being a Narration of the Adventures of the Author in Texas. Cincinnati: published by George Conclin, 1840. 1st edition; 367, (368 ad) pages; 2 illustrations, folding map; original calf, rebacked, original black spine label, binding somewhat worn but overall a clean copy, very good, illustrations quite crisp. Howes S998; Streeter Texas 1367; Raines pp. 195-96; Graff 3989. Michael D. Heaston 23-310 1996 $3,000.00

STIGAND, CHAUNCEY H. Hunting the Elephant in Africa and Other Recollections of Thirteen Years' Wanderings. New York: 1913. 1st American edition; 8vo; (16), 379 pages; illustrations; original cloth, ex-library. Edward Morrill 368-569 1996 $125.00

STILES, HENRY REED Bundling: Its Origin, Progress and Decline In America. Albany: Knickerbocker, 1871. 1st Knickerbocker edition; 16mo; 138 pages; original brown cloth, title in gilt on spine, fine but for few minor scratches on front boards; fine. Roy W. Clare XXIV-20 1996 $100.00

STILL, WILLIAM The Underground Rail Road. Philadelphia: Porter & Coates, 1872. 1st edition; cloth stamped in gilt, front hinge tender, couple of very short tears at extremities of spine, still near fine. Between the Covers 43-413 1996 $500.00

STILL, WILLIAM The Underground Rail Road. Philadelphia: Porter & Coates, 1872. 1st edition; skillfully repaired at edges of spine, evidence of some repair to hinges but tight and sound, very good copy with some separation of paper covering the boards along edge of rear gutter. Between the Covers 43-414 1996 $350.00

STILLWELL, RICHARD The Theatre. Princeton: ASCSA, 1952. Folio; x, 141 pages, 103 figures, 8 plates; original cloth, corner bumped. Archaeologia Luxor-3185 1996 $350.00

STIRLING, JOHN A System of Rhetorick, in a Method Entirely new. Dublin: printed by John Exshaw, 1786. contemporary sheep, spine chipped, hinges splitting, slightly spotted and embrowned; Alston VI.157. Jarndyce 103-346 1996 £120.00

STIRLING, PATRICK JAMES The Philosophy of Trade; or, Outlines of a Theory of Profits and Prices... Edinburgh: Oliver and Boyd, 1846. 1st edition; 8vo; half title, library stamp on lower blank margin of title and on endpapers; original cloth, uncut, unopened; nice. Kress C6975; Goldsmith 34541; Williams I p. 202. Anthony W. Laywood 108-236 1996 £85.00

STIRLING, WILLIAM ALEXANDER, 1ST EARL OF 1567?-1640 Recreations with the Muses. London: Tho. Harper, 1637. Folio; (8), 326 pages; frontispiece; early calf, neatly rebacked, gilt black morocco spine label; this copy lacks the rare portrait by Marshall only found in small part of edition. This copy with an extra-illustrated 18th century engraved portrait of Alexander. Kenneth Karmiole 1NS-5 1996 $650.00

STOBO, ROBERT Memoirs of Major Robert Stobo, of the Virginia Regiment. Pittsburgh: J. Davidson, 1854. 2nd edition; 16mo; (6 incl. fr.), (9)-92 pages, 12 x 18 folded plan; original cloth, gilt title; Howes S1015; Field 382; Haynes 17725. Bohling Book Co. 191-1015 1996 $200.00

STOCKDALE, FREDERICK WILLIAM LITCHFIELD Etchings...of Antiquities in the County of Kent. London: for the Proprietor, 1910. 4to; engraved title, 1 f., 1 f. subscribers, 23 ff. n.n., 1 f. list of plates, 39 engraved plates; boards, uncut, respined. Marlborough 162-92 1996 £350.00

STOCKDALE, JAMES Annales Caermoelenses; or Annals of Cartmel. Ulverston: 1872. 1st edition; thick 8vo; pages 595, vii, engraved frontispiece and 4 photographic plates; original blue cloth, gilt, over bevelled boards, extremities little rubbed; occasional spot, unusually sound, bright copy. R.F.G. Hollett & Son 78-1304 1996 £275.00

STOCKHAM, ALICE B. Karezza. Ethics of Marriage. Chicago: Alice B. Stockham & Co., 1897. Small 8vo; (viii), 10-136 pages, 6 publisher's ads; green cloth, fore edges browned, otherwise very good. Paulette Rose 16-310 1996 $100.00

STOCKLEY, C. H. Stalking in the Himalayas and Northern India. 1936. illustrations; original cloth, slightly rubbed, front endpaper bit stained. David Grayling J95Biggame-582 1996 £65.00

STOCKTON, FRANK RICHARD The Great Stone of Sardis. London: and New York: Harper & Bros., 1898. 1st English edition; 8vo; original brown cloth illustrated with argent, brown and gilt, some light rubbing and wear, some light spotting, else very good. BAL 18929n; Bleiler 187; Bolton, American Book Illustrators 113. James Cummins 14-198 1996 $250.00

STODART, M. A. Every-Day Duties; in Letters to a Young Lady. London: Seeley & Burnside, 1841. 2nd edition; half title, original pink cloth, very good. bookseller's ticket: George May, Evesham. Jarndyce 103-451 1996 £55.00

STODART, R. R. Scottish Arms Being a Collection of Armorial Bearings A.D. 1370-1678. Edinburgh: William Paterson, 1881. Limited to 300 numbered copies; folio; 2 volumes; 118 colored plates; original cloth. Charles W. Traylen 117-249 1996 £280.00

STODART, R. R. Scottish Arms Being a Collection of Armorial Bearings A.D. 1370-1678. Edinburgh: William Paterson, 1881. Limited to 300 numbered copies; folio; 2 volumes; 118 colored plates; covers stained and loose in case. Charles W. Traylen 117-249a 1996 £140.00

STODDARD, AMOS   Sketches. Historical and Descriptive, of Louisiana... Philadelphia: Published by Mathew Carey, 1812. 1st edition; (i)-viii, (1)-172, 175-488 pages; contemporary calf, marbled boards, red morocco spine label, rebacked with original spine, usual foxing, some staining; very good, pages 173-174 were omitted from pagination, there is no text missing. Bradford 5238; Clark II 168; Field 1505; Howes S1021. Michael D. Heaston 23-311 1996 $850.00

STODDARD, CHARLES WARREN   Poems. San Francisco: A. Roman and Co., 1867. 1st edition; one of 750 copies; 8vo; 123 pages; illustrations; original cloth, slight soiling and bubbling of cloth, but very good. With an early, possibly family inscription, dated San Fran. April 1868. BAL 18971 binding A.   M & S Rare Books 60-238 1996 $175.00

STODDARD, HERBERT L.   The Bobwhite Quail. New York: Scribner's, 1950. Later edition; 4to; originalb rown cloth in worn dust jacket; fine. Glenn Books 36-258 1996 $100.00

STODDARD, W. O.   The Great Union Pacific Railroad Excursion to the Hundredth Meridian: From New York to Platte City. Chicago: published by the Republican Co., 1867. 1st edition; frontispiece; original pictorial wrappers, fine. The copy of Hon. G. G. Fogg, former U.S. Senator from New Hamshire.   Michael D. Heaston 23-339 1996 $550.00

STODDART, THOMAS TOD   The Art of Angling, as Practised in Scotland. Edinburgh: 1835. 1st edition; small 8vo; illustrations; rebound in modern full dark geen morocco.   Petersfield Bookshop FH58-313 1996 £86.00

STOEVER, D. H.   The Life of Sir Charles Linnaeus, Knight of the Swedish Order of the Polar Star... London: printed by C. Hobson for B. and J. White, 1794. 1st English edition; 4to; engraved portrait, 4 page list of subscribers; contemporary sprinkled calf with coat of arms blindstamped on covers, rebacked preserving old spine label; some foxing of text; small ownership stamp of Ricardo Caminos. Soulsby 2627. Anthony W. Laywood 109-145 1996 £245.00

STOKER, BRAM 1847-1912   The Jewel of Seven Stars. New York: Harpers, 1904. 1st American edition; previous owner's bookplate on f.p.d. and previous owner's stamp on titlepage, upper inner rear hinge just starting, otherwise tight, very good copy.   Aronovitz 57-1129 1996 $125.00

STOKES, ANSON PHELPS   Church and State in the United States. New York: Harper and Bros., 1950. 1st edition; 3 volumes, lxx, 936, (vi), 799, (vi), 1042 pages; numerous plates; very good in very good dust jacket and original slipcase.   Metacomet Books 54-105 1996 $125.00

STOKES, ANSON PHELPS   Stokes Records: Notes Regarding the Ancestry and Lives of Anson Phelps Stokes and Helen Louisa (Phelps) Stokes. New York: privately printed for the family, 1910. Imperial 8vo; 2 volumes; plates, portraits, facsimiles; handsomely bound in original half crimson crushed levant morocco, spines gilt lettered, gilt tops, other edges untrimmed.   Howes Bookshop 265-2038 1996 £100.00

STOKES, GEORGE   A List of Books, Connected with the English Reformation and Chiefly in the English Language, in the Possession of George Stokes of Cheltenham. N.P.: Cheltenham?, 1844. 8vo; sewn as issued; fine.   Ximenes 109-177 1996 $225.00

STOKES, I. N. PHELPS   American Historical Prints, Early Views of American Cities, Etc. New York: New York Public Library, 1933. 1st edition; 8vo; frontispiece, xxxiii, 235 pages; 118 plates; cloth, minor rubbing on covers, else fine.   The Bookpress 75-465 1996 $175.00

STOKES, J. L.   Discoveries in Australia: During the Voyage of HMS Beagle in the Years 1837-43. Adelaide: 1969. 2 volumes; 521, 543 pages; illustrations; very good; the Meggitt copy.   Antipodean 28-405 1996 $150.00

STOKES, MAIVE   Indian Fairy Tales Collected and Translated. Calcutta: privately printed, 1879. 1st edition; one of 100 copies; 8vo; pages viii, 303; original ribbed blue cloth, rebacked, original backstrip laid down, lettering dulled, front cover gilt titled with double ruled border, border blind on rear cover, cloth faded, edges worn, yellow endpapers, soiled, sound. Author's inscription "Lady Strachey from Maive Stokes". Blackwell's B112-265 1996 £85.00

STOKES, WHITLEY   Gwreans an Bys. The Creation of the World, a Cornish Mystery. 1864. 1st edition; 8vo; 208 pages; cloth, very good. C. P. Hyland 216-808 1996 £85.00

STOKES, WHITLEY   The Tripartite Life of St. Patrick, with Other Documents Relating to...Saint. 1887. 8vo; 2 volumes; quarter cloth, small tear on volume 2 spine, ex-library, very good.   C. P. Hyland 216-806 1996 £200.00

STOKES, WILLIAM   The Life and Labours in Art and Archaeology of George Petrie. 1868. 1st edition; 8vo; cloth, spine worn, cover dull, text good.   C. P. Hyland 216-676 1996 £125.00

STOKES, WILLIAM   Treatise on the Diagnosis and Treatment of Diseases of the Chest... London: New Sydenham Soc., 1882. Portrait, 596 pages; cloth. GM 2213.   Argosy 810-463 1996 $300.00

STOKES, WILLIAM   A Treatise on the Diagnosis and Treatment of Diseases of the Chest, Part I. Diseases of the Lung and Windpipe. London: 1882. lv, 596 pages; frontispiece; cloth, spine ends worn; bookpate of Thomas Lewis.   Graham Weiner C2-534 1996 £50.00

STOLL, CASPAR   Representation Exactement Coloriee d'Apres Nature des Cigales... Amsterdam: Jan Christiaan Sepp, 1788. Large 4to; 124 pages, colored floral frontispiece, 29 copperplates, delicately colored by hand showing 171 specimens of cicadas, contemporary three quarter calf, joints slightly rubbed; fine, large copy. Nissen 3999; Hagen II 198; Horn Schenkling 21554.   Book Block 32-13 1996 $7,500.00

STONE, HERBERT STUART   First Editions of American Authors. Cambridge: Stone & Kimball, 1893. Large paper edition, limited to 50 numbered copies, signed by publisher; large 8vo; xxiv, 224 pages; lavender cloth, paper spine label; rare; E. B. Gould's copy (Chicago collector) with his bookplate. Kramer, Stone & Kimball 2.   Kenneth Karmiole 1NS-233 1996 $450.00

STONE, HERBERT STUART   First Editions of American Authors: a Manual for Book-Lovers. Cambridge: Stone & Kimball, 1893. 1st trade edition; 12mo; 19 page introduction by Eugene Field; titlepage printed in orange and black; original gilt stamped olive green cloth, bevelled edges, top edge gilt, uncut, partly unopened, very good.   George J. Houle 68-46 1996 $135.00

STONE, REYNOLDS   Reynolds Stone: Engravings. London: John Murray, printed at the Curwen Press, 1977. 1st edition; special issue, limited to 150 numbered copies, signed by Stone, with original engraving loosely inserted; imperial 8vo; pages xli, 151 pages of wood engravings; original blue buckram, spine blocked in gilt, top edge gilt, marbled endpapers; fine in marbled board slipcase.   Sotheran PN32-54 1996 £325.00

STONE, ROBERT   Dog Soldiers. Boston: Houghton Mifflin, 1974. Uncorrected proof, the second issue, in mustard brown wrappers with printed letter to bookseller from editor-in-chief, Austin Olney; signed, fine; almost as scarce as the first issue.   Bev Chaney, Jr. 23-653 1996 $265.00

STONE, ROBERT   Dog Soldiers. Boston: Houghton Mifflin Co., 1974. 1st edition; signed by author; bookplate front pastedown (under flap), else fine in dust jacket.   Thomas Dorn 9-241 1996 $120.00

STONE, ROBERT   A Hall of Mirrors. Boston: Houghton Mifflin, 1966. 1st edition; author's first book; near fine, light shelf wear, in price clipped very good plus dust jacket with wear at spinal crown; scarce. Thomas Dorn 9-240 1996 $300.00

STONE, ROBERT   A Hall of Mirrors. Boston: Houghton Mifflin, 1967. 1st edition; fine in much nicer than usual dust jacket with tiny edge tear at upper spine fold, very near fine.   Ken Lopez 74-425 1996 $400.00

STONE, ROBERT   A Hall of Mirrors. Boston: Houghton Mifflin, 1967. 1st edition; (5000 copies); author's first book; very good+ in price clipped dust jacket which has few short, internally mended tears. Steven C. Bernard 71-277 1996 $250.00

STONE, ROBERT   Helping. New York: Dim Gray Bar Press, 1987. One of only 100 copies of this short story numbeed and signed by author; tall quarto; quarter cloth and paper covered boards, publisher's paper covered slipcase; fine.   Lame Duck Books 19-510 1996 $200.00

STONE, ROBERT   Helping. N.P.: Dim Grey Bar Press, 1993. 1st separate edition; one of 100 numbered copies, signed by author; thin quarto; fine in slipcase, errata slip laid in.   Ken Lopez 74-426 1996 $200.00

STONE, ROBERT   Outerbridge Reach. New York: Ticknor and Fields, 1992. 1/250 signed and numbered copies; fine in slipcase.   Bev Chaney, Jr. 23-657 1996 $125.00

STONE, STUART   The Kingdom of Why. Indianapolis: Bobbs, Merrill, 1913. 4to; 6 black and white plates and numerous drawings in black and white by Peter Newell; olive cloth with pictorial onlay, spine lettering dulled, page with pale stain, 1 page corner with ink mark, else nice, very scarce.   Barbara Stone 70-160 1996 £95.00

STONE, WILLIAM   A Practical Treatise on Benefit Building Societies, Embracing Their Origin, Constitution and Change of Character... London: W. Maxwell, 1851. 1st edition; large 12mo; xiii, (3), 312 pages, library stamp on blank verso of title, small circular paper label with letter 'A' on title just partially covering a single letter of author's name; well bound in cloth with printed paper spine label; very good, very scarce.   John Drury 82-270 1996 £150.00

STONE, WILLIAM L.   Life of Joseph Brant - Thayendanegea. New York: George Dearborn, 1838. 1st edition; large 8vo; frontispiece, title leaf, xxiv, 425, (3), lviii pages, frontispiece, title leaf, viii, 537, (3), lxiv pages, 6 plates, publisher's cloth, slight chipping to extremities of spine an slight rubbing, else very nice, bookplates. Howes S1040.   The Bookpress 75-466 1996 $325.00

STOOKEY, BYRON   Surgical and Mechanical Treatment of Peripheral Nerves. Philadelphia: Saunders, 1922. 8vo; (5)-475 pages; illustrations, plus 2 colored plates; original binding, bit rubbed, internally good.   James Tait Goodrich K40-276 1996 $195.00

STOPES, MARIE   Contraception (Birth Control). Its Theory, History and Practice, a manual for the Medical and Legal Professions. London: 1924. 1st edition; 3rd printing; 418 pages; original binding.   W. Bruce Fye 71-2058 1996 $100.00

STORCK, KARL   Musik und Musiker in Karikatur. Oldenburg: Gerhard Stalling, ca. 1910. Large thick 4to; 502 caricature illustrations, numerous full page, folding and mounted plates, some in color, white vellum paper spine, cream boards, elaborate gilt pictorial border and lettering; uncommon.   Marilyn Braiterman 15-150 1996 $225.00

STORER, J.   Antiquarian and Topographical Cabinet. London: pub. for the proprietors by W. Clarke, New Bond St., J. Carpenter... 1807-11. 1st edition; 8vo; 10 volumes; 480 engraved copperplates, 10 vignettes to letterpress; half calf and marbled boards, corners bumped, few slightly worn, gilt title to spines and gilt rule to spines, worn, edges speckled; previous owner's stamp to front f.e.p. of all volumes; some very occasional and very slight foxing or offsetting, upper hinges to volumes I, V and IX all tender. Upcott xxxii, Lowndes V p. 2522.   Beeleigh Abbey BA56-24 1996 £350.00

STORER, J.   The Antiquarian Itinerary. London: pub. for the Proprietors by Wm. Clarke et al, 1815-18. 1st edition; 6 1/2 x 4 1/4 inches; 7 volumes; many woodcut headpieces and tailpieces, 336 plates; pleasing contemporary burgundy straight grain morocco, double gilt rule on covers framing blind foliate and inner gilt floral borders, spine with wide raised bands and gilt compartments in Regency style, narrow decorative gilt border on turn-ins, all edges gilt; slight wear to spine ends and bands, leather on spines evenly faded, otherwise bindings generally fine and quite pretty, with virtually no wear to joints, faint offsetting from plates onto facing text page, elaves just a shade less than bright, isolated very light foxing, but excellent internally, very smooth and clean and showing no significant signs of use.   Phillip J. Pirages 33-471 1996 $600.00

STORER, J.   Delineations Graphical and Descriptive of Fountains' Abbey, in the West Riding of the County of York. Ripon: H. Thirlway, n.d., c. 1840. Large paper copy; 4to; pages x, 1 f., tipped in errata notice, 158 pages, engraved frontispiece, 14 single and 1 double page plates, 2 vignettes, all on laid india paper, elaborately blindstamped green cloth, gilt lettered spine, corners very slightly bumped. UCBA p. 1936.   Marlborough 162-93 1996 £180.00

STORER, J.   History and Description of the Parish of Clerkenwell. The Historical Department... London: Longman... & J. & H. S. Storer, n.d. 1828. 8vo; title ruled in red (repaired at top blank section), engraved dedn. mounted, pages iii-viii, 448, v pages, index, 30 engraved plates and d/p map; recent half calf, some neat ms. notes and printed ephemera concerning Clerkenwell tipped in.   Marlborough 162-206 996 £150.00

STORER, JAMES   Cowper, Illustrated by a Series of Views in or Near the Park of Weston-Underwood, Bucks. London: 12mo; 51 pages; frontispiece, 12 plates; original boards, lacks backstrip, part uncut. Harris p. 42.   Marlborough 162-94 1996 £75.00

STORM, COLTON   A Catalog of the Everett D. Graff Collection of Western American. Chicago: The Newbery Library/University of Chicago Press, 1968. xvi, 854 pages; portrait frontispiece, maps; fine in dust jacket.   Rockland Books 38-211 1996 $125.00

THE STORY of the Fifty-Fifth Regiment Illinois Volunteer Infantry in the Civil War. Clinton: printed by W. J. Coulter, 1887. 1st edition; 9 1/4 x 6 1/4 inches; 519 pages; original cloth, front joint partly cracked, minor wear to cloth, but excellent copy, still quite firm and very clean internally. Phillip J. Pirages 33-131 1996 $175.00

STORY, JOSEPH   Commentaries on the Constitution of the United States... Boston: 1833. 1st edition; 8vo; 3 volumes; contemporary calf, scuffed, leather labels, new matching labels on volume 3, hinges tender, slight foxing, very good set, very clean, without any library markings (which is usually the case). Howes S1047; B&B 21380; Marvin 669; Sabin 92292.   M & S Rare Books 60-418 1996 $3,000.00

STORY, JOSEPH   Commentaries on the Law of Partnership, as a Branch of Commercial and Maritime Jurisprudence, with Occasional Illustrations from the Civil and Foreign Law. London: A. Maxwell, 1841. 1st English edition; patterned cloth, rebacked, very clean.   Meyer Boswell SL27-220 1996 $650.00

STOUT, G. D.   Shorebirds of North America. New York: 1967. Folio; 32 color plates, 270 pages; bound, dust jacket.   John Johnson 135-545 1996 $100.00

STOUT, PETER F.   Nicaragua: Past, Present and Future... Philadelphia: John E. Potter, 1859. 8vo; 372 pages; one large folding map; from the library of John T. Doyle, one mounted page of notes and extensive notes on rear endpaper, one mounted article, Doyle's "Dean of the California Bar"; original brown cloth, gilt, bookplate, library pocket. Kenneth Karmiole 1NS-148 1996 $175.00

STOUT, REX   And Be A Villain. New York: Viking, 1948. 1st edition; in book club dust jacket, very good with soiling on spine, in near fine dust jacket with tips lightly nicked and slight soiling.   Quill & Brush 102-1621 1996 $350.00

STOUT, REX   And Be a Villain. New York: Viking, 1948. 1st edition; fine in near fine dust jacket with light rubbing, light soiling, minor edge wear.   Quill & Brush 102-1622 1996 $250.00

STOUT, REX   And Be a Villain. New York: Viking Press, 1948. 1st edition; near fine in price clipped dust jacket with light soiling and minor edge wear.   Quill & Brush 102-1623 1996 $200.00

STOUT, REX   If Death Ever Slept. New York: Viking Press, 1957. 1st edition; spine extremities and corners lightly rubbed, otherwise fine in dust jacket with spine extremities and corners lightly creased and rubbed.   Quill & Brush 102-1625 1996 $100.00

STOUT, REX   Too Many Cooks. N.P.: American Magazine, 1938. 1st edition; gold box bound in red cloth cover with printed endpaper as titlepage and 36 card laid in; 34 recipe cards - in dust jacket with rear flap attached between box and cover, signed by Stout et al; dust jacket lightly soiled and rubbed with top and bottom (creased) edge of front flap split, few rubbed chips and tears;   Quill & Brush 102-1618 1996 $1,250.00

STOVALL, ALLAN   Nueces Headwater Country. San Antonio: Naylor, 1959. 1st edition; 468 pages; photos, dust jacket. CBC 1494.   Maggie Lambeth 30-490 1996 $135.00

STOW, JOHN   A Survay (sic) of London. London: Imprinted by Iohn Wolfe, 1599. 4to. in 8's; (viii), 483, (1 faults) pages; old calf, worn, rebacked, titlepage brittle at margins, last leaf defective, without loss of text, some pages darkened. With long history of ownership, including bookplates of Frank Staff; signatures of George Cage, George Manley, J. Millar, B. Castleton, Peter Smart, J. B. de V. Payen-Payne. Marlborough 162-207 1996 £1,100.00

STOWE, HARRIET ELIZABETH BEECHER 1811-1896   Dred: a Tale of the Great Dismal Swamp. Boston: Phillips, Sampson & Co., 1856. 1st edition; binding A, 1st printing; battered type on p. 209 though BAL states that most copies of the 1st printing are not damaged thus; 12mo; 2 volumes; black-brown cloth, spine tips with usual wear, moderate browning, some spotting. BAL 19389.   Charles Agvent 4-1059 1996 $225.00

STOWE, HARRIET ELIZABETH BEECHER 1811-1896   Dred: a Tale of the Great Dismal Swamp. Boston: Phillips, Sampson and Co., 1856. 1st edition; 2 volumes; brown cloth stamped with blind floral panel design on front and rear boards and titled in gilt, one eighth inch piece missing from left half of head of spine to volume one, very light rubbing to other spine ends and corners, otherwise fine.   Hermitage SP95-599 1996 $300.00

STOWE, HARRIET ELIZABETH BEECHER 1811-1896   A Key to Uncle Tom's Cabin. Boston: John P. Jewett & Co., 1853. 1st edition; 1st printing; 8vo; contemporary half leather, rubbed, edgeworn, light browning; very good. BAL 19359.   Charles Agvent 4-1060 1996 $175.00

STOWE, HARRIET ELIZABETH BEECHER 1811-1896   Little Pussy Willow. Boston: Houghton Mifflin, 1881. 1st edition thus; 8vo; decorated green cloth, light wear, contents bit darkened, very good; signed by author.   Charles Agvent 4-1061 1996 $1,500.00

STOWE, HARRIET ELIZABETH BEECHER 1811-1896   Men Of Our Times. Hartford: Hartford Publishing, 1868. 1st edition; 8vo; 19 steel engraved portraits; original binding, light wear, scattered foxing; very good; mounted to f.f.e.p. is an inscription from Stowe.   Charles Agvent 4-1063 1996 $550.00

STOWE, HARRIET ELIZABETH BEECHER 1811-1896   Palmetto Leaves. Boston: Houghton Mifflin, 1873. Reprint; 8vo; map and text cuts; signed by Stowe with inscription; decorated green cloth; covers bit soiled, occasional stain or tear to contents, very good.   Charles Agvent 4-1065 1996 $850.00

STOWE, HARRIET ELIZABETH BEECHER 1811-1896   Pink and White Tyranny. A Society Novel. Boston: Roberts Bros., 1871. 1st edition; octavo; pages (4 prelim ads), 331, 12 pages publisher's ads; many wood engraved illustrations; original brown cloth decorated in blind and gilt, binding somwhat rubbed; contents excellent. Hildreth p. 95. Hartfield 48-V45 1996 $135.00

STOWE, HARRIET ELIZABETH BEECHER 1811-1896   Queer Little People. Boston: Houghton Mifflin, 1867. 1st edition thus; 8vo; text cuts; decorated green cloth, very small crack in rear hinge, text with occasional stain, near fine. this rather scarce book is inscribed by Stowe.   Charles Agvent 4-1066 1996 $1,250.00

STOWE, HARRIET ELIZABETH BEECHER 1811-1896   Sunny Memories of Foreign Lands. Boston: Phillips, Sampson & Co., 1854. 1st edition; binding A, volume 2 is the 15th thousand; 12mo; 2 volumes; illustrations; black cloth, light wear, pencilled names on title and blank; near fine. Charles Agvent 4-1067 1996 $125.00

STOWE, HARRIET ELIZABETH BEECHER 1811-1896   Uncle Tom's Cabin. Boston: John P. Jewett & Co., 1852. 25th thousand; 12mo; 2 volumes; 6 plates; brown cloth, light wear to spine tips, moderate foxing, bright, very good; contemporary ownership signature of Catherine Putnam. BAL 19343 for 1st printing.   Charles Agvent 4-1069 1996 $350.00

STOWE, HARRIET ELIZABETH BEECHER 1811-1896   Uncle Tom's Cabin. London: John Cassell, 1852. 1st English edition, in parts; 8vo; No. I-XIII (all); 27 illustrations on wood by George Cruikshank; original printed wrappers, old tape repairs on verso in margins of front wrapper of part 1, back wrapper of part XIII trifle frayed, 2 leaves bound out of order, ads noted in Part VI by Cohn, not present; fine set, very unusual thus. Rare. Cohn, Cruikshank Cat. 777.   M & S Rare Books 60-240 1996 $2,750.00

STOWE, HARRIET ELIZABETH BEECHER 1811-1896   Uncle Tom's Cabin. London: Bohn, 1852. Early English edition; 8vo; illustrations; green cloth, front hinge with old glue repair, very good.   Charles Agvent 4-1070 1996 $150.00

STOWE, HARRIET ELIZABETH BEECHER 1811-1896   Uncle Tom's Cabin. London: John Cassell, 1852. 1st English edition; 8vo; portrait, 27 illustrations, pages 193-208 have short margins; contemporary half calf, slight rubbing; Sabin 92470.   Charles W. Traylen 117-201 1996 £80.00

STOWE, HARRIET ELIZABETH BEECHER 1811-1896   Oheim Tom's Hutte... Boston: John P. Jewett, 1853. 1st German-American edition; 8vo; 6, 176 pages; illustrations; contemporary calf backed boards, hinges weak, last leaf quite foxed. Very scarce edition; Sabin 92555; LCP/HSP Afro Amer. Cat. 9922.   M & S Rare Books 60-239 1996 $400.00

STOWE, HARRIET ELIZABETH BEECHER 1811-1896   Uncle Tom's Cabin; or Life Among the Lowly. London: T. Nelson, 1853. Original blue cloth gilt presentation binding, rubbed, inner hinges neatly repaired; very good, cloth case; inscribed and signed by author. PMM 332.   19th Century Shop 39- 1996 $4,500.00

STOWE, HARRIET ELIZABETH BEECHER 1811-1896   Uncle Tom's Cabin. New York: Limited Editions Club, 1938. Limited to 1500 copies; 4to; illustrations by Miguel Covarrubias, signed by artist; half red morocco, near fine in very good case, uncommon.   Charles Agvent 4-1071 1995 $325.00

STOWE, HARRIET ELIZABETH BEECHER 1811-1896   The Writings of Harriet Beecher Stowe. Boston: printed at the Riverside Press for Houghton Mifflin, 1896. Large paper edition, one of 250 copies with author's autograph; 16 volumes; three quarter crushed brown levant over marbled boards, raised bands, spine gilt, top edge gilt, others uncut, marbled endpapers; superb set. BAL 19508; Merle Johnson, American First Editions p. 483.   Paulette Rose 16-311 1996 $4,500.00

STOWE, JOHN   Annales, or, a Generall Chronicle of England. (with) An Appendix of Corollary of the Foundations and Descriptions of the Three Most Famous Universities of England... (with) The Third Universities of England... London: Impensis Richardi Meighen, 1631/32/31. Tall folio; old buckram (nice condition) with attractive leather spine (raised bands, title and date of 1631 in gilt), title leaf bit age darkened, outer margin and outer margin of following leaf strengthened, marginal waterstaining to outer margin of 2d, 3d and 4th leaves; only a number of leaves cut close and with a small number lightly embrowned. Cox III p. 380.   Roy W. Clare XXIV-72 1996 $500.00

STOWELL, MYRON   "Fort Frick" or the Siege of Homestead. Pittsburg: Pittsburg Pub. Co., 1893. xiii pages; plates; green cloth. Blue River Books 9-256 1996 $250.00

STRABO   (Greek title) Strabonis De Situ Orbis Librix XVII. Basel: Henrichum Petri, August, 1549. Folio; 548 leaves, Greek and Latin text printed in parallel columns, "Hammer-Mountain" printer's device at colophon; small woodcut map, woodcut historiated initials; contemporary full alum tawed pigskin over oak boards, elaborately tooled in blind, center panel of fleurons with interlaced vines, historiated roll depicting biblical figures, framed in wide border composed of the same tools as those used in center panel, morocco label. Adams S1905; Graesse VI 505.   Family Album Tillers-589 1996 $900.00

STRACHEY, RAY   Marching on. New York: 1923. 1st American edition; original cloth, outer edge of upper cover trifle damp marked, otherwise very good; inscribed by author to Giles Lytton Strachey.   Words Etcetera 94-1192 1996 £50.00

STRADA, FAMIANO   De Bello Belgico. The History of the Low-Countrey Warres. London: printed for Humphrey Moseley, 1650. 1st edition; folio; frontispiece, 12 engraved portraits, leaf of ads at end, small wormhole in gutter, not affecting text, waterstain on lower half of some leaves, plain contemporary calf, morocco label, sound. Wing S5777.   H. M. Fletcher 121-75 1996 £175.00

STRAFFORD, THOMAS WENTWORTH, 1ST EARL OF 1593-1641   La Harangve dv Vice-Roy d'Irlande...Decapite a Londres...le 12 May 1641. Paris: Michel Brunet, 1641. 1st edition thus; small 8vo; pages 14, large Roman letter, slightly faded in modern boards; not in BM STC. Fr. 17th cent. 1 copy in NUC.   A. Sokol XXV-93 1996 £295.00

STRAHAN, A.   The Geology of the Isle of Purbeck and Weymouth. London: 1898. 1st edition; 8vo; pages xi, 278, 5 plates, folding colored map, 5 folding sections of which 3 are colored; cloth, gilt, fine.   John Henly 27-609 1996 £85.00

STRAHORN, ROBERT   Gunnison and San Juan. A Late and Reliable Description of the wonderful Gold and Silver Belts... Omaha: New West Pub. Co., 1881. 1st edition; 48 pages; original printed wrappers, minor dampstain to lower right hand portion of text, very good in half morocco slipcase and chemise. Streeter Sale 2201. Not in Adams Herd. Michael D. Heaston 23-105 1996 $850.00

STRAHORN, ROBERT   The Hand-Book of Wyoming and Guide to the Black Hills and Big Horn Regions for Citizen, Emigrant and Tourist... Cheyenne: 1877. 1st edition; 249, 251-72 ads; illustrations; original printed wrappers, fine with minor chipping, laid in half morocco and chemise slipcase. Howes S1055; Adams Herd 2181; Streeter Sale 2248; Graff 4000.   Michael D. Heaston 23-312 1996 $650.00

STRAHORN, ROBERT   Idaho, the Gem of the Mountain, The Resources and Attractions of Idaho Territory, Facts Regarding Climate, Soil, Minerals, Agricultural and Grazing Lands, Forests, Scenery, Etc. Boise City: 1881. 1st edition; 88 pages + ads, illustrations, folded maps, pictorial wrappers chipped; very good. Howes S1056; Herd 2183.   T. A. Swinford   49-1122   1996 $200.00

STRAND, MARK   Prose: Four Poems. Printed for Charles Seluzicki at Ives Street Press, 1987. Limited to 187 copies, signed by author; wrappers, fine.   Words Etcetera 94-1194   1996 £50.00

STRAND, MARK   A Suite of Appearances: a Poem. Charles Seluzicki: 1993. Limited to 150 copies signed by author, this being one of just 30 copies printed on Velke Losiny handmade paper and specially bound in stiff decorated paste paper wrappers; fine.   Words Etcetera 94-1196   1996 £85.00

STRAND, PAUL   Ghana: an African Portrait. Aperture. 1976. 1st edition; folio; illustrations; dust jacket.   J. B. Muns 154-288a 1996 $125.00

STRAND, PAUL   Time in New England. New York: 1950. 1st edition; 106 photos; dust jacket.   J. B. Muns 154-288b 1996 $125.00

STRANG, WILLIAM   The Doings of Death. London: Essex House Press, 1901. One of just 140 copies; oblong folio; bound portfolio of 12 chiaroscuro prints, signed in blocks, each print with its lettered tissue guard printed from black and brown block with white paper allowed to show through to help define the image; publisher's rough natural linen, titled on cover. Brilliant copy.   Book Block 32-21 1996 $1,250.00

STRAPAROLA, GIOVANNI FRANCESO   The Nights of Straparola. London: Lawrence and Bullen, 1894. 1st edition in English, 1 of 210 copies; 4to; 2 volumes, xxviii, 276; ix, 323 pages, printed on Japan vellum; 20 full page images; original brown boards with white spines, covers slightly rubbed and soiled, else nice, unopened, very good. Translator's (W. G. Waters) copy with bookplate.   Chapel Hill 94-340 1996 $275.00

STRATHMORE, MARY ELEANOR BOWES, COUNTESS OF   The Confessions of the Countess of Strathmore: Written by Herself. London: printed for W. Locke, 1793. 1st edition; 8vo; modern calf, gilt, spine and inner dentelles, gilt, all edges gilt; nice copy, bound with half title.   Ximenes 109-275 1996 $300.00

STRATTON, CHARLES   Grandmamma Easy's General Tom Thumb. Boston: Brown Bozin & Co., Nashua: N. P. Greene, n.d., c. 1850. Large 8vo; original decorative wrappers, backstrip reinforced, colored woodcut frontispiece, 7 colored woodcuts to text. Saxon p.1 23.   Dramatis Personae 37-169 1996 $150.00

STRATTON, GEORGE   Defences of George Stratton, Esq. London: printed for T. Cadell, November, 1778. 4to; 53 pages; disbound.   Anthony W. Laywood 108-126 1996 £145.00

STRAUB, P.   Ghost Story. London: Cape, 1979. 1st British edition; uncorrected proof; signed by author; fine in very good+ dust jacket.   Aronovitz 57-1132 1996 $140.00

STRAUS, RALPH   The Unspeakable Curll, Being Some Account of Edmund Curll, Bookseller; to Which is Added a Full List of His Books. London: Chapman and Hall, 1927. Limited to 535 copies; frontispiece, 31 plates; dark blue buckram, top edge gilt, generally good; inscribed by author with some later ink annotations in handlist.   Maggs Bros. Ltd. 1191-121 1996 £72.00

STRAUS, RALPH   The Unspeakable Curll. New York: Robert McBride, 1928. 1st American edition, from the English sheets; 8vo; xii, 322 pages, frontispiece, 32 plates; cloth; fine, in dust jacket, very scarce thus.   The Bookpress 75-357 1996 $225.00

STREAMER, D.   Ruthless Rhymes for Heartless Homes. London: Edward Arnold, 1899. 1st edition; landscape format, titlepage and full page black and white illustrations; cloth backed pictorial boards, covers rubbed, marked and dusty, head and tail of spine and corners bumped and bruised, free endpapers browned; good.   Ulysses 39-566 1996 £75.00

STREATFEILD, R. A.   Samuel Butler: Records and Memorials. Cambridge: printed for Private Circulation, 1903. Original wrappers chipped and detached.   Jarndyce CII-135 1996 £50.00

STREATFIELD, T.   Lympsfield with Its Environs. Westerham: George, 1838. Large 8vo; half title, title, 1 f. contents, 12 litho plates with letterpress, fly title, 3 ff. with 4 woodcut vignettes by Cruikshank, morocco backed boards, dusty, corners bumped. Cohn 778; Abbey Scenery 265 (not proof plates as here).   Marlborough 162-95 1996 £250.00

STREET Sketches of London Life. London: Protheim, ca. 1890. Octavo; (10)ff; 10 chromolithographed pictures of London street vendors, each accompanied by an amusing poem; original illustrated wrappers, which are slightly smudged, otherwise fine.   Bromer Booksellers 90-142 1996 $350.00

STREET, ALFRED B.   A Digest of Taxation in the States, Under Three Heads. 1. Mode or Machinery of Taxation. 2. Standard of Valuation. 3. Property Liable to and Exempt fromm Taxation. Albany: Weed, Parsons and Co., 1863. Original embossed olive green cloth, quite well preserved.   Meyer Boswell SL26-223 1996 $250.00

STREETER, THOMAS WINTHROP   The Celebrated Collection of Americana Formed by the late Thomas Winthrop Streeter. New York: Parke-Bernet Galleries, 1966-69. 1st and only edition; 8 volumes, which includes index; plates; original blue stiff boards with title stamp in gilt on spines, index volume in blue cloth; fine set.   Michael D. Heaston 23-48 1996 $750.00

STRICKLAND, AGNES   Lives of the Queens of England. Philadelphia: printed only for subscribers by George Barrie & Sons, 1902. One of 1000 copies; 8 3/4 x 5 3/4 inches; 16 volumes, printed on Japanese vellum paper, 180 photogravure plates, partly printed in red; very fine highly dec. inlaid purple mor. flamboyantly gilt, by Harcourt Bindery, covers with oval panelling featuring delicate voluted ornaments & lg. rose of inlaid red morocco in each corner, spines similarly dec. in handsome compartments, 4 of them on each vol. containing a smaller inlaid rose, motif continued on wide gilt dec. turn-ins (inside of each cover with 2 more inlaid roses, making a total of 16 roses per vol.), marbled endpapers, top edge gilt, small portions of two joints very skillfully and almost invisibly repaired; one cover with couple of superficial scratches, 2 or 3 covers with sl. dulling, spines just sl. & uniformly faded, but very fine set in all other ways, almost entirely bright and clean & with scarcely any signs of use, virtually pristine internally; exceptionally pretty set.   Phillip J. Pirages 33-472 1996 $4,500.00

STRICKLAND, W.   El Paso in 1854. El Paso: Texas Western Press, 1969. Quarto; xv, 29 facsimile leaves, 31-44 pages, map, illustrations, cloth; signed by Strickland and Hertzog; with 30 page handwritten newsletter by Frederic Augustus Percy; fine but for name on endpaper. Lowman 250.   Bohling Book Co. 191-141 1996 $150.00

STRID, A.   Mountain Flora of Greece. London: 1986-91. 8vo; 2 volumes, 1854 pages, 97 illustrations; hardbound.   Wheldon & Wesley 207-1592 1996 £185.00

STRODE, WILLIAM   The Floating Island. London: printed by T. C. for H. Twiford...N. Brooke and J. Place... 1655. 1st edition; small 4to; A-F4, close cropped but no loss of text, browned throughout, tear in titlepage repaired without loss; modern quarter calf, marbled boards. Wing S5983. H. M. Fletcher 121-76 1996 £195.00

STROMMENGER, EVA   5000 Years of the Art of Mesopotamia. New York: Harry N. Abrams, 1964. Folio; 480 pages, 70 figures and 324 plates (44 in color); photos; original cloth.   Archaeologia Luxor-2746 1996 $250.00

STRONG, JAMES CLARK   Biographical Sketch of James Clark Strong, Colonel and Brigadier General, by Brevet. Los Gatos: 1910. (vi), 106 pages, portraits; maroon cloth; gilt title; Howes S1080; Graff 4013; Smith 3877; Cowan p. 621; Dornbusch NY 260.   Bohling Book Co. 192-74 1996 $350.00

STRONG, LEONARD ALFRED STRONG   The Hansom Cab and Pigeons. Waltham St. Lawrence: Golden Cockerel Press, 1935. 1st edition; number 69 of 212 special copies; 8vo; pages 43 + colophon; printed on Arnold handmade paper and signed by author; frontispiece, vignette and four repeated ornamental headpieces by Ravilious; original blue morocco backed silver and blue marbled boards, top edge gilt, others uncut, backstrip faded to green. Chanticleer 105.   Claude Cox 107-66 1996 £135.00

STRONG, ROY   The English Icon - Elizabethan and Jacobean Portraiture. London: Paul Mellon Foundation for British Art, 1969. 32 x 2 cm; xvi, 388 pages; illustrations; original cloth, dust jacket, slipcase. Rainsford A54-541 1996 £150.00

STROTHER, EDWARD   The Family Companion for Health, or the Housekeeper's Physician... London: printed for John and James Rivington, 1750. 3rd edition; 8vo; pages (12), 426, (26); contemporary unlettered gilt ruled calf, binding lightly rubbed, otherwise nice. Neat contemporary ownership inscription "Isabella Monck 1750" on titlepage. James Fenning   133-326   1996 £265.00

STROZZI, TITO VESPASIANO   Strozii Poetae Pater et Filius. Venice: Venetiis is Aedibus Aldi et Andreae Asulani Soceri, 1513/14. Edition princeps; 8vo; 2 parts; ff. (8), 99, (1), 152 leaves, printed throughout in italics, early illumination of A1, with frame crowned by dolphins, and elephant drawing an ancient carriage with arms and shields, the book was once damped throughout, and illumination is somewhat faded with offsetting; crimson morocco stamped in gilt with Aldine anchor and dolphin, entwined in naval rope, binding was probably executed by Messrs. Storr and Ridge of Grantham for Sir John Hayford Thorold, preserved in cloth box; Syston Park copy. Renouard p. 65.10; Adams S1956; UCLA I/93; Goldsmid 91; Isaac 12832.   Family Album Tillers-591   1996 $2,000.00

STRUTT, J. G.   Sylva Britannica; or Portraits of Forest Trees... London: 1830. Imperial 8vo; pages viii, 151, engraved titlepage, 49 engraved plates on India paper; original cloth, neatly repaired. Little spotted.   Wheldon & Wesley 207-1856   1996 £120.00

STRUTT, JOSEPH   A Complete View of the Dress and Habits of the People of England, from the Establishment of the Saxons in Britain to the Present Time. (with) The Regal and Ecclesiastical Antiquities of England... London: Henry G. Bohn, 1842. 2nd edition; 4to; 2 volumes, x, cxvii, 117; 279; 153 full page hand colored plates; 2nd title - 150 pages; 72 full page hand colored plates; 19th century three quarter olive morocco and marbled boards; private library bookplate, but clean, near fine set. Chapel Hill 94-89   1996 $1,250.00

STRUTT, JOSEPH   Glig Camena Angel-Deod, or the Sports and Pastimes of the People of England... London: printed by T. Bensley, 1810. 4to; 40 plates engraved in sepia tone; full tan calf boards, expertly rebacked, gilt panelled spine, raised bands, nice copy.   Appelfeld Gallery 54-169   1996 $250.00

STRUTT, JOSEPH   Queen-Hoo Hall, A Romance: and Ancient Times. Edinburgh: by James Ballantyne & Co., for John Murray, London & Archibald... 1808. 1st edition; 6 1/2 x 4 inches; 4 volumes; later red three quarter morocco by Riviere, linen sides, raised spine bands decorated with a stippled rule, spine panels lettered in gilt or stamped with gilt thistle ornament, marbled endpapers, all edges gilt, slight rubbing at top of spines, very minor wear to few corners but joints virtually unworn and bindings clean, bright and very pretty, tear on title of third volume through two words very artfully repaired without loss, inexpensive paper little darkened and somewhat foxed or spotted throughout (as probably the case with most copies of this imprint), despite defects, quite attractive set, rather scarce in the marketplace. Phillip J. Pirages   33-459   1996 $350.00

STRUTT, JOSEPH   The Regal and Ecclesiastical Antiquites of Engalnd. London: H. G. Bohn, 1842. Thick 4to; 60 most beautiful colored plates; half morocco, gilt top, mottled board sides, small perforated stamp on titlepage.   Charles W. Traylen 117-250   1996 £290.00

STRUTT, JOSEPH   The Sports and Pastimes of the People of England. London: William Reeves, 1830. 1st octavo edition, large paper copy; large 8vo; 420 pages; 140 full page and in text wood engravings; original publisher's half morocco, some rubbing to binding, else very good. Chapel Hill 94-397   1996 $200.00

STRUVE, CHRISTIAN AUGUSTUS   Asthenology; or, the Art of Preserving Feeble Life; and of Supporting the Constitution... London: 1801. 1st edition in English; 8vo; contemporary half calf.   Argosy 810-465   1996 $300.00

STRZELECKI, P. E. DE   Physical Description of New South Wales and Van Diemen's Land. London: Longman, Brown, Green and Longmsn, 1845. (xx), 462 pages, 32 pages ads dated Dec. 1848, frontispiece and 2 sepia litho plates, plus 19 engraved plates, folding map; secondary brown covers rebacked, very good; the Absolon copy. Presentation inscription from author to Edward Cane with his bookplate dated 1849. Ferguson 4168.   Antipodean 28-628   1996 $1,250.00

STUART, ANDREW   Considerations on the Present State of East-India Affairs and Examination of Mr. Fox's Bill; Suggesting Certain Material Alterations for Averting Dangers and Preserving the Benefits of that Bill. London: J. Stockdale, 1784. Half title, 66 pages; disbound, nice. Goldsmiths 12648.   C. R. Johnson 37-35   1996 £65.00

STUART, ANDREW   A Letter to the Right Honourable Lord Amherst, from Andrew Stuart, Esq. London: n.d. 1781. 1st edition; 4to; 48 pages; disbound.   Anthony W. Laywood 108-127   1996 £85.00

STUART, ANDREW   Letters to the Righ Honourable Lord Mansfield, from Andrew Stuart. London: privately printed, 1773. 1st edition; 4to; 63, 47, 47 pages; contemporary full polished calf, library bookplate and blindstamp, rear joint tender, otherwise very good; signed by Stuart at the conclusion of one of the letters.   Chapel Hill 94-361   1996 $300.00

STUART, E. J.   Land of Opportunities, Being an Account of the Author's Recent Expedition to Explore the Northern Territories of Australia. London: 1923. (xiv), 144 pages, frontispiece, 46 pages illustrations, 2 folding maps; cloth covers, discolored, but covered with a fine dust jacket; very good; the Absolon copy.   Antipodean 28-418 1996 $125.00

STUART, GILBERT   A View of Society in Europe, in Its Progress from Rudeness to Refinement; or, Inquiries Concerning the History of Law, Government and Manners. London: J. Murray, 1782. 2nd edition; 4to; name on title; contemporary tree calf, spine gilt, hinges cracked lacks label.   Anthony W. Laywood 108-128   1996 £75.00

STUART, GRANVILLE   Forty Years on the Old Frontier as Seen by Granville Stuart, Gold Miner, Trader, Merchant, Rancher and Politician. Cleveland: 1925. 1st edition; 272, 265 pages; frontispiece, plates; cloth. Fine. Howes S1096. Herd 2195; Mintz 450; Smith 9974; Adams 150 #133.   T. A. Swinford 49-1125   1996 $425.00

STUART, HENRY   The Planter's Guide; or, a Practical Essay on the Best Method to Giving Immediate Effect to Wood... Edinburgh & London: Murray, 1828. 2nd edition; 8vo; 527 pages; 6 engraved plates; uncut in original paper boards, skillful rebacking and original label; excellent copy. Second Life Books   103-182   1996 $275.00

STUART, JAMES 1764-1849   Three Years in North America. Edinburgh: Robert Cadell, 1833. 1st edition; 8vo; ix, 495, (1), vi, (1), 580 pages; large folding map in volume one; contemporary full calf, raised bands, gilt labels, rubber stamp on endpapers from an institution and scuff marks on spines from removal of what was probably stickers bearing shelf numbers, but still nice, attractive set. TPL 1013, lacking the map; Lande 817; Sabin 93170.   David Mason 71-127   1996 $400.00

STUART, LOUISA   Notes on George Selwyn and His Contemporaries. New York: and London: Oxford University Press, 1928. 1st edition; number 159 of 500 copies; tall wide octavo; pages xiii, 65, frontispiece, on laid paper; linen spine, marbled boards, uncut.   Hartfield 48-A18 1996 $165.00

STUART, ROBERT L.   Catalogue of the Library of Robert L. Stuart. New York: J. J. Little & Co., 1884. 1st edition; number 112 of a limited edition; small 4to; original cloth, uncut; presentation copy, inner hinge shaken.   Forest Books 74-261   1996 £65.00

STUART, RUTH MC ENERY   The Story of Babette, a Little Creole Girl. New York: and London: Harper, 1898. 1st edition thus; 8vo; (209) pages; frontispiece and 15 plates; red decorated cloth with gilt lettered spine and front; signature, otherwise fine.   Paulette Rose 16-312 1996 $100.00

STUART, W. J.   Forbidden Planet. FSC, 1956. 1st edition; very good+ in near fine dust jacket save for insignificant stain to upper section of front dust jacket flap; most uncommon.   Aronovitz 57-1134 1996 $450.00

STUBBS, CHARLES WILLIAM   The Land and the Labourers. London: W. Swan Sonnenschein & Co., 1884. 1st edition; 8vo; 186 pages; Working men's College labels, original cloth, gilt; very good.   John Drury 82-272   1996 £50.00

STUBBS, LUCAS PETER   A Guide to Pawnbroking Being the Statutes Regulating Pawns and Pawnbrokers. London: George Routledge and Sons, 1866. original cloth, worn, binding strained, but quite clean and fresh.   Meyer Boswell SL26-224   1996 $150.00

STUBBS, WILLIAM   Chronicles and Memorials of the Reign of Richard I. London: 1864-65. 8vo; 2 volumes, pages 650, 760; original cloth. Howes Bookshop 265-1581   1996 £55.00

STUBBS, WILLIAM   Chronicles of the Reigns of Edward I and Edward II. London: 1882-83. 8vo; 2 volumes, pages 500, 524; volume 1 dampstained, original cloth.   Howes Bookshop 265-1596   1996 £60.00

STUBBS, WILLIAM　　The Constitutional History of England In its Origin and Development. London: Oxford University Press, 1880. Library edition; demy 8vo; 3 volumes; original cloth, ex-library with one or two stamps, but good, sound set.　　Howes Bookshop　265-1168　1996 £75.00

THE STUDIO. Modern Book-bindings and Their Designers. London: Winter Number of the Studio, 1899-1900. Small folio; 5 color plates and numerous photographic illustrations, ads bound in at beginning and end; half cloth, spine gilt, original wrappers bound in, slightly faded and rubbed, ex-library with numbers in ink and stamps of plates.　　Maggs Bros. Ltd.　1191-28　1996 £70.00

THE STUDIO. Modern Book-Bindings and Their Designers. Special Winter Number 1899-1900. London: The Studio, 1900. 1st edition; 4to; 82 pages, 5 color lithograph plates, numerous illustrations; original printed wrappers, uncut; Ruari McLean's copy with signature.　　Forest Books　74-369　1996 £75.00

STUDLEY, VANCE　　Specimens of Handmade Botanical Papers. Los Angeles: ptd. by William & Victoria Dailey at the Press of the Pegacylce Lady, 1979. Limited to 50 copies, numbered and signed by author; 4 page separate introduction and 6 samples of various paper, each mounted within its own folder and accompanied by a fine etching of the plant from which the paper was made, and notes on paper making techniques, the whole contained within original brown half morocco foldover box, gilt; fine.　　Thomas Thorp　489-293　1996 £125.00

STURGEON, THEODORE　　Caviar. Ballantine, 1955. 1st edition; very good+ in very good dust jacket with some light chipping, wear and tear, very scarce in this hard cover issue.　　Aronovitz　57-1139　1996 $325.00

STURGEON, THEODORE　　The Dreaming Jewels. New York: Greenberg, 1950. 1st edition; author's second book; fine in dust jacket with some rubbing and wear at spine panel ends.　　Robert Gavora　61-210　1996 $100.00

STURGEON, THEODORE　　The Joyous Invasions. SFBC, 1966. 1st edition; fine in near fine dust jacket, signed by author, very scarce thus. Aronovitz　57-1146　1996 $175.00

STURGEON, THEODORE　　More than Human. FSY, 1953. 1st edition; near fine in very good+ dust jacket with some light wear and tear; inscribed by author.　　Aronovitz　57-1138　1996 $495.00

STURGEON, THEODORE　　A Touch of Strange. Garden City: Doubleday, 1958. 1st edition; signed, fine in dust jacket, very attractive copy. Robert Gavora　61-211　1996 $225.00

STURGEON, THEODORE　　A Way Home. New York: Funk & Wagnalls, 1955. 1st edition; signed; fine in bright and clean dust jacket.　　Robert Gavora　61-212　1996 $225.00

STURT, CHARLES　　Narrative of an Expedition Into Central Australia...During 1844, 5 and 6. London: T. W. Boone, 1849. 1st edition; (x), (iv), 5-416 pages (8), (2) (2) last blank; (vi), 308, 92, (ii), (8), (4) pages; 18 plates, 1 folding map; original green embossed cloth, rebacked with original spine laid down, good, internally nice and crisp; the Absolon copy. Ferguson 5202; Wantrup 119.　　Antipodean　28-421　1996 $1,450.00

STURT, CHARLES　　Two Expeditions into the Interior of Southern Australia during the Years 1828, 1829, 1830 and 1831. London: Smith, Elder & Co., 1833. 1st edition; 2 volumes, viii, (ix)-xxx, 220 pages (last blank); 5 engraved plates, folding map (couple of small tears repaired); viii, 272 pages (last blank), (15 pages ads), 9 plates; original purple pebble grain cloth, gilt decorated spines, spine sunned and dusty as usual, some discoloration of boards and top hinge starting, otherwise a pleasant copy; the Absolon copy, and with Edge Partington bookplate. Antipodean　28-122　1996 $1,750.00

STYRON, WILLIAM　　Admiral Robert Penn Warren and the Snows of Winter. North Carolina: Palaemon Press Ltd., 1978. 1/276 copies numbered and signed by author; frontispiece; wrappers; very fine.　　Left Bank Books　2-139　1996 $100.00

STYRON, WILLIAM　　Lie Down in Darkness. Indianapolis and New York: The Bobbs, Merrill Co., 1951. 1st edition; 8vo; near fine in very nice dust jacket just lightly creased at top of spine, author's very successful first book; contemporary presentation copy inscribed by author.　　Lakin & Marley　3-59　1996 $750.00

STYRON, WILLIAM　　Lie Down in Darkness. Indianapolis: Bobbs Merril 1951. 1st edition; very good in very good dust jacket with darkening to portion of white rear dust jacket panel and less so to spine; author's first book; signed by author.　　Revere Books　4-407　1996 $175.00

STYRON, WILLIAM　　Set This House on Fire. New York: Random, 1960. 1st edition; in second issue dust jacket, first issued reportedly ha fewer than a dozen copies; near fine in bright, unfaded dust jacket with touch of edge wear, signed.　　Anacapa House　5-293　1996 $135.00

STYRON, WILLIAM　　Sophie's Choice. Franklin Center: Franklin Library 1979. True 1st edition; signed; illustrations by Alan Reingold; fine in gilt stamped leather;　　Lame Duck Books　19-511　1996 $200.00

STYRON, WILLIAM　　Sophie's Choice. New York: Random House, 1979. 1st edition; fine in near fine dust jacket, little faded at extremities; signed by author.　　Between the Covers　42-418　1996 $150.00

STYRON, WILLIAM　　This Quiet Dust and Other Writings. New York: Random House, 1982. 1/250 copies, numbered and signed by author; very fine in slipcase.　　Left Bank Books　2-140　1996 $150.00

THE SUBSTANCE of a Charge Delivered to the Grand Jury of Wiltshire, at the Summer Assizes 1827, by the Lord Chief Justice Best. London: printed by Luke Hansard and Sons, for T. Cadell, 1827. 35 pages; later wrappers showing wear, but sound; from the library of Sir Thomas Phillipps, in Middle Hill wrappers and with its press mark.　　Meyer Boswell　SL27-227　1996 $175.00

SUBSTANCE of the Speech of Joseph Phillimore in the House of Commons On Moving for Leave to Bring in a Bill to Amend the Marriag Act. London: John Murray, 1822. Modern marbled boards, paper label; good fresh copy.　　Meyer Boswell　SL26-156　1996 $350.00

SUCKLING, JOHN　　A Ballad Upon a Wedding. Waltham St. Lawrence: Golden Cockerel Press, 1927. One of 375 numbered copies; 8vo; half buckram, batik sides, spine little darkened and sides slightly faded; but nice.　　Bertram Rota　272-171　1996 £95.00

SUCKLING, JOHN　　Fragmenta Aurea... London: Humphrey Moseley, 1658. 3rd edition; small 8vo; 135, 64, (2), (96), 145-190 pages; later ca bound by Zaehnsdorf, gold tooled spine panels, blind inside dentelles and roll tooled side panels in blind and gold, modern bookplate, very good in fine binding.　　The Bookpress　75-467　1996 $450.00

SUCKLING, JOHN　　The Works. Dublin: Nelson, 1766. 1st Dublin edition; tall 8vo; pages 462, (2); handsome binding by Stikeman, in thre quarter crushed morocco, gilt extra, panelled spine, top edge gilt, marbled endpapers, slight defect at bottom of titlepage, not affecting text, else fine, scarce. Bookplate of Joseph Knight, distinguished Dicken scholar.　　Hartfield　48-L82　1996 $295.00

SUDDEN Fiction. American Short Stories. Layton: Gibbs Smith, 1986. Uncorrected proof; wrappers; fine, uncommon.　　Ken Lopez　74-9　199 $150.00

SUE, EUGENE 1804-1857　　The Wandering Jew. London: Chapman an Hall, 1844. 1st English edition; 8vo; 3 volumes; three quarter contemporary green calf, minor wear at extremities, gilt panelled spines raised bands, red leather labels, marbled edges.　　Appelfeld Gallery 54-173　1996 $250.00

SUGDEN, ALAN VICTOR　　A History of English Wallpaper 1509-1914. London: B. T. Batsford, c. 1925. 4to; xiv, 281 pages; 70 tipped in color plates, 191 black and white plates; publisher's blue buckram, decoratec gilt, top edge gilt, others uncut, spine little faded and back cover slight scuffed, front free endpaper excised, some minor foxing in text; Thomas Thorp　489-294　1996 £300.00

SUGDEN, EDWARD BURTENSHAW　　A Series of Letters to a Man of Property, on the Sale, Purchase, Mortgaging, Leasing, Settling and Devising of Estates. London: printed for Reed and Hunter, 1815. 3rd edition; original boards, uncut, quite desirable, unsophisticated copy. Meyer Boswell　SL25-213　1996 $250.00

SUKENIK, E. L.　　The Third Wall of Jerusalem: an Account of Excavations. Jerusalem: University Press, 1930. 8vo; frontispiece, 76 pages, 42 illustrations, 10 folding plans; original cloth, signature, bottor edge bumped, small tear at bottom of spine.　　Archaeologia Luxor-2750　1996 $175.00

SULLIVAN, ARABELLA JANE   Tales of Peerage and Pesantry. London: Richard Bentley, 1835. 1st edition; 8vo; 3 volumes; original maroon cloth backed boards, spines worn, corners rubbed, printed paper labels, little soiled, 1 chipped, uncut. Wolff 1708.   Howard S. Mott 227-137 1996 $350.00

SULLIVAN, ELEANOR   Whodunit: a Biblio-Bio Anecdotal memoir of Frederic Dannay. New York: Targ Editions, 1984. 1st edition; one of 150 copies, signed by author; cloth and paper binding, fine.   Priscilla Juvelis 95/1-325 1996 $150.00

SULLIVAN, FRANCIS STOUGHTON   Lectures on the Constitution and Laws of England. London: for Edward and Charles Dilly...and Joseph Johnson, 1776. 2nd edition; 4to; xvi, xxxii, 415, (1) pages, contents leaves rather spotted, private library stamp on foot of title, otherwise good, crisp copy, complete with half title, contemporary calf with spine label, bit worn, joints split but holding firm.   John Drury 82-273 1996 £175.00

SULLIVAN, JOHN T.   Report of Historical and Technical Information Relating to the Problem of Interoceanic Communication by Way of the American Isthmus. Washington: GPO, 1883. 1st edition; tall 4to; 219 pages; 28 maps inserted in text, 5 foldout maps; blue cloth, gilt, near fine.   Freedom Bookshop 14-33 196 $175.00

SULLIVAN, MAURICE S.   The Travels of Jedediah Smith. Santa Ana: Fine Arts Press, 1934. 1st edition; limited; 195 pages, large folding map and plates; original pictorial white cloth, title in gilt on spine, fine. Zamorano 25 note; Howes S1127; Eberstadt Modern Overlands 441. Michael D. Heaston 23-152 1996 $500.00

SULLIVANT, WILLIAM S.   Icones Muscorum, or Figures and Descriptions of Most of Those Mosses Peculiar to Eastern North America. Cambridge and London: 1864/74. Large 8vo; 2 volumes, including supplement; pages viii, 216; viii, 109; 210 copper engraved plates; 19th century cloth, rebacked retaining original backstrip, endpapers renewed.   Raymond M. Sutton VII-37 1996 $1,150.00

SULLIVANT, WILLIAM S.   The Musci and Hepaticae of the United States East of the Mississippi River. New York: George P. Putnam, 1856. 1st edition; 8vo; 113 pages; 8 plates; original cloth, outer spine cracked, some chipping.   M & S Rare Books 60-480 1996 $275.00

SULLY, MAXIMILLIAN DE BETHUNE, DUC OF 1559-1641   Memoirs of... London: Rivington, 1778. Tall octavo; 5 volumes; frontispieces, full tan polished calf, red and black leather labels, gilt spines, some wear, but attractive set. Lowndes IV 1760.   Hartfield 48-L53 1996 $450.00

SUMMERING in Colorado. Denver: Richards and Co., 1874. Pages 158, (iv), photographic plates; bound in this copy are 14 photographic plates; light wear to original boards, binding tight, interior clean, very good, scarce. Dumont 28-52 1996 $625.00

SUMMERS, MONTAGUE   The Gothic Quest. London: Fortune Press, n.d. One of 910 numbered copies; original cloth, very good with rubbed joints and sunned spine,   Beasley Books 82-148 1996 $125.00

SUMMERS, MONTAGUE   A Popular History of Witchcraft. London: Kegan Paul, Trench, Trubner & Co., Ltd., 1937. 1st edition; 8 black and white plates; original binding, top edge dusty, spine browned, edges slightly spotted, bottom edges of covers rubbed, head and tail of spine slightly bumped, very good in nicked, spotted and dusty, slightly torn and rubbed, price clipped dust jacket browned at spine and edges. Ulysses 39-567 1996 £55.00

SUMMERS, MONTAGUE   Witchcraft and Black Magic. London: Rider & Co. Ltd., n.d. 1946. 1st edition; 16 plates and 8 other illustrations; original binding, top edge dusty, tail of spine and corners slightly bumped, very good in nicked, rubbed and dusty, very slightly creased dust jacket, slightly darkened at spine and edges.   Ulysses 39-568 1996 £55.00

SUMMERSON, JOHN   Georgian London. London: Pleiades Books, 1945. 1st edition; demy 8vo; (xii), (316) pages; plates; bound in smart recent half morocco banded and gilt, marbled sides, some faint spotting, mainly to edges, but attractive copy; neatly inscribed and dated by author on prelim blank.   Ash Rare Books Zenzybyr-87 1996 £85.00

SUMNER, CHARLES   Argument of Charles Sumner, Esq. Against the Constitutionality of Separate Colored Schools, in the Case of Sarah C. Roberts vs. the City of Boston. Before the Supreme Court of Mass. Dec. 4, 1849. Boston: B. F. roberts, 1849. 1st edition; 8vo; 32 pages; removed; stian in lower corner of lst few leaves, otherwise very good. Not in LCP/HSP Afro Amer. Cat. 7 copies in NUC.   M & S Rare Books 60-324 1996 $1,250.00

SUNDAY, WILLIAM   Gah Dah Gwa Stee. Pryor: 1953. 1st edition; 172 pages; photos, cloth; very scarce; long inscription by author. 6 Guns 2166; Herd 2203.   T. A. Swinford 49-1127 1996 $175.00

SUNSET COPPER MINING CO.   Prospectus of the Sunset Copper Mining Company of Everett, Washington. New York: Press of Harles & Wright, ca. 1900. 1st edition; 14, (1) pages; original printed blue wrappers, chipped with minor staining; very good. Not in Smith or Soliday Sale.   Michael D. Heaston 23-353 1996 $125.00

SUPPRESSION of the Taiping Rebellion in the Departments Around Shanghai. Shanghai: Kelly & Co., 1871. Only edition; 8vo; original printed wrappers, rebacked; inkstains on front wrapper, else very good, in pullout slipcase. Presentation copy, dated Shanghai 1871.   Trebizond 39-87 1996 $350.00

SUPRON, L. F.   Medical and Civil Defense in Total War. Jerusalem: 1961. 1st English translation; 406 pages; original binding, scarce.   W. Bruce Fye 71-2070 1996 $150.00

SURTEES, ROBERT SMITH 1803-1864   "Ask Mamma". London: Bradbury & Evans, 1857-58. 1st edition; 1st issue; 8vo; in original 13 monthly parts; 13 hand colored engraved plates and 69 wood engravings, with all wrappers, slips and ads, except for 4 page Ask Mamma Advertiser in Part XIII; original brick red pictorial wrappers by Leech (backstrips of some parts skilfully repaired, very small repair to punctures in upper wrapper of Part 1, some slight offsetting from plates, otherwise fine, preserved in modern cloth foldover drop back case. Tooley 472.   Thomas Thorp 489-296 1996 £1,200.00

SURTEES, ROBERT SMITH 1803-1864   The Horseman's Manual. London: Alfred Miller, 1831. 1st edition; 12mo; contemporary maroon morocco, gilt, spine gilt, all edges gilt, in the manner of T. Gosden, light rubbing, in half red morocco slipcase; fine; author's rare first book; early armorial bookplate of Henry Ralph Lambton who was no doubt related to book's dedicatee, Ralph John Lambton of Durham; later bookplate of George Gordon Massey. Mellon Collection 141; CBEL III 967.   Ximenes 108-333 1996 $1,250.00

SURTEES, ROBERT SMITH 1803-1864   Mr. Sponge's Sporting Tour. London: Bradbury & Evans, 1860. 1st edition; 8vo; 408 pages; hand colored plates by John Leech; contemporary half morocco and marbled boards, ornately gilt tooled spine, top edge gilt, binding lightly rubbed, but very attractive.   Chapel Hill 94-398 1996 $200.00

SURTEES, ROBERT SMITH 1803-1864   "Plain or Ringlets?" London: 1860. 1st edition in book form; viii pages, 1 f., 406 pages, 13 colored plates; illustrations by John Leech; full red morocco, gilt, decorations of hounds, foxes, etc., inner wide dentelles, top edge gilt; laid in is 2 page ALS from Leech to Mrs. Mclan (?); fine copy but outer joints beginning to weaken.   Jens J. Christoffersen SL94-191 1996 $185.00

SURTEES, ROBERT SMITH 1803-1864   Selected Works, Including: Ask Mamma; Plain or Ringlets; Hawbuck Grange; Mr. Sponge's Sporting Tour; Mr. Romford's Hounds; and Handley Cross. London: Bradbury, Agnew & Co., n.d. Subscriber's Edition; 8vo; 6 volumes; numerous hand colored plates, text illustrations; red cloth with gilt and black stamped designs, spines lightly faded, else nice, bright set.   James Cummins 14-201 1996 $450.00

SURTEES, ROBERT SMITH 1803-1864   Sporting Novels. London: ca. 1890's. Jorrocks Edition; 8vo; 5 volumes; half red morocco, gilt lettered, raised bands, gilt lined panels with gilt motifs of horses heads, fox, hound, etc., top edge gilt, colored and other illustrations; very good. K Books 441-477 1996 £200.00

SURTEES, VIRGINIA   Dante Gabriel Rossetti 1828-1882. The Paintings and Drawings. A Catalogue Raisonne. Oxford: Clarendon Press, 1971. 30 x 22.5 cm; xvi, 267 pages; x, 504 black and white plates; original cloth, dust jacket (rubber stamp on titlepages), ex-library.   Rainsford A54-503 1996 £475.00

SUSSEX ARCHAEOLOGICAL SOCIETY   Sussex Archaeological Collections. London: 1848-1980. 8vo; volumes 1-118 (lacking volumes 2 and 4) and 4 index volumes, together 120 volumes, plates and illustrations; original cloth, 5 volumes in original wrappers, some dampstaining of sides of about 20 early volumes, not affecting text, spine of 2 other volumes slightly worn, one volume rebacked.   Howes Bookshop 265-2259 1996 £500.00

SUSSEX ARCHAEOLOGICAL SOCIETY   Sussex Archaeological Collections. London: 1954-92. 8vo; volumes 92-130, plates and illustrations; original wrappers.   Howes Bookshop 265-2260 1996 £125.00

SUTCLIFF, ROBERT   Travels in Some Parts of North America, in the Years 1804, 1805 and 1806. York: Peacock for Alexander, 1811. 1st edition; 8vo; frontispiece, 5 full page plates; calf, rebacked. Rostenberg & Stern 150-11 1996 $250.00

SUTHERLAND HARRIS, ANN   Andrea Sacchi. London: Phaidon, 1977. 8vo; 264 pages, including 181 black and white plates, 4 color plates; buckram, dust jacket.   Rainsford A54-512 1996 £110.00

SUTHERLAND, JOHN   Other Canadians. Montreal: First Statement Press, 1946. 1st edition; 112 pages; printed wrappers; near fine; inscribed by author for John Metcalf, with his ownership signature. Very scarce.   Nelson Ball 118-177 1996 $550.00

SUTHERLAND, ROBERT Q.   The Book of Colt Firearms. Kansas City: Published by the author, 1971. 1st edition; large quarto; photos, reproductions, drawings, in addition there are 39 full page color plates; grey cloth with Colt seal and titling in gilt on front cover, fine in like dust jacket.   Glenn Books 36-262 1996 $600.00

SUTRO, ADOLPH   Closing Argument of Adolph Sutro on the Bill Before Congress to Aid the Sutro Tunnel... Washington: McGill, Witherow, Printers, 1872. 1st edition; 96 pages; original pictorial blue cloth over stiff boards with title in gilt on front cover, very minor dampstain to part of text, covers very bright and crisp, fine. Paher Nevada 1923.   Michael D. Heaston 23-258 1996 $125.00

SUTRO, ADOLPH   The Sutro Tunnel to the Comstock Lode in the State of Nevada. New York: John A. Gray and Green, 1866. 1st edition; 31 pages, folding map; map finely colored and quite crisp; original printed green glazed wrappers, minor soiling; very good. Paher Nevada 1927.   Michael D. Heaston 23-260 1996 $750.00

SUTTER, BARTON   Cedarhome. Bockport: Boa Editions, 1977. 1st edition; limited to 26 lettered copies, signed by author and W. D. Snodgrass who provided introduction; thin 8vo; cloth, marbled endpapers; fine.   James S. Jaffe 34-624 1996 $125.00

SUTTON, G.   The Life and Writings of Menlove Edwards. London: 1961. 1st edition; 8 plates; bookplates of the Rucksack and Manchester Central Library; very good+, very scarce, issued without dust jacket. Moutaineering Books 8-RS01 1996 £70.00

SUTTON, RICHARD L.   An Africa Holiday. St. Louis: The C. V. Mosby Co., 1924. 1st edition; front endpapers lightly soiled, two small stains to front cover, otherwise very good, warmly inscribed by Sutton. Hermitage SP95-892 1996 $100.00

SUTTON, RICHARD L.   An African Holiday. USA: 1924. illustrations; near fine.   David Grayling J95Biggame-196 1996 £60.00

SVEVO, ITALO   Confessions of Zeno. London: & New York: Putnam, 1930. 1st English edition; marbled cloth covered boards in spine darkened, near fine dust jacket, which has no chips or tears; very scarce; fine.   Thomas Dorn 9-242 1996 $400.00

SVOBODA, ANTONIN   Computing Mechanisms and Linkages. New York: McGraw Hill, 1948. 1st edition; 8vo; xii, 359 pages; illustrations, folding nomogram in back cover sleeve; original cloth, few spots on covers, but very good.   Edwin V. Glaser 121-304 1996 $200.00

SWAN, JOHN   Explanation of an Improved Mode of Tanning; Laid Down from Practical Results... London: printed for the author, and to be had only of him, 1821. 1st edition; 8vo; iv, (iii), 6-143, (1) pages; frontispiece (lightly offset onto title); contemporary tree patterned sheep, neatly rebacked, corners rubbed; rare; not in NUC.   James Burmester 29-132 1996 £180.00

SWAN, JOHN A.   A Trio to the Gold Miner of California in 1882. San Francisco: 1960. 1st edition; limited to 400 copies; illustrations; quarter leather, boards; fine, very scarce.   T. A. Swinford 49-1128 1996 $100.00

SWANN, H. K.   A Monograph of the Birds of Prey: Accipitres. London: 1924-45. Limited to 412 copies; 4to; 2 volumes; 39 colored plates, 17 photogravure plates; half red morocco; some very slight foxing here and there; anthropomorphic ownership stamp.   Wheldon & Wesley 207-106 1996 £750.00

SWANN, THOMAS BURNETT   Alas, in Lilliput. Worcester: 1964. Limited to 500 copies; 2 3/8 x 1 3/4 inches; 61 pages; elegantly printed in spectrum type; gilt stamped blue leather, all edges gilt; very fine. Bromer Booksellers 87-223 1996 $135.00

SWANSON, VERN G.   The Biography and Catalogue Raisonne of the Paintings of Sir Lawrence Alma-Tadema. London: Garton & Co., 1990. 1s edition; 536 pages; 436 plates in color and black and white; fine in publisher's slipcse.   Hermitage SP95-819 1996 $300.00

SWANWICK, MICHAEL   Stations of the Tide. New York: Morrow, 1991. Uncorrected proof; blue printed wrappers, slight spine curl from obviously being read, else fine.   Robert Gavora 61-216 1996 $125.00

SWARBRECK, S. D.   Sketches in Scotland Drawn from Nature and On Stone. London: C. Hullmandel, 1845. Large folio; lithograph title and 25 fine tinted lithograph views, as is usual, a little foxing in margins; contemporary diced cloth, red morocco spine. Abbey Scenery 492 for 1839 ed.   Charles W. Traylen 117-373 1996 £800.00

SWARBRICK, JOHN   Robert Adam and His Brothers: Their Lives, Wor and Influence on English Architecture, Decoration and Furniture. London: B. T. Batsford, 1915. 1st edition; 4to; 8 page list of subscrbers, x, 316 pages; 224 illustrations; cloth, gilt, two very small nail holes on back cover, otherwise very good.   Thomas Thorp 489-297 1996 £85.00

SWAYNE, H. G. C.   Through the Highlands of Siberia. 1904. 60 illustrations; folding map; near fine, with just very light marks to covers; scarce.   David Grayling J95Biggame-587 1996 £300.00

SWEDENBORG, EMANUEL   A Treatise on the Nature of Influx, or, of the Intercourse Between the Soul and Body, Which is Supposed to be Either by Physical Influx, or by spiritual Influx or by Pre-Established Harmony. Boston: I. Thomas and E. T. Andrews, 1794. 1st American edition; 12mo; pages xxviii, (29), 174; contemporary boards, front cover loose, but holding, spine worn; minor foxing, light dampstain on first few leaves; Evans 27765.   Howard S. Mott 227-138 1996 $125.00

SWEDENBORG, EMANUEL   Swedenborg's Works. London: Houghton Mifflin Co., n.d., ca. 1930. Rotch edition; small 8vo; 32 volumes, blue cloth, gilt, top edge gilt. Scarce set.   Kenneth Karmiole 1NS-228 199 $500.00

SWEDIAUR, FRANCOIS XAVIER 1748-1824   Practical Observations on Venereal Complaints. New York: Samuel Campbell, 1788. 1st American edition; 8vo; (iv), 128 pages; contemporary sheep, paper browned, as usual, binding lightly worn, but overall a desirable copy in contemporary binding. Austin 1841.   The Bookpress 75-468 1996 $650.00

SWEENEY, THOMAS W.   Military Occupation of California 1849-1853. Washington: 1907. One of 25 copies separately printed; 47 pages, frontispiece, map and illustrations; original printed grey wrappers, laid in folding slipcase; fine. Graff 4048; Cowan p. 627; Howes S1172; not in Tutorow.   Michael D. Heaston 23-26 1996 $750.00

SWIFT, GRAHAM   Waterland. London: Heinemann, 1983. 1st edition; fine in dust jacket.   Lame Duck Books 19-513 1996 $350.00

SWIFT, JONATHAN 1667-1745   The Conduct of the Allies and of the Late Ministry in Beginning and Carrying on the Present War, London: John Morphew, 1711. 5th edition, same year as first; small 8vo; pages 48; recent marbled wrappers, paper label, cropped but with no loss of text, nice; Teerink 539; Rothschild 2025.   Hartfield 48-L83 1996 $295.00

SWIFT, JONATHAN 1667-1745   Capitain Lemuel Gullivers Resor, Til Atskillige Langt Borte Balagna Land... Wasteras: Joh. Laur. Horn, 1772. 2nd edition in Swedish; 8vo; 2 parts in 1 volume, with separate titlepages, 4 fine copperplate engravings;, ad leaf, 3 pages ads; original blue stiff wrappers, uncut. Scarce. Front hinges carefully repaired, fine. Trebizond 39-51 1996 $450.00

SWIFT, JONATHAN 1667-1745   Gulliver's Travels. London: printed for J. Johnson et al, 1803. New edition; 160 x 96 mm; contemporary tree calf, boards, spine titled and compartmented in gilt; sines slightly cracked and scraped, else very good.   Marjorie James 19-204 1996 £125.00

SWIFT, JONATHAN 1667-1745　　Gulliver's Travels into Several Remote Nations of the World. London: Dent/New York: Dutton, 1909. 2nd Rackham edition, 230/750 copies; imperial 8vo; pages xv, 291; printed on large paper and signed by the artist, 13 color printed plates (that for the frontispiece with foxed tissue guard), each tipped to fawn card backing, 2 full page illustrations, several other text illustrations, all by Arthur Rackham, titlepage printed in green, 2 pages little spotted at tail; original white buckram, lettering on backstrip and front cover and design on front cover all gilt blocked, covers with patina of soiling and with some faint staining to rear cover, four silk ties, one lacking, blue and white marbled endpapers with Rackham design of elves blocked in gilt, bookplate, top edge gilt, others untrimmed. Riall p. 91.　　Blackwell's B112-238　1996　£600.00

SWIFT, JONATHAN 1667-1745　　The Hibernian Patriot: Being a Collection of the Drapier's Letters to the People of Ireland... London: reprinted and sold by A. Moor, 1730. 1st London edition; 8vo; pages (iv), 264; titlepage browned, ink shelfmark at head, contemporary brown calf, rebacked with raised bands between gilt rules, black leather label, sides darkened and rubbed, corners worn, hinges split, but very sound. Rothschild 2095; Teerinck 22.　　Blackwell's　B112-266　1996　£300.00

SWIFT, JONATHAN 1667-1745　　The Lady's Dressing Room. London: for J. Roberts, 1732. 1st edition; 4to; pages 19, l), quite closely trimmed (by approx. 20 mm. all round from the untrimmed size), just touching one page numeral at head, skilfully washed and resized, superbly rebound in full old style speckled calf. Teerink 720; Rothschild 2132.　　Simon Finch　24-219　1996　£7,500.00

SWIFT, JONATHAN 1667-1745　　The Life and Genuine Character of Doctor Swift. London: printed for J. Roberts, 1733. 1st edition; folio; later stiff wrappers, in cloth slipcase. fine copy, outer edges uncut, fine. Foxon S884; Teerink 727; Rothschild 2143.　　Ximenes　109-276　1996　$900.00

SWIFT, JONATHAN 1667-1745　　The Life and Genuine Character of Doctor Swift. London: for Roberts and sold at the Pamphlet Shops, 1733. 1st edition; folio; pages 19; half title; rebound in half brown crushed morocco, title in gilt up spine, marbled sides and endpapers, rubbed, half title lightly browned, creased where once folded in half. Teerink 727; Rothschild 2143; foxon S884.　　Simon Finch　24-220　1996　£500.00

SWIFT, JONATHAN 1667-1745　　Miscellaneous Poems. Waltham St. Lawrence: Golden Cockerel Press, 1928. Limited to 375 numbered copies; wood engravings by Robert Gibbings; very good in scarce dust jacket with chip on right hand corner and head of spine, with TLS from Robert Gibbings to Brian Roberts.　　Words Etcetera　94-492　1996　£135.00

SWIFT, JONATHAN 1667-1745　　On Poetry; a Rapsody. Printed at Dublin and reprinted at London: sold by J.. Huggonson, 1733. 1st edition; folio; disbound, cloth slipcase; Fine, outer edges uncut; Foxon S888; Teerink 741; Hayward 153; Rothschild 2147.　　Ximenes　109-277　1996　$750.00

SWIFT, JONATHAN 1667-1745　　The Poetical Works. London: William Pickering, 1853. 6 1/2 x 4 1/2 inches; 3 volumes; frontispiece of author in volume 1, vignette on title of each volume; frontispiece in volume 1, vignette on title of each volume; attractive contemporary apple green pebble grain morocco, handsomely gilt, covers framed with two gilt rules, elegant central panel twined with gilt floral vines, raised bands, spine compartments with delicate centered flower and leafy corner decorations, floral decorations on board edges and turn-ins, marbled endpapers, all edges gilt, spines slightly and evenly faded to pleasing olive green, just a hint of wear and soiling to leather, but bindings nevertheless very pretty and very well preserved, with no significant wear, not infrequent modest foxing, one or two minor stains, but fresh and smooth and generally excellent internally; extremely appleing set. Keynes p. 38.　　Phillip J. Pirages　33-423　1996　$225.00

SWIFT, JONATHAN 1667-1745　　A Proposal Humbly Offered to the P--------t, for the Most Effectual Preventing the Further Growth of Popery. Dublin: printed: London: re-printed for J. Roberts, 1731. 1st London edition; 8vo; half morocco; fine, very scarce. Teerink 37; Rothschild 2127; Williams pp. 572-4 and 575-6.　　Ximenes　109-278　1996　$1,500.00

SWIFT, JONATHAN 1667-1745　　Prose Works. Oxford: printed at the Shakespeare Head Press, 1939-68. 8vo; 14 volumes; frontispieces, plates; original green cloth, some backstrips faded as usual, top edge gilt, others untrimmed, dust jackets to volumes v and xiv; excellent. Blackwell's　B112-267　1996　£350.00

SWIFT, JONATHAN 1667-1745　　A Tale of a Tub. N.P.: 1711. Early edition; small 12mo; old calf, spine fairly dry, joints partly split but tight, quite good. Teerink 226.　　Charles Agvent　4-1075　1996　$125.00

SWIFT, JONATHAN 1667-1745　　Travels into Several Remote Nations of the World... London: B. Motte, 1726. Teerink's B (3rd) edition; 8vo; 2 volumes; 2 plans and 4 maps; contemporary gilt ruled calf, morocco gilt labels, small piece of leather lacking from front panel of volume 2, minor wear to spine tips, rebacked, occasional foxing, name inked out on titlepages, very good.　　Charles Agvent　4-1076　1996　$3,500.00

SWIFT, JONATHAN 1667-1745　　Travels into Several Remote Nations of the World, in Four Parts. London: for Benj. Motte, 1727. 8vo; 2 volumes, pages (xxiv), xii, 148, (vi), 164; (i) blank, (vii), 155, (i), blank, (viii), 199; engraved frontispiece (third state), 4 maps, 2 plans; contemporary tan half calf, spines lettered and numbered in gilt, marbled sides, bookplates, rubbed, some restoration to spines, occasional spot or mark, maps and plans very lightly browned, very good. Teerink 293.　　Simon Finch　24-218　1996　£600.00

SWIFT, JONATHAN 1667-1745　　Travels into Several Remote Nations of the World. Waltham St. Lawrence: Golden Cockerel Press, 1925. One of 450 numbered copies; small 4to; 2 volumes; printed on Antique deluxe paper; 40 wood engravings by David Jones, many hand colored; half white buckram, black paper sides, buckram slightly soiled, sides little scuffed (less so that many copies), internally nice, fresh copy. Bookplates.　　Bertram Rota　272-166　1996　£700.00

SWIFT, JONATHAN 1667-1745　　Verses on the Death of Doctor Swift. Written by Himself: Nov. 1731. London: for C. Bathurst, 1739. 1st edition; folio; (ii), 18, half title not called for; modern half brown morocco, marbled sides; good, clean copy.　　Simon Finch　24-221　1996　£400.00

SWIFT, JONATHAN 1667-1745　　A Voyage to Lilliput and a Voyage to Brobdingnag Made by Lemuel Gulliver. New York: Limited Editions Club, 1950. Limited to 1500 copies, signed by designer, Bruce Rogers; 18 1/2 x 13 1/2 inches and 3 1/2 x 2 1/2 inches; 2 volumes; printed in red and black; half red linen, slipcased in one box; near fine in slipcase. Charles Agvent　4-1077　1996　$350.00

SWIFT, JONATHAN 1667-1745　　The Works of Dr. Jonathan Swift, Dean of St. Patrick's, Dublin...(with) Letters Written by the Late Jonathan Swift...(and) The Life of the Rev. Dr. Jonathan Swift... London: printed for W. Bowyer et al, 1768-79/87. Mixed issues; 8vo; 26 volumes; half antique style autumn leaf calf with marbled combed cloth sides, spines decorated with gilt, 8 pointed stars containing flower petals in reverse, crimson and black morocco spine labels, gilt with lettering and floriated acorn patterns by Morrell, apart from some very minor shelf wear, a fine and beautiful set.　　James Cummins　14-202　1996　$3,000.00

SWIFT, JONATHAN 1667-1745　　Works. London: Johnson et al, 1803. New edition; 12mo; 24 volumes; half black calf, marbled boards, frontispiece, most gilt rubbed away, handful of leather labels remain, some edgewear, rubbed; very good.　　Charles Agvent　4-1079　1996　$325.00

SWINBURNE, ALGERNON CHARLES 1837-1909　　Chastelard: a Tragedy. London: Moxon, 1865. 1st edition; 12mo; 219 pages, plus 16 pages ads; contemporary full violet morocco, gracefully gilt tooled with flowering vines and areas of dense stippling, spine and turn-ins similary gilt, spine in 5 compartments with four raised bands, spine slightly faded, still very fine. Handsome binding.　　Bromer Booksellers　87-265　1996　$750.00

SWINBURNE, ALGERNON CHARLES 1837-1909　　Hide-and-Seek. London: Stourton Press, 1975. 1st edition; number 84 of 250 copies; small folio; printed on Batchelor's Kelmscott handmade paper, 16 pages, printed in Gill's Aries type in black and sepia within blue borders, original half leather, cloth sides; very good.　　Claude Cox　107-161　1996　£55.00

SWINBURNE, ALGERNON CHARLES 1837-1909　　Hymn to Proserpine. Waltham St. Lawrence: Golden Cockerel Press, 1944. Limited to 350 numbered copies; small 4to; 10 pages; pictorial titlepage, 6 wood engraved illustrations by J. Buckland-Wright; original buckram, green morocco label, edges uncut, spine very slightly faded.　　Thomas Thorp　489-298　1996　£65.00

SWINBURNE, ALGERNON CHARLES 1837-1909　　Laus Veneris. Waltham St. Lawrence: Golden Cockerel Press, 1948. One of 750 numbered copies; 8vo; printed in 14 pt. Perpetua; marbled boards with cloth spine, spine little faded and edges of leaves trifle discolored as usual, but nice. Bertram Rota　272-185　1996　£75.00

SWINBURNE, ALGERNON CHARLES 1837-1909　　Laus Veneris. Waltham St. Lawrence: Golden Cockerel Press, 1948. Limited edition, 703/650 copies (of an edition of 750); 8vo; pages 28, (1), printed on mouldmade paper, 4 full page wood engravings, 6 further engravings, all by John Buckland Wright; original quarter maroon cloth, gilt lettered backstrip lightly faded, red marbled boards, top edge gilt, others untrimmed. Cockalorum 178.　　Blackwell's　B112-130　1996　£60.00

SWINBURNE, ALGERNON CHARLES 1837-1909   The Letters of Algernon Charles Swinburne. New York: John Lane Co., 1919. 1st edition; 2 volumes; original binding, top edges dusty, spines darkened, covers slightly marked, cover edges slightly faded, heads and tails of spines and corners bumped, very good; with pencilled ownership signatures of Frederick Pottle.   Ulysses 39-715 1996 £60.00

SWINBURNE, ALGERNON CHARLES 1837-1909   Locrine a Tragedy. London: Chatto & Windus, 1887. 1st edition; 8vo; pages viii, 138, (ii), 32 pages ads; uncut in original dark blue-green cloth, spine gilt lettered, sides ruled in gilt, upper part of upper joint and lower part of lower joint just beginning to split, but very good, preserved in quarter green morocco folding case; presentation copy to Burne-Jones, with inscription in author's hand. Ashley VI p. 171.   Simon Finch 24-223 1996 £2,250.00

SWINBURNE, ALGERNON CHARLES 1837-1909   Miscellanies. London: Chatto & Windus, 1886. 1st edition; 8vo; 32 page publisher's ads at back dated March 1886; CC4 with stylized floral decoration not blank as stated in Tinker; original green cloth, gilt ruled and lettered, publisher's design in gilt at lower spine, some darkening, and rubbing; some browning and spotting, generally at front and back; good copy. Poet Lionel Johnson's copy with his signature; Willis Vickery's copy with bookplate. Tinker 2030; Wise 'Swinburne' I.80, 2.124-5.   James Cummins 14-203 1995 $350.00

SWINBURNE, ALGERNON CHARLES 1837-1909   A Note on Charlotte Bronte. London: Chatto & Windus, 1877. 1st edition; later issue; 7 1/2 x 5 inches; pages vi, 97, 32 pages publisher's ads dated Oct. 1883. dark green cloth, gilt titling backstrip, uncut, pale blue and grey floral patterned endpapers, uncut, very good, bookplate of Lord Battersea, slight foxing to prelims and edges of pages; very good. Wise 64, Wise pp. 71/72.   Ian Hodgkins 78-379 1996 £75.00

SWINBURNE, ALGERNON CHARLES 1837-1909   Pasiphae. Waltham St. Lawrence: Golden Cockerel Press, 1950. Limited to 500 numbered copies, of which this is one of 100 speciallly bound and with an extra illustration; 8vo; 40 pages; copper engraved frontispiece, pictorial titlepage and 5 other illustrations; publisher's wine colored vellum, top edge gilt, others uncut, by Sangorski & Sutcliffe, with original slipcase. Cock-a-Hoop 185.   Thomas Thorp 489-299 1996 £385.00

SWINBURNE, ALGERNON CHARLES 1837-1909   Pasiphae; a Poem. Waltham St. Lawrence: Golden Cockerel Press, 1950. One of 500 numbered copies; 8vo; blue and yellow buckram, pictorial design in gilt on upper cover, spine little faded and edges of leaves somewhat discolored as usual, but nice.   Bertram Rota 272-187 1996 £90.00

SWINBURNE, ALGERNON CHARLES 1837-1909   Poems and Ballads. London: Chatto & Windus, 1908. Pages x, 338; handsome contemporary binding in art nouveau style, full crimson morocco ruled and decorated in gold with plant device of five leaves on curving interwoven stems with dot background in corners of sides and reworked in smaller scale on four panels of backstrip and inner corners of turn-ins, upper cover slightly darkened but very good, attractive binding, all edges gilt, for Bumpus, probably by Sangorski & Sutcliffe.   Claude Cox 107-18 1996 £75.00

SWINBURNE, ALGERNON CHARLES 1837-1909   The Queen Mother. (and) Rosamund. London: Basil Montagu Pickering, 1860. 1st edition; 1st issue, one of fewer than 20 copies; 7 x 4 1/2 inches; 5 p.l., 160 pages, (1) leaf, (161)-217, (1) pages, (1) leaf, including half titles and errata leaf at end; extremely fine crimson crushed morocco, heavily gilt by Riviere, covers with frame of five plain and decorative rules enclosing lovely broad filigree border of closely spaced elaborate fleurons, spine handsomely gilt in compartments filled with floral and foliate stamps, especially pretty inner gilt dentelles, top edge gilt, other edges untrimmed, slipcase, faint soiling here and there in text, otherwise very fine in splendid and pristine binding; Wise 2.   Phillip J. Pirages 33-476 1996 $1,250.00

SWINBURNE, ALGERNON CHARLES 1837-1909   Songs Before Sunrise. London: Chatto & Windus for the Florence Press, 1909. Limited to 662 copies, this being number 3 of 12 copies on vellum; 4to; pages ix, (i0, 209, (ii), initials printed in red; original limp vellum, spine and upper cover lettered in gilt, silk ties, top edge gilt, others uncut, bookplate, excellent copy.   Simon Finch 24-88 1996 £725.00

SWINBURNE, ALGERNON CHARLES 1837-1909   The Springtide of Life: Poems of Childhood. London: 1918. 1st edition thus; color plates by Arthur Rackham; cloth, gilt, one gathering weak, top edge of spine rubbed and little frayed, otherwise very good.   Words Etcetera 94-1057 1996 £125.00

SWINBURNE, ALGERNON CHARLES 1837-1909   The Springtide of Life. Garden City: Doubleday, Page & Co., 1926. 4to; ix, (i), 132, (ii) pages; pictorial endpapers, title vignettes printed in green, black and white vignettes and head and tailpieces, 8 color plates by Arthur Rackham; green cloth titled in gilt in cream dust jacket, soiled, tiny tears at edges, titled with vignettes in green. Fine in very good dust jacket.   Blue Mountain SP95-79 1996 $150.00

SWINBURNE, ALGERNON CHARLES 1837-1909   The Tragedies. London: Chatto & Windus, 1905-06. 1st collected edition, one of 110 large paper copies; 9 x 6 inches; 5 volumes; photogravure frontispiece in final volume, titles printed in red and black; large paper copies, especially fine contemporary burgundy crushed morocco by Bumpus, covers and board edges with double gilt rule, spines very attractively and densely gilt in compartments filled with massed stippled volutes enclosing quatrefoil at center, elegant inner gilt dentelles, top edge gilt, other edges rough trimmed, entirely unopened; beautifully bound in splendid condition.   Phillip J. Pirages 33-478 1996 $1,500.00

SWINDLER, MARY HAMILTON   Ancient Painting. New Haven: Yale University Press, 1929. Thick 8vo; xiv, 488 pages; map, 15 plates, some color, 640 illustrations; buckram. Chamberlin 1206.   Rainsford A54-547 1996 £85.00

SWINDLER, MARY HAMILTON   Ancient Painting from the Earliest Times to the Period of Christian Art. New Haven: Yale University Press, 1929. 4to; xlv, 488 pages; map, 15 plates, 640 other illustrations; decorated cloth.   Thomas Thorp 489-300 1996 £65.00

SWISHER, JAMES   How I Know Or Sixteen Years Eventful Experience. Cincinnati: 1881. 384 pages; plates, illustrations; pictorial cloth, nice; scarce in any printing.   T. A. Swinford 49-1131 1996 $125.00

THE SWORN Book of Honorius the Magician.. Heptangle: 1977. Limited edition of 450 numbered copies, this being no.351 of 450, signed; xxiii, 111 pages; beautifully bound, fine, in very good dust jacket.   Middle Earth 77-262 1996 $195.00

SWYNNERTON, C. F. M.   The Tsetse Flies of East Africa. London: 1936. 616 pages, 22 photo plates, 7 maps; original wrappers, protected with brown paper; scarce.   David Grayling J95Biggame-197 1996 £70.00

SYDENHAM, THOMAS 1624-1689   Opera Medica; in Hae Novissima Editione Variis Variorum Praestantissimorum Medicorum Observation-ibus... Venice: Ex Typographia Remondiniana, 1762. Folio; xvi, 438 pages; one folding plate, title printed in red and black; lacking frontispiece; contemporary calf, gilt spine, somewhat worn.   Kenneth Karmiole 1NS-183 1996 $175.00

SYDENHAM, THOMAS 1624-1689   The Works of Thomas Sydenham, M.D., on Acute and Chronic Diseases. Philadelphia: 1809. 8vo; 473 pages, contemporary sheep, worn, covers detached. Austin 1845.   Argosy 810-470 1996 $150.00

SYDENHAM, THOMAS 1624-1689   Works... London: for the Sydenham Society, 1848-50. 1st edition thus; 8vo; 2 volumes, cvi, 276; vii, 395 pages; original cloth, volume one rebacked, original spine laid down, volume 2 spine extremities rubbed, occasional marginal annotations in pencil; good set. GM 64.   Edwin V. Glaser B122-138 1996 $225.00

SYDENHAM, THOMAS 1624-1689   The Works. London: Sydenham Soc., 1848-50. Translated from the Latin edition of Dr. Greenhill; 8vo; 2 volumes; green cloth, by Westley's, with their tickets, bit scuffed. GM 64.   Maggs Bros. Ltd. 1190-175 1996 £75.00

SYDENHAM, THOMAS 1624-1689   The Works of... London: Sydenham Soc., 1848-50. 8vo; 2 volumes; rebound in library buckram, ex-library but not an abused set. GM 64.   James Tait Goodrich K40-279 1996 $125.00

SYDNEY, ALGERNON   Discourses Concerning Government...with His Letters Trial Apology and Some Memoirs of His Life... London: A. Millar, 1763. 4to; (v), 46, (vii), 497, (i), 198 pages; frontispiece, contemporary red goatskin, single gilt rule, Hollis's cockerel device on front board and feather on lower board, spine in five compartments, morocco label on one, owl device on others, good copy, inscription from Thomas Hollis to Paul Celesia Genoese.   Robert Clark 38-207 1996 £600.00

SYDNEY, ALGERNON   Discourses Concerning Government. London: A. Miller, 1763. 4th edition; 497 pages; frontispiece; contemporary full calf, covers worn, joints broken, occasional foxing, thus good copy only, but clean internally.   Chapel Hill 94-229 1996 $125.00

SYDNEY, PHILIP   Sir Philip Sydney's Defence of Poetry, and Observations on Poetry and Eloquence from the Discoveries of Ben Jonson. London: printed for G. G. J. and J. Robinson and J. Walter, 1787. 1st edition; 8vo; pages iv, 144; early 19th century boards, spine worn.   Howard S. Mott 227-139 1996 $125.00

SYKES, ARTHUR ASHLEY   A Paraphrase and Notes Upon the Epistle to the Hebrews. London: printed for John and Paul Knapton, 19755. 1st edition; 4to; (iv), liv, 253, (ix) pages; original speckled calf, red morocco spine label, slight wear at top of spine, but fine crisp copy.   David Bickersteth 133-63 1996 £85.00

SYLVAN'S Pictorial Handbook to the English Lakes. London: John Johnstone, 1847. 1st edition; 8vo; pages (ii), 248, (iv), 24, engraved vignettes, text woodcuts, tables, maps, large folding map at end; contemporary half calf, gilt, trifle rubbed. Bicknell 139.1.   R.F.G. Hollett & Son 78-1310 1996 £130.00

SYMINGTON, J. ALEXANDER   Some Unpublished Letters of Walter Scott from the Collection in the Brotherton Library. Oxford: Basil Blackwell, 1932. 1st edition; large 8vo; pages xix, 195; uncut, 14 plates, 4 facsimiles; original cloth, gilt, dust jacket, prospectus and compliments slip from (and signed and dated by) the editor, both loosely inserted; fine.   R.F.G. Hollett 76-305 1996 £75.00

SYMMONS, JOHN   Thoughts On the Present Prices of Provisions, Their Causes and Remedies; Addressed to All Ranks of People. London: T. Reynolds, 1800. 1st edition; 8vo; (ii), 87 pages, wanting half title, little foxing at beginning and end; recently well bund in linen backed marbled boards lettered; very good. Kress B4293; Goldsmiths 17990; Black 2283.   John Drury 82-274 1996 £175.00

SYMONDS, B.   A Treatise on Field Diversions. Published in Yarmouth by W. Meggy, Quay, 1825. frontispiece; tastefully rebound in grey boards, spine label, apart from frontispiece being browned, with slight offsetting on title, very good, rare.   David A.H. Grayling 3/95-264 1996 £200.00

SYMONDS, EMILY MORSE d. 1936   B. R. Haydon and His Friends. London: Nisbet & Co. Ltd., 1905. 1st edition; 294 pages; original binding, bookplate, top edge dusty, prelims, edges and endpapers spotted, some sporadic internal spotting, head and tail of spine slightly bumped, covers slightly marked, cover edges rubbed, free endpapers browned, good.   Ulysses 39-277 1996 £65.00

SYMONDS, JOHN ADDINGTON   Anima Figura. London: Smith Elder, 1882. 1st edition; original binding, old catalog description on front pastedown and bookseller sticker on rear, upper corners slightly bumped, near fine.   Charles Agvent 4-1080 1996 $100.00

SYMONDS, JOHN ADDINGTON   The Letters 1844-1893. Wayne State University Press, 1967-69. Thick large 8vo; 3 volumes; 72 plates; pages 867, 1009, 931; original cloth.   Howes Bookshop 265-1189 1996 £85.00

SYMONDS, JOHN ADDINGTON   The Life of Michelangelo Buonarroti, Based on Studies of the Buonarrotti Family at Florence. London: 1893. 2 volumes; etched portrait, 50 reproductions, full brown morocco, richly gilt on spines and sides, inner ornate dentelles, gilt edges by Zaehnsdorf.   Jens J. Christoffersen SL94-83 1996 $225.00

SYMONDS, JOHN ADDINGTON   Our Life in the Swiss Highlands. London: 1892. 1st collected edition; 8vo; portrait, pages x, 366, (6 ads); original green cloth, gilt, very good/nice.   James Fenning 133-329 1996 £65.00

SYMONDS, JOHN ADDINGTON   Renaissance in Italy. London: Smith, elder, 1875-86. 23 x 15 cm; 7 volumes; original cloth, portrait frontispiece (loose) in volume 4.   Rainsford A54-549 1996 £50.00

SYMONDS, JOHN ADDINGTON   Renaissance in Italy. London: Smith, Elder, 1880-86. Demy 8vo; 7 volumes; portrait; bound c. 1900 in quarter niger morocco and buckram, spines gilt lettered, gilt tops, some spine extremities slightly rubbed.   Howes Bookshop 265-1190 1996 £150.00

SYMONS, ALPHONSE JAMES ALBERT   Emin. London: Fleuron, 1928. One of 300 copies; quarter bound in decorated boards, spine bumped and boards slightly rubbed, else excellent; inscribed by author for R. H. Carruthers, also laid in is autograph letter from author to Carruthers.   R. A. Gekoski 19-133 1996 £200.00

SYMONS, ALPHONSE JAMES ALBERT   An Episode in the Life of the Queen of Sheba. London: privately printed, 1929. One of 150 copies; decorated wrappers; half title and last page offset, but nice copy. Inscribed by author for Ralph Carruthers.   R. A. Gekoski 19-135 1996 £175.00

SYMONS, ARTHUR 1865-1945   Charles Baudelaire - a Study. London: Elkin Mathews, 1920. 100 copies, numbered and signed by author; 8 black and white plates, one line drawing reproduced; handmade paper; top edge gilt, pages unopened, original binding, head and tail of spine and corners bumped, spine creased, corners slightly bruised, covers slightly marked and dusty, cover edges browned and slightly spotted, front pastedown glue soiled where bookplate has been removed, free endpapers browned, very good.   Ulysses 39-570 1996 £150.00

SYMONS, ARTHUR 1865-1945   Studies in Strange Souls. London: Charles J. Sawyer, 1929. One of 100 copies on handmade paper, out of a total edition of 360 copies, signed by author, this copy being out of series; Kelmscott handmade paper; 3 black and white reproductions of portraits; buckram covers, top edge gilt, spine and cover edges faded, prelims, edges and endpapers spotted, very good in plain, unprinted dust jacket which is nicked, chipped and dusty, slightly rubbed, spotted and soiled, as well as darkened at spine and edge   Ulysses 39-572 1996 £185.00

SYMONS, ARTHUR 1865-1945   A Study of Walter Pater. London: Charles J. Sawyer, 1932. One of 100 copies, out of a total edition of 460, signed by author and printed on hnamade paper, this copy being out of series; black and white frontispiece, top edge gilt, pages unopened; free endpapers browned and slightly spotted, edges spotted, spine slightly faded, very good in plain, unprinted tissue dust jacket, which is torn, creased and chipped, as well as missing large piece at head of spine and bottom edge of lower panel.   Ulysses 39-573 1996 £185.00

SYMONS, ARTHUR 1865-1945   Thomas Hardy. London: Charles J. Sawyer, 1927. One of 100 copies, out of a total edition of 350 copies, signed by author and printed on handmade paper; black and white photo of Hardy by Alvin Langdon Coburn, signed by him; buckram covers, spine slightly faded, some pages slightly dusty, covers slightly bowed, recto of rear free endpaper partially browned through contact with newspaper cutting, very good.   Ulysses 39-571 1996 £240.00

SYMONS, JULIAN   The Second Man - Poems. London: George Routledge & Sons Ltd., 1943. 1st edition; cloth backed boards, edges spotted, head and tail of spine and corners bumped, endpapers slightly sellotape marked, covers slightly marked, spotted and dusty, very good in nicked, rubbed and dusty, slightly torn, marked, creased dust jacket browned at spine and edges; signed by author.   Ulysses 39-575 1996 £75.00

SYMPSON, SAMUEL   A New Book of Cyphers, More Compleat and Regular than Any Ever Publish'd. London: for John Bowles & Son, n.d. Reissue of a work first published in 1726; pott 4to; engraved throughout, 100 plates; contemporary sprinkled calf, few very minor marks, but very good, from the library of Brent Gration-Maxfield.   Ash Rare Books Zenzybyr-88 1996 £245.00

SYMPSON, SAMUEL   A New Book of Cyphers, More Compleat & Regular Than any Ever Publish'd. London: printed for John Bowles and Son, 1750? Small 4to; engraved titlepage, engraved ad leaf and 100 engraved plates; contemporary unlettered calf, with simple double ruled gilt borders and gilt banded spine, small old stain to titlepage.   Ken Spelman 30-7 1996 £360.00

SYNGE, JOHN MILLINGTON 1871-1909   Deidre of the Sorrows. New York: John Quinn, 1910. 1st American edition; although one of 50 copies (of which 5 were on vellum, Quinn reported that he had destroyed all but five vellum copies and five paper copies, this one of the paper copies, clothbound, paper over boards, very near fine, rare.   Ken Lopez 74-430 1996 $3,500.00

SYNGE, JOHN MILLINGTON 1871-1909   The Works. London: 1910. 1st edition; 4 volumes; buckram, little scratched, fore edges foxed, otherwise very good.   Words Etcetera 94-1202 1996 £50.00

SYRACUSE ORNAMENTAL CO., SYRACUSE, NEW YORK.   Period Carvings. Catalogue K, c. 1923. 13 x 10 inches; (6), 432 pages (no page 59/60); illustrations, original cloth; very good, rubbed edges.   Bohling Book Co. 191-311 1996 $110.00

SYRIACAE Linguae Prima Elementa. Antwerp: ex off. Christophor Plantini, 1572. 1st edition thus; 4to; pages viii, 23, (i), mostly double column, syriac in one, roman and italic in the other, Hebrew beneath; printer's woodcut device on title, light foxing; 18th (?) century quarter sheep, morocco label, marbled boards; good copy. BM STC Dutch p. 195; Adams W 139; Voet 1120.   A. Sokol XXV-94 1996 £950.00

A SYSTEM of Civil and Criminal Law for the District of Columbia and for the Organization of the Courts Therein. Washington: Printed by Duff, Green, 1833. contemporary sheep, very worn and embrowned, usable copy.   Meyer Boswell SL26-63 1996 $125.00

T

T., R.   The Mother the Best Governess. London: John W. Parker, 1839. 1st edition; 4 page catalog; small corner torn from head of title, original dark green cloth wrappers, all edges gilt, slight rubbing at edges. Jarndyce 103-576 1996 £60.00

T., R.   Tenants Law: a Treatise of Great Use, for Tenants and Farmers of All Kinds, and All Other Persons Whatsoever. London: printed for and sold by John Amery, 1674. 3rd edition; 12mo; name on title; contemporary sheep, rubbed, spine defective. Sweet and Maxwell p. 461, 14; Wing T52.   Anthony Laywood 108-19 1996 £225.00

TACITUS, CORNELIUS   The Annales. The Description of Germanie. (with) The End of Nero and Beginning of Galba. London: by Arnold Hatfield for Iohn Norton, 1612. Folio; pages (vi0, 271; (vi), 227, (1) (imprint); 1st title lacks prelim blank, early owner's name on titlepage; 2nd title with single wormhole through last 3 gatherings, lacks final blank; 2 parts bound together in contemporary brown calf, expertly rebacked, corners repaired, most of original backstrip relaid, unlettered, originally with single ornament in centre of each compartment, triple blind fillet border on sides, diamond shaped strapwork gilt ornament in centre, free endpapers renewed with old paper, 18th century owner's name, very good. STC 23646.   Blackwell's B112-268 1996 £200.00

TACITUS, CORNELIUS   De Moribus Germanorum et De Vita Agricolae; ex Editione Gabrielis Brotier ad Alteram Joh. Aug. Ernesti Collata. Londini: 1788. 8vo; pages (4), 39, (3), 48, (2); well printed on thick Whatman paper; contemporary straight grain crimson morocco, ruled and lettered in gold with simple wavy leaf roll on inner borders, marbled endpapers, all edges gilt; original ownership mark of 'J. Davies 1790' with (?his) pencilled notes on 20 pages. Lowndes p. 2567.   Claude Cox 107-165 1996 £100.00

TACITUS, CORNELIUS   De Vita Moribus Iulii Agricolae Liber. Hammersmith: Doves Press, 1900. One of 225 copies; small 4to; 33 pages; bound at the Doves Bindery in full flexible vellum, very slightly dusty, very nice.   Hermitage SP95-869 1996 $1,000.00

TACITUS, CORNELIUS   The Works of Cornelius Tacitus. London: Stockdale, 1805. New edition; tall octavo; 8 volumes, folding maps in volumes I, III, V and VII; original publisher's boards, spines renewed, printed paper labels, entirely uncut; handsome early set. Lowndes IV 1768; CBEL II 768.   Hartfield 48-A13 1996 $495.00

TACOMA. CHAMBER OF COMMERCE   Tacoma Illustrated. Chicago: Baldwin, Calcutt & Co., 1889. 1st edition; 97, (1) pages; frontispiece, illustrations, plates, maps and portraits; original green cloth over boards, title stamped in gold on front cover, some bumping and wear, very good. Not in Soliday or Smith.   Michael D. Heaston 23-356 1996 $300.00

TACQUET, ANDREAS   Arithmeticae Theory et Praxis. Antwerp: J. Meurs, 1682. 12mo; *8), 38, (4) pages; folding engraved plates; contemporary calf, very good. De Backer Sommervogel VII 1810 no. 6; Jeffrey Mancevice 20-80 1996 $550.00

TAGORE, SOURINDRO MOHUN   Victoria Samrajyan, or Sanskrit Stanzas (with a translation) on the Various Dependencies of the British Crown, Each Composed and Set to the Respective National Music, in Commemoration of the Assumption by Her Most Gracious Majesty the Queen Victoria... Calcutta: printed by I. C. Bose & Co., at the Stanhope Press... 1876. 1st edition; 8vo; contemporary full green morocco, covers elaborately decorated in gilt, spine and inner dentelles, gilt, all edges gilt; very fine in pretty Indian binding. 2 copies in NUC.   Ximenes 109-280 1996 $375.00

TAHSIN AL-DIN   The Loves of Camarupa and Camalta, an Ancient Indian Tale. London: printed for T. Cadell, 1793. 1st edition in English; 8vo; contemporary mottled calf, gilt, neatly rebacked, spine gilt; nice copy of a scarce book, complete with half title. Block p. 78.   Ximenes 108-334 1996 $650.00

TAILLANDIER, YVON   Indelible Miro. New York: Tudor Pub. Co., 1972. 1st edition; 115 reproductions of Miro's aquatints, drypoints, drawings, etchings and illustrations and with 2 original lithgoraphs pulled by hand for this publication; fine in near fine dust jacket. Publisher's slipcase. Hermitage SP95-798 1996 $200.00

TAINE, JOHN   Before the Dawn. Williams and Wilkins, 1934. 1st edition; tiny nick at head of spine, else fine in attractive dust jacket with several small chips.   Aronovitz 57-1155 1996 $125.00

TAINE, JOHN   The Forbidden Garden. Reading: Fantasy Press, 1947. 1st edition; one of 500 numbered copies, inscribed by author; light offsetting to endpapers and light foxing along upper paper edges, else fine in dust jacket, light edge wear.   Robert Gavora 61-218 1996 $150.00

TAINE, JOHN   G.O.G. 666. Reading: Fantasy Press, 1954. 1st edition; one of 300 numbered copies, signed by author; lightly foxing along upper edge, rear cover slightly scuffed, else fine in dust jacket showing some wear at corners and spine panel ends.   Robert Gavora 61-220 1996 $125.00

TAINE, JOHN   Quayle's Invention. New York: Dutton, 1927. 1st edition; 3 tiny punctures to spine, else bright tight, very good/very good+ copy in rear very good dust jacket with some wear and tear and chipping and fading to dust jacket spine, uncommon dust jacket.   Aronovitz 57-1153 1996 $195.00

TAINE, JOHN   Seeds of Life. Reading: Fantasy Press, 1951. 1st edition; one of 300 numbered copies, signed by author; near very fine in dust jacket with quarter inch closed tear.   Robert Gavora 61-221 1996 $175.00

TAINE, JOHN   The Time Stream. Buffalo Book Co., 1946. 1st edition; very good+ in like dust jacket; inscription by author.   Aronovitz 57-1156 1996 $125.00

TAKHTAJAN, A.   Floristic Regions of the World. London: 1986. 8vo; 4 maps, pages 548; cloth.   Wheldon & Wesley 207-1454 1996 £62.00

TALBOT, EDITH ARMSTRONG   Samuel Chapman Armstrong: a Biographical Study. New York: Doubleday Page, 1904. 1st edition; slight rubbing to base of spine, couple of pages roughly opened and hinges neatly repaired, still a bright, otherwise fine copy. Inscribed by Robert C. Ogden on Founder's Day 1904.   Between the Covers 43-416 1996 $250.00

TALBOT, FREDERICK A.   Making Good in Canada. London: Adam and Charles Black, 1912. 20cm; x, 282, (2) pages, frontispiece, illustrations; black stamped and decorated red cloth; fine, beautiful copy, scarce. Rockland Books 38-215 1996 $125.00

TALBOTT, JAMES   The Christian School-Master; or, the Duty of Those Who Are Employed in the Public Instruction of Children... London: F. C. and J. Rivington, 1811. New edition; 12mo; original tree calf with S.P.C.K blindstamp on front board, red label, very good, bright copy. Jarndyce 103-577 1996 £65.00

**TALES of the Classics: a New Delineation of the Most Popular Fables, Legends and Allegories Commemorated in the Works of Poets, Painters and Sculptors. London: Henry Colburn and Richard Bentley, 1830. 1st edition; large 12mo; 3 volumes; 19th century half red morocco, slight rubbing; very good, scarce. 5 copies in NUC; Block p. 232; Wolff 7652. Ximenes 109-142 1996 $350.00

TALESE, GAY   New York: a Serendipiter's Journey. New York: Harpe 1961. 1st edition; photos by Marvin Lichter; boards slightly bowed, else fine in fine dust jacket with tiny puncture to rear gutter; author's first book; inscribed by him in year of publication.   Between the Covers 42-420 1996 $125.00

TALIESIN   The Poems of Taliesin. Tern Press, 1989. One in an editio of 90 copies, signed by Nicholas and Mary Parry; 15.25 x 10.75 pages; blocks of original manuscript printed on Antik mould made paper, with 12 large etched lino printed heightened by watercolors; quarter bound with rough linen and lino printed boards, title in red on front cover, title in red on spine label; fine. Joshua Heller 21-240 1996 $250.00

**TALLIS'S London Street Views, Exhibiting Upwards of One Hundred Buildings in Each Number... London: John Tallis, ca. 1847. Oblong 8vo; parts 1-48 (ex 88); 27 original printed front wrappers retained, each par with double page plates, some slight staining, together in half crushed morocco. Rare.   Marlborough 162-208 1996 £2,000.00

TALMUD   The Living Talmud. New York: Limited Editions Club, 1960. One of 1500 copies; signed by artist; drawings by Ben-Zion; very good in publisher's slipcase.   Hermitage SP95-1007 1996 $225.00

TAN, AMY   The Joy Luck Club. New York: Putnam's, 1989. Advance reading copy, near fine in wrappers.   Ken Lopez 74-431 1996 $450.00

TAN, AMY   The Joy Luck Club. New York: Putnam, 1989. Advance reading copy; crease on rear wrapper, slight soiling to fore edge and some wear to extremities, not quite very good.   Between the Covers 42-422 1996 $200.00

TAN, AMY   The Joy Luck Club. New York: Putnam, 1989. 1st edition; fine in fine dust jacket, signed, with author's distinctive chop stamp. Book Time 2-435 1996 $350.00

TAN, AMY   The Joy Luck Club. New York: Putnam, 1989. 1st edition; very near fine in dust jacket with minor surface crinkling to head of spine. Scarce.   Lame Duck Books 19-514 1996 $300.00

TAN, AMY   The Joy Luk Club. New York: Putnam, 1989. 1st edition; as new in like dust jacket, author's first book; signed presentation on titlepage.   Sherwood 3-302 1996 $250.00

TAN, AMY   The Kitchen God's Wife. New York: Putnam, 1991. 1st edition; proof copy, signed; wrappers; fine.   Alice Robbins 15-321 1996 $125.00

TAN, AMY   The Kitchen God's Wife. New York: Putnam, 1991. Uncorrected proof; red wrappers; very good, signed by author.   Bud Schweska 12-733 1996 $100.00

TANG, W. C.   Chinese Drugs of Plant Origin. Berlin: 1992. 8vo; about 850 pages, 38 figures; hardcover.   Wheldon & Wesley 207-1916 1996 £110.00

TANNER, HEATHER   Wiltshire Village. London: 1939. 1st edition; 4to; illustrations by Robin Tanner; very good in dust jacket with repaired tear at bottom right corner of upper panel.   Words Etcetera 94-1204 1996 £125.00

TANNER, MATTHAIS   Societas Jesu Apostolorum Imitrix Sive Gesta Praeclara et Virtutes Eorum. Prague: A. G. Konias, 1694. Large 4to; 196 engravings; 19th century full crimson morocco with scalloped gilt outer border inside of which is a double gilt fillet border, upon which sits an inch wide elaborate border composed of alternating floral designs, including acorns and lilies, spine with seven raised bands and complimentary gilt tooling in six of the compartments, the second and third from the top being reserved for two morocco labels bearing title information, inner gilt dentelles, board edges gilt, marbled endleaves, all edges gilt, bound by J. Mackenzie, bookbinder to the king; with gilt stamped Huth bookplate (his sale, Sotheby's 8 Jul6 1919, lot 7206) and bookplate of Leonard and Lisa Baskin.   Book Block 32-67 1996 $7,500.00

TANQUEREL DES PLANCHES, LOUIS   Traite des Maladies de Plomb. Paris: 1838. 8vo; 2 volumes; original wrappers, near fine, uncut and partly unopened. Rare. GM 2098.   James Tait Goodrich K40-280 1996 $1,295.00

TAORMINA: Wilhelm von Gloeden. Pasadena: Twelve Tree Press, 1986. 1st edition; limited edition; folio; illustrations; dust jacket.   J. B. Muns 154-315 1996 $125.00

TAPLIN, GEORGE   Narrinyeri: an Account of the Tribes of South Australian Aborigines Inhabiting the Country Around the Lakes Alexandria, Albert and Coorong and the Lower Part of the River Murray, Their Manner and Customs. Adelaide: E. S. Wing, 1878. 2nd edition; (iv), (iv), 156 pages, 6 color lithographs; original embossed cloth showing slight discoloration, otherwise bright, clean copy; the Absolon copy. Ferguson 16707; Greenway 8980.   Antipodean 28-434 1996 $550.00

TAPLIN, WILLIAM   The Sporting Dictionary, and Rural Repository of General Information Upon Every Subject Appertaining to sports of the Field. London: 1803. 2 volumes; engraved plates foxed and title to volume 2 expertly repaired; finely bound in half scarlet levant morocco by Sangorski & Sutcliffe; most attractive.   David A.H. Grayling 3/95-227 1996 £150.00

TAPLIN, WILLIAM   The Sportsman's Cabinet; or, a Correct Delineation of the Various Dogs Used in the Sports of the Field... London: printed and published...by Cundee.. 1803-04. 1st edition; 4to; 2 volumes; pages viii, 276, (2), (4 ads); 310, (2); 2 engraved vignette titles, 2 engraved frontispieces, 24 engraved plates by J. Scott after Reinagle, 22 vignettes, tailpieces, etc., mostly good, clean impressions of the plates, though a few are just a little fox spotted in borders and some are browned on reverse side, but attractive copy; contemporary diced calf, gilt border to sides, gilt spines; armorial bookplate of John Forster. Hugo 185; Pease 114; Schwerdt II p. 248.   Sotheran PN32-78 1996 £1,350.00

TAPPLY, WILLIAM G.   Death at Charity's Point. New York: Scribners, 1984. 1st edition; author's first book; fine in near fine dust jacket with light rubbing and few very light creases.   Quill & Brush 102-1639 1996 $200.00

TAPPLY, WILLIAM G.   Death at Charity's Point. New York: Scribner's, 1984. 1st edition; author's first book; fine in price clipped dust jacket with slight rubbing.   Robert Gavora 61-402 1996 $150.00

TAPPLY, WILLIAM G.   The Dutch Blue Error. New York: Scribners, 1984. 1st edition; fine in dust jacket.   Quill & Brush 102-1640 1996 $175.00

TARG, WILLIAM   Abacus Now: Footnotes to Indecent Pleasure and Observations on Fine Book Printing, Book-Collecting and Matters Personal, Including How to Survive in the Computer Age. New York: Targ Editions, 1984. One of 200 copies, signed in colophon by author and each of the printers; 7.75 x 5.5 inches; printed on various colored papers in black with addition of color; black cloth spine and red paper boards, fine.   Joshua Heller 21-227 1996 $150.00

TARKINGTON, BOOTH 1869-1946   The Gentleman from Indiana. New York: Doubleday mcClure, 1899. 1st edition; bookplate and name, very near fine with touch of rubbing, very nice copy of author's first book. Between the Covers 42-423 1996 $150.00

TARKINGTON, BOOTH 1869-1946   Monsieur Beaucaire. New York: Limited Editions Club, 1961. Limited to 1500 copies, signed by artist/designer; 8vo; illustrations by T. M. Cleland; full damask, fine in like chemise and slipcase.   Charles Agvent 4-1083 1996 $125.00

TARR, RALPH STOCKMAN   Alaskan Glacier Studies of the National Geographic Society in the Yakutat Bay, Prince William sound and Lower Copper River Regions. Washington: the National Geographic Society, 1914. 26 cm; xxvii, 498 pages; frontispiece, illustrations, plates, maps; 9 color maps in rear pocket; gilt stamped burgundy cloth; very good. Rockland Books 38-216 1996 $150.00

TARRIN, W. A.   The Italian Confectioner. London: Routledge, Warne and Routledge, 1861. New edition; small 8vo; xxxiv, 35-298 + 22 pages ads, frontispiece, 2 folding plates, printed on glazed linen; modern cloth, spine lettered gilt, portrait and title spotted, several other leaves little browned.   Thomas Thorp 489-301 1996 £65.00

TARTT, DONNA   The Secret History. New York: Knopf, 1992. Advance reading copy; wrappers; near fine, signed by author.   Ken Lopez 74-432 1996 $150.00

TASHJIAN, VIRGINIA A.   Once There Was and Was Not - Armenian Tales Retold. Boston and Toronto: Little Brown and Co., 1966. 1st edition; color drawings by Nonny Hogrogian; decorated boards; head and tail of spine and corners bumped, very good in nicked, rubbed and dusty, slightly creased dust jacket slightly browned at spine and edges; from the library of William Saroyan, inscribed by author; loosely inserted author's compliments slip, stamped by Saroyan "Received Jun 28 1967. W.S."   Ulysses 39-22 1996 £55.00

TASMAN, ABEL JANSZOON   Abel Janzoon Tasman's Journal of His Discovery of Van Diemen's Land and New Zealand in 1642, with Documents Relating to His Exploration of Australia in 1644. Los Angeles: N. A. Kovach, 1965. Facsimile edition, limited to 225 copies; thick demy folio; pages x, 196; 2, 60 pages; blank, 2, 164 pages; blank, 2, 22 pages; blank, 5 folding charts, 53 pages of maps and illustrations, errata slip; volume and folding maps fine, dust jacket lightly worn, still in original shipping box.   Parmer Books 039/Nautica-047042 1996 $600.00

TASSI, ROBERTO   Graham Sutherland Complete Graphic Work. London: Thames & Hudson, 1978. Large 4to; 228 pages; 218 illustrations, 122 color plates; decorated cloth, dust jacket.   Rainsford A54-546 1996 $75.00

TASSO, BERNARDO   Li Tre Libri Delle Lettere...Alli Quali Nuovamente s'Aggiunto il Quarto Libro. Venice: P. Gironimo Giglio, 1559. 8vo; (8), 255, (3) leaves, woodcut printer's devices on title and last leaf, woodcut head and tailpieces and historiated initials; small tear in one leaf without loss and few leaves have small worm holes in blank margin which are neatly repaired; modern calf. Not in admas or BM STC Italian.   Jeffrey Mancevice 20-81 1996 $275.00

TASSO, TORQUATO 1544-1595   La Gerusalemme Liberata.... Genua: G. Pavoni for B. Castello, 1617. 1st edition; folio; 380 pages; 2 engraved titles, 20 full page engravings, woodcut ornaments; old full vellum, minor repairs and some wear; very good. NUC 583.515; Gamba 948; Raccolta Tassiana no. 198.   Bennett Gilbert LL29-84 1996 $4,500.00

TASSO, TORQUATO 1544-1595   Godfrey of Bullogine, or Jerusalem Delivered. London: printed by Bensley and Son for R. Triphook, 1817. One of 50 large paper copies, initialled by Triphook; 8vo; 2 volumes; portrait is a mounted proof on India paper, foxed, vignette head and tailpieces line cut on wood after J. Thurston, reproduction of titlepage for the original 1600 edition; full contemporary red English morocco gilt, all edges gilt, Brunet V 671.   Family Album Tillers-598 1996 $275.00

TASSO, TORQUATO 1544-1595   Ventiquattro Sonetti. Vienna: 1939. Not numbered but the edition size is 45 to 50 copies; 9 x 6.75 inches; metal engraving of Tasso by Victor Hammer in brown on titlepage, printed in black on handmade paper, grey paper boards, printed label on spine; very fine in grey dust jacket. Victor Hammer Artist & Printer p. 146.   Joshua Heller 21-138 1996 $250.00

TATE, ALLEN   Christ and the Unicorn. West Branch: Cummington Press, 1966. 1st edition; one of 125 copies printed; thin 8vo; wrappers, margin of one leaf lightly foxed, otherwise fine.   James S. Jaffe 34-651 1996 $100.00

TATE, ALLEN   Fragment of a Meditation/MCMXXVIII. Cummington: Cummington Press, 1947. 1st edition; 8vo; wrappers; front cover very lightly faded along edges, otherwise fine.   James S. Jaffe 34-646 1996 $175.00

TATE, ALLEN   The Golden Mean and Other Poems. Nashville: Privately printed, 1923. 1st edition; one of 200 copies, signed by Tate and Wills; 8vo; author's first book; original buff wrappers lightly dust soiled, one small stain to upper cover, otherwise very good, enclosed in half morocco folding box; rare; this copy additionally inscribed by Ridley Wills for Katherine Waits. With Waits' signature.   James S. Jaffe 34-636 1996 $3,000.00

TATE, ALLEN   Jefferson Davis: His Rise and Fall. New York: Minton Balch & Co., 1929. 1st edition; 1st issue; reproductions; very good+ in somewhat worn later issue price clipped dust jacket, author's rare 3rd book.   Pettler & Lieberman 28-237 1996 $100.00

TATE, ALLEN   The Mediterranean and other Poems. New York: Alcestis Press, 1936. 1st edition; limited to 165 copies (this one out of series), signed by Tate; thin 8vo; wrappers. Fine   James S. Jaffe 34-641 1996 $500.00

TATE, ALLEN   The Mediterranean and Other Poems. New York: Alcestis Press, 1936. 1st edition; limited to 165 copies (this one out of series), signed by Tate; thin 8vo; wrappers; fine.   James S. Jaffe 34-640 1996 $175.00

TATE, ALLEN   Mr. Pope and Other Poems. New York: Minton Balch, 1928. 1st edition; small 8vo; cloth with printed labels and printed glassine dust jacket; fine in jacket which is slightly rubbed at head and foot of spine.   James S. Jaffe 34-637 1996 $500.00

TATE, ALLEN   Poems: 1928-1931. New York: Scribner's, 1932. 1st edition; small 8vo; cloth, spine faded, otherwise fine; signed by author.   James S. Jaffe 34-640 1996 $175.00

TATE, ALLEN   Reactionary Essays on Poetry and Ideas. New York: Charles Scribner's Sons, 1936. 1st edition; original binding, top edge dusty, endpapers partially browned, title label on spine browned, edges and endpapers slightly spotted, very good in nicked, rubbed and dusty, slightly marked and creased dust jacket browned at spine and edges.   Ulysses 39-577 1996 £125.00

TATE, ALLEN   Reason in Madness. Critical Essays. New York: Putnam's, 1941. 1st edition; 8vo; cloth, dust jacket, signed by author, fine in jacket rubbed at head of spine.   James S. Jaffe 34-643 1996 $100.00

TATE, ALLEN   Reason in Madness. Critical Essays. New York: Putnam's, 1941. 1st edition; 8vo; signed by author; cloth, fine in dust jacket rubbed at head of spine.   James S. Jaffe 34-643 1996 $100.00

TATE, ALLEN   Selected Poems. New York: Scribner's, 1937. 1st edition; 8vo; cloth backed boards, dust jacket, light offsetting on front and back endpapers and previous bookseller's label on front endsheet, otherwise very good inslightly rubbed jacket chipped and worn at head of spine.   James S. Jaffe 34-642 1996 $100.00

TATE, ALLEN   Selected Poems. New York: Scribner's, 1937. 1st edition; 8vo; cloth backed boards, dust jacket, light offsetting on front and back endpapers and previous bookseller's label on front endsheet, otherwise very good in slightly rubbed jacket chipped and worn at head of spine.   James S. Jaffe 34-642 1996 $100.00

TATE, ALLEN   Sonnets at Christmas. Cummington: Cymmington Press, 1941. 1st separate printing, of a total edition of 150 copies, this one of only 50 lettered copies; saddle stitched wrappers; fine. Rare.   Between the Covers 42-423a 1996 $950.00

TATE, ALLEN   Stonewall Jackson, the Good Soldier, a Narrative. New York: 1928. 1st edition; viii, (2), 322 pages; with top of backstrip showing shelfwear.   Bookworm & Silverfish 276-56 1996 $125.00

TATE, ALLEN   Two Conceits for the Eye to Sing, if Possible. Cummington: Cummington Press, 1950. 1st edition; one of 300 copies; small thin 8vo; wrappers; mint.   James S. Jaffe 34-648 1996 $150.00

TATE, ALLEN   Who Owns America? Boston: Houghton Mifflin, 1936. 1st edition; 8vo; cloth, some offsetting and light foxing to front and back endpapers, light stains on back cover spine faded, still good, scarce.   James S. Jaffe 34-658 1996 $300.00

TATE, ALLEN   The Winter Sea: A Book of Poems. Cummington: Cummington Press, 1944. 1st edition; one of 300 copies printed, review copy with slip laid in; 8vo; cloth, unprinted dust jacket; fine in spine darkened jacket rubbed and slightly chipped at extremities; presentation copy inscribed by author for Malcolm Cowley.   James S. Jaffe 34-645 1996 $650.00

TATE, JAMES   Bewitched; Twenty-Five Poems. Embers Handpress, 1989. of 100 numbered copies, signed by author, this one of 20 on Barcham Green handmade; small folio; frontispiece; printed in handset Ehrhardt in black and two shades of brown; frontispiece and drawing reproduced on boards and slipcase, by Laruie Smith; half cloth, boards; fine in slipcase;   Bertram Rota 272-134 1996 £65.00

TATE, NAHUM   Characters of Vertue and Vice. London: printed for Francis Saunders, 1691. 1st edition; small 4to; disbound; titlepage lightly browned, but nice. Wing H372; CBEL II 775.   Ximenes 109-281 1996 $850.00

TATE, NAHUM   Dido and Aeneas. Bangor/Newark: Janues Press, April, 1989. One in an edition of 150 copies signed by Claire Van Vliet; 37 printed surfaces, 14.875 x 6.5 inches folded, 14.875 x 70.25 inches unfolded; accordion-fold pulp-painted base sheet with pulp-painted and shaped insert pages on which the text is printed, each opening of the accordion forms a stage set for one of the opera's five scenes; with wrap-around title sheet which forms the cover and spine, typographical design by Michael Alpert; book structure and box by Claire Van Vliet, pulp painting by Claire Van Vliet & Bernie Vinzani & Katie MacGregor, supplemented with other papers from MacGregor-Vinzani, Twinrocker and Barcham Green; text handset; enclosed i double tray box covered with Japanese cloth, with compact disc recording of the opera, enclosed in removable chemise located inside the box. Fine.   Joshua Heller 21-27 1996 $600.00

TATE, NAHUM   A Duke and No Duke. London: printed for Henry Bonwicke, 1685. 1st edition; 4to; 5 pages printed music at back, careful repair to first and final leaves, running headline of Dedication trimmed, half straight grained red morocco, marbled boards, some light rubbing, some light browning or offsetting, else very nice; Robert Hoe copy with bookplate. W&M 1196.   James Cummins 14-204 1996 $300.00

TATE, WILLIAM   The Modern Cambist; Forming a Manual of Foreign Exchanges, in the Direct, Indirect and Cross Operations of Bills of Exchange and Bullion... Paris: A. and W. Galignani; Liverpool J. & G. Robinson; London: Effingham... 1834. 2nd edition; 8vo; half title, name erased from upper blank margin of title, 20 pages of ads; original cloth, hinges partly torn, uncut and unopened, printed paper label. Goldsmith 28624.   Anthony W. Laywood 108-240 1996 $75.00

TATHAM, JOSEPH   Rules and Instructions for the Regular Management of the Seminary, Kept by Joseph Tatham, Leeds. Leeds: printed by Edward Baines, 1817. 30 pages; disbound.   Jarndyce 103-579 1996 £50.00

TATTERSALL, GEORGE   Tablets of an Itinerant. London: Sherwood & Co., 1836. 1st edition; 8vo; pages xii, 165, (24 ads), plus errata leaf; hand colored folding map, engraved title, 41 fine etched plates. Bicknell 116;   R.F.G. Hollett & Son 78-1312 1996 £110.00

TATTERSALL, GEORGE   Tablets of an Itinerant. London: Sherwood & Co., 1836. 1st edition; 8vo; pages xii, 165, (20 ads); hand colored folding map, 41 fine etched plates, title in facsimile.   R.F.G. Hollett & Son 78-1313 1996 £65.00

TAUBERT, SIGRED   Bibliopola. Hamburg & London: 1966. 4to; 2 volumes, 258 plates, numerous illustrations; beige cloth, red spine labels, good condition; booklabel of Alan Thomas.   Maggs Bros. Ltd. 1191-122 1996 £110.00

TAUBERT, SIGRED   Bibliopola: Pictures and Texts About the Book Trade. Hamburg/New York: Dr. Ernst Huaswedell & R. R. Bowker, 1966. 1st edition; folio; 2 volumes, xxvi, 126; x, 526 pages; 317 text illustrations in volume 1, 258 plates of which 42 are tipped in and in color, 2 facsimiles; linen with leather spine labels, fine in slipcase. Andrew Cahan 47-30 1996 $125.00

TAUT, BRUNO   Houses and People of Japan. Tokyo: The Sanseido Co. Ltd., 1937. 1st edition; 551 illustrations in line and photograph, including 9 original mounted color woodblock prints, brown linen, nearly imperceptible wear to foot of spine, otherwise fine in modern slipcase covered in Japanese handmade paper complimenting the endpapers. Hermitage SP95-1060 1996 $600.00

TAUT, BRUNO   Modern Architecture. London: Studio, n.d. 4to; x, 212 pages, numerous illustrations; original cloth, spine slightly faded, top edge gilt, endpapers slightly foxed and slight worming at front. Rainsford A54-664 1996 £85.00

TAVERNER, ERIC   The Making of a Trout Stream. London: 1953. Limited to 250 copies, signed by author; illustrations; original buckram in slipcase, book fine, case lightly rubbed.   David A.H. Grayling 3/95-519 1 996 £50.00

TAVERNER, ERIC   Trout Fishing from All Angles. London: Seeley, Service & Co., 1929. Limited deluxe edition of 375 copies, signed by author; this being out of series copy numbered 0; royal 8vo; 448 pages; with a collection of artificial tied flies mounted in a sunken panel on inside rear cover, 65 tipped in photographic plates, 118 text illustrations; publisher's dark blue morocco, gilt, top edge gilt, others uncut, corners rubbed, lacks 2 of the 30 artificial flies and few of the others slightly moth damaged.   Thomas Thorp 489-302 1996 £150.00

TAYLOR, A.   Birds of a County Palatine. London: 1913. Large 4to; tipped in and other photo plates; original buckram; excellent.   David A.H. Grayling MY95Orn-256 1996 £55.00

TAYLOR, ALFRED SWAINE   On Poisons in Relation to Medical Jurisprudence and Medicine. Philadelphia: Henry C. Lea, 1875. 3rd edition; contemporary? sheep, spine abraded and portions of four letters on title effaced, else clean, sound.   Meyer Boswell SL25-216 1996 $125.00

TAYLOR, ALRUTHEUS AMBUSH   The Negro in Reconstruction of Virginia. Washington: Assoc. for the Study of Negro Life and History, 1926. 1st edition; corners slightly worn and small pencilled owner name, else fine, bright copy lacking presumed dust jacket, nice.   Between the Covers 43-418 1996 $125.00

TAYLOR, ARTHUR   The Glory of Regality: an Historical Treatise of the Anointing and Crowning of the Kings and Queens of England. London: printed by and for R. and A. Taylor, Sold by... 1820. 1st edition; tall 8vo; xvi, 424 pages; contemporary half green morocco, elaborate gilt decoration on spine, all edges gilt, boards slightly rubbed, otherwise attractive.   David Mason 71-41 1996 $280.00

TAYLOR, BAYARD 1825-1878   A Book of Romances, Lyrics and Songs. Boston: Ticknor, Reed and Fields, 1852. 1st printing of only 1000 copies; 8vo; brown cloth, binding A with Sept. 1851 catalog, little spotting to cloth, sporadic foxing, near fine; fine association, George William Curtis's copy with his signature.   Charles Agvent 4-1085 1996 $175.00

TAYLOR, BAYARD 1825-1878   Eldorado, or, Adventures in the Path of Empire; Comprising a Voyage to California, via Panama.... New York: Putnam, 1850. 1st edition; 1st issue; 12mo; 2 volumes, pages xii, 251; 2, 247, 45 ads; 8 tinted plates; original cloth, rubbed, some light foxing. Howes T43; Wheat 204; Cowan p. 630; Sabin 94440; Graff 4073. Richard Adelson W94/95-169 1996 $585.00

TAYLOR, EDWARD SAMUEL   The History of Playing Cards, with Anecdotes of their Use in Conjuring, Fortune-Telling and Card-Sharping. London: John Camden Hotten, 1865. 1st edition; 8vo; xiv, 529, (16, 6, 10 ad) pages; colored frontispiece, 47 plates, colored vignette on title, partly unopened, occasional spotting, several leaves with clean tears; original red pictorial cloth, gilt.   James Burmester 29-133 1996 £250.00

TAYLOR, ELIZABETH   A Dedicated Man - and Other Stories. London: Chatto & Windus, 1965. 1st edition; original binding, top edge slightly dusty, prelims and endpapers slightly spotted, very good in nicked, creased and spotted, slightly rubbed and marked dust jacket, by Ionicus, browned at spine and edges; from the library of Ian Parsons, publisher of this book.   Ulysses 39-579 1996 £95.00

TAYLOR, ELIZABETH   The Devastating Boys and Other Stories. London: Chatto & Windus, 1972. 1st edition; original binding, top edge slightly dusty, head and tail of spine slightly faded, top corner of one page creased, very good in nicked and slightly creased dust jacket faded at spine and browned at edges; pencilled ownership signature of Ian Parsons, publisher of this book.   Ulysses 39-583 1996 £75.00

TAYLOR, ELIZABETH   Mossy Trotter. London: Chatto & Windus, 1967. 1st edition; numerous black and whtie drawings; original binding, tail of spine and corners slightly bumped, small stain on upper cover, very good in slightly nicked and dusty dust jacket, slightly darkened at spine and edges and slightly soiled on upper panel; from the library of Ian Parsons.   Ulysses 39-580 1996 £75.00

TAYLOR, ELIZABETH   The Sleeping Beauty. London: Peter Davies, Ltd., 1953. 1st edition; original binding, ownership name and address stamped twice on front free endpaper, first of all the wrong way up, then the right way up, top edge dusty, edges browned, spine faded and with offsetting from dust jacket, very good in nicked, rubbed and slightly chipped, creased and dusty dust jacket frayed at head of spine. Ulysses 39-578 1996 £95.00

TAYLOR, ELIZABETH   The Wedding Group. London: Chatto & Windus Ltd., 1968. 1st edition; original binding, tail of spine slightly bumped, cover edges slightly bumped, very good in nicked, spotted and slightly soiled and dusty dust jacket, slightly browned at edges and with ring stain on lower panel; from the library of Ian Parsons.   Ulysses 39-581 1996 £55.00

TAYLOR, G.   An Account of the Genus Meconopsis. London: 1934. Crown 4to; pages xxix, 130, frontispiece, 30 (on 24) plates and 12 maps; original buckram, interleaved with tissues and printed on superior paper to that of the cloth bound issue.   Wheldon & Wesley 207-1750 1996 £60.00

TAYLOR, G. L.   The Architectural Antiquities of Rome. London: the author, 1821-22. Folio; 2 volumes, frontispiece, xii, (ii), 66 pages, 62 plates; (iv), 62 pages, 65 plates; contemporary morocco, boards, ex-library with markings, binding worn, some foxing;   The Bookpress 75-242 1996 $750.00

TAYLOR, HENRY   Philip Van Artevelde; a Dramatic Romance. London: Edward Moxon, 1834. 1st edition; small 8vo; 2 volumes, half title discarded in volume i(?), pages xxxvi (for xxxiv), (iv), 287, (1); (iv), 306, (1); contemporary dark green morocco, slight rubbing to extremities, backstrip with raised bands, gilt lettered direct in second, third and fourth compartments, all panelled with single rule, double gilt fillet border on sides, single fillet on board edges, narrow scroll roll on turn-ins, pale blue endpapers, early ownership signature, green silk markers, gilt edges, very good.   Blackwell's B112-269 1996 £145.00

TAYLOR, HENRY   The Statesman. London: Longman, et al, 1836. 1st edition; small 8vo; pages xviii, 267, (1); original boards, cloth back, paper label; nearly fine with little lightening of cloth, darkening of label and rubbing of edges of boards, ownership signature twice of Foley author and Astor heir Charles Astor Bristed.   Howard S. Mott 227-163 1996 $150.00

TAYLOR, ISAAC 1759-1829   Scenes in America, for the Amusement and Instruction of Little Tarry-at-Home Travellers. London: Harris & Son, 1821. 1st edition; 16mo; frontispiece, viii, 122, (2) pages, 84 illustrations on plates; original quarter red morocco, printed boards, map repaired, contemporary inscriptions in ink, occasional foxing and browning, binding worn.   The Bookpress 75-469 1996 $150.00

TAYLOR, ISAAC 1759-1829   Scenes of Commerce, by Land and Sea. London: John Harris, n.d. 1830. 1st edition; 12mo; iv, 387, (1) pages, 24 pages publisher's catalog at end, 18 plates, each with 3 vignette illustrations; original roan backed marbled boards, title in gilt on spine, very good. Goldsmiths 26201; not in Kress.   John Drury 82-275 1996 £125.00

TAYLOR, ISAAC 1759-1829   Specimens of Gothic Ornaments Selected from the Parish Church of Lavenham in Sufolk. London: I. and J. Taylor, 1796. 1st edition; 4to; (ii) pages, 40 plates; contemporary quarter calf, hinges starting, some minor foxing.   Bookpress 75-126 1996 $250.00

TAYLOR, ISAAC 1787-1865   Fanaticism. London: Holdsworth and Ball, 1833. 1st edition; 8vo; contemporary polished calf, gilt, spine gilt, minor rubbing; fine copy; bookplate of France Mary Richardson Currer. Ximenes 108-336 1996 $250.00

TAYLOR, ISAAC 1787-1865   Fanaticism. London: Holdsworth and Ball, 1833. 1st edition; 8vo; viii, 515 pages; original blue boards, drab spine, printed label, top of spine little worn. cf. CBEL III 1604.   James Burmester 29-134 1996 £75.00

TAYLOR, ISAAC 1787-1865   Spiritual Despotism. London: Holdsworth and Ball, 1835. 1st edition; 8vo; contemporary polished calf, gilt, spine gilt, minor rubbing; possibly bound without half title, but fine, scarce; bookplate of Frances Mary Richardson Currer.   Ximenes 108-337 1996 $225.00

TAYLOR, J. J.   The Physician as a Business Man; or, How to Obtain the Best Financial Results in the Practice of Medicine. Philadelphia: 1892. 1st edition; 143 pages; original binding, ex-library; the original owner of this copy wrote his own fees in the section "An Average Fee-bill".   W. Bruce Fye 71-2082 1996 $125.00

TAYLOR, JANE 1783-1824   City Scenes or a Peep Into London, for Children. London: Darton Harvey & Darton, 1823. Large 12mo; engraved title, pages 1-72, 76 plates num. on 35 ff., red road backed boards, little worn (little worn);   Marlborough 162-209 1996 £250.00

TAYLOR, JEFFERYS   A Month in London. London: Harvey & Darton, 1832. 1st edition; post 12mo; (ii), 182, (vi) pages frontispiece, extra title and 4 plates; original quarter roan, slightly rubbed, lacks front free endpaper, some browning and spotting, mainly to plates, one plate torn and expertly repaired, still reasonable copy. Adams 171.   Ash Rare Books Zenzybyr-89 1996 £95.00

TAYLOR, JEREMY 1613-1667   The Worthy Communicant: or, a Discourse of the...Lords Supper. London: T.N. for John Martyn, 1678. 8vo; (xiv), 462 pages; frontispiece; contemporary calf, rebacked, old spine laid down, label; slightly rubbed, small repair to corner of titlepage, just touching border, little browning; good. Wing T420C.   Robert Clark 38-138 1996 £60.00

TAYLOR, JOHN   African Rifles and Cartridges. 1948. 1st edition; Many illustrations; excellent copy in frayed dust jacket, seldom found in this condition.   David Grayling J95Biggame-351 1996 £150.00

TAYLOR, JOHN   A Dog of War. London: Frederick Etchells & Hugh MacDonald, 1927. 1st edition; five full page colored illustrations by Hester Sainsbury; buckram backed boards, free endpapers browned, covers rubbed, marked, dusty and slightly soiled, cover edges darkened, head and tail of spine and corners bumped and rubbed, corners also bruised, good.   Ulysses 39-517 1996 £55.00

TAYLOR, JOSEPH H.   Kaleidoscopic Lives. Washburgn: 1902. 2nd edition; 206 pages + ads, photos; illustrations; pictorial cloth. Scarce. 6 Guns 2184; Howes T67. dustin 255.   T. A. Swinford 49-1139 1996 $125.00

TAYLOR, M. W.   The Old Manorial Halls of Westmorland and Cumberland. Kendal: T. Wilson, 1892. 1st edition; 8vo; pages xxi, 384, 54 , 27 folding plans; modern half levant morocco gilt, excellent copy. R.F.G. Hollett & Son 78-46 1996 £185.00

TAYLOR, M. W.   The Old Manorial Halls of Westmorland and Cumberland. Kendal: T. Wilson, 1892. 1st edition; 8vo; pages xxi, 384; 54 illustrations, 27 folding plans; original cloth, gilt.   R.F.G. Hollett & Son 78-44 1996 £150.00

TAYLOR, M. W.   The Old Manorial Halls of Westmorland and Cumberland. Kendal: T. Wilson, 1892. 1st edition; 8vo; pages xxi, 384, 54 illustrations and 27 folding plans; original brown cloth, gilt, extremities little rubbed, few spots to prelims, lower joint cracking. Attractive bookplate of Margaret Eleanor Thomson.   R.F.G. Hollett & Son 78-45 1996 £140.00

TAYLOR, MARLY L.   The Tiger's Claw. 1956. illustrations; frayed, protected dust jacket.   David Grayling J95Biggame-590 1996 £55.00

TAYLOR, MICHAEL   A Bibliography of St. Dominic's Press 1916-1937. London: Whittington Press, 1995. 1st edition; Deluxe edition, limited to 100 copies; folio; c. 200 pages; 4 pages color plates, half tone illustrations, facsimiles and other inserted material; printed in Caslon types on Zerkall mould made paper; quarter bound in morocco with original St. Dominic's leaf and facsimile of one of the books published by the Press.   Claude Cox 107-155b 1996 £265.00

TAYLOR, MICHAEL   A Bibliography of St. Dominic's Press 1916-1937. London: Whittington Press, 1995. 1st edition; limited to 250 copies (& 100 specials); folio; c. 200 pages, 4 pages color plates, half tone illustrations, facsimiles and other inserted material; printed in Caslon types on Zerkall mould-made paper; buckram backed printed paper sides and slipcase.   Claude Cox 107-155 1996 £135.00

TAYLOR, MICHAEL   St. Dominic's Press: a Bibliography. Herefordshire: Whittington Press, 1994. Of an edition of 350 copies, this one of 100 bound thus; 11 x 7.5 inches; approximately 22 pages, 4 pages of color plates, as well as black and white plates and other tipped in material, printed on Zerkall mould made paper; quarter bound in Oasis leather with pringed paper sides, including an original St. Dominic's leaf, facsimile of one of the titles; slipcase.   Joshua Heller 21-221 1996 $475.00

TAYLOR, MICHAEL   St. Dominic's Press: a Bibliography. Herefordshire: Whittington Press, 1994. Of 350 copies, this one of 250 copies bound thus; 11 x 7.5 inches; approximately 22 pages, 4 pages of color plates, as well as black and white plates and other tipped in material; printed on Zerkall mould made paper; quarter bound in buckram with printed paper sides, slipcase.   Joshua Heller 21-221 1996 $250.00

TAYLOR, N.   Ibex Shooting on the Himalayas. 1903. illustrations, frontispiece missing; some foxing to prelims, light rubbing; rare; presentation copy from author's parents to Rugby School Library. David Grayling J95Biggame-589 1996 £135.00

TAYLOR, PETER   The Collected Stories. New York: FSG, 1969. 1st edition; near fine in dust jacket with one inch tear to fore edge of front flap, signed by author.   Lame Duck Books 19-517 1996 $150.00

TAYLOR, PETER   Happy Families Are All Alike. New York: McDowell Obolensky, 1959. 1st edition; very good+ copy in dust jacket; superb association copy, inscribed by author to literary critic and poet Allen Tate and his wife Isabella in the year of publication and with typed 3 x 5 inch index card laid in.   Lame Duck Books 19-515 1996 $1,500.00

TAYLOR, PETER   A Long Fourth and Other Stories. New York: Harcourt Brace, 1947. 1st edition; author's first book; fine in very good dust jacket which is lightly chipped and somewhat faded at spine; signed by Taylor.   Captain's Bookshelf 38-207 1996 $300.00

TAYLOR, PETER   A Long Fourth and Other Stories. New York: Harcourt Brace, 1948. 1st edition; 8vo; author's first book; cloth, dust jacket; small stain on front free endpaper, otherwise fine in lightly dust soiled jacket somewhat faded along spine, much better than average copy, scarce.   James S. Jaffe 34-660 1996 $350.00

TAYLOR, PETER   A Long Fourth and Other Stories. New York: Harcourt, Brace & Co., 1948. 1st edition; author's first book, signed by author on special printed label pasted to flyleaf; near fine in very good dust jacket which is faded at spine and slightly chipped at top spine corners.   Steven C. Bernard 71-231 1996 $300.00

TAYLOR, PETER   Miss Leonora When Last Seen and 15 other Stories New York: Ivan Obolensky, 1963. 1st edition; very near fine in like dust jacket, uncommon thus, signed by Taylor.   Lame Duck Books 19-516 1996 $350.00

TAYLOR, PETER   Miss Leonora When Last Seen. New York: Obolensky, 1963. 1st edition; fine in fine dust jacket.   Ken Lopez 74-435 1996 $285.00

TAYLOR, PETER   The Old Forest. Garden City: Dial, 1985. 1st edition; fine in dust jacket, inscribed by author. Uncommon.   Lame Duck Books 19-520 1996 $150.00

TAYLOR, PETER   The Old Forest. London: Chatto & Windus, 1985. Uncorrected proof of the first English edition; printed wrappers; near fine, signed by author.   Lame Duck Books 19-521 1996 $100.00

TAYLOR, PETER   A Stand in the Mountains. New York: Frederic C. Beil, 1986. 1st edition; (1000 copies); signed by author on special printed label pasted to flyleaf; new, issued, without dust jacket, in flimsy cardboard slipcase.   Steven C. Bernard 71-232 1996 $100.00

TAYLOR, PETER   The Widow of Thornton. New York: Harcourt Brace, 1954. 1st edition; light wear to edges, still about near fine in modestly rubbed jacket, signed by author.   Ken Lopez 74-434 1996 $375.00

TAYLOR, PETER   A Woman of Means. New York: Harcourt, Brace & Co., 1950. 1st edition; signed by author on special printed label pasted to flyleaf, place and date written in ink on lower left corner of flyleaf, otherwise very good+ in dust jacket which is slightly worn at spine ends.   Steven C. Bernard 71-234 1996 $225.00

TAYLOR, PHILIP MEADOWS   Conressions of a Thug. London: Henry S. King, 1873. 2nd edition; 8vo; frontispiece; contemporary quarter calf, gilt, morocco label, boards; covers somewhat stained, some foxing, but good.   Trebizond 39-27 1996 $100.00

TAYLOR, ROBERT H.   Authors at Work: an Address Delivered by Robert H. Taylor at the Opening of an Exhibition of Literary Manuscripts at the Grolier Club Together with a Catalogue of the Exhibition by Herman W. Liebert and Facsimiles of Many of the Exhibits. New York: Grolier Club, 1957. One of 750 copies; 11 1/4 x 8 3/4 inches; 52 pages, (3) leaves; original dust jacket, very fine in very fine jacket.   Phillip J. Pirages 33-291 1996 $100.00

TAYLOR, ROBERT W.   A Clinical Atlas of Veneral And Skin Diseases Including Diagnosis, Prognosis and Treatment. Philadelphia: Lea, 1889. Small folio; 2 volumes; 22, (2), 19-172; (173)-427 pages; 58 chromolithograph plates; original three quarter morocco and cloth, boards worn and scuffed, joints weak and rear joint to volume 2 is coming detached.   James Tait Goodrich K40-117 1996 $595.00

TAYLOR, SAMUEL T.   Dress Cutting Simplified and Reduced to Science. Baltimore: John W. Woods, 1850. 1st edition; 18mo; 8 pages; original plain wrappers; foxed. Very scarce.   M & S Rare Books 60-436 1996 $175.00

TAYLOR, W. A.   Intermere. XXth Century Pub. Co., 1901. 1st edition; fine in very rare plain dust jacket which is little chipped and soiled.   Aronovitz 57-1160 1996 $125.00

TAYLOR, W. THOMAS   Twenty-One Years of Bird and Bull: a Bibliography 1958-1979. Bird & Bull Press, 1980. One of 350 copies; 9 3/4 x 6 3/4 inches; xii, 108 pages, (1) leaf; citron morocco backed boards, prospectus laid in; mint.   Phillip J. Pirages 33-83 1996 $225.00

TAYLOR, WILLIAM   Christian Adventures in South Africa. New York: Nelson and Phillips, 1879. Later edition; 8vo; xv, 557, (3) 3 pages ads; illustrations; original green cloth, spine cocked, touch of rubbing to spine ends, otherwise near fine;   David Mason 71-15 1996 $100.00

TAYLOR, WILLIAM   Scots Poems. Edinburgh: printed for the author, 1787. 1st edition; 8vo; 19th century half calf, slight wear, small later date sticker at foot of spine; very good, very scarce. Jackson p. 135.   Ximenes 109-282 1996 $650.00

TAYLOR, WILLIAM COOKE   The Natural History of Society in the Barbarous and Civilized State... London: Longman, Orme, Brown, Green and Longmans, 1840. 1st edition; large 12mo; 2 volumes, x, (2), 348; (4), 347 pages; original green cloth embossed in blind, spines lettered in gilt, short tear to head of spine of first volume, else very good. Goldsmiths 31369; not in Kress or Williams.   John Drury 82-276 1996 £125.00

TAYLOR, ZACHARY   A Sketch of the Life and Character of Gen. Taylor, the American Hero and People's Man... New York: S. French, 1847. 1st edition; 8vo; original yellow printed wrappers, slight wear, bit soiled; very good; Howes T80; not in Sabin.   Ximenes 108-338 1996 $225.00

TCHELITCHEW, PAVEL   Drawings. New York: H. Bittner & Co., 1947. 1st edition; 48 black and white plates; original binding, top edge slightly dust, head and tail of spine slightly bumped and rubbed, cover edges slightly faded, endpaper gutters browned, some pages slightly marked and thumbed, very good in nicked, rubbed, marked and dusty slightly creased and soiled, price clipped dust jacket browned at spine and edges.   Ulysses 39-585 1996 £95.00

THE TEA Cyclopaedia. Calcutta: E. C. Lazarus, 1881. 1st edition; 8vo; 5 hand colored lithographs after drawings by S. E. Peal, stamp on title, minor soiling; half leather, rebacked.   Maggs Bros. Ltd. 1190-18 1996 £110.00

THE TEA Planter's Vade Mecum... Calcutta: published at the office of the Tea Gazette, 1885. 1st edition; 8vo; half roan, somewhat worn and stained, date erased from title; minor marginal worming.   Maggs Bros. Ltd. 1190-19 1996 £90.00

TEBB, W. SCOTT   A Century of Vaccination and What it Teaches. London: 1899. 2nd edition; 452 pages; original cloth.   W. Bruce Fye 71-2084 1996 $100.00

TEGETMEIER, W. B.   Pheasants for Coverts and Aviaries. London: 1873. Large 4to; full page engraved plates, text illustrations; expertly restored in original pictorial cloth, all edges gilt, unobtrusive light stain to corners of about 4 leaves; scarce.   David A.H. Grayling MY95Orn-73 1996 £75.00

TEGETMEIER, W. B.   Pheasants for Coverts and Aviaries. London: 1873. Large 4to; full page plates; original pictorial cloth, expertly restored, very light stain to corner of 3 leaves; scarce.   David A.H. Grayling MY95Orn-257 1996 £65.00

TEISER, RUTH   Lawton Kennedy, Printer. San Francisco: Book Club of California, 1988. 1st edition; limited to 450 copies; 107 pages; numerous color facsimile titlepages; cloth backed gilt decorated boards, paper spine label; mint with plain grey dust jacket.   Argonaut Book Shop 113-388 1996 $125.00

TEIXEIRA, JOSE   Rervm ab Henrici Boronii Franciae Protoprincipis Majoribus Gestarum, Epitome... Paris: Leodegarius Delaz, 1598. 1st edition thus; 12mo; pages 237, (iii), 62, (ii), last blank, mostly Roman letter, some italic, nice woodcut headpieces and initials; title and outer blank margin of first leaf little dusty, some very light waterstaining, mostly at outer corners at head, nowhere really affecting text; contemporary vellum over boards, lacks first free endpaper, remains of ties; generally good.   A. Sokol XXV-95 1996 £385.00

TELLER, H. M.   Letter from the Secretary of the Interior...Relating to Leases of Lands in the Indian Territory to Citizens of the United States for Cattle-Grazing and Other Purposes. Washington: Senate Executive Document 54, 1884. 1st edition; 160 pages; 3 folding maps; half morocco and cloth with title in gilt on spine, very good. Reese Six Score 72 note.   Michael D. Heaston 23-91 1996 $250.00

TELLER, H. M.   Letter From the Secretary of the Interior...(a) Report Relatie to the Leasing of Indian Lands in the Indian Territory. Washington: Senate Executive Document No. 17, 1885. 1st edition; 220 pages; 2 folding maps; half morocco and cloth with title in gilt on spine, very good. Reese Six Score 72.   Michael D. Heaston 23-92 1996 $225.00

TELLIER, JULES   Abd-er-Rhaman in Paradise. Waltham St. Lawrence: Golden Cockerel Press, 1928. 1st edition in English, 319/400 copies; crown 8vo; pages (iii), 34, (1); printed on handmade paper, 3 full page wood engravings and wood engrved title vignette by Paul Nash; original quarter mid blue buckram, gilt lettered backstrip faded, black, orange and tan boards, insignificant free endpaper foxing, top edge gilt, others untrimmed; excellent. Chanticleer 60.   Blackwell's B112-131 1996 £140.00

TEMPLE, A. G.   Wantage Collection. A Catalogue of Pictures Forming the Collection of Lord and Lady Wantage. London: George bell, 1905. 35 x 25 cm; xvi, 196 pages; 108 plates; unbound, uncut sheets on handmade paper.   Rainsford A54-655 1996 £85.00

TEMPLE, RICHARD   Palestine Illustrated. London: W. H. Allen & Co., 1888. 1st edition; 4to; 296 pages; frontispiece, plates; original maroon cloth, cover lightly soiled, but very good.   Chapel Hill 94-282 1996 $150.00

TEN Little Negro Boys. New York: Charles E. Graham, ca. 1880. Octavo; (6)ff., chromolithographed paltes and black and white illustrations; colored self wrappers, very nice, owner's inscription and light wear to extremities.   Bromer Booksellers 90-143 1996 $375.00

TEN Tales. Huntington Beach: Cahill, 1994. Of a total edition of 276 copies, this one of 26 lettered copies; signed by each author, as well as Lawrence Block who provides introduction; three quarter leather, fine in fine slipcase. Ken Lopez 74-14 1996 $350.00

TEN Tales. Huntington Beach: Cahill, 1994. Limited to 276 copies, this copy designated 'author's copy' presumably intended for presentation to or by authors and is signed by all 12 contributors; half leather and paper covered boards, slipcase, as new. Between the Covers 42-15 1996 $250.00

TENCIN, CLAUDINE ALEXANDRINE GUERIN DE The Siege of Calais, an Historical Novel. London: printed by Charles Say, Jr. 1751. 1st edition of this translation; 8vo; 2 volumes in one, (140, 149) pages; engraved title in each volume; contemporary half calf over marbled boards, contrasting title label; fine; scarce; signature of M. Finlater and Cullen House bookplate. 2 copies in NUC; Raven 103. Paulette Rose 16-316 1996 $850.00

TENN, W. Of All Possible World. Ballantine, 1955. 1st edition; just about fine in very good+ dust jacket. Aronovitz 57-1162 1996 $185.00

TENNESSEE Report of James Y. Dunlap, Comptroller of the Treasury to the General Assembly of Tennessee, October 1861. Nashville: J. O. Griffith, Camp & Co., 1861. 1st edition; 69 pages; folding chart, original printed wrappers; very good. Rare. Parrish & Willingham 4138. McGowan Book Co. 65-112 1996 $650.00

TENNYSON D'EYNCOURT, CHARLES Eustace an Elegy. London: Saunders and Otley, 1851. 2nd edition; 8vo; original magenta cloth, front cover elaborately decorated in gilt; fine. Ximenes 109-284 1996 $450.00

TENNYSON, ALFRED TENNYSON, 1ST BARON 1809-1892 Idylls of the King. London: Edward Moxon, 1867. 8vo; page 167 paper eaten by insect with loss of a few words; contemporary red morocco, boards with gilt panels, upper board lettered in gilt, spine fully gilt, rubbed, all edges gilt, with water color painting on fore-edge of a coastal scene with various fishing boats and fishermen, sand, cliffs, &c. Ian Wilkinson 95/1-98 1996 £95.00

TENNYSON, ALFRED TENNYSON, 1ST BARON 1809-1892 In Memoriam. Boston: Ticknor, Reed and Fields, 1850. 1st American edition; 8vo; original binding, light fading, soiling to covers, spine tips worn, very good, neat contemporary owner signature. Charles Agvent 4-1099 1996 $150.00

TENNYSON, ALFRED TENNYSON, 1ST BARON 1809-1892 In Memoriam. Boston: Ticknor, Reed and Fields, 1850. 1st American edition; 8vo; 48 pages publisher's ads at back, slight spotting of endpapers, else very nice; original brown cloth, covers stamped in blind, spine lettered in gilt, chipping of head and tail of spine, some darkening and rubbing; James Cummins 14-205 1996 $100.00

TENNYSON, ALFRED TENNYSON, 1ST BARON 1809-1892 In Memoriam. London: Moxon, 1850. 1st edition; 1st issue, with 8 pages of prelim ads dated Feb. 1850; one of 5000 copies; 8 original purple cloth, spine and top edge evenly and not unattractively faded to light brown; fine, virtually no wear, only a trace of foxing, lovely copy in folding box. Lakin & Marley 3-61 1996 $1,000.00

TENNYSON, ALFRED TENNYSON, 1ST BARON 1809-1892 In Memoriam. London: Moxon, 1850. 1st edition; 1st issue; modern full red calf, light rubbing to spine and corners; near fine. Owner inscription. Charles Agvent 4-1098 1996 $450.00

TENNYSON, ALFRED TENNYSON, 1ST BARON 1809-1892 In Memoriam. London: Macmillan & Co., 1896. Later edition; 12mo; original green cloth, slightly worn; quarter morocco box; presentation copy from Edward Thomas to his future Mother-in-law, Mrs. Noble; important ALS to Mrs. Nobel; Edward Thomas letters are scarce; with two George Sims bookplates. Lakin & Marley 3-66 1996 $2,500.00

TENNYSON, ALFRED TENNYSON, 1ST BARON 1809-1892 In Memoriam. London: Nonesuch Press, 1933. Of 2000 numbered copies, this one of 125 with ornaments printed in gold leaf and specially bound; imperial 8vo; printed on Van Gelder; full vellum, gold thonged and with gold endpapers, fine in slipcase, scarce. Bertram Rota 272-329 1996 £300.00

TENNYSON, ALFRED TENNYSON, 1ST BARON 1809-1892 Maud, and Other Poems. London: Edward Moxon, 1855. 1st edition; 8vo; original green cloth, covers stamped in blind, spine lettered in gilt, some light rubbing, cream endpapers (offsetting from bookplates, one removed), 8 pages publisher's ads dated July 1855 at front, single leaf of author's ads at back, very nice in green morocco backed slipcase; with leather bookplate of Richard Montgomery Gilchrist Potter at front and signature of Emily Hodgekinson. Ashley vii 118; Hayward 248. Tinker 2080. James Cummins 14-206 1996 $150.00

TENNYSON, ALFRED TENNYSON, 1ST BARON 1809-1892 Maud. Kelmscott Press, 1893. One of 500 copies on paper (there were also five vellum copies, not for sale); 8 1/4 x 5 3/4 inches; 2 p.l., 69, (1) pages; large woodcut initials and decorative marginal extensions, device at end, printed in red and black, using Golden type; original limp vellum, gilt titling on spine, silk ties, in original very slightly worn publisher's green slipcase, titled in gilt, elaborate woodcut frontispiece and borders around first pages of text, as fine a copy as one could hope to find; bookplate of Leslie Benson. Sparling 17; Tomkinson p. 112. Phillip J. Pirages 33-323 1996 $1,400.00

TENNYSON, ALFRED TENNYSON, 1ST BARON 1809-1892 Poems. London: Edward Moxon, 1842. 1st edition; 8vo; 2 volumes; contemporary calf, gilt, spines and inner dentelles gilt, contrasting red and blue morocco labels, all edges gilt, little rubbed; very nice set, complete with half titles; Wise 12; CBEL III 414. Ximenes 109-283 1996 $800.00

TENNYSON, ALFRED TENNYSON, 1ST BARON 1809-1892 Poems. London: Macmillan & Co., 1893. New edition; square 8vo; xv, 376 pages; portrait, 54 illustrations, green cloth, ornately gilt with acorn design, all edges gilt. Robin Greer 94A-76 1996 £120.00

TENNYSON, ALFRED TENNYSON, 1ST BARON 1809-1892 Poems. London: George Bell & Sons, 1905. 1st edition; limited to 75 copies on Japanese vellum, this number 71; x, 402, 2 pages of ads, frontispiece and decorated title, 17 full page and 47 text illustrations by Eleanor Fortescue Brickdale. Green and red binding design from trade edition bound in, beige holland cloth, titled in black and red on spine; excellent copy, mainly unopened. Robin Greer 94A-37 1996 £300.00

TENNYSON, ALFRED TENNYSON, 1ST BARON 1809-1892 Poems. London: George Bell & Sons, 1905. 1st edition; 402 pages; titlepages, several full page black and white illustrations, numerous black and white decorations in text, endpapers and cover design by Eleanor Fortescue Brickdale; decorated cloth gilt, top edge gilt, inscription, head and tail of spine and corners slightly bumped, covers slightly marked and rubbed, prelims, edges and endpapers slightly spotted, free endpapers partially browned, some protruding page edges nicked, short tear to fore-edge of front free endpaper; very good. Ulysses 39-72 1996 £85.00

TENNYSON, ALFRED TENNYSON, 1ST BARON 1809-1892 The Poetical Works of Alfred Lord Tennyson, Poet Laureate. London: Kegan Paul & Co., 1878. 12mo; 12 volumes; beautifully bound in full dark blue morocco, gilt edges, by Riviere. Charles W. Traylen 117-209 1996 £390.00

TENNYSON, ALFRED TENNYSON, 1ST BARON 1809-1892 Seven Poems and Two Translations. London: printed by T. J. Cobden-Sanderson & Emory Walker at the Doves Press, 1902. One of 350 copies printed, 25 of them on vellum; small 4to; 56 pages, text printed in black and red; original limp vellum, spine lettered in gilt; bookplate, foxing spot affecting first few leaves, otherwise nice; inscribed by Cobden-Sanderson. Sotheran PN32-40 1996 £328.00

TENNYSON, ALFRED TENNYSON, 1ST BARON 1809-1892 12 Verses from "The Day Dream". London: 1995. One in an edition of 17 copies; 7 x 6 inches; designed, printed, illustrated & bound by Susan Allix; 65 ptd. pages, 35 of which have pochoir, lino-cut or a combination of both; printed in various colors on somerset mould made paper with cream Japanese title sheets; binding is tongue-in-slot construction with boards edged in wide strip of dark purple goatskin and covered in Japanese paper stenciled in pastel colors & varnished, w/ptd. title & aqua green lea. onalys, edges sponted w/watercolor, endpapers stenciled flyleaves ptd. allowing no visual interruption in looking at the book from its very beginning, book has curved top and is contained under a painted glass dome. Joshua Heller 21-41A 1996 $1,350.00

TENNYSON, ALFRED TENNYSON, 1ST BARON 1809-1892 12 Verses from "The Day Dream". London: 1995. One in an edition of 17 copies; 7 x 6 inches; designed, printed, illustrated and bound by Susan Allix, 65 printed pages, 35 of which have pochoir, lino-cut or a combination of both; printed in various colors on Somerset mould made paper with cream Japanese title sheets, binding is tongue-in-slot construction with boards edged in a wide strip of dark purple goatskin and covered in Japanese paper stenciled in pastel colors and varnished, with printed title and aqua green leather onlays, edges are sponged & watercolor, endpapers are stenciled, and flyleaves printed, allowing no visual interruption in looking at the book from its very beginning; book has curved top, in green cloth box with pink leather tie. Joshua Heller 21-41b 1996 $1,100.00

TENNYSON, ALFRED TENNYSON, 1ST BARON 1809-1892   Works. Boston: Estes & Lauriat, 1895. One of 100 numbered copies of the Edition des Amateurs; 8vo; 12 volumes; printed on Japan vellum; numerous plates; full morocco, 5 raised bands, inner gilt dentelles, bookplates, minor edgewear and scuffing, spines lightly and evenly faded.   Charles Agvent 4-1106 1996 $850.00

TENNYSON, ALFRED TENNYSON, 1ST BARON 1809-1892   Works. New York: Bryan Taylor, 1895. One of 25 numbered copies of author's autograph edition, signed by editor, William Rolfe; 8vo; numerous plates; full tree calf, 5 raised bands, inner gilt dentelles, gilt decorated spine panels with red and tan morocco labels, some of which are discolored, spine tips little worn, dry with 1 small chip, gorgeous covers.   Charles Agvent 4-1105 1996 $1,200.00

TEONGE, HENRY   The Diary of Henry Teonge, Chaplain on Board His Majesty's Ships Assitance, Bristol, & Royal Oak: Anno. 1675 to 1679. London: Charles Knight, 1825. 1st edition; 8vo; folding facsimile, 2 titlepages, xviii, half title, 327 pages, index; three quarter maroon goat and marbled paper over boards, marbled endpapers, repair to verso of titlepage, marginal staining through pages vii of preface.   Parmer Books 039/Nautica-047044 1996 $200.00

TERENTIUS AFER, PUBLIUS 180-159 BC   Comoedias Sex. Leipzig: Jacobi Bervaldi (Berwald) for Jacobi Apelij, 1577. Small 8vo; 304 leaves; contemporary binding of alum tawed vellumized pigskin over oak boards, boldly stamped on front cover is baroque portrait of Augustus I, elector of Saxony, rear cover bears his arms, binding retains original clasps, quite scarce.   Family Album Tillers-602 1996 $500.00

TERENTIUS AFER, PUBLIUS 180-159 BC   Comoediae. Venice: Apud Joan. Gryphium, 1586. Folio; title with large woodcut vignette, 6 woodcut illustrations in text, large woodcut initial letters; occasional light soiling, some worming, mainly to margins, slight foxing; old stamp of Royal Inst. of South Wales; full near contemporary vellum.   Ian Wilkinson 95/1-145 1996 £240.00

TERENTIUS AFER, PUBLIUS 180-159 BC   Comediae Sex ex Recensione Heinsiana. Amsterdam: Apud Henr. Wetstenium, ca. 1650. 24mo; 236 pages; engraved title, new vellum binding; good.   K Books 441-127 1996 £50.00

TERENTIUS AFER, PUBLIUS 180-159 BC   Comedies. London: 1749. 2nd edition; 12mo; 2 volumes, over 800 pages; portrait, full unlettered contemporary calf, very good.   K Books 442-143 1996 £50.00

TERENTIUS AFER, PUBLIUS 180-159 BC   Comoediae. Birmingham: Baskerville, 1772. Quarto; 364 pages; uncut, unopened, slight foxing; contemporary paper boards backed in morocco gilt. Gaskell 46; Brunet V 718.   Family Album Tillers-607 1996 $1,200.00

TERENTIUS AFER, PUBLIUS 180-159 BC   Comoediae. Birmingham: Baskerville, 1772. 4to; 364 pages; foxed; all edges gilt, full straight grain plum morocco binding, splendidly tooled in gilt and blind, boards tooled with wide gilt Greek key outer dentelle, enclosing archway (almost cathedral) frame, though unsigned, some aspects of the binding remind us of the work of Birdsall. engraved English armorial bookplate, ms. presentation from B. Drury, Eton. Gaskell 46.   Family Album Tillers-608 1996 $1,200.00

TERENTIUS AFER, PUBLIUS 180-159 BC   Comoediae. Birmingham: Baskerville, 1772. 12mo; pages (4), 308, cancellans at G2; all edges gilt, early full crushed red morocco gilt, floral decorated gilt spine, engraved ex-libris from the Scottish clan Gordon; Gaskell 47.   Family Album Tillers-609 1996 $350.00

TERENTIUS AFER, PUBLIUS 180-159 BC   Comediae... Birmingham: John Baskeverille, 1772. 4to; 364 pages; contemporary diced calf, title label inset on red morocco, gilt lines, respined neatly and expertly in same style; very good.   K Books 441-126 1996 £190.00

TERENTIUS AFER, PUBLIUS 180-159 BC   Comoediae. Birmingham: Baskerville, 1772. 12mo; pages (4), 308 pages, the edition without the cancellans at G2; some leaves in 2 gatherings smudged during printing (very unusual), contemporary sprinkled calf, gilt tulip roll on boards, spine ornamented with gilt crossed arrows, later ex-libris of John Rayner. Gaskell 47.   Family Album Tillers-610 1996 $325.00

TERENTIUS AFER, PUBLIUS 180-159 BC   Comoediae. Birmingham: Typis Johannis Baskerville, 1772. 8vo; 364 pages; tree calf, neatly and expertly respined, small tears on Dd3 and L2 neatly repaired, marginal tears with no loss, some minor browning but good.   K Books 442-145 1996 £140.00

TERENTIUS AFER, PUBLIUS 180-159 BC   Terentii Comoediae. Birmingham: Typis Johannis Baskerville, 1772. 1st edition thus; 12mo; 307 pages; original full mottled calf, rebacked at an early date with original spine and morocco spine label laid down, covers feature circular green designs with gilt borders and dentelles, spine chipped, expected wear to covers and corners, several decorative bookplates, still good, solid copy.   Chapel Hill 94-103 1996 $100.00

TERENTIUS AFER, PUBLIUS 180-159 BC   P. Terentius Afer A. M. Antonio Mureto Emendatus. Venice: Apud Aldum, 1560. 8vo; 271 leaves, Aldine device on title; old mottled calf; Not in UCLA; Renouard 180.11; Adams T357; Brunet V714.   Family Album Tillers-599 1996 $700.00

TERENTIUS AFER, PUBLIUS 180-159 BC   P. Terentius Afer A. M. Antonio Mureto Emendatvs Eiusdem. Mureti Argumenta et Scholia. Venice: Apud Aldum, 1575. 8vo; 271 leaves, Latin Italic with some Greek, oval woodcut device of Aldus Pius Manutius R on title; over title verso there appears a privilege device of Emperor Maximilian II, which includes Aldine anchor and dolphin; woodcut decorative initials, early ms. ownerships; modern quarter calf over marbled boards, ex-libris Harvard/Houghton Library (released). Renouard 219.13; Adams T368; Dibdin II471.   Family Album Tillers-601 1996 $600.00

TERENTIUS AFER, PUBLIUS 180-159 BC   Terentius, in Quem Triplex Edita est P. Antesignani. Lyons: Mathiam Bonhome, 1560. 2nd edition thus; 8vo; (43), 850 pages; contemporary full speckled calf, with raised bands, front hinge cracked internally, still tight, names on titlepage, else very good.   Chapel Hill 94-160 1996 $200.00

TERENTIUS AFER, PUBLIUS 180-159 BC   Terentius A. M. Antonio Mureto, Locis. (with) Annotationes. Antwerp: Plantin, 1565. 16mo; pages 316; 144; archtiectural woodcut title frames, closely trimmed; all edges gilt, handsomely bound in full 17th century morocco, on each board the large 1663 arms of Charles de Castellan, Abbe Commandataire de Saint-Epvre, Diocese of Toul, France, his monogram repeated 4 times on spine; scarce. Brunet V715; Voet 2285/2295; Annales p. 49-50; Olivier 802.   Family Album Tillers-600 1996 $750.00

TERKEL, STUDS   Giants of Jazz. New York: Crowell, 1957. 1st edition; original cloth, fine in very close to fine dust jacket; Inscribed by author. Beasley Books 82-251 1996 $125.00

THE TERRIBLE Tragedy at Washington, Assassination of President Lincoln. Philadelphia: 1865. 9.5 x 5.5 inches; 116 pages; pictorial wrappers, covers frayed and chipped, back cover with small cut. Monaghan 768; McDade 621; Howes L342.   John K. King 77-81 1996 $100.00

TERRY, DANIEL   The Antiquary; a Musical Play. London: printed for William Stockdale, 1820. 1st edition; 12mo; later blue morocco backed marbled boards, some rubbing, some light browning and spotting of text, especially at front and back, good.   James Cummins 14-176 1996 $150.00

TERRY, G. E.   Unknown North Queensland. Victoria: 1937. 60 pages; 2 black and white photos; light brown wrappers; presentation copy, light foxing on few pages, otherwise very good.   Antipodean 28-442 1996 $150.00

TERRY, MICHAEL   Across Unknown Australia. London: 1925. 311 pages, frontispiece and 24 plates; original green stamped buckram, several later pages slightly rubbed, light blue mark on spine, otherwise nice. Signed by Terry, with inscription for Mrs. Van Kirk.   Antipodean 28-443 1996 $295.00

TERRY, MICHAEL   Across Unknown Australia. London: 1926. 2nd impression; 311 pages, frontispiece, 24 plates; original green stamped buckram, very good.   Antipodean 28-444 1996 $175.00

TERRY, MICHAEL   Sand and Sun: with Camels in the Dry Lands of Central Australia. London: 1937. 288 pages; illustrations; good; the Meggitt copy.   Antipodean 28-445 1996 $145.00

TERTULLIAN   Q. Septimii Florentis Tertulliani (Opera). Basel: Froben, 1562. Folio; pages (12), 909, (52) + blanks, printer's device at title and colphon, Holbein woodcut initials, dampstain at lower right corner, not affecting text; old (French) leather backed paper boards, central arabesque lozenge on each board. Adams T411. 3 copies in NUC.   Family Album Tillers-614 1996 $550.00

TESLA, NIKOLA   Experiments with Alternate Currents of High Potential and High Frequency. New York: W. J. Johnston Co., 1896. Later edition; small octavo; ix, 146, (20 ads) pages; frontispiece, text illustrations; original dark green cloth stamped in gilt on spine, minor wear to extremities, otherwise fine.   Heritage Book Shop 196-185 1996 $300.00

TESSIER, THOMAS   In Sight of Chaos. London: Turret Books, 1971. 1st edition; limited to 100 copies, this one of an undetermined number of over run copies left unnumbered and unsigned; author's first book, 24 pages; wrappers, very fine, issued in printed dust jacket.   Robert Gavora 61-228 1996 $100.00

TESSIER, THOMAS   The Night Walker. New York: Athenaeum, 1980. 1st edition; fine in fine dust jacket.   Bud Schweska 12-739 1996 $125.00

TESSIER, THOMAS   Phantom. New York: Athenaeum, 1982. 1st edition; review slip laid in; fine in fine dust jacket.   Bud Schweska 12-738 1996 $100.00

TESSIER, THOMAS   Phantom. New York: Atheneum, 1982. 1st edition; fine in dust jacket with one bump to edge.   Robert Gavora 61-229 1996 $100.00

THE TESTAMENT of Charlotte B. Libanus Press, 1988. Of 220 numbered copies, this is one of 50 specially bound in half deep violet morocco, pictorial boards, laid into pale violet cloth folding box; fine.   Bertram Rota 272-255 1996 £160.00

THE TESTAMENT of Charlotte B. Libanus, 1988. One of 220 numbered copies; tall 8vo; printed in Monotype Garamond on Amatruda handmade, decorations in lavender grey; pictorial boards, with cloth spine; fine.   Bertram Rota 272-254 1996 £85.00

TESTE, A.   The Homoeopathic Materia Medica. Philadelphia: 1854 1st English translation; 634 pages; half leather.   W. Bruce Fye 71-2094 1996 $100.00

TEW, DAVID   The Oakham Canal. Wymondham: Brewhouse Press, 1968. 411/450 copies; small folio; pages 116, (1); double page color printed plate, 11 full page illustrations printed in one or more colors and 28 other black and white text illustrations, all by Rigby Graham, several facsimiles of maps and ephemeral pieces used by the canal company, titlepage printed in red and black; original mid-green cloth, backstrip lettering and Rigby Graham design on front cover, all gilt blocked, pale green and white illustrated endpapers, fine. Battye 13.   Blackwell's B112-47 1996 £65.00

TEXAS   General Regulations for the Government of the Army of the Republic of Texas. Houston: Intelligencer Office-S, Whiting Printer, 1839. 1st edition; leaf of title, verso blank, inserted leaf of errata, 187 pages, 2 plates, 16 pages, including half title; original muslin cloth with original printed spine label, binding somewhat worn and stained, minor chipping to label, plates crisp; very good. Streeter Texas 372A. Not in Eberstadt, Decker, Graff or Howes.   Michael D. Heaston 23-314 1996 $8,500.00

TEXAS.   Senate and House Journals of the Tenth Legislature...State of Texas. Austin: Texas State Library, 1965. 1 of 400 copies; 1st edition; Maggie Lambeth 30-96 1996 $300.00

TEXTOR, BENEDICTUS   Stirpium Differentiae... Paris: Colines, 1534. 1st edition; 16mo; 104 leaves; woodcut architectural title border; late 19th century red morocco, gilt, collector's bibliographic notes laid in; fine. Pritzel 10142; not in Adams, Renouard, Plesch, Hunt or Johnston. Bennett Gilbert LL29-85 1996 $5,250.00

THACKERAY, WILLIAM MAKEPEACE 1811-1863   The Adventures of Philip on His Way through the World. London: Smith, Elder and Co., 1862. 1st edition; 2nd binding (but first 'official' issue); 8vo; 3 volumes; original brown pebbled cloth (Sadlier binding 'i'); bookplate, institutional notice in third volume (though no other ex-libris markings); chipping and fraying to spine ends, hinges weak or cracked, couple of leaves with some minor marginal chipping and creasing, else very good. Sadlier 3186. Sadlier I 339.   James Cummins 14-208 1995 $300.00

THACKERAY, WILLIAM MAKEPEACE 1811-1863   The Adventures of Philip On His Way through the World. London: Smith, Elder and Co., 1862. 1st edition; 8 x 5 1/4 inches; 3 volumes; bound without half title in volume 1; original salmon brown embossed cloth, gilt titled spine, leaves unopened, as close to a perfect copy as one could hope to find; Van Duzer pp. 21-22; Sadlier 3186.   Phillip J. Pirages 33-479 1996 $750.00

THACKERAY, WILLIAM MAKEPEACE 1811-1863   The Adventures of Philip... London: Smith, Elder, 1862. 1st edition; 1st issue binding which is quite scarce in this condition, 8vo; purpe cloth, light wear, minor fading to covers, contents fresh, near fine; This copy has Thackeray's full name below the half title, but it does not appear to match either of his hands and is not being sold as his signature.   Charles Agvent 4-1108 1996 $850.00

THACKERAY, WILLIAM MAKEPEACE 1811-1863   Ballads. (with) Barry Lyndon. London: Bradbury & Evans, 1855/56. 1st edition; 8vo; 2 works bound in one volume; leaf of ads and half titles present in Ballads, terminal ads not present with Barry Lyndon, this one of the few, as noted by Van Duzer 11, without words "The right of Translation reserved' on titlepage; beautifully bound by Blackwell in full crushed crimson morocco with elaborate gold tooling on covers and spine, original yellow wrappers, bit dust soiled, few minor paper repairs, otherwise fine.   Charles Agvent 4-1109 1996 $425.00

THACKERAY, WILLIAM MAKEPEACE 1811-1863   History of Henry Esmond. New York: Limited Editions Club, 1956. One of 1500 copies; 8vo; illustrations by Edward Ardizzone, colored by hand, signed by Ardizzone; full brocade, fine in like case.   Charles Agvent 4-1110 1996 $100.00

THACKERAY, WILLIAM MAKEPEACE 1811-1863   The History of Samuel Titmarsh and The Great Hoggarty Diamond. London: Bradbury & Evans, 1849. 1st edition; small 8vo; original printed boards, worn and rebacked, brown morocco spine, spotting on plates.   Appelfeld Gallery 54-177 1996 $125.00

THACKERAY, WILLIAM MAKEPEACE 1811-1863   The Irish Sketch-Book. London: Chapman and Hall, 1843. 1st edition; large 12mo; 2 volumes; frontispiece, illustrations; original grey-green cloth, spines trifle faded, half brown morocco slipcase, case bit scuffed; particularly fine. Van Duzer 96; CBEL III 857.   Ximenes 109-285 1996 $1,500.00

THACKERAY, WILLIAM MAKEPEACE 1811-1863   The Irish Sketch-Book. London: Chapman and Hall, 1843. 1st edition; 8vo; 2 volumes; numerous engravings; original green cloth, spine ends showing little wear, spines lightly faded, three hinges renewed, chip in front free endpaper, some discoloring of frontispieces around edges, else unusually fine, fresh copy, relatively scarce; in green cloth slipcase with matching chemise, gilt stamped with Bachman's monogram; armorial bookplate of R. FitzGerald Uniacke, bookplates of Edwin Bachman.   James Cummins 14-209 1996 $300.00

THACKERAY, WILLIAM MAKEPEACE 1811-1863   The Kickleburys on the Rhine. London: Smith, Elder & Co., 1850. 1st edition; small 4to; 15 colored plates by author, including vignette title and frontispiece; later half dark green morocco, rubbed, some wear along joints, gutters of lower free endpaper and preceding blanks glue stained, some creasing and tears of same leaves, glue marks in gutters between title and frontispiece, very good.   James Cummins 14-210 1996 $200.00

THACKERAY, WILLIAM MAKEPEACE 1811-1863   The Loving Ballad of Lord Bateman. London: Bell and Daldy, 1871. 16mo; pages 40; wood engraved re-workings of Cruikshank's 11 etched illustrations of 1839, plate of music, plates and letterpress of poem printed on one side of leaf, eccentrically paginated, inscription at head of titlepage; original sand-grain blue cloth, spine unlettered, gilt titled in center of upper side, oblong panel in style of French type ornament at head and foot of both sides, very good; inscribed by Cruikshank for Mrs. William Stebbing. Blackwell's B112-84 1996 £125.00

THACKERAY, WILLIAM MAKEPEACE 1811-1863   Mrs. Perkins's Ball. London: Chapman & Hall, 1847. 3rd edition; 8vo; 22 hand colored plates; 22 hand colored plates, short tear to fold of folding plate; original pink glazed boards, backstrip lacking, some spotting to covers, contents near fine. Van Duzer (140).   Charles Agvent 4-1113 1996 $125.00

THACKERAY, WILLIAM MAKEPEACE 1811-1863   The Newcomes. London: Bradbury & Evans, Oct. 1853-Aug. 1855. 1st edition; 24 parts in 23; illustrations; original pictorial wrappers; set lacks 7 of the ads cited by Van Duzer (147), but includes 2 leaves not mentioned in bibliography; former owner's signatures on few covers, backstrips and wrappers with some wear and neat repairs, little soiled and worn, but good set in two very attractive full morocco solander cases; bookplates of Alex M. Hudnut.   David J. Holmes 52-120 1996 $750.00

THACKERAY, WILLIAM MAKEPEACE 1811-1863   The Newcomes. London: Bradbury & Evans, 1855. 1st edition in book form; 8vo; 2 volumes; engraved titlepages, 46 engraved plates by Richard Doyle, many text illustrations; contemporary quarter calf, spines gilt, marbled boards, front hinges of one volume repaired, margins of plates age darkened, nevertheless good. Van Duzer 147; Sterling Lib 971. Trebizond 39-52 1996 $175.00

THACKERAY, WILLIAM MAKEPEACE 1811-1863   The Newcomes. New York: Limited Editions Club, 1955. Limited to 1500 copies; 4to; 2 volumes; hand colored illustrations by Edward Ardizzone who signs; original binding, fine in very good case.   Charles Agvent 4-1114 1996 $100.00

THACKERAY, WILLIAM MAKEPEACE 1811-1863   Rebecca and Rowena. London: Chapman and Hall, 1850. 1st edition; 8 colored illustrations by Richard Doyle; rebound in full crushed maroon morocco, spine with raised bands, title and author compartments edged in single gold rule with remaining compartments, edges in double gold rule, front and rear boards edged in double gold rule, original wrappers, bound in at rear, original ad leaf present, bookplate to front pastedown with minor offsetting to front free endpapers, joints lightly rubbed with upper front joint just starting to split, still very good.   Hermitage SP95-611 1996 $300.00

THACKERAY, WILLIAM MAKEPEACE 1811-1863   The Rose and the Ring. New York: Limited Editions Club, 1942. Limited to 1500 copies, small folio; original illustrations, redrawn by Fritz Kredel, colored by hand; decorated buckram, near fine in bit worn chemise and quite worn case.   Charles Agvent 4-1115 1996 $125.00

THACKERAY, WILLIAM MAKEPEACE 1811-1863   Vanity Fair. London: Bradbury & Evans, 1848. 1st book edition, 1st issue; illustrations by author; all correct points, no ads; later half calf, leather label; light wear, rubbing, some spotting to plates, not severe, very good.   Charles Agvent 4-1117 1996 $650.00

THACKERAY, WILLIAM MAKEPEACE 1811-1863   Vanity Fair. Oxford: Limited Editions Club, 1931. Limited to 1500 copies; 4to; 2 volumes; lithographs by John Austen, colored by hand by Daniel Jacomet, signed by Austen; half magenta linen and paper, fine in near fine dust jackets and broken case.   Charles Agvent 4-1118 1996 $150.00

THACKERAY, WILLIAM MAKEPEACE 1811-1863   The Works of William Makepeace Thackeray. London: Smith, Elder & Co., 1878-79/86. Limited edition, limitation is stated to be 1000 sets; 52 volumes; original engraved titlepages and illustrations printed on India paper and laid down; occasional foxing to some pages; full green polished pigskin mottled in autumn colors, gilt, uniformly fine, with 6 panel spine with raised bands titled in gilt, compartments decorated with leaf sprays in corners and framed in double fillet, covers decorated with intricate design of triple and double fillets framing a complex ornamental border of trefoils, fleurons and arabesques of exceptionally delicate execution, finished inside with delicate dentelle border with stylized flower & leaf corner ornaments on leather turn-ins & green watered silk endleaves; spine color altered from green to brown.   Hermitage SP95-612 1996 $6,500.00

THAKUR, R. S.   Major Medicinal Plants of India. Lucknow: 1989. 8vo; x, 585 pages; numerous colored plates and line drawings; hardbound.   Raymond M. Sutton VI-1095 1996 $165.00

THE THAMES From Its Source to the Sea. London: Cassell & Co., 1892. 4to; viii, 148; 149-264; 265-368 pages; volumes by the insertion of 20 hand colored, 3 tinted and 344 uncolored plates and with 2 original 19th century watercolors; contemporary dark brown half morocco, spines extra gilt in 6 compartments, two of these being lettered and the remainder tooled with stylized flowers, leaves, etc., top edge gilt, extremities lightly rubbed; superb set.   Thomas Thorp 489-303 1996 £2,200.00

THANE, J.   British Autography. A Collection of Fac-Similes of the Hand Writing of Royal and Illustrious Personages, with Their Autahentic Portraits. London: published by J. Thane, n.d. 4to; 2 volumes, 2 frontispieces, 269 plates; half russia, quite rubbed at extremities, corners bit bumped; booklabel of Charles E. Kempe.   Maggs Bros. Ltd. 1191-164 1996 £85.00

THANE, J.   British Autography. A Collection of Fac-Similes of the Hand-writing of Royal and Illustrious Personages, with Their Authentic Portraits. London: Thane, n.d., ca. 1790. 4to; frontispiece, engraved title, pages iv, 16, 40, 102 engraved plates; contemporary dark blue morocco, covers gilt, outer border of double and single rules enclosing swags, cornerpieces with crimson morocco onlays, central panel with corners a l'eventail spine gilt in 6 panels, raised bands gilt, panels with massed small tools and crimson morocco onlays, head and foot of spine with red morocco onlays gilt, all edges gilt, marbled endpapers, by Benedict, London, with his ticket, joints weakening; Ramsden p. 37.   Marlborough 160-58 1996 £750.00

THAXTER, CELIA   Among the Isles of Shoals. Boston: James R. Osgood, 1873. 1st edition; 1st printing; one of 2060 copies; 12mo; on 75 lb. paper; green cloth, tips and front edge bit worn, spine slightly cocked, traces of glue on verso, very nice, scarce. BAL 19848.   Priscilla Juvelis 95/1-236 1996 $100.00

THAXTER, CELIA   Drift Weed. Boston: Houghton, Osgood and Co., 1879. 1st edition; one of 1004 copies; 12mo; green gilt stamped cloth with author and title on front panel and spine, early pencil all but completely faded from front lyleaf, but generlaly very good. BAL 19871.   Priscilla Juvelis 95/1-237 1996 $100.00

THAYER, ELISHA   Family Memorial. Hingham, 1835. pages 180, 100; original binding, paper label, spine and hinges cracked, text very good.   Stephen Lunsford 45-157 1996 $100.00

THAYER, EMMA HOMAN   Wild Flowers of Colorado. New York: Cassell and Co., 1885. Large quarto; pages 54, 24 color plates; original printed boards, all edges gilt, slight wear to extremities, short tear to spine repaired.   Dumont 28-59 1996 $195.00

THAYER, G. H.   Concealing Colouration in the Animal Kingdom. New York: 1918. New edition; 4to; pages xix, 260; 16 colored plates, 40 plain plates; original cloth, neatly refixed.   Wheldon & Wesley 207-593 1996 £95.00

THAYER, JOHN   An Account of the Conversion of the Reverend Mr. John Thayer, Lately a Protestant Minister at Boston in North America... Baltimore: reprinted and sold by William Goddard, 1788. 5th edition; 12mo; disbound, foxed, but very good; Evans 21491; Sabin 95233; Wheeler, Maryland Press 485.   Ximenes 108-339 1996 $300.00

THEOBALD, F. V.   Physiologue Theobaldi Episcopi De Naturis Duodecim Animalium. Bloomington: Indiana University Press, c. 1964. Number 182 of 325 copies, signed by artist; 20 x 14 inches; 41 pages of text; unbound signatures in folding box, as issued; 12 lithographs and 10 woodcuts, book designed by George Sadek; text handset in Emerson and print with woodcuts from original blocks on Rives and printed at the Spiral Press, lithographs printed in Italy; grey cloth clamshell box, illustrated paper title label on front; box lightly marked, else fine. Grolier Club, Amer. Illus. Books 194-1965, no. 26.   Joshua Heller 21-192 1996 $350.00

THEOBALD, F. V.   The Plant Lice or Aphididae of Great Britain. London: 1926-29. 8vo; 3 volumes, 591 text figures; rexine.   Wheldon & Wesley 207-1121 1996 £75.00

THEOBALD, LEWIS   The History of the Loves of Antiochus and Stratonice; In which are Interspers'd Some Accounts Relating to Greece and Syria. London: printed for Jonas Browne, 1717. 12mo; contemporary calf, gilt, rather worn, joints cracked; 2 clean tears without surface loss, otherwise, aside from binding wear, very good, scarce; McBurney 88; CBEL II 988 and 1745.   Ximenes 109-287 1996 $850.00

THEOBALD, LEWIS   Shakespeare Restored: or, a Specimen of the Many Errors, as well Commited, as Unamended by Mr. Pope in His Late edition of this Poet. London: by Sam Aris for R. Francklin, J. Woodman and D. Lyon and C. Davis, 1726. 1st edition; 1st issue; 4to; pages (6), viii, 194; contemporary half calf, spine with raised bands, double gilt rules, red morocco label (chipped), marbled paper sides, modern booklabel, lower joint just cracked, corners little worn, first and last leaves just browned at outer corners fromt turn-ins, small burnhole in gutter of title not affecting text, very good, clean and crisp. Jaggard p. 663.   Simon Finch 24-225 1996 £1,500.00

THEOCRITIUS   Commentari Vetera in Theocriti Eglogas...(Scholia to Theocritis). Venice: Apud Salamandrum (Bartholomaei de Zanettis), 1539. Small 8vo; ff. 112, Greek text, woodcut decorative initials and headpieces, printer's device of crowned 'dragon' in flames on first and last leaves; leather backed paper boards, ex-libris Harvard College. Brunet V 781; Adams T477.   Family Album Tillers-615 1996 $280.00

THEOCRITUS   Theocritus, Bion and Moschus. Idylls. London: Medici Society, 1922. Number 55 of 500 numbered sets; 4to; 2volumes, 30 tipped in color plates by William Russell Flint; tan cloth over blue/grey baords, printed paper labels on spines and upper covers, top edge gilt, uncut, fine.   George J. Houle 68-49 1996 $375.00

THEOCRITUS   Sixe Idyllia; the Anonymous English Translation Printed at Oxford in 1588. New York: Chilmark Press, 1971. One of 270 numbered copies; small folio; printed in handset 20 pt. Palatino italic on J. Green's mouldmade paper, plates printed by Studio Prints; quarter buckram, marbled boards, some faint offsetting to plates, but very nice in slipcase.   Bertram Rota 272-394 1996 £150.00

THEOPHRASTUS   The Moral Characters of Theophrastus. London: Jacob Tonson, 1714. 12mo; pages (34), 80, 4 pages, publisher's ad; worn contemporary full leather, old ms. notes.   Family Album Tillers-616 1996 $140.00

THEORY of Theatrical Dancing. London: 1888. 1st edition; 92 pages; 14 plates; three quarter calf, rubbed, otherwise very good clean copy; scarce. Lyman Books 21-434 1996 $100.00

THEROUX, ALEXANDER An Adultery. New York: S&S, 1987. Uncorrected proof of the first edition; blue-green wrappers; fine; signed by author. Lame Duck Books 19-531 1996 $150.00

THEROUX, ALEXANDER Darconville's Cat. Garden City: Doubleday, 1981. 1st edition; signed by author; near fine in dust jacket with light wear to extremities, signed by author. Lame Duck Books 19-529 1996 $150.00

THEROUX, ALEXANDER The Great Whealde Tragedy. Boston: Godine, 1975. 1st edition; oblong octavo; near fine in dust jacket, signed by author. Lame Duck Books 19-525 1996 $100.00

THEROUX, ALEXANDER History is Made at Night. West Chester: Aralia Press, 1992. One of a limited handprinted edition of 150 copies, this one signed by author though not called for; red cloth covered boards with publisher's announcement laid in; fine. Lame Duck Books 19-534 1996 $100.00

THEROUX, ALEXANDER The Lollipop Trollops and Other Poems. Naperville: Dalkey Archive, 1992. Uncorrected proof; illustrations by Edward Gorey; illustrated red wrappers; fine; signed by author and artist; Lame Duck Books 19-532 1996 $200.00

THEROUX, ALEXANDER The Lollipop Trollops and Other Poems. Normal: Dalkey Archive, 1992. Of a total limited edition of 100, one of 50 copies for sale, signed and numbered by author and artist; illustrations by Edward Gorey; fine in like dust jacket. Lame Duck Books 19-533 1996 $200.00

THEROUX, ALEXANDER The Primary Colors. New York: Holt, 1994. Uncorrected proof; cabernet wrappers; fine, signed by author. Lame Duck Books 19-535 1996 $150.00

THEROUX, ALEXANDER The Schinocephalic Waif. Boston: Godine, 1975. 1st edition; oblong octavo; fine in dust jacket, signed by author. Lame Duck Books 19-526 1996 $125.00

THEROUX, ALEXANDER Theroux Metaphrastes. Boston: Godine, 1975. 1st edition; stapled wrappers; fine, signed by author. Lame Duck Books 19-527 1996 $100.00

THEROUX, ALEXANDER Three Wogs. Boston: Gambit, 1972. 1 fine in near fine presumed first issue dust jacket with sepia-tone photo; signed by author. Lame Duck Books 19-524 1996 $350.00

THEROUX, ALEXANDER Watergraphs. Boston: Base Canard, 1994. Deluxe issue, one of 15 copies on handmade paper, Roman numeralled and signed by author; elegantly handbound by Sarah Creighton in quarter leather and marbled paper of her own design. Lame Duck Books 19-537 1996 $350.00

THEROUX, ALEXANDER Watergraphs. Boston: Base Canard, 1994. 1st edition; one of 100 copies on laid paper, each numbered and signed by author, from a total issue of 116; each illustrated with previously unpublished wood engraving by Fritz Eichenberg, executed as a gift to the author for his personal ex-libris in 1980; designed by Bruce Chandler; blue cloth, author and title stamped in gold on front panel and spine, new. Priscilla Juvelis 95/1-239 1996 $100.00

THEROUX, ALEXANDER Watergraphs. Boston: Base Canard, 1994. 1st book edition, one of 100 copies; bound in linen at the Harcourt bindery and signed by author. Lame Duck Books 19-536 1996 $100.00

THEROUX, PAUL 1941- Fong and the Indians. London: Hamish Hamilton, 1976. 1st edition; signed; fine in dust jacket. Bev Chaney, Jr. 23-685 1996 $175.00

THEROUX, PAUL 1941- Girls at Play. Boston: Houghton Mifflin Co., 1969. 1st edition; fine in dust jacket. Hermitage SP95-613 1996 $150.00

THEROUX, PAUL 1941- London Snow: a Christmas Story. London: 1973. Limited to 450 copies signed by author and artist; engravings by John Lawrence; patterned cloth gilt, fine in original glassine wrapper. Words Etcetera 94-1208 1996 £75.00

THEROUX, PAUL 1941- The Mosquito Coast. Boston: Houghton Mifflin Co., 1982. 1st edition; number 217 of 350 copies, signed by author; fine in lightly soiled slipcase. Hermitage SP95-616 1996 $125.00

THEROUX, PAUL 1941- The Mosquito Coast. Boston: Houghton Mifflin, 1982. 1/250 copies, signed and numbered; fine in slipcase. Bev Chaney, Jr. 23-688 1996 $100.00

THEROUX, PAUL 1941- The Mosquito Coast. Boston: Houghton Mifflin, 1982. Fine in dust jacket with slight sunning on spine and small section of lower front panel; presentation copy inscribed by author to James Hanley. R. A. Gekoski 19-139 1996 £125.00

THEROUX, PAUL 1941- My Secret History. London: Hamish Hamilton, 1989. One of 4 copies with printing mistake omitting the author's name on front panel on spine, with the exception of small blemish on spine, a fine copy. R. A. Gekoski 19-140 1996 £200.00

THEROUX, PAUL 1941- The Old Patagonian Express. Boston: Houghton Mifflin, 1979. Nice copy in slightly soiled dust jacket; presentation copy from author for James Hanley. R. A. Gekoski 19-138 1996 £125.00

THEROUX, PAUL 1941- Sinning With Annie. Boston: Houghton Mifflin Co., 1972. Advance uncorrected proof copy; red wrappers, publisher's information pasted to front cover; near fine, rare state. Lame Duck Books 19-538 1996 $350.00

THEROUX, PAUL 1941- V. S. Naipaul: an Introduction to His Work. London: Deutsch, 1972. Correct first edition, preceding the American flawless, scarce. Lame Duck Books 19-539 1996 $1,250.00

THEROUX, PAUL 1941- V. S. Naipaul: an Introduction to His Work. London: Andre Deutsch, 1972. Author's scarce second book; very slight spotting to top edge, otherwise fine in prie clipped dust jacket. R. A. Gekoski 19-137 1996 £500.00

THEROUX, PAUL 1941- Waldo. Boston: Houghton Mifflin, 1967. 1st edition; signed, superior copy with only a touch of light rubbing on verso. Bev Chaney, Jr. 23-693 1996 $175.00

THEROUX, PAUL 1941- Waldo. Boston: Houghton Mifflin Co., 1967. 1st edition; fine in lightly worn dust jacket with three quarter inch diagonal closed tear across head of spine panel. Author's first book. Hermitage SP95-617 1996 $125.00

THEROUX, PAUL 1941- Waldo. Boston: Houghton Mifflin Co., 1967. 1st edition; author's first book; nice copy in bright near fine dust jacket, with small closed tear on upper back panel. Left Bank Books 2-141 1996 $125.00

THESAURUS Dramaticus. London: printed by Sam. Aris, 1924. 12mo; 2 volumes, x, 240; (2), 358 pages; frontispieces, titlepages printed in red and black; contemporary speckled calf, decoratively blindstamped covers, gilt spines with raised bands tooled in compartments, blindstamped board edges, edges sprinkled red, front cover of volume 1 lightly scraped, light rubbing to corners and edges, minor wear to joints; very good, armorial bookplates. Heritage Book Shop 196-249 1996 $500.00

THESPIAN Dictionary, or Dramatic Biography of the Present Age, Containing Sketches of the Lives...Of All the Principal Dramatists, Composers, Commentators, Managers, Actors and Actresses of the United Kingdom. London: James Cundee, 1805. 2nd edition (same year as first); 12mo. in sixes; pages (i-iii), iv, 396 (5 ads); engraved titlepage and second title which calls for '22 elegant illustrations', except for 2 titlepage vignettes, however, ther is no indication of any illustrations having ever been present, tan polished calf, gilt in panels, raised bands, gilt on brown leather label, gilt fillets; some wear, but nice. LAR 43; CBEL II 394. Hartfield 48-11u 1996 $225.00

THE THESPIAN Preceptor; or, a Full Display of Scenic Art: Including Ample and Easy Instructions for Treading the Stage, Using Proper Action... Boston: for Elam Bliss, 1810. 1st edition; 12mo; original boards, worn, later quarter calf; scarce; some embrowning; bookplate of Eva LeGallienne. S&S 21479; LAR 717-718 (English editions of 1811 and 1818). Dramatis Personae 37-11 1996 $300.00

THICKNESSE, PHILIP   Memoirs and Anecdotes of Philip Thicknesse, Late Lieutenant Governor of Land Guard Fort and Unfortunately Father to George Touchet, Baron Audley. London: printed for the author, 1788. 1st edition; 8vo. in 4's; 2 volumes, pages xvi, (viii), 326, (2) (blank); (viii), 326; bound together in modern russet russia backed contemporary marbled boards, smooth backstrip divided by double gilt rules, contemporary gilt lettered red leather label re-laid, vellum tips to boards; early owner's name "D. Gell"; excellent.   Blackwell's B112-270 1996 £250.00

THIELEN, BETH   Why the Revolving Door: the Neighborhood, the Prisons. 1993. One of 20 copies, signed by artist; sculptural pop-up book made from mono-printed templates which vary in color and textual application, hand printed by artist on an Ettan etching press on 100 percent rag paper, acid free, white and black Arches Cover; each page hand cut and bound by artist, cover with etching, cover and slipcase boards are acid free, lignin free, binder's board, black linen book cloth for book spine and slipcase.   Joshua Heller 21-267 1996 $1,600.00

THIERS, LOUIS ADOLPHE   The History of the French Revolution. London: Richard Bentley and Son, 1881. New edition; 8vo; 5 volumes; 41 steel engravings; three quarter burgundy leather over marbled boards by Bayntun.   Glenn Books 36-265 1996 $450.00

THINGS By Their Right Names; a Novel. Boston: Munroe & Francis, Nov. 1812. Only American edition (same year as the London); 2 volumes in 1; original printed boards, uncut; spine very worn, covers present but detached, pervasive light foxing, in clamshell case; scarce. Gothic Bib. p. 533; Block p. 235. Shaw & Shoemaker 26869.   Trebizond 39-22 1996 $425.00

THIRTY-SECOND Infantry Division WWII. Blakely: 1955. 416 pages; fine in dust jacket.   Blue River Books 9-339 1996 $110.00

THOMA, KURT H.   Oral Roentgenology: a Roentgen Study of the Anatomy and Pathology of the Oral Cavity. Boston: 1922. 4to; 311 illustrations; cloth. GM 3690.   Argosy 810-476 1996 $125.00

THOMAS A KEMPIS 1380-1471   The Following of Christ... London: 1686. 24mo; (iv), 23, (xix), 474 pages; interesting later blindstamped morocco binding, signed and dated 'F.P. 1901', gilt lettering, rubbed, lacks clasps, some soiling; scarce miniature edition. Wing T953A. Clancy 953.   Robert Clark 38-139 1996 £160.00

THOMAS AQUINAS, SAINT 1225?-1274   Catena Aurea Super Omnia Evangelia Dominicalia et Ferialia. Venice: Joannes Rubeus Vercellensis, 29 April 1494. Quarto; 356 leaves (of 358, lacking 2 blanks, a1 and y4), gothic letter with some roman capitals, historiated woodcut initials, occasional annotations, some faint waterstaining; 19th century paper boards, worn. Goff T224; HC 1337*; BMC V 418; IGI 9520;   H. M. Fletcher 121-18 1996 £1,950.00

THOMAS AQUINAS, SAINT 1225?-1274   In Evangelium Beati Joannis Evageliste Aurea Expositio... Paris: Joanne de Porta, 1520. 4to. (in 6s); ff. 24, 147 leaves; elaborate emblematic woodcut titlepage, woodcut initials; early ms. annotations and ownerships, early binding of plain paper boards; very scarce. Apparently not in Adams, nor BMC STC French. Family Album Tillers-617 1996 $650.00

THOMAS AQUINAS, SAINT 1225?-1274   Opus Aureum Sancti Thome de Aquino Super Quatuor Evangelia. Venice: Bonetus Locatellus for Octavianus Scotus 4 June, 1493. Folio; 318 leaves, double column, gothic letter with roman capitals used for proper names, various floriated or historiated woodcut initials; Scotus's woodcut device on last leaf, extensively rubricated with paragraph marks, underlinings and capital strokes, all supplied in red (the diligent rubricator has painted the initials as well), small tear in blank margin of title, narrow (5mm) strip cut from head of fol. 2, old (probably early 16th century) sprinkled calf over reverse bevelled wooden boards, sewn on 4 double cords, two chased brass catches on front board, clasps missing, apart from split in lower front hinge, both binding and contents are in good, sound condition. Goff T232; H1336; BMC V 441; IGI 9519;   H. M. Fletcher 121-019 1996 £2,450.00

THOMAS AQUINAS, SAINT 1225?-1274   Selections from His Works. Limited Editions Club, 1969. Number 1029 of 1500 copies signed by artist; wood engravings by Reynolds Stone; fine in slipcase. Hermitage SP95-1029 1996 $125.00

THOMAS HERBERT   Chapters in American Obstetrics. Springfield: 1933. 1st edition; 90 pages; original binding.   W. Bruce Fye 71-2115 1996 $100.00

THOMAS, CASSIUS M.   Centennial Congress 1876. Washington: C. M. Thomas, 1876. 1st edition; large 4to; 24 pages; original printed wrappers; very rare. 2 copies in NUC.   M & S Rare Books 60-423 1996 $275.00

THOMAS, D. M.   Birthstone. London: Gollancz, 1980. 1st edition; fine in fine dust jacket and custom quarter leather clamshell box; author's own copy, signed by him with extensive holograph corrections.   Ken Lopez 74-436 1996 $1,250.00

THOMAS, D. M.   Personal and Possessive. London: Outposts Publications, 1964. 1st edition; author's first book; signed by author; wrappers, covers slightly marked and dusty, very good; nameplate of literary agent John Johnson.   Ulysses 39-587 1996 £75.00

THOMAS, DYLAN MARLAIS 1914-1953   Adventures in the Skin Trade and Other Stories. Norfolk: New Directions, 1955. 1st edition; original binding, top edge slightly dusty, head and tail of spine and corners slightly bumped and rubbed, edges and endpaper edges slightly browned, very good in nicked, chipped and dusty, slightly rubbed, torn and creased dust jacket slightly darkened at edges; ownership signature of William Meredith.   Ulysses 39-588 1996 £75.00

THOMAS, DYLAN MARLAIS 1914-1953   Collected Poems: 1934-1952. London: J. M. Dent, 1952. 1st edition; one of 4760 copies; 8vo; frontispiece, blue cloth, dust jacket; signed by author, cloth somewhat bubbled on covers, otherwise fine.   James S. Jaffe 34-662 1996 $1,250.00

THOMAS, DYLAN MARLAIS 1914-1953   18 Poems. London: Sunday Referee/Parton Bookshop, 1934. 1st edition; 1st issue (with flat spine); one of only 250 first issue copies; 8vo; remarkably fine in complete, though somewhat foxed and nicked rare dust jacket, endpapers and edges of book also have some foxing, otherwise this is a superb example; in black quarter morocco slipcase with silk moire chemise; presentation copy in the year of publication, jointly inscribed with fellow writer-translator, A. L. Lloyd for Lloyd's wife Ethel; laid in is autograph note from Lloyd presented the book.   Lakin & Marley 3-63 1996 $6,000.00

THOMAS, DYLAN MARLAIS 1914-1953   The Map of Love. London: 1939. 1st edition; 1st issue; excellent copy; presentation copy from author for Helen McMaster.   R. A. Gekoski 19-141 1996 £875.00

THOMAS, DYLAN MARLAIS 1914-1953   Under Milk Wood. London: J. M. Dent & Son, 1954. 1st edition; 8vo; pages x, 101; original brown cloth, dust jacket little torn and chipped, otherwise very good. Sotheran PN32-56 1996 £178.00

THOMAS, DYLAN MARLAIS 1914-1953   Under Milk Wood. London: J. M. Dent & Sons Ltd., 1954. 1st edition; 8vo; pages ix, (i) blank, 101; original cloth, spine lettered in gilt, dust jacket just a little chipped; bookplate, excellent.   Simon Finch 24-226 1996 £120.00

THOMAS, DYLAN MARLAIS 1914-1953   Under Milk Wood. New York: A New Directions Book, 1954. 1st American edition; fine in rubbed dust jacket with slightly crumpled back panel.   Hermitage SP95-618 1996 $100.00

THOMAS, EDWARD   Cloud Castle and Other Papers. London: Duckworth & Co., 1922. 1st edition; original binding, free endpapers partially browned, edges slightly spotted, head and tail of spine and corners slightly bumped and rubbed, very good in remains of dust jacket, remnants of which have been sellotaped together, large piece is missing at head of spine, surviving parts rubbed, chipped, frayed and slightly soiled, spine and cover edges are browned.   Ulysses 39-591 1996 £85.00

THOMAS, EDWARD   Collected Poems. London: 1920. 1st edition; spine and cover edges little darkened, otherwise very good.   Words Etcetera 94-1227 1996 £65.00

THOMAS, EDWARD   Horae Solitariae. London: Duckworth, 1902. Endpapers and pastedowns offset and spine slightly bumped at extremities, otherwise very good.   R. A. Gekoski 19-143 1996 £200.00

THOMAS, EDWARD   Selected Poems. Newtown: Gregynog Press, 1927. One of 25 copies specially bound of a total edition of 275; 9 1/4 x 6 1/4 inches; xix, (1), 95, (1) pages; device on title, red printer's device in colophon; title printed in blue and black, initials in red, ruled in blue; very fine polished blue levant morocco by the Gregynog Press Bindery (signed by R. Ashwin Maynard and George Fisher on rear turn-in), covers with 3 overlapping gilt lozenges made of leaf sprays, connected by gilt decoration to double gilt rule frame, raised bands, spine titled in gilt with similar gilt decoration at either end, double gilt rule on turn-ins, marbled endpapers, top edge gilt, other edges untrimmed, in blue cloth chemise and matching slipcase, blue morocco label on spine, spine leather perhaps just a shade lighter than covers, but remarkably fine copy copy otherwise of the first Gregynog book to be printed on Japanese vellum. Harrop 6.   Phillip J. Pirages 33-267 1996 $4,500.00

THOMAS, EDWARD   Six Poems... Pear Tree Press, c. 1921. 2nd state, one illustration added, one replaced with different version and two omitted, one of a total of 100 copies, numbered and signed by Guthrie; small folio; illustrations and decorations by James Guthrie; original grey wrappers with intaglio label on upper, overlapping edges of wrappers little creased and frayed, but internally very nice, fresh copy; rare; discreet bookplate.   Bertram Rota 272-366 1996 £2,500.00

THOMAS, EDWARD   Two Poems. London: Ingpen and Grant, 1927. Limited to 85 numbered copies, this copy being unnumbered; printed at the Curwen Press, this was the printers' own file copy "From the library of the Curwen Press London" on front pastedown; titlepage and cover decorations by Percy Smith; original binding, top edge dusty, head and tail of spine and bottom edges rubbed, very good in unprinted tissue dust jacket which is creased, torn, chipped and brown.   Ulysses 39-592 1996 £275.00

THOMAS, FREDERICK WILLIAM   The Emigrant, or Reflections While Descending the Ohio. Cincinnati: Alexander Flash, 1833. 1st edition; 12mo; 48 pages; later plain stiff wrappers, fore-edge of first few leaves cropped close, without loss, very good. B&B 21503; Streeter III 1370. Sabin 95393. Rusk I p. 347.   M & S Rare Books 60-244 1996 $425.00

THOMAS, N. W.   Kinship Organisations and Group Marriage in Australia. Cambridge: 1906. 1st edition; 163 pages, 3 maps, 1 folding table; original green gilt, buckram, very good. Scarce. Mervyn Meggitt's copy, signed.   Antipodean 28-454 1996 $145.00

THOMAS, N. W.   Natives of Australia. London: 1906. (xii), 256 pages, 1 folding map, 32 plates; some damp discoloration on boards not affecting gilt or bright spine, internally bright, clean copy; the Absolon copy.   Antipodean 28-455 1996 $125.00

THOMAS, R. S.   The Mountains. New York: Chilmark Press, 1968. One of 240 numbered copies; large 4to; printed in handset 18 pt. Palatino on Wookey Hole mouldmade; 10 drawings by John Piper, engraved on wood by Reynolds Stone; decorated paper boards with cloth back, fine in slipcase; scarce.   Bertram Rota 272-393 1996 £300.00

THOMAS, ROSS   The Backup Men. New York: Morrow, 1971. 1st edition; glue stains from sticker removal on front endpaper and following page, else near fine in dust jacket with several tiny tears and slight wear at corners and spine panel ends.   Robert Gavora 61-403 1996 $125.00

THOMAS, ROSS   The Brass Go-Between. New York: Morrow, 1969. 1st edition; fine in dust jacket with hint of rubbing and little tanning to edge.   Robert Gavora 61-404 1996 $300.00

THOMAS, ROSS   Briarpatch. New York: Simon & Schuster, 1984. 1st edition; slight darkening on bottom edge, otherwise fine in dust clipped dust jacket with minor edge creasing and few short closed tears; publisher's device on bottom page edges.   Quill & Brush 102-1658 1996 $100.00

THOMAS, ROSS   Cast a Yellow Shadlow. New York: Morrow, 1967. 1st edition; fine in dust jacket with price in ink to corner of front flap. Robert Gavora 61-406 1996 $275.00

THOMAS, ROSS   The Cold War Swap. New York: Morrow, 1966. 1st edition; author's first book, price in ink to corner of front endpaper, else near fine in dust jacket, very attractive.   Robert Gavora 61-407 1996 $650.00

THOMAS, ROSS   The Highbinders. New York: Morrow, 1974. 1st edition; fine in dust jacket.   Robert Gavora 61-408 1996 $250.00

THOMAS, ROSS   If You Can't Be Good. New York: Morrow, 1973. 1st edition; fine in dust jacket with slight bumping to heel of spine panel. Robert Gavora 61-409 1996 $250.00

THOMAS, ROSS   The Money Harvest. New York: Morrow, 1975. 1st edition; fine in dust jacket.   Robert Gavora 61-410 1996 $125.00

THOMAS, ROSS   Out On the Rim. New York: Mysterious Press, 1987. 1st edition; uncorrected and unedited version of the advance review copy; scarce; peach color printed paper wrappers, some minor creasing, othrwise fine.   Quill & Brush 102-1661 1996 $150.00

THOMAS, ROSS   The Porkchoppers. New York: Morrow, 1972. 1st edition; fine in dust jacket with several tiny tears and slight wear at heel of spine panel.   Robert Gavora 61-412 1996 $165.00

THOMAS, ROSS   The Porkchoppers New York: Wm. Morrow & Co., 1972. 1st edition; one corner very lightly bumped, otherwise fine in very lightly soiled dust jacket with onlyt wo tiny spots of minor edge wear. Quill & Brush 102-1654 1996 $125.00

THOMAS, ROSS   Protocol, for a Kidnapping. New York: Morrow, 1971. 1st edition; fine in dust jacket with line of lamination separation. Robert Gavora 61-413 1996 $250.00

THOMAS, ROSS   Protocol for a Kidnapping. New York: Wm. Morrow & Co., 1971. 1st edition; corners lightly bumped, otherwise near fine in dust jacket with minor soiling on rear panel and touch of creasing at head of spine.   Quill & Brush 102-1653 1996 $175.00

THOMAS, ROSS   The Seersucker Whipsaw. New York: Morrow, 1967. 1st edition; author's second book; previous owner's signature; near fine in dust jacket with some tanning along edge.   Robert Gavora 61-414 1996 $500.00

THOMAS, ROSS   The Singapore Wink. New York: Morrow, 1969. 1st edition; light wear to bottom edges of covers and bumped at rear corner, else near fine in dust jacket with slight wear at corners and spine panel ends and small stain to interior edge of rear panel. Robert Gavora 61-415 1996 $200.00

THOMAS, ROSS   Yellow-Dog Contract. New York: Morrow, 1977. 1st edition; fine in dust jacket.   Robert Gavora 61-416 1996 $150.00

THOMAS, WILLIAM   A Collection of Early Prose Romances. London: William Pickering, 1827/28. 8vo; 3 volumes; 13 parts, half titles, titles in red and black with vignette; modern calf backed marbled boards, morocco labels; very good, scarce. Keynes p. 92*.   Claude Cox 107-240 1996 £135.00

THOMAS, WILLIAM RUSSELL   Sunlight Views of Fort Collins and Surroundings. Fort Collins: Courier Print, 1907. 1st edition; 48 pages; illustrations; original black wrappers with title stamped in silver; fine. Wynar 1196.   Michael D. Heaston 23-106 1996 $125.00

THOMAS, WILLIAM S.   Hunting Big Game with Gun and Kodak. New York: 1906. illustrations; original pcitorial buckram; excellent copy. David Grayling J95Biggame-450 1996 £70.00

THOMASON, GEORGE   Catalogue of the Pamphlets, Books, Newspapers and Manuscripts Relating to the Civil War, the Commonwealth and Restoration Collected by George Thomason, 1640-1661. London: British Museum, 1908. 2 volumes; original cloth, headcaps slightly chipped, pencil ownership inscription of H. M. Nixon with couple of pencil annotations. De Ricci p. 29.   Maggs Bros. Ltd. 1191-89 1996 £145.00

THOMPSON, ALBERT   They Were Open Range Days, Annals of a Western Frontier. Denver: 1946. 1st edition; viii, 194 pages, photos, maps; nice, dust jacket, very scarce.   T. A. Swinford 49-1148 1996 $150.00

THOMPSON, ALICE   A Bibliography of Nursing Literature, 1859-1960, with An Historical Introduction. London: 1968. 4to; 132 pages; original cloth.   W. Bruce Fye 71-2106 1996 $150.00

THOMPSON, C. J. S.   The Mystery and Lore of Monsters with Account of Some Giants, Dwarfts, and Prodigies. New York: 1931. 1st American edition; 256 pages;   W. Bruce Fye 71-2108 1996 $100.00

THOMPSON, D'ARCY W.   On Growth and Form. Cambridge: 1942. New edition; 8vo; 2 plates, 554 text figures; cloth, rubbed; loosely inserted ALS from author.   Maggs Bros. Ltd. 1190-267 1996 £80.00

THOMPSON, DEBORAH   Stucco from Chal Tarkhan-Eshgabad Near Rayy. Warminster: Arais and Phillips, 1976. Folio; xvi, 328 pages, 36 plates, 1 map, 4 plans, 2 tables; original cloth.   Archaeologia Luxor-2760 1996 $150.00

THOMPSON, EDWARD H.   The Chultunes of Labna, Yucatan. Cambridge: Peabody Museum, 1897. Folio; 20 pages, 13 figures, 13 plates, tattered wrappers; ink mark at titlepage.   Archaeologia Luxor-4947 1996 $125.00

THOMPSON, FRANCIS BENJAMIN   The Universal Decorator. London: Houlston & Wright, n.d., ca. 1860. 2nd edition; 4to; frontispiece, xii, 512 pages, 237 plates of which 112 are printed in colored inks and 11 in two or more colors; contemporary half morocco, very good.   Bookpress 75-127 1996 $850.00

THOMPSON, GEORGE   Catharine and Clara; or the Double Suicide. Boston: Federhen and Co., 1854. 8vo; 46, (1) pages; full page woodcut; removed, some stains. Wright II 2480 for NY ed. 1853.   M & S Rare Books 60-245 1996 $125.00

THOMPSON, GEORGE   The Prison Bard; or Poems on Various Subjects. Hartford: William H. Burleigh, 1848. 1st edition; 12mo; 215 pages; contemporary calf backed boards; LCP/HSP Afro Amer. Cat. 10221.   M & S Rare Books 60-246 1996 $125.00

THOMPSON, GEORGE   Prison Life and Reflections. Hartford: A Work, 1849. 3rd edition; short tear to rear free endpaper, foxing to first and last few pages and some tiny spots of flaking to cloth, still fine, tight copy. Contemporary name "Perley King".   Between the Covers 43-239 1996 $225.00

THOMPSON, GEORGE   Travels and Adventures in Southern Africa. London: Henry Colburn, 1827. 1st edition; 4to; pages xviii, 2, 493, 2 ads; 20 plates, 2 plans, folding map; contemporary calf, rebacked, rubbed, small library blindstamp on title; Theal p. 303; Mendelssohn p. 493. Richard Adelson W94/95-170 1996 $1,085.00

THOMPSON, HARRY STEPHEN   Ireland in 1839 and 1869. London: Dorrell and Son, 1870. 1st edition; 8vo; (4), 115 pages, original blue cloth, gilt, upper cover embellished, with floral wreath in gilt; very good; inscribed 'With the author's kind regards'; Not in NUC.   John Drury 82-278 1996 £95.00

THOMPSON, HENRY   The Motor-Car, an Elementary Handbook On its Nature, Use and Management. London: 1902. 1st edition; 7 x 4.5 inches; illustrations; 108 pages, with index; cloth, label on spine rubbed, front hinge loose, soiled with minor tear at front hinge top.   John K. King 77-755 1996 $150.00

THOMPSON, HUNTER S.   Fear and Loathing in Las Vegas. New York: Random House, 1971. 1st edition; fine in dust jacket with nick at base of spine, very nice copy.   Ken Lopez 74-437 1996 $250.00

THOMPSON, HUNTER S.   Fear and Loathing on the Campaign Trail '72. San Francisco: Straight Arrow, 1973. 1st edition; 1st issue; photos and drawings by Ralph Steadman; light shelf wear to lower board edges, else near fine in first issue jacket with white border around photo on rear panel; scarce in first issue.   Lame Duck Books 19-541 1996 $300.00

THOMPSON, HUNTER S.   Fear and Loathing on the Campaign Trail '72. San Francisco: Straight Arrow, 1973. 1st edition; bottom of spine little bumped, thus a very good copy in very good plus, first issue dust jacket, price clipped with some rubbing and couple of short tears. Between the Covers 42-425 1996 $250.00

THOMPSON, HUNTER S.   Screwjack. Santa Barbara: Neville, 1991. One of numbered 300 copies (of a total edition of 326), signed by author; fine in gilt stamped cloth as issued.   Between the Covers 42-425a 1996 $150.00

THOMPSON, J. ERIC   An Archaeological Reconnaissance in the Cotzumalhuapa Region, Escuintla, Guatemala. Washington: Carnegie Inst., 1948. 4to; 56 pages; 63 figures; original printed wrpapers. Archaeologia Luxor-4952 1996 $175.00

THOMPSON, J. ERIC   Excavations at San Jose, British Honduras. Washington: Carnegie Inst. of Washington, 1939. 4to; xi, 292 pages, 100 figures, 33 plates, 18 tables; original printed wrappers, light staining to top and bottom of wrappers; with signature of J. A. Bennyhoff. Archaeologia Luxor-4950 1996 $250.00

THOMPSON, J. V.   Catalogue of Plants Growing in the Vicinity of Berwick upon Tweed. London: 1807. Pictorial hand colored title, one other hand colored plate; finely bound in modern half calf, gilt, some browning to contents; lovely copy, rare.   David A.H. Grayling MY95Orn-74 1996 £150.00

THOMPSON, J. W.   Sketches, Historical and Descriptive of Noted Maine Horses. Portland: Hoyt & Fogg/Canton, 1874/87. 1st printings; 8vo; volumes 1 and 2; original binding, edges worn, bindings much faded, tight, complete.   October Farm 36-312 1996 $135.00

THOMPSON, JAMES MAURICE   The Witchery of Archery: a Complete Manual of Archery. New York: Charles Scribner's Sons, 1878. 1st edition; small octavo; viii, 259 pages; illustrations; original dark green cloth decoratively stamped in gilt and black on front cover and in gilt on spine, light wear to extremities, paper slightly browned, otherwise near fine. Lake and Wright pp. 283-284.   Heritage Book Shop 196-205 1996 $200.00

THOMPSON, JERRY   Sabers on the Rio Grande. Austin: Presidial, 1974. 1st edition; 4to; 235 pages; illustrations; dust jacket.   Maggie Lambeth 30-501 1996 $150.00

THOMPSON, JIM   The Criminal. New York: Lion, 1953. Paperback original; scarce, crease on back cover, still at least very good.   Ken Lopez 74-438 1996 $175.00

THOMPSON, JIM   Ironside. New York: Popular Library, 1967. 1st edition; pages darkened and few page corners creased, very good. Between the Covers 42-426 1996 $150.00

THOMPSON, JIM   The Kill-Off. New York: Lion, 1957. Paperback original; creased along spine fold from reading, else near fine, pages much whiter than usually found in pulp paperbacks of this vintage. Ken Lopez 74-439 1996 $150.00

THOMPSON, JIM   The Nothing Man. New York: Dell, 1954. Dell First edition, paperback original; illustrated wrappers; fine.   Pettler & Lieberman 28-240 1996 $100.00

THOMPSON, JIM   The Undefeated. New York: Popular Library, 1969. 1st edition; pages uniformly darkened, few page corners bent and little darkening of edges of wrappers, very good plus.   Between the Covers 42-427 1 996 $100.00

THOMPSON, JOHN R.   Oration and Poem. Richmond: Macfarlane & Fergusson, 1856. 1st edition; 8vo; 40 pages; disbound, light foxing on last leaf, else very good.   The Bookpress 75-470 1996 $225.00

THOMPSON, KAY   Eloise in Paris. London: Max Rheinhardt, 1958. 1st edition; 4to; two tone illustrations by Hilary Knight; blue boards, gilt, fine in dust jacket.   Marjorie James 19-211 1996 £65.00

THOMPSON, LAWRANCE   Moby Dick; the Passion of Ahab. Barre: 1968. Limited to 500 copies; containing 26 offset lithographs (16 x 22 inches) by Benton Spruance and a separate text volume in a clamshell case;   Charles Agvent 4-890 1996 $600.00

THOMPSON, NATHANIEL   The Tryal of Nathaniel Thompson, William Pain and John Farwell...for Writing, Printing and Publishing Libels. London: Simmons, 1682. Folio; quarter calf; Wing T2207; Rostenberg Pub....in England II 315-343.   Rostenberg & Stern 150-150 1996 $450.00

THOMPSON, R. CAMPBELL   Late Baybionian Letters, Transliterations and Translations of a Series of letters Written in Babylonian Cuneiform, Chiefly During the Reigns of Nabonidus, Cyrus, Cambyses and Darius. London: Luzac, 1906. 8vo; frontispiece, xxxvi, 226 pages; original cloth. Archaeologia Luxor-2763 1996 $125.00

THOMPSON, RALPH   An Artist's Safari. London: 1970. Large oblong folio; many color and other plates; covers slightly warped and minute stain to fore edges of few leaves, dust jacket.   David A.H. Grayling MY95Orn-75 196 £50.00

THOMPSON, ROBERT FARRIS   African Art in Motion. Icon and Act in the Collection of Katherine Coryton White. Washington: National Gallery of Art, Berkeley, Univ. of Calif. Press, 1974. Original edition; 28cm; xv, 275 pages; color and black and white plates; decorated covers, stiff paper, small tear to front cover.   L. Clarice Davis 111-98 1996 $110.00

THOMPSON, ROBERT FARRIS   Black Gods and Kings. Yoruba Art at UCLA. 1971. 27.5 cm; maps, many color and black and white plates; stiff paper, light wear on spine, minor stain on edge of margin of last page. L. Clarice Davis 111-99 1996 $150.00

THOMPSON, SILVANUS P.   The Life of William Thomson, Baron Kelvin of Largs. London: Macmillan, 1910. 1st edition; 8vo; 2 volumes, xx, 584; xi, 585-1297, (2 ads) pages; frontispiece in each volume, 14 plates, several figures in text, titlepage to volume one torn without loss, faint trace of numbers removed from spine; original cloth, top edge gilt; very good, untrimmed set.   Edwin V. Glaser 121-173 1996 $150.00

THOMPSON, T. D.   Facts for the People, Relating to the Teeth... Boston: B. B. Mussey and Co., 1854. 1st edition; 12mo; 251 pages; frontispiece, other illustrations; original decorated cloth; fine. Campbell 559.   M & S Rare Books 60-452 1996 $225.00

THOMPSON, THEOPHILUS   Annals of Influenza or Epidemic Catarrhal Fever in Great Britain from 1510 to 1837. London: 1852. 1st edition; original binding. GM 5489. Bloomfield 390.   W. Bruce Fye 71-2113 1996 $150.00

THOMPSON, THOMAS H.   Official Historical Atlas Map of Fresno County. N.P.: n.d. Facsimile reprint of the rare 1891 edition; folio; 1 portrait, 16 views, 87 maps, red cloth, fine.   Argonaut Book Shop 113-266 1996 $175.00

THOMPSON, THOMAS H.   Official Historical Atlas Map of Fresno County. Tulare: Thomas H. Thompson, 1891. 1st edition; folio; 1 portrait, 16 views, 87 maps; new three quarter leatherette and cloth, original gilt and blindstamped cover laid down, first 4 leaves professionally reinforced at edges, minor stain to lower outer border of some leaves, overall very good, complete; rare. Cowan p. 255; Rocq 1840.   Argonaut Book Shop 113-265 1996 $1,000.00

THOMPSON, W.   Sedbergh Garsdale and Dent. Leeds: Richard Jackson, 1892. 1st edition; 8vo; pages xiv, 280 (iv, ads), 47 illustrations from drawings by J. A. Symington; original pictorial brown cloth, gilt, extremities trifle rubbed, corners little bumped, upper joint cracked. R.F.G. Hollett & Son 78-1321 1996 £120.00

THOMPSON, W.   Sedbergh Garasdale and Dent. Leeds: Richard Jackson, 1910. Number 61 of 100 copies; 8vo; pages xx, 291, (vii, ads), frontispiece, 43 plates; modern cream pigskin, contrasting green leather spine label, top edge gilt, uncut. Handsome copy.   R.F.G. Hollett & Son 78-1325 1996 £220.00

THOMPSON, W.   Sedbergh Garsdale and Dent. Leeds: Richard Jackson, 1910. 2nd edition, limited to 500 copies; 8vo; pages xx, 291, (viii, ads), colored frontispiece, 43 photographic plates; modern half levant morocco gilt, gilt title panel from original cloth laid in to upper board, top edge gilt, uncut.   R.F.G. Hollett & Son 78-1324 1996 £150.00

THOMPSON, W.   Sedbergh Garsdale and dent. Leeds: Richard Jackson, 1910. 2nd edition, limited to 500 copies; 8vo; pages xx, 291, (viii, ads); colored frontispiece, 43 photographic plates; top edge gilt, uncut, original red cloth, gilt; front flyleaf lightly spotted, otherwise excellent copy.   R.F.G. Hollett & Son 78-1322 1996 £140.00

THOMPSON, W.   Sedbergh Garsdale and Dent. Leeds: Richard Jackson, 1910. 2nd edition, limited to 500 copies; 8vo; pages xx, 291, (viii ads), colored frontispiece, 43 photographic plates; original green cloth, gilt, rather faded, very good.   R.F.G. Hollett & Son 78-1323 1996 £130.00

THOMPSON, WADDY   Recollections of Mexico. New York: wiley and Putnam, 1846. 1st edition; 304 pages;   Maggie Lambeth 30-381 1996 $100.00

THOMSON, ALLEN   History of the Walker Horse. The Morrills and the Hamilton Horses of Vermont. 1893. 8vo; 94 pages; photos; paperbound, back cover missing, edges worn; rare.   October Farm 36-262 1996 $225.00

THOMSON, ANDREW   The Hendersonian Testimony... Edinburgh, London and Dublin: A. Fullarton and Co., 1849. 1st edition; 8vo; xx, 203, (1) pages; frontispiece little offset onto title, original green cloth, gilt; good. scarce. Not in Goldsmiths or Williams. not in NUC.   John Drury 82-279 1996 £75.00

THOMSON, CHARLES WYVILLE 1830-1882   Report on the Scientific Results of the Voyage of H.M.S. Challenger During the Years 1873-76 Under the Command of Capt. George S. Nares, R.N., F.R.S. and Captain Frank Tourle Thomson. London: ptd. for Her Majesty's Stationery Office, 1882. 12.5 x 10 inches; viii, 385 pages, 48 plates, 192 pages, 13 plates; original heavy green cloth, gilt spine titles, some edgewear especially at base, paper cracked over front hinge, else very good, unopened copy. Parmer Books Nat/Hist-67432 1996 $250.00

THOMSON, CHARLES WYVILLE 1830-1882   The Voyage of the 'Challenger'. The Atlantic. A Preliminary Account of the Exploring Voyage of H.M.S. "Challenger" During the Year 1873 and the Early part of the Year 1876. London: 1877. 8vo; 2 volumes, pages xv, 424; 2, xiv, 396, 4 ads, with portrait, 43 plates of which 39 folding, 176 text figures; cloth, pictorial gilt, rebacked preserving spine.   John Henly 27-153 1996 £175.00

THOMSON, CHARLES WYVILLE 1830-1882   The Voyage of the "Challenger". The Atlantic. A Preliminary Account of the General Results of the Exploring Voyage of H.M.S. Challenger During the Year 1873 and the Early Part of the Year 1876. London: 1877. 2 volumes; folding maps, numerous illustrations.   Petersfield Bookshop FH58-415 1996 £160.00

THOMSON, CLARA J.   Samuel Richardson - a Biographical and Critical Study. London: Horace Marshall & Son, 1900. 1st edition; original binding, bookplate, top edge dusty, head and tail of spine and corners bumped, endpapers browned, covers rubbed and marked, spine darkened, good; with pencilled ownership signature of Frederick Pottle. Ulysses 39-711 1996 £55.00

THOMSON, DAVID CROAL   Life and Labours of Hablot Knight Browne, "Phiz". 1st edition; limited edition, number 58 of 200 copies; 4to; 245 pages; 130 illustrations; initialled by author; original cloth.   K Books 442-472 1996 £150.00

THOMSON, DONALD   Economic Structure and the Ceremonial Exchange Cycle in Arnhem Land. Melbourne: 1949. 106 pages black and white illustrations, 2 folding maps; original red and gilt buckram, good+ copy; the Meggitt copy.   Antipodean 28-460 1996 $125.00

THOMSON, GLADYS SCOTT   The Russells in Bloomsbury. London: Jonthan Cape, Inc., 1940. 1st edition; folding map, several black and white plates; original binding, top edge spotted, fore and bottom edges and endpapers slightly spotted, head and tail of spine slightly bumped, very good in rubbed and slightly spotted, marked and dusty dust jacket. Ulysses 39-55 1996 £55.00

THOMSON, JAMES 1700-1748   The Seasons. London: Samuel Richardson, 1730. 2nd collected edition, printed for subscribers in an edition of about 350 copies; 4 plates, engraved by Nicholas Tardieu after William Kent and title vignette and plate of Newton's monument engraved by P. Fourdrinier after William Kent; contemporary calf, gilt, very rubbed, rebacked, new endpapers, title printed in red and black, plate for 'Summer' inserted from a smaller copy, seven page list of subscribers; errata page; some marginal browning, last leaf soiled. Hammelmann/Boase p. 58; Rothschild 2423.   James Cummins 14-211 1996 $250.00

THOMSON, JAMES 1700-1748   The Seasons. London: 1852. Numerous fine engravings; finely bound in contemporary morocco, ornate gilt borders, inner dentelles and gilt extra spine, all edges gilt, light rubbing, contents totally free from foxing.   David A.H. Grayling MY95Orn-447 1996 £80.00

THOMSON, JAMES 1700-1748   The Seasons. London: 1927. one of 1500 copies; xx, (1),, bl., 198, (1) pages; 5 tinted copperplates; unopened, original marbled cloth; fine, uncut.   Bookworm & Silverfish 276-156 1996 $100.00

THOMSON, JAMES, weaver in Kenleith   Poems, in the Scottish Dialect. Edinburgh: W. Reid, for the author, 1801. 1st edition; 8vo; pages xxiii, 215, uncut, frontispiece, blindstamps to portrait, title and final leaf, library label on front pastedown, but very nice, unsophisticated copy; modern half leavnat morocco gilt solander box.   R.F.G. Hollett 76-308 1996 £295.00

THOMSON, JAMES, weaver in Kenleith   Poems, in the Scottish Dialect. Edinburgh: printed by J. Fillans and Sons, published by W. Reid, Leith for the... 1801. 1st edition; 8vo; pages xxiii, 215; frontispiece; original boards, some chipping at edges, rebacked with paper, new printed label; minor discoloration.   Howard S. Mott 227-140 1996 $275.00

THOMSON, JOHN   An Account of the Varioloid Epidemic Which Has Lately Prevailed in Edinburgh and Other Parts of Scotland; with Observations on the Identity of Chicken-Pox with Modified Small-Pox, in Letter to Sir James M'Grigor. London: 1820. 1st edition; 8vo; errata leaf at end, minor foxing, but crisp copy; unattractive binding of half roan, bit worn and stained.   Maggs Bros. Ltd. 1190-520 1996 £90.00

THOMSON, JOHN   Etymons of English Worlds. Edinburgh: Oliver & Boyd, 1826. 1st edition; 4to; contemporary half purple calf, rather rubbed, maroon label chipped at edges.   Jarndyce 103-347 1996 £160.00

THOMSON, RICHARD   An Antiquary, Chronicles of London Bridge. London: Smith, Elder and Co., 1827. Very good copy.   Limestone Hills 41-146 1996 $130.00

THOMSON, SAMUEL   Learned Quackery Exposed; or Theory According to Art. Boston: 1824. 1st edition; 16mo; 24 pages; new plain wrappers; rare.   M & S Rare Books 60-122 1996 $750.00

THOMSON, SAMUEL   New Guide to Health; or Botanic Family Physician. Boston: for the author, 1835. Small 8vo; 228 pages; some light foxing, otherwise very good, bound in moderately worn publisher's cloth and leather label.   Second Life Books 103-187 1996 $150.00

THORBURN, ARCHIBALD   British Birds. London: 1916. 2nd edition of volumes 1 and 2; 1st edition of volumes 3 and 4; 4to; 4 volumes; 82 colored paltes of aobut 500 figures; original red buckram; as usual, there is some foxing in volumes 3 and 4 due to quality of wartime paper;   Wheldon & Wesley 207-107 1996 £500.00

THORBURN, ARCHIBALD   British Birds. London: 1931-35. New edition, 2nd impression; 8vo; 4 volumes; 192 fine color plates; cloth; small stain on plate 132 just affecting engraved surface.   John Henly 27-30 1996 £100.00

THORBURN, ARCHIBALD   British Mammals. London: 1920-21. 4to; 2 volumes; 50 colored plates; original red cloth; inscritpion on flyleaf of volume 1 and small nick on both spines, but good, clean internally. Wheldon & Wesley 207-110 1996 £1,000.00

THORBURN, ARCHIBALD   British Mammals. London: 1920-21. 4to; 2 volumes bound in 1; pages vii, 84; vi, 105, 50 fine color plates; cloth, worn dust jacket, slight waterstain to top edge, othewise fine.   John Henly 27-46 1996 £350.00

THORBURN, ARCHIBALD   Game Birds and Wild-Fowl of Great Britain and Ireland. London: 1923. Folio; 30 colored plates; later red buckram, spine title bit uneven, endpapers foxed, but text and plates remarkably clean.   David A.H. Grayling MY95Orn-77 1996 £600.00

THORBURN, ARCHIBALD   Game Birds and Wild Fowl of Great Britain and Ireland. London: 1923. Imperial 4to; pages vii, 78, 30 colored plates of 58 species; original red buckram; attractive work, endpapers somewhat foxed, otherwise good.   Wheldon & Wesley 207-111 1996 £500.00

THORBURN, ARCHIBALD   A Naturalist's Sketch Book. London: 1919. Royal 8vo; pages viii, 72, 24 colored and 36 collotype plates; original red cloth; some very slight foxing, especially of endpapers.   Wheldon & Wesley 207-108 1996 £350.00

THORBURN, ARCHIBALD   A Naturalist's Sketchbook. London: 1919. 4to; 60 plates; minor foxing, cloth, trifle worn and marked.   Maggs Bros. Ltd. 1190-268 1996 £200.00

THOREAU, HENRY DAVID 1817-1862   Autumn: From the Journal of Henry David Thoreau. Boston & New York: Houghton, Mifflin & Co., 1892. 1st edition; 470 pages; original green cloth, gilt, near fine. BAL 20130.   Blue River Books 9-306 1996 $200.00

THOREAU, HENRY DAVID 1817-1862   Autumn. Boston: Houghton Mifflin, 1892. 1st edition; original green cloth, glt, very good. Borst A11.1.a. BAL 20130.   Mac Donnell 12-116 1996 $150.00

THOREAU, HENRY DAVID 1817-1862   Cape Cod. Boston: Ticknor & Fields, 1865. 1st edition, 1st printing of 2000 copies; binding variant 2 (no priority) with 24 page publisher's catalog dated Dec. 1864, at end; light fading and chipping to spine extremities, remains of a clipping pasted to endpaper, nonetheless, fine, unsophisticated copy. BAL 20115; Borst A5.1.a.1.   Bromer Booksellers 90-230 1996 $500.00

THOREAU, HENRY DAVID 1817-1862   Cape Cod. Boston: Ticknor & Fields, 1865. 1st edition; binding C, no priority; 2040 copies printed; 8vo; catalog dated 1864; original binding, some soiling internally, spine touch rubbed, but gilt still bright, near fine.   Charles Agvent 4-1124 1996 $850.00

THOREAU, HENRY DAVID 1817-1862   Early Spring in Massachusetts. Boston: Houghton Mifflin, 1881. 1st edition; original green cloth, gilt, very good; Boswell & Crouch 183. Borst A8.1.a. BAL 20123.   Mac Donnell 12-117 1996 $150.00

THOREAU, HENRY DAVID 1817-1862   Excursions. Boston: Ticknor & Fields, 1863. 1st edition; 1st printing of 1500 copies; octavo; binding variety 3 (no priority), frontispiece; green cloth with some wear to spine extremities otherwise fine unsophisticated copy. BAL 20111; Borst A3.1.a.1.   Bromer Booksellers 90-231 1996 $500.00

THOREAU, HENRY DAVID 1817-1862   Excursions. Boston: 1863. 1st edition; near fine and bright.   Stephen Lupack 83- 1996 $450.00

THOREAU, HENRY DAVID 1817-1862   Excursions. Boston: Ticknor & Fields, 1863. 1st edition; original green cloth, gilt, small area of fraying at crown, else fine, bright copy; Borst A3.1.a. BAL 5236 and 20111.   Mac Donnell 12-118 1996 $450.00

THOREAU, HENRY DAVID 1817-1862   Letters to Various Persons. Boston: Ticknor & Fields, 1865. 1st edition; 1st printing, binding A; original dark green cloth, gilt; fine, tight copy. Borst A6.1.a. BAL 5246 and 20116.   Mac Donnell 12-119 1996 $800.00

THOREAU, HENRY DAVID 1817-1862   Letters to Various Persons. Boston: Ticknor & Fields, 1865. 1st edition; 1st printing; octavo; (x), 229 pages; purple textured cloth; slight fading to spine and an early bookseller's ticket on endpaper, very fine. BAL 20116; Borst A6.1.a. Bromer Booksellers 90-232 1996 $850.00

THOREAU, HENRY DAVID 1817-1862   Letters. Boston: Ticknor & Fields, 1865. 1st edition; 2130 copies, binding A; 8vo; original binding, bit rubbed, spine still readable, frayed at head and heel.   Charles Agvent 4-1126 1996 $500.00

THOREAU, HENRY DAVID 1817-1862   The Maine Woods. Boston: Ticknor & Fields, 1864. 1st edition; 1650 copies printed, true 1st printing with list of Thoreau's books priced; 8vo; catalog dated June 1864 with last leaf advertising "the Fourteenth Volume"; green cloth, neat bookplate removal from front pastedown, spine tips bit frayed, gilt clear, about fine.   Charles Agvent 4-1127 1996 $1,250.00

THOREAU, HENRY DAVID 1817-1862   The Maine Woods. Boston: Ticknor and Fields, 1864. 1st edition; 1st printing of 1450 copies; octavo; (viii), 328, 23 pages of publisher's ads dated April, 1864. fading to spine and chipping to spine extremities, else fine, unsophisticated copy. BAL 20113; Borst A4.1.a.   Bromer Booksellers 90-233 1996 $600.00

THOREAU, HENRY DAVID 1817-1862   Men of Concord. Boston: Houghton Mifflin, 1936. 1st edition thus; small quarto; xi, 255 pages; 10 full page color plates by N. C. Wyeth; green cloth, lightly worn dust jacket, very fine.   Bromer Booksellers 90-246 1996 $200.00

THOREAU, HENRY DAVID 1817-1862   Sir Walter Raleigh. Boston: Bibliophile Society, 1905. 1st edition; limited to 489 copies; original three quarter brown morocco, gilt, uncut, boxed, minor rubbing and two inch piece chipped from lower edge of box, but fine, fresh, attractive copy of a book not often found in the box these days; Borst A19.1. BAL 20142 form A.   Mac Donnell 12-120 1996 $225.00

THOREAU, HENRY DAVID 1817-1862   Summer from the Journal of Henry David Thoreau. Boston and New York: Houghton, Mifflin and Co., 1894. New Riverside Edition; 8vo; volume 6, 382 pages; anonymous owner has drawn in the margins of approximately 90 pen and ink drawings illustrating underlined passages; dark green cloth, later printing; spine worn, good.   Robert F. Lucas 42-75 1996 $100.00

THOREAU, HENRY DAVID 1817-1862   Transmigration of the Seven Brahmans. New York: William Rudge, 1932. 1st trade edition, one of 1000 coies; preceded by a limited edition of 200 copies; original quarter cloth, gilt, dust jacket, fine, fresh copy in somewhat chipped but attractive jacket; Borst A27.1.b. BAL 20155 form 2.   Mac Donnell 12-122 1996 $125.00

THOREAU, HENRY DAVID 1817-1862   Unpublished Poems by Bryant and Thoreau. Boston: Bibliophile Society, 1907. 1st edition; one of 470 copies; original vegetable vellum boards, gilt, uncut, tiny nick at crown, else fine; Borst A21.1. BAL 1805 and 20146.   Mac Donnell 12-124 1996 $150.00

THOREAU, HENRY DAVID 1817-1862   Unpublished Poems by Bryant and Thoreau. Boston: Bibliophile Society, 1907. 1st edition; one of 470 copies printed; original vegetable vellum boards, gilt, uncut, with all of the interleaved laid-in tissue guards present, in publisher's box; very fine, fresh copy, label of outer box slightly rubbed, quite scarce in this condition. Borst A21.1. BAL 1805 and 20146.   Mac Donnell 12-123 1996 $275.00

THOREAU, HENRY DAVID 1817-1862   Walden, or, Life in the Woods. Boston: Ticknor and Fields, 1854. 1st edition; 1st printing of 2000 copies; octavo; 252, (7), 8 pages; 8 pages of ads dated June 1854; fine, unsophisticated copy. BAL 20106; Borst A2.1.a.   Bromer Booksellers 90-234 1996 $8,000.00

THOREAU, HENRY DAVID 1817-1862   Walden; or, Life in the Woods. Boston: Ticknor and Fields, 1854. 1st edition; April ads as desired; original brown cloth, very minor wear to spine ends, near fine, in half green morocco case; ALS signed by Ralph Waldo Emerson concerning Walden Pond tipped in. Grolier 100 American Books 63.   19th Century Shop 39- 1996 $12,500.00

THOREAU, HENRY DAVID 1817-1862   Walden; or, Life in the Woods. Boston: Ticknor & Fields, 1854. 1st edition; map at pae 307, May 1854 ads; original brown cloth, gilt, fine, tight copy, quite handsome, touch of rubbing at foot, two short cracks in crown expertly glued shut, faint spot on rear cover; with early ownership inscription dated 1854. Housed in black silk box. BAL 20106; Borst A2.1.a.   Mac Donnell 12-125 1996 $6,000.00

THOREAU, HENRY DAVID 1817-1862   Walden; or, Life in the Woods. Boston: Ticknor & Fields, 1854. 1st edition; 7 1/4 x 4 3/4 inches; 357 pages (bound without ads); vignette on title, one map; modern red mor. heavily gilt in unusual, remarkably animated & very pleasing pictorial design, both covers featuring a lg. leafy tree bending in wind, 3 geese in flight near top of tree, numerous flowers & thick blades of grass along lower edge, several fluttering butterflies, all within single gilt ruled frame, spine compartments with leafy sprays surrounding central butterfly ornament, densely gilt inner dentelles, patterned endpapers, gilt edges; titlepage bit darkened, soiled and wrinkled, old repair to fore edge of one leaf, with five letters affected, two of them obscured, one oepning with brown splattering, otherwise only trivial imperfections internally, leaves almost entirely fresh, clean and smooth, perhaps a hint of wear to joints and hint of soil to covers, but binding fine with leather and gilt very bright. BAL 20106.   Phillip J. Pirages 33-481 1996 $4,500.00

THOREAU, HENRY DAVID 1817-1862   Walden. Boston: Fields, Osgood & Co., 1869. 1st edition; 8th printing; 8vo; 357 pages; purple cloth, plan missing and appears to have never been bound in, cloth extremities slightly worn, very good.   Robert F. Lucas 42-74 1996 $300.00

THOREAU, HENRY DAVID 1817-1862   Walden or Life in the Woods. Boston: Bibliophile Society, 1909. One of 483 sets on Holland handmade paper with two facsimiles of a Thoreau ms.; small 4to; 2 volumes; engraved titlepage and frontispiece, 1 etching and 9 mounted original palladium prints, each with tissue guard with relevant passages from Walden; half vellum and boards, in publisher's lined double boxes with printed labels, binding very clean, engraved titlepage and several tissue guards foxed, scattered light foxing, photographic plates very fresh. Marilyn Braiterman 15-195 1996 $625.00

THOREAU, HENRY DAVID 1817-1862   Walden: or Life in the Woods. Boston: Limited Editions Club, 1936. Limited to 1500 copies, signed by photographer; octavo; xiii, 290 pages; numerous plates from photos by Edward Steichen; cloth backed decorative boards, slipcase; very slight wear to spine ends, else fine.   Bromer Booksellers 87-262 1996 $750.00

THOREAU, HENRY DAVID 1817-1862   A Week on the Concord and Merrimack Rivers. Boston: Ticknor & Fields, 1862. 1st edition; 2nd issue; original slate brown cloth, gilt, mild fading and spine ends slightly frayed, but nice, tight copy; Borst A1.1.a.2. BAL 20104 binding D (no priority). Mac Donnell 12-126 1996 $3,250.00

THOREAU, HENRY DAVID 1817-1862   A Week On the Concord and Merrimack Rivers. Boston: Ticknor & Fields, 1862. 1st edition; reissue of first printing sheets of Thoreau's first book with cancel title leaf; binding C; original binding, spine little sunned, but gilt still strong, some fraying to spine tips, attached to front pastedown is a clipping describing the history of the book; BAL 20104.   Charles Agvent 4-1131 1996 $1,500.00

THOREAU, HENRY DAVID 1817-1862   A Week on the Concord and Merrimack Rivers. Limited Editions Club, 1975. One of 2000 copies; signed by artist; 8vo; illustrations by Raymond Holden; original binding, fine in very good case.   Charles Agvent 4-1132 1996 $100.00

THOREAU, HENRY DAVID 1817-1862   Winter. Boston: Houghton Mifflin, 1888. 1st edition; original green cloth, gilt, top edge gilt, very good. Borst A10.1.a.1. BAL 20129.   Mac Donnell 12-127 1996 $150.00

THOREAU, HENRY DAVID 1817-1862   A Winter Walk. Bangor: Theodore Press, 1991. Limited to 140 copies, signed by artist/printer/binder, Michael Alpert; tall quarto; (30) pages; frenchfold; printed in blue and maroon, woodcuts by Michael Alpert, printed in complementary shades of blue, green and red; linen boards; mint. Bromer Booksellers 90-235 1996 $325.00

THOREAU, HENRY DAVID 1817-1862   A Yankee in Canada. Boston: Ticknor & Fields, 1866. 1st edition; 1st printing, 1st binding; original blue green cloth, gilt, remarkably fine, fresh copy, rarely found thus. Borst A7.1.a. BAL 5248 and 20117.   Mac Donnell 12-129 1996 $1,500.00

THOREAU, HENRY DAVID 1817-1862   A Yankee in Canada. Boston: Ticknor & Fields, 1866. 1st edition; 1st printing, 1st binding; original purple cloth, gilt, crown of spine frayed and general fading, but tight, clean copy. Borst A7.1.a. BAL 5248 and 20117; Downs, Books That Changed Amer. 8.   Mac Donnell 12-128 1996 $600.00

THOREAU, HENRY DAVID 1817-1862   A Yankee in Canada, with Anti-slavery and Reform Papers. Boston: Ticknor and Fields, 1866. 1st edition; 1st printing; 8vo; (iv), 286 pages; purple textured cloth; spine slightly faded and marginal waterstain to corner of several leaves and small tear to top of spine, still nice, unsophisticated copy. BAL 20117; Borst A7.1.a.   Bromer Booksellers 90-236 1996 $750.00

THOREAU, HENRY DAVID 1817-1862   A Yankee in Canada. Boston: Ticknor & Fields, 1866. 1st edition; 1546 copies printed; 12mo; three quarter green morocco, original cloth (binding A) bound at rear; old dampstaining causing some wrinkling of pages, quite good. BAL 20117. Charles Agvent 4-1134 1996 $600.00

THORER, ALBAN   De Re Medica. Basel: A. Cratander, 1528. 1st edition; folio; (12), 125, (1) leaves; woodcut printer's device on title and last leaf, two fine four piece woodcut borders (signed I.F.) by Jacob Faber after H. Holbein and numerous fine initials, some minor soiling to titlepage and one blank margin reinforced, modern vellum over boards, leather label; very good. Durling 4351; Choulant, Handbuch p. 406. Jeffrey Mancevice 20-82 1996 $2,850.00

THORESBY, RALPH   Ducatus Leodiensis; or, the Topography of the Ancient and Populous Town and Parish of Leedes and Parts Adjacent... London: B. Dewhirst, for Robinson, Son and Holdsworth, Leeds, and John Hurst.. 1816. 2nd edition; folio; (ii), xvi (=xvii), (i), xvii, (i), 86, 89-139, (144)-261 (=268), (ii), 123, (i), 159, (i), 11, (l) pages; pedigrees, decorated initial letters; recent quarter calf, marbled boards, label; good. Robert Clark 38-208 1996 £125.00

THORIUS, RAPHAEL   Hymnus Tabaci; a Poem in Honour of Tabaco. London: printed by T.N. for Humphrey Moseley, 1651. 1st English translation; small 8vo; pages 73, (7), 8; titlepage browned; late 18th century half brown russia, rubbed, smooth backstrip longitudinally gilt lettered, marbled boards, bookplate neatly removed, very good. Blackwell's B112-271 1996 £300.00

THORNDIKE, LYNN   A History of Magic and Experimental Science. New York: & London: Columbia University Press, 1964-66. Later printings; 8vo; 8 volumes; original green cloth, fine set in tissue jackets. Chapel Hill 94-321 1996 $350.00

THORNLEY, JOHN J.   The Ancient Church Registers of the Parish of Kirkoswald, Cumberland, Baptisms, Marriages, Burials, 1577-1812. Workington: G. H. Smith and Co., 1901. Small 4to; pages 75; original printed wrappers, rather chipped and creased, upper corners rather creased, very scarce.   R.F.G. Hollett & Son 78-584 1996 £85.00

THORNTON, ALFRED   The Adventures of a Post Captain. London: published by J. Johnston, 1817. 1st edition; 1st issue with imprint of J. & T. Agg on verso of titlepage; octavo; (4), 280, (2) pages, hand colored engraved title and 24 hand colored aquatint plates; bound by Root & Son in full red morocco, gilt single rule border on cvoers with gilt corner ornaments, gilt spine, tooled in compartments, gilt board edges and inner dentelles, top edge gilt, light foxing and soiling, few plates neatly repaired, armorial bookplate; very good. Abbey Life 347; Tooley 484.   Heritage Book Shop 196-196 1996 $1,100.00

THORNTON, EDWARD   India, Its State and Prospects. London: Parbury, Allen & Co., 1835. 1st edition; 8vo; xx, 354 pages; contemporary half calf, spine gilt, with label, bit rubbed; very good. Kress S6691; Goldsmiths 29033.   John Drury 82-280 1996 £125.00

THORNTON, ROBERT JOHN 1768?-1837   The British Flora; or, Genera and Species of British Plants... London: 1812. 8vo; 5 volumes in 2; pages x, 120; 122; 126; 100; 52; 345 engraved plates, 53 copper engraved charts; modern marbled boards (title to volume 1 partially loose, some offsetting from plates, marginal pencilled notations to a plate, two marginal tears to a plate.   Raymond M. Sutton VI-31 1996 $500.00

THORNTON, ROBERT JOHN 1768?-1837   Thornton's Temple of Flora with Plates Faithfully Reproduced from the Original Engravings. London: Collins, 1951. Limited edition, number 117 of only 250 copies of this spectacular facsimile; folio; pages 20, 32 collotype plates after the originals, 12 printed in colours, tissue guards, very fine internally and externally, with simply slight scratching to paper covered cloth slipcase, slipcase is also slightly sun lightened; original brown half morocco, spine titled in gilt with raised bands.   Sotheran PN32-99 1996 £498.00

THOUGHTS on Education in Ireland, and on National Education and Improvements Generally in the Present Times. London: W. HI Dalton, 1832. 1st edition; 8vo; 40 pages; disbound. 1 copy in NUC.   James Burmester 29-136 1996 £60.00

THRASHER, MAX BENNET   Tuskegee. Boston: Small Maynard, 1900. 1st edition; about fine, tipped onto free front endpaper is the conclusion of a letter signed by Booker T. Washington and dated 5 Jan. 1901, above the signature is written "Henry W. Sage/from.." It seems likely this was a presentation copy from Washington to Sage.   Between the Covers 43-422 1996 $425.00

THE THREE Bears. Portland: Chamberlain Press, 1983. Of an edition of 125 copies, this one of 25 deluxe copies, signed by Chamberlain, this copy additionally inscribed; octavo; (16) pages; designed, printed and illustrated by Sarah Chamberlain, 10 wood engravings, all engravings signed, the deluxe issue, including an extra signed print, there are also 9 inscribed proofs; bound by Barbara Blumenthal in pastepaper boards, painted to a pattern of paw prints; extremely fine, housed in dropback box of ivory buckram.   Bromer Booksellers 87-121 1996 $500.00

THREE Choruses from Opera Libretti, by Lou Harrison to Robert Duncan. Highlands: Jargon Society, 1960. 1st edition; one of 200 copies, issued hors commerce; 24mo; 4 pages; decorated wrappers; fine, very scarce. Captain's Bookshelf 38-124 1996 $200.00

THREE Early French Essays on Paper Marbling 1642-1765. Bird & Bull Press, 1987. One of 310 numbered copies; large 8vo; printed in Cochin on Umbria handmade; 13 original marbled samples; half dark green morocco, marbled sides, made by Wolfe; fine.   Bertram Rota 272-38 1996 £180.00

THREE Famous New Songs Called Effects of Whisky. The Valley Below. Larry O'Gaff. Paisley: printed by and for G. Caldwell, Jun. c. 1820. 16mo; pages 8; primitive woodcut on titlepage, cheap paper uniformly browned, unbound as issued (?); very good.   Blackwell's B112-261 1996 £50.00

THE THREE Little Kittens. London: George Routledge & Sons, ca. 1870. Folio; 24 pages; printed on one side only and backed with linen, 6 full page excellent illustrations by Harrison Weir and printed in colors by Leighton Bros.; some spoitting and occasional minor fraying of edges; original yellow chromolithograph covers (printed by Kronheim & Co.), worn at extremities and spine, short tears at edges with no loss, lower cover and ads for hair restorer and tooth powder; scarce.   Ian Wilkinson 95/1-77 1996 £50.00

THREE Speeches Spoken at Common-Hall, Thursday the 3 of July, 1645. By Mr. Lisle, Mr. Tate, Mr. Brown, Members of the House of Commons... London: printed for Peter Cole, 1645. 1st edition; 4to; title within woodcut border, 20 pages; padded with blanks, modern morocco, label with Fairfax coat of arms blocked in gold on upper cover, all edges gilt, bookplate of Fairfax of Cameron, nice. Wing T1121. Anthony Laywood 108-18 1996 £75.00

THRELKELD, C.   Synopsis Stirpium Hibernicarum Alphabetice Dispositarum... Dublin: 1727. 2nd issue; pages (22), 23-26, (176), 60; contemporary calf, worn, joints broken; good ex-library, perforated stamp in titlepage and release number on verso, leaf A has accession number stamped in upper margin; rare.   Wheldon & Wesley 207-1506 1996 £500.00

THUCYDIDES   The History of the Grecian War. London: printed by Andrew Clark for Charles Harper, 1676. 2nd edition by Hobbes; small folio; pages (46), 357, (10), engraved title, 4 (of 5?) engraved maps and plates, uncased; Wing T1134.   Family Album Tillers-621 1996 $200.00

THUCYDIDES   The History of the Grecian War. London: 1723. Hobbes revised 3rd edition; 8vo; 2 volumes, pages (84), 732, 22, folding map; contemporary full leather, tooled in blind, needs rebacking.   Family Album Tillers-622 1996 $150.00

THUCYDIDES   History of the Peloponnesian War Arundel Press, 1930. One of 260 copies; large folio; printed in Ptolemy, marginal summaries in red in Blado italic, opening lines and initials designed by Graily Hewitt and printed in red; full white pigskin, binding just little soiled and rubbed, essentially very nice, clean and bright.   Bertram Rota 272-19 196 £1,500.00

THUCYDIDES   History of the Peloponnesian War. Chelsea: University of Oxford, Ashendene Press, 1930. Limited edition, this being one of 260 copies printed on handmade paper; folio; text printed in black, with initials, side notes and openings in red, ii, 364 pages; publisher's white pigskin, spine lettered in gilt, edges uncut, torn remnants of original glassine dust jacket, faint trace of discoloration to binding, otherwise very fine.   Thomas Thorp 489-304 1996 £1,500.00

THUDICHUM, J. L. W.   The Spirit of Cookery. London: and New York: Frederick Warne and Co., 1895. 1st American edition; green cloth titled in gilt and black; fine with bookplate on front pastedown.   Hermitage SP95-875 1996 $150.00

THURBER, JAMES GROVER 1894-1961   The Beast in Me: and other Animals. New York: Harcourt Brace, 1948. 1st edition; 1st binding, 2nd state text; blue green cloth stamped in black to front cover and spine, in dust jacket which is slightly chipped to top edge, later owner's inscription also present; inscribed by author for Elizabeth Whiting. Bromer Booksellers 87-268 1996 $385.00

THURET, G.   Etudes Phycologiques... Paris: 1878. Limited to 200 copies; folio; pages iii, 105; 51 plates; half morocco (original wrappers bound in); extremely scarce, slight foxing at beginning and slight waterstain on lower blank corner, the Plesch copy.   Wheldon & Wesley 207-112 1996 £600.00

THURSTON, JOSEPH   The Toilette. London: for Benj. Motte, 1730. 1st edition; 8vo. in half sheets, pages 47; frontispiece by A. Motte, woodcut head and tailpieces and initials, title printed in red and black; 19th century black half morocco, gilt rules on sides, spine lettered and with ornaments, gilt, marbled boards and endpapers, slight wear, one or two trivial repairs, but excellent. Both title and F3 are cancels. Foxon T269. Simon Finch 24-227 1996 £300.00

THWAITE, LEO   Alberta: an Account of its Wealth and Progress. Chicago/New York: Rand McNally, 1912. 19.5 cm; 250 pages; frontispiece, plates, maps, tables, large folding map at rear, in color; near mint (dust jacket lightly worn), uncut, unopened. Peel 2348. Rockland Books 38-224 1996 $125.00

TIBULLUS   Elegies de Tibulle. Paris: an VI, 1798. 8vo; 3 volumes, half titles, 2 frontispiece portraits, 13 engraved plates; contemporary French quarter straight grain red morocco, brick red paper sides, vellum corners, spines with double gilt rules within crochet lines and twice repeated star and lyre motifs, lettered in gilt, bookplates in volumes 2 and 3; ownership signature in ink (1889) on half titles of same volumes, small library stamp of Hebrew letters within a triangle at foot of titlepage in volume 3 with evidence of same, erased in volume 1, some slight soiling and wear. Cohen/de Ricci 993.   Simon Finch 24-228 1996 £750.00

TICE, GEORGE A.   Paterson. Rutgers University Press, 1972. 1st edition; illustrations; dust jacket.   J. B. Muns 154-306 1996 $100.00

TICE, JOHN H.   Over the Plain, on the Mountains; or Kansas, Colorado and the Rocky Mountains; Agriculturally, Mineralogically and Aestehtically Described. St. Louis: 1872. 272, iv pages plus 2 pages ads, some illustrations; original cloth, 2 titlepages; should be recased, clean and tight, backstrip torn and chipped, middle portion missing, title remains, front hinge weak. Scarce, and but for the spine, a nice copy. Wynar 2065; Rader 2065.   Bohling Book Co. 192-230 1996 $200.00

TICEHURST, CLAUD B.   A History of the Birds of Suffolk. London: 1932. illustrations, folding map; fine in new half dark green morocco, lovely, scarce.   David A.H. Grayling MY95Orn-78 1996 £80.00

TIDCOMBE, MARIANNE   The Bookbindings of T. J. Cobden-Sanderson. London: British Library, 1984. 1st edition; 4to; 407 pages, many plates and illustrations; cloth, slipcase.   The Bookpress 75-360 1996 $115.00

TIEMANN, GEORGE, & CO.   American Armamentarium Chirurgicum. San Francisco: 1989. Centennial Edition, facsimile of 1889 edition; 4to; 65, 846 pages; original binding. GM 5620.1. Rutkow GS 140.1.   W. Bruce Fye 71-36 1996 $150.00

TIERNEY, GEORGE   The Real Situation of the English-India Company Considered, With Respect to Their Rights and Privileges... London: printed for J. Debrett, 1787. 1st edition; 8vo; 96 pages; disbound; signature of Dudley North on half title. Kress B6166; Goldsmith 20700. Anthony W. Laywood 109-150 1996 £135.00

TIERNEY, M. A.   The History and Antiquities of the Castle and Town of Arundel... London: 1834. Thick 4to; 8 engraved plates on India paper, 2 pedigrees and text illustrations; half brown morocco by Leighton, plate margins little foxed.   Petersfield Bookshop FH58-197 1996 £150.00

TILLI, M. A.   Catalogus Plantarum Horti Pisani. Florence: 1723. 1st edition; folio; portrait, 2 plants, 50 engraved plates; contemporary vellum, bit worn; good copy; stamp of Rafael Garreta of Barcelona on verso on half title. Hunt 457.   Maggs Bros. Ltd. 1190-146 1996 £1,100.00

TILLYARD, R. J.   The Insects of Australia and New Zealand. Sydney: 1926. Royal 8vo; pages xiii, 560; 44 plates, numerous text figures; cloth (trifle used); extremely scarce.   Wheldon & Wesley 207-1122 1996 £120.00

TILLYARD, R. J.   The Insects of Australia and New Zealand. Sydney: 1926. 8vo; pages xv, 560, 8 color and 36 plain plates; cloth, library stamps on titlepage and verso of plates.   John Henly 27-70 1996 £52.00

TILMAN, H. W.   The Ascent of Nanda Devi. London: 1937. 1st edition; 35 plates, 2 maps; fine in carefully restored dust jacket with some moderate soiling of cream colored portions and repairs to end of spine, very good, very scarce in dust jacket.   Moutaineering Books 8-T05 1996 £110.00

TILMAN, H. W.   Two Mountains and a River. 1949. 1st edition; 37 black and white plates, maps; very good+ on very good dust jacket with repaired chipping to spine and slight soiling.   Moutaineering Books 8-T07 1996 £50.00

TILNEY, EDMUND   A Brief and Pleasant Discourse of Duties in Mariage, etc. London: by Henrie Denham, 1568. 1st edition; variant issue? 8vo; 40 unnumbered leaves, black letter, Italic side notes, title within orante typographcial border, large woodcut of Roya arms on verso, couple of large initials; early and laat leaves somewhat soiled, running title and side notes occasionally shaved, paper restorations to blank portion of several pages, title possibly made up, intermittent early underlinings and doodles; modern crushed morocco gilt, preserved in folding box; unique copy of an exceedingly rare work.   A. Sokol XXV-96 1996 £3,500.00

TILNEY, ROBERT   My Life in the Army. Three Years and a Half with the Fifth Army Corps, Army of the Potomac 1862-1865. Philadelphia: 1912. 1st edition; 8vo; 247 pages; portrait; ex-library with no external marks. Coulter 447.   Edward Morrill 369-558 1996 $100.00

TILSON, JAKE   Excavator, Barcelona, Excavador. London: Woolley Dale Press, 1986. One of 150 copies, signed by artist/writer and numbered; page size 11 x 8 inches; tan wrappers with collage on upper cover, hand collaged color prints with type settting by Wandsowrth. Priscilla Juvelis 95/1-304 1996 $350.00

TILTON, THEODORE   The Two Hungry Kittens. New York: Tibbals & Whiting, 1866. Octavo; 8ff., 6 half page lithographs, titlepage and copyright page in red and gold, pictorial wrappers in blue and gold, light soil, traces of tape along spine, withal a nice copy. Scarce.   Bromer Booksellers 90-141 1996 $175.00

TIMM, WERNER   The Graphic Art of Edvard Munch. Greenwich: New York Graphic Society, 1969. 4to; 314 pages, 186 plates, some in color, illustrations; cloth, dust jacket. Freitag 6904.   Brannan 43-471 1996 $135.00

TIMPERLAKE, JAMES   Illustrated Toronto: Past and Present, Being an Historical and Descriptive Guide-Book... Toronto: Peter A. Gross, 1877. Large 8vo; xvi, 17-384 pages, 145 views on 60 color litho plates with guard sheets; rebaked with original decorated covers retained, new endpapers, pages 145-46 repaired with Japanese tissue, else very good. Hugh Anson-Cartwright 87-435 1996 $850.00

TIMPERLEY, CHARLES HENRY   A Dictionary of Printers and Printing with the Progress of Literature, Ancient and Modern. London: H. Johnson, 1939. vi, 996 pages; 11 plates, illustrations in text half calf, rebacked, gilt edges and boards bit worn, titles in red and black, ex-library with stamps on verso of plates and title.   Maggs Bros. Ltd. 1191-218 1996 £130.00

TIMPERLEY, CHARLES HENRY   Encyclopaedia of Literary and Typographical Anecdote... London: Henry G. Bohn, 1842. 2nd edition; small folio; plates, illustrations, inner hinge strengthened, original purple cloth, spine faded, very good.   Jarndyce 103-220 1996 £220.00

TINDAL, WILLIAM   The History and Antiquities of the Abbey and Borough of Evesham. Evesham: printed and sold by John Agg, 1794. 4to; viii, 363, (5) pages, 7 plates, 19th century half green calf, marbled boards, spine gilt with unidentified arms in bottom compartment, edges marbled, joints little worn, good copy, scarce.   H. M. Fletcher 121-123 1996 £275.00

TINDALE, NORMAN   Aboriginal Tribes of Australia... Berkeley: 1974. 1st U.S. edition; 4to; 1 volume text, 1 volume maps in slip box, xii, 404 pages, black and white illustrations and maps in text, 46 color plates, 92 black and white plates; bound in imitation leather in slipbox, otherwise very good.   Antipodean 28-466 1996 $295.00

TINDALE, THOMAS KEITH   The Handmade Papers of Japan. Vermont & Tokyo: Tuttle, 1952. No limitation indicated; folio; 4 volumes; first 3 volumes bound oriental-style in color woodblock-printed paper wrappers with silk head and tailpieces; the fourth volume is unbound and laid into a portfolio of matching paper with ivory clasps, the four volumes and envelope are housed together in a portfolio of rust-colored cloth with ivory clasps, portfolio is lightly rubbed, else very fine set, rare. Bromer Booksellers 87-247 1997 $7,500.00

TING, WALASSE   One Cent Life. Bern: E. W. Kornfeld, 1964. One of 2000 copies with lithographs; page size 16 1/4 x 11 3/8 inches; pink cloth over boards with jacket designed by Appel. Fine.   Priscilla Juvelis 95/1-240 1996 $3,000.00

TING, WALASSE   1 Cent Life. Bern: E. W. Kornfeld, 1964. One of 2000 numbered copies; 62 color lithographs, many folding, 19 reproductions, loose as issued; original pictorial and decorated cloth folder by Lichtenstein and Alechinsky in pictorial dust jacket and slipcase. From Manet to Hockney 135.   Marilyn Braiterman 15-164 1996 $2,500.00

TINGLEY, ELBERT R.   Poco Loco; Sketches of New Mexico Life. Blair: Danish Lutheran Pub. House, 1900. Pages 94; frontispiece; good, rare. Dumont 28-107 1996 $225.00

TINKER, CHAUNCEY BREWSTER   Addresses Commemorating the Hundredth Anniversary of the Birth of William Morris - Delivered Before the Yale Library Associates in the Sterling Memorial Library, XXIX October MCMXXXIV. N.P.: Overbrook Press, 1935. One of 450 copies; woodcut initials by Anna Simons, titlepage border designed by Valenti Angelo, printed on dampened Curfew paper by John F. Macnamara; original binding, top edge gilt, first few pages spotted, head and tail of spine and corners bumped, spine faded, covers slightly rubbed and marked, very good.   Ulysses 39-420 1996 £115.00

TIPPING, HENRY AVRAY   English Homes. Periods 1-6. London: 1921-26. 16 x 10.5 inches; 6 volumes, numerous photos; two-tone cloth, all edges gilt, covers soiled and rubbed, spines heavily worn.   John K. King 77-540 1996 $850.00

TIPPING, HENRY AVRAY   English Gardens. London: Country Life, 1925. 1st edition; folio; lxiv, 375 pages; cloth, partial dust jacket, some dampstaining to lower tips of second half of book, spine sunned, dust jacket lacks spine and is chipped.   The Bookpress 75-243 1996 $295.00

TIPPING, HENRY AVRAY   English Gardens. London: 1925. Folio; pages lxiv, 375; 590 photographic illustrations; cloth, gilt, all edges gilt, spine little faded, else fine.   John Henly 27-339 1996 £145.00

TIPPING, HENRY AVRAY   Gibbons and the Woodwork of His Age (1648-1720). London: Country Life, 1914. Folio; 16 pages of ads at back; numerous illustrations; ex-library, white cloth backstrip, corners bumped and worn.   Petersfield Bookshop FH58-8 1996 £120.00

TIPTREE, J.   Ten Thousand Light-Years from Home. London: Methuen, 1975. 1st edition; uncorrected proof; author's first book; wrappers; near fine.   Aronovitz 57-1169 1996 $100.00

TIRPITZ, VON   My Memoirs. London: Hurst, n.d. 1919. 1st edition; 8vo; 2 volumes, 500 pages; cloth, very good.   John Lewcock 30-131 1996 £50.00

TISCHNER, HERBERT   Oceanic Art. New York: 1954. 4to; 32 pages, 96 plates; tan cloth, dust jacket slightly chipped, otherwise very good+l owner's signature trimmed. Chamberlin 569.   Antipodean 28-470 1996 $125.00

TISSOT, SAMUEL AUGUSTE ANDRE DAVID   Advice to the People in General, with Regard to Their Health. London: printed for T. Becket and P. A. De Hondt, 1768. 3rd edition in English; 8vo; (xxxvi), 620 pages; contemporary calf, firm, clean copy.   John Gach 150-456 1996 $185.00

TITSINGH, M. ISAAC   Illusrations of Japan; Consisting of Private Memoirs and Anecdotes of the Djogouns, or, Sovereigns of Japan. London: Printed for R. Ackermann, 1822. 1st English edition; 4to; xvi, 325 pages; 13 hand colored engraved and aquatint plates, two of the plates have semi-circular piece burned out of margin measuring about half inch deep and 1 1/2" wide (not affecting either text on plate or image itself), large folding plate has closed tear extending 2 1/2" down a folding and running approx. 3 1/2" across the plate with no loss, in fact it does not detract from the image when plate is opened, folding plate has some light discoloration (soiling) in margin but not affecting image; in all, a lovely copy; rare. Abbey 557, Tooley 489; Prideaux p. 128; Hardie p. 113.   David Mason 71-61 1996 $6,800.00

TITUS and Vespasian or the Destruction of Jerusalem. London: printed for the Roxburghe Club by J.B. Nichols and Sons, 1905. 1st edition; 11 x 8 1/2 inches; (i)-xlvi, 242 pages; title printed in red and black; 2 color plates, partly printed in gold, reproducing illuminated manuscript pages; original roan backed reddish paper boards, top edge gilt, other edges untrimmed; one small abrasion and minor soiling to paper covers, corners and spine ends slightly worn, otherwise fine, beautiful copy internally; with bookplates of C. H. St. John Hornby and John Roland Abbey.   Phillip J. Pirages 33-451 1996 $550.00

TO Brokers, Attornies & Landlords. Oppression, Robbery and Neglect, Exemplified in the Distressing Case of Henry Smith vs. Charles Hall and the Conduct of J. Searle, Attorney at Law, Fetter Lane. London: printed by Seale & Bates, for the plaintiff, H. Smith, late of... c. 1815. 1st edition; 12mo; (ii), 43 pages, title frayed along outer edge, uncut, disbound.   James Burmester 29-19 1 996 £65.00

TO The Millers of the United States. Take Notice -- That Congress Did on the 21st of Jan. 1808, Pass the Following Act: An Act for the Relief of Oliver Evans. Philadelphia?: 1809. 1st edition; 4to. leaflet, printed on pages (1-3), signed twice by Evans at end of printed statement of fees for the use of his patents and at conclusion of a letter written in the margins to the Gov. of Ohio, Samuel Huntington.   M & S Rare Books 60-455 1996 $3,750.00

TOBIN, J.   Journal of a Tour Made in the Years 1828-1829, Through Syria, Carniola and Itlay, Whilst Accompanying the Last Sir Humphry Davy. London: W. S. Orr, 14 Paternoster Row, 1832. 1st edition; small 8vo; (iii-vi), 1-242 pages; frontispiece, 4 engraved plates, frontispiece crudely repaired to top edge margin, some dampstaining to margins of a couple of plates, library stamp on verso of title, library withdrawal stamp to rear endpaper, owner's bookplate, soiling to endpapers; ex-library, library style cloth, soiled and faded, gilt title to spine corners bumped.   Beeleigh Abbey BA/56-123 1996 £55.00

TODD, CHARLES W.   Woodville; or, the Anchoret Reclaimed. Knoxville: printed for the author by F. S. Heiskell, 1832. 1st edition; 12mo; (4), 278 pages, original muslin backed plain boards, printed paper label, spine worn, lacks front free endpaper; Rare. Wright I 2600; Tenn Imprints 247. B&B 15011.   M & S Rare Books 60-242 1996 $1,500.00

TODD, FRANK MORTON   Eradicating Plague from San Francisco. San Francisco: 1909. 1st edition; 313 pages, photographic illustrations; original red cloth, very good, plus; Herbert McLean, Evans and Harrison Horblit with their bookplates.   19th Century Shop 39- 1996 $225.00

TODD, W. B.   Tauchnitz International Editions in English 1841-1955. A Bibliographical History. New York: Bib. Soc. of America, 1988. frontispiece, several illustrations; red cloth, protective wrappers.   Maggs Bros. Ltd. 1191-125 1996 £65.00

TODD, W. E. C.   The Birds of the Santa Marta Region of Colombia, a Study in Altitudinal Distribution. Carnegie Mus., 1922. 8vo; 611 pages, map and 8 plates; half morocco, rubbed.   Wheldon & Wesley 207-879 1996 £70.00

TODHUNTER, I.   Researches in the Calculus of Variations Principally on the Theory of Discontinuous Solutions. London: 1871. vii, 278 pages; diagrams; cloth, little worn and soiled; scarce.   Graham Weiner C2-333 1996 £50.00

TOESCA, PIETRO   Florentine Painting of the Trecento. Florence: Pantheon and Pegasus Press, 1929. Large 4to; text set in Monotype Poliphilus and Blado by the Officina Bodoni, 119 plates; three quarter red morocco, gilt, bottom edges somewhat worn and some quite severe foxing, not affecting plates, otherwise nice in dust jacket, rubber stamp on endpaper, scarce.   Bertram Rota 272-341 1996 £200.00

TOESCA, PIETRO   The Mosaics in the Church of St. Mark in Venice. London: George Rainbird, 1958. 39 x 29 cm; 51 pages text, 32 text figures, xli color plates; original cloth, in dust jacket, corner slightly bumped.   Rainsford A54-554 1996 £48.00

TOFFTEEN, OLAF A.   Researches in Biblical Archaeology. Chicago: University of Chicago Press, 1907-09. 8vo; 2 volumes; xix, 302 pages, 8 plates; xxii, 339 pages, 4 plates; original cloth, top edge gilt, corners bumped.   Archaeologia Luxor-2773 1996 $125.00

THE TOKEN. Boston: Gray & Bowen, 1833. 1st edition; original maroon morocco, gilt, all edges gilt, mild foxing in text, fine copy; BAL 6126 and 7574; Clark C3.   Mac Donnell 12-105 1996 $200.00

THE TOKEN. Boston: Charles Bowen, 1838. 1st edition; original dark brown morocco, gilt, all edges gilt, remarkably fine, fresh copy. BAL 6816, 7583 and 8731. Clark C10.   Mac Donnell 12-104 1996 $200.00

THE TOKEN and Atlantic Souvenir. Boston: C. Bowen, 1837. 1st edition; 12mo; 9 (of 12) plates; original full roan, gilt borders/rules, owner's name in gilt on cover, some edgewear, foxing, lacking front blank; good.   Charles Agvent 4-641 1996 $150.00

THE TOKEN and Atlantic Souvenir. Boston: American Stationers, 1838. 1st edition; 9 plates, engraved title; full gilt decorated roan, all edges gilt, beautiful exemple of early American binding with only light rubbing at corners and edges, hinge crack before presentation palte, superby copy.   Charles Agvent 4-642 1996 $400.00

TOLENTINO, RAUL   De Luxe Catalogue of the Rare Artistic Properties Collected by Signor Raoul Tolentino. New York: April, 21st-27th, 1920. Large 8vo; illustrations; half cloth, marbled boards, leather labels;   Rainsford A54-657 1996 £130.00

TOLFREY, FREDERIC   The Sportsman in Canada. London: T. C. Newby, 1845. Large 12mo; 2 volumes, pages iii, 283, (4) (publisher's ads), frontispiece, 4 plates, pages 286, 8 (publisher's ads), frontispiece, 4 plates; original blindstamped cloth with binder's stamp "Marrow, 3 Cecil St. Strand" and bookseller's label, edges slightly scuffed, exterior dusty, else exceptionally clean, crisp set. TPL 2744.   Hugh Anson-Cartwright 87-410 1996 $750.00

TOLKIEN, JOHN RONALD REUEL 1892-1973   Farmer Giles of Ham. London: George Allen and Unwin ltd., 1949. 1st edition; 8vo; pages (vi), 7-78, 2 colored plates and line drawings by Pauline Baynes; original ochre cloth stamped in blue, preserved in white pictorial dust jacket, decorated endpapers; fine in wrapper with couple of very short closed tears and very slight wear at head of spine; Excellent copy in unusually fresh and clean jacket.   Sotheran PN32-156 1996 £168.00

TOLKIEN, JOHN RONALD REUEL 1892-1973   The Fellowship of the Ring. H-M, 1954. 1st American edition (from the English sheets); just about very good in like dust jacket with small chip gone from base of rear dust jacket panel.   Aronovitz 57-1174 1996 $450.00

TOLKIEN, JOHN RONALD REUEL 1892-1973   The Hobbit. H-M, 1938. 1st American edition (1st issue, without half title and with the bowing figure as opposed to the H-M logo on titlepage); illustrations by author; tiny nick at head of spine, else very good in bright, attractive near very good dust jacket save for some wear and tear and light chipping and some staining to dust jacket spine;   Aronovitz 57-1172 1996 $1,975.00

TOLKIEN, JOHN RONALD REUEL 1892-1973   The Hobbit. Boston: Houghton Mifflin, 1966. 1st printing, collector's edition; very fine in slipcase.   Bud Schweska 12-751 1996 $125.00

TOLKIEN, JOHN RONALD REUEL 1892-1973   The Lord of the Rings. London: George Allen & Unwin Ltd., 1954-55. 1st edition; 8vo; 3 volumes, map in volume 1 and folding map at end of each volume, original red cloth, spines lettered in gilt, dust jackets with some soiling and chipping, but not price clipped, ownership signature on front free endpapers, very good.   Simon Finch 24-229 1996 £3,200.00

TOLKIEN, JOHN RONALD REUEL 1892-1973   The Lord of the Rings. A&U, 1954/55/56. 1st editions; 3 volumes, just about fine in very good+ dust jackets save for some light wear and tear to head of slightly faded dust jacket spines and small stain to rear of volume 2; with TLS from author laid in.   Aronovitz 57-1173 1997 $7,500.00

TOLKIEN, JOHN RONALD REUEL 1892-1973   The Lord of the Rings. H-M, 1967/67/67. 1st revised American editions; 3 volumes; very fine in dust jackets, original slipcase.   Aronovitz 57-1178 1996 $295.00

TOLKIEN, JOHN RONALD REUEL 1892-1973   The Return of the King. A&U, 1955. 1st edition; fine in very good+/near fine dust jacket save for some light sunning to dust jacket spine.   Aronovitz 57-1175   1996 $750.00

TOLLER, ERNEST   Hinkerman. Potsdam: 1925. 7.5 x 4.5 inches; 61 pages; boards, spine gilt and cello-taped, covers rubbed; presentation copy, inscribed and signed by author.   John K. King   77-479   1996 $150.00

TOLLER, ERNST   Brockenbrow. London: Nonesuch Press, 1926. 1st English edition; small 4to; 50 pages; 6 litho plates of drawings by Grosz; original mottled decorated boards, paper label, overlapping edge at head of backstrip chipped away; good, uncut copy; from the library of Alastair Robb-Smith. Dreyfus 30.   Claude Cox   107-116   1996 £65.00

TOLSTOI, LEV NIKOLAEVICH 1828-1910   Anna Karenina. Cambridge: Limited Editions Club, 1951. Number 904 from 1500 copies, signed by artist; lithographs by Barnett Freedman; near fine in publisher's slipcase. Hermitage   SP95-1045   1996 $125.00

TOLSTOI, LEV NIKOLAEVICH 1828-1910   Anna Karenina. Cambridge: Limited Editions Club, 1951. Limited to 1500 copies; 8vo; illustrations by Barnett Freedman; original binding, slight foxing to edges and few pages, near fine in very good slipcase.   Charles Agvent   4-1139   1996 $100.00

TOLSTOI, LEV NIKOLAEVICH 1828-1910   Anna Karenina. Cambridge; Limited Editions Club, 1951. Limited to 1500 copies; signed by artist; 8vo; 2 volumes; lithos by Barnett Freedman; original binding, near fine in very good dust jackets and slipcase.   Charles Agvent   4-1138   1996 $125.00

TOLSTOI, LEV NIKOLAEVICH 1828-1910   Childhood, Boyhood, Youth. New York: Crowell, 1886. 1st American edition; 8vo; decorated cloth, minor rubbing, soiling, bright copy; institutional bookplate.   Charles Agvent   4-1141   1996 $125.00

TOLSTOI, LEV NIKOLAEVICH 1828-1910   Childhood, Boyhood, Youth. New York: Limited Editions Club, 1972. Limited to 1500 copies; signed by artist; 8vo; wood engravings by Fritz Eichenberg; quarter gold stamped buckram, fine in near fine slipcase.   Charles Agvent   4-1142   1996 $150.00

TOLSTOI, LEV NIKOLAEVICH 1828-1910   The Kreutzer Sonata. Boston: Benj. R. Tucker, 1890. 1st English language; one small spot to front cover, overall light rubbing, otherwise fine.   Hermitage   SP95-625   1996 $100.00

TOLSTOI, LEV NIKOLAEVICH 1828-1910   Resurrection. New York: Limited Editions Club, 1963. Limited to 1500 copies; tall 8vo; wood engravings by Fritz Eichenberg, signed by artist; blue and tan buckram, fine in fine slipcase.   Charles Agvent   4-1145   1996 $125.00

TOLSTOI, LEV NIKOLAEVICH 1828-1910   War and Peace. Glasgow: Limited Editions Club, 1938. Limited to 1500 copies; signed by artist; 8vo; 6 volumes; lithographs by Barnett Freedman; original binding, very good in very good slipcase.   Charles Agvent   4-147   1996 $200.00

TOM Thumb's Playbook to Teach Children Their Letters as Soon as They Can Speak... Newcastle: 1824. 48mo; woodcuts; except for light cover soil, this is an exceptional copy of a rare and fragile little book with virtually no wear. Osborne II p. 742.   Glenn Books   36-42   1996 $2,500.00

TOMBLESON, WILLIAM   Eighty Picturesque Views on the Thames and Medway. London: by Black and Armstrong 1834, but later Post 4to; (2), (vi), 84 pages, engraved vignette title, 80 plates, 2 folding panorama maps; later half calf, banded and gilt with ships by Riviere & Son, all edges gilt, few very minor marks, but very good. Adams 178.   Ash Rare Books   Zenzybyr-90   1996 £895.00

TOMKINSON, G. S.   A Select Bibliography of the Principal Modern Presses Public and Private in Great Britain and Ireland. London: First Edition Club, 1928. One of 1000 copies, this numbered and signed by Tomkinson; 4to; boards with holland back and leather label, corners little worn, otherwise very nice, clean copy.   Bertram Rota   272-101   1996 £160.00

TOMLINE, WILLIAM EDWARD PRETYMAN   A Speech on the Character of the Right Hon. William Pitt, Delivered at Trinity College Chapel Cambridge, Dec. 17, 1806. Cambridge: printed by R. Watts, at the University Press, 1806. 1st edition; 4to; "From the author" (copped) on title; contemporary diced calf, rebacked.   Anthony W. Laywood   108-241   1996 £75.00

TOMLINSON, CHARLES   Cyclopaedia of Useful Arts, Mechanical and Chemical, Manufactures, Mining and Engineering. London: George Virtue & Co., 1854. 2 volumes; 40 steel engravings, 2745 wood engravings; original blue decorated cloth, little rubbed, spines extra gilt.   Jarndyce   103-222   1996 £250.00

TOMLINSON, DAVID   African Wildlife in Art. 1991. Limited to 100 copies only, this copy has an original watercolor sketch by Mandy Shepherd tipped in; oblong folio; 90 fine colored plates, text sketches, etc; finely bound in full Chieftain morocco, silk marker, marbled endpapers.   David Grayling   J95Biggame-207   1996 £350.00

TOMLINSON, DAVID   African Wildlife in Art. London: 1991. Limited to 100 copies only; (only 30 have, in fact, been produced); oblong folio; 90 fine colored plates, text sketches, this copy has an original watercolor sketch by Mandy Shepherd tipped in; finely bound in full Chieftain morocco, silk marker, marbled endpapers.   David A.H. Grayling   MY95Orn-79   1996 £350.00

TOMLINSON, HENRY MAJOR 1873-1958   A Brown Owl. Garden City: Henry J. Longwell, 1928. 1st edition; one of 107 copies, signed by author and publishers; square 12mo; pages 19; flowered boards, paper label, fore and bottom edges uncut; fine.   Howard S. Mott   227-141   1996 $175.00

TOMLINSON, HENRY MAJOR 1873-1958   The Sea and the Jungle. London: Duckworth, 1930. One of 515 numbered copies, signed by author; 16 full page wood engravings by Clare Leighton, printed on handmade paper at the Camelot Press Ltd.; buckram covers, top edge gilt, bottom edges of few pages soiled, spine and top edge of upper cover faded, free endpapers browned, tail of spine and corners slightly bumped, very good.   Ulysses   39-367   1996 £55.00

TOMLINSON, HENRY MAJOR 1873-1958   The Sea and the Jungle. London: 1930. 1st edition; woodcuts by Clare Leighton, uncut and partly unopened, spine little faded, fine.   Polyanthos   22-859   1996 $100.00

TOMLINSON, HENRY MAJOR 1873-1958   The Sea and the Jungle. New York: Harper, 1930. 1st edition; ("H-E"); number 161 of 325 copies, signed by author; 8vo; frontispiece, chapter headings and full page woodcuts by Clare Leighton; gilt stamped beige cloth over light blue boards; very good to fine in glassine dust jacket. NCBEL 4 750. George J. Houle   68-82   1996 $175.00

TOMLINSON, HENRY MAJOR 1873-1958   Thomas Hardy. New York: Crosby Gaige, 1929. Signed, limited edition of 761 numbered copies, signed by Tomlinson and by artist; 8vo; lithograph frontispiece by Zhenya Gay; cloth, in acetate titlepage; fine.   Antic Hay   101-777   1996 $125.00

TOMPKINS, P. W.   To Her Royal Highness the Princess Amelia, This Book Representing the Birth-Day Gift or the Joy of a New Doll... London: Tomkins, 1796. Oblong quarto; 8ff.; engraved book with illustrated titlepage and 7 other engravings; 2 plates with slight dampstaining and spine somewhat worn yet a remarkable copy in original wrappers. Bromer Booksellers   90-145   1996 $950.00

TONER, J. M.   The Medical Men of the Revolution, With a Brief History of the Medical Department of the Continental Army... Philadelphia: Collins, 1876. 1st edition; 8vo; original quater cloth, small hole at head of spine, narrow stain on front board.   James Tait Goodrich   K40-282   1996 $145.00

TONGE, THOMAS   Denver by Pen and Picture. Denver: The Hamilton & Kendrick Stationery Co., 1900. (80) pages; frontispiece, profusely illustrated, map; original pictorial grey wrappers; very good.   Michael D. Heaston   23-107   1996 $100.00

TONNA, CHARLOTTE ELIZABETH   Derry, a Tale of the Revolution. London: James Nisbet, 1833. 1st edition; 8vo; (iv, 382) pages; contemporary tan morocco, gilt lettered spine, gilt decorated with panels and bands, contrasting title label, all edges marbled; fine. Block p. 237; this title not in Wolff.   Paulette Rose   16-322   1996 $300.00

TOOKE, JOHN HORNE 1736-1812   Epea Pteroenta. Or, The Diversions of Purley. London: printed for the author, a J. Johnson's, 1798-1805. 2nd edition, 1st edition of part 2; 4to; 2 volumes; frontispiece, slight spotting in prelims; handsome contemporary plain half pigskin; fine.   Jarndyce 103-348 1996 £320.00

TOOKE, JOHN HORNE 1736-1812   Epea Pteroenta, or the Diversions of Purley. London: printed by Richard Taylor for Thomas Tegg, 1829. New edition; 2 volumes, frontispiece in volume 1 slightly spotted with offsetting on title, contemporary calf, gilt spines, borders and dentelles, hinges rubbed with splits at head, but good.   Jarndyce 103-349 1996 £70.00

TOOKE, THOMAS   A History of Prices, and of the State of the Circulation from 1793 to 1837...(with) A History of Prices, and of the State of the Circulation in 1838 and 1839... London: Longman, 1838/40. 1st editions; 8vo; 3 volumes, viii, 376; iv, 420; iv, 298 pages, 32 page publisher's catalog at end; original black cloth, embossed in blind, spines lettered in gilt, some wear to joints and slight chipping of head and foot of spines, covers slightly damp marked. Kress C4744; Goldsmiths 30310 and 31370; Einaudi 5655.   John Drury 82-281 1996 £250.00

TOOKER, RICHARD   The Dawn Boy. Philadelphia: Penn Publishing, 1932. 1st edition; fine in dust jacket with very slight wear at spine panel ends and evidence of tape removal from front flaps and inside dust jacket, bright and clean copy.   Robert Gavora 61-235 1996 $125.00

TOOLE-SCOTT, R.   Circus and Allied Arts, a World Bibliography 1500-1957, Based Mainly On Circus Literature in the British Museum, the Library of Congress, the Bibliotheque Nationale and On His Own Collection. Derby: Harpur & Sons, 1958-71. 4to; 4 volumes; red contemporary, dust jackets (except volume 1), volume 4 signed by author.   Maggs Bros. Ltd. 1191-127 1996 £215.00

TOOMER, JEAN   Essentials. Chicago: Private Edition, 1931. 1st edition; printed in an edition of 1000 numbered copies, this copy unnumbered; 12mo; black cloth with printed labels of various tones of blue on spine and front board, dust jacket printed to match the labels, slight darkening to gutter of front pastedown, else fine, as new.   Andrew Cahan 47-195 1996 $650.00

TOPHAM, EDWARD   The Poetry of "The World". London: printed by John Bell, 1788. 1st separate edition; small 8vo; 2 volumes bound in 1; contemporary speckled calf, gilt, surface worming, some rubbing and chipping, some soiling and browning, mostly marginal and light, good copy; bookplate of Rev. John Phelps.   James Cummins 14-212 1996 $150.00

TOPHAM, W. F.   The Lakes of England. London: T. J. Allman, 1869. 1st edition; 8vo; pages 40; 18 colored plates, all with original tissues; original blindstamped cloth, gilt extra over bevelled boards, extremities minimally worn; lovely, bright and clean copy.   R.F.G. Hollett & Son 78-1328 1996 £160.00

TOPLADY, AUGUSTUS   The Scheme of Christian and Philosophical Necessity Asserted. London: Vallance and Simmons, 1775. 1st edition; 8vo; (vi), ix, (2), 10-216 pages, numbers on blank verso of title and on blank foot of A2; late 19th century maroon cloth, spine lettered in gilt, shelf numbert at foot, very good, crisp copy.   John Drury 82-282 1996 £175.00

TOPONCE, ALEXANER   Reminiscences of Alexander Toponce, Pioneer 1839-1923. Ogden: 1923. 1st edition; 248 pages; photos; morocco; nice. Howes T299; Smith 10262; 6 Guns 2225; Rittenhouse 580; Flake 8975. T. A. Swinford 49-1162 1996 $175.00

TOPP, CHESTER W.   Victorian Yellowbacks and Paperbacks 1849-1905, Volume One, George Routledge. Denver: Hermitage Antiquarian Bookshop, 1993. 1st edition; 557 pages; 32 color illustrations.   Hermitage SP95-847 1996 $135.00

TOPP, CHESTER W.   Victorian Yellowbacks and Paperbacks 1849-1905. Volume Two, Ward Lock. Denver: Hermitage Antiquarian Bookshop, 1995. 1st edition; 32 color illustrations.   Hermitage SP95-848 1 996 $135.00

TORCZYNER, HARRY   Magritte: Ideas and Images. New York: Abrams, 1977. 4to; 277 pages; 527 illustrations, 90 in color; cloth, dust jacket. Freitag 5891.   Brannan 43-369 1996 $165.00

TORELLI, LELIO   Raguaglio della Marciata, e Comparsa a' Uso di Guerra con L'Artiglieria... Urbino; Ghisoni, 1640. Sole edition, apparently unrecordded; 4to; 48 pages; corners missing without loss of text, to all but two numbers in date on title, heavy browning, fair copy; old wrpapers. Not in NUC, BM STC or Vinciana.   Bennett Gilbert LL29-86 1996 $750.00

TORMES, LAZARILLO DE   The Pleasant History of Lazarillo de Tormes. Gwasg Gregynog, 1991. One of 300 numbered copies; tall 8vo; printed in Monotype Garamond in black and several colors on Zerkall mouldmade; 16 woodcuts and wood engravings; pictorial boards, cloth spine; fine.   Bertram Rota 272-215 1996 £85.00

TORNE, L'ABBE   Sermons Preches Devant Le Roi, Pendant Le Careme de 1764. Paris: Chez Saillant, 1765 8vo; 2 volumes, titles with attractive woodcut vignettes, very clean and well margined copy; very finely bound in full contemporary French red morocco by Derome-le-Jeune, boards with wide and elaborate dentelle border in gilt, large central gilt armorial stamp, arms containing a lamb, surmounted by a gilt crown, spines elaborately gilt in compartments, all edges gilt, inner gilt dentelles, corners and insignificant wear; execllent armorial binding in fine condition. Ian Wilkinson 95/1-35 1996 £870.00

TORNIELLO, FRANCESCO   The Alphabet. Officina Bondoni, 1971. One of 160 numbered copies; small 4to; illustrations; quarter blue morocco with linson sides, bearing author's name printed on his letters; fine in slipcase.   Bertram Rota 272-352 1996 £600.00

TORONTO of To-day: to Commemorate the Twelfth International Geological Congress, Toronto. Toronto: Morang & Co., 1913. 4to; pages 112; richly illustrated; map; decorated paper covers, covers slightly dusty, else fine.   Hugh Anson-Cartwright 87-412 1996 $100.00

TORONTO. Toronto: 188-. 18 x 14 cm; concertina with total of 13 plates containing 23 illustrations, gilt stamped boards, covers scuffed and soiled, pictures fine.   Hugh Anson-Cartwright 87-411 1996 $100.00

TORONTONENSIS, 1900: A Yearly Record and Memorial of Student Life in the University of Toronto. Toronto: 1900. Oblong 8vo; pages x, 217, xlvi; illustrations; gilt cloth, shaken, bumped, else very good.   Hugh Anson-Cartwright 87-436 1996 $100.00

TORRE, NICHOLAS LEE   Translations of the Oxford and Cambridge Latin Prize Poems. Second Series. London: A. J. Valpy, 1831. Only edition; 8vo; contemporary quarter calf, spine gilt, marbled boards; very fine and attractive; armorial bookplate of Sir James Buller East. Trebizond 39-43 1996 $165.00

TORRE, NICHOLAS LEE   Translations of the Oxford Latin Prize Poems. First Series. London: A. J. Valpy, 1831. Only edition; 8vo; 12 page subscriber list; contemporary quarter calf, spine gilt, marbled boards; very fine; armorial bookplate of Sir James Buller East, a subscriber. Trebizond 39-42 1996 $125.00

TORRENCE, RIDGELY   Granny Maumee/The Rider of Dreams/Simon the Cyrenian: Plays for a Negro Theatre. New York: Macmillan, 1917. 1st edition; bit of darkening to edges of spine and neat contemporary bookplate on front pastedown, else about fine in dust jacket with several sizeable chips, worst of which affects some of the title on spine. Between the Covers 43-196 1996 $175.00

TORREY, JOHN   Explorations and Surveys for a Railroad Route from the Mississippi River... Washington: 1856. Offprint; 4to; 8 lithograph plates; title rather soiled, next leaf bit so, recent half cloth. Stafleu 14.763.   Maggs Bros. Ltd. 1190-148 1996 £65.00

TORSELLINO, ORAZIO   the History of Our B. Lady of Loreto. N.P.: n.p., St. Omer: English College Press, 1608. 1st edition; 2nd issue; small 8vo; pages (xxxii), 541 (misnumbered 540), (ix), roman letter, quotations in italic, printed side notes, title within fine engraved architectural border, rich full page engraving of the translation of the Holy House, both by Willim du Tielt, decorative initials and tailpieces, uniform very light browning; contemporary vellum, remains of ties; good, clean copy; STC 24141. Allison & Rogers 826.   A. Sokol XXV-97 1996 £325.00

TORY, GEOFFROY ca. 1480-1533   Champ Fleury. New York: Grolier Club, 1927. One of 390 copies; 12.5 x 8.5 inches; 208 pages; designed by Bruce Rogers; vellum spine with title in gilt, tan paste paper with fleur-de-lis in tan over boards, top edge gilt; fine, dust jacket with few repaired tears and marks; neat booklabel on front free endpaper. Joshua Heller 21-205 1996 $750.00

TOTT, FRANCOIS DE   Memoirs...on the Turks and the Tartars. London: J. Jarvis, 1785. 1st English edition; 8vo; 2 volumes; pages xxiv, 532; (ii), 382, (14); contemporary quarter tan calf, minor worm damage to front joint of volume i, rubbed, smooth backstrips divided by gilt rules, slight wear to heads, red leather gilt lettered labels, vellum tipped marbled boards; very good. early owner's name "P Gell". Cox I p. 234. Blackwell's B112-272 1996 £175.00

TOTTENHAM, GEORGE L.   The Peasant Proprietors of Norway. 1889. 1st edition; 16 pages; printed wrappers, very good.   C. P. Hyland 216-860 1996 £150.00

THE TOUCHSTONE of Precedents Relating to Judicial Proceedings at Common Law. London: printed for Awnsham Churchill at the Black Swan, 1682. contemporary sheep, very worn, joints cracking, usable only; with ownership signature on second blank of Isaac Story.   Meyer Boswell SL27-219 1996 $650.00

THE TOUR of Doctor Syntax through London, or the Pleasures and Miseries of the Metropolis. London: J. Johnson, 1820. 1st edition; 8vo; iv, (2), 319 pages; 20 hand colored aquatint plates; modern half vellum and boards, some plates out of order, but all present, some minor foxing and offsetting, otherwise near fine, untrimmed copy.   James Tait Goodrich K40-257 1996 $495.00

TOUR to the Loire and La Vendee in 1835. London: Effingham Wilson, 1836. 2nd edition; small 8vo; pages viii, 254, 1 f., litho frontispiece, cloth backed boards, old library stamp on title; from the library at St. Mary's College, Blairs.   Marlborough 162-260 1 996 £110.00

TOURGEE, ALBION WINEGAR 1838-1905   With Gauge & Swallow, Attorneys. Philadelphia: J. P. Lippincott Co., 1889. 1st edition; original brown cloth, decorated and lettered in gilt, some rubbing and slight fraying of extremities, decorated endpapers, some light marginal browning; bgood. Wright Fiction 3.5532.   James Cummins 14-213 1996 $250.00

TOURIST'S Guide to the English Lakes. London: T. Nelson and Sons, n.d., c. 1870. Oblong small 8vo; pages 61; map, text woodcuts and 12 highly finished chromolithographed plates; original cloth, gilt, few spots, but very attractive bright copy.   R.F.G. Hollett & Son 78-1331 1996 £65.00

TOUSSAINT, FRANCOIS V.   Manners. London: printed for W. Johnston, 1749. 1st English edition; 12mo; ink marks on 2 leaves, tear repaired on a1, contemporary calf, rubbed, upper hinge cracked. Anthony Laywood 108-46 1996 £125.00

TOWARDS a New American Poetics: Essays and Interviews. Santa Barbara: Black Sparrow Press, 1978. Limited edition, 16/125 copies only, signed by all contributors except Olson; top edge of rear cover slightly sunned, fine in acetate dust jacket. Polyanthos 22-860 1996 $100.00

THE TOWER of Babel: an Anthology. Janus Press, 1975. One of 100 press-numbered copies, all copies signed by artist; 12.5 x 10 inches; 17 lithographs and 1 wood engraving by Claire Van Vliet; 10 unbound folios and 10 loose sheets with titled slip sheets attached; designed and letterpress printed by Clair Van Vliet, lithographed printed from stone; titles and text handset, printed in black with acknowledgment page in tan on ivory Zerkall Butten with Kozu slip sheets and ivory Zerkall Butten wrapper, boxed in tan buckram. Fine.   Joshua Heller 21-8 1996 $850.00

TOWNE, ROSA M.   Plant Lore of Shakespeare. Louisville: 1974. Facsimile with addition of notes of the 1897 edition; folio; 73 colored plates by R. M. Towne, plus an additional suite of 8 colored plates in publisher's envelope; three quarter brown leather over marbled boards, light rubbing, slipcase.   Raymond M. Sutton VI-32 1996 $325.00

TOWNSEND, GEORGE A.   Campaigns of a Non-Combatant and His Roamings Abroad During the War. New York: 1866. 1st edition; 368 pages; decorated cloth, very good.   T. A. Swinford 49-1166 1996 $100.00

TOWNSEND, JOHN K.   Narrative of a Journey Across the Rocky Mountains to the Columbia River, and a Visit to the Sandwich Islands, Chili, &c. Philadelphia: Henry perkins, 1839. 1st edition; curious copy with original plum cloth faded on rear cover & spine, but with front cover dyed blue & a bit of red stain at head of spine, 3 inch split in cloth over head of front joint, but cover is sound, even with short splits in endpapers and over front hinge, light foxing throughout, but clean copy, ownership inscription from James Mott (possibly NY abolitionist and founder of Swathmore College) to cousin Isaac Willis. Howes T319; Wagner Cam Becker 79.1. Field 1558.   Magnum Opus 44-103 1996 $350.00

TOWNSEND, LUTHER T.   History of the 16th Regiment, New Hampshire Volunteers. 1897. 1st edition; 574 pages; frontispiece, photos, illustrations; decorated cloth, very good. Dornbusch NH 67.   T. A. Swinford 49-1167 1996 $125.00

TOWNSEND, RICHARD H.   Scenes at Washington; a Story of the Last Generation. New York: Harper & Bros., 1848. 1st edition; 8vo; 197, (1) pages; original cloth; Wright I 2319; Sabin 77460.   M & S Rare Books 60-247 1996 $100.00

TOWNSHEND, FREDERICK T.   Ten Thousand Miles of Travel, Sport and Adventure. London: Hurst and Blackett, 1869. 1st edition; 275 pages; frontispiece, half title and pictorial titlepage; original three quarter morocco and marbled boards, fine. Graff 4175; Howes T322; Phillips Sporting Books 379.   Michael D. Heaston 23-336 1996 $300.00

TOWNSHEND, GEORGE, MARQUESS OF   A Political and Satyrical History of the Years 1756, 1757, 1758 and 1759. London: for E. Morris, 1760. Small square 8vo; 2 parts, 15 pages, 75 engraved plates; 8 pages, 25 engraved plates (numbered 76-100), some general browning and spotting; contemporary calf, rebacked retaining original spine, new red gilt label, small square 8vo.   Ken Spelman 30-119 1996 £650.00

TOZER, HENRY FANSHAW   Lectures on the Geography of Greece. London: J. Murray, 1873. 1st collected edition; crown 8vo; folding map, pages xvi, 405; contemporary green prize calf, gilt, fully gilt spine, label, gilt, very good to nice.   James Fenning 133-341 1996 £55.00

TOZZER, ALFRED M.   Chichen Itza and its Cenote of Sacrifice: a Comparative Study of Contemporaneous Maya and Toltec. Cambridge: Peabody Museum, 1957. Folio; 2 volumes, viii, 316 pages, 709 figures, 27 tables; wrappers.   Archaeologia Luxor-4972 1996 $350.00

TOZZER, ALFRED M.   A Preliminary Study of the Prehistoric Ruins of Nakum Guatemala. Cambridge: the Museum, 1913. Folio; viii, pages 148-201 with 53 figures, 22 plates; wrappers.   Archaeologia Luxor-4974 1996 $250.00

TRAGICUM Theatrum Actorum & Casuum Tragicorum Londini Publice Celebratorum. Amsterdam: Janson, 1649. 8vo; title device, 8 full page portraits and 1 folding plate; crushed crimson morocco, crowned monogram in all corners, inner dentelles, gilt edges by Trautz-Bauzonnet; Valentin Uhink y Gomez Farias bookticket. Splendid copy. Barbier IV 1395-6; Abbot 422.   Rostenberg & Stern 150-111 1996 $1,250.00

TRAICE, W. H. J.   Hand-Book of Mechanics' Institutions, with Priced Catalogue of Books Suitable for Libraries and Periodicals for Reading Rooms. London: Longman, 1863. 2nd edition; half title, 2 pages ads; original purple cloth wrappers, very good, bright.   Jarndyce 103-584 1996 £60.00

TRAIL, WILLIAM   Account of the Life and Writings of Robert Simson. London: R. Cruttwell for G. W. Nicol, 1812. 1st edition; 4to; (6) leaves, 190, (1) pages, 1 folding engraved plate; stipple engraved portrait on titlepage; original boards, spine chipped and cracked; fine, uncut copy. Jeffrey Mancevice 20-83 1996 $475.00

TRAILL, CATHERINE PARR   The Backwoods of Canada: Being Leters from the Wife of an Emigrant Officer Illustrative of the Domestic Economy of British America. London: Charles Knight, 1836. 1st edition; 351 pages; 20 engravings on wood, ownership in ink on free endpaper, else very good, free of foxing and marginalia in slightly worn publisher's cloth, spine rebacked with original cloth laid down.   Hermitage SP95-850 1996 $250.00

TRAILL, CATHERINE PARR   The Backwoods of Canada: Being Letters from the Wife of an Emigrant Officer... London: Charles Knight, 1836. 1st edition; 2nd issue, with appendix B beginning on p. 326 and text finishing on p. 351; 12mo; wood engraved portrait, full page illustrations and map; contemporary half calf, lightly rubbed; Staton and Tremaine 1923; Sabin 96441.   James Burmester 29-137 1996 £125.00

TRAILL, CATHERINE PARR   The Backwoods of Canada: Being Letters from the Wife of an Emigrant Officer... London: Charles Knight, 1836. 12mo; pages viii, 351, frontispiece, portrait, 14 plates, 5 text illustrations, map; half calf, marbled boards, names on front endpapers, covers show wear, else very nice. TPL 1922.   Hugh Anson-Cartwright 87-438 1996 $200.00

TRAILL, CATHERINE PARR   Canada and the Oregon. The Backwoods of Canada. London: M. A. Nattali, 1846. 1st edition of the combined titles; 17.5 cm; viii, 351, (5), 78 pages; map; fine in blind and gilt stamped green cloth. Strathern 546; smith 10297; TPL 1925; Sabin 96441.   Rockland Books 38-227 1996 $375.00

TRAILL, CATHERINE PARR   Canadian Wild Flowers. Montreal: 1869. Folio; hand colored lithographed title and 10 hand colored lithographed plates (most tissue guards with later juvenile crayon tracing, but not affecting plates), original gilt decorated cloth, worn at corners, light soiling and some dulling to gilt, some soiling to dedication page, light browning to page margins, front inner hinge split apart at title, occasional marginal dampstaining, shaken.   Raymond M. Sutton VI-33 1996 $750.00

TRAILL, CATHERINE PARR   Studies of Plant Life in Canada; or Gleanings from Forest, Lake and Plain. Ottawa: 1885. 1st edition; royal 8vo; pages iii, ix, 288; portrait, 9 colored paltes; original decorated cloth, gilt, gilt edges; scarce, good, clean copy.   Wheldon & Wesley 207-1595 1996 £160.00

TRAILL, H. D.   The Building of Britain and the Empire. London: Waverley Book Co., 1914. 8vo; 6 volumes; plates, illustrations, maps; half maroon morocco, spines richly gilt decorated and lettered, gilt tops; very good set.   Howes Bookshop 265-1219 1996 £120.00

TRANSITION. No. 25. London: Fall, 1936. cover by Miro; very good, clean and bright, yapped edges, without a tear; near fine.   Words Etcetera 94-1241 1996 £50.00

TRAQUAIR, RAMSAY   The Old Architecture of Quebec, A Study of the Buildings Erected in New France from the Earliest Explorers to the Middle of the Nineteenth Century. Toronto: 1947. Quarto; pages xix, 324; profusely illustrated; original binding, nice.   Stephen Lunsford 45-158 1996 $400.00

TRAQUAIR, RAMSAY   The Old Architecture of Quebec: a Study of the Buildings Erected in New France from the Earliest Explorers to the Middle of the Nineteenth Century. Toronto: Macmillan Co. of Canada, 1947. 4to; pages xix, 324, 303 illustrations on 179 plates; cloth, review copy with inserts from publisher and editor, covers faded and scuffed, interior clean and crisp.   Hugh Anson-Cartwright 87-439 1996 $250.00

TRATTINNICK, LEOPOLD   Die Essbaren Schwamme des Oesterreichischen Kaiserstaates. Wien and Triest: 1809. 1st edition; 12mo; pages cxxiii, 174; 30 hand colored plates; marbled boards, with annotations to front pastedown, 1 plate accompanied by descriptie caption in photocopy. Rare.   Raymond M. Sutton VII-38 1996 $1,000.00

TRAVEN, B.   The Cotton Pickers. London: Rovert Hale Ltd., 1956. 1st edition; original binding, top edge dusty, head and tail of spine slightly bumped, very good in nicked, chipped and rubbed, torn, creased, marked and dusty dust jacket slightly browned at spine and edges and missing small piece at head of spine.   Ulysses 39-595 1996 £75.00

TRAVEN, B.   The Rebellion of the Hanged. New York: Knopf, 1952. 1st U.S. edition; bookplate to front pastedown, else near fine in attractively illustrated dust jacket with dampstain to verso of rear panel. Lame Duck Books 19-545 1996 $125.00

TRAVERS, P. L.   Mary Poppins Opens the Door. Davies, 1944. 1st edition; very good in dust jacket.   Aronovitz 57-1191 1996 $165.00

TRAVLOS, JOHN   Pictorial Dictionary of Ancient Athens. London: Thames and Hudson, 1971. 4to; xvi, 590 pages; 721 illustrations, original cloth.   Archaeologia Luxor-4087 1996 $175.00

TREMAIN, HENRY EDWIN   Last Hours of Sheridan's Cavalry. New York: Bonnell, Silver & Bowers, 1904. 1st edition; 563 pages; original cloth, very good to near fine, original publisher's prospectus laid in. Dornbusch III 1908; Haynes 18557; Nicholson p. 847.   McGowan Book Co. 65-94 1996 $150.00

TREMAINE, MARIE   A Bibliography of Canadian Imprints 1751-1800. Toronto: 1952. Pages xxvii, 705; ex-library, but very good otherwise. Stephen Lunsford 45-160 1996 $300.00

TRENDALL, A. D.   Early South Italian Vase-Painting. Mainz: Philipp von Zabern, 1974. Revised edition; 4to; (ii), 58 pages, 1 map, 32 plates; original cloth, stamp; signature of author.   Archaeologia Luxor-4088 1996 $150.00

TRENDALL, A. D.   The Red-Figured Vases of Apulia. Volume I: Early and Middle Apulian. Oxford: Clarendon Press, 1978. 4to; lix, 442 pages, 2 figures, 160 plates, 1 folding table; original cloth, tattered dust jacket. Archaeologia Luxor-4093 1996 $250.00

TRENDALL, A. D.   The Red-Figured Vases of Lucania, Campania and Sicily. Oxford and London: Clarendon Press and Institute of Classical Studies, 1967-83. Large 4to; 2 volumes and supplements 1-3; color frontispiece, xxix, 700 pages, 18 figures; frontispiece, pages 701-812 and 256 plates; xii, pages 145-294 and 44 plates; xxvi, 392 pages, 33 plates; stiff wrappers; signature of author volumes 1 and 2.   Archaeologia Luxor-4091 1 996 $1,500.00

TRENDALL, A. D.   The Red-Figured Vases of Paestum. London: British School at Rome, 1987. 8vo; xxxi, 452 pages, 242 plates; original cloth, dust jacket.   Archaeologia Luxor-4092 1996 $150.00

TRENT, COUNCIL OF, 1545-1563   Vera, et Catholica Doctrina, Qvod in Missa Vervm Sacrificivm et Propitiatorivm Offeratvr... Brescia: Jaaqob ben David Marcaria? ad Instantiam Io: Baptistae Bozolae, 1563. 1st edition; 4to; 6 unnumbered leaves, italic letter, large woodcut printer's device on titlepage, 1 woodcut initial, very lightly age yellowed, lower blank corners very slightly waterstained, unbound (as issued) in modern slipcase. not in BM STC It. Adams C2831. 1 copy in NUC.   A. Sokol XXV-86 1996 £325.00

TREVERS, JOSEPH   An Essay to the Restoring of Our Decayed Trade. London: printed for Giles Widdowes...John Sims and Will. Milward... 1675. Small 4to; title, 4 prelims, 59 pages, (3) pages, upper margin rather short, but still very good; 2 cm taller than Kress copy; vellum boards. The Huth copy, with his book label. Wing T2129; Kress 1390; Goldsmiths' 2120 (calls for 59pp. in error).   H. M. Fletcher 121-79 1996 £835.00

TRIAL for Murder. The People vs. James K. Polk. Counsel for the People, J. Q. Adams...for the Prisoner, John Tyler. Boston: S. Harris, 1847. 1st edition; 8vo; 16 pages; woodcut; removed, hole in title affecting one word, lower margins from first two leaves torn. Not in Sabin.   M & S Rare Books 60-374 1996 $325.00

TRIAL of Marshal Ney, Preceded by a Memoir of His Life... Glasgow: W. Stuart, Ingram St., 1829. Modern quarter calf, quite good, clean copy. Meyer Boswell SL27-172 1996 $350.00

THE TRIAL, Before the Lord President of the Court of Session, Lord MacKenzie and a Specail Jury, ... of the issues in the Action of Damages at the Instance of Lady Ramsay Widow of the Late Colonel Sir Thomas Ramsay. Edinburgh: printed by Ballantyne and Co., 1833. 1st edition; 4to; 234 pages, 80 pages; original cloth backed boards, spine torn, uncut. Anthony W. Laywood 108-242 1996 £60.00

TRIANA, JOSE MARIA MARTIN   Suite Lirica: en Homenaje a Wallace Stevens. Plain Wrapper Press, 1982. One of 90 copies, signed by author and artist; 14 x 8 3/4 inches; (14) leaves; vignette on title, 2 other vignettes and 2 plates by Leo Lionni, title printed in blue and black, blue initials; calf backed paitned pink boards, top edge gilt, other edges untrimmed, in publisher's fine folding cloth box; mint.   Phillip J. Pirages 33-427 1996 $325.00

A TRIBUTE to Huddie Ledbetter. London: Jazz Music Books, 1946. 1st edition; wrappers, near fine.   Beasley Books 82-234 1996 $100.00

A TRIBUTE to Jim Lowell. Cleveland: Ghost Press, 1967. 1st edition; wrappers, loosening from staples, otherwise near fine; scarce. Beasley Books 82-8 1996 $100.00

TRICHTERN, VALENTIN   Pferd-Buch... Pferd-Anatomie. Nuremberg: Frankfurt & Leipzig: 1716-17. 1st German and 2nd overall edition; 8vo; 2 volumes, 1218 pages, 9 folding and 41 full page engravings; earlier cream vellum, rich decoration in blind, intact clasps and catches; very rare; beautiful copy. GV 147.70; not in Menessier, Thebaud, Podeschi or Huth.   Bennett Gilbert LL29-87 1996 $4,000.00

THE TRICKS OF London Laid Open: Being a True Caution to Both Sexes in Town and Country. London: T. Sabine, n.d., c. 1780. 7th edition; small 8vo; frontispiece, title in red and black, offsetting from frontispiece; period sheep, tips worn, upper hinge tender, scattered light foxing, two small juvenile drawings to rear endpapers. Scarce. Not in LAR, Jessel, Horr, or Gardner.   Dramatis Personae 37-12 1996 $750.00

TRIER, EDUARD   The Sculpture of Marino Marini. New York: Praeger, 1961. 4to; 146 pages, 2 color and 150 monochrome illustrations, cloth, dust jacket.   Brannan 43-385 1996 $100.00

TRIER, JESPER   Ancient Paper of Nepal. Copenhagen: Jutland Archaeological Society Publications, 1972. Quarto; 271 pages; printed limp cloth, bumped at upper spine; fine.   Bromer Booksellers 87-248 1996 $350.00

TRIEWALD, MARTEN   Short Description of the Atmospheric Engine Published at Stockhom, 1734. London: for the Newcomen Society, 1928. 1st edition in English; 8vo; xii, (10), 61 pages, facsimile titlepage of the original 1734 edition in red and black and with large folding plate; original half vellum over linen boards, top edge gilt. Fine. Quite rare. Zeitlinger 15335.   Edwin V. Glaser 121-314 1996 $150.00

TRIMBLE, ISAAC P.   A Treatise on the Insect Enemies of Fruit and Fruit Trees... New York: William Wood, 1865. 1st edition; 4to; 139 pages; hand colored frontispiece and 8 uncolored pates; bound in little soiled publisher's cloth, little foxed, very good; Whitman Bennett p. 106. Second Life Books 103-194 1996 $350.00

TRIMBLE, WILLIAM TENNANT   The Trimbles and Cowens of Dalston, Cumberland. Carlisle: privately printed, 1935. Large 8vo; pages 64, 26; 20 plates; original cloth; presentation copy inscribed for C. Roy Hudleston, ALS to Hudleston from a Cowan descendant loosely inserted.   R.F.G. Hollett & Son 78-267 1996 £85.00

TRIMBLE, WILLIAM TENNAT   The Trimbles and Cowens of Dalston, Cumberland. Carlisle: privately printed, 1935. Large 8vo; pages 64, 26; 20 plates; original cloth, gilt, presentation copy, inscribed to Sir Mayson Beeton from author, further copy of the 'Supplement' in original wrappers, inscribed, laid in.   R.F.G. Hollett & Son 78-266 1996 £60.00

TRIMMER, SARAH   Fabulous Histories Designed for the Instruction of Children, Respecting Their Treatment of Animals. London: J. Johnson & Co., 1811. 9th edition; 12mo; few spots, contemporary sheep, covers rubbed, neatly rebacked, very good.   Jarndyce 103-585 1996 £110.00

TRIMMER, SARAH   The Teacher's Assistant; Consisting of Lectures in the Catechetical Form; Being Part of a Plan of Appropriate Instruction for the Children of the Poor. London: F. C. & J. Rivington, 1820. 10th edition; 2 volumes; original sheep, hinges weak, bookseller' tickets: John Stacy, Norwich.   Jarndyce 103-586 1996 £85.00

TRIO. First Poems by Gael Turnbull, Phyllis Webb, E. W. Mandel. N.P: Contact Press, c. 1954. 1st edition; unpaginated; printed wrappers; near fine, very scarce; inscribed by Phyllis Webb for F. R. Scott; recently inscribed to John Metcalf by Gael Turnbull.   Nelson Ball 118-173 1996 $800.00

TRIPLER, CHARLES S.   Hand-Book for the Military Surgeon. Cincinnati: Robert Calrke and Co., 1861. 1st edition; original cloth, edge worn, more so at head of spine, becoming quite scarce in any condition; small ink inscription.   Glenn Books 36-182 1996 $950.00

TRIPP, F. E.   British Mosses, Their Homes, Aspects, Structure and Uses. London: 1874. 2nd edition; royal 8vo; pages xxi, 124, 8 ads; 125-235, 8 ads, 2 colored title pages and 39 hand colored plates; original cloth, gilt, fine, clean copy, partly unopened.   John Henly 27-270 1996 £120.00

TRISTRAM, HENRY BAKER   The Land of Israel: a Journal of Travels in Palestine. London: Society for Promoting Christian Knowledge, 1865. 1st edition; demy 8vo; xx, (652) pages; plates, some colored, illustrations and maps; original cloth, gilt in attractive and unusual design, few minor signs of age and use, some foxing, mainly to plates, nonetheless very good.   Ash Rare Books Zenzybyr-91 1996 £195.00

TRISTRAM, HENRY BAKER   Scenes in the East, Consisting of Twelve Coloured Photographic Views of Places Mentioned in the Bible... London: Society for Promoting Christian Knowledge, 1880. 4to; 49 pages, 12 color plates; original gilt decorated cloth, all edges gilt, bookplate, boards stained. Inscribed "Greetings and best wishes, Olga Tufnell, Jan. '73".   Archaeologia Luxor-2775 1996 $125.00

TROGUS POMPEIUS   Justinus de Historiis Philippicis... London: 1798. 8vo; pages (8), 329, (102), titlepage printed in red and black, uncased.   Family Album Tillers-626 1996 $100.00

TROILI, GUILIO 1613-1685   Paradossi per Pratticare la Prospettiva Senza Saperla, Fiori, per Facilitare l'Intelligencia, Frutii, per non Operare alla Cieca (with) Parte Terza Divisa in Due Settioni. Bologna: Giuseppe Longhi, 1683. 1st complete edition; folio; 3 parts in 1, (8), 120; (4), 64 pages; woodcut armorial device on first title and woodcut device on third part, 67 full page woodcut illustrations and diagrams within decorative borders, several smaller woodcut diagrams and ornaments, faint dampstains on some leaves, early library stamp on titlepages, 19th century mottled sheep, gilt tooled. Schlosser Magnino pp. 620, 626; Berlin Cat. 4722; Cicognara 866.   Jeffrey Mancevice 20-84 1996 $1,850.00

TROLLOPE, ANTHONY 1815-1882   The American Senator. London: Chapman and Hall, 1877. 1st edition; 8vo; 3 volumes, with half titles; fine contemporary full dark green morocco, bound for the Earl of Carysfort with his arms in gilt on upper covers and his monogram at foot of the spine, raised bands, triple gilt rules, spines polished and gilt lettered in two panels and date in gilt at foot, marbled endpapers, gilt edges with Elton Hall bookplate dated 1894 and library shelf label on front pastedown; excellent set. Irwin p. 11; Sadleir 46; Tinker 2234; Wolff 6763.   Simon Finch 24-247 1996 £1,100.00

TROLLOPE, ANTHONY 1815-1882   Ayala's Angel. London: Chapman and Hall, 1881. 1st edition; 8vo; 3 volumes; original orange cloth, blocked in black and gilt, recently recased, new black endpapers, spines little faded, covers slightly marked, but very good set, no half titles were issued; bookplate of William Melville in each volume. Sadleir 60. Sotheran PN32-57 1996 £1,250.00

TROLLOPE, ANTHONY 1815-1882   Ayala's Angel... London: Chapman and Hall Ltd., 1881. 1st edition; 8vo; 3 volumes, no half titles called for; modern half red crushed morocco, red cloth sides, raised bands, spines gilt lettered direct, top edge gilt, by Sangorski & Sutcliffe, titles slightly spotted, good set, firmly and attractively rebound. Irwin p. 13; Sadleir 60; Tinker 2244; Wolff 6764.   Simon Finch 24-Simon Finch 24-248 1996 £500.00

TROLLOPE, ANTHONY 1815-1882   Barchester Towers... London: Longman, Brown, Green, Longmans and Roberts, 1857. 1st edition; 8vo; 3 volumes; without half titles or final ad leaf; contemporary half black polished calf, skilfully rebacked to match, brown morocco grain cloth, green endpapers, red sprinkled edges; corners worn, occasional mark, little light browning in margins; good set. Irwin p. 14; sadleir 5; Tinker 2172; Wolff 6766.   Simon Finch 24-232 1996 £1,100.00

TROLLOPE, ANTHONY 1815-1882   The Belton Estate. Philadelphia: J. B. Lippincott and Co., 1866. 1st American edition; the authorised edition; 8vo; pages iv, 392; original purple cloth, spine lettered in gold, pink endpapers (corner torn from front free endpaper); bookplate removed, later bookplate of Miss H. W. Seavey's Circulating Library, North Conway, N.H., pencilled inscription on titlepage, unobtrusive circulating library blindstamps on first and last leaf of text, spine sunned (as usual), occas. spot or stain, good copy   Simon Finch 24-239 1996 £350.00

TROLLOPE, ANTHONY 1815-1882   The Bertrams. London: Chapman & Hall, 1859. 1st edition; post 8vo; 3 volumes; recent half morocco, banded and gilt, marbled sides, top edge gilt, text somewhat browned and thumbed, some marks and spots, one leaf with 3 inch tear (without loss) but reasonable set in smart new binding. Sadleir 8.   Ash Rare Books Zenzybyr-92 1996 £1,750.00

TROLLOPE, ANTHONY 1815-1882   Can You Forgive Her? London: Chapman and Hall, 1864. 1st edition in book form; 8vo; 2 volumes; vi, (ii), 320; vi, (ii), 320 pages, 40 illustrations; modern half red crushed morocco, red cloth sides, raised bands, spines gilt lettered direct, top edge gilt, by Sangorski & Sutcliffe, very good, firmly and attractively rebound. Irwin p. 16; Sadlier 19; Tinker 2195; Wolff 6769.   Simon Finch 24-238 1996 £275.00

TROLLOPE, ANTHONY 1815-1882   Castle Richmond. London: Chapman and Hall, 1860. 1st edition; 8vo; 3 volumes; with half titles, 6 leaves in volume 2 from another copy, with library stamp; early 20th century half red crushed morocco, red cloth sides, raised bands, spines gilt lettered direct, top edge gilt, by Sangorski & Sutcliffe; very good, firmly and attractively rebound. Irwin p. 16; Sadleir 10; Tinker 2180; Wolff 6770.   Simon Finch 24-234 1996 £450.00

TROLLOPE, ANTHONY 1815-1882   The Claverings. New York: Harper & Bros., 1866/67? 1st edition in book form; 8vo; pages 211, (v), 24 woodcut illustrations, of which 12 are large and 12 vignettes; pink printed wrappers, spine defective at head and tail, lower cover torn across at head with some loss, last few gatherings stained at lower outer corner, ownership inscription of E. C. Williams, Charleston, S.C., bookseller's stamp of H. L. Schreiner, Savannah, Ga. Sadleir 27 (+Add); Wolff 6771a.   Simon Finch 24-241 1996 £250.00

TROLLOPE, ANTHONY 1815-1882   Cousin Henry. London: Chapman and Hall, 1881. 2nd edition; octavo, pages 355, plus 8 pages ads; "yellowack volume" color wood engravings to cover and spine; some wear, but better than usual shape for volumes in this series, contents, very good. Sadleir 56.   Hartfield 48-L84 1996 $265.00

TROLLOPE, ANTHONY 1815-1882   Dr. Thorne. New York: Harper, 1858. 1st American edition; octavo; pages 520 plus ads; original stamped cloth shows wear, scarce in any condition. Sadleir 7. Hartfield 48-L86 1996 $245.00

TROLLOPE, ANTHONY 1815-1882   An Editor's Tales. London: Strahan and Co., 1870. 1st edition in book form; 8vo; pages (vi), 375, (i), complete with half title and initial blank; fine contemporary binding of full dark green morocco, bound for the Earl of Carysfort, with his arms in gilt on upper cover and his monogram at foot of spine, raised bands, triple gilt rules, spine polished and gilt lettered in two panels and date in gilt at foot, marbled endpapers, gilt edges, Elton Hall bookplate dated 1894 and library shelf label, very lightly and evenly browned; very good; scarce. Irwin p. 41; Sadleir 34; Tinker 2217; Wolff 6774.   Simon Finch 24-243 1996 £375.00

TROLLOPE, ANTHONY 1815-1882   The Eustace Diamonds. New York: Harper & Bros., 1872. 1st edition in book form; 8vo; 351 pages, plus 4 pages of ads at front; original brick red cloth titled in gilt, corners slightly worn and one corner bumped, slight shelfwear and small bookplate on pastedown, but exceptionally clean, bright and attractive. Hermitage SP95-628 1996 $750.00

TROLLOPE, ANTHONY 1815-1882   The Eustace Diamonds. New York: Harper & Bros., 1872. 1st edition; royal 8vo; (1)-4, (ii), (9)-(352) pages; original cloth, gilt, little rubbed and worn, mainly tips of spine, some corner creases, minor marks, nick to rear endpaper, but good, copy; Ash Rare Books Zenzybyr-93 1996 £295.00

TROLLOPE, ANTHONY 1815-1882   Framley Parsonage... London: Smith, Elder & Co., 1861. 1st edition in book form; 8vo; 3 volumes; wood engraved frontispieces, 3 plates, 16 pages ads at end dated April 1861; original purple blindstamped cloth, rebacked with original spines laid down, lettered and decorated in gilt, new endpapers, somewhat soiled, ownership inscriptions deleted on recto of frontispieces, very good. Sadleir 11; Tinker 2181; Wolff 6777.   Simon Finch 24-235 1996 £1,250.00

TROLLOPE, ANTHONY 1815-1882   Framley Parsonage... London: Smith, Elder and Co., 1861. 1st edition; 8vo; 3 volumes; wood engraved frontispieces and 3 plates, tissue guards; contemporary half purple roan, pale tan morocco labels, wide raised bands, gilt, marbled endpapers, beige endpapers, red sprinkled edges, rubbed, few spots, good copy. Sadleir 11; Tinker 2181; Wolff 6777.   Simon Finch 24-236 1996 £750.00

TROLLOPE, ANTHONY 1815-1882   He Knew He Was Right. London: Strahan and Co., 1869. 1st edition; 8vo; 2 volumes, pages ix, (iii), 384; ix, (iii), 384, half titles; wood engraved frontispieces and illustrations; original green cloth, sides stamped in blind, spines lettered and decorated in gilt, bookplates, generally little worn, slight damage to one upper cover, but excellent. Sadleir 31; Tinker 2214; Wolff 6780.   Simon Finch 24-242 1996 £1,500.00

TROLLOPE, ANTHONY 1815-1882   Hunting Sketches, London: Chapman & Hall, 1865. 1st edition in book form; 8vo; iv, 116, 36 pages; cloth, joints and corners worn, occasional light spotting in text, signature on contents leaf; Sadleir 21.   Thomas Thorp 489-305 1996 £120.00

TROLLOPE, ANTHONY 1815-1882   Lady Anna. London: Chapman and Hall, 1874. 1st edition; 8vo; 2 volumes, pages viii, 317; viii, 314; half titles; modern half red crushed morocco, red cloth sides, raised bands, spines gilt lettered direct, top edge gilt, by Sangorski & Sutcliffe, some faint spotting in first volume, still good set, firmly and attractively rebound. Irwin p. 25; Sadleir 42; Tinker 2228.   Simon Finch 24-244 1996 £500.00

TROLLOPE, ANTHONY 1815-1882   The Landleaguers. London: Chatto & Windus, 1883. 1st edition; 8vo; 3 volumes, half titles, 32 pages of ads at end of volume 3; original green cloth, sides and spines decorated in yellow, spines lettered in gilt, little wear, especially at head and foot of spines, endpapers and half titles somewhat spotted, very good. Sadleir 68; Wolff 6783.   Simon Finch 24-251 1996 £1,850.00

TROLLOPE, ANTHONY 1815-1882   The Last Chronicle of Barset. London: Smith, Elder and Co., 1867. 1st edition; 8vo; 2 volumes; illustrations by George H. Thomas; half aqua morocco gilt, trimmed about one half inch, some light discoloration, else very good. Sadleir 26. James Cummins 14-214 1996 $600.00

TROLLOPE, ANTHONY 1815-1882   The Last Chronicle of Barset. London: Smith, Elder and Co., 1867. 1st edition; (with pale yellow endpapers); 8vo; 2 volumes, pages (iv), 384; (iv), 384, (2) ads; no half titles called for; frontispieces, 30 plates and illustrations in text after Millais; original blue cloth, lower covers ruled in blind, upper covers and sides decorated and lettered in gilt, worn, good copy only. Sadleir 26; Wolff 6784.   Simon Finch 24-240 1996 £300.00

TROLLOPE, ANTHONY 1815-1882   The Macdermots of Ballycloran. London: Thomas Cautley Newby, 1847. 1st edition; 12mo; 3 volumes; modern red half morocco, spines lettered in gilt, top edge gilt, by Sangorski & Sutcliffe, occasional slight spotting; excellent copy. rare. Sadleir 1; Tinker 2164.   Simon Finch 24-230 1996 £16,000.00

TROLLOPE, ANTHONY 1815-1882   Marion Fay. London: Chapman and Hall, 1882. 1st edition; 8vo; 3 volumes; half titles; original ochre cloth, decorated in black on upper covers and spines, spines lettered in gilt, quite soiled and slightly worn, title to volume 1 repaired at upper margin, first leaf of text in volume 2 loose, without final blank in volume 2, bookplate; very good. Sadleir 64; Wolff 6786.   Simon Finch 24-249 1996 £825.00

TROLLOPE, ANTHONY 1815-1882   Mr. Scarborough's Family. London: Chatto & Windus, 1883. 1st edition; 8vo; 3 volumes, half titles, 32 pages of ads at end of volume1; original blue green cloth, sides and spines decorated in brown, spines lettered in gilt, volume 1 little lighter than others, some soiling and wear, that to volume 1 little more severe, bookplates removed, endpapers and half titles spotted, lower hinges to volumes 2 and 3 split, very good. Sadleir 66; Tinker 2252.   Simon Finch 24-250 1996 £1,200.00

TROLLOPE, ANTHONY 1815-1882   New Zealand. London: Chapman and Hall, 1875. New edition; small 8vo; pages 166, index; yellowback, with pictorial covers, publisher's ads to prelims, large foldout color map; some wear, but better than usual condition for such scarce and fragile titles. Sadleir 40 and addenda pp. 5-6.   Hartfield 48-L85 1996 $195.00

TROLLOPE, ANTHONY 1815-1882   North America. New York: Harper, 1862. 1st Actual American edition; octavo; pages 623, plus 4 pages ads and appencies; original brown cloth, blind decorations, gilt title (faded), very skillfully rebacked; Scarce edition. Sadaleir pp. 44-5 and 274-5. Hartfield 48-L87. 1996 $395.00

TROLLOPE, ANTHONY 1815-1882   Orley Farm. London: Chapman and Hall, 1866. 1st one volume edition; 8vo; pages (vi), 320, 320; 40 plates by J. E. Millais, plates rather foxed, otherwise very good; contemporary half dark green calf, by Birdsall, marbled board sides, expertly rebacked, preserving original backstrip, recent red morocco lettering pieces, marbled edges; this copy has a strip of paper bearing author's signature pasted to front free endpaper. Sadleir 13.   Sotheran PN32-58 1996 £350.00

TROLLOPE, ANTHONY 1815-1882   The Prime Minister. London: Chapman and Hall, 1876. 1st edition in book form; 8vo; 4 volumes, half titles not called for; fine contemporary binding of full dark green morocco, bound for Earl of Carysfort, with his arms in gilt on upper covers and his monogram at foot of spine, raised bands, triple gilt rules, spines polished and gilt lettered in two panels and date in gilt at foot, marbled endpapers, gilt edges, with Elton Hall bookplate dated 1894 and library shelf-label on front pastedown, excellent set. Irwin p. 33; Sadleir 45; Tinker 2233.   Simon Finch 24-246 1996 £1,100.00

TROLLOPE, ANTHONY 1815-1882   Rachel Ray. London: Chapman and Hall, 1868. So called '10th edition'; tall 8vo; pages 347; attractive Victorian binding in three quarter olive green polished calf, gilt extra, marabled boards, nice, uncommon. Sadleir 17.   Hartfield 48-L88 1996 $195.00

TROLLOPE, ANTHONY 1815-1882   The Small House at Allington. London: Smith, Elder and Co., 1864. 1st edition; with one of some (presumably four) possible variants in volume I, with hobbledehoys' correctly spelt on p. 33 and the mispagination "O" for "70"; 8vo; 2 volumes; pages (iv), 312; (iv), 316; wood engraved frontispieces and 16 plates by Millais; fine contemporary binding of full dark green morocco, bound for the Earl of Carysfort, with his arms in gilt on upper covers and his monogram at foot of spine, raised bands, triple gilt rules, spines polished and gilt lettered in two panels, and date in gilt at foot, marbled endpapers, gilt edges and Elton Hall bookplate and library shelf label, original green cloth upper cover and spine of volume 1 laid down and bound in at end of volume 1, iny chip at head of spine of volume 1, excellent set. Irwin p. 35; Sadleir 18; Tinker 2194; Wolff 6795.   Simon Finch 24-237 1996 £1,500.00

TROLLOPE, ANTHONY 1815-1882   Travelling Sketches... London: Chapman and Hall, 1866. 1st edition in book form; 8vo; original scarlet cloth, title blocked in gold on front cover, gilt line at head and foot of spine, top edge gilt, uncut, spine faded, otherwise fine, bookseller's ticket of Edward Baker of Birmingham; the publisher's cat. dated 1 February 1866 bound in the earliest copies, not included in this volume. H. M. Fletcher 121-150 1996 £175.00

TROLLOPE, ANTHONY 1815-1882   La Vendee. London: Henry Colburn, 1850. 1st edition; 8vo; 3 volumes; bound without half titles, in early 20th century half red crushed morocco, red cloth sides, raised bands, spine gilt lettered direct, top edge gilt, by Sangorski & Sutcliffe; very good, firmly and attractively rebound. Irwin p. 38; Sadleir 3.   Simon Finch 24-231 1996 £4,800.00

TROLLOPE, ANTHONY 1815-1882   The Way We Live Now. London: Chapman and Hall, 1875. 1st edition; 8vo; 2 volumes, pages (viii), 320; (viii), 319, half titles; wood engraved frontispiece, 38 plates after Luke Fildes; original green cloth, upper cover decorated and ruled in black, lower cover in blind, spines lettered and decorated in gilt and black, the Sadleir copy with his bookplate and label of Barton Currie, joints and corners little rubbed, hinges to volume 1 split, but excellent copy. publisher's presentation copy, with blindstamp on titlepage to volume I "With publisher's compliments", the Sadleir copy. Sadleir 44; Tinker 2231; Wolff 6799.   Simon Finch 24-245 1996 £2,000.00

TROLLOPE, ANTHONY 1815-1882   The Way We Live Now. New York: Harper & Bros., 1875. 1st American edition; 408 pages, plus 8 pages of ads at back, 4 at front; printed in double columns; original brick red cloth stamped in blind and titled in gilt on spine, corners, crown and heel frayed or worn, joints and extremities faintly rubbed, but sound and bright copy.   Hermitage SP95-629 1996 $125.00

TROLLOPE, ANTHONY 1815-1882   The West Indies and the Spanish Main. London: Chapman and Hall, 1859. 1st edition; 8vo; pages iv, 395, without publishers ads; frontispiece colored map; fine contemporary full dark green morocco, bound for the Earl of Carysfort, with his arms in gilt on upper cover and his monogram at foot of spine, raised bands, triple gilt rules, spine polished and gilt lettered in two panels, date in gilt at foot, marbled endpapers, gilt edges, with Elton Hall bookplate dated 1894 and library shelf label on front pastedown, very lightly and evenly browned, very good. Irwin p. 40; Sadleir 9; Tinker 2179.   Simon Finch 24-233 1996 £675.00

TROLLOPE, FRANCES MILTON 1780-1863   The Mother's Manual or Illustrations of Matrimonial Economy. London: Treuttel and Wurtz and Richter, 1833. 1st edition; 20 illustrations by Hervieu, some spotting; original cloth covered boards, rebacked in calf, label.   Jarndyce 103-453 1996 £220.00

TROLLOPE, FRANCES MILTON 1780-1863   Jessie Phillips, a Tale of the Present Day. London: Henry Colburn, 1844. 1st one volume edition; 8vo; (352) pages; frontispiece; contemporary half brown calf over marbled boards, spine gilt decorated, black title label; very nice, clean copy. Sadleir 3223b; NCBEL III 419; Wolff 6814a.   Paulette Rose 16-328 1996 $300.00

TROLLOPE, FRANCES MILTON 1780-1863   The Widow Barnaby. Paris: A. and W. Galignani, 1840. 8vo; (371) pages; contemporary quarter green calf over marbled boards, spine gilt lettered, some scattered spotting, otherwise near fine.   Paulette Rose 16-329 1996 $150.00

TROLLOPE, THOMAS ADOLPHUS 1810-1892   A Decade of Italian Women. London: Chapman and Hall, 1859. 1st edition; tall octavo; 2 volumes, pages 410, 451; frontispiece and engraved portraits (tissue guards); three quarter brown crushed morocco, linen boards and endpapers, top edge gilt, gilt titling, raised bands. Attractive set in fine condition. CBEL III 510.   Hartfield 48-L89 1996 $295.00

THE TROLLOPIAN. A Journal of Victorian Fiction. London: 1945/49. 9 x 5 7/8 inches; volumes 1-3, bound in 2; maroon cloth, leather title label backstrips, top edge gilt, photocopies of the original titlepages to different parts inserted, backstrips faded, very good.   Ian Hodgkins 78-382 1996 £145.00

TROTTER, THOMAS   A View of the Nervous Temperament: Being a Practical Inquiry into the Increasing Prevalence, Prevention and Treatment of Those Diseases Commonly Called Nervous, Bilious, Stomach and Liver Complaints... New York: pub. by Wright, Goodenow & Stockwell, 1808. 1st American edition; 8vo; 338, (2) pages; contemporary calf, light foxing, front board detached, else clean, respectable copy. Hunter & Macalpine p. 588.   John Gach 150-458 1996 $495.00

TROUBETZKOY, PAUL   Exodus A.D. - A Warming to Civilians. London: Hutchinson & Co., Ltd., n.d. 1934. 1st edition; original binding, edges slightly spotted, head and tail of spine and corners slightly bumped, fore-edge of half titlepage nicked, bottom edge of upper cover slightly darkened, very good in remains of dust jacket, which are torn, worn and defective, on upper panel is C. R. W. Nevinson's painting "Homo Sapiens".   Ulysses 39-442 1996 £250.00

TROUSSEAU, ARMAND   Treatise on Therapeutics. New York: William Wood, 1880. 1st American edition; 8vo; 3 volumes; 980 pages; original cloth; very good.   Edwin V. Glaser B122-149 1996 $135.00

TROUT, PETER LAIRD   Prospectors' Manual Being a Full and Complete History and Description of the Newly Discovered Gold Mines on Granite Creek, the Canyon of the Tulameen River, and Other New Mineral Discoveries in the Similkameen Country... Victoria: 1886. Pages (2), 2 maps, 64, 8 colored leaves of advertising not included in pagination; original printed wrappers, title on front wrapper, ads on inner and outer covers, light dust soiling, few minor nicks on edges of wrappers, else remarkably fine. Lowther 726; Smith 10231.   Stephen Lunsford 45-161 1996 $1,450.00

TROVHERTIGHE Vermaninghe Aende Verheerde Nederlantsche Provintien. N.P.: 1586. 4to; stitched; STC books printed in the Netherlands 160. Rostenberg & Stern 150-99 1996 $425.00

TROWELL, S.   A New Treatise of Husbandry, Gardening and Other Matters Relating to Rural Affairs... London: 1739. 8vo; pages viii, 164; sprinkled calf, rebacked; bookplate of John Cator. Henrey 1440.   John Henly 27-373 1996 £198.00

TRUAX, CHARLES   The Mechanics of Surgery Comprising Detailed Descriptions, Illustrations and Lists of the Instruments, Appliances and Furniture Necessary in Modern Surgical Art. Chicago: 1899. 1st edition; 1024 pages; handsome woodcuts; inner hinges cracked, owner's name on fore edge. Very scarce.   W. Bruce Fye 71-2139 1996 $500.00

TRUCCHI, LORENZA   Francis Bacon. New York: Harry N. Abrams, Inc., 1975. 1st edition; 1st signature slightly loose with tear in gutter of page one, fine in lightly soiled dust jacket with abrasion to upper right corner of front panel, still a pleasant and respectable copy.   Hermitage SP95-820 1996 $150.00

A TRUE Account of What Was Transacted in the Assembly of the United Ministers of Devon and Cornwal... Exon: printed by G. Bishop, 1719. 1st edition; 8vo; 15 pages, title dusty, disbound; with list of ministers agreeing to the statement, annotated in a contemporary hand giving the towns they came from;   David Bickersteth 133-67 1996 £65.00

A TRUE and Faithful Account of the Island of Veritas; Together with the Forms of Their Liturgy... London: for C. Stalker, 1790? 1st and only edition; viii, 88, 87-171, (2) pages; contemporary calf backed and vellum tipped pastepaper boards, skillfully rebacked in period style, light cover wear, otherwise fine; Pruyn bookplate.   Joseph J. Felcone 64-41 1996 $900.00

A TRUE Narrative of the Proceedings at Guild-Hall, London, The Fourth of this Instant February, in Their Unanimous Election of Their Four Members to Serve in Parliament. London: printed for Francis Smith at the Elephant and Castle near the... 1681. Folio; 2 pages; disbound; Wing T 2809.   H. M. Fletcher 121-31 1996 £55.00

TRUEMAN, A.   British Carboniferous Non-Marine Lamellibranchia. London: 1946-68. 4to; pages lx, 449; 48 plates; cloth.   John Henly 27-791 1996 £60.00

TRUEMAN, R. H.   Views of Glacier House District Selkirk Mountains. Vancouver: ca. 1895. Linen covered portfolio containing 6 mounted 7 x 9 inch plantinum prints, portfolio slightly soiled, else near fine. Very rare. Stephen Lunsford 45-162 1996 $500.00

TRUEMAN, T., PSEUD.   The Unrivalled Adventures of that Great Aeronaut and Glum, Peter Wilkins... London: printed for T. Tegg and Co...T. Hurst...T. Brown and B. Dugdale, n.d. 1802. Crown 8vo; engraved frontispiece, text (2)-39, 1 page glossary, slightly soiled, lasat leaf browned, disbound.   H. M. Fletcher 121-151 1996 £175.00

TRUMAN, BEN C.   Tourists' Illustrated Guide to the Celebrated Summer and Winter Resorts of California Adjacent to and Upon the Lines of the Central and Southern Pacific Railroads. San Francisco: H. S. Crocker & Co., 1883. 1st edition; 9 7/8 x 6 5/8 inches; 240 pages, including numerous illustrations and ads; chromolithographed pictorial wrappers, spine ends bit chipped and mild wear to corners. Dawson's Books Shop 528-242 1996 $150.00

TRUMAN, HARRY S.   Memoirs. Garden City: Doubleday & Co., 1955-56. Kansas City Edition; 8vo; 2 volumes; fine in dust jacket which are faded and soiled on spines, signed by author, owner's name in ink on half titles.   Glenn Books 36-267 1996 $375.00

TRUMAN, HARRY S.   Memoirs by... Garden City: Doubleday, 1955/56. 1st edition; thick 8vo; dust jackets (few nicks, slight rubbing), very good. Signed and inscribed by author for Edward E. Elliott.   George J. Houle 68-145 1996 $500.00

TRUMBO, DALTON   Washington Jitters. New York: 1936. 1st edition; near fine and bright.   Stephen Lupack 83- 1996 $450.00

TRUMBO, DALTON   Washington Jitters. New York: Alfred A. Knopf, London, 1936. 1st edition; 8vo; original burgundy cloth, lettered and decorated in black, slight rubbing; original printed dust jacket, short tears along edges, some rubbing and discolroation, very good.   James Cummins 14-215 1996 $125.00

TRUMBULL, JOHN   Autobiography, Reminiscences and Letters of John Trumbull from 1756 to 1841. New York: Wiley & Putnam/New Haven: B. L. Hamlen, 1841. 8vo; pages xvi, 439; 21 plates, 2 folding maps; original cloth, rebacked, signed by author. Sabin 97249.   Richard Adelson W94/95-171 1996 $285.00

TRUMBULL, JOHN   Catalogue of Paintings by Colonel Trumbull: Including 8 subects of the American Revolution, with near 250 portraits... New Haven: printed by J. Peck, 1835. 2nd edition; 8vo; pages 36; original half roan over marbled boards, large paper label on front cover; fine. Sabin 97244.   Howard S. Mott 227-142 1996 $600.00

TRUSLER, JOHN   The Differences Between Words, Esteemed Synonymous, in the English Language; and the Proper Choice of Them Determined... London: printed for J. Dodsley, 1766. 1st edition; 12mo; 2 volumes, half titles in volume 1; contemporary speckled calf, gilt borders, spines worn at head and tail, hinges splitting, red label. Alston III 515. Jarndyce 103-352 1996 £350.00

TRUSLER, JOHN   Memoirs of the Life of the Rev. Dr. Trusler, with His Opinions On a Variety of Interesting Subjects, and His Remarks... (with) A Prospectus of a Work Which the Author Proposes to Publish, Under the Title of Sententiae Variorum, and the Conditions. Bath: printed and published by John Browne, 1806/c. 1800. 1st editions; 4to; 192; 8 pages; some foxing, contemporary half calf.   James Burmester 29-140 1996 £600.00

THE TRYALS of Henry Cornish, Esq; for Conspiring the Death of the King, and Raising a Rebellion in This Kingdom; and John Fernley, William King and Elizabeth Gaunt, for Harbouring and Maintaining Rebels...Oct. 19, 1685. London: George Croom, 1685. Folio; (ii), 42 pages; disbound, paper browned, some foxing. Wing T2250.   Robert Clark 38-142 1996 £55.00

THE TRYALS of Robert Green, Henry Berry & Lawrence Hill, for the Murder of Sr. Edmond-Bury Godfrey Knt..., Before the Right Honourable Sir William Scroggs...10th of February 1678/79. London: Robert Pawlet, 1679. folio; (iv), 92 pages, imprimatur leaf; minor browning and staining. Wing T2256.   Robert Clark 38-103 1996 £50.00

TRYE, JOHN   Jus Filizarii; or, the Filacer's Office in the Court of King's-Bench (etc.). London: printed by the Assigns of R. and E. Atkyns etc., 1684. Modern calf, binding strained, else sound.   Meyer Boswell SL25-222 1996 $650.00

TRYPANIS, C. A.   The Elegies of a Glass Adonis; a Poem. New York: Chilmark Press, 1967. One of 450 numbered copies, signed by author; 4to; printed in red and black; boards; fine.   Bertram Rota 272-392 1996 £100.00

TRYPANIS, C. A.   The Elegies of a Glass Adonis. New York: Ptd. by the Rampant Lions Press for the Chilmark Press, 1967. 1st edition; number 436 of 450 copies, signed by author; 8vo; original boards, spine gilt, uncut; Ruari McLean's copy with his bookplate.   Forest Books 74-372 1996 £95.00

TUCKER, E. S.   The Lawrence Memorial Album... Lawrence: E. S. Tucker and Geo. O. Foster, 1895. 1st edition; (68) pages; map and illustrations; original printed wrappers with title stamped in red on front cover, minor chipping; very good.   Michael D. Heaston 23-197 1996 $150.00

TUCKER, JOSIAH   Four Letters on Important National Subjects, Addressed to the Right Honourable the Earl of Shelburne, His Majesty's First Lord Commissioner of the Treasury. Glocester: printed by R. Raikes, 1783. 1st edition; 8vo; half title, perforation stamp on title and library accession number on blank margin of following leaf; calf backed marbled boards, hinges rubbed. Krss B661; Goldsmith 12535; Sabin 97343; Williams II p. 523.   Anthony W. Laywood 109-152 1996 £80.00

TUCKER, PATRICK T.   Riding the High Country. Caldwell: Caxton Printers, 1933. 1st edition; 8vo; frontispiece, pictorial endpapers by Joe De Young, 11 full page black and white illustrations,, dust jacket with few nicks, light foxing to edges; very good.   George J. Houle 68-131 1996 $125.00

TUCKER, PETER   Haslewood Books: The Books of Frederick Etchells & Hugh Macdonald. Hanborough Parrot Press, 1990. Of 170 numbered copies, signed by author, this one of only 25 largely pochoir colored by Sylvia Stokled; folio; numerous illustrations; marbled cloth, printed labels, fine in slipcase.   Bertram Rota 272-225 1996 £156.00

TUCKER, PETER   Haslewood Books. The Books of Frederick Etchells & Hugh Macdonald. Hanborough Parrot, Church Hanborough, Oxon: Haslewood Books: 1990. V/50 copies (of an edition of 170 copies); folio; pages 53, (1); numerous reproductions, a number color stenciled; multi-colored marbled linen, printed backstrip and front cover labels, that on front cover with a handcolored engraving, untrimmed, board slipcse incorporating a handcolored design, new.   Blackwell's B112-148 1996 £156.00

TUCKER, PETER   The Interpretation of a Classic, the Illustrated Editions of Candide. Oxon: Church Hanborough, 1993. Limited edition, 82/185 copies; small folio; pages (i), 70, printed in black and red on Zerkall mouldmade paper and signed by Giles Babber and Peter Tucker, numerous reproductions, some color printed plates tipped in; gilt floral patterned orange and red linen, printed labels on backstrip and front cover, tail edges untrimmed, illustrated board slipcase, new. Blackwell's B112-234 1996 £58.00

TUCKER, W.   Prison Planet. Krueger, 1947. 1st edition; wrappers; fine. Signed by author, quite scarce.   Aronovitz 57-1197 1996 $100.00

TUCKERMAN, ARTHUR LYMAN   A Short History of Architecture. New York: Scribner's, 1887. 1st edition; 8vo; 168 pages; illustrations; ca. 1930 prize binding of full polished tree calf by Wickers & Son, with raised bands, gilt tooled spine, morocco spine labels, gilt borders on covers, and gilt heraldic crest on front cover, prize award bookplate, light general wear to binding, but handsome, very good.   Chapel Hill 94-118 1996 $125.00

TUCKERMAN, FREDERICK GODDARD   The Complete Poems of Frederick Goddard Tuckerman. New York: Oxford University Press, 1965. 1st edition; fine in dust jacket slightly sunned at spine.   Captain's Bookshelf 38-166 1996 $100.00

TUCKERMAN, FREDERICK GODDARD   The Cricket. Cummington: Cummington Press, 1950. One of 290 copies; 11.25 x 7.25 inches; (8) page; woodcut by Wightman Williams; dust jacket over plain wrappers, yapped edges of dust jacket lightly rumpled at edges, repaired tear at foot of backstrip, generally very good.   Joshua Heller 21-115 1996 $125.00

TUCKETT, F.   A Pioneer in the High Alps. London: 1920. 1st edition; 6 plates, 2 folding maps; title on spine dull, but very good; bookplates of the Rucksack Club and the Manchester Central Library and presentation label of C. H. Pickstone.   Moutaineering Books 8-RT01 1996 £100.00

TUER, ANDREW WHITE 1838-1900   History of the Horn-Book. London: Leadenhall Press, 1896. 1st edition; 4to; 2 volumes; profusely illustrated, with facsimile horn-books and battledores as issued in pockets; uncut in original full decorated vellum, brown leather labels, top edge gilt, as issued; lovely copy; booklabel of Wm. Bernard Atherton; from the collection of Anne & Fernand Renier.   Jarndyce 103-587 1996 £750.00

TUER, ANDREW WHITE 1838-1900   Quads within Quads. London: Leadenhall Press, 1884. Limited to 500 sets; 1 5/8 x 1 inches; 2 volumes; full gilt titled vellum with silk ties, nested within hollowed out compartment built into rear of a larger version of the same book, also bound in gilt titled vellum (ties lacking), larger of the two books printed on regular paper, while its companion has been printed on Bank Note paper using Pearl and Brilliant types; scarce.   Book Block 32-51 1996 $750.00

TUKE, DANIEL HACK   Illustrations of the Influence of the Mind Upon the Body in Health and Disease. Philadelphia: Henry C. Lea, 1873. 1st American edition; 8vo; xvi, (17)-415, 32 (ads) pages; original cloth, binding worn at extremities, hinges starting; good. Zilboorg pp. 422-431. Cordasco 70-3680   Edwin V. Glaser B122-150 1996 $150.00

TUKE, DANIEL HACK   Illustrations of the Influence of the Mind Upon the Body in Health and Disease, Designed to Elucidate the Action of the Imagination. Philadelphia: Henry C. Lea's Son & Co., 1884. 2nd American edition; 8vo; (ii), (xx), 33)-482, (36) pages + 2 plates; panelled blue grey cloth.   John Gach 150-459 1996 $150.00

TUKE, DANIEL HACK   Rules and List of the Present Members of the Society for Improving the Condition of the Insane; and the Prize Essay Entitled The Progressive Changes Which Have Taken Place Since the Time of Pinel in the Moral Management of the Insane and the Various... London: published for the Society for Improving the Condition of the Insane... 1854. 1st edition; thin 8vo; (iv), 119, (3) pages; embossed mauve cloth, rare.   John Gach 150-460 1996 $250.00

TULASNE, LOUISE RENE   Fungi Hypogaei, Histoire et Monographie des Champignons Hypoges. Paris: 1841. 1st edition; limited to 100 numbered copies; folio; 21 engraved plates (first 9 hand colored); contemporary black quarter morocco (some wear at corners, fore-edes bumped, very scattered foxing, lightly affecting uncolored plates), bookplate; contemporary ms. laid in.   Raymond M. Sutton VII-39 1996 $2,400.00

TULL, JETHRO   The Horse-Hoeing Husbandry: or a Treatise on the principles of Tillage and Vegetaion... London: 1829. 8vo; pages xxiv, 466, 1 plate; original cloth, some slight spotting, largely unopened.   John Henly 27-374 1996 £135.00

TULL, JETHRO   The Horse-Hoeing Husbandry: or, a Treatise on the Principles of Tillage and Vegetation, Wherein is Taught a Method of Introducing a Sort of Vineyard Culture into the Corn-Fields... London: Cobbett, 1829. Later printing of collected edition; tall 8vo; 436 pages; original cloth, very good tight copy.   Second Life Books 103-195 1996 $175.00

TUNNICLIFFE, C. F.   Mereside Chronicle, with a Short Interlude of Lochs and Lochans. London: 1948. 4to; pages 200, over 200 illustrations from drawings by author; cloth, bookplate on flyleaf, dust jacket worn. Wheldon & Wesley 207-881 1996 £50.00

TUNNICLIFFE, C. F.   Shorelands Summer Diary. London: 1952. 4to; pages 160, 16 colored plates and 180 line drawings; cloth, very good, without dust jacket.   Wheldon & Wesley 207-882 1996 £85.00

TURGENEV, IVAN SERGEEVICH 1818-1883   Fathers and Sons. New York: Limited Editions Club, 1951. Limited to 1500 copies; 8vo; wood engravings by Fritz Eichenberg, signed by artist; half natural linen, fine in worn glassine and near fine slipcase.   Charles Agvent 4-1152 1996 $125.00

TURNBULL, GAEL   As from Fleece; a Long Poem. Circle Press, 1990. One of 120 numbered copies, signed by author and artist; imperial 8vo; text printed in dark green on left of a horizontal concertina, print approximately 4 1/2 inches wide and extending to some 11 feet in length down right hand margin; wrappers bearing further print; fine.   Bertram Rota 272-82 1996 £60.00

TURNBULL, GAEL   Land That I Knew. Toronto: Clo Chluain Tairbh, 1962. 1st edition; 8 pages; autographed by author; self wrappers; fine; from the library of John Metcalf, with his ownership signature.   Nelson Ball 118-182 1996 $275.00

TURNBULL, ROBERT   The Theatre in its Influence Upon Literature, Morals, and Religion. Boston: Gould, Kendall and Lincoln, 1839. 2nd edition; 18mo; 110 pages; original decorated cloth, very good.   Lyman Books 21-443 1996 $175.00

TURNBULL, ROBERT J.   A Visit to the Philadelphia Prison; Being an Accurate and Particular Account of the Wise and Humane Administration Adopted in Every Part of that Building. London: re-printed & sold by James Phillips & Son, 1797. 1st English edition; 8vo; 93 pages, folding table at end, later paper wrappers.   Anthony W. Laywood 108-133 1996 £150.00

TURNER, DAWSON 1775-1858   Descriptive Index of the Contents of Five Manuscript Volumes, Illustrative of the History of Great Britain, in the Library of Dawson Turner, Esq. Yarmouth: Charles Solman, 1851. 1st edition; 8vo; original cloth, spine little torn, uncut.   Forest Books 74-266 1996 £75.00

TURNER, DAWSON 1775-1858   Muscologiae Hibernicae Spicilegium. Yarmouth and London: 1804. 8vo; pages xi, 200, (i)-xiv; 16 hand colored plates; modern buckram, some edge chipping to title and last plate, slight dampstaining to prelim page, owner's name stamp on title and 1 text page. rare.   Raymond M. Sutton VII-380 1996 $350.00

TURNER, DAWSON 1775-1858   Sketch of the History of Caister Castle. London: Whittaker, 1842. Large 8vo; title, 144 pages, frontispiece and 11 engraved plates, mounted folding pedigree; cloth, spine faded, some offset and foxing.   Marlborough 162-96 1996 £90.00

TURNER, ERNEST   Hints to Househunters and Householders. London: B. T. Batsford, 1883. 1st edition; 12mo; frontispiece, xiv, 161, (23) pages; publisher's gilt cloth, occasional faint foxing, light wear along joints, else very good.   Bookpress 75-131 1996 $185.00

TURNER, HENRY GLYES   A History of the Colony of Victoria from Its Discovery to Its Absorption into the Commonwealth of Australia. London: 1904. 8vo; 2 volumes, over 750 pages; folding map, plan; original blue cloth, spines faded, otherwise very good.   K Books 442-476 1996 £80.00

TURNER, J. HORSFALL   Haworth Past and Present, a History of Haworth, Stanbury & Oxenhope. Brighouse, J. S. Jowett, 1879. 1st edition; later issue; 7 x 4 3/4 inches; pages (viii), 184, 3 pages ads; frontispiece and 19 illustrations; blue basket weave grain cloth, blind decoration to both covers and gilt titling front cover and backstrip, white endpapers; inscription; very good, clean copy, scarce.   Ian Hodgkins 78-422 1996 £65.00

TURNER, JOHN P.   The North-West Mounted Police, 1873-1893. Ottawa: 1950. 1st edition; 686, 516 pages; photos, folding map; stiff printed wrappers, nice, scarce. 6 Guns 2250.   T. A. Swinford 49-1179 1996 $125.00

TURNER, LUCIEN MC SHAW   Contributions to the Natural History of Alaska. Washington: GPO, 1886. 1st edition; 4to; 226 pages, index, 15 detail drawings, 11 color lithograph plates; some wear to head of spine, approximately 2 cm. square of cloth missing from base of spine, interior very good, plates lovely. Arctic Bib. 18092; Ricks p. 222; Wickersham 7836.   Parmer Books Nat/Hist-031469 1996 $165.00

TURNER-TURNER, J.   Three Years Hunting and Trapping in America and the Great North West. 1888. Imperial 8vo; illustrations by Constance Hoare, 8 plates, text illustrations; 2 maps (loose); original pictorial silver cloth, illustration of bear on upper cover, top and base of spine slightly frayed, otherwise excellent; very scarce.   David Grayling J95Biggame-453 1996 £220.00

TUROW, SCOTT   One L. New York: Putnam, 1977. 1st edition; fine in dust jacket with light edge wear; signed.   Quill & Brush 102-1685 1996 $225.00

TUROW, SCOTT   One L. New York: G. P. Putnam's, 1977. 1st edition; author's first book; name, otherwise near fine in price clipped dust jacket.   Steven C. Bernard 71-246 1996 $150.00

TUROW, SCOTT   One L. New York: Putnam, 1977. 1st edition; fine copy in very good+ dust jacket; small tear, edgewear; author's first book.   Book Time 2-832 1996 $125.00

TUROW, SCOTT   One L. New York: Putnam, 1977. 1st edition; author's first book; good copy in good dust jacket.   Book Time 2-448 1996 $100.00

TUROW, SCOTT   Presumed Innocent. New York: Farrar Straus and Giroux, 1987. 1st edition; fine in price clipped dust jacket, signed.   Quill & Brush 102-1686 1996 $100.00

TURPIN DE CRISSE, LANCELOT, COUNT   An Essay on the Art of War. London: printed by A. Hamilton for W. Johnston, 1761. Sole edition in English; 4to; 2 volumes, (viii), xvi, 303; (iv), 138, (xlii), (viii) pages, 25 folding engraved plates, original speckled calf, morocco spine labels, some joints just beginning to crack, new endpapers in each volume, but fine, crisp copy.   David Bickersteth 133-86 1996 £450.00

TURPIN, RICHARD   The Trial of the Notorious Highwayman Richard Turpin, at York Assizes, on the 22d day of March 1739... York: printed by Ward and Chandler, 1739. 1st edition; 8vo; half blue morocco, few leaves bit stained, generally very good. Very rare.   Ximenes 109-291 1996 $2,500.00

TURTON, W.   British Fauna. Swansea: 1807. 1st edition; 8vo; Volume 1, all published; original printed boards, uncut, bit worn, rebacked, backstrip defective; the Bradley Martin copy, bought from Wheldon in 1958 for $7.50.   Maggs Bros. Ltd. 1190-270 1996 £55.00

TURTON, W.   A Manual of the Land and Fresh Water Shells of the British Islands. London: 1840. New edition; post 8vo; pages ix, 324, 12 colored plates; half morocco, rubbed.   Wheldon & Wesley 207-1217 1996 £50.00

TUSON, E.   Myology Illustrated: a supplement to Myology. London: Callow & Wilson, 1825-28. 1st edition; folio; 2 volumes, 1st with 8 lithographed plates, the second with 9 lithograph plates, both after drawings by author, both with multiple overlays, considerable hand coloring in red and blue, both on plates and overlays; first volume somewhat soiled, several of the overlays creased, few short tears repaired, title washed to remove library stamps and inscription thereon rather faint 'presented by Raphael W. Read, asst. surgeon, 52nd Lt. infantry, Nov. 26th 1847'; contemporary half calf, rather worn, second volume with slight soiling and minor marginal fraying, small spot of damage by adhesion on one overlay, several creased, contemporary boards, printed label on front cover (rather worn), label scraped, rebacked with cloth; very rare, especially with supplement.   Maggs Bros. Ltd.   1190-527   1996 £2,200.00

TUSSER, THOMAS   ...Five Hundred Pointes of Good Husbandrie...Mixed in Everie Month with Huswiferie. London: for the Assignés of William Seres, 1590. 4to; 162, (2) pages, printed largely in black letter; leaves I8 and L2 supplied in neat pen facimile on period paper; contemporary sheep, skillfully rebacked with nearly all the original spine laid down, two blank margins of title reinforced, blank corners of several leaves with early reinforcing, some minor staining, but overall very good. STC 24383.   Joseph J. Felcone   64-40   1996 $1,000.00

TUSSER, THOMAS   Five Hundred Points of Good Husbandry. James Tregaskis & Son, 1931. Limited to 500 copies; 4to; printed on handmade paper; xiv, 336 pages; original Hermitage calf by Bain & Son, edges uncut, slipcase, very fine.   Thomas Thorp   489-306   1996 £150.00

TUTTLE, FRANCIS   Report of the Cruise of the U.S. Revenue Cutter Bear and the Overland Expedition for the Relief of the Whalers in the Arctic Ocean from Nov. 27, 1897 to Sept. 13, 1898. Washington: 1899. pages iv, 144, 48 plates, large folding map; original binding; near fine. Arctic 18402.   Stephen Lunsford   45-164   1996 $100.00

TWEEDIE, W. K.   Jerusalem and its Environs; or, the Holy City As It Was and Is. London: T. Nelson and Sons, 1860. Small octavo; viii, (9)-224 pages, 8 color printed plates, including frontispiece; original blue blindstamped cloth stamped in gilt on front cover and spine, spine faded, extremities lightly rubbed; very good.   Heritage Book Shop   196-263   1996 $250.00

21 Kapitel Aus Der Historia Von D. Johann Fausten. Raamin Presse, 1992. One of 190 copies, signed by artist (of 195 total); 13 1/2 x 9 1/2 inches; 77, (1) pages, (5) leaves; 8 full page color illustrations by Roswitha Quadflieg, many smaller grey illustrations in margins, small device on first leaf; printed in red and blue; very handsome publisher's maroon morocco, central panel of covers with beautifully blindpressed abstract design, title in blind on spine, slipcase; as new.   Phillip J. Pirages   33-4363   1996 $1,850.00

TWIGDEN, B. L.   Pisces Tropicani. Melbourne: 1978. Limited to 350 numbered and signed copies; folio; pages 92, 26 colored plates; half morocco.   Wheldon & Wesley   207-992   1996 £120.00

TWINING, HENRY   On the Philosophy of Painting; a Theoretical and Practical Treatise... London: Longman, Brown, 1849. 1st edition; large 8vo; xxviii, 443 pages; 10 plates, 23 text illustrations; complete with half title and errata slip; original blindstamped cloth; very good.   Ken Spelman   30-45   1996 £90.00

TWINING, RICHARD   An Answer to the Second Report of the East India Directors, Respecting the Sale and Prices of Tea. London: T. Cadell, 1785. (2), 102 pages; recent marbled wrappers; nice. Goldsmiths 12961.   C. R. Johnson   37-37   1996 £125.00

TWISS, HORACE   An Enquiry Into the Means of Consolidating and Digesting the Laws of England. London: printed for R. Pheney, Inner Temple Lane, 1826. New quarter calf, some embrowning, but attractive, presentation copy.   Meyer Boswell   SL27-231   1996 $350.00

TWISS, HORACE   The Public and Private Life of Lord Chancellor Eldon, with Selections from His Correspondence. Philadelphia: Carey and Hart, 1844. 2 volumes; original embossed cloth, gilt, rubbed, but sound. Meyer Boswell   SL27-75   1996 $150.00

TWISS, RICHARD   A Trip to Paris, in July and August, 1792. London: printed at the Minerva Press and sold by William Lane & by Mrs. Harlow 1793. 8vo; (6), 131, (1) pages, plate; contemporary red morocco, lower part of leading hinge splitting; the author's own copy with extensive ms. corrections and additions; with several printed cuttings inserted.   C. R. Johnson   37-44   1996 £1,350.00

TWISS, TRAVERS   On Certain Tests of a Thriving Population. London: Longman, 1845. 1st edition; 8vo; (4), 107, (1) pages, 32 page publisher's list at end dated March 31, 1845; original dark blue cloth, lettered in gilt on upper cover, front endpaper bit stained, otherwise very good. Scarce. Williams I 218; Kress C6742; Goldsmiths 34146. Not in Black or Einaudi John Drury   82-283   1996 £375.00

TWO Humble Petitions of the Apprentices of London & Parts Adjacent, for Lawful Recreations: the First Presented to the Rt. Hon. the Lords & Commons Assembled in Parliament on Tuesday, Feb. 9, 1646...The Other Presented to Rt. Hon. Lord Mayor Alderman... London: printed by J. Macocok, for Nathanael Webb, & Wm. Grantham... 1647. 4to; 8 pages; rebound in boards; very nice. Wing T. 3453.   C. R. Johnson   37-45   1996 £125.00

TWOHY LAND CO.   Twohy Land Company's Review of the Famous Yakima Valley. North Yakima: ca. 1909. 1st edition; (36) pages, including wrappers; illustrations; original pictorial wrpapers; fine. Not in Smith or Soliday.   Michael D. Heaston   23-357   1996 $150.00

TWYMAN, MICHAEL   Printing 1770-1970, an Illustrated History Of Its Development and Uses in England. London: Eyre & Spottiswoode, 1970. 1st edition; 4to; x, 283 pages; 880 illustrations; cloth, dust jacket rubbed.   The Bookpress   75-363   1996 $125.00

TYLER, ANNE 1941-   Celestial Navigation. New York: Knopf, 1974. 1st edition; fine in dust jacket, lovely copy.   Between the Covers   42-431   1996 $250.00

TYLER, ANNE 1941-   Celestial Navigation. New York: A. Knopf, 1974. 1st edition; near fine in price clipped dust jacket that is lightly rubbed and has small closed tear to top front cover.   Bud Schweska   12-754   1996 $135.00

TYLER, ANNE 1941-   The Clock Winder. New York: Knopf, 1972. 1st edition; this copy signed by author; thumbnail size spot of discoloration on upper front panel, otherwise fine, only traces of wear to white dust jacket.   Captain's Bookshelf   38-211   1996 $1,250.00

TYLER, ANNE 1941-   Earthly Possessions. New York: Knopf, 1977. 1st edition; fine in dust jacket.   Hermitage   SP95-632   1996 $150.00

TYLER, ANNE 1941-   If Morning Ever Comes. New York: Knopf, 1964. 1st edition; author's scarce first book; fine in very near fine jacket with one faint shadow on spine, with top stain still a bright, rich shade of orange.   Ken Lopez   74-444   1996 $1,750.00

TYLER, ANNE 1941-   If Morning Ever Comes. New York: Knopf, 1964. 1st edition; author's scarce first book; some fading to edges and top stain, overall very good in very good price clipped jacket with midl wear at extremities of spine, including chip at crown, signed by author, uncommon.   Ken Lopez   74-443   1996 $1,250.00

TYLER, ANNE 1941-   If Morning Ever Comes. New York: Knopf, 1964. 1st edition; author's scarce first book; near fine in very good dust jacket with mild darkening and wear at edges and along front flap fold, few small chips at spine extremities, still handsome.   Ken Lopez   74-445   1996 $750.00

TYLER, ANNE 1941-   If Morning Ever Comes. London: Chatto & Windus, 1965. 1st English edition; fine in fine dust jacket with little scuffing on spine, visible only afeter close scrutiny, very nice, scarce, fragile.   Between the Covers   42-429 1   1996 $850.00

TYLER, ANNE 1941-   Morgan's Passing. New York: Knopf, 1980. 1st edition; fine in dust jacket with single minuscule tear.   Between the Covers   42-432   1996 $150.00

TYLER, ANNE 1941-   A Slipping-Down Life. New York: Alfred A. Knopf, 1970. 1st edition; fine in lightly worn dust jacket.   Hermitage   SP95-634   1996 $300.00

TYLER, ANNE 1941-   A Visit with Eudora Welty. Chicago: Presswork, 1980. One of 100 not-for-sale copies; small quarto; stapled wrappers, fine, signed by Tyler and Welty, copies signed by both are rare.   Lame Duck Books   19-548   1996 $450.00

TYLER, GEORGE W.   History of Bell County. San Antonio: 1936. 1st edition; 425 pages, frontispiece, photos; cloth; very good+, scarce. 6 Guns 2256. Herd 2348.   T. A. Swinford   49-1182   196 $100.00

TYLER, GILLIAN   The Good Wine. Thetford: Cricket Press, 1965. One of 22 copies only, page size 11 x 11 1/2 inches; on Umbria paper for text and Japanese paper for wood engravings; bound in natural burlap over boards by artist, housed in publisher's slipcase; ex-libris on front pastedown; fine.   Priscilla Juvelis 95/1-244 1996 $300.00

TYLER, LYON G.   The Letters and Times of the Tylers. Richmond: Whittet & Shepperson, 1884-85. 1st edition; 8vo; 2 volumes, frontispiece, xiii, (iii), 633 pages, 1 plate; frontispiece, xiv, (ii), 736 pages, 3 plates; publisher's cloth, covers rubbed, corners of volume 2 torn and bruised, bookplates, all hinges internally cracked, ex-library with only bookplate. Howes T448.   The Bookpress 75-473 1996 $400.00

TYLER, LYON G.   The Letters and Times of the Tylers. New York: 1971. Reissue, first published in a small edition Richmond and Williamsburg 1884-96. Large 8vo; 3 volumes; illustrations and facsimiles; original cloth.   Howes Bookshop 265-2061 1996 £65.00

TYLER, LYON G.   Men of Mark in Virginia. Washington: 1906. 5 volumes, complete as issued; approximately 250 steel engravings; full forest green morocco with gilt, top edge gilt, near fine, one cover has 2 x 4 inch discolored area at bottom edge; scarce.   Bookworm & Silverfish 276-212 1996 $350.00

TYLER, MOSES COIT   The Literary History of the American Revolution 1763-1783. New York: & London: 1897. 1st edition; royal 8vo; 2 volumes, titles in red and black, pages 552 and 545; original cloth, gilt tops.   Howes Bookshop 265-1231 1996 £50.00

TYLOR, EDWARD B.   Anahuac; or Mexico and the Mexicans, Ancient and Modern. London: Longman, Green, Longman and Roberts, 1861. 8vo; frontispiece, xii, 344 pages, 26 figures, 3 color plates, 1 folding map; gilt pictorial cloth, endpapers removed, skillfully rebacked, light foxing, slight edgewear.   Archaeologia Luxor-4981 1996 $150.00

TYNAN, KENNETH   Bull Fever. London: Longmans, Green and Co., 1955. 1st edition; numerous black and white photos; original binding, top edge dusty, edges spotted, head and tail of spine and corners slightly bumped, very good in nicked, rubbed and slightly marked, spotted and dusty dust jacket, by Broom Lynne, browned internally and at edges. Ulysses 39-95 1996 £55.00

TYNDALL, JOHN   Essays on the Floating-Maatter of the Air in Relation to Putrefaction and Infection. New York: D. Appleton, 1882. 1st American edition; 8vo; xix, 338, (4) ads, pages; 24 figures; original decorated embossed cloth; near fine. Heirs of Hipp. 1881; GM 2495 for 1881 1st. Norman Lib. 2119.   Edwin V. Glaser 121-315 1996 $235.00

TYNER, J. W.   Our People and Where They Rest. Norman: 1969-78. 1st edition; viii, 121, viii, 120, viii, 114, viii, 120, ix, 124, ix, 136 ix, 124, x,, 127, ix, 141, viii, 147 pages; photos; stiff printed wrappers; fine.   T. A. Swinford 49-1188 1996 $175.00

TYPIS Sacrae Congregationis De Propoganda Fide, The Vatican. Regi Gustavo...Adfuerit Iterumque Ad Officinae Librariae Cognitionem...Litterarium formarum Omnigenearum Specimen Laeti Libentes Dedicant... Rome, the Vatican: Typis Sacrae Congregationis de Propoganda Fide, 1784. Small folio; dedication title with engraved medallion portrait of Gustavus III of Sweden, 23 leaves of 46 specimens of alphabets and scripts, a polyglot printed on rectos only, within woodcut borders, occasional slight spotting; modern half calf, spine gilt. Scarce. Birrell & Garnett pp. 4; Updike I 182ff.   Maggs Bros. Ltd. 1191-220 1996 £850.00

A TYPOGRAPHICAL Commonplace-Book. Harrison of Paris, 1932. One of 595 numbered copies; 8vo; printed on Montgolfier, printed in black, blue and red; blue buckram, gilt, spine slightly faded and little offsetting within, but very nice.   Bertram Rota 272-228 1996 £85.00

TYRRELL, HENRY   The History of the War With Russia... (with) The History of the Russian Empire... London: and New York: printed and pub. by the London Printing and Publishing Co., n.d., c.1860. 4to; 4 volumes; Directions to binder, steel engraved frontispiece to all volumes; 81 steel engraved plates, 9 double page colored steel engraved maps and plans and 1 single page map; half calf and black buckram boards, some scoring to calf, black morocco label to spines, raised bands to spines, corners worn, edges marbled; some foxing to few plates, one plate with neat marginal repair not affecting imprint.   Beeleigh Abbey BA/56-124 1996 £250.00

TYRRELL, JAMES W.   Across the Sub-Arctics of Canada: a Journey of 3200 Miles by Canoe and Snowshoe through the Hudson Bay Region. Toronto: William Briggs, 1908. 3rd edition; 8vo; pages viii, 10-280; frontispiece with tissue, photos, drawings, folding maps; original decorated cloth, name stamp on endpapers, cover slightly worn, else very good. AB 18138.   Hugh Anson-Cartwright 87-445 1996 $125.00

TYSON, JAMES L.   Diary of a Physician in California: Being the Results of Actual Experience, Including Notes of the Journey by Land and Water and Observations on the Climate, Soil, Resources of the Country, Etc. New York: 1850. 92 pages; original binding, front wrapper foxed, one half inch missing from corners of the first two leaves, corners of additional 10 leaves are wrinkled; rare. Atkinson 244.   W. Bruce Fye 71-2146 1996 $300.00

TYTLER, PATRICK FRASER   History of Scotland 1249-1603. Edinburgh: William Tair, 1841-43. 8vo; 9 volumes; original blindstamped cloth, gilt; excellent clean and sound set; armorial bookplate of Sir John Watson, Bart.   R.F.G. Hollett 76-312 1996 £85.00

TYTLER, SARAH   Jane Austen and Her Works. London: Cassell, Petter, Galpin and Co., n.d. 1880. 1st edition; 7 1/8 x 4 3/4 inches; pages viii, 386, 8 pages publisher's ads dated Sept. 1880; frontispiece; black boards with design of Daisies on both covers and backstrip, gilt titling to front cover and backstrip, black endpapers, all edges gilt. original backstrip laid down, slight foxing to prelims, very good, scarce. Gilson M146.   Ian Hodgkins 78-157 1996 £65.00

U

UKERS, W. H.   All About Coffee. New York: 1922. Royal 8vo; pages xxix, 796; numerous plates and figures; buckram; some very slight worming.   Wheldon & Wesley 207-1891 1996 £75.00

ULMANN, DORIS   A Book of Portraits of the Faculty of the Medical Department of the Johns Hopkins University Baltimore. Baltimore: 1922. 1st edition; folio; untrimmed; fine, very rare.   W. Bruce Fye 71-2147 1996 $750.00

ULMO, GIOVANNI FRANCESCO   Francisci Ulmi...De Liene Libellus. Paris: Apud Mamertum Patissonium Typographum Regium in officina Roberti... 1578. 24mo; ff. 27 (-terminal blank), text in Greek and Latin, Estienne printer's mark on title; full vellum. Scarce. Not in Screiber. Adams U47.   Family Album Tillers-628 1996 $245.00

THE UNDER-Sheriff: Containing the Office and Duty of High-Sheriffs, Under-Sheriffs and Bailiffs... London: printed by H. Woodfall and W. Strahan...for W. Owen, etc., 1766. Only edition; contemporary calf, joints cracking, but fresh, well preserved.   Meyer Boswell SL27-208 1996 $450.00

UNDERHILL, FRANCIS T.   Driving for Pleasure, or, the Hareness Stable and Its Appointments. New York: Appleton, 1897. 2nd edition; 4to; 158 pages, 124 full page photographic plates; rubbed three quarter calf and suede, front hinge tender, little internal staining, otherwise very good tight copy, name on front blank.   Second Life Books 103-198 1996 $250.00

UNDERHILL, HAROLD A.   Plan-on-Frame Models and Scale Masting and Rigging. Glasgow: 1958. 1st edition; 2 volumes, ix, 157 pages; several full page and many text illustrations, near fine in dust jacket with small tears and frays.   Bookworm & Silverfish 280-180 1996 $195.00

UNION PACIFIC RAILROAD   Guide to the Union Pacific Railroad Lands 12,000,000 Acres... Omaha: Omaha Herald Steam Printing Establishment, 1870. New edition; 44 pages; frontispiece, folding map; original printed wrappers, minor chipping, laid in half morocco folding case, fine. Michael D. Heaston 23-338b 1996 $750.00

UNION PACIFIC RAILROAD   Guide to the Union Pacific R. R. Lands. 12,000,000 Acres Best Farming and Mineral Lands in America... Omaha: Republican Steam Printing House, 1870. 36 pages, folding map, frontispiece map; original purple glazed printed wrappers, stained and chipped, good to very good, laid in half morocco slipcase. Nebraska Imprints Inventory 194.   Michael D. Heaston 23-338a 1996 $700.00

UNION PACIFIC RAILROAD   Guide to the Union Pacific Railroad Lands 12,000,000 Acres Best Farming, Grazing and Mineral Lands in America... Omaha: Land Department: Union Pacific Railroad Building, Omaha Herald... 1872. 5th edition; 48 pages; folding maps; original brown printed wrappers, laid in half morocco slipcase; very fine. Nebraska Imprints Inventory 283.   Michael D. Heaston 23-338d 1996 $650.00

UNION PACIFIC RAILROAD   Hand-Buch Zu Den Union-Pacific Eisenbahn-Landereien 12,000,000...in Dem Staate Nebraska Und Den Territorien Colorado, Wyoming Und Utah... Omaha: Land Bureau, Union Pacific, 1871. 1st edition of this issue; 23 pages, folding maps; original printed blue wrappers with map, minor repairs to wrappers, fine, laid in half morocco slipcase.   Michael D. Heaston 23-338c 1996 $1,200.00

UNION PACIFIC RAILROAD   The Resources and Attractions of Colorado. Council Bluffs: Nonpareil Printing and Pub., 1888. 1st edition; pages (iv), 91; map; front wrapper stained, interior slightly browned, else good.   Dumont 28-60 1996 $120.00

UNION PACIFIC RAILROAD   The Resources and Attractions of Colorado. Chicago: Rand McNally & Co., 1889. Stated second edition; pages (ii), 91; slight soil, else good.   Dumont 28-61 1996 $120.00

UNION PACIFIC RAILROAD   The Union Pacific R. R. Cheap Homes! Farms Nebraska, 3,000,000 Acres! Land Guide, 1880. Omaha: 1880. 1st edition; 16 pages, 2 maps; original printed pink wrappers with Union Pacific Depot and Hotel, Council Bluffs, featured on back wrapper; laid in half morocco slipcase, fine.   Michael D. Heaston 23-338 1996 $375.00

UNITED BROTHERHOOD OF CARPENTERS & JOINERS OF AMERICA By-laws of Butte Union No. 112 of the United Brotherhood of Carpenters and Joiners of America Organized Feb. 22, 1890. Butte: The Sunday Bystander, 1891. 1st edition; 14 pages; sewn as issued, tears neatly repaired, some soiling, very good.   Michael D. Heaston 23-251 1996 $200.00

UNITED STATES NATIONAL CENTER FOR HEALTH STATISTICS   The International Classification of Diseases 9th Revision Clinical Modification Icd.9.Cm. Volume 1: Diseases: Tabular List. 2: Procedures: Alphabetic List. 3: Procedures: Tabular List and Alphabetic Index. Ann Arbor: Commission on Professional and Hospital Activities, 1978. 1st edition; 8vo; 3 volumes, 2608 pages; printed ochre cloth, slight fraying to crown of volume 2, else very good set.   John Gach 150-462 1996 $100.00

UNITED STATES NAVAL ASTRONOMICAL EXPEDITION, 1849-1852   The U. S. Naval Astronomical Expedition to the Southern Hemisphere During the Years 1849-50-51-52. Washington: A. O. P. Nicholson, 1855. 1st edition; 4to; 2 volumes; xiii, 556 pages, 3 maps, 11 plates; ix, 300 pages, 2 maps, 35 plates, some plates colored; modern three quarter leather, marbled paper over boards, endpapers renewed, small tape repaired closed split in large folding panorama, binder who has done gilt spine titles has incorrectly dated '1885' on spines; very good. Sabin 27419; Hill p. 602.   Parmer Books Nat/Hist-067426 1996 $450.00

THE UNITED States Sanitary Commission. A Sketch of its Purposes and its Work. Boston: 1863. 1st edition; 299 pages; original binding.   W. Bruce Fye 71-2150 1996 $250.00

UNITED STATES. ARCHITECT OF THE CAPITOL - 1899   Annual Report of the Architect of the United States... Washington: GPO, 1899. 1st edition; 8vo; 44 pages, 53 plates, 9 are folding; wrappers chipped, internally very good.   The Bookpress 75-247 1996 $150.00

UNITED STATES. ARMY - 1813   Military Laws and Rules and Regulations for the Armies of the United States. Washington: Addjutant and Inspecctor General's Office, May 1st, 1813. 12mo; xx, (2), 272 pages; original brown calf over marbled boards, rubbed, top quarter of front free endpaper torn away. American Imprints 1813 30267.   Kenneth Karmiole 1NS-13 1996 $150.00

UNITED STATES. ARMY - 1851   Annual Report of the Quartermaster General, of the Operations of the Quartermaster's Department, for the Fiscal Year Ending on the 30th June, 1850. Washington: C. Alexander, 1851. 218 pages; 36 plates; original printed wrpapers laid in half morocco folding case; minor foxing, fine. Mintz The Trail 112; Howes C923; Becker Wagner Camp 181.3.   Michael D. Heaston 23-127 1996 $2,000.00

UNITED STATES. ARMY - 1866   Official Army Register for 1866 and 1867. Washington: 1866/67. 186, 347, 177, 5, 39 pages; cloth, very good+. Dustin 226.   T. A. Swinford 49-1191 1996 $125.00

UNITED STATES. ARMY - 1886   Annual Report of Brigadier General Nelson A. Miles, U.S. Army, Commanding Department of Arizona, 1886. Albuquerque: 1886. 1st edition; 22 pages; original printed grey wrappers; fine, laid in half morocco slipcase. Graff 2785.   Michael D. Heaston 23-24 1996 $2,500.00

UNITED STATES. BUREAU OF AMERICAN ETHNOLOGY - 1888 Sixth Annual Report of the Bureau of American Ethnology to the Secretary of the Smithsonian Inst. 1884-25. Washington: GPO, 1888. 4to; lviii, 675 pages; profusely illustrated; original cloth, lightly worn at extremities; front endpaper absent.   Archaeologia Luxor-4319 1996 $175.00

UNITED STATES. BUREAU OF AMERICAN ETHNOLOGY - 1891 Seventh Annual Report...1885-86. Washington: GPO, 1891. 1st edition; 409 pages; color plates;   Maggie Lambeth 30-30 1996 $125.00

UNITED STATES. BUREAU OF AMERICAN ETHNOLOGY - 1893 Tenth Annual Report of the Bureau of Ethnology to the Secretary of the Smithsonian Inst. 1888-89. Washington: GPO, 1893. 1st edition; 822 pages; illustrations; some signatures and pages loose.   Maggie Lambeth 30-32 1996 $150.00

UNITED STATES. BUREAU OF AMERICAN ETHNOLOGY - 1894
Twelfth Annual Report of the Bureau of American Ethnology....
Washington: GPO, 1894. 4to; xlviii, 742 pages; profusely illustrated; three
quarter calf, 5 raised bands, marbled boards and endpapers.
Archaeologia Luxor-4323 1996 $250.00

UNITED STATES. BUREAU OF AMERICAN ETHNOLOGY - 1894
Eleventh Annual Report of the...1889-'90. Washington: GPO, 1894. 1st
edition; 553 pages; many color plates, black and white photos;
Maggie Lambeth 30-31 1996 $250.00

UNITED STATES. BUREAU OF AMERICAN ETHNOLOGY - 1894
Twelfth Annual Report of the Bureau of Ethnology to the Secretary of the
Smithsonian Institution, 1890-1891. Washington: GPO, 1894. 4to; xlviii, 742
pages; profusely illustrated; original cloth, lightly worn at extremities,
corner bumped, shaken. Archaeologia Luxor-4322 1996 $200.00

UNITED STATES. BUREAU OF AMERICAN ETHNOLOGY - 1896
Fourteenth Annual Report of the Bureau of Ethnology to the Secretary of
the Smithsonian Inst. 1892-93. Washington: GPO, 1896. 1st edition; 637
pages; photos, folding maps; Maggie Lambeth 30-33 1996 $275.00

UNITED STATES. BUREAU OF AMERICAN ETHNOLOGY - 1904
Twenty-Second Annual Report of the Bureau of American Ethnology to
the Secretary of the Smithsonian Institution 1900-1901. Part I (only).
Washington: GPO, 1904. 8vo; xliiv, 320 pages; 170 figures, 82 plates;
original cloth, worn at extremities, ink stamps. Archaeologia
Luxor-4321 1996 $175.00

UNITED STATES. BUREAU OF AMERICAN ETHNOLOGY - 1912
Twenty-Eighth Annual Report of the Bureau of American Ethnology to the
Secretary of the Smithsonian Institution 1906-1907. Washington: GPO,
1912. 8vo; 308 pages, (xxxv), 68 figures, 102 plates, 1 map; original
cloth, top board bumped at lower edge. Archaeologia Luxor-4320
1996 $175.00

UNITED STATES. BUREAU OF AMERICAN ETHNOLOGY - 1922
Thirty-Fourth Annual Report of the.... Washington: GPO, 1922. 4to; 281
pages; profusely illustrated; original cloth, 2 corners lightly bumped;
Archaeologia Luxor-4317 1996 $125.00

UNITED STATES. BUREAU OF AMERICAN ETHNOLOGY - 1928
Forty-First Annual Report of the Bureau of American Ethnology to the
Secretary of the Smithsonian Inst. 1919-1924. Washington: GPO, 1928.
4to; x, 626 pages; 200 figures, 138 plates, 1 folding map; original cloth,
lightly worn at extremities. Archaeologia Luxor-4318 1996 $150.00

UNITED STATES. CONGRESS. HOUSE OF REPRESENTATIVES - 1812
Report, or Manifesto on the Causes and Reasons of War with Great
Britain. Presented to the House of Representatives by the Committee of
Foreign Relations, June 3, 1812. Washington: A. & G. Way, 1812. 17
pages, bound with filler leaves in three quarter leather and marbled
boards, gilt spine title, text leaves untrimmed and stained. S&S 27350.
Bohling Book Co. 192-21 1996 $150.00

UNITED STATES. CONGRESS. HOUSE OF REPRESENTATIVES - 1872
Report of the Commissioners and Evidence Taken by the Committee on
Mines and Mining of the House of Representatives of the United States,
In Regard to the Sutro Tunnel... Washington: M'Gill & Witherow Printers,
1872. 1st edition; 66, 988 pages; original pictorial blue cloth, all edges
gilt, repairs to spine, very good. Paher 2028. Michael D. Heaston
23-259 1996 $250.00

UNITED STATES. CONGRESS. SENATE - 1854 Report Of the
Select Committee of the Senate of the United States On the Sickness
and Mortality on Board Emigrant Ships. Washington: 1854. 1st edition;
147 pages; original binding, covers and backstrip worn, torn and stained,
scattered foxing. W. Bruce Fye 71-1752 1996 $125.00

UNITED STATES. CONGRESS. SENATE - 1906 Proceedings Before
the Committee on Privileges and Elections of the United States Senate in
the Matter of the Protests Against the Right of Hon. Reed Smoot, a
Senator from the State of Utah, to Hold His Seat. Washington: 1906. 4
volumes, 3433 pages, 2 bindings styles: three quarter leather and full
leather, depository rubberstamps, volume 4 hinges split, not used. Flake
9173. Bohling Book Co. 191-814 1996 $150.00

UNITED STATES. CONSTITUTION - 1987 Constitution of the United
States. Arion Press in Assoc. with the Library of Congress, 1987. One of
500 copies; 10 3/4 x 6 3/4 inches; 63, (1) pages; initials drawing and
illuminated in red, blue and gold by Thomas Ingmire; printed flexible
vellum covers, text sewn on exposed red vellum thongs laced through
covers and backstrip, untrimmed edges, blue cloth chemise and
matching slipcase with paper label. As new. Phillip J. Pirages 33-17
1996 $875.00

UNITED STATES. COURT OF CLAIMS - 1863 In the Court of
Claims. No. 1882. William S. Grant vs. the United States. Washington:
1863-64. 1st edition; original parts bound in later cloth. McGowan
Book Co. 65-97 1996 $250.00

UNITED STATES. DEPARTMENT OF AGRICULTURE - 1902 A Report
of the Secretary of Agriculture in Relation to the Forests, Rivers and
Mountains of the Southern Appalachian Region. Washington: 1902. 4to;
pages 210; 78 plates; original cloth, inner hinges cracked, embossed
library stamps on plate pages, ex-library. Raymond M. Sutton VII-711
1996 $125.00

UNITED STATES. DEPARTMENT OF THE INTERIOR - 1882 Letter
from the Secretary of the Interior...Concerning a Tract of Land in
Colorado Patented to Charles Beaubien. Washington: Senate Executive
Document 142, 1882. 1st edition; 64 pages, 5 folding maps; half
morcoco and cloth, title in gilt on spine, very good. Michael D.
Heaston 23-110 1996 $350.00

UNITED STATES. DEPARTMENT OF TREASURY - 1828 Letter from
the Secretary of the Treasury, Transmitting the Information Required by a
Resolution of the House of Presentations...in Relation to the Growth and
Manufacture of Silk. Washington: 1828. 8vo; pages 224; 5 plates;
contemporary boards, worn, backstrip perished, shaken, title browned,
foxed, corner of title missing. Raymond M. Sutton VII-963 1996
$165.00

UNITED STATES. GENERAL LAND OFFICE - 1869 Circular (No. 26)
from the General Land Office, Showing the Manner of Proceeding to
Obtain Title to Public Lands...Issued March 10, 1869. Washington: GPO,
1869. 1st edition; 25 pages; original pictorial wrappers, very good.
Michael D. Heaston 23-202 1996 $125.00

UNITED STATES. GENERAL LAND OFFICE - 1882 Letter from the
Secretary of the Interior, Transmitting...the Report of the Commissioner
of the General Land Office Upon the Survey of the Unites States and
Texas Boundary Commission. Washington: 1882. 309 pages; text
illustrations, 15 folding maps; removed, very good. Bohling Book Co.
191-174 1996 $120.00

UNITED STATES. LAWS, STATUTES, ETC. - 1794 Act Making
Appropriations for the Support of the Military Establishment of the United
States for the Year One Thousand Seven Hundred Ninety-Four.
Philadelphia: Chils & Swaine, 1794. 13 x 8 inches; 2 plages; nice, little
age toned; Evans 27838. Bohling Book Co. 191-670 1996 $600.00

UNITED STATES. LAWS, STATUTES, ETC. - 1832 An Act to
Provide for Liquidating and Paying Certain Claims of the State of Virginia.
Washington: 1832. 4to; unbound, (3) pages. The Bookpress 75-475
1996 $175.00

UNITED STATES. LIBRARY OF CONGRESS - 1901 A List of Maps
of America in the Library of Congress. Washington: GPO, 1901. Pages
1137; soiled boards faded, hinges repaired, interior good. Dumont
28-115 1996 $225.00

UNITED STATES. LIBRARY OF CONGRESS - 1914 List of
Geographical Atlases in the Library of Congress with Bibliographical
Notes - Volume 3 and 4. Washington: 1914/20. 1st edition; 2 volumes,
1030 pages, 629 pages; cloth, hinges weakened. W. M. Morrison
436-184 1996 $150.00

UNITED STATES. LIBRARY OF CONGRESS - 1975 Children's Books
in the Rare Book Division of the Library of Congress. Totowa: Rowman
& Littlefield, 1975. 4to; 2 volumes; blue cloth. Maggs Bros. Ltd.
1191-109 1996 £95.00

UNITED STATES. PRESIDENT - 1809 Message from the President
of the United States Transmitting Extracts from the Correspondence of
Mr. Pinkney. Washington: A. & G. Way, 1809. 1st edition; 8vo; 14 pages;
disbound. American Imprints 18975. The Bookpress 75-436 1996
$225.00

UNITED STATES. PRESIDENT - 1819 Message of the
President...Transmitting a Report to the Secretary of War, in Compliance
With a Resolution of the Senate of the 25th of January Last Requesting
Him "To Cause to Be Laid Before It, a Copy of the Rules and
Regulations Adopted for... Washington: ptd. by E. DeKrafft, 1819. 1st
edition; 13 pages plus 9 long folding tables; fine. Taurus Books
83-30 1996 $100.00

UNITED STATES. PRESIDENT - 1836   Condition of Texas. Message from the President of the U.S. Upon the Subject of the Political, Military, and Civil Condition of Texas. Washington: 1836. 33 pages; removed; light foxing. Howes M793; Streeter Texas 1255.   Bohling Book Co. 191-103 1996 $100.00

UNITED STATES. PRESIDENT - 1836   The Political, Military and Civil Condition of Texas. Washington: 1836. 36 pages; removed, light foxing, nice. Howes M793; Streeter TX 1255.   Bohling Book Co. 191-104 1996 $125.00

UNITED STATES. PRESIDENT - 1848   Message of the President...Communicating the Proceedings of the Court Martial in the Trial of Lieutenant Colonel Fremont. Washington: Senate Executive Document 33, 1848. 1st edition; half morocco, marbled boards, gilt title on spine; fine. Howes F369.   Michael D. Heaston 23-149 1996 $300.00

UNITED STATES. PRESIDENT - 1849   Message from the President of the United States to The Two Houses of Congress, at the Commencement of the First Session of the Thirty-First Congress, Dec. 24, 1849. Washington: 1849. 43, 850 pages; 6 folded charts, 6 folded plates, 1 folded plan; full leather, scuffed, spine top chipped, hinges splitting, foxing. Jenkins 234:1099.   Bohling Book Co. 191-674 1996 $200.00

UNITED STATES. PRESIDENT - 1853   Message from the President of the U. S...at the Commencement of the First Session of the 33rd Congress. Washington: 1853. 3 text volumes, 525, 583, 821 pages; and Part IV: maps and other illustrations; full leather, very good overall with some depository markings.   Bohling Book Co. 191-677 1996 $300.00

UNITED STATES. PRESIDENT - 1853   Message from the President of the U.S....at the Commencement of the First Session. 33d Congress. Part IV: Maps and Other Illustrations Belonging to Reports Accompanying the Message. Washington: 1853. 37 folded maps and charts, 5 litho views; full leather, leather quite scuffed, upper 2 inch of backstrip chipped away, interior generally nice and fresh, last map split along exposed fold.   Bohling Book Co. 191-679 1996 $200.00

UNITED STATES. PRESIDENT - 1854   Message from the President of the U.S...at the Commencement of the Second Session of the 33d Congress. Dec. 4, 1854. Washington: 1854. 8vo; 3 volumes; 22, 629; 22, 712 pages and part 3, illustrations, 8 folding maps; full leather, very good, nice set.   Bohling Book Co. 191-678 1996 $300.00

UNITED STATES. PRESIDENT - 1858   A Proclamation...Concerning the Utah War and Its Necessity. Washington: Office of the President, April 6, 1858. 1st edition; small folio; 3 pages of a 4 page folder, minor marginal tears expertly repaired; fine, overall copy. Flake 9220.   Michael D. Heaston 23-342 1996 $2,500.00

UNITED STATES. PRESIDENT - 1879   Message From the President of the United States...Information in Relation to an Alleged Occupation of a Portion of the Indian Territory by White Settlers. Washington: Senate Executive Document 20, 1879. 1st edition; 34 pages; folding amp, half morocco and marbled boards, title in gilt on spine; fine. Gilcrease Hargrett Cat. p. 286.   Michael D. Heaston 23-169 1996 $300.00

UNITED STATES. PRESIDENT - 1886   Message from...Transmitting a Report from the Secretary of State Relative to the Frontier Line Between Alaska and British Columbia. Washington: Senate Executive Doc. 143, 1886. 1st edition; 20 pages; folding maps, 3 other maps and charts; half morocco and marbled boards, title in gilt on spine; fine.   Michael D. Heaston 23-3 1996 $300.00

UNITED STATES. TREATIES, ETC. - 1848   The Treaty Between the U.S. and Mexico and the Proceedings of the Senate Thereon...From Which the Injunction of Secrecy Has Been Removed. Washington: Senate Executive Document 52, 1848. 1st American edition, Senate issue; 384 pages; half morocco and marbled boards, very good.   Michael D. Heaston 23-244 1996 $300.00

UNITED STATES. TREATIES, ETC. - 1868   Treaty With Russia. Washington: House of Representatives Report No. 37, 1868. 1st edition; 65 pages; sewn; very good.   Michael D. Heaston 23-14 1996 $125.00

UNITED STATES. WAR DEPARTMENT - 1834   Letter from the Secretary of War, Transmitting a Map and Report of Lieut. Allen and H. B. Schoolcraft's Visit to the Northwest Indians in 1832. Washington: 23rd Congress 1st session, Doc. No. 323, House of Reps., April 12, 1834. 8vo; 68 pages; large folding map; modern quarter red calf, lightly rubbed. Sabin 77847; Graff 3703.   Richard Adelson W94/95-148 1996 $485.00

UNITED STATES. WAR DEPARTMENT - 1837   Letter from the Secretary of War Transmitting Various Reports in Relation to the Protection of the Western Frontier. Washington: Dec. 30, 1837. 1st edition; 18 pages; disbound. Good.   Gene W. Baade 1094-147 1996 $100.00

UNITED STATES. WAR DEPARTMENT - 1840   Report from the Secretary of War, Transmitting...Copies of Reports, Plans, and Estimates for the Improvement of the Neenah, Wiskonsin and Rock Rivers; the Improvement of the Haven of Rock River; and the Construction of a Pier at the Northern Extremity... Washington: 1840. 29 pages, 17 maps and plans (part folded), stitched as issued, untrimmed; little edge worn and darkened, still very nice.   Bohling Book Co. 192-405 1996 $120.00

UNITED STATES. WAR DEPARTMENT - 1919   Manual of Neuro-Surgery Authorized by the Secretary of War. Washington: GPO, 1919. 8vo; 492 pages; original leather boards, newly rebacked, fore-edges chipped, internally very good.   James Tait Goodrich K40-98 1996 $275.00

UNSWORTH, BARRY   The Partnership. London: New Authors Limited, 1966. 1st British edition; author's first book; near fine in very good+ dust jacket.   Pettler & Lieberman 28-244 1996 $100.00

UNTERMYER, IRWIN   Chelsea and Other English Porcelain Pottery and Enamel in the Irwin Untermyer Collection. Cambridge: pub. for the Metropolitan Museum of Art, 1957. 4to; 146 colored black and white plates, slightly torn dust jacket, otherwise fine.   Petersfield Bookshop FH58-9 1996 £100.00

UNWIN, A. H.   West African Forests and Forestry. New York: 1920. 8vo; pages 527; 110 photos; original cloth, some wear to extremities, light soiling, endpapers foxed.   Raymond M. Sutton VII-775 1996 $150.00

UPCOTT, WILLIAM   A Bibliographical Account of Principal Works Relating to English Topography. London: printed by Richard and Arthur Taylor, 1818. Limited to 250 copies; 3 volumes, 2 plates; green half morocco, spine gilt in compartments with raised bands; bound for the Carlton Club with booklabel in each volume, rubbed and torn at joints and corners.   Maggs Bros. Ltd. 1191-130 1996 £180.00

UPCOTT, WILLIAM   A Bibliographical Account of the Principal Works Relating to English Topography. New York: Burt Franklin, 1968. Reprint of 1818 edition; 8vo; 3 volumes; frontispieces, original cloth.   Forest Books 74-268 1996 £75.00

UP DE GRAFF, F. W.   Head-Hunters of the Amazon. London: Herbert Jenkins, 1923. 1st English edition; 8vo; 316 pages, (4) pages of ads, photographs and folding map; original green cloth, very good. not in NUC.   Chapel Hill 94-368 1996 $150.00

UPDIKE, JOHN 1932-   The Afterlife; a Story. Leamington: Sixth Chamber Press, 1987. One of 175 numbered copies on Basingwerk Parchment, signed by author; small 4to; set in Monotype Ehrhardt at the Stellar Press, printed in black and rust; cloth, printed label; fine.   Bertram Rota 272-397 1996 £60.00

UPDIKE, JOHN 1932-   The Afterlife and Other Stories. New York: Knopf, 1994. 1st edition; wrappers; fine.   Ken Lopez 74-449 1996 $125.00

UPDIKE, JOHN 1932-   Buchanan Dying: a Play. New York: Knopf, 1974. 1st edition; fine in fine dust jacket.   Sherwood 3-323 1996 $100.00

UPDIKE, JOHN 1932-   The Carpentered Hen and other Tame Creatures. New York: Harper & Bros., 1956. 1st edition; fine in price clipped first issue dust jacket with 'two small children' on rear flap.   Sherwood 3-307 1996 $650.00

UPDIKE, JOHN 1932-   The Centaur. New York: Knopf, 1963. 1st edition; several small stains to boards, very good in somewhat wrinkled dust jacket.   Sherwood 3-312 1996 $150.00

UPDIKE, JOHN 1932-   A Child's Calendar. New York: 1965. 1st edition; illustrations in color by Nancy Burkert; gift inscription, tiny area lower edge front panel little sunned, near fine, dust jacket with few small edge tears, little edge rubbed; scarce; signed presentation copy from author.   Polyanthos 22-877 1996 $100.00

UPDIKE, JOHN 1932-   Couples. New York: Knopf, 1968. 1st edition; fine in fine dust jacket, former owner's signature on front pastedown. Sherwood 3-318 1996 $130.00

UPDIKE, JOHN 1932-   Ego and Art in Walt Whitman. New York: Bird & Bull Press, 1980. One of 350 copies, signed by author; 8vo; decorated paper over boards, linen spine, protective wrappers; new. Priscilla Juvelis 95/1-248 1996 $125.00

UPDIKE, JOHN 1932-   Going Abroad. Helsinki: Eurographica, 1988. limited edition, one of 350, each signed and dated by author on titlepage, fine in white wrappers and blue printed dust jacket; printed by Tipografia Nobili in Pesaro on Michelangelo paper made at Magnani Mills. Priscilla Juvelis 95/1-249 1996 $150.00

UPDIKE, JOHN 1932-   Hawthorne's Creed. New York: Targ Editions, 1981. 1st edition; one of 250 copies, signed by author; 8vo; on Nideggan paper, set in Bakserville; marbled paper over boards, maroon linen spine, repro of photo of Hawthorne on front cover, repeated as frontispiece in large format, grey protective wrapper; new. Priscilla Juvelis 95/1-250 1996 $125.00

UPDIKE, JOHN 1932-   Hawthorne's Creed. New York: Targ Editions, 1981. Limited to 250 copies only, signed by author; fine in dust jacket. Polyanthos 22-880 1996 $100.00

UPDIKE, JOHN 1932-   Hoping for a Hoopoe. London: Victor Gollanz, 1959. 1st English edition; author's first book; fine. Bev Chaney, Jr. 23-744 1996 $120.00

UPDIKE, JOHN 1932-   The Magic Flute. New York: Knopf, 1962. 1st edition; near fine in very good dust jacket with light wear at extremities of spine, signed by author. Ken Lopez 74-447 1996 $850.00

UPDIKE, JOHN 1932-   Midpoint and Other Poems. New York: Knopf, 1969. 1st edition; fine in fine dust jacket. Sherwood 3-319 1996 $125.00

UPDIKE, JOHN 1932-   A Month of Sundays. New York: Knopf, 1975. Copy number 2 of 250 numbered copies, signed by author; fine in dust jacket, slipcase. Between the Covers 42-435 1996 $175.00

UPDIKE, JOHN 1932-   A Month of Sundays. New York: Alfred A. Knopf, 1975. 1st edition; number 142 of 450 copies, signed by author; fine in dust jacket and slipcase. Hermitage SP95-638 1996 $150.00

UPDIKE, JOHN 1932-   A Month of Sundays. New York: Alfred A. Knopf 1975. 1/450 copies, signed and numbered, fine in slipcase. Bev Chaney, Jr. 23-734 1996 $125.00

UPDIKE, JOHN 1932-   A Month of Sundays. New York: Knopf, 1975. 1st edition; fine in fine dust jacket and signed by author. Ken Lopez 74-447 1996 $850.00

UPDIKE, JOHN 1932-   Museums and Women and Other Stories. New York: Knopf 1972. 1st edition; fine in fine dust jacket. Sherwood 3-322 1996 $100.00

UPDIKE, JOHN 1932-   The Music School. New York: Knopf, 1966. 1st edition; near fine in dust jacket. Sherwood 3-317 1996 $130.00

UPDIKE, JOHN 1932-   Of the Farm. New York: Knopf, 1965. 1st edition; several small stains to page edges, else fine in very good dust jacket. Sherwood 3-316 1996 $130.00

UPDIKE, JOHN 1932-   Picked-Up Pieces. New York: Knopf, 1975. One of 250 numbered copies, signed by author; fine in dust jacket and fine cardboard slipcase, with just a touch of sunning at extremities. Between the Covers 42-434 1996 $250.00

UPDIKE, JOHN 1932-   Pigeon Feathers and Other Stories. New York: Knopf, 1962. 1st edition; near fine in price clipped dust jacket with tape residue to margins and 1 small chip. Sherwood 3-311 1996 $250.00

UPDIKE, JOHN 1932-   The Poorhouse Fair. New York: Knopf, 1959. 1st edition; few tiny stains on front board, otherwise fine in fine dust jacket, with small bookstore label on rear flap. Sherwood 3-308 1996 $350.00

UPDIKE, JOHN 1932-   The Poorhouse Fair. New York: Alfred A. Knopf, 1959. Author's first novel; some creasing to price clipped dust jacket, which also has small tape repair to verso of front panel on lower edge, otherwise very good. R. A. Gekoski 19-144 1996 £150.00

UPDIKE, JOHN 1932-   Rabbit at Rest. New York: Knopf, 1990. Advance uncorrected proofs; wrappers, fine in fine cardboard slipcase; signed by author. Beasley Books 82-156 1996 $125.00

UPDIKE, JOHN 1932-   Rabbit Redux. New York: Knopf, 1971. 1st edition; near fine in like dust jacket. Sherwood 3-321 1996 $100.00

UPDIKE, JOHN 1932-   Rabbit, Run. New York: Knopf, 1960. 1st edition; 1 corner bumped, else fine in dust jacket, with couple of small chips. Sherwood 3-310 1996 $300.00

UPDIKE, JOHN 1932-   The Same Door. New York: Knopf, 1959. 1st edition; as new in like dust jacket. Sherwood 3-308 196 $375.00

UPDIKE, JOHN 1932-   The Same Door. New York: Knopf, 1959. 1st edition; fine in slightly shortened dust jacket with internally repaired tear and some negligible rubbing. Between the Covers 42-433 1 996 $185.00

UPDIKE, JOHN 1932-   Self Consciousness. New York: Aflred A. Knopf, 1989. 1/350 signed and numbered copies; very fine in slipcase. Bev Chaney, Jr. 23-741 1996 $135.00

UPDIKE, JOHN 1932-   Talk from the Fifties. Northridge: Lord John Press, 1979. 1st edition; limited to 300 copies, signed by author; cloth backed patterned boards; very fine. Bromer Booksellers 87-272 1996 $125.00

UPDIKE, JOHN 1932-   Telephone Poles and Other Poems. New York: Knopf, 1963. 1st edition; couple of dampstains to page edges running to prelims and margins, else very good in price clipped dust jacket. Sherwood 3-313 1996 $100.00

UPDIKE, JOHN 1932-   The Witches of Eastwick. Franklin Center: Franklin Library 1984. One of a limited edition; decorated full leather; fine. Lame Duck Books 19-550 1996 $125.00

UPDIKE, JOHN 1932-   The Witches of Eastwick. New York: Knopf, 1984. 1st edition; limited to 350 copies, signed by author; original decorated slipcase, extremely fine. Bromer Booksellers 87-273 19964 $175.00

UPDIKE, JOHN 1932-   The Young King. New York: Macmillan, 1962. 1st edition; quarto; illustrations by Sandro Nardini and Enrico Bagnoli; laminated paper covered boards, scarce, near fine. Lame Duck Books 19-549 1996 $350.00

UPTON, BERTHA   The Golliwogg's Air-Ship. London: Longmans, Green and Co., 1902. 1st edition; 64 pages; color title vignette, 30 color plates, 26 sepia text illustrations; extra color pictorial boards, small tear in corner of title, bottom of front board very worn. Robin Greer 94A-87 1996 £120.00

URBAN, MARTIN   Emil Nolde: Flowers and Animals, Watercolors and Drawings. London: Thames & Hudson, 1966. Square folio; 46 pages text, 5 color and 12 monochrome plates, 19 color plates; cloth backed boards, acetate dust jacket. Brannan 43-493 1996 $145.00

URE, DAVID   The History of Rutherglen and East-Kilbride. Glasgow: printed by David Niven, 1793. 1st edition; 8vo; pages vi, (ii), 334, (xxii, list of subscribers; uncut, complete with 21 plates, including aquatint, folding plate (often missing), and 11 plates of fossils; title waterstained, few spots and dampstains, original boards, spine little chipped and worn; but very good, unsophisticated copy. R.F.G. Hollett 76-313 1996 £175.00

URE-SMITH, SYDNEY   Adrian Feint: Flower Paintings. Sydney: 1948. Limited to 1500 copies on Georgian paper, signed by artist; 4to; 78 pages; 28 plates, including 12 in color tipped in; 20 decorations in text by artist, 18 of which are printed in color; printed on handmade paper by Waite & Bul of Sydney, in Monotype Baskerville type; cloth, gilt, dust jacket, slightly bumped;   Thomas Thorp 489-307 1996 £60.00

URIS, LEON M.   The Angry Hills. New York: Random House, 1955. 1st edition; slight rubbing to base of spine, still fine in dust jacket, becoming uncommon in this condition.   Between the Covers 42-438 1996 $350.00

URQUHART, B. L.   The Rhododendron. Sharpthorne, 1958-62. Folio; 2 volumes, pages 40; 36; 36 colored plates plus colored endpaper maps; cloth, dust jackets, some soiling, piece missing to corner of dust jacket of volume 1, one and one half inch tear to rear panel of dust jacket from volume 2.   Raymond M. Sutton VII-40 1996 $385.00

UTAMARO, KITAGAWA   Twelve Woodblock Prints of Kitagawa Utamaro Illustrating the Process of Silk Culture. San Francisco: Book Club of California, 1965. Limited to 4t0 copies; tall folio; 12 full page color reproductions from the originals; parchment backed decorated boards, spine lettered in gilt; very fine.   Argonaut Book Shop 113-291 1996 $250.00

UTTLEY, ALISON   Little Grey Rabbit's Party. London: Collins, 1936. Small octavo; 112 pages; 25 color plates; lightly rubbed to covers and two corners bumped, else near fine.   Bromer Booksellers 87-156 1996 $125.00

UZANNE, OCTAVE   French Bookbinders of the Eighteenth Century. Chicago: Caxton club, 1904. One of 252 copies printed at the Lakeside Press; quarto; 133 pages, text illustrations, color plates with printed tissue guards; cloth backed boards, mostly unopened, some foxing, printed spine label etched, upper corners slightly bumped, very good/very good+ overall.   Bohling Book Co. 192-713 1996 $350.00

V

VACCARESCO, HELENE   The Bard of the Dimbovitza Roumanian Folksongs Collected from the Peasants...(with).... Second Series. London: Osgood, McIlvaine & Co., 1892/97/96. 1st editions; 8vo; 2 volumes; pages viii, 130; viii, 146; well printed on thick paper; original green cloth, backstrips decorated in gold with varied design of hearts, flowers and angel wings against stipple ground by Ricketts, uncut.   Claude Cox 107-139   1996 £65.00

VAILLANT, ANNETTE   Bonnard. Greenwich: New York Graphic Society, 1965. Square 4to; 229 pages, 53 tipped in color and 92 monochrome plates, 79 line drawings, 6 in color; cloth, dust jacket. Lucas p. 126; Freitag 859.   Brannan Books 43-71   1996 $140.00

VAKHRAMEEV, V. A.   Jurassic and Cretaceous Floras and Climates of the Earth. London: 1991. Royal 8vo; 334 pages, 45 half tones, 3 tables, 20 text figures; hardback.   Wheldon & Wesley 207-1378   1996 £65.00

VALDEZ, R.   Wild Sheep and Wild Sheep Hunters of the Old World. 1983. Limited to 750 copies only, signed by author; imperial 8vo; colored frontispiece, many other illustrations; near fine in lightly frayed dust jacket.   David Grayling J95Biggame-598   1996 £50.00

VALENTINER, W. R.   Studies of Italian Renaissance Sculpture. London: Phaidon, 1950. 30 x 23 cm; xi, 239 pages; 250 illustrations; original cloth, dust jacket.   Rainsford A54-559   1996 £65.00

VALENTINI, MICHAEL   Novellae Medico-Legales Seu Responsa medico-Forensia. Frankfurt: 1711. 1st edition; 1250 pages, (38) pages; vellum, one quarter by one inch piece clipped from titlepage not affecting text; otherwise very good. GM 1728.   W. Bruce Fye 71-2156   1996 $1,000.00

VALERIUS FLACCUS, GAIUS   Argonautica. Venice: in Aedibus Aldi et Andreae Asulani Soceri... May 1523. 1st and only Aldine edition; 8vo; 148 leaves, Aldine devices on first and last leaves, handsome early 18th century red morocco, exquisitely tooled in gilt, ms. shelf title on bottom edge. Dibdin II 515; Renouard 97.3. Adams V77 UCLA II 192; Brunet V 1045.   Family Album Tillers-629   1996 $1,250.00

VALERIUS MAXIMUS   Valerio Massimo Volgare Novamente Coretto (sic). Venice: Gregorio de Gregorii, 1526. 5th recorded edition in Italian; small 8vo; ff. 215, italic letter, white on black woodcut border to titlepage, also early ms. ownership autographs of (D?) Flaminius Ruffinus & Jesuit College of Reggio(?), white on black woodcut initials; contemporary vellum with modern boards, modern gilt title label; occasional light yellow, rather good. BM STC Ital. p. 708; Aams V125; brunet V 1052.   A. Sokol XXV-98   1996 £395.00

VALERIUS MAXIMUS   Valerius Maximus Nuper Editus Index Copiosissimus Rerum Omnium, et Personarum, de Quibus in His Libris Agitur. Venice: in aedibvs haeredum Aldi, et Andreae Soceri, March 1534. 8vo; 228 leaves, italic, Aldine devices on first and last leaves; old limp vellum; Renouard 110.2. Adams V 104; UCLA IIIa/233; Dibdin II 521. Family Album Tillers-630   1996 $800.00

VALERY, PAUL   Le Cimetiere Marin. Paris: Emile Paul Freres, 1920. 1st edition; one of 556 numbered copies; original wrappers, with outer tissue wrapper, inner hinge loose due to dried glue, else near fine; presentation copy inscribed by author for Roland de Margerie.   19th Century Shop 39-   1996 $1,250.00

VALERY, PAUL   The Graveyard by the Sea. London: Martin Secker & Warburg, 1945. One of 500 copies, signed by C. Day Lewis, translator; wrappers, chemise; excellent.   R. A. Gekoski 19-145   1996 £175.00

VALERY, PAUL   The Graveyard by the Sea. London: Martin Secker & Warburg, 1946. One of 500 numbered copies, signed by translator, C. Day Lewis; printed by Hans Mardersteig at Officina Bodoni, Verona, on paper made by Fratelli Magnani of Pescia; parallel French and English texts; marbled paper covers, spine and cover edges slightly faded, very good, lacks brown card folder; from the library of Ian Parsons of Hogarth Press.   Ulysses 39-372   1996 £225.00

VALLANS, W.   A Tale of Two Swannes... London: Lion and Unicorn Press, 1953. Number 4 of 50 copies printed (not for sale). 8vo; 24 pages; frontispiece and 28 vignette wood engravings printed in green by David Gentleman; original pictorial printed boards with sheet of 3 of Gentleman's engravings laid in; very good, scarce.   Claude Cox 107-90   1996 £85.00

VALMIER, GEORGES   Collection Decors et Couleurs. Paris: Editions Albert Levy, n.d., but c. 1930. Folio; title, 20 finely colored pochoir plates; publisher's decorative portfolio with ties, title label to centre of upper board. Fine.   Sotheran PN32-198   1996 £4,500.00

VALMIN, M. N.   The Swedish Messenia Expedition. Lund: C. W. K. Gleerup, 1938. 4to; xv, 484 pages, 100 figures, 37 plates, 7 plans; original printed boards; very scarce; inscribed presentation copy to Gosta Saflund.   Archaeologia Luxor-4100   1996 $450.00

VALUABLE Secret Concerning Arts and Trades; or Approved Directions from the Best Artists for the Various Methods of Engraving on Brass, Copper, or Steel. London: printed and sold by Will. Hay, Printer and Bookseller to the... 1775. 1st edition; 12mo; contemporary mottled calf, label, nice.   Anthony W. Laywood 108-120   1996 £475.00

VALUABLE Secrets, Concerning Arts and Trades or Approved Directions from the Best Artists... Boston: J. Bumstead, 1798. 2nd edition; 12mo; 264 pages; contemporary calf, leather label, hinges repaired. Evans 34913; Rink 157; Lincoln Lowenstein 31a.   M & S Rare Books 60-449   1996 $850.00

VALUABLE Secrets in Arts and Trades; or, Approved Directions from the Best Artists. London: J. Barker...J. Cattermoul...and J. Parsons, n.d., ca. 1791? 12mo; vi, (2), 351, (1) pages; contemporary half calf, neatly rebacked and repaired, spine lettered in gilt; very good.   John Drury 82-284   1996 £275.00

VALUABLE Secrets in Arts, Trades, &c. Selected from the Best Authors and Adapted to the Situation of the United States. New York: Every Duyckinck, 1809. 1st edition; 16mo; 380, 20 pages; contemporary calf, split in spine repaired; Lincoln Lowenstein 48; Rink 163. S&S 19085. M & S Rare Books 60-450   1996 $650.00

VAN ALEN, W. K.   The Sutro Tunnel In Congress. Explanatory Remarks. N.P.: 1870. 1st edition; (1-3), 4-30, (2) pages; cover title in pagination, sewn as issued, fine. Not in Paher Nevada.   Michael D. Heaston 23-261   1996 $200.00

VAN BAAL, J.   Dema. Description and Analysis of Marind-Anim Culture (South New Guinea). The Hague: 1966. 1st English edition; thick 8vo; (xxviii), 988 pages; 25 plates; red cloth cover, spine sunned, front free endpaper stuck down causing some browning, some pencil marks, otherwise very good.   Antipodean 28-500   1996 $125.00

VAN BOEKEL, GEORGETTE MARIA EUGENIE CORNELIA   Roman Terracotta Figurines and Masks from the Netherlands. Groningen: Rijksuniversiteit te Groningen, 1987. 8vo; vi, 737 pages; profusely illustrated; wrappers.   Archaeologia Luxor-4101   1996 $150.00

VANBRUGH, JOHN   The Provok'd Wife: a Comedy. London: printed for Richard Wellington and William Lewis, 1709. 4to; publisher's ads on verso of half title, some light browning or spotting of text, but very pleasing copy; red morocco gilt, publisher's ads on verso of half title, some light browning or spotting of text, but very pleasing copy. Pforzheimer 1020; Wing V55 Woodward and McManaway 1258 for 1st. ed.   James Cummins 14-218   1996 $200.00

VANBRUGH, JOHN   The Complete Works of Sir John Vanbrugh. London: Nonesuch Press, 1927-28. Limited to 1300 numbered copies; 4to; 4 volumes, 9 plates; quarter buckram, paper labels, edges uncut, spines uniformly faded, but nice, partly unopened set.   Thomas Thorp 489-309   1996 £105.00

VANBRUGH, JOHN   The Complete Works of. Bloomsbury: Nonesuch Press, 1927. One of 1300 sets; post 4to; 4 volumes; spine sunned, otherwise fine set.   Lyman Books 21-444   1996 $125.00

VANBRUGH, JOHN   The Complete Works. London: Nonesuch Press, 1927. 1st edition; number 33 of 110 sets; 4to; printed on handmade paper; 4 volumes, each c. 450 pages, frontispiece and 8 plates in volume 4; bound in vellum backed batik boards, slight superficial flaking to vellum on volume 1, but good set. Meynell Nonesuch Century 49. Claude Cox 107-117   1996 £220.00

VAN BUREN, DOUGLAS E.   Clay Figurines of Babylonia and Assyria. New Haven: Yale University Press, 1930. 8vo; lxx, 288 pages, 68 plates; original cloth, signature.   Archaeologia Luxor-2784 1996 $350.00

VAN BUREN, DOUGLAS E.   Greek Fictile Revetments in the Archaic Period. London: John Murray, 1926. 8vo; xx, 208 pages; 39 plates; original gilt lettered cloth, several corners lightly bumped. Archaeologia Luxor-4102 1996 $150.00

VAN BUREN, MARTIN   Considerations in Favour of the Appointment of Rufus King, to the Senate of the United States. Submitted to the Republican Members of the Legislature of...New York. New York: 1819. 1st edition; 8vo; 32 pages, removed; lower portion of last leaf damaged affecting a few words on recto. S&S 49973; Sabin 98409.   M & S Rare Books 60-425 1996 $250.00

VAN CAPELLEVEEN, PAUL   Prototype. Phoenix Editions, 1991. One of 35 copies; 14 x 7 1/2 inches; (5) leaves of text; title printed in purple and black; original silk, front cover and spine purple, back cover cream colored, fore edge and tail edges untrimmed, in publisher's cream colored paper slipcase; mint.   Phillip J. Pirages 33-417 1996 $300.00

VANCE, ANDREW   The Green Book; or, Reading Made Easy of the Irish Statutes, Containing an Account of the Principal Reported Decisions at Law and in Equity, on the Irish Statues, Rules and Orders of Court, From Magna Charta to the Present Time. Dublin: Joseph White, 1862. Original green cloth, gilt, definitely rubbed, but quite sound.   Meyer Boswell SL25-225 1996 $175.00

VANCE, JACK   Big Planet. U&M, 1978. 1st illustrated edition, 1/111 copies, specially bound and signed by both author and artist; fine in dust jacket.   Aronovitz 57-1211 1996 $175.00

VANCE, JACK   Cadwal II: Ecce and Old Earth. Novato: Underwood/Miller, 1991. 1st edition; one of 26 lettered copies, signed by author; quarter bound in leather, marbled boards, very fine, issued without dust jacket, in slipcase.   Robert Gavora 61-244 1996 $250.00

VANCE, JACK   Cadwal III: Throy. Novato: Underwood-Miller, 1992. 1st edition; one of 26 lettered copies, signed by author; quarter bound in blue leather with marbled boards, very fine, issued without dust jacket, in slipcase.   Robert Gavora 61-246 1996 $250.00

VANCE, JACK   The Faceless Man. The Brave Free Men. The Asutra. San Francisco: Underwood/Miller, 1983. 1st hardcover edition, limited to 1000 sets, this one of 200 sets, each book numbered and signed by author; 3 volumes; all very fine in dust jackets within one slipcase. Robert Gavora 61-251 1996 $175.00

VANCE, JACK   The Five Gold Bands. Novato: Underwood/Miller, 1993. 1st edition; one of 26 lettered copies, signed by author; quarter bound in red leather with marbled covers, very fine, issued without dust jacket, in slipcase.   Robert Gavora 61-252 1996 $250.00

VANCE, JACK   Vandals of the Void. Winston, 1953. 1st edition; signed by author; very good+/near fine copy in bright very good+ dust jacket save for 4 small chips missing from upper margin of the rear dust jacket panel, nice, signed by author.   Aronovitz 57-1210 1996 $190.00

VANCE, JACK   When the Five Moons Rise. San Francisco: Underwood Miller, 1992. 1st edition; one o 26 lettered copies, signed by author; quarter bound in leather with cloth covers, very fine, issued without dust jacket in slipcase.   Robert Gavora 61-265 1996 $250.00

VAN COURT, DEWITT   The Making of Champions in California. Los Angeles: Press of the Premier Printing Co., 1926. 1st edition; small quarto; 160 pages; portraits, photos; brick cloth lettered in gilt on front cover, fine.   Argonaut Book Shop 113-88 1996 $150.00

VANCOUVER, GEORGE   A Voyage of Discovery to the North Pacific Ocean, and Round the World... Amsterdam: N. Isreal, 1967. 26 cmo; 3 volumes and map portfolio; various pagination; plates, maps and charts; gilt stamped cream and blue mock vellum; fine.   Rockland Books 38-232 1996 $325.00

VANDER ELST, JOANNES FRANCISCUS   Prael-Treyn Verrykt Door Ry-Benden, Prael-Wagens Zinne-Beelden en Andere Oppronkingen Toegeschikt Aen Het Duyzend-Jaerig Jubile... Mechelen: J. F. Vander Eslt, 1775. 1st Dutch edition; small folio; half title, title, (viii), 34 (actually 38, numbers 15-18 repeated in pagination), 17 folding plates; contemporary marbled paper wrappers, worn and soiled. Berlin Kat 3168. Lipperheide 2803.   Sotheran PN32-199 1996 £695.00

VAN DER POST, LAURENS   The Heart of the Hunter. London: Hogarth Press, 1961. 1st edition; numerous black and white drawings in text by Maurice Wilson; original binding, edges spotted, spine faded, head of spine nicked, very good in nicked, spotted and slightly rubbed and dusty dust jacket faded at spine. Presentation copy from author.   Ulysses 39-601 1996 £75.00

VAN DOREN, CARL   Benjamin Franklin. New York: Viking Press, 1938. Signed, limited edition, number 359 of 625 copies; 3 volumes; boxed set, blue cloth with red leather labels.   Blue River Books 9-140 1996 $100.00

VAN GIESON, JUDITH   Mercury Retrograde. Huntington Beach: Cahill, 1994. One of 6 uncorrected proof copies of this limited edition; quarter bound in leather and bound in marbled paper over boards; fine.   Ken Lopez 74-451 1996 $150.00

VAN GULIK, ROBERT   The Chinese Bell Murders. Three Cases Solved by Judge Dee. London: Heinemann, 1963. 1st edition; 15 plates drawn by author in Chinese style; fine in dust jacket slightly soiled on rear panel.   Quill & Brush 102-1708 1996 $200.00

VAN GULIK, ROBERT   The Emperor's Pearl. London: Heinemann, 1963. 1st edition; fine with small store sticker on front pastedown, in near fine dust jacket with slight soiling on inside flaps.   Quill & Brush 102-1710 1996 $100.00

VAN GULIK, ROBERT   The Haunted Monastery. New York: Scribners, 1969. 1st edition; 8 illustrations drawn by author in Chinese style, fine in near fine dust jacket with light edge wear and one small closed tear. Quill & Brush 102-1713 1996 $100.00

VAN GULIK, ROBERT   The Chinese Maze Murders. Hague and Bandung: W. Van. Hoeve Ltd., 1956. 1st edition; 19 plates drawn by author in Chinese style; minor bump in head of spine, otherwise fine in dust jacket slightly darkened on spine.   Quill & Brush 102-1707 1996 $400.00

VAN KAMPEN, N. G.   The History and Topography of Holland and Belgium. London: George Virtue, n.d., c. 1837. 8vo; engraved ttile, 61 engraved plates, 1 folding map, iv, 204 pages; contemporary dark green half morocco, spine gilt, gilt edges, most plates lightly spotted as usual, little wear to marbled paper on covers, but very nice.   Thomas Thorp 489-308 1996 £125.00

VAN PEEBLES, MELVIN   The Big Heart. San Francisco: Fearon Pub., 1957. 1st edition; thin quarto; photos; owner name, else fine in very good plus dust jacket with few small chips; signed by Van Peebles and by photographer.   Between the Covers 43-464 1996 $300.00

VAN PELT, GARRETT   Old Architecture of Southern Mexico. Cleveland: J. H. Jansen, 1926. 1st edition; small folio; 125 pages; photos, map; cloth, dust jacket.   The Bookpress 75-248 1996 $165.00

VAN RENSSELAER, MARIANA GRISWOLD 1851-1934   History of the City of New York in the 18th Century. New York: Macmillan, 1909. 1st edition; 2 volumes, xxx, 533, xiv, 640 pages; cloth, very good set. Metacomet Books 54-111 1996 $100.00

VAN RENSSELAER, SOLOMON   A Narrative of the Affair of Queenstown: in the War of 1812. New York: Leavitt Lord, 1836. 8vo; pages viii, 9-41, 2, 95, 22 ads; folding map; original cloth, paper label. Howes V40; Sabin 98548.   Richard Adelson W94/95-172 1996 $200.00

VAN ROYEN, P.   The Orchids of the High Mountains of New Guinea. London: 1980. 8vo; pages 784, text figures and 8 plates; cloth. Wheldon & Wesley 207-1813 1996 £86.00

VAN ROYEN, P.   The Orchids of the High Moutains of New Guinea. Vaduz: 1980. 8vo; pages vi, (51-) 834; 9 plates, 238 text figures; hardbound, light soiling and spotting.   Raymond M. Sutton VI-970 1996 $125.00

VAN SICHEM, CHRISTOFFEL   Bibels Tresor, Ofte dere Ziellen Lusthof, Vytgebeelt in Figueren, Door Verschyeden Meesters. Amsterdam: P. I. Paets, 1646. 1st edition; large thick 8vo; 740 woodcuts; contemporary vellum, little soiled and with some superficial scratches, with burgundy morocco title label added to spine, final blank lacking, very clean, handsome copy, scarce.   Book Block 32-70 1996 $2,750.00

VAN SOMEREN, G. R. C.   Van Somerens' Birds. Volume 2. London: 1994. 4to; 144 pages, 56 fine colored plates and other illustrations; full morocco, gilt edges.   Wheldon & Wesley 207-113 1996 £700.00

VAN SOMEREN, V. G. L.   The Birds of East Africa. Volume I. Ploceidae. London: 1973. Limited to 1000 copies; 4to; colored portrait, 93 colored plates, each with leaf of text; full blue morocco.   Wheldon & Wesley 207-885 1996 £10.00

VAN URK, J. BLAN   The Story of American Foxhunting. New York: Derrydale, 1940/41. Limited to 950 copies; 2 volumes; original binding, spines slightly faded, as is top edge of cover of volume 1, still very good in original glassine dust jackets; volume 1 is signed presentation copy, laid in signed Christmas card from author and ALS, volume 2 is signed.   October Farm 36-225 1996 $595.00

VAN URK, J. BLAN   The Story of Rolling Rock. New York: Scribner 1950. Limited to 750 copies; 4to; original binding, very good.   October Farm 36-226 1996 $295.00

VAN VECHTEN, CARL 1880-1964   Spider Boy: a Scenario for a Moving Picture. New York: Alfred A. Knopf, 1928. 1st edition; fine in beautiful, bright dust jacket.   Left Bank Books 2-146 1996 $150.00

VAN VOGT, A. E.   Masters of Time. Fantasy Press, 1950. 1st edition; 1/500 copies of plated edition signed by author; very good+ in near fine dust jacket.   Aronovitz 57-1207 1996 $125.00

VAN VOGT, A. E.   The Voyage of the Space Beagle. S&S, 1950. 1st edition; signed by author; fine in near fine dust jacket, save for light soiling to rear dust jacket panel.   Aronovitz 57-1208 1996 $110.00

VAN VOGT, A. E.   The Weapon Makers. Hadley, 1947. 1st edition; near fine in very good+ dust jacket save for some light soiling, signed by author.   Aronovitz 57-1206 1996 $135.00

VAN VOGT, A. E.   The Weapon Makers. Providence: Hadley, 1947. 1st edition; fine in dust jacket with half inch closed tear and hint of loss to head of spine panel.   Robert Gavora 61-243 1996 $135.00

VARCHI, BENEDETTO   De Sonetti...Parte Prima (and) Parte Secunda. Florence: Lorenzo Torrentino, 1555-57. 1st edition; 8vo; 2 volumes bound in 1; (8) leaves, 272, (24) pages; 224, (30) pages, (leaf ff2 is blank); woodcut Medici arms on titlepages, some minor handsoiling and stains; early vellum. Rare. Adams V258 & V259; Gamba 1016; Brunet V 1086.   Jeffrey Mancevice 20-86 1996 $800.00

VARDY, JOHN   Some Designs of Mr. Inigo Jones and Mr. William Kent. London: the author, 1744. 1st edition; folio; (vi) pages, 53 plates; contemporary mottled calf, rebacked, cloth clamshell box; binding appropriately rebacked and gold tooled, red morocco spine label, bookplates, else very clean, scarce.   The Bookpress 75-250 1996 $4,950.00

VAREKAMP, MARJOLEIN   Francesco. Groningen: La Stampa Chiara, 1987. One of 45 numbered copies, signed by author/artist; 4to; printed on Lana in handset Garamond with De Roos Open Kapitalen in black, red and blue; stiff wrappers, folding map laid in; fine in decorative slipcase.   Bertram Rota 272-440 1996 £120.00

VARGAS LLOSA, MARIO   The Real Life of Alejandro Mayta. New York: Farrar, Straus & Giroux, 1986. 1st American edition, number 72 of 175 copies signed by author; fine in slipcase.   Hermitage SP95-644 1996 $225.00

VARILLAS, ANTOINE 1624-1696   (Anekdota Eterouiaka (Greek Characters) or, the Secret History of the House of Medicis... London: printed for R.E. for R. Bentley and S. Magnes, 1686. 1st English edition; 8vo; pages (lxxviii), 470; title printed within double border, contemporary speckled calf, expertly rebacked to match, backstrip with low raised bands, gilt lettered red morocco label, hinges cracked but firm, mottled edges, excellent; early owner's name (Jno Eyre), "John Eyre His Booke 1694' on binder's prelim blank. Wing V111b.   Blackwell's B112-276 1996 £300.00

VARIOUS Methods to Prevent Fires in Houses and Shipping and for Preserving...Lives...an Account of Remarkable Accidents by Fire... London: printed and sold by T. Evans, 1775. 8vo; pages xii (including half title), 81, 1 leaf ad of 'J. Southern, Stataioner'; recent boards.   Peter Murray Hill 185-62 1996 £185.00

VARLEY, JOHN   Blue Champagne. Niles: Dark Harvest, 1986. 1st edition; one of 300 numbered copies, signed by author and artist; illustrations by Todd Cameron Hamilton; very fine in dust jacket with slipcase.   Robert Gavora 61-266 1996 $125.00

VARLEY, JOHN   The Gaean Trilogy, Being Titan, Wizard and demon. Putnam, 1979/80/84. 1st editions; fine in dust jackets.   Aronovitz 57-1217 1996 $175.00

VARLO, CHARLES   Nature Display'd a New Work. London: printed for the Editor, 1793. 3rd edition; 8vo; (iv), xii, (13)-320 pages; original tree calf, rebacked, original spine label and endpapers preserved.   David Bickersteth 133-87 1996 £185.00

VARRO, MARCUS TERENTIUS   Opera Quae Supersunt...De Re Rustica. Geneva: Henri Stephanus, 15181. 3rd Estienne edition; small 8vo; 5 parts in one volume, pages 143; 255, (76); 48; 129, (14); 77 + blanks, Estienne pritners device (12) on title; remains of old leather binding; engraved armorial bookplate of William Markham, Becca Lodge, Yorkshire. Schreiber 207; Renouard 148.2. Schweiger II 1116.   Family Album Tillers-631 1996 $450.00

VASARI, GIORGIO   Lives of the Most Eminent Painters. Limited Editions Club, 1966. One of 1500 numbered copies, signed by Mardersteig; small folio; 2 volumes; 45 woodcut portraits; cloth, fine in dust jackets and slipcase, bookplate.   Bertram Rota 272-443 1996 £150.00

VASARI, GIORGIO   Lives of the Most Eminent Painters. Verona: Limited Editions Club, 1966. Limited to 1500 copies; small folio; signed by printer, Giovanni Mardersteig; reproductions by the masters and woodcuts by the author and Fritz Kredel; original binding; fine in dust jacket and slipcase.   Charles Agvent 4-1155 1996 $250.00

VASEY, G.   Grasses of the Pacific Slope... Washington: 1890-91. 4to; 2 parts; pages viii, 100 plates; original cloth, worn at extremities, shaken, library stamps on prelim ppages, pages tanned.   Raymond M. Sutton VI-641 1996 $135.00

VASSE, A.   Souvenir de Beloeil, Dedie a Son Altesse Serenissime La Princesse de Ligne, nee Princesse Lubomirska. Brussels: Deltombe, 1853. Limited to 150 copies; oblong folio; 4ff., 17 pages, all with borders, 12 litho plates, all tinted except 1 in black and white; new cloth, roan spine, slipcase, original litho front wrapper (partly in facsimile) bound in. De Ganay 249.   Marlborough 162-262 1996 £900.00

VASSOS, RUTH   Humanities. New York: Dutton, 1935. 1st edition; 4to; 104 pages; illustrations by John Vassos; original aquamarine cloth; very good in dust jacket with couple of closed tears.   Chapel Hill 94-94 1996 $100.00

VATABLUS, FRANCISCUS   In Hoc Opere Continentvr Totivs Philosophiae Naturalis Paraphrases. Paris: Widow of Petit, 1533. Folio; title within fine Petit woodcut border, woodcut initials, woodcut diagrams in text, Petit device at end; calf; perforated ownership of Forbes Lib., Northampton Mass. on titlepage.   Rostenberg & Stern 150-100 1996 $1,250.00

VAUGHAN, BENJAMIN   Letters on the Subject of the Concert of Princes, and the Dismemberment of Poland and France. London: printed for G. G. and J. J. Robinson, 1793. 1st edition; 8vo; pages (8), lx, 231, 23; uncut; original boards, very fine.   Howard S. Mott 227-143 1996 $450.00

VAUGHAN, HENRY   Silex Scintillans, &c. Scared Poems and Pious Ejaculations... London: Bell and Daldy, 1858. 8vo; pages xlviii, 247, (i), engraved titlepage; contemporary black hard grain morocco, triple rules in blind, gilt lettered direct, gilt inner dentelles, gilt edges, autograph inscription of Robert Bridges to Gerard Manley Hopkins on initial blank, head and tail of spine and corners little worn, small tear in half title not affecting text, internally clean, good, attractive edtiion;   Simon Finch 24-252 1996 £1,850.00

VAUGHAN, JOHN   The Reports and Arguments of that Learned Judge Sir John Vaughan Kt. Late Chief Justice of His Majesties Court of Common Pleas. London: printed by Thomas Roycroft for Richard Marriott, etc., 1677. contemporary calf, rebacked, some leaves repaired and backed, sound.   Meyer Boswell SL25-227 1996 $350.00

VAUGHAN, SALLIE WERNER   Illusion of Two. Houston: Crystal Press, 1981. One of 40 copies only; page size 11 x 3 1/2 inches; printed on moulin du verger and moulin du verger china paper, each signed by author/artist; each copy handpainted by the artist; type is 14 pt. garamond by J. Brejoux who also made the paper; bound accordion fold laid into publisher's wrappers and slipcase;   Priscilla Juvelis 95/1-73 1996 $350.00

VAUGHAN, SALLIE WERNER   Seeds of Snow. Houston: Crystal Press, 1981. One of 100 copies, 50 hand colored by artist and 50 with engravings uncolored; each engraving hand numbered and initialled by the artist; page size 9 1/2 x 6 1/4 inches; paper handmade by Roger Powell; sewn into folding boards, closed with silk ribbon tie.   Priscilla Juvelis 95/1-74 1996 $600.00

VAURIE, C.   The Birds of the Palaearacitc Fauna. London: 1959-65. Crown 4to; 2 volumes; cloth, dust jackets, presentation copy, inscribed on half titles by author and 2 ALS's from him to his publisher loosely inserted.   Wheldon & Wesley 207-886 1996 £275.00

VAURIE, C.   Tibet and Its Birds. London: 1972. Limited to 65 copies, signed by author; Royal 8vo; pages xv, 407, frontispiece, map, 3 colored plates, 23 photos; half red morocco by Sangorski & Sutcliffe; nice copy. Wheldon & Wesley 207-887 1996 £180.00

VAUX, CALVERT   Villas and Cottages. A Series of Designs Prepared for Execution in the United States. New York: Harper & Bros., 1857. 8vo; frontispiece, (vi), 318 pages, 1 color plates; publisher's cloth, signature in pencil on front free endpaper, covers sunned, light edge wear, front hinge internally cracked, minor marginal spotting.   Bookpress 75-132 1996 $285.00

VAUX, ROBERTS   Memoirs of the Life of Anthony Benezet... Philadelphia: printed: York: reprinted...for W. Alexander, & sold by him, also by... 1817. Sole English edition; 12mo; pages (ii), 156; frontispiece, titlepage browned, unpressed; original boards, dulled and dusty, joints and printed paper label worn, edges rubbed, still very good. Blackwell's B112-31 1996 £95.00

VAVILOV, N. I.   Origin and Geography of Cultivated Plants. London: 1992. 8vo; 570 pages; 33 plates, 28 text figures; hardback.   Wheldon & Wesley 207-1457 1996 $75.00

VEEN, JAN VAN DER   Zinne-Beelden, oft Adams Appel...Mitsgagders Sijne en Nieuwe Ongemeene Bruylofs Zege-Zangen, Raetselen...Sijn Gulden en Yseren Eeuw... Amsterdam: J. J. Bouman, 1659. 1st edition; 8vo; (12) leaves (last blank), 456 pages, (3) leaves, 138 pages, engraving on titlepage and 50 half page engraved embelms in text, possibly by S. Savry; minor paper flaw in one leaf, without loss, few leaves lightly foxed, faint stain on few leaves and some traces of use; contemporary vellum; generally very good. Landwehr 845; Praz 523; Scheurleer 156.   Jeffrey Mancevice 20-87 1996 $875.00

VEITCH, J. H.   Hortus Vitchii: a History of the Rise and Progress of the Nurseries... London: 1906. Imperial 8vo; 542 pages; 50 plates; original cloth, good copy, with dust jacket.   Wheldon & Wesley 207-1758 1996 £190.00

VEITCH, JOHN   The Feeling for Nature in Scottish Poetry. London: William Blackwood and Sons, 1887. 1st edition; 8vo; 2 volumes, pages 353, 369; original cloth, gilt, spines rather darkened, trifle worn at head and tail, small labels at base, ex-library, armorial bookplate, few marginal blindstamps, but very good set, scarce.   R.F.G. Hollett 76-314 1996 £85.00

VENABLES, R.   The Experienced Angler. London: 1827. 2nd issue by Thomas Gosden; large paper copy, 19.25 x 12cm; original frontispiece and title in facsimile, fine text engravings on India paper; original half morocco, silk marker, light rubbing and bumping to corners; nice. David A.H. Grayling 3/95-618 1996 £175.00

VENERONI, GIOVANNI   The Italian Master; or, The Easiest and Best method for Attaining that Language. London: printed for J. Walthoe, R. Wilkin &c., 1729. 2nd edition; contemporary dark brown calf, gilt borders, spine rubbed, with slight split in leading hinge and small scars on following hinge; good, sound copy.   Jarndyce 103-353 1996 £110.00

VENESS, W. T.   El Dorado; or, British Guiana as a Field for Colonisation. London: Cassell, Petter & Galpin, 1867. 1st edition; 8vo; half title, sketch map, colored in outline and folding map; original crimson cloth, upper cover little marked. Not listed by Sabin.   Charles W. Traylen 117-424 1996 £130.00

VENUS Oceanica. New York: privately printed by the Oceanica Research Press, 1935. Limited to 925 copies; 412 pages; many illustrations; pictorial paper boards gilt spine, very good.   Antipodean 28-509 1996 $185.00

VERDICT of 13 a Detection Club Anthology. London: Faber, 1979. fine in pricce clipped dust jackets with light edge wear; signed by Dick Francis and P. D. James.   Quill & Brush 102-27 1996 $100.00

VERGANI, ANGELO   The Beauties of English Poetry, or a Collection of Poems Extracted from the Best Authors. Paris: printed for the Editor, 1803. 2nd edition; 12mo; vignette titlepage; contemporary French calf, spine richly gilt, morocco label; early bookstamps of the College des Sciences et Arts, otherwise very good, attractive. scarce.   Trebizond 39-44 1996 $180.00

VERGILIUS MARO, PUBLIUS 70-19 BC   L'Eneide Fidelement Traduite en Vers Francois: Parts I and II. Paris: Estienne Loyson, 1658. 4to; engraved title by Abraham Bosse, 6 additional half page plates, foldout map; newly bound in retrospective acid calf with triple blind borders on the covers, spine with five raised bands and period gilt tooling in all compartments save for the one with the title label, board edges gilt, marbled endleaves. Lessing Rosenwald Coll. 1393; STC V 492.   Book Block 32-69 1996 $2,650.00

VERGILIUS MARO, PUBLIUS 70-19 BC   The Aeneid of Virgil. Boston & New York: Houghton Mifflin, 1906. 1st edition thus, number 301 of 650 large paper copies; 4to; 2 volumes, xvi, 266; original full dark blue publisher's morocco with triple gilt fillet and gilt tooled rectangular panel on covers, gilt tooled spine with 6 compartments, turn-ins with triple gilt fillet, top edges gilt; beautiful set in fine condition.   Chapel Hill 94-119 1996 $250.00

VERGILIUS MARO, PUBLIUS 70-19 BC   The Aeneid. New York: Limited Edtiions Club, 1944. One of 1100 numbered copies, signed by artist; illustrations by Carlotta Petrina; small tasteful bookplate, else fine in tissue jacket and publisher's drop lid box.   Hermitage SP95-1047 1996 $125.00

VERGILIUS MARO, PUBLIUS 70-19 BC   Bucolica, Georgica, et Aneis. Edinburgh: Apud G. Hamilton & J. Balfour, 1743. Small 12mo; pages 335, 19; contemporary Scottish full red leather gilt, all edges gilt, ms. ownership of Henry John Caulfield, 1856; Brunet V 1291; Dibdin II 552. Family Album Tillers-640 1996 $230.00

VERGILIUS MARO, PUBLIUS 70-19 BC   Bucolica, Georgica, et Aeneis. Birmingham: Baskerville, 1757. 2nd Baskerville edition; 4to; pages (10), 432, with some slight variations from Gaskell in points and paper; all edges gilt, elegant full purple straight grained morocco, tooled in gilt and blind, boards with wide anthemion and palmette roll border, with corners of floral design on studded ground;   Family Album Tillers-644 1996 $1,650.00

VERGILIUS MARO, PUBLIUS 70-19 BC   Bucolica, Georgica, et Aeneis. Birmingham: Baskerville, 1757. 2nd Baskerville edition; 4to; pages (10), 432; full leather binding slightly broken at joints; Gaskell 2.   Family Album Tillers-645 1996 $1,000.00

VERGILIUS MARO, PUBLIUS 70-19 BC   Bucolica, Georgica, et Aeneis. Birmingham; Baskerville, 1757. 1st Baskerville edition; 4to; pages (10), 432, apparently with usual cancels; contemporary full calf, gilt, joints broken; Dibdin II 554-8; Brunet V 1292-3.   Family Album Tillers-643 1996 $2,000.00

VERGILIUS MARO, PUBLIUS 70-19 BC   Bucolica, Georgica et Aeneis. Birmingham: Baskerville, 1766. 8vo; pages (2), 388 (with all Cancellans), engraved frontispiece; all edges gilt, foxed, early full red crushed morocco, spine abundantly tooled in floral gilt, ex-libris of Douglass Maxwell Moffat. Gaskell 34.   Family Album Tillers-646 1996 $600.00

VERGILIUS MARO, PUBLIUS 70-19 BC   Bucolica et Georgica... London: John and Robert Pine, 1774. Tall 8vo; pages 15, 144, 3, numerous full page and folding engraved plates, engraved vignettes, culs-de-lampe, etc.; all edges gilt, very fine contemporary English crimson straight grained morocco, covers tooled with gilt palmetto dentelles, spine elaborately decorated; Hugh Walpole's with his leather bookplate. Dibdin II p. 561.   Family Album Tillers-647 1996 $550.00

VERGILIUS MARO, PUBLIUS 70-19 BC   Bucolica et Georgica... London: John and Robert Pine, 1774. Tall 8vo; illustrations, engraved full page and folding plates, vignettes, culs-de-lamp and other devices, old polished calf.   Family Album Tillers-648 1996 $400.00

VERGILIUS MARO, PUBLIUS 70-19 BC   Bucolica, Georgica, et Aeneis. Glasgow: Foulis, 1778. Large paper copy; folio; 2 volumes in one, pages 277; 308, subscription list; contemporary full leather, gilt arms of City of Edinburgh, elaborately gilt spine, front board detached; engraved armorial bookplate of John Wilkes (1727-1797). Gaskell 639.   Family Album Tillers-649 1996 $750.00

VERGILIUS MARO, PUBLIUS 70-19 BC   Bucolica, Georgica, et Aeneis. Glasgow: Foulis, 1778. Folio; 2 volumes, pages 277; 308, subscription list; full morocco, nicely decorated in gilt with interlocked square cornered double rule designs, wide floral gilt inner dentelles, engraved ex-libris of Hon. Joshua Maddox Wallace of Burlington, N.J. Gaskell 639. Family Album Tillers-650 1996 $650.00

VERGILIUS MARO, PUBLIUS 70-19 BC   Bucolica, Georgica, et Aeneis. Paris: Petrus Didot 'natu major', 1798. Number 190 of a edition of 251 large paper copies, signed by Didot; large folio; pages (11), 572, + 23 magnificent engraved plates, uncut, deckle edged; contemporary leather boards, spine weak. Ray, French Illus. Book 70; Cohen 514; Cohen de Ricci 1019.   Family Album Tillers-653 1996 $2,400.00

VERGILIUS MARO, PUBLIUS 70-19 BC   Bucolica, Georgica, et Aeneis. London: A. Dulau, 1800. Imperial 8vo. in 4's; pages (iv), 246; (iv), 276; 2 volumes, half titles; 15 engravings, text uniformly slightly browned, some faint foxing; contemporary straight grain red morocco in Greek revival style, backstrips darkened, rubbing to extremities, smooth backstrips divided by gilt rope rolls between rules, lettered direct in second and third compartments, single ornament in centre of remainder, sides with Greek-key and narrow flower and bolt rolls, zig-zag roll on board edges, Greek-key roll on turn-ins and morocco hinges, chalked green doublure and free endpapers, latter stained in gutter margins by hinges, broad pink silk markers, gilt edges; good. Dibdin p. 564; Ebert 23737. Blackwell's B112-277 1996 £185.00

VERGILIUS MARO, PUBLIUS 70-19 BC   Bucolica, Georgica, et Aeneis. London: Typis C. Corrall for William Pickering, 1821. 48mo. (in 8); 283 pages; engraved title and frontispiece (by Grave) + Ad for future miniature classics and corrigenda; crisp copy, full contemporary English pebbled morocco, gilt dentelles, all edges gilt, Keynes p. 63 and 93. Family Album Tillers-655 1996 $260.00

VERGILIUS MARO, PUBLIUS 70-19 BC   An English Version of the Eclogues of Virgil. London: Seeley & Co., 1883. 1st printing of this edition; 13 x 9 inches; xv, 102 pages; 14 distinctive etchings by Samuel and Herbert Palmer, half title and title printed in red and black, printed on fine paper, with untrimmed edges; original green cloth, gilt vignette on front cover, gilt titling on front cover and spine, small snag in cloth at top of front joint, hinges partly cracked, but nothing loose, free endpapers slightly browned, otherwise quite fine, text and binding remarkably clean.   Phillip J. Pirages 33-411 1996 $1,350.00

VERGILIUS MARO, PUBLIUS 70-19 BC   Les Eclogues. Cranach Press, 1926. One of 250 copies, of a total edition of 292; 13 1/2 x 10 1/2 inches; 106 pages, (1) leaf (colophon); many woodcut illustrations by Aristide Maillol; untrimmed and unbound, laid into original printed paper wrappers and contained in publisher's vellum backed board portfolio, cloth ties; portfolio little worn and bit smudged, couple of minor creases in printed wrapper, very few small faint spots in text, otherwise extremely fine, very fresh internally.   Phillip J. Pirages 33-145 1996 $5,000.00

VERGILIUS MARO, PUBLIUS 70-19 BC   Les Eclogues de Virgile. Weimar: Cranach Press, 1926. One of 250 copies of the French edition; 4to; printed on specially hand made paper on the Cranach Press hand press; titlepage and initial letters designed and cut by Eric Gill and ornamented by Maillol and 43 woodcuts by Aristide Maillol; loose signatures laid in stiff tan pictorial wrappers, enclosed in folding case of vellum backed boards with ties, lettered in red, fine. From Manet to Hockney 30; Artist and the Book 172.   Marilyn Braiterman 15-137 1996 $4,000.00

VERGILIUS MARO, PUBLIUS 70-19 BC   The Eclogues. New York: Limited Editions Club, 1960. Limited to 1500 copies, signed by artist; 4to; illustrations by Marcel Vertes; three quarter gold toned Shiki silk, fine in near fine slipcase.   Charles Agvent 4-1159 1996 $100.00

VERGILIUS MARO, PUBLIUS 70-19 BC   The Eclogues of Virgil. New York: Limited Editions Club, 1960. Limited to 1500 copies, signed by artist; 4to; xxvii, 96 pages; numerous color illustrations by Vertes; illustrated Shiki silk with cloth spine, housed in publisher's slipcase slightly soiled, else fine; bookplate;   Andrew Cahan 47-113 1996 $100.00

VERGILIUS MARO, PUBLIUS 70-19 BC   Georgica/Les Georgiques. Paris: Philippe Gonin, 1937-43-50. One of 750 copies; 13 x 9 1/2 inches; printed on luxurious thick textured paper made by artist; French and Latin texts on facing pages; 2 volumes; 122 woodcut tailpieces, marginal vignettes & large illustrations by Aristide Maillol; untrimmed and unbound folded signatures laid into fine textured printed wrappers, forming a volume that is contained in publisher's original vellum backed board chemises (spines titled in black), chemises each in a publisher's slipcase, the whole assemblage as issued; aside from some trivial soiling on vellum spines, a virtually pristine copy, with none of the foxing that is normally present in this book. Rauch 144; Artist and the Book 175.   Phillip J. Pirages 33-373 1996 $2,750.00

VERGILIUS MARO, PUBLIUS 70-19 BC   The Georgics. Verona: Limited Editions Club, 1952. Limited to 1500 copies; signed by artist, Bruno Bramanti and by designer, Giovanni Mardersteig; large 4to; wood engravings; original cloth, fine in like slipcase.   Charles Agvent 4-1160 1996 $135.00

VERGILIUS MARO, PUBLIUS 70-19 BC   The Works of Virgil. London: J. Brotherton, et al, 1731. 1st edition of this translation; 12mo; 3 volumes, 240, 420, 430 pages; frontispieces; contemporary full calf with gilt tooled borders and spine panels, spines little worn, covers little abraded, else handsome set.   Chapel Hill 94-162 1996 $300.00

VERGILIUS MARO, PUBLIUS 70-19 BC   The Works of Virgil. London: printed for J. Brotherton, J. Hazard, W. Meadows, T. Cox, ... 1735. 2nd edition; 12mo; 3 volumes; frontispiece in each volume; contemporary calf, gilt, spines elaborately gilt, bit rubbed, but quite sound; attractive set, scarce. Foxon p. 818; CBEL II 571 and 1502.   Ximenes 109-294 1996 $200.00

VERGILIUS MARO, PUBLIUS 70-19 BC   Opera. Amsterdam: Wetstenil, 1746. Large 4to; 4 volumes, pages (32), (82), 520; 706; 707; 360, (92), engraved frontispiece, vignettes, maps, etc., title in red and black, one of the few copies that were struck off on large paper; brilliant full red straight grained morocco Syston Park binding, all edges gilt, engraved ex-libris of Thorold's Syston Park Library. Dibdin II 552-3; Brunet V 1292. Family Album Tillers-641 1996 $2,000.00

VERGILIUS MARO, PUBLIUS 70-19 BC   Opera. Parma: Typis Bodonianis, 1793. Probably one of only 25 fine large paper copies, of a total edition that numbered less than 200; folio; pages 7, 340; 296; 41 + blanks; uncut and deckle edged; full red morocco gilt, boards stamped in gilt with the crowned cypher of Marie Louise, Empress Consort of Napoleon I and edged with gilt palmetto roll, one corner slightly chewed, fine large paper. Blumenthal Art of Ptd. Book p. 27; Brooks 486; Dibdin II 562.   Family Album Tillers-652 1996 $8,000.00

VERGILIUS MARO, PUBLIUS 70-19 BC   Opera Omnia... London: A. J. Valpy, 1819. 8vo; 9 volumes; full brown morocco with raised bands, bookplates in all volumes, extremities rubbed and some wear to covers, else very good, complete set. Handsome set.   Chapel Hill 94-163 1996 $375.00

VERGILIUS MARO, PUBLIUS 70-19 BC   The Works of Virgil. New York: 1823. 3rd American edition; 8vo; pages 956), 353; 478; original full mottled leather (roan), boards detached; AI 14772.   Family Album Tillers-656 1996 $100.00

VERGILIUS, POLYDORUS 1470-1555   Les Memoires et Histoire de l'Origine, Invention & Autheurs des Choses. Paris: Chez Robert le Mangnier, 1582. Small 8vo; pages (11), 863, (84); late full leather, rebacked and worn, early ms. ownerships. Brunet V 1137. Graesse VI 283.   Family Album Tillers-634 1996 $300.00

VERINO, UGOLINO 1438-1516   Vita di Santa Chiara Vergine. Arundel Press, 1921. One of 236 copies; 8vo; printed in Subiaco type in black and red, with some initials in blue, on handmade paper; silk ties, limp vellum; fine, preserved in cloth folder.   Bertram Rota 272-16 1996 £450.00

VERITY, FRANK T.   Flats, Urban Houses and Cottage Homes. London: Hodder & Stoughton, 1906. 1st edition; 4to; frontispiece, 160, (16) pages, 18 color plates; cloth, text lightly foxed, binding worn. The Bookpress 75-251 1996 $175.00

VERLARDE, PABLITA   Old Father. The Story Teller. Globe: Dale Stuart King, 1960. 1st edition; one of 400 copies, signed by author; color illustrations; original cloth, decorated slipcase shows minor shelf wear; fine.   Ken Sanders 8-285 1996 $150.00

VERLET, PIERRE   The James A. de Rothschild Collection at Waddesdon Manor: the Savonnerie, its History - The Waddlesdon Collection. Fribourg: for the national Trust by Office du Livre, 1982. Larg 4to; 220 illustrations, several in color; fine with dust jacket.   Petersfiel Bookshop FH58-19 1996 £60.00

VERMEULE, CORNELIUS C.   Roman Imperial Art in Greece and Asia Minor. Cambridge: Harvard University Press, 1968. 4to; xxiv, 548 pages; 184 figures and 3 plans; original cloth, dust jacket.   Archaeologia Luxor-4116   1996 $125.00

VERMEULE, EMILY D. T.   Toumba tou Skourou: a Bronze Age Potters' Quarter on Morphou Bay in Cyprus. Cambridge: Harvard University Press, 1990. 4to; frontispiece, xxxix, 442 pages; 46 figures, 11 illustrations, 183 plates, 2 plans; original cloth.   Archaeologia Luxor-4119   1996 $100.00

VERNE, JULES 1828-1905   From the Earth to the Moon and Around the Moon. New York: Limited Editions Club, 1970. Copy number 417 of 1500 signed by artist; 2 volumes; illustrations by Robert Shore; fine in publisher's slipcase.   Hermitage SP95-1046   1996 $135.00

VERNE, JULES 1828-1905   The Mysterious Island. New York: Heritage Press, 1959. 1st edition thus; small 4to; three quarter gilt stamped morocco over red cloth by Bayntun, spine with raised bands and gilt stamped devices within gilt ruled compartments, covers ruled in gilt, marbled endpapers, very good to fine.   George J. Houle 68-146   1996 $225.00

VERNE, JULES 1828-1905   A Voyage Around the World - South America. London: Routledge and Sons, 1876. 1st British edition; bright, very good.   Aronovitz 57-1218   1996 $235.00

VERNON, EDWARD   A Specimen of Naked Truth, from a British Sailor. London: W. Webb, 1746. 1st edition; 8vo; 30 pages; original half calf, marbled boards, hinges tender, very good.   John Lewcock 30-133   1996 £65.00

VERNON, EDWARD JOHNSTON   A Guide to the Anglo-Saxon Tongue: a Grammar... London: J. R. Smith, 1846. Errata leaf, 28 pages ads; original dark green cloth, fine.   Jarndyce 103-354   1996 £50.00

VERNON-HARCOURT, LEVESON FRANCIS   Rivers and Canals. The Flow, Control and Improvement of Rivers and the Design, Construction and Development of Canals Both for Navigation and Irrigation. Oxford: Clarendon Press, 1896. 2nd edition; 13 folding color plates and 14 woodcut in text, half titles; original coarse green cloth, gilt spines. Charles W. Traylen 117-353   1996 £160.00

VERPLANCK, GULIAN C.   The Influence of Moral Causes Upon Opinion, Science and Literature. (with) The Right Moral Infuence and Use of Liberal Studies. (with) Discourses and Addresses. New York: Harpers & Bros. and J. & J. Harper, 1834/33/33. 1st editions of all 3 works; full polished calf, spine attractively gilt, slightly rubbed and bit worn, but very good; contemporary ink ownership on first blank and scattered foxing to titles, else very good, clean copies, very slightly trimmed. Hermitage SP95-1071   1996 $250.00

VERRALL, G. H.   British Flies. Volume 8: Platypezidae, Pipunculidae and Syrphidae. London: 1901. Royal 8vo; pages 691, 121, portrait, 458 text figures; half red morocco, neat; very rare, fine.   Wheldon & Wesley 207-1125   1996 £100.00

VERSAILLES Illustrated, or Divers Views of the Several Parts of the Royal Palace... London: printed & sold by John Bowles at the Black Horse in Cornhill, n.d. c. 1740. Oblong folio; engraved title, 28 plates; new half calf, title stained, persistent foxing in margins. rare.   Marlborough 162-222   1996 £1,750.00

VERVE: an Artistic and Literary Quarterly. Paris: Dec. 1937. 4to; Volume 1, #1, this is the issue in English, with foil seal on titlepage and tipped in card advertising subscriptions to magazine; multi colored pictorial wrappers, just very mild soil, minimal wear; nice copy.   Magnum Opus 44-112   1996 $165.00

THE VERY Remarkable Trial of John Holloway, and Owen Haggerty...Guilty...of the Wilful Murder of Mr. J. C. Steele...to Which is added the Trial of Elizabeth Godfrey for the Murder of Richard Prince etc. London: pub. by R. Macdonald, 1807? Somewhat dusty and embrowned in attractive modern quarter morocco..   Meyer Boswell SL27-230   1996 $175.00

VERY, JONES   Essays and Poems. Boston: Charles C. Little and James Brown, 1839. 1st edition; 12mo; 7, (1), 175 pages; original cloth, faded, paper label rubbed, bottom of spine chipped, title foxed. Inscribed by author. BAL 20763 binding B & BAL 5188; Rinderknecht 59036.   M & S Rare Books 60-256   1996 $750.00

VERY, JONES   Essays and Poems. Boston: Little & Brown, 1839. 1st edition; original brown cloth, label; botom two inches gone, label chipped, else very good, solid copy, lightly foxed as always, tight with strong hinges; BAL 5188; Myerson F2.   Mac Donnell 12-145   1996 $125.00

VERY, LYDIA L. A.   Poems. Andover: W. F. Draper, 1856. 1st edition; 12mo; 222 pages; original cloth, spine darkened and rubbed. Inscribed by author.   M & S Rare Books 60-257   1996 $150.00

VESALIUS, ANDREAS   Opera Omnia Antomica and Chirurgica... Leiden: Apud Joannem du Vivie, et Joan. & Herm. Verbeek, Lugduni Batavorum, 1725. Large folio; 2 volumes, over 1200 pages, text illustrations, engraved title, fine portrait, 27 engraved copperplate illustrations, slight loss on first two leaves; contemporary leather backed paper boards, rubbed. GM 375; Cushing VI.D-8; Osler 579; Waller 9917.   Family Album Tillers-636   1996 $7,000.00

VESTAL, STANLEY   Warpath - The True Story of the Eighty Sioux, Told in a Biography of Chief White Bull. New York: 1934. 1st edition; 291 pages; photos, maps, map endpapers, dust jacket, very good+. Rader 3535; Luther 93; Dustin 263; Smith 10545.   T. A. Swinford 49-1202   1996 $100.00

VETALAPANCAVIMASTI   Vikram and the Vampire or Tales of Hindu Devilry. L-G, 1870. 1st edition by Richard Burton; illustrations; half leather and marbled boards; very good.   Aronovitz 57-217   1996 $250.00

VETALAPANCAVIMASTI   Vikram and the Vampire or Tales of Hindu Devilry. London: Longmans, Green, 1870. 12mo; pages xxiv, 319; 16 plates; rebound in modern cloth; Penzer p. 82.   Richard Adelson W94/95-217   1996 $145.00

VETH, CORNELIS   Comic Art in England. Amsterdam: M. Hertzberger, 1930. 4to; 206 pages; 56 plates, numerous text illustrations; buckram, slightly worn.   Thomas Thorp 489-319   1996 £60.00

VIAN, BORIS   L'Automne a Pekin. Paris: Minuit, 1956. 1st edition; wrappers and (probably supplied) glassine; near fine; inscribed by author, uncommon thus.   Lame Duck Books 19-554   1996 $1,000.00

VIANA, FRANCISCO JAVIER DE   Dairio Del Viage Explorador de Las Corbetas Espanolas "Descubierta" y "Atrevida" en Los Anos de 1789 a 1794, Llevado Por el Teniente de Anvio D. Francisco Janvier de viana, Y Ofrecido Para Su Publicacion, en Su Original Inedito... Cirrito de la Victoria: Imprenta del Ejercito, 1849. 20.5 cm; (iv), 3-360 pages; decorated wrappers, with wrappers and all pages framed in an ornamental border; fine, exceedingly rare. Strathern 586; Wickersham 6642.   Rockland Books 38-235   1996 $2,500.00

VICEDOM, GEORG F.   Die Mbowamb. Hamburg: 1943-48. Large 4to; 2 volumes out of 3; 264, 484 pages; 23 plates, 17 plates, many illustrations in text; paper wrappers, hinges loose, very good in original paper wrpapers; very scarce set.   Antipodean 28-511   1996 $1,200.00

VICERY, ELIZA   Emily Hamilton, a Novel. Worcester: printed and sold wholesale and retail by Isaiah Thomas Jun. 1803. 1st edition; 12mo; modern sheep, spine gilt, by Bennett, joints little rubbed; some light soiling, but very good. Wright I 2638; Shaw & Shoemaker 5504. Ximenes 109-293   1996 $475.00

VICK'S Flower and Vegetable Garden. Rochester: Vick, ca. 1900. 8vo; 166 pages; 6 full page chromolithographs; dust speckled cloth, very good, clean copy;   Second Life Books 103-202   1996 $100.00

VICKERS, C. L.   History of Arkansas Valley, Colorado. Chicago: 1881. 1st edition; vii, 889 pages; frontispiece, plates, illustrations; morocco/pictorial cloth, nice, scarce. Howes H314; 6 Guns 2272; Herd 2408.   T. A. Swinford 49-1203   1996 $675.00

VICKERS, LEONARD B.   The Loud Voice: Rev. X. 3, and Everlasting Gospel; Rev. XIV 6. New York: American News Co., n.d., ca. 1865. 1st edition; 8vo; 24 pages; original printed wrappers, very good to fine. Robert F. Lucas 42-62   1996 $150.00

VICKERS, ROY   Some Like the Dead. London: Hodder & Stoughton, 1960. 1st edition; signed by five of the 13 contributors, Margery Allingham, Roy Vickers, Anthony Gilbert, Edmund Crispin and Michael Gilbert; original binding, edges slightly spotted, tail of spine bumped, very good in slightly dusty and creased dust jacket rubbed at extremities, and slightly faded at spine.   Ulysses 39-16   1996 £175.00

VICTOR, METTA V., MRS.   Maum Guinea, and Her Plantation "Children" or, Holiday-Week on a Louisiana Estate. A slave Romance. New York: Beadle and Co., 141 William St., London: 44 Paternoster Row, 1861. 1st edition?; 12mo; (2), 215 pages; illustrations; original cloth; front covered stamped "Beadle's/Christmas Story/Maum Guinea." Publisher's presentation copy in ink; LCP/HSP Afro Amer. Cat. 10768 for what may be London edition.   M & S Rare Books 60-258 1996 $550.00

VICTORIA & ALBERT MUSEUM   Catalogue of Watercolor Paintings by British Artists and Foreigners Working in Great Britain. London: 1927. Revised edition; 22 x 14 cm; 2 volumes; xiv, 312 pages; pages 313-636, 20 pages with 118 small illustrations; each page interleaves with lined paper with annotations; bound in blue cloth;   Rainsford A54-568 1996 £65.00

VICTORIA County Hisstory. Sussex. Volume I. London: 1905. Original issue; thick 4to; 575 pages; many plates, maps and illustrations; original cloth, gilt, gilt top.   Howes Bookshop 265-2266 1996 £55.00

VICTORIA County History. Sussex. Volume II. London: 1907. Imperial 8vo; 496 pages; 13 plates, 20 illustrations; original half morocco, gilt top. Howes Bookshop 265-2267 1996 £60.00

VICTORIA UNIVERSITY OF MANCHESTER. LIBRARY   Catalogue of Medical Books in Manchester University Library 1480-1700. Manchester: 1972. 8vo; (5), 399 pages; original binding, dust jacket; mint.   James Tait Goodrich K40-41 1996 $145.00

VICTORIA, QUEEN OF GREAT BRITAIN 1819-1901   Leaves from the Journal of Our Life in the Highlands from 1848 to 1861. London: Smith Elder, 1868. 8vo; 6 plates and text sketches; pictorial souvenir binding, rebacked, gauffered edges gilt; bound by local binder T. Russell of Pitlochry; Henry Alexander Murray armorial bookplate.   Rostenberg & Stern 150-32 1996 $150.00

VICTORIA, QUEEN OF GREAT BRITAIN 1819-1901   The Letters of Queen Victoria. London: John Murray, 1907-32. Original edition; thick demy 8vo; 9 volumes; original red cloth, gilt, some spines faded; complete set now scarce.   Howes Bookshop 265-1238 1996 £250.00

VICTORIUS, PETRUS   Petri Victorii Variarum lectionum... Lyon: Bartholomaeus Frein, for Joannem Temporalem, Lugduni, May, 1554. 4to; pages (12), 486, (59) plus blanks, printers device, great historiated woodcut initials; Old French full leather, spine gilt, joints weak, titlepage with old repair at corner, ms. marginalia.   Family Album Tillers-637 1996 $220.00

VIDA, MARCO GIROLAMO, BP. OF ALBA d. 1566   Poemata Omnia... Cremona: G. Muzio and B. Locheta, Nov. 1550. 1st collected edition; 8vo; 292 leaves, engraved printer's device; contemporary limp vellum (cracking, small piecies missing), yapp edges (lacking ties), vellum ms. stubs; very good. BM STC 724; Adams V704; not in NUC (1 copy Cremona 1568 ed. only).   Bennett Gilbert LL29-88 1996 $1,800.00

VIDA, MARCUS GIROLAMO, BP. OF ALBA d. 1566   The Poetics of... Sunderland: Printed by T. Reed, 1793. 8vo; errata slip after contents, 7 page list of subscribers; contemporary calf, rebacked, gilt lettering on spine.   Anthony W. Laywood 109-154 1996 £75.00

VIDAL, GORE   Death in the Fifth Position. New York: E. P. Dutton, 1952. 1st edition; edges lightly rubbed, otherwise near fine in price clipped dust jacket with faint foxing on rear panel, folds lightly rubbed and few quarter to half inch chips and short closed tears.   Quill & Brush 102-1716 1996 $150.00

VIDAL, GORE   Death Before Bedtime. New York: E. P. Dutton, 1953. 1st edition; endpapers faintly foxed; previous owner's small address label on pastedown (under flap), cover edges slightly faded, still very good or better in lightly rubbed dust jacket with touch of soiling and tiny damp stain on rear panel, shallow chipping in tips & few short closed tears. Quill & Brush 102-1717 1996 $200.00

VIDAL, GORE   The Judgment of Paris. New York: E. P. Dutton, 1952. 1st edition; signed by author; name and date on flyleaf, otherwise near fine in dust jacket which is lightly soiled on rear panel.   Steven C. Bernard 71-247 1996 $150.00

VIDAL, GORE   Lincoln. Franklin Center: Franklin Library, 1984. Franklin Library signed, limited first edition; gilt stamped leather; fine.   Lame Duck Books 19-555 1996 $150.00

VIELE, TERESA GRIFFIN   Following the Drum: a Glimpse of Frontier Life. New York: Rudd & Carleton, 1858. Pges 256, (8), 4; original stamped boards, some fading and wear, generally good, tight copy. Howes V92; WC 312a.1.   Dumont 28-132 1996 $275.00

VIELLOT, LOUIS J. P.   Songbirds of the Torrid Zone. 1979. Limited to 1500 copies; large 4to; 70 fine colored plates; full morocco, gilt borders, spine and edges; mint.   David A.H. Grayling MY95Orn-81 1996 £170.00

VIEWS in Cheltenham. Cheltenham: Davies, n.d., ca. 1830. Oblong 8vo; 10 plates, title on upper wrapper dusty; attractive small plates. Marlborough 162-19 1996 £250.00

VIEWS of Denver Colorado 1889. Denver: O. O. Howard, Jr., 1889. 1st edition; (25) pages, each with illustrations on recto and descriptive text on verso, printed in sepia, original pictorial wrapprs; fine. Wynar 2351. Michael D. Heaston 23-102 1996 $225.00

VIEWS of Pompeii. London: printed for James Carpenter & Son, 1828. 1st edition; folio; 25 full page plates, text opposite, 2 page map of Pompeii prior to title, blind decorated green cloth covers which are detached and lack spine, plates and text very clean; scarce.   Freedom Bookshop 14-14 1996 $850.00

VIGEE-LEBRUN, MARIE LOUISE ELISABETH   Souvenirs of Madame Vigee le Brun. London: Richard Bentley, and Son, 1879. 1st English edition; 8vo; 2 volumes; original decorated green cloth, remarkably fine and appealing copy of a scarce book. 2 copies in NUC.   Paulette Rose 16-334 1996 $425.00

VIGNOLES, CHARLES   Statements Respecting the Method and Cost of Producing Coke from Turf. London: printed by J. and H. Cox, 1850. 1st edition; 8vo; name on title, large folding table at end; original cloth. Anthony W. Laywood 108-244 1996 £60.00

VILLA and Cottage Architecture: Select Examples of Country and Suburban Residences Recently Erected. London: Glasgow and Edinburgh: Blackie & Son, 1869. 15 1/4 x 11 1/4 inches; xii, 112 pages, (1) leaf; device on title, woodcut initials and 80 engraved plates, printed on thick paper; contemporary half morocco, cloth sides, spine with raised bands, blind rules, gilt titling, top third of front joint cracked, corners and spine ends bit rubbed (though skillfully refurbished), portions of cloth rather soiled, but binding still solid and otherwise perfectly satisfactory; penciled architectural plans on two front flyleaves, frequent (though never serious), light foxing to plates and tissue guards, otherwise excellent internally.   Phillip J. Pirages 33-16 1996 $375.00

VILLON, FRANCOIS   Le Lais, Le Testament et Sea Balaldes. The Hague: 1926. One of 110 copies; 8vo; printed in Lucien Pissaro's Disteltype, initials and ornaments in red and blue; full vellum, very nice, rare.   Bertram Rota 272-248 1996 £600.00

VILLON, FRANCOIS   The Lyrical Poems of... New York: Limited Editions Club, 1979. Limited to 2000 copies; 4to; calligraphy by S. Harvard; French and English text; signed by Harvard, with numbered signed engraving by Fritz Eichenberg laid in; green linen; fine in glassine and slipcase, with Monthly Letter.   Charles Agvent 4-1157 1996 $125.00

VILLON, FRANCOIS   The Lyrics of Francois Vilion. New York: Limited Editions Club, 1933. Limited to 1500 copies, signed by artist; 4to; wood-blocks cut by Howard Simon; original tan buckram, leather label on spine, slipcase; fine.   James S. Jaffe 34-703 1996 $150.00

VILLON, JACQUES   Cent Croquis 1894-1904. Paris: Pierre Beres, 1959. 4to; 100 plates, including 63 in color; all mounted on grey card, unbound as issued; original wrappers within board portfolio, preserved in publisher's slipcase, slipcase slightly worn, otherwise fine.   Thomas Thorp 489-311 1996 £75.00

VIMERCATI, FRANCESCO   In...Libros Aristotelis Meteorologicorum Commentarij (etc). Venice: ex off. Dominici Guerrei et Io. Baptistate fratrum 1565. 2nd edition; folio; ff. (vi), 217, (i), Roman and Greek letter, large woodcut printer's device on top edge gilt, woodcut diagrams, initials and ornaments, two old repairs to blank portion of titlepage, wormtrail to this and next leaf just touching couple of letters on latter, small cut in last two leaves without loss; contemporary limp vellum, some damages, loosening and exposing early Italian vernacular poetical 'waste'; Adams V646; 2 copies in NUC.   A. Sokol XXV-99 1996 £985.00

VINCENT, C. W.   Chemistry, Theoretical, Practical and Analytical as Applied to the Arts and Manufactures. London: William MacKenzie, 1882. 1st edition; 4to; 8 volumes, more than 2000 double column pages, 62 steel engraved plates and numerous woodcuts in text; very good, bright and attractive set. Sotheran 772; not in Duveen or Ferguson.   Edwin V. Glaser   121-62   1996 $450.00

VINCENT, JOHN   Fowling. A Poem. London: 1808. finely bound in half crushed morocco by Riviere; light foxing, otherwise most attractive. Very scarce.   David A.H. Grayling   3/95-393   1996 £100.00

VINCENT, JOHN   Fowling, a Poem. London: 1812. 2nd edition; finely bound in contemporary panelled calf; excellent copy.   David A.H. Grayling   3/95-234   1996 £75.00

A VINDICATION Of the Honourable the Sheriffs and Recorder of London, from Those Impudent Reflections Cast Upon them in Fitzharris's Libel, Entituled His Confession. London: printed for Rich. Baldwyn, 1681. Folio; 2 pages, uncut, disbound. Wing V 506.   H. M. Fletcher 121-32 1996 £75.00

VINE, BARBARA   Asta's Book. Bristol: Scorpion Press, 1993. 1/20 deluxe lettered copies, signed by author and Julian Symons who provided author appreciation; quarter bound in goatskin with raised bands; fine.   Quill & Brush   102-1719   1996 $450.00

VINES, RICHARD   The Hearse of the Renowned, the Right Honourable Robert Earle of Essex... London: by T. R. and E. M. for Abel Roper, 1646. Small 4to; portrait, 38 pages; disbound. Wing V554a.   H. M. Fletcher 121-80 1996 £50.00

VINETTE, A.   Buena Vista and Tributary Mining Camps: A Sketch of the Mines of Cottonwood and La Plata Districts, Chaffee County, Colorado. Buena Vista: Times Book and Job Rooms, 1882. 1st edition; 37 pages, (3) pages ads; original printed wrappers, some soiling, staining and chipping to wrappers, very good, very scarce, laid in half morocco slipcase. Not in Grabb, Eberstadt, Decker or Streeter. Michael D. Heaston 23-108 1996 $750.00

VINGE, VERNOR   A Fire Upon the Deep. New York: 1992. 1st edition; very fine in dust jacket.   Robert Gavora 61-271 1996 $150.00

VINTON, STALLO   John Colter, Discoverer of Yellowstone Park. New York: Edward Eberstadt, 1926. 1st edition; 114 pages, maps and plate; original boards and vellum spine, minor bumping to corners, otherwise fine. Howes V114; Smith 10603; Graff 4490.   Michael D. Heaston 23-347 1996 $500.00

VIRGINIA. CONVENTION   Virginia Bill of Rights, Passed June 12, 1776; Adopted Without Alteration by the Convention of 1829-30, and Re-adopted, with Amendments, by the Convention of 1850-51, and Now Re-adopted as Passed June 12, 1776. Richmond: Wyatt M. Elliott, Printer, 1861. 1st edition; 26 pages; original self wrappers, foxing, else very good. Parrish & Willingham 4356.   McGowan Book Co. 65-114 1996 $250.00

VISHNIAC, ROMAN   Polish Jews, a Pictorial Record. New York: 1947. 31 photos.   J. B. Muns 154-314 1996 $125.00

VITA De'Beati Gaspar e Niccolo... Turin: Briolo, 1788. 8vo; vignette title, pages iii-viii, 263, printed on blue paper; contemporary crimson morocco gilt, covers with gilt double outer border and intertwined leafy inner border, wreath cornerpieces, flat spine gilt in 6 panels, panels with star and sunburst, black label lettered gilt, all edges gilt, marbled endpapers, gilt arms of Victor Amadeus III, Duke of Savoy from 1773-1796, to whom the work is dedicated, presumably the unique dedication copy. Marlborough 160-59 1996 £1,200.00

VITRUVIUS POLLIO, MARCUS   The Civil Architecture of Vitruvius. London: printed by Thomas Davison, Whitfriars for Longman, et al, 1812. Folio; pages (8), 76, 93; 97-282, (1), 41 engraved architectural plates, lacks one sectional title, foxed, 2 volumes; uncased. Brunet V 1331. Family Album Tillers-661 1996 $375.00

VIVIAN, H. HUSSEY   Notes of a Tour in America from August 7th to November 17th 1877. London: 1878. 1st edition; 260 pages; folded map; half leather, raised bands, red leather label; nice. Rare. Flake 8545.   T. A. Swinford 49-1207 1996 $275.00

VIVISECTION. The Royal Society for the Prevention of Cruelty to Animals and the Royal Commission. London: Smith Elder & Co., 1876. Original embossed cloth, gilt, worn, but sound.   Meyer Boswell SL26-7 1996 $225.00

VIZETELLY, HENRY   A History of Champagne with Notes on the Other Sparkling Wines of France. London: Vizetelly & Co., 1882. 1st edition; 4to; 350 engravings, and over 200 original sketches; gilt pictorial green cloth, spine little rubbed, especially lower extremity, some foxing to prelims, gilt cover vignette bright, extremely nice. Simon Vinaria 105. Marilyn Braiterman 15-208 1995 $750.00

VLIET, R. G.   Sand is the Tool. New York: William Frederick Press, 1953. 1st edition; scarce first book; faint offsetting to endpapers, cloth covered boards, very good+.   Lame Duck Books 19-556 1996 $350.00

VLIET, R. G.   Solitude. New York: HBJ, 1977. 1st edition; fine in dust jacket with two very short, internally repaired tears, author's scarce second novel.   Between the Covers 42-441 1996 $125.00

VOCABULA Amatoria; a French-English Glossary of Words, Phrases and Allusions Occuring in the Works of Rabelais, Voltaire, Moliere, Rousseau, Beranger, Zola and Others... London: privately printed for subscribers only, 1896. 4to; half title, title in red and black; uncut in blue boards, cream paper spine and paper label dulled and chipped, hinges splitting; from the collection of Fernand & Anne Renier.   Jarndyce 103-112 1996 £65.00

VOGEL, GERTRUIDA   Spring Flowers. London: A. And C. Black, c. 1916. Oblong 4to; 14 colored plates by Rie Cramer; blue cloth, colored pictorial onlay; nice, scarce.   Barbara Stone 70-58 1996 £125.00

VOLBACH, W. F.   Early Christian Art. London: Thames & Hudson, 1961. 31 x 24 cm; 363 pages, 39 color plates, 271 monochrome plates, 30 text figures; original cloth, very slightly marked, very slight foxing on first and last leaves.   Rainsford A54-575 1996 £58.00

VOLK, ERNEST   The Archaeology of the Delaware Valley. Cambridge: Peabody Museum, 1911. 8vo; xvi, 258 pages, 26 figures, 125 plates, 2 maps; tattered wrappers, uncut.   Archaeologia Luxor-4998 1996 $125.00

VOLLMANN, WILLIAM T.   An Afghanistan Picture Show, or, How I Saved the World. New York: FSG, 1992. Advance review copy with publisher's material laid in, signed by author with half pge drawing by him, presumably a self portrait; fine in dust jacket.   Between the Covers 42-443 1996 $200.00

VOLLMANN, WILLIAM T.   Butterfly Stories. Andre Deutsch, 1993. One of 100 signed and numbered copies; fine in slipcase.   Book Time 2-458 1996 $500.00

VOLLMANN, WILLIAM T.   Butterfly Stories. Grove/Atlantic Press, 1994. Uncorrected proof; near fine, inscribed explaining revisions.   Book Time 2-459 1996 $130.00

VOLLMANN, WILLIAM T.   The Convict Bird. CoTangent Press, 1987. 1/100 copies; signed by author; hardbound in stiff wrappers; very fine. Left Bank Books 2-151 1996 $300.00

VOLLMANN, WILLIAM T.   The Convict Bird. CoTangent Press, 1987. Limited edition, number 77 of 100 copies; signed; hand sewn wrappers. Book Time 2-460 1996 $250.00

VOLLMANN, WILLIAM T.   The Grave of Lost Stories. Sacramento: CoTangent Press, 1993. One of 15 deluxe copies only, 13 of which are for sale, all on Johannot paper, each signed and numbered by artist/author and binder, from an edition of 200 (185 regular edition); page size 10 7/8 x 7 7/8 inches; 4 illustrations hand colored; letterpress by Alastair Johnston in Electra and Cochin with display in Caslon, Marbleheart, Rimmed Lith and Asatoria at Poltroon Press, t.p. in 3 colors, guards of black & gold gilt Japanese (?) paper; bound by Ben Pax - steel & grey marble box (tomb) fitted to custom steel hinge by means of a copper sheet riveted to the steel and then crimped upward to form a pan, hinge powder coated black as interior; front cover incised with title, author's initials & Poe's dated, the copy number appears in roman numeral on back cover, along fore edge, 13 teeth have been set in handmade silver bezels; inside covers each have 4 brass & copper rods (oxidized green); book itself bound in blue w/linen spine which are 'leafed, and variegated & painted in metallic fungoid patterns over which author has painted a female figure to represent one of the stories (author's description); gessoed bds. are copper colored & female in blue w/onlays of 4 sm. white bones (?) outlining skeleton. Boxed.   Priscilla Juvelis 95/1-254 1996 $4,500.00

VOLLMANN, WILLIAM T. The Grave of Lost Stories. Sacramento: Co-Tangent Press, 1993. Signed, limited edition, one of 200 copies, all on Johannot and each signed by Vollmann and Ben Pax, this is the regular edition (15 copies comprising the deluxe edition); page size 9 7/8 x 7 3/4 inches; titlepage printed in 3 colors. 4 hand colored illustrations and title glyph by author, set by Alastair Johnson in Electra and Cochin with display in Caslon, Marbleheart, Rimmed Litho, and Astoria and printed at Poltroon Press; sewn pages laid into black paper wrapper with illustration by Vollmann. Priscilla Juvelis 95/1-255 1996 $500.00

VOLLMANN, WILLIAM T. The Ice Shirt. Andre Deutsch, 1990. 1st edition; fine in fine dust jacket, signed. Book Time 2-462 1996 $165.00

VOLLMANN, WILLIAM T. The Ice Shirt. London: Deutsch, 1990. 1st edition; very fine in dust jacket signed by author. Left Bank Books 2-153 1996 $145.00

VOLLMANN, WILLIAM T. The Ice-Shirt. N.P.: Viking, 1990. Uncorrected proof of the first American edition; wrappers, signed by author; near fine. Ken Lopez 74-452 1996 $200.00

VOLLMANN, WILLIAM T. The Ice Shirt. New York: Viking, 1990. 1st edition; fine copy in fine dust jacket; signed. Book Time 2-461 1996 $110.00

VOLLMANN, WILLIAM T. The Rainbow Stories. Andre Deutsch, 1st edition; fine in fine dust jacket, signed with drawing. Book Time 2-463 1996 $180.00

VOLLMANN, WILLIAM T. The Rainbow Stories. New York: Atheneum, 1989. 1st U.S. edition; fine in dust jacket, signed by author, with drawing of a spider on facing page at ends of each of whose legs appears one letter of the acronym for the visible light spectrum. Lame Duck Books 19-557 1996 $200.00

VOLLMANN, WILLIAM T. Thirteen Stories and Thirteen Epitaphs. Andre Deutsch, 1991. 1st edition; near fine in fine dust jacket, slight crinkling to first pages, signed. Book Time 2-468 1996 $145.00

VOLLMANN, WILLIAM T. Thirteen Stories and Thirteen Epitaphs. London: Deutsch, 1991. 1st edition; 1000 copies, this copy signed by author. Revere Books 4-425 1996 $225.00

VOLLMANN, WILLIAM T. Thirteen Stories and Thirteen Epitaphs. London: Deutsch, 1991. Correct first edition, reportedly, one of 1000 copies; fine in dust jacket, scarce. Lame Duck Books 19-558 1996 $150.00

VOLLMANN, WILLIAM T. Thirteen Stories and Thirteen Epitaphs. London: Deutsch, 1991. 1st edition; very fine in dust jacket and signed by author. Left Bank Books 2-154 1996 $125.00

VOLLMANN, WILLIAM T. Thirteen Stories and Thirteen Epitaphs. London: Andre Deutsch, 1991. 1st edition; original cloth, fine but for slight rough fore-edge on first few pages, fine dust jacket. Beasley Books 82-159 1996 $100.00

VOLLMANN, WILLIAM T. Thirteen Stories and Thirteen Epitaphs. New York: Pantheon, 1991. 1st U.S. edition; fine in dust jacket, signed by author. Lame Duck Books 19-559 1996 $100.00

VOLLMANN, WILLIAM T. Whores for Gloria. New York: Pantheon, 1991. 1st edition; fine in dust jacket, signed by author with drawing. Lame Duck Books 19-560 1996 $150.00

VOLLMANN, WILLIAM T. Whores for Gloria. New York: Pantheon, 1992. Uncorrected proof; red wrappers; fine, scarce. Lame Duck Books 19-561 1996 $150.00

VOLLMANN, WILLIAM T. You Bright and Risen Angels. Andre Deutsch, 1987. 1st edition; fine in fine dust jacket, signed. Book Time 2-473 1996 $250.00

VOLLMANN, WILLIAM T. You Bright and Risen Angels. London: Deutsch, 1987. Only 2500 copies in the first printing; very fine in dust jacket, signed by author. Left Bank Books 2-152 1996 $200.00

VOLLMANN, WILLIAM T. You Bright and Risen Angels. New York: Atheneum, 1987. 1st U.S. edition; author's first book; portion of bottom rear cover slightly discolored from dampness, otherwise near fine in dust jacket which has slight discoloration at lower left spine corner. Steven C. Bernard 71-254 1996 $100.00

VOLNEY, CONSTANTIN FRANCOIS, COMTE DE The Law of Nature, or Principles of Morality, Deduced from the Physical Constitution of Mankind and the Universe. London: reprinted for D. Steel, 1796. 1st London edition; 12mo; pages (i)-x, (11)-171; oval stipple engraved portrait frontispiece; contemporary half red roan, smooth backstrip divided by gilt rules, lettered direct in second compartment, small gilt sunburst in centre of remainder, marbled boards, bookplate of Clifton baronetcy, pale green edges, rose silk marker; fine. Blackwell's B112-278 1996 £250.00

VOLNEY, CONSTANTIN FRANCOIS, COMTE DE Tableau du Climat et du Sol des Etats-Unis D'Amerique. Paris: Chez Coucier, Imprimeur-Libraire quai des Augustins No. 71, ... 1803. 1st edition; 1st issue; 8vo; 2 volumes; (i-xvi), 1-532 pages, errata leaf, Direction to Binder, 2 folding engraved copperplates and 2 large folding maps; half green calf and mottled boards, gilt titles to spines, corners bumped and worn, edges speckled, brown marbled endpapers, owner's bookplate to front pastedowns, very clean and crisp copy internally. Sabin 100692; Gagnon 3676; Stanton Tremaine 723. Beeleigh Abbey BA/56-126 1996 £700.00

VOLNEY, CONSTANTIN FRANCOIS, COMTE DE Travels through Syria and Egypt. In the Years 1783, 1784 and 1785. London: printed for G. G. J. and J. Robinson, 1788. 2nd English edition; 8vo; 2 volumes, 418, 500, (15) pages; 2 folding maps, plan, 2 folding engravings; original half speckled calf, bookplate, some foxing, not affecting text, still solid, very good. Chapel Hill 94-283 1996 $300.00

VOLTAIRE, FRANCOIS MARIE AROUET DE 1694-1778 Candide. New York: Random House, 1928. Limited to 95 copies; signed by Kent; octavo; 112 pages; exquisitely colored illustrations on every page by Rockwell Kent; quarter brown morocco and cloth patterned with Random House logo; gilt lettering to spine, extremely fine in morocco trimmed black linen slipcase. Johnson pp.3 04-341. Bromer Booksellers 90-157 1996 $2,000.00

VOLTAIRE, FRANCOIS MARIE AROUET DE 1694-1778 Candide, or Optimism. New York: Limited Editions Club, 1973. Limited to 1500 copies, signed by artist; 4to; illustrations by May Neama; quarter cowhide and linen, fine in glassine and lightly soiled case; fine, with Monthly letter. Charles Agvent 4-1162 1996 $100.00

VOLTAIRE, FRANCOIS MARIE AROUET DE 1694-1778 Essay on Milton. Cambridge University Press, 1954. One of 400 copies; 8vo; printed on Whatman paper with types and ornaments made by Deberny & Peignot from newly engraved copies of the original Baskerville punches; 8vo; marbled paper boards, cloth spine, edges little worn, but nice. Bertram Rota 272-65 1996 £70.00

VOLTAIRE, FRANCOIS MARIE AROUET DE 1694-1778 La Henriade. Londres: 1728. 2nd edition; 8vo; preserving the early form of M3, before cancellation; contemporary calf, rebacked, spine gilt; very uncommon in any state; very good complete with frontispiece; Foxon V114. Ximenes 108-342 1996 $500.00

VOLTAIRE, FRANCOIS MARIE AROUET DE 1694-1778 The History of Zadig, or Destiny. Paris: Limited Editions Club, 1952. Limited to 1500 copies; 8vo; illustrations by Sylvain Sauvage, hand colored by Etienne Giradot; brown linen decorated in gold, fine in lightly worn case. Charles Agvent 4-1163 1996 $100.00

VOLTAIRE, FRANCOIS MARIE AROUET DE 1694-1778 Irene. Paris: n.p. 1779. 1st edition; 8vo; 62 pages; half title; modern wrappers; excellent; contemporary ownership signature. Blackwell's B112-279 1996 £200.00

VOLTAIRE, FRANCOIS MARIE AROUET DE 1694-1778 Letters Concerning the English Nation. London: printed for C. Davis and A. Lyon 1733. 1st edition; 8vo; with ad leaf A8; contemporary calf, rebacked, label; nice, clean copy. Bengesco 11, p. 11; Evans 346; Sabin 100751; Babson 242. Anthony W. Laywood 109-155 1996 £250.00

VOLTAIRE, FRANCOIS MARIE AROUET DE 1694-1778 Letters from M. de Voltaire, to Several of His Friends. London: T. Davies and J. Wheble 1770. 12mo; (iv), 234 pages; contemporary calf, spine gilt, label, half title, spine ends worn, joints cracked but firm, corner clipped from endpaper, minor browning and foxing; sound, uncommon edition. Robert Clark 38-211 1996 £110.00

VOLTAIRE, FRANCOIS MARIE AROUET DE 1694-1778   Memoirs of the Life of Voltaire. London: Robinson, 1784. 1st English translation; 8vo; calf; Greaves ownership in title margin. CBEL II 804.   Rostenberg & Stern 150-33 1996 $175.00

VOLTAIRE, FRANCOIS MARIE AROUET DE 1694-1778   The Princess of Babylon. London: Nonesuch press, 1927. 1st edition; 11 full page black and white illustrations as well as other decorations by Thomas Lowinsky; half parchment backed marbled paper boards, top edge gilt, spine spotted, cover edges slightly rubbed, head and tail of spine slightly bumped, very good.   Ulysses 39-382 1996 £85.00

VOLTAIRE, FRANCOIS MARIE AROUET DE 1694-1778   A Treatise on Toleration; the Ignorant Philosopher... London: printed for Fielding and Walker, 1779. 8vo; library stamp on general titlepage, separate titles to each part, 19th century cloth, paper label.   Anthony W. Laywood 108-134 1996 £90.00

VOLTAIRE, FRANCOIS MARIE AROUET DE 1694-1778   Collection Complete des Oeuvres de Mr. De Voltaire. Geneva: 1768-77. Early collected edition; 4to; 30 volumes; 50 full page engraved portraits and illustrations; contemporary full sheep with raised bands, gilt tooled spine panels, gilt borders, fillets and dentelles, all edges gilt, couple of volumes slightly scuffed, few instances of marginalia in unkown early hand, but very attractive set in well preserved French binding; signature of Charles Willing Hare, bookplate of Jacob Solis Cohen.   Chapel Hill 94-416 1996 $1,800.00

VON BOTHMER, DIETRICH   The Amasis Painter and His World: Vase-Painting in Sixth Century B.C. Athens. New York: Thames and Hudson, 1985. 4to; 246 pages, 116 figures, numerous illustrations and 8 color plates; original cloth, dust jacket.   Archaeologia Luxor-4124 1996 $125.00

VON FALKE, JACOB   Art in the House. Historical, Critical and Aesthetical Studies on the Decoration and Furnishing of the Dwelling. Boston: L. Prang, 1879. Thick 4to; chromolithograph titlepage and 60 illustrations, plus 166 text illustrations; deep blue cloth with gilt pictorial illustration on front cover, gilt decorated spine, excellent copy. Hitchcock 436.   Marilyn Braiterman 15-200 1996 $300.00

VON HAGEN, VICTOR WOLFGANG   Jungle in the Clouds. New York: Duell, Sloan and Pearce, 1940. 1st edition; 8vo; frontispiece, x, 260 pages; 58 illustrations; original cloth, lightly chipped dust jacket; inscribed by author for Robert G. Stoddard.   Archaeologia Luxor-5009 1996 $125.00

VONNEGUT, KURT   Deadeye Dick. New York: Delacorte, 1982. 1st edition; near fine in fine dust jacket, signed by author.   Between the Covers 42-448 1996 $100.00

VONNEGUT, KURT   Galapagos. New York: Delacorte Press, 1985. 1st edition; number 184 of 500 copies signed by author; fine in slipcase. Hermitage SP95-649 1996 $125.00

VONNEGUT, KURT   God Bless You, Mr. Rosewater, or Pearls Before Swine. HRW, 1965. 1st edition; slight wear to bottom corner tips, else very good+/near fine in very good dust jacket with some soiling. Aronovitz 57-1225 1996 $175.00

VONNEGUT, KURT   Happy Birthday, Wanda June. New York: Delacorte, 1971. 1st edition; photos; owner's name and date to half title, else slightly spine cocked, near fine copy in slightly spine faded dust jacket.   Lame Duck Books 19-564 1996 $850.00

VONNEGUT, KURT   Jailbird. New York: Delacorte Press, 1979. 1st edition; number 449 of 500 copies, signed by author; fine in lightly edge sunned slipcase.   Hermitage SP95-650 1996 $125.00

VONNEGUT, KURT   Mother Night. New York: Harper, 1966. 1st edition; small name, else fine in fine dust jacket with two tiny tears on rear panel and little yellowing at extremities, fresher copy than usual; signed by author.   Between the Covers 42-447 1996 $350.00

VONNEGUT, KURT   Mother Night. New York: Harper & Row, 1966. 1st hardcover edition; fine in near fine jacket with one internally repaired tear on rear spine fold.   Ken Lopez 74-453 1996 $125.00

VONNEGUT, KURT   Nothing Is Lost Save Honor. Jackson: Nouveau Press for the Mississippi Civil Liberties Union, 1984. 1st edition; number 83 of 300 copies signed by author; fine in slipcase.   Hermitage SP95-652 1996 $125.00

VONNEGUT, KURT   Player Piano. New York: Scribner's, 1952. 1st edition; variant, bound in darker shade of green cloth with some foxing to endpapers, some marks and soiling to covers, otherwise very good in attractive dust jacket with some sunning and some wear and tear; author's first book.   Aronovitz 57-1223 1996 $125.00

VONNEGUT, KURT   Player Piano. London: Macmillan, 1953. 1st British edition; some soiling to covers, else very good copy in chipped dust jacket; most uncommon edition; author's first book.   Aronovitz 57-1224 1996 $125.00

VONNEGUT, KURT   The Sirens of Titan. New York: Dell, 1959. Paperback original; edges of pages slightly darkened, touch of rubbing and slight bump on rear wrapper, still somewhat nicer than usual. Between the Covers 42-446 1996 $100.00

VONNEGUT, KURT   Slapstick. Franklin Center: Franklin Library, 1976. Franklin Library first edition; illustrations by Robert Andrew Parker, fine in full gilt stamped leather and signed by author;   Lame Duck Books 19-565 1996 $100.00

VONNEGUT, KURT   Welcome to the Monkey House. New York: Delacorte, 1968. 1st edition; very lightly spotted on fore-edge, else very near fine in near fine dust jacket, nice copy, uncommon title, signed by author.   Lame Duck Books 19-562 1996 $850.00

VON RAUMER, FREDERICK   England in 1835: Being a Series of Letters. London: John Murray, 1836. 1st edition in English; 8vo; x, 280, vi, 310, vi, 318, (2) pages ads; marks on front pastedowns from removal of bookplates; contemporary half calf, marbled boards, some light rubbing, otherwise very good set.   David Mason 71-42 1996 $320.00

VON ROSENBERG, TOMLINSON   Von Rosenberg Family of Texas: a Record with Historical Facts and Legends. (with) The Von Rosenberg Family Record Book II. Boerne/Waco: 1949/1974. 1st editions; 2 volumes, 164, 341 pages; photos.   W. M. Morrison 436-364 1996 $200.00

VON WINNING, HASSO   Pre-Columbian Art of Mexico and Central America. New York: Harry N. Abrams, 1968. Folio; tipped in color frontispiece, xv, 388 pages, 595 plates (many tipped in and in color); original cloth, dust jacket, small owner's name stamped at upper and lower edges, bookplate.   Archaeologia Luxor-5015 1996 $350.00

VRIES, HUGO DE 1848-1935   Intracellular Pangenesis Including a Paper on Fertilization and Hybridization. Chicago: 1910. 1st English translation; 270 pages; original binding.   W. Bruce Fye 71-2185 1996 $100.00

VRIES, HUGO DE 1848-1935   Species and Varieties, Their Origin by Mutation, Lectures Delivered at the University of California. Chicago: 1906. 2nd edition; 8vo; pages xviii, 847; frontispiece; cloth, light soiling, owner's name.   Raymond M. Sutton VI-390 1996 $100.00

THE VULGARITIES of Speech Corrected: with Elegant Expressions for Provincial and Vulgar Scots and Irish... London: printed for F. C. Westley, 1829. 2nd edition; small 8vo; contemporary half calf, neatly rebacked, edges rubbed; rare. Very good.   Ximenes 108-237 1996 $150.00

W

W., S. A Visit to London Containing a Description of the Principal Curiosities in the British Metropolis. London: William Darton, 58 Holborn Hill, 1820. New edition; 140 x 85 mm; 212 pages, 1 page Darton booklist; frontispiece, 5 other full page copper engravings, folding panorama; marbled boards with red roan spine titled in gilt, edges and boards worn, prelims browned, else very good. From the collection of Geoffrey Gollin London collection. Marjorie James 19-218 1996 £150.00

W., W. Animadversions on the Late Vindication of Slingsby Bethel, Esq.; Wherein the Ancient and Laudable Customs of the City of London are Asserted... Hamborough: printed for the Use of the English Merchants, 1681. Folio; 4 pages; uncut, disbound. H. M. Fletcher 121-55 1996 £70.00

WADE, DAVID Pattern in Islamic Art. London: Studio Vista, 1976. 28 x 22 cm; 144 pages, 142 illustrations; original cloth, dust jacket. Rainsford A54-578 1996 £55.00

WAGNER, HENRY RAUP 1862-1957 The Plains and the Rockies. San Francisco: John Howell Books, 1982. 4th edition; 4to; frontispiece, plates; original buckram. Forest Books 74-271 1996 £95.00

WAGNER, HENRY RAUP 1862-1957 The Plains and the Rockies. San Francisco: 1982. 4th edition; royal 8vo; 745 pages; illustrations; cloth, light edge wear, very good+, no dust jacket, as issued. Gene W. Baade 1094-166 1996 $125.00

WAGNER, HENRY RAUP 1862-1957 Sir Francis Drake's Voyage Around the World: its Aims and Achievements. San Francisco: John Howell, 1926. 11 x 8 inches; xii, 543 pages, frontispiece, 12 full page photographic illustrations, other illustrations in text; red buckram, uncut and unopened. Dawson's Books Shop 528-244 1996 $225.00

WAGNER, HENRY RAUP 1862-1957 Spanish Voyages to the Northwest Coast of America in the Sixteenth Century. San Francisco: California Historical Society, 1929. viii, 571 pages; 20 plates; nicely bound in blue cloth with gilt spine titles; hint of bumping to corners, else near fine. Parmer Books 039/Nautica-039018 1996 $425.00

WAGNER, HENRY RAUP 1862-1957 Spanish Voyages to the Northwest Coast of America in the Sixteenth Century. Amsterdam: N. Israel, 1966. Facsimile edition; 25.5 cm; viii, 571 pages, maps and charts, some folding, facsimiles; gilt stamped blue buckram; very good to fine. Smith 10662. Rockland Books 38-238 1996 $135.00

WAGNER, KARL EDWARD Horrorstory: Volume III. Novato: Underwood/Miller, 1991/92. 1st edition, one of 300 numbered copies, signed by editor and 20 of the contributing authors; very fine in dust jacket. Robert Gavora 61-276 1996 $150.00

WAGNER, KARL EDWARD Horrorstory: Volume Four. Novato: Underwood/Miller, 1990. 1st hardcover edition, one of 350 numbered copies, signed by editor and 26 of the contributing authors; very fine in dust jacket with folding tray case. Robert Gavora 61-278 1996 $150.00

WAGNER, KARL EDWARD Horrorstory: Volume Five. Novato: Underwood/Miller, 1989. 1st hardcover edition, one of 350 numbered copies, signed by editor and a majority of the contributing authors; very fine in dust jacket with folding tray case. Robert Gavora 61-280 1996 $150.00

WAGNER, RICHARD 1813-1883 The Rhinegold & the Valkyrie. London: William Heinemann, 1910. 1st edition with these illustrations; 4to; pages (xiii), 3-159, 34 mounted colored plates by Arthur Rackham, tissue guards, by Arthur Rackham; original brown buckram, gilt, pictorial endpapers; little rubbed, very good, clean copy. Sotheran PN32-144 1996 £198.00

WAGNER, RICHARD 1813-1883 The Ring of the Niblung. London: 1939. 1st edition thus; color plates by Arthur Rackham; exceptionally good in clean, pictorial dust jacket with closed, repaired tear at one corner and with one tear at foot of spine with some loss, very uncommon in this good, bright condition. Words Etcetera 94-1058 1996 £175.00

WAHLENBERG, ANNA Old Swedish Fairy Tales. New York: Hampton, 1925. Octavo; 296 pages; 6 color plates and several figures in text by Jeanette Berkowtiz; red cloth with illustrated pasteon, very fine. Bromer Booksellers 90-147 1996 $100.00

WAILES, B. L. C. Report on the Agriculture and Geology of Mississippi... N.P.: 1854. 8vo; pages xx, (17)-371; 16 plates, folding map original cloth, wear to corners and ends of spine, half inch tear to head of spine, pencilled numbers on page, number sticker on spine, institutional bookplate. Raymond M. Sutton VII-1225 1996 $225.00

WAINEWRIGHT, LATHAM The Literary and Scientific Pursuits Which Are Encouraged and Enforced in the University of Cambridge... London: J. Hatchard, 1815. contemporary morocco, gilt spine and borders, rubbed at tail with one marginal wormhole, armorial bookplate; inscribed "From the Author". Jarndyce 103-590 1996 £110.00

WAINWRIGHT, ALFRED The Far Eastern Fells. Kentmere: Henry Marshall, 1957. 1st edition; small 8vo; unpaginated, illustrations; original cloth, gilt, edges little warped, dust jacket little worn. R.F.G. Hollett & Son 78-1430 1996 £95.00

WAINWRIGHT, ALFRED Fellwanderer. The Story Behind the Guidebooks. Kendal: Westmorland Gazette, 1966. 1st edition; oblong 8vo; illustrations by author with photos; original cloth, gilt, dust jacket, top of spine trifle creased, bottom edge little chipped. R.F.G. Hollett & Son 78-1414 1996 £75.00

WAINWRIGHT, ALFRED A Fifth Lakeland Sketchbook. Kendal: Westmorland Gazette, n.d. 1st edition; oblong 8vo; 80 illustrations; original cloth, gilt, dust jacket. R.F.G. Hollett & Son 78-1426 1996 £50.00

WAINWRIGHT, ALFRED A Furness Sketchbook. Kendal: Westmorland Gazette, c. 1979. 1st edition; oblong 8vo; 75 drawings; original cloth, gilt, dust jacket. Fine. R.F.G. Hollett & Son 78-1415 1996 £50.00

WAINWRIGHT, ALFRED Kendal in the Nineteenth Century. Kendal: Westmorland Gazette, n.d., c. 1977. 1st edition; oblong small 4to; 130 drawiangs; original cloth, gilt, dust jacket (price clipped); signed by author. R.F.G. Hollett & Son 78-1417 1996 £140.00

WAINWRIGHT, ALFRED Kendal in the Nineteenth Century. Kendal: Westmorland Gazette, n.d., c. 1977. 1st edition; oblong small 4to; original cloth, gilt, dust jacket (few short edge tears); signed by author. R.F.G. Hollett & Son 78-1418 1996 £120.00

WAINWRIGHT, ALFRED A Second Lakeland Sketchbook. Kendal: Westmorland Gazette, c. 1970. 1st edition; oblong 8vo; 80 illustrations; original cloth, gilt, dust jacket (with one short tear, head and tail of spine trifle frayed, inner flap a little creased). R.F.G. Hollett & Son 78-1421 1996 £50.00

WAINWRIGHT, ALFRED A Third Lakeland Sketchbook. Kendal: Westmorland Gazette, c. 1977. 1st edition; oblong 8vo; 80 drawings; original cloth, gilt, dust jacket. R.F.G. Hollett & Son 78-1423 1996 £50.00

WAINWRIGHT, ALFRED Wainwright in Lakeland. Kendal: Abbott Hall Art Gallery, 1983. Signed limited edition of 1000 copies; oblong 4to; large folding map in rear pocket; illustrations; unpaginated; original green rexine gilt, dust jacket, mint. Very scarce. R.F.G. Hollett & Son 78-1446 1996 £295.00

WAINWRIGHT, ALFRED Wainwright in Lakeland. Kendal: Abbott Hall Art Gallery, 1983. 1st trade edition; oblong 4to; large folding illustrated map in rear pocket; original green rexine gilt, dust jacket; mint. R.F.G Hollett & Son 78-1445 1996 £65.00

WAINWRIGHT, ALFRED Westmorland Heritage. Kendal: Westmorland Gazette, 1975. Signed limited edition, number 718 of 1000 copies; oblong 4to; pages 487; illustrations; original cloth, gilt, dust jacket in original card box; mint. R.F.G. Hollett & Son 78-1449 1996 £395.00

WAINWRIGHT, ALFRED   Westmorland Heritage. Kendal: Westmorland Gazette, 1975. Limited edition, number 9 of 1000 copies; signed; oblong 4to; 487 pages, illustrations; original cloth, gilt, dust jacket (edges rather reased with some short tears, 2 inch piece missing from top edge of upper panel).   R.F.G. Hollett & Son   78-1450   1996 £340.00

WAINWRIGHT, JOHN   The Medical and Surgical Knowledge of William Shakespeare with Explanatory Notes. New York: 1907. Limited edition (200 copies), autographed by author; original binding, backstrip lacking, corners bumped.   W. Bruce Fye   71-2189   1996 $175.00

WAINWRIGHT, JOHN   The Medical Knowledge of William Shakespeare with Explanatory Notes. New York: 1915. 1st edition; 4th printing; 81 pages; original binding.   W. Bruce Fye   71-2190   1996 $150.00

WAIT, A. E.   The Real History of the Rosicrucians. London: George Redway, 1887. 1st edition; forty pages of publisher's ads dated 1887 at rear; decorated cloth, gilt, top edge dusty, inscription, head and tail of spine bumped, rubbed and nicked, corners bumped and rubbed, spine darkened, covers slightly marked, good.   Ulysses   39-509   1996 £125.00

WAITE, ARTHUR E.   The Book of Ceremonial Magic: Including the Rites and Mysteries of Goetic Theurgy, Sorcery and Infernal Necromancy. London: 1911. 1st edition; frontispiece, xxxv, 337 pages, 9 plates, 60 illustrations; cover lightly rubbed, small stain, otherwise shapr, very good+.   Middle Earth   77-189   1996 $295.00

WAITE, OTIS F. R.   New Hamphsire in the Great Rebellion. Claremont: 1870. 1st edition; 608 pages; pictorial cloth, very good+.   T. A. Swinford   49-1211   1996 $100.00

WAKE, C. STANILAND   The Development of Marriage and Kinship. London: 1889. (xxii), 484 pages, 2 black and white charts; brown cloth, gitl, slightly marked, otherwise very good.   Antipodean   28-524   1996 $195.00

WAKEFIELD, D. R.   The Sporting Fishes of the British Isles. Chevington Press, 1985. Limited to only 100 copies, numbered and signed by artist; this copy 11; folio; 20 fine etched plates made by the compiler, most printed in color with accompanying letterpress, the whole printed on Barcham Green handmade paper; untrimmed loose sheets as issued, contained in original cloth box, box very slightly dust soiled, otherwise fine.   Thomas Thorp   489-313   1996 £360.00

WAKEFIELD, EDWARD GIBBON   The Trial in Full of Edw. Gibbon Wakefield and Others, for the Abduction of Miss Turner (etc). London: printed for Knight and Lacey, 55, Paternoster Row, 1827. Modern quarter calf over marbled boards, bit dusty, but quite nice.   Meyer Boswell   SL26-233   1996 $150.00

WAKEFIELD, EDWARD GIBBON   A View of the Art of Colonization with Present Reference to the British Empire; in Letters Between a Statesman and a Colonist. London: J. W. Parker, 1849. 1st edition; 8vo; 6 page publisher's catalog at end; original cloth, paper label (little damaged); Charles W. Traylen   117-56   1996 £295.00

WAKEFIELD, JOSEPHUS   History of Waupaca County, Wisconsin. Waupaca: D. L. Stinchfield, 1890. 17.5 cm; 219 pages; frontispiece, 2 other portraits; brown cloth, title in gilt on front cover and spine, some wear, personal bookplate and signature, one name underlined in text. Howes W20.   Bohling Book Co.   192-418   1996 $120.00

WAKEMAN, GEOFFREY   Functional Developments in Bookbinding. New Castle: Plough Press, Kidlington, Oxford, 1993. Number 65 of 180 copies; 4to; pages 94, (1); printed in black and red, 6 colored cards reproducing period binding designs tipped in, 2 tipped in plates, 29 other plates loosely inserted in pockets on 3 leaves at end; fawn canvas, brown morocco label, untrimmed, new.   Blackwell's   B112-228   1996 £150.00

WAKEMAN, STEPHEN   The Stephen H. Wakeman Collection of Books. New York: American Art Association, 1924. 1st edition; original green cloth, paper label, fine.   Mac Donnell   12-146   1996 $100.00

WAKEMAN, STEPHEN   The Stephen Wakeman Collection of Books. New York: American Art Association, 1924. 1st edition; original printed wrappers, some chipping to lower corner and fore edge of front wrap, but crisp, clean copy, unpriced.   Mac Donnell   12-147   1996 $100.00

WAKOSKI, DIANE   George Washington's Camp Cups. Madison: Red Ozier Press, 1976. 1st edition; one of 150 copies, signed by author; thin 8vo; original wrappers, dust jacket; mint; additionally inscribed by author with signed postcard from printer, Steve Miller, laid in.   James S. Jaffe   34-586   1996 $150.00

WAKOSKI, DIANE   Greed. Parts 8, 9, 11. Los Angeles: Black Sparrow Press, 1973. 1st edition; limited to 250 copies signed by author; thin 8vo; cloth backed boards, acetate dust jacket; mint.   James S. Jaffe   34-668   1996 $100.00

WAKOSKI, DIANE   The Ice Queen. Alabama: Parallel Editions, 1994. 1st edition; one of 70 copes signed by author; 4to; illustrations by Margaret Prentice; green cloth; new.   James S. Jaffe   34-669   1996 $250.00

WAKOSKI, DIANE   The Managed World. New York: Red Ozier Press, 1980. 1st edition; one of 15 specially bound copies, 12mo; quarter leather and pictorial boards, mint, rare issue; additionally inscribed by author.   James S. Jaffe   34-750   1996 $750.00

WAKOSKI, DIANE   The Managed World. New York: Red Ozier Press, 1980. 1st edition; one of 200 copies, signed by author and publishers; 12mo; original wrappers; mint; inscribed by author.   James S. Jaffe   34-589   1996 $150.00

WAKOSKI, DIANE   Overnight Projects with Wood. A Poem. Madison: Red Ozier Press, 1977. 1st edition; one of 170 copies, signed by author; 12mo; original wrappers; mint; additionally inscribed by author.   James S. Jaffe   34-587   1996 $100.00

WAKOSKI, DIANE   Thanking My Mother for Piano Lessons. Mount Horeb: Perishable press, 1969. 1st edition; one of 250 copies; oblong 12mo; printed wrappers; very fine.   Captain's Bookshelf   38-212   1996 $100.00

WALBERG, GISELA   Provincial Middle Minoan Pottery. Mainz amd Rhein: Philipp von Zabern, 1983. 4to; 232 pages, 55 plates; original cloth. Archaeologia   Luxor-4131   1996 $250.00

WALCOTT, C. D.   Cambrian Brachiopoda. Washington: 1912. 4to; 2 volumes; 872 pages, with atlas of 104 plates; cloth, bindings rather used and loose, contents loose.   Wheldon & Wesley   207-1379   1996 £60.00

WALCOTT, DEREK   Omeros. New York: FSG, 1993. Later printing, but special issue with tipped in page presenting the book to members of the 1993 graduating class of Boston University and signed by author; fine in dust jacket, scarce.   Between the Covers   43-199   1996 $125.00

WALCOTT, DEREK   Selected Poems. New York: FS, 1964. 1st edition; corners very slightly bumped, still fine in dust jacket; inscribed by author to fellow author Barry Beckham.   Between the Covers   43-199   1996 $275.00

WALCOTT, GEORGE   The George Walcott Collection of Used Civil War Patriotic Covers. New York: 1934. Tall 8vo; 261 pages; profusely illustrated.   Edward Morrill   369-458   1996 $150.00

WALCOTT, MACKENZIE E. C.   Scot-Monasticon. The Ancient Church of Scotland. London: Virtue, Spalding and Daldy, 1874. 4to; pages xxvii, 428, 24 steel three quarter, 29 tinted plans, colored map; original cloth, paper spine label, trifle soiled, corners little bumped; little scattered light spotting, otherwise very nice, clean and sound.   R.F.G. Hollett   76-320   1996 £140.00

WALDMAN, DIANE   Roy Lichtenstein. New York: Abrams, 1971. Square folio; 2489 pages, 283 illustrations, including 86 color plates; cloth, dust jacket. Freitag 5615.   Brannan   43-353   1996 $625.00

WALDO, SAMUEL PUTNAM   Biographical Sketches of Distinguished American Naval Heroes in the War of the Revolution. Hartford: Silas Andrus, 1823. 1st edition; 392 pages, 3 portraits; full calf, red label, very good. Howes W26.   Blue River Books   9-310   1996 $150.00

WALKEM, W. WYMOND   Stories of Early British Columbia. Vancouver: News Advertizer, 1914. 24cm; 287 pages; frontispiece, illustrations, portraits; mildly soiled pictorial cloth, last two leaves have bit of tape repair to edges, however this copy is unusually bright and clean; signed by author; very good; rare. Smith 10680; Lowther 1621.   Rockland Books   38-239   1996 $400.00

WALKER, A. EARL   A History of Neurological Surgery. Baltimore: Williams and Wilkins, 1951. Original edition; 8vo; xii, 583 pages; nicely illustrated; original binding, near fine, rarely seen as such.   James Tait Goodrich   K40-291   1996 $295.00

WALKER, ADAM   Remarks Made in a Tour from London to the Lakes of Westmoreland and Cumberland, in the Summer of MDCCXCI. London: G. Nichol and C. Dilly, 1792. 2nd edition; 8vo; 251 pages; lacks half title (not always present), otherwise very good; modern half calf, gilt with raised bands and spine label, marbled boards. Armorial bookplate of William Cuthbert Brian Tunstall. Bicknell p. 24.2.   R.F.G. Hollett & Son 78-1336   1996 £325.00

WALKER, ALICE 1944-   The Color Purple. New York: HBJ, 1970. 1st edition; near fine in price clipped dust jacket with one inch closed tear to rear panel.   Lame Duck Books 19-28   1996 $500.00

WALKER, ALICE 1944-   The Color Purple. New York: HBJ, 1982. 1st edition; small faint blemish on front board and little rubbing to spine, near fine in fine dust jacket.   Between the Covers 43-200 1996 $550.00

WALKER, ALICE 1944-   Good Night, Willie Lee, I'll See You In the Morning. New York: Dial Press, 1979. 1st edition; fine in fine dust jacket; inscribed and signed by author in year of publication.   Pettler & Lieberman 28-37 1996 $450.00

WALKER, ALICE 1944-   Her Blue Body Everything We Know. New York: HBJ, 1991. One of only 111 copies of the signed limited edition; fine in publisher's slipcase.   Lame Duck Books 19-34 1996 $375.00

WALKER, ALICE 1944-   Horses Make a Landscape More Beautiful. New York: HBJ, 1984. Uncorrected proof of 1st edition; wrappers, fine, signed by author.   Lame Duck Books 19-30 1996 $250.00

WALKER, ALICE 1944-   In Search Of Our Mother's Gardens. New York: HBJ, 1983. 1st edition; fine in dust jacket with slight wear at head of spine; signed by author.   Lame Duck Books 19-29 1996 $125.00

WALKER, ALICE 1944-   In Search of Our Mothers' Gardens. San Diego: New York; London: Harcourt Brace Jovanovich, 1983. 1st edition; signed by author; price clipped dust jacket; short non-authorial Christmas inscription, otherwise near fine.   Steven C. Bernard 71-45 1996 $100.00

WALKER, ALICE 1944-   Meridian. London: Deutsch, 1976. 1st British edition; fresh, fine copy in dust jacket.   Lame Duck Books 19-26 1996 $200.00

WALKER, ALICE 1944-   Meridian. New York: HBJ, 1976. Uncorrected proof; very scarce format, proof sheets bound in card-stock covers with black tape spine, several pieces of text tipped in, fine in wrappers and signed by author, rare.   Ken Lopez 74-454 1996 $1,000.00

WALKER, ALICE 1944-   Meridian. New York: HBJ, 1976. 1st edition; fine in dust jacket, signed by Walker.   Lame Duck Books 19-24 1996 $350.00

WALKER, ALICE 1944-   Meridian. New York: HBJ, 1976. 1st edition; very near fine in dust jacket.   Lame Duck Books 19-25 1996 $275.00

WALKER, ALICE 1944-   Possessing the Secret of Joy. HBJ, 1992. One of 250 signed copies of the first edition; fine in publisher's slipcase.   Lame Duck Books 19-35 1996 $200.00

WALKER, ALICE 1944-   Possessing the Secret of Joy. New York: HBJ, 1992. Limited to 250 numbered copies; fine in slipcase, signed by author.   Bella Luna 7-592 1996 $175.00

WALKER, ALICE 1944-   The Third Life of Grange Copeland. New York: HBJ, 1970. 1st edition; near fine in dust jacket, signed by author. Lame Duck Books 19-27 1996 $500.00

WALKER, ALICE 1944-   To Hell With Dying. New York: HBJ, 1988. 1st trade edition; uncommon; fine in dust jacket, signed by author.   Lame Duck Books 19-31 1996 $150.00

WALKER, ANNE   Rose Rose. Paris: 1993. One in an edition of 3 copies, signed and dated by Walker; 6.25 x 5 inches; pastel painting with black hand-written poetry on accordion folded two-sided book; individually bound with two end boards by Jill Oriane Tarlau, the front board is covered with finely worked metallic petit-point embroidery by Tarlau, with a plum leater surround, dark plum back baord has inlays and onlays of patchwork leather forming the letters of the word 'Rose' as well as 3 onlays of metallic embroidery, one of a rose, all laid in drop-back box of lilac, green and gold handmade paper trimmed with dark plum leather and lined with purple suede.   Joshua Heller 21-228 1996 $3,400.00

WALKER, D. E.   A Resume of the Story of 1st Battalion, the Saskatoon Light Infantry (MG) Canadian Army, Overseas. Saskatoon: General Printing and Bookbinding, 1946. 8vo; pages 139, illustrations, maps, music; paper, covers scuffed, else very good. Dornbusch 114.   Hugh Anson-Cartwright 87-289 1996 $100.00

WALKER, GEORGE   The Costume of Yorkshire. London: printed by T. Bensley for Longman et al, 1814. 1st edition; 14 1/2 x 10 1/2 inches; 4 p.l., 96 pages; 41 fine hand colored costume plates, including frontispiece, separate texts in English and French; unusual binding, probably contemporary, of marbled paper sides enclosed by calf border filled with a series of blindstamped botanical ornaments, recently rebacked and recornered, spine with raised bands, titling in gilt, decorations in blind, marbled endpapers; boards just a little marked, hint of wear to edges, but binding well restored and really rather appealing, text with occasional insignificant smudging, one plate with what appears to be a marginal wrinkle (but which could possibly be very artfully repaired tear), just into image, another plate with minor soiling, 3 plates with few pinpoints of foxing, two plates with offsetting from text (one of these with only trace of transfer, & no offsetting to any other plates), unusually clean copy, well colored negravings with only most trivial imperfections. Tooley 498; Abbey Life 432; Colas 3044; Hiler p. 890; Brunet II 325.   Phillip J. Pirages 33-505 1996 $4,500.00

WALKER, GEORGE   A New Treatise on Chess... London: published by Messrs. Walker and Son, 1832. 1st edition; 12mo; frontispiece; original dark green cloth, slight bubbling, mauve printed paper side label; author's first book; fine.   Ximenes 109-295 1996 $225.00

WALKER, J.   The History of Penrith, from the Earliest Period to the Present Time. Penrith: Hodgson, printer, n.d., c. 1865. 2nd edition; 8vo; pages (ii), 180, 8 engraved vignettes, little fignering in places; old half calf gilt, spine little chipped, upper hinge cracked; upper joint cracked.   R.F.G. Hollett & Son 78-1337 1996 £120.00

WALKER, J.   The History of Penrith, from the Earliest Period to the Present time. Hodgson: printer, n.d., 1857. 2nd edition; 8vo; pages (ii), 180, 8 engraved vignettes; original blindstamped cloth, gilt, recased, backstrip little scratched.   R.F.G. Hollett & Son 78-1338 1996 £125.00

WALKER, JOHN 1732-1807   The Academic Speaker; or, a Selection of Parliamentary Debates, Orations, odes, Scenes and Speeches. London: printed for the author, by A. Wilson &c., 1803. 5th edition; plates, 3 pages ads, few spots in text; contemporary tree sheep, spine cracked and chipped, hinges splitting, corners rubbed; Alston VI 423-425, 3rd ed, 1797.   Jarndyce 103-357 1996 £60.00

WALKER, JOHN 1732-1807   A Critical Pronouncing Dictionary and Expositor of the English Language... London: sold by G. G. and J. Robinson & T. Cadell, Junior, & W. Davies, 1797. 2nd edition; 4to; contemporary speckled calf, neatly rebacked retaining original red label, very good. Alston V338.   Jarndyce 103-226 1996 £180.00

WALKER, JOHN 1732-1807   A Critical Pronouncing Dictionary, and Expositor of the English Language... London: J. Johnson; G. Wilkie & J. Robinson, 1806. 4to; half title, with new ad to this edition, 1 page ads; tree calf, little rubbed, wear to base of spine, otherwise very good.   Jarndyce 103-227 1996 £140.00

WALKER, JOHN 1732-1807   A Dictionary of the English Language, Answering at Once the Purposes of Rhyming, Spelling and Pronouncing. London: printed for T. Becket, 1775. contemporary calf, slight rubbing at tail of spine, black label, nice; Granard booklabel. Alston VI.570.   Jarndyce 103-224 1996 £400.00

WALKER, JOHN 1732-1807   Elements of Elocution. London: printed for the author and sold by T. Cadell, &c., 1781. 1st edition; 2 volumes, half titles, folding plates; handsome contemporary tree calf, gilt spines and borders, corner repaired on front board of volume 2, but all edges gilt, attractive copy, red and green labels; Alston VI 416.   Jarndyce 103-355 1996 £150.00

WALKER, JOHN 1732-1807   A Rhyming Dictionary; Answering, at the Same Time, the Purposes of Spelling and Pronouncing the English Language... London: printed for J. Johnson, J. Walker &c., 1806. 2nd edition; contemporary half calf, dark brown label, very good.   Jarndyce 103-225 1996 £65.00

WALKER, MARY ADELAIDE   Through Macedonia to the Albanian Lakes. London: Chapman and Hall, 1864. 1st edition; 12 tinted lithographs, 3 of which have additional hand coloring; green cloth with costumed figure and decoration stamped in gilt; occasional foxing, heaviest to front prelims and only affecting one image, very good. Hermitage SP95-1116 1996 $950.00

WALKER, R.   The Flora of Oxfordshire, and its Contiguous Counties... Oxford: 1833. 8vo; pages cxxxv, 338, folding table, 12 plates; neatly rebacked, preserving spine.   John Henly 27-248 1996 £68.00

WALKER, WILLIAM 1824-1860   The War in Nicaragua. Mobile: S. H. Goetzel, 1860. 1st edition; 8vo; 432 pages; frontispiece, large folding map; original brown cloth, spine bit rubbed and soiled; very scarce. Kenneth Karmiole 1NS-149 1996 $300.00

WALKER, WILLIAM SIDNEY   Gustavus Vasa and Other Poems. London: for Longman, Hurst, Rees, Orme and Brown, 1813. 1st edition; 8vo; pages xxiii, (i) blank, 230, (xxxiv) notes; contemporary half calf, smooth spine gilt in compartments, gilt lettered direct, drab paper sides, marbled edges, tiny area of insect damage at foot of front joint, sides rubbed, attractive copy.   Simon Finch 24-253 1996 £80.00

WALL, ALFRED H.   A Manual of Artistic Colouring, as Applied to Photographs. London: Thomas Piper, 1861. 1st edition; 8vo; viii, 266, x pages ads, half title; blind and gilt stamped blue cloth; very good, scarce. Gernsheim 863.   Ken Spelman 30-49 1996 £220.00

WALL, WALTER   Spider Poems. Madison: Perishable Press, 1967. One in an edition of 250 copies; 9.5 x 6.5 inches; text handset Palatino and display is Michelangelo, printed in red, brown and black on Nideggen mould made paper; brown cloth over board with title blindstamped on front cover; fine. Hamady 11.   Joshua Heller 21-183 1996 $150.00

WALLACE NUTTING INC.   Wallace Nutting Windsors. Correct Windsor Furniture. N.P.: Saugus: Wallace Nutting Inc., 1918. 4to; 48 pages and (2) page price list tipped in; original printed wrappers, evidence of previous price list tipped in on rear inside wrapper, very good. 1 copy in NUC.   Robert F. Lucas 42-41 1996 $150.00

WALLACE'S American Trotting Register. Volume 3; original binding, back cover stained.   October Farm 36-313 196 $135.00

WALLACE'S American Trotting Register. New York: 1874. Volume 2; original binding, shelfworn, 3 inch tear in top of back hinge, interior tight and clean.   October Farm 36-313b 1996 $135.00

WALLACE, ALFRED RUSSEL 1823-1913   The Malay Archipelago; the Land of the Orang-Utan and the Bird of Paradise. London: Macmillan & Co., 1869. 2nd edition; 8vo; 2 volumes; xix, 312, 341, (2) pages; illustrations, large folding map at front of volume one; original medium green cloth with small pictorial decoration in gilt on upper cover; inner rear hinges cracked, some very minor war at spine ends, very faint, small spot on each spine from removal of label, still fine, bright set. David Mason 71-149 1996 $240.00

WALLACE, ALFRED RUSSEL 1823-1913   The Malay Archipelago. New York: 1869. 1st American edition; 8vo; pages 638, 8 plates and 43 illustrations, 2 folding maps and 8 maps; original cloth, trifle used, trifle loose; from the collection of Jan Coldewey.   Wheldon & Wesley 207-115 1996 £500.00

WALLACE, ALFRED RUSSEL 1823-1913   The Malay Archipelago. New York: Harper, 1869. 1st American edition, published the same year as the first edition; 8vo; 2 maps, 8 plates and numerous text illustrations; original purple cloth, bit worn, spine badly faded.   Maggs Bros. Ltd. 1190-272 1996 £75.00

WALLACE, ALFRED RUSSEL 1823-1913   A Narrative of Travels on the Amazon and Rio Negro, with an Account of the Native Tribes and Observations on the Climate, Geology and Natural History of the Amazon Valley. London: Reeve, 1853. 1st edition; 1st issue; 8vo; pages viii, 541, 2 pages undated ads, tinted frontispiece, map, 8 plates, folding table; original olive cloth, rebacked.   Richard Adelson W94/95-174 1996 $985.00

WALLACE, ALFRED RUSSEL 1823-1913   Palm Trees of the Amazon and Their Uses. London: 1853. 1st edition; 8vo; pages viiii, 129; 47 plain lithographic plates, lithographic map; original green blindstamped cloth, tear and split to head of spine, some dampstaining to front cover, back cover somewhat curled, most of the plates are dampstained, sometimes covering as much as a third of the plate, text is clean; author's first book, and one of his rarest.   Raymond M. Sutton VII-41 1996 $1,450.00

WALLACE, ALFRED RUSSEL 1823-1913   Tropical Nature and Other Essays. London: Macmillan, 1878. 1st edition; xiii, 356 pages, ad leaf; ex-library, newly rebound, corner torn from 1 page, not affecting text. John Johnson 135-93 1996 $100.00

WALLACE, ALFRED RUSSEL 1823-1913   The Wonderful Century. London: 1898. 1st edition; 8vo; pages xii, 400; portrait, 12 folding charts; cloth, gilt.   John Henly 27-155 1996 £65.00

WALLACE, D. MAC KENZIE   Russia. London: Cassell, Petter & Galpin, 1877. 5th edition; 8vo; 2 volumes, xiv, 466; viii, 472 pages, (12) pages ads; 2 large folding color maps; covers lightly soiled, bookplates; very good.   Chapel Hill 94-347 1996 $150.00

WALLACE, DAVID FOSTER   The Broom of the System. New York: Viking/Penguin, 1987. Uncorrected proof; 8vo; author's first book; pritned wrappers; as new, rare.   James S. Jaffe 34-671 1996 $225.00

WALLACE, F. W.   Roving Fisherman. An Autobiography. Gardenvale: 1955. Limited to 1000 numbered copies; quarto; pages xxi, 512, many illustrations; original binding, nice.   Stephen Lunsford 45-168 1996 $100.00

WALLACE, H. F.   British Deer Heads. 1913. Limited to 600 copies; 4to; illustrations; original white buckram, lightly soiled/browned as usual; bookplate of Gilfrid William Hartley.   David Grayling J95Biggame-328 1996 £150.00

WALLACE, H. F.   Stalks Abroad. Being Some Account of the Sport Obtained During a Two Years' Tour of the World. 1908. illustrations; original pictorial gilt cloth, light foxing to some pages; excellent copy. David Grayling J95Biggame-602 1996 £80.00

WALLACE, JAMES   Every Man His Own Letter Writer; or, the New and Complete Art of Letter-Writing. London: printed for J. Cooke, 1782? 12mo; frontispiece, 24 page catalog; contemporary sheep, rubbed, splits in hinges, contents sound. Not in Alston.   Jarndyce 103-298 196 £50.00

WALLACE, LEW 1827-1905   Ben-Hur. New York: Harper & Bros., 1880. 1st edition; 1st issue with early state of the dedication; 8vo; original blue cloth with 'aesthetic' floral design, rubbed and faded, spine repaired, 12 pages publisher's ads for 'Novels' at back, some browning and soiling, generally light, upper hinge starting, brown morocco backed slipcase; rare first issue; Grolier 'American' 82.   James Cummins 14-218 1996 $500.00

WALLACE, LEW 1827-1905   Ben Hur, a Tale of the Christ. New York: Harper & Bros., 1892. Garfield edition, number 304 of 350 copies; 8vo; 2 volumes; illustrations by William Martin Johnson, frontispiece and photogravures; original vellum gilt, some soiling and rubbing, generally light, some light browning of endpapers, else very good, attractive set. James Cummins 14-217 1996 $150.00

WALLACE, PATRICK MAXWELL STEWART   The Trials of Patrick Maxwell Stewart Wallace and Michael Shaw Stewart Wallace for Wilfully Destroying the Brig Dryad, Off Cuba, with Intent to Defraud the Marine Assurance Companies and Underwriters. London: printed and published by Williams and Son, 1841. Modern quarter morocco, quite clean, attractive copy.   Meyer Boswell SL26-84 1996 $450.00

WALLACE, ROBERT   A Dissertation on the Verb of the English Language, Its Moods, Tenses and Inflections, Delivered Before the Members of the Literary and Philosophical Society of Chesterfield, Dec. 7, 1832. Chesterfield: printed by J. and T. Woodhead, 1832. 1st and probably only edition; 8vo; 28 pages; recently well bound in cloth backed marbled boards, spine lettered in gilt; very good. Rare. Not in NUC.   John Drury 82-286 1996 £75.00

WALLER, EDMUND   The Works of Edmund Waller, Esq. London: J. Tonson, 1730. 2nd edition; 12mo; (14), 295, clxii pages; 2 frontispiece portraits and 2 plates, folding plate torn and chipped, otherwise very good; modern three quarter calf by Brentano's, with raised bands. Chapel Hill 94-418 1996 $150.00

WALLER, EDMUND   The Works...in Verse and Prose. London: Tonson, 1753. Octavo; pages (16), 272; frontispiece; original polished calf, spine profusely gilt decorated, leather label, marbled endpapers, all edges sprinkled, silk ribbon marker; wear to spine and hinges, text excellent; With 2 fine armorial bookplates on pastedown: Robert Walpole of Lincoln's Inn, on flyleaf W. Baylies, M.D. (physician to Frederick the Great). Lowndes IV 1892; CBEL II 455.   Hartfield 48-L90 1996 $295.00

WALLER, ERIK   Bibliotheca Walleriana. New York: 1990. Facsimile of 1955 edition; 2 volumes in 1, 471 pages, 494 pages, plus paltes; original binding; GM 6786.1.   W. Bruce Fye 71-1868 1996 $150.00

WALLER, JOHN FRANCIS   Pictures from English Literature. London: Cassell, Petter and Galpin, n.d. 2nd edition; 8vo; viii, 163, (1) pages, 19 pages; frontispiece; publisher's gilt cloth, all edges gilt, sporadic faint foxing, else fine.   Bookpress 75-136 1996 $225.00

WALLER, ROBERT JAMES   Bridges of Madison County. New York: Warner Books, 1992. 1st edition; fine copy in fine dust jacket; signed and dated 5/22/92.   Oracle Books 1-322 196 $350.00

WALLER, ROBERT JAMES   The Bridges of Madison County. New York: Warner, 1992. 1st edition; fine in fine dust jacket.   Alice Robbins 15-336 1996 $125.00

WALLER, WILLIAM   The Tragical History of Jetzer: or, a Faithful Narrative of the Feigned Visions, Counterfeit Revelations and False Miracles of the Dominican Fathers of the Covent of Berne in Switzerland... London: Nathanael Ponder, 1679. 8vo; (x), 38 pages, last leaf repeated, marginal staining. Wing W548.   Robert Clark 38-97 1996 £55.00

WALLIS, G. HARRY   Illustrated Catalogue of Classical Antiquities from the Site of the Temple of Diana, Nemi, Italy. Nottingham: Museum Art Gallery, 1893. 1st illustrated edition; 4to; frontispiece, 5 page list of subscribers, 69 pages, 19 plates; three quarter rubbed calf, 5 raised bands, crimson leather label, top edge gilt, nick at spine, top joint starting, rubbed; Very scarce.   Archaeologia Luxor-4134 1996 $350.00

WALLIS, HELEN   Carteret's Voyage Round the World 1766-1769. Cambridge: for the Hakluyt Society, 1965. 1st edition thus; 2 volumes; fine in lightly worn dust jackets.   Hermitage SP95-1117 1996 $100.00

WALLIS, JOHN   Grammatica Linguae Anglicanae. London: Millar Bowyer, 1765. 8vo; pages (35), 281, frontispiece, tooled ink stamp of Liberty on rear flyleaf; full red morocco binding executed by John Matthewman for Thomas Hollis, in center of front cover is gilt figure of Brittania, seated; lower cover has seated owl, spine tooled with title and Caduceus of Mercury, marbled edges;   Family Album Tillers-664 1996 $800.00

WALLIS, THOMAS WILKINSON   Autobiography of...Sculptor in Wood and Extracts from His Sixty Years' Journal... Louth: J. W. Goulding, & Son, 1899. 1st and only edition; 8vo; xv, 244 pages; 24 illustrations, 4 diagrams; red cloth, spine faded, otherwise very good.   K Books 442-482 1996 £65.00

WALPOLE, HORACE 1719-1797   Anecdotes of Painting in England... (with) A Catalogue of Engravers, who Have Been Born, or Resided in England. London: printed for J. Dodsley, 1782. 3rd edition; 2nd edition of volume 4; 8vo; 5 volumes; rebacked in contemporary tree calf; very good set.   Ken Spelman 30-17 1996 £360.00

WALPOLE, HORACE 1719-1797   The Castle of Otranto... London: Tho. Lownds, 1765/64. 1st edition; tall copy, 8vo; contemporary tree calf with red morocco lettering piece, board edges sprinkled, preserved in half morocco sliding case with inner chemise. Rothschild 2491; Hazen 17; Tinker 2274.   Book Block 32-60 1996 $5,750.00

WALPOLE, HORACE 1719-1797   The Castle of Otranto. London: Jones & Co., 1825. 12mo; 4 pages publisher's ads at rear; publisher's smooth pinkish cloth with printed paper spine label that reads Diamond Classics across top and with price, 1s.6.d. at bottom; preserved in exceptionally fine condition. Hazen p. 66.   Book Block 32-61 1996 $175.00

WALPOLE, HORACE 1719-1797   The Castle of Otranto. Westerham: Limited Editions Club, 1975. Limited to 2000 copies; tall 8vo; reproductions, designed by Ruari McLean; signed by Wilmarth Lewis, who provided introduction; quarter blue levant, owner blindstamp to titlepage, otherwise fine in fine case.   Charles Agvent 4-1164 1996 $100.00

WALPOLE, HORACE 1719-1797   A Catalogue of Horace Walpole's Library. (with) Horace Walpole's Library. London: 1969. Small 4to; 3 volumes, blue cloth, dust jackets.   Maggs Bros. Ltd. 1191-46 1996 £85.00

WALPOLE, HORACE 1719-1797   A Catalogue of the Royal and Noble Authors of England, Scotland and Ireland. London: printed for John Scott, No. 442, Strand, 1806. New edition; 8vo; 5 volumes; half titles, portrait frontispiece to volume 1, engraved frontispiece to volume 2, 148 stipple engraved plates, text and plates all in very good condition; full polished tan calf, double gilt rule border to boards with tiny gilt ornamental cornerpieces, green and brown morocco labels to spines, elaborate gilt tooling to panelled spines, upper board to volume 2 slightly scored, edges and endpapers uniformly marbled; handsome copy.   Beeleigh Abbey BA56-167 1996 £350.00

WALPOLE, HORACE 1719-1797   Essay on Modern Gardening. Strawberry Hill: T. Kirgate, 1785. 1st edition; one of 400 copies, 200 for presentation by Walpole and 200 for the Duc, none being for sale; 4to; pages 94; engraved vignette (offset onto endpaper), text nice and clean, with wide margins; modern full calf; very nice; no presentation on this copy, but notes on endpapers indicate that it came from both the "Burdett Coutts" and "Pinkerton" sales. Hazen, Strawberry Hill Press 31; Henrey 1475; Hunt 675.   Second Life Books 103-205 1996 $1,350.00

WALPOLE, HORACE 1719-1797   Historic Doubts on the Life and Reign of King Richard the Third. London: printed by J. Dodsley, 1768. 1st edition; one of 1200 copies; 4to; contemporary wrappers, spine repaired, some marginal soiling and short tears, some offsetting, some erased marginal pencilled marks, very good in blue cloth folding box. Hazen 19. James Cummins 14-165 1996 $250.00

WALPOLE, HORACE 1719-1797   Letters from Horace Walpole to George Montagu, from the Year 1736-1770. London: Rodwell & Martin, 1818. 1st edition; 4to; contemporary three quarter maroon calf, faded around spine, gilt lines and lettering on spine, marbled edges; fine, bright copy; binding bears the emblem of a horned ram atop a coronet with initials J.G.S. in gilt at bottom spine, fine, bright copy.   Appelfeld Gallery 54-179 1996 $500.00

WALPOLE, HORACE 1719-1797   Memoirs of the Reign of King George the Third. London: Richard Bentley, 1845. 1st edition; 8vo; 4 volumes, half titles; errata leaf, errata slip tipped in to volume 3; frontispiece to all volumes; full polished tan calf, double gilt rule border to boards, tiny gilt ornaments to corners, elaborate gilt tooling to panelled spines, green and brown morocco labels to spines, joints slightly rubbed, edges and endpapers uniformly marbled. Armorial bookplates to front pastedowns of all volumes.   Beeleigh Abbey BA56-166 1996 £250.00

WALPOLE, HORACE 1719-1797   The Mysterious Mother: a Tragedy. Dublin: J. Archer, W. Jones and R. White, 1791. Tall 8vo; contemporary calf with single decorated border on both covers, spine with five raised bands, gilt decoration and black morocco lettering piece, extremities lightly rubbed but sound, attractive copy, altogether unsophisticated; Rothschild 2494 (Strawberry Hill ed.); Tinker 2276; Hazen pp. 82-84. Book Block 32-62 1996 $475.00

WALPOLE, HORACE 1719-1797   The Mysterious Mother. Dublin: John Archer, 1791. Pirated copy, presumably from a Strawberry Hill copy; three quarter morocco, marbled boards and endpapers, spine gilt in compartments, Walpole's name written in on titlepage in an early hand; exceptionally nice, uncommon. Hazen 83.   Hartfield 48-L91 1996 $225.00

WALPOLE, HORATIO   The Complaints of the Manufacturers, Relating to the Abuses in Marking the Sheep, and Winding the Wool, Fairly Stated, and Impartially Considered, in a Letter to the Marquis of Rockingham. London: printed by W. Bowyer, 1742. 1st edition; 8vo; half titles; modern boards; nice. Kress 5190; Goldsmith 8705; Higgs 262.   Anthony W. Laywood 108-135 1996 £245.00

WALPOLE, HUGH   The Fortress. London: Macmillan, 1931. Limited larage paper edition, limited to 350 copies; signed; 8vo; pages x, 811; extending pedigree and folding map; original cloth backed blue boards, spine label.   R.F.G. Hollett & Son 78-479 1996 £85.00

WALPOLE, HUGH   Vanessa. London: Macmillan, 1933. Signed limited large paper edition of 315 copies; 8vo; pages xii, 852; extending pedigree and folding map; original cloth backed blue boards, spine label, lower board edges little worn;   R.F.G. Hollett & Son 78-495 1996 £85.00

WALPOLE-BOND, J.   A History of Sussex Birds. London: 1938. Royal 8vo; 3 volumes; 53 colored plates; original buckram, trifle faded, trifle marked; good, with slightly used dust jackets, author's signature pasted to front endpaper of volume 1.   Wheldon & Wesley 207-890 1996 £200.00

WALSH, JOHN HENRY   The   Dogs of the British Islands. London: Horace Cox, 1867. Reprinted from the "Field" Newspaper; 4to; viii, 148 pages; 29 wood engraved plates; publisher's dark green cloth, decorated in gilt and blind, gilt edges, corners very slightly worn and small stain on back cover, otherwise very good.   Thomas Thorp 489-314 1996 £295.00

WALSH, JOHN HENRY   The   Modern Sportsman's Gun and Rifle. London: 1988. Reprint; many illustrations, folding plates; quality buckram, with dust wrappers;   David A.H. Grayling 3/95-331 1996 £50.00

WALSH, ROBERT 1784-1859   A   Letter On the Genius and Dispositions of the French Government... Baltimore: P. H. Nicklin and Co. and several others, 1810. 1st edition; 1st issue; 8vo; iv, 253 pages; original boards, neatly rebacked; some foxing and light dampstaining, otherwise good, large, uncut copy. Kress B5763; Sabin 101165.   John Drury 82-287 1996 £125.00

WALSH, THOMAS   Journal of the Late Campaign in Egypt... London: Cadell and Davies, 1803. 4to; pages viii, 17,, 2, 261, 2, 150; 50 plates and maps (6 hand colored), modern half brown morocco, marbled boards, some light foxing. Abbey Travel 266.   Richard Adelson W94/95-175 1996 £425.00

WALSINGHAM, FRANCIS   A   Search Made Into Matters of Religion... St. Omer: English College Press, 1609. 1st edition; 4to; (xxiv), 284, 289-512, (viii) pages; 19th century divinity calf, ruled in blind, all edges gilt, bit rubbed and scuffed, titlepage frayed and repaired on outer edge, not affecting text, occasional minor staining. Good copy. STC 25002; A & R 875.   Robert Clark 38-124 1996 £175.00

WALSINGHAM, LORD   Shooting, Field and Covert, Moor and Marsh. London: 1886. 1st edition; plates and text illustrations; finely bound in half scarlet morocco, gilt sporting emblems on spine, marbled boards and endpapers by Stikeman. Choice copy.   David A.H. Grayling 3/95-236 1996 £75.00

WALSINGHAM, LORD   Shooting: Field and Covert. (and) Shooting: Moor and Marsh. London: Longmans, Green and Co., 1895/93. 5th edition; 4th edition; octavo; 2 volumes, xv, 357; xiii, 358 pages; numerous illustrations; original brown cloth pictorially stamped in brown and lettered in black and white on front cover and spine with additional gilt lettering on spine, light wear to extremities, occasional light foxing, very good, partially unopened.   Heritage Book Shop 196-206 1996 $150.00

WALTER, H.   Studies of Cattle from Nature. London: published by H. Walter, April 16, 1821. Oblong 4to; 4 lithograph plates, lithographed by Hullmandel after drawings by Walter; original wrappers with decorative printed title on upper cover, some marginal browning and backstrip worn, but good copy, very scarce.   Ken Spelman 30-35 1996 £95.00

WALTER, HENRY   A   History of England. London: printed for J. G. F. & Rivington, 1840. 8 x 5 1/4 inches; 7 volumes; engraved maps as frontispiece in 6 of the volumes; contemporary light brown polished half calf, marbled sides, edges and endpapers, raised bands, spines attractively gilt in compartments in antique style, red and green morocco labels, corners bit rubbed, outer edge of one volume little worn, paper sides somewhat chafed, but only trivial signs of wear, otherwise fine internally, pretty set in excellent condition; 19th century armorial bookplate of Ferdinand M. McVeagh in each volume.   Phillip J. Pirages 33-506 1996 $750.00

WALTER, of Coventry   The   Historical Collections. London: 1872-73. 8vo; 2 volumes, pages 512, 521; original cloth.   Howes Bookshop 265-1587 1996 £55.00

WALTER, RICHARD 1716?-1785   A   Voyage Round the World, in the Years MDCCXL, I, II,, III, IV. London: printed for the author by John and Paul Knapton, 1748. 1st edition; 4to; 42 folding engraved plates and maps, occasional foxing, 12 page list of subscribers, final leaf of direction to binder; contemporary red morocco, gilt borders, spine and inner dentelles gilt, all edges gilt, rebacked, original spine laid down, covers bit scratched, some rubbing; handsome copy on royal paper in binding appropriate for presentation; pres. copy neatly inscribed by recipient, 2nd Duke of Portland "Given to me by Anson at Aix la Chapelle June ye 7th, 1748. W. Bentinck"; early booklabel of Mary Boydell. Hill 317-8; Sabin 1625.   Ximenes 109-8 1996 $5,000.00

WALTER, RICHARD 1716?-1785   A   Voyage Round the World... London: John and Paul Knapton, 1748. 3rd edition; 3 folding maps; contemporary polished calf, gilt on spine; Sabin 1626; Cox I p. 49; Hill I p. 318.   Parmer Books 039Nautica-039011 1996 $650.00

WALTER, RICHARD 1716?-1785   A   Voyage Round the World in the Years MDCCXL, I, II, III, IV. London: printed for the author by John and Paul Knapton, 1749. 5th edition; 4to; 17 leaves, 417 pages, 1 leaf (directions to binder), 42 plates, some fat lateral wormholes in margins of last leaves not affecting text, very small wormhole in gutter of prelims, repair to folding chart at p. 237; with inconsequential loss, contemporary calf, rebacked.   H. M. Fletcher 121-83 1996 £350.00

WALTER, RICHARD 1716?-1785   A   Voyage Round the World in the Years MDXXKL, I, II, III, IV. London: printed for D. Browne, T. Osborne and J. Shipton...& H. Woodgate, 1756. 9th edition; 4to; 417 pages of text, 29 large folding plates, 13 maps, plates and maps all in good condition, with only very minor occasional offsetting to text; very neat repairs to tears in maps of Philippine and Pacific Ocean; full old speckled calf, triple gilt rule borders, hinges cracked, leaving upper joint tender, fully gilt panelled spine, brown morocco label, marbled edges. Hill, Pac. Voyages p. 318.   Beeleigh Abbey BA56-33 1996 £650.00

WALTER, RICHARD 1716?-1785   Anson's Voyage Round the World. London: Martin Hopkinson, 1928. 8vo; pages lxiv, 402; 44 plates, 4 folding maps; cloth backed boards.   Richard Adelson W94/95-211 1996 $120.00

WALTER, RYE   The   Norfolk Antiquarian Miscellany. Second Series. Parts 1, 2 and 3. Norwich: Gibbs and Waller, 1906/07/08. 1st edition; limited to 100 copies only; 8vo; 172 pages, illustrations; 161 pages, illustrations; 130 pages, illustrations and folding chart; cloth spine and stiff printed boards; spine cloth very worn, good to very good. Robert F. Lucas 42-10 1996 $125.00

WALTERS, H. B.   Marbles and Bronzes: Fifty-Two Plates from Selected Subjects in the Department of Greek and Roman Antiquities. London: British Museum, 1928. 3rd edition; large 4to; 8 pages, 5 figures, 52 collotype plates; original gilt lettered cloth.   Archaeologia Luxor-4140 1996 $350.00

WALTERS, H. B.   Select Bronzes, Greek, Roman and Etruscan in the Department of Antiquities. London: British Museum, 1915. Folio; 9 pages, 73 plates, 73 pages of descriptive text; original cloth, corners bumped, otherwise fine.   Archaeologia Luxor-4139 1996 $650.00

WALTERS, HENRY   Incunabula Typographica. A Descriptive Catalogue of the Books Printed in the Fifteenth Century (1450-1500) in the Library of Henry Walters. Baltimore: 1906. 4to; 542 pages; handsome full leather done on deckled edged rag paper, bound in 15th century style with fleur-de-lys tooling on boards, recently rebacked in original style; presentation copy with note on front pastedown "Presented with the compliments of the Trustees of the Walters Art Gallery".   James Tait Goodrich K40-164 1996 $225.00

WALTERS, HENRY   Incunabula Typographica. Baltimore: 1906. 4to; color frontispiece, plate and numerous facsimiles; later blue and grey cloth.   Maggs Bros. Ltd. 1191-222 1996 $80.00

WALTERS, JOHN   A   Dissertation on the Welsh Language, Pointing Out It's Antiquity, Copiousness, Grammatical Perception, with Remarks On it's Poetry... Cowbridge: printed for the author by R. & D. Thomas, 1771. 70 pages, lacking half title; uncut, stabbed almost as issued in dark drab wrappers, slight dusting and spotting with small tears at edges, but very good.   Jarndyce 103-90 1996 £220.00

WALTERS, MINETTE   The   Scold's Bridle. Bristol: Scorpion Press, 1994. 1/15 deluxe lettered copies, signed by author and by A. Taylor who provided author appreciation; quarter bound goatskin with raised bands; fine.   Quill & Brush 102-1722 1996 $500.00

WALTERS, MINETTE   The   Sculptress. London: Macmillan, 1993. 1st edition; signed; fine in fine dust jacket.   Book Time 2-737 1996 $100.00

WALTON, IZAAK 1593-1683   The   Compleat Angler. London: Henry Kent, 1750. 1st Moses Browne edition; small 12mo; fine engraved frontispiece, 5 full page plates, numerous woodcuts, lower margin of title cropped close wity some loss to imprint, occasionally cropped close in upper margin, without loss; near contemporary full red-brown morocco over thin boards, fold-over flap, color faded around spine; generally very good.   Ian Wilkinson 95/1-152 1996 £195.00

WALTON, IZAAK 1593-1683   The Complete Angler. London: printed for Samuel Bagster, 1808. Called the "Seventh Edition: on the engraved title leaf; 10 x 6 1/2 inches; 2 p.l., vi, 7-61, (1), (lxiii)-lxvi, 67-512 (i.e. 510) pages, (1) leaf (ads); vignette on engraved title, 17 plates, all but two of them engraved by P. Audinet, mostly after drawings by S. Wale, two large woodcuts and 17 illustrations of fish in text; original printed list of illustrations pasted inside front cover; original paper boards, apparently (though not certainly) rebacked some time ago, original paper label on spine, edges untrimmed and unopend, spine evenly sunned, little wear, as expected, to corners and eges, otherwise binding in remarkably fine condition, unusually solid and clean, slight browning to frontispiece and title, one leaf bit dampstained in margin, minor faint foxing here and there, but excellent internally and obviously never read; beautiful copy. Coigney 17.   Phillip J. Pirages   33-507   1996 $550.00

WALTON, IZAAK 1593-1683   The Complete Angler or Contemplative Man's Recreation. London: Samuel Bagster, 1815. 8vo; pages 514, (20); engraved half title with vignette frame, portrait frontispiece (foxed and offset to title), 13 plates, 35 engravings, ads discarded, foxed; modern half russia with old marbled boards, backstrip with raised wide bands between double gilt rules, gilt lettered polished russet labels, single ruled saltire in remainder, edges of boards rubbed, marbled endpapers, hinges split but firm, good; Coigney 21; Satchell pp. 10-11; Wood pp. 38-39.   Blackwell's   B112-281   1996   £165.00

WALTON, IZAAK 1593-1683   The Complete Angler. London: William Pickering, 1826. Miniature edition; 32mo; 325, (4) pages; original green cloth, bookplate, top of spine chipped, thus good copy only.   Chapel Hill   94-400   1996 $100.00

WALTON, IZAAK 1593-1683   The Complete Angler. London: J. Major, 1835. 3rd edition; 12mo; 416 pages; 15 plates and many woodcuts; gilt decorated full calf, very good. Coigney 43.   Robert F. Lucas   42-81   1996 $300.00

WALTON, IZAAK 1593-1683   The Compleat Angler. The Lives of Donne, Wotton, Hooker, Herbert and Sanderson, with Love and Truth and Miscellaneous Writings. London: Nonesuch Press, 1929. Limited edition of 1600 numbered copies; 8vo; x, 631 pages; 6 copperplate engraved portraits, 9 color stencilled wood engraved text illustrations from drawings by Thomas Poulton; publisher's full niger morocco, gilt "I.W." monogram on front cover, top edge rough gilt, edges uncut, binding slightly spotted, internally fine.   Thomas Thorp   489-315   1996   £140.00

WALTON, IZAAK 1593-1683   The Compleat Angler. London: George G. Harrap & Co. Ltd., 1931. One of 775 copies, signed by artist; 10 1/2 x 8 1/4 inches; 223, (1) pages; color frontispiece and 11 other color plates by Arthur Rackham, several illustrations in text, title in green and black; original vellum covered boards, gilt titling and decoration on front cover and spine, top edge gilt, other edges untrimmed and partly unopened, in original publisher's numbered slipcase with paper spine label; extremely fine, white boards unusually clean and original slipcase remarkably well preserved. Haskell p. 66.   Phillip J. Pirages   33-444   1996 $1,600.00

WALTON, IZAAK 1593-1683   The Compleat Angler, or the Contemplative Man's Recreation. London: George G. Harrap & Co., 1931. Limited to 775 numbered copies, signed by artist; quarto; 223 pages; 12 color plates with descriptive tissue guards, 25 drawings in black and white by Arthur Rackham; original full vellum over boards, stamped in gilt on front cover and spine, top edge gilt, others uncut, pictorial endpapers in brown and white, head and foot of spine lightly bumped, near fine, unopened, original publisher's cardboard box. Latimore & Haskell p. 66-67.   Heritage Book Shop   196-207   1996 $1,500.00

WALTON, IZAAK 1593-1683   The Compleat Angler. London: George C. Harrap, 1931. One of 775 numbered copies; 12 color plates, many text illustrations by Arthur Rackham; signed by artist; original vellum gilt, spine gilt, original pictorial endpapers by Rackham; very fine. Trebizond   39-48   1996 $650.00

WALTON, IZAAK 1593-1683   The Compleat Angler. London: George G. Harrap & Co., 1931. 1st edition illustrated by Arthur Rackham; 4to; pages (iv), 5-223, 12 colored plates by Arthur Rackham, guarded by tissue; original slate blue cloth, gilt, top edge gilt, others untrimmed, pictorial endpapers; excellent copy.   Sotheran   PN32-147   1996   £138.00

WALTON, IZAAK 1593-1683   The Life of Dr. Sanderson, Late Bishop of Lincoln. London: Richard Marriott, 1678. 1st edition; (242), 276 pages; frontispiece; old calf, rebacked, old spine laid down, outer corners rubbed, title bit soiled. Wing W667.   Kenneth Karmiole   1NS-255   1996 $350.00

WALTON, IZAAK 1593-1683   The Life of Mr. George Herbert... London: Tho. Newcomb for Rich. Marriott, 1670. 1st edition; 2nd issue; 8vo; (3)-146, (ii) pages; frontispiece; contemporary calf, neatly rebacked, spine gilt ruled; corners little worn, edges of F4 bit dusty, nice. Wing W669; Grolier 954; Butt 8b.   Robert Clark   38-143   1996   £550.00

WALTON, IZAAK 1593-1683   The Lives. London: John Major, 1825. 1st Major edition; 7 3/4 x 5 inches; xviii pages, (1) leaf, 503, (1) pages; large paper copy; 11 mounted copperplates on India paper, 52 woodcuts in text. animated exhibition binding of black morocco by Riviere, covers framed with multiple gilt rules enclosing a field of 9 vertical rows of curvilinear decorations in blind and gilt (featuring blindstamped lilies on delicate ascending stem) alternating with twining gilt ovoids, each of which contains a blindstamped daisy surrounded by massed gilt dots, the whole field flanked by rows of arching gilt lines, each enclosing a semi circle of gilt dots, spine with similar decoration but with greater concentration of gilt dots, gilt edges, simple gilt ruled turn-ins, deep maroon endpapers; beautiful copy in extraordinarily pleasing binding. Phillip J. Pirages   33-77   1996 $1,500.00

WALTON, IZAAK 1593-1683   The Works of that Learned and Judicious Divine, Mr. Richard Hooker. Oxford: at the University Press, 1850. 2 volumes; full dark blue calf, blind tooled border to boards, double gilt rule dentelles, elaborate gilt tooling to compartments, red morocco title labels and brown morocco volume labels to spines, edges and endpapers uniformly marbled, ink inscription, corners very slightly bumped, overall very handsome set.   Beeleigh Abbey   BA56-150   1996   £200.00

WALTON, JOHN   The Oxford Companion to Medicine. New York: 1986. 1st edition; 2 volumes, 1524 pages; original binding, dust jacket. W. Bruce Fye   71-2206   1996 $125.00

WALZ, ARTHUR   Presidents Boyhood Home. Austin: 1965. 1st edition; 1/200 copies with conveyance envelope; this copy number 199. signed by speakers;   W. M. Morrison   436-365   1996 $150.00

WANDREI, DONALD   The Eye and the Finger. Sauk City: Arkham House, 1944. 1st edition; illustrations by Howard Wandrei; pictorial dust jacket, very fine.   Bromer Booksellers   87-12   1996 $200.00

WANDREI, DONALD   The Eye and the Finger. Sauk City: Arkham House, 1944. 1st edition; very good in like dust jacket save for some light chipping to head of dust jacket spine and flap-fold extremities. Aronovitz   57-1234   1996 $145.00

WANDREI, DONALD   The Web of Easter Island. Sauk City: Arkham House, 1948. 1st edition; very fine in pictorial dust jacket designed by Audrey Johnson.   Bromer Booksellers   87-28   1996 $100.00

WARBASSE, JAMES   Medical Sociology: a Series of Observations Touching Upon the Sociology of Health and the Relations of Medicine to Society. London: 1878. 1st edition; 934 pages, 2 volumes; original binding. GM 2034.   W. Bruce Fye   71-2214   1996 $250.00

WARBURTON, PETER EGERTON   Journey Across the Western Interior of Australia. London: Sampson Lowe et al, 1875. (xii), 308 pages, (40) pages; frontispiece and 8 plates, 1 large folding map, some tears along folds; original green decorated cloth, front inner hinge starting, extremities and gilt on spine rubbed, otherwise good+; the Absolon copy. Ferguson 1817; Wantrup 201.   Antipodean   28-527   1996 $950.00

WARD, ADOLPHUS WILLIAM   A History of English Dramatic Literature to the Death of Queen Anne. London: Macmillan and Co., 1875. 1st edition; royal 8vo; half titles, 2 volumes, beautifully bound in three quarter green levant morocco, gilt, fully gilt panelled spines (faded), with inset red morocco flowers, top edges gilt, by Henderson and Bisset. Charles W. Traylen   117-215   1996   £180.00

WARD, ARTEMAS   The Grocer's Encyclopedia. New York: Artemus Ward, 1911. 4to; 80 beautiful color plates, numerous black and white photos; original sturdy green buckram with some general wear and soiling, on front cover is a large leather label stating this volume was compliments of the Ideal Cocoa and Chocolate Co. of New York:. Glenn Books   36-60   1996 $250.00

WARD, EDWARD   The Insinuating Bawd, and the Repenting Harlot. London?: printed in the year 1758. Scarce reissue; 20 pages; original blue wrappers, little crumpled, but very good in original state; exceedingly rare item.   C. R. Johnson   37-46   1996   £650.00

WARD, ELIZABETH STUART PHELPS 1844-1911   Chapters from a Life. Boston and New York: Houghton Mifflin, 1897. 1st edition; 8vo; (278) pages; frontispiece and additional 23 plates; original maroon cloth, gilt lettered front and spine, top edge gilt; except for previous owner's small label, this copy is as new; Ungar p. 348; BAL 20963, binding B (no priority).   Paulette Rose   16-243   1996 $150.00

WARD, HUMPHREY   A Biographical and Critical Essay with a Catalogue Raisonne of His Works. London: Thos. Agnew & Sons, 1904. Number 150 of 350 copies; 32 x 27 cm; 2 volumes, x, 131 pages, 46 illustrations; ix, 203 pages, 24 illustrations; quarter morocco, top edge gilt, cloth sides marked.   Rainsford A54-502   1996 £300.00

WARD, LYND   Mad Man's Drum: a Novel in Woodcuts. London: and Toronto: Jonathan Cape, 1930. 1st edition; 8 x 5 3/4 inches; (130) leaves; woodcut half title, woodcut title and 128 woodcut plates; original cloth backed pictorial paper boards, paper label on spine, edges untrimmed; slight fading to covers, spine label darkened, otherwise fine. Phillip J. Pirages 33-508   1996 $125.00

WARD, LYND   Madman's Drum: a Novel in Woodcuts. New York: Cape and Son, 1930. 1st edition; 2nd printing; 8vo; over 150 woodcuts and designs; black cloth over black and white patterned boards, printed paper spine label, black endpapers, top edge stained black, uncut, slight rubbing; very good.   George J. Houle 68-147   1996 $250.00

WARD, MARY AUGUSTA ARNOLD 1851-1920   Robert Elsmere. London: Smith, Elder & Co., 1888. Cabinet edition; 8vo; 2 volumes; original dark green cloth, gilt lettering on spine, some wear to extremities, otherwise very nice; inscribed presentation copy from author to Rev. T. A. Armstrong. McFarlin p. 108.   Paulette Rose 16-337   1996 $100.00

WARD, PATIENCE   The Speech of the Right Honourable Sir Patience Warade, Lord Mayor Elect, at Guild-Hall, London, September 29, 1680... London: printed for Thomas Collins and Brabazon Aylmer, 1680. Folio; 4 pages; uncut, disbound.   H. M. Fletcher 121-56   1996 £55.00

WARD, ROBERT PLUMER   Illustrations of Human Life. London: Henry Colburn, 1837. 1st edition; small 8vo; 3 volumes; contemporary half polished calf with raised bands and morocco spine labels, some rubbing, else very good. Sadleir 3299.   Chapel Hill 94-120 1996 $150.00

WARD, ROBERT PLUMER   Pictures of the World at Home and Abroad. London: Colburn, 1839. 1st edition; 8vo; 3 volumes; original boards, rebacked, new labels, uncut; bookplate of Earl of Lonsdale, inscribed by author.   Howard S. Mott 227-146   1996 $375.00

WARD, ROWLAND   Records of Big Game. 1899. 3rd edition; illustrations; lovely copy bound in modern half dark green morocco; fine. David Grayling J95Biggame-612   1996 £200.00

WARD, ROWLAND   Records of Big Game. 1907. 5th edition; illustrations; spine faded, covers very lightly marked, contents excellent. David Grayling J95Biggame-609   1996 £100.00

WARD, ROWLAND   Records of Big Game. 1910. 6th edition; illustrations; original cloth, bit rubbed, contents very good.   David Grayling J95Biggame-614   1996 £100.00

WARD, ROWLAND   Records of Big Game. 1922. 8th edition; illustrations; nice copy, near fine in repaired dust jacket.   David Grayling J95Biggame-611   1996 £180.00

WARD, ROWLAND   Records of Big Game. 1922. 8th edition; illustrations; recased in original cloth; good copy.   David Grayling J95Biggame-610   1996 £140.00

WARD, ROWLAND   Records of Big Game. 1928. 9th edition; illustrations; buckram, slightly rubbed and faded; contents fine, very good copy.   David Grayling J95Biggame-613   1996 £250.00

WARD, ROWLAND   Records of Big Game (Africa). 1962/64/66. Including 1st and 2nd addendum; colored frontispiece, numerous photos illustrations; matching green cloth, all 3 bit discolored on covers, otherwise fine.   David Grayling J95Biggame-209   196 £75.00

WARD, ROWLAND   The Sportsman's Handbook to Practical Collecting and Preserving Trophies. 1891. illustrations; original leather, pictorial gilt; excellent copy; with hand written letter from author regarding the book. David Grayling J95Biggame-607   1996 £70.00

WARD, THOMAS   The Bird Fancier's Recreation: Being Curious Remarks on the Nature of Song-Birds... London: John Smith, 1770. New edition; 8vo; 15 crude hand colored plates, rather soiled and stained copy; marbled boards, worn, later calf spine.   Maggs Bros. Ltd. 1190-623   1996 £160.00

WARD, THOMAS   England's Reformation: from the Time of King Henry VIII, to the End of Oates's Plot, a Poem in Four Canto's. London: for W. B. and sold by Thomas Bickerton, 1716. 8vo; pages (iv), 402, titlepage in red and black; contemporary panelled calf, raised bands, lacks label, red sprinkled edges, pastedowns lifted, spine rubbed at head and tail, corners lightly bumped, very good. Foxon W209.   Simon Finch 24-254 1996 £90.00

WARD, WILLIAM A.   The Role of the Phoenicians in the Interaction of Mediterranean Civilizations: Papers Presented to the Archaeological Symposium at the American University of Beirut: March 1967. Beirut: American University of Beirut, 1968. 4to; xi, 152 pages; numerous figures and 40 plates; original cloth, shelfworn dust jacket.   Archaeologia Luxor-2806 1996 $125.00

WARDE, F.   Printers Ornaments Applied to the Composition of Decorative Borders, Panels and Patterns. London: Lanston Monotype Corp. Ltd., 1928. 4to; 114 pages, original red and gilt cloth, headcaps mildly bumped; ink inscription from "BLW" (Beatrice Warde) to Ruari McLean. Appleton 277.   Maggs Bros. Ltd. 1191-223 1996 £80.00

WARDEN, C. F.   The Battle of Waterloo. London: printed for the author by Dean & Munday, 1817. Octavo; (4), 48 pages; frontispiece, 8 hand colored aquatint plates; original blue boards with printed paper label on front cover, spine reinforced with black cloth, occasional foxing, staining and offsetting, two corners torn away, previous owner's ink inscription; very good overall; Not in Abbey or Tooley.   Heritage Book Shop 196-197   1996 $600.00

WARDENBURG, FRED A.   Operation Safari. (with) Safari Encore. privately printed, 1948. 2nd printing, limited to 100 copies; & 1st edition, limited to 400 copies; fine set.   Bookworm & Silverfish 276-220 1996 $110.00

WARDROP, JAMES   The Morbid Anatomy of the Human Eye. London: John Churchill, 1834. 2nd edition; 8vo; 2 volumes, 2 leaves of ads, 18 plates; some light staining and foxing of text; original boards, uncut, new cloth spines, printed paper labels; Becker 400; GM 5340.   Anthony W. Laywood 108-246 1996 £450.00

WARE, HENRY   Papers on the Diaries of William Nicolson, Sometime Bishop of Carlisle. Kendal: Titus Wilson, 1905. Volumes 1-5, pages (ii), 236, 67, 78, 36; with separate title, 2 plates, 2 pages of facsimiles; contemporary full blind ruled roan gilt, head of spine little frayed; very scarce.   R.F.G. Hollett & Son 78-269 1996 £140.00

WARE, HENRY   A Sermon Delivered at the Ordination of Rev. Chandler Robbins, Over the Second Congreational Church in Boston, December 4, 1833. Boston: James W. Burditt, 1833. 1st edition; 8vo; 32 pages; removed, light foxing. BAL 5177; Howe Lib. RWE 11. B&B 22536. M & S Rare Books 60-328 1996 $175.00

WARE, WILLIAM ROTCH   The Georgian Period. New York: U.P.C. Book Co., 1901-08. folio; 451 plates and over 500 in text illustrations, cloth; extremely worn but complete.   The Bookpress 75-254 1996 $325.00

WARHOL, ANDY   Andy Warhol's Exposures. New York: Andy Warhol Books/Grosset & Dunlop, 1979. 1st edition; quarto; photos; very good+ in dust jacket; signed by author, inscribed.   Lame Duck Books 19-39 1996 $450.00

WARHOL, ANDY   The Philosophy of Andy Warhol. New York: Harcourt Brace Jovanovich, 1975. 1st edition; 241 pages; orange cloth spine, yellow paper covered boards, fine with tiny spot to top edge in fine dust jacket, inscribed, signed and initialled by artist with a drawing of Campbell's soup can.   Orpheus Books 17-12 1996 $650.00

WARHOL, ANDY   Portraits of the 70s. New York: Random House, 1979. 1st limited edition, one of 200 numbered copies, signed in black felt-tip pen by Warhol; small square 4to; 141 pages, 112 color plates from original acrylic and silkscreen enamels on canvas; black cloth, spine lettered in gilt, black endpapers, fine in lightly worn slipcase with partial crack at one edge.   Marilyn Braiterman 15-201 1996 $400.00

WARING, J. B.   Art Treasures of the United Kingdom, from the Art Treasures Exhibition, Manchester. London: Day and Son, 1858. 1st edition; folio; (xviii), 42, (1), 32, (1), (49)-80, (2), 27 pages; 50 plates; contemporary leather; edges rubbed, else very good. Bookplate of Alexander Lord Sultown. Friedman 176; Ray 236; Mclean p. 125. Bookpress 75-137 1996 $925.00

WARING, J. B.   Illustrations of Architecture and Ornament. London: Day & Son, 1865. Folio; 19 pages + 70 plates drawn and etched on copper; original cloth gilt.   Family Album Tillers-666 1996 $225.00

WARING, ROBERT LEWIS   As We See It. Washington: Press of C. F. Sudwarth, 1918. 1st edition; frontispiece; dampstain to tops of boards and lightly to edges of first and last few pages, only a fair, if sound, copy; very uncommon.   Between the Covers 43-203 1996 $275.00

WARING, THOMAS   A Treatise on Archery, or the Art of Shooting with the English Bow... London: R. Hamm, 1847. 9th edition; small thin 8vo; 2 engraved plates, contemporary aqua boards (tan rebacking, stains), very good.   George J. Houle 68-3 1996 $275.00

WARNER, CHARLES DUDLEY   The Complete Writings of... Hartford: American Pub, 1904. One of 612 numbered copies, signed by editor, Thomas Lounsbury, with original ms. leaf by Warner tipped in; 8vo; 15 volumes, portraits, plates, a number of the illustrations signed in pencil by the artists; original binding, some rubbing and chipping to extremities, very good.   Charles Agvent 4-1167 1996 $600.00

WARNER, G. F.   Illuminated Manuscripts in the British Museum. London: 1899-1903. Limited to 300 copies; folio; 1st to 4th series, in 4 volumes; 60 fine color and gilt plates; loose in green cloth backed portfolios as issued, some fading on first title, ties missing on first and third series, booklabels of Lord Kenyon   Maggs Bros. Ltd. 1191-167 1996 £500.00

WARNER, P. F.   Imperial Cricket. London: The London & Counties Press Assoc. Ltd., 1912. Subscriber's edition, limited to 900 numbered copies; 4to; pages xxi, 504; many photographic and other illustrations, including 6 photogravures and 3 colored plates, initials printed in red; original publisher's full morocco, gilt, all edges gilt; very good.   Sotheran PN32-73 1996 £248.00

WARNER, R.   Select Orchidaceous Plants. London: 1874. Folio; pages (ix, 80), 40 beautiful hand colored plates; original green cloth, neatly rebacked; small ink stain on half title and contents leaf.   Wheldon & Wesley 207-117 1996 £1,500.00

WARNER, R.   Select Orchidaceous Plants. Jacksonville: 1975. Facsimile edition, limited to 1000 copies, this is a display copy; small folio; pages 88 (unpaginated), 40 colored plates; simulated red leather.   Raymond M. Sutton VI-972 1996 $150.00

WARNER, RICHARD   A Tour through the Northern Counties of England and the Borders of Scotland. Bath: R. Crutwell, 1802. 1st edition; 8vo; 2 volumes; pages iv, 316; iv, 300; 2 titles, each with engraved vignette, 2 tinted plates after Becker and 2 maps in text; old half calf, gilt, little worn, head of one spine repaired. Bicknell 43.   R.F.G. Hollett & Son 78-1345 1996 £220.00

WARNER, RICHARD   A Tour through the Northern Counties of England, and the Borders of Scotland. Bath: R. Crutwell, 1802. 1st edition; 8vo; 2 volumes in 1; pages iv, 316, iv, 300, 2 titles, each with engraved vignette, 2 maps in text, lacks frontispiece to volume 1; old half calf, spine label lacking, head of spine frayed.   R.F.G. Hollett 76-325 1996 £130.00

WARNER, RICHARD   A Walk through Wales in August 1797. Bath: printed by R. Cruttwell, 1798. 2nd edition; tall 8vo; viii, 238 pages; full contemporary calf which has been professionally rebacked with new spine, new endpapers; some wear to corners, otherwise nice.   David Mason 71-156 1996 $200.00

WARNER, SUSAN BOGART   The Old Helmet. London: James Nisbet and Co., 1864. 1st English edition; 8vo; original green cloth, blindstamped on front with gilt helmet, gilt lettered spine; BAL 21275B.   Paulette Rose 16-338 1996 $450.00

WARNER, SYLVIA TOWNSEND   After the Death of Don Juan. London: Chatto & Windus, 1938. 1st edition; original binding, top edges slightly faded, prelims, edges and endpapers slightly spotted, tail of spine slightly bumped, very good in nicked, rubbed and dusty, slightly marked, spotted and creased dusty dust jacket browned at spine and edges   Ulysses 39-603 1996 £125.00

WARREN, EDWARD   The Life of John Warren, M.D. Boston: Noyes, Holmes and Co., 1874. 1st edition; xvi, 568 pages; cloth, bit of wear at spine tips, some minor spots on cover, otherwise very good.   Metacomet Books 54-115 1996 $135.00

WARREN, EDWARD H.   The Rights of Margin Customers Against Wrongdoing Stockbrokers and Some Other Problems in the Modern Law of Pledge. Norwood: Plimpton Press, 1941. Original brown cloth, gilt, fresh.   Meyer Boswell SL25-231 1996 $125.00

WARREN, EDWARD H.   Spartan Education. Boston: Houghton Mifflin Co., 1942. One of 1000 copies, of which this is number 156; inscribed by Professor Warren to Olney Raymond, whose ownership inscription dated Oct. 5 1942, found on first blank.   Meyer Boswell SL25-232 1996 $150.00

WARREN, ELIZA SPALDING   Memoirs of the West. Portland: ca. 1917. 1st edition; 153 pages; illustrations; original green cloth, title stamped in black on front cover and spine, fine; without dampstaining which appears in most copies; Howes W117; Smith 10731; Graff 4544.   Michael D. Heaston 23-348 1996 $225.00

WARREN, JOHN C.   Description of an Egyptian Mummy Presented to the Massachusetts General Hospital; With an Account of the Operation of Embalming, in Ancient and Modern Times. N.P.: n.p., 1821. 4to; 33 pages; 2 plates, offsetting; wrappers, sewn, near fine, scarce.   Freedom Bookshop 14-21 196 $750.00

WARREN, JOHN C.   Physical Education and the Preservation of Health. Boston: 1846. 1st edition; 90 pages; original binding, scarce.   W. Bruce Fye 71-2219 1996 $200.00

WARREN, JOHN C.   Remarks on Some Fossil Impression in the Sandstone Rocks of Connecticut River. Boston: Ticknor Fields, 1854. 1st edition; 8vo; 54 pages, 2 text figures, folding frontispiece (rather faded as usual), blue cloth bit scuffed, Boston PL stamp (and release stamp) on title and p. 21; bookplate bit defective, but clean copy, apparently donated by the Rev. G. Ellis, D.D. with his name on title verso. Truthful lens 81.   Maggs Bros. Ltd. 1190-316 1996 £575.00

WARREN, ROBERT PENN 1905-   All the Kings Men. London: Eyre & Spottiswode, 1948. 1st English edition, in red, second state dust jacket; about fine in very good dust jacket with some rubbing and light nicking at extremities and with short tear on rear panel.   Between the Covers 42-450 1996 $165.00

WARREN, ROBERT PENN 1905-   The Circus in the Attic. New York: HB, 1947. 1st edition; fine in near fine dust jacket with two short edge tears to rear panel.   Lame Duck Books 19-568 1996 $350.00

WARREN, ROBERT PENN 1905-   How Texas Won Her Freedom: The Story of Sam Houston and the Battle of San Jacinto. San Jacinto Monument Texas: San Jacinto Museum and History, 1959. 1st edition; cloth and papercovered boards as issued, very scarce hardcover issue, just a touch of rubbing to extremities, fine, nicely inscribed by designer.   Between the Covers 42-451 1996 $550.00

WARREN, ROBERT PENN 1905-   John Brown: the Making of a Martyr. New York: Payson & Clarke, 1929. 1st edition; about fine with very light wear, lacking dust jacket.   Between the Covers 42-449 1996 $250.00

WARREN, ROBERT PENN 1905-   A Place to Come To. New York: Random House, 1977. 1st edition; number 95 of 350 copies signed by author; fine in slipcase.   Hermitage SP95-655 1996 $150.00

WARREN, SAMUEL   Ten Thousand a Year. Philadelphia: Carey & Hart, 1840-1841. 1st edition; 1st issue, without any volume number on titlepage of volume 1; 12mo; 6 volumes; original boards, slight rubbing at edges, cloth backs (faded), paper labels; despite trifling binding defects, a fine copy.   Howard S. Mott 227-147 1996 $975.00

WARRINER, FRANCES   Cruise of the United States Frigate Potomac Round the World, During the Years 1831-34. New York: Leavitt, Lord & Co., Boston: Crocker & Brewster, 1835. 1st edition; 366 pages; engravings; original green cloth, half inch chip to top of spine, foxing, otherwise very good.   Blue River Books 9-313 1996 $150.00

WARTON, THOMAS   The History of English Poetry, from the Close of the Eleventh to the Commencement of the Eighteenth Century. London: 1774-78-81/1806 1st edition; 4to; 4 volumes, first 3 volumes uncut, in original paper backed boards, spines hand lettered, spines partly defective, one cover detached, last volume in contemporary tree calf, spine richly gilt, red and green morocco labels.   Simon Finch 24-255 1996 £380.00

WARTON, THOMAS   The Lives of those Eminent Antiquaries John Iceland, Thomas Hearne and Anthony a Wood... Oxford: Clarendon Press, for J. and J. Fletcher & Joseph Pote, 1772. 1st edition; 8vo; 2 volumes; (viii), (112), (ex), (22), iv, 139, (ix); (ii), (vi), 404, 58 pages; 11 engraved plates, 3 folding; 19th century calf, spines decorated gilt, double labels, all edges gilt, rubbed, corners bit worn, some insect damage to joints and edges of boards, scattered paper browning, otherwise very good internally, sound set.   Robert Clark 38-213 1996 £140.00

WARVILLE, J. P. BRISSOT DE   New Travels in the United States of America. Performed in 1788. Dublin: P. Byrne (et al), 1792. 1st Dublin edition, 8vo; half title, pages (iv), (i)-xliii, (i), 45-483, (4); contemporary sprinkled tan calf, backstrip dulled, slight loss at foot of lower joint, from the Gage library with Marcus Gage's signature; excellent.   Blackwell's B112-282 1996 £125.00

WASCHER-JAMES, SANDE   How Long? An Artists' Book by Sande Wascher-James. 1993. One in an edition of 125 copies; 9.5 x 5.5 inches; accordion fold, laminated color xerox cards taken from original cloth quilting blocks, printing done by hand with Gocco using gold metallic ink, front and back boards have stitched fabric bands; very attractive. Joshua Heller 21-277 1996 $160.00

WASCHER-JAMES, SANDE   How Long? Renton: 1993. One of 125 copies; signed by artist/author; printed with a Gocco using gold metallic ink, photos printed with a Gocco as well in gold and gilt; laminated card stock photocopying original hand made quilt blocks with stamp on each block, mounted on lavender blue Canson paper; museum board covered in hand sewn Liberty Lawn One-off fabric, with 3 different 'quilt blocks' on each of the covers, accordion-fold, opening flat reading right to left but pulling out to a quilt of images (text not visible) by pulling covers out flat.   Priscilla Juvelis 95/1-257 1996 $160.00

WASHBURN, EMORY   A Manual of Criminal Law, Including the Mode of Procedure by Which It is Enforced. Chicago: Callaghan & Co., 1878. contemporary sheep, worn and rubbed, good, sound copy.   Meyer Boswell SL25-233 1996 $125.00

WASHBURNE, E. B.   Sketch of Edward Coles, Second Governor of Illinois and of the Slavery Struggle of 1823-24. Chicago: Jansen, McClurg & Co., 1882. 1st edition; original cloth, very slight fraying at head and tail of spine, else fine.   Blue River Books 9-170 1996 $100.00

WASHINGTON County, Oklahoma. Industrial-Labor Review. Kansas City: Punton Reed Publishing Co., 1914. 1st edition; 48 pages; profusely illustrated; original pictorial glazed wrappers, title stamped in gilt on front cover, fancy string tied cord intact; minor chipping and dampstain. Michael D. Heaston 23-281 1996 $375.00

WASHINGTON, BOOKER T.   The Man Farthest Down: a Record of Observation and Study in Europe. Garden City: Doubleday Page, 1912. 1st edition; tiny tear to base of spine very near fine copy, lacking rare dust jacket; relatively uncommon.   Between the Covers 43-428 1996 $200.00

WASHINGTON, BOOKER T.   Putting the Most Into Life. New York: Crowell, 1906. 1st edition; offsetting to front fly from jacket flaps, else fine in very good example of the rare printed dust jacket, lacking a portion of the bottom inch of the spine, slight loss to the corner & with long tear on front panel, professionally and unobtrusively repaired. Rarely found in jacket.   Between the Covers 43-407 1996 $850.00

WASHINGTON, BOOKER T.   Up From Slavery. New York: Doubleday Page, 1901. 1st edition; couple of light bumps to edges of boards, one signature slightly sprung, but still tight, near fine, bright copy. Between the Covers 43-426 1996 $300.00

WASHINGTON, GEORGE 1732-1799   Washington's Farewell Address to the People of the United States the XIX Day of September MDCCXCVI. San Francisco: printed by Edwin & Robert Grabhorn & James McDonald, Sept. 1922. Number 81 of 175 copies; 13 x 8.5 inches; printed in black, red and blue, bound in full parchment with gilt spine title, very good, bumping damage to top of spine. Heller Magee 43.   Bohling Book Co. 191-692 1996 $150.00

WASHINGTON, GEORGE 1732-1799   The Writings. Boston: John B. Russell, 1834-37. 8vo; 12 volumes; numerous engraved portraits, maps and charts; contemporary three quarter green morocco over marbled boards, raised bands, gilt tops, attractive volumes.   Appelfeld Gallery 54-180 1996 $600.00

WASHINGTON, M. BUNCH   The Art of Romare Bearden: the Prevalence of Ritual. New York: Abrams, 1972. Folio; 230 pages; 91 illustrations, 46 in color; cloth, one front free endpaper removed, dust jacket. Freitag 483.   Brannan Books 43-43 1996 $245.00

WASSING, RENE S.   African Art. Its Background and Traditions. New York: Harry N. Abrams, 1968. 29.8 cm; xii, 285 pages, 244 plates, illustrations (24 tipped on color); maps; cloth, dust jacket top edge chipped.   L. Clarice Davis 111-105 1996 $150.00

WASSON, ROBERT GORDON   Maria Sabina and Her Mazatec Mushroom Velada. New York: & London: Harcourt Brace Jovanovich, 1974. 1st edition; 4to; 281 pages; numerous full page photos; complete as issued, with 4 cassette tape recordings of the ritual; also present is the printed musical score in wrappers; original Mexican patterned cloth, fine in publisher's cloth clamshell box.   Chapel Hill 94-10 1996 $300.00

WASSON, ROBERT GORDON   Soma: Divine Mushroom of Immortality. New York: Harcourt Brace & World, 1968. 1st edition; number 113 of 678 numbered copies; 4to; 381 pages; printed on handmade paper with stylized mushroom watermarks, designed by Giovanni Mardersteig; 2 pochoir plates and 22 additional plates, mostly color, as well as numerous in-text illustrations; original crushed blue quarter morocco, top edge gilt, fine, handsome copy in publisher's slipcase; with TLS from author dated 20 April 1974.   Chapel Hill 94-9 1996 $575.00

WASSON, ROBERT GORDON   Soma: Divine Mushroom of Immortality. New York: 1971. 8vo; 381 pages; chart, 5 plain and 17 colored plates, 3 maps, 10 text figures; cloth, good copy with dust jacket.   Wheldon & Wesley 207-1665 1996 £60.00

WASSON, V. P.   Mushrooms, Russia and History. New York: 1957. Limited to 512 copies; tall 4to; pages xxi, 433; 82 plates, plus 28 illustrations in text; original green buckram, small owner's stamp on lower blank area of titles, owner's circular sticker on lower corner of front cover of volume 2, red spine labels, gilt tops, cloth slipcase; half inch tear to upper inside edge.   Raymond M. Sutton VII-42 1996 $2,600.00

WATERHOUSE, BENJAMIN   The Botanist. Boston: Joseph T. Buckingham, 1811. 1st edition; 8vo; 263 pages; original green boards recently rebacked with paper spine, library bookplate and blindstamp, small piece torn from front flyleaf, some foxing, else very good. American Imprints 24380; Sabin 102055.   Chapel Hill 94-137 1996 $165.00

WATERHOUSE, BENJAMIN   An Essay on Junius and His Letters... Boston: 1831. 1st edition; large 8vo; 449 pages; contemporary cloth backed boards, uncut, partly unopened, moderate foxing. Cushing W68; Reynolds 4275.   Argosy 810-504 1996 $300.00

WATERHOUSE, BENJAMIN   The Rise, Progress and Present State of Medicine. Boston: 1792. 1st edition; small 8vo; 12, 31 pages, last two leaves reparied, without loss, good ex-library; new wrappers, clamshell case. Austin 2014; Evans 24978.   M & S Rare Books 60-482 1996 $600.00

WATERHOUSE, E. G.   Camellia Trail. Sydney: 1952. Limited to 1000 numbered copies, signed by author and artist; royal 4to; pages 44, 21 colored plates; cloth. Obituary of author taped to front.   Wheldon & Wesley 207-1866 1996 £200.00

WATERHOUSE, EDWARD   A Short Narrative of the Late Dreadful Fire in London... London: printed by W.G. for Rich. Thrale and James Thrale, 1667. 1st edition; 8vo; paper flaw in blank margin of title; old sheep, worn, upper hinge cracked; ownership inscription of Samuel Leigh. Wing W1050.   Anthony Laywood 108-20 1996 £75.00

WATERMAN, LEROY   Royal Correspondence of the Assyriad Empire. Ann Arbor: University of Michigan Press, 1930-1936. 4to; 4 volumes; ix, 492 pages; 524 pages; x, 376 pages; xiii, 282 pages; original green cloth, corners bumped, some pencil annotations.   Archaeologia Luxor-2808 1996 $1,250.00

WATERMAN, THOMAS TILESTON   The Early Architecture of North Carolina. Chapel Hill: UNC Press, ca. 1965. 2nd edition; small folio; 290 pages; original dark green and tan cloth, ring stains on covers, but very good in publisher's pictorial slipcase. Thornton 7029.   Chapel Hill 94-24 1996 $125.00

WATERS, ALAN   A Lotos Eater in Capri. London: Richard Bentley and Son, 1893. Tall 8vo; 377 pages; illustrations; original maroon cloth, pictorial gilt on upper cover, inner hinges cracked, spine ends bit worn, still near fine.   David Mason 71-107 1996 $100.00

WATERS, FRANK   The Man Who Killed the Deer. Flagstaff: Northland Press, 1965. Limited edition, number 178 of 1250 copies, signed, numbered; in clear acetate dust jacket and slipcase, signed by author. Very fine.   Ken Sanders 8-403 1996 $150.00

WATERS, FRANK   Masked Gods: Navajo and Pueblo Ceremonialism. Albuquerque: University of New Mexico Press, 1950. 1st edition; 438 pages; fine in worn dust jacket with some chipping and pieces missing along top edge of dust jacket.   Ken Sanders 8-404 1996 $100.00

WATERS, FRANK   The Yogi of Cockroach Court. New York: Rinehart, 1947. 1st edition; near fine in very good+ dust jacket with one small piece missing.   Ken Sanders 8-410   1996 $145.00

WATERSTON, JOHN JAMES   The Collected Scientific Papers. Edinburgh & London: 1928. lxviii, 709 pages; 5 plates, folding charts, diagrams; cloth marked, ex-BMA library.   Graham Weiner C2-788   1996 £50.00

WATERTON, CHARLES   Wanderings in South America, the North-West of the United States, and the Antilles, in the Years 1812, 1816, 1820 and 1824. London: J. Mawman, 1825. 1st edition; 4to; vii, 326 pages; frontispiece; some wear to boards and spine, occasional light foxing, overall very good; Hill p. 319; Howes W158; Sabin 102094.   Parmer Books Nat/Hist-063029   1996 $850.00

WATHEN, JONATHAN   The Conductor and Containing Splints; or, a Description of two Instruments, for the Safer Conveyance and More Perfect Cure of Fractured Legs. London: printed for T. Cadell, 1781. 3rd edition; 8vo; half title, 5 engraved plates; disbound.   Anthony W. Laywood 108-136   1996 £250.00

WATKINS, JOHN   A Biographical Dictionary of the Living Authors of Great Britain and Ireland... London: printed for Henry Colburn, 1816. 1st edition; 8vo; viii, 449 pages; contemporary marbled boards, neatly rebacked. Bentley, Blake Books p. 12 and no. 2929.   James Burmester 29-141   1996 £125.00

WATSON, GEORGE   Bygone Penrith. Penrith: J. Atkinson Sweeten, 1893. 8vo; pages x, 136; original wrappers, little worn, few corners creased, scarce.   R.F.G. Hollett & Son 78-1349   1996 £75.00

WATSON, HENRY   Narrative of Henry Watson, a Fugitive Slave. Boston: Bela Marsh, 1848. 1st edition; 12mo; 48 pages, 4 text woodcuts; original printed and pictorial wrappers. Blockson 9730.   M & S Rare Books 60-431   1996 $1,250.00

WATSON, JOHN   The Medical Profession in Ancient Times. An Anniversary Discourse Delivered Before the New York Academy of Medicine, November 7, 1855. New York: Baker & Godwin, 1856. 1st edition; 8vo; xii, (9)-222, (1 errata); original stiff printed wrappers, cloth back, covers soiled, some foxing; good. Osler 6525; Waller 15257; Cordasco 50-1906.   Edwin V. Glaser B122-157   1996 $150.00

WATSON, JOHN   Psychology: from the Standpoint of a Behaviorist. Philadelphia: J. B. Lippincott Co., 1919. 1st edition; ink name on front free endpaper, light overall wear, else very good. GM 4987.   Hermitage SP95-1085   1996 $100.00

WATSON, JOHN F.   Annals of Philadelphia and Pennsylvania in the Olden Time. Philadelphia: Leary, Stuart Co., 1927. 3 volumes; bookplate to each front free pastedown, light wear to head and foot of spine of volume 2, otherwise very clean, tight set.   Hermitage SP95-736   1996 $150.00

WATSON, LARRY   Montana 1948. Minneapolis: Milkweed, 1993. 1st edition; slight indentation on first couple of pages, still fine in dust jacket and signed by author.   Between the Covers 42-452a   1996 $100.00

WATSON, PETER WILLIAM   Dendrologia Britannia, or Trees and Shrubs That Will Live in the Open Air of Britain throughout the Year. London: 1825. 8vo; 2 volumes, pages (2), lxxii, 173, 30, (10); 172 hand colored engraved plates, slight offsetting onto text; 19th century calf with gilt decorated spines, hinges split, cords still holding.   Raymond M. Sutton VII-43   1996 $1,950.00

WATSON, RICHARD   Historicall Collections of Ecclesiastaick Affairs in Scotland and Politick Related to Them... London: printed by G.D. for John Garfield, 1657. Small 8vo; pages (x), 210, (ii ad leaf); early inscription on title and few marginalia; contemporary blind ruled calf, little rubbed, few scrapes to lower board; Wing W109.   R.F.G. Hollett 76-328   1996 £50.00

WATSON, ROBERT GRANT   Spanish and Portuguese South America During the Colonial Period. London: Trubner & Co., 1884. 8vo; 2 volumes, xvi, 308; viii, 320 pages; large folding map housed in rear pocket of volume 1; original tan cloth, gilt, bit soiled, bookplates, library pockets.   Kenneth Karmiole 1NS-150   1996 $100.00

WATSON, S. H.   A Folio of Old Songs. Waxahachie: Texas Division, U.D.C., 1912. 1st edition; 152 pages; original cloth; near fine.   McGowan Book Co. 65-101   1996 $150.00

WATSON, SERENO   Report of the Geological Exploration of the Fortieth Parallel. Volume V. Botany Washington: 1871. Large square 8vo; liii, 525 pages; 40 plates, folding map; spine torn, back joint breaking.   Graham Weiner C2-264   1996 £50.00

WATTERSON, GEORGE   The L... Family at Washington; or, a Winter in the Metropolis. Washington: printed and published by David and Force, 1822. 1st edition; 12mo; original printed boards, uncut, spine replaced, spotting and soiling of covers and text; S&S 11356; Wright Fiction 2682.   James Cummins 14-219   1995 $250.00

WATTS, ALAN W.   Beat Zen Square Zen and Zen. San Francisco: City Lights, 1959. 1st edition; waterstain to lower portion of front and rear panels, otherwise very good+ in stapled wrappers; inscribed by author in year of publication.   Lame Duck Books 19-571   1996 $200.00

WATTS, ALAN W.   Buddhism in the Modern World. Cecil Court: Watkins, n.d, c. 1930's. 1st edition; yellow wrappers, near fine.   Words Etcetera 94-247   1996 £75.00

WATTS, ALAN W.   Nature, Man and Woman. New York: Pantheon, 1958. 1st edition; fine in very good or better dust jacket with insect damage to edges and flap golds, inscribed by author and uncommon thus.   Lame Duck Books 19-570   1996 $250.00

WATTS, ALAN W.   An Outline of Zen Buddhism. London: Golden Vista Press, 1932. 1st edition; yellow wrappers; fine.   Words Etcetera 94-248   1996 £75.00

WATTS, ALAN W.   This Is It and Other Essays on Zen and Spiritual Experience. New York: Pantheon, 1960. 1st edition; whale stamp on front endpaper, otherwise fine in very good, slightly spine faded jacket with one edge tear on back panel; inscribed by author to noted Harvard psychologist, Henry A. Murray, particularly good association.   Ken Lopez 74-458   1996 $500.00

WATTS, ALAN W.   The Wisdom of Insecurity. New York: Pantheon, 1951. 1st edition; near fine in good, fragile dust jacket that is spine faded and chipped at corners and spine extremities and fold flaps; signed by author, uncommon thus; with gift note tipped to rear free endpaper.   Ken Lopez 74-457   1996 $400.00

WATTS, ALAN W.   Zen Buddihsm. London: the Buddhist Society, 1947. 1st edition; yellow wrappers, trifle soiled, otherwise very good.   Words Etcetera 94-249 1 996 £50.00

WATTS, ISAAC   Divine and Moral Songs for Children. London: J. Johnson, 72 St. Paul's Church-Yard, 1803. 4th edition; 110 x 100mm; pages (ix), ads, 96, 8 page catechisms and prayers; contemporary half sheep with marbled boards, skilful half page woodcuts to each song, binding worn, f.e.p. lacking, competent amateur hand coloring to two cuts, else very good.   Marjorie James 19-219   1996 £125.00

WATTS, ISAAC   Divine and Moral Songs. Derby: Thomas Richardson & Son, n.d., ca. 1840. 145 x 90mm; pages (x), 69; full page frontispiece on paste-down, other woodcuts are small without borders; green paper covered pictorial boards, red cloth spine; boards slightly grubby, else very good. Not in Pafford.   Marjorie James 19-220   1996 £95.00

WATTS, ISAAC   Divine Songs, Attempted in Easy Language for the Use of Children. London: James Bucklan, James Waugh, John Ward, Thomas Longman & Edward Dilly, 1777. 145 x 85 mm; pages (xii), 59; George II licence faces titlepage and is undated; brown canvas covered boards as issued, contents slightly grubby, else very good. Inscription dated 1780. Pafford B31.   Marjorie James 19-221   1996 £225.00 .

WATTS, ISAAC   Divine Songs, Attempted in Easy Language for the Use of Children. London: J. Buckland: J.F. & C. Rivington; T. Longman, W. Fenner, T. Field &... 1780. 150 X 91mm; pages (Xll), 58, with 2 page booklist; pruple paper covered boards, boards faded, else near fine. Pafford B35.   Marjorie James 19-223   1996 £195.00

WATTS, ISAAC   Divine Songs, Attempted in Easy Language for the Use of Children. London: Knott & Lloyd, 1804. 150 x 95 mm; pages (x), 58; no illustrations; dutch patterned boards, brown calf spine; boards worn and contents slightly grubbed, very good, scarce. Not in Pafford.   Marjorie James 19-222   1996 £125.00

WATTS, ISAAC   Divine Songs, Attempted in Easy Language for the Use of Children. Derby: Henry Mozley & Sons, 1840. 145 x 90mm; pages (viii), 71; full page frontispiece woodcut, woodcuts; yellow paper covered pictorial boards, red roan spine; boards slightly grubby, else very good; inscription 1841. Pafford B117.   Marjorie James 19-224   1996 £145.00

WATTS, ISAAC   The Improvement of the Mind or a Supplement to the Art of Logic in Two Parts. Berwick: printed by W. & H. Richardson, 1801. 351 pages; portrait; full tree calf, title label inset on black morocco; good copy.   K Books 442-484 1996 £56.00

WATTS, ISAAC   The Knowledge of the Heavens and the Earth Made Easy; or, the First Principles of Astronomy and Geography Explain'd by the Use of Globes and Maps. London: T. Longman, J. Buckland and W. Fenner, 1760. 6th edition; 8vo; xiii, (13), 222 pages, 6 engraved plates; contemporary calf (rubbed); very nice. Houzeau Lancaster 10936. Jeffrey Mancevice 20-91 1996 $250.00

WATTS, ISAAC   Logic; or, the Right Use of Reason, in the Enquiry After Truth... London: John Bumpus, 1822. 8vo; frontispiece, some spotting of prelims; full contemporary plum morocco, boards with wide gilt borders, little rubbed, spine gilt, all edges gilt, water color painting on fore-edge of a naval seascape, with several ships, with rowing boat in foreground with 3 naval officers in uniform of the period.   Ian Wilkinson 95/1-97 1996 £225.00

WATTS, ISAAC   Reliquiae Juveniles: Miscellaneous Thoughts in Prose and Verse, on Natural, Moral and Divine Subjects... London: printed for T. Longman, J. Buckland, J. Oswald, J. Waugh and... 1752. 4th edition; 12mo; xvi, (iv), 350 pages, ad leaf; all edges gilt, marbled endpaeprs, full contemporary red morocco, covers with broad tooled border in gilt, spine gilt in compartments, gilt dentelles, very slight wear at head and foot of spine, but very attractive binding; small booklabel of G. E. Gubbins, Wellington Street.   David Bickersteth 133-88 1996 £125.00

WAUGH, ALEC   The Year-Boke of the Sette of Odd Volumes. London: 1935. One of 133 numbered copies; decorated gilt parchment, pages unopened, covers dusty, spine and cover edges browned, head and tail of spine and corners slightly bumped, very good, presentation copy from the compiler.   Ulysses 39-608 1996 £55.00

WAUGH, EVELYN 1903-1966   Basil Seal Rides Again. Boston: Little Brown, 1963. Limited to 1000 copies, signed by author; buckram, gilt, very good in original acetate wrpaper which is little torn on back panel. Words Etcetera 94-1264 1996 £165.00

WAUGH, EVELYN 1903-1966   Black Mischief. London: Chapman & Hall, 1932. Book Society bookplate on front free endpaper, as often, top edge little dusty, otherwise excellent copy in very slightly soiled dust jacket, just a touch sunned at spine.   R. A. Gekoski 19-146 1996 £450.00

WAUGH, EVELYN 1903-1966   Helena, a Novel. London: Chapman & Hall, 1950. One of about 50 copies on large paper, specially printed for Waugh to give to his friends; large 8vo; pages xiii, 265; original white buckram, edges untrimmed, covers trifle soiled, but very nice; author's presentation copy, inscribed by author for Daniel Bolton.   Sotheran PN32-60 1996 £1,995.00

WAUGH, EVELYN 1903-1966   Labels: a Mediterranean Journal. London: Duckworth, 1930. 1st edition; this being one of 100 specially bound copies, signed by author, and with piece of original manuscript inserted; 8vo; pages 206; frontispiece, 3 plates of photos, 2 maps, edges little spotted, but very nice; original blue buckram, spine lettered in gilt, top edge gilt.   Sotheran PN32-59 1996 £1,598.00

WAUGH, EVELYN 1903-1966   Love Among the Ruins. London: Chapman and Hall, 1953. 1st edition; this being one of 350 numbered copies, signed by author; 8vo; pages (vi), 50; illustrations by author and others; original red buckram, gilt, top edge gilt, others untrimmed, spine slightly faded, otherwise fine.   Sotheran PN32-61 1996 £338.00

WAUGH, EVELYN 1903-1966   The Loved One. Boston: Little Brown and Co., 1948. 1st edition; fine in lightly sunned and soiled dust jacket. Hermitage SP95-660 1996 $100.00

WAUGH, EVELYN 1903-1966   The Loved One. London: Chapman and Hall, 1948. Large paper edition, limited to 250 numbered copies, signed by author and artist; viii, 144 pages; 7 full page illustrations and several decorative initials by Stuart Boyle, all printed in red-brown, pictorial titlepage; original sage green buckram, top edge gilt, others uncut, spine slightly faded, but fine with scarce printed glassine dust jacket, albeit slightly torn.   Thomas Thorp 489-317 1996 £320.00

WAUGH, EVELYN 1903-1966   Ninety Two Days. London: 1934. 1st edition; photos; very good, bright copy, very scarce thus.   Words Etcetera 94-1262 1996 £95.00

WAUGH, EVELYN 1903-1966   Waugh in Abyssinia. London: Longmans, 1936. 1st edition; very good, tight copy, clean interior covers, unmarked, gilt bright, small ownership bookplate, very tiny foxing on edge, dust jacket by John French, damaged with small pieces missing top front panel and top of spine slightly soiled and rubbed, some of the printing on inside flap of dust jacket scuffed, extremely scarce in dust jacket. Virgo Books 48-205 1996 £300.00

WAUGH, EVELYN 1903-1966   Wine in Peace and War. London: Saccone & Speed Ltd., 1949. 1st edition; 8vo; 78 pages; cover design and 2 text illustrations in color from drawings by Rex Whistler; original pictorial cream boards, covers very slightly dust soiled and with few small ink spots, endpapers slighty foxed, otherwise fine copy internally. Thomas Thorp 489-316 1996 £75.00

WAUGH, JULIA NOTT   Castroville and Henry Castro, Empresario. San Antonio: 1934. 1st edition; illustrations; wrappers, some wear. Signed by Adina de Zavala, this her copy.   W. M. Morrison 436-366 1996 $100.00

WAUGH, NORAH   Corsets and Crinolines. London: Batsford: 1954. 1st edition; 4to; 176 pages, 115 illustrations and line drawings, cloth, fine in slightly chipped pictorial dust jacket.   J. M. Cohen 35-109 1996 $100.00

WAY, THOMAS ROBERT 1816-   Memories of James McNeill Whistler. London: Bodley Head, 1912. 23 x 18 cm; xi, 150 pages; 38 lithograph illustrations; original cloth (slightly stained), top edge gilt, others uncut, some slight foxing, presentation copy signed by author.   Rainsford A54-581 1996 £75.00

WAYLAND, FRANCIS   A Memoir of the Life and Labors of the Rev. Adoniram Judson, D.D. Boston: Phillips, Sampson, 1853. 1st edition; 8vo; 2 volumes; frontispiece; original cloth, spines gilt, binding of second volume quite worn, otherwise very good. Not in Sabin or Hill. Trebizond 39-83 1996 $100.00

WAYSS, G. A.   Das System Monier. (Eisengerippe mit Cementumhullung) in Seiner Anwendung auf das Gesammte Bauwesen. Berlin: 1887. 8vo; vii, (i), 128 pages; text and photo illustrations; original printed wrapeprs, later linen reback, lower wrapper rather worn, boxed. Elton Engineering 10-109 1996 £850.00

WEALE, GEORGE   An Interesting Memoir of George Weale...From the Time of His Leaving His Father at the Age of Fourteen... Leamingon: printed for the author by J. Dewe, c. 1838. 1st edition; 12mo; 47 pages; original printed wrpapers; fine.   James Burmester 29-143 1996 £150.00

THE WEALTH Of Great Britain in the Ocean... London: printed for M. Cooper, W. Owen, Mr. Dodsley, Mr. Trye & Mr. Hodges, 1749. 3rd edition; 8vo; 71 pages; disbound, title little dusty. Kress 4994; Goldsmith 8400; Hanson 6232. mcCulloch p. 232.   David Bickersteth 133-89 1996 £85.00

WEARE, W. K.   Songs of the Western Shore. San Francisco: Bacon & Co., 1879. 1st edition; 16mo; 204 pages; original cloth, although lacking front flyleaf, very nice.   M & S Rare Books 60-261 1996 $125.00

WEATHERLY, FREDERIC   Punch and Judy and Some of Their Friends. London: Marcus Ward, n.d., ca. 1885. 4to; color printed illustrations; cloth backed color pictorial boards, boards and extremities rubbed, new endpapers, else very good.   Marjorie James 19-181 1996 £65.00

WEATHERLY, FREDERIC   Punch and Judy and Some of Their Friends. London: Marcus Ward and Co., n.d., c. 1885. 1st edition; small 4to; 12 color illustrations, line illustrations to text, slight offsetting, bit shaken; cloth backed pictorial boards, extremities bit worn.   Dramatis Personae 37-178 1996 $100.00

WEATHERS, J.   Commercial Gardening, a Practical and Scientific Treatise for Market Gardeners, Market Growers, Fruit, Flower & Vegetable Growers, Nurserymen etc. London: 1913. 8vo; 4 volumes; over 958 pages; 64 plates, 531 text figures; decorative cloth, some wear and soiling, small splits to spine ends, hinges starting, occasional foxing and smudging to pages.   Raymond M. Sutton VII-1236 1996 £110.00

WEAVER, RAYMOND   Herman Melville: Mariner and Mystic. New York: George Doran, 1921. 1st edition; 8vo; original binding, fine in beautiful dust jacket with short tear to rear; marvelous copy.   Charles Agvent 4-891 1996 $200.00

WEAVER, WILLIAM D.   Catalogue of the Wheeler Gift of Books, Pamphlets and Periodicals in the Library of the American Institute of Electrical Engineeers. New York: American Inst. of Electrical Engineers, 1909. 1st edition; 8vo; 2 volumes, vii, 504; 475 pages; 113 plates; original cloth bindings bit rubbed and soiled, volume one rebacked with original backstrip laid down; very good, sound set.   Edwin V. Glaser 121-319 1996 $450.00

WEAVER, WILLIAM D.   Catalogue of the Wheeler Gift of Books, Pamphlets and Periodicals in the Library of the American Institute of Electrical Engineers. New York: American Institute of Electrical Engineers, 1909. 1st edition; 8vo; 2 volumes; frontispieces, numerous facsimiles; original cloth.   Forest Books 74-275 1996 £195.00

WEBB, DANIEL   An Inquiry Into the Beauties of Painting; and Into the Merits of the Most Celebrated Painters, Ancient and Modern London: for J. Dodsley, 1769. 3rd edition; 8vo; xvi, 200 pages; rebacked in contemporary mottled calf; very good.   Ken Spelman 30-14 1996 £120.00

WEBB, DANIEL   Observations on the Correspondence Between Poetry and Music. (with) Remarks on the Beauties of Poetry. London: for J. Dodsley/London: for R. & J. Dodsley, 1769/62. 1st edition; 8vo; 2 volumes in one; vii, (i), 155, (1), (4) pages ads, half title; (4), 123, (1) pages, half title; rebacked in contemporary mottled calf; very good. Ken Spelman 30-13 1996 £180.00

WEBB, DANIEL   Remarks on the Beauties of Poetry. London: R. and J. Dodsley, 1762. 1st edition; 8vo; (iv), 123, (i) pages; contemporary calf, spine gilt ruled, label, half title, corners slightly worn, one joint cracked, but firm, few page edges dusty; nice.   Robert Clark 38-215 1996 £100.00

WEBB, FRANCIS   Friendship: a Poem Inscribed to a Friend; to Which is added, An Ode. London: printed for G. Kearsly and Johnson and Payne, 1779. 1st edition; 4to; 48 pages; engraved vignette on title; disbound.   Anthony W. Laywood 108-138 1996 £145.00

WEBB, GEORGE   The Practice of Quietness, Directing a Christian How to Live Quietly in this Troublesome World. 1705. 8vo; vignette titlepage, portrait, (i), vi, 156, (2) pages; contemporary calf, rebacked, good.   C. P. Hyland 216-892 1996 £95.00

WEBB, JAMES JOSIAH   Adventures in the Santa Fe Trade 1844-1847. Glendale: Arthur H. Clark Co., 1931. 9 3/8 x 6 1/4 inches; frontispiece, 301 pages, foldout map; dark red cloth.   Dawson's Books Shop 528-246 1996 $100.00

WEBB, MARIA   The Fells of Warthmoor Hall and Their Friends: With an Account of Their Ancestor, Anne Askew, the Martyr... London: Alfred W. Bennett, 1865. 1st edition; 8vo; pages xii, 434, (ii ads), 3 illustrations and 4 facsimiles; original blindstamped cloth, gilt, spine slightly faded, extremities little frayed, upper joint just cracking, trifle shaken.   R.F.G. Hollett & Son 78-271 1996 £75.00

WEBB, MARIA   The Penns and Peningtons of the Seventeenth Century, in Their Domestic and Religious Life... London: F. B. Kitto, 1867. 1st edition; 8vo; pages xiv, 430, 7 plates; original blindstamped cloth, gilt, spine faded, prelims spotted, lower joint cracked.   R.F.G. Hollett & Son 78-273 1996 £65.00

WEBB, SAMUEL B.   Records of North American Big Game. 1952. 2nd issue; colored frontispiece, many other illustrations; fine in torn and rather grubby dust jacket; presentation copy from J. Watson Webb to Lord Dalhousie.   David Grayling J95Biggame-457 1996 £105.00

WEBB, T.   A New Select Collection of Epitaphs, Panegyrical and Moral, Humorous, Whimsical, Satyrical and Inscriptive. London: S. Bladon, 1775. 1st edition; 8vo; 2 volumes; full contemporary brown calf, upper joints cracking but firm, spines little worn, all edges gilt; bookplates of Frances Mary Richardson Currer.   Ian Wilkinson 95/1-156 1996 £175.00

WEBB, THOMAS H.   Information for Kanzas Immigrants. Boston: printed by Alfred Mudge and Son, 1859/60. 15th edition; 120 pages; sewn as issued, first and last page somewhat soiled, text clean, very good. Howes W193.   Michael D. Heaston 23-198 1996 $1,500.00

WEBB, WALTER P.   Flat Top-a Story of Modern Ranching. El Paso: 1960. 1st edition; limited to 200 cloth bound copies; 38 pages, frontispiece, plates, photos; cloth, nice. Lowman 130.   T. A. Swinford 49-1226 1996 $125.00

WEBB, WALTER P.   Texas Rangers: a Century of Frontier Defense. Boston: 1935. 1st edition, 1st issue with incorrect identifications to photo on page 565; 584 pages; illustrations; cloth, fading to spine, owner's name. Howes W194; Jenkins BTB 212; Adams 150 #145.   W. M. Morrison 436-367 1996 $115.00

WEBB, WALTER P.   The Texas Rangers. New York: Houghton Mifflin Co., 1935. 1st edition; limited to 205 copies signed by author, this copy number 14; 583, (1) pages; illustrations; original half calf and white cloth boards, morocco spine label, slipcase, spine somewhat darkened, but very good and clean copy overall. Adams Six Guns 2333; Dobie p. 60; Howes W194; Jenkins BTB 212.   Michael D. Heaston 23-360 1996 $750.00

WEBB, WALTER P.   The Texas Rangers, a Century of Frontier Defense. New York: Houghton, 1935. 1st edition; 582 pages; illustrations; Basic 212; One Fifty 145.   Maggie Lambeth 30-523 1996 $100.00

WEBBER, ALEXANDER   Shooting: a Poem Comprising a General Description of Field Sports, Dependant on the Gun...Game... London: Rudolph Ackerman, 1841. 1st edition; 8vo; viii, 154 pages; frontispiece, title vignette, original cloth, gilt decorated.   K Books 441-509 1996 £60.00

WEBBER, CHARLES WILKINS   Jack Long; or, Shot in the Eye. New York: W. H. Graham, 1846. 1st edition; 8vo; 30, (2) pages; original printed wrappers, lower portions of last several leaves progressively browned, last two leaves of text and ad leaf especially so. Wright I 2688; Howes W197.   M & S Rare Books 60-259 1996 $750.00

WEBBER, SAMUEL   War, a Poem. Cambridge: Hilliard and Metcalf, 1823. 1st edition; 16mo; 48 pages; original printed wrappers. Ink inscription from Noah Worcester to President Kirkland of Harvard. Shoemaker 14854.   M & S Rare Books 60-212 1996 $175.00

WEBER, CARL J.   Fore-Edge Painting. A Historical Survey of a Curious Art in Decoration. London: Harvey House, 1966. 1st printing under this title; small 4to; colored mounted frontispiece, illustrations, original cloth, dust jacket, little torn.   Forest Books 74-276 1996 £200.00

WEBER, CARL J.   A Thousand and One Fore-Edge Paintings. Waterville: Colby College Press, 1949. 1st edition; limited to 1000 copies; buckram, near mint, in dust jacket.   Bromer Booksellers 90-37 1996 $475.00

WEBSTER, DANIEL 1782-1852   Mr. Webster's Address at the Laying of the Corner Stone of the Addition to the Capitol: July 4, 1851. Washington: Gideon, 1851. 29 pages; printed cream wrappers, minor soiling; very good.   George J. Houle 68-149 1996 $125.00

WEBSTER, DANIEL 1782-1852   Mr. Webster's Speech on the Greek Revolution. Washington City: John Meehan, 1824. 8vo; 50 pages; printed wrappers, holograph notation on upper wrapper, some soiling, lacking lower right corner of last page, not affecting text; very good, inscribed. "With the Respects of Dr. Sewall(?)".   George J. Houle 68-150 1996 $125.00

WEBSTER, DANIEL 1782-1852   Speech of the Hon. Daniel Webster to the Young Men of Albany Wednesday, May 28, 1851. Washington: Gideon & Co., 1851. 29 pages; printed salmon wrappers, minor soiling; very good.   George J. Houle 68-151 1996 $125.00

WEBSTER, DANIEL 1782-1852   The Works of Daniel Webster. Boston: Little Brown & Co., 1890. 20th edition; large 8vo; 6 volumes; 3 engraved portraits, 2 views; original blue cloth, gilt.   Kenneth Karmiole 1NS-229 1996 $125.00

WEBSTER, GEORGE C.   Around the Horn in '49. Journal of the Hartford Union Mining and Trading Company. Wethersfield: Rev. L. J. Hall, 1898. 2nd edition; 252 pages; 25 illustrations; maroon cloth, slight rubbing to joints, one small spot on spine, otherwise fine, scarce. Hermitage SP95-737 1996 $250.00

WEBSTER, JOHN   Love's Graduate: a Comedy. Daniel Press, 1885. One of 150 copies; 9 x 7 inches; 2 p.l., ix, (1) pages, (1) leaf, 69, (1) pages, (1) leaf (printer's device); printed on fine qualtiy thick paper; vellum backed paper boards, spine titled in gilt, 2 edges untrimmed; 2 bookplates on endpapers, titlepage with presentation inscription from editor, Stephen Edward Spring-Rice, to Henry Bradshaw dated 1885; also with ownership inscription of R. A. Neil, dated 1886 and with ms. note signed by Gosse tipped in after prefatory essay, corners bit worn, spine and covers somewhat soiled, but binding tight and otherwise pleasing; very fine internally. Madan 11.   Phillip J. Pirages 33-154 1996 $400.00

WEBSTER, JOHN   Love's Graduate. Oxford: printed at the Private Press of H. Daniel Fellow of Worcester College 1885. Limited to 150 copies; small 4to; pages (4), xii, 69, (2); uncut in original vellum backed boards, slightly spotted; inscribed by Edmund Gosse for Bessie Waterhouse. Madan 11.   Claude Cox 107-40 1996 £180.00

WEBSTER, JOHN   Metallographia: or, an History of Metals. London: printed by A. C. for Walter Kettilby, 1671. 1st edition; 388 pages, 2 pages ads; rebound in 19th century green calf over marbled boards, light to moderate foxing, boards slightly bowed, abrasion to spine from label removal, but all in all a nice copy. Ferguson II 534-2; Wing W1234; Honeyman 3096.   Hermitage SP95-1086 1996 $1,000.00

WEBSTER, JOHN   The Works. London: William Pickering, 1830. Only 250 copies printed, of which this is one of 12 on large paper; 8vo; 4 volumes; 19th century full dark green morocco, double gilt fillet border to sides, gilt crest with "R.F.G." (Fitzgerald) monogram at centre of upper and lower covers, flat spines with gilt fillet panels, inside dentelles, gilt edges, marbled endpapers, some marginal spotting, but handsome set; Vol. 1 inscribed, possibly by Picerking himself, "Large Paper, twelve copies only printed, No. 1. W. Pickeirng".   Sotheran PN32-62 1996 £1,250.00

WEBSTER, JOHN W.   A Description of the Island of St. Michael Comprising an Account of Its Geological Structure... Boston: R. P. & C. Williams, 1821. 8vo; 244 pages, 2 folding maps, folding chart, 3 engraved plates; original brown cloth over boards, spine worn, boards soiled, outer hinges starting, front free endpaper lacking, some text foxing. Worn copy, very scarce.   Kenneth Karmiole 1NS-256 1996 $150.00

WEBSTER, KIMBALL   The Gold Seekers of '49. Manchester: Standard Book Co., 1917. 1st edition; 240 pages, plates; original mustard cloth, pictorial paper label on front cover and title stamped in gilt on spine and cover; minor wear, fine. From the collection of Nathaniel S. Thomas, with his bookplate. Cowan p. 673; Graff 4571; Wheat Gold Rush 222; Mintz Trail 489.   Michael D. Heaston 23-361 1996 $175.00

WEBSTER, LYDIA GERTRUDE HAMILTON   When Dreams Come True. N.P.: Boston? 1925. (75) leaves, text printed on recto only, 27 tipped in photos and 15 other tipped in illustrations; new black cloth with gilt title, very good. Not in NUC.   Bohling Book Co. 192-248 1996 $120.00

WEBSTER, NOAH 1758-1843   American Dictionary of the English Language. New York: 1828. 1st edition; small 4to; 2 volumes; original suede, backstrips reseated, minor chipping to label.   Bookworm & Silverfish 276-222 1996 $4,400.00

WEBSTER, NOAH 1758-1843   The Elementary Spelling Book... New Brunswick: John Terhune, 1840. Linen backed blue/grey boards, front joint cracking, else clean, untrimmed copy.   Hermitage SP95-1087 1996 $100.00

WEBSTER, NOAH 1758-1843   Elements of Useful Knowledge. Hartford: Hudson & Goodwin, 1802. 1st edition; 12mo; 206 pages; original boards, sheep back, very good. AI 3519.   Howard S. Mott 227-148 1996 $200.00

WEBSTER, NOAH 1758-1843   A Letter to Dr. David Ramsay, of Charleston (S.C.) Respecting the Errors in Johnson's Dictionary and Other Lexicons. New Haven: printed by Oliver Steele & Co., 1807. 28 pages; slightly spotted, stabbed as issued, scarce.   Jarndyce 103-230 1996 £300.00

WEBSTER, NOAH 1758-1843   Webster's International Dictionary of the English Language. Springfield: George Bell, G. & C. Merriam, 1903. 4to; frontispiece, tears to lower corner of first few leaves; 2012 pages + 238 page supplement; full maroon morocco, hinges repaired, good sound copy.   Jarndyce 103-231 1996 £110.00

WEBSTER, REDFORD   Miscellaneous Remarks on the Police of Boston, as Respects Paupers; alms and Work House; Clases of Poor and Beggars... Boston: Cummings & Hillard, Feb. 1814. 1st edition; 8vo; 42 pages; removed. With several ink corrections to text. Sabin 102418; S&S 32141; Kress S6119.   M & S Rare Books 60-393 1996 $175.00

WEBSTER, WILLIAM   Narrative of a Voyage to the Southern Atlantic Ocean, in the Years 8128, 29, 30, Performed in H.M. Sloop Chanticleer, Under the Command of the Late Capt. Henry Foster... London: Richard Bentley, 1834. 1st edition; 8vo; 2 volumes; pages xii, 399; viii, 398; 2 maps, 5 aquatint plates; half green calf, red labels, rubbed, some light foxing to plates; Sabin 102429; De Moraes II p. 273; Abbey Travel II Mendelssohn II p596   Richard Adelson W94/95-176 1996 $675.00

WEDEL, GEORG WOLFGANG   Compendium Praxeos Clinicae Exemplaris Secundum Orinem Casuum Timaei a Guldenklee. Jena: Joh. Bielki, 1706. 1st edition; 4to; (8) leaves, 213, (11) pages, 2 folding tables, woodcut device on titlepage with small library stamp in blank margin, title printed in red and black; some light browning, long gift inscription dated 1719 on front endpaper; contemporary three quarter blindstamped pigskin; very good, rare. Blake p. 484; cf. Ferguson II 536; 1 copy in NUC.   Jeffrey Mancevice 20-92 1996 $1,250.00

WEDGWOOD, MRS.   Wind Along the Waste: Poems. Daniel Press, 1902. One of 130 numbered copies; small 4to; bound without original wrappers, in limp blue cloth; nice, bookplate.   Bertram Rota 272-123 1996 £90.00

WEED, FRANK   Military Hospitals in the United States. Washington: 1923. 857 pages; more than 200 illustrations; original binding.   W. Bruce Fye 71-2231 1996 $175.00

WEED, WILLIAM H.   To Texas and Back. New York: 1877. 1st and only edition; 51 pages; original brown stiff boards, title in gilt on front cover; fine.   Michael D. Heaston 23-362 1996 $650.00

WEEKS, A. G.   Illustrations of Diurnal Lepidoptera, with Descriptions. Boston: 1905-11. 2 volumes; 2 portraits, 6 photo plates, 66 colored plates; original half cloth, some inner margins in volume 2 stained, effect is slight, on the whole a good copy.   Wheldon & Wesley 207-1127 1996 £90.00

WEEKS, STEPHEN B.   Southern Quakers and Slavery: a Study in Institutional History. Baltimore: Johns Hopkins Press, 1896. 1st edition; 8vo; xiv, 400 pages, large folding map; light stains on edges, rubbed on extremities, bookplate removed from front pastedown, one page torn and creased, with no loss, occasional light staining, else very good, unopened. Thornton 14623.   Andrew Cahan 47-173 1996 $100.00

WEEVER, JOHN   Ancient Monuments With In the United Monarchie of Great Britaine, Ireland and the Lands Adjacent with the Dissolved Monasteries Therein Contained... London: ptd. by Tho. Harper, & are to be sold in Little Britayne by Laurence.. 1631. 1st edition; folio; errata leaf, 871 pages of text, 14 page index, frontispiece, 6 full plates; modern light brown morocco, triple gilt rule borders, gilt rule and floral tools to panelled spine, yellow edges, inner gilt dentelles, marbled endpapers, engraved bookplate, bound by J. Clarke. STC 25223; Cox III pp. 463-4; Upcott p. xx.   Beeleigh Abbey BA56-27 1996 £850.00

WEGMAN, WILLIAM   ABC. New York: Hyperion, 1964. Thin quarto; as new in dust jacket, signed by photographer with drawing of dog.   Between the Covers 42-530 1996 $125.00

WEIGHT, CAREL   The Curious Captain, War Artist 1939-1945: Letters to Helen Roeder. Camberwell Press, 1989. One of 200 numbered copies, signed by author and Helen Roeder; 4to; 33 black and white illustrations; white boards, printed labels; fine.   Bertram Rota 272-59 1996 £60.00

WEIGHTMAN, R. H.   To the Congress of the United States...Requesting the Passage of a Bill Declaring New Mexico One of the United States of America on Certain Conditions. Washington: printed by Gideon and Co., 1851. 1st edition; 25 pages; original printed wrpapers, minor chipping, fine copy; Howes W224; Streeter Sale 433.   Michael D. Heaston 23-275 1996 $500.00

WEINBERG, SAUL S.   Corinth. Volume I. Part V: The Southeast Building and Twin Basilicas, the Mosaic House. Princeton: ASCSA, 1960. 4to; xviii, 128 pages; 29 figures, 57 plates, 10 plans; original cloth, spine faded.   Archaeologia Luxor-3183 1996 $200.00

WEISMANN, A.   Essays Upon Heredity and Kindred Biological problems. Oxford: 1889. 8vo; pages xii, 455; cloth, rather tired copy.   Wheldon & Wesley 207-196 1996 £60.00

WEITZMANN, KURT   Age of Spirituality: Late Antique and Early Christina Art, Third to Seventh Century. New York: Metropolitan Museum of Art, 1979. 1st edition; 736 pages; fine in lightly worn dust jacket.   Hermitage SP95-821 1996 $100.00

WELCH, DENTON   I Left My Grandfather's House: an Account of His First Walking Tour. Limited Editions Club, 1958. Of 150 copies, this one only 20 specially bound by Grodon Acornley of the Royal College of Art Bindery; 4to; color lithographs; quarter black morocco, patterned cloth sides, gilt, edges of spine just a little scuffed, but very nice, scarce.   Bertram Rota 272-272 1996 $200.00

WELCH, DENTON   I Left My Grandfather's House. London: Lion and Unicorn Press, 1958. 1st edition; 108/200 copies; imperial 8vo; pages (viii), 82, (9) (letters), (1); double page plate and 11 other color printed plates, 9 uncolored illustrations and color printed endpaper illustrations, all by Leslie Jones, frontispiece of Welch is self portrait; original quarter mid brown reversed calf, pale green linen sides with overall illustration on front cover, blocked in black and repeated on rear cover, backstrip lettering and reproduction of Welch's signature on front cover, all gilt blocked, minor wear to backstrip tail, top edge gilt; good.   Blackwell's B112-283   1996 £100.00

WELCH, DENTON   A Lunch Appointment. Elysium Press, 1993. Limited to 150 copies; illustrations by Pierre Le-Tan; case bound in black Japanese silk, fine as issued.   Words Etcetera 94-1270 1996 £75.00

WELCH, DENTON   A Lunch Appointment. North Pomfret: Elysium Press, 1993. 1st edition; one of 150 copies, this one of the deluxe edition with an original etching and signed by Edmund White; illustrations by Pierre Le-Tan; black silk cloth.   Priscilla Juvelis 95/1-87A $475.00

WELCH, DENTON   A Lunch Appointment. North Pomfret: Elysium Press, 1993. 1st edition; one of 150 copies; 8vo; handset and printed in 14 pt. spiral on Arches; illustrations by Pierre Le-Tan; bound in black silk cloth.   Priscilla Juvelis 95/1-87 1996 $100.00

WELCH, JAMES   Fool's Crow. New York: Viking, 1986. 1st edition; 390 pages; white cloth spine, mauve paper covered boards, fine in fine dust jacket, signed by author.   Orpheus Books 17-232 1996 $125.00

WELCH, JAMES   Riding the Earthboy 40. New York: World: 1971. 1st edition; 54 pages; fine in near fine dust jacket, signed by author.   Ken Sanders 8-368 1996 $200.00

WELCH, JAMES   Winter in the Blood. New York: Harper & Row, 1974. 1st edition; 176 pages; near fine in dust jacket with some wear, one crease on inside panel; signed by author.   Ken Sanders 8-371 1996 $150.00

WELCH, JAMES   Winter in the Blood. New York: Harper, 1974. 1st edition; fine in dust jacket with just a touch of darkening at extremities, nice, author's first novel.   Between the Covers 42-453 1996 $100.00

WELCH, JAMES   Winter in the Blood. New York: Harper and Row, 1975. 1st edition; 176 pages; author's first novel; brown cloth spine, blue paper covered boards, fine in fine dust jacket with one tiny crease to front flap, superb copy, signed by author.   Orpheus Books 17-231 1996 $200.00

WELCH, JOSEPH   A List of Scholars at St. Peter's College, Westminster, as They were Seleted to Christ Church College, Oxford and Trinity College, Cambridge, from the Foundation by Queen Elizabeth. MDLXI to the Present Time. London: J. Nichols, 1788. 4to; pages v-vii, 190 pages, interleaves with ms. additions, p. 191 in ms., blanks, 13 ff. index interleaved with ms., 2 engraved plates; later half calf, rubbed. Marlborough 162-214 1996 £100.00

WELCH, ORRIN   Knights Templars' Tactics and Drill for the Use of Commanderies, and the Burial, Service of the Orders of Masonic Knighthood. New York: Masonic Pub. Co., 1872. 1st edition; 12mo; illustrations, tipped in at end 'ad' for the Low Twelve by Edward Ellis; original purple cloth with knight in gilt on front cover and spine with gilt lettering (corners very lightly bumped), fine.   Roy W. Clare XXIV-55 1996 $120.00

WELCH, S. L.   Southern California Illustrated, Containing an Epitome of the Growth and Industry of the Three Southern Counties. Los Angeles: Warner Bros., 1886-87. 10 1/4 x 6 3/4 inches; 154 pages + 3 ad leaves, 2 folding maps, numerous illustrations and ads in pagination; printed grey wrappers, front wrpaper lacking and rear detached.   Dawson's Books Shop 528-248 1996 $150.00

WELCH, WILLIAM   Papers and Addresses. Baltimore: 1920. 1st edition; 3 volumes; original binding; GM 86.2.   W. Bruce Fye 71-2240 1996 $300.00

WELD, CHARLES RICHARD   A History of the Royal Society with Memoirs of the Presidents. London: John W. Parker, 1848. 8vo; 2 volumes; frontispieces, 12 plates and illustrations; newly bound in half antique calf, original marbled boards, morocco labels, gilt.   Charles W. Traylen 117-351 1996 £120.00

WELD, EDWARD F.   The Ransomed Bride: a Tale of the Inquisition. New York: Burgess, Stringer andCo., 1846. 1st edition; 8vo; 86 pages; illustrations; removed. Wright I 2693 (2 copies).   M & S Rare Books 60-260 1996 $125.00

WELFORD, RICHARD GRIFFITHS   The Influences of the Game Laws; Being Classified Extracts from the Evidence Taken Before a Select Committe On the House of Commons on the Game Laws. London: 1846. 500 pages; original cloth, apart from fraying to top/base of spine, nice. David A.H. Grayling 3/95-239 1996 £150.00

WELFORD, RICHARD GRIFFITHS   the Influences of the Game Laws... London: R. Groombridge and Sons...and J. Gadsby, 1846. 1st edition; 8vo; 429, (3), lxxi pages, together with 8 pages of publisher's ads; neat inkstamp of private library on blank margin of title, original green cloth, embossed in blind, lettered in gilt, shelf number in ink on foot of spine, slight wear to head, else good. Goldsmiths 34569. Not in Williams or Kress.   John Drury 82-289 1996 £95.00

WELL Dressed Lines. Stripped from the Reels of Five New Englanders. New York: privately printed for the Anglers' Club of New York, 1962. 1st edition; one of 500 copies; 8vo; 82 pages; decorative initials by John C. Atherton; original light brown cloth with paper labels, fine, bright copy in publisher's slipcse with spine label;   Chapel Hill 94-402 1996 $150.00

WELLCOME HISTORICAL MEDICAL LIBRARY   A Catalogue of Printed Books in the Wellcome Historical Medical Library. Wellcome Historical Medical Library, 1962-76. 1st edition; 4to; 3 volumes; original cloth, volumes 1 and 2 ex-library.   Forest Books 74-277 1996 £345.00

WELLEK, RENE   Concepts of Criticism. New Haven and London: Yale University Press, 1963. 1st edition; original binding, head and tail of spine bumped, covers marked and rubbed, very good in nicked, rubbed and spotted, creased, torn and dusty dust jacket; presentation cropy from author for Cleanth Brooks.   Ulysses 39-601 1996 £65.00

WELLMAN, JOHN   Opera Brevis, a Play. Boston: Heron Press, 1977. One of 20 copies apart from 250 paperbound copies; 8 x 5.75 inches; signed by author; folded color frontispiece on Japanese paper, plus two text illustrations by Bruce Chandler; black quater leather and brown-gray marbled paper boards, printe don Velke-Losiny paper and bound by E. G. Parrot; fine. Printer's Choice 46.   Joshua Heller 21-143 1996 $125.00

WELLMAN, MANLY WADE   Lonely Vigils. Chapel Hill: Carcosa, 1981. 1st edition; one of 566 copies of the subscriber's issue with label signed by author and artist, George Evens; 28 illustrations; very fine in dust jacket.   Robert Gavora 61-290 1996 $150.00

WELLMAN, MANLY WADE   Worse Things Waiting. Chapel Hill: Carcosa, 1973. 1st edition; illustrations by Coye; fine in dust jacket. Robert Gavora 61-291 1996 $100.00

WELLS, GABRIEL   Edgar Allan Poe as a Mystic. Metuchen: 1934. One of only 99 numbered copies; 8vo; wrappers; scarce, fine.   Charles Agvent 4-956 1996 $125.00

WELLS, HERBERT GEORGE 1866-1946   The Adventures of Tommy. London: Harrap, 1929. 1st edition; 1st issue; illustrations by Wells; cloth backed printed boards, with original chipped dust jacket, narrow cloth back strip and gold dust jacket, extremities lightly rubbed, else fine. Bromer Booksellers 87-158 1996 $175.00

WELLS, HERBERT GEORGE 1866-1946   Anticipations of the Reaction of Mechanical and Scientific Progress Upon Human Life and Thought. London: Methuen, 1902. 1st edition; uncommon Colonial issue; some light soil to covers near fore edge, else tight, very good copy. Aronovitz 57-1255 1996 $175.00

WELLS, HERBERT GEORGE 1866-1946   The Country of the Blind and Other Stories. Nelson, 1911. 1st edition; birhgt, very good+ copy. Aronovitz 57-1259 1996 $150.00

WELLS, HERBERT GEORGE 1866-1946   The Invisible Man. London: C. A. Pearson, 1897. Supposed first issue, with page 1 misnumbered as page 2; previous owner's bookplate; very good, bumped at top and bottom of spine, which is faded and slightly soiled.   R. A. Gekoski 19-148 1996 £750.00

WELLS, HERBERT GEORGE 1866-1946   The Invisible Man. New York: Limited Editions Club, 1967. Number 417 of 1500 copies, signed by artist; illustrations by Charles Mozley; fine in slipcase.   Hermitage SP95-1048 1996 $100.00

WELLS, HERBERT GEORGE 1866-1946   The Island of Dr. Moreau. Chicago: Stone & Kimball, 1896. 1st American edition; author's youthful photo laid in; some slight rubbing to spine extremities, and unobtrusive staining to lower gutters of first several pages (not affecting text), else very good.   Aronovitz 57-1248 1996 $225.00

WELLS, HERBERT GEORGE 1866-1946   The Island of Dr. Moreau. London: Heinemann, 1896. 1st edition; but later issue with first edition sheets and cancelled titlepage dated 1906; good to very good copy in secondary binding.   Aronovitz 57-1247 1996 $110.00

WELLS, HERBERT GEORGE 1866-1946   The Outlook for Homo Sapiens... London: Martin Secker and Warburg Ltd., 1942. 1st edition; rebound in half morocco with raised bands, top edge gilt, marbled endpapers, spine rubbed, upper cover slightly creased; very good; presentation copy, inscribed by author for Emanuel Shinwell.   Ulysses 39-612 1996 £185.00

WELLS, HERBERT GEORGE 1866-1946   Phoenix - a Summary of the Inescapable Conditions of World Reorganisation. London: Secker & Warburg, 1942. 1st edition; publisher's copy with several pencilled corrections to text, slip of paper containing the new text fastened with paperclip to page 11; original binding, top edge dusty, head and tail of spine and corners bumped, very good in torn, creased, rubbed, soiled and dust dust jacket, browned at spine and edges. Loosely inserted APS from author to Roger Senhouse.   Ulysses 39-613 1996 £135.00

WELLS, HERBERT GEORGE 1866-1946   The Science of Life. Garden City: Doubleday, 1931. Limited to 750 numbered sets, signed by the three authors; 8vo; 4 volumes; plates, frontispiece to volume 4 tape repaired; cloth backed boards, spines sunned and soiled, very good. Charles Agvent 4-1175 1996 $225.00

WELLS, HERBERT GEORGE 1866-1946   The Science of Life. New York: Doubleday Doran, 1931. 2 volumes; some minor chipping to dust jackets, otherwise excellent set in defective slipcase; inscribed by Wells to Dr. Hella Czech.   R. A. Gekoski 19-149 1996 £175.00

WELLS, HERBERT GEORGE 1866-1946   The Sea Lady. New York: 1902. 1st edition; near fine.   Stephen Lupack 83- 1996 $125.00

WELLS, HERBERT GEORGE 1866-1946   The Stolen Bacillus. London: Methuen, 1895. 1st edition; publisher's most handsome highly decorated cloth; bright, very good copy with slight wear. Uncommon.   Aronovitz 57-1245 1996 $685.00

WELLS, HERBERT GEORGE 1866-1946   Tales of Life and Adventure. London: Collins, ca. 1923. 1st edition; very good/very good+ in attractive dust jacket with some wear and tear and chipping. uncommon. Aronovitz 57-1263 1996 $250.00

WELLS, HERBERT GEORGE 1866-1946   Tales of Space and Time. New York: Doubleday & McClure, 1899. 1st American edition; spine little darkened, front inner hinge starting, else near very good.   Aronovitz 57-1252 1996 $135.00

WELLS, HERBERT GEORGE 1866-1946   Tales of Time and Space. G. Bell & Sons, 1900. 1st edition; Colonial issue; some soiling to covers, otherwise very good with ads dated Aug. 1899; most rare issue. Aronovitz 57-1251 1996 $375.00

WELLS, HERBERT GEORGE 1866-1946   The Time Machine. London: Heinemann, 1895. 1st British edition, (1st state binding and 1st issue ads), some all around light dust soil, else tight, smart, very good+/near fine copy of author's first novel.   Aronovitz 57-1244 1996 $1,750.00

WELLS, HERBERT GEORGE 1866-1946   The Time Machine. London: William Heinemann, 1895. 1st British edition; foolscap 8vo; finely bound, recent full crimson morocco, banded and gilt, all edges gilt, by Bayntun-Riviere, few very minor internal marks, but very good.   Ash Rare Books Zenzybyr-95 1996 £950.00

WELLS, HERBERT GEORGE 1866-1946   The Time Machine: an Invention. London: Heinemann, 1895. 1st edition; some scattered foxing to endsheets, still very good, with coarse wove cloth somewhat soiled and spine darkened.   Captain's Bookshelf 38-214 1996 $1,000.00

WELLS, HERBERT GEORGE 1866-1946   The Time Machine. London: William Heinemann, 1895. 1st British edition; foolscap 8vo; recent full crimson morocco, banded and gilt, all edges gilt, by Bayntun-Riviere, few very minor internal marks, but very good.   Ash Rare Books Zenzybyr-94 1996 £395.00

WELLS, HERBERT GEORGE 1866-1946   The Time Machine: an Invention. New York: Random House, 1931. Limited to 1200 copies; octavo; 86 pages; designs and 7 full page color plates by Dwiggins; patterned boards and slightly soiled slipcase; very fine. Agner 31.07; AIGA Fifty Books.   Bromer Booksellers 90-31 1996 $150.00

WELLS, HERBERT GEORGE 1866-1946   Twelve Stories and a Dream. Macmillan, 1903. 1st edition; slight rubbing to corner tips and spine extremities, else tight, very good copy with gold-tip top page edges. Aronovitz 57-1257 1996 $175.00

WELLS, HERBERT GEORGE 1866-1946   When the Sleeper Wakes. New York: Harpers, 1899. 1st edition; spine little lightened, some light foxing, else solid, very good copy.   Aronovitz 57-1250 1996 $285.00

WELLS, HERBERT GEORGE 1866-1946   The Wonderful Visit. Macmillan, 1895. 1st American edition; very good, tight copy.   Aronovitz 57-1246 1996 $225.00

WELLS, HERBERT GEORGE 1866-1946   The Wonderful Visit. London: J. M. Dent, 1895. Considerable foxing to endpapers, sunned and soiled on spine, very good.   R. A. Gekoski 19-147 1996 £150.00

WELLS, HERBERT GEORGE 1866-1946   The Works of... London: T. Fisher Unwin Ltd., 1924-27. Limited to 626 sets; signed by author; 8vo; 28 volumes; original dark red buckram, lettered in gilt, top edge gilt, others uncut, frontispieces, spines uniformly faded, some covers little marked, but very good set, attractive bookplate in the style of Gordon Craig in each volume;   Sotheran PN32-63 1996 £1,485.00

WELLS, HERBERT GEORGE 1866-1946   The World Set Free. Macmillan, 1914. 1st edition; tight, very good copy; inscribed by author to fellow author Hilaire Belloc.   Aronovitz 57-1261 1996 $795.00

WELLS, JOHN G.   Wells' Hand-Book of Iowa: Past, Present and Prospective. New York: John G. Wells, Publishing Agent, 1857. 1st edition; 136 pages; 3 folding maps; original brown embossed cloth, gilt decoration and title stamped in gilt on front cover, very fine and bright copy. Streeter Sale 1910. Howes W250 and Graff 4583 note only 1 map. Michael D. Heaston 23-363 1996 $1,750.00

WELLS, POLK   Life and Adventures of Polk Wells, the Notorious Outlaw. N.P.: 1907. 1st edition; 259 pages; illustrations, decorated cloth, very good, Howes W243; 6 Guns 2342; Flake 9679.   T. A. Swinford 49-1234 1996 $125.00

WELLS, S. Y.   Testimonies Concering the Character and Ministry of Mother Ann Lee and the First Witnesses of the Gospel of Christ's Second Appearing; given by some of the Aged Brethern and Sisters of the United Society. Albany: Packard & Van Benthuysen, 1827. 1st edition; 12mo; 178 pages; original stiff printed wrappers, uncut; minor staining of cover, slight foxing, some chipping of spine,, but fine, rarely seen in printed wrappers. Richmond 1421; MacLean 98; Shoemaker 30577. Sabin 102603.   M & S Rare Books 60-407 196 $325.00

WELLS, WILLIAM CHARLES   Two Essays: One Upon Single Vision with Two Eyes; the Other On Dew. Edinburgh: printed for Archibald Constable and Co., 1818. 1st edition; 8vo; half title, perforation and cancellation stamps on blank verso of title; new half calf, spine gilt, label; nice. Osler 4210; Hirschberg Para 746; Becker 414.   Anthony W. Laywood 109-156 1996 £375.00

WELLS, WILLIAM CHARLES   Two Essays: One Upon Single Vision with Two Eyes; the Other on Dew. London: printed for Archibald Constable, Edinburgh: Longman & Hurst... 1818. 1st collected edition; 8vo; lxxiv, (ii), 439 pages, half title; short clean tear at inner margin of title and another in upper margin of prelim leaf (touching first line of text), original cloth backed drab boards, black morocco label, rubbed; GM 1604.   James Burmester 29-144 1996 £750.00

WELSTED, LEONARD   Epistles, Odes &c. Written on Several Subjects. London: for J. Walthoe and J. Peele, 1724. 1st edition; 8vo; pages lxiv, 255; contemporary panelled calf, unlettered, red sprinkled edges; front joint just starting at head and tail, but firm, some trivial surface insect damage to upper cvoer, still fine. Foxon p. 677.   Simon Finch 24-256 1996 £500.00

WELTY, EUDORA 1909-   Acrobats in a Park. N.P.: Delta, 1977. 1st separate edition, offprint; 8vo; printed white glossy wrappers, stapled; fine.   James S. Jaffe 34-679 1996 $750.00

WELTY, EUDORA 1909-   The Bride of Innisfallen. New York: Harcourt Brace and Co., 1955. 1st edition; with both states of the titlepage; faint soiling and trivial shelf wear, else very nice in slightly rubbed dust jacket; signed by author.   Hermitage SP95-665 1996 $600.00

WELTY, EUDORA 1909-   The Bride of Innisfallen and Other Stories. New York: Harcourt Brace & Co., 1955. 1st edition; 2nd issue, with five copyright dates and binding of green cloth backed boards, titled in silver; slightly shelf worn and bumped copy in lightly used dust jacket. With label signed by Welty glued to free endpaper.   Hermitage SP95-666 1996 $250.00

WELTY, EUDORA 1909-   The Bride of Innisfallen and Other Stories. New York: Harcourt, Brace and Co., 1955. 1st edition; inscription, head and tail of spine slightly bumped, lower endpaper gutter partially browned, very good in nicked, rubbed & dusty dust jacket browned at spine & edges, wormed slightly at lower flap fold & sl. frayed at head of spine.   Ulysses 39-614 1996 £125.00

WELTY, EUDORA 1909-   The Collected Stories of Eudora Welty. New York: Harcourt Brace Jovanovich, 1980. 1st trade edition; cloth backed boards, fine in slightly creased dust jacket.   Ulysses 39-616 1996 £65.00

WELTY, EUDORA 1909-   Delta Wedding. New York: Harcourt Brace, 1946. 1st edition; fine in fine dust jacket with very light wear at spine crown; attractive copy.   Ken Lopez 74-460 1996 $250.00

WELTY, EUDORA 1909-   Henry Green: a Novelist of the Imagination. 1961. Offprint 4to; 11 pages; edges of wrappers sunned, very good, scarce.   Captain's Bookshelf 38-215 1996 $350.00

WELTY, EUDORA 1909-   The Little Store. Newton: Tamazunchale Press, 1985. 1st edition; one of 250 numbered copies; 1 1/2 x 2 1/2 inches; green leather, all edges gilt; fine.   Captain's Bookshelf 38-216 1996 $100.00

WELTY, EUDORA 1909-   Losing Battles. New York: Random House, 1970. Advance review copy with slip and photo laid in; fine in dust jacket, very nicely inscribed by author.   Between the Covers 42-455 1996 $200.00

WELTY, EUDORA 1909-   Losing Battles. New York: Random House, 1970. 1st edition; fine in dust jacket, signed by author.   Hermitage SP95-667 1996 $125.00

WELTY, EUDORA 1909-   Losing Battles. New York: Random House, 1970. 1st edition; fine in very good+ dust jacket, signed; closed 1/8" in tear, minor spine end wear.   Book Time 2-479 1996 $120.00

WELTY, EUDORA 1909-   One Time, One Place. Mississippi in the Depression. New York: Random House, 1971. 1st edition; one of 300 copies signed by author; 8vo; cloth; fine, lacking slipcase.   James S. Jaffe 34-676 1996 $175.00

WELTY, EUDORA 1909-   One Writer's Beginnings. Cambridge: Harvard University Press, 1984. Uncorrected proof; printed green wrappers; fine. Bev Chaney, Jr. 23-762 1996 $195.00

WELTY, EUDORA 1909-   A Pageant of Birds. New York: Albondocani, 1974. Of a total edition of 326 copies, this one of 25 lettered copies, signed by author; fine in photographic self wrappers, publisher's prospectus laid in, scarce in lettered issue.   Between the Covers 42-456 1996 $500.00

WELTY, EUDORA 1909-   A Pageant of Birds. New York: Albondocani Press, 1974. 1st edition; one of 300 copies signed by Welty; small thin 8vo; black and white photos; original wrappers; mint.   James S. Jaffe 34-678 1996 $225.00

WELTY, EUDORA 1909-   A Pageant of Birds. New York: Albondocani, 1974. 1/300 copies, signed by author; self-wrappers; fine.   Ken Lopez 74-463 1996 $175.00

WELTY, EUDORA 1909-   Photographs. Jackson: University Press of Mississippi, 1989. One of 375 numbered copies, signed by author; this copy additionally signed by Reynolds Price, who provided introduction; fine in publisher's slipcase.   Lame Duck Books 19-572 1996 $450.00

WELTY, EUDORA 1909-   Place in Fiction. New York: House of Books, 1957. 1/300 numbered copies signed by author; very fine in original glassine dust jacket, missing tiny chips at spine extremities, otherwise fine.   Ken Lopez 74-461 1996 $550.00

WELTY, EUDORA 1909-   The Ponder Heart. New York: Harcourt, Brace and Co., 1954. 1st edition; signed by author; very good in lightly used dust jacket.   Priscilla Juvelis 95/1-262 1996 $200.00

WELTY, EUDORA 1909-   Retreat. Palaemon Press, 1981. Limited to 200 numbered copies, signed by author; 10.5 x 6 inches; buckram backed patterned boards, very good.   John K. King 77-510 1996 $125.00

WELTY, EUDORA 1909-   The Robber Bridegroom. Pennyroyal Press, 1987. One of 150 copies; signed by author and artist; 9 1/4 x 6 1/2 inches; 3 p.l., 134 pages, (1) leaf (colophon); vignette on title, colophon device, one text illustration, 21 fine woodcut plates, all by Barry Moser, title printed in maroon and black; very attractive maroon crushed levant morocco, vignette in blind on front cover showing a bird and full moon, spine titled in gilt, marbled endpapers; very slight soiling on back cover, otherwise very fine copy of quite lovely book.   Phillip J. Pirages 33-415 1996 $750.00

WELTY, EUDORA 1909-   The Robber Bridegroom. Garden City: Doubleday, 1942. 1st edition; near fine in near fine dust jacket and very light edgewear and surface soiling to rear panel, nice copy, uncommon. Ken Lopez 74-459 1996 $500.00

WELTY, EUDORA 1909-   The Shoe Bird. New York: Harcourt, Brace & World, 1964. 1st edition; illustrations by Beth Krush; fine in near fine dust jacket.   Steven C. Bernard 71-464 1996 $150.00

WELTY, EUDORA 1909-   Some Notes on Time in Fiction. Jackson: Mississippi Quarterly, 1973. 1st edition; offprint; signed by author; thin 8vo; printed wrappers; fine.   James S. Jaffe 34-677 1996 $350.00

WELTY, EUDORA 1909-   Three Papers on Fiction. Northampton: Smith College, 1962. 1st edition; stapled wrappers; fine, signed by author. Ken Lopez 74-462 1996 $275.00

WELTY, EUDORA 1909-   White Fruitcake. New York: Albondocani Press, 1980. 1st edition; one of 450 copies printed hors commerce; thin 12mo; cover drawing by Robert Dunn; original wrappers, inscribed by publisher, George Bixby. Mint.   James S. Jaffe 34-680 1996 $100.00

WELTY, EUDORA 1909-   Primo Amore. Milano: Longanesi & C., 1947. 1st Italian edition of the Wide Net. wrappers, dust jacket, short tear to front wrapper, pages uniformly browned, very good in about very good dust jacket with some chipping at top of front panel, but affecting no lettering, briefly inscribed by author.   Between the Covers 42-454 1996 $175.00

WERFEL, FRANZ   The Forty Days of Musa Dagh. New York: Modern Library, 1934. 1st Modern Library edition; very good+ in less than very good dust jacket; inscribed by author for Edith Snow.   Lame Duck Books 19-574 1996 $175.00

WERFEL, FRANZ   Hearken Unto the Voice. New York: Viking, 1938. 1st U. S. edition; near fine in dust jacket; inscribed by author for Edith Snow.   Lame Duck Books 19-577 1996 $500.00

WERFEL, FRANZ   The Pascarella Family. New York: Viking, 1935. 1st U.S. edition; V+ in very good dust jacket with chipping to extremities, inscribed by author for Edith Snow.   Lame Duck Books 19-575 1996 $250.00

WERFEL, FRANZ   Poems. Princeton: Princeton University, 1945. 1st edition; near fine in very good+ dust jacket with some minor chips and tears; this copy inscribed by translator, Edith Snow to her husband. Lame Duck Books 19-581 1996 $275.00

WERFEL, FRANZ   The Song of Bernadette. New York: Viking, 1942. 1st U.S. edition and 1st English translation; spine lightly tanned, else very good+ or better in very good dust jacket with chipping to extremities and couple of edge tears to rear panel; this copy inscribed by author for Edith Snow.   Lame Duck Books 19-580 1996 $850.00

WERFEL, FRANZ   The Twilight of a World. New York: Viking, 1937. 1st U.S. edition; near fine in very good dust jacket with several chips and tears; inscribed by author for Edith Snow.   Lame Duck Books 19-576 1996 $350.00

WERFEL, FRANZ   Verdi. New York: S&S, 1926. 3rd printing; very good+; inscribed by author to Edith Snow.   Lame Duck Books 19-573 1996 $100.00

WERNER, ARNO   One Man's Work: a Lecture. Easthampton: Warwick Press, 1872. One of 200 copies, signed by author and printer; 8vo; printed in Sans Serif Light 329 on Barcham Green handmade; tipped in colored plates, titlepage portrait; bound by Werner and Blinn in quarter russet morocco with paste paper sides; fine.   Bertram Rota 272-485 1996 £105.00

WERNER, CARL   Nile Sketches, Painted from Nature During the Travels through Egypt. London: Hildesheimer & Faulkner, 1871-75. Folio; map printed in blue and red titlepage printed in red and black, 24 chromolithographed plates; decorated cloth, gilt, slight rubbed. Blackmer 1947.   Charles W. Traylen 117-397 1996 £1,200.00

WESCHER, HERTA   Collage. New York: Harry N. Abrams, 1979. 4to; 418 pages; 396 illustrations (40 mounted color plates), yellow cloth stamped in black, dust jacket, fine.   Kenneth Karmiole 1NS-27 1996 $200.00

WESCOTT, GLENWAY   The Babe's Bed. Paris: Harrison of Paris, 1930. 1st edition; one of 375 copies on Pannekoek, from a total of 393, each signed by author on colophon; page size 8 3/4 x 6 3/4 inches; printed by Enschede in Zonen, Haarlem, designed by J. van Krimpen, the crator of the type face Lutitia in which the type is set; red silk with author and title in gilt on spine and housed in slightly soiled yellow publisher's box. Priscilla Juvelis 95/1-123 1996 $450.00

WESCOTT, GLENWAY   Good-Bye Wisconsin. New York: & London: Harper & Bros., 1928. 1st edition; number 99 of 250 copies; 8vo; original cloth backed boards, paper label, fore and bottom edges uncut; fine; inscribed to Ingle Barr from author.   Howard S. Mott 227-149 1996 $150.00

WESLEY, CHARLES H.   The History of Alpha Phi Alpha: a Development in Negro College Life. Washington: Howard University Press, 1929. 1st edition; photos; small tear to prelim page, little smudge on titlepage, otherwise near fine. Uncommon in first edition.   Between the Covers 43-432 1996 $175.00

WESLEY, CHARLES H.   Negro Labor in the United States 1850-1925. New York: Vanguard, 1927. 1st edition; slight soiling near fine, lacking the presumed dust jacket; signed by author and dated in year of publication.   Between the Covers 43-431 1996 $175.00

WESLEY, SAMUEL   Maggots; or, Poems on Several Subjects, Never Before Handled. London: John Dunton, 1685. 1st edition; 1st issue; 12mo; frontispiece; later Riviere style panelled morocco, spine gilt; leaves bit age darkened, small hole in leaf E3, excising few letters, otherwise very good, scarce, in modern pullout slipcase; armorial bookplate. Parks 52; Wing W1374; Wither to Prior 962.   Trebizond 39-56 1996 $975.00

WESLEY, SAMUEL   Poems on Several Occasions... London: printed for the author by E. Say... 1736. 1st edition; 4to; pages (ii), iv, (vi), 412; copper engraved coat of arms, wood engraved headpieces and ornaments, prelim and final leaves foxed; contemporary speckled calf, rebacked, raised bands between blind rules, original label relaid, blind ornaments in compartments, double gilt fillet border to sides, blind roll on board edges, corners rubbed, recased, good. Foxon W332; Lowndes IV p. 2876.   Blackwell's B112-284 1996 £195.00

WEST India Agricultural Distress, and a Remark on Mr. Wilberforce's Appeal. London: Sold by Edmund Lloyd, 1823. 1st edition; 8vo; 56 pages; disbound. Sabin 102770. Ragatz p. 276; Goldsmith 23833. Anthony W. Laywood 108-247 1996 £85.00

THE WEST Indian; or, the Happy Effects of Diligence and Self-Control; Exemplified in the History of Philip Montague. Wellington: printed by and for F. Houlston, 1827. 1st edition; 12mo; 154, (2 ad) pages, engraved frontispiece (offset onto title), original drab boards, rebacked, printed label; Osborne p. 956.   James Burmester 29-80 1996 £75.00

WEST, CHARLES   Lectures on the Diseases of Infancy and Childhood. London: 1859. 4th edition; 755 pages; boards, rubbed. GM 6344.   W. Bruce Fye 71-2247 1996 $100.00

WEST, LEONARD   The Natural Trout and Fly and Its Imitation. London: 1921. Color and other plates; original buckram, excellent copy. David A.H. Grayling 3/95-536 1996 £60.00

WEST, LEONARD   The Natural Trout Fly and It's Imitation. London: 1921. 2nd edition; color and other paltes; lightly rubbed/marked.   David A.H. Grayling 3/95-538 1996 £60.00

WEST, NANCY GLASS   Jose Vives-Atsara: His Life and His Art. Austin: 1976. Limited edition, signed by author and artist; oblong 4to; 28 color plates, 159 pages plus index.   W. M. Morrison 436-368 1996 $100.00

WEST, NATHANAEL   A Cool Million. New York: Covici Friede, 1934. 1st edition; 1st binding in light tan cloth; near fine in very good+ dust jacket with few minor chips; excellent association copy, inscribed by author for Jerry Sackheim, scarce inscribed.   Lame Duck Books 19-582 1996 $7,500.00

WEST, PAUL   The Growth of the Novel. Toronto: Canadian Broadcasting Corp., 1959. 1st edition; red wrappers, light crease to upper fore-corner of front panel, scarce, very good+.   Lame Duck Books 19-583 1996 $150.00

WEST, PAUL   The Spellbound Horses. Toronto: Ryerson Press, 1960. One of 250 copies; spine slightly faded, else very good+ in paper covered boards.   Lame Duck Books 19-584 1996 $250.00

WEST, REBECCA 1892-1983   The Return of the Soldier. New York: Century Co., 1918. Bookplate on front free endpaper, dust jacket chipped at top and bottom of spine, which is also rather discolored, but nice. R. A. Gekoski 19-150 1996 £225.00

WEST, THOMAS   The Antiquities of Furness; or an Account of the Royal Abbey of St. Mary. London: for the author, 1774. 1st edition; 4to; pages (xx), lvi (actually liv), 288, (138), 1 folding map as frontispiece, 3 engraved plates; contemporary full tree calf, finely tooled gilt decorative spine, red morocco label, marbled endpapers; few minor tears expertly repaired; bookplate of the Earl of Suffolk.   Sotheran PN32-200 1996 £295.00

WEST, THOMAS   The Antiquities of Furness... London: printed for the author by T. Spilsbury & sold by J. Johnson... 1774. 1st edition; 4to; pages (xx), lvi, 288, 3A-3R4 (appendices), extending frontispiece, folding map and plan and engraved plate; contemporary full calf, little rubbed and scraped, neatly rebacked in matching calf gilt, raised bands and contrasting spine label, edges of first three leaves little worn and neatly repaired, few spots and some pencilled notes and marginal lining, otherwise very good.   R.F.G. Hollett & Son 78-1387 1996 £275.00

WEST, THOMAS   The Antiquities of Furness... London: printed for the author by T. Spilsbury, 1774. 1st edition; 4to; pages (xx), lvi, 288, 3A-3R4 (appendices), folding engraved plan, folding plan, 2 engraved plates; contemporary full polished calf gilt, edges rather rubbed, rebacked in matching calf, gilt, raised bands, original spine label retained; attractive copy; attractive etched pictorial bookplate of James Frothingham Hunnewell.   R.F.G. Hollett & Son 78-1358 1996 £275.00

WEST, THOMAS   The Antiquities of Furness; or an Account of the Royal Abbey of St. Mary, in the Vale of Nightshade, Near Dalton in Furness... London: for the author by T. Spilsbury, 1774. 1st edition; 4to; pages (xx), lvi, (ii), 288, (136, appendix and conclusion), edges marbled, folding map, folding plan, 2 engraved plates, small tear to upper margin of b2; contemporary sprinkled calf, gilt, edges worn, little scraped, rebacked in blindstamped calf gilt, with raised bands and lettering piece; very good, sound copy. Upcott I p. 476.   R.F.G. Hollett & Son 78-1356 1996 £225.00

WEST, THOMAS   The Antiquities of Furness... Ulverston: George Ashburner, 1805. New edition; 8vo; pages (xxii), 426, (vi), engraved map, 5 aquatint plates, 3 hand colored plans and 2 engraved plates; fore-edge of one leaf of index soiled, corner torn away, otherwise a good copy; original boards, printed backstrip little defective.   R.F.G. Hollett & Son 78-1360 1996 £120.00

WEST, THOMAS   The Aniquities of Furness... Ulverston: George Ashburner, 1805. New edition; 8vo; pages xiv, 426, (vi), engraved map, 5 finely hand colored plates, 1 hand colored text plan, lacks frontispiece plate, title rather spotted, few leaves at end soiled and browned; modern cloth gilt.   R.F.G. Hollett & Son 78-1359 1996 £95.00

WEST, THOMAS   The Antiquities of Furness. Ulverston: Printed & sold by George Ashburner, 1822. New edition; 8vo; (xxi), 426 pages, index, map, engravings; tree calf, bit browned, otherwise very good, scarce. K Books 441-511 1996 £85.00

WEST, THOMAS   A Guide to the Lakes in Cumberland, Westmorland, and Lancashire. London: for B. Law, 1784. 3rd edition; 8vo; xii, 306 pages, ad leaf, engraved frontispiece and folding map, half title; wide margins, bound in contemporary half calf, rebacked; very good. Loosely inserted are 3 earlier engraved plates. Bicknell 13.3.   Ken Spelman 30-114   1996 £160.00

WEST, THOMAS   A Guide to the Lakes in Cumberland, Westmorland and Lancashire... London: W. Richardson (& 3 others), 1793. 5th edition; 8vo; xii, 311, (iii) pages; frontispiece, folding map, one other plate; half title, 3 pages ads at end; contemporary gree calf, neatly rebacked, spine gilt ruled, old label preserved; corners very slightly worn, nice.   Robert Clark 38-216   1996 £125.00

WEST, THOMAS   A Guide to the Lakes in Cumberland, Westmorland and Lancashire. Kendal: W. Pennington, 1812. 10th edition; 8vo; pages vi, (ii), 311, (i), uncut, complete with extending hand colored map frontispiece; original blue boards, rebacked in matching levant morocco, gilt. Bicknell 1310.   R.F.G. Hollett & Son   78-1362   1996 £135.00

WEST, THOMAS   A Guide to the Lakes in Cumberland, Westmorland and Lancashire. Kendal: W. Pennington, 1812. 10th edition; 8vo; pages vi, (ii), 311; uncut, complete with extending hand colored map frontispiece; modern half levant morocco gilt. Bicknell 1310.   R.F.G. Hollett & Son 78-1361   1996 £125.00

WEST, THOMAS   A Guide to the Lakes in Cumberland, Westmorland and Lancasahire. Kendal: W. Pennington, 1821. 11th edition; 8vo; pages v, (iii), 312, uncut, complete with hand colored aquatint frontispiece and extending hand colored map (offset); 20th century three quarter morocco gilt by New of Eton; Abbey 193; Bicknell 13.11.   R.F.G. Hollett & Son 78-1363   1996 £140.00

WEST, W.   A Monograph of the British Desmidiaceae. London: 1904-23. 8vo; volumes 1-5 (complete); pages xxxvi, 224; x, 204; xv, 274; xiv, 191; xxi, 300; recent buckram, perforated library stamp on titles, marginal ink notations on first preface page, small tear to a page, tears to an index page repaired with tape, pages tanned; rare.   Raymond M. Sutton VII-44   1996 $450.00

WEST, WILLIAM   The First Part of Symboleography. London: A. Islip, ptd. for the Companie of Stationers,/ ptd. by Thomas Wright, 1610/01. 1st edition; 4to in 8's; 2 volumes; 6 leaves + A1-(Qq8)-(RR6); 2 leaves + A1-Qq7; first part bound in contemporary vellum, second in somewhat later tooled calf with modern rebacking with leather label, volume 1 has following minor faults - short tear to text block of C2 without loss, tiny marginal burn holes to Dd4 & Ee2, running title to Rr3 & Rr4 cropped, some browning, foxing, edgewear and small marginal wormhole to first several leaves including titlepage, save for few quite minor edge tears, volume 2 essentially fine; STC 25272, 25278.   John Gach   150-469 1996 $850.00

WESTALL, W.   Views of Ragland Castle. London: Westall, 1843. Small folio; 6 engraved plates; sewn in wrappers, slight foxing, otherwise as issued.   Marlborough 162-97   1996 £300.00

WESTBY-GIBSON, JOHN   The Bibliography of Shorthand. London: Isaac Pitman, & Sons, 1887. 8 page catalog; original olive brown cloth, bevelled boards, one mark on front board, very good.   Jarndyce 103-358   1996 £65.00

WESTCOTT, THOMPSON   Centennial Portfolio. A Souvenir of the International Exhibition at Philadelphia. Philadelphia: Thomas Hunter, 1876. Oblong folio; large paper copy, unusual thus, with plates colored, titlepage, 3 leaves, ground plan and 52 color lithograph plates; publisher's brown morocco, gilt, scuffed at extremities, hinges of this heavy book weakening, gilt bright, plates fine. Hitchcock 1365.   Marilyn Braiterman 15-204   1996 $1,000.00

WESTCOTT, THOMPSON   Centennial Portfolio: a Souvenir of the International Exhibition. Philadelphia: Thomas Hunter, 1876. 1st edition; oblong 4to; viii pages, 52 plates, with accompanying text leaves, map; publisher's cloth rubbed at extremities, otherwise very good. Bookpress 75-99   1996 $650.00

WESTERMARCK, EDWARD   The History of Human Marriage. London: 1894. 2nd edition; 644 pages; original binding.   W. Bruce Fye 71-2248 1996 $100.00

WESTERN RAILROAD CORP.   Reports of the Engineers of the Western Rail Road Corporation, Made to the Directors in 1836-7. Springfield: Merriam Wood & Co., 1838. 120 pages, 2 folding maps; plain wrapper, rear wrapper tor and wrinkled, else very good. Thornton 2055; BRE p. 278.   Bohling Book Co. 192-720   1996 $125.00

THE WESTERN Sanitary Commission: a Sketch of Its Origin, History, Labors for the Sick and Wounded of the Western Armies, and Aid Given to Freedmen and Union Refugees, with Incidents of Hospital Life. St. Louis: 1864. 1st edition; original binding, head and tail of spine chipped, contents fine.   W. Bruce Fye 71-2249   1996 $300.00

WESTERVELT, W. D.   Hawaiian Legends of Gods and Ghosts. Boston/London: Ellis Press/Constable & Co., 1915. 1st edition; approximately 7.25 x 4.75 inches; 262 pages; illustrations; grey decorated cloth, spine faded, front hinge cracked, front free endpaper taped and marked.   Parmer Books   039/Nautica-039028   1996 $125.00

WESTGARTH, WILLIAM   Victoria and the Australian Gold Mines in 1857; with Notes on the Overland Route from Australia via Suez. London: Smith, Elder, 1857. 8vo; pages xvi, 466, 16 ads, 3 maps; original green embossed cloth, owner's signature on title. Ferguson 181st edition;8. Richard Adelson W94/95-177   1996 $425.00

WESTLAKE, DONALD E.   God Save the Mark. New York: Random House, 1967. 1st edition; fine in near fine dust jacket with few small closed tears and very light soiling; inscribed.   Quill & Brush 102-1730 1996 $100.00

WESTLAKE, HERBERT F.   Westminster Abbey; the Church, Convent, Cathedral and College of St. Peter, Westminster. London: Philip Allan, 1923. Only 350 copies printed in red and black on wove paper; 4to; 2 volumes; colored folding plan, 80 plates, mostly in photogravure and 12 text illustrations; original blue buckram, gilt, gilt tops, nice. Author's signature neatly affixed to title of each volume.   Howes Bookshop 265-732   1996 £150.00

WESTMACOTT, CHARLES MOLLOY 1787?-1868   Fitzalleyne of Berkeley. London: Sherwood and Co., 1825. 1st edition; 8vo; 2 volumes; original grey boards, marbled paper backs (chipped), paper labels (1 rubbed, the other chipped), uncut; Wolff 7136; Block p. 251; not in Sadleir. Howard S. Mott 227-150   1996 $450.00

WESTMAN, ERIK G.   The Swedish Element in America: a Comprehensive History of Swedish-American Achievements from 1638 to the Present Day. Chicago: Swedish-American Biographical Society, 1931. 1st edition; 3 volumes, (xvi), 492; (vi), 536, (vi), iv, 3-519 pages; profuse illustrations and portraits; cloth, pages bumped in volume 2, otherwise very good set.   Metacomet Books 54-119   1996 $110.00

THE WESTMORLAND Note-Book. Volume I 1888-1889. London: Elliot Stock and Kendal, Edward Gill, c. 1890. 8vo; All published, pages 382, tinted engraved vignette frontispiece of Kendal Parish Church by W. Banks and index; tinted engraved vignette frontispiece; modern cloth gilt, R.F.G. Hollett & Son 78-1369   1996 £130.00

WESTON, EDWARD   My Camera on Point Lobos. 1950. 1st edition; dust jacket, spiral bound, stiff wrpapers, dust jacket front cover present, but chipped, torn from rear dust jacket of which a part is laid in, uncommon in dust jacket.   J. B. Muns 154-324   1996 $400.00

WESTON, WILLIAM   Report of William Weston, Esquire, on the Practicability of Introducting the Water of the River Bonx into the City of New York: New York: printed by John Furman, 1799. 1st edition; 8vo; half dark blue morocco, gilt, by Bennett; fine, very scarce. Evans 36709; Sabin 103057; Rink Tech. Americana 2743.   Ximenes 108-344 1996 $750.00

WESTWOOD, JOHN OBADIAH 1805-1893   Illuminated Illustrations of the Bible... Wm. Smith, 1846. 4to; 37 chromolithograph plates finely printed in gold and colors, including title (only of 40, and lacking printed title); contemporary maroon morocco, gilt panelled sides, spine gilt in 6 comparments, inside edges gilt, slightly rubbed, but handsome copy, slightly foxed and lacks front free endpaper.   Thomas Thorp 489-319 1996 £80.00

WETMORE, PROSPER   Lexington, with Other Fugitive Poems. New York: G. & C. & H. Carvill, 1830. 1st edition; 8vo; 87, (1) pages; original muslin backed pink paper covered boards, printed paper label, slight chipping along spine edges; some pencil notes in text; fine. Cooper 5427.   M & S Rare Books 60-253   1996 $175.00

WETZEL, G.   Howard Phillips Lovecraft Memoirs Critiques & Bibliographies. SSR, 1955. 1st edition; 1/200 copies; some light wear to covers, but very good copy of this most fragile and uncommon booklet. Aronovitz 57-725   1996 $125.00

WEYMAN, STANLEY J.   A Gentleman of France. London: 1893. 1st edition; 3 volumes; original cloth, some foxing to text of each volume, library label removed from upper cover of each volume, but not unduly noticeable; very good. Sadleir 3307.   Words Etcetera 94-1280 1996 £65.00

THE WHALE and the Dangers of the Whale-Fishery. New Haven: S. Babcock, n.d. 110 x 70 mm; sewn as issued; decorative printed borders, illustrations; original fragile printed wrappers, soiled throughout, wrappers chipped and separating from text;   Parmer Books Nat/Hist-047331 1996 $100.00

WHALL, W. B.   Sea Songs and Shanties. Glasgow: Brown, Son, Ferguson Ltd., 1927. 6th edition; approximately 9.25 x 7 inches; xx, 154 pages; drawings and illustrations; green cloth, black spine and cover titles, bit of fading and wear, decorative bookplate.   Parmer Books 039/Nautica-039045 1996 $150.00

WHARBURTON, CHARLES   A Memoir of Charles Mordaunt Earl of Peterborough and Monmouth... London: Longman, Brown, Green and Longmans, 1853. 1st edition; 8vo; 2 volumes; vii, 261, 295 pages; original red blindstamped cloth, bookplates; else fine.   David Mason 71-44 1996 $140.00

WHARTON, EDITH 1862-1937   The Age of Innocence. New York: Limited Editions Club, 1973. One of 2000 numbered copies, signed by Lawrence Beall Smith; illustrations by Lawrence Beall Smith; fine in publisher's slipcase.   Hermitage SP95-1050 1996 $125.00

WHARTON, EDITH 1862-1937   Artemis to Actaeon. London: Macmillan, 1909. 1st British edition from American sheets with titlepage a cancel; one of only 250 copies; spine head chewed, occasional light foxing, else very good, lacking rare dust jacket. Inscribed by author to lifelong friend Daisy Chanler, scarce inscribed, but important association copies such as this are extremely rare.   Lame Duck Books 19-591 1996 $5,000.00

WHARTON, EDITH 1862-1937   Artemis to Actaeon and other Verse. New York: Charles Scribner's Sons, 1909. 1st edition; 12mo; dark green cloth stamped in gilt with shield design, two cherubs on either side, within flower frame surrounded by a single rule and lettered in gilt on spine, top edge gilt; nice, scarce, only touches of wear to tips of spine and corners, contemporary ink inscription dated Oct. 1909, else near fine. Garrison A17.1.a.   Priscilla Juvelis 95/1-263 1996 $250.00

WHARTON, EDITH 1862-1937   A Backward Glance. New York: D. Appleton Co., 1934. 1st edition; 8vo; smooth blue cloth stamped in gold, printed light green dust jacket, touch of wear to foot of spine and lower tips, jacket has some chipping with quarter inch lacking at head of spine and some darkening, jacket, however, is usually found in less than collectable condition, generally attractive, very good; Garrison A47.1.a. Priscilla Juvelis 95/1-264 1996 $275.00

WHARTON, EDITH 1862-1937   The Book of the Homeless. Le Livre des Sans-Foyer. New York: Charles Scribner's, 1916. 1st edition; one of 125 on Van Gelder paper; titlepage and other decorations by Rudolph Ruzicka; grey cloth over boards, stamped in gilt, tan cloth spine stamped in gilt, this copy unnumbered; bit of soiling to covers, generally very good in publisher's slipcase. Garrison D1.1.a.   Priscilla Juvelis 95/1-270 1996 $1,250.00

WHARTON, EDITH 1862-1937   The Buccaneers. New York: D. Appleton Century Co., 1938. 1st edition; 12mo; original navy blue cloth gilt in dust jacket; fine with jacket bright (2 minor scratches on cover), jacket shows some wear at edges and top of spine but rare in this condition.   Priscilla Juvelis 95/1-266 1996 $450.00

WHARTON, EDITH 1862-1937   The Buccaneers. New York: D. Appleton, 1938. 1st edition; minor offsetting to endpapers, near fine in very good jacket with some rubbing along edges and folds; nice, quite uncommon in dust jacket.   Ken Lopez 74-464 1996 $400.00

WHARTON, EDITH 1862-1937   Crucial Instances. New York: Scribners, 1901. 1st edition; decorated boards, front hinge lightly cracked, former owner signature, near fine.   Charles Agvent 4-1176 1996 $125.00

WHARTON, EDITH 1862-1937   The Custom of the Country. London: Macmillan and Co., 1913. 1st edition; 10 pages publisher's ads at rear; buckram covers, top edge gilt, head and tail of spine and corners bumped, covers slightly marked & partially faded, cover edges rubbed, spine faded, free endpapers browned, prelims, edges and endpapers spotted, very good.   Ulysses 39-617 1996 £75.00

WHARTON, EDITH 1862-1937   The Custom of the Country. New York: Scribner's, 1913. 1st edition; near fine with some rubbing to extremities. Garrison A21.1.a.   Priscilla Juvelis 95/1-269 1996 $175.00

WHARTON, EDITH 1862-1937   The Custom of the Country. New York: Charles Scribner's sons, 1913. 1st edition; fine, clean copy, bright. Left Bank Books 2-156 1996 $125.00

WHARTON, EDITH 1862-1937   The Descent of Man and Other Stories. New York: Scribners, 1904. 1st edition; slight wear to spine ends and little flecking to cloth, else nice, near fine.   Between the Covers 42-460 1996 $150.00

WHARTON, EDITH 1862-1937   The Fruit of the Tree. New York: Scribner's, 1907. 1st edition; near fine, with only one bit of spotting; Garrison A14.1.a.   Priscilla Juvelis 95/1-273 1996 $175.00

WHARTON, EDITH 1862-1937   A Gift from the Grave. London: John Murray, 1900. 1st English edition, 1st printing; 8vo; blue cloth over boards, with yap edges, green flower and vine pattern on spine and front join, author and title in gilt on front cover, title and publisher in gilt on spine, spine slightly discolored, some wear to edges, generally very good, very rare; inscribed by publisher, John Murray to Ms. Bonham Carter.   Priscilla Juvelis 95/1-274 1996 $750.00

WHARTON, EDITH 1862-1937   The God's Arrive. New York: Appleton, 1932. 1st edition; near fine in uncommonly bright and clean dust jacket with discreet, internally mended three quarter inch tear.   Anacapa House 5-323 1996 $225.00

WHARTON, EDITH 1862-1937   The Greater Inclination. New York: Charles Scribner's Sons, 1899. 1st edition; 2nd printing, holiday edition; 12mo; 254 pages; smooth white cloth stamped in gold (Garrison's Binding C), binding considerably worn and soiled, spotting to front cover and loss of gilt from elaborate design, genuine rarity despite its lesser condition; good. Garrison A3.1.b.   Priscilla Juvelis 95/1-275 1996 $650.00

WHARTON, EDITH 1862-1937   Hudson River Bracketed. New York: D. Appleton and Co., 1929. 1st edition; 1st printing; 12mo; 560 pages; black cloth stamped in gold front and spine, decorated mustard yellow dust jacket; this copy dusty with some fading to the lettering at the spine, owner's pencilled name and date to front flyleaf, dust jacket lacking quarter inch at head of spine (with loss of 'Hudson' from the title) and chipping at the foot with chip at front fore tip and two half inch tears (closed); about very good. Garrison A43.1.a.   Priscilla Juvelis 95/1-277 1996 $285.00

WHARTON, EDITH 1862-1937   In Morocco. New York: Charles Scribner's, 1920. 1st edition; 8vo; green cloth stamped in white, trade binding designed by Margaret Armstrong (signed) of brilliant green-yellow leaf and vine frame with pink stamped parrots in upper corners, gold stamped on spine, printed offset white dust jacket lettered in green with photograph at front panel, illustrated with half tones, in fine condition, gilt on spine completely undimmed and color stamping fresh and bright; jacket in white paper stamped in green, jacket very good with only few minor chips and short (half inch) tear at bottom, rarely found in good collector condition, to find it in a jacket is extremely unusual, housed in custom made clamshell box. Garrison A29.1.a.   Priscilla Juvelis 95/1-278 1996 $2,000.00

WHARTON, EDITH 1862-1937   Madame de Treymes. New York: Scribners, 1907. 1st edition; 8vo; color plates; original cloth, slightly cocked, very good, former owner signature, ink offsetting to f.f.e.p. Charles Agvent 4-1179 1996 $100.00

WHARTON, EDITH 1862-1937   The Marne. London: Macmillan and Co., 1918. 1st and only English edition, binding A; brick cloth, gilt stamped on front panel and spine with title and author, front panel lettering enclosed in fillet rondel, minor wear to edges and tips, generally very good; inscribed by author for Clarence Carrigan. Garrison A27.2.   Priscilla Juvelis 95/1-279 1996 $3,600.00

WHARTON, EDITH 1862-1937   The Marne. New York: D. Appleton, 1918. 1st edition; 2nd printing; original dust jacket, book is drab paper over boards with green cloth spine (exactly as first printing), dust jacket printed in green and red, jacket chipped and shows traces of tape removal on inside, Garrison A28.1.a.   Priscilla Juvelis 95/1-280 1996 $200.00

WHARTON, EDITH 1862-1937   The Mother's Recompense. New York: D. Appleton and Co., 1925. 1st edition; maroon gilt stamped cloth, rose and gilt paper printed in dark blue dust jacket, some wear to a fragile paper jacket including a tear (no paper loss) to top of front about 2 inches long, spine of jacket sunned to light pink; traces of tape removal from interior of jacket. Garrison A38.1.a.   Priscilla Juvelis 95/1-281 1996 $350.00

WHARTON, EDITH 1862-1937 The Mother's Recompense. New York: London: D. Appleton & Co., 1925. 1st edition; 1st printing, American issue, binding A, (no priority) in dust jacket C (no priority); 12mo; maroon cloth stamped in gilt front and spine, gilt spangled blue green dust jacket, near fine in fine jacket that shows sunning to spine and some minor chipping and some small tears at top, scarce in this condition. Garrison A37.1.a. Priscilla Juvelis 95/1-282 1996 $350.00

WHARTON, EDITH 1862-1937 A Son at the Front. New York: Charles Scribner's Sons, 1923. 1st edition; red gilt stamped cloth, gilt a shade dimmer on spine, generally very good in rare dust jacket that has some chips to bottom and top of spine. Priscilla Juvelis 95/1-283 1996 $250.00

WHARTON, EDITH 1862-1937 A Son at the Front. New York: Charles Scribner's Sons, 1923. 1st edition; red gilt stamped cloth, gilt dimmer on spine, generally very good in rare dust jacket that has some 1 1/4 x 1 3/8 inches missing from bottom of spine as well as some minor chipping to corners. Priscilla Juvelis 95/1-284 1996 $175.00

WHARTON, EDITH 1862-1937 The Touchstone. New York: Charles Scribner's Sons, 1900. 1st edition; 12mo; grey boards with gilt stamping to front and spine, top edge gilt, decorated titlepage; touch of foxing throughout text, last page roughly opened, unusually firm and crisp copy, very good. Garrison A4.1.a. Priscilla Juvelis 95/1-285 1996 $200.00

WHARTON, EDITH 1862-1937 The Valley of Decision. New York: Scribners, 1902. 1st edition; 1st state; 8vo; 2 volumes; cloth bit darkened at edges, scuffed rear of volume 1; owner signature dated March, a month after publication date; near fine. Charles Agvent 4-1180 1996 $150.00

WHARTON, EDITH 1862-1937 The Valley of Decision. New York: Charles Scribner's Sons, 1902. 1st edition; dark red cloth stamped in gold on spine, wear to edges of spine and tips, ink stains on front cover volume 1; still good. Garrison A6.1.a. Priscilla Juvelis 95/1-286 1996 $100.00

WHARTON, EDITH 1862-1937 The World Over. New York: D. Appleton Century Co., 1936. 1st edition; 12mo; 308 pages; dark blue stamped in gold to front and spine, black dust jacket with white lettering and green accents; bright, fresh copy, near fine. Garrison A48.1.a. Priscilla Juvelis 95/1-287 1996 $475.00

WHARTON, EDITH 1862-1937 The Writing of Fiction. London: Charles Scribner's Sons, 1925. 1st and only edition, 1st printing, English issue; 8vo; blue cloth over boards, author and title stamped in gilt on cover and spine, some discoloring to spine, small hold on front hinge (nail) and some wear to tips, but generally good, collectable copy; Scarce. Garrison A38.1.a.2. Priscilla Juvelis 95/1-288 1 996 $250.00

WHARTON, GRACE The Wits and Beaux of Society. London: J. W. Jarvis, 1890. New edition; tall 8vo; 2 volumes, xxxii, 262, (vi), 246 pages; original gree cloth, fine, bright copy. David Mason 71-45 1996 $120.00

WHARTON, THOMAS The Union; or Scots and English Poems. Dublin: printed for Richard Watts, 1761. 1st Dublin edition; 12mo; some slight soiling of text in places, final ad leaf; contemporary calf, spine gilt, label. Anthony W. Laywood 109-116 1996 £85.00

WHARTON, W. Franky Furbo. Holt, 1989. 1st edition; 1/250 copies, signed by author; as new in dust jacket, uncommon. Aronovitz 57-1268 1996 $135.00

WHARTON, WILLIAM A Midnight Clear. New York: Knopf, 1982. Uncorrected proof; wrappers; just about fine. Between the Covers 42-461 1996 $100.00

WHAT is to Be Done? Or Past, Present and Future. London: James Ridgway, 1844. 1st edition; 8vo; (iv), 123 pages; recent printed blue boards lettered; very good; from the contemporary library of Lord William Russell with his signature on titlepage. Goldsmiths 33622 (2nd ed.); Kress C6518 (2nd ed.); Black 5803 (3rd ed. John Drury 82-290 1996 £95.00

WHATELY, RICHARD Introductory Lectures on Political Economy, Delivered at Easter Term, MDCCCXXXI. London: printed for B. Fellowes, 1832. 2nd edition; 8vo; slight foxing at beginning and end, some quires sprung; original boards, uncut, lacking backstrip. Kress C3379; Goldsmith 27309. Anthony W. Laywood 109-157 1996 £90.00

WHATELY, RICHARD Miscellaneous Lectures and Reviews. London: Parker Sons and Bourn, 1861. 1st collected edition; 8vo; vii, (1), 339, (1) pages, 28 pages publisher's ads at end; original cloth, embossed in blind, spine lettered in gilt, trifle worn; very good. John Drury 82-291 1996 £75.00

WHEAT, CARL I. Mapping the Transmississippi West 1540-1861. Storrs-Mansfield: Maurizio Martino Pub., 1995. Reprint edition, limited to 350 copies; 5 volumes, with volume 5 having 2 parts; frontispieces, maps, some foldouts; original green cloth, title stamped in gilt on spine, very fine set. Michael D. Heaston 23-49 1996 $650.00

WHEAT, CARL I. The Pioneer Press of California. Oakland: Biobooks, 1948. Limited to 450 copies; folio; (38) pages; 3 tipped in facsimiles; printed in red and black; cloth backed boards, paper spine label. Grabhorn Press Bib. 459. Kenneth Karmiole 1NS-257 1996 $125.00

WHEATER, W. The History of the Parishes of Sherburn and Cawood with Notices of Wistow and Saxton, Towton, etc. London: 1882. 2nd edition; 8vo; (4), vi, 328 pages; colored plates, litho frontispiece and other illustrations; red cloth, bit dull, otherwise good. Scarce. K Books 442-494 1996 £70.00

WHEELER, A. O. The Selkirk Range. Ottawa: Government Printing Bureau, 1905. 24cmo; xvii, 459 pages; frontispiece, illustrations, portraits, drawings, errata page, gilt stamped decorated green cloth, few gatherings slightly loose; very good. Rockland Books 38-247 1996 $300.00

WHEELER, ANNE The Westmorland Dialect, with the Adjaceny of Lancashrie and Yorkshire, in four Familiar Dialogues. Kendal: M. & r. Branthwaite, 1821. 3rd edition; 8vo pages 120, 12, 12, (addenda), woodcut frontispiece, 2 woodcuts, original printed wrappers, worn and soiled, corners chipped and backstrip lacking. From the library of Dr. Arthur Raistrick, with his bookplate. R.F.G. Hollett & Son 78-501 1996 £95.00

WHEELER, ANNE The Westmorland Dialect... London: John Russell Smith, 1851. 8vo; 175 pages; original blind ruled cloth, gilt, very nice. R.F.G. Hollett & Son 78-503 1996 £55.00

WHEELER, ARTHUR OLIVER The Selkirk Range. Ottawa: Government Printing Bureau for Dept. of the Interior, 1905. 8vo; 2 volumes; pages xvii, (i) (errata), 459, illustrations; portfolio of 11 folding maps, panoramas, diagrams on 14 sheets; original uniform gilt stamped cloth, except for portfolio case beginning to tear at seams, text volume and maps in excellent condition. Hugh Anson-Cartwright 87-452 1996 $350.00

WHEELER, DANIEL Extracts from the Letters and Journal of Daniel Wheeler, Now Engaged in a Religious Visit to the Inhabitants of the Islands of the Pacific Ocean, Van Dieman's land, and New South Wales, Accomapnied by His Son, Charles Wheeler. London: Harvey and Darton, 1839. 1st collected edition; 8vo; 4 parts in one; 300 pages; original black cloth, slightly worn. Ferguson 2895; Sabin 103182. Anthony W. Laywood 108-248 1996 £110.00

WHEELER, GEORGE M. Report Upon United States Geographical Surveys West of the One Hundredth Meridian. Washington: 1889-79. 4to; over 5000 pages; 7 volumes in 8 (separate atlas volume not included); 258 plates, over 300 woodcuts and 6 folding maps; original cloth, wear to extremities, but generally sound, splitting to rear edge of backstrip of volume 7, small tear to rear cover of volume 7, tear to 1 text page, pages yellowed. Raymond M. Sutton VI-34 1996 $2,100.00

WHEELOCK, JULIUS The Boys in White: The Experience of a Hospital Agent in and Around Washington. New York: 1870. 1st edition; 268 pages; original binding, water stain affecting the first few leaves. W. Bruce Fye 71-2250 1996 $300.00

WHEELWRIGHT, H. W. Natural History Sketches by the Old Bushman (Australia). London: 187-. New edition; 8vo; pages xv, 272, 16 plates; cloth, trifle stained. Obtrusive signature on reverse of frontispiece. Wheldon & Wesley 207-460 1996 £55.00

WHEELWRIGHT, MARY C. The Myth and Prayers of the Great Star Chant and The Myth of the Coyote Chant. Santa Fe: Museum of Navajo Ceremonial Art, 1956. 190 pages; 22 serigraph color plates by Louie Ewing after sand paintings; teal cloth, no dust jacket; near fine. Ken Sanders 8-299 1996 $350.00

WHELER, R. B.   History and Antiquities of Stratford-upon-Avon: Comprising a Description of the Collegiate Church, the Life of Shakespeare, and Copies of Several Documents Relating to Him and His Family. Stratford-upon-Avon: n.d. 1806. 1st edition; 8vo; half title, 6 aquatint plates, 19 page list of subscribers; 19th century half morocco, top edge gilt, others uncut.   Anthony W. Laywood 109-158 1996 £65.00

WHELLAN, WILLIAM   The History and Topography of the Counties of Cumberland and Westmorland. Pontefract: W. Whellan and Co., 1860. 1st edition; thick 4to; 8vo; pages 896, viii, half title spotted, otherwise very good, sound copy; modern three quarter calf, gilt.   R.F.G. Hollett & Son 78-1371 1996 £120.00

WHERE the Two Came to Their Father: a Navaho War Ceremonial... Princeton: Princeton University Press, 1969. New edition; folio; 18 loose serigraph plates; portfolio in box with printed labels, text in separate booklet. Fine.   Marilyn Braiterman 15-152 1996 $450.00

WHEWELL, WILLIAM 1794-1866   Astronomy and General Physics, Considered with Reference to Natural Theology. London: William Pickering, 1834. 3rd edtiion, 8vo; 381 pages; rebound in modern blue cloth, gilt titling on spine, fore-edge lightly foxed, occasional light foxing to pages, pages slightly browned, otherwise a good copy.   Knollwood Books 70-197 1996 $130.00

WHEWELL, WILLIAM 1794-1866   English Hexameter Translations from Schiller, Goethe, Homer, Callinus and Meleager. London: John Murray, 1847. 1st edition; oblong 8vo; contemporary rose calf, rebacked to style, all edges gilt, with "English Hexameters" stamped in large capitals on top edge, original color printed pictorial wrappers bound in; very good, scarce. With large orange and yellow bookplate of William Stirling, later Stirling Maxwell. CBEL III 1282.   Ximenes 109-297 1996 $400.00

WHEWELL, WILLIAM 1794-1866   History of the Inductive Sciences, from the Earliest to the Present Times. London: John Parker, 1837. 1st edition; 8vo; 3 volumes, xxxvi, 437, (2); xi, (1), 534, (2); xii, 624 pages, complete with all half titles and errata leaves; modern three quarter calf over marbled boards, morocco spine labels, some scattered contemporary ink underlining and notations in volume one; bright, crisp copy, near fine.   Edwin V. Glaser 121-320 1996 $750.00

WHEWELL, WILLIAM 1794-1866   History of the Inductive Sciences... London: 1847. 2nd edition; 8vo; 3 volumes, some foxing; half cloth, bit worn and shaken, backstrip of last volume defective at foot.   Maggs Bros. Ltd. 1190-358 1996 £55.00

WHEWELL, WILLIAM 1794-1866   The Philosophy of the Inductive Sciences, Founded Upon Their History... London: John Parker, 1847. 8vo; 2 volumes, xxxii, (2), 708; xiv, (2), (3)-679 pages, large folding table; contemporary calf, elaborately gilt prize binding, five raised bands, marbled endpapers and edges; attractive, near fine; from the library of the medical historian John B. de C. M. Saunders, with his bookplate. Sotheran 5373; Duveen p. 617.   Edwin V. Glaser 121-321 1996 $450.00

WHICHER, GEORGE F.   Alas All's Vanity or a leaf from the First American Edition of Several Poems by Anne Bradstreet Printed at Boston anno 1678. New York: Collector's Bookshop, 1942. One of 105 numbered copies; page 219 is tipped in facing page 8, black and white reproductions of titlepages of the first English and 1st American editions; original binding, tail of spine slightly bumped, very good in plain unprinted tissue dust jacket, which is torn, chipped and creased, as well as browned at spine and edges slightly torn; from the library of James D. Hart.   Ulysses 39-64 1996 £155.00

WHISTLER, JAMES A. MC NEILL   Mr. Whistler's Ten O'Clock - Being a Talk Delivered by...in London February 1885. San Francisco: Black Vine Press, 1940. One of 300 copies; limp decorated gilt parchment covers, covers browned and slightly marked, pastedowns spotted, very good in slipcase faded at spine and edges.   Ulysses 39-619 1996 £55.00

WHISTLER, LAURENCE   The English Festivals. London: 1947. 1st edition; illustrations; extremely good copy in very good dust jacket with small piece of tape at head of lightly browned spine, signed by author.   Words Etcetera 94-1288 1996 £55.00

WHISTLER, LAURENCE   Sir John Vanbrugh, Architect and Dramtist 1664-1726. London: Cobden-Sanderson, 1938. 1st edition; 8vo; 327 pages, 14 plates; frontispiece; cloth, minor foxing on endpapers, light coverwear, else fine.   The Bookpress 75-249 1996 $120.00

WHISTLER, REX   The Konigsmark Drawings, Reproduced in Facsimile in Sepia and Colour. London: Richards Press, 1952. 1st edition; limited to 1000 numbered copies; 4to; pages 24, 10 tinted plates by Rex Whistler mounted at large, original red buckram, gilt, usual slight fading to spine, otherwise very nice, bookplate.   Sotheran PN32-65 1996 £198.00

WHISTLER, REX   The Konigsmark Drawings. London: Richards Press, 1952. Limited to 950 copies; large 4to; 10 full page illustrations by Whistler; red buckram, gilt, spine slightly faded, otherwise very good with remains of original acetate wrapper in slightly faded slipcase.   Words Etcetera 94-1285 1996 £90.00

WHISTLER, REX   The New Forget-Me-Not: a Calendar. London: Cobden-Sanderson, 1929. One of 360 numbered copies, signed by artist on limitation page; illustrations by Rex Whistler; some sunning to spine and edges of decorated boards, otherwise very good.   R. A. Gekoski 19-151 1996 £110.00

WHISTON, WILLIAM   Memoirs of the Life and Writings of Mr. William Whiston. London: printed for the author & sold by Mr. Whiston; and Mr. Bishop, 1749. 1st edition; 8vo; 622 pages; perforation and cancellation stamps on blank verso of title; new half calf, label, light browning of text, occasional marginal tears.   Anthony W. Laywood 109-160 1996 £145.00

WHISTON, WILLIAM   A New Theory of the Earth, from Its Original, to the Consummation of All Things. London: printed by R. Roberts, for Benj. Tooke, 1696. 1st edition; 8vo; engraved frontispiece, 7 plates, piece torn from outer margin of S2 with loss of few letters of the marginal notes, ad leaf and errata leaf at end; contemporary panelled calf, rebacked, label; bookplate of Henry Poley of Badley, 1703 on blank verso of title, nice. Wing W1696; Hoover 883; Norman 2229.   Anthony W. Laywood 109-159 1996 £485.00

WHISTON, WILLIAM   Sir Isaac Newton's Mathematick Philosophy More Easily Demonstrated; with Dr. Halley's Account of Comets Illustrated. London: printed for J. Senex and W. Taylor, 1716. 1st English edition; 8vo; half title, neat stamp on blank verso of title and last page, slight dampstaining in some blank margins; contemporary calf, rebacked, label. Babson 127; Wallis Newton and Newtoniana 168.   Anthony W. Laywood 109-161 1996 £375.00

WHISTON, WILLIAM   Whiston's Account of the Exact Time when Miraculous Gifts Ceas'd in the Church. London: printed for the Author & are to be sold by Mr. Noon; Mr. Whiston.. 1749. 1st edition; 8vo; 40 pages; disbound.   Anthony W. Laywood 109-162 1996 £75.00

WHITAKER, JOHN   The History of Manchester. London: printed for J. Murray, No. 32 Fleetstreet, Opposite St. Dunstan's... 1773. 2nd edition; 8vo; 2 volumes; (iii-x), (xiii-xvi), 1-385 pages, 1-276 pages, appendices 277-379 pages, index 381-427 pages, ad leaf, frontispiece to volume 1, 21 vignettes to letterpress; new endpapers and prelims, boards slightly soiled and worn. Cox III p. 210.   Beeleigh Abbey BA56-29 1996 £95.00

WHITAKER, JOHN   The History of Manchester. London: printed for J. Murray, 1773. 2nd edition; 8vo; 2 volumes; contemporary tree calf, slightly rubbed, spines gilt, hinges cracked, lacks 3 labels of 4; clean copy.   Anthony W. Laywood 108-140 1996 £95.00

WHITAKER, T. D.   The History and Antiquities of the Deanery of Craven, in the County of York. London: Cassell, Petter and Galpin, 1878. Large paper copy; thick folio; title in red and black, colored frontispiece, 27 other color plates, 32 black and white plates, 1 extra plate of Skipton Castle, 2 maps, 29 folding pedigrees and numerous text illustrations; finely bound in half red morocco, cloth sides to match, 5 raised bands to spine, gilt lettering and decorations to spine and date, top edge gilt.   Charles W. Traylen 117-384 1996 £600.00

WHITAKER, T. D.   The History and Antiquities of the Deanery of Craven, in the County of York. London: Cassell, Petter and Galpin and Leeds: Joseph Dodgson, 1878. 3rd edition; thick folio; 54 plates, 2 maps, 20 folding pedigrees and numerous text illustrations; original black blind ruled and gilt morocco over heavy bevelled boards.   Charles W. Traylen 117-385 1996 £280.00

WHITAKER, W.   Geology of London and Of Part of the Thames Valley. London: 1889. 8vo; 2 volumes; folding table and numerous text figures; cloth, trifle worn, few small library stamps.   Wheldon & Wesley 207-1381 1996 £90.00

WHITE, A.   The Stapelieae, an Introduction to the Study of the Tribe of Asclepiadaceae. Pasadena: 1933. 1st edition; 4to; pages xi, 206; colored frontispiece tipped in, portraits, 236 text figures; original cloth, some loss to silver lettering on covers, marginal yellowing to pages.   Raymond M. Sutton VI-1034 1996 $125.00

WHITE, ANTONIA   Frost in May. London: Desmond Harmesworth, 1933. 1st edition; binding soiled and little foxing, an about very good copy, lacking dust jacket; scarce; inscribed by author for Peggy Guggenheim, art patron.   Between the Covers 42-462 1996 $575.00

WHITE, CHARLES   Cases in Surgery with Remarks. London: 1770. 1st edition; 8vo; 7 folding engraved plates, marginal worming in first 20 or so leaves (one large hole a little obtrusive) and later in book, but text not affected, from the Bedford Medical Library, with several stamps; contemporary sheep, worn.   Maggs Bros. Ltd. 1190-534 1996 £145.00

WHITE, CHRISTOPHER   The Flower Drawings of Jan Van Huysum 1682-1749. Leigh-on-Sea: 1964. 29 x 22.5 cm; 23 pages text, 64 plates; original cloth, dust jacket.   Rainsford A54-330 1996 £55.00

WHITE, CHRISTOPHER   Rembrandt as an Etcher. London: A. Zwemmer Ltd., 1969. 30 x 23 cm; 2 volumes; xi, 243 pages; 20 pages, 348 illustrations; original cloth, dust jacket.   Rainsford A54-483 1996 £125.00

WHITE, DIANA   The Descent of Ishtar. Eragny Press, 1903. One of only 10 copies on vellum; 12mo; issued in sheets, newly bound in full white vellum by Bayntun-Riviere, lettering and decoration from half title being reproduced in gilt on upper cover, fine in slipcase.   Bertram Rota 272-138 1996 £5,000.00

WHITE, DIANA   The Descent of Ishtar. Eragny Pres, 1903. One of 226 copies 12mo; printed in black and red in the Brook type, with borders in green on Arches handmade paper; patterned boards, endpapers and patterned paper of upper cover discolored, as is often the case (by reaction to the binder's paste?), otherwise nice, bookplate.   Bertram Rota 272-137 1996 £300.00

WHITE, EDMUND   Noctures for the King of Naples. New York: St. Martin's Press, 1978. 1st edition; 8vo; cloth backed boards, dust jacket, fine; inscribed with short note by author.   James S. Jaffe 34-683 1996 $100.00

WHITE, EDWARD   Evansville and Its Men of Mark. Evansville: Historical Pub. Co., 1873. 1st edition; 420 pages; decorative green cloth, 1 inch tear to top of spine, otherwise very good.   Blue River Books 9-188 1996 $120.00

WHITE, ELIZA   Gertrude; or Thoughtlessness & Inattention Corrected. London: Harvey & Darton, 1823. 1st edition; 134 x 84mm; 161, 2 pages; marbled boards with maroon roan spine, compartmented and lettered in gilt, covers with light wear, else very good. Osborne 956.   Marjorie James 19-227 1996 £75.00

WHITE, ELWYN BROOKS   The Fox of Peapack. New York: Harper & Brothers, 1938. 1st edition; offsetting to endpapers, minor foxing to tope edge, still near fine in very good price clipped dust jacket with some edgewear and closed tears at rear spine and flap folds; attractive copy, scarce, particularly uncommon in dust jacket.   Ken Lopez 74-465 1996 $250.00

WHITE, ELWYN BROOKS   Stuart Little in the Schoolroom. H&R, ca. 1960. 1st edition thus; red paper boards, without dust jacket as issued, fine, signed by famous illustrator Garth Williams, most uncommon. Aronovitz 57-1270 1996 $225.00

WHITE, EUGENE E.   Service on the Indian Reservations. Little Rock: Diploma Press Arkanasas Democrat Co., 1893. 1st edition; 336 pages; illustrations; original green cloth, title stamped in gilt on spine and front cover, rubbing and some discoloration to cloth, overall very good. Flake Supplement 9729a; not in Graff, Decker, Ebserstadt, Howes.   Michael D. Heaston 23-364 1996 $850.00

WHITE, GEORGE FRANCIS   Views in India, Chiefly Among the Himalaya Mountains... London: Fisher, Son and Co., n.d., c. 1838. 4to; 37 steel engraved plates, all in good condition, (appear to have been washed), no offsetting; modern half red morocco, gilt rule and title to panelled spine, marbled boards and endpapers, new prelim and final blanks.   Beeleigh Abbey BA/56-127 1996 £300.00

WHITE, GILBERT 1720-1793   The Natural History and Antiquities of Selborne, in the County of Southampton. London: 1789. 1st edition; 4to; vignette half title, (iii-v), 1-430 pages, 431-468 pages, index, (12) pages, list of plates, errata leaf, large folding linen backed frontispiece, 6 full page engraved copperplates, 1 large folding, and vignette half title to Antiquities of Selborne; neat repair to small tear to title, further neat repairs to few other pages, no loss to text, previous catalog description loosely inserted to rear; bound by Bayntun, full green calf, triple gilt rule border, red and brown morocco labels to spine, decorative gilt tooled birds, butterfuly and hare to panelled spine, joints very slightly rubbed, all edges gilt, marbled endpapers.   Beeleigh Abbey BA56-30 1996 £800.00

WHITE, GILBERT 1720-1793   The Natural History (Antiquities) of Selborne. London: 1813. 1st edition; 4to; 2 vignettes, 10 plates (one colored by hand); from the collection of Robert Leigh, with his booklabel, later in the W. H. Mullens collection, with his bookplate, bound for him in half green morocco, uncut, original printed label (defective) and front wrapper (? or was it orginally a board) preserved. Maggs Bros. Ltd. 1190-275 1996 £110.00

WHITE, GILBERT 1720-1793   The Natural History of Selborne, to Which are Added, The Naturalist's Calendar... London: 1825. 8vo; 2 volumes, pages 352; 2, 364, 4 plates; original boards, uncut, binding and labels slightly worn.   John Henly 27-159 1996 £90.00

WHITE, GILBERT 1720-1793   The Natural History and Antiquities of Selborne and a Garden Kalendar. London: 1900. 8vo; 2 volumes; 99 plates, 69 text figures; original cloth, gilt top.   Wheldon & Wesley 207-462 1996 £180.00

WHITE, GILBERT 1720-1793   The Natural History of Selbourne. London: John Lane, The Bodley Head, 1902. 1st edition thus; 8vo; 552 pages; illustrations; original half levant morocco by Birdsall, featuring inlaid owl, gilt back and top edge gilt, bookplate, spine browned, still near fine.   Chapel Hill 94-121 1996 $200.00

WHITE, GILBERT 1720-1793   The Natural History of Selborne. Ipswich: Limited Editions Club, 1972. 1500 copies, signed by artist; 4to; illustrations by John Nash; quarter gold stamped calfskin; fine in glassine and slipcase.   Charles Agvent 4-1181 1996 $175.00

WHITE, GILBERT 1720-1793   A Naturalist's Calendar with Observations in Various Branches of Natural History. London: 1795. 1st edition; crown 8vo; pages iv, 170, v, one ad, hand colored plate; later polished calf, gilt, little spotting.   John Henly 27-157 1996 £148.00

WHITE, GLEESON   Children's Books and Their Illustrators. London: the Studio, 1897. 1st edition; 4to; 68 pages, plates, illustrations in text; cloth, paper label. Some foxing, light spotting to cover.   The Bookpress 75-368 1996 $110.00

WHITE, HENRY   Geology, Oil Fields and Minerals of Canada West: How and Where to Find Them. Toronto: W. C. Chewett, 1865. 1st edition; 12mo; 109 pages; 2 enormous colored folding maps, lithograped by Chewett; original cloth, black paper label on front cover, as one might accept, some tears in folding maps, but sight and maps are complete and intact; excellent copy. Staton & Tremaine 4461 (wanting 2 maps).   M & S Rare Books 60-433 1996 $1,750.00

WHITE, J.   An Essay on the Indigenous Grasses of Ireland. Dublin: 1808. 8vo; pages xxix, (1), 156; 2 folding hand colored plates (2 small tears); contemporary half calf, rubbed, some wear, pages yellowed. Raymond M. Sutton VI-842 1996 £135.00

WHITE, JAMES   English Country Life. London: Richard Bentley, 1843. 1st edition; 8vo; original green cloth, decorated in gilt; fine, scarce. 5 copies in NUC.   Ximenes 109-298 1996 $125.00

WHITE, JOHN   The Birth and Rebirth of Pictorial Space. London: Faber & Faber, 1967. 2nd edition; 25.5 x 16 cm; 289 pages, 64 plates; cloth, dust jacket, ex-library copy, rubber stamp on reverse titlepage. Rainsford A54-582 1996 £55.00

WHITE, LUKE   The Complete Dublin Catalogue of Books In All Arts and Sciences. (Printed in Ireland) from the Beginning of this Century, to the Present Time. Dublin: 1786. 54 pages; marbled paper backed paper wrappers, bit worn, lower wrapper and final leaf torn (affecting c.p. of text);   Maggs Bros. Ltd. 1191-62 1996 £210.00

WHITE, PATRICK 1912-   The Aunt's Story. London: Routledge & kevan Paul, 1948. Slight soiling to boards, otherwise excellent in chipped dust jacket; signed by author, signed copies of White's books are exceedingly scarce.   R. A. Gekoski 19-152 1996 £600.00

WHITE, PATRICK 1912-   The Burnt Ones. London: Eyre & Spottiswoode, 1964. 1st edition; fine in dust jacket.   Lame Duck Books 19-592 1996 $200.00

WHITE, PATRICK 1912-   Four Plays. London: Eyre & Spottiswoode, 1965. front board slightly bumped at lower edge, otherwise fine in dust jacket; inscribed by author.   R. A. Gekoski 19-156 1996 £950.00

WHITE, PATRICK 1912-   Riders in the Chariot. London: Eyre & Spottiswoode, 1961. 1st English edition; signed by author; fine copy in bright, fine dust jacket; signed copies are exceedingly scarce.   Thomas Dorn 9-246 1996 $1,500.00

WHITE, PATRICK 1912-   Riders in the Chariot. London: Eyre & Spottiswoode, 1961. dust jacket little creased at top and bottom of spine, some trifling soiling to outside edge; excellent copy, signed by author.   R. A. Gekoski 19-155 1996 £450.00

WHITE, PATRICK 1912-   The Tree of Man. London: Eyre & Spottiswoode, 1956. 2nd impression, signed by author on titlepage; spine slightly cocked and dust jacket chipped at top and bottom of spine, otherwise excellent.   R. A. Gekoski 19-153 1996 £200.00

WHITE, PATRICK 1912-   Voss. London: Eyre & Spottiswoode, 1957. 3rd impression; signed by author, endpapers very slightly offset and dust jacket tron at top of spine, still very good.   R. A. Gekoski 19-154 1996 £300.00

WHITE, RICHARD GRANT   Poetry, Lyrical, Narrative and Satirical of the Civil War. New York: American News Co., 1866. 1st edition; 8vo; 22, 334 pages; original beveled cloth, very nice.   M & S Rare Books 60-262 1996 $100.00

WHITE, TERENCE HANBURY 1906-1964   Gone to Ground. London: Collins, 1935. Some offsetting, but nice in later issue green binding stamped in black, slightly browned dust jacket.   R. A. Gekoski 19-157 1996 £140.00

WHITE, TERENCE HANBURY 1906-1964   Loved Helen and Other Poems. London: Chatto & Windus, 1929. 1st edition; original binding, inscription, top edge dusty, head and tail of spine and corners bumped, cover edges slightly rubbed, endpapers partially browned, very good, no dust jacket; signed by author.   Ulysses 39-621 1996 £325.00

WHITE, TERENCE HANBURY 1906-1964   The Once and Future King. London: Collins, 1958. 1st edition; faint offsetting from flaps, still fine in near fine dust jacket with touch of darkening to extremities of the white portions of jacket, nice.   Between the Covers 42-463 1996 $350.00

WHITE, TERENCE HANBURY 1906-1964   The Once and Future King. London: Collins, 1958. Good plus in like (lightly stained) dust jacket.   Limestone Hills 41-143 1996 $135.00

WHITE, TERENCE HANBURY 1906-1964   The Sword in the Stone. London: Collins, 1938. 1st edition; 8vo; 339 pages; numerous line illustrations; cloth, dust jacket, top of spine very slightly bumped and small piece chipped from dust jacket, crease in one leaf, otherwise very nice, fresh copy.   Thomas Thorp 489-320 1996 £150.00

WHITEHALL in Cumberland. London: privately published, 1865. 8vo; pages 28, 3 colored lithographs; original blindstamped blue cloth, gilt, extremities trifle rubbed; scarce.   R.F.G. Hollett & Son 78-1374 1996 £95.00

WHITEHALL in Cumberland. London: privately published, 1865. 8vo; pages 28, 3 colored lithographs; original stiff card wrappers, edges worn, backstrip defective; scarce.   R.F.G. Hollett & Son 78-1375 1996 £75.00

WHITEHEAD, ALFRED NORTH 1861-1947   Symbolism its Meaning and Effect. Cambridge: Cambridge University Press, 1928. 1st edition; tan printed cloth, tan printed jacket, near fine.   Priscilla Juvelis 95/1-294 1996 $150.00

WHITEHEAD, C. E.   The Camp-Fires of the Everglades, or Wild Sports in the South. Edinburgh: 1891. Plates and taext sketches; nicely bound in quartaer morocco, marbled boards.   David A.H. Grayling 3/95-241 1996 £75.00

WHITEHEAD, G. K.   The Deer of Great Britain and Ireland. London: 1964. Many illustrations, lacks fr. endpaper and half title, otherwise fine in frayed dust jacket.   David A.H. Grayling MY95Orn-83 1996 £65.00

WHITEHEAD, G. K.   Deer of the World. 1972. 1st edition; color and other illustrations; fine copy in dust jacket.   David Grayling J95Biggame-336 1996 £70.00

WHITEHEAD, G. K.   The Whitehead Encyclopedia of Deer. London: 1993. 4to; 609 pages; 124 colored and numerous plain illustrations; cloth.   Wheldon & Wesley 207-615 1996 £75.00

WHITEHEAD, P. J. P.   Clupeoid Fishes of the World. Rome: 1985-88. 4to; volume 7 parts 1, 2; numerous figures, 579 pages; wrappers.   John Johnson 135-593 1996 $100.00

WHITELOCKE, BULSTRODE   The Diary. London: 1989. Large 8vo; pages 920; 16 plates; original cloth.   Howes Bookshop 265-1273 1996 £60.00

WHITELOCKE, BULSTRODE   Memorials of the English Affairs; or, an Historical Account of What Passed from the Beginning of the Reign of King Charles the First, to King Charles the Second His Happy Restauration. London: Nathaniel Ponder, 1682. 1st edition; folio; (viii), 704, (xvi) pages; 18th century calf, label, some wear at extremities, joints cracked, but secure, minor soiling; sound. Wing W1986.   Robert Clark 38-144 1996 £185.00

WHITESIDE, J.   Sharpe in Bygone Days. Kendal: Titus Wilson, 1904. 1st edition; 8vo; pages xvi, 395; frontispiece, 20 plates; modern half levant morocco, gilt;   R.F.G. Hollett & Son 78-1379 1996 £125.00

WHITFIELD, CHRISTOPHER   Mr. Chambers and Persephone. Waltham St. Lawrence: Golden Cockerel Press, 1937. 1st edition; number 28 of 150 special copies, printed on Arnold's handmade paper, signed by author and artist; 8vo; 63 pages; five full page engravings by Dorothea Braby; original green morocco backed cloth, backstrip faded to tan, sides little soiled, otherwise very good, top edge gilt, others uncut; Pertelote 125.   Claude Cox 107-67 1996 £65.00

WHITFIELD, CHRISTOPHER   Together and Alone. Waltham St. Lawrence: Golden Cockerel Press, 1945. 1st edition; number 96 of 100 copies specially bound; 8vo; pages 109 + colophon; signed by author and artist; 10 wood engravings by O'Connor, printed in Blado italic on Arnold's handmade paper, top edge gilt, others uncut; very good.   Cockalorum 165.   Claude Cox 107-68 1996 £85.00

WHITFIELD, CHRISTOPHER   Together and Alone. Waltham St. Lawrence: Golden Cockerel Press, 1945. 1st edition; 399/400 copies (of an edition of 500 copies); signed by artist; 8vo; pages 109, (1); printed on Arnold's mouldmade paper; 10 wood engravings by John O'Connor; original quarter cream cloth, backstrip gilt lettered, marbled cloth sides, top edge gilt, others untrimmed, fine.   Blackwell's B112-132 1996 £80.00

WHITFIELD, CHRISTOPHER   Together and Alone. London: Golden Cockerel Press, 1945.. Limited to 500 copies; of which this is one of only 100 signed by both author and artist and bound thus; octavo; 109 pages; printed on mould made paper; printed in italics, several wood engravings by John O'Conor; one quarter white morocco with marbled cloth, top edge gilt; fine.   Bromer Booksellers 90-47 1996 $450.00

WHITING, SAMUEL   The Connecticut Town-Officer...Containing...the Powers and Duties of Towns...Town Officers (and) Religious and School Societies. Danbury: printed by Nthaniel L. skinner, 1814. contemporary sheep, bit rubbed, exceptionally well preerved.   Meyer Boswell SL27-245 1996 $225.00

WHITLAW, CHARLES   A Treatise on the Causes and Effects of Inflammation, Fever, Cancer, Scrofula, and Nervous Affections... London: published by the author, 1831. 1st edition; 8vo; pages (4), xxxi, 304; original cloth, printed paper label, rubbed; very good.   James Fenning 133-361 1996 £95.00

WHITMAN, SARAH   Edgar Poe and His Critics. New York: Rudd & Carleton, 1860. 1st edition; printing B (probable sequence); 8vo; maroon cloth, spine tips chipped to text block, spine faded, very good; early inscription on front blank.   Charles Agvent 4-1182 1996 $250.00

WHITMAN, SARAH   Hours of Life and Other Poems. Providence: Whitney, 1853. 1st edition; binding A; 8vo; original binding; light wear to spine, near fine; signature of Ellen Sawyer on f.f.e.p. BAL 21366.   Charles Agvent 4-1184 1996 $150.00

WHITMAN, WALT 1819-1892   Calamus. A Series of Letters Written During the Years 1868-1880...to a Young Friend (Peter Doyle). Boston: Laurens Maynard, 1897. 1st issue of the trade edition; 12mo; frontispiece; green cloth, very good. BAL 21446.   Marilyn Braiterman 15-206 1996 $300.00

WHITMAN, WALT 1819-1892   Criticism: an Essay. Newark; The Carteret Book Club, 1913. 1st edition; one of 100 numbered copies; gray boards, paper label; small chip from head of fragile spine, otherwise near fine.   Captain's Bookshelf 38-219 1996 $125.00

WHITMAN, WALT 1819-1892   Democratic Vistas, and Other Papers. London: Walter Scott, 1888. 1st edition; top edge gilt, decorated cloth, gilt, head and tail of spine and corners slightly bumped and rubbed, covers slightly marked and rubbed, prelims, edges and endpapers spotted, fore-edges of some pages nicked, one page slightly creased, very good.   Ulysses 39-623 1996 £65.00

WHITMAN, WALT 1819-1892   Good-Bye My Fancy. Philadelphia: David McKay, 1891. 1st edition; Binding E; portrait; green cloth, faint offsetting to pastedowns and endpapers as if a jacket at some point were present, hinges lightly cracked, slight rubbing to spine tips, near fine; inscribed by Horace Traubel to R. W. Gilder stating "This book (?) (?) bound this way in green covers was made by W.W. at the (?) not for the market but for distribution among his friends". Fine association. BAL 21440.   Charles Agvent 4-1187 1996 $1,200.00

WHITMAN, WALT 1819-1892   Good-Bye My Fancy. Philadelphia: David McKay, 1891. 1st edition; 8vo; 66 pages; frontispiece; original maroon cloth, slight rubbing, but very nice.   M & S Rare Books 60-263 1996 $250.00

WHITMAN, WALT 1819-1892   The Half Breed. New York: Columbia University Press, 1927. Limited to 155 copies; 8vo; illustrations by Allen Lewis; cloth/boards, fine in original worn glassine; former owner signature. BAL 21467 printing A.   Charles Agvent 4-1188 1996 $150.00

WHITMAN, WALT 1819-1892   Hymn on the Death of President Lincoln. London: Edward Arnold, 1900. Limited to 125 copies; octavo; 18 pages, printed entirely on vellum; frontispiece and initial letters by C. R. Ashbee; full vellum over boards, blindstamped with rose logo and motto of the series "Soul is Form", very fine. Crawford pp. 384-85; Ashbee p. 68.   Bromer Booksellers 87-63 1996 $650.00

WHITMAN, WALT 1819-1892   Leaves of Grass. Brooklyn: 1856. 2nd edition; 12mo; recased in original green cloth with spine laid down, gilt lettering somewhat dull, some mild foxing, but very good, scarce edition; housed in attractive quarter green morocco slipcase; the Doheny copy. Captain's Bookshelf 38-217 1996 $1,750.00

WHITMAN, WALT 1819-1892   Leaves of Grass. Boston: Thayer & Eldridge, 1860-65. 3rd edition, 2nd printing, pirated edition; 8vo; state 3 of the portrait frontispiece; state C purple cloth, pink endpapers, cloth spotted, gilt on spine still clear for title, rubbed away on Whitman's name, inner front hinge repaired, former owner signature, 1 page torn in gutter, good +.   Charles Agvent 4-1191 1996 $250.00

WHITMAN, WALT 1819-1892   Leaves of Grass. Philadelphia: Rees Welsh & Co., 1882. 1st Philadelphia edition; 8vo; decorated cloth, minor rubbing and soiling, bright copy; BAL 21419.   Charles Agvent 4-1192 1996 $450.00

WHITMAN, WALT 1819-1892   Leaves of Grass. Philadelphia: David McKay, 1891-92. 9th edition; printing 2, binding C, "Deathbed" edition; 8vo; original binding, trifle wear, beautiful copy, uncut, partly unopened; BAL 21441.   Charles Agvent 4-1193 1996 $750.00

WHITMAN, WALT 1819-1892   Leaves of Grass. Philadelphia: David McKay, 1891-92. 1st edition; 2nd issue (clothbound) of the 'Deathbed' edition; front hinge bit tender, minor rubbing to green cloth, but very good, top edge gilt.   Captain's Bookshelf 38-218 1996 $400.00

WHITMAN, WALT 1819-1892   Leaves of Grass. Grabhorn Press for Random House, 1930. One of 400 copies, signed by Edwin Grabhorn and Valenti Angelo; 14 3/4 x 10 1/2 inches; 11 p.l. (6 blank), 423, (1) pages, (5) leaves (blanks); vignette on title and 36 other woodcuts in text by Valenti Angelo; original red niger backed Philippine mahogany boards, Random House vignette carved on lower corner of front cover, raised bands, blindstamped spine titling, in publisher's fine fleece lined slipcase with morocco lips, one opening somewhat foxed, few shallow marks to wooden boards, otherwise extraordinarily fine, showing virtually no signs of use; Heller & Magee 138.   Phillip J. Pirages 33-256 1996 $3,500.00

WHITMAN, WALT 1819-1892   Leaves of Grass Comprising All the Poems Written by Walt Whitman Following the Arrangement of the Edition of 1891-'2. New York: Random House, 1930. Number 77 of 400 copies; 14 1/2 x 9 3/4 inches; woodcuts by Valenti Angelo; red niger over Philippine mahogany, flawless, housed in modern custom cloth slipcase with leather label, matching spine color and type. Heller & Magee 138.   Hermitage SP95-886 1996 $3,000.00

WHITMAN, WALT 1819-1892   Leaves of Grass. New York: Random House, 1930. One of 400 copies; large folio; x 423 pages; leather spine, mahogany boards; spine, while faded with a few maraks of wear, is much better than most copies we have seen, paper has almost no foxing, but edges on longer untrimmed sheets is browned, as usual; overall very good copy.   The Bookpress 75-300 1996 $1,250.00

WHITMAN, WALT 1819-1892   Leaves of Grass. New York: Heritage Press, 1937. Octavo; xli, 527 pages; illustrations by Rockwell Kent; gilt stamped blue-green cloth, faintly rubbed slipcse; extremely fine. Bromer Booksellers 87-163 1996 $135.00

WHITMAN, WALT 1819-1892   New York Dissected - a Sheaf of Recently Discovered Newspaper Articles by the Author of Leaves of Grass. London: Rufus Rockwell Wilson, 1936. One of 750 numbered copies; 8 black and white plates; original binding, top edge dusty, spine slightly faded, one corner slightly bumped, pastedowns browned, very good; from the library of James Hart.   Ulysses 39-624 1996 £65.00

WHITMAN, WALT 1819-1892   Notebook used Along the New Jersey Coast September & October 1883. Montclair: Caliban Press, 1992. 1st edition; one of 125 copies only, signed by Mark McMurray, designer and printer; paper with linen spine, label on spine, mint.   Priscilla Juvelis 95/1-295 1996 $140.00

WHITMAN, WALT 1819-1892   Notebook Used Along the New Jersey Coast, September & October 1883. Montclair: Caliban Press, 1992. One of 125 numbered copies, signed by McMurry; small 4to; printed on five different handmade papers; flexible boards, cloth spine; fine.   Bertram Rota 272-56 1996 £90.00

WHITMAN, WALT 1819-1892   November Boughs. Philadelphia: David McKay, 1888. 1st edition; printing 1, binding D (probable sequence); 8vo; frontispiece; maroon cloth, top edge gilt, others untrimmed, small nick on front spine edge, possibly a binding defect; near fine.   Charles Agvent 4-1195 1996 $600.00

WHITMAN, WALT 1819-1892   November Boughs. Philadelphia: David McKay, 1888. 1st edition; printing 1, binding D (probable sequence); 8vo; maroon cloth, spine and portion of rear cover sunned, near fine, former owner signature.   Charles Agvent 4-1196 1996 $500.00

WHITMAN, WALT 1819-1892   November Boughs. Philadelphia: David McKay, 1888. 1st edition; 8vo; green cloth, front hinge repaired, f.f.e.p. removed, still a nice copy.   Charles Agvent 4-1197 1996 $250.00

WHITMAN, WALT 1819-1892   November Boughs. London: Alexander Gardner, 1889. 1st English edition; 8vo; 140 pages; frontispiece; original cloth, spine faded; BAL 21430 British issue "sheets of printing 1".   M & S Rare Books 60-264 1996 $300.00

WHITMAN, WALT 1819-1892   November Boughs. 1891. 1st edition; printing 3 (Winship believes this is one of 400 copies printed in 1891 intended by Whitman to be bound with Goodbye My Fancy until illness prevented him from pursuing his plans); signed by author; green cloth, few small stains on front cover, front hinge lightly cracked, near fine; inscribed by Horace Traubel in 1903 to Larson Butler with initialled note below inscription by Traubel stating that "this edn. of N.B. bound in green was designed by W.W. for his friends, not for market, + was never anywhere but on sale." Fine association.   Charles Agvent 4-1198 1996 $3,500.00

WHITMAN, WALT 1819-1892   Poems. London: 1868. 1st English edition of Leaves of Grass; frontispiece; original blue cloth, rebacked with original spine laid on, original gilt imprint is bright, near fine, without any foxing, uncommon.   Stephen Lupack 83- 1996 $450.00

WHITMAN, WALT 1819-1892   President Lincoln's Funeral Hymn London: Essex House Press for Edward Arnold, 1900. One of 135 numbered copies; 18.4 x 12.2 cm; 18 pages, with frontispiece and captials, all drawn and hand colored by C. R. Ashbee, interleaved throughout with tissue guards; original full vellum stamped in blind and titled in gilt along spine, original cloth dust jacket, fine in slightly rubbed publisher's slipcase.   Hermitage SP95-872 1996 $1,750.00

WHITMAN, WALT 1819-1892   Selected Poems. New York: Charles Webster, 1892. 1st edition; decorated cloth; near fine; BAL 21638, issue A.   Charles Agvent 4-1200 1996 $150.00

WHITMAN, WALT 1819-1892   Selected Poems. Snake River Press, 1979. One of only 20 numbered copies; folio; printed in handset 16 pt. Walbaum; 9 colored drawings by Geoffrey Trenaman; half brown morocco by Adrian Pasotti; fine.   Bertram Rota 272-435 1996 £100.00

WHITMAN, WALT 1819-1892   Songs At Parting... San Francisco: privately printed, 1930. Limited to 200 copies, folio; (28) pages; unopened sheets, unbound and laid into gilt titled grey-green wrappers, fine.   Andrew Cahan 47-210 1996 $150.00

WHITMAN, WALT 1819-1892   Specimen Days and Collect. Philadelphia: Rees Welsh, 1882-83. 1st edition; binding C (no sequence established); 8vo; portrait; decorated cloth, old clipping pasted to f.f.e.p. below former owner signature dated 1883; near fine.   Charles Agvent 4-1201 1996 $350.00

WHITMAN, WALT 1819-1892   Wrenching Times; Poems from Drum Taps. Gwasg Gregynog, 1991. One of 450 numbered copies; folio; printed in 14 pt. Monotype Basakerville on Zerkall mouldmade; 8 large colored wood engravings and a tailpiece by Gaylord Schanilec; half dark blue goatskin, ruled and lettered in red, grey handmade paper boards lettered in blind; fine.   Bertram Rota 272-216 1996 £200.00

WHITMAN, WALT 1819-1892   The Complete Writings. New York: G. P. Putnam, 1902. Camden Edition limited to 500 sets; 8vo; 10 volumes, printed on handmade paper; numerous illustrations printed on Japanese vellum; blue boards, other vellum spines and corners, gilt floral tooling on spines, gilt tops, fresh, bright set with original linen wrappers; Appelfeld Gallery 54-181 1996 $850.00

WHITNEY, CASPAR   Jungle Trails and Jungle People. New York: Scribner's, 1905. 1st edition; 8vo; 310 pages, (4) pages ads; original gilt stamped blue cloth, early ownership signature, otherwise exceptionally bright, fine copy. Scarce.   Chapel Hill 94-403 1996 $165.00

WHITNEY, CASPAR   Of Snow-Shoes to the Barren Grounds. 1896. Plates and illustrations; original pictorial cloth, very light rubbing. Rare.   David Grayling J95Biggame-460 1996 £200.00

WHITTIER, JOHN GREENLEAF 1807-1892   At Sundown. Cambridge: Riverside Press, 1892. 1st edition thus; large paper issue limited to 250 numbered copies printed on rectos only; 8vo; portrait, illustrations; white vellum, fine in very good, rubbed and uncommon dust jacket. BAL 22158.   Charles Agvent 4-1209 1996 $150.00

WHITTIER, JOHN GREENLEAF 1807-1892   The Life and Letters of John Greenleaf Whittier. Boston: Houghton Mifflin, 1894. 1st trade edition; 8vo; 2 volumes; plates and facsimile; green cloth, near fine; tipped to f.f.e.p. is a 3 page ALS from Pickard.   Charles Agvent 4-1220 1996 $100.00

WHITTIER, JOHN GREENLEAF 1807-1892   The Literary Remains of John G. C. Brainard, with a Sketch of His Life. Hartford: P.B. Goodsell, 1832. 1st edition; 8vo; 228 pages; later half leather. Bookplate and ink signature of literary critic, William Winter. BAL 1332 (Brainard); 21678 (Whittier); Howe Lib. JGW 22; B&B 11485.   M & S Rare Books 60-266 1996 $250.00

WHITTIER, JOHN GREENLEAF 1807-1892   Miriam. Boston: Fields, Osgood, 1871. 1st edition; binding 1; 8vo; frontispiece and vignettes; green cloth, superb copy. BAL 21889.   Charles Agvent 4-1213 1996 $100.00

WHITTIER, JOHN GREENLEAF 1807-1892   Moll Pitcher, a Poem. Boston: Carter and Hendee, 1832. 1st edition; 8vo; original printed blue wrappers, uncut, slight chipping of spine, Massachusetts Library stamp at top of cover of titlepage; great rarity in wrappers. The Estelle Doheny copy. BAL 214677; Howes Lib. V, JGW 20; B&B 17076.   M & S Rare Books 60-265 1996 $14,000.00

WHITTIER, JOHN GREENLEAF 1807-1892   Narrative of James Williams, an American Slave, Who Was for Several Years a Driver on a Cotton Plantation in Alabama. New York: Pub. Isaac Knapp, 1838. 2nd edition; 12mo; 108 pages; fine lithographic portrait; original cloth backed printed green boards, lacking paper label, some minor wear to cloth spine, printed boards in excellent, unrubbed condition. Howes W396; Rinderknecht 53637?   M & S Rare Books 60-434 1996 $1,750.00

WHITTIER, JOHN GREENLEAF 1807-1892   The Panorama and Other Poems. Boston: Ticknor & Fields, 1856. 1st edition; 8vo; original brown cloth, particularly fine. BAL 21792. Currier pp. 78-9.   Ximenes 108-345 1996 $150.00

WHITTIER, JOHN GREENLEAF 1807-1892   Saint Gregory's Guest and Recent Poems. Cambridge: Riverside Press, 1886. 1st edition; 1558 copies; 8vo; gold stamped vellum wrappers, paper little aged, covers darkened, soiled, very good; tipped to f.f.e.p. is small card signed by author; on another blank is a note by former owner stating how the book came from Dr. D. Neale, an old friend and admirer of Whittier.   Charles Agvent 4-1216 1996 $200.00

WHITTIER, JOHN GREENLEAF 1807-1892   Snow-Bound. A Winter Idyll. Boston & New York: Houghton Mifflin & Co., 1892. 1st edition thus, with new preface, limited to 250 copies; 8vo; vii, (iii), 43 pages, printed on one side, printed on vellum, title printed in 2 colors, title device, frontispiece, 9 plates decorated initials in green; full natural vellum titled in gilt on spine with gilt title above elaborate gilt floral decoration within gilt gilt double ruled frame on front cover, top edge gilt, fine. BAL 22152.   Blue Mountain SP95-122 1996 $250.00

WHITTIER, JOHN GREENLEAF 1807-1892   Songs of Three Centuries. Boston: Osgood, 1876. Household edition; 8vo; original binding, moderate wear, fair amount of offsetting from old clippings; inscribed to Mary E. Carter from the author, dated Dec. 23, 1875, only 20 days after it was issued. BAL 21933 & 11341.   Charles Agvent 4-1218 1996 $475.00

WHITWORTH, CHARLES   An Account of Russia As It Was in the Year 1710. Strawberry Hill: 1758. 1st edition; one of 700 copies; 8vo; boards; few stains. Hazen 42.5. Minzloff 121.13; Brunet V 1440 f.   Rostenberg & Stern 150-149 1996 $525.00

WHITWORTH, CHARLES   An Account of Russia As It Was in the Year 1710. Strawberry Hill: 1758. 1st edition; 8vo; contemporary calf, rebacked, original red morocco label preserved in cloth slipcase; very good, errata leaf; signature of scholar-collector Richard Farmer. CBEL II 1420 and 1590. Hazen 5; Nerhood, to Russia & Return 75.   Ximenes 109-299 1996 $600.00

WHO Stole My Nest? New York: R. Shugg, ca. 1870-80. Octavo; 16 pages; illustrations by W. Momberger, with full page colored lithographs and wood engravings; rare and fragile, original pictorial wrappers; very fine. Hamilton p. 186.   Bromer Booksellers 90-140 1996 $325.00

WHO'S Who in Cumberland and Westmorland. London: 1937. Limited edition, number 129; tall 8vo; 246 pages; original cloth, gilt, trifle marked and faded, uncut, little spotting to fore-edge and endpapers.   R.F.G. Hollett & Son 78-277 1996 £50.00

THE WHOLE FAMILY: a Novel by Twelve Authors. New York: Harpers, 1908. 1st edition; 8vo; illustrations; decorated blue cloth, owner's inscription dated 1908 on pastedown; near fine.   Charles Agvent 4-741 1995 $150.00

WHY the Sea Is Salt - and Other Fairy Stories. London: Peter Lunn, 1946. 1st edition; 8 full page color illustrations, 13 black and white illustrations in text by R. A. Brandt; pictorial boards, covers repeat two of the color plates; spine worn and slightly defective, covers slightly marked and dusty, cover edges rubbed; good.   Ulysses 39-70 1996 £85.00

WHYMPER, EDWARD   The Ascent of the Matterhorn. London: 1880. Abridged 3rd edition of 'Scrambles Amongst the Alps', but this is the first in this form with a different binding; 2 maps have been removed, repaired and inserted in a new pocket; inscribed "J. A. Murray/from his loving Father/Dec. 25, 1879", also signed on another page "J.A. Murray, (the publisher); gilt lettering and design on dark blue cloth, some slight internal marking, aminly of the (blank) rears of the half title and titlepages, ends of spine little rubbed, but generally good sound, very good copy with gilt lettering & decoration still bright.   Moutaineering Books 8-EWO1 1996 £110.00

WHYMPER, EDWARD   How to Use the Aneroid Barometer. London: John Murray, 1891. 1st edition; 8vo; (ii), 61 pages; original limp cloth, spine faded; library stmap of the Philosophical Society of Glasgow on title; very uncommon.   James Burmester 29-145 1996 £225.00

WHYMPER, EDWARD   Scrambles Amongst the Alps in the Years 1860-69. London: John Murray, 1871. 1st edition; 4th thousand; 8vo; xviii, (ii), 432 pages, 23 plates, 92 text illustrations, 5 folding maps; original green cloth, spine gilt, recased, preserving original endpapers, slightly defective top of spine repaired; clean tears in maps repaired, without loss, light spotting on endpapers, half title and title. Neate W65.   David Bickersteth 133-174 1996 £145.00

WHYMPER, EDWARD   Scrambles Amongst the Alps in the Years 1860-69. London: 1900. 5th edition; 5 folding maps, 22 plates, numerous illustrations; blue cloth with gilt lettering and page edges; some foxing and traces of rubbing on spine ends, generally fine.   Moutaineering Books 8-EW02 1996 £120.00

WHYMPER, EDWARD   Travels Amongst the Great Andes of the Equator. 1892. 1st U.S. edition; 25 plates, illustrations, 4 maps, 2 folding, with 1 in pocket; attractive silver lettering on blue boards, slight foxing of front endpaper and half titles, generally nice, clean, near fine copy.   Moutaineering Books 8-EW03 1996 £120.00

WHYMPER, EDWARD   Travels Amongst the Great Andes of the Equator... London: 1892/91. Royal 8vo; 2 volumes; pages xxiv, 456, 20 full page illustrations, 118 text figures, 4 maps; pages xxii, 147, 14 plates and 42 text figures; original cloth, scarce, used copy, neatly repaired. Wheldon & Wesley 207-466 1996 £150.00

WHYMPER, FREDERICK   Travel and Adventure in the Territory of Alaska, Formerly Russian America-Now Ceded to the United States--and in Various Other Parts of the North Pacific. New York: Harper, 1869. 1st edition; 8vo; 353 pages, (2) pages ads; folding map and numerous handsome engravings. original orange cloth, some general wear to binding, but very good;   Chapel Hill 94-8 1996 $125.00

WHYTE, FREDERIC   The Life of W. T. Stead. New York: Houghton Mifflin Co., 1925. 1st edition; 2 volume set, 345, 368 pages; cloth, near fine.   Middle Earth 77-198 1996 $135.00

WHYTE-MELVILLE, G. J.   Novels. London: 1890, etc. Foolscap 8vo; 26 volumes; choicely bound in half polished calf, mottled board sides, panelled spines with sporting emblems in gold, by Riviere; fine set from the library of Lord Rootes, with his bookplate in each volume.   Charles W. Traylen 117-218 1996 £400.00

WHYTT, ROBERT   Observations on the Nature, Causes and Cure of Those Diseases Which Have Been Commonly Called Nervous Hypochondriac, or Hysteric... Edinburgh: Ptd. for T. Becket & P. A. De Hondt, London and J. Balfour, Edin., 1765/64. 2nd corrected edition; 8vo; (xiv), 520, (2) pages; contemporary calf, leather spine label, joints repaired, very good, clean copy.   John Gach 150-476 1996 $1,000.00

WICKHOFF, FRANZ   Roman Art: Some Of Its Principles and Their Application to Early Christian painting. London: William Heinemann, 1900. Folio; frontispiece, xv, 198 pages, 31 figures, 13 plates; original cloth. Archaeologia Luxor-4169 1996 $150.00

WIDEMAN, JOHN EDGAR   Damballah. London: Allison & Busby, 1984. 1st English edition, as well as first hardcover; fine in dust jacket, inscribed by author.   Between the Covers 43-210 1996 $125.00

WIDEMAN, JOHN EDGAR   A Glance Away. New York: HBW, 1967. 1st edition; fine in dust jacket, beautiful copy, author's first book. Between the Covers 43-206 1996 $250.00

WIDEMAN, JOHN EDGAR   Hiding Place. London: Allison & Busby, 1984. 1st English edition; fine in dust jacket, inscribed by author, uncommon thus.   Between the Covers 43-209 1996 $125.00

WIDEMAN, JOHN EDGAR   Hurry Home. New York: HBW, 1970. 1st edition; fine in dust jacket with trace of wear, author's scarce second book, lovely copy.   Between the Covers 43-207 1996 $175.00

WIDEMAN, JOHN EDGAR   The Lynchers. New York: HBJ, 1973. 1st edition; tiny creases to page edges, else fine in dust jacket, attractive copy, scarce.   Between the Covers 43-208 1996 $100.00

WIDEMAN, JOHN EDGAR   Philadelphia Fire. New York: Holt, 1990. Uncorrected proof; fine in oversized proof dust jacket with unprinted flaps and with publisher's material and author photo laid in.   Between the Covers 43-211 1996 $125.00

WIDEMAN, JOHN EDGAR   The Stories of John Edgar Wideman. New York: Pantheon, 1992. Advance reading copy; wrappers; fine; briefly inscribed by author.   Between the Covers 43-212 1996 $100.00

WIENERS, JOHN   Unhired. Mt. Horeb: Perishable Press, 1968. One of 250 copies; 7.75 x 5.75 inches; 12 page surfaces, 6 printed, handset in Palatino and printed on variegated Shadwell handmade; brown Fabriano cover wrpapers sewn; fine. Hamady 18 - this is a variant binding. Joshua Heller 21-185 1996 $110.00

WIESEL, ELIE   The Golem. New York: Summit Books, 1983. 1st edition; one of 250 specially bound copies signed by author and artist; 8vo; illustrations by Mark Podwal; cloth, pictorial endpapers, slipcase; mint.   James S. Jaffe 34-684 1996 $125.00

WIGGIN, KATE DOUGLAS   A Child's Journey with Dickens. Boston: 1912. 1st edition; 12mo; frontispiece, original printed boards, cloth back; fine; inscribed by author for Laura Fisher.   Howard S. Mott 227-151 1996 $135.00

WIGGIN, KATE DOUGLAS   A Child's Journey with Dickens. Boston: Houghton Mifflin Co., 1922. 12mo; 31 pages; original color pictorial wrpapers; inscribed by author; fine in blue cloth portfolio.   Heritage Book Shop 196-292 1996 $250.00

WIGHAM, ELIZA   The Anti-Slavery Cause in America and Its Martyrs. London: A. W. Bennett (printed by H. Armour, Edinburgh), 1863. 1st edition; 8vo; viii, 168 pages; original green cloth.   James Burmester 29-146 1996 £60.00

WIGHT, T.   A History of the...People Called Quakers in Ireland from..1653 to (1751). Dublin: 1751. 1st edition; 4to; full contemporary calf, generous margins, very good.   C. P. Hyland 216-902 1996 £135.00

WIJDEVELD, H. T.   The Life-Work of the American Architect Frank Lloyd Wright. Santpoort: C. A. Mees, 1925. 1st edition in book form; square folio; 164 pages; original cloth, red spine label; two inch tear on right margin of titlepage, inscription in ink, rear endpaper lightly marked and smudged, light cover wear, else very good. Sweeney 165.   The Bookpress 75-263 1996 $1,250.00

WILBERFORCE, WILLIAM   A Letter on the Abolition of the Slave-Trade; addressed to the Freeholders and Other Inhabitants of Yorkshire. London: T. Cadell and W. Davies and J. Hatchard, 1807. 1st edition; issue with half title, but no list of content; 8vo; (4), 396 pages, half title laid down, ink monogram on title, neat small university stamp on verso of title and foot of last leaf; modern half calf, gilt, labels; good copy. Goldsmiths 19505; Kress B5282; Ragatz p. 569; Williams II 431. John Drury 82-292 1996 £200.00

WILBUR, K. M.   Physiology of Mollusca. London: 1964-66. 8vo; 2 volumes; numerous text figures; cloth.   Wheldon & Wesley 207-1221 1996 £60.00

WILBUR, RICHARD   The Beautiful Changes - And Other Poems. New York: Reynal & Hitchcock, 1947. 1st edition; original binding, top edge dusty, head and tail of spine and corners slightly bumped, covers slightly spotted, very good in nicked, rubbed and duty, slightly chipped and marked dust jacket browned at spine and edges. Presentation copy inscribed by author.   Ulysses 39-627 1996 £325.00

WILCOCKE, SAMUEL HULL   A Narrative of Occurrences in the Indian Countries of North America, Since the Connexion of the Right Hon. the Earl of Selkirk with the Hudson's Bay Company and His Aattempt to Establish a Colony on the Red River. London: 1817. Pages xiv, 152, 87; original pprinted wrappers, head and foot of backstrip worn away, label intact, fine, ucntu copy, though a noted collector's morocco bookplate has offset onto titlepage, preserved in quarter morocco slipcase. TPL 1108; Streeter VI 3675.   Stephen Lunsford 45-171 1996 $1,750.00

WILCOCKE, SAMUEL HULL   Report of the Proceedings Connected with the Disputes Between the Earl of Selkirk and the North-West Company, at the Assizes, Held at York, un Upper Canada, October 1818. London: 1819. 1st London edition; pages xxv, 225, 203, 48; uncut, largely unopened in original printed wrappers, slightest chipping to hinges, fine, preserved in quarter morocco clamshell box; fine; inscribed by Simon McGillivray for John W. Croker. TPL 1146; Peel68; cf. Streeter VI 3687. Stephen Lunsford 45-170 1996 $2,500.00

WILCOX, THOMAS   A Right Godly and Learned Exposition, Upon the Whole Booke of Psalmes... London: T. Man and W. Brome, 1586. 1st edition; 4to. in 8's; (iv), 112, 111-379 390-550 pages; titlepage border, titlepage little soiled, minor soiling & staining, some early marginalia. 18th century calf, spine gilt, label, neatly rebacked and recornered, original spine and label laid down; Very good. STC 25625.   Robert Clark 38-145 1996 £385.00

WILDE, JOHN   44 Wilde 1944: Being a Selection of 44 Images from a Sketchbook Kept by John Wilde Mostly in 1944. Mount Horeb: Perishable Press, 1984. One in an edition of 200 copies, signed and dated by artist in brown ink on last illustration; 10 x 7.25 inches; 52 page surfaces, 47 printed, 44 reproduced images, printed in black, grey and pastels; 14 signatures are French-folded Mohawk vellum cream; 14 images achieved offset in 3 colors and 9 runs, the rest letterpress from 11 pt. metal plates; binding handsewn on thin ribbons tucked into blank shadwell end signatures that received matching printed wrapper, title in brown on front cover, prospectus laid in; fine.   Joshua Heller 21-187 1997 $125.00

WILDE, OSCAR 1854-1900   The Ballad of Reading Gaol. London: Leonard Smithers, 1898. Number 20 of 99 copies, signed by author, third edition; 8vo; pages (viii), (64), original white and purple linen, gilt design by Charles Ricketts on upper cover, spine lettered in gilt, light dust soiling and little cockling to white linen towards head of lower cover, uncut and unopened; very good. Mason 374.   Simon Finch 24-258 1996 £2,500.00

WILDE, OSCAR 1854-1900   The Ballad of Reading Gaol. East Aurora: Roycrofters, 1905. Limited edition, 67/100 copies only, signed by Hubbard; printed on Japanese vellum; half leather, gilt spine, spine and edges little rubbed, fine.   Polyanthos 22-441 1996 $100.00

WILDE, OSCAR 1854-1900   The Ballad of Reading Gaol. London: Methuen & Co., 1924/25. Limited to 50 numbered copies; royal 8vo; 66 pages; illustrations by Frans Masereel, with frontispiece, 6 other full page woodcuts and 30 smaller woodcuts in text; maroon half calf, top edge gilt, others uncut, spine and corners rubbed.   Thomas Thorp 489-321 1996 £280.00

WILDE, OSCAR 1854-1900   The Ballad of Reading Gaol. New York: Limited Editions Club, 1937. Limited to 1500 copies; 4to; original lithographs by Zhenya Gay who signs; full granite-gray sheepskin; near fine in like case, adhesive remnant from bookplate, with Monthly Letter. Charles Agvent 4-1224 1996 $175.00

WILDE, OSCAR 1854-1900   The Ballad of Reading Gaol. New York: Limited Editions Club, 1937. Number 904 from 1500 copies, signed by artist; lithographs by Zhenya Gay; full leather, near fine in publisher's slipcase.   Hermitage SP95-1051 1996 $100.00

WILDE, OSCAR 1854-1900   The Ballad of Reading Gaol. Old Stile Press, 1994. One of 225 numbered copies, signed by artist; tall 8vo; printed in Baskerville on Zerkall mouldmade; boards, "C.3.3." in blind on upper cover; fine in stout pictorial slipcse.   Bertram Rota 272-361 1996 £85.00

WILDE, OSCAR 1854-1900   The Critic as Artist: a Dialogue. Utrecht: De Roos Society, 1957. One of 175 numbered copies; large 8vo; printed by Thieme, Nijmegen in Poliphilus in black and red on Zerkall; cloth, gilt, very nice.   Bertram Rota 272-127 1996 £75.00

WILDE, OSCAR 1854-1900   De Profundis. London: Methuen & Co., 1905. 1st edition; 8vo; x, 11-151 + 40 pages publisher's ads dated March 1905; cloth, gilt, top edge gilt, others uncut, slightly faded, small mark on spine. Mason 388.   Thomas Thorp 489-322 1996 £75.00

WILDE, OSCAR 1854-1900   The Happy Prince and Other Tales. London: David Nutt, 1888. 1st edition; one of 75 numbered large paper copies, signed by author and publisher; folio; 116 pages; 4 wood engraved plates by Walter Crane present in duplicate, as mounted India paper proofs printed in black and brown, 5 wood engraved headpieces, printed in black on India paper and mounted; original Japanese vellum boards with front cover printed in red and black with vignette after Jacomb Hood and spine printed in black, some rubbing and wear to boards, endpapers slightly foxed, previous owner's ink signature, very good with text clean and bright. Mason 314.   Heritage Book Shop 196-224 1996 $7,500.00

WILDE, OSCAR 1854-1900   Hellenism. Edinburgh: The Tragara Press, 1979. 1st edition; one of 99 copies; 8vo; blue cloth in original protective glassine as issued; fine.   Priscilla Juvelis 95/1-296 1996 $150.00

WILDE, OSCAR 1854-1900   The House of Judgement. Utrecht: Catharijne Press, 1986. Limited to 150 copies; 2 5/8 x 2 1/16 inches; printed in four colors after a calligraphed original by J. H. Moesman; brown cloth with title label on front cover, prospectus laid in; extremely fine.   Bromer Booksellers 87-200 1996 $125.00

WILDE, OSCAR 1854-1900   A House of Pomegranates. London: James R. Osgood McIlvaine, 1891. 1st edition; small 4to; pages (viii), 158; 4 full page illustrations by C. H. Shannon, decorations by Charles Ricketts, slight wear to spine,, but very good, uncommon in nice condition; original cream colored linen boards with moss green linen spine, upper cover printed in light red and stamped and gilt designs of a peacock, running fountain and basket of split pomegranates, decorated endpapers, all of these designs by Charles Ricketts; slight wear to spine. Mason 347.   Sotheran PN32-69 1996 £675.00

WILDE, OSCAR 1854-1900   An Ideal Husband. London: Smithers, 1899. 1st edition; one of 100 copies on large paper, signed by Wilde; slight fading to spine, marginal soiling, but nice. Mason 386.   R. A. Gekoski 19-161 1996 £3,500.00

WILDE, OSCAR 1854-1900   The Importance of Being Ernest. London: presented by Mr. George Alexander as a Souvenir of His 20th...Feb. 1 1910. Limited to 1000 copies; top edge gilt.   Lyman Books 21-651 1996 $125.00

WILDE, OSCAR 1854-1900   The Importance of Being Earnest. New York: New York Public Library, 1956. Limited to 500 numbered copies; 4to; 2 volumes, text volume, 5 plates, xxxviii, 187 pages; facsimile volume containing reproduction of the complete typescripts of Acts I, III and IV and the manuscript of Act II; publisher's white boards, decorated gilt, glassine dust jackets, fine set in original slipcase.   Thomas Thorp 489-323 1996 £150.00

WILDE, OSCAR 1854-1900   Lady Windemere's Fan: a Play About a Good Woman. Paris: Leonard Smithers, 1903. One of 250 numbered copies of this piracy; mauve cloth; near fine. Mason 597.   Captain's Bookshelf 38-220 1996 $175.00

WILDE, OSCAR 1854-1900   Lady Wildermere's Fan and The Importance of Being Earnest. London: Limited Editions Club, 1973. Limited to 1500 copies; signed by artist; 8vo; illustrations by Tony Walton; original binding, bookplates; fine in case, Monthly Letter. Charles Agvent 4-1226 1996 $100.00

WILDE, OSCAR 1854-1900   Phrases and Philosophies for the Use of the Young. London: privately printed for presentation, 1894, i.e. 1902? 1st edition; 8vo; original brown printed wrappers, in half calf, slipcase; fine, scarce. 4 copies in NUC; Mason 599.   Ximenes 109-300 1996 $500.00

WILDE, OSCAR 1854-1900   Phrases and Philosophies for the Use of the Young. London: privately printed for presentation, 1894, i.e. 1905? Piracy by Leonard Smithers; limited to 75 numbered copies; 8vo; original blue grey printed wrappers; fine. Mason 602.   Ximenes 109-301 1996 $150.00

WILDE, OSCAR 1854-1900   The Picture of Dorian Gray. London: Ward Lock, 1891. 1st English edition; spine somewhat sunned, some foxing to upper board, but very good in rare dust jacket, which is somewhat rubbed and soiled, neatly restored at base of spine.   R. A. Gekoski 19-160 1996 £3,500.00

WILDE, OSCAR 1854-1900   The Picture of Dorian Gray. New York: Horace Liveright, 1930. Limited to 1500 numbered copies, though not called for, this copy signed by artist under frontispiece; large 8vo; viii, 281, (i) pages; 8 color plates by Majeska; black cloth titled in gilt within peach rectangle on spine, floral decorations in gilt adorn spine, top edge gilt; Near fine in very good black slipcase with printed peach paper label. Blue Mountain SP95-74 1996 $150.00

WILDE, OSCAR 1854-1900   Poems. London: David Bogue, 1881. 2nd edition; 1st printing; 8vo; pages x, 236, colophon; recently rebound in half dark green morocco, spine and top edges gilt; slight spotting of a few leaves, but very nice copy; with bookplate of writer, theatre critic and literary agent, Giles Alexander Esme Gordon. Mason 305. Sotheran PN32-68 1996 £598.00

WILDE, OSCAR 1854-1900   Ravenna. Oxford: Thos. Shrimpton & Son, 1878. 1st edition; 12mo; original printed wrappers; covers little soiled and worn, front wrapper neatly mended, creased down middle, otherwise good, with few neat markings in ink in text, in half morocco slipcase, little worn. Inscribed by author. Mason 301.   David J. Holmes 52-126 1996 $3,500.00

WILDE, OSCAR 1854-1900   Salome. Paris: Lib. de l'Art Independandant/Londres: Elkin Mathews et John Lane... 1893. Limited to 600 copies; octavo; 84 pages; original purple wrappers printed in silver on front cover, wrappers considerably faded, some minor professional restoration to spine, little light foxing and browning, very good, rare, fragile piece. Housed in quarter purple morocco clamshell case. Presentation copy inscribed by author. Mason 348.   Heritage Book Shop 196-250 1996 $6,500.00

WILDE, OSCAR 1854-1900   Salome: Drame en un Acte. Paris: Les Editions G. Cres, 1923. Early edition; square 8vo; spine bit sunned, otherwise very good in pictorial wrappers.   Captain's Bookshelf 38-221 1996 $100.00

WILDE, OSCAR 1854-1900   Salome. New York: Limited Editions Club, 1938. Limited to 1500 copies, signed by artist; small quarto; 2 volumes, 107, 72 pages; gouache drawings on black paper, reproduced by pochoir; virst volume is very fine in cloth, second shows some wrinkling to printer wrappers, internally very fine, housed together in slipcase. Bromer Booksellers 90-27 1996 $200.00

WILDE, OSCAR 1854-1900   Salome. Paris & London: Limited Editions Club, 1938. Limited to 1500 copies, signed by Andre Dearain; 4to; 2 volumes; illustrations by Aubrey Beardsley; gilt decorated cloth and printed black wrappers, slipcase faded; fine copy.   James S. Jaffe 34-704 1996 $650.00

WILDE, OSCAR 1854-1900   Salome. London: Folio Society, 1957. 1st edition thus; thin 8vo; engravings by Frank Martin, illustrations, titlepage and text printed in blue and black; gilt stamped peacock patterned green and blue silk brocade; fine, in publisher's black board box.   George J. Houle 68-154 1996 $125.00

WILDE, OSCAR 1854-1900   The Short Stories Of... Burlington: Limited Editions Club, 1968. 1st edition thus; 1500 copies; signed by artist; 4to; illustrations by James Hill; full silk cloth; fine in worn glassine and fine case.   Charles Agvent 4-1229 1996 $100.00

WILDE, OSCAR 1854-1900   The Sphinx. London: Elkin Mathews and John Lane, 1894. One of 250 copies on Arnold handmade paper with Vale Press watermark, part of the edition destroyed by fire; 8vo; pictorial titlepage and 9 illustrations by Ricketts printed in dark red with initials in green; full vellum gilt stamped on both covers with designs by Ricketts, very mild soil, gentle bowing to boards and less than usual fine pinpoint foxing to few leaves in rear; handsome copy, preserved in plain custom chemise and slipcase.   Marilyn Braiterman 15-174 1996 $5,000.00

WILDE, OSCAR 1854-1900   The Works of... London: Dawsons, 1969. Reprint of Carrington-Methuen edition; 8vo; 15 volumes; original white buckram in imitation of the binding on the edition of 1908, with gilt decorations after Charles Ricketts, very nice fresh set, with original glassine wrappers.   Sotheran PN32-67 1996 £775.00

WILDE, OSCAR 1854-1900   The Young King and Other Fairy Tales. New York: Macmillan, 1962. 1st edition; folio; illustrations in color; original pictorial boards, spine very slightly faded, otherwise fine. James S. Jaffe 34-666 1996 $250.00

WILDENSTEIN, GEORGES   Ingres. London: Phaidon, 1926. 4to; viii, 66 pages; frontispiece, 79 photogravure or collotype plates; buckram, gilt, top edge gilt.   Rainsford A54-334 1995 £95.00

WILDENSTEIN, GEORGES   Ingres. London: Phaidon, 1956. 2nd edition; 31 x 23 cm; 246 pages, 119 plates, 22 drawings, 200 figures; original cloth; bookplate.   Rainsford A54-336 1996 £150.00

WILDER, MITCHELL A.   Santos: the Religious Folk Art of New Mexico. Colorado Springs: the Taylor Museum of the Colorado Springs Fine Arts Center, 1943. 1st edition; 4to; 50 pages; plus 64 full page black and white plates; illustrated cloth, slightly faded along spine and edges, anonymous inscription on endpaper; very good.   Andrew Cahan 47-145 1996 $125.00

WILDER, THORNTON 1897-1976   The Bridge of San Luis Rey. New York: Albert & Charles Boni, 1929. Limited to 1100 copies, signed by Kent; tall 8vo; 120, (iii) pages; color illustrations by Rockwell Kent; color pictorial green cloth, soiled, joints rubbed, lacks slipcase, gilt lettered brown leather label on spine, label chipped; very good.   Blue Mountain SP95-71 1996 $175.00

WILDER, THORNTON 1897-1976   Our Town. Avon: Limited Editions Club, 1974. Limited to 2000 copies; quarto; 118 pages; signed by Wilder and by artist, Robert J. Lee; bound in corduroy and in slipcase; fine. Bromer Booksellers 90-165 1996 $150.00

WILDMAN, THOMAS   A Treatise on the Management of Bees. London: printed for the author and sold by T. Cadell, 1768. 1st edition; 4to; list of subscribers, 3 folding engraved plates, occasional spotting, original boards, lacking backstrip, uncut, nice. British Bee Books 119. Anthony W. Laywood 108-141 1996 £285.00

WILEY, HUGH   The Prowler. New York: Knopf, 1924. 1st edition; couple of tiny spots of foxing to front endpaper, else fine in beautiful white dust jacket.   Between the Covers 43-213 1996 $200.00

WILFORD, JOHN   Memorials and Characters, Together with the Lives of Divers Eminent and Worthy Persons...from the Year One Thousand Six Hundred to the Present Time... London: John Wilford, 1741. 1st edition; folio; (iv), iv, (viii), 780, (779)-(780), 781-788, 42, (ii) pages; titlepage in red and black, 4 page subscriber list; 19th century calf, rebacked, with old decorated gilt spine laid down, new label; slight wear to lower corners; good.   Robert Clark 38-217 1996 £100.00

WILHELM, G. T.   Unterhaltungen aus der Naturgeschichte des Pflanzenreichs. Augsburg: 1810-14. 1st edition; 8vo; volumes 1-6 (of 10); 6 volumes text, with 6 engraved frontispieces; 6 volumes plates, with 384 hand colored plates, all mounted on card and contained in 6 book boxes, without sectional title to volume 4 or a possible portrait, the internal card wrapping for volume 2 of the plates defective, otherwise very nice set, uniformly bound in 12 volumes, half vellum, neat; from the Fugger library with pencil note by a 19th century librarian explaining the make up of the set.   Maggs Bros. Ltd. 1190-151 1996 £850.00

WILKES, MAURICE V.   Automatic Digital Computers. New York: John Wiley & Sons, 1956. 1st American edition; 8vo; x, 305 pages; 9 plates, numerous tables and figures in text; original cloth, near fine.   Edwin V. Glaser 121-324 1996 $250.00

WILKIE, FRANC B.   Davenport Past and Present: Including the Early History and Personal and Anecdotal Reminiscences of Davenport. Davenport: Luse, Lane & Co., 1858. 1st edition; 333 pages, plus errata; many engraved plates and portraits, including double page frontispiece of Davenport, College library gift bookplate on free endpaper, but no ex-library markings, original blindstamped brown cloth, spine titled in gilt, corners worn and extremities of spine evenly chipped, else very clean and tight copy.   Hermitage SP95-702 1996 $165.00

WILKINS, H. ST. CLAIR   Reconnoitering in Abyssinia, a Narrative of the Proceedings of the Reconnoitiring Party (for the) Expeditionary Field Force. London: Smith, Elder & Co., 1870. 1st edition; 8vo; 409 pages; 10 chromolithographs and large folding map, library stamp on titlepage and in margins of two of the plates, slightly intruding on the iamges, professionally rebacked with original spine laid down, original maroon cloth over bevelled boards, endpapers and flyleaves renewed, linen backed folding map present in pocket at back; other than faults noted, a very good copy.   Hermitage SP95-1120 1996 $450.00

WILKINS, JOHN   The Autobiography of an English Gamekeeper. London: 1892. 1st edition; illustrations; original pictorial cloth; scarce, most excellent.   David A.H. Grayling 3/95-103 1996 £50.00

WILKINS, JOHN, BP. OF CHESTER 1614-1672   The Mathematical and Philosophical Works of... London: 1802. Note on endpaper states "a few copies of this edition was (sic) produced on paper made from wood of which this is one..." 2 volumes; on remarkably high quality paper, very free of foxing; original half olivined vellum and pink paper, now a bit faded, over boards, corners with some wear, untrimmed;   Bookworm & Silverfish 276-225 1996 $900.00

WILKINS, JOHN, BP. OF CHESTER 1614-1672   Of the Principles and Duties of Natural Religion. London: printed for R. Chiswell, W. Battersby and C. Brome, 1699. 4th edition; 8vo; portrait, contemporary panelled calf, morocco label, joints expertly repaired. Wing W2208.   H. M. Fletcher 121-81 1996 £65.00

WILKINS, W. H.   The Romance of Isabel Lady Burton. The Story of Her Life. London: Hutchinson, 1897. 8vo; 2 volumes; pages xvi, 374; viii, 375-778; 43 plates; original cloth, rubbed. Penzer p. 311.   Richard Adelson W94/95-250 1996 $135.00

WILKINSON, E. S.   Shanghai Birds. Shanghai: 1929. Royal 8vo; xxi, 243 pages, 24 plates; cloth.   Wheldon & Wesley 207-895 1996 £140.00

WILKINSON, GEORGE THEODORE   An Authentic History of the Cato-Street Conspiracy... London: printed for Thomas Kelly, 1820. 1st edition; 8vo; viii, (ii), (I, paged 'v'), (ii), 6-434 pages, engraved portrait, 7 engraved plates with additional plates (trimmed) not called for, titlepage browned, contemporary marbled boards, new calf spine.   James Burmester 29-147 1996 £58.00

WILKINSON, HUGH   Sunny Lands and Seas. 1883. Folding map, engraved plates, text illustrations; contemporary half calf, gilt, light rubbing; nice.   David Grayling J95Biggame-617 1996 £75.00

WILKINSON, TATE   Memoirs of His Own Life... York: printed for the author, by Wilson, Spence and Mawman; & sold by... 1790. 1st edition; 12mo; 4 volumes; xxiv, 240; (ii), 266; (ii), 266; (ii), 274, (ii) pages; half title in each volume, final errata leaf in volume IV, 12 page subscriber list; contemporary calf, spines decorated gilt, double labels; 3 spines very slightly chipped at head, one corner little worn, some faint marginal dampstaining in volume 1, localised marginal worming in early leaves of volume 4, well clear of text; handsome set. From the Granard library. A&R 3637   Robert Clark 38-218 1996 £480.00

WILKINSON, TATE   Memoirs of His Own Life. York: printed for the author by Wilson, Spence & Mawman, 1790. 1st edition; 12mo; 4 volumes, no half title in volume 1 (not called for in other volumes), 12 page list of subscribers, errata leaf end of volume 4; 19th century calf, all edges gilt, bound by Riviere and Son, recently rebacked, labels. Arnott & Robinson 3637.   Anthony W. Laywood 109-163 1996 £350.00

WILKINSON, TATE   The Wandering Patentee; or, a History of the Yorkshire Theatres, from 1770 to the Present Time... York: printed for the author, by Wilson, Spence and Mawman, sold by... 1795. 1st edition; 12mo; 4 volumes; (ii), xi, (iii), (13)-312; 268; 268; (3)-(268) pages; half titles present in volumes I-III; contemporary speckled calf, spines gilt ruled, double labels; localised wear to some corners and edges, 3 boards bit scuffed, volume 4 titlepage mounted, repairing closed tear (no loss); good set, with Granard library bookplates. A&R 3640.   Robert Clark 38-219 1996 £450.00

WILKINSON, THOMAS   Tours to the British Mountains, with the Descriptive Poems of Lowther and Emont Vale. London: printed for Taylor and Hessey, 1824. 1st (only) edition; 8vo; pages viii, 320; original grey paper boards with patterned cloth spine, paper spine label, rather worn and soiled. Bicknell 103.   R.F.G. Hollett & Son 78-1383 1996 £275.00

WILLARD, MARGARET WHEELER   Letters on the American Revolution 1774-1776. Boston & New York: Houghton Mifflin Co., 1925. 1st edition, limited to 1040 copies; xix, 370 pages; 3 maps; light green cloth, some light spotting to spine, else very good to slipcase.   Blue River Books 9-15 1996 $125.00

WILLCOCKS, J.   From Kabul to Kumassi. Twenty-Four Years of Soldiering and Sport. 1904. Pages xiv, 440; illustrations; light rubbing, very small snag on spine.   David Grayling J95Biggame-618 1996 £60.00

WILLDENOW, D. C.   The Principles of Botany, and Of Vegetable Physiology. Edinburgh: 1805. 1st English edition; 508 pages, 10 plages, 1 of color samples; contemporary calf, very worn, rebacked, small library stamp on title. Pritzel 10277 pp. 409-471.   Graham Weiner C2-657 1996 £50.00

WILLEFORD, CHARLES   Cockfighter Journal. Santa Barbara: Neville, 1989. One of 300 numbered copies (of a total edition of 326), signed by Burke; fine in cloth, as issued.   Between the Covers 42-464 1996 $125.00

WILLEFORD, CHARLES   Everybody's Metamorphosis. Missoula: Dennis McMillan, 1988. 1/400 numbered copies, signed by Willeford; fine in jacket. This copy also signed by publisher.   Janus Books 36-339 1996 $125.00

WILLEFORD, CHARLES   A Guide for the Undehemorrhoided. Boynton Beach: Star Publishing, 1977. 1st edition; fine in dust jacket, signed.   Quill & Brush 102-1739 1996 $100.00

WILLEFORD, CHARLES   Kiss Your Ass Good-bye. Miami Beach: Dennis McMillan, 1987. 1st edition; 1/400 numbered copies, signed by Willeford; fine in jacket, this copy also signed by publisher.   Janus Books 36-338 1996 $125.00

WILLEFORD, CHARLES   New Hope for the Dead. New York: St. Martin's Press, 1985. 1st edition; fine in dust jacket with touch of rubbing at head of spine, inscribed copies scarce.   Quill & Brush 102-1741 1996 $200.00

WILLEFORD, CHARLES   New Hope for the Dead. New York: St. Martin's Press, 1985. 1st edition; fine in very good+ dust jacket which has an internally mended tear at top right spine corner, very unobtrusive and slightly creased near top edge of front panel.   Steven C. Bernard 71-368 1996 $150.00

WILLEFORD, CHARLES   New Hope For the Dead. New York: St. Martin's Press, 1985. 1st edition; fine in dust jacket.   Quill & Brush 102-1742 1996 $150.00

WILLEFORD, CHARLES   Off the Wall. Montclair: Pegasus Rex Press, 1980. 1st edition; dust jacket.   Quill & Brush 102-1740 1996 $100.00

WILLEFORD, CHARLES   Proletarian Laughter. The Alicat Chapbooks, No. XII, 1948. 1st edition; titlepage separated from binding, small tears at staples, paper slightly darkened, otherwise fine.   Book Time 2-740 1996 $100.00

WILLEFORD, CHARLES   Proletarian Laughter. Yonkers: Alicat Bookshop Press, 1948. 1st edition; 1 of 1000 copies; pages browning due to acidic quality of paper used, otherwise fine; stiff wrappers.   Janus Books 36-337 1996 $100.00

WILLEFORD, CHARLES   Sideswipe. New York: St. Martin's, 1987. 1st edition; fine in dust jacket, signed by author.   Lame Duck Books 19-381 1996 $200.00

WILLEFORD, CHARLES   The Way We Die Now. N.P.: Ultramarine, 1988. One of 10 lettered copies; signed by author; full leather; fine.   Ken Lopez 74-477 1996 $750.00

WILLEFORD, CHARLES   The Woman Chaser. Chicago: Newsstand Library, 1960. 1st edition; small pictorial paper wrappers; fine.   Quill & Brush 102-1738 1996 $125.00

WILLETT, EDWARD   Cat's Cradle. London: Strahan and Co., n.d., ca. 1880. 1st edition; 48 pages; color frontispiece, color pictorial title, 3 plates, 46 color text illustrations; blue decorated endpaper, green glazed boards, extra color pictorial, all edges red; light foxing, light wear.   Robin Greer 94A-59 1996 £110.00

WILLETT, MARY   A History of West Bromwich. West Bromwich: printed and published by the Free Press co., 1882. 1st edition; 8vo; 8 pedigrees at end; original cloth, nice.   Anthony W. Laywood 109-164 1996 £50.00

WILLIAM Morris and the Art of the Book. New York: Pierpont Morgan Library, 1976. 1st edition; 4to; 140, (2) pages; 114 plates; cloth, dust jacket; fine.   The Bookpress 75-328 1996 $125.00

WILLIAM, PRINCE OF SWEDEN   Among Pygmies and Gorillas. 1921/23. Many photo illustrations; original cloth, just very light foxing to few pages, spine dulled; excellent copy.   David Grayling J95Biggame-214 1996 £65.00

WILLIAMS, A. F.   The Genesis of the Diamond. London: 1932. Royal 8vo; 2 volumes, pages xv, 352, vi; pages xii, 353-636, iv, 221 plates of which 30 are colored, numerous text figures, folding map; cloth, gilt, very fine.   John Henly 27-717 1996 £300.00

WILLIAMS, AMELIA W.   The Writings of Sam Houston: 1821-1847. Austin: University of Texas, 1938-41. 1st editions; limited to 500 copies; 6 volumes of 8 published; Basic 96.   Maggie Lambeth 30-273 1996 $400.00

WILLIAMS, ARTHUR ANDERSON   The Registers of Colton Parish Church, in Furness Fells. London: Elliot Stock, and Kendal: Atkinson & Pollitt, 1891. 8vo; pages 282; original boards, trifle rubbed, rebacked in matching buckram, gilt, very scarce.   R.F.G. Hollett & Son 78-575 1996 £95.00

WILLIAMS, ARTHUR ANDERSON   The Registers of Colton Parish Church in Furness Fells. London: Elliot Stock and Kendal: Atkinson and Pollitt, 1891. 8vo; pages 282; half levant morocco gilt, rather spotted at beginning and end; scarce; armorial bookplate of Paul Collinson.   R.F.G. Hollett & Son 78-576 1996 £85.00

WILLIAMS, BENJAMIN SAMUEL   The Orchid-Growers Manual... London: Victoria and Paradise Nurseries, 1885. 6th edition; 8vo; 659 pages, ad for orchids to be purchased; green cloth stamped in gold and black, hinges loose, very good.   Second Life Books 103-214 1996 $150.00

WILLIAMS, BENJAMIN SAMUEL   The Orchid Grower's Manual. London: 1894. 7th edition; 8vo; pages xix, 796, (1); buckram, retaining original decorated cover, original cover scuffed, title and prelim pages foxed, light dampstaining of lower page fore edges.   Raymond M. Sutton VI-977 1996 $150.00

WILLIAMS, BENJAMIN SAMUEL   The Orchid Grower's Manual. London: 1961. 7th edition; 815 pages; over 300 illustrations;   Wheldon & Wesley 207-1814 1996 £64.00

WILLIAMS, C.   Zoological Gardens, Regent's Park. London: C. Tilt, ca. 1835. 3 X 2 1/2 inches; 191 pages; 48 woodcut illustrations; original gilt stamped cloth, very slightly faded, all edges gilt. Bondy pp. 66-7.   Bromer Booksellers 90-196 1996 $350.00

WILLIAMS, CHARLES   Divorce. London: Humphrey Milford/Oxford University Press, 1920. 1st edition; original binding, top edge dusty, tail of spine and top and bottom edges of upper cover slightly bumped, lower cover slightly creased, very good in nicked, chipped and slightly creased, marked, rubbed and dusty dust jacket browned at spine and edges.   Ulysses 39-628 1996 £125.00

WILLIAMS, CHARLES   Many Dimensions. London: Gollancz, 1931. 1st edition; several tiny spots of foxing to leading edges, else fine in dust jacket with two tiny chips to head of spine, superior copy, elusive. Robert Gavora 61-303 1996 $500.00

WILLIAMS, CHARLES   Poetry at Present. London: 1930. 1st edition; cloth, gilt, fine; dedication copy, inscribed by author. Words Etcetera 94-1301 1996 £375.00

WILLIAMS, GARDNER F.   The Diamond Mines of South Africa. New York: Macmillan, 1902. 1st edition; 8vo; pages xix, 681; folding map, 30 plates (5 colored); original cloth, lightly rubbed. Mendelssohn II p. 614; Theal p. 333. Richard Adelson W94/95-178 1996 $200.00

WILLIAMS, GEORGE   Bullet and Shell. War as the Soldiers Saw It: Camp, March and Picket, Battlefield and Bivouac; Prison and Hospital. New York: 1882. 1st edition; 454 pages; original binding. W. Bruce Fye 71-2265 1996 $150.00

WILLIAMS, H. M.   The Gray Man. Privately printed, 1911. 1/125 copies, 1st edition;; some rubbing to top edge of front board, else tight, very good copy with tipped in photos on tissue. scarce. Aronovitz 57-1278 1996 $125.00

WILLIAMS, H. W.   Travels in Italy, Greece and the Ionian Islands, in a Series of Letters, Descriptive of Manners, Scenery and the Fine Arts... Edinburgh: Archibald Constable and Co. and Hurst, Robinson and Co., London, 1820. 1st edition; 8vo; 2 volumes; half title, 399 pages, 437 pages; errata leaf to rear of volume I, frontispieces to both volumes, 17 plates, 1 page of facsimile music; half calf, blind rule borders, blind embossed spine, gilt rule and title, moddled paper boards, speckled edges, printed paper label. Beeleigh Abbey BA/56-128 1996 £350.00

WILLIAMS, HENRY T.   William's Pacific and Guide Across the Continent. New York: 1879. 1st edition; 342 pages; illustrations, large color map in rear; pictorial cloth, spine fading. T. A. Swinford 49-1261 1996 $150.00

WILLIAMS, J.   The Northern Almanac for 1837, Being the First After Bissextile, or Leap Year and the Eighth of the Reign of His Present Majesty... (with) Companion to the Northern Almanac for 1837. Penrith: printed and sold by James Brown, 1387. 8vo; pages 24, 60, original lavender endpapers, original cloth, base of spine little worn. R.F.G. Hollett & Son 78-1386 1996 £85.00

WILLIAMS, JAMES   Imposed Rebellion. Fresno: Fabian Books, 1959. Paperback original; faint dampstain visible only at inside edges of paper wrappers, slight bowing to body of book, presumably reversible, attractive, very good plus copy. Extremely uncommon. Between the Covers 43-214 1996 $175.00

WILLIAMS, JOHN   The Life of the Late Earl of Barrymore. London: printed for H. D. Symonds, 1793. 3rd edition; 8vo; 119 pages; half title, etched portrait printed in sepia; stitched as issued, uncut. Arnott & Robinson 2422. Anthony W. Laywood 109-165 1996 £110.00

WILLIAMS, JOHN   A Narrative of Missionary Enterpises in the South Sea Islands... London: John Snow, 1839. 12mo; pages xx, 506; colored frontispiece, folding map, 5 plates; blindstamped red morocco, all edges gilt, rubbed. Snow 9032; Taylor p. 83; Hill p. 326. Richard Adelson W94/95-180 1996 $275.00

WILLIAMS, JOHN A.   Night Song. New York: FSC, 1961. 1st edition; small ink number front fly, otherwise fine in very good plus dust jacket that is tanned on spine and lightly soiled, uncommon. Between the Covers 43-215 1996 $100.00

WILLIAMS, JONATHAN   Descant on Rawthey's Madrigal - Conversations with Basil Bunting. Lexington: Gnomon Press, 1968. One of 500 copies; wrappers, covers slightly marked and dusty, yapp edges creased, very good, signed and dated 1982 on titlepage by Basil Bunting. Ulysses 39-83 1996 £75.00

WILLIAMS, JONATHAN   Epitaphs for Lorine. Penland: Jargon Society, 1973. 1st edition; one of 1000 copies; thin 12mo; wrappers, dust jacket, fine. James S. Jaffe 34-510 1996 $100.00

WILLIAMS, JONATHAN   La Vie Entre les Gadaraenes (Infinity First, Not Last). Black Mountain: Grapnel Press, 1951. 1st edition; one of 'under 150 copies' printed on 'varying scrappaper', initialled by J. W. Jaffe; 8vo; poem leaflet; fine, rare. Jonathan Williams 6. James S. Jaffe 34-685 1996 $450.00

WILLIAMS, JONATHAN   Letters to Mencken from the Land of Pink Lichen. New York: Dim Gray Bar Press, 1994. 1st edition; limited to 75 copies signed by author and Guy Davenport; 8vo; tipped in color photo by Williams and caricature of Mencken by Guy Davenport; cloth backed boards; new. James S. Jaffe 34-686 1996 $125.00

WILLIAMS, JONATHAN   Strung Out with Elgar on a Hill. Urbana: Finial Press, 1970. 1st edition; number one of 101 copies handbound; oblong folio; drawings by Peter Bodnar; decorated red cloth, issued without dust jacket; signed by author and A. D. Moore. Captain's Bookshelf 38-223 1996 $350.00

WILLIAMS, KENNETH POWERS   Lincoln Finds a General: a Military Study of the Civil War. New York: Macmillan, 1949-59. 1st printings of volumes 1-3 and 5, 2nd printing of volume 4; 5 volumes; original cloth; very good, presentation inscription from author. Union Bookshelf 113; Nevins I 48. McGowan Book Co. 65-104 1996 $150.00

WILLIAMS, MARY F.   History of the San Francisco Committee of Vigilance of 1851. Berkeley: University of California, 1921. 1st edition; 543 pages; plates; original navy blue cloth with title in gilt on spine, very fine, unopened copy. Cowan p. 687. Michael D. Heaston 23-366 1996 $125.00

WILLIAMS, MARY FLOYD   History of the San Francisco Committee of Vigilance of 1851... Berkeley: University of California Press, 1921. 1st edition; xii, 543 pages, 4 plates; cloth, owner's name on endpaper, but bright, attractive copy. Metacomet Books 54-127 1996 $125.00

WILLIAMS, O. W.   Letters to J. C. Williams. Fort Stockton: 1925. 14 pages; self wrappers; very good+, rare. 6 Guns 2408. T. A. Swinford 49-1262 1996 $125.00

WILLIAMS, PAUL R.   The Small Home of Tomorrow. Hollywood: Murray & Gee, 1945. 10 7/8 x 8 3/8 inches; 95 pages, printed in green; illustrations; green stamped light green cloth, bottom tips bumped. Dawson's Books Shop 528-251 1996 $100.00

WILLIAMS, R. T.   The Williams' Official British Columbia Directory 1897-98. Victoria: 1897. 744 pages; ads; plates; original binding and boards, some edges chipped, foot of backstrip darkened, else very good. Stephen Lunsford 45-175 1996 $400.00

WILLIAMS, ROBERT P.   Modern and Valuable Books, for Sale Wholesale and Retail, Cornhill Square, May 21, 1819. Boston: 1819. 12mo; 48 pages; disbound; some foxing,b ut very good. Ximenes 108-27 1996 $650.00

WILLIAMS, S. W.   American Medical Biography. Greenfield: 1845. 1st edition; 8vo; 9 portraits lithographed by W. C. Sharp of Boston; some foxing; cloth, spine worn and repaired, corners stubbed, errata slip tipped in at end; contemporary signature of J. P. Avery, later bookplate of Charles Willmarth, M.D. Maggs Bros. Ltd. 1190-535 1996 £75.00

WILLIAMS, SAMUEL   The Natural and Civil History of Vermont. Burlington: Samuel Mills, 1809. 2nd edition; 8vo; 2 volumes, pages 514, errata; 488; large folding map; modern half tan calf, red labels, some light foxing; Howes W478; Sabin 104350; Larned 1038. Richard Adelson W94/95-179 1996 $225.00

WILLIAMS, STEPHEN   American Medical Biography; or, Memoirs of Eminent Physicians, Embracing principally Those Who Have Died Since the Publication of Dr. Thatcher's Work on the Same Subject. Greenfield: 1845. 1st edition; 664 pages; original binding. W. Bruce Fye 71-2268 1996 $175.00

WILLIAMS, TENNESSEE 1911-1983   Cat On a Hot Tin roof. New York: New Directions, 1955 1st edition; 8vo; xiii, (i), 197 pages; 1 plate; tan cloth, titled in black on spine in printed dust jacket (top edge slightly chipped), theatrical bookplate partially removed from front pastedown, illustrated with 1 plate, near fine in very good dust jacket. Blue Mountain SP95-173 1996 $125.00

WILLIAMS, TENNESSEE 1911-1983   The Glass Menagerie: a Play. New York: Random House, 1945. 1st edition; 8vo; xii, 124 pages; photos; rust cloth, rear cover dampstained, titled in gilt within black rectangle on spine in printed dust jacket, chipped at edges, dampstained; very good. Blue Mountain SP95-176 1996 $125.00

WILLIAMS, TENNESSEE 1911-1983   Hard Candy, a Book of Stories. New York: 1954. 1st edition; 10 x 6 inches; 220 pages; cloth backed boards, very good in rubbed slipcase. John K. King 77-516 1996 $125.00

WILLIAMS, TENNESSEE 1911-1983   Steps Must Be Gentle: a Dramatic Reading for Two Performers. New York: Targ Editions, 1980. 1st edition; limited to 350 copies signed by author; 8vo; 22 pages plus colophon; light grayish blue cloth backed marbled blue boards titled in gilt on spine, in tissue dust jacket; fine.   Blue Mountain SP95-174 1996 $150.00

WILLIAMS, TENNESSEE 1911-1983   A Streetcar Named Desire. New York: New Directions, 1947. 1st edition; 4to; fine and beautiful copy in fine dust jacket, jacket is lightly sunned, as seems inevitable, along the spine and very top of panels, with two very small closed tears; trace of offsetting to front endpaper; signed by author.   Lakin & Marley 3-68 1996 $2,500.00

WILLIAMS, TENNESSEE 1911-1983   Summer and Smoke. New York: New Directions, 1948. 1st edition; 1st issue; light fading to spine of both jacket and book, otherwise fine in lightly worn dust jacket.   Hermitage SP95-674 1996 $100.00

WILLIAMS, THOMAS   Ceremony of Love. Indianapolis: Bobbs Merrill, 1955. 1st edition; author's first book; spine slant and mild dampstaining, overall very good in dust jacket; inscribed by author.   Ken Lopez 74-470 1996 $250.00

WILLIAMS, THOMAS   Ceremony of Love. Indianapolis: Bobbs Merrill, 1955. 1st edition; author's first book; fine in very near fine jacket, uncommon first book.   Ken Lopez 74-471 1996 $150.00

WILLIAMS, THOMAS D.   Cohesion. New York: Vantage, 1982. 1st edition; owner name, slight spotting to boards, otherwise near fine in like dust jacket with few small spots on front panel; nicely inscribed by author; scarce.   Between the Covers 43-216 1996 $150.00

WILLIAMS, W. MATTIEU   Through Norway with a Knapsack. London: Smith, Elder & Co., 1859. 2nd edition; 8vo; xii, 340 pages, 5 plates in color and folding map; original blue cloth with decoration in gilt on upper cover; bookplate, wear to spine ends and corners, otherwise very good.   David Mason 71-134 1996 $120.00

WILLIAMS, WILLIAM   A Vocabulary of Familier (sic) Dialogues in English and Welsh... Carnarvon: Lewis Evan Jones, 1837. 4th edition; 60 pages; stitched as issued in grey wrappers bearing offsetting from a poster (?) in Welsh.   Jarndyce 103-91 1996 £60.00

WILLIAMS, WILLIAM CARLOS 1883-1963   The Clouds, Aigeltinger, Russia, &c. Cummington: Wells College Press and Cummington Press, 1948. 1st edition; one of 310 copies; thin 8vo; cloth, printed label on spine; fine. Wallace A26.   James S. Jaffe 34-688 1996 $450.00

WILLIAMS, WILLIAM CARLOS 1883-1963   The Collected Later Poems of William Carlos Williams. New York: New Directions Book, 1950. 1st edition; 2nd issue; very good in lightly worn and sun faded dust jacket, with two short closed tears on rear panel.   Hermitage SP95-676 1996 $100.00

WILLIAMS, WILLIAM CARLOS 1883-1963   The Desert Music. New York: RH, 1954. One of a first edition of 100 numbered copies, signed by author; fine in quarter cloth and paper covered boards in glassine dust jacket and acetate protector, in publisher's paper covered slipcase with shelf wear to extremities.   Lame Duck Books 19-599 1996 $950.00

WILLIAMS, WILLIAM CARLOS 1883-1963   In the Money, White Mule -- Part II. Norfolk: 1940. 1st edition; 8 x 5 inches; 382 pages; cloth, very good in dust jacket with minor tear and slight extremity fray.   John K. King 77-517 1996 $125.00

WILLIAMS, WILLIAM CARLOS 1883-1963   The Knife of the Times and Other Stories. Ithaca: Dragon Press, 1932. One of only 500 copies; very fine, scarce, in both printed and glassine publisher's dust jackets; usually found in poor condition.   Lame Duck Books 19-598 1996 $850.00

WILLIAMS, WILLIAM CARLOS 1883-1963   Make Light of It. New York: Random House, 1950. Advance review copy; cloth very slightly frayed at spine extremities, very good in good dust jacket, chipped along front spine fold and with significant chipping at spine extremities, though not affecting text, author photo laid in; inscribed by author to Edward Parone.   Ken Lopez 74-478 1996 $350.00

WILLIAMS, WILLIAM CARLOS 1883-1963   Paterson (Books 1-5). New York: New Directions, 1946-58. 1st editions, the first four parts limited to 1000 copies, fifth to 3000; 8vo; 5 volumes; cloth, dust jackets, somewhat worn and soiled dust jackets.   James S. Jaffe 34-687 1996 $1,250.00

WILLIAMS, WILLIAM CARLOS 1883-1963   The Pink Church. Columbus: Golden Goose Press, 1949. Limited to 400 copies, signed by author; printed blue wrappers which are slightly toned at edge, otherwise fine.   Bromer Booksellers 90-242 1996 $425.00

WILLIAMS, WILLIAM CARLOS 1883-1963   Sour Grapes. A Book of Poems. Boston: Four Seas, 1921. One of 1000 copies of the first edition; contemporary ownership signature, pages roughly opened, else fine in rare dust jacket with small chip to head of spine; inscribed by author for Dave McDowell, editor at New Directions.   Lame Duck Books 19-597 1996 $2,500.00

WILLIAMS, WILLIAM CARLOS 1883-1963   A Voyage to Pagany. New York: Macaulay Co., 1st edition; author's first novel; original binding, top edge slightly dusty, head and tail of spine and corners bumped, covers slightly rubbed, free endpapers partially and faintly browned, very good in nicked, chipped, rubbed, marked and dusty, slightly soiled and creased dust jacket slighty browned at spine and edges.   Ulysses 39-630 1996 £225.00

WILLIAMS-ELLIS, CLOUGH   Architecture Here and Now. London: Thomas Nelson and Sons Ltd., 1934. 1st edition; black and white photos, drawings and designs; original binding, top edge dusty, tail of spine sl. bumped, bottom edges of covers slightly rubbed, very good in nicked, spotted and slightly rubbed and dusty, internally repaired dust jacket darkened at spine and edges.   Ulysses 39-631 1996 £75.00

WILLIAMSON, GEORGE C.   Lady Anne Clifford. Countess of Dorset, Pembroke and Montgomery, 1590-1676. London: S. R. Publishers, 1967. 2nd edition; 8vo; pages xxii, 548, 61 plates and pedigrees; original cloth, gilt, hinges little frayed, names erased from endpapers, piece cut from bottom of titlepage.   R.F.G. Hollett & Son 78-279 1996 £60.00

WILLIAMSON, HENRY   The Wet Flanders Plain. London: Beaumont Press, 1929. 1st edition; 363/320 copies (of an edition of 400 copies); crown 8vo; pages (v), 96, (1), printed on handmade paper, large 2 color printed title design and cover design by Randolph Schwabe; original quarter cream buckram, sunned backstrip gilt lettered, black and red patterned pale grey boards, untrimmed, excellent.   Blackwell's B112-26 1996 £50.00

WILLIAMSON, J.   Darker Than You Think. Fantasy Press, 1948. 1st edition; 1/500 copies; fine in very good+ dust jacket, some light dust soiling and tiny chip missing from rear dust jacket panel; very fine.   Aronovitz 57-1280 1996 $250.00

WILLIAMSON, J.   The Legion of Space. Fantasy Press, 1947. 1st edition; 1/500 copies; near fine in dust jacket; inscribed by author.   Aronovitz 57-1279 1996 $185.00

WILLIAMSON, J.   The Legion of Time. Fantasy Press, 1950. 1st edition; 1/350 copies, signed by author; near fine in dust jacket.   Aronovitz 57-1284 1996 $160.00

WILLIAMSON, R. W.   Religion and Social Organizaition in Central Polynesia. Cambridge: Cambridge University Press, 1937. Royal 8vo; 340 pages; green cloth, gilt, very good, scarce.   Antipodean 28-578 1996 $225.00

WILLIAMSON, R. W.   The Way of the South Sea Savage. London: Seeley Serv., 1914. 308 pages, 32 plates, folding map; green pictorial cloth, very good.   Antipodean 28-579 1996 $175.00

WILLIAMSON, THOMAS   The Complete Angler's Vade-Mecum. London: for Payne & Mackinlay and Cuthell & Martin, 1808. 1st edition; royal 12mo; (xii), 316 pages; 10 etched plates; later half morocco, banded and gilt, touch sunned, few faint marks and nicks, some spotting and browning, but good.   Ash Rare Books Zenzybyr-96 1996 £195.00

WILLIAMSON, THOMAS   Oriental Field Sports: Being a Complete Detailed and Accurate Description of the Wild Sports of the East. London: printed by W. Bulmer and Co. for Edward Orme and B. Crosby and Co., 1808. 2nd edition; 11 1/4 x 9 1/2 inches; 2 volumes, lacking pages 299-302 in text volume 1, 42 fine hand colored plates (including frontispiece in each volume); modern brown coarse grain morocco (ca. 1920?), spine with titling in blind, front covers with elaborate hand carved scene of mounted hunter subduing a wild boar with lance, whole done in vaguely art deco style; one cover with several small spots from damp spill, leather with other minor stains and discoloration, but curious bindings (probably executed by a skilled amateur), generally quite appealing and with almost no signs of wear, slight offsetting on some plates, one plate with two small brown spots, text with several faint diagonal creases at upper corners, leaves generally a shade less than bright (as often with this book), but plates and text clean and fresh, aquatints brightly colored, apart from missing leaves of text, an excellent copy.   Phillip J. Pirages   33-511   1996 $1,350.00

WILLIAMSON, W. C.   The Recent Foraminifera of Great Britain. London: Ray Society, 1858. Large thin 4to; 7 plates; limp boards, paper label, binding little rubbed, contents very good.   Petersfield Bookshop FH58-293   1996 £60.00

WILLIS, BROWNE   Notitia Parlaimentaria; or, an History of the Counties, Cities and Boroughs in England and Wales. London: Robert Gosling, 1730. 2nd edition; 8vo. in 4's; 2 volumes, half title in volume i (all called for), title printed within double ruled border, single wormhole through bottom margins pages 212, pages (xii), xliv, 212, (32); (vi), xii, 558, 10; contemporary panelled calf, backstrip with raised bands, red leather, gilt lettered in second compartment, volume number lettered direct in third, sides sprinkled but with panel border plain, edged with blind fillets and rolls, gilt roll on board edges, very good.   Blackwell's B112-288   1996 £80.00

WILLIS, NATHANIEL PARKER 1806-1867   American Scenery; or Land, Lake and River Illustrations of Transatlantic Nature. (with Canadian Scenery. London: pub. for the Prorpietors by G. Virtue, 26, Ivy Lane, 1840-42. 1st edition; 4to: (8), 140, 106; 128, 116 pages; 241 engraved plates; original roan backed printed and illustrated green boards, some foxing to text and plates, but very sound, some rubbing to roan and bumping of corners, but very nice with large vignette of Capitol building in Washington on front cover of all volumes. Howes B209; Sabin 3784; Staton & Tremaine 2424. Sabin 3786.   M & S Rare Books   60-283   1996 $4,250.00

WILLIS, NATHANIEL PARKER 1806-1867   Canadian Scenery. London: George Virtue, 1842. 11 x 8 1/2 inches; 2 volumes, added engraved titles, map and 117 scenic plates by W. H. Bartlett; contemporary (publisher's?) maroon half morocco, textured cloth sides, large morocco lettering piece, with intricate gilt decoration on front cover of each volume, spines handsomely gilt in compartments, filled with swirling foliage, gilt edges; few insignificant scuffs to leather, two or 3 plates with very modest traces of foxing, but extraordinarily fine in bright, attractive binding and with plates as clean as one will every find them; not especially scarce book, but almost never found without significant amounts of foxing. Neat 19th century presentation inscription.   Phillip J. Pirages   33-512   1996 $1,750.00

WILLIS, NATHANIEL PARKER 1806-1867   Sketches. Boston: S. G. Goodrich, 1827. 1st edition; 8vo; 96 pages; original printed boards, cloth back, trifling signs of wear to binding, printed paper label; fine. BAL 22713, binding B;   Howard S. Mott   227-153   1996 $175.00

WILLIS, THOMAS   The Anatomy of the Brain and Nerves. Montreal: McGill University Press, 1965. Limited to 2000 sets; small folio; 2 volumes; printed on Spanish mould-made paper made by L. Guarro Casas, Barelona; slipcase, light soiling to box and spines, internally fine.   James Tait Goodrich   K40-293   1996 $250.00

WILLIS, THOMAS   Cerebri Anatome: Cui Accessit Nervorum Descriptio et Usus. London: Tho. Roycroft, for Jo. Martyn & Ja. Allestry, 1664. 1st edition; 2nd impression; 8vo; 240 pages, 15 folding copperplates and rare Imprimatur leaf dated Jan. 20, 1663 present in this copy; in full contemporary (original?) vellum (bit soiled), yapped edges, text bit foxed and browned in parts, overall very clean, tight, crisp copy.   James Tait Goodrich   K40-292   1996 $3,950.00

WILLIS, WILLIAM JOHN   Successful Exploration through the Interior of Australia, from Melbourne to the Gulf of Carpentaria, from the Journals and Letters of... London: Richard Bentley, 1863. (xii), 396 pages, (32) pages, frontispiece and 1 plate, folding map; original embossed green cloth, covers and gilt on spine rubbed, corners bumped, internally bright, clean copy, overall in good condition; Edge Partington bookplate; the Absolon copy. Ferguson 18622; Wantrup 172.   Antipodean   28-629 1996 $750.00

WILLIUS, FREDRICK   Cardiac Classis: a Collection of Classic Works in the Heart and Circulation with Comprehensive Biographical Accounts of the Authors. St. Louis: 1941. 1st edition; 858 pages; original binding; scarce. GM 3158.   W. Bruce Fye   71-2272   1996 $100.00

WILLIUS, FREDRICK   Classics of Cardiology; A Collection of Classic Works in the Heart and Circulation, with Comprehensive Biographical Accounts of the Authors. Malabar: 1983. 858 pages, 1077 pages; 581 pages; 623 pages; 399 pages; 4 volumes in five; original binding. GM 3158.   W. Bruce Fye   71-2271   1996 $100.00

WILLSHIRE, WILLIAM HUGHES   An Introduction to the Study and Collection of Antique Prints. Ellis & White, 1877. 2 volumes, xx, 373; viii, 305 pages; 3 plates; contemporary maroon morocco, top edge gilt, others uncut, slightly rubbed, spines faded, one frontispiece slightly spotted, otherwise nice, crisp copy internally. Thomas Thorp   489-324   1996 £100.00

WILLSON, BECKLES   The Great Company, Being a History of the Honourable Company of Merchants-Adventurerers Trading Into Hudson's Bay. Toronto: Copp, Clark Co., 1899. 24cm; xxii, 17-541 pages; frontispiece, illustrations, portraits, lists and tables, tipped in folding map; fine in near fine dust jacket. Trotter 112; Peel 1567.   Rockland Books 38-251   1996 $150.00

WILLUGHBY, FRANCIS   The Ornithology. London: printed by A. C. for John Martyn, 1678. 1st edition in English; small folio; title in red and black, (xii), 441, (vi) pages, 2 inserted printed leaves at pages 55 and 273, 78 engraved plates, 2 engraved plates; original panelled calf, rebacked, original endpapers preserved; good, clean copy. Keynes p. 52, 54.   David Bickersteth   133-220   1996 £1,250.00

WILMERSING, LUCIUS   A Catalogue of an Exhibition of Renaissance Bookbindings Held at the Grolier Club ... New York: Grolier Club, 1937. 1st edition; one of 200 copies printed on rag paper, 8vo; frontispiece, 16 plates; 68 pages; original printed wrappers.   Forest Books   74-281 1996 £75.00

WILSON, A.   The Flora of Westmorland. London: 1938 Photographic plaes; original cloth; excellent, very scarce.   David A.H. Grayling MY95Orn-84   1996 £75.00

WILSON, A.   Sport and Service in Assam and Elsewhere. 1924. illustrations; fading to spine and some foxing.   David Grayling J95Biggame-395   1996 £55.00

WILSON, A. PHILIPS   A Treatise on Febrile Diseases... Hartford: 1809. 1st American edition; 8vo; 5 volumes in 2; contemporary calf, first few pages waterstained, hinges repaired. Austin 1542.   Argosy   810-521 1996 $200.00

WILSON, ADRIAN   The Making of the Nuremberg Chronicle. Amsterdam: Nico Israel, 1976. 1st printing; folio; 255 pages; cloth, dust jacket. Fine.   The Bookpress   75-369   1996 $165.00

WILSON, ADRIAN   The Making of the Nuremberg Chronicle. Amsterdam: Nico Israel, 1978. 1st edition; 2nd printing; 13 3/4 x 9 3/4 inches; 255, (1) pages; many illustrations, some in color; original cloth and dust jacket; virtually mint.   Phillip J. Pirages   33-513   1996 $150.00

WILSON, ADRIAN   The Medieval Mirror: Speculum Humanae Salvationis 1324-1500. Berkeley: Los Angeles: & London: University of California Press, 1984. 1st edition; 13 3/4 x 9 3/4 inches; 4 p.l., (one blank), 9-229, (1) pages; numerous illustrations, some in color; original cloth and dust jacket, mint in extremely fine jacket.   Phillip J. Pirages 33-514   1996 $200.00

WILSON, ADRIAN   Printing for Theater. San Francisco: Adrian Wilson, 1957. Limited to 250 numbered copies; folio; 57 pages, chapter heading and binding blocks by Nuiko Haramaki, numerous tipped-in original theater programs designed by Wilson, additional programs laid in pocket inside back cover, printed in Linotype Caslon and Trajanus on handmade Tovil paper; bound by Perry G. Davis in natural linen decoratively stamped in green on front cover and lettered in red on spine, programs for Hamlet used as endpapers, spine very slightly darkened, occasional offsetting from specimens; fine overall.   Heritage Book Shop 196-251 1996 $1,500.00

WILSON, ANGUS   As If by Magic. London: Martin Secker & Warburg Ltd., 1973. 1st edition; original binding, head and tail of spine and top corners bumped, upper cover slightly marked, very good in nicked and slightly creased, rubbed, dusty dust jacket darkened at spine and edges; presentation copy from author for Jim and Ruth Hart, inscribed in addition, by Tony Garrett who took photo of author on dust jacket. Ulysses   39-633   1996 £75.00

WILSON, ANGUS   Laughing Matter. New York: Viking Press, 1967. 1st edition; original binding, head and tail of spine and top corners slightly bumped, spine and cover edges slightly faded,, very good in nicked and slightly creased, rubbed and dusty dust jacket faded at spine, slightly fyraed at head and tail of spine and with short tear in centre of spine; presentation copy from author, inscribed, for Jim and Ruth Hart; loosely inserted photo of a Lignum Vitae planted by Princess Margaret. Ulysses 39-632 1996 £65.00

WILSON, CAROL A.   Catalogue of the Collection of Samuel Butler (of Erewhon) in the Chapin Library, Williams College, Williamstown, Mass. Portland: Southworth-Anthoensen Press, 1945. Blue cloth, paper label. Jarndyce CII-136 1996 £50.00

WILSON, CHARLOTTE ELEANOR   Somersetshire Dialogues, or, Reminiscences of the Old Farmhouse at Weston-Super-Mare (in 1826). Weston-super-Mare: C. Robbins, 1822. 8vo; 20 pages, litho frontispiece, 4 litho plates, numerous litho text illustrations; original printed wrappers, blue cloth back, covers and endpapers bit foxed.   Marlborough 162-98 1996 £55.00

WILSON, COLIN   Ritual in the Dark. London: Victor Gollancz, 1960. 1st edition; few minor spots on page edges, still near fine in lightly soiled, price clipped dust jacket slightly dakened on spine with small chip and minor crease on front top corner.   Quill & Brush 102-1744 1996 $100.00

WILSON, DANIEL   The Archaeology and Prehistoric Annals of Scotland. Edinburgh: Sutherland and Knox, 1851. Large thick 8vo; pages xxvi, 714, 6 engraved plates, 195 text woodcuts; original decorated cloth, gilt, neatly rebacked in levant morocco, gilt; from the library of Dr. Arthur Raistrick, with his bookplate.   R.F.G. Hollett 76-337 1996 £85.00

WILSON, DANIEL   Preshistoric Annals of Scotland. London: Macmillan, 1863.. 2nd edition; tall 8vo; 2 volumes, xxxv, 504, x, 556 pages; illustrations; contemporary half calf, raised bands, gilt compartments, labels, binding rubbed on corners, otherwise fine, attractive set.   David Mason 71-144 1996 $240.00

WILSON, DAVID   A Catalogue of the Manuscripts and Printed Books Collected by David Wilson, M.D., Glasgow. Southport: printed for private circulation, 1925. 1st edition; one of 50 copies; 8vo; frontispiece, bound in half morocco by Morrell, gilt, uncut, top edge gilt.   Forest Books 74-282 1996 £75.00

WILSON, E. H.   Aristocrats of the Trees. Boston: 1930. 1st edition; 4to; pages xxi, 279; cloth, few light spots on edges and scuff marks on rear cover; ink name on pastedown.   Raymond M. Sutton VII-798 1996 $135.00

WILSON, EDMUND 1895-1972   The Boys in the Back Room. San Francisco: Colt Press, 1941. One of 1500 copies; cloth jacket decorated paper boards, top edge slightly dusty, spine and cover edges slightly browned, bottom corners slightly bumped, one corner also slightly bruised, covers slightly marked and spotted, top edge of lower cover browned, very good, no dust jacket; from the library of James D. Hart. Ulysses 39-634 1996 £75.00

WILSON, EDMUND 1895-1972   Corrections and Comments (by Edmund Wilson to Sherman Paul's Book Edmund Wilson: a study of Literary Vocation In Out Time. Iowa City: Windhover Press, c. 1976. (The University of Illinois Press, 1965); one of 175 copies; 6.25 x 9.5 inches; brown wrappers attached to brown paste paper boards; fine.   Joshua Heller 21-284 1996 $100.00

WILSON, G. H.   The Eccentric Mirror; Reflecting a Faithful and Interesting Delineation of Male and Female Characters, Ancient and Modern... London: J. and J. Cundee, 1813. 1st edition; 12mo; 4 frontispieces, 4 engraved additional titlepages, 36 plates; original grey boards, printed paper labels, untrimmed, excellent.   Blackwell's B112-289 1996 £425.00

WILSON, HENRY   The Book of Wonderful Characters. London: Hotten, 1870. Sole edition under this title; 8vo; xx, 2 leaves, 23-416 pages, colored frontispiece loose (very old scotch tape repair to frontispiece gutter and left side of title without any surface problems, 61 full page engravings (all fine); half leather and marbled boards plus library cloth addition, original spine laid down, binding very good, contents very nice. Roy W. Clare XXIV-26 1996 $125.00

WILSON, J.   A Descriptive Catalogue of the Prints of Rembrandt. London: J. F. Setchel & H. G. Bohn, 1836. 22 x 114 cm; vi, 266 pages plus errata and addenda leaf, (369 etchings described, and their states); half morocco, slightly worn, marbled sides and edges, some slight foxing.   Rainsford A54-484 1996 £70.00

WILSON, J. OLIVER   Birds of Westmorland and the Northern Pennines. London: Hutchinson, 1933. 1st edition; 8vo; pages 319, 153 illustrations; original black cloth, gilt, top of spine rather dulled, dust jacket creased and rather defective.   R.F.G. Hollett & Son 78-554 1996 £85.00

WILSON, J. OLIVER   Birds of Westmorland and the Northern Pennines. London: Hutchinson, 1933. 1st edition; 8vo; 319 pages; original black cloth, gilt, spine rather dulled, lettering faded.   R.F.G. Hollett & Son 78-555 1996 £75.00

WILSON, JAMES   The Monumental Inscription of the Churchyard and Cemetery, of S. Michael's Dalston, Cumberland. Dalston: W. R. Beck, 1890. 8vo; pages xvi, 163, (iii, subscribers), title and endpapers rather spotted, marginal annotations and additions, possibly in editor's hand; contemporary half calf, gilt, contrasting spine label.   R.F.G. Hollett & Son 78-566 1996 £85.00

WILSON, JAMES   The Monumental Inscription of the Churchyard, and Cemetery of S. Michael's Dalston, Cumberland. Dlaston: W. R. Beck, 1890. 8vo; pages xvi, 163, (iii, subscribers); original cloth, paper labels, spine faded and little worn, unopened; inscribed by publisher on title. R.F.G. Hollett & Son 78-567 1996 £65.00

WILSON, JAMES   The Register of the Priory of St. Bees... Kendal: Titus Wilson, 1915. Thick 8vo; pages xxxix, 663, prelims little spotted, lower joint cracked; original cloth, gilt, extremities trifle rubbed.   R.F.G. Hollett & Son 78-592 1996 £145.00

WILSON, JAMES   A Treatise on Quadrupeds. Edinburgh: 1836. 4to; 17 engraved plates by Geo. Aikman; contemporary half cloth, bit worn and soiled, small tear in one joint; inscribed by author to the Royal Society of Edinburgh and with his ms. title as quoted.   Maggs Bros. Ltd. 1190-727 1996 £60.00

WILSON, JAMES   The Victoria History of the County of Cumberland. London: Constable, 1905. 1st edition; 4to; volume 2; pages xvii, 507, 14 plates and 2 maps, half title rather spotted, old stamps erased from titlepage; handsomely rebound in half crimson levant morocco gilt, arms from original cloth laid on to upper board. From the library of Daniel Scott of Penrith, with his label.   R.F.G. Hollett & Son 78-1388 1996 £85.00

WILSON, JAMES 1795-1856   The Rod and The Gun. London: 1840. engraved plates, foxed, text illustrations; original cloth, expertly restored, spine faded, nice.   David A.H. Grayling 3/95-246 1996 £50.00

WILSON, JAMES HARRISON 1837-1925   Under the Old Flag Recollections of Military Operations in the War for the Union, The Spanish War, The Boxer Rebellion, etc. New York: D. Appleton & Co., 1912. 1st edition; 2 volumes; original cloth, very good to near fine set. Nevins I 180; Dornbusch II 2556.   McGowan Book Co. 65-105 1996 $275.00

WILSON, JOHN MAC KAY   The Land of Burns, a Series of Landscapes and Portraits, Illustrative of the Life and Writings of the Scottish Poet. London: Blackie & Son, 1840. 4to; 2 volumes; pages vi, 105; vi, 72; 2 engraved titles and 80 steel engraved plates, little spotting to frontispiece and engraved title to volume on dampstained; full morocco gilt by J. Dewar of Perth, boards with unusual design and panelled in blind and gilt fillets, spine panels bordered with multiple gilt fillets, trifle rubbed.   R.F.G. Hollett 76-340 1996 £150.00

WILSON, JOHN MAC KAY   The Rural Cyclopaedia, or a General Dictionary of Agriculture, and of the Arts, Sciences, Instruments and Practice, Necessary to the Farmer, Stockfarmer, Gardener, Forester, Landsteward, Farrier &c. Edinburgh: A. Fullerton & Co., 1847. Thick royal 8vo; 4 volumes; 67 full page plates, including 7 colored plates; contemporary half calf.   Charles W. Traylen 117-57 1996 £190.00

WILSON, JOHN MAC KAY   Tales of the Borders and Of Scotland. Gateshead-on-Tyne: Adam and Co., n.d., c. 1870. 4to; 3 volumes; full page tinted plates; half green morocco gilt, trifle marked, all edges gilt, nice.   R.F.G. Hollett 76-339 1996 £95.00

WILSON, JOSEPH T.   The Black Phalanx: a History of the Negro Soliders of the United States in the Wars of 1775-1812, 1861-65. Hartford: American Pub. Co., 1888. 1st edition; couple of faint spots of foxing, otherwise lovely, fine, with very slight fading to spine; especially bright.   Between the Covers 43-436 1996 $500.00

WILSON, JOYCE LANCASTER   The Swing. ptd. by Adrian Wilson at the Press in Tuscany Alley, 1981. Limited edition, number 125 of 300 copies, signed by printer and artist; 4to; 8 full page colored illustrations; colored pictorial wrappers; fine.   Barbara Stone 70-212 1996 £55.00

WILSON, O. S. The Larvae of the British Lepidoptera and Their Food Plants. London: 1880. Royal 8vo; pages xxix, 367, 40 colored plates; binder's cloth, backstrip and gilt device from original binding bound in at end. Wheldon & Wesley 207-1132 1996 £120.00

WILSON, R. L. Winchester, The Golden Age of American Gun Smithing and the Winchester of 1000. Cody: 1983. 1st edition; one of the limited (500 copies), numbered edition, signed by author; 144 pages, black and white color photos; book and dust jacket very fine. Early West 22-416 1996 $125.00

WILSON, ROBERT Bibliography of Gertrude Stein. Quill & Brush, 1994. 1/50 copies, signed by Wilson, numbered, deluxe copies; illustrations, photo laid in; special binding; fine. Bev Chaney, Jr. 23-633 1996 $100.00

WILSON, ROBERT THOMAS History of the British Expedition to Egypt. London: printed by C. Rowroth, Bell Yard, Fleet St. & Sold by T. Egerton... 1803. 2nd edition; 4to; pages xxi, 387; frontispiece, 1 folding map, 3 folding plans; contemporary calf, spine gilt, spine little rubbed, otherwise very attractive. Blackmer 1819; Ibrahim Hilmy p. 337. Sotheran PN32-169 1996 £350.00

WILSON, SELDEN L. Recollections and Experiences, During the Civil War, 1861-1865, in the 15th Penna. Vol. Cavalry, Better Known as the Anderson Cavalry. Washington: 1913. 1st edition; 168 pages; original printed wrappers, chipping along backstrip, else very good to near fine; formerly the copy of Sgt. John W. Eckman who contributed to the work. Dornbusch I PA 94. McGowan Book Co. 65-106 1996 $450.00

WIND, HERBERT WARREN The Complete Golfer. London: William Heinemann, 1954. 1st British edition; demy 8vo; (xxvi), 398 pages; plates; bound in smart modern half morocco by Bayntun-Riviere, titlepage, couple of very minor marks, but very good. Donovan & Murdoch 40320. Ash Rare Books Zenzybyr-97 1996 £225.00

WINGATE, EDMUND An Exact Abridgment of All Statutes in Force and Use from the Beginning of Magna Charta Untill...1675. London: printed by John Streater, Eliz. Flesher, and Henry Twyford, 1675. contemporary calf, binding strained and defective, usable. Meyer Boswell SL25-245 1996 $150.00

WINKLER, E. W. Manuscript Letters and Documents of Early Texians: 1821-1845. Austin: Steck, 1937. 1st edition; 314 pages; map endpapers. Maggie Lambeth 30-545 1996 $200.00

WINNETT, FRED V. The Excavations at Dibon (Dhiban) in Moab. New Haven: ASOR, 1964-72. 8vo; 2 volumes; plates, plans; original cloth. Archaeologia Luxor-2826 1996 $125.00

WINSLOW, C. E. A. Nursing and Nursing Education in the United States. Report of the Committee for the Study of Nursing Education. New York: 1923. 1st edition; 585 pages; original binding, scarce. W. Bruce Fye 71-2278 1996 $125.00

WINSLOW, DON The Trail to Buddha's Mirror. New York: St. Martin's, 1992. 1st edition; author's second book; fine in fine dust jacket, signed by author. Bella Luna 7-625 1996 $100.00

WINSLOW, FORBES BENIGNUS The Anatomy of Suicide. London: Henry Renshaw, 1840. 8vo; (xvi), (340) pages + frontispiece, embossed brown cloth, head and foot of spine and joints chipped, covers bumped and somewhat rubbed, good copy; bookplate and gilt titlepage stamp of Hartford Retreat. John Gach 150-482 1996 $275.00

WINSLOW, FORBES BENIGNUS The Plea of Insanity in Criminal Cases. London: Henry Renshaw, 1848. 1st edition; thin 12mo; viii, 78, (2) pages; embossed printed green cloth, front board detached, some early marginal pencil lining, edges bit worn, good copy, presentation copy. John Gach 150-483 1996 $250.00

WINSLOW, J. B. Exposition Anatomique de la Structure du Corps Humain. London: 1732. 1st edition; 4to; 4 folding engraved plates (slight tears at fold, blank upper margin of first defective), with 4 pages of errata (some 250!), minor browning, contemporary French mottled calf, clumsily repaired with part of the original spine missing, bit worn, bookplate of A. Louis (1723-92), name, perhaps Henry Brewer, partly erased from flyleaf. Maggs Bros. Ltd. 1190-536 1996 £525.00

WINTERBOTHAM, WILLIAM An Historical, Geographical, Commercial, and Philosophical View of the United States of America, and of the European Settlements in America and the West-Indies. New York: John Reid, 1796. 1st U.S. edition; Volume III (of 4) only; 519, 4 engravings (1 colored); original calf, considerable cover wear rear panel detached, but present; very good internally. Evans 31647; Howes W581. Taurus Books 83-31 1996 $275.00

WINTERS, IVOR The Magpie's Shadow. Chicago: Musterbookhouse, 1922. 1st edition; ad inside back cover; printed wrappers; some rubbing to spine and corners of covers, otherwise fine. Inscribed by author. Bromer Booksellers 90-244 1996 $500.00

WINTROBE, MAXWELL Blood, Pure and Eloquent: a Story of Discovery of People and Of Ideas. New York: 1980. 1st edition; 771 pages; original binding; GM 3161.5. W. Bruce Fye 71-2283 1996 $100.00

WINZET, NINIANE Certane Tractatis for Reformatioun of Doctryne and Maneris in Scotland... MDLXII-MDLXIII. Edinburgh: for the Maitland Club, 1835. One of 96 copies; 4to; (xxiv), 184 pages; partly printed in black letter, woodcut; contemporary calf, spine gilt, double albels; scarce. Robert Clark 38-148 1996 £90.00

WIONI, PSEUD. Songs of the Wye, and Poems, by Wioni. London: Simpkin, Marshall and Co., 1859. 1st edition; 8vo; pages viii, 131; original green blindstamped cloth, spine and upper cover lettered and richly decorated in gilt with large wreath on upper cover, urn, bird and flowers on spine, unopened; fine. Simon Finch 24-259 1996 £60.00

WIRSING, ADAM LUDWIG Abbildungen der Marmor-Arten Mamora et Adfines Lapides... Nurnberg: auf Kosten des Verlegers, 1775. 1st edition; tall 4to; 56 plates; morocco back with contrasting gilt title label over old speckled boards, fine, tall brilliantly colored copy. Book Block 32-14 1996 $16,500.00

WIRT, ELIZABETH WASHINGTON GAMBLE Flora's Dictionary. Baltimore: Fielding Lucas, 1830? 1st edition; 4to; 133, 87 pages; leather backed printed boards, interleaved with blank leaves for saving specimens. Second Life Books 103-215 1996 $125.00

WISCONSIN (TERRITORY). CONSTITUTIONAL CONVENTION Journal of the Convention to Form a Constitution for the State of Wisconsin: Begun and Held at Madison, on the Fifth Day of October, 1846. Madison: Beriah Brown, printer, 1847. 506 pages; leather backed boards, hinges split, cords still intact, though front cover is loosening, tight paper darkened, some foxing; numerous marginal check marks in pencil, many next to the name Doty in the text and in some places where the delegate making a motion is not identified, "Doty" is written in; Delegate James Duane Doty had been territorial governor. All Wisc. 370; McMurtrie 263; Shearer 674; Bohling Book Co. 192-465 1996 $250.00

WISCONSIN RAILROAD COMMISSION Opinions and Decisions of the Railroad Commission of the State of Wisconsin. Madison: 1908-12. Volumes 1-8; 850-1040 pages each; original cloth, morocco spine labels, soiled exteriors, not used, with Franklin Institute markings. Bohling Book Co. 192-437 1996 $100.00

WISE, FRANCIS A Letter to Dr. Mead, Concerning some Antiquities in Berkshire. Oxford: Thomas Wood, 1737. 4to; 58 pages, 1 f. (blank), 2 folding engraved plates; modern half calf, foxing. Anderson p. 50. Marlborough 162-99 1996 £100.00

WISE, GEORGE History of the Seventeenth Virginia Infantry. Baltimore: Kelly, Piet & Co., 1870. 1st edition; 312 pages; original cloth, inner hinges starting, minor wear to extremities, else very good or better; scarce. Coulter 482. Dornbusch II 1398. Howes W592; Nicholson p. 938. McGowan Book Co. 65-107 1996 $450.00

WISE, JENNINGS CROPPER The Military History of the Virginia Military Institute from 1839 to 1865. Lynchburg: 1915. 576 pages; 16 plates; untrimmed, unopened, bound in modern cloth with gilt stamped leather spine label, fine, good looking binding. Nevins II 206; Haynes 21681. Bohling Book Co. 191-1057 1996 $125.00

WISE, JOHN R.   The New Forest: Its History and Scenery. London: and Manchester: Ballantyne Press for Henry Sotheran & Co., 1883. Apparently One of 350 copies, 'Artist's Edition'; 11 1/4 x 8 1/4 inches; xi, (1) pages, (2) leaves, 335, (1) pages; title in red and black, printed as a large paper copy on fine quality thick and untrimmed leaves; 12 etched plates by Heywood Sumner, 2 maps, frontispiece and more than 60 mounted illustrations, by Walter Crane; publisher's original special black morocco, sides covered with wood veneer, front cover with titling and sylvan vignette in black, flat spine with gilt titling, top edge gilt, other edges untrimmed; wood veneer little warped and blistered, board edges and corners bit worn, slight rubbing to joints and few marks to spine, but binding still very much intact, and, in a quirky way, quite pleasing, very fine copy internally. With armorial bookplate of Sir Arthur Conan Doyle and with his signature. Nissen 2173 (earlier editions).   Phillip J. Pirages 33-194 1996 $550.00

WISE, THOMAS JAMES 1859-1937   A Bibliography of the Writings in Verse and Prose of George Gordon Noel, Baron Byron. London: Dawsons, 1972. Reprint of 1933 edition; 8vo; 2 volumes, numerous facsimiles; original cloth, dust jacket.   Forest Books 74-287 1996 £95.00

WISEMAN, JAMES   Studies in the Antiquities of Stobi. Beograd: University of Texas at Austin and the National Mus. of Titov Veles, 1973-81. 8vo; 3 volumes, xxxvi, 781 pages; 329 illustrations and 8 plates, 2 fold-out plans; original cloth.   Archaeologia Luxor-4178 1996 $125.00

WISHART, GEORGE   A Complete History of the Wars in Scotland; Under the Conduct of the Illustrious James Marquis of Montrose. London: printed in the Year, 1720. 8vo; (xvi), 200, xlvi, xlix-lvi, 24 pages; old calf, rebacked, new old style free endpapers.   David Bickersteth 133-90 1996 £75.00

WISLIZENUS, FREDERICK A.   A Journey to the Rocky Mountains in the Year 1839. St. Louis: Missouri Historical Society, 1912. Number 138 of 500 copies; 162 pages; frontispiece, folded map; cloth backed boards, light top, edge wear and soiling, faint marginal dampstain on some leaves, good to very good. Howes W596; Rittenhouse SFT 655. Bohling Book Co. 192-257 1996 $160.00

WISTER, OWEN 1860-1938   The Jimmyjohn Boss and Other Stories. New York: Harper, 1900. 1st edition; illustrations; very good, covers only very slightly worn, lettering and cover illustration clean and bright. Sherwood 3-347 1996 $200.00

WISTER, OWEN 1860-1938   Lin Mc Lean. New York: Harper, 1898. 1st edition; 8 Remington illustrations; somewhat worn, corners bumped, otherwise very good, tight, clean copy.   Sherwood 3-346 1996 $200.00

WISTER, OWEN 1860-1938   The New Swiss Family Robinson. New York: Duffield, 1922. 2nd edition; pictorial boards, with dust jacket (soiled and worn, but complte); near fine.   Sherwood 3-359 1996 $100.00

WISTER, OWEN 1860-1938   The Virginian. New York: Macmillan, 1902. 1st edition; near fine, clean, bright printing in custom slipcase, faint owner's name on f.f.e.p., splendid copy of increasingly rare book. Sherwood 3-348 1996 $750.00

WISTER, OWEN 1860-1938   The Virginian. New York: MacMillan, 1902. 1st edition; 8vo; illustrations by Arthur keller; original binding; soiled, rubbed, good+; owner's signature dated June 1902.   Charles Agvent 4-1231 1996 $125.00

WISTER, OWEN 1860-1938   Watch Your Thirst: a Dry Opera in Three Acts. New York: Macmillan, 1923. 1st limited edition of 1000 copies; fine in very good+ dust jacket, signed limitation page.   Sherwood 3-360 1996 $300.00

WITHER, GEORGE   A Christmas Carroll: a Poem. Village Press, 1915. One of 85 copies; 10 1/4 x 7 3/4 inches; 2 p.l., 3-8 pages, (1) leaf (colophon); printed blue paper wrappers, edges untrimmed. faint creases to wrappers and text, but fine copy of this fragile item. Cary 113. Phillip J. Pirages 33-504 1996 $250.00

WITHERBY, H. F.   The Handbook of British Birds. London: 1943-45. volumes 1 and 2 are 2nd impression, volumes 3-5 are 3rd impression; 8vo; 5 volumes, 156 plates, mostly colored; cloth, dust jackets.   John Henly 27-33 1996 £95.00

WITHERBY, H. F.   The Handbook of British Birds. London: 1948. 5th impression; 8vo; 5 volumes; 157 colored and other plates; cloth. Wheldon & Wesley 207-896 1996 £90.00

WITHERBY, H. F.   The Handbook of British Birds. London: 1949. Reprint; 5 volumes;numerous colored plates and other illustrations; mint, with dust jackets.   Petersfield Bookshop FH58-210 1996 £110.00

WITHERS, GEORGE   A Rich Store-House; or, Treasury for the Diseased. London: John Clowes, 1650. 8th edition; 4to; (22), 274 pages; contemporary sheep, rebacked, with corners restored, some text browning, else very nice, very rare.   James Tait Goodrich K40-290 1996 $895.00

WITHINGTON, WILLIAM   Modern Ideas in Prose and Poetry, Dictated by the True Spirit. Portland: Brown Thurston, 1854. 1st edition; 18mo; 36 pages; original printed and pictorial front wrapper.   M & S Rare Books 60-192 1996 $125.00

WITTKE, CARL   The History of the State of Ohio in Six Volumes. Columbus: 1941-44. 8vo; 6 volumes; maps and illustrations; original cloth, very nice.   Edward Morrill 369-356 1996 $135.00

WITTON, P. H.   Views of the Ruins of the Principal Houses Destroyed During the Riots at Birmingham, 1791. London: J. Johnston, 1792. Oblong 4to; 8ff., text in English and French, 8 uncolored aquatint plates by William Ellis after Witton; original printed bufff wrappers, edges little frayed and dusty; rare. Abbey Scenery 48.   Marlborough 162-276 1996 £600.00

WODARCH, CHARLES   An Introduction to the Study of Conchology. London: Longman, Hurst, Rees, Orme & Browne, 1820. 1st edition; post 8vo; xxiv, (124), (ii) pages, 4 hand colored plates; original boards, hinges and extremities rubbed and slightly split, although boards still firm, few minor marks, but good copy.   Ash Rare Books Zenzybyr-98 1996 £75.00

WODEHOUSE, PELHAM GRENVILLE 1881-1975   Bill the Conqueror: His Invasion of England in the Springtime. New York: George H. Doran, 1924. 1st American edition; very light soiling, otherwise fine.   Hermitage SP95-681 1996 $125.00

WODEHOUSE, PELHAM GRENVILLE 1881-1975   My Man Jeeves. London: George Newnes, Ltd., 1919. 1st edition; 1st issue; small 8vo; pages (5)-251, (1) blank, (2) ads; original blindstamped salmon pink cloth, spine lettered and decorated in black (slightly faded), little soiling to sides, upper hinge cracked, some spotting internally as usual, ownership signature on front pastedown, but very good; McIlvaine A22a. Simon Finch 24-260 1996 £500.00

WODEHOUSE, PELHAM GRENVILLE 1881-1975   Quick Service. London: Herbert Jenkins, 1940. 1st edition; crown 8vo; McIlvaine's primary bindin of red cloth and in first issue jacket; some slight marks, some browning of endpapers, but nice in slightly chipped and worn dust jacket. McIlvaine A63a.   Ash Rare Books Zenzybyr-99 1996 £295.00

WODEHOUSE, PELHAM GRENVILLE 1881-1975   The Return of Jeeves. New York: Simon and Schuster, 1954. 1st edition; fine in lightly worn dust jacket;   Hermitage SP95-682 1996 $200.00

WODHULL, MICHAEL   The Equality of Mankind, a Poem. London: 1798. 2nd edition; 8vo; disbound; very good copy printed on thick paper, presentation inscription trimmed by binder. Not in Jackson.   Ximenes 108-346 1996 $225.00

WOHL, HELMUT   The Paintings of Domenico Veneziano, c. 1410-1461. New York: New York University Press, 1980. 27 x 21 cm; xxv, 412 pages, frontispiece, 254 illustrations; original cloth.   Rainsford A54-562 1996 £100.00

WOLCOT, JOHN 1738-1819   The Poetical Works of Peter Pindar. Philadelphia: Spotswood & Rice, 1792. New edition; 12mo; 2 volumes; original diced calf, leather labels, light rubbing, occasional foxing, darkening; early signature, near fine.   Charles Agvent 4-1232 1996 $300.00

WOLCOTT, ELIZA   The Two Sisters' Poems and Memoirs. New Haven: Baldwin & Treadway, 1830. 1st edition; 174 pages; frontispiece, signed "J.W.B."; contemporary calf, very rubbed. Cooper 5527.   M & S Rare Books 60-254 1996 $125.00

WOLCOTT, OLIVER   An Address, to the People of the United States on the Subject of the Report of a Committee of the House of Representatives, Appointed to "Examine...Whether Monies Drawn from the Treasury, Have Been Faithfully Applied to the Objects..." Boston: 1802. 1st edition; 8vo; 112 pages; removed. S&S 3576; Kress B4622. M & S Rare Books 60-435 1996 $250.00

WOLF Hunting in Lower Brittany. 1875. 2nd edition; woodcut illustrations; original cloth, some wear, some pages bit grubby.   David Grayling J95Biggame-474   1996 £75.00

WOLF, EDWIN   Rosenbach: a Biography. Cleveland and New York: World Publishing Co., 1960. 1st edition; 8vo; cloth, dust jacket; fine in slightly rubbed and price clipped dust jacket; signed by Wolf and Fleming.   James S. Jaffe   34-74   1996 $150.00

WOLF, GARY   Who Censored Roger Rabbit? New York: St. Martin's, 1981. 1st edition; very slight rubbing to corners, else fine in near fine dust jacket, little rubbed at extremities; very scarce book in first edition. Between the Covers   42-507   1996 $150.00

WOLF, J.   Monograph of the Pheasants: the Original Sketches... London: 1988. Copy E of an edition limited to 10 copies, lettered A-J. folio; 95 charcoal drawings, 79 colored plates; half morocco, slipcase. Wheldon & Wesley   207-118   1996 £750.00

WOLFE, EDWIN   Rosenbach: a Biography. Cleveland & New York: World Publishing Co., 1960. 1st edition; one of 250 copies signed by authors; 9 1/2 x 6 3/4 inches; 1 p.l., 616 pages, (2) leaves; frontispiece, 8 plates, title in green and black; original cloth, in publisher's slipcasse, very slightly rubbed, one seam neatly repaired with tape), very fine. Phillip J. Pirages   33-104   1996 $250.00

WOLFE, GENE   Bibliomen. New Castle: Cheap St., 1984. 1st edition; one of 57 numbered copies, signed by author and artist; illustrations by George Barr; quarter Niger goat, very fine, issued without dust jacket, laid into traycase.   Robert Gavora   61-320   1996 $230.00

WOLFE, GENE   The Boy Who Hooked the Sun. Cheap Street, 1985. 1st edition; approximately 100 copies produced, signed by author; wrappers and envelope, as issued; fine.   Aronovitz   57-1301   1996 $175.00

WOLFE, GENE   The Castle of the Otter. Ziesing, 1982. 1st edition; one of 520 copies, this is 1/100 specially bound and signed; fine in dust jacket.   Aronovitz   57-1298   1996 $300.00

WOLFE, GENE   The Claw of the Concilliator. S&S, 1981. 1st edition; uncorrected proof; wrappers; very good+/near fine; inscribed by author. Aronovitz   57-1297   1996 $200.00

WOLFE, GENE   Empires of Foliage and Flower. New Castle: Cheap St., 1987. 1st edition; one of 60 numbered copies of the Publisher's edition, signed by author and artist; illustrations by Judy King-Rieniets; hand bound in Japanese cloth with inlaid illustrated panel on front board, very fine, issued without dust jacket, laid into traycase.   Robert Gavora 61-326   1996 $230.00

WOLFE, GENE   Peace. New York: Harper & Row, 1975. Uncorrected proof, gold printed wrappers; very fine; short inscription by author. Robert Gavora   61-334   1996 $250.00

WOLFE, GENE   The Shadow of the Torturer. New York: Simon & Schuster, 1980 1st edition; fine in dust jacket, inscription by author. Robert Gavora   61-337   1996 $175.00

WOLFE, GENE   The Shadow of the Torturer. New York: Simon & Schuster, 1980. Uncorrected proof; yellow printed wrappers; very fine, inscribed.   Robert Gavora   61-336   1996 $500.00

WOLFE, GENE   Soldier of the Mist. New York: 1986. Uncorrected proof; green printed wrappers, very fine with dust jacket laid in, bumped at head of spine panel.   Robert Gavora   61-339   1996 $100.00

WOLFE, GENE   The Urth of the New Sun. Ultramarine Press, 1987. 1st limited edition utilizing the first issue sheets of the American edition, of 125 such copies, this 1/21 bound thus and signed by author; full leather.   Aronovitz   57-1303   1996 $600.00

WOLFE, GENE   The Urth of the New Sun. London: Gollancz, 1987. 1st edition; uncorrected proof; signed by author; wrappers; fine.   Aronovitz 57-1304   1996 $125.00

WOLFE, GENE   The Wolfe Archipelago. Willimantic: Ziesing, 1983. 1st edition; one of 200 numbered copies, signed by author and artists; illustrations by Carl Lundgren and Rick Demaraco; very fine in dust jacket.   Robert Gavora   61-351   1996 $150.00

WOLFE, GENE   Young Wolfe. U.M. Press, 1992. 1st edition; 1/100 copies, signed by author; as new, without dust jacket as issued. Along with "Orbital Thoughts" a 32 page booklet, not offered for sale separately;   Aronovitz   57-1307   1996 $250.00

WOLFE, HUMBERT   Humoresque. London: Ernest Benn Ltd., 1926. 3rd impression; original binding, top edge dusty, head and tail of spine and corners bumped, covers marked, free endpapers browned; ownership signature of Ian Fleming.   Ulysses   39-693   1996 £125.00

WOLFE, HUMBERT   The Unknown Goddess. London: Methuen & Co. Ltd., 1925. 1st edition; original binding, top edge dusty, head and tail of spine and corners bumped, title label on spine rubbed, chipped, creased and browned, cover edges faded and rubbed, endpaper edges browned; good; ownership signature of Ian Fleming.   Ulysses   39-692   1996 £125.00

WOLFE, RICHARD J.   Louis Herman Kinder and Fine Bookbinding in America. Bird & Bull Press, 1985. One of 325 numbered copies; large 8vo; 14 colored plates, 18 black and white illustrations; printed in Van Dijck on Arches mouldmade; half dark blue morocco, decorated boards; fine.   Bertram Rota   272-37   1996 £180.00

WOLFE, RICHARD J.   On Improvements in Marbling the Edges of Books and Paper. Bird & Bull Press, 1983. One of 350 copies; 4 1/2 x 6 1/4 inches; 64 pages, (1) leaf (colophon); 14 mounted specimens of marbled paper; original turquoise half morocco, marbled paper sides, gilt titling on spine, fore edge and tail edge untrimmed, 14 mounted specimens of marbled paper; virtually mint.   Phillip J. Pirages   33-84 1996 $190.00

WOLFE, RICHARD J.   On Improvements in Marbling the Edges of Books and Paper. A Nineteenth Century Account. Newtown: Bird and Bull Press, 1983. Limited to 350 numbered copies; oblong 12mo; 14 original marbled paper samples tipped in, blue half morocco, gilt lettering and border, marbled paper boards; booklabel of Ruari McLean.   Maggs Bros. Ltd.   1191-225   1996 £225.00

WOLFE, RICHARD J.   On Improvements in Marbling the Edges of Books and Paper. Newtown: Bird & Bull Press, 1983. Limited to 350 copies; oblong 12mo; 64 pages, (14)ff; marbled boards, backed with gilt stamped blue morocco; extremely fine. Heany A37.   Bromer Booksellers   87-33   1996 $200.00

WOLFE, THOMAS CLAYTON 1900-1938   From Death to Morning. New York: Scribner's, 1935. 1st edition; small dampspot to top page edges, else fine in very good dust jacket with chipping to top of spine panel and front panel.   Sherwood   3-372   1996 $175.00

WOLFE, THOMAS CLAYTON 1900-1938   From Death to Morning. New York: Scribners, 1935. 1st edition; original cloth, fine in very good dust jacket.   Beasley Books   82-163   1996 $125.00

WOLFE, THOMAS CLAYTON 1900-1938   From Death to Morning. New York: Scribner's, 1935. 1st edition; 8vo; maroon cloth, as issued; fine in slightly marked dust jacket.   Appelfeld Gallery   54-183   1996 $100.00

WOLFE, THOMAS CLAYTON 1900-1938   Gentlemen of the Press. Chicago: Black Archer Press, 1942. Limited to 350 copies; fine, issued without dust jacket.   Sherwood   3-380   1996 $250.00

WOLFE, THOMAS CLAYTON 1900-1938   The Hills Beyond. New York: Harper, 1941. 1st edition; slight wear to head of spine, else near fine in dust jacket showing wear to head and foot of spine panel and other edges.   Sherwood   3-379   1996 $150.00

WOLFE, THOMAS CLAYTON 1900-1938   Mannerhouse. New York: 1948. 1st edition; limited to 500 numbered copies; 9 x 5.5 inches; 183 pages; portrait, facsimiles; cloth, very good in dust jacket with slight discolored and spotted spine, else good in slightly soiled dust jacket. John K. King   77-523   1996 $200.00

WOLFE, THOMAS CLAYTON 1900-1938   Mannerhosue: a Play in a Prologue and Three Acts. New York: Scribners, 1948. 1st edition; fine in price clipped dust jacket.   Sherwood   3-362   1996 $125.00

WOLFE, THOMAS CLAYTON 1900-1938   Mannerhouse. New York: Harper Bros., 1948. 1st edition; fine in dust jacket.   Bev Chaney, Jr. 23-780 1996 $100.00

WOLFE, THOMAS CLAYTON 1900-1938   Of Time and the River: a Legend of Man's Hunger in In His Youth. New York: Scribners, 1935. 1st edition; very fine in dust jacket, only very slightly worn at edges. Sherwood 3-371 1996 $500.00

WOLFE, THOMAS CLAYTON 1900-1938   Of Time and the River. New York: Scribner, 1937. 1st edition; near fine in dust jacket with some rubbing to extremities; inscribed by author.   Captain's Bookshelf 38-224 1996 $1,500.00

WOLFE, THOMAS CLAYTON 1900-1938   The Story of a Novel. New York: Scribner's, 1936. 1st edition; review copy; very good+ in dust jacket with review slip laid in; inscribed by author, quite uncommon thus. Lame Duck Books 19-604 1996 $2,250.00

WOLFE, THOMAS CLAYTON 1900-1938   The Story of a Novel. New York: Scribners, 1936. 1st edition; one page carelessly opened, else fine in beautiful, unworn dust jacket.   Sherwood 3-373 1996 $150.00

WOLFE, THOMAS CLAYTON 1900-1938   You Can't Go Home Again. New York: Scribner's, 1940. 1st edition; very good with light wear to spine, dust jacket has about 1 inch piece missing top of spine panel, other wear and chipping, former owner's bookplate on front pastedown. Sherwood 3-377 1996 $100.00

WOLFE, TOM   In Our Time. New York: FSG, 1980. 1st edition; fine in fine dust jacket and signed by author.   Ken Lopez 74-480 1996 $100.00

WOLFE, TOM   The Kandy-Kolored Tangerine-Flake Streamline Baby. New York: FSG, 1965. 1st edition; author's first book; near fine in dust jacket with occasional light soiling to front panel.   Lame Duck Books 19-605 1996 $200.00

WOLFE, TOM   The Kandy-Kolored Tangerine Flake Streamline Baby. New York: Farrar Straus & Giroux, 1965. 1st printing; author's first book. near fine with quarter inch closed tear to lower front panel;   Sherwood 3-384 1996 $185.00

WOLFE, TOM   The New Journalism. New York: Harper & Row, 1973. 1st edition; small bookstore sticker on endpaper, else near fine in near fine price clipped dust jacket.   Pettler & Lieberman 28-263 1996 $100.00

WOLFE, TOM   The Pump House Gang. New York: Farrar Straus & Giroux, 1968. 1st edition; 1st printing; fine in dust jacket with few scuff marks on front panel.   Sherwood 3-385 1996 $100.00

WOLFE, TOM   Radical Chic and Mau Mauing the Flak Catchers. New York: FSG, 1970. 1st edition; long galleys, strign tied and printed on rectos only; nicely inscribed for Burt Britton.   Between the Covers 42-467 1996 $650.00

WOLFF, TOBIAS   Back in the World. Boston: Houghton Mifflin, 1985. Uncorrected proof copy; wrappers; fine; signed by author.   Ken Lopez 74-483 1996 $175.00

WOLFF, TOBIAS   Back in the World. Boston; Houghton Mifflin, 1985. Uncorrected proof; blue printed wrappers; fine; signed by author. Lame Duck Books 19-610 1996 $125.00

WOLFF, TOBIAS   In the Garden of North American Martyrs. New York: Ecco, 1981. 1st edition; fine in fine dust jacket with just a touch of rubbing to front panel; signed by author.   Ken Lopez 74-482 1996 $250.00

WOLFF, TOBIAS   In the Garden of the North American Martyrs. New York: Ecco Press, 1981. 1st edition; near fine in like jacket with traces of rubbing; signed.   Alice Robbins 15-347 1996 $100.00

WOLFF, TOBIAS   The Other Miller. Babcock & Koontz, 1990. 1/40 deluxe copies, signed by author and artist and numbered I-XL (total edition 240); very fine.   Alice Robbins 15-348 1996 $225.00

WOLFF, TOBIAS   This Boy's Life: a Memoir. New York: Atlantic Monthly, 1989. 1st edition; slight rubbing to base of boards, else fine in dust jacket, signed by author.   Between the Covers 42-468 1996 $125.00

WOLFF, TOBIAS   Ugly Rumours. London: George Allen Unwin, 1975. 1st edition; fine in dust jacket, signed by author. Exceedingly scarce. Ken Lopez 74-481 1996 $750.00

WOLFF, TOBIAS   Ugly Rumors. London: Allen & Unwin, 1975. 1st edition; signed by author, scarce thus. Lopez 25.   Lame Duck Books 19-606 1996 $850.00

WOLFF, TOBIAS   Ugly Rumours. London: Allen & Unwin, 1975. 1st edition; author's first book; fine in near fine dust jacket with traces of wear, inscribed and dated 1994.   Alice Robbins 15-346 1996 $750.00

WOLFF, TOBIAS,   In the Garden of the North American Martyrs. New York: Ecco, 1981. 1st edition; near fine in dust jacket with couple of short scrapes along fore-edge of front panel, signed by author.   Lame Duck Books 19-607 1996 $200.00

WOLLASTON, A. F. R.   Pygmies and Papuans. New York: 1912. Small 4to; (xvii), 352 pages, 54 black and white illustrations, 6 color illustrations, 2 map; brick red cloth boards, gilt title, upper spine chipped, light foxing, otherwise good+.   Antipodean 28-595 1996 $195.00

WOLLASTON, WILLIAM   The Religion of Nature Delineated. London: printed for J. and P. Knpaton, 1750. 7th edition; 8vo; contemporary calf, red morocco label, rubbed, some scuffing and chipping, lower joint starting, signature removed from upper outer corner of title, marginal browning, generally light.   James Cummins 14-221 1996 $125.00

WOLLE, F.   Desmids of the United States and List of American Pediastrums. Bethlehem: 1884. 1st edition; 8vo; pages 168; 53 colored plates and 800 illustrations, embossed stamp on corner of a plate; original cloth, wear to corners and ends of spine, marginal stain to title, pages tanned, ex-library.   Raymond M. Sutton VII-399 1996 $275.00

WOLLE, F.   Fresh Water Algae of the United States. Bethlehem: 1887. 8vo; 2 volumes, pages 364; 157 colored plates; original cloth, light wear to extremities, some white staining to lower edges of covers and pages, hinges starting, pages tanned. Rare.   Raymond M. Sutton VII-45 1996 $475.00

WOLLE, F.   Fresh Water Algae of the United States Exclusive of the Diatomaceae, Complemental to Desmids of the United States. Bethlehem: 1887. 8vo; text volume only; pages xix, (21-), 364; cloth.   Raymond M. Sutton VII-400 1996 $125.00

WOLLSTONECRAFT, MARY 1759-1797   A Vindication of the Rights of Woman. London: printed for J. Johnson, 1792. 1st edition; 8vo; contemporary drab paper boards, neatly rebacked to style, recent paper label; fine, uncut, very fresh condition; Early signature of G. Dyer, possibly the eccentric poet George Dyer. PMM 242; Windle 5; CBEL II 1255.   Ximenes 108-347 1996 $4,750.00

WOLLSTONECRAFT, MARY 1759-1797   A Vindication of the Rights of Woman... London: J. Johnson, 1792. 1st edition; 8vo; xix, (1), 452 pages, some occasional spotting and paper discolorations, 3 early ownership names partially erased on title; in handsome late 19th century crushed black morocco, fully gilt with raised bands, spine ornately gilt in compartments, gilt ruled borders to sides with corner fleurons, all edges gilt, inner gilt dentelles, joints skilfully repaired; good in handsome binding. Goldsmiths 15366; PMM 242; Einaudi 2631. Stammhammer I 263. John Drury 82-294 1996 £2,000.00

WOLSELEY, FRANCES   The Story of Marlborough. London: tol in 52 pictures colored and black and white by Caran d'Ache, pictorial cvoers, gilt, spine little rubbed, bookplate; fine; with 2 page ALS from Wolseley. Polyanthos 22-449 1996 $100.00

WOMAN In All Ages and In All Countries. Philadelphia: G. Barrie & Sons, 1907-08. Limited edition, one of 1000 numbered sets; 8vo; 10 volumes, printed on Japan vellum, with all plates in 2 states, including hand colored frontispieces; three quarter morocco over marbled boards, elaborate gilt decorated and lettered spines, all edges gilt;   Paulette Rose 16-343 1996 $1,000.00

THE WONDER Book of Freaks and Animals in the Barnum and Bailey Greatest Show on Earth. London: Walter Hill, n.d., c. 1898. Small 4to; illustrations, ads; color pictorial wrappers; very good. Toole Stott 1317. Dramatis Personae 37-35 1996 $200.00

THE WONDERS of Nature and Art; Being an Account of Whatever Is Most Curious and Remarkable Throughout the World... London: Newberry and Carnan, 1768. 2nd edition; 17.5cm; iii, 176 pages, plates; full calf, front cover loose but attached; very good. Rockland Books 38-253 1996 $150.00

WONG, K. CHIMIN   History of Chinese Medicine. Tientsin: Tientsin Press, 1932. Thick large 8vo; original blue cloth, spine bit sun faded. James Tait Goodrich K40-297 1997 $495.00

WONG-QUINCEY, J.   Chinese Hunter. 1939. illustrations; nice, slightly soiled covers; scarce.   David Grayling J95Biggame-621 1996 £120.00

WONG-QUINCEY, J.   Chinese Hunter. New York: 1939. illustrations; original yellow buckram; near fine.   David Grayling J95Biggame-623 1996 £130.00

WOOD, A. B.   Fifty Years of Yesterdays. Gering: 1945. 1st edition; 204 pages; frontispiece, photos, maps; cloth; V+. Herd 2550.   T. A. Swinford 49-1276 1996 $125.00

WOOD, ANN MARIA MICHELL   Verses and Imitations and Translations. N.P.: London: 1842. 1st edition; 8vo; original tan morocco, gilt, spine and inner dentelles, gilt, all edges gilt, trifle rubbed; very good. Ximenes 109-303 1996 $100.00

WOOD, ANTHONY   The History and Antiquities of the Colleges and Halls in the University of Oxford. Oxford: at the Clarendon Press, printed for the editor, 1786-90. 1st edition in English; large 4to; 2 volumes bound in 1; pages (16), 692 (recte 690); (4), 330, (55), with (8) page subscriber list; strongly bound in 19th century half morocco, very good to nice.   James Fenning 133-372 1996 £245.00

WOOD, C. A.   The Fundus Oculi of Birds Especially as Viewed by the Ophthalmoscope... Chicago: 1917. Royal 4to; pages 180, 61 colored plates, 145 text figures; cloth, slightly bumped; margins of one or two plates slightly damaged by adhesion but good; presentation copy from author.   Wheldon & Wesley 207-897 1996 £80.00

WOOD, C. A.   An Introduction to the Literature of Vertebrate Zoology. Hildesheim: 1974. 8vo; 662 pages; cloth.   Wheldon & Wesley 207-298 1996 £60.00

WOOD, EDWARD J.   Curiosities of Clocks and Watches from the Earliest Times. London: Richard Bentley, 1866. frontispiece and vignette to titlepage; new half balck morocco, gilt.   Petersfield Bookshop FH58-116 1996 £56.00

WOOD, ELLEN PRICE 1814-1887   East Lynne. London: Richard Bentley, 1861. 1st edition; small 8vo; 3 volumes; contemporary half calf, some slight foxing, each volume has contemporary inscription of "M. Ogilvie". Charles W. Traylen 117-220 1996 £400.00

WOOD, GEORGE   Introductory Lectures and Addresses on Medical Subjects. Philadelphia: 1859. 1st edition; 460 pages; recent quarter leather, waterstain affecting most leaves. Scarce.   W. Bruce Fye 71-2296 1996 $150.00

WOOD, J. MAXWELL   Smuggling in the Solway and Around the Galloway Sea-Board. Dumfries: J. Maxwell & Son, 1908. 8vo; pages (viii), 208, xvi, frontispiece, 12 plates, 11 tailpieces, 5 charts and route map; original pictorial cloth over bevelled boards, little rubbed and faded, few marks to upper fore edge.   R.F.G. Hollett 76-341 1996 £65.00

WOOD, JOHN   A Description of the Exchange of Bristol... Bath: printed by Thomas Boddeley for James leake, 1743. 8vo; title, 38 pages, 2 double page plates; later quarter calf, with long MS letter from two 'rough Masons' dated 1745.   Marlborough 162-100 1996 £1,500.00

WOOD, JOSEPHINE   Indian Costumes of Guatemala. Graz: Akademische Druck, 1966. 1st edition; 60 plates in color by Josephine Wood; as new, in original shipping carton.   Hermitage SP95-862 1996 $150.00

WOOD, NICHOLAS   A Practical Treatise on Rail-Roads, and Interior Communications in General... London: 1838. 3rd edition; thick 8vo; folding frontispiece, 12 folding plates, 4 folding tables, errata slip and 16 pages of publisher's ads; original embossed green cloth, gilt; presentation copy, with author's inscription on titlepage.   Charles W. Traylen 117-58 1996 £240.00

WOOD, SALLY S. K.   Ferdinand & Elmira; a Russian Story. Baltimore: Samuel Butler, 1804. 1st edition; 12mo; 311, (4) pages; contemporary calf, (needs rebinding), lacks front endpaper,, lower portion of title torn away, affecting portions of date and street adress of publisher; Wright I 2756; S&S 7795.   M & S Rare Books 60-267 1996 $950.00

WOOD, T. W.   Curiosities of Ornithology. London: 1871. 10 colored lithographic plates, text drawings; original cloth, spine faded, light rubbing, stitching slightly defective, needs light restoration.   David A.H. Grayling MY95Orn-86 1996 £75.00

WOOD, WILLIAM 1774-1857   General Conchology, or a Description of Shells arranged According to the Linnean System. London: 1835. Re-issue of the work of 1815, omitting the 'Vol. 1" from the titlepage; 8vo; pages iv, 7, lxi, 246 and 60 hand colored plates; new half morocco, gilt, gilt edges; very small stain on inner lower corner of few leaves of text and plates, otherwise nice.   Wheldon & Wesley 207-119 1996 £300.00

WOOD, WILLIAM 1774-1857   Illustrations of the Linnean Genera of Insects. London: 1821. 1st edition; 8vo; 2 volumes; 86 hand colored plates, few minor smudges; calf, bit worn, several sections starting. Maggs Bros. Ltd. 1190-182 1996 £285.00

WOOD, WILLIAM MAXWELL   Fankwei; or the San Jacinto in the Seas of India, China and Japan, New York: Harper & Bros., 1859. 1st edition; 8vo; viii, (9)-545, (2) pages ads; some occasional foxing; original blue cloth, rubbed with wear at corners and spine ends, still very good. David Mason 71-62 1996 $120.00

WOOD-MARTIN, W. G.   History of Sligo, County and Town (1603-1688). 1889. 1st edition; 8vo; (xvi), 323 pages; illustrations; cloth; very good.   C. P. Hyland 216-917 1996 £125.00

WOODHOUSE, L. G. O.   The Butterfly Fauna of Ceylon. Colombo: 1942. Original issue; 4to; pages xiv, (4), 153, (18), colored frontispiece and colored map, 14 plain and 36 colored plates; original blue cloth, bevelled edges, trifle used; rare; this copy stamped "Presentation Copy" inside front cover.   Wheldon & Wesley 207-1133 1996 £250.00

WOODHOUSE, ROBERT   An Elementary Treatise on Astronomy. Cambridge: 1812. 1st edition; 9 x 5.5 inches; 471 pages, with index; boards, ink inscrition, scattered foxing, spine poor, covers detached. John K. King 77-731 1996 $195.00

WOODHOUSE, ROBERT   The Principles of Analytical Calculation. Cambridge: at the University Press, 1803. 1st edition; 4to; (8), xxxiv, 219 pages; diagrams; contemporary tree calf, rebacked, raised bands, red morocco spine label; title browned at edges, text lightly browned, very good.   Edwin V. Glaser 121-325 1996 $475.00

WOODHOUSE, ROBERT   A Treatise on Astronomy. Cambridge: 1821/23. New edition; 9 x 6 inches; 2 volumes, 875 pages; cloth backed boards, covers worn and soiled, scattered foxing.   John K. King 77-731a 1996 $150.00

WOODRUFF, DOUGLAS   Plato's American Republic. London: Kegan Paul, Trench, Trubner & Co., Ltd., 1926. Reprint; original binding, top edge dusty, head and tail of spine and corners bumped, covers marked and dusty, cover edges worn, title label on spine browned, good; ownership signature of Ian Fleming.   Ulysses 39-694 1996 £125.00

WOODS, J. E.   Geological Observations in South Australia... London: 1862. 8vo; pages xviii, 404, frontispiece, map, 5 plates and 32 text figures; cloth, neatly rebacked and refixed.   Wheldon & Wesley 207-1384 1996 £140.00

WOODS, JOSEPH   Thoughts On the Slavery of the Negroes. London: printed and sold by James Philips, 1784. 1st edition; 8vo; half title, 32 pages; disbound. Sabin 105126; Ragatz p. 570. Goldsmith 12772; Anthony W. Laywood 109-166 1996 £300.00

WOODS, MARGARET L.   Songs. Oxford: Daniel Press, 1896. 1st edition; number 145 of 200 copies on Rives handmade paper; 12mo; pages 28 (4); original printed grey wrappers, exceptional copy.   Claude Cox 107-41 1996 £110.00

WOODS, ROBERT ARCHEY   English Social Movements. New York: Scribners, 1891. 1st edition; original cloth, fine but for slightly marked spine; inscribed by author.   Beasley Books 82-365 1996 $150.00

WOODSON, CARTER GODWIN   The Negro Heads of Families in the United States in 1830, Together with a Brief Treatment of the Free Negro. Washington: Association for the Study of Negro Life and History, 1925. 1st edition; slight wrinkle at top of spine, otherwise unusually fine and bright uncommon title to find in this condition.   Between the Covers 43-441 1996 $375.00

WOODSON, CARTER GODWIN   The Rural Negro. Washington: Association for the Study of Negro Life and History 1930. 1st edition; slight foxing to the titlepage, else usually fine and bright copy lacking the rare dust jacket.   Between the Covers 43-441 1996 $275.00

WOODSON, HENRY M.   Historical Genealogy of the Woodsons and Their Connections. Memphis: 1915. 1st edition; massive quarto; 760 pages; later library binding, worn, some pages loose, very scarce. Bookworm & Silverfish 280-278 1996 $150.00

WOODWARAD, DAVID   The Narrative of Capt. David Woodard and Four Seamen, Who Lost Their Ship While in a Boat at Sea and Surrendered Themselves Up to the Malays in the Island of Celebes... London: J. Johnson, 1805. 2nd edition; 8vo; pages xxxi, 234; portrait, 2 folding maps, 2 plates; new tan cloth, red morocco label, title and portrait washed, one map repaired. Hill I p. 331; Ferguson 399. Richard Adelson W94/95-182 1996 $325.00

WOODWARD, GEORGE E.   Woodward's National Architect. New York: American News Co., 1869. 4to; x, 47, (1) pages; Volume 1; publisher's cloth, minor occasional foxing, margins lightly browned, binding worn. Hitchcock 1436.   Bookpress 75-139 1996 $275.00

WOODWARD, JOSEPH   The Medical and Surgical History of the War of Rebellion 1861-65. The Three Surgical Volumes. Washington: 1870-83. 1st edition; volumes 1 and 2 are first printing; 3 volumes; original green cloth, inner hinges cracked, as usual in this heavy set, four inches of outer hinge of one volume cracked, otherwise very good to fine set. GM 2171.   W. Bruce Fye 71-365 1996 $1,500.00

WOODWARD, JOSEPH   The Medical and Surgical History of the War of Rebellion, 1861-65. Washington: 1870-88. 1st edition; 1st and 2nd printings; 6 volumes; original green cloth, some inner hinges cracked as usual, very good.   W. Bruce Fye 71-363 1996 $2,500.00

WOODWARD, LLEWELLYN   British Foreign Policy in the Second World War. London: 1970-76. Royal 8vo; 5 volumes; original cloth, dust jackets. Howes Bookshop 265-1522 1996 £125.00

WOODWARD, SAMUEL   Reports and Other Documents Relating to the State Lunatic Hospital at Worcester, Mass. Boston: 1837. 1st edition; 200 pages; cloth backed boards, ex-library, no marks on titlepage, outer hinges cracked with tears on backstrip, contents fine. Rare.   W. Bruce Fye 71-2305 1996 $350.00

WOOLF, LEONARD   The Hotel London: Hogarth Press, 1939. 1st edition; original binding, top edge dusty, head and tail of spine and corners slightly bumped, very good in slightly dusty dust jacket slightly darkened at spine and edges.   Ulysses 39-639 1996 £75.00

WOOLF, LEONARD   Socialism and Co-Operation. London: and Manchester: National Labour Press, Ltd., 1921. 1st edition; wrappers, top edge dusty, covers dusty and slightly marked, cover edges rubbed, spine darkened, very good.   Ulysses 39-638 1996 £65.00

WOOLF, VIRGINIA 1882-1941   Beau Brummell. New York: Rimington & Hooper, 1930. 1st edition thus; this copy is number 387 of 550 copies, signed in purple ink by Woolf; royal 4to; 18 pages; designed and embellished by W. A. Dwiggins; red cloth spine and gilt lettering, beige paper covered boards with paper label image of pink peacock pasted down to front panel, top edge gilt, green paper covered slipcase worn all around missing two inch piece at top edge, repeated image of peacock in blue on front panel of slipcase, overall near fine in worn slipcase. Kirkpatrick A15.   Hermitage SP95-687 1996 $575.00

WOOLF, VIRGINIA 1882-1941   Between the Acts. London: Hogarth Press, 1941. dust jacket designed by Vanessa Bell, free endpapers offset, dust jacket slightly sunned on spine and rubbed on rear panel, otherwise nice.   R. A. Gekoski 19-165 1996 £180.00

WOOLF, VIRGINIA 1882-1941   Between the Acts. New York: Harcourt Brace, n.d. 1941. 1st American edition; endpapers browned, covers slightly faded at top edge and spine, otherwise very good in slightly browned dust jacket with chips from corners and ends of spine. Kirkpatrick A26b.   Virgo Books 48-216 1996 £80.00

WOOLF, VIRGINIA 1882-1941   The Captain's Death Bed. London: Hogarth Press, 1950. 1st U.K. edition; offsetting to endpapers, edges of pages slightly spotted; inscription, top edge of covers slightly faded, otherwise very good in browned and slightly soiled dust jacket with chips from ends of spine and corners, price clipped, designed by Vanessa Bell.   Virgo Books 48-217 1996 £50.00

WOOLF, VIRGINIA 1882-1941   The Captain's Death Bed and Other Essays. New York: 1950. 1st edition; lower edges slightly rubbed, fine, price clipped dust jacket by Vanessa Bell.   Polyanthos 22-956 1996 $100.00

WOOLF, VIRGINIA 1882-1941   The Captain's Death Bed and Other Essays. London: Hogarth Press, 1950. 1st edition; extremities of spine slightly rubbed, fine in dust jacket by Vanessa Bell, spine sunned, top little chipped.   Polyanthos 22-955 1996 $100.00

WOOLF, VIRGINIA 1882-1941   The Common Reader. London: Hogarth Press, 1925. 1st edition; white paper covered boards, grey cloth spine, upper cover illustrated by Vanessa Bell, edges and covers slightly spotted, slight foxing internally, endpapers browned, else very good, lacks dust jacket. Kirkpatrick A8a.   Virgo Books 48-212 1996 £140.00

WOOLF, VIRGINIA 1882-1941   The Diaries of Virginia Woolf. London: The Hogarth Press, 1977-84. 1st edition; 8vo; 5 volumes; maroon cloth boards, gilt lettered spines, several unobtrusive tiny pencil annotations on rear endpapers of some volumes, otherwise fine in like dust jackets. Kirkpatrick A48, 52.   Paulette Rose 16-349 1996 $325.00

WOOLF, VIRGINIA 1882-1941   The Diary of Virginia Woolf. London: Hogarth Press, 1977/84. 1st edition; 5 volumes; all very good in dust jackets, volume 1 price clipped, very good set.   Virgo Books 48-230 1996 £150.00

WOOLF, VIRGINIA 1882-1941   The Essays of Virginia Woolf. London: Hogarth Press, 1986/87/88/94. 1st editions; 4 volumes; volume 1 has slight mark on f.e.p., otherwise fine in dust jackets.   Virgo Books 48-227 1996 £100.00

WOOLF, VIRGINIA 1882-1941   Granite and Rainbow. London: Hogarth Press, 1958. 1st edition; very good in lightly worn and darkened dust jacket, one short closed tear to rear panel.   Hermitage SP95-685 1996 $100.00

WOOLF, VIRGINIA 1882-1941   Granite and Rainbow. London: Hogarth Press, 1958. 1st edition; very nice in slightly soiled and browned dust jacket with chips from ends of spine and corners, one 2 inch closed tear from top edge; jacket designed by Vanessa Bell.   Virgo Books 48-219 1996 £50.00

WOOLF, VIRGINIA 1882-1941   Hours in a Library. New York: Harcourt Brace, 1958. 1st separate edition; foolscap 8vo; frontispiece, pages 24; original quarter pale blue cloth, black linen cloth sides with author's initials blindstamped and with title and her name also gilt lettered on front cover. Kirkpatrick A33.   Blackwell's B112-291 1996 £65.00

WOOLF, VIRGINIA 1882-1941   Hours in a Library. New York: Harcourt, 1958. 1st edition; privately printed for friends of the publisher as a New Year's greeting; near fine in worn glassine dust jacket.   Alice Robbins 15-351 1996 $100.00

WOOLF, VIRGINIA 1882-1941   The Letters. London: Hogarth Press, 1975-80. Proof copies; 6 volumes, 2 with dust jackets, volume 1 has rubbing at base of spine, otherwise very good set.   Virgo Books 48-222 1996 £300.00

WOOLF, VIRGINIA 1882-1941   The Letters of Virginia Woolf. London: Hogarth Press, 1975-80. 1st edition; 8vo; 6 volumes; blue cloth, several unobtrusive tiny pencil annotations on rear endpapers of some volumes, otherwise fine in like dust jackets; Kirkpatrick A44, 47, 51, 53-54. Paulette Rose 16-350 1996 $350.00

WOOLF, VIRGINIA 1882-1941   The Letters of Virginia Woolf. London: Hogarth Press, 1976/80. 1st editions; 6 volumes; name of previous owner on f.e.p.', otherwise very good in dust jackets which are slightly faded in places and corners of volume 1 nicked; very good.   Virgo Books 48-221 1996 £200.00

WOOLF, VIRGINIA 1882-1941   The Moment: and Other Essays. London: Hogarth Press, 1947. 1st edition; 8vo; dust jacket with cover illustration by Vanessa Bell, chipped at top of spine and upper cover, very good. Kirkpatrick A29a; NCBEL 4.474.   George J. Houle 68-156 1996 $150.00

WOOLF, VIRGINIA 1882-1941   On Being Ill. London: printed and published by Leonard & Virginia Woolf at Hogarth Press, 1930. 1st edition; 152/250 copies signed by author; crown 8vo; 35 pages; faint browning to first and final blank pages; original quarter white vellum, backstrip gilt lettered, blue-green linen sides, marbled endpapers, untrimmed, excellent. Kirkpatrick A14; Woolmer A Checklist of Hogarth Press 245.   Blackwell's   B112-293   1996 £750.00

WOOLF, VIRGINIA 1882-1941   Orlando - a Biography. London: Hogarth Press, 1928. 1st edition; original binding, top edge dusty, prleims, edges and endpapers spotted, covers slightly bowed, spine and cover edges faded, very good in nicked, rubbed and dusty, slightly creased dust jacket slightly darkened at spine and edges.   Ulysses 39-640 1996 £375.00

WOOLF, VIRGINIA 1882-1941   A Room of One's Own. London: Hogarth Press, 1929 1st edition; original binding, front free endpaper partially browned, rear endpaper browned at gutter, head of spine very slightly faded, near fine in chipped, dusty and slightly rubbed dust jacket darkened at spine and defective at head and tail of spine.   Ulysses 39-641 1996 £325.00

WOOLF, VIRGINIA 1882-1941   Virginia Woolf and Lytton Strachey: Letters. London: Hogarth Press/Chatto & Windus, 1956. 1st edition; very slight shelf wear, otherwise very good in very good dust jacket with only very slight wear at corners and ends of spine, dust jacket designed by Vanessa Bell.   Virgo Books   48-232   1996 £80.00

WOOLF, VIRGINIA 1882-1941   The Voyage Out. London: Duckworth & Co., 1915. 1st edition; very light rubbing to bottom edge, otherwise exceptionally clean copy with bright gilt and black stamping. Author's first book.   Hermitage   SP95-688   1996 $1,500.00

WOOLF, VIRGINIA 1882-1941   The Waves. London: Hogarth Press, 1931. 1st edition; first and last few pages and edges little spotted, ends of spine and corners slighty rubbed, otherwise very good in browned, slightly soiled and internally slightly stained dust jacket nicked and chipped at corners and ends of spine, with a 1 1/2 inch closed tear at top edge of spine, dust jacket designed by Vanessa Bell.   Virgo Books 48-213 1996 £350.00

WOOLF, VIRGINIA 1882-1941   A Writer's Diary. London: Hogarth Press, 1963. 1st edition; endpapers and fore-edges slightly spotted, otherwise very good in soiled and browned dust jacket slightly nicked at edges, dust jacket designed by Vanessa Bell.   Virgo Books 48-218 1996 £50.00

WOOLF, VIRGINIA 1882-1941   The Years. London: Hogarth Press, 1937. Excellent copy only in marginally browned dust jacket by Vanessa Bell.   R. A. Gekoski 19-164 1996 £350.00

WOOLF, VIRGINIA 1882-1941   The Years. London: Hogarth Press, 1937. 1st edition; pale jade green cloth with dust jacket by Vanessa Bell; bright and clean copy. Some light foxing to dust jacket, else very fine, modern owner's bookplate. Kirkpatrick A22.   Bromer Booksellers 87-279 1996 $475.00

WOOLF, VIRGINIA 1882-1941   The Years. London: Hogarth Press, 1937. 1st edition; pages slightly browned at edges, slight offsetting and spotting to endpapers, covers little soiled and rubbed, spine slightly faded and rubbed, otherwise very good in browned and spotted dust jacket with chips from corners and ends of spine, frayed at top edge, dust jacket designed by Vanessa Bell.   Virgo Books 48-215 1996 £200.00

WOOLF, VIRGINIA 1882-1941   The Years. London: Hogarth Press, 1937. 1st edition; crown 8vo; pages (iv), 469; original sea green cloth, backstrip gilt lettered, owner's name on front free endpaper, faint browning to free endpapers, excellent.   Blackwell's   B112-294   1996 £100.00

WOOLLEY, CHARLES LEONARD 1880-1960   The Development of Sumerian Art. New York: Charles Scribner, 1935. 4to; 140 pages; 72 illustrations; original cloth, tattered dust jacket, signature at flyleaf, corner bumped.   Archaeologia Luxor-2835   1996 $150.00

WOOLLEY, CHARLES LEONARD 1880-1960   The Old Babylonian Period. New York: Joint Expedition of the British Museum and the Museum of the Univ... 1976. Small folio; 278 pages; 44 figures, 129 plates; boards.   Archaeologia Luxor-2857   1996 $250.00

WOOLLEY, CHARLES LEONARD 1880-1960   The Royal Cemetery: a Report on the Predynastic and Saragonid Graves Excavated Between 1926 and 1931. New York: Joint Expedition of the British Museum and the Museum of the Univ... 1934. Small folio; 2 volumes, 604 pages, 81 figures, 273 plates; original printed wrappers; fine set.   Archaeologia Luxor-2842   1996 $650.00

WOOLLEY, CHARLES LEONARD 1880-1960   Ur Excavations. The Royal Cemetery. A Report on the Predynastic and Saragonid Graves Excavated Between 1926 and 1931. N.P.: Publications of the Joint Expedition of the British Museum... 1934. Heavy folio; 2 volumes, one volume of text, the other with 274 plates in color and black and white; cloth and boards, few smudges on spine of one volume, else fine.   Marilyn Braiterman 15-209   1996 $575.00

WOOLLEY, CHARLES LEONARD 1880-1960   The Ziggurat and its Surroundings. Oxford: British Museum and University of Pennsylvania, 1939. Small folio; xiv, 150 pages, 10 figures and 88 plates; original cloth backed printed boards, signature, corners rubbed.   Archaeologia Luxor-2856   1996 $650.00

WOOLMAN, JOHN 1720-1772   A Journal of the Life and Travels of John Woolman in the Service of the Gospel. Essex House Press, 1901. One of 250 copies; 6 1/4 x 4 3/4 inches; 2 p.l., 387, (1) pages, (1) leaf (colophon); frontispiece, decorative woodcut initials, device in colophon, printed in red and black; original stiff vellum, wallet edges, untrimmed; vellum bit smudged, but fine otehwise; armorial bookplate of Charles Wm. Swainston Goodger. Tomkinson p. 72.   Phillip J. Pirages   33-210 1996 $250.00

WOOLNOTH, WILLIAM   A Graphical Illustration of the Metropolitan Cathedral Church of Canterbury... London: T. Cadell and W. Davies, 1816. 1st edition; large 4to; engraved titlepage and 20 engraved plates by Woolnoth after drawings by T. Hastings; extra illustrated with the insertion of 43 hand illumianted coats-of-arms (attributed to C. R. Cotton) in margins alongside biographies of various bishops; full early 19th century olive calf, spine with raised bands, gilt and blindstamped compartments, gilt leonine device and gilt stamped red morocco label, covers with blindstamped decorative borders with gilt stamped floral devices at corners, gilt ruled inner dentelles, marbled edges and endpapers, dark blue silk bookmark, some rubbing, foxing to title, slight foxing or offsetting to some plates; very good; mid 19th century bookplate of C. R. Cotton, ex-libris H. R. Kavanagh.   George J. Houle 68-157 1996 $850.00

WOOLWARD, F. H.   The Genus Masevallia, Issued by the Marquess of Lothian chiefly from Plants in His Collection of Orchids at Newbattle Abbey. London: 1890-96. Limited to 250 copies; folio; colored map, 87 hand colored plates; half morocco, gilt, trifle worn; Good, clean copy. Wheldon & Wesley   207-120   1996 £6,000.00

WOOTEN, DUDLEY G.   A Comprehensive History of Texas: 1685-1897. Dallas: William G. Scarff, 1898. 1st edition; 2 volumes, 890, 851 pages; lacks large map called for, photos, text maps; newly bound in handsome gilt stamped red morocco with spine dentelles and marbled endpapers. Howes W673; Larned 3342. Rader 3737.   Maggie Lambeth 30-558 1996 $875.00

WORCESTER STATE HOSPITAL   Annual Report of the Trustees of...41st, 42nd, 44th, 60th, 61st, 65-69th, 77th, 78th, 84th, 85th. Boston: 1874-1918. 8vo; 14 volumes; printed wrappers, several issues lacking covers, generally very good.   John Gach 150-486 1996 $200.00

WORCESTER, A.   Small Hospitals. Establishment and Maintenance. New York: 1985. 114 pages; original binding, scarce.   W. Bruce Fye 71-2310   1996 $100.00

WORCESTER, EDWARD SOMERSET, 2ND MARQUIS OF 1601-1667   A Century of the Names and Scantlings of Such Inventions, as at Present I Can Call to Mind to Have Tried and Perfected... London: Printed in the Year 1663, reprinted & sold by T. Payne, 1746. 2nd edition; 12mo; no half title, with final ad, leaf D12, 19th century buckram, top edge gilt, others uncut; nice copy; bookplate of the Sixth Duke of Portland. Anthony W. Laywood   108-123   1996 £165.00

WORDS, Weather and Wolfmen: Conversations with Tony Hillerman. Gallup: Southwesterner Books, 1989. Of a total edition of 400 copies, this one of 10 copies designated as an Advance proof copy, and signed by author, artist and publisher; art by Ernest Franklin. Quarter leather and cloth in slipcase.   Between the Covers 42-492 1996 $650.00

WORDSWORTH, CHRISTOPHER   Greece: Pictorial, Descriptive and Historical. London: William S. Orr and Co., 1840. 1-356 pages text; steel engraved frontispiece, 24 full page steel engravings, 2 engraved maps, numerous woodcut illustrations and vignettes to text, some foxing to a few plates, including frontispiece; full green straight grain morocco, slightly scuffed and worn, gilt ruled border, gilt title to spine, raised bands to spine, all edges gilt, bound by Clarke of Bedford, hinges cracked, but still a good tight copy. Bookplate. Binder's ticket. Beeleigh Abbey BA/56-129 1996 £250.00

WORDSWORTH, DOROTHY   Journals of... London: Macmillan and Co., 1897. 1st edition; small 8vo; 2 volumes, frontispieces in each volume; maroon cloth, crown and foot of spine lightly bumped, otherwise fine and bright. NCBEL III 1310; Ungherini II 561.   Paulette Rose 16-352 1996 $275.00

WORDSWORTH, DOROTHY   Journals. London: Macmillan, 1938. 8vo; pages xvii, 544; frontispiece and title vignette; original cloth, gilt, spine rather faded; from the library of the late Norman Nicholson, Lake District poet and author, with his bookplates and signature, and numerous pencilled marginal lines, notes, etc.   R.F.G. Hollett & Son 78-282 1996 £65.00

WORDSWORTH, WILLIAM 1770-1850   A Guide through the District of the Lakes, in the North of England... Kendal: John Hudson, 1835. 5th edition; 8vo; pages xxiv, 140, (ii, ad leaf), engraved folding map; original publisher's patterned cloth, spine and edges rather faded, paper spine label, rubbed, few scattered spots, but very nice; inscribed "Eliza Jane Fletcher from A. Preston Esre, August 1839".   R.F.G. Hollett & Son 78-1395 1996 £175.00

WORDSWORTH, WILLIAM 1770-1850   A Guide through the District of the Lakes, in the North of England... Kendal: John Hudson, 1835. 5th edition; 8vo; pages xxiv, 140, (ii, ad leaf), engraved folding map (1 panel torn across, but complete); original publisher's pebble grained cloth gilt, paper spine label; nice. Bicknell 95.5.   R.F.G. Hollett & Son 78-1396 1996 £160.00

WORDSWORTH, WILLIAM 1770-1850   Lyrical Ballads, with Other Poems. London: for T. N. Longman and O. Rees, by Biggs & Co., Bristol, 1800. 2nd edition; small 8vo; pages xlvi, (ii) blank, 210, (v) notes; (iv), 227, (i) errata; contemporary tree calf, relaid and recently rebacked, with occasional trivial spot or mark, good copy. Tinker 2330; Cornell Wordsworth Coll. 6-11.   Simon Finch 24-261 1996 £3,100.00

WORDSWORTH, WILLIAM 1770-1850   Lyrical Ballads. London: Oxford, 1924. Reprint of 1798 volume; very good without dust jacket, with gift inscription presenting the book to poet Merrill Moore and then inscribed by Moore to Donald Davidson.   Ken Lopez 74-327 1996 $275.00

WORDSWORTH, WILLIAM 1770-1850   Ode on the Intimations of Immortality. London: Edward Arnold, 1903. Limited to 150 copies; octavo; 12 pages, printed entirely on vellum; hand colored wood engraved frontispiece by Walter Crane, full vellum over boards, blindstamped with rose logo and motto of the series "Soul is Form"; very fine. Ashbee p. 73;   Bromer Booksellers 87-64 1996 $650.00

WORDSWORTH, WILLIAM 1770-1850   Poems...Including Lyrical Ballads... London: printed for Longman, etc., 1815. 1st edition; 8vo; 2 volumes; frontispiece in each volume, some foxing, as always; leaves Q1-4 in volume 1, and 2A5 in volume 2 are cancels, as usual; later 19th century half green calf and marbled boards spines gilt, spines faded, minor rubbing; fine; Cornell Wordsworth Collection 30.   Ximenes 109-304 1996 $1,500.00

WORDSWORTH, WILLIAM 1770-1850   Poems...Including Lyrical Ballads, and the Miscellaneous Pieces of the Author. London: 1815. 1st collected edition; 8.5 x 5 inches; 2 volumes; frontispieces, 375, 440 pages, 3 pages with clean cuts (Q cancel) in volume 1, ends foxed, cover extremities well worn, else nice set; recently rebacked fancy diced calf.   John K. King 77-526 1996 $750.00

WORDSWORTH, WILLIAM 1770-1850   Poems, Chiefly of Early and Late Years, Including the Borderers, a Tragedy. London: Edward Moxon, 1842. 1st edition; 8vo; pages xi, (i) errata; 406 + ad leaf, also with additional series half title and titlepage; uncut in original publisher's cloth, very neatly rebacked with original spine laid down, lettered in gilt, new endpapers, but retaining original free endpapers; very good; presentation copy, inscribed by author, excellent association copy, also signed by George Taylor (1772-1851), and by his son Henry Taylor.   Simon Finch 24-262 1996 £1,600.00

WORDSWORTH, WILLIAM 1770-1850   Poems of William Wordsworth. London: George Routledge & Co., 1859. 1st edition thus; royal 8vo; pages (16), 388; original blue cloth, gilt, edges gilt, signed "A.W." by Leighton, Son & Hodge, with ticket, inside joints cracked, binding sound and otherwise nice.   James Fenning 133-373 1996 £55.00

WORDSWORTH, WILLIAM 1770-1850   The Complete Poetical Works of... Boston: Houghton Mifflin, 1911. Grasmere Edition; 8vo; 10 volumes; photogravures; half green morocco, spines unevenly sunned, few quite scuffed, internally fine.   Charles Agvent 4-1234 1996 $250.00

WORDSWORTH, WILLIAM 1770-1850   The Prelude. Doves Press, 1915. One of 10 copies on vellum (there were also 155 on paper); 9 1/4 x 6 1/2 inches; 301, (1) pages; extraordinarily fine russet morocco, elaborately and beautifully gilt by the Doves Bindery (signed '19 C-S 19' on rear turn-in), covers framed by multiple gilt rules and featuring lovely intricate cornerpieces consisting of a rose surrounded by criclets and four sprigs of five oak leaves, there corner decorations connected by tendrils (which support 8 additional, smaller sprigs of oak), front cover with titling and dates, spine densely gilt in compartments filled with the same decoration as used for the cornerpieces, turn-ins with four parallel gilt rules and with oak leaves and circlets at corners, vellum pastedowns and flyleaves, all edges gilt, binding identical to Tidcombe 795; front flyleaf with tiny ownership stamp of Ernst Kyriss. Only mostr tirivial imperfections, virtually pristine.   Phillip J. Pirages 33-190 1996 $15,000.00

WORDSWORTH, WILLIAM 1770-1850   The Prose Works. London: Edward Moxon, 1876. 1st edition; 8vo; 3 volumes, pages xxxviii, (1), 360; (4), 347; xii, 516 (2 ads), (2 blank); original green cloth, fine, bright, fresh and attractive copy.   James Fenning 133-374 1996 £350.00

WORDSWORTH, WILLIAM 1770-1850   Selected Poems. Snake River Press, 1987. One of 30 numbered copies; folio; printed in handset 14 pt. Garamond on Arches, 2 lithographs on a softer tinted sheet; 3 double page lithographs by Geoffrey Trenaman; half morocco; fine.   Bertram Rota 272-437 1996 £90.00

WORDSWORTH, WILLIAM 1770-1850   The Waggoner a Poem. London: printed by Strahan and Spottiswoode for Longman, etc., 1819. 1st edition; 8vo; full dark green morocco, gilt, spine and inner dentelles gilt, top edge gilt, by Wood, joints little rubbed; attractive copy; booklabel of Herschel V. Jones. Cornell Wordsworth Collection 49; Wise p. 22.   Ximenes 109-305 1996 $600.00

WORDSWORTH, WILLIAM 1770-1850   The White Doe of Rylstone; or the Fate of the Nortons. London: Longman, Hurst, Rees, Orme and Brown, 1815. 1st edition; 4to; (xii), 162 pages; frontispiece, half title; original boards, old reback, paper label, untrimmed, corners and edges worn, joints cracked but secure, internally clean, reasonable uncut copy.   Robert Clark 38-264 1996 £385.00

WORDSWORTH, WILLIAM 1770-1850   Yarrow Revisited, and Other Poems. London: printed for Longman, etc., and Edward Moxon, 1835. 1st edition; 12mo; original grey boards, rebacked, original spine and paper label preserved, spine bit scuffed, cloth folding case; nice; presentation copy, inscribed by author's wife Mary, to M. Elliott; Borowitz booklabel. Wing W3658; CBEL II 1832.   Ximenes 109-307 1996 $600.00

WORKERS COMMUNIST PARTY   The 4th National Convention of the Workers (Communist) Party of America. Chicago: Daily Worker Pub., 1925. 1st edition; 166 pages; original cloth, pencilling, very good, with owner's name.   Beasley Books 82-366 1996 $100.00

WORLIDGE, JOHN   Systema Agriculturae... London: T. Dring, 1675. 2nd edition; folio; 3 parts in one volume; pages 324, iv (misnumbered 134), vi; old calf, front cover almost separate; some marginal worming, nice clean copy. Armorial bookplate of Charles Viscount Bruce of Ampthill. Fussell pp. 68-70; Perkins 1947; McDonald pp. 116-121; Hunt 361.   Second Life Books 103-219 1996 $700.00

WORSHAM, WILLIAM JOHNSTON   The Old Nineteenth Tennessee Regiment, C.S.A. June, 1861. April 1865. Knoxville: Press of Paragon Print, 1902. 1st edition; 235 pages; plans, plates, original cloth, little soiled, spine darkened, rubbing to extremities, yet very good, scarce. Dornbusch II 1021. Howes W681; Nevins I 183; Smith p. 126.   McGowan Book Co. 65-108 1996 $450.00

WORTLEY, EMMELINE CHARLOTTE ELIZABETH MANNERS STUART, LADY 1806-1855   Travels in the United States, etc., During 1849 and 1850. New York: Harper, 1851. 1st U.S. edition; 8vo; 463 pages; original cloth, head of spine chipped, spine faded, otherwise very good;   David Mason 71-128 1996 $100.00

WOTTON, HENRY   Reliquiae Wottonianae: a Collection of Lives, Letters, Poems, with Characters of Sundry Personages. London: Marriott, Tyton, etc., 1672. 3rd edition; octavo; 582 pages; frontispiece; original calf, sometime rebacked, raised bands, gilt on red leather label, some wear but nice. Lowndes IV 1987-88. CBEL I 426.   Hartfield 48-L92 1996 $395.00

WOUK, HERMAN   The Hope. Boston: Little Brown, 1993. 1/300 copies, numbered and signed; fine in matching royal blue slipcase. Bev Chaney, Jr.   23-782   1996 $150.00

WOUK, HERMAN   Marjorie Moringstar. Garden City: Doubleday, 1955. 1st edition; fine in dust jacket with just a touch of rubbing, rarely found in this condition, beautiful copy.   Between the Covers   42-469   1996 $150.00

WRAGG, J.   Improved Flute Preceptor or the Whole Art of Playing the German Flute, Op 6. Clementi, Collard, Davids & Collard, 1818. 15th edition; 72 pages, no covers.   William Reeves   309-9708   1996 £123.00

WRANGHAM, FRANCIS   A Charge Delivered in July 1822, at Stokesley, Thirsk and Malton to the Clergy of the Archdeaconry of Cleveland; and Published at Their Particular Desire. York: ptd. by Thomas Wilson, sold by Messrs. Baldwin & Co. & Messrs... 1822. 1st edition; 8vo; (iv), 65 pages; disbound; Sadleir, Wrangham 54.   James Burmester   29-149   1996 £125.00

WRAXHALL, NATHANIEL WILLIAM, BART. 1751-1831   Historical Memoirs of My Own Time. London: T. Cadell and W. Davies, 1815. 1st edition; 8vo; 549, 583 pages, 2 volumes; 19th century half polished calf with raised bands and maroon morocco spine labels, couple of scuff marks, else very good.   Chapel Hill   94-122   1996 $150.00

WRIFFORD, ANSON   A New Plan of Writing Copies with Accompanying Explanations. Boston: W. Hooker, 1810. 1st edition; oblong 12mo; 6 engraved plates; side stitched into blue/grey wrappers with printed paper label; especially desirable in original condition. Book Block   32-76   1996 $575.00

WRIGHT, CHARLES   Colphons: Poems. Iowa City: Windhover Press, 1973. 1st edition; 6 1/2 x 8 3/4 inches; unpaginated (64); paper over boards, cloth spine, paper label on spine; mint; signed by author. William A. Graf   186-191   1996 $100.00

WRIGHT, CHARLES   Yard Journal. Richmond: Laurel Press, 1986. 1st edition; portfolio issue (also issued in bound format), one of 30 copies (the entire edition); signed by author and artist; 4to; printed on Rives; 7 colored intaglio etchings by David Freed; loose sheets in portfolio, slipcase; as new.   James S. Jaffe   34-691   1996 $750.00

WRIGHT, E. PERCEVAL   The Book of Trinity College Dublin, 1591-1891. Belfast: Marcus Ward, 1892. 4to; 70 illustrations in text; original green cloth, gilt, parchment spine, gilt, top edge gilt.   Charles W. Traylen   117-365   1996 £95.00

WRIGHT, FRANK LLOYD 1869-1959   An American Architecture. New York: Horizon Press, 1955. 1st edition; 269 pages; illustrations; very good in slightly worn and faded dust jacket.   Hermitage   SP95-750   1996 $150.00

WRIGHT, FRANK LLOYD 1869-1959   An Autobiography. London: Faber, 1945. 1st English edition; 8vo; 76 black and white photos; dust jacket, nicks, light soiling; very good.   George J. Houle   68-158   1996 $225.00

WRIGHT, FRANK LLOYD 1869-1959   Drawings for a Living Architecture. New York: Horizon Press, 1959. 1st edition; oblong folio; 255 pages; 200 illustrations; cloth, dust jacket tattered, else very good. Sweeney 1265.   The Bookpress   75-261   1996 $950.00

WRIGHT, FRANK LLOYD 1869-1959   The Life-Work of American Architect Frank Lloyd Wright... Santpoort: C. A. Mees, 1925. 1st edition; oblong small folio; original cloth designed by Wright, very good, slightly soiled, red leather spine label bit rubbed where it extends to covers but gilt lettering is bright. Sweeney 165.   Marilyn Braiterman   15-210   1996 $1,950.00

WRIGHT, FRANK LLOYD 1869-1959   The Natural House. New York: Horizon, 1954. 1st edition; slightly musty, but fairly nice copy, cloth still white and text fresh (aside from light offset on titlepage and darkening of endpapers), dust jacket has few very small chips and short tears, but at least very good; ownership signature dated Dec. 20, 1954. Sweeney 992. Magnum Opus   44-118   1996 $115.00

WRIGHT, FRANK LLOYD 1869-1959   Studies and Executed Buildings. Palos Park: Prairie School Press, 1975. 1st edition; oblong folio; (xxxii) pages, 60 plates; cloth, dust jacket chipped and rubbed, text, however, is very good.   The Bookpress   75-262   1996 $250.00

WRIGHT, FRANK LLOYD 1869-1959   V. C. Morris. N.P.: n.p., ca. 1948. 4to; buff wrappers with circular motif echoing the building described in gilt and red and lettered in red; fine. Sweeney 799.   Marilyn Braiterman   15-211   1996 $350.00

WRIGHT, G. N.   An Historical Guide to Ancient and Modern Dublin. 1821. 1st edition; 8vo; 442 pages; 16 plates, lacks plan and view of St. Patric's; some foxing, original boards, modern spine, else very good. C. P. Hyland   216-918   1996 £70.00

WRIGHT, HEZEKIAH HARTLEY   Desultory Reminiscences of a Tour through Germany, Switzerland and France. Boston: William D. Ticknor, 1838. 1st edition; tall 8vo; xx, 364 pages, new endpapers; recently rebound in medium blue cloth; fine.   David Mason   71-77   1996 $180.00

WRIGHT, J. E.   The Genus Tulostoma (Gasteromycetes) a World Monograph. London: 1987. Revised edition; 8vo; 338 pages; 50 plates and 156 text figures; wrpapers.   Wheldon & Wesley   207-1667   1996 £68.00

WRIGHT, J. M. F.   A Commentary on Newton's Principia. 1833. 8vl; 2 volumes; x, 458; cii, 415 pages; original calf, rubbed, blind round library stamp on each titlepage. Babson 130; Wallis 171.2.   David Bickersteth   133-213   1996 £140.00

WRIGHT, JOSEPH   English Dialect Dictionary. London: 1898. Thick 4to; 6 volumes; library binding of blue leather, rubbed.   Charles W. Traylen   117-221   1996 £125.00

WRIGHT, M.   Svenska Faglar Efter Naturen. Stockholm: 1927-29. Imperial 4to; 3 volumes; 364 colored plates; full mottled calf, gilt design on upper covers; nice, from the collection of Jan Coldewey.   Wheldon & Wesley   207-121   1996 £2,000.00

WRIGHT, MARTIN   Introduction to the Law of Tenures. London: 1768. 3rd edition; royal 8vo; pages iv, 133, 135-222 (3 blank), (7 appendix); contemporary calf, label, worn at corners, but strong, few openings little dusty, but large, very good copy on thick paper, with Hodder bookplate. James Fenning   133-375   1996 £95.00

WRIGHT, NATHANIEL H.   The Fall of Palmyra; and Other Poems. Middlebury: 1817. 1st edition; 24mo; 18, (3), (25)-143 pages; c calf backed boards. S&S 42979; McCorison 1977; Wegelin 1225.   M & S Rare Books   60-255   1996 $125.00

WRIGHT, R. G.   The Ducks of India. London: 1925. Royal 8vo; pages 231; 22 colored plates; original buckram, slightly faded.   Wheldon & Wesley   207-898   1996 $75.00

WRIGHT, RICHARD 1908-1960   The Color Curtain. A Report on the Bandung Conference. Cleveland: 1956. 1st edition; fine in dust jacket. Polyanthos   22-112   1996 $100.00

WRIGHT, RICHARD 1908-1960   Native Son. New York: Harper & Bros., 1940. 1st edition; fine in very good, internally tape repaired dust jacket that has moderate edgewear and few tiny chips.   Ken Lopez   74-486   1996 $950.00

WRIGHT, RICHARD 1908-1960   Native Son. New York: Harper, 1940. 1st edition; fine in near fine first issue dust jacket with few tears, tiny chip and slightly faded spine.   Captain's Bookshelf   38-225   1996 $450.00

WRIGHT, ROBERT M.   Dodge City, the Cowboy Capital. Wichita: Kansas, 1913. 1st edition; 344 pages; colored frontispiece, 40 illustrations; original pictorial green cloth, title in gilt on spine and stamped in black on front cover, very fine in slipcase. Graff 4756; Howes W706; Adams Six Guns 2456; Dobie p. 125.   Michael D. Heaston   23-368   1996 $350.00

WRIGHT, STEPHEN   Meditations in Green. New York: Scribner, 1983. Uncorrected proof copy; author's first book; fine copy in wrappers. Ken Lopez   74-488   1996 $150.00

WRIGHT, SYDENY FOWLER   Dream or the Simian Maid. Harrap, 1931. 1st edition; just about fine in very good/very good+ dust jacket, save for some slight sunning to d spine.   Aronovitz   57-1314   1996 $125.00

WRIGHT, SYDNEY FOWLER   Elfwin. Longmans, 1930. 1st American edition; near fine in just about very good dust jacket.   Aronovitz 57-1313   1996 $125.00

WRIGHT, SYDNEY FOWLER   The World Below. Chicago: Shasta, 1949. One of 500 copies of the limited edition, autographed, signed by author; fine in new dust jacket where fold crease was touched up and bled through to inside, superb copy.   Robert Gavora 61-357   1996 $200.00

WRIGHT, THOMAS   The Anglo-Latin Satirical Poets and Epigrammatists of the Twelfth Century. London: 1872. 8vo; 2 volumes, pages 995; original cloth.   Howes Bookshop 265-1588   1996 £60.00

WRIGHT, THOMAS   The Antiquities of the Town of Halifax in Yorkshire, Wherein Is Given an Account of the Town, Church and Twelve Chapels... Leeds: by James Lister, 1738. 2nd edition; large 12mo; title, pages vi, 207; contemporary panelled calf, worn, joints almost gone; Boyne 126.   Marlborough 162-101   1996 £175.00

WRIGHT, THOMAS   Le Keux's Memorials of Cambridge: A Series of Views of the Colleges, Halls and Public Buildings, Engraved by J. Le Keux... London: Tilt and Bogue, 1841. 1st edition; 4to; 2 volumes; engraved vignette titlepages, printed titlepages, 74 engraved plates, 77 vignettes in text and engraved plan; brown morocco with large gilt central cover ornament, other gilt decorations, gilt banded and decorated spine, clumsily mended horizontal tear on spine of one volume, joints rubbed but sound, some scattered marginal foxing, but desirable large paper set.   Marilyn Braiterman 15-132   1996 $500.00

WRIGHT, THOMAS   The Political Songs of England, from the Reign of John to that of Edward II. Edinburgh: privately printed by Unwin Bros., London and Chilworth, 1884. One of 75 large paper copies (there were also 275 small paper copies); 7 x 4 1/2 inches; printed as a large paper copy on good quality paper, partly in red; quite pleasing contemporary tawny morocco, covers with simple gilt rule border, flat spines with gilt titling and simple gilt ornaments, double gilt rule on turn-ins, patterned silvered endpapers, top edge gilt; covers with slight soiling and variation in color, just a hint of wear to joints and extremities, but bindings absolutely sound, generally well preserved, quite pretty; lightly mottled on flyleaves, otherwise lovely copy internally; contemporary gift inscription on front fly leaf in volume 1.   Phillip J. Pirages 33-518   1996 $250.00

WRIGHT, WILLARD HUNTINGTON 1888-1939   The Dragon Murder Case. New York: Scribners, 1933. 1st edition; 8vo; near fine in chipped and lightly used pictorial jacket in black with red dragon on front panel. Priscilla Juvelis 95/1-326   1996 $100.00

WRIGHT, WILLIAM 1829-1898   History of the Big Bonanza: an Authentic Account of the Discovering History and Working of the World Renowned Comstock Silver Lode of Nevada. Hartford: 1871. 1st edition; 569 pages; frontispiece, plates; decorated cloth, map endpapers, very good+. Very scarce. Graff 4157; Howes W710.   T. A. Swinford 49-291 1996 $250.00

WRIGHT, WILLIAM 1829-1898   Snow-Shoe Thompson. Los Angeles: Glen Dawson, 1954. Limited to 210 copies; 16mo; 64 pages; printed by L-D Allen Press on Arches paper, printed in red and black; 64 pages, linoleum block illustrations on title, printed in green; illustrated boards; fine, rare. Allen Press Bib. 14.   Kenneth Karmiole 1NS-6   1996 $400.00

WUNDERLICH, CAROL REINHOLD AUGUST   On the Temperature in Diseases. London: New Sydenham Society, 1871. 1st English edition; 8vo; new cloth, very good, clean copy. GM 2677 for first German ed. 1868.   James Tait Goodrich K40-301   1996 $125.00

WYATT, GEORGE   A Compendious Description of a Design for a Theatre; Made in Pursuance of an Order (and Now Published Under Permission) from the Committee of Subscrbers for Carrying into Effect the Project of Erecting a Third Theatre in the Metropolis. London: J. Taylor, 1812. 4to; pages 22, frontispiece, 4 folding plates, fold to one plate expertly repaired; original wrappers, restitched; scarce.   Sotheran PN32-201   1996 £495.00

WYATT, M. DIGBY   Fine Art, a Sketch of its History, Theory, Practice... London: Macmillan, 1870. 1st edition; 8vo; viii, 375 pages; publisher's cloth, text foxed, inscription in ink, both hinges internally cracked, light cover wear, occasional pencilling.   Bookpress 75-140 1996 $150.00

WYATVILLE, JEFFRY   Illustrations of Windsor Castle. London: published for the son in law and executors of Sir Jeffry Wyatville, 1841. Elephant folio; 2 volumes; 40 fine plates on India paper, (6 folding, one of which has a slight marginal repairs); few text illustrations; extra illustrated with 4 plates; contemporary half green morocco, slightly rubbed.   Charles W. Traylen 117-355 1 996 £1,200.00

WYCHERLEY, WILLIAM   The Plain Dealer. London: R. Bentley and M. Magnes, 1677. 3rd edition; 4to; green morocco backed marbled boards, some rubbing and chipping, stitch marks in inner margins, publisher's ads on recto of "The Persons" leaf, some browning and soiling, endpaper spotted, few short marginal tears or losses, else nice. The Robert Hoe-Herbert F. Griffiths copy with bookplates. Wing W 3751; Woodward & McManaway 1335; Pforzheimer 1102 (1st ed.).   James Cummins 14-222   1996 $250.00

WYCHERLEY, WILLIAM   The Complete Works. London: Nonesuch Press, 1924. 1st edition; number 496 of 900 sets (+75 specials); 4to; 4 volumes; original buckram backed boards, paper labels, one chipped, one backstrip, slightly darker brown (as issued), uncut and partly unopened; good set. Dreyfus 17.   Claude Cox 107-118   1996 £110.00

WYCHERLEY, WILLIAM   Works. Soho: Nonesuch Press, 1924. One of 900 numbered copies; crown 4to; printed on antique paper; 4 volumes; cloth backed boards, partly unopened, minor edgewear, foxing to endpapers, spine labels chipped, very good; prospectus.   Charles Agvent 4-1240   1996 $100.00

WYCOFF, EDITH   Bibliogaphical Contributions from the Lloyd Library. Numbers 1-14. 1911/14. Number 6 supplied in xerox facsimile; wrpapers, some wrappers torn and detached. Scarce.   W. Bruce Fye 71-1413 1996 $100.00

WYETH, ANDREW   Andrew Wyeth. Boston: Houghton Mifflin Co., 1968. 2nd edition; large oblong folio; 165 pages + index; beautiful reproductions; very good in dust jacket.   Parker Books of the West 30-187   1996 $195.00

WYLIE, ANDREW   Sectarianism Is Heresy, in Three Parts, in Which is Shewn, Its Nature, Evils and Remedy. Bloomington: 1840. 8vo; viii, 132 pages; plain paper wrappers, edge chipped and frayed along spine, light scattered foxing, very good. American Imprints 40-7157; Sabin 65667; Byrd & Peckham 894.   Andrew Cahan 47-91   1996 $125.00

WYLIE, ELINOR HOYT 1885-1928   The Orphan Angel. New York: Knopf, 1926. 1st edition; #42/190 large paper copies, signed by author; some light chipping to spine label, although new unused label in redy tipped to r.p.d.), some light wear to base spine, else very good+/near fine in worn slipcase.   Aronovitz 57-1316   1996 $165.00

WYLIE, ELINOR HOYT 1885-1928   The Orphan Angel. New York: Alfred A. Knopf, 1926. 1st edition; number 13 of 30 on Shidzuoka Japan vellum from an edition of 190 copies, signed by author; gilt stamped vellum, slight darkening to spine, otherwise fine in modern cloth slipcase. Hermitage SP95-691   1996 $350.00

WYLLIE, JOHN   Tumours of the Cerebellum. London: H. K. Lewis, 1908. 8vo; 109 pages; original boards, text bit browned, otherwise very good.   James Tait Goodrich K40-302   1996 $195.00

WYLLIE, ROBERT   A Letter Concerning the Union, with Sir George Mackenzie's Observations and Sir John Nisbet's Opinion Upon the Same Subject. N.P.: Edinbrugh? printed in the year, 1706. One of 2 recorded editions, both 32 pages, this one with catchword on p. 5 "mentals" (as opposed to "vern" in the other edition); small 8vo; disbound; very good, rare. McLeod 192; Kress 2517.   Ximenes 109-308   1996 $150.00

WYNDHAM, CHARLES   Sketches of Cockermouth Castle in the County of Cumberland. Carlisle: n.d., c. 1845. Small folio; pages 9, 9 tinted lithographs by C. Moody after Wyndham; original cloth gilt, boards panelled with decorative fillet and double rule in gilt, edges little darkened, handsomely rebacked in matching levant morocco, gilt, original decorative endpapers retained; scattered foxing, but very sound, rare. Presentation copy inscribed and dated 1849.   R.F.G. Hollett & Son 78-1400   1996 £375.00

WYNDHAM, JOHN   Consider Her Ways and Others. London: Michael Joseph, 1961. 1st edition; near fine in very good jacket with small chip at crown.   Ken Lopez 74-489   1996 $100.00

WYNDHAM, JOHN   The Day of the Triffids. New York: Doubleday, 1951. 1st edition; just about fine in bright dust jacket with some light shelf wear.   Aronovitz 57-1317   1996 $225.00

WYNDHAM, JOHN   Jizzle. London: Dobson, 1954. 1st edition; fine in dust jacket with tad of bumping at head of spine panel.   Robert Gavora 61-361   1996 $200.00

WYNDHAM, JOHN   The Kraken Wakes. M. Joseph, 1953. 1st edition; some light dust soil to cvoers, else very good/very good+ in like dust jacket.   Aronovitz 57-1318   1996 $110.00

WYNDHAM, JOHN   The Midwich Cuckoos. London: Michael Joseph, 1957. 1st edition; light, near transparent stain to bottom section of covers, else very good+ in near fine dust jacket with some light soil to rear dust jacket panel.   Aronovitz 57-1319   1996 $100.00

WYNDHAM, JOHN   Out of the Deeps. New York: Ballantine, 1953. 1st U.S. edition; fine in dust jacket, clean and bright copy.   Robert Gavora 61-362   1996 $225.00

WYNDHAM, JOHN   Re-Birth. New York: Ballantine, 1955. 1st edition; some browning to pages, else fine in dust jacket, with light bumping to spine panel ends and some foxing to edges.   Robert Gavora 61-363 1996 $325.00

WYNDHAM, JOHN   Trouble with Lichen. London: Michael Joseph, 1960. 1st edition; fine in price clipped dust jacket.   Robert Gavora 61-364   1996 $100.00

WYNDHAM, JOHN   Trouble with Lichen. New York: Walker, 1960. 1st U.S. hardcover edition; review slip laid in; very fine copy of a very difficult book in dust jacket.   Robert Gavora 61-365   1996 $100.00

WYNDHAM, MARGARET   Catalogue of the Collection of Greek and Roman Antiquities in the Possession of Lord Leconfield. London: Medici Society, 1915. Number 42 of 200 copies printed for private circulation; small 4to; frontispiece, xxiii, 142 pages, 86 plates; original printed wrappers, wrappers lightly soiled, boxed in half dark blue morocco case; very scarce.   Archaeologia Luxor-4187   1996 $450.00

WYNNE, JOHN HUDDLESTONE   Tales for Youth; in Thirty Poems; to Which are Annexed Historical Remarks and Moral Applications in Prose. London: Newbery, 1794. Octavo; x, 158 pages, plus (2) pages ads; 30 vignettes plus frontispiece by John Bewick; contemporary speckled calf, gilt ruling to spine and edges of binding, spine shows some areas of worm damage and front joint is cracked but firm; Hugo 73; Roscoe J391; Osborne p. 88.   Bromer Booksellers 90-85   1996 $750.00

WYSS, JOHANN DAVID 1743-1818   The Family Robinson Crusoe; or Journal of a Father Shipwrekced, with His Wife and Children, on an Uninhabited Island. London: printed for M. J. Godwin and Co., 1814-16. 1st English edition, 2nd issue of volume 1, 1st English edition of volume 2; 12mo; 2 volumes, xxiv, 346, (2); iv, 380 pages; frontispiece, 5 engraved plates after H. Corbould, engraved folding map; contemporary tree calf, each spine with 7 horizontal gilt rules, faint blindstamping of title on spine of volume 1, gilt volume number on spine of volume 2, binding somewhat rubbed and worn, occasional light foxing and browning, some offsetting from plates, small marginal tear to plate facing p. 135 on volume 1 repaired, small tears to two flyleaves repaired, thumb-size piece torn from leaf C7 in volume 2, with loss of few words; early ink ownership inscription on front flyleaf of each volume, very good, housed in dark blue morocco folding box; rare. Osborne Coll. p. 318.   Heritage Book Shop 196-240   1996 $4,000.00

WYSS, JOHANN DAVID 1743-1818   The Swiss Family Robinson. Ipswich: Limited Editions Club, 1963. Limited to 1500 copies; signed by artist; 4to; wood engravings in 1 and 2 colors by David Gentleman; imported grass cloth; fine in soiled slipcase; with Monthly Letter. Charles Agvent   4-1242   1996 $100.00

X Y Z

XENOPHON De Cyri Institutione, Libri Octo. Philadelphia: printed by John Watts for Ex Officina Classica Impensis Wm. Poyntell.. 1806. 1st American edition of Cyropaedia; 8vo; 547 pages; soiled and wormed; rubbed contemporary full roan leather, blue printed American ex-libris of Maris Gibson. Al 11903.   Family Album Tillers-670 1996 $400.00

XENOPHON Cyrupaedia: the Institution and Life of Cyrus, the First of that Name, King of the Persians. Newtown: Gregynog Press, 1936. One of 150 copies, printed and signed by Haberly; folio; decorated hand colored initials by Loyd Haberly; full grey morocco with emblematic center medallion and corner fleurons inlaid in red and green leather, gilt panelled spine, raised bands, gilt top by Gregynog Bindery.   Appelfeld Gallery 54-110 1996 $1,500.00

YABLON, G. A. A Bronte Bibliography. London: Hodgkins & Meckler, 1978. 1st edition; limited to 25 signed and numbered copies; 10 x 6 3/4 inches; xii, 151 pages; maroon calf backed maroon cloth, raised bands and gilt titling backstrip, top edge gilt; mint.   Ian Hodgkins 78-432 1996 £50.00

YADIN, YIGAEL The Art of Warfare in Biblical Lands in Light of Archaeological Study. New York: McGraw Hill, 1963. 4to; 2 volumes, 484 pages, 464 illustrations; half cloth, slipcase.   Archaeologia Luxor-2865 1996 $175.00

YADIN, YIGAEL The Finds from the Bar Kokhba period in the Cave of letters. Jerusalem: Israel Exploration Society, 1963. Folio; xix, 279 pages; 94 figures, 108 plates (12 in color), 21 tables; original cloth, dust jacket.   Archaeologia Luxor-2868 1996 $225.00

YADIN, YIGAEL Hazor I-IV. Jerusalem: Magnes P., 1958-89. Folio; 4 volumes in 4 parts; frontisportrait, frontispiece, xxiv, 160 pages, 184 plates; colored frontispiece, xxiv, 174 pages, 5 figures, 210 plates; frontisportrait, xxii, 362 pages, numerous figures, 46 plans; plate volume: xxvi, 365 plates; original cloth, lightly chipped dust jackets (jacket of volume 2 lacking and covers lightly soiled), corners lightly bumped.   Archaeologia Luxor-2871 1996 $850.00

YAHUDA, A. S. The Language of the Pentateuch in Its Relation to Egyptian. London: Oxford University Press, 1933. large 8vo; volume I (all published), xxxviii, 310 pages, 16*; original cloth, dust jacket.   Archaeologia Luxor-2872 1996 $175.00

YALE & TOWN MANUFACTURING CO. Album of Crane Designs. New York: 1887. 3.5 x 5 inches; 408, 89, (pl) pages.   Bookworm & Silverfish 276-228 1996 $125.00

YARRELL, WILLIAM A History of British Birds. London: 1837-43-45. 8vo; 3 volumes, 520 wood engravings, and supplement 53 pages, 11 wood engravings; half calf, gilt, trifle used; signature on titlepages of volumes 2 and 3, otherwise nice.   Wheldon & Wesley 207-900 1996 £100.00

YARRELL, WILLIAM A History of British Birds. London: 1843. 1st edition; 3 volumes, 520 fine woodcut engravings; contemporary calf, gilt, fine.   John Henly 27-34 1996 £120.00

YARRELL, WILLIAM A History of British Birds. London: 1871-75. 8vo; 4 volumes; 564 wood engravings; original cloth. Spines trifle worn; fromt he library of Arthur Lister, with ALS from his daughter, Gulielma.   Wheldon & Wesley 207-901 1996 £80.00

YARRELL, WILLIAM A History of British Fishes. London: 1836. 1st edition; 2 volumes; 383 woodcut illustrations and vignettes, cloth, rebacked preserving spines, occasional slight foxing.   John Henly 27-52 1996 £75.00

YARRELL, WILLIAM A History of British Fishes. London: John Van Voorst, 1856-59. 3rd edition; royal 8vo; 5 volumes; very fine contemporary green morocco, edges gilt, 5 raised bands, fully gilt spine, endpapers little foxed. Beautifully bound.   Charles W. Traylen 117-345 1996 £750.00

YATES, RICHARD William Styron's Life Down in Darkness: a Screenplay. Watertown: Ploughshares Books, 1985. 1st edition; fine in dust jacket, signed by Styron and Yates.   Captain's Bookshelf 38-206 1996 $150.00

YATES, ROBERT Secret Proceedings and Debates of the Convention Assembled at Philadelphia in the year 1787, for the Purpose of Forming the Constitution of the United States of America. Albany: printed by Websters and Skinners, 1821. 1st edition; front board detached, spine chipped, ex-library, working copy.   Meyer Boswell SL25-53 1996 $150.00

YATO, TAMOTSU Young Samurai. New York: Grove Press, 1967. 1st American edition; 4to; photos; cloth, dust jacket; fine.   James S. Jaffe 34-500 1996 $150.00

YEATMAN, J. P. The Early Genealogical History of the House of Arundel...Account of the Origin of the Families of Montgomery, Albini, Fitzalan and Howard...from the Conquest of Normand. London: 1882. Number 4 of a very limited edition; folio; frontispiece, few other illutrations; original morocco, trifle rubbed, one inner joint sprung.   Charles W. Traylen 117-383 1996 £120.00

YEATS, JACK BUTLER 1871-1957 La La Noo. Dublin: Cuala Press, 1943. One of 250 copies; fine in original tissue dust jacket; owner's bookplate.   R. A. Gekoski 19-166 1996 £220.00

YEATS, JACK BUTLER 1871-1957 La La Noo. Dublin: Cuala Press, 1943. 1st edition; limited to 250 copies, numbered on colophon and dust jacket; unopened, cloth backed boards, original glassine dust jacket with chips; very fine.   Bromer Booksellers 90-22 1996 $185.00

YEATS, JACK BUTLER 1871-1957 A Little Book of Drawings. Dublin: Cuala Press, 1971. One of 1000 copies; (of which 200 were hand colored); titlepage drawing, 1 headpiece and 9 full page drawings by artist, printed on Irish paper from original blocks, wrappers; near fine; from the library of James D. Hart.   Ulysses 39-663 1996 £55.00

YEATS, WILLIAM BUTLER 1865-1935 Celtic Twilight. London: Lawrence Bullen, 1893. Spine sunned, some foxing to front and rear free endpapers and pastedowns, but very good; inscribed by Andrew Lang.   R. A. Gekoski 19-167 1996 £450.00

YEATS, WILLIAM BUTLER 1865-1935 Four Plays for Dancers. London: Macmillan, 1921. 1st edition; 8vo; illustrations by Edmund Dulac; pictorial boards, offsetting to endpapers, dust jacket spine chipped at head and heel, rear portion neatly separated but looks handsome in protective mylar cover, scarce in dust jacket; "Presentation copy" blindstamped on titlepage.   Charles Agvent 4-1245 1996 $300.00

YEATS, WILLIAM BUTLER 1865-1935 Full Moon in March. London: Macmillan, 1935. 1st edition; 8vo; original binding, corners bumped, small chip on dust jacket spine; Wade 182.   Charles Agvent 4-1246 1996 $175.00

YEATS, WILLIAM BUTLER 1865-1935 The Hour-Glass, Catahleen ni Houlihan, the Pot of Broth... London: A. H. Bullen, 1904. 1st edition; cloth backed boards, top edge dusty, head and tail of spine and corners bumped, covers slightly marked and dusty, cover edges rubbed, prelims, edges and endpaeprs spotted; very good. Presentation copy from author for John Masefield.   Ulysses 39-664 1996 £2,000.00

YEATS, WILLIAM BUTLER 1865-1935 The King's Threshold. New York: printed for private circulation, 1904. 1st edition; limited to 100 copies; octavo; 58 pages; plain boards, original glassine dust jacket, slipcasae; extremely fine. Wade 55.   Bromer Booksellers 90-247 1996 $3,000.00

YEATS, WILLIAM BUTLER 1865-1935 The Lake of Innesfree. London: printed by John Henry Nash, 1924. 1st separate printing; folio; 6 leaves, including blanks, with text finely printed in red and black and facsimile of poem in Yeats' hand tipped in, all within beautiful formal decorated green borders; green cloth backed marbled boards, bottom front corners stained; fine internally. Wade 143.   Blue Mountain SP95-125 1996 $175.00

YEATS, WILLIAM BUTLER 1865-1935   The Land of the Heart's Desire. London: Fisher Unwin, 1912. 7th edition; author's presentation copy inscribed for Nugent Monck.   R. A. Gekoski 19-170 1996 £750.00

YEATS, WILLIAM BUTLER 1865-1935   The Player Queen. London: Macmillan, 1922. 1st separate appearance; very light overall dust soiling, otherwise fine in wrappers.   Ken Lopez 74-490 1996 $125.00

YEATS, WILLIAM BUTLER 1865-1935   Poems. London: Fisher Unwin, 1904. Elaborate gilt stamped cover designs by Althea Gyles, little light scattered foxing to prelims, spine very slightly faded, but excellent.   R. A. Gekoski 19-169 1996 £175.00

YEATS, WILLIAM BUTLER 1865-1935   Poems of Place. Market Drayton: Tern Press, March, 1991. One of 10 specials thus in edition of 175 copies, signed by Nicholas Parry; 10 x 6.5 inches; 67 pages; printed on Arches but with 12 original watercolor paintings instead of etchings by Nicholas Parry; drop back box; fine.   Joshua Heller 21-247 1996 $500.00

YEATS, WILLIAM BUTLER 1865-1935   Poems of Place. Market Drayton: Tern Press, March, 1991. One of 165 copies thus in total edition of 175 copies, signed by Nicholas and Mary Parry; 10 x 6.5 inches; 67 pages; 12 etching relief prints in black, printed in 12 pt. Bell, set by Bill Hughes in Monotype and printed on Arches; bound in buff linen and printed paper with colored relief etched print; fine.   Joshua Heller 21-246 1996 $125.00

YEATS, WILLIAM BUTLER 1865-1935   The Secret Rose. London: Lawrence & Bullen, 1897. frontispiece and 6 other illustrations by Jack B. Yeats; blue cloth with gold stamped cover designs by Althea Gyles; offsetting to front and rear pastedowns and free endpapers, corners bumped, otherwise excellent copy, gilt particularly fresh and bright.   R. A. Gekoski 19-168 1996 £500.00

YEATS, WILLIAM BUTLER 1865-1935   Stories of Red Hanrahan. Dundrum: the Dun Emer Press, 1904. 1st edition; one of 500 copies; 8vo; pages (vi), 56, (1), printed in red and black; woodcut by Robert Gregory; original quarter linen, blue paper boards, printed label on upper cover, but without that on spine, uncut and unopened; excellent copy. Wade 59.   Simon Finch 24-263 1996 £1,750.00

YEATS, WILLIAM BUTLER 1865-1935   Tables of the Law; and The Adoration of the Magi. Stratford-upon-Avon: Shakespeare Head Press, 1914. 1st edition thus, one of 510 numbered copies; 8vo; original binding, very good.   Charles Agvent 4-1251 1996 $125.00

YEATS, WILLIAM BUTLER 1865-1935   Three Things. London: Faber & Faber, 1929. One of 500 numbered copies, signed by author; drawings by Gilbert Spencer; some light soiling and rubbing to boards at extremities, but very good.   R. A. Gekoski 19-171 1996 £225.00

YEATS, WILLIAM BUTLER 1865-1935   The Tower. London: Macmillan, 1928. 1st edition; small 8vo; decorated cloth, dust jacket; fine in jacket which is chipped at head of spine and somewhat split along front fold at top and bottom.   James S. Jaffe 34-692 1996 $450.00

YEIVIN, S.   The Israelite Conquest of Canaan. Istanbul: Nederlands Historisch-Archaeologisch Inst., 1971. 8vo; xviii, 302 pages, 12 figures (9 in back pocket as issued), 2 plates; wrappers; inscribed presentation copy in Hebrew.   Archaeologia Luxor-2875 1996 $150.00

YELVERTON, HENRY   The Reports of... In the Savoy: printed by E. and R. Nutt, 1735. 1st edition in English; folio; pages (14), 228, (24), with licence leaf; contemporary calf, label, gilt, slightest of wear at headbands and sides lightly scratched, otherwise fine, bright, crisp copy. James Fenning 133-376 1996 £125.00

YERBY, FRANK   Benton's Row. New York: Dial, 1954. 1st edition; slight tanning to pastedown, else fine in very good dust jacket with somewhat jagged tear on rear panel, very warm full page inscription to author's literary agent.   Between the Covers 43-219 1996 $250.00

YERBY, FRANK   The Foxes of Harrow. New York: Dial, 1946. 9th printing, in the year of publication; cheap paper browned, otherwise near fine in internally repaired, very good plus dust jacket with several small chips. Nicely inscribed by author in year of publication, additionally this copy inscribed on dedication page by dedicatee, Murial Fuller; Between the Covers 43-217 1996 $185.00

YGLESIAS, JOSE   One German Dead. Leeds: Eremite Press, 1988. 1st edition; one of 115 copies, signed by artist and author; page size 9 3/4 x 5 5/8 inches; one original etched portrait of author by Baskin; blue paste paper over boards by Gray Parrot.   Priscilla Juvelis 95/1-90 1996 $350.00

YOM-TOV, Y   The Zoogeography of Israel... The Hague: 1988. 8vo; 560 pages; cloth.   Wheldon & Wesley 207-468 1996 £160.00

YONGE, CHARLOTTE MARY 1823-1901   Heartsease; or the Brother's Wife. New York: D. Appleton, 1871. 8vo; 2 volumes, (303, 8 ads); 315, 8 ads); frontispiece in each volume; original green ripple cloth with floral design on front and back, gilt decorated and lettered spines;   Paulette Rose 16-353 1996 $125.00

YONGE, CHARLOTTE MARY 1823-1901   History of Christian Names. London: Macmillan, 1878. 1st edition; 2 volumes; 2 pages as volume 1; original maroon cloth, spines slightly faded.   Jarndyce 103-363 1996 £80.00

YONGE, CHARLOTTE MARY 1823-1901   Magnum Bonum or Mother Carey's Brood. London: Macmillan and Co., 1879. 1st edition; 3 volumes, no half titles called for, ad leaf at end of volume 3; original green cloth, blocked in gilt and blind, lettered gilt on spines, ink inscription top margin of titlepages of volumes 2 and 3, light red ink stain in upper margin of page (iii) (contents list) in volume 1.   David Bickersteth 133-175 1996 £55.00

YORK, EDWARD, 2ND DUKE OF   The Master of Game by Edward, Second Duke of York. The Oldest English Book on Hunting. London: 1904. Limited to 600 numbered copies; folio; frontispiece, 51 plates; suede, gilt inner dentelles on top edge, spotting throughout, not affecting plates, slight marks on some plates only on margins, mildly shaken; booklabel of Lord Kenyon.   Maggs Bros. Ltd. 1191-136 1996 £125.00

YOSHIDA, KOGORO   Tanrokubon, Rare Books of Seventeenth Century Japan. Tokyo: Kodansha International, 1984. 1st edition; small 4to; 228 pages; cloth, slipcase; fine.   The Bookpress 75-371 1996 $110.00

YOST, KARL   A Bibliography of the Published Works of Charles M. Russell. New York: Dodd, Mead and Co., 1971. 1st edition; 4to; linen backed, leatherette gilt, fine in like dust jacket.   Glenn Books 36-285 1996 $125.00

YOUNG & MARTEN   Illustrated General Catalogue... London: Caledonian Works, n.d., ca. 1897. 1st edition; 4to; (ii), 432 pages; xvi, (i), 414 pages; 2 volumes; 42 chromolithographic plates; publisher's cloth; bookplates removed, titlepages are marked, back hinge of volume 2 internally cracked, some cover wear.   Bookpress 75-141 1996 $1,500.00

YOUNG, ANDREW   Crystal and Flint: Poems. Snake River Press, 1991 One of only 30 numbered copies; folio; printed in handset Walbaum on Fabriano; 1 full and 2 double page colored lithographs by Geoffrey Trenaman; half morocco; fine.   Bertram Rota 272-438 1996 £125.00

YOUNG, ANDREW   The Natural History and Habits of the Salmon, &c London: 1854. Pasted in rear is 3 page prospectus (1840) for Jardine's Salmonidae; original cloth, spine faded, attractive copy.   David A.H. Grayling 3/95-550 1996 £120.00

YOUNG, ARTHUR 1741-1820   The Farmer's Calendar. London: Richard Phillips, 1809. 8th edition; 8vo; xi, (i), 663 pages; near contemporary half calf, marbled boards; very good.   Ken Spelman 30-117 1996 £85.00

YOUNG, ARTHUR 1741-1820   The Farmer's Guide in Hiring and Stocking Farms. London: printed for W. Strahan, 1770. 8vo; 2 volumes, (20, ii, viii, 458, (2) pages ads; (2), ii, 500 pages, 14 folding plates; contemporary calf, expertly rebacked with new gilt labels, some occasional foxing.   Ken Spelman 30-115 1996 £280.00

YOUNG, ARTHUR 1741-1820   The Farmer's Guide in Hiring and Stocking Farms. Dublin: Exshaw et al, 1771. 1st Dublin edition; 8vo; 2 volumes, pages 336, 380; 4 figures, 8 engraved plates; contemporary calf, hinge little tender, very good, Fussell pl 157; Macdonald p. 212. Second Life Books 103-223 1996 $425.00

YOUNG, ARTHUR 1741-1820   The Farmer's Letters to the People of England... London: printed for W. Nicoll, 1768. 2nd edition; 8vo; perforation stamp on title, library accession number on lower blank margin of A2; modern half calf, label.   Anthony W. Laywood 108-145 1996 £145.00

YOUNG, ARTHUR 1741-1820   General View of the Agriculture of the County of Essex. London: ptd. for Richard Phillips, Bridge Street, Blackfriars... 1807. 8vo; 2 volumes; (vii)-x), (xi-xv), errata leaf, 1-400 pages, 2, 2, catalog; frontispiece to volume 1, 58 plates, 3 illustrations, all plates bound to rear of both volumes rather than placed in text per binder's directions, plates as called for, plus duplicate of plate 26 not called for, plates numbered I-LVIII but plates XLI, XLII and LIII are repeats of earlier plates and so do not reappear; some offsetting to title of volume 1, partial loss to title of volume 2, not affecting text, some sporadic light foxing, hinges cracked, lower board of volume 2 worn through at edges; quarter cloth and paper backed boards, remains of original paper labels to spines, corners bumped and worn, volume 1 joints rubbed and worn through at head and foot of spine.   Beeleigh Abbey BA56-31 1996 £200.00

YOUNG, ARTHUR 1741-1820   General View of the Agriculture of the County of Sussex... London: 1793. 4to; 97 pages, folding hand colored map, 3 plates, 2 hand colored; morocco backed boards; the two colored plates of ploughs cropped with some loss of text.   John Henly 27-375 1996 £110.00

YOUNG, ARTHUR 1741-1820   A Six Weeks Tour, through the Southern Counties of England and Wales. Salisbury: printed for B. Collins; J. Balfour at Edinburgh & W. Strahan... 1769. 2nd edition; 8vo; perforation stamp on title, library accession number on lower blank margin of ad leaf follwing the title; folding engraved plate; new half calf, label, nice, clean copy.   Anthony W. Laywood 108-144 1996 £150.00

YOUNG, ARTHUR 1741-1820   A Tour in Ireland in 1776 and 1779. 1892. 8vo; 2 volumes; cloth, ex-library, but very good.   C. P. Hyland 216-935 1996 £85.00

YOUNG, ARTHUR 1741-1820   Travels During the Years 1787, 1788, 1789; Undertaken More Particularly with a View of Ascertaining the Cultivation, Wealth, Resources, and Prosperity of the Kingdom of France. London: for W. Richardson, 1794. 2nd edition; large 4to; 2 volumes; 3 larage folding maps; three quarter blue morocco, wear at extremities, richly gilt panelled spines, raised bands, gilt tops, apart from occasional foxing; good, sound copy.   Appelfeld Gallery 54-99 1996 $400.00

YOUNG, BETTY LOU   Rustic Canyon and the Story of the Uplifters. Santa Monica: Casa Vieja Press, 1975. 11 x 8 3/8 inches; (x), 160, (6) pages; photographic illustrations; grey cloth in dust jacket with 1 short tear, book bowed.   Dawson's Books Shop 528-253 1996 $125.00

YOUNG, DANIEL   Young's Demonstrative Translation of Scientific Secrets; or a Collection of Above 500 Useful Receipts on a Variety of Subjects. Toronto: printed by Rowsell & Ellis, 1861. 12mo; pages iv, (5), 300; original blindstamped cloth, soiled and shaken, text fine. TPL 5994.   Hugh Anson-Cartwright 87-464 1996 $150.00

YOUNG, EDWARD 1683-1765   The Brothers, a Tragedy. London: John Bell, 1777. Small 8vo; pages 63; fine engraved frontispiece; nice recent marbled paper binding, paper labels, very good, uncommon. CBEL II 292.   Hartfield 48-L93 1996 $175.00

YOUNG, EDWARD 1683-1765   The Centaur Not Fabulous. London: printed for A. Millar and R. and J. Dodsley, 1755. 2nd edition; 8vo; frontispiece, xvi, 384 pages; original calf, rebacked, original endpapers preserved.   David Bickersteth 133-91 1996 £80.00

YOUNG, EDWARD 1683-1765   The Complaint; or Night-Thoughts. Newburyport: printed by John Mycall for the Proprietor of the Boston Book Store, c.1789. 12mo; 408 pages; foxed and browned, new old style half calf. Scarce. Evans 23098; NCBEL 2.494 (gives date as 1790).   K Books 442-516 1996 £80.00

YOUNG, ERNEST A.   Walt Wheeler, the Scout Detective. New York: J. S. Ogilvie, 1884. 1st edition; 12mo; 124 pages plus ads; original cloth; not in Wright.   M & S Rare Books 60-268 1996 $150.00

YOUNG, FRANCIS BRETT   Dr. Bradley Remembers. London: William Heinemann, 1938. 1st edition; original binding, top edge dusty, head and tail of spine and corners slightly bumped, covers dusty and slightly marked, edges slightly browned, good; ownership signature of Ian Fleming.   Ulysses 39-695 1996 £125.00

YOUNG, FRANCIS BRETT   Woodsmoke. Severn Edition, 1939. 1st edition; trifle shaken in binding, otherwise very good; inscribed by author to David Lloyd George who has annotated the flyleaf with what appears to be his initials and date 30.7.39.   Words Etcetera 94-1340 1996 £55.00

YOUNG, GEORGE   A Treatise on Opium, Founded on Practical Observations. London: printed for A. Millar, 1753. 1st edition; 8vo; xv, (i), 182 pages, ad leaf; original calf, rebacked, original spine label and original endpapers preserved.   David Bickersteth 133-222 1996 £330.00

YOUNG, JOHN   The Letters of Agricola on the Principles of Vegetation and Tillage, Written for Nova Scotia... Halifax: printed by Holland and Co., 1822. 8vo; pages xvi, 17-462, (10) index; uncut, original boards, paper label at spine, some foxing, boards soiled, spine worn with most of label missing; very good, scarce. TPL 1271.   Hugh Anson-Cartwright 87-465 19964 $450.00

YOUNG, JOHN   Letters of Agricola on the Principles of Vegetation and Tillage, Written for Nova Scotia... Halifax: printed by Holland & Co., 1822. 1st edition; 8vo; 402, (10) index pages; original boards, front hinge repaired, edges rubbed, little soiled, printed paper label; some foxing and spotting, TPL 1271; Sabin 106083; Gagnon I 3739.   Howard S. Mott 227-155 1996 $400.00

YOUNG, JOHN P.   San Francisco: a History of the Pacific Coast Metropolis. San Francisco: S. J. Clarke Publishing Co., 1912. Number 262 of a limited edition (number unspecified); signed and dated by author; 4to; 2 volumes, xxx, 473; 474-969 pages; frontispiece, 150 monochrome plates; publisher's dark green half morocco gilt, spines gilt in five compartments, top edge gilt, others uncut, extremities rubbed.   Thomas Thorp 489-326 1996 £150.00

YOUNG, MARGUERITE   Miss MacIntosh, My Darling. New York: Scribner's, 1965. 1st U.S. edition; near fine in price clipped dust jacket, signed by author.   Lame Duck Books 19-613 1996 $250.00

YOUNG, MARY JULIA   Voltairiana. London: printed by D. N. Shury, for J. F. Hughes, 1805. 1st edition; small 8vo; 4 volumes; contemporary half red morocco, gilt, spine gilt, slight rubbing, spines trifle dark; very good set, uncommon.   Ximenes 108-349 1996 $350.00

YOUNG, OTIS E.   The West of Philip St. George Cooke 1809-1895. Glendale: 1955. 1st edition; 393 pages, frontispiece, plates, maps; cloth, very good+.   T. A. Swinford 49-1300 1996 $125.00

YOUNG, ROLAND   Not for Children: Pictures and Verse. Garden City: Doubleday, 1930. 1st edition; small folio; illustrations, color endpapers and jacket design by Young; black cloth over yellow pictorial boards, some rubbing at extremities; very good; signed and inscribed by author. Bruccoli C23.   George J. Houle 68-159 1996 $175.00

YOUNG, THOMAS   Outlines of Experiments and Inquiries Respecting sound and Light in a Letter to Edward Whitaker Gray, M.D. London: W. Bulmer, 1800. 1st edition; 8vo; 47 pages, 5 folding plates; modern stiff wrappers; fine; rare. PMM 259; GM 1488 and Dibner 152; Blake p. 497.   Edwin V. Glaser 121-326 1996 $950.00

YOUNG, WILLIAM   Picturesque Architectural Studies and Practical Designs... London: E. & F. N. Spon, 1872. 1st edition; 4to; viii, 37, (1) pages, 50 plates; publisher's gilt cloth; front hinge internally cracked, light foxing on early leaves and margins of illustrations, slight wear along edges and joints, else very good.   Bookpress 75-142 1996 $475.00

YOUNG, WILLIAM 1749-1815   A Journal of a Summer's Excursion by the Road of Montescasino to Naples, and from Thence Over All the Southern Parts of Italy, Sicily and Malta in the Year 1772. London: ca. 1774. 8vo; (iv), 141 pages; contemporary calf, spine gilt, little worn; signed by author with corrections in his hand. Pine Coffin 772.   Marlborough 162-264 1996 £1,400.00

YOUNGHUSBAND, FRANCIS EDWARD   The Heart of a Continent. London: John Murray, 1896. 1st edition; royal 8vo; (xx), (410) pages; plates, maps, folding map in pocket; original decorative cloth, gilt, expertly refurbished and restored, endpapers rejointed, some minor wear, few marks, small repair to one map, but good.   Ash Rare Books Zenzybyr-100 1996 £245.00

Z., A.   An Epistle to I. G. the author of a Pamphlet Entitled, "Some Account of the Free Grammar School of Highgate...With Remarks on the Origin and Nature of the Recent Inquiry Into the Management of that Institution." London: printed by C. Baldwin, 1823. 1st edition; 8vo; 68 pages; folding plan; uncut in original plain blue wrappers, backstrip worn.   James Burmester 29-73 1996 £65.00

ZADKIEL   The Handbook of Astrology: Containing the Doctrine of Nativities. In a Form Free of All Mystery...and Learn His Own Natural Character and Proper Destiny. Volume II. London: 1863. xii, 75 pages, 33 pages; decorated cover, worn, near very good.   Middle Earth 77-431 1996 $145.00

ZADOKS-JOSEPHUS JITTA, A. H.   Roman Bronze Statuettes fromt he Netherlands I-II. Groningen: J. B. Wolters, 1967-69. 4to; 2 volumes, xxviii, 356 pages; profusely illustrated; original cloth, dust jacket. Archaeologia Luxor-4193 1996 $150.00

ZAEHNSDORF, JOSEPH W.   The Art of Bookbinding. London: George Bell & Sons, 1880. 1st edition; 8vo; contemporary full rose polished calf, covers gilt in 4 compartments, central lozenge, spine and inner dentelles gilt, top edge gilt, by Zaehnsdorf; traces of rubbing; Fine; booklabel of Charles L. Dana, later bookplate of Nell Rose Wheeler and Charles Van Lise Wheeler.   Ximenes 108-350 1996 $500.00

ZANGWILL, ISRAEL   Dreamers of the Ghetto. London: Heinemann, 1898. 1st English edition; 8vo; original binding, endpapers darkened, minor wrinkling, very good; inscribed by Zangwill.   Charles Agvent 4-1255 1996 $175.00

ZANGWILL, ISRAEL   The Works of Israel Zangwill. London: Globe Publishing Co., 1925. Edition deluxe; 14 volumes, colored plates (1 per volume); half leather; some uneven wear to spines, but mostly nice, volume 1 lacks f.f.e.p.; very good set.   Ian Patterson 9-319 1996 £250.00

ZAPF, HERMANN 1918-   Pen and Graver. Alphabets and Pages of Calligraphy. New York: Museum Books, 1952. 1st edition; one of 2000 copies; oblong 4to; publicity leaflet laid in; quarter vellum bnad boards, one corner slightly bumped, otherwise fine.   James S. Jaffe 34-664 1996 $450.00

ZEISLER, SIGMUND   Reminiscences of the Anarchist Case. Chicago: Chicago Literary Club, 1927. 1st edition; wrappers, near fine but for tiny corner chip and edge tears.   Beasley Books 82-318 1996 $125.00

ZEISLOFT, E. IDELL   The New Metropolis. 1600-1900. Memorable Events of Three Centuries. New York: D. Appleton, 1899. Thick oblong 4to; 16 color maps and 1000 illustrations; modern full brown linen. Appelfeld Gallery 54-145 1996 $450.00

ZELAZNY, ROGER   The Changing Land: a Novel of Dilvish the Damned. San Francisco: Underwood/Miller, 1981. 1st hardcover edition; one of a small number of presentation copies stamped as such and signed by author and by Thomas Canty, dust jacket illustrator; very fine in dust jacket.   Robert Gavora 61-376 1996 $100.00

ZELAZNY, ROGER   Creatures of Light and Darkness. London: Faber, 1970. 1st British edition; signed by author; fine in dust jacket, uncommon.   Aronovitz 57-1326 1996 $150.00

ZELAZNY, ROGER   The Last Defender of Camelot. San Francisco: Underwood/Miller, 1981. 1st edition; one of 17 copies with signed label tipped in and stamped "Presentation Copy"; very fine, issued without dust jacket.   Robert Gavora 61-380 1996 $125.00

ZELAZNY, ROGER   Nine Princes in Amber. London: Faber, 1972. 1st British edition; signed by author; just about fine in like dust jacket, with some rubbing to rear dust jacket panel.   Aronovitz 57-1327 1996 $275.00

ZELAZNY, ROGER   A Rhapsody in Amber. New Castle: Cheap Street, 1981. 1st edition; one of 64 copies of the 'Special Edition', numbered and signed by author and artist, Duncan Eagleson; plain stiff wrappers, very fine in dust jacket with slipcase.   Robert Gavora 61-382 1996 $150.00

ZELAZNY, ROGER   A Rose for Ecclesiastes. RHD, 1969. 1st British and 1st hard covere edition; signed by author; near fine in dust jacket. Aronovitz 57-1325 1996 $475.00

ZERI, FEDERICO   Italian Paintings in the Walters Art Gallery. Baltimore: 1976. 4to; 2 volumes; pages xx, 312, 4 color and 142 black and white plates; vi,3 13-647 and 4 color and 143-299 black and white plates; cloth.   Rainsford A54-608 1996 £110.00

ZERVOS, CHRISTIAN   Catalan Art from the Ninth to the Fifteenth Centuries. London: 1937. Royal 8vo; 36 pages; 223 plates; buckram, dust jacket (worn), slipcase.   Rainsford A54-611 1996 £75.00

ZEVI, BRUNO   Towards an Organic Architecture. London: Faber & Faber, 1950. 1st British edition; 8vo; 180 pages; cloth, ex-library, few markings, spine sunned, else very good.   The Bookpress 75-264 1996 £110.00

ZIEGLER, HENRY BRYAN   Six Views of Ludlow... Ludlow: R. Jones, 1846. Oblong folio; title and 6 ff. letterpress, engraved vignette on titlepage, 6 mezzotint plates on steel (very slight foxing); original printed wrappers, slight stianing.   Marlborough 162-102 1996 £350.00

ZIEMSSEN, HUGO VON   Acute Infectious Diseases. New York: 1874. 1st English translation; 2 volumes, 708, 751 pages; full leather.   W. Bruce Fye 71-2320 1996 $125.00

ZIENKOWICZ, LEON   Les Costumes du Peuple Polonais, Suivis d'une Description Exacte de ses Moeurs, de ses Usages et de ses Habitudes. Paris: La Librairie Polonaise, 1841. Large 4to; (4), 126, 2 pages, 39 brilliantly hand colored costume plates, 2 leaves of lithographed music; contemporary red calf over boards, extremities bit rubbed, verall very choice copy. Very scarce. Colas 3115. Lipperheid 1391.   Kenneth Karmiole 1NS-83 1996 $2,500.00

ZIMMERMAN, E. C.   Insects of Hawaii. Honolulu: 1948-58. Royal 8vo; volumes 1-8; original wrappers.   Wheldon & Wesley 207-1136 1996 £95.00

ZOLA, EMILE   The Attack on the Mill. London: William Heinemann, 1895. 1st edition; tissue guarded color plates and numerous black and white drawaings in text by E. Courboin; decorated cloth, gilt, top edge gilt, spine darkened, head and tail of spine and corners bumped, covers marked, rubbed and slightly cocked, prelims, edges and endpaepr slightly spotted, free endpapers browned, very good.   Ulysses 39-667 1996 £125.00

ZOLA, EMILE   Les Rougon-Macquart, Histoire Naturelle et Sociale d'une Famille Sous le Second Empire. Paris: G. Charpentier et Cie, 1886. 1st edition; 12mo. in half sheets, pages (iv), 491; quarter morocco, spine in compartments with raised bands, gilt rules and lettering, original wrappers bound in, some spotting, very good. Presentation copy from author to Henry Bauer, with ALS by Zola about the book, bound in. Simon Finch 24-265 1996 £1,400.00

ZOLA, EMILE   The Trial of Emile Zola Containing M. Zola's Letter to President Faure Relating to the Dreyfus Case and a Full Report of the Fifteen Days' Proceedings in the Assize Court of the Seine... New York: Benj. R. Tucker, 1898. 1st edition; 12mo; 355 pages; old calf backed marbled boards, rebacked. Rare.   M & S Rare Books 60-439 1996 $425.00

ZOLA, EMILE   Une Campagne 1880-1881. Paris: G. Charpentier, 1882. 1st edition; 12mo. in half sheets, pages x, 408; contemporary green half morocco, green marbled boards, raised bands, gilt tooled compartments, gilt lettered direct, marbled endpapers, small modern bookplate, original yellow printed paper wrapper folded and bound in, autograph presentation inscription to Ivan Turgenev on half title, uncut, some gatherings unopened, light foxing, remarkable presentation copy; Simon Finch 24-264 1996 £2,200.00

ZOLA, EMILE   Work. London: Chatto & Winds, 1901. 1st edition; original binding, edges spotted, head and tail of spine slightly bumped, gilt titles on spine starting to oxidise, very good in very scarce dust jacket which is slightly faded at spine, slightly rubbed and very slightly nicked with small burn hole to fold of upper flap.   Ulysses 39-668 1996 £325.00

ZOOLOGICAL SOCIETY OF LONDON   Transactions. London: 1866-1965. 4to; Volumes 5 to 30, 26 volumes; numerous colored and plain plates; half morocco, different styles, 2 volumes buckram, remainder in cloth and original wrappers (2 volumes need rebinding). Plates 21 and 22 and titlepage and index of volume 24 slightly torn in upper margin. Wheldon & Wesley 207-123 1996 £3,500.00

ZORN, ANDERS LEONARD ZORN   Zorn Engravings. A Complete Catalogue. Hjert & Hjert, 1980. 30 x 21.5 cm; 192 pages; frontispiece, 289 illustrations; original cloth, in dust jacket.   Rainsford A54-612 1996 £75.00

ZUKOFSKY, LOUIS   Some Time. Short Poems. Stuttgart: Jonathan Williams, 1956. 1st edition; "Author's Edition", one of 50 special copies numbered and signed by author; 8vo; wrappers designed by Celiz Zukofsky, glassine dust jacket, slipcase; fine.   James S. Jaffe 34-693 1996 $750.00

ZWEIG, PAUL   Images and Footsteps, a Poem. Plain Wrapper Press, 1971. One of 200 copies, signed by author and artist; 13 1/4 x 10 1/4 inches; (9) leaves of text, plus blanks and 5 etched plates by Berta Moltke, beautifully printed on damp handmade sized Umbria paper from Miliani Fabriano; green morocco backed tan paper boards, gilt titling on spine, in publisher's matching paper slipcase; mint.   Phillip J. Pirages 33-428 1996 $550.00

ZWEIG, PAUL   The River. Plain Wrapper Press, 1981. One of 120 copies, signed by author and artist; 11 x 8 1/4 inches; 4 p.l., 7, (1) pages; (1) leaf (colophon); titlepage in red and black, page numbers in red; original dark blue morocco backed paper boards, etching inset in front cover, fore edge and tail edge untrimmed, in fine publisher's folding cloth box, mint.   Phillip J. Pirages   33-429   1996 $175.00

Association Copies

ASSOCIATION COPIES

ASSOCIATION - A'ROY

SANTORIO, SANTORIO 1561-1636   (Opera Omnia)...Commentaria in Prima Fen Primi Libri Canonis Avicennae.../...Methodi Vitandorum.../...Commentaria in Artem Medicinalem Galeni... Venice: Franciscum Brogiollum, 1660. Small 4to; 5 works in 3 volumes, pages (20), 1120; (16), 336; (36); (52), 464; (38), 763; fine woodcut medical illustrations plus engraved portrait; old vellum; engraved armorial bookplate of Corn. Henr. A'Roy. Rare. GM 2668; 2 copies in NUC. Family Album Tillers-561 1996 $750.00

ASSOCIATION - JOHN ROLAND ABBEY

ABBEY, JOHN ROLAND   Life in England in Aquatint and Lithography, 1770-1860. London: Curwen Press, 1953. 1st edition; limited to 400 numbered copies; 4to; colored frontispiece, 32 collotype plates, 50 illustrations in text; original brown cloth, red morocco spine label, headcaps and corners mildly bumped, upper hinge slightly cracked, Major Abbey's own copy with his booklabel.   Maggs Bros. Ltd. 1191-63 1996 £320.00

ACHILLES TATIUS   De Dlitophontis et leucippes Amoribus Libri VIII. Heidelberg: Commelin, 1606. 8vo; title within border, 1 f., 396 ff. num.; contemporary Parisian crimson morocco, covers panelled gilt with outer and inner triple rule, border empty, panel decorated to a fanfare pattern of compartments outlined by a single and double fillet and filled with small tools, background of gyrate and leafy spray tools, central oval panel empty, flat spine similarly patterned, titled later at head and foot, all edges gilt, later endpapers, corners soft, two pairs of ties gone, preserved in cloth box. From the collection of "Potier, Paris, 1853"; Sir Edward Sullivan with his ex-libris, his sale, lot 14 Sotheby's May 19, 1890; J. R. Abbey with his ex-libris, his sale lot, Sotheby's June 21, 1965 to H. M. Fletcher.   Marlborough 160-11 1996 £2,100.00

THE BOKE of Noblesse. London: printed for the Roxburghe Club, by J. B. Nichols and Sons, 1890. 1st edition; 10 1/2 x 8 inches; 4 p.l., lx, 95, (1) pages; original roan backed reddish paper boards, gilt titling on spine, corners of paper boards slightly worn, just a tiny bit of rubbing to spine ends and chafing to covers, but binding entirely sound and pleasing, fine internally. Bookplates of C. H. St. John Hornby and John Roland Abbey.   Phillip J. Pirages 33-450 1996 $600.00

JUVENALIS, DECIMUS JUNIUS 55-140   Satyrae. Birmingham: Baskerville Press, 1761. 4to; 240 pages; plain calf, flat spine gilt in 7 panels, spine and covers stamped with arms of Pembroke Hall, Cambridge, all edges white, marbled endpapers; from the collection of the Rivers family with their 19th century bookplate and from the collection of J. R. Abbey with his bookplate.   Marlborough 160-44 1996 £450.00

LACTANTIUS FIRMIANUS, LUCIUS CAELIUS   Opera. Lyons: Soubron, 1594. 16mo; 879 pages, 21ff; contemporary Roman brown calf, covers gilt with outer double rules, enclosing panels at head and foot, centre decorated with large and small gyrate, leafy and other small tools, central panel with arms below a helmet and leafy spray, spine gilt in 4 panels, plain endpapers, all edges gilt, gilt and gauffered, upper cover lettered B. Curtus: R/Acad. Parth, lower cover N. Nucctus/Acad. Parth. Small repairs to tie-holes and spine, corners soft, most unusual Roman binding with some elements of fanfare, coats of arms (each different) are those of B. Curtus and N. Nucctus of the Parthenopean Academy; later the copy of J. R. Abbey, Abbey Sale 22 vi. 1965 lot 426 to E. P. Goldschmidt.   Marlborough 160-4 1996 £2,250.00

TITUS and Vespasian or the Destruction of Jerusalem. London: printed for the Roxburghe Club by J.B. Nichols and Sons, 1905. 1st edition; 11 x 8 1/2 inches; (i)-xlvi, 242 pages; title printed in red and black; 2 color plates, partly printed in gold, reproducing illuminated manuscript pages; original roan backed reddish paper boards, top edge gilt, other edges untrimmed; one small abrasion and minor soiling to paper covers, corners and spine ends slightly worn, otherwise fine, beautiful copy internally; with bookplates of C. H. St. John Hornby and John Roland Abbey.   Phillip J. Pirages 33-451 1996 $550.00

ASSOCIATION - FRANKLIN ABBOTT

BONE, DAVID W.   Merchantman Rearmed. London: Chatto & Windus, 1949. 1st edition; number 43 of 160 copies signed by David Bone; 4to; (2), 331, (1) pages; original drypoint etched frontispiece portrait signed by artist Muirhead Bone, who did the full page and in-text illustrations; original blue quarter morocco and cloth, top edge gilt, couple of small light damp spots on front cover, but very good; this copy with signed inscription from David Bone for Franklin Abbott laid in on separate sheet, dated 1949.   Chapel Hill 94-39 1996 $150.00

ASSOCIATION - LASCELLES ABERCROMBIE

BOTTOMLEY, GORDON   Chambers of Imagery, Together with Chambers of Imagery (Second Series). London: Elkin Mathews, 1907-12. 1st editions; small 8vo; 2 volumes; original wrappers, those of first volume slightly soiled, spine of second volume chipped. 1st volume initialled "L(ascelles) A(bercrombie) and signed and dated by author at end, some underlining by Abercrombie, 2nd volume inscribed by author for Abercrombie.   R.F.G. Hollett & Son 78-323 1996 £85.00

ASSOCIATION - PETER ABRAHAMS

ALLFREY, PHYLLIS SHAND   In Circles. Poems. London: Raven Press, 1940. Number 261 of an edition of 300, signed by poet; 20 pages; wrappers, sewn; nice, scarce; with additional inscription in her hand to Peter Abrahams.   Ian Patterson 9-23 1996 £75.00

PADMORE, GEORGE   How Russia Transformed Her Colonial Empire. London: Dennis Dobson, 1946. 1st edition; xx, 178 pages; cloth, nice in nicked red and black dust jacket; inscribed by author for Peter (Abrahams).   Ian Patterson 9-230 1996 £50.00

ASSOCIATION - ABSOLON

FORREST, JOHN   Explorations in Australia. London: Sampson Low, Marston, Low & Searle, 1875. (vii), 351 pages, (iii) pages, 4 folding maps, frontispiece, 7 illustrations by G. F. Angas; prize leather binding, raised bands, gold gilt, marbled edges and endpapers and endpaper, small tear on hinge restored, good plus condition; the Absolon copy. Ferguson 9681; Wantrup 200.   Antipodean 28-618 1996 $950.00

MC KINLAY, JOHN   McKinlay's Journal of Exploration in the Interior of Australia (Burke Relief Expedtiion). Melbourne: F. F. Bailliere, 1861. 136 pages, 3 large folding maps; late 19th century plain cloth, with pocket for maps, gold gilt on spine, text lightly browned and little spotted, otherwise good+. Some cracks and failures at some folds in some of the maps; the Absolon copy. Ferguson 12057; Wantrup 177. Antipodean 28-626 1996 $750.00

MASLEN, T. J.   The Friend of Australia; or, a Plan for Exploring the Interior and for Carrying on a Survey of the Whole Continent of Australia. London: Smith Elder & Co., 1836. 2nd edition; (xxiv), 428 pages, (8) pages ads; folding map, 5 folding aquatint plates; original blue cloth, spine rebacked with 1920's plain black cloth, stamped on old endpaper South Aus. Rooms A; Gole & Co.; James Partington bookplate; very nice. The Absolon copy. Ferguson 2145; Wantrup 117b.   Antipodean 28-625 1996 $1,450.00

MASSON, ELSIE R.   An Untamed Territory, the Northern Territory of Australia. London: 1915. (xii), 181 pages & 2 pages ads, frontispiece and 3 1 pages illustrations; green cloth; very good; Absolon copy. Antipodean 28-37 1996 $145.00

MITCHELL, T. L.   Three Expeditions into the Interior of Eastern Australia. London: T. & W. Boone, 1838. 2 volumes, (xxii), 352 pages, 16 pages ads & (viii), (ii), 406 pages, 50 plates, large folding hand colored map; engraved folding map loose in volume 1, otherwise good+ condition; original embossed and decorated cloth, rebacked, o laid down; Absolon copy. Ferguson 2553; Wantrup 124a.   Antipodean 28-88 1996 $1,750.00

NICOLAY, C. G.   Notes on the Aborigines of Western Australia. London: William Clowes & Sons, The Colonial & Indian Exhibition, 1886. 18 page pamphlet; original printed wrappers, bound in papered boards, leather spine label; fine, scarace; Edge-Partington bookplate, the Absolon copy. Ferguson 13373; Greenway 7213.   Antipodean 28-147 1996 $350.00

SADLEIR, RICHARD   The Aborigines of Australia. Sydney: Thomas Richards, 1883. 4to; 69 pages, 5 full page plates, 2 color illustrations; red pictorial cloth, covers stamped in gilt and black some marking to front cover, otherwise good + condition; the Absolon copy; Charlotte Fabris copy with her signature. Ferguson 15343; Greenway 8227. Antipodean 28-301 1996 $550.00

ASSOCIATION - ABSOLON

SMITH, GEOFFREY   A Naturalist in Tasmania. Oxford: 1909. 151 pages, 16 pages ads, frontispiece and 20 pages illustrations and illustrations in text, folding map; original decorated cloth, some light rubbing to spine of dust jacket, otherwise fine copy; the Absolon copy. Antipodean 28-360 1996 $110.00

SMYTH, R. BROUGH   The Aborigines of Victoria: with Notes Relating to the Habits of the Natives of Other Parts of Australia and Tasmania. London: 1878. Volume 1 only, (lxxii), 483 pages, illustrations, large map; pictorial gilt blue buckram, hinges loose, otherwise good+. The Absolon copy. Ferguson 15882.   Antipodean 28-367 1996 $250.00

SPENCER, BALDWIN   Across Australia. London: Macmillan, 1912. 1st edition; 2 volumes, (xiv), 254 pages, 105 illustrations and 5 color, folding map; (xvii), 255-525 pages, 2 pages ads, illustrations, 106-356 pages, 2 color, 1 folding map, red gilt buckram with gilt title and stamped decoration, light spotting on lower boards, corners slightly bumped, else very good; the Absolon copy.   Antipodean 28-377 1996 $650.00

STRZELECKI, P. E. DE   Physical Description of New South Wales and Van Diemen's Land. London: Longman, Brown, Green and Longmsn, 1845. (xx), 462 pages, 32 pages ads dated Dec. 1848, frontispiece and 2 sepia litho plates, plus 19 engraved plates, folding map; secondary brown covers rebacked, very good; the Absolon copy. Presentation inscription from author to Edward Cane with his bookplate dated 1849. Ferguson 4168.   Antipodean 28-628 1996 $1,250.00

STUART, E. J.   Land of Opportunities, Being an Account of the Author's Recent Expedition to Explore the Northern Territories of Australia. London: 1923. (xiv), 144 pages, frontispiece, 46 pages illustrations, 2 folding maps; cloth covers, discolored, but covered with a fine dust jacket; very good; the Absolon copy.   Antipodean 28-418 1996 $125.00

STURT, CHARLES   Narrative of an Expedition Into Central Australia...During 1844, 5 and 6. London: T. W. Boone, 1849. 1st edition; (x), (iv), 5-416 pages (8), (2) (2) last blank; (vi), 308, 92, (ii), (8), (4) pages; 18 plates, 1 folding map; original green embossed cloth, rebacked with original spine laid down, good, internally nice and crisp; the Absolon copy. Ferguson 5202; Wantrup 119.   Antipodean 28-421 1996 $1,450.00

STURT, CHARLES   Two Expeditions into the Interior of Southern Australia during the Years 1828, 1829, 1830 and 1831. London: Smith, Elder & Co., 1833. 1st edition; 2 volumes, viii, (iv), (ix)-xxx, 220 pages (last blank), 5 engraved plates, folding map (couple of small tears repaired); viii, 272 pages (last blank), (15 pages ads), 9 plates; original purple pebble grain cloth, gilt decorated spines, spine sunned and dusty as usual, some discoloration of boards and top hinge starting, otherwise a pleasant copy; the Absolon copy, and with Edge Partington bookplate. Antipodean 28-122 1996 $1,750.00

TAPLIN, GEORGE   Narrinyeri: an Account of the Tribes of South Australian Aborigines Inhabiting the Country Around the Lakes Alexandria, Albert and Coorong and the Lower Part of the River Murray, Their Manner and Customs. Adelaide: E. S. Wing, 1878. 2nd edition; (iv), (iv), 156 pages, 6 color lithographs; original embossed cloth showing slight discoloration, otherwise bright, clean copy; the Absolon copy. Ferguson 16707; Greenway 8980.   Antipodean 28-434 1996 $550.00

THOMAS, N. W.   Natives of Australia. London: 1906. (xii), 256 pages, 1 folding map, 32 plates; some damp discoloration on boards not affecting gilt or bright spine, internally bright, clean copy; the Absolon copy.   Antipodean 28-455 1996 $125.00

WARBURTON, PETER EGERTON   Journey Across the Western Interior of Australia. London: Sampson Lowe et al, 1875. (xii), 308 pages, (40) pages; frontispiece and 8 plates, 1 large folding map, some tears along folds; original green decorated cloth, front inner hinge starting, extremities and gilt on spine rubbed, otherwise good+; the Absolon copy. Ferguson 1817; Wantrup 201.   Antipodean 28-527 1996 $950.00

WILLIS, WILLIAM JOHN   Successful Exploration through the Interior of Australia, from Melbourne to the Gulf of Carpentaria, from the Journals and Letters of... London: Richard Bentley, 1863. (xii), 396 pages, (32) pages, frontispiece and 1 plate, folding map; original embossed green cloth, covers and gilt on spine rubbed, corners bumped, internally bright, clean copy, overall in good condition; Edge Partington bookplate; the Absolon copy. Fergsuon 18622; Wantrup 172.   Antipodean 28-629 1996 $750.00

ASSOCIATION - FLORENCE ACTON

MORRIS, FRANCIS ORPEN 1810-1893   A Natural History of British Moths. London: Bell and Daldy, 1872. 3rd edition; 8vo; 4 volumes; 132 hand colored plates; green cloth gilt, dust jackets, very rare survival, the dust jackets have few slight tears and small holes, but are generally in sound condition; ownership inscriptions of Florence Acton, 3 Dean's Yard, Westminster, dated August 1878, booklabel of Ruari McLean. Maggs Bros. Ltd. 1190-169 1996 £350.00

ASSOCIATION - ROBERT ADAMS

BRIN, D.   Startide Rising. Phantasia Press, 1985. 1st hardcover edition; fine in dust jacket, inscribed by author to fellow writer Robert Adams and his wife.   Aronovitz 57-177 1996 $120.00

NORTON, ANDRE   Gryphon in Glory. Atheneum, 1981. 1st edition; fine in dust jacket; inscribed by author to fellow writer, Robert Adams, laid in is holograph letter to Adams from artist (for this dust jacket) Jack Gaughan.   Aronovitz 57-891 1996 $125.00

NORTON, ANDRE   Merlin's Mirror. S&J, 1976. 1st hardcover edition, fine in dust jacket; inscribed by author to fellow writer Robert Adams. Uncommon.   Aronovitz 57-881 1996 $125.00

NORTON, ANDRE   Octagon Magic. World, 1967. 1st edition; fine in dust jacket, inscribed by author to fellow writer Robert Adams. Aronovitz 57-873 1996 $150.00

NORTON, ANDRE   Ordeal in Otherwhere. World, 1964 1st edition; fine in very good+/near fine dust jacket save for some light rubbing to the dust jacket spine and rear panel; inscribed by author to fellow writer Robert Adams.   Aronovitz 57-870 1996 $150.00

NORTON, ANDRE   Wolfshead. Hale, 1977. 1st hard cover edition; fine in dust jacket, inscribed by author to fellow writer Robert Adams; quite scarce.   Aronovitz 57-887 1996 $150.00

NORTON, ANDRE   The X Factor. H-B, 1965. 1st edition; near fine in very good+ dust jacket with some light wear to head of dust jacket spine, inscribed by author for fellow writer Robert Adams.   Aronovitz 57-871 1996 $150.00

ASSOCIATION - M. ADYE

SOUTHERNE, THOMAS   The Maids Last Prayer: or, Any, Rather Than Fail. London: R. Bentley and J. Tonson, 1693. 1st edition; issue with 'upon' on page I line 3; 4to; half calf, marbled boards, joints rubbed, text browned; the Robert Hoe copy with his bookplate, contemporary signature of "M. Adye" on title. Wing S4760; W&M 1166; Pforzheimer 958.   James Cummins 14-191 1995 $300.00

ASSOCIATION - MADELEINE AGNINI

OE, KEZABURO   A Personal Matter. New York: Grove Press, 1968. 1 edition; original binding, top edge dusty, very good in slightly darkened dust jacket; presentation copy from author, inscribed for Mrs. Madeleine Agnini.   Ulysses 39-449 1996 £325.00

ASSOCIATION - AKE AKERSTROM

BOETTICHER, ERNST   La Troie de Schliemann. Une Necropole a Incineration a la Maniere Assyro-Babylonienne. Louvain: Lefever, 1889. Offprint; 8vo; vii, 115 pages, 12 plates; half calf with 5 raised bands, marbled boards, spine chipped, bottom joint cracked but holding; from the collection of Heinrich Schliemann, and was acquired by Professor Akerstrom; with facsimile letter about acquisition; with remnants of Schliemann's paper private library label at foot of spine.   Archaeologia Luxor-3982 1996 $4,500.00

BURNOUF, EMILE   Memoires sur l'Antiquite: l'Age du Bronze, Troie, Santorin, Delos, Ycenes, le Parthenon, les Courbes, les Propylees, un Faubourg d'Athenes. Paris: Masionneuve, 1879. 8vo; 340 pages, 4 plate half calf, rubbed, 5 raised bands, marbled boards, bottom joint starting but holding; from the collection of Heinrich Schliemann, and was acquired by Professor Akerstrom; with facsimile letter about acquisition inscribed "....Schliemann admiration et affection, Em. Burnouf." (closely cut at top edge by Schoemann's bookbinder), also noted on same pag as acquired at "Athens Sept. 1955" in hand of Akerstrom. Archaeologia Luxor-3983 1996 $1,250.00

ASSOCIATION - AKE AKERSTROM

EVANS, JOHN   The Ancient Stone Implements, Weapons and Ornaments of Great Britain. London: Longmans, Green, Reader and Dyer, 1872. 1st edition; 8vo; xvi, 640 pages; 476 figures, 2 folding plates; original gilt pictorial cloth, spine faded, chipped and torn; from the collection of Heinrich Schliemann, and was acquired by Professor Akerstrom; with facsimile letter about acquisition; inscribed by author for Schliemann, with traces of Schliemann's private paper library label at foot of spine.   Archaeologia Luxor-3984 1996 $650.00

SALISBURY, STEPHEN   Troy and Homer. Remarks on the Discovers of Dr. Heinrich Schliemann in the Troad. Worcester: privately printed by Charles Hamilton, 1875. 8vo; 52 pages; original gilt lettered cloth, light shelfwear at spine; from the collection of Heinrich Schliemann, and was acquired by Professor Akerstrom; with facsimile letter about acquisition; with traces of Schliemann's paper private library stamp at foot of spine; inscribed by Scliemann by author.   Archaeologia Luxor-3986 1996 $650.00

SCHLIEMANN, HEINRICH   Trojanischer Alterthumer. Bericht uber Die Ausgrabungen in Troja. Leipzig: F. A. Brockhaus, 1874. 1st edition; 8vo; lx, 320 pages, 1 plate; 19th century half calf with 4 raised bands, gilt lettered spine, initials "S.S." (for Sophia Schliemann at foot, original wrappers bound in (light rubbing at etremities), remnants of Schliemann's paper private label label at foot of spine; from the library of Ake Akerstrom.   Archaeologia Luxor-3981 1996 $15,000.00

SNIDER, DENTON J.   A Walk in Hellas, or the Old in the New. St. Louis: privately printed, 1881. 8vo; 350 pages; original publisher's gilt lettered cloth, spine with light shelfwear and tears, label no longer present; from the collection of Heinrich Schliemann, and was acquired by Professor Akerstrom; with facsimile letter about acquisition; inscribed by Charles Parsons for Schliemann.   Archaeologia Luxor-3988 1996 $450.00

ASSOCIATION - L. CLIFFORD ALBERT

SHAW, GEORGE BERNARD 1856-1950   The Doctor's Dilemma: Getting Married, the Shewing-Up of Blanco Posnet. London: Constable, 1911. 1st edition; original pale green cloth; near fine, fine half morocco case; presentation copy inscribed by author for Sir L. Clifford Albert.   19th Century Shop 39- 1996 $2,800.00

ASSOCIATION - CARLO ALBERTINELLI

LUCIANUS SAMOSATENSIS   I Dialoi Piacevoli, le Vere Narrationi, le Facete Epitole... Venice: Giovanni de Farri & Fratelli, 1541. Small 8vo; ff. 224, (some errors in foliation), italic letter, woodcut printer's device on titlepage, 30 woodcuts in text; contemporary limp vellum, bit soiled, ties removed; few light early marginal marks and 1 correction in text; good; autographs of Carlo Albertinelli 1576 & Stefano Pergamasci 1605. BM STC It. p. 396; Adams L1632; Brunet III 1213.   A. Sokol XXV-59 1996 £1,850.00

ASSOCIATION - SIDNEY ALBERTS

JEFFERS, ROBINSON 1887-1962   Such Counsels You Gave to Me and Other Poems. New York: Random House, 1937. 1st edition; one of 300 specially bound copies, signed by author; 8vo; quarter leather, decorated boards, glassine dust jacket, slipcase; light offsetting on front and black endpapers, as usual, otherwise fine in somewhat worn glassine; from the collection of Jeffers' bibliographer, Sidney Alberts, with his ownership inscription.   James S. Jaffe 34-328 1996 $350.00

ASSOCIATION - JOSEPH ALBREE

MILL, JOHN STUART 1806-1873   The Subjection of Women. New York: Appleton, 1869. 1st American edition; 8vo; original cloth, Joseph Albree 1869 bookticket.   Rostenberg & Stern 150-117 1996 $750.00

ASSOCIATION - ALDENHAM

SALLUSTIUS CRISPUS, C.   The Two Most Worthy and Notable Histories... London: W. Jaggard for J. Jaggard, 1608-09. Apparently the first edition of Thomas Heywood's translation; 4to; pages (22), 60, (5), 110 plus errata and blanks, printer's device on title, historiated initials; later full leather, front board detached, ms. ownership and engraved armorial ex-libris of Henry H(ucks) Gibbs, Lord Aldenham, book collector. STC 21625.   Family Album Tillers-546 1996 $500.00

ASSOCIATION - BRIAN ALDISS

KESEY, KEN 1935-   Kesey's Garage Sale. New York: Viking, 1973. 1st edition; fine in dust jacket; inscribed by Kesey for Brian Aldiss.   Aronovitz 57-617 1996 $275.00

ASSOCIATION - CHARLES DEXTER ALLEN

PATMORE, COVENTRY   Florilegium Amantis. London: George Bell & Sons, n.d. 1879. 1st edition; 12mo; printed presentation slip from author tipped in at front and Robert Louis Stevenson's "Sherryvore" bookplate on front pastedown; original cloth, paper spine label (partially worn away); covers glazed (as was the case with many of Stevenson's books), inner hinges cracked, else good in half morocco slipcase (spine little rubbed); also bookplate of noted collector, Charles Dexter Allen.   David J. Holmes 52-115 1996 $850.00

ASSOCIATION - AMHERST

CASTIGLIONE, BALDASSARE 1475-1529   Il Cortegiano. Lyons: Guillaume Rouille, 1553. 16mo; titlepage, 7 ff. n.n., pages 1-"457", 6 ff. n.n., ruled in red; a Parisian binding c. 1560, red mor. over stiff pasteboards, tooled in silver (now oxydised) to a pre-fanfare pattern of compartments outlined by a continuous fillet & w/azured tools, spine w/4 double bands, compartments dec. w/azured tools, title label added in 18th century, edges of bds. dec. w/lines & tooling in silver, edges black (originally silver?), pastedown w/2 endleaves at front (two at back), no watermark; covers are divided into compartments by a continuous fillet, as on fanfare bindings, but do no have the leafy sprays of the true fanfare; note by W. Kerney, 15.11. (18)88; Lord Amherst of Hackney, his sale, Sotheby's, 3 December 1908, lot 173.   Marlborough 160-2 1996 £4,800.00

ASSOCIATION - JEFFREY AMHERST

DAWSON, HENRY   Reminiscences of the Park and its Vicinity. New York: 1855. Limited to 25 copies, signed and dated by authors; 8vo; 64 pages of text; this copy extra illustrated, with 17 tipped in plates; three quarter green morocco and marbled red boards, slightly rubbed at head of joints, spine in 6 panels with raised bands, triple ruled gilt frames and gilt lettered black leather label, top edge gilt; near fine, very attractive; with ALS by Jeffrey Amherst mounted on thick stock.   Blue Mountain SP95-13 1996 $1,250.00

ASSOCIATION - J. P. ANDERSON

BUTLER, SAMUEL 1835-1902   Erewhon or Over the Range. London: Longmans, Green & Co., 1890. 8th edition; half title, original brown cloth, fine; inscribed by author for J. P. Anderson. Hoppe 5 p. 12.   Jarndyce CII-17 1996 £200.00

ASSOCIATION - J. REDWOOD ANDERSON

BLUNDEN, EDMUND 1896-   Retreat. London: Richard Cobden Sanderson, 1928. 1st trade edition; original red cloth, label on spine, spine sunned, else fine in dust jacket, spine darkened and worn; inscribed for poet J. Redwood Anderson.   Priscilla Juvelis 95/1-34 1996 $150.00

ASSOCIATION - JOHN ANDERSON

DARWIN, CHARLES ROBERT 1809-1882   On the Origin of Species by Means of Natural Selection. London: 1859. 1st edition; 8vo; folding diagram, with half title, but without inserted ads, usually found; late 19th century half green morocco, date tooled at foot of spine (which is faded to brown), little worn and scuffed, signature of John Anderson, later in the collection of Dr. Warren G. Smirl, bought from Quaritch in 1978 for $1700.   Maggs Bros. Ltd. 1190-231 1996 £4,200.00

ASSOCIATION - POUL ANDERSON

HEINLEIN, ROBERT ANSON 1907-1988   Time Enough for Love. Putnam, 1973. 1st edition; very good in dust jacket with some slight wear and tear; from the library of Poul Anderson with his ownership signature, nice association.   Aronovitz 57-536 1996 $185.00

ASSOCIATION - JOHN ANDREWS

GREENWOOD'S Pictures of Hull. Hull & London: published by J. Greenwood, t Bowlalley Lane, Hull; colophon: Driffield: printed by B. Fawcett, 1835. 1st edition; 8vo; viii, 206 pages, 66 of 70 engravings; new old style quarter calf, good. Presentation copy from author to John Andrews. K Books 441-254 1996 £140.00

ASSOCIATION - THOMAS ANDREWS

ALGAROTTI, FRANCESCO An Essay on Painting. London: L. Davis & C. Reymers, 1764. 1st English edition; small8vo; vii, (i), 186, (4) pages ads; recent quarter calf, marbled boards; very good; signature of Wm. Curran at head of titlepage and second signature of Thos. Andrews. Ken Spelman 30-10 1996 £220.00

ASSOCIATION - QUEEN ANNE

CHURCH OF ENGLAND. BOOK OF COMMON PRAYER Book of Common Prayer. Oxford: by the University Printers, 1701. Large folio; ruled in red and black; contemporary black morocco, covers gilt and blindstamped with broad outer border of floral drawer handle and small tools, central panel with blindstamped leafy sprays and flowers, monograms gilt in each corner, centre gilt with Royal Arms (Queen Anne, Davenport p. 51), spine gilt in 8 panels with raised bands and one panel lettered direct, all edges gilt, corner soft, some gilt faded, but generally fresh, fine binding with both Royal Arms and monograms almost certainly by Robert Steel. Marlborough 160-31 1996 £2,250.00

ASSOCIATION - A. N. ANTRIM

HALIFAX, GEORGE SAVILE, 1ST MARQUIS OF 1633-1695 The Lady's New-Years' Gift: or, Advice to a Daughter, Under these Following Heads... London: Matt. Gillyflower & James Partridge, 1688. 3rd edition; 12mo; frontispiece; contemporary speckled calf, very good; signature on title of A. N. Antrim, and neat contemporary handwriting on blank prelims. Wing H305a. Jarndyce 103-440 1996 £480.00

ASSOCIATION - CATHERINE ARCHER

KILNER, DOROTHY Letters from a Mother to her Children, on Various Important Subjects. London: by John Marshall and Co., 1780? 1st edition; 24mo. in sixes; 2 volumes, pages 178; 179; with half titles and 3 pages of ads at end of volume 2; contemporary quarter calf, volume numbers in gilt on spines, marbled sides, worn, spines restored, especially at head of volume 1, small area of leather missing on same volume, rustmarks to volume 1 prelims, still good set; contemporary ownership inscriptions of Catherine Archer at beginning of each volume. Osborne I p. 153 has only 2nd edition of 1787. Simon Finch 24-141 1996 £750.00

ASSOCIATION - GEORGE ARDEN

PERCY, THOMAS, BP. OF DROMORE 1729-1811 Reliques of Ancient English Poetry... London: printed for J. Dodsley, 1767. 2nd edition; 8vo; 3 volumes; contemporary calf, worn, half titles, frontispiece, engraved vignettes, unsigned, but probably after Wale, E6 torn (volume 1), some short marginal tears, engraved leaf of music at end of volume 2, leaf of publisher's ads at back of volume 3; some browning and staining, well red copy; signatures of Nathaniel Bristed, gift inscriptions from Miss Bristed to George Arden dated 1830; Courtney-Nichol Smith p. 111; Chapman & Hazen p. 148; Rothschild 1521. (all for 1st ed.). James Cummins 14-155 1996 $150.00

ASSOCIATION - MERLE ARMITAGE

HERODOTUS History. London: Nonesuch Press, 1935. One of 675 copies; 12 x 7 1/2 inches; xxvi, 778 pages; woodcut title illustration and 9 half page woodcuts by V. Le Campion, 9 maps and plans by T. L. Poulton, title in red and black; original blue vellum backed cloth boards, backstrip lettered and attractively decorated in gilt, top edge gilded on rough, other edges untrimmed, hint of fading to spine (as usual), cloth somewhat soiled, corners ittle bumped, binding completely solid and showing no significant wear; fine internally; bookplate of Merle Armitage. Phillip J. Pirages 33-401 1996 $450.00

ASSOCIATION - T. A. ARMSTRONG

WARD, MARY AUGUSTA ARNOLD 1851-1920 Robert Elsmere. London: Smith, Elder & Co., 1888. Cabinet edition; 8vo; 2 volumes; original dark green cloth, gilt lettering on spine, some wear to extremities, otherwise very nice; inscribed presentation copy from author to Rev. T. A. Armstrong. McFarlin p. 108. Paulette Rose 16-337 1996 $100.00

ASSOCIATION - HERB ARNOLD

LUMLEY, BRIAN The Caller of the Black. Sauk City: Arkham House, 1971. 1st edition; illustrations by Herb Arnold; very fine in dust jacket, inscribed by Arnold and with original drawing by him. Bromer Booksellers 87-2 1996 $150.00

ASSOCIATION - SAMUEL ARNOLD

BIBLE. ENGLISH - 1823 The Holy Bible, Containing the Old and New Testaments; Together with the Apocrypha. New York: Daniel D. Smith, 1823. Daniel Smith's Stereotype Edition; thick quarto; 770 pages; numerous engraved plates; contemporary full red morocco, spine gilt stamped, orange endpapers, flyleaves becoming loose), two scratches on back cover, but spectacular contemporary American period binding; very rare, extremely handsome, signatures and inscriptions, indicating early and long ownership by prominent Rhode Island family of Samuel Arnold. Hills 459; Shoemaker 11816. M & S Rare Books 60-286 1996 $750.00

PHILADELPHIA SOCIETY FOR ALLEVIATING THE MISERIES OF PUBLIC PRISONS. Constiution. Philadelphia: Joseph Cruikshank, 1806. 1st edition; 16mo; 8 pages; contemporary marbled wrappers, fine. With signature of Samuel G. Arnold, wealthy Providence businessman. S&S 11155. M & S Rare Books 60-402 1996 $250.00

ASSOCIATION - HAL ASHBY

HUNTER, KRISTIN The Landlord. New York: Scribners, 1966. 1st edition; small number on front free endpaper and little fading at extremities of cloth; very good in about very good dust jacket with couple of short tears and small stain at top edge of spine; although there is no tangible evidence, this was Hal Ashby's copy. Ashby directed the film made from this book. Between the Covers 43-125 1996 $100.00

KESEY, KEN 1935- Kesey's Garage Sale. New York: Viking, 1973. Softcover edition; wrappers; not quite very good; Hal Ashby's copy with complimentary slip from publisher laid in. Ken Lopez 74-242 1996 $150.00

ASSOCIATION - SAMUEL ASHBY

JOHNSON, SAMUEL 1709-1784 A Dictionary of the English Language... London: printed for J. Knapton, C. Hitch and L. Hawes, A. Millar, W. Strahan.. 1760. 2nd octavo edition; 8vo; 2 volumes; contemporary calf, gilt, spines gilt, bit worn, some cracking of joints; very good, early armorial bookplates of Samuel Ashby, Trinity College, Cambridge. Courtney p. 62; Alston V 194. Ximenes 108-225 1996 $450.00

ASSOCIATION - ASQUITH

FIELDING, HENRY 1707-1754 The Works. London: and Edinburgh: fo F. C. and R. Rivington, 1821. 8 3/4 x 5 1/2 inches; 10 volumes; frontispiece in vol. 1, diagram in vol. 8; fine retrospective binding of flamed calf (ca. 1915?), flat spines with wide & narrow gilt bands forming compartments w/lg. gilt sunburst ornament in center, black morocco double labels, gilt hatching on board edges, text block edges gilt, marbled endpapers, lower inch of one joint wormed, two inch abrasion in one cover, otherwise only trivial defects to this very attractively bound set, volume 1 with few minor repaired tears (and one 3 inch tear into text, with slight displacement of letters, but no loss), text with isolated minor discoloration, final two volumes with slightly creased upper corners, otherwise fine, internally quite clean, smooth and fresh. Bookplate of English politician Neil Primrose in each volume, with presentation to him, inscribed and signed by British Prime Minister H. H Asquith. Phillip J. Pirages 33-235 1996 $1,250.00

ASSOCIATION - FRED ASTAIRE

GREEN, STANLEY   Starring Fred Astaire. New York: Dodd, Mead, 1973. 1st edition; 4to; numerous black and white illustrations; dust jacket, very good; taped down on front free endpaper is ALS from Astaire to actress Lana Wood.   George J. Houle 68-5 1996 $275.00

ASSOCIATION - ATHERTON

TUER, ANDREW WHITE 1838-1900   History of the Horn-Book. London: Leadenhall Press, 1896. 1st edition; 4to; 2 volumes; profusely illustrated, with facsimile horn-books and battledores as issued in pockets; uncut in original full decorated vellum, brown leather labels, top edge gilt, as issued; lovely copy; booklabel of Wm. Bernard Atherton; from the collection of Anne & Fernand Renier.   Jarndyce 103-587 1996 £750.00

ASSOCIATION - BUDDLE ATKINSON

HIGGINS, BRYAN   Experiments and Observations with the View of Improving the Art of composing and Applying Calcareous Cements, and of Preparing Quick-Lime... London: T. Cadell, 1780. 8vo; viii, 232 pages; contemporary marbled boards with seemly new calf spine and corners; bookplates of Buddle Atkinson and Gilbert Redgrave. Harris & Savage No. 347.   Elton Engineering 10-73 1996 £450.00

ASSOCIATION - ATKISON

HUNTER, ALEXANDER   Outlines of Agriculture, Addressed to Sir John Sinclair, Bart, President of the Baord of Agriculture. York: printed by Wilson, Spence & Mawman & sold by Cadell Jun. & Davies... 1797. 2nd edition; 47, (1) pages; plates; contemporary calf, rebacked; good; inscribed presentation copy from author to Fr. Atkison. Goldsmith's 16249.   C. R. Johnson 37-18 196 £150.00

ASSOCIATION - JAMES ST. AUBYN

JOHNSON, SAMUEL 1709-1784   Prayers and Meditataions. London: Cadell & Davis, 1807. 4th edition; tall octavo; pages 230, 1 page ads; fine full polished morocco binding, raised bands, blind fillets, gilt in panels, gilt on red leather label; fine; armorial bookplate of Sir James St. Aubyn who has made some interesting notes. Courtney p. 160. Hartfield 48-L46 1996 $295.00

ASSOCIATION - AUCHINLECK

HORATIUS FLACCUS, QUINTUS 65-8 BC   Opera. Leiden: Elzevier, 1629. 12mo; 3 parts in one; 1f., (30), 239; 296 (i.e. 286) pages, 1 blank f; 250 pages, 3 blank ff.; full contemporary vellum with wallet edges and blue silk ties, stamped in gilt on both covers is the Auchinleck Library mark, spine with horizontal gilt bands and brown morocco title label, Lord Auchinleck's library mark is also stamped at the foot of the engraved title, on first blank at end (Q6) there are 8 lines of verse in praise of Horace, believed to be in the hand of Alexander Boswell, Lord Auchinleck; very fine copy with an excellent association. Copinger 2396; Willems 314;   Book Block 32-56 1996 $1,750.00

ASSOCIATION - AUCKLAND

SHEFFIELD, JOHN BAKER HOLYROYD, 1ST EARL OF 1735-1821 Strictures on the Necessity of Inviolably Maintaining the Navigation and Colonial System of Great Britain. London: J. Debrett, 1804. 1st edition; 8vo; iv, 65 (3) pages, including final leaf of ads, with few ms notes added in ink, in contemporary hand; recently well bound in cloth backed marbled boards gilt, very good; presentation copy from author to Lord Auckland. Williams I 407; Kress B48491 Goldsmiths 18858; not in Einaudi. John Drury 82-255 1996 £95.00

ASSOCIATION - AUGUSTUS I, ELECTOR OF SAXONY

TERENTIUS AFER, PUBLIUS 180-159 BC   Comoedias Sex. Leipzig: Jacobi Bervaldi (Berwald) for Jacobi Apelij, 1577. Small 8vo; 304 leaves; contemporary binding of alum tawed vellumized pigskin over oak boards, boldly stamped on front cover is baroque portrait of Augustus I, elector of Saxony, rear cover bears his arms, binding retains original clasps, quite scarce.   Family Album Tillers-602 1996 $500.00

ASSOCIATION - AULD

GOLDSMITH, OLIVER 1730-1774   The Miscellaneous Works. Perth: printed by R. Morison Jr. for R. Morison and Son, 1792. 8vo in half sheets; 7 volumes; frontispiece and engraved additional titlepage to volume 1, frontispiece in each volume, these browned; contemporary tree calf, smooth backstrips divided by ball and bolt roll between rules, gilt lettered and red leather title labels in second compartments, dark blue circular volume labels in fourth; contemporary ownership signature of Rb. Auld, Edinb. 1796, sprinkled and polished edges, small chip to head of two backstrips and tail of another, otherwise excellent. Blackwell's B112-134 1996 £250.00

ASSOCIATION - AUSTIN

BLAND, WILLIAM   Experimental Essays on the Principles of Construction in Arches, Piers, Buttresses &c. London: John Weale, 1839. 1st edition; 8vo; viii, 103, (1) pages, 8 page publisher catalog, many text illustrations; publisher's cloth, neatly rebacked; presentation inscription by author to a Mr. Austin, probably Henry Austin, the civil engineer, from the library of J. G. James.   Elton Engineering 10-14 1996 £135.00

ASSOCIATION - AVERY

WILLIAMS, S. W.   American Medical Biography. Greenfield: 1845. 1st edition; 8vo; 9 portraits lithographed by W. C. Sharp of Boston; some foxing; cloth, spine worn and repaired, corners stubbed, errata slip tipped in at end; contemporary signature of J. P. Avery, later bookplate of Charles Willmarth, M.D.   Maggs Bros. Ltd. 1190-535 1996 £75.00

ASSOCIATION - E. B. AVERY

GRAY, ASA   Letters of Asa Gray. Boston: 1893. 1st edition; 8vo; pages (4), 838; 2 volumes, 6 illustrations; original cloth, some corner rubbing and wear to spine ends, piece missing from page margin, light foxing to frontispiece; included are 2 ALS's by Gray, the recipient is E. B. Avery.   Raymond M. Sutton VI-12 1996 $450.00

ASSOCIATION - JOHN AVERY

JENNINGS, HENRY CONSTANTINE   Summary and Free Reflections, In Which the Great Outline Only, and Principal Features, of the Following Subjects are Impartially Traced and Candidly Examined. Chelmsford: printed by Clachar, Frost and Gray, for the author, 1783. 8vo; xvii, (1), 115, (1), 31, (1), 64, iv, vi, 82, 6, (4), 7-34, 142-178, iv, 68 pages, few annotations in pencil; bound in modern maroon morocco, raised bands, spine lettered in gilt; contemporary signature of Hary Le Dieu on title and bookplate of John Avery; inscribed by author.   John Drury 82-124 1996 £500.00

ASSOCIATION - EDWARD AYER

CAMPBELL, JOHN L.   Idaho: Six Months in the New Gold Diggings. New York: Published by J. L. Campbell, 1864. 1st edition; (1)-52, 53-63 ads, (1-4 ads on mauve paper, vignette and four full page illustrations, frontispiece map; original yellow pictorial front wrapper with back wrapper having ad, wrappers printed yellow and are semi-glazed, title printed in red and black, slightly soiled, with few minor tears, cloth slipcase. From the collection of Edward Ayer with his booklabel. Smith 580; Streeter Sale 3301; Graff 560; Flake 1117; Mintz Trail 75.   Michael D. Heaston 23-78 1996 $12,500.00

GEBOW, JOSEPH A.   A Vocabulary of the Snake, Or Sho-Sho-Nay Dialect... Green River City: Freeman and Bros. print, 1868. 2nd edition; 24 pages; original printed front wrapper only bound in three quarter morocco, very good. From the library of Edward Ayer with his booklabel. Graff 1533; Streeter Sale 2232. Pilling 1487;   Michael D. Heaston 23-154 1996 $6,500.00

ASSOCIATION - EDWIN BACHMAN

THACKERAY, WILLIAM MAKEPEACE 1811-1863   The Irish Sketch-Book. London: Chapman and Hall, 1843. 1st edition; 8vo; 2 volumes; numerous engravings; original green cloth, spine ends showing little wear, spines lightly faded, three hinges renewed, chip in front free endpaper, some discoloring of frontispieces around edges, else unusually fine, fresh copy, relatively scarce; in green cloth slipcase with matching chemise, gilt stamped with Bachman's monogram; armorial bookplate of R. FitzGerald Uniacke, bookplates of Edwin Bachman.   James Cummins 14-209 1996 $300.00

ASSOCIATION - BADEN

SALMON, THOMAS   A New Historical Account of St. George for England and the Original of the most Noble Order of the Garter. London: R. Janeway for Nath. Dancer, 1704. 8vo; title, 3ff., 109 pages, 2 ff (contents to part II), 113 pages, 2 portraits and 1 view; slight browning, pencil underlinings, later morocco; with Baden-Powell bookplate. Lowndes p. 2179.   Marlborough 162-198 1996 £125.00

ASSOCIATION - A. W. BAHR

SIREN, OSVALD   Early Chinese Paintings from A. W. Bahr Collection. London: Chiswick Press, 1938. Limited to 750 numbered copies; folio; 116 pages; 27 tipped in plates, including 13 in color; buckram, gilt, top edge gilt, others uncut, covers very slightly dust soiled. Inscribed by A. W. Bahr to A. J. Kiddell.   Thomas Thorp 489-282 1996 £125.00

ASSOCIATION - BAILLIE

ANDERSON, WALTER   The History of Coresus in IV Parts. Edinburgh: printed by Hamilton, Balfour and Neill, 1755. 1st edition; 12mo; contemporary calf, spine gilt; very fine; rare; early armorial bookplate of George Baillie and signed on titlepage by Grizel (Grisell) Baillie, daughter of the well-known Scottish poetess.   Ximenes 109-7 1996 $900.00

ASSOCIATION - ROBERT GEORGE TEESDALE BAKER-CARR

HEDIN, SVEN   Central Asia and Tibet. Towards the Holy City of Lassa. London: Hurst & Blackett Ltd., 1903. 1st edition; royal 8vo; 2 volumes, 5 folding maps and over 420 illustrations; publisher's cloth, gilt, slightly dust stained and faded at fore-edge of both volumes, otherwise good. Tipped into front of volume 1 is holograph note by author on notepaper bearing his arms to Captain Baker-Carr. The recipient was Robert George Teesdale Baker-Carr.   H. M. Fletcher 121-155 1996 £300.00

ASSOCIATION - ALFRED BALDWIN

LANG, ANDREW   The Book of Dreams and Ghosts. London: Longmans, Green & Co., 1897. 1st edition; crown 8vo; xviii, (304), 32 pages; original enammeled cloth in striking art nouveau design by Paul Woodroffe, top edge gilt, spine slightly darkened, some browning of prelims and edges, but nice; 1893 bookplate of Alfred Baldwin.   Ash Rare Books Zenzybyr-59 1996 £95.00

ASSOCIATION - FAITH BALDWIN

DE VRIES, PETER   But Who Wakes the Bugler? Boston; Houghton Mifflin, 1940. 1st edition; illustrations by Charles Addams; very slight soiling, faint offsetting on rear board, near fine lacking dust jacket; author's first book; inscribed by author for Faith Baldwin.   Between the Covers 42-132 1996 $550.00

ASSOCIATION - ROGER SHERMAN BALDWIN

ABERT, JAMES WILLIAM   Report of the Secretary of War...A Report and Map of the Examination of New Mexico. Washington: Senate Executive Document 23, 1848. 1st edition; 132 pages; 24 plates, large folding map; original printed yellow wrappers, minor chipping and neatly rebacked; tall, untrimmed copy, some foxing to map, plates quite crisp and clean; fine; formerly the copy of Lindley Eberstadt; presentation copy from U.S. Senator Roger Sherman Baldwin to Yale Library. Goetzmann pp. 144-49; Streeter Sale 168; Howes A11; Graff 5. Michael D. Heaston 23-1 1996 $1,850.00

ASSOCIATION - WILLIAM HENRY BALDWIN

THE NEGRO Problem. New York: James Pott 1903. 1st edition; very slight rubbing to boards, still fine, bright copy; bookplate of William Henry Baldwin on front pastedown, Baldwin was a railroad executive, very scarce and nice association.   Between the Covers 43-253 1996 $650.00

ASSOCIATION - GEORGE BALL

HELLER, JOSEPH   Catch-22: a Dramatization. New York: Delacorte, 1973. Fine in near fine dust jacket with just a trace of wear, this copy inscribed by author for George Ball, Under Secretary of State Under Kennedy and Johnson.   Between the Covers 42-212 1996 $450.00

ASSOCIATION - SIDNEY BALL

PATER, WALTER 1839-1894   Imaginary Portraits. London: Macmillan, 1887. 1st edition; 8vo; original binding, bookplates of Sidney Ball and Morse Peckham, rear endpaper foxed, near fine.   Charles Agvent 4-932 1996 $125.00

ASSOCIATION - CHARLES BALLANTYNE

LUTHER, MARTIN 1483-1546   The Way to Prayer. London: William Pickering, 1846. 1st edition in English; 6 1/4 x 5 1/4 inches; xxvi pages, (1) leaf, 68 pages; frontispiece, device on title, decorative headpieces and initials; quite appealing slightly later dark brown morocco by Riviere for B. M. Pickering, covers panelled in gilt and blind, corner fleurons between raised bands, marbled endpapers, all edges gilt (with Pickering booksellers' ticket at front), slight rubbing to joints, spine bands and extremities, inner margin of frontispiece, skillfully repaired without loss, otherwise fine and attractive copy. Modern bookplates of Charles Ballantyne and H. C. Wace, owner's signature of E. Arnett on flyleaf dated 1861. Rare edition. Keynes p. 65.   Phillip J. Pirages 33-421 1996 $325.00

ASSOCIATION - BAMFORD

BLATCHFORD, ROBERT   Merrie England: a Series of Letters on the Labour Problem. London: Clarion Office and Walter Scott, 1893. 1st edition; small quarto; 101 pages; half leather, all edges gilt, head and tail of spine slightly chipped, edges of boards slightly marked; nice; inscribed "To Mr. S. Bamford with the compliments of the Clarion Board' and separately signed by author.   Ian Patterson 9-37 1996 £75.00

ASSOCIATION - JOHN KENDRICK BANGS

DOWDEN, EDWARD   Robert Southey. New York: Harper & Bros., Publishers, 1880. 1st edition; 197 page study; original binding; top ede dusty, spine slightly faded, head and tail of spine and corners slightly bumped, cover edges slightly rubbed; very good; with bookplate of John Kendrick Bangs on front pastedown; subsequently from the library of James D. Hart who has pencilled at top corner of the recto of the rear free endpaper the name of bookshop he bought the book in, with date & price.   Ulysses 39-157 1996 £55.00

ASSOCIATION - RUSSELL BANKS

MORGAN, ROBERT   Zirconia Poems. Northwood Narrows: Lillabulero Press, 1969. 1st edition; pictorial wrappers; poet's first book, fine; with ALS from Russell Banks to Jim Harrison recommending this book. Captain's Bookshelf 38-168 1996 $100.00

ASSOCIATION - BANNERMAN

MATTHEWS, HENRY   The Diary of an Invalid, Being the Journal of a Tour in Pursuit of Health in Portugal, Italy, Switzerland and France in the Years 1817, 1818 and 1819. London: John Murray, 1820. 2nd edition; 8vo; contemporary full calf, elaborate gilt borders on both covers, spine gilt, original morocco label; spine somewhat faded, but very clean and attractive copy; fine armorial bookplate of Bannerman of Elsick. Trebizond 39-108 1996 $175.00

ASSOCIATION - MAFFEO BARBERINI

RUBEUS, THEODOSIUS   Discursus Circa Literas Apostolicas in Forma Brevis S.D.M. Urvani Papae VIII. Rome: Typis Vaticanis, 1639. Folio; title in red and black with woodcut device, pages 3-56; Roman limp vellum, covers panelled gilt with double inner and outer rules, flat spine lettered in ink, gilt arms of Cardinal Maffeo Barberini, later Pope Urban VIII, with Barberini bee at each corner of the central panel.   Marlborough 160-23 1996 £1,250.00

ASSOCIATION - PHILIP BARD

HALES, STEPHEN   Statical Essays. London: 1731-33. 1st edition; 2 volumes, 376, 361 pages, plus index; recent quarter leather; Philip Bard's copies with his signature. GM 765.   W. Bruce Fye 71-893 1996 $2,750.00

ASSOCIATION - RICHARD HARRIS BARHAM

NICOLAS, HARRIS   A Treatise on the Law of Adulterine Bastardy, with a Report of the Banbury Case, and All Other Cases Bearing Upon the Subject. London: William Pickering, 1836. 1st edition; 8vo; half title, 588 pages, 9 pages ads at end, original cloth, leather label; presentation inscription for Revd. R. H. Barham.   Anthony W. Laywood 109-106 1996 £135.00

ASSOCIATION - SAMUEL BARLOW

HARRISSE, HENRY   Christopher Columbus and the Bank of Saint George: Two Letters Addressed to Samuel L. M. Barlow, Esquire. New York: privately printed, 1888. 1st edition; one of 150 copies; 12 1/2 x 10 inches; quarter leather over boards, front hinges cracked, boards and spine rubbed, bottom of spine torn and crinkled, very scarce. This copy inscribed by Samuel Barlow.   Hermitage SP95-1103 1996 $250.00

ASSOCIATION - THOMAS OLDHAM BARLOW

DICKENS, CHARLES 1812-1870   Works. London: Chapman and Hall, 1874-76. Illustrated Library Edition; 8vo; 30 volumes; original illustrations by Phiz; original green cloth, bevelled boards, blocked in black and gilt; with some Dickens centenary stamps and other ephemeral items pasted in; from the collection of mezzotint engraver Thomas Oldham Barlow, with his bookplate in several volumes.   Sotheran PN32-8 1996 £998.00

ASSOCIATION - INGLE BARR

WESCOTT, GLENWAY   Good-Bye Wisconsin. New York: & London: Harper & Bros., 1928. 1st edition; number 99 of 250 copies; 8vo; original cloth backed boards, paper label, fore and bottom edges uncut; fine; inscribed to Ingle Barr from author.   Howard S. Mott 227-149 1996 $150.00

ASSOCIATION - CLIFTON WALLER BARRETT

ROWSON, CHARLOTTE   Charlotte. A Tale of Truth. Philadelphia: printed for Mathew Carey, Oct. 9 1794. 2nd Philadelphia edition; 12mo; 169, (1) pages; full contemporary calf, leather label, spot below label on spine chipped, outer front hinge cracked above this spot; browning and handsoiling throughout to varying degrees, one leaf torn through horizontally without loss; with Clifton Waller Barrett bookplate. Wright I 2160; Evans 276550.   M & S Rare Books 60-225 1996 $2,500.00

ASSOCIATION - ELIZABETH BARRETT

LONGFELLOW, HENRY WADSWORTH 1807-1882   The Seaside and the Fireside. Boston: Ticknor, Reed and Fields, 1850. 1st edition; 8vo; original boards, spine lacking, some loosening of stitching and wear of edges, faint offprint from publisher's ads dated Dec. 1849 on front endpapers and signature of Elizabeth B. Barrett on blank at front, generally pleasant copy internally. BAL 12099; Caroll A. Wilson Cat. 232.   James Cummins 14-127 1996 $100.00

ASSOCIATION - BARRINGTON

AUBREY, JOHN   The Topographical Collections. Devizes, Bull, 1862. 1st edition; 4to; half title, pages xiii, 491, (1 p. errata), frontispiece, 42 engraved plates, 3 folding pedigrees and 2 folding plans, 1 hand colored text plan; contemporary half morocco, trifle rubbed, one or two tears to the folding plates; presentation copy with ink ms. corrections by J. E. Jackson to Viscount Barrington, tipped in at back is Jackson's printed appeal "Ten Pounds Reward. Folio Volume of Aubrey's Wiltshire Antiquities: an Original Manuscript Missing".   Marlborough 162-268 1996 £250.00

ASSOCIATION - REDMOND BARRY

HARGRAVE, FRANCIS   A Collection of Tracts Relative to the Law of England, from Manuscripts.. London: printed by T. Wright..., 1787. 1st edition; 4to; pages (6), lii, 578, errata leaf; contemporary calf, label, gilt, headband and corner of label worn, lower joint cracked, but binding very strong, otherwise nice copy; attractive armorial bookplate of Redmond Barry.   James Fenning 133-151 1996 £245.00

ASSOCIATION - BARTLETT

STEVENSON, ROGER   Military Instructions for Officers Detached in the Field: Containing a Scheme for Forming a Corps of a Partisan. Philadelphia: R. Aitken, 1775. 1st edition; (8), vii, (1), 232, (4) pages; 12 engraved plates; contemporary sheep, hinges very skilfully restored, other than small piece torn from upper blank corner of one plate, this is a remarkably fine, fresh copy, completely free of foxing and in handsome original binding, signed "Josiah Bartlett's Book 1776"; beneath is are 3 other signatures of later 18th and 19th century members of Bartlett's family; bookplate of William S. Greenough. In attractive cloth clamshell box with leather label. Howes S981; Evans 14475.   Joseph J. Felcone 64-39 1996 $4,000.00

ASSOCIATION - JACOB BARTOL

PAULDING, JAMES KIRKE 1778-1860   Koningsmarke, the Long Finne, a Story of the New World. New York: Charles Wiley, 1823. 1st edition; 12mo; 2 volumes; contemporary mottled sheep, red morocco labels, some rubbing, especially of joints; very attractive copy; with signature of Jacob W. Bartol on each, final blank in second volume, some spotting and offsetting, generally light; scarce. BAL 15697; Wright Fiction I.2012.   James Cummins 14-151 1996 $425.00

ASSOCIATION - BRIAN BARTTELOT

SEALSFIELD, CHARLES   The Cabin Book; or, National Characteristics. London: Ingram, Cooke, 1852. 8vo; 8 plates and ads at end; original cloth; Brian B. Barttelot ownership inscription of 1852.   Rostenberg & Stern 150-8 1996 $250.00

ASSOCIATION - BASKIN

HEMINGWAY, ERNEST MILLAR 1899-1961   (Yiddish Title): The Old Man and the Sea. London: New York: Der Kval, 1958. 1st edition in Yiddish; illustrations by Leonard Baskin; yellow cloth and original unprinted tissue dust jacket; fine, very uncommon; inscribed by Baskin.   Between the Covers 42-214 1996 $275.00

TANNER, MATTHAIS   Societas Jesu Apostolorum Imitrix Sive Gesta Praeclara et Virtutes Eorum. Prague: A. G. Konias, 1694. Large 4to; 196 engravings; 19th century full crimson morocco with scalloped gilt outer border inside of which is a double gilt fillet border, upon which sits an inch wide elaborate border composed of alternating floral designs, including acorns and lilies, spine with seven raised bands and complimentary gilt tooling in six of the compartments, the second and third from the top being reserved for two morocco labels bearing title information, inner gilt dentelles, board edges gilt, marbled endleaves, all edges gilt, bound by J. Mackenzie, bookbinder to the king; with gilt stamped Huth bookplate (his sale, Sotheby's 8 Jul6 1919, lot 7206) and bookplate of Leonard and Lisa Baskin.   Book Block 32-67 1996 $7,500.00

ASSOCIATION - SALLIE K. BATES

LONGFELLOW, HENRY WADSWORTH 1807-1882   The Divine Tragedy. Boston: James R. Osgood and Co., 1871. 1st edition; the 8vo. format (also published in 12mo); BAL does not give priority; original purple cloth gilt, faded, some rubbing with fraying and losses at head and tail of spine, ownership stamp on title and blank, some marginal browning, generally light; contemporary gift inscription "Miss Sallie K. Bates with the best wishes of her friend Mrs. R. Cambridge Christmas 1871."   James Cummins 14-126 1996 $150.00

ASSOCIATION - BATTERSEA

SWINBURNE, ALGERNON CHARLES 1837-1909   A Note on Charlotte Bronte. London: Chatto & Windus, 1877. 1st edition; later issue; 7 1/2 x 5 inches; pages vi, 97, 32 pages publisher's ads dated Oct. 1883. dark green cloth, gilt titling backstrip, uncut, pale blue and grey floral patterned endpapers, uncut, very good, bookplate of Lord Battersea, slight foxing to prelims and edges of pages; very good. Wise 64, Wise pp. 71/72.   Ian Hodgkins 78-379 1996 £75.00

ASSOCIATION - HENRY BAUER

ZOLA, EMILE   Les Rougon-Macquart, Histoire Naturelle et Sociale d'une Famille Sous le Second Empire. Paris: G. Charpentier et Cie, 1886. 1st edition; 12mo. in half sheets, pages (iv), 491; quarter morocco, spine in compartments with raised bands, gilt rules and lettering, original wrappers bound in, some spotting, very good. Presentation copy from author to Henry Bauer, with ALS by Zola about the book, bound in.   Simon Finch 24-265 1996 £1,400.00

ASSOCIATION - BAYLIES

WALLER, EDMUND   The Works...in Verse and Prose. London: Tonson, 1753. Octavo; pages (16), 272; frontispiece; original polished calf, spine profusely gilt decorated, leather label, marbled endpapers, all edges sprinkled, silk ribbon marker; wear to spine and hinges, text excellent; With 2 fine armorial bookplates on pastedown: Robert Walpole of Lincoln's Inn, on flyleaf W. Baylies, M.D. (physician to Frederick the Great). Lowndes IV 1892; CBEL II 455.   Hartfield 48-L90 1996 $295.00

ASSOCIATION - BARTH BEALE

THE LAW of Commons and Commoners. London: Atkins for J. Walthoe, 1698. 1st edition; octavo; contemporary calf, worn, rebacked, some foxing, 2 leaves of prelims with blank corners torn away, with 3 publisher's ads; inscription "Barth Beale, 1706". Wing L634.   Maggs Bros. Ltd. 1190-3 1996 £200.00

ASSOCIATION - BENJAMIN LLOYD BEALL

FLETCHER, JOHN   Studies on Slavery, in Easy Lessons. Natchez: published by Jackson Warner, 1852. 8vo; xiv, 637 pages; contemporary calf with morocco spine label, marbled endpapers, light soiling and moderate wear, scattered foxing, very good. the copy of Benjamin Lloyd Beall. Sabin 24729.   Andrew Cahan 47-181 1996 $125.00

ASSOCIATION - AUBREY BEARDSLEY

ROSSETTI, CHRISTINA 1830-1894   Poems. London: Macmillan and Co. and New York, 1891. New edition; 8vo; pages xiv, (2), 450, (2) ads, frontispiece and 3 plates after D. G. Rossetti; original blue cloth, gilt rules and small circles on sides and spine to a geometric design after D. G. Rossetti, spine lettered in gilt, uncut; excellent copy; Aubrey Beardsley's copy, signed by him.   Simon Finch 24-197 1996 £1,500.00

ASSOCIATION - BEAUFORT

MONRO, ROBERT   His Expedition with the Worthy Scots Regiment. London: William Jones, 1637. 1st edition; folio; pages (xvi), 89, (xxiii), 224, (xviii), 3 parts in 1; paginated as two; Roman letter, attractive woodcut initials and head and tailpieces; general light age yellowing, faintest waterstain to inner upper corner of early leaves, good clean copy; 17th century panelled calf, spine gilt; armorial bookplate, 1705 of Henry, Duke of Beaufort. STC 18022. Lowndes 1585.   A. Sokol XXV-66 1996 £750.00

ASSOCIATION - CYRIL BEAUMONT

DE LA MARE, WALTER 1873-1956   The Sunken Garden and Other Poems. London: Beaumont Press, 1917. 1st edition; one of 6 copies, printed for presentation (of an edition of 276 copies); crown 8vo; printed in black and red on handmade paper; original quarter fawn buckram, printed backstrip and front cover labels, that on backstrip trifle darkened, floral patterned pale grey boards, faint free endpaper browning, untrimmed; good. Presentation copy inscribed by Cyril Beaumont to George Sutcliffe of Sangorski & Sutcliffe. Beaumont 2.   Blackwell's B112-17 1996 £95.00

ASSOCIATION - EDWIN BECHTEL

PERCY, WILLIAM ALEXANDER   The Collected Poems of William Alexander Percy. New York: Knopf, 1943. 1st edition; fine in dust jacket with few very small chips, tipped in is one page TLS from Percy to Edwin Bechtel; with recipient's attractive bookplate and ink notation. Captain's Bookshelf 38-184 1996 $250.00

ASSOCIATION - BECKFORD

ROBERT, of Gloucester fl. 1260-1300   Robert of Gloucester's Chronicle. Oxford: printed at the Theater, 1724. 8vo; 2 volumes; xciv, (ii), 364; (365)-800 pages; contemporary panelled calf, spines decorated gilt, labels; lightly rubbed, spines slightly chipped at head, little dampstaining in volume 1, insignificant marginal worming; nice set, according to old note on front endpaper "The Beckford copy".   Robert Clark 38-59 1996 £120.00

ASSOCIATION - BARRY BECKHAM

AWOONOR, KOFI   This Earth, My Brother... Garden City: Doubleday, 1971. 1st edition; near fine in attractive dust jacket, despite two inch edge-tear to front panel; inscribed by author to African-American Novelist Barry Beckham.   Lame Duck Books 19-7 1996 $150.00

FORREST, LEON   The Bloodworth Orphans. New York: Random House, 1977. 1st edition; fine in lightly soiled, about fine dust jacket; very warmly inscribed to fellow novelist Barry Beckham and dated 1979. Between the Covers 43-79 1996 $125.00

WALCOTT, DEREK   Selected Poems. New York: FS, 1964. 1st edition; corners very slightly bumped, still fine in dust jacket; inscribed by author to fellow author Barry Beckham.   Between the Covers 43-199 1996 $275.00

ASSOCIATION - BEDFORD

BLACKWELL, MISS   Poverty and Affluence. Brussels: imp. de G. Stapleaux, 1851. 1st edition; 12mo; 2 volumes in one, pages 190, (i), errata: 192; half titles; some foxing, chiefly marginal in first volume; contemporary red hard grain morocco, richly gilt, marbled endpapers, gilt edges, by Dodd and Peeling, Woburn; from the ducal library at Woburn with bookplate of Anna Maria, Duchess of Bedford. Rare.   Simon Finch 24-8 1996 £950.00

BOYS, JOHN   A General View of the Agriculture of the County of Kent... London: for G. Nicol, 1796. 8vo; xiv, (2), 206 pages, errata leaf, folding hand colored map, 2 engraved plates, folding table; contemporary half russia; very good; Duke of Bedford's copy with Woburn Abbey bookplate.   Ken Spelman 30-62 1996 £225.00

BYRON, GEORGE GORDON NOEL, 6TH BARON 1788-1824   Sunset from the Parthenon. N.P.: Chevening?: 1875. 1st edition; 4to; contemporary half calf and marbled boards, spine gilt, trifle rubbed; leaf of heavily corrected ms. from an early version of Byron's "Curse of Minerva" reproduced in photographic facsimile, along with letterpress titlepage, leaf of explanation, fine copy; from the library of Duke of Bedford at Woburn Abbey. Not in Wise or NCBEL.   Ximenes 108-55 1996 $400.00

EVELYN, JOHN 1620-1706   Silva: or, a Discourse of Forest-Trees and the Propogation of Timber In His Majesty's Dominions. London: 1786. 2nd Hunter edition; 4to; 2 volumes; (xlvi), 311, (ix); (ii), 343, (x); (viii), 72, (iv); portrait, 42 plates, 3 folding tables; calf, rebacked; bookplate of the Duke of Bedford.   John Henly 27-351 1996 £250.00

HOWARD, JAMES   Continental Farming and Peasantry. London: William Ridgeway, 1870. 1st edition; 8vo; iv, 104 pages; original gilt lettered green cloth, fine; few pencil notes in margins; although without any marks of provenance, this is the Duke of Bedford's copy.   Ken Spelman 30-86 1996 £75.00

JACKSON, JOHN   A Defense of Human Liberty, in Answer to the Principal Arguments Which Have Been Alledged Against It. London: J. Noon, 1725. 1st edition; 8vo; (8), 207, (1) pages, ads on verso of last leaf; contemporary calf, gilt, joints cracked, otherwise very good, crisp copy; the Woburn Abbey copy with contemporary armorial bookplate of Duke of Bedford, blue circular Woburn Abbey shelf label and Bedford arms in gilt on each cover.   John Drury 82-122 1996 £350.00

ASSOCIATION - WILLIAM BEDFORD

GLOVER, ROBERT   Nobilitas Poltica Vel Civilis. London: William Jaggard, 1608. 1st edition; 4to; 190, (1) pages; 9 full page engravings; contemporary full limp vellum, covers soiled, text leaf R4 wanting, one plate trimmed and mounted, various notices tipped to front endpaper, thus fair only; with ownership signatures of William Bedford and Charles Kirkpatrick Sharpe, with Bedford's bookplate.   Chapel Hill 94-222 1996 $125.00

ASSOCIATION - MAYSON BEETON

TRIMBLE, WILLIAM TENNAT   The Trimbles and Cowens of Dalston, Cumberland. Carlisle: privately printed, 1935. Large 8vo; pages 64, 26; 20 plates; original cloth, gilt, presentation copy, inscribed to Sir Mayson Beeton from author, further copy of the 'Supplement' in original wrappers, inscribed, laid in.   R.F.G. Hollett & Son 78-266 1996 £60.00

ASSOCIATION - OLIVE BEHRENDT

KRAFT, WILLIAM   The Dream Tunnel: a Magical Journey through the Music of America: for Narrator and Orchestr. N.P.: n.p., 1976. Folio; 71 page musical score; spiral bound, together with 7 4to. sheets of text by Barbara Kraft; stiff blue wrappers; very good; signed and inscribed by author to Olive Behrendt.   George J. Houle 68-78 1996 $395.00

PRICE, VINCENT   The Vincent Price Treasury of American Art. Waukesha: Country Beautiful Corp. 1972. 1st edition; 4to; 150 plates in color, over 300 black and white illustrations; dust jacket (few chips and tears), good to very good. Signed by Price and inscribed to Olive Behrendt.   George J. Houle 68-123 1996 $125.00

ASSOCIATION - DAVID BELASCO

GUITRY, SACHA   Deburau. Published by Belasco, 1925. 1st edition; 178 pages; 34 plates with tissue; stiff boards with jacket, fine in board box. Inscribed by David Belasco to Dr. Arthur Hobson Quinn.   Lyman Books 21-493 1996 $100.00

ASSOCIATION - HELEN STRONG BELKNAP

BRISTED, JOHN   The Resources of the United States of America; or, a View of the Agricultural, Commercial, Manufacturing, Financial, Political, Literary, Moral and Religious Capacity and Character of the American People. New York: James Eastburn & Co., 1818. 1st edition; 8vo; xvi, 505, (1) pages; occasional unobtrusive spotting, original half calf, gilt, sometime rebacked with original backstrip preserved, marbled sides; very good; from the library of Helen Strong Belknap and William Burke Belknap with their bookplate. Sabin 8050; Kress C24; not in Einaudi, Hollander, McCulloch or Masui.   John Drury 82-33 1996 £150.00

ASSOCIATION - WILLIAM BURKE BELKNAP

BRISTED, JOHN   The Resources of the United States of America; or, a View of the Agricultural, Commercial, Manufacturing, Financial, Political, Literary, Moral and Religious Capacity and Character of the American People. New York: James Eastburn & Co., 1818. 1st edition; 8vo; xvi, 505, (1) pages; occasional unobtrusive spotting, original half calf, gilt, sometime rebacked with original backstrip preserved, marbled sides; very good; from the library of Helen Strong Belknap and William Burke Belknap with their bookplate. Sabin 8050; Kress C24; not in Einaudi, Hollander, McCulloch or Masui.   John Drury 82-33 1996 £150.00

ASSOCIATION - BENJAMIN BELL

CORRIE, EDGAR   Letters on the Subject of the Scotch Distillery Laws. Liverpool: M'Creery, 1796. Half title, 23 pates; recent marbled wrappers; nice, inscribed presentation copy from author to Benjamin Bell.   C. R. Johnson 37-7 1996 £150.00

ASSOCIATION - THOMAS BELL

JOHNSTONE, CHEVALIER DE   Memoirs of the Rebellion in 1745 and 1746. London: Longman, Hurst etc., 1822. 3rd edition; 8vo; pages lxxii, 456, folding plan, 2 engraved portraits (little spotted and stained); old roan backed boards gilt, little rubbed. Woodcut bookplate of Thomas Bell, 1797.   R.F.G. Hollett 76-139 1996 £120.00

ASSOCIATION - WALTER LEONARD BELL

ROSE, D. MURRAY   Historical Notes and Essays on the '15 and '145. Edinburgh: William Brown, 1897. Limited edition (150); 8vo; pages xii, 198, 2 portraits and 10 facsimiles; original buckram, gilt; armorial bookplate of Walter Leonard Bell.   R.F.G. Hollett 76-260 1996 £65.00

ASSOCIATION - HILAIRE BELLOC

WELLS, HERBERT GEORGE 1866-1946   The World Set Free. Macmillan, 1914. 1st edition; tight, very good copy; inscribed by author to fellow author Hilaire Belloc.   Aronovitz 57-1261 1996 $795.00

ASSOCIATION - BELMORE

MASON, HENRY JOSEPH MONCK   Reasons and Authorities and Facts Afforded by the History of the Irish Society, Respecting the Dusty of Employing the Irish Language, as a More General Medium for Conveying Scriptural Instruction to the Native Peasantry of Ireland. Dublin: printed by M. Goodwin and Co., 1835. 3rd edition; 8vo; 32 pages; original plain brown paper wrappers; nice; inscribed (twice) "For Earl Belmore" (?by the author).   James Fenning 133-229 1996 £65.00

SAUNDERSON, FRANCIS   The Case Stated of Education As It Was and Ought to Be Restored; and As It Now and Ought to be Discontinued. Dublin: George Herbert, 1862 1st (?only) edition; large 12mo; 103 pages; original cloth, large printed paper label on upper cover, nice/fine copy with 6 line inscription by author to Earl of Belmore. Remarkably scarce.   James Fenning 133-298 1996 £85.00

ASSOCIATION - BELPER

BRUTON, JOHN HILL   Life and Correspondence of David Hume. Edinburgh: William Tait, 1846. 1st edition; 8vo; 2 volumes, xvii, (1), 480; vii, (1), 534 pages, bound without half titles; frontispiece, folding facsimile letter in volume 1, 2 facsimiles of Hume's holograph in volume 2; contemporary calf, gilt and panelled, contrasting labels and marbled edges by Hayday; fine; from the 19th century library of Lord Belper with his bookplate. Jessop p. 46; Mossner p. 636; not in Chuo.   John Drury 82-117 1996 £275.00

ASSOCIATION - ELMER BELT

ABBOTT, MAUDE E.   Classified and Annotated Bibliography of Sir William Osler's Publications. Montreal: Medical Museum, McGill University, 1939. 2nd edition; 8vo; xiii, (ii), 163 pages; frontispiece, plate, 16 figures; blue cloth, very good; bookplate of Elmer Belt.   Jeff Weber 31-102 1996 $120.00

MUIRHEAD, ARNOLD   Grace Revere Osler, a Brief Memoir. London: printed for private circulation at Oxford University Press, 1931. 1st edition; 8vo; 35 pages, frontispiece, 2 plates; original vellum backed grey baords; fine, rare; bookplate of Elmer Belt.   Jeff Weber 31-101 1996 $150.00

OSLER, WILLIAM 1849-1919   An Alabama Student and Other Biographical Essays. New York: Oxford University Press, London: Henry Frowde, 1908. 1st edition; 8vo; (iv), 334 pages; frontispiece, illustrations; red cloth; very good; signed by S. Hamilton Jr. Nov. 1908, bookplate of Dr. Elmer Belt.   Jeff Weber 31-29 1996 $175.00

OSLER, WILLIAM 1849-1919   Bibliotheca Osleriana. A Catalogue of Books Illustrating the History of Medicine and Science...Bequeathed to McGill University. Oxford: Clarendon Press, 1929. 1st edition; limited to 761 copies; 4to; xxxv, 785 pages; navy blue cloth, hinges and spine repaired; bookplate of Elmer Belt. GM 6772; Golden & Roland 1073.   Jeff Weber 31-33 1996 $700.00

OSLER, WILLIAM 1849-1919   The Growth of Truth, As Illustrated in the Discovery of the Blood. London: Henry Frowde, Oxford University Press, 1906. 1st separate printing; 8vo; 44 pages; grey printed wrappers, blue cloth slipcase, red leather spine label; scarce; occasional pencil notes in margin, otherwise very good; bookplate of Elmer Belt.   Jeff Weber 31-47 1996 $145.00

OSLER, WILLIAM 1849-1919   Lectures on Angina Pectoris and Allied States. New York: D. Appleton, 1897. 2nd edition; 8vo; vi, 160, ads (8) pages; dark green embossed cloth; very scarce; bookplate of Elmer Belt. Bedford 627; Golden & Roland 669.   Jeff Weber 31-50 1996 $300.00

OSLER, WILLIAM 1849-1919   Lectures on Angina Pectoris and Allied States. New York: D. Appleton, 1897. 2nd edition; 8vo; vi, 160, ads (8) pages; brown embossed cloth, signature of C. H. Bunting and bookplate of Elmer Belt. Golden & Roland 669.   Jeff Weber 31-51 1996 $200.00

OSLER, WILLIAM 1849-1919   Lectures on the Diagnosis of Abdominal Tumors. New York: D. Appleton, 1894. 2nd edition; 8vo; (iii), 192 ads (2) pages; 43 figures; brown cloth, fine; bookplate and stamps of Elmer Belt. Golden & Roland 643.   Jeff Weber 31-52 1996 $250.00

OSLER, WILLIAM 1849-1919   The Principles and Practice of Medicine. New York: D. Appleton, 1892. 1st edition; 2nd state, "Georgias" corrected to read "Gorgias" and other internal corrections. 8vo; xvi, 1079, ads (vi), 8 page index; ads dated March 1892; modern quarter brown morocco and marbled boards, new endleaves, fine, bookplate of Elmer Belt. GM 2231; Golden & Roland 1378.   Jeff Weber 31-70 1996 $750.00

ASSOCIATION - ELMER BELT

OSLER, WILLIAM 1849-1919   The Principles and Practice of Medicine. New York: D. Appleton, 1896. 2nd edition; 8vo; xvi 1143, ads, (4), 8 pages, 19 charts, 11 figures, ads dated June 1896; later quarter black leather, green cloth, leather corners; very good; signature of Albert E. Brown, 1896; bookplate of Elmer Belt.   Jeff Weber 31-73 1996 $275.00

ASSOCIATION - OLIVIA BENARD-SPARROW

BRITISH & FOREIGN BIBLE SOCIETY   Reports of the British and Foreign Bible Society, with Extracts of Correspondence, &c... London: printed for the Society by J. Tilling, 1805-16. 22cm; various pagination; gilt and blindstamped dark blue calf, all edges gilt; very good. This set given by the Society to (lady?) Olivia Bernard-Sparrow (came from Kimbolton Castle Lib).   Rockland Books 38-29 1996 $1,500.00

ASSOCIATION - J. T. BENNETT-POE

JEKYLL, GERTRUDE   Wall and Water Gardens. London: Country Life/George Newnes, n.d. 1901. 1st edition; light foxing, inscribed by author for J. T. Bennett-Poe, horticulturist.   Between the Covers 42-185 1996 $950.00

ASSOCIATION - BENNYHOFF

ANDERSON, ARTHUR J. O.   Florentine Codex. Santa Fe: School of American Research and the University of Utah, 1950-69. Limited to 1000 copies; 4to; 13 parts in 11 volumes; 1669 pages, over 1700 illustrations; original cloth, several corners bumped; very scarce; J. A. Bennyhoff's light pencil annotations in several volumes, his stamp in most volumes. Archaeologia Luxor-4214 1996 $650.00

KELLY, ISABEL   The Archaeology of the Autlan-Tuxcacuesco Area of Jalisco. I-II. Berkeley: University of California Press, 1945-49. 8vo; 2 volumes, 390 pages, 73 figures and 29 plates, 8 maps; lightly worn wrpapers, with ink stamp of Bennyhoff.   Archaeologia Luxor-4591 1996 $150.00

LINNE, S.   Mexican Highland Cultures: Archaeological Researches at Teotihuacan, Calpulalpan and Chalchicomula in 1934/35. Stockholm: Ethnographic Museum, 1942. 4to; 223 pages, 333 figures and 6 plates; chipped wrappers; with ink stamp and pencil annotations of Bennyhoff. Archaeologia Luxor-4639 1996 $250.00

MASON, J. ALDEN   Archaeology of Santa Marta Colombia; The Tairona Culture, Part I-II: 2. Chicago: Field Museum, 1931-39. 8vo; 3 volumes, 418 pages, 26 figures, 248 plates, 2 maps; wrappers. With signature of J. A. Bennyhoff.   Archaeologia Luxor-4681 1996 $250.00

RICKETSON, OLIVER G.   Uaxactun, Guatemala. Group E --- 1926-1931. Washington: Carnegie Inst. of Washington, 1937. 8vo; xiii, 314 pages, 198 figures, 88 plates, 1 folding map in pocket at rear; original printed wrappers, scarce; with stamp of J. A. Bennyhoff at foot of spine. Archaeologia Luxor-4817 1996 $275.00

SHOOK, EDWIN M.   Tikal Reports Numbers 1-11 in 3 Parts. Philadelphia: University Museum, 1958-61. Small 4to; 2 volumes of text and 1 volume of maps loose in portfolio; 344 pages, 99 figures; iv, 26 pages, 1 figure, 3 tables, 9 large folding maps loose in portfolio; wrappers. Ink stamps of Bennyhoff.   Archaeologia Luxor-4890 1996 $125.00

THOMPSON, J. ERIC   Excavations at San Jose, British Honduras. Washington: Carnegie Inst. of Washington, 1939. 4to; xi, 292 pages, 100 figures, 33 plates, 18 tables; original printed wrappers, light staining to top and bottom of wrappers; with signature of J. A. Bennyhoff. Archaeologia Luxor-4950 1996 $250.00

ASSOCIATION - J. L. BENSON

KENNA, V. E. G.   Cretan Seals, with a Catalogue of the Minoan Gems in the Ashmolean Museum. Oxford: Clarendon Press, 1960. Folio; 163 pages, 72 figures and 23 plates; original cloth, torn dust jacket. With signature of J. L. Benson.   Archaeologia Luxor-3554 1996 $350.00

ASSOCIATION - LESLIE BENSON

TENNYSON, ALFRED TENNYSON, 1ST BARON 1809-1892   Maud. Kelmscott Press, 1893. One of 500 copies on paper (there were also five vellum copies, not for sale); 8 1/4 x 5 3/4 inches; 2 p.l., 69, (1) pages; large woodcut initials and decorative marginal extensions, device at end, printed in red and black, using Golden type; original limp vellum, gilt titling on spine, silk ties, in original very slightly worn publisher's green slipcase, titled in gilt, elaborate woodcut frontispiece and borders around first pages of text, as fine a copy as one could hope to find; bookplate of Leslie Benson. Sparling 17; Tomkinson p. 112.   Phillip J. Pirages 33-323 1996 $1,400.00

ASSOCIATION - BENTHAM

GRAY, ASA   Characters of Some New Genera and Species of Plants of the Natural Order Compositae. Boston: Journal Nat. History, 1845. Offprint; 8vo; pages 8; plate; later plain wrappers, staples bit rusted; inscribed by author to Bentham (one great botanist to another). Maggs Bros. Ltd. 1190-9 1996 £75.00

ASSOCIATION - B. BENTHAM

BYNG, JOHN   The Trial of the Honoruable Admiral John Byng, at a Court Martial, as Taken by Mr. Charles Fearne, Judge Advocate of His Majesty's Fleet. London: R. Manby, 1757. 1st edition; tall folio; 130, 19 pages; full contemporary calf, upper joint cracked but firm, red morocco label; signature of B. Bentham dated 1757 to verso of title and final leaf; engraved bookplate of Sir Strafford N. Northcote (private secretary to Gladstone).   Ian Wilkinson 95/1-147 1996 £240.00

ASSOCIATION - BENZ

BUCHANAN, ROBERT   The Piper of Hamelin: Fantastic Opera in Two Acts. London: Chiswick Press, 1893. 1st edition; 7 1/4 x 5 1/2 inches; 1 p.l., 63, (1) pages; added engraved title and 12 plates by Hugh Thomson; fine chestnut brown morocco by Sangorski & Sutcliffe, front cover with gilt titling above charming gilt vignette of two dancing rats, their tales entwining a musical pipe, spine with raised bands, gilt ruled compartments, gilt titling, blind ruled extensions of the raised bands terminating on covers in finial of 3 leaves, turn-ins with triple gilt fillets, all edges gilt, in fine plush lined folding morocco case by Zaehnsdorf with raised bands and gilt spine titling; from the distinguished collections of Doris Benz and Paul Chevalier with their bookplates. Virtually flawless copy   Phillip J. Pirages 33-69 1996 $600.00

ASSOCIATION - REBECCA BERGER

SIMMS, WILLIAM GILMORE 1806-1870   The Wigwam and the Cabin. First (and Second) Series. New York: Wiley and Putnam, 1845. 1st edition; 8vo; 2 parts in one volume; contemporary half black morocco, marbled boards, quite rubbed, discoloring from leather, short crack at top of upper joint, some browning and staining of endpapers, else light browning, half titles without ad leaves which determine printings, partial image of an ad leaf offset on blank at front; signatures of Rebecca Berger and E. E. Knapp on endpapers. BAL 18093, 18094; Barzun & Taylor Cat. of Crime 3461.   James Cummins 14-181 1996 $750.00

ASSOCIATION - BERKELEY

HUSSEY, A. M.   Illustrations of British Mycology. London: 1847-55. 4to; Series 1 and 2, 2 volumes, 90 hand colored plates, 50 hand colored plates; contemporary half green roan; nice complete copy, some very limited foxing, especially of endpapers; presentation inscription to Revd. M. J. Berkeley with compliments of author and publisher.   Wheldon & Wesley 207-52 1996 £2,250.00

ASSOCIATION - W. TURNER BERRY

FOURNIER, PIERRE SIMON 1712-1768   Fournier on Typefounding. London: the Fleuron Books, Published by Soncino Press, 1930. Limited to 260 copies; 8vo; pages xxxviii, (4), 323; frontispiece, 16 double page plates; original buckram backstrip faded little marked, but good; inscribed "W. Turner Berry for his indispensable library. J.R." and subsequently in the collection of Walter Tracy with his ownership signature.   Claude Cox 107-268 1996 £75.00

ASSOCIATION - BETHUNE

KETTELL, SAMUEL   Manual of the Practical Naturalist; or, Directions for Collecting, Preparing and Preserving Subjects of Natural History. Boston: 1831. 1st edition; 8vo; frontispiece, bit browned and foxed; original cloth, worn, covers off; pencil inscription by M. Bethune; the Bradley Martin copy.   Maggs Bros. Ltd. 1190-247 1996 £85.00

ASSOCIATION - JOHN BEWLEY

MARK, JOHN   Genealogy of the Family of Mark or Marke, Cumberland, Pedigree and Arms of the Bowscale Branch of the Family. Manchester: privately printed, 1898. 4to; pages 285; 16 engraved plates; original quarter navy morocco and cloth, gilt, gilt top. Presentation copy, inscribed by author to John Bewley of Stanwix, Carlisle.   Howes Bookshop 265-1908 1996 £75.00

ASSOCIATION - A. C. BICKNELL

DWYER, CHARLES P.   The Economy of Church, Parsonage and School Architecture, Adapted to Small Societies and Rural Districts. Buffalo: Phinney & Co., 1856. 1st and only edition; 8vo; vi, (7)-95 pages, 40 plates; publisher's cloth, sporadic foxing, else very good; with A. C. Bicknell's rubber stamp on endpaper.   Bookpress 75-46 1996 $500.00

ASSOCIATION - BIENNAIOS

BAIF, LAZARE DE   Annotationes in L. II. De Captivis, et Postliminio Reversis. In Quibus Tractatur De Re Navali. Paris: Robert Estienne 31 August, 1536. 1st edition; 4to; (4) leaves, 168 pages, (4) leaves, 203, (13) pages, Estienne's printer device on title, several fine large crible initials; 29 large woodcuts; 19th century half calf; wide margined copy with two early ms. entries at foot of title, one consisting of a presentation in Greek from Joseph Biennaios, probably a hellenization of the name 'Bienne'; Renouard, Estienne 44: 19; Brun p. 116; Armstrong 110.   Jeffrey D. Mancevice 20-8 1996 $1,650.00

ASSOCIATION - BIENNE

BAIF, LAZARE DE   Annotationes in L. II. De Captivis, et Postliminio Reversis. In Quibus Tractatur De Re Navali. Paris: Robert Estienne 31 August, 1536. 1st edition; 4to; (4) leaves, 168 pages, (4) leaves, 203, (13) pages, Estienne's printer device on title, several fine large crible initials; 29 large woodcuts; 19th century half calf; wide margined copy with two early ms. entries at foot of title, one consisting of a presentation in Greek from Joseph Biennaios, probably a hellenization of the name 'Bienne'; Renouard, Estienne 44: 19; Brun p. 116; Armstrong 110.   Jeffrey D. Mancevice 20-8 1996 $1,650.00

ASSOCIATION - JOHN BIGELOW

PLUTARCHUS   Plutarch's Lives. Philadelphia: William Brown for Hickman and Hazzard, 1822. New edition; 8vo; 4 volumes; frontispiece; contemporary full mottled roan, spine gilt, morocco labels, some joints weak; ms. ownerships of John P. Bigelow and Prescott Bigelow. Family Album Tillers-511 1996 $140.00

ASSOCIATION - PRESCOTT BIGELOW

PLUTARCHUS   Plutarch's Lives. Philadelphia: William Brown for Hickman and Hazzard, 1822. New edition; 8vo; 4 volumes; frontispiece; contemporary full mottled roan, spine gilt, morocco labels, some joints weak; ms. ownerships of John P. Bigelow and Prescott Bigelow. Family Album Tillers-511 1996 $140.00

ASSOCIATION - BIRD

MAJOR, RICHARD HENRY   India in the Fifteenth Century: Being a Collection of Narratives... London: printed for the Hakluyt Society, by T. Richards, 1857. 1st edition; 8vo; 8 pages ads at end; original blue cloth, spine and upper cover stamped gilt and blind, blindstamped lower cover, yellow endpapers (slight fading to spine, slight foxing), good to very good; inscribed by author for W. O'Moore Bird.   George J. Houle 68-90 1996 $150.00

ASSOCIATION - BIRKENHEAD

SECRET Anecdotes of the Revolution of the 18th Fructidor: (September 4th, 1797) and New Memoirs of the Persons Deported to Guiana, Written by Themselves... London: printed for J. Wright, 1799. 1st English edition; 8vo; little spotting of text; 19th century marbled boards, leather label; bookplate of Viscount Birkenhead. Sabin 67633.   Anthony W. Laywood 109-58 1996 £95.00

ASSOCIATION - GEORGE BIXBY

WELTY, EUDORA 1909-   White Fruitcake. New York: Albondocani Press, 1980. 1st edition; one of 450 copies printed hors commerce; thin 12mo; cover drawing by Robert Dunn; original wrappers, inscribed by publisher, George Bixby. Mint.   James S. Jaffe 34-680 1996 $100.00

ASSOCIATION - WILLIAM BIXBY

BURNS, ROBERT 1759-1796   Poems and Letters in the Handwriting of Robert Burns. Saint Louis: printed for the Burns Club, 1908. Limited edition of 300 numbered copies; folio; printed on Dutch handmade paper; numerous tipped in plates or ms. facsimiles; original half paper parchment and boards; very good, some browning to spine; signed presentation copy from William K. Bixby, the principal owner of the manuscripts reproduced herein, to the Hon. Albert Douglass.   Antic Hay 101-262 1996 $185.00

ASSOCIATION - EDWARD BLACKETT

HUDDESFORD, GEORGE   Salmagundi: a Miscellaneous Combination of Original Poetry...(with) Topsy Turvy; With Anecdotes and Observations Illustrataive of the Leading Characters in the Present Government of France. London: ptd. by E. Hodson for J. Anderson/London: ptd. for the author... 1793/93. 3rd edition of the first title, re-issue of the sheets of the second edition of 1792 with new titlepage; 2nd edition of the 2nd title, reissue of sheets of the 1st edition; 8vo; 2 volumes in one; engraved titlepage and 2 other plates (one in sepia); contemporary blue morocco, gilt, spine gilt, all edges gilt, pink endpapers by Kalthoeber, with his orange ticket (some scuffing of spine); half title present. Presentation copies, inscribed by author for Sir Edward Blackett, Bart. CBEL II 660.   Ximenes 109-160 1996 $275.00

ASSOCIATION - ANTHONY BLACKWALL

GAY, JOHN 1685-1732   Trivia; or, the Art of Walking the Streets of London. London: printed for Bernard Lintot, n.d. 1716. 2nd eidtion; 8vo; disbound; very good; signed on titlepage by Anthony Blackwall, the classical scholar and schoolmaster. Foxon G83; CBEL II 498.   Ximenes 108-154 1996 $150.00

ASSOCIATION - HENRY BLAKE

PLOT, ROBERT   The Natural History of Oxford-Shire, Being an Essay Toward the Natural History of England. at the theater in Oxford, 1677. 1st edition; folio; (10), 358, 1 f. errata, (10) page index, prelim imprimatur leaf, vignette titlepage, folding map and 16 engraved plates; contemporary calf, blind ruled panel, expertly rebacked with new gilt label; near contemporary ms. insdex on prelim blank and chapter numbers added by hand to the upper margin of each leaf; contemporary signature of Taylor Russell to front endpaper and Henry Blake to titlepage; good copy.   Ken Spelman 30-101 1996 £580.00

ASSOCIATION - ALFRED BLALOCK

HALSTED, WILLIAM   Surgical Papers by William Stewart Halsted. Baltimore: 1924. 1st edition; 2 volumes, 586, 603 pages; skilfully recased, white library adhesive label at bottom of each spine; remarkable association set, presentation from Halsted's sister to Alfred Blalock, with Blalock's signature in both volumes. GM 863.   W. Bruce Fye 71-906 1996 $600.00

ASSOCIATION - WILLIAM BLAND

ESMONDE, THOMAS   Hunting Memories of Many Lands. 1925. Many illustrations; spine and upper cover slightly discolored, contents fine. Presentation copy inscribed to William Bland.   David Grayling J95Biggame-512 1996 £55.00

ASSOCIATION - BLISS

SILLAR, DAVID   Poems. Kilmarnock: printed by John Wilson, 1789. 1st edition; 8vo; pages (i)-viii, (9)-247; titlepage and prelim leaves lightly browned, title within typographic border; early 20th century half tan calf by Bayntun, joints rubbed, short splits at head, very firm, gilt milled low bands, green morocco label in second compartment, remainder gilt panelled, fawn glazed cotton boards, marbled endpapers, top edge gilt, generally excellent; bookplates of Robert Woods Bliss and Mildred Bliss. Egerer 14; ECSB 400; Johnson, Provincial Poetry 832.   Blackwell's B112-257   1996 £350.00

ASSOCIATION - MILDRED BLISS

GREAT BRITAIN. COURT OF STAR CHAMBER - 1884   A Decree of Star Chamber Concerning Printing, Made July 11, 1637. New York: Grolier Club, 1884. One of 150 copies; 9 x 6 inches; (48) leaves, including initial blank; color device on title, full page woodcut coat of arms, decorative headpieces, tailpieces and initials; original printed paper wrappers, apparently original tissue jacket, in cloth chemise and slipcase, tissue little wrinkled (as expected), hint of soiling to wrappers, occasional light foxing to text, surprisingly fine, quite fragile; armorial bookplates of Robert Woods Bliss and Mildred Bliss, both stamped withdrawn. Phillip J. Pirages   33-282   1996 $600.00

ASSOCIATION - PHILIP BLISS

ORRERY, ROGER BOYLE, 1ST EARL OF 1621-1679   English Adventures. London: printed by T. Newcomb, for H. Herringman, 1676. 1st edition; 8vo; contemporary tree calf, nicely rebacked, spine gilt; occasional light stains, otherwise very good; the copy of Rev. Philip Bliss (1787-1857); Also the copy of David Garrick. Wing O476; Esdaile p. 167; Mish p. 51; CBEL II 770.   Ximenes   109-50   1996 $6,000.00

SHAKESPEARE, WILLIAM 1564-1616   Titus Andronicus, or the Rape of Lavinia. London: printed by J. B. for J. Hindmarsh, 1687. 1st edition thus; 4to; disbound; uncommon; from the library of Philip Bliss. Wing S2949; Bartlett (1922) 178; CBEL II 771.   Ximenes   109-259   1996 $1,500.00

ASSOCIATION - ROBERT WOODS BLISS

GREAT BRITAIN. COURT OF STAR CHAMBER - 1884   A Decree of Star Chamber Concerning Printing, Made July 11, 1637. New York: Grolier Club, 1884. One of 150 copies; 9 x 6 inches; (48) leaves, including initial blank; color device on title, full page woodcut coat of arms, decorative headpieces, tailpieces and initials; original printed paper wrappers, apparently original tissue jacket, in cloth chemise and slipcase, tissue little wrinkled (as expected), hint of soiling to wrappers, occasional light foxing to text, surprisingly fine, quite fragile; armorial bookplates of Robert Woods Bliss and Mildred Bliss, both stamped withdrawn. Phillip J. Pirages   33-282   1996 $600.00

ASSOCIATION - S. T. BLOOMLINE

AGRICOLA, GEORGIUS   De Re Metallica. London: 1912. Folio; pages xxxi, 640; 270 woodcut illustrations, many full page, short split in upper hinge, otherwise fine, bound in vellum; inscribed by H. C. Hoover to S. T. Bloomline, Esq.   John Henly   27-636   1996 £550.00

ASSOCIATION - BLUMENBACH

LAWRENCE, W.   Lectures on Physiology, Zoology and the Natural History of Man, Delivered at the Royal College of Surgeons. London: 1819. 1st edition; 8vo; pages xxiv, 579, 12 engraved plates; original boards, rebacked in calf; dedication copy, with manuscript inscription to dedicatee, Blumenbach, by Lawrence, in addition Blumenbach's letter of acknowledgement has been loosely inserted.   Wheldon & Wesley 207-56   1996 £950.00

ASSOCIATION - ANTHONY BLUNT

PHILBY, KIM   A Handbook of Marxism. London: Gollancz, 1935. Spine faded and soiled, but very good in sunned dust jacket; Bearing ownership signature "Anthony Blunt September 1935"; from the library of Philby, though without indication of his ownership of the book.   R. A. Gekoski   19-110   1996 £800.00

ASSOCIATION - WILFRED BLUNT

LINDLEY   The Lindley Library. Catalogue of Books, Pamphlets, Manuscripts and Drawings. London: Royal Horticultural Society, 1927. blue cloth, gilt lettering on spine, bit rubbed at extremities, ownership inscription of Wilfred Blunt.   Maggs Bros. Ltd.   1191-49   1996 £55.00

ASSOCIATION - JOHN BLYTH

CERVANTES SAAVEDRA, MIGUEL DE 1547-1616   Journey to Parnassus. London: Kegan Paul, Chiswick Press printed, 1883. Crown 8vo; portrait, pages (2), lxxv, (2), 387; original binding, gilt, edges gilt, metal clasp, very good to nice; inscribed to John Blyth by James Gibson.   James Fenning   133-52   1996 £55.00

ASSOCIATION - DANIEL BOLTON

WAUGH, EVELYN 1903-1966   Helena, a Novel. London: Chapman & Hall, 1950. One of about 50 copies on large paper, specially printed for Waugh to give to his friends; large 8vo; pages xiii, 265; original white buckram, edges untrimmed, covers trifle soiled, but very nice; author's presentation copy, inscribed by author for Daniel Bolton.   Sotheran PN32-60   1996 £1,995.00

ASSOCIATION - PAUL HYDE BONNER

MOYLLUS, DAMIANUS   A Newly Discovered Treatise on Classic Letter Design Printed at Parma by Damianus Moyllus Circa 1480. Officina Bodoni, 1923. One of 222 copies; 11 1/2 x 8 inches; 38 pages, (1) leaf (colophon); device in colophon, printed in blue-gray and black; original vellum over stiff boards, titled in gilt on spine, gilt device on front cover, edges untrimmed and unopened, hint of soil and discoloration to binding, very slight browning of leaves right at edges, but these defects quite minor and an extremely fine copy in general; bookplates of Paul Hyde Bonner and of Colton Storm, compiler of the catalog of the Graff collection.   Phillip J. Pirages   33-407   1996 $1,250.00

ASSOCIATION - ELWOOD BONNEY

DELLENBAUGH, FREDERICK S.   A Canyon Voyage. New Haven: Yale University Press, 1926. 2nd edition; 8vo; xxxviii, 277 pages; color frontispiece with tissue guard, numerous photos illustrations, chapter head and tailpieces (by author), maps, 4 folding; occasional light foxing, else very good; inscribed to Elwood Bonney on endpaper with sketch of a canoe dated March 6th, 1932, New York, with lengthy inscription; with initialled annotations by author and Bonney.   Andrew Cahan   47-64   1996 $350.00

ASSOCIATION - BORDEN

CONSTABLE, HENRY   The Poems and Sonnets. Vale Press, 1897. One of 210 copies; 9 1/4 x 6 inches; ci, (1) pages, (1) leaf (colophon, limitation), elaborate woodcut vine border on first page of text as well as fine decorative woodcut initials by Charles Ricketts; absolutely splendid crimson morocco, heavily gilt, by Riviere & Son (very possibly contemporary), covers with very wide and animated borders of circulating gilt vines terminating in deeply gouged broad leaves & groups of flowers & emanating from a semis ground, raised bands decorated with 3 large gilt dots, six spine panels, two with titling, rest with leafy gilt vines like those on covers, turn-ins gilt ruled and with corner ornaments, top edge gilt, others untrimmed; nearly perfect copy in sumptuous binding. Armorial bookplate of M. C. D. Borden. Tomkinson p. 165.   Phillip J. Pirages   33-490   1996 $1,800.00

ASSOCIATION - BEATRICE BORLAND

KEATS, JOHN 1795-1821   Endymion: a Poetic Romance. London: for Taylor and Hesey, 1818. 1st edition; 8vo; pages ix, (x-xii), 207, with half title but without ad leaf sometimes found, with five line errata; this copy has a little additional material bound in: engraved portrait of Keats by Henry Meyer after Severn, on india paper, mounted & bound as frontispiece, & 3 critical notices from the Boston Mercury, another from London Athenaeum, cut down & mounted on p. 5; 19th century red half morocco, gilt rules on sides, spine in compartments with raised bands, gilt rules, lettering and date and leafy ornament, top edge gilt, others uncut, marbled boards, endpapers; bookplate of Beatrice Borland, somewhat spotted, otherwise excellent. Ashley III p. 13; Mac Gillvray 2; Hayward 232; Tinker 1419.   Simon Finch   24-135   1996 £3,750.00

ASSOCIATION - BOROWITZ

FLATMAN, THOMAS   Poems and Songs. London: printed by S. & B.G. for Benjamin Took & Jonathan Edwin, 1674. 1st edition; 8vo; contemporary sheep, half morocco slipcase; particularly fine copy, complete with two original blanks at beginning (one signed "A"), and two at end. The Greenhill-Borowitz-Slater copy. Wing F1151; Grolier 356; Hayward 131; CBEL II 473.   Ximenes 109-127 1996 $2,500.00

ASSOCIATION - BOULTON

GODWIN, WILLIAM 1756-1836   Things As They Are; or, the Adventures of Caleb Williams... London: for G. G. and J. Robinson, 1796. 2nd edition; 12mo; 3 volumes, half titles; contemporary half russia, marbled boards, from the Boulton Library with labels, extremities rubbed, spines in compartments with gilt rules and lettering, one cracked, one with pieces missing, few leaves clumsily opened, but internally very clean, fresh copy.   Simon Finch 24-93 1996 £650.00

ASSOCIATION - MATTHEW BOULTON

HORNE, HENRY   Essays Concerning Iron and Steel. London: T. Cadell, 1773. 1st edition; 12mo; iii, 223 pages; later polished calf; rebacked using original spine as overlay; from the library of Matthew Boulton. The Bookpress 75-418 1996 $2,500.00

ASSOCIATION - EDWARD BOURNE

BOYLE, ROBERT 1627-1691   Occasional Reflections Upon Several Subjects. London: by W. wilson for Henry Herringman, 1665. 1st edition; small 8vo; (40), 80, 161-264, 230, (10) pages; title in red and black; contemporary calf, rebacked, original spine laid down; early portrait of Boyle tipped in on imprimatur leaf; very good; signature of Edward Bourne, dated 1768. Fulton 64; Wing B4005; Honeyman Sale I 464; Waller 19434; Neu 657.   Edwin V. Glaser 121-41 1996 $950.00

ASSOCIATION - CLIFFORD BOWER

ARNOLD, E. C.   The Birds of Eastbourne. Eastbourne: 1936. Imperial 8vo; 10 colored plates, other illustrations; original buckram, top of spine, very slightly snagged, contents lightly foxed; very scarce; inscribed by author to Clifford Bower.   David A.H. Grayling MY95Orn-89 1996 £65.00

ASSOCIATION - RALPH BOYD

JOHNSON, SAMUEL 1709-1784   A Dictionary of the English Language. Dublin: printed for Thomas Ewing, 1775. 4th edition; 4to; 2 volumes; contemporary speckled calf, neatly rebacked retaining original red and green labels, very good. Signature of Reid, Ralph Boyd and bookplate of John Stafford Reid Byers. Alston V184.   Jarndyce 103-168 1996 £480.00

ASSOCIATION - MARY BOYDELL

WALTER, RICHARD 1716?-1785   A Voyage Round the World, in the Years MDCCXL, I, II,, III, IV. London: printed for the author by John and Paul Knapton, 1748. 1st edition; 4to; 42 folding engraved plates and maps, occasional foxing, 12 page list of subscribers, final leaf of direction to binder; contemporary red morocco, gilt borders, spine and inner dentelles gilt, all edges gilt, rebacked, original loose label down, covers bit scratched, some rubbing; handsome copy on royal paper in binding appropriate for presentation; pres. copy neatly inscribed by recipient, 2nd Duke of Portland "Given to me by Anson at Aix la Chapelle June ye 7th, 1748. W. Bentinck"; early booklabel of Mary Boydell. Hill 317-8; Sabin 1625.   Ximenes 109-8 1996 $5,000.00

ASSOCIATION - CECIL BOYLE

LA MOTTE FOUQUE, FRIEDRICH HEINRICH KARL, FREIHERR DE 1777-1843   Undine and Other Tales. Leipzig: 1867. Small 8vo; pages (6), 361; full green crushed morocco (backstrip and edges faded to tan), 6 sections of backstrip lettered and decorated in gold wtih four groups of three 3 pointed leaves connected by intertwined stems within ogee border, in each compartment, edges ruled and turn-ins triple-ruled with leaf and dot decoration at corners, signed "The Doves Bindery 1894"; contemporary inscripiton to Cecil Boyle with his bookplate carelessly pasted to endpaper.   Claude Cox 107-17 1996 £180.00

ASSOCIATION - COURTENAY BOYLE

HAMILTON, RICHARD VESEY   Letters and Papers of Sir Thos. Byam Martin. London: 1903-1898. 8vo; 3 volumes; portrait, 3 lithos, portrait, 2 lithos, portrait, 1 litho; blue/white loth, very good, ex-library. With Sir Courtenay Boyle's bookplate.   John Lewcock 30-90 1996 £90.00

ASSOCIATION - HENRY BRADSHAW

WEBSTER, JOHN   Love's Graduate: a Comedy. Daniel Press, 1885. One of 150 copies; 9 x 7 inches; 2 p.l., ix, (1) pages, (1) leaf, 69, (1) pages, (1) leaf (printer's device); printed on fine qualtiy thick paper; vellum backed paper boards, spine titled in gilt, 2 edges untrimmed; 2 bookplates on endpapers, titlepage with presentation inscription from editor, Stephen Edward Spring-Rice, to Henry Bradshaw dated 1885; also with ownership inscription of R. A. Neil, dated 1886 and with ms. note signed by Gosse tipped in after prefatory essay, corners bit worn, spine and covers somewhat soiled, but binding tight and otherwise pleasing; very fine internally. Madan 11.   Phillip J. Pirages 33-154 1996 $400.00

ASSOCIATION - WILLIAM BRAGGE

HERODOTUS   Historiae Libri VIIII Musarum Nominibus Inscripti...De Genere Vitaque Homeri Libellus. Lyons: Heirs of Seb. Gryphius, 1558. 16mo; pages (1)-892, 65ff. n.n., 2 ff. blank; stiff vellum, sewn through the vellum in account-book style, yapp edges, sides decorated with cornerpieces of arabesque ornament on a gilt ground and a large centrepiece of interlaced fillets and arabesque flowers also on a gilt ground , the field seme with triple dots, flat spine with three concealed bands marked by lines of gilt tooling, gilt quatrefoil in each compartment, edges handsome gauffered with large foliate ornament and parcel-gilt, pastedown and one endleaf at each end, in very sound unrestored condition; a contemporary Lyonnese binding; the copy of William Bragge, his sale Sotheby's 10 Nov. 1880 lot 457; the copy of Arthur Ram, his sale Sotheby's 25 May 1906, lot 81.   Marlborough 160-3 1996 £2,250.00

ASSOCIATION - SAMUEL BRENTON

MOUNTAINE, WILLIAM   The Seaman's Vade-Mecum and Defensive War by Sea... London: printed for W. and J. Mount, T. and T. Page, 1757. 12mo; 2 part folding plate, 2 other folding plates (one tear repaired, without loss), early signatures on front flyeaves of various seamen, beginning with Samuel Brenton of Portsmouth; contemporary unlettered calf, gilt, spine gilt; some foxing and few minor stains, but fine; all early edtions are exceedingly uncommon.   Ximenes 108-273 1996 $1,500.00

ASSOCIATION - OLIVER BRETT

BRIDGES, ROBERT 1844-1930   Peace. Printed for the first anniversary June 1st, 1903. 1st edition; c. 100 copies; 4to; pages (8); printed on Van Gelderhandmade paper, original printed blue-grey wrappers and later maroon linen, uncut; bookplate of Oliver Brett & his pencilled initials dated Dec. 1921. Madan 55.   Claude Cox 107-38 1996 £95.00

ASSOCIATION - HENRY BREWER

WINSLOW, J. B.   Exposition Anatomique de la Structure du Corps Humain. London: 1732. 1st edition; 4to; 4 folding engraved plates (slight tears at fold, blank upper margin of first defective), with 4 pages of errata (some 250!), minor browning, contemporary French mottled calf, clumsily repaired with part of the original spine missing, bit worn, bookplate of A. Louis (1723-92), name, perhaps Henry Brewer, partly erased from flyleaf.   Maggs Bros. Ltd. 1190-536 1996 £525.00

ASSOCIATION - HENRY CHARDON DE BRIALLES

LACTANTIUS FIRMIANUS, LUCIUS CAELIUS   Divinaru(m) Institutionu(m). Lyon: Jean de Tournes, 1587. 16mo; pages 785, (45), title set within wide woodcut floral border, slight worming and soiling; all edges gilt and beautifully guaffred with wide interlaced floral design, accentuated with red paint, early full red morocco, tooled in blind, each board with blind ownership stamp of an unidentified Cardinal, old repairs to spine; from the library of Count Henry Chardon de Brialles.   Family Album Tillers-377 1996 $400.00

ASSOCIATION - ROBERT BRIDGES

LE GALLIENNE, RICHARD 1866-1947   Religion of a Literary Man. London: Mathews and Lane, 1893. One of 250 larage paper copies; 8vo; original binding, very good; inscribed by publisher, John Lane to American poet, Robert Bridges.   Charles Agvent 4-819 1996 $185.00

ASSOCIATION - ROBERT BRIDGES

VAUGHAN, HENRY Silex Scintillans, &c. Scared Poems and Pious Ejaculations... London: Bell and Daldy, 1858. 8vo; pages xlviii, 247, (i), engraved titlepage; contemporary black hard grain morocco, triple rules in blind, gilt lettered direct, gilt inner dentelles, gilt edges, autograph inscription of Robert Bridges to Gerard Manley Hopkins on initial blank, head and tail of spine and corners little worn, small tear in half title not affecting text, internally clean, good, attractive edtiion; Simon Finch 24-252 1996 £1,850.00

ASSOCIATION - D. G. BRIDSON

MILTON, JOHN 1608-1674 Comus: a Mask. printed by the Cambridge Univ. Press for Ernest Benn Ltd., 1926. Limited to 300 copies; 4to; printed on handmade paper, 8 plates; original buckram gilt, covers with borders of type ornaments, very slightly rubbed, uncut, top edge gilt. Bookplates of Ruari McLean and D. G. Bridson. Forest Books 74-344 1996 £65.00

ASSOCIATION - RICHARD BRILLIANT

BLAKE, MARION ELIZABETH Roman Construction in Italy from Tiberius through the Flavians. Washington: Carnegie Inst. of Washington, 1959. 4to; xvii, 195 pages, 31 plates, 6 plans; stiff wrappers; with signature and stamp of Richard Brilliant at flyleaves. Archaeologia Luxor-3016 1996 $125.00

ASSOCIATION - JOHN MALCOLM BRINNIN

ROETHKE, THEODORE The Waking. New York: Doubleday and Co., 1953. 1st edition; 8vo; near fine in bright, but lightly creased dust jacket, more so at extremities; inscribed presentation copy for John Malcolm Brinnin. Lakin & Marley 3-51 1996 $1,000.00

ASSOCIATION - BRISSAC

SEAGER, JOHN A Supplement to Dr. Johnson's Dictionary of the English Language... London: printed by A. J. Valpy, 1819. 1st edition; 4to; uncut in original blue boards, marked and worn at corners, spine recently neatly rebacked; inscribed as a gift from Captain Brissac to John Budd, 1821. Jarndyce 103-187 1996 £220.00

ASSOCIATION - CHARLES ASTOR BRISTED

TAYLOR, HENRY The Statesman. London: Longman, et al, 1836. 1st edition; small 8vo; pages xviii, 267, (1); original boards, cloth back, paper label; nearly fine with little lightening of cloth, darkening of label and rubbing of edges of boards, ownership signature twice of Foley author and Astor heir Charles Astor Bristed. Howard S. Mott 227-163 1996 $150.00

ASSOCIATION - NATHANIEL BRISTED

PERCY, THOMAS, BP. OF DROMORE 1729-1811 Reliques of Ancient English Poetry... London: printed for J. Dodsley, 1767. 2nd edition; 8vo; 3 volumes; contemporary calf, worn, half titles, frontispiece, engraved vignettes, unsigned, but probably after Wale, E6 torn (volume 1), some short marginal tears, engraved leaf of music at end of volume 2, leaf of publisher's ads at back of volume 3; some browning and staining, well red copy; signatures of Nathaniel Bristed, gift inscriptions from Miss Bristed to George Arden dated 1830; Courtney-Nichol Smith p. 111; Chapman & Hazen p. 148; Rothschild 1521. (all for 1st ed.). James Cummins 14-155 1996 $150.00

ASSOCIATION - BRITTAIN

SIMPSON, JAMES YOUNG Acupressure, a New Method of Arresting Surgical Haemorrahge and of Accelerating the Healing of Wounds. Edinburgh: 1864. 1st edition; 8vo; 42 text illustrations, light waterstain on lower portion of book throughout, becoming more noticeable towards end; green cloth by Burn, with their ticket, binding little worn and stained, front joint beginning to split; inscribed "Mr. Brittain with author's kind regards". Russel & Forster p. 50. Maggs Bros. Ltd. 1190-508 1996 £225.00

ASSOCIATION - BURT BRITTON

WOLFE, TOM Radical Chic and Mau Mauing the Flak Catchers. New York: FSG, 1970. 1st edition; long galleys, strign tied and printed on rectos only; nicely inscribed for Burt Britton. Between the Covers 42-467 1996 $650.00

ASSOCIATION - BRITWELL

CIBBER, THEOPHILUS The Lives and Characters of the Most Eminent Actors and Actresses of Great Britain and Ireland... London: printed for R. Griffiths, 1753. 8vo; pages xcix, xiv, 89, final blank leaf; original boards, uncut, large unopened, cloth folding case, minor wear to covers, but fine, unsophisticated copy; evidently the Britwell copy, with pencil shelfmark. LAR 2503. Peter Murray Hill 185-38 1996 £475.00

ASSOCIATION - BRODIE

PHILLIPS, JOHN 1800-1874 The Geology of Oxford and the Valley of the Thames. Oxford: 1871. 8vo; pages xxiv, 523, 12 publishers ads, 2 geological maps, 2 sections, all hand colored, 2 plain sections, 11 plates, 210 text figures; cloth, rebacked preserving spine; presentation copy from author for Rev. P. B. Brodie, pencilled marginal notes by Brodie. John Henly 27-537 1996 £110.00

ASSOCIATION - T. DAWSON BRODIE

MAC KENZIE, GEORGE 1636-1691 Memoirs of the Affairs of Scotland from the Restoration of King Charles II. Edinburgh: 1821. Large paper; 4to; pages xii, 332; old diced calf, gilt, edges very rubbed and scraped, sometime rebacked in matching calf gilt, raised bands, upper joint cracking. Armorial bookplate, signed, of T. Dawson Brodie. R.F.G. Hollett 76-182 1996 £60.00

ASSOCIATION - DANIEL BRODY

BROCH, HERMANN James Joyce und die Gegenwart. Zurich: Reichner, 1936. 1st edition; wrappers; near fine; inscribed by author to Daniel Brody. Lame Duck Books 19-94 1996 $1,500.00

ASSOCIATION - J. S. BROMELY

NEALE, JOHN The Elizabethan House of Commons. 1949. Elizabeth I and Her Parliaments 1559-1581. Elizabeth I and Her Parliaments 1584-1601. London: 1949-57. 1st editions; 8vo; 3 volumes; plates; original cloth, dust jackets. Professor J. S. Bromley's set with ownership. Howes Bookshop 265-878 1996 £65.00

ASSOCIATION - B. H. BRONSON

BOSWELL, JAMES 1740-1795 The Journal of a Tour to Corsica & Memoirs of Pascal Paoli. Cambridge: Cambridge University Press, 1923. 1st edition; black and white portrait; cloth backed patterned paper boards, spare title label, top edge dusty, head and tail of spine and corners bumped and bruised, covers marked, rubbed, dusty and slightly soiled, free endpapers browned, very good; with pencilled ownership signature of B. H. Bronson, who has marked off several passages in the book, again in pencil. Ulysses 39-60 1996 £55.00

ASSOCIATION - RUPERT BROOKE

ELIOT, CHARLES Turkey in Europe. London: Edward Arnold, 1908. New edition; 8vo; 2 folding maps; worn; enclosed in attractive black cloth box with blue labels; Rupert Brooke's copy, boldly inscribed less than two months before his death. Lakin & Marley 3-3 1996 $1,250.00

ASSOCIATION - CAROLINE BROOKS

EMERSON, RALPH WALDO 1803-1882 Nature. Boston: James Munroe, 1836. 1st edition; 1st state of page 94 (no priority). Original green coral pattern embossed cloth, gilt, minor rubbing and foxing, but fine, from the library of Caroline D. Brooks, who married E. R. Hoar in 1840. Myerson A3.a.a. (frame A cloth 2); BAL 5181. Mac Donnell 12-35 1996 $3,000.00

ASSOCIATION - CLEANTH BROOKS

WELLEK, RENE   Concepts of Criticism. New Haven and London: Yale University Press, 1963. 1st edition; original binding, head and tail of spine bumped, covers marked and rubbed, very good in nicked, rubbed and spotted, creased, torn and dusty dust jacket; presentation cropy from author for Cleanth Brooks.   Ulysses 39-601 1996 £65.00

ASSOCIATION - VAN WYCK BROOKS

SCHWARTZ, DELMORE   The World is a Wedding. Norfolk: New Directions, 1948. Uncorrected proof, string tied signatures in unprinted wrappers, light stain and slight crease to one corner of the front wrapper, little darkening to extremities of wrappers, very good; Van Wyck Brooks's copy with his ownership signature, titled in his hand and with some of his notes on front wrap and few in text.   Between the Covers 42-389 1996 $750.00

ASSOCIATION - WALTER BROOKS

BOSWELL, JAMES 1740-1795   Life of Samuel Johnson. Oxford: Clarendon Press/New York: Macmillan, 1887. 1st of this important edition; tall 8vo; original green cloth, gilt titles, uncut, 14 portraits, maps and facsimiles, some folding; some wear but very good. Bookplate of Walter Brooks. Pottle 98.   Hartfield 48-V4a 1996 $395.00

ASSOCIATION - BROUGHAM & VAUX

PORSON, RICHARD 1759-1808   Letters to Mr. Archdeacon Travis, in Answer to His Defence of the Three Heavenly Witnesses. London: T. and J. Egerton, 1790. 8vo; (ii), xxxix, (i), 406, pages; 11th century morocco backed boards, spine gilt, rubbed, little foxing; tipped in to this copy is leaf inscribed "To Henry Lord Brougham and Vaux...from Edward Chichester (=Maltby), A.D. 1833"; Brougham's gilt coronet and monogram on spine.   Robert Clark 38-199 1996 £150.00

ASSOCIATION - JAMES BROUGHAM

PUGH, JOHN   A Treatise on the Science of Muscular Action. London: 1794. 1st edition; 8vo; engraved title, 15 engraved plates by Kirk, each with key plate, minor browning, ruled border of several plates cut into, several plates mounted and with tears repaired (in case of plate 1 just touching the figure), few other minor repairs, 5 plates with duplicate descriptions mounted on versos (cut from second quire of prelims), contemporary half calf, bit worn; 19th century bookplate of James Brougham.   Maggs Bros. Ltd. 1190-488 1996 £345.00

ASSOCIATION - ALBERT BROWN

OSLER, WILLIAM 1849-1919   The Principles and Practice of Medicine. New York: D. Appleton, 1896. 2nd edition; 8vo; xvi 1143, ads, (4), 8 pages, 19 charts, 11 figures, ads dated June 1896; later quarter black leather, green cloth, leather corners; very good; signature of Albert E. Brown, 1896; bookplate of Elmer Belt.   Jeff Weber 31-73 1996 $275.00

ASSOCIATION - EDITH BROWN

EARHART, AMELIA   20 Hours. 40 Minutes: our Flight in the Friendship. New York: Putnam/Knickerbocker Press, 1928. 1st edition; 8vo; frontispiece, numerous photos; gilt stamped maroon cloth, facsimile ms. endpapers (slight rubbing); very good Signed and inscribed by author for Edith R. Brown.   George J. Houle 68-8 1996 $1,500.00

ASSOCIATION - JOHN BROWN

RUSKIN, JOHN 1819-1900   Praeterita. Outlines of Scenes and Thoughts Perhaps Worthy of Memory in My Past Life. Sunnyside, Orpington, Kent: George Allen, 1886-89. 1st edition; one of 600 large paper copies, with extra plate not found in ordinary copies, and with all 3 of the plates printed on India paper; 4to; 3 volumes; bound from original parts, including all four of the original titles to parts I-IV of volume 3, which was never completed; this set with extra engraved portrait of Ruskin; three quarter morocco, gilt spines in compartments, marbled endpapers, top edge gilt; extremities and edges bit scuffed and worn, otherwise good set. Presentation copy inscribed by author for John Brown. Wise 258.   David J. Holmes 52-95 1996 $1,250.00

ASSOCIATION - JOHN MASON BROWN

CRAIG, EDWARD GORDON 1872-1966   Books and Theatres. London: 1925. 1st edition; 164 pages, 32 plates and 3 illustrations; moderate wear, but very good, acceptable copy; ownership signature of John Mason Brown. Note pasted in; signed by author.   Lyman Books 21-94 1996 $175.00

FLANAGAN, HALLIE   Shifting Scenes of Modern European Theatre. New York: 1928. 1st edition; 280 pages; illustrations; pasted in autograph letter by Flanagan to critic John Mason Brown; sunned, very good.   Lyman Books 21-146 1996 $125.00

ASSOCIATION - LES BROWN

RULE, BOB   Champions Golf Club 1957-1976. Houston: Graphics Unlimited, 1976. 1st edition; small 4to; color frontispiece, numerous illustrations; dust jacket (some rubbing); very good, signed and inscribed by Jack Burke and Jimmy Demaret to bandleader Les Brown.   George J. Houle 68-54 1996 $125.00

ASSOCIATION - OSWALD BROWN

PEARSON, ALEXANDER   The Doings of a Country Solicitor. Kendal: Titus Wilson, 1947. Signed limited edition, number 50 of 500 signed copies; tall 8vo; pages xvii, 198, 32 illustrations; original cloth, gilt, dust jacket, rather worn and repaired; presentation copy inscribed to Oswald and Phyliis Brown of Grange-over Sands), loosely inserted 2 sm. original photos of author, P.c.s. and ALS, both from author to Browns.   R.F.G. Hollett & Son 78-230 1996 £55.00

ASSOCIATION - PHYLIIS BROWN

PEARSON, ALEXANDER   The Doings of a Country Solicitor. Kendal: Titus Wilson, 1947. Signed limited edition, number 50 of 500 signed copies; tall 8vo; pages xvii, 198, 32 illustrations; original cloth, gilt, dust jacket, rather worn and repaired; presentation copy inscribed to Oswald and Phyliis Brown of Grange-over Sands), loosely inserted 2 sm. original photos of author, P.c.s. and ALS, both from author to Browns.   R.F.G. Hollett & Son 78-230 1996 £55.00

ASSOCIATION - ROBERT BROWNING

BROWNING, ELIZABETH BARRETT 1806-1861   A Selection from the Poetry....First Series (-Second Series). London: Smith, Elder & Co., 1884. New edition; 8vo; 2 volumes; original brown cloth, some rubbing, spines bit dull; first volume bit shaken, but very good set; presentation copy, inscribed by Robert Browning for William G. Kingsland, who has added another inscription passing the set on to his grandson. Barnes E145.   Ximenes 108-367 1996 $450.00

ASSOCIATION - ELIZABETH BROWNLOW

BUTLER, ELIZABETH   A Memoir of the Very Rev. Richard Butler, Vicar of Trim. 1863. 8vo; quarter leather, good. Presentation copy to Lady Elizabeth Brownlow.   C. P. Hyland 216-71 1996 £110.00

ASSOCIATION - THOMAS BROWNRIGG

CARLISLE, ANTHONY   An Essay on the Disorders of Old Age, and On the Means for Prolonging Human Life. London: printed for Longman, Hurst, 1817. 1st edition; 8vo; titlepage printed in red and black, pages iv, 103; some foxing, but very good, contemporary half calf; armorial bookplate of Thomas Brownrigg.   James Fenning 133-48 1996 £145.00

ASSOCIATION - BRUCE

RAWLINSON, RICHARD   The English Topographer. London: T. Jauncy, 1720. 1st edition; 8vo; (viii), xliv, 275, (13) pages; contemporary calf, nice, light chipping at extremities of spine, hinges strong but starting. With bookplate of Charles Bruce of Ampthill and later bookplate of G. H. Wyatt.   The Bookpress 75-347 1996 $600.00

ASSOCIATION - BRUCE

SPENSER, EDMUND 1552-1599 The Fairie Queen: The Shepheards Calendar: Together with the Other Works of England's Arch Poet. London: H. L. for Mathew Lownes, 1611-09-12. 1st collected edition; folio; woodcut illustrations, head and tailpieces, decorated title; 18th century mottled calf with armorial crest on covers of lion rampant loading a cannon, rebacked, new lower endpapers and corners, joints worn, some chipping, especially along lower edges, final blanks Ii4 and F4 present, upper corner torn A2, minor worming in blank upper margins, underlinings on one leaf, loss of lower outer corners of last gathering, some staining, browning and soiling, mostly light; good. From the library of Charles Viscount Bruce of Ampthill and Baron Bruce of Whorleton, with his dated bookplate of 1712. James Cummins 14-193 1996 $1,500.00

WORLIDGE, JOHN Systema Agriculturae... London: T. Dring, 1675. 2nd edition; folio; 3 parts in one volume; pages 324, iv (misnumbered 134), vi; old calf, front cover almost separate; some marginal worming, nice clean copy. Armorial bookplate of Charles Viscount Bruce of Ampthill. Fussell pp. 68-70; Perkins 1947; McDonald pp. 116-121; Hunt 361. Second Life Books 103-219 1996 $700.00

ASSOCIATION - JOHN BRUNNER

DICK, PHILIP K. Do Androids Dream of Electric Sheep. New York: Doubleday, 1968. 1st edition; just about fine in very good+ dust jacket with some light wear to dust jacket spine extremities; John Brunner's copy with his personal bookplate, nice association. Aronovitz 57-338 1996 $1,375.00

NIVEN, LARRY A Gift from Earth. MacDonald, 1969. 1st British and 1st hardcover edition, review copy with accompanying review slip laid in; fine in near fine dust jacket; nice association, from the collection of John Brunner with his bookplate. Aronovitz 57-852 1996 $375.00

NIVEN, LARRY Neutron Star. MacDonald, 1969. 1st British and 1st hardcover edition; review copy with accompanying review slip laid in; fine in near fine dust jacket; from the collection of John Brunner, with his bookplate. Aronovitz 57-853 1996 $185.00

NIVEN, LARRY World of Ptavvs. MacDonald, 1969. 1st British and 1st hard cover edition, review copy with accompanying review slip laid in; fine in near fine dust jacket; nice association, the copy of John Brunner with his bookplate. Aronovitz 57-852 1996 $375.00

ASSOCIATION - ASHLEY BRYAN

DUNBAR, PAUL LAURENCE I Greet the Dawn. New York: Atheneum, 1978. 1st edition; illustrations; fine in near fine dust jacket, slighty faded on spine and with some light soiling, very nicely inscribed by Ashley Bryan who provided introduction. Between the Covers 43-228 1996 $125.00

ASSOCIATION - WILLIAM CULLEN BRYANT

BRYANT, WILLIAM CULLEN 1794-1878 Poems. New York: & London: D. Appleton & Co., 1872. 8vo; 590 pages; illustrations; brown cloth, bumped, rubbed and soiled, rebacked with upper portion of original spine laid down, titled in gilt on spine with title within gilt device on front cover, all edges gilt, lacks rear endpaper, front endpaper chipped, hinges reinforced with black tape, few page edges creased and chipped, text printed within red ruled frame; good; inscribed to a namesake William Cullen Bryant. Blue Mountain SP95-91 1996 $125.00

ASSOCIATION - JOHN BUCKLAND-WRIGHT

SHAKESPEARE, WILLIAM 1564-1616 The Passionate Pilgrim and the Songs in Shakespeare's Plays. Vale Press, 1896. One of 310 copies; 8vo; printed in Vale type, woodcut illustrations, border and initials by Charles Ricketts; original boards with printed labels, backstrip darkened and worn at head and foot, corners bruised, internally nice fresh copy; from the library of John Buckland-Wright with his neat pencilled initials and notes on endpaper; warm signed autograph presentation inscription from T. J. Cobden-Sanderson. Bertram Rota 272-479 1996 £150.00

ASSOCIATION - GEORGE BUCKLEY

MEZERAY, FRANCOIS A General Chronological History of France... London: Thomas Basset, 1683. 1st English edition; thick folio; 3 parts in 1; fine additional engraved title, laid down with slight loss, printed title laid down with signature of George Buckley dated 1698, first couple of leaves of prelims little soiled, full contemporary panelled calf, old rebacked with red morocco label; Ian Wilkinson 95/1-121 1996 £220.00

ASSOCIATION - JOHN BUDD

SEAGER, JOHN A Supplement to Dr. Johnson's Dictionary of the English Language... London: printed by A. J. Valpy, 1819. 1st edition; 4to; uncut in original blue boards, marked and worn at corners, spine recently neatly rebacked; inscribed as a gift from Captain Brissac to John Budd, 1821. Jarndyce 103-187 1996 £220.00

ASSOCIATION - GEORGE BULL

GOGARTY, OLIVER ST. JOHN 1878-1957 An Offering of Swans. London: 1924. 1st Public edition; 8vo; portrait; cloth, very good. Presentation ALS from Gogarty's son to Sir George Bull. C. P. Hyland 216-276 1996 £85.00

ASSOCIATION - THOMAS BULL

JOHNSON, SAMUEL 1709-1784 The Lives of the Most Eminent English Poets. London: Bathurst et al, 1781. 1st London edition; 8vo; 4 volumes; state of portrait without publisher's imprint, signature of Tho. E Bull on f.f.e.p.; sheep, lacks ad leaf and leaf with paper labels, as customary, all but one of the leather labels lacking, joints split but tight except on volume IV where front cover is detached, scattered foxing, some pencil notes. Charles Agvent 4-754 1996 $400.00

ASSOCIATION - BUNTING

OSLER, WILLIAM 1849-1919 Lectures on Angina Pectoris and Allied States. New York: D. Appleton, 1897. 2nd edition; 8vo; vi, 160, ads (8) pages; brown embossed cloth, signature of C. H. Bunting and bookplate of Elmer Belt. Golden & Roland 669. Jeff Weber 31-51 1996 $200.00

ASSOCIATION - BASIL BUNTING

WILLIAMS, JONATHAN Descant on Rawthey's Madrigal - Conversations with Basil Bunting. Lexington: Gnomon Press, 1968. One of 500 copies; wrappers, covers slightly marked and dusty, yapp edges creased, very good, signed and dated 1982 on titlepage by Basil Bunting Ulysses 39-83 1996 £75.00

ASSOCIATION - W. H. BURBANK

INSTRUCTIONS for Officers and Non-Commissioned Officers On Outpost and Patrol Duty and Troops in Campaign. Washington: GPO, 1863. 1st edition; 8vo; 88 pages; printed wrappers; rear wrapper missing, approximately 1 1/2 inch of blank bottom of final leaf torn off, affecting two words 'shall still', front wrapper soiled and stained, oil stain on first few leaves, overall condition fair; scarce. Ink signature of "W.H. Burbank" repeated approximately 8 times scattered through the manual, pencil signature and information of E. B. Holt, of 3rd Regt. N.H. V. Robert F. Lucas 42-19 1996 $200.00

ASSOCIATION - DE BURE

NATTER, LAURENT Traite de la Methode Antique de Graver en Pierres Fines, Comparee avec la methode Moderne... London: Haberkorn for the author, 1754. Small folio; pages xxxix, 1 f., eng. dedn., 37 engraved plates (one extra plate of Sirius, from another work, tipped in); contemporary dark green morocco, triple fillet gilt, spine gilt in compartments with floral device and dog tooth and fillet borders, gilt inner dentelle, comb marbled endpapers, all edges gilt, bound by Antoine Michel Padeloup, called "Le Jeune"; from the De Bure library, with the MS shelf mark of Madame Guillaume, possibly part of the small collection formed by De Bure for her, from the collection of J. J. de Bure, from the collection of Arthur Hamilton Smith, with his bookplate with long letter (presumably to him) from de Bure. Fine, scarce. Marlborough 160-49 1996 £2,500.00

ASSOCIATION - EDWARD BURNE-JONES

SWINBURNE, ALGERNON CHARLES 1837-1909   Locrine a Tragedy. London: Chatto & Windus, 1887. 1st edition; 8vo; pages viii, 138, (ii), 32 pages ads; uncut in original dark blue-green cloth, spine gilt lettered, sides ruled in gilt, upper part of upper joint and lower part of lower joint just beginning to split, but very good, preserved in quarter green morocco folding case; presentation copy to Burne-Jones, with inscription in author's hand. Ashley VI p. 171.   Simon Finch 24-223 1996 £2,250.00

ASSOCIATION - J. C. BURNS

BURNS, R. F.   The Life and Times of the Rev. Robert Burns, D.D. Toronto: James Campbell & Son, 1872. 8vo; pages xvi 462, (ii); steel engraved frontispiece (offset on to title), engraved title, 2 woodcuts; original cloth, gilt extra over bevelled boards, spine little faded, all edges gilt, presentation copy from publisher to Rev. J. C. Burns (descendant of the subject). With APS from James C. Burns.   R.F.G. Hollett 76-50 1996 £65.00

ASSOCIATION - BUTE

FLEETWOOD, WILLIAM   Chronicon Preciosum; or, an Account of English Money, the Price of Corn, and Other Commodities for the Last 600 Years. London: Charles Harper, 1707. 1st edition; 8vo; (16), 181, (11) pages, complete with final 5 pages of Charles Harper's ads; contemporary cottage panelled calf, gilt label on spine; fine, crisp copy; from the contemporary library of James Earl of Bute, with his armorial bookplate. Kress 2553; Goldsmiths 4403; hanson 823; Hollander 635. McCulloch p192   John Drury 82-82 1996 £250.00

ASSOCIATION - CHARLES BUTLER

HENRY VIII, KING OF GREAT BRITIAN   A Necessary Doctrine and Ervidition for any Christen Man, set Furthe by the Kynges Maiestie of Englande &c. London: Thomas Barthelet, 1543. Small 4to; 118 unnumbered leaves, black letter with Roman and italic titlepage, the latter with woodcut architectural border, woodcut initials, contemporary ms. annotations on 3 pages, title and laste page bit dusty, small repairs without loss to edges of titlepage and 5 other leaves, occasional light margina stain; 18th century red morocco richly gilt, rebacked, spine remounted, all edges gilt; good copy; bookplates of Viscount Mersey and Charles Butler of Hatfield. STC 5168.7. Lowndes 1040.   A. Sokol XXV-50 1996 £1,350.00

ASSOCIATION - CLEMENTINE BUTLER

PATON, JAMES   Missioanry to the New Hebrides. London: Hodder & Stoughton, 1890. 6th edition; 2 volumes, 376 pages, frontispiece; 382 pages, frontispiece; blue gilt buckram, very bright set. ALS loosely inserted from John G. Paton to Miss Clementine Butler.   Antipodean 28-176 1996 $195.00

ASSOCIATION - ELEANOR BUTLER

ROBERTSON, MANNING   Dun Laoghaire: the History, Scenery and Developemtn of the District. 1936. 1st edition; 8vo; maps, photos; cloth, very good; signed presentation copy to Eleanor Butler, loose insert, 3 page ALS to her husband from a friend discussing architectural education.   C. P. Hyland 216-724 1996 £100.00

ASSOCIATION - HARRY BUTLER

COX, ISAAC   The Annals of Trinity County. Eugene: printed for Harold C. Holmes, 1940. One of 350 copies; xxix, 265 pages; half cloth, boards, paper spine label, bookplate, owner's ink notation, otherwise fine with slipcase; presentation signed by printer, John Henry Nash, to Harry Butler, ink notation by Butler under presentation. Howes C819; Rocq 15151.   Argonaut Book Shop 113-150 1996 $165.00

ASSOCIATION - LARSON BUTLER

WHITMAN, WALT 1819-1892   November Boughs. 1891. 1st edition; printing 3 (Winship believes this is one of 400 copies printed in 1891 intended by Whitman to be bound with Goodbye My Fancy until illness prevented him from pursuing his plans); signed by author; green cloth, few small stains on front cover, front hinge lightly cracked, near fine; inscribed by Horace Traubel in 1903 to Larson Butler with initialled note below inscription by Traubel stating that "this edn. of N.B. bound in green was designed by W.W. for his friends, not for market, + was never anywhere but on sale." Fine association.   Charles Agvent 4-1198 1996 $3,500.00

ASSOCIATION - THOMAS BUTLER

BUTLER, SAMUEL 1835-1902   A First Year in Canterbury Settlement. London: Longman, Green, Longman, Roberts and Green, 1863. half title, folding map, 32 page catalog (Jan. 1863); original plum cloth, affected by damp; inscribed by Butler's father, Thomas Butler. Hoppe 2. Hoppe 48 for 1914 ed.   Jarndyce CII-8 1996 £300.00

ASSOCIATION - W. RUSSELL BUTTON

ACKERMANN, RUDOLPH 1764-1834   The History of the Charter-House. London: Ackermann, 1816. Large 4to; title, 332 pages, engraved aquatint portrait proof to frontispiece in laid india paper, 5 hand colored aquatint plates; red straight grain morocco, marbled boards (worn), contemporary red morocco label, gilt lettered, gilt roll tool border; some offsetting, otherwise finely coored early issue. Pencil note suggests this is "The Rev. P. Fisher's copy, master of the Charter-House to whom this work is dedicated". Bookplate of W. Russell Button.   Marlborough 162-1 1996 £350.00

ASSOCIATION - JOHN STAFFORD REID BYERS

JOHNSON, SAMUEL 1709-1784   A Dictionary of the English Language. Dublin: printed for Thomas Ewing, 1775. 4th edition; 4to; 2 volumes; contemporary speckled calf, neatly rebacked retaining original red and green labels, very good. Signature of Reid, Ralph Boyd and bookplate of John Stafford Reid Byers. Alston V184.   Jarndyce 103-168 1996 £480.00

ASSOCIATION - GEORGE CAGE

STOW, JOHN   A Survay (sic) of London. London: Imprinted by Iohn Wolfe, 1599. 4to. in 8's; (viii), 483, (1 faults) pages; old calf, worn, rebacked, titlepage brittle at margins, last leaf defective, without loss of text, some pages darkened. With long history of ownership, including bookplates of Frank Staff; signatures of George Cage, George Manley, J. Millar, B. Castleton, Peter Smart, J. B. de V. Payen-Payne. Marlborough 162-207 1996 £1,100.00

ASSOCIATION - JOHN CALDWELL

MORRIS, WILLIAM 1834-1896   The Pilgrims of Hope: a Poem in Thirteen Books. London: brought together from the Commonweal, 1886. 1st collected edition; 7 1/2 x 5 3/4 inches; 69 pages; original printed paper wrappers, in cloth chemise and morocco backed slipcase with raised bands and gilt spine titling, wrapper beginning to come away from text block at top, slight fading to wrapper, two integral leaves creased during printing, otherwise very fine copy of a fragile item; with neat signature of John Caldwell.   Phillip J. Pirages 33-393 1996 $450.00

ASSOCIATION - CAMBRIDGE

LONGFELLOW, HENRY WADSWORTH 1807-1882   The Divine Tragedy. Boston: James R. Osgood and Co., 1871. 1st edition; the 8vo. format (also published in 12mo); BAL does not give priority; original purple cloth gilt, faded, some rubbing with fraying and losses at head and tail of spine, ownership stamp on title and blank, some marginal browning, generally light; contemporary gift inscription "Miss Sallie K. Bates with the best wishes of her friend Mrs. R. Cambridge Christmas 1871." James Cummins 14-126 1996 $150.00

ASSOCIATION - RICARDO CAMINOS

STOEVER, D. H.   The Life of Sir Charles Linnaeus, Knight of the Swedish Order of the Polar Star... London: printed by C. Hobson for B. and J. White, 1794. 1st English edition; 4to; engraved portrait, 4 page list of subscribers; contemporary sprinkled calf with coat of arms blindstamped on covers, rebacked preserving old spine label; some foxing of text; small ownership stamp of Ricardo Caminos. Soulsby 2627. Anthony W. Laywood 109-145 1996 £245.00

ASSOCIATION - CHARLES CAMP

MOSELEY, HENRY N.   Notes by a Naturalist, an Account of Observations Made During the Voyage of the H.M.S. "Challenger" Round the World in the Yars 1872-1876. New York: London: G. P. Putnam's/John Murray, 1892. 8vo; 540 pages, plus 4 pages ads, illustrations; tan cloth, spine label; spine and boards darkened, library blindstamp on titlepage, decorative bookplate of James Clark White, small signature of Chas. L. Camp Dec. 1919, else very good.   Parmer Books Nat/Hist-077042 1996 $195.00

ASSOCIATION - CAMPBELL

DURIE, JOHN   Confvtatio Responsionis Gvlielmi VVitakeri. Paris: Brumennius, 1582. Thick 8vo; calf and vellum; Revd. H. Campbell and Bib. Mai. Heythrop booktickets.   Rostenberg & Stern 150-82 1996 $425.00

ASSOCIATION - LORING CAMPBELL

KING, FRANK M.   Wranglin' the Past. Trails End Pub. Co., 1946. Revised edition; fine, very good dust jacket, presentation copy from author to well known collector, Loring Campbell. Six Guns 1239.   Early West 22-151 1996 $150.00

ASSOCIATION - ALBERT CAMUS

BLANCHOT, MAURICE   Celui Qui ne m'Accompagnait Pas. Paris: Gallimard, 1953. 1st edition; review copy; wrappers with some foxing to lower border of front panel, in publisher's glassine; near fine, this copy warmly inscribed by author for Albert Camus, superb association. Lame Duck Books 19-79 1996 $1,500.00

ASSOCIATION - EDWARD CANE

STRZELECKI, P. E. DE   Physical Description of New South Wales and Van Diemen's Land. London: Longman, Brown, Green and Longmsn, 1845. (xx), 462 pages, 32 pages ads dated Dec. 1848, frontispiece and 2 sepia litho plates, plus 19 engraved plates, folding map; secondary brown covers rebacked, very good; the Absolon copy. Presentation inscription from author to Edward Cane with his bookplate dated 1849. Ferguson 4168.   Antipodean 28-628 1996 $1,250.00

ASSOCIATION - GIOVANNI BATTISTA CAPPONI

FRACASTORO, GIROLAMO   Opera Omnia, in vnum Proxime Post Illius Mortem Collecta. Venetiis: Apud Ivntas, 1555. 1st edition; 4to; 1 full page woodcut (slightly damaged), several text woodcuts, 6, 281, 32 leaves; contemporary vellum, spine slightly worn at tail, several leaves misnumbered as usual, front free endpaper lacking, slight worming of last leaf and lower hinge, slight marginal waterstaining on first few leaves; neat contemporary marginalia in Latin, Fracastoro's name in ink on lower edge and leather ex-libris of Charles L. Dana. Crisp, wide margined copy; several inscriptions, indicating the volume belonged to Givoanni Battista Capponi, doctor.   Argosy 810-185 1996 $3,250.00

ASSOCIATION - DE CARAVA

ALINDER, J.   Roy De Carava Photographs. Friends of Photo, 1981. 1st edition; large square 4to; illustrations, dust jacket slightly chipped, signed and inscribed by De Carava.   J. B. Muns 154-91 1996 $100.00

ASSOCIATION - CAREW

BARRERA, A. DE   Memoirs of Rachel. London: Hurst and Blackett, 1858. 1st edition; 8vo; 2 volumes; engraved portrait (spotted); contemporary green half calf; very nice; with contemporary bookplates of Lord Carew.   James Burmester 29-10 1996 £100.00

ASSOCIATION - ROBERT CAREY

RILEY, JAMES WHITCOMB 1849-1916   Old-Fashioned Roses. London: Longmans, Green, 1888. 1st edition; 8vo; vellum backed cloth, very good in cloth slipcase; inscribed by author to Robert Carey in 1891 with 15 line poem.   Charles Agvent 4-971 1996 $325.00

ASSOCIATION - CARLINGFORD

BAGEHOT, WALTER   The English Constitution... London: Henry S. King & Co., 1872. 2nd edition; 8vo; lxxi, (i), 291, (5) pages, complete with 2 final ad leaves; original blue cloth lettered in gilt and with geometric designs in black; very good, with Carlingford armorial bookplate.   John Drury 82-12 1996 £200.00

ASSOCIATION - CARLINGFORD

REED, ISAAC   The Repository: a Select Collection of Furitive Pieces of Wit and Humour... London: for C. Dilly, 1790. 8vo; 4 volumes, 19th century half tan morocco, green cloth sides, spines richly gilt in compartments, dark green double lettering-pieces, sides with double gilt rules, green endpapers, top edge gilt, others uncut, second letterin piece on volume 4 defective, a most attractive set. with Carlingford engraved bookplates.   Simon Finch 24-194 1996 £180.00

ASSOCIATION - CARLISLE

FERGUSON, RICHARD S.   Cumberland and Westmorland M.P.'s (sic) from the Restoration to the Reform Bill of 1867, (1660-1867). London: J. Bell and Daldy and Carlisle: C. Thurman, 1871. Large paper limited edition (20 copies only); 4to; pages xix, 478; frontispiece; frontispiece; three quarter levant morocco gilt by Riviere, with 5 flattened raised bands and marbled boards, spine trifle mellowed, front flyleaf foxed, some occasional foxing and light spotting elsewhere, but generally very nice, scarce; printed memo affixed to flyleaf lists 15 recipients of the large paper copies, and a further 4 recipients are added in Ferguson's hand, including this Naworth Castle library copy; presentation copy from author for Mr. Howard (Earl of Carlisle).   R.F.G. Hollett & Son 78-152 1996 £275.00

FERGUSON, RICHARD S.   A Short Historical and Architectural Account of Lanercost, a Priory of Black Canons, 8 miles from Carlisle... London: Bell and Daldy; Carlisle:....n.d., c. 1870. Square 4to; 56 pages; lithographed title and plan, 2 large photographic plates mounted on card, flyleaf and card mounts foxed; full blind ruled tan calf, gilt, edges little rubbed and scaped; presentation copy inscribed by author for George Howard, Lord Carlisle; loosely inserted 6 page ALs from author to Lord Carlisle.   R.F.G. Hollett & Son 78-921 1996 £160.00

ASSOCIATION - A. CARLISLE

HASLAM, JOHN   A Letter to the Governors of Bethlem Hospital Containing an Account of Their management of that Insitution for the Last Twenty Years... London: Taylor and Hessey, 1818. 8vo; (2), 58, (2) pages, ads; original boards, paper label; inscribed presentation from author "A. Carlisle, Esq., from his friend the author", first blank leaf has signature also of Robert Wilfred Skeffington Lutwidge dated 1844, Lutwidge was Commissioner for Lunacy 1842-45.   C. R. Johnson 37-82 1996 £350.00

ASSOCIATION - CARMICHAEL

POPE, ALEXANDER 1688-1744   The Works. Edinburgh: A. Donaldson, 1767. 12mo in half sheets; 6 volumes; titles within typographic borders, 10 engraved plates, 2 as frontispieces; contemporary sprinkled calf, spines with raised bands, double gilt rules and ornaments, numbered in gilt, red morocco labels, red sprinkled edges; lightly rubbed in places, occasional very light spotting, 2 leaves loose in prelims of volume IV, generally an excellent, bright set; armorial bookplate of Carmichael of Eastend.   Simon Finch 24-191 1996 £350.00

ASSOCIATION - ROCCO DI CARMINATI

BLONDUS, FLAVIUS   Roma Instaurata. De Origine et Gestis Venetorum. Italia Instaurata. Verona: Boninus de Bonini, I, 20 Dec. 1481/ II, 7 February, 1482. 1st collected edition; folio; 2 volumes in one; modern quarter vellum antique style, first several pages embrowned, minor mend to blank outer edge of first leaf, blank margins with some worming, last leaves with small wormholes, piercing text but not affecting legibility, else tall and clean with scattered notes by the early humanist Rocco di Carminati, whose ownership inscription occurs beneath the colophons and has been effaced, but is still Adentifiable. Hain Copinger 3243; GW 4423; Goff B702.   G. W. Stuart 59-53 1996 $6,750.00

ASSOCIATION - CARNARVON

BOYLE, ROBERT 1627-1691   The Martyrdom of Theodora and of Didymus. London: printed by H. Clark, for John Taylor, and Christopher Skegnes, 1687. 1st edition; 8vo; the issue with single rules beneath "Didymus" and "honour" on titlepage; contemporary calf, covers with gilt coronet and initials "M.C.", spine prettily gilt (light rubbing); very fine, scarce; complete with genuine blanks at beginning and end; signature of M. Carnarvon dated 1687. Wing B3986; Fulton 173; Esdaile p. 166; Mish p. 71.   Ximenes 109-47 1996 $5,000.00

ASSOCIATION - ANDREW CARNEGIE

HARE, AUGUSTUS J. C.   Life and Letters of Frances Bunsen, Baroness. London: 1879. 1st edition; small 8vo; 2 volumes; choicely bound in three quarter blue levant morocco, gilt panelled spines, gilt tops; from the library of Andrew Carnegie.   Charles W. Traylen 117-79 1996 £65.00

HILL, ROWLAND 1795-1879   The Life of Sir Rowland Hill and the History of the Penny Postage. London: Thomas de la Rue, 1880. 8vo; 2 volumes, 6 plates; choicely bound in half red morocco, gilt tops; superb copy from the library of Andrew Carnegie.   Charles W. Traylen 117-50 1996 £190.00

ROGERS, JAMES EDWIN THOROLD 1823-1890   Cobden and Modern Political Opinion. London: Macmillan and Co., 1873. 1st edition; 8vo; xvi, (4), 382 pages; rather later brown half morocco, spine gilt, raised bands, top edge gilt, fine; from the library of Andrew Carnegie. Williams I 145.   John Drury 82-246 1996 £125.00

SMITH, GOLDWIN   The United Kingdom: a Political History. London: Macmillan, 1899. 1st edition; 8vo; 2 volumes; choicely bound in half red levant morocco, gilt tops, panelled spines; from the library of Andrew Carnegie.   Charles W. Traylen 117-197 1996 £65.00

ASSOCIATION - LOUISE CARNEGIE

STEPHEN, LESLIE   Hours in a Library. New York: & London: 1894. New edition; 8vo; 3 volumes extended to 6, extra illustrated by the insertion of 235 extra plates, mainly portraits; beautifully bound in 1948 in three quarter brown levant morocco, gilt panelled spines, gilt tops; choice copy from the library of Louise Whitefield Carnegie with her bookplate.   Charles W. Traylen 117-199 1996 £650.00

ASSOCIATION - CURT CARPENTER

JONES, FRED R.   An Uneventful Tramp. N.P.: Flexible Flyer Press, 1975. Limited to 41 copies; 12mo; 20 pages; woodcuts by Curt L. Carpenter, who also made the paper from old beach towels; light spot on back cover, else very fine. inscribed and signed by artist "For Fr. Catich April 1977".   Bromer Booksellers 90-36 1996 $150.00

ASSOCIATION - G. D. H. CARPENTER

DARWIN, CHARLES ROBERT 1809-1882   The Different Forms of Flowers on Plants of the Same Species. London: 1892. 4th thousand; 8vo; pages xxiv, 352, 15 text figures; original cloth, G.D.H. Carpenter's copy. Freeman 1286.   Wheldon & Wesley 207-1409 1996 £60.00

DARWIN, CHARLES ROBERT 1809-1882   The Movements and Habits of Climbing Plants. London: 1891. 5th thousand; 8vo; pages x, 208; original cloth; G. D. H. Carpenter's copy with his signature.   Wheldon & Wesley 207-1407 1996 £60.00

DARWIN, CHARLES ROBERT 1809-1882   The Variation of Animals and Plants Under Domestication. London: 1899. 8th impression of the 2nd edition; 8vo; 2 volumes; text figures; original cloth; G.D.H. Carpenter's copy with his signature.   Wheldon & Wesley 207-151 1996 £60.00

ASSOCIATION - CLARENCE CARRIGAN

WHARTON, EDITH 1862-1937   The Marne. London: Macmillan and Co., 1918. 1st and only English edition, binding A; brick cloth, gilt stamped on front panel and spine with title and author, front panel lettering enclosed in fillet rondel, minor wear to edges and tips, generally very good; inscribed by author for Clarence Carrigan. Garrison A27.2.   Priscilla Juvelis 95/1-279 1996 $3,600.00

ASSOCIATION - RALPH CARRUTHERS

SYMONS, ALPHONSE JAMES ALBERT   Emin. London: Fleuron, 1928. One of 300 copies; quarter bound in decorated boards, spine bumped and boards slightly rubbed, else excellent; inscribed by author for R. H. Carruthers, also laid in is autograph letter from author to Carruthers. R. A. Gekoski 19-133 1996 £200.00

ASSOCIATION - RALPH CARRUTHERS

SYMONS, ALPHONSE JAMES ALBERT   An Episode in the Life of the Queen of Sheba. London: privately printed, 1929. One of 150 copies; decorated wrappers; half title and last page offset, but nice copy. Inscribed by author for Ralph Carruthers.   R. A. Gekoski 19-135 1996 £175.00

ASSOCIATION - CARROLL CARSTAIRS

MOORE, GEORGE 1852-1933   Memoirs of My Dead Life. London: Wilson Heinemann, 1906. 1st edition; 8vo; pages vii, (i), 335, (i); original dark blue cloth, spine gilt lettered, sides panelled in blind, lower edges uncut, joints very lightly rubbed, otherwise fine, protected in quarter grey morocco slipcase; author's presentation inscription to Carroll Cartsairs. Simon Finch 24-175 1996 £250.00

ASSOCIATION - ANGELA CARTER

FEINSTEIN, ELAINE   The Ecstasy of Miriam Garner. London: 1976. 1st edition; presentation copy from author to Angela Carter; small stian on flyleaf, otherwise very good in dust jacket.   Words Etcetera 94-418 1996 £50.00

ASSOCIATION - BONHAM CARTER

WHARTON, EDITH 1862-1937   A Gift from the Grave. London: John Murray, 1900. 1st English edition, 1st printing; 8vo; blue cloth over boards, with yap edges, green flower and vine pattern on spine and front join, author and title in gilt on front cover, title and publisher in gilt on spine, spine slightly discolored, some wear to edges, generally very good, very rare; inscribed by publisher, John Murray to Ms. Bonham Carter.   Priscilla Juvelis 95/1-274 1996 $750.00

ASSOCIATION - E. F. CARTER

DAVIS, JOHN KING   Willis Island: a Storm Warning Station in the Coral Sea. Melbourne: Critchley Parker, 1923. 1st edition; 21.4 cm x 14 cm; 119 pages, frontispiece, 15 plates; blue cloth, blindstamped on front cover, gilt spine titles. Mark from paperclip on front pastedown, free endpaper and recto of frontispiece; this copy inscribed by author for E. F. Carter.   Parmer Books Nat/Hist-039380 1996 $150.00

DAVIS, JOHN KING   Willis Island: a Storm Warning Station in the Coral Sea. Melbourne: Critchley Parker, 1923. 1st edition; 21.4 x 14 cm; 119 pages; frontispiece, 15 plates; blue cloth, blindstamped on front cover, gilt spine titles, mark from paper clip on front pastedown, free endpaper and recto of frontispiece, else light wear; inscribed by author fo E. F. Carter.   Parmer Books 039Nautica-039380 1996 $150.00

ASSOCIATION - JOHN CARTER

HART-DAVIS, RUPERT   Edmund Blunden - 1896-1974 - an Address. London: 1974. One of 75 copies; wrappers, very good; inscribed presentation from author, apparently to John Carter.   Ulysses 39-275 1996 £125.00

PERUCCI, FRANCESCO   Pompe Funebri di Tutte Le Nationi Del Mondo. Verona: Francesco Rossi, 1639. Folio; pages 97, (90, engraved title; 30 engravings, numerous woodcut devices and illustrations; worn 18th century French full leather, each board stamped in gilt with large and impressive arms of the notorious Louis Francois Armand du Plessis, Duc de Richelieu; early engraved armorial ex-libris of a French Bishop, B. H. De Fourey, 18th century ms. ownership of John Carter. Brunet IV 524; Michel & Michel V. 6, p. 102.   Family Album Tillers-477 1996 $800.00

ASSOCIATION - MARY CARTER

WHITTIER, JOHN GREENLEAF 1807-1892   Songs of Three Centuries. Boston: Osgood, 1876. Household edition; 8vo; original binding, moderate wear, fair amount of offsetting from old clippings; inscribed to Mary E. Carter from the author, dated Dec. 23, 1875, only 20 days after it was issued. BAL 21933 & 11341.   Charles Agvent 4-1218 1996 $475.00

ASSOCIATION - MARY GREY BONHAM CARTER

GRAHAME, KENNETH 1859-1932   The Wind in the Willows. London: Methuen and Co., 1908. 1st edition; 8vo; pages (ii) blank, (vi0, 302, (ii) blank, imprint; frontispiece by Graham Robertson, some spotting; original pictorial cloth, gilt, top edge gilt, others uncut, little wear, short tears at head and foot of spine, hinges cracked; good copy; bookplate of Mary Grey Bonham Carter.   Simon Finch   24-97   1996 £1,200.00

ASSOCIATION - WILL CARTER

CLERIHEWS. Cambridge: Rampant Lions Press, 1938. Wrappers very slightly rubbed, spine moderately wrinkled, but excellent; autograph letter from Will Carter to John Rayner laid in.   R. A. Gekoski   19-116   1996 £75.00

ASSOCIATION - CARTWRIGHT

PHILIPS, JOHN 1676-1709   Cyder. London: for Jacob Tonson, 1708. 1st edition; ordinary paper (i.e. first) issue; 8vo; pages (iv), 89; frontispiece; contemporary panelled calf, red morocco label, red sprinkled edges, front joint cracked, endpapers browned, otherwise very clean, fresh copy; from the library of Thomas Cartwright at Aynho, with his bookplate Hayward 143; I.A. Williams p. 92; Rothschild 1535; Foxon p. 237.   Simon Finch   24-182   1996 £120.00

ASSOCIATION - RAYMOND CARVER

GARDNER, JOHN   On Becoming a Novelist.. New York: Harper & Row, 1983. 1st edition; fine in fine dust jacket, signed by Raymond Carver, who provided foreword.   Revere Books   4-145   1996 $225.00

ASSOCIATION - JOYCE CARY

LAMB, CAROLINE 1785-1828   Glenarvon. London: printed for Henry Colburn, 1816. 3rd edition; 12mo; 3 volumes; engraved half titles in each volume; contemporary maroon half calf, spines gilt decorated with floral frame, contrasting green title labels, marbled boards, with 2 leaves of engraved music in volume 2 and final ad leaf in volume 3; very nice in lovely 'lady's binding'; the Joyce Cary copy, (with his? notes on free endpapers). NCBEL III 740.   Paulette Rose   16-204   1996 $850.00

ASSOCIATION - CARYSFORT

TROLLOPE, ANTHONY 1815-1882   The American Senator. London: Chapman and Hall, 1877. 1st edition; 8vo; 3 volumes, with half titles; fine contemporary full dark green morocco, bound for the Earl of Carysfort with his arms in gilt on upper covers and his monogram at foot of the spine, raised bands, triple gilt rules, spines polished and gilt lettered in two panels and date in gilt at foot, marbled endpapers, gilt edges with Elton Hall bookplate dated 1894 and library shelf label on front pastedown; excellent set. Irwin p. 11; Sadleir 46; Tinker 2234; Wolff 6763.   Simon Finch   24-247   1996 £1,100.00

TROLLOPE, ANTHONY 1815-1882   An Editor's Tales. London: Strahan and Co., 1870. 1st edition in book form; 8vo; pages (vi), 375, (i), complete with half title and initial blank; fine contemporary binding of full dark green morocco, bound for the Earl of Carysfort, with his arms in gilt on upper cover and his monogram at foot of spine, raised bands, triple gilt rules, spine polished and gilt lettered in two panels and date in gilt at foot, marbled endpapers, gilt edges, Elton Hall bookplate dated 1894 and library shelf label, very lightly and evenly browned; very good; scarce. Irwin p. 41; Sadleir 34; Tinker 2217; Wolff 6774.   Simon Finch   24-243   1996 £375.00

TROLLOPE, ANTHONY 1815-1882   The Prime Minister. London: Chapman and Hall, 1876. 1st edition in book form; 8vo; 4 volumes, half titles not called for; fine contemporary binding of full dark green morocco, bound for Earl of Carysfort, with his arms in gilt on upper covers and his monogram at foot of spine, raised bands, triple gilt rules, spines polished and gilt lettered in two panels and date in gilt at foot, marbled endpapers, gilt edges, with Elton Hall bookplate dated 1894 and library shelf-label on front pastedown, excellent set. Irwin p. 33; Sadleir 45; Tinker 2233.   Simon Finch   24-246   1996 £1,100.00

ASSOCIATION - CARYSFORT

TROLLOPE, ANTHONY 1815-1882   The Small House at Allington. London: Smith, Elder and Co., 1864. 1st edition; with one of some (presumably four) possible variants in volume I, with hobbledehoys' correctly spelt on p. 33 and the mispagination "O" for "70"; 8vo; 2 volumes; pages (iv), 312; (iv), 316; wood engraved frontispieces and 16 plates by Millais; fine contemporary binding of full dark green morocco, bound for the Earl of Carysfort, with his arms in gilt on upper covers and his monogram at foot of spine, raised bands, triple gilt rules, spines polished and gilt lettered in two panels, and date in gilt at foot, marbled endpapers, gilt edges and Elton Hall bookplate and library shelf label, original green cloth upper cover and spine of volume 1 laid down and bound in at end of volume 1, iny chip at head of spine of volume 1, excellent set. Irwin p. 35; Sadleir 18; Tinker 2194; Wolff 6795.   Simon Finch   24-237   1996 £1,500.00

TROLLOPE, ANTHONY 1815-1882   The West Indies and the Spanish Main. London: Chapman and Hall, 1859. 1st edition; 8vo; pages iv, 395, without publishers ads; frontispiece colored map; fine contemporary full dark green morocco, bound for the Earl of Carysfort, with his arms in gilt on upper cover and his monogram at foot of spine, raised bands, triple gilt rules, spine polished and gilt lettered in two panels, date in gilt at foot, marbled endpapers, gilt edges, with Elton Hall bookplate dated 1894 and library shelf label on front pastedown, very lightly and evenly browned, very good. Irwin p. 40; Sadleir 9; Tinker 2179.   Simon Finch   24-233   1996 £675.00

ASSOCIATION - WALTER CASH

CASH, J.   The British Freshwater Rhizopoda and Heliozoa. London: 1905-19. 8vo; volumes 1-4 (of 5), 63 plates; original cloth; slight waterstaining but contents unaffected; volumes 1 and 2 with presentation inscription by Cash to his son Walter.   Wheldon & Wesley   207-1242   1996 £175.00

ASSOCIATION - ROBERT CASSIDY

SENEFLEDER, ALOIS 1771-1834   A Complete Course of Lithography: Containing Clear and Explicit Instructions in all the Different Branches and Manners of that Art... London: printed for R. Ackermann, 1819. 4to; 14 lithographic plates, some very mild browning to a few of the plates, 2 small dampstains on 2 of them, but not with usual heavy foxing, found on plates in this work, text clean and crisp; contemporary half calf, spine gilt in compartments with raised bands, Cassidy arms in top compartment, marbled boards (bit torn and rubbed), headcaps chipped, corners bumped; remarkably good, clean copy; booklabel of Robert Cassidy. Bigmore & Wyman II p. 340; Bridson & Wakeman D13.   Maggs Bros. Ltd.   1191-215   1996 £850.00

ASSOCIATION - NIDRIE CASTEL

EVELYN, JOHN 1620-1706   A Philosophical Discourse on Earth, Relating to the Culture and Improvement of It for Vegetation, and the Propagation of Plants, Etc., As It Was Presented to the Royal Society, April 29, 1675. London: printed for John Martyn, 1676. 1st edition; small 8vo; contemporary mottled calf, spine gilt, some rubbing of spine; some of gilt on spine rubbed away, but very fine and fresh; complete with prelim leaf giving order to print from the Royal Society; ownership inscripiton of Nidrie Castel, Tues. 18 Octo. 1681. later Hopetoun bookplate. Keynes 93; wing E3507.   Ximenes   109-112   1996 $3,500.00

ASSOCIATION - CHARLES DE CASTELLAN

TERENTIUS AFER, PUBLIUS 180-159 BC   Terentius A. M. Antonio Mureto, Locis. (with) Annotationes. Antwerp: Plantin, 1565. 16mo; pages 316; 144; archtiectural woodcut title frames, closely trimmed; all edges gilt, handsomely bound in full 17th century morocco, on each board the large 1663 arms of Charles de Castellan, Abbe Commandataire de Saint-Epvre, Diocese of Toul, France, his monogram repeated 4 times or spine; scarce. Brunet V715; Voet 2285/2295; Annales p. 49-50; Olivier 802.   Family Album   Tillers-600   1996 $750.00

ASSOCIATION - CASTLE FREKE LIBRARY

JOHNSON, SAMUEL 1709-1784   The Poetical Works of Samuel Johnson, LL.D. Dublin: printed for L. White, P. Byrne, and R. Marchbank, 1785. 1st Dublin edition; 12mo; contemporary calf, spine gilt; fine, scarce; bookplates of the Castle Freke Library and Robert William Rogers. Courtney p. 157; CBEL II 1126.   Ximenes   108-228   1996 $400.00

ASSOCIATION - CATICH

JONES, FRED R. An Uneventful Tramp. N.P.: Flexible Flyer Press, 1975. Limited to 41 copies; 12mo; 20 pages; woodcuts by Curt L. Carpenter, who also made the paper from old beach towels; light spot on back cover, else very fine. inscribed and signed by artist "For Fr. Catich April 1977". Bromer Booksellers 90-36 1996 $150.00

ASSOCIATION - JOHN CATOR

CRULL, JODOCUS A Compleat History of the Affairs of Spain, From the First Treaty of Partition, to this Present Time. London: Jos. Barns, 1708. 2nd edition; 8vo; frontispiece; full contemporary panelled calf, joints repaired; annotations of Peter Collinson on front free endpaper, bookplate of John Cator. Ian Wilkinson 95/1-86 1996 £175.00

THE FLOWER-Piece: a Collection of Miscellany Poems. London: printed for J. Walthoe and H. Wlathoe, 1731. 1st edition; 12mo; contemporary panelled calf, rebacked, most of original spine laid down; very good, scarce; early armorial bookplate of John Cator. Case 367; CBEL II 360 and 541. Ximenes 109-229 1996 $900.00

TROWELL, S. A New Treatise of Husbandry, Gardening and Other Matters Relating to Rural Affairs... London: 1739. 8vo; pages viii, 164; sprinkled calf, rebacked; bookplate of John Cator. Henrey 1440. John Henly 27-373 1996 £198.00

ASSOCIATION - HENRY JOHN CAULFIELD

VERGILIUS MARO, PUBLIUS 70-19 BC Bucolica, Georgica, et Aneis. Edinburgh: Apud G. Hamilton & J. Balfour, 1743. Small 12mo; pages 335, 19; contemporary Scottish full red leather gilt, all edges gilt, ms. ownership of Henry John Caulfield, 1856; Brunet V 1291; Dibdin II 552. Family Album Tillers-640 1996 $230.00

ASSOCIATION - CAYZER

NIMMO, WILLIAM History of Stirlingshire, Corrected and Brought Down to the Present Time by Rev. William M. Stirling. London: printed by John Fraser for Andrew Bean etc., 1817. 2nd edition; 8vo; 2 volumes, pages (viii), 385; 386-772, uncut, complete with folding hand colored map, 1 plan and 1 plate, map with short repaired tear slightly offset on to title, but very nice set; late 19th century half morocco, gilt, raised bands and decorative rolls. Armorial bookplate of Sir Charles Cayzer, Bart, in each volume; ms. notes relating to Garvarton Castle, 14 page article on Merchiston Castle tipped in. R.F.G. Hollett 76-221 1996 £160.00

ASSOCIATION - DAVID CECIL

GATHORNE-HARDY, ROBERT A Month of Years: Poems. Mill House Press, 1956. One of only 50 copies; 4to; blue cloth, covers little faded and bubbled, but internally very nice, crisp copy; with author's signed autograph presentation inscription to David Cecil. Bertram Rota 272-293 1996 £60.00

ASSOCIATION - MANUEL CERVANTES

GUILLERMUS, EPISCOPUS PARISIENSIS Rhetorica Divina. Basel: Johan Froben, ca. 1492. Octavo; 19th century boards under handsome 18th century vellum antiphonal leaf in red and black, light thumbing, few small waterstains at blank lower edge, quite decent; minor mends to blank portion including repairs to tiny wormholes which also pierce the Tabula with slight loss but disappear before the Beginning of the text proper; the Manuel Cervantes copy with bookplate, title soiled, few early ms. notes on title and small booklabel of former owner. Hain Copinger 8305; Goff G715. G. W. Stuart 59-60 1996 $2,950.00

ASSOCIATION - B. CHADWICK

SPELMAN, HENRY Glossarium Archaiologicum: Continens Latino-Barbara...Scholiis and Commentariis Illustrata. London: Alice Warren, 1664. Folio in 4's; pages (xii), 576; imprimatur leaf, titlepage printed in black and red within double ruled frame; mid 19th century half tan russia, backstrip darkened, front joint weak, slight wear to head, raised bands, gilt compartments, morocco grain maroon cloth sides, marbled endpapers; early ownership signature, lengthy 19th century ms. note on verso, owner's name "B. Chadwick" stamped on head margin of titlepage. Ex-libris of John Henry Johnson; good. Cordell p. 158; Wing S4925. Blackwell's B112-263 1996 £200.00

ASSOCIATION - CHAMBERLAIN

KEATE, GEORGE An Account of the Pelew Islands...from the Journals and Communications of Captain Henry Wilson... London: G. Nicol, 1788. 2nd edition; small folio; frontispiece, xxvii, (i), 378 pages; 16 plates; uncut, contemporary half calf, binding rubbed, rubberstamp on bottom edge of leaf v, some pencilling and leaves crudely repaired, text foxed. The Chamberlain family copy. The Bookpress 75-428 1996 $550.00

ASSOCIATION - SARAH CHAMBERLAIN

BROWNING, ROBERT 1812-1889 The Pied Piper of Hamlin. Portland: Chamberlain Press, 1980. Limited to 150 copies signed by artist, this copy inscribed by her as well; octavo; (16) pages; illustrations by Sarah Chamberlain, with 11 wood engravings; with prospectus; marbled boards, leather spine label stamped in black, extremely fine. Bromer Booksellers 87-119 1996 $250.00

LEAR, EDWARD 1812-1888 The New Vestments. Portland: Chamberlain Press, 1978. Limited to 100 copies, signed by artist, this copy additionally inscribed; octavo; (6) pages, french fold; illustrations by Sarah Chamberlain; printed in two colors on beige japanese paper, 2 full page wood engravings, the two illustrations each signed by Chamberlain; printed wrappers, extremely fine. Bromer Booksellers 87-118 1996 $150.00

THE THREE Bears. Portland: Chamberlain Press, 1983. Of an edition of 125 copies, this one of 25 deluxe copies, signed by Chamberlain, this copy additionally inscribed; octavo; (16) pages; designed, printed and illustrated by Sarah Chamberlain, 10 wood engravings, all engravings signed, the deluxe issue, including an extra signed print, there are also 9 inscribed proofs; bound by Barbara Blumenthal in pastepaper boards, painted to a pattern of paw prints; extremely fine, housed in dropback box of ivory buckram. Bromer Booksellers 87-121 1996 $500.00

JONES, KENNETH Stone Soup. Portland: Chamberlain Press, 1985. One of 150 copies; signed by artist, both book and laid in prospectus are additionally inscribed by artist; octavo; (26) pages; designed, printed and illustrated by Sarah Chamberlain; bound by Barbara Blumenthal in marbled boards, leather spine label stamped in black; extremely fine. Bromer Booksellers 87-120 1996 $200.00

ASSOCIATION - DAISY CHANLER

WHARTON, EDITH 1862-1937 Artemis to Actaeon. London: Macmillan, 1909. 1st British edition from American sheets with titlepage a cancel; one of only 250 copies; spine head chewed, occasional light foxing, else very good, lacking rare dust jacket. Inscribed by author to lifelong friend Daisy Chanler, scarce inscribed, but important association copies such as this are extremely rare. Lame Duck Books 19-591 1996 $5,000.00

ASSOCIATION - W. E. CHANNING

MAISTRE, FRANCOIS XAVIER, COMTE DE The Leper of Aost. Boston: Cummings, Hilliard, 1825. 1st American edition; 12mo; pages 37; original brown boards, printed paper label on front cover, uncut; fine; inscribed by translator for Revd. Dr. W. E. Channing; below this in later hand has pencilled "May have been by Rev. Henry Ware?" Howard S. Mott 227-94 1996 $200.00

ASSOCIATION - JOSIAH CHAPIN

HOFLAND, BARBARA WREAKS HOOLE 1770-1844 The Young Cadet; or, Henry Delamere's Voyage to India, His Travels in Hindostan, His Account of the Burmese War, and Wonders of Elora. New York: Orville A. Roorbach, 1828. 12mo; x, 206 pages plus 12 engraved illustrations; original maroon calf over green boards, bit rubbed, leather label of "Josiah Chapin" on front cover, some text foxing. Not in Osborne. Kenneth Karmiole 1NS-70 1996 $100.00

ASSOCIATION - R. W. CHAPMAN

AUSTEN, JANE 1775-1817 Lady Susan. London: Oxford University Press, 1925. Limited to 250 copies; 7 3/4 x 5 inches; large paper copy, pages vii, 173, 15 pages; white linen backed grey boards, printed paper title label, backstrip, spare label rear, uncut, title label slightly discolored; fine; initialled presentation copy from editor, R. W. Chapman to John Sparrow. Gilson F5; Keynes 176; Chapman 28. Ian Hodgkins 78-13 1996 £125.00

ASSOCIATION - CHATSWORTH

ANGELIO, PIETRO DA BARGA   Poemata Omnia. Diligenter ab Ipso Recognita... Rome: ex typogr. Francisci Zannetti, 1585. 2nd edition; 8vo; 2 volumes in 1; pages (xxii), 424 (p. 424 misnumbered 124), (xvi), 180, italic letter, 5 pages Greek, Roman dedications and index, separate titlepage to each volume, large engraved woodcut printer's device (stag) on each, 1 full page engraving signed Aliprandus Capriolus, large woodcut initials and ornaments; 17th century polished calf, rebacked, later gilt spine remounted; old owner's autograph on second titlepage, wormtrail through blank lower margin in last third of volume, text untouched, final leaf lightly foxed, otherwise very good; bookplate of Chatsworth library. BM STC It. p. 28; Adams A1105; Index Aurel 105.684 and 105.685.   A. Sokol XXV-5 1996 £850.00

ASSOCIATION - EDWARD CHENEY

JUVENALIS, DECIMUS JUNIUS 55-140   Paraphrasi Nella Sesta Satira di Givvenale. Venice: Curtio Naso e Fratelli, 1538. 1st edition; small 4to; 62 unnumbered leaves, italic letter; 19th century straight grainedd morocco (by Tuckett?), gilt double fillets, corner fleurons, spine and inner dentelles, all edges gilt, marbled endpapers; early ms. page numbers and marginal strokes, very few light spots in margins; very good; 19th century bookplate of Edward Cheyney. BM STC It. p. 365; Adams J 769; Brunet II 792. Fontainin II 117.   A. Sokol XXV-55 1996 £1,450.00

ASSOCIATION - JOHN MILTON CHENEY

HAWTHORNE, NATHANIEL 1804-1864   Mosses from an Old Manse. New York: Wiley & Putnam, 1846. 1st edition; 1st printing of both volumes; 2 volumes bound as one, as issued; original faded slate cloth, gilt, quite rubbed, with splits at joints neatly reglued; from the library of John Milton Cheney, with his signature on titlepage. BAL 7598; Clark A15.1.a.b.   Mac Donnell 12-71 1996 $225.00

ASSOCIATION - BEVERLY CHEW

PASSE, CRISPJIN VAN DE 1593 or 4-1667   XII Sibyllarum Icones Elegantissimi... N.P.: 1601. 8vo; wuite of 16 plates, brilliant impressions; simply (yet elegantly) bound in green pastepaper over flexible boards with single gilt fillet on both covers and title gilt within oval cartouche, spine with spare gilt decoration & red morocco title label, top edge gilt, preserved in half morocco clamshell case, also preserved are the leather bookplates of 3 previous owners: Beverly Chew, John Camp Williams and Robert Hoe; pencil note indicating that this had also been the copy of William Beckford.   Book Block 32-68 1996 $7,250.00

ASSOCIATION - MARIO DEL CHIARO

GJERSTAD, EINAR   Early Rome. Lund: C. W. K. Gleerup, 1953-73. 4to; volumes I-IVI (complete; illustrations; volumes I-IV in uniform three quarter cloth with leather labels, volumes V-VI in original printed wrappers, several corners bumped, otherwise fine. Volumes I and III are inscribed by author, Mario A. Del Chiaro's signature appears in volumes I, III and IV.   Archaeologia Luxor-3367 1996 $1,500.00

ASSOCIATION - ALEXANDER ROBERT CHISHOLM

SCOTT, ROBERT N.   The War of the Rebellion: a Compilation of the Union and Confederate Armies. Series I - Volumes I & II. Washington: GPO, 1880. 1st edition; 8vo; v, 752 pages, v, 1101 pages; tears to spine cloth repaired, bottom edge of volume 1 rubbed, marginal dampstain to volume 2, else good; the copies of Lieut. Col. Alexander Robert Chisholm, with his ownership signature. Very fine association.   Andrew Cahan 47-49 1996 $500.00

ASSOCIATION - WINSTON CHURCHILL

LAMB, CHARLES 1775-1834   The Works. London: Methuen & Co., 1903-05. 8vo; 7 volumes; frontispiece to each volume, numerous plates and illustrations; original red cloth, paper labels to spines, top edge gilt, spines sunned and slightly rubbed, paper labels soiled, otherwise very good set with spare labels tipped in at rear of each volume; from the library of Algernon Charles Swinburne, also from the collections of Sir James Stevenson, Sir Winston Churchill and Randolph Churchill, with bookplates.   Sotheran PN32-5 1996 £1,995.00

ASSOCIATION - JOY CHUTE

SINGER, ISAAC BASHEVIS   The Fearsome Inn. New York: Charles Scribner's Sons, 1967. 4to; illustrations by Nonny Hogrogian; original purple cloth, decorated in black, some light fading, illustrated dust jacke some light browning and offsetting and wear to spine; very good; inscribed by author to Marchette and Joy Chute.   James Cummins 14-184 1996 $100.00

ASSOCIATION - MARCHETTE CHUTE

SINGER, ISAAC BASHEVIS   The Fearsome Inn. New York: Charles Scribner's Sons, 1967. 4to; illustrations by Nonny Hogrogian; original purple cloth, decorated in black, some light fading, illustrated dust jacke some light browning and offsetting and wear to spine; very good; inscribed by author to Marchette and Joy Chute.   James Cummins 14-184 1996 $100.00

ASSOCIATION - MARIA CIMINO

BROWN, MARCIA   Felice. New York: Scribner's, 1958. 1st edition; 4to; water color illustrations by author; beige coth stamped in pink and black, lower end of spine slightly rubbed, else very fresh in pictorial du jacket; laid in is compliments card from author and small original watercolor drawing; inscribed dedication copy for Maria Cimino and her husband Will Lipkind.   Barbara Stone 70-40 1996 £250.00

DUVOISIN, ROGER   The Happy Hunter New York: Lothrop, Lee and Shepard, 1961. 1st edition; small oblong 4to; colored illustrations by Duvoisin; colored pictorial boards; fine in original pictorial dust jacket. Inscribed by Roger Duvoisin to Maria Cimino.   Barbara Stone 70-87 1996 £65.00

ASSOCIATION - A. CLARK

BEAUMONT, WILLIAM 1785-1853   Experiments and Observations on the Gastric Juice and the Physiology of Digestion. Plattsburgh: F. P. Allen, 1833. 1st edition; 8vo; 280 pages, 3 wood engravings in text; 3 wood engravings in text; original boards, rebacked in cloth, paper spine label, replicating original; half morocco folding clamshell box; usual light foxing to prelims; early ownership signature of A. Clark; very good. GM 989; Norman Lib. 152.   Edwin V. Glaser B122-15 1996 $2,400.00

ASSOCIATION - VAN CLEAVER

GOLDING, WILLIAM 1911-1993   The Inheritors. London: Faber, 1955. 1st edition; very good+ in like dust jacket with some slight fading to dust jacket spine; formerly Van Cleaver's copy with his ownership signature.   Aronovitz 57-455 1996 $285.00

ASSOCIATION - MILDRED CLEMENS

PAINE, ALBERT BIGELOW   Dwellers in Arcady. New York: Harpers, 1919. 1st edition; illustrations by Thomas Fogarty; original binding, near fine in scarce dust jacket with wear at spine head and short tear on rear; with ownership signature and address of Mildred Clemens; Charles Agvent 4-925 1996 $125.00

ASSOCIATION - WILLIAM CLEMENTS

CLINTON, HENRY   Narrative of: Relative to His Conduct During Part His Command of the King's Troops in North America; Particularly to tha Which Respects the Unfortunate Issue of the Campaign in 1781. London printed for J. Debrett, 1783. 6th edition; 112 pages; one third black leather and boards, bookplate of William L. Clements. Howes C496. Blue River Books 9-12 1996 $350.00

RUNDLE, T.   A Sermon Preached at St. George's Church, Hanover Square, On Sunday Feb. 17, 1733-34. To Recommend the Charity for Establishing the New Colony of Georgia. London: printed for T. Woodward...and J. Brindley, 1734. 24 pages; half morocco; bookplate c William Clements.   Blue River Books 9-149 1996 $850.00

ASSOCIATION - THOMAS CLOWES

HORNE, T. H.   A Catalogue of the Library of the College of St. Margaret & St. Bernard, Commonly Called Queen's College in the University of Cambridge. London: for the Society of Queen's College, 1827. 2 volumes; original cloth backed boards, paper spine labels, worn, spines partly detached and boards of volume 2 coming loose, mild spotting to first and last few leaves; ownership inscription of Dawson Turner with ALS dated 21st Nov. 1827 presenting it to him from Thomas Clowes of Queen's College.   Maggs Bros. Ltd.   1191-48   1996 £290.00

ASSOCIATION - THOMAS GLEN COATS

MAC PHERSON, H. A.   Vertebrata Fauna of Lakeland Including Cumberland and Westmorland and Lancashire North of the Sands. Edinburgh: David Douglas, 1892. 1st edition; large 8vo; pages civ, 552, (ss ads), folding map, 8 plates, 9 text woodcuts; original ribbed cloth, gilt, spine faded, upper joint trifle tender, but excellent, clean and sound copy; armorial bookplate of Sr. Thomas G. Glen Coats, bart.   R.F.G. Hollett & Son   78-533   1996 £120.00

ASSOCIATION - COBBOLD

BRADSTREET, ROBERT   The Sabine Farm, a Poem:.... London: printed for J. Mawman,, 1810. 1st edition; 8vo; 7 etched plates; contemporary half red morocco, gilt, spine gilt; nice, uncommon; signature "Cobbold, Holy Wells", presumably the Ipswich poet Elizabeth Cobbold (or her husband). Jackson p. 344; not in Mills.   Ximenes   108-34   1996 $225.00

ASSOCIATION - COBDEN-SANDERSON

BULLEN, HENRY LEWIS   Nicolas Jenson, Printer of Venice: His Famous Type Designs and Some Comment Upon the Printing Types of Earlier Printers. San Francisco: Printed by John Henry Nash, 1926. One of 207 copies; 16 1/2 x 10 3/4 inches; with leaf from the Jenson Printing of Plutarch's 'Lives' of 1478 laid in, leaf bit foxed, faint dampstain in lower margin, bottom edge little frayed and creased; original vellum backed marbled paper boards, leather spine label, the volume with foxing to endpapers and with portions of edges of binding darkened, top edge of text leaves also with two small grey spots, otherwise the leaf and volume in excellent condition, without any appreciable signs of use; inscribed by John Henry Nash for Mrs. T. J. Cobden-Sanderson. Goff P832; BMC V 178 (for leaf).   Phillip J. Pirages   33-339   1996 $450.00

ASSOCIATION - THOMAS JAMES COBDEN-SANDERSON

SHAKESPEARE, WILLIAM 1564-1616   The Tragedie of Anthony and Cleopatra. London: Doves Press, 1912. One of 200 copies; small 4to; printed in black and red on handmade paper; limp vellum; nice; inscribed by Thomas James Cobden-Sanderson to Madeline Whyte.   Bertram Rota   272-129   1996 £400.00

SHAKESPEARE, WILLIAM 1564-1616   The Tragicall Historie of Hamlet Prince of Denmarke. Hammersmith: Doves Press, 1909. Small quarto; 158, (2), 23, (1) pages, printed in red and black, with opening initial flourished in green by Edward Johnson; full dark blue morocco elaborately stamped in gilt, gilt board edges and inner dentelles, all edges gilt and gauffered with dotted fillet, dentelles offsetting to endpapers, fine; beautiful unsigned binding, appears to be the product of the Doves Bindery. Inscribed by Thomas James Cobden-Sanderson for Edmond Holmes.   Heritage Book Shop   196-247   1996 $3,500.00

SHAKESPEARE, WILLIAM 1564-1616   The Passionate Pilgrim and the Songs in Shakespeare's Plays. Vale Press, 1896. One of 310 copies; 8vo; printed in Vale type, woodcut illustrations, border and initials by Charles Ricketts; original boards with printed labels, backstrip darkened and worn at head and foot, corners bruised, internally nice fresh copy; from the library of John Buckland-Wright with his neat pencilled initials and notes on endpaper; warm signed autograph presentation inscription from T. J. Cobden-Sanderson.   Bertram Rota   272-479   1996 £150.00

TENNYSON, ALFRED TENNYSON, 1ST BARON 1809-1892   Seven Poems and Two Translations. London: printed by T. J. Cobden-Sanderson & Emory Walker at the Doves Press, 1902. One of 350 copies printed, 25 of them on vellum; small 4to; 56 pages, text printed in black and red; original limp vellum, spine lettered in gilt; bookplate, foxing spot affecting first few leaves, otherwise nice; inscribed by Cobden-Sanderson.   Sotheran PN32-40   1996 £328.00

ASSOCIATION - FRANK COCHRAN

MASEFIELD, JOHN 1878-1967   The Faithful - a Tragedy in Three Acts. London: William Heinemann, 1915. 1st edition; original binding, pictorial endpapers, top edge dusty, head and tail of spine and corners bumped, spine slightly darkened, first blank torn and repaired with sellotape, prelims, edges and endpapers spotted; good only; loosely inserted ALS from author to presentee, presentation copy inscribed by author to Frank Cochran, producer of the play.   Ulysses   39-393   1996 £75.00

ASSOCIATION - SYDNEY COCKERELL

EVANS, ABEL   Vertumnus. An Epistle to Mr. Jacob Bobart, Botany Professor to the University of Oxford and Keeper of the Physick-Garden. Oxford: printed by L. L. for Stephen Fletcher, 1713. 1st edition; 8vo; 33 pages; frontispiece, little light foxing of text, short tear in last leaf expertly repaired; modern marabled boards; Sir Sydney Cockerell's copy with inscriptions, with letter to Sir Sydney tipped in, inscribed "B. S. Cron from SCC 31 Jan. 1960". Foxon E530.   Anthony W. Laywood   109-53   1996 £150.00

ASSOCIATION - JACOB SOLIS COHEN

VOLTAIRE, FRANCOIS MARIE AROUET DE 1694-1778   Collection Complete des Oeuvres de Mr. De Voltaire. Geneva: 1768-77. Early collected edition; 4to; 30 volumes; 50 full page engraved portraits and illustrations; contemporary full sheep with raised bands, gilt tooled spine panels, gilt borders, fillets and dentelles, all edges gilt, couple of volumes slightly scuffed, few instances of marginalia in unkown early hand, but very attractive set in well preserved French binding; signature of Charles Willing Hare, bookplate of Jacob Solis Cohen.   Chapel Hill 94-416   1996 $1,800.00

ASSOCIATION - HENRY COLBURN

AINSWORTH, WILLIAM HARRISON 1805-1882   Rookwood: a Romance. London: Richard Bentley, 1834. 1st edition; octavo; 3 volumes; bound without half titles to volumes 2 and 3, note on flyleaf of volume 1, name on title to volumes 2 and 3, author's presentation inscription to Henry Colburn, his former publisher on half title of volume 1, bookplate removed from each volume; contemporary half calf, scuffed; interesting presentation set. Sadleir 26.   G. W. Stuart   59-3   1996 $650.00

ASSOCIATION - JAN COLDEWEY

ALSTON, E. R.   Biologia Centrali-Americana: Mammalia. London: 1879-82. 4to; pages xx, 220, 22 plates; buckram; now very scarce; from the collection of Jan Coldewey.   Wheldon & Wesley   207-11   1996 £800.00

ARCHER, G.   The Birds of British Somaliland and the Gulf of Aden. London: 1937-61. Imperial 8vo; 4 maps, 23 plain and 34 colored plates; half red morocco, gilt; very fine, very scarce; from the collection of Jan Coldewey.   Wheldon & Wesley   207-4   1996 £1,000.00

DRESSER, H. E.   A History of the Birds of Europe. London: 1871-96. Royal 4to; 9 volumes, 2 plain and 632 hand colored plates, 89 hand colored plates; half red morocco; complete set, some rather obtrusive foxing of plates in volume 4, some limited slight foxing in volumes 3 and 5, otherwise good set; from the collection of Jan Coldewey.   Wheldon & Wesley   207-26   1996 £8,500.00

GODMAN, F. DU CANE   A Monograph of the Petrels (Order Tubinares). London: 1907-10. Limited to 225 numbered copies; royal 4to; paes iv, 381, 106 hand colored plates by Keulemans; full brown morocco gilt, uncut; some limited marginal staining, especially towards end, some very slight offsetting, still good copy; from the collection of Jan Coldewey.   Wheldon & Wesley   207-38   1996 £3,500.00

HUME, A. O.   Contributions to Indian Ornithology. No. 1 Cashmere Ladak. Yarkand. London: 1873. Royal 8vo; pages (vi), 152; 32 fine hand colored plates by Keulemans; cloth. Narrow waterstain on margins of plates; from the collection of Jan Coldewey.   Wheldon & Wesley 207-51   1996 £750.00

LAYARD, E. L.   The Birds of South Africa. London: 1875-84. New edition; royal 8vo; pages xxvii, 890, 12 hand colored plates; original half green morocco, spine trifle faded and joints rubbed; very scarce, first 2 plates very slightly stained, but good, from the collection of Jan Coldewey.   Wheldon & Wesley   207-57   1996 £650.00

ASSOCIATION - JAN COLDEWEY

LEGGE, W. V.   A History of the Birds of Ceylon. London: 1878-80. Royal 4to; 3 volumes; pages xlvi, 1237, colored map, plain outline plate, 34 hand colored plates by Keulemans; recent half red morocco, gilt, top edge gilt, one or two minor stains, but nice; from the collection of Jan Coldewey.   Wheldon & Wesley 207-59 1996 £3,000.00

LILFORD, THOMAS LITTLETON POWYS, 4TH BARON 1833-1896 Coloured Figures of the Birds of the British Islands. London: 1891-97. 2nd edition; royal 8vo; 7 volumes; portrait, 421 colored plates; contemporary maroon morocco, spines faded, gilt top; exceptionally clean, entirely free from usual foxing; from the collection of Jan Coldewey.   Wheldon & Wesley 207-60 1996 £3,000.00

MILNE-EDWARDS, A.   Notice Sur Quelques Especes d'Oiseaux Actuellement Eteintes Qui se Trouvent Representees dans les Collections du Museum d'Histoire Naturelle. Paris: 1893. Reprint; 4to; pages 68, 5 hand colored plates; half cloth, one inner plate margin cracked, library stamps removed from verso of plates; some (mostly slight) foxing of text and plates, last 2 plates rather browned; from the collection of Jan Coldewey.   Wheldon & Wesley 207-66 1996 £500.00

MIVART, ST. G.   Dogs, Jackals, Wolves and Foxes. London: 1890. 4to; pages xxvi, 216, text figures, 45 hand colored plates by Keulemans; recent fullb rown morocco; fine, clean copy; from the collection of Jan Coldewey.   Wheldon & Wesley 207-68 1996 £1,600.00

MIVART, ST. G.   A Monograph of the Lories, or Brush-Tongued Parrots, Comprising the Family Loriidae. London: 1896. Original issue; royal 8vo; pages liii, 193, 4 maps, hand colored plates; original brown cloth, bevelled edges; good copy; formerly the copy of W. E. Oates, from the collection of Jan Coldewey, with bookplate.   Wheldon & Wesley 207-69 1996 £3,950.00

NAUMANN, J. F.   Iconographie d'Oiseaux d'Europe et de Leurs Oeufs. Paris: 1910. 4to; 4 volumes; pages 24, 409 colored and 5 plain plates; quarter leather; good copy; from the collection of Jan Coldewey. Wheldon & Wesley 207-74 1996 £3,000.00

OORT, E. D. VAN   Ornithologia Neerlandica, De Vogels van Nederland. The Hague: 1918-22-35. Imperial 4to; 5 volumes; 407 colored plates; half dark green morocco, spines faded. From the collection of Jan Coldewey. Wheldon & Wesley 207-76 1996 £1,300.00

SCLATER, P. L.   The Book of Antelopes. London: 1894-1900. 4to; 4 volumes; 100 fine hand colored plates by Wolf and Smit, 121 illustrations in text; blue buckram; good, rare, well rebound to match spines of original binding, some very limited slight foxing and obituary of G. Rosenboom in Dutch pasted on flyleaf volume 1, from the collection of Jan Coldewey.   Wheldon & Wesley 207-92 1996 £5,000.00

SCLATER, P. L.   A Monograph of the Jacamars and Puff Birds, or Families Galbulidae and Bucconidae. London: 1879-82. Limited to 250 copies; royal 4to; pages liii, 171, 55 hand colored plates; contemporary half morocco. bind trifle rubbed and some extremely limited slight staining; from the collection of Jan Coldewey.   Wheldon & Wesley 207-91 1996 £3,800.00

SHARPE, RICHARD BOWLDER   Monograph of the Paradiseidae, or Birds of Paradise, and Ptilonorhynchidae, or Bower-Birds. London: 1891-98. Imperial folio; 2 volumes; 79 fine hand colored plates; contemporary full green morocco, gilt, gilt edges; binding trifle rubbed and inside covers trifle marked, still very fine, contents excellent; from the collection of Jan Coldewey.   Wheldon & Wesley 207-96 1996 £28,000.00

SHARPE, RICHARD BOWLDER   On the Birds Collected by Professor J. B. Steere in the Philippine Archipealgo. London: 1877. 4to; 49 pages, 9 hand colored plates; modern cloth, from the collection of Jan Coldewey. Wheldon & Wesley 207-94 1996 £675.00

SHELLEY, G. E.   A Monograph of the Nectariniidae or Family of Sun Birds. London: 1876-80. Only 250 copies printed; royal 4to; cviii, 393 pages, 121 fine hand colored plates; contemporary full brown morocco, gilt, gilt inside borders by Porter, gilt top; rare. Fine, clean copy, beautifully colored, with author's bookplate, from the collection of Jan Coldewey.   Wheldon & Wesley 207-98 1996 £10,000.00

WALLACE, ALFRED RUSSEL 1823-1913   The Malay Archipelago. New York: 1869. 1st American edition; 8vo; pages 638, 8 plates and 43 illustrations, 2 folding maps and 8 maps; original cloth, trifle used, trifle loose; from the collection of Jan Coldewey.   Wheldon & Wesley 207-115 1996 £500.00

ASSOCIATION - JAN COLDEWEY

WRIGHT, M.   Svenska Faglar Efter Naturen. Stockholm: 1927-29. Imperial 4to; 3 volumes; 364 colored plates; full mottled calf, gilt design on upper covers; nice, from the collection of Jan Coldewey.   Wheldon & Wesley 207-121 1996 £2,000.00

ASSOCIATION - DERWENT COLERIDGE

D'ISRAELI, ISAAC 1776-1848   Amenities of Literature, Consisting of Sketches and Characters of English Literature. London: Edward Moxon, 1841. 1st edition; large 8vo; 3 volumes; later 19th century vellum, gilt, spines gilt, black morocco labels; fine and attractive copy, with half titles; this copy has the ownership inscription and calling card of Samu Taylor Coleridge's grand-daughter, Edith Coleridge, 1887, who has adde the note "from the books of dear Uncle Derwent Coleridge". CBEL III 1278.   James Burmester 29-42 1996 £250.00

ASSOCIATION - EDITH COLERIDGE

D'ISRAELI, ISAAC 1776-1848   Amenities of Literature, Consisting of Sketches and Characters of English Literature. London: Edward Moxon, 1841. 1st edition; large 8vo; 3 volumes; later 19th century vellum, gilt, spines gilt, black morocco labels; fine and attractive copy, with half titles; this copy has the ownership inscription and calling card of Samu Taylor Coleridge's grand-daughter, Edith Coleridge, 1887, who has adde the note "from the books of dear Uncle Derwent Coleridge". CBEL III 1278.   James Burmester 29-42 1996 £250.00

ASSOCIATION - WILLIAM COLGATE

ROUS AND MANN   Toronto: The Capital of Ontario. Eleven Reproductions of Etchings Made in the Art Department of Rous and Mann. Toronto: Rous & Mann, Designers and Printers, 1921. 8vo; 13 leaves; 11 plates tipped in; decorated paper wrapper over boards, wrappers scuffed with stain on front cover, else very good. Very scarc signed by William Colgate.   Hugh Anson-Cartwright 87-431 1996 $125.00

ASSOCIATION - PAUL COLLINSON

WILLIAMS, ARTHUR ANDERSON   The Registers of Colton Parish Church in Furness Fells. London: Elliot Stock and Kendal: Atkinson and Pollitt, 1891. 8vo; pages 282; half levant morocco gilt, rather spotted a beginning and end; scarce; armorial bookplate of Paul Collinson. R.F.G. Hollett & Son 78-576 1996 £85.00

ASSOCIATION - PETER COLLINSON

CRULL, JODOCUS   A Compleat History of the Affairs of Spain, From the First Treaty of Partition, to this Present Time. London: Jos. Barns, 1708. 2nd edition; 8vo; frontispiece; full contemporary panelled calf, joints repaired; annotations of Peter Collinson on front free endpaper, bookplate of John Cator.   Ian Wilkinson 95/1-86 1996 £175.00

ASSOCIATION - J. L. COLTER

BIBLE. CREE - 1876   The New Testament Translated Into the Cre Language. London: printed for the British and Foreign Bible Society, 1876. 8vo; pages (iii), 425; contemporary calf, hinges broken, section spine missing, interior clean and crisp; inscribed by J. L. Colter, Ruper House, 1877 to Prof. John Galbraith. Banks p. 38; Evans 80; Peel 437. Hugh Anson-Cartwright 87-309 1996 $275.00

ASSOCIATION - SIDNEY COLVIN

KEATS, JOHN 1795-1821   Lamia, Isabella, The Eve of St. Agnes and Other Poems. London: for Taylor and Hessey, 1820. 1st edition; 12mo; pages (vi), 199, (1), without half title and ad leaves sometimes found end; contemporary brown calf, triple fillet gilt border to sides around elaborate blind roll, triple fillets and cornerpieces, spine in compartmer with raised bands, gilt rules, place and date, and blind ornament, red morocco label, little rubbed, just a few spots, excellent copy; at one time the copy of scholar Sidney Colvin, signed notes by him, along wi another later inscription; presentation copy, inscribed to poet George Darley from his cousin Maria. Ashley III p. 15-16; MacGillivray 3; Hayward 233; Tinker 1420.   Simon Finch 24-136 1996 £5,500.00

ASSOCIATION - COMERFORD

RICCI, SEYMOUR DE 1881-1942   English Collectors of Books and Manuscripts (1530-1930) and Their Marks of Ownership. New York: 1930. 1st edition; American issue; 203 pages, 8 plates, 4 figures in text; blue cloth, paper spine label, dust jacket, booklabel of Comerford.   Maggs Bros. Ltd. 1191-79 1996 £80.00

ASSOCIATION - JAMES COMERFORD

DALLAWAY, JAMES   History of the Western Division of the County of Sussex, Including the Rapes of Chichester, Arundel and Bramber, with the City and Diocese of Chichester. London: 1815-32. Large 4to; 4 volumes; numerous engraved maps and plates; contemporary polished calf gilt, neatly rebacked, volume 1 with original spine, remainders bound to match, gilt edges. with armorial ex-libris of James Comerford, noted collector of topographic books. Lowndes pp. 580-582.   Marlborough 162-17 1996 £2,400.00

ASSOCIATION - CONINGSBY

POZZO, ANDREA   Rules and Examples of Perspective Proper for Painters and Architects... London: Benjamin Motte, 1707. 1st English language edition; folio; frontispiece, (xx), 130 pages, 103 plates; contemporary calf; spine darkened, hinges beginning to crack, otherwise exceptionally nice; subscriber's copy, belonging to Earl of Coningsby whose arms are stamped on binding.   The Bookpress 75-224 1996 $3,500.00

ASSOCIATION - EUGENE CONNETT

BUCKINGHAM, NASH   Mark Right! Tales of Shooting and Fishing. New York: Derrydale Press, 1936. 1st edition; number 770 of 1250 copies; full page photograpic illustrations; original maroon cloth with color pictorial centerpiece depicting quail, spine lightly rubbed and some page edges trifle browned, else bright, near fine, housed in custom cloth slipcase. Bookplate of Eugene V. Connett, owner of Derrydale Press. Chapel Hill 94-375 1996 $450.00

ASSOCIATION - VERA CONNOLLY

STERLING, GEORGE   The Testimony of the Suns. San Francisco: Robertson, 1907. 3rd edition; one of 1000 copies; 8vo; decorated cloth, near fine; inscribed across title from author to his mistress, Vera Connolly, with 2 sonnets to Vera in Sterling's hand and signed by him. Charles Agvent 4-1030 1996 $375.00

ASSOCIATION - CONOLLY

FIELDING, HENRY 1707-1754   The Works... London: for A. Millar, 1762. 1st edition; 4to; 4 volumes; frontispiece; contemporary sprinkled calf, single fillet gilt border to sides, spines in compartments, raised bands, top compartments with device of Thomas Conolly, the others with black leather labels and ornaments, with Conolly's bookplate and shelf label, marbled endpapers, rubbed at extremities, hinges reinforced, little slight spotting, but very good. Cross III 328-9.   Simon Finch 24-85 1996 £750.00

ASSOCIATION - JACK CONROY

BONTEMPS, ARNA   Slappy Hooper, the Wonderful Sign Painter. Boston: Houghton Mifflin, 1946. 1st edition; illustrations by Ursula Koering; original cloth, fine, with pieces of dust jacket laid in; this copy inscribed by Jack Conroy.   Beasley Books 82-182 1996 $100.00

ASSOCIATION - CONWAY

HOWELLS, WILLIAM DEAN 1837-1920   Suburban Sketches. Boston: Osgood, 1875. Reprint; original binding; near fine; inscribed by Howells to Mrs. W. D. Conway.   Charles Agvent 4-686 1996 $150.00

ASSOCIATION - CONYNGHAM

MATURIN, CHARLES ROBERT 1782-1824   Women; or, Pour et Contre. Edinburgh: by James Ballantyne & Co. for Arch. Constable & Co., Edinb. &... 1818. 1st edition; 12mo; 3 volumes; fly-title in each volume; contemporary half polished calf, double black lettering pieces, drab paper sides and endpapers, spines worn, corners rubbed; good, clean set; ink monogram stamp of the Marquess of Conyngham (of Slane Castle, Ireland).   Simon Finch 24-166 1996 £1,000.00

ASSOCIATION - E. B. COOK

COOK, E. B.   American Chess-Nuts: a Collection of Problems, by Composers of the Western World. New York: Adelmour W. King, 1868. 1st edition; 8vo; x, 527 pages, errata; full contemporary brown morocco, gilt, hinges rubbed with short split at top of front hinge, small chip to front free fly, else very good; presentation from editor, E. B. Cook; the owner of this volume has placed two small paper game boards at opposition to form an 8 pointed star ex-libris with his initials.   Andrew Cahan 47-45 1996 $285.00

ASSOCIATION - COOTE

DUTTON, HELY   Statistical Survey of the County Clare. London: 1808. 1st edition; map; half calf, very good; ex-library C. Coote, author, of a number of other 'Stat Surveys'.   C. P. Hyland 216-195 1996 £300.00

ASSOCIATION - CORK & ORRERY

BOYLE, ROBERT 1627-1691   Of the Reconcileableness of Specifick Medicines to the Corpuscular Philosophy. London: printed for Sam. Smith, 1685. 1st edition; 8vo; early 18th century black morocco, elaborate gilt borders, spine gilt in five compartments, with coronet in middle, all edges gilt; splendid copy in handsome binding; some light bornwing, but most appealing association copy, binding executed for John Boyle, 5th Earl of Cork and Orrery, in exceptional condition. Wing B4013; Fulton 166.   Ximenes 109-48 1996 $5,000.00

ASSOCIATION - FRANCIS WARRE CORNISH

MILL, JOHN STUART 1806-1873   England and Ireland. London: Longmans, 1868. 1st edition; 8vo; 44 pages; disbound. Ownership inscription of Francis Warre Cornish, teacher, classicist & writer on education.   James Burmester 29-97 1996 £200.00

ASSOCIATION - CORNWALLIS

CORK & ORREY, JOHN BOYLE, 5TH EARL OF 1707-1762   Letters from Italy, in the Years 1754 and 1755. London: printed for B. White, 1773. 1st edition; small 8vo; 267 pages; half tan calf and cloth boards, ca. 1900, with morocco spine label, one corner slightly skinned, still tight, near fine; a distinguished copy, with bookplate of noted Revolutionary figure Earl Charles Cornwallis, later owner's bookplate.   Chapel Hill 94-197 1996 $250.00

ASSOCIATION - NORMAN CORWIN

LEWIS, CLIVE STAPLES 1898-1963   The Screwtape Letters. Macmillan, 1943. 1st American edition; just about fine in near very good dust jacket, save for some light wear and tear and chipping & sunning to dust jacket spine, still a most collectable copy; the copy of Norman Corwin, with his signature.   Aronovitz 57-698 1996 $250.00

ASSOCIATION - COTES

BROWNE, MOSES   Angling Sports: in Nine Piscatory Eclogues. London: Edward and Charles Dilly, 1773. 3rd edition; 8vo; frontispiece, 2 ms. marginal notes, pages xxxvii, (iii), 136; contemporary speckled calf, upper joint split, but still frim, smooth backstrip divided by gilt bands and dotted rolls, slight loss at head, red leather label, dated at foot, Bewick bookplate of Revd. H. Cotes Vicar Bedlington 1802. Excellent. Westwood and Satchell p. 43.   Blackwell's B112-48 1996 £150.00

ASSOCIATION - MERTON RUSSELL COTES

GOLDSMITH, OLIVER 1730-1774   The Poetical Works. London: printed by Ellerton and Henderson for Suttaby, Evance and Co., 1811. 1st printing of this edition; 11 1/4 x 9 inches; iv, 182 pages, 6 quite pleasing yellow tinted aquatint plates by Samuel Alken after drawings by R. H. Newell; contemporary smooth calf by E. Paul of Southampton (with his ticket at front), covers framed with blind and gilt foliate borders, raised bands, spine compartments pleasantly gilt, maroon calf label, new endpapers, joints lightly rubbed, tiny cracks just starting at top, covers slightly marked, small loss of leather in bottom spine compartment, but very good, sturdy original binding, small paper repair below titlepage imprint, minor foxing and offsetting, but excellent internally; bookplate of Merton Russell Cotes. Abbey Scenery 456.   Phillip J. Pirages   33-254   1996 $175.00

ASSOCIATION - COTTLE

STEFANSON, VIHJALMUR   Hunters of the Great North. New York: Harcourt Brace, 1922. 1st edition; 8vo; 26 black and white illustrations, 2 black and white folding maps at end, dust jacket (small chips to spine, nicks), very good. Signed and inscribed by author to Mrs. S. F. Cottle.   George J. Houle   68-140   1996 $150.00

ASSOCIATION - COTTON

WOOLNOTH, WILLIAM   A Graphical Illustration of the Metropolitan Cathedral Church of Canterbury... London: T. Cadell and W. Davies, 1816. 1st edition; large 4to; engraved titlepage and 20 engraved plates by Woolnoth after drawings by T. Hastings; extra illustrated with the insertion of 43 hand illumianted coats-of-arms (attributed to C. R. Cotton) in margins alongside biographies of various bishops; full early 19th century olive calf, spine with raised bands, gilt and blindstamped compartments, gilt leonine device and gilt stamped red morocco label, covers with blindstamped decorative borders with gilt stamped floral devices at corners, gilt ruled inner dentelles, marbled edges and endpapers, dark blue silk bookmark, some rubbing, foxing to title, slight foxing or offsetting to some plates; very good; mid 19th century bookplate of C. R. Cotton, ex-libris H. R. Kavanagh.   George J. Houle   68-157   1996 $850.00

ASSOCIATION - COULTON

GILL, ERIC 1882-1940   Art and Manufacture. Fanfare Press for the New Handworkers' Gallery, 1929. 7 3/4 x 5 inches; 43-56 pages, (1) leaf, device on title and 2 illustrations in text; original white paper self wrappers, first and last leaves slightly creased and soiled, otherwise fine. Inscribed presentation copy from Eric Gill to G. Coulton. Gill 19.   Phillip J. Pirages   33-241   1996 $750.00

ASSOCIATION - VERN COUNTRYMAN

DOUGLAS, WILLIAM O.   The Right of the People. Garden City: Doubleday & Co., 1958. Very well preserved copy in slightly embrowned dust jacket; Presentation copy from Justice Douglas to Vern Countryman, one of his earliest law clerks.   Meyer Boswell SL25-72   1996 $250.00

ASSOCIATION - SAMUEL AUGUSTINE COURTAULD

DICKENS, CHARLES 1812-1870   Bleak House. London: Bradbury & Evans, 1853. 1st edition in book form; 8 1/2 x 5 3/4 inches; xvi, 624 pages; frontispiece, added engraved title, 38 engraved plates by Phiz; bound up from parts, fine medium brown straight grain morocco gilt, covers with French fillet as well as inner dotted frame in blind, raised bands, spine handsomely gilt in compartments in antique style, complex floral ornament at center and elaborate scrolling stamps in corners, two maroon and one olive colored lettering pieces, turn-ins with densely gilt decoration, all edges gilt, front joint little worn (nothing loose), one small scar on back cover, otherwise binding virtually unworn as well as very bright, clean and attractive, slight mottling and faint darkening to some of the plates, otherwise excellent copy; armorial bookplate of Samuel Augustine Courtauld.   Phillip J. Pirages   33-164   1996 $750.00

ASSOCIATION - COURVILLE

BROWNE, THOMAS 1605-1682   Religio Medici. Lugd. Batavorum: Apud Francifcum, 1650. 12mo; 120 leaves, engraved frontispiece; full contemporary calf, raised bands, tooled spine, armorial gilt stamp on front board, all edges gilt, front blanks loose, nice, clean copy; bookplate of Garth Huston and Courville Collection. Keynes 62.   James Tait Goodrich   K40-68   1996 $395.00

ASSOCIATION - BURDETT COUTTS

WALPOLE, HORACE 1719-1797   Essay on Modern Gardening. Strawberry Hill: T. Kirgate, 1785. 1st edition; one of 400 copies, 200 fo presentation by Walpole and 200 for the Duc, none being for sale; 4to; pages 94; engraved vignette (offset onto endpaper), text nice and clear with wide margins; modern full calf; very nice; no presentation on this copy, but notes on endpapers indicate that it came from both the "Burdett Coutts" and "Pinkerton" sales. Hazen, Strawberry Hill Press 31 Henrey 1475; Hunt 675.   Second Life Books   103-205   1996 $1,350.0

ASSOCIATION - THOMAS COUTTS

FOOT, JESSE   The Life of John Hunter. London: T. Becket, 1794. 28 pages; contemporary tree calf, red label, spine slightly rubbed, otherwi very nice, handsome copy. Thomas Coutts's copy with his bookplate. Wellcome III p. 39.   C. R. Johnson   37-79   1996 £350.00

ASSOCIATION - MIGUEL COVARRUBIAS

MARAN, RENE   Batouala. New York: Limited Editions Club, 1932. Limited to 1500 numbered copies, signed by artist; folio; (2), xiv, (2), 117, (3) pages; profusely illustrated with 6 color plates and numerous text drawings by Miguel Covarrubias; full brown morocco, extremities t rubbed, slipcase, bookplate; extremities bit rubbed; this copy inscribed by Covarrubias in 1939 with original sketch by Covarrubias.   Kenneth Karmiole   1NS-158   1996 $250.00

ASSOCIATION - ROBERT ERNEST COWAN

HARTE, BRET 1836-1902   Fac-Simile of the Original Manuscript of th Heathen Chinee, as Written for the Overland Monthly... San Francisco: John H. Carmany & Co., 1871. 1st facsimile edition; 9 leaves (1 blank), printed and lithographed on one side only; original printed wrappers; v scarce; from the collection of bibliographer Robert Ernest Cowan, with his bookplate. BAL 7248J; Cowan p. 266.   Argonaut Book Shop 113-333   1996 $225.00

ASSOCIATION - MALCOLM COWLEY

CHEEVER, JOHN 1912-1984   Homage to Shakespeare. Stevenson: Country Squires Books, 1968. One of 50 copies of the first edition of 1st separate publication of this early Cheever story; fine in dust jacket inscribed by author for Malcolm and Muriel Cowley.   Lame Duck Books   19-138   1996 $1,500.00

TATE, ALLEN   The Winter Sea: A Book of Poems. Cummington: Cummington Press, 1944. 1st edition; one of 300 copies printed, review copy with slip laid in; 8vo; cloth, unprinted dust jacket; fine in spine darkened jacket rubbed and slightly chipped at extremities; presentatio copy inscribed by author for Malcolm Cowley.   James S. Jaffe 34-6 1996 $650.00

ASSOCIATION - MURIEL COWLEY

CHEEVER, JOHN 1912-1984   Homage to Shakespeare. Stevenson: Country Squires Books, 1968. One of 50 copies of the first edition of 1st separate publication of this early Cheever story; fine in dust jacket inscribed by author for Malcolm and Muriel Cowley.   Lame Duck Books   19-138   1996 $1,500.00

ASSOCIATION - COX

SPENSER, EDMUND 1552-1599   Thalamos or the Brydall Boure Beir the Epithalamion and Prothalamion... At the sign of the Boar's Head, Manaton, Devon, 1932. Number 2 of 200 copies; octavo; pages 36; 4 full page wood engravings and tailpiece by Lettice Sandford, printed ir Baskerville on Millbourn handmade paper; original sheepkskin backed Cockerell marbled boards, top edge gilt, others uncut; inscribed at so length to Edwin & Margery Cox, from Christopher and Lettice Sandfor Claude Cox   107-23   1996 £85.00

ASSOCIATION - CHARLES COX

SENECA, LUCIUS ANNAEUS   The Workes of Lucius Annaeus Seneca. London: printed by Willi Stansby, 1620. Early English edition; folio in 6s; pages 928), 921, (22), engraved title, 2 divisional titles; fine woodcut initials and devices, apparently lacks 3 prelim leaves, but includes Lipsius' "Life of ...Seneca". Original boards, detached, but decorated with central arabesque medallion stamp painted(?) in gilt, requires rebacking, ex-libris of Charles F. Cox, New York.   Family Album Tillers-568 1996 $360.00

ASSOCIATION - CRAHAN

PETRONIO, ALESSANDRO TRAJANO d. 1585   De Victu Romanorum et de Sanitate Tuenda Libri Quinque. Rome: In Aedibus Populi Romani, 1581 (1582). 1st edition; folio; 340 pages (12) leaves, engraved device on titlepage and woodcut device on last leaf, dampstaining at beginning and end of text, brown stain on titlepage and through about a third of the volume (mostly marginal), library stamp in blank margins; contemporary limp vellum gilt tooled; Crahan copy with his bookplate. Adams P858; Bitting 368; Simon 1158; Bibl. Bacchia 498. Brunet IV 577.   Jeffrey Mancevice 20-67 1996 $1,850.00

ASSOCIATION - MARCUS CRAHAN

LIEBIG, JUSTUS VON   Researches on the Motion of the Juices in the Animal body. London: for Taylor and Walton, 1848. 1st edition in English; 8vo; xiv, 109, (3) pages; plus 16 page publisher's catalog; woodcut illustrations in text; original embossed cloth; fine bright copy; with Marcus Crahan bookplate. Wellcome III 516.   Edwin V. Glaser 121-188 1996 $300.00

ASSOCIATION - CRAVEN

BURNEY, FRANCES   Tragic Dramas... London: printed by Thomas Davison, for the author and sold by J. Murray, 1818. 1st edition; 8vo; contemporary calf, panelled in blind, gilt borders, spine and inner dentelels gilt, marbled edges, some rubbing, spine dull; half title present, very good; bookplate of the Earl of Craven and later bookplate of Robert William Rogers. Stratman 719.   Ximenes 108-51 1996 $275.00

ASSOCIATION - JAMES CRAWFURD

BARBOUR, JOHN   The Life and Acts of the Most Victorious Conqueror Robert Bruce, King of Scotland. Edinburgh: 1758. Small 4to; pages 443, uncut, printed in black letter with head and tailpieces, few leaves rather browned; old binders cloth, gilt, lower corners of boards damped; nice, unsophisticated copy. Inscription of William Ingram 1788, on title; signature of James Crawfurd on pastedown & inscription below of George Arbuthnot dated Feb. 1st 1831.   R.F.G. Hollett 76-13 1996 £95.00

ASSOCIATION - JOHN CRERAR

A FULL Relation Concerning the Wonderful and Wholesome Fountain. At First Discovered in Germany, Two Miles from the City of Halberstadt, by a Certain Youth Upon the Fifth of March 1646, as He Was Coming from Schoole. London: printed by T. W. for Joshua Kirton, 1646. 4to; (2), 21, (1) pages; neatly rebound in quarter calf, marbled boards; excellent copy, uncut on fore and lower edges; ex-libris of John Crerar, with neat perforation stamp on titlepage and small neat de-accession stamp on reverse. Wing F2355; Krivatsy 4462.   C. R. Johnson 37-80 1996 £450.00

MC MURTRIE, DOUGLAS C.   The First Printers of Chicago with a Bibliography of the Issues of the Chicago Press 1836-1850. chicago: the Cuneo Press, 1927. Limited to 650 numbered copies; 4to; 42 pages; 9 illustrations; black cloth backed marbled boards, gilt lettering on spine, headcaps and corners very mildly bumped, presentation copy with ink inscription from author to Ella M. Salmonsen; ex-John Crerar Library with booklabel.   Maggs Bros. Ltd. 1191-192 1996 £50.00

MORISON, STANLEY 1889-1967   Four Centuries of Printing. London: Ernest Benn, 1924. Limited to 390 copies for sale (in addition there were 3 special copies and 100 copies in German); 641 illustrations; half canvas, black cloth boards bit grubby, headcaps slightly bumped, uncut, shelf number on spine; booklabel and perforated stamp on title, ex-John Crerar Library copy. Appleton 35. Fleuron III p. 107-116.   Maggs Bros. Ltd. 1191-199 1996 £285.00

ASSOCIATION - JOHN CRERAR

PALMER, S.   A General History of Printing; from the First Invention of It In the City of Mentz, to Its Propagation and Progress... London: printed for A. Bettesworth, C.Hitch & C. Davis 1733. 2nd printing; 4to; xii, 400 pages (pages after p.312 beginning a new pagination at pp. 121-144, then they are counted in and pagination made continuous by taking it up at pp. 337); brown cloth, headcaps and corners bumped, bit scuffed and grubby, lettering and shelf mark on spine in gilt, title in red and black, some browning between Rr and Ss, otherwise, clean, crisp copy; ex-John Crerar Library copy with booklabel and perforated stamps. Maggs Bros. Ltd. 1191-211 1996 £200.00

ASSOCIATION - J. CRESSWELL

CROFT, JOHN   Memoirs of Harry Rowe; Constructed from Materials in an Old Box, After His Decease. York: ptd. by Wilson & Spence, sold by all booksellers...n.d. 1805. 1st edition; 12mo; portrait, 8 page subscribers, old half calf, gilt; very good, complete with half title; bookplate of J. Cresswell. 5 copies in NUC; LAR 1703 (not seen). Ximenes 109-93 1996 $750.00

ASSOCIATION - LIONEL CRESSWELL

BROWNING, ROBERT 1812-1889   Bells and Pomegranates. No. I Pippa Passes. (No. II-No. VIII). London: Edward Moxon, 1841-46. 8vo; 8 numbers in 1 volume, original black cloth, very fine; large Victorian bookplate of Lionel Cresswell. Hayward 253.   Ximenes 108-374 1996 $2,750.00

ASSOCIATION - R. N. CRESSWELL

ENGLEHEART, N. B.   A Concise Treatise on Eccentric Turning. London: 1952. 1st edition; 4to; 50 figures on 16 plates, few text figures, slightly soiled copy, contemporary cloth, stained, repaired; inscribed by author in rather tremulous hand, to R. N. Cresswell. Abell 91.   Maggs Bros. Ltd. 1190-628 1996 £185.00

ASSOCIATION - CREWE

SNODGRASS, JOHN JAMES   Narrative of the Burmese War... London: John Murray, 1827. 1st edition; 8vo; pages xii, 319, (8) ads, 1 plate and large folding map, small fold tear with no loss, uncut; original boards, hinges starting, but firm, paper label; some rubbing to edges, excellent copy, seldom found in original condition; bookplate of John, 1st Baron Crewe.   Howard S. Mott 227-158 1996 $450.00

ASSOCIATION - JOHN CRICKETT

IRELAND, SAMUEL d. 1800   Picturesque Views, with an Historical Account of the Inns of Court in London and Westminster. London: C. Clark, 1800. 8vo; xvi, 254, (i errata) pages, 21 aquatint plates, 2 text illustrations; contemporary half calf, slightly scuffed. Inscribed "John Crickett, Esqr. & From the Extors of the late Saml. Ireland". Adams 81; Abbey Scenery 207.   Marlborough 162-156 1996 £360.00

ASSOCIATION - JOHN CROFT

GREAT BRITAIN. LAWS, STATUTES, ETC. - 1556   Magna Charta, Cum Statius Quae Antiqua Vocantur... London: Richardum Totelum, 1556. 1st Tottel edition; 12mo; 2 parts in 1, 172, 72ff; contemporary full calf, corners bumped and spine ends chipped, some general wear, but remarkably well preserved; the John Croft copy, with his bookplate. Chapel Hill 94-253 1996 $1,750.00

ASSOCIATION - THOMAS CROFTS

CARACCIOLUS, ROBERTUS   Sermones Quadragesimales de Peccatis. Venice: Joannes & Gregorius de Gregoriis, de Forlivio 11 May, 1490. Quarto; 158 leaves, double column, gothic letter, first 6 lines at head of text printed in red, initial spaces with guide letters, printer's device on fol. 158 recto, some page numerals slightly cropped, slight browning on first and last leaves; 18th century vellum boards; from the collection of Thomas Crofts, then Michael Wodhull. Goff C162; Hain 4441; GKW 083; IGI 2466; not in BMC.   H. M. Fletcher 121-6 1996 £1,800.00

ASSOCIATION - JOHN CROKER

WILCOCKE, SAMUEL HULL   Report of the Proceedings Connected with the Disputes Between the Earl of Selkirk and the North-West Company, at the Assizes, Held at York, un Upper Canada, October 1818. London: 1819. 1st London edition; pages xxv, 225, 203, 48; uncut, largely unopened in original printed wrappers, slightest chipping to hinges, fine, preserved in quarter morocco clamshell box; fine; inscribed by Simon McGillivray for John W. Croker. TPL 1146; Peel68; cf. Streeter VI 3687. Stephen Lunsford 45-170 1996 $2,500.00

ASSOCIATION - CROMER

DIGESTORUM Seu Pandectarum Libri Quinquaginta Ex Florentinis Pandectis Repraesentati. Florence: in Officina Laurentii Torrentini, 1553. 1st edition; folio; 2 volumes (volumes 1 and 2, of 3); large well margined copy, title and half page detailed woodcut vignette, very large detailed illustrative woodcut initial letters, full 18th century blue French morocco (a pencil note suggest by Derome-le-Jeune), boards with triple gilt fillet, spines elaborately gilt in compartments with gilt lettering direct, spines browned, all edges gilt; very fine, clean and fresh copy. Bookplates of the Earl of Cromer and Viscount Mersey, Bignor Park. Ian Wilkinson 95/1-90 1996 £295.00

ASSOCIATION - B. S. CRON

EVANS, ABEL   Vertumnus. An Epistle to Mr. Jacob Bobart, Botany Professor to the University of Oxford and Keeper of the Physick-Garden. Oxford: printed by L. L. for Stephen Fletcher, 1713. 1st edition; 8vo; 33 pages; frontispiece, little light foxing of text, short tear in last leaf expertly repaired; modern marabled boards; Sir Sydney Cockerell's copy with inscriptions, with letter to Sir Sydney tipped in, inscribed "B. S. Cron from SCC 31 Jan. 1960". Foxon E530.   Anthony W. Laywood 109-53 1996 £150.00

ASSOCIATION - F. CROSBY

HOLMES, OLIVER WENDELL 1809-1894   Astraea; the Balance of Illusions. A Poem. Boston: Ticknor, Reed and Fields, 1850. 1st edition; 1st printing, state A and binding A; 12mo; 39 pages; original glazed printed boards; fine, early owner's signature (F. Crosby) Oct. 9, 1850. BAL 8757. Tryon & Charvat A189b. Carroll Wilson p. 500.   M & S Rare Books 60-172 1996 $300.00

ASSOCIATION - HARRY CROSBY

JOYCE, JAMES 1882-1941   Anna Livia Plurabelle. New York: Crosby Gaige, 1928. One of 800 copies; touch of fraying to cloth at spine extremtieis, still near fine; signed by Joyce, this copy inscribed by Harry Crosby to Aldous Huxley.   Ken Lopez 74-236 1996 $8,500.00

ASSOCIATION - GEORGE CRUIKSHANK

THACKERAY, WILLIAM MAKEPEACE 1811-1863   The Loving Ballad of Lord Bateman. London: Bell and Daldy, 1871. 16mo; pages 40; wood engraved re-workings of Cruikshank's 11 etched illustrations of 1839, plate of music, plates and letterpress of poem printed on one side of leaf, eccentrically paginated, inscription at head of titlepage; original sand-grain blue cloth, spine unlettered, gilt titled in center of upper side, oblong panel in style of French type ornament at head and foot of both sides, very good; inscribed by Cruikshank for Mrs. William Stebbing. Blackwell's B112-84 1996 £125.00

ASSOCIATION - GEORGE CUKOR

ARCE, HECTOR   Groucho. New York: Putnam, 1979. 1st edition; thick 8vo; illustrations; dust jacket, very good; from Cukor's library with his Paul Landacre bookplate.   George J. Houle 68-92 1996 $175.00

HOYNINGEN-HUENE, GEORGE   Baalbek Palmyra. New York: Augustin, 1946. 1st edition; ('October 1946'); 4to; 55 black and white photos, 2 plans; dust jacket, rubbed, few nicks, very good. Signed and inscribed by Hoyningen-Huene to George Cukor with Cukor's Paul Landacre bookplate.   George J. Houle 68-113 1996 $225.00

ASSOCIATION - COUNTEE CULLEN

DILLON, GEORGE   Boy in the Wind. New York: Viking, 1927. 1st edition; rubbing to edges of paper spine label, else solid, very good copy, lacking dust jacket; author's first book; Countee Cullen's copy wit his large bookplate and signature, and few pencilled notes.   Between the Covers 43-58 1996 $250.00

GROOM, C. LAURENCE   The Singing Sword. Lees: The Swan Press, 1927. 1st edition; lightly soiled, very good, with no remarkable flaws, without dust jacket presumably as issued; Countee Cullen's copy with h ownership signature and one pencil notation in text.   Between the Covers 43-59 1996 $175.00

ASSOCIATION - CULLEN HOUSE

TENCIN, CLAUDINE ALEXANDRINE GUERIN DE   The Siege of Calais, an Historical Novel. London: printed by Charles Say, Jr. 1751. 1st editio of this translation; 8vo; 2 volumes in one, (140, 149) pages; engraved title in each volume; contemporary half calf over marbled boards, contrasting title label; fine; scarce; signature of M. Finlater and Cullen House bookplate. 2 copies in NUC; Raven 103.   Paulette Rose 16-31 1996 $850.00

ASSOCIATION - SCOTT CUNNINGHAM

BATES, HERBERT ERNEST 1905-1974   Seven Tales and Alexander: Stories. London: Scholartis Press, 1929. 1st edition; cloth backed boards, near fine in dust jacket; bookplate of Scott Cunningham. Words Etcetera 94-91 1996 £75.00

ASSOCIATION - WILLIAM CURRAN

ALGAROTTI, FRANCESCO   An Essay on Painting. London: L. Davis & C. Reymers, 1764. 1st English edition; small8vo; vii, (i), 186, (4) pages ads; recent quarter calf, marbled boards; very good; signature of Wm. Curran at head of titlepage and second signature of Thos. Andrews. Ken Spelman 30-10 1996 £220.00

ASSOCIATION - CURRER

ADAMS, JOHN 1735-1826   A Defence of the Constitutions of Government of the United States of America, Against the Attack of M. Turgot in His Letter to Dr. Price, Dated the Twenty-Second Day of March, 1778. London: John Stockdale, 1794. New edition; 8vo; 3 volumes, plate, portrait, 8, xxxii, 392; (2), 451, (1); (2), 528, (36) pages, bound without half titles; early 19th century calf, from the library of Francies Mary Richardson Currer with her bookplate in each volume. Sabin 235; Goldsmiths 15903.   C. R. Johnson 37-49 1996 £350.00

BULL, ROGER, PSEUD.   Grobianus; or the Compleat Booby. London: printed for T. Cooper, 1739. 1st edition; 8vo; contemporary mottled calf spine gilt, joints neatly repaired; very good; bookplate of Frances Mary Richardson Currer. Foxon B564; Teerink 1318; Rothschild 513; Cagle, Matter of Taste 645.   Ximenes 108-46 1996 $750.00

FERRIER, SUSAN EDMONDSTONE 1782-1854   The Inheritance. Edinburgh: William Blackwood and T. Cadell, London, 1824. 1st edition; 8vo; 3 volumes; half titles present; contemporary half rose calf, gilt, spines elaborately gilt. Fine attrative set, from the library of Frances Mary Richardson Currer. Wolff 2235; Block p. 74; CBEL III 720. Ximenes 108-129 1996 $450.00

GORHAM, GEORGE CORNELIUS   The History and Antiquities of Eynesbury and St. Neot's in Huntingdonshire and of St. Neot's in the County of Cornwall. London: T. Davison for Lackington, etc. 1820-24. 8vo; 2 volumes in 1; (2), xii, (4), 340; (2), clxxxvii pages, engraved frontispiece, 10 plates, wood engravings in text, slightly later half morocco, gilt, top edge gilt. P. A. Hanrott's copy with his note on flyleaf, probably purchased in his sale in 1830 by Frances Richardson Currer.   Marlborough 162-33 1996 £290.00

HOFLAND, BARBARA WREAKS HOOLE 1770-1844   A Descriptive Account of the Mansion and Gardens of White-Knights... London: printe for His Grace the Duke of Marlborough, by W. Wilson, 1819. folio; (8) 152 pages; 23 engraved plates on india paper (mounted); later half gre morocco, little rubbed, some slight foxing in margins; from the library Frances Mary Richardson Currer, with her armorial ex-libris. Abbey Scenery 425; Tooley 268.   Marlborough 162-45 1996 £1,850.00

ASSOCIATION - CURRER

HOOD, THEODORE EDWARD   Maxwell. London: Henry Colburn and Richard Bentley, 1830. 1st edition; 12mo; 3 volumes, contemporary half blue calf, gilt, spines ornately gilt, traces of rubbing; half titles present in volumes 1 and 2 (all required), 14 line errata slip at end of first volume; occasional foxing, bound without publisher's ads at end of 3rd volume, but a pretty set; from the library of Frances Mary Richardson Currer; Sadleir 1207; Wolff 3256; CBEL III 732.   Ximenes 108-204 1996 $450.00

HOUTTUYN, MARTINUS   Hotkunde, Behelzende de Abfeeldingen van Meest Alle Bekund, in-en Uitlandsche Houten. Amsterdam: J. C. Sepp, 1773-91. 4to; titles and text in Dutch, German, French, English and Latin; 100 hand colored engraved plates, 50 leaves describing timbers dealt with on the 100 copperplates; later gilt stamped diced calf, rubbed, all edges gilt; signature of William Forsyth, 1808; Currer bookplate. Raymond M. Sutton VII-16 1996 $8,500.00

IRVING, WASHINGTON 1783-1859   A History of New York, from the Beginning of the World to the End of the Dutch Dynasty. London: John Murray, 1821. New edition; 8vo; pages (vi), (i)-xxxi, (i), (33)-341, (1); (vi), 282; 2 volumes; contemporary red calf, backstrips with gilt ruled raised bands, gilt lettered direct in second and fifth compartments, remainder decorated with gilt lozenge blocked pane, slightly dulled, sides with wide border of 'Celtic' plait roll between fillets, roll on board edges and turn-ins, brown chalked endpapers, blue silk markers, gilt edges, excellent; bookplate of Frances Mary Richardson Currer.   Blackwell's B112-161 1996 £75.00

KENNET, WHITE   Parochial Antiquities Attempted in the History of Ambrosden, Burcester and Other Adjacent Parts in the Counties of Oxford and Bucks... Oxford: at the Theatre, 1695. 4to; vignette title, 7 ff., 703 (recte 701) pages, 15 ff. index, 58 ff. glossary, 9 engraved plates, contemporary calf, rebacked; good copy, form the library of Frances Richardson Currer, with her ex-libris. Wing K302.   Marlborough 162-56 1996 £850.00

PANVINO, ONOFRIO   Antiquitatum Veronensium, Libri Octo. Padua: P. Frambotti, 1647. 1st and only edition; folio; (xii), 236, (8) pages, 33 plates; contemporary gilt vellum, lacking ties; fine; rare. Bookplate of Miss Richardson Currer, later sold to Sir Mathew Wilson, with his bookplate. Cicognara 4059.   The Bookpress 75-222 1996 $5,800.00

TAYLOR, ISAAC 1787-1865   Fanaticism. London: Holdsworth and Ball, 1833. 1st edition; 8vo; contemporary polished calf, gilt, spine gilt, minor rubbing; fine copy; bookplate of France Mary Richardson Currer. Ximenes 108-336 1996 $250.00

TAYLOR, ISAAC 1787-1865   Spiritual Despotism. London: Holdsworth and Ball, 1835. 1st edition; 8vo; contemporary polished calf, gilt, spine gilt, minor rubbing; possibly bound without half title, but fine, scarce; bookplate of Frances Mary Richardson Currer.   Ximenes 108-337 1996 $225.00

WEBB, T.   A New Select Collection of Epitaphs, Panegyrical and Moral, Humorous, Whimsical, Satyrical and Inscriptive. London: S. Bladon, 1775. 1st edition; 8vo; 2 volumes; full contemporary brown calf, upper joints cracking but firm, spines little worn, all edges gilt; bookplates of Frances Mary Richardson Currer.   Ian Wilkinson 95/1-156 1996 £175.00

ASSOCIATION - GEORGE WILLIAM CURTIS

TAYLOR, BAYARD 1825-1878   A Book of Romances, Lyrics and Songs. Boston: Ticknor, Reed and Fields, 1852. 1st printing of only 1000 copies; 8vo; brown cloth, binding A with Sept. 1851 catalog, little spotting to cloth, sporadic foxing, near fine; fine association, George William Curtis's copy with his signature.   Charles Agvent 4-1085 1996 $175.00

ASSOCIATION - KATHLEEN SPENCER CURWEN

CURWEN, J. SPENCER   Memorials of John Curwen. London: J. Curwen & sons, 1882. 8vo; pages xii, 320; frontispiece; original cloth, gilt; scarce; signature of Kathleen Spencer Curwen on flyleaf.   R.F.G. Hollett & Son 78-144 1996 £85.00

ASSOCIATION - CUTHBERT

DEFOE, DANIEL 1661?-1731   The Novels... Edinburgh: by James Ballantyne and Co. for John Ballantyne and Co. and Brown &... 1810. Foolscap 8vo; 12 volumes; woodcut illustrations; contemporary red straight grain half morocco, spines decorated in blind and in gilt and lettered in gilt, green paper sides and endpapers, green sprinkled edges, extremities rubbed, attractive set; bookplates of F. I. Cuthbert.   Simon Finch 24-67 1996 £350.00

ASSOCIATION - J. W. CUTHBERT

BACON, FRANCIS, VISCOUNT ST. ALBANS 1561-1626   The Works of Francis Bacon... London: printed for a. Millar, 1765. 4to; 5 volumes; 4 steel engraved frontispieces, folding table; near contemporary full polished tan calf, spines with twin lettering pieces and 6 raised bands, panels with overall diaper pattern in gilt; each volume inscribed "To the Hawkshead Instiute, John Ruskin, Brantwood, Candlemasm 1883"; each volume with armorial bookplate of J. W. Cuthbert.   R.F.G. Hollett & Son 78-318 1996 £1,200.00

ASSOCIATION - HELLA CZECH

WELLS, HERBERT GEORGE 1866-1946   The Science of Life. New York: Doubleday Doran, 1931. 2 volumes; some minor chipping to dust jackets, otherwise excellent set in defective slipcase; inscribed by Wells to Dr. Hella Czech.   R. A. Gekoski 19-149 1996 £175.00

ASSOCIATION - AUGUSTUS D'ESTE

SIMPSON, GEORGE   Narrative of a Journey Round the World, During the Years 1841 and 1842. London: Henry Colburn, 1847. 1st edition; 8vo; 2 volumes; original grey purple cloth, spines quite faded, some spotting; bookplates removed, but a fine set, despite faded bindings, scarce in cloth; presentation copy inscribed by author for Col. Sir Augustus D'Este. Sabin 81343; Howes S495; Wagner Camp 140.1. TPL 2548; Hill p. 274.   Ximenes 109-267 1996 $1,250.00

ASSOCIATION - GEORGE D'OYLY

BYRON, GEORGE GORDON NOEL, 6TH BARON 1788-1824   English Bards and Scotch Reviewers. London: printed for Charles Cawthorn, n.d. 1809. 1st edition; 12mo; half blue calf, traces of rubbing fine; signed on half title by George D'Oyly (1778-1846). Wise I 21; Hayward 219; CBEL III 277.   Ximenes 108-53 1996 $750.00

ASSOCIATION - LUCIEN D'URSIN

SIMEONI, GABRIELE   Epitome de l'Origine et Svccession de la Dvche de Ferrare. Paris: Corrozet, 1553. 8vo; woodcut portrait of Simeoni on titlepage, gilt calf, bookpate of Collection Lucien d'Ursin. STC French 402. Rostenberg & Stern 150-98 1996 $1,200.00

ASSOCIATION - EDWARD DAHLBERG

DECHARME, PAUL   Euripides and the Spirit of His Dramas. New York: 1906. 1st edition; 378 pages; very good in slipcase; Edward Dahlberg's copy with anntoations by him, and 20 line original poem.   Lyman Books 21-104 1996 $275.00

ASSOCIATION - DALHOUSIE

WEBB, SAMUEL B.   Records of North American Big Game. 1952. 2nd issue; colored frontispiece, many other illustrations; fine in torn and rather grubby dust jacket; presentation copy from J. Watson Webb to Lord Dalhousie.   David Grayling J95Biggame-457 1996 £105.00

ASSOCIATION - JOHN DALTON

A DOZEN All Told. London: Blackie, 1894. 1st edition; fine; from the collection of John H. Dalton.   Harland H. Eastman 10/94-89 1996 $225.00

FENN, G. MANVILLE   George Alfred Henty, the Story of an Active Life. London: Blackie, 1907. 1st edition; frontispiece in facsimile, otherwise very good+. from the collection of John H. Dalton.   Harland H. Eastman 10/94-8 1996 $150.00

ASSOCIATION - JOHN DALTON

HENTY, GEORGE ALFRED 1832-1902　　At the Point of the Bayonet. London: Blackie, 1902. 1st edition; fine; from the collection of John H. Dalton.　　Harland H. Eastman 10/94-11 1996 $100.00

HENTY, GEORGE ALFRED 1832-1902　　Bonnie Prince Charlie. London: Blackie, 1888. 1st edition; edges worn, soiling, front free endpaper out, good plus; from the collection of John H. Dalton.　Harland H. Eastman 10/94-13 1996 $100.00

HENTY, GEORGE ALFRED 1832-1902　　The Brahmins' Treasure. Philadelphia: Lippincott, 1900. 1st edition; binding with Brhamin peering from a curtained doorway (one of two bindings for this edition); fine; from the collection of John H. Dalton.　　Harland H. Eastman 10/94-84 1996 $175.00

HENTY, GEORGE ALFRED 1832-1902　　Brains and Bravery. W. & R. Chambers, 1903. 1st edition; minor rubbing; very good-fine; from the collection of John H. Dalton.　　Harland H. Eastman 10/94-85 1996 $250.00

HENTY, GEORGE ALFRED 1832-1902　　Bravest of the Brave. London: Blackie, 1887. 1st edition; near fine; from the collection of John H. Dalton.　　Harland H. Eastman 10/94-14 1996 $250.00

HENTY, GEORGE ALFRED 1832-1902　　Bravest of the Brave. London: Blackie, 1887. 1st edition; spine bit darkened, stain on front cover, otherwise very good+; from the collection of John H. Dalton.　　Harland H. Eastman 10/94-15 1996 $200.00

HENTY, GEORGE ALFRED 1832-1902　　Bravest of the Brave London: Blackie, 1887. 1st edition; rubbed, spine ends worn, nevertheless very good copy; from the collection of John H. Dalton.　　Harland H. Eastman 10/94-16 1996 $150.00

HENTY, GEORGE ALFRED 1832-1902　　By England's Aid. London: Blackie, 1891. 1st edition; very slight soiling, nevertheless about fine; from the collection of John H. Dalton.　Harland H. Eastman 10/94-18 1996 $165.00

HENTY, GEORGE ALFRED 1832-1902　　By Pike and Dyke. London: Blackie, 1890. 1st edition; top of spine slightly chipped, minor soiling, very good+; from the collection of John H. Dalton.　　Harland H. Eastman 10/94-19 1996 $140.00

HENTY, GEORGE ALFRED 1832-1902　　By Right of Conquest. London: Blackie, 1891. 1st edition; fine; from the collection of John H. Dalton. Harland H. Eastman 10/94-20 1996 $165.00

HENTY, GEORGE ALFRED 1832-1902　　By Sheer Pluck. London: Blackie, 1884. 1st edition; inner hinges somewhat cracked, otherwise fine, absolutely brilliant copy; from the collection of John H. Dalton. Harland H. Eastman 10/94-21 1996 $375.00

HENTY, GEORGE ALFRED 1832-1902　　A Chapter of Adventures. London: Blackie, 1891. 1st edition; minor edge wear, very good+; from the collection of John H. Dalton.　　Harland H. Eastman 10/94-23 1996 $135.00

HENTY, GEORGE ALFRED 1832-1902　　Colonel Thorndyke's Secret. London: Chatto & Windus, 1899. Presentation edition; very good; from the collection of John H. Dalton.　　Harland H. Eastman 10/94-118 1996 $100.00

HENTY, GEORGE ALFRED 1832-1902　　Condemned as a Nihilist. London: Blackie, 1893. 1st edition; near fine; from the collection of John H. Dalton.　　Harland H. Eastman 10/94-24 1996 $100.00

HENTY, GEORGE ALFRED 1832-1902　　Curse of Carne's Hold. Spencer Blackett, 1st one volume edition, with Oct. 1890 catalog; very good; from the collection of John H. Dalton.　　Harland H. Eastman 10/94-87 1996 $350.00

HENTY, GEORGE ALFRED 1832-1902　　Cuthbert Hartington. S. W. Partridge, 1st edition; 6 illustrations; fine, from the collection of John H. Dalton.　　Harland H. Eastman 10/94-88 1996 $185.00

ASSOCIATION - JOHN DALTON

HENTY, GEORGE ALFRED 1832-1902　　Cuthbert Hartington. S. W. Partridge, fine; from the collection of John H. Dalton.　　Harland H. Eastman 10/94-121 1996 $100.00

HENTY, GEORGE ALFRED 1832-1902　　The Dragon and the Raven. London: Blackie, 1886. 1st edition; bit rubbed and soiled, nevertheless very good; from the collection of John H. Dalton.　　Harland H. Eastman 10/94-25 1996 $175.00

HENTY, GEORGE ALFRED 1832-1902　　Facing Death. London: Blackie, 1883. 2nd edition, with 1883 catalog announcing "New Series for Season 1884"; near fine; from the collection of John H. Dalton.　　Harland H. Eastman 10/94-26 1996 $300.00

HENTY, GEORGE ALFRED 1832-1902　　The Fall of Sebastopol. Charles E. Brown Co., red cloth; fine; from the collection of John H. Dalton. Harland H. Eastman 10/94-128 1996 $125.00

HENTY, GEORGE ALFRED 1832-1902　　Fighting the Saracens. Charles E. Brown, 1st edition; bit soiled and rubbed, nevertheless a very good copy; from the collection of John H. Dalton.　　Harland H. Eastman 10/94-96 1996 $150.00

HENTY, GEORGE ALFRED 1832-1902　　Fighting the Saracens. Charles E. Brown Co., red cloth; fine; from the collection of John H. Dalton. Harland H. Eastman 10/94-129 1996 $125.00

HENTY, GEORGE ALFRED 1832-1902　　For Name and Fame. London: Blackie, 1887. 1st edition; fine; from the collection of John H. Dalton. Harland H. Eastman 10/94-28 1996 $300.00

HENTY, GEORGE ALFRED 1832-1902　　For the Temple. London: Blackie, 1888. 1st edition; very good+; from the collection of John H. Dalton.　　Harland H. Eastman 10/94-29 1996 $200.00

HENTY, GEORGE ALFRED 1832-1902　　Friends Though Divided. Griffith & Farran, 1883. 1st edition; 1st issue, with publisher's 32 page catalog dated 9/83; brown cloth, very good, near fine; from the collection of John H. Dalton.　　Harland H. Eastman 10/94-96 1996 $350.00

HENTY, GEORGE ALFRED 1832-1902　　Friends though Divided. Griffith & Farran, 1883. 1st edition; 1st issue, with publisher's 32 page catalog dated 9/83; green cloth, very good plus; from the collection of John H. Dalton.　　Harland H. Eastman 10/94-97 1996 $325.00

HENTY, GEORGE ALFRED 1832-1902　　A Girl of the Commune. R. F. Fenno, 1895. 1st edition; very good+; from the collection of John H. Dalton.　　Harland H. Eastman 10/94-98 1996 $125.00

HENTY, GEORGE ALFRED 1832-1902　　Held Fast for England. London: Blackie, 1892. 1st edition; fine, from the collection of John H. Dalton. Harland H. Eastman 10/94-31 1996 $125.00

HENTY, GEORGE ALFRED 1832-1902　　In the Hands of the Cave-Dwellers. New York: Harper & Bros., 1900. 1st edition; small oval stamp on titlepage, indicating former ownership by private library, otherwise very fine; from the collection of John H. Dalton.　　Harland H. Eastman 10/94-102 1996 $125.00

HENTY, GEORGE ALFRED 1832-1902　　In the Heart of the Rockies. London: Blackie, 1895. 1st edition; fine; from the collection of John H. Dalton.　　Harland H. Eastman 10/94-34 1996 $110.00

HENTY, GEORGE ALFRED 1832-1902　　In the Reign of Terror. London: Blackie, 1888. 1st edition; near fine; from the collection of John H. Dalton.　　Harland H. Eastman 10/94-35 1996 $250.00

HENTY, GEORGE ALFRED 1832-1902　　Jack Archer. Roberts Bros., 1884. 1st American edition; minor edge wear, very good; from the collection of John H. Dalton.　　Harland H. Eastman 10/94-103 1996 $175.00

HENTY, GEORGE ALFRED 1832-1902　　A Knight of the White Cross. London: Blackie, 1896. 1st edition; fine; from the collection of John H. Dalton.　　Harland H. Eastman 10/94-38 1996 $100.00

ASSOCIATION - JOHN DALTON

HENTY, GEORGE ALFRED 1832-1902   The Lion of St. Mark. London: Blackie, 1889. 1st edition; near fine, from the collection of John H. Dalton.   Harland H. Eastman 10/94-40 1996 $200.00

HENTY, GEORGE ALFRED 1832-1902   The Lion of the North. London: Blackie, 1886. 1st edition; edge wear, front hinge reglued, rubbed, nevertheless nar very good copy of a difficult title to find; from the collection of John H. Dalton.   Harland H. Eastman 10/94-41 1996 $125.00

HENTY, GEORGE ALFRED 1832-1902   Maori and Settler. London: Blackie, 1891. 1st edition; fine; from the collection of John H. Dalton. Harland H. Eastman 10/94-43 1996 $225.00

HENTY, GEORGE ALFRED 1832-1902   March to Coomassie. London: Tinsley, 1874. 1st edition; spine professionally relaid, very good; from the collection of John H. Dalton.   Harland H. Eastman 10/94-5 1996 $1,000.00

HENTY, GEORGE ALFRED 1832-1902   March to Coomassie. London: Tinsley, 1874. 2nd edition; very good plus, scarce as the first edition; from the collection of John H. Dalton.   Harland H. Eastman 10/94-6 1996 $1,000.00

HENTY, GEORGE ALFRED 1832-1902   March to Magdala. London: Tinsley, 1868. 1st edition; very good; from the collection of John H. Dalton.   Harland H. Eastman 10/94-4 1996 $1,000.00

HENTY, GEORGE ALFRED 1832-1902   Orange and Green. London: Blackie, 1888. 1st edition; minor rubbing at edges, otherwise fine copy of a very difficult title; from the collection of John H. Dalton.   Harland H. Eastman 10/94-48 1996 $250.00

HENTY, GEORGE ALFRED 1832-1902   Out of the Pampas. London: Griffith & Farran, 1871. 1st edition; author's first book for boys; very good; from the collection of John H. Dalton.   Harland H. Eastman 10/94-7 1996 $650.00

HENTY, GEORGE ALFRED 1832-1902   Out with Garibaldi. London: Blackie, 1901. 1st edition; fine, with summary slip laid in; from the collection of John H. Dalton.   Harland H. Eastman 10/94-49 1996 $100.00

HENTY, GEORGE ALFRED 1832-1902   Peril and Prowess. New York: E. P. Dutton, 1st American edition; minor rubbing, near fine; from the collection of John H. Dalton.   Harland H. Eastman 10/94-104 1996 $100.00

HENTY, GEORGE ALFRED 1832-1902   The Queen's Cup. London: Chatto & Windus, 1897. 1st edition; (publisher's records show only 350 copies were printed); 3 volumes; original cloth, some edge wear and soiling, overall very good set; from the collection of John H. Dalton. Harland H. Eastman 10/94-2 1996 $3,000.00

HENTY, GEORGE ALFRED 1832-1902   Redskin and Cowboy. London: Blackie, 1892. 1st edition; near fine copy of a difficult to find title in nice condition; from the collection of John H. Dalton.   Harland H. Eastman 10/94-52 1996 $125.00

HENTY, GEORGE ALFRED 1832-1902   A Roving Commission. London: Blackie, 1900. 1st edition; spine slow slightly faded as to be hardly noticeable (this title is notorious for spine fading); fine; from the collection of John H. Dalton.   Harland H. Eastman 10/94-53 1996 $125.00

HENTY, GEORGE ALFRED 1832-1902   Rujub the Juggler. London: Chatto & Windus, 1899. Presentation edition; very good+; from the collection of John H. Dalton.   Harland H. Eastman 10/94-142 1996 $100.00

HENTY, GEORGE ALFRED 1832-1902   St. Bartholomew's Eve. London: Blackie, 1894. 1st edition; fine; from the collection of John H. Dalton. Harland H. Eastman 10/94-54 1996 $100.00

HENTY, GEORGE ALFRED 1832-1902   St. George for England. London: Blackie, 1885. 1st edition; first 3 pages once folded, leaving slight creases; otherwise fine copy of early Blackie title; from the collection of John H. Dalton.   Harland H. Eastman 10/94-55 1996 $250.00

HENTY, GEORGE ALFRED 1832-1902   A Search for a Secret, Gall and Inglis. 1st one volume edition; new endpapers, near fine. from the collection of John H. Dalton.   Harland H. Eastman 10/94-106 1996 $115.00

HENTY, GEORGE ALFRED 1832-1902   A Tale of Waterloo. Worthington, 1st edition; fine copy, scarce; from the collection of John H. Dalton.   Harland H. Eastman 10/94-108 1996 $200.00

HENTY, GEORGE ALFRED 1832-1902   A Tale of Waterloo. Worthington, Later issue, with 2 battle plans and 9 page catalog as in first edition, but not the 8 illustrations called for; binding less ornate than first; near fine; from the collection of John H. Dalton.   Harland H. Eastman 10/94-144 1996 $100.00

HENTY, GEORGE ALFRED 1832-1902   Those Other Animals. Henry & Co. 1st edition; fine, from the collection of John H. Dalton.   Harland H. Eastman 10/94-109 1996 $145.00

HENTY, GEORGE ALFRED 1832-1902   The Tiger of Mysore. London: Blackie, 1896. 1st edition; fine copy; from the collection of John H. Dalton.   Harland H. Eastman 10/94-59 1996 $100.00

HENTY, GEORGE ALFRED 1832-1902   True to the Old Flag. London: Blackie, 1885. 1st edition; quarter inch cut in spine, otherwise near fine copy, difficult to find early title; from the collection of John H. Dalton. Harland H. Eastman 10/94-62 1996 $225.00

HENTY, GEORGE ALFRED 1832-1902   Two Sieges. S. W. Partridge, 1st edition; minor soiling, front free endpaper out, otherwise near fine, exceedingly scarce; from the collection of John H. Dalton.   Harland H. Eastman 10/94-110 1996 $150.00

HENTY, GEORGE ALFRED 1832-1902   Under Drake's Flag. London: Blackie, 1883. 1st edition; fine; from the collection of John H. Dalton. Harland H. Eastman 10/94-63 1996 $300.00

HENTY, GEORGE ALFRED 1832-1902   Under Wellington's Command. London: Blackie, 1899. 1st edition; fine, from the collection of John H. Dalton.   Harland H. Eastman 10/94-64 1996 $100.00

HENTY, GEORGE ALFRED 1832-1902   Venture and Valour. London: W. & R. Chambers, 1900. 1st edition; bit soiled, nevertheless very good+; from the collection of John H. Dalton.   Harland H. Eastman 10/94-111 1996 $100.00

HENTY, GEORGE ALFRED 1832-1902   With Clive in India. London: Blackie, 1884. 1st edition; fine, from the collection of John H. Dalton. Harland H. Eastman 10/94-67 1996 $300.00

HENTY, GEORGE ALFRED 1832-1902   With Frederick the Great. London: Blackie, 1898. 1st edition; fine, from the collection of John H. Dalton.   Harland H. Eastman 10/94-70 1996 $100.00

HENTY, GEORGE ALFRED 1832-1902   With Lee in Virginia. London: Blackie, 1890. 1st edition; very good+/near fine, from the collection of John H. Dalton.   Harland H. Eastman 10/94-72 1996 $150.00

HENTY, GEORGE ALFRED 1832-1902   With Moore at Corunna. London: Blackie, 1898. 1st edition; fine, from the collection of John H. Dalton.   Harland H. Eastman 10/94-73 1996 $100.00

HENTY, GEORGE ALFRED 1832-1902   With Wolfe in Canada. London: Blackie, 1887. 1st edition; bit rubbed and soiled, nevertheless very good; from the collection of John H. Dalton.   Harland H. Eastman 10/94-77 1996 $175.00

HENTY, GEORGE ALFRED 1832-1902   A Woman of the Commune. F. W. White & Co., 1895. 1st edition; spine bit faded, endpapers brittle and chipped, otherwise very good+; from the collection of John H. Dalton. Harland H. Eastman 10/94-113 1996 $150.00

HENTY, GEORGE ALFRED 1832-1902   Wulf the Saxon. London: Blackie, 1895. 1st edition; fine; from the collection of John H. Dalton. Harland H. Eastman 10/94-79 1996 $100.00

ASSOCIATION - JOHN DALTON

HENTY, GEORGE ALFRED 1832-1902   Yarns on the Beach. London: Blackie, 1886. 1st edition; minor edge wear, otherwise very good+, near fine, almost impossible to find Blackie first; from the collection of John H. Dalton.   Harland H. Eastman 10/94-83 1996 $300.00

HENTY, GEORGE ALFRED 1832-1902   The Young Carthaginian. London: Blackie, 1887. 1st edition; blue cloth; very good+; from the collection of John H. Dalton.   Harland H. Eastman 10/94-81 1996 $200.00

HENTY, GEORGE ALFRED 1832-1902   The Young Carthaginian. London: Blackie, 1887. 1st edition; rust cloth; very good+, from the collection of John H. Dalton.   Harland H. Eastman 10/94-82 1996 $200.00

ASSOCIATION - DALZIEL

ENGLISH Rustic Pictures Drawn by Frederick Walker and G. J. Pinwell and Engraved by the Brothers dalziel. India Proofs. London: George Routledge and Sons, 1882. Limited to 300 copies; folio; pages (14), 30 plates (15 of each artist), printed on india paper from the original blocks, each with accompanying leaf of letterpress; bound by Burn in original full japon decorated and lettered in gold and browns; inscribed by the Dalziels for Edith Warne.   Claude Cox 107-36 1996 £135.00

FOSTER, BIRKET   Pictures of English Landscape. London: George Routledge & Sons, 1881. Number 671 of 1000 copies; folio; pages (18), + 30 plates, printed by hand on india paper from original wood blocks, each with accompanying leaf of verse (all printed on rectos only); engraved by Brothers Dalziel. original full japon decorated and lettered in gold and browns, lightly soiled, uncut, by Burn and Co.; inscribed by the Brothers Dalziel for Miss Edith Warne.   Claude Cox 107-35 1996 £135.00

ASSOCIATION - CHARLES DANA

FRACASTORO, GIROLAMO   Opera Omnia, in vnum Proxime Post Illius Mortem Collecta. Venetiis: Apud Ivntas, 1555. 1st edition; 4to; 1 full page woodcut (slightly damaged), several text woodcuts, 6, 281, 32 leaves; contemporary vellum, spine slightly worn at tail, several leaves misnumbered as usual, front free endpaper lacking, slight worming of last leaf and lower hinge, slight marginal waterstaining on first few leaves; neat contemporary marginalia in Latin, Fracastoro's name in ink on lower edge and leather ex-libris of Charles L. Dana. Crisp, wide margined copy; several inscriptions, indicating the volume belonged to Givoanni Battista Capponi, doctor.   Argosy 810-185 1996 $3,250.00

ZAEHNSDORF, JOSEPH W.   The Art of Bookbinding. London: George Bell & Sons, 1880. 1st edition; 8vo; contemporary full rose polished calf, covers gilt in 4 compartments, central lozenge, spine and inner dentelles gilt, top edge gilt, by Zaehnsdorf; traces of rubbing; Fine; booklabel of Charles L. Dana, later bookplate of Nell Rose Wheeler and Charles Van Lise Wheeler.   Ximenes 108-350 1996 $500.00

ASSOCIATION - DANIEL

BINYON, LAURENCE 1869-1943   Poems. Oxford: Daniel Press, 1895. 1st edition; number 45 of 200 copies; large 8vo; pages (8), 52, (4); printed with Fell italic type on French (Rives, Isere) handmade paper; slight spotting on edges, otherwise very good, uncut in original printed grey wrappers with prospectus slip laid in; 2 ALS's from Dr. Daniel preserved in original postal envelope with penny violet stamp franked 'Oxford 11.45am SP 30 95'. Madan 35   Claude Cox 107-37 1996 £220.00

ASSOCIATION - GEORGE DARLEY

KEATS, JOHN 1795-1821   Lamia, Isabella, The Eve of St. Agnes and Other Poems. London: for Taylor and Hessey, 1820. 1st edition; 12mo; pages (vi), 199, (1), without half title and ad leaves sometimes found at end; contemporary brown calf, triple fillet gilt border to sides around elaborate blind roll, triple fillets and cornerpieces, spine in compartments with raised bands, gilt rules, place and date, and blind ornament, red morocco label, little rubbed, just a few spots, excellent copy; at one time the copy of scholar Sidney Colvin, signed notes by him, along with another later inscription; presentation copy, inscribed to poet George Darley from his cousin Maria. Ashley III p. 15-16; MacGillivray 3; Hayward 233; Tinker 1420.   Simon Finch 24-136 1996 £5,500.00

ASSOCIATION - RALPH DARLING

SELECT Portions of the Psalms of David, According to the Version of Dr. Brady and Mr. Tate...Hymns for..Church Holy-Days and Festivals. Sydney: printed by R. Howe, Government Printer, 1828. 12mo. (but signed in 4's) contemporary sheep, blind tooled borders, head of spine chipped, but nce; inscribed by Lt. General Sir Ralph Darling, Governor of New South Wales for Mrs. Dumaresq.   Peter Murray Hill 185-2 1996 £450.00

ASSOCIATION - CLARENCE DARROW

BACON, EDWIN N.   Historic Pilgrimages in New England, Among Landmarks of Pilgrim and Puritan Days and of the Provincial and Revolutionary Periods. Boston: Silver, Burdett & Co., 1898. original pictorial cloth, showing definite wear but sound; Clarence Darrow's copy with his bookplate.   Meyer Boswell SL27-59 1996 $750.00

ASSOCIATION - WHITNEY DARROW

FITZGERALD, FRANCIS SCOTT KEY 1896-1940   This Side of Paradise. New York: Charles Scribner's Sons, 1920. 1st edition; 1st printing, with dedicatee's name misspelled on page (v); original dark green cloth, better than good copy, slightly discolored and dusty, without much wear but without much freshness either; enclosed in lovely black morocco box with marbled paper sides; presentation inscription from author for Whitney Darrow.   Lakin & Marley 3-13 1996 $8,000.00

ASSOCIATION - DARTREY

SIDNEY, PHILIP 1554-1586   The Countess of Pembroke's Arcadia. London: for George Calvert, 1674. 13th edition; folio; (32), 624, (26) pages; portrait; full brown polished calf, covers panelled, spine richly gilt in compartments, dentelles gilt, by Riviere; some page numbers cropped, front hinge just beginning to crack, else fine, Dartrey bookplate. Wing S3770.   Joseph J. Felcone 64-38 1996 $450.00

ASSOCIATION - DARWIN

LAMB, CHARLES 1775-1834   The Letters of Charles Lamb, with a Sketch of His Life. London: Edward Moxon, 1837. 1st edition; 8vo; 2 volumes, x, 335; (iv), 338 pages; engraved portraits, contemporary dark green mottled calf, gilt spines, spines very lightly rubbed and faded; nice set with ownership inscriptions of L Darwin (possibly Leonard, Charles Darwin's Son) and E. Catherine Darwin.   James Burmester 29-85 1996 £90.00

ASSOCIATION - CHARLES DASHWOOD

GROSE, FRANCIS 1731-1791   The Antiquities of England and Wales. London: printed for Hooper & Wigstead,... n.d., c. 1783-97. New edition; 4to; 8 volumes; vignette title to all volumes, County Index to all volumes, (iii-iv), preface 1-142 pages, addenda to preface 143-160 pages, text, to the Public (i-iv) to volume VIII, General Index 165-172 pages, Directions to Binder to final leaf volume VIII, engraved frontispiece to all volumes, 589 engraved plates, and 1 extra plate not called for, 88 maps and plans and 1 extra plan not called for, 88 maps and plans and 1 extra plate not called for; full diced calf, gilt rule border to boards, gilt titles and tooling to spines, few joints rubbed, corners slightly bumped, very fine and handsome set; plates in near mint condition with no foxing or offsetting, signature O to volume 1 heavily browned, only light foxing to few other pages, uniformly marbled endpapers & edges, bookplate of Charles Vere Dashwood & E. N. Thornton.   Beeleigh Abbey BA/56-10 1996 £950.00

ASSOCIATION - CHARLES LEWES DASHWOOD

BAYLEY, JOHN   The History and Antiquities of the Tower of London, with Memoirs of Royal and Distinguished persons, Deduced from Records, State Papers and Manuscripts... London: for T. Cadell, 1821-25. Large 8vo; 2 volumes, half title, title, dedn., list of paltes, title and dedn. repeated, pages vii-xiv, list of plates repeated, pages 272, xxiv, 1 f. ad, frontispiece, double page map, 28 engraved plates (3-27, 3 n.n.); half title, title 2 ff., pages 273-674, xxxv-cxxviii, 9 ff. index; half brown morocco, spines faded and scuffed, top edge gilt. bookplates of Charles Dashwood. Adams 136.   Marlborough 162-110 1996 £550.00

ASSOCIATION - DAUX

RICHTER, GISELA M. A.   Catalogue of Engraved Gems: Greek, Etruscan and Roman. Roma: L'Erma di Bretschneider, 1956. 4to; xliii, 143 pages, 75 plates; half calf with marbled boards, spine faded and rubbed; scarce. Daux's copy.   Archaeologia Luxor-3887 1996 $450.00

ASSOCIATION - CHARLES DAVENANT

DAVENANT, WILLIAM 1606-1668   Gondibert: an Heroick Poem. London: printed by Tho. Newcomb for John Holden, 1651. 1st edition; 4to; woodcut device on title, (2), 88, (4), 322, (8) pages; collating correctly A-3K4 with 3K4 blank present; occasional slight soiling and edge fingermarks, few pencilled reader's emphasis marks; contemporary ruled sheep, sometime neatly rebacked, lettered in gilt; good, crisp copy. From the library of Charles Davenant, author's son, this copy with at least 32 author's ms. corrections. MacDonald & Hargreaves p. 24. John Drury 82-63 1996 £450.00

ASSOCIATION - DONALD DAVIDSON

WORDSWORTH, WILLIAM 1770-1850   Lyrical Ballads. London: Oxford, 1924. Reprint of 1798 volume; very good without dust jacket, with gift inscription presenting the book to poet Merrill Moore and then inscribed by Moore to Donald Davidson.   Ken Lopez 74-327 1996 $275.00

ASSOCIATION - GEORGE DAVIDSON

CALIFORNIA. STATE BOARD OF HEALTH   Second Biennial Report of the State Board of Health of California, for the Years 1871, 1872 and 1873. Sacramento: State Board of Health, 1873. 8 3/4 x 5 1/2 inches; (viii), 235 pages, 5 folding tables, 3 maps, 3 lithographic plates; dark blue cloth. On titlepage is ownership stamp of George Davidson of the U.S. Coast Survey.   Dawson's Books Shop 528-19 1996 $100.00

DAVIS, ANDREW MC FARLAND   The Journey of Moncacht-Ape, an Indian of the Yazoo Tribe, Across the Continent, About the Year 1700. Worcester: printed by Charles Hamilton, 1883. 1st separate edition; 30 pages; printed wrappers, fore-edges of wrappers chipped, some pencil annotations, else fine; presentation copy, signed by author, signed by George Davidson. Howes D103.   Argonaut Book Shop 113-171 1996 $125.00

ASSOCIATION - DAVIES

SCRATCHLEY, J.   The London Dissector; or System of Dissection Practised in the Hospitals and Lecture Rooms of the Metropolis. London: 1816. 1st edition; 8vo; boards, uncut, worn, joints cracked and printed label defective, 24 page publisher catalog of J. Callow, medical books bound at end; signataure of Danl. Owen Davies, surgeon, on title. Maggs Bros. Ltd. 1190-503 1996 £65.00

ASSOCIATION - HOWELL DAVIES

BUTLER, SAMUEL 1835-1902   Butleriana. Bloomsbury: Nonesuch Press, 1932. Number 658 of 800 copies; half green calf by Sangorski & Sutcliffe, top edge gilt, booklabel of Howell L. Davies.   Jarndyce CII-98 1996 £85.00

ASSOCIATION - J. DAVIES

TACITUS, CORNELIUS   De Moribus Germanorum et De Vita Agricolae; ex Editione Gabrielis Brotier ad Alteram Joh. Aug. Ernesti Collata. Londini: 1788. 8vo; pages (4), 39, (3), 48, (2); well printed on thick Whatman paper; contemporary straight grain crimson morocco, ruled and lettered in gold with simple wavy leaf roll on inner borders, marbled endpapers, all edges gilt; original ownership mark of 'J. Davies 1790' with (?his) pencilled notes on 20 pages. Lowndes p. 2567.   Claude Cox 107-165 1996 £100.00

ASSOCIATION - ANNIE DAVIS

HEMINGWAY, ERNEST MILLAR 1899-1961   A Farewell to Arms. New York: Charles Scribner's Sons, 1929. 1st edition; 2nd issue, with legal disclaimer; original blue cloth, paper labels, good plus, labels browned, with complete dust jacket which is chipped at top of spine and boasts quite a few small closed tears; overall effect is not at all unpleasant; enclosed in elegant black cloth box; presentation copy from author for Annie Daivs, wife of his old friend Nathan "Bill" Davis.   Lakin & Marley 3-18 1996 $7,500.00

ASSOCIATION - JOSEPH DAWSON

DETROSIER, ROWLAND   Lecture On the Utility of Political Unions, for the Diffusion of Sound Moral and Political Information Amongst the People. London: John Brooks, 1832. 1st edition; 8vo; 24 pages; recently well bound in linen backed marbled boards lettered, very good, presentation copy, inscribed by author for Joseph Dawson. Kress C3122; Goldsmiths 27698; not in Black or Williams.   John Drury 82-64 1996 £250.00

ASSOCIATION - ARTHUR BLISS DAYTON

OSLER, WILLIAM 1849-1919   Cancer of the Stomach. Philadelphia: P. Blakiston's Son, 1900. 1st American edition; 8vo; iv, 157, ads, 40, (8) pages, 25 figures; dark blue blind stamped cloth, inner hinge cracked signature of Arthur Henry Morse who inscribed the book to Arthur Bliss Dayton, 1921. Bookplate of Elmer Belt. Abbott p. 72; Golden & roland 727.   Jeff Weber 31-36 1996 $325.00

ASSOCIATION - ROBIN DE BEAUMONT

BAYNES, ROBERT H.   The Illustrated Book of Sacred Poems. London: Cassell, Petter and Galpin, n.d. ca. 1867. 1st edition; 8vo; viii, 391, (1) pages; illustrations; publisher's cloth, all edges gilt; spine lightly sunned, otherwise very good; from the library of Robin de Beaumont. Bookpress 75-5 1996 $145.00

ASSOCIATION - L. S. DE CAMP

HOWARD, ROBERT E.   Conan the Conqueror. The Sword of Conan. King Conan. The Coming of Conan. Conan the Barbarian. Tales of Conan. Gnome Press, 1950-55. 1st editions; 6 volumes; all very good+ to fine in like dust jackets; Tales of Conan is inscribed by co-author, L. S. De Camp.   Aronovitz 57-565 1996 $750.00

ASSOCIATION - TED DE GRAZIA

BRANDES, RAY   Troopers West: Military and Indian Affairs on the American Frontier. San Diego: Frontier Heritage Press, 1970. 1st edition; limited to 1000 numbered copies; quarto; xii, 206 pages; photos, maps, numerous drawings and color plates by Ted De Grazia; original cloth; fine, with dust jacket; presentation copy, signed and dated by De Grazia. Argonaut Book Shop 113-190 1996 $150.00

ASSOCIATION - JAMES DE KAY

CLINTON, DE WITT   A Discourse Delivered at Schenectady, July 22nd, 1823, Before the New York Alpha of the Phi Beta Kappa. New York: Websters and Skinners, 1823. 1st edition; 8vo; 47 pages; removed; foxed. Inscribed "from the author" to the naturalist (James E) De Kay. Shoemaker 12185.   M & S Rare Books 60-306 1996 $150.00

ASSOCIATION - DE RENNE

GEORGIA. (COLONY). LAWS STATUTES ETC.   Acts Passed by the General Assembly of the Colony of Georgia 1755-1774. Wormsloe: privately printed, 1881. 1st and only edition, limited to 49 copies; large folio; 427 pages; original green patterned cloth, red morocco spine label, minor repairs to spine, some foxing to several pages, otherwise fine, tight copy; presentation copy from Mrs. George De Renne. Quite rare. Michael D. Heaston 23-156 1996 $2,500.00

ASSOCIATION - DE THOU

APHTHONIUS   Progymnasmata...cum Scholiss R. Lorichii. Amsterdam: L. Elzevir, 1642. 12mo; engraved title, printed title, 5 ff. index, 1 f. blank, 400 pages; contemporary plain calf, covers gilt with arms of F. A. de Thou, spine gilt in five panels, raised bands, de Thou monogram in four panels, all edges red, plain endpapers;   Marlborough 160-12 1996 £900.00

DOMINICY, MARC ANTOINE   Assertor Gallicvs, Contra Vindicias Hispanicas Ioannes Iacobi Chiffletii. Paris: Typographia Regis, 1616. Large4to; title arms, fine head and tailpieces and 3 full page plates; calf, gilt impressed on both covers the arms of Jacques-Auguste de Thou II; fine. Brunet 24008.   Rostenberg & Stern 150-45 1996 $1,875.00

ASSOCIATION - DE VERNACCIA

GELLI, GIOVANNI BATISTA   La Circe Di Giovan-Batista Gelli. Firenze: Lorenzo Torrentino, 1549. 1st edition; octavo; late 17th or early 18th century polished grained sheep, gilt spine with contrasting title labels of tan and black morocco gilt; joints slightly rubbed, cracked at head and foot of spine with excellent restoration to top of spine, tiny chip at top back joint, light soiling tot title and final leaf, small collector's stamp at foot of title, very respectable copy of a very rare book; several bookplates, including De Vernaccia and Landau bookplates. Adams G333; Gamba 491.   G. W. Stuart 59-43 1996 $750.00

ASSOCIATION - WALTER DEAN

SMITH, WALTER   Art Education, Schoalstic and Industrial. Boston: James R. Osgood, 1872. 1st edition; 8vo; 40 full page, inserted illustrations; cloth, gilt, very good; copy of the Boston and Gloucester artist, Walter Dean, with his signature.   Freedom Bookshop 14-16 1996 $125.00

ASSOCIATION - FRANK DEARDEN

LUCAS, EDWARD VERRALL   All the World Over. London: Grant Richards, 1898. 1st edition; oblong folio; original pictorial boards, edges rubbed, cloth back; with the Frank J. Dearden pencilled note, with comment, "Very rare.".   Howard S. Mott 227-90 1996 $120.00

ASSOCIATION - JIMMY DEMARET

RULE, BOB   Champions Golf Club 1957-1976. Houston: Graphics Unlimited, 1976. 1st edition; small 4to; color frontispiece, numerous illustrations; dust jacket (some rubbing); very good, signed and inscribed by Jack Burke and Jimmy Demaret to bandleader Les Brown.   George J. Houle 68-54 1996 $125.00

ASSOCIATION - DERBY

STATIUS, PUBLIUS PAPINIUS   Statii Sylvarum Libri V./ Achilleidos Libri XII./ Thebaidos Libri II./ Orthographia et Flexus Dictionum Graecarum Omnium... Venice: In aedibvs Aldi, et Andreae Soceri (Andrea Torresano), 1519. 1st Aldine edition; 8vo; 296 leaves, italic, Aldine devices on first and last leaves; red morocco binding by Bozerian le jeune, with gilt arms of Edward George Geoffrey Smith Stanley, 14th Earl of Derby, statesman and Greek scholar, silk doublures, tooled in gilt, all edges gilt, very clean and handsome copy. Renouard 88/12; Adams S1672; UCLA II/153; Brunet V512.   Family Album Tillers-587 1996 $1,600.00

ASSOCIATION - JACQUES DERRIDA

HUSSERL, EDMUND   L'Origine de la Geometrie. Paris: Presses Universitaires de France, 1962. 1st edition translated by Jacques Derrida. Wrappers; near fine; exceptional association copy, inscribed by Derrida to American critic and novelist Susan Sontag.   Lame Duck Books 19-460 1996 $1,500.00

ASSOCIATION - GEORGE DERRY

SCOTT, TEMPLE   The Silver Age and Other Dramatic Memories. New York: Scott & Seltzer, 1919. 1st edition; 8vo; crushed dark burgundy morocco du cap with two gilt fillet borders and elaborate corner pieces made up of groupings of individual floral tools, spine with five raised bands and similar floral decoration within compartments, board edges gilt, inner dentelles, top edge gilt, stamped with name of binder on lower front turn in: The Atelier Bindery; the dedication copy, with presentation inscription to dedicatee D. George Derry, Esq. dated Christmas 1919; laid in is one page ALS from Scott to Derry.   Book Block 32-44 1996 $395.00

ASSOCIATION - DESCHAMPS

BARBUT, JAMES   The Genera Vermium Exemplified by Various Specimens of the Animals Contained in the Orders of the Intestina at Mollusca Linnaei. Drawn from Nature. London: printed for the author by James Dixwell, 1783. 1st edition; 4to; frontispiece, 2 page list of subscribers, 11 hand colored plates, some offsetting in text, text in English and French; contemporary tree calf, spine gilt, label, with Deschamps bookplates; nice copy. Nissen ZBI 221.   Anthony W. Laywood 109-6 1996 £425.00

ASSOCIATION - ANDRE DEUTSCH

RHYS, JEAN   Voyage in the Dark. London: Andre Deutsch, 1967. 1st edition; near fine in dust jacket; presentation copy from author to her publisher, Andre Deutsch.   Words Etcetera 94-1086 1996 £250.00

ASSOCIATION - PETER DEVRIES

FAULKNER, WILLIAM HARRISON 1897-1962   The Reivers. New York: Random House, 1962. 1st edition; fine in price clipped, very near fine dust jacket with little rubbing to edge of spine; nicer copy than usual; the copy of Peter DeVries with his pencil ownership.   Between the Covers 42-166 1996 $250.00

POWELL, ANTHONY DYMOKE 1905-   A Question of Upbringing. New York: Scribners, 1951. 1st American edition; fore edges slightly tanned, else fine in near fine dust jacket with small nicks and tears at extremities and touch of darkening to extremities, still nice. Author Peter DeVries's copy with his pencil ownership.   Between the Covers 42-358 1996 $375.00

STAFFORD, JEAN   A Mother in History. New York: FSG, 1966. 1st edition; fine in dust jacket with tiny tear and faint spot on rear panel; inscribed by author for Peter DeVries and his wife.   Between the Covers 42-409 1996 $275.00

ASSOCIATION - CHARLES DICKENS

MENKEN, ADAH ISAACS   Infelicia. London: Paris: New York: Published by the author, 1868. Small 8vo; publisher's green cloth over beveled boards with gilt decoration on cover and spine, cloth slightly bubbled in few spots, all edges gilt, gilt mostly missing along top and lower edges, first gathering bit loose with small piece chipped off the fore-edge of content's page; dedication copy, dedicated to Charles Dickens, with his bookplate; in old cloth chemise (for a slipcase) with two labels. Podeschi pp. 207-208; Wolff 4738; Modern Lib. at Watlington Park p.199   Book Block 32-57 1996 $1,350.00

ASSOCIATION - BENJAMIN DICKINSON

MOORE, JOHN 1729-1802   A Journal During a Residence in France...to the Middle of December 1792. London: for G. G. J. & J. Robinson/ G.G. & J. Robinson, 1793. 1st edition; demy 8vo; 2 volumes; (iv), 502; (vi), (618) pages; folding colored map; contemporary half calf gilt, numbers in roundels, lemon edges, some wear, slight chipping, few marks, little tender, but good set, contemporary bookplates of Benjamin Dickinson. Ash Rare Books Zenzybyr-70 1996 £200.00

POEMS, Moral, Elegant and Pathetic. London: printed for E. Newbery, and Vernor and Hood, 1796. 1st edition; 12mo; frontispiece, 5 other plates; contemporary tree calf, spine gilt (labelled "Williams's Poems"); uncommon; early armorial bookplate and signature of Benjamin Dickinson, of Tiverton. Roscoe A411(1); CBEL III 423 and 693. Ximenes 108-291 1996 $450.00

ASSOCIATION - M. H. DICKINSON

DARLINGTON, W.   Memorials of John Bartram and Humphry Marshall, with Notices of Their Botanical Contemporaries. Philadelphia: 1849. 1st edition; 8vo; 2 plates of facsimile ms., 2 plates of houses; cloth, bit worn, rebacked; signature of M. H. Dickinson on title.   Maggs Bros. Ltd. 1190-230 1996 £55.00

ASSOCIATION - ANN DILLWYN

CRESSON, JOSHUA   Meditations Written During the Prevalence of the Yellow Fever in the City of Philadelphia in the Year 1793. London: W. Phillips, 1803. 1st edition; 8vo; pages x, 26; original marbled wrappers; signature of Ann Dillwyn of the Quaker family. Not in Wellcome. Maggs Bros. Ltd. 1190-392 1996 £85.00

ASSOCIATION - CHARLES DOBLE

POOLE, JACOB   A Glossary, with some Pieces of Verse, of the Old Dialect of the English Colony in the Baronies of Forth and Bargy, County of Wexford, Ireland. London: J. Russell Smith, 1867. Half title; original green cloth, slightly rubbed; bookplates of Charles Doble & John Sparrow.   Jarndyce 103-92 1996 £110.00

ASSOCIATION - DODSON

HUGHES, LANGSTON   Famous Negro Music Makers. New York: Dodd, Mead, 1955. 1st edition; some underlining in text, else fine in very good dust jacket with light chipping to extremities; signed by author; uncommon; ownership signature of Edith Dodson, wife of author Owen Dodson.   Between the Covers 43-119 1996 $425.00

ASSOCIATION - DOHENY

FORSTER, JOHN   The Life and Adventures of Oliver Goldsmith. London: Chapman and Hall, 1848. 1st edition; illustrations; original pictorial cloth, all edges gilt, in cloth folding box (also little worn); inner hinges cracked as usual on this thick book, covers somewhat faded and worn; presentation copy, inscribed "M. W. Savage (probably the Irish-born novelist and editor, Marmion W. Savage) from his old and attached friend J.F." Bookplate of Estelle Doheny.   David J. Holmes 52-36 1996 $550.00

PEACOCK, THOMAS LOVE   The Misfortunes of Elphin. London: Thomas Hookham, 1829. 1st edition; 12mo; pages (viii), 240, half title; original drab boards, uncut, largely unopened; cloth box, upper joint starting at foot, head of spine very slightly damaged, otherwise fine; rare uncut in original boards; the Doheny copy with her morocco booklabel. Sadleir 1957; Wolff 5481.   Simon Finch 24-179 1996 £900.00

RYAN, ABRAM J.   Father Ryan's Poems. Mobile: 1879. 1st edition; 8vo; 262, (1) pages; frontispiece; original cloth, very good; two part slipcase; bookplate of Estelle Doheny. BAL 17107.   M & S Rare Books 60-228 1996 $250.00

SHELLEY, PERCY BYSSHE 1792-1822   The Masque of Anarchy: a Poem. London: Edward Moxon, 1832. 1st edition; 6 3/4 x 4 1/4 inches; xxx, 47 pages, (1) leaf ads; original buff paper boards, paper spine label, edges of leaves untrimmed, contained in folding box lined with watered silk and plush velvet and covered in full red levant morocco, French fillets on sides, spine with raised bands, gilt ruled compartments and gilt titling, front joint of box little worn, part of paper spine label missing (with all the printed letters affected but none of them completely lost), but only very minor smudging or wear to binding, two leaves faintly creased (apparently during binding), otherwise fine, fragile, exceptionally clean internally. Leather bookplate of Estelle Doheny. Granniss 80; Wise p. 71.   Phillip J. Pirages 33-461 1996 $2,500.00

WHITMAN, WALT 1819-1892   Leaves of Grass. Brooklyn: 1856. 2nd edition; 12mo; recased in original green cloth with spine laid down, gilt lettering somewhat dull, some mild foxing, but very good, scarce edition; housed in attractive quarter green morocco slipcase; the Doheny copy. Captain's Bookshelf 38-217 1996 $1,750.00

WHITTIER, JOHN GREENLEAF 1807-1892   Moll Pitcher, a Poem. Boston: Carter and Hendee, 1832. 1st edition; 8vo; original printed blue wrappers, uncut, slight chipping of spine, Massachusetts Library stamp at top of verso of titlepage; great rarity in wrappers. The Estelle Doheny copy. BAL 214677; Howes Lib. V, JGW 20; B&B 17076.   M & S Rare Books 60-265 1996 $14,000.00

ASSOCIATION - WILLIAM DONDESNELL

LUCANUS, MARCUS ANNAEUS 39-68   Lucanus. Venice: In Aedibus Aldi, et Andreae Soceri, 1515. 2nd Aldine edition; 8vo; 140 leaves, Italic; early 18th century full leather, boards, detached, all edges gilt; engraved armorial Bookplate of William Dondesnell Esq. of Pull Cort. Renouard 72.6. Adams L1564; UCLA II 117; Brunet III 1199.   Family Album Tillers-402 1996 $700.00

ASSOCIATION - DOTRENGE

BERNOULLI, JAKOB   Ars Conjectandi, Opus Posthumum. Basel: Impensis Thurnisiorum, Fratrum, 1713. 1st edition; small quarto; (4), 306, 35, (1 errata) pages; 2 folding tables, 1 folding plate; 19th century full green calf, gilt single rule border on covers, gilt decorated spine with red morocco label, gilt board edges, few leaves slightly browned, otherwise excellent; ink signature of Theod. Dotrenge, and his handwritten notes at foot of page 78 and on recto and verso of back free endpaper. Dibner 110; Horblit 12; PMM 179.   Heritage Book Shop 196-177 1996 $9,500.00

ASSOCIATION - GEORGE DOUGLAS

HOBHOUSE, JOHN CAM   A Journey through Albania, and Other Provinces of Turkey in Europe and Asia, to Constantinople, During the Years 1809 and 1810. London: printed for James Cawthorn, 1833. 3rd edition; 11 x 8 3/4 inches; 2 volumes; 24 plates, including 2 folding maps and 18 hand colored aquatints; old probably contemporary half calf, marbled sides, red morocco spine labels, gilt rules and volume numbers, joints and extremities somewhat rubbed (one joint partly cracked, with board just slightly wobbly), sides little chafed and leather bit marked, but early bindings still rather bright and pleasing, despite defects, very faint marginal dampstain on 20 leaves in first volume, slight browning to text, few leaves of volume 2 with small stain at inner margin, plates very clean with pleasing color; front pastedowns with engraved bookplate of Sir George Douglas and paper shelf label of Springwood Park, Kelso. Abbey 202 (1813 ed.). Blackmer Sale Cat. 688. Phillip J. Pirages 33-307 1996 $1,750.00

ASSOCIATION - JOHN DOUGLAS

AYLING, STEPHEN   Photographs from Sketches by Augustus Welby N. Pugin. London: S. Ayling, 1865. 1st edition; large 8vo; title leaf, 4 pages, 250 mounted photos; frontispiece; publisher's cloth, top edge gilt, light wear to covers, but very good set overall; bookplate of John Douglas. Gernsheim 274.   Bookpress 75-103 1996 $1,825.00

ASSOCIATION - ALBERT DOUGLASS

BURNS, ROBERT 1759-1796   Poems and Letters in the Handwriting of Robert Burns. Saint Louis: printed for the Burns Club, 1908. Limited edition of 300 numbered copies; folio; printed on Dutch handmade paper; numerous tipped in plates or ms. facsimiles; original half paper parchment and boards; very good, some browning to spine; signed presentation copy from William K. Bixby, the principal owner of the manuscripts reproduced herein, to the Hon. Albert Douglass.   Antic Hay 101-262 1996 $185.00

ASSOCIATION - ARTHUR CONAN DOYLE

WISE, JOHN R.   The New Forest: Its History and Scenery. London: and Manchester: Ballantyne Press for Henry Sotheran & Co., 1883. Apparently One of 350 copies, 'Artist's Edition'; 11 1/4 x 8 1/4 inches; xi, (1) pages, (2) leaves, 335, (1) pages; printed as a large paper copy on fine quality thick and untrimmed leaves; 12 etched plates by Heywood Sumner, 2 maps, frontispiece and more than 60 mounted illustrations, by Walter Crane; publisher's original special black morocco, sides covered with wood veneer, front cover with titling and sylvan vignette in black, flat spine with gilt titling, top edge gilt, other edges untrimmed; wood veneer little warped and blistered, board edges and corners bit worn, slight rubbing to joints and few marks to spine, but binding still very much intact, and, in a quirky way, quite pleasing, very fine copy internally. With armorial bookplate of Sir Arthur Conan Doyle and with his signature. Nissen 2173 (earlier editions).   Phillip J. Pirages 33-194 1996 $550.00

ASSOCIATION - J. M. DOYLE

FITZPATRICK, WILLIAM JOHN   The Life of Charles Lever. London: Chapman and Hall, 1879. 1st edition; large 8vo; 2 volumes; original dark green cloth, very minor rubbing; fine set. Presentation copy, inscribed on first titlepage from author for J. M. Doyle. CBEL III 944.   Ximenes 109-126 1996 $250.00

ASSOCIATION - JOHN DOYLE

STOUT, PETER F.   Nicaragua: Past, Present and Future... Philadelphia: John E. Potter, 1859. 8vo; 372 pages; one large folding map; from the library of John T. Doyle, one mounted page of notes and extensive notes on rear endpaper, one mounted article, Doyle's "Dean of the California Bar"; original brown cloth, gilt, bookplate, library pocket. Kenneth Karmiole 1NS-148 1996 $175.00

ASSOCIATION - H. E. DRESSER

POYNTING, F.   Eggs of British Birds with an Account of Their Breeding Habits: Limicolae. London: 1895-96. 4to; 2 plain and 55 fine colored plates; new buckram, unique copy, the copy of H. E. Dresser, there are 3 extra plates and few cuttings inserted; one plate is inscribed "With kind regards from H. E. Dresser." The owner has noted "Given to me by Mr. Dresser on Saturday June 5th 1909 - before this plate appeared in his work on Palearctic Eggs." Little foxed, heavily on few leaves. Wheldon & Wesley 207-86 1996 £500.00

ASSOCIATION - JOHN DRINKWATER

JENYNS, SOAME   Poems. London: printed for R. Dodsley, 1752. 1st edition; 8vo; contemporary calf, spine gilt, some rubbing, but sound; very good; from the library of John Drinkwater, with his book label and note of acquisition dated 1923, purchased from Hodgson's sale of the library of Eliza Tollet, this volume signed twice by her nephew George Tollet. Foxon P387; CBEL II 554.   Ximenes 108-222 1996 $250.00

LANDOR, WALTER SAVAGE 1775-1864   Pericles and Aspasia. London: Saunders and Otley, 1836. 1st edition; 8vo; 2 volumes; original green backed boards, uncut, printed paper labels; very good set without major fault and quite tight of case, in lush crimson morocco box; boards and labels show rub and wear which is usual to this period of publisher's binding, still very good; the superior H. Bradley Martin-John Drinkwater copy, orginally Edward Fitzgerald's copy with his ownership inscription in each volume.   Lakin & Marley 3-28 1996 $1,000.00

MUSAEUS   The Loves of Hero and Leander. London: printed for and sold by T. Osborne, et al, 1747. 1st edition; quarto; modern quarter cloth over boards, housed in lovely quarter morocco slipcase with elaborate floral motifs in red, green and gilt in compartments; John Drinkwater's copy with his small, distinctive leather bookplate and owenrship signature.   Captain's Bookshelf 38-171 1996 $350.00

ASSOCIATION - HENRY DRUMMOND

BANNATYNE CLUB   The Bannatyne Miscellany.... Edinburgh: printed 1827-36-55. 4to; complete set, 3 volumes; contemporary half red morocco, top edge gilt; fine; bookplates of Henry Drummond, Albury Park, Surrey. CBEL III 679.   Ximenes 108-14 1996 $650.00

ASSOCIATION - DRURY

TERENTIUS AFER, PUBLIUS 180-159 BC   Comoediae. Birmingham: Baskerville, 1772. 4to; 364 pages; foxed; all edges gilt, full straight grain plum morocco binding, splendidly tooled in gilt and blind, boards tooled with wide gilt Greek key outer dentelle, enclosing archway (almost cathedral) frame, though unsigned, some aspects of the binding remind us of the work of Birdsall. engraved English armorial bookplate, ms. presentation from B. Drury, Eton. Gaskell 46.   Family Album Tillers-608 1996 $1,200.00

ASSOCIATION - DU PLESSIS

BIBLE. FRENCH - 1738   Version du Nouveau Testament Selon La Vulgate... Paris: Chez J. B. Garnier, 1738. New edition; 8vo; 2 volumes, engraved frontispiece to volume 1, each page ruled in red, well margined; handsomely bound in full 18th century French brown morocco, triple gilt fillet to boards enclosing stylised fleurons at corners each board with large round elaborate gilt stamp of dual coat-of-arms, corners little worn, flat spines elaborately gilt in compartments with lettering direct, tiny wormhole to base of spine of volume 2, large red morocco doublures on inside of all boards, wide and elaborate gilt dentelle border, all edges gilt, marbled endpapers, magnificent contemporary French armorial bindings; bookplates of Mr. A. G-du Plessis and P de La Morandiere.   Ian Wilkinson 95/1-36 1996 £580.00

ASSOCIATION - G. DUCHARME

BRASS, JOHN   The Art of Ready Reckoning; or Mental and Practical Arithmetic. Toronto: printed by Lovell and Gibson, 1851. 8vo; pages 80; original paper covered boards, cloth strip at spine, paper label, boards warped and stained, else very good. Bookplate of G. Ducharme, noted Canadian book collector.   Hugh Anson-Cartwright 87-378 1996 $100.00

ASSOCIATION - DUCIE

HELPS, ARTHUR   Thoughts Upon Government. London: Bell and Daldy, 1872. 1st edition; 8vo; viii, 245 pages, contemporary brown half morocco, gilt, raised bands, marbled edges and endpapers; very fine; from the library of the Earl of Ducie with his signature on title.   John Drury 82-104 1996 £60.00

ASSOCIATION - MARY DUDGEON

ROTHERY, MARY C. HUME   The Bridesmaid, Count Stephen and other Poems. London: John Chapman, 1853. 1st edition; large 12mo; pages v, (2), 362, (2 blank) and 10, (2 ads) dated June 1853; original blue cloth, by Westleys with ticket, very good to nice; inscribed by author for her cousin Mrs. Mary Dudgeon.   James Fenning 133-168 1996 £65.00

ASSOCIATION - THOMAS BASIL DUGUID

STARK, JAMES   Scenery of the Rivers of Norfolk, Comprising the Yare, the Waveney and the Bure. Norwich & London: 1834. Large paper copy with india paper proofs; imperial quarto; 24 full page and 12 vignette steel engravings, all on india paper; bound in at end are original printed paper wrappers for the four parts, an "Address to Subscribers" dated 1830 and another dated 1831, two prospectuses containing various states of the "List of Subscribers", the latter carefully inlaid to size, full hard grain red morocco, narrow gilt border, fully gilt spine, inner dentelles gilt, top edge gilt, others uncut, by F. Bedford, very fine, uncommon; the copy of Thomas Basil Duguid with engraved armorial bookplate.   H. M. Fletcher 121-148 1996 £500.00

ASSOCIATION - DUMARESQ

SELECT Portions of the Psalms of David, According to the Version of Dr. Brady and Mr. Tate...Hymns for..Church Holy-Days and Festivals. Sydney: printed by R. Howe, Government Printer, 1828. 12mo. (but signed in 4's); contemporary sheep, blind tooled borders, head of spine chipped, but nce; inscribed by Lt. General Sir Ralph Darling, Governor of New South Wales for Mrs. Dumaresq.   Peter Murray Hill 185-2 1996 £450.00

ASSOCIATION - DUNCAN

BRITISH MUSEUM.   Catalogue of the Fossil Sponges in the Geological Department of the British Museum (Natural History). London: 1883. 4to; pages viii, 248; 38 plates; cloth, rebacked; inscribed "From the author to P. Martin Duncan".   John Henly 27-728 1996 £60.00

ASSOCIATION - DUNLOP

LUCRETIUS CARUS, TITUS 99-55 BC   Titi Lucretii Cari De Rerum Natura Libri Sex. Glasgow: Robert and Andrew Foulis, 1759. Small 8vo; pages (16), 269; attractive full contemporary dark green morocco binding, spine gilt; early ms. ownership of G. Dunlop and ms. notes of Lionel B. C. L. Muirhead. Gaskell 370; Brunet III 1220.   Family Album Tillers-413 1996 $260.00

ASSOCIATION - J. A. DUTHIE

BRUCE, GEORGE   The Land Birds In and Around St. Andrews, Including a Condensed History of the British Land Birds... Dundee: John Leng & Co., 1895. 8vo; pages vii, 563; little spotting to first and final leaves; original pictorial cloth gilt, extremities minimally rubbed, little spotting to first and final leaves; inscribed by son of author for Mrs. J. A. Duthie.   R.F.G. Hollett 76-45 1996 £65.00

ASSOCIATION - W. R. S. DWYER

LOCKE, JOHN 1632-1704   Some Thoughts on the Conduct of the Understanding in the Search of Truth. N.P.: 1741. 1st separate edition; 12mo; contemporary sheep, cracked, some rubbing, and chipping, circular mark on upper cover as if an onlay, endpapers removed, without "Advertisement" leaves at front, dated signature of W. R. S. Dwyer, 1844 on title, browned.   James Cummins 14-124 1996 $150.00

ASSOCIATION - DYER

WOLLSTONECRAFT, MARY 1759-1797   A Vindication of the Rights of Woman. London: printed for J. Johnson, 1792. 1st edition; 8vo; contemporary drab paper boards, neatly rebacked to style, recent paper label; fine, uncut, very fresh condition; Early signature of G. Dyer, possibly the eccentric poet George Dyer. PMM 242; Windle 5; CBEL II 1255.   Ximenes 108-347 1996 $4,750.00

ASSOCIATION - JAMES BULLER EAST

TORRE, NICHOLAS LEE   Translations of the Oxford and Cambridge Latin Prize Poems. Second Series. London: A. J. Valpy, 1831. Only edition; 8vo; contemporary quarter calf, spine gilt, marbled boards; very fine and attractive; armorial bookplate of Sir James Buller East.   Trebizond 39-43 1996 $165.00

TORRE, NICHOLAS LEE   Translations of the Oxford Latin Prize Poems. First Series. London: A. J. Valpy, 1831. Only edition; 8vo; 12 page subscriber list; contemporary quarter calf, spine gilt, marbled boards; very fine; armorial bookplate of Sir James Buller East, a subscriber.   Trebizond 39-42 1996 $125.00

ASSOCIATION - MARGOT EATES

HODIN, J. P.   John Milne: Sculptor - Life and Work. London: Latimer New Dimensions Ltd., 1977. 1st edition; illustrations in color and black and white; wrappers, slightly soiled, very good, head and tail of spine and corners slightly bumped, free endpapers slightly rubbed, very good in nicked, rubbed and slightly chipped and creased dust jacket; presentation copy from artist to engraved plates. H. Ramsden and Margot Eates.   Ulysses 39-410   1996 £95.00

READ, HERBERT   Lord Byron at the Opera - a Play for Broadcasting. North Harrow: Philip Ward, 1963. 1st edition; wrappers, covers spotted and slightly soiled and creased, cvoer edges faded, some slight internal spotting; good. Presentation copy from author to E. H. Ramsden and Margot Eates.   Ulysses 39-496   1996 £80.00

ASSOCIATION - RICHARD EBERHART

GINSBERG, ALLEN   Iron Horse. Toronto: Coach House Press, 1972. 1st edition; one of 1000 copies; bolong 8vo; pictorial wrappers; fine; inscribed by author for Richard Eberhart.   Captain's Bookshelf 38-91 1996 $100.00

ASSOCIATION - LINDLEY EBERSTADT

ABERT, JAMES WILLIAM   Report of the Secretary of War...A Report and Map of the Examination of New Mexico. Washington: Senate Executive Document 23, 1848. 1st edition; 132 pages; 24 plates, large folding map; original printed yellow wrappers, minor chipping and neatly rebacked; tall, untrimmed copy, some foxing to map, plates quite crisp and clean; fine; formerly the copy of Lindley Eberstadt; presentation copy from U.S. Senator Roger Sherman Baldwin to Yale Library. Goetzmann pp. 144-49; Streeter Sale 168; Howes A11; Graff 5. Michael D. Heaston 23-1 1996 $1,850.00

ASSOCIATION - JOHN ECKMAN

WILSON, SELDEN L.   Recollections and Experiences, During the Civil War, 1861-1865, in the 15th Penna. Vol. Cavalry, Better Known as the Anderson Cavalry. Washington: 1913. 1st edition; 168 pages; original printed wrappers, chipping along backstrip, else very good to near fine; formerly the copy of Sgt. John W. Eckman who contributed to the work. Dornbusch I PA 94.   McGowan Book Co. 65-106 1996 $450.00

ASSOCIATION - EDGE

MORGAN, JOHN   The Life and Adventures of William Buckley; Thirty-Two Years a Wanderer Amongst the Aborigines of the Then Unexplored Country Round Port Phillip, Now the Province of Victoria. Tasmania: Archibald MacDougall, 1852. (xiv), (ii), 208 pages; frontispiece little foxed, couple of marks; original cloth boards, rebacked, original spine laid down, chipped paper title piece; fully signed presentation copy dated June 11, 1852. Edge-Partington bookplate. Ferguson 12813. Antipodean 28-102 1996 $750.00

NICOLAY, C. G.   Notes on the Aborigines of Western Australia. London: William Clowes & Sons, The Colonial & Indian Exhibition, 1886. 18 page pamphlet; original printed wrappers, bound in papered boards, leather spine label; fine, scarace; Edge-Partington bookplate, the Absolon copy. Ferguson 13373; Greenway 7213.   Antipodean 28-147 1996 $350.00

OXLEY, JOHN   Journals of Two Expeditions Into the Interior of New South Wales, Under-Taken by Order of the British Government in the Years 1817-1818. London: John Murray, 1820. Quarto; (xv), 408 pages, 6 aquatint engravings, 3 folding maps, 2 folding tables (the two large folding maps have long ago been expertly mounted on folding linen; finely rebound (signed Morrell, London) in half morocco and linen boards, gilt decorated spine, all edges gilt, text is quite clean and bright; very pretty copy; old pen signature in titlepage partially removed with some staining, otherwise very good+; from the Edge-Partington collection, the Absolon copy. Ferguson 796; Wantrup 107.   Antipodean 28-160 1996 $5,500.00

SMITH, JAMES, MRS.   The Booandik Tribe of South Austrlian Aborigines. Adelaide: E. spiller, 1880. Small 8vo; (xi), 139 pages, 6 illustrations; leather spine and printed wrapper boards, leather spine rubbed, corners bumped, browning affects lower fore edge of text for first 30 od pages, otherwise good+; presentation copy from Rev. F. H. Robinson to his brother. James Edge Partington bookplate; Ferguson 15823; Greenway 8565.   Antipodean 28-364 1996 $225.00

ASSOCIATION - EDMOND

SIBSON, FRANCIS   Medical Anatomy. London: 1869. 1st edition; folio; text illustrations, 21 hand colored lithographed plates; minor soiling and slight creases, but sound copy; half calf, rebacked, by J. Edmond of Aberdeen, with his ticket, flyleaves creased.   Maggs Bros. Ltd. 1190-507 1996 £1,400.00

ASSOCIATION - H. W. EDWARDS

BIBLIOGRAPHICA. Papers on Books, Their History and Art. London: Kegan Paul, 1895-97. Thick 4to; 12 parts in 3 volumes, 65 plates and numerous illustrations; quarter morocco, bound by Zaehnsdorf (original wrappers bound in); fine set from the library of the late bookseller H. W. Edwards.   Charles W. Traylen 117-2 1996 £330.00

ASSOCIATION - EGERTON

GRAFER, JOHN   A Descriptive Catalogue of Upwards of Eleven Hundred Species and Varities of Herbaceous or Perenial Plants... London: printed and sold by J. Smeeton, n.d. 1794. 3rd edition; 8vo; contemporary half calf, spine gilt, some rubbing, but sound; blank strip clipped from foot of titlepage, just touching last line of publisher's ads, very good, scarce; inscribed to Mrs. Egerton with Mr. Vanbrugh's respects.   Ximenes 108-169 1996 $600.00

ASSOCIATION - EGMONT

HOPE, WILLIAM H. ST. JOHN   Cowdray and Easebourne Priory in the County of Sussex. London: Country Life, 1919. Limited to 400 numbered copies; folio; pages 158; frontispiece, 53 plates; original half parchment, gilt top, binding trifle dust soiled; armorial bookplate of Charles, 9th Earl of Egmont.   Howes Bookshop 265-2248 1996 £120.00

ASSOCIATION - A. EHRMAN

BLAKE, WILLIAM 1757-1827   The Ladies Charity School-House Roll of Highgate; or a Subscription of Many Noble, Well Disposed Ladies for the Easie Carrying of It On. London: 1670. 8vo; drophead title, 292 pages, 1 f., lacks the 4 plates; contemporary black morocco, richly gilt, all over repeating pattern of 'drawer-handles', tulips, rosettes, dots, pointed leaves, etc., spine gilt in comparments, with presentation inscription "TO MAD'm SEMENS" in gilt in a panel on upper cover, all edges gilt, comb marbled endpapers, edges and hinges little worn; with stamp in blue of A. Ehrman, who formed the famous Broxbourne Library.   Marlborough 160-88 1996 £750.00

ASSOCIATION - ELIOCK

PETER MARTYR ANGELERIUS   De Rebus Oceanicis et Novo Orbe, Decades Tres... Cologne: 1574. Small 8vo; pages (48), 655, (30); early half vellum, marginal worming in first signatures, not affecting text; some contemporary ms. marginalia, early German and English ownerships including Lord Eliock. Sabin 1558; Brunet I.293; Alden I 574/1; Medina 235.   Family Album Tillers-478 1995 $1,200.00

ASSOCIATION - ELKIND

CLEMENS, SAMUEL LANGHORNE 1835-1910   The Jumping Frog. Cheloniidae Press, 1985. One of 20 specially bound copies (of a total edition of 325), signed by binder; 8 3/4 x 5 3/4 inches; (26) leaves, on of them folding, printed in green & black; 15 signed or initialled wood engravings by Alan James Robinson, including frontispiece; including an additional complete suite of engravings, an additional suite of state-proof and working proof prints, & another paperbound copy of the book, with every engraving in the two separate suites inscribed "To Arnold and Mimi"; prospectus laid in; inscribed by artist to Arnold and Mimi Elkind; bound by Daniel Kelm in fine & whimsical tan crushed mor., both covers w/lg. inlaid recumbent mor. frog, in 2 colors, each doubtlure w/similar onlaid leaping frog, vol. contained in book well inside attractive & cleverly designed burlap folding box, which also has a pull out chemise (containing the extra engravings), housed in recess under book well; as new.   Phillip J. Pirages 33-123 1996 $2,250.00

ASSOCIATION - MIMI ELKIND

BLUMENTHAL, JOSEPH   Typographic Years: a Printer's Journey through a Half Century 1925-1975. Steinhour Press for the Grolier Club, 1982. One of 300 copies, signed by author; 9 1/2 x 6 1/4 inches; 6 p.l., 153, (1) pages, (1) leaf (colophon); device on title, several illustrations in text, some in brown, grey and black; very fine, inscribed and signed by author for Mimi Elkind, an impression of the Grolier Club 'centennial mark' laid in as well as printed note from publisher regarding slipcase;   Phillip J. Pirages   33-278   1996 $125.00

ASSOCIATION - ALBERT ELKUS

SESSIONS, ROGER   Quintet (for 2 Violins, 2 Violas and Cello). New York: Marks, 1959. 1st printing; tall octavo; stapled wrappers, near fine. This is the dedication copy, inscribed to Berkeley Music professor Albert Elkus from Sessions.   Lame Duck Books   19-350   1996 $275.00

ASSOCIATION - EDWARD ELLIOTT

TRUMAN, HARRY S.   Memoirs by... Garden City: Doubleday, 1955/56. 1st edition; thick 8vo; dust jackets (few nicks, slight rubbing), very good. Signed and inscribed by author for Edward E. Elliott.   George J. Houle   68-145   1996 $500.00

ASSOCIATION - M. ELLIOTT

WORDSWORTH, WILLIAM 1770-1850   Yarrow Revisited, and Other Poems. London: printed for Longman, etc., and Edward Moxon, 1835. 1st edition; 12mo; original grey boards, rebacked, original spine and paper label preserved, spine bit scuffed, cloth folding case; nice; presentation copy, inscribed by author's wife Mary, to M. Elliott; Borowitz booklabel. Wing W3658; CBEL II 1832.   Ximenes   109-307   1996 $600.00

ASSOCIATION - ARTHUR ELLIS

REID, HUGO   The Indians of Los Angeles County. Los Angeles: Arthur M. Ellis, 1926. One of 200 copies; 9 1/2 x 6 1/4 inches; (viii), 70 pages; patterned grey baords with paper spine label, chipping to spine ends and label, paper over front joint cracked. Inscription from Ellis to a San Francisco publisher of Limited Edition reprints of rare California, Thomas Russell.   Dawson's Books Shop   528-201   1996 $135.00

ASSOCIATION - CHARLES ELST

RELY, JEHAN DE   L'Ordre Tenv et Garde en L'Assemblee des Trois Estats.. Paris: Galliot du Pre, 1558. 8vo; fine large Galliot du Pre device at end; vellum; extremely rare, few blank margins wormed and repaired. Charles V. D. Elst bookticket. Adams R342.   Rostenberg & Stern   150-95   1996 $625.00

ASSOCIATION - JACK EMDEN

MC PHEE, JOHN   The Pine Barrens. New York: Farrar, Straus, Giroux, 1968. 1st edition; 8vo; cloth, dust jacket; fine in price clipped dust jacket, uncommon, seldom found inscribed. Presentation copy inscribed by author for Jack Emden.   James S. Jaffe   34-478   1996 $250.00

ASSOCIATION - RALPH WALDO EMERSON

THOREAU, HENRY DAVID 1817-1862   Walden; or, Life in the Woods. Boston: Ticknor and Fields, 1854. 1st edition; April ads as desired; original brown cloth, very minor wear to spine ends, near fine, in half green morocco case; ALS signed by Ralph Waldo Emerson concerning Walden Pond tipped in. Grolier 100 American Books 63.   19th Century Shop   39-   1996 $12,500.00

ASSOCIATION - R. M. ENGBERG

SPEISER, E. A.   Excavations at Tepe Gawra. Philadelphia: ASOR, 1935. 4to; volume I (only): Levels I-VIII; frontispiece, xvi, 220 pages; 86 plates; original cloth; R. M. Engberg copy with his scholarly annotations in pencil.   Archaeologia   Luxor-2731   1996 $150.00

ASSOCIATION - ERNST AUGUST, KING OF HANOVER

BROCKMAN, CARL HEINRICH   Die Metallurgischen Krankheiten des Oberharzes. Osterode: Sorge, 1851. 1st edition; large 8vo; pages xiv, 376; dedication copy, contemporary red morocco, gilt crowned monogram of Ernst August, of Hanover, on upper cover, his arms, onlaid in color, on lower cover, both within ornamental rococo gilt and silvered borders, flat spine, gilt lettered within scrolling floral border, glazed endpapers, all edges gilt, fine royal binding of the period, enchanced by the use of silver.   Marlborough   160-63   1996 £1,350.00

ASSOCIATION - ESHER

AKENSIDE, MARK 1721-1770   An Ode to the Country Gentlemen of England. London: printed for R. and J. Dodsley, and sold by M. Cooper, 1758. 1st edition; 4to; modern panelled calf, spine and inner dentelles gilt, by Dulau & Co. (slight rubbing); very good, bookplate of Lord Esher. Rothschild 25; Iolo Williams p. 93; CBEL II 637.   Ximenes   109-3   1996 $125.00

BROWNING, ROBERT 1812-1889   Gold Hair: a Legend of Pornic. N.P.: London: 1864. Wise forgery, probably printed ca. 1890; 8vo; folded sheets as issued, one short split, cloth folding case; bookplate of Oliver Brett, later Lord Esher, above which is penciled note "Bought Gorfin 1924". Nice. Todd 86f.   Ximenes   108-377   1996 $450.00

BROWNING, ROBERT 1812-1889   Helen's Tower. N.P.: London: April 26, 1870, i.e. ca. 1897. Wise forgery; 4to; 2 leaves folded; cloth folding case; fine; from the collection of Oliver Brett, later Lord Esher. Not in Todd.   Ximenes   108-378   1996 $600.00

BUTLER, SAMUEL 1835-1902   Shakespeare's Sonnets Reconsidered. London: Longmans, Green and Co., 1899. Reprint of original 1609 edition; original green cloth; very good; inscribed presentation copy from author to T. T. Greg, who occupied rooms beneath Butler's at 15 Clifford's Inn Dated Dec. 1st. 1899; Booklabel of Robert P. Greg, later Lord Esher's copy, with bookplate, 2 small ms. corrections in Butler's hand on p. 15.   Jarndyce   CII-63   1996 £250.00

GAY, JOHN 1685-1732   Two Epistles; One, to the Right Honourable Richard Earl of Burlington; the Other to a Lady. London: printed for Bernard Lintot, n.d. 1717. 1st edition; 8vo; modern mottled calf, gilt, spine and inner dentelles gilt, top edge gilt, slight rubbing; bound without half title, 2 leaves of ads are present at end; very good, scarce; bookplate of Oliver Brett, Lord Esher. Foxon G88; Rothschild 913 (lacking ads); CBEL II 498.   Ximenes   108-155   1996 $600.00

ASSOCIATION - GERMAN ESPINOZA

GARCIA MARQUEZ, GABRIEL 1928-   La Mala Hora. Madrid: Esso, 1962. illustrated wrappers with surface loss and short edge tear to spine folds; very good or better, inscribed by author to Colombian poet German Espinoza.   Lame Duck Books   19-208   1996 $4,000.00

ASSOCIATION - ETTINGHAUSEN

GIBSON, R. W.   St. Thomas More: a Preliminary Bibliography of His Works and of Moreana to the Year 1750, with a Bibliography of Utopiana. New Haven and London: Yale University Press, 1961. Numerous illustrations; red cloth, black and gilt on spine, dust jacket mildly defective; inscribed copy from Gibson to Dr. Ettinghausen.   Maggs Bros. Ltd.   1191-92   1996 £120.00

ASSOCIATION - FREDERICK EVANS

ROSSETTI, CHRISTINA 1830-1894   Sing-Song. A Nursery Rhyme Book. London: Routledge, 1872. 1st edition; 8vo; drawings by Arthur Hughes; decorated blue cloth, spine with large chips, corners worn, hinges repaired rather crudely, good only; but a great association copy, with bookplate of photographer Frederick H. Evans.   Charles Agvent   4-974   1996 $175.00

ASSOCIATION - HERBERT MCLEAN EVANS

OSLER, WILLIAM 1849-1919   Thomas Linacre. Cambridge: University Press, 1908. 1st edition; 8vo; 64 pages, frontispiece, 10 plates; variant binding of light brown boards, upper cover and spine stamped in black; bookplate of Herbert McLean Evans. Golden & Roland 981.   Jeff Weber   31-57   1996 $125.00

ASSOCIATION - OLIVER EVANS

TO The Millers of the United States. Take Notice -- That Congress Did on the 21st of Jan. 1808, Pass the Following Act: An Act for the Relief of Oliver Evans. Philadelphia?: 1809. 1st edition; 4to. leaflet, printed on pages (1-3), signed twice by Evans at end of printed statement of fees for the use of his patents and at conclusion of a letter written in the margins to the Gov. of Ohio, Samuel Huntington.   M & S Rare Books 60-455 1996 $3,750.00

ASSOCIATION - EVELYN

BROOKE, FULKE GREVILLE   The Remains...Being Poems of Monarchy and Religion. London: printed by T. N. Herringman, 1670. 1st edition; 8vo; contemporary mottled calf, spine gilt, spine bit rubbed. Fine copy; from the Evelyn family library, complete with leaf of imprimatur. Wing B4900; Grolier 408; CBEL I 1057.   Ximenes 109-147 1996 $1,250.00

MAINWARING, THOMAS   A Defence of Amicia, Daughter of Hugh Cyveliok, Wherein It is Proved That Sir Peter Leicester Baronet... London: Sam. Lowndes, 1673. 1st edition; 8vo; (x), 80, (vi) pages; titlepage in red and black, 3 page catalog at end, final blank leaf; old calf, label; rubbed, boards bit bowed, minor staining; sound; from the Evelyn Library, with modern booklabel indicating provenance. Wing M300.   Robert Clark 38-80 1996 £100.00

ASSOCIATION - JOHN EVELYN

BOYLE, ROBERT 1627-1691   Some Considerations About the Reconcileableness of Reason and Religion. London: printed by T. N. for H. Herringman, 1675. 1st edition; 8vo; contemporary sprinkled sheep, lightly rubbed; John Evelyn's copy, inscribed by Evelyn on blank facing titlepage. With signature of William Upcott dated 1816. Fulton 122; Wing B4024.   Ximenes 109-49 1996 $4,500.00

DELLA BELLA, STEFANO   Recueil de Douze Cartouches. Paris: F. L. D. Ciartres, 1643. Oblong 4to; 12 plates, each with its outer border entirely untrimmed, tipped into an album on handmade sheets; included are two counter proofs, plates 5 and 6; each plate is signed with monogram of Stefano Della Bella; bound in three quarter green morocco over marbled boards. From the collection of John Evelyn.   Book Block 32-66 1996 $5,500.00

GODOLPHIN, JOHN   Repertorium Carnonicum; or an Abridgment of the Ecclesiasatical Laws of This Realm... London: printed by S. Roycroft, for Christopher Wilkinson, 1680. 2nd edition; 4to; licence leaf before title, with signature of John Evelyn (junior) on title, press mark G54 (deleted) in his father's hand; contemporary mottled calf, hinges slightly rubbed, spine gilt, label; this copy passed from John Evelyn Jr. to his father, after the former's death in 1699. Wing G950.   Anthony Laywood 108-9 1996 £345.00

ASSOCIATION - EVERSLEY

BORROW, GEORGE HENRY 1803-1881   Lavengro; the Scholar - the Gypsy - the Priest. London: John Murray, 1851. 1st edition; 12mo; 3 volumes; frontispiece, half titles, 32 pages ads at end of volumes 1 and 2; original cloth, spines somewhat faded and nicked at head and foot, labels little chipped, uncut, occasional spotting; very good; bookplate of first Viscount Eversley; Wolff 598; Wise 11.   Simon Finch 24-14 1996 £175.00

CENNINI, CENNINO   A Treatise on Painting, Written in the Year 1437 and First Published in Italian in 1821. London: Edward Lumley, 1844. Royal 8vo; illuminated titlepage, fine illuminated plate in gold and colors and 8 plates in outline; contemporary morocco, gilt edges, presentation copy from the translator, Signor Tambroni, from the library of Viscount Eversley.   Charles W. Traylen 117-227 1996 £225.00

ASSOCIATION - MARY EWART

ELIOT, GEORGE, PSEUD. 1819-1880   George Eliot's Life as Related in Her Letters and Journals. Edinburgh and London: William Blackwood and Sons, 1885. 8vo; 3 volumes, errata slip at end of volume 3; original lilac-grey diagonally fine ribbed cloth, sides decorated in black within single black rule, spines numbered and lettered in gilt and ruled and decorated in black, dark brown endpapers, bottom edges trimmed, others uncut, as issued; fine; Mary A. Ewart's copy, with her ownership inscription dated 27 Jan. 1885 on first half title verso and her note "Mr. Cross read the proofs of this book to Barbara Bodichon at Grafse(?) in Feby 1884 when I was with her'. Parrish p. 47; Tinker 1018.   Simon Finch 24-83 1996 £475.00

ASSOCIATION - JOHN EYRE

VARILLAS, ANTOINE 1624-1696   (Anekdota Eterouiaka (Greek Characters) or, the Secret History of the House of Medicis... London: printed for R.E. for R. Bentley and S. Magnes, 1686. 1st English edition; 8vo; pages (lxxviii), 470; title printed within double border, contemporary speckled calf, expertly rebacked to match, backstrip with low raised bands, gilt lettered red morocco label, hinges cracked but firm, mottled edges, excellent; early owner's name (Jno Eyre), "John Eyre His Booke 1694' on binder's prelim blank. Wing V111b.   Blackwell's B112-276 1996 £300.00

ASSOCIATION - CHARLOTTE FABRIS

SADLEIR, RICHARD   The Aborigines of Australia. Sydney: Thomas Richards, 1883. 4to; 69 pages, 5 full page plates, 2 color illustrations; red pictorial cloth, covers stamped in gilt and black some marking to front cover, otherwise good + condition; the Absolon copy; Charlotte Fabris copy with her signature. Ferguson 15343; Greenway 8227.   Antipodean 28-301 1996 $550.00

ASSOCIATION - FAIRFAX

CARTER, MATTHEW   A Most Trve and Exact Relation of that Unfortunate Expedition of Kent, Essex and Colchester. London: 1650. 1st edition; pott 8vo; (x), 214 pages; contemporary sheep, with label and date later additions, spine repaired at tips, but still little split along hinge, some wear, some marks, some chips, some browning, but good; with Fairfax of Cameron bookplate. Wing C662.   Ash Rare Books Zenzybyr-20 1996 £195.00

GOODWIN, ARTHUR   Two Letters of Great Consequence to the House of Commons: the One from Alisbury in Buckinghamshire Dated March 22, 1642... London: printed for Edw. Husbands, 1642. 1st edition; 4to; title within woodcut border, some browning of text, 8 pages; modern calf backed boards; bookplate of Fairfax of Cameron. Wing G1144b.   Anthony Laywood 108-10 1996 £135.00

THE HUMBLE Petition and Representation of the Gentry, Ministers and Others of the Counties of Cumberland and Westmorland, to His Sacred Majestie; with His Majesties Answer Thereunto. York 5th Julii 1642. London: printed by Robert Barker and the Assignes of John Bill, 1642. 4to; pages 5, title with typographic border, page 1 with decorated initial, last two pages in black letter with decorated initial and typographic headpiece; old half crimson morocco, gilt, marbled boards; attractive copy, with armorial bookplate of Fairfax of Cameron. Wing 3442/3. Thomason Trats: E1541 (46).   R.F.G. Hollett & Son 78-413 1996 £150.00

JONSON, BEN 1573?-1637   The Workes... (with) The Second Volume. Containing These Playes, Viz. 1. Bartholomew Fayre. 2 The Staple of Newes. 3 The Divell Is an Asse. (and with Walkley's Third Volume, issued without volume title, as always) London: by Richard Bishop.../London: for Richard Meighen; 1640/31-40. 1st Canonical collected edition; folio; 3 volumes bund in 2, volume 1 with frontispiece portrait by robert Vaughan (3rd state, as usual), engraved title by William Hole; fine binding of red crushed morocco, sides with one-line outer gilt rules, panelled in gilt with an intersecting two-line border and lozenge, semicircles at sides, spines with raised bands, lettered in gilt, other panels with gilt border-and-lozenge pattern to match sides, gilt inner dentelels, marbled endpapers, gilt edges by Zaehnsdorf, titles of volumes I and II with early ownership inscriptions of J. Fairfax at head, endpapers with bookplates of the Fairfax family, Earl of Jersey at Osterley Park, the Shakespearian Library of Marsden J. Perry and Stuart Bennett; occasional trivial spot or mark, first A6 of volume 2 extended at inner margin, generally clean and fresh. STC 14753 & 14754; greg III 1073, 1076 & 1079; Pforzheimer 560.   Simon Finch 24-133 1996 £7,500.00

THREE Speeches Spoken at Common-Hall, Thursday the 3 of July, 1645. By Mr. Lisle, Mr. Tate, Mr. Brown, Members of the House of Commons... London: printed for Peter Cole, 1645. 1st edition; 4to; title within woodcut border, 20 pages; padded with blanks, modern morocco, label with Fairfax coat of arms blocked in gold on upper cover, all edges gilt, bookplate of Fairfax of Cameron, nice. Wing T1121. Anthony Laywood 108-18 1996 £75.00

ASSOCIATION - FALCON

BROWNING, ELIZABETH BARRETT 1806-1861   Aurora Leigh. London: Chapman and Hall, 1857. 2nd edition; 8vo; original red cloth, spine evenly faded; contemporary booklabel of T. W. Falcon; fine, scarce. Barnes E12.   Ximenes 108-352 1996 $150.00

ASSOCIATION - JEAN FANCHETTE

MATHEWS, HARRY   Tlooth. Garden City: Doubleday/Paris Review, 1966. 1st edition; Couple of small waterstains to top edge of pages, else very good+ in very good spine faded dust jacket with several edge tears to front and spine panels; this copy inscribed by author in French to Jean Fanchette.   Lame Duck Books   19-310   1996 $200.00

ASSOCIATION - VALENTIN UHINK Y GOMEZ FARIAS

TRAGICUM Theatrum Actorum & Casuum Tragicorum Londini Publice Celebratorum. Amsterdam: Janson, 1649. 8vo; title device, 8 full page portraits and 1 folding plate; crushed crimson morocco, crowned monogram in all corners, inner dentelles, gilt edges by Trautz-Bauzonnet; Valentin Uhink y Gomez Farias bookticket. Splendid copy. Barbier IV 1395-6; Abbot 422.   Rostenberg & Stern   150-111   1996 $1,250.00

ASSOCIATION - RICHARD FARMER

WHITWORTH, CHARLES   An Account of Russia As It Was in the Year 1710. Strawberry Hill: 1758. 1st edition; 8vo; contemporary calf, rebacked, original red morocco label preserved in cloth slipcase; very good, errata leaf; signature of scholar-collector Richard Farmer. CBEL II 1420 and 1590. Hazen 5; Nerhood, to Russia & Return 75.   Ximenes 109-299   1996 $600.00

ASSOCIATION - FRANCIS FARQUHAR

MC ARTHUR, HARRIET NESMITH   Recollections of the Rickreall. Portland: privately printed, 1930. 1st edition; 24 pages; frontispiece, plates; original stiff boards, green cloth spine with printed paper label on front cover, minor bumping; presentation copy from McArthur to Francis P. Farquhar; fine. Smith 6177 locating only 3 copies; Soliday Sale II 934. Michael D. Heaston   23-207   1996 $500.00

ASSOCIATION - FAUCONBERG

PLUTARCHUS 45-125   The Lives of the Noble Grecians and Romanes, Compared Together... London: by Thomas Vautroullier and for John Wight, 1579. 1st edition in English; there is another state of the imprint in which Wight's name is omitted; priority between the two, if any, is not known; folio in sixes; pages (xiv), 1175; Vautrollier's woodcut printer's device on title (McK. 170) and at colophon, woodcut medallion portraits within ornamental borders at beginning of each Life, woodcut initials, head and tailpieces; 17th century panelled calf, neatly rebacked with old spine laid down, later red morocco label, rather browned, scattered tears without loss, small rusthole in 4G5 affecting five letters, good; with ownership inscriptions of Thomas Belasyse, Earl Fauconberg, Oliver Cromwell's son-in-law, dated 1677 on titlepage; Richard Man, 1724 on recto of *2; Josa. Jacques 1731 on title; T. Crowe on title, James Hunter Jr., the Bradley Martin copy with his sale booklabel. STC 20066; Bartlett 226; Pforzheimer 801; PMM 48.   Simon Finch   24-187   1996 £7,800.00

ASSOCIATION - FERGUSON

SALLUSTIUS CRISPIUS, C.   C. Crispi Sallustii Belli Catilinarii et Jugurthini Historiae. Edinburgh: Guielmus Ged, Aurifaber Edinensis, on typis mobilibus, ut vulgo... 1739. 12mo; contemporary calf, spine gilt, front cover loose, lower joint cracked, in cloth folding case; booklabel of F.S. Ferguson; aside from worn binding, an excellent copy.   Ximenes 109-135   1996 $2,500.00

ASSOCIATION - FRANCIS FERGUSSON

SCHWARTZ, DELMORE   In Dreams Begin Responsibilities. Norfolk: New Directions, 1938. 1st edition; only 1000 copies printed; 8vo; good copy, somewhat marked and faded, married, with bright dust jacket, just lightly chipped at extremities; presentation copy from author for Francis Fergusson, with Fergusson's pencilled notes.   Lakin & Marley 3-54 1996 $2,750.00

ASSOCIATION - LAWRENCE FERLINGHETTI

EHRLICH, J. W.   Howl of the Censor, The Four Letter Word on Trial. San Carlos: Nourse Pub. Co., 1961. Lawrence Ferlinghetti's copy with his signature on first blank.   Meyer Boswell   SL27-74   1996 $150.00

ASSOCIATION - M. L. FILLEY

CROFF, G. B.   Model Suburban Architecture, Embodying Designs for Dwellings of Moderate Cost, Varying from $1400 to $5000, Together with Extensive and Elaborate Villas, Banking Houses, Club Houses, Hotels, Engine Houses and a Variety of Architectural Features... Saratoga Springs: 1870. 1st edition; large 4to; lithographic title, 43 lithographic plates; original green cloth, upper cover lettered in gilt; very good; Loosely inserted is a short ALS from author to Mr. M. L. Filley. Hitchcock 293.   John Drury   82-62   1996 £500.00

ASSOCIATION - FINCHAM

BOAKE, BARCROFT   Where the Dead men Lie and Other Poems. Sydney: Angus and Robertson, 1896. 1st edition; 8vo; pages xiv, (ii), 208, 8 pages ads; original pale blue moire fine ribbed cloth, spine lettered across in gold, top edge gilt, bookseller's ticket of Dymock's Book Arcade, Sydney and neat ownership inscription of W. Fincham dated 1897; spine lightly rubbed, very good.   Simon Finch   24-10 1996 £260.00

ASSOCIATION - JIMMY FINDLAY

NALDRET, PERCY   Collected Magic Series. Numbers 1-8. Portsmouth: 1920-27. Numbers 1-8; numerous text figures; 8 volumes; wrappers (slightly worn); all but the first number inscribed by Naldret for Jimmy Findlay.   Thomas Thorp   489-229   1996 £120.00

ASSOCIATION - FINLATER

TENCIN, CLAUDINE ALEXANDRINE GUERIN DE   The Siege of Calais, an Historical Novel. London: printed by Charles Say, Jr. 1751. 1st edition of this translation; 8vo; 2 volumes in one, (140, 149) pages; engraved title in each volume; contemporary half calf over marbled boards, contrasting title label; fine; scarce; signature of M. Finlater and Cullen House bookplate. 2 copies in NUC; Raven 103.   Paulette Rose   16-316 1996 $850.00

ASSOCIATION - RICASOLI FIRIDOLFI

MOORE, EDWARD   The World. London: Dodsley, 1782. 8vo; 4 volumes; stencilled tree calf covers with narrow leafy small tool border, a central oval of plain calf with large urn and stand in stencilled outline, flat spines gilt with four panels and two lettering pieces, all between red and green or blue onlay, gilt flowers in each corner, all edges yellow, marbled endpapers, some corners soft, occasional small abrasions on covers, overall an excellent set; from the collection of Ficasoli Firidolfi with his label.   Marlborough   160-48   1996 £2,200.00

ASSOCIATION - FISHER

PAULUS AEGINETA   Opera a Ioanne Guinterio Andernaco... Strassburg: W. Rihelius, 1542. Folio; 2 parts in 1 volume, woodcut device on title, minor browning, but good copy with two blank leaves; contemporary limp green vellum, bit worn, ties missing; 17th century inscription 'di Calvina Peri de Roppa, later in the Dr. O. Fisher medical collection, sold at Swann 5 April 1978 lot 744 ($520.00). Durling 3554. Maggs Bros. Ltd.   1190-478   1996 £1,800.00

ASSOCIATION - A. M. FISHER

GALLAUDET, THOMAS H.   A Discourse, Delivered at the Dedication of the American Asylum, for the Education of Deaf and Dumb Persons, May 22nd, 1821. Hartford: Hudson and Co., 1821. 1st edition; 8vo; 15 pages, removed, library stamp at foot of title; inscribed by author to friend A. M. Fisher. Shoemaker 5419.   M & S Rare Books   60-316   1996 $275.00

ASSOCIATION - J. T. FISHER

LONGFELLOW, HENRY WADSWORTH 1807-1882   The Song of Hiawatha. Boston: Ticknor and Fields, 1855. 1st American edition; 8vo; some chipping of spine and slight spotting of text, otherwise light wear and nice copy; from the collection of J. T. Fisher. BAL 12112; Carroll Wilson Cat. p. 239.   James Cummins   14-128   1995 $150.00

ASSOCIATION - JAMES FISHER

JOHNSON, SAMUEL 1709-1784   The Idler. London: printed for T. Davies, etc., 1767. 3rd edition; 12mo; 2 volumes; old calf rebacked; armorial bookplates of James Fisher, Corpus Christi Oxford. Courtney pp. 83-4; Chapman & Hazen 142.   Peter Murray Hill 185-91 1996 £140.00

ASSOCIATION - LAURA FISHER

WIGGIN, KATE DOUGLAS   A Child's Journey with Dickens. Boston: 1912. 1st edition; 12mo; frontispiece, original printed boards, cloth back; fine; inscribed by author for Laura Fisher.   Howard S. Mott 227-151 1996 $135.00

ASSOCIATION - OTTO ORREN FISHER

PEPYS, SAMUEL 1633-1703   Memoirs of Samuel Pepys, Esq. London: 1825. 1st edition; large 4to; 2 volumes, xlii, (2), 498, (2), xlix, (2) pages; (4), 348, vii, (1), 311 pages; engraved plates, half titles and ad leaf, uncut; later half calf, spines gilt, red and green labels by Sangorski & Sutcliffe; beautiful set, fine and fresh, with just the lightest rubbing at extremities, in fleece lined cloth slipcase; Otto Orren Fisher bookplate. Superb condition.   Joseph J. Felcone 64-31 1996 $1,800.00

ASSOCIATION - P. FISHER

ACKERMANN, RUDOLPH 1764-1834   The History of the Charter-House. London: Ackermann, 1816. Large 4to; title, 332 pages, engraved aquatint portrait proof to frontispiece in laid india paper, 5 hand colored aquatint plates; red straight grain morocco, marbled boards (worn); contemporary red morocco label, gilt lettered, gilt roll tool border; some offsetting, otherwise finely coored early issue. Pencil note suggests this is "The Rev. P. Fisher's copy, master of the Charter-House to whom this work is dedicated". Bookplate of W. Russell Button.   Marlborough 162-1 1996 £350.00

ASSOCIATION - SAMUEL FISHER

DARWIN, CHARLES ROBERT 1809-1882   The Formation of Vegetable Mould through the Action of Worms. London: 1881. 5th thousand; 8vo; pages vii, 326, (2); original cloth; from the collection of Samuel J. Fisher, then of Walter Garstang with his bookplate; some marginal annotation in pencil.   Wheldon & Wesley 207-1247 1996 £60.00

ASSOCIATION - EARL FISK

JACKSON, HOLBROOK   A Cross-Section of English Printing: the Curwen Press 1918-1934. London: Curwen Press, 1935. One of 60 copies for sale (of a total of 75); 10 1/4 x 7 1/2 inches; 4 p.l., 24 pages; numerous illustrations, some in color; original cloth, publisher's patterned paper slipcase; very fine; bookplate of Earl E. Fisk.   Phillip J. Pirages 33-152 1996 $250.00

ASSOCIATION - EDWARD FITZGERALD

LANDOR, WALTER SAVAGE 1775-1864   Pericles and Aspasia. London: Saunders and Otley, 1836. 1st edition; 8vo; 2 volumes; original green backed boards, uncut, printed paper labels; very good set without major fault and quite tight of case, in lush crimson morocco box; boards and labels show rub and wear which is usual to this period of publisher's binding, still very good; the superior H. Bradley Martin-John Drinkwater copy, originally Edward Fitzgerald's copy with his ownership inscription in each volume.   Lakin & Marley 3-28 1996 $1,000.00

ASSOCIATION - FRANCIS SCOTT FITZGERALD

DURNING-LAWRENCE, EDWIN   Bacon is Shakespeare. New York: McBride, 1910. 1st edition; page 95 torn and tape repaired by F. Scott Fitzgerald, a fact acknowledged and apologized for by him in his hand on appropriate page "F Scott Fitzgerald did this and is very sorry"; well worn, hinges cracked, at least one endpaper missing; overall, at best, a good copy.   Ken Lopez 74-138 1996 $1,500.00

ASSOCIATION - FITZWILLIAM

SCOT, REYNOLDE REGINALD   A Perfite Platform of a Hop Garden. London: Henrie Denham at the Signe of the Starre, 1574. 1st edition; 4to; pages xvi, 54 (of 56), (lacking last leaf of epilogue (photocopy laid in), decorated initials and 15 woodcuts; very tall, bound with first blank leaf with ornament, marbled boards, modern rebacking in calf, some interior soiling, especially to final leaf; circular indistinct pencil rubbings of coins on front flyleaf, still quite attractive. Bookplate of Earl Fitzwilliam, early ownership signatures of Robert and Tho. Glover. STC 21865; Hunt 128; Henrey 337;   Second Life Books 103-168 1996 $2,200.00

ASSOCIATION - FLECKEISEN

HENRY, JAMES   Poems Chiefly Philosophical, in Continuation of My Book and a Half Year's Poems. Dresden: C. C. Meinhold and Sons, 1856. Only edition; 8vo; 1 p.l., pages 285, (1), 15; frontispiece; contemporary German marbled boards, leather label, presentation copy inscribed by author for Professor Fleckeisen, Frankfurt. With later ownership signature and bookplate.   Howard S. Mott 227-161 1996 $275.00

ASSOCIATION - J. D. FLEEMAN

GRAY, THOMAS 1716-1771   The Correspondence... Oxford: Clarendon Press, 1971. Reprint; 8vo; 3 volumes; 3 portrait frontispieces, other illustrations and facsimiles; pages lx, 1-453; xxxiv, 455-909; xxxiv, 911-1369; original dark blue cloth, gilt lettered, dust jackets, excellent; J.D. Fleeman's copy with his signature.   Blackwell's B112-138 1996 £150.00

HUME, DAVID 1711-1776   The Letters. Oxford: Clarendon Press, 1969. Reprint; 8vo; 2 volumes; 2 frontispieces, 3 plates, pages xxxii, 532; vi, 498; original blue cloth, gilt lettered, excellent; J.D. Fleeman's copy with some marginalia by him.   Blackwell's B112-159 1996 £150.00

SHERIDAN, RICHARD BRINSLEY BUTLER 1751-1816   The Letters... Oxford: Clarendon Press, 1966. 8vo; 3 portrait frontispieces; pages lix,(i), 271, (1); (vi), 311, (1); (vi), 417, (1); original blue cloth, gilt lettered, excellent; J. D. Fleeman's copy with his signature in each volume. Blackwell's B112-255 1996 £150.00

ASSOCIATION - IAN FLEMING

BAX, CLIFFORD   The Traveller's Tale. Oxford: 1921. 1st edition; original binding, top edge dusty, free endpapers browned, pastedowns partially browned, head and tail of spine and corners bumped, covers marked and slightly dusty; good; ownership signature of Ian Fleming. Ulysses 39-671 1996 £125.00

BRIDGES, ROBERT 1844-1930   The Testament of Beauty - a Poem in Four Books. Oxford: Oxford University Press, 1929. 1st edition; original binding, pages unopened, top edge dusty, head and tail of spine slightly bumped, spine browned, covers marked and dusty, cover edges slightly rubbed; very good; ownership signature of Ian Fleming.   Ulysses 39-672 1996 £160.00

CARP, AUGUSTUS   Augustus Carp, by Himself. London: William Heinemann, 1924. 1st edition; several black and white illustrations; original binding, top edge dusty, head of spine split and worn, head and tail of spine and corners bumped, covers marked and slightly soiled, cover edges rubbed, free endpapers browned, good. With ownership signataure of Ian Fleming.   Ulysses 39-673 1996 £125.00

DRINKWATER, JOHN 1882-1937   Abraham Lincoln - A Play. London: Sidgwick & Jackson Ltd., 1923. Reprint; original binding, top edge dusty, head and tail of spine and corners bumped, covers marked and slightly soiled, free endpapers browned, good; ownership signature of Ian Fleming; mounted on front free endpaper are remains of label "House Library E. V. Slater's, Esq. D.D." after the letters "D.D." Fleming has written his name.   Ulysses 39-674 1996 £125.00

EMERSON, RALPH WALDO 1803-1882   Moments with Emerson. London: Henry Frowde, n.d. 1st edition; 16mo; original binding, top edge gilt, upper cover soiled, head and tail of spine and corners slightly bumped, endpaper gutters browned, front free endpaper and fore-edge slightly soiled; good; ownership signature of Ian Fleming.   Ulysses 39-675 1996 £125.00

ASSOCIATION - IAN FLEMING

FLECKER, JAMES ELROY   Hassan: the Story of Hassan of Bagdad and How He Came to Make the Golden Journey to Samarkand. London: William Heinemann, 1922. 1st edition; original binding, top edge dusty, free endpapers browned, head and tail of spine and corners bumped, top corners of few pages creased, spine darkened, covers rubbed and partially faded, good; ownership signature of Ian Fleming.   Ulysses 39-678 1996 £125.00

FRANCE, ANATOLE   Penguin Island. London: John Lane, Bodley Head, 1924. Reprint; original binding, top edge dusty, head and tail of spine and corners bumped, free endpapers browned, covers marked and dusty; good; ownership signature of Ian Fleming.   Ulysses 39-679 1996 £125.00

FRANCE, ANATOLE   The Seven Wives of Bluebeard. London: John Lane, Bodley Head, 1925. Reprint; original binding, top edge dusty, head and tail of spine and corners bumped, spine darkened, covers marked and dusty, good; ownership signature of Ian Fleming.   Ulysses 39-680 1996 £125.00

GILBERT, WILLIAM SCHWENCK 1836-1911   Fifty "Bab" Ballads - Much Sound and Little Sense. London: George Routledge & Sons Ltd., n.d. Reprint; 12mo; full leathetr covers, top edge gilt, cover edges worn, head and tail of spine and corners bumped and worn, good only; ownership signature of Ian Fleming.   Ulysses 39-682 1996 £125.00

GREENE, GRAHAM 1904-1991   A Visit to Morin. London: Heinemann, 1959. One of only 250 copies; very good+ in rather soiled dust jacket with ink squiggle to upper front panel; extraordinary association copy, inscribed by author to Ian Fleming.   Lame Duck Books 19-228 1996 $3,750.00

OMAR KHAYYAM   The Rubaiyat of Omar Khayyam. Edinburgh & London: W. P. Nimmo, Hay & Mitchell Ltd., n.d. 1st edition; color frontispiece and color endpapers by Alice Ross, decorated leather wrappers, top edge dusty, spine and cover edges darkened, frayed and chipped; good only; ownership signature of Ian Fleming.   Ulysses 39-677 1996 £125.00

ONIONS, OLIVER   The Compleat Bachelor. London: John Murray, 1900. Reprint; original binding, top edge dusty, free endpapers browned, covers marked and slightly soiled, cover edges rubbed, spine browned, head and tail of spine and corners bumped, remains of labels on upper cover and front free endpaper, good; top edge gilt; ownership signature of Ian Fleming.   Ulysses 39-686 1996 £125.00

RYAN, KATHRYN WHITE   Golden Pheasant - Poems. New York: & London: G. P. Puntam's Sons, 1925. 1st edition; original binding, top edge dusty, head and tail of spine and corners bumped, spine darkened, covers marked, endpaper edges browned, top corners of few pages slightly creased, good; ownership signature of Ian Fleming.   Ulysses 39-687 1996 £180.00

SAFRONI-MIDDLETON, A.   Gabrielle of the Lagoon - a Romance of the South Seas. London: Grant Richards Ltd., 1919. 1st edition; original binding, top edge dusty, head and tail of spine and corners bumped, spine faded, covers marked and slightly soiled, cover edges rubbed, endpapers browned, upper hinge partially cracked, bottom corners of few pages slightly creased; good; ownership signature of Ian Fleming.   Ulysses 39-688 1996 £125.00

SHAKESPEARE, WILLIAM 1564-1616   The Comedy of Errors. London: J. M. Dent & Sons, 1909. Reprint; 12mo; full leather, cover edges worn, head and tail of spine and corners bumped and worn, upper cover creased, good only; ownership signature of Ian Fleming.   Ulysses 39-689 1996 £125.00

SHAKESPEARE, WILLIAM 1564-1616   The Taming of the Shrew. London: J. M. Dent and Sons, 1909. Reprint; 12mo; full leather covers, edges rubbed, head and tail of spine and corners bumped and worn, very good; ownership signature of Ian Fleming.   Ulysses 39-690 1996 £125.00

STEVENS, SAMUEL   A Wilding Posy. London: Selwyn & Blount Ltd., 1925. 1st edition; original binding, top edge dusty, head and tail of spine and corners bumped, covers marked, cover edges darkened, spine faded, title label on spine worn and browned, edges spotted, endpaper edges browned; good; ownership signature of Ian Fleming.   Ulysses 39-691 1996 £275.00

WOLFE, HUMBERT   Humoresque. London: Ernest Benn Ltd., 1926. 3rd impression; original binding, top edge dusty, head and tail of spine and corners bumped, covers marked, free endpapers browned; ownership signature of Ian Fleming.   Ulysses 39-693 1996 £125.00

ASSOCIATION - IAN FLEMING

WOLFE, HUMBERT   The Unknown Goddess. London: Methuen & Co. Ltd., 1925. 1st edition; original binding, top edge dusty, head and tail of spine and corners bumped, title label on spine rubbed, chipped, creased and browned, cover edges faded and rubbed, endpaper edges browned; good; ownership signature of Ian Fleming.   Ulysses 39-692 1996 £125.00

WOODRUFF, DOUGLAS   Plato's American Republic. London: Kegan Paul, Trench, Trubner & Co., Ltd., 1926. Reprint; original binding, top edge dusty, head and tail of spine and corners bumped, covers marked and dusty, cover edges worn, title label on spine browned, good; ownership signature of Ian Fleming.   Ulysses 39-694 1996 £125.00

YOUNG, FRANCIS BRETT   Dr. Bradley Remembers. London: William Heinemann, 1938. 1st edition; original binding, top edge dusty, head and tail of spine and corners slightly bumped, covers dusty and slightly marked, edges slightly browned, good; ownership signature of Ian Fleming.   Ulysses 39-695 1996 £125.00

ASSOCIATION - ELIZA JANE FLETCHER

WORDSWORTH, WILLIAM 1770-1850   A Guide through the District of the Lakes, in the North of England... Kendal: John Hudson, 1835. 5th edition; 8vo; pages xxiv, 140, (ii, ad leaf), engraved folding map; original publisher's patterned cloth, spine and edges rather faded, paper spine label, rubbed, few scattered spots, but very nice; inscribed "Eliza Jane Fletcher from A. Preston Esre, August 1839".   R.F.G. Hollett & Son 78-1395 1996 £175.00

ASSOCIATION - FRANK FLETCHER

SCOTT, WALTER 1771-1832   Halidon Hill: a Dramatic Sketch. Edinburgh: printed for Archibald Constable & Co., and Hurst, Robinson & Co.,... 1822. 1st edition; 8vo; original grey brown printed wrappers, uncut, rubbed, some chipping and tearing along spine, inner hinges strengthened, discreet reinforcement of upper cover, pastedown on lower cover is a page of text from a report on smallpox epidemic in Wicks in early 1822, some light browning or soiling of text, else very good in royal blue cloth box; bookplate of Frank Fletcher.   James Cummins 14-175 1996 $300.00

ASSOCIATION - ERROL FLYNN

KIPLING, RUDYARD 1865-1936   Kim. Garden City: Doubleday, ca. 1935. 8vo; color frontispiece, 9 full page plates; gilt and blindstamped dark blue cloth, spine with gilt stamped Indian scenes, top edge stained blue, uncut, dust jacket (nicked, rubbed), very good, tipped in on verso of frontispiece is photo of an unidentified female cast member. Signed and inscribed by Errol Flynn and over 60 cast & crew members.   George J. Houle 68-77 1996 $2,500.00

ASSOCIATION - G. G. FOGG

STODDARD, W. O.   The Great Union Pacific Railroad Excursion to the Hundredth Meridian: From New York to Platte City. Chicago: published by the Republican Co., 1867. 1st edition; frontispiece; original pictorial wrappers, fine. The copy of Hon. G. G. Fogg, former U.S. Senator from New Hamshire.   Michael D. Heaston 23-339 1996 $550.00

ASSOCIATION - HENRY FOLKARD

KIRKWOOD, JAMES   Proposals Made by Rev. James Kirkwood in 1699, to Found PUblic Libraries in Scotland. London: privately printed by William Blades, 1889. Limited edition, number 1 of 100 copies for presentation; small square 4to; pages 9, (15, facsimile, pritned on handmade paper); modern half levant morocco gilt, marbled boards, few faint marginal blindstamps; this copy presented to the Wigan Public Library by the historian Henry T. Folkard.   R.F.G. Hollett 76-27 1996 £185.00

ASSOCIATION - FONTHILL

RUSSEL, JAMES   Letters from a Young Painter Abroad to His Friends in England. London: printed for W. Russel, 1750. 2nd edition of volume 1, 1st edition of volume 2; large 8vo; 2 volumes; 13 plates, occasional light spotting, but very good set on large paper; contemporary calf, gilt, rebacked, edges and corners restored; early note identifies this as the Fonthill copy. Pine-Coffin 740.1. CBEL ii 1419.   Ximenes 108-315 1996 $450.00

ASSOCIATION - BENJAMIN FOOTE

LYTTELTON, GEORGE LYTTELTON, 1ST BARON 1709-1773   Dialogues of the Dead. London: for W. Sandby, 1760. 1st edition; demy 8vo; 18th century tree calf, prettily gilt with variety of devices, lemon edges, lightly rubbed and worn, faintest of cracks in upper hinge, but most attractive copy; contemporary bookplate of Benjamin Foote.   Ash Rare Books Zenzybyr-63   1996 £200.00

ASSOCIATION - CHARLES FOOTE

HAWTHORNE, NATHANIEL 1804-1864   Twice-Told Tales. Boston: James Munroe, 1842. 1st edition thus, 1st issue; full green morocco, gilt panels, raised bands, gilt compartments, inner dentelles gilt, silk markers, uncut, signed by Stikeman; fine, fresh set with only the slightest rubbing; from the library of Charles B. Foote; extremely rare book. Dickinson p. 121-2; BAL 7594; Clark A2.3.1.   Mac Donnell 12-86 1996 $850.00

ASSOCIATION - ADELAIDE FORBES

DIBDIN, THOMAS FROGNALL 1776-1847   Bibliomania; or Book Madness; A Bibliographical Romance in Six Parts. London: ptd. for the author by J. McCreery, Longman, Hurst, Rees, Orme & Brown 1811. 2nd edition; ix, 782 pages, plus errata; frontispiece, title vignette, several plates and illustrations in text, first page of each part with decorated border, calf, gilt and blind tooled inner panel, spine blind tooled in compartments with raised bands, few small scuff marks, volume 2 title bound in case owner wanted to bind in 2 volumes; ownership inscription of one Adelaide Forbes of Dublin; attractive copy. Jackson 18.   Maggs Bros. Ltd. 1191-81 1996 £170.00

ASSOCIATION - H. REGINALD FORBES

DIBDIN, THOMAS FROGNALL 1776-1847   An Introduction to the Knowledge of Rare and Valuable Editions of the Greek and Latin Classics, Including an Account of the Polyglot Bibles. London: Longman, Hurst, Rees & Orme, 1808. 3rd edition; 2 volumes, 1 folding plate; diced calf, gilt and blind tooled outer borders, inner gilt borders, spine gilt in compartments with raised bands, some scuffing and marking, very small hole at base of joint of volume 1, still an attractive copy, light browning to title of volume 1, dampstain on first few leaves of volume 2 (not affecting text), ownership inscription of F. Reginald Forbes.   Maggs Bros. Ltd. 1191-80 1996 £155.00

ASSOCIATION - FORMAN

COLERIDGE, SAMUEL TAYLOR 1772-1834   Sibylline Leaves: a Collection of Poems. London: Rest Fenner, 1817. 1st edition; (4), x, (2), 303 pages, (20) page Hatchard catalogue; original tan paper covered boards and spine, printed spine label, front cover detached, top of spine chipped, else fine, uncut. In gilt morocco backed slipcase. H. Buxton Forman's copy with his bookplate and signature. Wise, Coleridge 45.   Joseph J. Felcone 64-11 1996 $1,400.00

ASSOCIATION - EDWARD MORGAN FORSTER

SASSOON, SIEGFRIED LORRAINE 1886-1967   The Daffodil Murderer. London: John Richmond Ltd., 1913. One of 1000 copies; wrappers little rubbed, otherwise excellent; presentation copy from author for E. M. Forster, with Forster's bookplate.   R. A. Gekoski 19-123 1996 £1,000.00

ASSOCIATION - JOHN FORSTER

TAPLIN, WILLIAM   The Sportsman's Cabinet; or, a Correct Delineation of the Various Dogs Used in the Sports of the Field... London: printed and published...by Cundee.. 1803-04. 1st edition; 4to; 2 volumes; pages viii, 276, (2), (4 ads); 310, (2); 2 engraved vignette titles, 2 engraved frontispieces, 24 engraved plates by J. Scott after Reinagle, 22 vignettes, tailpieces, etc., mostly good, clean impressions of the plates, though a few are just a little fox spotted in borders and some are browned on reverse side, but attractive copy; contemporary diced calf, gilt border to sides, gilt spines; armorial bookplate of John Forster. Hugo 185; Pease 114; Schwerdt II p. 248.   Sotheran PN32-78 1996 £1,350.00

ASSOCIATION - W. E. FORSTER

FRIENDS, SOCIETY OF   Transactions of the Central Relief Committee During the Famine in Ireland. 1846 and 1847. 1852. 1st edition; 8vo; xxiii, 481 pages; half leather; presentation copy from Committee to W. E. Forster, bound for him.   C. P. Hyland 216-242 1996 £170.00

ASSOCIATION - WILLIAM FORSYTH

HOUTTUYN, MARTINUS   Hotkunde, Behelzende de Afbeeldingen van Meest Alle Bekund, in-en Uitlandsche Houten. Amsterdam: J. C. Sepp, 1773-91. 4to; titles and text in Dutch, German, French, English and Latin; 100 hand colored engraved plates, 50 leaves describing timbers dealt with on the 100 copperplates; later gilt stamped diced calf, rubbed, all edges gilt; signature of William Forsyth, 1808; Currer bookplate. Raymond M. Sutton VII-16 1996 $8,500.00

ASSOCIATION - FOX

MERVAULT, PETER   The Last Famous Siege of the city of Roche; Together with the Edict of Nantes. London: Wickins, 1680. 8vo; 2 parts in 1; 3 page publisher's catalog at end; calf; Ilchester-Fox copy with bookplates. Wing M1879. Haag VII 393.   Rostenberg & Stern 150-58 1996 $450.00

ASSOCIATION - FRANCIS FREDERICK FOX

MILTON, JOHN 1608-1674   The Poetical Works of John Milton. London: printed by W. Bulmer & Co. for John and Josiah Boydell and George ... 1749-97. Folio; 3 volumes; stipple engraved portraits and fine plates, some plates foxed, text offsetting; though it requires some restoration, elaborate straight grained full red morocco gilt binding by Riley is notable; fine paper, wide margins; engraved ex-libris of Francis Frederick Fox.   Family Album Tillers-442 1996 $450.00

ASSOCIATION - MORTIMER FRANK

BOYLE, ROBERT 1627-1691   Medicinal Experiments; or, a Collection of Choice and Safe Remedies for the Most Part Simple, and Easily Prepar'd... London: printed for w. Innys, 1712. 5th edition; 12mo; engraved portrait laid down, perforation stamp on title, accession number on A2, 12 pages of ads; modern cloth; bookplate of Mortimer Frank. Fulton 184.   Anthony Laywood 108-30 1996 £85.00

MEDICINA Flagellata; or, the Doctor Scarified. London: printed for J. Bateman and J. Nicks, 1721. 1st edition; 8vo; engraved and printed titles, both with perforation stamp and de-accession stamps on blank verso; contemporary panelled calf, rebacked with morocco, rubbed, upper hinge partly cracked; bookplate of Mortimer Frank. Waller 6421; Blake p. 297; Heirs of Hippocrates 948.   Anthony W. Laywood 108-90 1996 £345.00

ASSOCIATION - AUGUSTUS FRANKS

BERNAL, RALPH   Illustrated Catalogue of the Distinguished Collection of Works of Art and Vertu, from the Byzantine Period to that of Louis Seize Collected by the Late Ralph Bernal, Esq. London: for J. H. Burn, 1855. 4to; Large paper copy printed on thick paper, with additional general titlepage and frontispiece, (2), 357, (1), 66, (2) pages, frontispiece, plates, loosely inserted is a printed petition from P. Le Neve Foster of the Society for the Encouragement of Arts, Manufactures and Commerce, Requesting for the Collection to be Purchased for the Nations; there is also an associated letter from P. Le Neve Foster to Augustus Franks, keeper of the Dept. of British & Medieval Antiquities at the British Museum; although unsigned, this would suggest this is Frank's copy of the catalog; some occasional foxing, but good copy, bound by Riviere in later 19th century half brown morocco, several small repairs to joints and corners and also to the marbled paper on board edges.   Ken Spelman 30-46 1996 £360.00

ASSOCIATION - WILLIAM FRASER

LYSONS, SAMUEL   A Collection of Gloucestershire Antiquities. London: Cadell & Davies, 1791-1804. One of 12 copies on large paper, with all but two plates colored by hand within wash borders; large folio; engraved title, 1 f., iv, 38 pages, 2 ff., 110 plates, drawn and etched by Lysons, 108 colored by hand, 1 in 2 states; plate 81 uncolored and inlaid to size, plate 84 in 2 states (colored and uncolored), title and following leaf bit foxed, occasional offset onto text but very handsome. contemporary dark blue morocco, gilt inner borders, gilt edges. ex-libris of Sir William Fraser, Lindsay Fleming and W. R. Jeudwine. Lowndes 1425.   Marlborough 162-63 1996 £2,200.00

ASSOCIATION - WILLIAM AUGUSTUS FRASER

COOK, HENRY   Pride, or The Heir of Craven. London: John W. Parker, 1841. 1st edition; 8vo; author's own copy, with his bookplate; pages (iii)-viii, 139, (i) blank, (i) ad; contemporary calf with double fillet gilt border to sides with rosette at each corner, spine decorated in compartments with floral ornaments, leaf sprays, etc., green morocco label, marbled endpapers, gilt edges, some wear to upper joint and head of spine skilfully repaired; bookplates of author and Sir William Augustus Fraser Bart. and leather booklabel of Joseph Widener.   Simon Finch 24-55 1996 £450.00

ASSOCIATION - CLAUDE FREDERICKS

DONNE, JOHN 1571-1631   A Prayer. Banyan Press, 1947. Limited edition of 120 numbered copies; 8vo; 6 leaves, including blanks, title printed in 2 colors; title printed in 2 colors; decorative paper wrappers, 6 leaves, including blanks, fine in publisher's original mailing envelope. Though not called for, this copy inscribed by the printers, Claude Fredericks and Milton Saul to the bookman Paul Standard; laid in is prospectus for the Banyan Press edition of Spender's "Returning to Vienna 1974'.   Blue Mountain SP95-48 1996 $175.00

ASSOCIATION - FRENCH

THE NEW Hampshire Book: Being Specimens of the Literature of the Granite State. Nashua: David Marsahll, 1842. 1st edition; 391 pages; original gift binding, full brown morocco, some rubbing and foxing; attractive American binding; fine association copy, inscribed by Franklin Pierce for Mrs. B. B. French.   19th Century Shop 39- 1996 $3,200.00

ASSOCIATION - ASA FRENCH

THE SCOUNDREL'S Dictionary, or an Explantion of the Cant Words Used by the Thieves, Horse-Breeders, Street-Robbers and Pick-Pockets About Town. London: printed for J. Brownell, 1754. pages 32; small corner tear from margin of pages 15-16; original boards, marked, recently neatly rebacked. Small stamp of Williams's Library Cheltenham, bookplate of Asa French (1912). Alston IX 322.   Jarndyce 103-5 1996 £1,250.00

ASSOCIATION - JIM FRENKEL

SIMMONS, DAN   Song of Kali. Bluejay, 1985. 1st edition; author's first book; fine; signed by author; publisher Jim Frenkel's copy with business card laid in.   Aronovitz 57-1062 1996 $425.00

ASSOCIATION - MURIAL FULLER

YERBY, FRANK   The Foxes of Harrow. New York: Dial, 1946. 9th printing, in the year of publication; cheap paper browned, otherwise near fine in internally repaired, very good plus dust jacket with several small chips. Nicely inscribed by author in year of publication, additionally this copy inscribed on dedication page by dedicatee, Murial Fuller; Between the Covers 43-217 1996 $185.00

ASSOCIATION - ALEXANDER FULLERTON

ADAIR, ROBERT   Sketch of the Character of the Late Duke of Devonshire. London: printed by William Bulmer, 1811. One of 50 copies; 4to; pages 28; mezzotint portrait offset on tile; printed on Furness & Co. paper dated 1804; contemporary dark blue straight grained morocco, elaborately decorated in gold and blind, blue watered silk endpapers similarly decorated, all edges gilt, hinges and edges worn, upper hinge cracked and weak, but held on cords; very good; bookplate and stamp of the Writers Library to which it was donated by Alexander Fullerton. Claude Cox 107-25 1996 £65.00

ASSOCIATION - THOMAS FUTCHER

DANA, CHARLES   Poetry and Doctors: a Catalogue of Poetical Works Written by Physicians with Biographical Notes. Woodstock: 1916. 1st edition; 83 pages; illustrations; original binding; inscribed by Henry Barton Jacobs to Thomas B. Futcher; rare.   W. Bruce Fye 71-484 1996 $250.00

ASSOCIATION - GAGE

JOHNSTON, ALEXANDER KEITH   Atlas to Alison's History of Europe. Edinburgh & London: Wm. Blackwood, 1848. Small oblong 4to; frontispiece and 98 maps all with colored definitions (map 57 was not issued); contemporary calf, loose in case. Bookplate of Viscount Gage. Charles W. Traylen 117-425 1996 £120.00

ASSOCIATION - MARCUS GAGE

APHORISMS for Youth, with Observations and Reflections, Religious, Moral, Critical and Characteristic... London: Lackington, Allen, 1801. Sole edition; small 8vo; 200 pages; frontispiece, tissue guard, early owner's name, lacks half title (?); finely bound in contemporary marbled brown calf, smooth backstrip divided by wide gilt roundel and lozenge bands, between dotted rolls, red morocco label in second compartment, remaining compartments with dotted line saltire and central foliate stars, seme other small tools, sides with border of fillet, lozenge and star roll, fillet and open twist roll, fillet on board edges, ball roll on turn-ins, marbled endpapers and edges, lilac silk marker, fine. Scarce. From the library of Marcus Gage.   Blackwell's B112-64 1996 £250.00

WARVILLE, J. P. BRISSOT DE   New Travels in the United States of America. Performed in 1788. Dublin: P. Byrne (et al), 1792. 1st Dublin edition, 8vo; half title, pages (iv), (i)-xliii, (i), 45-483, (4); contemporary sprinkled tan calf, backstrip dulled, slight loss at foot of lower joint, from the Gage library with Marcus Gage's signature; excellent.   Blackwell's B112-282 1996 £125.00

ASSOCIATION - CROSBY GAIGE

COBDEN-SANDERSON, THOMAS JAMES 1840-1922   The Arts and Crafts Movement Hammersmith: Hammersmith Pub. Society, 1905. 1st edition; (40) pages; vellum backed boards, spine backed boards, some browning to paste-down and front free endpaper, otherwise fine, bright copy; with bookplate of publisher, Crosby Gaige.   Hermitage SP95-769 1996 $400.00

KENNEDY, MARGARET   Dewdrops. London: Heinemann, 1928. Signed limited edition of 525 numbered copies; 8vo; cloth and boards, dust jacket, enclosed in custom made blue morocco, leather and cloth slipcase; fine, small tear in dust jacket; bookplate of publisher Crosby Gaige.   Antic Hay 101-929 1996 $135.00

ASSOCIATION - F. F. GAINES

POPE, ALEXANDER 1688-1744   Pope's Poetical Works. Princeton: D. A. Borrestein, Pub., Princeton Press, 1828. 12mo; 3 volumes; frontispiece; original tan cloth backed boards, printed paper labels (chipped), rubbed, some fraying and water staining of spines, half titles, engravd titles, browning and spotting, staining at back of volume 2; library label of F. F. Gaines.   James Cummins 14-158 1996 $150.00

ASSOCIATION - JOHN GALBRAITH

BIBLE. CREE - 1876   The New Testament Translated Into the Cree Language. London: printed for the British and Foreign Bible Society, 1876. 8vo; pages (iii), 425; contemporary calf, hinges broken, section of spine missing, interior clean and crisp; inscribed by J. L. Colter, Ruperts House, 1877 to Prof. John Galbraith. Banks p. 38; Evans 80; Peel 437. Hugh Anson-Cartwright 87-309 1996 $275.00

ASSOCIATION - EDWIN GALLUP

THE SOLDIER'S Hymn Book. Chicago: Chicago Young Men's Christian Association, ca. 1863. 39th thousand; 24mo; 62, (2) pages; original cloth backed colored pictorial boards. fine; pencil signature of Edwin A. Gallup, Co. H, 9th Vt. Volunteers.   M & S Rare Books 60-303 1996 $250.00

ASSOCIATION - ADRIEN GAMBET

SEVERINO, MARCO AURELIO   Il Filosofia Overo il Perche Degli Scacchi...(with) Dell'Antica Pettia Overo che Palamede non e Stato L'Inentor Degli Sacchi... Napoli: Antonio Bulifon, 1690. 1st editions; 4to; 2 volumes in 1; (6), 120, (6), 82 (i.e. 64), 2 portraits, illustrations; later vellum backed boards, bookplate, two small and unobtrusive library blindstamps and release stamps, first signature slightly browned, otherwise very attractive copy; from the library of chess collector Adrien Gambet, with his signature.   Joseph J. Felcone 64-10 1996 $700.00

ASSOCIATION - E. S. GANNETT

DIX, D. L.   Remarks on Prisons and Prison Discipline in the United States. Boston: Munroe & Francis, 1845. 1st edition; 8vo; 104 pages; original printed wrappers, wrappers little dusty, but excellent copy. With ink signature of Rev. E. S. Gannett, conservative Unitarian minister.   M & S Rare Books 60-319 1996 $750.00

ASSOCIATION - ISABELLA GARDNER

HILL, GEOFFREY   Preghiere. Leeds: Northern House Pamphlet Poets, 1964. 1st edition; white glossy printed wrappers;; fine; presentation copy, inscribed by author to Allen Tate and his wife Isabella Gardner. James S. Jaffe 34-248 1996 $1,000.00

ASSOCIATION - ALEXANDER GARDYNE

CROMARTY, GEORGE MAC KENZIE, 1ST EARL OF 1630-1714   A Vindication of Robert III, King of Scotland... Edinburgh: printed by the Heirs and Successors to Andrew Anderson, 1695. Small 4to; pages (iv), 48, 3 decorated initials, final leaf incorrectly paginated and small hole inserted to remove incorrect printing, title little soiled, library stamp of Alexander Gardyne, 1883 on verso; modern quarter calf, gilt, marbled boards. Wing C7027; Aldiss 3454.   R.F.G. Hollett 76-70 1996 £185.00

ASSOCIATION - DAVID GARNETT

BUTLER, SAMUEL 1835-1902   Alps and Actuaries of Piedmont and the Canton Ticino. London: David Bogue, 1882. Longmans reissue with cancel title and binding in lighter shade of brown; half title, frontispiece, illustrations; original brown cloth, bevelled edges; David Garnett's copy with his bookplate. With inscription "Given by Samuel Butler to Robert Singleton Garnett and Martha Garnett (nee Roscoe) on their marriage 25th June 1896". Hoppe 13 pp. 35-36.   Jarndyce CII-33 1996 £250.00

ASSOCIATION - EDWARD GARNETT

BONAVENTURA, PSEUDO   Diaeta Salutis. Paris: Pierre le Dru for Denis Roce, c. 1500. Crown 8vo; 152 leaves (1)-58), gothic letter, rubricated throughout, large woodcut device of Denis Roce, on titlepage, 18th century panelled calf; bookplate of Edward Garnett, inscribed "N. Irelondi' in rubrricator's ink. Capinger 1154; GKWW 4735; not in Goff, BMC, Polain or Oates.   Petersfield Bookshop FH58-44 1996 £2,500.00

ASSOCIATION - ROBERT GARNETT

BUTLER, SAMUEL 1835-1902   Alps and Actuaries of Piedmont and the Canton Ticino. London: David Bogue, 1882. Longmans reissue with cancel title and binding in lighter shade of brown; half title, frontispiece, illustrations; original brown cloth, bevelled edges; David Garnett's copy with his bookplate. With inscription "Given by Samuel Butler to Robert Singleton Garnett and Martha Garnett (nee Roscoe) on their marriage 25th June 1896". Hoppe 13 pp. 35-36.   Jarndyce CII-33 1996 £250.00

ASSOCIATION - GEORGE GARNIER

FIELDING, HENRY 1707-1754   The Journal of a Voyage to Lisbon. London: A. Millar, 1755. 1st published edition; 8vo; half title; contemporary calf, spine gilt, original morocco label; in modern pullout slipcase, hinges rather worn but firm, internally fine, crisp copy; early bookplate of George Garnier. Cross III p. 326; Sterling Lib. 363. Trebizond 39-14 1996 $625.00

ASSOCIATION - RAFAEL GARRETA

TILLI, M. A.   Catalogus Plantarum Horti Pisani. Florence: 1723. 1st edition; folio; portrait, 2 plants, 50 engraved plates; contemporary vellum, bit worn; good copy; stamp of Rafael Garreta of Barcelona on verso on half title. Hunt 457.   Maggs Bros. Ltd. 1190-146 1996 £1,100.00

ASSOCIATION - GEORGE GARRETT

THE POET'S of Today IV. New York: Scribner's, 1957. 1st edition; fine in very good dust jacket, with some wear along spine and fore edge; signed by contributor, George Garrett, his first book.   Thomas Dorn 9-126 1996 $125.00

ASSOCIATION - TONY GARRETT

WILSON, ANGUS   As If by Magic. London: Martin Secker & Warburg Ltd., 1973. 1st edition; original binding, head and tail of spine and top corners bumped, upper cover slightly marked, very good in nicked and slightly creased, rubbed, dusty dust jacket darkened at spine and edges; presentation copy from author for Jim and Ruth Hart, inscribed in addition, by Tony Garrett who took photo of author on dust jacket. Ulysses 39-633 1996 £75.00

ASSOCIATION - DAVID GARRICK

ORRERY, ROGER BOYLE, 1ST EARL OF 1621-1679   English Adventures. London: printed by T. Newcomb, for H. Herringman, 1676. 1st edition; 8vo; contemporary tree calf, nicely rebacked, spine gilt; occasional light stains, otherwise very good; the copy of Rev. Philip Bliss (1787-1857); Also the copy of David Garrick. Wing O476; Esdaile p. 167; Mish p. 51; CBEL II 770.   Ximenes 109-50 1996 $6,000.00

ASSOCIATION - NICHOLAS GARRY

O'REILLY, BERNARD   Greenland and the Adjacent Seas, and the North-West Passage to the Pacific Ocean, Illustrated in a Voyage to Davis's Strait, During the Summer of 1817. London: printed for Baldwin, Cradock and Joy, 1818. 1st edition; 4to; contemporary red straight grained moroccco, covers elaborately decorated in blind and gilt, all edges gilt, slight wear, but sound; attractive copy; from the library of Sir. Thomas Phillipps, with his shelfmark; armorial bookplate of Nicholas Garry. Sabin 57576; Hill p. 219 (American reprint); Abbey, Travel 633. Ximenes 109-208 1996 $1,500.00

ASSOCIATION - WALTER GARSTANG

DARWIN, CHARLES ROBERT 1809-1882   The Formation of Vegetable Mould through the Action of Worms. London: 1881. 5th thousand; 8vo; pages vii, 326, (2); original cloth; from the collection of Samuel J. Fisher, then of Walter Garstang with his bookplate; some marginal annotation in pencil.   Wheldon & Wesley 207-1247 1996 £60.00

LANKESTER, E. R.   A Treatise on Zoology. London: 1900-09. 8vo; parts 1, 2, 4, 7 and 9 in 6 volumes; parts 6 and 8 were never issued; original cloth and buckram. Formerly the property of Walter Garstang and Alistair G. Hardy.   Wheldon & Wesley 207-499 1996 £120.00

ASSOCIATION - PHILIP GASKELL

THE CAMBRIDGE Economic History of Europe. Cambridge University Press, 1963-67. Thick large 8vo; 4 volumes in 5; buckram, dust jacket; from the library of Philip Gaskell, librarian of Trinity.   Howes Bookshop 265-124 1996 £175.00

ASSOCIATION - MIRIAM GASKING

MORISON, STANLEY 1889-1967   American Copybooks. An Outline of Their History from Colonial to Modern Times. Philadelphia: Wm. F. Fell Co., 1951. This copy number 238 (total copies printed unknown); Small 8vo; 13 illustrations; printed paper boards, bit rubbed at extremities, inscribed by author to his secretary Miriam Gasking, booklabel of Ruari Mclean, pencil note saying the book was bought from Tony Appleton in 1978.   Maggs Bros. Ltd. 1191-160 1996 £88.00

ASSOCIATION - GATHORNE-HARDY

GAY, JOHN 1685-1732   The What D'Ye Call It: a Tragi-Comi-Pastoral Farce. London: Bernard Lintott, n.d. 1715. 1st edition; octavo; modern boards, cover detached, final leaf rehinged with few letters supplied; very rare; the Gathorne-Hardy copy with bookplate.   G. W. Stuart 59-41 1996 $685.00

ASSOCIATION - JACK GAUGHAN

NORTON, ANDRE   Gryphon in Glory. Atheneum, 1981. 1st edition; fine in dust jacket; inscribed by author to fellow writer, Robert Adams, laid in is holograph letter to Adams from artist (for this dust jacket) Jack Gaughan.   Aronovitz 57-891 1996 $125.00

ASSOCIATION - PIERRE GAUTHIER

ARETINO, PIETRO   La Vita di Maria Vergine. Venice: Francesco Marcolini, c. 1540? Small 8vo; 180 unnumbered leaves, italic letter, woodcut medallion on titlepage repeated at end, corner of 1 leaf repaired without loss; 18th century French crushed red morocco, gilt triple fillets, edges and spine, marbled endpapers, all edges gilt; very good; autograph of Pierre Gauthier, Aretino's biographer on fly. Index Aurel 107.069. Brunet 1416.   A. Sokol XXV-7   1996 £1,950.00

ASSOCIATION - JOHN GAWSWORTH

SITWELL, EDITH 1887-1964   Wheels 1917. Oxford: B. H. Blackwell, 1917. Pastedowns and endpapers offset, boards rubbed, top edge rather dusty, otherwise very good; inscribed by author for John Gawsworth. R. A. Gekoski   19-125   1996 £120.00

ASSOCIATION - GAY

STEWART, CHARLES S.   A Visit to the South Seas in U.S. Ship Vincennes, During the Years 1829 and 1830. New York: John P. Haven, 1833. Small 8vo; 2 volumes, (xii), 323 pages; (v), 312 pages; slight foxing throughout; original green embossed cloth, gilt title on spine, bit faded, rubbed and bit bumped on extremities, but quite pleasant overall; inscribed by John Gay for W. Gay, St. Louis Sept. 1843.   Antipodean 28-401   1996 $400.00

ASSOCIATION - GELL

BOSWELL, JAMES 1740-1795   The Principal Corrections and Additions to the First Edition of Mr. Boswell's Life of Dr. Johnson. London: Henry Baldwin for Charles Dilly, 1793. 1st edition; 4to; pages (ii), 42; contemporary speckled calf, gilt Greek key border to sides, flat spine with gilt rules, lacks label, rubbed, spine worn at head and tail, front joint cracked at head; very good copy; the Gell copy with ownership inscirption of Philip and Dorothy Gell, Hopton, dated 2 Jan. 1793, few ms. corrigenda; Pottle 113.   Simon Finch   24-17   1996 £1,500.00

CHESTERFIELD, PHILIP DORMER STANHOPE, 4TH EARL OF 1694-1773   Letters...to His Son, Philip Stanhope, Esq... London: J. Dodsley, 1774. 1st edition; 4to; 2 volumes, pages (iv), vii, (i), 568; (iv), 606, (1); oval portrait frontispiece in volume 1 (offset), half titles with early owner's name printed at head (P. Gell, Hopton), errata leaf at end of volume 2, 1 underlining and ink marginal note; contemporary sprinkled tan calf, expertly rebacked in sprinkled russia to match, raised bands between double gilt rules, original red morocco title and green volume labels laid down, blind fillet border on sides, hinges split but very firm, endpapers stained by turn-ins, overall excellent; Gulick 2; Rothschild 596. Blackwell's B112-63 1996 £500.00

COWPER, WILLIAM 1731-1800   Poems... London: J. Johnson, 1786. 2nd edition; 8vo; 2 volumes bound together; half title in volume 2 (not called for in volume 1), pages (iv), 367, (1) blank; (viii), 359, (1); contemporary quarter dark brown calf, rubbed, smooth backstrip divided by gilt rules, red leather gilt lettered label, slight loss at head, marbled boards, modern calf tips, early owner's name on upper pastedown (D. Gel, Hopton), early owner's name (S. Gell, Hopton); generally excellent. Blackwell's B112-80 1996 £150.00

COWPER, WILLIAM 1731-1800   Poems. London: J. Johnson, 1798. 1st illustrated edition; foolscap 8vo; no half titles, as issued, 2 volumes; pages (iv), x, 324; iv, (iv), 335, (1); 10 engraved plates; contemporary marbled calf, smooth backstrips divided by gilt rules, red and blue title and volume labels, crest and name (P. Gell) stamped on upper pastedown within wash shield surround, speckled edges; excellent. Russell 83.   Blackwell's B112-81 1996 £85.00

DARWIN, ERASMUS 1731-1802   The Botanic Garden; a Poem. London: for J. Johnson, 1791. 1st edition; 4to; 2 volumes bound in one; pages xii, 214 (actually 216), 126 ('Additional Notes'), (ii); (12), v-vii, (i), 184 (actualy 186), directions to the binder on two slips, one inserted between volume I and II, the other laid down below text at end of volume 2; frontispiece in each volume, 15 engraved plates, 1 engraved vignette half title in volume 2 only, as issued; contemporary tree calf, rebacked, old spine laid down, red morocco label, gilt in compartments, corners neatly repaired, marbled endpapers, pale yellow edges, occasional light spotting or staining, two of the four plates of the Portland Vase very slightly cropped at one edge (as often), good copy; the Gell copy, with Gell family ownership inscription. Blake 450A; Nissen 451.   Simon Finch   24-64   1996 £680.00

DOSSIE, ROBERT   The Elaboratory Laid Open; or, the Secrets of Modern Chemistry and Pharmacy Revealed... London: printed for J. Nourse, 1768. 2nd edition; 8vo; xviii, (ii), 456, (viii) pages; original sheep, covers rubbed, spine worn at head and foot, joints cracked; signature of Philip Gell, of Hopton House, Derbyshire.   David Bickersteth 133-185 1996 £220.00

ASSOCIATION - GELL

GRAVES, RICHARD   The Spiritual Quixote; or, the summer's Ramble of Mr. Geoffrey Wildgoose. London: J. Dodsley, 1774. 2nd edition; 12mo; 3 volumes; frontispieces in each volume, half titles present; pages xxiv, 352; viii, 287; xii, 323; contemporary tan calf, backstrips and raised bands, red and green albels in second and third compartments, remainder gilt, but rubbed, expert repairs at head and foot of all joints, board edges gilt hatched, printed book ticker in volume II (D. Gell, Hopton 1776); very good.   Blackwell's B112-135 1996 £180.00

GRAY, THOMAS 1716-1771   The Poems of Mr. Gray. London: printed by H. Hughs; and sold by J. Dodsley...and J. Todd 1775. 4to; pages (iv), 416; 109, (1); frontispiece, small waterstains in outer corners, titlepage lightly browned; contemporary marbled tan calf, 20th century tan russia reback, with raised bands, original label laid down, lower corners of boards bumped, corners repaired, extensive ms. note no prelim pages; good; contemporary owner's signature of D. Gell at head.   Blackwell's B112-139 1996 £225.00

GRIFFITH, RICHARD   The Triumvirate; or, the Authentic Memoirs of A.B. and C. London: W. Johnston, 1764. 1st edition; 12mo; pages xxvii, (i), 264, (ii), 5; 338, (1) (errata); bound together in contemporary brown sheep, backstrip faded, lightly rubbed, red morocco label 'D. Gell, Hopton Hall' on front pastedown; owner's name of D. Gell at head of titlepage, F7-F12 opened carelessly with slight damage to fore-edges, excellent.   Blackwell's B112-143 1996 £750.00

HOMERUS   The Iliad and Odyssey of Homer. London: for J. Johnson, 1791. 1st edition; 4to; 2 volumes, xvii, (xi), 668; (iv), 583 pages; early 19th century polished tan calf, spines richly gilt in compartments, green lettering and numbering pieces, sides with triple gilt rules, blindstamped inner dentelles, marbled endpapers and edges, scattered light spotting but generally very clean and fresh internally, excellent copy; bookplates of Philip Lyttelton Gell. Rothschild 684.   Simon Finch 24-117 1996 £350.00

PATRICK, SIMON   The Christian Sacrifice. London: printed by R.N. for R. Royston, 1671. 1st edition; 8vo; pages (xiv), 509; frontispiece, additional titlepage; contemporary polished black morocco, backstrip faded, raised bands, unlettered, compartments gilt panelled with single central ornament in each, sides panelled with inner and outer double fillet borders, with poppy-head and arabesque gilt ornaments at corners of central panel, marbled pastedowns; presentation inscription; excellent; from the Gell family library. Wing P760.   Blackwell's B112-220 1996 £85.00

PIOZZI, HESTER LYNCH SALUSBURY THRALE 1741-1821   Anecdotes of the Late Samuel Johnson... London: T. Cadell, 1786. 2nd edition; 8vo; half title present, pages viii, 306, (1); contemporary marbled calf, some surface wear, smooth backstrip with wavy, pointille, foliate rolls, gilt dulled, red label with rope roll border, 'hound's tooth' roll border on sides, board edges gilt hatched, marbled endpapers, very good; half title present, signature of early owner D. Gell.   Blackwell's B112-226 1996 £175.00

ROBIN HOOD   Robin Hood. A Collection of all the Antient Poems, Songs, and Ballads, Now Extant Relative to that Celebrated English Outlaw... London: T. Egerton and J. Johnson, 1795. 1st edition; 8vo; 2 volumes, half titles present, wood engraved head and tailpieces, by Thomas and John Bewick, K1 volume 2 torn with loss of text, first gathering of volume 2 starting; pages (iv), cxviii, (ii), 167; (viii), 220, (4); contemporary quarter blue roan, slight loss at head of backstrip of volume i, joints rubbed, smooth backstrips divided by gilt rules and open twist rolls, gilt lettered direct in second and fourth compartments, vellum tipped marbled boards, crest and name of 'P. Gell' printed on front pastedowns, with ms. note below 'given by my Brother Dec. 1st 1795' in both volumes, endpapers and binder's blanks lightly foxed, blue speckled edges, very good. Hugo 86.   Blackwell's B112-244 1996 £450.00

SMOLLETT, TOBIAS GEORGE 1721-1771   The Adventures of Peregrine Pickle. London: printed for the author, 1751. 1st edition; 12mo; 4 volumes; pages ix, (i), 288; x, 322; v, (i), 205; vii, (i), 315; titlepages stained by turn-ins, L12 (pp. 227/28) in volume ii cancelled (as often); contemporary tan calf, rebacked, raised bands between double gilt rules, gilt lettered red leather labels, double gilt fillet border on sides, some corners repaired, endpapers stained by turn-ins, hinges strengthened, generally very good; early owner's name 'P. Gell', Hopton stamped at tail of titlepage. Ashley Lib. V p. 185/86; Rothschild 1910; Tinker 1927. Blackwell's B112-259 1996 £550.00

SMOLLETT, TOBIAS GEORGE 1721-1771   The Expedition of Humphry Clinker. London: printed for W. Johnston...and B. Collins, 1771. 2nd edition; 12mo; 3 volumes; half titles present, hinges strengthened, pages xv, (i0, 250; (iv), 249; (iv), 275; contemporary sprinkled calf, edges darkened, rebacked with raised bands between gilt bands, gilt lettered red labels, endpapers browned, early owner's name "D. Gell" on cut out scrap bouquet of holly within wreath, surmounted by cut out eagle crest. Blackwell's B112-260 1996 £250.00

ASSOCIATION - GELL

STEELE, RICHARD 1672-1729   The Theatre...To Which are added, the Anti-Theatre; The Character of Sir John Steel's Case with the Lord Chamberlain the Crisis of Property, with the Sequel, Two Pasquins &c. &c. London: printed by and for the editor, 1791. 8vo; 2 volumes, pages vii, (i), (1)-314; iv, 315-615, (1); additional engraved portrait vignette titlepage volume i, early owner's name at head of titlepages; modern half russet calf with contemporary marbled boards, smooth backstrips divided by gilt rules, contemporary red morocco labels, early ownership name on front pastedowns "D. Gell - Hopton-Hall", excellent. Arnott & Robinson 4069; Lowe pp. 321/22.   Blackwell's B112-264 1996 £200.00

STERNE, LAURENCE 1713-1768   The Life and Opinions of Tristram Shandy, Gentleman. York & London: for R. and J. Dodsley, & for T. Becket and P. A. DeHondt, 1760-69. 1st edition; small 8vo; 9 volumes bound in 5; volumes IV, V, VI and IX with half titles, as called for, volume III with frontispiece; Sterne's signature in ink, as usual, inscribed at head of chapter one in volumes V, VII and IX; uncut, contemporary quarter calf, marbled sides, green morocco spine labels, reamins of paper library spine labels, binding on volume IX slightly variant, scarce and desirable in uncut state; spines worn, few trivial tears not affecting text, very good copy, protected in folding polished calf backed book-form. The Gell copy, with contemporary ownership stamps of P. Gell, Hopton on titles of first work in each volume except last. Rothschild 1970.   Simon Finch 24-214 1996 £9,500.00

THICKNESSE, PHILIP   Memoirs and Anecdotes of Philip Thicknesse, Late Lieutenant Governor of Land Guard Fort and Unfortunately Father to George Touchet, Baron Audley. London: printed for the author, 1788. 1st edition; bound in 4's; 2 volumes, pages xvi, (viii), 326, (2) (blank); (viii), 326; bound together in modern russet russia backed contemporary marbled boards, smooth backstrip divided by double gilt rules, contemporary gilt lettered red leather label re-laid, vellum tips to boards; early owner's name "D. Gell"; excellent.   Blackwell's B112-270 1996 £250.00

TOTT, FRANCOIS DE   Memoirs...on the Turks and the Tartars. London: J. Jarvis, 1785. 1st English edition; 8vo; 2 volumes; pages xxiv, 532; (ii), 382, (14); contemporary quarter tan calf, minor worm damage to front joint of volume i, rubbed, smooth backstrips divided by gilt rules, slight wear to heads, red leather gilt lettered labels, vellum tipped marbled boards; very good. early owner's name "P Gell". Cox I p. 234. Blackwell's B112-272 1996 £175.00

ASSOCIATION - LEO GENN

MORGAN, CHARLES   The Flashing Stream. London: Macmillan & Co., 1938. Limited to 15 copies, signed by author and specially bound, this being a presentation copy from author; 8vo; xxii, 264, 2 ad pages; full niger morocco, gilt panelled sides, gilt edges, spine slightly rubbed and faded; this is copy number 3, inscribed for Leo Genn; loosely inserted is 4 page ALS to Genn from author.   Thomas Thorp 489-222 1996 £125.00

ASSOCIATION - PAUL CELESIA GENOESE

SYDNEY, ALGERNON   Discourses Concerning Government...with His Letters Trial Apology and Some Memoirs of His Life... London: A. Millar, 1763. 4to; (v), 46, (vii), 497, (i), 198 pages; frontispiece, contemporary red goatskin, single gilt rule, Hollis's cockerel device on front board and feather on lower board, spine in five compartments, morocco label on one, owl device on others, good copy, inscription from Thomas Hollis to Paul Celesia Genoese.   Robert Clark 38-207 1996 £600.00

ASSOCIATION - DAVID LLOYD GEORGE

YOUNG, FRANCIS BRETT   Woodsmoke. Severn Edition, 1939. 1st edition; trifle shaken in binding, otherwise very good; inscribed by author to David Lloyd George who has annotated the flyleaf with what appears to be his initials and date 30.7.39.   Words Etcetera 94-1340 1996 £55.00

ASSOCIATION - DAN GERBER

BERRYMAN, JOHN 1914-1972   77 Dream Songs. London: Faber & Faber, 1964. 1st British edition; fine in dust jacket, laid in is a 1967 Dublin Poetry Season program featuring Berryman; inscribed by author to poet Dan Gerber in 1967.   Captain's Bookshelf 38-16 1996 $300.00

BRAUTIGAN, RICHARD   Dreaming of Babylon: a Private Eye Novel 1942. New York: Delacorte, 1977. 1st edition; fine in dust jacket with few tiny nicks, complimentary author card laid in, splendid association copy with author's warm contemporary presentation inscription to the Dan Gerbers on titlepage.   Captain's Bookshelf 38-24 1996 $750.00

ASSOCIATION - JOHN GERE

RICHARDS, FRANK   Old-Soldier Sahib. London: Faber & Faber, Ltd., 1936. 1st edition; original binding, top edge dusty, tail of spine bumped, corners very slightly bumped, cover edges slightly rubbed, very good in nicked, rubbed and dusty, slightly marked dust jacket frayed and slightly chipped at head of spine and browned at spine and edges; bookplate of John Gere, who was keeper of books & drawings at the British Museum.   Ulysses 39-244 1996 £450.00

ASSOCIATION - PAOLINO GERLI

POTANUS, JOANNES JOVIANUS   Opera Omnia. Venice: Aldus & Asulanus, June 1518 - April 1519 - September 1519. 4to; 3 volumes; Aldine Anchor on titlepage of first volume and at end of 3rd volume; vellum; owner's stamp cut out o title leaf of volume 3 affecting few letters of text on verso; Di Veroli & Paolino Gerli booktickets in all volumes, ownership stamps in title margins of volumes 2 and 3; ownership inscription of Magnoccavalli in volume II. Renouard 82.3, 87.6 and 7; Adams P1860; Brunet IV 808.   Rostenberg & Stern 150-76 $2,750.00

ASSOCIATION - WILLIAM GERY

CARTER, ELIZABETH   Poems on Several Occasions. London: printed for John Rivington, 1762. 1st edition; small 8vo; pages vii, 104; contemporary calf serviceably rebacked; bookplate of Wm. Gery, of Bushmead.   Peter Murray Hill 185-29 1996 £95.00

ASSOCIATION - FRANCISCUS GIANIBELLUS

MALIPIERO, GIROLAMO   Il Petrarcha Spirituale. Venice: Francesco Marcolini, Sept. 1538. 2nd edition; 8vo; titlepage, ff. 2-153, 10ff. n.n., woodcut portrait on titlepage; red mor. over pasteboards, richly gilt, lacks 4 pairs of ties, sides dec. inside upper cover the title II PE/TRARCHA/SPIR and originally on lower one the (intended) first owner's name MACRO/ANOTIMO(?), subsequently obliterated (by the original binder) by over-tooling, spine with 3 raised bands alternating with four false bands, compartments dec. w/line-ornament in blind & w/motto CONSTANTIA gilt downwards, edges of bds. scored at right angles w/groups of 3 lines, edges gilt & gauffered w/sm. knotwork tools, pastedown and 2 endleaves (origina?) at each end, no watermark; the copy of Franciscus Gianibellus, 16th century signature on titlepage; William Bateman, F.A.S. of Middleton-by-Yolgrave in the County of Derby, with armorial bookplate. A contemporary Bolognese binding by a man whom the late Dr. Schunke called the "Binder of the Acts of the Cabinetmakers' Guild.   Marlborough 160-6 1996 £7,500.00

ASSOCIATION - ROBERT GIBBINGS

SWIFT, JONATHAN 1667-1745   Miscellaneous Poems. Waltham St. Lawrence: Golden Cockerel Press, 1928. Limited to 375 numbered copies; wood engravings by Robert Gibbings; very good in scarce dust jacket with chip on right hand corner and head of spine, with TLS from Robert Gibbings to Brian Roberts.   Words Etcetera 94-492 1996 £135.00

ASSOCIATION - EDWARD GIBBON

BARRINGTON, DAINES 1727-1800   Miscellanies. London: printed by J. Nichols; sold by B. White and J. Nichols, 1781. 1st edition; 4to; 2 plates, 2 maps, 5 genealogical tables; contemporary tree calf, spine gilt, neatly rebacked, original spine laid down; very desirable copy, from the library of historian Edward Gibbon with his booklabel. Sabin 3628; Howes B177; Hill pp. 13-14; Lada Mocarski 34.   Ximenes 109-27 1996 $2,500.00

ASSOCIATION - ELISA GIBSON

RUSH, BENJAMIN 1745-1813   Essays, Literary, Moral and Philosophical. Philadelphia: printed by Thomas and Samuel F. Bradford, 1798. 1st edition; 8vo; (ii), (viii), 378 pages; modern tooled calf with raised bands and leather spine label, fine, untrimmed copy; inscribed by author for Miss Elisa Gibson, rare thus. Norman Cat. 1863.   John Gach 150-405 1996 $2,500.00

ASSOCIATION - JAMES GIBSON

CERVANTES SAAVEDRA, MIGUEL DE 1547-1616   Journey to Parnassus. London: Kegan Paul, Chiswick Press printed, 1883. Crown 8vo; portrait, pages (2), lxxv, (2), 387; original binding, gilt, edges gilt, metal clasp, very good to nice; inscribed to John Blyth by James Gibson.   James Fenning 133-52 1996 £55.00

ASSOCIATION - MARIS GIBSON

XENOPHON   De Cyri Institutione, Libri Octo. Philadelphia: printed by John Watts for Ex Officina Classica Impensis Wm. Poyntell.. 1806. 1st American edition of Cyropaedia; 8vo; 547 pages; soiled and wormed; rubbed contemporary full roan leather, blue printed American ex-libris of Maris Gibson. AI 11903.   Family Album Tillers-670 1996 $400.00

ASSOCIATION - JOE GIGANTI

MITCHELL, JOHN   Organized Labor. Philadelphia: American Book and Bible House, 1903. 1st edition; 436 pages; photos; original cloth, very good+; nice association, the copy of Joe Giganti.   Beasley Books 82-331 1996 $100.00

ASSOCIATION - RICHARD GILBERTSON

HUGHES, TED 1930-   The Martyrdom of Bishop Farrar. Bow, Crediton, Devon: the Manuscript Series, 1970. 1st separate edition; 1st issue, withdrawn owing tot he transposition of two lines of the poem and the poet's disapproval of the wrappers, one of 'probably somewhat more than 100'; 4to; frontispiece; pictorial marbled wrappers, riveted; fine; inscribed by publisher, Richard Gilbertson. Sagar & Tabor A21.   James S. Jaffe 34-269 1996 $150.00

ASSOCIATION - R. W. GILDER

WHITMAN, WALT 1819-1892   Good-Bye My Fancy. Philadelphia: David McKay, 1891. 1st edition; Binding E; portrait; green cloth, faint offsetting to pastedowns and endpapers as if a jacket at some point were present, hinges lightly cracked, slight rubbing to spine tips, near fine; inscribed by Horace Traubel to R. W. Gilder stating "This book (?) (?) bound this way in green covers was made by W.W. at the (?) not for the market but for distribution among his friends". Fine association. BAL 21440.   Charles Agvent 4-1187 1996 $1,200.00

ASSOCIATION - ARTHUR TIDMAN GILL

GILL, ERIC 1882-1940   Sculpture. An Essay. Ditchling: Saint Dominic's Press, 1918. 1st edition; one of 400 copies; crown 8vo; pages (i), 22, (4) (ads); printed on handmade paper, pagination on page 5 present and misspelling 'frll' on page 10, typographical rule border present on titlepage; original pale brown wrappers, front cvoer printed in black, price is printed "Price One Shilling" and is unaltered, faint edges fading, rear cover, because of brittle nature of paper, is almost detached, untrimmed and almost entirely unopened; good. Superb association copy, given by Gill to his father the Revd. Arthur Tidman Gill and inscribed by Gill. Later in Gill's library with bookplate; Sewell 17; Gill, Eric Gill Bib. 5.   Blackwell's B112-247 1996 £450.00

ASSOCIATION - LEONARD GILLESPIE

ORTA, GARCIA DE   Aromatum, et Simplicium Aliquot Medicamentorum Apud Indos Nascentium Historia... Antwerp: Ex officina Christophori Plantani, Arachitypographi Regii, 1579. 3rd Plantin edition; small 8vo; pages 217, (6), 28 woodcuts by Peter van der Borcht and Arnold Nicolai, old paper faults, repaired, with slight loss, title soiled, later full vellum; numerous old ownerships including presentation to William Reynaud from Leonard Gillespie, Fort Royal Naval Hospital, Martinique, 1802.   Family Album Tillers-460 1996 $750.00

ASSOCIATION - THOMAS GISBORNE

JOHNSON, SAMUEL 1709-1784   A Journey to the Western Islands of Scotland. London: printed for W. Strahan and T. Cadell, 1775. 1st edition; 8vo; 384 pages, complete with errata slip; contemporary quarter calf and marbled boards with vellum corner tips, morocco spine label, bookplate, front board nearly detached, blanks missing, but near very good. Interesting association copy, with signature of Thomas Gisborne, the elder.   Chapel Hill 94-241 1996 $250.00

ASSOCIATION - ALGERNON GISSING

STERNBERG, THOMAS   The Dialect and Folk-lore of Northamptonshire. London: John Russell Smith, 1851. 1st edition; original red cloth, spine slightly dulled, very good; with signature of Algernon Gissing, 1887, with few pencil notes and cutting about author inserted. Jarndyce 103-80 1996 £65.00

ASSOCIATION - GJERSTAD

OPUSCULA Romana. Volume IV. Lund: C. W. K. Gleerup, 1962. 4to; frontisportrait, 248 pages, numerous illustrations; three quarter green calf with 4 raised bands, original wrappers bound in; the first copy, inscribed by the publisher, specially bound for Gjerstad.   Archaeologia Luxor-3780 1996 $200.00

ASSOCIATION - MARY GLASCOCK

POINTZ, ROBERT   Testimonies for the Real Presence of Christes Body and Blood in the Blessed Scarament of the Aultar. Louvain: Jean Fouler, 1566. 8vo; title, 7 ff., n.n., ff. 1-200 (lacking ff. 155-158); sides of original binding laid down on a new binding in 1885, they are of brown goatskin decorated in gilt with border formed by repeated impressions of lacework took, a plaque of arabesque foliate ornament blocked in centre between the name GLASCOK/MARI (the words reversed on lower cover), lacks two slit ties, upper edge dark green, others show traces of guilding; this binding may be Roman, of about the same date as the book; the book was bound for Mary Glascock; the copy of Bartholomew Wicker with early scribblings in margins.   Marlborough 160-10 1996 £1,750.00

ASSOCIATION - GLENTWORTH

DICKENS, CHARLES 1812-1870   Nicholas Nickleby. London: Chapman and Hall, 1839. 1st edition; bound from parts; frontispiece, illustration by Phiz, with extra illustrations: two series, one by Peter Palette, and also portraits by Onwhyn; bound in period style in three quarter polished calf, marbled boards and endpapers, red and black labels, slight wear, but nice. From the library of Lady Glentworth. Eckel pp. 64-66.   Hartfield 48-L28 1996 $595.00

ASSOCIATION - GLOVER

SCOT, REYNOLDE REGINALD   A Perfite Platform of a Hop Garden. London: Henrie Denham at the Signe of the Starre, 1574. 1st edition; 4to; pages xvi, 54 (of 56), (lacking last leaf of epilogue (photocopy laid in), decorated initials and 15 woodcuts; very tall, bound with first blank leaf with ornament, marbled boards, modern rebacking in calf, some interior soiling, especially to final leaf; circular indistinct pencil rubbings of coins on front flyleaf, still quite attractive. Bookplate of Earl Fitzwilliam, early ownership signatures of Robert and Tho. Glover. STC 21865; Hunt 128; Henrey 337;   Second Life Books 103-168 1996 $2,200.00

ASSOCIATION - LEROY GOBLE

JUNGE, CARL S.   Ex Libris. New York: H. L. Lindquist, 1935. 1st edition; number 97 of 500 copies signed by Junge; 4to; (51) leaves, original cloth backed printed boards, fine in very good glassine jacket with few pieces missing; with sardonic penciled inscription on colophon from Leroy Goble to noted Americana bibliographer Wright Howes. Nice association.   Chapel Hill 94-126 1996 $100.00

ASSOCIATION - HERB GOLD

PALEY, GRACE   Enormous Changes at the Last Minute. New York: FSG, 1973. Uncorrected proof copy; scarce proof; very good in tall wrappers; the copy of novelist Herb Gold.   Ken Lopez 74-366 1996 $275.00

ASSOCIATION - JOHN GOLD

BOTTOMLEY, GORDON   Laodice and Danae. London: privately printed, 1909. 1st edition; 8vo; original wrappers, slightly creased and chipped at edges; few spots; presentation copy inscribed in author's hand to Daisy Rigby and John Gold.   R.F.G. Hollett & Son 78-326 1996 £55.00

ASSOCIATION - GOLDWATER

DIODORUS, SICULUS   Bibliothecae Historicae Libri VI. Venice: Joannis Tacuinis, de Tridino 20 September 1496. Folio; later vellum, inner blank margin of title leaf restored, some smudges, stains, ink imprint of three leaves (two with twigs), some light watermarks and faint stains throughout, neat contemporary marginalia; Goldwater bookplate, very nice. Hain 6191; GW 8377; Goff D 213.   G. W. Stuart 59-56 1996 $3,100.00

ASSOCIATION - JOHN GOODALL

FULLER, RONALD   The Work of Rex Whistler. London: Batsford, 1960. 1st edition; 600 copies printed; 4to; pages xxiv, 112 illustrations on 68 pages, (ii), 122; 9 of the illustrations are in color, numerous other illustrations in text; original green buckram, decorated in gilt, with dust jacket, lower cover little marked, dust jacket slightly frayed, very good. Loosely inserted autograph letter from Laurence Whistler to artist John Goodall.   Sotheran PN32-66 1996 £498.00

ASSOCIATION - GOODGER

WOOLMAN, JOHN 1720-1772   A Journal of the Life and Travels of John Woolman in the Service of the Gospel. Essex House Press, 1901. One of 250 copies; 6 1/4 x 4 3/4 inches; 2 p.l., 387, (1) pages, (1) leaf (colophon); frontispiece, decorative woodcut initials, device in colophon, printed in red and black; original stiff vellum, wallet edges, untrimmed; vellum bit smudged, but fine othewise; armorial bookplate of Charles Wm. Swainston Goodger. Tomkinson p. 72.   Phillip J. Pirages 33-210 1996 $250.00

ASSOCIATION - GOODWIN

SHAKESPEARE, WILLIAM 1564-1616   The Tragedy of Richard the Third. Grabhorn Press, 1953. One of 180 copies; 10 1/2 x 7 3/4 inches; 3 p.l., 190, (1) pages; printed in red and black; 6 original colored woodcuts in text, including vignette on title by Mary Grabhorn, original limp vellum, linen ties, edges untrimmed, spine with gilt lettering; only the most trivial imperfections, extremely fine, especially clean inside and out. Signed, dated (1958 and inscribed by Jane Grabhorn to Elaine(?) Goodwin.   Phillip J. Pirages 33-255 1996 $550.00

ASSOCIATION - WILLARD GOODWIN

BLOGG, MINNIE WRIGHT   Bibliography of the Writings of Sir William Osler. Baltimore: Lord Baltimore Press, 1921. 1st separate edition; 8vo; 96 pages, frontispiece, blue cloth; fine; inscribed by author to Willard Goodwin, with his bookplate.   Jeff Weber 31-125 1996 $125.00

OSLER, WILLIAM 1849-1919   An Alabama Student and Other Biographical Essays. London: Humphrey Milford, 1929. 1st edition; 2nd impression; 8vo; (iii), 334 pages, frontispiece, illustrations; red cloth, spine soiled; inscribed to Willard E. Goodwin from Howard A. Kelly and Goodwin's signature and bookplate.   Jeff Weber 31-31 1996 $100.00

ASSOCIATION - GORDON

TERENTIUS AFER, PUBLIUS 180-159 BC   Comoediae. Birmingham: Baskerville, 1772. 12mo; pages (4), 308, cancellans at G2; all edges gilt, early full crushed red morocco gilt, floral decorated gilt spine, engraved ex-libris from the Scottish clan Gordon; Gaskell 47.   Family Album Tillers-609 1996 $350.00

ASSOCIATION - GEORGE GORDON

DINKINS, JAMES   1861 to 1865, by an Old Johnnie. Personal Recollections and Experiences in the Confederate Army. Cincinnati: Robert Clark Co., 1897. 1st edition; 280 pages; original cloth, near fine, scarce. General George Gordon's copy with marks delienating references made to him in the book. Harwell In Tall Cotton 44; Howes D346; Nicholson p. 241;   McGowan Book Co. 65-25 1996 $650.00

ASSOCIATION - GILES ALEXANDER ESME GORDON

WILDE, OSCAR 1854-1900   Poems. London: David Bogue, 1881. 2nd edition; 1st printing; 8vo; pages x, 236, colophon; recently rebound in half dark green morocco, spine and top edges gilt; slight spotting of a few leaves, but very nice copy; with bookplate of writer, theatre critic and literary agent, Giles Alexander Esme Gordon. Mason 305. Sotheran PN32-68 1996 £598.00

ASSOCIATION - GOSFORD

BEMBO, PIETRO, CARDINAL 1470-1547   Historiae Venetae Libri XII. Venice: Sons of Aldus, 1551. Folio; fine title woodcut of Mercury & Pallas within frame of Cupids and Angels, Aldine Anchor at end, woodcut initials; gilt calf, rebacked, Aldine Anchors gilt impressed on both covers, "vigilantibus" bookticket of 3rd Earl of Gosford; large paper copy; The Renouard copy. Adams B597. Renouard 152 no. 17.   Rostenberg & Stern 150-75 1996 $3,500.00

ASSOCIATION - EDMUND GOSSE

BARCLAY, JOHN   John Barclay, His Argenis. London: Felix Kyngston for Richard Meighen and Henry Seile, 1628. 1st edition of this new translation; 4to; (8), 490 pages; engraved headpieces, initials; old mottled calf, rebacked, morocco spine label, gilt, extremities lightly rubbed; bookplate of Edmund Gosse. STC 1393.   Kenneth Karmiole 1NS-37 1996 $450.00

WEBSTER, JOHN   Love's Graduate. Oxford: printed at the Private Press of H. Daniel Felllow of Worcester College 1885. Limited to 150 copies; small 4to; pages (4), xii, 69, (2); uncut in original vellum backed boards, slightly spotted; inscribed by Edmund Gosse for Bessie Waterhouse. Madan 11.   Claude Cox 107-40 1996 £180.00

ASSOCIATION - E. B. GOULD

STONE, HERBERT STUART   First Editions of American Authors. Cambridge: Stone & Kimball, 1893. Large paper edition, limited to 50 numbered copies, signed by publisher; large 8vo; xxiv, 224 pages; lavender cloth, paper spine label; rare; E. B. Gould's copy (Chicago collector) with his bookplate. Kramer, Stone & Kimball 2.   Kenneth Karmiole 1NS-233 1996 $450.00

ASSOCIATION - A. S. F. GOW

CAMPBELL, ARCHIBALD 1726-1780   Lexiphanes, a Dialogue. London: printed for R. Faulder and J. Fielding, 1783. 3rd edition; 12mo; contemporary tree calf, neatly rebacked retaining original gilt spine strip and slightly chipped red label; armorial bookplate and booklabel of A. S. F. Gow, the classicist. Alston III 281.   Jarndyce 103-39 1996 £180.00

ASSOCIATION - JOHN GRABAU

CHANNING, WILLIAM ELLERY   Poems. Boston: 1843. 1st edition; 12mo; 151 pages; full 20th century turquoise morocco binding, original paper label preserved on back endleaf; inscribed by author for Emma Lazaraus; beneath is 1916 inscription "This vol. that came to me on the death of Josephine Lazarus from her private library I inscribed to my brother John f. Grabau."   M & S Rare Books 60-193 1996 $4,500.00

ASSOCIATION - JANE GRABHORN

SHAKESPEARE, WILLIAM 1564-1616   The Tragedy of Richard the Third. Grabhorn Press, 1953. One of 180 copies; 10 1/2 x 7 3/4 inches; 3 p.l., 190, (1) pages; printed in red and black; 6 original colored woodcuts in text, including vignette on title by Mary Grabhorn, original limp vellum, linen ties, edges untrimmed, spine with gilt lettering; only the most trivial imperfections, extremely fine, especially clean inside and out. Signed, dated (1958 and inscribed by Jane Grabhorn to Elaine(?) Goodwin.   Phillip J. Pirages 33-255 1996 $550.00

ASSOCIATION - ALICE GRACE

LENNOX, CHARLOTTE RAMSEY 1720-1804   The Female Quixote; or, the Adventures of Arabella. Dublin: printed for W. Whitestone, 1763. 3rd edition; 12mo; 2 volumes; contemporary calf, bit worn, lacks one label; very good, complete with final leaf of ads in volume 1, scarce printing; early armorial bookplates of Mrs. Alice Grace. cf. Hazen pp. 94-98; cf. Courtney p. 38.   Ximenes 108-242 1996 $300.00

ASSOCIATION - PAMELA GRADON

plummer, charles   Bethada Naem nEreenn: Lives of irish Saints. London: Oxford University Press, 1922. 8vo; 2 volumes, pages 390, 404; original cloth, very scarce. ownership signatures of E. S. Procter, hispanist, St. Hugh's College; and Pamela Gradon, medievalist, St. Hugh's College.   Howes Bookshop 265-980 1996 £120.00

ASSOCIATION - GRAFF

ESTRACTO de Noticias Del Puerto De Monterey, De La Mission, Y Presido Que Se Han Establecido En El Con La Denominacion De San Carlos, Y Del Sucesso De Las Dos Expediciones De Mar, Y Tierra Que A este Fin Se Despacharon En Al Ano Proxima... Mexico: En la Imprenta del Superior Govierno 16 de Agosto de 1770. Small folio; (5) pages; later marbled wrappers, slight browning, else exceptionally fine, with contemporary note of '31' at top of first leaf, in half morocco slipcase; the Everett Graff copy with his bookplate. Cowan p. 199; Graff 1264; Wagner Spanish Southwest 150.   Michael D. Heaston 23-290 1996 $45,000.00

ASSOCIATION - GRAFF

REYNOLDS, JOHN　　Friendship's Offering: a Sketch of the Life of Dr. John Mason Peck. Belleville: Advocate Book and Job Office, Print, 1858. 1st edition; 34 pages; original glazed yellow binding, minor chipping; fine, slipcase; Graff copy with his bookplate. Eberstadt Cat. 168 231. Michael D. Heaston　23-288　1996　$2,250.00

ASSOCIATION - CHRISTINE ALEXANDER GRAHAM

SHAKESPEARE, WILLIAM 1564-1616　　The Tempest. London: n.d. 1908. Limited to 500 numbered copies, signed by artist; 11.5 x 8.5 inches; 144 pages; 40 tipped in color plates by Edmund Dulac, on green art paper, with lettered tissue guards; full vellum, top edge gilt, covers slightly rubbed and spotted, spine heavily spotted, slightly warped covers, lacking original ties, text tight and clean; bookplate of Christine Alexander Graham.　John K. King　77-594　1996　$950.00

ASSOCIATION - GRANARD

JONES, WILLIAM TODD　　Authentic Detail of an Affair of Honour, Between William Todd Jones, Esq. and Sir Richard Musgrave. Dublin: 1802. 8vo; (ii), 9, (i) pages; disbound, small paper flaw in lower corner of B1, affecting a few letters; good, clean copy, uncommon; inscribed "For the Countess of Granard".　Robert Clark　38-238　1996　£85.00

PHILLIPS, EDWARD　　The New World of Words; or, Universal English Dictionary. London: for J. Phillips, H. Rhodes, J. Taylor, 1706. 6th edition; folio; fine frontispiece, some browning towards end of text; contemporary calf, old reback, hinges slightly weakened, red label, good, sound copy; Granard booklabel. Alston V61.　Jarndyce 103-607　1996　£550.00

PIOZZI, HESTER LYNCH SALUSBURY THRALE 1741-1821　　British Synonymy; or, an Attempt at Regulating the Choice of Words in Familiar Conversation... Dublin: William Porter for P. Byrne & W. Jones, 1794. 1st Dublin edition; contemporary speckled calf, spine with double bands in gilt, red label, handsome copy; Granard booklabel. Alston III. 535. Jarndyce 103-Jarndyce 103-323　1996　£380.00

SIDNEY, JOHN APSLEY　　A Scheme For Improving Small Sums of Money... Rochester: printed by W. Epps, Troy-Town, 1801. 1st and probably only edition; 8vo; (ii), 45, (1) pages, complete with half title; original boards, gilt morocco lettering piece on upper cover, fine; from the library of the Rt. Hon. the Earl of Granard at Castle Forbes. Goldsmiths 18292; Not in Kress, Black, Williams, NUC or BLC.　John Drury　82-258　1996　£250.00

WALKER, JOHN 1732-1807　　A Dictionary of the English Language, Answering at Once the Purposes of Rhyming, Spelling and Pronouncing. London: printed for T. Becket, 1775. contemporary calf, slight rubbing at tail of spine, black label, nice; Granard booklabel. Alston VI.570. Jarndyce 103-224　1996　£400.00

WILKINSON, TATE　　Memoirs of His Own Life... York: printed for the author, by Wilson, Spence and Mawman; & sold by... 1790. 1st edition; 12mo; 4 volumes; xxiv, 240; (ii), 266; (ii), 266; (ii), 274, (ii) pages; half title in each volume, final errata leaf in volume IV, 12 page subscriber list; contemporary calf, spines decorated gilt, double labels; 3 spines very slightly chipped at head, one corner little worn, some faint marginal dampstaining in volume 1, localised marginal worming in early leaves of volume 4, well clear of text; handsome set. From the Granard library. A&R 3637　Robert Clark　38-218　1996　£480.00

WILKINSON, TATE　　The Wandering Patentee; or, a History of the Yorkshire Theatres, from 1770 to the Present Time... York: printed for the author, by Wilson, Spence and Mawman, sold by... 1795. 1st edition; 12mo; 4 volumes; (ii), xi, (iii), (13)-312; 268; 268; (3)-(268) pages; half titles present in volumes I-III; contemporary speckled calf, spines gilt ruled, double labels; localised wear to some corners and edges, 3 boards bit scuffed, volume 4 titlepage mounted, repairing closed tear (no loss); good set, with Granard library bookplates. A&R 3640.　Robert Clark　38-219　1996　£450.00

ASSOCIATION - CHARLES GRANT

MC CAULEY, KIRBY　　Dark Forces. New York: Viking Press, 1980. 1st edition; fine in dust jacket with very slight tear to front panel, inscribed by Charles L. Grant and Joe Haldeman and dated Nov. 1980.　Bud Schweska　12-454　1996　$135.00

ASSOCIATION - THOMAS GRANT

BLOOMFIELD, ROBERT　　The Farmer's Boy; a Rural Poem. London: printed for Vernor and Hood, 1800. 3rd edition; 8vo; xxxii, 128 pages, wood engraved frontispiece, 5 other plates, wood engraved vignettes at beginning of each part of the poem, uncut, original boards, pink paper spine largely defective, but fine, fresh copy, inscribed "From the author to Tho. Grant. 1800" and with loosely inserted letter, 3 pages from Grant to his mother.　David Bickersteth　133-138　1996　£160.00

ASSOCIATION - GRANTHAM

KRUSENSTERN, IEVAN FEDOROVICH　　Voyage Round the World in the Years 1803, 1804, 1805 and 1806, by Order of His Imperial Majesty Alexander the First on Board the Ships Nadeshda and Neva, Under the Comman of Captain A. J. von Krusenstern of the Imperial Navy. London: printed by C. Roworth, for John Murray, 1813. 1st edition in English; 4to; 2 volumes in one, as issued; hand colored frontispiece in each volume, folding map, plate; contemporary half calf, spine gilt ("Newby Hall" lettered in gilt on front cover); fine copy, rare; early armorial bookplate of Grantham. Sabin 38331; Howes K272; Hill p. 167; Lada Mocarski 61-62.　Ximenes 109-172　1996　$8,500.00

ASSOCIATION - BRENT GRATION-MAXFIELD

LESSIUS, LEONARDUS　　Hygiasticon; or, the Right Course of Preserving Life and Health unto Extream old Age... Cambridge: R. Daniel & T. Buck, printers to the University, 1634. 2nd English edition; 24mo. in 12's; mainly Roman letter, woodcut titlepage border, initials and ornaments, 1st blank missing, titlepage lightly discolored and bit frayed on fore edge, 18th century library stamp of Sion College on verso, 3 or 4 wormholes with very little loss, small pieces torn from 2 leaves with no loss of consequence, otherwise good; modern blindstamped calf, gilt spine, inner edge stamped with gilt ex-libris of Brent Gration-Maxfield, a.e.r. STC 15521; not in GM.　A. Sokol　XXV-57　1996　£475.00

SHOWER, JOHN　　Practical Reflections on the Late Earthquakes in Jamaica, England, Sicily, Malta &c. Anno 1692. London: printed for John Salusbury...and Abraham Chandler, 1693. 1st edition; 8vo; titlepage printed within double ruled border, final blank present, pages xvi, 206, (2); modern dark brown stained calf, by C. E. Smart, backstrip with raised bands between gilt rules and pointille rolls, red labels in second and third compartments, gilt flower in centre of remainder, narrow blind roll and fillet border on sides, gilt lettered on turn-in at tail of rear cover "Ex Libris Brent Gration-Maxfield", excellent. Sabin 80740; Wing S3680. Blackwell's　B112-256　1996　£650.00

SYMPSON, SAMUEL　　A New Book of Cyphers, More Compleat and Regular than Any Ever Publish'd. London: for John Bowles & Son, n.d. Reissue of a work first published in 1726; pott 4to; engraved throughout, 100 plates; contemporary sprinkled calf, few very minor marks, but very good, from the library of Brent Gration-Maxfield.　Ash Rare Books　Zenzybyr-88　1996　£245.00

ASSOCIATION - JOSEPH GRATZ

BURNS, ROBERT 1759-1796　　Reliques...Consisting Chiefly of Original Letters, Poems and Critical Observataions on Scottish Songs. Philadelphia: pub. by R. H. Cromek, 1809. 12mo; 20, 294 pages; contemporary tree calf, leather label, slightly scuffed, but very nice. Ink signature of Jo(seph) Gratz, brother of Rebecca. S&S 17127.　M & S Rare Books　60-186　1996　$200.00

ASSOCIATION - JOHN GRAY

ROSSETTI, DANTE GABRIEL 1828-1882　　The Blessed Damozel: a Poem. Vale Press, 1898. One of 210 copies; oblong 16mo; woodcut initials by Charles Ricketts; printed in black and red in Vale type; patterned boards, printed label on spine, nice bright copy; bookplate of Fr. John Gray partially removed.　Bertram Rota　272-481　1996　£200.00

ASSOCIATION - GREAVES

VOLTAIRE, FRANCOIS MARIE AROUET DE 1694-1778　　Memoirs of the Life of Voltaire. London: Robinson, 1784. 1st English translation; 8vo; calf; Greaves ownership in title margin. CBEL II 804.　Rostenberg & Stern　150-33　1996　$175.00

ASSOCIATION - JOSEPH HENRY GREEN

SIMON, JOHN   General Pathology as Conducive to the Establishment of Rational principles for the Diagnosis and Treatment of Disease. Philadelphia: 1852. 1st American edition; 8vo; boards; inscribed to Joseph Henry Green. Osler 3978 (London ed. 1850).   Argosy 810-446 1 1996 $200.00

ASSOCIATION - GREEN-ARMYTAGE

BUTLER, SAMUEL 1835-1902   God the Known and God the Unknown. London: A. C. Fifeld, 1909. Half title; original blue cloth; booklabel and signature of R. N. Green-Armytage. Hoppe 46.   Jarndyce CII-89 1996 £60.00

ASSOCIATION - VIVIEN GREENE

GREENE, GRAHAM 1904-1991   Doctor Fischer of Geneva or the Bomb Party. London: Bodley Head, 1980. 1st edition; crown 8vo; pages 140; original mid green linen backstrip gilt lettered, dust jacket; fine; superb association copy, inscribed by author for his wife Vivien.   Blackwell's B112-142 1996 £700.00

ASSOCIATION - RICHARD GREENHAM

HAYWOOD, ELIZA FOWLER 1693-1756   The Husband. In Answer to The Wife. (with) The Wife. London: for T. Gardner, 1756/56. 1st editions; 8vo; 2 works in one volume, pages (ii), v, (i) ad, 279, (i) ads; pages (iv), half title and title, v, (i) blank, 282, first leaf of contents of second work torn across with loss of lower half of leaf; contemporary calf, red morocco label, spine gilt in compartments, rubbed, gilt faded, occasional neglible spotting in margins, very good; ownership inscription of Richard Greenham.   Simon Finch 24-115 1996 £580.00

ASSOCIATION - GREENHILL

FLATMAN, THOMAS   Poems and Songs. London: printed by S. & B.G. for Benjamin Took & Jonathan Edwin, 1674. 1st edition; 8vo; contemporary sheep, half morocco slipcase; particularly fine copy, complete with two original blanks at beginning (one signed "A"), and two at end. The Greenhill-Borowitz-Slater copy. Wing F1151; Grolier 356; Hayward 131; CBEL II 473.   Ximenes 109-127 1996 $2,500.00

ASSOCIATION - WILLIAM GREENOUGH

STEVENSON, ROGER   Military Instructions for Officers Detached in the Field: Containing a Scheme for Forming a Corps of a Partisan. Philadelphia: R. Aitken, 1775. 1st edition; (8), vii, (1), 232, (4) pages; 12 engraved plates; contemporary sheep, hinges very skilfully restored, other than small piece torn from upper blank corner of one plate, this is a remarkably fine, fresh copy, completely free of foxing and in handsome original binding, signed "Josiah Bartlett's Book 1776"; beneath is are 3 other signatures of later 18th and 19th century members of Bartlett's family; bookplate of William S. Greenough. In attractive cloth clamshell box with leather label. Howes S981; Evans 14475.   Joseph J. Felcone 64-39 1996 $4,000.00

ASSOCIATION - FREDERICK GREENWOOD

HARDY, THOMAS 1840-1928   Tess of the D'Urbervilles. London: James R. Osgood, McIlvaine & Co., 1892. 1st one volume edition, called 'Fifth' edition; original decorated cloth, designed by Charles Ricketts, covers little worn, spine trifle faded, else very good in attractive full morocco solander case (just bit worn); inscribed by author for Frederick Greenwood.   David J. Holmes 52-52 1996 $6,500.00

ASSOCIATION - GREG

BUTLER, SAMUEL 1835-1902   Shakespeare's Sonnets Reconsidered. London: Longmans, Green and Co., 1899. Reprint of original 1609 edition; original green cloth; very good; inscribed presentation copy from author to T. T. Greg, who occupied rooms beneath Butler's at 15 Clifford's Inn Dated Dec. 1st. 1899; Booklabel of Robert P. Greg, later Lord Esher's copy, with bookplate, 2 small ms. corrections in Butler's hand on p. 15. Jarndyce CII-63 1996 £250.00

BUTLER, SAMUEL 1835-1902   The Way of All Flash. London: Grant Richards, 1903. 1500 copies were printed; half title; original red cloth, very slight marking, otherwise very good; pencil inscription for E. W. Greg from T. T. Greg.   Jarndyce CII-77 1996 £350.00

ASSOCIATION - ROBERT HYDE GREG

PITKIN, TIMOTHY   A Statistical View of the Commerce of the United States of America... Hartford: printed by Charles Hosmer, 1816. 1st edition; 8vo; xii, 407, (1), xix, (1) pages, errata on verso of final leaf; contemporary calf, gilt, rather worn, head and foot of spine chipped, joints cracked; 19th century armorial bookplate of Robert Hyde Greg (1795-1875), the economist and politician.   John Drury 82-220 1996 £150.00

ASSOCIATION - W. W. GREG

BRITISH MUSEUM.   Catalogue of the Fifty Manuscripts and Printed Books Bequeathed to the British Museum by Alfred H. Huth. London: printed for the Trustees, 1912. 4to; xvi, 130 pages; frontispiece, 18 plates, facsimiles in text; original red cloth, gilt lettering, rebacked, old backstrip laid down; cloth faded, edges slightly rubbed. W. W. Greg's copy with his signature.   Robert Clark 38-266 1996 £65.00

ASSOCIATION - FRANCIS GREGG

HORATIUS FLACCUS, QUINTUS 65-8 BC   The Works of Horace... London: ptd. for W. Flexney, Mess. Johnson & Co. and T. Caslon, 1767. 1st edition; 8vo; 4 volumes; half title in each volume; contemporary calf, gilt, rebacked, spines gilt, contrasting morocco labels, edges bit rubbed; some foxing, but very good set; early armorial bookplates of Francis Gregg. Mahony & Rizzo 158. CBEL II 591.   Ximenes 108-327 1996 $900.00

ASSOCIATION - GOERGE DE LIGNE GREGORY

A NEW and General Biographical Dictionary... London: T. Osborne, J. Whiston & B. White, 1761-67. 12 volumes, licence leaf in volume 1; contemporary sprinkled calf, brown and green labels, some slight rubbing, handsome set; armorial booklabels of George de Ligne Gregory. Jarndyce 103-109 1996 £450.00

ASSOCIATION - TOM GREGORY

LONDON, JACK 1876-1916   John Barleycorn. New York: Century Co., 1913. 1st edition; 1st printing with one blank leaf following page 343; (6), 3-343 pages, frontispiece, 7 full page illustrations by H. T. Dunn; gilt lettered dark green cloth, contemporary owner's name in ink on inner front cover, upper front corner slightly jammed, overall fine. Laid in is ALS by author to Tom Gregory.   Argonaut Book Shop 113-422 1996 $1,250.00

ASSOCIATION - LOREN GREY

GREY, ZANE 1872-1939   Majesty's Rancho. New York: Harper, 1938. 1st edition; 297 pages; gray cloth lettered in black; fine and clean with pictorial dust jacket, housed in later slipcase; signed by author's son, Loren.   Argonaut Book Shop 113-298 1996 $275.00

ASSOCIATION - ROMER GREY

GREY, ZANE 1872-1939   Desert Gold: A Romance of the Border. London: Nelson, 1926. Small 8vo; dust jacket with few chips; very good. Boldly signed by author, his son's copy (Romer Grey) with his signature. George J. Houle 68-56 1996 $350.00

ASSOCIATION - WILLAIM SCURFIELD GREY

ATKINSON, J. C.   A Glossary of the Cleveland Dialect; Explanatory, Derivative and Critical. London: John Russell Smith, 1868. 1st edition; 4to; 8 pages subscribers' list; original purple cloth, spine faded and slightly worn at head and tail; clean and sound, armorial bookplate of Wm. Scurfield Grey.   Jarndyce 103-61 1996 £95.00

ASSOCIATION - ELIZABETH DE GREYS

DAVENANT, WILLIAM 1606-1668   The Works... London: printed by T. N. for Henry Herringman, 1673. 1st edition; folio; contemporary mottled calf, gilt, spine gilt, some rubbing, completely sound; wholly unrestored binding, text crisp and fresh; inscribed "Mrs. Elizabeth de Greys booke, given her by John Knyvett Esq. ye yeere he was High Sheriff of Norfolke, 1681/2." Wing D320; Greg III 1057-8; CBEL I 1208; Woodward & McManaway 309.   Ximenes 109-97 1996 $2,500.00

ASSOCIATION - HERBERT GRIFFITHS

WYCHERLEY, WILLIAM   The Plain Dealer. London: R. Bentley and M. Magnes, 1677. 3rd edition; 4to; greeen morocco backed marbled boards, some rubbing and chipping, stitch marks in inner margins, publisher's ads on recto of "The Persons" leaf, some browning and soiling, endpaper spotted, few short marginal tears or losses, else nice. The Robert Hoe-Herbert F. Griffiths copy with bookplates; Wing W 3751; Woodward & McManaway 1335; Pforzheimer 1102 (1st ed.).   James Cummins 14-222 1996 $250.00

ASSOCIATION - ROBERT GRISWOLD

HARRING, HARRO   Dolores: a Novel of South America. New York: author: Motevideo: Hernandez; New York: Marrenner, Lockwood, 1846. 4to; 4 parts as issued; front printed wrappers on parts 2-4, browned and stained; extremely rare in original parts; presentation inscription from author to Capt. Robert Griswold. Rostenberg & Stern, Connections 108-9. Rostenberg & Stern   150-20   1996 $875.00

ASSOCIATION - EUSTACE GRUBBE

BOSWELL, JAMES 1740-1795   Carminum Rariorum Macaronicarum Delectus: In Usum Ludorum Apollinarum... Edinburgi: Ex Typographia G. Ramsay, 1813. 8vo; pages 144, 14; blind tooled calf, rebacked. Theodore Martin's copy, with his presentation ALS to Eustace Grubbe.   Peter Murray Hill   185-12   1996   £95.00

ASSOCIATION - WALTER GRUENINGER

CULLEN, COUNTEE   Caroling Dusk: An Anthology of Verse by Negro Poets. New York: Harper, 1927. 1st edition; decorataions by Aaron Douglas; slight scuffing to boards and some chipping to spine label, clean, very good plus copy, lacking dust jacket. Nicely inscribed by editor for Walter Grueninger.   Between the Covers   43-56   1996 $950.00

ASSOCIATION - PEGGY GUGGENHEIM

WHITE, ANTONIA   Frost in May. London: Desmond Harmesworth, 1933. 1st edition; binding soiled and little foxing, an about very good copy, lacking dust jacket; scarce; inscribed by author for Peggy Guggenheim, art patron.   Between the Covers   42-462   1996 $575.00

ASSOCIATION - JAMES GUILD

ROBIN HOOD   Robin Hood's Garland: Being a Complete History of All the Notable and Merry Exploits Performed by Him and His Men on Many Occasions. Kidderminster: printed at the Office of G. Gower, 17--? 12mo; 96 pages light marginal pencil marks, 31 fine woodcuts; original printed self wrappers bound into green calf backed marbled boards, with 2 raised bands, title vertically in gilt along a burgundy leather label on spine, original wrappers soiled and darkened, slightly chipped along front edge, 1 1/2 inch vertical tear along bottom of inner edge affecting 1 word. Armorial bookplate of James Wyllie Guild. Rare.   Blue Mountain SP95-40   1996 $750.00

ASSOCIATION - JOHN GULSON

ADDISON, JOSEPH 1672-1719   The Miscellaneous Works in Verse and Prose... London: for J. and R. Tonson, 1765. 8vo; 4 volumes; frontispiece in volume 1, frontispiece in volume 2, contemporary finely spirnkled tan calf, smooth spines ruled across in gilt, red morocco lettering pieces, black oval numbering pieces, blue sprinkled edges; little rubbing, unobtrusive marks to foot of spine of volumes 3 and 4 where old shelf labels removed, excellent set; ex-Coventry City Libraries with bookplates etc. on front and back pastedowns (no borrowing recorded) and with ink library stamp on blank verso of each title, presented to the library by John Gulson.   Simon Finch   24-1   1996   £200.00

ASSOCIATION - SELINA GUNN

DICTIONARY of Quotations, in Most Frequent Use. London: G. G. & J. Robinson, 1799. 3rd edition; contemporary speckled calf, green label, very good, booklabel; signature of Selina Gunn on title.   Jarndyce 103-105   1996   £85.00

ASSOCIATION - GYLDENSTOLPE

RADCLIFFE, ANN WARD 1764-1823   The Mysteries of Udolpho, a Romance... London: for G. G. and J. Robinson, 1794. 1st edition; large 12mo; 4 volumes, with half titles, but without final blank in volume 2; contemporary Swedish calf, spines with raised bands, pale tan morocco labels, oval black numbering-pieces, extremities little worn, sides rubbed, one or two trivial stains, nice contemporary set. From the library of Swedish Count Nils Gyldenstolpe with his initials and coronet blindstamped on endpapers of 2 volumes, and his large monogram inkstamp on each title, also with later oval lib. inkstamp of C. Fr. Wernher on e.p.'s. Rothschild 1710; Summers p. 434.   Simon Finch 24-193   1996   £950.00

ASSOCIATION - EDWARD HAILSTONE

LE LOYER, PIERRE, SIEUR DE LA BROSSE 1550-1634   A Treatise of Specters or Straunge Sights, Visions and Apparitions, Appearing Sensibly Unto Men. London: by Val S(immes) for Mathew Lownes, 1605. 1st edition in English; 4to; (8), 145, (1) leaves; errata leaf in very skilfll pen facsimile on old paper, title soiled, two or three leaves with early paper reinforcement at gutter; 19th century calf, very nice, tight copy, extensive contemporary marginal notes in hand of one Daniel Hughes; leather bookplate of Edward Hailstone. STC 15448.   Joseph J. Felcone   64-25   1996 $1,200.00

MACAULEY, ELIZABETH WRIGHT   The Wrongs of Her Royal Highness the Princess Olive of Cumberland... Purkess: 1833. 8vo; 26 pages; old marbled boards, rebacked in modern calf gilt; original lavender printed wrappers (worn and soiled) bound in; some browning in places; very scarce. Circular armorial bookplate of Edward Hailstone.   R.F.G. Hollet & Son   78-421   1996   £95.00

ASSOCIATION - JOE HALDEMAN

MC CAULEY, KIRBY   Dark Forces. New York: Viking Press, 1980. 1st edition; fine in dust jacket with very slight tear to front panel, inscribed by Charles L. Grant and Joe Haldeman and dated Nov. 1980.   Bud Schweska   12-454   1996 $135.00

ASSOCIATION - FAIRFAX HALL

SHEPARD, RUPERT   Passing Scene: Eighteen Images of Southern Africa. London: Stourton Press, 1966. One of 200 numbered copies, signed by artist; folio; brightly colored plates; orange buckram, two color pictorial design on upper cover, fine, laid in is a slip bearing signed autograph presentation inscription of Fairfax Hall.   Bertram Rota 272-456   1996   £90.00

ASSOCIATION - MERE HALL

GODWIN, WILLIAM 1756-1836   Life of Geoffrey Chaucer, the Early English Poet... London: by T. Davison for Richard Phillips, 1803. 1st edition; 4to; 2 volumes; pages xxxvi, 489; vii, (i), 642, (32); frontispiece; contemporary green straight grain morocco, smooth spines richly decorated and lettered in gilt, sides with gilt border enclosing central panel of marbled paper, red marbled edges; spines rubbed, sides little stripped; attractive copy in unusual Regency binding. Bookplate of Mere Hall.   Simon Finch   24-94   1996   £575.00

ASSOCIATION - JAMES MOTT HALLOWELL

HALLOWELL, ANNA DAVIS   James and Lucretia Mott. Life and Letters Boston: Houghton Mifflin Co., c. 1884. 1st edition; 8vo; frontispiece with tissue guarad, 5 illustrations; brown cloth, uncut and unopened, fine; inscribed by James Mott Hallowell for Carl Pforzheimer.   James Cummins   14-139   1996 $100.00

ASSOCIATION - WALTER HAMADY

BLACKBURN, PAUL   Two New Poems. Mt. Horeb: Perishable Press, 1969. 1st edition; one of only 10 copies printed in Palatino handmade Shadwell paper "none are for public distribution, but rather are for the poet and printer evenly divided"; oblong 8vo; embossed grey wrappers, very fine, rare. Inscribed by author, although not stated, this copy belonged to Walter Hamady, the printer-publisher.   James S. Jaffe 34-537   1996 $2,750.00

ASSOCIATION - HAMILTON

OSLER, WILLIAM 1849-1919   An Alabama Student and Other Biographical Essays. New York: Oxford University Press, London: Henry Frowde, 1908. 1st edition; 8vo; (iv), 334 pages; frontispiece, illustrations; red cloth; very good; signed by S. Hamilton Jr. Nov. 1908, bookplate of Dr. Elmer Belt.   Jeff Weber 31-29 1996 $175.00

SMITH, CHARLES   Elegiac Sonnets. London: Printed by R. Noble, for T. Cadell, 1792. 6th edition; 12mo; author's first book; 5 engraved plates; contemporary tree calf, gilt, red morocco initial label centered on covers, some rubbing, upper joint cracked; bookplate, initial label for the Duke of Hamilton (Brandon); very attractive.   James Cummins 14-186 1996 $150.00

ASSOCIATION - CHARLES HAMILTON

PIERS PLOWMAN   The Vision and the Creed of Piers Ploughman. London: William Pickering, 1842. 8vo; 2 volumes, pages xlix, (3), 272; (4), (273-) 629, title and folding frontispiece printed in red and black; original cloth, rubbed and little worn at extremities, paper labels (browned); good set; Bookplate of Col. Sir Charles J. Hamilton. Claude Cox 107-201 1996 £85.00

ASSOCIATION - JOAN HANCOCK

BATES, HERBERT ERNEST 1905-1974   Spella Ho: a Novel. London: 1938. 1st edition; presentation inscription from author to Joan Hancock, Joan's own name written alongside a number of town names on endpapers, otherwise very good in scarce and bright dust jacket with wrap around band.   Words Etcetera 94-103 1996 £160.00

ASSOCIATION - G. M. A. HANFMANN

COMSTOCK, MARY   Greek, Etruscan and Roman Bronzes in the Museum of Fine Arts. Greenwich: New York Graphic Society, 1971. 8vo; xxvii, 511 pages, profusely illustrated; original cloth, dust jacket; with signature of G. M. A. Hanfmann.   Archaeologia Luxor-3169 1995 $150.00

ASSOCIATION - JAMES HANLEY

THEROUX, PAUL 1941-   The Mosquito Coast. Boston: Houghton Mifflin, 1982. Fine in dust jacket with slight sunning on spine and small section of lower front panel; presentation copy inscribed by author to James Hanley.   R. A. Gekoski 19-139 1996 £125.00

THEROUX, PAUL 1941-   The Old Patagonian Express. Boston: Houghton Mifflin, 1979. Nice copy in slightly soiled dust jacket; presentation copy from author for James Hanley.   R. A. Gekoski 19-138 1996 £125.00

ASSOCIATION - W. HANNAH

STEVENSON, ROBERT LOUIS BALFOUR 1850-1894   The Best Thing in Edinburgh: an Address... San Francisco: John Howell, 1923. 1st edition; number 48 of 250 copies on handmade paper; linen backed boards with paper label, light overall soiling, end of paper label chipped, otherwise very good; inscribed by John Howell to W. Hannah.   Hermitage SP95-885 1996 $150.00

ASSOCIATION - P. A. HANROTT

GORHAM, GEORGE CORNELIUS   The History and Antiquities of Eynesbury and St. Neot's in Huntingdonshire and of St. Neot's in the County of Cornwall. London: T. Davison for Lackington, etc. 1820-24. 8vo; 2 volumes in 1; (2), xii, (4), 340; (2), clxxxvii pages, engraved frontispiece, 10 plates, wood engravings in text, slightly later half morocco, gilt, top edge gilt. P. A. Hanrott's copy with his note on flyleaf, probably purchased in his sale in 1830 by Frances Richardson Currer.   Marlborough 162-33 1996 £290.00

ASSOCIATION - J. H. HANSON

OMAR KHAYYAM   Rubaiyat of Omar Khayyam. London: Vale Press, 1901. Limited to 310 copies; 8vo; printed in red and black Vale type on handmade paper, pages xxx, (2), frontispiece, borders and initials by Ricketts, faint browning in bottom margin of first opening, otherwise very good; uncommon; original holland backed boards, paper label, uncut; from the library of Will Ransom with his label. Bookplate of J. H. Hanson. Tomkinson 32.   Claude Cox 107-176 1996 £150.00

ASSOCIATION - LUCY HARDCASTLE

BOOTT, FRANCIS   A Letter Addressed to William Pratt, Esq... N.P.: Derby?: 1819. 1st edition; 8vo; recent half calf, very good. Appears to be the dedication copy (for Lucy Hardcastle of Derby) whom Boott married the following year, with pres. inscription, with few ms. corrections.   Ximenes 108-28 1996 $250.00

ASSOCIATION - MARTIN HARDIE

EXAMPLES of San Bernardino of Siena. Gerald Howe, 1926. 8vo; illustrations by Robert Austin; buckram, very nice in slightly marked dust jacket, on prelim blank artist has made a small pen and ink drawing, signed and tipped in his Autograph Letter presenting the book to Martin Hardie.   Bertram Rota 272-61 1996 £70.00

ASSOCIATION - ERNEST HARDING

RAWSON, MRS.   Notes of Eastern Travel: Being Selections from the Diary of a Lady. Manchester: Johnson and Rowson, printed in aid of the Bazaar for the Blackley... 1864. 1st edition; small 4to; (viii), 107 pages, original red cloth, blocked in gilt and blind, fine. inscribed to Ernest C. Harding, from author. Not found in NUC.   James Burmester 29-112 1996 £100.00

ASSOCIATION - GEORGE HARDING

LEWIS, OSCAR   The Big Four. The Story of Huntington, Stanford, Hopkins and Crocker and of the Building of the Central Pacific. New York: Knopf, 1938. 1st edition; 418 pages, plus foreword and index; numerous illustrations; light offsetting to front endpaper, else extremely fine and bright with perfect dust jacket; very scarce, especially in this condition; presentation inscription signed by author for George Harding. Argonaut Book Shop 113-411 1996 $150.00

ASSOCIATION - HARDY

ROTHSCHILD, MIRIAM   Dear Lord Rothschild. Birds, Butterflies and History. London: 1983. 8vo; 426 pages; 18 colored and 152 plain illustrations, 2 family trees and several text figures; cloth; signed on titlepage by Miriam Rothschild and inscribed by her to Alistair and Sylvia Hardy, whose copy it was; inserted is a photo of Ashton Mill. Wheldon & Wesley 207-272 1996 £75.00

ASSOCIATION - ALISTAIR G. HARDY

LANKESTER, E. R.   A Treatise on Zoology. London: 1900-09. 8vo; parts 1, 2, 4, 7 and 9 in 6 volumes; parts 6 and 8 were never issued; original cloth and buckram. Formerly the property of Walter Garstang and Alistair G. Hardy.   Wheldon & Wesley 207-499 1996 £120.00

ASSOCIATION - AUGUSTUS HARE

HOBBES, THOMAS 1588-1679   Decameron Physiologicum; or Ten Dialogues of Natural Philosophy... London: printed by J.C. for W. Crook, 1678. 1st edition; 8vo; pages (viii), 136, (8); folding plate, 3 engravings on letterpress, license leaf before title, small worm hole in bottom margin of last four leaves (ads); contemporary sheep, rebacked, smooth backstrip, divided by black rules, gilt lettered in second compartment, dated at foot, sides with blind border, hinges strengthened, small area of insect damage on front pastedown, generally very good; bookplate of Augustus Hare. Macdonald & Hargreaves 84; Wing 2226.   Blackwell's B112-154 1996 £650.00

ASSOCIATION - CHARLES WILLING HARE

VOLTAIRE, FRANCOIS MARIE AROUET DE 1694-1778   Collection Complete des Oeuvres de Mr. De Voltaire. Geneva: 1768-77. Early collected edition; 4to; 30 volumes; 50 full page engraved portraits and illustrations; contemporary full sheep with raised bands, gilt tooled spine panels, gilt borders, fillets and dentelles, all edges gilt, couple of volumes slightly scuffed, few instances of marginalia in unkown early hand, but very attractive set in well preserved French binding; signature of Charles Willing Hare, bookplate of Jacob Solis Cohen.   Chapel Hill 94-416   1996 $1,800.00

ASSOCIATION - EDWARD HARGITT

SHARPE, RICHARD BOWLDER   Matabele Land and the Victoria Falls, from the Letters and Journals of the Late Frank Oates, F.R.G.S. London: 1882. Original offprint from the book; 8vo; 2 fine hand colored plates, folding hand colored map, grey printed wrappers, signature (bit indistinct) of Edward Hargitt (1835-95, ornithologist).   Maggs Bros. Ltd.   1190-605 1996 £125.00

ASSOCIATION - HARPER

COUES, ELLIOTT   On the Trail of a Spanish Pioneer: The Diary and Itinerary of Francisco Garces. New York: Francis P. Harper, 1900. One of 950 copies; 8 7/8 x 6 1/4 inches; 2 volumes, 18 maps, views and facsimiles; blue cloth, light wear to extremities, scratches to rear cover of volume 2; presentation inscription from publisher Harper and his son Lathrop Harper.   Dawson's Books Shop   528-66   1996 $325.00

ASSOCIATION - ANNE HARRIS

HOLME, C. GEOFFREY   Decorative Art 1930. London: The Studio, 1930. 4to; pages viii, 180, illustrations; cloth; slightly scuffed, spine darkened, else fine; signature of Anne Harris, one of the first professional decorators in Toronto.   Hugh Anson-Cartwright   87-376 1996 $150.00

ASSOCIATION - JIM HARRISON

MORGAN, ROBERT   Zirconia Poems. Northwood Narrows: Lillabulero Press, 1969. 1st edition; pictorial wrappers; poet's first book, fine; with ALS from Russell Banks to Jim Harrison recommending this book. Captain's Bookshelf   38-168   1996 $100.00

ASSOCIATION - HART

WILSON, ANGUS   Laughing Matter. New York: Viking Press, 1967. 1st edition; original binding, head and tail of spine and top corners slightly bumped, spine and cover edges slightly faded,, very good in nicked and slightly creased, rubbed and dusty dust jacket faded at spine, slightly fyraed at head and tail of spine and with short tear in centre of spine; presentation copy from author, inscribed, for Jim and Ruth Hart; loosely inserted photo of a Lignum Vitae planted by Princess Margaret. Ulysses   39-632   1996 £65.00

ASSOCIATION - CHARLES HENRY HART

PAGE, THOMAS NELSON   Two Little Confederates. New York: Charles Scribner's Sons, 1889. 1st edition; 2nd printing with pages 157-8 blank; 8vo; grey pictorial cloth, gilt lettering, bookplate, small unobtrusive inked library stamp on p. 156, aside from only some minor shelf wear, very bright copy; inscribed by author for Mrs. Frederic Taylor, laid in are two TLS's, one to Charles Henry Hart and one to Frederic W. Speirs. BAL 15364.   James Cummins   14-149   1996 $200.00

ASSOCIATION - JAMES HART

AGNER, DWIGHT   The Books of WAD - A Bibliography of the Books Designed by W. A. Dwiggins. Baton Rouge: The Press of Nightowl, 1974. One of approximately 190 numbered copies, printed on 70 pound Curtis Colophon - there were also 16 copies on damped Worthy Hand and Arrows paper; handset in Eric Gill's Monotype Joanna; titlepage and decorations by W. A. Dwiggins; bound by Robert Burlen and Son, cloth backed marbled paper boards, tail of spine and bottom corners slightly bumped, near fine. From the library of James D. Hart.   Ulysses 39-165   1996 £185.00

ASSOCIATION - JAMES HART

THE BENEDICTINES of Stanbrook. Worcester: Stanbrook Abbey Press, 1957. Reprint; hand set in Perpetua type and printed on WSH handmade paper, hand painted initials in gold and 3 colors; parchment wrappers, titlepage very slightly creased and marked (production fault, near fine in bumped slipcase; loosely inserted is the Press's Christmas list for 1959, together with an order form; from the library of James D. Hart. Ulysses   39-552   1996 £65.00

BENNETT, PAUL A.   Bouquet for B. R. New York: Typophiles, 1950. One of 600 copies; reproductions of 7 pages designed by Bruce Rogers, 6 black and white photos; original binding, very good in plain, unprinted tissue dust jacket which is nicked, creased and slightly torn and browned at spine and edges; from the library of James D. Hart, loosely inserted is postcard to him from Tyophiles.   Ulysses   39-506   1996 £55.00

CHAUCER, GEOFFREY 1340-1400   The Booke of the Duchesse... Lexington: Anvil Press, 1954. One of 225 numbered copies; handset and printed by Jacob Hammer, handmade paper, pages unopened; unprinted covers with title label on spine, original binding, top edge slightly dusty, spine browned, endpapers slightly browned and spotted, very good; from the library of James D. Hart.   Ulysses   39-261   1996 £100.00

CLEMENS, SAMUEL LANGHORNE 1835-1910   Wapping Alice... Berkeley: Friends of the Bancroft Library, 1981. 1st edition; specially tipped in is an extra leaf bearing the printed legend "To James D. Hart in appreciation of all your efforts on behalf of Mark Twain project - May 1981" quarter morocco, loosely inserted slip of paper signed by staff of the Mark Twain Project; fine.   Ulysses   39-598   1996 £155.00

DAVIES, H. W.   Devices of the Early Printers - 1457-1560 - Their History and Development... London: Grafton & Co., 1935. 1st edition; numerous black and whtie reproductions of printer's devices; original binding, spine slightly faded, covers slightly marked, head and tail of spine and corners slightly bumped, very good; with pencilled ownership signature of James Hart.   Ulysses   39-483   1996 £95.00

DOWDEN, EDWARD   Robert Southey. New York: Harper & Bros., Publishers, 1880. 1st edition; 197 page study; original binding; top ede dusty, spine slightly faded, head and tail of spine and corners slightly bumped, cover edges slightly rubbed; very good; with bookplate of John Kendrick Bangs on front pastedown; subsequently from the library of James D. Hart who has pencilled at top corner of the recto of the rear free endpaper the name of bookshop he bought the book in, with date & price.   Ulysses   39-157   1996 £55.00

DREYFUS, JOHN   William Caxton and His Quincentenary. San Francisco: Book Club of California, 1976. One of 400 copies, there were also 700 copies for the Typophiles; original binding, one corner slightly bumped, fine, without dust jacket, as issued; presentation copy from author inscribed for James Hart; loosely inserted prospectus for this book, together with first day cover postmarked 12th Nov. 1976, of the William Caxton stamps issued by the British G.P.O.   Ulysses   39-159 1996 £65.00

ELIOT, THOMAS STEARNS 1888-1965   Ezra Pound - His Metric and Poetry. New York: Alfred A. Knopf, 1917, i.e 1918. Only 1000 copies were printed; original binding, spine and cover edges faded, head and tail of spine and corners bumped, covers slightly marked, very good in quarter morocco custom made slipcase, which is faded at spine and slightly faded. Bookplate of James D. Hart.   Ulysses   39-170   1996 £485.00

FARRELL, DAVID   The Stinehours Press - A Bibliographical Checklist of the First Thirty Years. Lunenburg: Meriden-Stinehour Press, 1988. One of 1200 numbered copies; 12 pages of color illustrations; original binding, fine in dust jacket; presentation copy from compiler to James D Hart; loosely inserted ALS from compiler to presentee.   Ulysses 39-564   1996 £75.00

HALL, CARROLL D.   Bierce and the Poe Hoax. San Francisco: Book Club California, 1934. One of 250 numbered copies; quarto; original binding, title label on spine browned, head and tail of spine and corners slightly rubbed, free endpapers browned, covers slightly marked; very good; from the library of James D. Hart.   Ulysses   39-292   1996 £75.00

HITTELL, THEODORE H.   El Triunfo de la Cruz - a Description of the Building by Father Juan Ugarte of the First ship Made in California. San Francisco: 1930. One of 50 copies; titlepage and decorations by Valenti Angelo; loosely inserted woodcut by Angelo, signed and titled by him; boards, front endpapers slightly browned, covers very slightly marked, spine and title label on spine browned; very good. Inscribed by Angelo for James Hart, sometime publisher.   Ulysses   39-14   1996 £175.00

ASSOCIATION - JAMES HART

JAMES, HENRY 1843-1916 The Notebooks of Henry James. London: George Brazillier, Inc., 1955. 1st edition; original binding, top edge dusty, head and tail of spine and bottom edge of upper cover slightly bumped, very good in nicked, chipped and dusty, slightly rubbed and torn dust jacket browned at spine and edges. From the library of James Hart. Ulysses 39-314 1996 £55.00

JUDGES, A. V. The Elizabethan Underworld - a Collection of Tudor and Early Stuart Tracts and Ballads Telling of the Lives and Misdoings of Vagabonds, Thieves, Rogues and Cozeners, and Giving Account of the Operation of the Criminal Law. London: George Routledge & Sons, Ltd., 1930. 1st edition; original binding, top edge slightly marked and dusty, head and tail of spine and corners bumped, covers slightly rubbed and marked, very good. From the library of James Hart. Ulysses 39-329 1996 £75.00

KINDERSLEY, DAVID Mr. Eric Gill - Recollections. San Francisco: Book Club of California, 1967. One of 400 copies; 28 black and white reproductions of Eric Gill's drawings and sculpture; original binding, fine; loosely inserted prospectus for this book and a Christmas card bearing a wood engraving by Eric Gill and printed for Duncan Houx Olmsted by Arlen Philpott, Fairfax in an edition of 250 copies; from the library of James D. Hart. Ulysses 39-230 1996 £65.00

LOWES, JOHN LIVINGSTON The Road ot Xanadu - a Study in the Ways of the Imagination. Boston and New York: Houghton Mifflin, 1927. 1st edition; signed by author; 432 pages, 153 pages of notes; original binding, top edge dusty, covers slightly marked, spine darkened, head and tail of spine and corners slightly bumped and rubbed, very good; presentation copy from Gale Noyes to James D. Hart. Ulysses 39-381 1996 £85.00

MATTHIESSEN, F. O. Translation - an Elizabethan Art. Cambridge: Harvard University Press, 1931. 1st edition; original binding, top edge gilt, head and tail of spine and corners slightly bumped, traces of removal of bookplate on front pastedown, covers slightly marked, cover edges rubbed, very good with pencilled ownership signature of James Hart. Ulysses 39-394 1996 £55.00

MERRYMOUNT PRESS A Selection of Type Ornaments - the Merrymount Press Collection of Daniel Berkeley Updike Now at the Bancroft Library. Berkeley: Bancroft Library Press, University of California, 1984. One of 25 copies; wrappers; fine; from the library of James D. Hart, director of the Bancroft Library. Ulysses 39-407 1996 £125.00

MORRIS, WILLIAM 1834-1896 Under an Elm-Tree; or, Thoughts in the Countryside. Aberdeen: James Leatham, 1891. 1st edition; wrappers, two sheets, folded and stitched to make 16 pages, upper outer panel being titlepage, lower outer panel being the final page of text, on verso of titlepage there is a list of publisher's "Penny Pamphlets', covers dusty, cover edges browned and slightly rubbed and spotted; very good; from the library of James D. Hart. Ulysses 39-418 1996 £155.00

NOYES, ROBERT GALE Ben Jonson on the English Stage 1660-1776. Cambridge: Harvard University Press, 1935. 1st edition; original binding, top edge gilt, endpaper edges slightly browned, covers slightly marked and dusty, very good; presentation copy from author inscribed for James Hart; loosely inserted Christmas card from author, newspaper article on author, programme for a performance of Bartholomew Fair in 1933; Ulysses 39-324 1996 £75.00

PARKINSON, THOMAS Hart Crane and Yvor Winters - Their Literary Correspondence. Berkeley: Los Angeles: & London: University of California Press, 1978. 1st edition; original binding, tail of spine very slightly rubbed, covers very slightly rubbed at extremities in very slightly creased and rubbed dust jacket; dedication copy, inscribed by author for James D. Hart; loosely inserted are clippings of two reviews of the book and an offprint of an article by author on Hart Crane. Ulysses 39-125 1996 £95.00

PARTRIDGE, ERIC The Spectator - the Story of Addison & Steele's Famous Paper. San Francisco: Book Club of California, 1939. One of 455 copies; quarto; cloth backed marbled paper boards; tipped in is an original issue of The Spectator for 12th Dec. 1711 (no. 246); top corners slightly bumped and bruised, near fine; from the collection of James D. Hart. Ulysses 39-459 1996 £250.00

PEPLER, HILARY DOUGLAS CLARK d. 1951 The Hand Press - an Essay Written and Printed by Hand for the Society of Typographic Arts, Chicago... Ditchling: 1934. One of 250 numbered copies, signed by author; hand printed by author and Mark Pepler on a Stanhope Press, Joseph Batchelor & Son handmade paper; wrappers, spine and cover edges browned, cover edges slightly rubbed and creased, tail of spine split, covers slightly marked and dusty, small tear to bottom edges of lower cover; very good; from the library of James D. Hart. Ulysses 39-146 1996 £275.00

ASSOCIATION - JAMES HART

PISSARRO, LUCIEN The Gentle Art - A Collection of Books and Wood Engravings by Lucien Pissarro. Zurich: L'Art Ancien S.A., 1974. One of 350 copies; illustrations in black and white; boards, spine slightly faded, head and tail of spine and top edge of upper cover slightly bumped, very good; loosely inserted is a price list for the exhibits; from the library of James D. Hart. Ulysses 39-466 1996 £65.00

RANSOM, WILL d. 1955 Kelmscott, Doves and Ashendene - the Private Press Credos. New York: The Typophiles, 1952. One of 400 copies for Typophile subscribers and contributors, there were a further 300 copies for the Book Club of California, San Francisco; loosely inserted prospectus for this book and related material; spine slightly faded, head and tail of spine slightly bumped, covers slightly browned; very good; from the library of James D. Hart, loosely inserted is an APS from Humphrey Stone to Hart. Ulysses 39-494 1996 £75.00

ROBERTS, S. C. The Evolution of Cambridge Publishing. Cambridge: Cambridge University Press, 1956. 1st edition; 14 black and white plates; decorated cloth gilt, fine in slightly marked and dusty, price clipped dust jacket browned at spine and edges; loosely inserted publisher's compliments slip; fromt he library of James Hart. Ulysses 39-504 1996 £55.00

SCHORER, MARK Sinclair Lewis - an American Life. New York: McGraw Hill Book Co., 1961. 1st edition; 16 pages of black and white photos; original binding, head and tail of spine slightly bumped, near fine in nicked and slightly rubbed, marked and creased dust jacket slightly darkened at spine and edges; presentation copy inscribed by author for James D. Hart. Ulysses 39-374 1996 £55.00

SOBY, JAMES THRALL Tchelitchew - Paintings - Drawings. New York: Museum of Modern Art, 1942. 1st edition; 2 color plates and 72 black and white reproductions; wrappers, top edge slightly dusty, spine faded, covers slightly marked, very good; from the library of James Hart. Ulysses 39-584 1996 £55.00

SPARLING, H. HALLIDAY The Kelmsoctt Press and William Morris Master-Craftsman. London: Macmillan and Co., 1924. 1st edition; 16 black and white plates; linen backed boards, top edge dusty, covers slightly marked, spine browned, head and tail of spine and corners slightly bumped, pastedown edges browned, some page edges nicked, very good. From the library of James Hart. Ulysses 39-334 1996 £185.00

SPENDER, STEPHEN 1909- The Generous Days. Boston: David R. Godine, 1969. One of 250 numbered copies, cloth backed marbled paper boards, bottom corners slightly bumped, near fine; presentation copy, signed and inscribed by author "(printer's copy) Stephen Spender"; inscribed by author for Jim and Ruth Hart. Loosely inserted are two newspaper cuttings and top panel of envelope in which this book had been posted from author to Hart. Ulysses 39-550 1996 £100.00

SPENDER, STEPHEN 1909- Recent Poems. London: Anvil Press Poetry, 1978. One of 400 numbered copies, signed by author; original binding, spine faded, bottom corner of upper cover slightly creased, very good; presentation copy inscribed by author for James Hart. Ulysses 39-551 1996 £75.00

STEIN, GERTRUDE 1874-1946 What Are Masterpieces. Los Angeles: Conference Press, 1940. 1st edition; 2 full page line drawings by Francis Picabia; original binding, top edge dusty, endpapers partially browned, very good in nicked, rubbed, faded and dusty, slightly marked dust jacket; loosely inserted prospectus for this book, folded twice; from the library of James D. Hart. Ulysses 39-556 1996 £125.00

STEVENS, WALLACE 1879-1955 A Primitive Like an Orb - a Poem. New York: Gotham Book Mart, 1948. One of 500 copies; text pages on Etruria paper, 4 drawings by Kurt Seligmann, on Zebu paper; wrappers, spine and cover edges browned, covers slightly marked, bottom corner of upper cover creased and slightly torn, very good; from the library of James D. Hart. Ulysses 39-562 1996 £125.00

WHICHER, GEORGE F. Alas All's Vanity or a leaf from the First American Edition of Several Poems by Anne Bradstreet Printed at Boston anno 1678. New York: Collector's Bookshop, 1942. One of 105 numbered copies; page 219 is tipped in facing page 8, black and white reproductions of titlepages of the first English and 1st American editions; original binding, tail of spine slightly bumped, very good in plain unprinted tissue dust jacket, which is torn, chipped and creased, as well as browned at spine and edges slightly torn; from the library of James D. Hart. Ulysses 39-64 1996 £155.00

ASSOCIATION - JAMES HART

WHITMAN, WALT 1819-1892   New York Dissected - a Sheaf of Recently Discovered Newspaper Articles by the Author of Leaves of Grass. London: Rufus Rockwell Wilson, 1936. One of 750 numbered copies; 8 black and white plates; original binding, top edge dusty, spine slightly faded, one corner slightly bumped, pastedowns browned, very good; from the library of James Hart.   Ulysses 39-624 1996 £65.00

WILSON, ANGUS   As If by Magic. London: Martin Secker & Warburg Ltd., 1973. 1st edition; original binding, head and tail of spine and top corners bumped, upper cover slightly marked, very good in nicked and slightly creased, rubbed, dusty dust jacket darkened at spine and edges; presentation copy from author for Jim and Ruth Hart, inscribed in addition, by Tony Garrett who took photo of author on dust jacket. Ulysses 39-633 1996 £75.00

WILSON, EDMUND 1895-1972   The Boys in the Back Room. San Francisco: Colt Press, 1941. One of 1500 copies; cloth jacket decorated paper boards, top edge slightly dusty, spine and cover edges slightly browned, bottom corners slightly bumped, one corner also slightly bruised, covers slightly marked and spotted, top edge of lower cover browned, very good, no dust jacket; from the library of James D. Hart. Ulysses 39-634 1996 £75.00

YEATS, JACK BUTLER 1871-1957   A Little Book of Drawings. Dublin: Cuala Press, 1971. One of 1000 copies; (of which 200 were hand colored); titlepage drawing, 1 headpiece and 9 full page drawings by artist, printed on Irish paper from original blocks, wrappers; near fine; from the library of James D. Hart.   Ulysses 39-663 1996 £55.00

ASSOCIATION - GILFRID WILLIAM HARTLEY

WALLACE, H. F.   British Deer Heads. 1913. Limited to 600 copies; 4to; illustrations; original white buckram, lightly soiled/browned as usual; bookplate of Gilfrid William Hartley.   David Grayling J95Biggame-328 1996 £150.00

ASSOCIATION - GORDON CECIL HARTLEY

CARLYLE, THOMAS 1795-1881   Sartor Resartus; the Life and Opinions of Herr Teufelsdrockh. London: Saunders and Otley, 1838. 1st English published edition; contemporary morocco or pebble grained blue-green cloth lettered only on spine and doesn't match any of the binding variants noted by Tarr A5.4, either a trial, or more likely, a remainder binding; small chip or erosion at heel of spine, possibly recased as endpapers seem more recent, text doesn't seem cropped, though, and is relatively clean, few scattered fingermarks and stray foxy stains to the contrary, front hinge looks shaken, but feels okay; ownership signatures of Gordon Cecil Hartley (1923) and one other. Scarce.   Magnum Opus 44-23 1996 $250.00

ASSOCIATION - HASTINGS

JAMIESON, JOHN   An Etymological Dictionary of the Scottish Language; in Which the Words are Explained In their Different Senses... Edinburgh: Archibald Constable 1818. 8vo; pages x, unpaginated; 4; contemporary vellum, gilt, flyleaves and half title lightly spotted; armorial bookplate of Hon. Marchioness of Hastings.   R.F.G. Hollett 76-136 1996 £75.00

ASSOCIATION - CARL HAVERLIN

HAMILTON, IAIN   Variations on an Original Theme for Strings. Op. 1. London: Schott, 1953. 1st edition; 8vo; 38 pages; stiff grey wrappers; very good; miniature score, signed and inscribed on titlepage to noted author and radio broadcaster Carl Haverlin.   George J. Houle 68-60 1996 $200.00

HOVHANESS, ALAN   The Burning House: Opus 185. New York: C. F. Peters, 1960. Manuscript facsimile; 4to; black cloth over stiff brown wrappers, very good; dedication copy, the copy of dedicatee Carl Haverlin; with TLS from Walter Hinrichsen to Haverlin. Extra ms. pages laid in loose.   George J. Houle 68-68 1996 $850.00

HOVHANESS, ALAN   Magnificat for Soli, Chorus and Ochestra. New York: C. F. Peters, 1961. 1st edition; 4th printing; small 4to; stiff light green wrappers, very good; signed and inscribed by author for Carl Haverlin.   George J. Houle 68-69 1996 $295.00

ASSOCIATION - CARL HAVERLIN

KAY, ULYSSES   Symphony. N.P.: n.p., 1967. Manuscript facsimile; small folio; stiff black wrappers, paper label on upper cover, spiral bound; very good; dedication copy, the copy of Carl Haverlin, inscribed to Haverlin by author.   George J. Houle 68-75 1996 $750.00

PINKHAM, DANIEL   Symphony No. 1 for Orchestra. New York: Peters 1961. 1st edition; small 4to; 72 pages; stiff cream wrappers, very good; publisher's complimentary copy (stamped on upper cover); signed and inscribed on titlepage by Pinkham to dedicatee Carl Haverlin.   George J. Houle 68-116 1996 $375.00

ASSOCIATION - NATHANIEL HAWTHORNE

RICHTER, J.   Flower, Fruit and Thorn Pieces. Leipzig: Tauchnitz, 1871 1st edition thus (?); 2 volumes bound in 1; original binding, front hinge cracked, old tape repair; good; both titlepages signed by Nathaniel Hawthorne, with addditional note 'from his Wife/Jan. 5th, 1874/Dresden"; f.f.e.p. also signed by Hawthorne.   Charles Agvent 4-630 1996 $150.00

ASSOCIATION - A. L. HAYWARD

HEWETT, SARAH   The Peasant Speech of Devon with Other Matters Connected Therewith. London: Elliot Stock, 1892. Half title; uncut in original blue cloth, dulled; with signature of A. L. Hayward and some ms. additions in pencil.   Jarndyce 103-66 1996 £55.00

ASSOCIATION - HEATH

HARTE, WALTER 1709-1774   The History of the Life of Gustavus Adolphus, King of Sweden, Surnamed the Great. London: J. Hinton, 1767 2nd edition; 8vo; 2 volumes; pages (ii), xxxiv, 328; (iv), 385, (1), (60), (54); frontispiece to volume i, 3 folding plans, 2 with tipped in explanatory leaf, folding diagram, some creasing to few fore-edges in volume i; contemporary tan calf, backstrips raised bands between double gilt rules, red title label in second compartment, volume number lettered direct in third, darkened, blind roll on board edges, endpapers stained by turn-ins, contemporary; very good; contemporary bookplate of Nic. Heath U.C. Oxon.   Blackwell's B112-147 1996 £115.00

ASSOCIATION - HEBER

MIDDLETON, THOMAS   A Tragi-Coomodie, called The Witch... London privately printed by John Nichols for Isaac Reed, 1778. 1st edition; 8vo; pages 111, (i) colophon, early MS not on blank facing title; full red crushed morocco, spine richly gilt between raised bands, sides ruled in gilt with a french fillet, gilt inner dentelles, all edges gilt, by Sangorski & Sutcliffe; fine copy; the Heber - Chalmers - Holgate - Bridgewater - Huntington - Clawson - Spiegelberg copy, with most bookplates; Simon Finch 24-168 1996 £1,000.00

ASSOCIATION - ARTHUR HELPS

MILL, JOHN STUART 1806-1873   Essays on Some Unsettled Questions of Political Economy. London: John W. Parker, 1844. 1st edition; 8vo; vi, (ii), 164, 4 pages, complete with half title, 2 final ad leaves; cancelled bookplate of Queen's College, Cambridge on verso of title; original cloth backed boards with paper spine label, bit worn, dust soiled, else very good. Sir Arthur Helps' copy with his signature. Einaudi 3899; Goldsmith 33591; Kress C6398. MacMinn et al p. 57.   John Drury 82-183 1996 £700.00

ASSOCIATION - MARY HENDRIE

LAMB, CHARLES 1775-1834   Tales from Shakespeare. London: T. C. and E. C. Jack/Toronto: Morgan and Co., 1905. 8vo; pages xii, 324; frontispiece, 20 color paltes by N. M. Price; decorated endpapers and gilt and blind stamped covers, covers slightly scuffed, else very good; signed by artist on half title, with ALS from artist on Carlton Studio letterhead to Mary M. Hendrie of Hamilton.   Hugh Anson-Cartwright 87-354 1996 $200.00

ASSOCIATION - HENRY IV, KING OF FRANCE

HIERONYMUS, SAINT   Epistolae Selectae. Paris: Nivel, 1602. 12mo; 417ff. num., 48 ff. n.n.; contemporary brown calf, covers gilt with triple outer rule and seme of fleur-de-lys, corners with crowned H and laurel wreath, flat spine gilt in similar fashion with central Maltese cross, all edges gilt, later endpapers, gilt armos of Henry IV, King of France, corners and covers worn and rubbed, Henry IV bindings are of some rarity in commerce.   Marlborough 160-19 1996 £2,100.00

ASSOCIATION - BARBARA HEPWORTH

BROWSE, LILLIAN   Barbara Hepworth - Sculptress. London: pub. for the Shenval Press by Faber & Faber, Ltd., 1946. 1st edition; 50 black and white plates; original binding, top edge dusty, head and tail of spine, corners and cover edges slightly bumped, spine and cover edges darkened, covers slightly marked and bowed, page edges slightly browned, good only, no dust jacket. Presentation copy from artist to E. H. Ramsden and Margot Eates, inscribed by her.   Ulysses 39-286 1996 £175.00

ASSOCIATION - RICARDO HEREDIA

PEZZI, LORENZO   Vinea Domini. Cum Brevi Descriptione Sacramentorum et Paradisi, Limbi Purgatorij, Atque Inferni a Catechismo Catholicisque Patribus Excerpta. Venice: Girolamo Porro, 1588. 1st edition; Porro issue, with large plate partly unshaded; portrait in second state; 8vo; 12ff., n.n., pages 1-186, engraved titlepage, portrait, double page plate, 12 large engraved illustrations; ruled in mauve throughout; brown mor. over stiff pasteboards, lacks two pairs of ties, sides & spine richly gilt, border of leafy tendrils issuing from corners, centre dec. with 6 rows each of five oval frames outlined by leafy tendrils, each frame containing 1 of 4 monograms, flat spine with continuous ornament of leafy tendrils, edges plain gilt, rebacked with old spine laid down and very skilfully restored, new pastedowns and endleaves; a Parisian binding of c. 1590-1600; the copy of G. Garcia sale Paris 27 April 1868, lot 118; the copy of Ricardo Heredia, the poet, his sale, Paris 22 May 1891, lot 165 with illustration in sale catalog, the copy of Lord Amherst of Hackney, sale Sotheby's 24 March 1909 lot 679. It was suggested in the Heredia cat. that the initials on binding indicate joint ownership of Francois de Coligny, & his wife Marguerite d'Ailly;   Marlborough 160-9 1996 £6,800.00

ASSOCIATION - JOSEPH HERGESHEIMER

BEERBOHM, MAX 1872-1956   And Even Now. London: Heinemann, 1920. 1st edition; 8vo; green cloth with paper spine label, very good or better; Joseph Hergesheimer's copy with his name and address stamped in gilt on lower right hand corner of front cover.   Antic Hay 101-149 1996 $125.00

ASSOCIATION - WILLIAM HERICK

OVIDIUS NASO, PUBLIUS 43 BC - AD 17   Publii Ovidii Nasonis Opera Omnia. Amsterdam: Changuion, 1727. 4to; 4 volumes; pages (24), 863; 1102, (4); 900; 263, (144), 582, engraved plates, vignettes; title in red and black, foxed; full red straight grained morocco in the Syston Park style, all edges gilt; engraved ex-libris of William Herick. Fine copy. Dibdin II 268-9. Brunet IV 273.   Family Album Tillers-462 1995 $1,400.00

ASSOCIATION - MELVIN HERSHKOWITZ

OSLER, WILLIAM 1849-1919   Lectures on Diagnosis of Abdominal Tumors. New York: D. Appleton, 1898. Reprinted from NY Medical Journal 1894; 8vo; (6), 192, ads (dated April 1899), (2), 8 pages; 43 illustrations; dark green cloth, front inner hinge split, back starting, spine ends frayed, rather ugly label pasted over early signature on front flyleaf, title leaf loose; good; signature of Melvin Hershkowitz.   Jeff Weber 31-54 1996 $150.00

ASSOCIATION - HERSHOLT

EVERGREEN Tales. New York: 1949. One of 2500 numbered copies; quarto; 15 volumes; lavishly illustrated in color; glassine wrapper to each volume, in five slipcases, one of which has a chip; very fine; inscribed by editor, Jean Hersholt.   Bromer Booksellers 90-111 1996 $500.00

ASSOCIATION - GERTA HERZ

MAUPASSANT, GUY DE 1850-1893   Claire de Lune. Leipzig: privately printed for Erik-Ernst Schwabach, 1916. Number 7 of 7 copies; numbered in the press, this 'reserve pour M. Schwabach'; small 4to; full red morocco, gilt, backstrip repaired and darkened and sides somewhat sprung, but internally nice, slightly foxed; presentation from Schwabach presenting this to Gerta Herz, with Schwabach's bookplate.   Bertram Rota 272-130 1996 £110.00

ASSOCIATION - MAURICE HEWLETT

HUDSON, WILLIAM HENRY 1841-1922   Far Away and Long Ago: a History of My Early Life. London: J. M. Dent, 1918. 1st edition; 8vo; decorative green cloth, some wear to ends of spine and edges; bookplate of English author, Maurice Hewlett.   Antic Hay 101-852 1996 $135.00

ASSOCIATION - ANDREW HICHENS

READE, CHARLES 1814-1884   White Lies. London: Trubner & Co., 1857. 1st English edition; 8vo; 3 volumes; contemporary half calf, brown and black morocco labels on gilt spines, marbled boards, some rubbing and minor discoloration, some knocking of a few corners; bookplates of Andrew K. Hichens, dated 1888, with his small initial blindstamp on titles, some spotting at front and back, else quite clean, pleasant copies. Parrish p. 197; not in Sadleir or Wolff.   James Cummins 14-163 1996 $425.00

ASSOCIATION - MARY WORDSWORTH HIGGINBOTHAM

CALVERLEY, WILLIAM SLATER   Notes On the Early Sculptured Crosses, Shrines and Monuments in the Present Diocese of Carlisle. Kendal: T. Wilson, 1899. 8vo; pages xviii, 319, portrait, numerous plates and illustrations; original brown cloth, gilt; scarce; labe reads "This book belonged to William Paton Ker, All Souls College, Oxford and in memory of him was given to Mary Wordsworth Higginbotham Dec. 1923."   R.F.G. Hollett & Son 78-12 1996 £95.00

ASSOCIATION - CHESTER HIGGINS

COOMBS, ORDE   Drums of a Life: a Photographic Essay on the Black Man in America. Garden City: Anchor/Doubleday, 1974. 1st edition; photos by Chester Higgins; perfect bound wrappers as issued, couple of mild blemishes on front wrapper and little rubbing at extremities, thus very good; very nicely inscribed by the photographer.   Between the Covers 43-458 1996 $100.00

ASSOCIATION - HIGGINSON

LEAHY, JOHN   The Art of Swimming in the Eton Style. Nottingham: Shepherd Bros., 1875. frontispiece, folding plate; original mauve cloth, slightly faded, very good; inscribed presentation copy from author to Colonel Higginson.   Jarndyce 103-522 1996 £50.00

ASSOCIATION - G. F. HILDER

BUTLER, SAMUEL 1835-1902   Gavottes, Minuets, Fugues and Other Short Pieces for the Piano by Samuel Butler. London: and New York: Novello, Ewer and Co., 1885. Original blue-grey mottled paper wrappers, as issued, backstrip worn, otherwise good. Signed presentation from Henry Festing Jones to G. F. Hilder. Hoppe 19.   Jarndyce CII-40 1996 £150.00

BUTLER, SAMUEL 1835-1902   Narcissus. London: Weekes and Co., 1888. Without wrappers mentioned by Hoppe; loosely inserted is an ALS from Festing Jones (presumably to G. F. Hilder). Signed presentation from Jones to Hilder; Hoppe 22.   Jarndyce CII-49 1996 £120.00

BUTLER, SAMUEL 1835-1902   Ulysses: a Dramatic Oratorio in Vocal Score... London: Weekes and Co., 1904. Original light brown paper wrappers slightly faded, otherwise very good, signed presentation from Festing Jones to G. F. Hilder. Hoppe 45.   Jarndyce CII-88 1996 £110.00

ASSOCIATION - P. HILDEW

COWPER, HENRY SWAINSON   Hawkshead. London: Bemrose & Sons, 1899. 1st edition; large 8vo; pages xvi, 580; 2 colored folding maps, 32 illustrations; original buckram gilt, little rubbed, spine and edges rather faded; joints strengthened, but very good, sound copy; ALS from P. Hildew loosely inserted.   R.F.G. Hollett & Son 78-833 1996 £195.00

ASSOCIATION - HILL

KEYNES, JOHN MAYNARD, 1ST BARON 1883-1946   Indian Currency and Finance. London: Macmillan, 1913. 1st edition; original rust brown cloth, shelf number on spine, minor wear to spine ends, near fine; presentation copy from author to his sister and her husband M.N. and A. V. Hill, Keynes presentation copies of this significance are extremely scarce.   19th Century Shop 39- 1996 $7,500.00

ASSOCIATION - MAURICE HILL

GRIMBLE, A.   More Leaves from My Game Book. 1917. Limited to 250 copies; illustrations; original half vellum, top of spine slightly frayed, corners lightly rubbed; contents excellent; inscribed by author to Maurice Hill.   David Grayling J95Biggame-260 1996 £80.00

ASSOCIATION - HILLSBOROUGH

GALLOWAY, JOSEPH   A Reply to the Observations of Lieut. Gen Sir William Howe, on a Pamphlet Entitled Letters to a Nobleman (On the Conduct of the War in the Middle Colonies). London: printed for G. Wilkie, 1780. 1st edition; 8vo; half title, 2 pages of ads at end, 149 pages; disbound; presentation inscription from author for the Earl of Hillsborough.   Anthony Laywood 108-66 1996 £235.00

ASSOCIATION - C. HINES

RICH, CHARLES H.   Specimens of the Art of Ornamental Turning, In Eccentric and Concentric Patterns... Southampton: E. Skelton, c. 1825. 2nd edition; 4to; half title, title, pages (iii), iv-v (vi), (7), 8-33 (34), 6 engraved plates, 4 folding; boards, uncut, somewhat worn and spotted; inscription, C. Hines, Norwich 1841 on front pastedown. Very rare. Maggs Bros. Ltd. 1190-650 1996 £420.00

ASSOCIATION - RALPH HINMAN

STEPHENS, ANN S.   The Portland Sketch Book. Portland: Colman and Chisholm, 1836. 1st edition; engraved title; original binding, some loss of cloth along spine edges, light to moderate foxing, name on pastedown scratched out; inscribed twice by Stephens in 1840 to R. Ralph Hinman, in addition the author has changed two words in one of her works. Charles Agvent 4-1026 1996 $350.00

ASSOCIATION - WALTER HINRICHSEN

HOVHANESS, ALAN   The Burning House: Opus 185. New York: C. F. Peters, 1960. Manuscript facsimile; 4to; black cloth over stiff brown wrappers, very good; dedication copy, the copy of dedicatee Carl Haverlin; with TLS from Walter Hinrichsen to Haverlin. Extra ms. pages laid in loose.   George J. Houle 68-68 1996 $850.00

ASSOCIATION - RENATE HIRSCH

FITZWILLIAM MUSEUM   Catalouge. An Exhibition of Printing at the Fitzwilliam Museum, 6 May to 23 June 1940. Cambridge: 1940. Blue quarter morocco, marbled boards, original wrappers with Reynolds Stone's red insignia on upper cover bound in, bound for Schuster by his daughter Renate Hirsch, wife of Paul, with ink inscription "Bound for Papa, Christmas 1940, Renate Hirsch". Bookplate of Renate Schuster. Maggs Bros. Ltd. 1191-194 1996 £140.00

ASSOCIATION - HIRSEL

SIEMIENOWICZ, CASIMIR   Artis Magnae Artilleriae. Amsterdam: J. Jansson, 1650. 1st edition; tall 4to; (16), 284, (4) pages, complete with half title, engraved titlepage, 22 full page copperplate engravings, 1 double page depicting 229 figures; modern panelled calf, morocco spine label, occasional marginal notes in contemporary hand, extreme outer edges of first four leaves strengthened, some marginal browning, particularly to the last few leaves; with shelfmark and engraved armorial bookplate of the Hirsel Library; very good copy. Graesse VI 401; Partington Hist. of Greek fire & Gunpowder p. 168.   Edwin V. Glaser 121-286 1996 $3,800.00

ASSOCIATION - HENRY RUSSELL HITCHCOCK

MADDOX, WILLES   Views of Landsdown Tower, Bath... London: Edmund English and others, 1844. 1st edition; folio; (vi), 10 pages; 12 plates; contemporary half black morocco, satin covers, some cover wear, tips repaired, still respectable copy, scarce; Henry Russell Hitchcock's copy.   Bookpress 75-86 1996 $4,250.00

ASSOCIATION - HOAR

EMERSON, RALPH WALDO 1803-1882   Representative Men. Boston: Phillips, Sampson, 1850. 1st edition; 1st printing, 1st binding; original black cloth, gilt, fine, front free endpaper neatly excised and brief note pasted in forwarding the book signed by Judge E. R. Hoar. BAL 5219. Mac Donnell 12-38 1996 $450.00

ASSOCIATION - GEOFFREY HOBSON

QUARTICH, BERNARD   A Catalogue of Illuminated and Other Manuscripts Together with Some Works on Palaeography. London: Bernard Quaritch, 1931. 4to; color frontispiece, 65 plates; original boards extremities slightly worn, ownership inscription of Lord Kenyon, few annotations in pencil, copy of letter to Maggs offering 3 items for sale, with their descriptions, bill of sale of 3 items to Bernard Quaritch from Kenyon and letter from Geoffrey Hobson to Kenyon about a ms. sold at Sothebys in 1913 inserted loose.   Maggs Bros. Ltd. 1191-35 1996 £65.00

ASSOCIATION - SANDRA HOCHMAN

LOWELL, ROBERT 1917-1977   For the Union Dead. New York: Farrar, Straus & Giroux, 1964. 1st edition; 8vo; green cloth, dust jacket, custom made folding box; front cover slightly rubbed along bottom edge, otherwise a fine copy in slightly dust soiled jacket with small closed tear; presentation inscribed by author to his lover, poet Sandra Hochman.   James S. Jaffe 34-429 1996 $1,250.00

ASSOCIATION - HODDER

BLACKSTONE, WILLIAM 1723-1780   An Analysis of the Laws of England. Oxford: printed at the Clarendon Press, 1762. 5th edition; 8vo; pages lxxvii, (7), 189, (15); contemporary calf, label supplied, nice, fresh copy; contemporary signature of William Hodder.   James Fenning 133-25 1996 £115.00

BLACKSTONE, WILLIAM 1723-1780   Commentaries on the Laws of England. Dublin: printed for John Exshaw, 1766-67-69-70. 1st Irish edition 8vo; 4 volumes, 2 folding engraved plates, pages (4), iii, (4), 473; (8), 520, xix; (8), 455, xxvii; (60, 436, vii, (46), with half title to volume one (none others called for); contemporary calf, labels supplied, very good to nice. Contemporary signature of William Hodder.   James Fenning 133-26 1996 £1,250.00

FOSTER, MICHAEL   A Report of Some Proceedings on the Commission for the Trial of the Rebels in the Year 1746 in the County of Surry... London: printed for E. and R. Brooke, 1792. 3rd edition; royal 8vo; pages xxxvi, 441, (19); contemporary calf, with label, binding rubbed and worn, but sound and strong, internally fine; with Hodder bookplate. Pargellis & Medley 630.   James Fenning 133-114 1996 £125.00

JONES, WILLIAM   An Essay on the Law of Bailments. London: 1781. 1st edition; 8vo; pages (4), 130, (2), with half title and errata; contemporary calf, label, gilt, slight wear at corners, but binding strong and otherwise, nice, fresh copy; with W. H. M. Hodder bookplate. James Fenning 133-185 1996 £350.00

ASSOCIATION - HODDER

WRIGHT, MARTIN   Introduction to the Law of Tenures. London: 1768. 3rd edition; royal 8vo; pages iv, 133, 135-222 (3 blank), (7 appendix); contemporary calf, label, worn at corners, but strong, few openings little dusty, but large, very good copy on thick paper, with Hodder bookplate. James Fenning 133-375 1996 £95.00

ASSOCIATION - EMILY HODGEKINSON

TENNYSON, ALFRED TENNYSON, 1ST BARON 1809-1892   Maud, and Other Poems. London: Edward Moxon, 1855. 1st edition; 8vo; original green cloth, covers stamped in blind, spine ruled in blind, lettered in gilt, some light rubbing, cream endpapers (offsetting from bookplates, one removed), 8 pages publisher's ads dated July 1855 at front, single leaf of author's ads at back, very nice in green morocco backed slipcase; with leather bookplate of Richard Montgomery Gilchrist Potter at front and signature of Emily Hodgekinson. Ashley vii 118; Hayward 248. Tinker 2080.   James Cummins 14-206 1996 $150.00

ASSOCIATION - JOHN HODGSON

CURLE, RICHARD   The Personality of Joseph Conrad. London: privately printed, 1925. One of 100 copies; wrappers, titlepage and edges slightly spotted, slightly creased; very good; presentation copy from author inscribed for John Hodgson.   Ulysses 39-122 1996 £135.00

ASSOCIATION - HOE

DOBSON, AUSTIN 1840-1921   Proverbs in Porcelain: to Which is Added "Au Revoir" a Dramatic Vignette. London: Kegan Paul, Trench, Trubner & Co., 1895. Large paper edition of 175 numbered copies for distribution in England, another 75 copies - in a different binding - were prepared for America; quarto; 25 illustrations by Bernard Partridge; white cloth, good, binding somewhat worn and browned; ALS from Dobson tipped to front endpaper to Mr. Hoe.   Antic Hay 101-453 1996 $125.00

ASSOCIATION - ROBERT HOE

CATHOLIC CHURCH. LITURGY & RITUAL. OFFICE   Officium B. Mariae Virginis, Nuper Reformatum... Antwerp: Ex Architypographia Plantiniana, 1731. 8vo; title in red and black with engraved vignette, 21 f., 741 pages, 2 ff. index, 16 engraved plates; contemporary crimson morocco covers gilt with five fold outer border, central panel with swags, arabesque corner-pieces and central lozenge w/similar tools filled with star, flower and other small tool decoration, spine gilt in 6 panels, raised bands, gilt, panels with stars and arabesques, all edges gilt and gauffered, marbled endpapers, corners little soft, some aging of paper, attractive and striking Low Countries binding - having some affinity with H. Davis Gift II 311 and Culot, Quatre Siecles de Reliure en Belgique 1500-1900 no. 54; with contemporary illegible signature, later in the library of Robert Hoe with his label.   Marlborough 160-50 1996 £1,200.00

FOURNIER, PIERRE SIMON 1712-1768   Manuel Typographique. Paris: Fournier, 1764-66. 8vo; 2 volumes, 2 frontispieces, portrait of Fournier, 21 folding and double page plates; with half title (usually missing) in volume 1; full brown morocco, gilt edges, detnelle, bound by A. Motte; Robert Hoe bookticket in each volume. Bigmore & Wyman I 228; Updike Printing Types I 260 ff; Brunet II 1359.   Rostenberg & Stern 150-128 1996 $8,500.00

SILLAR, DAVID   Poems. Kilmarnock: by John Wilson, 1789. 1st edition; 8vo; 247 pages; printed on blueish paper; fine binding of full green straight grain morocco, sides with triple gilt rules, spine lettered in gilt, double gilt rules, purple coated endpapers, top edge gilt, others uncut; protected in modern green morocco backed folding case; the Hoe copy with Robert Hoe's leather booklabel, later label of Herschel V. Jones. Egerer 14; Johnson Provincial Poetry 832.   Simon Finch 24-211 1996 £1,000.00

SOUTHERNE, THOMAS   The Maids Last Prayer: or, Any, Rather Than Fail. London: R. Bentley and J. Tonson, 1693. 1st edition; issue with 'upon' on page I line 3; 4to; half calf, marbled boards, joints rubbed, text browned; the Robert Hoe copy with his bookplate, contemporary signature of "M. Adye" on title. Wing S4760; W&M 1166; Pforzheimer 958.   James Cummins 14-191 1995 $300.00

TATE, NAHUM   A Duke and No Duke. London: printed for Henry Bonwicke, 1685. 1st edition; 4to; 5 pages printed music at back, careful repair to first and final leaves, running headline of Dedication trimmed, half straight grained red morocco, marbled boards, some light rubbing, some light browning or offsetting, else very nice; Robert Hoe copy with bookplate. W&M 1196.   James Cummins 14-204 1996 $300.00

ASSOCIATION - ROBERT HOE

WYCHERLEY, WILLIAM   The Plain Dealer. London: R. Bentley and M. Magnes, 1677. 3rd edition; 4to; greeen morocco backed marbled boards, some rubbing and chipping, stitch marks in inner margins, publisher's ads on recto of "The Persons" leaf, some browning and soiling, endpaper spotted, few short marginal tears or losses, else nice. The Robert Hoe-Herbert F. Griffiths copy with bookplates; Wing W 3751; Woodward & McManaway 1335; Pforzheimer 1102 (1st ed.).   James Cummins 14-222 1996 $250.00

ASSOCIATION - CHARLES BEECHER HOGAN

AUSTEN, JANE 1775-1817   Persuasion. Philadelphia: Carey & Lea, 1832. 1st American edition; 7 1/4 x 4 1/2 inches; 2 volumes, pages 204, 36 page publisher's catalogue, 204; heavy foxing of section 4, pages 74/75 carelessly opened at top and two pages at top corners, ocassional light foxing contents of both volumes, rare in original brown linen backed drab boards (lacking title labels on backstrips), uncut, small leather booklabel of Charles Beecher Hogan, backstrips and boards marked and worn at corners and edges, volume 1 loose in its binding and has small piece torn from fore edge of title, lower edge of p. 133 at top corner page 119, sections 6, 8 and 9 foxed and occasional slight waterstain top corner of some pages, volume 2 has front free endpaper caught by glue at top edge and slightly torn, lacks 2nd front free e.p. & one of rear free e.p. Gilson B3 1250.   Ian Hodgkins 78-26 1996 £3,750.00

BARTLETT, HENRIETTA C.   A Census of Shakespeare's Plays in Quarto 1594-1709. New Haven: Yale University Press, 1916. 1st edition; one of 500 copies; folio; original boards, cloth back, paper label, fore and bottom edges uncut; fine; with Charles Beecher Hogan bookplate. Howard S. Mott 227-125 1996 $200.00

ASSOCIATION - FRANK HOGAN

RICHARDSON, SAMUEL 1689-1761   The History of Sir Charles Grandison. (with) Clarissa. Suffield: printed by Havila & Oliver Farnsworth, for Oliver D. & I. Cooke... 1798. 12mo; 2 volumes in one, 143, 138, (1) pages; full contemporary calf, original leather label on spine reading "Novels for Youth"; fine copy, with gilt stamped red leather label of Frank Hogan. Splendid copy. Welch 1104.5. Evans 34465 & 34463.   M & S Rare Books 60-189 1996 $450.00

ASSOCIATION - HOGG

EYRE, EDWARD JOHN   Journals of Expeditions of Discovery into Central Australia and Overland from Adelaide to King Georges Sound in the Years 1840-41. London: T. W. Boone, 1845. Primary edition pagination and binding; 2 volumes, (ii), (xx), 448 pages, 4 pages ads, frontispiece, 10 litho plates, 1 loose map in front pocket (lacks 1 loose map); (iv), (vi), 512 pages, 8 pages ads, frontispiece and 10 litho plates; original green ribbed and embossed cloth, spines lettered and decorated in gilt, several folds of the Arrowsmith map strengthened at folds, otherwise crisp, neatly recased with original cloth, gilt slightly faded, otherwise very nice. Presentation copy from author for Rev. Hogg. Wantrup 133a.   Antipodean 28-617 1996 $3,500.00

ASSOCIATION - J. WOOLSTEN HOLEM

LUCRETIUS CARUS, TITUS 99-55 BC   Titi Lucretii Cari De Rerum Natura... Birmingham: Baskerville, 1773. 12mo; pages (2), 214, (i.e. 218); worn 19th century full leather, foxed, ms. ownerships of H. Mansfield and J. Woolsten Holme. Gaskell 50.   Family Album Tillers-415 1996 $275.00

ASSOCIATION - THOMAS HOLLIS

SYDNEY, ALGERNON   Discourses Concerning Government...with His Letters Trial Apology and Some Memoirs of His Life... London: A. Millar, 1763. 4to; (v), 46, (vii), 497, (i), 198 pages; frontispiece, contemporary red goatskin, single gilt rule, Hollis's cockerel device on front board and feather on lower board, spine in five compartments, morocco label on one, owl device on others, good copy, inscription from Thomas Hollis to Paul Celesia Genoese.   Robert Clark 38-207 1996 £600.00

WALLIS, JOHN   Grammatica Linguae Anglicanae. London: Millar Bowyer, 1765. 8vo; pages (35), 281, frontispiece, tooled ink stamp of Liberty on rear flyleaf; full red morocco binding executed by John Matthewman for Thomas Hollis, in center of front cover is gilt figure of Brittania, seated; lower cover has seated owl, spine tooled with title and Caduceus of Mercury, marbled edges;   Family Album Tillers-664 1996 $800.00

ASSOCIATION - EDMOND HOLMES

SHAKESPEARE, WILLIAM 1564-1616   The Tragicall Historie of Hamlet Prince of Denmarke. Hammersmith: Doves Press, 1909. Small quarto; 158, (2), 23, (1) pages, printed in red and black, with opening initial flourished in green by Edward Johnson; full dark blue morocco elaborately stamped in gilt, gilt board edges and inner dentelles, all edges gilt and gauffered with dotted fillet, dentelles offsetting to endpapers, fine; beautiful unsigned binding, appears to be the product of the Doves Bindery. Inscribed by Thomas James Cobden-Sanderson for Edmond Holmes.   Heritage Book Shop 196-247 1996 $3,500.00

ASSOCIATION - MICHAEL HOLROYD

COLERIDGE, SAMUEL TAYLOR 1772-1834   Notes and Lectures Upon Shakespeare and some of the Old Poets and Dramatists. London: William Pickering, 1849. 1st edition; small 8vo; 2 volumes; full crushed green morocco, decorative gilt to spines, spines faded to brown, panelled gilt, decorative gilt dentelles and inner dentelles, bit of rubbing to extremities, all edges gilt, internally fine; handsomely bound set, inscribed to Michael Holroyd on dedication page. Jaggard p. 55. Keynes p. 59.   Dramatis Personae 37-37 1996 $150.00

ASSOCIATION - E. B. HOLT

INSTRUCTIONS for Officers and Non-Commissioned Officers On Outpost and Patrol Duty and Troops in Campaign. Washington: GPO, 1863. 1st edition; 8vo; 88 pages; illustrations; printed wrappers; rear wrapper missing, approximately 1 1/2 inch of blank bottom of final leaf torn off, affecting two words 'shall still', front wrapper soiled and stained, oil stain on first few leaves, overall condition fair; scarce. Ink signature of "W.H. Burbank" repeated approximately 8 times scattered through the manual, pencil signature and information of E. B. Holt, of 3rd Regt. N.H. V.   Robert F. Lucas 42-19 1996 $200.00

LE GRAND, LOUIS   The Military Hand-Book, and Soldier's Manual of Information, the Official Articles of War...Regulations for Camp and Service...Health Department, with Valuable Remedies, Etc... New York: Beadle & Co., 1862. 12mo; 125 pages; printed wrappers, crude 'cardboard' boards sewn on; very good; front wrapper intact, rear wrapper missing; signature of Edward B. Holt 3rd Regt. Co. E. N.H.V., Concord, N.H.   Robert F. Lucas 42-20 1996 $150.00

ASSOCIATION - LISTER HOLTE

MORE, CRESACRE   The Life of Sir Thomas More, Kt. Lord High Chancellour of England Under K. Henry the Eighth... London: Woodman and Lyon, 1726. 8vo; finey engraved frontispiece, title in red and black, publisher's list at end; calf, rebacaked; Lister Holte armorial bookplate. Gibson 108.   Rostenberg & Stern 150-90 1996 $375.00

ASSOCIATION - HONEYMAN

EUCLIDES   Elementorvm Evclidis Libri Tredecim. London: Excudebat Gulielmus Iones, 1620. 1st edition published in England of the original Greek text. Folio in 4's; pages (ii), 250, final blank missing, Greek & roman letter in parallel columns, woodcut vignette on titlepage and initials at beginning of each book, diagrams in text, lightly yellowed, few small light lamp oil spots on last 2 leaves; contemporary calf, rebacked, blindstamped fleurons, covers worn, front hinge beginning to crack; owner's autograph of Thos. Middleton 1668, W. Stanley Jevons 1879 & Robert Honeyman 1963; good copy. STC 10559; Lowndes 755; Graesse II 510; Honeyman 1030.   A. Sokol XXV-35 1996 £985.00

ASSOCIATION - EDWIN HONIG

BISHOP, ELIZABETH 1911-   The Complete Poems. New York: 1970. 3rd printing; fine/near fine. Inscribed by author to poet Edwin Honig. Stephen Lupack 83- 1996 $150.00

ASSOCIATION - JOSEPH SYMONDS HOOKER

ANDERSON, JOHN 1833-1900   Mandalay to Momien: a Narrative of the Two Expeditions to Western China of 1868 and 1875. London: Macmillan & Co., 1876. 1st edition; demy 8vo; xvi, (480) pages; plates, folding maps; original decorative cloth, gilt, by Burn and Co., with their ticket, covers little worn, nicked and marked, but good copy still, bookplate of Hooker's Son, Joseph Symonds Hooker.   Ash Rare Books Zenzybyr-3 1996 £450.00

ASSOCIATION - JOSEPH SYMONDS HOOKER

HEDIN, SVEN   Adventures in Tibet. London: Hurst & Blackett, 1904. 1st edition; demy 8vo; xvi, (488) pages; numerous illustrations, original cloth, pictorial onlay, little rubbed and worn at extremities of spine, little shaken, lacks front fly, but good; bookplate of Hooker's son, Joseph Symonds Hooker.   Ash Rare Books Zenzybyr-48 1996 £185.00

ASSOCIATION - W. J. HOOKER

PRIOR, R. C. A.   On the Popular Names of British Plants, an Explanation of the Origin and meaning of the Names of the Indigenous and Most Commonly Cultivated Species. London: 1879. 3rd edition; small 8vo; original cloth, little faded; presentation copy with inscription; with 4 page letter from W. J. Hooker.   Charles W. Traylen 117-327 1996 £100.00

ASSOCIATION - JOHN HOOPER

LEVER, CHARLES JAMES 1806-1872   The Fortunes of Glencore. London: Chapman and Hall, 1857. 1st edition; 8vo; 3 volumes; original green blindstamped cloth, spines lettered in gilt, occasional spotting or soiling, ownership signature on front free endpapers, but excellent; bookplate of John Hooper. Sadleir 1405.   Simon Finch 24-155 1996 £300.00

ASSOCIATION - HERBERT HOOVER

AGRICOLA, GEORGIUS   De Re Metallica. London: 1912. Folio; pages xxxi, 640; 270 woodcut illustrations, many full page, short split in upper hinge, otherwise fine, bound in vellum; inscribed by H. C. Hoover to S. T. Bloomline, Esq.   John Henly 27-636 1996 £550.00

AGRICOLA, GEORGIUS   De Re Metallica. London: published for the translators by the Mining Magazine, 1912. 4to; 640 pages; 270 woodcut illustrations; uncut, bound in full vellum, soiled, 2 inch cut to lower hinge, endpaper soiled, possibly a bookplate removed, internally nice, clean copy. Inscribed by Herbert Hoover.   Second Life Books 103-6 1996 $600.00

ASSOCIATION - W. H. ST. J. HOPE

FERGUSON, RICHARD S.   A Short Historical and Architectural Account of Lanercost, a Priory of Black Canons... London: Bell and Daldy, Carlisle C. Thurnam, n.d., before 1868. Large paper copy; 4to; pages 56, 2 lithographed plans and 2 large photographic plates, first leaf of text misbound; presentation copy inscribed on title to W. H. St. J. Hope, with author's compliments.   R.F.G. Hollett & Son 78-919 1996 £120.00

ASSOCIATION - HOPETOUN

EVELYN, JOHN 1620-1706   A Philosophical Discourse on Earth, Relating to the Culture and Improvement of It for Vegetation, and the Propagation of Plants, Etc., As It Was Presented to the Royal Society, April 29, 1675. London: printed for John Martyn, 1676. 1st edition; small 8vo; contemporary mottled calf, spine gilt, some rubbing of spine; some of gilt on spine rubbed away, but very fine and fresh; complete with prelim leaf giving order to print from the Royal Society; ownership inscirpiton of Nidrie Castel, Tues. 18 Octo. 1681. later Hopetoun bookplate. Keynes 93; wing E3507.   Ximenes 109-112 1996 $3,500.00

ASSOCIATION - CLARK HOPKINS

CASSON, STANLEY   Macedonia, Thrace and Illyria: Their Relations to Greece from the Earliest Times Down to the Time of Philip, Son of Amyntas. Oxford: Oxford University Press, 1926. 8vo; xx, 357 pages; 106 illustrations, 19 maps; original cloth; scarce; with signature of Clark Hopkins.   Archaeologia Luxor-3142 1996 $150.00

ASSOCIATION - GERARD MANLEY HOPKINS

PRATT, ANNE   Things of the Sea Coast. London: Society for Promoting Christian Knowledge, 1853. 1st edition; 8vo; original cloth, somewhat worn; enclosed in brown cloth box with matching labels; Gerard Manley Hopkins' copy, inscribed by him to his Aunt Maria. Lakin & Marley 3-20 1996 $750.00

ASSOCIATION - GERARD MANLEY HOPKINS

VAUGHAN, HENRY   Silex Scintillans, &c. Scared Poems and Pious Ejaculations... London: Bell and Daldy, 1858. 8vo; pages xlviii, 247, (i), engraved titlepage; contemporary black hard grain morocco, triple rules in blind, gilt lettered direct, gilt inner dentelles, gilt edges, autograph inscription of Robert Bridges to Gerard Manley Hopkins on initial blank, head and tail of spine and corners little worn, small tear in half title not affecting text, internally clean, good, attractive edtiion;   Simon Finch 24-252 1996 £1,850.00

ASSOCIATION - RICHARD HOPTON

MATHIAS, THOMAS JAMES   The Pursuits of Literature. (with) A Translation of the Passages from Greek, Latin, Italian and French Writers, Quoted in the Prefaces and Notes to the Pursuit of Literature... London: for T. Becket, 1799/98. 10th edition, 3rd edition of 2nd title; 8vo; pages (ii), iv, 445, (1); (ii), lxxv, (i) blank, (iv) fly-title, ad, 104, bound without half titles; contemporary diced calf, gilt roll border to sides, spine in compartments with gilt rolls, ornaments and lettering, little sunned and rubbed at head and foot, marbled edges and endpapers, by T. B. Watkins of Hereford, occasional slight spotting, otherwise an excellent copy; bookplate of Richard Hopton.   Simon Finch 24-165 1996 £95.00

ASSOCIATION - HARRISON HORBLIT

NORWOOD, RICHARD   Norwood's Epitome: Being the Application of the Doctrine of Triangles...The Use of the Plain Sea Chart, and Meractor's Chart... London: William Fisher, Sarah Passinger and Elizabeth Smith, 1690. Small 8vo; (ii), 34, (3)-94, (72) pages; contemporary sheep, headband chipped, hinges beginning to crack; with bookplate of Hugh Cecil, Earl of Lonsdale and label of Harrison D. Horblit.   The Bookpress 75-443 1996 $1,250.00

TODD, FRANK MORTON   Eradicating Plague from San Francisco. San Francisco: 1909. 1st edition; 313 pages, photographic illustrations; original red cloth, very good, plus; Herbert McLean, Evans and Harrison Horblit with their bookplates.   19th Century Shop 39- 1996 $225.00

ASSOCIATION - EMMETT HORINE

ROLLESTON, HUMPHRY   Cardio-Vascular Diseases Since Harvey's Discvoery. Cambridge: 1928. 1st edition; 149 pages; original binding; inscribed by author to Warfield Longcope. Later inscribed by Emmett Horine to Carleton Chapman. GM 3156   W. Bruce Fye 71-1801 1996 $100.00

ASSOCIATION - C. H. ST. JOHN HORNBY

THE BOKE of Noblesse. London: printed for the Roxburghe Club, by J. B. Nichols and Sons, 1890. 1st edition; 10 1/2 x 8 inches; 4 p.l., lx, 95, (1) pages; original roan backed reddish paper boards, gilt titling on spine, corners of paper boards slightly worn, just a tiny bit of rubbing to spine ends and chafing to covers, but binding entirely sound and pleasing, fine internally. Bookplates of C. H. St. John Hornby and John Roland Abbey.   Phillip J. Pirages 33-450 1996 $600.00

TITUS and Vespasian or the Destruction of Jerusalem. London: printed for the Roxburghe Club by J.B. Nichols and Sons, 1905. 1st edition; 11 x 8 1/2 inches; (i)-xlvi, 242 pages; title printed in red and black; 2 color plates, partly printed in gold, reproducing illuminated manuscript pages; original roan backed reddish paper boards, top edge gilt, other edges untrimmed; one small abrasion and minor soiling to paper covers, corners and spine ends slightly worn, otherwise fine, beautiful copy internally; with bookplates of C. H. St. John Hornby and John Roland Abbey.   Phillip J. Pirages 33-451 1996 $550.00

ASSOCIATION - ST. JOHN HORNBY

BIBLE. ENGLISH - 1904   A Book of Songs and Poems from the Old Testament and the Apocrypha. Chelsea: Ashendene Press, 1904. Limited to 150 copies, this being a presentation copy signed by St. John Hornby, Christmas 1908. 8vo; 62, (2) pages, printed in red, blue and black; original vellum, gilt spine. Ashendene Bib. 18.   Kenneth Karmiole 1NS-28 1996 $1,250.00

ASSOCIATION - HORODISCH

ENGLISH Bijou Almanac for 1836. London: Schloss, 1835. 11/16 x 9/16 inches; (64) pages; stiff paper covers with gilt floral stamp, protected by paper case with matching gilt stamp; ribbon bookmark frayed; bookplate of A. Horodisch. Bondy pp. 165-7; Welh 2654-6.   Bromer Booksellers 90-189 1996 $375.00

ASSOCIATION - ABRAHAM HORODISCH

ABC for Tiny Schools. Los Angeles: 1975. 3/4 x 1/2 inches; (30)ff; large calligraphic style letters, burnt orange leather with gilt title on spine; very fine, tiny bookplate of Abraham Horodisch.   Bromer Booksellers 87-202 1996 $150.00

CHURCH OF ENGLAND. BOOK OF COMMON PRAYER   The Book of Common Prayer...Together with the Psalter... London: Oxford University Press, 1898. 2 3/8 x 1 7/8 inches; 688 pages; full gilt stamped black morocco with intricate gilt dentelles red edges gilt, housed in original velvet lined morocco fitted case; contemporary inscription and bookplate of Abraham Horodisch. Bondy p. 117; Welsh 1856.   Bromer Booksellers 87-208 1996 $225.00

ASSOCIATION - CHARLES HORSEY

SHERWELL, JOHN W.   A Descriptive and Historical Account of the Guild of Saddlers of the City of London. London: printed...for private circulation, 1889. 8vo; xxiv, 240 pages, text printed with red ruled borders, 16 plates, text printed within red ruled borders, contemporary full red morocco, gilt panelled sides and spine, with arms of the Guild on the front cover, gilt dentelles, gilt edges, slightly rubbed, some very minor foxing in places. Presentation copy to Charles Horsey.   Thomas Thorp 489-279 1996 £150.00

ASSOCIATION - ROBERT WILMOT HORTON

BURKE, EDMUND 1729-1797   Reflections on the Revolution in France, and On the Proceedings in Certain Societies in London Relative to that Event. Dublin: W. Watson (etc), 1790. iv, 356 pages; contemporary tree calf, red label; fine and attractive copy. Bookplate of Robert Wilmot Horton and extensively annotated throughout in ink in margins by Robert Wilmot Horton, bookplate is probably that of Wilmot Horton's father, Wilmot added surname Horton when he married Anne Horton in 1806.   C. R. Johnson 37-51 196 £750.00

ASSOCIATION - PHILIP J. C. HOWARD

HOWARD, CHARLES   Historical Anecdotes of the Howard Family. London: printed by G. Scott for J. Robson, 1769. 8vo; pages (vi), 201, engraved vignette on title; old speckled calf, edges worn and little scraped, sometime rebacked, spine worn at head and tail. signed on flyleaf by Daniel Scott of Penrith. Loosely inserted 4 page ALS from Philip J. C. Howard of Corby Castle, a pres offprint concerning the latter's Golden Wedding and an example of Corby Castle headed notepaper.   R.F.G. Hollett & Son 78-181 1996 £120.00

ASSOCIATION - CHARLES AUGUSTUS HOWELL

ROSSETTI, DANTE GABRIEL 1828-1882   Hand and Soul. Colophon: London: Strangeways and Walden, printers, n.d. 1869. 1st edition; 8vo; original buff printed wrappers (slight wear); very scarce, very good; with monogram "C.A.H." (most surely Charles Augustus Howell) and "T.H.T. B."? Fredeman 23.6; Tinker 1813; CBEL III 491.   Ximenes 109-252 1996 $2,750.00

ROSSETTI, DANTE GABRIEL 1828-1882   Hand and Soul. London: privately printed by Strangeways and Walden, 1869. 1st separate edition; 12mo; pages 24, title (manuscript coat-of-arms on verso), text (pages (3)-22, imprint at foot of last page), final blank; original drab wrappers, letterpress title on upper cover within one line ms. border, slightly soiled, backstrip slightly split; monograms " C.A.H.(owell)? and T.H.T.B? in same hand dated 23 July 1872 on upper cover, ink inscription on inside upper cover 'Bought of Sotheran 10 dec. 1886...", probably the copy of Charles Augustus Howell. Ashley IV 122.   Simon Finch 24-198 1996 £1,000.00

ASSOCIATION - JOHN HOWELL

STEVENSON, ROBERT LOUIS BALFOUR 1850-1894   The Best Thing in Edinburgh: an Address... San Francisco: John Howell, 1923. 1st edition; number 48 of 250 copies on handmade paper; linen backed boards with paper label, light overall soiling, end of paper label chipped, otherwise very good; inscribed by John Howell to W. Hannah.   Hermitage SP95-885 1996 $150.00

ASSOCIATION - WRIGHT HOWES

JUNGE, CARL S.   Ex Libris. New York: H. L. Lindquist, 1935. 1st edition; number 97 of 500 copies signed by Junge; 4to; (51) leaves, original cloth backed printed boards, fine in very good glassine jacket with few pieces missing; with sardonic pencilled inscription on colophon from Leroy Goble to noted Americana bibliographer Wright Howes. Nice association.   Chapel Hill 94-126 1996 $100.00

ASSOCIATION - JOHN SALLOWS HUBBARD

BRONTE, THE SISTERS   Poems by Currer, Ellis and Acton Bell. London: Smith, Elder and Co., 1846/48. 1st edition; 2nd issue, with Smith, Elder titlepage; 8vo; pages iv, 165, (i) imprint, (i) ads; uncut in original olive green vertically ribbed cloth, covers stamped in blind with double line rectangular border enclosing decorative floral designs, harp in centre, spine with bands in blind, lettered in gold, cream endpapers; spine worn at head and tail, corners just bumped, extremities slightly sunned; good copy; early ownership inscription of Miss Lowe, bookplate of John Sallows Hubbard; Walter Smith, Bronte Sisters pp. 6-14. Simon Finch 24-18 1996 £650.00

ASSOCIATION - C. ROY HUDLESTON

EWBANK, JANE M.   Antiquary on Horseback. Kendal: Titus Wilson, 1963. 8vo; pages xvi, 163; illustrations; original cloth, gilt, dust jacket (little worn, some loss to top edge). C. Roy Hudleston's copy with autograph postcard signed from author.   R.F.G. Hollett & Son 78-904 1996 £50.00

FOSTER, JOSEPH   Pedigree of Sir Josslyn Pennington, Fifth Baron Muncaster of Muncaster and Ninth Baronet. London: privately printed, Chiswick Press, 1878. Tall 4to; pages v, 73 leaves, uncut, 3 page pedigree; flyleaves rather browned; original cloth, gilt, little scratched, corners repaired and neatly recased; flyleaves rather browned; very scarce. C. Roy Hudleston's copy with his Mss. annotations to the pedigree, 2 letters to him and a typescript copy of a Pennington deed in Manchester Cent. Lib. loosely inserted.   R.F.G. Hollett & Son 78-157 1996 £180.00

MORRIS, W. P.   The Records of Patterdale. Kendal: T. Wilson, 1903. 1st edition; 8vo; pages 161, 8 plates; original cloth, gilt, extremities little rubbed, partly unopened, scarce; C. Roy Huddleston's copy, with some marginal notes and annotations in places.   R.F.G. Hollett & Son 78-1125 1996 £120.00

ROBINSON: Some Account of the Family of Robinson of the White House, Appleby, Westmoreland. London: privately printed, Nichols and Sons, 1874. 8vo; pages 101; lithographed plate; contemporary half roan, gilt with raised bands, little rubbed, flyleaves rather spotted, some marginal notes in hand of C. Roy Hudleston to a few leaves, extremely scarce.   R.F.G. Hollett & Son 78-242 1996 £185.00

TRIMBLE, WILLIAM TENNANT   The Trimbles and Cowens of Dalston, Cumberland. Carlisle: privately printed, 1935. Large 8vo; pages 64, 26; 20 plates; original cloth; presentation copy inscribed for C. Roy Hudleston, ALS to Hudleston from a Cowan descendant loosely inserted.   R.F.G. Hollett & Son 78-267 1996 £85.00

ASSOCIATION - ALEX HUDNUT

THACKERAY, WILLIAM MAKEPEACE 1811-1863   The Newcomes. London: Bradbury & Evans, Oct. 1853-Aug. 1855. 1st edition; 24 parts in 23; illustrations; original pictorial wrappers; set lacks 7 of the ads cited by Van Duzer (147), but includes 2 leaves not mentioned in bibliography; former owner's signatures on few covers, backstrips and wrappers with some wear and neat repairs, little soiled and worn, but good set in two very attractive full morocco solander cases; bookplates of Alex M. Hudnut.   David J. Holmes 52-120 1996 $750.00

ASSOCIATION - E. W. HUDSON

JONES, HENRY FESTING   Samuel Butler, author of Erewhon (1835-1902). London: Macmillan and Co., 1919. 2 volumes; original red cloth, dulled; E. W. Hudson's copy, signed by him, enclosed are 2 letters, one typed, the other in autograph and both signed by Henry Festing Jones to Hudson.   Jarndyce CII-126 1996 £110.00

ASSOCIATION - ROBERT ARUNDEL HUDSON

FRASER, CLAUD LOVAT 1890-1921   Sixty-Three Unpublished Designs. London: printed at the Curwen Press for the First Edition Club, 1924. 1st edition; 87/50 copies; foolscap 8vo; pages xii, 63; printed on yellow dyed Ingres handmade paper, 63 drawings, one repeated on titlepage; original quarter black cloth, gilt lettered lightly faded backstrip, white boards with overall purple, orange and black design by Lovat Fraser; untrimmed, good; bookplate of Robert Arundel Hudson and bookticket of Raymond Lister.   Blackwell's B112-111 1996 £70.00

ASSOCIATION - DANIEL HUGHES

LE LOYER, PIERRE, SIEUR DE LA BROSSE 1550-1634   A Treatise of Specters or Straunge Sights, Visions and Apparitions, Appearing Sensibly Unto Men. London: by Val S(immes) for Mathew Lownes, 1605. 1st edition in English; 4to; (8), 145, (1) leaves; errata leaf in very skilfil pen facsimile on old paper, title soiled, two or three leaves with early paper reinforcement at gutter; 19th century calf, very nice, tight copy, extensive contemporary marginal notes in hand of one Daniel Hughes; leather bookplate of Edward Hailstone. STC 15448.   Joseph J. Felcone 64-25 1996 $1,200.00

ASSOCIATION - LANGSTON HUGHES

BAKER, DOROTHY   Young Man with a Horn. Boston: Houghton Mifflin Co., 1938. Later printing; moderately worn and soiled, about very good, lacking dust jacket; Langston Hughes' copy with his ownership signature. Between the Covers 43-21 1996 $200.00

RANSOM, JOHN CROWE   Selected Poems. New York: Knopf, 1952. 2nd printing; ink stains to edges of several pages and on back board; only fair copy, lacking dust jacket; inscribed by Langston Hughes. Between the Covers 43-122 1996 $200.00

ASSOCIATION - TED HUGHES

PLATH, SYLVIA 1932-1963   Ariel. London: Faber and Faber, 1965. 1st edition; 8vo; fine in fine dust jacket; Presentation copy "The brown stains on top edge and cover are thatch-drip from leaking roof of Court Green (where SP had lived) in the winter of 1965/6. Ted Hughes". Lakin & Marley 3-47 1996 $650.00

ASSOCIATION - JAMES FROTHINGHAM HUNNEWELL

WEST, THOMAS   The Antiquities of Furness... London: printed for the author by T. Spilsbury, 1774. 1st edition; 4to; pages (xx), lvi, 288, 3A-3R4 (appendices), folding engraved plan, folding plan, 2 engraved plates; contemporary full polished calf gilt, edges rather rubbed, rebacked in matching calf, gilt, raised bands, original spine label retained attractive copy; attractive etched pictorial bookplate of James Frothingham Hunnewell.   R.F.G. Hollett & Son 78-1358 1996 £275.00

ASSOCIATION - LEIGH HUNT

BUCKE, CHARLES   Amusements in Retirement; or, the Influence of Science, Literature and the Liberal arts, on the Manners and Happiness of Private Life. London: printed for Henry Colburn, 1818. 2nd edition; 8vo; xvii, (iii), 320, (2 ad) pages; later black half morocco, top edge gilt others uncut, joints slightly rubbed; ownership inscription on title of Leigh Hunt, and his marginal annotations throughout.   James Burmester 29-22 1996 £375.00

ASSOCIATION - EDWARD HUNTER

DIBDIN, THOMAS FROGNALL 1776-1847   The Library Companion; or, the Young Man's Guide, and the Old Man's Comfort in the Choice of a Library. London: by W. Nicol for Harding, Triphook and Lepard and J. Major, 1824. 1st edition; 1st issue; 8 x 5 1/2 inches; 2 volumes, complete with half titles and with ad leaves at front of volume 1 and back of volume 2; original cloth (Smith's variant form with Roman numeral "I" on spine), very artful minor repairs at top of spines, substantial custom made cloth covered slipcase, as always, spines and edges of covers slightly faded, gilt titling rendered a bit indistinct, because of fading, few trivial imperfections in text, but an extraordinarily fine copy otherwise, with hinges in perfect order, with cloth exceptional clean and with text showing no significant signs of use; armorial bookplates of Samuel Parker and of Edward Hunter in each volume (an earlier owner, no doubt Parker, has pasted a matching sheet of coated paper over the existing pastedown in the first volume, with opening that frames Parker's bookplate this redecoration presumably intended to obscure other marks of ownership. Eckel p. 108; Sabin 19996; Smith II 8-15.   Phillip J. Pirages 33-161 1996 $1,450.00

ASSOCIATION - F. D. HUNTINGTON

DOWNING, A. J.   The Fruits and Fruit Trees of America; or, the Culture, Propagation and Management in the Garden and Orchard, of Fruit Trees Generally... New York: 1845. 1st edition; 8vo; pages xiv, 594, (14 page ads); 214 engraved illustrations; original cloth, gilt decorated spine, worn at corners and edges, spine ends partially perished, inch piece missing at head of spine, spot on front cover, small tear to titlepage, some page browning, mostly marginal, missing pages vii-x in preface. Signed presentation from author for Rev. F. D. Huntington. Raymond M. Sutton VII-8 1996 $650.00

ASSOCIATION - SAMUEL HUNTINGTON

TO The Millers of the United States. Take Notice -- That Congress Did on the 21st of Jan. 1808, Pass the Following Act: An Act for the Relief of Oliver Evans. Philadelphia?: 1809. 1st edition; 4to. leaflet, printed on pages (1-3), signed twice by Evans at end of printed statement of fees for the use of his patents and at conclusion of a letter written in the margins to the Gov. of Ohio, Samuel Huntington.   M & S Rare Books 60-455 1996 $3,750.00

ASSOCIATION - HUSSEY

CLARE, JOHN 1793-1864   The Village Minstrel, and Other Poems... London: for Taylor and Hessey and E. Drury, Stamford, 1821. 1st edition; 12mo; 2 volumes, pages xxviii, 216, (iv) ads; (viii), 211, (v) ads; frontispiece in volume 1; uncut in original blue boards, skilfully rebacked, new printed spine labels, some occasional spotting and marking internally; early bookplates of P. Hussey. Tinker 673.   Simon Finch 24-40 1996 £700.00

ROBINSON, DR.   Magistrate's Pocket-Book; or an Epitome of the Duties and Practice of a Justice of the Peace, Out of Sessions. London: 1837. 2nd edition; 8vo; xviii, 466, (40) pages; old mellow calf, title label inset on red morocco; very good; with bookplate of A. & F. Renier and lettered in gilt on front board J. Hussey.   K Books 442-417 1996 £60.00

ASSOCIATION - GARTH HUSTON

BROWNE, THOMAS 1605-1682   Religio Medici. Lugd. Batavorum: Apud Francifcum, 1650. 12mo; 120 leaves; engraved frontispiece; full contemporary calf, raised bands, tooled spine, armorial gilt stamp on front board, all edges gilt, front blanks loose, nice, clean copy; bookplate of Garth Huston and Courville Collection. Keynes 62.   James Tait Goodrich K40-68 1996 $395.00

ASSOCIATION - HUTH

TREVERS, JOSEPH   An Essay to the Restoring of Our Decayed Trade. London: printed for Giles Widdowes...John Sims and Will. Milward... 1675. Small 4to; title, 4 prelims, 59 pages, (3) pages, upper margin rather short, but still very good; 2 cm taller than Kress copy; vellum boards. The Huth copy, with his book label. Wing T2129; Kress 1390; Goldsmiths' 2120 (calls for 59pp. in error).   H. M. Fletcher 121-79 1996 £835.00

ASSOCIATION - THOMAS HUTTON

PARNELL, THOMAS   Poems on Several Occasions...With the Life of Zoilus and His Remarks on Homer's Battle of the Frogs and Mice... Dublin: Thomas Ewing, 1773. 4to; engraved portrait headpiece, some waterstaining to upper portion of text, mostly of front and back, else light browning; contemporary mottled calf gilt, with crest of Thomas Hutton on a morocco label, joints worn, rubbed; pleasant edition. James Cummins 14-150 1996 $150.00

ASSOCIATION - ALDOUS HUXLEY

JOYCE, JAMES 1882-1941   Anna Livia Plurabelle. New York: Crosby Gaige, 1928. One of 800 copies; touch of fraying to cloth at spine extremtieis, still near fine; signed by Joyce, this copy inscribed by Harry Crosby to Aldous Huxley.   Ken Lopez 74-236 1996 $8,500.00

KRUTCH, JOSEPH   Samuel Johnson. New York: Holt, 1944. 1st edition; plates; original binding, very good in worn dust jacket; wonderful association copy, Anita Loos's copy with her bookplate and estate stamp, the book was given her by Aldous Huxley, with inscription. Charles Agvent 4-762 1996 $375.00

ASSOCIATION - J. K. HUYSMANS

GONCOURT, EDMOND   Les Freres Zemganno. Paris: Charpentier, 1879. 1st edition; starting to front inner hinge, else very good+ in contemporary percaline with leather spine label, with original yellow wrappers bound in; inscribed by author for J. K. Huysmans.   Lame Duck Books 19-224 1996 $3,500.00

ASSOCIATION - ILCHESTER

MERVAULT, PETER   The Last Famous Siege of the city of Roche; Together with the Edict of Nantes. London: Wickins, 1680. 8vo; 2 parts in 1; 3 page publisher's catalog at end; calf; Ilchester-Fox copy with bookplates. Wing M1879. Haag VII 393.   Rostenberg & Stern 150-58 1996 $450.00

ASSOCIATION - JOHN INGILBY

ASCHAM, ROGER   Toxophilus, the Schole, or Partitions, of Shooting. Wrexham: Reprinted by R. Marsh, 1788. 8vo; contemporary tree calf, spine rubbed, upper hinge cracked, small piece missing from head of spine, arms of Sir John Ingilby, Bart in gilt on upper cover.   Anthony Laywood 108-22 1996 £110.00

CHARACTERS And Anecdotes of the Court of Sweden. London: printed for Elizabeth Harlow, 1790. 1st edition; 8vo; 2 volumes; some foxing of text, contemporary half calf, rubbed, hinges cracked, piece measuring 1 inch missing from spine of volume 2, bookplates of Sir John Ingilby. Anthony W. Laywood 108-129 1996 £50.00

ASSOCIATION - EDWARD INGRAHAM

MARRYAT, FREDERICK 1792-1848   Peter Simple. London: Saunders and Otley, 1834. 1st English edition; with author's calling card (oxidized & with offsetting) tipped in, several penned notations annotating the clippings or inserts, including an inserted portrait & 3 illustrations by R.W. Buss; ALS by author to Edward Ingraham, Ingraham signed 1st vol; contemporary half calf, marbled boards, uncut, some rubbing, generally light, half title in volume 2 only as issued, errata slip to third volume inserted in volume 1 following contents, blank and leaves through the title in volume 1 loose, some offsetting of inserts, some light soiling, browning and spotting, mostly at front and back, few ms. markings, newspaper clippings relating to Marryat inserted on blanks & endpapers, without publisher's ads at back of volume 3; brown morocco folding box. Block 153; Sadleir 1592a; Wolff 517a.   James Cummins 14-131 1996 $1,000.00

ASSOCIATION - WILLIAM INGRAM

BARBOUR, JOHN   The Life and Acts of the Most Victorious Conqueror Robert Bruce, King of Scotland. Edinburgh: 1758. Small 4to; pages 443, uncut, printed in black letter with head and tailpieces, few leaves rather browned; old binders cloth, gilt, lower corners of boards damped; nice, unsophisticated copy. Inscription of William Ingram 1788, on title; signature of James Crawfurd on pastedown & inscription below of George Arbuthnot dated Feb. 1st 1831.   R.F.G. Hollett 76-13 1996 £95.00

ASSOCIATION - HENRY BATCHELLOR INMAN

BARCLAY, JOHN   The Mirror of Minds or Barclay's Icon Animorum. London: I.B. for Thomas Walkley, 1633. 12mo; pages (xii), 380, roman letter, title backed long since, couple of minor tears not affecting text, perfectly acceptable copy; early 19th century calf gilt, upper cover loosening; armorial bookplates of W. Combes and Henry Batchellor Inman, autograph of "J. Mitford 1832" (probably the writer John Mitford 1781-1859). STC 1400. Lowndes 112.   A. Sokol XXV-10 1996 £500.00

ASSOCIATION - WILLIAM VAN RENSSELAER IRVING

ASHLEY, CLIFFORD W.   Whaleships of New Bedford. Sity Plates. Boston & New York: Houghton Mifflin, 1929. One of 1035 copies; 10.5 x 8.5 inches; red cloth, bit of wear at head of spine; interesting bookplate of William Van Rensselaer Irving.   Parmer Books O39Nautica-039139 1996 $275.00

ASSOCIATION - R. H. ISHAM

DOUGLAS, JOHN   Pandaemonium; or, a New Infernal Expedition. London: printed for W. Owen, 1750. 1st edition; 4to; full polished marbled calf, gilt, spine gilt, by Zaehnsdorf; very rare; fine; from the library of R. H. Isham. Foxon P28.   Ximenes 108-112 1996 $2,250.00

FIELDING, HENRY 1707-1754   The Journal of a Voyage to Lisbon. London: A. Millar, 1755. 1st published edition; 8vo; complete with half title; contemporary calf spine with five raised bands and red morocco label, over marbled boards, slight strengthening to spine bardely visible, all edges sprinkled, in protective slipcase with inner chemise, bookplate of Col. R. H. Isham. Rothschild I pp. 207-208; Cross III 84-88.   Book Block 32-55 1996 $700.00

JOHNSON, SAMUEL 1709-1784   Samuel Johnson's Prologue Spoken at the Opening of the Theatre in Drury-Lane in 1747, with Garrick's Epilogue. New York: Dodd, Mead and Co., 1902. 1st edition thus; large 4to; original blue grey boards, printed paper side label, some wear to spine; very good; presentation copy inscribed by A. S. W. Rosenbach for Colonel Ralph Isham.   Ximenes 108-231 1996 $600.00

ASSOCIATION - AMBROSE ISTED

FIELDING, HENRY 1707-1754   The History of Tom Jones. London: A. Millar, 1749. 1st edition; 8vo; 6 volumes; original calf, joints cracked, minor chipping, attracctive set, preserved in fine quarter morocco gilt slipcases, this set has all the cancels as per the Rothschild set and volume 6 is true first edition (not the close reprint) and volume 5 has the first issue titlepage; contemporary bookplate of Ambrose Isted; Rothschild 850; Cross Fielding II 122.   G. W. Stuart 59-33 1996 $4,100.00

ASSOCIATION - JAMES IVISON

HARWOOD, J.   Harwood's Views of the Lakes. London: J. & F. Harwood, c. 1852. Oblong 8vo; 24 engraved plates, few trifle spotted, some numbered and dated between 1842 and 1846; original cloth backed color printed boards, blindstamp of James Ivison, bookseller of Keswick on flyleaf.   R.F.G. Hollett & Son 78-974 1996 £85.00

ASSOCIATION - HOLBROOK JACKSON

FRANCE, ANATOLE   Stendhal. London: 1926. One of 110 numbered copies, this copy being additionally inscribed; wrappers, first two pages and final page partially browned, covers slightly marked and spotted; very good; inscribed by Holbrook Jackson for E. A. Ratcliffe.   Ulysses 39-134 1996 £85.00

ASSOCIATION - J. E. JACKSON

AUBREY, JOHN   The Topographical Collections. Devizes, Bull, 1862. 1st edition; 4to; half title, pages xiii, 491, (1 p. errata), frontispiece, 42 engraved plates, 3 folding pedigrees and 2 folding plans, 1 hand colored text plan; contemporary half morocco, trifle rubbed, one or two tears to the folding plates; presentation copy with ink ms. corrections by J. E. Jackson to Viscount Barrington, tipped in at back is Jackson's printed appeal "Ten Pounds Reward. Folio Volume of Aubrey's Wiltshire Antiquities: an Original Manuscript Missing".   Marlborough 162-268 1996 £250.00

ASSOCIATION - SYLVINA JACKSON

EMERSON, RALPH WALDO 1803-1882   May-Day and Other Pieces. Boston: Ticknor & Fields, 1867. 1st edition; one of 100 copies, specially bound for presentation purposes; original white cloth, gilt, spine browned, spine ends lightly chafed, covers somewhat aged, else tight, clean copy; housed in cloth folding case, leather labels; inscribed by author for Mrs. Sylvina Jackson. BAL 5250; Myerson A28.1.a.   Mac Donnell 12-28 1996 $1,850.00

ASSOCIATION - CARL JACOBI

SMITH, CLARK ASHTON   The Double Shadow and Other Fantasies. Auburn Press Journal, 1933. 1st edition; 1/1000 copies; some staining to front cover, else very good in wrappers; inscribed by author to fellow writer Carl Jacobi.   Aronovitz 57-1074 1996 $875.00

ASSOCIATION - HENRY BARTON JACOBS

DANA, CHARLES   Poetry and Doctors: a Catalogue of Poetical Works Written by Physicians with Biographical Notes. Woodstock: 1916. 1st edition; 83 pages; illustrations; original binding; inscribed by Henry Barton Jacobs to Thomas B. Futcher; rare.   W. Bruce Fye 71-484 1996 $250.00

ASSOCIATION - JAFFRAY

COPPETTA DE' BECCUTI, FRANCESCO   Rime. Venice: D. & G. B. Guerra for Aldo Manuzio, 1580. 1st edition; small 8vo; pages (xvi), 190, lacking final blank, italic letter with Roman Index, woodcut printer's device on titlepage and at end, woodcut initials and ornaments, few early ms. annotations, fore edge of titlepage bit soiled, top outer corner of this and following leaf repaired, occasional spot, finger mark or similar blemish, good copy in attractive neo-Classical binding c. 1800, vellum over boards, gilt borders and title, morocco lettering pieces; engraved armorial bookplate of Jaffray. BM STC It. p. 77; Adams C2606; Gamba 372; Brunet II 261.   A. Sokol XXV-24 1996 £625.00

ASSOCIATION - HARRY JAMES

EYRE, ALICE   The Famous Fremonts and Their America. N.P.: 1948. 374 pages; illustrations and maps; nice inscription, laid in is printed book mark card of Western authority and author Harry C. James. Fine in moderately soiled, lightly worn dust jacket.   Gene W. Baade 1094-54 1996 $125.00

ASSOCIATION - J. G. JAMES

BERLIN IRON BRIDGE CO.   The Berlin Iron Bridge Company. A Trade Catalogue. East Berlin: Berlin Iron Bridge Co., 1889. Oblong 8vo; 127, (3) pages, final leaf in facsimile, many wood engraved illustrations; limp crimson leather boards, very worn, original printed front wrpaper bound in, original back wrapper in facsimile; from the library of J. G. James. Elton Engineering 10-10 1996 £150.00

BLAND, WILLIAM   Experimental Essays on the Principles of Construction in Arches, Piers, Buttresses &c. London: John Weale, 1839. 1st edition; 8vo; viii, 103, (1) pages, 8 page publisher catalog, many text illustrations; publisher's cloth, neatly rebacked; presentation inscription by author to a Mr. Austin, probably Henry Austin, the civil engineer, from the library of J. G. James.   Elton Engineering 10-14 1996 £135.00

BOOTH, G. R.   A Popular Treatise on the Strength and Application of Materials Used in Buildings in General Shewing the Advantages to Be Derived from the Principles of the Patent of Messrs. R. Witty & Co. in All Architectural and Engineering... London: Weale, 1836. 8vo; vi, 35, (1) pages, 1 engraved plate; seemly modern cloth; from the library of J. G. James.   Elton Engineering 10-15 1996 £195.00

CLEGG, SAMUEL   Architecture of Machinery: an Essay on Propriety of Form and Proportion, with a View to Assist and Improve Design. London: John Weale, Architectural Library, 1842. 4to; (xiii), 64 pages, 40 page publisher's catalog; 8 engraved plates, many wood engraved text figures; publisher's cloth, neatly rebacked, from the library of J. G. James.   Elton Engineering 10-30 1 996 £2,800.00

CLEGG, SAMUEL   Architecture of Machinery: an Essay on Propriety of Form and Proportion, with a View to Assist and Improve Design. London: John Weale, Architectural Library, 1842. 4to; (xiii), 64 pages, 40 page publisher's catalog, 8 engraved plates, many wood engraved text figures; publisher's cloth, neatly rebacked. From the library of J. G. James.   Elton Engineering 10-30 1996 £2,800.00

DREDGE, JAMES   Thames Bridges from the Tower to the Source. London: Offices of 'Engineering', 1897. Oblong 4to; (iv), 255, (1) pages, 77 photo engraved plates numbered 1-75, 1, 44 and some text illustrations; contemporary quarter morocco; from the library of J. G. James.   Elton Engineering 10-39 1996 £550.00

HOSKING, WILLIAM   Treatises on Architecture, Building, Masonry, Joinery and Carpentry. Edinburgh: Black, 1846. 7th edition; 4to; (ii), 157, (1) pages, 36 engraved plates (last one browned); publisher's cloth, rebacked. From the library of J. G. James.   Elton Engineering 10-77 1996 £130.00

ASSOCIATION - J. G. JAMES

KRAFFT, J. C.   Plans, Coupes et Elevations de Diverses Productions de l'Art de la Charpente Executees Tant en France que Dans les Pays. Paris: Levrault, 1805. Folio; 4 parts in 2 volumes; (iv), 27, (1) pages, engraved dedication leaf, engraved frontispiece, 31 engraved plates; 27, (1), 82 engraved plates; (ii), 18 pages, 63 engraved plates; 9, (1) pages, 28 engraved plates; quarter calf; library stamp of Reading Public Library on title and few plates; fromt he library of J. G. James.   Elton Engineering 10-87 1996 £1,250.00

MAYNARD, HENRY N.   The Viaduct Works' Handbook; Being a Collection of Examples from Actual Practice of Viadcuts, Bridges, Roofs, and Other Structures in Iron... London: Spon, 1868. 8vo; 108 pages, some full page wood engraved plates and many wood engraved text illustrations, folding tinted litho frontispiece (slightly stained), publisher's cloth; presentation inscription from author to civil engineer, H. D. Martin, from the library of J. G. James.   Elton Engineering 10-102 1996 £170.00

ASSOCIATION - H. W. JANSON

ENTWISLE, E. A.   French Scenic Wallpapers 1800-1860. Leigh-On-Sea: E. Lewis, Publishers, Ltd., 1972. 1st edition; limited to 500 copies; 11 1/8 x 8 5/8 inches; numerous black and white plates; fine in original publisher's glassine wrapper. With card laid in from noted historian H. W. Janson reading "From the library of H. W. Janson".   Hermitage SP95-776 1996 $150.00

ASSOCIATION - CHARLES JARRELL

LOWELL, ROBERT 1917-1977   Land of Unlikeness. Cummington: Cummington Press, 1944. 1st edition; one of 250 copies; 8vo; original blue cloth lettered in red, virtually unworn, but faded unevenly to light brown along spine and edges, one small scuff to lower cover; in attractive blue cloth box with black labels; presentation copy from Randall Jarrell to his brother Charles.   Lakin & Marley 3-33 1996 $3,500.00

ASSOCIATION - RANDALL JARRELL

LOWELL, ROBERT 1917-1977   Land of Unlikeness. Cummington: Cummington Press, 1944. 1st edition; one of 250 copies; 8vo; original blue cloth lettered in red, virtually unworn, but faded unevenly to light brown along spine and edges, one small scuff to lower cover; in attractive blue cloth box with black labels; presentation copy from Randall Jarrell to his brother Charles.   Lakin & Marley 3-33 1996 $3,500.00

ASSOCIATION - R. C. JEBB

SMITH, A. H.   A Catalogue of Engraved Gems in the British Museum. London: British Museum, 1888. 1st edition; 12mo; ix, 244 pages, 9 plates; original gilt lettered cloth, 2 corners bumped; inscribed by co author A.S. Murray for R. C. Jebb.   Archaeologia Luxor-4032 1996 $450.00

ASSOCIATION - GWEN JEFFERSON

LANDOR, WALTER SAVAGE 1775-1864   Epicurus, Leontion and Ternissa. London: Hacon & Ricketts, 1896. Limited to 210 copies; 8vo; pages xcix, printed in red and black on handmade paper with elaborate woodcut initials and borders (in red) by Ricketts, slight rubbing at extremities, but very good, unopened; original boards, paper labels; bookplate of Gwendolen Jefferson. Tomkinson 32.   Claude Cox 107-177 1996 £130.00

ASSOCIATION - JELLIFFE

BINACHI, LEONARDO   A Text-Book of Psychiatry for Physicians and Students. New York: William Wood and Co., 1906. 1st American edition; thick 8vo; (xvi), 904 pages, 106 illustrations; panelled black cloth with gilt spine, titlepage stamp and spine numbers of the Hartford Retreat, rear pocket removed; with Jelliffe's name stamp to titlepage and front paste-down.   John Gach 150-41 1996 $125.00

BLACKBURN, ISAAC WRIGHT   Intracranial Tumors Among the Insane: a Study of Twenty-Nine Intracranial Tumors Found in Sixteen Hundred and Forty-Two Autopsies in Cases of Mental Disease. Washington: GPO, 1903. 1st edition; 8vo; 94, (2) pages, 71 plates; pebbled ruled green cloth with gilt spine, with spine numbers and titlepage stamp of Hartford Retreat; with author's printed complimentary slip and Jelliffe's name stamp and bookplate.   John Gach 150-47 1996 $125.00

ASSOCIATION - JELLIFFE

BLEULER, PAUL EUGEN   Dementia Praecox Oder Gruppen der Schizophrenien. Handbuch der Psychiatrie, Herausgegeben von G(ustav) Aschaffenburg Spezieller Teil, 4. Abteilung, 1. Halfte. Leizig und Wien: Franz Deuticke, 1911. 1st edition; 8vo; xii, 420 pages; early red buckram with leather spine label, titlepage stamp of Hartford Retreat; with Jelliffe's name stamp to titlepage and bookplate; GM Cat. 5 4957; Norman Catalog 245.   John Gach 150-53 1996 $1,000.00

BRODIE, BENJAMIN COLLINS   Lectures Illustrative of Certain Local Nervous Affections. London: printed for Longman, Rees, Orme, Brown, Green & Longman, 1837. 1st edition; 8vo; iv, 88 pages, plus Longman catalog dated Feb. 1837 inserted at front; original drab boards, spine chipped (wtih base erose for about an inch), fine, uncut in original condition; scarce; with titlepage stamp of the Hartford Retreat; with Jelliffe's name stamp to titlepage and his bookplate. Norman Cat. 346.   John Gach 150-76 1996 $375.00

GRIESINGER, WILHELM   Die Pathologie und Therapie der Psychischen Krankheiten, fur Arzte und Studirende. Stuttgart: Verlag von Adolf Krabbe, 1845. 1st edition; 8vo; viii, 396, (2) pages; original patterned boards, paper spine label, boards rubbed, shelfwear to joints and edges, very nice, pleasing copy in original condition; rare; Jelliffe's copy with his name stamp. Norman Cat. 948; Zilboorg pp. 275-277; GM 4930.   John Gach 150-188 1996 $1,750.00

IRELAND, WILLIAM WOTHERSPOON   The Mental Affections of Children: Idiocy, Imbecility and Insanity. Philadelphia: P. Blakiston's Son & Co., 1900. 1st U.S. edition; 8vo; (xii), 450 pages, 14 pages of ads, 21 plates, 11 text illustrations, panelled thatched blue-green cloth,f ront flyleaf detached; good to very good, with titlepage stamp and spine numbers of Hartford Retreat; with Jelliffe's bookplate. Cordaso 00-1670.   John Gach 150-221 1996 $100.00

JANET, PIERRE   The Major Symptoms of Hysteria: Fifteen Lectures Given in the Medical School of Harvard University. New York: Macmillan Co., 1907. 1st edition; 12mo; (xii), 345, (1) pages; blue cloth, slight cover soiling and rubbing to joints, very good, titlepage stamp and spine call numbers of Hartford Retreat, with Jelliffe's bookplate.   John Gach 150-222 1996 $125.00

JANET, PIERRE   Mental State of Hystericals: a Study of Mental Stigmata and Mental Accidents. New York: London: G. P. Putnam's Sons/Knickerbocker Press, 1901. 1st edition in English; thick 8vo; xviii, 535, (7) pages; green cloth, recased, label removed from spine, very good, usually turns up in poor condition; very scarce; with Jelliffe's name stamp.   John Gach 150-223 1996 $200.00

KRAEPELIN, EMIL   Clinical Psychiatry: a Text Book for Students and Physicians Abstracted and Adapted from the Seventh German Edition of Kraepelin's "Lehrbuch der Psychiatrie"... New York: Macmillan Co./London: Macmillan & Co., Ltd., 1902. 8vo; (xii), 420 pages + 10 pages of ads; blue cloth, titlepage stamp, rear pocket and whited spine numbers of the Hartford Retreat; with Jelliffe's name stamps.   John Gach 150-247 1996 $125.00

KRAEPELIN, EMIL   Dementia Praecox and Paraphrenia. Edinburgh: E. & S. Livingstone, 1919. 1st edition in English; 8vo; (ii), x, (332) pages; rebound in red library buckram, right edge of titlepage and two ensuing leaves chipped, good, scarce; titlepage stamp and spine label of The Hartford Retreat, rear pocket removed, Jelliffe's copy, signed on titlepage.   John Gach 150-248 1996 $250.00

KRAEPELIN, EMIL   Lectures on Clinical Psychiatry. New York: William Wood & Co., 1913. 3rd edition in English; 8vo; (xviii), 368 pages; panellbed blue buckram, spine label deftly removed, very good, stamp of Hartford Retreat to title and several other pages, uncommon; Jelliffe's copy, signed on titlepage with his bookplate.   John Gach 150-250 1996 $150.00

KRAEPELIN, EMIL   Psychologische Arbeiten. Leipzig: Verlag von Wilhelm Engelmann, 1896-1928. 1st edition; 8vo; 6080 pages, 26 plates, 18 folding; early 20th century maroon cloth, crown to volume 2 shelfworn, otherwise very good, clean copies, rare; with titlepage stamp, rear pocket and spine call numbers of Hartford Retreat; with Jelliffe's name stamp and bookplate in every volume.   John Gach 150-256 1996 $1,250.00

MAUDSLEY, HENRY   The Physiology and Pathology of the Mind. New York: D. Appleton and Co., 1867. 1st U.S. edition; 8vo; (xvi), 442, (8) pages; pebbled mauve cloth, faded spine and edges; very good, with titlepage stamp, rear pocket & call numbers of the Hartford Retreat, with Jelliffe's name stamp and bookplate.   John Gach 150-313 1996 $150.00

ASSOCIATION - JELLIFFE

PAVLOV, IVAN PETROVICH   Conditioned Reflexes: an Investigation of
the Physiological Activity of the Cerebral Cortex. London: Oxford
University Press/Humphrey Milford, 1927. 1st edition in English; large
8vo; (xvi), 430, (2) pages; pebbled black cloth, crisp, tight copy with
spine numbers artfully removed, titlepage stamp of Hartford Retreat; with
Jelliffe's name stamp and bookplate.   John Gach 150-357 1996
$200.00

RACHFORD, BENJAMIN KNOX   Neurotic Disorders of Childhood
Including a study of Auto and Intestinal Intoxications, Chronic Anaemia,
Fever, Eclampsia, Epilepsy, Migraine, Chorea, Hysteria, Asthma, etc. New
York: E. B. Treat & Co., 1905. 8vo; 440, (8) pages; olive cloth with gilt
spine, gold titlepage stamp and spine call numbers of the Hartford
Retreat; with Jelliffe's name stamp and bookplate.   John Gach
150-376 1996 $150.00

SOUTHARD, ELMER ERNEST   Shell-Shock and Other Neuropsychiatric
Problems Presented in 589 Histories from the War Literature 1914-1918.
Boston: W. M. Leonard, 1919. 1st edition; 8vo; (viii), (xxviii), 982, 21, (5)
pages; + 3 half tones; brown buckram with painted spine labels, good
used copy with some shelfwear, with titlepage stamp and spine call
numbers of Hartford Retreat; inscribed by author for Jelliffe, with Jelliffe's
bookplate.   John Gach 150-439 1996 $175.00

ASSOCIATION - SMITH ELY JELLIFFE

ADLER, ALFRED   The Neurotic Constitution: Outlines of a Comparative
Individualistic Psychology and Psychotherapy. New York: Moffat, Yard
and Co., 1916. 1st edition in English; 8vo; blue cloth, gilt spine; very
good; Smith Ely Jelliffe's copy, signed on titlepage, with his bookplate
and long note opposite titlepage about translation. Grinstein 405.   John
Gach 150-4 1996 $125.00

ASSOCIATION - JENKINS

CHURCH OF ENGLAND. BOOK OF COMMON PRAYER   The Book of
Common Prayer, and Administration of the Sacraments and Other Rites
and Ceremonies of the Church, According to the Use of the Church of
England... London: Printed by Thomas Baskett, Printer to the King's most
Excellent... 1751. Folio; 1-19 pages; frontispiece, text and title rubricated
by hand; full black morocco, elaborate gilt tooled border to boards, gilt
coat of arms of George II to both bds., gilt title St. James's Chapel
1752, to upper bd., corners bumped, jts. sl. worn, crown & GR
monograph to compartments, raised bands to spine, marbled endpapers;
owner's bookplate, owner's pen inscription, some sproadic foxing; ms.
inscription "This book which belonged originally to the Princess of
Wales, was used by Members of the Royal Family in the Chapel of St.
James, was bought of Mr. Bohn at Canterbury in June 1847 by Robert
Jenkins, M.A. Rector & Vicar of Lyminge...June 1847 and given by him to
Helen Constable Jenkins Easter Monday (March 29th) 1880."   Beeleigh
Abbey BA56-140 1996 £550.00

ASSOCIATION - FRANCIS JENKS

PEIXOTTO, DANIEL L. M.   Anniversary Discourse, Pronounced before
the Society for the Education of Orphan Children and the Relief of
Indigent Persons of the Jewish Persuasion. New York: J. Seymour, 1830.
1st edition; 8vo; 47 pages; original printed wrappers, sewn, uncut; very
nice, ink presentation inscription from 'the author' to Francis Jenks,
editor of the Christian Examiner.   M & S Rare Books 60-355 1996
$3,500.00

ASSOCIATION - ELIZABETH JENNINGS

ENRIGHT, D. J.   Poems of the 1950s an Anthology of New English
Verse. Tokyo: Kenkyusha Ltd., 1955, i.e. 1956. 1st edition; original
binding, free endpapers partially browned, head and tail of spine and
corners slightly bumped, covers slightly bowed, very good in nicked,
rubbed, chipped and dusty, slightly torn, creased, spotted and marked
dust jacket browned at spine and edges and missing small piece at
head of spine. With ownership signataure of Elizabeth Jennings.
Ulysses 39-343 1996 £350.00

ASSOCIATION - JEUDWINE

LYSONS, SAMUEL   A Collection of Gloucestershire Antiquities.
London: Cadell & Davies, 1791-1804. One of 12 copies on large paper,
with all but two plates colored by hand within wash borders; large folio;
engraved title, 1 f., iv, 38 pages, 2 ff., 110 plates, drawn and etched by
Lysons, 108 colored by hand, 1 in 2 states; plate 81 uncolored and
inlaid to size, plate 84 in 2 states (colored and uncolored), title and
following leaf bit foxed, occasional offset onto text but very handsome.
contemporary dark blue morocco, gilt inner borders, gilt edges. ex-libris
of Sir William Fraser, Lindsay Fleming and W. R. Jeudwine. Lowndes
1425.   Marlborough 162-63 1996 £2,200.00

ASSOCIATION - JEVONS

EUCLIDES   Elementorvm Evclidis Libri Tredecim. London: Excudebat
Gulielmus Iones, 1620. 1st edition published in England of the original
Greek text. Folio in 4's; pages (ii), 250, final blank missing, Greek &
roman letter in parallel columns, woodcut vignette on titlepage and
initials at beginning of each book, diagrams in text, lightly yellowed, few
small light lamp oil spots on last 2 leaves; contemporary calf, rebacked,
blindstamped fleurons, covers worn, front hinge beginning to crack;
owner's autograph of Thos. Middleton 1668, W. Stanley Jevons 1879 &
Robert Honeyman 1963; good copy. STC 10559; Lowndes 755; Graesse
II 510; Honeyman 1030.   A. Sokol XXV-35 1996 £985.00

ASSOCIATION - ARMINE WODEHOUSE JOHNSON

BAILEY, NATHAN   An Universal Etymological English Dictionary.
London: Ware, Innys and many others, 1753. 15th edition; very thick
octavo; unpaginated, final leaf of book ads present; full sprinkled
morocco, original panelled boards, nice blind fillets and decorations,
professionally rebacked, raised bands, original gilt on red leather label
laid down, two (partially overlapping) engraved armorial bookplates of Sir
Armine Wodehouse Johnson and a later family member. Excellent copy.
Cordell p. 10; CBEL II 930.   Hartfield 48-V11A 1996 $385.00

ASSOCIATION - GUY JOHNSON

DU BOIS, W. E. B.   Encyclopedia of the Negro: Prepatory Volume with
Reference Lists and Reports. New York: Phelps-Stokes Fund, 1946. 2nd
edition; 8vo; 216, (2) pages, photo; cloth; near fine; the copy of Guy B.
Johnson and signed by him.   Andrew Cahan 47-1 1996 $200.00

REDDING, J. SAUNDERS   To Make a Poet Black. Chapel Hill:
Unviersity of North Carolina Press, 1939. 8vo; x, 142 pages; cloth; very
good, presentation from author to Guy Johnson. Thornton 11607.
Andrew Cahan 47-5 1996 $150.00

ASSOCIATION - JOHN JOHNSON

ALLISON, DRUMMOND   The Poems of Drummond Allison.
Whiteknights Press, University of Reading, 1978. One of 200 numbered
copies; original binding, patterned endpapers, loosely inserted are: a
slightly soiled publicity leaflet for this book and an 'editorial errata' slip,
listing errors arising from misreading of the original manuscripts;
fore-edge of upper cover darkened, covers very slightly marked, cover
edges very slightly rubbed, very good, issued without dust jacket.
Bookplate of the literary agent John Johnson.   Ulysses 39-9 1996
£65.00

ALLISON, DRUMMOND   The Yellow Night - Poems - 1940-41-42-43.
London: Fortune Press, 1944. 1st edition; frontispiece, 3 other drawings;
original binding, gilt lettering on spine oxidised, covers slightly marked,
head and tail of spine & corners bumped, bottom edges of covers
slightly worn, front free endpaper partially browned from insertion of
small newspaper clipping, very good in nicked, rubbed and spotted,
slightly creased, chipped, marked and dusty dust jacket browned at
spine; bookplate of literary agent John Johnson.   Ulysses 39-654
1996 £155.00

DAVIDSON, JOHN   In a Music Hall and Other Poems. London: Ward
and Downey, 1891. 1st edition; buckram covers, top edge dusty, covers
dusty and slightly soiled, spine browned, head and tail of spine and
corners bumped, free endpapers browned, edges of some pages nicked,
prelims, edges and endpapers spotted, some internal spotting; good.
Presentation copy from author; with bookplate of literary agent John
Johnson.   Ulysses 39-137 1996 £650.00

DOUGLAS, KEITH   The Collected Poems of Keith Douglas. London:
Editions Poetry, 1951. 1st edition; black and white frontispiece; original
binding, top edge slightly dusty, prelims, edges and endpapers spotted,
free endpapers browned, spine slightly darkened, very good, no dust
jacket; bookplate of literary agent John Johnson.   Ulysses 39-155
1996 £80.00

HARRISON, TONY   The Loiners. London: London Magazine Editions,
1970. 1st edition; original binding, head of spine slightly bumped, very
good in nicked and slightly rubbed and dusty dust jacket slightly torn
and creased at head of spine; bookplate of literary agent John Johnson.
Ulysses 39-269 1996 £55.00

HENNELL, THOMAS   Poems. Oxford University Press/Humphrey
Milford, 1936. 1st edition; original binding, top edge slightly dusty, edges
slightly spotted, head and tail of spine and corners bumped, covers
slightly marked, very good, no dust jacket; with ownership signature of
William Rothenstein; bookplate of literary agent John Johnson.
Ulysses 39-284 1996 £75.00

ASSOCIATION - JOHN JOHNSON

HENNELL, THOMAS   Six Poems. Tunbridge Wells: School of Arts and Crafts, 1947. 1st edition; hand printed on crown folio 'Arab' platen machine, 14 pages of text, handmade paper; wrappers, top edge dusty, edges slightly spotted, top edges of covers slightly creased and browned, covers slightly spotted and dusty, very good. Loosely inserted is single leaf with note by headmaster of the school, E. Owen Jennings; bookplate of literary agent John Johnson.   Ulysses 39-285 1996 £125.00

HOMERUS   The Odyssey. London: Oxford University Press, 1935. 1st edition translated by T. E. Lawrence; decorated buckram gilt, top edge gilt, top edge dusty, edges spotted, spine faded, head and tail of spine and one corner slightly bumped, covers slightly marked, very good, no dust jacket; bookplate of the literary agent John Johnson.   Ulysses 39-354 1996 £45.00

MAC LEOD, JOSEPH GORDON   The Ecliptic. London: Faber & Faber, 1930. 1st edition; original binding, top edge dusty, bottom corners bumped, covers slightly marked, creased and dusty, cover edges worn and browned, very good, bookplate of literary agent, John Johnson; loosely inserted is a printed circular letter dated July 25th 1933 from author.   Ulysses 39-391 1996 £85.00

MOLIERE, JEAN BAPTISTE POQUELIN DE 1622-1673   The Misanthrope. London: Rex Collings Ltd., 1973. 1st edition; wrappers, covers slightly marked and rubbed, very good; bookplate of literary agent John Johnson.   Ulysses 39-270 1996 £65.00

RACINE, JEAN   Phaedra Britannica. London: Rex Collings Ltd., 1975. 1st edition; wrappers, covers slightly marked, spotted and dusty, spine browned, small stain at fore-edge of half titlepage, very good; bookplate of literary agent John Johnson.   Ulysses 39-271 1996 £65.00

ROSENBERG, ISAAC   The Collected Works of Isaac Rosenberg - Poetry - Prose - Letters - and Some Drawings. London: Chatto & Windus, 1937. 1st edition; 8 black and white plates; original binding, top edge dusty, prelims, edges and endpapers slightly spotted, spine faded, covers slightly marked and dusty, free endpapers faintly browned, tail of spine and corners very slightly bumped, top corners of last few pages slightly creased, very good, no dust jacket. Bookplate of library agent John Johnson.   Ulysses 39-508 1996 £75.00

SORLEY, CHARLES HAMILTON   Marlborough and Other Poems. Cambridge: Cambridge University Press, 1916. 1st edition; black and white frontispiece photo of author; titlepage, buckram, top edge dusty, prelims, edges and endpapers spotted, covers slightly marked and rubbed, free endpapers browned, head and tail of spine and corners slightly bumped, very good; Cambridge University Press's onw copy, bookplate of literary agent John Johnson.   Ulysses 39-643 1996 £250.00

SPENCER, BERNARD   Agean Islands and Other Poems. London: Editions Poetry/Nicholson and Watson, 1946. 1st edition; original binding, top edge dusty and slightly spotted, covers dusty, head and tail of spine and corners bumped and worn as usual, covers cocked, very good in nicked and slightly rubbed, marked and dusty dust jacket, by Nicols Engonopoulos, darkened at spine and edges; bookplate of literary agent John Johnson.   Ulysses 39-547 1996 £75.00

SPENDER, STEPHEN 1909-   Poems. London: Faber & Faber Ltd., 1934. 2nd edition; original binding, top edge dusty, head and tail of spine slightly bumped, head of spine slightly split, prelims, edges and endpaper spotted, covers slightly marked and dusty, good, no dust jacket; signed by author; loosely inserted ALS from author to literary John Johnson, with Johnson bookplate.   Ulysses 39-549 1996 £75.00

THOMAS, D. M.   Personal and Possessive. London: Outposts Publications, 1964. 1st edition; author's first book; signed by author; wrappers, covers slightly marked and dusty, very good; nameplate of literary agent John Johnson.   Ulysses 39-587 1996 £75.00

ASSOCIATION - JOHN HENRY JOHNSON

SPELMAN, HENRY   Glossarium Archaiologicum: Continens Latino-Barbara...Scholiis and Commentariis Illustrata. London: Alice Warren, 1664. Folio in 4's; pages (xii), 576; imprimatur leaf, titlepage printed in black and red within double ruled frame; mid 19th century half tan russia, backstrip darkened, front joint weak, slight wear to head, raised bands, gilt compartments, morocco grain maroon cloth sides, marbled endpapers; early ownership signature, lengthy 19th century ms. note on verso, owner's name "B. Chadwick" stamped on head margin of titlepage. Ex-libris of John Henry Johnson; good. Cordell p. 158; Wing S4925.   Blackwell's B112-263 1996 £200.00

ASSOCIATION - LIONEL JOHNSON

SWINBURNE, ALGERNON CHARLES 1837-1909   Miscellanies. London: Chatto & Windus, 1886. 1st edition; 8vo; 32 page publisher's ads at back dated March 1886; CC4 with stylized floral decoration not blank as stated in Tinker; original green cloth, gilt ruled and lettered, publisher's design in gilt at lower spine, some darkening, and rubbing; some browning and spotting, generally at front and back; good copy. Poet Lionel Johnson's copy with his signature; Willis Vickery's copy with bookplate. Tinker 2030; Wise 'Swinburne' I.80, 2.124-5.   James Cummins 14-203 1995 $350.00

ASSOCIATION - LYNDON JOHNSON

MOONEY, BOOTH   The Lyndon Johnson Story. New York: FS&C, 1956. 1st edition; book very good in dust jacket has numerous small tears; nice inscription from Johnson to Karl Wyler (El Paso publisher). Parker Books of the West 30-128 1996 $350.00

ASSOCIATION - REGINALD BRIMLEY JOHNSON

AUSTEN, JANE 1775-1817   The Letters of... London: Richard Bentley & Son, 1884. 1st edition; 7 7/8 x 5 1/2 inches; 2 volumes, frontispiece in each volume, pages xv, 374, 2 pages ads; v, 366, 2 pages ads; dark olive green cloth, Austen's monogram in gilt on front covers, gilt titling to backstrip, bevelled boards, doneky brown endpapers, uncut, backstrips worn at top and bottom, slight trace of label to front covers, corners slightly worn, contents very good. Reginald Brimley Johnson's copy with his bookplate. Gilson g1; Keynes 165; Chapman 95.   Ian Hodgkins 78-66 1996 £180.00

ASSOCIATION - MARGARET ELIZA JOHNSTONE

ROGERS, SAMUEL   Italy, a Poem. London: Edward Moxon, 1844. 8vo; illustrations, vignettes; 8 pages of publisher's ads dated Oct. 1, 1844 at back following single leaf ad, stain on fore-edge; brown morocco gilt, slight rubbing and soiling; very attractive copy; presentation copy from author to Margaret Eliza Johnstone.   James Cummins 14-169 1996 $150.00

ASSOCIATION - HANS JONAS

HEIDEGGER, MARTIN   Zur Sache des Denkens. Tubingen: Niemeyer, 1969. 1st edition; fine, lacking dust jacket; superb association, inscribed by author to great scholar of Gnosticism, Hans Jonas.   Lame Duck Books 19-240 1996 $1,500.00

ASSOCIATION - FESTING JONES

BUTLER, SAMUEL 1835-1902   Gavottes, Minuets, Fugues and Other Short Pieces for the Piano by Samuel Butler. London: and New York: Novello, Ewer and Co., 1885. Original blue-grey mottled paper wrappers, as issued, backstrip worn, otherwise good. Signed presentation from Henry Festing Jones to G. F. Hilder. Hoppe 19.   Jarndyce CII-40 1996 £150.00

BUTLER, SAMUEL 1835-1902   Narcissus. London: Weekes and Co., 1888. Without wrappers mentioned by Hoppe; loosely inserted is an ALS from Festing Jones (presumably to G. F. Hilder). Signed presentation from Jones to Hilder; Hoppe 22.   Jarndyce CII-49 1996 £120.00

BUTLER, SAMUEL 1835-1902   Seven Sonnets and a Psalm of Montreal. Cambridge: printed for Private Circulation, 1904. Original wrappers, chipped and detached; inscribed by Festing Jones to Charles Strachey, with ALS from Festing Jones to Strachey.   Jarndyce CII-87 1996 £150.00

BUTLER, SAMUEL 1835-1902   Ulysses: a Dramatic Oratorio in Vocal Score... London: Weekes and Co., 1904. Original light brown paper wrappers slightly faded, otherwise very good, signed presentation from Festing Jones to G. F. Hilder. Hoppe 45.   Jarndyce CII-88 1996 £110.00

JONES, HENRY FESTING   Samuel Butler, author of Erewhon (1835-1902). London: Macmillan and Co., 1919. 2 volumes; origina red cloth, dulled; E. W. Hudson's copy, signed by him, enclosed are 2 letters, one typed, the other in autograph and both signed by Henry Festing Jones to Hudson.   Jarndyce CII-126 1996 £110.00

ASSOCIATION - H. A. JONES

LEMOINE, H. History, Origin and Progress of the Art of Printing, From Its First Invention in Germany to the End of the Seventeenth Century. London: 1797. 1st edition; 12mo; 156 pages; later library cloth, some browning throughout, first blank very brittle, title flaking little at edges (not affecting text); ex-John Crerar Library copy with booklabel, perforated stamps on first 3 leaves, with release stams; presentation inscription to Ellis Williams, Printer from Miss H. A. Jones. Bigmore & Wyman p. 431. Maggs Bros. Ltd. 1191-188 1996 £115.00

ASSOCIATION - H. LANGLEY JONES

STEPHENSON, BLAKE & CO. Lining Type Borders, Brass Rule, &c. Material and Machinery. London: Stephenson Blake & Co. ltd., 1915/19. 2nd issue; 4to; pages xviii, 144, 72 (machinery) + 8 inserted pages; original cloth, gilt, dated 1915 but with new price list and inserted slips dated 1919; very good; contemporary ownership signature of H. Langley Jones, subsequently in the library of Walter Tracy, with few pencilled marginal notes by him. Claude Cox 107-237 1996 £65.00

ASSOCIATION - HERSCHEL JONES

SILLAR, DAVID Poems. Kilmarnock: by John Wilson, 1789. 1st edition; 8vo; 247 pages; printed on blueish paper; fine binding of full green straight grain morocco, sides with triple gilt rules, spine lettered in gilt, double gilt rules, purple coated endpapers, top edge gilt, others uncut; protected in modern green morocco backed folding case; the Hoe copy with Robert Hoe's leather booklabel, later label of Herschel V. Jones. Egerer 14; Johnson Provincial Poetry 832. Simon Finch 24-211 1996 £1,000.00

WORDSWORTH, WILLIAM 1770-1850 The Waggoner a Poem. London: printed by Strahan and Spottiswoode for Longman, etc., 1819. 1st edition; 8vo; full dark green morocco, gilt, spine and inner dentelles gilt, top edge gilt, joints little rubbed; attractive copy; booklabel of Herschel V. Jones. Cornell Wordsworth Collection 49; Wise p. 22. Ximenes 109-305 1996 $600.00

ASSOCIATION - HUGH JONES

LAWSON, JOHN PARKER The Book of Perth: an Illustration of the Moral and Ecclesiastical State of Scotland Before and After the Reformation. Edinburgh: Thomas G. Stevenson, 1847. Limited edition (251); 8vo; pages xl, 318, (ii), 3 engraved plates, woodcut; little spotting; original cloth, gilt, rather faded, tear across top of spine repaired. Presentation copy from William Turnbull, to whomt he work is dedicated, to Hugh Jones. R.F.G. Hollett 76-152 1996 £75.00

ASSOCIATION - BEN JONSON

LECTIUS, JACOBUS Poetae Graeci Veteres Carminis Heroici Scriptores Qui Extant, Omnes. Aureliae Allobrogum (i.e. Geneva): sumptibus Caldorianae Societatis, 1606. Folio; pages (vi), (ii) blank, (xvi), 739, (i) blank, 624, (xxii), apparently lacks rT8 (final blank), titlepage in red and black, title in Greek at head of titlepage, parallel Greek and Latin texts; late 19th century tan morocco with embossed relief dec. by Mrs. A. S. Macdonald of the Guild of Women Binders, depicting on the upper cover Hermes descending, surrounded by the sacred fire of Olympus and on the lower cover a portrait of Ben Jonson, (this was his copy) within a surround of his ownership inscription, bookplates, binding, lightly rubbed, titlepage dusty and reinforced on verso at inner margin at time of rebinding, some edges little frayed, occasional marginal worming; Simon Finch 24-134 1996 £2,250.00

ASSOCIATION - CORNELIA JORDAN

MILLER, RICHARD L. Travels Abroad: Embracing Holland, England, Belgium, France, Sandwich Islands, New Zealand, Australia &c... Lynchburg: J. P. Bell Co., Stationers and Printers, 1891. 1st edition; 8vo; 121 pages; author's only book; original full brown pebbled calf with gilt title and inner dentelles, all edges gilt, some edgewear, front outer joint starting at bottom, but very good; rare; with pencilled ALS from author presenting the book to Cornelia Jordan. Haynes 12265. Chapel Hill 94-412 1996 $150.00

ASSOCIATION - KAMES

BRADLEY, RICHARD d. 1732 New Improvements of Planting and Gardening, Both Philosophical and Practical, Explaining the Motion of the Sap and Generation of Plants... London: Mears, 1717/17/18. 1st edition; 8vo; pages (xvi), 70, (2), 1 plate; (xvi), 136, 3 plates; (xii), 290, (2), 3 plates; title printed in red and black, some foxing and light staining; contemporary panelled calf, worn, especially on spine; very good, tight copy; bookplate of Henry Home Lord Kames; Henrey 494, 495, 496; PMM 356 (note). Second Life Books 103-31 1996 $1,800.00

ASSOCIATION - E. MC KNIGHT KAUFFER

HUXLEY, ALDOUS LEONARD 1894-1936 Themes and Variations. New York: Harper, 1950. 1st American edition; spine decoration bit rubbed, thus a very good copy, lacking dust jacket; this copy inscribed to British artist E. McKnight Kauffer and his wife Marion. Between the Covers 42-232 1996 $375.00

ASSOCIATION - KAVANAGH

WOOLNOTH, WILLIAM A Graphical Illustration of the Metropolitan Cathedral Church of Canterbury... London: T. Cadell and W. Davies, 1816. 1st edition; large 4to; engraved titlepage and 20 engraved plates by Woolnoth after drawings by T. Hastings; extra illustrated with the insertion of 43 hand illuminated coats-of-arms (attributed to C. R. Cotton) in margins alongside biographies of various bishops; full early 19th century olive calf, spine with raised bands, gilt and blindstamped compartments, gilt leonine device and gilt stamped red morocco label, covers with blindstamped decorative borders with gilt stamped floral devices at corners, gilt ruled inner dentelles, marbled edges and endpapers, dark blue silk bookmark, some rubbing, foxing to title, slight foxing or offsetting to some plates; very good; mid 19th century bookplate of C. R. Cotton, ex-libris H. R. Kavanagh. George J. Houle 68-157 1996 $850.00

ASSOCIATION - HOWARD KELLY

OSLER, WILLIAM 1849-1919 An Alabama Student and Other Biographical Essays. London: Humphrey Milford, 1929. 1st edition; 2nd impression; 8vo; (iii), 334 pages, frontispiece, illustrations; red cloth, spine soiled; inscribed to Willard E. Goodwin from Howard A. Kelly and Goodwin's signature and bookplate. Jeff Weber 31-31 1996 $100.00

ASSOCIATION - CHARLES KEMPE

THANE, J. British Autography. A Collection of Fac-Similes of the Hand Writing of Royal and Illustrious Personages, with Their Autahentic Portraits. London: published by J. Thane, n.d. 4to; 2 volumes, 2 frontispieces, 269 plates; half russia, quite rubbed at extremities, corners bit bumped; booklabel of Charles E. Kempe. Maggs Bros. Ltd. 1191-164 1996 £85.00

ASSOCIATION - KENNEY

KAUFFMAN, C. H. The Dictionary of Merchandize, and Nomenclature in All Languages... London: printed for the author, sold by T. Boosey, 1803. 1st edition; 8vo; iv, 380 pages, piece torn from upper margin of X1 with loss of one word of text, lightly browned; contemporary half calf, neatly rebacked; from the Kenney collection. Kress B4690; 4 copies in NUC. James Burmester 29-81 1996 £300.00

ASSOCIATION - STAN KENTON

GATES, WILLIAM G. Illustrated History of Portsmouth. Portsmouth: Charpentier & Co., 1900. Hampshire Telegraph Centenary Edition; thick 4to; 734 pages; contemporary half black morocco, upper joint cracked; presentation inscription to Stan Kenton. Howes Bookshop 265-451 1996 £85.00

ASSOCIATION - KENYON

BURLINGTON FINE ARTS CLUB Illustrated Catalogue of Illuminated Manuscripts. Exhibition Catalogue 269. London: 1908. Folio; 162 plates; brown cloth, gilt lettering on spine and upper cover, bit scuffed, spine bit faded, some very slight browning only to edges, crease on f.f.e.p., pencil annotations beside few exhibits referring to particular lots in the Aldenham sale 19371 Ownership inscription of Lord Kenyon. Maggs Bros. Ltd. 1191-141 1996 £360.00

ASSOCIATION - KENYON

JAMES, MONTAGUE RHODES   The Apocalypse in Latin. Ms. 10 in the Collection of Dyson Perrins. Oxford: 1927. Folio; color frontispiece, 42 plates; green half morocco, gilt lettering on spine, pencil ownership inscription and booklabel, both of Lord Kenyon, attractive volume. Maggs Bros. Ltd. 1191-155 1996 £100.00

JAMES, MONTAGUE RHODES   A Descriptive Catalogue of the Manuscripts in the Fitzwilliam Museum. Cambridge: 1895. Plates; blue cloth, gilt, bit worn at extremities, booklabel of Lord Kenyon.   Maggs Bros. Ltd. 1191-152 1996 £100.00

JAMES, MONTAGUE RHODES   A Descriptive Catalogue of the Manuscripts in the Library of Lambeth Palace. Cambridge: 1930-32. 3 volumes, 357 mss. described, original wrappers, spines slightly torn. Lord Kenyon's copy.   Maggs Bros. Ltd. 1191-151 1996 £80.00

OLDHAM, J. BASIL   English Blind-Stamped Bindings and Blind Panels of English Binders. Cambridge: 1952-58. Folio; 2 volumes, several plates; blue cloth, red leather spine labels, ownership inscription of Lord Kenyon, offprint of Festschrift for Ernst Kyriss, Oldham's English Fifteenth Century Binding, inscribed from author presumably to Kenyon inserted loose, along with few notes on loose leaf & bill for second volume from Quaritch;   Maggs Bros. Ltd. 1191-21 1996 £340.00

OWEN, HUGH   A History of Shrewsbury. London: Pub. by Harding, Lepard and Co., 1825. 1st edition; 4to; 2 volumes; engraved frontispieces (foxed), half titles in pictorial borders, 48 engraved and lithograph plates (some foxed), contemporary half calf, slightly rubbed, spines gilt. Bookplates of Lord Kenyon.   Anthony W. Laywood 108-216 1996 £395.00

QUARITCH, BERNARD   A Catalogue of Illuminated and Other Manuscripts Together with Some Works on Palaeography. London: Bernard Quaritch, 1931. 4to; color frontispiece, 65 plates; original boards, extremities slightly worn, ownership inscription of Lord Kenyon, few annotations in pencil, copy of letter to Maggs offering 3 items for sale, with their descriptions, bill of sale of 3 items to Bernard Quaritch from Kenyon and letter from Geoffrey Hobson to Kenyon about a ms. sold at Sothebys in 1913 inserted loose.   Maggs Bros. Ltd. 1191-35 1996 £65.00

RICCI, SEYMOUR DE 1881-1942   A Hand List of a Collection of Books and Manuscripts Belonging to the Rt. Hon. Lord Amherst of Hackney at Didlington Hall, Norfolk. Cambridge: privately printed, 1906. 4to; frontispiece, 4 plates; cloth backed boards, spine missing, edges bit bumped, printed on rectos only; Lord Kenyon's booklabel and ownerhsip inscription, few pencil annotations in his hand, compliments slip from Lord Amherst tipped in.   Maggs Bros. Ltd. 1191-4 1996 £60.00

SIX Views of the Scenery at Nesscliff. London: Hullmandel, 1824. Folio; 6 uncolored lithographic plates, 44 x 34 cm. sheet size; original wrappers; Lord Kenyon's copy. Not in Abbey.   Marlborough 162-49 1996 £700.00

WARNER, G. F.   Illuminated Manuscripts in the British Museum. London: 1899-1903. Limited to 300 copies; folio; 1st to 4th series, in 4 volumes; 60 fine color and gilt plates; loose in green cloth backed portfolios as issued, some fading on first title, ties missing on first and third series, booklabels of Lord Kenyon   Maggs Bros. Ltd. 1191-167 1996 £500.00

YORK, EDWARD, 2ND DUKE OF   The Master of Game by Edward, Second Duke of York. The Oldest English Book on Hunting. London: 1904. Limited to 600 numbered copies; folio; frontispiece, 51 plates; suede, gilt inner dentelles on top edge, spotting throughout, not affecting plates, slight marks on some plates only on margins, mildly shaken; booklabel of Lord Kenyon.   Maggs Bros. Ltd. 1191-136 1996 £125.00

ASSOCIATION - LLOYD KENYON

DIBDIN, THOMAS FROGNALL 1776-1847   The Bibliographical Decameron; or, Ten Days Pleasant Discourse Upon Illuminated Manuscripts, and Subjects... London: printed for the author by W. Bulmer and Co., Shakespeare Press... 1817. 1st edition; 4to; 3 volumes, large paper copy;, 410, 535, 484 pages of text, without half titles; 54 plates, numerous vignettes, some on India paper, some colored, full diced calf, gilt rule and decorative borders, gilt bands, rule and title to panelled spines, all edges gilt, narrow inner gilt dentelles, marbled endpapers, armorial bookplate, later printed book label of Lloyd Kenyon to volume 1. Lowndes II p. 640.   Beeleigh Abbey BA56-143 1996 £750.00

ASSOCIATION - WILLIAM PATON KER

CALVERLEY, WILLIAM SLATER   Notes On the Early Sculptured Crosses, Shrines and Monuments in the Present Diocese of Carlisle. Kendal: T. Wilson, 1899. 8vo; pages xviii, 319, portrait, numerous plates and illustrations; original brown cloth, gilt; scarce; labe reads "This book belonged to William Paton Ker, All Souls College, Oxford and in memory of him was given to Mary Wordsworth Higginbotham Dec. 1923." R.F.G. Hollett & Son 78-12 1996 £95.00

ASSOCIATION - A. J. KIDDELL

JOHN, W. D.   Pontypool and Usk Japanned Wares: with the Early History of the Iron and Tinplate Industries at Ponypool. Newport: Ceramic Book Co., 1953. 4to; xii, 88 pages; map and 26 plates, including 4 in color; publisher's scarlet calf, top edge gilt, very slightly rubbed; inscribed presentation copy from author to A. J. B. Kiddell.   Thomas Thorp 489-172 1996 £50.00

SIREN, OSVALD   Early Chinese Paintings from A. W. Bahr Collection. London: Chiswick Press, 1938. Limited to 750 numbered copies; folio; 116 pages; 27 tipped in plates, including 13 in color; buckram, gilt, top edge gilt, others uncut, covers very slightly dust soiled. Inscribed by A. W. Bahr to A. J. Kiddell.   Thomas Thorp 489-282 1996 £125.00

ASSOCIATION - KIMBOLTON

REID, THOMAS 1710-1796   Essays on the Active Powers of Man. Edinburgh: printed for John Bell, 1788. 1st edition; 4to; vii, 493, (3) pages; bound without half title and ad leaf; near contemporary full green morocco by Hering with his ticket, some very minor scuffing and scratching, but a handsome copy; the Kimbolton Library copy with bookplate. Jessop p. 165.   C. R. Johnson 37-76 1996 £900.00

ASSOCIATION - KIMBOLTON CASTLE

BRITISH & FOREIGN BIBLE SOCIETY   Reports of the British and Foreign Bible Society, with Extracts of Correspondence, &c... London: printed for the Society by J. Tilling, 1805-16. 22cm; various pagination; gilt and blindstamped dark blue calf, all edges gilt, very good. This set given by the Society to (lady?) Olivia Bernard-Sparrow (came from Kimbolton Castle Lib).   Rockland Books 38-29 1996 $1,500.00

ASSOCIATION - R. D. KING

MELVILLE, HERMAN 1819-1891   White-Jacket; or the World in a Man-of-War. New York: Harper & Bros., 1850. 1st American edition, 1st printing; original brown cloth, ornately stamped in blind, spine lettered in gilt (BAL first cloth binding), fraying and wearing to joints and spine ends, some repair, rubbed, upper joint cracked, title nearly detached, spotting throughout, staining, mostly at front, ads at back; blue morocco backed case (damaged); with signature of R. D. King 1850 on endpaper. BAL 13662.   James Cummins 14-135 1996 $750.00

ASSOCIATION - RICHARD POOLE KING

SEALY, HENRY NICHOLAS   A Treatise on Coins, Currency and Banking, with Observations on the Bank Act of 1844 and on the Reports of the Committees of the House of Lords and of the House of Commons on the Bank Acts. London: Longman, 1858-67. 1st edition; 8vo; 2 volumes; original brown calf, neatly repaired; presentation copy, inscribed in each volume by author for Richard Poole King Esq. Very good, uncommon.   James Burmester 29-124 1996 £400.00

ASSOCIATION - WILLIAM KINGSLAND

BROWNING, ELIZABETH BARRETT 1806-1861   A Selection from the Poetry....First Series (-Second Series). London: Smith, Elder & Co., 1884. New edition; 8vo; 2 volumes; original brown cloth, some rubbing, spines bit dull; first volume bit shaken, but very good set; presentation copy, inscribed by Robert Browning for William G. Kingsland, who has added another inscription passing the set on to his grandson. Barnes E145. Ximenes 108-367 1996 $450.00

ASSOCIATION - H. J. KIRBY

AN ACCURATE Account of the Trial of William Corder for the Murder of Maria Marten...To Which are Added, An Explantory Preface and Fifty-Three of the Letters Sent by Various Ladies, in Answer to Corder's Matrimonial Advertisements... London: Pubished by George Foster, n.d., c. 1828. 2nd edition; 12mo; the printer appears to have left off the page number 14 as the consecutive pages are 13 to 15 and text appears continuous, pages 52 to 57 are out of order, some light spotting and browning; contemporary calf, red morocco label, upper joint starting, some knocking of corners and rubbing, generally light, without portrait; signature and address of H. J. Kirby on free endpaper, cropped signature of Jane Waldo on title.   James Cummins 14-140 1995 $200.00

ASSOCIATION - JOSHUA KIRBY

KIRBY, JOHN   The Suffolk Traveller; or a Journey through Suffolk... Ipswich: Bagnall, 1735. 1st edition; 8vo; 2ff., 206 pages, 1 f., blanks at end, contemporary calf, rubbed, title grubby; with signature of Joshua Kirby, author's son.   Marlborough 162-58 1996 £250.00

ASSOCIATION - KIRKLAND

WEBBER, SAMUEL   War, a Poem. Cambridge: Hilliard and Metcalf, 1823. 1st edition; 16mo; 48 pages; original printed wrappers. Ink inscription from Noah Worcester to President Kirkland of Harvard. Shoemaker 14854.   M & S Rare Books 60-212 1996 $175.00

ASSOCIATION - JACOB KITTREDGE

CULLEN, WILLIAM   Lectures on the Materia Medica... Philadelphia: Robert Bell, 1775. 1st American edition; 4to; viii, 512 pages; later calf, foxed, contemporary notes on endpapers; Jacob Kittredge's copy. Evans 14000; Austin 577.   The Bookpress 75-405 1996 $500.00

ASSOCIATION - GEORGE KLOSS

PIUS II, POPE 1405-1464   Epistolae Familiares. Nuremberg: Anton Koberger 17 July, 1486. Quarto; 246 leaves (first blank), gothic letter, initials spaces, initials supplied in alternate blue and red, paragraph marks in red, corner torn from first blank leaf and patched, insignificant wormhole in gutter of few leaves but generally good, clean copy; 19th century half sheep, marbled boards; from the collection of George Kloss, with his bookplate and ink note of the Panzer no. and Manhattan College, New York with bookplate.   H. M. Fletcher 121-15 1996 £2,300.00

ASSOCIATION - E. E. KNAPP

SIMMS, WILLIAM GILMORE 1806-1870   The Wigwam and the Cabin. First (and Second) Series. New York: Wiley and Putnam, 1845. 1st edition; 8vo; 2 parts in one volume; contemporary half black morocco, marbled boards, quite rubbed, discoloring from leather, short crack at top of upper joint, some browning and staining of endpapers, else light browning, half titles without ad leaves which determine printings, partial image of an ad leaf offset on blank at front; signatures of Rebecca Berger and E. E. Knapp on endpapers. BAL 18093, 18094; Barzun & Taylor Cat. of Crime 3461.   James Cummins 14-181 1996 $750.00

ASSOCIATION - BARTHOLOMEW KNEELAND

SECCOMBE, JOSEPH   Some Occasional Thoughts on the Influence of the Spirit. Boston: S. Kneeland, and T. Green, 1742. 1st edition; 8vo; (2), 2, 16 pages; modern plain wrappers, lacks half title, foxed. With oxidized signature of Bartholomew Kneeland, presumably a relative of the printer. M & S Rare Books 60-405 1996 $300.00

ASSOCIATION - ARNOLD KNIGHT

HOLLAND, JOHN   The History, Antiquities and Description of the Town and Parish of Worksop. Sheffield: J. Blackwell, 1826. One of 150 copies; 4to; x pages, 1 f., 204 pages, 32 engraved text illustrations; original boards, joints cracked; subscriber's copy with ex-libris of Sir Arnold Knight. Anderson p. 238.   Marlborough 162-46 1996 £220.00

ASSOCIATION - JOSEPH KNIGHT

SUCKLING, JOHN   The Works. Dublin: Nelson, 1766. 1st Dublin edition; tall 8vo; pages 462, (2); handsome binding by Stikeman, in three quarter crushed morocco, gilt extra, panelled spine, top edge gilt, marbled endpapers, slight defect at bottom of titlepage, not affecting text, else fine, scarce. Bookplate of Joseph Knight, distinguished Dickens scholar.   Hartfield 48-L82 1996 $295.00

ASSOCIATION - THOMAS KNOWLTON

ALPINUS, PROSPER   De Plantis Aegyptis Liber...De Balsamo, Dialogvs (etc.). Venice: Francesco Franceschi, 1592. 1st edition of first work, 2nd edition of the second; 4to; ff. (iv), 80, (viii), Roman letter, woodcut printer's device on main titlepage (repeated on 2nd), many woodcuts of plants, mostly full page, woodcut initials and ornaments, titlepage bit dusty, frayed at edges and reinforced in gutter, light yellowing in parts, some outer margins lightly waterstained, small pieces torn from upper edges of last 4 leaves, without loss; contemporary calf, neatly rebacked, gilt double fillets & spine, outer corners worn; inscription recording gift by Richard Richardson of North Bierley to Thos. Knowlton 7.2. 1748/9 on endpaper. BM STC It. p. 20; Adams A803; Index Aurel 103.853; Pritzel 163;   A. Sokol XXV-3 1996 $2,850.00

ASSOCIATION - JOHN KNYVETT

DAVENANT, WILLIAM 1606-1668   The Works... London: printed by T. N. for Henry Herringman, 1673. 1st edition; folio; contemporary mottled calf, gilt, spine gilt, some rubbing, completely sound; wholly unrestored binding, text crisp and fresh; inscribed "Mrs. Elizabeth de Greys booke, given her by John Knyvett Esq. ye yeere he was High Sheriff of Norfolke, 1681/2." Wing D320; Greg III 1057-8; CBEL I 1208; Woodward & McManaway 309.   Ximenes 109-97 1996 $2,500.00

ASSOCIATION - ABRAM KROL

BIBLE. FRENCH - 1952   Cantique des Cantiques. Paris: A. Krol, 1952. Limited to 236 copies; oblong octavo; 57 copies; engravings and woodcut initials by Burins de Abram Krol; bound in full Chinese red morocco by Denise Lubett in 1975, spine gilt tooled with design of grape vines, front cover with gilt tooled chalice, grape vines and deer, gilt tooled turquoise morocco doublures, all edges gilt, housed in felt lined morocco backed chemise with morocco trimmed slipcase, spine of chemise slightly faded, else extremely fine; presentation inscription from Krol.   Bromer Booksellers 87-166 1996 $2,000.00

ASSOCIATION - ERNST KYRISS

GOETHE, JOHANN WOLFGANG VON 1749-1832   Iphigenie auf Tauris: Ein Schauspiel. Doves Press, 1912. One of 32 copies on vellum (12 of which had gold initials, there were 200 copies printed on paper); 9 1/4 x 6 3/4 inches; 110 pages, (1) leaf (colophon); printed in red and black, with tiny stamped cipher of Ernst Kyriss; bound by Doves Bindery in 1913 in Russet morocco, covers and turn-ins with simple gilt rule borders, raised bands, spine compartments ruled and titled in gilt, all edges gilt, except for inevitable slight discoloration of the vellum flyleaves where they touch the facing leather turn-ins, this is a virtually mint copy in unworn and extremely pleasing Doves binding.   Phillip J. Pirages 33-187 1996 $8,750.00

WORDSWORTH, WILLIAM 1770-1850   The Prelude. Doves Press, 1915. One of 10 copies on vellum (there were also 155 on paper); 9 1/4 x 6 1/2 inches; 301, (1) pages; extraordinarily fine russet morocco, elaborately and beautifully gilt by the Doves Bindery (signed '19 C-S 19' on rear turn-in), covers framed by multiple gilt rules and featuring lovely intricate cornerpieces consisting of a rose surrounded by criclets and four sprigs of five oak leaves, there corner decorations connected by tendrils (which support 8 additional, smaller sprigs of oak), front cover with titling and dates, spine densely gilt in compartments filled with the same decoration as used for the cornerpieces, turn-ins with four parallel gilt rules and with oak leaves and circlets at corners, vellum pastedowns and flyleaves, all edges gilt, binding identical to Tidcombe 795; front flyleaf with tiny ownership stamp of Ernst Kyriss. Only mostr tirivial imperfections, virtually pristine.   Phillip J. Pirages 33-190 1996 $15,000.00

ASSOCIATION - RICHARD LA GALLIENNE

HINKSON, KATHARINE TYNAN 1861-1931   Shamrocks. London: Kegan Paul, Trench & Co., 1st edition; soiled beige cloth with gilt lettering and shamrock design on front panel; overall very good, showing very litte if any wear; bookplate of Richard LaGallienne. Colby College Library bookplate.   Hermitage SP95-637 1996 $150.00

ASSOCIATION - MARSHALL LAIRD

LIVINGSTONE, DAVID 1813-1873   Missionary Travels and Researches in South Africa... London: John Murray, 1857. 1st edition; 8vo; pages ix, (i), 711, (1), 8 (ads dated Nov. 1 1857); folding wood engraved frontispiece, steel engraved portrait with tissue guard; 24 plates, 2 folding maps; original blindstamped cloth, backstrip gilt lettered direct, rear cover dampstained at edge, brown chalked endpapers, hinges split but firm; bookplate of Marshall Laird, early owner's name, and ticket of 'Edmond and Remnants'.   Blackwell's B112-178 1996 £120.00

ASSOCIATION - CHARLES LAMB

HILLIAR, ANTHONY   A Brief and Merry History of Great Britain... London: printed for J. Roberts; J. Shuckburgh; J. Jackson; J. Penn, n.d. 1730. 1st edition; 8vo; early 19th century half red morocco, top edge gilt, some rubbing, in red half morocco slipcase; from the library of Charles Lamb, with his signature on titlepage, presented by Lamb to his good friend Henry Crabb Robinson. Outside rather dusty, but uncut and essentially in very good condition.   Ximenes 109-157 1996 $3,500.00

ASSOCIATION - LAMBART

JOHNSON, SAMUEL 1709-1784   Letters to and From the Late Samuel Johnson, LL.D. London: for A. Strahan, and T. Cadell, 1788. 1st edition; 8vo; 2 volumes; pages (ii), xv, (i) blank, (397); xi, (i) blank, without errata slip found in some copies; contemporary tan calf, skilfully rebacked to style and corners repaired, edges of boards worn, with occasional spot or stain; presentation copy from editor, Hester Lynch Piozzi to her friend Mrs. Lambart, with later Lambart family ownership inscriptions. Rotschild 1270; Courtney & Nichol Smith p. 168; Chapman & Hazen p.165.   Simon Finch 24-185 1996 £850.00

ASSOCIATION - LAMBERT

OATES, FRANK   Matabele Land and the Victoria Falls. London: Kegan, Paul, Trench & Co., 1889. 2nd edition; thick 8vo; original grey-green pictorial cloth, spine dull, slight restoration; very good, presentation copy inscribed by editor C.G. Oates to Miss Lambert. Theal p. 219.   Ximenes 109-207 1996 $450.00

ASSOCIATION - HENRY RALPH LAMBTON

SURTEES, ROBERT SMITH 1803-1864   The Horseman's Manual. London: Alfred Miller, 1831. 1st edition; 12mo; contemporary maroon morocco, gilt, spine gilt, all edges gilt, in the manner of T. Gosden, light rubbing, in half red morocco slipcase; fine; author's rare first book; early armorial bookplate of Henry Ralph Lambton who was no doubt related to book's dedicatee, Ralph John Lambton of Durham; later bookplate of George Gordon Massey. Mellon Collection 141; CBEL III 967.   Ximenes 108-333 1996 $1,250.00

ASSOCIATION - J. LAMONT

KOLDEWEY, CAPTAIN   The German Expedition of 1869-70, and Narrative of the Wreck of the 'Hansa' In the Ice. London: 1874. 1st English edition; royal 8vo; 4 chromolithographs, 2 steel engraved portraits, 2 colored maps and numerous woodcuts in text; contemporary half calf, gilt spine, red morocco label, gilt; extremely scarce; bookplate of J. Lamont of Knockddow.   Charles W. Traylen 117-419 1996 £600.00

ASSOCIATION - HARRY LANDA

KRUEGER, M.   Pioneer Life in Texas. N.P.: n.d., San Antonio: ca. 1930. 1st edition; 225 pages; presentation copy from author's family to Harry Landa. Howes K269; Herd 1289.   Maggie Lambeth 30-315 1996 $250.00

ASSOCIATION - LANDAU

FRANCO, NICCOLO   La Philena. Historia Amorosa Vltimamente Composta. Mantua: Jacomo Ruffinelli, 1547. 1st edition; 8vo; ff. 470, italic leetter, woodcut portrait of author on titlepage, woodcut printer's device and repeated portrait at end, slight foxing in places; faded contemporary ex-libris on titlepage; 19th century straight grained green morocco by C. Smith, gilt fillets and corner fleurons and richly gilt spine, all edges gilt, very good; bookplate of Baron Landau on pastedown. A. Sokol XXV-40 1996 £1,650.00

ASSOCIATION - LANDAU

GELLI, GIOVANNI BATISTA   La Circe Di Giovan-Batista Gelli. Firenze: Lorenzo Torrentino, 1549. 1st edition; octavo; late 17th or early 18th century polished grained sheep, gilt spine with contrasting title labels of tan and black morocco gilt; joints slightly rubbed, cracked at head and foot of spine with excellent restoration to top of spine, tiny chip at top back joint, light soiling tot title and final leaf, small collector's stamp at foot of title, very respectable copy of a very rare book; several bookplates, including De Vernaccia and Landau bookplates. Adams G333; Gamba 491.   G. W. Stuart 59-43 1996 $750.00

ASSOCIATION - EDWIN LANDSEER

BELL, CHARLES 1774-1842   Essays on the Anatomy of Expression in Painting. London: printed for Longman, Hurst, Rees, and Orme, 1806. 1st edition; 4to; xii, 186 pages, 6 engraved plates, 26 engravings in text; contemporary calf, rebacked, original spine label and endpapers preserved, without half title and without final ad leaf, little light spotting near inner joint of front fly, titlepage and following two pages, and on endpapers; the copy of Sir Edwin Landseer". Gordon Taylor 6.   David Bickersteth 133-179 1996 £465.00

ASSOCIATION - JOHN LANE

LE GALLIENNE, RICHARD 1866-1947   Religion of a Literary Man. London: Mathews and Lane, 1893. One of 250 larage paper copies; 8vo; original binding, very good; inscribed by publisher, John Lane to American poet, Robert Bridges.   Charles Agvent 4-819 1996 $185.00

ASSOCIATION - ANDREW LANG

YEATS, WILLIAM BUTLER 1865-1935   Celtic Twilgiht. London: Lawrence Bullen, 1893. Spine sunned, some foxing to front and rear free endpapers and pastedowns, but very good; inscribed by Andrew Lang. R. A. Gekoski 19-167 1996 £450.00

ASSOCIATION - HENRY PHILIP LANGDON

SENTENTIAE et proverbia ex Poetis Latinis. His Adiecimus. Leosthenis Colvandri Sententias Prophanas... Venice: Ioannes Patauinus, c. 1550. 8vo; pages 216, italic letter, woodcut printer's device on title, frequent contemporary underlining and few ms. annotations in first half of volume, light age yellow, good copy contemporary vellum; bookplate of Henry Philip Langdon. Not in BM STC. This ed. not in Adams.   A. Sokol XXV-91 1996 £425.00

ASSOCIATION - PHILIP LARKIN

DONNE, JOHN 1571-1631   Poems. London: J. M. Dent, 1931. some fading to cloth on spine, otherwise very good; ownership signature "Philip Larkin - Christmas 1939", later ownership signataure underneath with numerous annotations by Larkin.   R. A. Gekoski 19-89 1996 £650.00

ASSOCIATION - LASCELLES

BEVERIDGE, W. H.   Unemployment - a Problem of Industry. London: Longmans, Green and Co., 1931. Reprint; original binding, top edge dusty, covers rubbed and marked, free endpapers browned, spine darkened, head and tail of spine slightly bumped, free endpaeprs browned and spotted, very good; with ownership signature of J. H. Lascelles, dated Balliol 3.8.32. Bookplate of late owner.   Ulysses 39-53 1996 £65.00

ASSOCIATION - FRANCIS LASHER

SMITH, ADAM 1723-1790   An Inquiry into the Nature and Causes of the Wealth of Nations. Philadelphia: Dobson, 1789-96-89. 1st American editions of volumes I and 3; 8vo; 3 volumes; original uniform calf, scuffed; ownership signatures of Francis Lasher in volume 1 and Jacob Lasher 1798 in volume 2.   Rostenberg & Stern 150-9 1996 $1,400.00

ASSOCIATION - JACOB LASHER

SMITH, ADAM 1723-1790   An Inquiry into the Nature and Causes of the Wealth of Nations. Philadelphia: Dobson, 1789-96-89. 1st American editions of volumes I and 3; 8vo; 3 volumes; original uniform calf, scuffed; ownership signatures of Francis Lasher in volume 1 and Jacob Lasher 1798 in volume 2.   Rostenberg & Stern 150-9 1996 $1,400.00

ASSOCIATION - JOHN LATROBE

LAWS and Ordinances Relating to the Baltimore and Ohio Rail Road. Baltimore: John Murphy, 1850. 1st edition thus; very worn old roan covers, spine has perished and is covered by eugly old red cloth tape, front hinge entirely broken, but text is hanging together, old markings and brief notes in text, possibly by the owner John H. B. Latrobe (who was legal counsel for the B & O), Latrobe's name stamped on covers. Magnum Opus 44-89 1996 $100.00

ASSOCIATION - T. LATTER

CAREY, WILLIAM   A Grammar of the Mahratta Language to Which are Added Dialogues on Familiar Subjects. Serampore: printed at the Mission Press, 1825. 3rd edition; 8vo; half title; modern cloth, morocco spine label; prevasive light dampstaining, but very good, uncommon; early armorial bookplate of T. Latter, Bengal Army.   Trebizond 39-106 1996 $325.00

ASSOCIATION - DAVID HERBERT LAWRENCE

DAVIES, WILLIAM HENRY 1871-1940   Foliage Various Poems. London: Elkin Mathews, 1913. Small 8vo; pages 63, (1); original cloth, lettered in gilt on upper cover and spine, cloth box lettered in gilt, somewhat spotted, otherwise excellent; D. H. Lawrence's copy, presentation copy, inscribed by author to Lawrence and dated 1913, with 2 original sketches by Lawrence on rear free endpaper.   Simon Finch 24-152 1996 £1,250.00

ASSOCIATION - THOMAS EDWARD LAWRENCE

CELLINI, BENVENUTO   The Life of Benvenuto Cellini. London: Ballantyne/Vale Press, 1900. Folio; 2 volumes in 1; 2 titlepages, 187, 188 pages of text; woodcut border and initial to first page of text; bound by C. and C. McLeish, full maroon morocco, gilt rule borders with decorative gilt cornerpieces, gilt panelled spine, top edge gilt, others untrimmed, inner gilt rule and repeat cornerpieces; T. E. Lawrence's copy with his pencilled initials to top right hand corner of front free endpaper. Beeleigh Abbey BA56-139 1996 £450.00

ASSOCIATION - FRANK LAWSON

BOYLE, ELEANOR VERE   A Garden of Pleasure. London: Elliot Stock, 1895. 3rd edition; 175 x 105mm; pages xvi, 220, (2), frontispiece and other illustrations in line; contemporary full tan morocco, sides ruled into 9 sections with gold lines and dot at intersections, backstrip lettered and double ruled in compartments with small triple leafe ornaments in blind extending from 3 raised band, all edges gilt on the rough, signed "D(ouglas) C(ockerell) 1900", little rubbed but sound; bookplate of Frank Lawson of Ewelme Down.   Claude Cox 107-14 1996 £110.00

ASSOCIATION - ROBERT LAWSON

LEAF, MUNRO   The Story of Ferdinand the Bull. New York: Viking Press, 1938. drawings in black and white by Robert Lawson; red pictorial boards backed in grey cloth, pictorial endpapers, covers little faded, else fresh copy; inscribed by Robert Lawson with small ink drawing of posy of flowers.   Barbara Stone 70-137 1996 £135.00

ASSOCIATION - LAWTON

BOYCE, CHARLES WILLIAM   A Brief History of the Twenty-Eighth Regiment New York State Volunteers First Brigade, FirstDivision, Twelfth Corps, Army of the Potomac... Buffalo: Matthews Northrup Co., 1896? 1st edition; 194 pages; original cloth; near fine; with long presentation from Wilbur J. Lawton, a member of Co. K. to his Son. Dornbusch I NY 286; Nicholson p. 95.   McGowan Book Co. 65-12 1996 $275.00

ASSOCIATION - EMMA LAZARUS

CHANNING, WILLIAM ELLERY   Poems. Boston: 1843. 1st edition; 12mo; 151 pages; full 20th century turquoise morocco binding, original paper label preserved on back endleaf; inscribed by author for Emma Lazaraus; beneath is 1916 inscription "This vol. that came to me on the death of Josephine Lazarus from her private library I inscribed to my brother John f. Grabau."   M & S Rare Books 60-193 1996 $4,500.00

ASSOCIATION - HENRI LE COURT

SENAULT, LOUIS   Hevres Nouvelles Dediees A Madame La Davphine. Paris: the author, Versailles: Duval, 1680. 1st edition; 8vo; illustrated with vignettes, borders, initials, head and tailpieces; contemporary black sharkskin with silver clasps and studs intact. Henry Le Court bookticket. Univ. Cat. of Books on Art III 56.   Rostenberg & Stern 150-110 1996 $1,750.00

ASSOCIATION - LE DIEU

JENNINGS, HENRY CONSTANTINE   Summary and Free Reflections, In Which the Great Outline Only, and Principal Features, of the Following Subjects are Impartially Traced and Candidly Examined. Chelmsford: printed by Clachar, Frost and Gray, for the author, 1783. xvii, (1), 115, (1), 31, (1), 64, iv, vi, 82, 6, (4), 7-34, 142-178, iv, 68 pages, few annotations in pencil; bound in modern maroon morocco, raised bands, spine lettered in gilt; contemporary signature of Hary Le Dieu on title and bookplate of John Avery; inscribed by author.   John Drury 82-124 1996 £500.00

ASSOCIATION - W. R. LE FANU

BURGESS, RENATE   Portraits of Doctors & Scientisits in the Wellcome Institute of the History of Medicine. Wellcome Inst., 1973. 1st edition; 4to; numerous illustrations; original cloth, dust jacket; from the library of W. R. Le Fanu, with Le Fanu's typescript review for "Medical History" and a TLS from author to Le Fanu.   Forest Books 74-30 1996 £55.00

MOORAT, S. A. J.   Catalogue of Western Manuscripts on Medicine and Science in the Wellcome Historical Medical Library. Wellcome Historical Medical Library, 1962-73. 1st edition; 4to; 3 volumes; hand colored frontispiece, original buckram; from the library of W. R. Le Fanu with few notes on endpapers.   Forest Books 74-185 1996 £110.00

POYNTER, F. N. L.   A Catalouge of Incunabula in the Wellcome Historical Medical Library. London: Oxford University Press, 1954. 1st edition; 4to; 12 plates; original cloth, dust jacket little foxed; presentation copy from author to W. R. Le Fanu.   Forest Books 74-221 1996 £80.00

ASSOCIATION - LE PELLETIER

GENLIS, STEPHANIE FELICITE DUCREST DE ST. AUBIN, COMTESSE DE 1746-1830   Adelaide and Theodore; or Letters on Education... London: T. Cadell, 1788. 3rd edition; 12mo; 3 volumes contemporary tree calf, spines in compartments with raised bands, gilt rules and delicate ornamentation, red and black morocco labels, lettered in gilt; slight spotting to just a few leaves, otherwise fine; bookplate of Count le Pelletier, inscription presenting the book to Mary Pottinger on rear pastedowns, one little chipped.   Simon Finch 24-23 1996 £285.00

ASSOCIATION - TOM LEA

LEA, TOM 1907-   The Hands of Cantu. Boston and Toronto: Little, Brown and Co., 1964. 1st edition; number 40 of only 100 numbered copies; 244 pages; specially printed on mouldmade Arches paper and signed by author; illustrations by author, including mounted frontispiece in color; bound by Harcourt Bindery in full brown crushed levant morocco, raised bands, gilt lettered spine, marbled endpapers, top edge gilt, mint, uncut, in publisher's cloth slipcase; accompanied by a signed and dated print by Lea, additionally, the print with his copy has a presentation inscription signed by Lea. Rare.   Argonaut Book Shop 113-403 1996 $3,000.00

ASSOCIATION - LECONFIELD

BLOUNT, THOMAS 1618-1679   Boscobel; or, the Compleat History of the most Miraculous Preservation of King Charles II. After the Battle of Worcester (and) Claustrum Regale Reseratum; or, the King's Concealment at Trent. London: printed for J. Wilford, 1725. 4th edition; 12mo; fine engraved title, portrait, printed title, 2 folding plates, neatly linen backed; sheep, rebacked; with Petworth House bookplate (?ca. 1910) of Viloet (Wyndham, nee Rawson, Lady) Leconfield.   Peter Murray Hill 185-35 1996 £65.00

ASSOCIATION - JOHN LEECH

SURTEES, ROBERT SMITH 1803-1864   "Plain or Ringlets?" London: 1860. 1st edition in book form; viii pages, 1 f., 406 pages, 13 colored plates; illustrations by John Leech; full red morocco, gilt, decorations of hounds, foxes, etc., inner wide dentelles, top edge gilt; laid in is 2 page ALS from Leech to Mrs. Mclan (?); fine copy but outer joints beginning to weaken.   Jens J. Christoffersen SL94-191 1996 $185.00

ASSOCIATION - EVA LEGALLIENNE

THE THESPIAN Preceptor; or, a Full Display of Scenic Art: Including Ample and Easy Instructions for Treading the Stage, Using Proper Action... Boston: for Elam Bliss, 1810. 1st edition; 12mo; original boards, worn, later quarter calf; scarce; some embrowning; bookplate of Eva LeGallienne. S&S 21479; LAR 717-718 (English editions of 1811 and 1818).   Dramatis Personae 37-11 1996 $300.00

ASSOCIATION - R. LEGARD

SELDEN, JOHN 1584-1654   Joannis Seldeni I. C. de Dis Syris Syntagmata. London: Excudebat Gulielmus Stansbeius, 1617. 1st edition; 8vo; contemporary calf; fine; contemporary signatures of R. Legard and Joshua Meen. STC 22167; CBEL I 2331.   Ximenes 108-321 1996 $750.00

ASSOCIATION - JOHN LEHMANN

COOMBES, B. L.   These Poor Hands - the Autobiography of a Miner Working in South Wales. London: Victor Gollancz Ltd., 1939. 1st edition; original binding, head and tail of spine and one corner slightly bumped, gilt titles on spine oxidising, very good; presentation copy from author, inscribed, dedication copy, for John Lehmann.   Ulysses 39-123 1996 £85.00

ASSOCIATION - LEIGH

MILTON, JOHN 1608-1674   Paradise Lost. London: by Miles Flesher for Jacob Tonson, 1688. 4th edition; folio; pages (iv), 343, (i) blank, (vi) list of subscribers, frontispiece, 12 engraved plates; Regency diced russia, sides panelled in gilt and blind, spine with double raised bands, decorated in gilt and in blind, inner dentelles with blind border between double gilt rules, drab green endpapers, joints restored, frontispiece skilfully laid down, g. lightly browned, few trivial spots or stains, chiefly marginal, small repair to blank recto of plate illustrating book IV; very good, large paper copy with bunch of grapes watermark and ample margins, both around text and plates; Leigh bookplate. Coleridge 93b; Wing M2147; Grolier W-P 607.   Simon Finch 24-171 1996 £1,750.00

WATERHOUSE, EDWARD   A Short Narrative of the Late Dreadful Fire in London... London: printed by W.G. for Rich. Thrale and James Thrale, 1667. 1st edition; 8vo; paper flaw in blank margin of title; old sheep, worn, upper hinge cracked; ownership inscription of Samuel Leigh. Wing W1050.   Anthony Laywood 108-20 1996 £75.00

ASSOCIATION - ROBERT LEIGH

WHITE, GILBERT 1720-1793   The Natural History (Antiquities) of Selborne. London: 1813. 1st edition; 4to; 2 vignettes, 10 plates (one colored by hand); from the collection of Robert Leigh, with his booklabel, later in the W. H. Mullens collection, with his bookplate, bound for him in half green morocco, uncut, original printed label (defective) and front wrapper (? or was it orginally a board) preserved. Maggs Bros. Ltd. 1190-275 1996 £110.00

ASSOCIATION - PAUL LEMPERLY

CARMAN, BLISS 1861-1929   By the Aurelian Wall and Other Elegies. Boston, New York & London: Lamson, Wolffe and Co., 1898. 1st edition; 1st state; 8vo; 132 pages; title in 2 colors; green cloth titled in gilt on spine with title in gilt and black on front cover above gilt and black vignette, single ruled black frame, vertical slit along top half of inner edge of titlepage; otherwise near fine. From the library of Paul Lemperly, founder of Rowfant Club.   Blue Mountain SP95-92 1996 $150.00

ASSOCIATION - JOHN LENNON

AMIS, KINGSLEY 1922-   One Fat Englishman. London: Penguin Books, 1966. Paperback; 12mo; pages 173, (iv) ads, autograph inscription of John Lennon and Yoko Ono Lennon on first page, loosely inserted memo on headed writing paper "Waiting for a plane at Heathrow on 29th December 1969 to take us to Moscow, we met John Lennon & Yoko. They very kindly signed the book..."   Simon Finch 24-153 1996 £185.00

ASSOCIATION - POPE LEO XII

SACRORUM Rituum Congreagtione...Beatificationis et Canonizationis...Roberti Bellarmini Societatis Iesu. Rome: Typis Reverendae Camerae Apostolicae, 1712. Folio; 2 volumes; portrait, 18 sections variously paginated; later polished brown calf, covers gilt with broad double border of acanthus and vine leaves, central panel with IHS corner-pieces, flat spine gilt with green and red labels, all edges gilt, green endpapers, gilt arms of Pope Leo XII, unobtrusively rebacked preserving spine. From the collection of R. M. Beverley with his ex-libris. Marlborough 160-53 1996 £650.00

ASSOCIATION - PAT LEONARD

CUSHING, H.   Consecratio Medici and Other Papers. Boston: 1928. 2nd printing; 8vo; cloth, bit worn, elaborate inscription from author to Pat Leonard, July 16, 1919. with small ink sketch.   Maggs Bros. Ltd. 1190-395 1996 £75.00

ASSOCIATION - SOL LESTER

HILL, JOSEPH J.   The History of Warner's Ranch and Its Environs. Los Angeles: John Treanor, 1927. One of 300 copies; 11 x 7 7/8 inches; xii, 221 pages, 2 etchings by Loren Barton; brown boards with linen spine and tips and paper spine label, small spot to tail of spine; inscribed by Treanor to Sol Lesser.   Dawson's Books Shop 528-108 1996 $100.00

ASSOCIATION - LEVERHULME

MAC PHERSON, H. A.   The Birds of Cumberland Critically Studied, Including Some Notes on the Birds of Westmorland. Carlisle: Chas. Thurnam, 1886. 8vo; pages xx, 206, colored lithograph frontispiece, folding colored map; original cloth, gilt. armorial bookplate of W. H. Mullens; presentation copy to P. Leverhulme, with 4 page ALS from Rev. MacPherson tipped in.   R.F.G. Hollett & Son 78-535 1996 £160.00

ASSOCIATION - PAUL LEVERKUHN

SCHRENCK, P. L. VON   Vogel des Amur-Landes. St. Petersberg: 1860. 1st edition; small folio; 7 hand colored lithographs by W. Pape, some browning; half leather, repaired; Paul Leverkuhn's copy with his signature, later in Bradley Martin collection. Very rare.   Maggs Bros. Ltd. 1190-597 1996 £650.00

ASSOCIATION - RICHARD LEVEY

HAWKES, JOHN   Lunar Landscapes. Stories and Short Novels 1949-1963. New York: New Direction, 1969. One of 150 numbered copies, signed by author; fine in near fine slipcase with small sticker ghost top of back; from the collection of Richard Levey with bookplate from Poet's House Library.   Thomas Dorn 9-136 1996 $125.00

ASSOCIATION - PHILIP LEVINE

LOWELL, ROBERT 1917-1977   Land of Unlikeness. Poems. Cummington: Cummington Press, 1944. 1st edition; limited to 250 copies (the entire edition); 8vo; blue boards printed in blue; covers faded and worn, but good copy; author's rare first book; unusual association copy, inscribed facetiously by poet Robert Mezey to Philip Levine, with Levine's ownership signature.   James S. Jaffe 34-419 1996 $1,750.00

ASSOCIATION - HAL LEVINSON

ALDRIN, EDWIN E.   Return to Earth. New York: Random House, 1973. 1st edition; 8vo; black and white photos and facsimiles; very good in dust jacket; signed by Aldrin for Hal Levinson.   George J. Houle 68-6 1996 $150.00

ASSOCIATION - LEWIS

NANSEN, FRIDTJOF 1861-1930   In Northern Mists. London: William Heinemann, 1911. 1st English edition; royal 8vo; 2 volumes; xi, 384; (8), 416 pages; mounted color frontispieces, numerous text illustrations; original cloth, gilt vignettes on upper covers; fine. 1st volume inscribed by author for Mrs. G. Lewis.   Thomas Thorp 489-231 1996 £350.00

ASSOCIATION - THOMAS LEWIS

STOKES, WILLIAM   A Treatise on the Diagnosis and Treatment of Diseases of the Chest, Part I. Diseases of the Lung and Windpipe. London: 1882. Iv, 596 pages; frontispiece; cloth, spine ends worn; bookpate of Thomas Lewis.   Graham Weiner C2-534 1996 £50.00

ASSOCIATION - THEODORE LILIENTHAL

BROMFIELD, LOUIS   Twenty-Four Hours. New York: Stokes, 1930. 1st edition; limited to 500 copies, signed by author; red cloth with white cloth spine and stamped in gold, dust jacket and endpapers have an Art Deco montage in black on silver background of New York City by P. S. Jobst; very fine in dust jacket and original slipcase, also in silver and black with red label. Bookplate of Theodore Lilienthal.   Bromer Booksellers 90-10 1996 $250.00

ASSOCIATION - LINDSAY

COLLINS, ANTHONY 1676-1729   A Philosophical Enquiry Concerning Human Liberty. London: Robinson, 1717. Corrected version of the first edition of 1715; 8vo; title, pages vi, 1f., 114, 1 f., ruled in red; red morocco panelled gilt, with centre and side pieces built up from small tools, spirals, acorns, small drawer handles and others, spine gilt in 6 compartments, all edges gilt, comb-marbled endpapers, perhaps by Brindley. Armorial bookplate of Lindsay of Kirkforther.   Marlborough 160-37 1996 £1,100.00

ASSOCIATION - ELIZABETH LYNN LINTON

LINTON, WILLIAM J.   Poems and Translations. London: John C. Nimmo, 1889. 1st edition; number 96 of 780 copies for England and America; 8vo; pages x, 202, (1); frontispiece; uncut, original boards, sheep back; presented by author to his wife, Elizabeth Lynn Linton. Boards somewhat soiled and spine little rubbed, still very good. Howard S. Mott 227-86 1996 $150.00

ASSOCIATION - WILL LIPKIND

BROWN, MARCIA   Felice. New York: Scribner's, 1958. 1st edition; 4to; water color illustrations by author; beige coth stamped in pink and black, lower end of spine slightly rubbed, else very fresh in pictorial dust jacket; laid in is compliments card from author and small original watercolor drawing; inscribed dedication copy for Maria Cimino and her husband Will Lipkind.   Barbara Stone 70-40 1996 £250.00

ASSOCIATION - ARTHUR WILMER LISSAUER

DUMAS, ALEXANDRE 1825-1895   Camile. Ptd. by the Curwen Press for Members of the Limited Editions Club, 1937. One of 1500 copies, signed by the artist; 11 x 9 inches; xi, (1) (blank) pages, (1) leaf, 213, (1) (blank) pages, (1) leaf (colophon); 12 watercolors by Marie Laurencin, printed in process collotype by Chiswick Press, tissue guards; original white linen, gilt rose on front cover, titled in gilt on spine, in publisher's (slightly soiled but sound) slipcase; very fine; small oval leather bookplate of Arthur Wilmer Lissauer. Quarto Millenary 93.   Phillip J. Pirages 33-357 1996 $350.00

ASSOCIATION - ARTHUR LISTER

YARRELL, WILLIAM   A History of British Birds. London: 1871-75. 8vo; 4 volumes; 564 wood engravings; original cloth. Spines trifle worn; fromt he library of Arthur Lister, with ALS from his daughter, Gulielma. Wheldon & Wesley 207-901 1996 £80.00

ASSOCIATION - ERIC LISTER

PERELMAN, S. J.   Acres and Plains. New York: Simon & Schuster, 1972. Later edition; excellent in dust jacket; inscribed by author for Eric Lister.   R. A. Gekoski 19-108 1996 £100.00

PERELMAN, S. J.   Eastward Ha!. London: Eyre Methuen, 1977. Excellent copy in dust jacket; inscribed by author for Eric Lister.   R. A. Gekoski 19-109 1996 £100.00

PERELMAN, S. J.   Strictly from Hunger. New York: Random House, 1937. Some soiling to cloth on front panel, else excellent; inscribed by author for Eric Lister, owner of Portal Gallery.   R. A. Gekoski 19-107 1996 £100.00

ASSOCIATION - PAMELA LISTER

CAREW, THOMAS 1595-1639   A Rapture. Waltham St. Lawrence: Golden Cockerel Press, 1927. One of 375 copies; 7 3/4 x 5 1/4 inches; 14 pages, (1) leaf (colophon); 2 engraved plates by J. E. Laboureur, device in colophon; original cloth backed patterned paper boards, dust jacket, fore edge and tail edge untrimmed, virtually perfect copy in extremely fine jacket that has one small tear neatly repaired on verso; small bookplate of Pamela Lister. Chanticleer 47.   Phillip J. Pirages 33-244 1996 $250.00

ASSOCIATION - RAYMOND LISTER

FRASER, CLAUD LOVAT 1890-1921   Sixty-Three Unpublished Designs. London: printed at the Curwen Press for the First Edition Club, 1924. 1st edition; 87/50 copies; foolscap 8vo; pages xii, 63; printed on yellow dyed Ingres handmade paper, 63 drawings, one repeated on titlepage; original quarter black cloth, gilt lettered lightly faded backstrip, white boards with overall purple, orange and black design by Lovat Fraser; untrimmed, good; bookplate of Robert Arundel Hudson and bookticket of Raymond Lister.   Blackwell's B112-111 1996 £70.00

ASSOCIATION - LUTHER LIVINGSTON

LONGFELLOW, HENRY WADSWORTH 1807-1882   Hyperion. New York: S. Colman, 1839. 1st edition; 1st printing, 1st published edition; 8vo; purple cloth, spine sunned, little frayed, very good. Longfellow bibliographer Luther Livingston's copy with signed note by him on front blank stating the numerous ms. corrections he made in this copy show the differences between the published edition and the earlier private printing of only 10 copies.   Charles Agvent 4-841 1996 $350.00

ASSOCIATION - THOMAS LLEWELYN

HURD, RICHARD   Dialogues on the Uses of Foreign Travel... London: printed by W.B. for A. Millar...; and W. Thurlbourn and J. Woodyer... 1764. 1st edition; 8vo; title printed in red and black, (4), 201, (1) pages, few inoffensive spots at beginning and end, author's name and shelf number supplied in red ink on title; contemporary quarter calf, neatly rebacked, label on spine; very good, large copy, entirely uncut; late 18th century armorial label of Thomas Llewelyn and early 19th century label of the Bristol Education Society.   John Drury 82-118 1996 £200.00

ASSOCIATION - LLOYD

THOMAS, DYLAN MARLAIS 1914-1953   18 Poems. London: Sunday Referee/Parton Bookshop, 1934. 1st edition; 1st issue (with flat spine); one of only 250 first issue copies; 8vo; remarkably fine in complete, though somewhat foxed and nicked rare dust jacket, endpapers and edges of book also have some foxing, otherwise this is a superb example; in black quarter morocco slipcase with silk moire chemise; presentation copy in the year of publication, jointly inscribed with fellow writer-translator, A. L. Lloyd for Lloyd's wife Ethel; laid in is autograph note from Lloyd presented the book.   Lakin & Marley 3-63 1996 $6,000.00

ASSOCIATION - EDWARD LLOYD

KOOPS, M.   Historical Account of the Substances Which Have Been Used to Describe Events. London: Jaques & co., 1801. 2nd edition; one of 510 issues, this issue was printed on de-inked waste paper, the other printed on straw; frontispiece lacking; appendix printed on purpe wood pulp paper; half calf, gilt bands, rebacked, original marbled boards, faint stamp on title. Ownership inscription of Edward Lloyd.   Maggs Bros. Ltd. 1191-187 1996 £200.00

ASSOCIATION - NATHANIEL LLOYD

CRUNDEN, JOHN   Convenient and Ornamental Architecture Consisting of Original Designs... London: I. Taylor, 1785. 4to; viii, 26 pages, 70 plates; contemporary calf, respined, lacking dedication leaf, endpapers renewed, corners worn, some light spots or marks, else very good; bookplate of Nathaniel Lloyd.   Bookpress 75-172 1996 $1,350.00

EASTLAKE, CHARLES L.   A History of the Gothic Revival. London: Longmans, Green and Co., 1872. 1st edition; 4to; xvi, 427, (3) pages, 35 plates; publisher's blindstamped gilt cloth; minor wear along edges, occasional spotting, rear hinge internally cracked, else very good; Nathaniel Lloyd's copy.   Bookpress 75-47 1996 $350.00

ASSOCIATION - NOEL LLOYD

BECKETT, SAMUEL 1906-1989   The North. London: Enitharmon Press, 1972. Number 6 of 125 copies numbered in press and signed by author, there were a further 12 ad personam copies; folio; 3 full page etchings by Avigdor Arikha; loose gatherings in folding wrapper and cloth case; fine in slightly dusty slipcase; presentation copy from author for Noel Lloyd and Geoffrey Palmer. Fine in slightly dusty slipcase.   Ulysses 39-38 1996 £650.00

ASSOCIATION - VINCENT LLOYD-RUSSELL

HIGGINS, GODFREY   The Celtic Druids: an Attempt to Shew, That the Druids Were the Priests of Oriental Colonies Who Emigrated from India. London: R. Hunter, 1829. (Engraved title reads 1827); small folio; lxxxi, 324 pages; frontispiece map, engraved title and 45 plates on India paper, all laid down, 14 wood engravings; modern three quarter dark brown morocco over matching cloth, spines with raised bands and gilt stamped red morocco label, minor foxing; very good. Bookplate of Vincent Lloyd-Russell.   George J. Houle 68-65 1996 $650.00

ASSOCIATION - LONDESBOROUGH

THE ANCIENT British Drama. (with) The Modern British Drama. London: William Miller, 1810/11. Sole editions(?). royal 8vo. in fours; 8 volumes; half titles, pages xi, (i) 595; (iv), 614; (iv), 598, (2); half titles, pages vi, (ii), 688; iv, 602; (iv), vii, (i), 668; (vi), 648; viii, 668; uniformly bound in contemporary half white vellum, minor wear to some extremities, smooth backstrips darkened, divided into compartments by narrow arrow head rolls, red leather title label in second compartments, dark blue volume labels in fourth, remainder with small concave sided octagonal ornament in centre, drab boards, blue sprinkled edges, light damage to front endpaper of volume i, bookplate of Lord Londesborough in each volume, generally excellent.   Blackwell's B112-88 1996 £350.00

ASSOCIATION - LONDON

LONDON, JACK 1876-1916   Theft. New York: Macmillan, 1910. 1st edition; original cloth, near fine; choice presentation copy, inscribed by author to his mother.   19th Century Shop 39- 1996 $8,500.00

ASSOCIATION - WARFIELD LONGCOPE

ROLLESTON, HUMPHRY   Cardio-Vascular Diseases Since Harvey's Discvoery. Cambridge: 1928. 1st edition; 149 pages; original binding; inscribed by author to Warfield Longcope. Later inscribed by Emmett Horine to Carleton Chapman. GM 3156   W. Bruce Fye 71-1801 1996 $100.00

ASSOCIATION - HENRY WADSWORTH LONGFELLOW

BRETON DE LA MARTINIERE, J. B.   La Chine en Miniature, ou Choix de Costumes, Arts et Metiers de cet Empire Representes par 74 Gravures...a l'Usage de la Jeunesse. Paris: Nepveu, 1811. Small 8vo; 4 volumes; suite of colored plates; elegant black straight grain morocco with decorative gilt border on covers, smooth rounded spines with 6 compartments formed by double gilt rules, the second from top containing the title and fourth containing the volume numbers, other compartments are filled with dense combination of delicate tools and pointelles, all edges gilt, marbled and tinted endleaves, on pastedown of all four volumes are the bookplates of Henry W. Longfellow. Brunet I 1225.   Book Block 32-8 1996 $4,750.00

ASSOCIATION - ALICE ROOSEVELT LONGWORTH

HUXLEY, ALDOUS LEONARD 1894-1936   The Doors of Perception. New York: Harper, 1954. 1st American edition; slight crease on front board, else fine in near fine dust jacket, bit soiled and with one short tear; Alice Longworth's copy with her pencil signature.   Between the Covers 42-233 1996 $125.00

ASSOCIATION - LONSDALE

AIKIN, JOHN 1747-1822   Essays On Song-Writing: with a Collection of Such English Songs as are Most Eminent for Poetical Merit. London: printed for Joseph Johnson, 1772. 8vo; contemporary sheep, spine and joints worn, some rubbing, usual marginal browning of endpapers, otherwise very clean and pleasant copy; from the Lonsdale Library with her bookplate.   James Cummins 14-189 1996 $250.00

COWPER, WILLIAM 1731-1800   The Poetical Works... London: Henry G. Bohn, 1851. 8vo; pages xxiv, 516; frontispiece, extra engraved title (both foxed), 2 portraits and one view (slightly foxed), 18 engraved plates; contemporary green hard grained morocco, sides tooled with wide gilt dentelle order made up of a large number of individual tools, spine divided into six panels by raised bands, elaborately tooled in gilt, lettered in second panel, gilt inner dentelles, pale yellow endpapers, gilt edges, spine slightly darkened and rubbed at head and tail, handsome binding by John Wright; contemporary presentation inscription to Arthur Pemberton Lonsdale on his leaving Eton on front blank.   Simon Finch 24-61 1996 £180.00

NORWOOD, RICHARD   Norwood's Epitome: Being the Application of the Doctrine of Triangles...The Use of the Plain Sea Chart, and Meractor's Chart... London: William Fisher, Sarah Passinger and Elizabeth Smith, 1690. Small 8vo; (ii), 34, (3)-94, (72) pages; contemporary sheep, headband chipped, hinges beginning to crack; with bookplate of Hugh Cecil, Earl of Lonsdale and label of Harrison D. Horblit.   The Bookpress 75-443 1996 $1,250.00

PARRY, WILLIAM EDWARD 1790-1855   Journal of a Second Voyage for the Discovery of a North West Passage...Performed in the Years 1821-22-23 in His Majesty's Ships Fury and Hecla... London: John Murray, 1824. 1st edition; 4to; 37 plates, maps, plans, occasional very light foxing on few plates, contemporary diced calf, narrow gilt border, centre of each cover carries the Earl of Lonsdale's gilt ex-libris stamp, a monogrammed 'Lowther' within an oak leaf wreath surmounted by an Earl's coronet, fine; Lonsdale bookplate. The Lowther Castle copy.   H. M. Fletcher 121-144 1996 £400.00

A SELECTION from the Harleian Miscellany of Tracts, Which Principally Regard the English History... London: printed for C. and G. Kearsley, 1794. 1st edition; 4to; contemporary red morocco, elaborately ruled in gilt, Lowther arms in gilt on each cover, spine and inner dentelles gilt, all edges gilt, bit rubbed; sumptuously bound and extra illustrated with more than 50 portraits and other engravings; good, early example of a 'grangerized' book in excellent condition; later armorial bookplate of Hugh Cecil (Lowther), Earl of Lonsdale.   Ximenes 108-182 1996 $500.00

WARD, ROBERT PLUMER   Pictures of the World at Home and Abroad. London: Colburn, 1839. 1st edition; 8vo; 3 volumes; original boards, rebacked, new labels, uncut; bookplate of Earl of Lonsdale, inscribed by author.   Howard S. Mott 227-146 1996 $375.00

ASSOCIATION - ANITA LOOS

KRUTCH, JOSEPH   Samuel Johnson. New York: Holt, 1944. 1st edition; plates; original binding, very good in worn dust jacket; wonderful association copy, Anita Loos's copy with her bookplate and estate stamp, the book was given her by Aldous Huxley, with inscription. Charles Agvent 4-762 1996 $375.00

ASSOCIATION - LOUDOUN

ANDERSON, HENRY   An Enquiry Into the Natural Right of Mankind to Debate Freely Concerning Religion. London: C. Davis and G. Hawkins, 1737. 1st and only edition; 8vo; viii, (2), 357, (1) page, errata at foot of last page of text, ads on verso; contemporary calf, gilt, raised bands, label, bit worn, joints cracking, otherwise good. From the 18th century library of John Campbell, 4th Earl of Loudoun. 3 copies in NUC.   John Drury 82-7 1996 £300.00

ASSOCIATION - A. LOUIS

WINSLOW, J. B.   Exposition Anatomique de la Structure du Corps Humain. London: 1732. 1st edition; 4to; 4 folding engraved plates (slight tears at fold, blank upper margin of first defective), with 4 pages of errata (some 250!), minor browning, contemporary French mottled calf, clumsily repaired with part of the original spine missing, bit worn, bookplate of A. Louis (1723-92), name, perhaps Henry Brewer, partly erased from flyleaf.   Maggs Bros. Ltd. 1190-536 1996 £525.00

ASSOCIATION - LOUIS XV

BELLIN, JACQUES NICOLAS   Essai Geographique sur les Isles Britanniques Contenant une Description de l'Angleterre... Paris: De L'Imprimrie de Didot, 1757. 1st edition; small 4to; 1-471 pages, 22 vignette plates to letterpress, 18 maps, city plans, 2 large folding maps, map of Ireland detached and loosely inserted, royal library stamp to engraved title, small part of upper right corner of front f.e.p. missing; full French mottled calf, gilt coat of arms of Louis XV and library stamp of Versailles to boards, triple gilt rule borders, gilt tooling to compartments, corners worn and bumped, marbled endpapers. Cox III p. 92.   Beeleigh Abbey BA/56-3 1996 £650.00

ASSOCIATION - LOVELACE

DARWIN, CHARLES ROBERT 1809-1882   On the Origin of Species by Means of Natural Selection or the Preservation of Favoured Races in the Struggle for Life. London: John Murray, 1860. 2nd edition; 5th thousand; 8vo; x, 502 pages, 32 pages ads; original green cloth, gilt, front inner hinge starting, outer hinges frayed, spine quite bright, stamp and signature of the Earl of Lovelace in 1860. Freeman 376, ads dated Jan. 1860. Binding variant A.   Kenneth Karmiole 1NS-85 1996 $1,000.00

ASSOCIATION - LOWE

BRONTE, THE SISTERS   Poems by Currer, Ellis and Acton Bell. London: Smith, Elder and Co., 1846/48. 1st edition; 2nd issue, with Smith, Elder titlepage; 8vo; pages iv, 165, (i) imprint, (i) ads; uncut in original olive green vertically ribbed cloth, covers stamped in blind with double line rectangular border enclosing decorative floral designs, harp in centre, spine with bands in blind, lettered in gold, cream endpapers; spine worn at head and tail, corners just bumped, extremities slightly sunned; good copy; early ownership inscription of Miss Lowe, bookplate of John Sallows Hubbard; Walter Smith, Bronte Sisters pp. 6-14. Simon Finch 24-18 1996 £650.00

ASSOCIATION - JAMES RUSSELL LOWELL

LOWELL, ANNA CABOT   Seed-Grain for Thought and Discussion. Boston: Ticknor & Fields, 1856. 1st edition; 8vo; original brown cloth, bit rubbed; very good condition; fine presentation copy, inscribed from author to her brother-in-law, James Russell Lowell.   Ximenes 109-178 1996 $250.00

ASSOCIATION - LOWNDES

A NEW History of the Holy Bible. Ipswich: printed and sold by Charles Punchard sold also by Messrs. Rivington... n.d. not later than 1783; apparently the first and only edition; 8vo; vi, 229 pages, errata slip pasted on to blank verso of final leaf, occasional very light spotting, contemporary calf, gilt, recently rebacked, spine gilt with label, good; from the contemporary library of I. K. Lowndes with his armorial bookplate and signature.   John Drury 82-198 1996 £150.00

ASSOCIATION - LOWTHER

GILCHRIST, OCTAVIUS GRAHAM   Rhymes. London: 1805. 1st edition; 8vo; contemporary red straight grained morocco, gilt, gilt Lowther monograms on each cover, all edges gilt, spine bit faded, very slight rubbing; elegant copy; presentation copy, inscribed by recipient William Lowther, later 2nd Earl of Lonsdale also from the library of John Sparrow.   Ximenes 108-159 1996 $750.00

A SELECTION from the Harleian Miscellany of Tracts, Which Principally Regard the English History... London: printed for C. and G. Kearsley, 1794. 1st edition; 4to; contemporary red morocco, elaborately ruled in gilt, Lowther arms in gilt on each cover, spine and inner dentelles gilt, all edges gilt, bit rubbed; sumptuously bound and extra illustrated with more than 50 portraits and other engravings; good, early example of a 'grangerized' book in excellent condition; later armorial bookplate of Hugh Cecil (Lowther), Earl of Lonsdale.   Ximenes 108-182 1996 $500.00

ASSOCIATION - LOWTHER CASTLE

PARRY, WILLIAM EDWARD 1790-1855   Journal of a Second Voyage for the Discovery of a North West Passage...Performed in the Years 1821-22-23 in His Majesty's Ships Fury and Hecla... London: John Murray, 1824. 1st edition; 4to; 37 plates, maps, plans, occasional very light foxing on few plates, contemporary diced calf, narrow gilt border, centre of each cover carries the Earl of Lonsdale's gilt ex-libris stamp, a monogrammed 'Lowther' within an oak leaf wreath surmounted by an Earl's coronet, fine; Lonsdale bookplate. The Lowther Castle copy.   H. M. Fletcher 121-144 1996 £400.00

ASSOCIATION - LUDWIG II, KING OF BAVARIA

GONCOURT, EDMOND   Salon de 1852. Paris: Levy, 1852. One of only 10 copies; original wrappers, chip to rear panel split to length of spine and half of front spine fold; presentation copy from Goncourt Brothers to Ludwig II, King of Bavaria.   Lame Duck Books 19-225 1996 $1,000.00

ASSOCIATION - ROBERT WILFRED SKEFFINGTON LUTWIDGE

HASLAM, JOHN   A Letter to the Governors of Bethlem Hospital Containing an Account of Their management of that Insitution for the Last Twenty Years... London: Taylor and Hessey, 1818. 8vo; (2), 58, (2) pages, ads; original boards, paper label; inscribed presentation from author "A. Carlisle, Esq., from his friend the author", first blank leaf has signature also of Robert Wilfred Skeffington Lutwidge dated 1844, Lutwidge was Commissioner for Lunacy 1842-45.   C. R. Johnson 37-82 1996 £350.00

ASSOCIATION - EDWARD LYDALL

GREW, NEHEMIAH 1628-1711   Museum Regalis Societatis. London: by W. Rawlins for the author, 1681. 1st edition; folio; (12), 386, (2), index, 1 f. blank, (2) titlepage to part II, 43 pages, frontispiece, 31 engraved plates (several folding); contemporary calf, expertly rebacked and with new red gilt label and corners also neatly repaired, some old and faint waterstaining to lower margin, but very good; contemporary note of purchase on front free endpaper, and 19th century bookplate of Edward Lydall. LeFanu III 2; Wing G1952; G&M 297; Babson 406.   Ken Spelman 30-1 1996 £650.00

ASSOCIATION - D. LYDDELL

LOWNDES, WILLIAM 1652-1724   A Report Containing an Essay for the Amendment of the Silver Coins. London: printed by Charles Bill, and the executrix of Thomas Newcomb, 1695. 1st edition; 8vo; contemporary black morocco, gilt rules, central gilt panels with floral ornaments at corners, spine gilt in six compartments, all edges gilt; magnificent copy, no doubt bound for presentation (and possibly on fine paper); with 2 ms. corrections (pp. 19 and 22), no doubt authorial; signature of D. Lyddell dated Nov. 21, Wing L3323; Kress 1908.   Ximenes 109-179 1996 $3,500.00

ASSOCIATION - EDWARD DEAN LYMAN

HARDING, GEORGE L.   Don Agustin V. Zamorano: Statesman, Soldier, Craftsman and California's First Printer. Los Angeles: Zamorano Club, 1934. 1st edition; although not indicated, limited to 325 copies; 308 pages, frontispiece, large folding map, numerous facsimiles; offsetting to 2 blank flyleaves from newspaper articles, otherwise fine with lightly soiled and slightly chipped dust jacket. From the collection of Edward Dean Lyman, with his card laid in.   Argonaut Book Shop 113-323 1996 $275.00

ASSOCIATION - ROBIE MACAULEY

JARRELL, RANDALL   Little Friend, Little Friend. New York: Dial Press, 1945. 1st edition; not stated; dark blue boards blindstamped with stars, spine printed in gold and blue, fine in very good dust jacket with several small chips and normal wear, from the library of Robie Macauley, Jarrell's friend and advisor.   Bev Chaney, Jr. 23-338 1996 $250.00

ASSOCIATION - MALCOLM MACDONAD

THE POLITICAL History of England. London: 1906-10. Thick small 8vo; 12 volumes; maps, original cloth, booklabel of Malcolm MacDonald. Howes Bookshop 265-983 1996 £75.00

ASSOCIATION - W. S. MACDONALD

SCADDING, HENRY   Toronto of Old: Collections and Recollections. Toronto: Willing and Williamson, 1878. Reissue of the 1873 first edition; 8vo; pages xii, 594; frontispiece, 14 plates, folding map; original black and gold stamped brown cloth; with ALS and inscription from author to W. S. MacDonald.   Hugh Anson-Cartwright 87-432 1996 $300.00

ASSOCIATION - ANDREW MACK

MASON, JOHN 1706-1763   The Student and Pastor, or Directions How to Attain to Eminence and Usefulness In those Respective Characters. Exeter: from the Press of Thomas Odiorne, 1794. 1st American edition; 12mo; contemporary sheep, spine gilt, rubbed, upper joint cracked; very good; early bookplate of Andrew Mack. Evans 27275.   Ximenes 109-188 1996 $100.00

ASSOCIATION - J. A. MACKAY

CHURCH OF ENGLAND. BOOK OF COMMON PRAYER   The Book of Common Prayer, and Administration of the Sacraments, and Other Rites and Ceremonies of the Church According to the Use of the Church of England in Canada. London: Society for Promoting Christian Knowledge, 1917. Small 8vo; pages viii, 299; translated into the Cree language; (mixed roman and syllabic characters). full calf, all edges gilt, inscribed, with ALS by revisor, J. A. Mackay; near mint.   Hugh Anson-Cartwright 87-305 1996 $300.00

ASSOCIATION - JOHN MACKENZIE

COWPER, WILLIAM 1731-1800   Poems. London: printed for J. Johnson and Co., 1812. 6 3/4 x 4 1/4 inches; 2 volumes; very pleasing contemporary blond straight grain morocco, sides framed with lovely latticework border in gilt and blind, raised bands, spines attractively gilt in compartments featuring multiple plain and decorative rules and large scrolling and floral ornament at center, all edges gilt, spines evenly darkened to pleasing honey brown, very slight rubbing at spine ends, otherwise an ornate and charming contemporary set in fine condition, nearly immaculate internally; armorial bookplate of John Mackenzie of Dunvegan and with presentation inscription from Lydia to Alice Rigby. Phillip J. Pirages 33-140 1996 $165.00

ASSOCIATION - AVERIL MACKENZIE-GRIEVE

FRYER, MARY ANN   John Fryer of the Bounty. Waltham St. Lawrence: Golden Cockerel Press, 1939. 1st edition; 78/300 copies; small folio; pages 53, (1); printed on Arnold's handmade paper, signed by author and artist; 12 wood engravings, 3 full page by Averil Mackenzie-Grieve, included is a greeting card printed at the Golden Cockerel Press, an illustration by Averil Mackenzie-Grieve, signed and inscribed by her; original mid-blue canvas, backstrip lettering and Mackenzie-Grieve design on front cover, all gilt blocked, endpapers lightly foxed, top edge gilt, others untrimmed, original tissue jacket; excellent. Blackwell's B112-125 1996 £300.00

ASSOCIATION - JOHN MACKEY

HEMINGWAY, ERNEST MILLAR 1899-1961   Death in the Afternoon. New York: Charles Scribner's Sons, 1932. 1st edition; color frontispiece of Juan Gris painting; original cloth, some wear and uneven fading, front inner hinge tender; important copy in attractive dust jacket (supplied); superb presentation copy, inscribed by author for John H. Mackey. 19th Century Shop 39- 1996 $12,500.00

ASSOCIATION - JAMES MACKINTOSH

PRIESTLEY, JOSEPH 1733-1804   Letters to the Right Honourable Edmund Burke, Occasioned by His Reflections on the Revolution in France &c. London: 1791. 2nd edition; 8vo; xiii, (3), 155, (1) pages, perforated stamp on margin of title and another leaf, small marginal tear on leaf M1 (not touching printed surface), title bit soiled; old half cloth, rather worn, label on spine, uncut. From the library of Sir James Mackintosh (1765-1832) the philosopher, with his bookplate. Crook 305. John Drury 82-230 1996 £175.00

ASSOCIATION - DONALD MACLACHLAN

MALTHUS, THOMAS ROBERT 1766-1834   An Essay on the Principle of Population; or, a View of its Past and Present Effects on Human Happiness... London: J. Johnson, 1806. 3rd edition; 8vo; 2 volumes, xvi, 505, (61); vii, (1), 559, (1) pages, bound without half titles; contemporary calf, flat spine ruled in gilt with labels; fine; contemporary ownership inscription of Donald Maclachlan and his armorial bookplate. Kress B5067; Goldsmiths 19210; Einaudi 3669.   John Drury 82-171 1996 £575.00

ASSOCIATION - MAGARICK

ANGELOU, MAYA   I Know Why the Caged Bird Sings. New York: Random House, 1969. 1st edition; 8 1/2 x 5 3/4 inches; 3 p.l., (1) pages; original cloth, dust jacket, with Christmas card from author laid in; very fine in like jacket; inscribed and signed by author for Pat Magarick.   Phillip J. Pirages 33-12 1996 $150.00

ELLISON, RALPH   Invisible man. New York: Random House, 1952. 1st edition; 8 1/2 x 5 3/4 inches; 4 p.l., 439 pages; original cloth and dust jacket, front endpapers with shadow of previously laid in paper, otherwise fine in very good jacket that is bit frayed at edges and neatly tape repaired on verso in several places; inscribed and signed by author for P. Magarick.   Phillip J. Pirages 33-199 1996 $500.00

ASSOCIATION - DAVID MAGEE

HART, JAMES D.   An Original leaf from the First Edition of Alexander Barclay's English translation of Sebastian Grant's "Ship of Fools", printed by Richard Pynson in 1509. San Francisco: printed for David Magee by the Grabhorn Press, 1938. One of 260 copies, this copy being one of 115 copies, with an original leaf bearing a woodcut; printed in Deepdene text on heavy American mould made paper; cloth backed decorated paper boards, top edge slightly dusty, covers very slightly marked, cloth spine very slightly spotted, very good; loosely inserted also is the prospectus for this book; Hart's own copy, loosely inserted ALS from Magee to Hart.   Ulysses 39-357 1996 £385.00

ASSOCIATION - JOHN MAJORIBANKS

KERR, R.   Memoirs of the Life, Writings and Correspondence of William Smellie. Edinburgh: 1811. 1st edition; 8vo; 2 volumes; portrait, plate; calf, rebacked; inscribed by Alexander Smellie (the son) to Sir John Majoribanks, Lord Provost.   Maggs Bros. Ltd. 1190-246 1996 £120.00

ASSOCIATION - PETER MAKAROFF

MAUDE, AYLMER   A Peculiar People. The Doukhobors. New York: 1904. Pages xi, 338, 15 photo illustrations, 2 maps; original binding, near fine, laid in is one page TLS from Peter Makaroff of the Society of Independent Doukhobors, dated 1937.   Stephen Lunsford 45-107 1996 $325.00

ASSOCIATION - ALFRED MALHERBE

GOULD, JOHN 1804-1881   An Introduction to the Birds of Australia. London: printed for the author, 1848. Printed from the proof sheets of the great folio edition, at end is 6 page prospectus for the folio, with list of subscribers, and note that 250 copies were printed, of which 180 were subscribed; original cloth, spine faded, bit worn, two rather inappropriate leather labels added; presentation copy inscribed by Gould to Alfred Malherbe of Metz.   Maggs Bros. Ltd. 1190-570 1996 £215.00

ASSOCIATION - STEPHANE MALLARME

BECKFORD, WILLIAM 1760-1844   Vathek. Paris: Perrin, 1893. 2nd edition; wrappers; very good+ or better; this copy inscribed by Stephane Mallarme.   Lame Duck Books   19-300   1996 $950.00

ASSOCIATION - EDWARD MALTBY

PORSON, RICHARD 1759-1808   Letters to Mr. Archdeacon Travis, in Answer to His Defence of the Three Heavenly Witnesses. London: T. and J. Egerton, 1790. 8vo; (ii), xxxix, (i), 406, pages; 11th century morocco backed boards, spine gilt, rubbed, little foxing; tipped in to this copy is leaf inscribed "To Henry Lord Brougham and Vaux...from Edward Chichester (=Maltby), A.D. 1833"; Brougham's gilt coronet and monogram on spine.   Robert Clark   38-199   1996 £150.00

ASSOCIATION - H. MANSFIELD

LUCRETIUS CARUS, TITUS 99-55 BC   Titi Lucretii Cari De Rerum Natura... Birmingham: Baskerville, 1773. 12mo; pages (2), 214, (i.e. 218); worn 19th century full leather, foxed, ms. ownerships of H. Mansfield and J. Woolsten Holme. Gaskell 50.   Family Album   Tillers-415   1996 $275.00

ASSOCIATION - ROLAND DE MARGERIE

VALERY, PAUL   Le Cimetiere Marin. Paris: Emile Paul Freres, 1920. 1st edition; one of 556 numbered copies; original wrappers, with outer tissue wrapper, inner hinge loose due to dried glue, else near fine; presentation copy inscribed by author for Roland de Margerie.   19th Century Shop   39-   1996 $1,250.00

ASSOCIATION - MARIE LOUISE, EMPRESS

VERGILIUS MARO, PUBLIUS 70-19 BC   Opera. Parma: Typis Bodonianis, 1793. Probably one of only 25 fine large paper copies, of a total edition that numbered less than 200; folio; pages 7, 340; 296; 41 + blanks; uncut and deckle edged; full red morocco gilt, boards stamped in gilt with the crowned cypher of Marie Louise, Empress Consort of Napoleon I and edged with gilt palmetto roll, one corner slightly chewed, fine large paper. Blumenthal Art of Ptd. Book p. 27; Brooks 486; Dibdin II 562.   Family Album   Tillers-652   1996 $8,000.00

ASSOCIATION - CLEMENTS MARKHAM

HENDERSON, G.   Lahore to Yarkand. London: 1873. Royal 8vo; pages xiv, 370, map, 16 plain and 38 colored plates; original cloth, neatly rebacked; signature of Sir Clements Markham on titlepage, few pencil annotations in text.   Wheldon & Wesley   207-43   1996 £900.00

ASSOCIATION - WILLIAM MARKHAM

VARRO, MARCUS TERENTIUS   Opera Quae Supersunt...De Re Rustica. Geneva: Henri Stephanus, 15181. 3rd Estienne edition; small 8vo; 5 parts in one volume, pages 143; 255, (76); 48; 129, (14); 77 + blanks, Estienne pritners device (12) on title; remains of old leather binding; engraved armorial bookplate of William Markham, Becca Lodge, Yorkshire. Schreiber 207; Renouard 148.2. Schweiger II 1116.   Family Album   Tillers-631   1996 $450.00

ASSOCIATION - MARLBOROUGH

BERKELEY, GEORGE MONCK 1763-1793   Literary Relics: Containing Original Letters from King Charles II. King James II. The Queen of Bohemia, Swift, Berkeley, Addison, Steele, Congreve, the Duke of Ormond and Bishop Rundle. London: for C. Elliot and T. Kay and C. Elliot, Edinburgh, 1789. 1st edition; 8vo; pages lvi, 415, half title; uncut in original blue-grey paper boards, skilfully rebacked to style; presentation copy to the fourth Duke of Marlborough, with Berkeley's autograph inscription; presentation copy; bookplate and added ownership inscription of the fourth Duke's youngest son, Lord Francis Almeric Spencer. Teerink 120; Rothschild 385.   Simon Finch   24-222   1996 £175.00

RADCLYFFE, C. W.   The Palace of Blenheim. Oxford: James Wyatt & Son, 1842. Large folio; tinted lithographic title, litho dedication, 18 tinted litho plates on 16 ff., rebacked with green morocco, original cloth covered boards, original green morocco label on upper cover. Excellent copy, rare. Inscribed by the Duchess of Marlborough.   Marlborough   162-275   1996 £2,500.00

ASSOCIATION - JOHN MARSHALL

GILBERT, GEOFFREY   The History and Practice of the High Corut of Chancery. London: printed by Henry Lintot for J. Worral and W. Owen, 1758. 1st edition; 8vo; (x), 347 pages, (xlvii); contemporary tan calf, red morocco label, light browning, joints neatly reinforced, handsome copy in fine half morocco case; from the law library of John Marshall, Chief Justice of the Supreme Court; books from Marshall's Library are extremely rare on the market.   19th Century Shop   39-   1996 $22,500.00

ASSOCIATION - BRADLEY MARTIN

BIERCE, AMBROSE 1842-1914   Black Beetles in Amber. San Francisco & New York: Western Authors Pub. Co., 1892. 1st edition; 8vo; 280 pages; frontispiece; original grey cloth, two part cloth box. The very fine Swann-Bradley Martin copy. Swann Sale 21 (1960).   M & S Rare Books   60-121   1996 $950.00

BIGLAND, JOHN   A Natural History of Animals... Philadelphia: 1828. 1st edition; 8vo; 2 volumes; colored vignette titles, 22 hand colored plates, rather browned, as often; contemporary half roan, worn, one backstrip off, and cover detached; bookplate of Frances Meyers, later in the Bradley Martin collection.   Maggs Bros. Ltd.   1190-223   1996 £85.00

BREE, C. R.   A History of the Birds of Europe. London: 1875-76. 2nd edition; 8vo; 5 volumes, 253 plates, all but one colored; original purple cloth, dust jackets, printed in black on grey, front covers with vignette title the same as blocked in gilt on cloth, surrounded by a geometrical pattern ditto (but the effect is quite different), on the back ads for other Bell publications, volume numbers lettered on spines, one cloth spine faded, stamped signature of Thomas Bableton(?) on titles, later in the Bradley Martin collection.   Maggs Bros. Ltd.   1190-549   1996 £650.00

COWPER, WILLIAM 1731-1800   Poems. (with) The Task. London: Johnson, 1782/85. 1st editions; octavo; 2 volumes, 367, 359 pages; beautifully bound by Riviere and son in full dark blue morocco, covers outlined with a triple gilt rule, spine gilt in 6 compartments, showing elaborate floral devices, turn-ins richly gilt with floral border; housed together in morocco backed pull-off box; very fine; bookplates of H. Bradley Martin. Rothschild 681; Hayward I 191; Grolier English II 60.   Bromer Booksellers   90-21   1996 $1,000.00

CRANE, STEPHEN 1871-1900   The Black Riders and Other Lines. Boston: Copeland and Day, 1895. 1st edition; one of 500 copies; 12mo; white paper boards beautifully decorated with a lily motif in an art deco style, head of spine little rubbed, binding very slightly dusty, otherwise a fine copy, housed in quarter morocco clamshell slipcase; the Bradley Martin copy with his bookplate.   Captain's Bookshelf   38-47   1996 $1,500.00

KETTELL, SAMUEL   Manual of the Practical Naturalist; or, Directions for Collecting, Preparing and Preserving Subjects of Natural History. Boston: 1831. 1st edition; 8vo; frontispiece, bit browned and foxed; original cloth, worn, covers off; pencil inscription by M. Bethune; the Bradley Martin copy.   Maggs Bros. Ltd.   1190-247   1996 £85.00

PLUTARCHUS 45-125   The Lives of the Noble Grecians and Romanes, Compared Together... London: by Thomas Vautroullier and for John Wight, 1579. 1st edition in English; there is another state of the imprint in which Wight's name is omitted; priority between the two, if any, is not known; folio in sixes; pages (xiv), 1175; Vautrollier's woodcut printer's device on title (McK. 170) and at colophon, woodcut medallion portraits within ornamental borders at beginning of each Life, woodcut initials, head and tailpieces; 17th century panelled calf, neatly rebacked with old spine laid down, later red morocco label, rather browned, scattered tears without loss, small rusthole in 4G5 affecting five letters, good; with ownership inscriptions of Thomas Belasyse, Earl Fauconberg, Oliver Cromwell's son-in-law, dated 1677 on titlepage; Richard Man, 1724 on recto of *2; Josa. Jacques 1731 on title; T. Crowe on title, James Hunter Jr., the Bradley Martin copy with his sale booklabel. STC 20066; Bartlett 226; Pforzheimer 801; PMM 48.   Simon Finch   24-187   1996 £7,800.00

POPE, ALEXANDER 1688-1744   A Key to the Lock. London: printed for J. Roberts, 1715. 1st edition; 8vo; stitcched as issued, in cloth slipcase; splendid copy, entirely uncut, rare. From the collection of H. Bradley Martin with his booklabel. Griffith 37; not in Rothschild.   Ximenes   108-297   1996 $2,500.00

SCHRENCK, P. L. VON   Vogel des Amur-Landes. St. Petersberg: 1860. 1st edition; small folio; 7 hand colored lithographs by W. Pape, some browning; half leather, repaired; Paul Leverkuhn's copy with his signature, later in Bradley Martin collection. Very rare.   Maggs Bros. Ltd.   1190-597   1996 £650.00

ASSOCIATION - BRADLEY MARTIN

STEPHENS, JAMES 1882-1950   The Insurrection in Dublin. Dublin and London: Maunsel & Co. Ltd., 1916. 1st edition; 16 pages publisher's ads dated Sept. 1916 at rear; original binding, bottom edges of covers slightly rubbed, head and tail of spine slightly bumped, very good in torn, rubbed, marked and dusty dust jacket browned at spine and edges, price on spine has been altered in ink; preserved in custom made quarter morocco slipcase, spine of slipcase rubbed and browned; bookplate of H. Bradley Martin.   Ulysses 39-558 1996 £195.00

TURTON, W.   British Fauna. Swansea: 1807. 1st edition; 8vo; Volume 1, all published; original printed boards, uncut, bit worn, rebacked, backstrip defective; the Bradley Martin copy, bought from Wheldon in 1958 for $7.50.   Maggs Bros. Ltd. 1190-270 1996 £55.00

ASSOCIATION - H. D. MARTIN

MAYNARD, HENRY N.   The Viaduct Works' Handbook; Being a Collection of Examples from Actual Practice of Viaducts, Bridges, Roofs, and Other Structures in Iron... London: Spon, 1868. 8vo; 108 pages, some full page wood engraved plates and many wood engraved text illustrations, folding tinted litho frontispiece (slightly stained), publisher's cloth; presentation inscription from author to civil engineer, H. D. Martin, from the library of J. G. James.   Elton Engineering 10-102 1996 £170.00

ASSOCIATION - THEODORE MARTIN

BOSWELL, JAMES 1740-1795   Carminum Rariorum Macaronicarum Delectus: In Usum Ludorum Apollinarum... Edinburgi: Ex Typographia G. Ramsay, 1813. 8vo; pages 144, 14; blind tooled calf, rebacked. Theodore Martin's copy, with his presentation ALS to Eustace Grubbe.   Peter Murray Hill 185-12 1996 £95.00

ASSOCIATION - GROUCHO MARX

ROSTEN, LEO   People I Have Loved, Known or Admired. New York: McGraw Hill, 1970. 1st edition; 8vo; dust jacket, very good; signed and inscribed by author to Groucho Marx.   George J. Houle 68-93 1996 $150.00

ASSOCIATION - JOHN MASEFIELD

BELL, WILLIAM   Poetry from Oxford in Wartime. London: Fortune Press, 1945. 1st edition; original binding, top edge dusty, edges slightly spotted, front pastedown very slightly soiled, tail of spine and one corner very slightly bumped, very good in nicked, dusty and slightly rubbed, marked, spotted and soiled dust jacket browned at spine and edges; mounted on front pastedown is printed slip, denoting this book to have been from the library of John Masefield.   Ulysses 39-345 1996 £195.00

YEATS, WILLIAM BUTLER 1865-1935   The Hour-Glass, Cathaleen ni Houlihan, the Pot of Broth... London: A. H. Bullen, 1904. 1st edition; cloth backed boards, top edge dusty, head and tail of spine and corners bumped, covers slightly marked and dusty, cover edges rubbed, prelims, edges and endpaeprs spotted; very good. Presentation copy from author for John Masefield.   Ulysses 39-664 1996 £2,000.00

ASSOCIATION - WILLIAM MASON

SMART, CHRISTOPHER 1722-1771   Poems on Several Occasions. London: for the author, by W. Strahan, and sold by J. Newbery, 1752. 1st edition; 4to; pages (xvi), 203, engraved f by Grignion after Hayman, 1 engraved plate; contemporary quarter calf, raised bands, lacks label, marbled sides, front joint cracked, but holding firm, some stripping and rubbing of sides, first four leaves very lightly spotted; good; William Mason's copy with his engraved booklabel. Tinker 1919.   Simon Finch 24-212 1996 £900.00

ASSOCIATION - GEORGE GORDON MASSEY

SURTEES, ROBERT SMITH 1803-1864   The Horseman's Manual. London: Alfred Miller, 1831. 1st edition; 12mo; contemporary maroon morocco, gilt, spine gilt, all edges gilt, in the manner of T. Gosden, light rubbing, in half red morocco slipcase; fine; author's rare first book; early armorial bookplate of Henry Ralph Lambton who was no doubt related to book's dedicatee, Ralph John Lambton of Durham; later bookplate of George Gordon Massey. Mellon Collection 141; CBEL III 967.   Ximenes 108-333 1996 $1,250.00

ASSOCIATION - HAROLD MASSINGHAM

BLUNDEN, EDMUND 1896-   To Nature. New Poems. London: Beaumont Press, 1923. 1st edition; 115/310 copies (of an edition of 390 copies); crown 8vo; printed on handmade paper, pages (x), 50, (1) pages; titlepage printed in blue and brown, 2 color wood engraved medallion design on titlepage, initial letter to each poem, endpaper and cover designs, all by Randolph Schwabe; original quarter fawn buckram, sunned backstrip gilt lettered, pale grey boards, overall apttern of flowers in green and yellow, endpapers lightly foxed, untrimmed, good. Inscribed by Blunden to Harold Massingham and his first wife. Blackwell's B112-13 1996 £75.00

ASSOCIATION - MASTERMAN

STEVENSON, ROBERT LOUIS BALFOUR 1850-1894   Kidnapped. London: Cassell & Co., 1886. 1st edition; 1st issue; crown 8vo; text 1-311 pages, publisher's ad, 16 page publisher's catalog to rear, half title; large folding colored map frontispiece; rebound in half crimson morocco and red cloth boards, gilt panelled spine, gilt titles to compartments, top edge gilt, marbled endpapers, new prelims, original crimson cloth spine and board bound in rear; fine and handsome copy, blue crayon/pencil ownership inscription of J. S. Masterman.   Beeleigh Abbey BA56-164 1996 £350.00

ASSOCIATION - LEO MATARASSO

ASTURIAS, MIGUEL ANGEL   The Talking Machine. Garden City: Doubleday, 1971. 1st U.S. edition; illustrations by Jacqueline Duheme; near fine in very good+ dust jacket; this copy inscribed by Asturias to one Leo Matarasso.   Lame Duck Books 19-43 1996 $1,500.00

ASSOCIATION - ROBERT MAUNSELL

SALT, HENRY   A Voyage to Abyssinia, and Travels into the Interior of that Country...in 1809 and 1810. London: for F. C. and J. Rivington, 1814. 1st edition; large 4to; printed on thick paper, 34 plates and charts, lower margin of first leaf leaf of text repaired; contemporary half russia, with decorated paper boards, joints very skilfully repaired; inscribed "To the Lady Hester Stanhope from the Author" below in another hand 'purchased at sale of Lady Hester Stanhope's books by E. Kilby(?) at Beirout in 1840" followed by notes signed by "John Maconchy, surgeon. HMS Hecate" & Robert Maunsell, Capt. HMS Rodney"   H. M. Fletcher 121-146 1996 £2,500.00

ASSOCIATION - STIRLING MAXWELL

WHEWELL, WILLIAM 1794-1866   English Hexameter Translations from Schiller, Goethe, Homer, Callinus and Meleager. London: John Murray, 1847. 1st edition; oblong 8vo; contemporary rose calf, rebacked to style, all edges gilt, with "English Hexameters" stamped in large capitals on top edge, original color printed pictorial wrappers bound in; very good, scarce. With large orange and yellow bookplate of William Stirling, later Stirling Maxwell. CBEL III 1282.   Ximenes 109-297 1996 £400.00

ASSOCIATION - HENRI THOMASSIN DE MAZANGUES

CATHOLIC CHURCH. LITURGY & RITUAL. BREVIARY   Dirunal du Breviarie Romain. Lyon: Valfray, 1740. 4to; contemporary crimson morocco, covers gilt with wide floral border and corner-pieces, arms of Henri Thomassin de Mazangues, spine gilt in 6 panels with floral decoration, all edges gilt, rubbed, corners worn, old reback now cracked at foot of one joint.   Marlborough 160-38 1996 £450.00

ASSOCIATION - MC IAN

SURTEES, ROBERT SMITH 1803-1864   "Plain or Ringlets?" London: 1860. 1st edition in book form; viii pages, 1 f., 406 pages, 13 colored plates; illustrations by John Leech; full red morocco, gilt, decorations of hounds, foxes, etc., inner wide dentelles, top edge gilt; laid in is 2 page ALS from Leech to Mrs. Mclan (?); fine copy but outer joints beginning to weaken.   Jens J. Christoffersen SL94-191 1996 $185.00

ASSOCIATION - W. N. MCCLEAN

MATHEWS, C.   The Annals of Mont Blanc. London: 1898. 1st edition; 30 plates, folding map; grey cloth, gilt lettering and illustrations, top edge gilt; fine; small attractive bookplate of W. N. McClean.   Moutaineering Books 8-EM01 1996 £220.00

ASSOCIATION - DAVE MCDOWELL

WILLIAMS, WILLIAM CARLOS 1883-1963　Sour Grapes. A Book of Poems. Boston: Four Seas, 1921. One of 1000 copies of the first edition; contemporary ownership signature, pages roughly opened, else fine in rare dust jacket with small chip to head of spine; inscribed by author for Dave McDowell, editor at New Directions.　Lame Duck Books　19-597　1996 $2,500.00

ASSOCIATION - SIMON MCGILLIVRAY

M'DONNELL, ALEXANDER GREENFIELD　A Narrative of Transactions in the Red River Country... London: 1819. Pages xix, 85, large folding hand colored map; untrimmed, original printed wrappers; fine, crisp copy; preserved in quarter morocco clamshell box; inscribed by Simon McGillivray on front wrapper. Peel 59; Streeter VI 3682; TPL 1100; Wagner Camp Becker 15c.　Stephen Lunsford　45-100　1996 $4,500.00

WILCOCKE, SAMUEL HULL　Report of the Proceedings Connected with the Disputes Between the Earl of Selkirk and the North-West Company, at the Assizes, Held at York, un Upper Canada, October 1818. London: 1819. 1st London edition; pages xxv, 225, 203, 48; uncut, largely unopened in original printed wrappers, slightest chipping to hinges, fine, preserved in quarter morocco clamshell box; fine; inscribed by Simon McGillivray for John W. Croker. TPL 1146; Peel68; cf. Streeter VI 3687. Stephen Lunsford　45-170　1996 $2,500.00

ASSOCIATION - GORDON MCKENZIE

PRITCHETT, V. S.　When My Girl Comes Home. New York: Alfred A. Knopf, 1961. 1st edition; original binding, spine slightly faded, tail of spine bumped, very good in nicked and slightly rubbed, very slightly creased dust jacket browned at spine and edges; presentation copy from author inscribed for Jane and Gordon McKenzie.　Ulysses 39-487　1996 £75.00

ASSOCIATION - JANE MCKENZIE

PRITCHETT, V. S.　When My Girl Comes Home. New York: Alfred A. Knopf, 1961. 1st edition; original binding, spine slightly faded, tail of spine bumped, very good in nicked and slightly rubbed, very slightly creased dust jacket browned at spine and edges; presentation copy from author inscribed for Jane and Gordon McKenzie.　Ulysses 39-487　1996 £75.00

ASSOCIATION - WILLIAM MCKIM

MARIN, JOHN　Letters of John Marin. New York: privately printed for an American Place, 1931. One of an issue of 350 numbered copies (of a total edition of 400), although only the issue of 50 copies was issued, signed; fine in cloth; this copy inscribed by author for William L. McKim. Between the Covers　42-286　1996 $1,500.00

ASSOCIATION - DAVID MCKITTERICK

SALAMAN, MALCOLM C.　French Colour Prints of the XVIII Century. London: William Heinemann, 1913. 1st edition; 4to; 49 mounted colored plates; original gilt decorated cloth, top edge gilt, inner hinges sightly shaken; Ruari McLean's copy with bookplate, with ALS from David McKitterick to McLean.　Forest Books　74-364　1996 £95.00

ASSOCIATION - HERBERT MCLEAN

TODD, FRANK MORTON　Eradicating Plague from San Francisco. San Francisco: 1909. 1st edition; 313 pages, photographic illustrations; original red cloth, very good, plus; Herbert McLean, Evans and Harrison Horblit with their bookplates.　19th Century Shop　39-　1996 $225.00

ASSOCIATION - RUARI MCLEAN

CARTER, HARRY　Fournier on Typefounding. London: printed at the Curwen Press for Soncino Press, 1930. 1st edition; one of 260 copies; 8vo; portrait, 16 double page facsimiles, original cloth, slightly faded and stained. Bookplate of Ruari McLean.　Forest Books　74-301　1996 £85.00

ASSOCIATION - RUARI MCLEAN

DREYFUS, JOHN　The Work of Jan Van Krimpen: a Record in Honour of His Sixtieth Birthday. Haarlem: Joh. Enschede en Zonen, 1952. 1st edition; 4to; numerous illustrations, original buckram, title gilt on spine and upper cover; Ruari McLean's copy with bookplate.　Forest Books 74-319　1996 £120.00

FRANKLIN, COLIN　Emery Walker. Some Light on His Theories of Printing and On His Relations with William Morris and Cobden-Sanderson. Cambridge: 1973. 1st edition; limited to 500 copies; folio; pages x, 36; portrait, 2 facsimile pages plus 3 items in pocket at end, original morocco backed boards, decorated with reduced version of a Morris wallpaper; fine; from the library of Ruari McLean, with his booklabel. Claude Cox　107-28　1996 £130.00

HELLINGA, W.　Copy and Print in the Netherlands. An Atlas of Historical Bibliography. Amsterdam: 1962. Folio; numerous plates; cloth, gilt; inscribed to and with booklabel of Ruari McLean.　Maggs Bros. Ltd.　1191-181　1996 £100.00

MILTON, JOHN 1608-1674　Comus: a Mask. printed by the Cambridge Univ. Press for Ernest Benn Ltd., 1926. Limited to 300 copies; 4to; printed on handmade paper, 8 plates; original buckram gilt, covers with borders of type ornaments, very slightly rubbed, uncut, top edge gilt. Bookplates of Ruari McLean and D. G. Bridson.　Forest Books　74-344 1996 £65.00

MORISON, STANLEY 1889-1967　American Copybooks. An Outline of Their History from Colonial to Modern Times. Philadelphia: Wm. F. Fell Co., 1951. This copy number 238 (total copies printed unknown); Small 8vo; 13 illustrations; printed paper boards, bit rubbed at extremities, inscribed by author to his secretary Miriam Gasking, booklabel of Ruari Mclean, pencil note saying the book was bought from Tony Appleton in 1978.　Maggs Bros. Ltd.　1191-160　1996 £88.00

MORISON, STANLEY 1889-1967　'Black Letter' Text. Cambridge: University Press, 1942. Limited to 100 copies; folio; iv, 40 pages; frontispiece, illustrations on title, 43 illustrations in text; original printed wrappers, headcaps bit worn, edges slightly faded; bookplate of Ruari McLean. Appleton 162.　Maggs Bros. Ltd.　1191-196　1996 £220.00

MORISON, STANLEY 1889-1967　A Fifteenth Century Modus Scribendi from the Abbey of Melk. Cambridge: at the University Press, 1940. Limited to 50 copies; 16 pages of facsimile, title vignette, introduction, transcription and translation; original black cloth, headcaps and corners tiny bit bumped; booklabel of Ruari McLean. Appleton 155.　Maggs Bros. Ltd.　1191-161　1996 £100.00

MORISON, STANLEY 1889-1967　Notes Towards a Specimen of the Ancient Typographical Materials Principally Collected and Bequeated to the Unviersity of Oxford by Dr. John Fell d. 1686. Oxford: privately printed, 1953-57. One of 50 copies; 4to; 3 volumes, 15 pages of specimens; blue papers, crease on upper cover of volume 1, extra set of the text of volume 1 on loose pages inserted. Ruari McLean's copy with booklabels.　Maggs Bros. Ltd.　1191-205　1996 £235.00

MORISON, STANLEY 1889-1967　Politics and Script. Aspects of Authority and Freedom in the Development of Graeco-Latin Script from the Sixth Century B.C. to the Twentieth Century. Oxford: Clarendon Press, 1972. Tall 8vo; 186 illustrations; blue cloth, dust jacket; booklabel of Ruari Mclean. Appleton 205a.　Maggs Bros. Ltd.　1191-206　1996 £60.00

MORISON, STANLEY 1889-1967　Printing "The Times" Since 1785. London: Printing House Square, 1953. 1st edition; limited to 250 copies; large folio; 52 plates, numerous line engravings; original cloth, dust jacket slightly soiled; with McLean's signature and bookplate. Appleton 187.　Forest Books　74-346　1996 £175.00

MORISON, STANLEY 1889-1967　Typographic Design in Relation to Photographic Composition. San Francisco: Ptd. at the Black Vine Press for the Book Club of California, 1959. 1st edition; one of 400 copies; 8vo; original parchment backed marbled (Cockerell boards, title gilt on spine, preserved in wrapper; Ruari McLean's copy with bookplate and critical pencilled annotations.　Forest Books　74-349　1996 £95.00

MORRIS, FRANCIS ORPEN 1810-1893　A Natural History of British Moths. London: Bell and Daldy, 1872. 3rd edition; 8vo; 4 volumes; 132 hand colored plates; green cloth gilt, dust jackets, very rare survival, the dust jackets have few slight tears and small holes, but are generally in sound condition; ownership inscriptions of Florence Acton, 3 Dean's Yard, Westminster, dated August 1878, booklabel of Ruari McLean. Maggs Bros. Ltd.　1190-169　1996 £350.00

ASSOCIATION - RUARI MCLEAN

NASH, R.   Calligraphy and Printing in the Sixteenth Century. Antwerp: Plantin-Moretus Museum, 1964. 2nd edition, limited to 500 copies; small 8vo; 39 pages; cloth backed pictorial boards, dust jacket, booklabel of Ruari McLean & inscription to him from Rocky Stinehour.   Maggs Bros. Ltd.   1191-210   1996 £40.00

PLATO   Crito. Paris: printed at the Officina Bodoni, Montagnola for, Pleiad, 1926. Number 64 of 470 copies; 8vo; printed on Binda handmade paper (5 on Japanese vellum); pages xxxvi, (2); original marbled boards, paper label, vellum caps at head and tail of backstrip, uncut, hinges rubbed and corners just bumped, generally well preserved. From the library of Ruari McLean. Mardersteig 16.   Claude Cox 107-120   1996 £180.00

PLOMER, HENRY R.   English Printers' Ornaments. London: Grafton & Co., 1924. 1st edition; one of 500 copies; 4to; frontispiece, facsimiles; original cloth backed boards, corners bumped, uncut, top edge gilt; Ruari McLean's copy with signature and bookplate.   Forest Books 74-356   1996 £95.00

SALAMAN, MALCOLM C.   French Colour Prints of the XVIII Century. London: William Heinemann, 1913. 1st edition; 4to; 49 mounted colored plates; original gilt decorated cloth, top edge gilt, inner hinges sightly shaken; Ruari McLean's copy with bookplate, with ALS from David McKitterick to McLean.   Forest Books 74-364   1996 £95.00

SCHONFIELD, H. J.   The New Hebrew Typography. London: Denis Archer, 1932. 4to; 17 plates; white cloth backed black baords, gilt lettering, some slight soiling to cloth, booklabel and ownership inscription of Ruari McLean. Appleton 125.   Maggs Bros. Ltd. 1191-214   1996 £135.00

THE STUDIO. Modern Book-Bindings and Their Designers. Special Winter Number 1899-1900. London: The Studio, 1900. 1st edition; 4to; 82 pages, 5 color lithograph plates, numerous illustrations; original printed wrappers, uncut; Ruari McLean's copy with signature.   Forest Books 74-369   1996 £75.00

TRYPANIS, C. A.   The Elegies of a Glass Adonis. New York: Ptd. by the Rampant Lions Press for the Chilmark Press, 1967. 1st edition; number 436 of 450 copies, signed by author; 8vo; original boards, spine gilt, uncut; Ruari McLean's copy with his bookplate.   Forest Books 74-372   1996 £95.00

WARDE, F.   Printers Ornaments Applied to the Composition of Decorative Borders, Panels and Patterns. London: Lanston Monotype Corp. Ltd., 1928. 4to; 114 pages, original red and gilt cloth, headcaps mildly bumped; ink inscription from "BLW" (Beatrice Warde) to Ruari McLean. Appleton 277.   Maggs Bros. Ltd.   1191-223   1996 £80.00

WOLFE, RICHARD J.   On Improvements in Marbling the Edges of Books and Paper. A Nineteenth Century Account. Newtown: Bird and Bull Press, 1983. Limited to 350 numbered copies; oblong 12mo; 14 original marbled paper samples tipped in, blue half morocco, gilt lettering and border, marbled paper boards; booklabel of Ruari McLean.   Maggs Bros. Ltd.   1191-225   1996 £225.00

ASSOCIATION - HELEN MCMASTER

THOMAS, DYLAN MARLAIS 1914-1953   The Map of Love. London: 1939. 1st edition; 1st issue; excellent copy; presentation copy from author for Helen McMaster.   R. A. Gekoski 19-141   1996 £875.00

ASSOCIATION - DENNIS MCMILLAN

BROWN, FREDRIC   Before She Kills. San Diego: Dennis McMillan, 1984. 1st edition; publisher's copy; fine in jacket, inscribed to publisher with drawing by William Nolan.   Janus Books 36-102   1996 $150.00

BURKE, JAMES LEE   Two for Texas. New York: Pocket Books, 1982. 1st edition; pictorial paper wrappers with light edge wear, light rubbing and soiling; very good+, owner's "to do" list on inside front panel; inscribed to Dennis McMillan, from author.   Quill & Brush 102-162 1996 $100.00

CRUMLEY, JAMES   Whores. Missoula: Dennis McMillan Publications, 1988. One of 26 (of 501 total), signed, lettered copies; cover and endpapers by Joe Servello; bound in full goatskin morocco with gold stamped lettering and design and page edges marbled; fine; this copy inscribed to publisher from author.   Quill & Brush 102-408 1996 $750.00

ASSOCIATION - FERDINAND MCVEAGH

WALTER, HENRY   A History of England. London: printed for J. G. F. & Rivington, 1840. 8 x 5 1/4 inches; 7 volumes; engraved maps as frontispiece in 6 of the volumes; contemporary light brown polished half calf, marbled sides, edges and endpapers, raised bands, spines attractively gilt in compartments in antique style, red and green morocco labels, corners bit rubbed, outer edge of one volume little worn, paper sides somewhat chafed, but only trivial signs of wear, otherwise fine internally, pretty set in excellent condition; 19th century armorial bookplate of Ferdinand M. McVeagh in each volume.   Phillip J. Pirages 33-506   1996 $750.00

ASSOCIATION - MEAKIN

SMITH, W.   A Synopsis of the British Diatomaceae. London: 1853. 2 volumes in 1, 69 plates; half morocco, trifle rubbed, somewhat foxed, as usual; from the library of S. H. Meakin with a number of insertions, including a small correction to Sowerby English Botany.   Wheldon & Wesley 207-1658   1996 £200.00

ASSOCIATION - GEORGE MEEK

SOUTHEY, ROBERT 1774-1843   The Doctor, &c. London: Longman, Rees, Orme, Brown, Green and Longman, 1834-47. 1st edition; 8vo; 7 volumes, titles printed in red with pyramid motif printed in black, with half titles; contemporary half pink polished calf, spines decorated in compartments with intersecting circles in blind, double black morocco lettering pieces, marbled edges and endpapers, top edge gilt, spines slightly soiled and rubbed, sides rubbed, endpapers spotted, early marginalia in volume I, correctly identifying the author, good set; contemporary bookplates of George Meek.   Simon Finch 24-213 1996 £750.00

ASSOCIATION - JOSHUA MEEN

SELDEN, JOHN 1584-1654   Joannis Seldeni I. C. de Dis Syris Syntagmata. London: Excudebat Gulielmus Stansbeius, 1617. 1st edition; 8vo; contemporary calf; fine; contemporary signatures of R. Legard and Joshua Meen. STC 22167; CBEL I 2331.   Ximenes 108-321 1996 $750.00

ASSOCIATION - MEGGITT

PRATT, A. E.   Two Years Among New Guinea Cannibals... London: Seeley & Co., 1906. 360 pages, black and white plates, folding map; rebound in attracative black half gilt morocco, nice; Mervyn Meggitt's copy.   Antipodean 28-209   1996 $175.00

RECLUS, ELISEE   The Earth and Its Inhabitants: Oceanica. New York: 1890. 4to; 512 pages; woodcut illustrations; rubbed half morocco, otherwise good+; the Meggitt copy.   Antipodean 28-232   1996 $145.00

ROTH, H. LING   The Aborigines of Tasmania. Hobart: n.d. Facsimile of 1899 2nd edition; map, 228 pages, ciii vocabulary and appendix; original green cloth and yellow dust jacket, good+ copy. Mervyn Meggitt's copy.   Antipodean 28-279   1996 $125.00

SEMON, RICHARD   In the Australian Bush and on the Coast of the Coreal Sea. London: 1899. (xvi), 552 pages, 4 folding maps; original green gilt ribbed cloth, slightly shaken, small split side of spine, good+ overall. The Meggitt copy. Ferguson 15574.   Antipodean 28-331 1996 $350.00

SMITH, W. RAMSAY   Myths and Legends of the Australian Aboriginals. London: Geo. Harrap, 1930. 356 pages; many plates in black and white and 16 in color; original pictorial grey stamped and gilt cloth, spine very slightly faded, otherwise pristine; Mervyn Meggitt's copy, signed on endpaper.   Antipodean 28-365   1996 $125.00

SPENCER, BALDWIN   The Arunta. A Study of a Stone Age People. London: Macmillan, 1927. Large 8vo; 2 volumes, 390 pages and black and white illustrations; 256 pages, 4 color plates and black and white illustrations; original green cloth, gilt; pristine in original printed dust jackets; Mervyn Meggitt's copy.   Antipodean 28-386   1996 $750.00

STOKES, J. L.   Discoveries in Australia: During the Voyage of HMS Beagle in the Years 1837-43. Adelaide: 1969. 2 volumes; 521, 543 pages; illustrations; very good; the Meggitt copy.   Antipodean 28-405   1996 $150.00

ASSOCIATION - MEGGITT

TERRY, MICHAEL   Sand and Sun: with Camels in the Dry Lands of Central Australia. London: 1937. 288 pages; illustrations; good; the Meggitt copy.   Antipodean 28-445 1996 $145.00

THOMAS, N. W.   Kinship Organisations and Group Marriage in Australia. Cambridge: 1906. 1st edition; 163 pages, 3 maps, 1 folding table; original green gilt, buckram, very good. Scarce. Mervyn Meggitt's copy, signed.   Antipodean 28-454 1996 $145.00

THOMSON, DONALD   Economic Structure and the Ceremonial Exchange Cycle in Arnhem Land. Melbourne: 1949. 106 pages black and white illustrations, 2 folding maps; original red and gilt buckram, good+ copy; the Meggitt copy.   Antipodean 28-460 1996 $125.00

ASSOCIATION - MELVILLE

BRUCE, JOHN   Report on the Arrangements Which Were Made...When Spain, By Its Armada, Projected the Invasion. London: State Paper Office, 1798. Demy 8vo; (iv), (98), (xiv), cccxxviii pages, 2 folding tables; bound in elegant recent full morocco, top edge gilt, trimmed close, shaving few sidenotes, otherwise very good state. Presentation copy signed by Bruce and inscribed to Henry Dundas, 1st Viscount Melville, Secretary of War. Ash Rare Books Zenzybyr-16 1996 £450.00

ASSOCIATION - WILLIAM MELVILLE

TROLLOPE, ANTHONY 1815-1882   Ayala's Angel. London: Chapman and Hall, 1881. 1st edition; 8vo; 3 volumes; original orange cloth, blocked in black and gilt, recently recased, new black endpapers, spines little faded, covers slightly marked, but very good set, no half titles were issued; bookplate of William Melville in each volume. Sadleir 60. Sotheran PN32-57 1996 £1,250.00

ASSOCIATION - SCOTT MEREDITH

CLARKE, ARTHUR C.   Interplanetary Flight. New York: Harpers, 1950. 1st edition; 3rd impression; tight, bright, very good+ copy; signed by author with his agent, Scott Meredith's bookplate, author's first book. Aronovitz 57-263 1996 $150.00

ASSOCIATION - WILLIAM MEREDITH

THOMAS, DYLAN MARLAIS 1914-1953   Adventures in the Skin Trade and Other Stories. Norfolk: New Directions, 1955. 1st edition; original binding, top edge slightly dusty, head and tail of spine and corners slightly bumped and rubbed, edges and endpaper edges slightly browned, very good in nicked, chipped and dusty, slightly rubbed, torn and creased dust jacket slightly darkened at edges; ownership signature of William Meredith.   Ulysses 39-588 1996 £75.00

ASSOCIATION - MERSEY

CICERO, MARCUS TULLIUS 106-43 BC   Phippicae. Francisci Mantvrantii Enarrationes in Philippicas. Venice: Ioannes Tacuinus de Tridino, 22nd March 1494. 2nd edition; small folio; 78 unnumbered leaves a-n6, Roman letter in 2 sizes, white on black woodcut initials, woodcut printer's device; contemporary scholarly annotations throughout, later ownership autograph of St. Peter's College, Strasbourg on titlepage, slight age yellowing, 3 tiny wormholes affecting single letters but not legibility in few leaves, otherwise very good; 17th century English polished speckled calf panelled in blind, spine gilt; bookplate of Viscount Mersey, Bignor Park. BMC V 528; Hain Coppinger 5139; Goff C557; GKW 6797. Graesse II 165.   A. Sokol XXV-22 1996 £2,250.00

HENRY VIII, KING OF GREAT BRITIAN   A Necessary Doctrine and Ervidition for any Christen Man, set Furthe by the Kynges Maiestie of Englande &c. London: Thomas Barthelet, 1543. Small 4to; 118 unnumbered leaves, black letter with Roman and italic titlepage, the latter with woodcut architectural border, woodcut initials, contemporary ms. annotations on 3 pages, title and laste page bit dusty, small repairs without loss to edges of titlepage and 5 other leaves, occasional light margina stain; 18th century red morocco richly gilt, rebacked, spine remounted, all edges gilt; good copy; bookplates of Viscount Mersey and Charles Butler of Hatfield. STC 5168.7. Lowndes 1040.   A. Sokol XXV-50 1996 £1,350.00

ASSOCIATION - W. S. MERWIN

NERUDA, PABLO   Selected Poems. New York: Delacorte, 1972. 1st edition; review copy with slip and photo laid in. fine in slightly spine tanned dust jacket, scarce; inscribed by one of the translators, W. S. Merwin.   Lame Duck Books 19-414 1996 $100.00

ASSOCIATION - DE MESMES

POLYBIUS   Histoire de Polybe, Depuis la Seconde Guerre Punique Jusqu'a Celle de Macedoine. Paris: Lamesle for Gandouin (& others), 1727-30. 4to; 6 volumes; over 125 engraved plates, maps and plans, hundreds of woodcut typographic ornaments; fine contemporary French full leather gilt, some joints cracked, red edges; on boards of each volume are the gilt arms of Jean Jacques IV, Comte de Mesmes. Brunet IV 791; Jahns 1461-2; Olivier 1328.   Family Album Tillers-519 1996 $2,000.00

ASSOCIATION - JOHN METCALF

BIRNEY, EARLE   The Beginnings of Chaucer's Irony (an Essay). New York: Modern Language Association, n.d. ... Sept. 1939. Reprint; printed wrpapers; fine, rare; from the library of John Metcalf, with his ownership signature.   Nelson Ball 118-2 1996 $300.00

BIRNEY, EARLE   David and Other Poems. Toronto: Ryerson Press, 1942. Reprint; boards, dust jacket, fine in good jacket; from the library of John Metcalf, with his ownership signature.   Nelson Ball 118-8 1996 $100.00

BIRNEY, EARLE   Near False Creek Mouth (Poems). Toronto and Montreal: McClelland and Stewart, c. 1964. 1st edition; unpaginated; cloth, in dust jacket, scarce in cloth; fine; from the library of John Metcalf, with his ownership signature.   Nelson Ball 118-18 1996 $100.00

BIRNEY, EARLE   Now Is the Time (Poems). Toronto: Ryerson Press, 1945. 1st edition; 56 pages; boards, in dust jacket; author's signed presentation, inscribed with two lines of a poem in the book, author has changed a word in poem on page 49; about very good; from the library of John Metcalf, with his ownership signature.   Nelson Ball 118-19 1996 $150.00

BIRNEY, EARLE   The Strait of Anian. Selected Poems. Toronto: Ryerson Press, 1948. 1st edition; viii, 84 pages; boards, in dust jacket; inscribed and signed by author, fine in good jacket; from the library of John Metcalf, with his ownership signature.   Nelson Ball 118-24 1996 $100.00

DUDEK, LOUIS   East of the City (Poems). Toronto: Ryerson Press, 1946. 1st edition; 51 pages; boards, dust jacket; fine in near fine jacket; author's first book; with ownership signature of Wesley Scott; author's signed presentation to John Metcalf.   Nelson Ball 118-43 1996 $450.00

DUDEK, LOUIS   Patterns of Recent Canadian Poetry (an Essay). Quebec: Culture, 1958. Reprint; printed wrappers; very good, scarce; from the library of John Metcalf, with his ownership signature.   Nelson Ball 118-51 1996 $150.00

HAMBLETON, RONALD   Unit of Five. Toronto: Ryerson, 1944. 1st edition; (x), 87 pages; cloth, in dust jacket; inscribed by author to John Metcalf. Near fine.   Nelson Ball 118-62 1996 $500.00

NEWLOVE, JOHN   Moving in Alone. Toronto: Contact Press, c. 1965. 1st edition; issued in printed wrappers, autographed by author, dated 12 May, 1965; about fine; from the library of John Metcalf, with his ownership signature.   Nelson Ball 118-80 1996 $300.00

NOWLAN, ALDEN   A Darkness in the Earth. Eureka: Hearse Press, n.d. 1959. 1st edition; printed wrappers; fine; rare, author's second book; from the library of John Metcalf, with his ownership signature.   Nelson Ball 118-96 1996 $1,500.00

NOWLAN, ALDEN   The Rose and the Puritan. Fredericton: Fiddlehead Poetry Books, 1958. 1st edition; 16 pages; printed wrappers; fine copy of author's first book; from the library of John Metcalf, with his ownership signature.   Nelson Ball 118-105 1996 $150.00

ASSOCIATION - JOHN METCALF

NOWLAN, ALDEN   The Things Which Are. Toronto: Contact Press, c. 1962. 1st edition; 1st issue; 71 pages; printed wrappers, printed card covers in printed jacket; fine, very scarce; from the library of John Metcalf, with his ownership signature.   Nelson Ball 118-107 1996 $200.00

NOWLAN, ALDEN   Wind in a Rocky Country. Toronto: Emblem Book, 1960/61. 1st edition; (23) pages; designed, illustrated and printed by Robert Rosewarne at his Blue R Press, Ottawa; printed wrappers; fine, very scarce. from the library of John Metcalf, with his ownership signature.   Nelson Ball 118-110 1996 $450.00

PURDY, AL   Morning and it's Summer: a Memoir. Dunvegan: Quadrant Editions, 1983. 1st edition; issue in unbound sheets laid into boards, one of 50 copies so housed, numbered and signed by author; in board slipcase with paper label; fine; from the library of John Metcalf, with his ownership signature.   Nelson Ball 118-122 1996 $250.00

PURDY, AL   Morning and it's Summer: a Memoir. Dunvegan: Quadrant Edtiions, 1983. 1st edition; one of 300 copies of the cloth issue, numbered and signed by author; mounted photos; fine in dust jacket; from the library of John Metcalf, with his ownership signature.   Nelson Ball 118-123 1996 $100.00

PURDY, AL   No Second Spring. Coatsworth: Black Moss Press, 1977. 1st edition; one of 100 copies, numbered and signed by author; quarto; (8) pages; cloth and boards, paper label; fine; from the library of John Metcalf, with his ownership signature.   Nelson Ball 118-127 1996 $100.00

PURDY, AL   On the Bearpaw Sea. Burnaby: Blackfish Press, 1973. 1st edition; one of 25 numbered and signed copies; unpaginated; signed by author and artist; this copy number 4; bound in full calfskin, board slipcase; fine; from the library of John Metcalf, with his ownership signature.   Nelson Ball 118-130 1996 $250.00

PURDY, AL   On the Bearpaw Sea. Burnaby: Blackfish Press, 1973. One of 100 numbered and signed copies, bound thus, signed by author, this number 74; Japanese binding and Mulberry covers; fine; inscribed by author for John Newlove, with his ownership signature dated 1973; from the library of John Metcalf, with his ownership signature.   Nelson Ball 118-131 1996 £125.00

PURDY, AL   Pressed on Sand. Toronto: Ryerson, c. 1955. 1st edition; one of 250 copies; 16 pages; boards; fine; inscribed by author; from the library of John Metcalf, with his ownership signature.   Nelson Ball 118-135 1996 $125.00

ROSENBLATT, JOE   Dream Craters. Erin: Press Porcepic, 1974. 1st edition; 1st issue with editor's name printed on front cover; 86 pages; fine; inscribed by author to editor, John Newlove; from the library of John Metcalf, with his ownership signature.   Nelson Ball 118-151 1996 $100.00

SOUSTER, RAYMOND   As Is. Toronto: Oxford University Press, 1967. 1st edition; of the last 75 copies, one of 62 each with a different unpublished poem written on front flyleaf, signed and dated August 1971 on back flyleaf; cloth, dust jacket; fine; with John Newlove's ownership signature, from the library of John Metcalf, with his ownership signature. Nelson Ball 118-155 1996 $150.00

SOUSTER, RAYMOND   City Hall Street. Toronto: Ryerson, c. 1951. 1st edition; near fine; author's copy with his pencilled notations and revisions; from the library of John Metcalf, with his ownership signature. Nelson Ball 118-157 1996 $200.00

SOUSTER, RAYMOND   The Colour of the Times: the Colleccted Poems. Toronto: Ryerson Press, c. 1964. 1st edition; 121 pages; cloth, dust jacket; about fine, autographed by author; from the library of John Metcalf, with his ownership signature.   Nelson Ball 118-158 1996 $100.00

SOUSTER, RAYMOND   Go to Sleep, World. Toronto: Ryerson, 1947. 1st edition; vii 59 pages; boards; fine in dust jacket; from the library of John Metcalf, with his ownership signature.   Nelson Ball 118-160 1996 $400.00

SOUSTER, RAYMOND   A Local Pride. Toronto: Contact Press, 1962. 1st edition; 131 pages; issued in printed card covers, printed dust jacket; fine; from the library of John Metcalf, with his ownership signature.   Nelson Ball 118-163 1996 $250.00

ASSOCIATION - JOHN METCALF

SOUSTER, RAYMOND   Shake Hands with the Hangman: Poems 1940-1952. Toronto: Contact Press, 1953. 1st edition; mimeographed; one of 100 copies; (i), 24 pages, mimeographed cover; internally fine, covers good; with Henry Moscovitch's ownership signature; from the library of John Metcalf, with his ownership signature.   Nelson Ball 118-165 1996 $1,000.00

SOUSTER, RAYMOND   When We Are Young. Montreal: First Statement, 1946. 1st edition; unpaginated; plain card covers in printed jacket, edges of front cover time darkened, one short closed tear, about very good copy of author's first book; inscribed by author for Wesley Scott, from the library of John Metcalf, with his ownership signature. Nelson Ball 118-167 1996 $1,250.00

SUTHERLAND, JOHN   Other Canadians. Montreal: First Statement Press, 1946. 1st edition; 112 pages; printed wrappers; near fine; inscribed by author for John Metcalf, with his ownership signature. Very scarce.   Nelson Ball 118-177 1996 $550.00

TURNBULL, GAEL   Land That I Knew. Toronto: Clo Chluain Tairbh, 1962. 1st edition; 8 pages; autographed by author; self wrappers; fine; from the library of John Metcalf, with his ownership signature.   Nelson Ball 118-182 1996 $275.00

ASSOCIATION - FRANCES MEYERS

BIGLAND, JOHN   A Natural History of Animals... Philadelphia: 1828. 1st edition; 8vo; 2 volumes; colored vignette titles, 22 hand colored plates, rather browned, as often; contemporary half roan, one backstrip off, and cover detached; bookplate of Frances Meyers, later in the Bradley Martin collection.   Maggs Bros. Ltd. 1190-223 1996 £85.00

ASSOCIATION - ROBERT MEZEY

LOWELL, ROBERT 1917-1977   Land of Unlikeness. Poems. Cummington: Cummington Press, 1944. 1st edition; limited to 250 copies (the entire edition); 8vo; blue boards printed in blue; covers faded and worn, but good copy; author's rare first book; unusual association copy, inscribed facetiously by poet Robert Mezey to Philip Levine, with Levine's ownership signature.   James S. Jaffe 34-419 1996 $1,750.00

ASSOCIATION - JOHN MIDDLETON

LA FONTAINE, JEAN DE 1621-1695   The Amours of Cupid and Psyche. London: printed for R. Withy, at the Dunciad in Cornhill, 1749. Crown 8vo; 2 volumes, 31 copper engravings; contemporary sprinkled calf, very fine; armorial bookplate of John Middleton.   H. M. Fletcher 121-100 1996 £2,750.00

ASSOCIATION - L. MILAZZO

GARDNER, JOHN   On Moral Fiction. New York: Basic Books, 1978. 1st edition; advance review copy with publisher's slip; fine in fine dust jacket; inscribed by author to prominent critic, L. Milazzo, thanking him for his kind review of On Moral Fiction. Nice association.   Thomas Dorn 9-123 1996 $175.00

ASSOCIATION - JOSEPHINE MILES

LYNCH, JAMES J.   Box, Pit and Gallery - Stage and Society in Johnson's London. University of California Press, 1953. 1st edition; black and white frontispiece and 6 black and white plates; original binding, top edge slightly dusty, head and tail of spine slightly faded, very good in nicked, torn, creased, rubbed and slightly marked, chipped and dusty dust jacket, faded at spine and browned at edges. Presentation copy from author for Josephine Miles.   Ulysses 39-320 1996 £55.00

ASSOCIATION - NOLAN MILLER

SEXTON, ANNE   To Bedlam and Part Way Back. Boston: Houghton, Mifflin Co., 1960. 1st edition; 8vo; fine presentation copy to Nolan Miller of The Antioch review.   Lakin & Marley 3-55 1996 $1,250.00

ASSOCIATION - MINTO

BRAND, JOHN   Observataions on Popular Antiquities. London: Rivington and Many Others, 1813. 1st edition; very tall, wide quarto; Large paper edition; 2 volumes; half titles and index, pages xxvi, 486; xi, 731; elegant binding in full tan polished calf, spines skillfully rehinged, gilt extra, gauffered edges, elaborately gilt panelled in compartments; gilt crests of the Earl of Minto on front and back covers of both volumes, marbled edges and endpapers, splendid set. Lowndes I 241.   Hartfield 48-L12   1996 $695.00

ASSOCIATION - DAVID MITCHELL

ANGELOU, MAYA   Gather Together in My Name. New York: Random House, 1974. 1st edition; 8 1/2 x 5 3/4 inches; 3 p.l., 214 pages, (1) leaf; original cloth, dust jacket; signed and inscribed by author for David Mitchell. Very fine in like jacket.   Phillip J. Pirages 33-10 1996 $100.00

ANGELOU, MAYA   Oh Pray My Wings Are Gonna Fit Me Well. New York: Random House, 1975. 1st edition; 8 1/2 x 5 3/4 inches; ix, (1) 67 pages; original cloth backed boards, dust jacket; extremely fine in like jacket; inscribed and signed by author for David Mitchell.   Phillip J. Pirages 33-13 1996 $100.00

ASSOCIATION - S. P. MITCHELL

SAY, THOMAS 1787-1834   American Entomology, or Descriptions of the Insects of North America. Philadelhia: Samuel Agustus Mitchell, 1824-25/28. 1st edition; tall 8vo; 3 volumes, (2), viii, 18 hand colored engraved plates with unpaginated explanatory text (3 index); (2), 18 hand colored engraved plates with unpaginated explantory text, (3 index); (2), 18 hand colored engraved plates with unpaginated explanatory text (3 index) pages; tissue guards intact; original green pictorial label on front cover of volume 1, original pink spine label on volume 2, with extra engraved title in volume 1; some moderte foxing and occational spotting; lovely fresh set, entirely untrimmed and uncut in nearly original condition; 19th century bookplate of S. P. Mitchell. Nissen ZBI 3612; Bennett Amer. Colo Books p. 95; Sabin 77370.   Edwin V. Glaser 121-275 1996 $3,000.00

ASSOCIATION - JOHN MITFORD

BARCLAY, JOHN   The Mirror of Minds or Barclay's Icon Animorum. London: I.B. for Thomas Walkley, 1633. 12mo; pages (xii), 380, roman letter, title backed long since, couple of minor tears not affecting text, perfectly acceptable copy; early 19th century calf gilt, upper cover loosening; armorial bookplates of W. Combes and Henry Batchellor Inman, autograph of "J. Mitford 1832" (probably the writer John Mitford 1781-1859). STC 1400. Lowndes 112.   A. Sokol XXV-10 1996 £500.00

ASSOCIATION - DOUGLASS MAXWELL MOFFAT

VERGILIUS MARO, PUBLIUS 70-19 BC   Bucolica, Georgica et Aeneis. Birmingham: Baskerville, 1766. 8vo; pages (2), 388 (with all Cancellans), engraved frontispiece; all edges gilt, foxed, early full red crushed morocco, spine abundantly tooled in floral gilt, ex-libris of Douglass Maxwell Moffat. Gaskell 34.   Family Album   Tillers-646 1996 $600.00

ASSOCIATION - FRANCIS MOHUN

MAXWELL-LYTE, H. C.   A History of Dunster and of the Families of Mohun and Luttrell. London: St. Catherine's Press, 1909. Crown 8vo; 2 volumes, xxi, (ii), 328 pages; (iv), 329-596 pages; text illustrations and plates; original black cloth, gilt, shelf wear and edges bit faded. Francis Mohun's copy.   Marlborough 162-68 1996 £90.00

ASSOCIATION - MOLESWORTH

BRIDGES, ROBERT 1844-1930   Prometheus the Firegiver. Oxford: printed at the Private Press of H. Daniel, 1883. 1st edition; number 35 of 100 copies; 4to; pages (4), 72, hand miniated initial F in red, printed in small pica roman on Van Gelder handmade paper, uncut in original vellum backed blue boards, little scuffed; scarce; ownership signature of G. Molesworth of Simla.   Claude Cox 107-39 1996 £135.00

ASSOCIATION - WILLIAM MOLESWORTH

MILL, JOHN STUART 1806-1873   Principles of Political Economy with Some of Their Applications to Social Philosophy... London: John W. Parker and Son, 1852. 3rd edition; 8vo; 2 volumes, xx, 604; xv, (1), 571, (1) pages, complete with 4 pages of ads in volume 2; original green cloth, printed paper labels, slightly rubbed, but overall very good, largely unopened; from the contemporary library of Sir William Molesworth with his armorial bookplate. Hollander 2818.   John Drury 82-184 1996 £275.00

ASSOCIATION - PERRY MOLSTAD

BENNET, E. ARNOLD   A Man From the North. London: & New York: John Lane, 1989. 1st edition; author's first book; elusive white lettering on spine and cover intact; brick red cloth showing only light soil and small faint dampspot, one chip in top margin of one leaf, otherwise text is fresh, housed in morocco backed slipcase with folding wrapper, some rubbing, still dignified, on slipcase spine. Nice copy, scarce; bookplate of Perry Molstad. Wolff 391; John Quinn 461.   Magnum Opus 44-39 1996 $225.00

ASSOCIATION - ISABELLA MONCK

STROTHER, EDWARD   The Family Companion for Health, or the Housekeeper's Physician... London: printed for John and James Rivington, 1750. 3rd edition; 8vo; pages (12), 426, (26); contemporary unlettered gilt ruled calf, binding lightly rubbed, otherwise nice. Neat contemporary ownership inscription "Isabella Monck 1750" on titlepage. James Fenning 133-326 1996 £265.00

ASSOCIATION - NUGENT MONCK

YEATS, WILLIAM BUTLER 1865-1935   The Land of the Heart's Desire. London: Fisher Unwin, 1912. 7th edition; author's presentation copy inscribed for Nugent Monck.   R. A. Gekoski 19-170 1996 £750.00

ASSOCIATION - EDWARAD MONCKTON

DESCARTES, RENE   Epistolae...in Quibus Omnis Generis Questiones Philosophicae Tractantur... London: Impensis Joh. Dunmore & Octavian Pulleyn, 1668. Small 4to; 2 volumes bound in 1, 4 leaves, 368 pages, 10 folding plates, 2 leaves, 404 pages, 2 leaves; contemporary calf, rebacked, worn; bookplate of Hon. Edward Monckton, Sumerford Hall, Staffs.   H. M. Fletcher 121-61 1996 £400.00

ASSOCIATION - JOHN MONTAGUE

HUGHES, TED 1930-   A Few Crows. Exeter: Rougemont Press, 1970. 1st edition; one of 150 copies; thin square 8vo; illustrations by Reiner Burger; full leather, dust jacket; foot of spine bumped, otherwise fine in slightly soiled jacket chipped at foot of spine; inscribed by author to poet John Montague.   James S. Jaffe 34-266 1996 $375.00

ASSOCIATION - WALTER MONTGOMERY

RUSSELL, WILLIAM CLARK   "Fra" Angelo: a Tragedy. London: for the author; John Camden Hotten, 1865. 1st edition; 8vo; original green cloth, bit rubbed, old library blindstamp on covers, front inner hinge weak; exceedingly rare first book; with fine inscription by Walter Montgomery to member of the original cast. not in CBEL or BM Cat. Wolff 6016. Ximenes 108-317 1996 $1,500.00

ASSOCIATION - CLEMENT CLARKE MOORE

KINGSLEY, CHARLES 1819-1875   Two Years Ago. Boston: Ticknor and Fields, 1857. 1st American edition, called the "Author's Edition"; original green cloth shows some soil and fading, with some odd wear at heel of spine and rubbing at other extremities, 2 inch split at top of front joint has been glue repaired, text shows light dampstains and foxing in foremargin almost throughout, though there is no evident correspondent marking of cloth; Clement Clarke Moore's copy with his signature (in rather faded ink) dated June 1857 on front free endpaper and again (bit stronger) on titlepage.   Magnum Opus 44-68 1996 $195.00

ASSOCIATION - ELIZABETH MOORE

NIN, ANAIS   House of Incest. London: Edwards Bros., 1958. 1st edition; wrappers, very good; presentation copy from author for Elizabeth Moore.   Words Etcetera 94-992 1996 £55.00

NIN, ANAIS   Solar Barque. London: Edwards Bros., 1958. 1st edition; wrappers; very good; presentation copy from author for Elizabeth Moore.   Words Etcetera 94-991 1996 £55.00

ASSOCIATION - ELLEN MOORE

BROWNING, ELIZABETH BARRETT 1806-1861   Aurora Leigh. London: Chapman and Hall, 1859. 4th edition; 8vo; frontispiece (some foxing) original green cloth; signatuare at front of Ellen Moore, dated Dec. 1859; fine, uncommon. Barnes A11b.   Ximenes 108-354 1996 $175.00

ASSOCIATION - JOHN MOORE

HENDERSON, WILLIAM   My Life as an Angler. London: W. Satchell, Peyton & Co., 1879. 2nd edition; large paper copy, this being number 1, numbered and signed yb publisher; royal 8vo; xvi, 312 pages; woodburytype portrait, 6 full page wood engraved plates on India paper, 59 wood engravings in text engraved by Edmund Evans; contemporary dark green half morocco gilt, gilt edges, rubbed, very slight spotting throughout text; presentation inscription from angling bibliographer Thomas Satchell to John Moore.   Thomas Thorp 489-145 1996 £200.00

ASSOCIATION - MERRILL MOORE

WORDSWORTH, WILLIAM 1770-1850   Lyrical Ballads. London: Oxford, 1924. Reprint of 1798 volume; very good without dust jacket, with gift inscription presenting the book to poet Merrill Moore and then inscribed by Moore to Donald Davidson.   Ken Lopez 74-327 1996 $275.00

ASSOCIATION - NORMAN MOORE

CURRY, EUGENE   Cath Mhuighe Leana, or The Battle of Magh Leana. London: 1855. 1st edition; 8vo; cloth, spine cloth chipped top and bottom, otherwise very good, 2 ALS's from Norman Moore to unnamed correspondent.   C. P. Hyland 216-133 1996 £125.00

ASSOCIATION - JOHN MORGAN

RICKETTS, CHARLES 1866-1931   A Defence of the Revival of Printing. Vale Press, 1899. One fo 250 copies; 7 3/4 x 5 1/4 inches; 37, (1) pages, (1) leaf; prospectus for book laid in, very elaborate white on black woodcut border occupying most of first page of text, woodcut initial and evice at end; original paper boards, paper labels on front cover and spine, usual browning to endpapers, otherwise especially fine. Large woodcut bookplate of John Morgan, designed by Charles Ricketts. Phillip J. Pirages 33-493 1996 $750.00

ASSOCIATION - ARTHUR HENRY MORSE

OSLER, WILLIAM 1849-1919   Cancer of the Stomach. Philadelphia: P. Blakiston's Son, 1900. 1st American edition; 8vo; iv, 157, ads, 40, (8) pages, 25 figures; dark blue blind stamped cloth, inner hinge cracked signature of Arthur Henry Morse who inscribed the book to Arthur Bliss Dayton, 1921. Bookplate of Elmer Belt. Abbott p. 72; Golden & roland 727.   Jeff Weber 31-36 1996 $325.00

ASSOCIATION - SAMUEL MORSE

SHILLABER, BENJAMIN   Partingtonian Patchwork. Boston: Lee and Shepard, 1873. 2nd edition; 8vo; frontispiece, 7 plates; decorated blue cloth, light wear to spine tips, front hinge partly cracked; inserted loosely is a carte-de-visite of the author's daughter, to whom he refers in the letter. Laid down on pastedown and f.f.e.p. is an ALS from author to inventor Samuel Morse. BAL 17578.   Charles Agvent 4-1011 1996 $150.00

ASSOCIATION - JOHN MORTON

HANKINS, SAMUEL W.   Simple Story of a Soldier. Nashville: 1912. 1st edition; 63 pages, plate; original printed wrpapers; bit of chipping about edges, else very good; housed in custom made clamshell case with leather spine and antique marbled sides; rare; presentation to John W. Morton, Forrest's chief of artillery. Dornbusch II 572; not in Nevins; Nicholson p. 354.   McGowan Book Co. 65-38 1996 $950.00

ASSOCIATION - SAMUEL MORTON

HOLMES, OLIVER WENDELL 1809-1894   Poems. London: O. Rich & sons, 1846. 1st English edition; 12mo; original cloth, quite worn, especially the spine. With Bradley's embossed stamp on front flyleaf; Inscribed by Holmes for Dr. Samuel G. Morton and Holmes' signature on titlepage, inserted ALS; bookplates of William Harris Arnold & Stephen Wakeman. BAL 8743 binding B (Ticknor).   M & S Rare Books 60-173 1996 $550.00

ASSOCIATION - HENRY MOSCOVITCH

SOUSTER, RAYMOND   Shake Hands with the Hangman: Poems 1940-1952. Toronto: Contact Press, 1953. 1st edition; mimeographed; one of 100 copies, mimeographed cover; internally fine, covers good; with Henry Moscovitch's ownership signature; from the library of John Metcalf, with his ownership signature.   Nelson Ball 118-165 1996 $1,000.00

ASSOCIATION - BARRY MOSER

BLY, ROBERT   The Whole Moisty Night. New York: Red Ozier Press, 1983. 1st edition; one of 300 copies, signed by author and artist; small thin 8vo; illustration by Barry Moser; original wrappers; mint, with separate titlepage and colophon leaf signed by Bly and Moser laid in; inscribed by Moser.   James S. Jaffe 34-562 1996 $100.00

ASSOCIATION - HOWARD MOSS

ACKROYD, PETER   Country Life. London: Ferry Press, 1978. One of 350 copies; tall stapled wrappers, little rust on staples and one corner little bumped, still very near fine; inscribed by author to American Poet Howard Moss.   Between the Covers 42-3 1996 $475.00

ASSOCIATION - W. E. MOSS

KEYNES, GEOFFREY 1887-1982   William Pickering, Publisher. A Memoir and a Hand-List of His Editions. London: at the Office of the Fleuron, 1924. Limited to 350 copies, 1st edition; 37 facsimile reproductions of titlepages; maroon cloth, top edge gilt, paper spine label, extra label on inside lower cover, headcaps mildly bumped, slightly scuffed, slight spotting on first and last few leaves; ALS from author to Col. W. E. Moss, the collector and scholar. Besterman 4863.   Maggs Bros. Ltd. 1191-106 1996 £110.00

ASSOCIATION - JAMES MOTT

TOWNSEND, JOHN K.   Narrative of a Journey Across the Rocky Mountains to the Columbia River, and a Visit to the Sandwich Islands, Chili, &c. Philadelphia: Henry perkins, 1839. 1st edition; curious copy with original plum cloth faded on rear cover & spine, but with front cover dyed blue & a bit of red stain at head of spine, 3 inch split in cloth over head of front joint, but cover is sound, even with short splits in endpapers and over front hinge, light foxing throughout, but clean copy, ownership inscription from James Mott (possibly NY abolitionist and founder of Swathmore College) to cousin Isaac Willis. Howes T319; Wagner Cam Becker 79.1. Field 1558.   Magnum Opus 44-103 1996 $350.00

ASSOCIATION - MIKE MOUTON

ONDAATJE, MICHAEL   Coming Through Slaughter. New York: Norton, 1976. 1st U.S. edition; near fine in price clipped dust jacket; inscribed by author to poet Mike Mouton with ALS to him laid in.   Lame Duck Books 19-444 1996 $375.00

ASSOCIATION - EDWARD MOXON

HOOD, THOMAS 1799-1845   Whims and Oddities, in Prose and
Verse... (with) Whims and Oddities...(Second Series). London: Lupton
Relfe/ London: Hurst, Chance and Co., 1827/29. 2nd edition; 8vo; 2
works; pages xiv, 146; viii, 150, each with 40 humorous illustrations by
Hood; uniformly bound in 19th century half green hard grain morocco,
spines gilt lettered direct, combe marbled sides and endpapers, gilt
edges, rubbed, one or two trivial spots or stains; very good;
presentation copies from author to Edward Moxon.   Simon Finch
24-118 1996 £500.00

ASSOCIATION - LIONEL MUIRHEAD

LUCRETIUS CARUS, TITUS 99-55 BC   Titi Lucretii Cari De Rerum
Natura Libri Sex. Glasgow: Robert and Andrew Foulis, 1759. Small 8vo;
pages (16), 269; attractive full contemporary dark green morocco
binding, spine gilt; early ms. ownership of G. Dunlop and ms. notes of
Lionel B. C. L. Muirhead. Gaskell 370; Brunet III 1220.   Family Album
Tillers-413 1996 $260.00

ASSOCIATION - W. H. MULLENS

MAC PHERSON, H. A.   The Birds of Cumberland Critically Studied,
Including Some Notes on the Birds of Westmorland. Carlisle: Chas.
Thurnam, 1886. 8vo; pages xx, 206, colored lithograph frontispiece,
folding colored map; original cloth, gilt. armorial bookplate of W. H.
Mullens; presentation copy to P. Leverhulme, with 4 page ALS from Rev.
MacPherson tipped in.   R.F.G. Hollett & Son 78-535 1996 £160.00

WHITE, GILBERT 1720-1793   The Natural History (Antiquities) of
Selborne. London: 1813. 1st edition; 4to; 2 vignettes, 10 plates (one
colored by hand); from the collection of Robert Leigh, with his
booklabel, later in the W. H. Mullens collection, with his bookplate,
bound for him in half green morocco, uncut, original printed label
(defective) and front wrapper (? or was it orginally a board) preserved.
Maggs Bros. Ltd. 1190-275 1996 £110.00

ASSOCIATION - R. I. MURCHISON

MAWE, THOMAS   The Universal Gardener and Botanist; or, a General
Dictionary of Gardening and Botany. London: 1778. 1st edition; 4to; calf,
rebacked, two small stamps on titlepage; bookplates of Sir R. I.
Murchison and the Museum of Practical Geology stating presented
Murchison in May 1862.   John Henly 27-312 1996 £150.00

ASSOCIATION - ROYAL MURDOCH

EBERHART, RICHARD   Burr Oaks. London: Chatto & Windus, 1947. 1st
edition; precedes American edition; 8vo; viii, 68 pages; yellow cloth,
soiled, slightly warped, titled in gilt on spine; near fine internally;
presentation copy for Royal Murdoch, inscribed by poet with 3 or 4
corrections in poet's hand; tipped in TLS by poet on verso of a first
edition of his 1947 broadside 'Ruminations'.   Blue Mountain SP95-97
1996 $250.00

ASSOCIATION - JOHN MURPHY

BORDEN, W. C.   The Use of the Roentgen Ray by the Medical
Department of the United States Army in the War with Spain.
Washington: 1900. 1st edition; 4to; 98 pages, plus 38 x-ray plates;
original binding; John B. Murphy's copy with his autograph and
bookplate. Kelly Burrage 892; Norman 267.   W. Bruce Fye 71-206
1996 $500.00

ASSOCIATION - MURRAY

BRADFORD, ROARK   Ol' Man Adam An' His Chillun. New York:
London: Harper & Bros., 1928. 1st edition; author's first book; drawings
by A. B. Walker; very good+ in very good price clipped dust jacket
which is moderately chipped at folds and with several mended tears;
signed by author for Mrs. B. G. Murray.   Steven C. Bernard 71-54
1996 $125.00

ASSOCIATION - A. S. MURRAY

SMITH, A. H.   A Catalogue of Engraved Gems in the British Museum.
London: British Museum, 1888. 1st edition; 12mo; ix, 244 pages, 9
plates; original gilt lettered cloth, 2 corners bumped; inscribed by co
author A.S. Murray for R. C. Jebb.   Archaeologia Luxor-4032 1996
$450.00

ASSOCIATION - DAVID MURRAY

MAC KINNON, WILLIAM ALEXANDER   History of Civilisation and Public
Opinion. London: Henry Colburn, 1849. 3rd edition; 8vo; 2 volumes; (ii),
xxviii, 388; xii, 402 pages, complete with half title in each volume;
contemporary morocco, fully gilt with raised bands and silk markers by
Holloway of London, little wear to upper joints, else fine; from the library
of David Murray, novelist and journalist, presentation copy inscribed by
author.   John Drury 82-164 1996 £100.00

ASSOCIATION - FRANCIS EDWIN MURRAY

BLAKE, WILLIAM 1757-1827   Poetical Sketches. London: Hacon &
Ricketts, 1899. Limited to 210 copies on handmade paper; 8vo; pages
xciii, + colophon, frontispiece, pictorial initials, 2 full page and one half
page borders designed and cut on wood by Charles Ricketts', original
blue boards, paper labels, backstrip darkened and little rubbed, but
good, uncut copy. Etched pictorial library bookplate of Francis Edwin
Murray.   Claude Cox 107-171 1996 £135.00

ASSOCIATION - HENRY MURRAY

VICTORIA, QUEEN OF GREAT BRITAIN 1819-1901   Leaves from the
Journal of Our Life in the Highlands from 1848 to 1861. London: Smith
Elder, 1868. 8vo; 6 plates and text sketches; pictorial souvenir binding,
rebacked, gauffered edges gilt; bound by local binder T. Russell of
Pitlochry; Henry Alexander Murray armorial bookplate.   Rostenberg &
Stern 150-32 1996 $150.00

WATTS, ALAN W.   This Is It and Other Essays on Zen and Spiritual
Experience. New York: Pantheon, 1960. 1st edition; whale stamp on front
endpaper, otherwise fine in very good, slightly spine faded jacket with
one edge tear on back panel; inscribed by author to noted Harvard
psychologist, Henry A. Murray, particularly good association.   Ken
Lopez 74-458 1996 $500.00

ASSOCIATION - J. A. MURRAY

WHYMPER, EDWARD   The Ascent of the Matterhorn. London: 1880.
Abridged 3rd edition of 'Scrambles Amongst the Alps', but this is the
first in this form with a different binding; 2 maps have been removed,
repaired and inserted in a new pocket; inscribed "J. A. Murray/from his
loving Father/Dec. 25, 1879", also signed on another page "J.A. Murray,
(the publisher); gilt lettering and design on dark blue cloth, some slight
internal marking, aminly of the (blank) rears of the half title and
titlepages, ends of spine little rubbed, but generally good sound, very
good copy with gilt lettering & decoration still bright.   Moutaineering
Books 8-EW01 1996 £110.00

ASSOCIATION - PAULI MURRAY

MURRAY, FLORENCE   The Negro Handbook 1944. New York: Current
Reference Pub., 1944. 2nd issue; extremities worn,hinges tender, but
sound, good copy lacking dust jacket; this is Pauli Murray's copy with
her contemporary ownership stamp. Nice Association.   Between the
Covers 43-376 1996 $150.00

ASSOCIATION - JOHN HENRY NASH

BULLEN, HENRY LEWIS   Nicolas Jenson, Printer of Venice: His
Famous Type Designs and Some Comment Upon the Printing Types of
Earlier Printers. San Francisco: Printed by John Henry Nash, 1926. One
of 207 copies; 16 1/2 x 10 3/4 inches; with leaf from the Jenson Printing
of Plutarch's 'Lives' of 1478 laid in, leaf bit foxed, faint dampstain in
lower margin, bottom edge little frayed and creased; original vellum
backed marbled paper boards, leather spine label, the volume with
foxing to endpapers and with portions of edges of binding darkened, top
edge of text leaves also with two small grey spots, otherwise the leaf
and volume in excellent condition, without any appreciable signs of use;
inscribed by John Henry Nash for Mrs. T. J. Cobden-Sanderson. Goff
P832; BMC V 178 (for leaf).   Phillip J. Pirages 33-339 1996 $450.00

COX, ISAAC   The Annals of Trinity County. Eugene: printed for Harold
C. Holmes, 1940. One of 350 copies; xxix, 265 pages; half cloth, boards,
paper spine label, bookplate, owner's ink notation, otherwise fine with
slipcase; presentation signed by printer, John Henry Nash, to Harry
Butler, ink notation by Butler under presentation. Howes C819; Rocq
15151.   Argonaut Book Shop 113-150 1996 $165.00

ASSOCIATION - PAUL NASH

BIBLE. ENGLISH - 1924   Genesis. London: Nonesuch Press, 1924. 1st edition; 12 woodcuts by Paul Nash; boards, head and tail of spine and corners bumped and worn, covers marked, good, no dust jacket; presentation copy from Nash to his wife.   Ulysses 39-435 1996 £2,250.00

ASSOCIATION - JANET NATHAN

LEWIS, SINCLAIR 1885-1951   Kingsblood Royal. New York: Random House, 1947. 1st edition; book is very good in dust jacket; inscribed by author in year of publication to Janet Nathan, wife of author Robert Nathan, with two ALS's from Lewis to Janet Nathan; excellent association.   Ken Lopez 74-265 1996 $750.00

ASSOCIATION - EARL NATION

OSLER, WILLIAM 1849-1919   Men and Books. Pasadena: 1959. 1st edition; limited to 200 copies; 675 pages; original binding; autographed by Earl Nation who provided introduction.   W. Bruce Fye 71-1568 1996 $150.00

ASSOCIATION - NEATE

DODGSON, CHARLES LUTWIDGE 1832-1898   Doublets a Word-Puzzle. London: Macmillan and Co., 1879. 1st edition; 16mo; 39 pages; original red cloth, sides ruled in blind, upper cover with publisher's blindstamp and lettered in gilt, in original envelope, preserved in maroon cloth and morocco slipcase lettered and ruled in gilt, title somewhat browned as often the case, cloth little soiled, small stain from cloth to rear pastedown, but an excellent copy. Presentation copy inscribed by author in purple ink to Mrs. Neate. Williams and Madan 130.   Simon Finch 24-31 1996 £3,500.00

ASSOCIATION - W. L. NECKER

JUETTNER, OTTO   Daniel Drake and His Followers. Cincinnati: Harvey Pub., 1909. 1st edition; tall 8vo; 496 pages; illustrations; original cloth, trifle rubbed at spine ends; near fine; With W. L. Necker bookplate. Cordasco 00-1804.   Edwin V. Glaser B122-84 1996 $150.00

ASSOCIATION - NEHRU

NUCLEAR Explosions and Their Effects. Delhi: The Publications Division, Ministry of Information & Broadcasting... 1958. Revised edtiion; large 8vo; xvi, 276, 64 pages; 4 folding charts, folding map, numerous tables; orange cloth with blue printed paper label on cover, dust jacket (slightly chipped); this copy signed by Nehru.   Kenneth Karmiole 1NS-199 1996 $300.00

ASSOCIATION - LORD NEWARK

ALLWOOD, PHILIP   Literary Antiquities of Greece; as Developed in an Attempt to Ascertain Principles for a New Analysis of the Greek Tongue...(with) Remarks On some Observations Edited in "The British Critic" Relating to a Work Lately Published... London: ptd. by J. Davis... 1799/1800. 1st editions; 4to; 2 volumes in one; 1st title with 4 plates & leaf of errata; the 4 page list of subscribers not preserved; 2nd title with half title, frontispiece map and errata leaf; contemporary tree calf, covers with attractive red mottled borders framed in gilt, spine stained dark and ruled in gilt, red morocco label (slight cracking of joints); both titles very scarce; fine in striking and very handsome binding; armorial bookplate of Lord Newark. not in Blackmer.   Ximenes 109-4 1996 $650.00

ASSOCIATION - NEWCASTLE

LYTE, H. C. MAXWELL   A History of Eton College (1440-1910). London: Macmillan and Co. Ltd., 1911. 4th edition; royal 8vo; half title, vignette, 627 pages of text, frontispiece, 9 plates, 63 illustrations to text, one colored folding map; full dark blue morocco, triple gilt rule borders, gilt corner ornaments, gilt stamped arms and motto of Eton College to upper board gilt rule, title, date and ornaments to panelled spine all edges gilt, inner gilt rule borders with engraved bookplate of the Seventh Duke of Newcastle, bound by Bumpus; very fine.   Beeleigh Abbey BA/56-14 1996 £250.00

ASSOCIATION - ROGER NEWDIGATE

CROUCH, NATHANIEL 1632?-1725?   A New View and Observations on the Ancient and Present State of London and Westminster... London: A. Bettesworth, Charles Hitch and J. Batley, 1730. 12mo; woodcut frontispiece, title, 2 ff., 1-240, 265-312, 145-240, 380-468, text woodcuts; contemporary mottled calf, joints cracking but firm, this coy lacks 2 final leaves of ads; armorial bookplate of Sir Roger Newdigate. Marlborough 162-125 1996 £220.00

ASSOCIATION - JOHN NEWLOVE

PURDY, AL   The Blur in Between: Poems 1960-61. Toronto: Emblem Books, 1962. 1st edition; limited to 300 copies; (iv), 21, (ii) pages; printed wrappers; very good; inscribed by author to John Newlove, with Newlove's ownership signature.   Nelson Ball 118-114 1996 $350.00

PURDY, AL   On the Bearpaw Sea. Burnaby: Blackfish Press, 1973. One of 100 numbered and signed copies, bound thus, signed by author, this number 74; Japanese binding and Mulberry covers; fine; inscribed by author for John Newlove, with his ownership signature dated 1973; from the library of John Metcalf, with his ownership signature.   Nelson Ball 118-131 1996 £125.00

ROSENBLATT, JOE   Dream Craters. Erin: Press Porcepic, 1974. 1st edition; 1st issue with editor's name printed on front cover; 86 pages; fine; inscribed by author to editor, John Newlove; from the library of John Metcalf, with his ownership signature.   Nelson Ball 118-151 1996 $100.00

SOUSTER, RAYMOND   As Is. Toronto: Oxford University Press, 1967. 1st edition; of the last 75 copies, one of 62 each with a different unpublished poem written on front flyleaf, signed and dated August 1971 on back flyleaf; cloth, dust jacket; fine; with John Newlove's ownership signature, from the library of John Metcalf, with his ownership signature. Nelson Ball 118-155 1996 $150.00

ASSOCIATION - HARRY NEWTON

HABERLY, LOYD   The Boy and the Bird. Long Crendon: Seven Acres Press, 1932. Limited to 155 numbered copies; 8vo; (8), 18, (2) pages; 19 hand colored woodcuts by author, text printed in red and black; original full brown niger morocco, spine lettered gilt, top edge gilt, others uncut; from the library of dedicatee, Sir Harry K. Newton, with his bookplate.   Thomas Thorp 489-128 1996 £350.00

ASSOCIATION - NICHOLAS NICHOLAS

GIBBON, EDWARD 1737-1794   Miscellaneous Works. London: A. Strahan and T. Cadell Jun. and W. Davies, 1796. 1st edition; 4to; 2 volumes; silhouette portrait frontispiece in volume 1, offset to titlepage, as usual; pages xxv, (i),703; viii, 726, (2), errata and ad; contemporary quarter calf, rubbed and marked, smooth backstrip divided by double gilt rules, gilt lettered red morocco labels, calf tipped marbled boards, contemporary owner's signature (Nicholas Nicholas), contents unpressed and untrimmed, very good. Norton 131 & 136; Rothschild 949. Blackwell's B112-116 1996 £350.00

ASSOCIATION - E. H. NICHOLL

NICHOLL, JOHN   Some Account of the Worshipful Company of Ironmongers. London: Privately printed, 1866-1916. 2nd edition; very thick 4to; (2), xii, (2), 621, (4), 8, (2), 4, (2), 6, (2), 3, (2), 11, (2), 7, (2), 52, 10, xlviii (623)-657, (1) pages; numerous illustrations, some as folding plates, some in color; photographic illustrations mounted on heavy paper; additional materials realting to Ironmongers bound in; three quarter morocco, top edge gilt, marbled endpapers, binding rubbed, joints tender, very good; with ms. presentation from E. H. Nicholl, Honorary Librarian to the Company laid in.   Edwin V. Glaser 121-234 1996 $475.00

ASSOCIATION - H. S. NICHOLS

BROWNING, ROBERT 1812-1889   Letters from Robert Browning to Various Correspondents. London: privately printed, 1895-96. 1st edition; 8vo; 2 volumes; original plum cloth; fine set, armorial bookplates of Henry Cabot Lodge. Presentation copy, inscribed by Thomas James Wise for H. S. Nichols. Todd 87d; CBEL III 445.   Ximenes 108-379 1996 $500.00

ASSOCIATION - F. NICHOLSON

ROBINSON, JACOB   Wrestling and Wrestlers: Biographical Sketches of Celebrated Atheletes of the Northern Ring. London: Bemrose & Sons, 1893. 8vo; pages xlvii, 251, 2 woodcut headpieces; little scattered foxing, but excellent copy; inscribed by F. Nicholson for R. W. Thompson. R.F.G. Hollett & Son 78-649 1996 £120.00

ASSOCIATION - NORMAN NICHOLSON

BLACK'S Picturesque Guide to the English Lakes. Edinburgh: 1858. 9th edition; 8vo; pages xxiv., 232, 64, 26 illustrations by Birket Foster; original blindstamped green cloth, gilt, trifle shaken. From the library of Norman Nicholson, Lake District poet and author.   R.F.G. Hollett & Son 78-700 1996 £55.00

GREEN, WILLIAM   The Tourist's New Guide Containing a Description of the Lakes, Mountains and Scenery in Cumberland, Westmorland and Lancashire. Kendal: R. Lough and Co., 1819.. 1st edition; 8vo; 2 volumes; pages 461; ix, 507, lv, with 1 half title, folding map and 33 plates, volume 1 lacks folding map, preface (pages v-xii), index (iii-viii) and errata leaf, volume 2 lacks half title, errata leaf and 2 aquatints (Ilse of Windermere and Derwentwater); old half calf, gilt, neatly recased; little spotting in places, small tear neatly repaired, but good sound set, rarely found complete. From the library of Norman Nicholson.   R.F.G. Hollett & Son 78-949 1996 £850.00

OTLEY, JONATHAN   A Descriptive Guide to the English Lakes, and Adjacent Mountains... Keswick: pub. by the author, 1842. 7th edition; 8vo; pages viii, 220, folding map, hand colored in outline, 13 outlines of mountains and 33 woodcuts plus 33 plates; original blindstamped cloth, gilt, spine and edges faded. From the library of the late Norman Nicholson. Bicknell 102.6.   R.F.G. Hollett & Son 78-1167 1996 £125.00

ROBINSON, THOMAS   An Essay Towards a Natural History of Westmorland and Cumberland. London: printed by J. L. for W. Freeman, 1709. 1st edition; 8vo; pages (xiv), 95, 118, (ii ads), trifle used; contemporary paneled calf, very rubbed and worn, spine defective at tail; very scarce. Inscribed "Ex Dono Thomae Robinson"; from the library of Norman Nicholson, Lake District poet and author.   R.F.G. Hollett & Son 78-547 1996 £195.00

WORDSWORTH, DOROTHY   Journals. London: Macmillan, 1938. 8vo; pages xvii, 544; frontispiece and title vignette; original cloth, gilt, spine rather faded; from the library of the late Norman Nicholson, Lake District poet and author, with his bookplates and signature, and numerous pencilled marginal lines, notes, etc.   R.F.G. Hollett & Son 78-282 1996 £65.00

ASSOCIATION - THOMAS NICHOLSON

BURTON, ROBERT 1577-1640   The Anatomy of Melancholy, What It Is. Oxford: John Lichfield and James Short for Henry Cripps, 1621. 1st edition; small 4to; pages (iv), 783, (8); contemporary Oxford calf, sides with triple rule border and central arabesque in blind, spine in compartments with raised bands, slightly rubbed, joints repaired at head and foot, headcaps and corners repaired, Gg3-6 and Rr8 from another copy, some worming at margins, occasionally affecting sidenotes; contemporary signature of Thomas Nicholson on rear pastedown endpaper, ms. annotations in outer margins and few underlinings, last leaf of text, errata leaf, rear free endpaper copiously annotated. STC 4159; Pforzheimer 119; PMM 120.   Simon Finch 24-25 1996 £12,000.00

ASSOCIATION - GEORGE NICOL

REED, ISAAC   Bibliotheca Reediana. London: J. Barker, printer, 1807. 8vo; frontispiece; full polished calf, gilt, spine gilt, marbled edges, by Pratt, slight rubbing; fine copy on large paper; tipped in is letter May 2 1808 from auctioneer Thomas King, pres. this copy to noted antiquarian bookseller George Nicol; neatly priced and ruled throughout; fine. LAR 124; De Ricci p. 63.   Ximenes 108-12 1996 $1,250.00

ASSOCIATION - THOMAS NICOLL

OTWAY, THOMAS 1652-1685   The Atheist; or, the Second Part of the Souldiers Fortune. London: printed for R. Bentley and J. Tonson, 1684. 1st edition; 4to; later wrappers, the 'F' gathering not used with pagination jumping from page 32 to 41 as usual, leaf l2 torn with loss of few words on either page, most of the words have been written into the margins, browning, some staining, else good copy copy contemporary signature and markings of Thomas Nicoll on final leaf, nice black morocco backed case; Wing O541; W&M 872.   James Cummins 14-147 1996 $200.00

ASSOCIATION - HOWARD NIXON

COCKERELL, SYDNEY M.   The Repairing of Books. London: Sheppard Press, 1958. 1st edition; 8vo; frontispiece, 33 illustrations; original cloth, dust jacket; Howard M. Nixon's copy.   Forest Books 74-48 1996 £55.00

THOMASON, GEORGE   Catalogue of the Pamphlets, Books, Newspapers and Manuscripts Relating to the Civil War, the Commonwealth and Restoration Collected by George Thomason, 1640-1661. London: British Museum, 1908. 2 volumes; original cloth, headcaps slightly chipped, pencil ownership inscription of H. M. Nixon with couple of pencil annotations. De Ricci p. 29.   Maggs Bros. Ltd. 1191-89 1996 £145.00

ASSOCIATION - ANDREW NOBLE

FARADAY, MICHAEL 1791-1867   Experimental Researches in Chemistry and Physics. London: Richard Taylor & William Francis, 1859. 1st collected edition; 8vo; viii, 496 pages, 3 plates, 1 folding and a number of illustrations in text; errataum slip at p. 445; embossed cloth, spine lightly sunned, bit of wear to top and bottom of spine, front hinge starting, very good, partially unopened copy; armorial bookplate of Sir Andrew Noble. Duveen p. 208; Norman 765.   Edwin V. Glaser 121-104 1996 $600.00

ASSOCIATION - WILLIAM NOLAN

BROWN, FREDRIC   Before She Kills. San Diego: Dennis McMillan, 1984. 1st edition; publisher's copy; fine in jacket, inscribed to publisher with drawing by William Nolan.   Janus Books 36-102 1996 $150.00

ASSOCIATION - HUBERT NORMAN

FULTON, JOHN F.   Sir Kenelm Digby. Writer, Bibliophile and Protagonist of William Harvey. New York: Peter & Katharine Olvier, 1937. Limited edition of 300 copies; 8vo; 75 pages; original binding; author's presentation copy with presentation to Hubert Norman, with TLS from Fulton to Norman. Nice association item.   James Tait Goodrich K40-134 1996 $395.00

ASSOCIATION - NORMANBY

BURTON, JOHN   Monasticon Eboracense; and the Ecclesiastical History of Yorkshire. York: printed for the author by N. Nickson, 1758. 1st edition; folio; 3 engraved folding plates, small hole in b1 and c1 with loss of a word; contemporary calf, slightly worn, hinges cracked, label chipped; bookplate of Hon. Constantine John Phipps, Marquess of Normanby.   Anthony W. Laywood 109-19 1996 £245.00

ASSOCIATION - NORMANDY

LEVER, CHARLES JAMES 1806-1872   The Fortunes of Glencore. London: Chapman and Hall, 1857. 1st edition; 8vo; 3 volumes; original green blindstamped cloth, spines lettered in gilt, cloth box, morocco label, lettered in gilt; just a few spots, but fine, bright copy; inscribed by author on titlepage for the Marchioness of Normandy; the Sadleir copy with his and other booklabels. Sadleir 1405; Wolff 4088.   Simon Finch 24-154 1996 £2,000.00

ASSOCIATION - DUDLEY NORTH

BENTHAM, JEREMY 1748-1832   Supply Without Burthen; or Escheat Vice Taxation: Being a Proposal for a Saving in Taxes by an Extension of the law of Escheat... to which is prefixed A Protest Against Law Taxes, Shewing the Peculiar Mischievousness of All Such Impositions... London: printed for J. Debrett, 1795/93. 1st edition; 8vo; disbound; scarce, complete and in excellent condition; signed on titlepage by Dudley North (1748-1829). Kress B2287.   Ximenes 108-17 1996 $1,500.00

COURTENAY, JOHN   Juvenile Poems. London: printed by J. Jones, 1795. 1st edition; 8vo; disbound; fine, very rare; presentation copy inscribed to Dudley North. Jackson p. 200.   Ximenes 109-88 1996 $450.00

HAMILTON, ALEXANDER   A New Account of the East Indies. London: printed for C. Hitch, 1744. Apparently 2nd London edition, though not so designated; 8vo; 2 volumes; 8 folding maps and 11 plates; contemporary calf, spines gilt; very rare; very fine set; early signatures of Dudley North. CBEL II 1437.   Ximenes 108-178 1996 $1,500.00

ASSOCIATION - DUDLEY NORTH

JENYNS, SOAME   Disquisitions on Several Subjects. London: printed for J. Dodsley, 1782. 1st edition; 8vo; disbound; very good; contemporary signature on titlepage of Dudley North. CBELii 554. Ximenes   108-221   1996 $150.00

JOHNSON, SAMUEL 1709-1784   Political Tracts. Containing, The False Alarm. Falkland's Islands. The Patriot. and Taxation No Tyranny. London: printed for W. Strahan and T. Cadell, 1776. 1st collected edition; 750 copies printed; 8vo; contemporary calf, spine gilt; as often the case, binder has not preserved the fly-title to the first tract, otherwise fine and attractive; contemporary signature of Dudley Long, later North. Courtney p 127; Chapman and Hazen p. 152; Sabin 36302; Adams 76-71a. Ximenes   108-229   1996 $400.00

PRICE, UVEDALE   Thoughts on the Defence of Property. Addressed to the County of Hereford. Heredord: sold by J. Allen and all other booksellers, 1797. 8vo; (2), 28 pages; with half titles; recent wrappers, very nice; signature of Dudley North (1748-1829), a prominent Whig and close associate of Fox.   C. R. Johnson   37-68   1996 £250.00

TIERNEY, GEORGE   The Real Situation of the English-India Company Considered, With Respect to Their Rights and Privileges... London: printed for J. Debrett, 1787. 1st edition; 8vo; 96 pages; disbound; signature of Dudley North on half title. Kress B6166; Goldsmith 20700. Anthony W. Laywood   109-150   1996 £135.00

ASSOCIATION - STAFFORD NORTHCOTE

BYNG, JOHN   The Trial of the Honoruable Admiral John Byng, at a Court Martial, as Taken by Mr. Charles Fearne, Judge Advocate of His Majesty's Fleet. London: R. Manby, 1757. 1st edition; tall folio; 130, 19 pages; full contemporary calf, upper joint cracked but firm, red morocco label; signature of B. Bentham dated 1757 to verso of ttile and final leaf; engraved bookplate of Sir Strafford N. Northcote (private secretary to Gladstone).   Ian Wilkinson   95/1-147   1996 £240.00

COLERIDGE, SAMUEL TAYLOR 1772-1834   Poems. London: by N. Biggs for J. Cottle, Bristol and Messrs. Robinsons, London, 1797. 2nd edition; small 8vo; pages xx, 278; contemporary tree calf, spine gilt, black morocco label, rubbed, spine with vertical crack and chipped at foot, front joint cracked but held firm by cords, front free endpaper detached, stain at upper outer corner affecting first few leaves, still good; bookplate of Stafford C. Northcote, and earlier Northcote family inscription. Ashley I p. 199.   Simon Finch   24-44   1996 £400.00

FORTESCUE, HUGH   Public Schools for the Middle Classes. London: Longman, 1864. 1st edition; half title; original brown cloth, very good; inscribed presentation copy to Stafford Northcote, with author's compliments.   Jarndyce   103-474   1996 £75.00

LYELL, CHARLES 1797-1875   Principles of Geology: Being an Enquiry How Far the Former Changes of the Earth's Surface are Referable to causes Now in Operation. London: 1837. 5th edition; 12mo; 4 volumes, 16 maps and plates, some colored, some folding; calf, skilfully rebacked preserving spines; bookplate of Stafford H. Northcote.   John Henly   27-507   1996 £280.00

ASSOCIATION - NORTHUMBERLAND

BOYLE, ELEANOR VERE   A Dream Book. London: Sampson Low, Son and Marston, 1870. Folio; 12 drawings; three quarter crushed green morocco over pebbled green cloth, spine, slightly sunned with five raised bands and title in gilt, rare; stamped on front free endleaf "C. Gross, Binder to the Queen." The Duke of Northumberland's bookplate. Reid p. 253; Baskin p. 55.   Book Block   32-22   1996 $825.00

ASSOCIATION - FETTIPLACE NOTT

RAY, JOHN   Travels through the Low-Countries, Germany, Italy and France... London: printed for J. Walthoe, (and 16 other booksellers), 1738. 2nd edition; 8vo; 2 volumes; half titles and titles printed in red and black, 3 engraved plates in volume 1; original mottled calf, both volumes rebacked, original endpapers preserved; nice 18th century bookplate of Fettiplace Nott inside front cover of each volume. Keynes 22, 96. David Bickersteth   133-58   1996 £320.00

ASSOCIATION - GALE NOYES

LOWES, JOHN LIVINGSTON   The Road ot Xanadu - a Study in the Ways of the Imagination. Boston and New York: Houghton Mifflin, 1927. 1st edition; signed by author; 432 pages, 153 pages of notes; original binding, top edge dusty, covers slightly marked, spine darkened, head and tail of spine and corners slightly bumped and rubbed, very good; presentation copy from Gale Noyes to James D. Hart.   Ulysses 39-381   1996 £85.00

ASSOCIATION - ELIZABETH NREMAN

BRONTE, EMILY 1818-1848   Gondal's Queen. Austin: University of Texas, 1955. 1st edition; 9 x 6 1/8 inches; pages (xxxviii), 207; frontispiece, 4 illustrations; cream buckram, gilt titling on blue panel backstrip, very good; Elizabeth Nreman's copy with her bookplate and signature on endpapers.   Ian Hodgkins   78-222   1996 £68.00

ASSOCIATION - NUGENT-DUNBAR

BROUGHAM & VAUX, HENRY PETER BROUGHAM, 1ST BARON 1778-1868 Installation Address (as Chancellor of the University of Edinburgh) Delivered in the 18th May. Edinburgh: Adam and Charles Black, 1860. 8vo; 70 pages; original cloth, gilt, spine faded; short ALS from author with stamped envelope addressed in his hand and signed, dated May 1861, loosely inserted; armorial bookplate of R. I. Nugent-Dunbar of Machemore.   R.F.G. Hollett & Son   78-340   1996 £75.00

ASSOCIATION - GERTRUDE NUSSEY

BRONTE, CHARLOTTE 1816-1855   Jane Eyre. London: Smith, Elder and Co., 1847. 1st edition; 7 3/4 x 4 3/4 inches; 3 volumes, pages iv, 304, 32 pages publisher's ads dated October 1847; iv, 304, 32 pages ads dated Oct. 1847; iv, 304; iv, 311; maroon cloth with blindstamped decorated borders on covers, gilt titling to backstrips, rebound with original cloth sides laid down, red leather title label on backstrips, rebound with original cloth sides laid down, red leather title label on backstrips, contents have usual foxing, good, sound copy, very scarce; pencil signature of Gertrude Nussey on half title of each volume. Smith 2.   Ian Hodgkins   78-190   1996 £6,750.00

ASSOCIATION - MARY VORSE O'BRIEN

LEWIS, SINCLAIR 1885-1951   Our Mr. Wrenn. The Romantic Adventures of a Gentle Man. New York: Harper & Bros., 1914. 1st edition; 8vo; frontispiece; original grey cloth, gilt, rubbed, some browning and spotting of text, generally light; very nice association copy, inscribed twice by Lewis to Mary Vorse O'Brien and Joseph O'Brien, the first signed only with initials, the other with inscription.   James Cummins 14-123   1996 $1,250.00

ASSOCIATION - JOSEPH O'BRIEN

LEWIS, SINCLAIR 1885-1951   Our Mr. Wrenn. The Romantic Adventures of a Gentle Man. New York: Harper & Bros., 1914. 1st edition; 8vo; frontispiece; original grey cloth, gilt, rubbed, some browning and spotting of text, generally light; very nice association copy, inscribed twice by Lewis to Mary Vorse O'Brien and Joseph O'Brien, the first signed only with initials, the other with inscription.   James Cummins 14-123   1996 $1,250.00

ASSOCIATION - JAMES O'BYRNE

BARON, JOHN   Scudamore Organs, Practical Hints Respecting Organs. London: Bell and Daldy, 1862. 2nd edition; 8vo; frontispiece, xxii, (ii), 112, (8) pages, 7 plates; publisher's cloth, light foxing on a few leaves, spine slighly sunned, else very good. From the library of architect James O'Byrne.   Bookpress 75-125   1996 $265.00

ASSOCIATION - P. F. O'CARROLL

DAWSON, CHARLES   Finola: an Opera, Chiefly Composed of Moore's Irish Melodies. Dublin: M. H. Gill, 1879. 1st and apparently only edition; large 12mo; 64 pages; original green cloth, gilt, very good; inscribed by author for P. F. O'Carroll.   James Fenning   133-83   1996 £75.00

ASSOCIATION - ROSS O'CONNELL

PRIVILEGGI e Statuti Della Venerabile Archiconfraternita dell'Anime Piu' Bisognose del Purgatorio eretta in Roma Sotto il Patrocino di Gesu Maria, e S. Giuseppe dal Venerabile Servo di Dio Papa Innocenzo XI. Rome: 1734. 4to; 46 pages, 1 f., woodcut device on titlepage; slightly later brown morocco, ornate ruled borders with swags, gathers and floral festoons; floral cornerpieces, central panel with arms of a cardinal (very similar to Belmas, Chauvelin, cf. Guigard Amateurs Ecclesiastqie), a snake climbing a tree, surmounted by a Maltese Cross, cardinals hat, rope and tassle borders, etc., spine flat, gilt a la repetition panels, alternated with urns in ruled compartments (one or two wormholes to head of spine, slight rubbing to extremities), old all edges gilt, later endpapers; bookplate of Sir Ross O'Connell, 1897, and his marks. Marlborough 160-51 1996 £650.00

ASSOCIATION - ROSE O'CONNOR

DODGSON, CHARLES LUTWIDGE 1832-1898 The Hunting of the Snark an Agony in Eight Fits. London: Macmillan and Co., 1876. 1st edition; one of 100 copies in red cloth; 8vo; pages xiv (including frontispiece), 83, (iii), imprint, ad leaf, wood engraved frontispiece, 9 full page illustrations after Holiday, 'chart'; original red pictorial cloth, densely gilt, gilt edges, spotting to endpapers and half title, little to title, ad and rear free endpaper browned where what was presumably a news cutting was inserted; inscriptions on half title, externally bright copy; bookplate of Rose O'Connor. Williams and Madan 115. Simon Finch 24-30 1996 £1,500.00

ASSOCIATION - LULU RASMUSSEN O'NEAL

EDWARDS, E. I. Lost Oases Along the Carrizo. Los Angeles: Westernlore Press, 1961. 1st edition; one of 500 copies; xvi, 126 pages; 8 plates after photos; very fine with dust jacket; presentation inscription, signed author for Lulu Rasmussen O'Neal. Edwards p.73; Miller p. 78. Argonaut Book Shop 113-224 1996 $150.00

ASSOCIATION - OATES

OATES, FRANK Matabele Land and the Victoria Falls. London: Kegan, Paul, Trench & Co., 1889. 2nd edition; thick 8vo; original grey-green pictorial cloth, spine dull, slight restoration; very good, presentation copy inscribed by editor C.G. Oates to Miss Lambert. Theal p. 219. Ximenes 109-207 1996 $450.00

ASSOCIATION - ROBERT WASHINGTON OATES

PEPYS, SAMUEL 1633-1703 The Life, Journals and Correspondence of Samuel Pepys, Esq. London: Richard Bentley, 1841. 1st edition; 2 volumes; original binding, top edges dusty, heads and tails of spines and corners bumped and bruised, prelims and contents sporadically spotted, covers marked and rubbed, spines browned, spine of volume 2 slightly worn, lower hinge of volume 1 cracked; good; 3 bookplates in each volume, one belonging to Robert Washington Oates. Ulysses 39-463 1996 £375.00

ASSOCIATION - W. E. OATES

MIVART, ST. G. A Monograph of the Lories, or Brush-Tongued Parrots, Comprising the Family Loriidae. London: 1896. Original issue; royal 8vo; pages liii, 193, 4 maps, hand colored plates; original brown cloth, bevelled edges; good copy; formerly the copy of W. E. Oates, from the collection of Jan Coldewey, with bookplate. Wheldon & Wesley 207-69 1996 £3,950.00

ASSOCIATION - THOMAS ODDYS

GODWIN, FRANCIS Rerum Anglicarum Henrico VIII, Edwardo VI et Maria Regnantibus Annales. London: John Bill, 1628. 2nd edition; 4to; pages (viii), 246, (ii), Roman letter, side notes in italic, printer's woodcut device on title, colophon within typographical border on recto of last leaf, else blank, woodcut initials and headpieces; small light waterstain in extreme upper inner corner of first few leaves; contemporary limp vellum; good, clean copy, contemporary autograph of Thomas Oddys on fly. STC 11946; Lowndes 905; Hazlitt II 697. A. Sokol XXV-44 1996 £395.00

ASSOCIATION - ROBERT OGDEN

TALBOT, EDITH ARMSTRONG Samuel Chapman Armstrong: a Biographical Study. New York: Doubleday Page, 1904. 1st edition; slight rubbing to base of spine, couple of pages roughly opened and hinges neatly repaired, still a bright, otherwise fine copy. Inscribed by Robert C. Ogden on Founder's Day 1904. Between the Covers 43-416 1996 $250.00

ASSOCIATION - THOMAS OGDEN

JOHNSON, SAMUEL 1709-1784 A Dictionary of the English Language. London: printed for J. F. and C. Rivington, L. Davis, T. Payne & Sons, &c., 1785. 7th edition; folio; title slightly creased and spotted at edges; contemporary calf, superbly rebacked retaining spine, rubbed, red label slightly chipped, small lot label on front board; armorial bookplate with signature of Thomas Ogden, 12 July 1787. Jarndyce 103-166 1996 £620.00

ASSOCIATION - OGILVIE

WOOD, ELLEN PRICE 1814-1887 East Lynne. London: Richard Bentley, 1861. 1st edition; small 8vo; 3 volumes; contemporary half calf, some slight foxing, each volume has contemporary inscription of "M. Ogilvie". Charles W. Traylen 117-220 1996 £400.00

ASSOCIATION - BASIL OLDHAM

GARDINER, S. R. History of England, from the Accession of James I to the Outbreak of the Civil War 1603-1642. London: 1899-1901. Crown 8vo; 10 volumes; original cloth, printed labels; from the lirary of J. Basil Oldham, with bookplate. Howes Bookshop 265-393 1996 £200.00

ASSOCIATION - LEO OLSCHKI

SMITH, ADAM 1723-1790 Essays on Philosophical Subjects. London: T. Cadell and W. Davies, 1795. 1st edition; 4to; xcv, (1), 244 pages; modern half calf and marbled boards, green morocco label, minor offsetting as usual, fine; bookplate of Leo Olschki. Rothschild 1902. Vanderblue p. 43. 19th Century Shop 39- 1996 $6,500.00

ASSOCIATION - YOKO ONO

AMIS, KINGSLEY 1922- One Fat Englishman. London: Penguin Books, 1966. Paperback; 12mo; pages 173, (iv) ads, autograph inscription of John Lennon and Yoko Ono Lennon on first page, loosely inserted memo on headed writing paper "Waiting for a plane at Heathrow on 29th December 1969 to take us to Moscow, we met John Lennon & Yoko. They very kindly signed the book..." Simon Finch 24-153 1996 £185.00

ASSOCIATION - CAS OORTHUYS

REZAC, J. 96 Photographs. Artia, 1964. 1st edition; English, French and German; dust jacket; rare. From the collection of Dutch photographer, Cas Oorthuys, signed by him. J. B. Muns 154-298 1996 $650.00

ASSOCIATION - JOEL OPPENHEIMER

SPELLMAN, A. B. The Beautiful Days. New York: Poets Press, 1965. 1st edition; white stapled wrappers, slight crease to bottom corner of front wrapper, else near fine; inscribed by author to fellow poet Joel Oppenheimer. Nice association. Between the Covers 43-191 1996 $135.00

ASSOCIATION - ROBERT ORCHARD

HUNTER, DARD 1883-1966 Papermaking through Eighteen Centuries. New York: Rudge, 1930. 1st edition; octavo; xvii, 358 pages; 214 illustrations; folding frontispiece; linen, morocco spine label; some chipping to label, otherwise fine; with presentation from Dard Hunter Jr. to Robert Orchard. Laid in are TLS from Hunter to Robert Orchard's father, and watermarked portrait specimen of D.H. Bromer Booksellers 90-73 1996 $350.00

ASSOCIATION - ROBERT H. ORCHARD

HUNTER, DARD 1883-1966   Paper-making in the Classroom. Peoria: Manual Arts Pres, 1931. 1st edition; 80 pages; fully illustrated; light soiling to tan cloth, else near fine; inscribed by Hunter for Robert H. Orchard.   Bromer Booksellers 90-69 1996 $250.00

ASSOCIATION - KARL OREND

DURRELL, LAWRENCE GEORGE 1912-1990   Nurse and Mistress of the Crossroads; Arles and the Alyscamps. London: privately printed, Alyscamps Press, 1993. Limited to 50 copies; mint in dust jacket; signature of Karl Orend who provides introduction.   Virgo Books 48-69 1996 £60.00

ASSOCIATION - ORLEANS

PLINIUS CAECILIUS SECUNDUS, C. 61-112   Epistolarum Libri X and Panegyricus. Leiden: Ex Officina Elseviriorum Lugd. Batavorum, 1640. Small 24mo; pages (24), 414, (14), with lacunae, Solitaire printer's mark; lovely full polished French calf, gilt cipher of the Dukes of Orleans(?), spine handsomely gilt, all edges gilt, old marginalia. Dibdin II 331; Willems 506; Brunet IV 722.   Family Album Tillers-507 1996 $325.00

ASSOCIATION - ORLEBAR

HOADLY, BENJAMIN   The Original and Institution of Civil Government, Discuss'd. London: James Knapton, 1710. 2nd edition; 8vo; (2), xiv, 200, 204, 11, (1) pages; contemporary panelled calf, recent paper labels on spine, joints cracked, but very good. with contemporary ownership and John Orlebar's bookplate. Sweet & Maxwell I 608(39); not in Goldsmiths. John Drury 82-109 1996 £175.00

ASSOCIATION - CHARLES OSBORNE

CONNOLLY, CYRIL 1903-1974   The Unquiet Grave. Horizon, 1944. 1st edition; wrappers, little browned around edges and with nick at foot of spine, otherwise very good; Charles Osborne's copy with his signature on half title.   Words Etcetera 94-316 1996 £60.00

ASSOCIATION - EDWARD OSBORNE

MANUTIUS, ALDUS 1547-1597   Phrases Linguae Latinae...Nunç Primum in Ordinem Abecedarium Adductae, & in Anglicum Sermonem Conversae... London: Excusum pro Societate Stationorum, 1636. Small 8vo; pages (6), 256, (22), printer's device on title crudely colored in gold, text in English and Latin; contemporary full leather with slight old repair, edges stained red, top and bottom edges with ms. lettered ownerships of Edward Osborne and Thomas Osborne.   Family Album Tillers-431 1995 $900.00

ASSOCIATION - THOMAS OSBORNE

MANUTIUS, ALDUS 1547-1597   Phrases Linguae Latinae...Nunc Primum in Ordinem Abecedarium Adductae, & in Anglicum Sermonem Conversae... London: Excusum pro Societate Stationorum, 1636. Small 8vo; pages (6), 256, (22), printer's device on title crudely colored in gold, text in English and Latin; contemporary full leather with slight old repair, edges stained red, top and bottom edges with ms. lettered ownerships of Edward Osborne and Thomas Osborne.   Family Album Tillers-431 1995 $900.00

ASSOCIATION - JOHN OWEN

LONGFELLOW, HENRY WADSWORTH 1807-1882   Tales of a Wayside Inn. Boston: Ticknor and Fields, 1863. 1st edition; original blue cloth, very good in blue half morocco case; fine presentation copy inscribed by author for John Owen, who published Longfellow's first books of poetry.   19th Century Shop 39- 1996 $4,500.00

ASSOCIATION - ELIZABETH OXENHAM

LAFAYETTE, MARIE MADELEINE PLOCHE DE LA VERGNE, COMTESSE DE   The Princess of Cleves. London: printed for R. Bentley and M. Mages, 1679. 1st edition in English; 8vo; (359 pages, 6 pages ads); contemporary mottled calf, spine gilt, some overall wear, few small paper flaws, expert minor repair to several pages and back cover, all in all, a very good copy, bound without blanks or flyleaves at beginning and end, but complete with a prelim license leaf and 3 terminal leaves of ads; rare; signature on titlepage of Elizabeth Wroth, dated dec. 24, 1680; 18th century ownership inscription of Elizabeth Oxenham. Rare. Bazin 59; Wing L169.   Paulette Rose 16-200 1996 $4,000.00

ASSOCIATION - H. R. PAKENHAM

POPE, ALEXANDER 1688-1744   The Works. London: Bernard Lintot, 1717. 1st edition; 1st issue; half title, titlepage in red and black, numerous finely engraved head and tail pieces and large initial letters by Gribelin, lacks frontispiece; finely bound in full contemporary red morocco, boards with several gilt panels, floral devices at corners and sides, enclosing different gilt rolls and more floral devices, outer gilt fillet border with small gilt leaves in corners, upper joint cracking but firm, spine elaborately gilt in compartments, all edges gilt, attractive early 18th century English binding; with signature of Joseph Sanford (or Sandford) dated 1717, the scholar & book collector; bookplates of John Sparrow & H.R. Pakenham.   Ian Wilkinson 95/1-136 1996 £450.00

ASSOCIATION - FRANCIS PALMER

NATTES, JOHN CLAUDE   Bath, Illustrated by a Series of Views... London: W. Bulmer for W. Miller and W. Sheppard, Bristol, 1806. Folio; title, iv, 56 pages, large color aquatint vignette on title and another on lasata page, 28 color aquatint plates; dark blue morocco, gilt, covers and spine tooled to a geometrical design, gilt inner borders, gilt edges, by Bayntun of Bath for E. H. Wells & Co., New York; original morocco label pasted onto rear endleaf; handsome copy. Ex-libris Francis Palmer, James Comerford and Mildred Davey.   Marlborough 162-72 1996 £5,750.00

ASSOCIATION - GEOFFREY PALMER

BECKETT, SAMUEL 1906-1989   The North. London: Enitharmon Press, 1972. Number 6 of 125 copies numbered in press and signed by author, there were a further 12 ad personam copies; folio; 3 full page etchings by Avigdor Arikha; loose gatherings in folding wrapper and cloth case; fine in slightly dusty slipcase; presentation copy from author for Noel Lloyd and Geoffrey Palmer. Fine in slightly dusty slipcase.   Ulysses 39-38 1996 £650.00

ASSOCIATION - PANDULPHINI

AUGUSTINUS, AURELIUS, SAINT, BP. OF HIPPO   Explantio Psalmorum. Venice: Bernardinus Benalius 4 August, 1493.. Folio; 372 leaves, gothic letter, wormholes in first two leaves expertly mended, but affecting few letters, clean, tall and crisp copy in sympathetic binding of antique style blindstamped brown morocco over bevelled boards. On fol. 16 there are early records of ownership by members of the Pandulphini family, old library stamp of Museo Cavaleri. Goff A1273; BMC V 374; GKW 2910. H. M. Fletcher 121-3 1996 £2,200.00

ASSOCIATION - PANMURE

BUCKINGHAM, GEORGE VILLIERS, 2ND DUKE OF 1628-1687   Miscellaneous Works... London: printed for Sam. Briscoe and sold by J. Nutt, 1705. 2nd edition of the 1st volume (as often), 1st edition of second volume; 8vo; 2 volumes; frontispiece in each; contemporary calf, slight rubbing; fine set with signature on each titlepage of the Earl of Panmure. Case 232; Macdonald 313; CBEL III 343 and 758.   Ximenes 109-55 1996 $500.00

ASSOCIATION - WOODBINE PARISH

MORIER, JAMES JUSTINIAN 1780?-1849   An Oriental Tale... Brighton: Printed (not published) by W. Leppard, 1839. 1st edition; 8vo; half morocco, worn, upper cover detached, spine defective, without frontispiece described in Sadleir, some browning, mostly light and to endpapers; inscribed by author for Sir Woodbine Parish (1796-1882). Sadleir 1800; Wolff 4931.   James Cummins 14-138 1996 $250.00

ASSOCIATION - CATHERINE JANE PARKENHAM

GISBORNE, THOMAS   An Enquiry Into the Duties of the Female Sex. London: T. Cadell & W. Davies, 1801. 5th edition; contemporary half maron morocco, very good signature on title of Catherine Jane Parkenham.   Jarndyce 103-439 1996 £85.00

ASSOCIATION - SAMUEL PARKER

DIBDIN, THOMAS FROGNALL 1776-1847   The Library Companion; or, the Young Man's Guide, and the Old Man's Comfort in the Choice of a Library. London: by W. Nicol for Harding, Triphook and Lepard and J. Major, 1824. 1st edition; 1st issue; 8 x 5 1/2 inches; 2 volumes, complete with half titles and with ad leaves at front of volume 1 and back of volume 2; original cloth (Smith's variant form with Roman numeral "I" on spine), very artful minor repairs at top of spines, substantial custom made cloth covered slipcase, as always, spines and edges of covers slightly faded, gilt titling rendered a bit indistinct, because of fading, few trivial imperfections in text, but an extraordinarily fine copy otherwise, with hinges in perfect order, with cloth exceptionally clean and with text showing no significant signs of use; armorial bookplates of Samuel Parker and of Edward Hunter in each volume (an earlier owner, no doubt Parker, has pasted a matching sheet of coated paper over the existing pastedown in the first volume, with opening that frames Parker's bookplate this redecoration presumably intended to obscure other marks of ownership. Eckel p. 108; Sabin 19996; Smith II 8-15.   Phillip J. Pirages 33-161 1996 $1,450.00

ASSOCIATION - EDWARD PARONE

WILLIAMS, WILLIAM CARLOS 1883-1963   Make Light of It. New York: Random House, 1950. Advance review copy; cloth very slightly frayed at spine extremities, very good in good dust jacket, chipped along front spine fold and with significant chipping at spine extremities, though not affecting text, author photo laid in; inscribed by author to Edward Parone.   Ken Lopez 74-478 1996 $350.00

ASSOCIATION - IAN PARSONS

DAY-LEWIS, CECIL 1904-   Collected Poems - 1929-1933 - Transitional Poem. London: Hogarth Press, 1935. 1st edition; original binding, top edge dusty, free endpapers browned, spine and top edge of lower cover slightly darkened, very good in nicked, rubbed and dusty, slightly torn and soiled dust jacket browned at spine and edges and wormed along almost the entire length of the upper flap fold and slightly at lower flap fold; leonard Woolf's copy; from the library of Ian Parsons who inherited Leonard Woolf's library.   Ulysses 39-300 1996 £175.00

EDEL, LEON   Henry James - the Master - 1901-1916. London: Hart-Davis Ltd., 1972. 1st edition; original binding, top edge faded, head and tail of spine slightly bumped, very good in slightly creased, soiled, rubbed and dusty dust jacket faded at spine; presentation copy from author, inscribed for Trekkie and Ian Parsons.   Ulysses 39-315 1996 £75.00

FRY, ROGER ELIOT 1866-1934   A Sampler of Castile. London: Hogarth Press, 1923. One of 550 numbered copies; quarto; 16 black and white plates by author; cloth backed decorated paper boards, covers slightly bowed, free endpapers partially browned, prelim edges and endpapers spotted, very good in torn, creased and chipped, rubbed and dusty, internally repaired dust jacket, which repeats cover design, faded at spine and edges; From the library of Ian Parsons, who worked at Hogarth Press and inherited Leonard Woolf's library.   Ulysses 39-214 1996 £395.00

GARNETT, DAVID   Aspects of Love. London: Chatto & Windus Ltd., 1955. 1st edition; original binding, edges spotted, spine faded and with offsetting from dust jacket, very good in nicked, spotted and slightly creased, rubbed and dusty dust jacket, by Angelica Garnett, browned at spine and edges; from the library of Ian Parsons.   Ulysses 39-218 1996 £55.00

GREEN, HENRY   Concluding. London: Hogarth Press, 1948. 1st edition; original binding, top edge dusty, prelims, edges and endpapers slightly spotted, head of spine slightly bumped, very good in nicked, torn, marked and heavily spotted, slightly creased, rubbed and dusty dust jacket, browned at spine and edges; from the library of Ian Parsons.   Ulysses 39-251 1996 £85.00

MURDOCH, IRIS   The Bell. London: Chatto & Windus Ltd., 1958. 1st edition; original binding, top edge dusty, free endpapers partially browned, edges spotted, very good in nicked, spotted, rubbed and dusty, slightly marked dust jacket, browned at spine and edges; from the library of Ian Parsons, publisher of this book.   Ulysses 39-429 1996 £85.00

ASSOCIATION - IAN PARSONS

MURDOCH, IRIS   The Flight from the Enchanter. London: Chatto & Windus, 1956. 1st edition; original binding, top edge dusty, head and tail of spine and corners slightly bumped, bottom edge partially browned, fore-edge spotted, very good in nicked, spotted and slightly rubbed, soiled, marked and dusty dust jacket by Edward Bawden, browned at spine and edges; with pencilled ownership signature of publisher of this book, Ian Parsons.   Ulysses 39-428 1996 £355.00

MURDOCH, IRIS   The Flight from the Enchanter. London: Chatto & Windus Ltd., 1956. 1st edition; original binding, top edge dusty, head and tail of spine and corners slightly bumped, bottom edge partially browned, fore-edge spotted, very good in nicked, spotted and slightly rubbed, soiled, marked and dusty dust jacket, by Edward Bawden, browned at spine and edges, with pencilled ownership signature of publisher of this book, Ian Parsons.   Ulysses 39-428 1996 £355.00

MURDOCH, IRIS   Under the Net. London: Chatto & Windus, 1954. 1st edition; original binding, top edge slightly dusty, head of spine slightly bumped, edges spotted, rear free endpaper slightly creased, very good in nicked, spotted and dusty, slightly creased dust jacket faded at spine and slightly darkened at edges; fomr the library of Ian Parsons, publisher of this book.   Ulysses 39-427 1996 £375.00

TAYLOR, ELIZABETH   A Dedicated Man - and Other Stories. London: Chatto & Windus, 1965. 1st edition; original binding, top edge slightly dusty, prelims and endpapers slightly spotted, very good in nicked, creased and spotted, slightly rubbed and marked dust jacket, by Ionicus, browned at spine and edges; from the library of Ian Parsons, publisher of this book.   Ulysses 39-579 1996 £95.00

TAYLOR, ELIZABETH   The Devastating Boys and Other Stories. London: Chatto & Windus, 1972. 1st edition; original binding, top edge slightly dusty, head and tail of spine slightly faded, top corner of one page creased, very good in nicked and slightly creased dust jacket faded at spine and browned at edges; pencilled ownership signature of Ian Parsons, publisher of this book.   Ulysses 39-583 1996 £75.00

TAYLOR, ELIZABETH   Mossy Trotter. London: Chatto & Windus, 1967. 1st edition; numerous black and whtie drawings; original binding, tail of spine and corners slightly bumped, small stain on upper cover, very good in slightly nicked and dusty dust jacket, slightly darkened at spine and edges and slightly soiled on upper panel; from the library of Ian Parsons.   Ulysses 39-580 1996 £75.00

TAYLOR, ELIZABETH   The Wedding Group. London: Chatto & Windus Ltd., 1968. 1st edition; original binding, tail of spine slightly bumped, cover edges slightly bumped, very good in nicked, spotted and slightly soiled and dusty dust jacket, slightly browned at edges and with ring stain on lower panel; from the library of Ian Parsons.   Ulysses 39-581 1996 £55.00

VALERY, PAUL   The Graveyard by the Sea. London: Martin Secker & Warburg, 1946. One of 500 numbered copies, signed by translator, C. Day Lewis; printed by Hans Mardersteig at Officina Bodoni, Verona, on paper made by Fratelli Magnani of Pescia; parallel French and English texts; marbled paper covers, spine and cover edges slightly faded, very good, lacks brown card folder; from the library of Ian Parsons of Hogarth Press.   Ulysses 39-372 1996 £225.00

ASSOCIATION - PARTINGTON

HODGKINSON, CLEMENT   Australia, from Port MacQuarie to Moreton Bay.... London: T. and W. Boone, 1845. 8vo; (xi), 244 pages, vi), (8) pages, (last pages colophon), frontispiece and 6 sepia aquatint plates, 1 engraved maps, (iv), and 8 pages ads; oriignal tight grained green coth, extra blind borders and decorations on boards, gilt decoration and titles on spine; with James Edge Partington bookplate. Bright, clean copy. Ferguson 4067; Wangraup 158a.   Antipodean 28-620 1996 $3,000.00

MASLEN, T. J.   The Friend of Australia; or, a Plan for Exploring the Interior and for Carrying on a Survey of the Whole Continent of Australia. London: Smith Elder & Co., 1836. 2nd edition; (xxiv), 428 pages, (8) pages ads; folding map, 5 folding aquatint plates; original blue cloth, spine rebacked with 1920's plain black cloth, stamped on old endpaper South Aus. Rooms A; Gole & Co.; James Partington bookplate; very nice. The Absolon copy. Ferguson 2145; Wantrup 117b.   Antipodean 28-625 1996 $1,450.00

MORGAN, JOHN   The Life and Adventures of William Buckley; Thirty-Two Years a Wanderer Amongst the Aborigines of the Then Unexplored Country Round Port Phillip, Now the Province of Victoria. Tasmania: Archibald MacDougall, 1852. (xiv), (ii), 208 pages; frontispiece little foxed, couple of marks; original cloth boards, rebacked, original spine laid down, chipped paper title piece; fully signed presentation copy dated June 11, 1852. Edge-Partington bookplate. Ferguson 12813.   Antipodean 28-102 1996 $750.00

ASSOCIATION - PARTINGTON

OXLEY, JOHN   Journals of Two Expeditions Into the Interior of New South Wales, Under-Taken by Order of the British Government in the Years 1817-1818. London: John Murray, 1820. Quarto; (xv), 408 pages, 6 aquatint engravings, 3 folding maps, 2 folding tables (the two large folding maps have long ago been expertly mounted on folding linen; finely rebound (signed Morrell, London) in half morocco and linen boards, gilt decorated spine, all edges gilt, text is quite clean and bright; very pretty copy; old pen signature in titlepage partially removed with some staining, otherwise very good+; from the Edge-Partington collection, the Absolon copy. Ferguson 796; Wantrup 107.   Antipodean 28-160   1996 $5,500.00

SMITH, JAMES, MRS.   The Booandik Tribe of South Austrlian Aborigines. Adelaide: E. spiller, 1880. Small 8vo; (xi), 139 pages, 6 illustrations; leather spine and printed wrapper boards, leather spine rubbed, corners bumped, browning affects lower fore edge of text for first 30 od pages, otherwise good+; presentation copy from Rev. F. H. Robinson to his brother. James Edge Partington bookplate; Ferguson 15823; Greenway 8565.   Antipodean 28-364 1996 $225.00

SPENCER, BALDWIN   Notes on Certain of the Initiation Ceremonies of the Arunta Tribe, Central Australia. Melbourne: 1898. Offprint from the Proceedings of the Royal society of Victoria; original printed wrappers bound in attractive linen and boards binding, very good; presentation copy from author to J. Edge Partington. Greenway 8678; Ferguson 16073.   Antipodean 28-382 1996 $175.00

STURT, CHARLES   Two Expeditions into the Interior of Southern Australia during the Years 1828, 1829, 1830 and 1831. London: Smith, Elder & Co., 1833. 1st edition; 2 volumes, viii, (iv), (ix)-xxx, 220 pages (last blank), 5 engraved plates, folding map (couple of small tears repaired); viii, 272 pages (last blank), (15 pages ads), 9 plates; original purple pebble grain cloth, gilt decorated spines, spine sunned and dusty as usual, some discoloration of boards and top hinge starting, otherwise a pleasant copy; the Absolon copy, and with Edge Partington bookplate. Antipodean 28-122 1996 $1,750.00

WILLIS, WILLIAM JOHN   Successful Exploration through the Interior of Australia, from Melbourne to the Gulf of Carpentaria, from the Journals and Letters of... London: Richard Bentley, 1863. (xii), 396 pages, (32) pages, frontispiece and 1 plate, folding map; original embossed green cloth, covers and gilt on spine rubbed, corners bumped, internally bright, clean copy, overall in good condition; Edge Partington bookplate; the Absolon copy. Fergsuon 18622; Wantrup 172.   Antipodean 28-629 1996 $750.00

ASSOCIATION - BLANCHE PATCH

COWARD, NOEL 1899-1973   The Vortex, a Play in Three Acts. London: Ernest Benn Ltd., 1925. 1st edition; 8vo; original blue cloth with printed labels on spine and upper cover; appears to have been issued without a protective dust jacket; lovely, near fine copy with light and even browning to pages and just little darkening to spine and spine label; presentation copy, inscribed to George Bernard Shaw's secretary, Blanche Patch, from Coward.   Lakin & Marley 3-8 1996 $850.00

ASSOCIATION - ALAN PARK PATON

BROWNING, ELIZABETH BARRETT 1806-1861   An Essay on Mind, With Other Poems. London: James Duncan, 1826. 1st edition; contemporary tree calf, gilt, spine gilt, little rubbed, slight crack in upper joint; very good; the copy of Alan Park Paton, signed by him. Barnes A2; Hayward 238.   Ximenes 108-358 1996 $2,500.00

ASSOCIATION - JOHN PATON

PATON, JAMES   Missioanry to the New Hebrides. London: Hodder & Stoughton, 1890. 6th edition; 2 volumes, 376 pages, frontispiece; 382 pages, frontispiece; blue gilt buckram, very bright set. ALS loosely inserted from John G. Paton to Miss Clementine Butler.   Antipodean 28-176 1996 $195.00

ASSOCIATION - WILLIAM AGNEW PATON

SANNAZARO, JACOPO 1458-1530   Arcadia Del Sannazaro. (wtih) Sonetti, E Canzoni del Sannazaro. Venice: Paulum Manutium et Andrea Socero (Torresano), July 1534. 8vo; ff. 92; 52 leaves; Aldine devices on first and last leaves; early 18th century blindstamped vellum with complex central florette shield on each cover, framed in line fillets and corner stamps; ms. ownership signature of "Wm. Agnew Paton 1899", old ownership stamp on title obscured, ancient signature clipped from tail of A2. Renouard 112.5 and 6; Adams S320 & S338; UCLA IIIa/236/237.   Family Album Tillers-560 1996 $1,200.00

ASSOCIATION - LINDSAY PATTERSON

HUGHES, LANGSTON   The Book of Negro Humor. New York: Dodd, Mead, 1966. 1st edition; somewhat worn, fair only, corners bumped and several tears to cloth spine lacking dust jacket; inscribed by author to author Lindsay Patterson, pleasing association.   Between the Covers 43-21 1996 $450.00

ASSOCIATION - CHARLES KEGAN PAUL

SHELLEY, PERCY BYSSHE 1792-1822   Shelley Memorials: from Authentic Sources. London: Smith, Elder and Co., 1859. 2nd edition; 8vo; pages x, (2), 290, (i) errata, frontispiece; contemporary half vellum, spine gilt, red morocco labels, red sides, endpapers and edges; inscribed by Lady Shelley for Charles Kegan Paul   Simon Finch 24-209 1996 £150.00

ASSOCIATION - JAMES PAYN

A GUIDE to the English Lake District Intended Principally for the Use of Pedestrians. London: Simkin, Marshall and Co. and Windermere: J. Garnett, c. 1865. 2nd edition; 8vo; pages viii, 123, viii (Garnett's ads), with colored frontispiece and 4 folding maps, printed in blue, 2 woodcut plates and several tables; original blindstamped cloth, gilt; label of "The People's Library" and signature of James Payn.   R.F.G. Hollett & Son 78-966 1996 £65.00

ASSOCIATION - CAROLINE NESTMANN PECK

LUCKENBEILL, DANIEL DAVID   Ancient Records of Assyria and Baylonia. Chicago: University of Chicago Press, 1926-27. 8vo; 2 volumes, (complete), xxviii, 801 pages; original cloth; with annotations and signataures of Caroline Nestmann (Peck).   Archaeologia Luxor-2396 1996 $275.00

LUCKENBILL, DANIEL DAVID   Inscriptions from Adab. Chicago: University of Chicago Press, 1930. 8vo; x, 8 pages, 87 plates; half cloth; with annotations and signature of Caroline Nestmann (Peck).   Archaeologia Luxor-2398 1996 $125.00

ASSOCIATION - FREDERICK PECK

BYRON, GEORGE GORDON NOEL, 6TH BARON 1788-1824   The Island, or Christian and His Comrades. London: by C. H. Rennell for John Hunt, 1823. 1st edition; 8vo; 94 pages, with half title, without final ad leaf F8; full green straight grain morocco, sides with single gilt fillet, spine with raised bands, gilt motifs, lettered in gilt in two compartments, inner dentelles with double gilt fillet, comb marbled endpapers, top edge gilt, others uncut, by Bedford; fine copy; bookplate of Frederick S. Peck, bookseller's catalog description and note of acquisition by "J.H.S." dated 14 may 1946 tipped on binder's blank; fine, scarce.   Simon Finch 24-28   1996 £600.00

ASSOCIATION - MORSE PECKHAM

PATER, WALTER 1839-1894   Imaginary Portraits. London: Macmillan, 1887. 1st edition; 8vo; original binding, bookplates of Sidney Ball and Morse Peckham, rear endpaper foxed, near fine.   Charles Agvent 4-932 1996 $125.00

ASSOCIATION - C. PEERS

SMYTH, WILLIAM   English Lyricks. Liverpool: printed by J. M'Creery and sold by Cadell and Davies, 1797. 8vo; contemporary calf, gilt ruled borders, spine decorated in gilt, rubbed; very attractive; with inscription "M. M. White. The gift of Mr. C. Peers."   James Cummins 14-188 1996 $225.00

ASSOCIATION - BOIES PENROSE

NATTES, JOHN CLAUDE   Bath Illustrated by a Series of Views from the Drawings of John Claude Nattes... London: published by William Miller, Albemarle St. and Wm. Sheppard, Bristol, 1806. 1st edition; later issue; folio; half title, tissue guarded hand colored aquatint frontispiece, title with hand colored vignette, (i-iii), 56 leaves of text, 27 hand colored aquatint plates and 1 hand colored vignette, large paper copy; half red straight grained morocco and marbled boards, edges scuffed, slight damage to top right hand corner of upper marbled board, red morocco label to upper board, raised bands to spine, gilt tooling to compartments, gilt title to second compartment, all edges gilt, new marbled endpapers and new prelims; ink inscription removed from verso front f.e.p. leaving slight mark, very minor oxidisaton to first plates, rest in excellent condition, very minor occasional offset to text only; bound by Bayntun; bookplates of Boies Penrose, another armorial bookplate.
Beeeleigh Abbey   BA56-17   1996   £7,000.00

PURCHAS, SAMUEL 1575?-1695   Purchas His Pilgrimes. (with) Purchase His Pilgrimage. London: ptd. by William Stansby for Henry Fetherstone, 1625/26. 1st edition of the 1st four volumes and 4th edition of volume 5; folio; 5 volumes; engraved title in volume 1, 7 folding maps, 81 smaller maps, numerous engraved and woodcut illustrations; text maps in volume 1 have been delicately hand colored at an early date; engraved title is in its very rare first state, dated 1624 (most are 1625), map of Virginia in Volume IV is in Tooley's 10th state, last volume is the usual second issue, with title beginning with 'Purchas'; late 18th century russia, panelled in gilt, beautifully rebacked, spines gilt in compartments, all edges gilt; engraved title skilfully remarginal, not touching the engraved surface, volume 1 lacks a blank R4 and has one blank lower margin restored; from the library of Boies Penrose; earlier bookplates of Henry Perkins and Lucy Wharton Drexel. STC 20508.5 & 20509; Sabin 66682-6. Church 401a.   Ximenes 109-242   1996 $52,500.00

RALEIGH, WALTER 1552-1618   The Discoverie of the Large, Rich and Bewtiful Empyre of Guiana, with a Relation of the Great and Golden Citie of Manoa... London: by Robert Robinson, 1595. 1st edition; 3rd issue; 4to; (16), 112 pages; full polished calf, spine richly gilt in compartments by Riviere, upper edge of title very skilfully extended, with 3 letters and parts of 10 other letters in almost imperceptible pen facsimile, two or three repairs to blank margins, else fine; with Boies Penrose bookplates. Church 254; JCB III 1.349; Sabin 67554; STC 20636.   Joseph J. Felcone 64-33   1996 $5,500.00

ASSOCIATION - EDWARD PENTON

DEGREVANT. (ROMANCE)   Sire Degrevaunt. Kelmscott Press, 1896. One of 350 copies on paper, there were also 8 on vellum; 8 1/4 x 6 inches; 2 p.l., 81, (1) pages; frontispiece and first page of text with elaborate borders by Sir Edward Burne-Jones, decorative initials, device on colophon; printed in red and black; original holland backed blue grey paper boards, edges untrimmed; trivial foxing and soiling only to spine, but very fine. Armorial bookplate of Edward Penton.   Phillip J. Pirages 33-322   1996 $1,250.00

ASSOCIATION - STEFANO PERGAMASCI

LUCIANUS SAMOSATENSIS   I Dialoi Piacevoli, le Vere Narrationi, le Facete Epitole... Venice: Giovanni de Farri & Fratelli, 1541. Small 8vo; ff. 224, (some errors in foliation), italic letter, woodcut printer's device on titlepage, 30 woodcuts in text; contemporary limp vellum, bit soiled, ties removed; few light early marginal marks and 1 correction in text; good; autographs of Carlo Albertinelli 1576 & Stefano Pergamasci 1605. BM STC It. p. 396; Adams L1632; Brunet III 1213.   A. Sokol XXV-59   1996   £1,850.00

ASSOCIATION - HENRY PERKINS

PURCHAS, SAMUEL 1575?-1695   Purchas His Pilgrimes. (with) Purchase His Pilgrimage. London: ptd. by William Stansby for Henry Fetherstone, 1625/26. 1st edition of the 1st four volumes and 4th edition of volume 5; folio; 5 volumes; engraved title in volume 1, 7 folding maps, 81 smaller maps, numerous engraved and woodcut illustrations; text maps in volume 1 have been delicately hand colored at an early date; engraved title is in its very rare first state, dated 1624 (most are 1625), map of Virginia in Volume IV is in Tooley's 10th state, last volume is the usual second issue, with title beginning with 'Purchas'; late 18th century russia, panelled in gilt, beautifully rebacked, spines gilt in compartments, all edges gilt; engraved title skilfully remarginal, not touching the engraved surface, volume 1 lacks a blank R4 and has one blank lower margin restored; from the library of Boies Penrose; earlier bookplates of Henry Perkins and Lucy Wharton Drexel. STC 20508.5 & 20509; Sabin 66682-6. Church 401a.   Ximenes 109-242   1996 $52,500.00

ASSOCIATION - AMOS PERRY

HIBBERD, SHIRLEY   New and Rare Beautiful Leaved Plants. London: 1870. Royal 8vo; pages viii, 144, 54 colored plates; original cloth, refixed, trifle worn; bookplate of Amos Perry, with inscription from author for Perry.   Wheldon & Wesley 207-1701 196 £120.00

ASSOCIATION - THOMAS ALOYSIUS PERRY

BROWNING, ELIZABETH BARRETT 1806-1861   Aurora Leigh. London: Chapman and Hall, 1857. 3rd edition; 8vo; original green cloth, very slight rubbing, slight foxing at beginning and end, but fine, scarce; contemporary bookplate of Thomas Aloysius Perry.   Ximenes 108-353 1996 $100.00

ASSOCIATION - WILLIAM PERRY

LEAVITT, JONATHAN   A Summary of the Laws of Massachusetts, Relative to the Settlement, Support, Employment and Removal of Paupers. Greenfield: Printed by John Denio, 1810. 1st edition; 8vo; original sheep backed marbled newsprint boards, text showing through the marbling, printed paper label on upper cover, edges chipped with tears, rubbed, text browned; signatures of William Perry on endpaper and Dr. J. W. Proctor of Malden, Mass. on title, with note at foot of title reading "State Board of Charity, April 1, 1901". Marvin p. 456; S&S 20533; Sabin 39559.   James Cummins 14-152   1996 $200.00

ASSOCIATION - JOHN PETERS

MOXON, JOSEPH   Mechanick Exercises on the Whole Art of Pritning (1683-84). Oxford: 1958. 1st edition; 8vo; pages lxiv, 480; 58 pages, plates, 17 figures in text; original cloth; fine. Booklabel of CUP designer and founder of the Vine Press, John Peters.   Claude Cox 107-323 1996 £85.00

ASSOCIATION - F. PETERSON

LAENNEC, R.   A Treatise On the Diseases of the Chest and On Mediate Ausculation... New York: S. & W. Wood; Philadelphia: Thomas, Cowperwaite & Co., 1838. 4th and final American edition, from the 3rd French edition; 8vo; 2 lithographed plates, rather foxed; recent half calf; signature of Fredk. Peterson on title.   Maggs Bros. Ltd. 1190-444 1996 £220.00

ASSOCIATION - PETWORTH HOUSE

BLOUNT, THOMAS 1618-1679   Boscobel; or, the Compleat History of the most Miraculous Preservation of King Charles II. After the Battle of Worcester (and) Claustrum Regale Reseratum; or, the King's Concealment at Trent. London: printed for J. Wilford, 1725. 4th edition; 12mo; fine engraved title, portrait, printed title, 2 folding plates, neatly linen backed; sheep, rebacked; with Petworth House bookplate (?ca. 1910) of Viloet (Wyndham, nee Rawson, Lady) Leconfield.   Peter Murray Hill 185-35   1996   £65.00

ASSOCIATION - J. WATTS DE PEYSTER

COLES, ELISHA   An English Dictionary. London: printed by F. Collins for R. Bonwick et al, 1713. 4th edition; 8vo; original full sheep, joints repaired with tissue and inner margin of titlepage and first text leaf similarly repaired; else very good. Bookplate of General J. Watts de Peyster.   Chapel Hill 94-170   1996 $175.00

ASSOCIATION - CARL PFORZHEIMER

HALLOWELL, ANNA DAVIS   James and Lucretia Mott. Life and Letters Boston: Houghton Mifflin Co., c. 1884. 1st edition; 8vo; frontispiece with tissue guarad, 5 illustrations; brown cloth, uncut and unopened, fine; inscribed by James Mott Hallowell for Carl Pforzheimer.   James Cummins 14-139 1996 $100.00

ASSOCIATION - JAMES D. PHELAN

DWINELLE, JOHN W.   The Colonial History of the City of San Francisco... San Francisco: Towne and Bacon, 1866. 3rd edition; xlv, (1), 34, (2), 106, 391 pages, with pages 363*-(370*) inserted after p. (366); 3 lithographed plates, one single map; with 2 errata slips preceding pages xlv and 365; original three quarter black morocco, gilt lettered spine, marbled boards, very slight rubbing to extremities, corners lightly worn, inner front hinge cracked (cords strong), overall fine; with bookplate of James Phelan (mayor of San Francisco & U.S. Senator); Cowan p. 75-76; Graff 1189; Howes D614; Rocq 7961; Zamorano 80 32.   Argonaut Book Shop   113-220 1 996 $1,500.00

ASSOCIATION - JOHN PHELPS

TOPHAM, EDWARD   The Poetry of "The World". London: printed by John Bell, 1788. 1st separate edition; small 8vo; 2 volumes bound in 1; contemporary speckled calf, gilt, surface worming, some rubbing and chipping, some soiling and browning, mostly marginal and light, good copy; bookplate of Rev. John Phelps.   James Cummins   14-212 1996 $150.00

ASSOCIATION - KIM PHILBY

PAGE, LEITCH   Philby: The Spy Who Betrayed and Generation. London: Andrew Deutsch, 1968. Signed by author's on half title, though Leitch's is printed; fine in torn dust jacket; Kim Philby's own copy with his annotations, altogether there are marks by Philby on 37 pages.   R. A. Gekoski   19-111 1996 £2,000.00

ASSOCIATION - GEORGE PHILIPS

FORTEGUERRI, NICOLO   Ricciardetto di Niccolo Carteromaco. Paris (in fact Venice): A spese di Francesco Pitteri, 1738. 1st edition; 4to; portrait, xxxvi, 420 apges, 2 leaves, 412 pages, 1 leaf (errata), historiated initials and finely engraved title vignette and head and tailpieces by F. Zucchi, Cattini, M. Pitteri and P. Monaco... contemporary vellum boards, engraved armorial bookplate of George Philips. Gamba 2241; Brunet I 1604.   H. M. Fletcher   121-99 1996 £550.00

ASSOCIATION - PHILLIPPS

FALCONER, W.   An Account of the Epidemical Catarrahl Fever Commonly called the Influenza, As It Appeared at Bath in the Winter and Spring of the Year 1803. Bath: Cruttwell, 1803. 1st edition; 8vo; pages 46; old brown paper wrappers, inscribed by author, but name of recipient cut from upper blank margin of title, additional ms. note about the spread to Paris on p. 45 apparently in author's hand, later in Phillipps collection, with pressmark.   Maggs Bros. Ltd.   1190-407 1996 £120.00

ASSOCIATION - THOMAS PHILLIPPS

BEDLOE, WILLIAM   The Excommunicated Prince; or the False Relic. London: printed for Tho. Parkhurst, D. Newman, Tho. Cockerill and Tho... 1679. 1st edition; folio; prelim license leaf; half calf; very good; the Sir Thomas Phillipps copy, with "M.H.C." in pencil on front flyleaf. Wing B1676.   Ximenes   109-29 1996 $350.00

O'REILLY, BERNARD   Greenland and the Adjacent Seas, and the North-West Passage to the Pacific Ocean, Illustrated in a Voyage to Davis's Strait, During the Summer of 1817. London: printed for Baldwin, Cradock and Joy, 1818. 1st edition; 4to; contemporary red straight grained moroccco, covers elaborately decorated in blind and gilt, all edges gilt, slight wear, but sound; attractive copy; from the library of Sir Thomas Phillipps, with his shelfmark; armorial bookplate of Nicholas Garry. Sabin 57576; Hill p. 219 (American reprint); Abbey, Travel 633. Ximenes   109-208 1996 $1,500.00

THE SUBSTANCE of a Charge Delivered to the Grand Jury of Wiltshire,, at the Summer Assizes 1827, by the Lord Chief Justice Best. London: printed by Luke Hansard and Sons, for T. Cadell, 1827. 35 pages; later wrappers showing wear, but sound; from the library of Sir Thomas Phillips, in Middle Hill wrappers and with its press mark.   Meyer Boswell SL27-227 1996 $175.00

ASSOCIATION - B. M. PICKERING

BAKER, RICHARD   A Chronicle of the Kings of England from the Time of the Romans Government unto the Raigne of Our Soveraigne Lord King Charles. London: for Daniel Frere, 1643. 1st edition; folio; (10), 181, (1), 163, (1), 108, 163, (36) pages, errata leaf present; portrait, engraved title; late 19th century full sprinkled calf, gilt, small repair at upper blank edge of portrait, fore-edge of engraved title bit darkened and neatly strengthened on verso, two margins neatly extended, few minor marginal repairs, clean and desirable copy, in very attractive binding; with 2 interesting B. M. Pickering letters laid in relating to Baker's book. Wing B501.   Joseph J. Felcone   64-3 1996 $800.00

ASSOCIATION - FRANKLIN PIERCE

THE NEW Hampshire Book: Being Specimens of the Literature of the Granite State. Nashua: David Marsahll, 1842. 1st edition; 391 pages; original gift binding, full brown morocco, some rubbing and foxing; attractive American binding; fine association copy, inscribed by Franklin Pierce for Mrs. B. B. French.   19th Century Shop   39- 1996 $3,200.00

ASSOCIATION - LUIGI FORTUNATO PIERI

PETRARCA, FRANCESCO 1304-1374   Il Petrarcha. Venice: Aldus, August, 1514. 2nd Aldine edition; 8vo; 208 leaves; 19th century quarter calf over marbled boards, gilt spine; owner's name trimmed from two leaves, some old staining; bookplate of Luigi Fortunato Pieri, with armorial stamps. Renouard 68.6. Adams P790; UCLA I 107; Brunet IV 545.   Family Album   Tillers-479 1996 $850.00

ASSOCIATION - PIEROTT

MENETRIES, E.   Monographie de la Famille des Myiotherinae...Extrait des Memoires de l'Academie Imperiale des Sciences. St. Petersburg: 1836. Author's offprint from the third volume of the sixth series of 'Memoires'. folio (the text 4to. stilted); pages (ii), 102, 16 lithographed plates of which 15 are fine hand colored plates of the birds by F. Davignon, the final plate a diagram; contemporary half vellum, bit worn; inscribed by author to his friend Florent Pierott (?).   Maggs Bros. Ltd. 1190-582 1996 £750.00

ASSOCIATION - PIGOTTS

HAWKINS, JOHN   The Life of Samuel Johnson, LL.D. London: for J. Buckland (& 39 others in London), 1787. 1st separate edition; large 8vo; pagaes (ii), 602, (xv) index, final leaf of index pasted onto inside back board, uncut, probably original boards, re-covered sometime during the early 19th century with plain paper, spine with painted gold lines and stars on black paper background cut out and pasted on in imitation of comartments, the whole a pleasing amateur construct, possibly the work of Miss Pigotts of Underdale whose signature is at the head of the titlepage; attractive and unusual copy.   Simon Finch 24-109 1996 £340.00

ASSOCIATION - JOHN PILLARD

DARIOT, CLAUDE   Dariotus Redivivus; or a Briefe Introduction to the Judgement of the Stars. London: for Andrew Kemb, 1653. 4to; (12), 303 pages, including woodcut frontispiece, 1 plate, many woodcut charts and diagrams including 3 with volvelles, title in red and black; very skillful period style modern full calf, imprint cut into, neat repair on A2, few small spots, otherwise very attractive; calligraphic signature of John Pillard, 1789. Wellcome II p. 432; Wing D257.   Joseph J. Felcone   64-1 1996 $1,000.00

ASSOCIATION - PINKERTON

WALPOLE, HORACE 1719-1797   Essay on Modern Gardening. Strawberry Hill: T. Kirgate, 1785. 1st edition; one of 400 copies, 200 for presentation by Walpole and 200 for the Duc, none being for sale; 4to; pages 94; engraved vignette (offset onto endpaper), text nice and clean, with wide margins; modern full calf; very nice; no presentation on this copy, but notes on endpapers indicate that it came from both the "Burdett Coutts" and "Pinkerton" sales. Hazen, Strawberry Hill Press 31; Henrey 1475; Hunt 675.   Second Life Books   103-205 1996 $1,350.00

ASSOCIATION - HESTER LYNCH PIOZZI

JOHNSON, SAMUEL 1709-1784   Letters to and From the Late Samuel Johnson, LL.D. London: for A. Strahan, and T. Cadell, 1788. 1st edition; 8vo; 2 volumes; pages (ii), xv, (i) blank, (397); xi, (i) blank, without errata slip found in some copies; contemporary tan calf, skilfully rebacked to style and corners repaired, edges of boards worn, with occasional spot or stain; presentation copy from editor, Hester Lynch Piozzi to her friend Mrs. Lambart, with later Lambart family ownership inscriptions. Rotschild 1270; Courtney & Nichol Smith p. 168; Chapman & Hazen p.165.   Simon Finch 24-185 1996 £850.00

ASSOCIATION - ROBERT PITCAIRN

NICHOLSON, WILLIAM   A Collection of Papers Scatter'd Lately About the Town in the Daily-Fourant, St. James's Post, &c... London: printed for B. Barker and C. King, both in Westminster Hall, 1717. Small 8vo; half leather, marbled boards, front cover separated, collector blindstamp on title, very good. Bookplate of Robert Pitcairn. Lampeter 6191.   Freedom Bookshop 14-24 1996 $115.00

ASSOCIATION - PITKIN

STEFANSSON, VIHJALMUR   The Friendly Arctic: The Story of Five Years in Polar Regions. New York: Macmillan, 1921. 1st edition; ("November 1921"); thick 8vo; 103 black and white illustrations, 7 text maps, 2 folding maps in pocket at end; full dark blue cloth, gilt stamped spine and upper cover; very good; acetate dust jacket. Signed and inscribed by Stefansson to Dr. C. E. Pitkin on front free endpaper.   George J. Houle 68-139 1996 $175.00

ASSOCIATION - PITT

SPENCE, JOSEPH 1699-1768   A Parallel: in the Manner of Plutarch: Between a Most Celebrated Man of Florence, and One, Scarce Ever Heard of, In England. Strawberry Hill: Robinson, 1758. 1st edition; one of 700 copies; 8vo; vignette; ad at end; gilt calf, joints weak; contemporary engraved armorial bookplate of Pitt family. Hazen 44.6.   Rostenberg & Stern 150-148 1996 $450.00

ASSOCIATION - PIXERECOURT

GRECOURT, JEAN BAPTISTE JOSEPH   Oeuvres Completes. Paris: Chaignieu, 1796. 8vo; 4 volumes; portrait, 8 engraved plates by Gragonand fils; contemporary vellum gilt by Bozerian Jeune (with his name in gilt on spine), gilt roll tooled borders, flat spine, gilt in compartments, lettered and dated in gilt, turquoise marbled endpapers, all edges gilt; the Pixerecourt copy, with engraved, green label.   Marlborough 160-39 1996 £1,500.00

ASSOCIATION - PLESCH

DAVIES, H.   Welsh Botanology...Native Plants of Anglesey... London: 1813. 1st edition; 8vo; 2 parts in 1 volume; engraved plate; original boards, uncut, bit stained and worn; the Plesch copy with booklabel.   Maggs Bros. Ltd. 1190-71 1996 £90.00

PHILLIPS, HENRY   Pomarium Britannicum: an Historical and Botanical Account of Fruits Known in Great Britain. London: 1823. 3rd edition; 8vo; pages ix, 372, 3 hand colored paltes; straight grained morocoo, slightly rubbed, plates slightly foxed; Plesch copy with bookplate.   John Henly 27-321 1996 £120.00

THURET, G.   Etudes Phycologiques... Paris: 1878. Limited to 200 copies; folio; pages iii, 105; 51 plates; half morocco (original wrappers bound in); extremely scarce, slight foxing at beginning and slight waterstain on lower blank corner, the Plesch copy.   Wheldon & Wesley 207-112 1996 £600.00

ASSOCIATION - ROBERT S. POEHLER

KENT, ROCKWELL 1882-   Of Men and Mountains, Being an Account of the European Travels of the Author and His Wife, Sally... Ausable Forks: Asgaard Press,, 1959. One of 250 copies; octavo; 46 pages; illustrated and signed by author; very fine and partially unopened, in cloth backed marbled boards, with original glassine dust jacket; inscribed by kent for Robert S. Poehler.   Bromer Booksellers 90-154 1996 $450.00

ASSOCIATION - HENRY POLEY

WHISTON, WILLIAM   A New Theory of the Earth, from Its Original, to the Consummation of All Things. London: printed by R. Roberts, for Benj. Tooke, 1696. 1st edition; 8vo; engraved frontispiece, 7 plates, piece torn from outer margin of S2 with loss of few letters of the marginal notes, ad leaf and errata leaf at end; contemporary panelled calf, rebacked, label; bookplate of Henry Poley of Badley, 1703 on blank verso of title, nice. Wing W1696; Hoover 883; Norman 2229.   Anthony W. Laywood 109-159 1996 £485.00

ASSOCIATION - GRAHAM POLLARD

BROWN, ROBERT   The Book of the Landed Estate. Edinburgh: William Blackwood and Sons, 1869. 1st edition; 8vo; xiii, (i), 505, (1), 16 pages; contemporary quarter black calf, covers slightly sunned, else very good; Graham Pollard's copy.   The Bookpress 75-391 1996 $385.00

ASSOCIATION - JOHN POLLOCK

JOHNSON, J.   A View of the Jurisprudence of the Isle of Man... Edinburgh: sold by Thomas Bryce and Co., 1811. 1st edition; 8vo; viii, 234, vi, 15 pages; slightly spotted at beginning; contemporary red half morocco, spine gilt and lettered, marbled edges; fine. Contemporary armorial bookplate of John Pollock, Esq.   John Drury 82-127 1996 £195.00

ASSOCIATION - RICHARD POLWHELE

POLWHELE, RICHARD 1760-1838   Traditions and Recollections; Domestic, Clerical and Literary. London: John Nichols and Son, 1826. 1st edition; 8vo; 2 volumes bound in 1; vi, 820 pages; frontispiece, 5 plates; recent black half calf, spine gilt, marbled boards; minor foxing and staining; good copy; bookplate of Richard G. Polwhele.   Robert Clark 38-256 1996 £75.00

ASSOCIATION - CLEMENT DU PONTET

THE OXFORD University and City Guide... Oxford: c. 1870. New edition; 12mo; pages vi, (ii), 278, (2); frontispiece, and engraved additional titlepage (waterstain in gutter margin), folding map (little frayed at fore-edge), 7 plates; original morocco grain dark green cloth, backstrip gilt titled direct, sides with blindstamped border, gilt vignette of University Museum on front cover, yellow chalked endpapers, front free endpaper removed; modern bookplate of Clement Du Pontet and entry clipped from bookseller's catalog on front pastedown, generally very good   Blackwell's B112-216 1996 £40.00

THE OXFORD Visitor; or Picturesque Views of all the Colleges and Halls of the University: Public Buildings of the City; and Representations of Curious Works of Art,... London: Sherwood, Neely and Jones, 1822. 12mo; pages vi, 114, (6); engraved frontispiece, 55 plates, one with small amateur repair to verso of margin, foxed, tissue guards; original 'Cathedral' binding in green morocco, extremities little rubbed, backstrip with wide raised bands, gilt lettered direct in second and fourth compartments, remainder with Gothic tracery decoration, gilt dulled, sides panelled with border of wide gilt diamond pattern roll, diamonds filled with tracery, centre of sides blindstamped with Gothic window of complicated design, green endpapers, large modern bookplate of Clement du Pontet, entry clipped from booksellers catalog, gilt edges, very good.   Blackwell's B112-217 1996 £150.00

ASSOCIATION - J. LAWRENCE POOL

ELSBERG, CHARLES   Tumors of the Spinal Cord and the Symptons of Irritation and Compression of the Spinal Cord and Nerve Roots. New York: Paul Hoeber, 1925. 8vo; 421 pages; 354 illustrations; original binding; J. Lawrence Pool's copy with his signature.   James Tait Goodrich K40-126 1996 $350.00

ASSOCIATION - LUCIUS POOLE

PRY, PAUL, PSEUD.   Oddities of London Life. London: Richard Bentley, 1838. 8vo; 2 volumes, 316, 234 pages; 22 engraved plates; 19th century three quarter morocco by F. P. Hathaway, Boston, with original green cloth covers and spine titles tipped to pastedowns, near fine, with bookplate of Lucius Poole, Boston.   Chapel Hill 94-49 1996 $200.00

ASSOCIATION - POOR

BROWNING, ROBERT 1812-1889   Strafford: an Historical Tragedy. London: printed for Longman, Rees, Orme, Brown, Green & Longman, 1837. 1st edition; 8vo; full brown crushed levant, covers decorated in gilt with elaborate interlocking ruled border enclosed withing light brown inlaid morocco strips, intricate tan morocco doublures, with all over floral pattern in gilt, spine gilt, all edges gilt, by the Club Bindery, original drab wrappers, printed paper side label, bound in at end; fine in handsome binding. From the library of H. W. Poor, additional bookplate of Christine Alexander Graham. CBEL III 442.   Ximenes 108-391 1996 $850.00

ASSOCIATION - PORTLAND

WALTER, RICHARD 1716?-1785   A Voyage Round the World, in the Years MDCCXL, I, II,, III, IV. London: printed for the author by John and Paul Knapton, 1748. 1st edition; 4to; 42 folding engraved plates and maps, occasional foxing, 12 page list of subscribers, final leaf of direction to binder; contemporary red morocco, gilt borders, spine and inner dentelles gilt, all edges gilt, rebacked, original spine laid down, covers bit scratched, some rubbing; handsome copy on royal paper in binding appropriate for presentation; pres. copy neatly inscribed by recipient, 2nd Duke of Portland "Given to me by Anson at Aix la Chapelle June ye 7th, 1748. W. Bentinck"; early booklabel of Mary Boydell. Hill 317-8; Sabin 1625.   Ximenes 109-8 1996 $5,000.00

WORCESTER, EDWARD SOMERSET, 2ND MARQUIS OF 1601-1667   A Century of the Names and Scantlings of Such Inventions, as at Present I Can Call to Mind to Have Tried and Perfected... London: Printed in the Year 1663, reprinted & sold by T. Payne, 1746. 2nd edition; 12mo; no half title, with final ad, leaf D12, 19th century buckram, top edge gilt, others uncut; nice copy; bookplate of the Sixth Duke of Portland. Anthony W. Laywood 108-123 1996 £165.00

ASSOCIATION - DAVID POSNER

GRAVES, ROBERT 1895-1985   Treasure Box. London: privately printed for the author at the Chiswick Press, 1919. 1st edition; 15 pages; titlepage illustration and further illustrations in text by Nancy Nicholson; original pale blue sewn wrappers; fine; presentation inscription from Graves to fellow poet David Posner. Higginson & Williams A4. Blackwell's B112-137 1996 £1,650.00

ASSOCIATION - MONTGOMERY GILCHRIST POTTER

TENNYSON, ALFRED TENNYSON, 1ST BARON 1809-1892   Maud, and Other Poems. London: Edward Moxon, 1855. 1st edition; 8vo; original green cloth, covers stamped in blind, spine ruled in blind, lettered in gilt, some light rubbing, cream endpapers (offsetting from bookplates, one removed), 8 pages publisher's ads dated July 1855 at front, single leaf of author's ads at back, very nice in green morocco backed slipcase; with leather bookplate of Richard Montgomery Gilchrist Potter at front and signature of Emily Hodgekinson. Ashley vii 118; Hayward 248. Tinker 2080.   James Cummins 14-206 1996 $150.00

ASSOCIATION - POTTINGER

GENLIS, STEPHANIE FELICITE DUCREST DE ST. AUBIN, COMTESSE DE 1746-1830   Adelaide and Theodore; or Letters on Education... London: T. Cadell, 1788. 3rd edition; 12mo; 3 volumes contemporary tree calf, spines in compartments with raised bands, gilt rules and delicate ornamentation, red and black morocco labels, lettered in gilt; slight spotting to just a few leaves, otherwise fine; bookplate of Count le Pelletier, inscription presenting the book to Mary Pottinger on rear pastedowns, one little chipped.   Simon Finch 24-23 1996 £285.00

ASSOCIATION - FREDERICK POTTLE

HICKS, EDWARD   Sir Thomas Malory - His Turbulent Career - a Biography. Cambridge: Harvard University Press, 1928. 1st edition; 8 black and white plates; buckram backed boards, top edge gilt, page and endpaper edges slightly browned, head and tail of spine slightly bumped, covers slightly marked, cover edges faded, very good; with ownership signature of Frederick Pottle.   Ulysses 39-710 1996 £55.00

HOUTCHENS, CAROLYN WASHBURN   The English Romantic Poets and Essayists - A Review of Research and Criticism. New York: Modern Language Association of America, 1957. 1st edition; original binding, top edge slightly dusty, head and tail of spine slightly bumped, very good in nicked, chipped, torn, rubbed, frayed and dusty, slightly creased and marked dust jacket browned at spine and edges; pencilled ownership signature of Frederick A. Pottle.   Ulysses 39-696 1996 £75.00

ASSOCIATION - FREDERICK POTTLE

LONGAKER, MARK   English Biography in the Eighteenth Century. Philadelphia: University of Pennsylvania Press, 1931. 1st edition; original binding, top edge dusty, head and tail of spine, corners and bottom edges of covers bumped and bruised, covers marked, cover edges rubbed, very good; with pencilled ownership signature of Frederick Pottle.   Ulysses 39-707 1996 £75.00

MC LAREN, MORAY   Corsica Boswell - Paoli, Johnson and Freedom. London: Martin Secker & Warburg, 1966. 1st edition; 6 black and white plates; original binding, top edge dusty, front free endpaper slightly browned through contact with TLS (review of this book) clipping; head and tail of spine, corners and bottom edge of lower cover bumped, very good in nicked and slightly creased, rubbed and dusty dust jacket; with pencilled ownership signature of Frederick Pottle.   Ulysses 39-709 1996 £55.00

NORMAN, CHARLES BERNARD 1887-1947   Mr. Oddity - Samuel Johnson LL.D. Drexel Hill: Bell Pub. 1951. 1st edition; advance review slip loosely inserted; original binding, top edge dusty, head and tail of spine slightly bumped, very good in nicked, chipped and dusty, slightly rubbed, torn and creased dust jacket slightly faded at spine and slightly browned at edges; with pencilled ownership signature of Frederick Pottle. Ulysses 39-705 1996 £55.00

SALPETER, HOWARD   Dr. Johnson and Mr. Boswell. New York: Coward McCann, 1929. 1st edition; 16 black and white plates; original binding, top edge dusty, spine darkened, head and tail of spine and corners slightly bumped, covers slightly marked and rubbed; very good; pencilled ownership signature of Frederick Pottle.   Ulysses 39-704 1996 £65.00

SHERWOOD, MARGARET   Undercurrents of Influence in English Romantic Poetry. Cambridge: Harvard University Press, 1934. 1st edition; original binding, bottom corners slightly bumped, free endpapers partially browned, upper cover very slightly soiled, very good; with pencilled ownership signature of Frederick Pottle.   Ulysses 39-714 1996 £85.00

SWINBURNE, ALGERNON CHARLES 1837-1909   The Letters of Algernon Charles Swinburne. New York: John Lane Co., 1919. 1st edition; 2 volumes; original binding, top edges dusty, spines darkened, covers slightly marked, cover edges slightly faded, heads and tails of spines and corners bumped, very good; with pencilled ownership signatures of Frederick Pottle.   Ulysses 39-715 1996 £60.00

THOMSON, CLARA J.   Samuel Richardson - a Biographical and Critical Study. London: Horace Marshall & Son, 1900. 1st edition; original binding, bookplate, top edge dusty, head and tail of spine and corners bumped, endpapers browned, covers rubbed and marked, spine darkened, good; with pencilled ownership signature of Frederick Pottle. Ulysses 39-711 1996 £55.00

ASSOCIATION - POWELL

SALMON, THOMAS   A New Historical Account of St. George for England and the Original of the most Noble Order of the Garter. London: R. Janeway for Nath. Dancer, 1704. 8vo; title, 3ff., 109 pages, 3ff. (contents to part II), 113 pages, 2 portraits and 1 view; slight browning, pencil underlinings, later morocco; with Baden-Powell bookplate. Lowndes p. 2179.   Marlborough 162-198 1996 £125.00

ASSOCIATION - WALTER MERRIAM PRATT

SHILLABER, BENJAMIN   Knitting-Work: a Web of Many Textures Wrought by Ruth Partington. Boston: Brown, 1859. 1st edition; blue cloth, binding A, minor wear to spine tips, rear cover with small bruise, about very good. Bookplate of Lt. Col. Walter Merriam Pratt.   Charles Agvent 4-1009 1996 $125.00

ASSOCIATION - BRUCE PRICE

PRICE, WILLIAM   Clement Falconer; or, the Memoirs of a Young Whig. Baltimore: N. Hickman, 1838. 1st edition; 12mo; 2 volumes in 1; later half red morocco, very worn, some spotting of text, identification of author written on title; the copy of Bruce Price, with signature, great-grandson of author, on title. Wright Fiction 2072.   James Cummins 14-159 1996 $150.00

ASSOCIATION - BYRON PRICE

HAWTHORNE, NATHANIEL 1804-1864   The House of the Seven Gables. Boston: Ticknor, Reed & Fields, 1851. 1st edition; 3rd printing; original brown cloth with March 1851 catalog at front (formerly accepted as a 'first issue'), mild rubbing, little shaken, but nice copy; bookplate of Byron Price (prominent newspaper editor). Clark A17.1.c. BAL 7604. Mac Donnell 12-61 1996 $450.00

ASSOCIATION - CHARLES PRICE

MC ELRATH, THOMSON P.   A Press Club Outing. New York: the League, 1893. Quarto; 150 pages; illustrations; original cloth, gilt title; nice; inscribed by Chas. W. Price, a delegate.   Bohling Book Co. 191-368 1996 $200.00

ASSOCIATION - NORMAN PRICE

LAMB, CHARLES 1775-1834   Tales from Shakespeare. London: T. C. and E. C. Jack/Toronto: Morgan and Co., 1905. 8vo; pages xii, 324; frontispiece, 20 color paltes by N. M. Price; decorated endpapers and gilt and blind stamped covers, covers slightly scuffed, else very good; signed by artist on half title, with ALS from artist on Carlton Studio letterhead to Mary M. Hendrie of Hamilton.   Hugh Anson-Cartwright 87-354 1996 $200.00

ASSOCIATION - HERBERT PRIESTLEY

MC GOWAN, EDWARD   Narrative of Edward McGowan, Including a Full Account of the Author's Adventures and Perils While Persecuted by the San Francisco Vigilance Committee of 1856. San Francisco: Printed by Thomas C. Russell, 1917. Reprint of 1857 edition, one of 200 numbered copies; 12mo; pages viii, 9-250, tinted frontispiece, numerous full page tinted illustrations, title in red and black; original light brown boards, paper spine label, very fine, clean copy; presentation inscription from printer, Thomas C. Russell to Herbert I. Priestley.   Argonaut Book Shop 113-439 1996 $300.00

ASSOCIATION - NEIL PRIMROSE

FIELDING, HENRY 1707-1754   The Works. London: and Edinburgh: for F. C. and R. Rivington, 1821. 8 3/4 x 5 1/2 inches; 10 volumes; frontispiece in vol. 1, diagram in vol. 8; fine retrospective binding of flamed calf (ca. 1915?), flat spines with wide & narrow gilt bands forming compartments w/lg. gilt sunburst ornament in center, black morocco double labels, gilt hatching on board edges, text block edges gilt, marbled endpapers, lower inch of one joint wormed, two inch abrasion in one cover, otherwise only trivial defects to this very attractively bound set, volume 1 with few minor repaired tears (and one 3 inch tear into text, with slight displacement of letters, but no loss), text with isolated minor discoloration, final two volumes with slightly creased upper corners, otherwise fine, internally quite clean, smooth and fresh. Bookplate of English politician Neil Primrose in each volume, with presentation to him, inscribed and signed by British Prime Minister H. H. Asquith.   Phillip J. Pirages 33-235 1996 $1,250.00

ASSOCIATION - E. S. PROCTER

plummer, charles   Bethada Naem nEreenn: Lives of Irish Saints. London: Oxford University Press, 1922. 8vo; 2 volumes, pages 390, 404; original cloth, very scarce. ownership signatures of E. S. Procter, hispanist, St. Hugh's College; and Pamela Gradon, medievalist, St. Hugh's College.   Howes Bookshop 265-980 1996 £120.00

ASSOCIATION - J. W. PROCTOR

LEAVITT, JONATHAN   A Summary of the Laws of Massachusetts, Relative to the Settlement, Support, Employment and Removal of Paupers. Greenfield: Printed by John Denio, 1810. 1st edition; 8vo; original sheep backed marbled newsprint boards, text showing through the marbling, printed paper label on upper cover, edges chipped with tears, rubbed, text browned; signatures of William Perry on endpaper and Dr. J. W. Proctor of Malden, Mass. on title, with note at foot of title reading "State Board of Charity, April 1, 1901". Marvin p. 456; S&S 20533; Sabin 39559.   James Cummins 14-152 1996 $200.00

ASSOCIATION - FREDERIC PROKOSCH

COPPARD, ALFRED EDGAR 1878-1957   Nixey's Harlequin. London: Cape, 1931. Limited edition, this number 89 copies from an edition of 304, signed; printed on handmade paper, top edge gilt; full vellum, edges of pages slightly browned, covers spotted otherwise very good in glassine wrapper; from the library of Frederic Prokosch with his signature and bookplate   Virgo Books 48-56 1996 £60.00

ASSOCIATION - PRUYN

A TRUE and Faithful Account of the Island of Veritas; Together with the Forms of Their Liturgy... London: for C. Stalker, 1790? 1st and only edition; viii, 88, 87-171, (2) pages; contemporary calf backed and vellum tipped pastepaper boards, skillfully rebacked in period style, light cover wear, otherwise fine; Pruyn bookplate.   Joseph J. Felcone 64-41 1996 $900.00

ASSOCIATION - PULL COURT

LUCANUS, MARCUS ANNAEUS 39-68   Lucanus. Venice: In Aedibus Aldi, et Andreae Soceri, 1515. 2nd Aldine edition; 8vo; 140 leaves, Italic; early 18th century full leather, boards, detached, all edges gilt; engraved armorial Bookplate of William Dondesnell Esq. of Pull Cort. Renouard 72.6. Adams L1564; UCLA II 117; Brunet III 1199.   Family Album Tillers-402 1996 $700.00

ASSOCIATION - CATHERINE PUTNAM

STOWE, HARRIET ELIZABETH BEECHER 1811-1896   Uncle Tom's Cabin. Boston: John P. Jewett & Co., 1852. 25th thousand; 12mo; 2 volumes; 6 plates; brown cloth, light wear to spine tips, moderate foxing, bright, very good; contemporary ownership signature of Catherine Putnam. BAL 19343 for 1st printing.   Charles Agvent 4-1069 1996 $350.00

ASSOCIATION - JONATHAN PYTTS

BOSWELL, JAMES 1740-1795   The Life of Samuel Johnson, LL.D. Comprehending an Account of His Studies and Numerous Works, in Chronological Order... London: by Henry Baldwin, for Charles Dilly, 1791. 1st edition; 4to; 2 volumes, xii, (xvi), 516; (iv), 588; this copy has the misprint 'gve' on p. 135, indicating that the inner forme of sheet S in that volume is in an earlier uncorrected state; frontispiece, 2 engraved facsimile plates; contemporary mottled calf, sides with narrow gilt borders, spines divided into panels with a metope and pentaglyph roll, gilt blazons in each panel, black morocco lettering pieces, circular numbering pieces, marbled endpapers; spines lightly rubbed and gilt slightly faded, but fine in modern brown morocco backed folding case; engraved armorial bookplates of Jonathan Pytts. Courtney & Nichol Smith pp. 172-173; Pottle 79; Rothschild 463.   Simon Finch 24-16 1996 £5,500.00

EDWARDS, THOMAS   The Canons of Criticism and Glossary; the Trial of the Letter Y(upsilon)), Alias Y, and Sonnets. London: for C. Bathurst, 1765. 1st edition thus; 8vo; pages 351, (xvii), index and ads; contemporary calf, rather worn; good, firm copy. Bookplate of Jonathan Pytts. Jaggard p. 90.   Simon Finch 24-80 1996 £140.00

ASSOCIATION - ARTHUR HOBSON QUINN

GUITRY, SACHA   Deburau. Published by Belasco, 1925. 1st edition; 178 pages; 34 plates with tissue; stiff boards with jacket, fine in board box. Inscribed by David Belasco to Dr. Arthur Hobson Quinn.   Lyman Books 21-493 1996 $100.00

ASSOCIATION - JOHN QUINN

SHELLEY, PERCY BYSSHE 1792-1822   A Philosophical View of Reform. London: Humphrey Milford, Oxford University Press, 1920. 1st edition; 4to; pages xi, 94, 1 plate; frontispiece, original boards, cloth back. Fine in little chipped and stained dust jacket, inscribed "John Quinn from T. W. Rolleston Sept. 23 1920". Bookplate of Great American collector Gordon Craig.   Howard S. Mott 227-128 1996 $135.00

ASSOCIATION - RADFORD

SCOTT, WILLIAM   Picturesque Scenery in the County of Sussex, sketched from Nature, Drawn on Stone... London: Rodwell and Martin, 1821. Oblong 4to; 6 lithographic plates; stitched as issued, original buff colored paper wrappers. Pristine copy; presentation, inscribed to Miss Radford.   Marlborough 162-87 1996 £650.00

ASSOCIATION - EDWARD RAHIR

BADIUS ASCENCIUS, JODOCUS 1462-1535   Stultiferae Naves Sensus Animosque Trahentes Mortis in Exitium. Paris: Thielmann Kerver for E. J. and G. Marnef, 1500. 1st edition; small 4to; 6 large woodcut illustrations; full crushed burgundy morocco du cap, spine with five raised bands and gilt titling, board edges gilt, inner gilt dentelles, all edges gilt, by Riviere, very top of front joint slightly cracked, nearly invisible paper remargining to few leaves; bookplates of Edward Rahir and Henri Burton.   Book Block 32-29 1996 $7,500.00

ASSOCIATION - PHILLIP RAHV

JARRELL, RANDALL   Little Friend, Little Friend. New York: Dial Press, 1945. 1st edition; 8vo; very good and tight copy in well chipped dust jacket; presentation copy inscribed by author for Phillip Rahv, founder of The Partisan Review.   Lakin & Marley 3-26 1996 $750.00

ASSOCIATION - RAISTRICK

SINCLAIR, JOHN 1754-1835   An Account of the Systems of Husbandry Adopted in the More Improved Districts of Scotland. Edinburgh: printed for Arch. Constable and Co... G. Nicol, 1812. 1st edition; 8vo; pages xii, 432, 152, 77, 16 (ad leaves), uncut, 13 engraved plates and plans; original boards, spine and edges little chipped and worn, very good in original state. From the library of Dr. Arthur Raistrick with his bookplate. Rothamsted p. 135.   R.F.G. Hollett 76-279 1996 £275.00

WHEELER, ANNE   The Westmorland Dialect, with the Adjaceny of Lancashrie and Yorkshire, in four Familiar Dialogues. Kendal: M. & r. Branthwaite, 1821. 3rd edition; 8vo pages 120, 12, 12, (addenda), woodcut frontispiece, 2 woodcuts, original printed wrappers, worn and soiled, corners chipped and backstrip lacking. From the library of Dr. Arthur Raistrick, with his bookplate.   R.F.G. Hollett & Son 78-501 1996 £95.00

WILSON, DANIEL   The Archaeology and Prehistoric Annals of Scotland. Edinburgh: Sutherland and Knox, 1851. Large thick 8vo; pages xxvi, 714, 6 engraved plates, 195 text woodcuts; original decorated cloth, gilt, neatly rebacked in levant morocco, gilt; from the library of Dr. Arthur Raistrick, with his bookplate.   R.F.G. Hollett 76-337 1996 £85.00

ASSOCIATION - E. H. RAMSDEN

BROWSE, LILLIAN   Barbara Hepworth - Sculptress. London: pub. for the Shenval Press by Faber & Faber, Ltd., 1946. 1st edition; 50 black and white plates; original binding, top edge dusty, head and tail of spine, corners and cover edges slightly bumped, spine and cover edges darkened, covers slightly marked and bowed, page edges slightly browned, good only, no dust jacket. Presentation copy from artist to E. H. Ramsden and Margot Eates, inscribed by her.   Ulysses 39-286 1996 £175.00

BUONAROTTI, MICHEL ANGELO 1475-1564   The Letters of Michelangelo. London: Peter Owne Ltd., 1963. One of 500 sets; quarto; 2 volumes; decorated gilt buckram covers, bottom corners of two pages in volume 2 slightly creased, one of the corners is also very slightly torn, heads and tails of spine and 3 corners slightly bumped, covers slightly rubbed, near fine in slightly torn, bumped and worn slipcase, top edge gilt; presentation inscription from E. H. Ramsden, the editor. Ulysses 39-409 1996 £195.00

HODIN, J. P.   John Milne: Sculptor - Life and Work. London: Latimer New Dimensions Ltd., 1977. 1st edition; illustrations in color and black and white; wrappers, slightly soiled, very good, head and tail of spine and corners slightly bumped, free endpapers slightly rubbed, very good in nicked, rubbed and slightly chipped and creased dust jacket; presentation copy from artist to engraved plates. H. Ramsden and Margot Eates.   Ulysses 39-410 1996 £95.00

ASSOCIATION - E. H. RAMSDEN

NASH, PAUL   Paul Nash - a Portfolio of Colour Plates. London: Soho Gallery Ltd., 1937. 1st edition; folio; 10 mounted color plates, one of which is one upper cover, 2 black and white reproductions in text; wrappers, covers soiled and dusty, cover edges rubbed, creased and darkened, head and tail of spine and corners bumped and worn, prelims spotted, good; presentation copy from artist to art critic and companion of Margot Eates, E. H. Ramsden, inscribed.   Ulysses 39-438 1996 £950.00

NASH, PAUL   Paul Nash. Harmondsworth: Penguin Books Ltd., 1944. 1st edition; 16 color and 16 black and white plates; landscape format, wrappers; covers dusty, slightly soiled and creased and internally spotted, cover edges rubbed, staples rusted away; good; presentation copy from author to the art critic and companion of Margot Eates, E. H. Ramsden.   Ulysses 39-439 1996 £750.00

OLSON, RUTH   Naum Gabo and Antoine Pevner. New York: Museum of Modern Art, 1948. 1st edition; wrappers; covers worn and creased, some corners slightly creased; good. Presentation copy from Herbert Reed for E. H. Ramsden and Margot Eates.   Ulysses 39-495 1996 £95.00

READ, HERBERT   Lord Byron at the Opera - a Play for Broadcasting. North Harrow: Philip Ward, 1963. 1st edition; wrappers, covers spotted and slightly soiled and creased, cvoer edges faded, some slight internal spotting; good. Presentation copy from author to E. H. Ramsden and Margot Eates.   Ulysses 39-496 1996 £80.00

ASSOCIATION - THOMAS RAMSDEN

ACKERMANN, RUDOLPH 1764-1834   A History of the University of Oxford, Its Colleges, Halls and Public Buildings. London: R. Ackermann, 1814. 4to; 2 volumes; pages xiv, (ii), 275, (1) (blank), (6) (index); (iv), 262, (6) (index); 2 frontispieces, 62 plates, aquatints, 6 with double views, all hand colored, 17 colored line and stipple plates, uncolored stipple engraved portrait, half titles present, plates and text in excellent state, although plates offset, expert paper repair to blank fore-margins of two leaves in gathering Hh, volume 2, corner of last leaf volume 2 creased, wide margins; early 20th century three quarter crushed polished blue morocco, for Henry Sotheran, backstrips with gilt decorated raised bands, lettered direct in second and third compartments, remainder gilt panelled, pale blue cloth sides, marbled endpapers, red markers, entirely untrimmed; excellent; bookplate of Thomas Ramsden of Middton Tower, King's Lynn. Abbey Scenery 278-280; Clary 113; Cordeaux-Merry Univ. 25; Tooley 5.   Blackwell's B112-219 1996 £3,200.00

ASSOCIATION - A. PHILIP RANDOLPH

BRAZEAL, BRAILSFORD R.   The Brotherhood of Sleeping Car Porters. New York: Harper, 1946. Early later printing; fine in dust jacket with couple of very small nicks and tears; signed by A. Philip Randolph, the president of the Union.   Between the Covers 43-395 1996 $450.00

ASSOCIATION - WILL RANSOM

OMAR KHAYYAM   Rubaiyat of Omar Khayyam. London: Vale Press, 1901. Limited to 310 copies; 8vo; printed in red and black Vale type on handmade paper, pages xxx, (2), frontispiece, borders and initials by Ricketts, faint browning in bottom margin of first opening, otherwise very good; uncommon; original holland backed boards, paper label, uncut; from the library of Will Ransom with his label. Bookplate of J. H. Hanson. Tomkinson 32.   Claude Cox 107-176 1996 £150.00

ASSOCIATION - RATCLIFFE

LYTTON, EDWARD GEORGE EARLE LYTTON BULWER-LYTTON, 1ST BARON 1803-1873   England and the English. London: Richard Bentley, 1833. 1st edition; large 12mo; xii, 399, (1); and xi, (1), 355, (1) pages, no half titles (not called for?); 2 volumes; contemporary half calf, spines gilt with raised bands and double labels, marbled sides and edges by S. Ratcliffe of Faversham; very good. New CBEL III 918.   John Drury 82-35 1996 £250.00

ASSOCIATION - E. A. RATCLIFFE

FRANCE, ANATOLE   Stendhal. London: 1926. One of 110 numbered copies, this copy being additionally inscribed; wrappers, first two pages and final page partially browned, covers slightly marked and spotted; very good; inscribed by Holbrook Jackson for E. A. Ratcliffe.   Ulysses 39-134 1996 £85.00

ASSOCIATION - WILLIAM RATHBONE

MILL, JOHN STUART 1806-1873　　Inaugural Address Delivered to the University of St. Andrews Feb. 1st 1867. London: Longmans, 1867. 1st edition; 8vo; 99, (1) pages; original maroon cloth, lettered in gilt on upper cover, neatly rebacked. From the library of William Rathbone (1787-1868) the Liverpool educationist and philanthropist.　　John Drury 82-186　1996　£125.00

ASSOCIATION - HARRIET RAUCH

KENT, ROCKWELL 1882-　　Salamina. New York: Harcourt Brace, 1935. 1st edition; 8vo; 336 pages; 80 illustrations; original blue cloth, nearly fine in dust jacket; inscribed by Kent for Harriet and Herbert Rauch. Chapel Hill　94-64　1996　$150.00

ASSOCIATION - HERBERT RAUCH

KENT, ROCKWELL 1882-　　Salamina. New York: Harcourt Brace, 1935. 1st edition; 8vo; 336 pages; 80 illustrations; original blue cloth, nearly fine in dust jacket; inscribed by Kent for Harriet and Herbert Rauch. Chapel Hill　94-64　1996　$150.00

ASSOCIATION - HARDWICKE DRUMMOND RAWNSLEY

BUTLER, SAMUEL 1835-1902　　Ex Voto; an Account of the Sacro Monte or New Jerusalem at Varallo Sesia... London: Longmans, Green and Co., 1890. Longman's reissue; original brown cloth slightly rubbed; Hardwicke Drummond Rawnsley's copy with his bookplate and his ms. description on his Crosthwaite Vicarage, Keswick headed notepaper. Jarndyce CII-46　1996　£75.00

ASSOCIATION - BRONSON RAY

DANDY, WALTER　　Intracranial Arterial Aneurisms. Ithaca: 1945. 2nd printing; 8vo; viii, 146 pages, 5 folding charts, numerous text illustrations; original binding; nice association copy, Bronson Ray's copy with his signature. Walker pp. 112-13.　　James Tait Goodrich K40-109　1996　$395.00

ASSOCIATION - OLNEY RAYMOND

WARREN, EDWARD H.　　Spartan Education. Boston: Houghton Mifflin Co., 1942. One of 1000 copies, of which this is number 156; inscribed by Professor Warren to Olney Raymond, whose ownership inscription dated Oct. 5 1942, found on first blank.　　Meyer Boswell SL25-232 1996　$150.00

ASSOCIATION - JOHN RAYNER

CLERIHEWS. Cambridge: Rampant Lions Press, 1938. Wrappers very slightly rubbed, spine moderately wrinkled, but excellent; autograph letter from Will Carter to John Rayner laid in.　　R. A. Gekoski 19-116　1996 £75.00

TERENTIUS AFER, PUBLIUS 180-159 BC　　Comoediae. Birmingham: Baskerville, 1772. 12mo; pages (4), 308 pages, the edition without the cancellans at G2; some leaves in 2 gatherings smudged during printing (very unusual), contemporary sprinkled calf, gilt tulip roll on boards, spine ornamented with gilt crossed arrows, later ex-libris of John Rayner. Gaskell 47.　　Family Album Tillers-610　1996　$325.00

ASSOCIATION - RAPHAEL READ

TUSON, E.　　Myology Illustrated: a supplement to Myology. London: Callow & Wilson, 1825-28. 1st edition; folio; 2 volumes, 1st with 8 lithographed plates, the second with 9 lithograph plates, both after drawings by author, both with multiple overlays, considerable hand coloring in red and blue, both on plates and overlays; first volume somewhat soiled, several of the overlays creased, few short tears repaired, title washed to remove library stamps and inscription thereon rather faint 'presented by Raphael W. Read, asst. surgeon, 52nd Lt. infantry, Nov. 26th 1847'; contemporary half calf, rather worn, second volume with slight soiling and minor marginal fraying, small spot of damage by adhesion on one overlay, several creased, contemporary boards, printed label on front cover (rather worn), label scraped, rebacked with cloth; very rare, especially with supplement.　　Maggs Bros. Ltd.　1190-527　1996　£2,200.00

ASSOCIATION - GILBERT REDGRAVE

HIGGINS, BRYAN　　Experiments and Observations with the View of Improving the Art of composing and Applying Calcareous Cements, and of Preparing Quick-Lime... London: T. Cadell, 1780. 8vo; viii, 232 pages; contemporary marbled boards with seemly new calf spine and corners; bookplates of Buddle Atkinson and Gilbert Redgrave. Harris & Savage No. 347.　　Elton Engineering　10-73　1996　£450.00

ASSOCIATION - HERBERT REED

OLSON, RUTH　　Naum Gabo and Antoine Pevner. New York: Museum of Modern Art, 1948. 1st edition; wrappers; covers worn and creased, some corners slightly creased; good. Presentation copy from Herbert Reed for E. H. Ramsden and Margot Eates.　　Ulysses　39-495　1996 £95.00

ASSOCIATION - REES

MAITLAND, JOHN　　Observations on the Impolicy or Permitting the Exploration of British Wool, and of Preventing the Free Importation of Foreign Wool. London: printed and published by William Phillips, 1818. 1st edition; 8vo; original boards, uncut; presentation inscription by author for Revd. Dr. Rees. Kress C116; Goldsmith 22072.　　Anthony W. Laywood　109-94　1996　£95.00

ASSOCIATION - CLARA REEVE

BARCLAY, JOHN　　Barclay, His Argenis. London: printed for Henry Seile, 1636. 2nd edition of this translation; 4to; 23 plates; contemporary calf, spine worn, front cover detached; the copy of Clara Reeve, 18th century novelist), with signature. Aside from binding, in very good condition. STC 1392.5. Esdaile p. 18; Mish p. 21.　　Ximenes　109-24 1996　$750.00

ASSOCIATION - JOYCE REEVES

RAY, MAN　　Man Ray: Photographs 1920-1934 Paris. Hartford: Soby, 1934. 2nd edition; spiral bound with color illustration on cover. The copy of translator, Joyce Reeves, signed by her.　　J. B. Muns　154-247 1996　$1,650.00

ASSOCIATION - ROBIE REID

GREAT BRITAIN. COLONIAL OFFICE - 1863　　Vancouver Island..."Copies or Extracts of Correspondence Between Mr. Langford and the Colonial Department, Rleative to Alleged Abuses in the Government of Vancouver's Island... London: Colonial Office, 1863. 33 cm; 52 pages; gilt stamped quarter leather and cloth, bit of scuffing to leather; very good. Bookplate of Robie Reid. Lowther 200.　　Rockland Books　38-87　1996　$450.00

ASSOCIATION - RENIER

DODSLEY, ROBERT 1703-1764　　The Preceptor; Containing a General Course of Education. London: printed for J. Dodsley, 1775. 6th edition; 2 volumes; frontispiece, folding plates, 3 pages ads in volume 1; contemporary calf, hinges splitting, but sound, red labels; from the library of Anne and Fernand Renier. Alston VII.202.　　Jarndyce 103-460 1996　£120.00

ROBINSON, DR.　　Magistrate's Pocket-Book; or an Epitome of the Duties and Practice of a Justice of the Peace, Out of Sessions. London: 1837. 2nd edition; 8vo; xviii, 466, (40) pages; old mellow calf, title label inset on red morocco; very good; with bookplate of A. & F. Renier and lettered in gilt on front board J. Hussey.　　K Books　442-417　1996 £60.00

TUER, ANDREW WHITE 1838-1900　　History of the Horn-Book. London: Leadenhall Press, 1896. 1st edition; 4to; 2 volumes; profusely illustrated, with facsimile horn-books and battledores as issued in pockets; uncut in original full decorated vellum, brown leather labels, top edge gilt, as issued; lovely copy; booklabel of Wm. Bernard Atherton; from the collection of Anne & Fernand Renier.　　Jarndyce　103-587　1996 £750.00

ASSOCIATION - ANNE RENIER

FORRESTER, ALFRED HENRY 1804-1872   The Tutor's Assistant, or Comic Figures of Arithmetic... London: J. and F. Harwood, 1843. frontispiece, illustrations; original dark green cloth, slight rubbing at head of spine, all edges gilt; very good, bright, from the collection of Anne and Fernand Renier with label.   Jarndyce 103-456 1996 £50.00

GREENWOOD, THOMAS   Free Public Libraries, Their Organisation, Uses and Management. London: Simpkin, Marshall, 1886. 1st edition; frontispiece, illustrations, ads; original dark green cloth, slightly defective at head of spine; from the collection of Anne and Fernand Renier. Jarndyce 103-483 1996 £75.00

GROSE, FRANCIS 1731-1791   A Classical Dictionary of the Vulgar Tongue. London: printed for Hooper & Co., 1796. 3rd edition; uncut in original blue boards, brown paper spine chipped, hinges splitting, paper label chipped; from the collection of Fernand & Anne Renier.   Jarndyce 103-153 1996 £130.00

GROSE, FRANCIS 1731-1791   Lexicon Balatronicum. London: printed for C. Happel, 1811. Reprint; half title; contemporary tree sheep, rubbed at corners, hinges splitting, red label; from the collection of Fernand & Anne Renier.   Jarndyce 103-154 1996 £85.00

GROSE, FRANCIS 1731-1791   A Provincial Glossary, with a Collection of Local Proverbs and Popular Superstitions London: Printed for S. Hooper, 1787. 1st edition; 2 parts; 19th century half calf, red label, rubbed, leading hinge splitting; from the collection of Fernand & Anne Renier. Alston IX 58.   Jarndyce 103-55 1996 £110.00

JONES, STEPHEN   Sheridan Improved. London: printed by and for J. W. H. Payne, &c., 1812. Stereotype edition; oblong 8vo; slight stain at end of text, contemporary sheep with stain on back board, neatly rebacked; from the collection of Fernand & Anne Renier.   Jarndyce 103-191 1996 £65.00

KNIGHT, CHARLES   The Bridal of the Isles; a Mask. London: Effingham Wilson, 1817. 2nd edition; color frontispiece; contemporary half calf, gilt spine, black label; attractive, very good; from the collection of Anne and Fernand Renier, with booklabel.   Jarndyce 103-507 1996 £120.00

VOCABULA Amatoria; a French-English Glossary of Words, Phrases and Allusions Occuring in the Works of Rabelais, Voltaire, Moliere, Rousseau, Beranger, Zola and Others... London: privately printed for subscribers only, 1896. 4to; half title, title in red and black; uncut in blue boards, cream paper spine and paper label dulled and chipped, hinges splitting; from the collection of Fernand & Anne Renier.   Jarndyce 103-112 1996 £65.00

ASSOCIATION - FERNAND RENIER

FORRESTER, ALFRED HENRY 1804-1872   The Tutor's Assistant, or Comic Figures of Arithmetic... London: J. and F. Harwood, 1843. frontispiece, illustrations; original dark green cloth, slight rubbing at head of spine, all edges gilt; very good, bright, from the collection of Anne and Fernand Renier with label.   Jarndyce 103-456 1996 £50.00

GREENWOOD, THOMAS   Free Public Libraries, Their Organisation, Uses and Management. London: Simpkin, Marshall, 1886. 1st edition; frontispiece, illustrations, ads; original dark green cloth, slightly defective at head of spine; from the collection of Anne and Fernand Renier. Jarndyce 103-483 1996 £75.00

GROSE, FRANCIS 1731-1791   A Classical Dictionary of the Vulgar Tongue. London: printed for Hooper & Co., 1796. 3rd edition; uncut in original blue boards, brown paper spine chipped, hinges splitting, paper label chipped; from the collection of Fernand & Anne Renier.   Jarndyce 103-153 1996 £130.00

GROSE, FRANCIS 1731-1791   Lexicon Balatronicum. London: printed for C. Happel, 1811. Reprint; half title; contemporary tree sheep, rubbed at corners, hinges splitting, red label; from the collection of Fernand & Anne Renier.   Jarndyce 103-154 1996 £85.00

GROSE, FRANCIS 1731-1791   A Provincial Glossary, with a Collection of Local Proverbs and Popular Superstitions London: Printed for S. Hooper, 1787. 1st edition; 2 parts; 19th century half calf, red label, rubbed, leading hinge splitting; from the collection of Fernand & Anne Renier. Alston IX 58.   Jarndyce 103-55 1996 £110.00

ASSOCIATION - FERNAND RENIER

JONES, STEPHEN   Sheridan Improved. London: printed by and for J. W. H. Payne, &c., 1812. Stereotype edition; oblong 8vo; slight stain at end of text, contemporary sheep with stain on back board, neatly rebacked; from the collection of Fernand & Anne Renier.   Jarndyce 103-191 1996 £65.00

KNIGHT, CHARLES   The Bridal of the Isles; a Mask. London: Effingham Wilson, 1817. 2nd edition; color frontispiece; contemporary half calf, gilt spine, black label; attractive, very good; from the collection of Anne and Fernand Renier, with booklabel.   Jarndyce 103-507 1996 £120.00

VOCABULA Amatoria; a French-English Glossary of Words, Phrases and Allusions Occuring in the Works of Rabelais, Voltaire, Moliere, Rousseau, Beranger, Zola and Others... London: privately printed for subscribers only, 1896. 4to; half title, title in red and black; uncut in blue boards, cream paper spine and paper label dulled and chipped, hinges splitting; from the collection of Fernand & Anne Renier.   Jarndyce 103-112 1996 £65.00

ASSOCIATION - RENOUARD

BEMBO, PIETRO, CARDINAL 1470-1547   Historiae Venetae Libri XII. Venice: Sons of Aldus, 1551. Folio; fine title woodcut of Mercury & Pallas within frame of Cupids and Angels, Aldine Anchor at end, woodcut initials; gilt calf, rebacked, Aldine Anchors gilt impressed on both covers, "vigilantibus" bookticket of 3rd Earl of Gosford; large paper copy; The Renouard copy. Adams B597. Renouard 152 no. 17.   Rostenberg & Stern 150-75 1996 $3,500.00

EURIPIDES   Tres Tragoediae, Phoenissae, Hippolytvs Coronatvs, atqve Andromacha... Antwerp: Ex officina Christophori Plantini, 1581. 16mo; paes 248, mainly italic letter, woodcut printer's compass device on titlepage, fairly uniform light age browning, paper flaw in 1 leaf with slight loss, later calf, rebacked, gilt triple border fillets, edges, inner dentelles and spine, corners and edges only very slightly worn, vellum endpapers; good copy. 19th French bibliographer Renouard had vellum endpapers in any Classical texts which he had rebound, & this vol. is likely to have come from his own collection. BM Dutch p. 73; Adams E1050; Voet 1145; Buelens/De Backer 224.8.   A. Sokol XXV-37 1996 £385.00

ASSOCIATION - CHARLES RENOUVIER

JAMES, WILLIAM 1842-1910   What Is An Emotion? N.P.: n.d., but 1884. 1st separate printing; 8vo; 18 pages; original stapled wrappers, in fine, fresh condition with just one light vertical crease, as if it were folded once for a brief pocket-journey home; presentation copy, inscribed by author for Charles Renouvier, French philosopher. Rare. Lakin & Marley 3-24 1996 $1,250.00

ASSOCIATION - WILLIAM REYNAUD

ORTA, GARCIA DE   Aromatum, et Simplicium Aliquot Medicamentorum Apud Indos Nascentium Historia... Antwerp: Ex officina Christophori Plantini, Arachitypographi Regii, 1579. 3rd Plantin edition; small 8vo; pages 217, (6), 28 woodcuts by Peter van der Borcht and Arnold Nicolai, old paper faults, repaired, with slight loss, title soiled, later full vellum; numerous old ownerships including presentation. to William Reynaud from Leonard Gillespie, Fort Royal Naval Hospital, Martinique, 1802.   Family Album Tillers-460 1996 $750.00

ASSOCIATION - CHARLES REZNIKOFF

BARNES, DJUNA 1892-   The Antiphon: a Play. London: Faber & Faber, 1958. 1st edition; some rubbing to spine, very good plus, lacking the dust jacket; inscribed by author to poet Charles Reznikoff. Between the Covers 42-29 1996 $1,000.00

ASSOCIATION - ANNE RICE

MC ELROY, JOSEPH   A Smuggler's Bible. New York: Harcourt Brace, 1966. Advance reading copy; author's first book; printed tan wrappers, very good; signature of Anne Rice on front panel (perhaps she review it?).   Pettler & Lieberman 28-171 1996 $135.00

ASSOCIATION - M. C. RICHARDS

OLSON, CHARLES　　Apollonius of Tyana. A Dance, With Some Words, for Two Actors. Black Mountain: Black Mountain College, 1951. 1st edition; one of only 50 copies printed, of which 30 were bound in wrappers and 20 in boards; 8vo; silk screen map by Stanley Vanderbeek; original decorated wrappers very slightly soiled, otherwise fine; rare. Excellent association copy, the copy of Olson's fellow Black Mountain College colleague, M. C. Richards, with her signature.　James S. Jaffe　34-523　1996　$3,500.00

OLSON, CHARLES　　Projective Verse. New York: Totem, 1959. 1st edition; 8vo; cover drawing by Matsumi Kanemitsu; original wrappers, lightly sunned along spine, otherwise fine, with errata slip; presentation copy, inscribed by author for MC (Richards).　James S. Jaffe　34-525　1996　$650.00

OPPENHEIMER, JOEL　　The Dutiful Son. N.P.: Jonathan Williams, 1956. 1st edition; one of 200 copies; 8vo; lithograph frontispiece by Joe Fiore, original printed buff wrappers, scarce; wrappers somewhat soiled; presentation copy inscribed by author for M. C.(Richards).　James S. Jaffe　34-527　1996　$500.00

ASSOCIATION - RALPH RICHARDSON

BOWLES, PAUL　　The Hours After Noon. London: Heinemann, 1959. 1st English edition; near fine in very good plus dust jacket with light surface chipping at spinal extremities, else bright; scarce; this copy came from the library of English actor Sir Ralph Richardson, and 2 pages of his pencil written notes on last blank page & back free e.p.　Thomas Dorn　9-41　1996　$750.00

ASSOCIATION - RICHARD RICHARDSON

ALPINUS, PROSPER　　De Plantis Aegyptis Liber...De Balsamo, Dialogvs (etc.). Venice: Francesco Franceschi, 1592. 1st edition of first work, 2nd edition of the second; 4to; ff. (iv), 80, (viii), Roman letter, woodcut printer's device on main titlepage (repeated on 2nd), many woodcuts of plants, mostly full page, woodcut initials and ornaments, titlepage bit dusty, frayed at edges and reinforced in gutter, light yellowing in parts, some outer margins lightly waterstained, small pieces torn from upper edges of last 4 leaves, without loss; contemporary calf, neatly rebacked, gilt double fillets & spine, outer corners worn; inscription recording gift by Richard Richardson of North Bierley to Thos. Knowlton 7.2. 1748/9 on endpaper. BM STC It. p. 20; Adams A803; Index Aurel 103.853; Pritzel 163;　A. Sokol XXV-3　1996　$2,850.00

ASSOCIATION - RICHELIEU

PERUCCI, FRANCESCO　　Pompe Funebri di Tutte Le Nationi Del Mondo. Verona: Francesco Rossi, 1639. Folio; pages 97, (90, engraved title; 30 engravings, numerous woodcut devices and illustrations; worn 18th century French full leather, each board stamped in gilt with large and impressive arms of the notorious Louis Francois Armand du Plessis, Duc de Richelieu; early engraved armorial ex-libris of a French Bishop, B. H. De Fourey, 18th century ms. ownership of John Carter. Brunet IV 524; Michel & Michel V. 6, p. 102.　Family Album Tillers-477　1996　$800.00

ASSOCIATION - OLIFFE RICHMOND

HOUSMAN, ALFRED EDWARD 1859-1936　　Last Poems. London: Richards, 1922. 1st edition; foolscap 8vo; 79 pages; original dark blue buckram, backstrip and front cvoer gilt lettered, backstrip lightly faded, good; Professor Oliffe Richmond's copy with 2 page letter dated 6th Feb. 1923 from Houseman to Richmond.　Blackwell's B112-157　1996　£500.00

ASSOCIATION - RIGBY

COWPER, WILLIAM 1731-1800　　Poems. London: printed for J. Johnson and Co., 1812. 6 3/4 x 4 1/4 inches; 2 volumes; very pleasing contemporary blond straight grain morocco, sides framed with lovely latticework border in gilt and blind, raised bands, spines attractively gilt in compartments featuring multiple plain and decorative rules and large scrolling and floral ornament at center, all edges gilt, spines evenly darkened to pleasing honey brown, very slight rubbing at spine ends, otherwise an ornate and charming contemporary set in fine condition, nearly immaculate internally; armorial bookplate of John Mackenzie of Dunvegan and with presentation inscription from Lydia to Alice Rigby.　Phillip J. Pirages　33-140　1996　$165.00

ASSOCIATION - DAISY RIGBY

BOTTOMLEY, GORDON　　Laodice and Danae. London: privately printed, 1909. 1st edition; 8vo; original wrappers, slightly creased and chipped at edges; few spots; presentation copy inscribed in author's hand to Daisy Rigby and John Gold.　R.F.G. Hollett & Son 78-326　1996　£55.00

ASSOCIATION - RIPLEY CASTLE

STEDMAN, JOHN　　Laelius and Hortensia; or, Thoughts on the Nature and Objects of Taste and Genius, in a Series of Letters to Two Friends. Edinburgh: ptd. for J. Balfour and T. Cadell, London, 1782. 8vo; xiv, 536 pages, with errata slip bound in at end; contemporary tree calf, neatly rebacked, fine; from the library of Ripley castle.　C. R. Johnson 37-77　1996　£450.00

ASSOCIATION - D. G. RIPPINGALE

MAUGHAM, WILLIAM SOMERSET 1874-1965　　Christmas Holiday. London: Heinemann, 1939. Spine cocked and slight foxing to outside edge, otherwise excellent in slightly chipped dust jacket; inscribed by author for D. G. Rippingale.　R. A. Gekoski　19-103　1996　£250.00

MAUGHAM, WILLIAM SOMERSET 1874-1965　　The Painted Veil. London: Heinemann, 1925. spine cocked and some offsetting to endpapers, otherwise very good copy; inscribed by author for D. Rippingale.　R. A. Gekoski　19-101　1996　£200.00

MAUGHAM, WILLIAM SOMERSET 1874-1965　　Theatre. London: Heinemann, 1937. Second free endpaper excised, spine slightly cocked and trifle foxing to outside edge, otherwise very good in slightly chipped and foxed dust jacket; signed by author for D. G. Rippingale.　R. A. Gekoski　19-102　1996　£120.00

ASSOCIATION - ALICE RITCHIE

SMITH, STEVIE　　A Good Time Was Had by All. London: Jonathan Cape Ltd., 1937. 1st edition; original binding, top edge dusty and partially faded, prelims, edges, endpapers and contents spotted, covers slightly marked, spine and cover edges darkened, head and tail of spine and corners bumped, very good, no dust jacket. Presentation copy from author for novelist Alice Ritchie.　Ulysses 39-542　1996　£185.00

ASSOCIATION - DAVID RITCHIE

MILLS, JOHN　　The Flyers of the Hunt. London: The Field and Ward and Lock, 1859. 1st edition; 7 1/4 x 5 inches; 5 p.l., 114, (1) pages; 6 etched plates (including frontispiece) by John Leech; fine honey colored polished calf by Riviere, spine attractively gilt in compartments featuring equestrian ornaments, red and green morocco labels, board edges attractively hatched in gilt, densely gilt inner dentelles, marbled endpapers, top edge gilt, original cloth bound in at back; top of back cover faintly faded, otherwise binding extremely bright entirely free of wear and very pleasing, fine internally. Modern signed engraved bookplate of David M. Ritchie. Podeschi 196.　Phillip J. Pirages　33-386　1996　$225.00

MILLS, JOHN　　Stable Secrets; or, Puffy Doddles, His Sayings and Sympathies. London: Ward and Lock, 1863. 1st edition; 7 1/2 x 5 1/4 inches; 112, (1) pages; vignette on title, 3 etched plates, including frontispiece; fine honey colored polished calf by Riviere, spine attractively gilt on compartments featuring equestrian ornaments, red and green morocco labels, board edges attractively hatched in gilt, densely gilt inner dentelles, marbled endpapers, top edge gilt, original cloth bound in at rear, text little darkened (because of inferior paper stock) and slightly soiled, otherwise excellent internally, one small spot on front cover, but handsome binding in fine, unworn condition, very attractive. Bookplate of David M. Ritchie. Podeschi 203.　Phillip J. Pirages　33-387　1996　$200.00

ASSOCIATION - RIVERS

ADAMS, JULIUS J.　　Challenge: a Study in Negro Leadership. New York: Wendell Malliet Co., 1949. 1st edition; fine in lightly worn, very good plus dust jacket with few small chips; inscribed by author to Justice Frances E. Rivers.　Between the Covers 43-240　1996　$165.00

ASSOCIATION - RIVERS

LINCOLN, C. ERIC   The Black Muslims in America. Boston: Beacon Press, 1961. 1st edition; some underlining, mostly in pencil and several pages dog eared thus, very good in like dust jacket with some general wear, internal tape repair and small stain on front flap; very uncommon in first edition; Justice Francis E. Rivers copy with his ownership stamp and presumably his underlining.   Between the Covers 43-357 1996 $125.00

ASSOCIATION - GEORGE BARCLAY RIVES

BAILLIE-GROHMAN, W. A.   Fifteen Years' Sport and Life in the Hunting Grounds of Western America and British Columbia. London: Horace Cox, 1900. 1st edition; 13 7/8 x 10 1/2 inches; 77 photos, 3 specially prepared maps, frontispiece, 3 color folding maps in rear pocket; green cloth shows light soiling and slight tan on spine, but little wear, endpapers split over rear hinge (no doubt owing to map pocket) and browned, photographic plate leaves foxed, mainly in margins, with stain or two in text and two text illustrations marked, overall sound, very good; armorial bookplate of George Barclay Rives, by Jos. Rith of Vienna. Riling (1951 ed.) 1488.   Magnum Opus 44-16 1996 $200.00

ASSOCIATION - ALASTAIR ROBB-SMITH

TOLLER, ERNST   Brockenbrow. London: Nonesuch Press, 1926. 1st English edition; small 4to; 50 pages; 6 litho plates of drawings by Grosz; original mottled decorated boards, paper label, overlapping edge at head of backstrip chipped away; good, uncut copy; from the library of Alastair Robb-Smith. Dreyfus 30.   Claude Cox 107-116 1996 £65.00

ASSOCIATION - JOHN ROBBINS

OVIDIUS NASO, PUBLIUS 43 BC - AD 17   P. Ovidii Nasonis Metamorphoseon Libri X. Philadelphia: William Spotswood, 1790. 1st American edition; small 8vo; pages (32), 328; old American leather backed boards; ms. ownership of John K. Robbins. Evans 22753.   Family Album Tillers-465 1996 $260.00

ASSOCIATION - BRIAN ROBERTS

SWIFT, JONATHAN 1667-1745   Miscellaneous Poems. Waltham St. Lawrence: Golden Cockerel Press, 1928. Limited to 375 numbered copies; wood engravings by Robert Gibbings; very good in scarce dust jacket with chip on right hand corner and head of spine, with TLS from Robert Gibbings to Brian Roberts.   Words Etcetera 94-492 1996 £135.00

ASSOCIATION - ELIZABETH MADOX ROBERTS

FORD, FORD MADOX 1873-1939   New York Essays. New York: William Edwin Rudge, 1927. 1st edition; limited to 750 copies; 8vo; cloth backed boards, lacking dust jacket with faint offsetting from clipping on half title, otherwise fine; inscribed by author for Elizabeth Madox Roberts.   James S. Jaffe 34-158 1996 $275.00

ASSOCIATION - ALAN JAMES ROBINSON

BROWNE, THOMAS 1605-1682   Pseudodoxia Epidemica: of Unicornes Hornes. Williamsburg: Cheloniidae Press, 1984. 1st edition thus, state proof issue, one of 15 copies only, all on obsolete Whatman paper (blue white laid ca. 1962) from a total issue of 225, all signed by the artist, as follows: 15 state proof copies in full vellum nonadhesive limp binding with an original drawing and an extra suite of proofs of the etching, 60 deluxe copies in vellum binding and an extra suite, 150 regular copies on T.H. Saunders Laid; page size 9 1/2 x 7 inches; bound by Gray Parrot in full vellum, matching quarter vellum sleeve for extra suites, all housed in vellum and linen clamshell box. Illustrated with 16 wood engravings and one etching by Alan James Robinson. Text is set and cast in Van Dijk Monotype in black and blue; this copy inscribed by Robinson to the noted collectors Mimi and Arnold Elkind and is signed on colophon by printer and binder as well as Robinson.   Priscilla Juvelis 95/1-53 1996 $1,500.00

ASSOCIATION - HENRY CRABB ROBINSON

HILLIAR, ANTHONY   A Brief and Merry History of Great Britain... London: printed for J. Roberts; J. Shuckburgh; J. Jackson; J. Penn, n.d. 1730. 1st edition; 8vo; early 19th century half red morocco, top edge gilt, some rubbing, in red half morocco slipcase; from the library of Charles Lamb, with his signature on titlepage, presented by Lamb to his good friend Henry Crabb Robinson. Outside rather dusty, but uncut and essentially in very good condition.   Ximenes 109-157 1996 $3,500.00

ASSOCIATION - HENRY SCHRODER ROBINSON

MERRITT, BENJAMIN DEAN   The Athenian Calendar in the Fifth Century Based on a Study of the Detailed Accounts of Money Borrowed by the Athenian State. Cambridge: Harvard University Press, 1928. 4to; 324, vii, 138 pages, 6 illustrations, 2 folding plates (in pocket at rear); original cloth; bookplate of Henry Schroder Robinson.   Archaeologia Luxor-3699 1996 $150.00

ASSOCIATION - SELMA ROBINSON

HEYWARD, DU BOSE   Jasbo Brown and Selected Poems. New York: Farrar & Rinehart, 1931. 1st edition; fine in lightly soiled, near fine pictorial dust jacket; inscribed by author for Selma Robinson.   Captain's Bookshelf 38-108 1996 $375.00

ASSOCIATION - ESTHER ROBSON

FERGUSON, RICHARD S.   Cumberland and Westmorland M.P.'s (sic) from the Restoration to the Reform Bill of 1867 (1660-1867). London: Bell and Daldy and Carlisle: C. Thurman, 1871. 1st edition; 8vo; pages xix, 478; frontispiece; modern half green levant morocco gilt, occasional spots, but very good; presentation copy inscribed by author for Miss Esther Robson.   R.F.G. Hollett & Son 78-154 1996 £150.00

ASSOCIATION - ROCK

HAMILTON, AUGUSTUS   The Art Workmanship of the Maori Race in New Zealand. Dunedin: New Zealand Inst., 1896. 4to; 448 pages; 65 plates, 78 other illustrations; green half morocco, covers slightly discolored in places; scarce; inked presentation from author for Dr. Ch. Rock.   Thomas Thorp 489-140 1996 £280.00

ASSOCIATION - LOUIS RODDIS

ROSE, A.   Napoleon's Campaign in Russia Anno 1812, Medico-Historical. New York: 1913. 1st edition; 212 pages; original binding; Louis Roddis's copy with his bookplate.   W. Bruce Fye 71-1815 1996 $125.00

ASSOCIATION - HIERONYMI REGII RODIEN

MANUZIO, PAOLO 1512-1574   Epistolarum Pauli Manutii Libri V. Venice: Paulus Manutius, 1561. 8vo; 248 leaves, italic; contemporary limp vellum; early ms. ownership of Hieronymi Regii Rodien, interesting and extensive early ms. notes on flyleaves. Renouard 184.19; Adams M485; UCLA IIIb/498.   Family Album Tillers-432 1996 $750.00

ASSOCIATION - ROBERT WILLIAM ROGERS

BURNEY, FRANCES   Tragic Dramas... London: printed by Thomas Davison, for the author and sold by J. Murray, 1818. 1st edition; 8vo; contemporary calf, panelled in blind, gilt borders, spine and inner dentelels gilt, marbled edges, some rubbing, spine dull; half title present, very good; bookplate of the Earl of Craven and later bookplate of Robert William Rogers. Stratman 719.   Ximenes 108-51 1996 $275.00

JOHNSON, SAMUEL 1709-1784   The Poetical Works of Samuel Johnson, LL.D. Dublin: printed for L. White, P. Byrne, and R. Marchbank, 1785. 1st Dublin edition; 12mo; contemporary calf, spine gilt; fine, scarce; bookplates of the Castle Freke Library and Robert William Rogers. Courtney p. 157; CBEL II 1126.   Ximenes 108-228 1996 $400.00

ASSOCIATION - WILL ROGERS

RUSSELL, CHARLES MARION 1864-1926   Trails Plowed Under. Garden City: Doubleday, 1927. 1st edition; small 4to; 5 plates in color, 5 black and white plates, 46 black and white illustrations; dust jacket with few chips, very good to fine; boldly signed and inscribed by Will Rogers.   George J. Houle 68-130 1996 $1,250.00

ASSOCIATION - ROGERSON

POTTER, BEATRIX 1866-1943   The Tale of Little Pig Robinson. London:
Frederick Warne & Co. Ltd., 1930. Early reprint; illustrations by author;
original pictorial cloth, dust jacket (extremities and corners somewhat
frayed, bit worn and soiled); very nice; presentation, inscribed by author
for Mrs. Rogerson. Very nice.   David J. Holmes 52-88 1996
$2,950.00

ASSOCIATION - ROLLE

NATTA, MARCO ANTONIO   Marci Antonii Nattae Astensis De Deo Libri
XV. Venice: Apud Paulum Manutium, 1560. Folio; 170 leaves, printer's
devices; 18th century full sprinkled calf, rubbed; despite some slight
staining, an attractive later Aldine folio; early engraved English Rolle
family armorial bookplate. Renouard 177.1. Adams N67; UCLA IIIb/481.
Family Album Tillers-455 1996 $750.00

REA, JOHN   Flora; seu de Florum Cultura. Or, a Complete Florilege,
Furnished with all Requisites Belonging to a Florist. London: by J. G. for
Richard Marriott, 1665. 1st edition; folio; (24), 239, (4) pages, including
"Mind of the front" leaf, added engraved title, 8 engraved plates,
woodcut initials and headpieces, title printed in red and black; calf, spine
gilt by Thomas Fowler, with his printed label "Bound for the library/of
the/ right Honorable Lord Rolle/ at Stevenstone/, by Thomas Fowler,
printer & bookbinder,/ Great Torrington. Anno Domini 1834". Absolutely
pristine, wide margined copy in very good, very slightly rubbed, ticketed
binding. Hunt 301; Wing R421.   Joseph J. Felcone 64-35 1996
$2,800.00

ASSOCIATION - T. W. ROLLESTON

SHELLEY, PERCY BYSSHE 1792-1822   A Philosophical View of Reform.
London: Humphrey Milford, Oxford University Press, 1920. 1st edition;
4to; pages xi, 94, 1 plate; frontispiece, original boards, cloth back. Fine
in little chipped and stained dust jacket, inscribed "John Quinn from T.
W. Rolleston Sept. 23 1920". Bookplate of Great American collector
Gordon Craig.   Howard S. Mott 227-128 1996 $135.00

ASSOCIATION - WILLIAM ROOTS

AUBREY, JOHN   The Natural History and Antiquities of the County of
Surrey; Begun in the Year 1673...and Continued to the Present Time.
London: printed for E. Curll, 1718-23. 1st edition; 5 volumes, extra
illustrated with 252 engraved, etched and aquatint plates; some offsetting
and spotting, pages 3-16 in volume 3 supplied in ms.; contemporary calf,
slightly rubbed, volumes 2 and 3 rebacked with original spines, all edges
gilt, bookplates and ownership inscriptions on titles of William Roots.
Note at beginning states "26 April/42 Lot. 59 - at Strawberrry Hill.." bt.
by Bohn".   Anthony W. Laywood 109-5 1996 £850.00

ASSOCIATION - DI CALVINA PERI DE ROPPA

PAULUS AEGINETA   Opera a Ioanne Guinterio Andernaco...
Strassburg: W. Rihelius, 1542. Folio; 2 parts in 1 volume, woodcut
device on title, minor browning, but good copy with two blank leaves;
contemporary limp green vellum, bit worn, ties missing; 17th century
inscription 'di Calvina Peri de Roppa, later in the Dr. O. Fisher medical
collection, sold at Swann 5 April 1978 lot 744 ($520.00). Durling 3554.
Maggs Bros. Ltd. 1190-478 1996 £1,800.00

ASSOCIATION - MARABEL RORISON

RILEY, JAMES WHITCOMB 1849-1916   Old Fashioned Roses. London:
Longmans, Green and Co., 1896. 16th edition; 12mo; frontispiece; original
parchment backed blue cloth, blue label lettered in gilt, some light soiling
and rubbing, endpapers and pages 82-3 are browned from offsetting
from inserts (removed). Inscribed to Miss Marabel Rorison with two
pleasant quatrains of verse in Hoosier dialect from author.   James
Cummins 14-167 1996 $100.00

ASSOCIATION - ROSEBERY

DAVIS, HENRY GEORGE   The Memorials of the Hamlet of
Knightsbridge. London: J. Russell Smith, 1859. 8vo; pages xi, 282, tinted
litho frontispiece, 7 tinted litho plates, text illustrations; original mauve
cloth, spine faded; Rosebery bookplate.   Marlborough 162-129 1 996
£80.00

ASSOCIATION - ABRAHAM SIMON WOLF ROSENBACH

JOHNSON, SAMUEL 1709-1784   Samuel Johnson's Prologue Spoken at
the Opening of the Theatre in Drury-Lane in 1747, with Garrick's Epilogue.
New York: Dodd, Mead and Co., 1902. 1st edition thus; large 4to;
original blue grey boards, printed paper side label, some wear to spine;
very good; presentation copy inscribed by A. S. W. Rosenbach for
Colonel Ralph Isham.   Ximenes 108-231 1996 $600.00

ASSOCIATION - PAUL ROSENFELD

CRANE, HART 1899-1932   The Bridge. New York: Horace Liveright,
1930. 1st trade edition, 2nd edition, extensively revised and corrected;
8vo; frontispiece by Walker evans; original blue cloth, covers slightly
rubbed, but very good; presentation copy inscribed by author for Paul
Rosenfeld, important association copy.   James S. Jaffe 34-120 1996
$12,000.00

ASSOCIATION - FRED ROSENSTOCK

ROGERS, JOHN WILLIAM   Finding Literature on the Texas Plains.
Dallas: Southwest Press, 1931. 12mo; 57 pages, frontispiece; cloth
backed boards, title in gilt on spine and front cover; very good+ with
pencilled marginalia by Fred Rosenstock. Dobie 10; McVicker, Dobie B14;
Jenkins BTB 167.   Bohling Book Co. 191-127 1996 $125.00

ASSOCIATION - WILLIAM ROTHENSTEIN

HENNELL, THOMAS   Poems. Oxford University Press/Humphrey
Milford, 1936. 1st edition; original binding, top edge slightly dusty, edges
slightly spotted, head and tail of spine and corners bumped, covers,
slightly marked, very good, no dust jacket; with ownership signature of
William Rothenstein; bookplate of literary agent John Johnson.
Ulysses 39-284 1996 £75.00

ASSOCIATION - BERTON ROUCHE

DE VRIES, PETER   The Blood of the Lamb. Boston: Little Brown,
1961. 1st edition; foxing to endpapers and edges of pages, thus ner fine
in like dust jacket foxed on flaps and with little tanning to spine;
inscribed by author for Berton Rouche and his Wife Kay.   Between the
Covers 42-133 1996 $250.00

ASSOCIATION - KAY ROUCHE

DE VRIES, PETER   The Blood of the Lamb. Boston: Little Brown,
1961. 1st edition; foxing to endpapers and edges of pages, thus ner fine
in like dust jacket foxed on flaps and with little tanning to spine;
inscribed by author for Berton Rouche and his Wife Kay.   Between the
Covers 42-133 1996 $250.00

ASSOCIATION - WILLIAM ROUGHEAD

DONELLAN, JOHN   The Trial of John Donellan, Esq. for the Wilful
Murder of Sir Theodosius Edward Allesley Boughton... London: sold by
George Kearsley...and Martha Gurney, 1781. 2nd edition; contemporary
quarter calf, rebacked, embrowning but well preserved; William
Roughead's copy with his bookplate and elaborate notes.   Meyer
Boswell SL27-229 1996 $650.00

ASSOCIATION - ROUSE

SCHLIEMANN, HEINRICH   Tiryns: the Prehistoric Palace of the Kings
of Tiryns. London: John Murray, 1886. 8vo; lxiv, 385 pages; 188
illustrations, 24 chromolithographic plates, 1 map, 4 plans; gilt pictorial
cloth, titlepage, worn at extremites, spine soiled and chipped, bookplate
removed; with signature of W.H.D. Rouse.   Archaeologia Luxor-3994
1996 $250.00

ASSOCIATION - CHARLES ROWLEY

MARRYAT, FREDERICK 1792-1848   Mr. Midshipman Easy. London:
Saunders and Otley, Conduit ST., 1836. 1st edition; 3 volumes; pages
(vii), 291; (vii), 306; (viii), 314 pages; uniformly bound by Hering in
marbled boards, half black roan with red gilt titles, extremities rubbed
and spines scraped, spine to volume III cracked, some page corners
missing, no loss, else very nice; all volumes inscribed by Sir Charles
Rowley.   Marjorie James 19-147 1996 £125.00

ASSOCIATION - ROXBURGH

MAC KENZIE, GEORGE 1636-1691   The Laws and Customs of Scotland, in Matters Criminal. Edinburgh: the Heirs & successors of Andrew Anderson for Mr. Andrew Symson, 1699. 2nd edition; folio; (viii), (292), (vi), 30, (ii), 31-32, (iv), 33-66, (iv), 62 pages; titlepage in red and black, 4 secondary titlepages; contemporary calf, rebacked, corners repaired; edges rubbed, closed tears in titlepage neatly repaired, without loss, paper uniformly browned, some minor soiling. Sound copy, early (1703) bookplate of Earl (later First Duke) of Roxburgh. Wing M168; Aldis 3866.   Robert Clark 38-74 1996 £380.00

ASSOCIATION - JOHN RUSKIN

BACON, FRANCIS, VISCOUNT ST. ALBANS 1561-1626   The Works of Francis Bacon... London: printed for a. Millar, 1765. 4to; 5 volumes; 4 steel engraved frontispieces, folding table; near contemporary full polished tan calf, gilt, spines with twin lettering pieces and 6 raised bands, panels with overall diaper pattern in gilt; each volume inscribed "To the Hawkshead Instiute, John Ruskin, Brantwood, Candlemasm 1883"; each volume with armorial bookplate of J. W. Cuthbert.   R.F.G. Hollett & Son 78-318 1996 £1,200.00

SHAKESPEARE, WILLIAM 1564-1616   The Works. London: Chapman and Hall, 1875-76. 3rd edtiion; 8vo; 9 volumes; 2 engraved portraits, plate of facsimile signatures; contemporary red hard grain morocco, spines divided in six panels by raised bands, gilt lettered in 3 panels, double blind rules, green silk markers, comb marbled endpapers, inner dentelles and edges gilt, little trivial rubbing, excellent set; John Ruskin's copy with his booklabel, 4 line ms. pencilled note in his hand on p. 363 vol. V.   Simon Finch 24-203 1996 £1,200.00

ASSOCIATION - JOHN JAMES RUSKIN

MITFORD, MARY RUSSELL 1787-1855   Recollections of a Literary Life. London: Richard Bentley, 1852. 1st edition; crown 8vo; 3 volumes; original cloth, gilt by Remnant & Edmonds, with their ticket, some very minor external wear, but very good; pleasing literary association, each volume bards contemporary ownership signatures of John James Ruskin, wine merchant and father of the Victorian sage.   Ash Rare Books Zenzybyr-68 1996 £195.00

ASSOCIATION - JOANNA RUSS

LE GUIN, URSULA   The Dispossessed. H&R, 1974. 1st edition; fine in near fine dust jacket; the copy of SF writer Joanna Russ, with her namd sticker, and this copy inscribed by author for Russ, fully annotated by Russ.   Aronovitz 57-677 1996 $500.00

ASSOCIATION - ANNIE RUSSELL

EGERTON, GEORGE, PSEUD.   Flies in Amber. London: Hutchison & Co., 1905. 1st edition; original cloth, covers little soiled and stained, endpapers somewhat browned as usual, edges foxed; scarce; presentation copy inscribed by author for Annie Russell (who wrote fiction under the name of "Annie Carruthers".   David J. Holmes 52-42 1996 $250.00

ASSOCIATION - HERBRAND RUSSELL

HAYES, ISAAC ISRAEL   The Open Polar Sea. London: Sampson Low, Son & Marston, 1867. 1st British edition; demy 8vo; xxiv, (456), 16 pages; plates and colored maps; original cloth, gilt, expertly restored and refurbished, endpapers rejointed, little dull and bumped, few slight marks, but good; bookplate of Herbrand Russell.   Ash Rare Books Zenzybyr-44 1996 £250.00

ASSOCIATION - TAYLOR RUSSELL

PLOT, ROBERT   The Natural History of Oxford-Shire, Being an Essay Toward the Natural History of England. at the theater in Oxford, 1677. 1st edition; folio; (10), 358, 1 f. errata, (10) page index, prelim imprimatur leaf, vignette titlepage, folding map and 16 engraved plates; contemporary calf, blind ruled panel, expertly rebacked with new gilt label; near contemporary ms. insdex on prelim blank and chapter numbers added by hand to the upper margin of each leaf; contemporary signature of Taylor Russell to front endpaper and Henry Blake to titlepage; good copy.   Ken Spelman 30-101 1996 £580.00

ASSOCIATION - THOMAS RUSSELL

MC GOWAN, EDWARD   Narrative of Edward McGowan, Including a Full Account of the Author's Adventures and Perils While Persecuted by the San Francisco Vigilance Committee of 1856. San Francisco: Printed by Thomas C. Russell, 1917. Reprint of 1857 edition, one of 200 numbered copies; 12mo; pages viii, 9-250, tinted frontispiece, numerous full page tinted illustrations, title in red and black; original light brown boards, paper spine label, very fine, clean copy; presentation inscription from printer, Thomas C. Russell to Herbert I. Priestley.   Argonaut Book Shop 113-439 1996 $300.00

REID, HUGO   The Indians of Los Angeles County. Los Angeles: Arthur M. Ellis, 1926. One of 200 copies; 9 1/2 x 6 1/4 inches; (viii), 70 pages; patterned grey baords with paper spine label, chipping to spine ends and label, paper over front joint cracked. Inscription from Ellis to a San Francisco publisher of Limited Edition reprints of rare California, Thomas Russell.   Dawson's Books Shop 528-201 1996 $135.00

ASSOCIATION - WILLIAM RUSSELL

REMARKS by a Junior to His Senior, On an Article in the Edinburgh Review of January, 1844 on the State of Ireland, and the Measures for Its Improvement. London: James Ridgway, 1844. 1st edition; 8vo; 83 pages, few contemporary annotations in pencil; recent printed blue boards lettered; very good; from the contemporary library of Lord William Russell with his signature. Black 5761; Goldsmiths 33602; not in Kress.   John Drury 82-240 1994 £95.00

WHAT is to Be Done? Or Past, Present and Future. London: James Ridgway, 1844. 1st edition; 8vo; (iv), 123 pages; recent printed blue boards lettered; very good; from the contemporary library of Lord William Russell with his signature on titlepage. Goldsmiths 33622 (2nd ed.); Kress C6518 (2nd ed.); Black 5803 (3rd ed.   John Drury 82-290 1996 £95.00

ASSOCIATION - JERRY SACKHEIM

WEST, NATHANAEL   A Cool Million. New York: Covici Friede, 1934. 1st edition; 1st binding in light tan cloth; near fine in very good+ dust jacket with few minor chips; excellent association copy, inscribed by author for Jerry Sackheim, scarce inscribed.   Lame Duck Books 19-582 1996 $7,500.00

ASSOCIATION - EDWARD SACKVILLE-WEST

SACKVILLE-WEST, VICTORIA MARY 1892-1962   Orchard and Vineyard. London: John Lane, Bodley Head, 1921. Boards slightly bowed and some wear to title plate on spine, otherwise excellent; bookplate of Edward Sackville-West, inscribed to him from author.   R. A. Gekoski 19-119 1996 £800.00

ASSOCIATION - SACVILE

BACON, FRANCIS, VISCOUNT ST. ALBANS 1561-1626   Of the Advancement and Proficiencie of Learning; or the Partitions of Sciences... London: printed for Thomas Williams, 1674. Folio; frontispiece, final printer's note, library stamps; excellently rebound in full calf, label, very good. With contemporary signature of R. Sacvile ap. 15.75 pre. 6s. Wing B312; Gibson 142.   Jarndyce 103-388 1996 £240.00

ASSOCIATION - SADLEIR

LEVER, CHARLES JAMES 1806-1872   The Fortunes of Glencore. London: Chapman and Hall, 1857. 1st edition; 8vo; 3 volumes; original green blindstamped cloth, spines lettered in gilt, cloth box, morocco label, lettered in gilt; just a few spots, but fine, bright copy; inscribed by author on titlepage for the Marchioness of Normandy; the Sadleir copy with his and other booklabels. Sadleir 1405; Wolff 4088.   Simon Finch 24-154 1996 £2,000.00

TROLLOPE, ANTHONY 1815-1882   The Way We Live Now. London: Chapman and Hall, 1875. 1st edition; 8vo; 2 volumes, pages (viii); (viii), 319, half titles; wood engraved frontispiece, 38 plates after Luke Fildes; original green cloth, upper cover decorated and ruled in black, lower cover in blind, spines lettered and decorated in gilt and black, the Sadleir copy with his bookplate and label of Barton Currie, joints and corners little rubbed, hinges to volume 1 split, but excellent copy. publisher's presentation copy, with blindstamp on titlepage to volume I "With publisher's compliments", the Sadleir copy. Sadleir 44; Tinker 2231; Wolff 6799.   Simon Finch 24-245 1996 £2,000.00

ASSOCIATION - GOSTA SAFLUND

VALMIN, M. N.   The Swedish Messenia Expedition. Lund: C. W. K. Gleerup, 1938. 4to; xv, 484 pages, 100 figures, 37 plates, 7 plans; original printed boards; very scarce; inscribed presentation copy to Gosta Saflund.   Archaeologia Luxor-4100 1996 $450.00

ASSOCIATION - HENRY W. SAGE

THRASHER, MAX BENNET   Tuskegee. Boston: Small Maynard, 1900. 1st edition; about fine, tipped onto free front endpaper is the conclusion of a letter signed by Booker T. Washington and dated 5 Jan. 1901, above the signature is written "Henry W. Sage/from.." It seems likely this was a presentation copy from Washington to Sage.   Between the Covers 43-422 1996 $425.00

ASSOCIATION - JAM SAHIB

PATMORE, COVENTRY   The Angel in the House. The Bethroal. London: John W. Parker and Son, 1854. 1st edition; 8vo; pages viii, 191; fine binding of aquamarine crushed morocco, spine divided in six panels by raised bands, gilt lettered direct in second, others with red heart shaped onlays within floral borders, place and date in gilt at foot, sides ruled around with dog tooth roll and double fillet enclosing deep border built up from leaf sprays, floral motifs, dosts, etc. and 6 red onlays of fans, inner dentelles rulled all round in gilt, cream watered silk doublures and endpapers, gilt borders, gilt edges by Sangorski & Sutcliffe, folding cloth box, lea. label; from the lib. of Maharajah Jam Sahib.   Simon Finch 24-178 1996 £380.00

ASSOCIATION - JOHN SAKS

ROSSETTI, DANTE GABRIEL 1828-1882   Hand and Soul. Hammersmith: Kelmscott Press, 1895. One of 525 copies; 16mo; printed in black and orange-red in Golden type on handmade paper, this copy being one of the American issue printed for Way and Williams, Chicago; woodcut double page title within vine and floral border and many decorated initials; bound in maroon morocco, covers set with panels of red and gold persian floral William Morris silk brocade, fine; from the library of John Saks with his bookplate and ink note.   Marilyn Braiterman 15-120 1996 $950.00

ASSOCIATION - ELLA SALMONSEN

MC MURTRIE, DOUGLAS C.   The First Printers of Chicago with a Bibliography of the Issues of the Chicago Press 1836-1850. chicago: the Cuneo Press, 1927. Limited to 650 numbered copies; 4to; 42 pages; 9 illustrations; black cloth backed marbled boards, gilt lettering on spine, headcaps and corners very mildly bumped, presentation copy with ink inscription from author to Ella M. Salmonsen; ex-John Crerar Library with booklabel.   Maggs Bros. Ltd. 1191-192 1996 £50.00

ASSOCIATION - HARRY SALZBERG

SINCLAIR, UPTON 1878-1968   100%. The Story of a Patriot. Pasadena: Published by author, 1920. 1st edition; 8vo; brick red cloth, spine ends and corners with slight wear, else about fine. inscribed by author for Harry J. Salzberg.   James Cummins 14-182 1996 $500.00

ASSOCIATION - NICK SAMPAS

KEROUAC, JACK 1922-1969   Satori in Paris. New York: Grove, 1966. 1st edition; very good+ in not quite very good dust jacket with rather large mostly closed tear to front panel; excellent presentation to author's brother-in-law, Nick Sampas.   Lame Duck Books 19-275 1996 $3,850.00

ASSOCIATION - SANDFORD

SPENSER, EDMUND 1552-1599   Thalamos or the Brydall Boure Being the Epithalamion and Prothalamion... At the sign of the Boar's Head, Manaton, Devon, 1932. Number 2 of 200 copies; octavo; pages 36; 4 full page wood engravings and tailpiece by Lettice Sandford, printed in Baskerville on Millbourn handmade paper; original sheepskin backed Cockerell marbled boards, top edge gilt, others uncut; inscribed at some length to Edwin & Margery Cox, from Christopher and Lettice Sandford. Claude Cox 107-23 1996 £85.00

ASSOCIATION - WILLIAM SANDYS

MILTON, JOHN 1608-1674   Paradise Lost...Paradise Regain'd...Samson...Poems. Birmingham: John Baskerville, 1758. 1st Baskerville edition; octavo; 2 volumes; original calf, now worn, joints and extremities rubbed and chipped, joints cracked and near breaking; signature of William Sandys dated March 1, 1759. Gaskell 4(a) and 5(a). G. W. Stuart 59-9 1996 $350.00

ASSOCIATION - WINTHROP SARGENT

STATIUS, PUBLIUS PAPINIUS   Statii Sylvarum Libri V./ Achilleidos Libri XII./ Thebaidos Libri II./ Orthographia et Flexus Dictionum Graecarum Omnium... Venice: In Aedibvs Aldi, et Andreae Soceri (Andrea Torresano), 1502. Small 8vo; last 20 leaves with slight dampstains, otherwise quite clean, worn 18th century calf; the copy of historian Winthrop Sargent. Renouard 35.7; Adams S1670; STC IT 646; UCLA I/49.   Family Album Tillers-585 1996 $1,000.00

ASSOCIATION - WILLIAM SAROYAN

HACOBIAN, M. P.   The Armenian Church - History, Ritual and Communion Service. Sydney: Robert Dey, Son & Co., 1947. 1st edition; 39 pages of text, black and white drawings; wrappers; spine slightly browned, cover edges slightly bumped; very good; presentation copy from author, inscribed for William Saroyan.   Ulysses 39-21 1996 £65.00

OLSON, CHARLES   Call Me Ishmael. New York: Reynal & Hitchcock, 1947. 1st edition; very good in good jacket that is edgeworn and spine faded, with several small closed triangular tears along spine; the copy of William Saroyan.   Ken Lopez 74-361 1996 $400.00

TASHJIAN, VIRGINIA A.   Once There Was and Was Not - Armenian Tales Retold. Boston and Toronto: Little Brown and Co., 1966. 1st edition; color drawings by Nonny Hogrogian; decorated boards; head and tail of spine and corners bumped, very good in nicked, rubbed and dusty, slightly creased dust jacket slightly browned at spine and edges; from the library of William Saroyan, inscribed by author; loosely inserted author's compliments slip, stamped by Saroyan "Received Jun 28 1967. W.S."   Ulysses 39-22 1996 £55.00

ASSOCIATION - THOMAS SATCHELL

HENDERSON, WILLIAM   My Life as an Angler. London: W. Satchell, Peyton & Co., 1879. 2nd edition; large paper copy, this being number 1, numbered and signed yb publisher; royal 8vo; xvi, 312 pages; woodburytype portrait, 6 full page wood engraved plates on india paper, 59 wood engravings in text engraved by Edmund Evans; contemporary dark green half morocco gilt, gilt edges, rubbed, very slight spotting throughout text; presentation inscription from angling bibliographer Thomas Satchell to John Moore.   Thomas Thorp 489-145 1996 £200.00

ASSOCIATION - CALUDE DE SAUMAISE

HOTMAN, FRANCOIS   Brutum Fulmen. N.P.: n.p., n.d., Leyden? 1585. 1st edition; 8vo; pages 234, (xi), Roman letter, quotations in italic, woodcut of the seal of Sixtus V; contemporary calf, spine gilt, worn in usual places; light age yellowing, generally good; autograph of Claude de Saumaise. not in BMC STC Fr. or Dutch; Adams H1056; Haag V 537. 1 copy in NUC.   A. Sokol XXV-52 1996 £750.00

ASSOCIATION - SAUNDERS

WHEWELL, WILLIAM 1794-1866   The Philosophy of the Inductive Sciences, Founded Upon Their History... London: John Parker, 1847. 8vo; 2 volumes, xxxii, (2), 708; xiv, (2), (3)-679 pages, large folding table; contemporary calf, elaborately gilt prize binding, five raised bands, marbled endpapers and edges; attractive; near fine; from the library of the medical historian John B. de C. M. Saunders, with his bookplate. Sotheran 5373; Duveen p. 617.   Edwin V. Glaser 121-321 1996 $450.00

ASSOCIATION - THEODORE SAUZIER

NEWTON, A.   President's Address to the Norfolk and Norwich Naturalist's Society. Norwich: 1888. Offprint; 8vo; 8 leaves; contemporary half leather, inscribed by author to Theodore Sauzier and with his annotations.   Maggs Bros. Ltd. 1190-589 1996 £55.00

ASSOCIATION - SAVAGE

FORSTER, JOHN   The Life and Adventures of Oliver Goldsmith. London: Chapman and Hall, 1848. 1st edition; illustrations; original pictorial cloth, all edges gilt, in cloth folding box (also little worn); inner hinges cracked as usual on this thick book, covers somewhat faded and worn; presentation copy, inscribed "M. W. Savage (probably the Irish-born novelist and editor, Marmion W. Savage) from his old and attached friend J.F." Bookplate of Estelle Doheny.   David J. Holmes 52-36 1996 $550.00

ASSOCIATION - JOHN SAVILE

MIEGE, GUY   A Relation of Three Embassies from...Charales II to the Great Duke of Muscovie, The King of Sweden, and the King of Denmark. Performed by the...Earle of Carlisle in the Years 1663 and 1664. London: Starkey, 1669. 8vo; full page portrait, publisher's list at end; calf, rebacked, scuffed, hinged; extremely rare English version; ownership signature of John Savile on titlepage. Wing M 2025.   Rostenberg & Stern 150-59 1996 $385.00

ASSOCIATION - SAVOY

VITA De'Beati Gaspar e Niccolo... Turin: Briolo, 1788. 8vo; vignette title, pages iii-viii, 263, printed on blue paper; contemporary crimson morocco gilt, covers with gilt double outer border and intertwined leafy inner border, wreath cornerpieces, flat spine gilt in 6 panels, panels with star and sunburst, black label lettered gilt, all edges gilt, marbled endpapers, gilt arms of Victor Amadeus III, Duke of Savoy from 1773-1796, to whom the work is dedicated, presumably the unique dedication copy. Marlborough 160-59 1996 £1,200.00

ASSOCIATION - ELLEN SAWYER

WHITMAN, SARAH   Hours of Life and Other Poems. Providence: Whitney, 1853. 1st edition; binding A; 8vo; original binding; light wear to spine, near fine; signature of Ellen Sawyer on f.f.e.p. BAL 21366. Charles Agvent 4-1184 1996 $150.00

ASSOCIATION - JOHN SCHIFF

STEPHEN, GEORGE   The Adventures of a Gentleman in Search of a Horse. Philadelphia: John W. Moore, 1857. 1st American edition, from the 6th edition; 8vo; illustrations; original red cloth, decorated and lettered in gilt and blind, some rubbing and soiling; some spotting, offsetting and browning, generally light; from the John Schiff collection with his bookplate.   James Cummins 14-195 1996 $150.00

ASSOCIATION - MORTIMER SCHIFF

BURTON, ROBERT 1577-1640   The Anatomy of Melancholy. Oxford: J. Litchfield & J. Short for H. Cripps, 1621. 1st edition; small 4to; with errata leaf (Ddd4) which is un folio'd, and the preceding leaf Ddd3; tiny hole in Hh6 affecting a few words; full crushed morocco with outer gilt fillet border inside of which is a blind fillet border, three quarter of an inch inside this outermost border are two sets of gilt and blind fillet borders, about one quarter inch apart and on the corners of this inner set of borders are four gilt fleurons, spine divided into six compartments by five raised bands, second and third of which contain the title information, others each contain a gilt fleuron and some gilt border decoration, board edges gilt with single gilt fillet, inner gilt fillets stamped at bottom of front turn-in, bound by Riviere & Son; in half morocco slipcase with inner chemise; with bookplates of T. G. Arthur and Mortimer L. Schiff. Grolier English 18; PMM 120; Maden/Oxford Books I, 115. II 90.   Book Block 32-52 1996 $14,500.00

ASSOCIATION - HEINRCIH SCHLIEMANN

BOETTICHER, ERNST   La Troie de Schliemann. Une Necropole a Incineration a la Maniere Assyro-Babylonienne. Louvain: Lefever, 1889. Offprint; 8vo; vii, 115 pages, 12 plates; half calf with 5 raised bands, marbled boards, spine chipped, bottom joint cracked but holding; from the collection of Heinrich Schliemann, and was acquired by Professor Akerstrom; with facsimile letter about acquisition; with remnants of Schliemann's paper private library label at foot of spine.   Archaeologia Luxor-3982 1996 $4,500.00

ASSOCIATION - HEINRCIH SCHLIEMANN

BURNOUF, EMILE   Memoires sur l'Antiquite: l'Age du Bronze, Troie, Santorin, Delos, Ycenes, le Parthenon, les Courbes, les Propylees, un Faubourg d'Athenes. Paris: Masionneuve, 1879. 8vo; 340 pages, 4 plates; half calf, rubbed, 5 raised bands, marbled boards, bottom joint starting but holding; from the collection of Heinrich Schliemann, and was acquired by Professor Akerstrom; with facsimile letter about acquisition; inscribed "....Schliemann admiration et affection, Em. Burnouf." (closely cut at top edge by Schoemann's bookbinder), also noted on same page as acquired at "Athens Sept. 1955" in hand of Akerstrom.   Archaeologia Luxor-3983 1996 $1,250.00

EVANS, JOHN   The Ancient Stone Implements, Weapons and Ornaments of Great Britain. London: Longmans, Green, Reader and Dyer, 1872. 1st edition; 8vo; xvi, 640 pages; 476 figures, 2 folding plates; original gilt pictorial cloth, spine faded, chipped and torn; from the collection of Heinrich Schliemann, and was acquired by Professor Akerstrom; with facsimile letter about acquisition; inscribed by author for Schliemann, with traces of Schliemann's private paper library label at foot of spine.   Archaeologia Luxor-3984 1996 $650.00

SALISBURY, STEPHEN   Troy and Homer. Remarks on the Discovers of Dr. Heinrich Schliemann in the Troad. Worcester: privately printed by Charles Hamilton, 1875. 8vo; 52 pages; original gilt lettered cloth, light shelfwear at spine; from the collection of Heinrich Schliemann, and was acquired by Professor Akerstrom; with facsimile letter about acquisition; with traces of Schliemann's paper private library stamp at foot of spine; inscribed by Scliemann by author.   Archaeologia Luxor-3986 1996 $650.00

SNIDER, DENTON J.   A Walk in Hellas, or the Old in the New. St. Louis: privately printed, 1881. 8vo; 350 pages; original publisher's gilt lettered cloth, spine with light shelfwear and tears, label no longer present; from the collection of Heinrich Schliemann, and was acquired by Professor Akerstrom; with facsimile letter about acquisition; inscribed by Charles Parsons for Schliemann.   Archaeologia Luxor-3988 1996 $450.00

ASSOCIATION - SOPHIA SCHLIEMANN

SCHLIEMANN, HEINRICH   Trojanischer Alterthumer. Bericht uber Die Ausgrabungen in Troja. Leipzig: F. A. Brockhaus, 1874. 1st edition; 8vo; lx, 320 pages, 1 plate; 19th century half calf with 4 raised bands, gilt lettered spine, initials "S.S." (for Sophia Schliemann at foot, original wrappers bound in (light rubbing at etremities), remnants of Schliemann's paper private label label at foot of spine; from the library of Ake Akerstrom.   Archaeologia Luxor-3981 1996 $15,000.00

ASSOCIATION - WILLIAM SCHROEDER

ROYLE, JOHN FORBES   An Essay on the Antiquity of Hindoo Medicine, Including an Introductory Lecture to the Course of Materia Medica and Therapeutics, Delivered at King's College. London: Wm. H. Allen & Co., and J. Churchill, 1837. 1st edition; 8vo; contemporary half morocco, hinges cracked; presentation inscription "To the editor of the Atlas from the Author", with signature and stamp of William Schroeder. Osler 109.   Anthony W. Laywood 108-229 1996 £175.00

ASSOCIATION - SCHUSTER

FITZWILLIAM MUSEUM   Catalouge. An Exhibition of Printing at the Fitzwilliam Museum, 6 May to 23 June 1940. Cambridge: 1940. Blue quarter morocco, marbled boards, original wrappers with Reynolds Stone's red insignia on upper cover bound in, bound for Schuster by his daughter Renate Hirsch, wife of Paul, with ink inscription "Bound for Papa, Christmas 1940, Renate Hirsch". Bookplate of Renate Schuster. Maggs Bros. Ltd. 1191-194 1996 £140.00

ASSOCIATION - RENATE SCHUSTER

PARRY, H.   The Art of Bookbinding: Containing a Description of the Tools, forwarding, Gilding and Finishing &c. Cambridge: ptd. by Thomas Wayte in Burton-upon-Trent, London: Baldwin, Cradock... 1818. frontispiece, title vignette; half calf, spine gilt in compartments, green morocco spine label, marbled boards, bit worn and rubbed at edges; booklabel of Renate Schuster (daughter of Paul Hirsch), bookseller's label of W. Heffer of Cambridge.   Maggs Bros. Ltd. 1191-24 1996 £850.00

ASSOCIATION - SCHWABACH

MAUPASSANT, GUY DE 1850-1893　Claire de Lune. Leipzig: privately printed for Erik-Ernst Schwabach, 1916. Number 7 of 7 copies; numbered in the press, this 'reserve pour M. Schwabach'; small 4to; full red morocco, gilt, backstrip repaired and darkened and sides somewhat sprung, but internally nice, slightly foxed; presentation from Schwabach presenting this to Gerta Herz, with Schwabach's bookplate.　Bertram Rota　272-130　1996 £110.00

ASSOCIATION - DELMORE SCHWARTZ

POUND, EZRA LOOMIS 1885-1972　Poems 1918-1921. New York: Boni & Liveright, 1921. 1st edition; 8vo; original quarter vellum and boards, spine cracking, boards slightly worn, not unattractive, but good copy only, in handsome quarter morocco slipcase; Delmore Schwartz's copy, complete with extensive annotations and one original Schwartz poem. Lakin & Marley　3-48　1996 $1,250.00

ASSOCIATION - DANIEL SCOTT

HOPE, WILLIAM H. ST. JOHN　The Abbey of St. Mary in Furness, Lancashire. Kendal: T. Wilson, 1902. Limited to 200 copies; large 4to; pages 82, 18 steel engraved plates on thick paper tipped on to guards, 12 collotypes, etc., 4 maps; prospectus for work loosely inserted; original buckram gilt, little soiled and rubbed; from the library of Daniel Scott of Penrith, with his booklabel.　R.F.G. Hollett & Son　78-998 1996 £180.00

HOWARD, CHARLES　Historical Anecdotes of the Howard Family. London: printed by G. Scott for J. Robson, 1769. 8vo; pages (vi), 201, engraved vignette on title; old speckled calf, edges worn and little scraped, sometime rebacked, spine worn at head and tail. signed on flyleaf by Daniel Scott of Penrith. Loosely inserted 4 page ALS from Philip J. C. Howard of Corby Castle, a pres offprint concerning the latter's Golden Wedding and an example of Corby Castle headed notepaper.　R.F.G. Hollett & Son　78-181　1996 £120.00

INSCRIPTIONS on the Great Picture at Appleby Castle, Painted for the Right Honourable George Clifford, Third Earl of Cumberland. Appleby: J. Whitehead, 1877. Small 4to; pages 27, margins ruled in red; original cloth, spine and edges faded; extremely scarce; from the library of Daniel Scott of Penrith, with his label and pencilled signature.　R.F.G. Hollett & Son　78-57　1996 £175.00

WILSON, JAMES　The Victoria History of the County of Cumberland. London: Constable, 1905. 1st edition; 4to; volume 2; pages xvii, 507, 14 plates and 2 maps, half title rather spotted, old stamps erased from titlepage; handsomely rebound in half crimson levant morocco gilt, arms from original cloth laid on to upper board. From the library of Daniel Scott of Penrith, with his label.　R.F.G. Hollett & Son　78-1388　1996 £85.00

ASSOCIATION - F. R. SCOTT

TRIO. First Poems by Gael Turnbull, Phyllis Webb, E. W. Mandel. N.P: Contact Press, c. 1954. 1st edition; unpaginated; printed wrappers; near fine, very scarce; inscribed by Phyllis Webb for F. R. Scott; recently inscribed to John Metcalf by Gael Turnbull.　Nelson Ball　118-173 1996 $800.00

ASSOCIATION - WESLEY SCOTT

DUDEK, LOUIS　East of the City (Poems). Toronto: Ryerson Press, 1946. 1st edition; 51 pages; boards, dust jacket; fine in near fine jacket; author's first book; with ownership signature of Wesley Scott; author's signed presentation to John Metcalf.　Nelson Ball　118-43　1996 $450.00

SOUSTER, RAYMOND　When We Are Young. Montreal: First Statement, 1946. 1st edition; unpaginated; plain card covers in printed jacket, edges of front cover time darkened, one short closed tear, about very good copy of author's first book; inscribed by author for Wesley Scott, from the library of John Metcalf, with his ownership signature. Nelson Ball　118-167　1996 $1,250.00

ASSOCIATION - HARRIET ELIZABETH SEARS

SMITH, SAMUEL B.　The Wonderful Adventures of a Lady of French Nobility, and the Intrigues of a Popish Priest, Her Confessor, to Seduce and Murder Her. New York: Office of the Downfall of Babylon, 1836. Probable first edition; 12mo; woodcut frontispiece; very attractive contemporary American red sheep gilt binding, rubbed along edges, small worm holes on front cover and along lower inner cover, blue coated endpapers, some spotting of text; with contemporary signature of Harriet Elizabeth Sears of Troy, with her stamp. Not in Shaw or Shoemaker.　James Cummins　14-187　1996 $275.00

ASSOCIATION - JOHN SAUNDERS SEBRIGHT

PENNANT, THOMAS 1726-1798　The Journey to Snowdon. London: printed by Henry Hughes, 1781. 1st edition; 4to; engraved vignette titlepage with ink inscription "A gift of my worthy Friend the Author", 197 pages of text (p. 173 misnumbered 137), 2 vignettes to letterpress, 11 engraved copperplates, plates in excellent condition; old speckled calf boards, slight surface wear in places, double gilt rule borders, gilt bands, tools and armorial device to panelled spine, red morocco label, speckled edges, marbled endpapers; armorial bookplate of Sir John Saunders Sebright.　Beeleigh Abbey　BA56-18　1996 £250.00

ASSOCIATION - JEAN SEGUIER

EUTHYMIUS ZIGABENUS　Commentarii in Omnes Psalmos. Paris: Charlotte Guillard, for J. de Roigny, 1543. 8vo; (31) leaves (of 32: fol. A5 of index missing, last blank present), 407, (1) leaves (last blank); italic for the text, roman for the commentary, with use of Greek in side notes and occasionally in the commentary, crible initials, ruled in red, 18th century sprinkled calf, flat spine handsomely gilt; on title are 2 early ownership inscriptions, incuding that of Jean Seguier ("Joannis Seguier & amicorum"); 2nd leaf lacking, otherwise fine copy; rare.　Jeffrey D. Mancevice　20-29 1　1996 $450.00

ASSOCIATION - KATE SELLARS

LOWELL, JAMES RUSSELL 1819-1891　The Vision of Sir Launfal. Boston: Fields, Osgood, 1870. Reprint; 8vo; illustrations by S. Eytinge; original binding, near fine. signed by author with inscription below in another hand, to Miss Kate M. Sellars; books signed by Lowell are not terribly common.　Charles Agvent　4-894　1996 $175.00

ASSOCIATION - DAVID SELZNICK

FITZGERALD, FRANCIS SCOTT KEY 1896-1940　Taps at Reville. New York: Scribner's, 1935. 1st edition; near fine in very good dust jacket with light edgewear; inscribed warmly by author to David O. Selznick in 1939.　Ken Lopez　74-137　1996 $25,000.00

PURDY, JAMES　Don't Call Me by My Right Name and Other Stories. New York: William Frederick Press, 1956. 1st edition; author's first book; wrappers, some faint creasing to covers, otherwise fine. Inscribed by author for David O. Selznick, laid in is a TLS from Purdy to Selznick presenting the book.　Left Bank Books　2-125　1996 $250.00

ASSOCIATION - SEMENS

THE LADIES Charity School-House Roll of Highgate; or a Subscription of Many Noble, Well Disposed Ladies for the Easie Carrying Of It On. London: 1670. 8vo; 292, (2) pages, drophead title, wanting the four plates; very attractive contemporary London binding in black morocco, richly gilt with all over gilt tooling of 'drawer-handles', tulips, rosettes, dots, pointed leaves, etc. repeated on lower cover, spine gilt in compartments, with presentation "To MADM SEMENS" in gilt in panel on upper cover, joints little rubbed.　John Drury　82-23　1996 £500.00

ASSOCIATION - RICHARD SENHOUSE

SCOTT, JOHN　Poetical Works. London: printed for J. Buckland, 1782. 1st edition; 8vo; illustrations; contemporary tree calf, nicely rebacked; very good; from the library of Richard Senhouse with his booklabel. Bentley 494; CBEL II 681.　Ximenes　108-320　1996 $600.00

ASSOCIATION - ROGER SENHOUSE

HAZLITT, WILLIAM 1778-1830   Political Essays, with Sketches of Public Characters. London: printed for William Hone, 1819. 1st edition; 8vo; contemporary half calf, spine gilt, bit scuffed, edges rubbed; very good; bookabel of Roger Senhouse. Keynes 49.   Ximenes 108-191 1996 $400.00

WELLS, HERBERT GEORGE 1866-1946   Phoenix - a Summary of the Inescapable Conditions of World Reorganisation. London: Secker & Warburg, 1942. 1st edition; publisher's copy with several pencilled corrections to text, slip of paper containing the new text fastened with paperclip to page 11; original binding, top edge dusty, head and tail of spine and corners bumped, very good in torn, creased, rubbed, soiled and dust dust jacket, browned at spine and edges. Loosely inserted APS from author to Roger Senhouse.   Ulysses 39-613 1996 £135.00

ASSOCIATION - ALEXANDRI SERITECOLO

PLUTARCHUS 45-125   Vitae Illustrium Virorum. Venice: Bartholomaeus de Zanis, 8 June, 1496. Folio; 290 leaves, roman letter, 62 lines and headline, woodcut capitals, woodcut border on a2r; later vellum, old paper repairs at lower corners of a1, marginal worming to last four leaves, touching one letter only, slight dampstain at head and beginning of second part, fol. 23. evenly browned, still good, fresh copy; library stamps of Alexandri Seritecolo on recto of first and verso of last leaf, inscription erased at foor of a24; HC 13130*; Proctor 5335; BMC V 432 (IB 23719); Goff P 834.   Simon Finch 24-186 1996 £3,500.00

ASSOCIATION - SERLE

SCLATER, W. L.   Systema Avium Ethiopicarum... London: 1924-30. 8vo; 2 volumes; interleaved; cloth, worn; from the library of Dr. W. Serle, with numerous notes.   Wheldon & Wesley 207-853 1996 £85.00

ASSOCIATION - DE SERZA

HOLLAND, HENRY RICHARD VASSALL FOX, 3RD BARON 1773-1840   A Dream. London: printed by Bensley & Sons, 1818. 1st edition; uncut as issued in drab wrappers, slightly creased and chipped at edges, library label; inscribed by Lady Holland for Mde. de Serza.   Jarndyce 103-491 1996 £120.00

ASSOCIATION - R. S. SETON

AUDLJO, JOHN   Journal of a Visit to Constantinople and some of the Greek Islands, in the Spring and Summer of 1833. London: Longmans, Rees, Orme, Brown, Green, Longman, 1835. 8vo; pages xii, 259; engraved titlepage, 2 (of 7) plates and 1 illustration in text; recent half morocco; very good; bookplate of Major R. S. Seton and of Larchmont Yacht Club.   Worldwide Antiquarian 151-60 1996 $165.00

ASSOCIATION - JOHN SEVERINO

NIXON, RICHARD MILHOUS 1913-1994   1999: Victory Without War. New York: Simon & Schuster, 1988. 1st edition; 2nd printing; 8vo; dust jacket; very good to fine. Signed and inscribed by Nixon to actor John Severino.   George J. Houle 68-106 1996 $350.00

ASSOCIATION - ERIC SEXTON

CYPRIANUS, SAINT, BP. OF CARTHAGE   Opera. Stuttgart: printer of the Erwahlung Maximilians, n.d., c. 1486. Folio; repairs to last leaf, without loss of text, some worming towards end, mostly minor; contemporary calf over wooden boards, upper cover stamped with floral pattern within triple fillet, a hop-vine roll tool, interesting outer frame of a dog, deer, another dog and a dragon chasing through flowering shrubs, lower cover, with same floral pattern in larger panel, surrounded by two stylized rolls and an outer frame of intersecting triple fillets, rebacked, preserving some of the original spine, brass clasps and catches, spine bit worn; essentially a large fresh copy; the Eric Sexton copy. Goff C1014; GKW 7887; HC *5895; Proctor 2750; BMC III p. 675.   Ximenes 109-94 1996 $6,000.00

ASSOCIATION - WILLIAM KEAN SEYMOUR

CLARKE, AUSTIN 1896-1974   Two Great a Vine - Poems and Satires - Second Series. Dublin; The Bridge Press, 1958. 2nd impression; wrappers; head and tail of spine and corners slightly bumped, cover edges browned, very good; presentation from author for William Kean Seymour, loosely inserted 2 page TLS from author.   Ulysses 39-112 1996 £115.00

ASSOCIATION - ROBERT SHACKLETON

BLACKWELL, THOMAS   An Enquiry Into the Life and Writings of Homer. London: printed in the Year 1735. 1st edition; 8vo; (iv), 335, (lxxxi) pages; frontispiece, folding map, 12 engravings in text, rubbed, extremities bit worn, closed tears in map and p. 54; both repaired, without loss; contemporary calf, old reback, label; some minor soiling; sound copy; bookplate of classical scholar Robert Shackleton.   Robert Clark 38-159 1996 £100.00

ASSOCIATION - R. E. DUNCOMBE SHAFTO

SILIUS ITALICUS, GAIUS   De Bello Punico Secundo XVII Libri Nuper Diligentissime Castigati. Venice: In Aedibvs Aldi, et Andreae Auslani Soceri (Andrea Torresano), July 1523. 1st Aldine edition; 8vo; 212 leaves; Italic Aldine devices on first and last leaves, blank portion of titlepage with old repair, otherwise really clean and tight; attractive half calf, gilt, marbled boards; engraved armorial Ex-libris of R. E. Duncombe Shafto; Dibdin II 405; Renouard 98.6. Adams S1134; UCLA II/194. Brunet V383.   Family Album   Tillers-571 1996 $1,250.00

ASSOCIATION - CHARLES SHARP

CAINE, HALL   The Bondman Play. London: Daily Mail, 1906. 1st edition; small 8vo; 6 of the 15 photographic plates are signed by the respective performer of the original production at London's Theatre Royal, including Frank Cooper, Henry Neville, Marie Illington, Lionel Brough, Marjorie Day and Austin Melford; red cloth; very good, occasional foxing. Signed presentation from author to Charles Sharp. Antic Hay   101-264 196 $175.00

ASSOCIATION - CHARLES KIRKPATRICK SHARPE

GLOVER, ROBERT   Nobilitas Poltica Vel Civilis. London: William Jaggard, 1608. 1st edition; 4to; 190, (1) pages; 9 full page engravings; contemporary full limp vellum, covers soiled, text leaf R4 wanting, one plate trimmed and mounted, various notices tipped to front endpaper, thus fair only; with ownership signatures of William Bedford and Charles Kirkpatrick Sharpe, with Bedford's bookplate.   Chapel Hill 94-222 1996 $125.00

ASSOCIATION - JOHN SHEEPSHANKS

BRYDGES, SAMUEL EGERTON, BART 1762-1837   Letters From the Continent. Kent: printed at the private press of Lee Priory by John Warwick, 1821. 1st edition; 8vo; 2 volumes in 1; 177, (178)-362 pages, 7 pages ads; full speckled calf by Riviere with a decorative gilt border, spine richly gilt in 6 compartments with 5 raised bands, extremities slightly rubbed, bookplates and short tipped in clipping, else tight, very good, one of the bookplates is that of John Sheepshanks, famous English art collector; very scarce, most likely issued in an edition of 250 copies.   Chapel Hill 94-255 1996 $450.00

ASSOCIATION - ROBERT PEEL SHELDON

STEVENSON, ROBERT LOUIS BALFOUR 1850-1894   Island Night's Entertainments. London: Cassell & Co., 1893. 1st edition; 1st issue; illustrations; decorated cloth; moderate edgewear, very good; price corrected in ink, ads dated March 1893; bookplate of Robert Peel Sheldon dated Sept. 1893; moderate edgewear, very good.   Charles Agvent 4-1041 1996 $185.00

ASSOCIATION - WILLIAM SHELDON

GABRIELSON, IRA N.   Birds of Alaska. Harrisburg/Washington: Stackpole Co./Wildlife Management Inst., 1959. Thick heavy 8vo; 922 pages; full color illustrations; very good in worn dust jacket. William Sheldon's copy.   Parmer Books Nat/Hist-091142 1996 $395.00

ASSOCIATION - SHELLEY

SHELLEY, PERCY BYSSHE 1792-1822   Shelley Memorials: from Authentic Sources. London: Smith, Elder and Co., 1859. 2nd edition; 8vo; pages x, (2), 290, (i) errata, frontispiece; contemporary half vellum, spine gilt, red morocco labels, red sides, endpapers and edges; inscribed by Lady Shelley for Charles Kegan Paul   Simon Finch 24-209 1996 £150.00

ASSOCIATION - JOANNA SHEPARD

HOWELLS, WILLIAM DEAN 1837-1920   Indian Summer. Boston: Ticknor & Co., 1886. 1st edition; decorated brown cloth, minor wear to spine tips, pages bit darkened, near fine; inscribed by author for his sister Joanna M. Shepard. BAL 9624.   Charles Agvent 4-675 1996 $1,200.00

HOWELLS, WILLIAM DEAN 1837-1920   The Mouse-Trap. New York: Harpers, 1889. 1st edition; 8 plates; original binding, slight hinge crack, spine sunned, soiled; very good; inscribed by author for his sister Joanna Shepard.   Charles Agvent 4-687 1996 $1,000.00

ASSOCIATION - PHILIP SHERIDAN

LYTTON, EDWARD ROBERT BULWER-LYTTON, 1ST EARL OF 1831-1891 Lucile. Boston: Osgood, 1873. 1st edition; light rubbing at extremities, else near fine in publisher's deluxe leather binding; inscribed by Civil War General, Philip Sheridan.   Between the Covers 42-393 1996 $650.00

ASSOCIATION - SHINWELL

BOOTHBY, ROBERT   Recollections of a Rebel. London: Hutchison & Co. Ltd., 1978. 1st edition; color frontispiece and numerous black and white photos; original binding, top edge slightly dusty, head and tail of spine slightly bumped, very good in nicked and slightly creased and frayed dust jacket. Inscribed presentation from author for Manny Shinwell.   Ulysses 39-57 1996 £75.00

CHURCHILL, WINSTON LEONARD SPENCER 1874-1965   Defending the West. London: Maurice Temple Smith Ltd., 1981. 1st edition; 4 maps, 8 figures, 3 tables and 4 black and white photos; original binding, fine in very slightly creased and marked dust jacket; presentation copy from author inscribed for Lord Shinwell.   Ulysses 39-110 1996 £55.00

CHURCHILL, WINSTON LEONARD SPENCER 1874-1965   Great Contemporaries. London: Macmillan & Co., 1942. Re-issue; rebound in half morocco with raised bands, marbled endpapers and top edge gilt, inscribed by Churchill for Emmanuel Shinwell.   Ulysses 39-108 1996 £2,500.00

CHURCHILL, WINSTON LEONARD SPENCER 1874-1965   Secret Session Speeches. London: Cassell & Co., 1946. 1st edition; 16 black and white photos; original binding, top edge dusty, head and tail of spine and corners bumped, covers bowed and slightly marked, cover edges rubbed and darkened; good, no dust jacket; presentation copy from author for Emmanuel Shinwell.   Ulysses 39-109 1996 £2,500.00

GREAT BRITAIN. LAWS, STATUTES, ETC. - 1946   Coal Industry Nationalization Act, 1946. London: HMSO, 1946. 1st edition; interleaved throughout with blank leaves; full vellum covers, bound by Hatchards, the words "The Rt. Hon. Emanuel Shinwell M.P." are stamped in gilt on upper cover, top edge gilt, covers bowed and slightly marked and soiled, spine and cover edges darkened, front free endpaper slightly creased, edges slightly browned; very good. Signed by all members of the first National Coal Board.   Ulysses 39-113 1996 £475.00

MONTGOMERY OF ALAMEIN, BERNARD LAW MONTGOMERY, 1ST VISCOUNT 1887-   Normandy to the Baltic. London: privately printed for private circulation... 1946. 1st edition; 279 pages, 46 folding maps, 3 diagrams; original binding, page edges browned, spine browned, worn and chipped, tail of spine and bottom edge of upper cover dampstained, covers slightly marked, good. presentation copy to the Secretary of State for War, Manny Shinwell.   Ulysses 39-416 1996 £600.00

WELLS, HERBERT GEORGE 1866-1946   The Outlook for Homo Sapiens... London: Martin Secker and Warburg Ltd., 1942. 1st edition; rebound in half morocco with raised bands, top edge gilt, marbled endpapers, spine rubbed, upper cover slightly creased; very good; presentation copy, inscribed by author for Emanuel Shinwell.   Ulysses 39-612 1996 £185.00

ASSOCIATION - LOUIS EVAN SHIPMAN

PINERO, ARTHUR   The Enchanted Cottage. London: William Heinemann, 1922. 1st published edition; 8vo; original printed wrappers, some creasing, tear repaired on upper cover, upper cover detached, light marginal browning, else very good; inscribed by author for Louis Evan Shipman, tipped in TLS sending the volume to Shipman.   James Cummins 14-156 1996 $350.00

ASSOCIATION - PHILIP SHIRLEY

PETRIE, ADAM   Rules of Good Deportment, or of Good Breeding. Edinburgh: n.p., 1835. One of 45 copies; 4to; (iv), iii, (9), 136 pages; full calf, all edges gilt; bookplate of Philip Shirley.   The Bookpress 75-448 1996 $1,200.00

ASSOCIATION - J. SHORT

MACHIAVELLI, NICCOLO 1469-1527   The Florentine History in VII Books. London: printed for Charles Harper and John Amery, 1674. 1st edition of this translation. Small 8vo; 654 pages, frontispiece, each book separately paginated; repaired hole in titlepage, rebound, German style full leather; early ms. ownerships of J. Short.   Family Album Tillers-421 1995 $220.00

ASSOCIATION - CLEMENT SHORTER

STEVENSON, ROBERT LOUIS BALFOUR 1850-1894   The Waif Woman. London: Chatto & Windus, 1916. 1st edition; 24mo; drab boards, purple cloth spine, some wear to edges, but generally very good copy of this fragile book; ex-libris of Clement Shorter with his bookplate. Prideaux 74.   Priscilla Juvelis 95/1-226 1996 $150.00

ASSOCIATION - LOUIS SIMPSON

COHEN, LEONARD   Selected Poems. New York: Viking, 1968. Uncorrected proof; spiral bound in wrappers, slight darkening to edge of pages, else about fine; this is poet Louis Simpson's copy with his pencil ownership signature, very scarce proof.   Between the Covers 42-106 1996 $375.00

ASSOCIATION - GEORGE SIMS

TENNYSON, ALFRED TENNYSON, 1ST BARON 1809-1892   In Memoriam. London: Macmillan & Co., 1896. Later edition; 12mo; original green cloth, slightly worn; quarter morocco box; presentation copy from Edward Thomas to his future Mother-in-law, Mrs. Noble; important ALS to Mrs. Nobel; Edward Thomas letters are scarce; with two George Sims bookplates.   Lakin & Marley 3-66 1996 $2,500.00

ASSOCIATION - HUGH MACDONALD SINCLAIR

FULTON, JOHN F.   A Bibliography of the Honourable Robert Boyle. N.P.: n.d. Early galley copy of the Oxford University Press 1932 edition; 8vo; 172 pages; uncut, bound in plain blue linen, heavily annotated in the hand of Hugh MacDonald Sinclair, significant collector of Boyle; choice association, with TLS from Fulton to Sinclair.   James Tait Goodrich K40-36 1996 $795.00

ASSOCIATION - CHARLES SINGER

CREIGHTON, C.   A History of Epidemics in Britian. Cambridge: 1891-94. 1st edition; 8vo; 2 volumes; cloth, bit worn and scuffed; Charles Singer's copy with his signature.   Maggs Bros. Ltd. 1190-391 1996 £80.00

ASSOCIATION - ISAAC SINGER

BOGAN, LOUISE   Selected Criticism - Poetry & Prose. London: Noonday Press, 1955. 1st edition; original binding, top edge dusty, front gutter slightly spotted, head and tail of spine and corners slightly bumped, very good in nicked, chipped, rubbed, marked and dusty, slightly creased dust jacket darkened at spine and edges; presentation copy from author to Isaac Singer.   Ulysses 39-56 1996 £135.00

ASSOCIATION - ISAAC SINGER

JOHNSTON, JENNIFER   The Christmas Tree. London: Hamish Hamilton, 1981. 1st edition; original binding, head and tail of spine and corners bumped, very good in very slightly marked and dusty dust jacket. Presentation copy from author, inscribed for Isaac Bashevis Singer.   Ulysses 39-321 1996 £75.00

ASSOCIATION - SIDNEY SKOLSKY

GABLE, KATHLEEN   Clark Gable: a Personal Portrait. Englewood Cliffs: Prentice Hall, 1961. 1st edition; frontispiece, black and white photos, dust jacket (few nicks); very good. Signed and inscribed by author to columnist Sidney Skolsky.   George J. Houle 68-52 1996 $150.00

ASSOCIATION - ALEXANDER SMELLIE

KERR, R.   Memoirs of the Life, Writings and Correspondence of William Smellie. Edinburgh: 1811. 1st edition; 8vo; 2 volumes; portrait, plate; calf, rebacked; inscribed by Alexander Smellie (the son) to Sir John Majoribanks, Lord Provost.   Maggs Bros. Ltd. 1190-246 1996 £120.00

ASSOCIATION - WARREN SMIRL

DARWIN, CHARLES ROBERT 1809-1882   On the Origin of Species by Means of Natural Selection. London: 1859. 1st edition; 8vo; folding diagram, with half title, but without inserted ads, usually found; late 19th century half green morocco, date tooled at foot of spine (which is faded to brown), little worn and scuffed, signature of John Anderson, later in the collection of Dr. Warren G. Smirl, bought from Quaritch in 1978 for $1700.   Maggs Bros. Ltd. 1190-231 1996 £4,200.00

ASSOCIATION - CLARK ASHTON SMITH

LOVECRAFT, H. P.   The Outsider and Others. Sauk City: Arkham House, 1939. 1st edition; first book from this publisher; near fine in most attractive very good dust jacket with some light wear and tear; laid into this copy is an envelope addressed to Clark Ashton Smith in Lovecraft's hand.   Aronovitz 57-720 1996 $2,250.00

ASSOCIATION - DOC SMITH

HOWARD, ROBERT E.   Skull Face and Others. Sauk City: Arkham House, 1946. 1st edition; very good+ in very good dust jacket with some wear and tear; Doc Smith's copy with his hand printed name and address, and his hand printed pencil notations on contents page and verso.   Aronovitz 57-566 1996 $500.00

LEINSTER, M.   Operation: Outer Space. Fantasy Press, 1954. 1st edition; 1/300 copies of the signed/plated edition; inscribed to Doc smith; near fine in dust jacket.   Aronovitz 57-691 1996 $750.00

ASSOCIATION - JOHN PYE SMITH

COLERIDGE, SAMUEL TAYLOR 1772-1834   The Plot Discovered; or an Address to the People Against Minsterial Treason. Bristol: 1795. 1st edition; small 8vo; 52 pages; preserved in full brown crushed morocco folding case, title slightly dusty, tiny mark in lower outer corner affecting first four leaves, very good. Presentation copy with author's autograph inscription for John Pye Smith (1774-1851) non-conformist divine. Wise 4; Tinker 675.   Simon Finch 24-42 1996 £5,000.00

ASSOCIATION - FRANK SMYTHE

RUTTLEDGE, H.   Everest 1933. London: 1934. 1st edition; 59 sepia plates, 4 maps, 3 diagrams; very good/fine; inscribed by Frank Smythe.   Moutaineering Books 8-R32 1996 £100.00

ASSOCIATION - DUDLEY SNELGROVE

LARKIN, PHILIP 1922-   All What Jazz - a Record Diary 1961-68. London: Faber & Faber, 1970. 1st edition; original binding, head and tail of spine & corners slightly bumped, spine and cover edges slightly faded, some offsetting to covers from dust jacket, very good in slightly creased and dusty dust jacket; presentation copy from author to Dudley Snelgrove, loosely inserted 2 page ALS from author to presentee.   Ulysses 39-350 1996 £985.00

ASSOCIATION - WILLIAM SNOOKE

JOHNSON, SAMUEL 1709-1784   A Dictionary of the English Language. London: printed by W. Strahan, for J. & P. Knapton, T. & T. Longman, &c., 1755-56. 2nd edition; folio; 2 volumes; titles in red and black, unpaginated; handsomely rebound in half calf, marbled boards, red and black labels, library stamps on title versos, tiny ink stain on top edge volume 1, slight worming in early leaves volume 2, but very good, clean copy. Inscription of William Snooke, 1758; early bookseller's ticket for John Levery, Poultry, London, with small Gloucester library stamps.   Jarndyce 103-164 1996 £2,800.00

ASSOCIATION - EDITH SNOW

WERFEL, FRANZ   The Forty Days of Musa Dagh. New York: Modern Library, 1934. 1st Modern Library edition; very good+ in less than very good dust jacket; inscribed by author for Edith Snow.   Lame Duck Books 19-574 1996 $175.00

WERFEL, FRANZ   Hearken Unto the Voice. New York: Viking, 1938. 1st U. S. edition; near fine in dust jacket; inscribed by author for Edith Snow.   Lame Duck Books 19-577 1996 $500.00

WERFEL, FRANZ   The Pascarella Family. New York: Viking, 1935. 1st U.S. edition; V+ in very good dust jacket with chipping to extremities, inscribed by author for Edith Snow.   Lame Duck Books 19-575 1996 $250.00

WERFEL, FRANZ   Poems. Princeton: Princeton University, 1945. 1st edition; near fine in very good+ dust jacket with some minor chips and tears; this copy inscribed by translator, Edith Snow to her husband.   Lame Duck Books 19-581 1996 $275.00

WERFEL, FRANZ   The Song of Bernadette. New York: Viking, 1942. 1st U.S. edition and 1st English translation; spine lightly tanned, else very good+ or better in very good dust jacket with chipping to extremities and couple of edge tears to rear panel; this copy inscribed by author for Edith Snow.   Lame Duck Books 19-580 1996 $850.00

WERFEL, FRANZ   The Twilight of a World. New York: Viking, 1937. 1st U.S. edition; near fine in very good dust jacket with several chips and tears; inscribed by author for Edith Snow.   Lame Duck Books 19-576 1996 $350.00

WERFEL, FRANZ   Verdi. New York: S&S, 1926. 3rd printing; very good+; inscribed by author to Edith Snow.   Lame Duck Books 19-573 1996 $100.00

ASSOCIATION - SOMERSET

STERLING, WILLIAM   Annals of the Artists of Spain. London: John Ollivier, 1848. 1st edition;one of 25 extra illustrated sets; thick octavo; 2 volumes; pages 1480 in all; 52 illustrations, plus an additonal 6 noted by Stirling on holograph page; bound by Leighton in red striated morocco, raised bands, all edges gilt, 7 coats of arms in gilt on front covers, gilt monograms on backs, marbled endpapers, bound for Duke of Somerset, with his fine armorial bookplate in volume 1.   Hartfield 48-L81 1996 $850.00

ASSOCIATION - SUSAN SONTAG

HUSSERL, EDMUND   L'Origine de la Geometrie. Paris: Presses Universitaires de France, 1962. 1st edition translated by Jacques Derrida. Wrappers; near fine; exceptional association copy, inscribed by Derrida to American critic and novelist Susan Sontag.   Lame Duck Books 19-460 1996 $1,500.00

ASSOCIATION - SOTHEBY

NEWELL, R. H.   Letterwriters on the Scenery of Wales... London: for Baldwin Cradock and Joy, 1821. 8vo; xiv, (2), 192 pages, half title, vignette titlepage, 10 aquatint plates; contemporary half calf; very good; bookplate of C. W. H. Sotheby.   Ken Spelman 30-97   1996 £160.00

ASSOCIATION - W. SOWERBY

SOWERBY, JAMES 1757-1822   A New Elucidation of Colours, Original Prismatic and Material... London: 1809. 4to; pages (iv), 51, 1 plain and 6 colored plates; original boards, uncut, spine worn, contents good; bookplate of W. Sowerby.   Wheldon & Wesley 207-103   1996 £600.00

ASSOCIATION - JOHN SPARROW

AUSTEN, JANE 1775-1817   Charades Etc. London: Pub. Spottiswoode & Co., n.d. 1895. 1st edition; 9 x 5 1/2 inches; 34 pages, illustrations; cream wrappers lettered in black and red on front, cased in dark red rexine backed paper covered boards; fine, scarce; John Sparrow's copy with his bookplate and signature. Gilson F2; Keynes 169; Chapman 31. Ian Hodgkins 78-4   1996 £130.00

AUSTEN, JANE 1775-1817   Lady Susan. London: Oxford University Press, 1925. Limited to 250 copies; 7 3/4 x 5 inches; large paper copy, pages vii, 173, 15 pages; white linen backed grey boards, printed paper title label, backstrip, spare label rear, uncut, title label slightly discolored; fine; initialled presentation copy from editor, R. W. Chapman to John Sparrow. Gilson F5; Keynes 176; Chapman 28.   Ian Hodgkins 78-13 1996 £125.00

AUSTEN, JANE 1775-1817   The Watsons. London: Oxford University Press, 1927. Limited to 250 copies; 7 1/2 x 5 inches; pages vii, 121, 42; printed on handmade paper; frontispiece; white linen backed grey boards, printed paper title label backstrip, uncut and unopened, title label slightly discolored, corners very slightly bruised; fine; John Sparrow's copy with his bookplate. Gilson F10; Keynes 180; Chapman 26.   Ian Hodgkins 78-54   1996 £120.00

BERLIN, ISAIAH   Historical Inevitability. London: Oxford University Press, 1954. 1st edition; wrappers, yapp edges creased, nicked and slightly chipped, covers slightly marked and creased, head and tail of spine and corners bumped; very good; presentation copy from author to John Sparrow.   Ulysses 39-48   1996 £95.00

CATULLUS, C. VALERIUS   (Opera). Caius Valerius Catullus et in Eum Isaaci Vossi Observationes. N.P.: Leyde: Prostat apud Isaacum Littleburii Bibilioplam Londinensem, 1684. 1st edition by Vossius; and first edition of Catullus to be published in England; small 4to; 18th century French red morocco, gilt, spine and inner dentelles gilt, all edges gilt (attributed in pencil note to Derome); some foxing and light browning, but fine in elegant early binding; from the library of John Sparrow. Wing C1526. Ximenes 109-74   1996 $600.00

CLEVELAND, JOHN   Poems... (with) Cleveland Revived: Poems, Orations, Epistles and Other of His Genuine Incomparable Pieces. London: ptd. by S. G. for John Williams/London: ptd. for Nathaniel Brooks, 1668. 4th edition; 8vo; 2 volumes in one; contemporary calf, rebacked, front joint quite weak; very good, booklabel of John Sparrow. Wing C4697 and 4677; Morris P16 and CR4.   Ximenes 108-77   1996 $300.00

COKE, EDWARD 1552-1634   La Size Part des Reports Sr. Edw. Coke Chiualer,, Chief Iustice del Common Banke (etc.). London: printed for the Societie of Stationers, 1607. contemporary vellum, worn, else very fresh; John Sparrow's copy.   Meyer Boswell SL26-47   1996 $1,250.00

GILCHRIST, OCTAVIUS GRAHAM   Rhymes. London: 1805. 1st edition; 8vo; contemporary red straight grained morocco, gilt, gilt Lowther monograms on each cover, all edges gilt, spine bit faded, very slight rubbing; elegant copy; presentation copy, inscribed by recipient William Lowther, later 2nd Earl of Lonsdale also from the library of John Sparrow.   Ximenes 108-159   1996 $750.00

GILPIN, WILLIAM 1724-1804   Three Dialogues on the Amusements of Clergymen. London: printed for B. and J. White, 1796. 1st edition; 8vo; original pale blue wrappers, rebacked to match at an early date; half title present, fine, uncut copy, scarce; booklabel of John Sparrow. CBEL II 1561.   Ximenes 108-162   1996 $300.00

HUNTER, JOHN   A Tribute to the Manes of Unfortunate Poets; in Four Cantos. London: printed for T. Cadell, Junior and W. Davies, 1798. 1st edition; small 8vo; original pink boards, drab paper backstrip, very slight wear; fine, very scarce; booklabel of John Sparrow. Ximenes 108-212   1996 $500.00

ASSOCIATION - JOHN SPARROW

JOHNSON, SAMUEL 1709-1784   The Life of Samuel Johnson, LL.D.... (with) The Poetical Works... London: G. Kearlsey, 1785/85. 2nd edition; 12mo; iv, 209, (iii) pages; viii, 196, (iv) pages, 4 pages ads at end, A2-N2-4 cancels as usual; frontispiece; bound together in contemporary tiger striped half calf, marbled boards, spine gilt, corners little worn, spine rather rubbed, internally very good. With John Sparrow's booklabel.   Robert Clark 38-185   1996 £550.00

LETTSOM, J. C.   The Naturalist's and Traveller's Companion... London: 1799. 3rd edition; 8vo; engraved title with hand colored vignette, hand colored frontispiece, 3 plates; original boards, uncut, worn, front cover nearly off; John Sparrow's copy.   Maggs Bros. Ltd. 1190-248   1996 £75.00

MOON, ANNA MARIA   In Memoriam. The Rev. W. Leeves, Author of the Air of 'Audl Robin Gray''. N.P.; printed for private circulation, 1873. 8vo; pages xvi, (ii), 185, viii, 11, (12); frontispiece, plate, half title; contemporary dark blue morocco, double and single fillet borders to sides, enclosing ornaments and lettered on upper cover, spine in compartments with raised bands, gilt rules and lettering, gilt edges and inner dentelles, white silk endpapers; few ms. corrections in pencil, extremities rubbed, but very good; booklabel of John Sparrow; presentation copy inscribed by author.   Simon Finch 24-174   1996 £90.00

POOLE, JACOB   A Glossary, with some Pieces of Verse, of the Old Dialect of the English Colony in the Baronies of Forth and Bargy, County of Wexford, Ireland. London: J. Russell Smith, 1867. Half title; original green cloth, slightly rubbed; bookplates of Charles Doble & John Sparrow.   Jarndyce 103-92   1996 £110.00

POPE, ALEXANDER 1688-1744   The Works. London: Bernard Lintot, 1717. 1st issue; half title, titlepage in red and black, numerous finely engraved head and tail pieces and large initial letters by Gribelin, lacks frontispiece; finely bound in full contemporary red morocco, boards with several gilt panels, floral devices at corners and sides, enclosing different gilt rolls and more floral devices, outer gilt fillet border with small gilt leaves in corners, upper joint cracking but firm, spine elaborately gilt in compartments, all edges gilt, attractive early 18th century English binding; with signature of Joseph Sanford (or Sandford) dated 1717, the scholar & book collector; bookplates of John Sparrow & H.R. Pakenham.   Ian Wilkinson 95/1-136   1996 £450.00

ASSOCIATION - ALEXANDER SPEIRS

BYRON, GEORGE GORDON NOEL, 6TH BARON 1788-1824   Marino Faliero, Doge of Venice an Historical Tragedy. London: John Murray, 1821. 1st edition; 1st issue; 8 1/2 x 5 1/2 inches; xxi, (1), 261, (1) pages, (1) leaf (ads); pleasing probably contemporary diced calf, sides framed with double gilt fillets and decorative floral blind rule, central panel in blind with large arabesque at middle, raised bands, spine gilt in compartments, featuring large foliate stamp, dark blue double labels, marbled edges; leather little faded and slightly soiled, joints and extremities with minor rubbing, but solid and attractive binding in excellent condition, very fine internally; bookplate of Alexander Speirs of Elderslie.   Phillip J. Pirages 33-118   1996 $165.00

ASSOCIATION - ARCHIBALD SPEIRS

MERCIER, LOUIS SEBASTIEN   Paris In Miniature: Taken from...Tableau de Paris... London: Kearsly, 1782. Tall 8vo; publisher's list at end; quarter calf; armorial bookplate of Archibald Speirs of Elerslee. Halkett & Laing IV 300.   Rostenberg & Stern 150-24   1996 $385.00

ASSOCIATION - SPENCER

BERKELEY, GEORGE MONCK 1763-1793   Literary Relics: Containing Original Letters from King Charles II. King James II. The Queen of Bohemia, Swift, Berkeley, Addison, Steele, Congreve, the Duke of Ormond and Bishop Rundle. London: for C. Elliot and T. Kay and C. Elliot, Edinburgh, 1789. 1st edition; 8vo; pages lvi, 415, half title; uncut in original blue-grey paper boards, skilfully rebacked to style; presentation copy to the fourth Duke of Marlborough, with Berkeley's autograph inscription; presentation copy; bookplate and added ownership inscription of the fourth Duke's youngest son, Lord Francis Almeric Spencer. Teerink 120; Rothschild 385.   Simon Finch 24-222   1996 £175.00

DOUGLAS, M.   Notes of a Journey from Berne to England through France, Made in the Year 1796. London: 1797. 8vo; 2nd part only; 56 pages; contemporary calf, gilt, by C. Kalthoeber, with his binder's ticket, rebacked. This copy fromt he Althorp Library with its label and Spencer bookplate.   Thomas Thorp 489-89   1996 £135.00

ASSOCIATION - T. J. SPENCER

COOKE, WILLIAM   The Elements of Dramatic Criticism. London: for G. Kearsley and G. Robinson, 1775. 1st edition; engraved vignette to title; disbound, half title embrowned and chipped at edges, T. J. Spencer's copy with his bookticket and annotations.   Dramatis Personae 37-49 1996 $100.00

ASSOCIATION - ALBERT SPERISEN

FORDE, H. A.   The Fruit of the Spirit. London: De La More Press, n.d. 1919. Number 7 of 21 copies printed on vellum; 8vo; 23 pages, printed on rectos only, wood engraved frontispiece of George and the Dragon within elaborate Morris-style border as it is facing the titlepage, contemporary morocco backed Cockrell marbled boards, lettered in gold; very good; bookplate of Albert Sperisen. Ridler 26(1).   Claude Cox 107-44 1996 £220.00

ASSOCIATION - HELEN SPIERS

CIPRIANI, G. B.   Cipriani's Rudiments of Drawing. London: Edward Orme, 1815. Re-issue of the 1786 issue of engraved titlepage; oblong folio; 6 stipple engraved plates by Bartolozzi, but with plates still dated Jan. 1st 1786, augmented with 3 plates of hands and legs dated Jan. 1st 1792, and 2 further plates dated Jan. 20th 1793; original grey wrappers, paper label on upper wrapper titled "Cipriani & Bartolozzi's Drawing Book of the Human Figure. New Edition - 1815", spine expertly repaired; inscription "Helen Spiers, from Mrs. Spiers, March 1824 Hinckly".   Ken Spelman 30-32 1996 £280.00

ASSOCIATION - ARTHUR SPINGARN

FORD, FORD MADOX 1873-1939   Some Do Not... London: Duckworth, 1924. 1st edition; 8vo; green cloth, pictorial dust jacket; top of spine faded, extremities of spine trifle worn, otherwise very good in rare dust jacket which is chipped and somewhat soiled; inscribed by author for Arthur Spingarn.   James S. Jaffe 34-157 1996 $1,500.00

ASSOCIATION - AGNES WRIGHT SPRING

FRINK, MAURICE W.   When Grass Was King. Boulder: University of Colorado Press, 1956. 1st edition; one of 1500 numbered copies; xv, 465 pages, 35 illustrations, map endpapers; fine in dust jacket; presentation inscription signed by Agnes Wright Spring. Adams 853; Reese Six Score 45; Six Guns 777.   Argonaut Book Shop 113-267 1996 $150.00

ASSOCIATION - STEPHEN EDWARD SPRING-RICE

WEBSTER, JOHN   Love's Graduate: a Comedy. Daniel Press, 1885. One of 150 copies; 9 x 7 inches; 2 p.l., ix, (1) pages, (1) leaf, 69, (1) pages, (1) leaf (printer's device); printed on fine qualtiy thick paper; vellum backed paper boards, spine titled in gilt, 2 edges untrimmed; 2 bookplates on endpapers, titlepage with presentation inscription from editor, Stephen Edward Spring-Rice, to Henry Bradshaw dated 1885; also with ownership inscription of R. A. Neil, dated 1886 and with ms. note signed by Gosse tipped in after prefatory essay, corners bit worn, spine and covers somewhat soiled, but binding tight and otherwise pleasing; very fine internally. Madan 11.   Phillip J. Pirages 33-154 1996 $400.00

ASSOCIATION - RAYMOND SPRUANCE

DOUGLAS, WILLIAM O.   North from Malaya, Adventure on Five Fronts. Garden City: Doubleday & Co., 1953. Quite good copy, in chipped dust jacket; presentation copy from Justice Douglas to Raymond A. Spruance, then U.S. ambassador to the Philippines.   Meyer Boswell SL27-69 1996 $350.00

ASSOCIATION - A. R. SQUIRE

GILL, ERIC 1882-1940   Engravings 1928-1933. London: Faber & Faber, 1934. 1st edition; of which only 400 copies were pritned; 4to; pages xvi, 102; 133 wood engravings, all but 2 printed from original blocks; original green cloth, spine lettered in gilt, dust jacket, spine of jacket repaired internally, occasional slight foxing, otherwise very nice in original slipcase; this copy inscribed by Eric Gill for A. R. Squire. Evan Gill 27.   Sotheran PN32-14 1996 £998.00

ASSOCIATION - FRANK STAFF

STOW, JOHN   A Survay (sic) of London. London: Imprinted by Iohn Wolfe, 1599. 4to. in 8's; (viii), 483, (1 faults) pages; old calf, worn, rebacked, titlepage brittle at margins, last leaf defective, without loss of text, some pages darkened. With long history of ownership, including bookplates of Frank Staff; signatures of George Cage, George Manley, J. Millar, B. Castleton, Peter Smart, J. B. de V. Payen-Payne.   Marlborough 162-207 1996 £1,100.00

ASSOCIATION - PAUL STANDARD

DONNE, JOHN 1571-1631   A Prayer. Banyan Press, 1947. Limited edition of 120 numbered copies; 8vo; 6 leaves, including blanks, title printed in 2 colors; title printed in 2 colors; decorative paper wrappers, 6 leaves, including blanks, fine in publisher's original mailing envelope. Though not called for, this copy inscribed by the printers, Claude Fredericks and Milton Saul to the bookman Paul Standard; laid in is prospectus for the Banyan Press edition of Spender's "Returning to Vienna 1974'.   Blue Mountain SP95-48 1996 $175.00

ASSOCIATION - HESTER STANHOPE

SALT, HENRY   A Voyage to Abyssinia, and Travels into the Interior of that Country...in 1809 and 1810. London: for F. C. and J. Rivington, 1814. 1st edition; large 4to; printed on thick paper, 34 plates and charts, lower margin of first leaf leaf of text repaired; contemporary half russia, with decorated paper boards, joints very skilfully repaired; inscribed "To the Lady Hester Stanhope from the Author" below in another hand 'purchased at sale of Lady Hester Stanhope's books at Beirout in 1840" followed by notes signed by "John Maconchy, surgeon HMS Hecate" & Robert Maunsell, Capt. HMS Rodney"   H. M. Fletcher 121-146 1996 £2,500.00

ASSOCIATION - DOROTHEA STANLEY

BROWNING, ELIZABETH BARRETT 1806-1861   The Seraphim and Other Poems. London: Saunders and Otley, 1838. 1st edition; 12mo; contemporary half green calf, spine gilt, slightly rubbed, bound without half title, but nice; armorial bookplates of Dorothea Stanley and Conon Williams. Baranes A4; CBEL III 436.   Ximenes 108-368 1996 $400.00

ASSOCIATION - STEBBING

THACKERAY, WILLIAM MAKEPEACE 1811-1863   The Loving Ballad of Lord Bateman. London: Bell and Daldy, 1871. 16mo; pages 40; wood engraved re-workings of Cruikshank's 11 etched illustrations of 1839, plate of music, plates and letterpress of poem printed on one side of leaf, eccentrically paginated, inscription at head of titlepage; original sand-grain blue cloth, spine unlettered, gilt titled in center of upper side, oblong panel in style of French type ornament at head and foot of both sides, very good; inscribed by Cruikshank for Mrs. William Stebbing. Blackwell's B112-84 1996 £125.00

ASSOCIATION - ALAN STEELE

BATES, HERBERT ERNEST 1905-1974   The Black Boxer. London: 1932. 1st edition; slight foxing to fore edges, otherwise very good in dust jacket browned on spine and minimally chipped at its head; inscribed by author for Alan W. Steele.   Words Etcetera 94-97 1996 £150.00

BATES, HERBERT ERNEST 1905-1974   Catherine Foster. New York: Viking Press, 1929. 1st American edition; cloth backed boards, gilt, slight discoloration at head of both covers, otherwise very good in dust jacket little browned on spine and with one closed tear, loosely inserted is a small 3 x 2 1/2 inch studio photo of Bates; inscribed by author for A. W. Steele.   Words Etcetera 94-90 1996 £160.00

BATES, HERBERT ERNEST 1905-1974   Charlotte's Row. London: 1931. 1st edition; near fine in dust jacket, superb copy, inscribed by author for Alan W. Steele.   Words Etcetera 94-94 196 £160.00

BATES, HERBERT ERNEST 1905-1974   Cut and Come Again. London: 1935. 1st edition; beautiful bright copy in dust jacket with minimal rubbing to extremities of lower edge of upper panel and head of spine. Inscribed by author for Alan W. Steele.   Words Etcetera 94-99 1996 £150.00

BATES, HERBERT ERNEST 1905-1974   Day's End and Other Stories. London: 1928. 1st edition; very good in dust jacket with browned spine and little chipped at head; inscribed by author for A. W. Steele.   Words Etcetera 94-89 1996 £150.00

ASSOCIATION - ALAN STEELE

BATES, HERBERT ERNEST 1905-1974   The Fallow Land. London: 1932. 1st edition; minimal foxing, otherwise fine in dust jacket, rare thus; warmly inscribed by author for Alan W. Steele, with APCs Christmas Greeting from author.   Words Etcetera 94-96 1996 £150.00

BATES, HERBERT ERNEST 1905-1974   The Flying Goat. London: 1939. 1st edition; very good in dust jacket with few short closed tears and minimal rubbing to head and foot of spine; Alan W. Steele's copy with his signature. Words Etcetera 94-104 1996 £100.00

BATES, HERBERT ERNEST 1905-1974   A House of Women. London: 1936. 1st edition; rust mark on inner hinge, otherwise very good in dust jacket worn on spine and chipped at head and foot and rubbed on two corners; inscribed by author for Alan W. Steele.   Words Etcetera 94-100 1996 £160.00

BATES, HERBERT ERNEST 1905-1974   Seven Tales and Alexander; Stories. London: Scholartis Press, 1929. 1st edition; cloth backed boards, somewhat worn and browned, dust jacket torn and defective, newscuttings of reviews, one by Arnold Bennett, loosely inserted, also loosely inserted 8 page pamphlet entitled Mr. H. E. Bates which has been reprinted from the Times of Jan. 24th 1935; inscribed at length by author for Alan W. Steele; with ALS to Steele.   Words Etcetera 94-92 1996 £160.00

BATES, HERBERT ERNEST 1905-1974   Seven Tales and Alexander. New York: 1930. 1st American edition; canvas backed boards, very good in browned and chipped dust jacket; inscribed by author of Alan W. Steele.   Words Etcetera 94-93 1996 £150.00

ASSOCIATION - ALFRED STEIGLITZ

FRANK, WALDO   America and Alfred Steiglitz. Garden City: Doubleday, Doran, 1934. 1st edition; couple of short tears to foot of spine and wear to cloth of remaining extremities, overall very good in dust jacket with chipping to extremities; this copy belonged to Steiglitz, with his ownership signature and bookplate. Inscribed by Steiglitz for Mildred Wilson.   Lame Duck Books 19-507 1996 $2,500.00

ASSOCIATION - STEPHENS

BACON, FRANCIS, VISCOUNT ST. ALBANS 1561-1626   Letters of Sr. Francis Bacon, Baron of Verulam, Viscount St. Albany, and Lord High Chancellor of England. London: printed for Benj. Tooke, 1702. 1st edition; 4to; contemporary mottled calf, gilt, neatly rebacked, original label preserved, all edges gilt, corners worn; large paper; very good with errata leaf at end, few copies are known with leaf of dedication to the king, not present here, but it was meant to be called as William III died before publication. Presentation copy inscribed by Rob. Stephens for Edward Ward. Gibson 245   Ximenes 109-20 1996 $600.00

ASSOCIATION - GEORGE STEPHENS

MONTAGU, EDWARD WORTLEY 1713-1776   Reflections on the Rise and Fall of the Ancient Republicks. London: printed for J. Rivington and Sons, T. Longman, S. Crowder, T. Cadell.. 1778. 4th edition; 8vo; half title; contemporary sheep, rubbed, label, bookplate of George Stephens, signed by him.   Anthony W. Laywood 109-100 1996 £55.00

ASSOCIATION - EDWARD KEPPEL STEPHENSON

BOWMAN, S. M.   Sherman and His Campaigns: a Military Biography. New York: Charles B. Richardson, 1865. 1st edition; thick 8vo; frontispiece, other full page engrave dplates, infrequent spotting; original brown buckram, rubbed, black morocco label, gilt; generally very good; bookplate of Edward Keppel Stephenson of Langham Hall, Suffolk.   Ian Wilkinson 95/1-4 1996 £65.00

ASSOCIATION - STEVENS

STEVENS, HENRY   An Account of the Proceedings at the Dinner Given by Mr. George Peabody to the Americans Connected with the Great Exhibition. London: Pickering, 1851. 8vo; 114 pages, 1 f., blue cloth, top of spine chipped; presentation copy from Mrs. Henry Stevens. Marlborough 162-205 1996 £135.00

ASSOCIATION - ROBERT LOUIS STEVENSON

BIBLE. ENGLISH -   The Large-Print Paragraph Bible...The New Testament. London: Samuel Bagster and Sons, n.d. 8vo; numerous colored maps and colored view; original publisher's roan, spine lettered in gilt, gilt edges, covers worn, preserved in black cloth fall-down back box with leather label; Robert Louis Stevenson's copy with his Skerryvore bookplate and with his mother's inscription.   Sotheran PN32-53 1996 £998.00

GOSSE, EDMUND 1849-1928   Gray. London: Macmillan and Co., 1882. 1st edition; Presentation copy inscribed by author for Robert Louis Stevenson; original cloth, paper spine label; inner hinges cracked, covers glazed (as were many of the books from Stevenson's library), with preservative varnish which has darkened a little with age, little worn, in handsome full morocco solander case.   David J. Holmes 52-114 1996 $1,000.00

PATMORE, COVENTRY   Florilegium Amantis. London: George Bell & Sons, n.d. 1879. 1st edition; 12mo; printed presentation slip from author tipped in at front and Robert Louis Stevenson's "Sherryvore" bookplate on front pastedown; original cloth, paper spine label (partially worn away); covers glazed (as was the case with many of Stevenson's books), inner hinges cracked, else good in half morocco slipcase (spine little rubbed); also bookplate of noted collector, Charles Dexter Allen. David J. Holmes 52-115 1996 $850.00

ASSOCIATION - STEWART

BROWN, THOMAS   Brighton; or, the Styne. London: for the author, sold by Sherwood, Neely and Jones, 1818. 1st edition; 8vo; 3 volumes, half titles; contemporary half straight grain citron morocco, smooth spines with gilt bands, black morocco labels, marbled sides and endpapers, green sprinkled edges, sides lightly rubbed; excellent set, clean and fresh; engraved bookplates with baronial arms of the Stewart family, Charles William Stewart, Baron Stewart Block p. 28; not in Wolff. Simon Finch 24-20 1996 £750.00

ASSOCIATION - JAMES STEWART

FALCONER, WILLIAM   The Shipwreck, a Poem. London: printed for William Miller by T. Bensley, 1804. 9 1/4 x 6 1/4 inches; 8 p.l., xiii-xlvi pages, (1) leaf, 220 pages; 5 vignettes and 3 plates engraved by J. Fittler from paintings by N. Pocock; fine contemporary diced russia bound from James Stewart of Killymoon, sides with gilt frame of thick and thin rules, spine with gilt decorated broad raised bands, pretty gilt floral rows at spine ends, top and bottom compartments with intricate blindstamping, gilt titling, marbled edges and endpapers; covers little variegated, but virtually pristine;   Phillip J. Pirages 33-214 1996 $250.00

ASSOCIATION - ROCKY STINEHOUR

NASH, R.   Calligraphy and Printing in the Sixteenth Century. Antwerp: Plantin-Moretus Museum, 1964. 2nd edition, limited to 500 copies; small 8vo; 39 pages; cloth backed pictorial boards, dust jacket, booklabel of Ruari McLean & inscription to him from Rocky Stinehour.   Maggs Bros. Ltd. 1191-210 1996 £40.00

ASSOCIATION - WILLIAM STITH

DU FRESNOY, CHARLES ALPHONSE 1611-1665   The Art of Painting. London: printed for Bernard Lintott, 1716. 2nd edition; small 8vo; lxviii, (4), 397, (7) pages; contemporary brown calf, decoratively blind tooled and with spine in 6 compartments, modest external wear, bookplates, else good, internally very clean; with engraved heraldic bookplate and ownership signature of early Virginia historian William Stith. Interesting association.   Chapel Hill 94-53 1996 $500.00

ASSOCIATION - ROBERT STODDARD

VON HAGEN, VICTOR WOLFGANG   Jungle in the Clouds. New York: Duell, Sloan and Pearce, 1940. 1st edition; 8vo; frontispiece, x, 260 pages; 58 illustrations; original cloth, lightly chipped dust jacket; inscribed by author for Robert G. Stoddard.   Archaeologia Luxor-5009 1996 $125.00

ASSOCIATION - HUMPHREY STONE

RANSOM, WILL d. 1955   Kelmscott, Doves and Ashendene - the Private Press Credos. New York: The Typophiles, 1952. One of 400 copies for Typophile subscribers and contributors, there were a further 300 copies for the Book Club of California, San Francisco; loosely inserted prospectus for this book and related material; spine slightly faded, head and tail of spine slightly bumped, endpaper gutters slightly browned; very good; from the library of James D. Hart, loosely inserted is an APS from Humphrey Stone to Hart.   Ulysses 39-494 1996 £75.00

ASSOCIATION - COLTON STORM

MOYLLUS, DAMIANUS   A Newly Discovered Treatise on Classic Letter Design Printed at Parma by Damianus Moyllus Circa 1480. Officina Bodoni, 1923. One of 222 copies; 11 1/2 x 8 inches; 38 pages, (1) leaf (colophon); device in colophon, printed in blue-gray and black; original vellum over stiff boards, titled in gilt on spine, gitl device on front cover, edges untrimmed and unopened, hint of soil and discoloration to binding, very slightl browning of leaves right at edges, but these defects quite minor and an extremely fine copy in general; bookplates of Paul Hyde Bonner and of Colton Storm, compiler of the catalog of the Graff collection.   Phillip J. Pirages 33-407 1996 $1,250.00

ASSOCIATION - ISAAC STORY

THE TOUCHSTONE of Precedents Relating to Judicial Proceedings at Common Law. London: printed for Awnsham Churchill at the Black Swan, 1682. contemporary sheep, very worn, joints cracking, usable only; with ownership signature on second blank of Isaac Story.   Meyer Boswell SL27-219 1996 $650.00

ASSOCIATION - HARRIET BEECHER STOWE

CROWFIELD, CHRISTOPHER   The Chimney Corner. Boston: Houghton Mifflin, 1888. Reprint; 12mo; green cloth, fine; signed by Harriet Beecher Stowe with inscription.   Charles Agvent 4-1057 1996 $850.00

CROWFIELD, CHRISTOPHER   House and Home Papers. Boston: Ticknor and Fields, 1865. 1st edition; 8vo; three quarter calf, moderate rubbing; very good, tipped in sheet with inscription from Harriet Beecher Stowe.   Charles Agvent 4-1058 1996 $600.00

ASSOCIATION - STRACHEY

FERDOOSEE   Episodes from the Shah Nameh; or Annals of the Persian Kings; by Ferdoosee. London: printed for the author, 1815. 8vo; frontispiece, ad leaf at end; original boards, uncut; fine; presentation inscription "From the author to Sir H. Strachey Bt.".   Anthony W. Laywood 108-171 1996 £120.00

LEAR, EDWARD 1812-1888   Later Letters...to Chichester Fortescue (Lord Carlingford), Frances Countess Waldegrave and Others. London: T. Fisher Unwin, 1911. 1st edition; 8vo; 392 pages; 2 colored plates, numerous black and white plates and text illustrations; original two colored cloth, gilt, top edges gilt, dust jacket; half title spotted, other light spotting; presentation copy with Lady Strachey's visting card pasted to front free endpaper inscribed "With the editors kindest remembrances & thans, Sutton Court".   Sotheran PN32-91 1996 £68.00

SOUVESTRE, EMILE   Translations from the French of Emile Souvestre. N.P.: privately printed, 1856. Small 4to; 2 volumes; full dark blue crushed morocco over beveled boards, spine & covers heavily ornamented with gilt & blind relief decoration, far too elaborate to describe, at top & bottom (on edges of outer gilt fillet borders) are two gilt lines "To the Memory of Elizabeth Strachey and Coelum Non Animum; board edges gilt, inner gilt dentelles, all edges gilt, on inside rear pastedown is binder's ticket of Leighton, Son & Hodge, on front flyleaf is inscription "Constance Strachey from E. S. 1 June, 1887". Fine.   Book Block 32-45 1996 $1,250.00

STOKES, MAIVE   Indian Fairy Tales Collected and Translated. Calcutta: privately printed, 1879. 1st edition; one of 100 copies; 8vo; pages viii, 303; original ribbed blue cloth, rebacked, original backstrip laid down, lettering dulled, front cover gilt titled with double ruled border, border blind on rear cover, cloth faded, edges worn, yellow endpapers, soiled, sound. Author's inscription "Lady Strachey from Maive Stokes".   Blackwell's B112-265 1996 £85.00

ASSOCIATION - CHARLES STRACHEY

BUTLER, SAMUEL 1835-1902   Seven Sonnets and a Psalm of Montreal. Cambridge: printed for Private Circulation, 1904. Original wrappers, chipped and detached; inscribed by Festing Jones to Charles Strachey, with ALS from Festing Jones to Strachey.   Jarndyce CII-87 1996 £150.00

ASSOCIATION - LYTTON STRACHEY

STRACHEY, RAY   Marching on. New York: 1923. 1st American edition; original cloth, outer edge of upper cover trifle damp marked, otherwise very good; inscribed by author to Giles Lytton Strachey.   Words Etcetera 94-1192 1996 £50.00

ASSOCIATION - STRADBALLY

CHURCH OF ENGLAND. BOOK OF COMMON PRAYER   Book of Common Prayer. London: by the Assigns of His Majesty's Printer & of Henry Hills, deceased, 1729. large folio; engraved title (undated, but 1713/14), title, 12 ff. prelims, 278 ff. n.n., ruled in red throughout; dark blue morocco, covers gilt with broad double border, inner of alternating crowns and flowers spine gilt in 8 panels, raised bands gilt, panels with royal monogram, crowns and flowers, all edges gilt, marbled endpapers, gilt arms of King George I (d. 1727) on covers, corners little rubbed, ties gone, a fine royal binding on large paper; from the library of Dudley Alexander Sydney Cosby, Baron of Stradbally (Ireland) with his ex-libris and signature, ca. 1730.   Marlborough 160-33 1996 £1,250.00

ASSOCIATION - STRADBROKE

RICHARDSON, JONATHAN 1665-1745   The Works. Strawberry Hill: sold by B. White and Son & others, 1792. 1st edition; 4to; pages vii, 287, 12 etched, stipple and line engraved plates printed on pink washed paper; titlepage in first state described by Hazen p. 65; large copy in contemporary speckled calf, upper hinge cracked but side securely held; very good; bookplate and ownership signature of Earl of Stradbroke, 1827. Hazen p. 83, p. 65.   Claude Cox 107-163 1996 £165.00

ASSOCIATION - JOSHUA STRANGER

BUSH, JAMES   The Choice: or Lines on the Beatitudes. London: R. Saywell; Cockermouth: Bailey & Sons; Carlisle: C. Thurman, 1841. Square 8vo; pages 102; frontispiece foxed; full polished calf, gilt, edges rubbed; presentation copy inscribed by author to Mrs. Joshua Stranger.   R.F.G. Hollett & Son 78-342 1996 £65.00

ASSOCIATION - STRAWBERRY HILL

AUBREY, JOHN   The Natural History and Antiquities of the County of Surrey; Begun in the Year 1673...and Continued to the Present Time. London: printed for E. Curll, 1718-23. 1st edition; 5 volumes, extra illustrated with 252 engraved, etched and aquatint plates; some offsetting and spotting, pages 3-16 in volume 3 supplied in ms.; contemporary calf, slightly rubbed, volumes 2 and 3 rebacked with original spines, all edges gilt, bookplates and ownership inscriptions on titles of William Roots. Note at beginning states "26 April/42 Lot. 59 - at Strawberry Hill.." bt. by Bohn".   Anthony W. Laywood 109-5 1996 £850.00

ASSOCIATION - THOMAS WINTHROP STREETER

LUNDY, BENJAMIN   The Origin and True Causes of the Texas Insurrection Commenced in the Year 1835. Philadelphia: 1836. Reprinted from the Philadelphia 'National Gazette'; 32 pages; removed, trimmed, darkened/foxed, lacking original bright yellow wrappers; Streeter's duplicate copy, with his pencilled notes. Raines p. 141. Streeter TX 1216.   Bohling Book Co. 191-87 1996 $700.00

MILLER, BENJAMIN S.   Ranching in the Southwest: Ranch Life in Southern Kansas and the Indian Territory. New York: Fless & Ridge Printing Co., 1896. 1st edition; 163 pages; portrait; original pictorial wrappers, title stamped in blue on spine and front cvoer, minor chipping, laid in folding slipcase; fine; the Thomas Streeter copy with his bookplate and several pencil notes. Choice copy, rare; Streeter Sale 2387; Graff 2795; Howes M602; Adams Herd 1485.   Michael D. Heaston 23-90 1996 $2,000.00

ASSOCIATION - RICHARD SHUTTLEWORTH STRETFEILD

REGULATIONS and Instructions for the Cavalry Sword Exercise. London: Clowes, 1819. Tall 8vo; 2 plates, including on large folding plate, 4 page publisher's list of military books at end; calf, front hinge weak, slight foxing; armorial bookplate of Richard Shuttleworth Stretfeild & ownership inscription of Lt. John Watson on p. 3.　　Rostenberg & Stern 150-108 1996 $140.00

ASSOCIATION - GEORGE STRICKLAND

JOHNSTONE, CHARLES 1719?-1800?　　The History of Arsaces, Prince of Betlis. London: printed for T. Becket, 1774. 1st edition; 12mo; 2 volumes; contemporary calf, gilt spines, red and green morocco labels; some wear at head of volume 1, still fine; engraved armorial bookplate of Sir George Strickland, bt.　　H. M. Fletcher 121-105 1996 £1,800.00

ASSOCIATION - SAMUEL STRODE

MOLIERE, JEAN BAPTISTE POQUELIN DE 1622-1673　　Select Comedies...in French and English. London: printed for John Watts, 1732. 1st edition; 12mo; 8 volumes; contemporary calf, gilt, spines gilt, contrasting morocco labels, slight wear. Very good; early armorial bookplates of Samuel Strode. Paulson Hogarth's Graphic Works 222-3. Ximenes 108-269 1996 $900.00

ASSOCIATION - LEONARD STRONG

O'CONNOR, FRANK 1903-1966　　The Saint and Mary Kate. London: Macmillan, 1932. Advance reading copy with slip tipped in; corners slightly bumped, spine little faded and small tape remnant on front pastedown from an old booksellers description, sound, very good copy, lacking the dust jacket; inscribed by author to Irish novelist L.A.G. Strong.　　Between the Covers 42-342 1996 $450.00

ASSOCIATION - OTTO STRUVE

FINE, ORONCE　　Quadratura Circuli, Tandem Inventa & Clarissime Demonstrata. De Circuli Mensura, & Ratione Circumferentiae ad Diametrum... Paris: Simon de Colines, 1544. 1st edition; folio; (12), 107 pages, illustrations, woodcut initials and ornaments, title with woodcut border; 3 leaves scorched at upper edge of outer margin; new limp vellum, titled on spine in calligraphy, very good, wide margined copy. Otto Struve's copy with his neat signature. Norman Lib 795. Mortimer French 16th Cent. Books 229; Adams F479.　　Edwin V. Glaser 121-107 1996 $3,000.00

ASSOCIATION - F. H. STUBBINGS

KOSMOPOULOS, LESLIE WALKER　　The Prehistoric Inhabitation of Corinth. Munich: F. Bruckmann, 1948. Limited to 500 copies; 4to; xxii, 73 pages, 51 figures, 4 color plates; wrappers; with signature of F. H. Stubbings, 1949.　　Archaeologia Luxor-3575 1996 $150.00

ASSOCIATION - SUFFOLK

DRAYTON, MICHAEL 1563-1631　　Poems... London: printed by W. Stansby for John Methwicke, 1613. 4th edition; 8vo; 19th century black morocco, wide gilt borders, spine and inner dentelles gilt, all edges gilt, by Winstanley of Manchester, joints bit rubbed; titlepage bit dusty, slight scattered foxing and couple of minor wormholes near end, but very good; flyleaf preserved bears the contemporary signature of Charles Brandon, Duke of Suffolk. STC 7221; Pforzheimer 305.　　Ximenes 109-104 1996 $850.00

WEST, THOMAS　　The Antiquities of Furness; or an Account of the Royal Abbey of St. Mary. London: for the author, 1774. 1st edition; 4to; pages (xx), lvi (actually liv), 288, (138), 1 folding map as frontispiece, 3 engraved plates; contemporary full tree calf, finely tooled gilt decorative spine, red morocco label, marbled endpapers; few minor tears expertly repaired; bookplate of the Earl of Suffolk.　　Sotheran PN32-200 1996 £295.00

ASSOCIATION - SULTOWN

WARING, J. B.　　Art Treasures of the United Kingdom, from the Art Treasures Exhibition, Manchester. London: Day and Son, 1858. 1st edition; folio; (xviii), 42, (1), 32, (1), (49)-80, (2), 27 pages; 50 plates; contemporary leather; edges rubbed, else very good. Bookplate of Alexander Lord Sultown. Friedman 176; Ray 236; Mclean p. 125. Bookpress 75-137 1996 $925.00

ASSOCIATION - A. G. SUMMER

LIEBIG, JUSTUS VON　　Animal Chemistry, or Organic Chemistry in Its Application to Physiology and Pathology. Cambridge: 1842. 1st American edition; 8vo; pages xl, 347, (8); contemporary half calf, very rubbed, boards scuffed, foxing and some page browning; scarce; A. G. Summer's copy (publisher of Southern Agriculturalit).　　Raymond M. Sutton VII-1038 1996 $275.00

ASSOCIATION - WILLIAM SUMMER

BOUSSINGAULT, J. B.　　Rural Economy, In its Relations with Chemistry, Physics and Meteorology... New York: 1845. 8vo; pages iv, 507; contemporary half calf, rubbed, worn at corners and edges, spine ends partially perished, with foxing and page browning, some minor marginal dampstaining. From the library of William Summer (1815-1878). Raymond M. Sutton VII-844 1996 $125.00

ASSOCIATION - SUSSEX

MACHIAVELLI, NICCOLO 1469-1527　　Historie. (with) Libro dell'Arte Della Guerra. Venice: Comin da Trino, 1540/41. 8vo; 2 works in 1 volume, titlepage, ff. 2-243, 1 f. blank; titlepage, 1 f., ff 1-108, 9 ff., woodcut portrait on titles, woodcut diagrams at end of second work, ruled in red. Light brown calf over stiff pasteboards, gilt, sides decorated with a plaque of illusionistic three dimensional strapwork, an azured 'stirrup' tool repeated upright and reversed in the centre, original sides laid down on a 19th century binding, edges plain gilt, 19th century marbled endleaves; a Parisian binding of c. 1545-50; early ownership inscription on titlepage scribbled over "Gu. Lyly", at foot of titlepage; H.R.H. Augustus Frederick, Duke of Sussex, sixth son of King George III, his sale, evans pt. IV, 30 Jan. 1845 lot 1016, bought by Payne. Marlborough 160-5 1996 £1,950.00

ASSOCIATION - GEORGE SUTCLIFFE

DE LA MARE, WALTER 1873-1956　　The Sunken Garden and Other Poems. London: Beaumont Press, 1917. 1st edition; one of 6 copies, printed for presentation (of an edition of 276 copies); crown 8vo; printed in black and red on handmade paper; original quarter fawn buckram, printed backstrip and front cover labels, that on backstrip trifle darkened, floral patterned pale grey boards, faint free endpaper browning, untrimmed; good. Presentation copy inscribed by Cyril Beaumont to George Sutcliffe of Sangorski & Sutcliffe. Beaumont 2.　　Blackwell's B112-17 1996 £95.00

ASSOCIATION - ALFRED SUTRO

ROSSETTI, DANTE GABRIEL 1828-1882　　Ballads and Narrative Poems. Hammersmith: Kelmscott Press, 1893. One of 310 paper copies; octavo; 227 pages; printed in red and black in Golden type; decorative woodcut borders and initials; full limp vellum with reddish brown silk ties, spine lettered in gilt, edges lightly foxed, near fine; bookplate of Alfred Sutro. Clark Lib. Kelmscott & Doves p. 29; Peterson A20; Sparling 20. Heritage Book Shop 196-162 1996 $1,750.00

ASSOCIATION - SWANN

BIERCE, AMBROSE 1842-1914　　Black Beetles in Amber. San Francisco & New York: Western Authors Pub. Co., 1892. 1st edition; 8vo; 280 pages; frontispiece; original grey cloth, two part cloth box. The very fine Swann-Bradley Martin copy. Swann Sale 21 (1960).　　M & S Rare Books 60-121 1996 $950.00

ASSOCIATION - GLORIA SWANSON

BRASSAI　　Seville en Fete. Paris: n.p., 1954. 1st edition; photos; cloth edges fading, near fine in very good dust jacket with uneven horizontal chip at spine crown and upper front panel; inscribed by author to Gloria Swanson in year of publication.　　Ken Lopez 74-41 1996 $1,250.00

ASSOCIATION - ALGERNON CHARLES SWINBURNE

LAMB, CHARLES 1775-1834　　The Works. London: Methuen & Co., 1903-05. 8vo; 7 volumes; frontispiece to each volume, numerous plates and illustrations; original red cloth, paper labels to spines, top edge gilt, spines sunned and slightly rubbed, paper labels soiled, otherwise very good set with spare labels tipped in at rear of each volume; from the library of Algernon Charles Swinburne, also from the collections of Sir James Stevenson, Sir Winston Churchill and Randolph Churchill, with bookplates.　　Sotheran PN32-5 1996 £1,995.00

ASSOCIATION - WILLIAM HALES SYMONS

COLERIDGE, SAMUEL TAYLOR 1772-1834   Poems on Various Subjects... London: for G. G. and J. Robinson and J. Cottle, Bristol, 1796. 1st edition; small 8vo; pages (iii)-xvi, 188, (2) errata, verso blank, (1) ads; bound without half title; contemporary green half morocco, spine with triple gilt bands, lettered in gilt, gilt lyre motifs in compartments, marbled sides, extremities slightly rubbed; very good; bookplate of William Hales Symons. Wise 8; Hayward 206; Tinker 678. Simon Finch 24-43 1996 £1,200.00

ASSOCIATION - SYNGE

SHAKESPEARE, WILLIAM 1564-1616   Mr. William Shakespear's Comedies, Histories and Tragedies. London: for H. Herringman, E. Brewster and R. Bentley, 1685. 4th folio edition, this copy with the variant setting of the title omitting Chiswell's name from the imprint; folio in sixes, printed in double columns within ruled borders, pages (xii), 96, 99-160, 163-254, (253)-(273), (i), 328, 303; without frontispiece and final leaf of text with titlepage, C2-5, Qq3-4 and Eee8 supplied in excellent facsimile; contemporary calf, some wear, rebacked in 19th century, spine in compartments with raised bands, gilt rules and label lettered in gilt, small piece cut from 9 leaves at blank margin, tear to H2 without loss, small hole affecting 3 letters to Ddd3, occasional rustmarks, but very good, clean copy; signature of Robert Synge on front free endpaper and Markree Library label on pastedown. Wing S2915; Bartlett 123A; greg III p. 1119; Pforzheimer 910.   Simon Finch 24-201 1996 £7,200.00

ASSOCIATION - SYSTON PARK

LUCRETIUS CARUS, TITUS 99-55 BC   De Rerum Natura Sex, ad Optimorum Exemplarium Fidem Recensiti. London: Tonson, 1712. Large folio; (4), 282 pages, engraved frontispiece and 6 plates, head and tailpieces, and initials; contemporary gilt panelled red morocco with triple fillet and cornerpieces, gilt roll tooled inner dentelle, spine gilt in compartments, raised gilt bands, all edges gilt, comb marbled endpapers, skilfully rebacked preserving original spine, corners little soft, elegantly understated binding, from Syston Park library.   Marlborough 160-45 1996 £800.00

VERGILIUS MARO, PUBLIUS 70-19 BC   Opera. Amsterdam: Wetstenil, 1746. Large 4to; 4 volumes, pages (32), (82), 520; 706; 707; 360, (92), engraved frontispiece, vignettes, maps, etc., title in red and black, one of the few copies that were struck off on large paper; brilliant full red straight grained morocco Syston Park binding, all edges gilt, engraved ex-libris of Thorold's Syston Park Library. Dibdin II 552-3; Brunet V 1292. Family Album Tillers-641 1996 $2,000.00

ASSOCIATION - TALLEYRAND-PERIGORD

HILL, JOHN 1716?-1775   The Actor. London: for R. Griffiths, 1750. 1st edition; 12mo; pages (x), 326; contemporary calf, unlettered, double gilt rules, worn; from the library of Charles Maurice de Talleyrand-Perigord, bookplate of Bibliotheque du Chateau de Valencay.   Simon Finch 24-116 1996 £500.00

ASSOCIATION - TAMBRONI

CENNINI, CENNINO   A Treatise on Painting, Written in the Year 1437 and First Published in Italian in 1821. London: Edward Lumley, 1844. Royal 8vo; illuminated titlepage, fine illuminated plate in gold and colors and 8 plates in outline; contemporary morocco, gilt edges, presentation copy from the translator, Signor Tambroni, from the library of Viscount Eversley.   Charles W. Traylen 117-227 1996 £225.00

ASSOCIATION - ALLEN TATE

HILL, GEOFFREY   Preghiere. Leeds: Northern House Pamphlet Poets, 1964. 1st edition; 8vo; white glossy printed wrappers;; fine; presentation copy, inscribed by author to Allen Tate and his wife Isabella Gardner. James S. Jaffe 34-248 1996 $1,000.00

TAYLOR, PETER   Happy Families Are All Alike. New York: McDowell Obolensky, 1959. 1st edition; very good+ copy in dust jacket; superb association copy, inscribed by author to literary critic and poet Allen Tate and his wife Isabella in the year of publication and with typed 3 x 5 inch index card laid in.   Lame Duck Books 19-515 1996 $1,500.00

ASSOCIATION - ISABELLA TATE

TAYLOR, PETER   Happy Families Are All Alike. New York: McDowell Obolensky, 1959. 1st edition; very good+ copy in dust jacket; superb association copy, inscribed by author to literary critic and poet Allen Tate and his wife Isabella in the year of publication and with typed 3 x 5 inch index card laid in.   Lame Duck Books 19-515 1996 $1,500.00

ASSOCIATION - TAYLOR

BARLOW, THOMAS   The Case Concerning Setting Up Images or Painting of them in Churches. London: James Roberts, 1714. Large 12mo; (2), 22 pages, interleaved and bound in marbled wrappers at the beginning of the 19th century; head of titlepage clipped but not affecting text; signature of Anth. Taylor, 1811, and leaf of manuscript transcriptions from Dugdale.   Ken Spelman 30-2 1996 £220.00

FROST, ROBERT LEE 1874-1963   North of Boston. New York: Holt, 1915. Later printing of second edition; some rubbing and fraying to spine, overall very good, without dust jacket; remarkable copy; inscribed by author for Mrs. Bruce Taylor, with poem "Reluctance" 24 lines long in author's hand and initilled by him, and Misgining" which consists of 16 lines and is also initialled by author.   Ken Lopez 74-144 1996 $650.00

PAGE, THOMAS NELSON   Two Little Confederates. New York: Charles Scribner's Sons, 1889. 1st edition; 2nd printing with pages 157-8 blank; 8vo; grey pictorial cloth, gilt lettering, bookplate, small unobtrusive inked library stamp on p. 156, aside from only some minor shelf wear, very bright copy; inscribed by author for Mrs. Frederic Taylor, laid in are two TLS's, one to Charles Henry Hart and one to Frederic W. Speirs. BAL 15364.   James Cummins 14-149 1996 $200.00

ASSOCIATION - GEORGE TAYLOR

WORDSWORTH, WILLIAM 1770-1850   Poems, Chiefly of Early and Late Years, Including the Borderers, a Tragedy. London: Edward Moxon, 1842. 1st edition; 8vo; pages xi, (i) errata, 406 + ad leaf, also with additional series half title and titlepage; uncut in original publisher's cloth, very neatly rebacked with original spine laid down, lettered in gilt, new endpapers, but retaining original free endpapers; very good; presentation copy, inscribed by author, excellent association copy, also signed by George Taylor (1772-1851), and by his son Henry Taylor.   Simon Finch 24-262 1996 £1,600.00

ASSOCIATION - HENRY TAYLOR

WORDSWORTH, WILLIAM 1770-1850   Poems, Chiefly of Early and Late Years, Including the Borderers, a Tragedy. London: Edward Moxon, 1842. 1st edition; 8vo; pages xi, (i) errata, 406 + ad leaf, also with additional series half title and titlepage; uncut in original publisher's cloth, very neatly rebacked with original spine laid down, lettered in gilt, new endpapers, but retaining original free endpapers; very good; presentation copy, inscribed by author, excellent association copy, also signed by George Taylor (1772-1851), and by his son Henry Taylor.   Simon Finch 24-262 1996 £1,600.00

ASSOCIATION - LESLEY TAYLOR

FROST, ROBERT LEE 1874-1963   North of Boston. New York: Holt, 1926. Later edition; good copy, lacking the dust jacket, but again with lengthy and thoughtful inscription from author to Lesley Taylor in 1927; owner's attractive bookplate and offsetting to the first page of text from an additional Frost poem, on newsprint, laid in. Spine cloth on rear joint sliced for 2 inches from base, and some wear to extremities and corners.   Ken Lopez 74-145 1996 $450.00

ASSOCIATION - LESLIE TAYLOR

FROST, ROBERT LEE 1874-1963   Mountain Interval. New York: Holt, 1924. 2nd edition; spine gilt largely rubbed away, still about very good without dust jacket; inscribed by author; with attractive bookplate of Leslie Taylor.   Ken Lopez 74-146 1996 $400.00

ASSOCIATION - S. TAYLOR

NICHOLSON, NORMAN   The Fire of the Lord. London: Nicholson and Watson, 1944. 1st edition; 8vo; pages 222; original cloth, spine faded as usual; presentation copy, inscribed by author for Rev. S. Taylor. R.F.G. Hollett & Son 78-430 1996 £65.00

ASSOCIATION - CHRISTOPHER TEESDALE

SHELLEY, PERCY BYSSHE 1792-1822   The Poetical Works... London: Edward Moxon, 1839. 1st edition; small 8vo; 4 volumes; frontispiece in volume 1 (foxed, as often); contemporary vellum, green morocco labels, marbled endpapers, red edges; excellent set; bookplate of Christopher Teesdale. Wise p. 87; Granniss 88; Dunbar, Shelley Studies 345. Simon Finch 24-208   1996 £580.00

ASSOCIATION - EDWARD TELLER

SMYTH, HENRY DE WOLF   Atomic Enery for Military Purposes a General Account of the Scientific Research and Technical Development That Went into the Making of Atomic Bombs. Princeton; Princeton University Press, 1945. 1st edition; signed by Dr. Edward Teller; good/very good in like dust jacket.   Aronovitz 57-1105   1996 $150.00

ASSOCIATION - TEMPLER

BRETT, THOMAS   An Account of Church-Government and Governours. London: John Wyat, 1701. 1st edition; 8vo; reddish brown turkey morocco in triple panel design wtih 2 line fillet and rolls, second panel contains ornamental fleurons in corners from which a single acorn tool is suspended, there are four larger fleurons midway along each side, innermost panel is intersected at each corner, spine with five raised bands and closely stamped decoration within the compartments (without title), board edges gilt decorated, inner gilt dentelles, all edges gilt, marbled endleaves, in absolutely fine condition; bookplate of J. L. Templer, Torrhill, Devon.   Book Block 32-33   1996 $875.00

ASSOCIATION - CHARLES TENNANT

HOOD, THOMAS 1799-1845   Odes and Addresses to Great People. London: Baldwin, Cradock and Joy, 1825. 1st edition; octavo; later polished tan calf, gilt, top edge gilt, by Bedford, edges untrimmed; very fine; Charles Tennant bookplate.   G. W. Stuart 59-47   1996 $325.00

ASSOCIATION - DYLAN MARLAIS THOMAS

ERNST, MAX   At Eye Level and Paramyths. Beverley Hills: Copley Galleries, 1949. One of 513 copies; some waterstaining to lower margins of early pages, front hinge rather fragile, but very good; presentation copy from Ernst for Dylan and Caitlin Thomas.   R. A. Gekoski 19-142   1996 £875.00

ASSOCIATION - EDWARD THOMAS

TENNYSON, ALFRED TENNYSON, 1ST BARON 1809-1892   In Memoriam. London: Macmillan & Co., 1896. Later edition; 12mo; original green cloth, slightly worn; quarter morocco box; presentation copy from Edward Thomas to his future Mother-in-law, Mrs. Noble; important ALS to Mrs. Nobel; Edward Thomas letters are scarce; with two George Sims bookplates.   Lakin & Marley 3-66   1996 $2,500.00

ASSOCIATION - NATHANIEL THOMAS

WEBSTER, KIMBALL   The Gold Seekers of '49. Manchester: Standard Book Co., 1917. 1st edition; 240 pages, plates; original mustard cloth, pictorial paper label on front cover and title stamped in gilt on spine and cover; minor wear, fine. From the collection of Nathaniel S. Thomas, with his bookplate. Cowan p. 673; Graff 4571; Wheat Gold Rush 222; Mintz Trail 489.   Michael D. Heaston 23-361   1996 $175.00

ASSOCIATION - R. W. THOMPSON

ROBINSON, JACOB   Wrestling and Wrestlers: Biographical Sketches of Celebrated Atheletes of the Northern Ring. London: Bemrose & Sons, 1893. 8vo; pages xlvii, 251, 2 woodcut headpieces; little scattered foxing, but excellent copy; inscribed by F. Nicholson for R. W. Thompson. R.F.G. Hollett & Son 78-649   1996 £120.00

ASSOCIATION - W. H. THOMPSON

SOUTHARD, ELMER ERNEST   Neurosyphylis: Modern Systematic Diagnosis and Treatment Presented in One Hundred and Thirty-Seven Case Histories. Boston: W. M. Leonard, Pub., 1917. 1st edition; 8vo; 496 pages + 25 halftones; panelled green cloth with painted spine labels, lightly shelfworn, with stamp of Hartford Retreat to titlepage and several over leaves; with one page TLS from publisher to W. H. Thompson presenting the book.   John Gach 150-440   1996 $125.00

ASSOCIATION - WILLIAM THOMPSON

FRANKFURTER, FELIX   The Labour Injunction. New York: Macmillan Co., 1930. Olive green cloth, showing wear, but fresh copy. With presentation in author's hand to William G. Thompson, lawyer for Sacco and Vanzetti.   Meyer Boswell SL25-85   1996 $500.00

ASSOCIATION - A. THOMSON

BOULENGER, G. A.   Catalogue of the Lizards. London: 1885-87. 1st edition; 8vo; 3 volumes; 96 lithographed plates, last few plates of volume 1 bit stained, just touching figure on last plate; cloth, worn and used, backstrips flapping, one rear endpaper missing, signature of A. Thomson on titles.   Maggs Bros. Ltd. 1190-668   1996 £145.00

ASSOCIATION - MARGARET ELEANOR THOMSON

TAYLOR, M. W.   The Old Manorial Halls of Westmorland and Cumberland. Kendal: T. Wilson, 1892. 1st edition; 8vo; pages xxi, 384, 54 illustrations and 27 folding plans; original brown cloth, gilt, extremities little rubbed, few spots to prelims, lower joint cracking. Attractive bookplate of Margaret Eleanor Thomson.   R.F.G. Hollett & Son 78-45   1996 £140.00

ASSOCIATION - HELEN THOREAU

OSGOOD, FRANCES S.   The Poetry of Flowers and Flowers of Poetry. New York: J. C. Riker, 1841. 1st edition; octavo; 276 pages; hand colored title and 12 hand colored full page floral plates; pictorial boards, all edges gilt, light foxing and rebacking to soiled boards. Inscribed in pencil to H. D. Thoreau's sister Helen from a member of Prudence Ward's family.   Bromer Booksellers 90-211   1996 $450.00

ASSOCIATION - T. THORNHILL

FOX, CHARLES JAMES   A History of the Early Part of the Reign of James the Second. London: printed for William Miller by William Savage, 1808. 1st edition; 11 x 8 3/4 inches; 2 p.l., li, (1), 277, (1) pages, (1) leaf, clviii pages, (1) leaf (blank), 8 pages (ads); frontispiece; errata slip tipped in; fine contemporary marbled calf, sides framed with 4 closely spaced gilt fillets, raised bands flanked by multiple gilt rules, spine compartments with large and elegant gilt foliate ornament in center, black morocco label, marbled edges and endpapers; trivial marks on covers, offsetting from frontispiece onto titlepage, occasional very minor foxing in text, but very fine and handsome copy. Armorial bookplate of T. Thornhill.   Phillip J. Pirages 33-238   1996 $450.00

ASSOCIATION - E. N. THORNTON

GROSE, FRANCIS 1731-1791   The Antiquities of England and Wales. London: printed for Hooper & Wigstead,... n.d., c. 1783-97. New edition; 4to; 8 volumes; vignette title to all volumes, County Index to all volumes, (iii-iv), preface 1-142 pages, addenda to preface 143-160 pages, text, to the Public (i-iv) to volume VIII, General Index 165-172 pages, Directions to Binder to final leaf volume VIII, engraved frontispiece to all volumes, 589 engraved plates, and 1 extra plate not called for, 88 maps and plans and 1 extra plan not called for, 88 maps and plans and 1 extra plate not called for; full diced calf, gilt rule border to boards, gilt titles and tooling to spines, few joints rubbed, corners slightly bumped, very fine and handsome set; plates in near mint condition with no foxing or offsetting, signature O to volume 1 heavily browned, only light foxing to few other pages, uniformly marbled endpapers & edges, bookplate of Charles Vere Dashwood & E. N. Thornton.   Beeleigh Abbey BA/56-10   1996 £950.00

ASSOCIATION - THOROLD

BIBLE. GREEK - 1723   Novum Testamentum Graecum. Leipzig: Gleditsch, 1723. Folio; crimson morocco by Walther, with his label, all edges gilt, the Syston Park copy, with Thorold's pencil note "Chart Max/Walther" in front flyleaves.   Marlborough 160-29   1996 £500.00

ASSOCIATION - THOROLD

STROZZI, TITO VESPASIANO   Strozii Poetae Pater et Filius. Venice: Venetiis is Aedibus Aldi et Andreae Asulani Soceri, 1513/14. Edition princeps; 8vo; 2 parts; ff. (8), 99, (1), 152 leaves, printed throughout in italics, early illumination of A1, with frame crowned by dolphins, and elephant drawing an ancient carriage with arms and shields, the book was once damped throughout, and illumination is somewhat faded with offsetting; crimson morocco stamped in gilt with Aldine anchor and dolphin, entwined in naval rope, binding was probably executed by Messrs. Storr and Ridge of Grantham for Sir John Hayford Thorold, preserved in cloth box; Syston Park copy. Renouard p. 65.10; Adams S1956; UCLA I/93; Goldsmid 91; Isaac 12832.   Family Album Tillers-591 1996 $2,000.00

VERGILIUS MARO, PUBLIUS 70-19 BC   Opera. Amsterdam: Wetstenil, 1746. Large 4to; 4 volumes, pages (32), (82), 520; 706; 707; 360, (92), engraved frontispiece, vignettes, maps, etc., title in red and black, one of the few copies that were struck off on large paper; brilliant full red straight grained morocco Syston Park binding, all edges gilt, engraved ex-libris of Thorold's Syston Park Library. Dibdin II 552-3; Brunet V 1292. Family Album Tillers-641 1996 $2,000.00

ASSOCIATION - RAYMOND HENRY THRUPP

CLODE, C. M.   Memorials of the Guild of Merchant Taylors of the Fraternity of St. John the Baptist, in the City of London... London: Harrison and sons, 1875. 1st edition; royal 8vo; title printed in red and black, xxxi, (1), 746 pages, 29 plates and plans; original blue half morocco, gilt, rubbed at edges and joints, otherwise very good. Presentation copy to Raymond Henry Thrupp.   John Drury 82-47 1996 £50.00

ASSOCIATION - TICHBORNE

RUSSEL, JAMES   Letters from a Young Painter Abroad to His Friends in England. London: printed for W. Russel, 1750. 2nd edition of volume 1, 1st edition of volume 2; 8vo; 2 volumes; printed on ordianry paper; 13 plates; occasional light spotting, contemporary calf, gilt, reacked, very good set; early engraved bookplates of Mrs. Tichborne. Pine Coffin 740.1. CBEL II 1419.   Ximenes 108-316 1996 $300.00

ASSOCIATION - TITTERTON

CHESTERTON, GILBERT KEITH 1874-1936   The Return of Don Quixote. London: Chatto & Windus, 1927. 1st edition; 312 pages; original binding, top edge dusty, prelims, edges and endpapers spotted, head and tail of spine and corners bumped, covers marked, cover edges rubbed, free endpapers browned, spine slightly darkened, some semi-erased pencillings on rear pastaedown; inscription; good; with ALS from author to W. R. Titterton.   Ulysses 39-105 1996 £145.00

ASSOCIATION - WILLIAM C. TODD

DANTE, ALIGHIERI 1265-1321   Dante's Hell. Boston: Ticknor & Fields, 1857. 1st edition of this translation; 12mo; original quarter black roan and marbled boards, bit worn; some foxing at beginning and end, but very good; presentation copy, inscribed from translator to William C. Todd.   Ximenes 108-101 1996 $100.00

ASSOCIATION - N. TOLL

PFISTER, R.   The Excavations at Dura-Europos. Final Report IV. Part II: The Textiles. New Haven: Yale University Press, 1945. Large 4to; color frontispiece, vi, 64 pages, 8 figures, 33 plates; original cloth, fine. With signature of N. Toll.   Archaeologia Luxor-3273 1996 $175.00

ASSOCIATION - TOLLET

JENYNS, SOAME   Poems. London: printed for R. Dodsley, 1752. 1st edition; 8vo; contemporary calf, spine gilt, some rubbing, but sound; very good; from the library of John Drinkwater, with his book label and note of acquisition dated 1923, purchased from Hodgson's sale of the library of Eliza Tollet, this volume signed twice by her nephew George Tollet. Foxon P387; CBEL II 554.   Ximenes 108-222 1996 $250.00

ASSOCIATION - SERGE TOMKEIEFF

BUTLER, SAMUEL 1835-1902   The Humour of Homer and Other Essays. London: A. C. Fifeld, 1913. Portrait in photogravure; original blue cloth, dust jacket; inscribed presentation copy from editor to Serge Tomkeieff, 7th Jan. 1921. Hoppe 26 p. 56; Hoppe III 5.   Jarndyce CII-52 1996 £60.00

ASSOCIATION - HENRY MAJOR TOMLINSON

DOUGHTY, CHARLES MONTAGU 1843-1926   Wanderings in Arabia. London: Duckworth, 1908. 1st edition; 8vo; 2 volumes, prelims in volume 1 slightly foxed; original cloth, slightly soiled, library labels removed from front covers, inscription on each front free endpaper "Philip Tomlinson from H. M. T." (H. M. Tomlinson to his brother).   H. M. Fletcher 121-154 1996 £650.00

ASSOCIATION - PHILIP TOMLINSON

DOUGHTY, CHARLES MONTAGU 1843-1926   Wanderings in Arabia. London: Duckworth, 1908. 1st edition; 8vo; 2 volumes, prelims in volume 1 slightly foxed; original cloth, slightly soiled, library labels removed from front covers, inscription on each front free endpaper "Philip Tomlinson from H. M. T." (H. M. Tomlinson to his brother).   H. M. Fletcher 121-154 1996 £650.00

ASSOCIATION - ARNOLD TOYNBEE

LAL, MOHAN   Life of the Amir Dost Mohammed Khan of Kabul; with His Political Proceedings Towards the English, Russian and Persian Governments... London: Longman, Brown, Green and Longmans, Paternoster Row, 1846. 1st edition; 8vo; 2 volumes; 1-399, 1-498 pages; frontispiece to volume 1, 18 engraved portraits on India paper and 1 large folding map; half calf and marbled boards, rebacked, corners and joints worn, morocco labels to spines, edges and endpapers uniformly marbled; ex-libris Arnold Toynbee with his ink signature to prelim of both volumes, some offsetting to title of volume 1, armorial bookplate to front pastedown.   Beeleigh Abbey BA56-86 1996 £450.00

ASSOCIATION - WALTER TRACY

FOURNIER, PIERRE SIMON 1712-1768   Fournier on Typefounding. London: the Fleuron Books, Published by Soncino Press, 1930. Limited to 260 copies; 8vo; pages xxxviii, (4), 323; frontispiece, 16 double page plates; original buckram backstrip faded little marked, but good; inscribed "W. Turner Berry for his indispensable library. J.R." and subsequently in the collection of Walter Tracy with his ownership signature.   Claude Cox 107-268 1996 £75.00

MEYNELL, FRANCIS   Typography, the Written Word and the Printed Word... London: prepared, printed and published by the Pelican Press, 1923. 1st edition; 500 copies printed; 8vo; pages lxv, 30 leaves of type specimens and titlepages french folded and printed on one side only, large folding title and plate of Pelican devices; printed in black and colors; original blue boards, paper label, good, uncut copy. ownership signature of Walter Tracy. Appleton 19; Meynell My Lives p. 144. Clark Cox 107-231 1996 £85.00

STEPHENSON, BLAKE & CO.   Lining Type Borders, Brass Rule, &c. Material and Machinery. London: Stephenson Blake & Co. ltd., 1915/19. 2nd issue; 4to; pages xviii, 144, 72 (machinery) + 8 inserted pages; original cloth, gilt, dated 1915 but with new price list and inserted slips dated 1919; very good; contemporary ownership signature of H. Langley Jones, subsequently in the library of Walter Tracy, with few pencilled marginal notes by him.   Claude Cox 107-237 1996 £65.00

ASSOCIATION - OSWALD TRAIN

BROWN, FREDRIC   Here Comes a Candle. New York: Dutton, 1950. 1st edition; near fine, in very good price clipped dust jacket with soiling, light chipping, few small closed tears and light creases; near fine with bookplate of publisher Oswald Train.   Quill & Brush 102-102 1996 $250.00

GERRARE, W.   Phantasms. Roxburghe Press, 1985. 1st edition; spine darkened, else just about very good; the copy of Oswald Train, with his bookplate; quite scarce.   Aronovitz 57-445 1996 $295.00

KIP, L.   Hannibal's Man and Other Tales. Argus Christmas Stories, 1878. 1st edition; some slight soil resulting in a lightening of the green cloth along fore-edge of rear cloth panel, else bright, very good+; from the collection of Oswald Train with bookplate.   Aronovitz 57-632 1996 $125.00

ASSOCIATION - HORACE TRAUBEL

WHITMAN, WALT 1819-1892   Good-Bye My Fancy. Philadelphia: David McKay, 1891. 1st edition; Binding E; portrait; green cloth, faint offsetting to pastedowns and endpapers as if a jacket at some point were present, hinges lightly cracked, slight rubbing to spine tips, near fine; inscribed by Horace Traubel to R. W. Gilder stating "This book (?) (?) bound this way in green covers was made by W.W. at the (?) not for the market but for distribution among his friends". Fine association. BAL 21440.   Charles Agvent 4-1187 1996 $1,200.00

WHITMAN, WALT 1819-1892   November Boughs. 1891. 1st edition; printing 3 (Winship believes this is one of 400 copies printed in 1891 intended by Whitman to be bound with Goodbye My Fancy until illness prevented him from pursuing his plans); signed by author; green cloth, few small stains on front cover, front hinge lightly cracked, near fine; inscribed by Horace Traubel in 1903 to Larson Butler with initialled note below inscription by Traubel stating that "this edn. of N.B. bound in green was designed by W.W. for his friends, not for market, + was never anywhere but on sale." Fine association.   Charles Agvent 4-1198 1996 $3,500.00

ASSOCIATION - TREANOR

HILL, JOSEPH J.   The History of Warner's Ranch and Its Environs. Los Angeles: John Treanor, 1927. One of 300 copies; 11 x 7 7/8 inches; xii, 221 pages, 2 etchings by Loren Barton; brown boards with linen spine and tips and paper spine label, small spot to tail of spine; inscribed by Treanor to Sol Lesser.   Dawson's Books Shop 528-108 1996 $100.00

ASSOCIATION - ELLEN TREE

KNOWLES, JAMES SHERIDAN   The Beggar's Daughter of Bethnal Green. London: Basil Stewart and J. Ridgway, 1828. 1st edition; half blue morocco, scuffed at points, marbled boards, spine gilt, untrimmed, inscribed presentation copy from author for Ellen Tree who played Bess. Dramatis Personae 37-108 1996 $200.00

ASSOCIATION - BAKER TRISTRAM

MORRIS, WILLIAM 1834-1896   Love Is Enough, or the Freeing of Pharamond: a Morality. Kelmscott Press, 1897. One of 300 copies on paper (there were also 8 on vellum); 11 1/2 x 8 1/2 inches; 2 p.l., 90 pages; 2 full page woodcut illustrations designed by Edward Burne-Jones & engraved by W.H. Hooper, 1 as frontispiece, other at end, woodcut initials in black or blue, elaborate woodcut full border on 1st page of text, smaller borders on many other pages; ptd. in red, blue & black; fine cont. brown mor., handsomely gilt by Douglas Cockerell (signed "19 DC 01" on rear turn-in), covers w/broad frame of linked rectangles & stylized interlaced floral ornaments in corners (front cover w/central panel giving author, title & pub. in lg. letters), spine in very attractive compartments filled w/twining tendrils & many broadleaf stamps, gilt dec. turn-ins w/clusters of sm. inlaid green leaves at corners, edges gilded on rough; covers w/hint of soiling & few marks (one 3/4" superficial scratch on front board), otherwise very fine inside and out, especially appealing binding. Armorial bookplate of Baker Tristram. Sparling 52; Tomkinson p. 121.   Phillip J. Pirages 33-320 1996 $6,500.00

ASSOCIATION - JOHN TROLLOPE

BOILEAU-DESPREAUX, NICHOLAS   Oevvres. Glasgow: De L'Imprimerie De R. et A. Foulis, 1759. Octavo; 2 volumes; contemporary calf, spine ends chipped, joints cracked, one label gone from spine; bookplate of Sir John Trollope. Gaskell 364.   G. W. Stuart 59-18 1996 $195.00

ASSOCIATION - WILLIAM TRUMBULL

BIBLE. GREEK - 1568   Nouum Testamentum. Paris: Robert Estienne, 1568, 1569 at end; 7th Estienne edition; small 8vo; 2 volumes; pages (xxxii), 494, 342, (sl), Greek letter in 2 sizes, Roman dedication, woodcut printer's basilisk device on titlepages, 'Noli altum' device at end of volume 2, woodcut initials & ornaments, single line red borders throughout volume 2, fairly light waterstain in gutter of first 60 or so leaves of volume 1, light age yellowing, generally very good set; English red morocco richly gilt, c. 1700, all edges gilt; 18th century bookplates of William Trumbull; BMSTC Fr. p. 62; Adams B1670; Renouard 171.1. Brunet V 737.   A. Sokol XXV-68 1996 £985.00

ASSOCIATION - OLGA TUFNELL

TRISTRAM, HENRY BAKER   **Scenes** in the East, Consisting of Twelve Coloured Photographic Views **of Places** Mentioned in the Bible... London: Society for Promoting Christian Knowledge, 1880. 4to; 49 pages, 12 color plates; original gilt decorated cloth, all edges gilt, bookplate, boards stained. Inscribed "Greetings and best wishes, Olga Tufnell, Jan. '73". Archaeologia Luxor-2775 1996 $125.00

ASSOCIATION - WILLIAM CUTHBERT BRIAN TUNSTALL

WALKER, ADAM   Remarks Made in a Tour from London to the Lakes of Westmoreland and Cumberland, in the Summer of MDCCXCI. London: G. Nichol and C. Dilly, 1792. 2nd edition; 8vo; 251 pages, lacks half title (not always present), otherwise very good; modern half calf with raised bands and spine label, marbled boards. Armorial bookplate of William Cuthbert Brian Tunstall. Bicknell p. 24.2.   R.F.G. Hollett & Son 78-1336 1996 £325.00

ASSOCIATION - IVAN TURGENEV

ZOLA, EMILE   Une Campagne 1880-1881. Paris: G. Charpentier, 1882. 1st edition; 12mo. in half sheets, pages x, 408; contemporary green half morocco, green marbled boards, raised bands, gilt tooled compartments, gilt lettered direct, marbled endpapers, small modern bookplate, original yellow printed paper wrapper folded and bound in, autograph presentation inscription to Ivan Turgenev on half title, uncut, some gatherings unopened, light foxing, remarkable presentation copy; Simon Finch 24-264 1996 £2,200.00

ASSOCIATION - EDWIN TURNBULL

ROBINSON, FRANCIS KILDALE   A Glossary of Yorkshire Words and Phrases. London: John Russell Smith, 1855. 1st edition; post 12mo; (2), x, 204, 16 pages; original cloth, just slightly worn and sunned, good copy nonetheless, with bookabel of Edwin Turnbull, also of Whitby. Ash Rare Books Zenzybyr-78 1996 £65.00

ASSOCIATION - WILLIAM TURNBULL

LAWSON, JOHN PARKER   The Book of Perth: an Illustration of the Moral and Ecclesiastical State of Scotland Before and After the Reformation. Edinburgh: Thomas G. Stevenson, 1847. Limited edition (251); 8vo; pages xl, 318, (ii), half title, 3 engraved plates, woodcut; little spotting; original cloth, gilt, rather faded, tear across top of spine repaired. Presentation copy from William Turnbull, to whomt he work is dedicated, to Hugh Jones.   R.F.G. Hollett 76-152 1996 £75.00

ASSOCIATION - DAWSON TURNER

HORNE, T. H.   A Catalogue of the Library of the College of St. Margaret & St. Bernard, Commonly Called Queen's College in the University of Cambridge. London: for the Society of Queen's College, 1827. 2 volumes; original cloth backed boards, paper spine labels, worn, spines partly detached and boards of volume 2 coming loose, mild spotting to first and last few leaves; ownership inscription of Dawson Turner with ALS dated 21st Nov. 1827 presenting it to him from Thomas Clowes of Queen's College.   Maggs Bros. Ltd. 1191-48 1996 £290.00

ASSOCIATION - STANELY TWARDOWICZ

KEROUAC, JACK 1922-1969   Satori in Paris. New York: 1966. 1st edition; fine in dust jacket; with signed presentation inscription from Kerouac's friend, Stanley Twardowicz.   Polyanthos 22-488 1996 $125.00

ASSOCIATION - TWEEDDALE

BUCHANAN, GEORGE 1506-1582   Rervm Scoticarvm Historia. Edimbvrgi (but London?) ad exemplar Alexandri Arbuthneti Editum, 1583. Folio; 17th century mottled calf, very nice; contemporary bookplate of Marquess of Tweeddale. STC 3992.   G. W. Stuart 59-21 1996 $850.00

ASSOCIATION - ANNE TYLER

BLACKBURN, WILLIAM   A Duke Miscellany. Durham: Duke University, 1970. 1st edition; signed by Anne Tyler at her entry, The Feather Behind the Rock; unobtrusive bump to fore-edge of a number of pages, else fine in dust jacket.   Lame Duck Books 19-546 1996 $175.00

ASSOCIATION - MICHAEL TYSON

MILTON, JOHN 1608-1674   Paradise Lost...Paradise Regain'd...Samson...Poems. Birmingham: John Baskerville, 1760. 3rd and final Baskerville edition; tall octavo; 2 volumes; contemporary diced russia finely gilt, joints cracked, spine ends chipped, all edges gilt; contemporary bookplate of Michael Tyson. Gaskell 9 and 10.   G. W. Stuart 59-11 1996 $285.00

ASSOCIATION - FRED UHLMAN

FOWLES, JOHN 1926-   The Collector. Boston: Little Brown, 1963. 1st American edition; 8vo; pages 305; cloth, dust jacket by Tom Adams (wrapper very slightly worn at extremities), otherwise fine; inscribed by author for Fred Uhlman.   Thomas Thorp 489-105 1996 £180.00

ASSOCIATION - JULIUS UNGER

SMITH, EDWARD E.   The Skylark of Space. Hadley, 1947. 2nd edition; 1/1000 copies; very good+ in dust jacket with small piece missing from lower right corner of front dust jacket; inscribed by author to Julius Unger.   Aronovitz 57-1085 1996 $135.00

SMITH, EDWARD E.   The Skylark of Valeron. Fantasy Press, 1949. 1st edition; fine in near fine dust jacket; inscribed by author to Julius Unger.   Aronovitz 57-1088 1996 $135.00

ASSOCIATION - R. FITZGERALD UNIACKE

THACKERAY, WILLIAM MAKEPEACE 1811-1863   The Irish Sketch-Book. London: Chapman and Hall, 1843. 1st edition; 8vo; 2 volumes; numerous engravings; original green cloth, spine ends showing little wear, spines lightly faded, three hinges renewed, chip in front free endpaper, some discoloring of frontispieces around edges, else unusually fine, fresh copy, relatively scarce; in green cloth slipcase with matching chemise, gilt stamped with Bachman's monogram; armorial bookplate of R. FitzGerald Uniacke, bookplates of Edwin Bachman.   James Cummins 14-209 1996 $300.00

ASSOCIATION - LOUIS UNTERMEYER

MEW, CHARLOTTE   The Farmer's Bride. London: Poetry Bookshop, 1921. New edition; original pictorial boards, pictorial dust jacket (faded chipped and worn); Louis Untermeyer's copy with his bookplate and 3 autograph letters to him from author, envelopes of which are neatly pasted to front and rear endpapers; book in very good condition, letters fine.   David J. Holmes 52-72 1996 $1,250.00

ASSOCIATION - WILLIAM UPCOTT

BOYLE, ROBERT 1627-1691   Some Considerations About the Reconcileableness of Reason and Religion. London: printed by T. N. for H. Herringman, 1675. 1st edition; 8vo; contemporary sprinkled sheep, lightly rubbed; John Evelyn's copy, inscribed by Evelyn on blank facing titlepage. With signature of William Upcott dated 1816. Fulton 122; Wing B4024.   Ximenes 109-49 1996 $4,500.00

ASSOCIATION - JOHN USHER

STEVENSON, ROBERT LOUIS BALFOUR 1850-1894   The Letters to His Family and Friends. London: Methuen, 1900. 1st edition; large 8vo; 2 volumes, pages xliv, 375; xiii, 384; 2 portraits; original cloth, gilt, little rubbed and scratched, paper spine labels, top edge gilt, uncut. from Sir John Usher's library.   R.F.G. Hollett 76-357 1996 £65.00

ASSOCIATION - HORACE ANNESLEY VACHELL

LECKY, WILLIAM EDWARD HARTPOLE   A History of England in the Eighteenth Century. New York: D. Appleton, 1888-90. 8vo; 8 volumes; original cloth. From the library of Horace Annesley Vachell with presentation inscription from his mother.   Howes Bookshop 265-648 1996 £120.00

ASSOCIATION - DE VALMY

HOOPER, GEORGE   Waterloo: the Downfall of the First Napoleon: a History of the Campaign of 1815. London: Smith, Elder, 1862. Thick 8vo; extra illustrated with 28 folded, full page and in-set engravings, 2 color lithograph views, original small watercolor bust portrait of Louis XVIII, and 5 folding maps; also tipped in signed document: Divsion de Paris, 1817, 1 printed note to Marshal Francois Etienne de Kellerman, Duc De Valmy on folded quarto sheet with contemporary hand written note by subordinate, and signed by Duc de Valmy, with orig. red wax seal & postmarked address to Duc de Valmy on verso of second leaf; later full crushed navy mor. gilt by Sangorski & Sutcliffe of Charles J. Sawyer Ltd., alternating motif of crowns & bees, initial 'N' with crowns at corners, crimson morocco at pastedown under bevelled glass with brass frame is a very fine miniature on enamel of Napoleon on the deck of the 'Belellrophon", deck rigging and ropes in background with sea in distance; binding in perfect condition in fleece lined blue cloth box.   Marilyn Braiterman 15-151 1996 $3,750.00

ASSOCIATION - MARTIN VAN BUREN

MORRIS, GEORGE P.   The Deserted Bride; and Other Poems. New York: 1838. 8vo; original blue cloth, fine, two part half morocco slipcase; earliest known copy, presentation copy to President Martin Van Burne, inscribed in ink by Morris. Rinderknecht 51776; BAL 14355.   M & S Rare Books 60-248 1996 $1,750.00

STEPHENS, JOHN LLOYD 1805-1852   Incidents of Travel in the Yucatan. New York: Harper & Bros., 1843. 1st edition; 8vo; 2 volumes; 937 pages, 124 illustrations, 1 folding map; original gilt pictorial cloth, light chipping and small tears at spines, scattered foxing and browning; inscribed by author for President Martin Van Buren.   Archaeologia Luxor-4914 1996 $2,500.00

ASSOCIATION - VAN KIRK

TERRY, MICHAEL   Across Unknown Australia. London: 1925. 311 pages, frontispiece and 24 plates; original green stamped buckram, several later pages slightly rubbed, light blue mark on spine, otherwise nice. Signed by Terry, with inscription for Mrs. Van Kirk.   Antipodean 28-443 1996 $295.00

ASSOCIATION - VANBRUGH

GRAFER, JOHN   A Descriptive Catalogue of Upwards of Eleven Hundred Species and Varities of Herbaceous or Perenial Plants... London: printed and sold by J. Smeeton, nd. 1794. 3rd edition; 8vo; contemporary half calf, spine gilt, some rubbing, but sound; blank strip clipped from foot of titlepage, just touching last line of publisher's ads, very good, scarce; inscribed to Mrs. Egerton with Mr. Vanbrugh's respects.   Ximenes 108-169 1996 $600.00

ASSOCIATION - DI VEROLI

POTANUS, JOANNES JOVIANUS   Opera Omnia. Venice: Aldus & Asulanus, June 1518 - April 1519 - September 1519. 4to; 3 volumes; vellum; Aldine Anchor on titlepage of first volume and at end of 3rd volume; owner's stamp cut out o title leaf of volume 3 affecting few letters of text on verso; Di Veroli & Paolino Gerli booktickets in all volumes, ownership stamps in title margins of volumes 2 and 3; ownership inscription of Magnoccavalli in volume II. Renouard 82.3, 87.6 and 7; Adams P1860; Brunet IV 808.   Rostenberg & Stern 150-76 $2,750.00

ASSOCIATION - WILLIS VICKERY

SWINBURNE, ALGERNON CHARLES 1837-1909   Miscellanies. London: Chatto & Windus, 1886. 1st edition; 8vo; 32 page publisher's ads at back dated March 1886; CC4 with stylized floral decoration not blank as stated in Tinker; original green cloth, gilt ruled and lettered, publisher's design in gilt at lower spine, some darkening, and rubbing; some browning and spotting, generally at front and back; good copy. Poet Lionel Johnson's copy with his signature; Willis Vickery's copy with bookplate. Tinker 2030; Wise 'Swinburne' I.80, 2.124-5.   James Cummins 14-203 1995 $350.00

ASSOCIATION - HENRY VIRTUE-TEBBS

CATHOLIC CHURCH. LITURGY & RITUAL. OFFICE   Officium Beatae Mariae Virginis. Brescia: Policreto Turlino, 1583. 12mo; title, 16ff., n.n., pp. 1-578, 1 f. printed in red and black, 5 full page and many smaller woodcuts; brown goatskin, sides stamped with plaque of arabesque ornament on a gilt ground around an empty oval centre, spine with 3 double bands outlined by continuous foliate ornament in gilt, gilt rosette in each compartment, edges of boards plain, lacks two pairs of blue fabric ties, edges plain gilt, pastedown and one endleaf at each end, front endleaf detached, in sound unrestored condition, the binding may be from Lombardy or from Brescia; the copy of Henry Virtue-Tebbs, his sale, Sotheby's 25 June, 1900, lot 318.   Marlborough 160-7 1996 £2,100.00

ASSOCIATION - VON STEDINGKS BOKBAND

DECRETALES   Gregorii Papae IX. Venice: s.n. 1600. Large 4to; vignette title, 26 ff. n.n., 2 full page woodcuts, 2 ff., 1388 pages; red morocco elaborately gilt broad outer borders w/arabesque & heraldic tools, sq. corners w/dragons & winged putti, oval centre-piece w/the combined, quartered arms of Caffarelli (lions) & Borghese (dragons rampant & spread eagles), surmounted by a Cardinal's hat, broad spine gilt in 5 panels, single raised bands, middle 3 panels w/dragon, lion & eagle, respectively, flanked by salamanders & arabesques, later labels to first and last panels, all edges gilt & gauffered, plain endpapers, spine skilfully repaired with restoration at head, foot and lower band, corners also sympathetically restored, edges little worn, in half morocco folding case; from the collection of Victor von Stedingks Bokband. A Fine Soresini binding.   Marlborough 160-17 1996 £4,500.00

ASSOCIATION - HOWARD VYSE

SHAW, THOMAS   Travels, or Observations Relating to Several Parts of Barbary and the Levant. London: for A. Millar and W. Sandby, 1757. 2nd edition; quarto; xviii pages, 1 leaf, 5136 pages; 38 maps and plates; contemporary calf, rebacked in brown morocco, gilt, new endpapers, sound copy. Bookplate of Howard Vyse.   H. M. Fletcher 121-121 1996 £420.00

ASSOCIATION - WALTER WADE

DAVY, HUMPHRY 1778-1829   Elements of Agricultural Chemistry in a Course of Lectures for the Board of Agriculture. London: W. Bulmer for Longman, Hurst et al, 1813. 1st edition; 4to; viii, 323, lxiii, (4) pages; 10 copper engraved plates, 1 folding; contemporary boards, rebacked in early binders cloth, some wear to boards and top and bottom of spine, several plates bit foxed, in all very nice, wide margined, untrimmed copy; with early 19th century bookplate of Walter Wade, the Dublin physician and botanist. Fullmer p 70. Kress B6111.   Edwin V. Glaser 121-79 1996 $500.00

ASSOCIATION - WAHLENBERG

RICORD, PHILIPPE   Traite complet des Maldies Veneriennes. Clinique Iconographique de l'Hopital des Veneriens. London: J. Rouvier, 1851. 1st edition; folio; vignette title, 66 hand colored lithographed plates, text somewhat foxed and bit browned and plates generally in good state; half black leather, bit scuffed and worn, flyleaf chipped, faint inscription of Dr. Wahlenberg on half title.   Maggs Bros. Ltd. 1190-492 1996 £1,100.00

ASSOCIATION - KATHERINE WAITS

TATE, ALLEN   The Golden Mean and Other Poems. Nashville: Privately printed, 1923. 1st edition; one of 200 copies, signed by Tate and Wills; 8vo; author's first book; original buff wrappers lightly dust soiled, one small stain to upper cover, otherwise very good, enclosed in half morocco folding box; rare; this copy additionally inscribed by Ridley Wills for Katherine Waits. With Waits' signature.   James S. Jaffe 34-636 1996 $3,000.00

ASSOCIATION - STEPHEN WAKEMAN

HOLMES, OLIVER WENDELL 1809-1894   Poems. London: O. Rich & sons, 1846. 1st English edition; 12mo; original cloth, quite worn, especially the spine. With Bradley's embossed stamp on front flyleaf; Inscribed by Holmes for Dr. Samuel G. Morton and Holmes' signature on titlepage, inserted ALS; bookplates of William Harris Arnold & Stephen Wakeman. BAL 8743 binding B (Ticknor).   M & S Rare Books 60-173 1996 $550.00

ASSOCIATION - STEPHEN WAKEMAN

LOWELL, JAMES RUSSELL 1819-1891   Four Poems: The Ballad Of The Stranger, King Retro, The Royal Pedigree, and a Dream I Had. Village Press, 1906. One of 50 copies; 9 1/4 x 6 inches; 32 pages, (1) leaf colophon; original holland backed blue printed paper boards, edges untrimmed, especially fine, almost faultless copy; prospectus and letter from bookseller dated 1906 laid in. Modern bookplate of Stephen H. Wakeman. Cary 33.   Phillip J. Pirages 33-502 1996 $350.00

ASSOCIATION - JANE WALDO

AN ACCURATE Account of the Trial of William Corder for the Murder of Maria Marten...To Which are Added, An Explantory Preface and Fifty-Three of the Letters Sent by Various Ladies, in Answer to Corder's Matrimonial Advertisements... London: Publshed by George Foster, n.d., c. 1828. 2nd edition; 12mo; the printer appears to have left off the page number 14 as the consecutive pages are 13 to 15 and text appears continuous, pages 52 to 57 are out of order, some light spotting and browning; contemporary calf, red morocco label, upper joint starting, some knocking of corners and rubbing, generally light, without portrait; signature and address of H. J. Kirby on free endpaper, cropped signature of Jane Waldo on title.   James Cummins 14-140 1995 $200.00

ASSOCIATION - PRINCESS OF WALES

CHURCH OF ENGLAND. BOOK OF COMMON PRAYER   The Book of Common Prayer, and Administration of the Sacraments and Other Rites and Ceremonies of the Church, According to the Use of the Church of England... London: Printed by Thomas Baskett, Printer to the King's most Excellent... 1751. Folio; 1-19 pages; frontispiece, text and title rubricated by hand; full black morocco, elaborate gilt tooled border to boards, gilt coat of arms of George II to both bds., gilt title St. James's Chapel 1752, to upper bd., corners bumped, jts. sl. worn, crown & GR monogram to compartments, raised bands to spine, marbled endpapers; owner's bookplate, owner's pen inscription, some sproadic foxing; ms. inscription "This book which belonged originally to the Princess of Wales, was used by Members of the Royal Family in the Chapel of St. James, was bought of Mr. Bohn at Canterbury in June 1847 by Robert Jenkins, M.A. Rector & Vicar of Lyminge...June 1847 and given by him to Helen Constable Jenkins Easter Monday (March 29th) 1880."   Beeleigh Abbey BA56-140 1996 £550.00

ASSOCIATION - CORNELIUS WALFORD

FALCONER, THOMAS   On Surnames and the Rules of Law Affecting Their Change. London: Charles W. Reynell, 1862. Patterned cloth, later?, lalbel, dusty, but still sound and clean; presentation copy with armorial bookplate of Cornelius Walford, the Middle Temple barrister.   Meyer Boswell SL27-78 1996 $150.00

ASSOCIATION - DAVID WALLACE

FITZGERALD, FRANCIS SCOTT KEY 1896-1940   The Vegetable, or From President to Postman. New York: Charles Scribner's, 1923. 1st edition; 1st printing; octavo; 145 pages; original green cloth stamped in blind on front cover and in gilt on spine, front hinge cracked after front endpaper, light browning to margins, very good, in dust jacket with spine creased and with some tears mended with tape; with ALS by Fitzgerald to broadway producer and manager, David Wallace, and playbill for the production of the play at Princeton. The three items housed together in quarter brown morocco pull off case.   Heritage Book Shop 196-242 1996 $6,000.00

ASSOCIATION - JOSHUA MADDOX WALLACE

VERGILIUS MARO, PUBLIUS 70-19 BC   Bucolica, Georgica, et Aeneis. Glasgow: Foulis, 1778. Folio; 2 volumes, pages 277; 308, subscription list; full morocco, nicely decorated in gilt with interlocked square cornered double rule designs, wide floral gilt inner dentelles, engraved ex-libris of Hon. Joshua Maddox Wallace of Burlington, N.J. Gaskell 639. Family Album Tillers-650 1996 $650.00

ASSOCIATION - PICKFORD WALLER

BEAUMONT, C.   New Paths. London: Beaumont, 1918. One of 30 copies (of a total edition of 130), with original color woodcut frontispiece signed and in 2 states and the decorations hand colored; this is copy number 4 signed by Rice; decorations by Anne Estelle Rice; original binding, spine frayed along edges seemingly a result of a binding defect, large bookplate of Pickford Waller designed by Haldane Macfall. Charles Agvent 4-1239 1996 $200.00

ASSOCIATION - WALPOLE

CHATTERTON, THOMAS 1752-1770   Poems, Supposed to Have Been Written at bristol by Thomas Rowley, and Others in the Fifteenth Century. London: for T. Payne and Son, 1778. 3rd edition; 1st edition; with Tyrwhitt's appendix; 8vo; pages (ii), xxvii, (i), 333; facsimile plate facing p. 288; contemporary full russia, flat spine gilt lettered direct, gilt edges, spine slightly darkened and rubbed, front joint tender at head, good firm copy; with ownership of Elizabeth Walpole and bookplate of Lord Walpole of Woolterton. Warren 4.   Simon Finch 24-35 1996 £120.00

ASSOCIATION - HUGH WALPOLE

BUTLER, SAMUEL 1835-1902   The Authoress of the Odyssey. London: Longmans, Green and Co.; 1897. Scarce 1st issue with uncancelled ad showing John Murray as publisher of Butler's Life and Letters of Dr. Samuel Butler, this correction was made prior to publication; original light purple cloth, spine faded; Brackenburn bookplate of Hugh Walpole. Jarndyce CII-57 1996 £120.00

STEVENSON, ROBERT LOUIS BALFOUR 1850-1894   A Footnote to History. London: Cassell & Co., 1892. 1st edition; published simultaneously with the American edition; 8vo; ads dated May 1892; original binding, slight foxing of endpapers, very mild edgewear, near fine. Hugh Walpole's bookplate.   Charles Agvent 4-1039 1996 $125.00

VERGILIUS MARO, PUBLIUS 70-19 BC   Bucolica et Georgica... London: John and Robert Pine, 1774. Tall 8vo; pages 15, 144, 3, numerous full page and folding engraved plates, engraved vignettes, culs-de-lampe, etc.; all edges gilt, very fine contemporary English crimson straight grained morocco, covers tooled with gilt palmetto dentelles, spine elaborately decorated; Hugh Walpole's with his leather bookplate. Dibdin II p. 561.   Family Album Tillers-647 1996 $550.00

ASSOCIATION - ROBERT WALPOLE

WALLER, EDMUND   The Works...in Verse and Prose. London: Tonson, 1753. Octavo; pages (16), 272; frontispiece; original polished calf, spine profusely gilt decorated, leather label, marbled endpapers, all edges sprinkled, silk ribbon marker; wear to spine and hinges, text excellent; With 2 fine armorial bookplates on pastedown: Robert Walpole of Lincoln's Inn, on flyleaf W. Baylies, M.D. (physician to Frederick the Great). Lowndes IV 1892; CBEL II 455.   Hartfield 48-L90 1996 $295.00

ASSOCIATION - WARD

OSGOOD, FRANCES S.   The Poetry of Flowers and Flowers of Poetry. New York: J. C. Riker, 1841. 1st edition; octavo; 276 pages; hand colored title and 12 hand colored full page floral plates; pictorial boards, all edges gilt, light foxing and rebacking to soiled boards. Inscribed in pencil to H. D. Thoreau's sister Helen from a member of Prudence Ward's family.   Bromer Booksellers 90-211 1996 $450.00

ASSOCIATION - EDWARD WARD

BACON, FRANCIS, VISCOUNT ST. ALBANS 1561-1626   Letters of Sr. Francis Bacon, Baron of Verulam, Viscount St. Albany, and Lord High Chancellor of England. London: printed for Benj. Tooke, 1702. 1st edition; 4to; contemporary mottled calf, gilt, neatly rebacked, original label preserved, all edges gilt, corners worn; large paper; very good with errata leaf at end, few copies are known with leaf of dedication to the king, not present here, but it was meant to be called as William III died before publication. Presentation copy inscribed by Rob. Stephens for Edward Ward. Gibson 245   Ximenes 109-20 1996 $600.00

ASSOCIATION - BEATRICE WARDE

WARDE, F.   Printers Ornaments Applied to the Composition of Decorative Borders, Panels and Patterns. London: Lanston Monotype Corp. Ltd., 1928. 4to; 114 pages, original red and gilt cloth, headcaps mildly bumped; ink inscription from "BLW" (Beatrice Warde) to Ruari McLean. Appleton 277.   Maggs Bros. Ltd. 1191-223 1996 £80.00

ASSOCIATION - JAMES WARDROP

MORISON, STANLEY 1889-1967   Notes on the Development of Latin Script from Early to Modern Times. Cambridge: 1949. Limited to 50 copies; folio; 2 plates; original wrappers, ink inscription from Morison to James Wardrop dated 16 Aug. 1949. Appleton 178.   Maggs Bros. Ltd. 1191-204 1996 £345.00

ASSOCIATION - JOHN WARE

EMERSON, RALPH WALDO 1803-1882   Essays: Second Series. Boston: James Munroe, 1844. 1st edition; 1st printing, 1st state of binding; original olive grey-green cloth, gilt, fine, tight copy of a very scarce book. From the library of John Ware (brother of Henry Ware, whom Emerson replaced as pastaor of Second Church); Rusk Life p. 136; BAL 5198; Myerson A16.1.a.b.   Mac Donnell 12-20 1996 $1,000.00

ASSOCIATION - CLEMENTINE WARING

FRANKAU, GILBERT   One Of Us. London: Chatto & Windus, 1917. 1st illustrated edition, number 48 of 110 copies signed by author and artist; small 4to; 173 pages; frontispiece, vignette titlepage and 8 plates by A. H. Fish; original full parchment, top edge gilt, some soiling to cover, else very good, Clementine Waring's copy with her bookplate.   Chapel Hill 94-57 1996 $165.00

ASSOCIATION - JAMES WARING

FAHIE, J. J.   Memorials of Galileo Galilei, 1564-1642. Leamington & London: for the author, 1929. 1st edition; complete with limitation slip stating only 200 copies printed, of which 105 were for sale; tall square 8vo; xxiv, 172 pages; frontispiece, 46 plates; original cloth; fine. Bookplate of James J. Waring.   Edwin V. Glaser 121-121 1996 $285.00

SMYTH, HENRY DE WOLF   Atomic Energy for Military Purposes. Princeton: Princeton University Press, 1945. 1st public edition; fine in dust jacket with small, neat private library numbers on spine; bookplate of James J. Waring.   Hermitage SP95-1083 1996 $150.00

ASSOCIATION - EDITH WARNE

ENGLISH Rustic Pictures Drawn by Frederick Walker and G. J. Pinwell and Engraved by the Brothers dalziel. India Proofs. London: George Routledge and Sons, 1882. Limited to 300 copies; folio; pages (14), 30 plates (15 of each artist), printed on india paper from the original blocks, each with accompanying leaf of letterpress; bound by Burn in original full japon decorated and lettered in gold and browns; inscribed by the Dalziels for Edith Warne.   Claude Cox 107-36 1996 £135.00

FOSTER, BIRKET   Pictures of English Landscape. London: George Routledge & Sons, 1881. Number 671 of 1000 copies; folio; pages (18), + 30 plates, printed by hand on india paper from original wood blocks, each with accompanying leaf of verse (all printed on rectos only); engraved by Brothers Dalziel. original full japon decorated and lettered in gold and browns, lightly soiled, uncut, by Burn and Co.; inscribed by the Brothers Dalziel for Miss Edith Warne.   Claude Cox 107-35 1996 £135.00

ASSOCIATION - WARNER

HERRMANN, GOTTFRIED   De Metris Poetarum Graecorum et Romanorum Libri III. Leipzig: Fleischer, 1796. 8vo; 461 pages; contemporary vellum, covers panelled with blue double rules, upper cover with full length portrait, flat spine in 6 panels, gilt rules, blue title and imprint lables, all edges gilt, marbled endpapers, preserved in drop side cloth box within morocco backed slipcase, a German binding in the style of Edwards of Halifax; from the libraries of F. Lee Warner, the gift of Dr. Butler and thus inscribed and Ham Court, Upton-on Severn, with bookplate.   Marlborough 160-41 1996 £1,950.00

ASSOCIATION - JACK WARNER

BEAVERBROOK, WILLIAM MAXWELL AIKEN   Don't Trust to Luck. London: London Express, ca. 1950. Revised; small 8vo; frontispiece; very good in dust jacket with few nicks and tears; signed and inscribed by author for Jack Warner.   George J. Houle 68-13 1996 $175.00

ASSOCIATION - RICHARD WARNER

SPENSER, EDMUND 1552-1599   The Faerie Queen; The Shepherds
Calendar; Together with the Other Works. H. L. for Mathew Lownes,
1611. 1st collected edition, variant issue; folio; paes (iv), 363, (xix), (x),
56, (ii), (iv), 5-16, (cxxxvi), double column, roman letter, general title
within elaborate woodcut border incoporating an Arcadian shepherd and
Amazon (McKerrow & Ferguson 212); 12 separate title with devices in
text, extensive woodcut head and tailpieces and other ornaments, 12
large cuts; 18th century calf, rebacked; uniform paper yellowing, some
minor inoffensive old stains and thumb marks, overall good; fine 18th
century armorial bookplate on pastedown of Richard Warner of
Woodford Row, Essex, the celebrated Shakespearean scholar. STC
23084; Lowndes 2477; Grolier, Langland to Wither 239.   A. Sokol
XXV-92   1996 £1,150.00

ASSOCIATION - BOOKER T. WASHINGTON

THRASHER, MAX BENNET   Tuskegee. Boston: Small Maynard, 1900.
1st edition; about fine, tipped onto free front endpaper is the conclusion
of a letter signed by Booker T. Washington and dated 5 Jan. 1901,
above the signature is written "Henry W. Sage/from.." It seems likely this
was a presentation copy from Washington to Sage.   Between the
Covers 43-422 1996 $425.00

ASSOCIATION - BESSIE WATERHOUSE

WEBSTER, JOHN   Love's Graduate. Oxford: printed at the Private
Press of H. Daniel Felllow of Worcester College 1885. Limited to 150
copies; small 4to; pages (4), xii, 69, (2); uncut in original vellum backed
boards, slightly spotted; inscribed by Edmund Gosse for Bessie
Waterhouse. Madan 11.   Claude Cox 107-40 1996 £180.00

ASSOCIATION - HELEN C. WATERHOUSE

CHURCH OF ENGLAND. BOOK OF COMMON PRAYER   The Book of
Common Prayer Together with the Psalter or Psalms of David. London:
Peacock, Mansfield & Britton, n.d., ca. 1885. 8vo; full calf, front cover
achieved in cuir-cisele with words DEVS DANTE OMNIA AMANDVS above
an heraldic coat of arms featuring a lion holding a hatchet, the date 1 8
8 5 in four corners, and the initials HCW below; background is covered
in blind pointelles and raised letters tinted with gilt, spine with 4 raised
bands and cuir-cisele panels, 8 silver corner bosses and silver clasp
with leather strap extending from lower cover to a stud on upper cover
to a stud on upper cover, all edges handsomely gilt and gauffered, gilt
decorated vellum pastedowns and free endleaves in seme of
pomegranates on a leafy stem, on lower edge of rear cover is a sm.
cuir-cisele panel with words, ME FEC, and initials O.H., above and below
a stylized binding, bird with both wings extended, the initials & logotype
of Otto Hupp, graphic designer & publisher; laid in is ANS from former
owner, Helen C. Waterhouse, whose initials appear on cover; splendid
binding example.   Book Block 32-42 1996 $1,175.00

ASSOCIATION - W. G. WATERS

MASUCCIO   The Novellino of Masuccio. London: Lawrence & Bullen,
1895. 1st edition in English, number 1 of 210 copies; 4to; 2 volumes,
printed on Japan vellum; xxxi, 294; x, 352; 20 full page images by E. R.
Hughes; original brown boards with white spines, covers lightly rubbed
and soiled, else nice, unopened, very good set; translator's (W. G.
Waters) own copy with his bookplate.   Chapel Hill 94-364 1996
$275.00

STRAPAROLA, GIOVANNI FRANCESO   The Nights of Straparola.
London: Lawrence and Bullen, 1894. 1st edition in English, 1 of 210
copies; 4to; 2 volumes, xxviii, 276; ix, 323 pages, printed on Japan
vellum; 20 full page images; original brown boards with white spines,
covers slightly rubbed and soiled, else nice, unopened, very good.
Translator's (W. G. Waters) copy with bookplate.   Chapel Hill 94-340
1996 $275.00

ASSOCIATION - WATKINS

CHAMBERLAIN, HENRY   A New and Compleat History and Survey of
the Cities of London and Westminster, the Borough of Southark and
parts Adjacent... London: J. Cooke, 1770. Folio; 4 ff., pages 5-682, 1 f.
appendix, 4 ff. index, 68 engraved plates; contemporary calf, gilt spine,
raised bands, label, bit worn, one or two scuff marks; signataure on
titlepage for R. Watkins, 1774. Adams 48.   Marlborough 162-120
1996 £500.00

ASSOCIATION - EDWARD WATKINS

BAUDOUIN, ALEXANDRE   The Man of the World's Dictionary. London:
J. Appleyard, 1822. 12mo; half title; half calf neatly rebacked; armorial
bookplate of Sir Edward Watkins.   Jarndyce 103-123 1996 £75.00

ASSOCIATION - JOHN WATSON

TYTLER, PATRICK FRASER   History of Scotland 1249-1603. Edinburgh:
William Tair, 1841-43. 8vo; 9 volumes; original blindstamped cloth, gilt;
excellent clean and sound set; armorial bookplate of Sir John Watson,
Bart.   R.F.G. Hollett 76-312 1996 £85.00

ASSOCIATION - ISAAC WATTS

MILTON, JOHN 1608-1674   Poems &c., Upon Several Occasions...Both
English and Latin... London: for Tho. Dring at the Blue Anchor, 1673. 2nd
edition; 8vo; pages (viii), 165, (1) blank, 117, (5) ads, lacking title,
supplied in early ms. facsimile, with conjugate initial blank and early ms.
copies of Milton's four political sonnets on 2 extra leaves inserted at
end; 19th century divinity calf, extremties little rubbed, trivial tear to D8,
some page numbers shaved, little soiling, very good; Isaac Watt's copy,
inscribed by Watts. Fine association copy. Wing M2161; Turnbull 85.
Simon Finch 24-170 1996 £1,000.00

ASSOCIATION - WEBB

MITFORD, MARY RUSSELL 1787-1855   Christina, the Maid of the
South Seas; Narrative Poems on the Female Character...; Our Village...
London: 1811/13/24. 1st editions; 8vo; 3 volumes; uniformly bound in gilt
tooled green calf, minor edgewear, front endpapers from poetry volumes
lacking; very good; with 2 page AMS, a 56 line poem inscribed to
James Webb, the Narrative Poems has a presentation inscription from
author to the Miss Webbs.   Charles Agvent 4-901 1996 $475.00

ASSOCIATION - J. WATSON WEBB

WEBB, SAMUEL B.   Records of North American Big Game. 1952. 2nd
issue; colored frontispiece, many other illustrations; fine in torn and
rather grubby dust jacket; presentation copy from J. Watson Webb to
Lord Dalhousie.   David Grayling J95Biggame-457 1996 £105.00

ASSOCIATION - JOE WEBB

OSLER, WILLIAM 1849-1919   An Alabama Student and Other
Biographical Essays. New York: Oxford University Press American
Branch/London: Henry Frowde, 1909. 1st edition; 2nd impression; 8vo;
(iv), 334, ads (16) pages; frontispiece, illustrations; red cloth; very good;
booklabel of Joe Webb, Johns Hopkins University.   Jeff Weber 31-30
1996 $100.00

ASSOCIATION - PHLLYS WEBB

TRIO. First Poems by Gael Turnbull, Phyllis Webb, E. W. Mandel. N.P:
Contact Press, c. 1954. 1st edition; unpaginated; printed wrappers; near
fine, very scarce; inscribed by Phyllis Webb for F. R. Scott; recently
inscribed to John Metcalf by Gael Turnbull.   Nelson Ball 118-173
1996 $800.00

ASSOCIATION - PAUL FRANCIS WEBSTER

GOLDSMITH, OLIVER 1730-1774   The Traveller or, a Prospecct of
Society. London: printed for J. Newbery, 1765 1st published edition; 4to;
half title (neat repair to small hole at fore edge), 22 pages text, 2 pages
publisher's ads; full polished calf, triple gilt rule borders, tiny corner
ornaments, fully gilt panelled spine, red morocco label, all edges gilt,
inner gilt dentelles, marbled endpapers, brown paper book label of Paul
Francis Webster; bound by F. Bedford. Very fine copy. Rothschild 1024;
Tinker 1101.   Beeleigh Abbey BA56-144 1996 £1,500.00

ASSOCIATION - WEILMANN

GIBBON, EDWARD 1737-1794   Histoire de la decadence et de la Chute de l'Empire Romain... Paris: Chez Les Freres Debure; Moutard, 1786. 12mo; 4 parts in 2 volumes; contemporary calf, sides with border tooled in blind, spine with ornately gilt tooled compartmetns between raised bands, double contrasing beige and brown morocco labels, blue edges, marbled endpapers; fine; contemporary ownership inscription of A. Weilmann in ink on titlepages. Norton 80.   Simon Finch 24-91 1996 £575.00

ASSOCIATION - ANN WENDELL

PUMPHREY, STANLEY   Indian Civilization: a Lecture. Philadelphia: Bible & Tract Dist. Soc., 1877. 1st edition; 8vo; plates; original binding, light wear, old dampstain to bottom margin of all pages; signed and dated by Whittier though date is hard to make out; signature of Ann Wendell on title & pencil note dated 1883 on verso of leaf Whittier has signed which is a lighter paper but does not appear to have been tipped in; laid in 64 line poem in another hand.   Charles Agvent 4-1222 1996 $375.00

ASSOCIATION - JOHN WENGER

FORNARO, CARLO DE   John Wenger. New York: Joseph Lawren, 1925. Limited to 1000 copies; small 4to; 24 pages, plus 50 plates, including color frontispiece; boards, very good; this copy inscribed by Wenger.   J. M. Cohen 35-112 1996 $125.00

ASSOCIATION - HENRY WENNING

ANTONINUS, BROTHER 1912-   The Blowing of the Seed. New Haven: Henry W. Wenning, One of 218 copies, signed by Everson; quarter calf, batik boards, fine; inscribed by well known bookseller and publisher, Henry Wenning, to a book scout.   Bev Chaney, Jr. 23-198 1996 $200.00

ASSOCIATION - WERNHER

RADCLIFFE, ANN WARD 1764-1823   The Mysteries of Udolpho, a Romance... London: for G. G. and J. Robinson, 1794. 1st edition; large 12mo; 4 volumes, with half titles, but without final blank in volume 2; contemporary Swedish calf, spines with raised bands, pale tan morocco labels, oval black numbering-pieces, extremities little worn, sides rubbed, one or two trivial stains, nice contemporary set. From the library of Swedish Count Nils Gyldenstolpe with his initials and coronet blindstamped on endpapers of 2 volumes, and his large monogram inkstamp on each title, also with later oval lib. inkstamp of C. Fr. Wernher on e.p.'s. Rothschild 1710; Summers p. 434.   Simon Finch 24-193 1996 £950.00

ASSOCIATION - WESTPORT HOUSE

WALKER, WILLIAM SIDNEY   Gustavus Vasa and Other Poems. London: for Longman, Hurst, Rees, Orme and Brown, 1813. 1st edition; 8vo; pages xxiii, (i) blank, 230, (xxxiv) notes; contemporary half calf, smooth spine gilt in compartments, gilt lettered direct, drab paper sides, marbled edges, tiny area of insect damage at foot of front joint, sides rubbed, attractive copy.   Simon Finch 24-253 1996 £80.00

ASSOCIATION - CARL WHEAT

BAYARD, SAMUEL J.   A Sketch of the Life of Com. Robert F. Stockton; with...Extracts from the Defence of Col. J. C. Fremont. New York: Derby & Jackson, 1856. 1st edition; 131 pages, plus one leaf of ads, frontispiece; original brown embossed cloth, title in gilt on spine, minor fading to spine and some wear, fine; from the collection of Carl Wheat, with his bookplate. Howes B259; Becker Wagner Camp 271b. Tutorow Mex. Amer. War 3743.   Michael D. Heaston 23-39 1996 $250.00

FORBES, ALEXANDER   California: a History of Upper and Lower California. London: Smith, Elder and Co., 1839. 1st edition; 8 3/4 x 5 1/2 inches; xvi, 352 pages, folding map, frontispiece, 9 other lithographed plates, 32 page publisher's catalouge (dated Jan. 1848) at end; blindstamped plum cloth, tips bumped, some foxing to map and plates (generally confined to margins); bookplate of Carl I. Wheat. Zamorano 80 38.   Dawson's Books Shop 528-84 1996 $1,000.00

ASSOCIATION - CARL WHEAT

MARRYAT, FRANK   Mountains and Molehills, or Recollections of a Burnt Journal. London: Longman, Brown, Green and Longmans, 1855. 8 3/4 x 5 1/2 inches; xii, 443 pages, 24 page's publisher's catalog at end, frontispiece, 7 other chromolithographed plates, woodcuts in text; blindstamped salmon cloth, recased preserving original endpapers, rear free endpaper lacking, some light marginal stain, stain unobtrusively touching frontispiece image; Bookplate of Carl Wheat. Zamorano 80 52. Dawson's Books Shop 528-166 1996 $600.00

ASSOCIATION - WILLIAM MORTON WHEELER

LINNE, CARL VON 1707-1778   Species Plantarum, Exhibentes Plantas Rite cognitas, ad Genera Relatas, Cum Differentiis Specificis Nominibus Trivialibus... Stockholm: 1762-63. 2nd edition; 8vo; 2 volumes; (16), 1684, (64) pages; without portrait sometimes found; contemporary half calf, minor wear to edges and corners, cracking to outer hinges, but solid, some browning to endpaper, light dampstaining to back pages of volume 1, occasional old marginal notation in ink, head of spine of volume 1 chipped; leather spine labels, titles printed in red and black. With signatures of zoologist and entomologist William Morton Wheeler. Raymond M. Sutton VI-17 1996 $2,500.00

ASSOCIATION - LAURENCE WHISTLER

FULLER, RONALD   The Work of Rex Whistler. London: Batsford, 1960. 1st edition; 600 copies printed; 4to; pages xxiv, 112 illustrations on 68 pages, (ii), 122; 9 of the illustrations are in color, numerous other illustrations in text; original green buckram, decorated in gilt, with dust jacket, lower cover little marked, dust jacket slightly frayed, very good. Loosely inserted autograph letter from Laurence Whistler to artist John Goodall.   Sotheran PN32-66 1996 £498.00

ASSOCIATION - WHITBREAD

DICKENS, CHARLES 1812-1870   A Christmas Carol. London: Chapman & Hall, 1843. 1st edition; 1st impression, 1st issue, with 14-15mm. between closest points of blindstamping and gilt wreath on upper cover, the "D" of "Dickens" unbroken on upper cover, text uncorrected, yellow e.p.'s, half title printed in blue, title in red & blue, 'Stave I' on p. 1; 8vo; pages (viii), 166, (2) ads, hand colored etched frontispiece, 3 plates, illustrations after Leech; original brown cloth, gilt, spine and edges of boards slightly faded as usual, spine just nicked at head, title with two trivial marks, very good. Ownership inscription of Mrs. Whitbread dated Jan. 1844 on half title. Smith Part II 4; Eckel pp. 110-5. Simon Finch 24-72 1996 £3,800.00

ASSOCIATION - CHARLES WHITE

BENNETT, LERONE   The Shaping of Black America. Chicago: Johnson Pub. Co., 1975. 1st edition; illustrations by Charles White; fine in attractive Charles White dust jacket with couple of short tears. Inscribed by Bennett and White. Great copy.   Between the Covers 43-268 1996 $500.00

ASSOCIATION - HENRY WHITE

PEDANTIVS. Comoedia, Olim Cantabrig. Acta in Coll. Trin. London: William Stansby (?) Impensis Robert Mylbourn, 1631. 1st edition; 12mo; pages 168; Roman letter, woodcut titlepage border, double page engraved printed on verso of titlepage and recto of following leaf, 1 woodcut initial; 19th century red half morocco, a.e.r.; early ms. annotations or autographs above title (deleted) and on following leaf (pasted over), autograph of Henry White "Lichfield (sic) Octob.. 27 1807". STC 19524; Greg L9; Lowndes 1814.   A. Sokol XXV-73 1996 £485.00

ASSOCIATION - JAMES CLARK WHITE

MOSELEY, HENRY N.   Notes by a Naturalist, an Account of Observations Made During the Voyage of the H.M.S. "Challenger" Round the World in the Yars 1872-1876. New York: London: G. P. Putnam's/John Murray, 1892. 8vo; 540 pages, plus 4 pages ads, illustrations; tan cloth, spine label; spine and boards darkened, library blindstamp on titlepage, decorative bookplate of James Clark White, small signature of Chas. L. Camp Dec. 1919, else very good.   Parmer Books Nat/Hist-077042 1996 $195.00

ASSOCIATION - M. M. WHITE

SMYTH, WILLIAM   English Lyricks. Liverpool: printed by J. M'Creery and sold by Cadell and Davies, 1797. 8vo; contemporary calf, gilt ruled borders, spine decorated in gilt, rubbed; very attractive; with inscription "M. M. White. The gift of Mr. C. Peers."   James Cummins 14-188   1996 $225.00

ASSOCIATION - ELIZABETH WHITING

THURBER, JAMES GROVER 1894-1961   The Beast in Me: and other Animals. New York: Harcourt Brace, 1948. 1st edition; 1st binding, 2nd state text; blue green cloth stamped in black to front cover and spine, in dust jacket which is slightly chipped to top edge, later owner's inscription also present; inscribed by author for Elizabeth Whiting.   Bromer Booksellers 87-268   1996 $385.00

ASSOCIATION - JOHN GREENLEAF WHITTIER

PUMPHREY, STANLEY   Indian Civilization: a Lecture. Philadelphia: Bible & Tract Dist. Soc., 1877. 1st edition; 8vo; plates; original binding, light wear, old dampstain to bottom margin of all pages; signed and dated by Whittier though date is hard to make out; signature of Ann Wendell on title & pencil note dated 1883 on verso of leaf Whittier has signed which is a lighter paper but does not appear to have been tipped in; laid in 64 line poem in another hand.   Charles Agvent 4-1222   1996 $375.00

ASSOCIATION - WHITTUCK

DICKENS, CHARLES 1812-1870   Little Dorrit. London: Bradbury & Evans, 1855-57. 1st edition; 1st issue with 'Rigaud' for 'Blandois' in part XV and slip correcting errors in part XVI; this copy has all the slips and ads and all but first part have ownership signature of Miss Whittuck on upper wrapper; 8vo; in original 19/20 parts; etched frontispiece, additional title, 38 plates by Phiz; original blue printed wrappers, red cloth folders and morocco pull of cases, spines with raised bands lettered numbered in gilt, few minor repairs to wrappers, backstrip with only very slight wear, small label on upper wrapper of last part, some plates little spotted, but excellent; Hatton and Cleaver pp. 307-30; Eckel p. 82-85.   Simon Finch 24-74   1996 £1,800.00

ASSOCIATION - MADELINE WHYTE

SHAKESPEARE, WILLIAM 1564-1616   The Tragedie of Anthony and Cleopatra. London: Doves Press, 1912. One of 200 copies; small 4to; printed in black and red on handmade paper; limp vellum; nice; inscribed by Thomas James Cobden-Sanderson to Madeline Whyte.   Bertram Rota 272-129   1996 £400.00

ASSOCIATION - JAMES WICKERSHAM

MAYNE, R. C.   Four Years in British Columbia and Vancouver Island. London: John Murray, 1862. 23cm; xi, 468, (32) pages; frontispiece, illustrations, folding map outlined in color; gilt stamped and illustrated russet cloth, neatly rebacked; fine. From the collection of Alaskan judge and bibliographer James Wickersham. Lowther 178; TPL 4076.   Rockland Books 38-149   1996 $375.00

ASSOCIATION - JOSEPH WIDENER

COOK, HENRY   Pride, or The Heir of Craven. London: John W. Parker, 1841. 1st edition; 8vo; author's own copy, with his bookplate; pages (iii)-viii, 139, (i) blank, (i) ad; contemporary calf with double fillet gilt border to sides with rosette at each corner, spine decorated in compartments with floral ornaments, leaf sprays, etc., green morocco label, marbled endpapers, gilt edges, some wear to upper joint and head of spine skilfully repaired; bookplates of author and Sir William Augustus Fraser Bart. and leather booklabel of Joseph Widener.   Simon Finch 24-55   1996 £450.00

ASSOCIATION - OSBORNE WIGHT

PRIESTLEY, JOSEPH 1733-1804   An Appeal to the Public, on the Subject of the Riots in Birmingham. Birmingham: printed by J. Thompson, sold by J. Johnson, London, 1792. 2nd edition; 8vo; xxxix, (1), 184 pages, wanting leaf before title (presumably a half title), numerous ms. annotations in pencil, mostly in margins, some of these notes cropped by binder; contemporary calf backed marbled boards, neatly rebacked, spine lettered in gilt, very good; ownership inscription of 'Osborne Wight 1792" on title.   John Drury 82-233   1996 £150.00

ASSOCIATION - WIGTOUNE

DEFOE, DANIEL 1661?-1731   The Political History of the Devil, as Well Ancient as Modern. London: printed for T. Warner, 1726. 1st edition; 8vo; frontispiece, pages (viii), 408; contemporary panelled calf, rebacked bookplate of Lord Wigtoune. Moore 480.   Peter Murray Hill 185-49   1996 £250.00

ASSOCIATION - SAMUEL WILBERFORCE

QUARLES, FRANCIS   Divine Poems, Containing the History of Jonah, Ester, Job, Sampson. Together with Sions Sonnets, Elegies. London: Benj. Tooke, and Tho. Sawbridge, 1674. Variant issue; 8vo; (xvi), 471, (i) pages; old sheep,s pine decorated gilt, label, rubbed, upper joint cracked but firm, minor adhesion at inner margin of engraved title, scattered foxing. Good copy, ownership signature of Samuel Wilberforce. Wing Qu4a.   Robert Clark 38-119   1996 £200.00

ASSOCIATION - WILLIAM WILBERFORCE

CHURCH OF ENGLAND. BOOK OF COMMON PRAYER   The Book of Common Prayer and Administration of the Sacraments, and Other Rites and Ceremonies of the Church. Cambridge: 1760. 1st edition; 2nd impression; 8vo; text unpaginated; text surrounded by border of lozenge and star ornaments; full burgundy morocco, gilt tool scrolled border, elaborate gilt tooling to panelled spine, black morocco label to spine, joints rubbed, corners worn, all edges gilt; hinges cracked, library identification plate to front pastedown. Bookplate of William Wilberforce, ownership inscription.   Beeleigh Abbey BA56-133   1996 £250.00

ASSOCIATION - OSCAR WILDE

RODD, RENNELL   Rose Leaf and Apple Leaf. Philadelphia: J. M. Stoddart & Co., 1882. 1st edition under this title, the edition deluxe issue of which the publisher recalled the total number of copies printed was 'not over 250'; 12mo; illustrations; original printed full parchment, text printed in brown ink (rectos only) on thin transparent handmade paper, with deckled edges, interleaved with thin leaves of green tissue, top edge gilt, white moire endpapers, covers little soiled and worn, as usual, but very good, in slightly rubbed half morocco slipcase; laid in is ALS from Rodd to Oscar Wilde.   David J. Holmes 52-127   1996 $2,250.00

ASSOCIATION - BELL WILEY

CARTER, ROBERT GOLDTHWAITE   Four Brothers in Blue or Sunshine and Shadows of the War of the Rebellion a Story of the Great Civil War from Bull Run to Appomatox. Washington: Gibson Bros., 1913. True 1st edition, limited to only 80 copies; xiii, (v)-509 pages; scarce issue; original cloth; very good to near fine; formerly the copy of Bell Wiley. Dornbusch I Mass. 5; Howes C191; Nevins I 67.   McGowan Book Co. 65-18   1996 $2,250.00

ASSOCIATION - JOHN WILKES

MACHIAVELLI, NICCOLO 1469-1527   The Works of the Famous Nicholas Machiavel, Citizen and Secretary of Florence. London: by T. W. for A. Churchill, (and 10 others), 1720. 3rd edition in English; folio; (24), 543, (i.e. 545) pages; contemporary panelled calf, hinges cracking slightly but held secure by cords, spine ends bit chipped; fine, clean copy in attractive binding; 18th century signature of John Wilkes.   Joseph J. Felcone 64-29   1996 $650.00

VERGILIUS MARO, PUBLIUS 70-19 BC   Bucolica, Georgica, et Aeneis. Glasgow: Foulis, 1778. Large paper copy; folio; 2 volumes in one, pages 277; 308, subscription list; contemporary full leather, gilt arms of City of Edinburgh, elaborately gilt spine, front board detached; engraved armorial bookplate of John Wilkes (1727-1797). Gaskell 639.   Family Album Tillers-649   1996 $750.00

ASSOCIATION - C. H. WILKINSON

BUCHAN, JOHN 1875-1940   Sir Walter Scott. London: 1932. 1st edition; near fine in dust jacket with some slight soiling and minor repairs, bookplate of C. H. Wilkinson, with inscription by author for Wilkinson; very scarce with inscription and dust jacket.   Bannatyne Books 19-S22   1996 £100.00

ASSOCIATION - C. H. WILKINSON

LAMB, CHARLES 1775-1834   The Works. London: Volume I. by Marchant; Volume II by Renell, for C. and J. Ollier, 1818. 1st collected edition; small 8vo; 2 volumes, pages ix, (iii), 291, (i); (vi), 259, (i), (ii) publisher's ads dated June 1818; later blue crushed morocco, sides ruled in gilt with French fillet, quatrefoils in corners, spines gilt with quatrefoil designs in compartments, gilt lettered direct, date at foot, gilt inner dentelles, marbled endpapers, silk bookmarks, top edge gilt, others uncut, by W. Root & Son; spines slightly sunned, one or two trivial spots; very good copy; bookplate of C. H. Wilkinson. Thomson SLI; Ashley III 49.   Simon Finch 24-146 1996 £350.00

PEACOCK, THOMAS LOVE   The Genius of the Thames: a Lyrical Poet in Two Parts. London: printed by T. Bensley for T. Hookham Jun. and E. T. Hookham... 1810. 1st edition; 8vo; attractive brown morocco, gilt, uncut, half title, minor soiling, very nice, from the library of C. H. Wilkinson with his bookplate. NCBEL 3.701.   James Cummins 14-154 1996 $325.00

PEACOCK, THOMAS LOVE   Maid Marian. London: printed for T. Hookham and Longman, etc., 1822. 1st edition; 12mo; half red morocco, top edge gilt, very good, scarce; bookplate of C. H. Wilkinson. Block p. 181; CBEL III 701.   Ximenes 109-220 1996 $650.00

PEACOCK, THOMAS LOVE   Maid Marian. London: Printed for T. Hookham, and Longman, Hurst, Rees, Orme and Brown, 1822. 1st edition; 12mo; with leaf stating that the work was written in the autumn of 1818 following the title; attractive simple half red morocco; minor spotting and browning, attractive copy; from the C. H. Wilkinson library with his bookplate. NCBEL 3.701.   James Cummins 14-153 1996 $325.00

ASSOCIATION - WILLIAM IV

GLEIG, G. R.   The Soldier's Help to the Knowledge of Divine Truth. London: J. G. & F. Rivington, 1835. 8vo; full purple crushed morocco with a Scotch-rule gilt fillet border inside of which is a border composed of leafy vines and flower heads, at top of the central panel on both covers, is a gilt crown beneath which are entwined rustic initials "WR", spine with five raised bands and gilt decoration within compartments, board edges gilt, inner gilt dentelles, all edges gilt, signed at bottom of front turn in: bound by J. Mackenzie Bookbinder to the King, very attractive royal binding. Bound of William IV.   Book Block 32-40 1996 $950.00

ASSOCIATION - A. P. WILLIAMS

HAWTHORNE, NATHANIEL 1804-1864   Mosses from an Old Manse. New York: Wiley & Putnam, 1846. 1st edition; 1st printing with Craighead and Smith imprints below copyright notice in both volumes, state 1 of the front wrappers, state 3 of back wrapper present; 12mo; 2 volumes; original printed wrappers, lacking back wrapper of volume 2, ends o spine chipped (textually complete), bookplate on half title of each volume, some glue show through, light waterstaining in lower corner of first 100 pages of second volume; very good set. Entirely unsophisticated, early pencilled signature in each volume of A. P. Williams of Augusta, Me. BAL 759 state A. Clark A15.1.a1. Bradley Martin Sale 2064.   M & S Rare Books 60-166 1996 $3,500.00

ASSOCIATION - CONON WILLIAMS

BROWNING, ELIZABETH BARRETT 1806-1861   The Seraphim and Other Poems. London: Saunders and Otley, 1838. 1st edition; 12mo; contemporary half green calf, spine gilt, slightly rubbed, bound without half title, but nice; armorial bookplates of Dorothea Stanley and Conon Williams. Baranes A4; CBEL III 436.   Ximenes 108-368 1996 $400.00

ASSOCIATION - E. C. WILLIAMS

TROLLOPE, ANTHONY 1815-1882   The Claverings. New York: Harper & Bros., 1866/67? 1st edition in book form; 8vo; pages 211, (v), 24 woodcut illustrations, of which 12 are large and 12 vignettes; pink printed wrappers dated 1867, spine defective at head and tail, lower cover torn across at head with some loss, last few gatherings stained at lower outer corner, ownership inscription of E. C. Williams, Charleston, S.C., bookseller's stamp of H. L. Schreiner, Savannah, Ga. Sadleir 27 (+Add); Wolff 6771a.   Simon Finch 24-241 1996 £250.00

ASSOCIATION - ELLIS WILLIAMS

LEMOINE, H.   History, Origin and Progress of the Art of Printing, From Its First Invention in Germany to the End of the Seventeenth Century. London: 1797. 1st edition; 12mo; 156 pages; later library cloth, some browning throughout, first blank very brittle, title flaking little at edges (not affecting text); ex-John Crerar Library copy with booklabel, perforated stamps on first 3 leaves, with release stams; presentation inscription to Ellis Williams, Printer from Miss H. A. Jones. Bigmore & Wyman p. 431.   Maggs Bros. Ltd. 1191-188 1996 £115.00

ASSOCIATION - JOHN WILLIAMS

PRICE, RICHARD 1723-1791   Observations on the Nature of Civil Liberty, the Principles of Government and the Justice and Policy of the War With America.... (with) Additional Observations on the Nature and Value of Civil Liberty, and the War with America... London: printed for T. Cadell, 1776/77. 7th edition, 1st edition respectively; 8vo; 2 volumes in 1; pages (viii), 134; xvi, 176; recent quarter calf, utilizing contemporary marbled boards, little rubbed, red leather label, very good; with armorial bookplate of John Williams. Kress B71.   Sotheran PN32-39 1996 £498.00

ASSOCIATION - JOHN CAMP WILLIAMS

PASSE, CRISPJIN VAN DE 1593 or 4-1667   XII Sibyllarum Icones Elegantissimi... N.P.: 1601. 8vo; wuite of 16 plates, brilliant impressions; simply (yet elegantly) bound in green pastepaper over flexible boards with single gilt fillet on both covers and title gilt within oval cartouche, spine with spare gilt decoration & red morocco title label, top edge gilt, preserved in half morocco clamshell case, also preserved are the leather bookplates of 3 previous owners: Beverly Chew, John Camp Williams and Robert Hoe; pencil note indicating that this had also been the copy of William Beckford.   Book Block 32-68 1996 $7,250.00

ASSOCIATION - JONATHAN WILLIAMS

DICKEY, JAMES   Buckdancer's Choice. Poems. Middletown: Wesyleyan, 1965. 1st edition; fine in dust jacket with few tiny nicks; inscribed by author to poet Jonathan Williams.   Captain's Bookshelf 38-51 1996 $225.00

DICKEY, JAMES   Helmets. Poems. Middletown: Wesleyan, 1964. 1st edition; fine in dust jacket; inscribed by author to poet Jonathan Williams.   Captain's Bookshelf 38-51 1996 $225.00

ASSOCIATION - JOSHUA WILLIAMS

CLARENDON, EDWARD HYDE, 1ST EARL OF 1609-1674   The Proceedings in the House of Commons, Touching the Impeachment of Edward Late Earl of Clarendon, Lord High Chancellour of England... N.P.: London:? 1700. Mottled calf, very worn, repaired, usable copy; with ownership signature on first blank of Joshua Williams, noted scholar on rearl property.   Meyer Boswell SL27-45 1996 $350.00

ASSOCIATION - PENRY WILLIAMS

GARRICK, DAVID 1717-1779   The Poetical Works... London: George Kearsley, 1785. 1st edition; 8vo; contemporary calf, spines gilt, morocco labels, half titles, 3 pages ads in volume 2; fine early armorial bookplates of Penry Williams; signatures on flyleaf of early owner. Fine in modern slipcase. Rothschild 901; NCBEL II 801.   Trebizond 39-18 1996 $285.00

ASSOCIATION - THEODORE WILLIAMS

JEBB, SAMUEL   The Life of Robert Earl of Leicester, the Favourite of Queen Elizabeth. London: printed for Woodman and Lyon and C. Davis, 1727. 1st edition; 8vo; frontispiece; early 19th century full polished tree calf, wide gilt borders enclosing gilt crests, spine elaborately gilt, all edges gilt, by John Clarke; pretty copy; from the handsome library of Rev. Theodore Williams, with his characteristic crest on front cover containing initials "T.W." within an oval.   Ximenes 108-219 1996 $330.00

LONGINUS   Dionysii Longini de Sublimitate Libellus. Oxford: Wilmot, 1718. Large paper copy; 8vo; pages (13), 163, (32), full leather, from the library of the great book collector, Rev. Theodore Williams, probably bound by Clarke for Williams, with Williams' gilt stamps on each board, gilt dentelles, all edges gilt. Dibdin II 177; Brunet III 1152.   Family Album Tillers-398 1995 $300.00

ASSOCIATION - W. F. WILLIAMS

STARBUCK, ALEXANDER   History of the American Whale Fishery From
Its Earliest Inception to the Year 1876. Waltham: 1878. Pages 767, 6
plates, extra pencil drawing of a whale; original binding, backstrip
repaired, some shelf wear, some pencilling; fully signed by W. F.
Williams with three quarter page ms. note by him. Arctic 16698.
Stephen Lunsford 45-153 1996 $950.00

ASSOCIATION - G. C. WILLIAMSON

THE GENEALOGIST'S Pocket Library. London: 1908-10. Foolscap 8vo; 8
volumes; original cloth; from the library of art historian G. C. Williamson
with his book label in each volume.   Howes Bookshop 265-1792
1996 £65.00

ASSOCIATION - ISAAC WILLIS

TOWNSEND, JOHN K.   Narrative of a Journey Across the Rocky
Mountains to the Columbia River, and a Visit to the Sandwich Islands,
Chili, &c. Philadelphia: Henry perkins, 1839. 1st edition; curious copy with
original plum cloth faded on rear cover & spine, but with front cover
dyed blue & a bit of red stain at head of spine, 3 inch split in cloth over
head of front joint, but cover is sound, even with short splits in
endpapers and over front hinge, light foxing throughout, but clean copy,
ownership inscription from James Mott (possibly NY abolitionist and
founder of Swathmore College) to cousin Isaac Willis. Howes T319;
Wagner Cam Becker 79.1. Field 1558.   Magnum Opus 44-103 1996
$350.00

ASSOCIATION - WILLMARTH

WILLIAMS, S. W.   American Medical Biography. Greenfield: 1845. 1st
edition; 8vo; 9 portraits lithographed by W. C. Sharp of Boston; some
foxing; cloth, spine worn and repaired, corners stubbed, errata slip
tipped in at end; contemporary signature of J. P. Avery, later bookplate
of Charles Willmarth, M.D.   Maggs Bros. Ltd. 1190-535 1996 £75.00

ASSOCIATION - RIDLEY WILLS

TATE, ALLEN   The Golden Mean and Other Poems. Nashville: Privately
printed, 1923. 1st edition; one of 200 copies, signed by Tate and Wills;
8vo; author's first book; original buff wrappers lightly dust soiled, one
small stain to upper cover, otherwise very good, enclosed in half
morocco folding box; rare; this copy additionally inscribed by Ridley
Wills for Katherine Waits. With Waits' signature.   James S. Jaffe
34-636 1996 $3,000.00

ASSOCIATION - ROBERT WILMOT

BURKE, EDMUND 1729-1797   Reflections on the Revolution in France,
and On the Proceedings in Certain Societies in London Relative to that
Event. Dublin: W. Watson (etc), 1790. iv, 356 pages; contemporary tree
calf, red label; fine and attractive copy. Bookplate of Robert Wilmot and
extensively annotated throughout in ink in margins by Robert Wilmot
Horton, bookplate is probably that of Wilmot Horton's father, Wilmot
added surname Horton when he married Anne Horton in 1806.   C. R.
Johnson 37-51 196 £750.00

ASSOCIATION - J. RIMINGTON WILSON

EGAN, PIERCE 1772-1849   Every Gentleman's Manual. A Lecture on
the Art of Self-Defence. London: Flintoff, 1851. 12mo; iv, 199 pages, 6
full page wood engraved illustrations; original blue ribbed cloth, printed
paper labels on upper cover and spine; little rubbed and faded, but nice,
very uncommon book, ownership inscription of J. Rimington Wilson.
Magriel 43 (1st ed.); Hartley 597.   James Burmester 29-48 1996
£375.00

ASSOCIATION - JOHN WILSON

FOSTER, JAMES   Discourses On All the Principal Branches of Natural
Religion and Social Virtue. London: printed for the author and sold by
Mr. Noon in Cheapside... 1749-52. 1st edition; 4to; 2 volumes; viii, 391
and xxxix; (1), 400, (1) pages, including final errata leaf; contemporary
polished calf, spines fully gilt with raised bands and labels, red edges;
fine; from the contemporary library of John Wilson, M.A., Fellow &
Bursar of Trinity College, Cambridge. Lowndes 824; New CBEL II 1675;
not in Chuo.   John Drury 82-86 1996 £450.00

ASSOCIATION - LANGFORD WILSON

SHAFFER, PETER   Five Finger Exercise; a Play. London: 1958. 1st
edition; very good in trifle creased and scuffed dust jacket; inscribed by
author to American playwright Langord Wilson.   Words Etcetera
94-1119 1996 £65.00

ASSOCIATION - MATHEW WILSON

PANVINO, ONOFRIO   Antiquitatum Veronensium, Libri Octo. Padua: P.
Frambotti, 1647. 1st and only edition; folio; (xii), 236, (8) pages, 33
plates; contemporary gilt vellum, lacking ties; fine; rare. Bookplate of
Miss Richardson Currer, later sold to Sir Mathew Wilson, with his
bookplate. Cicognara 4059.   The Bookpress 75-222 1996 $5,800.00

ASSOCIATION - MILDRED WILSON

FRANK, WALDO   America and Alfred Steiglitz. Garden City: Doubleday,
Doran, 1934. 1st edition; couple of short tears to foot of spine and wear
to cloth of remaining extremities, overall very good in dust jacket with
chipping to extremities; this copy belonged to Steiglitz, with his
ownership signature and bookplate. Inscribed by Steiglitz for Mildred
Wilson.   Lame Duck Books 19-507 1996 $2,500.00

ASSOCIATION - ROBERT WILSON

ALBEE, EDWARD   Who's Afraid of Virginia Woolf? New York:
Atheneum, 1962. 1st edition; 8 1/2 x 5 1/2 inches; 6 p.l., 242 pages, (1)
leaf; original cloth, dust jacket; particularly fine and desirable copy, in
very fine jacket. inscribed by author for Robert A. Wilson.   Phillip J.
Pirages 33-4 1996 $150.00

ASSOCIATION - WILLIAM WINTER

WHITTIER, JOHN GREENLEAF 1807-1892   The Literary Remains of
John G. C. Brainard, with a Sketch of His Life. Hartford: P.B. Goodsell,
1832. 1st edition; 8vo; 228 pages; later half leather. Bookplate and ink
signature of literary critic, William Winter. BAL 1332 (Brainard); 21678
(Whittier); Howe Lib. JGW 22; B&B 11485.   M & S Rare Books
60-266 1996 $250.00

ASSOCIATION - THOMAS JAMES WISE

BROWNING, ROBERT 1812-1889   Letters from Robert Browning to
Various Correspondents. London: privately printed, 1895-96. 1st edition;
8vo; 2 volumes; original plum cloth; fine set, armorial bookplates of
Henry Cabot Lodge. Presentation copy, inscribed by Thomas James
Wise for H. S. Nichols. Todd 87d; CBEL III 445.   Ximenes 108-379
1996 $500.00

ASSOCIATION - WILLIAM WITTLIFF

DOBIE, BERTHA MC KEE   Growing Up in Texas. Austin: Encino Press,
1972. 1st edition; one of only 44 copies, signed by all the contributors;
153 pages; woodcuts; two-tone cloth; very fine and bright with pictorial
dust jacket; presentation inscription signed by William D. Wittliff, owner
of the Encino Press on colophon page.   Argonaut Book Shop 113-202
1996 $300.00

ASSOCIATION - BELLA WITZNER

LENSKI, LOIS   Indian Captive - the Story of Mary Jemison. New York:
Stokes, 1941. illustrations by Lenski, with colored lithographed
frontispiece and black and white lithographs; beige cloth pictorially
printed in red and green; very nice; inscribed by Lenski to Bella Witzner.
Barbara Stone 70-143 1996 £125.00

ASSOCIATION - WOBURN ABBEY

BEDFORDSHIRE GENERAL LIBRARY   Catalogue of the Bedfordshire
General Library: Established in July, 1830. Bedford: Chas. F. Timaeus,
1831. 64 pages; half vellum, very worn, some very mild browning;
booklabel of Woburn Abbey.   Maggs Bros. Ltd. 1191-32 1996
£225.00

ASSOCIATION - WOBURN ABBEY

BOYS, JOHN   A General View of the Agriculture of the County of Kent... London: for G. Nicol, 1796. 8vo; xiv, (2), 206 pages, errata leaf, folding hand colored map, 2 engraved plates, folding table; contemporary half russia; very good; Duke of Bedford's copy with Woburn Abbey bookplate.   Ken Spelman 30-62 1996 £225.00

BYRON, GEORGE GORDON NOEL, 6TH BARON 1788-1824   Sunset from the Parthenon. N.P.: Chevening?: 1875. 1st edition; 4to; contemporary half calf and marbled boards, spine gilt, trifle rubbed; leaf of heavily corrected ms. from an early version of Byron's "Curse of Minerva" reproduced in photographic facsimile, along with letterpress titlepage, leaf of explanation, fine copy; from the library of Duke of Bedford at Woburn Abbey. Not in Wise or NCBEL.   Ximenes 108-55 1996 $400.00

JACKSON, JOHN   A Defense of Human Liberty, in Answer to the Principal Arguments Which Have Been Alledged Against It. London: J. Noon, 1725. 1st edition; 8vo; (8), 207, (1) pages, ads on verso of last leaf; contemporary calf, gilt, joints cracked, otherwise very good, crisp copy; the Woburn Abbey copy with contemporary armorial bookplate of Duke of Bedford, blue circular Woburn Abbey shelf label and Bedford arms in gilt on each cover.   John Drury 82-122 1996 £350.00

ASSOCIATION - P. G. WODEHOUSE

HAWKINS, ANTHONY HOPE 1863-   Comedies of Courtship. New York: Charles Scribner's Sons, 1896. spine bumped, otherwise very good; ownership signature of P. G. Wodehouse.   R. A. Gekoski 19-163 1996 £120.00

ASSOCIATION - LANA WOOD

GREEN, STANLEY   Starring Fred Astaire. New York: Dodd, Mead, 1973. 1st edition; 4to; numerous black and white illustrations; dust jacket, very good; taped down on front free endpaper is ALS from Astaire to actress Lana Wood.   George J. Houle 68-5 1996 $275.00

ASSOCIATION - RUTH MARTIN WOODHOUSE

DODGSON, CHARLES LUTWIDGE 1832-1898   Sylvie and Bruno. (with) Sylvie and Bruno Concluded. London: and New York: Macmillan and Co./London: Macmillan and Co., 1889/93. 1st editions; 8vo; pages xxiii (including frontispiece), (i), blank, 400, (4) ads, wood engraved frontispiece and illustrations in text after Furniss; pages xxxi including frontispiece (i) blank, 423, (1) blank, (6) ads; wood engraved frontispiece and illustrations after Furniss; loosely inserted rare single-leaf ad expressing author's outrage at the poor printing of the sixtieth thousand of "Through the Looking Glass"; original red cloth, 1st title triple fillet gilt border and central meadllion to sides, spine lettered and ruled in gilt, gilt edges, little worn, occasional slight soiling, but very good; 2nd title with triple fillet border gilt to sides, sides with medallion portrait gilt at centre, spine ruled, lettered and decorated in gilt, gilt edges, dust jacket torn with some slight loss, '8/6 Net' label on spine, the 2 volumes together in maroon quarter morocco slipcase, ruled and lettered in gilt; excellent copy; Pres. copy of first book inscribed by author for Ruth Martin Woodhouse   Simon Finch 24-32 1996 £1,500.00

ASSOCIATION - MICHAEL WOODHULL

CALLIMACHUS   The Hymns of Callimachus. London: printed for the translator, 1755. Only edition; large 4to; engraved vignette on titlepage, 6 engraved headpieces; contemporary mottled calf, spine gilt, morocco label; fine; signature of Michael Woodhull dated 1760; bookplate. NCBEL II 652.   Trebizond 39-9 1996 £600.00

CARACCIOLUS, ROBERTUS   Sermones Quadragesimales de Peccatis. Venice: Joannes & Gregorius de Gregoriis, de Forlivio 11 May, 1490. Quarto; 158 leaves, double column, gothic letter, first 6 lines at head of text printed in red, initial spaces with guide letters, printer's device on fol. 158 recto, some page numerals slightly cropped, slight bronwing on first and last leaves; 18th century vellum boards; from the collection of Thomas Crofts, then Michael Wodhull. Goff C162; Hain 4441; GKW 083; IGI 2466; not in BMC.   H. M. Fletcher 121-6 1996 £1,800.00

ASSOCIATION - CHARLES WOODRUFF

BILLROTH, CHRISTIAN ALBERT THEODOR   General Surgical Pathology and Therapeutics in Fifty-One Lectures. New York: 1883. 8vo; 169 wood engraved woodcut prints; half sheepskin, rebacked; signature of Charles E. Woodruff, well known American surgeon and ethnologist. GM 5608 (Berlin 1863 ed.).   Argosy 810-60 1996 $200.00

ASSOCIATION - MARY WOODWARD

SHERIDAN, THOMAS   A Complete Dictionary of the English Language Both with Regard to Sound and Meaning... London: printed for Charles Dilly, 1789. 4to; half title; frontispiece (slightly stained in margins), contemporary tree calf, excellent repair to head and tail of spine. signature of Mary Woodward. Alston V315.   Jarndyce 103-215 1996 £280.00

ASSOCIATION - WOOL

MARCY, RANDOLPH BARNES 1812-1887   The Prairie Traveler. New York: Harper & Bros., 1859. 1st edition; 340 pages; frontispiece, illustrations, folding map; original black cloth, title in gilt on spine, fine, bright copy. Major General Wool's copy with his signature. Choice copy of a fine association. Howes M279; Smith 6509; Graff 2676; Streeter Sale 2123.   Michael D. Heaston 23-241 1996 $1,250.00

ASSOCIATION - LEONARD WOOLF

DAY-LEWIS, CECIL 1904-   Collected Poems - 1929-1933 - Transitional Poem. London: Hogarth Press, 1935. 1st edition; original binding, top edge dusty, free endpapers browned, spine and top edge of lower cover slightly darkened, very good in nicked, rubbed and dusty, slightly torn and soiled dust jacket browned at spine and edges and wormed along almost the entire length of the upper flap fold and slightly at lower flap fold; leonard Woolf's copy; from the library of Ian Parsons who inherited Leonard Woolf's library.   Ulysses 39-300 1996 £175.00

ASSOCIATION - NOAH WORCESTER

WEBBER, SAMUEL   War, a Poem. Cambridge: Hilliard and Metcalf, 1823. 1st edition; 16mo; 48 pages; original printed wrappers. Ink inscription from Noah Worcester to President Kirkland of Harvard. Shoemaker 14854.   M & S Rare Books 60-212 1996 $175.00

ASSOCIATION - MARY WORDSWORTH

WORDSWORTH, WILLIAM 1770-1850   Yarrow Revisited, and Other Poems. London: printed for Longman, etc., and Edward Moxon, 1835. 1st edition; 12mo; original grey boards, rebacked, original spine and paper label preserved, spine bit scuffed, cloth folding case; nice; presentation copy, inscribed by author's wife Mary, to M. Elliott; Borowitz booklabel. Wing W3658; CBEL II 1832.   Ximenes 109-307 1996 $600.00

ASSOCIATION - DE WORMS

FELLOWES, ROBERT   The History of Ceylon, from the Earliest Period to the Year MDCCCXV... London: printed for Joseph Mawman, 1817. 4to; 2 parts in one volume, engraved portrait, folding map, 15 plates; half calf, marbled boards, rubbed, top edge gilt, others uncut; bookplate of Baron de Worms.   H. M. Fletcher 121-138 1996 £450.00

ASSOCIATION - JONATHAN WRIGLEY

CAESAR, GAIUS JULIUS 100-44 BC   The Eyght Bookes of Caius Iulius Caesar... London: Willyam Seres, 1565. 1st edition in English; octavo; modern polished calf antique style, blind tooled and roll stamped, minor soiling and embrowning within, with few side notes, page numerals and headlines cropped, leaf Eg with signature 'Jonathan Wrigley' dated 1711. Attractive copy. STC 18962; Pforzheimer 411.   G. W. Stuart 59-26 1996 $3,500.00

ASSOCIATION - ELIZABETH WROTH

LAFAYETTE, MARIE MADELEINE PLOCHE DE LA VERGNE, COMTESSE DE   The Princess of Cleves. London: printed for R. Bentley and M. Mages, 1679. 1st edition in English; 8vo; (359 pages, 6 pages ads); contemporary mottled calf, spine gilt, some overall wear, few small paper flaws, expert minor repair to several pages and back cover, all in all, a very good copy, bound without blanks or flyleaves at beginning and end, but complete with a prelim license leaf and 3 terminal leaves of ads; rare; signature on titlepage of Elizabeth Wroth, dated dec. 24, 1680; 18th century ownership inscription of Elizabeth Oxenham. Rare. Bazin 59; Wing L169.   Paulette Rose 16-200 1996 $4,000.00

ASSOCIATION - WROTTESLEY

ARBUTHNOT, JOHN   Tables of the Grecian, Roman and Jewish
Measures, Weights and Coins. London: Ralph Smith, n.d. 1705? 1st
edition; small oblong 4to; 14 leaves, engraved throughout, title within a
cartouche and signed 'Sturt sculpsit', 29 tables; contemporary cottage
panelled calf, neatly rebacked, very good; early 18th century ownership
inscriptions of Thomas and Elizabeth Wrottesley. Not in Goldsmith or
Kress.   John Drury 82-9 1996 £250.00

ASSOCIATION - G. H. WYATT

RAWLINSON, RICHARD   The English Topographer. London: T. Jauncy,
1720. 1st edition; 8vo; (viii), xliv, 275, (13) pages; contemporary calf,
nice, light chipping at extremities of spine, hinges strong but starting.
With bookplate of Charles Bruce of Ampthill and later bookplate of G. H.
Wyatt.   The Bookpress 75-347 1996 $600.00

ASSOCIATION - ANDREW WYETH

FORESTER, CECIL SCOTT 1899-1966   Lord Hornblower. Boston: Little,
Brown & Co., 1946. 1st edition; 8vo; 322 pages; teal cloth, bumped,
slightly soiled, in color pictorial dust jacket, chipped and creased at
edges with small piece out from tail of spine, dust jacket illustration by
Andrew Wyeth; near fine in good dust jacket; inscribed by Andrew
Wyeth.   Blue Mountain SP95-82 1996 $375.00

ASSOCIATION - KARL WYLER

MOONEY, BOOTH   The Lyndon Johnson Story. New York: FS&C,
1956. 1st edition; book very good in dust jacket has numerous small
tears; nice inscription from Johnson to Karl Wyler (El Paso publisher).
Parker Books of the West 30-128 1996 $350.00

ASSOCIATION - YARBOROUGH

RALEIGH, WALTER 1552-1618   Judicious and Select Essayes and
Observations. London: printed by T. W. for Humphrey Mosele, 1650. 1st
collected edition; 8vo; frontispiece, title printed within border of
typographical fleur-de-lys, (1), 42, (2), 4, (72), (2), 46, (2), 69, (1) pages;
mid 19th century calf, gilt, tear at foot of spine, otherwise very good;
from the library of the Earl of Yarborough with his bookplate.   John
Drury 82-236 1996 £600.00

ASSOCIATION - JANES YATES

SCOTT, WALTER 1771-1832   The Life of Napoleon Buonaparte,
Emperor of the French... Edinburgh: printed by Ballantyne and Co. for
Longman et al, 1827. 2nd edition; 7 1/4 x 4 3/4 inches; 9 volumes;
especially appealing contemporary fawn colored polished half calf in
regency style, marbled paper sides, raised bands, spine panels
attractively decorated with blind and gilt rules and centered blind floral
ornament, elegant gilt latticework at spine ends, red morocco double
labels, paper sides bit chafed, 3 or 4 corners with slight wear, binding
exceptionally fine, very bright and virtually without wear, first and last
few leaves of most volumes freckled with foxing, isolated light foxing or
minor stains, otherwise excellent internally quite clean and fresh,
extremely pretty set; bookplate of Jane Yates, Irwell House in each
volume.   Phillip J. Pirages 33-456 1996 $750.00

ASSOCIATION - YATTON COURT

COLERIDGE, SAMUEL TAYLOR 1772-1834   The Friend: a Series of
Essays to Aid in the Formation of Fixed Principles in Politics, Morals and
Religion. London: William Pickering, 1837. 3rd edition; 8vo; 3 volumes;
original pebble grain blue cloth, printed paper spine labels, edges uncut;
spines rubbed, good firm set; bookplates of Yatton Court, Herefordshire.
Wise 23.   Simon Finch 24-45 1996 £150.00

ASSOCIATION - WILLIAM BUTLER YEATS

RUSSELL, GEORGE WILLIAM 1867-1935   By Still Waters, Lyrical
Poems Old and New. Dundrum: Dun Emer Press, 1906. One of 200
copies; 8vo; pages (viii), 33, text printed in black and red; original linen
backed boards, lettered in dark blue on upper cover, edges uncut and
unopened; this may have been W. B. Yeats's copy, as it has his
signature on verso of half title.   Sotheran PN32-47 1996 £450.00

ASSOCIATION - YEOMAN

ENGLISH, THOMAS H.   A Memoir of the Yorkshire Esk Fishery
Association. London: 1925. Privately printed, it is likely that around 50
copies were produced; 4to; original buckram; this copy has a letter
from the author to a Miss Yeoman; book is also inscribed to Miss
Yeoman by author on dedication leaf.   David A.H. Grayling 3/95-433
1996 £350.00

ASSOCIATION - OWEN YOUNG

ROBERTSON, JOHN W.   Francis Drake and Other Early Explorers
Along the Pacific Coast. San Francisco: Grabhorn Press, 1927. One of
1000 copies; 26 x 17.5 cm; 290 pages; 28 maps, vellum spine, paper
over boards, bit of darkening to spine, slipcase worn; this copy with
warm inscription by author for Owen D. Young Jr.   Parmer Books
039/Nautica-039148 1996 $450.00

ASSOCIATION - SUSAN YOUNG

JOHNSON, SAMUEL 1709-1784   A Dictionary of the English Language.
London: printed for J. Johnson, C. Dilly, G. G. & J. Robinson, &c., 1799.
11th edition; half title; contemporary tree calf, slightly scarred and
recently neatly rebacked with red label; Signature of Susan Young 1800.
Alston V210, variant on laid paper.   Jarndyce 103-177 1996 £160.00

ASSOCIATION - ADINA DE ZAVALA

WAUGH, JULIA NOTT   Castroville and Henry Castro, Empresario. San
Antonio: 1934. 1st edition; illustrations; wrappers, some wear. Signed by
Adina de Zavala, this her copy.   W. M. Morrison 436-366 1996
$100.00

ASSOCIATION - JAKE ZEITLIN

MAXWELL, JAMES CLERK 1831-1879   An Elementary Treatise on
Electricity... Oxford: at the Clarendon Press, 1881. 1st edition; 8vo; xvi,
208, 36 (ads), (8 ads) pages, 6 plates, 53 figures in text; original cloth,
scuffed and frayed at spine ends; former owner's stamp on titlepage,
very good; personal booklabel of Jake Zeitlin on front pastedown.
Wheeler Gift I 2243.   Edwin V. Glaser 121-212 1996 $300.00

ASSOCIATION - EMILE ZOLA

MENDES, CATULLE   Petits Poemes Russes Mis en Vers Francais.
Paris: Charpentier et Fasquelle, 1893. 1st edition; 77 pages, (1) index;
contemporary half brown morocco, spine gilt, original yellow wrappers
bound in, upper joint rubbed, printed on poor paper, else very good;
presentation copy inscribed and signed by Mendes for Emile Zola.
19th Century Shop 39- 1996 $1,800.00

Fine Bindings

FINE BINDINGS

BINDING - 15TH CENTURY

AUGUSTINUS DE ANCONA 1243-1328   Summa de Potestate Ecclesiasatica. Augsburg: Johann Schussler 6 March, 1473. 1st edition; folio; 470 leaves (first blank) and 4 line printed slip at fol. 153, gothic letter, initials, paragraph marks and initial strokes all supplied in red, broad margins with many uncut edges, pinholes still visible and last leaves and gutter of lower margin, but tall, clean and crisp copy; contemporary South German binding of blindstamped pigskin stained red over wooden boards, brass clasps and catches, ms. title in ink on lower edge, expertly rebacked, straps renewed. Goff A1363; Hain 960; BMC II 329; GKW 3050.   H. M. Fletcher 121-4 1996 £8,800.00

BINDING - 16TH CENTURY

BIBLE. LATIN - 1567   Novum I. C. Testamentum. Antwerp: Plantin, 1567. 16mo; 244ff. num., 20 ff. n.n.; contemporary brown calf, covers and spine a la fanfare, all edges gilt, worn, ties gone, attractive and still bright small scale fanfare binding.   Marlborough 160-1 1996 £1,500.00

CASTIGLIONE, BALDASSARE 1475-1529   Il Cortegiano. Lyons: Guillaume Rouille, 1553. 16mo; titlepage, 7 ff. n.n., pages 1-"457", 6 ff. n.n., ruled in red; a Parisian binding c. 1560, red mor. over stiff pasteboards, tooled in silver (now oxydised) to a pre-fanfare pattern of compartments outlined by a continuous fillet & w/azured tools, spine w/4 double bands, compartments dec. w/azured tools, title label added in 18th century, edges of bds. dec. w/lines & tooling in silver, edges black (originally silver?), pastedown w/2 endleaves at front (two at back), no watermark; covers are divided into compartments by a continuous fillet, as on fanfare bindings, but do no have the leafy sprays of the true fanfare; note by W. Kerney, 15.11. (18)88; Lord Amherst of Hackney, his sale, Sotheby's, 3 December 1908, lot 173.   Marlborough 160-2 1996 £4,800.00

CATHOLIC CHURCH. LITURGY & RITUAL. OFFICE   Officium Beatae Mariae Virginis. Brescia: Policreto Turlino, 1583. 12mo; title, 16ff., n.n., pp. 1-578; 1 f. printed in red and black, 5 full page and many smaller woodcuts; brown goatskin, sides stamped with plaque of arabesque ornament on a gilt ground around an empty oval centre, spine with 3 double bands outlined by continuous foliate ornament in gilt, gilt rosette in each compartment, edges of boards plain, lacks two pairs of blue fabric ties, edges plain gilt, pastedown and one endleaf at each end, front endleaf detached, in sound unrestored condition, the binding may be from Lombardy or from Brescia; the copy of Henry Virtue-Tebbs, his sale, Sotheby's 25 June, 1900, lot 318.   Marlborough 160-7 1996 £2,100.00

HERODOTUS   Historiae Libri VIIII Musarum Nominibus Inscripti...De Genere Vitaque Homeri Libellus. Lyons: Heirs of Seb. Gryphius, 1558. 16mo; pages (1)-892, 65ff. n.n., 2 ff. blank; stiff vellum, sewn through the vellum in account-book style, yapp edges, sides decorated with cornerpieces of arabesque ornament on a gilt ground and a large centrepiece of interlaced fillets and arabesque flowers also on a gilt ground , the field seme with triple dots, flat spine with three concealed bands marked by lines of gilt tooling, gilt quatrefoil in each compartment, pages handsome gauffered with large foliate ornament and parcel-gilt, pastedown and one endleaf at each end, in very sound unrestored condition; a contemporary Lyonnese binding; the copy of William Bragge, his sale Sotheby's 10 Nov. 1880 lot 457; the copy of Arthur Ram, his sale Sotheby's 25 May 1906, lot 81.   Marlborough 160-3 1996 £2,250.00

LACTANTIUS FIRMIANUS, LUCIUS CAELIUS   Opera. Lyons: Soubron, 1594. 16mo; 879 pages, 21ff; contemporary Roman brown calf, covers gilt with outer double rules, enclosing panels at head and foot, centre decorated with large and small gyrate, leafy and other small tools, central panel with arms below a helmet and leafy spray, spine gilt in 4 panels, plain endpapers, all edges gilt, gilt and gauffered, upper cover lettered B. Curtus: R/Acad. Parth, lower cover N. Nucctus/Acad. Parth. Small repairs to tie-holes and spine, corners soft, most unusual Roman binding with some elements of fanfare, coats of arms (each different) are those of B. Curtus and N. Nucctus of the Parthenopean Academy; later the copy of J. R. Abbey, Abbey Sale 22 vi. 1965 lot 426 to E. P. Goldschmidt.   Marlborough 160-4 1996 £2,250.00

BINDING - 16TH CENTURY

MACHIAVELLI, NICCOLO 1469-1527   Historie. (with) Libro dell'Arte Della Guerra. Venice: Comin da Trino, 1540/41. 8vo; 2 works in 1 volume, titlepage, ff. 2-243, 1 f. blank; titlepage, 1 f., ff 1-108, 9 ff., woodcut portrait on titles, woodcut diagrams at end of second work, ruled in red. Light brown calf over stiff pasteboards, gilt, sides decorated with a plaque of illusionistic three dimensional strapwork, an azured 'stirrup' tool repeated upright and reversed in the centre, original sides laid down on a 19th century binding, edges plain gilt, 19th century marbled endleaves; early ownership inscription on titlepage scribbled over "Gu. Lyly", at foot of titlepage; H.R.H. Augustus Frederick, Duke of Sussex, sixth son of King George III, his sale, evans pt. IV, 30 Jan. 1845 lot 1016, bought by Payne.   Marlborough 160-5 1996 £1,950.00

MALIPIERO, GIROLAMO   Il Petrarcha Spirituale. Venice: Francesco Marcolini, Sept. 1538. 2nd edition; 8vo; titlepage, ff. 2-153, 10ff. n.n., woodcut portrait on titlepage; red mor. over pasteboards, richly gilt, lacks 4 pairs of ties, sides dec. inside upper cover the title II PE/TRARCHA/SPIR and originally on lower one the (intended) first owner's name MACRO/ANOTIMO(?), subsequently obliterated (by the original binder) by over-tooling, spine with 3 raised bands alternating with four false bands, compartments dec. w/line-ornament in blind & w/motto CONSTANTIA gilt downwards, edges of bds. scored at right angles w/groups of 3 lines, edges gilt & gauffered w/sm. knotwork tools, pastedown and 2 endleaves (origina?) at each end, no watermark; the copy of Franciscus Gianibellus, 16th century signature on titlepage; William Bateman, F.A.S. of Middleton-by-Yolgrave in the County of Derby, with armorial bookplate. A contemporary Bolognese binding by a man whom the late Dr. Schunke called the "Binder of the Acts of the Cabinetmakers' Guild.   Marlborough 160-6 1996 £7,500.00

PETRARCA, FRANCESCO 1304-1374   Il Canzoniere. Venice: Giovanni Antonio dei Nicolini da Sabbio and Brothers, 1541. 4to; 23ff. n.n. (with the blank leaf C8); ff. I-CCCLXXXIV, 80 ff.; recased in binding of brown morocco over pasteboards, lacks 4 pair of ties, richly gilt with narrow border of a lacework tool and large centre arabesque plaque, blindfold Cupid with bow and arrows, in centre of upper cover and Fortune with her sail in same position on lower one, spine with 3 double bands alternating with four false bands, compartments cross hatched in blind, edges gilt and gauffered with small knotwork tools, new pastedowns and endleaves; a Bolognese binding of c. 1550, the plaque is akin to one owned by the "Binder of the Acts of the Cabinetmakers' Guild".   Marlborough 160-8 1996 £1,500.00

PEZZI, LORENZO   Vinea Domini. Cum Brevi Descriptione Sacramentorum et Paradisi, Limbi Purgatorij, Atque Inferni a Catechismo Catholicisque Patribus Excerpta. Venice: Girolamo Porro, 1588. 1st edition; Porro issue, with large plate partly unshaded; portrait in second state; 8vo; 12ff., n.n., pages 1-186, engraved titlepage, portrait, double page plate, 12 large engraved illustrations; ruled in mauve throughout; brown mor. over stiff pasteboards, lacks two pairs of ties, sides & spine richly gilt, border of leafy tendrils issuing from corners, centre dec. with 6 rows each of five oval frames outlined by leafy tendrils, each frame containing 1 of 4 monograms, flat spine with continuous ornament of leafy tendrils, edges plain gilt, rebacked with old spine laid down and very skilfully restored, new pastedowns and endleaves; a Parisian binding of c. 1590-1600; the copy of G. Garcia sale Paris 27 April 1868, lot 118; the copy of Ricardo Heredia, the poet, his sale, Paris 22 May 1891, lot 165 with illustration in sale catalog, the copy of Lord Amherst of Hackney, sale Sotheby's 24 March 1909 lot 679. It was suggested in the Heredia cat. that the initials on binding indicate joint ownership of Francois de Coligny, & his wife Marguerite d'Ailly;   Marlborough 160-9 1996 £6,800.00

POINTZ, ROBERT   Testimonies for the Real Presence of Christes Body and Blood in the Blessed Scarament of the Aultar. Louvain: Jean Fouler, 1566. 8vo; title, 7 ff., n.n., ff. 1-200 (lacking ff. 155-158); sides of original binding laid down on a new binding in 1885, they are of brown goatskin decorated in gilt with border formed by repeated impressions of lacework took, a plaque of arabesque foliate ornament blocked in centre between the name GLASCOK/MARI (the words reversed on lower cover), lacks two ld ties, upper edge dark green, others show traces of guilding; this binding may be Roman, of about the same date as the book; the book was bound for Mary Glascock; the copy of Bartholomew Wicker with early scribblings in margins.   Marlborough 160-10 1996 £1,750.00

BINDING - 17TH CENTURY

ACHILLES TATIUS   De Dlitophontis et leucippes Amoribus Libri VIII. Heidelberg: Commelin, 1606. 8vo; title within border, 1 f., 396 ff. num.; contemporary Parisian crimson morocco, covers panelled gilt with outer and inner triple rule, border empty, panel decorated to a fanfare pattern of compartments outlined by a single and double fillet and filled with small tools, background of gyrate and leafy spray tools, central oval panel empty, spine similarly patterned, titled later at head and foot, all edges gilt, later endpapers, corners soft, two pairs of ties gone, preserved in cloth box. From the collection of "Potier, Paris, 1853"; Sir Edward Sullivan with his ex-libris, his sale, lot 14 Sotheby's May 19, 1890; J. R. Abbey with his ex-libris, his sale lot, Sotheby's June 21, 1965 to H. M. Fletcher.   Marlborough 160-11 1996 £2,100.00

BINDING - 17TH CENTURY

ALLESTREE, RICHARD   The Government of the Tongue. Oxford: at the Theater, 1674. 1st edition; 2nd impression; 8vo; in half sheets, pages (xvi), 224; contemporary 'sombre' binding, dark brown morocco, elaborately decorated in blind with a background of fine parallel lines and some cross-hatching forming a 'cottage-roof' pattern, then decorated with tulips, fruit, rosettes and other tools, spine in compartments with darkened maroon morocco label gilt, some wear at joints and corners, marbled endpapers, inner hinges split, imprimatur leaf pasted to front free endpaper and with inscription erased, some light staining and soiling, but very good, and interestingly bound copy. Wing A1134; Madan 3002.   Simon Finch 24-2   1996 £550.00

APHTHONIUS   Progymnasmata...cum Scholiss R. Lorichii. Amsterdam: L. Elzevir, 1642. 12mo; engraved title, printed title, 5 ff. index, 1 f. blank, 400 pages; contemporary plain calf, covers gilt with arms of F. A. de Thou, spine gilt in five panels, raised bands, de Thou monogram in four panels, all edges red, plain endpapers;   Marlborough 160-12   1996 £900.00

AUBESPIN, NICOLAS   La Cordeliere ou Tresor des Indulgences du Cordon St. Francois. Paris: Jean le Bouc, 1610. Very small 8vo; engraved title, 11 fine engraved plates by L. Gaultier, p. 97 torn without loss, very good with final colophon leaf; full early 17th brown morocco, boards elaborately gilt with outer panel enclosing large floral scrolls at corners surrounding a central symmetrical gilt arabesque, corners worn, flat spine symmetrically gilt, small wear at head. Good example of an early French binding.   Ian Wilkinson 95/1-32   1996 £260.00

BLAKE, WILLIAM 1757-1827   The Ladies Charity School-House Roll of Highgate; or a Subscription of Many Noble, Well Disposed Ladies for the Easie Carrying of It On. London: 1670. 8vo; drophead title, 292 pages, 1 f., lacks the 4 plates; contemporary black morocco, richly gilt, all over repeating pattern of 'drawer-handles', tulips, rosettes, dots, pointed leaves, etc., spine gilt in comparments, with presentation inscription "TO MAD'm SEMENS" in gilt in a panel on upper cover, all edges gilt, comb marbled endpapers, edges and hinges little worn; with stamp in blue of A. Ehrman, who formed the famous Broxbourne Library.   Marlborough 160-88   1996 £750.00

CATHOLIC CHURCH. LITURGY & RITUAL. OFFICE   L'Officio di Maria Vergine. Vienna: Voigt, 1672. 8vo; engraved title, printed title, portrait on verso, 18ff. n.n. with 1 full page text illustration, 595 pages (16 full pae engraved text illustrations); brown morocco gilt, all edges gilt, gauffered, (worn, corners soft, clasps gone). Covers gilt with broad outer border, central panel with corner decoration a l'evantail and central 25 part wheel within arabesque and other ornament, flat spine with repeated small tool ornaments, all edges gilt and gauffered, plain endpapers, unusual binding, possibly italian.   Marlborough   160-22   1996 £550.00

HIERONYMUS, SAINT   Epistolae Selectae. Paris: Nivel, 1602. 12mo; 417ff. num., 48 ff. n.n.; contemporary brown calf, covers gilt with triple outer rule and seme of fleur-de-lys, corners with crowned H and laurel wreath, flat spine gilt in similar fashion with central Maltese cross, all edges gilt, later endpapers, gilt armos of Henry IV, King of France, corners and covers worn and rubbed, Henry IV bindings are of some rarity in commerce.   Marlborough   160-19   1996 £2,100.00

THE LADIES Charity School-House Roll of Highgate; or a Subscription of Many Noble, Well Disposed Ladies for the Easie Carrying Of It On. London: 1670. 8vo; 292, (2) pages, drophead title, wanting the four plates; very attractive contemporary London binding in black morocco, richly gilt with all over gilt tooling of 'drawer-handles', tulips, rosettes, dots, pointed leaves, etc. repeated on lower cover, spine gilt in compartments, with presentation "To MADM SEMENS" in gilt in panel on upper cover, joints little rubbed.   John Drury 82-23   1996 £500.00

LE CONTE, MICHEL   Les Trophees de l'Amour Divin au Tres-Sainct Sacrement de l'Autel. Charleville: Raoult et Poncelet, 1645. 8vo; title, pages 3-15, 2ff., 1-364; brown morocco gilt, broad outer border of repeated small tools enclosing a central panel with small tool cornerpeices and a lozenge shaped centre-piece enclosing a simple crowned letter "C", flat spine is gilt in 8 panels, all edges gilt, comb-marbled endpapers, bookplate.   Marlborough 160-21   1996 £750.00

RUBEUS, THEODOSIUS   Discursus Circa Literas Apostolicas in Forma Brevis S.D.M. Urvani Papae VIII. Rome: Typis Vaticanis, 1639. Folio; title in red and black with woodcut device, pages 3-56; Roman limp vellum, covers panelled gilt with double inner and outer rules, flat spine lettered in ink, gilt arms of Cardinal Maffeo Barberini, later Pope Urban VIII, with Barberini bee at each corner of the central panel.   Marlborough 160-23   1996 £1,250.00

BINDING - 18TH CENTURY

ALMANACH. Paris: Le Breton, 1778. contemporary crimson morocco, covers gilt with placque by Dubuisson, spine with five raised bands, panels with gilt fleur-de-lys or lettering, all edges gilt, blue silk endpapers, the bookseller Larcher's striking engraved (1756) label on blank leaf before title, head of spine neatly repaired.   Marlborough 160-25   1996 £600.00

BIBLE. ENGLISH - 1715   The Holy Bible. Edinburgh: Watson, 1715, colophon 1714. 8vo; engraved title, 348 ff. n.n.; black morocco panelled gilt, all edges gilt, corners little worn, edges little rubbed, some foxing, presumably a Scottish binding, but the distinctive cornerpieces are without record known to the N.L.S.; D&M 729.   Marlborough 160-28   1996 £90.00

BIBLE. ENGLISH - 1780.   The Bible in Miniuture (sic), or a Concise History of the Old and New Testaments. London: E. Newbery, 1780. 42 x 30mm; 256 pages; 2 engraved titlepages, 14 plates; contemporary black morocco, gilt dog-tooth roll border with floral cornerpieces, central oval red onlay, with sacred monogram in gilt, smooth spine divided into three gilt decorated panels, spot marbled endpapers, all edges gilt; early issue in good condition and in the scarcer variant black binding.   Marlborough 160-27   1996 £950.00

BIBLE. FRENCH - 1738   Version du Nouveau Testament Selon La Vulgate... Paris: Chez J. B. Garnier, 1738. New edition; 8vo; 2 volumes, engraved frontispiece to volume 1, each page ruled in red, well margined; handsomely bound in full 18th century French brown morocco, triple gilt fillet to boards enclosing stylised fleurons at corners each board with large round elaborate gilt stamp of dual coat-of-arms, corners little worn, flat spines elaborately gilt in compartments with lettering direct, tiny wormhole to base of spine of volume 2, large red morocco doublures on inside of all boards, wide and elaborate gilt dentelle border, all edges gilt, marbled endpapers, magnificent contemporary French armorial bindings; bookplates of Mr. A. G-du Plessis and P de La Morandiere.   Ian Wilkinson 95/1-36   1996 £580.00

BRETT, THOMAS   An Account of Church-Government and Governours. London: John Wyat, 1701. 1st edition; 8vo; reddish brown turkey morocco in triple panel design wtih 2 line fillet and rolls, second panel contains ornamental fleurons in corners from which a single acorn tool is suspended, there are four larger fleurons midway along each side, innermost panel is intersected at each corner, spine with five raised bands and closely stamped decoration within the compartments (without title), board edges gilt decorated, inner gilt dentelles, all edges gilt, marbled endleaves, in absolutely fine condition; bookplate of J. L. Templer, Torrhill, Devon.   Book Block 32-33   1996 $875.00

CAMERON, CHARLES   The Baths of the Romans Explained and Illustrated... London: George Scott for the Author, 1772. 1st edition; Large folio; text in English and French, engraved title, English title with engraved vignette, engraved dedication f., iv, 65 pages, French title, iv + 68 pages, 20 engraved text illustrations in duplicate, 76 plates, errata slip pasted on verso of last plate; sumptuously bound in near cont. Russian red mor., covers gilt panelled w/roll-tooled borders and corner ornaments, spine gilt in 7 compartments w/neo-classical motifs, green label, inner borders gilt, marbled endpapers, gilt edges, upper cover w/gilt stamp of arms, crest, supporters & motto: PRO RIGE (sic) ET PATRIA, of Cameron of Lochiel (to which Charles Cameron was not entitled) & the initials C.C.A.M.I.R. (Charles Cameron Architecte a Sa Majeste Imperiale Russe); Cameron's own copy, covers little rubbed and scratched, otherwise fine, sound and unrestored condition.   Marlborough 160-35   1996 £15,000.00

CATHOLIC CHURCH. LITURGY & RITUAL. OFFICE   Officium B. Mariae Virginis, Nuper Reformatum... Antwerp: Ex Architypographia Plantiniana, 1731. 8vo; title in red and black with engraved vignette, 21 f., 741 pages, 2 ff. index, 16 engraved plates; contemporary crimson morocco covers gilt with five fold outer border, central panel with swags, arabesque corner-pieces and central lozenge w/similar tools filled with star, flower and other small tool decoration, spine gilt in 6 panels, raised bands, gilt, panels with stars and arabesques, all edges gilt and gauffered, marbled endpapers, corners little soft, some aging of paper, attractive and striking Low Countries binding - having some affinity with H. Davis Gift II 311 and Culot, Quatre Siecles de Reliure en Belgique 1500-1900 no. 54; with contemporary illegible signature, later in the library of Robert Hoe with his label.   Marlborough 160-50   1996 £1,200.00

CATHOLIC CHURCH. LITURGY & RITUAL. BREVIARY   Dirunal du Breviarie Romain. Lyon: Valfray, 1740. 4to; contemporary crimson morocco, covers gilt with wide floral border and corner-pieces, arms of Henri Thomassin de Mazangues, spine gilt in 6 panels with floral decoration, all edges gilt, rubbed, corners worn, old reback now cracked at foot of one joint.   Marlborough 160-38   1996 £450.00

BINDING - 18TH CENTURY

CATHOLIC CHURCH. LITURGY & RITUAL. MISSAL   Missale Romanum. Venice: Apud Nicolaum Pezzana, 1763. Tall large thick 8vo; title in red and black with large copper plate engraving, 3 full page three quarter, woodcut initial letters, printed in red and black throughout, several pages of musical notation in red and black, 2 or 3 leaves with slight marginal soiling, rest in very good condition; handsomely bound in full contemporary brown morocco, boards with outer gilt roll border, foliate cornerpieces in gilt, center of boards stamped with large and elaborate gilt heraldic coat of arms enclosing 2 griffins surmounted by 2 cherubs and a crown, elaborate foliate outer border, spine gilt in compartments with repeated acorn devices, upper cover with slight staining and gilt rubbed, lower cover extremely good and bright; magnificent 18th century armorial binding, probably Venetian.   Ian Wilkinson 95/1-34 1996 £690.00

CATHOLIC CHURCH. LITURGY & RITUAL. MISSAL   Missale Romanum ex Decreto Sacrosancti Concilii Tridentini Restitutum... Venice: Balleone, 1766. Folio; vignette title, pages v-xxxv, 436, cviii, engraved frontispiece, 2 other plates; boards, cvoers gilt w/multi-colored mor., calf & paper onlays in form of a broad crimson outer border gilt w/leafy sprays, L-shaped black corner-pieces, circular brown inlays, central panel w/mottled brown broad borders, blue corner & centre pieces, enclosing a blue background & sunken red & green oval centre-piece w/crimson surrounds gilt w/flower & other sm. tools, 6 brass corner & centre studs, spine w/4 raised bands, alternate red & brown panels similarly gilt, all edges gilt, marbled pastedowns, sl. rubbed, unobtrusively & skillfully rebacked, remarkable binding using at least 50 pieces of leather on each cover to produce a design which is at once technically proficient & refreshingly exuberant.   Marlborough 160-47 1996 £6,000.00

CHURCH OF ENGLAND. BOOK OF COMMON PRAYER   Book of Common Prayer. Oxford: at the Theatre, 1680. 8vo; fine engraved architectural titlepage of the inteiror of a church, top edge cut close occasionally touching running title, 3 leaves with lower right hand corner torn away with loss of a few letters only, generally fine, crisp and clean; finely bound in full 18th century black morocco, boards with gilt key-roll border, spine elaborately gilt with stars and urn devices, insignificant wear at extremities. Scarce. Wing B3660.   Ian Wilkinson 95/1-37 1996 £95.00

CHURCH OF ENGLAND. BOOK OF COMMON PRAYER   Book of Common Prayer. London: 1717. 8vo; 85 pages, engraved, frontispiece, portrait, 2 small and 16 half page text illustrations; contemporary black morocco, panelled blind with outer leafy border and central panel with arabesque and other small tools, spine with five raised bands, panels with repeated small tools, all edges gilt, endpapers marbled, covers with centre and cornerpieces of filigree silver.   Marlborough 160-56 1996 £1,500.00

CHURCH OF ENGLAND. BOOK OF COMMON PRAYER   The Book of Common Prayer, and Administration of the Sacraments...with the Psalter or Psalms of David... Oxford: printed at the Clarendon Press, 1791. tall 8vo; (196)ff; contemporary full red straight grained morocco with gilt tooled spine and inner dentelles, gilt ruled borders, all edges gilt, bookplate removed, but crisp, near fine in lovely binding showing only minimal wear; very scarce.   Chapel Hill 94-106 1996 £175.00

GOLDSMITH, JOHN   An Almanack for the Year of OUr Lord 1701. London: Mary Clarke, 1701. 16mo; red and black printed title, 23ff., interleaved with blanks (some excised, pages shaved with some loss of text towards back), 2 woodcuts; contemporary brown morocco gilt a l'eventail, 'wheel' centre-piece surmounted by birds, ruled border, spine with running pattern, ruled head and foot, marbled endpapers, clasps lost, all edges gilt.   Marlborough 160-24 1996 £500.00

HERRMANN, GOTTFRIED   De Metris Poetarum Graecorum et Romanorum Libri III. Leipzig: Fleischer, 1796. 8vo; 461 pages; contemporary vellum, covers panelled with blue double rules, upper cover with full length portrait, flat spine in 6 panels, gilt rules, blue title and imprint lables, all edges gilt, marbled endpapers, preserved in drop side cloth box within morocco backed slipcase, a German binding in the style of Edwards of Halifax; from the libraries of F. Lee Warner, the gift of Dr. Butler and thus inscribed and Ham Court, Upton-on Severn, with bookplate.   Marlborough 160-41 1996 £1,950.00

JUVENALIS, DECIMUS JUNIUS 55-140   Satyrae. Birmingham: Baskerville Press, 1761. 4to; 240 pages; plain calf, flat spine gilt in 7 panels, spine and covers stamped with arms of Pembroke Hall, Cambridge, all edges white, marbled endpapers; from the collection of the Rivers family with their 19th century bookplate and from the collection of J. R. Abbey with his bookplate.   Marlborough 160-44 1996 £450.00

BINDING - 18TH CENTURY

LONDON Almanack for the Year of Christ 1774. London: printed for the Company of Stationers, n.d. 1773. 59 x 33 mm; 12 ff. engraved throughout, folding plate mounted as one leaf; original red morocco, gilt, all edges gilt, gold patterned printed endpapers with sponge applied coloring, covers gilt, ruled in squares, dog-tooth border, pointille saltires interspersed with flower-heads and scrollwork, spine gilt with running pattern, (clasp lost, small loss to foot of spine, edges little worn), within colored and embossed paper covered card pull-off case, with marbled paper interior, worn with some loss to pull-off top; top left corner of first page bears the red partial imprint of the penny 'stamp duty'.   Marlborough 160-26 1996 £250.00

LUCRETIUS CARUS, TITUS 99-55 BC   De Rerum Natura Sex, ad Optimorum Exemplarium Fidem Recensiti. London: Tonson, 1712. Large folio; (4), 282 pages, engraved frontispiece and 6 plates, head and tailpieces, and initials; contemporary gilt panelled red morocco with triple fillet and cornerpieces, gilt roll tooled inner dentelle, spine gilt in compartments, raised gilt bands, all edges gilt, comb marbled endpapers, skilfully rebacked preserving original spine, corners little soft, elegantly understated binding, from Syston Park library.   Marlborough 160-45 1996 £800.00

MOORE, EDWARD   The World. London: Dodsley, 1782. 8vo; 4 volumes; stencilled tree calf covers with narrow leafy small tool border, a central oval of plain calf with large urn and stand in stencilled outline, flat spines gilt with four panels and two lettering pieces, all between red and green or blue onlay, gilt flowers in each corner, all edges yellow, marbled endpapers, some corners soft, occasional small abrasions on covers, overall an excellent set; from the collection of Ficasoli Firidolfi with his label.   Marlborough 160-48 1996 £2,200.00

PRIVILEGGI e Statuti Della Venerabile Archiconfraternita dell'Anime Piu' Bisognose del Purgatorio eretta in Roma Sotto il Patrocino di Gesu Maria, e S. Giuseppe dal Venerabile Servo di Dio Papa Innocenzo XI. Rome: 1734. 4to; 46 pages, 1 f., woodcut device on titlepage; slightly later brown morocco, ornate ruled borders with swags, gathers and floral festoons; floral cornerpieces, central panel with arms of a cardinal (very similar to Belmas, Chauvelin, cf. Guigard Amateurs Ecclesiastqie), a snake climbing a tree, surmounted by a Maltese Cross, cardinals hat, rope and tassle borders, etc., spine flat, gilt a la repetition panels, alternated with urns in ruled compartments (one or two wormholes to head of spine, slight rubbing to extremities), old all edges gilt, later endpapers; bookplate of Sir Ross O'Connell, 1897, and his marks.   Marlborough 160-51 1996 £650.00

PROSI e Versi per Onorare la Memoria de Livia Doria Caraffa... Parma: Stamperia Reale, 1784. 4to; 4 ff., 407 pages, 2 ff. (colophon and errata), 2 engraved portraits, 6 engraved plates, 168 vignettes and initials; contemporary crimson morocco, triple gilt fillet, simple fleuron corner pieces, gilt raised bands, spine gilt in 6 compartments, using only a few tools, including poppy beads (and - on the turn ins - strawberries), black morocco label, gilt lettered, all edges gilt, skly-blue silk endpapers, but lacking f.f.e.p., somewhat restrained binding, but, given the contents, exactly what is called for. Excellent copy. Brooks 250; Geering 39; Updike II 172.   Marlborough 160-52 1996 £3,300.00

SACRORUM Rituum Congreagtione...Beatificationis et Canonizationis...Roberti Bellarmini Societatis Iesu. Rome: Typis Reverendae Camerae Apostolicae, 1712. Folio; 2 volumes; portrait, 18 sections variously paginated; later polished brown calf, covers gilt with broad double border of acanthus and vine leaves, central panel with IHS corner-pieces, flat spine gilt with green and red labels, all edges gilt, green endpapers, gilt arms of Pope Leo XII, unobtrusively rebacked preserving spine. From the collection of R. M. Beverley with his ex-libris.   Marlborough 160-53 1996 £650.00

SMART, JOHN   Tables of Time. London: for the author, 1710. 12mo; vignette title, engraved throughout, 17 unnumbered leaves; contemporary black morocco, double gilt fillet, spine gilt in compartments, double ruled, raised bands, comb marbled endpapers, all edges gilt, elegant.   Marlborough 160-55 1996 £450.00

VITA De'Beati Gaspar e Niccolo... Turin: Briolo, 1788. 8vo; vignette title, pages iii-viii, 263, printed on blue paper; contemporary crimson morocco gilt, covers with gilt double outer border and intertwined leafy inner border, wreath cornerpieces, flat spine gilt in 6 panels, panels with star and sunburst, black label lettered gilt, all edges gilt, marbled endpapers, gilt arms of Victor Amadeus III, Duke of Savoy from 1773-1796, to whom the work is dedicated, presumably the unique dedication copy.   Marlborough 160-59 1996 £1,200.00

BINDING - 19TH CENTURY

ALMANACK for the Year of Christ 1850. London: 1849. 58 x 33 mm; 13 ff., engraved throughout, folding plate mounted at 2 leaves; original brown morocco, gilt, all edges gilt, covers gilt with beige, green and red onlays, spine gilt with knot and cord pattern, matching contemporary slipcase; excellent condition.   Marlborough 160-60 1996 £225.00

BINDING - 19TH CENTURY

APHORISMS for Youth, with Observations and Reflections, Religious, Moral, Critical and Characteristic... London: Lackington, Allen, 1801. Sole edition; small 8vo; 200 pages; frontispiece, tissue guard, early owner's name, lacks half title (?); finely bound in contemporary marbled brown calf, smooth backstrip divided by wide gilt roundel and lozenge bands, between dotted rolls, red morocco label in second compartment, remaining compartments with dotted line saltire and central foliate stars, seme other small tools, sides with border of fillet, lozenge and star roll, fillet and open twist roll, fillet on board edges, ball roll on turn-ins, marbled endpapers and edges, lilac silk marker, fine. Scarce. From the library of Marcus Gage.   Blackwell's B112-64 1996 £250.00

BIBLE. ENGLISH - 1823   The Holy Bible, Containing the Old and New Testaments; Together with the Apocrypha. New York: Daniel D. Smith, 1823. Daniel Smith's Stereotype Edition; thick quarto; 770 pages; numerous engraved plates; contemporary full red morocco, spine gilt stamped, orange endpapers, flyleaves becoming loose), two scratches on back cover, but spectacular contemporary American period binding; very rare, extremely handsome, signatures and inscriptions, indicating early and long ownership by prominent Rhode Island family of Samuel Arnold. Hills 459; Shoemaker 11816.   M & S Rare Books 60-286 1996 $750.00

BROCKMAN, CARL HEINRICH   Die Metallurgischen Krankheiten des Oberharzes. Osterode: Sorge, 1851. 1st edition; large 8vo; pages xiv, 376; dedication page, contemporary red morocco, gilt crowned monogram of Ernst August, of Hanover, on upper cover, his arms, onlaid in color, on lower cover, both within ornamental rococo gilt and silvered borders, flat spine, spine lettered within scrolling floral border, glazed endpapers, all edges gilt, fine royal binding of the period, enchanced by the use of silver.   Marlborough 160-63 1996 £1,350.00

BYRON, GEORGE GORDON NOEL, 6TH BARON 1788-1824   The Poetical Works of Lord Byron. New York: Johnson Fry, 1867. 1st edition thus; 4to; xxviii, 740 pages; 48 lovely full page steel engravings; original publisher's full red morocco with gilt decorated covers and gilt spine in 6 compartments, volume has been personalized with gilt lettering at foot of spine, extremities slightly darkened, small embossed library stamps, else very good.   Chapel Hill 94-108 1996 $150.00

COMINES, PHILIPPE DE, SIEUR D'ARGENTON 1445-1511   The Memoirs of Philip De Commines, Lord of Argenton. London: Henry G. Bohn, 1855. 2nd, but preferred edition; small 8vo; 2 volumes, 399, 444 pages; frontispiece portraits; contemporary three quarter green polished calf with heavily gilt tooled spine panel florets, light and dark red morocco spine labels, raised bands, top edge gilt, slight discoloration on couple of covers, otherwise near fine. Lowndes p. 505.   Chapel Hill 94-110 1996 $125.00

L'ECHO des Bardes ou Le Menestrel. Dedie Aux Dames. Paris: Le Fuel, 1821. 12mo; frontispiece, title, 68 ff. with 14 vignette headpieces, 6 ff., 4 ff. letterpress; gold covered boards with multi colored silk onlays, neo-classical borders around central winged figures, flat spine with matching onlaid backstrip decorated in four compartments, all edges gilt, matching silk covered slipcase (slipcase little darkened), attractive and unusual binding in remarkably fine state of preservation.   Marlborough 160-71 1996 £500.00

ELIOT, GEORGE, PSEUD. 1819-1880   Romola. Boston: Estes and Lauriat, 1890. One of 250 copies of the edition deluxe; 8 3/4 x 6 1/4 inches; 2 volumes; frontispiece in each volume, 60 other plates, each with printed tissue guard, titles in red and black; very fine olive green onlaid morocco, covers framed with multiple plain and stippled rules and an onlaid strip of ochre morocco, especially pretty large cornerpieces featuring onlaid blue morocco flower amidst delicate gilt stems and leaves, raised bands, spine gilt in compartments with simple floral corner ornaments, butterscotch morocco doublures, elegant gilt cornerpieces similar to those on covers, but larger, patterned flyleaves, gilt edges; faint mark to one cover, otherwise a very fine copy, handomsely bound. Virtually faultless inside and out.   Phillip J. Pirages 33-63 1996 $450.00

FINDEN, WILLIAM   The Ports, Harbours, Watering Places, Fishing Villages and Picturesque Scenery of Great Britain. London: Virtue and Co., n.d., ca. 1845. 4to; 2 volumes, extra engraved title, titlepage, 145 pages, extra engraved title, titlepage, 143 pages, 71 and 71 engraved plates and tissue guards; navy blue morocco, ornate borders roll tooled in gilt and blind with large gilt neo-classical urn at centre of each panel, spines gilt in compartments, raised bands, gilt inner dentelle, all edges gilt; magnificently bound.   Marlborough 162-30 1996 £975.00

GREVILLE, CHARLES CAVENDISH FULKE 1794-1865   A Journal of the Reign of Queen Victoria from 1837 to 1852. London: Longmans, Green & Co., 1885. 1st edition; 8vo; 3 volumes; contemporary half black morocco with raised bands, lightly rubbed, former owner's name clipped from top of title, not affecting lettering, else very good.   Chapel Hill 94-112 1996 $100.00

BINDING - 19TH CENTURY

LONGFELLOW, HENRY WADSWORTH 1807-1882   The Poetical Works. Boston: Houghton Mifflin, 1881. Later edition; small folio; 2 volumes; xvi, 488; xvi, 489-928 pages; profusely illustrated with engravings; original full red morocco with richly gilt turn-ins, library bookplate and blindstamp, extremities lightly rubbed, but nice, very good; BAL 12601.   Chapel Hill 94-115 1996 $150.00

LYTTON, EDWARD ROBERT BULWER-LYTTON, 1ST EARL OF 1835-1891   Poems. Boston: Houghton Mifflin, 1881. New revised edition; 8vo; 406 pages; numerous full page illustrations; contemporary full tree calf with ornately gilt tooled borders, inner dentelles, and spine panel florets, red and green morocco spine labels, raised bands, all edges gilt, beautiful binding in virtually fine condition.   Chapel Hill 94-107 1996 $120.00

RATHBONE, HANNAH MARY   The Poetry of Birds, Selected from Various Authors... Liverpool: George Smith...and Ackermann & Co., London, 1833. 4to; 21 hand colored lithographs, vi, (i +) 136 pages; contemporary green morocco, panelled and lettered in gilt, very slightly scuffed; extremely rare.   Marlborough 160-74 1996 £1,500.00

RUGGIERI, CLAUDE   Precis Historique sur les Fetes, les Spectacles et les Rejouissances Publiques. Paris: Chez l'Auteur, 1830. 8vo; 2ff., pages viii, 380; contemporary green calf, triple gilt fillet, elaborate scrolling leaf-work, blindstamped covers, central blank panel with blindstamped egg and dart border, flat spine, 2 ornate fleuron gilt panels and central gilt lettered black calf label, all edges gilt, crease marbled endpapers. Most attractive.   Marlborough 160-75 1996 £650.00

SKELTON, JOSEPH   Engraved Illustrations of the Principal Antiquities of Oxfordshire... Oxford: Skelton, 1823, plates dated 1823-27. Large paper, probably a subscriber's copy; large folio; engraved title, 4 ff., 140 pages, variously paginated, 2 ff. index, engraved frontispiece, map, 48 engraved illustrations on India paper, numerous text engravings; green morocco gilt with single fillet cathedral pattern on covers and flat spine, all edges gilt, purple silk liners (spine darkened), most unusual, cathedral bindings were normally embossed from a single block, here the unknown binder has used small tools and single rules to create a similar effect.   Marlborough 160-79 1996 £850.00

WARD, ROBERT PLUMER   Illustrations of Human Life. London: Henry Colburn, 1837. 1st edition; small 8vo; 3 volumes; contemporary half polished calf with raised bands and morocco spine labels, some rubbing, else very good. Sadleir 3299.   Chapel Hill 94-120 1996 $150.00

WRAXHALL, NATHANIEL WILLIAM, BART. 1751-1831   Historical Memoirs of My Own Time. London: T. Cadell and W. Davies, 1815. 1st edition; 8vo; 549, 583 pages, 2 volumes; 19th century half polished calf with raised bands and maroon morocco spine labels, couple of scuff marks, else very good.   Chapel Hill 94-122 1996 $150.00

BINDING - 20TH CENTURY

GODEY'S Lady's Book and Magazine. Philadelphia: Louis A. godey, 1851/54. 1st printings; 8vo; 3 volumes; numerous full page engraved plates, many hand colored; early 20th century half red morocco with raised bands, all edges gilt, library bookplate and blindstamp, former owner's inscriptions, else lovely set.   Chapel Hill 94-111 1996 $200.00

LOCKER-LAMPSON, FREDERICK 1821-1895   London Lyrics. London: Macmillan, 1904. 8vo; full crushed green morocco with all-over design featuring a large central arabesque pattern filled with small tools used in combination; fields of pointelles and small trefoils fill most of the remaining space, spine with five raised bands and matching decoration in all but two of the compartments which carry the title information, spine gilt stamped in the manner of Sarah Prideaux, board edges gilt, inner gilt dentelles, marbled endleaves, all edges gilt, binding unsigned, stamped on blind on titlepage "Presentation Copy" (within circle); fine.   Book Block 32-37 1996 $375.00

PRIDEAUX, SARA T.   Bookbinders and Their Craft. New York: 1903. One of 500 signed and numbered copies, nicely bound; viii, (4), 298, (2) pages; illustrations; attractively bound in full brown morocco, covers, spine and turn-ins stamped in blind with geometric rosette design, spine lettered in gilt, pastedowns of marbled paper, all edges gilt, by "A.P." and dated 1904 on rear turn-in, tiny three quarter inch crack at top of front hinge, tiny scuff marks on bottom edge, endpapers discolored from turn-ins, very attractive, in practically fine condition.   Joseph J. Felcone 64-5 1996 $1,000.00

BINDING - 20TH CENTURY

READE, CHARLES 1814-1884   The Works. London: Grolier Society, ca. 1910. One of only 5 copies of L'Edition des Aquarelles; 8 1/2 x 6 inches; 25 volumes; few illustrations in text and 114 plates by F.T. Merrill each in colored & uncolored states (for a total of 228 plates, 6 left uncolored), printed tissue overlays, titles printed in red and black; 4 page ALS by Reade tipped in; elaborately inlaid & gilt dec. lavender crushed mor., each cover framed by double gilt fillet, gilt foliate cornerpieces w/heart-shaped inlays of red calf, lg. & beautiful gilt & onlaid floral centerpiece featuring 2 lilies in white calf & 5 buds in green mor., raised bands, spine compartments dec. in gilt w/2 of the compartments featuring sm. onlaid flower of red calf, morocco doublures, w/multiple plain & stippled rules as well as antique fleuron cornerpieces framing a central panel of green mor. featuring lg. architectural ornament composed of elaborate gilt leaves & ribbons & scrolling inlaid red calf, green silk e.p.'s, mor. hinges, marbled flyleaves, a.e.g., handful of plates bit darkened, spines rather faded to grayish lilac color, some covers bit faded, else remarkably fine.   Phillip J. Pirages 33-68   1996 $6,500.00

VERGILIUS MARO, PUBLIUS 70-19 BC   The Aeneid of Virgil. Boston & New York: Houghton Mifflin, 1906. One of 650 large paper copies; 4to; 2 volumes, xvi, 266; vii, 283 pages; handsomely illustrated with color frontispieces and several black and white plates; original full dark blue publisher's morocco with triple gilt fillet and gilt tooled rectangular panel on covers, gilt tooled spine with 6 compartments, turn-ins with triple gilt fillet, top edges gilt; beautiful set in fine condition.   Chapel Hill 94-119   1996 $250.00

BINDING - 20TH CENTUY

GARGAZ, PIERRE ANDRE   A Project of Universal and Perpetual Peace. New York: George Simpson Eddy, 1922. One of 1250 copies; 8vo; printed in Monotype Caslon by W.E. Rudge to Bruce Roger's design; full crushed navy blue morocco with series of five gilt borders joined at the corners by an elaborate gilt fleuron, spine with five raised bands and gilt decoration with compartments, except the two that carry the title information, full morocco doublures that more or less repeat the cover design, top edge gilt, other edges untrimmed; fine; handsome copy in very handsome binding. Warde 159.   Book Block 32-41   1996 $265.00

BINDING - GORDON ACORNLEY

WELCH, DENTON   I Left My Grandfather's House: an Account of His First Walking Tour. Limited Editions Club, 1958. Of 150 copies, this one of only 20 specially bound by Grodon Acornley of the Royal College of Art Bindery; 4to; color lithographs; quarter black morocco, patterned cloth sides, gilt, edges of spine just a little scuffed, but very nice, scarce.   Bertram Rota 272-272   1996 £200.00

BINDING - ADAMS

BERNERS, JULIANA   A Treatyse of Fysshynge wyth an Angle. Ashendene Press, 1903. One of 20 copies for sale on vellum (there were also 150 on paper); 7 3/4 x 5 1/2 inches; 48 pages, plus 5 vellum blanks at front and 5 at back; one nearly full page reproduction of a 15th century woodcut, one initial in red, several small illustrations in text, device in colophon; contemporary black morocco by Katherine Adams (signed "K/A 1904" on rear turn-in), spine almost invisibly repaired (nature and extent of restoration are uncertain because the work is so skillfully done), raised bands, front cover and top spine compartment with gilt titling, gilt ruled turn-ins; fine.   Phillip J. Pirages 33-24   1996 $4,500.00

BINDING - JAMES ADAMS

HIERONYMUS, SAINT   Vitae Sanctorum Patrum, Sive Vitas Patrum. Venice: Octavianus Scotus, 14 Feb. 1483/84. 251 of 252 leaves, lacking initial blank a1; in highly unusual early 19th century Irish binding of dark maroon morocco, spine fully gilt in panels, covers with central arabesque design blocked in blind within an ornamental gilt and blind border, gilt edges and turn-ins, cloth endleaves printed with tiny sunburst pattern, yellow and blue silk endbands, signed in gilt along front fore-edge turn (and visible with book closed) "Bibliotheca Conoviana Dublinii. M.D.CCC.XXXIV. James Adams Binder Dublin." Very slightest of rubbing to covers, else fine, clean copy. BMC V 279; Goff H 206; Hain Copinger 8599.   Joseph J. Felcone 64-24   1996 $3,500.00

BINDING - ALLIX

TENNYSON, ALFRED TENNYSON, 1ST BARON 1809-1892   12 Verses from "The Day Dream". London: 1995. One in an edition of 17 copies; 7 x 6 inches; designed, printed, illustrated & bound by Susan Allix; 65 ptd. pages, 35 of which have pochoir, lino-cut or a combination of both; printed in various colors on somerset mould made paper with cream Japanese title sheets; binding is tongue-in-slot construction with boards edged in wide strip of dark purple goatskin and covered in Japanese paper stenciled in pastel colors & varnished, w/ptd. title & aqua green lea. onalys, edges sponted w/watercolor, endpapers stenciled flyleaves ptd. allowing no visual interruption in looking at the book from its very beginning, book has curved top and is contained under a painted glass dome.   Joshua Heller 21-41A   1996 $1,350.00

TENNYSON, ALFRED TENNYSON, 1ST BARON 1809-1892   12 Verses from "The Day Dream". London: 1995. One in an edition of 17 copies; 7 x 6 inches; designed, printed, illustrated and bound by Susan Allix, 65 printed pages, 35 of which have pochoir, lino-cut or a combination of both; printed in various colors on Somerset mould made paper with cream Japanese title sheets; binding is tongue-in-slot construction with boards edged in a wide strip of dark purple goatskin and covered in Japanese paper stenciled in pastel colors and varnished, with printed title and aqua green leather onlays, edges are sponged & watercolor, endpapers are stenciled, and flyleaves printed, allowing no visual interruption in looking at the book from its very beginning; book has curved top, in green cloth box with pink leather tie.   Joshua Heller 21-41b   1996 $1,100.00

BINDING - ALTERMAN

MELVILLE, HERMAN 1819-1891   Billy Budd Sailor. Mount Holly; Married Mettle Press, 1987. One of 5 copies from a total edition of 185; page size 9 1/8 x 6 1/8 inches; set in 13 point Van Dijck and Caslon for the display, headpiece/tailpiece engravings; 9 letterpress and wood engraving broadsides, with extra suite of the wood engravings, each signed by the artist, Deborah Alterman; bound by Benjamin and Deborah Alterman with champleve bronze spine with wooden boards riveted to the spine with handmade hinges and the sections of the book sewn with herringbone stitch onto doubled linen cords laced through, cross laminated teakwood and mahogany boards, title raised in relief by etching away the bronze, which has blue-grey patina, housed in clear hand blown leaded glass drop back box; book, extra suite, catalog and broadsides housed in specially made clamshell box.   Priscilla Juvelis 95/1-172   1996 $5,000.00

BINDING - MARGARET ARMSTRONG

REED, MYRTLE   The Master Violin. New York: G. P. Putnam's Sons, 1904. 1st edition; 8vo; (315 pages, 2 publisher's ads); mauve and gold on pale grey vertically ribbed cloth with printer's ornament of a gladiolus, designed by Margaret Armstrong, except for short marginal tear on page 303, that has been skillfully repaired, this is a beautiful copy free of bookplates and signatures, in original publisher's decorated box; Paulette Rose 16-255   1996 $100.00

BINDING - ATELIER BINDERY

SCOTT, TEMPLE   The Silver Age and Other Dramatic Memories. New York: Scott & Seltzer, 1919. 1st edition; 8vo; crushed dark burgundy morocco du cap with two gilt fillet borders and elaborate corner pieces made up of groupings of individual floral tools, spine with five raised bands and similar floral decoration within compartments, board edges gilt, inner dentelles, top edge gilt, stamped with name of binder on lower front turn in: The Atelier Bindery; the dedication copy, with presentation inscription to dedicatee D. George Derry, Esq. dated Christmas 1919; laid in is one page ALS from Scott to Derry.   Book Block 32-44   1996 $395.00

BINDING - BABCOCK

GRAHAM, RIGBY   Holt Mill Papers. Santa Cruz: Donna and Peter Thomas, 1994. 1st edition; one of 50 copies, signed by the author and by the Thomas's; page size 15 x 11 3/8 inches; handset in Centaur types, paper handmade using cotton rag and 'a few other fibers' by Peter Thomas with the help of Joanna Gibson; tipped into each copy of the book are two samples of paper made at the Holt Mill in 1958; Coptic binding with handmade paper boards by John Babcock, by Donna and Peter Thomas.   Priscilla Juvelis 95/1-109   1996 $235.00

BINDING - BAGGULEY

SALT, T. J.   Trentham Hymnal. Newcastle-under-Lyme: n.d. 1894. 4to; 64 pages; sumptuously bound, perhaps for presentation, by Bagguley, full brown morocco, covers panelled in blind and gilt, upper cover gilt lettered, spine ruled in blind and gilt, gilt lettered, raised bands, wide gilt rolled inner dentelle, brown satin doublures and endpapers, binder's stamp on lower doublure, all edges gilt;   Marlborough 160-80   1996 £350.00

BINDING - BAIN

SHAKESPEARE, WILLIAM 1564-1616　　The Works of Shakespeare. New York: Random House, 1929-33. Limited edition of 1050 sets for Great Britain and Ireland, 550 sets for America, this number 1031; 7 volumes; full tan morocco with slight edgewear, three of the spines uniformly darkened somewhat. Bound by A. W. Bain. Dreyfus 58.　　Glenn Books 36-198　1996 $1,500.00

SHAKESPEARE, WILLIAM 1564-1616　　The Works of William Shakespeare. New York: Nonesuch Press, 1929-33. Limited edition of 1050 copies for sale in Great Britain and Ireland and 550 copies for sale in the USA. This copy number 1076. 8vo; 7 volumes; errata leaf to volume 7; full tan morocco, double gilt rule borders, gilt titles to panelled spines, top edge gilt, uncut, inner gilt rule borders, covers rubbed and worn in places, unevenly sunned; nice set bound by A. W. Bain. Beeleigh Abbey BA56-163　1996 £750.00

TUSSER, THOMAS　　Five Hundred Points of Good Husbandry. James Tregaskis & Son, 1931. Limited to 500 copies; 4to; printed on handmade paper; xiv, 336 pages; original Hermitage calf by Bain & Son, edges uncut, slipcase, very fine.　　Thomas Thorp 489-306　1996 £150.00

BINDING - BANYTUN

EMERSON, RALPH WALDO 1803-1882　　An Address Delivered Before the Senior Class in Divinity College. Boston: James Munroe, 1838. 1st edition; 1000 copies printed; three quarter tan calf, raised bands, gilt, by Bayntun; fine. BAL 5184; Myerson A7.1.　　Mac Donnell 12-9　1996 $275.00

BINDING - BAYNTUN

ARNOLD, EDWIN　　The Light of Asia; or the Great Renunciation. London: Ballantyne Press for Trubner & Co., 1889. One of 126 large paper copies; 7 1/4 x 5 3/4 inches; xviii, (2), (21)-240 pages; frontispiece, decorative initials and number of small illustrations in text, title printed in red and black; bookplate on flyleaf; very appealing auburn crushed levant morocco by Bayntun (for Brentano's), raised bands, gilt titling on spine, wide turn-ins deocrated with triple gilt rules and corner ornaments, marbled endpapers, all edges gilt; very fine, only the most trivial imperfections, binding quite bright and essentially unworn;　Phillip J. Pirages　33-57　1996 $175.00

BRAY, ANNA ELIZA　　Life of Thomas Stothard. London: John Murray, 1851. 4to; 1 volume bound in 2, xxiv, 128; 129-246, 16 page catalog; 55 illustrations, extra illustrated with 147 engravings by Stothard, including some with handwashed borders, 2 water colors, 8 pen and ink sketches; 2 original wrappers bound in, later crimson full levant morocco by Bayntun, gilt panelled sides and spines gilt in 6 compartments, gilt edges; fine.　　Thomas Thorp 489-291　1996 £480.00

BROWNING, ELIZABETH BARRETT 1806-1861　　The Battle of Marathon. London: for private distribution only, 1891. 1st edition thus; one of only 50 copies printed (along with 4 more on vellum); 8vo; half red morocco, spine gilt, top edge gilt, by Bayntun; fine. Barnes E191; cf. Barnes A1; CBEL III 436.　　Ximenes 108-356　1996 $400.00

CHURCHILL, WINSTON LEONARD SPENCER 1874-1965　　Ian Hamilton's March. London: Longman, 1900. 1st edition; small 8vo; choicely bound in half crimson levant morocco, cloth sides, 5 raised bands, gold lettering and gold lion design, gilt top, bound by Bayntun.　　Charles W. Traylen 117-88　1996 £280.00

CHURCHILL, WINSTON LEONARD SPENCER 1874-1965　　London to Ladysmith via Pretoria. London: Longmans, 1900. 1st edition; small 8vo; 4 maps, 1 folding, also 4 plans, 32 pages of ads at end; choicely bound in half red levant morocco, cloth sides to match, 5 raised bands, gold lion ornaments on spine, gilt top, by Bayntun. Woods A4 p. 29. Charles W. Traylen 117-89　1996 £320.00

DANIEL, SAMUEL　　The Collection of the History of England. London: by F. Leach, for Benj. Tooke, and Thomas Sawbridge, 1685. 5th edition; folio; (6), 262, (10), 263 pages; modern half calf, spine heavily gilt, by Bayntun, neat repair at inner margin of title, light overall foxing, occasional browning, otherwise very nice in fine binding. Wing D208. Joseph J. Felcone 64-16　1996 $650.00

DICKENS, CHARLES 1812-1870　　A Christmas Carol. London: King Penguin Books, 1946. Small octavo; 138 pages; illustrations by John Leech; bound by Bayntun of Bath in full red crushed levant morocco, gilt decorative border on covers, front cover set with vignette, executed in multicolored morocco onlays, gilt spine, tooled in compartments, gilt board edges and turn-ins, all edges gilt, marbled endpapers, fine in red cloth slipcase.　　Heritage Book Shop 196-280　1996 $600.00

BINDING - BAYNTUN

DORAN, JOHN　　"Their Majesties' Servants": Annals of the English Stage from Thomas Betterton to Edmund Kean. London: William H. Mallen & Co., 1864. 1st edition; 8 1/2 x 5 3/4 inches; 2 volumes extended to four; extra illustrated with a total of 252 plates, two of them double page, 42 of them in color, many of them inlaid to size, almost all with tissue guards, titles and dedications printed in red and black; almost bound by Bayntun in handsome crushed moroccco in dark honey brown color, sides with simple gilt rule frame, central panel in gilt and black in geometric design with pointed ears in corners, raised bands ornamented with gilt disks, spine compartment decoration similar to cover panels, gilt ruled turn-ins, marbled endpapers, all edges gilt; a number of the plates lightly foxed, isolated cases of more noticeable foxing, adjacent pages sometimes slightly affected, otherwise very fine and attractive set, bright, clean bindings virtually unworn.　Phillip J. Pirages 33-179　196 $1,750.00

DOYLE, ARTHUR CONAN 1859-1930　　Adventures of Gerard. London: Newnes, 1903. 1st edition; full red box calf, double gilt rule on front and back panels, spine with five raised bands, red morocco label, gilt titling on spine, marbled endpapers, all edges gilt; fine. Bound by Bayntun.　　Priscilla Juvelis 95/1-311　1996 $450.00

EMERSON, RALPH WALDO 1803-1882　　The Method of Nature, an Oration Delivered Before the Society of the Adelphi. Boston: Samuel Simpkins, 1841. 1st edition; one of 500 copies; three quarter tan calf, raised bands, gilt, by Bayntun; fine, rare. BAL 5190; Myerson A11.1. Mac Donnell　12-30　1996 $350.00

GOSSE, PHILIP　　Sir John Hawkins. London: John Lane, Bodley Head, 1930. 1st edition; demy 8vo; (xiv), 290 pages; plates; bound in later half blue calf, banded and gilt with ships, by Bayntun, top edge gilt, few faint marks, but very good.　　Ash Rare Books　Zenzybyr-38　1996 £85.00

IBSEN, HENRIK　　Peer Gynt. London: George G. Harrap & Co., 1936. One of 450 copies, signed by artist; 10 3/4 x 8 1/4 inches; 255, (1) pages, (1) leaf (colophon); color frontispiece & 11 other color plates by Arthur Rackham, each with printed tissue guard, color vignettes on title and half title, several other illustrations in text, mostly as tailpieces; very handsome cinnamon colored crushed morocco by Bayntun, covers framed with French fillet and featuring ealborate floral cornerpieces, raised bands, spine densely gilt in compartments, marbled endpapers, wide turn-ins decorated like covers, top edge gilt, other edges untrimmed, extremely fine in quite handsome binding.　　Phillip J. Pirages 33-443　1996 $1,600.00

KOHL, JAHNN G.　　Wanderings Round Lake Superior. London: Chapman and Hall, 1860. 1st English edition; 8vo; wood engraved illustrations; new half calf and cloth, gilt panelled spine, red morocco label, gilt top and marbled endpapers, by Bayntun; Sabin 38215. Howes 5798.　　Charles W. Traylen　117-418　1996 £270.00

LATROBE, CHARLES JOSEPH　　The Rambler in Mexico: 1834. London: Published by R. B. Seeley and W. Burnside and sold by L. & G. Seeley, 1836. 1st edition; 8 x 5 1/4 inches; viii, 309 pages; folding engraved map; contemporary owner's name top of title; light brown half calf by Bayntun, linen sides, simple gilt rules, ornaments and titling on spine, marbled endpapers, top edge gilt, tiny tear in map, leaves a shade less than bright because of inexpensive paper stock, but fine, clean, fresh copy in bright, unworn binding. Sabin 39221.　　Phillip J. Pirages 33-329 1996 $250.00

MANDEVILLE, JOHN　　The Travels of... London: Macmillan, 1900. 1st edition thus; 8vo three quarter blue calf over matching cloth by Bayntun, spine with raised bands, red morocco label and gilt floral tooling withing gilt ruled compartments, marbled endpapers, top edge gilt; fine. George J. Houle　68-91　1996 $150.00

NATTES, JOHN CLAUDE　　Bath Illustrated by a Series of Views from the Drawings of John Claude Nattes... London: published by William Miller, Albemarle St. and Wm. Sheppard, Bristol, 1806. 1st edition; later issue; folio; half title, tissue guarded hand colored aquatint frontispiece, title with hand colored vignette, (i-iii), 56 leaves of text, 27 hand colored aquatint plates and 1 hand colored vignette, large paper copy; half red straight grained morocco and marbled boards, edges scuffed, slight damage to top right hand corner of upper marbled board, red morocco label to upper board, raised bands to spine, gilt tooling to compartments, gilt title to second compartment, all edges gilt, new marbled endpapers and new prelims; ink inscription removed from verso front f.e.p. leaving slight mark, very minor oxidisaton to first plates, rest in excellent condition, very minor occasional offset to text only; bound by Bayntun; bookplates of Boies Penrose, another armorial bookplate. Beeleigh Abbey BA56-17　1996 £7,000.00

BINDING - BAYNTUN

NATTES, JOHN CLAUDE   Bath, Illustrated by a Series of Views...
London: W. Bulmer for W. Miller and W. Sheppard, Bristol, 1806. Folio;
title, iv, 56 pages; large color aquatint vignette on title and another on
lasata page, 28 color aquatint plates; dark blue morocco, gilt, covers
and spine tooled to a geometrical design, gilt inner borders, gilt edges,
by Bayntun of Bath for E. H. Wells & Co., New York: original morocco
label pasted onto rear endleaf; handsome copy. Ex-libris Francis Palmer,
James Comerford and Mildred Davey.   Marlborough 162-72 1996
£5,750.00

NEWMAN, JOHN HENRY, CARDINAL 1801-1890   Apologia Pro Vita
Sua... London: Longman, Green, 1864. 1st edition; 8vo; three quarter
morocco by Bayntun, margins trimmed in rebinding, owner name faded
from title, gilt decorated spine, all edges gilt, rubbing to joints and
edges, near fine.   Charles Agvent 4-918 1996 $325.00

NIXON, ROBERT   The Original Predictions or Prophecies of Robert
Nixon, the Cheshire Prophet... London: J. Bailey, c. 1810. 12mo; 28
pages; etched frontispiece, light foxing, padded at end with 12 blank
leaves foxed; modern half dark tan mottled sheep by Bayntun, lightly
rubbed, backstrip with dark red longitudinal label, gilt lettered, small gilt
tools, marbled boards and endpapers, thin paper guard supplied for
frontispiece, excellent.   Blackwell's B112-201 1996 £60.00

SCOTT, WALTER 1771-1832   The Poetical Works of Sir Walter Scott.
London: Frederick Warne, 1893. Thick 8vo; full blue polished calf,
armorial coat of arms and head of man in gilt on front and rear cover
respectively, richly gilt paneled spine, raised bands, edges gilt, by
Bayntun; with fine quality painting on fore-edge of volume depicting
harvesters in a field with landscape in background, fine, bright example.
Appelfeld Gallery 54-98 1996 $650.00

SILLAR, DAVID   Poems. Kilmarnock: printed by John Wilson, 1789. 1st
edition; 8vo; pages (i)-viii, (9)-247; titlepage and prelim leaves lightly
browned, title within typographic border; early 20th century half tan calf
by Bayntun, joints rubbed, short splits at head, very firm, gilt milled low
bands, green morocco label in second compartment, remainder gilt
panelled, fawn glazed cotton boards, marbled endpapers, top edge gilt,
generally excellent; bookplates of Robert Woods Bliss and Mildred Bliss.
Egerer 14; ECSB 400; Johnson, Provincial Poetry 832.   Blackwell's
B112-257 1996 £350.00

SOME Account of the English Stage, from the Restoration in 1660 to
1830. Bath: printed by H. E. Carrington, 1832. Octavo; 10 volumes, with
377 extra illustrations, 192 of which are hand painted; bound by Bayntun
in full red morocco, covers decoratively stamped in gilt, gilt spine with
raised bands tooled in compartments, gilt board edges and inner
dentelles, all edges gilt, marbled endpapers, small stains to some
covers, armorial bookplate, handsome set.   Heritage Book Shop
196-248 1996 $3,000.00

STEELE, RICHARD 1672-1729   Essays. London: Macmillan, 1914. 6 1/4
x 4 1/4 inches; xv, (1), 358 pages, (1) leaf (colophon); frontispiece;
bookplate; very appealing dark green crushed morocco by Bayntun (for
Brentano's), spine with raised bands and gilt titling, turn-ins ruled and
ornamented in gilt, marbled endpapers, all edges gilt; hint of sunning to
spine, but extremely clean, binding very bright and showing virtually no
wear.   Phillip J. Pirages 33-74 1996 $100.00

STEPHEN, LESLIE   Hours in a Library. (First Series-Third). London:
Smith, Elder & Co., 1874-79. 1st edition; 8vo; 3 volumes, half titles; half
morocco by Bayntun of Bath, volume 3 slightly faded, uncut, top edge
gilt.   Forest Books 74-257 1996 £75.00

THIERS, LOUIS ADOLPHE   The History of the French Revolution.
London: Richard Bentley and Son, 1881. New edition; 8vo; 5 volumes; 41
steel engravings; three quarter burgundy leather over marbled boards by
Bayntun.   Glenn Books 36-265 1996 $450.00

VERNE, JULES 1828-1905   The Mysterious Island. New York: Heritage
Press, 1959. 1st edition thus; small 4to; three quarter gilt stamped
morocco over red cloth by Bayntun, spine with raised bands and gilt
stamped devices within gilt ruled compartments, covers ruled in gilt,
marbled endpapers, very good to fine.   George J. Houle 68-146 1996
$225.00

WHITE, GILBERT 1720-1793   The Natural History and Antiquities of
Selborne, in the County of Southampton. London: 1789. 1st edition; 4to;
vignette half title, (iii-v), 1-430 pages, index, (12) pages,
list of plates, errata leaf, large folding linen backed frontispiece, 6 full
page engraved copperplates, 1 large folding, and vignette half title to
Antiquities of Selborne; neat repair to small tear to title, further neat
repairs to few other pages, no loss to text, previous catalog description
loosely inserted to rear; bound by Bayntun, full green calf, triple gilt rule
border, red and brown morocco labels to spine, decorative gilt tooled
birds, butterfly and hare to panelled spine, joints very slightly rubbed,
all edges gilt, marbled endpapers.   Beeleigh Abbey BA56-30 1996
£800.00

BINDING - BAYNTUN-RIVIERE

ALLEN, H. WARNER   A History of Wine. London: Faber & Faber,
1961. 1st edition; demy 8vo; 304 pages; plates; bound in elegant recent
half morocco by Bayntun-Riviere of Bath, top edge gilt, fine.   Ash Rare
Books Zenzybyr-2 1996 £195.00

DESCLOZEAUX, ADRIEN   Gabrielle D'estrees. London: Arthur L.
Humphreys, 1907. 1st edition in English; 8 1/4 x 6 inches; vi, 330 pages;
title printed in red and black; pleasing green smooth calf by Bayntun
(Riviere), covers with double gilt rule frame, raised bands, spine densely
gilt in compartments featuring many floral stamps, morocco labels of
blue and orange, gilt edges, marbled endpapers; very fine.   Phillip J.
Pirages 33-157 1996 $195.00

DICKENS, CHARLES 1812-1870   Bleak House. London: Bradbury and
Evans, 1853. 1st edition in book form; 9 x 5 3/4 inches; 2 volumes; xvi,
624 pages (pagination continues in second volume); frontispiece, added
engraved title and 38 plates by Phiz, with the majority of wrappers and
ads from original parts bound in at back of each volume; bound up
from parts (stab holes visible), fine rich brown crushed morocco by
Bayntun-Riviere, bound for Charles Sawyer, sides with double gilt rule,
spine attractively gilt in compartments with large floral ornament at
center, headcaps and board edges decorated in gilt, broad turn-ins with
multiple gilt rules, all edges gilt, marbled endpapers; small portion of
corner 3 leaves skillfully renewed, few trivial marks to covers, but
extraordinarily fine, with text and plates remarkably clean.   Phillip J.
Pirages 33-163 1996 $850.00

DICKENS, CHARLES 1812-1870   The Chimes. London: Chapman and
Hall, 1845. 1st edition; 1st issue; 12mo; beautifully bound by Bayntun
(Riviere) in full scarlet morocco, gilt strapwork, all edges gilt, gilt inner
dentelles; lovely copy. Smith II 6.   Glenn Books 36-85 1996 $400.00

DICKENS, CHARLES 1812-1870   The Adventures of Oliver Twist.
London: pub. for the author by Bradbury and Evans, 1846. New edition;
8vo; 24 illustrations on steel by George Cruikshank; frontispiece, half
title; full red morocco by Bayntun-Riviere, single line gilt border with
blindstamped bust to upper boards and facsimile signature to back
board, full gilt spine with five raised bands. Sadleir 696c.   Charles W.
Traylen 117-97 1996 £350.00

DOYLE, ARTHUR CONAN 1859-1930   The Hound of the Baskervilles.
London: George Newnes, 1902. 1st edition; 8vo; frontispiece, 15 full
page illustrations by Sidney Paget; full dark red calf by Bayntun-Riviere,
spine with raised bands and gilt stamped floral designs within gilt ruled
compartments, contrasting blue and green gilt stamped morocco labels,
covers double ruled in gilt, gilt stamped floral inner dentelles, marbled
endpapers, all edges gilt; very good to fine in red cloth slipcase; scarce.
George J. Houle 68-43 1996 $1,750.00

GEORGE, JOHN NIGEL   English Guns and Rifles. Plantersville:
Small-Arms Technical Pub. Co., 1947. 1st edition; royal 8vo; (x), (346)
pages; plates and illustrations; bound in elegant modern half morocco,
banded and gilt with rifles by Bayntun-Riviere, top edge gilt, very good.
Ash Rare Books Zenzybyr-37 1996 £250.00

LAWRENCE, DAVID HERBERT 1885-1930   Lady Chatterley's Lover.
Florence Privately printed by Tipografia Giuntina, 1928. 1st edition; one of
1000 copies; signed by author; 9 x 6 1/2 inches; 2 p.l., 365 pages; very
fine simple but elegant forest green crushed morocco by Bayntun-Riviere,
spine with raised bands and gilt titling, broad turn-ins with multiple gilt
borders, including an animated floral design, marbled endpapers, top
edge gilt, other edges untrimmed, isolated trivial spots internally, but
extremely fine in unworn binding. Roberts A42a.   Phillip J. Pirages
33-330 1996 $2,950.00

M'GREGOR, JOHN   British America. Edinburgh: William
Blackwood/London: T. Cadell, 1832. 1st edition; 8 1/2 x 5 1/4 inches; 2
volumes; folding maps as frontispiece in each volume, one other folding
map, 6 full page maps, 2 small engravings in text, half title in second
(though not in first) volume; attractive red half morocco by
Bayntun-Riviere, cloth sides, raised bands, spine with gilt ruled
compartments and gilt titling, marbled endpapers, top edge gilt; very fine
in appealing unworn binding. Sabin 43280.   Phillip J. Pirages 33-372
1996 $450.00

WELLS, HERBERT GEORGE 1866-1946   The Time Machine. London:
William Heinemann, 1895. 1st British edition; foolscap 8vo; finely bound,
recent full crimson morocco, banded and gilt, all edges gilt, by
Bayntun-Riviere, few very minor internal marks, but very good.   Ash
Rare Books Zenzybyr-95 1996 £950.00

WELLS, HERBERT GEORGE 1866-1946   The Time Machine. London:
William Heinemann, 1895. 1st British edition; foolscap 8vo; recent full
crimson morocco, banded and gilt, all edges gilt, by Bayntun-Riviere, few
very minor internal marks, but very good.   Ash Rare Books
Zenzybyr-94 1996 £395.00

BINDING - BAYNTUN-RIVIERE

WHITE, DIANA   The Descent of Ishtar. Eragny Press, 1903. One of only 10 copies on vellum; 12mo; issued in sheets, newly bound in full white vellum by Bayntun-Riviere, lettering and decoration from half title being reproduced in gilt on upper cover, fine in slipcase.   Bertram Rota 272-138 1996 £5,000.00

WIND, HERBERT WARREN   The Complete Golfer. London: William Heinemann, 1954. 1st British edition; demy 8vo; (xxvi), 398 pages; plates; bound in smart modern half morocco by Bayntun-Riviere, titlepage, couple of very minor marks, but very good. Donovan & Murdoch 40320. Ash Rare Books Zenzybyr-97 1996 £225.00

BINDING - BEDFORD

BACON, FRANCIS, VISCOUNT ST. ALBANS 1561-1626   The Essayes, or Counsels, Civill and Moral... London: by John Haviland for Hanna Barret, and Richard Whitaker, 1625. 1st complete edition, 1st issue (last lifetime edition); 4to; (10), 340 pages; woodcut initials and headpieces; lacks initial blank A1, as usual, neat repair to running head of 2G3, with loss of a few letters; sprinkled calf, gilt, by Bedford; clean, fresh copy with good margins; Gibson 13; Pforzheimer 30 (2nd issue); STC 1147. Joseph J. Felcone 64-2 1996 £3,000.00

BYRON, GEORGE GORDON NOEL, 6TH BARON 1788-1824   The Island, or Christian and His Comrades. London: by C. H. Rennell for John Hunt, 1823. 1st edition; 8vo; 94 pages, with half title, without final ad leaf F8; full green straight grain morocco, sides with single gilt fillet, spine with raised bands, gilt motifs, lettered in gilt in two compartments, inner dentelles with double gilt fillet, comb marbled endpapers, top edge gilt, others uncut, by Bedford; fine copy; bookplate of Frederick S. Peck, bookseller's catalog description and note of acquisition by "J.H.S." dated 14 may 1946 tipped on binder's blank; fine, scarce.   Simon Finch 24-28 1996 £600.00

GOLDSMITH, OLIVER 1730-1774   The Traveller or, a Prospecct of Society. London: printed for J. Newbery, 1765 1st published edition; 4to; half title (neat repair to small hole at fore edge), 22 pages text, 2 pages publisher's ads; full polished calf, triple gilt rule borders, tiny corner ornaments, fully gilt panelled spine, red morocco label, all edges gilt, inner gilt dentelles, marbled endpapers, brown paper book label of Paul Francis Webster; bound by F. Bedford. Very fine copy. Rothschild 1024; Tinker 1101.   Beeleigh Abbey BA56-144 1996 £1,500.00

HOOD, THOMAS 1799-1845   Odes and Addresses to Great People. London: Baldwin, Cradock and Joy, 1825. 1st edition; octavo; later polished tan calf, gilt, top edge gilt, by Bedford, edges untrimmed; very fine; Charles Tennant bookplate.   G. W. Stuart 59-47 1996 $325.00

KEATS, JOHN 1795-1821   Lamia, Isabella, the Eve of St. Agnes and Other Poems. London: printed for Taylor and Hessey, 1820. 1st edition; 12mo; half title present, 8 page catalog of Taylor and Hessey ads at end; full green morocco, gilt, spine and inner dentelles gilt, by Bedford, few traces of rubbing; uncut, fine. Hayward 233.   Ximenes 109-169 1996 $7,500.00

LAMB, CHARLES 1775-1834   Album Verses, with a Few Others. London: Edward Moxon, 1830. 1st edition; 8vo; pages vii, (i) blank, 150, (i) ad; 19th century brown morocco, French fillet gilt border to sides, spine in compartments, raised bands, gilt rules, lettering and date, 4 compartments with urn with bird perched on top and leafy sprays gilt, top edge gilt, inner dentelles, gilt, by Bedford, bookplates; excellent copy. Ashley III p. 52.   Simon Finch 24-147 1996 £420.00

MIDDLETON, THOMAS   Works. London: Edward Lumley, Chancery Lane, 1840. 8vo; 5 volumes; beautifully bound in full morocco, 3 line gilt border, fully gilt spines, gilt edges, by Francis Bedford. Superb set. Charles W. Traylen 117-168 1996 £350.00

MORE, THOMAS 1478-1535   De Optimo Reip. Statu Deque Nova Insula Utopia Libellus... Basel: Johann Froben, March 1518. 3rd edition, 1st Froben edition; small quarto; 3 parts in 1 volume, roman types with occasional greek, title within fine woodcut border by Ambrosius Holbein, dedication & divisional titles within fine woodcut borders by Hans Holbein, full page woodcut view of Utopia on b2 verso and woodcut historiated headpiece on d1 recto, both by A. Holbein, woodcut initials by A. and H. Holbein, Froben's device at end of each part; full crimson morocco, gilt and blind fillets, floral centerpieces, edges gilt, by Francis Bedford; superb, tall, clean copy. PMM 47 note; Gibson 3; Adams M1756.   H. M. Fletcher 121-26 1996 £16,000.00

PERRINCHIEF, RICHARD   The Sicilian Tyrant; or, The Life of Agathocles. London: printed for J. Grover and R. Royston, 1676. 1st edition; 8vo; engraved pportrait, engraved vignette on title, folding plate, small hole in E1-E5 repaired, with loss of a few letters; 19th century calf, spine gilt, label, all edges gilt, bound by F. Bedford; nice copy. Wing P1607.   Anthony W. Laywood 109-112 1996 £225.00

BINDING - BEDFORD

ROWLANDSON, THOMAS   The World in Miniature. London: published by R. Ackermann, 101 Strand, sold by all Respectable Book .. 1817. Tall 8vo; lacks title, 40 hand colored etched plates, no text and not titles to plates; full polished calf, ruled gilt dentelles, decorative gilt tooling to spine, raised bands to spine, red morocco label to spine, all edges gilt, marbled endpapers, armorial bookplate to front pastedown and one other loosely inserted, binders stamp to front free endpaper; margins slightly cropped with occasional partial loss of imprint, plates all in fine, clean state, coloring bright, plates watermarked J. Whatman 1816; preserved in red cloth chemise, within quarter red morocco & cloth box, gilt title to spine, bound by Bedford. Tooley 437.   Beeleigh Abbey BA56-162 1996 £2,000.00

SOMNER, WILLIAM   The Antiquities of Canterbury in Two Parts. London: printed for R. Knaplock, 1703. 2nd edition; folio; 2 volumes in 1, large paper copy; 192 pages of text, 80 page appendix, 4 page table to part 1, 178 pages of text, 70 page appendix, 3 page table to part 2, with errata to both parts on verso of last leaf; frontispiece, 13 engraved plates, 6 maps, city plans, ground plans; full red morocco, triple gilt rule borders enclosing central gilt rule rectangle with ornate conerpieces to both covers, fully gilt panelled spine, top edge gilt, inner gilt dentelles, marbled endpapers, bound by F. Bedford. Cox III p. 187; Upcott pp. 388-90; Lowndes V2442.   Beeleigh Abbey BA56-23 1996 £900.00

STARK, JAMES   Scenery of the Rivers of Norfolk, Comprising the Yare, the Waveney and the Bure. Norwich & London: 1834. Large paper copy with india paper proofs; imperial quarto; 24 full page and 12 vignette steel engravings, all on india paper; bound in at end are original printed paper wrappers for the four parts, an "Address to Subscribers" dated 1830 and another dated 1831, two prospectuses containing various states of the "List of Subscribers", the latter carefully inlaid to size, full hard grain red morocco, narrow gilt border, fully gilt spine, inner dentelles gilt, top edge gilt, others uncut, by F. Bedford, very fine, uncommon; the copy of Thomas Basil Duguid with engraved armorial bookplate.   H. M. Fletcher 121-148 1996 £500.00

BINDING - BENEDICT

THANE, J.   British Autography. A Collection of Fac-Similes of the Hand-writing of Royal and Illustrious Personages, with Their Authentic Portraits. London: Thane, n.d., ca. 1790. 4to; frontispiece, engraved title, pages iv, 16, 40, 102 engraved plates; contemporary dark blue morocco, covers gilt, outer border of double and single rules enclosing swags, cornerpieces with crimson morocco onlays, central panel with corners a l'eventail spine gilt in 6 panels, raised bands gilt, panels with massed small tools and crimson morocco onlays, head and foot of spine with red morocco onlays gilt, all edges gilt, marbled endpapers, by Benedict, London, with his ticket, joints weakening; Ramsden p. 37. Marlborough 160-58 1996 £750.00

BINDING - BENNETT

THE FORTUNATE Orphan; or, Memoirs of the Countess of Marlou. London: printed for F. Needham, 1745. 1st edition; 12mo; modern calf, gilt, spine gilt, by Bennett, joints rubbed. Margins little marked by damp, bit limp throughout, but sound copy of a rare novel.   Ximenes 109-120 1996 $750.00

LOLLIUS, ANTONIUS   Oratio Circumcisionis Dominicae Coram Innocentis VIII Habita. Rome: Stephen Plannck, after 1 Jan. 1485. Quarto; modern green quarter morocco gilt by Bennett, lovely copy. Hain 10180; Goff I 275.   G. W. Stuart 59-64 1996 $2,100.00

VICERY, ELIZA   Emily Hamilton, a Novel. Worcester: printed and sold wholesale and retail by Isaiah Thomas Jun. 1803. 1st edition; 12mo; modern sheep, spine gilt, by Bennett, joints little rubbed; some light soiling, but very good. Wright I 2638; Shaw & Shoemaker 5504. Ximenes 109-293 1996 $475.00

WESTON, WILLIAM   Report of William Weston, Esquire, on the Practicability of Introducting the Water of the River Bonx into the City of New York: New York: printed by John Furman, 1799. 1st edition; 8vo; half dark blue morocco, gilt, by Bennett; fine, very scarce. Evans 36709; Sabin 103057; Rink Tech. Americana 2743.   Ximenes 108-344 1996 $750.00

BINDING - BICKERS

BARING, THOMAS   Catalogue of the Library of Thomas Baring, Esq. at Sunninghill Park (later at Baring Court). London: 1914. 8vo; over 200 pages of typescript; full red morocco by Bickers & Son, gilt, all edges gilt.   Forest Books 74-168 1996 £110.00

BINDING - BICKERS

BONER, CHARLES   Chamois Hunting in the Mountains of Bavaria. London: Chapman and Hall 193, Piccadilly, 1853. 1st edition; 8vo; (iii-iv) (v-viii), 1-410 pages; chromo litho frontispiece, 5 chromo litho plates, 6 woodcut vignettes to letterpress; foxing to frontispiece and chromo lithographs, ms. ink inscription to prelim, binders stamp to front f.e.p., hinges cracked; bound by Bickers & Son, full strawberry calf, rebacked, original spine laid down, double gilt rule borders to boards, some wear to upper board, some slight loss of original backstrip, endpapers and edges uniformly marbled.   Beeleigh Abbey   BA56-38   1996 £125.00

CARLYLE, THOMAS 1795-1881   History of Friedrich II of Prussia, Called Frederick the Great. London: Chapman & Hall, c. 1890. Crown 8vo; 6 volumes in 3; portrait; full blue prize calf gilt by Bickers, gilt crest of University College school on sides.   Howes Bookshop 265-136 1996 £50.00

GERSTAECKER, FRIEDRICH WILHELM CHRISTIAN 1816-1872   Western Lands and Western Waters. London: S. O. Beeton, 1864. 1st English edition; xii, 388 pages; text engravings; bound by Bickers and Son, London in full dark blue morocco, marbled edges and endleaves, gilt ruling on edges, elaborate gilt tooling on spine; very good/fine light rubbing of edges, in later slipcase; 1st. English ed. of Howes G140. Bohling Book Co.   192-152   1996 $350.00

LA FONTAINE, JEAN DE 1621-1695   Oeuvres Complettes... Paris: chez Lefevre, 1814. 8vo; 6 volumes; all half titles present, frontispiece, 23 copperplates; half green straight grain morocco, green cloth sides, spines attractively decorated in gilt, top edge gilt, marbled endpapers, by Bickers; very nice.   Sotheran   PN32-25   1996 £598.00

SCOTT, WALTER 1771-1832   The Waverley Novels. Edinburgh: Robert Cadell, 1842. 17 volumes; hundreds of steel plate and wood engravings; elegantly bound by Bickers and Son in full crushed green morocco with raised bands forming 6 compartments; two compartments contain title and volume labels of tan morocco with simple gilt double border and cornerpieces, other compartments elaborately gilt with same double rule but surrounding very ornate floral corner and center pieces on background of circles and stars, boards panelled with both simple rule and decorative roll and elaborate floral pattern surrounding open panel just inside last double rule, fancy gilt dentelles. Beautiful condition. Hermitage   SP95-557   1996 $3,500.00

BINDING - BICKNELL

BIDPAI   A Fable of Bidpai. Janus Press, 1974. One of 270 copies thus, in an edition of 300 copies, signed by artist; 10 x 7 inches; 20 pages; 14 wood engravings by Helen Siegl; designed and letterpress printed by Claire Van Vliet, text printed in black with title and colophon pages in blue, wood engravings printed in dark blue, light blue, green, orange or lavender on French-folded Hosokawa and handsewn into mustard Strathmore Beau Brilliant cover glued over light boards, binding and boxes by Claire Van Vliet and James Bicknell. Fine.   Joshua Heller 21-6   1996 $175.00

BINDING - BIRDSALL

CROMWELL, THOMAS KITSON   Excursions in the County of Essex... London: printed for Longman, Hurst, Rees, Orme and Brown,... 1818-19. Small 8vo; 2 volumes; (iii-iv), 1-216 pages, 217-224 pages, directions to binder, errata leaf, directions to binder, errata leaf, 1-190 pages, 191-197 pages; large folding map frontispiece to volume 1, 96 engraved copperplates and 1 large folding city plan of Colchester; half strawberry calf and marbled boards, corners worn, joints rubbed with slight loss to lower joint of volume 1, gilt tooling to compartments, black morocco labels to spines, board edges and endpapers, all uniformly marbled; bound by Birdsall; armorial bookplates, binder's ticket.   Beeleigh Abbey BA56-236   1996 £150.00

MAYHEW, AUGUSTUS   Paved with Gold. London: Chapman & Hall, 1858. 8vo; viii, 408 pages, added illustrated titlepage, frontispiece and 24 full page illustrations; half brown morocco by Birdsall over marbled boards, original cloth bound in.   Kenneth Karmiole 1NS-172 1996 $125.00

TROLLOPE, ANTHONY 1815-1882   Orley Farm. London: Chapman and Hall, 1866. 1st one volume edition; 8vo; pages (vi), 320, 320; 40 plates by J. E. Millais, plates rather foxed, otherwise very good; contemporary half dark green calf, by Birdsall, marbled board sides, expertly rebacked, preserving original backstrip, recent red morocco lettering pieces, marbled edges; this copy has a strip of paper bearing author's signature pasted to front free endpaper. Sadleir 13.   Sotheran   PN32-58   1996 £350.00

BINDING - BIRDSALL

WHITE, GILBERT 1720-1793   The Natural History of Selbourne. London: John Lane, The Bodley Head, 1902. 1st edition thus; 8vo; 552 pages; illustrations; original half levant morocco by Birdsall, featuring inlaid owl, gilt back and top edge gilt, bookplate, spine browned, still near fine.   Chapel Hill 94-121   1996 $200.00

BINDING - BLACKWELL

SKELTON, JOHN   Charles I. London: Paris: & Edinburgh: Goupil & Co., et al, 1898. 1st edition; 12 3/4 x 10 inches; 4 p.l., v, (1), 185, (1) pages, (1) leaf (colophon), device on title, decorative initials, handsomely hand colored frontispiece and 41 engravings, 23 plates; each with printed tissue overlay; appealing contemporary red morocco by Blackwell for Brentano's, covers with double gilt rule borders and floral cornerpieces, front cover with very large central arabesque enclosing coat-of-arms, raised bands, spine gilt in compartments containing large floral ornaments as well as leaves, stars and circlets, turn-ins decorated with gilt tendril, unusual pastedowns and free endpapers of brown and orange brocaded cloth, morocco hinges, all edges gilt, rubbing to spine ends (very shallow chip across top of spine), joints slightly eroded (and growing tender in two places, though boards still snugly attached), covers sightly marked and slightly soiled, frontispiece partly offset onto title, otherwise fine internally.   Phillip J. Pirages   33-121   1996 $150.00

THACKERAY, WILLIAM MAKEPEACE 1811-1863   Ballads. (with) Barry Lyndon. London: Bradbury & Evans, 1855/56. 1st edition; 8vo; 2 works bound in one volume; leaf of ads and half titles present in Ballads, terminal ads not present with Barry Lyndon, this one of the few, as noted by Van Duzer 11, without words "The right of Translation reserved" on titlepage; beautifully bound by Blackwell in full crushed crimson morocco with elaborate gold tooling on covers and spine, original yellow wrappers, bit dust soiled, few minor paper repairs, otherwise fine.   Charles Agvent   4-1109   1996 $425.00

BINDING - BLINN

DUNCAN, HARRY   Doors of Perception; Essays in Book Typography. Austin: W. Thomas Taylor, 1983. One of 325 copies, signed by author; 8vo; designed by Carol J. Blinn at Warwick Press and printed in perpetua in black and brown on Frankfurt Cream by Daniel Keleher; hand bound by Sarah Creighton and C. J. Blinn in quarter grey Niger goatskin with boards covered in Blinn's pasted papers. Fine.   Bertram Rota 272-487 1996 £75.00

WERNER, ARNO   One Man's Work: a Lecture. Easthampton: Warwick Press, 1872. One of 200 copies, signed by author and printer; 8vo; printed in Sans Serif Light 329 on Barcham Green handmade; tipped in colored plates, titlepage portrait; bound by Werner and Blinn in quarter russet morocco with paste paper sides; fine.   Bertram Rota   272-485 1996 £105.00

BINDING - BLUMENTHAL

JONES, KENNETH   Stone Soup. Portland: Chamberlain Press, 1985. One of 150 copies; signed by artist, both book and laid in prospectus are additionally inscribed by artist; octavo; (26) pages; designed, printed and illustrated by Sarah Chamberlain; bound by Barbara Blumenthal in marbled boards, leather spine label stamped in black; extremely fine. Bromer Booksellers   87-120   1996 $200.00

THE THREE BEARS. Portland: Chamberlain Press, 1983. Of an edition of 125 copies, this one of 25 deluxe copies, signed by Chamberlain, this copy additionally inscribed; octavo; (16) pages; designed, printed and illustrated by Sarah Chamberlain, 10 wood engravings, all engravings signed, the deluxe issue, including an extra signed print, there are also 9 inscribed proofs; bound by Barbara Blumenthal in pastepaper boards, painted to a pattern of paw prints; extremely fine, housed in dropback box of ivory buckram.   Bromer Booksellers   87-121   1996 $500.00

BINDING - BONE

HOTTEN, JOHN CAMDEN 1832-1873   A Dictionary of Modern Slang, Cant and Vulgar Words, Used at the Present Day in the Streets of London... London: John Camden Hotten, 1859. 1st edition; late issue; half title, 2 pages ads; original dull purple cloth by Bone & Son, very good.   Jarndyce   103-160   1996 £120.00

BINDING - BOOKLOVER'S BINDERY

HAWTHORNE, NATHANIEL 1804-1864   Tanglewood Tales for Boys and Girls: Being a Second Wonder-Book. Boston: Ticknor, Reed and Fields, 1853. 1st American edition, 1st printing; small octavo; 366 pages; engraved vignette title and six engraved plates, 8 page publisher's Catalog inserted at front in Blanck's A printing, dated July 1853 with 'Tanglewood Tales' listed as "In Press"; full red levant morocco by the Booklover's Bindery, New York, gilt lettered spine with raised bands, gilt board edges and turn-ins, top edge gilt, marbled endpapers, original red cloth bound in at back, original front free endpaper bearing previous owner's ink signature has been preserved by binder, bookplate; occasional foxing and browning to text, otherwise fine.   Heritage Book Shop 196-218 1996 $500.00

BINDING - BOURBEAU

GOULD, ROBERT   The Twelve of Hearts. Boston: 1982. Limited to just 36 copies; 2 11/16 x 2 1/16 inches; 12 original watercolor designs on soft gray paper by Gould, calligraphy by Colleen; full vellum with exposed bands of red ribbon by David Bourbeau of the Thistle Bindery; title stamped in gold on spine; extremely fine.   Bromer Booksellers 90-178 1996 $350.00

JOYCE, JAMES 1882-1941   Epiphanies. New York: Vincent Fitz Gerald, 1988. One of 52 copies only, all on Rives du Gue paper; page size 12 x 14 inches; over 150 plates, original watercolors, collage and hand cutting, Letterpress by Dan Kelher's Wild Carrot Letterpress in 40 colors; bound loose in publisher's wrappers in handmade box by David Bourbeau at the Thistle Bindery in Japanese handmade silk woven for this box, with incised line of Japanese tea paper showing profile of Joyce.   Priscilla Juvelis 95/1-142 1996 $15,000.00

BINDING - BOZERIAN

GRECOURT, JEAN BAPTISTE JOSEPH   Oeuvres Completes. Paris: Chaignieu, 1796. 8vo; 4 volumes; portrait, 8 engraved plates by Gragonand fils; contemporary vellum gilt by Bozerian Jeune (with his name in gilt on spine), gilt roll tooled borders, flat spine, gilt in compartments, lettered and dated in gilt, turquoise marbled endpapers, all edges gilt; the Pixerecourt copy, with engraved, green label. Marlborough 160-39 1996 £1,500.00

STATIUS, PUBLIUS PAPINIUS   Statii Sylvarum Libri V./ Achilleidos Libri XII./ Thebaidos Libri II./ Orthographia et Flexus Dictionum Graecarum Omnium... Venice: In aedibvs Aldi, et Andreae Soceri (Andrea Torresano), 1519. 1st Aldine edition; 8vo; 296 leaves, italic, Aldine devices on first and last leaves; red morocco binding by Bozerian le jeune, with gilt arms of Edward George Geoffrey Smith Stanley, 14th Earl of Derby, statesman and Greek scholar, silk doublures, tooled in gilt, all edges gilt, very clean and handsome copy. Renouard 88/12; Adams S1672; UCLA II/153; Brunet V512.   Family Album Tillers-587 1996 $1,600.00

BINDING - BRADLEY

DOWNING, A. J.   The Fruits and Fruit Trees of America... New York: 1845. 1st edition; 8vo; pages xiv, 594, (14 pages ads); 214 engraved illustrations; original cloth with gilt decorated spine, wear to ends and edges of spine, corners worn, rubbing to boards, bookplate, 3 signatures loose or partially loose, pages tanned; signed in blindstamp Bradley Binder Boston.   Raymond M. Sutton VII-906 1996 $300.00

BINDING - BRAMHALL & MENZIES

BUTLER, SAMUEL 1835-1902   Seven Sonnets and a Psalm of Montreal. Cambrdige: printed for Private Circulation, 1904. contemporary purple morocco by Bramhall and Menzies with green printed wrappers bound in; fine. Hoppe 44.   Jarndyce CII-86 1996 £150.00

BUTLER, SAMUEL 1835-1902   Seven Sonnets and a Psalm of Montreal. Cambridge: printed for Private Circulation, 1904. contemporary purple morocco by Bramhall and Menzies with green printed wrappers bound in; fine.   Jarndyce CII-86 1996 £150.00

BINDING - HORACE BRAY

PEACOCK, THOMAS LOVE   The Misfortunes of Elphin. Newtown: Gregynog Press, 1928. One of 25 specially bound copies of a total edition of 250; 9 3/4 x 6 1/2 inches; 2 p.l., 119, (1) pages; 21 wood engravings as headpieces and tailpieces, by H. W. Bray, device in colophon; lovely crimson morocco by Gregynog (signed in gilt by Horace Bray and George Fisher on rear turn-in); covers with single gilt rule frame, upper cover with gilt design of two hand-held goblets with wine pouring from one to the other (though with considerable gilt spillage), gilt ruled spine compartments between raised bands, one compartment with gilt titling, turn-ins with double gilt rule, top edge gilt, other edges untrimmed; a faultless copy. Harrop 12.   Phillip J. Pirages 33-264 1996 $4,500.00

BINDING - BRENTANO

WALLER, EDMUND   The Works of Edmund Waller, Esq. London: J. Tonson, 1730. 2nd edition; 12mo; (14), 295, clxii pages; 2 frontispiece portraits and 2 plates, folding plate torn and chipped, otherwise very good; modern three quarter calf by Brentano's, with raised bands. Chapel Hill 94-418 1996 $150.00

BINDING - BRINDLEY

COLLINS, ANTHONY 1676-1729   A Philosophical Enquiry Concerning Human Liberty. London: Robinson, 1717. Corrected version of the first edition of 1715; 8vo; title, pages vi, 1f., 114, 1 f., ruled in red; red morocco panelled gilt, with centre and side pieces built up from small tools, spirals, acorns, small drawer handles and others, spine gilt in 6 compartments, all edges gilt, comb-marbled endpapers, perhaps by Brindley. Armorial bookplate of Lindsay of Kirkforther.   Marlborough 160-37 1996 £1,100.00

BINDING - BROWN

WALTON, IZAAK 1593-1683   The Complete Angler or Contemplative Man's Recreation. London: Samuel Bagster, 1815. 8vo; pages 514, (20); engraved half title with vignette frame, portrait frontispiece (foxed and offset to title), 13 plates, 35 engravings, ads discarded, foxed; modern half russia with old marbled boards, by C. & E. Brown, backstrip with raised wide bands between double gilt rules, gilt lettered polished russet labels, single ruled saltire in remainder, edges of boards rubbed, marbled endpapers, hinges split but firm, good; Coigney 21; Satchell pp. 10-11; Wood pp. 38-39.   Blackwell's B112-281 1996 £165.00

BINDING - BRUGALLA

SENECA, LUCIUS ANNAEUS   Cinco Libros de Seneca. Seville: Meynardus Ungut & Stanislaus Polonus, 28 May 1491. 1st edition in Spanish; folio; 129 leaves (of 132, lacking 3 blanks), gothic letter, text surrounded by commentary, 5 lines of title and decorated woodcut initial on a2 printed in red, smaller woodcut initials, printer's device at end, blind impressions of lines of barer type at foot of title and last leaf, 6 leaves neatly remargined, g8 (blank) present but not genuine, few light stains, early inscription on titlepage deleted; modern spanish vellum by Brugalla, 1946; Goff S374; HC 14596; BMC X38; Davies Printers Devices no. 10a.   H. M. Fletcher 121-16 1996 £13,500.00

BINDING - BUMPUS

ARNOLD, MATTHEW 1822-1888   Poems. London: Macmillan & Co., 1888. Crown 8vo; 3 volumes; slightly later white calf, for Bumpus, gilt and enamelled with roses, inner gilt dentelles, all edges gilt, few faint marks and scratches, little discolored with age, but still very pretty set. Ash Rare Books Zenzybyr-6 1996 £125.00

BUTLER, SAMUEL 1835-1902   Erewhon or Over the Range. London: 1872. 2nd edition; half dark blue morocco by Bumpus, top edge gilt. Jarndyce CII-13 1996 £75.00

GRESWELL, WILLIAM PARR   Annals of Parisian Typography. London: Cadell and Davies, et al, 1818. 1st edition; one of an unspecified number of large paper copies; 8vo; 356 pages; 12 full page plates; 19th century three quarter green morocco and cloth by L. & F. Bumpus with gilt spine and raised bands, spine faded to brown, covers little bowed, else very good, quite nice internally.   Chapel Hill 94-328 1996 $250.00

BINDING - BUMPUS

LYTE, H. C. MAXWELL   A History of Eton College (1440-1910). London: Macmillan and Co. Ltd., 1911. 4th edition; royal 8vo; half title, vignette, 627 pages of text, frontispiece, 9 plates, 63 illustrations to text, one colored folding map; full dark blue morocco, triple gilt rule borders, gilt corner ornaments, gilt stamped arms and motto of Eton College to upper board gilt rule, title, date and ornaments to panelled spine all edges gilt, inner gilt rule borders with engraved bookplate of the Seventh Duke of Newcastle, bound by Bumpus; very fine.   Beeleigh Abbey BA/56-14 1996 £250.00

SWINBURNE, ALGERNON CHARLES 1837-1909   The Tragedies. London: Chatto & Windus, 1905-06. 1st collected edition, one of 110 large paper copies; 9 x 6 inches; 5 volumes; photogravure frontispiece in final volume, titles printed in red and black; large paper copies, especially fine contemporary burgundy crushed morocco by Bumpus, covers and board edges with double gilt rule, spines very attractively and densely gilt in compartments filled with massed stippled volutes enclosing quatrefoil at center, elegant inner gilt dentelles, top edge gilt, other edges rough trimmed, entirely unopened; beautifully bound in splendid condition.   Phillip J. Pirages 33-478 1996 $1,500.00

BINDING - BURLEN

AGNER, DWIGHT   The Books of WAD - A Bibliography of the Books Designed by W. A. Dwiggins. Baton Rouge: The Press of Nightowl, 1974. One of approximately 190 numbered copies, printed on 70 pound Curtis Colophon - there were also 16 copies on damped Worthy Hand and Arrows paper; handset in Eric Gill's Monotype Joanna; titlepage and decorations by W. A. Dwiggins; bound by Robert Burlen and Son, cloth backed marbled paper boards, tail of spine and bottom corners slightly bumped, near fine. From the library of James D. Hart.   Ulysses 39-165 1996 £185.00

BINDING - BURN

ANDERSON, JOHN 1833-1900   Mandalay to Momien: a Narrative of the Two Expeditions to Western China of 1868 and 1875. London: Macmillan & Co., 1876. 1st edition; demy 8vo; xvi, (480) pages; plates, folding maps; original decorative cloth, by Burn and Co., with their ticket, covers little worn, nicked and marked, but good copy still, bookplate of Hooker's Son, Joseph Symonds Hooker.   Ash Rare Books Zenzybyr-3 1996 £450.00

ELIOT, GEORGE, PSEUD. 1819-1880   The Mill on the Floss. Edinburgh and London: William Blackwood and Sons, 1860. 1st edition; in Carter's A binding, indicating an early issue; 3 volumes, 16 page undated publisher's catalog at end of volume 3; original bright brown ripple grain cloth, sides blocked in blind, spine lettered in gold and with gold designs, deep cream endpapers, top and fore-edges uncut, bottom cut as issued, Binder's ticket of Burn at end of volume 1, cloth very slightly cockled on spine of volume 1, tiny area of front joint of volume 3 worn, skilful and minimal restoration not detracting from an excellent set, clean and fresh; Parrish pp. 14-15; Carter pp. 110-11; Sadleir 816.   Simon Finch 24-81 1996 £600.00

KINGSLEY, CHARLES 1819-1875   Hereward the Wake "Last of the English". London: Macmillan, 1867. 8vo; 2 volumes in 1, pages xii, 365, (1); 402, (2 ads); original blue cloth, by Burn, with ticker, very good. James Fenning 133-195 1996 £65.00

KINGSLEY, CHARLES 1819-1875   Town Geology. London: Strahan & Co., 1872. 1st edition; crown 8vo; pages (2), lvi, 239, (6 ads); original blue cloth, by Burn, with his ticket; fine.   James Fenning 133-196 1996 £55.00

LEE, FREDERICK GEORGE   The Other World, or, Glimpses of the Supernatural. London: Henry S. King and Co., 1875. 8vo; 2 volumes; 72 pages publisher's ads at back of volume 2; original brown cloth by Burn and Co., with their label on lower pastedown, decorated in black, lettered in gilt, some rubbing and soiling; some light browning and spotting, mostly of fore-edges, else very good.   James Cummins 14-200 1996 $325.00

MORRIS, WILLIAM 1834-1896   Love is Enough. London: Ellis & White, 1873 but 1872. 1st edition; imperial 16mo; original decorative cloth, gilt in a delightful Morris willow-and-myrtle design by Burn & Co., with their ticket, few minor marks, front endpaper very slightly cracked, few tiny nicks, but very attractive copy still. Forman 37.   Ash Rare Books Zenzybyr-71 1996 £195.00

BINDING - BURN

SIMPSON, JAMES YOUNG   Acupressure, a New Method of Arresting Surgical Haemorrahge and of Accelerating the Healing of Wounds. Edinburgh: 1864. 1st edition; 8vo; 42 text illustrations, light waterstain on lower portion of book throughout, becoming more noticeable towards end; green cloth by Burn, with their ticket, binding little worn and stained, front joint beginning to split; inscribed "Mr. Brittain with author's kind regards". Russel & Forster p. 50.   Maggs Bros. Ltd. 1190-508 1996 £225.00

BINDING - CAMPBELL-LOGAN

HALL, EDWIN   Sweynheym and Pannartz and the Origins of Printing in Italy: German Technology and Italian Humanism in Renaissance Rome. Minnville: printed by the Bird and Bull Press for Phillip J. Pirages, 1991. 1st edition; one of 231 copies (of 239 total); 9 1/4 x 6 1/4 inches; 131 pages; text with 4 nine-line initials in red and blue, two pages of typographic facsimiles; with a large folio Sweynheym and Pannartz leaf from the 1471 printing of Nicholas of Lyra's "Postilla super totam Bibliam"; a Campbell-Logan Co. binding of purple quarter morocco using marbled papers, especially designed for this edition by Iris Nevins, paper label on front cover, two edges untrimmed, the book and leaf (which is secured in mylar envelope behind a hinged cloth mat) contained in impressive 15 1/2 x 11 3/4 inch navy blue folding cloth box constructed of acid-free materials by Nancy Cuthbert.   Phillip J. Pirages 33-341 1996 $450.00

BINDING - CAPE

CHURCH OF ENGLAND. BOOK OF COMMON PRAYER   The Book of Common Prayer. London: William Pickering, 1853. 7 1/4 x 5 inches; (360) leaves, every page of text with wide panel borders, title leaf with elaborate border on recto, all in imitation of Richard Day's "Booke of Christian Prayers", commonly known as "Queen Elizabeth's Prayerbook" first printed in 1569; title in red and black; extremely attractive ornately gilt & blindstamped contemporary dark brown morocco by Cape, covers dominated by large diapered field of blindstamped fleurs-de-lis, spine similarly decorated in compartments between raised bands, one compartment titled in gilt, very handsome densely gilt inner dentelles, marbled endpapers, all edges gilt, light mottling or foxing here and there, otherwise very fine, lovely binding bright, clean and virtually unworn; Keynes p. 74.   Phillip J. Pirages 33-418 1996 $650.00

BINDING - CARSS

COLERIDGE, SAMUEL TAYLOR 1772-1834   Biographia Literaria; or Biographical Sketches of My Literary Life and Opinions. London: Rest Fenner, 1817. 1st edition; 8vo; 2 volumes bound in one; pages (iv), 296; (vi), 309, (i) ads; contemporary full calf, maroon morocco label, sides ruled in blind, spine with gilt bands, red sprinkled edges, by J. Carss & Co., Glasgow with their ticket, spine rubbed in places, first two leaves spotted; excellent copy. Wise, Coleridge 40; Tinker 696.   Simon Finch 24-47 1996 £900.00

EDEN, EMILY   The Semi-Attached Couple. London: Richard Bentley, 1860. 1st edition; 8vo; 2 volumes, bound without half titles, pages iv, 266; (ii), 259, (1); 2 volumes; foxed, one gathering in volume 1 starting; contemporary half tan calf by Carss & Co., little rubbed, backstrip with gilt ruled raised bands between black rules, red labels, marbled boards and edges, endpapers foxed, blue silk markers, good. Sadleir 760; Wolff 1982.   Blackwell's B112-91 1996 £350.00

EDEN, EMILY   The Semi-Detached House. London: Richard Bentley, 1859. 1st edition; 12mo; half title discarded, pages (ii), 327; contemporary half tan calf by Carss & Co., backstrip rubbed, raised bands, red labels, marbled boards, hinges split but firm, blue silk marker, good. Sadleir 761; not in Wolff.   Blackwell's B112-92 1996 £250.00

LAMB, CHARLES 1775-1834   Satan in Search of a Wife: With the Whole Process of His Courtship and Marriage, and Who Danced at the Wedding. London: Edward Moxon, 1831. 1st edition; 8vo; 2 volumes; engraved frontispiece, engraved plates, owner's bookplate to front pastedown of both volumes, binders ticket to front f.e.p. of volume 2, bound by Carss & Co., Glasgow, half green morocco and green buckram boards, corners slightly bumped, elaborate gilt tooling to compartments of panelled spine, raised bands, marbled edges; fine, handsome copy. Sadleir 1400.   Beeleigh Abbey BA56-156 1996 £65.00

BINDING - CAUMONT

SCOTT, WALTER 1771-1832   The Lay of the Last Minstrel. London: Longman, 1807. 6th edition; lg. 8vo; 340 pages; 3 contemporary ink and wash drawings by Sophia Merrick Hoare bound in; dark blue morocco gilt by Comte Caumont, with his label, gilt & blind roll tooled borders, single fillet panel with small fleuron cornerpieces, spine gilt in compartments, lettered and dated, double raised bands, turn-ins, olive silk doublures and endpapers with gilt roll tooled borders, all edges gilt, exemplary binding.   Marlborough 160-77 1996 £450.00

BINDING - DE CAUMONT

COLLIER, JANE   An Essay on the Art of Ingeniously Tormenting. London: Millar, 1753. 8vo; title, pages 234, etched plate by Gillray dated 1804, mounted before title; slightly later calf, covers decorated with single gilt rule, enclosing stencilled intertwining snakes in plain calf on mottled calf background, flat spine gilt, 3 labels missing, edges speckled beneath blue diamond pattern, marbled endpapers, by the Count de Caumont (ca. 1804) with his pink Gerrard St. label, covers worn and pitted, some loss of surface; worn and shabby, acid has removed much of the surface of the cover and spine is worn, but enough survives to make clear the imaginative purpose and some of the dramatic effect of this unique and historically important binding.   Marlborough 160-36 1996 £550.00

BINDING - CHARRIERE

BEARD, MARK   Manhattan Third Year Reader. New York: Vincent Fitz Gerald & Co., 1984. Out of series copy, one of 30 copies only, each signed by author; 35 linocuts pulled and assembled by the artist and publisher on 28 different papers; specially bound by Gerard Charriere in green morocco with rondel onlays on front and back panel, rondel is of white box calf with onlays including a smashed trash can on both covers.   Priscilla Juvelis 95/1-23 1996 $13,000.00

BINDING - CHEN

O'BANLON, NANCE   Domestic Science: Pop-Up Icons. Domestic Science: Idioms. Berkeley: Flying Fish Press, 1990. One of 150 copies from a total edition of 165; page size 6 1/8 x 12 inches; printed on Fabriano Rosaspina paper, each copy signed and numbered by artist; at least 58 linoleum cuts, five of which are pop-ups, many in color; text was handset in 12 point Gill Sans; bound by Julie Chen with the assistance of many hands, black and white linoleum cut paper, Sandy Tilcock produced the boxes of black and white checked linoleum cut paper with gold label, title printed in black on front cover and spine; the book structure is accordion fold front-to-back and back-to-front. Priscilla Juvelis 95/1-95 1996 $575.00

BINDING - CHIVERS

COLLINGWOOD, W. G.   The Life and Work of John Ruskin. London: Methuen & Co., 1893. Number 208 of 300 numbered copies; square 4to; 2 volumes; pages xiv, 243; vi, 285; on handmade paper; mounted color frontispiece, 20 plates; contemporary three quarter tan speckled calf gilt by Cedric Chivers of Bath, spines tooled in blind, with elaborate art nouveau sunflower design within a single vertical panel bordered with single and dotted rule, top edge gilt; handsome set.   R.F.G. Hollett & Son 78-133 1996 £275.00

HOLE, S. REYNOLDS   Our Gardens. London: Dent, 1901. 4th edition; 8vo; 1 f., titlepage, 3 ff., 304 pages, frontispiece, 8 plates, text illustrations, top edge gilt; a vellucent binding by Cedric Chivers of Bath, signed on lower turn-in; vellum, running "Art Nouveau" motif of stylised roses, thorns and leaves, gilt studded, framing a central hand colored panel of a garden scene, with the pattern repeated on the spine, executed and lettered by hand in colored inks, gilt fillets on turn-ins, top edge gilt, marbled lemon endleaves.   Marlborough 160-82 1996 £650.00

BINDING - CLAESSENS

RABELAIS, FRANCOIS 1494?-1553   Les Oevvres. Antwerp: Jean Fuet, 1605-8. 2nd of the 3 (or possibly 4) editions of the works which pruport to have been printed at Antwerp by Jean Fuet; 12mo; pages 347, (vii), 469 (recte 465) (ix), 166 (xvi), some pages misnumbered, final blank missing, separate titlepage to Book V, roman and Italic letter, 1 full page woodcut of the Bottle, woodcut initials and ornaments, light age yellowing, 3 small rust holes affecting the odd letter, early owner's autograph, neatly erased on titlepage, 19th century orange morocco by Claessens, gilt fillets, inner dentelles and spine, all edges gilt, marbled endpapers, good copy; 19th century bookplate. BM STC Fr. 17th R56; Low Countries 1601-21 R1; Tchemerzine V 315.   A. Sokol XXV-79 1996 £950.00

BINDING - CLARKE

LONGINUS   Dionysii Longini de Sublimitate Libellus. Oxford: Wilmot, 1718. Large paper copy; 8vo; pages (13), 163, (32), full leather, from the library of the great book collector, Rev. Theodore Williams, probably bound by Clarke for Williams, with Williams' gilt stamps on each board, gilt dentelles, all edges gilt. Dibdin II 177; Brunet III 1152.   Family Album Tillers-398 1995 $300.00

WEEVER, JOHN   Ancient Monuments With In the United Monarchie of Great Britaine, Ireland and the Lands Adjacent with the Dissolved Monasteries Therein Contained... London: ptd. by Tho. Harper, & are to be sold in Little Britayne by Laurence.. 1631. 1st edition; folio; errata leaf, 871 pages of text, 14 page index, frontispiece, 6 full plates; modern light brown morocco, triple gilt rule borders, gilt rule and floral tools to panelled spine, inner gilt dentelles, marbled endpapers, engraved bookplate, bound by J. Clarke. STC 25223; Cox III pp. 463-4; Upcott p. xx.   Beeleigh Abbey BA56-27 1996 £850.00

WORDSWORTH, CHRISTOPHER   Greece: Pictorial, Descriptive and Historical. London: William S. Orr and Co., 1840. 1-356 pages text; steel engraved frontispiece, 24 full page steel engravings, 2 engraved maps, numerous woodcut illustrations and vignettes to text, some foxing to a few plates, including frontispiece; full green straight grain morocco, slightly scuffed and worn, gilt ruled border, gilt title to spine, raised bands to spine, all edges gilt, bound by Clarke of Bedford, hinges cracked, but still a good tight copy. Bookplate. Binder's ticket. Beeleigh Abbey BA/56-129 1996 £250.00

BINDING - CLEMENTS

HOMERUS   Iliad. Munich: Bremer Press, 1923. Limited to 615 numbered copies; folio; text finely printed in Greek in Monachos type; superbly bound by Jeff Clements in full brown morocco, blind tooled, geometrically designed inlays in blue, red, grey and black colored moroccos, black morocco doublures, suede endpapers, gilt edges, preserved in drop down cloth box. Outstanding copy.   Thomas Thorp 489-157 1996 £1,250.00

BINDING - CLUB BINDERY

BROWNING, ROBERT 1812-1889   Strafford: an Historical Tragedy. London: printed for Longman, Rees, Orme, Brown, Green & Longman, 1837. 1st edition; 8vo; full brown crushed levant, covers decorated in gilt with elaborate interlocking ruled border enclosed withing light brown inlaid morocco strips, intricate tan morocco doublures, with all over floral pattern in gilt, spine gilt, all edges gilt, by the Club Bindery, original drab wrappers, printed paper side label, bound in at end; fine in handsome binding. From the library of H. W. Poor, additional bookplate of Christine Alexander Graham. CBEL III 442.   Ximenes 108-391 1996 $850.00

BINDING - DOUGLAS COCKERELL

BOYLE, ELEANOR VERE   A Garden of Pleasure. London: Elliot Stock, 1895. 3rd edition; 175 x 105mm; pages xvi, 220, (2), frontispiece and other illustrations in line; contemporary full tan morocco, sides ruled into 9 sections with gold lines and dot at intersections, backstrip lettered and double ruled in compartments with small triple leafe ornaments in blind extending from 3 raised band, all edges gilt on the rough, signed "D(ouglas) C(ockerell) 1900", little rubbed but sound; bookplate of Frank Lawson of Ewelme Down.   Claude Cox 107-14 1996 £110.00

MORRIS, WILLIAM 1834-1896   Love Is Enough, or the Freeing of Pharamond: a Morality. Kelmscott Press, 1897. One of 300 copies on paper (there were also 8 on vellum); 11 1/2 x 8 1/2 inches; 2 p.l., 90 pages; 2 full page woodcut illustrations designed by Edward Burne-Jones & engraved by W.H. Hooper, 1 as frontispiece, other at end, woodcut initials in black or blue, elaborate woodcut full border on 1st page of text, smaller borders on many other pages; ptd. in red, blue & black; fine cont. med. brown mor., handsomely gilt by Douglas Cockerell (signed "19 DC 01" on rear turn-in), covers w/broad frame of linked rectangles & stylized interlaced floral ornaments in corners (front cover w/central panel giving author, title & pub. in lg. letters), spine in very attractive compartments filled w/twining tendrils & many broadleaf stamps, gilt dec. turn-ins w/clusters of sm. inlaid green leaves at corners, edges gilded on rough; covers w/hint of soiling & few marks (one 3/4" superficial scratch on front board), otherwise very fine inside and out, especially appealing binding. Armorial bookplate of Baker Tristram. Sparling 52; Tomkinson p. 121.   Phillip J. Pirages 33-320 1996 $6,500.00

BINDING - COHEN

BALDWIN, JAMES 1924-   Gypsy and Other Poems. Leeds: Gehenna Press, 1989. Limited edition of 325 copies, this one of 275 copies containing one etching of Baldwin by Baskin signed and numbered by artist; printed on Magnani paper; bound by Claudia Cohen in grey paper over boards, red morocco label on spine and front cover, signed by Baskin.   Priscilla Juvelis 95/1-13 1996 $375.00

BASKIN, LEONARD   Jewish Artists of the Early and Late Renaissance. Northampton: Gehenna Press, 1993. Limited to 26 copies; 4to; portraits; geometric texts have been set in van Krimpen's Spectrum types and have been printed on a variety of Europgean handmade papers using an Albion handpress, portraits have been pulled on the same sheets as the letterpress; full green morocco with various color morocco onlays and gilt tooling and titling, matching clamshell case (by Claudia Cohen). Book Block 32-49 1996 $7,500.00

DANTE, ALIGHIERI 1265-1321   Dantes Inferno. Hopewell: Ecco Press, 1993. 1st edition; deluxe issue, limited to 125 copies, signed by each of the translators and with the original etching signed by Francesco Clemente laid in; small folio; frontispiece by Francesco Clemente; text was set in Monotype Dante & printed letterpress by Michael & Winifred Bixler on Rives heavyweight paper; quarter black calf and red silk over boards, slipcase by Claudia Cohen; handsome book, as new.   James S. Jaffe 34-244 1996 $1,500.00

BINDING - COLLEY

AESOPUS   The Little Esop. London: Tilt and Bogue, ca. 1835. 2 15/16 x 2 1/2 inches; 191 pages; 48 wood engravings; half speckled calf by Arthur S. Colley, with gold tooling, spine in five compartments and morocco label, all edges gilt, original cloth cover with gilt stamp showing Aesop telling a tale to a child, bound in; Bondy p. 67; Welsh 62.   Bromer Booksellers 90-194 1996 $500.00

FAMOUS Men of Britain. London: Tilt & Bogue, ca. 1835. 2 15/16 x 2 1/2 inches; 191 pages; 48 wood engravings; half speckled calf by Arthur S. Colley, with gilt tooling, spine in compartments and morocco label, all edges gilt, original cloth cover bound in; Bondy p. 67; Welsh 2772. Bromer Booksellers 90-195 1996 $550.00

MAY, W.   The Little Book of British Birds. London: C. Tilt, ca. 1835. 2 15/16 x 2 1/2 inches; 191 pages, wood engravings; half speckled calf by Arthur S. Colley, with gilt stamping, spine in five compartmnts and morocco label, original gilt stamped cloth cover and pines bound in all edges gilt; Bondy pp. 66-67; Welsh 4889.   Bromer Booksellers 90-192 1996 $450.00

MAY, W.   The Little Book of British Quadrupeds. London: C. Tilt, ca. 1835. 2 15/16 x 2 1/2 inches; 191 pages, 48 wood engraved illustrations; half speckled calf by Arthur S. Colley, gilt tooling, spine in five compartments, morocco label, all edges gilt, original gilt stamped cloth cover and spine are bound in; Bondy pp. 66-7; Welsh 4890.   Bromer Booksellers 90-193 1996 $450.00

BINDING - COMMIN

KIRKMAN, F. B.   The British Bird Book: an Account of All the Birds. London: T. C. and E. C. Jack, 1911-13. 1st edition; 4to 4 volumes; pages 449, 540, 609, 1602; with 280 colored plates; contemporary green half morocco gilt, by Horace C. Commin; occasional mainly light spotting to beginning and end of volumes, spines slightly faded.   Sotheran PN32-90 1996 £398.00

BINDING - CONANT

DREYFUS, JOHN   A Typographical Masterpiece. London: Bain and Williams, (prtd. by Meriden Stinehour Press, Vermont), 1993. 1st edition; limited to 200 copies (+499 for the Book Club of California); large 4to; pages 120; 41 illustrations; full red cloth by Judi Conant with Fabriano endpapers.   Claude Cox 107-61A 1996 £95.00

BINDING - CONDLE

HOWISON, JOHN   Sketches of Upper Canada, Domestic, Local and Characteristic. Edinburgh: Oliver & Boyd, High Street, G. & W. B. Wittaker, Ave Maria Ln. London 1821. 1st edition; 8vo; half title, (v-vii), (ix-xvi), 1-339 pages, half title; full polished tan calf, gilt tooled borders to boards, maroon morocco labels to spines, gilt tooling to compartments of panelled spine, edges and endpapers marbled; bound by James Condle of Paisley. Sabin 33366; Gagnon 1710; Stanton & Tremaine 1200.   Beeleigh Abbey BA56-81 1996 £295.00

BINDING - CORDAVAU

HORATIUS FLACCUS, QUINTUS 65-8 BC   (Opera) Quae Supersunt Recensuit et Notulis Instruxit Giblertus Wakefield. London: Kearsley, 1794. Large 8vo; 2 volumes in 1; pages viii, 186, 4 ff., 2 engraved plates, title, pages 168, 5 ff., errata slip on final blank; large paper copy of this scarce edition; crimson morocco gilt, relatively plain, covers panelled with two single fillets, one straight and one indented and looped at corners, spine with repeated gilt pattern within double raised bands, binder's ticket "Bound by L. Cordavau".   Marlborough 160-42 1996 £800.00

BINDING - DE COVERLY

GOLDSMITH, OLIVER 1730-1774   The Citizen of the World. London: printed for J. Newbery, 1762. 1st edition; 12mo; 2 volumes; polished calf, spines and inner dentelles gilt, all edges gilt, by R. de Coverly, traces of rubbing, small worn spot in one lower joint; very nice, clean copy. Rothschild 1021; Iolo Williams pp. 123-4; Roscoe A190; Raven 717. Ximenes 108-165 1996 $800.00

BINDING - CREIGHTON

DUNCAN, HARRY   Doors of Perception; Essays in Book Typography. Austin: W. Thomas Taylor, 1983. One of 325 copies, signed by author; 8vo; designed by Carol J. Blinn at Warwick Press and printed in perpetua in black and brown on Frankfurt Cream by Daniel Keleher; hand bound by Sarah Creighton and C. J. Blinn in quarter grey Niger goatskin with boards covered in Blinn's pasted papers. Fine.   Bertram Rota 272-487 1996 £75.00

SHELLEY, MARY WOLLSTONECRAFT GODWIN 1797-1851   Frankenstein or, The Modern Prometheus. West Hatfield: Pennyroyal Press, 1984. One of 300 copies; 13 3/4 x 10 inches; 255 pages, 52 wood engravings by Barry Moser, printed in several colors in Poliphilus and Wilhelm Klingsporschrift on Strathmore Pulegium, specially made for the Press; specially bound by Sarah Creighton in full grey niger goatskin with white and rust leather onlays, blind and palladium tooling, graphite head edge, sewn rust silk endbands with silver teachest flyleaves; one of four so bound, with additional suite of prints in quarter leather traycase, 36 x 36 cm.   Taurus Books 83-125 1996 $3,000.00

BINDING - SARAH CREIGHTON

THEROUX, ALEXANDER   Watergraphs. Boston: Base Canard, 1994. Deluxe issue, one of 15 copies on handmade paper, Roman numeralled and signed by author; elegantly handbound by Sarah Creighton in quarater leather and marbled paper of her own design.   Lame Duck Books 19-537 1996 $350.00

BINDING - CUZIN

MILTON, JOHN 1608-1674   The Sonnets. London: printed by Ballantyne, Hanson & Co. for Kegan, Paul Trench & Co., 1883. One of 50 large paper copies, signed by printer; 8 x 5 1/4 inches; 1 p.l., 222, (1) pages, (1) leaf; frontispiece, vignette on title, title printed in red and black; very attractive contemporary olive brown morocco by Cuzin, covers with French fillet frame, gilt rose in each corner, raised bands, spine compartments handsomely gilt with similar rose in center and with floral sprays in corners, fine beige morocco doublures bordered with multiple plain and decorative gilt rules and featuring large and elegant gilt floral designs at center and each corner, marbled flyleaves, all edges gilt, slight variation in color to one cover, hint of rubbing to joints, otherwise very fine, handsomely bound and virtually pristine internally.   Phillip J. Pirages 33-388 1996 $650.00

BINDING - D'AMBROSIO

BRADBURY, RAY 1920-   Long After Ecclesiastes; New Biblical Texts by Ray Bradbury. Santa Ana: Gold Stein Press, 1985. 1st edition; limited to 75 copies, signed by author and by D'Ambrosio; 2 13/16 x 2 1/2 inches; illustrated with embossed images and with serigraphs, poems printed over some of these images; bound, printed and designed by Joseph D'Ambrosio; bound in full gray morocco with silver foil inset, which resembles a stained glass window and is embossed with Hebrew lettering; extremely fine, with marbled slipcase.   Bromer Booksellers 87-206 1996 $450.00

BINDING - D'AMBROSIO

POE, EDGAR ALAN 1809-1849   Al Aaraff. Phoenix: D'Ambrosio, 1995.
One of 50 copies; 12 x 4 3/4 x 7 inches high, including book stand; 5
p.l., 45, (1) pages, (1) leaf (colophon); illustrated and decorated in
various ways, including some paste-ons, illustrations printed from
handmade paper plates made by D'Ambrosio, letterpress printed from
magnesium plates in blue and black in distinctive "Black Chancery" face,
with separate 16 page booklet of notes, contained in pocket inside back
cover; imaginative trapezoidal binding of blue niger-backed boards,
plexiglas mirror mounted on each cover and framed with blue Japanese
paper, book set down into grooved platform and retained by matching
lid (of Japanese papaer and 7 plexiglas mirros) latched into the platform,
this cover with two open sides, revealing the mirrored sides of the
book, the whole forming a truncated reflecting pyramid (with spine of
book at top, under cover).   Phillip J. Pirages 33-153 1996 $800.00

BINDING - DAVID

IMITATIO CHRISTI   L'Imitation de Jesus-Christ. Paris: Curmer, 1856-58.
4to; 2 volumes, 4 full page plates, ca. 400 pages, all with
chromolithographic borders by Lemercier; purple morocco, richly gilt,
buff onlays, inner borders gilt and stamped by binder, David, the spines
gilt in compartments, raised bands, all edges gilt, watered green silk
endpapers.   Marlborough 160-65 1996 £1,250.00

BINDING - DAVIS

WILSON, ADRIAN   Printing for Theater. San Francisco: Adrian Wilson,
1957. Limited to 250 numbered copies; folio; 57 pages, chapter heading
and binding blocks by Nuiko Haramaki, numerous tipped-in original
theater programs designed by Wilson, additional programs laid in pocket
inside back cover, printed in Linotype Caslon and Trajanus on handmade
Tovil paper; bound by Perry G. Davis in natural linen decoratively
stamped in green on front cover and lettered in red on spine, programs
for Hamlet used as endpapers, spine very slightly darkened, occasional
offsetting from specimens; fine overall.   Heritage Book Shop 196-251
1996 $1,500.00

BINDING - DE COVERLY

BORROW, GEORGE HENRY 1803-1881   Works. London: John Murray,
1923-26. 8vo; 7 volumes; frontispieces and other illustrations; half red
morocco, gilt panel spines, marbled endpapers, top edge gilt, by De
Coverly; handsome set.   Sotheran PN32-3 1996 £750.00

THE HYMNARY. A Book of Church Song. London: Novello, 1872. 2nd
edition; large 8vo; pages xlv, 618; crimson morocco gilt, covers
decorated by a seme of VA ciphers, each encircled by four s fernes, the
borders carrying a verse between gilt fillets; spine in more restrained
style, double gilt and blind ruled compartments, raised bands, all edges
gilt, marbled endpapers. Bound by De Coverley.   Marlborough 160-69
1996 £200.00

STANLEY, HENRY MORTON 1841-1904   In Darkest Africa. London:
Sampson Low, Marston, Searle and Rivington, Ltd... St. Dunstan's... 1890.
1st edition; 8vo; 2 volumes; frontispiece to volume 1, photogravure
portrait frontispiece to volume 2, 39 full page illustrations, 85 illustrations
to text, 21 maps; bound by Roger de Coverly & Sons, half crimson
morocco and buckram boards, corners slightly worn, gilt titles, raised
bands to spines, top edge gilt, marbled endpapers, owner's bookplate to
front pastedown of both volumes, new endpapers and prelims; fine,
handsome copy in excellent condition.   Beeleigh Abbey BA/56-121
1996 £275.00

BINDING - DELRUE

ROBERTS, KATE   Two Old Men and Other Stories. Newtown: Gwasg
Gregynog, 1981. Part of a printing of 265 copies (15 on handmade paper
by Wookey Hole Mill with frontispiece hand colored, 250 on Zerkall
mould made paper); out of series copy, specially signed by artist; 10
1/2 x 7 inches; xi, (1), 80 pages, (1) leaf (colophon); frontispiece in 2
colors, each of the six stories with plate in two colors, title vignettes,
headpieces, other illustrations, all by Kyffin Williams; title partly printed in
blue-grey; a flamboyant expressionistic inlaid binding of gray morocco by
Paul Delrue, front cover with long worm shaped orange inlays, back
cover with large black onlaid irregularly shaped patches (themselves
decorated with several light brown onlaid slivers), front cover highlighted
with very many thin black onlays, top edge of text block delightfully
painted in complementary colors (giving the impression of a landscape),
other edges untrimmed, in very fine folding cloth box, partly lined with
matching morocco, similar onlaid morocco spine label; very fine.
Phillip J. Pirages 33-265 1996 $1,950.00

BINDING - DEROME

CATULLUS, C. VALERIUS   (Opera). Caius Valerius Catullus et in Eum
Isaaci Vossi Observationes. N.P.: Leyde: Prostat apud Isaacum Littleburii
Bibilioplam Londinensem, 1684. 1st edition by Vossius; and first edition
of Catullus to be published in England; small 4to; 18th century French
red morocco, gilt, spine and inner dentelles gilt, all edges gilt (attributed
in pencil note to Derome); some foxing and light browning, but fine in
elegant early binding; from the library of John Sparrow. Wing C1526.
Ximenes 109-74 1996 $600.00

DIGESTORUM Seu Pandectarum Libri Quinquaginta Ex Florentinis
Pandectis Repraesentati. Florence: in Officina Laurentii Torrentini, 1553.
1st edition; folio; 2 volumes (volumes 1 and 2, of 3); large well
margined copy, title and half page detailed woodcut vignette, very large
detailed illustrative woodcut initial letters, full 18th century blue French
morocco (a pencil note suggest by Derome-le-Jeune), boards with triple
gilt fillet, spines elaborately gilt in compartments with gilt lettering direct,
spines browned, all edges gilt; very fine, clean and fresh copy.
Bookplates of the Earl of Cromer and Viscount Mersey, Bignor Park.
Ian Wilkinson 95/1-90 1996 £295.00

TORNE, L'ABBE   Sermons Preches Devant Le Roi, Pendant Le Careme
de 1764. Paris: Chez Saillant, 1765 8vo; 2 volumes, titles with attractive
woodcut vignettes, very clean and well margined copy; very finely bound
in full contemporary French red morocco by Derome-le-Jeune, boards
with wide and elaborate dentelle border in gilt, large central gilt armorial
stamp, arms containing a lamb, surmounted by a gilt crown, spines
elaborately gilt in compartments, all edges gilt, inner gilt dentelles,
corners and insignificant wear; execllent armorial binding in fine condition.
Ian Wilkinson 95/1-35 1996 £870.00

BINDING - DEWAR

WILSON, JOHN MAC KAY   The Land of Burns, a Series of
Landscapes and Portraits, Illustrative of the Life and Writings of the
Scottish Poet. London: Blackie & Son, 1840. 4to; 2 volumes; pages vi,
105; vi, 72; 2 engraved titles and 80 steel engraved plates, little spotting
to frontispiece and engraved title to volume on dampstained; full
morocco gilt by J. Dewar of Perth, boards with unusual design and
panelled in blind and gilt fillets, spine panels bordered with multiple gilt
fillets, trifle rubbed.   R.F.G. Hollett 76-340 1996 £150.00

BINDING - DODD & PEELING

BLACKWELL, MISS   Poverty and Affluence. Brussels: imp. de G.
Stapleaux, 1851. 1st edition; 12mo; 2 volumes in one, pages 190, (i),
errata: 192; half titles; some foxing, chiefly marginal in first volume;
contemporary red hard grain morocco, richly gilt, marbled endpapers, gilt
edges, by Dodd and Peeling, Woburn; from the ducal library at Woburn
with bookplate of Anna Maria, Duchess of Bedford. Rare.   Simon Finch
24-8 1996 £950.00

BINDING - DORFNER

DE MARGERIE, PIERRE   Eloge de La Typographie. Cranach Press,
1931. One of 115 copies on paper, (there were also 14 on vellum); 11
1/4 x 7 1/4 inches; 12 pages, (1) leaf (colophon); raised historiated initial
in blue, orange and gold, engraved by Eric Gil after a drawing by
Aristide Maillol, headlines printed in red; fine scarlet crushed morocco by
O. Dorfner of Weimar, covers framed with single gilt rule, gilt titling on
front cover, raised bands, top edge gilt, other edges untrimmed, fine felt
lined folding cloth box with red morocco spine label; especially fine in
handsome, unworn binding. Schroder p. 11.   Phillip J. Pirages 33-143
1996 $7,800.00

MARGERIE, PIERRE DE   Eloge de la Typographie. Weimar: Cranach
Press, for Editions de Cluny, Paris, 1931. One of 115 copies on Monval
from a total issue of 129; 115 on Monval (this copy) and 14 on vellum;
page size 11 1/8 x 7 inches; initial engraved by Eric Gill, original
woodcut of Aristide Maillol, hand gilded by Max Goertz; paper handmade
by Caspard and Raffael Maillol, type set by Walter Tanz and Hans
Schulze and book was printed by Max Kopp under the direction of
Kessler and Max Goertz; bound by Otto Dorfner in full red morocco with
gilt fillet on front and back cover, fillet on both edges and double fillet
repeated on inside covers, spine panelled, top edge gilt, title and author
tooled in gilt on front cover, grey paper slipcase, outstanding copy;
signed on back turn-in Dorfner-Weimar.   Priscilla Juvelis 95/1-72 1996
$5,000.00

BINDING - DOVES BINDERY

BROWNING, ROBERT 1812-1889   Dramatis Personae. Doves Press, 1910. One of 250 copies on paper (there were also 15 on vellum); 9 1/4 x 6 1/2 inches; 4 p.l., (2 of them blank), (9)-202 pages, (1) leaf (colophon); printed in black and red; fine deep blue morocco, elaborately decorated in gilt, covers with many cloverleafs (outlined in gold or else gouged out and filled with gold), emanating from swirling stalks and tendrils, author's name enclosed by wreath at center, spine compartments and turn-ins similarly decorated, purportedly a Doves Binding (signed "The Doves Bindery/19C-S12" on tear turn-in), but actually a fake.   Phillip J. Pirages   33-62   1996 $4,500.00

BROWNING, ROBERT 1812-1889   Dramatis Personae. London: T. J. Cobden-Sanderson at the Doves Press, 1910. Limited to 250 copies, large 8vo; 204 pages; printed in red and black; original vellum (Doves Bindery), gilt spine, slipcase.   Kenneth Karmiole 1NS-93   1996 $475.00

COBDEN-SANDERSON, THOMAS JAMES 1840-1922   London, A Paper Read at a Meeting of the Art Workers Guild...March 6, 1891. Doves Press, Presented to the Subscribers, 1906. One of 300 copies on paper (there were also five on vellum); 9 1/4 x 6 1/2 inches; 7, (1) pages; bound in fine deep blue morocco by Doves Bindery, cover frames of two spaced gilt fillets, enclosing a double strapwork panel, spine with raised bands, simple gilt ruled compartments and gilt lettering turn-ins with two gilt rules, rear turn-in signed '19 C-S 19'; slight mottling to text, otherwise an excellent copy in bright, appealing binding, without any significant wear.   Phillip J. Pirages   33-184   1996 $650.00

GOETHE, JOHANN WOLFGANG VON 1749-1832   Iphigenie auf Tauris: Ein Schauspiel. Doves Press, 1912. One of 32 copies on vellum (12 of which had gold initials, there were 200 copies printed on paper); 9 1/4 x 6 3/4 inches; 110 pages, (1) leaf (colophon); printed in red and black, with tiny stamped cipher of Ernst Kyriss; bound by Doves Bindery in 1913 in Russet morocco, covers and turn-ins with simple gilt rule borders, raised bands, spine compartments ruled and titled in gilt, all edges gilt, except for inevitable slight discoloration of the vellum flyleaves where they touch the facing leather turn-ins, this is a virtually mint copy in unworn and extremely pleasing Doves binding.   Phillip J. Pirages   33-187   1996 $8,750.00

LA MOTTE FOUQUE, FRIEDRICH HEINRICH KARL, FREIHERR DE 1777-1843   Undine and Other Tales. Leipzig: 1867. Small 8vo; pages (6), 361; full green crushed morocco (backstrip and edges faded to tan), 6 sections of backstrip lettered and decorated in gold wtih four groups of three 3 pointed leaves connected by intertwined stems within ogee border, in each compartment, edges ruled and turn-ins triple-ruled with leaf and dot decoration at corners, signed "The Doves Bindery 1894"; contemporary inscripiton to Cecil Boyle with his bookplate carelessly pasted to endpaper.   Claude Cox   107-17   1996   £180.00

MORRIS, WILLIAM 1834-1896   Signs of Change: Seven Lectures Delivered On Various Occasions. London: Reeves and Turner, 1888. 1st edition; 7 1/2 x 5 1/3 inches; viii, (2), 202 pages; very pleasing apple green crushed morocco, handsomely gilt by the Doves Bindery (signed and dated 1903 on rear turn-in), covers with ususal single gilt rule frame accompanied by spaced gilt dots, spine handsomely gilt in compartments densely occupied by large and small oak leaves and circlets, wide turn-ins with triple gilt fillet and gilt foliate ornament at corners, edges gilt and gauffered, spine just slightly and evenly sunned, free endpapers with shadow from turn-ins (as always), otherwise fine in extremely attractive binding; scarce; with slip laid in reading "61. Signs of Change by William Morris. London, 1888...Lent by Mrs. George M. Millard". Forman 104; Tidcombe 555 (for binding).   Phillip J. Pirages   33-61   1996 $1,500.00

SHELLEY, PERCY BYSSHE 1792-1822   Poems. London: Doves Press, 1914. One of 212 copies, one of 200 on paper. 4to; pages 181; printed in red and black, original limp vellum, spine lettered in gilt, by the Doves Bindery, uncut, excellent.   Simon Finch   24-78   1996   £550.00

TACITUS, CORNELIUS   De Vita Moribus Iulii Agricolae Liber. Hammersmith: Doves Press, 1900. One of 225 copies; small 4to; 33 pages; bound at the Doves Bindery in full flexible vellum, very slightly dusty, very nice.   Hermitage   SP95-869   1996 $1,000.00

WORDSWORTH, WILLIAM 1770-1850   The Prelude. Doves Press, 1915. One of 10 copies on vellum (there were also 155 on paper); 9 1/4 x 6 1/2 inches; 301, (1) pages; extraordinarily fine russet morocco, elaborately and beautifully gilt by the Doves Bindery (signed '19 C-S 19' on rear turn-in), covers framed by multiple gilt rules and featuring lovely intricate cornerpieces consisting of a rose surrounded by criclets and four sprigs of five oak leaves, there corner decorations connected by tendrils (which support 8 additional, smaller sprigs of oak), front cover with titling and dates, spine densely gilt in compartments filled with the same decoration as used for the cornerpieces, turn-ins with four parallel gilt rules and with oak leaves and circlets at corners, vellum pastedowns and flyleaves, all edges gilt, binding identical to Tidcombe 795; front flyleaf with tiny ownership stamp of Ernst Kyriss. Only mostr tirivial imperfections, virtually pristine.   Phillip J. Pirages   33-190   1996 $15,000.00

BINDING - DULAU

AKENSIDE, MARK 1721-1770   An Ode to the Country Gentlemen of England. London: printed for R. and J. Dodsley, and sold by M. Cooper, 1758. 1st edition; 4to; modern panelled calf, spine and inner dentelles gilt, by Dulau & Co. (slight rubbing); very good, bookplate of Lord Esher. Rothschild 25; Iolo Williams p. 93; CBEL II 637.   Ximenes 109-3   1996 $125.00

BINDING - EDMONDS & REMNANTS

DAVIS, NATHAN   Ruined Cities Within the Numidian and Carthaginian Territories. London: John Murray, 1862. 1st edition; demy 8vo; (xvi), (392), 12 pages; illustrations, plates, folding map; original binding, gilt, by Edmonds & Remnants, with their ticket, expertly restored, cloth repaired, endpapers replaced, good.   Ash Rare Books   Zenzybyr-24   1996   £125.00

ELIOT, GEORGE, PSEUD. 1819-1880   The Mill on the Floss. London: William Blackwood and Sons, 1860. 1st edition; 8vo; 3 volumes; (viii), 362; (320), (viii), (314) pages, 16 page catalog; original brown blindstamped cloth, spines gilt, Carter's "B" binding with Edmonds & Remnants' ticket, though without the integral ad leaf and blank found in some copies; very slight wear to a couple of corners, cloth marked and bit darkened, stitching of volume 1 little loose, spine of volume 3 faded; good.   Robert Clark   38-239   1996   £270.00

LIVINGSTONE, DAVID 1813-1873   Missionary Travels and Researches in South Africa. London: John Murray, 1857. 1st edition; 1st issue, with colored frontispiece; demy 8vo; (x), 688), 8 pages, folding frontispiece, plates, some colored, illustrations, maps; original cloth by Edmonds & Remnants, with their ticket, little light wear, frontispiece slightly worn and spotted, endpapers strained, few minor marks, but very good in original binding.   Ash Rare Books   Zenzybyr-62   1996   £350.00

BINDING - EDMONDSON

SHERIDAN, THOMAS   A Course of Lectures on Elocution; Together with Two Dissertations on Language; and Some Other Tracts Relative to those Subjects. London: printed for J. Dodsley, 1781. Uncut in 19th century half calf by Edmondson & Co., Skipton, brown label, very good. Alston VI 359.5.   Jarndyce 103-338   1996   £80.00

BINDING - EDWARDS

NICHOLS, JOHN   Miscellaneous Tracts by the Late William Bowyer, Printer, F.S.A. and Several of His Learned Friends... Edinburgh: printed by and for the editor, 1775. 1st edition; 4to; vignette on title; contemporary "Etruscan" calf by Edwards of Halifax bindery, with central tree calf panel, surrounded by a border of stained classical palmette, and gilt Greek-key pattern roll, rebacked, spine gilt, label, all edges gilt, nice. Anthony W. Laywood   108-98   1996   £175.00

BINDING - EMBROIDERED

BIBLE. ENGLISH - 1635   The Whole Booke of Psalmes Collected into English Meeter by T. Sternhold, I. Hopkins and Others. London: Imprinted for the Company of Stationers, 1635. 32mo; roman letter; contemporary ivory stain embroidered with scrolling and raised flowers in silver thread covered in colored silks, enhanced with sequins, few missing, all edges gilt, apart from some minor tear at extremities and some yellowing of satin through age, this delicate binding is in very fine condition; preserved in velvet lined cloth box.   H. M. Fletcher 121-78   1996   £2,000.00

CARROTHERS, JULIA D.   Japan's Year. Tokyo: T. Hasegawa, 1905. 1st edition; 9 3/4 x 7 1/4 inches; 76 pages, printed on one side only and unopened at fore edge; hand painted illustrations on nearly every page, many of them full leaf, as well as 3 inserted color plates on highly textured paper, done by 'Japanese artists'; fine original embroidered silk binding, featuring many bright flowers in several colors and considerable gold on black background, boards laced on with purple tasseled cords, double slipcases (somewhat worn and with obvious tape repairs); portions of the black silk background bit threadbare at some edges, but flowers in fine, bright condition, internally excellent.   Phillip J. Pirages 33-316   1996 $300.00

BINDING - EVETTS

FITZGERALD, FRANCIS SCOTT KEY 1896-1940   The Great Gatsby. New York: Limited Editions Club, 1980. One of 2000 numbered copies, signed by artist; illustrations by Fred Meyer; pictorial cloth by Deborah M. Evetts; fine in publisher's slipcase.   Hermitage SP95-982   1996 $125.00

BINDING - FAZAKERLEY

OMAR KHAYYAM   The Rubaiyat of Omar Khayyam. Boston: Riverside Press/London: Bernard Quaritch, n.d. 1884. Folio; illustrated titlepage, frontispiece and 50 full page plates, from drawings by Elihu Vedder (some very sight foxing); superbly bound in full crimson morocco, elaborate gilt design on both covers of the tree of life surrounded by an archway of two pillars with 12 oval ornaments rising and meeting at a peak, outer margins are four and one line with wide leafy border, spine similarly decorated, wide inside morocco doublures, silk endpapers, bound by Fazakerley of Liverpool, enclosed in silk lined box case. Charles W. Traylen 117-175 1996 £1,800.00

BINDING - FINE BINDERY

GANT, ROLAND   Steps to the River. Lower Marston, Risbury, Herefordshire: Whittington Press, 1995. One of 40 special copies thus, from an edition of 200 copies, numbered and signed by poet and artist; with set of signed artist's proofs of engravings laid in matching green folder; all in dark green slipcase; fine; bound by the Fine Bindery with green cloth spine, paper title label, green plant patterned paper over board sides printed from wood engraving by artist. Joshua Heller 21-280 1996 $270.00

BINDING - FISHER

BROOKE, FULKE GREVILLE, 1ST BARON 1554-1628   Caelica. Newtown: Gregynog Press, 1936, i.e. 1937. One of 15 copies specially bound (of a total edition of 225); 9 1/4 x 6 1/4 inches; xiii, (1), 149, (1) pages, (1) leaf (colophon); title printed in red and black, initials and colophon in red; lovely heavy grained slate blue levant morocco by Gregynog Press Bindery (signed in gilt on rear turn-in by Blair Hughes-Stanton and George Fisher), dec. in all over design featuring a total of 16 inset vellum stars on covers and spine, vellum stars stained a sublte shade pink and connected by gilt and blind fillets, raised bands, top edge gilt, other edges untrimmed, in somewhat faded and soiled folding cloth box, with paper label on spine, except for faint shadow of leather turn-ins on facing flyleaves, an extremely fine copy, especially clean inside and out, showing no signs of use. Harrop 36. Phillip J. Pirages 33-260 1996 $6,500.00

DAVIES, WILLIAM HENRY 1871-1940   The Lovers' Song-Book. Newtown: Gregynog Press, 1933. One of 19 copies specially bound, of a total edition of 250; 9 1/4 x 6 1/4 inches; v, (1), 30 pages, (1) leaf (colophon); printed on Japanese vellum, green initials, ruled in green; printer's device in green on title; bound by the Gregynog Press Bindery (signed in gilt by George Fisher on rear turn-in) in fine Emerald green polished levant morocco, two raised bands, covers, spine and turn-ins tooled in gilt with foliate sprays rising vertically from double line of lozenges, spine titled in gilt, top edge gilt, other edges untrimmed, in custom made folding cloth box with paper labels (somewhat soiled), a choice copy, virtually as bright and clean as when it was produced. Harrop 28. Phillip J. Pirages 33-261 1996 $4,250.00

GRUFFYDD, W. J.   Caniadau. Newtown: Gregynog Press, 1932. One of 25 specially bound copies, of a total edition of 25; 10 1/4 x 7 1/2 inches; vii, (1), 101, (1) pages, (1) leaf (colophon); printed in russet and black on stone colored handmade paper; 4 full page wood engravings as well as shadow initials by Blair Hughes-Stanton; very handsome brown crushed levant morocco by the Gregynog Press Bindery (signed in gilt by Blair Hughes-Stanton and George Fisher on turn-in), panel of 24 closely spaced gilt lines connecting the covers across the spine with half panels on each cover continuing around board edges onto turn-ins, raised bands, spine titled in gilt, top edge gilt, other edges untrimmed; remarkably fine, especially bright and clean. Harrop 21. Phillip J. Pirages 33-262 1996 $5,500.00

OMAR KHAYYAM   Penillion. (Rubaiyat in Welsh). Newtown: Gregynog Press, 1928. One of 25 copies specially bound, out of a total edition of 210; 10 x 7 1/4 inches; xvi, 30 pages; printer's device on title, 10 wood engravings in text by R. A. Maynard, printed in blue and black; bound by Gregynog Press Bindery in fine deep blue polished levant morocco (signed by George Fisher in gilt on rear turn-in), raised bands, spine with gilt titling, two gilt rules on turn-ins, top edge gilt, other edges untrimmed; perhaps very slight variation in color of leather, but an extremely fine copy, virtually pristine internally. Harrop 13. Phillip J. Pirages 33-263 1996 $3,750.00

PEACOCK, THOMAS LOVE   The Misfortunes of Elphin. Newtown: Gregynog Press, 1928. One of 25 specially bound copies of a total edition of 250; 9 3/4 x 6 1/2 inches; 2 p.l., 119, (1) pages; 21 wood engravings as headpieces and tailpieces, by H. W. Bray, device in colophon; lovely crimson morocco by Gregynog (signed in gilt by Horace Bray and George Fisher on rear turn-in); covers with single gilt rule frame, upper cover with gilt design of two hand-held goblets with wine pouring from one to the other (though with considerable gilt spillage), gilt ruled spine compartments between raised bands, one compartment with gilt titling, turn-ins with double gilt rule, top edge gilt, other edges untrimmed; a faultless copy. Harrop 12. Phillip J. Pirages 33-264 1996 $4,500.00

BINDING - FISHER

ROSSETTI, CHRISTINA 1830-1894   Poems Chosen By Walter De La Mare. Newtown: Gregynog Press, 1930. One of 25 copies, specially bound, of a total edition of 300; 9 1/4 x 6 1/2 inches; xliii, (1), 107, (1) pages; initial openings and frontispiece portrait by Maynard after drawings by Dante Gabriel Rossetti, shoulder notes printed in red; fine very animated scarlet morocco by Gregynog Press Bindery (signed by R. Ashwin Maynard and George Fisher on rear turn-in), covers tooled in gilt with 2 large cruciform foliate ornaments elaborated with diagonal blind and gilt decoration (something like evergreen leaves), ornaments on field of gold dots, covers framed by gilt and blind rules, fomr which emanate a series of similar gilt and blind evergreen decorations, spine with raised bands, panels in blind and gilt ttling, board edges ruled in gilt, turn-ins with double gilt rule, top edge gilt, other edges untrimmed, in substantial and attractive morocco backed folding cloth box, fleece lined, spine with raised bands; extremely fine. Harrop 15. Phillip J. Pirages 33-266 1996 $5,500.00

THOMAS, EDWARD   Selected Poems. Newtown: Gregynog Press, 1927. One of 25 copies specially bound of a total edition of 275; 9 1/4 x 6 1/4 inches; xix, (1), 95, (1) pages; device on title, red printer's device in colophon; title printed in blue and black, initials in red, ruled in blue; very fine polished blue levant morocco by the Gregynog Press Bindery (signed by R. Ashwin Maynard and George Fisher on rear turn-in), covers with 3 overlapping gilt lozenges made of leaf sprays, connected by gilt decoration to double gilt rule frame, raised bands, spine titled in gilt with similar gilt decoration at either end, double gilt rule on turn-ins, marbled endpapers, top edge gilt, other edges untrimmed, in blue cloth chemise and matching slipcase, blue morocco label on spine, spine leather perhaps just a shade lighter than covers, but remarkably fine copy otherwise of the first Gregynog book to be printed on Japanese vellum. Harrop 6. Phillip J. Pirages 33-267 1996 $4,500.00

BINDING - FORNARO

BORGES, JORGE LUIS   Siete Poemas Sajones. Seven Saxon Poems. Verona: Plain Wrapper Press, 1974. Limited to 120 copies, signed by author and artist; folio; 37 pages; low relief images by Arnaldo Pomodor; binding by Marcello Fornaro of unbleached vellum, inset with 3 striking gold plated bronze bas-relief plates by Pomodoro, mounted in recessed panels on front cover, housed in cloth covered wooden box, which also displays relief-etched brass panel by Pomodoro on front cover. Smyth 14. Bromer Booksellers 87-253 1996 $8,000.00

BINDING - THOMAS FOWLER

REA, JOHN   Flora; seu de Florum Cultura. Or, a Complete Florilege, Furnished with all Requisites Belonging to a Florist. London: by J. G. for Richard Marriott, 1665. 1st edition; folio; (24), 239, (4) pages, including "Mind of the front" leaf, added engraved title, 8 engraved plates, woodcut initials and headpieces, title printed in red and black; calf, spine gilt by Thomas Fowler, with his printed label "Bound for the library/of the/ right Honorable Lord Rolle/ at Stevenstone/, by Thomas Fowler, printer & bookbinder,/ Great Torrington. Anno Domini 1834". Absolutely pristine, wide margined copy in very good, very slightly rubbed, ticketed binding. Hunt 301; Wing R421. Joseph J. Felcone 64-35 1996 $2,800.00

BINDING - JOHN FOX

HAMILTON, THOMAS   The Youth and Manhood of Cyril Thornton. Edinburgh: William Blackwood, and T. Cadell, London, 1827. 1st edition; 8vo; 3 volumes; contemporary half red morocco, gilt, spines gilt, binder's tickets of John Fox and Son of Pontefract. Spines bit faded and rubbed, nice set, complete with half titles; Ramsden p. 75; Sadleir 1101; Wolff 2948; Block p. 96; CBEL III 730. Ximenes 109-149 1996 $450.00

BINDING - FROST

ACKERMANN, RUDOLPH 1764-1834   The History of the Colleges of Winchester, Eton and Westminster, with the Charter-House, the Schools of St. Paul's, Merchant Taylor's and Rugby and the Free-School of Christ's Hospital. London: Ackermann, 1816. 4to; 3ff. (lacks binder's leaf), pages 56, 72, 40, 32, 43, 34, 27, 22, 48 hand colored aquatint plates, plate 26 in second state, few plates offset, as usual; later red straight grain morocco gilt, all edges gilt, by Frost. Abbey scenery 438. Marlborough 162-2 1996 £3,500.00

BINDING - GARCIA-GUTIERREZ

GRAVES, ROBERT 1895-1985   Across the Gulf. Deja, Mallorca: 1992. Limited to 175 copies; signed by editors, printer and binder; printed on handmade paper; bound by Carmen Garcia-Gutierrez, fine in protective wrapper. Words Etcetera 94-527 1996 £95.00

BINDING - GARCIA-GUTIERREZ

GRAVES, ROBERT 1895-1985   Across the Gulf; Late Poems. Deya: New Seizin Press, 1992. i.e. 1994. One of 175 numbered copies; signed by all 3 editors, printer and binder; large 8vo; handset 18 pt Bembo by Tomas Graves on paper specially made by Lluis Morera; double title spread in blue and black; decorated boards by Carmen Garcia-Gutierrez; fine.   Bertram Rota 272-313 1996 £80.00

BINDING - LOUISE GENEST

ERTE   Erte Maquettes. Hyattsville: Rebecca Press, 1984. Limited to 2200 copies, signed by Rebecca Bingham, the publisher; 1 1/2 x 2 1/8 inches; 58 pages, 42 color design reproductions; in 1994 designer binding of aqua morocco by Louise Genest, a Canadian binder, on each cover, there are four rectangular onlays of metallic foils in tones of gold, bronze, copper and red, one rectangle on each cover cut out to shape of a fashion plate, leaving silhouette of female form showing through to aqua cover; foil fashion plate is then onlaid to another part of the cover, doublures are of mottled gold foil on paper, housed in box of handmade aqua paper, accented with metallic foil. Mint.   Bromer Booksellers 87-183 1996 $1,200.00

BINDING - GOSDEN

DEKKER, THOMAS   The Gull's Hornbook. Bristol: Gutch, 1812. 4to; title printed in red and black, vii pages, 2 ff., 177 pages, 6 ff; calf, covers gilt and blindstamped with single rule and broad roll tool borders spine gilt in seven panels with broad raised bands, all edges gilt, blue silk endpapers, by Thomas Gosden, with his engraved label inside upper cover, joints little weak, preserved in recent cloth slipcase. Marlborough 160-66 1996 £250.00

BINDING - GRAY

BUNYAN, JOHN 1628-1688   The Pilgrim's Progress. London: Cassell, Petter and Galpin, 4to; engraved illustrations and decorations by H. C. Selous and M. Paolo Priolo; contemporary binding by Gray of Cambridge in full dark blue calf, spine in compartments, double gilt ruled, elaborately tooled in gilt on spine; fresh copy; armorial binding. Gleeson White, English Ills. The Sixties 123.   Barbara Stone 70-43 1996 £75.00

MILLER, JEFFREY   Paul Bowles: a Descriptive Bibliography. Santa Barbara: Black Sparrow, 1986. One of 26 lettered copies; fine in unprinted glassine as issued; handbound by Earle Gray; signed by author and by Bowles; uncommon issue.   Between the Covers 42-63 1996 $450.00

BINDING - GREENHILL

RIDLEY, MARK   A Short Treatise of Magneticall Bodies and Motions. London: Printed by Nicholas Okes, 1613. 1st edition; 2nd issue with errata on recto of leaf X3; small quarto; (14), 157, (1) pages; without initial and final blanks, engraved title by R. Elstrak, engraved portrait, 21 engravings, 2 maps, without volvelle on T1; bound by Elizabeth Greenhill in full red morocco, gilt single rule border on covers, gilt spine with raised bands, gilt board edges and turn-ins, all edges gilt, closely trimmed, cutting into a few lines of text, some headlines and catchwords, shaving a few platemarks, few leaves with very skillful paper restoration, overall very good. Very rare. Honeyman 2649; Sabin 71297; STC 21045.5. Wheeler Gift 86.   Heritage Book Shop 196-182 1996 $6,000.00

BINDING - GREGYNOG BINDER

HOPKINS, GERARD MANLEY   Pied Beauty. London: Simon King Press, 1994. Limited to 100 numbered copies; folio; pages (22), four full page linocut illustrations, printed in 18 pt. Baskerville of 176gsm Mohawk paper; with an additional set of the prints, signed and numbered in stiff paper folder; bound by Alan Wood at the Gregynog Bindery in quarter blue morocco lettered in gold, paste paper boards, with an additional set of prints, signed and numbered, in stiff paper folder.   Claude Cox 107-74B 1996 £150.00

BUTLER, SAMUEL 1835-1902   Erewhon. Newtown: Gregynog Press, 1923. Number 59 of 300 copies; pages (2), 266, (1); 27 illustrations by Blair Hughes-Stanton; original brown calf, by Gregynog bindery, binding lightly scratched, otherwise very good to nice.   James Fenning 133-140 1996 £135.00

BINDING - GREGYNOG BINDER

XENOPHON   Cyrupaedia: the Institution and Life of Cyrus, the First of that Name, King of the Persians. Newtown: Gregynog Press, 1936. One of 150 copies, printed and signed by Haberly; folio; decorated hand colored initials by Loyd Haberly; full grey morocco with emblematic center medallion and corner fleurons inlaid in red and green leather, gilt panelled spine, raised bands, gilt top by Gregynog Bindery.   Appelfeld Gallery 54-110 1996 $1,500.00

BINDING - GREGYNOG PRESS BINDERY

DAVIES, WILLIAM HENRY 1871-1940   The Lovers' Song-Book. Newtown: Gregynog Press, 1933. One of 19 copies specially bound, of a total edition of 250; 9 1/4 x 6 1/4 inches; v, (1), 30 pages, (1) leaf (colophon); printed on Japanese vellum, green initials, ruled in green; printer's device in green on title; bound by the Gregynog Press Bindery (signed in gilt by George Fisher on rear turn-in) in fine Emerald green polished levant morocco, two raised bands, covers, spine and turn-ins tooled in gilt with foliate sprays rising vertically from double line of lozenges, spine titled in gilt, top edge gilt, other edges untrimmed, in custom made folding cloth box with paper labels (somewhat soiled), a choice copy, virtually as bright and clean as when it was produced. Harrop 28.   Phillip J. Pirages 33-261 1996 $4,250.00

OMAR KHAYYAM   Penillion. (Rubaiyat in Welsh). Newtown: Gregynog Press, 1928. One of 25 copies specially bound, out of a total edition of 210; 10 x 7 1/4 inches; xvi, 30 pages, (1) leaf; printer's device on title, 10 wood engravings in text by R. A. Maynard, printed in blue and black; bound by Gregynog Press Bindery in fine deep blue polished levant morocco (signed by George Fisher in gilt on rear turn-in), raised bands, spine with gilt titling, two gilt rules on turn-ins, top edge gilt, other edges untrimmed; perhaps very slight variation in color of leather, but an extremely fine copy, virtually pristine internally. Harrop 13.   Phillip J. Pirages 33-263 1996 $3,750.00

BINDING - GRIEVE

MORRIS, FRANCIS ORPEN 1810-1893   A Natural History of British Moths, Accurately Delineating Every Known Species. Edinburgh: 1871. 1st edition; royal 8vo; 4 volumes; titles in red and black, 132 hand colored plates, some 1933 figures; beautiful set in half brown straight grained morocco, mottled sides, gilt spines, ornaments, gilt tops, bound by Andy Grieve.   Charles W. Traylen 117-322 1996 £300.00

BINDING - GROSS

BOYLE, ELEANOR VERE   A Dream Book. London: Sampson Low, Son and Marston, 1870. Folio; 12 drawings; three quarter crushed green morocco over pebbled green cloth, spine, slightly sunned with five raised bands and title in gilt, rare; stamped on front free endleaf "C. Gross, Binder to the Queen." The Duke of Northumberland's bookplate. Reid p. 253; Baskin p. 55.   Book Block 32-22 1996 $825.00

BINDING - GUETANT

DELLOYE, H. L.   Chants et Chansons Populaires de la France... Paris: Felix Locquin, imprimeur, Librairie de Garnier, freres, 1843. 1st edition; super royal 8vo; 3 volumes; steel engraved illustrations, musical notation; late 19th century dark green straight grain full morocco, sides ruled in gilt with triple fillet, spines lettered and decorated in gilt, gilt inner dentelles, spot marbled endpapers, silk bookmarks, gilt edges, by L. Guetant (spines evenly sunned); excellent set.   Simon Finch 24-68 1996 £1,500.00

BINDING - GUILD OF WOMEN BINDERS

BROWNING, ROBERT 1812-1889   Paracelsus. London: published by Effingham Wilson, 1835. 1st edition; small 8vo; full tan morocco, covers elaborately decorated with all over gilt floral pattern, spine and inner dentelles, all edges gilt, by the League of Women Binders; very rare, half title removed, otherwise very good. Hayward 252.   Ximenes 108-382 1996 $750.00

LECTIUS, JACOBUS   Poetae Graeci Veteres Carminis Heroici Scriptores Qui Extant, Omnes. Aureliae Allobrogum (i.e. Geneva): sumptibus Caldorianae Societatis, 1606. Folio; pages (vi), (ii) blank, (xvi), 739, (i) blank, 624, (xxii), apparently lacks rT8 (final blank), titlepage in red and black, title in Greek at head of titlepage, parallel Greek and Latin texts; late 19th century tan morocco with embossed relief dec. by Mrs. A. S. Macdonald of the Guild of Women Binders, depicting on the upper cover Hermes descending, surrounded by the sacred fire of Olympus and on the lower cover a portrait of Ben Jonson, (this was his copy) within a surround of his ownership inscription, bookplates, binding, lightly rubbed, titlepage dusty and reinforced on verso at inner margin at time of rebinding, some edges little frayed, occasional marginal worming; Simon Finch 24-134 1996 £2,250.00

BINDING - GUILD OF WOMEN BINDERS

MORRIS, WILLIAM 1834-1896   Love is Enough, or the Freeing of Pharamond: a Morality. Hammersmith: Kelmscott Press, 1897/98. Limited to 308 copies, this one of 300; folio; pages (iv), 90, (1), printed in Troy and Chaucer types in red and black, woodcut initials in blue and black, first page of text in wise woodcut border, numerous partial borders, frontispiece and another full page woodcut at end by W. H. Hooper after Burne-Jones; light brown morocco, spine and sides decorated in dark brown with flowers on long stems, spine lettered in brown, wise inner dentelles with border of small circles gilt, top edge gilt, others uncut, marbled endpapers by the Guild of Women Binders, some soiling, extremities bumped, internally an excellent copy. Cockerell 52.   Simon Finch   24-139   1996 £1,750.00

BINDING - HADDON CRAFTSMEN

BERRY, WENDELL   November Twenty-Six Nineteen Hundred Sixty Three. New York: Braziller, 1964. 1st edition; one of an unspecified number of copies, signed by Shahn and Berry; oblong large 8vo; 1 tipped in color plate, 12 black and white illustrations by Ben Shahn, white cloth, stamped black on spine and upper cover, fine, publisher's black cloth slipcase, with printed paper label. Bound by Haddon Craftsmen.   George J. Houle   68-76   1996 $350.00

BINDING - ROBERT HADRILL

CAMPBELL, KEN   Night Feet on Earth: a Poem. 1987. One of 50 copies, numbered and signed by Campbell; folio; printed in 4 colors on Saunders mouldmade; handbound in boards by Robert Hadrill; fine in slipcase.   Bertram Rota   272-74   1996 £200.00

BINDING - HARCOURT BINDERY

LEA, TOM 1907-   The Hands of Cantu. Boston and Toronto: Little, Brown and Co., 1964. 1st edition; number 40 of only 100 numbered copies; 244 pages; specially printed on mouldmade Arches paper and signed by author; illustrations by author, including mounted frontispiece in color; bound by Harcourt Bindery in full brown crushed levant morocco, raised bands, gilt lettered spine, marbled endpapers, top edge gilt, mint, uncut, in publisher's cloth slipcase; accompanied by a signed and dated print by Lea, additionally, the print with his copy has a presentation inscription signed by Lea. Rare.   Argonaut Book Shop   113-403   1996 $3,000.00

SAHAGUN, FRAY BERNADINO DE   Historia General de las Cosas de Nueva Espana. Mexico: Fomento Cultural Benemex, 1982. Limited to 500 copies; large quarto; 2 volumes, xxii, 745 pages, numbered consecutively; 80 full page colorplates reproduced from original ms.; morocco backed red silk covered boards by the Harcourt Bindery, housed in original slipcases. Mint.   Bromer Booksellers   87-259   1996 $2,500.00

STRICKLAND, AGNES   Lives of the Queens of England. Philadelphia: printed only for subscribers by George Barrie & Sons, 1902. One of 1000 copies; 8 3/4 x 5 3/4 inches; 16 volumes, printed on Japanese vellum paper, 180 photogravure plates, partly printed in red; very fine highly dec. inlaid purple mor. flamboyantly gilt, by Harcourt Bindery, covers with oval panelling featuring delicate voluted ornaments & lg. rose of inlaid red morocco in each corner, spines similarly dec. in handsome compartments, 4 of them on each vol. containing a smaller inlaid rose, motif continued on wide gilt dec. turn-ins (inside of each cover with 2 more inlaid roses, making a total of 16 roses per vol)., marbled endpapers, top edge gilt, small portions of two joints very skillfully and almost invisibly repaired; one cover with couple of superficial scratches, 2 or 3 covers with sl. dulling, spines just sl. & uniformly faded, but very fine set in all other ways, almost entirely bright and clean & with scarcely any signs of use, virtually pristine internally; exceptionally pretty set.   Phillip J. Pirages   33-472   1996 $4,500.00

THEROUX, ALEXANDER   Watergraphs. Boston: Base Canard, 1994. 1st book edition, one of 100 copies; bound in linen at the Harcourt bindery and signed by author.   Lame Duck Books   19-536   1996 $100.00

BINDING - HATCHARDS

DICKENS, CHARLES 1812-1870   The Battle of Life. London: Bradbury & Evans, 1846. 1st edition; (fourth state); foolscap 8vo; frontispiece and vignette titlepage and 11 illustrations finely bound in half crimson morocco, gilt top, for Hatchards. Brilliant copy. Eckels p. 127-130.   Charles W. Traylen   117-98   1996 £150.00

BINDING - HATCHARDS

DICKENS, CHARLES 1812-1870   Oliver Twist; or, The Parish Boy's Progress. London: Richard Bentley, 1838. 1st edition; 1st issue with the Boz titlepages and the 'Fireside' plate facing p. 313 in volume 3, r pages of publisher's ads at end of volume 1 & leaf of ads beginning of volume 3; 8vo; 3 volumes; frontispiece to each volume, 21 etchings by George Cruikshank; half red morocco, lettered in gilt on spine, gilt tops, choicely bound for Hatchards. Exceptionally fine; Eckels p. 52.   Charles W. Traylen   117-104   1996 £1,500.00

GREAT BRITAIN. LAWS, STATUTES, ETC. - 1946   Coal Industry Nationalization Act, 1946. London: HMSO, 1946. 1st edition; interleaved throughout with blank leaves; full vellum covers, bound by Hatchards, the words "The Rt. Hon. Emanuel Shinwell M.P." are stamped in gilt on upper cover, top edge gilt, covers bowed and slightly marked and soiled, spine and cover edges darkened, front free endpaper slightly creased, edges slightly browned; very good. Signed by all members of the first National Coal Board.   Ulysses   39-113   1996 £475.00

HAWKER, PETER   Instructions to Young Sportsmen in all that Relates to Guns and Shooting. London: printed for Longman, Hurst, Rees, Orme, Brown and Green, 1824. 3rd edition; royal 8vo; pages xxii, 470, 16 page publisher's catalog, 10 aquatint or engraved plates, 4 of which are hand colored, fine; handsomely bound (for Hatchards) in full green morocco, spine with raised bands, and lettered and ruled in gilt, marbled endpapers, edges uncut; fine. Tooley 256; Abbey Life 389; Schwerdt I p. 235.   Sotheran   PN32-75   1996 £850.00

HERVEY, JOHN   Memoirs of the Reign of George the Second... London: John Murray, 1848. 1st edition; 8vo; 2 volumes, lxvi, 520; vii, 593 pages; contemporary three quarter maroon morocco by Hatchards of Picadilly with raised bands, top edge gilt, attractive set.   Chapel Hill   94-223   1996 $175.00

IRELAND, ALEXANDER   The Book-Lover's Enchiridion. London: and New York: Macmillan, 1894. 7 x 5 inches; xviii, 511 pages; largely unopened, title in red and black; very pretty green straight grain half morocco by Hatchards, pale green cloth sides, spine compartments and broad raised bands, ruled in gilt, marbled endpapers, top edge gilt, very fine.   Phillip J. Pirages   33-314   1996 $100.00

JACKSON, CATHERINE HANNAH CHARLOTTE   Works (On French History). London: John C. Nimmo, 1899. 8 3/4 x 6 1/4 inches; 14 volumes; 113 plates, printed tissue guards, titles printed in red and black, plates printed on fine Japanese vellum; fine burnt orange straight grain morocco by Hatchards, covers simply panelled in gilt, flat spines titled and attractively decorated in gilt with elongated compartments at top and bottom, featuring antique volutes, marbled endpapers, top edge gilt, other edges untrimmed, spines slightly and uniformly faded, few tiny paint flecks on one cover, bit of wear to corners, small offensive dent at top of one spine, little soiling to boards, but all these imperfections minor, the set generally in fine condition, with joints showing scarcely any wear and with the bindings quite handsome.   Phillip J. Pirages   33-315   1996 $1,250.00

PRAED, WINTHROP MACKWORTH   The Poems. London: Edward Moxon & Co., 1864. 2nd edition; small 8vo; 2 volumes; half red morocco, spines decorated in compartments to an art nouveau design, gilt lettered in second and third compartments and with date in gilt at foot, pink cloth sides, marbled endpapers, top edges gilt, others uncut; for Hatchards.   Simon Finch   24-192   1996 £110.00

BINDING - HATHAWAY

PRY, PAUL, PSEUD.   Oddities of London Life. London: Richard Bentley, 1838. 8vo; 2 volumes, 316, 234 pages; 22 engraved plates; 19th century three quarter morocco by F. P. Hathaway, Boston, with original green cloth covers and spine titles tipped to pastedowns, near fine, with bookplate of Lucius Poole, Boston.   Chapel Hill   94-49   1996 $200.00

BINDING - HAYDAY

BRUTON, JOHN HILL   Life and Correspondence of David Hume. Edinburgh: William Tait, 1846. 1st edition; 8vo; 2 volumes, xvii, (1), 480; vii, (1), 534 pages, bound without half titles; frontispiece, folding facsimile letter in volume 1, 2 facsimiles of Hume's holograph in volume 2; contemporary calf, gilt and panelled, contrasting labels and marbled edges by Hayday; fine; from the 19th century library of Lord Belper with his bookplate. Jessop p. 46; Mossner p. 636; not in Chuo.   John Drury   82-117   1996 £275.00

BINDING - HAYDAY

CHURCH OF ENGLAND. BOOK OF COMMON PRAYER   The Book of Common Prayer...Together with the Psalter. Oxford: University Press, 1840. 8vo; crushed red morocco over bevelled boards decorated in blind, with panels and rules extending from the four sets of double raised bands on spine, which has title information stamped thereon in gilt, the top and bottom and fore edge have been elaborately decorated through the application of gilt, guaffering and illumination, each end contains a religious admonition lettered on a medieval style banderole, the painting and gauffering with its wide selection of tools and fields of pointelles, is of high quality and the decoration is in wonderfully fresh condition owing to presence of original leather slipcase, binding is signed Hayday on lower front turn-in.   Book Block 32-24 1996 $975.00

HERBERT, GEORGE   The Works in Prose and Verse. London: William Pickering, 1853. 9 x 6 inches; 2 volumes; frontispiece in each volume 2 small woodcut seals, woodcut device on each title, woodcut headpieces, tailpieces and initials; frontispieces and endpapers bit foxed and darkened, barely perceptible wear to leather, but bindings and text almost flawless; fine original black morocco (probably by Hayday), covers with double gilt rule frame and elaborate blind tooled center panel, spines with gilt decorated raised bands and compartments elaborately stamped in blind, board edges and turn-ins densely gilt in an antique floral pattern, all edges gilt; frontispieces and endpapers bit foxed and darkened, barely perceptible wear to leather, but bindings and text are almost flawless. Keynes p. 60.   Phillip J. Pirages 33-420 1996 $375.00

HISTORY of the Foundations in Manchester of Christ's College, Chetham's Hospital, and the Free Grammar School. London: Thomas Agnew and Joseph Zentti, 1828-33. 4to; 3 volumes; frontispieces to all volumes, 32 engraved plates, extra plate 'Northwest view of Chetham's College' not called for to volume 3, 2 full page wood engravings, 3 groundplans and several woodcuts to text; old tree calf boards, decorative gilt borders, skilfully rebacked, red and green labels, yellow edges, inner gilt dentelles, marbled endpapers with bookplate to front pastedowns, some surface damage to upper board of volume 2; bound by Hayday. some sporadic foxing to few pages, dampstain to frontispiece in volume 2. Halkett & Laing III p. 81.   Beeleigh Abbey BA56-26 1996 £375.00

PETIT, J. L.   Remarks on Church Architecture. London: John Petheram, 1841. 1st edition; 8vo; 2 volumes; large number of full page and textual lithographs; contemporary morocco, gilt extra, gilt edges by Hayday; extremely scarce. Not in Abbey Cat.   Charles W. Traylen 117-243 1996 £150.00

POPE, ALEXANDER 1688-1744   The Poetical Works. London: William Pickering, 1835. Small 8vo; 3 volumes; pages clxiii, (i), 168; viii, 311; vii, (i), 363; steel engraved portrait frontispiece in volume i, tissue guard and half titles present, titlepage to volume i lightly browned; dark green morocco by Hayday, backstrips with raised bands, gilt lettered direct, blind triple fillet border on sides, yellow chalked endpapers (slight foxing), green silk markers, gilt edges, excellent.   Blackwell's B112-230 1996 £50.00

BINDING - HENDERSON & BISSET

NAPIER, WILLIAM FRANCIS PATRICK   History of the War in the Peninsula and in the South of France from the Year 1807 to the Year 1814. London: John Murray (vol. 1), Thomas & William Boone (vols. 2-6), 1828-40. 1st edition; 9 x 5 3/4 inches; 6 volumes; 55 plates; very attractive 19th century smooth calf by Henderson & Bisset, covers framed with rule of blind dots inside double gilt fillet, handsomely gilt spine compartments occupied by 10 plain and decorative rules & central field of stippled scales, raised bands ornamented with twining roll, red calf and green morocco labels, marbled endpapers and edges, variable foxing to perhaps half the maps with offsetting onto facing pages, flyleaves little spotted, isolated small stains or nicks to two or three covers, slightest talking to few joints but text generally clean and bindings both extremely pleasing and very well preserved, contemporaneous presentation inscription at front in first 3 volumes, ownership inscription;   Phillip J. Pirages 33-395 1996 $1,500.00

WARD, ADOLPHUS WILLIAM   A History of English Dramatic Literature to the Death of Queen Anne. London: Macmillan and Co., 1875. 1st edition; royal 8vo; half titles, 2 volumes, beautifully bound in three quarter green levant morocco, gilt, fully gilt panelled spines (faded), with inset red morocco flowers, top edges gilt, by Henderson and Bisset. Charles W. Traylen 117-215 1996 £180.00

BINDING - HERING

CORYATE, THOMAS 1577?-1617   Coryats Crudities Hastily gobbled Up in Five Moneths Travells In France, Savoy, Italy, Rhetia Commonly Called the Grisons Country, Helvetia Alias Switzerland, Some Parts of High Germany and the Netherlands. London: by William Stansby, 1611. 1st edition; thick 4to; engraved title (shaved slightly at head), engraved plates skillfully inlaid, and engraved plate of clock at Strasburg (shaved at head and foot), woodcut of Prince of Wales' feathers, text portrait of Emperor Frederick IV; errata leaf present; portrait of Prince Henry inserted; late 18th or early 19th century straight grain red morocco, blind tooled panel and gilt fillet on covers, spine tooled in gilt and blind, inner dentelles tooled in gilt and blind, edges gilt, by Charles Hering, with his binder's ticket on endpaper, neat marginal repair to F2; unusually nice. Pforzheimer 218; Grolier Langland to Wither 49; STC 5808.   Joseph J. Felcone 64-15 1996 $7,500.00

MARRYAT, FREDERICK 1792-1848   Mr. Midshipman Easy. London: Saunders and Otley, Conduit ST., 1836. 1st edition; 3 volumes; pages (vii), 291; (vii), 306; (viii), 314 pages; uniformly bound by Hering in marbled boards, half black roan with red gilt titles, extremities rubbed and spines scraped, spine to volume III cracked, some page corners missing, no loss, else very nice; all volumes inscribed by Sir Charles Rowley.   Marjorie James 19-147 1996 £125.00

REID, THOMAS 1710-1796   Essays on the Active Powers of Man. Edinburgh: printed for John Bell, 1788. 1st edition; 4to; vii, 493, (3) pages; bound without half title and ad leaf; near contemporary full green morocco by Hering with his ticket, some very minor scuffing and scratching, but a handsome copy; the Kimbolton Library copy with bookplate. Jessop p. 165.   C. R. Johnson 37-76 1996 £900.00

BINDING - HOLLOWAY

MAC KINNON, WILLIAM ALEXANDER   History of Civilisation and Public Opinion. London: Henry Colburn, 1849. 3rd edition; 8vo; 2 volumes; (ii), xxviii, 388; xii, 402 pages, complete with half title in each volume; contemporary morocco, fully gilt with raised bands and silk markers by Holloway of London, little wear to upper joints, else fine; from the library of David Murray, novelist and journalist, presentation copy inscribed by author.   John Drury 82-164 1996 £100.00

BINDING - BLAIR HUGHES-STANTON

BROOKE, FULKE GREVILLE, 1ST BARON 1554-1628   Caelica. Newtown: Gregynog Press, 1936, i.e. 1937. One of 15 copies specially bound (of a total edition of 225); 9 1/4 x 6 1/4 inches; xiii, (1), 149, (1) pages, (1) leaf (colophon); title printed in red and black, initials and colophon in red; lovely heavy grained slate blue levant morocco by Gregynog Press Bindery (signed in gilt on rear turn-in by Blair Hughes-Stanton and George Fisher), dec. in all over design featuring a total of 16 inset vellum stars on covers and spine, vellum stars stained a sublte shade pink and connected by gilt and blind fillets, raised bands, gilt titling on spine, wide turn-ins with one blind and one gilt rule, top edge gilt, other edges untrimmed, in somewhat faded and soiled folding cloth box, with paper label on spine, except for faint shadow of leather turn-ins on facing flyleaves, an extremely fine copy, especially clean inside and out, showing no signs of use. Harrop 36.   Phillip J. Pirages 33-260 1996 $6,500.00

GRUFFYDD, W. J.   Caniadau. Newtown: Gregynog Press, 1932. One of 25 specially bound copies, of a total edition of 25; 10 1/4 x 7 1/2 inches; vii, (1), 101, (1) pages, (1) leaf (colophon); printed in russet and black on stone colored handmade paper; 4 full page wood engravings as well as shadow initials by Blair Hughes-Stanton; very handsome brown crushed levant morocco by the Gregynog Press Bindery (signed in gilt by Blair Hughes-Stanton and George Fisher on turn-in), panel of 24 closely spaced gilt lines connecting the covers across the spine with half panels on each cover continuing around board edges onto turn-ins, raised bands, spine titled in gilt, top edge gilt, other edges untrimmed; remarkably fine, especially bright and clean. Harrop 21.   Phillip J. Pirages 33-262 1996 $5,500.00

BINDING - OTTO HUPP

CHURCH OF ENGLAND. BOOK OF COMMON PRAYER   The Book of Common Prayer Together with the Psalter or Psalms of David. London: Peacock, Mansfield & Britton, n.d., ca. 1885. 8vo; full calf, front cover achieved in cuir-cisele with words DEVS DANTE OMNIA AMANDVS above an heraldic coat of arms featuring a lion holding a hatchet, the date 1 8 8 5 in four corners, and the initials HCW below; background is covered in blind pointelles and raised letters tinted with gilt, spine with 4 raised bands and cuir-cisele panels, 8 silver corner bosses and silver clasp with leather strap extending from lower cover to a stud on upper cover to a stud on upper cover, all edges handsomely gilt and gauffered, gilt decorated vellum pastedowns and free endleaves in seme of pomegranates on a leafy stem, on lower edge of rear cover is a sm. cuir-cisele panel with words, ME FEC, and initials O.H., above and below a stylized binding, bird with both wings extended, the initials & logotype of Otto Hupp, graphic designer & publisher; laid in is ANS from former owner, Helen C. Waterhouse, whose initials appear on cover; splendid binding example.   Book Block 32-42 1996 $1,175.00

BINDING - HYNES

GILPIN, WILLIAM 1724-1804   Observations Relative Chiefly to Picturesque Beauty, Made in the Year 1772, on Several Parats of England. London: R. Blamire, 1788. 2nd edition; 8vo; 2 volumes, (2), xvi, 238; (2), 268, xiv pages; 30 aquatint plates; very good, later 19th century half morocco, marbled boards, raised and gilt banded spines; binder's ticket of R. Hynes of Dover.   Ken Spelman 30-83 1996 £260.00

BINDING - IRISH

GRAVES, RICHARD   The Festoon: a Collection of Epigrams, Ancient and Modern. London: for Mess. Robinson and Roberts and W. Frederick, Bath, 1766/65. 1st edition; 12mo; pages xx, 200; full green calf, spine with gilt floral motifs between gilt bands, sides bordered in gilt, with gilt motifs in corners; very attractive Irish binding, ca. 1780. Simon Finch 24-98 1996 £350.00

BINDING - ANGELA JAMES

IRVING, WASHINGTON 1783-1859   The Legend of Sleepy Hollow. Hyattsville: Rebecca Press, 1983. Limited to 150 copies signed by Rebecca Bingham, publisher; 2 1/4 X 2 7/8 inches; (114) pages; wood engravings by Sarah Chamberlain, includes proof of one of the wood engravings signed by Chamberlain; designer binder by Angela James, signed and dated 1994 by her; full dark purple mor. inlaid on both covers with geometric pieces of white sheepskin, which are speckled with inks either in blue and purple or in yellow, other inlays surrounding these colored sections show black ink drawing on white sheepskin, these pieces laminated with transparent vellum, edges alternately treated w/gold, palladium & blue acrylic, doublures are of white sheepskin, speckled in a range from yellow to purple, and flyleaves are of correspondingly dyed paper, housed in matchbox container consisting of tray and sleeve, tray is of purple mor., lined w/matching suede, while sleeve is of purple speckled sheepskin, w/gilt titled purple mor. label. Bromer Booksellers 87-184 1996 $1,750.00

BINDING - ARTHUR JOHNSON

MULLER, JOSEPH EMILE   Petite Encyclopedie de L'Art. Klee (Picasso, Bonnard, Matisse). Paris: Hazan, 1956-71. 6 x 4 inches; 4 volumes; in different designer bookbindings by Arthur Johnson after the styles of four of the most important artists of the late 19th and 20th century, all with multi-color onlays and blind tooling on covers, spines with the artists' name elegantly stamped in gilt, housed in quarter morocco clamshell case with its own striking design employing onlays and gilt tooling, each signed with binder's initials on lower rear turn-in, dated 1983; absolutely fine.   Book Block 32-32 1996 $2,250.00

BINDING - JUNCKER

NEANDER, MICHAEL   Opus Aureum et Scholasticum... Leipzig: Steinman, 1577. 1st edition of this collection; 4to; 1,268 pages; printer's device; original full pigskin over wooden boards, dated, with fine, well preserved panels representing medicine, astronomy, theology and jurisprudence, signed by Wittenberg binder, Mathias Juncker; fine. Adams P2311; BM STC 646. NUC 409.55.   Bennett Gilbert LL29-52 1996 $1,850.00

BINDING - KALTHOEBER

DOUGLAS, M.   Notes of a Journey from Berne to England through France, Made in the Year 1796. London: 1797. 8vo; 2nd part only; 56 pages; contemporary calf, gilt, by C. Kalthoeber, with his binder's ticket, rebacked. This copy fromt he Althorp Library with its label and Spencer bookplate.   Thomas Thorp 489-89 1996 £135.00

HUDDESFORD, GEORGE   Salmagundi: a Miscellaneous Combination of Original Poetry...(with) Topsy Turvy; With Anecdotes and Observations Illustratalve of the Leading Characters in the Present Government of France. London: ptd. by E. Hodson for J. Anderson/London: ptd. for the author... 1793/93. 3rd edition of the first title, re-issue of the sheets of the second edition of 1792 with new titlepage; 2nd edition of the 2nd title, reissue of sheets of the 1st edition; 8vo; 2 volumes in one; engraved titlepage and 2 other plates (one in sepia); contemporary blue morocco, gilt, spine gilt, all edges gilt, pink endpapers by Kalthoeber, with his orange ticket (some scuffing of spine); half title present. Presentation copies, inscribed by author for Sir Edward Blackett, Bart. CBEL II 660.   Ximenes 109-160 1996 $275.00

BINDING - KELLY

BENTHAM, JEREMY 1748-1832   Plan of Parliamentary Reform, in the form of a Catechism, with Reasons for Each Article, with an Introduction, Shewing the Necessity of Radical... London: printed for R. Hunter, 1817. 1st edition; 8vo; slightly later 19th century half calf, spine gilt, by J. Kelly, with his miniscule ticket; slight rubbing; very good.   Ximenes 108-16 1996 $750.00

SCHWERDT, C. F. G. R.   Hunting, Hawking, Shooting. London: privately ptd. for the author by Waterlow & Sons, 1928-37. Limited to 300 copies, numbered and signed by author; large 4to; 4 volumes, xxiv, 324; xvi, 359; x, 256; xx, 260 pages; 380 plates; original dark green half morocco gilt, top edge gilt, others uncut, by Kelly & Sons (volumes 1 and 2 neatly rebacked), original backstrips relaid, extremities slightly rubbed, tiny piece chipped from head of volume 3, occasional light dust soiling in upper margin of few leaves.   Thomas Thorp 489-270 1996 £2,000.00

BINDING - KELM

CLEMENS, SAMUEL LANGHORNE 1835-1910   The Jumping Frog. Cheloniidae Press, 1985. One of 20 specially bound copies (of a total edition of 325), signed by binder; 8 3/4 x 5 3/4 inches; (26) leaves, on of them folding, printed in green & black; 15 signed or initialled wood engravings by Alan James Robinson, including frontispiece; including an additional complete suite of engravings, an additional suite of state-proof and working proof prints, & another paperbound copy of the book, with every engraving in the two separate suites inscribed "To Arnold and Mimi"; prospectus laid in; inscribed by artist to Arnold and Mimi Elkind; bound by Daniel Kelm in fine & whimsical tan crushed mor., both covers w/lg. inlaid recumbent mor. frog, in 2 colors, each doublure w/similar onlaid leaping frog, vol. contained in book well inside attractive & cleverly designed burlap folding box, which also has a pull out chemise (containing the extra engravings), housed in recess under book well; as new.   Phillip J. Pirages 33-123 1996 $2,250.00

CLEMENS, SAMUEL LANGHORNE 1835-1910   The Jumping Frog. Easthampton: Cheloniidae Press, 1985. Out of series copy with same binding that appears on State Proof Edition, which is limited to five copies only and one extra suite of the woodengravings and portrait etching of Twain as in the deluxe edition, which is limited to 50 copies, each signed and numbered by the artist, and has an inscribed copy of the prospectus, an inscribed drawing of the frog and is signed on the colophon by the artist and binder, the regular edition was limited to 250 copies and was bound in green paper wrappers, all edges were signed and numbered by the artist, Alan James Robinson; printed on Saunders paper in Centaur and Arrighi types, page size 22 x 14 cm; bound by Daniel Kelm, full undyed Oasis with onlays of the frog in repose-before the jump on the front panel and after the jump on the back panel, onlays in green oasis of the frog jumping are on front and back pastedowns; housed in linen clamshell box with pull-out portfolio for extra suite and drawing and prospectus with paper label on spine. Beautiful copy.   Priscilla Juvelis 95/1-57 1996 $2,250.00

BINDING - KERR & RICHARDSON

BURNS, ROBERT 1759-1796   Aloway Kirk; or Tam o'Shanter. N.P.: Glasgow?: n.d. 1796? 8vo; this variant has 'doon' as the last word on page 2; half brown morocco gilt, spine gilt by Kerr & Richardson, Glasgow; fine.   Ximenes 109-58 1996 $750.00

COLERIDGE, SAMUEL TAYLOR 1772-1834   Specimens of the Table Talk of the Late Samuel Taylor Coleridge. London: John Murray, 1835. 1st edition; 8vo; 2 volumes, pages lxxi, 267; 364; frontispiece in each volume; contemporary half maroon morocco, marbled boards, edges and endpapers by Kerr and Richardson of Glasgow, extremities worn; bookplates; good set. Wise 78; Tinker 709.   Simon Finch 24-51 1996 £120.00

BINDING - KERSTEN

NIEMEYER, WILHELM   Nicola Tuldo und Santa Catarina Im Kerker Zu Siena. Rupprecht-Presse, 1918-19. One of 200 copies; 9 3/4 x 7 1/2 inches; 2 p.l., (1 blank), xxxvi pages; (4) leaves; device on colophon; expressive inlaid black morocco by P. Kersten, covers framed with multiple plain and decorative gilt rules, large round complex sunburst ornament at center of each board featuring 8 inlaid purple tulips, flat spine titled and decorated in gilt, batik endpapers, fanciful flyleaves in colorful and jagged pattern, top edge gilt, very fine.   Phillip J. Pirages 33-452 1996 $2,800.00

BINDING - LARKINS

MANSEL, HENRY LONGUEVILLE   Letters, Lectures and Reviews, Including the Phrontisterion, or, Oxford in the 19th Century... London: John Murray, 1873. 1st edition; 8vo; vii, (1), 408 pages; contemporary polished calf, raised bands fully gilt with inner gilt dentelles by Larkins, handsome. Rand p. 364.   John Drury 82-174 1996 £100.00

BINDING - LARKINS

OLIPHANT, LAURENCE 1829-1888   Narrative of the Earl of Elgin's Mission to China and Japan in the Years 1857, 58, '59. Edinburgh: Wm. Blackwood, 1859. 1st edition; tall 8vo; 2 volumes; with half titles; 20 colored and tinted lithographs, five folding maps, many text wood engravings; three quarter red crushed morocco over marbled sides, spines with five raised bands and elaborate gilt tooling, top edge gilt, by J. Larkins; particularly fine set.   Book Block 32-79 1996 $750.00

BINDING - LEIGHTON

ARBLAY, FRANCES BURNEY D' 1752-1840   Diary and Letters of Madame D'Arblay. London: Colburn, 1854. Octavo; 7 volumes; portrait frontispiece, holograph ms. foldout in volume 1; bound by Leighton in dark blue cloth, pretty set. CBEL II 527.   Hartfield 48-A3 1996 $295.00

THE BRIDAL Souvenir. London: Griffith & Farran, 1857. Small 4to; printed in colors and gold on 21 leaves, complete with mounted photo portrait frontispiece, now always present; original richly gilt cloth, edges gilt, designed by John Leighton, signed "J.L.", trivial wear at headbands, otherwise bright, fresh and attractive copy.   James Fenning 133-322 1996 £95.00

LOCKHART, JOHN GIBSON 1794-1854   Ancient Spanish Ballads. London: John Murray, 1841. 1st of this edition; tall thick quarto; unpaginated, with 8 pages of publisher's ads; 4 splendid titlepages by Owen Jones, lavishly gilt in the Morrish style, the first to use 4 color chromolithography, every page with wood engraved illustrations in many colors & color lithographped borders or tailpieces; bound by Leighton (& probably designed by Jones) in red pebbled morocco, elaborate gilt and blind decorations to coers & spine, gilt & black floral endpapers; with forepedge painting: a bright, impressionistic view of Gibraltar, with several sailing ships in foreground, book and fore-edge painting in excellent condition, laid in is a glassine envelope with clippings about this historic instance of fine book-making. VBD 58-59 and 125. Hartfield 48-F7 1996 $1,950.00

LYRA Germanica. London: Longmans, Green, Reader & Dyer, 1868. 1st illustrated edition; royal 8vo; pages xvi, 254, ad leaf; frontispiece, other illustrations; original dark green cloth, gilt, red inlays, gilt, edges gilt, by Edmonds & Remnants with ticket, nice, elaborate signed binding by Leighton.   James Fenning 133-208 1996 £65.00

LYRA Germanica: Hymns for the Sundays and Chief Festivals of the Christian Year. London: Longman, Green, Longman and Roberts, 1861. 1st English Language edition; small 4to; xx, 272 pages; publisher's cloth binding designed by John Leighton and is the same as the publisher's deluxe morocco covers; very bright, very good, save for light edge wear.   Bookpress 75-77 1996 $225.00

NAPIER, MARK   Memorials and Letters Illustrative of the Life and Times of John Graham of Claverhouse, Viscount Dundee. Edinburgh: Thomas G. Stevenson, 22 Frederick St., London: Hamilton, Adams & Co., 1859. 1st edition; 8vo; 2 volumes; 1-388; 1-430 pages; frontispiece to both volumes, 3 engraved plates, 2 chromolithos, 3 facsimiles; binder's tamp, bound by Leighton of Brewer Street; half green morocco and green buckram boards, elaborate gilt tooling to compartments with Scottish thistles enclosed within gilt scrolling, gilt titles to spines, owern's name in gilt to foot of spines, endpapers and edges uniformly marbled; some foxing to couple of plates and few pages, owner's inscription to titles, this copy appears to have been specially bound for the owner as the name on the titles is the same as the name gilt stamped to spine, owner's bookplate.   Beeleigh Abbey BA56-159 1996 £125.00

STERLING, WILLIAM   Annals of the Artists of Spain. London: John Ollivier, 1848. 1st edition;one of 25 extra illustrated sets; thick octavo; 2 volumes; pages 1480 in all; 52 illustrations, plus an additonal 6 noted by Stirling on holograph page; bound by Leighton in red striated morocco, raised bands, all edges gilt, 7 coats of arms in gilt on front covers, gilt monograms on backs, marbled endpapers, bound for Duke of Somerset, with his fine armorial bookplate in volume 1.   Hartfield 48-L81 1996 $850.00

WORDSWORTH, WILLIAM 1770-1850   Poems of William Wordsworth. London: George Routledge & Co., 1859. 1st edition thus; royal 8vo; pages (16), 388; original blue cloth, gilt, edges gilt, signed "A.W." by Leighton, Son & Hodge, with ticket, inside joints cracked, binding sound and otherwise nice.   James Fenning 133-373 1996 £55.00

BINDING - LEIGHTON, SON & HODGE

CRAIK, DINAH MARIA MULOCK 1826-1887   John Halifax, Gentleman. London: Hurst and Blackett, 1586. 1st edition; 8vo; 3 volumes, no half titles, but none called for, 3 pages ads, and 24 page undated publisher's catalog at end of volume 1, one page of ads at end of volume 2, and one leaf of ads end of volume 3; drab endpapers; original brown wavy grain cloth blocked in blind on covers, lettered gilt on spines, Leighton Son & Hodge's ticket inside back cover of volume 1, small hole in outer side margins of one leaf of volume 3, just touching one letter at end of one line only, slight wear at head and foot of each spine, but excellent copy, without ownership marks or traces of labels. Sadleir 1812. Wolff 4996; Carter's A Binding.   David Bickersteth 133-160 1996 £260.00

PALGRAVE, FRANCIS TURNER 1824-1897   Gems of English Art. London: George Routledge, 1869. 1st edition; 4to; viii, 144 pages, 24 plates; publisher's cloth, all edges gilt, light rubbing to binding, else very nice. Binding by Leighton, Sons and Hodge.   Bookpress 75-95 1996 $325.00

SOUVESTRE, EMILE   Translations from the French of Emile Souvestre. N.P.: privately printed, 1856. Small 4to; 2 volumes; full dark blue crushed morocco over beveled boards, spine & covers heavily ornamented with gilt & blind relief decoration, far too elaborate to describe, at top & bottom (on edges of outer gilt fillet borders) are two gilt lines "To the Memory of Elizabeth Strachey and Coelum Non Animum; board edges gilt, inner gilt dentelels, all edges gilt, on inside rear pastedown is binder's ticket of Leighton, Son & Hodge, on front flyleaf is inscription "Constance Strachey from E. S. 1 June, 1887". Fine.   Book Block 32-45 1996 $1,250.00

BINDING - LEWIS

THE BEAUTIES of the Court of King Charles the Second. London: for Henry Colburn by Richard Bentley, 1833. 1st edition; extra tall, wide folio; pages ix, 222; 21 engraved portraits after Sir Peter Lely, on India paper, 17 marked PROOF; splendid full red Turkey morocco binding by C. Lewis, elaborately gilt panels and spine decorations, wide gilt tooled dentelles, all edges gilt, marbled endpapers, slight wear, but elegant copy; nice. CBEL III 674.   Hartfield 48-L8 1996 $695.00

BINDING - LINDRIDGE

SINCLAIR, GEORGE   Hortus Gramineus Woburnensis: or, an Account of the Results of Experiments on the Produce and Nutritive Qualities of Different Grasses and Other Plants Used as the Food of the More Valuable Domestic Animals. London: printed for James Ridgway, 1825. 2nd octavo edition; 8vo; 438 pages, (6) pages ads; 60 hand colored plates; contemporary full calf with binder's ticket of Lindridge of Maidstone, featuring gilt borders and gilt tooled spine with morocco label, library bookplate and unobtrusive blindstamp on titlepage and plates; otherwise very good.   Chapel Hill 94-7 1996 $200.00

BINDING - LOCK

JOHNSON, SAMUEL 1709-1784   Know Thyself. Kingston: Locks' Press, 1992. One of 85 numbered copies, signed by artist; oblong small 4to; larage titlepage woodcut by Margaret Lock, printed in handset 18 and 14 pt. Bembo on Twinrocker handmade; bound by Margaret Lock in marbled boards, cloth back, printed labels; fine.   Bertram Rota 272-280 1996 £80.00

BINDING - LUBETT

BIBLE. FRENCH - 1952   Cantique des Cantiques. Paris: A. Krol, 1952. Limited to 236 copies; oblong octavo; 57 pages; engravings and woodcut initials by Burins de Abram Krol; bound in full Chinese red morocco by Denise Lubett in 1975, spine gilt tooled with design of grape vines, front cover with gilt tooled chalice, grape vines and deer, gilt tooled turquoise morocco doublures, all edges gilt, housed in felt lined morocco backed chemise with morocco trimmed slipcase, spine of chemise slightly faded, else extremely fine; presentation inscription from Krol.   Bromer Booksellers 87-166 1996 $2,000.00

BINDING - LUMSDEN

FAWCETT, GRAHAM   Poems for Shakespeare 2. London: Globe Playhouse Trust Publications, 1973. 1st edition; one of 100 copies, printed (hors commerce), signed by 14 contributin poets; 8vo; quarter calf and red cloth, all edges gilt, red cloth slipcase, bound by A. W. Lumsden; fine   James S. Jaffe 34-243 1996 $450.00

BINDING - MACDONALD

HAWTHORNE, NATHANIEL 1804-1864　　The Scarlet Letter. New York: Privately printed, 1904. Limited edition, one of only 126 copies; 10 1/2 x 7 1/4 inches; 4 p.l., 333 pages; 15 original plates, each in two states, hand colored and uncolored, for a total of 30 plates by A. Robaudi and C. Graham, each plate with printed tissue guard, printed on fine Japanese vellum; sumptuous crimson morocco by MacDonald, heavily gilt in 18th century French design, covers bordered with multiple plain and decorative gilt rules and lavish foliate dentelles, raised bands, spine attractively gilt in compartments, similar ornaments at corners of broad gilt ruled turn-ins, marbled endpapers, top edge gilt, other edges untrimmed; evidence of bookplate removal, perhaps a hint of fading to binding, but extremely fine in handsome binding.　　Phillip J. Pirages 33-302　1996 $325.00

BINDING - MACKENZIE

GLEIG, G. R.　　The Soldier's Help to the Knowledge of Divine Truth. London: J. G. & F. Rivington, 1835. 8vo; full purple crushed morocco with a Scotch-rule gilt fillet border inside of which is a border composed of leafy vines and flower heads, at top of the central panel on both covers, is a gilt crown beneath which are entwined rustic initials "WR", spine with five raised bands and gilt decoration within compartments, board edges gilt, inner gilt dentelles, all edges gilt, signed at bottom of front turn in: bound by J. Mackenzie Bookbinder to the King, very attractive royal binding. Bound of William IV.　　Book Block　32-40　1996 $950.00

STATIUS, PUBLIUS PAPINIUS　　Statii Sylvarum Libri V./ Achilleidos Libri XII./ Thebaidos Libri II./ Orthographia et Flexus Dictionum Graecarum Omnium... Venice: in aedibvs Aldi, et Andreae Soceri (Andrea Torresano), 1502. Small 8vo;; light age stain, all edges gilt, full black morocco by Mackenzie, with repaired spine.　　Family Album　Tillers-586　1996 $1,000.00

TANNER, MATTHAIS　　Societas Jesu Apostolorum Imitrix Sive Gesta Praeclara et Virtutes Eorum. Prague: A. G. Konias, 1694. Large 4to; 196 engravings; 19th century full crimson morocco with scalloped gilt outer border inside of which is a double gilt fillet border, upon which sits an inch wide elaborate border composed of alternating floral designs, including acorns and lilies, spine with seven raised bands and complimentary gilt tooling in six of the compartments, the second and third from the top being reserved for two morocco labels bearing title information, inner gilt dentelles, board edges gilt, marbled endleaves, all edges gilt, bound by J. Mackenzie, bookbinder to the king; with gilt stamped Huth bookplate (his sale, Sotheby's 8 Jul6 1919, lot 7206) and bookplate of Leonard and Lisa Baskin.　　Book Block　32-67　1996 $7,500.00

BINDING - MANDERSON

PRICE, UVEDALE　　Essays on the Picturesque, as Compared with the Sublime and the Beautiful; and, on the Use of Sudying Pictures for the Purpose of Improving Real Landscape. London: 1810. 1st edition; 8vo; 3 volumes; mid 19th century half purple calf, faded and bit worn and scraped, by (William) Manderson of Brighton, with his ticket; some foxing.　　Maggs Bros. Ltd.　1190-43　1996 £300.00

BINDING - MANSELL

AMMAN, JOST　　Stand Und Orden der H. Romischen Catholischen Kirchen, Darinn aller Geistlichen Personen, H. Ritter und Dero Verwandten Herkommen, Constitution Regeln, Habit und Kleidung, Beneben Schonen und Kunstlichen Figurn Fleissig Beschrieben... Frankfurt a.m.: Sigmund Feyerabend, 1585. 1st German edtilon; small 4to; 102 fine woodcuts; full crushed dark brown morocco with triple gilt fillet borders, spine with five raised bands and one small tool in each of four compartments, the other two reserved for the title, board edges gilt, inner gilt dentelles, all edges gilt, by Mansell, successors to Hayday, fine, exceedingly scarce. Splendid copy. Becker 40a; Brunet I 234; Colas 120; Fairfax Murray German Books p.33.　　Book Block　32-71　1996 $4,500.00

BINDING - MARROW

TOLFREY, FREDERIC　　The Sportsman in Canada. London: T. C. Newby, 1845. Large 12mo; 2 volumes, pages iii, 283, (4) (publisher's ads), frontispiece, 4 plates, pages 286, 8 (publisher's ads), frontispiece, 4 plates; original blindstamped cloth with binder's stamp "Marrow, 3 Cecil St. Strand" and bookseller's label, edges slightly scuffed, exterior dusty, else exceptionally clean, crisp set. TPL 2744.　　Hugh Anson-Cartwright　87-410　1996 $750.00

BINDING - MATTHEWMAN

WALLIS, JOHN　　Grammatica Linguae Anglicanae. London: Millar Bowyer, 1765. 8vo; pages (35), 281, frontispiece, tooled ink stamp of Liberty on rear flyleaf; full red morocco binding executed by John Matthewman for Thomas Hollis, in center of front cover is gilt figure of Brittania, seated; lower cover has seated owl, spine tooled with title and Caduceus of Mercury, marbled edges;　　Family Album　Tillers-664　1996 $800.00

BINDING - MAUCHLINE

SCOTT, WALTER 1771-1832　　Rokeby. Edinburgh: Charles and Adam Black, 1869. 16mo; delightful Mauchline binding of Stuart tartan over wooden boards, backed in forest green morocco, gilt, all edges gilt, with the exception of a few light scratches, this is a fine exmaple of a uniquely Scottish bookbinding technique.　　Glenn Books　36-27　1996 $225.00

BINDING - MAYNARD

ROSSETTI, CHRISTINA 1830-1894　　Poems Chosen By Walter De La Mare. Newtown: Gregynog Press, 1930. One of 25 copies, specially bound, of a total edition of 300; 9 1/4 x 6 1/2 inches; xliii, (1), 107, (1) pages; initial openings and frontispiece portrait by Maynard after drawings by Dante Gabriel Rossetti, shoulder notes printed in red; fine very animated scarlet morocco by Gregynog Press Bindery (signed by R. Ashwin Maynard and George Fisher on rear turn-in), covers tooled in gilt with 2 large cruciform foliate ornaments elaborated with diagonal blind and gilt decoration (something like evergreen leaves), ornaments on field of gold dots, covers framed by gilt and blind rules, fomr which emanate a series of similar gilt and blind evergreen decorations, spine with raised bands, panels outlined in blind and gilt ttling, board edges ruled in gilt, turn-ins with double gilt rule, top edge gilt, other edges untrimmed, in substantial and attractive morocco backed folding cloth box, fleece lined, spine with raised bands; extremely fine. Harrop 15.　　Phillip J. Pirages 33-266　1996 $5,500.00

THOMAS, EDWARD　　Selected Poems. Newtown: Gregynog Press, 1927. One of 25 copies specially bound of a total edition of 275; 9 1/4 x 6 1/4 inches; xix, (1), 95, (1) pages; device on title, red printer's device in colophon; title printed in blue and black, initials in red, ruled in blue; very fine polished blue levant morocco by the Gregynog Press Bindery (signed by R. Ashwin Maynard and George Fisher on rear turn-in), covers with 3 overlapping gilt lozenges made of leaf sprays, connected by gilt decoration to double gilt rule frame, raised bands, spine titled in gilt with similar gilt decoration at either end, double gilt rule on turn-ins, marbled endpapers, top edge gilt, other edges untrimmed, in blue cloth chemise and matching slipcase, blue morocco label on spine, spine leather perhaps just a shade lighter than covers, but remarkably fine copy copy otherwise of the first Gregynog book to be printed on Japanese vellum. Harrop 6.　　Phillip J. Pirages　33-267　1996 $4,500.00

BINDING - MCLEISH

CELLINI, BENVENUTO　　The Life of Benvenuto Cellini. London: Ballantyne/Vale Press, 1900. Folio; 2 volumes in 1; 2 titlepages, 187, 188 pages of text; woodcut border and initial to first page of text; bound by C. and C. McLeish, full maroon morocco, gilt rule borders with decorative gilt cornerpieces, gilt panelled spine, top edge gilt, others untrimmed, inner gilt rule and repeat cornerpieces; T. E. Lawrence's copy with his pencilled initials to top right hand corner of front free endpaper. Beeleigh Abbey　BA56-139　1996 £450.00

DRYDEN, JOHN 1631-1700　　Of Dramatick Poesie, an Essay. London: printed By T. Warren for Henry Herringman, 1693. 4to; upper margins cropped close with loss or partial loss of some headlines, full 19th century calf by C. and C. McLeish; Wing D2329; MacDonald 127c. Jaggard p. 85. Lee, Shekespeareiana 256.　　Anthony Laywood　108-7 1996 £125.00

BINDING - MIDDLETON

AUSTEN, JANE 1775-1817　　Emma: a Novel. London: printed for John Murray, 1816. 1st edition; 12mo; 3 volumes; rebound by Bernard Middleton in period style full calf, spines fully gilt and with red morocco lettering pieces, inside dentelles, lacks half titles, some foxing, ownership inscription on titles, very good in sympathetic modern binding; Gilson A8. Sotheran　PN32-2　1996 £1,250.00

BINDING - MIDDLETON

BOYLE, ROBERT 1627-1691   Some Considerations Touching the Usefulnesse of Experimental Naturall Philosophy, Propos'd in Familiar Discourses to a Friend, by Way of Invitation to the Study Of It. Oxford: printed by Hen. Hall, Printer to the University, for Ric. Davis, 1663. 1st edition; 4to; 2 parts in 1 volume, as issued; (xvi), 127, (viii), 417, (xvi index), errata leaf, collation as in Fulton with all half titles and part titles called for, except the longitudinal label and half title to part 1, which are both lacking, small marginal holes in R4 and S1 (not affecting text), otherwise very good. Contemporary calf, rebacked and recornered in period style by Bernard Middleton. Fulton 50; Wing B4029; Madan 2634; Wellcome II p. 221.   Sotheran PN32-4 1996 £2,995.00

COMBE, WILLIAM 1742-1823   The English Dance of Death. London: published at R. Ackermann's Repository of Arts, 101, Strand, 1815-16. 1st edition; 8vo; 2 volumes; pages viii, (iv index), 296; (ii), (iv index); + 300; hand colored aquatint frontispiece, hand colored aquatint vignette on engraved titlepage, 72 fine hand colored aquatint plates by Thomas Rowlandson; contemporary marbled calf, rebacked to style, by Bernard Middleton; Tooley 411; Abbey Life 263.   Sotheran PN32-46 1996 £1,250.00

FAIRFIELD, SUMNER LINCOLN   The Last Night of Pompeii: a Poem; and Lays and Legends. New York: Elliot and Palmer, 1832. 1st edition; 8 1/2 x 5 1/2 inches; 309 pages; impressive recent replica binding by Bernard Middleton of black half morocco and marbled sides, spine with broad raised bands and multiple wide decorative gilt rules, as well as centered lyre ornaments; very slight yellowing to text, but very fine, rare. Phillip J. Pirages 33-213 1996 $125.00

BINDING - MONASTERY HILL BINDERY

JANSON, CHARLES WILLIAM   The Stranger in America: Containing Observations Made During a Long Residence in that Country, on the Genius, Manners and Customs... London: James Cundee, 1807. 1st edition; engraved title, plan of Philadelphia, 9 tinted full page engravings; handsomely bound at Monastery Hill Bindery in one half maroon morocco, spine with raised bands bordered by blindstamp rules tapering on to boards ending a fleur-de-lis, title and date in gilt, light foxing, heavier to prelims. Howes J59;   Hermitage SP95-712 1996 $1,250.00

BINDING - MONASTIC

BIBLE. ARABIC - 1776   (Arabic Gospels). Lebanon: Convent of Mar Jouana, Mt. Kerouan, 1776. Folio; 2ff., 315 pages, printed in red and black with numerous ornaments, 4 engraved portraits; contemporary red goatskin, gilt and blindstamped (slightly rubbed); rare Lebanese monastic binding.   Marlborough 160-30 1996 £1,750.00

BINDING - MOORE

BRATHWAITE, RICHARD 1588-1673   Drunken Barnaby's Four Journeys to the North of England. London: printed for J. Harding, 1805.. 8vo; pages xix, 160, 6 engraved illustrations; old polished panelled calf, gilt extra, by R. P. Moore of Bedford.   R.F.G. Hollett & Son 78-337 1996 £120.00

BINDING - MORRELL

ARNOLD, MATTHEW 1822-1888   The Works... London: Macmillan and Co., Ltd., Smith, Elder and Co., 1903. 1st complete collected edition, limited to 775 copies only; 8vo; 15 volumes; frontispiece in volume 1, general title and titles printed in red and black; contemporary half red crushed morocco, spines divided in 6 compartments, gilt lettered direct in two, others with gilt devices, red cloth sides, marbled endpapers, top edge gilt, others uncut, by Morrell; occasional very light spotting; fine. Simon Finch 24-4 1996 £950.00

CATULLUS, C. VALERIUS   The Carmina... London: printed for the translators...for private subscribers only, 1894. 1 of 4 copies on Japanese vellum; royal 8vo; pages xxiii, (i), 313; 3 states of frontispiece, mounted on linen guards, each with light paper guard, half title with limitation statement on verso; excellent copy; red silk marker; contemporary crushed and polished red morocco, by Morrell, backstrip with raised bands, gilt lettered direct in second compartment, and at foot, remaining panels gilt with arabesque tools, joints slightly rubbed, and upper joint tender, sides panelled with outer and inner triple fillet border, inner panel expanded at corners to contain arabesque corner ornaments & masks, single fillet on board edges, wide turn-ins & hinges with 3 fillets, pointille roll & corner ornaments, pale turquoise watered silk doublures & free endpapers, top edge gilt, remainder untrimmed. Blackwell's B112-53 1996 £550.00

BINDING - MORRELL

GRONOW, REES HOWELL 1794-1865   Reminiscences of Captain Gronow, Formerly of the Grenadier Guards, and M.P. for Stafford. London: Smith, Elder and Co., 1862. Mixed set; octavo; 4 volumes; bound by Morrell in full red polished calf, gilt double rule border on covers, gilt spines, tooled in compartments, gilt board edges and turn-ins, all edges gilt; handsome set.   Heritage Book Shop 196-188 1996 $500.00

GUERBER, HELENE ADELINE   Myths of the Norsemen, from the Eddas and Sagas. London: George G. Harrap & Co., 1911. 8 3/4 x 6 inches; xvi, 397 pages; partly unopened, 64 plates, including frontispiece; very pleasing red morocco gilt, by Morrell, covers framed by triple gilt rules, large and graceful impressionistic art nouveau floral ornament in corners, raised bands, spine attractively gilt in compartments with similar art nouveau decoration, gilt inner dentelles, top edge gilt, other edges untrimmed; hint of soiling to covers, but fine in attractive binding. Phillip J. Pirages 33-293 1996 $165.00

OXBERRY, WILLIAM   The Actor's Budget of Wit and Merriment... London: Simpkin, & Marshall, n.d. 1st of this edition; morocco spine, gilt, by Morrell.   Hartfield 48-L65 1996 $195.00

SWIFT, JONATHAN 1667-1745   The Works of Dr. Jonathan Swift, Dean of St. Patrick's, Dublin...(with) Letters Written by the Late Jonathan Swift...(and) The Life of the Rev. Dr. Jonathan Swift... London: printed for W. Bowyer et al, 1768-79/87. Mixed issues; 8vo; 26 volumes; half antique style autumn leaf calf with marbled combed cloth sides, spines decorated with gilt, 8 pointed stars containing flower petals in reverse, crimson and black morocco spine labels, gilt with lettering and floriated acorn patterns by Morrell, apart from some very minor shelf wear, a fine and beautiful set.   James Cummins 14-202 1996 $3,000.00

WILSON, DAVID   A Catalogue of the Manuscripts and Printed Books Collected by David Wilson, M.D., Glasgow. Southport: printed for private circulation, 1925. 1st edition; one of 50 copies; 8vo; frontispiece, bound in half morocco by Morrell, gilt, uncut, top edge gilt.   Forest Books 74-282 1996 £75.00

BINDING - MOTTE

FOURNIER, PIERRE SIMON 1712-1768   Manuel Typographique. Paris: Fournier, 1764-66. 8vo; 2 volumes, 2 frontispieces, portrait of Fournier, 21 folding and double page plates; with half title (usually missing) in volume 1; full brown morocco, gilt edges, detnelle, bound by A. Motte; Robert Hoe bookticket in each volume. Bigmore & Wyman I 228; Updike Printing Types I 260 ff; Brunet II 1359.   Rostenberg & Stern 150-128 1996 $8,500.00

BINDING - MUDIE

MAURY, MATTHEW FONTAINE 1806-1873   The Physical Geography of the Sea, and its Meteorology. London: Sampson Low, Marston, Low and Searle, 1874. 15th edtiion; small octavo; xx, 487 pages, folding plates; bound by Mudie in half calf over marabled boards, gilt spine with raised bands, black morocco label, marbled edges and endpapers, light dampstaining to upper margin of last several leaves; overall, very good, clean copy.   Heritage Book Shop 196-172 1996 $125.00

BINDING - FRANK MURRAY

PUGH, DAVID   London: Being an Accurate History and Description of the British Metropolis and Its Neighbourhood, to Thirty Miles Extent, from an Actual Perambulation. London: printed by W. Stratford, Crown Court, Temple Bar, for J. Stratford... 1805-09. New edition; 8vo; 6 volumes; steel engraved vignettes half titles to all volumes; steel engraved frontispiece to volume 1, 165 steel engraved plates, 111 woodcut vignettes to letterpress, 6 large folding maps and plans, all linen backed; half blue morocco and marbled boards, gilt tooling to panelled spines, gilt titles and volume numbers to spines, joints rubbed, top edge gilt, marbled endpapers, binder's ticket of Frank Murray of Nottingham. Upcott 659.   Beeleigh Abbey BA/56-11 1996 £650.00

BINDING - NEIL

MURRAY, HUGH   An Historical and Descriptive Account of China. Edinburgh: Oliver & Boyd, 1843. 3rd edition; 12mo; 3 volumes; folding map, full page and in-text illustrations; contemporary full calf by Neil, with blind tooled arabesque centerpieces, gilt tooled fillets and spines and raised bands, lightly scuffed in spots, still very good or better. Chapel Hill 94-153 1996 $200.00

BINDING - NEW

WEST, THOMAS   A Guide to the Lakes in Cumberland, Westmorland and Lancasahire. Kendal: W. Pennington, 1821. 11th edition; 8vo; pages v, (iii), 312, uncut, complete with hand colored aquatint frontispiece and extending hand colored map (offset); 20th century three quarter morocco gilt by New of Eton; Abbey 193; Bicknell 13.11.   R.F.G. Hollett & Son 78-1363   1996 £140.00

BINDING - OMEGA

GOLDSMITH, OLIVER 1730-1774   The Poems of Oliver Goldsmith. London: George Routledge and Co., 1859. 1st edition thus; large 8vo; xvi, 160 pages; full green morocco by Omega, sunned along spine and edges, otherwise very nice. Scarce. McLean, Publishers Book Bindings p. 82.   Bookpress 75-27   1996 $325.00

BINDING - PADELOUP

LUCANUS, MARCUS ANNAEUS 39-68   Lucanus. Venice: Apud Aldum, April, 1502. 1st Aldine edition; 8vo; 140 leaves, Italic; 18th century red morocco, spine heavily gilt, joints weak, signed with paper label of binder, Padeloup, all edges gilt. Dibdin II 184; Renouard 33.3. Adams L1557; UCLA I/44; Brunet III 1198.   Family Album Tillers-401   1996 $1,400.00

NATTER, LAURENT   Traite de la Methode Antique de Graver en Pierres Fines, Comparee avec la methode Moderne... London: Haberkorn for the author, 1754. Small folio; pages xxxix, 1 f., eng. dedn., 37 engraved plates (one extra plate of Sirius, from another work, tipped in); contemporary dark green morocco, triple fillet gilt, spine gilt in compartments with floral device and dog tooth and fillet borders, gilt inner dentelle, comb marbled endpapers, all edges gilt, bound by Antoine Michel Padeloup, called "Le Jeune"; from the De Bure library, with the MS shelf mark of Madame Guillaume, possibly part of the small collection formed by De Bure for her, from the collection of J. J. de Bure, from the collection of Arthur Hamilton Smith, with his bookplate with long letter (presumably to him) from de Bure. Fine, scarce. Marlborough 160-49   1996 £2,500.00

BINDING - PAINTED

BROWNING, ELIZABETH BARRETT 1806-1861   Sonnets from the Portuguese. Venice: S. Rosen, 1906. 2 3/4 x 2 1/8 inches; 104 pages, printed in two colors, with attractive type ornaments decorating each sonnet; full vellum, hand painted in 3 colors and gold with title and fleur-de-lys, later white calf ties, covers lightly soiled, else fine. Bondy p. 122; Welsh 1481.   Bromer Booksellers 87-194   1996 $125.00

MORTON, THOMAS, BP. OF COVENTRY & LICHFIELD   Of the Institution of the Sacrament of the Blessed Bodie and Blood of Christ. London: by W. Stansby for Robert Mylbourne, 1631. Folio; 10 leaves + 255 pages, 143 pages, 16 pages; contemporary sprinkled calf, 5 raised bands, double fillet border in blind on each cover, upper cover with coat of arms painted in heraldic colors in centre; bookplate of Hickman Barrt (sic). Joints rubbed, head of spine tape renewed. Painted arms on English bindings are rare. STC 18189.   H. M. Fletcher 121-67   1996 £850.00

SCALIGER, JOSEPH JUSTUS   Notitia Galliae. Amsterdam: Ex Musaeo Pauli Terhaarii, 1697. Thick 8vo; pages 501-862, (50), 224, plus engraved folding map, engraved portrait plate, edges colored brown; early full vellum, decorated with small, bold pen drawings of ships sailing below a seven line motto in Latin, painted under fore-edge, and visible only when fanned is the following text "Tullium M. C. Julius Caesar/ Ciceronem ob E Grecias Ejus/ Domitum Salvum et Incolumem/ Esse Jobemus C. Jaboienus/ Nostris Armis Virtuteque". Later ms. vellum spine label "Incerta" (Meaning uncertain or doubtful);   Family Album Tillers-562   1996 $650.00

BINDING - PARROT

BALLOU, ADIN   After Reading Thoreau. Seal Harbor: the Printing Office at High Loft, 1979. One of 140 copies; octavo; 59 pages; drawings; bound by Gray Parrot in pictorial green paper boards with morocco label going the full length of the spine. Fine.   Bromer Booksellers 90-65   1996 $125.00

BASKIN, LEONARD   Grotesques. Leeds: Gehenna Press, 1991. Limited to 26 copies; this one of 8 deluxe copies with an extra suite on ohter papers, a copperplate and watercolor; page size 9 5/8 x 12 7/8 inches; 41 original etchings, all but 3 printed in color; bound by Gray Parrot in green gilt stamped vellum, housed in black cloth clamshell box. Priscilla Juvelis 95/1-102A   1996 $12,000.00

BINDING - PARROT

BASKIN, LEONARD   Grotesques. Lees: Gehenna Press, 1991. Limited to 26 copies, this one of 13 regular copies; page size 9 5/8 x 12 7/8 inches; on handmade Italian and French papers, each signed by the artist/author; 41 original etchings, all but 3 printed in color, bound by Gray Parrot, gilt stamped marbled paper over boards, designed by Baskin.   Priscilla Juvelis 95/1-102   1996 $7,500.00

BASKIN, LEONARD   Grotesques: Etchings and a Panegyrical Note. Northampton: Gehenna Press, 1991. One of 26 copies; large 4to; with a total of 48 etchings in various colors, printed on French and Italian papers, laid in is an original mounted watercolor grotesque signed by Mr. Baskin; hand marbled paper over boards with geometric gilt design on upper cover, incorporating the name of the book, spine with gilt lettered morocco label, preserved in sturdy cloth clamshell case with matching morocco label, binding and box by Gray Parrot.   Book Block 32-48   1996 $8,500.00

BROWNE, THOMAS 1605-1682   Pseudodoxia Epidemica: of Unicornes Hornes. Williamsburg: Cheloniidae Press, 1984. 1st edition thus, state proof issue, one of 15 copies only, all on obsolete Whatman paper (blue white laid ca. 1962) from a total issue of 225, all signed by the artist, as follows: 15 state proof copies in full vellum nonadhesive limp binding with an original drawing and an extra suite of proofs of the etching, 60 deluxe copies in vellum binding and an extra suite, 150 regular copies on T.H. Saunders Laid; page size 9 1/2 x 7 inches; bound by Gray Parrot in full vellum, matching quarter vellum sleeve for extra suites, all housed in vellum and linen clamshell box. Illustrated with 16 wood engravings and one etching by Alan James Robinson. Text is set and cast in Van Dijk Monotype in black and blue; this copy inscribed by Robinson to the noted collectors Mimi and Arnold Elkind and is signed on colophon by printer and binder as well as Robinson.   Priscilla Juvelis 95/1-53   1996 $1,500.00

CLEMENS, SAMUEL LANGHORNE 1835-1910   Adventures of Huckleberry Finn. West Hatfield: Pennyroyal Press, 1985. Limited to 350 copies, signed by Barry Moser and by Gray Parrot; this copy number one, with each illustration signed by Moser, a signed prospectus, and an original, inscribed full page pencil drawing of Samuel Clemens as frontispiece; large quarto; xxiii, (8), 419 pages; 49 wood engravings by Moser, with an extra suite of plates; bound by Parrot in gilt stamped dark green morocco, extra suite is in a buckram chemise, book and sutie being housed together in slipcase of matching buckram; extremely fine.   Bromer Booksellers 87-250   1996 $2,500.00

GOETHE, JOHANN WOLFGANG VON 1749-1832   Fancies Bizarreries & Ornamented Grotesques. leeds: Eremite Press, 1989. One of 27 copies, from a total of 35; page size 15 3/4 x 10 1/2 inches; 24 etchings by Leonard Baskin; bound by Gray Parrot in half red morocco with marbled paper over boards, title on black morocco label on spine, housed in half morocco black clamshell box.   Priscilla Juvelis 95/1-89   1996 $6,000.00

KORN, ERIC   Lepidoptera Fantastica. Leeds: Gehenna Press, 1993. One of 40 copies, this one of 10 deluxe copies with an extra set of proofs in black painted in watercolor by Baskin and an original copperplate and a watercolor; page size 12 5/8 x 10 5/8 inches; printed on various European and Japanese handmade papers, all copies signed by Baskin and Korn; 16 etchings by Leonard Baskin, text printed letterpress in Centaur & Arrighi by Arthur Larson; bound by Gray Parrot with morocco spine and hand marbled paper over boards, title in gilt on cover, housed in custom clamshell box.   Priscilla Juvelis 95/1-103   1996 $10,000.00

ROBINSON, ALAN JAMES   Roadkills. Easthampton: Cheloniidae Press, 1981. Signed, limited edition, one of 250 copies each signed and numbered by the artist from a total edition of 300; 4to; printed on handmade Japanese paper; etching and 11 wood engravings by Robinson, text handset in 18pt. Arrighi and Centaur letterpress; bound by Gray Parrot in quarter grey Moroccan goat and Japanese paper in custom quarter leather clamshell box.   Priscilla Juvelis 95/1-56   1996 $750.00

YGLESIAS, JOSE   One German Dead. Leeds: Eremite Press, 1988. 1st edition; one of 115 copies, signed by artist and author; page size 9 3/4 x 5 5/8 inches; one original etched portrait of author by Baskin; blue paste paper over boards by Gray Parrot.   Priscilla Juvelis 95/1-90   1996 $350.00

BINDING - PARRY

BEST, THOMAS   A Concise Treatise on the Art of Angling. London: 1992. One of 175 copies; 2 color plates, text drawings; cloth backed boards title labels on spine and upper cover, printed on handmade paper; bound by Mary Parry.   David A.H. Grayling 3/95-571 1996 £75.00

BINDING - PARRY

BIBLE. ENGLISH - 1988   Saint Matheu. Shropshire: Tern Press, 1988. One in an edition of 140 copies signed by Nicholas and Mary Parry; 11.5 x 8.25 inches; 121 pages; illustrations by Nicholas Parry; titlepage border in blue, title in shades of blue and green, handcut capitals for chapter headings in different colors, 24 etched lino and combined technique prints in different colors, set in Baskerville, printed on T. H. Saunders handmade paper; bound by Mary Parry in white woven linen, paper title label in green on spine. Fine.   Joshua Heller 21-236   1996 $275.00

BIBLE. ENGLISH - 1991   Cantica Canticori. Salamons Lovelist Song. Market Drayton: Tern Press, 1991. One of 100 thus, in a total edition of 110 copies, signed by Nicholas Parry and Mary Parry; 5.25 x 6.5 inches; etchings printed in relief in black and shades of brown by Nicholas Parry on Arches paper; bound by Mary Parry in floral printed cloth; fine. Joshua Heller 21-244   1996 $135.00

BINDING - PASOTTI

WHITMAN, WALT 1819-1892   Selected Poems. Snake River Press, 1979. One of only 20 numbered copies; folio; printed in handset 16 pt. Walbaum; 9 colored drawings by Geoffrey Trenaman; half brown morocco by Adrian Pasotti; fine.   Bertram Rota 272-435 1996 £100.00

BINDING - PAUL

GOLDSMITH, OLIVER 1730-1774   The Poetical Works. London: printed by Ellerton and Henderson for Suttaby, Evance and Co., 1811. 1st printing of this edition; 11 1/4 x 9 inches; iv, 182 pages, 6 quite pleasing yellow tinted aquatint plates by Samuel Alken after drawings by R. H. Newell; contemporary smooth calf by E. Paul of Southampton (with his ticket at front), covers framed with blind and gilt foliate borders, raised bands, spine compartments pleasantly gilt, maroon calf label, new endpapers, joints lightly rubbed, tiny cracks just starting at top, covers slightly marked, small loss of leather in bottom spine compartment, but very good, sturdy original binding, small paper repair below titlepage imprint, minor foxing and offsetting, but excellent internally; bookplate of Merton Russell Cotes. Abbey Scenery 456.   Phillip J. Pirages 33-254 1996 $175.00

BINDING - PAX

VOLLMANN, WILLIAM T.   The Grave of Lost Stories. Sacramento: CoTangent Press, 1993. One of 15 deluxe copies only, 13 of which are for sale, all on Johannot paper, each signed and numbered by artist/author and binder, from an edition of 200 (185 regular copies); page size 10 7/8 x 7 7/8 inches; 4 illustrations hand colored; letterpress by Alastair Johnston in Electra and Cochin with display in Caslon, Marbleheart, Rimmed Lith and Asatoria at Poltroon Press, t.p. in 3 colors, guards of black & gold gilt Japanese (?) paper; bound by Ben Pax - steel & grey marble box (tomb) fitted to custom steel hinge by means of a copper sheet riveted to the steel and then crimped upward to form a pan, hinge powder coated black as interior; front cover incised with title, author's initials & Poe's dated, the copy number appears in roman numeral on back cover, along fore edge, 13 teeth have been set in handmade silver bezels; inside covers each have 4 brass & copper rods (oxidized green), book itself bound in bds. w/linen spine which are 'leafed, and variegated & painted in metallic fungoid patterns over which author has painted a female figure to represent one of the stories (author's description); gessoed bds. are copper colored & female in blue w/onlays of 4 sm. white bones (?) outlining skeleton. Boxed.   Priscilla Juvelis 95/1-254 1996 $4,500.00

BINDING - PEARSON

JONES, SHIRLEY   Impressions; Eight Aquatints to Accompany Eight Poems and Prose Pieces. Red Hen Press, 1984. Of 40 numbered copies, signed by artist, this is one of 15 'for fine binding' printed entirely on Barcham Green Waterleaf, text handset 18 pt. Baskerville; folio; unique binding by John Pearson of full calf dyed light and darker blues with stripes and stars, upper board further embellished in blind with title lettering and rules and with outline map of America, stars roughly marking the locations of five of the texts; fine state.   Bertram Rota 272-234 1996 £1,750.00

BINDING - HUGO PELLER

SHAKESPEARE, WILLIAM 1564-1616   The Passionate Pilgrim and the Songs in Shakespeare's Plays. Vale Press, 1896. One of 310 copies; 8 x 5 1/2 inches; 79 pages (plus 4 blanks at each end); woodcut border, vignette, initials by Charles Ricketts; gray inlaid and onlaid morocco signed by the Swiss binder Hugo Peller, front cover with thin white morocco onlays forming an abstract design suggesting three sinewy trees (three onlays in orange or maroon represent perhaps animals perched in trees), gilt leaves at base of tree and gilt disk above no doubt representing sun, spine lettered in blind capitals, top edge gilt and gauffered., in very nice matching fleece lined morocco backed folding box, virtually flawless copy.   Phillip J. Pirages 33-495 1996 $2,250.00

BINDING - PERCIVAL

LUBBOCK, JOSEPH G.   From Garden to Galaxy. London: Bertram Rota, 1980. 1st edition; number 11 of 80 copies, signed; small folio; 50 pages, 12 prints (6 of which are doublepage) from copperplates worked by engraving, etching and aquatint in various colours, some which are added by hand, printed on handmade paper by Will Carter; full morocco decorated in gold by George Percival, in glacine wrapper and matching slipcase, top edge gilt, others uncut, shelf mark on endpaper.   Claude Cox 107-91 1996 £220.00

LUBBOCK, JOSEPH G.   From the Snows to the Seas. 1986. One of 95 numbered copies, signed by author/artist; folio; 3 page foldout combined process illustrations by author; printed on handmade paper in blue and black by Will Carter; bound by George Percival in quarter morocco, silk boards, stamped in gilt with design by artist; fine in slipcase.   Bertram Rota 272-281 1996 £300.00

LUBBOCK, JOSEPH G.   From the Snows to the Seas. London: Rota, 1986. One of 95 copies only, each copy signed by artist/author; page size 14 x 10 1/2 inches; printed on R.W.S. handmade paper; 4 triple fold-out copperplates worked by etching and aquatint; colors printed in intaglio and relief, and additional color applied to some pages by hand; bound by George Percival in gilt stamped blue silk after a design by the artist, blue morocco spine; mylar jacket and publisher's slipcase. Priscilla Juvelis 95/1-159 1996 $500.00

LUBBOCK, JOSEPH G.   Landscapes of the Spirit. 1994. One of only 65 numbered copies, signed by author; 4to; printed on handmade paper in black and brown by Sebastian Carter; five full page colored prints, two double page, one vertical foldout and 3 page horizontal foldout by author; hand bound by George Percival in quarter purple morocco, ochre silk sides, design by Lubbock in gilt on upper cover, fine in slipcase. Bertram Rota 272-283 1996 £210.00

LUBBOCK, JOSEPH G.   Love for Earth. 1990. One of 95 numbered copies, signed by author; 4to; text designed and printed in black and deep rose by Will Carter; 5 double page and 6 full page colored illustrations hand printed by author; hand bound by George Percival in quarter red morocco, silk sides with design by Lubbock in gilt on upper cover, fine in marbled slipcase.   Bertram Rota 272-282 1996 £210.00

LUBBOCK, JOSEPH G.   Love for the Earth. Cambridge: Printed by Will Carter at the Rampant Lions Press for Bertram Rota, 1990. One of 95 copies, signed by author; 11 1/2 x 9 3/4 inches; 52 pages, (2) leaves; 11 expressive colored prints; maroon morocco backed silk over boards by George Percival, gilt stamped with design by artist; original marbled slipcase. Mint.   Phillip J. Pirages 33-370 1996 $550.00

BINDING - PERIOD BINDERY

PEROTTUS, NICCOLAUS   In Hoc Volumine Habentur Haec - Cornucopiae, Sive Linguae Latinae Com(m)entarii Diligentissime Recogniti... Venice: In Aedibus Aldi, et Andreae Soceri, 1513//17. Folio in 8s; 439 (of 440) leaves, lacks last leaf, blank except for device on verso, Aldine device appears on titlepage and on K8v, italic text in double column, last signatures with some marginal dampstaining; 2nd issue of November 1513 edition; modern sprinkled calf by Period Bindery, Bath. Renouard 81.10. Adams P721; UCLA II 132.   Family Album Tillers-476 1996 $1,750.00

BINDING - PERIOD BOOKBINDERS

ERSKINE, JOHN ELPHINSTONE   Journal of a Cruise Among the Islands of the Western Pacific, Including the Feejees and Others Inhabited by the Polynesian Negro Races, in Her Majesty's Ship Havannah. London: John Murray, 1853. 1st edition; 8vo; folding map, 7 plates, 4 are tinted lithographs; half maroon morocco, gilt, spine gilt, by Period Bookbinders of Bath; fine. Hill p. 98; Abbey Travel 602.   Ximenes 109-110 1996 $500.00

BINDING - PHOENIX BINDERY

HOLY Songs and Sonnets. Groningen: La Stampa Chiara, 1985. Each one of 50 numbered copies, signed by artist; narrow folio; text in Bembo and ornamental borders printed in 6 color silkscreen on Simili Japon, 2 volumes; etchings by Marjolein Varekamp; fine grey cloth by Phoenix Bindery, Amsterdam; fine in dust jackets.   Bertram Rota 272-439 1996 £130.00

BINDING - PORTER

SHELLEY, G. E.   A Monograph of the Nectariniidae or Family of Sun Birds. London: 1876-80. Only 250 copies printed; royal 4to; cviii, 393 pages, 121 fine hand colored plates; contemporary full brown morocco, gilt, gilt inside borders by Porter, gilt top; rare. Fine, clean copy, beautifully colored, with author's bookplate, from the collection of Jan Coldewey.   Wheldon & Wesley 207-98 1996 £10,000.00

BINDING - POUJADE

HORATIUS FLACCUS, QUINTUS 65-8 BC   Opera. Leyden & Rotterdam: Ex Officina Hackiana, 1670. 8vo; engraved title, 7 ff., 832 pages, 28ff. n.n.; black calf gilt by Poujade of Millau and with his ticket, ornate richly gilt and red painted neo-gothic central plaque, gilt and blind outer borders, spine with raised gilt bands enclosing blind stamped compartments, red label, all edges gilt; eye catching binding, little marred by inaccurate tool placement.   Marlborough 160-18 1996 £450.00

BINDING - PRATT

REED, ISAAC   Bibliotheca Reediana. London: J. Barker, printer, 1807. 8vo; frontispiece; full polished calf, gilt, slight rubbing; fine copy on large paper; tipped in is letter May 2 1808 from auctioneer Thomas King, pres. this copy to noted antiquarian bookseller George Nicol; neatly priced and ruled throughout; fine. LAR 124; De Ricci p. 63.   Ximenes 108-12 1996 $1,250.00

BINDING - PRIZE

COGAN, THOMAS   Ethical Questions; or Speculations on the Principal Subjects of Controversy in Moral Philosophy. London: T. Cadell and W. Davies, 1817. 1st edition; 8vo; vi, (2), 439, (1) pages; contemporary calf, gilt, marbled edges and gilt armorial stamp of Glasgow University on sides; very good, prize binding.   John Drury 82-51 1996 £250.00

TUCKERMAN, ARTHUR LYMAN   A Short History of Architecture. New York: Scribner's, 1887. 1st edition; 8vo; 168 pages; illustrations; ca. 1930 prize binding of full polished tree calf by Wickers & Son, with raised bands, gilt tooled spine, morocco spine labels, gilt borders on covers, and gilt heraldic crest on front cover, prize award bookplate, light general wear to binding, but handsome, very good.   Chapel Hill 94-118 1996 $125.00

BINDING - RAMAGE

PALGRAVE, FRANCIS TURNER 1824-1897   The Golden Treasury Selected fromt he Best Songs and Lyrical Poems in the English Language... London: Macmillan and Co. Ltd., New York: The Macmillan Co., 1900. Revised; small 8vo; pages (x), 381, (1); fine green morocco, elaborately and densely gilt, with large variety of ornaments, forming a large central wheel on sides surrounded by a seme of dots and numerous other tools, borders of a single filelt and two rolls, spine in compartments with raised bands, also densely gilt, gilt lettering, inner dentelles, richly gilt with series of roll borders, edges gilt, white silk endpapers, little spotted, otherwise fine. Delightful example of the work of John Ramage.   Simon Finch 24-177 1996 £550.00

BINDING - REMNANT & EDMONDS

MITFORD, MARY RUSSELL 1787-1855   Recollections of a Literary Life. London: Richard Bentley, 1852. 1st edition; crown 8vo; 3 volumes; original cloth, gilt by Remnant & Edmonds, with their ticket, some very minor external wear, but very good; pleasing literary association, each volume bards contemporary ownership signatures of John James Ruskin, wine merchant and father of the Victorian sage.   Ash Rare Books Zenzybyr-68 1996 £195.00

BINDING - RENOUF

KIPLING, RUDYARD 1865-1936   The Five Nations. London: Methuen, 1903. 2nd edition; 8vo; full polished acid calf with an abstract 'tree' design on both covers, within a leafy outer border, spine with five raised bands with elegant gilt tooling, red morocco title label, binder's name, Renouf, stamped in gilt at foot, ticket on front pastedown: Publisher, E.M. Renouf, Montreal; fine. Livingston pp. 265-69.   Book Block 32-39 1996 $225.00

BINDING - RIVIERE

ADOLPHUS, JOHN   Memoirs of John Bannister. London: Richard Bentley, 1839. Thick 8vo; 2 volumes; extra illustrated with approximately 140 plates, an original wash drawing of the Surrey Theatre by Thomas H. Shepherd; choicely bound in full crimson morocco, 3 line gilt border, fully gilt spine in 6 compartments, morocco doublures, all edges gilt, by Riveire.   Charles W. Traylen 117-60 1996 £950.00

AINSWORTH, WILLIAM HARRISON 1805-1882   Jack Sheppard. London: Richard Bentley, 1839. 1st edition; 8 x 5 1/4 inches; 3 volumes; 27 engraved plates by George Cruikshank, as well as portrait of Ainsworth in volume 1, with half title in volume 3 (no others called for), fly title from 1 mistakenly bound at front as a half title; half title somewhat soiled, few additional leaves slightly smudged, small nick on one spine, one or two other quite trivial imperfections; lovely crimson crushed morocco by Riviere & Son, French fillet frame on covers, spines beautifully gilt in compartments, with central floral ornament surrounded by circles, stars, flowers and folaige, top edge gilt, other edges untrimmed, fine filligree gilt inner dentelles, front hinge of volume 1 with neat cosmetic repair, original cloth covers and spines bound in at rear of each volume; fine copy in extremely handsome binding.   Phillip J. Pirages 33-3 1996 $575.00

BACON, FRANCIS, VISCOUNT ST. ALBANS 1561-1626   Essays. London: Longmans, Green and Co., 1873. New edition; 8 3/4 x 6 inches; xxiv, 620 pages; extremely pretty contemporary flamed calf, gilt, by Riviere, covers with delicate twining floral border, raised bands, spine compartments handsomely gilt in antique style with large floral stamps at middle and scrolling foliage in corners, black morocco lettering piece, marbled edges and endpapers; especially fine, handsome binding bright with only negligible wear and virtually pristine internally.   Phillip J. Pirages 33-34 1996 $150.00

BADIUS ASCENCIUS, JODOCUS 1462-1535   Stultiferae Naves Sensus Animosque Trahentes Mortis in Exitium. Paris: Thielmann Kerver for E. J. and G. Marnef, 1500. 1st edition; small 4to; 6 large woodcut illustrations; full crushed burgundy morocco du cap, spine with five raised bands and gilt titling, board edges gilt, inner gilt dentelles, all edges gilt, by Riviere, very top of front joint slightly cracked, nearly invisible paper remarging to few leaves; bookplates of Edward Rahir and Henri Burton.   Book Block 32-29 1996 $7,500.00

BARHAM, RICHARD HARRIS 1788-1845   Martin's Vagaries; Being a Sequel to "A Tale of a Tub"... London: A. H. Baily & Co., 1843. 1st edition; 8 x 5 inches, 48 pages; 2 plates, 1 textual illustration by George Cruikshank, text illustration repeated on original printed wrappers bound in at back; finely bound by Riviere in medium brown crushed morocco, covers framed with French fillet, spine handsomely gilt in compartments (with vertical title in elongated center compartment), turn-ins covered with lovely gilt filigree, gilt top, two edges rough trimmed, short portions at top of joints showing first signs of cracking, covers with few faint spots, slight wrinkling of a few leaves at fore edge, otherwise fine in very appealing binding. Cohn 516.   Phillip J. Pirages 33-149 1996 $250.00

BERKELEY, GRANTLEY F.   Reminiscences of a Huntsman. London: Longman, Brown, Green and Longmans, 1854. 1st edition; octavo; xi, 415 pages, plus 24 pages ads; hand colored frontispiece and 3 engraved plates; bound by Riviere & Son, in full red levant morocco, gilt lettered spine with raised bands, gilt board edges and inner dentelles, top edge gilt, marbled endpapers, scattered light foxing; armorial bookplate; very good. Schwerdt I p. 61.   Heritage Book Shop 196-198 1996 $400.00

BERNAL, RALPH   Illustrated Catalogue of the Distinguished Collection of Works of Art and Vertu, from the Byzantine Period to that of Louis Seize Collected by the Late Ralph Bernal, Esq. London: for J. H. Burn, 1855. 4to; Large paper copy printed on thick paper, with additional general titlepage and frontispiece, (2), 357, (1), 66, (2) pages, frontispiece, plates, loosely inserted is a printed petition from P. Le Neve Foster of the Society for the Encouragement of Arts, Manufactures and Commerce, Requesting for the Collection to be Purchased for the Nations; there is also an associated letter from Le Neve Foster to Augustus Franks, keeper of the Dept. of British & Medieval Antiquities at the British Museum; although unsigned, this would suggest this is Frank's copy of the catalog; some occasional foxing, but good copy, bound by Riviere in later 19th century half brown morocco, several small repairs to joints and corners and also to the marbled paper on board edges.   Ken Spelman 30-46 1996 £360.00

BINDING - RIVIERE

BRYDGES, SAMUEL EGERTON, BART 1762-1837 Letters From the Continent. Kent: printed at the private press of Lee Priory by John Warwick, 1821. 1st edition; 8vo; 2 volumes in 1; 177, (178)-362 pages, 7 pages ads; full speckled calf by Riviere with a decorative gilt border, spine richly gilt in 6 compartments with 5 raised bands, extremities slightly rubbed, bookplates and short tipped in clipping, else tight, very good, one of the bookplates is that of John Sheepshanks, famous English art collector; very scarce, most likely issued in an edition of 250 copies. Chapel Hill 94-255 1996 $450.00

BURNABY, FREDERICK On Horseback through Asia Minor. London: Sampson Low, Marston, Searle & Rivington, Crown Buildings, 188... 1877. 1st edition; 2 volumes; (v-vii), (ix-xliii), (xv-xxxii), 1-352 pages; (v-xix), 1-322, 323-399; frontispiece to volume 1, 3 maps, errata slip tipped in, binders stamp to front f.e.p.; bound by Riviere, full polished tan calf, double gilt rule border to boards, elaborate gilt tooling to panelled spines, morocco labels to spines, corners bumped and worn, all edges gilt, marbled endpapers. Beeleigh Abbey BA56-47 1996 £425.00

BURTON, ROBERT 1577-1640 The Anatomy of Melancholy. Oxford: J. Litchfield & J. Short for H. Cripps, 1621. 1st edition; small 4to; with errata leaf (Ddd4) which is un folio'd, and the preceding leaf Ddd3; tiny hole in Hh6 affecting a few words; full crushed morocco with outer gilt fillet border inside of which is a blind fillet border, three quarter of an inch inside this outermost border are two sets of gilt and blind fillet borders, about one quarter inch apart and on the corners of this inner set of borders are four gilt fleurons, spine divided into six compartments by five raised bands, second and third of which contain the title information, others each contain a gilt fleuron and some gilt border decoration, board edges gilt with single gilt fillet, inner gilt fillets stamped at bottom of front turn-in, bound by Riviere & Son; in half morocco slipcase with inner chemise; with bookplates of T. G. Arthur and Mortimer L. Schiff. Grolier English 18; PMM 120; Maden/Oxford Books I, 115. II 90. Book Block 32-52 1996 $14,500.00

BYRON, GEORGE GORDON NOEL, 6TH BARON 1788-1824 Hours of Idleness, a Series of Poems. Newark: printed and sold by S. and J. Ridge; sold also by B. Crosby & Co... 1807. 1st edition; crown 8vo; pages (iii-xiii), (i) errata, 187; rebound without half title, skilfully washed and resized, full dark blue crushed morocco, sides ruled in gilt with triple fillet, spine richly gilt between raised bands, gilt lettered in two panels and with date at foot, inner dentelles richly gilt, marbled endpapers, gilt edges; by Riviere. Wise I pp. 7-8. Simon Finch 24-26 1996 £975.00

CHATTERTON, THOMAS 1752-1770 The Rowley Poems. London: Hacon and Ricketts at the sign of the Dial, 1898. Limited to 210 copies; large 8vo; 2 volumes; full red morocco, extra wide gilt floral borders on upper covers, gold panelled spines in 6 compartments, gilt tops, other edges uncut, bound by Riviere for Henry Sotheran. Charles W. Traylen 117-87 1996 £450.00

CICERO, MARCUS TULLIUS 106-43 BC Cicero's Books of Friendship, Old Age and Scipio's Dream. London: Chatto & Windus/Boston: John W. Luce and Co., 1907. 6 x 4 3/4 inches; xviii, 217, (1) pages; frontispiece; very pretty burgundy morocco, heavily gilt by Riviere and Son (for Brentano's), covers with intricate frame featuring elegant roses on elongated stems reaching into the corners, large massed clump of a dozen roses at center of each cover, with tendrils extending to the four sides of the front cover fame, spine with raised bands, gilt to fur sides of the cover frame, spine with raised bands, gilt decorated compartments, gilt titling, turn-ins with simple gilt rules and corner ornaments, marbled endpapers, gilt edges; couple of minor marks to covers, spine a shade darker than boards, otherwise fine, attractively bound, virtually pristine internally. Phillip J. Pirages 33-60 1996 $175.00

COMBE, WILLIAM 1742-1823 The History of Johnny Quae Genus... London: Ackermann, 1822. 1st edition; 24 hand colored plates by Rowlandson, some brown offsetting onto text from some plates, otherwise exceptionally fine copy; full blue niger morocco with gilt borders on covers and gilt decorative panels on spine, by Riviere, all edges gilt, fine. Words Etcetera 94-1096 1996 £385.00

CONSTABLE, HENRY The Poems and Sonnets. Vale Press, 1897. One of 210 copies; 9 1/4 x 6 inches; ci, (1) pages, (1) leaf (colophon, limitation), elaborate woodcut vine border on first page of text as well as fine decorative woodcut initials by Charles Ricketts; absolutely splendid crimson morocco, heavily gilt, by Riviere & Son (very possibly contemporary), covers with very wide and animated borders of circuling gilt vines terminating in deeply gouged broad leaves & groups of flowers & emanating from a semis ground, raised bands decorated with 3 large gilt dots, six spine panels, two with titling, rest with leafy gilt vines like those on covers, turn-ins gilt ruled and with corner ornaments, top edge gilt, others untrimmed; nearly perfect copy in sumptuous binding. Armorial bookplate of M. C. D. Borden. Tomkinson p. 165. Phillip J. Pirages 33-490 1996 $1,800.00

COOPER, B. B. The Life of Sir Astley Cooper, Bart. London: 1843. 1st edition; 8vo; 2 volumes; portrait; slightly later calf, gilt spines, marbled edges and endpapers (similar pattern marble), by Riviere, trifle worn. Maggs Bros. Ltd. 1190-388 1996 £90.00

BINDING - RIVIERE

COWPER, WILLIAM 1731-1800 Poems. (with) The Task. London: Johnson, 1782/85. 1st editions; octavo; 2 volumes, 367, 359 pages; beautifully bound by Riviere and son in full dark blue morocco, covers outlined with a triple gilt rule, spine gilt in 6 compartments, showing elaborate floral devices, turn-ins richly gilt with floral border; housed together in morocco backed pull-off box; very fine; bookplates of H. Bradley Martin. Rothschild 681; Hayward I 191; Grolier English II 60. Bromer Booksellers 90-21 1996 $1,000.00

CRAIG, WILLIAM MARSHALL Description of the Plates Representing the Intinerant Traders of London in Their Ordinary Costume... London: n.d., c. 1804. Small 4to; 31 hand colored etched plates each with facing page of descriptive text, all bar seven plates have a grey wash border, plates all in very good condition with no foxing, light offsetting to letterpress only, text watermarked 1803 & majority of plates watermarked Whatman 1804, plate 3 'Baskets' watermarked E. & P. 1801, title to plate 12 'Green Hasteds' rather than 'Green Hastings' given in Abbey, new endpapers and prelims; bound by Riviere, full modern French styled mottled calf, triple gilt rule borders to boards, elaborate gilt tooling to panelled spine, green morocco labels to spine raised bands, grey speckled endpapers, very handsome copy. Abbey Life 271. Beeleigh Abbey BA56-235 1996 £1,500.00

CROLY, GEORGE May Fair. London: Ainsworth, 1827. 1st edition; octavo; pages 194, (2); handsome binding by Riviere in full mottled calf, gilt extra, panelled spine, gilt decorated dentelles and panels, double leather labels, marbled endpapers, all edges gilt; unusually attractive copy. CBEL III 231. Hartfield 48-L27 1996 $195.00

DEFOE, DANIEL 1661?-1731 The Life and Strange Surprizing Adventures of Robinson Crusoe...(and) The Farther Adventures of Robinson Crusoe. London: printed for W. Taylor, 1719. 1st edition of volume 2, 2nd edition of volume 1; 2 volumes, 364; 373 pages, (11) ads, 6 ads; frontispiece in volume 1, folding map in volume 2, in fine full dark green morocco, spines gilt, by Riviere, all edges gilt, some soiling (washed), few minor defects, very good, scarce; PMM 180; Grolier 100 English 41. 19th Century Shop 39- 1996 $3,800.00

DICKENS, CHARLES 1812-1870 American Notes for General Circulation. London: Chapman and Hall, 1842. 1st edition; 1st issue (first pagination of "Contents" page in volume I); 8vo; 2 volumes; half titles, ad leaf in volume I, 6 pages ads in volume 2; full gilt bordered morocco, spines gilt, top edge gilt, by Riviere, original cloth covers and spines bound in; fine set, bookplates. Smith 3; Eckel pp. 113-5; Tinker Lib. 821; Sterling 261. Trebizond 39-6 1996 $850.00

DICKENS, CHARLES 1812-1870 The Posthumous Papers of the Pickwick Club. London: Chapman and Hall, 1887. Limited to 2000 copies; this one of 500 with plates on India paper; thick royal 8vo; 2 volumes bound in 4; original illustrations; extra illustrated with the insertion of 326 extra illustrations; full green morocco, elaborate gilt corner pieces, gilt spines, gilt tops, gilt leather doublures, silk endpapers; bound by Riviere. Charles W. Traylen 117-108 1996 £3,750.00

EASTLAKE, CHARLES L. Materials for a History of Oil Painting. London: Longman, 1847. 1st edition; 8vo; xii, 561, (i) pages, bound without final 32 pages of ads; bound by Riviere in later 19th century polished tree calf, gilt panelled spine, joints expertly repaired; most handsome copy. Ken Spelman 30-44 1996 £140.00

EVENINGS At Haddon Hall. London: Henry G. Bohn, 1850. Small octavo; viii, 432 pages; 24 plates by George Cattermole; contemporary tan polished calf by Riviere & Son, gilt double rule border on covers, gilt spine, tooled in compartments with black morocco label, gilt board edges and turn-ins, all edges gilt, marbled endpapers, minor wear to covers, scattered light foxing, near fine. Heritage Book Shop 196-215 1996 $300.00

FERGUSON, RICHARD S. Cumberland and Westmorland M.P.'s (sic) from the Restoration to the Reform Bill of 1867, (1660-1867). London: J. Bell and Daldy and Carlisle: C. Thurman, 1871. Large paper limited edition (20 copies only); 4to; pages xix, 478; frontispiece; frontispiece; three quarter levant morocco gilt by Riviere, with 5 flattened raised bands and marbled boards, spine trifle mellowed, front flyleaf foxed, some occasional foxing and light spotting elsewhere, but generally very nice, scarce; printed memo affixed to flyleaf lists 15 recipients of the large paper copies, and a further 4 recipients are added in Ferguson's hand, including this Naworth Castle library copy; presentation copy from author for Mr. Howard (Earl of Carlisle). R.F.G. Hollett & Son 78-152 1996 £275.00

FIELDING, HENRY 1707-1754 The History of the Adventures of Joseph Andrews, and Of His Friend Mr. Abraham Adams. London: A. Millar, 1742. 1st edition; octavo; 2 volumes; full red morocco gilt, all edges gilt, by Riviere, bookplate, nice. Rothschild 844. G. W. Stuart 59-34 1996 $1,750.00

BINDING - RIVIERE

FORRESTER, ALFRED HENRY 1804-1872   Pictures Picked from the Pickwick Papers. London: 1838. 40 fine hand colored plates; full coarse grained morocco by Riviere with triple gilt rules on panels and with extra gilt floral devices in compartments, gilt dentelles, top edge gilt, original front wrapper bound in at rear.   Captain's Bookshelf 38-48 1996 $375.00

GRAY, THOMAS 1716-1771   Poems and Letters. London: printed at th Chiswick Press, 1867. 4to; actual photograph as frontispiece, 3 oval photos; contemporary calf, spine gilt, slightly worn, all edges gilt, by Riviere.   Anthony W. Laywood 108-176 1996 £60.00

GRIMM, THE BROTHERS   German Popular Stories. London: Pub. by. C. Baldwyn/ London: James Robins & Co. & Joseph Robins Dublin 1823/26. 1st edition, 1st issue of volume 1, without umlaut in word "marchen" on titlepage; 12mo; 2 volumes; xii, 240; iv, 256, (2) pages; 22 etched plates by George Cruikshank, including 2 vignette titles, plates in volume I printed in brown, without publisher's ads called for at end of volume 1 and at beginning of volume 2, but otherwise complete, with all first issue points called for by Cohn; full red crushed levant morocco by Riviere & Son, gilt triple rule border on covers, gilt spines, tooled in compartments, gilt board edges and turn-ins, all edges gilt; occasional light soiling, browning or offsetting, few expert marginal repairs in volume 2, overall very good, handsomely bound in red cloth slipcase. Cohn 369; Morgan Lib. Early Children's Books 197.   Heritage Book Shop 196-217 1996 $7,500.00

IRVING, WASHINGTON 1783-1859   A Chronicle of the Conquest of Granada. London: John Murray, 1829. 1st English edition; 8vo; 2 volumes; beautifully bound by Riviere in three quarter maroon morocco with fine gilt detail on spines, fine. BAL 10126.   Charles Agvent 4-709 1996 $400.00

KINGLAKE, ALEXANDER WILLIAM 1809-1891   The Invasion of the Crimea; Its Origin and an Account of Its Progress Down to the Death of Lord Raglan. London: 1863. 8vo; plates and maps; well bound in half red morocco, gilt top, by Riviere, small library numbers on spines.   Charles W. Traylen 117-144 1996 £390.00

LA FONTAINE, JEAN DE 1621-1695   Tales and Novels in Verse. Paris: J. Lemonnyer, 1884. Re-issue of the Fermier Genereaux edition; 8vo; 2 volumes; 85 engravings after drawings by Eisen; three quarter maroon morocco, gilt emblematic tooling on spines, raised bands, gilt tops by Riviere; attractive set.   Appelfeld Gallery 54-128 1996 $300.00

LEVER, CHARLES JAMES 1806-1872   Barrington. London: Chapman and Hall, 1862-63. 1st edition in original monthly parts; 8vo; 13 parts in 12 numbers; numerous inserted ads; original pink printed wrappers (evenly faded), in full green morocco solander case, by Riviere & Son (slight rubbing); fine set. Brown, Ireland in Fiction 935; CBEL III 943. Ximenes 108-244 1996 $750.00

LUTHER, MARTIN 1483-1546   The Way to Prayer. London: William Pickering, 1846. 1st edition in English; 6 1/4 x 5 1/4 inches; xxvi pages, (1) leaf, 68 pages; frontispiece, device on title, decorative headpieces and initials; quite appealing slightly later dark brown morocco by Riviere for B. M. Pickering, covers panelled in gilt and blind, corner fleurons between raised bands, marbled endpapers, all edges gilt (with Pickering booksellers' ticket at front), slight rubbing to joints, spine bands and extremities, inner margin of frontispiece, skillfully repaired without loss, otherwise fine and attractive copy. Modern bookplates of Charles Ballantyne and H. C. Wace, owner's signature of E. Arnett on flyleaf dated 1861. Rare edition. Keynes p. 65.   Phillip J. Pirages 33-421 1996 $325.00

MAC KAY, CHARLES   The Scenery and Poetry of the English Lakes. London: Longman, Brown, etc., 1846. 8vo; pages xvi, 235; 8 full page vignettes, 52 text illustrations; full polished calf, gilt, by Riviere, extremities little rubbed; margins faintly browned, flyleaves trifle spotted, but handsome copy. Bicknell 138.1.   R.F.G. Hollett & Son 78-1089 1996 £165.00

MACAULAY, THOMAS BABINGTON MACAULAY, 1ST BARON 1800-1859 The History of England from the Accession of James the Second. London: Longman, Brown, Green & Longmans/Longman, Green, Longman & Roberts, 1849-61. Mixed set, volumes i and ii fourth editions (although dating from 1849, the original year of publication), remainder first editions; demy 8vo; 5 volumes; bound in later half polished calf by Riviere & Son, banded and gilt, top edge gilt, little very light wear, few minor marks, but still in very good state.   Ash Rare Books Zenzybyr-64 1996 £245.00

MARRYAT, FREDERICK 1792-1848   Peter Simple. London: Saunders & Otley, 1834. 1st English edition (same year as Philadelphia); 12mo; 3 volumes, errata slip in volume 3, wanting half title in volume 2 (others not called for) and ads in volume 3; later Riviere style quarter calf, spines gilt, morocco labels, marbled boards; fine, attractive. Sadleir 1592a; wolff 4531.   Trebizond 39-40 1996 $190.00

BINDING - RIVIERE

MILLS, JOHN   The Flyers of the Hunt. London: The Field and Ward and Lock, 1859. 1st edition; 7 1/4 x 5 inches; 5 p.l., 114, (1) pages; 6 etched plates (including frontispiece) by John Leech; fine honey colored polished calf by Riviere, spine attractively gilt in compartments featuring equestrian ornaments, red and green morocco labels, board edges attractively hatched in gilt, densely gilt inner dentelles, marbled endpapers, top edge gilt, original cloth bound in at back; top of back cover faintly faded, otherwise binding extremely bright entirely free of wear and very pleasing, fine internally. Modern signed engraved bookplate of David M. Ritchie. Podeschi 196.   Phillip J. Pirages 33-386 1996 $225.00

MILLS, JOHN   Stable Secrets; or, Puffy Doddles, His Sayings and Sympathies. London: Ward and Lock, 1863. 1st edition; 7 1/2 x 5 1/4 inches; 112, (1) pages; vignette on title, 3 etched plates, including frontispiece; fine honey colored polished calf by Riviere, spine attractively gilt on compartments featuring equestrian ornaments, red and green morocco labels, board edges attractively hatched in gilt, densely gilt inner dentelles, marbled endpapers, top edge gilt, original cloth bound in at rear, text little darkened (because of inferior paper stock) and slightly soiled, otherwise excellent internally, one small spot on front cover, but handsome binding in fine, unworn condition, very attractive. Bookplate of David M. Ritchie. Podeschi 203.   Phillip J. Pirages 33-387 1996 $200.00

RALEIGH, WALTER 1552-1618   The Discoverie of the Large, Rich and Bewtiful Empyre of Guiana, with a Relation of the Great and Golden Citie of Manoa... London: by Robert Robinson, 1595. 1st edition; 3rd issue; 4to; (16), 112 pages; full polished calf, spine richly gilt in compartments by Riviere, upper edge of title very skillfully extended, with 3 letters and parts of 10 other letters in almost imperceptible pen facsimile, two or three repairs to blank margins, else fine; with Boies Penrose bookplates. Church 254; JCB III 1.349; Sabin 67554; STC 20636.   Joseph J. Felcone 64-33 1996 $5,500.00

RICHARDSON, SAMUEL 1689-1761   The Novels. New York: Croscup and Sterling, 1901. Founder's Edition, strictly limited to 15 numbered sets, with frontispieces in 2 states (colored and uncolored) and plates in 3 states; 8vo; 20 volumes; half dark blue morocco, gilt panelled spines, top edge gilt, by Riviere.   Charles W. Traylen 117-184 1996 £400.00

SCOT, REGINALD   The Discoverie of Witchcraft, Wherein the Lewde dealing of Witches and Witchmongers is Notablie detected... London: by William Brome, 1584. 1st edition; 4to; (28), 560, (16) pages, 2 unpagianted leaves signed * between 2C8 and 2D1 and between 2D5 and 2D6, 4 full page woodcuts of magical apparatus, diagrams, large woodcut initials and other woodcuts, Black letter; full red crushed levant morocco, covers with gilt fillets and cornerpieces, spine richly gilt in compartments, inner dentelles gilt, gilt edges by Riviere, absolutely flawless and beautiful copy, with excellent margins, measuring 18.8 x 13.8 cm; STC 21864. Hall, Old Conjuring Books pp. 47-62.   Joseph J. Felcone 64-37 1996 $12,000.00

SHAKESPEARE, WILLIAM 1564-1616   Comedies, Histories, and Tragedies... London: printed by Tho. Cotes for Robert Allot, 1632. 2nd edition, 1st issue of the second folio; 12 3/4 x 8 3/8 inches; titlepage with engraved portrait; finely bound in full blue morocco gilt by Riviere, minor restoration, affecting only a few leaves, occasional stains and minor flaws, significantly better than other copies appearing for sale in the past few years, this copy does not have the extensive facsimile work and remargined and inlaid leaves present in almost all copies which have recently appeared, very good and attractive copy.   19th Century Shop 39- 1996 $90,000.00

SHELLEY, PERCY BYSSHE 1792-1822   (Laon and Cythna). The Revolt of Islam.. London: for John Brooks, 1829. Re-issue with original sheets; 8vo; pages (ii), v-xxxii, (ii), fly-title to dedication and list of errata, 270, without initial and final blanks; 19th century green calf, sides with double fillet gilt border with roundels at corners, spine in compartments, with raised bands, gilt rules, rolls and floral ornaments, morocco labels, inner dentelles gilt, marbled endpapers, top edge gilt, others uncut, by Riviere & Son, joints cracked, spine with burn mark, rubbed in places and discolored, still very good. Forman 50; Granniss 45; Wise p. 50. Simon Finch 24-207 1996 £750.00

SHELLEY, PERCY BYSSHE 1792-1822   Prometheus Unbound, a Lyrical Drama in Four Acts With Other Poems. London: C. and J. Ollier, 1820. 1st edition; genuinely scarce first issue with misprint 'Misellaneous' in the 'Contents' list; this leaf (A3) was cancelled and a corrected leaf substituted in the second issue; 8vo; pages (i)-xv, (i) (blank), (17)-222, (2); half title and final (integral) leaf of ads present, half title, title and margins lightly browned; late 19th century polished blue morocco by Riviere, front joint slightly tender, backstrip with raised bands and gilt compartments, dulled, lettered direct in second, triple gilt fillet borders on sides, abrasion on upper side, double fillet on board edges, wide gilt dentelle decoration turn-ins, burgundy chalked endpapers, top edge gilt, overall excellent. Tal copy. Granniss p. 54; Tinker 1898; Wise p. 55/56. Blackwell's B112-254 1996 £2,750.00

BINDING - RIVIERE

SHELLEY, PERCY BYSSHE 1792-1822   Works in Verse and Prose. London: Reeves and Turner, 1876. 8vo; 8 volumes; portrait; finely bound in half blue levant morocco, mottled board sides, 5 raised bands, gilt tops, bound by Riviere, choice set.   Charles W. Traylen 117-194   1996 £850.00

SIDNEY, PHILIP 1554-1586   The Countess of Pembroke's Arcadia. London: for George Calvert, 1674. 13th edition; folio; (32), 624, (26) pages; portrait; full brown polished calf, covers panelled, spine richly gilt in compartments, dentelles gilt, by Riviere; some page numbers cropped, front hinge just beginning to crack, else fine, Dartrey bookplate. Wing S3770.   Joseph J. Felcone 64-38 1996 $450.00

STRUTT, JOSEPH   Queen-Hoo Hall, A Romance: and Ancient Times. Edinburgh: by James Ballantyne & Co., for John Murray, London & Archibald... 1808. 1st edition; 6 1/2 x 4 inches; 4 volumes; later red three quarter morocco by Riviere, linen sides, raised spine bands decorated with a stippled rule, spine panels lettered in gilt or stamped with gilt thistle ornament, marbled endpapers, all edges gilt, slight rubbing at top of spines, very minor wear to few corners but joints virtually unworn and bindings clean, bright and very pretty, tear on title of third volume through two words very artfully repaired without loss, inexpensive paper little darkened and somewhat foxed or spotted throughout (as probably the case with most copies of this imprint), despite defects, quite attractive set, rather scarce in the marketplace. Phillip J. Pirages 33-459 1996 $350.00

SWINBURNE, ALGERNON CHARLES 1837-1909   The Queen Mother. (and) Rosamund. London: Basil Montagu Pickering, 1860. 1st edition; 1st issue, one of fewer than 20 copies; 7 x 4 1/2 inches; 5 p.l., 160 pages, (1) leaf, (161)-217, (1) pages, 1 leaf, including half titles and errata leaf at end; extremely fine crimson crushed morocco, heavily gilt by Riviere, covers with frame of five plain and decorative rules enclosing lovely broad filigree border of closely spaced elaborate fleurons, spine handsomely gilt in compartments filled with floral and foliate stamps, especially pretty inner gilt dentelles, top edge gilt, other edges untrimmed, slipcase, faint soiling here and there in text, otherwise very fine in splendid and pristine binding; Wise 2.   Phillip J. Pirages 33-476 1996 $1,250.00

TENNYSON, ALFRED TENNYSON, 1ST BARON 1809-1892   The Poetical Works of Alfred Lord Tennyson, Poet Laureate. London: Kegan Paul & Co., 1878. 12mo; 12 volumes; beautifully bound in full dark blue morocco, gilt edges, by Riviere.   Charles W. Traylen 117-209 1996 £390.00

TOMBLESON, WILLIAM   Eighty Picturesque Views on the Thames and Medway. London: by Black and Armstrong 1834, but later Post 4to; (2), (vi), 84 pages, engraved vignette title, 80 plates, 2 folding panorama maps; later half calf, banded and gilt with ships by Riviere & Son, all edges gilt, few very minor marks, but very good. Adams 178.   Ash Rare Books Zenzybyr-90 1996 £895.00

VINCENT, JOHN   Fowling. A Poem. London: 1808. finely bound in half crushed morocco by Riviere; light foxing, otherwise most attractive. Very scarce.   David A.H. Grayling 3/95-393 1996 £100.00

WALTON, IZAAK 1593-1683   The Lives. London: John Major, 1825. 1st Major edition; 7 3/4 x 5 inches; xviii pages, (1) leaf, 503, (1) pages; large paper copy; 11 mounted copperplates on India paper, 52 woodcuts in text. animated exhibition binding of black morocco by Riviere, covers framed with multiple gilt rules enclosing a field of 9 vertical rows of curvilinear decorations in blind and gilt (featuring blindstamped lilies on delicate ascending stem) alternating with twining gilt ovoids, each of which contains a blindstamped daisy surrounded by massed gilt dots, the whole field flanked by rows of arching gilt lines, each enclosing a semi circle of gilt dots, spine with similar decoration but with greater concentration of gilt dots, gilt edges, simple gilt ruled turn-ins, deep maroon endpapers; beautifiul copy in extraordinarily pleasing binding. Phillip J. Pirages 33-77 1996 $1,500.00

WHYTE-MELVILLE, G. J.   Novels. London: 1890, etc. Foolscap 8vo; 26 volumes; choicely bound in half polished calf, mottled board sides, panelled spines with sporting emblems in gold, by Riviere; fine set from the library of Lord Rootes, with his bookplate in each volume.   Charles W. Traylen 117-218 1996 £400.00

WILKINSON, TATE   Memoirs of His Own Life. York: printed for the author by Wilson, Spence & Mawman, 1790. 1st edition; 12mo; 4 volumes, no half title in volume 1 (not called for in other volumes), 12 page list of subscribers, errata leaf end of volume 4; 19th century calf, all edges gilt, bound by Riviere and Son, recently rebacked, labels. Arnott & Robinson 3637.   Anthony W. Laywood 109-163 1996 £350.00

BINDING - ROOT

EDWARDS, RICHARD   The Book! Or, the Proceedings and Correspondence Upon the Subject of the Inquiry Into the Conduct of Her Royal Highness the Princess of Wales, Under a Commission Appointed by the King In the Year 1806. London: printed by and for Richard Edwards, 1813. 1st edition thus; 8vo; 248, 133 pages; early 20th century half mottled calf and marbled boards by Root & Son with morocco spine labels, top edge gilt; signatures of "W. P. Williams, Mar. 19th 1813" and later owner, else very good to near fine.   Chapel Hill 94-220 1996 $150.00

HARDY, THOMAS 1840-1928   The Woodlanders. London: Macmillan and Son, 1887. 1st edition; 8vo; 3 volumes, half title to each volume, 2 pages of publisher's ads in volume 1, finely bound in half crimson morocco, two line gilt borders, gilt panelled spines, top edge gilt by Root & Son. Purdy p. 54; Sadlier 1120.   Charles W. Traylen 117-128 1996 £485.00

LAMB, CHARLES 1775-1834   Final Memorials...Consisting Chiefly of His Letters Not Before Published, with Sketches of Some of His Companions. London: Edward Moxon, 1848. 1st edition; 8vo; 2 volumes, pages xii, 223, (i); (iv), 239; late 19th century half red crushed morocco, red cloth sides, spines gilt lettered direct "Lamb's Works" above title and volume numbers, marbled endpapers, top edge gilt, by Root and son, joints rubbed; good copy.   Simon Finch 24-148 1996 £85.00

LAMB, CHARLES 1775-1834   The Works. London: Volume I. by Marchant; Volume II by Renell, for C. and J. Ollier, 1818. 1st collected edition; small 8vo; 2 volumes, pages ix, (iii), 291, (i); (vi), 259, (i), (ii) publisher's ads dated June 1818; later blue crushed morocco, sides ruled in gilt with French fillet, quatrefoils in corners, spines gilt with quatrefoil designs in compartments, gilt lettered direct, date at foot, gilt inner dentilles, marbled endpapers, silk bookmarks, top edge gilt, others uncut, by W. Root & Son; spines slightly sunned, one or two trivial spots; very good copy; bookplate of C. H. Wilkinson. Thomson SLI; Ashley III 49.   Simon Finch 24-146 1996 £350.00

MAYHEW, HENRY   The Comic Almanack. London: 1839-42/45-50. 1st edition; 12mo; 10 volumes in 5; numerous full page and folding illustrations by George Cruikshank and H. G. Hine; late 19th century three quarter blue morocco and cloth by Root and Son, gilt tooled spines, top edge gilt, couple of spine ends worn, else near fine.   Chapel Hill 94-47 1996 $375.00

STAEL-HOLSTEIN, ANNE LOUISE GERMAINE NECKER, BARONNE DE 1766-1817   Corinne, or Italy. London: J. M. Dent, 1894. One of 100 numbered copies, large paper edition; 8vo; frontispiece, decorated titlepage and 2 additional illustrations in each volume by H. S. Greig; frontispiece, decorated titlepage, 2 additional illustrations in each volume; contemporary tan calf, gilt decorated spine with contrasing labels, raised bands, top edge gilt; fine and extremely handsome copy, bound by Root & Son.   Paulette Rose 16-304 1996 $300.00

THORNTON, ALFRED   The Adventures of a Post Captain. London: published by J. Johnston, 1817. 1st issue with imprint of J. & T. Agg on verso of titlepage; octavo; (4), 280, (2) pages, hand colored engraved title and 24 hand colored aquatint plates; bound by Root & Son in full red morocco, gilt single rule border on cvoers with gilt corner ornaments, gilt spine, tooled in compartments, gilt board edges and inner dentelles, top edge gilt, light foxing and soiling, few plates neatly repaired, armorial bookplate; very good. Abbey Life 347; Tooley 484.   Heritage Book Shop 196-196 1996 $1,100.00

BINDING - ROSWELL BINDERY

CURTIS, EDWARD S.   The North American Indian: the Southwest. Santa Fe: Classic Gravure, 1980. 1st edition thus, limited to 228 copies; folio; frontispiece; full leather by Roswell Bindery in Phoenix.   Parker Books of the West 30-45 1996 $250.00

BINDING - ROWLEY

PALEY, WILLIAM 1743-1805   A View of the Evidences of Christianity. London: Rivington (and 14 others), 1829. Reprint; 8vo; pages 439; cathedral style embossed calf, flat spine lettered gilt, all edges marbled, brown endpapers, bound by Rowley.   Marlborough 160-73 1996 £300.00

BINDING - ROYAL

CHURCH OF ENGLAND. BOOK OF COMMON PRAYER   Book of Common Prayer. London: by the Assigns of His Majesty's Printer & of Henry Hills, deceased, 1729. large folio; engraved title (undated, but 1713/14), title, 12 ff. n.n. prelims, 278 ff. n.n. ruled in red throughout; dark blue morocco, covers gilt with broad double border, inner of alternating crowns and flowers spine gilt in 8 panels, raised bands gilt, panels with royal monogram, crowns and flowers, all edges gilt, marbled endpapers, gilt arms of King George I (d. 1727) on covers, corners little rubbed, ties gone, a fine royal binding on large paper; from the library of Dudley Alexander Sydney Cosby, Baron of Stradbally (Ireland) with his ex-libris and signature, ca. 1730.   Marlborough 160-33 1996 £1,250.00

BINDING - ROYAL COLLEGE OF ART BINDERY

WELCH, DENTON   I Left My Grandfather's House: an Account of His First Walking Tour. Limited Editions Club, 1958. Of 150 copies, this one of only 20 specially bound by Grodon Acornley of the Royal College of Art Bindery; 4to; color lithographs; quarter black morocco, patterned cloth sides, gilt, edges of spine just a little scuffed, but very nice, scarce.   Bertram Rota 272-272 1996 £200.00

BINDING - ROYAL SCHOOL OF NEEDLEWORK

BYRON, GEORGE GORDON NOEL, 6TH BARON 1788-1824   Poetical Works. London: Henry Frowde, 1896. 8vo; 924 pages, printed on India paper; full natural vellum over slightly flexible boards, upper cover and spine hand painted in bright colors and gold to a medieval design with birds, flowers and intertwined leaves forming a most agreeable all over pattern (lower cover is unadorned), all edges gilt, although without their ticket, the binding appears to be the work of the Royal School of Needlework; in absolutely fine condition.   Book Block 32-34 1996 $675.00

BINDING - RUNTING

BRITTON, JOHN   Graphic Illustration, with Historical and Descriptive Accounts of Toddington, Gloucestershire, the Seat of Lord Sudeley... London: for the author, 1840. One of only 23 copies with proof plates according to subscription list; 4to; (title with vignette), pages xvi, 46, viii, 3 text illustrations, 28 etched plates and plans, (proofs), tinted litho frontispiece, foxing to frontispiece and most plates); contemporary purple blindstamped gilt lettered cloth by Runting, spine faded, repaired splits at head and foot of spine. Harris p. 42.   Marlborough 162-12 1996 £190.00

BINDING - RUSSELL

VICTORIA, QUEEN OF GREAT BRITAIN 1819-1901   Leaves from the Journal of Our Life in the Highlands from 1848 to 1861. London: Smith Elder, 1868. 8vo; 6 plates and text sketches; pictorial souvenir binding, rebacked, gauffered edges gilt; bound by local binder T. Russell of Pitlochry; Henry Alexander Murray armorial bookplate.   Rostenberg & Stern 150-32 1996 $150.00

BINDING - DE SAMBLANX

PASSERAT, JEAN   Recveil des Oevvres Poetiqves. Paris: Claude Morel, 1606. 1st complete edition; 8vo; 2 parts in 1 volume, pages (viii), 464, (viii); (xvi), 248, (vi), 8 pages misnumbered, mainly italic letter, woodcut printer's device on each titlepage, 2 identical engraved potraits by Thos. de Leu, woodcut initials & ornaments, blank corner of 1st titlepage repaired, tiny rust holes touching one letter of one headline; crushed red morocco by De Samblanx & J. Weckesser richly gilt dentelle borders and dentelle fan motif at corners, gilt spine and turn-ins, all edges gilt, marbled endpapers; from the library of Hecotr de Backer, with modern bookplates of Alfred Cliericeau and Henri Burton. BM STC Fr. 17th 631; Tchemerzine V113; Cioranesco 17247 & 17259.   A. Sokol XXV-72 1996 £1,650.00

BINDING - SANGORSKI

ACKERMANN, RUDOLPH 1764-1834   A History of the University of Oxford, Its Colleges, Halls and Public Buildings. London: Ackermann, 1814. 4to; (lacks half title i/ii), iii-xiv, 1 f. first issue list of plates, xxv, 275 pages, 3 ff. index (lacks half title), title, 262 pages, 3 ff. index, 115 plates (all hand colored aquatints, except pl. 2, 65 are views and the rest costume plates and portraits of the Founders), plates 1, 39, 50, 74 an d78 are 1st state plates, 15, 84 and 94 in second state; half burgundy morocco by Sangorski, all edges gilt. Abbey Scenery 280; Tooley p. 14.   Marlborough 162-4 1996 £3,500.00

BINDING - SANGORSKI

PAPWORTH, JOHN BUONAROTTI 1775-1847   Select Views of London, with Historical and Descriptive Sketches...of Its Public Buildings... London: J. Diggens for R. Ackermann, 1816. Large 8vo; 4 ff., 159 pages, 79 hand colored aquatint or engraved plates; full red morocco, gilt, gilt inner borders, top edge gilt, others uncut by Sangorski; Adams 177; Abbey Scenery 21.   Marlborough 162-184 1996 £2,500.00

BINDING - SANGORSKI & SUTCLIFFE

ARABIAN NIGHTS   Stories from the Arabian Nights. London: Hodder & Stoughton, 1907. Limited to 350 copies, numbered and signed by artist; quarto; xvi, 133 pages; 50 mounted color plates by Edmund Dulac; with descriptive tissue guards; bound by Sangorski & Sutcliffe in full orange morocco decoratively stamped in gilt on front cover, gilt lettered spine with raised bands, gilt board edges and turn-ins, top edge gilt, others uncut, marbled endpapers; fine.   Heritage Book Shop 196-210 1996 $2,250.00

BACON, FRANCIS, VISCOUNT ST. ALBANS 1561-1626   The Essays: Colors of Good and Evil and Advancement of Learning. London: Macmillan, 1900. 8vo; titlepage printed in red and black; full dark blue calf by Sangorski & Sutcliffe, spine with raised bands, gilt stamped devices within gilt ruled compartments and gilt stamped red morocco label, covers triple ruled in gilt with floral designs in corners, gilt ruled edges and gilt stamped inner dentelles, grey silk bookmark, marbled endpapers, all edges gilt, slight rubbing to extremities; very good. George J. Houle 68-11 1996 $175.00

BIBLE. FRENCH - 1931   Cantique des Cantiques de Salomon. Cranach Press, 1931. One of 55 copies on Imperial Japanese paper, of a total edition of 163; 10 1/2 x 5 1/2 inches; 1 p.l. (blank), (3)-32 pages, (1) leaf (colophon); 7 full page and 4 smaller woodcuts as well as woodcut initials, all by Eric Gill, printed in blue and black; prospects for the English version laid in; fine sky blue levant morocco by Sangorski & Sutcliffe, gilt rule border on covers, front cover titled in gilt, top edge gilt, other edges untrimmed, in vellum backed suede lined folding cloth box, titled in gilt on spine, leather slightly faded right at edges of boards, very faint mottling to text (on most pages, but not at all noticeable, otherwise in extremely fine condition.   Phillip J. Pirages 33-142 1996 $5,500.00

BROWNE, THOMAS 1605-1682   Urne Buriall and The Garden of Cyrus. London: Cassell, 1932. One of 215 numbered copies; folio; printed in Monotype Bembo, Centaur and New Hellenic on Barcham Green handmade; full vellum with brown morocco inlays, gilt, designed by Nash, executed by Sangorski & Sutcliffe; fine in slipcase.   Bertram Rota 272-102A 1996 £2,000.00

BUCHANAN, ROBERT   The Piper of Hamelin: Fantastic Opera in Two Acts. London: Chiswick Press, 1893. 1st edition; 7 1/4 x 5 1/2 inches; 1 p.l., 63, (1) pages; added engraved title and 12 plates by Hugh Thomson; fine chestnut brown morocco by Sangorski & Sutcliffe, front cover with gilt titling above charming gilt vignette of two dancing rats, their tales entwining a musical pipe, spine with raised bands, gilt ruled compartments, gilt titling, blind ruled extensions of the raised bands terminating on covers in finial of 3 leaves, turn-ins with triple gilt fillets, all edges gilt, in fine plush lined folding morocco case by Zaehnsdorf with raised bands and gilt spine titling; from the distinguished collections of Doris Benz and Paul Chevalier with their bookplates. Virtually flawless copy   Phillip J. Pirages 33-69 1996 $600.00

BUTLER, SAMUEL 1835-1902   Butleriana. Bloomsbury: Nonesuch Press, 1932. Number 658 of 800 copies; half green calf by Sangorski & Sutcliffe, top edge gilt, booklabel of Howell L. Davies.   Jarndyce CII-98 1996 £85.00

CHAUCER, GEOFFREY 1340-1400   The Canterbury Tales. Waltham St. Lawrence: Golden Cockerel Press, 1929-31. One of 485 copies on paper (there were also 15 copies printed on vellum); 12 1/2 x 8 inches; 4 volumes, red and blue initials and very pleasing wood engraved borders (frequently historiated) by Eric Gill on every page except in last part of volume 4; original morocco backed patterned paper boards by Sangorski & Sutcliffe, raised bands, gilt titling, top edge gilt, others untrimmed; tips of corners artfully refurbished, spine of first volume bit darker than the others, small spot on one spine and several tiny faint spots on another, quite a small abrasion at very bottom of one cover, otherwise fine, virtually no wear to joints and spine ends, gilt still bright and with text virtually without defects. Excellent copy. Chanticleer 63; Gill 281.   Phillip J. Pirages 33-245 1996 $5,000.00

BINDING - SANGORSKI & SUTCLIFFE

CHAUCER, GEOFFREY 1340-1400   The Canterbury Tales. Waltham St. Lawrence: Golden Cockerel Press, 1929-31. One of 485 numbered copies on Batachelor handmade paper, out of a total edition of 500 copies; folio; 4 volumes; 1 full page illustration, 29 half page illustrations, 269 decorative borders, tailpieces and line fillers and 61 initial letters (printed in black, red or blue), all engraved on wood by Eric Gill; bound by Sangorski & Sutcliffe in quarter niger morocco over patterned boards, gilt lettered spine with raised bands, top edge gilt, others uncut, light wear to extremities, slight discoloration to boards, small glue stains to endpapers where they touch the leather, little minor foxing, still near fine set overall, housed together in quarter reddish brown morocco slipcase. Chanticleer 63; Gill 281.   Heritage Book Shop 196-214 1996 $4,500.00

CHAUCER, GEOFFREY 1340-1400   Troilus and Criseyde. Waltham St. Lawrence: Golden Cockerel Press, 1927. One of 225 copies; 12 1/2 x 7 3/4 inches; xi, (1), 310 pages, (1) leaf (blank), (1) p. (colophon); 5 full page wood engravings, fore margins of every text page with wood engraved borders, all by Eric Gill, printed in red, blue and black; original quarter russet moroccco by Sangorski & Sutcliffe, patterned paper sides, vellum tips, top edge gilt, slipcase, paper on front cover with small abrasions, spine slightly nicked and with portions of the leather darkened (as often happens with this book), but binding otherwise unworn, and a virtually faultless copy internally. Chanticleer 50; Ransom p. 297.   Phillip J. Pirages 33-246 1996 $5,500.00

COPPARD, ALFRED EDGAR 1878-1957   Tapster's Tapestry. Waltham St. Lawrence: Golden Cockerel Press, 1938. One of 75 copies, signed by author and artist; 8 3/4 x 6 1/2 inches; 3 p.l., (two blank), 5-58 pages, (1) leaf (colophon); device on title, 10 wood engravings by Gwenda Morgan; original morocco backed buckram boards by Sangorski & Sutcliffe, gilt titling on spine, top edge gilt, other edges untrimmed, extremely fine. Pertelote 137.   Phillip J. Pirages 33-249 1996 $225.00

THE CORONATION of Her Majesty Queen Elizabeth II, 1953. Worcester: 1953. Limited to 2000 copies; 2 3/4 x 1 15/16 inches; printed in red and black; luxuriously bound in red crushed morocco with double gilt rule and stamping by Sangorski & Sutcliffe, all edges gilt; very fine. Bromer Booksellers 87-225 1996 $175.00

DRYDEN, JOHN 1631-1700   Songs and Poems. Waltham St. Lawrence: Golden Cockerel Press, 1957. One of 100 special copies hand bound (out of a total edition of 500 copies); 15 x 10 1/4 inches; 64 pages; 8 full page illustrations and several black and white drawings and vignettes by Lavinia Blythe; this copy (no. 36), should have an extra suite of illustrations, but none is present; bound by Sangorski & Sutcliffe in original full morocco, half of each cover dyed russet and half dyed green, large stylized gilt vignettes on covers, gilt spine titling, hint of soil to binding, otherwise very fine.   Phillip J. Pirages 33-250 1996 $375.00

GRIMALDI, STACEY   The Toliet. London: Rock Brothers & Payne, n.d. 12mo; full blue crushed morocco du cap with single gilt fillet border, with gilt titling and decoration on spine, board edges gilt, inner gilt dentelles, front cover and spine lightly sunned, all edges gilt, signed on lower turn-in: Sangorski & Sutcliffe; rare in any edition. Not in Abbey. 10 1996 $1,250.00

HAWKINS, RICHARD   The Observations of Sir Richard Hawkins Knight, in His Voiage Into the South Sea. London: printed by I. D. for John Jaggard, 1622. 1st edition; small folio; full red morocco by Sangorski & Sutcliffe, some very pale waterstains in lower margins, but fine, crisp copy. STC 12962; Sabin 30957; Hill p. 140; Borba de Moraes p. 395. Ximenes 109-153 1996 $17,500.00

HEYWOOD, THOMAS   Gunaikeion; or, Nine Bookes of Various History Concerninge Women. London: by Adam islip, 1624. 1st edition; folio; (8), 466 pages, engraved title, woodcut head and tailpieces; full brown levant morocco, gilt fillets, spine richly gilt in compartments, gilt dentelles, by Sangorski & Sutcliffe, lacking front and rear blanks, couple of tiny rust holes repaired, superb copy, fine and clean in elegant, flawless binding. Grolier L-W 142; STC 13326.   Joseph J. Felcone 64-42 1996 $3,200.00

HOLWELL, JOHN ZEPHANIAH   A Genuine Narrative of the Deplorable Deaths of the English Gentlemen and Others, Who Were Suffocated in the Black Hole in Fort William, at Calcutta in the Kingdom of Bengal... London: printed for A. Millar, 1758. 1st edition; 8vo; title and last page dusty, modern half calf by Sangorski & Sutcliffe; uncut.   Anthony Laywood 108-72 1996 £275.00

BINDING - SANGORSKI & SUTCLIFFE

HOOPER, GEORGE   Waterloo: the Downfall of the First Napoleon: a History of the Campaign of 1815. London: Smith, Elder, 1862. Thick 8vo; extra illustrated with 28 folded, full page and in-set engravings, 2 color lithograph views, original small watercolor bust portrait of Louis XVIII, and 5 folding maps; also tipped in signed document: Divsion de Paris, 1817, 1 printed note to Marshal Francois Etienne de Kellerman, Duc De Valmy on folded quarto sheet with contemporary hand written note by subordinate, and signed by Duc de Valmy, with orig. red wax seal & postmarked address to Duc de Valmy on verso of second leaf; later full crushed navy mor. gilt by Sangorski & Sutcliffe of Charles J. Sawyer Ltd., alternating motif of crowns & bees, initial 'N' with crowns at corners, crimson morocco at pastedown under bevelled glass with brass frame is a very fine miniature on enamel of Napoleon on the deck of the 'Belelrophon', deck rigging and ropes in background with sea in distance; binding in perfect condition in fleece lined blue cloth box. Marilyn Braiterman 15-151 1996 $3,750.00

IMITATIO CHRISTI   The Imitation of Christ. London: Chapman and Hall, n.d. 1st edition; 8vo; full calf, beautifully bound by Sangorski & Sutcliffe, inscription, light rubbing, near fine.   Charles Agvent 4-1121 1996 $175.00

IRVING, WASHINGTON 1783-1859   Old Christmas. London: Macmillan & Co., 1925. 4th edition, reprinted; small octavo; xiv, 165 pages; 106 illustrations designed by Randolph Caldecott; bound by Sangorski & Sutcliffe in full green polished calf, covers decoratively bordered in gilt, gilt spine, tooled in compartments, with red morocco labels, gilt board edges and turn-ins, all edges gilt, decorative endpapers, bookplate; fine. Heritage Book Shop 196-283 1996 $225.00

JONES, GWYN   The Green Island. Waltham St. Lawrence: Godlen Cockerel Press, 1946. 1st edition; number 82 of 100 copies specially bound; 8vo; 84 pages; frontispiece, 10 other wood engravings by John Petts; original two tone full morocco blocked in gold, top edge gilt, others uncut, by Sangorski & Sutcliffe; very good. Cockalorum 169. Claude Cox 107-64 1996 £85.00

LAWRENCE, THOMAS EDWARD 1888-1935   Secret Despatches from Arabia. Waltham St. Lawrence: Golden Cockerel Press, n.d. Number 959 of 1000 copies; bound by Sangorski & Sutcliffe in quarter niger, top edge gilt, endpapers and edges slightly foxed and browned at edges, cream cloth covers soiled and spotted, lower corners bumped, otherwise good.   Virgo Books 48-124 1996 £400.00

LAWRENCE, THOMAS EDWARD 1888-1935   Shaw - Ede. T. E. Lawrence's Letters to H. S. Ede 1927-1935. Waltham St. Lawrence: Golden Cockerel Press, 1942. 1st edition; no. 354 of 500 copies; 4to; 62 pages; original dark blue morocco backed cream boards, by Sangorski & Sutcliffe, top edge gilt, others uncut. Pertelote 151.   Claude Cox 107-65 1996 £280.00

LUCAS, F. L.   The Golden Cockerel Greek Anthology. Waltham St. Lawrence: Golden Cockerel Press, 1937. Limited to 206 numbered copies on handmade paper; small folio; 82 pages; titlepage illustration, tailpiece and 12 plates line engraved on zinc by Lettice Sandford, title printed in carmine; original black morocco backed boards, top edge gilt, others uncut by Sangorski & Sutcliffe, few minor spots on covers.   Thomas Thorp 489-198 1996 £150.00

MIDDLETON, THOMAS   A Tragi-Coomodie, called The Witch... London: privately printed by John Nichols for Isaac Reed, 1778. 1st edition; 8vo; pages 111, (i) colophon, early MS not on blank facing title; full red crushed morocco, spine richly gilt between raised bands, sides ruled in gilt with a french fillet, gilt inner dentelles, all edges gilt, by Sangorski & Sutcliffe; fine copy; the Heber - Chalmers - Holgate - Bridgewater - Huntington - Clawson - Spiegelberg copy, with most bookplates; Simon Finch 24-168 1996 £1,000.00

MILTON, JOHN 1608-1674   Paradise Lost. London: by S. Simmons and are to be sold by H. Helder, 1669. 1st edition; small 4to; collates complete as issued; modern brown calf by Sangorski & Sutcliffe, paper flaw on title just affecting lower bar of 'L' in Milton's name, quite closed trimmed, occasionally affecting upper frame and once or twice the headline, some browning, occasional stains, good. Amory 4; Wing M2143.   Simon Finch 24-169 1996 £3,800.00

NIDER, JOHANNES   Formicarius. Augsburg: Anton Sorg, c. 1484. Folio; 192 leaves (first and last blank), signatures, gothic letter, initial spaces with guide letters, some marginal annotations in 16th century hand, minor soiling; few wormholes mainly in last few leaves; modern blindstamped brown morocco by Sangorski & Sutcliffe, morocco edged slipcase. Good, tall, clean copy. Goff N 176; HC 11832; BMC II 351. H. M. Fletcher 121-13 1996 £5,000.00

BINDING - SANGORSKI & SUTCLIFFE

PATER, WALTER 1839-1894   Appreciations: With an Essay on Style. London: and New York: Macmillan, 1901. One of 775 copies; 9 x 6 1/4 inches; 2 p.l., 261, (1) pages; one volume, only (of 8) of an edition of the Works of Walter Pater; half title and title printed in red and black; handsome onlaid black morocco by Sangorski & Sutcliffe, sides framed with parallel gilt rules, two of them enclosing spaced onlaid red circlets, very fine corner decoration of onlaid green leaves and red berries on gilt stems, front cover with beautiful circular onlaid cluster of the same elements, along with gilt leaves and dots, spine with raised bands and gilt ruled compartments, featuring gilt and onlaid red disks, gilt ruled turn ins, all edges gilt, very slight wear at spine top, shadow on free endpaper, opposite leather turn-ins, otherwise very fine in lovely binding. Phillip J. Pirages   33-70   1996 $450.00

PATER, WALTER 1839-1894   Imaginary Portraits and Gaston De La Tour: an Unfinished Romance. London: and New York: Macmillan, 1900. One of 775 copies; 9 x 6 1/4 inches; 2 p.l., 321, (1) pages, one volume (of 8 fromt he Works); half title and title printed in red and black; especially attractive elaborately gilt and onlaid dark brown morocco by Sangorski & Sutcliffe, covers framed by parallel rules with broad gilt leaves in corners, rules on front cover enclosing the author's name and titles of the works as well as gilt clusters of leaves and berries, linked squares and rectangles surrounding a very beautiful central panel with many onlaid green leaves and large and small red flowers, massed on twining gilt stems and with gilt berries, spine with raised bands, compartments gilt ruled and divided into smaller rectangles with gilt disks and red onlaid circlets, gilt ruled turn-ins, gilt edges; spine uniformly faded to pleasing light brown, otherwise in very fine condition. Phillip J. Pirages   33-71   1996 $500.00

PATMORE, COVENTRY   The Angel in the House. The Bethroal. London: John W. Parker and Son, 1854. 1st edition; 8vo; pages viii, 191; fine binding of aquamarine crushed morocco, spine divided in six panels by raised bands, gilt lettered direct in second, others with red heart shaped onlays within floral borders, place and date in gilt at foot, sides ruled around with dog tooth roll and double fillet enclosing deep border built up from leaf sprays, floral motifs, dosts, etc. and 6 red onlays of fans, inner dentelles rulled all round in gilt, cream watered silk doublures and endpapers, gilt borders, gilt edges by Sangorski & Sutcliffe, folding cloth box, lea. label; from the lib. of Maharajah Jam Sahib.   Simon Finch 24-178   1996 £380.00

PEPYS, SAMUEL 1633-1703   Memoirs of Samuel Pepys, Esq. London: 1825. 1st edition; large 4to; 2 volumes, xlii, (2), 498, (2), xlix, (2) pages; (4), 348, vii, (1), 311 pages; engraved plates, half titles and ad leaf, uncut; later half calf, spines gilt, red and green labels by Sangorski & Sutcliffe; beautiful set, fine and fresh, with just the lightest rubbing at extremities, in fleece lined cloth slipcase; Otto Orren Fisher bookplate. Superb condition.   Joseph J. Felcone   64-31   1996 $1,800.00

STEVENSON, ROBERT LOUIS BALFOUR 1850-1894   Kidnapped. London: Cassell & Co. Ltd. 1886. 1st edition; 2nd issue; 7 1/2 x 5 inches; viii, 311, (17) pages, including ads at back; colored folding map as frontispiece; pleasing slate blue crushed levant three quarter morocco by Sangorski & Sutcliffe, blue cloth sides, raised spine bands with stippled rule and flanked by plain gilt rules, spine panels with gilt titling or lage centered ornament, marbled endpapers, top edge gilt, spine evenly faded to light blue green, minor tear in map, otherwise very fine. Phillip J. Pirages   33-470   1996 $375.00

STEVENSON, ROBERT LOUIS BALFOUR 1850-1894   Prayers Written at Valima. London: Chatto & Windus, 1910. 4to; illuminations by Alberto Sangorski; full citron morocco, gilt borders on covers, corner fleurons, 2 raised bands, gilt top by Sangorski & Sutcliffe.   Appelfeld Gallery 54-172   1996 $250.00

SWINBURNE, ALGERNON CHARLES 1837-1909   Pasiphae. Waltham St. Lawrence: Golden Cockerel Press, 1950. Limited to 500 numbered copies, of which this is one of 100 speciallly bound and with an extra illustration; 8vo; 40 pages; copper engraved frontispiece, pictorial titlepage and 5 other illustrations; publisher's wine colored vellum, top edge gilt, others uncut, by Sangorski & Sutcliffe, with original slipcase. Cock-a-Hoop 185.   Thomas Thorp   489-299   1996 £385.00

SWINBURNE, ALGERNON CHARLES 1837-1909   Poems and Ballads. London: Chatto & Windus, 1908. Pages x, 338; handsome contemporary binding in art nouveau style, full crimson morocco ruled and decorated in gold with plant device of five leaves on curving interwoven stems with dot background in corners of sides and reworked in smaller scale on four panels of backstrip and inner corners of turn-ins, upper cover slightly darkened but very good, attractive binding, all edges gilt, for Bumpus, probably by Sangorski & Sutcliffe.   Claude Cox   107-18   1996 £75.00

TAPLIN, WILLIAM   The Sporting Dictionary, and Rural Repository of General Information Upon Every Subject Appertaining to sports of the Field. London: 1803. 2 volumes; engraved plates foxed and title to volume 2 expertly repaired; finely bound in half scarlet levant morocco by Sangorski & Sutcliffe; most attractive.   David A.H. Grayling 3/95-227   1996 £150.00

BINDING - SANGORSKI & SUTCLIFFE

TROLLOPE, ANTHONY 1815-1882   Ayala's Angel... London: Chapman and Hall Ltd., 1881. 1st edition; 8vo; 3 volumes, no half titles called for; modern half red crushed morocco, red cloth sides, raised bands, spines gilt lettered direct, top edge gilt, by Sangorski & Sutcliffe, titles slightly spotted, good set, firmly and attractively rebound. Irwin p. 13; Sadleir 60; Tinker 2244; Wolff 6764.   Simon Finch 24-Simon Finch 24-248 1996 £500.00

TROLLOPE, ANTHONY 1815-1882   Can You Forgive Her? London: Chapman and Hall, 1864. 1st edition in book form; 8vo; 2 volumes; vi, (ii), 320; vi, (ii), 320 pages, 40 illustrations; modern half red crushed morocco, red cloth sides, raided bands, spines gilt lettered direct, top edge gilt, by Sangorski & Sutcliffe, very good, firmly and attractively rebound. Irwin p. 16; Sadlier 19; Tinker 2195; Wolff 6769.   Simon Finch 24-238   1996 £275.00

TROLLOPE, ANTHONY 1815-1882   Castle Richmond. London: Chapman and Hall, 1860. 1st edition; 8vo; 3 volumes; bound with half titles, 6 leaves in volume 2 from another copy, with library stamp; early 20th century half red crushed morocco, red cloth sides, raised bands, spines gilt lettered direct, top edge gilt, by Sangorski & Sutcliffe; very good, firmly and attractively rebound. Irwin p. 16; Sadleir 10; Tinker 2180; Wolff 6770.   Simon Finch 24-234   1996 £450.00

TROLLOPE, ANTHONY 1815-1882   Lady Anna. London: Chapman and Hall, 1874. 1st edition; 8vo; 2 volumes, pages viii, 317; viii, 314; half titles; modern half red crushed morocco, red cloth sides, raised bands, spines gilt lettered direct, top edge gilt, by Sangorski & Sutcliffe, some faint spotting in first volume, still good set, firmly and attractively rebound. Irwin p. 25; Sadleir 42; Tinker 2228.   Simon Finch 24-244 1996 £500.00

TROLLOPE, ANTHONY 1815-1882   The Macdermots of Ballycloran. London: Thomas Cautley Newby, 1847. 1st edition; 12mo; 3 volumes; modern red half morocco, spines lettered in gilt, top edge gilt, by Sangorski & Sutcliffe, occasional slight spotting; excellent copy. rare. Sadleir 1; Tinker 2164.   Simon Finch 24-230   1996 £16,000.00

TROLLOPE, ANTHONY 1815-1882   La Vendee. London: Henry Colburn, 1850. 1st edition; 8vo; 3 volumes; bound without half titles, in early 20th century half red crushed morocco, red cloth sides, raised bands, spine gilt lettered direct, top edge gilt, by Sangorski & Sutcliffe; very good, firmly and attractively rebound. Irwin p. 38; Sadleir 3.   Simon Finch 24-231   1996 £4,800.00

VAURIE, C.   Tibet and Its Birds. London: 1972. Limited to 65 copies, signed by author; Royal 8vo; pages xv, 407, frontispiece, map, 3 colored plates, 23 photos; half red morocco by Sangorski & Sutcliffe; nice copy. Wheldon & Wesley   207-887   1996 £180.00

BINDING - SCHUBERTH BOOKBINDERY

HEYECK, ROBIN   Marbling at the Heyeck Press. California: Heyeck Press, 1986. Limited to only 150 numbered copies; 4to; 68 pages printed on handmade paper; 28 examples of marbled paper tipped in, including frontispiece; publisher's dark grey morocco backed marbled boards, edges uncut, slipcase; mint, bound by Schuberth Bookbindery. Thomas Thorp   489-152   1996 £200.00

NIEBAUER, ABBY   Three Windows; Poems. Woodside: Heyeck Press, 1980. One of 100 numbered copies, signed by author; 4to; printed in handset Centaur and Arrighi in black and sepia on Barcham Green handmade; half brown cloth, marbled boards, by the Schuberth Bookbindery; fine.   Bertram Rota   272-230   1996 £55.00

BINDING - SCOTT

BREEN, HUGH   A Treatise on the Summation of Series. Belfast: printed by Joseph Smyth, 1827. 1st and only edition; 8vo; pages 104, 104 (bis)-163, including 3 page list of Armagh, Belfast, Dublin and Newry subscribers; contemporary half calf, gilt spine, by Scott of Armagh, with his ticket, nice. Remarkably scarce.   James Fenning 133-33   1996 £395.00

BINDING - SEMET & PLUMELLE

COCTEAU, JEAN   Picasso. Les Contemporains. Paris: Chez Delamain, Boutelleau et Cie, 1923. 1st edition; small 8vo; pages 32, 15 black and white photo plates; quarter black calf by Semet & Plumelle, preserving original wrappers; inscribed by Cocteau.   Sotheran PN32-181   1996 £550.00

BINDING - SIZER

FORBES, DUNCAN   A Grammar of the Hindustani Language. London: Wm. H. Allen & Co., 13 Waterloo Place, S.W... 1862. New edition; 8vo; (v-viii), 1-148, vocabulary (1-40 pages), (41-48), 49-56; frontispiece, and 15 plates; ms. ink ownership inscription, some pencil notations to few pages, some light foxing; bound by Sizer, half maroon morocco and maroon embossed cloth, gilt title to spine, raised bands, new endpapers and prelims.   Beeleigh Abbey BA56-67 1996 £125.00

BINDING - CLARE SKELTON

DREYFUS, JOHN   A Typographical Masterpiece. London: Bain & Williams, 1993. Deluxe edition, limited to 40 copies; proof from one of the original wood blocks, printed by hand by Graham Williams; hand bound in a design using 3 cloths, leather backed, by Clare Skelton; slipcase.   Claude Cox 107-61B 1996 £285.00

BINDING - SLOCOMBE & SIMMS

HOGG, JAMES   The Private Memoirs and Confessions of a Justified Sinner. London: printed for Longman, Hurst, Rees, Orme, Brown and Green, 1834. 1st edition; 8vo; 390 pages of text, frontispiece (fore-edge margin cropped, offset to title), final leaf blank but not the original; half black straight grain morocco, gilt bands and title to panelled spine, marbled edges and endpapers, bound by Slocombe & Simms, Leeds; armorial bookplate. Block English Novel p. 111; Sadleir 1198.   Beeleigh Abbey BA56-148 1996 £2,500.00

BINDING - SMART

SHOWER, JOHN   Practical Reflections on the Late Earthquakes in Jamaica, England, Sicily, Malta &c. Anno 1692. London: printed for John Salusbury...and Abraham Chandler, 1693. 1st edition; 8vo; titlepage printed within double ruled border, final blank present, pages xvi, 206, (2); modern dark brown stained calf, by C. E. Smart, backstrip with raised bands between gilt rules and pointille rolls, red labels in second and third compartments, gilt flower in centre of remainder, narrow blind roll and fillet border on sides, gilt lettered on turn-in at tail of rear cover "Ex Libris Brent Gration-Maxfield", excellent. Sabin 80740; Wing S3680.   Blackwell's B112-256 1996 £650.00

BINDING - SMITH

BATTY, ELIZABETH FRANCES   Italian Scenery. From Drawings Made in 1817. London: Rodwell & Martin, 1820. 1st edition; 11 3/4 x 9 1/2 inches; 5 p.l., 197, (1) pages; eng. title, vignette on final leaf, 60 fine engraved plates, all with tissue guards; very handsome contemporary rose colored hard grain mor., extra gilt by C. Smith, covers handsomely framed with 3 sets of parallel fillets enclosing 2 elegant scrolling floral borders, flat spines beautifully gilt in 2 compartments, top one with titling, elongated lower one composed of central vertical band of urn-like roll-tool flanked by gilt rules and pretty borders of acanthus leaves, board edges with triple gilt fillets, turn-ins with four gilt rules and corner ovals, endpapers of deep green coated stock, all edges gilt, spine evenly sunned to terra cotta color, minor scuffing or rubbing to edges, otherwise binding in excellent condition, with only trivial defects, very well executed, completely solid, and quite pretty; the majority of the plates with foxing, almost always very minor, but occasionally more noticeable (without ever being serious), otherwise fine internally, text clean & smooth.   Phillip J. Pirages 33-482 1996 $1,259.00

BATTY, ROBERT d. 1848   French Scenery, from Drawings Made in 1819. London: Rodwell & Martin, 1822. 1st edition; 11 3/4 x 9 1/2 inches; (64) leaves, half title called for in list of plates, not present; engraved title and 65 plates, tissue guards, separate texts in English and French; very handsome cont. rose colored hard grain mor. extra gilt by C. Smith, covers handsomely framed w/3 sets of parallel fillets enclosing 2 elegant scrolling floral borders, flat spines beautifully gilt in 2 compartments, top one with titling, elongated lower one composed of central and vertical band of urn-like roll-tool flanked by gilt rules & pretty borders of acanthus leaves, board edges with triple gilt fillets, turn-ins 2/4 gilt rules & corner ovals, endpapers of deep green coated stock, a.e.g.; most plates free from foxing; spine evenly faded to a terra cotta color, minor scuffing or rubbing to edges, otherwise binding in excellent condition, with only trivial defects.   Phillip J. Pirages 33-483 1996 $1,250.00

BINDING - SMITH

BATTY, ROBERT d. 1848   German Scenery. From Drawings made in 1820. London: Rodwell & Martin, 1823. 1st edition; 11 3/4 x 9 1/2 inches; (65) leaves; 61 fine engraved plates of views by Batty, tissue guards, with text in English and French; very handsome contemporary rose colored hard grain morocco, extra gilt by C. Smith, covers handsomely framed with 3 sets of parallel fillets enclosing two elegant scrolling floral borders, flat spines beautifully gilt in 2 compartments, top one with titling, elongated lower one composed of central vertical band of urn-like roll-tool flanked by gilt rules and pretty borders of acanthus leaves, board edges with triple gilt fillets, turn-ins with four gilt rules and corner ovals, endpapers of deep green coated stock, all edges gilt, spine evenly sunned to terra cotta color, minor scuffing or rubbing to edges, otherwise binding in excellent condition, with only trivial defects.   Phillip J. Pirages 33-484 1996 $3,500.00

BATTY, ROBERT d. 1848   Scenery of the Rhine, Belgium and Holland. London: Robert Jennings, 1826. 1st edition; 11 3/4 x 9 1/2 inches; (65) leaves; engraved title, 61 fine engraved plates, tissue gaurds, text in English and French; very handsome cont. rose colored hard grain morocco, extra gilt by C. Smith, covers handsomely framed with 3 sets of parallel fillets enclosing two elegant scrolling floral borders, flat spines beautifully gilt in 2 compartments, top one with titling, elongated lower one composed of central vertical band of urn-like roll-tool flanked by gilt rules and pretty borders of acanthus leaves, board edges with triple gilt filets, turn-ins with four gilt rules and corner ovals, endpapers of deep green coated stock, all edges gilt; spine evenly sunned to terra cotta color, minor scuffing or rubbing to edges, otherwise binding in excellent condition.   Phillip J. Pirages 33-485 1996 $3,000.00

BIBLE. ENGLISH - 1815   The Holy Bible Containing the Old and New Testaments, and the Apocrypha. London: White, Cochrane & Co., 1815/14. 4to; 3 volumes; engravings by Richard Westall, engraved by Charles Heath, printed on heavy laid paper which is lightly foxed; full black straight grained morocco with pair of triple gilt fillet borders surrounding a decorative roll, inner central frame is composed of four corner flowerheads with leafy sprays radiating therefrom, connected to each other by three spaced gilt fillets, spine has five wide raised bands with gilt tooling and rather complex arabesque gilt tooling in four of the six compartments, handsome set with some minor superficial rubbing, board edges gilt, inner gilt dentelles, all edges gilt, signed with name of binder on verso of front free endleaf of volume 1: "CHARLES SMITH"; fine, bindings very handsome and extremely well executed.   Book Block 32-46 1996 $1,650.00

CAMDEN, WILLIAM   Reges, Reginae Nobiles & Alii in Ecclesia Collegiata B. Petri Westmonasterii Sepulti, Usque ad Annum Reparatae Salutis 1600. London: excudebat E. Bollifantus, 1600. 1st edition; small 4to; 19th century calf, gilt spine, all edges gilt, by C. Smith (minor rubbing); fine. STC 4518.   Ximenes 109-61 1996 $900.00

COCKBURN, JAMES PATTISON   Swiss Scenery. London: Rodwell & Martin, 1820. 1st edition; 11 3/4 x 9 1/2 inches; vii, (1), 200 pages; engraved title, vignette on final page and 61 fine paltes, tissue guards; very handsome cont. rose colored hard grain morocco, extra gilt by C. Smith, covers handsomely framed with 3 sets of parallel fillets enclosing two elegant scrolling floral borders, flat spines beautifully gilt in 2 compartments, top one with titling, elongated lower one composed of central vertical band of urn-like roll-tool flanked by gilt rules & pretty borders of acanthus leaves, board edges with triple gilt fillets, turn-ins with four gilt rules and corner ovals, endpapers of deep green coated stock, all edges gilt, spine evenly sunned to terra cotta, minor scuffing or rubbing to edges, otherwise binding in excellent condition. Foxing to plates.   Phillip J. Pirages 33-486 1996 $1,800.00

FRANCO, NICCOLO   La Philena. Historia Amorosa Vltimamente Composta. Mantua: Jacomo Ruffinelli, 1547. 1st edition; 8vo; ff. 470, italic leetter, woodcut portrait of author on titlepage, woodcut printer's device and repeated portrait at end, slight foxing in places; faded contemporary ex-libris on titlepage; 19th century straight grained green morocco by C. Smith, gilt fillets and corner fleurons and richly gilt spine, all edges gilt, very good; bookplate of Baron Landau on pastedown.   A. Sokol XXV-40 1996 £1,650.00

HOMERUS   The Odyssey. London: ptd. & published by Sir Emery Walker, Wilfred Merton & Bruce Rogers, 1932. 1st edition; one of 530 copies; small folio; set in 16 point Monotype Centaur with 2 point leading, paper specially handmade grey toned paper from J. Barcham Green Mill with watermark of Greek Galley; 25 black on gold leaf roundels as title vignette and headpieces designed by Bruce Rogers; bound by W. H. Smith and Son, black niger morocco, spine gilt, top edge gilt, others uncut, original publisher's board slipcase (slightly worn), edges of turn-ins browned as usual, else lovely copy (edge of one page slight bit ruffled); O'Brien A141.   Priscilla Juvelis 95/1-128 1996 $1,250.00

BINDING - SMITH

LIGHT, WILLIAM   Sicilian Scenery. London: Rodwell & Martin, 1823. 1st edition; 11 3/4 x 9 1/2 inches; (64) leaves, including engraved title and half title, 61 fine plates, tissue guards; text in English and French; very handsome cont. rose colored hard grain morocco, extra gilt by C. Smith, covers handsomely framed with 3 sets of parallel fillets enclosing two elegant scrolling floral borders, flat spines beautifully gilt in 2 compartments, top one with titling, elongated lower one composed of central vertical band of urn-like roll-tool flanked by gilt rules and pretty borders of acanthus leaves, board edges with triple gilt fillets, turn-ins with four gitl rules and corner of ovals, endpapers of deep green coated stock, all edges gilt, spine evenly sunned to a terra cotta, minor scuffing or rubbing to edges, otherwise binding in excellent condition. Plates especially clean.   Phillip J. Pirages   33-487   1996 $1,250.00

NASH, FREDERICK   Picturesque Views of the City of Paris and Its Environs. London: printed by James Moyes for Longman, et al, 1823. 11 3/4 x 9 1/2 inches; 2 volumes in 1, without titlepage to volume 2; 57 fine engraved plates, tissue guards, text in English and French; very handsome cont. rose colored hard grain morocco, extra gilt by C. Smith, covers handsomely framed with 3 sets of parallel fillets enclosing two elegant scrolling floral borders, flat spines beautifully gilt in 2 compartments, top one with titling, elongated lower one composed of central vertical band of urn-like roll-tool flanked by gilt rules and pretty borders of acanthus leaves, board edges with triple gilt fillets, turn-ins with four gilt rules and corner ovals, endpapers of deep green coated stock, all edges gilt, spine evenly sunned to terra cotta color, minor scuffing or rubbing to edges, otherwise binding in excellent condition; plates especially clean.   Phillip J. Pirages   33-488   1996 $950.00

SCOTT, WALTER 1771-1832   Waverley Novels. Edinburgh: Adam and Charles Black, 1852-53. 8 3/4 x 6 inches; 25 volumes; frontispiece and engraved title in each volume; well bound in contemporary red half morocco by C. S. Smith of Edinburgh, buckram sides, spines with raised bands and gilt rules, ornaments and titling, marbled edges and endpapers, only the slightest signs of wear to bindings, which are especially bright and elegant; faint dampstain in 1 vol. at top and 1st four leaves, another vol. w/dark brown acidic stain (size of quarter) evident on 4 leaves, otherwise no significant faults internally, text especially smooth & clean, very fine and attractive set.   Phillip J. Pirages   33-458   1996 $1,650.00

BINDING - SORESINI

DECRETALES   Gregorii Papae IX. Venice: s.n. 1600. Large 4to; vignette title, 26 ff. n.n., 2 full page woodcuts, 2 ff., 1388 pages; red morocco elaborately gilt broad outer borders w/arabesque & heraldic tools, sq. corners w/dragons & winged putti, oval centre-piece w/the combined, quartered arms of Caffarelli (lions) & Borghese (dragons rampant & spread eagles), surmounted by a Cardinal's hat, broad spine gilt in 5 panels, single raised bands, middle 3 panels w/dragon, lion & eagle, respectively, flanked by salamanders & arabesques, later labels to first and last panels, all edges gilt & gauffered, plain endpapers, spine skilfully repaired with restoration at head, foot and lower band, corners also sympathetically restored, edges little worn, in half morocco folding case; from the collection of Victor von Stedingks Bokband. A Fine Soresini binding.   Marlborough   160-17   1996   £4,500.00

BINDING - SOTHERAN

GOLDSMITH, OLIVER 1730-1774   The Works of Oliver Goldsmith. London: John Murray, Albemarle St., 1854. 8vo; 4 volumes; full polished calf, gilt rule dentelles to boards, gilt tooling to compartments, green morocco title and volume labels to spines, all edges gilt, marbled endpapers; bound by Sotheran with binders stamp to front pastedown of all volumes, booksellers ticket to rear endpaper of volume 1; owner's stamp to front f.e.p. of all volumes, some light foxing to prelims and endpapers of all volumes, bookseller's ticket to rear endpaper of volume 1.   Beeleigh Abbey   BA56-146   1996   £250.00

BINDING - SOUTHWORTH

KAFKA, FRANZ 1883-1924   Ein Landarzt/A Country Doctor. Printed at the Philadelphia College of Art, 1962. Limited to 250 copies numbered and signed by artist; 12.25 x 8.75 inches; 32 pages; printed in black on Rives cuve velin; 12 relief etchings by Claire Van Vliet; unsatisfactorily bound by a Commercial Binder, William Marley Co., in Philadelphia in 1962; Claire Van Vliet, Nancy Southworth and Stephanie Westnedge have disbound di-acidified, sized and repaired 20 copies, of which 5 only are for sale; the new binding is sewn through alum tawed pigskin spine with wooden boards that have the snow storm of the story scratched and painted on them, boxed.   Joshua Heller   21-2   1996 $850.00

BINDING - STEEL

CHURCH OF ENGLAND. BOOK OF COMMON PRAYER   Book of Common Prayer. Oxford: by the University Printers, 1701. Large folio; ruled in red and black; contemporary black morocco, covers gilt and blindstamped with broad outer border of floral drawer handle and small tools, central panel with blindstamped leafy sprays and flowers, monograms gilt in each corner, centre gilt with Royal Arms (Queen Anne, Davenport p. 51), spine gilt in 8 panels with raised bands and one panel lettered direct, all edges gilt, corner soft, some gilt faded, but generally fresh, fine binding with both Royal Arms and monograms almost certainly by Robert Steel.   Marlborough   160-31   1996   £2,250.00

SANDFORD, FRANCIS   A Genealogical History of the Kings and Queens of England. London: Nicholson, 1707. One of 25 large paper copies; folio; on large paper, title in red and black, 3 ff., 878 pages, (pages 372, 495-8 exfoliated; pages 84-95 foliated), 13 ff. index, 1 f. errata; 71 full page or folding engraved plates; cont. red mor. gilt, elaborate gilt tooled covers arranged in panels, outer gilt triple fillet, wide border w/semi-circles & fleurons, middle border w/floral compartments of massed sm. tools, urns, roll-tools & lg. & sm. crowned cypher AR used 30 times on each cover, at centre, the Royal Arms, spine gilt in compartments, raised gilt bands, each compartments w/royal cypher (1 lg. & 4 sm.), gilt ruled, gilt inner dentelle, marbled endpapers, all edges gilt, rubbed, some scuff marks, rebacked preserving original compartments, corners sympathetically strengthened, large and impressive binding by Robert Steel, fine.   Marlborough   160-54   1996   £2,500.00

BINDING - STERN

SMALL World Alphabet. Seattle: Grey Spider Press, 1992. One of 75 copies signed by artist, Michael Dal Cerro; woodcuts by Michael Dal Cerro, printed from the blocks on Mohawk Letterpress paper, printed and bound by Christ Stern, decorated endpapers, green cloth boards, paper title label on spine, larger title label with illustration on front cover; fine.   Joshua Heller   21-44   1996 $125.00

BINDING - STIKEMAN

HAWTHORNE, NATHANIEL 1804-1864   Twice-Told Tales. Boston: James Munroe, 1842. 1st edition thus, 1st issue; full green morocco, gilt panels, raised bands, gilt compartments, inner dentelles gilt, silk markers, uncut, signed by Stikeman; fine, fresh set with only the slightest rubbing; from the library of Charles B. Foote; extremely rare book. Dickinson p. 121-2; BAL 7594; Clark A2.3.1.   Mac Donnell   12-86   1996 $850.00

HYDE, CATHERINE   Secret Memoirs of the Royal Family of France During the Revolution. London: H. S. Nichols, 1895. Later edition, one of 500 copies; 8vo; 2 volumes, 332, 307 pages; contemporary three quarter brown morocco by Stikeman & Co., with gilt tooled spine panels, raised bands, top edges gilt, bookplate, boards little mottled, still very good. Chapel Hill   94-113   1996 $100.00

LONGFELLOW, HENRY WADSWORTH 1807-1882   Tales of a Wayside Inn. Boston: Ticknor and Fields, 1863. 1st American edition; 12mo; illustrated titlepage; half purple morocco gilt by Stikeman, some light rubbing, light browning and spotting of some leaves of text, without publisher's ads; attractive copy. BAL 12136.   James Cummins   14-125   1996 $250.00

POE, EDGAR ALLAN 1809-1849   The Narrative of Arthur Gordon Pym. New York: Harper & Bros., 1838. 1st edition; 12mo; 201 pages, plus 14 pages publisher's ads, complete with 2 pages of ads at front dated May 1838; handsomely bound by Stikeman and Co. in full brown morocco, covers decoratively panelled in gilt, gilt spine, tooled in compartments, gilt board edges and turn-ins, top edge gilt, marbled endpapers, light wear to extremities, text exceptionally bright, fine. BAL 16128.   Heritage Book Shop   196-239   1996 $1,500.00

STEVENSON, ROBERT LOUIS BALFOUR 1850-1894   An Inland Voyage. London: C. Kegan Paul & Co., 1878. 1st edition; 8vo; author's first book; bound by Stikeman in three quarter black morocco and marbled boards with original sky blue covers and spine bound in rear, binding rubbed along edges, especailly spine, with head of spine peeling back; very good.   Charles Agvent   4-1040   1996 $350.00

SUCKLING, JOHN   The Works. Dublin: Nelson, 1766. 1st Dublin edition; tall 8vo; pages 462, (2); handsome binding by Stikeman, in three quarter crushed morocco, gilt extra, panelled spine, top edge gilt, marbled endpapers, slight defect at bottom of titlepage, not affecting text, else fine, scarce. Bookplate of Joseph Knight, distinguished Dickens scholar.   Hartfield   48-L82   1996 $295.00

WALSINGHAM, LORD   Shooting, Field and Covert, Moor and Marsh. London: 1886. 1st edition; plates and text illustrations; finely bound in half scarlet morocco, gilt sporting emblems on spine, marbled boards and endpapers by Stikeman. Choice copy.   David A.H. Grayling   3/95-236   1996   £75.00

BINDING - STOAKLEY

BRYAN, MICHAEL   Dictionary of Painters and Engravers. London: George Bell, 1909-10. 4to; 5 volumes; xii, 364; x, 292; xvi, 394; xvi, 310; xviii, 426 pages, including 5 pages of artist's monograms at end; modern half calf, spines richly gilt in 6 compartments, red and brown morocco double lettering pieces, top edge gilt, by Stoakley of Cambridge, slight fading to spines, otherwise superb set.   Thomas Thorp 489-46 1996 £350.00

BINDING - STONEHOUSE BINDERY

CONGREVE, WILLIAM 1670-1729   The Way of the World, a Comedy. London: for Jacob Tonson, 1700. 1st edition; 4to; (10), 89, (3) pages, wanting half title, minor worming in blank bottom margins, with bottom margins of last two leaves extended, with loss of type on final page (Tonson ad) only; in handsome modern design binding of full crimson goat, each cover with panel made up of blind tooled circles, marbled endpapers, by the Stonehouse Bindery; slightly imperfect, but very pleasing copy in tasteful design binding. Grolier English 100, 37; Tinker 734. Wing C5878.   Joseph J. Felcone 64-12 1996 $900.00

BINDING - STORR

ROBERTSON, WILLIAM 1721-1793   The Works... Chiswick: printed by C. Whittingham for Thomas Tegg, 1824. 12mo; additional titlepages, with wood engraved illustrations; contemporary green calf by R. Storr, Grantham, with his ticket on each rear pastedown, smooth backstrips, divided into compartments by narrow gilt rolls, polished morocco title label in third compartment, volume label in fifth, square foliage and flower ornaments in first and seventh, second, fourth and sixth with rope rolls and trellis pointille rolls, marbled boards lightly rubbed, endapers and edges, blank endleaves foxed, excellent.   Blackwell's B112-243 1996 £250.00

BINDING - STORR & RIDGE

STROZZI, TITO VESPASIANO   Strozii Poetae Pater et Filius. Venice: Venetiis is Aedibus Aldi et Andreae Asulani Soceri, 1513/14. Edition princeps; 8vo; 2 parts; ff. (8), 99, (1), 152 leaves, printed throughout in italics, early illumination of A1, with frame crowned by dolphins, and elephant drawing an ancient carriage with arms and shields, the book was once damped throughout, and illumination is somewhat faded with offsetting; crimson morocco stamped in gilt with Aldine anchor and dolphin, entwined in naval rope, binding was probably executed by Messrs. Storr and Ridge of Grantham for Sir John Hayford Thorold, preserved in cloth box; Syston Park copy. Renouard p. 65.10; Adams S1956; UCLA I/93; Goldsmid 91; Isaac 12832.   Family Album Tillers-591 1996 $2,000.00

BINDING - SUTTABY

SCOTLAND: Her Sons and Scenery, as Sung by Her Bards, and Seen in the Camera. London: A. W. Bennett, 1868. 1st edition; 8vo; (viii), 192 pages; 14 original mounted albumen photos; full navy blue morocco gilt, with four raised bands to spine and gilt medallion on front and rear covers surrounding an inlay of salmon morocco, gilt, covers have floral designs in blind, fine and bright in fine binding of the period, with bevelled edges, all edges gilt, front hinge shows slight wear, else fine, binding signed by R. & A. Suttaby, London.   Andrew Cahan 47-180 1996 $485.00

BINDING - TARLAU

CHAR, RENE   Elizabeth Petite Fille. Ales: P.A.B., 1958. Ales: P.A.B., 1958. 1st edition; one of 75 copies only; numbered and paragraphed by publisher, Pierre Andre Benoit; page size 3 3/8 x 3 1/4 inches; printed on Rives, color drawing after Chart; bound by Jill Tarlau in full turquoise and bordeaux mottled snakeskin with onlays in same mottled snakeskin and turquoise box calf forming pinwheel on center of front panel with a bordeaux 'jewel' in center of pinwheel, simplified binding structure in center of pinwheel; original wrappers bound in, signed on lower front turn-in, housed in bordeaux and turquoise pastepaper over boards clamshell box, with turquoise spine, lined in bordeaux suede and morocco.   Priscilla Juvelis 95/1-51 1996 $1,750.00

CROMBIE, JOHN   Cette Galere. Paris: 1991. Number 97 in an edition of 115 copies; 8 x 7.5 inches; colored illustrations, French text; specially bound by Jill Oriane Tarlau in light green leather with various colored leather onlays and inlays, with pieces of metallic embroidery and colored stones, various colored endpapers, all edges green, green decorated paper board chemise with light and dark green leather edges, slipcase of green decorated paper board with dark green leather trim, fine. Joshua Heller 21-229 1996 $1,400.00

BINDING - TARLAU

PERRAULT, CHARLES 1628-1703   Histoire de Peau d'Ane. Hammersmith: Eragny Press, 1902. One of 230 copies; page size 5 1/8 x 8 inches; printed on Arches paper watermarked for the Press; 3 original wood engravings by T. Sturge Moore and borders, frontispiece and initial letters by Lucien & Esther Pissarro; this copy in unique binding by Jill Tarlau, pale rose and bordeaux iridescent trellis patterned cloth with daisy-shaped rondel on upper panel of bordeaux onlays with lighter pink box calf onlaid on silver box calf to form center of flower, rose/lime green lizard, bordeaux suede surrounding rose/lime green rhinestone in center of rondel, matching chemise and etui edged in pale rose box calf, gilt lettering.   Priscilla Juvelis 95/1-88 1996 $2,000.00

SAGE, KAY   Mordicus. Paris: Ales PAB, 1962. One of 259 copies only; page size 8 1/16 x 6 15/16 inches; 10 full page drawings after Jean Dubuffet; bound by Jill Tarlau, full royal blue ostrich with onlays of red bordeaux, black and blue calf, silver and iridescent snakeskin, blue on blue striped plastic, blue and black dotted plastic, paste paper guards, blue suede lined chemise with blue ostrich spine, paste paper, author, title, and date on spine in lower case red letters, matching blue calf edge etui, original wrappers bound in, top edge gilt, signed on lower front turn-in.   Priscilla Juvelis 95/1-81 1996 $1,250.00

WALKER, ANNE   Rose Rose. Paris: 1993. One in an edition of 3 copies, signed and dated by Walker; 6.25 x 5 inches; pastel painting with black hand-written poetry on accordion folded two-sided book; individually bound with two end boards by Jill Oriane Tarlau, the front board is covered with finely worked metallic petit-point embroidery by Tarlau, with a plum leater surround, dark plum back baord has inlays and onlays of patchwork leather forming the letters of the word 'Rose' as well as 3 onlays of metallic embroidery, one of a rose, all laid in drop-back box of lilac, green and gold handmade paper trimmed with dark plum leather and lined with purple suede.   Joshua Heller 21-228 1996 $3,400.00

BINDING - TARRANT

LA TOUR LANDRY, GEOFFREY DE   The Book of the Knight of La Tour Landry. London: Alcuin Press for the Verona Society, 1930. One of 500 copies, this copy not numbered; 10 x 7 3/4 inches; xii, 172 pages; fine large dec. capitals in the style of the 16th century crible initials, printed in red & black; very appealing recent exhibition binding by Alan Tarrant of inlaid and onlaid black oasis mor., front bd. with stylized vignette at lower left showing a flowering tree made up of onlaid mor. in olive & blue, tree emananting from a shadowed ground represented by 8 oval orange mor. inlays and 22 especially imaginative pebble-shaped silver studs, upper left corner of back cover featuring a full moon (represented by a silver disk) & illuminated clouds (inlaid slender ovoids of gray & pink mor.), gray mor. doublures w/similar multicolored oval mor. inlays, free endpapers of gray suede, flat spine w/simple gilt titling, a.e.g., in substantial black folding buckram box, plushed lined, w/gilt lettered mor. label, slight wear to box, otherwise in extremely fine condition.   Phillip J. Pirages 33-75 1996 $950.00

BINDING - TATE

PEARSON, ANTHONY   The Great Gase of Tithes Truly Stated, Clearly Open'd and Fully Resolv'd... Dublin: by and for Isaac Jackson, 1756. 8vo; xvi, 130, (i) pages; old calf, gilt, by J. Tate, Belfast, rather rubbed; label of Friends' Library, Belfast.   R.F.G. Hollett & Son 78-453 1996 £85.00

BINDING - THIELEN

THIELEN, BETH   Why the Revolving Door: the Neighborhood, the Prisons. 1993. One of 20 copies, signed by artist; sculptural pop-up book made from mono-printed templates which vary in color and textual application, hand printed by artist on an Ettan etching press on 100 percent rag paper, acid free, white and black Arches Cover; each page hand cut and bound by artist, cover with etching, cover and slipcase boards are acid free, lignin free, binder's board, black linen book cloth for book spine and slipcase.   Joshua Heller 21-267 1996 $1,600.00

BINDING - THIERRY & DE PETIT-SIMIES

SHAKESPEARE, WILLIAM 1564-1616   The Passionate Pilgrim and the Songs in Shakespeare's Plays. London: Vale Press, 1896. One of 310 copies; 12mo; full olive-green levant morocco, ribbed spine in 6 compartments, all tooled in gilt, covers with elaborate gilt tooled borders composed of large foliate quadrilobe centerpieces with similar designs in gilt along all edges with gilt birds, torches and flower urns, all within border of gilt solid and dotted rules with outer border of repeated C-shaped devices, red morocco doublures similarly bordered in gilt with hightly decorative gilt panel, floral silk endpapers, binding signed 'Thierry & De Petit-Simies', tiny scuffs to spine ribs, else very fine.   Marilyn Braiterman 15-188 1995 $1,750.00

BINDING - THIERSCH

BIBLE. GERMAN - 1926   Biblia, das 1st; Die Gantze Heilige Schrifft-Deudsch D. Martin Luther. Bremer Presse, 1926-28. One of 365 copies; 14 1/4 x 10 1/4 inches; 5 volumes; titles and initials by Anna Simons; one of a limited number of copies very finely bound in stately vellum by Frieda Thiersch (signed by her on rear turn-in), covers with single gilt rule frame, raised bands, gilt titling on backstrips, spine compartments ruled in gilt, top edge gilt, other edges untrimmed, in rather faded and partly defective paper slipcases, very slight discoloration in few places on vellum, but very fine, showing no signs of wear and virtually pristine internally.   Phillip J. Pirages 33-110 1996 $8,500.00

BORCHARDT, RUDOLF   Gartenphantasie. Bremer Presse, 1925. One of 300 copies; 9 3/4 x 6 3/4 inches; 3 p.l. (1 blank), 7-36 pages, (2) leaves (colophon blank); black and red decorated initial by Anna Simons, who also designed title, printed in black and red; very fine burgundy crushed morocco by Frieda Thiersch (signed on rear turn-in), simple gilt fillet on covers, raised bands, gilt ruled spine compartments, turn-ins ruled in gilt, edges gilt, in very nice fleece lined slipcase with matching morocco lip, exceptionally fine copy.   Phillip J. Pirages 33-111 1996 $1,850.00

BINDING - THISTLE BINDERY

GOULD, ROBERT   The Twelve of Hearts. Boston: 1982. Limited to just 36 copies; 2 11/16 x 2 1/16 inches; 12 original watercolor designs on soft gray paper by Gould, calligraphy by Colleen; full vellum with exposed bands of red ribbon by David Bourbeau of the Thistle Bindery; title stamped in gold on spine; extremely fine.   Bromer Booksellers 90-178 1996 $350.00

JOYCE, JAMES 1882-1941   Epiphanies. New York: Vincent Fitz Gerald, 1988. One of 52 copies only, all on Rives du Gue paper; page size 12 x 14 inches; over 150 plates, original watercolors, collage and hand cutting, Letterpress by Dan Kelher's Wild Carrot Letterpress in 40 colors; bound loose in publisher's wrappers in handmade box by David Bourbeau at the Thistle Bindery in Japanese handmade silk woven for this box, with incised line of Japanese tea paper showing profile of Joyce.   Priscilla Juvelis 95/1-142 1996 $15,000.00

BINDING - THOMAS

GRAHAM, RIGBY   Holt Mill Papers. Santa Cruz: Donna and Peter Thomas, 1994. 1st edition; one of 50 copies, signed by the author and by the Thomas's; page size 15 x 11 3/8 inches; handset in Centaur types, paper handmade using cotton rag and 'a few other fibers' by Peter Thomas with the help of Joanna Gibson; tipped into each copy of the book are two samples of paper made at the Holt Mill in 1958; Coptic binding with handmade paper boards by John Babcock, by Donna and Peter Thomas.   Priscilla Juvelis 95/1-109 1996 $235.00

BINDING - THURKOW

BIBLE. ENGLISH - 1985   The Song of Songs by Solomon. Utrecht: Catharijne Press, 1985. Limited to 155 copies, signed by artist; 2 1/2 x 1 11/16 inches; 51 pages; engraved frontispiece; 6 large hand colored initial letters; bound in full vellum with title gilt stamped on cover by Luce Thurkow, top edge red, very fine.   Bromer Booksellers 87-201 1996 $100.00

BINDING - TOUT

BIRCH, JONATHAN   Fifty-One Original Fables, with Morals and Ethical Index. London: Hamilton Adams, 1833. 1st edition; octavo; 251 pages; 85 original wood engravings designed by Robert Cruikshank, including full page frontispiece; bound by Tout in tan calf, gilt stamped to covers and elaborately gilt stamped to spine and dentelles, faint wear to edges of spine, else very fine, all edges gilt.   Bromer Booksellers 90-92 1996 $475.00

DEFOE, DANIEL 1661?-1731   The Life and Strange Surprizing Adventures of Robinson Crusoe. (with) The Farther Adventures of Robinson Crusoe. (with) Serious Relfections During the Life and Surprising Adventures of Robinson Crusoe... London: for W. Taylor, 1719/19/20. 1st editions of 2nd and 3rd parts, 3rd edition of first part, all three are first issues; 8vo; 3 works, volume 1 with frontispiece, volume 2 with folding map at beginning of text (laid down on linen), volume 3 with folding map (laid down on linen); all 3 volumes with final ads; uniformly bound in modern dark blue crushed morocco, sides ruled in blind, spines in comaprtments with raised bands, gilt lettering, edges and inner dentelles gilt, marbled endpapers, by Tout and Son, corners little bumped, some slight spotting, browning or soiling, but very good. PMM 180.   Simon Finch 24-66 1996 £2,350.00

BINDING - TOUT

GAY, JOHN 1685-1732   Fables by John Gay. London: John Stockdale, 1793. 1st of this edition; tall octavo; wide margined copy; pages xi, 225; vii, 187, (1); 2 volumes; titlepage vignettes, 70 fine engraved plates by William Blake, tissue guards and subscriber list present; elegantly bound by Tout in three quarter morocco, marbled boards and endpapers, raised bands, spines elaborately gilt in compartments, all edges gilt, slight wear to covers, spines uniformly sunned, but beautiful set. Lowndes II 772; CBEL II 293.   Hartfield 48-L33 1996 $1,295.00

LE SAGE, ALAIN RENE 1668-1747   The Adventures of Gil Blas of Santillana. Edinburgh: William Paterson, 1886. 9 3/4 x 6 1/2 inches; 3 volumes; title vignettes, 21 fine etched plates by Adolphe Lalauze; three quarter vellum over sturdy boards by Tout, textured cloth sides, flat spines heavily gilt in compartments in antique style, brown morocco triple labels, marbled endpapers, gilt top, top corners of volume 1 little bumped, turn-ins little spotted (trivial spots and superficial marks elsewhere to covers and spines), otherwise excellent set, with no significant wear, and with gilt still bright and attractive, slight offsetting from plates, but very fine internally. Large attractive engraved bookplate in each volume.   Phillip J. Pirages 33-343 1996 $450.00

MAC LAREN, ARCHIBALD   The Fairy Family. London: Longmans, Brown, Green, Longmans & roberts, 1857. 1st edition; crown 8vo; (xvi), (284) pages; later half morocco by Tout, top edge gilt, spine tanned, damage to marbled sides neatly restored, endpapers gummed and adhesion damaged, little internal browning, one leaf slightly chipped, but looks better than it sounds.   Ash Rare Books Zenzybyr-65 1996 £195.00

MATTHEWS, THOMAS   Advice to the Young Whist Player. London: B.C. Collins (Salisbury): and Messrs. Norton and Son, Bristol, 1806. 2nd edition; 12mo; full dark green morocco, front wrapper reproduced in gilt on front cover, spine and inner dentelles gilt, all edges gilt, by Tout and Sons, very slightly rubbed, original light blue printed wrappers bound in; fine; rare. Jessel 1156.   Ximenes 109-190 1996 $300.00

MAYHEW, HENRY   1851; or, the Adventures of Mr. and Mrs. Sandboys and Family, Who Came Up to London to "Enjoy Themselves", and to See the Great Exhibition. London: David Bogue, n.d. 1851. 1st edition in book form, 1st issue with hiatus between pages 62 and 65; 8vo; folding frontispiece, engraved title, 10 plates by George Cruikshank, folding plates expertly backed with linen, contemporary half calf, hinges slightly rubbed, spine gilt, all edges gilt, by Tout. Cohn 548.   Anthony W. Laywood 108-214 1996 £110.00

THE RAMBLES and Surprising Adventures of Captain Bolio. London: ptd. for Thomas Tegg; Tegg & Co. Dublin, R. Griffin & Co. Glasgow... 1839. 1st edition; 12mo; half blue morocco, gilt, spine gilt, top edge gilt, by Tout (traces or rubbing); fine, scarce. Not in block; not in Wolff.   Ximenes 108-131 1996 $250.00

SHELLEY, PERCY BYSSHE 1792-1822   Rosalind and Helen, a Modern Eclogue; with Other Poems. London: printed for C. and J. Ollier, 1819. 8vo; full brown crushed levant, gilt, spine and inner dentelles gilt, top edge gilt, by Tout; fine, outer edges uncut, complete with half title and 2 leaves of ads at end; Granniss 49.   Ximenes 108-322 1996 $1,750.00

BINDING - TRAUTZ-BAUZONNET

TRAGICUM Theatrum Actorum & Casuum Tragicorum Londini Publice Celebratorum. Amsterdam: Janson, 1649. 8vo; title device, 8 full page portraits and 1 folding plate; crushed crimson morocco, crowned monogram in all corners, inner dentelles, all edges by Trautz-Bauzonnet; Valentin Uhink y Gomez Farias bookticket. Splendid copy. Barbier IV 1395-6; Abbot 422.   Rostenberg & Stern 150-111 1996 $1,250.00

BINDING - TRUSLOVE

EPPS, JAMES   The Cacao Plant: a Trip to the West Indies. Croydon: 1897-1903. 8vo; 2 offprints in 1 volume, 6 plates in the first item, extra illustrated with 75 plates, (1 real photo, 74 photographic plates, possibly collotype); contemporary half leather, gilt edges, by Truslove and Bray of West Norwood (bit worn, front joint cracked).   Maggs Bros. Ltd. 1190-236 1996 £400.00

BINDING - UPHAM LIBRARY

HALL, BASIL 1788-1844   Extracts from a Journal, Written on the Coasts of Chili, Peru and Mexico, in the Years 1820, 1821, 1822. Edinburgh: ptd. for Arch. Constable & Co., & Hurst, Robinson & Co., London, 1824. 1st edition; 8vo; 2 volumes; folding map; contemporary half dark blue calf, spines gilt, binder's tickets of Upham's Library in Bath; fine set in attractive provincial ticketed binding. Sabin 29718.   Ximenes 109-148 1996 $300.00

BINDING - VAN VLIET

BIDPAI   A Fable of Bidpai. Janus Press, 1974. One of 270 copies thus, in an edition of 300 copies, signed by artist; 10 x 7 inches; 20 pages; 14 wood engravings by Helen Siegl; designed and letterpress printed by Claire Van Vliet, text printed in black with title and colophon pages in blue, wood engravings printed in dark blue, light blue, green, orange or lavender on French-folded Hosokawa and handsewn into mustard Strathmore Beau Brilliant cover glued over light boards, binding and boxes by Claire Van Vliet and James Bicknell. Fine.   Joshua Heller 21-6 1996 $175.00

CAPETANAKIS, DEMETROIS   The Poetry of Demetrois Capetanakis... Janus Press, 1966. One of 100 numbered copies; 11 x 8 inches; 20 pages; designed, set and printed on Vandercook proofing press at the University of Wisconsin, Madison and bound by Claire Van Vliet; titles handset, printed in black with silver titles on Rives cuve velin and handsewn into grey Fabriano wrappers; fine.   Joshua Heller 21-3 1996 $125.00

DOVE, RITA   Lady Freedom Among Us. West Burke: Janus Press, 1994. One in an edition of 100 copies, plus 10 hors commerce signed by artist and author; 10.5 x 6.25 inches; images and design by Claire Van Vliet, handprinted and bound by Van Vliet on various handmade papers of brown, blue and black, text on white card between two cut-out profiles and fold-out face in black with three cut-out brown stars, blue card wrappers with wrap-around white ard relief of the Capitol, black reproduction of "Freedom" on spine where white card relief and blue wrappers meet; opaque plastic chemise, blue cloth slipcase with red, white and blue paper title label on spine.   Joshua Heller 21-38 1996 $300.00

JOHNSON, W. R.   Anno Domini. Janus Press, 1970. One of 140 copies; 6.75 x 6 inches; designed, set, printed and bound by Claire Van Vliet, titles and text handset, printed in black with old wood type, star and half title printed in silver on Rives cuve velin BFK Blue Fabriano half titles, Rives flyleaf into which star is handcut at center (front and back) and handsewn into red Fabriano wrapper with silver star printed on front; fine.   Joshua Heller 21-4 1996 $100.00

KAFKA, FRANZ 1883-1924   Ein Landarzt/A Country Doctor. Printed at the Philadelphia College of Art, 1962. Limited to 250 copies numbered and signed by artist; 12.25 x 8.75 inches; 32 pages; printed in black on Rives cuve velin; 12 relief etchings by Claire Van Vliet; unsatisfactorily bound by a Commercial Binder, William Marley Co., in Philadelphia in 1962; Claire Van Vliet, Nancy Southworth and Stephanie Westnedge have disbound di-acidified, sized and repaired 20 copies, of which 5 only are for sale; the new binding is sewn through alum tawed pigskin spine with wooden boards that have the snow storm of the story scratched and painted on them, boxed.   Joshua Heller 21-2 1996 $850.00

BINDING - VICTORIAN

BAINES, EDWARD   Yorkshire, Past and Present: a History and a Description of the Three Ridings of the Great County of York from the Earliest Ages to the Year 1870, with an Account of Its Manufactures, Commerce and Civil and Mechanical Engineering... London: 1863. 1st edition; 4to; 4 volumes; numerous finely engraved plates; elaborate gilt decorated purple cloth, fine example of a Victorian binding; very good. K Books 441-25 1996 £100.00

GOETHE, JOHANN WOLFGANG VON 1749-1832   Faust. A Tragedy. London: Frederick Bruckmann, 1877. Atlas folio; numerous detailed wood engravings to text, 14 fine mounted photographic plates, some margins occasionally little soiled, leaves somewhat loose as usual with this very large and heavy book; magnificently bound in original full morocco, upper board very elaborately embossed and gilt decorated, large central panel surrounded by 20 smaller panels, 8 large and elaborate silver corner pieces to boards, upper board with 6 large silver circular embossed portraits onlaid, little rubbed at extremities, very minor wear to upper joint, all edges gilt. Magnificent example of Victorian bookbinding.   Ian Wilkinson 95/1-102 1996 £490.00

BINDING - VILLA

SILIUS ITALICUS, GAIUS   De Bello Punico Libri Septemdecim... Paris: Colines, 1531. 8vo; title with device, ff. 2-223, (repair with text loss to f. 7), red stained edges; brown morocco, borders ruled in blind, gilt tooling and the Apollo and Pegasus plaquette added by Villa in the late 19th century; spine little worn, few wormholes; a fake 'Canevari' binding by Vittorio Villa.   Marlborough 160-78 1996 £1,500.00

BINDING - VILLA

SPANDUGINO, THEODORO   I Commentari di Theodoro Spandugino Cantacuscino Gentilhumomo Costantinopolitano, Dell'Origine de Principi Turchi... Florence: Lorenzo Torrentino, Impressor Ducale, Aug. 1551. Octavo; 8 leaves, 202 pages, 1 leaf, foremargin of first gathering stained and frayed; bound in contemporary red morocco with, on each cover, a panelled design of stylised leaves and flowers, and the Apollo and Pegasus palcquette at centre, added about 1890, this is one of the celebrated fake 'Canevari' bindings made by Vittorio Villa at end of the last century. Inscription at lower margin of title torn away (perhaps by the forger?). Adams S1531;   H. M. Fletcher 121-27 1996 £1,500.00

BINDING - WAGNER

PASQUIER, ESTIENNE   Des Recherches de La France, Livres Premier et Second. Paris: Pierre l'Huillier, 1570. 3rd combined edition; small 8vo; ff. 239 (xvii), roman & italic letter, woodcut titlepage border, initials and ornaments; age yellowed, upper edge of titlepage torn without loss, occasional headline shaved, 1 leaf loosening; 19th century calf by Wagner, richly gilt spine, gilt fillets and inner dentlles, marbled endpapers; This ed. not in BM STC Fr., Adams, Brunet, Tchemerzine, NUC.   A. Sokol XXV-71 1996 £550.00

BINDING - WALTHER

BIBLE. GREEK - 1723   Novum Testamentum Graecum. Leipzig: Gleditsch, 1723. Folio; crimson morocco by Walther, with his label, all edges gilt, the Syston Park copy, with Thorold's pencil note "Chart Max/Walther" in front flyleaves.   Marlborough 160-29 1996 £500.00

BINDING - WATKINS

MATHIAS, THOMAS JAMES   The Pursuits of Literature. (with) A Translation of the Passages from Greek, Latin, Italian and French Writers, Quoted in the Prefaces and Notes to the Pursuit of Literature... London: for T. Becket, 1799/98. 10th edition, 3rd edition of 2nd title; 8vo; pages (ii), iv, 445, (1); (ii), lxxv, (i) blank, (iv) fly-title, ad, 104, bound without half titles; contemporary diced calf, gilt roll border to sides, spine in compartments with gilt rolls, ornaments and lettering, little sunned and rubbed at head and foot, marbled edges and endpapers, by T. B. Watkins of Hereford, occasional slight spotting, otherwise an excellent copy; bookplate of Richard Hopton.   Simon Finch 24-165 1996 £95.00

BINDING - WEATHERBY WOOLNOUGH

THE GARDEN of the Night - Twenty-six Sufi Poems. Andoversford: Whittington Press, 1979. One of 35 specially bound copies, signed by editor and artist and numbered with Roman numerals, total edition comprised 235 copies; quarto; lacks extra etching by artist; printed on BFV Rives paper; full decorated gilt Nigerian goatskin by Weatherby Woolnough with Whittington marbled endpapers, top edge gilt, spine darkened, covers very slightly marked, very good in slipcase, which is slightly faded at edges and slightly marked and dusty.   Ulysses 39-625 1996 £450.00

BINDING - WECKESSER

PASSERAT, JEAN   Recveil des Oevvres Poetiqves. Paris: Claude Morel, 1606. 1st complete edition; 8vo; 2 parts in 1 volume, pages (viii), 464, (viii); (xvi), 248, (vi), 8 pages misnumbered, mainly italic letter, woodcut printer's device on each titlepage, 2 identical engraved potraits by Thos. de Leu, woodcut initials & ornaments, blank corner of 1st titlepage repaired, tiny rust holes touching one letter of one headline; crushed red morocco by De Samblanx & J. Weckesser richly gilt dentelle borders and dentelle fan motif at corners, gilt spine and turn-ins, all edges gilt, marbled endpapers; from the library of Hecotr de Backer, with modern bookplates of Alfred Clericeau and Henri Burton. BM STC Fr. 17th 631; Tchemerzine V113; Cioranesco 17247 & 17259.   A. Sokol XXV-72 1996 £1,650.00

BINDING - WERNER

WERNER, ARNO   One Man's Work: a Lecture. Easthampton: Warwick Press, 1872. One of 200 copies, signed by author and printer; 8vo; printed in Sans Serif Light 329 on Barcham Green handmade; tipped in colored plates, titlepage portrait; bound by Werner and Blinn in quarter russet morocco with paste paper sides; fine.   Bertram Rota 272-485 1996 £105.00

BINDING - WESTLEYS

LONGFELLOW, HENRY WADSWORTH 1807-1882   Hyperion: a Romance. London: Alfred William Bennett, 1865. 1st edition thus; 4to; 24 mounted albumen prints of views, pages x, (2), 270, (1); original purple cloth, gilt extra, edges gilt, by Westleys with ticket, little wear at joints and headbands, one small section starting, still very good to nice, rarely found in nice state.   James Fenning 133-121 1996 £195.00

MASON, J. A.   A Treatise on the Climate and Meteorology of Madeira... London: John Churchill, Liverpool: Deighton and Laughton, 1850. 1st edition; medium 8vo; large paper copy; 386 pages text, 5 climate graphs on 3 plates; original green cloth, elaborately decorated gilt covers and spine, top edge gilt, inner gilt dentelles, yellow endpapers, bound by Westleys & Co., upper and lower hinges cracked, corners bumped.   Beeleigh Abbey BA56-94 1996 £250.00

SYDENHAM, THOMAS 1624-1689   The Works. London: Sydenham Soc., 1848-50. Translated from the Latin edition of Dr. Greenhill; 8vo; 2 volumes; green cloth, by Westley's, with their tickets, bit scuffed. GM 64.   Maggs Bros. Ltd. 1190-516 1996 £75.00

BINDING - WHITESEL

MASON, BOBBIE ANN   With Jazz. Monterey: Larkspur, 1994. One of 50 copies; printed on dampened Johannot, signed by author and artist; illustrations by LaNelle Mason; hand bound by Carolyn Whitesel, fine in illustrated boards.   Bella Luna 7-360 1996 $125.00

BINDING - WICKERS

TUCKERMAN, ARTHUR LYMAN   A Short History of Architecture. New York: Scribner's, 1887. 1st edition; 8vo; 168 pages; illustrations; ca. 1930 prize binding of full polished tree calf by Wickers & Son, with raised bands, gilt tooled spine, morocco spine labels, gilt borders on covers, and gilt heraldic crest on front cover, prize award bookplate, light general wear to binding, but handsome, very good.   Chapel Hill 94-118 1996 $125.00

BINDING - MICHAEL WILCOX

LES GRANDES Merveilles d'Amour. France? n.d. Limited to 35 copies, signed by artist; 1 3/4 x 1 11/16 inches; (26) pages; printed in blue by Sergent Fulbert, surrounded by dark green engraved border by Francis Righi, who also illustrated the book with 2 full page color images; in unique binding by Michael Wilcox, dated 1994, of full salmon morocco, onlays of purple morocco form two open roses on each cover, which are accented with circular purple onlays and with gilt tooled dots, circles and other geometric shapes, doublures show reverse of covers with rectangular purple onlays silhouetting the salmon colored flowers, circular salmon onlays and corresponding gilt tooling; handsome binding, housed in buckram dropback box with gilt titled spine label in purple morocco, lined w/purple velvet & latched w/thread and buttom.   Bromer Booksellers 87-186 1996 $1,750.00

BINDING - WINSTANLEY

DRAYTON, MICHAEL 1563-1631   Poems... London: printed by W. Stansby for John Methwicke, 1613. 4th edition; 8vo; 19th century black morocco, wide gilt borders, spine and inner dentelles gilt, all edges gilt, by Winstanley of Manchester, joints bit rubbed; titlepage bit dusty, slight scattered foxing and couple of minor wormholes near end, but very good; flyleaf preserved bears the contemporary signature of Charles Brandon, Duke of Suffolk. STC 7221; Pforzheimer 305.   Ximenes 109-104 1996 $850.00

BINDING - WOOD

COLERIDGE, SAMUEL TAYLOR 1772-1834   Christabel; Kubla Khan, a Vision; the Pains of Sleep. London: for John Murray by William Bulmer and Co., 1816. 1st edition; 1st printing; 8vo; pages vii, (i) blank, 64; with half title, without inserted ad leaves sometimes found at end; well rebound in full red crushed morocco, spine lettered in gilt with date at foot, raised bands, one line gilt rules, gilt inner dentelles, top edge gilt, by Wood of London; bookplate, ownership inscription, blindstamps on endleaves; fine. Ashley I 204; Corns & Sparke p. 56; Hayward 207; Tinker 693.   Simon Finch 24-46 1996 £1,600.00

BINDING - WOOD

HOPKINS, GERARD MANLEY   Pied Beauty. London: Simon King Press, 1994. Limited to 100 numbered copies; folio; pages (22), four full page linocut illustrations, printed in 18 pt. Baskerville of 176gsm Mohawk paper; with an additional set of the prints, signed and numbered in stiff paper folder; bound by Alan Wood at the Gregynog Bindery in quarter blue morocco lettered in gold, paste paper boards, with an additional set of prints, signed and numbered, in stiff paper folder.   Claude Cox 107-74B 1996 £150.00

WORDSWORTH, WILLIAM 1770-1850   The Waggoner a Poem. London: printed by Strahan and Spottiswoode for Longman, etc., 1819. 1st edition; 8vo; full dark green morocco, gilt, spine and inner dentelles gilt, top edge gilt, by Wood, joints little rubbed; attractive copy; booklabel of Herschel V. Jones. Cornell Wordsworth Collection 49; Wise p. 22.   Ximenes 109-305 1996 $600.00

BINDING - WORSFOLD

ROE, THOMAS   Sir Thomas Rowe His Speech at the Councell-Table Touching Brasse-Money, or Against Brasse Money... London: printed Anno, 1641. 1st edition; 4to; (2), 351-358 pages, i.e. a total of 6 leaves including the blank before title, occasional light soiling, woodcut device on title; handsomely bound in late 19th century mottled calf, fully gilt, inner gilt dentelles, by Worsfold, blindstamp on title, in most respects a fine copy. Wing R1778a. Massie 575; Goldsmiths 760; Kress S708.   John Drury 82-244 1996 £350.00

BINDING - WRIGHT

CHAUNCY, HENRY   The Historical Antiquities of Hertfordshire... London: for B. Griffin etc., 1700. 1st edition; limited to 500 copies; folio; title, 4 ff., 601 pages, 11 ff., engraved portrait, folding map, 44 plates; early 19th century dark blue morocco gilt, gilt inner borders, gilt edges by J. Wright; extremities rubbed; very handsome. Wing C3741; Lowndes p. 430.   Marlborough 162-14 1996 £2,200.00

COWPER, WILLIAM 1731-1800   The Poetical Works... London: Henry G. Bohn, 1851. 8vo; pages xxiv, 516; frontispiece, extra engraved title (both foxed), 2 portraits and one view (slightly foxed), 18 engraved plates; contemporary green hard grained morocco, sides tooled with wide gilt dentelle order made up of a large number of individual tools, spine divided into six panels by raised bands, elaborately tooled in gilt, lettered in second panel, gilt inner dentelles, pale yellow endpapers, gilt edges, spine slightly darkened and rubbed at head and tail, handsome binding by John Wright; contemporary presentation inscription to Arthur Pemberton Lonsdale on his leaving Eton on front blank.   Simon Finch 24-61 1996 £180.00

MONTSTRELET, ENGUERRAND DE   The Chronicles of... N.P.: James Henderson at the Hafod Press, 1809. Folio; 5 volumes bound in 4; engravings; contemporary russia boards by J. Wright, rebacked in brown morocco, spines with raised bands, gilt tooling and dark brown gilt stamped labels, covers triple ruled in gilt with decorative floral corner devices, gilt stamped floral inner dentelles, marbled endpapers, edges extra gilt; very good.   George J. Houle 68-103 1996 $1,250.00

BINDING - ZAEHNSDORF

ANDERSEN, HANS CHRISTIAN 1805-1875   Stories from Hans Andersen. London: Hodder & Stoughton, 1911. Edition deluxe, limited to 750 numbered copies, signed by artist; large quarto; viii, 250 pages; 28 mounted color plates by Edmund Dulac; bound by Zaehnsdorf in full green morocco, front cover decoratively stamped in gilt, gilt lettered spine with raised bands, gilt board edges and turn-ins, top edge gilt, others uncut, marbled endpapers, little light foxing and browning, otherwise fine.   Heritage Book Shop 196-208 1996 $2,250.00

BARRIE, JAMES MATTHEW 1860-1937   Sentimental Tommy: the Story of His Boyhood. London: Paris: & Melbourne: Cassell and Co., 1896. 1st edition; 7 1/2 x 5 1/2 inches; viii, 452 pages, (2) leaves (ads, but without final, separate, 8 leaf section of ads); very pretty contemporary honey-brown three quarter calf by Zaehnsdorf, marbled sides and endpapers, spine densely gilt in compartments, top edge gilt; very fine copy, handsomely bound. Cutler 46.   Phillip J. Pirages 33-37 1996 $150.00

BEAUFORT, DUKE OF   Driving. London: 1889. Limited to 250 copies; small 4to; large paper edition; portrait and numerous illustrations; beautifully bound in half red levant morocco, gilt top, by Zaehnsdorf.   Charles W. Traylen 117-279 1996 £150.00

BINDING - ZAEHNSDORF

BIBLIOGRAPHICA. Papers on Books, Their History and Art. London: Kegan Paul, 1895-97. Thick 4to; 12 parts in 3 volumes, 65 plates and numerous illustrations; quarter morocco, bound by Zaehnsdorf (original wrappers bound in); fine set from the library of the late bookseller H. W. Edwards.   Charles W. Traylen 117-2 1996 £330.00

BLUNT, WILFRED 1901-   Flora Superba. London: 1971. Limited to 406 copies, signed by author, this copy un-numbered; folio; 16 colored plates; original morocco backed vellum boards by Zaehnsdorf (with cellotape stains around edges of pastedowns), all edges gilt. Raymond M. Sutton VI-16 1996 $600.00

BROWN, THOMAS 1663-1704   The Works of Mr. Thomas Brown, Serious and Comical, in Prose and Verse. London: Edward Midwinter, 1730. 7th edition; small 8vo; 4 volumes; frontispieces, full page illustrations; headpieces and devices in text; three quarter gilt stamped brown morocco over marbled boards by Zaehnsdorf, spines with raised bands, gilt stamped floral devices, gilt ruled covers, matching marbled endpapers, minor rubbing; very good.   George J. Houle 68-18 1996 $375.00

BULLEN, A. H.   Speculum Amantis: Love Poems of the 17th century, from Rare Song Books and Miscelalnies. London: privately printed, 1902. 1st edition; number 8 of 400 copies; octavo; pages 129; printed on fine laid paper; titlepage in red and black; beautiful binding by Zaehnsdorf in full polished maroon morocco, double gilt fillets, gilt extra to spine panels, raised bands, top edge gilt, uncut, marbled endpapers, inner gilt dentelles; fine. CBEL II 258.   Hartfield 48-V44 1996 $135.00

CARTWRIGHT, FAIRFAX L.   The Mystic Rose from the Garden of the King. London?: privately printed, 1898. 1st edition; small 4to; 315 pages; contemporary full polished calf by Zaehnsdorf, with raised bands, gilt tooled spine panels and borders, 19th century bookplate, but nice copy. Chapel Hill 94-109 1996 $200.00

COPE, THOMAS   The Smokers's Text Book. Liverpool: Cope, 1889-90. 2 volumes (Nos. 1-14, complete); illustrations; three quarter gilt stamped brown morocco over marbled boards by Zaehnsdorf, spines with raised bands and decorative devices stamped in gilt and black within double gilt ruled compartments, gilt ruled covers, marbled endpapers, top edge gilt, uncut, very good to fine, scarce. With all original gilt decorated wrappers bound in.   George J. Houle 68-144 1996 $450.00

DICKENS, CHARLES 1812-1870   Oliver Twist. London: Richard Bentley, 1838. 1st edition; this would apear to be a later issue because the 'fireside' plate has been replaced by the 'church' plate in volume 3, howeve, leaf containing a list of illustrationss (which Eckel says signifies a later pringing) is not present, 7 3/4 x 5 inches; 3 volumes; 24 plates by George Cruikshank, including frontispiece in each volume; beautiful polished calf by Zaehnsdorf, French fillet on covers, spines very handsomely gilt in compartments with delicate scrolling stamps, dark blue and ochre lettering pieces, gilt edges, marbled endpapers, modern bookplate in each volume; extraordinarily fine.   Phillip J. Pirages 33-170 1996 $1,750.00

DICKENS, CHARLES 1812-1870   The Posthumous Papers of the Pickwick Club. London: Chapman and Hall, 1837. 1st edition; 43 illustrations by Seymour and Phiz, plus 2 additional cancelled plates by Buss; three quarter crimson polished calf, marbled boards, endpapers, raised bands, leather labels, top edge gilt, silk ribbon marker, most attractive copy. Elegantly bound by Zaehnsdorf. Eckel pp. 17-18. Hartfield 48-L29 1996 $950.00

DOBIE, ROWLAND   The History of the United Parishes of St. Giles in the Fields and St. George, Bloomsbury. London: for the author, 1829. 8vo; pages viii, 432, 3 ff. index, folding map; half calf by Zaehnsdorf, scuffed, spine head damaged; author's complimentary copy, inscribed on titlepage and with few ms. corrections.   Marlborough 162-132 1996 £100.00

DOBSON, AUSTIN 1840-1921   Fielding. London: Macmillan, 1883. 1st edition; octavo; pages 196; extra illutrated with dozens of fine, professionally mounted engravings; bound by Zaehnsdorf in full tan polished calf, raised bands, gilt extra in panels, double labels, triple fillets front and back, gilt inner dentelles, marbled endpapers, all edges gilt, with most unusual period dust jacket.   Hartfield 48-V13 1996 $275.00

DU MAURIER, GEORGE 1834-1896   Works. London: 1892-98. 1st uniform edition, 1st edition; 8vo; 3 volumes; illustrations by author; choicely bound in full blue calf, red leather labels, gilt tops by Zaehnsdorf; original cloth covers bound in; superb set.   Charles W. Traylen 117-114 1996 £250.00

BINDING - ZAEHNSDORF

EGAN, PIERCE 1772-1849   Real Life in Ireland; or, the Day and Night Scenes, Rovings, Rambles and Sprees, Bulls, Blunders, Bodderation and Blarney of Brian Boru, Esq. and His Elegant Friend Sir Shawn O'Dogherty. London: ptd. by B. Bensley, Bolt Court, Fleet St., Pub. by Jones & Co... 1821. 1st edition; 8vo; 5-296 pages; hand colored aquatint frontispiece, 18 hand colored aquatints by Alken and others, some plates shaved at margins, no watermarks, bound by Zaehnsdorf, handsome copy, full crimson morocco, triple gilt rule borders to boards, gilt tie to spine and tooling to compartments, raised bands, all edges gilt, marbled endpapers. Tooley 201; Abbey Life 282.   Beeleigh Abbey BA/56-8 1996 £525.00

EMERSON, RALPH WALDO 1803-1882   An Oration Delivered Before the Literary Societies of Dartmouth College. Boston: Charles C. Little and James Brown, 1838. 1st edition; 1000 copies printed; three quarter tan calf, raised bands, gilt, by Zaehnsdorf, very fine. Myerson A8.1. BAL 5185.   Mac Donnell 12-36 1996 $275.00

FACSIMILES of Choice Examples of the Art of Book-Illumination During the Middle Ages/Facsimiles of Choice Examples Selected from Illuminated Manuscripts, Unpublished Drawings and Illustrated Books of Early Date. London: Bernard Quaritch, 1889-92. 4to; 10 parts in one volume; 113 mostly colored chromolithographic plates by William Griggs, including 5 folding plates; original wrappers bound into handsome red morocco by Zaehnsdorf, hinges expertly repaired, gilt ruled raised bands with gilt ruled framed panels, titled in gilt on spine, quadruple gilt ruled frame within single gilt ruled frame on covers, all edges gilt, marbled endpapers; near fine.   Blue Mountain SP95-26 1996 $650.00

FARADAY, PHILIP MICHAEL   "Amasis", an Egyptian Princess. A Comic Opera in 2 Acts. London: Metzler & Co., 1906. 1st edition; 45o; 152 pages, (4) pages ads; contemporary full cream morocco by Zaehnsdorf, with raised bands, gilt turn-ins, red silk endpapers and doublures, all edges gilt, some soiling, else very good. Rare.   Chapel Hill 94-291 1996 $150.00

FARMER, JOHN   Merry Songs and Ballads. London: privately printed for subscribers only, 1897. 8vo; 5 volumes, titles printed in red and black; contemporary dark brown half morocco, spines gilt with an ornate Art Nouveau design of a rose flower on a leafy stem surrounded by a decorative border, top edge gilt, others uncut, by Zaehnsdorf, corners slightly bumped.   Thomas Thorp 489-98 1996 £250.00

GORE, CATHERINE   The Snow Storm: a Christmas Story. London: Willoughby & Co., n.d. Reissue (first published in 1845); small octavo; 253 pages; 4 etched plates by George Cruikshank, bound by Zaehnsdorf in full red polished calf, gilt triple rule border on covers, gilt spine, tooled in compartments, with burgundy calf labels, gilt board edges and turn-ins, top edge gilt, marbled endpapers, corners, joints lightly rubbed, little light foxing, very good. Cohn 356 (first ed.).   Heritage Book Shop 196-282 1996 $150.00

HAZLITT, WILLIAM 1778-1830   Winterslow: Essays and Characters Written There. London: David Bogue, 1850. 1st edition; small 8vo; (vi), 314 pages; later olive morocco by Zaehnsdorf, spine gilt, lightly rubbed; Keynes 111; CBEL III 1233.   James Burmester 29-69 1996 £95.00

HERRICK, ROBERT 1591-1674   Poetical Works. London: George Bell, 1900. 8vo; 2 volumes; handsome three quarter tan polished calf over marbled boards, richly gilt panelled spines, raised bands, leather labels, gilt tops by Zaehnsdorf. Fine, attractive bindings.   Appelfeld Gallery 54-121 1995 $200.00

HOLMES, RICHARD   Queen Victoria by Richard R. Holmes, Librarian to the Queen. London: Boussod, Valadon & Co... 1897. Proof specimen copy, 4to; large paper copy; title on japan vellum, 4 tipped in letters, pencilled specimen of 3 dedication leaves, half title facsimile color portrait frontispiece, additional printed title, (i-ii), 1-195 pages, list of illustrations 199-200, publisher's colophon, 44 full page plates, all tissue guarded, 15 vignettes to letterpress, all tissue guarded, 4 facsimiles and decorative letterpieces; this copy contains a duplicate set of plates and facsimiles on japan vellum; bound by Zaehnsdorf, full red morocco with gilt royal coat of arms to both boards, gilt crown and Tudor rose emblem to all corners of both boards, gilt ruled dentelles to boards, gilt title and crowns to compartments, raised bands to spine, top edge gilt, rest untrimmed, watered silk endpapers; very handsome copy. Beeleigh Abbey BA56-149 1996 £650.00

HUGHES, TED 1930-   Orts. London: Rainbow Press, 1978. 1st edition; one of 200 copies; small 8vo; printed on Italian paper; signed by author; drawing by Leonard Baskin; bound by Zaehnsdorf, decorated endpapers, full black leather, slipcase; fine.   James S. Jaffe 34-278 1996 $175.00

BINDING - ZAEHNSDORF

HUNT, LEIGH 1784-1859   A Jar Of Honey from Mount Hybla. London: Smith, Elder and Co., 1848. 1st edition; 8 x 5 1/2 inches; 4 p.l., viii, xxiv, 200 pages, (8) leaves ads; frontispiece, title page vignette and 24 vignettes in text by Richard Doyle, with half title; text on acidic paper that has evenly browned, closed tear on one leaf from bottom well into text (no loss), otherwise fine copy; lovely and animated light brown crushed morocco exhibition binding by Zaehnsdorf, dated 1895, and with Zaehnsdorf emblem, normally reserved for the firm's better work, impressed at back, both covers filled with large panel of inlaid black tulips on long gilt foliated stems, flowers within diapered compartments and with a background of gilt dots, flat spine similarly decorated (there are a total of 54 inlaid tulips on sides and spine), fine inner gilt dentelles, silk pastedowns and free endpapers, gilt edges, in fine cloth folder and morocco backed slipcase with gilt stamped spine; virtually no external wear.   Phillip J. Pirages 33-65 1996 $1,250.00

INNES, HAMMOND The Conquistadors. London: Collins, 1969. 1st edition; limited to 265 numbered copies, signed by author; crown 4to; (ii), 336 pages, numerous illustrations, many in color; bound by Zaehnsdorf, original full morocco with colored onlay to an Aztec design, all edges gilt, few very minor marks, but very good, in original box.   Ash Rare Books Zenzybyr-55 1996 £195.00

JONSON, BEN 1573?-1637   The Workes... (with) The Second Volume. Containing These Playes, Viz. 1. Bartholomew Fayre. 2 The Staple of Newes. 3 The Divell is an Asse. (and with Walkley's Third Volume, issued without volume title, as always) London: by Richard Bishop.../London: for Richard Meighen; 1640/31-40. 1st Canonical collected edition; folio; 3 volumes bound in 2, volume 1 with frontispiece portrait by robert Vaughan (3rd state, as usual), engraved title by Wiliam Hole; fine binding of red crushed morocco, sides with one-line outer gilt rules, panelled in gilt with an intersecting two-line border and lozenge, semicircles at sides, spines with raised bands, lettered in gilt, other panels with gilt border-and-lozenge pattern to match sides, gilt inner dentelels, marbled endpapers, gilt edges by Zaehnsdorf, titles of volumes I and II with early ownership inscriptions of J. Fairfax at head, endpapers with bookplates of the Fairfax family, Earl of Jersey at Osterley Park, the Shakespearian Library of Marsden J. Perry and STuart Bennett; occasional trivial spot or mark, first A6 of volume 2 extended at inner margin, generally clean and fresh. STC 14753 & 14754; greg III 1073, 1076 & 1079; Pforzheimer 560.   Simon Finch 24-133 1996 £7,500.00

LATH BURY, THOMAS A History of the Nonjurors; their Controversies and Writings... London: William Pickering, 1845. 1st edition; 8vo; Aldine device on titlepage; half brown morocco by Zaehnsdorf, early Zaehnsdorf binding.   Charles W. Traylen 117-151 1996 £90.00

MARRYAT, FREDERICK 1792-1848   The Settlers in Canada. London: Longmans, 1844. 1st edition; foolscap 8vo; 2 volumes; frontispieces; bound by Zaehnsdorf in half light blue morocco, gilt tops, trifle faded.   Charles W. Traylen 117-159 1996 £60.00

MEE, MARGARET Flowers of the Brazilian Forests. London: 1968. Number 286 of 506 copies; folio; 32 colored plates, 32 vignettes and double page colored map; half morocco over marbled boards by Zaehnsdorf, top edge gilt, cloth slipcase (light staining, some wear and insect markings to backstrip and edges).   Raymond M. Sutton VI-20 1996 $1,850.00

MEREDITH, GEORGE 1828-1909   Lord Ormont and His Aminta. London: Chapman and Hall, 1894. 1st edition; limited to 1500 copies; small 8vo; 3 volumes; half brown morocco, gilt top, by Zaehnsdorf, slight foxing; complete with half titles.   Charles W. Traylen 117-162 1996 £70.00

MEREDITH, GEORGE 1828-1909   One of Our Conquerors. London: Chapman and Hall, 1891. 1st edition; small 8vo; 3 volumes; half brown morocco, gilt tops, by Zaehnsdorf.   Charles W. Traylen 117-165 1996 £70.00

BINDING - ZAEHNSDORF

MEREDITH, GEORGE 1828-1909   Rhoda Fleming. London: Tinsley Bros., 1865. 1st edition; 8vo; 3 volumes; half titles; half brown morocco by Zaehnsdorf; very good; rare; Collie VI; Sadleir 1702; not in Wolff; CBEL III 890.   Ximenes 109-191 1996 $600.00

OMAR KHAYYAM The Rubaiyat. London: Macmillan, 1920. 6 x 4 1/4 inches; 3 p.l., 111 pages; title printed in red and black; quite pretty deep blue morocco by Zaehnsdorf, covers dominated by a large and intricate gilt arabesque (with unusual onlaid oval of marbled calf at center), raised bands, spine with gilt floral ornaments, rules and titling, very pretty elaborate gilt inner dentelles, all edges gilt, top of spine with tiny chip, backstrip very slightly sunned, otherwise fine in charming binding. Bookplate.   Phillip J. Pirages 33-66 1996 $125.00

PALLISER, FANNY MARRYAT 1805-1878   A History of Lace. London: Sampson, Low, Son and Marston, 1869. 2nd edition; 9 x 6 inches; viii, 442 pages; frontispiece, decorative title page, many illustrations in text; gift inscription dated 1901 on front flyleaf; very fine handsomely gilt and onlaid tan crushed morocco by Zaehnsdorf, covers and spine compartments outlined with onlaid maroon morocco, covers with very board densely gilt dentelles (composed of many complex antique fleurons), spine compartments similarly decorated, elegant inner gilt dentelles, silk pastedowns and flyleaves, all edges gilt, extremely fine inside and out, in splendid binding.   Phillip J. Pirages 33-67 1996 $850.00

PLEY, ARTHUR F. E.   St. Paul's Cathedral. London: For the author, 1927. Folio; pages xvi, 29, viii appendices, 22 numbered plates, including frontispiece; bound by Zaehnsdorf in half morocco over cloth boards, gilt stamped design to centre of upper board showing the west elevation of the cathedral, top edge gilt, marbled endpapers. Good, clean copy.   Sotheran PN32-191 1996 £298.00

SMOLLETT, TOBIAS GEORGE 1721-1771   The Works. London: Gibbings & Co., ca. 1910. Limited edition; small 8vo; 12 volumes; handsome three quarter brown levant morocco, gilt panelled spines with floral inlays, raised bands, gilt top, by Zaehnsdorf. Fine, attractive set.   Appelfeld Gallery 54-167 1996 $600.00

SUCKLING, JOHN Fragmenta Aurea... London: Humphrey Moseley, 1658. 3rd edition; small 8vo; 135, 64, (2), (96), 145-190 pages; later calf, bound by Zaehnsdorf, gold tooled spine panels, blind inside dentelles and roll tooled side panels in blind and gold, modern bookplate, very good in fine binding.   The Bookpress 75-467 1996 $450.00

SYMONDS, JOHN ADDINGTON The Life of Michelangelo Buonarroti, Based on Studies of the Buonarroti Family at Florence. London: 1893. 2 volumes; etched portrait, 50 reproductions, full brown morocco, richly gilt on spines and sides, inner ornate dentelles, gilt edges by Zaehnsdorf.   Jens J. Christoffersen SL94-83 1996 $225.00

ZAEHNSDORF, JOSEPH W. The Art of Bookbinding. London: George Bell & Sons, 1880. 1st edition; 8vo; contemporary full rose polished calf, covers gilt in 4 compartments, central lozenge, spine and inner dentelles gilt, top edge gilt, by Zaehnsdorf; traces of rubbing; Fine; booklabel of Charles L. Dana, later bookplate of Nell Rose Wheeler and Charles Van Lise Wheeler.   Ximenes 108-350 1996 $500.00

BINDING - ZUCKER

MITCHELL, DONALD GRANT 1822-1908   American Lands and Letters. New York: Scribner's, 1901. Later edition; 8vo; 402 pages; this copy contains 40 extra plates bound in, in addition to the 94 illustrations called for; contemporary three quarter morocco by Hyman Zucker, top edge gilt, very slight rubbing to spine ends and edges, bookplate, else fine and bright. BAL 13980.   Chapel Hill 94-174 1996 $225.00

Fore-edge Paintings

FORE-EDGE PAINTINGS

FORE-EDGE - 1820

GAY, JOHN 1685-1732   The Poems. Chiswick: printed by Chas. Whittingham, College House, n.d., ca. 1820. 8vo; 2 volumes, pages 252, 250; elegantly bound in full striated crimson morocco, elaborate gilt titles and decorations, gilt inner, all edges gilt, cased in specially made linen box; with 2 fine early fore-edge paintings: Volume 1 a split scene showing Gay's portrait in an oval frame and Lincoln's Inn Gate, Chancery Lane, the whole in a surround of grapes and vines; volume II offers a similarly designed painting with a portrait of Richard Steele in an oval frame, & depiction of Covent Garden in 1660 in a surround of masks of comedey & tragedy w/laurel ribbon & decorations. Small bookplate. Hartfield 48-F2 1996 $2,800.00

FORE-EDGE - 1822

WATTS, ISAAC   Logic; or, the Right Use of Reason, in the Enquiry After Truth... London: John Bumpus, 1822. 8vo; frontispiece, some spotting of prelims; full contemporary plum morocco, boards with wide gilt borders, little rubbed, spine gilt, all edges gilt, water color painting on fore-edge of a naval seascape, with several ships, with rowing boat in foreground with 3 naval officers in uniform of the period.   Ian Wilkinson 95/1-97 1996 £225.00

FORE-EDGE - 1823

CRABBE, GEORGE 1754-1832   The Works of the Rev. George Crabbe. London: John Murray, 1823. Small 8vo; 8 volumes; full black straight grain morocco, decorative gilt borders to covers, inner blind rule and corner ornaments, fully gilt decorated spines, gilt edges, narrow inner gilt dentelles, red endpapers, ink inscriptions to all volumes; each volume with a fore-edge painting of London, all paintings in bright clean state and in excellent condition; upper hinges cracked to volumes 2 and 8. Beeleigh Abbey BA/56-6 1996 £3,000.00

FORE-EDGE - 1841

LOCKHART, JOHN GIBSON 1794-1854   Ancient Spanish Ballads. London: John Murray, 1841. 1st of this edition; tall thick quarto; unpaginated, with 8 pages of publisher's ads; 4 splendid titlepages by Owen Jones, lavishly gilt in the Morrish style, the first to use 4 color chromolithography, every page with wood engraved illustrations in many colors & color lithographped borders or tailpieces; bound by Leighton (& probably designed by Jones) in red pebbled morocco, elaborate gilt and blind decorations to coers & spine, gilt & black floral endpapers; with forepedge painting: a bright, impressionistic view of Gibraltar, with several sailing ships in foreground, book and fore-edge painting in excellent condition, laid in is a glassine envelope with clippings about this historic instance of fine book-making. VBD 58-59 and 125. Hartfield 48-F7 1996 $1,950.00

FORE-EDGE - 1847

MOORE, THOMAS   The Life of Lord Byron, with His Letters and Journals. London: John Murray, 1847. New edition in one volume; large octavo; 735 pages; frontispiece and five pportraits, engraved titlepage with vignette; green pebbled morocco, triple gilt and blind fillets, raised bands, gilt extra in panels, all edges gilt; appropriately elegant fore-edge painting with portrait of Byron and a view of the Acropolis in Athens; some wear and slight foxing, but nice copy, handsome, with finely detailed fore-edge painting under gilt.   Hartfield 48-F6 1996 $950.00

FORE-EDGE - 1851

JAMESON, ANNA BROWNELL MURPHY 1794-1860   Memoirs of the Beauties of the Court of Charles II. London: Bohn, 1851. Quarto; 350 pages; 21 splendid stipple engravings in perfect condition, all tissue guards present; full polished calf, raised bands, spine gilt in panels, gilt on black leather title, gilt fillets, marbled endpapers, gauffered edges; with colorful triple portrait fore-edge painting of Charles II, flanked by Nell Gwynne & Catherine of Braganza, each in oval frame, with six cupids supporting the portraits at top and bottom.   Hartfield 48-F4 1996 $1,400.00

FORE-EDGE - 1865

BACON, FRANCIS, VISCOUNT ST. ALBANS 1561-1626   Bacon's Essays and Colours of Good and Evil with Notes and Glossarial Index... Cambridge & London: Macmillan and Co., 1865. Golden Treasury Edition, Fourth Thousandth Impression; small 8vo; 388 pages of text; full red straight grain morocco, gilt rule borders, tiny corner ornaments to boards, gilt rule, title and small gilt leaf tools to panelled spine, all edges gilt, narrow inner gilt dentelles, marbled endpapers, ink inscription (Eton 1817), last leaf of text lightly foxed; a fine fore-edge painting of Eton College.   Beeleigh Abbey BA56-132 1996 £275.00

FORE-EDGE - 1867

TENNYSON, ALFRED TENNYSON, 1ST BARON 1809-1892   Idylls of the King. London: Edward Moxon, 1867. 8vo; page 167 paper eaten by insect with loss of a few words; contemporary red morocco, boards with gilt panels, upper board lettered in gilt, spine fully gilt, rubbed, all edges gilt, with water color painting on fore-edge of a coastal scene with various fishing boats and fishermen, sand, cliffs, &c.   Ian Wilkinson 95/1-98 1996 £95.00

FORE-EDGE - 1871

MOIR, DAVID MAC BETH   Domestic Verses. Edinburgh: Blackwood, 1871. Small octavo; pages 174; full black crushed morocco, fillets decorated in blind, raised bands, gilt titles, guaffered edges gilt, doublures, all edges gilt; patterned silk striped endpapers, echo the unusual honeycomb and floral needlework pattern of the fore-edge painting, which is signed with the initials "A.N."; name on flyleaf, else very pretty copy. CBEL III 410.   Hartfield 48-F5 1996 $895.00

FORE-EDGE - 1893

SCOTT, WALTER 1771-1832   The Poetical Works of Sir Walter Scott. London: Frederick Warne, 1893. Thick 8vo; full blue polished calf, armorial coat of arms and head of man in gilt on front and rear cover respectively, richly gilt paneled spine, raised bands, edges gilt, by Bayntun; with fine quality painting on fore-edge of volume depicting harvesters in a field with landscape in background, fine, bright example. Appelfeld Gallery 54-98 1996 $650.00

FORE-EDGE - 1910

EMERSON, RALPH WALDO 1803-1882   Essays. London: Macmillan, 1910. Octavo; 538 pages; full crushed dark green morocco, double gilt and blind fillets, raised bands, gilt, inner gilt dentelles, all edges gilt; with skilfully rendered fore-edge painting depicting Christopher Columbus and the Santa Maria on stormy seas; slight wear, old writing on flyleaf, generally an excellent copy.   Hartfield 48-F1 1996 $695.00